For Reference

Not to be taken from this room

The Almanac of American Politics

2020

Members of Congress and Governors:
Their Profiles and Election Results,
Their Districts and States

Richard Cohen
Charlie Cook

Senior Authors
Louis Jacobson
Louis Peck

Founding Author
Michael Barone

Columbia Books & Information Services
National Journal

ISBN-13: 978-1-938939-88-4 (paper)

ISBN-13: 978-1-938939-89-1 (hardback)

ISBN-13: 978-1-938939-93-8 (e-book)

THE ALMANAC OF
AMERICAN POLITICS
2020

Chief Author	Richard Cohen
Co-author	Charlie Cook
Managing Editor	Emma Gorman Griffin
Editorial Director	Duncan Bell
Senior Authors	Louis Jacobson, Louis Peck
Senior Contributing Authors	James A. Barnes, Michael Barone (Founding Author)
Senior Editors	John Bicknell, Judah Taylor
Data Editor	Dr. Emil Pitkin
Contributing Writers	Jennifer Duffy, Brent Griffiths, Cam Joseph, Abby Livingston, Jessica Taylor, David Wassserman
Director of Research	Charles Aull
Researchers	Rob Oldham (researcher-writer), Jackie Beran; Marielle Bricker; David Luchs; Sara Reynolds
Research consultant	Matthew Pinkus
Election Results	Dave Leip's Atlas of U.S. Presidential Elections (uselectionatlas.org)
District Maps	Polidata

Columbia Books & Information Services
President: Brittany Carter

About the Authors

Richard Cohen has been chief author of The Almanac of American Politics since 2015 and was co-author from 2001 through 2010. Rich has written about Congress for National Journal, Politico and Congressional Quarterly. Rich is the author of several books, including Washington at Work: Back Rooms and Clean Air, a case study of the 1990 Clean Air Act, and Rostenkowski: The Pursuit of Power and the End of the Old Politics. He co-authored The Partisan Divide, with former Reps. Tom Davis of Virginia and Martin Frost of Texas. In 1990, Rich won the prestigious Everett McKinley Dirksen Award for distinguished reporting on Congress.

Charlie Cook is the Editor and Publisher of The Cook Political Report, a political analyst for the National Journal Group, and an analyst for NBC News. Over the years, Charlie has served as an Election Night analyst for CBS, CNN, and since 1996 on NBC News Election Night Decision Desk in New York. In 2010, Charlie was the co-recipient of the American Political Science Association's prestigious Carey McWilliams award to honor "a major journalistic contribution to our understanding of politics." In 2013, Charlie served as a Resident Fellow at the Institute of Politics at Harvard's Kennedy School of Government.

Louis Jacobson is the Senior Correspondent for PolitiFact. Since 2002, Louis has handicapped political races, including races for Congress, governor, state legislature, other state offices, and the electoral college, currently for Governing magazine. Louis has served as deputy editor of Roll Call and as the founding editor of its legislative wire service, CongressNow. Earlier, Louis spent more than a decade as a reporter covering Congress, politics and lobbying for National Journal.

Louis Peck is politics editor for Bethesda magazine and a co-founder of Maryland Matters, which provides online coverage of politics and government in that state. Since 1978, Louis has been a Washington-based journalist who has written extensively on Congress and national politics. For nearly two decades, he was editor-in-chief of National Journal's Congress Daily. Earlier, Louis was editor of Campaigns and Elections magazine and a national political correspondent for the Washington bureau of Gannett newspapers, as well as collaborating on two books on campaign finance reform with the late Professor Herbert Alexander of the University of Southern California.

James A. Barnes has covered every presidential election and national party convention since 1984. He is a consultant to CNN, where he projects the outcome of presidential, congressional and gubernatorial races for its election and primary night coverage. He was the chief political correspondent for National Journal and found of the National Journal Insiders Poll. He was a contributor to The State of American Politics.

Michael Barone is Senior Political Analyst for the Washington Examiner, a Resident Fellow at the American Enterprise Institute and a contributor to Fox News Channel. He was co-author of The Almanac of American Politics 1972-2016. He is also the author of Our Country: The Shaping of America from Roosevelt to Reagan, The New Americans: How the Melting Pot Can Work Again, and many other publications in the United States and several other countries. Mr. Barone received the Bradley Prize from the Lynde and Harry Bradley Foundation in 2010, the Barbara Olsen Award from The American Spectator in 2006 and the Carey McWilliams Award from the American Political Science Association in 1992.

Acknowledgements

The authors owe their customary debt of gratitude to several people and organizations that have made essential contributions to the 2020 edition of The Almanac of American Politics and sustained it for a half-century. Most notably, Michael Barone co-founded and authored the original 1972 Almanac and since then his insights and prodigious knowledge of American politics and government have been the heart and soul of this vital work. John Fox Sullivan, the former president and publisher of National Journal, and David Bradley, the owner of National Journal's parent company, Atlantic Media, nurtured the Almanac for three decades. Ballotpedia, led by its president Leslie Graves and editor in chief Geoff Pallay, have provided essential research and editorial support for the 2020 Almanac, without which this edition would not have been possible. Charlie Cook and his staff at the Cook Political Report made significant contributions to this latest edition. The Brookings Institution graciously allowed usage of key figures from their report, "Vital Statistics on Congress." Dave Leip provided election and other data. Clark Benson, at Polidata, contributed updated congressional district maps. Beth Hahn, historical editor at the Senate Historical Office, gave vital research assistance. We are grateful to Brittany Carter, Matthew Barnes, Sami McPadden, Allison Rosenstock and the staff of Columbia Books and Information Services for their efforts in getting this book to press.

TABLE OF CONTENTS

GUIDE TO USAGE

The following guide explains the information sources used by The Almanac of American Politics. Major sources of information include the U.S. Census Bureau, Ballotpedia, the Center for Responsive Politics, The Cook Political Report and the Almanac's writers and researchers. The 2020 Almanac offers significant updates from the previous edition of the book, published in 2017. Figures released by the Census Bureau may vary slightly from those used by the Almanac due to different methods of data aggregation or tabulation. Percentages used in the book may not add up to 100% because of rounding.

Biography

This section lists the date each governor, senator, and representative was elected or appointed, the date and place of birth, academic degrees earned, religion, marital status, and, if applicable, spouse's name and number of children. Also provided is a brief outline of the subject's past elected offices, professional career and military service, and office addresses, telephone numbers, and websites. Committee and subcommittee assignments are current as of June 2019. (Note: On many committees, the chairman and ranking minority member are ex officio members of subcommittees. Leaders in the House typically do not serve on committees.)

Group Ratings

The congressional ratings by 10 interest groups provide insight into a legislator's general ideology and the degree to which he or she reflects the group's point of view. Some organizations provided just one rating for 2017 and 2018, the two sessions of the 115th Congress.

ADA: Americans for Democratic Action

Liberal: Since ADA's founding in 1947, the Annual Voting Records have served as the standard measure of political liberalism. Rating is calculated by combining 20 key votes on a wide range of social and economic issues, both domestic and international. Only 2017 ratings were available at the time of publication.

ACLU: American Civil Liberties Union

Pro-individual liberties: ACLU seeks to protect individuals from what it views as legal, executive, and congressional infringements on civil liberties. The ACLU compiles a combined score for each two-year Congress. (C = Combined)

AFL-CIO: American Federation of Labor Congress of Industrial Organizations

Liberal labor: The AFL-CIO is a federation of 56 unions representing some 12.5 million members that advocates for social and economic justice and improved working conditions through collective bargaining. Its analysis is based on roll call votes in 2017. Its 2018 analysis was not available at press time.

LCV: League of Conservation Voters

Environmental: Formed in 1970, LCV is the arm of the environmental movement that works to elect pro-environmental protection candidates to Congress. LCV ratings are based on key votes on energy, environment, and natural resources legislation in 2017 and 2018

ITI: Information Technology Industry Council

High-tech industry: ITI represents the leading U.S. providers of information technology products and services. It compiles a combined score for each two-year Congress. (C = Combined)

COC: U.S. Chamber of Commerce

Pro-business: Founded in 1912, COC represents local, regional, and state chambers of commerce in addition to trade and professional organizations. It promotes free market policies and ranks members of Congress for key business votes.

HAFA: Heritage Action for America

Conservative: HAFA advocates for conservative policies, many of which are developed by its sister organization, the Heritage Foundation. Key votes in this rating encompass a broad range of conservative issues. It compiles a combined score for each two-year Congress. (C = Combined)

ACU: American Conservative Union

Conservative: Since 1971, ACU ratings have provided a means of gauging the conservatism of members of Congress on foreign policy, social, and budget issues. Its scores are annual.

CFG: Club for Growth

Pro-tax limitation: CFG supports limited government, lower taxes, and policies it deems favorable to economic growth. CFG's annual ratings are based on key votes on taxes, trade, and the economy.

FRC: Family Research Council

Social conservative: The FRC promotes traditional marriage and family and advocates for policies that uphold Judeo-Christian values. Its annual ratings are based on votes on abortion and family issues. It compiles a score annually for each member of Congress.

Almanac Vote Ratings

Emil Pitkin, CEO of GovPredict, has computed the Almanac congressional vote ratings for 2018. Almanac editors have selected a list of key congressional roll call votes and classified them as economic, social, or foreign policy-related. Within each issue area, a principal component analysis (PCA) is applied to the votes. PCA is a general statistical procedure that reduces a complex data set with many dimensions into its most descriptive constituent parts, called principle components. This blind statistical procedure found that the most salient, one-number summary of how a legislator voted across dozens of votes corresponds to the liberalism or conservatism of each Member of Congress. That one number is known as the score of the first principal component.

The Members of Congress have been ranked according to their score, and their scores are normalized to fit in the 0 to 100 range, both for the "conservative score" and for their "liberal score." The liberal score is simply 100 minus the conservative score, and vice versa. The composite score is an average of a member's three issue-based scores.

Only Members of Congress who participate in at least half of the votes in an issue area receive ratings. Absences are not scored, while abstentions are scored as a 0.5, with an aye vote scored as a 1 and a nay vote as an 0.

Key Votes

The key votes section presents the positions of Senators and House members on important issues. The following key votes, selected by the Almanac staff, took place during the 115th Congress (2017-2018). There are 12 votes in the Senate and 12 votes in the House, which are split among economic, foreign policy, and social issues. A member who was absent or declined to vote receives NV for "not voting." The letter P signifies a vote of "present." No listings are provided for members who were not in office at the time. Roll-call data were obtained from the clerk of the House and Secretary of the Senate.

Senate Votes

- *Obama-care revision:* (Senate Vote 179, H.R. 1628) Repeal and revise the Affordable Care Act. July 28, 2017. Defeated 49-51. (R: 49-3; D: 0-46, I: 0-2)
- *Tax cuts:*(Senate Vote 303, H.R. 1) Reduce tax rates and reform Internal Revenue Code. Dec. 2, 2017. Passed 51-49. (R: 51-1; D: 0-46, I: 0-2)
- *Dodd-Frank revision:* (Senate Vote 54, S. 2155) Revise parts of the 2010 Dodd-Frank financial regulatory law. March 14, 2018. Passed 67-31. (R: 50-0; D: 16-30, I: 1-1)
- *Omnibus appropriations:* (Senate Vote 63, H.R. 1625) Appropriate funds for federal agencies for the remainder of Fiscal 2018. March 23, 2018. Passed 65-32. (R: 25-23; D: 39-8, I: 1-1)
- *Gun regulations:* (Senate Vote 66, H.J. Res 40) Disapprove regulations for sale of firearms to mentally incapable individuals by the Health and Human Services Department. Feb. 15, 2017. Passed 57-43 (R: 52-0; D: 4-42; I: 1-1)

* *Family planning regs:* (Senate Vote 101, H.J. Res. 43) Disapprove family-planning regulations by the Health and Human Services Department. March 30, 2017. Passed 50-50. (R: 50-2; D: 0-46, I: 0-2, Vice President Pence broke the tie)
* *Gorsuch confirmation:* (Senate Vote 111) Confirm Neil Gorsuch to the Supreme Court. April 7, 2017. Passed 54-45. (R: 52-0; D: 2-46; I: 1-1)
* *Immigration restrictions:* (Senate Vote 36, H.R. 2579) Limit debate on a bill to continue a tax credit for individuals who have lost their job. Feb. 15, 2018. Defeated 39-60. (R: 36-14; D: 3-44, I: 0-2)
* *Kavanaugh confirmation:* (Senate Vote 223) Confirm Brett Kavanaugh to the Supreme Court. Oct. 6, 2018. Passed 50-48 (R: 49-0; D: 1-46, I: 0-2)
* *Saudi arms sales:* (Senate Vote 143, S.J. Res. 42) Prohibit transfer of military weapons to Saudi Arabia. June 13, 2017. Defeated 47-53. (R: 4-48; D: 43-3; I: 0-2)
* *FISA rules:* (Senate Vote 11, S. 139) Limit debate on a bill to require the FBI to issue standards for steps to analyze DNA samples of criminal offenders. Jan. 16, 2018. Passed 60-38. (R: 41-8; D: 18-28, I: 1-1)
* *Military aid in Yemen:* (Senate Vote 266, S.J. Res. 54) Direct the removal of U.S. military force from Yemen. Dec. 13, 2018. Passed 56-41. (R: 7-41; D: 47-0, I: 2-0)

House Votes

* *Obama-care revision:* (House Vote 256, H.R. 1628) Repeal and revise the Affordable Care Act. May 4, 2017. Passed 217-213. (R: 217-20; D: 0-193)
* *Tax cuts:* (House Vote 637, H.R. 1) Reduce tax rates and reform Internal Revenue Code. Nov. 16, 2017. Passed 227-205. (R: 227-13; D: 0-192)
* *Omnibus appropriations:* (House Vote 127, H.R. 1625) Appropriate funds for federal agencies for the remainder of Fiscal 2018. March 22, 2018. Passed 256-167. (R: 145-90; D: 111-77)
* *Dodd-Frank revision:* (House Vote 216, S. 2155) Revise parts of the 2010 Dodd-Frank financial regulatory law. May 22, 2018. Passed 258-159. (R: 225-1; D: 33-158)
* *Family planning regs:* (House Vote 99, H.J. Res. 43) Disapprove family-planning regulations by the Health and Human Services Department. Feb. 16, 2017. Passed 230-188. (R: 228-2; D: 2-186)
* *Body cameras/immigration:* B (House Vote 461, H.R. 3354) Approve $10 million for body-worn cameras for immigration agents. Sept. 7, 2017. Defeated 203-211. (R: 17-210; D: 186-1)
* *Abortion ban:* (House Vote 549, H.R. 36) Impose criminal penalties to perform an abortion if the fetus is at least 20 weeks. Oct. 3, 2017. Passed 237-189. (R: 234-2; D: 3-187)
* *Concealed carry:* (House Vote 663, H.R. 38) Allow an individual to carry a concealed handgun to another state that allows such firearms. Nov. 14, 2017. Passed 231-198. (R: 225-14; D: 6-184)
* *Guantanamo prisoners:* (House Vote 359, H.R. 2810) Prohibit funds to transfer prisoners from Guantanamo Bay, Cuba. July 13, 2017. Defeated 167-257 (R: 3-232; D: 164-25)
* *Ground missiles, limit:* (House Vote 360, H.R. 2810) Limit development of a ground-launched missile system. July 13, 2017. Defeated 173-249. (R: 1-234; D: 172-15)
* *Ground missiles, limit:* (House Vote 360, H.R. 2810) Limit development of a ground-launched missile system. July 13, 2017. Defeated 173-249. (R: 1-234; D: 172-15)
* *Defense Dept. spending:* (House Vote 378, H.R. 2810) Authorize Defense Department spending for Fiscal Year 2018. July 14, 2017. Passed 344-81. (R: 227-8; D: 117-73)
* *FISA rules:* (Senate Vote 179, H.R. 1628) Require the FBI to issue standards for steps to analyze DNA samples of criminal offenders. Jan. 11, 2018. Passed 256-164. (R: 191-45; D: 65-119)

NOTE: Freshman members of the House, because they took office in January 2019, do not have key votes, vote scores from the interest groups, or ratings from the Almanac for the 115th Congress (2017-2018). Freshman senators have vote scores if they served in the House. Freshmen who won in a special election to fill a vacancy may have some key votes and vote scores from some interest groups.

Election Results

The most recent election results are listed for senators and governors. For House members, the results are from the 2018 primary and general elections, as well as any runoffs in 2018 or special elections held since November 2016. Candidates in primaries receiving less than 5% (before rounding) of the total vote and candidates in general elections receiving less than 2% (before rounding) of the total were excluded. Election results were supplied by Ballotpedia and Secretary of State websites. Prior Winning percentages: The incumbent's winning percentages in earlier elections.

Campaign Finance

Campaign finance data in the Almanac was sourced from the Federal Elections Commission (FEC) website. The FEC makes bulk campaign finance data available in several reports, however principally two were used for the purposes of the Almanac: Operating Expenditures and Independent Expenditures. The Operating Expenditures file was referenced to gather all spending activity for each candidate's principal campaign committee during the relevant election cycle; the Independent Expenditures file was referenced to gather all spending from outside groups attempting to influence an election result.

In the "Election Results" section of each Senator and Member profile, campaign finance data can be found in the 3 columns aligned to the right of each candidate election result. "Cand. Spent" provides the spending total for the principal campaign committee of the candidate during the election cycle in question. "Ind. Exp. Support" and "Ind. Exp. Oppose" both relate to the Intendent Expenditures file, which reports any spending from outside groups to impact an election outcome. The FEC requires that these filers indicate the relevant candidate, as well as whether they "support" or "oppose" the election of that candidate. "Outside groups" may include Super PACs, social welfare 501(c)(4) organizations, trade associations, unions, political parties, corporations, individuals or other groups. However, the monies may not account for all outside money spent in a race, as some outside spending is subject to different federal campaign finance disclosure rules.

The FEC Operating Expenses file for the 2017-2018 cycle was downloaded in May of 2019; the Independent Expenditures file for the 2017-2018 cycle was downloaded in May of 2019. These were mapped to the Candidate Master and Committee Master files, downloaded in May of 2019. Campaign finance data for 2018 special elections was downloaded from the FEC website in June 2019.

Demographics

Population: Figures are from the 2017 American Community Survey (ACS) one-year estimates reported by the U.S. Census Bureau.

Born in state: Percent of entire population of the district that was born in the state in which that district is located.

Race and ethnicity: Figures are from the 2017 ACS reported by the Census Bureau. As defined by the Census Bureau, race reflects individual respondents' perception of their racial identity. Latino origin is defined as an ethnicity. The Census Bureau initially reports data for whites, blacks, and other racial groups that include both Latinos and non-Latinos, but traditionally will follow this initial report with figures that breaks racial and ethnic data into results that are more useful for political analysis. As a result, this version of the Almanac uses the following definitions:

- *White* refers to people who describe their race as white and who say they are not of Latino ancestry or descent.
- *Black* refers to people who describe their race as black or African-American and who say they are not of Latino ancestry or descent.
- *Latino* refers to people who say they are of Latino or Hispanic ancestry, regardless of how they answer questions about their racial identity.
- *Asian* refers to people who describe their race as Asian and who say they are not of Latino ancestry or descent.
- *Two races* refer to people who choose more than one racial category (white, black, Asian, American Indian or Pacific Islander) to describe themselves. This does not include people who describe themselves as Latino.

- *Other* is comprised of the following groups: American Indian, Pacific Islander and those who report "Other".
- *American Indian* refers to people who describe their race as American Indian or Alaska Native and who say they are not of Latino ancestry or descent.
- *Pacific Islander* refers to people who describe their race as black or Native Hawaiian or "other Pacific Islander" and who say they are not of Latino ancestry or descent.

Education: H.S. grad or less refers to people who did not attend college. Some college refers to people who attended college but did not receive a diploma, or who received an associate's degree but not a bachelor's degree. College degree, 4 yr. refers to people who received a bachelor's degree but did not receive a graduate or professional degree after attending college. Post-grad study refers to people who received a graduate or professional degree. All groups are a percentage of people 25 years and older.

Veteran: This category includes both men and women in the civilian population who served in the U.S. military.

Active duty: This category refers to men and women currently employed in the U.S. armed forces.

Median income: This figure represents the median income (not the average income) for all households in the congressional district (or state) for 2017. The numbers in parentheses immediately below indicates where the district ranks among all 435 districts, with the richest district indicated by (1 of 435) and the poorest by (435 of 435).

Income: Each category represents the number of households in each district (or state) with a reported income that fell within that bracket in 2017. Poverty rate: This figure indicates the poverty rate computed by the Census Bureau for 2017 for each district using the definition outlined in the Office of Management and Budget's (OMB) Statistical Policy Directive 14.

Work: The Census Bureau asks all respondents over the age of 16 who are employed in the civilian workforce about their occupation and assigns each respondent to one of five occupation codes defined by the federal government.

- *White collar* refers to civilian workers assigned to the category titled "Management, Business, Science and Arts occupations."
- *Blue collar* refers to workers assigned to two categories: "Natural Resources, Construction and Maintenance occupations" and "Production, Transportation and Material Moving occupations."
- *Sales and service* refers to workers assigned to the final two categories: "Service occupations" and "Sales and Office occupations."
- *Govt. workers* refers to the percentage of respondents over the age of 16 who are employed in the civilian government workforce.

Language: This is percentage of households in the nation speaking a certain language as a percentage of people 5 years and older. The abbreviation other European refers to other Indo-European languages.

Place of Birth: The Census asks people if they are native or foreign born, and if they currently reside in the state in which they were born or if they were born in a different state.

Foreign-born Citizenship Status: This category shows the percentage of foreign-born residents in the U.S. who are citizens.

Region of Foreign Born: This category shows the regions of the world where foreign-born residents were born.

Abbreviations

ACLU	American Civil Liberties Union	HSOB	Hart Senate Office Building
ACU	American Conservative Union	I	Independent
ADA	Americans for Democratic Action	IAP	Independent American Party (NV)
AFDC	Aid to Families with Dependent Children	IC	Independent Conservative
AFL-CIO	American Federation of Labor and Congress of Industrial Organizations	ID	Independent Democrat
		IG	Independent Green
		Ind	Independence Party
AID	Agency for International Development	ITI	Information Technology Industry Council
ANWR	Arctic National Wildlife Refuge	IVP	Independent Voters Party
BL	Better Life Party	LCV	League of Conservation Voters
C	Conservative Party (NY	LHOB	Longworth House Office Building
CAFE	Corporate Average Fuel Economy	Lib	Libertarian Party
		Mod	Moderate Party
CAFTA	Central America Free Trade Agreement	NAFTA	North American Free Trade Agreement
CFG	Club for Growth	NARAL	NARAL Pro-Choice America
CHMN	Chairman	NL	Natural Law Party
CHOB	Cannon House Office Building	NP	Non-Partisan
CIA	Central Intelligence Agency	NPA	No Party Affiliation
CNP	Constitution Party	NRSC	National Republican Senatorial Committee
COC	United States Chamber of Commerce	NSA	National Security Agency
COLA	Cost of Living Adjustment	NTU	National Taxpayers Union
D	Democratic Party	PF	Peace and Freedom Party
DCCC	Democratic Congressional Campaign Committee	PNP	New Progressive Party (PR) (Spanish: Partido Nuevo Progresista)
DCS	District of Columbia Statehood	POP	Populist Party
DFL	Democratic-Farmer-Labor Party (MN)	PPD	Popular Democratic Party (PR) (Spanish: Partido Popular Democrático)
DLC	Democratic Leadership Council		
DNC	Democratic National Committee		
DSCC	Democratic Senatorial Campaign Committee	PRG	Progressive Party
		R	Republican Party
DSOB	Dirksen Senate Office Building	Ref	Reform Party
EMILY	EMILY's List (Early Money is Like Yeast)	RHOB	Rayburn House Office Building
		RMM	Ranking Minority Member
ERISA	Employee Retirement Income Security Act	RNC	Republican National Committee
		RSOB	Russell Senate Office Building
FEC	Federal Election Commission	RTL	Right-to-Life Party
FERC	Federal Energy Regulatory Commission	S	Capitol Building Room (Senate side)
FRC	Family Research Council	SOC	Socialist Party
GOP	Republican Party (Grand Old Party)	SW	Socialist Workers Party
		UAW	United Auto Workers
G	Green Party	UMJ	United States Marijuana Party
H	Capitol Building Room (House side)	WF	Working Families
HAFA	Heritage Action for America		

From 2016 to 2020

By Charlie Cook

In looking ahead to the 2020 elections it is important to look back four years and ask what has become a fundamental question for American politics: What did the 2016 presidential election mean? Was President Donald Trump's election a sign that Americans felt that the U.S. had lost its moorings, and drifted away from its traditional values and historic strengths? Was it a sign that the electorate wanted to restore the country to its former glory; a collective decision to "Make America Great Again?"

Or, alternatively, was the Trump victory simply an outlier? Was it the confluence of developments and circumstances that created the political equivalent of a perfect storm, one with an improbable result, unlikely to be replicated anytime soon? To what extent was the election as much about Hillary Clinton, and the political baggage she had accumulated over the last 25 years, as it was about the mood of America?

It is true that, at least until the #MeToo movement arrived, it was as if former President Bill Clinton had been coated with Teflon, -- negatives just did not stick to him. But if that was true, was Hillary Clinton covered in Velcro, things stuck to her that didn't adhere to him or wouldn't to someone else? If so, was this the product of gender bias or just unique to her? There is little doubt that the 2016 Democratic nominee brought substantial negatives into the race and was a polarizing figure, with the various controversies around her emails and private server and Wikileaked campaign and Democratic National Committee emails only exacerbating those problems. That had to matter at least to some extent in an election settled by fewer than 89,000 votes in three states out of 137 million cast nationwide. Was the election outcome more of a reflection of the specific choice voters were given?

Americans were presented a choice between a Republican nominee with the highest unfavorable ratings in exit poll history at 60 percent, against a Democratic nominee with the highest unfavorable ratings, 54 percent, of any nominee of her party. And who might have guessed that among the 18 percent of voters who told exit pollsters that they had unfavorable views of both Clinton and Trump, that they would end up voting for Trump by a 17-point margin, 47 to 30 percent?

That question, "what drove the 2016 election outcome," is a pivotal one in terms of how one sees American politics today. Arguably the answer was "yes." It was about both -- it was about a growing divide in our country, but it was also about the specific choice voters were given.

Ron Brownstein of The Atlantic and CNN, perhaps the most insightful observer of American politics today has argued since 2012 that we are seeing "powerful cultural and demographic currents" that are creating a historical reconfiguration of American politics. The two parties are aligning themselves in what he calls, "the coalition of transformation," that would be Democrats, and a "coalition of restoration," the GOP.

Brownstein's theory is that Democrats have come to embrace the cultural and demographic changes that are taking place in America, while Republicans are reflecting their party's base, people deeply unsettled by those changes, as personified by the pre-2016 tea party movement and its oft used slogan, "take back our country." Brownstein suggests that underlying this movement is a desire to restore "the political dominance of married, churchgoing white families." At first, Brownstein theorized that this looked "just about social, cultural and demographic factors, but now economics, the changes that have and continue to drive our economy, both job creation and destruction." Brownstein fears an increase in the distance and antagonism between the two parties, between "a Democratic coalition centered in racially diverse, largely secular, and post-industrial metropolitan centers and a Republican coalition grounded in small-town and rural communities that remain mostly white, Christian and rooted in traditional manufacturing, agriculture and resource extraction."

"One reason small-town and rural areas tilt so much more toward the GOP than urban areas," Brownstein argues, is "because their demographic composition leans so much more toward the groups that now most favor Republicans: older, blue-collar and evangelical whites." A notable study by the Pew Research Center "found that non-whites comprised over half the population in the largest urban centers, about one-third in suburban communities, and only about one-fifth in small town and rural places. Whites without a college degree represented about three-in-10 urban residents, exactly four-in-ten in suburbs and nearly six-in-10 in rural places."

The old adage about where you stand depends upon where you sit increasingly seems true about American politics. The 2008 book, The Big Sort: Why the Clustering of Like-Minded Americans is Tearing Us Apart, by Bill Bishop, explores how the self-sorting of our population -- people living, socializing and working with people much like themselves -- has created ideological and partisan echo chambers, reinforcing and enhancing political and social viewpoints. This self-sorting, combined with talk radio, cable television and social media is highly combustible, fanning partisan flames.

Changes in society and demographics were threatening enough for some Americans, but the transformation in the U.S. economy over the last 40 years was of equal or greater importance, particularly in the swath of industrial states from Pennsylvania through Michigan, Wisconsin and to a certain extent into Minnesota. For generations, many white males, who had not graduated from college could count on finding well-paying, often union jobs, particularly in the manufacturing sector, enabling them to enjoy a middle-class income and lifestyle that constituted the post-World War II American dream. If their spouse chose not to work outside the home but raise kids instead, that was an option, as was buying a fishing boat or a camp on the lake, taking good vacations, or sending kids to college. These dreams were often all possible in the three or four decades after the end of the war, all with no college degree required.

But as the U.S. economy shifted from skills-based to knowledge-based, a combination of increased trade and new technology jobs eliminated many of these jobs, decreased the skill-levels required for other jobs, while still more positions shifted to the south, often to non-union and lower wage jobs. The opportunities available for these non-college graduates whose world had been their oyster often evaporated, making that kind of middle-class income and lifestyle a memory and life more of a struggle. In some cases, the culprit really was trade, goods produced abroad by lower cost workers. But in other cases, it was technology, with robotics the source of the job destruction. While the cost of many goods dropped, some of the jobs that enabled their purchase were gone. Many of the affected men felt emasculated by these changes.

Simultaneously opportunities for women, minorities and other previously marginalized groups improved dramatically. These working-class white men saw things as a zero-sum proposition. More and better opportunities for others meant less opportunity for themselves. They interpreted the situation as others were cutting into the line ahead of them, or that the government and politicians were escorting others to the head of the line. The refrain, "I am working harder and harder but seem to be falling behind," was increasingly heard in focus groups and told to pollsters and anyone else who would listen.

At the same time the farm economy became more mechanized and fewer jobs were needed to grow crops and raise cattle, but the cities and surrounding metropolitan areas seemed to prosper. Small town and rural America seemed to be left behind. The people in the heartland and deep South began to see urban and suburban America as well as the two coasts as benefitting from these changes that were coming at the expense of those sometimes bitterly describing themselves as living in "fly-over country."

These working-class, small town and rural Americans did not see themselves as practicing grievance politics, but they were, just as other constituencies had done for some time.

A final divide, one among whites along religious lines, not so much pitting one religion against another as much between white, evangelical America and a secular America, between those who attend church faithfully and those who rarely, if ever went. Democrats and liberals were increasingly seen as at war with traditional values while Republicans and conservatives were perceived as defending the family and long-standing American principles. One side was seen as God-less, the other God-fearing. During the 2008 presidential campaign, when Sen. Barack Obama diagnosed one group of Americans as resentful and said, "They get bitter, they cling to guns or religion or antipathy to people who aren't like them or anti-immigrant sentiment or anti-trade sentiment as a way to explain their frustrations," these old-fashioned Americans saw that as a declaration of war against people like themselves and what they held dear. This might explain the unusual paradox of Donald Trump, someone who might not conventionally be perceived as an ally of evangelical Christians and moral conservatives, having impressive levels of support among those same people. Seen as "on our side," and appointing judges and making policies that support our cause, his personal life and history is less relevant. Or maybe it is as simple as the old adage that, "the enemy of my enemy is my friend."

This is hardly an esoteric, philosophical or religious argument, or idle cocktail party conversation. One of the biggest issues in American politics today is President Trump's push to build a border wall between the U.S. and Mexico. Brownstein and others argue that the wall represents a broader debate about immigration, both legal and illegal. The fact that 40 percent of undocumented people come into the U.S. legally, then overstay their visas is beside the point. This is about demographic change, about what is America and who are Americans, what this country is about and identity. It is as if to say, "we are Americans, and they are not."

Some, particularly those younger and in metropolitan areas welcome change, embrace diversity and see immigration as infusing our country with fresh blood, a continuation of something that has happened since America's earliest days. Others see the new arrivals as alien, as different, tearing the fabric of our country and society, changing the makeup of our country in irreversible and destructive ways. They fear the adoption of different values and traditions that fly in the face of our heritage and national identity, of who we are.

An April 2019 report from the Gallup Organization pointed to a trend -- that whites without a four-year college degree had begun identifying increasingly as Republicans long before Donald Trump's entry into politics, indeed dating back to the late 1990s interrupted only briefly by the controversy around the Iraq War, about the time of the 2006 election, and by the financial crisis of 2008. By early 2019, 59 percent of these non-college whites (NCW's) identify as Republicans, just 34 percent as Democrats. Conversely, whites with a four-year college degree, in early 2019, identified themselves as Democrats over Republicans by a 13-point margin, 54 to 31. Non-whites identified as Democrats by a 45-point margin, 66 to 21, four-year college degrees among non-whites having little impact on their party preference.

In both 1999 and the 2006-2009 periods, the parties ran about even with NCWs. Michael Podhorzer, political director of the AFL-CIO, points out that Democrats lost their position with NCWs in the South a generation ago, it was the more recent movement among those in the North that made it more noticeable. Podhorzer is also quick to point out that among NCWs who identify as evangelicals, Republican voting is incredibly strong, Democrats need not apply. But among those NCWs who are not evangelicals, the numbers are more competitive. But there is no question that NCWs are central to the Trump coalition.

Arguably the best book explaining what happened and why in 2016 was Identity Crisis: The 2016 Presidential Campaign and the Battle for the Meaning of America, by political scientists John Sides, Michael Tesler and Lynn Vavreck, who offer a fascinating look at the motivations of voters that lead to Donald Trump's nomination and subsequent election and the role of white identity politics. Others, notably SUNY-Buffalo political scientist James E. Campbell push back, arguing that anger mattered less and ideological polarization and economic concerns, notably a downtick in the economy during 2016, mattered more.

2018 MIDTERM ELECTIONS

Any party holding the White House and heading into a midterm election would be well advised to expect, indeed plan for the worst, and hopefully be pleasantly surprised. For Republicans in 2018, the outcome represented both the best and close to the worst-case scenarios. Picking up two seats in the Senate, expanding their majority from 51-49 before the midterm to 53-47, was as good as they could possibly hope for. But losing 40 seats and their House majority was more like a worst-case scenario, though actually a highly favorable 2011 redistricting may well have prevented GOP losses from something quite worse. Cook Political Report House Editor David Wasserman estimates that redistricting made an eight to ten seat difference, reducing GOP losses. Republicans suffered losses at the gubernatorial and state legislative levels as well, though those were not close to worst case-scenarios either. The 2018 election could have been much worse for Republicans.

It was against this backdrop of two Americas that we had the 2018 midterm campaign, as if the elections were held in two very different Americas. As in most midterm elections, it was a referendum on the current occupant of the White House, on President Trump. In one America, in much of blue, urban and in purple suburban areas and among younger and more culturally diverse Americans, Trump was very unpopular, hurting his party badly as is often the case in midterm elections. But in the other, in red, small town and rural America, and in the outer-ring of exurbs, well beyond the closer-in denser suburbs, among the white working class and particularly among evangelical whites, Trump still had strong support and was an asset to his party.

In the 2018 edition of The Almanac of American Politics, this essay began with the question, "If 2016 was the year when the political rulebook was thrown out, whether it will apply in 2017 and 2018 is a good question." As it turned out, the rulebook seemed to apply in the 2018 midterm elections after all. Republicans, the party holding the White House, largely had the losses history suggested they would. In the Senate, where Democrats had far greater exposure to potential losses, both in terms of the numbers of seats they had at risk and which states had Senate seats up, they suffered the losses one might expect, given such a difference in exposure.

Anyone reading an opening essay of an Almanac of American Politics will likely know that parties holding the White House generally have had tough midterm elections. Heading into 2018, whichever party occupied the White House had suffered a net loss in House seats in 35 out of the 38 (92 percent) midterm elections since the end of the Civil War. The National Conference of State Legislatures' Tim Storey, the nation's undisputed expert on state elections, has calculated that the party in the White House has suffered net losses of governorships in 26 of the 29 midterm elections since 1902 and of state legislative seats in 27 of the 29 midterms during that same period, 90 and 93 percent, respectively. The president's party has gained state legislative seats in only two midterms since the beginning of the 20th Century, in 1934 (Franklin Roosevelt's first midterm election) and 2002, just over a year after 9/11 with George W. Bush's approval ratings still sky-high.

For better or worse, midterm elections are referenda on the incumbent president and, as history shows, it usually turns out, worse. Though rarely heard in civics classes, the truth is that hate is a much stronger emotion in politics than love. In fact there is a relatively new term for this, negative partisanship, people hating the opposition party and candidates even more than they love their own party and candidates. It is not unusual for the members of a party that is not in the White House to be angry and hypermotivated, while those in the President's party might be either complacent or disappointed, but less motivated to turn out. At the same time, the mood of those in the middle, not part of either side's base, tends to be critical of the presidents midway through a term. In each of the past four midterm elections, independent voters cast their ballots for the "out-party," the party not holding the White House, by double-digits. Whether the first or second term, the midterm is an opportunity for anyone unhappy to vent their spleens. With the president's name not on the ballot, voters looking to send a message vote against candidates of that same party are guilty by association.

It is important to note that the 2018 midterm elections had the largest midterm election turnout in 104 years, since 1914. Emory University political scientist Alan I. Abramowitz points out that in the previous midterm election, in 2014, voter turnout was the lowest of any midterm election since 1942, while the country was at war and many Americans abroad or otherwise engaged. The 2018 midterm election was one that featured an enormous amount of interest, passion and money.

If anything, midterm elections have gotten even more explosive in recent years. With an increasing level of hyper-partisanship, control of the House, Senate or both has changed hands in four of the last six midterm elections, which is unprecedented in American politics. Democrats under President Clinton lost both the House and Senate in 1994, his first-term, midterm election. Republicans lost both chambers in 2006, which was President George W. Bush's second midterm election. Democrats lost the House President Obama's first-term, midterm in 2010 and the Senate in his second-term, midterm in 2014. There were two exceptions, with no change of control in the last six midterms. In 1998, there was a backlash against Republicans after their impeachment of Clinton, Democrats managed a wash in the Senate and actually picked up four seats in the House. The other exception was in the 2002 election, 14 months after the 9/11 attacks, when a very popular George W. Bush helped his party gain one Senate and eight House seats.

America entered the 2018 election campaign as polarized along party lines as at any point in modern history and, for better and worse, Trump turbocharged these emotions. Typically Trump's approval ratings among Republicans have been near 90 percent, among Democrats it is usually in single-digits, among Independents often in the high 30's. There has been little volatility in Trump's numbers, from his inauguration into the Spring of 2019, his Gallup job approval rating has not dropped below 35 percent or exceeded 46 percent. This is the narrowest 'trading range' of any president in polling history. As University of California-San Diego political scientist Gary C. Jacobson argues that "Democrats and others appalled by his (Trump's) character and objectives (before the election) have seen their worst expectations confirmed." Meanwhile Jacobson observes that, "Trump has also largely met the expectations of the Republicans who voted for him, and they, like Democrats, also continue to regard him pretty much as they did before he was elected."

Republicans entered the 2018 midterm campaign with a lot at risk, holding more elective offices than they have at any time since the 1922 election. Add in the fact that President Trump's job approval ratings have very consistently trailed those of his modern predecessors, and it was easy to say that the GOP faced the possibility of a catastrophic outcome.

2018 Senate Elections

The pattern of Senate midterm losses is strong, but not as potent as at other levels. Since the enactment of the 17th Amendment in 1913 calling for the direct election of senators, the party in the White House had a net loss in seats in 19 out of 26 midterms (73 percent). The difference between outcomes in the House, governorships and state legislative seats on the one hand, and the Senate on the other, is a real one and highly relevant to what happened in 2018. In the Senate, with its six-year terms, only a third of the chamber is up in any given election. It matters which third happens to be up. That means that what happened in the two preceding elections, six and 12 years earlier is important.

The class of Senate seats up in 2018 were previously up in 2006 and 2012, and a product of what happened in both of those elections. In 2006, as the increasingly unpopular Iraq War weighed heavily on President George W. Bush's poll numbers and hurt his party, a disastrous second-term, midterm election ensued. The GOP suffered a net loss of six Senate seats. In 2012, the contest between incumbent Barack Obama and Mitt Romney was relatively close, with a three percentage point margin, and Obama mounted a 50-state campaign, arguably the most sophisticated in history. And his party's candidates benefited, as Democrats picked up two more Senate seats.

As a result of these back-to-back, big years of 2006 and 2012 for Senate Democrats, Democrats would have gone into the 2018 with 25 seats up to just eight for Republicans, but each party had a special election seat up: Democrats with Tina Smith, who was appointed to fill the place of resigned Sen. Al Franken in Minnesota; Republicans with an appointee, Cindy Hyde-Smith, who took the Mississippi seat after the resignation of longtime incumbent Thad Cochran (he has since died), meaning that Democrats were defending 26 seats to nine for Republicans. Beyond simply greater numerical exposure, the fact that 10 of the 26 Senate Democrats up in 2018 represented states Donald Trump won just two years earlier constituted a real challenge. Conversely, of the nine Republican seats facing the voters, only one was in a state where Clinton prevailed. Still worse for Democrats, five of their 10 Senate seats up in Trump states were in states that Trump won by 19 points or more. The only GOP seat in a Clinton state was Dean Heller's in Nevada, where Clinton won by 2.4 points.

In the end, geography seemed to be destiny. Democrats lost four of their own seats, while claiming two from the GOP. Three of the five Democratic incumbents up in the states Trump carried by 19 points or more ended up losing: Joe Donnelly in Indiana, North Dakota's Heidi Heitkamp and Claire McCaskill in Missouri. Another Democratic incumbent, Bill Nelson, lost his seat in Florida, a state that Trump won by just one point. Democrats managed to hold onto scandal-damaged New Jersey's Robert Menendez, as well as the other two incumbents up in Trump +19-point states, Joe Manchin in West Virginia and Jon Tester of Montana.

At the same time, Democrats picked off two GOP seats, keeping their net loss to just a pair of seats, by beating Heller in Nevada and picking up the open Republican seat in Arizona, a state that Trump had carried by three and a half points. In the Tennessee open seat contest, GOP Rep. Marsha Blackburn beat former Democratic Gov. Phil Bredesen by an unexpectedly wide margin of almost 11 points while incumbent Ted Cruz beat back a spirited challenge from Rep. Beto O'Rourke by just 2.5 points.

One of the most interesting aspects of the 2018 Senate races was the crosscurrents at work. The political environment helped Democrats, but the map gave Republicans an advantage. These partially offsetting factors broke a two-decade pattern in Senate races. Jennifer Duffy, senior editor of the Cook Political Report and specialist on Senate and gubernatorial races, points out that in each election from 1998 through 2016, an average of 80 percent of the contests rated by the Cook Political Report as "Toss Ups" going into Election Day each election fell in the same direction. In 2016, Republicans won five out of seven (71 percent) Toss Up contests, eight out of nine in both 2014 and 2004 (89 percent) and six out of nine in 2002, while Democrats won eight out of 10 (80 percent) in both 2012 and 2008, five out of seven in 2010 (71 percent), seven out of nine in 2000 (78 percent) and six out of seven (86 percent) in 1998. But in 2018, Duffy points out that the Toss Up contests split more evenly. Republicans won five out of nine (56 percent), the only time in the last 11 elections that fewer than two-thirds broke in the same direction.

The UC-SD's Jacobson notes that five of the six Senate seats that changed parties in 2018 went for the party that won the state in 2016. Jacobson points out that 89 of the 100 senators now represent a state won by their respective party's presidential nominee in the last election, an all-time high. Perhaps geography is destiny.

Duffy argues that within the Senate, the institution will became even more ideologically polarized as a result of the 2018 election, with three of the least liberal Democrats in the Senate -- Donnelly, Heitkamp and McCaskill -- replaced by very conservative Republicans, businessman Mike Braun in Indiana, Rep. Kevin Cramer in North Dakota and Missouri Attorney General Josh Hawley. In the Tennessee open seat contest, one of the most centrist Republicans in the Senate and one of the most critical of President Trump, Bob Corker, was replaced by very conservative Rep. Marsha Blackburn, one of the President's strongest allies. As a result of the 2018 election, the center of gravity among Senate Democrats moved left while the midpoint of Republicans moved right.

2018 State Elections

Many people are surprised to learn that midterm elections have profound results for the president's party, even down-ballot in gubernatorial and state legislative races, contests for jobs not in proximity to the White House and dealing mostly with a different issue agenda.

Keep in mind that three-quarters (36) of our nation's governorships and four-fifths (82 percent) 6,066 of the nation's 7,383 state legislative seats are on the ballot in midterm, not presidential, election years. Worth remembering also is that 48 out of 50 states now have four-year gubernatorial terms. Only New Hampshire and Vermont still have two-year terms, both on the even-numbered cycles. New Jersey and Virginia have their gubernatorial elections in the odd-numbered years after presidential elections are held while Kentucky, Louisiana and Mississippi hold theirs in the odd-numbered years preceding a presidential election year. Regularly scheduled state legislative elections in these five states are also in odd-numbered years.

The stakes in the states are always high in midterm elections but the impressive GOP gains in the two Obama midterm elections of 2010 and 2014 created an exposure problem for Republicans as they had to defend all these newly acquired seats in what, in many states, was a challenging political environment. This is of no small importance given that congressional and legislative redistricting for the next decade will take place in 2021, after the 2020 census.

Also worth noting is that the increased nationalization of politics, a far more polarizing partisan environment including negative partisan (discussed previously), high energy levels on each side and the kind of population sorting that has become so important on the federal level is affecting state races as well. State elections are not immune to this trend.

2018 Gubernatorial Elections

When analyzing the Senate with its six-year terms, it is important to consider what happened six and 12 years before. For governors in the 48 states with four-year terms, it is important to consider what was going on four and eight years before. The two Obama midterm elections that had disastrous consequences for Democrats and resulted in huge gains for the GOP were a big factor in the layout of the 2018 gubernatorial playing field. Republicans headed into 2018 holding a total of 33 governorships to just 16 for Democrats, with one, Alaska held by an independent. On the ballot in 2018 were 36 governorships, with the GOP defending 26, Democrats just nine, plus the one independent in Alaska.

In the end, Democrats unseated Republican incumbents Bruce Rauner in Illinois and Scott Walker in Wisconsin, then picked up five GOP open seats in Kansas, Maine, Michigan, Nevada and New Mexico for a total of seven seats switching from Republicans to Democrats. No Democratic governorships flipped into GOP hands. Republicans were able to unseat the independent Bill Walker in Alaska. Democrats picked up seven governorships and Republicans had a net loss of six.

Republicans were able to hold onto six highly endangered governorships. Incumbent Kim Reynolds in Iowa survived a very strong challenge to win a full term in office (she was elevated from lieutenant governor after her predecessor, Terry Branstad, was named ambassador to China). The GOP also successfully defended five hotly contested open governorships in Florida, Georgia, Ohio, Oklahoma and South Dakota. It was unusual that the normally reliably Republican South Dakota had such a competitive race. Rep. Kristi Noem ended up winning by just over three percentage points, preserving the longest-running continuous string of GOP governors in the country, going back to

1979 (Oregon has had Democratic governors going back to 1985). When the dust settled after the 2018 elections, Republicans held a 27 to 23 advantage over Democrats in governorships. Given that all six of those Republican retentions were seen as toss-ups going into Election Day, it's not hard to see how this election could have been significantly worse for the GOP.

Worth noting: Three moderate Republican governors in a trio of the most Democratic states in the country were easily reelected, despite a challenging political environment -- Larry Hogan in Maryland, Massachusetts' Charlie Baker and Phil Scott in Vermont. For a time, the three had the highest job approval ratings of any governors of either party. Hogan, Baker and Scott successfully cracked the code of how a Republican can get elected and reelected, in even the bluest of states. By triangulating, charting a course roughly midway between where Republicans normally are (and where the legislators of their party may be) and Democrats, particularly Democrats in their state legislatures.

2018 State Legislative Elections

In 46 states, a total of 87 out of 99 state legislative chambers had regularly scheduled elections in 2018. With redistricting coming in 2021, the high stakes for the GOP in governorships existed in the legislatures as well. Republicans entered the 2018 election holding both state legislative chambers in 32 states, Democrats controlled both in 14. The other four were evenly split, counting Nebraska's nonpartisan, unicameral legislature as Republican, which it effectively is.

While Republicans had the benefit of friendly redistricting maps drawn in 2011 in many states, the political environment gave them concern about turnout. The chance that Republicans, whether complacent or disillusioned, might stay home, while energized Democrats might flock to the polls gave GOP strategists great angst. After the election, Republicans still held majorities in both chambers in 31 states, Democrats had both in 18, with one split. Democrats captured a total of six legislative chambers nationwide. In the Empire State, while Democrats technically had a majority in the Senate prior to the 2018, a rump group of Democrats teamed up with Republicans, giving the GOP effective control of the body. That situation reversed with strong gains for more loyal Democrats in November 2018. In terms of House chambers, the Minnesota House and both the House and Senate in New Hampshire changed into Democratic hands while Republicans wrested control the Alaska House, which previously had a Democratic majority and turned it into a power-sharing arrangement. In Connecticut, the state Senate had been evenly split with 18 seats for each party, but Democrats effectively controlled it thanks to holding the lieutenant governor's post. In the election, Democrats gained five seats.

In legislative bodies, if a party has a super-majority (in some states that is three-fifths of the seats, in others, two-thirds), it can override gubernatorial vetoes and often rule at will with little if any input from the minority party. According to the terrific resource, Ballotpedia, Democrats picked up supermajority status in California, Illinois and Oregon, bringing their total of supermajorities from four to seven states. Republicans lost their super-party status in North Carolina, taking them down one state from 17 to 16.

Just as in the gubernatorial races, Republicans were quite fortunate that they held their state legislative losses down. The GOP held onto the very endangered state Senate in Wisconsin and both the House and Senate chambers in Arizona. All three had been considered toss-ups before the election. Given the size of the Democratic wave, there were those before the election who speculated that Republicans might lose House chambers in Michigan, Minnesota and Pennsylvania, the Senate in Florida and both the House and Senate in Iowa.

Overall there was a 23 percent turnover in the 7,383 state legislative seats. And 28.7 percent of all state legislative seats are now held by women, an increase from 25.3 before the 2018 election.

Republicans began 2018 with complete control of state government -- that is, holding the governorship as well as both state legislative chambers -- in 26 states. Democrats had everything in seven states, while 17 had split control of some kind. After the election, Republicans still had total control in 23 states, a loss of three, Democrats had 14, a gain of seven, with 13 states having split control, a drop of four states. In this sense, Republicans went in dramatically over-exposed and came away with losses, but not as bad as it could have been.

Heading into the election it was thought that Republicans could lose as many as 450-500 state legislative seats and 10 or 11 governorships and state legislative chambers. In the end, Ballotpedia's count shows the GOP lost 295 seats, fewer than the 415 post-World War II average, Democrats gained 309, plus a half dozen governorships and legislative chambers – tough, but not nearly as bad as it could have been. Net changes in state legislative seats are a metric that should be used with caution.

In New Hampshire, for example, the 400 state House members had district populations averaging 3,291 in the 2010 census) while 31 members of the Texas state Senate had an average population of 811,147.

Why were the GOP losses less than expected? First, Republicans had spent the previous decade investing heavily into building state parties and fortifying their local political operations, while Democrats had spent considerably less. That GOP investment paid off when the political environment turned against them. While Democrats in 2018 did spend what for them was an unprecedented amount of money on state races and were better organized than they ever had been, they were playing catch up.

Republicans also benefited enormously from the legislative boundaries they were able to draw in 2011, thanks in no small part to their strong gains in the previous year's midterm elections.

Those lines helped mitigate the Democratic wave and minimize the damage. Another factor that the NCSL's Storey points to is that it wasn't just that the national economy was improving so much, but that state finances had bounced back. Voters saw the austerity that necessarily followed the 2008 recession and financial crisis was easing up. With Republicans in power in so many states, holding the governorships and state legislative chambers, they benefited from the improving financial conditions of those states.

2018 House

The brightest spot in the election for Democrats was in the House, with Democrats needing a 23-seat net gain to capture control. They ended up picking up 40 seats, with one last seat undecided. North Carolina's disputed open 9th District will be determined by a special election scheduled for Sept. 10, so the gain could edge up to 41.

Democrats won the national popular vote for the House by 8.4 percentage points, garnering 53 percent of the vote for the House to 45 percent for Republicans. Cook Political Report House Editor David Wasserman points out that Republicans won the national House vote by seven points in their banner years of 1994 and 2010, and Democrats won by eight points in their strong year of 2006.

While an eight-point national win is an impressive one and while the Democratic gain of 40 seats was on the high end of the 30-40 seat projection that the Cook Political Report forecast in the weeks before the election, the reality is that this could have been far worse for Republicans. The big national Democratic vote was somewhat mitigated by congressional district boundaries drawn in 2011, in the aftermath of their disastrous 2010 showing. Though the large number of GOP open seats worked against Republicans, many of the open GOP seats were in safely Republican districts.

Political gerrymandering, drawing Congressional and legislative districts in a way to benefit one candidate or party at the expense of another has been around since the earliest days of the republic. But with the increasingly hyper-partisan political environment creating a greater audacity among partisan redistricting artists, along with technological advances, the effectiveness of partisan gerrymandering has hit new levels. It is irrelevant whether the pens are wielded by Democrats or Republicans.

For much of this decade, the Republican majority in the House seemed impenetrable. As a result of huge GOP gains in the 2010 midterm elections, Republicans were in control of the redistricting process in 16 states with a total of 199 Congressional districts, drawing boundaries that definitely benefited their party, according to Wasserman. Democrats were in charge and drew lines designed to benefit their party in the four states where they could, a total of 40 districts. This effectively meant that only a very large political wave could endanger the GOP majority, a situation that could occur only in a midterm election with an unpopular Republican president. For most of this decade, and well into the 2018 election cycle, it looked like Republicans would likely hold onto their House majority. But as President Trump's approval ratings remained low and the election drew nearer, that majority became increasingly endangered.

Republican Congressional Gerrymanders	Democratic Congressional Gerrymanders
16 States (199 districts)	4 States (40 districts)
Alabama	Connecticut
Florida	Illinois
Georgia	Maryland
Michigan	Massachusetts
Mississippi	
Missouri	
Nebraska	
North Carolina	
Ohio	
Pennsylvania*	
South Carolina	
Tennessee	
Texas	
Utah	
Virginia	
Wisconsin	

*Plan struck down by Pennsylvania Supreme Court on Jan. 22, 2018; new map put into place Feb. 19, 2018.

Source: David Wasserman, The Cook Political Report

These maps constituted a wall, one that seemed likely to mitigate anything but a very large Democratic wave in 2018. The question was which was going to be stronger, the wave or the wall?

For what could be the first time in history, the political spotlight was on the House of Representatives. As the cycle unfolded, the Republican majority seemed in increasing jeopardy. The fight for the House became front and center with Democrats raising an unprecedented amount of money. Democratic candidates outspent their Republican rivals in 59 of the 75 most competitive House races, according to data compiled by OpenSecrets.org, in some cases by margins of two to one or even three to one, Wasserman points out.

While any party with an unpopular president should be concerned heading into a midterm election, there was one factor that proved decisive, even in states with maps carefully drawn to maximize Republican performance. It was in the suburban congressional districts where Republicans paid the price, losing seats they had held for decades in the suburbs of Atlanta, Dallas, Houston, Kansas City, Oklahoma City, Richmond and coastal South Carolina. These districts had one thing in common: substantial suburban populations, particularly ones with a high proportion of college graduates. If the theme of the 2016 election was the year of the angry, working-class white man, Wasserman suggests that 2018 was the year of the "fired-up female college graduate." This will be the first Congress in history with more than 100 women.

While Alexandria Ocasio-Cortez immediately became the most visible member of the freshman Democratic class after her primary upset of Rep. Joe Crowley in New York City, the more telling story of the election was the Democrats elected in those longtime, Sun Belt Republican districts (one in coastal South Carolina), as well as their near sweep winning 11 of New Jersey's 12 districts and picking up four Republican seats in Orange County California.

As David Wasserman explains, it was mostly a suburban revolt, Democrats winning high-income suburban districts by beating Republican incumbents like Mimi Walters (CA-45), Mike Coffman (CO-06), Peter Roskam (IL-06), Kevin Yoder (KS-03), Erik Paulsen (MN-03), Leonard Lance (NJ-07) and Barbara Comstock (VA-10), all by comfortable margins. In these kinds of districts, Democratic ads that these incumbents voted with President Trump "95 percent of the time" proved toxic. But Wasserman also points to well-funded Democrats who broke through in outer, middle-class suburbs that Trump carried by single digits, beating Randy Hultgren in Illinois' 14th, David Young in Iowa's 3rd, Mike Bishop in Michigan's 8th and an open seat in Michigan's 11th and incumbents Scott Taylor and Dave Brat in Virginia's 2nd and 7th, respectively. Underscoring the importance of Trump in this election, Wasserman points out that Democrats didn't win a single Republican seat where Trump cracked 55 percent of the vote in 2016. They fell short in Florida's 6th, Kansas' 2nd and Kentucky's 6th, despite multiple polls depicting competitive races. They also failed to hold onto two rural open seats in Minnesota (MN-01 and MN-08) and failed to knock off either Duncan Hunter or Chris Collins, both indicted GOP incumbents in very Republican districts, California's 50th and New York's 27th. Of the Republicans who survived in tough districts, they tended to be those who had established their own moderate reputations, Wasserman points out, before Trump took office. Members like Fred Upton (MI-06), John Katko (NY-24), Brian Fitzpatrick (PA-01) and Will Hurd (TX-23) all hung onto their seats by cultivating nonpartisan images a long time ago, much like the few younger, more moderate Democrats who hung on in 2010.

In 2015, UC-SD's Jacobson argued that the value of congressional incumbency on reelection, which had increased in the 1950s, 1960s and 1970s, began to decline in 2012 with the increased nationalization of congressional elections. Jacobson theorizes that traditional party loyalties weakened, or "decoupled" during that 1950s-1970s period, enabling members of Congress to establish their own "personal" relationship with voters and insulating them from the impact of national forces. Furthermore, the typical spending advantage made it even more difficult to unseat an incumbent. But starting in 2012, this nationalization of congressional voting reversed that trend. The "vote the party not the person" dynamic began to fade, national party spending and independent expenditures also worked to level the campaign spending field, eroding the financial advantage that incumbents used to enjoy.

Jacobson also reminds us that even apart from gerrymandering, there is a natural tendency for Democratic-tilting voters to concentrate in urban areas, in effect, "wasting votes," while Republican-oriented voters are more evenly spread out, more efficiently allocated, giving the GOP something of an advantage.

Role of Intensity

The last twist in the election cycle was the result of the fight over Court of Appeals Judge Brett Kavanaugh's nomination to the Supreme Court. Prior to the Kavanaugh fight in September, Republicans had an intensity problem. There is an old expression in politics that over the last month or two before an election, partisans "come home." Whether they had not been paying attention to the campaign or toying with the idea of either not voting or casting a ballot for the opposition party candidate, in the closing weeks of a campaign partisans tend to return to their respective corners. One thing that was unique about 2018 was that there wasn't much "coming home" for Democrats to do. They never left. Democrats had remained so angry about Trump's election that they had remained in an agitated state ever since November 2016. Conversely, Republicans seemed complacent. "In the minds of many Republicans, with Trump having proven the experts wrong, that polls had understated his strength in Michigan, Pennsylvania and Wisconsin in 2016, many Republicans seemed serenely confident that there was not really a problem in 2018."

Republicans seemed serenely confident that there was not really a problem in 2018. It got to the point that alarmed Republican National Committee officials in early September leaked the results of a national survey they had commissioned from Public Opinion Strategies to Bloomberg Business Week reporter Joshua Green showing that half of self-identified Republicans did not believe that Democrats were likely to win the House and that within that group, the 57 percent who described themselves as "strong Trump supporters" didn't believe that Democrats would take the House, 37 percent believed they would.

Other polls illuminated the challenge for many Republican voters. Polling conducted for NBC News and the Wall Street Journal by Democratic polling firm Hart Research and the same Republican polling firm that had done the RNC poll, Public Opinion Strategies, quantified the challenge that Republicans faced entering the fall campaign. All year, the NBC/WSJ polls had asked voters to assess their interest in the upcoming election on a scale of 1 to 10, with 9 and 10 representing the highest levels of interest. In the aggregated polls from January through August, while 63 percent of Democrats assigned their interest levels as 9 or 10, just 51 percent of Republicans did, a 12-point interest differential. Only 55 percent of people who voted for Trump two years earlier said they were 9s or 10s, while 64 percent of Clinton voters were.

The Kavanaugh fight changed all that. In some ways it was a "color enhancing event," making the reds redder and the blues bluer. Democrats were already motivated, so they couldn't get much more motivated. But Republicans sure could. The fight over Kavanaugh enhanced the normal "coming home" phenomenon. A late September NBC/WSJ poll showed that the 12-point January-August gap between the interest levels of the two parties had shrunk to just four points, 65 percent of Democrats as 9s or 10s, 61 percent of Republicans. The October poll also showed the gap was down to four points. In the final NBC/WSJ poll, the gap was down to a single point, 73 percent for Democrats, 72 percent for Republicans. Interest in the election had increased to the point that it far surpassed the numbers for previous midterms and was approaching presidential levels. This proved prescient and was corroborated by voter turnout, which was the highest for any midterm election since 1914. While some closure from Republicans "coming home" would have occurred anyway, I am convinced that the Kavanaugh fight put the coming-home dynamic on steroids and made a particular difference in some of those key Senate races in states that Trump had carried in 2016. The Kavanaugh fight highlighted Trump's placement of conservatives on the federal bench and the television coverage of the boisterous anti-Kavanaugh demonstrators in the halls of the Capitol and Senate Office Buildings effectively reminded Republicans and conservatives why they were Republicans and conservatives. Any Democrat who needed to win Republican votes to get reelected was suddenly in even more trouble than they thought, not only badly damaging incumbents like Donnelly in Indiana, McCaskill in Missouri and Heitkamp in North Dakota, but even former Tennessee Gov. Phil Bredesen, whose close Senate race quickly turned into a rout. Similarly, in the House, it may well have made a difference as well in keeping GOP losses in that chamber down. Wasserman also points out that 23 Republicans won their House races by less than five percentage points. Had the Kavanaugh fight not awoken the GOP base, he estimates that this could easily have been a 50-seat loss.

So for Republicans, while losing the House majority that they had held since 2010 was tough, the reality is that their House losses, indeed losses for governor and state legislature, could have been much worse, and their strong Senate performance had much more to do with how many and where each party had seats up in the 2018 political climate.

2020 ELECTIONS

2020 Presidential Race

University of Virginia political scientist Larry Sabato is fond of saying that "he who lives by the crystal ball ends up eating ground glass." Needless to say, there was a lot of ground glass ingested by political prognosticators in 2016, both in terms of the fight for the Republican presidential nomination as well as the general election outcome. A generous dose of humility never hurt anyone, but it is with this understanding that we look forward to the 2020 elections.

Since this essay in the 2018 Almanac began with the question, "If 2016 was the year when the political rulebook was thrown out, whether it will apply in 2017 and 2018 is a good question," a logical question might be whether 2020 will behave "normally," with the traditional political rules of the road, as we saw in the 2018 midterm elections, or "abnormally," with odd developments and unique plot twists unlike any before in U.S. politics, like 2016.

Is President Trump the Presumptive Favorite in this Race?

It is understandable that many looking ahead to 2020 begin with an assumption, among some a conviction, that President Trump will be reelected. In part this is premised on history: six of the eight post-World War II elected presidents successfully won reelection four years later, suggesting there is an incumbency advantage (political scientists have estimated the advantage to be about 2.5 percentage points). The other basis for this assumption seems to be based on Trump defying the experts and winning a race that few expected him to, particularly after the disclosure of the Access Hollywood tape of Trump engaged in a bawdy and sexually explicit conversation seemed to cinch the election for Hillary Clinton. That Trump proved the experts and polls wrong suggest to some that he can do it again, and win an Electoral College, if not a national popular vote victory.

Trump may pull off another win, but if he does, it would require overcoming some challenges at least as great as those faced by any of those eight previous elected presidents seeking reelection in the post-World War II-era. For the most part, Trump's presidential job approval ratings have trailed not just those of the six who were successful, but in many ways, the two that didn't win re-election. The Gallup Organization is the only polling entity that has been conducting polls measuring presidential job approval rating going back to just after World War II. In the two years of weekly Gallup tracking in 2017 and 2018 and monthly since the start of 2019, Trump has not only never had a job approval rating of 50 percent or higher, as every other president had, as of the end of May 2019 it had never exceeded 46 percent. He has averaged 40 percent since taking office, and his disapprovals consistently have run higher than his approvals, a situation pollsters refer to as "upside down," or "underwater."

To be sure, previous presidents had suffered bad months and several dropped below Trump's averages, but they all started with honeymoons and, during good times, enjoyed job approvals well over 50 percent and averages above 40 percent. Even in the second quarter of 2018, when real gross domestic product hit a blisteringly hot 4.2 percent growth rate, his approval rating reached 45 percent just one week that quarter, one of only five since taking office that his approval rating climbed as high as 46 percent.

Beyond the 108 Gallup Polls between the inauguration and mid-April 2019, in 12 ABC News/ Washington Post Polls, 17 by CBS News, 22 for CNN, 22 NBC News/Wall Street Journal Polls and 12 Pew Research Polls, all national samples, in not a single one was his job approval rating as high as his disapproval ratings. The same can be said for 23 polls for the Kaiser Family Foundation, 30 Marist University, 16 Monmouth University and 45 Quinnipiac polls, in which his approval numbers have been upside down. During that time Fox News conducted 24 national polls. In just one, taken in February 2017, did his approval ratings meet or exceed his disapprovals, with 48 percent approve, 47 percent disapprove, the month after taking office. In 330 out of 331 national polls by well-regarded pollsters, his approval numbers were upside down.

Beyond Trump's overall approval numbers is the intensity of the disapprove ratings. Since the earliest months of his presidency, for every person that strongly approved of his performance, there was between 1.4 and 2.0 who strongly disapproved; generally, between 70 and 75 percent either approved or disapproved strongly. Some of this is that Trump evokes strong emotions among both his fans and detractors. But there is also the high degree of ultra-partisanship that exists these days. The Gallup Organization has found an unprecedented difference between the approval and disapproval ratings of partisans on both ends of the spectrum. Previous first-term presidents have not been as enthusiastically embraced by members of their own party nor as thoroughly rejected by those in the opposition party, contributing to both the intensity and the lack of volatility. When the news is good, Trump's numbers move up very little, when the news is bad, they don't go down much either. Because they have changed so little in the first half of this term, there is good reason to believe that they may not deviate from that pattern much in the remaining half. If his approval ratings are consistently lower than his eight elected predecessors, both those reelected and those defeated, is that presumption still valid?

Trump fooled the experts and the polls once, he can do it again?

Then there is the argument that Trump fooled the experts and won in 2016, why can't he do that again? Can't we assume that there is a good chance that he replicates that result? Perhaps, but there are plenty of reasons why the 2016 outcome could be considered highly unusual, and unlikely to be repeated.

There have been 58 presidential elections in American history, and in 53 (91 percent), the candidate with the largest number of popular votes was elected. In one of the other five, in the 1824 election, Andrew Jackson won the popular vote, but no candidate received a majority in the Electoral College. The House elected John Quincy Adams president. In two other elections, one candidate won the popular vote by a percentage point or less, but another prevailed in the Electoral College: Grover Cleveland won the popular vote in 1888 by eight-tenths of a point, but Benjamin Harrison won the electoral vote; in 2000, Al Gore won the popular vote by a half-percentage point, about a half million votes, but George W. Bush won the electoral vote.

Just two of the 58 presidential elections, have had a candidate win the popular vote by two or more percentage points, but lose the Electoral College. In 2016, Hillary Clinton won the popular vote by 2.1 percentage points, 48.12 to 46.09 percent, but Donald Trump prevailed in the Electoral College, winning 30 states and 304 electoral votes while Clinton won 20 states (21 if you count D.C.) and 227 electoral votes (there were seven "faithless electors" who voted for other candidates, three from Washington state cast ballots for Collin Powell and another for Faith Spotted Eagle, two in Texas, one for John Kasich the other for Rand Paul, one in Hawaii voted for Bernie Sanders). This was the first time in 140 years that there had been a divergence of two points or more. In 1876 Samuel Tilden won more votes, but Rutherford B. Hayes won the electoral vote (and that under dubious circumstances).

Can we believe the polls?

One element in this "he did it once, he can do it again" argument is something that many have said: that "the polls were all wrong in 2016, maybe the polls are still wrong and will be in 2020 as well." First, the polls were not "all wrong." National polls showed Hillary Clinton ahead by a narrow margin, averaging a three-point lead in the RealClearPolitics.com average of major national polls going into Election Day, and she ended up winning the national popular vote, which is what national polls attempt to measure, by 2.1 percentage points. National polls do not attempt to project the outcome in any individual states. The national polls were actually a bit closer to the final outcome in 2016 than they had been in 2012 when the polls suggested that the Obama-Romney race would be a bit closer than the three-point final margin. National polls being a point or two off is not far off, and as previously discussed, in only one previous election had a candidate won the national popular vote by two or more percentage points and lost the Electoral College.

In terms of individual states, roughly 40 voted in precisely the direction widely anticipated, the way polls predicted. In a handful of others, Florida for example, a state that Obama won by a percentage point, it was expected to be very close and it was. Trump won by a percentage point.

There were just three states that were surprises: Michigan, Pennsylvania and Wisconsin, where in fact there were epic polling errors. Interestingly, the Clinton campaign didn't do traditional polling in those three states in the closing weeks, compounding the surprise. No alarm bells were sounding in the closing days of the campaign. Had the Clinton campaign taken measurements in those three states, it is not certain what they would have found as there were traditional polls conducted by pollsters in both parties in all three states on behalf of candidates for other offices that did not catch the upset in the making.

Some mistakenly attribute the polling challenge to the widespread and increasingly almost universal use of cell phones. But the truth is, high quality telephone polls by both parties and news organizations are already conducting a high percentage of their interviews with respondents who are on mobile phones. The biggest challenge for telephone surveys is a plummeting response rate. Now it is not uncommon for a pollster to attempt 100 calls in order to complete six interviews. Widespread use of caller ID and voice mail is making it very hard and extremely expensive to use telephone polling. The cost has been more in price and public confidence in the polls than quality of results.

At the same time, many argue that online polling, generally considered to be the wave of the future, has not yet been perfected. Some pollsters have had impressive results with very carefully supervised online polling, though in the hands of many pollsters, it is still a blunt and highly imperfect instrument, one that will certainly evolve and improve. Worth noting however is that polling, including traditional telephone surveys, performed very in 2018. There was not a single upset in any Senate or gubernatorial general election in the country, while the RealClearPolitics.com average of national polls gave Democrats an eight-point lead in the national vote for the House, and that average was off by only four-tenths of a percentage point. Some degree of skepticism in polling is healthy and justified, but to assume that the polls were or are all wrong seems highly unwarranted and, in many cases, a sign of denial.

Why the surprise?

This essay has already discussed the uniqueness of having two major party nominees of unparalleled levels of unfavorable ratings facing off against one another. There were also some notable mistakes by the Clinton campaign, beyond the abandonment in the closing weeks of individual state polling. Clinton was the first major party nominee since 1972 to not step foot in the state of Wisconsin, then unexpectedly lost the state by seven-tenths of a point. Prior to the election, Michigan Democrats complained of a lack of commitment of resources to their state. The lack of a strong voter turnout in Detroit undoubtedly made a difference in a state that their party lost by two-tenths of a percentage point. On a more strategic level, there was an assumption in the higher echelons of the Clinton campaign that the country had sufficiently changed that all they needed to do was get out the vote of those who had elected and reelected Obama, that persuading undecided voters and competing strong beyond urban and suburban areas was not necessary to win. That also can be called into question. Many Democrats attribute the loss of Pennsylvania to a failure to seriously contest the considerable space between the Philadelphia and Pittsburgh suburbs as a key factor in that state. As previously discussed, small town, rural and exurban and working-class white voters have and are trending away from Democrats and Trump and Republicans have effectively tapped into grievances felt by these groups. But to cede these groups entirely might not have been wise.

While some Democrats blame Clinton personally and her campaign for the loss, others want to put the blame squarely on Russian interference or then-FBI Director James Comey. In an election with 137 million voters and an outcome determined by fewer than 78,000 votes in three states, no doubt there are dozens of things that may well have made the difference, Russians and Comey being just two.

Whatever did take place and made a difference in Michigan, Pennsylvania and Wisconsin in 2016 did not seem to be at work in 2018. Democrats captured the governorships in Michigan and Wisconsin, the former winning an open seat, the latter upsetting incumbent Scott Walker, while holding onto the governorship of Pennsylvania. Democrats also held Senate seats in all three. In 2016 Trump prevailed in the three states by a total of just under 78,000 votes. In 2018, Democrats won the vote for the House in those three states with over 850,000 votes to spare, picking up two House seats in Michigan and three in Pennsylvania.

None of this is intended to question the legitimacy of Donald Trump's victory, but only to suggest that the circumstances of that win are so unusual, that assuming that something like that will happen again in 2020 might be a bit presumptuous.

The Bases and the Swing Voters.

A close examination of national polling suggests that roughly 35 percent of the vote is absolutely securely in the Trump camp, and it's hard to imagine any circumstances in which this base will not remain secure. As candidate Trump said during the campaign, he could shoot someone on Fifth Avenue and his base would stick with him. An equally adamant 45 percent seems to be locked into the opposition. Trump could find a cure for both cancer and the common cold, ensure peace and tranquility for eternity and eliminate all unemployment and this 45 percent would remain militantly opposed. That leaves about 20 percent up for grabs. Keeping in mind that a 2.1 percent popular vote edge for Clinton in 2016 was not sufficient to carry states with 270 electoral votes, though usually just a one-point plurality is enough, let's say that a Democrat needs to win the popular vote by three percentage points to be sure of winning an Electoral College majority. President Trump would still need to win between two-thirds and three-quarters of that 20 percent to stay within three points of a Democrat, a pretty tall order. While he has perfected the art of talking to his base of support, he seems unwilling or unable to reach or even talk to those beyond that base, those situated between his core support and the opposition camp. When U.S. unemployment hit a 49-year low in April 2019, Trump's approval rating barely moved.

A good question is how many of these 20 percent in the middle are truly conflicted, see both positive and negative things about Trump and are genuinely undecided, and how many just don't follow news or think much about politics until just before an election? Finally, how many are real voters who actually cast a ballot in 2014, 2016 or 2018?

Certainly, there are plenty of Republicans who would rather the president stay off Twitter, talk and behave differently, and disagree with him on various issues. But many of them have enjoyed the economic growth over the last two years, like their tax cuts, appreciate a less intrusive regulatory agenda and love the more conservative judges. Most may not be ecstatic about Trump and his table manners but politically speaking, remain on board, seeing the alternative as not a different Republican but instead an increasingly leftward-moving Democratic Party.

The 2020 presidential general election is quite likely to turn on three factors. In no particular order, the first is if there an element of Trump Fatigue among that quintile of voters in the middle, those that neither love nor reject him, and if so, how pervasive is it? Among some there seems to be a perception of chaos reigning through his administration, to others a question of competence, and still others about his temperament. This is not to suggest that this group turns against him en bloc as much as there could be a resistance to his ability to win between the two-thirds and three-quarters he needs to close enough in the popular vote to be within striking distance in states with 270 electoral votes.

Second, while the U.S. economy grew at an impressive rate during his first two years, real GDP growth of 2.2 percent in 2017 and 2.9 percent in 2018, as of spring 2019 the world economy is definitely slowing down and with it, likely the demand for U.S. exports will diminish.

Historically presidential elections have been much more closely linked to economic performance than midterm elections. But attitudes, both positive and negative, toward this Obama and Trump president seem less linked to the public perception of the economy. . In "Identity Politics," Sides, Tesler and Vavreck point out that "Obama's approval rating was also lower than expected given positive evaluations of the economy. Indeed, Obama was the only president since John F. Kennedy whose approval ratings did not increase alongside consumer sentiment. In fact, in Obama's case, the relationship between consumer sentiment and his approval rating was actually negative. If presidential approval were a function of consumer sentiment and nothing else, Obama should have been more popular than he was---approximately 5 percentage points more popular than in the third quarter of 2016." Since "Identity Politics" was published, it would seem that the de-linkage has continued under Trump, that his approval ratings have not tracked with either the economy itself or with consumer sentiment. His approval ratings certainly did not move up that much during the second quarter of 2018 when GDP was growing at a blistering 4.2 percent rate, so perhaps a slowdown wouldn't hurt it much

In the past, while the level of economic growth was important, the trend line was even more critical. If the trend is pointing upward, voters are more likely to feel optimistic and hopeful, which is helpful to a sitting president. If the trendline is pointing more downward, voters feeling pessimistic or just concerned about the economy, that can be a real problem for a president. How is their personal economy doing? What happened in the first two years of a president's term is ancient history. How are things now?

Though real GDP was improving during Obama's second term, from 1.8 in 2013, 2.5 percent in 2014 and 2.9 percent in 2015, during 2016, the year of the election, growth slumped to 1.6 percent, with the party holding the White House losing the presidency, possibly a factor though obviously not the only factor. In President Trump's first two years, the economy picked up to 2.2 percent for 2017 and 2.9 percent in 2018, but the hot 4.2 percent growth rate of the 2nd quarter of 2018 dipped to a still impressive 3.4 percent in the 3rd quarter, then dropped again to 2.2 percent in the 4th 1uarter of 2018. The Commerce Department's Bureau of Economic Analysis first estimate for the 1st Quarter of 2019, released on April 26, was 3.2 percent. Around Labor Day of 2020, when the general election campaign unofficially kicks off, will real GDP be growing at closer to the 2.9 percent level of 2018 or 1.6 percent, the level in 2016 when Democrats were losing the presidency in 2016 (the 3rd quarter, leading into the election quarter was 1.9 percent, the 4th quarter, the quarter in which the election was held, was 1.8 percent)? Will the linkage be return, or will the level and direction of the economy be subordinate to identity and tribal politics, and of course, partisanship?

For President Trump, winning between two-thirds and three-quarters of that fifth in the middle is a pretty tall order. If the economy is slowing, that will make it a more daunting task, no matter what happened in his first two years in office.

A third factor is who Democrats will nominate for president. Do Democrats choose someone who is an acceptable alternative or do they nominate someone who is as or more polarizing than President Trump? Is the alternative to Trump offered by Democrats considered a greater or lesser risk? Just as investment advisors seek to ascertain the risk tolerance of new clients, Democrats have to decide what their risk tolerance level is, a more delicate way of asking, how self-indulgent do they want to be?

Considering that Trump's approval rating among Democrats typically runs in single digits and attitudes toward him among Democrats and liberals could hardly be more contemptuous, it would seem that only an asteroid hitting and destroying Earth would be considered worse to them than Trump's reelection. The desire among Democrats is incredibly intense, and there seems to be little desire in the party to do anything or nominate anyone who would seem to have a poor chance of winning. But then again, we are talking about Democrats here and, as former President Obama has observed, their party has been known to form circular firing squads before.

An age-old question within both parties is whether it is better to nominate someone who can energize the party base and maximize base turnout, or to pick someone who can reach into the middle, winning a disproportionate share of the swing voters not loyal to either party? My own view is that just as people have to learn to walk and chew gum at the same time, this should not be an either/or question. A party should nominate someone who can do both, who can row on both sides of the boat.

There is no doubt that President Trump is the single most unifying force in the Democratic Party. My Cook Political Report colleague Amy Walker argues that this year Democrats may have preferences but few attachments, there is very little "my way or the highway" resistance to any alternatives, certainly not as much as was seen in 2016 when there were very strong elements within both the Clinton and Sanders camps resisting the idea of the other as nominee.

On a related note, while electability is rarely a primary factor in presidential primary voter decision-making, Democratic pollster Geoff Garin asks whether "unelectability" might be. If a Democratic voter is absolutely committed to trying to beat Trump, if they suspected that their first choice for the party's nomination might not be as strong as a second or third choice, might that affect their vote? While Sanders backers might say that the electability argument made for Clinton obviously didn't play out as some had thought, the animus toward Trump is so great, it could be that at least the perception of electability or unelectability could for once be key.

Who are the Democrats?

The Democratic Party is obviously more progressive today than it was during Bill Clinton's presidency. Some of the shift to the left in the Democratic Party is due to the departure of the non-college whites from the party; they had been the most conservative bloc. The center of gravity of the party subsequently shifted left. It is no accident that the centrist, pro-business Democratic Leadership Council he helped found no longer exists. But just how far to the left has the Democratic Party actually moved? In the aftermath of the 2018 election, Republicans and Trump backers have worked overtime to establish freshmen Reps. Alexandria Ocasio-Cortez (D-N.Y.), Rashida Tlaib (D-Mich.) and Ilhan Omar (D-Minn.), Sens. Bernie Sanders and Elizabeth Warren as the collective faces of the Democratic Party. Democratic socialism, single-payer health insurance, "Medicare for All" and a "Green New Deal" are portrayed as the party platform. At one point in early 2019, Fox News and Fox Business mentioned Ocasio-Cortez's name on air an average of 75 times per day, and in a February 2019 Gallup Poll, more Republicans were familiar enough to have an opinion of her than Democrats. Is AOC the face of the Democratic Party or what is portrayed as the face of the party?

Democratic leaders privately acknowledge that to the extent that the GOP is allowed to succeed in painting that picture, they will deserve to lose. They argue that an alternative face of the party should be the Democrats who unseated Republicans in suburban districts long held by the GOP outside of Atlanta, Dallas, Houston, Kansas City, Richmond, in Oklahoma City and across New Jersey, Pennsylvania, and in Orange County California. Democrats point to the 10 of their freshman House members elected who have either military or intelligence backgrounds, as more representative face of the new Democratic Congress. But this is a struggle that will play out over the next year and for once, many in the media are echoing the messages that Republicans are seeking to project. To the extent that any party is able to paint a pejorative face on the other, that will likely win. But who Democrats end up nominating will also go a long way in determining what direction the party is going and what face they are projecting.

The 2020 Democratic Presidential Nomination

While it is true that early presidential race polls are mostly about name recognition and often overstate the lead for better known, more established candidates, these polls are not without meaning. Some presidential candidates catch the eye of party activists and voters early on and gain traction, others are never able to draw that attention or get the footing needed to effectively compete for the nomination. Polls are not determinative, but when combined with money, crowd sizes and now social media hits, they are important metrics in determining who really is contending for the party nomination, and who is wasting their time.

There are as many ways to look at the unfolding Democratic nomination contest as there are people watching it. For decades, the Dean of the Washington political press corps was the late David Broder of the Washington Post. Broder's long-time protégé at the Post was Dan Balz, who has now assumed the role that Broder once played, the wise one. In a 2018 year-end analysis, looking ahead to 2020, Balz wrote that, "most recent Democratic nominating contests have been binary choices featuring a mainstream liberal versus a progressive or insurgent. In 2008, though there were others in the field, the campaign always was, fundamentally, one that pitted then-Sen. Obama against then-Sen. Clinton. That model applied to 2016 as well, a race between Clinton and Sen. Bernie Sanders (I-Vt.) despite the presence of others."

Balz continued, "that was true in 2000 as well, when then-vice president Al Gore took the establishment lane and former senator Bill Bradley ran as a progressive reformer. In 2004, though others figured into some of the early maneuvering, the contest became largely between then-senator John F. Kerry, the establishment choice, and former Vermont governor Howard Dean, the antiwar insurgent."

Balz concluded that, "There will be nothing binary about the battle that is about to unfold, at least not for many months. The field will be bigger than it has been in many cycles, bigger likely even than 1992 or 1988. There are two dozen or more names on handicapping charts and while many of them will not enter the race, the field could number in double digits by the time everyone makes their decisions." By June 1, there were 23 Democrats running.

It's helpful to have a framework, a way to look at the race, a theory of the case, but it is also important to remember that real people don't fit into tidy boxes. There are people who voted for Obama in 2008 or 2012, then for Trump in 2016, or cast a ballot for Sanders in the Democratic primary but then for Trump in the general election.

But there is some value in trying to organize thinking about how a race is shaping up. One approach is to first sort Democrats into two groups: the first, insurgent candidates, those seeking to disrupt the status quo. The second, the establishment, those running but fundamentally not rejecting the party's status quo. Of the major candidates, Sens. Bernie Sanders and Elizabeth Warren are the insurgent/disruption candidates, the rest of the major candidates are more or less establishment in their broad orientation. The establishment candidates can then be segmented into three relatively distinct groups: conventional, aspirational/inspirational and identity.

Along with former Vice President Joe Biden, the following can be seen as more conventional, establishment candidates: Sens. Michael Bennet and Amy Klobuchar, Governors Steve Bullock and Jay Inslee, former Gov. John Hickenlooper, Reps. Seth Moulton, Tim Ryan, Eric Swalwell, former Rep. John Delaney and New York City Mayor Bill de Blasio. They are running as alternatives to the chaos and strife that surround Donald Trump's presidency.

The second group might be inspirational and aspirational establishment candidates, ones pushing charisma and force of personality: South Bend Mayor Pete Buttigieg and former Rep. Beto O'Rourke are certainly in that group, a case can be made that Sen. Cory Booker is in this camp but as of this writing, hadn't quite made it yet.

The third element of establishment candidates are those who are identity-driven. Not to disparage or demean them in any way, all have sterling credentials, but for Sens. Cory Booker, Kirsten Gillibrand and Kamala Harris and former HUD Secretary Julian Castro, their gender and/or ethnicity are part of the essence of their appeal. Gillibrand, Klobuchar and Warren are all women, but only Gillibrand has made gender a central theme of her campaign. Booker, Gillibrand and Castro fit more cleanly into this box, Harris leverages her former post of attorney general in California more than the others, as if to put a foot in one of the other establishment camps.

It would be foolhardy to try to handicap a presidential nomination a year before the national convention. At the beginning of the summer of 2019, a plausible guess, but not a prediction, would be that Biden very likely has one of the Final Four slots and that either Bernie Sanders or Elizabeth Warren, but not both, would occupy a second. There is clearly sufficient support among Democrats to support one pure progressive, but it seems unlikely that there are sufficient numbers to grab two of the four positions. Watch for a Sanders-Warren battle for progressive supremacy, a good clue might be the primary in New Hampshire, in the backyards of both Sanders' Vermont and Warren's Massachusetts. The victor there would likely have the edge. Given that California is the largest state with the biggest block of delegates, that African-Americans make up a quarter of the Democratic primary vote nationwide and that roughly 60 percent of those voting in primaries are women, Harris would seem to have an inside track on the third position. That leaves the fourth and remaining slot as the wild card position, the one most contested. Arguably, Buttigieg has the edge a year out, as the first LGBTQ major party candidate; one could argue that he is in the identity lane as well. Buttigieg is a historic, groundbreaking candidate, just as Obama was as the first African-American major party nominee and Hillary Clinton the first woman. Nobody knows what share of the national Democratic primary vote is made up of LGBTQ voters. But with estimates of between five and ten percent of the overall population, it is not an inconsequential share of Democrats. Before the end of the primaries and the July 2020 convention, so much can and will happen. But these would seem to be decent guesses. What happened in the 2016 GOP nomination contest and the general election should remind us of that.

The 2020 Presidential General Election

The 2020 election may well be a continuation of the clash over cultural issues, the changing demography, economy and the geographic struggle between urban and suburban America, on the one hand, and small town, and rural and exurban America on the other. But it also could simply be a referendum on President Trump and his issue agenda and unorthodox style, or a choice of two vastly different visions of the county. It's a good bet that Republicans may favor the former, with a strong dose of portraying his opposition as proponents of democratic socialism. Democrats would probably prefer to keep it a referendum.

The Big Ten States

Where will the general election be settled? In 2016 the presidency was effectively settled by Michigan, Pennsylvania and Wisconsin. But Clinton's margins in New Hampshire and Minnesota were so small that they could easily have been the story as well. In terms of the two-party vote, factoring out all votes cast for independent candidates, there were 10 states settled by less than two points, six won by Trump: Michigan (.1 percent), Pennsylvania and Wisconsin (each .4 percent), Florida (.6 percent), Arizona and North Carolina (each 1.9 percent); four won by Clinton, New Hampshire (.2 percent, Minnesota (.8 percent), Nevada (1.3 percent) and Maine (1.6 percent). These should be the first 10 states to watch in the fall of 2020, and some might want to add two Clinton states, Colorado (2.7 percent) and Virginia (2.8 percent) or Georgia (2.7 percent), a Trump state, to come up with a Baker's Dozen of states to keep an eye on.

2020 House Elections

Republicans will need a net gain of 18 seats to capture a bare 218-seat majority in the House, or 19 should Democrats win the special election for the remaining unsettled seat in the House, in North Carolina's 9th District. With presidential voting a strong factor in House and Senate election outcomes, the fact that Democrats have 31 seats in districts that Trump carried in 2016, with just three Republicans left in districts that Clinton won should give Republicans some hope to win back the majority they lost in 2018.

The major factors in determining how a party will do in House elections are exposure, the political climate, recruiting and turnout. In terms of exposure, the larger number of seats a party has up, the more exposure they have, where those seats are, in what kind of districts and what are the partisan voting patterns in those districts. Particularly important is the number of open seats, with no incumbent running for re-election in competitive districts. The second factor is the political climate. Is the political environment favorable or unfavorable to a party, whether a party enjoy tailwinds or headwinds, is the incumbent president popular or unpopular is one bell-weather. With American politics getting increasingly nationalized, this is an increasingly important factor. Closely related is the third factor, recruiting and retention. A strong political environment for a party usually makes it easier to retain incumbents -- minimizing open seats -- and to recruit strong non-incumbents to challenge opposition party incumbents or for open seats. Finally, there is turnout, which party has a more motivated base, which has an advantage in intensity.

Cook Political Report House Editor David Wasserman points out that Democrats have history on their side. Control of the House has not flipped in consecutive elections since 1954 and has not changed hands in a presidential election year since 1952. Wasserman also points out that Democrats have gained House seats in five of the last six presidential election years, the exception being 2004 when newly drawn maps in Texas boosted GOP fortunes in that state.

As discussed earlier, the 2011 redistricting benefited Republicans enormously over this decade but it seemed to come unraveled in 2018. President Trump was a major liability for his party in the House in 2018 and unless his approval ratings improve considerably, it would seem hard for his party to score significant gains.

At a time when the political process seems awash in cash with a law of diminishing returns seemingly applying to political campaigns as well, one party having more money is usually not as big of an advantage as many people would expect, but it may well have been a factor in 2018 and would be something to watch in 2020 as well.

One historical pattern worth watching for is whether there is a large number of House retirements in 2020, and if they are disproportionately Republican. In the election immediately after a party loses control of the House, they tend to have a lot of retirements, while a party that has been in the minority and moves into majority status usually has few.

In the recent past, when the balance of power has shifted, the minority party has struggled to get some members to run again. In the 1994 GOP sweep, Democrats saw 24 retirements; two years later they saw the same number again. In 2008, two years after Democrats took back control, Republican retirements spiked to 24 as Democrats saw only three members not run again. So one factor to watch in 2020 is whether Republicans will have many more retirements than Democrats and if so, how many are in competitive districts.

2020 Senate Elections

The Republican net gain of two Senate seats in 2018 lifted the GOP from 51 to 53 seats, Democrats down from 49 to 47 seats. Unlike the 2018 election when Democrats had 26 seats up and at risk, to just nine for Republicans, in 2020, it's almost the reverse, Republicans have 22 seats up, Democrats 12. But while Senate Republicans have greater numerical exposure than Democrats, none of their seats up in 2020 are nearly as vulnerable as at least five of the Democrats up in 2018: Joe Donnelly (Indiana), Heidi Heitkamp (North Dakota), Joe Manchin (West Virginia), Claire McCaskill (Missouri) or Jon Tester (Montana). All had to run in states that Trump had won two years earlier by 19 points or more. That is not to say that Democrats don't have targets, and some chance to capture the majority they lost in 2014, but none appear to face the magnitude of the challenge that those Democrats faced in 2018. In fact, while the numbers put Republicans mostly on the defensive, the single most vulnerable Senate incumbent up is a Democrat, Doug Jones in Alabama.

To recapture in 2020 the majority that Democrats lost in Obama's second-term, midterm election in 2014, the party would have to score a net gain of three seats if they win the presidential race and a Democratic vice president could break a 50-50 tie in their favor, or a four-seat gain if they are unsuccessful in their attempt to win the White House. The Senate subplot is that Democrats know that even though they seem to have an advantage in holding onto their House majority and that Trump's low job approval ratings suggest that he might be an underdog for reelection, that as long as Republicans have a Senate majority, there is a real limit to what Democrats could accomplish. Conversely for Republicans, with the House not looking good and their hold on the White House in serious jeopardy, the Senate is effectively their firewall, what could be the only thing standing in the way of total Democratic control of both ends of Pennsylvania Avenue. It doesn't take much of an imagination to realize that these are going to be the talking points to donors for both Senate Majority Leader Mitch McConnell and Minority Leader Chuck Schumer as they try to raise money for the 2020 Senate elections.

The increasingly partisan voting behavior seen in recent years has made it clear that the single most important factor in Senate and House races is not incumbency but how that state or district voted in the most recent presidential election. As cited previously, University of California-San Diego political scientist Gary Jacobson's observation that five of the six Senate seats that changed parties in 2018 fell to the party that won the state in 2016, and that now, 89 of 100 Senators represent a state won by their respective party's presidential nominee in the last election, an all-time high.

Democrats are likely to target six Republican-held seats, starting with two states that were won by Clinton in 2018, freshman Cory Gardner in Colorado, a state Clinton carried by five points and Susan Collins, who is seeking a fifth term in Maine, a state where Clinton prevailed by three points. Then come the five in states Trump won by single digits: Iowa's Joni Ernst (Trump +9), appointed Sen. Martha McSally in Arizona (Trump +3.5), freshmen Thom Tillis in North Carolina (Trump + 3.7 points) and David Perdue in Georgia (Trump +5), plus John Cornyn (Trump +9), in the Lone Star State that featured one of the closest Senate races in 2018.

Republicans will be defending at least two open seats, Kansas (Trump +21), where Pat Roberts is retiring, and Tennessee (Trump +26), where Lamar Alexander is retiring. But given the tilt in those states, both would be considerably more difficult for Democrats to win than the half-dozen previously mentioned. No doubt there will be many Democrats pushing for a challenge to Senate Majority Leader Mitch McConnell in Kentucky. But given that Trump won the state by 30 points, it would be a contest driven more by spite than real opportunity.

Alabama's (Trump +28) Doug Jones is the undisputed most vulnerable Senate Democratic incumbent. The only other seemingly plausible targets for Republicans to go after are two freshman Democrats, Tina Smith in Minnesota (Clinton +1.5), Gary Peters (Trump +.2), plus Jeanne Shaheen, who is seeking a third-term in New Hampshire (Clinton +.4). More of a longshot is an open seat in New Mexico (Clinton +8), where Tom Udall is retiring.

Keep in mind that incumbency means far less than it used to. The strong relationship between presidential voting and Senate race outcomes, at least in this era of hyper-partisanship, is of paramount importance. Whether the Republican majority in the Senate is truly in doubt in 2020 will depend on the political climate, the strength of the two national tickets, retirements and candidate recruitment.

2019-2020 State Elections

With three-quarters of the gubernatorial and four-fifths of the state legislative seats on the ballot in midterms and just New Hampshire and Vermont with two-year gubernatorial terms, presidential election cycles are considerably quieter for state elections, though Kentucky, Louisiana and Mississippi have theirs in 2019. These will be the last state elections before the pivotal 2021 congressional and state legislative redistricting take place, with huge implications for the next decade.

2019-2020 Gubernatorial Elections

Kentucky, Louisiana and Mississippi have their gubernatorial races in 2019. Republicans are defending Kentucky incumbent Matt Bevin and an open governorship in Mississippi, while Democrats are defending Louisiana incumbent John Bel Edwards. For 2020, Democrats have five governorships up, but only Montana is term limited thus necessarily open. Republicans have nine gubernatorial seats up.

Democrats are defending two governorships in states that Trump won by about 20 points, Edwards in Louisiana and the open governorship in Montana. A second incumbent Democrat, Roy Cooper, is up in North Carolina, a state Trump carried by just over 3.5 points but will likely be a battleground in 2020. One Republican incumbent, Chris Sununu, is up in New Hampshire, a state Clinton won, though by only .4 of a point.

2019-2020 State Legislative Elections

As in the gubernatorial races, this is a lighter cycle in state legislative races. For 2019, the action is in Virginia, where the Republican majorities in both the Senate and House are very tight; Republicans hold a single seat majority in each chamber, with control very much in question. Scandals in Virginia involving both the governor and lieutenant governor have obviously thrown Virginia Democrats into disarray, it remains to be seen whether former Gov. Terry McAuliffe will be able to fill the void in terms of fundraising and organizing. In 2020, the National Conference of State Legislatures' Tim Storey counts the state Senate chambers in play in Colorado, Florida, Maine and Minnesota, the House chamber in Iowa and both chambers in Arizona, Michigan and New Hampshire in play. He adds that the Pennsylvania House and Nevada Senate could become competitive as well.

Impact on 2021 Reapportionment

The redistricting process is getting far more attention than ever. Ballot initiatives passed in 2018 will attempt to make the process less partisan in Colorado, Michigan, Ohio and Utah. But before redistricting comes reapportionment, the determination of how many House seats each state will have for the next decade based upon the results of the 2020 census. Based on current populations from Election Data Services, David Wasserman sees Texas in line to pick up three seats after the 2021 reapportionment, Florida gaining two seats while Arizona, Colorado, Montana, North Carolina and Oregon appear in line to gain one each.

New York seems likely to lose two seats while Alabama, Illinois, Michigan, Minnesota, Ohio, Pennsylvania, Rhode Island and West Virginia appear likely to lose one each. Minnesota seems closest to the edge. Wasserman believes it is possible that California could lose a seat for the first time in its history. In effect, California and Minnesota are competing to hang onto a seat, though Illinois could possibly lose two instead of just one. It all depends upon late decade population growth (or decline) and how the count goes.

REALIGNMENT

We are now seeing something of a realignment taking place in American politics, simultaneous shifts in opposite directions. We see a clear trend among whites with less than four-year college degrees trending away from the Democratic Party and toward the GOP, voters in small town and rural America are trending in the same direction, in each case this is even more true with men, but applicable to women as well. Non-college whites in the South abandoned Democrats some time ago. But outside of the South, particularly in manufacturing areas, the trend away from Democrats toward Republicans accelerated more recently. White evangelicals have now become virtually a no-fly zone for Democrats. At the same time, we are seeing equally clear movement among whites with college degrees, particularly in suburban areas and most specifically women, moving away from Republicans and toward Democrats. The numbers among younger voters are similarly trending toward Democrats, an ominous trend for Republicans if it goes unchecked. These are trends that began before President Trump was elected but have intensified since he took office. The 2020 elections will be very interesting to see if these trends continue and whether they intensify.

In 2014, we saw the lowest midterm election turnout since 1942, but in 2018, it was the highest since 1914 -- something that Emory University political scientist Alan I. Abramowitz suggests was a surge in political engagement that was driven by three factors: increasingly nationalized congressional elections, an intensity of opinions held by voters, and Trump seemed to do everything he could to make the election a referendum on his own performance, something that in the House was extremely detrimental to his party. What does this mean for 2020?

CONCLUSION

Major League Baseball catcher and manager Yogi Berra famously said, "it's tough to make predictions, especially about the future." In terms of elections, the fact that we are talking about anticipating human behavior makes it particularly challenging. Then, factor in the unusually tumultuous nature of American politics over the last few years, and things become particularly confounding. There will be a long campaign between the summer of 2019, when this book will hit bookstores and doorsteps, and the two major party conventions a year later and the Labor Day to Election Day general election sprint. Hundreds of events, retirements and developments that can't possibly be expected will likely be decisive. Even with the factors that today seem likely to be important, it's impossible to know how much weight to put on each factor. That's why politics is so fascinating and frustrating, and why so many of us love it. We hope this 2020 Almanac of American Politics will be a useful guide to this wild ride we have ahead of us.

***

In 1972, not quite 50 years ago, Michael Barone, Grant Ujifusa and Doug Matthews had the foresight to write and publish the first edition of the Almanac of American Politics, a book that has become an institution in American politics. What a contribution these three visionaries have made to our understanding of politics on both a macro and a micro level. Everyone who continues to use and rely upon The Almanac of American Politics owes a debt of gratitude to them and more recently to Rich Cohen, who quarterbacks this unique book, truly a mammoth undertaking. Rich is to the Almanac what Tom Brady is to the New England Patriots, an appropriate comparison given that Massachusetts happens to be Rich's home state. In 2015, Joel Poznansky, then president of Columbia Books, made a new home for the Almanac. More recently, his successor, Brittany Carter, has embraced it. Both are to be commended for keeping this vital institution alive as it approaches the beginning of its second half-century. With the change and uncertainty in American politics today, some things become even more important. The Almanac of American Politics is one of those things.

Congress: The Polarization Deepens

By Richard Cohen

In both the Senate and House, the 2018 election results were another step in the deepening polarization of national politics. Because of the structural differences between the two chambers, that pattern has had some contrasting results. But the bottom line in each case has been similar — a decline in the battlefield of competitive campaigns, which has taken on alarming dimensions.

Each party has become increasingly entrenched in its separate geographic and demographic strongholds. As a corollary, neither party has had comfortable control in either the House or Senate — nor the immediate likelihood of gaining such control. Because the majority in each chamber has become so ephemeral in recent years, the relatively few competitive campaigns in each cycle have had disproportionate impact in shaping the frequent shifts in party control and the relatively slim majorities of each party.

These recent trends surely have some limitations. They have been affected by additional factors such as redistricting in the House, plus the impact of the six-year term and the influence of less-populated states in the Senate.

Some seats have remained competitive, of course. In the House in 2018, 44 seats switched party control — as a 23-seat Republican majority became an 18-seat Democratic majority. Quite likely, many of those seats will be in play in 2020. In the Senate, five incumbents were defeated and a sixth seat switched party control, as Republicans scored a net two-seat gain. As with the House, partisan control of the Senate will be up for grabs in 2020 — though, perhaps barely. In each case, however, those incremental shifts have been outweighed by the broader entrenchment.

One dramatic way to demonstrate the trends is with the use of maps. The following three maps show: 22 states with two Republican senators, 19 states with two Democratic senators, and nine states with one senator from each party, as of January 2019. For these maps, the Independent Senators from Maine and Vermont are included with the Democrats, with whose Senate caucus they affiliate.

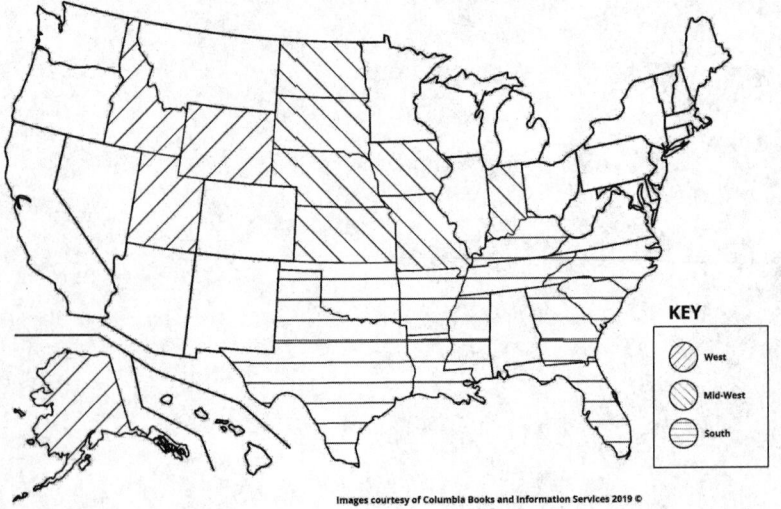

KEY

West

Mid-West

South

Images courtesy of Columbia Books and Information Services 2019 ©

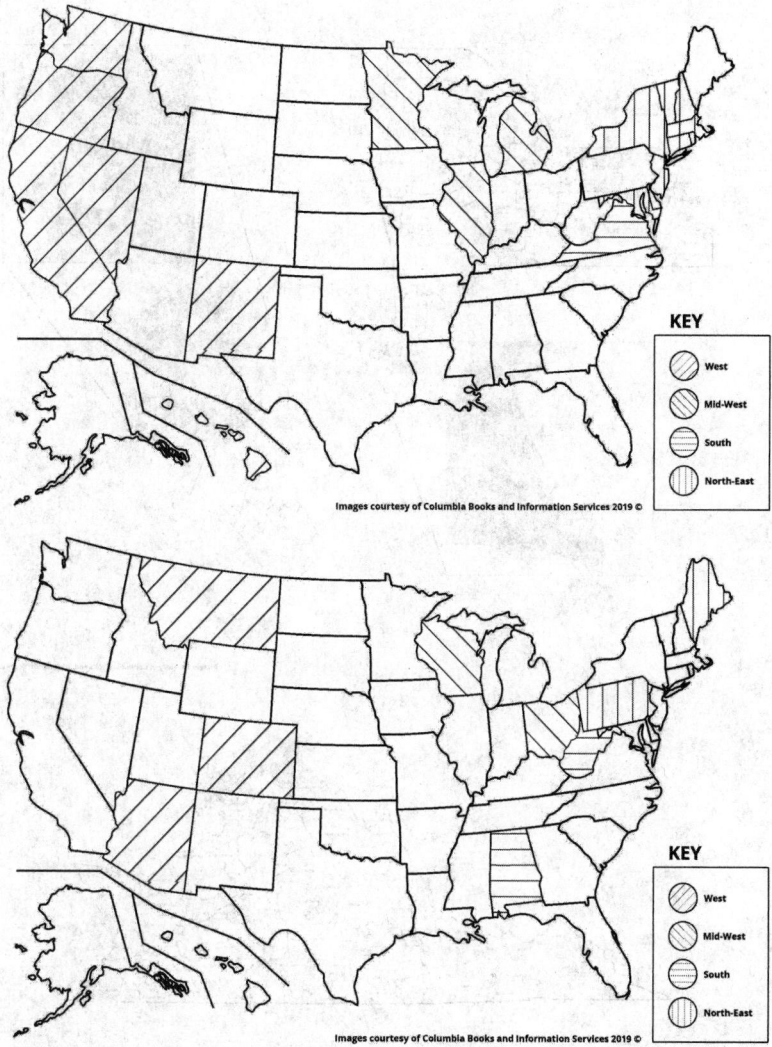

Images courtesy of Columbia Books and Information Services 2019 ©

The patterns are obvious. Senate Democrats are centered in two large and mostly contiguous blocks -- in the Northeast and the West — plus three states that surround the Great Lakes. Senate Republicans control the South and the Great Plains. The nine swing states are scattered throughout the four regions, though they are chiefly in the Great Lakes and Mountain West regions.

Next, consider the following maps of five metro areas with the nation's largest number of House seats. From east to west, they are: New York/northern New Jersey; Maryland/northern Virginia; Chicagoland; the San Francisco Bay Area; and Los Angeles/Orange/San Diego counties along the Pacific Coast.

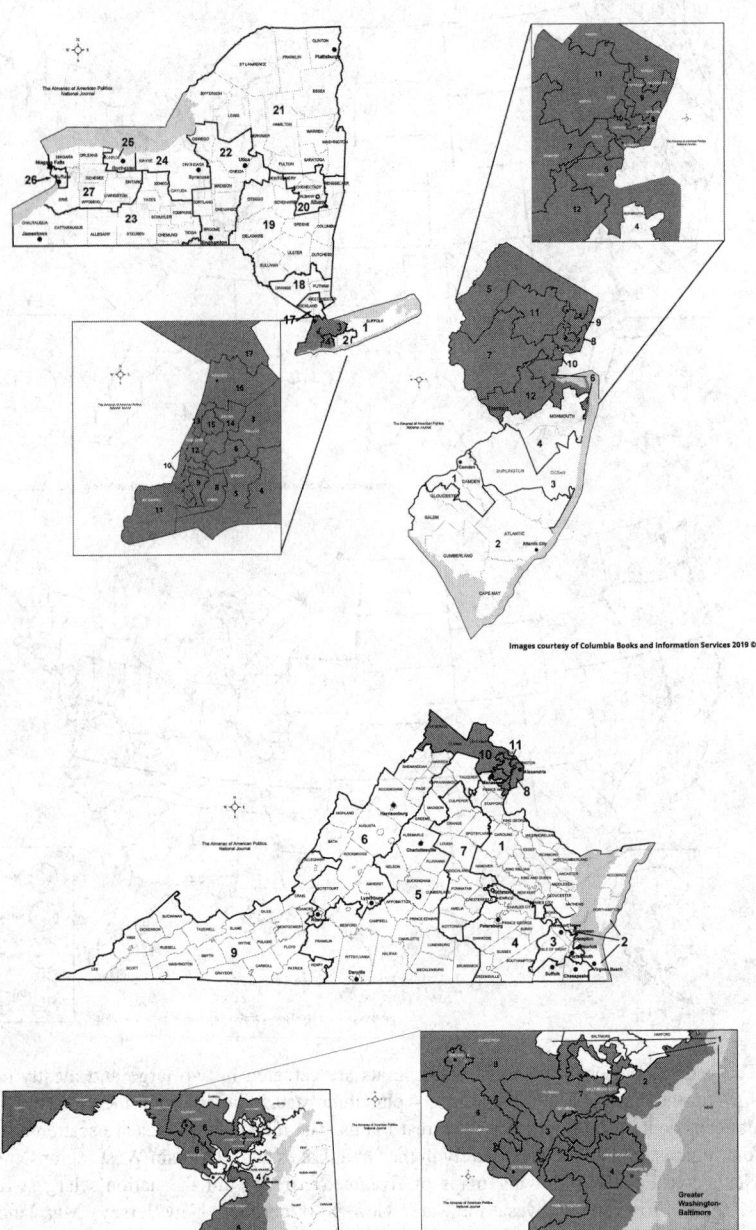

Images courtesy of Columbia Books and Information Services 2019 ©

Images courtesy of Columbia Books and Information Services 2019 ©

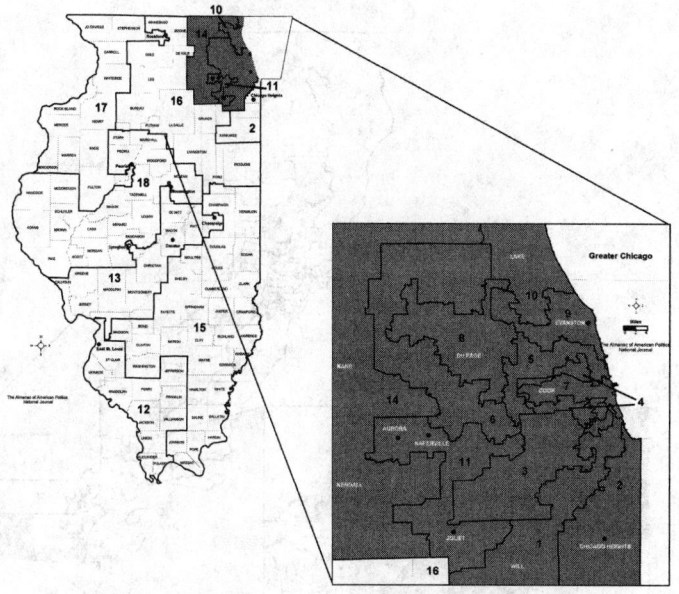

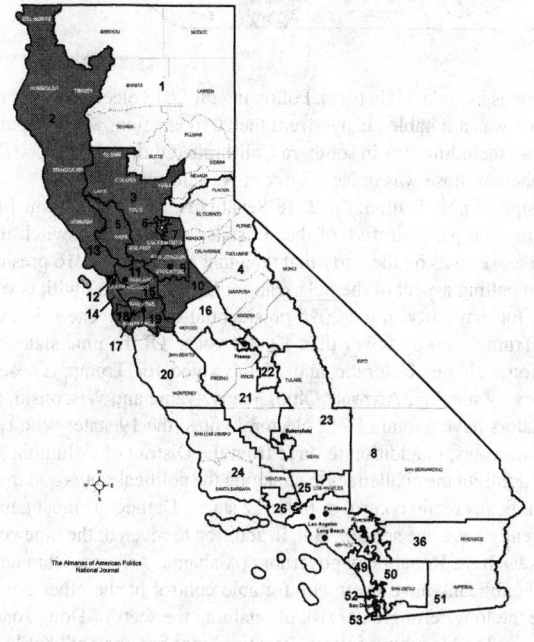

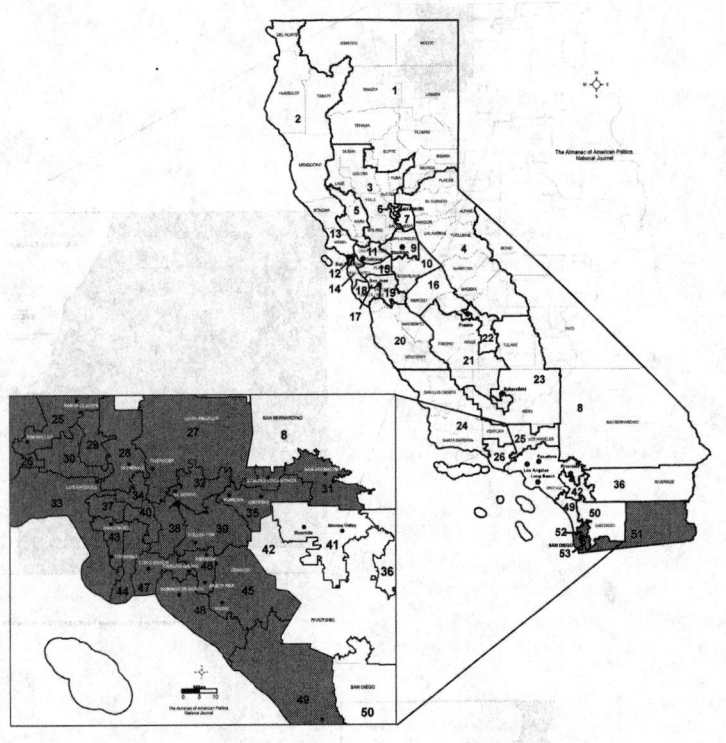

Those five areas include 85 districts. Following the 2018 election, every one of them was held by a Democrat. That was a notable change from the 2016 election, when Republicans won 13 of those House districts — including five in southern California. Of the 85 districts, Donald Trump won only three in 2016; each of those was in New York or New Jersey.

In another sign of polarization, the 2018 Senate results reduced from 14 to nine the states with one senator from each party. In five of the six states with a party switch in the Senate (all except Arizona), the takeover was by the party that won that state in the 2016 presidential election.

Another compelling aspect of the polarization: Of the 41 states with two senators from the same party, 40 voted for that party in the 2016 presidential election. The sole exception was Michigan, which Donald Trump won by fewer than 12,000 votes. Of the nine states with politically divided Senate delegations, all but Colorado and Maine voted for Trump. Those seven states were his margin of victory — notably, Arizona, Ohio, Pennsylvania and Wisconsin. (The 22 states with two Republican senators have a total of 212 electoral votes; the 19 states with two Democratic senators have 233 electoral votes, in addition to three from the District of Columbia.)

These data highlight the challenges to changing the political status quo in Congress. In the Senate, so long as Republicans retain control of those 22 states, Democrats must gain seats in the nine states where they currently have one senator. But, in addition to seven of the nine voting for Trump in 2016, four of those states have Republican governors (Alabama, Arizona, Ohio and West Virginia). In all but Arizona, Republicans have taken comfortable control of the other Senate seat. Consequently, Democrats face the long-term greater risk of retaining the seats of Doug Jones of Alabama, Sherrod Brown of Ohio and Joe Manchin of West Virginia; Jones has an uphill battle to hold his seat in 2020.

Arguably, Republicans have the greater long-term challenge in retaining their single Senate seat in Colorado and Maine; both Cory Gardner and Susan Collins face reelection in 2020. That leaves Montana, Pennsylvania and Wisconsin — where Democrat Jon Tester (whose term expires in 2024) and Republicans Pat Toomey and Ron Johnson (both of whom face reelection in 2022) have had the closer reelections in recent cycles.

Taking this political hypothesis to its limits: Republican takeovers in Alabama, Montana, Ohio and West Virginia would give them 26 states where they have both senators; Democratic takeovers in Colorado, Maine, Pennsylvania and Wisconsin would give them 23 states. For now, Arizona appears to be the state whose Senate seats are most up for grabs. In any case, the margin of control for one party or the other in the Senate appears likely to remain thin.

Of course, Democrats have opportunities to break the Republican lock in states such as Georgia, Iowa or North Carolina; the GOP's best options for additional Senate seats might be in Michigan and New Hampshire. Each of those five states has a potentially competitive contest in 2020.

In the House, Democratic seats have centered increasingly on metro areas. Aside from the 85 seats in the five areas in the above maps, Democrats have gained solid control in six other metro areas, with 33 House seats: Philadelphia/southern New Jersey (9); Detroit (6), Minneapolis/St. Paul (4), Denver (4), Las Vegas (3) and Seattle (7). They also control most, if not all, seats in eight other Democratic bastions, with 62 House seats: New England (21), Richmond/Tidewater (4), Atlanta (4), Orlando/Tampa (5), south Florida (7), parts of Texas (13), Phoenix/Tucson (5) and Portland (3). Democrats gained about 20 of those seats in 2018; many could be at risk in 2020.

For Republicans, their House seats have become increasingly centered in exurban and rural areas. These eight largest groups total 111 seats: large parts of Texas (23); non-urban areas of Kentucky/Tennessee/Arkansas/Oklahoma (20); non-urban areas of Alabama/Mississippi/Louisiana (14); large parts of Florida (14); Ohio (12); North Carolina (10, pending elections in two vacant seats in 2019); Georgia (9) and Pennsylvania (9). Redistricting has been a factor in some of those states, as also has been the case with a smaller number of states controlled by Democrats. Another 42 Republican-controlled House seats are centered in 7 states: the interior of California, Indiana and Michigan (7 each); Missouri (6); downstate Illinois, South Carolina and Wisconsin (5 each).

Setting aside those House clusters, that leaves 102 other House seats. Each party has solid control of about 30 of them. Those Democratic seats are mostly in urban areas, with large minority populations. Those largely safe Republicans seats are chiefly in rural areas. That leaves about 40 seats that are potentially House battlegrounds.

These political trends have grown more pronounced in the past quarter-century — especially following the Republican takeover of Congress in 1994. Previously, Democrats had unbroken control of the House for four decades; they held the Senate for 34 of those 40 years.

The President: Rhetoric and Reality

By Michael Barone

President

Donald J. Trump (R)

Elected 2016, term expires Jan. 2021, 1st term; b. June. 14, 1946, New York, NY; University of Pennsylvania Wharton School of Business (PA), B.A.; Presbyterian; married (Melania Trump); 5 children (4 from previous marriages), 8 grand-children.

Professional Career: Real estate developer & Owner, The Trump Organization, 1971-2016; Television Producer, "The Apprentice", 2004-2015.

Every American president has been unique — and, to a greater or lesser extent, different from what was expected when he was elevated to the office. George Washington, elected unanimously, was a symbol of the new nation's unity — and yet two philosophically and personally polarized political parties quickly emerged not just in the states and in Congress, but in the president's own Cabinet. Abraham Lincoln, elected with the thinnest credentials, least formal education and the lowest popular vote percentage of any president before or since, would bind together a nation riven by civil war with words of unsurpassable eloquence.

Donald Trump's presidency, in this respect if not in many others, resembles those of Washington and Lincoln. He brought to the office a curriculum vitae starkly different from that of almost any other president. He had never held (or sought) elective office nor had he served in the military; the only other president of which those things could be said was Herbert Hoover, who made a fortune as a mining engineer and investor and who won international fame supervising famine-relief in Belgium and Russia during World War I. Hoover achieved national and international fame for his efforts, comparable perhaps to the fame or notoriety Trump earned as a real estate developer/entrepreneur/ reality TV host. He did serve as a Cabinet member for Presidents Harding and Coolidge.

Nonetheless, Trump did put his opinions on policy in public view longer than Hoover. In the 1980s, he was opining on the unwisdom of free trade deals and mass immigration, and he flirted with running for president in 2000. He stepped off that escalator in the Trump Tower in June 2015 with more strengths as a political candidate than almost any established political expert reckoned. Those strengths were combined with more than one generous dollop of luck. With 16 rivals for the Republican nomination, he was able to win primaries and caucuses with pluralities despite antagonizing majorities (he failed to top 50 percent until he got to New York on April 19), and he was saved from early attacks by opponents' hesitation to antagonize Trump enthusiasts whose support they supposed must inevitably evaporate. He ran worst among college graduates and in areas with high social connectedness (as defined by scholars Robert Putnam and Charles Murray) and best in areas with those less educated and less socially connected. Overall he won 44 percent of primary and caucus votes and clinched the nomination when he won Indiana (despite Gov. Mike Pence's endorsement of Ted Cruz) on May 3. Meanwhile, Hillary Clinton's battle against Bernie Sanders for the Democratic nomination continued up through the last primaries in June. Clinton won the popular vote in primaries and caucuses by a less than overwhelming 55%-43% margin.

Going into the general election, Clinton led in most polls and had the advantage by just about every conventional measure. She raised and spent far more money; she had a more successful and less fraught national convention; she was supported heartily by the incumbent president, whose job approval hovered (just) above 50 percent; she was supported, though not always with enthusiasm, by just about everyone in the press. She performed better, according to media critics and polls, in all three presidential debates and in most target state polls. Democrats crowed about their blue wall — states with 242 electoral votes went Democratic in the six most recent presidential elections — and about their inevitably emerging demographic majority, as non-whites were on their way to outnumbering whites in the electorate.

Nevertheless, as became clear on election night between 9 and 10 p.m. Eastern, Donald Trump was elected the 45th president. In effect the author of The Art of the Deal made a trade. He traded away the votes of white college graduates: the exit poll showed him leading among them only 49%-45%, well short of Mitt Romney's 56%-42% in 2012. That lowered Republican percentages in California, Arizona, Colorado, Texas and Georgia, but changed no electoral votes. In return, presumably in response to his unorthodox positions on immigration, trade and foreign policy, he gained votes among non-college whites, carrying them by a 67%-28% margin, significantly better than Romney's 61%-36% among that group. Moreover, as New York Times psephologist Nate Cohn argued persuasively in June, non-college whites were a larger share of the electorate than indicated by exit polls: they outnumbered by roughly 2-1 the Hispanic and Asian voters who Democratic pundits had assumed were the key to victory — and among whom Trump's percentages were statistically indistinguishable from Romney's. The net result was that Trump carried 100 electoral votes that had gone for Barack Obama four years before, in Florida, Pennsylvania, Ohio, Michigan, Wisconsin, Iowa and the 2nd congressional district of Maine.

Just as Trump was not the first to be elevated to the presidency against widespread expectations, so as president he was not the first to govern contrary to what his campaign rhetoric suggested. (And, contrary to Democrats' expectations, he was not driven from office by charges triggered by the Clinton-campaign-financed Steele memorandum.) On his signature issues of immigration, on which he had taken stands contrary to those of presidents of both parties going back to the 1980s or even 1940s, he made only limited progress going into the first months of his third year. On trade, he persuaded the presidents of Mexico and Canada to accept modest modifications (and a renaming) of the NAFTA treaty he had excoriated on the campaign trail; given their nations' dependence on U.S. markets, they could scarcely have refused. He withdrew from the Trans-Pacific Partnership, as Hillary Clinton also promised to do, but also seemed to stop short of major changes in trade with China. On immigration, the author of The Art of the Deal failed to get agreement on a plausible bargain — legalizing DACA recipients in return for construction of a wall (or renamed barrier) — from a Republican-majority Congress and in his third year in office was trying to gain something less sweeping from a Democratic-majority House and not entirely sympathetic Republican-majority Senate. A sympathetic observer might add that Democrats failed to obtain from their congressional supermajorities in 2009 and 2010 changes in carbon reduction and immigration policies they have been saying are national necessities ever since, and many of their 2020 presidential candidates have said that the health insurance bill they did pass must be replaced now by much more drastic changes. But drastic change in policies long in place in a mostly prosperous and mostly peaceful nation is hard to achieve. It is hard to persuade people to improve on success.

Where the Trump administration has achieved more is when the president has pursued what are thought of as traditional Republican policies. The major legislative success of the 2017-18 Congress was a major tax bill, which did the work regarded as necessary by Trump and his predecessor to lower the world's highest corporate tax, and also eliminated subsidies for public employee unions and retirees by limiting federal deductions for state and local taxes. That raised taxes on $500,000-plus earners in heavily Democratic states while lowering them on virtually everyone else. On legal issues, which include the politically sensitive issue of abortion, Trump has largely subcontracted his judicial selections to the Federalist Society, with the Republican-majority Senate confirming Justices Neil Gorsuch and Brett Kavanaugh and numerous federal appeals court judges in largely partisan roll call votes.

On domestic regulation issues, Trump appointees have mostly followed conventional Republican approaches. On foreign policy, where presidents typically have the greatest leeway, he has pursued some policies that he advocated in his campaign and that differ from previous administrations — withdrawing the bulk of U.S. troops in Syria and Afghanistan, negotiating directly with North Korea's Kim Jong Un, withdrawing from the (non-mandatory) Paris Climate Accords. His loud and repeated insistence that NATO allies increase defense spending to agreed-on levels has produced more results than the muted diplomatic demands of previous administrations of both parties.

Trump's Democratic opponents, and his Republican and conservative critics, have done less in the way of criticizing his ideas or advancing feasible alternatives than they have in trying to oust him from office. Their assumption seemed to be that he would be removed from office, forthwith or at least as rapidly as Richard Nixon was in his second term. Such hopes proved unrealized. Nixon resigned less than 19 months after his second inauguration; Trump, as this is written, remained in office 26 months after his inauguration, with no indication that the special counsel had any evidence of criminal collusion with the Russians, as so many of his opponents assumed. Of course, his critics continued to search for such evidence , with profound consequences for his presidency. But it also may turn out that Democrats' pursuit of Trump diverted their psychic energy to what turned out to be a wild goose chase.

But not without some gains in the meantime. In the 2018 election, Democrats won control of the House of Representatives, gaining 40 or 41 (depending on the re-run of North Carolina 9, where a Republican lead was tainted by election fraud). The 241-194 Republican House elected in 2016 became a 235-199 Democratic House elected in 2018. The House popular vote switched from 48%-47% Republican in 2016 to 53%-45% Democratic in 2018. If the critical vote switchers that elected Donald Trump in 2016 were non-college whites, the critical vote switchers that elected a solidly Democratic House in 2018 were white college graduates in high-income suburban neighborhoods. Almost every district gained by Democrats falls into that category, including seats that almost no one saw as marginal, like South Carolina 1 and Oklahoma 5. What used to be reliable Republican constituencies are now, at least temporarily, Democratic. Comparison of the 2018 House exit poll with its 2016 counterpart shows Democrats gaining 2 percentage points among non-whites, 6 percentage points among non-college whites and 9 percentage points among white college graduates; Democratic gains were especially notable among young and low-income voters. There is a case to be made for anointing, as the press seems to have done in the early months of 2019, Rep. Alexandria Ocasio-Cortez of New York as the personification of the Democratic victory, even though she won not by defeating a Republican in November but by ousting a senior Democrat in a low-turnout primary in June.

At the same time Republicans were losing control of the House, and losing some governorships in key states like Michigan and Wisconsin as well, they were gaining a net two seats in the Senate, raising their majority from a tenuous 51-49 (effectively reduced to 50-49 during the long illness of the late John McCain) to a slightly more comfortable 53-47. This Republican success was due in part to the fact that only one-third of Senate seats are up in any election year, and those up in 2018 tended to favor Republicans — and to a greater extent than those up in 2020.

But of course, the election on which all eyes will be focused in that perhaps aptly named year will be the presidency, and whether Donald Trump — now that he seems almost certain not to be ejected Nixon-like from office — will be re-elected, as his three predecessors were, to a second term. There are signs that his chances are slim. He lost the popular vote, 48%-46%, to Hillary Clinton in 2016, and picked the Electoral College lock only after every tumbler hesitantly clicked into place. Republican losses in the House of Representatives suggest he cannot count on duplicating his 2016 narrow (49%-45%) majority among white college graduates. His job approval rating since March 2017 has stayed well below 50 percent, hovering between 37 percent (in December 2017) and 44 percent (in June and October 2017 and February 2018), while disapproval has remained above 50 percent.

Such stasis is perhaps odd, amid so much vivid (and furious) political debate; in our long period, going back to the middle 1990s, of polarized partisan parity, job approval of Bill Clinton and George W. Bush varied much more widely, and in tandem with macro events and trends. In contrast, positive economic statistics and attitudes have had minimal effect on Trump's ratings. Most Americans seem to have settled attitudes toward him, based on his persona and policy preferences. Even his more solemn performances — his Poland speech in 2017, his second State of the Union in 2019 — or blunders — the Charlottesville response, sexual misconduct allegations — have had little visible effect on those who love or loathe him. Not since December 2017 has his job approval fallen below 40 percent.

Before counting Trump out, it may be useful to remember that at midpoint in their first terms Clinton, Bush and Obama seemed headed to defeat, and yet they became the second trio of American two-term presidents (after Jefferson, Madison and Monroe in 1801-25). And if Trump hasn't reaped the political benefits of economic growth, he could be helped by his opposition. There was talk in early 2019 of a challenge in the Republican primaries — talk quickly discounted by polls showing near-unanimous Republican support. As for the Democrats, in early 2019 it seemed they would have an even larger field of candidates than the 17 Republicans had in 2016, with all the potential for intra-party strife. Moreover, the leftward movement of Democratic voters and Democratic politicians had already led well-known candidates to endorse measures like Ocasio-Cortez's Green New Deal, reparations for the descendants of slaves and legalizing some ninth-month abortions.

Vice President

Mike Pence (R)

Elected 2016, term expires Jan. 2021, 1st term; b. June. 7, 1959, Columbus, IN; Hanover College, B.A., 1981, Indiana University School of Law, J.D. 1986; Disciples of Christ; married (Karen Batten); 3 children.

Elected Office: U.S House, 2001-2003 (IN 2nd District), 2003-2013 (IN 6th District); IN Governor, 2013-2017.

Professional Career: Practicing attorney; President, Indiana Policy Review Foundation 1991-1994; Network Indiana talk show host, 1994-2000.

The United States of America

Population		Place of Birth		Age Groups	
Total	327,167,434	Native	86.6%	Under 18	22.9%
% change since 2010	5.6%	Born in US	85.1%	18-34	23.4%
Land area (sq. miles)	3,797,000	State of residence	58.5%	35-64	38.8%
Pop/ sq mi	86.2	Different state	26.6%	Over 64	14.9%
		Puerto Rico, U.S			
Race and Ethnicity		Islands or abroad to		**18 years and over**	
White	61.5%	american parent	1.5%	Male	48.7%
Black	12.3%	Foreign Born	13.4%	Female	51.3%
Latino	17.6%				
Mexican	11.1%	**Foreign-born Citizenship Status**		**65 years and over**	
Puerto Rican	1.7%	Naturalized U.S citizen	48.1%	Male	44.1%
Cuban	0.7%	Not a U.S citizen	51.9%	Female	55.9%
Other Hispanic or					
Latino	4.1%	**Region of Foreign Born**		**Income**	
Asian	5.3%	Europe	11.1%	Median Income	$57,652
Pacific Islander	0.2%	Asia	30.5%	Under $50,000	34.5%
American Indian and		Africa	4.7%	$50,000-$99,999	32.5%
Alaska Native	0.7%	Oceania	0.6%	$100,000-$199,999	24.8%
Two or more races	2.3%	Latin America	51.2%	$200,000 or more	8.2%
Other	0.2%	Northern America	1.9%	Poverty Rate	14.6%
Language		**Education**		**Health Insurance**	
English only	78.7%	H.S grad or less	39.9%	With health insurance	89.5%
Spanish	13.2%	Some college	29.1%	coverage	
Other European	3.6%	College Degree, 4 yr	19.1%		
Asian	3.5%	Post grad	11.8%	**Public Assistance**	
				Cash public assistance	2.6%
Work		**Military**		income	
White Collar	37.4%	Veteran	7.7%	Food stamp/SNAP	12.6%
Sales and Service	41.5%	Active Duty	0.4%	benefits	
Blue Collar	21.1%				
Government	13.8%				

2016 Presidential Vote				2012 Presidential Vote			
Hillary Clinton (D)	65,853,652	(48%)		Barack Obama (D)	65,915,795	(51%)	
Donald Trump (R)	62,985,134	(46%)		Mitt Romney (R)	60,933,504	(47%)	
Gary Johnson (L)	4,489,235	(3%)					

ALABAMA

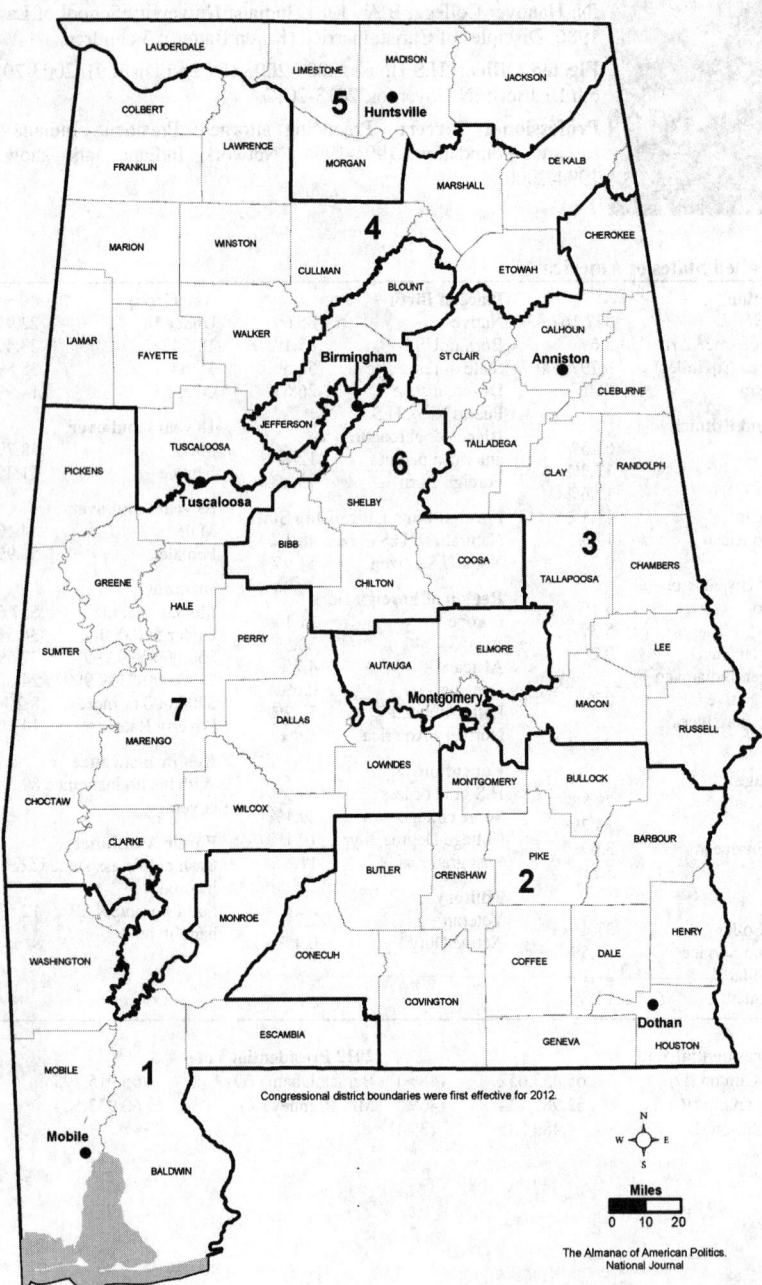

Congressional district boundaries were first effective for 2012.

Miles
0   10   20

The Almanac of American Politics,
National Journal

The past hangs over Alabama like its tall yellow pines: Refrains from decades-old civil rights struggles recur in the debate on gay marriage and Confederate memorials, and the state's manufacturing base has once again been built with the help of outsiders. The state continues to struggle with poverty and low rates of education, and while Alabama's dominant political party has changed, populists and "big mules" remain – and in the recent past, every branch of state government has been tainted by corruption or scandal.

The French founded Mobile near the Gulf of Mexico in 1702, but the interior of Alabama remained Indian country until 1814, when Andrew Jackson defeated the Red Stick band of the Creek Indians at Horseshoe Bend, ending the two-year Creek War. Jackson imposed a treaty on the Red Sticks and on his own Indian allies, expropriating almost all of what five years later became the state of Alabama. With the Indians removed, the first white settlers poured in. Farmers from Tennessee swept into the red clay hills in the north, bringing the folkways of the Scots-Irish, with their fierce determination to avenge any perceived insult or threat. The second wave of settlement came a decade later, when planters brought slaves to pick cotton in south central Alabama's Black Belt (named for its fertile soil, which had been enriched by the deposited remains of Cretaceous-era sea creatures). The interplay between the yeoman farmers and the plantation grandees has run through Alabama politics ever since. Both sought secession after the election of Abraham Lincoln; the first Confederate Congress assembled in Montgomery in February 1861, with Jefferson Davis taking the oath of office as president of the Confederacy in the Greek Revival state capitol atop Goat Hill.

After the Civil War and Reconstruction, Alabama, like other Southern states, became solidly Democratic, with a populist accent. With its solid-iron Red Mountain, steel manufacturing grew up around Birmingham in the late 1880s, thanks to northern bankers who helped finance it and Yankee engineers who built the blast furnaces. Birmingham, site of Dixie's first steel production, became known as the "Pittsburgh of the South," and the industry's growth gave birth to the nearby city of Bessemer and later Fairfield, a company town of U.S. Steel.

In the first half of the 20th century, Alabama politics pitted Black Belt planters, timber barons and economic potentates in Birmingham and Mobile called "the Big Mules" against populists who favored the New Deal. The latter included some influential and colorful figures: Gov. Bibb Graves; Sen. and future Supreme Court Justice Hugo Black; Rep. Lister Hill, who authored Tennessee Valley Authority legislation in the House of Representatives; 1952 vice presidential nominee John Sparkman; and Gov. James E. "Big Jim" Folsom Sr.

Alabama went on to become one of the birthplaces of the civil rights movement. From the Dexter Avenue Baptist Church, the 26-year-old Martin Luther King Jr. led the Montgomery bus boycott after seamstress Rosa Parks refused to give up her bus seat to a white passenger. A hundred miles north in Birmingham, two weeks after King penned his Letter from Birmingham Jail in 1963, Birmingham Police Commissioner Eugene "Bull" Connor, then Alabama's Democratic National Committeeman who had helped lead the walkout of southern delegates at the party's 1948 national convention, ordered police dogs and fire hoses to be turned on peaceful demonstrators. Four months later, four girls were killed when a bomb exploded in Birmingham's 16th Street Baptist Church. (The bombers were convicted in 1977, 2001 and 2002, the latter two defendants prosecuted by Doug Jones, who would later win an underdog race for a U.S. Senate seat.) In March 1965, scores of marchers who had been catalyzed by the murder of civil rights advocate Jimmie Lee Jackson in Marion were severely beaten by police at Selma's Edmund Pettus Bridge en route to Montgomery, including future Rep. John Lewis.

But while Parks and King were leading the nation forward on race, Alabama's most prominent politician of the time, George Wallace, was pushing back. In June 1963, during his first term as governor, Wallace made national news by standing in the schoolhouse door at the University of Alabama to defy a federal court desegregation order. In 1964, Wallace ran in the Democratic presidential primaries and got strong support in Indiana, Maryland and Wisconsin. In the 1968 general election, running as a third-party candidate, he won 13.5 percent of the popular vote and carried five southern states with 46 electoral votes. He ran in the Democratic primaries again in 1972 before being shot and partially paralyzed while campaigning in Laurel Maryland. He dominated Alabama politics, winning the governorship in 1962, running his wife to succeed him in 1966 (she died while in office), regaining the governorship in 1970 and 1974, then running and winning one last time in

1982. He spent the final years before his death in 1998 apologizing for his earlier acts. "The South has changed, and for the better," he said.

Today, civil rights tourism is a major business. Not far from the state capitol, Montgomery boasts sculptor-architect Maya Lin's circular Civil Rights Memorial, Troy University's Rosa Parks Museum, the Dexter Parsonage, and a new national memorial to the victims of lynching. The Selma to Montgomery National Historic Trail runs along U.S. Highway 80, and the Alabama Civil Rights Museum Trail includes the Tuskegee Airmen National Historic Site and the 16th Street Baptist Church. But conflict over remembrance of the pre-civil rights era has spiked, as it has elsewhere in the South. In May 2017, Gov. Kay Ivey signed legislation to ban "relocation, removal, alteration, renaming or other disturbance of any architecturally significant building, memorial building, memorial street or monument located on public property which has been in place for 40 or more years."

Economically, Alabama lost ground during the Wallace years. While Atlanta was peacefully desegregating and beginning decades of white-collar growth, Birmingham was violently resisting the civil rights movement, only to see its blue-collar base in the steel industry shrink and its most talented residents of all races flee to calmer climes. Agriculture remains a significant industry, including the third-highest percentage of timber acreage in the Lower 48, behind Oregon and Georgia. But where the state has really gained ground is in manufacturing.

Automobiles are now a major part of Alabama's economy – so much so that in 2018, Ivey criticized President Donald Trump, despite his popularity among Alabama voters, over his pursuit of tariffs on steel and aluminum. Mercedes opened its first U.S. assembly line in 1997 near Tuscaloosa, while Honda has a major plant in Lincoln and Hyundai has one in Montgomery. These operations spawned dozens of supplier and subcontractor firms. Alabama ranked fifth among states in vehicle production, producing 9 percent of U.S. output, even before the announcement of a new, $1.6 billion joint facility for Toyota and Mazda in Huntsville that is projected to build 300,000 vehicles annually, with production starting in 2021.

Aerospace has been another key to Alabama's economy. The Marshall Space Flight Center in Huntsville has attracted Boeing, which is developing NASA's Space Launch System, and Raytheon, which has opened a missile integration facility. In conventional aviation, Airbus selected Mobile as the location of its first U.S. assembly plant for A320 aircraft. A new sector flocking to the state is technology, including data centers that require cheap and environmentally friendly sources of electricity – something that TVA hydropower provides in abundance. In 2018, Facebook announced a $750 million data center in Huntsville, while Google is building a $600 million data facility northeast of the city. The economic growth around Huntsville boosted population in Madison County by 7.4 percent between 2010 and 2017, at a time when the state's overall population growth had been just 1.8 percent.

Manufacturing gains have been driven by weaker unionization than in the north, although Alabama does rank first among the former Confederate states with 7.4 percent of workers holding union cards in 2017. (Most members are public employees, including teachers in the politically potent Alabama Education Association.) In October 2018, the unemployment rate was 4.1 percent, historically low but slightly higher than the national average. Still, prosperity has largely eluded rural Alabama, where joblessness and grinding poverty persist. The state has the sixth-lowest median income in the country, and the trade publication Education Week ranked Alabama's K-12 education system 41st in the nation in 2018. "Our education system in this state sucks," opined Gov. Robert Bentley in 2016.

In the 30-plus years since Wallace's name last appeared on the Democratic ballot line, the state has become solidly Republican. For a while, many of the talented state politicians remained Democrats who, along with their allies — the AEA, major black political associations and trial lawyers — could defeat less-experienced Republicans with regularity. But even these canny Democratic survivors were overcome amid a disciplined and relentless Republican offensive. The local Democratic machinery atrophied, and the party's longstanding control of the state legislature disappeared in 2010 — the first GOP majorities in Montgomery since Reconstruction.

In short order, power proved corrupting. By 2016, the leaders of each of the three branches of state government – all Republicans – were mired in troubles of one kind or another. Taken together, these scandals turned Alabama into a national poster child for dysfunctional government. In the judicial branch, Roy Moore -- chief justice of the Alabama Supreme Court who had in 2003 defied a federal judge's order to remove a 5,280-pound granite monument to the Ten Commandments that he had installed in his Montgomery courthouse, leading to his ouster – was once again removed from his position, this time for defying federal court orders on same-sex marriage.

In 2017, Moore proved too radioactive even for Alabama voters. In a special election to fill the Senate seat given up by U.S. Attorney General-designate Jeff Sessions, Moore, backed by the party's socially conservative base, defeated Rep. Mo Brooks and the appointed senator, Luther Strange, in the GOP primary and runoff. This gave Jones, the former prosecutor who had won the Democratic nomination, a surprising opening in a state that Trump won by 28 points just a year before. Moore's challenge intensified with revelations about his past sexual indiscretions with underage girls. This led many national Republicans and suburban Republicans in the state to refuse to support him, though Trump stuck with Moore. Even as most Moore supporters told exit pollsters that they disbelieved the accusers' testimony, "upscale, Republican-leaning suburbs" were "blanketed in Jones signs," wrote Time magazine's Molly Ball. The weak suburban support, combined with a supercharged African-American turnout, enabled Jones to win – though by fewer than 22,000 votes out of more than 1.3 million cast, enough to win just one of the state's seven congressional districts. While Democrats celebrated Jones' victory, they acknowledged that it stemmed from unusual circumstances. "I don't think we're out dancing in the streets saying this is a totally new day," former Gov. Jim Folsom Jr. told the New York Times. "We're all realistic enough to know that party identification leans heavily Republican, and probably will for the foreseeable future."

Indeed, Alabama's social conservatives were undeterred by Moore's loss. In May 2019, the state enacted a nearly total ban on abortion, without any exceptions for rape and incest. It was widely seen as a way to encourage the Supreme Court to overturn the Roe v. Wade decision, but the new law also seemed to energize abortion supporters. It even drew criticism from some conservatives who said its broad scope would be a tactical mistake.

Population		Race and Ethnicity		Income	
Total	4,850,771	White	65.9%	Median Income	$46,472
Land area (sq. miles)	50,645	Black	26.4%	State Income Rank	47
Pop/ sq mi	95.8	Latino	4.1%	Poverty Rate	18.0%
Born in state	69.9%	Asian	1.3%	With health insurance	89.3%
		Two or more races	1.7%	Cash public assistance	1.7%
Age Groups		Other	0.6%	Food stamp/SNAP	15.0%
Under 18	22.7%				
18-34	22.6%	**Education**		**Work**	
35-64	39.0%	H.S grad or less	45.6%	White Collar	34.1%
Over 64	15.7%	Some college	29.9%	Sales and Service	40.3%
		College Degree, 4 yr	15.4%	Blue Collar	25.6%
Military		Post grad	9.1%	Government	15.6%
Veteran/ Active Duty	9.4%				

Presidential Politics

2016 Primary (D)	Clinton (D)	311,141 (78%)	Sanders (D)	76,878 (19%)			
2016 Primary (R)	Trump (R)	373,721 (43%)	Cruz (R)	181,479 (21%)	Rubio (R)	160,606 (19%)	
	Carson (R)	88,094 (10%)					
2016 Pres. Vote	Trump (R)	1,318,255 (62%)	Clinton (D)	729,547 (34%)	Johnson (L)	44,467	(2%)
2012 Pres. Vote	Romney (R)	1,255,925 (61%)	Obama (D)	795,696 (38%)			

Alabama has been a reliably Republican state in presidential races since 1980. Jimmy Carter, a son of the South, in 1976 was the last Democratic nominee to carry Alabama, winning 60 of its 67 counties. But in 2015, a huge August rally at Ladd-Peebles Stadium outside of Mobile for Donald Trump's nascent bid for the 2016 GOP presidential nomination attracted some 30,000 boisterous supporters and signaled the candidate's unique appeal to many Republican voters who had become alienated from the party establishment. GOP Sen. Jeff Sessions praised Trump's stance on halting illegal immigration and was the first senator to endorse the New York real estate developer, who handily won the state's March 1 primary with 43 percent over Texas Sen. Ted Cruz, the runner-up with 21 percent. Trump's victory in Alabama and elsewhere in the South that day was a major blow to Cruz. who had been counting on a strong showing in the region to bolster his candidacy. The Democrats' primary between former Secretary of State Hillary Clinton and Vermont Sen. Bernie Sanders was even more lopsided. Clinton trounced Sanders 78%-19%, with overwhelming support from African Americans, who made up a majority of the state's Democratic primary voters. According to the television network exit poll, Clinton won African Americans by roughly 15-to-1 over Sanders, who campaigned lightly in the state. In 2008, Clinton lost the Alabama primary to Illinois Sen. Barack Obama, 56%-42%. Turnout in the Democratic primary was down from 2008, while Republicans saw record turnout in their presidential primary.

The general election was a foregone conclusion: Trump bested Clinton 62%-34%, winning 54 of the state's 67 counties. Clinton won 12 counties in the state's Black Belt, named for the rich dark soil that was once worked by cotton plantation slaves and sharecroppers. The region has a high share of African-American voters. Clinton also captured Jefferson County (Birmingham), marking the third consecutive time that a Democratic presidential nominee carried the state's largest vote-producing county. But Jefferson's share of the statewide vote was less than 14 percent in 2016, down from 19 percent in 1980. That decline reflects the growth of Birmingham's Republican suburbs and exurbs in Shelby and St. Clair counties, where Trump swamped Clinton. Like other GOP presidential candidates, Trump dominated faster-growing counties, including Limestone, which encompasses suburban Huntsville, and Baldwin, a recreational haven on the Gulf Coast that includes suburbs of Mobile. Republican Gov. Robert Bentley, who endorsed Ohio Gov. John Kasich in the GOP primary, said he would not vote for Trump or Clinton in the general election.

Congressional Districts

116th Congress Lineup	1D 6R	115th Congress Lineup	1D 6R

Alabama's shift to its predominantly Republican delegation came more slowly than in other southern states. As recently as 2010, it was split between four Republicans and three Democrats. But that year's election eliminated the final white Democrats (in the Montgomery and Huntsville-area districts), and the subsequent redistricting further entrenched the Democrats' hold on the African-American 7th District by adding most of Montgomery's black precincts to its Birmingham-area black population. The prospect of a competitive partisan congressional election has become remote and the delegation has locked in with six Republicans and one Democrat.

Another way in which Alabama has contrasted with most of the South has been its shrinking number of House districts. As recently as 1960, it had nine seats. Current Census Bureau population forecasts project that it will drop to six seats after the 2020 reapportionment. That loss almost surely would be a Republican seat. With the likelihood that the GOP will control districts in the urban centers of Mobile, Montgomery, Birmingham and Huntsville, that likely would result in elimination of one of the two remaining districts in the central part of Alabama, which are mostly rural. They have been held by veteran Reps. Mike Rogers, who has become the senior Republican on the Homeland Security Committee, and Robert Aderholt, who failed in his bid to take that slot on the Appropriations Committee. Aderholt's continuing interest in a Senate seat might circumvent what otherwise looms as a musical-chairs contest in the center of the state.

Kay Ivey (R)

Assumed office in 2017, term expires 2023, 1st term; b. Oct. 15, 1944, Camden; Auburn U 1967; Baptist; Single.

Elected Office: AL House, 1980-1982; AL Treasurer, 2002-2010; AL Lt. Governor, 2011-2017.

Professional Career: High School teacher; Assistant Vice President, Merchants National Bank/Regions Bank, 1970-1979; Consultant, American Bankers Association, 1979; Reading Clerk, Assistant Director, Alabama Development Office, 1982-1985; Director of Government Affairs, Alabama Commission on Higher Education, 1985-1998.

Office: 600 Dexter Avenue, Montgomery, 36130; 334-242-7100; Fax: 334-353-0004; Website: alabama.gov.

Lt. Gov.: Will Ainsworth (R) **Atty. Gen:** Steve Marshall (R) **Sec. of State:** John Merrill (R)

State Legislature: Senate: 27D, 8R **House:** 28D, 76R, 1V

Election Results

Election	Name (Party)	Vote (%)
2018 General	Kay Ivey (R)	1,022,457 (59%)
	Walt Maddox (D)	694,495 (40%)
2018 Primary	Kay Ivey (R)	331,739 (56%)
	Tommy Battle (R)	147,207 (25%)
	Scott Dawson (R)	79,546 (14%)
	Bill Hightower (R)	29,367 (5%)

Republican Kay Ivey became governor of Alabama in April 2017, ending a long, soap-opera-like sex scandal involving fellow Republican Robert Bentley, who resigned under the threat of impeachment. Ivey took office at age 72, becoming only the second woman to serve as governor of Alabama, after Lurleen Burns Wallace, the wife of four-time Gov. George Wallace. Then, bolstered by a strong economy and a lack of scandal, Ivey was elected to a term of her own in 2018, coasting to a 59%-40% victory in this solidly Republican state.

Ivey was raised on a family cattle farm in Camden, served as lieutenant governor at Alabama Girls State while in high school, and earned a degree from Auburn University in 1967. While a student, she helped the Wallace campaign organize on campus. She received additional education at Duke University's Governor's Center for Public Policy, the Alabama Banking School and the University of Colorado School of Banking. She worked as a high school teacher, as assistant vice president of Merchants National Bank/Regions Bank, as a reading clerk in the state House, as assistant director of the Alabama Development Office, and as director of government affairs for the Alabama Commission on Higher Education. In 1982, she ran as a Democrat (as most Alabamians did at the time) for her first statewide office – state auditor – but lost.

Two decades later, Ivey began a more successful phase of her electoral career, as a Republican, a label that was becoming advantageous in the state. She was elected state treasurer in 2002 and 2006, then, after a brief flirtation with a gubernatorial bid in 2010, ran for lieutenant governor. Ivey's biggest albatross was her past leadership of the state's Prepaid Affordable College Tuition program, which closed in 2008 due to financial pressures. Still, she was able to narrowly defeat Democratic incumbent Jim Folsom Jr. to win the lieutenant governorship, and she was reelected in 2014 before being elevated to governor on Bentley's resignation.

Bentley's ethical problems were separate from -- but occurred at roughly the same time as -- serious troubles within the leadership of the other two branches of Alabama government. House Speaker Mike Hubbard, architect of the Republicans' legislative majority, was sentenced to four years in prison after being convicted on 12 felony ethics counts, while state Supreme Court Justice Roy Moore's refusal to follow orders from the federal bench led to his removal as chief justice (for the second time). At her swearing-in, Ivey said, "Today is a dark day in Alabama but also one of opportunity. Together we steady the ship of state and improve the image of the state. These are my two priorities as governor."

In 2017, Alabama's political scene was dominated by the open-seat Senate race that emerged when President Donald Trump named longtime Republican Sen. Jeff Sessions to be attorney general. Bentley appointed state Attorney General Luther Strange to the seat, but Strange ended up losing the GOP nomination to Moore. Initially, Ivey said she would "hold judgment" until more facts came out about allegations against Moore of past sexual improprieties with underage girls, but by mid-November, a few weeks before the election, she announced that she would vote for her fellow Republican over Democrat Doug Jones. While Ivey said she had "no reason" to doubt Moore's accusers, she cited a need to preserve the Republican majority in the Senate. In the end, Jones narrowly defeated Moore, giving Democrats a rare statewide win.

In 2018, Ivey turned her attention to her own election. She pursued a risk-averse "Rose Garden" strategy – a non-confrontational approach to the legislature, interactions mainly with friendly audiences, and support for policies popular with the GOP base. For instance, Ivey aired an ad in the primary touting her signing of a bill to protect historical monuments that featured images of two Confederate monuments; she also called for giving Trump the Nobel Peace Prize, citing his overtures to North Korea. (In a rare break with the president, Ivey warned that tariffs imposed by Trump threatened the state's $21.7 billion export economy.) In the June primary, Ivey easily defeated Huntsville Mayor Tommy Battle, preacher Scott Dawson, and several lesser-known candidates.

In their primary, Democrats chose Tuscaloosa Mayor Walt Maddox. He promised to expand Medicaid under the Affordable Care Act on his first day in office, and he advocated a special legislative session to enact a lottery to fund education. But while Maddox was a credible candidate, any Democrat running statewide in Alabama faces an enormous challenge. Bolstered by a fundraising advantage, Ivey easily won a term of her own. Maddox won his home county of Tuscaloosa by the slimmest of margins, along with Jefferson County (Birmingham), Montgomery County (Montgomery), and a smattering of more lightly populated counties. But Ivey won everywhere else; her relative lack of controversy enabled her to perform more strongly than Moore had in historically Republican suburban areas.

In May 2019, Ivey signed a near-total ban on abortion -- without exceptions for rape and incest -- that drew national attention. "To the bill's many supporters, this legislation stands as a powerful testament to Alabamians' deeply held belief that every life is precious and that every life is a sacred gift from God," Ivey said in explaining her decision to sign the law.

Richard Shelby (R)

Elected 1986, term expires 2022, 6th term, b. May 06, 1934; Birmingham; University of Alabama, B.A., 1957; University of Alabama School of Law, LL.B., 1963; Presbyterian; Married (Annette Nevin Shelby); 2 children; 2 grandchildren.

Elected Office: AL Senate, 1970-1978; U.S. House, 1979-1987.

Professional Career: Practicing attorney, 1963-1978; City prosecutor, Tuscaloosa, 1963-1971; U.S magistrate, 1966-1970; Spec. Assistant to Alabama Attorney General, 1969-1971.

DC Office: 304 RSOB 20510, 202-224-5744, Fax: 202-224-3416, shelby.senate.gov

State Offices: Birmingham, 205-731-1384; Huntsville, 256-772-0460; Mobile, 251-694-4164; Montgomery, 334-223-7303; Tuscaloosa, 205-759-5047.

Committees: *Appropriations (Chmn)*: Ex Officio membership on all subcommittees. *Banking, Housing & Urban Affairs*: Financial Institutions & Consumer Protection; Housing, Transportation & Community Development; Securities, Insurance & Investment. *Environment & Public Works*: Fisheries, Water, and Wildlife; Superfund, Waste Management, & Regulatory Oversight; Transportation & Infrastructure. *Rules & Administration*.

Group Ratings

	ADA	ACLU	AFL-CIO	LCV	ITI	COC	HAFA	ACU	CFG	FRC
2018	-	5%	-	7%	-	90%	62%	68%	45%	88%
2017	0%	C	0%	0%	C	86%	C	80%	79%	100%

Almanac Ratings 2017-18

	Economy	Social	Foreign	Composite
Liberal	0%	0%	0%	0%
Conservative	100%	100%	100%	100%

Key Votes of the 115th Congress

1. Obama-care revision	Y	5. Gun regulations	Y	9. Kavanaugh confirmation	Y
2. Tax Cuts	Y	6. Family planning regs	Y	10. Saudi arms sales	N
3. Dodd-Frank revision	Y	7. Gorsuch confirmation	Y	11. FISA rules	Y
4. Omnibus appropriations	Y	8. Immigration restrictions	Y	12. Military aid in Yemen	N

Election Results

Election	Name (Party)	Vote (%)		Cand. Spent	Ind. Exp. Support	Ind. Exp. Oppose
2016 General	Richard Shelby (R)	1,335,104	(64%)	$11,473,078	$479,359	
	Ron Crumpton (D)	748,709	(36%)	$22,060		
2016 Primary	Richard Shelby (R)	505,586	(65%)			
	Jonathan McConnell (R)	214,770	(28%)			
	John Martin (R)	23,558	(3%)			

Prior winning percentages: 2010 (65%), 2004 (68%), 1998 (63%), 1992 (65%), 1986 (50%); House: 1984 (97%), 1982 (97%), 1980 (73%), 1978 (94%)

By the spring of 2018, after nearly one-third of a century in the Senate, Republican Richard Shelby, Alabama's senior senator, had the distinction of having chaired three different standing committees. As chair of the Intelligence Committee, he tangled with the nation's spy chiefs; later, heading the Banking, Housing and Urban Affairs panel in separate stints nearly a decade apart, Shelby battled against bank bailouts, while also resisting stiffer regulation of the nation's banking industry in the wake of the 2008 financial crisis. Although Senate Republican Conference rules shuttled him to a lower profile post chairing the Rules and Administration Committee at the end of 2016, he would realize his fourth — and most influential — chairmanship a little more than a year later, when the early retirement of Mississippi Sen. Thad Cochran gave Shelby the Appropriations Committee gavel in April 2018.

In the face of intense polarization on Capitol Hill, Shelby worked throughout the 115th Congress with his Democratic counterpart on that panel, Patrick Leahy of Vermont, to restore "regular order" to an annual appropriations process that had gone off track in recent years — often resulting in the government being funded by short-term "continuing resolutions." Notwithstanding his longtime conservative credentials, Shelby was at odds with conservative hard-liners in his own party at times because of the effort.

If there is a feat responsible for Shelby's political longevity in the heart of Dixie — where he has been elected to the Senate twice as a Democrat and four times as a Republican — it has been the ability to steer federal funds to his home state from his Appropriations Committee perch. A half-dozen buildings that bear Shelby's name can be found on the campuses of the University of Alabama, Auburn University and the University of South Alabama. In the 2016 Republican primary, facing his first significant political challenge since first being elected to the Senate in 1986, Shelby emphasized the benefits of his seniority, while touting the prospect that he would soon ascend to the Appropriations Committee chairmanship. But Shelby had set his cap on chairing the appropriations panel well before that. Andrew Gray, a managing director of communications at JPMorgan Chase who was an aide to Shelby starting in 1998, told The Washington Post that even back then "and even probably further, Sen. Shelby was counting who had to lose, retire, or otherwise get out of the way to allow him to rise to the chairmanship of the Appropriations Committee."

On the surface, Shelby is much in the mold of Southern politicians of another era, quick to backslap and recount political war stories during downtime on the Senate floor. During a 2018 meeting with President Donald Trump not long after becoming appropriations chairman, Shelby — facing the task of telling the president that the Senate would not give him the amount he requested for a southern border wall — kept a difficult conversation amiable by opening with a long chat about college football. But Shelby is a tough negotiator, known for keeping his cards close to his chest and preserving his legislative options for as long as possible. His junior in-state colleague, Democrat Doug Jones, described Shelby to the Post as "a nice gentleman, that's just his nature," quickly adding, "Look, I've seen him, he can cut somebody off at the knees if he feels like they need it."

At 85, Shelby has honed his skills in a public career that goes back a half-century. He grew up the son of a steelworker in Birmingham, and, after earning both an undergraduate and law degree at the University of Alabama, remained in Tuscaloosa and practiced law with future Democratic Rep. Walter Flowers — who was part of an informal group of conservative Democrats and Republicans who were instrumental in the 1974 impeachment of President Richard Nixon.

Shelby was elected to the state Senate in 1970 as a Democrat, and, when Flowers unsuccessfully sought to join the U.S. Senate in 1978, Shelby ran for his House seat. The critical contest was the Democratic runoff against Chris McNair, an African-American state legislator whose daughter was one of the four girls killed in the 1963 Birmingham church bombing. Although the district had the most black residents of any in the state, Shelby won 59%-41%. In the House, Shelby had a conservative voting record, opposing the Voting Rights Act extension and the Martin Luther King Jr. Day. He was part of a bloc of conservative Democrats primarily from the South, known at the time as the "boll weevils," that was often allied with House Republicans.

Shelby ran for the Senate in 1986 and won a five-way Democratic primary with 51 percent of votes after then-Alabama secretary of state and later governor Don Siegelman withdrew. In the general election, he took on Republican Sen. Jeremiah Denton, a retired admiral and former Vietnam prisoner of war who had been swept into office by President Ronald Reagan's landslide victory six years earlier. Shelby slammed Denton for voting to cut Social Security and owning two Mercedes-Benz cars. He won a slim majority, coming out on top by 7,000 votes. As one of a half-dozen or so conservative Southern Democrats in the Senate in the mid-1980s, Shelby at first attracted little notice. He was re-elected in 1992 by a nearly 2-1 margin, as Democrat Bill Clinton won the presidency — but ran nearly 25 points behind Shelby in Alabama.

Soon after Clinton took office, Shelby broke ranks with the new administration. At a meeting with Vice President Al Gore, Shelby turned to the television cameras and criticized the Clinton program as "high on taxes, low on spending cuts." The administration retaliated, announcing that a multimillion-dollar space facility would be in Texas instead of Alabama (although it eventually was built in Alabama). The more he defied Clinton, the better Shelby's favorability ratings were at home. The day after Republicans regained control of the Senate in 1994, Shelby announced he was switching parties, increasing the GOP majority to 53 members. Republicans allowed him to keep his seniority on the banking committee and gave him the seat on appropriations panel and its defense subcommittee. In an interview with CNN several years later, Shelby said he switched parties because of the Democratic Party's leftward shift and rejected the idea that he made the move to gain power. "What I did didn't cause a political earthquake here," he said. "I just crossed the aisle and voted just like I've always been voting."

The switch paid dividends in 1997 when Shelby assumed the chairmanship of the Intelligence Committee. One of his first acts was to scuttle the nomination of Clinton's national security adviser, Anthony Lake, to be director of the CIA. By Sept. 11, 2001, the Senate was back in Democratic hands, but Shelby, as the ranking Republican on the committee, was an important player in the aftermath. He had an adversarial posture toward the intelligence agencies during the Clinton and Bush presidencies, and soon after 9/11, Shelby stopped just short of calling for the resignation of then-CIA Director George Tenet. But Shelby was mostly supportive of the Bush administration's conduct in the war on terrorism. Three months after Sept. 11, he was 1 of 10 senators to sign a letter calling for a plan "to eliminate the threat from Iraq." He led the call for the creation of a director of national intelligence, a position Congress created in 2004.

Republicans retook the Senate after the 2002 elections, opening the way for Shelby, over the next decade and a half, to exert substantial influence over the nation's financial and housing industries during a time of crisis for both. He chaired the banking committee from 2003 to 2007 and 2015 to 2017. While noted for his opposition to the 2010 Dodd-Frank financial reforms — Shelby believes the bill overreached in setting rules for regional and smaller community banks — he has exhibited a populist streak when it comes to Wall Street and the country's largest financial institutions.

As far back as 1999, Shelby was the only Senate Republican to vote against a financial-services deregulation bill that repealed the Glass-Steagall Act, a Depression-era law that separated commercial and investment banking.

During the 2008 financial crisis, Shelby opposed the $700 billion rescue of the financial markets. Not long afterward, Shelby protested the massive government loan for the Big Three domestic automakers, which he called "dinosaurs." He threatened to filibuster; the bill did not pass the Senate, but President Barack Obama bailed out the auto industry anyway. Shelby later drew praise from the Troubled Asset Relief Program special inspector general, Neil Barofsky. In a 2012 book generally criticizing Congress and the Treasury Department for their handling of the issue, Barofsky singled out Shelby for being more interested in substance than many of his colleagues. Of one briefing with the senator, Barofsky wrote, "I probably covered more in fifteen minutes of rapid-fire questions and answers than in most hour-long meetings with other members of Congress."

As efforts to reform the nation's financial-regulatory system geared up in 2009, Shelby and the Democratic chairman of the banking committee, Connecticut Sen. Chris Dodd, agreed, at least in theory, on the creation of a consumer financial protection division or agency. But a sticking point surfaced over its structure. While Dodd and Obama wanted the agency to be housed within the Federal Reserve and given more independence — a provision partly designed to prevent Republicans from blocking its funding — Shelby called for making it a division of the Federal Deposit Insurance Corp. His substitute plan failed on the Senate floor, and when the final Dodd-Frank bill was passed in May 2010, Shelby voted against it. Ultimately, the objections of Shelby and other Republicans were ameliorated with the change in administrations: When Trump named Office of Management and Budget Director Mick Mulvaney as the bureau's acting director, publicly announced enforcement actions dropped by a reported 75 percent.

Returning to the banking committee as chairman in 2015, Shelby sought to pass a Dodd-Frank overhaul. But Shelby's bill, after clearing the banking panel, went no further, with Democrats on the panel expressing concerns about Shelby's handling of the issue. Democratic ranking member Sherrod Brown voiced barely concealed pleasure that Shelby would be departing because of term limits in late 2016. With Trump in the White House, legislation loosening Dodd-Frank regulations on all but the largest banks was ultimately signed into law in May 2018.

Shelby has enjoyed a warmer relationship with his Appropriations Committee colleagues — most recently Leahy, and earlier, Democrat Barbara Mikulski of Maryland, who chaired the committee during Shelby's stint as ranking member. In 2014, Mikulski agreed to boost spending for NASA's Space Launch System, a major project at the Marshall Space Flight Center in Huntsville. Critics have derided SLS as a "rocket to nowhere," arguing its technology is outmoded and much costlier than using private alternatives to propel heavy payloads into space. But Shelby and Mikulski, with her own home-state interest at the Goddard Space Flight Center, worked collaboratively to fund NASA programs. "He's a true partner," the avowedly liberal Mikulski said of Shelby at a hearing that year.

Shelby also forged a partnership with another leading Senate liberal, Leahy, upon assuming the appropriations chairmanship in 2018. Trump had just signed "omnibus" legislation in which the 12 annual appropriations bills funding departments and agencies were merged into one hastily passed measure totaling 2,200 pages. Trump called the process "ridiculous" and vowed not to sign such legislation again. But Shelby and Leahy shared longer-term concerns that the breakdown of the appropriations process had concentrated power to cut last-minute deals with congressional leaders at the expense of increasingly frustrated rank-and-file legislators. "We took a couple of trips together and we talked about it, and just said unless we get this back, the Senate is really screwed," Leahy told The New York Times in relating his discussions with Shelby. "We have to get back to doing it the regular way."

The upshot was that Shelby and Leahy persuaded their respective party leaders to keep poison-pill "policy riders" off appropriations bills. Democrats credited Shelby for holding up his part of the bargain — often to the consternation of his fellow Republicans seeking to advance pet causes, and even when it meant Shelby had to vote against policy riders he personally supported. "If we're going to avoid another omnibus, and instead pass individual spending bills and send them to the president's desk, we have to work in a bipartisan fashion, which I'm going to try hard to do," Shelby told the Appropriations Committee shortly after becoming chairman.

Following a decade with few individual spending bills clearing the Senate floor, Shelby shepherded nine of the 12 annual appropriations measures to Senate passage on bipartisan votes in 2018. It was an accomplishment overshadowed by Trump's periodic threats to shut down the government over funding for a southern border wall — an approach with which Shelby pointedly took issue. "Both sides, Democrats and Republicans, realize that shutting down the government, the specter of shutting down the government ... is not in anyone's political interests," Shelby told the Times.

While he boasts that he has biennially introduced a balanced-budget constitutional amendment, Shelby makes no apologies for the amount of federal money he has sought to direct to his home state. When it came to earmarking, the now-banned practice that allowed individual lawmakers to tuck special provisions into spending bills, Shelby "made a kind of art form out of it," former Alabama GOP Rep. Jack Edwards — a longtime House Appropriations Committee member — told the Mobile Press-Register. Shelby bemoans the Senate earmark ban; after it was adopted in November 2010, he complained it would put a significant crimp in his long-term goal of securing $1 billion for science, engineering, and research projects at his state's colleges. Such efforts are one reason he easily won re-election for three decades. Another is the massive campaign treasury that, until the 2016 primary, scared off competitive challengers — with lawyers and law firms the biggest single source of campaign contributions during Shelby's career, according to the Center for Responsive Politics. Despite his party switch, Shelby has remained friendly with trial lawyers, who usually support Democrats in Alabama.

By the end of 2014, Shelby had amassed a campaign treasury of $18 million. He took hits that fall in the media for directing a fraction of that, a little over $17,000, to the National Republican Senatorial Committee while his party was seeking to recapture the Senate. But Shelby objected on principle to senators financing the NRSC and other campaigns, despite receiving the committee's assistance himself. After easily dispensing of a primary opponent in 2010 by a more than 5-1 margin, Shelby faced a significant threat in 2016 from former Marine Capt. Jonathan McConnell, an owner of a maritime security company. McConnell said Shelby was "too old" and had been in Washington for "too long," while taking aim at Shelby's role as an appropriator. "People are sick of his big spending ways," McConnell said. But, five days before the primary, the Tea Party Patriots Citizens Fund endorsed Shelby, citing his 2008 opposition to the TARP legislation; groups ranging from the National Rifle Association to the National Right to Life Committee had earlier endorsed the incumbent. Shelby outspent McConnell by 15-1, and defeated him by 65%-28%, with the remaining vote spread among three other candidates. In November, Shelby won a sixth term by 64%-36%.

Shelby will be 88 when he faces re-election in 2022. "I've got five years to go," he told the Post a year into his current term. "If I ... am blessed to live and am effective, that would be a good five years." Perhaps out of a lack of concern about future electoral repercussions, Shelby has not hesitated to differ from Trump — who is highly popular in Alabama — on issues ranging from Trump's imposition of tariffs on steel and aluminum to the president's call for banning transgender individuals from serving in the military.

Shelby's most visible split from Trump — as well as his home-state Republican Party — came in late 2017, when he withheld support from former Alabama Chief Justice Roy Moore, the controversial Republican nominee in the special Senate election for the seat now held by Jones. Shelby called the allegations against Moore — involving sexual contact with teenage girls when Moore was in his 30s — "believable;" he opted to vote for a write-in candidate rather than for Moore. "I think Alabama deserves better," he said of Moore. Shelby said Moore's election would have set back the image of the state which, while remaining one of the poorest in the nation, he has sought to transform by directing federal largesse. "I think the image of anything matters," he told the Post. "It's not 1860. It's not 1900. It's not 1940. It's not 1964 or 1965. ... And Alabama in a lot of ways is on the cutting edge, on the cusp of a lot of good things."

Doug Jones (D)

Won special election, December 2017, term expires 2020, 1st term, b. May 04, 1954; Fairfield; University of Alabama, B.S., 1976; Samford University Cumberland School of Law (AL) Cumberland School of Law, J.D., 1979; Methodist; Married (Louise F. Jones); 3 children; 2 grandchildren.

DC Office: 330 HSOB 20510, 202-224-4124, Fax: 202-224-3149, jones.senate.gov

State Offices: Birmingham, 205-731-1500; Dothan, 334-792-4924; Huntsville, 256-533-0979; Mobile, 251-414-3083; Montgomery, 334-230-0698.

Committees: *Aging. Armed Services*: Airland; Readiness & Management Support; Strategic Forces. *Banking, Housing & Urban Affairs*: Economic Policy; Financial Institutions & Consumer Protection; Housing, Transportation & Community Development. *Health, Education, Labor & Pensions*: Employment & Workplace Safety; Primary Health & Retirement Security.

Group Ratings

	ADA	ACLU	AFL-CIO	LCV	ITI	COC	HAFA	ACU	CFG	FRC
2018	-	42%	-	79%	-	60%	24%	14%	11%	14%

Key Votes of the 115th Congress

1. Obama-care revision	N/A	5. Gun regulations	N/A	9. Kavanaugh confirmation	N
2. Tax Cuts	N/A	6. Family planning regs	N/A	10. Saudi arms sales	N/A
3. Dodd-Frank revision	Y	7. Gorsuch confirmation	N/A	11. FISA rules	Y
4. Omnibus appropriations	Y	8. Immigration restrictions	N	12. Military aid in Yemen	Y

Election Results

Election	Name (Party)	Vote (%)		Cand. Spent	Ind. Exp. Support	Ind. Exp. Oppose
2017 Special	Doug Jones (D)	673,896	(50%)	$22,898,815	$3,943,038	$1,551,458
	Roy Moore (R)	651,972	(48%)	$5,239,066		
2017 Primary	Doug Jones (D)	109,105	(66%)			
	Robert Kennedy Jr. (D)	29,215	(18%)			
	Michael Hansen (D)	11,105	(7%)			

The December 2017 election of Democrat Doug Jones set off shock waves on the national political scene. Occurring in one of the country's reddest states, it was seen as a stinging defeat for President Donald Trump, who gave a full-throated endorsement in the special election – called to replace Sen. Jeff Sessions, who'd become U.S. attorney general – to Jones' controversial Republican opponent, former Alabama Supreme Court Chief Justice Roy Moore. Jones' victory cut the GOP advantage in the Senate to 51-49, raising Democrats' hopes that they could recapture a majority of that chamber the following year. But on Election Day 2018, the Democrats' hoped-for Senate gains failed to materialize. It left Jones' narrow win looking like little more than a fluke against a flawed GOP candidate; Moore's campaign was sent reeling in the closing weeks by allegations that he had repeatedly made sexual advances to teenage women while in his 30s.

The upshot was that Jones entered the 2020 cycle – and a bid for a full term – as the most vulnerable Senate Democratic incumbent up for re-election. Republicans confidently predicted that Jones – whose positions in favor of abortion rights and the Obama administration's Affordable Care Act were at apparent odds with many in a state with some of the nation's most restrictive abortion laws, and where President Barack Obama never received more than 39 percent of the vote – would fall easily to a candidate lacking Moore's baggage. A "Republican will win the seat so long as that Republican is not named Roy Moore," former Sen. Luther Strange, appointed to the seat after Sessions joined the Trump Cabinet, told Politico. But Strange's appointment also had stirred controversy, and his defeat by Moore in a September 2017 Republican runoff came amid a year of intraparty warfare that pitted Senate Majority Leader Mitch McConnell of Kentucky against the GOP's populist outsider wing. It opened a path for Jones – whose prosecution of Klu Klux Klan members for one of the most horrific crimes of the civil rights era had earned him strong support among Alabama's sizable African-American electorate – to build a coalition that also included college-educated and suburban whites, many of them independent or Republican voters.

Gordon Douglas Jones grew up near Birmingham in Fairfield, site of a U.S. Steel plant where his father worked. In the early 1960s, "I was … a white kid living out in suburbia, and so my life was a very segregated life, a sheltered life," Jones told the Los Angeles Times. "When I went to seventh grade, I, for the first time, went to a school that was integrated." Jones told FiveThirtyEight that he was "very socially conservative at the time" and voted for Richard Nixon in 1972, shortly after turning 18. But he grew disillusioned during Watergate, which coincided with his years as an undergraduate at the University of Alabama; he did field organizing for Jimmy Carter's 1976 presidential campaign. As a law student at Samford University's Cumberland Law School, Jones would cut classes to watch then-Alabama Attorney General Bill Baxley successfully prosecute a Ku Klux Klan member who was the ringleader of the 1963 bombing of Birmingham's 16th Street Baptist Church. Nationwide outrage over that bombing, in which four young black girls were killed, helped spur the civil rights movement. It went unprosecuted at the time, largely because of the reluctance of then-FBI Director J. Edgar Hoover to issue arrest warrants. Two decades after that was rectified by Baxley, Jones would further pursue the case in what he would later term "the most important thing I have done."

In 1978, Jones worked for the campaign of conservative Democrat Howell Heflin, who would go on to serve three terms in the Senate seat that Jones now holds. He spent 1979 and 1980 on Capitol Hill as a counsel to Heflin and then returned to Alabama as an assistant U.S. attorney for four years before going into private practice. Jones was back in public life in 1997, when President Bill Clinton nominated him to be U.S. attorney for the Northern District of Alabama. The 16th Street Baptist Church bombing case had been reopened four years earlier; as a U.S. attorney, Jones brought charges against two more suspects in the case. As a specially appointed state prosecutor, he won a conviction against one of them in 2001. Jones left the U.S. attorney's post shortly after that, but was reappointed state special prosecutor and led the successful prosecution against the second. With his new prominence, Jones contemplated taking on Sessions – who had succeeded Heflin upon the latter's retirement in 1996, and was preparing to seek a second term in 2002. "And then 9/11 hit," Jones told FiveThirtyEight. In the political atmosphere following the attack, Jones decided a race against an incumbent Republican in a deep-red state was too much of a reach. He remained in private law practice until May 2017, when he announced his bid for the Senate seat shortly after his 63rd birthday.

Three months earlier, then-Gov. Robert Bentley appointed the state's attorney general, Strange – a onetime college basketball player who, at 6 feet, 9 inches tall, would earn a footnote as the tallest senator in history – to replace Sessions. "Big Luther" was a creature of the Republican establishment: He ran the Washington, D.C. lobbying office of an Alabama-based energy holding company for nearly a decade before returning home to become a partner in one of the state's leading corporate law firms. Such credentials opened him up to a primary challenge from an outsider, a role that would be filled by Moore. Elected chief justice of Alabama's highest court in 2000, Moore drew national attention three years later when he was dismissed from office for ignoring a federal court order to remove a 5,000-pound Ten Commandments monument he had installed in the state judicial building. Elected chief justice again in 2012, Moore was discharged a second time – this time for instructing local judges not to issue marriage licenses to same-sex couples, in defiance of a U.S. Supreme Court order.

Strange's vulnerability as an insider was compounded by the circumstances of his appointment – bestowed by a governor engulfed in a sex scandal. In March 2016, the ousted head of the Alabama Law Enforcement Agency alleged that the then-married Bentley had misused state funds in carrying on an affair with a political adviser. A leaked phone recording in which the governor can be heard making sexually suggestive comments to the aide led to demands for his impeachment. As state attorney general, Strange in late 2016 asked the Alabama House of Representatives to delay impeachment hearings due to "related work" by his office. His appointment by Bentley just a few months later prompted accusations of political payback. "It's grimly problematic that the attorney general who blocked the impeachment investigation and who has not gone forward with the Bentley criminal investigation is rewarded with the U.S. Senate appointment," State Auditor Jim Zeigler, a Republican, told The New York Times. Citing the cost, Bentley declined to schedule a vote to fill the remainder of Sessions' term until the 2018 primary and general elections – a decision that critics said could have worked to Strange's benefit. But two months after appointing Strange, Bentley resigned from office to avoid prosecution and was succeeded by Lt. Gov. Kay Ivey – who moved up the special election by a year.

Jones had little trouble winning the August 2017 Democratic primary. But the Republican contest was forced into a runoff between Moore and Strange. The GOP primary was, on the surface, a competition to demonstrate who was the most supportive of the president in one of the few states where Trump's approval rating has consistently registered above 60 percent. But Trump's "complete and total endorsement" of Strange via Twitter before the primary sparked outcry among the president's base. The Senate Leadership Fund, a super PAC with close ties to McConnell, waged a multimillion-dollar TV effort to ensure Strange reached the runoff – even as Trump was attacking McConnell for the Senate's failure to repeal the Affordable Care Act. Moore finished first with 39 percent; Strange took 33 percent and Rep. Mo Brooks – who campaigned in a bus bedecked with a "Ditch Mitch" banner – took 20 percent. The banner echoed Moore's stance toward McConnell. He went on to defeat Strange by 10 points in the Sept. 26 runoff.

With national attention focused on the Dec. 12 special election, money began pouring into the Jones campaign. Jones outraised Moore by more than 4-1, with about $10 million coming in the campaign's final month. Publicly, Jones kept his distance from the national Democratic Party, and one of the few surrogates to campaign for him was former Vice President Joe Biden, whom Jones described as a friend. (Jones was Alabama chairman for Biden's short-lived bid for the party's 1988 presidential nomination.) But the national party sought to quietly boost Jones. A super PAC called Highway 31 pumped in more than $4 million, much of it for TV ads. Although the PAC took advantage of a legal loophole that allowed it to avoid disclosing donors until after the election, Politico reported prior to voting to that Highway 31 was a joint project of two national Democratic super PACs that had played major roles on behalf of Obama in 2012 and Hillary Clinton in 2016.

Jones avoided direct attacks on Trump and proclaimed himself a "Second Amendment guy." Moore sought to make an issue of Jones' support of abortion rights. But efforts to cast Jones as being significantly to the left of the state electorate were overshadowed by a Washington Post report in early November – in which four women on the record described sexual advances by Moore nearly 40 years earlier when they were teens. One of them, Leigh Corfman, described a sexual encounter with Moore when she was just 14 and he was 32. McConnell and several other GOP senators suggested that Moore should step aside, and the Republican National Committee and National Republican Senatorial Committee cut off support. Moore issued a statement calling the allegations "completely false" and "a desperate political attack by the National Democrat Party and the Washington Post." But as similar allegations continued to surface, Moore largely disappeared from the campaign trail. In a move that put him at odds with several Senate Republicans, Trump sought to rescue Moore's candidacy with a strong endorsement the week before the election, followed by a rally on Moore's behalf in Pensacola, Fla., a short distance from the Alabama border. The Republican National Committee also announced it was resuming financial support for Moore, although the NRSC held firm in its refusal to aid the nominee.

On Election Day, Jones capitalized on the split in the GOP ranks to eke out a 50%-48.3% victory. It was aided by more than 20,000 voters – most thought to be Republican-leaning – who wrote in candidates' names. Among them: the state's senior senator, Richard Shelby, who said earlier that Moore should "seriously consider dropping out." Jones became the first Democrat elected to the Senate from Alabama since Shelby – who switched to the GOP in 1994 – won a second term in 1992.

Jones' voting record in support of Trump's positions ranked fourth among Senate Democrats during 2018, according to vote ratings compiled by FiveThirtyEight. While Trump had attacked him repeatedly via Twitter in the closing phase of the special election, Jones refrained from directly attacking the president – although he was critical of one of Trump's signature achievements: the tax cut legislation approved shortly before Jones was sworn in. Three weeks after taking office, Jones was among only a half-dozen Senate Democrats to support a Republican-sponsored stopgap measure to extend government funding; it narrowly failed to pass, leading to a government shutdown that lasted several days. He also broke from his party in voting to confirm Mike Pompeo as secretary of State, despite Pompeo's history of anti-Muslim comments and anti-gay stances. (One of Jones' sons is gay, and the senator voiced support for gay rights on the campaign trail.) In addition, Jones was among a handful of Democrats who voted to roll back portions of the 2010 Dodd-Frank financial reforms. Serving on the Banking, Housing and Urban Affairs Committee, he contended that many small community banks in Alabama were overburdened by regulations.

At the same time, Jones' first Senate floor speech was seen as politically risky. He chose to focus on gun control, an issue that is anathema in much of the South – even if it was consistent with his support for universal background checks as a candidate. "Frankly, I … enjoy guns. I enjoy shooting them," Jones said. But, speaking shortly after the deaths of 17 students at a high school in Parkland, Fla., he added: "In the wake of yet another mass shooting, and the rising voices of young people across the country, it is our responsibility – our duty – to have a serious discussion about guns and gun safety. … On many levels, we fail our children and grandchildren every morning when we pack their backpacks and send them into harm's way."

Jones took another political risk when he joined all but one of his Democratic colleagues in voting against the Supreme Court confirmation of Brett Kavanaugh in late 2018. He urged Senate Republican leaders to "hit the pause button" after Christine Blasey Ford accused Kavanaugh of sexually assaulting her when the two were in high school. In comments to AL.com, Jones made note of the role that similar allegations had played in his election less than a year earlier. "We had some people that said it was a last-ditch effort to derail [Moore's] candidacy, but those allegations had serious credibility and disqualified Roy Moore from being in the U.S. Senate," he said. Following Ford's testimony before the Senate Judiciary Committee, Jones announced his "No" vote, saying: "The Kavanaugh nomination process has been flawed from the beginning and incomplete at the end.

Dr. Ford was credible and courageous, and I am concerned about the message our vote will be sending to our sons and daughters, as well as victims of sexual assault."

To the discomfiture of many Republicans -- including Trump -- a Jones vs. Moore rematch in 2020 became a real possibility when Moore announced in June 2019 that he was a candidate. Three months earlier, he had told a radio interviewer the special election had been "stolen." He was alluding to a New York Times disclosure in late 2018 of Democratic efforts -- reportedly funded by billionaire LinkedIn co-founder Reid Hoffman -- to establish a fake conservative Facebook page and encourage visitors to write in candidates in place of Moore. Jones denied any connection to the social media effort and called on federal authorities to investigate whether crimes had been committed. Other announced Republican candidates included Rep. Bradley Byrne and former Auburn University football coach Tommy Tuberville. Sessions did not appear interested in a comeback, although he stopped short of closing the door. When asked whether he missed the Senate, Sessions told Politico, "No. I mean, no," adding: "I could go back and spend time in the woods. I've got 10 grandchildren, oldest is 11." Alabama Republican leaders were ambivalent about a Sessions comeback, fearful that his strained relations with Trump could lead to another divisive Republican primary battle.

Bradley Byrne (R)

Elected 2013, 3rd full term, b. Feb 16, 1955; Mobile; University Military School (AL), 1973; Duke University (NC), B.A., 1977; University of Alabama School of Law, J.D., 1980; Episcopalian; Married (Rebecca Dukes); 4 children; 2 grandchildren.

Elected Office: AL Senate, 2002-2007.

Professional Career: Practicing attorney, 1980-1994, 2010-2013; AL State Board of Ed., 1994-2002; Chancellor of AL Department of Postsecondary Ed., 2007-2009.

DC Office: 119 CHOB 20515, 202-225-4931, Fax: 202-225-0562, byrne.house.gov

State Offices: Mobile, 251-690-2811; Summerdale, 251-989-2664.

Committees: *Armed Services*: Seapower & Projection Forces; Strategic Forces. *Education & Labor*: Workforce Protections (RMM).

Group Ratings

	ADA	ACLU	AFL-CIO	LCV	ITI	COC	HAFA	ACU	CFG	FRC
2018	-	4%	-	0%	-	82%	69%	84%	59%	100%
2017	0%	C	8%	0%	C	93%	C	93%	86%	100%

Almanac Ratings 2017-18

	Economy	Social	Foreign	Composite
Liberal	2%	3%	0%	2%
Conservative	99%	97%	100%	98%

Key Votes of the 115th Congress

1. Obama-care revision	Y	5. Family planning regs	Y	9. Guantanamo prisoners	N
2. Tax Cuts	Y	6. Body cameras/immigration	N	10. Ground missiles, limit	N
3. Omnibus appropriations	Y	7. Abortion ban	Y	11. Defense Dept. spending	Y
4. Dodd-Frank revision	Y	8. Concealed carry	Y	12. FISA rules	Y

Election Results

Election	Name (Party)	Vote (%)	Cand. Spent	Ind. Exp. Support	Ind. Exp. Oppose
2018 General	Bradley Byrne (R)............................ 153,228	(63%)	$732,655		
	Robert Kennedy Jr. (D)..................... 89,226	(37%)	$39,098		
2018 Primary	Bradley Byrne (R)..	(100%)			

Prior winning percentages: 2016 (96%), 2014 (68%), 2013 special (71%)

Republican Bradley Byrne, elected in 2013, has been a skillful back-room operator who cooperated with party leaders. Amid the continuing turmoil among Alabama Republicans, Byrne fell short in one statewide bid and has shown interest in another contest. He was the early GOP frontrunner to challenge democratic Sen. Doug Jones in 2020.

Byrne was born and raised in Mobile, where he practiced law for 14 years. He began his political career in 1994, successfully seeking a seat on the Alabama State Board of Education. He ran as a Democrat but left to join the Republican Party in 1997. "I learned there was no place for a conservative in the Alabama Democratic Party," Byrne told a reporter in 2013. After serving a second term on the state's Board of Education, he was elected to two terms in the state Senate. He stepped aside in 2007 when he was appointed chancellor of the Alabama Community College System, where he drew high marks for cleaning up a corrupt system.

Byrne didn't stay away from electoral politics for long, resigning in 2009 to launch a campaign for governor in 2010. With much of the state's Republican establishment and business community behind him, Byrne was the early frontrunner. He finished first in a tight four-way June Republican primary with 28 percent of the vote, but lost the runoff to state Rep. Robert Bentley, 56%-44%.

Byrne returned to practicing law in Mobile, but didn't hide his itch to seek elected office again. In 2013, Byrne got the opening he needed when Republican Rep. Jo Bonner took a high-ranking state education post. Once again, Byrne was the GOP favorite with strong support from the business community and Mobile-area establishment. In a nine-candidate Republican field, he finished first with 35 percent of the primary vote. His opponent in the run-off was businessman Dean Young, an outspoken social conservative, who got 23 percent. Young called for President Barack Obama's impeachment, said he would not support House Speaker John Boehner, and objected to "homosexuals pretending like they're married." The U.S. Chamber of Commerce spent more than $185,000 on late ads to boost Byrne. In an unexpectedly narrow outcome, the far better-funded Byrne won the runoff, 52.5%-47.5%. A month later, he handily won the general election with 71 percent against real-estate agent Burton LeFlore, grandson of Alabama civil-rights leader John LeFlore.

In the House, Byrne served on committees consistent with his local and personal interests -- Armed Services, and Education and the Workforce. He teamed with other Republicans on reforms in elementary and secondary education that would restore local control and empower parents and teachers.

Following an intensive push by Mobile business interests, Byrne successfully led opposition to a plan by the Obama administration to reduce the number of the Navy's littoral combat ships, relatively small vessels that are built at the Austral Shipyard in Mobile. In 2017, Byrne worked to include additional LCS construction in the House-passed defense-spending bill. The Trump administration placed orders for four of those ships from Austral.

Byrne voiced concern about the adverse impact on Alabama-based auto plants from tariffs imposed by President Donald Trump, which he called, "a pretty blunt tool." He led opposition by Alabama lawmakers to a Trump administration proposal to temporarily house illegal immigrants at Navy bases in Baldwin County.

Byrne responded to constituent concerns as a co-chair of the bipartisan Congressional Coastal Communities Caucus. He supported steps for off-shore oil and gas leasing in areas off the Atlantic Coast. In July 2018, the House approved his amendment to protect revenues paid to states from oil and gas leases in the Gulf of Mexico. He has joined other Gulf Coast lawmakers seeking to increase those revenues.

At home, Byrne remained active in internal GOP politics. In a 2016 rematch with Young in the Republican primary, he had a more comfortable — but not overwhelming — victory, 60%-40%. Following the resignation of Sen. Jeff Sessions to become attorney general, Byrne joined other Alabama Republicans who voiced interest in the seat. He may have damaged his prospects when he said in October 2016 that Donald Trump should step aside as Republican presidential nominee following the release of a 2005 tape in which Trump made lewd comments about women. Following the GOP chaos that led to the December 2017 special-election victory of Jones to fill the remainder of Sessions' term, Byrne sought support across the state for challenging the incumbent in 2020 and became the early favorite of many state and national party leaders. But Byrne initially faced the prospect of another divisive primary—including the continuing presence of former state Supreme Court Chief Justice Roy Moore, who narrowly lost to Jones.

AL-1: Southwest Alabama   Cook Partisan Voting Index: R+15

Population		Race and Ethnicity		Income	
Total	702,730	White	65.2%	Median Income	$46,449
Land area (sq. miles)	6,067	Black	27.5%	District Income Rank	360
Pop/ sq mi	115.8	Latino	3.1%	Poverty Rate	18%
Born in State	68.4%	Asian	1.4%	With health insurance	88.1%
		Two or more races	1.6%	Cash public assistance	1.6%
Age Groups		Other	1.2%	Food stamp/SNAP	14.8%
Under 18	23.2%				
18-34	21.6%	**Education**		**Work**	
35-64	38.8%	H.S grad or less	45.6%	White Collar	16.4%
Over 64	16.4%	Some college	30.3%	Sales and Service	43.2%
		College Degree, 4 yr	15.9%	Blue Collar	24.2%
Military		Post grad	8.2%	Government	13.5%
Veteran/ Active Duty	9.9%				

2012 Pres. Vote	Romney	184,743	(62%)	Obama	11,712	(37%)		
2016 Pres. Vote	Trump	192,633	(63%)	Clinton	103,363	(34%)	Johnson	6,153 (2%)

Mobile Bay: Mobile, the port where the Tombigbee and Alabama rivers flow into the Gulf of Mexico, was a strategic point on the American frontier. Spanish after the Revolutionary War, it was wrested away by threats of war from Secretary of State John Quincy Adams. During the Civil War, it was one of the major Confederate ports. In 1864, Admiral David Farragut, while steaming into the harbor lashed to his ship's rigging, cried, "Damn the torpedoes! Full speed ahead." Today, Mobile is full of graceful signs of its turbulent past. Behind the docks and rail lines are downtown buildings and old houses with Spanish motifs, French accents or tropical Art Deco lines. Further inland are neighborhoods with spacious houses, often with double porches, overhung by huge live oaks graced with Spanish moss. Mobile is a Gulf Coast version of Charleston or a smaller, more comfortable New Orleans, with a taste for shellfish and spicy food and an even older Mardi Gras, which the locals have been celebrating since 1703. As befits a frontier city with a martial past, Mobile is bristling with arms: One of the city's proudest possessions is the battleship USS Alabama, moored at the head of Mobile Bay, with its guns aimed out toward the Gulf.

Mobile's economy was based originally on docks and shipyards, factories and terminals, but with a determination to impose touches of beauty on its hot, flat landscape. The continuing expansion of the container terminal serves Alabama's booming auto factories. Three recent developments have attracted more business to the port: expansion of the Panama Canal; the local assembly line by European aircraft manufacturer Airbus for its A320 airline and a second assembly line for a smaller Bombardier passenger jet; and the return of Carnival Cruise Lines, which was a boost for local tourism. Although Huntsville has passed Mobile as the third-largest city in Alabama, four cities in neighboring Baldwin County ranked among the fastest-growing in the state.

In August 2005, Hurricane Katrina struck Mobile and its beaches with Category 4 intensity. On Dauphin Island, the 14-mile spit of land south of Mobile Bay, 300 homes were swept away, and a one-mile gash created a new island. Disaster struck the area again in 2010. After the explosion of BP's Deepwater Horizon offshore drilling rig, oil washed up on beaches and into Mobile Bay, prompting concerns that neighboring Louisiana was receiving more cleanup attention.

Mobile is the focus of Alabama's 1st Congressional District, which extends north along the usually lazy Tombigbee and Alabama rivers, with their old forts and mansions. There are surviving backcountry settlements of blacks and Cajans (who may or may not be descended from Louisiana Cajuns) and Creek Indians. Once cotton fields, this is now timberland, a major contributor to Alabama's economy. East of Mobile Bay, along the shores of the Gulf of Mexico, are condominium communities in Baldwin County. The area hosts the annual National Shrimp Festival, and its glorious Gulf beaches are among the South's best. For years, this southern seaboard of the Confederacy has been among the most hawkish parts of America, and today it is solidly Republican in national elections. Donald Trump made early appearances here during his 2016 campaign and was well-received.

Martha Roby (R)

Elected 2010, 5th term, b. Jul 26, 1976; Montgomery; New York University, B.M., 1998; Samford University Cumberland School of Law (AL) Cumberland School of Law, J.D., 2001; Presbyterian; Married (Riley Roby); 2 children.

Elected Office: Montgomery City Council, 2003-2010.

Professional Career: Practicing attorney, 2002-2004.

DC Office: 504 CHOB 20515, 202-225-2901, Fax: 202-225-8913, roby.house.gov

State Offices: Andalusia, 334-428-1129; Dothan, 334-794-9680; Montgomery, 334-262-7718.

Committees: *Appropriations*: Commerce, Justice, Science & Related Agencies; Military Construction, Veterans Affairs & Related Agencies; State, Foreign Operations & Related Programs. *Judiciary*: Courts, Intellectual Property & Internet (RMM).

Group Ratings

	ADA	ACLU	AFL-CIO	LCV	ITI	COC	HAFA	ACU	CFG	FRC
2018	-	3%	-	6%	-	83%	56%	70%	50%	100%
2017	0%	C	5%	0%	C	93%	C	85%	74%	100%

Almanac Ratings 2017-18

	Economy	Social	Foreign	Composite
Liberal	4%	3%	0%	2%
Conservative	96%	97%	100%	98%

Key Votes of the 115th Congress

1. Obama-care revision	Y	5. Family planning regs	Y	9. Guantanamo prisoners	N
2. Tax Cuts	Y	6. Body cameras/immigration	N	10. Ground missiles, limit	N
3. Omnibus appropriations	Y	7. Abortion ban	Y	11. Defense Dept. spending	Y
4. Dodd-Frank revision	Y	8. Concealed carry	Y	12. FISA rules	Y

Election Results

Election	Name (Party)		Vote (%)		Cand. Spent	Ind. Exp. Support	Ind. Exp. Oppose
2018 General	Martha Roby (R)	138,879	(61%)		$2,106,595	$370,620	
	Tabitha Isner (D)	86,931	(38%)		$508,913		
2018 Primary	Martha Roby (R)	48,277	(68%)				
runoff	Bobby Bright (R)	22,767	(32%)				
2018 Primary	Martha Roby (R)	36,708	(39%)				
	Bobby Bright (R)	26,481	(28%)				
	Barry Moore (R)	18,177	(19%)				
	Rich Hobson (R)	7,052	(8%)				
	Tommy Amason (R)	5,763	(6%)				

Prior winning percentages: 2016 (49%), 2014 (67%), 2012 (64%), 2010 (51%)

Alabama 2nd District Republican Martha Roby was one of the fastest-rising members of the 2010 Republican class, securing prime committee assignments and establishing herself as a leadership ally. An oft-mentioned contender for the U.S. Senate, Roby hit rough political waters in 2016. Years-long tea party complaints that she is not adequately conservative accelerated when she disavowed Donald Trump late in the 2016 campaign. The subsequent, unexpected drop in her voter support set her up with a tough 2018 re-election campaign.

Roby grew up with a political pedigree, but initially aspired to work on the business-side of the Nashville musical industry. She is the daughter of Joel Dubina, a senior judge on the U.S. Court of Appeals for the 11th Circuit. She grew up in Montgomery and received a bachelor's degree in music from New York University in 1998. After earning a law degree from Samford University in Birmingham, she returned to her hometown to practice law. In 2003, she was elected to the Montgomery City Council. In that role, she led efforts to adopt an ordinance barring city businesses from hiring undocumented workers.

National Republicans zeroed in on Roby as a 2010 top recruit for the seat occupied by freshman Democratic Rep. Bobby Bright, one of his party's most endangered incumbents. A former mayor of Montgomery, Bright criticized Roby for moving too slowly on her undocumented workers initiative. Roby and the Republicans kept Bright on the partisan defensive. He announced that he would not vote again to elect California liberal Nancy Pelosi as Speaker of the House. He also played up his endorsements from the National Rifle Association and the National Right to Life PAC. The Democratic Congressional Campaign Committee spent about $1 million for Bright, but that was not enough to save him. Roby pulled out a close win, 51%-49%.

On the Armed Services Committee during her first term, she worked on behalf of Maxwell-Gunter Air Force Base and the Army's Fort Rucker in her district. Politico named her the most underrated member of the freshman class, saying, "If she's able to win reelection, she could be a leader of her party." But a few conservative activists weren't satisfied with some of her votes. Erick Erickson of the influential RedState.com charged, "She has carried water for the leadership" and "betrayed her conservative constituents."

After the 2012 election, Roby made a bid to join the House Republican leadership as GOP conference vice chair. She lost to the slightly more senior Lynn Jenkins of Kansas, but she earned an impressive consolation prize in 2013 with a seat on the Appropriations Committee. Given her age, 36, at the time of that assignment and thanks to House GOP term limits in committee leadership, it is not an unreasonable consideration that she could ascend to that committee's chairmanship. She displayed her conservative credentials by joining the Select Committee on Benghazi, where she criticized the State Department's failure to upgrade security at its Libyan facility. She remained a hawk on defense, joining with Democratic Rep. Tulsi Gabbard of Hawaii to warn of the "devastating" effect if automatic military spending cuts took effect in 2016. Also that year, she backed the proposed shift of about 18 F-35s to the 187th Fighter Wing at Montgomery's Dannelly Field Air Guard Station.

Roby is friendly with a fellow Alabaman elected in 2010, Democratic Rep. Terri Sewell. The pair cooperated as co-sponsors of the March 2015 commemoration of the 50th anniversary of the Selma to Montgomery civil rights march. Roby organized significant participation by other House Republicans, plus former President George W. Bush. And she passed legislation giving the Congressional Gold Medal to the 1965 marchers.

Redistricting shifts in 2012 seemed to ensure that Roby was secure for another decade. In her next two campaigns, she sailed to reelection with 64 percent and 67 percent of the vote. But everything changed for Roby in 2016. A month before Election Day, Roby said that Trump's language was "unacceptable" for a presidential candidate and that she would not vote for him, following the release of a 2005 video in which he made crude sexual comments about women. She did not back down, even when other congressional Republicans later toned down their criticism of Trump. Her remarks sparked a furor at home. "I cannot look my children in the eye [Margaret, age 11, and George, age 7] and justify a vote for a man who promotes and boasts about sexually assaulting women," Roby responded.

The local Tea Party launched a write-in campaign against her, but Roby won re-election a month later. Roby stood by her criticism, while saying that she was "eager" to work with Trump and his administration.

Local critics raised the possibility of a primary challenge in 2018. Roby then spent the first half of 2017 courting President Trump, with frequent trips to the White House. The aim, Politico reported at the time, was to fend off presidential wrath on Twitter. She eventually earned his endorsement over that channel, thanks in part to a House GOP leadership lobbying effort.

A clear target remained on her back, and a five-candidate primary field forced Roby into a 2018 runoff. But Roby's primary opponent was an old, flawed foe: Bobby Bright. The ex-congressman switched parties and campaigned against Roby with charges that she was insufficiently supportive of Trump. Roby easily dispatched those attacks by underscoring Bright's 2009 vote to support Pelosi for Speaker. Roby dominated Bright in the July runoff, 68%-32%. In the fall, she coasted to a fourth term, defeating Democrat Tabitha Isner, 61%-38%.

AL-2: Southeast Alabama   **Cook Partisan Voting Index: R+16**

Population		Race and Ethnicity		Income	
Total	681,443	White	62.1%	Median Income	$44,765
Land area (sq. miles)	10,142	Black	31%	District Income Rank	377
Pop/ sq mi	67.2	Latino	3.5%	Poverty Rate	18.8%
Born in State	69.6%	Asian	1.1%	With health insurance	89.2%
		Two or more races	1.8%	Cash public assistance	1.4%
Age Groups		Other	0.5%	Food stamp/SNAP	16.3%
Under 18	22.9%				
18-34	22.8%	**Education**		**Work**	
35-64	38.5%	H.S grad or less	48.1%	White Collar	15.8%
Over 64	15.8%	Some college	29.9%	Sales and Service	41.1%
		College Degree, 4 yr	13.7%	Blue Collar	27%
Military		Post grad	8.4%	Government	18.3%
Veteran/ Active Duty	12.3%				

2012 Pres. Vote	Romney	182,146	(63%)	Obama	105,636	(36%)
2016 Pres. Vote	Trump	185,504	(64%)	Clinton	94,300	(33%)

Montgomery, Dothan: Thick green countryside blankets southern Alabama. Even in Montgomery, the stone and brick buildings of the downtown district do not mask the contours of the hills or hide the lush foliage. One can look downhill from the restored Greek Revival capitol toward Dexter Avenue King Memorial Baptist Church, where the young Martin Luther King Jr. was pastor in the 1950s, or out past the impressive Carolyn Blount Theatre, host of the Alabama Shakespeare Festival, toward new subdivisions and shopping malls, and easily imagine when this land was covered with cotton fields and pine trees, and a young Wilson Pickett was still performing in Baptist church choirs in Prattville. The atmosphere is especially rural in southeast Alabama's Wiregrass region, named for the stiff native grass. There is the fishing town of Eufaula, along the Chattahoochee River; the Army's Fort Rucker, home of Army aviation flight training; Maxwell-Gunter Air Force Base, which is the largest employer in the Montgomery area; and Enterprise, site of the Boll Weevil Monument that commemorates the insect that destroyed two-thirds of the cotton crop in 1915 and then spread throughout the South.

Timber is an important resource here, and peanuts replaced cotton as the main crop in the area surrounding Dothan, which calls itself the "peanut capital of the world." Each fall, Dothan holds the National Peanut Festival, the largest of its kind, to celebrate growers and the harvest season. A statue of peanut innovator George Washington Carver can be found here. Dothan also is the home of the expanded Wayne Farms chicken processing plant, which handles 1.3 million chickens weekly.

The area's industrial diversification has been led by the automobile industry. Hyundai, the world's fifth largest automaker, built its first U.S. assembly plant in southwest Montgomery County, with about 3,100 jobs and more than 400 robots to meet annual production capacity of 395,000 cars. The company calls the facility one of the most advanced in the North American auto industry, producing Sonata and Elantra sedans. Despite the economic growth, Montgomery's population continued to retract in recent years. In April 2018, the National Memorial for Peace and Justice, better known as "the lynching museum," opened in downtown Montgomery.

The 2nd Congressional District of Alabama covers 14 counties in the southeast corner of the state. It includes a thin link in the heart of Montgomery, but shares the surrounding metropolitan area with the 3rd and 7th districts to the east and west. The more heavily black precincts in west Montgomery, as well as mostly African-American Lowndes County, have become part of the sprawling majority-minority 7th. The remaining Montgomery County precincts in the 2nd district vote heavily Republican, as do suburban Elmore and Autauga counties and Houston County in the Wiregrass region; each gave Donald Trump more than 70 percent of the vote in 2016. These areas outvote the district's "Black Belt" counties, including Bullock, with a large black majority and the only Democratic county in the district, and Barbour on the Georgia border, which was George Wallace's home base. Like all of Alabama except for the 7th, this district is solidly Republican.

Mike Rogers (R)

Elected 2002, 9th term, b. Jul 16, 1958; Hammond, IN; Jacksonville State University (AL), B.A., 1981; Jacksonville State University (AL), M.P.A., 1984; Birmingham School of Law (AL), J.D., 1991; Baptist; Married (Beth Rogers); 3 children.

Elected Office: Calhoun County Commission, 1986-1990; AL House, 1994-2002; Min. Leader, 1998-2000.

Professional Career: Practicing attorney, 1991-2002.

DC Office: 2184 RHOB 20515, 202-225-3261, Fax: 202-226-8485, mikerogers.house.gov

State Offices: Anniston, 256-236-5655; Opelika, 334-745-6221.

Committees: *Armed Services*: Readiness; Strategic Forces. *Homeland Security (RMM)*: Ex Officio membership on all subcommittees.

Group Ratings

	ADA	ACLU	AFL-CIO	LCV	ITI	COC	HAFA	ACU	CFG	FRC
2018	-	4%	-	3%	-	83%	59%	72%	53%	100%
2017	5%	C	13%	0%	C	93%	C	78%	68%	100%

Almanac Ratings 2017-18

	Economy	Social	Foreign	Composite
Liberal	7%	3%	0%	3%
Conservative	93%	97%	100%	97%

Key Votes of the 115th Congress

1. Obama-care revision	Y	5. Family planning regs	Y	9. Guantanamo prisoners	N
2. Tax Cuts	Y	6. Body cameras/immigration	N	10. Ground missiles, limit	N
3. Omnibus appropriations	Y	7. Abortion ban	Y	11. Defense Dept. spending	Y
4. Dodd-Frank revision	Y	8. Concealed carry	Y	12. FISA rules	Y

Election Results

Election	Name (Party)	Vote (%)		Cand. Spent	Ind. Exp. Support	Ind. Exp. Oppose
2018 General	Mike Rogers (R)	147,770	(64%)	$1,189,467		
	Mallory Hagan (D)	83,996	(36%)	$419,679		
2018 Primary	Mike Rogers (R)		(100%)			

Prior winning percentages: 2016 (67%), 2014 (66%), 2012 (64%), 2010 (59%), 2008 (53%), 2006 (59%), 2004 (61%), 2002 (50%)

Republican Mike Rogers, elected in 2002, has been active on three House committees that deal with national security and agriculture issues. In the southern tradition, he gained seniority and became the top Republican on the Homeland Security panel.

Rogers is a fifth-generation resident of Calhoun County, the son of a textile worker and a fireman. At the age of 28, he was the first Republican elected to the county commission. In 1994, he won a seat in the Alabama House and, in his second term, became minority leader. Running for the House in 2002, he had stiff competition from Democrat Joe Turnham Jr., who served three years as state party chairman. Rogers touted his working-class values, support from the National Rifle Association and backing of a constitutional amendment permitting prayer in public schools. Turnham did not risk bringing in national Democrats to campaign for him in the socially conservative district, while Rogers got frequent visits from national Republican leaders. The contrast in national party support was evident in Rogers's big fundraising advantage. He won, but only 50%-48%.

On the Armed Services Committee, Rogers sought to protect Anniston Army Depot as well as Maxwell-Gunter Air Force Base and Fort Benning just across the state line in Georgia. He is a leading Republican hawk on defense issues, including his call for increased attention to missile defense. After Sen. Dianne Feinstein of California said that current spending for nuclear weapons is "unsustainable," Rogers wrote that her comment shows a disregard for reality. "Nuclear weapons are not undermining other national security priorities—they are undergirding them." President Donald Trump later picked up on that theme. Rogers has advocated space defense technology as a vital feature of American military strength, and has taken the lead in Congress in seeking to create the Space Force as the sixth service branch of the military. "We are heavily dependent on space now in warfare and with our national security," he said in October 2018. He criticized Air Force leaders as "in denial" for their resistance to the plan.

Rogers has sought to enhance Alabama's role in domestic protection against terrorism. His district includes the Federal Emergency Management Agency's Center for Domestic Preparedness. Following the 2018 election, as the most senior Republican eligible for the top slot on the Homeland Security Committee, he easily defeated a challenge from Rep. John Katko of New York. Rogers narrowly lost to Rep. Mike McCaul of Texas in 2012, when he competed to fill a vacancy as chairman of the committee. He has been outspoken in describing security threats facing the nation. With the Islamic State, he said during a meeting in his district, "We can't put our head in the sand because all of us are tired of war."

Rogers has shown populist leanings on economic issues. He bucked the Bush administration and won local praise by opposing a free trade agreement with Morocco on the grounds that it would reduce local textile and apparel jobs. Following the 2016 election, he stirred discussion among House Republicans to revive the practice of legislative earmarks for members of Congress to direct federal spending to their constituents. House Speaker Paul Ryan objected and shut down that internal debate for the next two years. Still, Rogers mostly has been a reliable Republican vote, including the showdown 2015 vote to give trade promotion authority to the president. His Almanac vote ratings in 2017-18 placed him among conservative House Republicans.

Rogers has worked hard to entrench himself and raise money to discourage Democratic opposition in this ancestrally Democratic district, with a 25 percent African-American population. In 2018, he faced his first serious challenger in a decade: Mallory Hagan, an Opelika native and winner of the Miss America pageant in 2013, who later was a television news reporter in Columbus Georgia. Hagan mostly avoided discussion of Trump. Instead, she said in an interview that she sought to be a "role model and leader to young people."

In a pre-election editorial, the Anniston Star described Hagan as "smart and passionate about several of the district's core issues, such as poverty, health care and the closing of rural hospitals." After writing that many local residents viewed Rogers as "unresponsive," but that "his experience and ability to protect the district's interests" were "undeniable," the newspaper concluded that it had no recommendation on the contest. Hagan raised nearly $500,000, but she had scant national party support and was outspent nearly 3-to-1. Rogers won, 64%-36%, and took 11 of the 13 counties, trailing only in Macon and neighboring Russell.

AL-3: Eastern Alabama   **Cook Partisan Voting Index: R+16**

Population		Race and Ethnicity		Income	
Total	703,772	White	68%	Median Income	$44,725
Land area (sq. miles)	7,544	Black	25.3%	District Income Rank	379
Pop/ sq mi	93.3	Latino	3%	Poverty Rate	18.7%
Born in State	65.4%	Asian	1.7%	With health insurance	90.2%
		Two or more races	1.7%	Cash public assistance	1.6%
Age Groups		Other	0.3%	Food stamp/SNAP	15.5%
Under 18	22.2%				
18-34	23.8%	**Education**		**Work**	
35-64	38.6%	H.S grad or less	47.7%	White Collar	15.4%
Over 64	15.4%	Some college	30.7%	Sales and Service	39.1%
		College Degree, 4 yr	12.8%	Blue Collar	28.2%
Military		Post grad	8.8%	Government	16.9%
Veteran/ Active Duty	10%				

2012 Pres. Vote	Romney	174,620	(62%)	Obama	103,089	(37%)		
2016 Pres. Vote	Trump	188,476	(65%)	Clinton	93,301	(32%)	Johnson	5,766	(2%)

Auburn, Anniston: The 3rd Congressional District of Alabama is centered geographically and philosophically in Lineville. The small town's progress from Ku Klux Klan country to an integrated community where crowds regularly cheer mixed black and white high school teams and people of all races work together echoes that of America's most integrated institution, the military. The local military presence is unmistakable: Calhoun County is home to Anniston Army Depot. Horseshoe Bend is where Andrew Jackson won a climactic battle against the Upper Creek Indians. Fort Mitchell, a 19th-century frontier military outpost, is the site of a national military cemetery sometimes referred to as the "Arlington of the South." Phenix City, across the Chattahoochee River from Georgia's Fort Benning, served as a "sin city" in the 1940s and 1950s, a place so sleazy that Gen. George Patton threatened to level it with his tanks. Today, the huge military installation plays a more constructive role in the local economy.

There are other places of distinction in the district: Tuskegee is the home of Booker T. Washington's Tuskegee University, training ground for the Tuskegee Airmen, the first black pilots trained to fly for the U.S. military. Auburn is the home of Auburn University and its renowned sports teams and veterinary school. Talladega is the site of the Alabama Institute for the Deaf and Blind and is perhaps America's most user-friendly city for people with disabilities. NASCAR fans know it as the home of a famed speedway and for the International Motorsports Hall of Fame — the Cooperstown of auto racing—where a $50 million "transformation" was scheduled for completion in 2019.

This looks and feels like rural country, though few people here make a living off their farms. An economy once dependent on cotton mills is today more diverse, and interstates have brought in new businesses. The Honda assembly plant in Talladega County employed more than 4,500 workers, who built 350,000 minivans, SUVs and pick-up trucks in 2017.

Politically, this was long one of the heartlands of the conservative wing of the Democratic Party, with a large population of African-American descendants of slaves from plantations. Tuskegee's Macon County is the only remaining Democratic County in the district. St. Clair County, close to Birmingham and solidly Republican, has been among the fastest-growing in the state. Redistricting changes in 2012 boosted Republicans, and Democrats have had a more difficult time competing here. Donald Trump won the district with 65 percent of the vote.

Robert Aderholt (R)

Elected 1996, 12th term, b. Jul 22, 1965; Haleyville; Birmingham-Southern College (AL), B.A., 1987; Samford University Cumberland Law School (AL), J.D., 1990; Methodist; Married (Caroline McDonald Aderholt); 2 children.

Professional Career: Haleyville Municipal Judge, 1992-1995; Assistant legal advisor, Gov. Fob James, 1995-1996.

DC Office: 1203 LHOB 20515, 202-225-4876, Fax: 202-225-5587, aderholt.house.gov

State Offices: Cullman, 256-734-6043; Gadsden, 256-546-0201; Jasper, 205-221-2310; Tuscumbia, 256-381-3450.

Committees: *Appropriations*: Agriculture, Rural Development, FDA & Related Agencies; Commerce, Justice, Science & Related Agencies (RMM); Defense.

Group Ratings

	ADA	ACLU	AFL-CIO	LCV	ITI	COC	HAFA	ACU	CFG	FRC
2018	-	4%	-	0%	-	83%	56%	72%	52%	100%
2017	0%	C	14%	0%	C	92%	C	81%	65%	100%

Almanac Ratings 2017-18

	Economy	Social	Foreign	Composite
Liberal	5%	3%	0%	3%
Conservative	95%	97%	100%	97%

Key Votes of the 115th Congress

1. Obama-care revision	Y	5. Family planning regs	Y
2. Tax Cuts	Y	6. Body cameras/immigration	N
3. Omnibus appropriations	Y	7. Abortion ban	Y
4. Dodd-Frank revision	Y	8. Concealed carry	Y

9. Guantanamo prisoners	N
10. Ground missiles, limit	N
11. Defense Dept. spending	Y
12. FISA rules	Y

Election Results

Election	Name (Party)	Vote (%)		Cand. Spent	Ind. Exp. Support	Ind. Exp. Oppose
2018 General	Robert Aderholt (R)......................	184,255	(80%)	$1,235,449		
	Lee Auman (D)..............................	46,492	(20%)	$73,193		
2018 Primary	Robert Aderholt (R)......................	93,959	(82%)			
	Anthony Blackmon (R)...................	21,366	(19%)			

Prior winning percentages: 2016 (99%), 2014 (99%), 2012 (74%), 2010 (100%), 2008 (75%), 2006 (70%), 2004 (75%), 2002 (87%), 2000 (61%), 1998 (56%), 1996 (50%)

Robert Aderholt, a Republican first elected in 1996, is a senior member of the Appropriations Committee who lost his bid to become its ranking minority member. He remained an influential player on agriculture and defense spending and considers obtaining federal money for the state to be an essential part of his job. He explored options for running for senator.

Aderholt is from Winston County, the one ancestrally Republican county in north Alabama; it opposed secession in the Civil War and declared itself the Free State of Winston. His father was a circuit judge for more than 30 years; his wife's father was a state senator and state commissioner of Agriculture and Industry. In 1992, Aderholt was appointed Haleyville municipal judge. Three years later, he became a top aide to Republican Gov. Fob James.

With that pedigree, he decided to run for Congress when 30-year veteran Rep. Tom Bevill, a Democrat and a pork-barrel spending appropriator, retired. As the Republican nominee, he faced state Sen. Bob Wilson Jr., who called himself a Democrat "in the Tom Bevill tradition." In this culturally conservative district, Aderholt emphasized social issues, opposing abortion rights, gun control, same-sex marriage and prohibitions on school prayer. "We want to go to Washington to deliver a message, and that is, don't mess with our traditional family values," he said. He attacked Wilson for his support from labor unions and trial lawyers. Aderholt won 50%-48%. The outcome was a landmark in the Republican takeover of rural southern districts.

Aderholt's voting record is generally conservative, and he was among the first House Republicans to join the Tea Party Caucus in 2010. His Almanac vote ratings in 2017-18 were among GOP conservatives. Aderholt has often sided with labor and economic populists on trade issues, mainly because of local imperatives. He has supported quotas on steel imports. He voted against normalizing trade relations with China and opposed free-trade agreements with Chile, Morocco and Singapore. In 2015, he was one of 50 Republicans to vote against the measure giving fast-track authority to negotiate trade deals to President Barack Obama and his successors. In another populist leaning, he was the only House member from Alabama in 2008 to vote against the $700 billion rescue of the financial markets. He cited the need for a more market-based approach.

Republican leaders put Aderholt on the Appropriations Committee, where he has secured more highway and water projects money than most of his GOP colleagues. In the old-style southern tradition, he has worked his way up the ranks by learning how deals are made and trading favors. After Republicans assumed House control in 2011, he became chairman of the Homeland Security Subcommittee. On behalf of Alabama's aerospace industry, Aderholt has worked with delegation members to have a new NASA heavy-lift rocket designed to carry astronauts into deep space built at Huntsville's Marshall Space Flight Center.

For six years, Aderholt chaired the Agriculture Appropriations Subcommittee, an area of interest for many of his constituents. His panel faced the limitation that about $120 billion under its nominal control is for "mandatory" programs — chiefly food stamps — and therefore subject to limited appropriations tinkering. He lists his priorities as "cuttingedge" agricultural research, vibrant rural communities, nutrition for the most vulnerable, competitive markets in the global economy and the safest food and drug supply in the world. He also was mindful of agri-business needs. When a federal advisory panel urged consideration of the environmental impact of nutrition plans, Aderholt criticized "politicallymotivated" steps such as taxes on certain foods that he said were at odds with sound science.

At Appropriations, he retained his interest in social issues. In 2012, Aderholt added an amendment to the department's spending bill specifying that none of the funds provided to Immigration and Customs Enforcement could be used to pay for an abortion, except under certain circumstances. In response to President Barack Obama's executive actions on immigration, he prepared House Republican legislation in 2015 to nullify presidential action and toughen enforcement against undocumented immigrants, especially the surge of unaccompanied children who have crossed the southern border. When Alabama Chief Justice Roy Moore called for a new law to prevent federal judges from interfering with public displays of the Ten Commandments, Aderholt filed a bill toward that goal. "The acknowledgment of God is not a legitimate subject of review by the federal courts," Aderholt said. In July 2018, the House approved an Aderholt rider to a spending bill that permitted adoption agencies to have separate standards for same-sex couples. That provision was deleted in September when the Senate and House agreed on the broader bill.

Aderholt was positioned as the next Republican to lead the Appropriations Committee after Rep. Rodney Frelinghuysen of New Jersey in early 2018 announced his retirement. Rep. Kay Granger of Texas, who entered the House the same year as Aderholt, waged a hard-fought campaign. She benefited from the support of the largest state delegation in the House, plus pressure to increase the influence of women among House Republicans. Some Republicans contended that Aderholt suffered because another Alabaman, Richard Shelby, chaired the Senate Appropriations Committee.

When President-elect Donald Trump tapped Alabama Sen. Jeff Sessions for attorney general, Aderholt said that he would like to be appointed as his successor. "I would be someone who could hit the ground running," he told the Yellowhammer News. Although he didn't get the appointment, Aderholt, with his relatively young age, could have other opportunities for the Senate. Following the 2018 election, he explored but soon ruled out a challenge to Democratic Sen. Doug Jones, who planned to seek a six-year term in 2020.The prospect that Aderholt's district might be squeezed by redistricting in 2022 raised the option of campaigning for the Senate that year if Shelby retires at age 88.

AL-4: North-Central Alabama   Cook Partisan Voting Index: R+30

Population		Race and Ethnicity		Income	
Total	683,508	White	83.7%	Median Income	$41,822
Land area (sq. miles)	8,889	Black	6.9%	District Income Rank	402
Pop/ sq mi	76.9	Latino	6.4%	Poverty Rate	18.5%
Born in State	74.9%	Asian	0.6%	With health insurance	88.2%
Age Groups		Two or more races	1.5%	Cash public assistance	1.4%
		Other	0.8%	Food stamp/SNAP	14.9%
Under 18	22.9%				
18-34	20.4%	**Education**		**Work**	
35-64	39.2%	H.S grad or less	53.1%	White Collar	17.5%
Over 64	17.5%	Some college	30%	Sales and Service	37.8%
		College Degree, 4 yr	10.4%	Blue Collar	33.5%
Military		Post grad	6.5%	Government	14.6%
Veteran/ Active Duty	8%				

2012 Pres. Vote	Romney	205,589	(75%)	Obama	65,852	(24%)	
2016 Pres. Vote	Trump	233,662	(80%)	Clinton	50,722	(17%)	

Gadsden: The Appalachian Mountains' corduroy ridges, dividing the Atlantic coast from the interior, make up America's coal-and-steel industrial spine, from the black coal country of western Pennsylvania to the red hill country of northern Alabama. Here rose America's two premier steel cities, Pittsburgh and Birmingham. Around both, and for many miles in between, is countryside settled by feisty Scots-Irish farmers in the years between the Revolution and the Civil War. In valley land accessible to railroads, great steel factories were built in the 80 years after the Civil War, along with smaller factories that produced socks, tires, glass and chemicals, and that butchered chickens. Northern Alabama was solidly Democratic through the 1950s. It was populist on economics, conservative on cultural issues. Since then, the region has become firmly Republican even as it has benefited from massive federal public works programs.

Alabama's 4th Congressional District is a collection of small towns — Cullman, Jasper, Russellville, Fort Payne and Albertville. The last is the home of a military helicopter plant and other aerospace facilities. Sandwiched between Huntsville to the north and Birmingham to the south, the 4th District crosses the state and the Appalachian ridges, from the Georgia line to Mississippi. Decades of coal mining scarred 150 square miles of landscape, about one-fourth of which has been reclaimed, with pockets of jobs. Gritty Gadsden (pop. 35,400) the biggest city, is losing population, like many parts of this area. Its Goodyear tire plant, built in 1929, has about 1,550 workers and daily production of 20,000 tires. In 2016, the company spent $30 million to expand the aging facility and its operations. The plant's most famous employee was activist Lilly Ledbetter, who waged a nine-year battle on behalf of equal pay for women. President Barack Obama in 2009 signed into law the Lilly Ledbetter Fair Pay Act extending the statute of limitations on equal-pay discrimination lawsuits. In Jasper, Japanese-based Yoruzu Automotive opened in March 2018 a $110 million plant to manufacture stamped parts for nearby auto companies, with 300 employees expected by 2020.

The 4th is Alabama's premier Scots-Irish district, with the lowest African-American population percentage of the state's seven congressional districts. In 2016, the 80 percent for Donald Trump was his highest in the nation. Census Bureau population estimates project that Alabama will lose a seat in the reapportionment following the 2020 census. The 4th district could be at risk because it's the only one in Alabama without an urban population center. Parts could be sliced and diced into four adjacent districts.

Mo Brooks (R)

Elected 2010, 5th term, b. Apr 29, 1954; Charleston, SC; Duke University (NC), B.A., 1975; University of Alabama School of Law, J.D., 1978; Christian Church; Married (Martha Brooks); 4 children; 8 grandchildren.

Elected Office: AL House, 1983-1992; Madison County Commissioner, 1996-2010.

Professional Career: Tuscaloosa County prosecutor, 1978-1980; Clerk, Circuit Ct. Judge John Snodgrass, 1980-1982; Madison County district Attorney, 1991-1993; AL special Assistant Attorney General, 1995-2002; practicing Attorney, 1993-2010.

DC Office: 2246 RHOB 20515, 202-225-4801, brooks.house.gov

State Offices: Decatur, 256-355-9400; Florence, 256-718-5155; Huntsville, 256-551-0190.

Committees: *Armed Services*: Readiness; Strategic Forces. *Science, Space & Technology*: Space & Aeronautics.

Group Ratings

	ADA	ACLU	AFL-CIO	LCV	ITI	COC	HAFA	ACU	CFG	FRC
2018	-	11%	-	20%	-	75%	86%	84%	75%	100%
2017	5%	C	6%	6%	C	90%	C	96%	97%	100%

Almanac Ratings 2017-18

	Economy	Social	Foreign	Composite
Liberal	7%	12%	3%	7%
Conservative	93%	88%	98%	93%

Key Votes of the 115th Congress

1. Obama-care revision	Y	5. Family planning regs	Y
2. Tax Cuts	Y	6. Body cameras/immigration	N
3. Omnibus appropriations	N	7. Abortion ban	Y
4. Dodd-Frank revision	Y	8. Concealed carry	Y

9. Guantanamo prisoners	N
10. Ground missiles, limit	N
11. Defense Dept. spending	Y
12. FISA rules	Y

Election Results

Election	Name (Party)	Vote (%)		Cand. Spent	Ind. Exp. Support	Ind. Exp. Oppose
2018 General	Mo Brooks (R)	159,063	(61%)	$1,986,583		
	Peter Joffrion (D)	101,388	(39%)		$558,640	
2018 Primary	Mo Brooks (R)	54,928	(61%)			
	Clayton Hinchman (R)	34,739	(39%)			

Prior winning percentages: 2016 (67%), 2014 (74%), 2012 (65%), 2010 (58%)

Mo Brooks, who in 2010 became the first Republican elected to the seat since 1868, has a boisterous style that has been accompanied by some legislative successes. A member of the maverick Freedom Caucus, he gained celebrity status as the third candidate during the contentious Republican primary in 2017 for the special election to fill the remainder of the term of former Sen. Jeff Sessions. The GOP's second-guessing over that outcome had mixed consequences for Brooks.

Brooks was born in Charleston South Carolina. His father was raised "dirt poor" in Chattanooga Tennessee, and later worked as an electrical engineer. His mother grew up without electricity or indoor plumbing, and later taught high school economics and government in Huntsville. "Out of that poverty, my parents learned that you'd better work, and work hard," Brooks said. He studied economics and political science at Duke University and got his law degree from the University of Alabama. As one of 11 Republicans in the state House, the Alabama Taxpayers' Defense Fund gave him its No. 1 ranking for opposing tax increases. He served two years as district attorney, lost reelection, then in 1996 was elected to the Madison County Commission.

Brooks won his House seat in two hard-fought battles. In the Republican primary, he defeated first-term Rep. Parker Griffith, who had been elected as a Democrat but switched parties in December 2009. Brooks campaigned on the theme that the district "deserves a congressman who acts honorably." He defeated Parker, 51%-33%. In the general election, he was opposed by Steve Raby, the longtime chief of staff to former Sen. Howell Heflin of Alabama. The Democrat shunned his party label, focusing almost exclusively on local issues. Brooks took on hot-button issues, declaring that he favored repealing President Barack Obama's health care legislation and deporting all illegal immigrants. He won, 58%-42%.

He made a quick impression. Within four months, he charged in a House speech that the United States is at "risk of insolvency and bankruptcy because the socialist members of this body choose to spend money that we do not have." Several months later, at a forum back home, Brooks said he supported any measure "short of shooting them" to force illegal immigrants back to their home countries. Latino lawmakers and groups condemned his remarks.

Brooks landed in an even bigger controversy in 2014. Asked by conservative radio host Laura Ingraham about a statement that the Republican Party was alienating non-white voters, Brooks responded: "This is a part of the war on whites that's being launched by the Democratic Party." Democrats blasted Brooks for playing the race card. But he was unapologetic.

His committee assignments have matched up well with his district. On Science, Space and Technology, Brooks has been part of a bipartisan coalition that has sought to reshape space policy with a stepping-stone approach to exploration. That plan featured access by American astronauts on American rockets to an international space station, and envisioned long-term plans for planetary destinations such as Mars. On the Armed Services Committee, he said that the United States should spend what it takes to fight terrorism. Following House passage in 2016 of the defense spending bill, he claimed credit for provisions that support Redstone Arsenal programs for military capability in space and small satellite technology development. He urged the Trump administration to base the Space Force at Redstone.

In what had been an entrenched Democratic district less than a decade ago, Brooks secured his House seat. In the 2012 primary, he again dispatched Griffith in the Republican primary, with 71 percent of the vote. He endorsed Ted Cruz and kept his distance from Donald Trump during the 2016 presidential primary. He used terms such as "serial adultery," "notorious flip-flopper" and "gutter mouth" to describe Trump and said that he would never endorse him. After Trump won the nomination, Brooks said that he was supporting the entire Republican ticket without mentioning Trump by name.

In May 2017, Brooks joined the campaign to succeed Sessions, after he quit the Senate to become Trump's attorney general. With a Super PAC linked to Senate Majority Leader Mitch McConnell spending millions of dollars on behalf of Sen. Luther Strange, who had been appointed to the seat by Gov. Robert Bentley, and attacking Brooks as anti-Trump, Brooks positioned himself as a political outsider and "grassroots conservative." He stressed his support for Trump's "America First" agenda, though he criticized the president for his "public water-boarding" of Sessions in his management of the Justice Department. He described McConnell as "head of the swamp" and said that he has "got to go." The attacks on Brooks accomplished their objective of weakening the outsider candidate, who ran third with 20 percent of the vote in the July primary. But the consequence was that former state Chief Justice Roy Moore and Strange faced each other in the GOP runoff, which led to Moore's nomination and his subsequent defeat by Democrat Doug Jones. Later that year, Brooks had surgery for prostate cancer.

Brooks faced a competitive Republican challenger in his 2018 reelection campaign. Clayton Hinchman, an Iraq war veteran, criticized Brooks for his support for Cruz in 2016 and for insufficient funding for Redstone. Brooks won the primary, 61%-39%. Against Democrat Peter Joffrion, the former city attorney for Huntsville, Brooks had the same victory margin. Though his 2018 victories were comfortable, they were his closest contests since Brooks was elected to the House—a likely residue of the bitter Senate primary.

AL-5: North Alabama

Cook Partisan Voting Index: R+18

Population		Race and Ethnicity		Income	
Total	708,691	White	72.9%	Median Income	$52,874
Land area (sq. miles)	3,677	Black	17.2%	District Income Rank	258
Pop/ sq mi	192.7	Latino	5%	Poverty Rate	15%
Born in State	61.5%	Asian	1.7%	With health insurance	89.7%
		Two or more races	2.3%	Cash public assistance	1.8%
Age Groups		Other	0.9%	Food stamp/SNAP	12.1%
Under 18	22.2%				
18-34	22.3%	**Education**		**Work**	
35-64	40.1%	H.S grad or less	39.9%	White Collar	15.4%
Over 64	15.4%	Some college	29.2%	Sales and Service	37.9%
		College Degree, 4 yr	19.5%	Blue Collar	22.8%
Military		Post grad	11.3%	Government	17%
Veteran/ Active Duty	10.6%				

2012 Pres. Vote	Romney	189,838	(64%)	Obama	103,601	(35%)		
2016 Pres. Vote	Trump	200,570	(64%)	Clinton	97,159	(31%)	Johnson	10,223	(3%)

Huntsville, Decatur: After the Soviets put up Sputnik in 1957, the Redstone Arsenal in Huntsville became the nation's foremost missile development center. Then a sleepy town huddled around a well-preserved, early-19th-century settlement, Huntsville grew to become the center of Alabama's northern tier. Residents are fond of referring to their hometown as "Rocket City." The first of the large U.S. ballistic missiles were developed here. On the grounds of Redstone, NASA built its Marshall Space Flight Center in the 1960s, and the Huntsville-Decatur area soon achieved high-tech critical mass. With leadership from Wernher von Braun and other German engineers, Redstone and Marshall built Explorer 1, the first American orbiting satellite; the Mercury-Redstone vehicle that boosted astronaut Alan Shepard into suborbital flight; and the Saturn V rocket that sent men to the moon. Later, Marshall produced Skylab and developed the space shuttle's main engines and solid-rocket boosters. The Obama administration, wary of large-scale space exploration programs funded entirely by the government, scuttled the Constellation program. Still, the Arsenal has more than 35,000 employees.

Huntsville has diversified its high-tech economy in recent years, and space-related jobs have evolved with a broader defense focus. In 2018, the Boeing facility won a $6.6 billion contract for missile-defense development and support. The FBI opened a terrorist explosive device analytical center at the Arsenal and planned more than 1,500 jobs by 2021, including relocations from the Washington D.C. area. Over several decades, city leaders carefully cultivated Cummings Research Park, which is the second-largest research park in the nation and home to more than 300 companies and 26,000 employees specializing in technology-based manufacturing, biotechnology and pharmaceutical firms that transform research into business opportunities. Blue-collar jobs also are increasing. In November 2018, Mazda and Toyota broke ground on an assembly plant in Huntsville that is scheduled to open in 2021, with 4,000 workers who build 300,000 cars annually.

Huntsville, which has annexed land in Limestone and Morgan counties, in 2017 surpassed Mobile as the third largest city in Alabama. Demographers predict that it will replace Birmingham as number-one by 2024. Like high-tech centers in places like Cambridge, Austin and Silicon Valley, Huntsville has attracted many educated and motivated people who also are socially liberal. After a federal judge in 2015 ruled that same-sex marriages were legal in Alabama, the city became a destination wedding site for gays in the South.

The 5th Congressional District of Alabama takes in most of the space counties. For decades, most voters here were staunch New Deal Democrats, liberal on economics and not much interested in race issues. Sen. John Sparkman, who taught school and practiced law in Huntsville, was the party's vice presidential nominee in 1952. Professional and technical people in the space business tended to be conservative, and this made much of northern Alabama marginal-to-Republican country in the 1990s. The district has voted Republican for president since 1980 but did not elect a Republican to Congress until 2010. Of the five counties in the district, Huntsville-based Madison County has nearly 60 percent of the voters. With the more corporate lifestyle in Madison, Donald Trump got a relatively small 55 percent of its vote. In the district's other four counties, his vote share ranged between 71 and 84 percent.

Gary Palmer (R)

Elected 2014, 3rd term, b. May 14, 1954; Hackleburg; Northwest Alabama Junior College, Att., 1974; University of Alabama, B.S., 1977; Presbyterian; Married (Ann Cushing); 3 children.

Professional Career: Engineer, 1977-1989; Founder/President, AL Policy Institute (formerly AL Family Alliance), 1989-2013; Founding board member, State Policy Network, 1992-1998.

DC Office: 207 CHOB 20515, 202-225-4921, Fax: 202-225-2082, palmer.house.gov

State Offices: Birmingham, 205-968-1290; Clanton, 205-280-6846; Oneonta, 205-625-4160.

Committees: House Republican Policy Committee Chairman. *Select Committee on the Climate Crisis. Transportation & Infrastructure*: Economic Dev't, Public Buildings & Emergency Management; Highways & Transit; Water Resources & Environment.

Group Ratings

	ADA	ACLU	AFL-CIO	LCV	ITI	COC	HAFA	ACU	CFG	FRC
2018	-	7%	-	0%	-	75%	88%	92%	84%	100%
2017	0%	C	3%	0%	C	93%	C	100%	95%	100%

Almanac Ratings 2017-18

	Economy	Social	Foreign	Composite
Liberal	0%	6%	6%	4%
Conservative	100%	94%	95%	96%

Key Votes of the 115th Congress

1. Obama-care revision	Y	5. Family planning regs	Y	9. Guantanamo prisoners	N
2. Tax Cuts	Y	6. Body cameras/immigration	N	10. Ground missiles, limit	N
3. Omnibus appropriations	N	7. Abortion ban	Y	11. Defense Dept. spending	Y
4. Dodd-Frank revision	Y	8. Concealed carry	Y	12. FISA rules	Y

Election Results

Election	Name (Party)	Vote (%)		Cand. Spent	Ind. Exp. Support	Ind. Exp. Oppose
2018 General	Gary Palmer (R).............................	192,542	(69%)	$1,071,440		
	Danner Kline (D).................................	85,644	(31%)	$281,687		
2018 Primary	Gary Palmer (R)..		(100%)			

Prior winning percentages: 2016 (75%), 2014 (76%)

Republican Gary Palmer, elected in 2014 as a political outsider, allied with conservative and free-spirited Republicans. He later earned his party stripes and won a lower-level GOP leadership position

Palmer grew up on a small farm in Hackleburg Alabama. He was the first in his family to go to college, where he studied engineering. He started his career in the private sector before cofounding the Alabama Policy Institute (API) in 1989. As president of the think tank with ties to the right-leaning American Legislative Exchange Council, Palmer engaged for years in state-level policy issues, including tax and regulatory affairs.

Following the retirement of Rep. Spencer Bachus, a former chairman of the House Financial Services Committee, there was a wide-open contest to succeed him. The path to victory focused on the party primary, which began with a seven-candidate field. Palmer came in second in the initial vote, trailing GOP state Rep. Paul DeMarco, 33%-19%. In the run-off, the Club for Growth weighed in for Palmer after deeming DeMarco pro-tax. Palmer got the Club's endorsement, along with $250,000 for ads that helped him go on the offensive. He also won the backing of prominent national Republicans such as Indiana Gov. Mike Pence. Palmer won the runoff handily, 64%-36%. He didn't need to break a sweat to defeat Democrat Mark Lester, 76%-24%.

Palmer joined forces with several incoming GOP members who said they would not back John Boehner for another term as Speaker in 2015. He told a local audience: "I cannot in good conscience support John Boehner because I think he lost his legitimacy to lead" after bringing to the House floor bills that most Republican members opposed. Palmer later said he regretted making that pledge because it jeopardized his ability to land good committee assignments. But he had told Boehner before the election that he would need to keep his word to his constituents. As he later recounted his conversation with the Speaker, "not only would I lose their confidence, but I would lose his. I think he respected that." As he predicted, Palmer fell short on influential committee posts. In a delegation where each of the other five Republicans served on either the Appropriations or Armed Services committees, Palmer was assigned to Science, Space and Technology (potentially useful for Alabama), plus the Budget and Oversight and Government Reform panels.

Palmer has remained outspoken. Summarizing his first term, Palmer told a local reporter that he had become "one of the top policy thinkers in our [Republican] conference." He cited his participation with a handful of Budget Committee members who crafted a compromise on the annual budget resolution with Majority Leader Kevin McCarthy. He also contributed to the party's "Better Way" policy agenda, which included eliminating the Environmental Protection Agency's authority to regulate greenhouse gasses. During debate in April 2017 of their proposal to repeal the Affordable Care Act, House Republicans included a plan prepared by Palmer for a $15 billion federal high-risk pool for people with pre-existing conditions. The plan, which he termed "invisible risk-sharing," would give states a block grant with more flexibility to meet the needs of Medicaid-eligible beneficiaries.

Palmer occasionally distanced himself from Donald Trump. In October 2016, during the closing weeks of the presidential campaign, Palmer condemned as "offensive and inappropriate" the lewd remarks that Trump made on a 2005 video recording. But he subsequently added that supporting Trump over Hillary Clinton "is not a difficult choice." A long-time friend of former Sen. Jeff Sessions, Palmer in August 2018 told Politico that there were other officials at the Justice Department who the then-attorney general was "not being well-served by." Trump ousted Sessions that November.

Following the 2018 election, Palmer successfully ran for the open position of Republican Policy Committee chairman against Rep. Dave Schweikert of Arizona, who had more seniority. He cited his career-long experience as a problem-solver and in "developing and promoting sound policies." Palmer became the first Freedom Caucus member to take a GOP leadership position.

In this district, Palmer's chief reelection concern has been a contest with a more "establishment" Republican candidate. In his two reelection campaigns, he got a free pass in the primary and faced modest Democratic challenges. Danner Kline, a craft-beer industry entrepreneur, opposed Palmer in 2018 and attacked Trump's character. Palmer outspent Kline 5-to-1 and won, 69%-31%. Palmer was among the early group of Republicans listed as potential challengers to Democratic Sen. Doug Jones in 2020.

AL-6: Central Alabama   **Cook Partisan Voting Index: R+26**

Population		Race and Ethnicity		Income	
Total	698,968	White	76.7%	Median Income	$63,009
Land area (sq. miles)	4,171	Black	14.8%	District Income Rank	149
Pop/ sq mi	167.6	Latino	4.9%	Poverty Rate	10.7%
Born in State	70.5%	Asian	1.7%	With health insurance	91.8%
		Two or more races	1.5%	Cash public assistance	1.3%
Age Groups		Other	0.4%	Food stamp/SNAP	7.9%
Under 18	23.6%				
18-34	21.2%	**Education**		**Work**	
35-64	40.1%	H.S grad or less	35.6%	White Collar	15.1%
Over 64	15.1%	Some college	28.4%	Sales and Service	39%
		College Degree, 4 yr	22.2%	Blue Collar	19%
Military		Post grad	13.7%	Government	13.1%
Veteran/ Active Duty	7.9%				

2012 Pres. Vote	Romney	233,803	(74%)	Obama	77,235	(25%)		
2016 Pres. Vote	Trump	233,494	(70%)	Clinton	86,117	(26%)	Johnson	8,709	(3%)

Birmingham Suburbs, Shelby County: Birmingham, once one of America's booming industrial cities, was better known in the middle of the 20th century as a center of white resistance to the civil rights movement. Its prospects in the 21st century have been more hopeful. This is a new city by Southern standards. Before the Civil War, there was nothing here but a few creeks running below Red Mountain. But Red Mountain is almost pure iron ore. With the additional mining of coal, Birmingham — the self-styled Magic City — had by 1890 the South's largest steel mills. In the early 20th century, as the statue of Vulcan, the Roman god of fire and metalworking, looked out over the smokestack-filled valley, Birmingham seemed prosperous and the most progressive city in the South. But the worldwide overcapacity of steel and technological obsolescence at home sent the American steel industry into long-term decline starting in the 1950s.

Meanwhile, Birmingham's political leaders plotted to avoid desegregation. The city's violent reaction to the civil rights movement made a vivid impression on the rest of the country. Police Commissioner (and Democratic National Committeeman at the time) Bull Connor set dogs and fire hoses against peaceful demonstrators, and Ku Klux Klansmen bombed the 16th Street Baptist Church, killing four young girls in 1963. Those images haunted Birmingham for a generation. As the more civic-minded Atlanta became the new heart of the South, Birmingham suffered from uninspired business leadership and it downsized as a regional force.

In recent years, Birmingham has worked to improve race relations and develop a new economic base. Health care is a major industry. The city has some of the largest and most advanced medical care centers in the South and is renowned for its sports medicine facilities and specialists who tend to the ailments of famous athletes. While Atlanta's banks foundered and were acquired by outsiders, Birmingham became the largest Southern banking center outside Charlotte North Carolina. But city leaders have worried that the viability of the downtown area and white movement to newer suburbs have continued the racial polarization.

Whites have been moving out of Birmingham's Jefferson County to Shelby County, which grew 44 percent in the 1990s, 36 percent in the next decade and 10 percent from 2010 to 2017 — the fastest growth in the state. (The African-American population in Shelby has increased as well, though the county is about 83 percent white.) Jefferson County, once more Republican than most of Alabama, votes Democratic in close statewide elections, while Shelby County is overwhelmingly Republican. Metropolitan planners projected continuing large increases for Shelby County, but little change for Jefferson, where physical expansion is limited by the hills and growth has slowed even in prosperous neighborhoods. Shelby County played a vital role in a civil rights debate, to the dismay of many local and national activists, when it challenged the constitutionality of a provision of the Voting Rights Act that required most southern states to report ballot changes to the Justice Department. In a landmark 2013 ruling, the U.S. Supreme Court agreed with Shelby County that it was no longer required to get "preclearance" of each voting change. Critics blamed lawmakers for the bipartisan failure to update the law — both before and after the ruling.

The 6th Congressional District of Alabama is the suburban Birmingham-area district and strongly Republican. It includes Shelby County and more than half of Jefferson County, including prosperous Hoover with upscale estates and shopping malls, and stretches southwest toward Tuscaloosa and south along Interstate 65 halfway to Montgomery. Jefferson retains a slight majority of the district vote and Shelby has 30 percent. This has been one of the most Republican districts in the nation. Mitt Romney got 74 percent in 2012, his ninth-best in the nation. In 2016, the vote for Donald Trump dipped to 70 percent.

Terri Sewell (D)

Elected 2010, 5th term, b. Jan 01, 1965; Huntsville; Princeton University (NJ), A.B., 1986; Oxford University (England), M.A., 1988; Harvard University Law School (MA), J.D., 1992; Protestant - Unspecified Christian; Divorced.

Professional Career: Clerk, U.S. District Court judge, 1993-1994; practicing Attorney, 1994-2010.

DC Office: 2201 RHOB 20515, 202-225-2665, Fax: 202-226-9567, sewell.house.gov

State Offices: Birmingham, 205-254-1960; Montgomery, 334-262-1919; Selma, 334-877-4414; Tuscaloosa, 205-752-5380.

Committees: *Permanent Select on Intelligence*: Defense Intelligence & Warfighter Support (Chmn); Intelligence Modernization & Readiness. *Ways & Means*: Health; Trade; Worker & Family Support.

Group Ratings

	ADA	ACLU	AFL-CIO	LCV	ITI	COC	HAFA	ACU	CFG	FRC
2018	-	79%	-	71%	-	80%	4%	11%	9%	0%
2017	85%	C	97%	91%	C	54%	C	4%	0%	11%

Almanac Ratings 2017-18

	Economy	Social	Foreign	Composite
Liberal	92%	98%	78%	89%
Conservative	8%	2%	22%	11%

Key Votes of the 115th Congress

1. Obama-care revision	N	5. Family planning regs	N	9. Guantanamo prisoners	N
2. Tax Cuts	N	6. Body cameras/immigration	Y	10. Ground missiles, limit	Y
3. Omnibus appropriations	Y	7. Abortion ban	N	11. Defense Dept. spending	Y
4. Dodd-Frank revision	Y	8. Concealed carry	N	12. FISA rules	Y

Election Results

Election	Name (Party)	Vote (%)		Cand. Spent	Ind. Exp. Support	Ind. Exp. Oppose
2018 General	Terri Sewell (D)	185,010	(98%)	$868,663		
2018 Primary	Terri Sewell (D)		(100%)			

Prior winning percentages: 2016 (98%), 2014 (98%), 2012 (76%), 2010 (73%)

Soon after Democrat Terri Sewell was elected in 2010, The Washington Post lauded her as "the breakout star" of the Congressional Black Caucus. Sewell has a lifelong knack for making friends who become powerful political allies.

Sewell was born in Huntsville and raised in Selma, a hotbed of activity for the civil rights movement. She grew up near the famed Edmund Pettus Bridge, site of the "Bloody Sunday" clash between protest marchers and state troopers. Sewell's family offered shelter for wayward travelers making the march from Selma to Montgomery in 1965. Hailing from such a place, "you appreciate the significance of your elders' fight for voting rights and civil rights," said Sewell, who was two months old at the time of the march. Her mother, Nancy Sewell, was the first African-American woman elected to the Selma City Council.

Sewell earned her undergraduate degree from Princeton University. During that time, she took part in a Big Sister program and drew inspiration from the mentor assigned to her, Michelle Robinson, later first lady Michelle Obama. While Sewell was writing her senior thesis at Princeton, she met former Democratic Rep. Shirley Chisholm of New York, the first African-American woman elected to Congress and a 1972 candidate for president, who was retired by then and teaching at Mount Holyoke College. "I don't know if anybody could ever follow in Shirley Chisholm's footsteps, but I can tell you that I was inspired by her whole life story," Sewell said.

Sewell later studied politics at Oxford University on a scholarship, earning a master's degree. A theater buff, she dabbled in drama while at Oxford, directing and starring in the play For Colored Girls Who Have Considered Suicide When the Rainbow is Enuf by Ntozake Shange, which also starred fellow Oxonian and future Obama national security adviser Susan Rice. Later, while earning her law degree from Harvard, Sewell was a classmate of future President Barack Obama. At Harvard, she took a year off to turn her master's thesis into a book called Black Tribunes: Race and Representation in British Politics.

After law school, Sewell clerked for a U.S. District Court judge in Birmingham. In 1994 she moved to New York City to work at the Davis, Polk & Wardwell law firm. There, she befriended a fellow associate, Tina Rutnik, who would be better known for her married name: Sen. Kirsten Gillibrand of New York. Sewell eventually returned home to Alabama to care for her ailing father, working as a bond lawyer and a partner in a Birmingham law firm.

When Democratic Rep. Artur Davis decided to leave the House to run for governor, House Democratic women brainstormed female recruits for the open seat. Gillibrand recruited her old friend. Sewell eventually jumped into the primary contest against eight other candidates. They included prominent local figures Earl Hilliard Jr., son of former Rep. Earl Hilliard, and Jefferson County Commissioner Shelia Smoot. Sewell had lower name recognition than Hilliard or Smoot, but she made up for it by outraising the other candidates with both a local and national fundraising network that included the support of EMILY's List. She finished first in the Democratic primary with 37 percent of the vote. Smoot snagged second place with 29 percent, setting up a runoff. Smoot got the endorsement of House Majority Whip James Clyburn. Sewell outspent her by nearly $1 million. In a relatively congenial runoff, Sewell won, 55%-45%. She has not faced a competitive contest since.

Once in Congress, she was elected freshman class president. Sewell moved into the Washington townhouse owned by Rep. Carolyn Maloney, a longtime boarding house for female members. She hit it off with her classmate from Alabama, Republican Martha Roby. They worked jointly on a slew of issues, most notably organizing the 50th anniversary commemoration of the Selma to Montgomery march.

In the House, Sewell has been more of a centrist than most of her Black Caucus colleagues. She serves as vice-chair of the New Democrat Coalition — moderate House Democrats who work on job creation and innovation, often with business groups. In 2013, Minority Whip Steny Hoyer of Maryland named Sewell as a chief deputy whip.

With increased seniority, Sewell gained influential committee assignments. At Ways and Means, she brought a unique voice as an African-American woman with the perspective of underserved communities in the industrial and rural South. Intelligence became the center of her world in the Trump era. Sewell participated in the investigation into Russian interference in the 2016 election. Occasionally, she explained the Democratic worldview but she generally left the political commentary to other Democrats.

On other issues, she worked with a bipartisan group to file a bill to restore a provision of the Voting Rights Act that the Supreme Court negated in 2013. At her urging, Obama designated parts of downtown Birmingham as a national historic monument, which made some of the sites eligible for renovation and tourist promotion.

AL-7: Central Alabama

Cook Partisan Voting Index: D+20

Population		Race and Ethnicity		Income	
Total	671,659	White	31.8%	Median Income	$35,059
Land area (sq. miles)	10,156	Black	63.3%	District Income Rank	431
Pop/ sq mi	66.1	Latino	2.7%	Poverty Rate	26.6%
Born in State	80%	Asian	0.8%	With health insurance	87.6%
Age Groups		Two or more races	1.1%	Cash public assistance	3.1%
Under 18	22%	Other	0.3%	Food stamp/SNAP	23.7%
18-34	26.9%	**Education**		**Work**	
35-64	36.7%	H.S grad or less	49.6%	White Collar	14.4%
Over 64	14.4%	Some college	30.8%	Sales and Service	44.6%
Military		College Degree, 4 yr	12.7%	Blue Collar	26.5%
Veteran/ Active Duty	7.5%	Post grad	6.9%	Government	15.9%

2012 Pres. Vote	Obama	228,468	(73%)	Romney	85,106	(27%)
2016 Pres. Vote	Clinton	204,585	(69%)	Trump	83,916	(28%)

Birmingham, Tuscaloosa, Parts of Montgomery: Alabama has learned to celebrate its black heritage, building striking memorials to the civil rights movement in Montgomery and Birmingham, while acknowledging its history as ground zero of white resistance to the empowerment of blacks in the 1950s and 1960s. Blacks first came here as slaves. The last slave ship to the United States, the Clotilde, docked in Mobile in 1859, where its cargo was then set free. Blacks were part of the great migration into the cotton lands after the Jacksonians swept the Indians out of the Southeast and sent them on their Trail of Tears to what is now Oklahoma. Today, Alabama's rural African Americans are still clustered in the Black Belt of fertile dark soil across the center of the state. All 11 of Alabama's majority-black counties are in the rich farm country of the Black Belt, but most Alabama blacks now live in urban areas — one-quarter of them in metropolitan Birmingham.

After decades of decline, Birmingham pulled itself out of the spiral of abandoned neighborhoods, soaring joblessness and crime through the savvy use of public-private partnerships and other incentives. Numerous vacant and boarded up buildings have been supplanted by lofts and cafes for young professionals and empty-nesters, slowing migration to the suburbs. Crime zones like the Metropolitan Gardens public housing project were leveled and replaced with mixed-income apartments. 2015 brought new hotels and an entertainment district downtown. But change has come too slowly to fully stem the exodus from the city. Birmingham's population declined 12.6 percent from 2000 to 2010, though it has remained steady since.

The 7th Congressional District of Alabama, which was created in 1992, is a majority African-American district that sprawls from Birmingham and Tuscaloosa to the western black precincts of Montgomery and nearly to Mobile County. Republican redistricting in 2011 made the 2nd and 3rd districts whiter and safer for the GOP, and further solidified the 7th for the Democrats.

The Alabama River flows on the district's eastern edge, while the Tombigbee River straddles the western border. The area is filled with old plantations and a thriving catfish industry. The district takes in part of Tuscaloosa, home of the University of Alabama, and nearby Vance, site of a Mercedes factory. In 2017, company officials announced a $1 billion electric SUV expansion at the Vance plant that will raise employment by 600. Birmingham received an additional boost when President Barack Obama, in one of his final official actions, signed a proclamation designating the Birmingham Civil Rights District a national monument. Even with some recent economic progress, this remains one of the poorest districts in the nation. Growth in Birmingham continues to be outpaced by other southern metro areas. Birmingham voters in 2017 elected former school board president Randall Woodfin as mayor. He defeated the incumbent, William Bell, who served seven years.

With its 63 percent African-American population, this is the only district in Alabama where Democrats have an expectation of victory. The 7th formed the backbone of Sen. Doug Jones' support, voting for him, 78%-21% against Republican Roy Moore. In her losing campaign in 2016, Hillary Clinton won the eight Black Belt counties and 69 percent of the district vote.

ALASKA

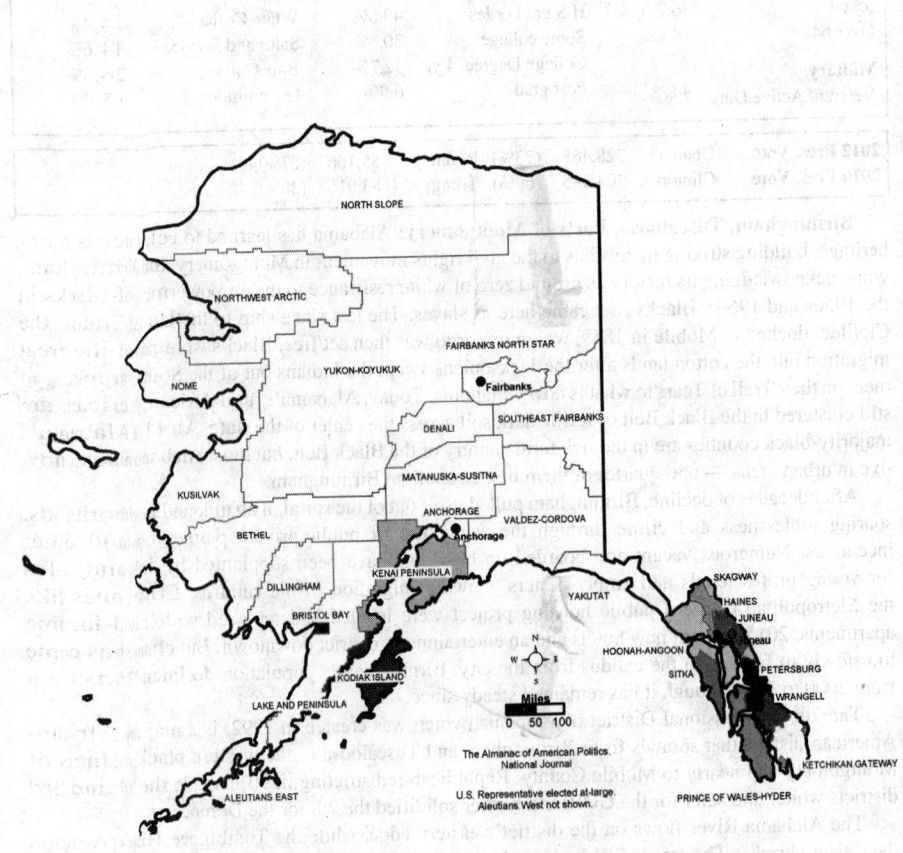

The Almanac of American Politics.
National Journal

U.S. Representative elected at-large.
Aleutians West not shown.

Alaska -- far removed from the Lower 48, what Alaskans sometimes refer to as "Outside" -- maintains an individualistic culture that has responded with creativity to its unique conditions. But while it is dependent on Washington for federal largesse, the relationship between Washington and Alaska is often fraught. Alaska at once depends on subsidies and special treatment and is resentful of what it considers Washington's heavy-handed intervention.

The father of Alaska was Secretary of State William Seward, who took advantage of an opportunity in 1867 to create an American Pacific empire by purchasing the region from Russia for $7.2 million. The Alaska territory owes much of its early growth to federal decisions. While the state burst into national consciousness with the Klondike Gold Rush of 1897, its largest city, Anchorage, had its beginnings in 1914 as the chief worksite for the federal government's Alaska Railroad, completed in 1923. Its famous sled dog race, the Iditarod, started in 1973 on a trail originally cleared and graded by the Army after Congress established the Alaska Road Commission in 1905. The race honors the 1925 emergency 20-team relay that delivered medicine from Nenana almost 700 miles to icebound Nome in 127 hours, saving hundreds of lives from a diphtheria outbreak. Alaska became strategic territory in World War II, when the Aleutian Islands of Attu and Kiska were invaded by a small force of Japanese, the only part of the United States occupied by a foreign enemy since the War of 1812. Alaska, with only 72,000 people when the war began, was connected to the states by the Army's Alcan Highway, completed in 1942; by 1943, there were 152,000 troops in the territory. Alaska is the only state abutting Russia, across the Bering Strait and over the North Pole—you can see Russia from part of Alaska—and the state maintains a strategic geographic position. The military is a major presence at Joint Base Elmendorf-Richardson near Anchorage and at Fort Wainwright and Eielson Air Force Base near Fairbanks, with interceptors for the national missile defense system not far to the south at Fort Greely. The state also has the highest per capita rate of military veterans in the nation.

The third least-populated state and the least densely populated state, Alaska's 741,000 people amount to less than one-quarter of one 1 percent of the nation's population, yet Alaska's land area is equal to one-fifth of the Lower 48. If superimposed on the continental United States, Alaska would stretch from Florida to California. The westernmost Aleutians are closer to Tokyo than to Juneau and farther west than Wellington New Zealand. Many Alaskans have no access to state roads and are reachable only by boat, airplane, dog sleds and snowmachines; its insularity enabled Blockbuster Video to last a decade longer than almost anywhere else before its final store closed in 2018. About two-thirds of the population resides in Anchorage and the nearby Kenai Peninsula and Matanuska-Susitna ("Mat-Su") Valley. This plus the Fairbanks area, accounting for about one-eighth of the population, are the fastest-growing parts of Alaska. The Panhandle, with about one-tenth of the population, is the old Alaska, its towns settled by Russians and built up against steep mountains on inlets from the Pacific. This includes the state capital of Juneau, which is inaccessible by road—you have to ferry or fly in. The rest of the population lives in the Bush and the Aleutians, scattered in small towns, Native settlements and the wilderness. (Only in Alaska does the term "Bush Democrat" not refer to a cross-party supporter of the presidential dynasty.)

Alaska became a state in January 1959. While this technically ended federal dominance, Washington remains the largest landowner in Alaska, with roughly 60 percent of the state's total area under the supervision of more than a dozen federal agencies, including national parks, wildlife refuges, national forests, military bases and the North Slope National Petroleum Reserve. Alaskans continue to seek federal subsidies for intrastate air service, loan guarantees for the fishing industry and funding for the Alaska Railroad. The state's special needs, its longtime Sen. Ted Stevens used to argue, justify its special treatment. Sometimes the state and the federal government agree – in 2015, President Barack Obama acted to rename Mount McKinley, the nation's highest peak, "Denali," its ancestral name, and the state's two Republican senators successfully lobbied President Donald Trump not to change it back, as Trump had promised as a candidate. But such agreement is not always the case.

Alaska's forbidding terrain is responsible for some of its economic assets. In 1959, Alaska's economy depended on fishing and the military, and they continue to be important. For 20 consecutive years, Alaska has reeled in the highest volume of fish of any state. It has more aircraft per capita than any other state; private contractors provide much of the Postal Service's deliveries to the Bush.

Tourism, the No. 2 private employer, has been on the rise, with cruise ships prowling the intra-coastal inlets amid glaciers and grizzlies and docking in Anchorage for side trips to Denali National Park and Preserve; warming of the Bering Sea has opened new ports of call.

Alaska has major mines producing gold, copper, coal and zinc. Twelve Native corporations created by the Alaska Native Claims Settlement Act have proved to be successful, not only in providing dividend income, elderly benefits and scholarships and employment opportunities for Natives, but also in helping them preserve Native traditions and adapt to Alaska's market economy. But not all is rosy. Native villages in the Bush have little in the way of a private-sector economy, and alcoholism, domestic violence and suicide rates remain high. Just 64 percent of Alaska Natives graduated from high school on time in 2016, almost 17 points below the rate for white students.

But something else has transformed Alaska —something not fully envisioned by those who obtained statehood in 1959. Within a decade, Alaska's economy and public life were reshaped by the discovery of North Slope oil. It began suddenly, almost accidentally, as Arco chief executive Robert Anderson, after seven dry wells on Prudhoe Bay, decided to use a nearby drilling rig to make another try — and a natural gas flare shot 30 feet in the air. The 12-billion barrel North Slope oil field proved to be the greatest single strike in U.S. history.

It was not clear in 1968 who owned the oil or how it could be taken out. The Statehood Act of 1959 gave the state the right to choose its own public lands, but only after settling Native land claims. Because the Arctic Ocean ice broke up in late July back then, and for only six weeks, the only feasible way to get the oil out was a pipeline. But environmentalists opposed that option for fears – which proved unfounded -- that it would destroy the delicate permafrost and interfere with caribou migrations. Development-minded Alaskans got a pipeline bill through Congress in 1973, but the pipeline had to be built on stilts and wasn't opened until 1977. Then in 1980, after astute lobbying by environmentalists, Congress passed — over the objections of Alaska's two senators and Rep. Don Young—the Alaska National Interest Lands Conservation Act, which set aside 159 million acres as national parks, national monuments or wilderness: one-third of the state was kept from development. It has paid environmental dividends; though the size of Western Arctic herd of caribou has fluctuated, it has grown from 75,000 in 1976 to 259,000 in 2017.

Oil provides most of Alaska's revenue –about 85 percent – and this enabled the state to abolish its income tax in 1980. (Alaska doesn't have a state sales tax, either.) In 1976, Republican Gov. Jay Hammond persuaded the legislature to establish a Permanent Fund for petroleum revenues. Each year, every qualified resident – man, woman and child –receives a dividend based on a five-year rolling average of the Permanent Fund's financial performance, which is now largely generated by stock, bond and real estate investments, rather than oil revenue. "The dividend has turned Alaska into a shivering paradox," Mark Oppenheimer wrote in Politico. "Despite its proud libertarian streak, they are the only Americans living the socialist dream of a guaranteed income." However, fluctuations in the oil markets have squeezed the state budget, and in 2016, independent Gov. Bill Walker moved to cap the dividend at about half of what it would have been otherwise, which allowed lawmakers to plug budget holes. Residents, however, were unhappy, and they remained so; in 2018, just weeks before a likely general election loss, Walker quit his reelection bid.

For years, efforts to develop Alaska's energy resources beyond the North Slope were stymied, causing no end of friction. The state's congressional delegation, despite its relative seniority, was unable to overcome the opposition to oil drilling in the Arctic National Wildlife Refuge (ANWR) east of Prudhoe Bay. Congress was on the verge of approving ANWR drilling in 1989 when the Exxon Valdez ran aground in Prince William Sound. In January 2015, President Obama proposed the largest-ever wilderness designation in ANWR, which would place its potentially oil-rich coastal plain and millions of additional acres off-limits to future oil and gas development. Obama also ordered an indefinite ban on oil and gas drilling in Alaska's Bristol Bay and, in December 2016, ordered 125 million acres of the Arctic Ocean, holding perhaps 27 billion barrels of oil, closed to future development.

But the Trump administration worked quickly to green-light exploration, with a loosening of drilling restrictions passed as part of the December 2017 tax bill. In October 2018, the Interior Department approved a plan to drill offshore in the Beaufort Sea, and the administration began the process of expanding exploration in half of the 22.1million acre National Petroleum Reserve, despite concerns about caribou and bird habitat adjoining the freshwater Teshekpuk Lake. "Decades of protections are unwinding with extraordinary speed as Republicans move to lock in drilling opportunities before the 2020 presidential election," the New York Times reported. One Alaska Native company, the Arctic Slope Regional Corporation, aggressively sought drilling opportunities, fueled by $7.5 billion in federal contracts over 10 years. But other Alaska Native groups, such as the Gwich'in, worried about the potential environmental impact.

The state's petro-fueled hayride has been hampered by the fluctuation in petroleum prices, which fell from $100 a barrel in 2014 to $27 in 2016 before rising to $80 in 2018. In late 2018, as the rest of the country was feeling like the Great Recession was finally in the rear-view mirror, Alaska was stuck with the nation's highest unemployment rate – 6.4 percent at a time when the national rate was 3.7 percent. A longer-term challenge for the state is climate change. While global warming has had some positives locally, such as the emergence of newly ice-free paths for high-speed internet cables to be laid to Asia and Europe, the negative impacts – from thawing permafrost to inundated coastal communities to declining fish stocks -- have become sufficiently worrisome for the state to begin weighing such options as emissions cuts and a boost to the state's renewable-energy mandate.

Alaska's congressional delegation has been notable for its longevity. Young won his House seat in a 1973 special election and, despite occasional turbulence, has been reelected ever since. Meanwhile, despite the fact that the state is about one-third non-white, the intense focus on the oil sector and its rural, gun-friendly nature has helped make Alaska Republican. It does, however, have a maverick streak: Walker, an independent, won the governorship with a Democratic running mate in 2014, and a coalition of 17 Democrats, two independents and three Republicans forged a majority in the state House after the 2016 election. A similar democratic-led coalition majority elected a speaker after the 2018 election. On the GOP side, Sen. Lisa Murkowski has been one of the likeliest in her conference to break ranks and join Democrats. But despite the favorable political environment for Democrats in 2018, the Alaska governorship was the only one in the nation to flip to Republican control.

Cook Partisan Voting Index: R+9

Population		Race and Ethnicity		Income	
Total	738,565	White	61.5%	Median Income	$76,114
Land area (sq. miles)	570,641	Black	3.1%	State Income Rank	3
Pop/ sq mi	1.3	Latino	6.8%	Poverty Rate	10.2%
Born in state	41.6%	Asian	6.1%	With health insurance	84.5%
Age Groups		Two or more races	7.4%	Cash public assistance	6.3%
Under 18	25.2%	Other	15.2%	Food stamp/SNAP	10.3%
18-34	26.4%	**Education**		**Work**	
35-64	38.3%	H.S grad or less	35.2%	White Collar	36.7%
Over 64	10.1%	Some college	35.8%	Sales and Service	40.0%
Military		College Degree, 4 yr	18.6%	Blue Collar	23.2%
Veteran/ Active Duty	15.5%	Post grad	10.4%	Government	25.2%

Presidential Politics

2016 Caucus (D)	Sanders (D)	8,447 (80%)	Clinton (D)	2,146 (20%)			
2016 Caucus (R)	Cruz (R)	8,369 (36%)	Trump (R)	7,740 (34%)	Rubio (R)	3,488 (15%)	
	Carson (R)	2,492 (11%)					
2016 Pres. Vote	Trump (R)	163,387 (51%)	Clinton (D)	116,454 (37%)	Johnson (L)	18,725 (6%)	
2012 Pres. Vote	Romney (R)	164,676 (55%)	Obama (D)	122,640 (41%)	Johnson (L)	7,392 (2%)	

Donald Trump handily won the state 51%-37%. That 14-percentage point advantage matched the margin that Mitt Romney defeated Barack Obama by four years earlier. While federal resources flow to the state, Alaska's voters also have a healthy suspicion of Washington, particularly when it comes to the federal government's oversight of the state's natural resources. Many Alaskans chafed at Obama administration environmental orders limiting oil and gas extraction. Trump's comfortable victory came despite the vows of the state's two GOP senators that they wouldn't vote for him in

November, after a 2005 tape surfaced in which Trump made lewd comments about women to Access Hollywood host Billy Bush.

Both parties hold caucuses to allocate their national convention delegates. With just over 23,000 participants, Texas Sen. Ted Cruz edged out Trump in the GOP caucuses, 36%-34%. Vermont Sen. Bernie Sanders overwhelmed Hillary Clinton 80%-20% among 10,593 Democratic caucus attendees. Alaska gave Sanders his second-largest margin of victory in the Democratic nominating contest, eclipsed only by his showing in his home state.

Alaska has traditionally been hospitable to third-party candidates: in 1992 Ross Perot won 28 percent here, his second-best showing in the country; and in 2000, Ralph Nader captured 10 percent of the vote, his best showing. In 2016, Libertarian nominee Gary Johnson won about 6 percent—up from 2 percent in 2012—and Green Party standard-bearer Jill Stein managed almost 2 percent.

When Alaska and Hawaii were admitted to the union in 1959, it was expected that Alaska would vote Democratic and Hawaii Republican. The opposite occurred: Alaska has voted for the GOP nominee in every presidential election except for 1964, the LBJ landslide year. Rural areas in the northern and western regions of the state, including hundreds of tiny settlements of Native Alaskans, are the most Democratic, while Republicans are strongest in the Mat-Su Valley, containing the northern suburbs of Anchorage.

Neither Trump nor Clinton made a 2015-16 campaign stop in Alaska.

Congressional Districts

116th Congress Lineup	1R	115th Congress Lineup	1R

Mike Dunleavy (R)

Elected 2018, term expires 2022, 1st term; b. May 5, 1961, Scranton, PA; Misericordia University, B.A., 1963 ; University of Alaska Fairbanks, M.Ed., 1991; Catholic; Married (Rose); 3 children.

Elected Office: AK Senate, 2012-2018.

Professional Career: Educational consultant; Program Manager, Alaska Statewide Mentor Project; Director, K-12 Outreach, University of Alaska; Logging camp employee.

Office: PO Box 110001, Juneau, 99811; 907-465-3500; Fax: 907-465-3532; Website: gov.alaska.gov

Lt. Gov.: Kevin Meyer (R)

State Legislature: Senate: 7D, 13R **House:** 15D, 23R, 2I

Election Results

Election	Name (Party)	Vote (%)
2018 General	Mike Dunleavy (R)	145,631 (51%)
	Mark Begich (D)	125,739 (44%)
	Bill Walker (I)	5,757 (2%)
2018 Primary	Mike Dunleavy (R)	43,802 (62%)
	Mead Treadwell (R)	22,780

Mike Dunleavy won back the Alaska governorship for Republicans in 2018, defeating former Democratic Sen. Mark Begich after the incumbent – independent Gov. Bill Walker – quit the three-way race just weeks before Election Day. Dunleavy's victory became the sole gubernatorial seat the Republicans were able to flip in the 2018 midterm election.

Dunleavy grew up in Scranton Pennsylvania. His father was a mailman and a World War II veteran; his mother was a city clerk. Dunleavy received his bachelor's degree at nearby Misericordia University, then settled in Alaska, attracted by its hunting and fishing. He earned a master's in education from the University of Alaska-Fairbanks and worked in education for most of his career, including seven years as a classroom teacher. For a time, he was the only teacher in the small coastal town of Koyuk. "It's a tricky endeavor to be teaching multiple grade levels at one time in multiple subjects, and you have to be able to organize and do it the right way to get the outcomes that you want," Dunleavy told Alaska Public Media. He settled in Noorvik, a predominantly Inupiat village in the state's vast interior that was the home of his wife, Rose. In 2004, the family moved to Wasilla, later famous as the home of Gov. Sarah Palin, who was mayor of the city; Dunleavy served on the Matanuska-Susitna Borough school board, then ran successfully for state Senate in 2012.

In the legislature, Dunleavy chaired the chamber's Education Committee, State Affairs Committee and Labor and Commerce Committee, but his relationship with other lawmakers was sometimes fraught. He was kicked out of the majority caucus and stripped of his chairmanships after voting against the Republican budget, having sought deeper spending cuts. Dunleavy was the first majority senator in three decades not to see one of his own bills pass. "My goal wasn't to pass a lot of bills," Dunleavy told the Anchorage Daily News. "My goal was to go down there, and in many cases, ensure that certain things didn't happen to Alaskans, such as taxes." He announced his gubernatorial bid in July 2017, briefly dropped out for medical reasons, then returned to the race. He resigned from the legislature in January 2018 to focus on his campaign.

The state's big challenge during Walker's tenure was grappling with the falling price of oil, which had squeezed the state's finances. Walker acted to fill budget holes by capping the Permanent Fund dividend, an annual payout to all qualifying Alaskans funded by investment gains from state oil revenues. This drew the ire of a broad cross-section of Alaskans, ranging from anti-tax Republicans to lower-income Alaska Natives for whom the annual dividend was important for keeping families afloat. During the first half of 2017, the GOP Senate and the Democratic coalition-led House failed to agree on the scope of cuts and the possibility of new revenues. With a government shutdown looming, legislators and the governor agreed to a stopgap measure that combined an end to oil-industry tax credits with increased withdrawals from the state's Constitutional Budget Reserve. In the meantime, a burgeoning opioid addiction problem led to a spike in property crimes. By 2018, Walker's approval ratings were far under water.

Walker's prospects worsened further as a three-way contest developed. Walker had initially considered running as a Democrat, but Begich, a one-term U.S. senator and the scion of an Alaskan political dynasty, effectively elbowed him out of the way. On the Republican side, Dunleavy won the August 2018 primary over former Lt. Gov. Mead Treadwell by a 2-to-1 margin, bolstered by an independent expenditure campaign partly funded by his brother Francis, a former high-ranking executive with JPMorgan Chase. While Walker pitched himself as someone willing to make tough financial decisions, both of his general-election opponents criticized his handling of the Permanent Fund dividend and the growth of crime on his watch. Dunleavy charged that "Alaskans are under siege from violent criminals and property thieves" and that on his watch, "criminals will no longer have free run on our streets." He also promised to cut government and beef up Permanent Fund dividends, though without many specifics. In polls, Dunleavy easily led the field, with Walker and Begich splitting the state's moderate-to-liberal vote.

Three weeks before Election Day, Walker decided to quit the race, throwing his support to Begich, who had supported Walker's earlier expansion of Medicaid. Walker's departure came just days after his Democratic lieutenant governor, Byron Mallott, resigned, citing inappropriate comments to a woman. This #metoo casualty robbed the Democrats of a leading politician of Alaska Native ancestry. On Election Day, Dunleavy defeated Begich, 51%-44%, with 2% for Walker, whose name remained on the ballot.

Dunleavy had planned to take the oath of office in Noorvik, more than 1,000 miles from the state capital, but a dense fog kept him 43 miles away in Kotzebue. So in a hastily arranged ceremony, he was inaugurated in Kotzebue, as Walker stayed in Anchorage to handle the response to a 7.0-magnitude earthquake. Despite the uncooperative weather, Dunleavy became the first governor of a state to be sworn in above the Arctic Circle. "We never forgot about rural Alaska," Dunleavy said at the ceremony. "You're not going to be an afterthought."

After taking office, Dunleavy sought a $3,000 permanent fund dividend while proposing deep cuts to balance the state budget. The cuts, however, ran into opposition in the state House, where 15 Democrats, four Republicans and two independents teamed up to elect a speaker and split up control of key posts. (The state Senate remained in GOP hands.)

Lisa Murkowski (R)

Elected 2002, term expires 2022, 4th term, b. May 22, 1957; Ketchikan; Willamette University (OR), Att., 1977; Georgetown University (DC), B.A., 1980; Willamette University College of Law (OR), J.D., 1985; Roman Catholic; Married (Verne Martell); 2 children.

Elected Office: AK House, 1998-2002.

Professional Career: Anchorage Dist. Court Clerk's Office, Attorney, 1987-1989; Practicing attorney, 1989-1998.

DC Office: 522 HSOB 20510, 202-224-6665, Fax: 202-224-5301, murkowski.senate.gov

State Offices: Anchorage, 907-271-3735; Fairbanks, 907-456-0233; Juneau, 907-586-7277; Ketchikan, 907-225-6880; Soldotna, 907-262-4220; Wasilla, 907-376-7665.

Committees: *Appropriations*: Commerce, Justice, Science & Related Agencies; Department of Defense; Department of Homeland Security; Department of the Interior, Environment & Related Agencies (Chmn); Energy & Water Development; Military Construction & Veteran Affairs & Related Agencies. *Energy & Natural Resources (Chmn)*: Ex Officio membership on all subcommittees. *Health, Education, Labor & Pensions*: Children & Families; Primary Health & Retirement Security. *Indian Affairs*.

Group Ratings

	ADA	ACLU	AFL-CIO	LCV	ITI	COC	HAFA	ACU	CFG	FRC
2018	-	52%	-	14%	-	89%	38%	36%	40%	50%
2017	15%	C	13%	0%	C	71%	C	52%	48%	50%

Almanac Ratings 2017-18

	Economy	Social	Foreign	Composite
Liberal	34%	34%	10%	26%
Conservative	66%	66%	90%	74%

Key Votes of the 115th Congress

1. Obama-care revision	N	5. Gun regulations	Y	9. Kavanaugh confirmation	P
2. Tax Cuts	Y	6. Family planning regs	N	10. Saudi arms sales	N
3. Dodd-Frank revision	Y	7. Gorsuch confirmation	Y	11. FISA rules	N
4. Omnibus appropriations	Y	8. Immigration restrictions	N	12. Military aid in Yemen	N

Election Results

Election	Name (Party)	Vote (%)		Cand. Spent	Ind. Exp. Support	Ind. Exp. Oppose
2016 General	Lisa Murkowski (R)	138,149	(44%)	$5,905,748	$147,178	
	Joe Miller (L)	90,825	(29%)	$727,527		
	Margaret Stock (I)	41,194	(13%)	$708,297		
	Ray Metcalfe (D)	36,200	(12%)	$12,355		
2016 Primary	Lisa Murkowski (R)	39,545	(72%)			
	Bob Lochner (R)	8,480	(15%)			
	Paul Kendall (R)	4,272	(8%)			
	Thomas Lamb (R)	2,996	(5%)			

Prior winning percentages: 2010 (39%), 2004 (49%)

As one of the few centrist senators in either party, Republican Lisa Murkowski has emerged as a powerful force in the narrowly divided chamber. With a freedom that has been enhanced by narrow election victories, plus the hostility of many voters in her own party, she has enjoyed pursuing her own course. She has shown a shrewd sense of timing and understanding of Senate folkways. And, not incidentally, she has worked with her own party to score big gains for her home state.

Since the first Congress 230 years ago, there have been no fewer than 45 sons who followed their fathers into Senate service. To date, there has been only one woman in this category: Murkowski, now Alaska's senior senator, who was appointed in 2002 by her father, then-Gov. Frank Murkowski, to fill the Senate vacancy created when he resigned to become governor. Father and daughter have occupied not only the same Senate seat for nearly 40 years, but now also the same committee chairmanship: Energy and Natural Resources, whose legislative jurisdiction is crucial to their vast, sparsely populated home state, where more than 60 percent of the land is owned by the federal government and 90 percent of the state's revenues are derived from the oil industry. Lisa Murkowski assumed the chairmanship of energy panel in 2015; Frank Murkowski claimed the chairman's gavel 20 years earlier, in 1995, and held it for more than six years.

Philosophically, Lisa Murkowski often has not been her father's daughter. If Frank Murkowski was largely a traditional conservative, his daughter has been more of a Republican moderate with a decidedly libertarian streak: She supports abortion rights, while her father was an abortion opponent, and she has been at odds with conservatives on issues ranging from gay rights to health care. Such independence has at times created political problems for her back home. Lisa Murkowski, in three statewide general election campaigns, has never won more than 49 percent of the vote. In fact, she is the only Senator never to have done so.

Murkowski has established a reputation for a willingness to reach across the aisle throughout her Senate tenure. As energy chairman, she crafted a bipartisan energy bill in 2015 that cleared the Senate with 85 votes. Murkowski does hew to a hard line in terms of what she sees as the economic prerogatives of her home state, resisting efforts by the federal government to restrict Alaska's ability to access its energy resources. But if state's longtime senior senator, the late Republican Ted Stevens, was known for berating colleagues on the Senate floor while wearing a tie emblazoned with the Incredible Hulk, the personable Murkowski is known more for her calm albeit steely resolve. "Channeling my inner #Hulk while meeting with the press," she once posted on her Instagram account, according to a profile in High Country News.

Murkowski, the first Alaskan-born U.S. senator, was born in Ketchikan, at the southern end of Alaska's Panhandle, in 1957, two years before Alaska achieved statehood. The family moved up the Panhandle in the early 1960s to Wrangell, then known as the timber capital of Alaska, where Frank Murkowski — a native of Seattle, Washington — managed a bank. A decade later, the Murkowskis moved 900 miles further north, to Fairbanks, reaping the economic benefits of construction of the Trans-Alaska pipeline, which opened in 1977.

Lisa Murkowski graduated from Georgetown University in 1980, the year her father was first elected to the Senate, and went on to earn a law degree from the Willamette University College of Law in Salem, Oregon, in 1985. She settled in Anchorage, serving as a district court attorney before going into private law practice. In 1998, Murkowski launched her political career. Motivated to run in part by concern about declines in two mainstays of the Alaskan economy— oil and timber— she was elected to the state House.

The independent streak that Murkowski has displayed throughout her political career was evident during her state legislative tenure. When Alaska faced a $1.1 billion budget shortfall in 2002, she was a leader in the bipartisan Fiscal Policy Caucus that pushed for a tax hike, including raising the alcohol tax from 3 cents to 10 cents a drink. It put her at odds with her father, then running for governor on a pledge of no new taxes. Her bill was enacted, making Alaska the state with the highest alcohol tax in the country. Some conservatives derisively referred to her and her allies as "RIMs"— "Republican Invertebrate Moderates." Facing a conservative challenger in the 2002 primary, Murkowski was renominated by a margin of just 57 votes. Nonetheless, after the general election, she was chosen as the House majority leader.

She was not in that leadership position for long. Alaskans elected her father to the governorship by a wide margin, though he had two years left in his Senate term. Frank Murkowski compiled a long list of possible successors, saying he was looking for someone whose views on Alaska issues were in sync with his, had legislative experience and was young enough to serve many years. Among the candidates: then-state Sen. Ben Stevens, Ted Stevens' son, and a rising political star named Sarah Palin, the former mayor of Wasilla. In an interview more than a decade afterward, Frank Murkowski recalled putting the candidates' names on a spreadsheet to compare qualifications. At first, he wasn't particularly serious about his daughter as a potential appointee — but, as he studied the spreadsheet, she began moving up the list.

It was the only time in U.S. history that a governor had appointed his or her child to the Senate. "Lisa, who's your daddy?" read the derisive bumper stickers at the time. Even though most Republicans and many Democrats praised her abilities, others said her selection was all about nepotism. In response, Murkowski sought to highlight her political differences with the man who had appointed her. "We have always maintained very separate identities, at least for the time I have been in the legislature," she said. "I haven't called him for counseling, and typically he doesn't offer."

Still, Murkowski knew that, as she completed her father's term, critics would be watching to see if she was up to the job. In learning the ropes, Murkowski got significant help from Ted Stevens, whose senior position on the Appropriations Committee made him one of Capitol Hill's most influential lawmakers. Murkowski pushed through a bill, with Stevens' help, that included federal loan guarantees for a 3,500-mile pipeline that would bring natural gas from the North Slope to the lower 48 states—a major venture for Alaska.

Nonetheless, as Murkowski entered the 2004 campaign, she was vulnerable. She turned back a challenge from the right, 58%-37%, in the primary, but in the general election, she faced a tough challenge from Tony Knowles. A Vietnam veteran and Yale University classmate and friend of President George W. Bush, Knowles had twice been elected mayor of Anchorage and twice won gubernatorial races. The nepotism issue loomed over the campaign. Fifty-thousand voters signed a ballot measure to ban governors from appointing senators, and it later passed with 56 percent of the vote. This strongly red state voted to give Bush a second term by a 25-point margin, helping Murkowski to eke out victory, 49%-46%. Frank Murkowski ended up paying the political price for the nepotism controversy. Seeking re-election in 2006, he finished third in a three-way primary, as Sarah Palin toppled him and went on to win the general election.

Following Ted Stevens' re-election defeat in 2008 — eight days after his conviction on corruption charges for concealing gifts — Murkowski assumed a much larger role in the Senate on Alaska-centric issues. With Stevens gone, she secured a seat on the Appropriations Committee, a critical post for a state so dependent on federal spending. Also in her first full term, she joined the GOP leadership as a counsel to then-Minority Leader Mitch McConnell. When there was a reshuffling in the leadership structure in 2009, Murkowski become vice chair of the Senate Republican Conference.

Murkowski continued to demonstrate her independent streak. She joined just three other Republican senators to seek more civil liberties protections in the Patriot Act. And, after President Barack Obama took office in 2009, Murkowski was one of just five Senate Republicans to help pass into law the Matthew Shepard Act, expanding the federal hate crimes statute to cover a victim's sexual orientation and gender identity.

Murkowski's work on state issues and frequent trips home to showcase her growing influence were not enough to stave off Joe Miller's vigorous primary challenge in 2010. A graduate of West Point and Yale Law School, the self-described "constitutional conservative" charged that Murkowski was a Washington insider who had abandoned Republican values by supporting abortion rights and higher taxes. His candidacy was backed by Palin, two years after her 2008 stint as the Republican vice presidential nominee. Miller also was boosted by an anti-abortion referendum on the ballot that brought thousands of voters to the polls. He narrowly prevailed, 51%-49%.

Murkowski conceded, and, for a time, appeared ready to move back to Alaska with her husband, Verne Martell, and their two sons. But after repeated urgings from friends and supporters, she announced seven weeks before the general election that she would pursue a long-shot write-in effort. Using the slogan "Let's Make History," she waged a spirited campaign, pointing to the considerable seniority that federally dependent Alaska would forsake if she lost. Her GOP colleagues in the Senate, prohibited by party rules from endorsing her as an independent, lined up behind Miller because, they said, Republican voters had spoken in the primary. But many were not enthusiastic, and Miller's campaign suffered from numerous missteps. With the support of some Democrats seeking to block Miller from the Senate, Murkowski won a three-way contest with 39 percent of the vote. Miller got 35 percent and the Democratic candidate, Scott McAdams, finished a distant third with 23 percent. She became only the second senator to win via write-in, matching an electoral feat that Strom Thurmond, as a Democrat, had accomplished in South Carolina more than a half-century earlier.

For the most part, Murkowski's difficult victory appeared to accelerate her march to the political middle. In the 2010 lame-duck session, she was among just seven Republican senators to support the repeal of the military's "don't ask, don't tell" policy. In 2013, she became the third GOP senator to voice support for gay marriage. Two years later, Murkowski was the lead Republican on a bill designed to restore several provisions of the Voting Rights Act ruled unconstitutional by the Supreme Court. That stance reflected the strong support that Alaska Natives had given her in the 2010 write-in effort. "Impediments to voting in many of our rural communities because of distance and language need to be addressed, and my hope is that this legislation will resolve these issues," Murkowski said.

When Republicans regained control of the Senate in 2014, Murkowski would find herself chairing not only the Energy and Natural Resources Committee but also the Appropriations Subcommittee on Interior, Environment and Related Agencies, adding to her leverage over federal departments and agencies that wield broad jurisdiction within her home state. She showed her independence by supporting the Obama administration on several fronts. In 2015, she was one of only seven GOP senators not to sign an open letter intended to undermine Obama's efforts to reach a nuclear deal with Iran. She was among a handful of Republicans to support holding hearings on Obama's 2016 nomination of Merrick Garland to the fill the Supreme Court vacancy created by the death of Antonin Scalia, although she later retreated from that position as Senate Republican leaders held firm to not allow Obama to fill the seat during his last year in office.

One source of repeated confrontation with the Obama administration was the state delegation's long-standing goal of opening the Alaska National Wildlife Refuge to oil and gas exploration— a popular idea in the state, but one that was rebuffed repeatedly in Washington. While the area is home to a wide array of wildlife, it also is thought to hold large oil and gas reserves. Murkowski was incensed when Obama in 2015 said that he would ask Congress to designate 12 million of the refuge's 19 million acres as wilderness. She blasted the move as "a stunning attack on our sovereignty." Murkowski likewise was enraged when Obama, a month before leaving office, invoked a 1953 law to bar new oil leases in most of the Arctic offshore waters by executive fiat. "The only thing more shocking than this reckless, short-sighted, last-minute gift to the extreme environmental agenda is that President Obama had the nerve to claim he is doing Alaska a favor," Murkowski said.

Such rhetoric tended to mask the collaborative manner in which Murkowski operated within the Energy and Natural Resources Committee as chairwoman and, prior to that, during six years as ranking minority member. In early 2015, Murkowski and the committee's ranking Democrat, Maria Cantwell of Washington, went to work on comprehensive energy legislation. Environmental advocates, while complaining it did nothing to address climate change, liked its provisions for energy research and modernizing the electric grid. Congressional Democrats praised its inclusion of a permanent reauthorization of the Land and Water Conservation Fund for public land acquisition, while Republicans liked provisions to expedite the processing for liquefied natural gas terminals. But, after clearing the Senate in the spring of 2016 on an overwhelmingly bipartisan vote, it ran into a far more partisan House counterpart bill. The legislation died in conference committee at the end of 2016.

Murkowski entered the 2016 election in an unfamiliar position — heavily favored to win a third term. But, while far from a repeat of 2010, it was short of a cakewalk. Former Anchorage Mayor Dan Sullivan (no relation to Murkowski's junior colleague, GOP Sen. Dan Sullivan) filed to take on Murkowski, but then dropped his bid. Murkowski, taking no chances this time, started earlier and spent more money, winning the primary with 72 percent. She benefitted from a split in the Democratic ranks: Democratic nominee Ray Metcalfe was a longtime critic of former Sen. Mark Begich, who returned the favor by endorsing independent candidate Margaret Stock. Miller, who opted not to challenge Murkowski in the primary, ran on the Libertarian Party line in the general election. Several officers of the state Republican Party resigned their posts to back him. Miller garnered 29 percent, second to Murkowski's victorious 44 percent.

During the campaign, Murkowski kept her distance from Republican presidential nominee Donald Trump. She never endorsed him, and, after the videotape surfaced of Trump making lewd comments about women, Murkowski called on him to step aside, saying he had "forfeited the right to be our party's nominee." After the election, Murkowski was conciliatory; Trump's aggressive stance on energy exploration could help further her goal of increasing oil and gas drilling at home. "When they want to work with us to do good things for Alaska, we'll be working together," Murkowski told Alaska Public Media about Trump. "So yes, I can absolutely [work] with anyone."

In 2017, she made clear that cooperation would be on her terms. With Sens. Susan Collins of Maine and John McCain of Arizona, she was one of three Republican Senators who voted against— and defeated—the GOP proposal to repeal Obamacare. That came in the face of presidential tweets and angry party stalwarts in Washington and at home. "The Affordable Care Act remains a flawed law that I am committed to reforming," she said in July. "But to do that, the Senate must fully devote itself to an effort to improve the health care system in this country." The state GOP chairman in Alaska said that local Republicans were unanimous in their unhappiness with Murkowski. Her vote,

Murkowski told The Washington Post a year later, brought "an emotional outpouring that made it just — intense is the best word."

Murkowski also went her own way in September 2018, when she opposed the nomination of Brett Kavanaugh to the Supreme Court. "We are dealing with issues right now that are bigger than a nominee," she told reporters, in an apparent reference to allegations of sexual assault against the nominee. "In my view he's not the right man for the court at this time." In that case, Kavanaugh was confirmed and her vote proved less consequential—in the short term, at least. Palin tweeted: "Hey @LisaMurkowski— I can see 2022 from my house." Murkowski responded that she wasn't worried.

One reason for her reaction might have been the huge legislative victory that Murkowski scored between the healthcare and Kavanaugh votes: Approval of the proposal, sought for decades by Alaska Republicans, to permit oil and natural gas drilling in part of the Arctic National Wildlife Refuge. Working with McConnell and Trump, Murkowski included that legislative action as a rider to the GOP's big tax cut bill. As Carl Hulse wrote in The New York Times, the victory had "a symbolic significance that is almost impossible to overstate, pitting the nation's leading environmental groups against Alaskan lawmakers and energy companies over a slice of tundra on the North Slope of Alaska that is home to abundant wildlife." Murkowski said, with under-statement, "We have come to a good place."

Murkowski faced many questions about her future in the Senate, including her re-election prospects in 2022 and the possibility that she will be in line in a few years to chair the Appropriations Committee—a position once held by Ted Stevens. Even with her continuing independence, she had achieved results on which her powerful predecessors from Alaska had fallen short.

Dan Sullivan (R)

Elected 2014, term expires 2020, 1st term, b. Nov 13, 1964; Fairview Park, OH; Harvard University, Bach. Deg., 1987; Georgetown University Law Center (DC), J.D., 1993; Georgetown University Law Center (DC), M.S., 1993; Roman Catholic; Married (Julie Fate); 3 children.

Military Career: U.S. Marine Corps and Reserves 1993-pres. (Afghanistan)

Professional Career: Law clerk, U.S Court of Appeals for the Ninth Circuit, 1997-1998; Law clerk, AK Supreme Court, 1998-1999; Assistant Secretary of State for Economic, Energy, and Business Affairs, U.S Department of State, 2006-2009; AK Attorney General, 2009-2010; Commissioner, AK Department of Natural Resources, 2010-2013.

DC Office: 302 HSOB 20510, 202-224-3004, Fax: 202-224-6501, sullivan.senate.gov
State Offices: Anchorage, 907-271-5915; Fairbanks, 907-456-0261; Juneau, 907-586-7277; Ketchikan, 907-225-6880; Soldotna, 907-283-4000; Wasilla, 907-357-9956.

Committees: *Armed Services*: Airland; Readiness & Management Support (Chmn); Strategic Forces. *Commerce, Science & Transportation*: Communications, Technology, Innovation & the Internet; Manufacturing, Trade & Consumer Protection; Subcommittee on Science, Oceans, Fisheries & Weather; Subcommittee on Security (Chmn). *Environment & Public Works*: Clean Air & Nuclear Safety; Fisheries, Water, and Wildlife; Transportation & Infrastructure. *Veterans' Affairs*.

Group Ratings

	ADA	ACLU	AFL-CIO	LCV	ITI	COC	HAFA	ACU	CFG	FRC
2018	-	21%	-	7%	-	80%	69%	86%	62%	100%
2017	0%	C	0%	0%	C	86%	C	76%	81%	100%

Almanac Ratings 2017-18

	Economy	Social	Foreign	Composite
Liberal	0%	0%	6%	2%
Conservative	100%	100%	94%	98%

Key Votes of the 115th Congress

1. Obama-care revision	Y	5. Gun regulations	Y	9. Kavanaugh confirmation	Y
2. Tax Cuts	Y	6. Family planning regs	Y	10. Saudi arms sales	N
3. Dodd-Frank revision	Y	7. Gorsuch confirmation	Y	11. FISA rules	NV
4. Omnibus appropriations	N	8. Immigration restrictions	Y	12. Military aid in Yemen	N

Election Results

Election	Name (Party)	Vote (%)	Cand. Spent	Ind. Exp. Support	Ind. Exp. Oppose
2014 General	Dan Sullivan (R)............................ 135,445	(48%)	$7,797,250	$4,548,858	$15,791,064
	Mark Begich (D)............................ 129,431	(46%)	$11,082,246	$7,103,335	$13,709,045
	Mark Fish (L)................................... 10,512	(4%)			
	Ted Gianoutsos (I)............................ 5,636	(2%)			
2014 Primary	Dan Sullivan (R)............................. 44,740	(40%)			
	Joe Miller (R)................................... 35,904	(32%)			
	Mead Treadwell (R)......................... 27,807	(25%)			

Dan Sullivan, the junior senator from Alaska, has kept his head down as a party loyalist and focused on issues of interest to him and his constituents, especially military topics. Holding his first elected office, he kept a low profile—compared to recent Republican elected officials from Alaska who have sought or attracted the public spotlight. He has voiced selective opposition to President Donald Trump, in particular on international trade issues that are vital to his coastal state. Early indications were that Sullivan was in good shape for re-election in 2020.

Until his election in 2014, Sullivan was sometimes referred to in his home state as the "other" Dan Sullivan — so as not to confuse him with former Anchorage Mayor Dan Sullivan, an Alaska native. Foes of the Senate candidate sometimes derided him as "Ohio Dan," an allusion to his upbringing in a Cleveland suburb and a continuing debate over precisely how long he had resided in Alaska. As a Marine officer with a long resume of state and federal jobs, Sullivan overcame two high-profile opponents in the Republican primary. And, in a bad year for Democrats, he proved too formidable for Democratic incumbent Mark Begich, another former Anchorage mayor who was the second generation of a prominent Alaska political family; Sullivan triumphed by a narrow margin after a bruising campaign.

Sullivan grew up in Fairview Park, Ohio, in prominent family. His paternal grandfather started a business just after World War II that has employed more than 10,000 workers in the manufacture of commercial and residential paints, coatings and sealants. Sullivan's father later ran and grew the firm. Sullivan chose a different course. He got a bachelor's degree in economics from Harvard University and earned a joint law and foreign service degree from Georgetown University. At Georgetown, he met Julie Fate, a staffer for then-Sen. Ted Stevens and part of a prominent Alaska Native family. They married in Fairbanks.

Sullivan enlisted in the Marine Corps and was commissioned a second lieutenant. He then moved to Alaska, where he clerked for a federal appeals court judge and for the chief justice of the state Supreme Court. After spending a couple of years in the Anchorage office of the Seattle-based Perkins Coie law firm, he left Alaska for what he said was good reason. Sullivan told the Alaska Dispatch News during the Senate campaign: "9/11 happened and that changed everything." He spent more than two years on a White House fellowship with President George W. Bush, working for the National Security Council and the National Economic Council. After Condoleezza Rice left the White House and became secretary of State, Sullivan joined her as assistant secretary of State for economic, energy and business affairs.

He returned to Alaska in early 2009 and Gov. Sarah Palin appointed him state attorney general a month before she resigned. Palin's successor, Republican Sean Parnell, chose Sullivan to head the Department of Natural Resources. He resigned in September 2013 to run for the Senate. In the GOP primary, he faced Lt. Gov. Mead Treadwell and Fairbanks attorney Joe Miller, a tea party favorite who had defeated Sen. Lisa Murkowski in the 2010 primary but lost to her in the general. Treadwell sought to depict Sullivan as a carpetbagger — "I've got a jar of mayonnaise in my refrigerator that's been there longer than Dan Sullivan's been in Alaska," Treadwell gibed to Politico — while Palin endorsed Miller. But the prospect of the GOP retaking Senate control prompted national conservative groups—including the Club for Growth and U.S. Chamber of Commerce—to support Sullivan as the best candidate to defeat Begich. Sullivan won the primary with 40 percent, to 32 percent for Miller and 25 percent for Treadwell.

As a Democrat from a deep-red state, Begich focused on parochial issues and worked to show his independence from President Barack Obama and his congressional colleagues. He was one of only four Senate Democrats to vote against a bill ending tax breaks for oil companies and opposed a ban on so-called earmark spending — a device that Stevens had used to steer appropriations to his huge, sparsely populated state.

Democrats began raising the carpetbagger theme against Sullivan during the primary and continued to use it until the general election. Sullivan committed an early gaffe when he criticized Begich in an ad filmed atop an Anchorage convention center, saying Alaskans wanted someone who delivered real results; construction of the center was a significant achievement for Begich when he was mayor. Otherwise, he ran a carefully managed campaign whose overriding goal was to tie Begich to Obama, who was deeply unpopular in Alaska. The bitter battle consumed $61 million, making it the most expensive race in Alaska history. Republicans had a superior ground game and Sullivan eked out a 48%-46% victory, with about 6,000 votes separating them; Begich declined to throw in the towel until all votes were tallied, calling Sullivan two weeks after Election Day to congratulate him.

During the campaign, Begich sought to appear nonpartisan by running an ad that featured the image of Murkowski and touted their close relationship. Murkowski told Begich to stop using her image and made clear that she supported Sullivan. Nonetheless, in the Senate, the more conservative Sullivan and Murkowski have differed on both policy and political matters. Sullivan, unlike Murkowski, endorsed Donald Trump after he emerged as the Republican presidential nominee. Both senators condemned Trump's behavior and called for him to step aside as the nominee after the release of the "Access Hollywood" video containing lewd comments about women. Sullivan went a step further and urged that Trump be replaced by his running mate, Mike Pence, a leading social conservative. During the 2014 campaign, Sullivan had staked out positions at odds with Murkowski on abortion and same-sex marriage, saying that he opposed both.

On Capitol Hill, Sullivan landed a seat on the Armed Services Committee and served notice that he would bring his hawkish views to defense issues. During a committee hearing in 2015, he accused Obama of holding an "almost delusional view of the world environment" after the president suggested in his State of the Union address that the shadow of crisis had passed on various threats, from ISIS's advance to Russia's aggression and Iran's nuclear program. Sullivan repeatedly took aim at what he saw as the Obama White House's downplaying of the battle against ISIS. In 2016, when ISIS forces killed a Navy SEAL who was advising Kurdish forces in Iraq, an Obama spokesman told reporters that the SEAL had not been on a combat mission. "The White House continues to diminish the service and sacrifice of our troops serving in Iraq, Syria, Afghanistan and elsewhere by peddling the fiction that they are not engaged in combat," snapped Sullivan, who has been called up for three tours of active duty as Marine reservist, most recently a six-week stint in Afghanistan in 2013.

Sullivan has been the only senator serving in the military reserves. He was promoted in March 2018 to the rank of colonel in the Marine Corps Forces Reserve, though he was forced to give up command of a California-based reserve unit after he became a senator. At issue was the clause of the Constitution prohibiting members of Congress from holding office in the executive branch. While his military experience was regarded as a significant political asset in his campaign for Senate, Sullivan contended it had given him a legislative edge as well. "Having first-hand experience, being able to talk about just how incredible Alaska is for military training, I think, gives me a lot of credibility as a senator to make the case to not only my fellow senators but to senior administration officials," he told Alaska Public Media.

On the Armed Services Committee, in September 2018, he became chairman of the Readiness Subcommittee following the reorganization that resulted from the death of Sen. John McCain. In describing his responsibilities for military bases and personnel, he focused on the role that Alaska plays as the military "rebalances" its attention to the Pacific Ocean, including the importance of its local installations. In the defense spending bill that Congress enacted a month earlier, he won approval of six polar-class icebreakers for the Coast Guard and a provision requiring the Pentagon to update its "Arctic strategy."

Sullivan's other committee assignments have enabled him to look out for Alaskan interests as well: He has chaired subcommittees that have jurisdiction over fisheries on both the Commerce Committee and Environment and Public Works Committee. About 60 percent of the seafood caught in the United States comes from Alaskan waters. With Sen. Sheldon Whitehouse, the Rhode Island Democrat, he enacted in October 2018 the "Save Our Seas" bill to address the problem of plastic trash in oceans.

Despite his reservations about Trump during the campaign, Sullivan approved of the president's actions on behalf of Alaska. "In terms of a federal government that is finally working to help grow Alaska's economy, we are making significant progress," he said in a February 2018 speech to the state Legislature, citing oil exploration in the Arctic Refuge and construction of a natural gas pipeline from the North Slope. Sullivan said that critics of the plans for oil drilling had not "kept up with Alaska's world-class environmental standards or advancements in technology," plus the jobs and "energy security" that would result. In his speech, he voiced concern about the cultural effects of violent movies and video games "that glorify killing people."

Sullivan parted company with Trump on his tariff increases on imports, especially for steel and aluminum. "I do worry about retaliation," he said in a March 2018 interview with Alaska Public Media. "We're a huge exporter, particularly of fish and natural resource products."

In Senate campaign prospects for 2020, Sullivan was low in the priorities for Democrats—a significant shift from six years earlier.

Don Young (R)

Elected 1973, 23rd full term, b. Jun 09, 1933; Meridian, CA; Yuba Junior College (CA), A.A., 1952; California State University, Chico, B.A., 1958; Episcopalian; Married (Anne Garland Walton); 2 children; 14 grandchildren; 1 great-grandchild.

Military Career: U.S. Army 1955-1957

Elected Office: Fort Yukon City Council, 1960-1964; Fort Yukon Mayor, 1964-1968; AK House, 1966-1970; AK Senate, 1970-1973.

Professional Career: School teacher, Fort Yukon, 1960-1968; Riverboat captain, 1968-1972.

DC Office: 2314 RHOB 20515, 202-225-5765, Fax: 202-225-0425, donyoung.house.gov

State Offices: Anchorage, 907-271-5978; Fairbanks, 907-456-0210.

Committees: *Natural Resources*: Indigenous Peoples of the United States; National Parks, Forests & Public Lands (RMM). *Transportation & Infrastructure*: Aviation; Coast Guard & Maritime Transportation; Highways & Transit.

Group Ratings

	ADA	ACLU	AFL-CIO	LCV	ITI	COC	HAFA	ACU	CFG	FRC
2018	-	15%	-	6%	-	80%	43%	54%	-	100%
2017	0%	C	47%	0%	C	93%	C	72%	51%	100%

Almanac Ratings 2017-18

	Economy	Social	Foreign	Composite
Liberal	10%	4%	5%	6%
Conservative	90%	97%	95%	94%

Key Votes of the 115th Congress

1. Obama-care revision	Y	5. Family planning regs	Y	9. Guantanamo prisoners	N
2. Tax Cuts	Y	6. Body cameras/immigration	N	10. Ground missiles, limit	N
3. Omnibus appropriations	Y	7. Abortion ban	Y	11. Defense Dept. spending	Y
4. Dodd-Frank revision	Y	8. Concealed carry	Y	12. FISA rules	Y

Election Results

Election	Name (Party)	Vote (%)		Cand. Spent	Ind. Exp. Support	Ind. Exp. Oppose
2018 General	Don Young (R)	149,779	(53%)	$1,371,705	$2,229	$2,406
	Alyse Galvin (D)	131,199	(47%)	$1,888,689	$5,047	$75,000
2018 Primary	Don Young (R)	49,667	(71%)			
	Thomas John Nelson (R)	10,913	(16%)			
	Jed Whittaker (R)	9,525	(14%)			

Prior winning percentages: 2016 (50%), 2014 (51%), 2012 (64%), 2010 (69%), 2008 (50%), 2006 (57%), 2004 (71%), 2002 (75%), 2000 (70%), 1998 (63%), 1996 (59%), 1994 (57%), 1992 (47%), 1990 (52%), 1988 (63%), 1986 (57%), 1984 (55%), 1982 (71%), 1980 (74%), 1978 (55%), 1976 (71%), 1974 (54%), 1973 special (56%)

Don Young has been Alaska's congressman-at-large since 1973. He became the most-senior member of the House following the resignation in December 2017 of Democrat John Conyers of Michigan. As of March 2019, he passed Speaker Joe Cannon, who retired in 1923 after 46 years, as the longest-serving Republican in the history of the House. Young's long political career was nearly destroyed by an influence-peddling scandal in 2008. After having served six years each as chairman of two House committees that are vital to his home state, he lost much of his internal clout, though he retained his frequently ornery manner.

Young grew up on his family's farm in the Sacramento Valley of California, served in the Army, and graduated from college. He had a thirst for adventure and the rugged outdoors: He remembers that The Call of the Wild by Jack London was a favorite book growing up. He moved to Alaska in 1959, the year that the vast, untamed U.S. territory became a state. Young worked in construction, fishing, trapping and gold prospecting. He taught elementary school to indigenous Alaskan children in Fort Yukon, population 700. After spring thaws, he worked as a tugboat captain on the Yukon. He is a licensed mariner, which, in his words, is definitely not a typical profession of "one of these smooth, namby-pamby politicians." Young was elected mayor of Fort Yukon in 1964, to the state House in 1966, and to the state Senate in 1970. He ran for Congress in 1972. His opponent, incumbent Democrat Nick Begich, was killed in a plane crash in October and reelected posthumously. Young won the March 1973 special election to succeed him. Young is not a free-market conservative and has voted with liberals on some cultural issues, but he is a consistent, fierce advocate for Alaska's interests. He is temperamental and salty-tongued. To critics who once proposed shifting money for Alaska bridges to Hurricane Katrina recovery efforts, he said, "They can kiss my ear."

Soon after taking his seat in the House, Young voted to build the Alaska oil pipeline. He often found that his aggressive pursuit of economic development for his state conflicted with the environmental lobby and its interest in preserving wildlife. He called his critics a "self-centered bunch, the waffle-stomping, Harvard-graduating, intellectual idiots."

When Republicans controlled the House, Young occupied power positions that allowed him to work around his adversaries. He chaired the Resources Committee from 1995 to 2001 and the Transportation and Infrastructure Committee from 2001 to 2007. In each case, his tenure was limited by the House GOP term-limits rule for committee chairmen. He steered to House passage bills allowing oil drilling in the Arctic National Wildlife Refuge in 1995, 2001, and 2006, only to see them defeated or bottled up in the Senate. On the Resources Committee, his attempts to roll back environmental rulings, such as the one that barred logging in the Tongass National Forest, were frustrated in the 1990s by Democratic President Bill Clinton or by adverse votes cast by moderate Republicans. In 2000, he got Congress to pass the Conservation and Reinvestment Act to dedicate royalties from offshore oil and gas wells to state purchases of land.

On the Transportation and Infrastructure Committee, he led arguably the most bipartisan panel in the House because its chairmen traditionally larded their bills to make sure every cooperating committee member received plenty of highway or mass transit projects for his or her district. In 2003, Young proposed a surface transportation bill with $375 billion in spending, financed with a gas tax increase. The Bush administration and House Republican leaders stoutly opposed any such hike. In 2005, he got the House to pass a $284 billion bill. There was harsh criticism of the bill's earmarks — special projects for certain lawmakers — particularly two bridges in Alaska. One was from Anchorage to largely uninhabited land across the Knik Arm at a cost of $230 million; the other, for $220 million, was from the town of Ketchikan (pop. 14,000) to the island of Gravina (pop. 50), whose airport could be reached by local ferry. They were derisively dubbed the "bridges to nowhere." In July, both chambers passed by near-unanimous votes a $286 billion bill with more than 6,300 earmarks.

That likely would have been the end of the earmark controversy, except that Hurricane Katrina struck the Gulf Coast in August 2005. Suddenly, there were demands that money be shifted from Alaska's "bridges to nowhere" to New Orleans and other parts of the devastated region. "That is the dumbest thing I ever heard," Young said. But criticism of earmarks and the bridges continued. Conservative Republicans as well as Democrats chimed in, and profligate spending, symbolized by the two spans, emerged as an issue in the 2006 election. The punch lines helped wipe out the Republican majorities that year.

For an incumbent with his lengthy seniority, Young has had a bumpy history with Alaska voters and has frequently drawn serious challengers. His acerbic personality has been accompanied by ethical problems. In April 2007, a former Young aide pleaded guilty to accepting cash from disgraced lobbyist Jack Abramoff in exchange for inside government information. Records showed 120 contacts between Young and his staff with Abramoff and his clients. The next month, Rick Smith, an associate of Young's and a former lobbyist with the oil services firm VECO, a major Young contributor since 1989, pleaded guilty to bribing Alaska state legislators. In 2008, House Speaker Nancy Pelosi ordered an ethics investigation; the Justice Department conducted its own review. Following lengthy inquiries, no charges were lodged against Young.

That year, Republican Lt. Gov. Sean Parnell announced he would challenge Young in the primary. Parnell was endorsed by GOP Gov. Sarah Palin. Polls in summer 2008 showed Young trailing, but he professed to be unfazed. During a debate with Parnell, he said: "I've been accused of being arrogant, being a bully, and sometimes I'll plead to being both of those. Most of the time and every time I've done that is because I'm fighting for this state." Parnell spent $572,000, with strong support from the anti-tax Club for Growth. "We're tired of being the nation's symbol of excess and greed," Parnell said in a debate. Young beat Parnell by just 304 votes.

His battle was far from over. Former Alaska House Minority Leader Ethan Berkowitz, a Democrat, ran against him in the general election. Berkowitz was well funded, with $1.6 million, while Young's resources were depleted by legal fees and by the primary contest. Berkowitz framed the choice as one of style, contrasting his consensus-building approach to Young's tendency to "bully and intimidate." He said he would seek earmarks if communities and citizens asked for them, but not for lobbyists. Young responded during a debate, tongue in cheek, that he is "one of the nicest, kindest persons in the world." He added, "But when you mess with the state, you're messing with me." Young defeated Berkowitz 50%-45%.

Young remained under a political cloud. He lost the ranking minority member position on Resources. Young issued a press release saying he would regain the post when "my name is cleared." For one reason or another, that has not happened. Ethics problems lingered for Young. In 2014, the House Ethics Committee rebuked him for "improperly accepting nearly $60,000 in hunting trips, rides on private planes and other gifts and failing to report them on his financial disclosure forms." The gifts dated back to 2001. Young repaid the donors of the gifts, plus his campaign account. "I've been under a cloud all my life," Young told reporters in Juneau. "It's sort of like living in Juneau. It rains on you all the time. You don't even notice it."

He has remained an active legislator. He introduced a sweeping bill — with long odds of passage and designed to make a political point — that would have required the Obama administration to review and justify every regulation implemented in the past 20 years. In 2017, he won enactment of a bill to expand a hydroelectric project in the Kodiak Island National Wildlife Refuge, plus a resolution to nullify an Obama administration regulation to restrict hunting in Alaska's wildlife refuges. Democrats and environmentalists opposed the hunting measure, which was approved on an expedited procedure. His Almanac vote ratings on social issues have placed him near the center of the House.

Young has remained as feisty and vocal as ever. In a 2013 radio interview in Alaska, he referred to Latino immigrants as "wetbacks." Other Republicans swiftly condemned him, and Young apologized for what he acknowledged was an "insensitive" term. Speaking out against gun control in early 2018, he said that the Jews could have resisted the Holocaust more effectively if they had owned firearms.

In 2018, Democrats were enthusiastic about Alyce Galvin, an education activist and campaign novice who opposed the Trump administration. She outspent Young, $1.9 million to $1.4 million. He was reelected, 53%-46%.

At age 85 when he set the longevity record for House Republicans, Young had no plans to retire. "Not to run, as long as you enjoy what you're doing and you're, frankly, good at it, why would you quit? Most people retire because they don't like their jobs," he told the Anchorage Daily News in June 2018. His real enthusiasm is no longer legislation, he said in an earlier interview, but "helping people that have problems." Next in line behind Young in seniority is Rep. Jim Sensenbrenner, the Wisconsin Republican, who was first elected in 1978.

ARIZONA

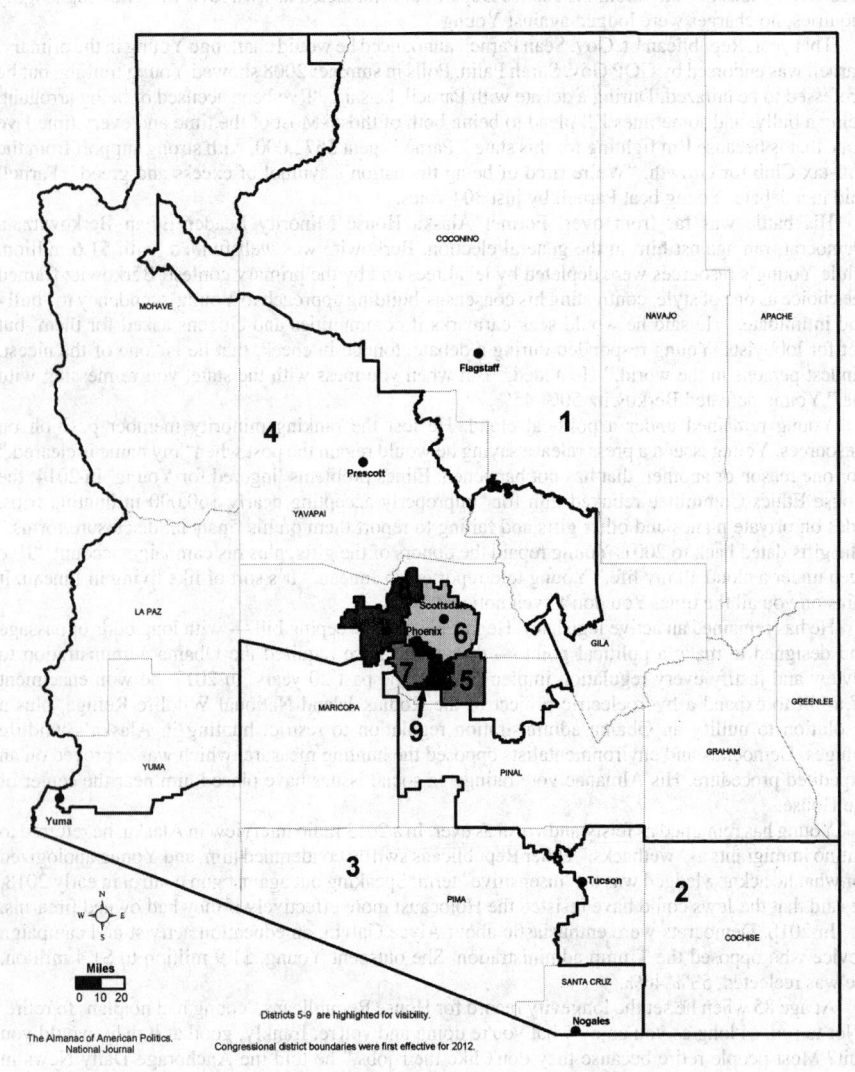

COCONINO

MOHAVE

NAVAJO

APACHE

Flagstaff

4

1

Prescott

YAVAPAI

LA PAZ

Scottsdale

Phoenix

6

GILA

7

5

MARICOPA

GREENLEE

9

GRAHAM

YUMA

PINAL

Yuma

3

2

Tucson

PIMA

COCHISE

Miles

0 10 20

SANTA CRUZ

N
W   E
S

Districts 5-9 are highlighted for visibility.

Congressional district boundaries were first effective for 2012.

Nogales

Arizona is at the crossroads of some of America's most urgent demographic and political trends – migration from colder states to the sunbelt, the impact of immigration, and the increase in Hispanic influence on politics. After years of dashed hopes, Democrats made tangible gains in the state in 2018, particularly in winning a hard-fought Senate race. As the 2020 presidential race approaches, Arizona could become a battleground.

Though Arizona has changed rapidly in recent decades, it is also home to the Hopi Indians, who have lived as shepherds on the plateaus east of the Grand Canyon for more than 900 years -- the oldest continuous community in the United States. They have spurned Christianity since 1680, when they killed the local Franciscan priests and burned their churches. Their land disputes with the more numerous Navajo have dragged on for centuries. Efforts by the federal government to get the two tribes to share lands came to naught, and it has cost more than $500 million to relocate families, primarily the Navajo, to new homes. Today, Arizona has 21 federally recognized Native American tribes who collectively control more than a quarter of the state's land.

Beyond the Native American population, Arizona, with its rugged desert, mountains and forests, was sparsely populated when the United States obtained it as part of the treaty that ended the Mexican War in 1848 (and another chunk a few years later to provide land for a southern route for a transcontinental railroad). Arizona was made a separate territory in 1863 after some locals tried to join the Confederacy. Nearly half a century later, in 1912, it became the 48th state.

Back then, few imagined that Arizona would transcend its frontier roots. For decades it relied on the five Cs, memorialized in the state seal. The first C was copper: The dome of the state Capitol is encased in copper, and one of the state's leading public figures was Lewis Douglas -- scion of a prominent Arizona mining family, a congressman, Franklin D. Roosevelt's first budget director, and Harry Truman's ambassador to Britain. The second C was cattle: As late as the mid-1960s a dozen or so cattle barons ran the state legislature. The third C was cotton: The signature achievement of Carl Hayden, a Democratic senator from 1927 to 1969, was the Central Arizona Project, a massive water project that brought irrigated cotton farms to the flatlands around Phoenix. The water also helped with the fourth C: citrus. The fifth C was climate: Dry, clear air drew visitors seeking its therapeutic benefits, though the scorching summer heat deterred permanent transplants for many years.

Then came air conditioning, which brought waves of retirees. In the years after World War II, Arizona became less dependent on federal largesse, except for its military bases and defense contracts. Businessmen, lawyers, developers and water companies, notably the Salt River Project, built Arizona and fostered an environment that welcomed new technological ideas. Their political champion was Barry Goldwater, a Phoenix City Council member, senator and the 1964 GOP presidential nominee who was the nation's most recognizable conservative for much of the 1950s and 1960s (and someone who today would be considered a libertarian, a strain of Republicanism with especially strong roots in the West). Goldwater helped to make Arizona solidly Republican, the only state to vote Republican for president in every election between 1952 and 1992. Later, Republican Sen. John McCain took up the mantle (but not the libertarianism) of Arizona's political giant; he died in 2018.

Arizona ranks third in the nation for producing market vegetables, and has significant uranium reserves (though in 2018, the U.S. Supreme Court upheld a ban on uranium mining near Grand Canyon National Park.) Still, Arizona's growth has long been based on high-tech and low taxes. Phoenix began attracting technology industries when Motorola built a research center for military electronics there in 1948. Other major employers followed: Honeywell, Raytheon, Intel, Avnet and General Dynamics. The state counts two Air Force bases and a Marine air station, plus the huge Barry M. Goldwater Range, where many of America's pilots have trained. Private companies have invested as well, including in recent years a cloud storage project by Apple; a manufacturing hub for Nikola Motor Co.'s hydrogen-powered trucks; an artificial intelligence facility for India-based company Infosys; and a Bill Gates-backed proposal for a "smart city" complex near Phoenix. While 25 percent of the energy consumed in Arizona homes is for air conditioning -- about four times the national average -- the state's per capita energy consumption is among the nation's lowest. The state is coming to grips with a changing climate, which could include a mix of rising temperatures, smaller snow packs, reduced Colorado River flow and more frequent wildfires; since 1984, more than 2 percent of Arizona has burned per decade. Arizona's Renewable Energy Standard requires 15 percent of the state's electricity consumption to come from renewables by 2025. Currently, Arizona ranks third in installed solar capacity behind California and North Carolina, and it has the nation's largest nuclear power plant, the Palo Verde Nuclear Generating Station.

Arizona has been one of the nation's boom states, driven by the relocation of retirees from the Midwest and elsewhere. Its population nearly doubled from 3.7 million in 1990 to 7.1 million in 2018, and is projected to reach 8.1 million by 2026, with metro Phoenix accounting for 5.5 million. The influx of newcomers led developers to buy out the cotton farms, making construction and real estate about a third of the state's economy. But the Great Recession torpedoed the housing market, and Arizona became a national leader in home foreclosures.

Arizona has been a focal point for the battle over illegal immigration. With strong border enforcement in Texas and a border fence near San Diego, the hilly Arizona desert in Cochise and Santa Cruz counties became a major entry point. Anger at the flood of illegals contributed to the passage of ballot propositions denying welfare benefits and requiring government employees to report illegal residents. Other ballot measures, supported by some 40 percent of Hispanic voters, declared English Arizona's official language and barred in-state tuition for illegal residents at state colleges. In 2010, the legislature passed Senate Bill 1070, authorizing law enforcement officials to check the immigration status of people stopped for other reasons. President Barack Obama denounced the law, saying it encouraged racial profiling, and Hispanic organizations called for a boycott of the state, which led to cancellation of some conventions and lower hotel bookings. The Justice Department brought a lawsuit to stop enforcement and won at the trial and appellate levels. But in June 2012, the Supreme Court upheld the main provision requiring law enforcement officers to check immigration status of people stopped for other reasons. Gradually, the crisis atmosphere in the state ebbed. In 2011, the heavily Republican state Senate, heeding the opposition from businesses, rejected several new measures that would have cracked down further on illegal immigration.

Latino voters have been the big story in Arizona in recent election cycles. For some time, Arizona, fueled by demographic changes and an increase in independent voters, has seemed to be on the verge of becoming more competitive. Democrats have hoped that the increasing Hispanic population — currently 31 percent — would tip the state their way in presidential contests. But John Kerry and Barack Obama lost by nearly identical 10-point margins. The conflict over immigration made Latinos more Democratic and whites more Republican. In 2004 and 2008, George W. Bush and John McCain – both of whom were in favor of immigration reform -- captured more than 40 percent of the Hispanic vote. But Mitt Romney lost Latinos 74%-25% while winning whites, 66%-32%, running ahead of Bush and McCain.

These trends came to a head in 2016, with Trump's aggressive rhetoric on illegal immigration. Cementing the issue's place at center stage was the presence on the ballot of Joe Arpaio, the fiercely anti-illegal-immigrant Maricopa County Sheriff seeking a seventh term. Ultimately, Trump, with slightly higher support from Latinos than Romney, won the state, though by 3.5 percentage points, about one-third of Romney's margin over Obama in 2012. In populous Maricopa County, Clinton came within about 40,000 votes of defeating Trump, and Arpaio lost by a double-digit margin.

In the Trump era, Arizona continued edging away from its small-government past. In early 2018, teachers staged a walkout that closed 1,000 schools under the banner #RedForEd. They ended their strike when Republican Gov. Doug Ducey signed a bill to boost teacher pay 20 percent by 2020, plus $100 million for support staff. It wasn't all the teachers had asked for, but it was considered a victory. In the midterm elections, Ducey won an easy reelection over an unabashed progressive. But Democrats otherwise performed well in Arizona, particularly female candidates. Former Rep. Ann Kirkpatrick flipped a GOP-held House seat; state Senate Minority Leader Katie Hobbs won the open Secretary of State seat; political novice Kathy Hoffman won the open state education superintendent seat; and Democrats gained ground in the legislature. The biggest victory was by Democratic Rep. Kyrsten Sinema. Steering a moderate course, she won an open Senate seat over GOP Rep. Martha McSally, who touted her tough stance on immigration and her support from Trump. McSally turned off some suburban voters; while Ducey won Maricopa County, Sinema defeated McSally there by 60,000 votes, 51%-49%, giving Democrats hope of making a serious play for Arizona in the 2020 presidential race.

Population		Race and Ethnicity		Income	
Total	6,809,946	White	55.6%	Median Income	$53,510
Land area (sq. miles)	113,594	Black	4.1%	State Income Rank	30
Pop/ sq mi	59.9	Latino	30.9%	Poverty Rate	17.0%
Born in state	39.3%	Asian	3.0%	With health insurance	87.8%
		Two or more races	2.2%	Cash public assistance	2.0%
Age Groups		Other	4.2%	Food stamp/SNAP	12.5%
Under 18	23.8%				
18-34	23.4%	Education		Work	
35-64	36.6%	H.S grad or less	37.7%	White Collar	35.7%
Over 64	16.2%	Some college	33.9%	Sales and Service	45.5%
		College Degree, 4 yr	17.8%	Blue Collar	18.8%
Military		Post grad	10.7%	Government	14.0%
Veteran/ Active Duty	9.7%				

Presidential Politics

2016 Primary (D)	Clinton (D)	262,459 (56%)	Sanders (D)	192,962 (41%)		
2016 Primary (R)	Trump (R)	286,743 (46%)	Cruz (R)	172,294 (28%)	Rubio (R)	72,304 (12%)
	Kasich (R)	65,965 (11%)				
2016 Pres. Vote	Trump (R)	1,252,401 (48%)	Clinton (D)	1,161,167 (45%)	Johnson (L)	106,327 (4%)
2012 Pres. Vote	Romney (R)	1,233,654 (54%)	Obama (D)	1,025,232 (45%)		

As the Arizona electorate becomes more diverse, the state is becoming more of a presidential battleground state. While Donald Trump kept the state in the Republican column, his 48%-45% victory over Hillary Clinton was a much slimmer margin than GOP nominees had garnered in recent White House contests.

Clinton made Arizona a competitive race by cutting the margin in Maricopa County to roughly three percentage points. Barack Obama lost it by nine points in both 2008 and 2012. Maricopa, which contains metro Phoenix with its fast-growing suburbs and exurbs such as Surprise, Buckeye, Goodyear and Gilbert, and large cities such as Glendale, Mesa and Scottsdale, cast some 60 percent of the state's votes in 2016. The county overall tilts Republican, but Tempe, home to Arizona State University, provides Democratic votes. Pima County, dominated by Tucson, the state's second largest city, is a Democratic stronghold, but only about one-sixth of the state's ballots were cast there in 2016. Arizona's largely rural territory had been home to conservative ranchers and others who were once known as "Pinto" or "Goldwater" Democrats. Today it is strong GOP turf, except for Apache County with its tribal reservations; Coconino County, with Flagstaff and Northern Arizona University; and Santa Cruz County, where four of five residents are Hispanic. This largely rural portion of the state (Mohave County now includes Las Vegas exurbs) delivered heavily for Trump, backing him 56%-39%, better than Mitt Romney did in 2012 or home-state Sen. John McCain performed in 2008. To prevail, a Democratic presidential candidate needs to battle a Republican at least close to a draw in Maricopa, score a big turnout in Pima, and hold down losses in the rest of the state. That was essentially the formula Bill Clinton followed in 1996, when he became the first Democrat to carry Arizona since Harry Truman in 1948.

Immigration has roiled the state's politics and one of Trump's early Arizona backers was Maricopa County Sheriff Joe Arpaio, who advocated a crackdown on illegal border crossers. In the late March Republican primary, Arpaio's support, along with the backing of former GOP governor Jan Brewer, helped Trump romp over his rivals with 46 percent of the vote, followed by Texas Sen. Ted Cruz, who captured 28 percent. In a winner-take-all contest, Trump claimed all the state's GOP convention delegates. Clinton won the Democratic primary handily, defeating Sen. Bernie Sanders 56%-41%. She did well in counties with large Hispanic populations and won all nine of the state's congressional districts; Sanders was most competitive in the 4th and 9th Districts, containing Phoenix suburbs and exurbs.

The primary was marred by long voting lines in Maricopa, in part because officials there reduced the number of polling places from 200 in the 2012 primary to 60. Lawsuits by Democrats and voting rights advocates helped prompt moves to ease long waits at polling places in November.

Congressional Districts

116th Congress Lineup	5D 4R	115th Congress Lineup	4D 5R

Arizona has become a competitive battleground for House seats. Its nine-member delegation includes four relatively secure Republican districts, two solidly Democratic districts (with large Hispanic majorities), and three districts that started the decade as "toss-ups" but are now held by Democrats. Those three districts are: the 1st, in the sprawling rural eastern part of the state; the 2nd, anchored in Tucson; and the 9th, in the university bastion of Tempe.

That map was drawn by a five-member Independent Redistricting Commission, which was created by a statewide referendum in 2000. It is composed of two Democrats, two Republicans and an ostensibly independent member picked by the other four. The commission's map resulted in a delegation of six Republican and two Democrats after the 2002 election, but it shifted to five Democrats and three Republicans in 2008. The GOP wave of 2010 restored Republicans to a 5-3 majority. When Arizona gained a seat from the 2010 census, replicating its pattern of increasing its delegation by at least one seat following each decennial count since 1960, Democrats emerged from a state dominated by a Republican governor and legislature with the map of their dreams and five of the state's nine House seats.

The Democrats' good fortune resulted when the commission's Republicans agreed to select as the panel's chair Colleen Coyle Mathis, a Tucson health care administrator who described herself as a "post-partisan" ex-Republican. She quickly sided with the commission's Democrats on the need to draw more competitive districts. The map infuriated Republicans: Not only did it maximize Democratic opportunities, it forced Republicans David Schweikert and Ben Quayle to run against each other even though the state was gaining a seat. GOP Gov. Jan Brewer chose to void the map and accused Mathis of "gross misconduct." The state Senate removed her from the commission on a 21-6 vote, with several Democrats abstaining in protest. The Arizona Republic slammed Brewer for running "roughshod over the public."

Less than three weeks after Mathis' removal, the Arizona Supreme Court rebuked Brewer and reinstated Mathis. The commission again approved its map. Schweikert and Quayle were forced to duel in an ugly primary and Democrats picked up both the 1st and 9th districts in November. In 2014, Democrats narrowly lost the 2nd, but they regained it in 2018.

The Republican-controlled legislature, meanwhile, challenged the map in federal court. Its lawyers contended that the 2000 referendum violated the Constitution by removing its authority over the congressional district map. A three-judge federal court ruled against the legislature in 2014, with two of the judges dismissing the complaint on the grounds that the Arizona's constitution reserved the initiative power to its people, and that the federal Constitution permits "legislative" power to be exercised through a referendum. The U.S. Supreme Court, in a 5-4 decision, ruled that Arizona voters had the authority to create a redistricting commission. Its ruling could encourage citizen referenda in other states, though both political parties likely will remain reluctant to relinquish their control.

With Republicans having retained control of the governorship and legislature in 2018, they could seek other steps to limit the authority of the commission. The Census Bureau's projection that Arizona will gain a tenth seat after the 2020 census means that the opening likely will be in the Phoenix area. Maricopa County is home to 60 percent of the state's residents and includes the entirety of five current districts. Hispanics, who are 30 percent of the population, likely will seek a third seat; they currently hold one in Phoenix, and the second is split between Phoenix and Tucson. The three other Democratic-held seats likely will be in play during the next redistricting, though even the most partisan Republicans likely would be satisfied to end up with 6 of the 10 new districts.

Doug Ducey (R)

Elected 2014, term expires 2023, 2nd term; b. Apr. 9, 1964, Toledo, OH; Arizona State U., B.S. 1986; Catholic; Married (Angela); 3 children.

Elected Office: AZ Treasurer, 2010-2014.

Professional Career: Beer Distributorship Marketing Coordinator, Hensley & Co., 1982-1986; Sales and Marketing Executive, Proctor & Gamble, 1986-1993; CEO and Chairman, Cold Stone Creamery, 1996-2007; Chairman, iMemories, 2008-2012.

Office: 1700 W. Washington St., Phoenix, 85007; 602-542-4331; Fax: 602-542-7601; Website: azgovernor.gov.

Atty. Gen: Mark Brnovich (R) **Sec. of State:** Katie Hobbs (D)

State Legislature: Senate: 13D, 17R **House:** 29D, 31R

Election Results

Election	Name (Party)	Vote (%)
2018 General	Doug Ducey (R)	1,330,863 (56%)
	David Garcia (D)	994,341 (42%)
	Angel Torres (G)	50,962 (2%)
2018 Primary	Doug Ducey (R)	463,672 (71%)
	Ken Bennett (R)	191,775 (29%)

Republican Doug Ducey, a self-professed "conservative ice cream guy," won the governorship in 2014 and was reelected four years later, even as several Democrats were winning statewide offices amid a national Democratic tide.

Ducey grew up in Toledo Ohio and graduated from St. John's Jesuit High School in 1982. He drove west in his Datsun B210, leaving his recession-ravaged state to attend Arizona State University and seek his fortune in the Sunbelt. He found it in a Tempe ice cream store. After graduating with a degree in finance in 1986, and a brief stint in marketing at Procter & Gamble, Ducey joined up with the founder of Cold Stone Creamery and helped turn it into a global brand with more than 1,400 stores. He eventually became CEO. In 2007, at the age of 43, Ducey helped engineer a merger with another Arizona franchising heavyweight, Kahala Corp. He got rich in the process, but that corporate marriage didn't work out, an experience Ducey described to Bloomberg Business as "incredibly frustrating and disappointing, but equally liberating all at once." Ducey took some time off, refocused, and became the lead investor and chairman of the board of iMemories, a friend's technology startup in Scottsdale, which helps people digitize their home movies and share them online.

Ducey made his first foray into elective politics by seeking the state treasurer's post, vowing to utilize his business background to promote economic growth. That's not a core function of the state treasurer's office, and at the time many viewed his bid for the treasurer's job as a warm-up for a Senate or gubernatorial run. Nevertheless, with his connections to the Phoenix business elite, Ducey significantly outraised and outspent his more credentialed GOP opponents, including a conservative favorite, handily won the primary and prevailed in the fall. While he was treasurer, Ducey laid the groundwork for higher office by leading a successful fight to defeat a 2012 ballot initiative that would have funded increased education spending by making a temporary one-cent sales tax increase permanent.

In 2014, he jumped into the spirited Republican contest to succeed Republican Gov. Jan Brewer. Ducey once again played up his business know-how, but this time he had plenty of backing from prominent conservatives, including Sen. Ted Cruz of Texas, former Alaska Gov. Sarah Palin, and Maricopa County Sheriff Joe Arpaio, an immigration hardliner who had supported one of Ducey's GOP primary rivals four years prior. Ducey's stewardship of Cold Stone Creamery was criticized for a high default rate on Small Business Administration loans used to finance franchises, but he easily won the nomination.

In the general election, Ducey faced former Board of Regents member Fred DuVal, a centrist Democrat, former Clinton White House staffer and longtime adviser to former Arizona Democratic Gov. Bruce Babbitt. Ducey campaigned for cuts in state regulations and in business and personal income taxes. He also campaigned against Common Core education standards, favored limiting the definition of marriage to that between a man and a woman, and opposed benefits to domestic partners of gay state employees, but added that he would comply with the law. Ducey pumped about $5 million of his own money into the campaign which, along with allied groups, resulted in more than $10 million being spent on his behalf in the election, compared with about $3 million spent by DuVal and his outside backers. Ducey won by nearly 12 percentage points and Arizonans extended their streak of electing governors not native to the state. (The last was Babbitt in 1982.)

In office, and confronting a yawning state deficit, Ducey pushed through a budget that cut nearly $100 million in funding to higher education, borrowed more than $100 million from the state's rainy day fund and clawed back some $220 million in unspent agency funds. Ducey backed off a plan to prune non-classroom K-12 education spending and negotiated a deal with legislators giving schools more flexibility. To the chagrin of his more conservative backers, Ducey steered clear of some controversial topics. He rejected demands to scrap Common Core standards, and when he learned that the Arizona Department of Child Safety had stopped granting joint foster care licenses and adoptions to same-sex couples while the U.S. Supreme Court was weighing the issue of same-sex marriage — the U.S. Court of Appeals for the 9th Circuit had overturned Arizona's ban in 2014 — the governor quickly stepped in and ordered the state agency to allow all legally married couples in Arizona to serve as foster parents and adopt.

In 2016, Ducey demanded that the federal government stop sending Syrian refugees to the state; Arizona had become the third most-common destination, behind Michigan and California. And he signed legislation that would allow the state to withhold funding from local jurisdictions that pursue policies at odds with the state. Given Arizona's unified Republican government at the state level and the predominance of Democratic governance in many of the state's big cities, this law held the potential for sinking liberal policies on the minimum wage, sick leave, gun restrictions and other issues. At the same time, Ducey sought to smooth the rough edges of Donald Trump's call to renegotiate NAFTA, a trade deal that made possible $8.32 billion in Arizona exports and $7.45 billion in imports, according to the University of Arizona. After Trump's election, Ducey visited Mexico, noting that it is "our No. 1 trading partner, times four, for the state of Arizona. We've built that relationship."

Ducey's relationship with Trump ran hot and cold in 2016, particularly compared with his predecessor, Brewer, who was all in for Trump early on. In March, Ducey didn't explicitly endorse Trump but pledged to support whoever won the GOP nomination. At the Republican National Convention in Cleveland, Ducey led the state's delegation and said, "I'm proud to be here." But it took until Aug. 31 for Ducey to appear in person alongside Trump, when he spoke at a rally in Phoenix touting Trump's promises to nominate conservative judges and toughen border security. Then, when the tape of Trump's sexually explicit comments to Billy Bush became public in early October, Ducey called the remarks "insulting and terribly demeaning to women" and said he disavowed them "100 percent." Even so, just days before the election, Ducey addressed a Trump rally in Mesa.

During the 2017 legislative session, Ducey signed tax breaks for small and big businesses; exempted the sale of U.S. gold coins from state capital gains taxes; partially restored cuts in cash payments to welfare recipients as long as they worked or enrolled in job training; signed some of the tightest requirements on what actions doctors must take if a baby is born alive during an attempted abortion; and vetoed legislation to legalize industrial hemp. The following year, Ducey signed a bill that exempted coal from sales taxes in Arizona, a change seen as crucial for securing a buyer for the Navajo Generating Station, a power plant that buys coal from the Kayenta Mine on Navajo and Hopi land.

But the big battle of 2018 pitted Ducey against striking teachers. The teachers, wearing red and carrying the banner of #RedForEd, followed labor actions by their colleagues in West Virginia, Oklahoma and Kentucky that sought to increase spending and boost pay in red states. Arizona's per-pupil expenditures in 2015 were lower than any state except Idaho and Utah. The teachers agreed to call off their strike as the legislature secured a Ducey proposal to increase teacher pay 20 percent by 2020 and expand the budget by $100 million for support staff and non-salary items.

Boasting an approval rating that was positive but not wildly so, Ducey faced a GOP primary challenge from the right by former Secretary of State Ken Bennett. Bennett attacked Ducey for "caving" to striking teachers, but the incumbent largely ignored his challenger and won, 71%-29%. Within weeks, Ducey tapped former GOP Sen. Jon Kyl to fill the U.S. Senate seat left vacant with the death of John McCain. In December 2018, Kyl announced his departure, clearing Ducey to choose outgoing Rep. Martha McSally, who had just narrowly lost a Senate race to Democrat Kyrsten Sinema, as Kyl's successor.

In the general election, Ducey faced David Garcia, an Arizona State University professor who had served as an Army infantryman and had narrowly lost a 2014 race for state education superintendent. Garcia, a fourth-generation Mexican-American, had only mastered Spanish as an adult and after a concerted effort to do so, but he took pains to boost turnout among younger, less-frequent Latino voters who had a stronger sense of ethnic nationality and a more progressive outlook. Asked about calls by some on the Democratic left to "abolish ICE," Garcia told the New Yorker, "We need to replace ICE with an immigration system that works. It's more than about an agency. It's about a system that's problematic." Ducey and Garcia clashed over Trump's proposal for a border wall and about Trump himself. In October 2018, Ducey joined Trump onstage at a rally, praising him for putting "public safety first" and "securing our southern border." Ducey was bolstered by a sizable fundraising advantage and ads that portrayed Garcia as soft on illegal immigration.

Sinema, the highest-profile Democrat running in Arizona in 2018, kept Garcia at arm's length, seemingly worried that a close alliance would scare off moderate Republican voters she needed to win. That strategy paid dividends on Election Day, as Sinema won and Garcia lost. Statewide, Ducey won 56%-42% -- an improvement of a few points over 2014, even though 2018 was a worse environment for Republicans. In populous Maricopa County, Ducey won, 56%-42%, even as Sinema was winning the county, 51%-49%. In one of every five precincts in Maricopa County, voters split their votes between Sinema and Ducey, the Arizona Republic found, a pattern that was especially true in Sinema's old district, the 9th. In a coda to his first term and perhaps a sign of Arizona's changing political environment, Ducey after the election named his 2014 Democratic rival, DuVal, to an eight year-term on the Board of Regents that oversees state universities.

Kyrsten Sinema (D)

Elected 2018, term expires 2024, 1st term, b. Jul 12, 1976; Tucson; Brigham Young University (UT), Bach. Deg., 1995; Arizona State University, M.S., 1999; Arizona State University Law School, J.D., 2004; Harvard University Kennedy School of Government (MA), Att., 2008; Harvard University Kennedy School of Government, 2010; Arizona State University, Ph.D., 2012; None; Single.

Elected Office: AZ House, 2004-2010; AZ Senate, 2010-2012; U.S. house 2013-2019.

Professional Career: Social worker, 1995-2002; Practicing lawyer, 2005-present; Instructor, Center for Progressive Leadership, 2006-present.

DC Office: 317 HSOB 20510, 202-224-4521, sinema.senate.gov

State Offices: Phoenix, 602-598-7327.

Committees: *Aging. Banking, Housing & Urban Affairs*: Economic Policy; National Security &International Trade & Finance; Securities, Insurance & Investment. *Commerce, Science &Transportation*: Communications, Technology, Innovation & the Internet; Manufacturing, Trade & Consumer Protection; Aviation & Space (RMM); Security. *Homeland Security & Government Affairs*: Federal Spending Oversight & Emergency Management; Regulatory Affairs & Federal Management (RMM). *Veterans' Affairs.*

Group Ratings (House)

	ADA	ACLU	AFL-CIO	LCV	ITI	COC	HAFA	ACU	CFG	FRC
2018	-	64%	-	74%	-	75%	10%	19%	25%	25%
2017	65%	C	69%	80%	C	75%	C	4%	6%	0%

Key Votes of the 115th Congress (House)

1. Obama-care revision	N	5. Family planning regs	N	9. Guantanamo prisoners	N
2. Tax Cuts	N	6. Body cameras/immigration	Y	10. Ground missiles, limit	N
3. Omnibus appropriations	Y	7. Abortion ban	N	11. Defense Dept. spending	Y
4. Dodd-Frank revision	Y	8. Concealed carry	N	12. FISA rules	Y

Election Results

Election	Name (Party)	Vote (%)	Cand. Spent	Ind. Exp. Support	Ind. Exp. Oppose
2018 General	Kyrsten Sinema (D)............................ 1,191,100	(50%)	$24,309,295	$9,050,763	$24,740,811
	Martha McSally (R)....................... 1,135,200	(48%)	$20,514,746	$3,054,086	$25,569,266
	Angela Green (G)................................. 57,442	(2%)			
2018 Primary	Kyrsten Sinema (D)............................. 404,170	(79%)			
	Deedra Abboud (D)............................. 105,800	(21%)			

Prior winning percentages: House: 2016 (61%), 2014 (55%), 2012 (49%)

Democrat Kyrsten Sinema won a hard-fought race in 2018 to become the first openly bisexual senator in U.S. history, the first female senator from Arizona and the first Democrat to win a Senate race in the state in three decades. In her political career, she's transformed from Green Party-supporting activist to one of the more moderate, bipartisan members of Congress. What's been consistent throughout her life has been a singular drive that's taken her from an impoverished childhood to Congress.

Sinema grew up in Tucson. Her parents divorced, and her mother married a teacher. When her stepfather lost his job, the family took shelter for two years in a former gas station on his parents' Florida property that she said lacked electricity and running water — a period she's described as homelessness, though some family members have said she's exaggerated how dire the living conditions were. The family relied on food donations from the close-knit Latter-day Saints community; her mother is Mormon. They eventually moved into a home but remained poor.

Those tough early years shaped her life — and play a key role in her political narrative. "For nearly three years, we lived in an old, abandoned gas station without running water or electricity," Sinema said in her Senate campaign launch video. "Sometimes, we didn't have enough food to eat, but we got by thanks to help from family, church and, sometimes, even the government."

At 16, Sinema graduated as her high school's valedictorian and went on to earn a bachelor's degree in social work from Brigham Young University. She also earned a master's degree in social work, a law degree and a doctorate in justice studies from Arizona State University — all while working full time. After graduating from BYU at 18, she became a social worker in a central Phoenix school district. Before her election to Congress, she worked as a lawyer, an adjunct professor at Arizona State, and an instructor at the Center for Progressive Leadership, a Washington-based institute that trains activists in progressive policies. Sinema is a fitness fiend: She has run more than 10 marathons, including Boston, and is the first member of Congress to have completed a triathlon. She has taught spin classes to colleagues in the House gym and has recruited a bipartisan group to join her for bootcamp-like Solidcore workout classes. Another congressional first for Sinema, according to U.S. News & World Report: She describes her religion as "none."

Sinema, who said she overcame adversity by using Helen Keller as a role model, was motivated to enter politics to help people with backgrounds like hers. "I'm a Democrat today ... because they taught me the best of both ideas: help each other when you're struggling, but work very hard on your own," she told National Journal. After serving as the state spokeswoman for the Green Party during Ralph Nader's 2000 presidential run and honing her political chops as an anti-war activist, she lost her first bid for the Arizona House running as an independent in 2002. She ran as a Democrat and won in 2004, serving there until 2010, when she was elected to the state Senate. As a liberal advocate in the Legislature, she promoted LGBT rights and sponsored several bills aimed at reining in Maricopa County Sheriff Joe Arpaio's tough and sometimes extralegal crackdowns on illegal immigration. She also worked with Republicans to pass legislation on human trafficking and other issues.

She ran for a competitive House district in suburban Phoenix in 2012, voicing frustration with the partisan divide in Congress and winning a three-way Democratic primary with 41% of the vote. Her general election opponent was Vernon Parker, a former Paradise Valley mayor who served in both Bush administrations. They fought for the independent vote, each painting the other as extreme in attack ads. Sinema supported closing corporate tax loopholes and protecting payroll tax cuts for working families. Parker followed the national GOP playbook in vowing to repeal the Affordable Care Act and rein in runaway spending. Sinema won 49%-45%. It was her only competitive House race in a fast-growing district that leaned Blue.

The former liberal firebrand joined the centrist Democratic Blue Dog Coalition and bipartisan Problem Solvers Caucus and co-founded the United Solutions Caucus, a bipartisan House group seeking consensus policies. Sinema hewed close to the center during her time in the House, breaking occasionally with her party on fiscal issues and voting against keeping Nancy Pelosi as Democratic leader in both 2015 and 2017. She routinely ranked as one of the most conservative Democrats in the Almanac's annual vote ratings. "I'm just doing my thing," she told Roll Call in February 2015. "I know my thing's a little bit different than other people, but I don't think there's anything wrong with that at all. And, you know what? I don't mind if some people like it or don't like it. That's OK."

In the House, Sinema worked on housing and consumer issues on the Financial Services Committee. The panel approved several of her proposals, including a 2016 measure to help law enforcement officials track down financial criminals who target seniors. Her actions have been unpredictable. She joined organizations of moderate Democrats, occasionally criticized then-President Barack Obama and worked across the aisle with House Republicans, voting with them to repeal some parts of Obamacare and the Dodd-Frank financial regulations. She also worked on legislation to protect victims of sexual violence on school campuses.

She tacked to the center on immigration, a hot-button issue in her home state, taking some votes that infuriated Hispanic groups. In 2017, she was one of just 24 House Democrats to vote for "Kate's Law," which would have guaranteed jail time for undocumented immigrants who re-entered the U.S. after being deported and increased penalties for undocumented immigrants who'd committed other crimes. She was one of just 11 Democrats who voted for GOP legislation that same year that would have made it easier to deport immigrants suspected of having gang ties. She voted against House Republicans' more hawkish and expansive immigration reform efforts.

Arizona operatives had long expected Sinema to run for statewide office. And she took the plunge in late 2017, announcing her bid to challenge Republican Sen. Jeff Flake that September. But Flake had emerged as one of President Trump's most vocal critics and was facing a tough primary challenge from conservative iconoclast Kelli Ward, a former state senator who'd put a scare into Sen. John McCain two years earlier. Flake admitted that there was no way for him to win re-election and announced he wouldn't seek another term one month after Sinema had announced her campaign.

Rep. Martha McSally received strong encouragement from Senate Majority Leader Mitch McConnell and other establishment Republicans to run and soon jumped in herself. But while McSally and Sinema had some commonalities — impressive personal stories, long-held ambitions to run statewide and moderate profiles — McSally was hamstrung throughout the campaign by her need to ward off primary challengers and spent much of the campaign pivoting to the right to defeat Ward and Arpaio. This allowed Sinema to dominate the center.

McSally was forced to fight a two-front war through the late August primary and navigate a state where the GOP base, strongly behind President Donald Trump, was distrustful of her former brand as a moderate and furious at its pair of senators — Flake and McCain — for regularly bucking the party. To shore up her base, she dropped her support for legislation on behalf of undocumented immigrants who entered the United States as children; she embraced Trump on the campaign trail.

Sinema ran campaign ads touting her independence and bipartisan values throughout the summer. Those spots heavily featured her talking about her tough upbringing and her work on education and veterans issues — including one memorable spot featuring her brother, a police officer and Marine veteran, touting her independence. She also vowed to support new leadership in the Senate, a promise she broke early after her election when Senate Minority Leader Chuck Schumer was reelected without opposition in late 2018.

When McCain died from brain cancer just days before the late August primary, McSally, a former protege of the senator, stayed silent about his death, seemingly worried her party's anti-McCain base would turn on her if she mourned him too vocally. Sinema heaped praise on the former senator, embracing his maverick persona and praising his lifetime of service.

But Sinema's past offered McSally plenty of fodder. As the primary wound down her campaign unleashed some brutal ads spotlighting Sinema's past hard-line liberalism, including ads featuring her in a pink tutu protesting the war in Afghanistan. McSally's allies later unearthed a pair of 2011 videos of Sinema mocking her home state, calling its population "crazy" and joking it "is clearly the meth lab of democracy" because of its attempted crackdowns on immigrants.

But McSally went too far in their one debate, accusing Sinema of treason — comments that drew rebukes in local media. Sinema earned the endorsement of the Arizona Republic, the state's largest paper, which historically has almost always backed Republicans.

After the primary, McSally did little to steer back to the center, worried she'd offend the state's hard-line conservative base. That allowed Sinema to position herself as the natural heir to Arizona's long line of maverick politicians, like McCain and Flake, rather than as a party-line Democrat.

The election in the GOP-leaning state tightened in the final month, with McSally leading a number of surveys. The Republican led on election night and for two days afterward, as Arizona's slow mailvoting dragged out the count. But Sinema took the lead, leading some national Republicans, including Trump, to claim voter fraud without evidence.

The race was called in Sinema's favor six days after the election. She ran well ahead of her state's gubernatorial nominee, liberal Democrat David Garcia, who struggled with fundraising against popular center-right Gov. Doug Ducey. Sinema and Garcia never endorsed one another.

Sinema repeatedly name-checked McCain in her victory speech, as she positioned herself to assume his mantle of independent voting in the Senate. She secured a spot on the Senate banking committee, where her pro-business views on regulation and the economy could have an effect. Ducey appointed McSally to the Senate after caretaker Sen. Jon Kyl resigned at the end of 2018, putting the old rivals in the same chamber and making Sinema the state's senior senator.

Martha McSally (R)

Appointed 2019, term expires 2020, 1st term, b. Mar 22, 1966; Warwick, RI; National Air War College, Mast. Deg.; St. Mary Academy, Bayview (RI), 1984; United States Air Force Academy, B.S., 1988; John F. Kennedy School of Government, Harvard University, M.P.P., 1990; Christian Church; Single.

Military Career: U.S. Air Force 1988-2001 (Operation Southern Watch, Operation Allied Force, Operation Enduring Freedom)

Elected Office: U.S. House, 2015-2019.

Professional Career: Legislative fellow, 1999-2000; National Security Studies professor, George C. Marshall Ctr, 2011-2012.

DC Office: B40D DSOB 20510, 202-224-2235, Fax: 202-228-2862, mcsally.senate.gov

State Offices: Phoenix, 602-952-2410; Tucson, 520-670-6334.

Committees: *Aging. Armed Services*: Airland; Personnel; Readiness & Management Support. *Banking, Housing & Urban Affairs*: Housing, Transportation & Community Development; National Security & International Trade & Finance; Securities, Insurance & Investment. *Energy & Natural Resources*: Energy; Public Lands, Forests & Mining; Water & Power (Chmn). *Indian Affairs*.

Group Ratings (House)

	ADA	ACLU	AFL-CIO	LCV	ITI	COC	HAFA	ACU	CFG	FRC
2018	-	7%	-	9%	-	92%	53%	84%	58%	100%
2017	0%	C	8%	11%	C	93%	C	85%	76%	89%

Key Votes of the 115th Congress (House)

1. Obama-care revision	Y	5. Family planning regs	Y	9. Guantanamo prisoners	N
2. Tax Cuts	Y	6. Body cameras/immigration	N	10. Ground missiles, limit	N
3. Omnibus appropriations	Y	7. Abortion ban	N	11. Defense Dept. spending	Y
4. Dodd-Frank revision	Y	8. Concealed carry	Y	12. FISA rules	Y

Prior winning percentages: House: 2016 (57%), 2014 (50%)

Republican Martha McSally was appointed to the Senate in January 2019, less than two months after losing a close race for the state's other seat in the upper chamber. The former Air Force fighter pilot made history by being the first woman to fly and command an Air Force squadron in combat and has carried that drive over to her political career. Two years after a narrow loss to Democratic Rep. Ron Barber in 2012, she campaigned on her extensive military background to win a rematch that wasn't decided for more than six weeks after polls closed. In her two terms in the House, she became a player on security issues — a role she planned to continue on the Senate Armed Services Committee as one of the chamber's few female veterans. She and Sen. Kyrsten Sinema, who defeated her in 2018, are the first two female senators in Arizona history and are the only bipartisan female pair in the Senate.

A Rhode Island native, McSally came to Tucson in the early 1990s when she was assigned to Davis-Monthan Air Force Base. She had graduated from the Air Force Academy in 1988 with a biology degree. Two years later, she received a master's in public policy from Harvard University. In 1999, McSally was selected for a Washington-based fellowship program, where she served as a national security adviser for Sen. Jon Kyl of Arizona. She later replaced him in the Senate. Kyl served a place-holding appointment of a few months after Sen. John McCain's death in late August before resigning in December, opening the seat for her.

McSally retired as a colonel in the Air Force with more than 2,600 flight hours, including 325 combat hours. She has served tours in the Middle East and supervised an air campaign based in Saudi Arabia during the Iraq War. She led a combat deployment to Afghanistan and taught senior military officials. In 2007, McSally received her second master's degree, this one from the Air Force Air War College.

She drew national attention after she filed — and won — a 2001 lawsuit against the Defense Department, *McSally v. Rumsfeld*, to overturn a policy that required U.S. servicewomen in Saudi Arabia to wear a body-covering Muslim abaya and headscarf. Her initiative also resulted in subsequent legislation. In an interview on CBS's "60 Minutes" in 2002, she criticized discrimination in conservative Saudi Arabia. "I can fly a single-seat aircraft in enemy territory, but [in Saudi Arabia] I can't drive a vehicle," she said. The kingdom lifted its ban on female drivers in 2018.

McSally has a history of close races — and has lost more than she's won. Things are unlikely to get easier for her in 2020, when she will run for the final two years of McCain's term in the purple-trending state. If she wins that race, McSally will need to run again for a full term in 2022.

She first lost a special election primary for the GOP nomination to fill the rest of Rep. Gabby Giffords' term after the congresswoman was grievously wounded in a 2011 mass shooting in Tucson. McSally went on to win the primary for the full term in 2012, setting her up to face Barber, a former Giffords aide who also was wounded in the shooting. That race drew controversy: The Democratic-backed House Majority PAC aired an ad that showed McSally in a kitchen cooking "a recipe for disaster," which she described as sexist. McSally was criticized for saying, "I resemble Gabby Giffords more than the man who worked for her." Barber prevailed by a 2,454-vote margin.

In their rematch, Barber and McSally sparred over gun control laws, with McSally criticizing an ad by Giffords' Americans for Responsible Solutions PAC that said the Republican "opposes making it harder for stalkers to get a gun." McSally revealed that she was a victim of stalking and called the ad "horrendous." Giffords' group spent more than $2 million on behalf of Barber in one of the most expensive House races of the year. McSally raised about $4.8 million compared to Barber's $4 million. Spending by outside groups exceeded $10 million, and was roughly equal for each side.

Election night didn't end the skirmishing. Just over a week after the election, McSally held a lead of fewer than 200 votes and declared victory. But the narrow margin triggered a mandatory recount under Arizona law. McSally eventually prevailed by just 161 votes — not the last time she'd have a close race and not the last time she wouldn't know her fate on election night. The pair of races left bad blood between McSally and the Giffords family.

In the House, McSally won a seat on the Armed Services Committee even before she was declared the election winner. She vowed to be a strong voice for both the military and Raytheon's missile programs in Tucson. In 2015, she praised the Pentagon's decision to lift its ban on women taking on combat roles as "long overdue."

She won re-election in 2016 by a 57%-43% margin over Democrat Matt Heinz, an emergency-room physician and former state representative, outspending him by a wide margin. A month before the election, she condemned as "disgusting" and "unacceptable" Donald Trump's lewd comments about women in a 2005 video. She never endorsed him during the campaign. That approach helped her in that race, as Trump lost the district. But it would come back to haunt her in her 2018 Senate race, as she'd spend the entirety of the campaign struggling to balance appeals to the hard-line conservative base and the state's large number of independent voters. In that effort, she fell short.

McSally had been viewed as a likely 2020 Senate candidate and a rising star in her party. But her chance at the upper chamber came early when Republican Sen. Jeff Flake, a frequent critic of Trump who had drawn the president's ire, said he had no chance of winning re-election and announced his retirement in late 2017.

National establishment Republicans encouraged McSally to run, and she announced her candidacy in January 2018. She spent the next year struggling to square her former brand as an independent-minded lawmaker with a skeptical conservative base. Sinema was already in the race, as was hard-line conservative and former state Sen. Kelli Ward, who had been leading Flake in primary polls before he dropped out and was a serious threat to McSally's chances.

Maricopa County's controversial former Republican sheriff, Joe Arpaio, joined the race not long after Trump had pardoned him for his conviction for criminal contempt related to his harsh tactics against undocumented immigrants.

Arpaio's entrance in the race was a gift for McSally, splitting the hard-line conservative vote and giving her an easier path to the nomination. But she still had to spend considerable time and effort convincing primary voters she was supportive enough of their hard-line views, especially on immigration, to get through the primary. That included a campaign-long embrace of all things Trump and a decision to rescind her earlier support of a bill to give legal status to undocumented immigrants brought to the country as children, known as Dreamers.

McSally spent all spring and summer wooing the GOP base ahead of the August primary, while Sinema ran a bevy of ads highlighting her centrist voting record and promising to be an independent voice for Arizona, a state that's appears to be moving into swing-state status. McSally also had to walk a tightrope as national attention focused on McCain's final months. McCain was a hero to many but hated by many base conservatives in Arizona for his independent streak and longtime support of a comprehensive immigration overhaul. Appearing with Trump at a signing ceremony of a defense authorization bill named in honor of McCain shortly before his death — and shortly before the primary — McSally didn't utter the ailing senator's name, a move that McCain's daughter Meghan called "disgraceful" in a tweet.

McSally won the primary with a majority of the vote, but didn't tack hard back to the center afterward. And she didn't have much time to pivot: Because of Arizona's late primary and heavy emphasis on mail voting, there were just six weeks between the primary and the real start of the general election.

McSally began the general campaign behind in the polls, but she unleashed a series of withering attacks highlighting Sinema's past as a liberal activist and attacking Sinema's immigration views that helped pull her into a near tie. National Democrats responded by flaying McSally for supporting Obamacare's repeal with a heavy focus on its protections for people with preexisting conditions. That was a core argument for national Democratic groups in nearly every 2018 race. Sinema herself stayed positive on the airwaves.

McSally held a narrow lead in the election night vote count, but with hundreds of thousands of mail-in ballots left to be counted the race was far from over. Sinema overtook her in the count later that week and built on her lead in subsequent vote counts. Republicans, including Trump, made baseless claims of voter fraud, but McSally refused to join in on those calls. When the Associated Press called the race six days after the election, McSally conceded, perhaps with an eye on Arizona's other Senate seat.

McSally didn't have to wait long. Kyl had come out of retirement to serve as a caretaker after McCain's death and announced in mid-December that he would leave the Senate that month.

McSally became the immediate front-runner for the appointment — but not without Gov. Doug Ducey considering others, including his former chief of staff. Some Arizona and national Republicans wondered if it was the best move to appoint someone who'd just lost a statewide race and struggled to bridge the divide between the Trump wing of the party and the GOP-leaning independents who often make the difference in close races in the state.

A memo written by her campaign advisers that blamed the loss on the national environment, party divisions, McSally's tough primary and lopsided spending in the race didn't help either. "Local media consistently focused on the tensions between the McCain/Flake and Trump wings of the party in AZ, making it more difficult to unify Republicans of all ideological identifications. The who do you side with, Trump or McCain, media narrative continued throughout the general election," the advisers wrote. The memo drew criticism that the campaign was avoiding blame for the loss.

McSally also had to make up with the McCain family, many of whom had remained furious at her for keeping the longtime senator at arm's length during her campaign. She met privately with McCain's widow, Cindy, in an attempt to patch things up in mid-December. The meeting seemed to go well enough, as Ducey, a McCain ally, appointed McSally afterward. McSally is the ninth senator to receive an appointment to the Senate after losing a Senate contest, according to an analysis by Smart Politics. She had to wait the shortest time — just 55 days between the election and the appointment.

McSally got a seat on the Armed Services Committee, which had been chaired by McCain. The committee's portfolio has long been her main legislative focus and its work is important to her state, which has many military bases and veterans. McSally also got seats on Banking, Housing and Urban Affairs; Energy and Natural Resources; Indian Affairs and Aging committees. All assignments made sense in a state with many energy issues and large populations of Native Americans and older Americans.

McSally faced the prospect of a tough 2020 campaign in a state that has been increasingly competitive. National Democrats saw her as the second-most vulnerable GOP incumbent after Colorado's Cory Gardner. Former astronaut Mark Kelly, Giffords' husband, was the first Democrat to announce a challenge. He quickly was embraced by Senate Democratic leaders and showed strong early fundraising. Other prospective Democratic contenders, including Rep. Ruben Gallego, stepped aside.

Tom O'Halleran (D)

Elected 2016, 2nd term, b. Jan 24, 1946; Chicago, IL; Lewis University, Att., 1966; DePaul University, Att., 1993; Catholic; Married (Pat O'Halleran); 3 children; 3 grandchildren.

Elected Office: AZ House, 2001-2007; AZ Senate, 2007-2009.

Professional Career: Police officer, 1966-1979; Bond trader/ business owner.

DC Office: 324 CHOB 20515, 202-225-3361, Fax: 202-225-3462, ohalleran.house.gov

State Offices: Casa Grande, 520-316-0839; Flagstaff, 928-286-5338; Tucson, 928-304-0131.

Committees: *Agriculture*: Conservation & Forestry. *Energy & Commerce*: Communications & Technology; Consumer Protection & Commerce; Energy.

Group Ratings

	ADA	ACLU	AFL-CIO	LCV	ITI	COC	HAFA	ACU	CFG	FRC
2018	-	68%	-	83%	-	83%	8%	17%	15%	0%
2017	70%	C	82%	91%	C	64%	C	4%	6%	11%

Almanac Ratings 2017-18

	Economy	Social	Foreign	Composite
Liberal	56%	76%	33%	55%
Conservative	44%	24%	67%	45%

Key Votes of the 115th Congress

1. Obama-care revision	N	5. Family planning regs	N	9. Guantanamo prisoners	N
2. Tax Cuts	N	6. Body cameras/immigration	Y	10. Ground missiles, limit	N
3. Omnibus appropriations	Y	7. Abortion ban	N	11. Defense Dept. spending	Y
4. Dodd-Frank revision	Y	8. Concealed carry	N	12. FISA rules	Y

Election Results

Election	Name (Party)	Vote (%)		Cand. Spent	Ind. Exp. Support	Ind. Exp. Oppose
2018 General	Tom O'Halleran (D)	143,240	(54%)	$2,694,663	$532,303	$51,974
	Wendy Rogers (R)	122,784	(46%)	$1,412,057	$453,948	$2,471,753
2018 Primary	Tom O'Halleran (D)		(100%)			

Prior winning percentages: 2016 (51%)

Democrat Tom O'Halleran, a former Republican state legislator who switched parties to run for the House, was elected in 2016 to an open seat in Arizona. In this competitive district, he initially defeated an ethically flawed opponent whom national Republicans refused to support and was reelected in 2018 when the GOP was preoccupied with protecting its own seats. O'Halleran has emphasized his independence and political centrism.

O'Halleran was born in Chicago. His father grew up on a dairy farm that his family lost during the Great Depression, and he worked in a steel foundry and later was a janitor. He joined the Chicago police department in 1966, serving as an officer and later a sergeant in a special operations unit. He received numerous department awards. O'Halleran became a government bond trader and served on the Chicago Board of Trade's executive board of directors. He retired and moved with his family to Arizona, where he became involved in local politics. He was elected as a Republican to the state House in 2000, where he was chairman of the Natural Resources and Agriculture Committee. In 2006, he was elected to the state Senate, where he chaired the Higher Education Committee, but was defeated in 2008.

Citing Republicans' inability to legislate on issues such as education, child welfare and water problems, O'Halleran became an independent in 2014 and ran again unsuccessfully that year for the Senate. When Democratic Rep. Ann Kirkpatrick challenged Sen. John McCain, O'Halleran ran for the open seat. Republicans nominated Paul Babeu, who got 31 percent of the vote in a six-candidate field. Babeu was well-known as the Sheriff of Pinal County, where he has been outspoken on illegal immigration. "I'm for enforcing the law, securing the border and protecting America. I don't feel our nation is more secure or more safe than it was eight years ago," Babeu said. O'Halleran called for improved security at the border, with the best technology and experts.

The campaign was overwhelmed by charges against Babeu, stemming from reports of alleged abuses while he was headmaster of a private Massachusetts school for troubled children, which subsequently was shut down; a state investigation concluded that the school's disciplinary practices were abusive and inhumane. The National Republican Congressional Committee decided to steer clear of the contest and spent no money in this competitive district. National Democratic groups and their allies spent $3 million, chiefly on ads attacking Babeu's personal history. O'Halleran won, 51%-43%. He led, 2-to-1, in Apache and Coconino counties.

Age 70 when he entered the House, O'Halleran sought bipartisanship and often kept his distance from national Democrats. In the Almanac vote ratings for the House in 2017, he ranked as the fourth most-conservative Democrat. The FiveThirtyEight website showed that he voted that year with President Donald Trump on 10 of the 11 key votes. The bipartisan legislation enacted in October 2018 to reduce opioid addiction included an amendment by O'Halleran that allowed states with high addiction rates to receive added Medicaid funds. "There is still a great deal of work to do that requires a strong partnership with local and state leaders who are at the forefront of this battle," he said. O'Halleran was the chief House sponsor of a bill signed by Trump that improved the water supply on the White River for the White Mountain Apache Tribe.

When Democrats took control of the House in 2019, O'Halleran was a leader of the party's moderates. He became the policy co-chair of the House Blue Dog Coalition and pledged to give moderate Democrats "a seat at the table." He was among the Democrats on the bipartisan Problem Solvers Caucus who agreed to support Nancy Pelosi for Speaker after she reached agreement with them on House rules changes for more open debate. He was awarded a seat on the Energy and Commerce Committee.

O'Halleran's initial bid for reelection generated some concern among House Democrats and their allies, who spent more than $3 million on his behalf in 2018. He was challenged by Wendy Rogers, a retired Air Force pilot and officer. News reports said that Rogers declined to meet with local reporters and editorial boards. The Arizona Republic, in endorsing O'Halleran, described Rogers as "another rock-throwing partisan." In the final campaign ratings by the Cook Political Report, O'Halleran was listed as the most vulnerable House Democrat, with a "lean Democrat" forecast. He won, 54%-46%. His lead of over 25,000 votes in Apache and Coconino counties was more than enough to cover the small lead by Rogers in Pinal and Pima counties. In this competitive district, Republicans continue to search for the right combination of candidate and political climate.

AZ-1: Northeast/Central Arizona   Cook Partisan Voting Index: R+2

Population		Race and Ethnicity		Income	
Total	741,377	White	48.9%	Median Income	$50,317
Land area (sq. miles)	55,040	Black	2.1%	District Income Rank	305
Pop/ sq mi	13.5	Latino	22.4%	Poverty Rate	20.9%
Born in State	52.5%	Asian	1.5%	With health insurance	87.4%
		Two or more races	2.3%	Cash public assistance	2.4%
Age Groups		Other	22.8%	Food stamp/SNAP	15.1%
Under 18	24.4%				
18-34	23.1%	**Education**		**Work**	
35-64	35.5%	H.S grad or less	40.7%	White Collar	17%
Over 64	17%	Some college	35.2%	Sales and Service	45.5%
Military		College Degree, 4 yr	14.4%	Blue Collar	21.4%
Veteran/ Active Duty	9.8%	Post grad	9.7%	Government	23.3%

2012 Pres. Vote	Romney	131,115	(50%)	Obama	124,550	(48%)		
2016 Pres. Vote	Trump	135,928	(47%)	Clinton	132,874	(46%)	Johnson	11,732 (4%)

Southern Phoenix, Navajo Nation, Flagstaff: Beyond Phoenix, Arizona is a vast state of stunning beauty: the awe-inspiring Grand Canyon, the subtle pastel hues of the Painted Desert, the sheer cliff walls of Canyon de Chelly, the majestic spires of Monument Valley, the still waters of Lake Powell, the mountainous pine forests around Flagstaff, and the rust-and-rose red rocks of Sedona. It also has man-made landmarks. The celebrated U.S. 66, now mostly superseded by Interstate 40, traverses the district, and it's dotted with old copper mining towns like Globe.

All of these places are in the 1st Congressional District in northeastern Arizona, an area larger than Pennsylvania and the tenth largest district in the nation. It encompasses Flagstaff, with rapid growth at Northern Arizona University, a gateway to the Grand Canyon and a growing tourism and retirement mecca that has lured snowbirds with its climate and affordable housing. In Casa Grande, between Phoenix and Tucson, Phoenix Mart was scheduled to open in 2019 as a 1.6-million square foot commercial complex over 585 acres that styles itself as "North America's most complete global product marketplace," designed to connect manufacturers, distributors, wholesalers and retailers; the opening was delayed by an FBI investigation of overseas investors. Also in Casa Grande, Lucid Motors — with $1 billion invested by Saudi Arabia -- moved ahead with a $1 billion plant to manufacture 130,000 luxury electric vehicles annually by 2022, as a competitor to Tesla Motors. Nikola Motor Co. planned to build a commercial-truck factory in Coolidge. In October 2018, the Supreme Court rejected a bid by mining companies to overturn the ban on extracting uranium at the Grand Canyon.

The 1st is home to the nation's largest Indian population. A full 23 percent of its residents identify themselves as Native Americans, who slightly outnumber Hispanics in the district. Redistricting after the 2010 census united the Navajo and Hopi reservations in the same congressional district for the first time in the state's history. The two tribes, historic enemies, concluded they could wield more political clout together than apart. Other tribes with a presence here are the Fort Apache, San Carlos, Havasupai, Hualapai, Kaibab, Gila River and Zuni.

By far the largest is the Navajo Nation. Most of the Navajo are in Apache County and others are on parts of the reservation that extend into New Mexico and Utah. There are about 286,000 Navajo in the three states, of whom an estimated 73 percent speak the language, and many still practice the traditional Navajo lifestyle. They have a history of fiercely contested tribal elections and considerable social problems. Alcoholism and drug abuse are rampant, violent crime is a problem, and there is little economic development. After a failed $500 million effort to encourage the Navajo and Hopi to share land, the federal government decided to remove members of each tribe from the property of the other. Another local setback was the plan by utility companies to close in 2019 a Navajo-owned power-generating plant; its use of coal was expensive and inefficient.

The 1st District was drawn to be competitive politically. With its diversity and huge size, it is one of the most difficult in the nation to manage. The district has leaned slightly Republican in recent presidential elections. Apache County, with its Navajo majority, is heavily Democratic. Flagstaff-based Coconino County has moved in that direction. South of Phoenix, Pinal County, which has the most voters, leans Republican, as does the sliver of Pima County included in the 1st.

Ann Kirkpatrick (D)

Elected 2018, 4th term, b. Mar 24, 1950; McNary; University of Arizona, B.A., 1972; University of Arizona James E. Rogers College of Law (AZ), J.D., 1979; Roman Catholic; Married (Roger Curley); 2 children.

Elected Office: AZ House, 2005-2007; U.S. House, 2009-2011, 2013-2017.

Professional Career: Attorney & Co-founder, Kirkpatrick & Harris, Law Firm; Business Law and Ethics Instructor, Coconino Community College; Coconino County Deputy County Attorney; Sedona City Attorney.

DC Office: 309 CHOB 20515, 202-225-2542

State Offices: Sierra Vista, 520-459-3115; Tucson, 520-881-3588.

Committees: *Agriculture*: Commodity Exchanges, Energy & Credit. *Appropriations*: Defense; Energy & Water Development & Related Agencies; Financial Services & General Government.

Election Results

Election	Name (Party)	Vote (%)		Cand. Spent	Ind. Exp. Support	Ind. Exp. Oppose
2018 General	Ann L. Kirkpatrick (D)	161,000	(55%)	$4,422,672		
	Lea Marquez Peterson (R)	133,083	(45%)	$1,435,325	$9,226	$2,114,754
2018 Primary	Ann L. Kirkpatrick (D)	33,938	(42%)			
	Matt Heinz (D)	23,992	(30%)			
	Mary Matiella (D)	7,606	(9%)			
	Bruce Wheeler (D)	6,814	(8%)			
	Billy Kovacs (D)	5,350	(7%)			

Prior winning percentages: 2014 (53%), 2012 (49%), 2008 (56%)

Democrat Ann Kirkpatrick returned to the House as a "freshman" for the third time—and in a new district. She had served three terms in Arizona's sprawling 1st District, losing reelection in 2010 and then a challenge to Republican Sen. John McCain in 2016. In 2018, she faced a competitive Democratic primary, but had a relatively easy time in November. She replaced GOP Rep. Martha McSally, who ran unsuccessfully for the Senate. Fun fact: For each of her three arrivals in the House, Kirkpatrick won an open seat that had been held by a Republican.

Kirkpatrick hails from the White Mountain Apache Nation reservation in eastern Arizona. After getting her bachelor's degree from the University of Arizona, she taught for two years in Tucson. She earned a law degree and worked as a prosecutor for the Coconino County Attorney's Office. In 2004, Kirkpatrick was elected to the state House from a district where two-thirds of the registered voters were Native Americans. She defeated the incumbent, who was a Navajo and political independent.

She made her first bid for the House in 2008 after GOP freshman Rep. Rick Renzi was the target of misconduct charges. (He opted not to seek reelection and was convicted in 2013 on charges related to a land deal that allegedly benefited one of his former business partners.) Kirkpatrick won a four-way Democratic primary with 47 percent of the vote, then soundly defeated GOP antitax activist Sydney Hay in November. In the House, she mostly supported President Barack Obama's agenda. Running for reelection, she was challenged by Republican Paul Gosar, a dentist and political newcomer. He attacked her support of the 2010 health care law and took a hard line on immigration. Kirkpatrick refused to distance herself from Obama, and she lost, 50%-44%.

After redistricting in 2012 made the 1st District more favorable to a Democrat but still competitive, Gosar decided to run in the GOP-friendly 4th District. In mounting her comeback, Kirkpatrick faced Republican Jonathan Paton, a former state legislator. Democrats attacked Paton for the brief work he did as a lobbyist for the payday-lending industry, while he hammered Kirkpatrick for spending too much taxpayer money on her staff. She pulled out a 49%-45% win. In 2014, she survived a stiff challenge from state House Speaker Andy Tobin, who sought to make the campaign a referendum on Obama.

That led to Kirkpatrick's challenge to the iconic McCain. After he won his three-way primary with 51 percent of the vote, Kirkpatrick sought to tie McCain to GOP presidential nominee Donald Trump, while suggesting that he was no longer the outspoken independent he had once been. McCain renounced his endorsement of Trump a month before the election, following the release of the decade-old videotape in which Trump made lewd comments about women. Kirkpatrick lost 54%-41%.

When McSally created the open seat, Kirkpatrick was the frontrunner among the seven Democratic candidates. In the primary, she described herself as "the most progressive candidate in this race who has a track record of getting things done." Former state Rep. Matt Heinz, her chief opponent, compared her to a "meth addict" in her eagerness to return to Congress and criticized her as an outsider with a centrist record. "Ann Kirkpatrick: Not from here. Not progressive," his ads claimed. In 2016, Heinz—an emergency-room physician—had lost to McSally, 57%-43%. Kirkpatrick, with the backing of the Democratic Congressional Campaign, won the primary with 42 percent of the vote to 30 percent for Heinz.

Republicans initially were enthusiastic about their nominee, Lea Marquez-Peterson, a conservative Latina and chief executive of the Tucson Hispanic Chamber of Commerce. But Kirkpatrick's experience and the enthusiasm among Democrats for women candidates became obstacles for Republicans in this swing district. The National Republican Congressional Committee abandoned its funding of the contest in early October.

With her previous service, Kirkpatrick had an advantage in the large freshman class—which resulted in a seat on the Appropriations Committee. But history shows that her latest victory is no guarantee of a secure seat.

AZ-2: Southeast Arizona   **Cook Partisan Voting Index: R+1**

Population		Race and Ethnicity		Income	
Total	717,718	White	61.3%	Median Income	$50,270
Land area (sq. miles)	7,838	Black	3.7%	District Income Rank	308
Pop/ sq mi	91.6	Latino	28.1%	Poverty Rate	15.9%
Born in State	36.6%	Asian	2.9%	With health insurance	90.9%
Age Groups		Two or more races	2.6%	Cash public assistance	2.2%
Under 18	20.6%	Other	1.4%	Food stamp/SNAP	12.5%
18-34	22.9%	**Education**		**Work**	
35-64	36.3%	H.S grad or less	30.3%	White Collar	20.2%
Over 64	20.2%	Some college	35.8%	Sales and Service	45.9%
Military		College Degree, 4 yr	19.4%	Blue Collar	15%
Veteran/ Active Duty	14.7%	Post grad	14.4%	Government	18.8%

2012 Pres. Vote	Romney	149,651	(50%)	Obama	144,966	(48%)			
2016 Pres. Vote	Clinton	156,676	(49%)	Trump	141,196	(44%)	Johnson	12,989	(4%)

Tucson Metro: Arizona's first frontier was just south of today's Tucson, where Franciscan friars built Mission San Xavier del Bac in the 18th century. To the east, the late-19th century mining towns of Tombstone and Bisbee sprang up on mountainsides, where miners dug up gold, silver and much of America's copper. In those wild and wicked mining days, the Earp brothers waged their famous gunfight against a gang of outlaws at the O.K. Corral in Tombstone. A 1957 movie starring Burt Lancaster and Kirk Douglas told that tale and helped put the city on the tourism map. Here the rebellion of the land-starved American Indian was quashed, when the Apache leader Geronimo surrendered in 1886.

In recent years, Cochise County became an active frontier again. After the Border Patrol reduced illegal crossings in California and Texas, Mexicans trying to enter the United States illegally began coming to Agua Prieta, just across the border from the town of Douglas. There they fanned out, crossed the border and used the area's numerous roads, mountain trails and ranch lands to get to Tucson and Phoenix. The Tucson sector became the Border Patrol's most active in both apprehensions and illegal drug seizures. Stepped-up border enforcement and a reduced flow of illegal immigrants have significantly decreased these metrics: down to 65,000 in 2016, about half what it had been just six years earlier. But the bodies of many who didn't make it are still found in the mountains and desert. Drug trafficking remains active. Local law enforcement officials worry that legalization of marijuana in western states will increase business for illegal cartels, including more powerful drugs. The Border Patrol in the Tucson area, chiefly Cochise County, reported that it seized more than 360 tons of marijuana in 2016; that was a 30 percent decline since 2011.

Tucson is Arizona's second metropolis. It is much smaller, poorer and politically more progressive than Phoenix. Tucson is a high-tech city and home to the University of Arizona. Defense giant Raytheon Co. has a huge missile plant at Tucson International Airport, which is in the 3rd District. Raytheon's hiring of 2,000 employees since 2016 increased the total to nearly 12,000 at its local headquarters. Davis-Monthan Air Force base near downtown is home to F-16 fighter jets and drone pilot training; with 11,000 service members, it contributes more than $1 billion a year to the area economy. TuSimple, a Chinese-based developer of self-driving commercial trucks, planned a local facility with 500 workers by 2020. Amazon planned to open in 2019 a new fulfillment center, with 1,500 employees.

The 2nd Congressional District includes most of Tucson, except the Latino-dominated west and south sides. It also includes the eastern half of surrounding Pima County. Also here are southeastern Arizona high desert real estate, including all of mountainous Cochise County, the small, border-crossing town of Douglas, and the city of Sierra Vista near Fort Huachuca, the site of the Army Military Intelligence Center, where military interrogators are trained. The population of Sierra Vista-Douglas dropped more than 5 percent from 2010 to 2017, the fourth-largest decrease in the nation. About 85 percent of the district is in Pima. Politically, it is very closely divided, voting for Arizona GOP favorite son John McCain by less than a percentage point in 2008 and for Republican Mitt Romney by just two points in 2012. Donald Trump lost much of the swing vote in 2016, and Hillary Clinton won the district by five points. This remains among the most competitive districts in the nation, a place where political centrism often is rewarded.

Raul Grijalva (D)

Elected 2002, 9th term, b. Feb 19, 1948; Tucson; University of Arizona, B.A., 1986; Roman Catholic; Married (Ramona Grijalva); 3 children.

Elected Office: Tucson Unified School District Governing Board, 1974-1986; Pima County Board of Supervisors, 1988-2002.

Professional Career: Assistant dean of Hispanic Affairs, University of AZ., 1987.

DC Office: 1511 LHOB 20515, 202-225-2435, Fax: 202-225-1541, grijalva.house.gov

State Offices: Avondale, 623-536-3388; Somerton, 928-343-7933; Tucson, 520-622-6788.

Committees: *Education & Labor*: Civil Rights & Human Services; Higher Education & Workforce Investment. *Natural Resources (Chmn)*: Ex Officio membership on all subcommittees.

Group Ratings

	ADA	ACLU	AFL-CIO	LCV	ITI	COC	HAFA	ACU	CFG	FRC
2018	-	89%	-	94%	-	50%	9%	4%	18%	0%
2017	100%	C	100%	100%	C	31%	C	4%	5%	0%

Almanac Ratings 2017-18

	Economy	Social	Foreign	Composite
Liberal	99%	98%	99%	99%
Conservative	1%	2%	1%	1%

Key Votes of the 115th Congress

1. Obama-care revision	N	5. Family planning regs	N	9. Guantanamo prisoners	Y
2. Tax Cuts	N	6. Body cameras/immigration	Y	10. Ground missiles, limit	Y
3. Omnibus appropriations	N	7. Abortion ban	N	11. Defense Dept. spending	N
4. Dodd-Frank revision	N	8. Concealed carry	N	12. FISA rules	N

Election Results

Election	Name (Party)	Vote (%)		Cand. Spent	Ind. Exp. Support	Ind. Exp. Oppose
2018 General	Raul Grijalva (D)	114,650	(64%)	$687,150	$13,751	
	Nicolas Pierson (R)	64,868	(36%)	$78,614		
2018 Primary	Raul Grijalva (D)		(100%)			

Prior winning percentages: 2016 (99%), 2014 (56%), 2012 (58%), 2010 (50%), 2008 (63%), 2006 (61%), 2004 (62%), 2002 (59%)

Raul Grijalva, a Democrat first elected in 2002, took over as chairman of the Natural Resources Committee. As one of the most liberal committee chairmen, and the only Hispanic, he has voiced his outspoken progressive views that often feature a border perspective. Even before Democrats returned to the majority, top officials of the Trump administration launched unusual attacks against him.

Grijalva was born and grew up in Tucson, the son of a bracero, or guest worker, who emigrated from Mexico in 1945. He graduated from the University of Arizona and has deep roots in the immigrant community on the city's southwest side. He was director of El Pueblo Neighborhood Center and assistant dean for Hispanic student affairs at the university. In 1974, he was elected to the Tucson school board and served 12 years. In 1988, he was elected a Pima County supervisor and served 14 years. As supervisor, he backed an effort to extend medical and dental benefits to same-sex domestic partners of county employees and focused on affordable health care, family and children services, and economic growth. Developers and builders helped elect him to office, but his support for planned growth and impact fees later alienated them. He won election to the House in a new seat created by redistricting. His chief opponent was state Sen. Elaine Richardson, who was endorsed by EMILY's List, which spent more than $500,000 on ads. Mocking his opponent's national funding, Grijalva created "Adelita's List," an allusion to the independent women who fought in the Mexican Revolution. He won the primary, 41%-21% and swept the general election in the heavily Democratic district.

In 2008, Grijalva was elected co-chair of the Progressive Caucus. In that position, he initially insisted that any health care overhaul include a government-run insurance option to compete with private insurers, but he later backed away from that demand. He espoused a "war tax" to finance military operations in Afghanistan, an effort he considered immoral. His Almanac vote rating has been among the most liberal in the House.

He has focused consistently on immigration policy. He has co-sponsored bills to raise the number of low-skill visas from 5,000 to 400,000 and to allow legalization for some illegal immigrants, provided they pay a $500 civil fine. After Arizona state lawmakers passed an immigration bill in 2010 expanding law enforcement's powers to detain suspected immigrants, Grijalva took the unusual step of urging a boycott of his state, calling on sympathetic organizations to refrain from using Arizona as a convention site. He abandoned the boycott after a federal judge halted implementation of most of the immigration law, although the central provision was later upheld by the U.S. Supreme Court. He has encouraged Congress to find common ground on a bipartisan plan to approve immigration changes that he viewed as "low-hanging fruit."

His initial efforts on environmental and energy issues were at home. He worked to stop uranium mining in the Kaibab National Forest and on federal lands near the Grand Canyon, and he was behind efforts to create a Sonoran Desert conservation system. Grijalva sponsored legislation to protect parts of Pima and Santa Cruz counties from future mining claims, and he has stuck up for the San Carlos Apache Tribe in battling copper-mining operations around its lands. Combining his interests in the environment and immigration, he has implored Homeland Security Department officials to take into account protecting native plants and species when building security checkpoints at the border.

At the Natural Resources Committee, where he became the top Democrat in 2015, Grijalva worked with party leaders in opposing Republican efforts to approve the Keystone XL pipeline. He urged environmentalists to view issues from the viewpoint of Hispanics and other minority groups. After Donald Trump became president, Grijalva filed a lawsuit with the Center for Biological

Diversity to highlight the environmental hazards of an expanded border wall. In September 2017, he was arrested for disorderly conduct during a protest of immigration policy in front of Trump Tower in New York City.

As chairman, Grijalva said "we're not going to waste time on" legislation that rips apart environmental laws. He promised more attention to climate change, which he said had been "scrubbed from the discussion." Grijalva repeatedly clashed with Interior Secretary Ryan Zinke, a former House colleague, over the use of scientific data, management of public lands and what he called the "culture of corruption" at the department. In response to Grijalva's call on him to resign, Zinke said that it was hard for the chairman "to think straight from the bottom of the bottle." That swipe was a reference to news reports that Grijalva in 2015 reached a severance agreement with a former female aide over her claims of drunkenness and a hostile workplace. He later said that the agreement prevented him from discussing the specifics.

Despite the strongly Democratic lean of his district, Grijalva has faced reelection challenges. In 2010, Republican Ruth McClung, a 28-year-old physicist, voiced the slogan "Boycott Grijalva, not Arizona." She got help from tea party groups, along with a televised endorsement from Republican Sen. John McCain, and pulled nearly even in polls. But national Democrats raced to Grijalva's assistance with ads, and he eked out a 50%-44% victory. When the Arizona Republic reported in 2014 that Grijalva had missed 13 percent of the previous year's votes, giving him one of the worst attendance records in Congress, he shrugged it off. "I had perfect attendance in the fifth grade," he told the newspaper. "That didn't make me the smartest kid in the class." In a 2014 challenge from conservative activist Gabriela Saucedo Mercer, he won with 56 percent. In Pima County, which cast nearly half the total vote, Grijalva led 61%-39%. But he trailed narrowly in Maricopa County and barely led in Yuma. He has been reelected easily since then, but those results showed the potential risk of redistricting.

In the 2016 presidential campaign, Grijalva was the first member of Congress to endorse Bernie Sanders and he was a key ally when Sanders and Hillary Clinton sought to reconcile their differences on the Democratic platform. "The positions he has taken and the values he holds are ones I share," Grijalva told The New York Times. He likely will continue to seek opportunities to shape the national debate.

AZ-3: Southwest Arizona   Cook Partisan Voting Index: D+13

Population		Race and Ethnicity		Income	
Total	751,029	White	27.4%	Median Income	$44,332
Land area (sq. miles)	15,689	Black	4.3%	District Income Rank	385
Pop/ sq mi	47.9	Latino	61.9%	Poverty Rate	22.5%
Born in State	47.8%	Asian	1.6%	With health insurance	84.2%
		Two or more races	1.4%	Cash public assistance	2.7%
Age Groups		Other	3.4%	Food stamp/SNAP	21.6%
Under 18	27.4%				
18-34	27.3%	**Education**		**Work**	
35-64	34.5%	H.S grad or less	51.8%	White Collar	10.8%
Over 64	10.8%	Some college	32.2%	Sales and Service	48%
		College Degree, 4 yr	10.5%	Blue Collar	26.6%
Military		Post grad	5.4%	Government	17.2%
Veteran/ Active Duty	7.2%				

2012 Pres. Vote	Obama	108,902	(61%)	Romney	65,482	(37%)		
2016 Pres. Vote	Clinton	130,466	(62%)	Trump	67,952	(32%)	Johnson	7,197 (3%)

Tucson West, Western Phoenix Exurbs, Yuma: Southern Arizona, although technically part of Mexico for hundreds of years, was never a home to Latin American civilization the way southern New Mexico has been. Here the hot desert land was inhabited mainly by Native American tribes such as the Apache and Cocopah. They kept their culture and language alive in the region until they were uprooted by English-speaking whites who came in on cavalry horses and in miners' wagons and railroad cars in the late 19th century. In 1854, the Gadsden Purchase — $10 million to Mexico for 30,000 square miles of desert — cleared the way for a southern transcontinental railroad. Today's Hispanic Arizonans are mostly descendants of later emigrants from Mexico, some of whom came over the border in the sleepier days before World War II, when la frontera was scarcely patrolled. Many more came in the 1980s to partake in the dazzling economic growth in the region. The continuing influx of mostly illegal immigrants has increased the national focus on this area.

The 3rd Congressional District is one of the state's two Hispanic-majority districts, with a population that is 63 percent Hispanic and 21 percent foreign-born. One of the two overwhelmingly Democratic districts in the state, it shares a 293-mile border with Mexico. The district is a collection of four distant communities connected by many square miles of uninhabited Sonoran desert.

One is the suburb of Avondale, west of downtown Phoenix, the site of the Palo Verde Nuclear Generating Station, the nation's largest nuclear power plant and the only one not located by a large body of water. Nearby Buckeye, with inexpensive housing for workers in the Phoenix area, in 2017 was the fifth fastest-growing city in the nation. The second community is the heavily Latino and mostly low-income west and south sides of Tucson, where the University of Arizona, the largest employer in southern Arizona, is located. The third is the Mexican border town of Nogales, which is 95 percent Hispanic and located near many maquiladora plants. It is one of the busiest cargo terminals along the Mexican border, but it also has long been an entry point for the drug trade and the scene of many illegal border crossings in recent years. The twin smuggling tides — drugs and people — have inflicted damage on the fragile desert ecosystem. The fourth is Yuma, located on the California border at a Colorado River crossing in an irrigated agricultural valley that is often the hottest place in the nation. In winter, the Yuma area produces 90 percent of the nation's leafy green vegetables — including 500 million heads of lettuce -- on more than 90,000 acres, with an estimated 30,000 Mexican workers crossing the border daily. In October 2018, the unemployment rate of 22 percent in Yuma was the highest in the nation.

In the desert you find the Organ Pipe Cactus National Monument, the Sonoran Desert National Monument, the Tohono O'odham Indian Reservation, and the Barry M. Goldwater Air Force Range, the largest aerial gunnery range after Nevada's Nellis Air Force Range. Near Nogales, unique forms of wildlife are found in the Tumacacori Highlands, including endangered species such as the jaguar, peregrine falcon, Chiricahua leopard frog and the Mexican spotted owl. For the 12 months ending in September 2018, the Border Patrol reported more than 26,000 "apprehensions" of Central American families and unaccompanied minors entering the country illegal in the Yuma area, which more than doubled the previous year. Federal agencies in 2019 planned to build 32 miles of wall along the border between Yuma and Nogales, at a cost of $32 4 million.

In 2016, Hillary Clinton defeated Donald Trump, 62%-32%. That margin was a few points higher than Barack Obama's local performance in 2012.

Paul Gosar (R)

Elected 2010, 5th term, b. Nov 27, 1958; Rock Springs, WY; Creighton University, B.S., 1981; Creighton Boyne School of Dentistry (NE), D.D.S., 1985; Roman Catholic; Married (Maude Gosar); 3 children.

Professional Career: Owner, dental practice.

DC Office: 2057 RHOB 20515, 202-225-2315, Fax: 202-226-9739, gosar.house.gov

State Offices: Gold Canyon, 480-882-2697; Kingman, 928-445-1683; Prescott, 928-445-1683.

Committees: *Natural Resources*: Energy & Mineral Resources (RMM); Oversight & Investigations. *Oversight & Reform*: National Security; Subcommittee on Environment.

Group Ratings

	ADA	ACLU	AFL-CIO	LCV	ITI	COC	HAFA	ACU	CFG	FRC
2018	-	29%	-	6%	-	83%	96%	88%	100%	100%
2017	5%	C	6%	0%	C	93%	C	96%	95%	100%

Almanac Ratings 2017-18

	Economy	Social	Foreign	Composite
Liberal	8%	19%	3%	10%
Conservative	92%	82%	97%	90%

Key Votes of the 115th Congress

1. Obama-care revision	Y	5. Family planning regs	Y	9. Guantanamo prisoners	N
2. Tax Cuts	Y	6. Body cameras/immigration	N	10. Ground missiles, limit	N
3. Omnibus appropriations	N	7. Abortion ban	Y	11. Defense Dept. spending	Y
4. Dodd-Frank revision	Y	8. Concealed carry	Y	12. FISA rules	N

Election Results

Election	Name (Party)	Vote (%)		Cand. Spent	Ind. Exp. Support	Ind. Exp. Oppose
2018 General	Paul Gosar (R)....................................... 188,842	(68%)		$557,845	$8,462	
	David Brill (D)................................ 84,521	(31%)		$562,975	$3,136	
2018 Primary	Paul Gosar (R)..	(100%)				

Prior winning percentages: 2016 (72%), 2014 (70%), 2012 (67%), 2010 (50%)

Republican Paul Gosar, first elected in 2010, survived two competitive elections. He then settled into the Republican-friendly 4th District and signed on with other party renegades in the House. His interest in an appointment to the Senate stirred negative reaction in Arizona. With an interest in western and mining issues, his legislative record has been modest.

Gosar grew up in Pinedale Wyoming. His father was often away working on rigs as a geologist, and an uncle, who was a dentist, stepped in as a role model during those absences. Gosar studied dentistry at Creighton University with the expectation that he would return to Wyoming to enter practice with his uncle. His father advised him to seek a more vibrant locale. After receiving his dental degree, Gosar settled in Flagstaff. Appealing to a local banker for financing to launch his practice, Gosar emphasized his frugality, vowing to eat nothing but peanut-butter-and-jelly sandwiches until his business was established.

When he challenged freshman Democratic Rep. Ann Kirkpatrick in 2010, Gosar sharply criticized her votes for President Barack Obama's agenda. He took a hard line on immigration. Kirkpatrick's ads highlighted her support for Obama's initiatives and cast Gosar as an irresponsible millionaire who was late paying business and property taxes 12 times. Gosar received help from the American Dental Association and other medical groups that opposed the 2010 health care law. The national GOP wave in high-growth areas like this district helped to seal his 50%-44% victory.

On the Oversight and Government Reform Committee, he became one of the first House members to call on Attorney General Eric Holder to resign because of the failed "Operation Fast and Furious," a program that facilitated the sale of thousands of weapons to Mexican drug cartels. The House voted in 2012 to cite the attorney general for contempt of Congress. In 2014, Congress approved as part of its annual defense spending bill Gosar's proposal to swap 2,400 acres of Tonto forest land — which includes the San Carlos Apache reservation — to make way for a new $4 billion copper mine. In exchange, the Resolution Copper Co. gave up land scattered across the state.

Faced with new redistricting lines, Gosar in 2012 ran in the more Republican-leaning 4th District. Pinal County Sheriff Paul Babeu, a strong foe of illegal immigration, initially was considered the frontrunner in the primary, but his momentum halted when a former boyfriend (and illegal immigrant) accused him of threatening deportation to keep their relationship quiet. That left Gosar with two challengers in the GOP primary: state Sen. Ron Gould of Lake Havasu City and radio station owner Rick Murphy of Bullhead City. Gould, one of the legislature's most conservative members, attacked Gosar for being the only House Republican from Arizona to support the 2011 deal to raise the federal debt limit. Gosar won with 51 percent to Gould's 32 percent.

In January 2015, Gosar was 1 of 25 House Republicans who opposed giving John Boehner another term as Speaker. Instead, he voted for Rep. Daniel Webster of Florida. "Our leadership in D.C. should be bold and determined," Gosar said. "We do not need more status quo." He became active in the House GOP's Freedom Caucus, which prepared conservative strategy and policy alternatives. In September, Boehner announced his resignation as Speaker under pressure from that faction. A month later, Gosar was one of nine House Republicans who voted against Paul Ryan as the new Speaker.

On the Natural Resources Committee, Gosar chaired the Energy and Mineral Resources Subcommittee. He chaired the Congressional Western Caucus, where he sought to protect the interests of western and rural communities, including their opposition to expansion of public lands without local input. In 2018, the House passed his bill to increase the transparency of the Western Area Power Administration, which delivers hydropower from federal facilities. He won House approval of his legislation to transfer federal and county lands in Cottonwood and elsewhere in Yavapai County.

Gosar's independence riled some of his constituents. When Ray Strauss, a local pastor, challenged him in the 2016 primary, the contest gained added attention when Washington-based business groups spent $300,000 to run ads critical of Gosar. That group's biggest contributor was the Western Growers Association, an agri-business group that advocates immigration reform, in part to provide foreign workers to aid farmers. Gosar won the primary, 71%-29%, and he defeated a token Democratic challenger in November.

Gosar stirred the ire of some Arizona Republicans when, following the hospitalization of Sen. John McCain for brain cancer, his chief of staff texted that Gosar was interested in securing the appointment of Gov. Doug Ducey if McCain's seat became open. Ducey responded harshly: "To anyone who uses this as an opportunity to speculate or fan the rumor mill: Washington D.C.'s obsession with this when there is no issue to be discussed is disgraceful." Gosar further distanced himself from party regulars when he endorsed Kelli Ward in the 2018 GOP primary against Rep. Martha McSally for the seat of retiring Sen. Jeff Flake. "We cannot afford another establishment patsy who promises one thing and votes differently," Gosar said.

He breezed to reelection in 2018 without a GOP challenger. During his otherwise uneventful contest, six of Gosar's siblings ran an online ad opposing their brother's strongly conservative views and speaking out to "stand up for our good name." Gosar responded that they were "liberal Democrats who hate President Trump" and added, "you can't pick your family."

AZ-4: Western Arizona   Cook Partisan Voting Index: R+21

Population		Race and Ethnicity		Income	
Total	749,187	White	74.5%	Median Income	$47,671
Land area (sq. miles)	33,199	Black	1.8%	District Income Rank	344
Pop/ sq mi	22.6	Latino	18.9%	Poverty Rate	15%
Born in State	28.2%	Asian	1.2%	With health insurance	89.3%
		Two or more races	1.9%	Cash public assistance	1.8%
Age Groups		Other	1.8%	Food stamp/SNAP	11.5%
Under 18	19.7%				
18-34	17.6%	**Education**		**Work**	
35-64	36.4%	H.S grad or less	43.2%	White Collar	26.3%
Over 64	26.3%	Some college	37.9%	Sales and Service	48.4%
		College Degree, 4 yr	11.8%	Blue Collar	21.8%
Military		Post grad	7%	Government	15.6%
Veteran/ Active Duty	14.6%				

2012 Pres. Vote	Romney	173,394	(67%)	Obama	80,035	(31%)		
2016 Pres. Vote	Trump	202,043	(67%)	Clinton	82,192	(27%)	Johnson	10,965	(4%)

Eastern Phoenix Exurbs, Prescott, Lake Havasu City: Beyond the cities of Phoenix and Tucson, much of Arizona looks as it did a century ago. Some places maintain a timeless western look, like Wickenburg, the oldest Arizona town north of Tucson. Others preserve antiquated ways of life, such as the polygamist community of Colorado City, just south of Utah. In some cases, nature and settlement juxtapose jarringly: The real London Bridge was transplanted to Lake Havasu City, a retirement community on the Colorado River and a popular spring break destination for college students.

The expansive 4th Congressional District stretches from the Hoover Dam and Lake Mead in the northwest corner of the state to the outskirts of Yuma, and it spans east to Prescott and beyond to the Phoenix exurbs in Pinal County. The district covers La Paz County, most of Mohave and Yavapai counties, and parts of Yuma, Gila and Pinal counties, along with a tiny slice of Maricopa. Its population center is in fast-growing Prescott, where Barry Goldwater announced his presidential campaign in 1964. Once a gold mining camp, Prescott has been home since 1888 to America's oldest annual rodeo and it retains the charming markers of an older city. The American Planning Association described the Yavapai County Courthouse Plaza as "a majestic, man-made urban forest in the heart of a historic commercial district." A firm tied to Microsoft founder Bill Gates reportedly invested in building a solar-powered "smart" community west of Phoenix, in Belmont.

The district's economy is fueled by tourism, with visitors coming to explore western folklore. Jerome, a mining town built improbably on hillside stilts, has been reborn as an artist colony. Bullhead City is home to the annual River Regatta, where participants take an eight-mile float down the Colorado. Arizona highway planners have discussed upgrading Route 93 between Phoenix and Las Vegas to an interstate highway. The district is a retirement haven and a mecca for second homes. According to the Census Bureau, Lake Havasu City has become the "remarriage capital" of the nation; in this self-styled "party town," 42 percent of women and 41 percent of men have married at least twice. The area is infused with a cultural and political conservatism, placing it among the top 10 percent Republican districts nationwide. Its rapid growth has increased demands for additional water supply. Donald Trump won 67 percent of the vote in 2016, by far his strongest district in Arizona.

Andy Biggs (R)

Elected 2016, 2nd term, b. Nov 07, 1958; Tucson; Brigham Young University (UT), B.A., 1982; University of Arizona Rogers College of Law, J.D., 1984; Arizona State University, M.A., 1999; Mormon; Married (Cindy Biggs); 6 children.

Elected Office: AZ house, 2003-2011; AZ Senate, 2011-2016, Majority Leader, 2011-2012, Senate President, 2013-2016.

Professional Career: Practicing attorney.

DC Office: 1318 LHOB 20515, 202-225-2635, biggs.house.gov

State Offices: Mesa, 480-699-8239.

Committees: *Judiciary*: Courts, Intellectual Property & Internet; Immigration & Citizenship. *Science, Space & Technology*: Energy; Investigations & Oversight.

Group Ratings

	ADA	ACLU	AFL-CIO	LCV	ITI	COC	HAFA	ACU	CFG	FRC
2018	-	26%	-	11%	-	83%	92%	92%	100%	100%
2017	10%	C	13%	6%	C	93%	C	93%	100%	89%

Almanac Ratings 2017-18

	Economy	Social	Foreign	Composite
Liberal	14%	3%	3%	7%
Conservative	86%	97%	97%	93%

Key Votes of the 115th Congress

1. Obama-care revision	N	5. Family planning regs	Y	9. Guantanamo prisoners	N
2. Tax Cuts	Y	6. Body cameras/immigration	N	10. Ground missiles, limit	N
3. Omnibus appropriations	N	7. Abortion ban	Y	11. Defense Dept. spending	Y
4. Dodd-Frank revision	Y	8. Concealed carry	Y	12. FISA rules	N

Election Results

Election	Name (Party)	Vote (%)		Cand. Spent	Ind. Exp. Support	Ind. Exp. Oppose
2018 General	Andy Biggs (R)	186,037	(59%)	$506,614	$3,309	
	Joan Greene (D)	127,027	(41%)	$194,126		
2018 Primary	Andy Biggs (R)		(100%)			

Prior winning percentages: 2016 (64%)

Andy Biggs, elected in 2016, joined the strong conservatives in the House Freedom Caucus and defended President Donald Trump from investigations of his alleged wrongdoing. With his lengthy experience in state government, he was an active lawmaker during his two years in the majority, hough his willingness to go his own way on repeal of the Affordable Care Act resulted in a clash with Trump and House Republican leaders. After winning his House seat by 27 votes in a GOP primary, Biggs secured his political status at home.

A native of Tucson, Biggs got his undergraduate degree in Asian studies from Brigham Young University, his master's degree in political science from Arizona State University and a law degree from the University of Arizona. After practicing law in Phoenix and then Gilbert, he was elected to the state House, where he served eight years. He moved to the Senate in 2010, and became majority leader and then president of the Senate. He was a hardliner on illegal immigration, and a conservative icon. Americans for Prosperity's Arizona Chapter named him a "Champion of the Taxpayer;" the Goldwater Institute tapped him as a "Friend of Liberty;" and the American Conservative Union gave him its "Conservative Excellence Award." In 1993, he won $10 million in the Publishers Clearing House sweepstakes.

After Republican Rep. Matt Salmon announced his retirement, Biggs was the initial frontrunner among four candidates in the GOP primary. He survived the closest contest that determined a House election in 2016, when he defeated Christine Jones, a former legal counsel with GoDaddy, an internet domain company. Jones ran as an outsider who emphasized her business record, and contributed $1.9 million to her own campaign. Biggs, who was endorsed by Salmon, spent nearly $1 million on the campaign and received another $560,000 in support from the Club for Growth. Maricopa County Supervisor Don Stapley identified with the GOP establishment and advocated controls on federal spending.

Jones was the leader in the vote count on the evening of the Aug. 30 primary, and she delivered a victory speech. The tight result led to an automatic recount by Maricopa County election officials and a court review. The recount showed that as many as 728 voters had gone to the wrong voting precinct and then cast a provisional ballot. When Superior Court Judge Joshua Rogers announced the official result, he conceded that many voters had been "disenfranchised."

In a bitter statement during that court hearing, Jones said, "I do want to say this for the record. This has been a very eye-opening experience." The official results of the primary showed that Biggs defeated Jones, 25,244 to 25,217. Each received 29.5 percent of the vote, while Stapley had 20.7 percent. In the pro forma general election, Biggs defeated Democrat Talia Fuentes, a single mother who had supported Bernie Sanders for president; he won, 64%-36%.

When House Republicans in May 2017 passed their American Health Care Act, Biggs was among the few conservatives who voted against it. He called the proposal "an ill-considered, ill-defined, and an almost certainly ill-fated three-stage plan to completely repeal Obamacare at an unspecified later date." He dismissed pressure from Trump and other party leaders. "I'm here to do a job and represent my constituents," he said. Biggs was more productive in other areas with House Republicans. He was the chief House sponsor of the "Right to Try" bill, signed by Trump, which makes it easier for patients with life-threatening conditions to use treatments that haven't received final Food and Drug Administration approval. He enacted a bill that extended to tribal areas the emergency Amber Alert system for missing children.

Biggs was an outspoken critic of Robert Mueller, the special counsel investigating Trump, and cosponsored a resolution that called for his removal. "Mueller's investigation is clearly careening far beyond the scope of his original charge," he wrote in USA Today. "His witch hunt must end."

Against Democrat Joan Greene, Biggs was reelected, 59%-41%--the best showing of the three Phoenix-area House Republicans.

AZ-5: Eastern Phoenix Suburbs   Cook Partisan Voting Index: R+15

Population		Race and Ethnicity		Income	
Total	782,680	White	71%	Median Income	$70,934
Land area (sq. miles)	293	Black	2.9%	District Income Rank	88
Pop/ sq mi	2667	Latino	17.9%	Poverty Rate	9%
Born in State	36.4%	Asian	4.6%	With health insurance	91.9%
		Two or more races	2.3%	Cash public assistance	1.3%
Age Groups		Other	1.2%	Food stamp/SNAP	6.2%
Under 18	26.4%				
18-34	19.7%	**Education**		**Work**	
35-64	37.9%	H.S grad or less	29%	White Collar	16%
Over 64	16%	Some college	35.8%	Sales and Service	42%
		College Degree, 4 yr	22.7%	Blue Collar	14.9%
Military		Post grad	12.5%	Government	11.2%
Veteran/ Active Duty	9.4%				

2012 Pres. Vote	Romney	187,304	(64%)	Obama	101,511	(35%)		
2016 Pres. Vote	Trump	191,432	(56%)	Clinton	121,280	(36%)	Johnson	15,845	(5%)

Eastern Mesa, Gilbert: The city of Phoenix is exceedingly young. In the early 20th century, local people remembered when the Valley of the Sun — or the Valley, as most people say — was virtually empty, with a few parched settlements set above a dry riverbed. As late as 1950, only 107,000 people lived in Phoenix and 332,000 in all of Maricopa County. But the air conditioner and military technology transformed Phoenix into today's high-rise studded metropolis, with 1.6 million city dwellers and 4.3 million people in Maricopa County, as of 2017. From 2000 to 2010, Maricopa's population grew by 26 percent. After a slowdown early in the new decade, following the collapse of the local housing market and the state's crackdowns on illegal immigration, it regained in 2017 its title as the fastest-growing county in the nation. Phoenix is not, as some people think, a giant retirement village, nor is it overrun by crooked land salesmen and fast-buck artists, though the area has attracted its share of each.

Maricopa's second-largest city is Mesa, south of the Salt River and east of Phoenix. It was founded by Mormons in 1878 on one square mile and was laid out Salt Lake City-style on broad streets with large lots. A gleaming white Mormon temple was built in 1927, one of the few in the United States then. In 1950, Mesa had 17,000 people, and more than half of its residents earned their living from farming, primarily citrus and cotton. In 2017, it had 496,000 people, more than Kansas City or Atlanta. A former Air Force base is now the Phoenix-Mesa Gateway Airport, with service by five passenger airlines; its joint customs-clearance center between the U.S. and Mexico is designed to speed cargo shipments. Valley Metro, the regional transit authority planned to open in 2019 a 2-mile light-rail extension from Mesa to Gilbert, with further additions planned.

The 5th Congressional District of Arizona is made up of Phoenix's East Valley suburbs: Mesa, Chandler, Gilbert and Queen Creek. Nicknamed the Silicon Desert, Chandler has become one of the fastest-growing tech centers in the country, with companies drawn to relatively cheap real estate and semiconductor chip maker Intel's longstanding presence. After it was forced to abandon plans to manufacture additional chips at its Fab 42 facility, Intel, the largest employer in Arizona, redesigned its operations to produce microprocessors, with 3,000 workers expected by 2021. In its largely hidden 1.3 million-square-foot data center in Mesa, which the Arizona Republic termed "The Fortress," Apple monitors the company's operations from its "global data command center."

The 5th has the highest median income in Arizona, though the district's cultural tone is resolutely middle class. Donald Trump won 56 percent of the vote here in 2016, compared with Mitt Romney's 64 percent in 2012.

David Schweikert (R)

Elected 2010, 5th term, b. Mar 03, 1962; Los Angeles, CA; Scottsdale Community College (AZ), A.A., 1985; Arizona State University, B.S., 1988; Arizona State University, M.B.A., 2005; Roman Catholic; Married (Joyce Schweikert); 1 child.

Elected Office: AZ House, 1989-1994; Treasurer, Maricopa County, 2004-2006.

Professional Career: Member, AZ State Board of Equalization, 1995-2003; Owner, Sheridan Equities & Sheridan Equities Holdings.

DC Office: 1526 LHOB 20515, 202-225-2190, Fax: 202-225-0096, schweikert.house.gov

State Offices: Scottsdale, 480-946-2411.

Committees: *Joint Economic. Ways & Means:* Select Revenue Measures; Trade.

Group Ratings

	ADA	ACLU	AFL-CIO	LCV	ITI	COC	HAFA	ACU	CFG	FRC
2018	-	18%	-	3%	-	75%	94%	96%	88%	100%
2017	0%	C	3%	0%	C	93%	C	100%	98%	100%

Almanac Ratings 2017-18

	Economy	Social	Foreign	Composite
Liberal	0%	13%	0%	4%
Conservative	100%	87%	100%	96%

Key Votes of the 115th Congress

1. Obama-care revision	Y	5. Family planning regs	Y	9. Guantanamo prisoners	N
2. Tax Cuts	Y	6. Body cameras/immigration	Y	10. Ground missiles, limit	N
3. Omnibus appropriations	N	7. Abortion ban	Y	11. Defense Dept. spending	Y
4. Dodd-Frank revision	Y	8. Concealed carry	Y	12. FISA rules	Y

Election Results

Election	Name (Party)	Vote (%)	Cand. Spent	Ind. Exp. Support	Ind. Exp. Oppose
2018 General	David Schweikert (R)............ 173,140	(55%)	$1,479,594	$23,259	
	Anita Malik (D)............ 140,559	(45%)	$379,919	$34,258	$3,575
2018 Primary	David Schweikert (R)............	(100%)			

Prior winning percentages: 2016 (62%), 2014 (65%), 2012 (61%), 2010 (52%)

Republican David Schweikert, elected in 2010, is a wonkish fiscal conservative who settled into his work following clashes with Republican leaders. He was rehabilitated with a seat on the Ways and Means Committee, where he became more of a team player. In 2018, he survived an ethics investigation and a tough reelection challenge in his once-safe seat. He lost a bid for a House leadership position.

Schweikert was born in a Catholic home for unwed mothers in downtown Los Angeles; he was adopted and raised by a family in Arizona. As an undergraduate at Arizona State University, where he later got an MBA, Schweikert focused on finance and real estate. He acquired a real estate license at age 18, worked full-time while taking classes at night and graduated in six years.

Growing up in Scottsdale, he credits his early affinity for politics to former President Ronald Reagan. He ventured into the political arena at 26, when he lost a bid for the Arizona House. Two years later, he won an open seat in the Scottsdale area, and at the end of his freshman term, he became majority whip at age 30. He worked to pass legislation that laid the foundation for tax cuts, tort reform and charter schools, as well as a bill shortening the legislative session from 170 to 98 days. He next was elected as Maricopa County treasurer. In that role, he managed a $4 billion budget, created a program to help low-income seniors pay their property taxes and corrected thousands of deed errors.

In 2008, Schweikert challenged Democratic Rep. Harry Mitchell, who had taken a GOP seat two years earlier. Schweikert lost by 9 percentage points in an inhospitable year for Republicans. Two years later, their rematch told the larger tale of the 2010 election. It featured an incumbent under fire for supporting the Obama administration agenda and a conservative challenger touting his outsider credentials. Schweikert made Mitchell's vote for President Barack Obama's $787 billion economic stimulus bill a central theme, and his campaign signs called Mitchell a "lap dog" for liberal House Speaker Nancy Pelosi. Mitchell countered that he had been among the Democrats most likely to buck his party and he raised about twice as much money. Schweikert won convincingly, 53%-42%.

In the House, Schweikert became known for his studiousness. In May 2011, he told The Washington Post that he spent five hours a day as a member of the Financial Services Committee learning about government-sponsored mortgage giants Fannie Mae and Freddie Mac. That summer , he strongly opposed raising the federal debt ceiling. He accused Treasury Secretary Tim Geithner of having "his hair on fire. ... It's absolutely silly. We have plenty of cash flow to pay debt." He proposed a constitutional amendment that would force Congress to get approval from a majority of the states before increasing the debt limit in the future.

After the 2010 census, the state's independent redistricting commission lumped Schweikert in a district with Rep. Ben Quayle, son of former Vice President Dan Quayle. The younger Quayle represented two-thirds of the new district. House Republican leaders and outgoing Arizona Sen. Jon Kyl lined up to support Quayle, whom they considered the more loyal Republican. Schweikert ran as a self-styled reformer against the GOP establishment. The acrimony peaked when Schweikert's campaign sent out a mailer claiming that Quayle "goes both ways" on conservative issues. Quayle and his supporters, including Sen. John McCain, angrily accused Schweikert of sexual innuendo, a charge that the congressman denied. Schweikert prevailed, 51%-49%. The general-election race was a formality.

In 2013, House Republican leaders took the rare step of booting Schweikert off Financial Services. His aides claimed that it resulted from his challenges to the leadership, although the bitterness of his race with Quayle may have been a factor. He left the Republican whip team. Still, Schweikert did not make a complete break. He moved to the Science, Space and Technology Committee and quietly reestablished his party credentials. Following the 2016 election, Speaker Paul Ryan closed the book on his earlier transgressions by awarding Schweikert a seat on the blue-ribbon Ways and Means Committee.

Instead of blocking legislation, as he and others had occasionally done in the past, he said that they should work with President Donald Trump and the Republican-controlled Congress. "If you have someone who's not necessarily an ideologue, be the first one to show up with the details worked out and all of a sudden your idea becomes the base of the discussion," he told Buzzfeed. He worked with other Republicans at Ways and Means to pass the party's American Health Care Act. He was an outspoken advocate of the tax cuts enacted in 2017. As he told the House, "Tax reform is fair to individuals. It is simpler. ... This is not a win for Republicans. It is a win for society."

Schweikert's ethics problems followed allegations from an Arizona Democrat that payments to his chief of staff for campaign work in 2014 exceeded House limits on outside income and that he misused official funds. Less than a month after the House Ethics Committee in June 2018 created an investigative subcommittee to review their actions, the aide resigned.

The inquiry spurred Democratic challengers to Schweikert's reelection. "The incumbent is reeling [and] has been shrouded in suspicion," the Arizona Republic wrote in an editorial prior to the August primary, with three Democratic candidates. Anita Malik, a tech executive who won the primary with 42 percent of the vote, attacked Schweikert's support for Trump's agenda, which she said "is not supporting the middle class." She rejected Schweikert's defense that the ethics problem was merely a matter of "paperwork." Unlike other House Democratic challengers in 2018, Malik was outspent 4-to-1. In what might have been a missed opportunity for Democrats, Schweikert prevailed, 55%-45%.

Following the election, Schweikert sought the chairmanship of the Republican Policy Committee. In one of only two contested GOP leadership races, he lost to Rep. Gary Palmer of Alabama — another member of the conservative House Freedom Caucus — in what reportedly was a 130-63 vote. In the House minority for the first time, Schweikert faced a potential reelection threat in 2020 in his evolving suburban district.

AZ-6: Northeastern Phoenix Suburbs   **Cook Partisan Voting Index: R+9**

Population		Race and Ethnicity		Income	
Total	762,220	White	72.1%	Median Income	$67,405
Land area (sq. miles)	625	Black	2.5%	District Income Rank	113
Pop/ sq mi	1219.4	Latino	16.8%	Poverty Rate	11.6%
Born in State	31.2%	Asian	4.7%	With health insurance	90.4%
		Two or more races	2.3%	Cash public assistance	1.3%
Age Groups		Other	1.6%	Food stamp/SNAP	7.1%
Under 18	20.6%				
18-34	20.7%	**Education**		**Work**	
35-64	41.1%	H.S grad or less	25.8%	White Collar	17.6%
Over 64	17.6%	Some college	30.7%	Sales and Service	42.7%
		College Degree, 4 yr	27%	Blue Collar	12.5%
Military		Post grad	16.4%	Government	9.2%
Veteran/ Active Duty	8%				

2012 Pres. Vote	Romney	186,537	(60%)	Obama	121,661	(39%)		
2016 Pres. Vote	Trump	177,332	(52%)	Clinton	143,571	(42%)	Johnson	13,891 (4%)

Scottsdale: In May 1998, conservative trailblazer Barry Goldwater died at his home in the Phoenix suburb of Paradise Valley. When he returned from military service in World War II, Paradise Valley was still undeveloped, and Phoenix — founded after the Civil War as a hay market for cavalry horses at Fort McDowell — was not much more than a tiny outpost of American civilization, a metropolitan area of fewer than 300,000 in the sizzling desert. By 2018, there were 4.3 million people in Maricopa County. And the city had been transformed from a frontier outpost to a diversified high-tech center, an example of how creativity and ingenuity can build a sophisticated city even in the most unwelcoming environs.

Like Los Angeles and San Francisco, Phoenix is dotted with mountains that rise grandly from the valley and are preserved as undeveloped parkland. From the landmark Camelback Mountain, 1,800 feet above Phoenix and Paradise Valley, one can appreciate with comparable awe what the land was originally like and how impressively Phoenix has grown. Over the mountains, east of the affluent part of Phoenix and north of Tempe and the Salt River Indian Reservation, is Scottsdale, a city that grew from 130,000 in 1990 to 250,000 in 2017. Scottsdale is home to Frank Lloyd Wright's Taliesin West, the architect's onetime winter home and studio, which was beyond the reach of electricity and telephone lines when built in the McDowell Mountain foothills in the 1940s. Today, the city boasts luxury shopping malls, resorts and the most expensive real estate market in Arizona. As part of what has been described as a biomedical corridor in north Phoenix, the Mayo Clinic in September 2018 announced plans to double its local campus. San Francisco-based McKesson Corp., a health care services firm, moved into a new facility with more than 2,000 workers. Scottsdale touts its reputation as one of the most retiree-friendly cities in the country. Twenty percent of its residents are 65 and older, the largest percentage among cities with 100,000 or more people. Only 4 percent are younger than five years old.

The 6th Congressional District of Arizona includes the northern part of Phoenix, most of Scottsdale, plus Paradise Valley, Cave Creek and Carefree, so named in 1955 by developers who hoped to lure snowbird retirees. Of the five Arizona districts contained entirely in Maricopa County, the 6th has the most college graduates and is the only one that borders each of the other four. This has been an affluent and comfortably Republican district. Donald Trump won 52 percent of the vote in 2016, only his fourth-best district in Arizona and a notable dip from the 60 percent that Mitt Romney took in 2012.

Ruben Gallego (D)

Elected 2014, 3rd term, b. Nov 20, 1979; Chicago, IL; Harvard University, B.A.; Catholic; Divorced.

Military Career: U.S. Marine Corps 2000-2006 (Iraq)

Elected Office: AZ House, 2010-2014.

Professional Career: Public affairs consultant 2007-2008; Delegate, DNC 2008; Vice chair, AZ Democratic Party, 2009.

DC Office: 1131 LHOB 20515, 202-225-4065, rubengallego.house.gov

State Offices: Phoenix, 602-256-0551.

Committees: *Armed Services*: Military Personnel; Tactical Air & Land Forces. *Natural Resources*: Indigenous Peoples of the United States (Chmn); National Parks, Forests & Public Lands.

Group Ratings

	ADA	ACLU	AFL-CIO	LCV	ITI	COC	HAFA	ACU	CFG	FRC
2018	-	89%	-	100%	-	50%	12%	4%	21%	0%
2017	95%	C	94%	91%	C	43%	C	4%	9%	11%

Almanac Ratings 2017-18

	Economy	Social	Foreign	Composite
Liberal	99%	98%	82%	93%
Conservative	1%	2%	18%	7%

Key Votes of the 115th Congress

1. Obama-care revision	N	5. Family planning regs	N	9. Guantanamo prisoners	Y
2. Tax Cuts	N	6. Body cameras/immigration	Y	10. Ground missiles, limit	Y
3. Omnibus appropriations	N	7. Abortion ban	N	11. Defense Dept. spending	Y
4. Dodd-Frank revision	N	8. Concealed carry	N	12. FISA rules	N

Election Results

Election	Name (Party)	Vote (%)		Cand. Spent	Ind. Exp. Support	Ind. Exp. Oppose
2018 General	Ruben Gallego (D)	113,044	(86%)	$752,138	$2,547	
	Gary Swing (G)	18,706	(14%)			
2018 Primary	Ruben Gallego (D)	32,231	(75%)			
	Catherine H. Miranda (D)	10,856	(25%)			

Prior winning percentages: 2016 (75%), 2014 (75%)

Democrat Ruben Gallego, a first-generation American with an impressive bio, was easily elected in 2014. With his experience in the military and local politics plus his engaging persona, he quickly gained notice in the House and showed a willingness to rock the boat among House Democrats. He was an early prospect in the 2020 contest against Sen. Martha McSally but decided not to run. At 39, Gallego likely would have another opportunity for a prime spot on the national political stage.

Gallego's life story is made for a political candidate, including a hardscrabble upbringing, a Harvard degree and military service in Iraq. Born in Chicago to Hispanic immigrant parents, Gallego and his family struggled after his father left home. He got his undergraduate degree in international relations. While attending Harvard, he enlisted in the Marine Corps. He served in Iraq as an assistant machine gunner and fought in more than 10 combat operations in urban areas; his best friend died in combat. That experience, including his anger over the quality of the troops' equipment, led him to get involved in politics and to help veterans.

Gallego was elected to the Arizona Senate in 2010, rising to assistant minority leader in 2012. When Democratic Rep. Ed Pastor retired, Gallego ran in this ultra-blue district, where the Democratic nominee was considered a shoo-in. His chief competitor in the primary was Mary Rose Wilcox, a Latina with high name recognition as a Maricopa County supervisor. She was endorsed by Pastor but may have suffered because she was 30 years older than Gallego. A Wilcox supporter challenged

Gallego's nominating petitions for not using his legal name. The suit was withdrawn when Gallego explained he had changed his name in 2008 from Ruben Marinelarena (his father's name) to Ruben Marinelarena Gallego to honor the mother who raised him.

Gallego opposed the Arizona law requiring police officers in some circumstances to determine the immigration status of arrested or detained persons. He combined a social media presence with aggressive door-to-door campaigning, and out-raised Wilcox by about $300,000. In the five-candidate field, Gallego defeated Wilcox, 48%-36%. In November, he won without Republican opposition. He said that he hoped to serve his career in the House. "I'll be trying to work my way fast into leadership," he told a local reporter.

On the Armed Services Committee, he got off to a quick start. He opposed additional U.S. military action in Iraq, which he described as "a horrible sequel to a horrible movie." He cited the many men and women who died because of the decisions of officials in Washington and at the Pentagon, and said that additional steps to assist Iraq should not come at the risk of losing more American lives. The United States "should support our allies in the region but limit the scope of our involvement on the ground," he said in response to President Barack Obama's request to authorize the use of force against the Islamic State. Gallego joined a congressional caucus of lawmakers who had served in the military since 2001. On the defense spending bill the House passed in June 2018, he won approval of his amendment to bar the Pentagon from purchasing goods from Chinese-based companies that have been listed as threats to U.S. national security.

Gallego was an early supporter of Hillary Clinton in 2016, calling her "our best-known, most experienced, most electable candidate." Following the election, he was among the first congressional Democrats to oppose the required waiver for recently retired Marine Corps Gen. James Mattis to serve as secretary of Defense. "As a veteran, I believe strongly in the principle of civilian leadership of the military," he said. Gallego was a harsh critic of President Donald Trump. When Trump complained following the February 2018 school shootings in Florida that FBI agents had been distracted by their work on the Russia probe, Gallego tweeted, "You are such a psychopath that you have to make even the death of 17 children about you." He added, "America will regret the day you were ever born."

Gallego was an outspoken proponent of replacing Democratic Leader Nancy Pelosi following House Democrats' poor performance in the 2016 election and was an early supporter of Rep. Tim Ryan of Ohio in his bid to replace Pelosi as party leader. The 63 votes cast for Ryan in the Democratic Caucus were "a message directly to leadership to be more responsive and actually make the Democratic Caucus more democratic," Gallego said.

Cited as a rising political star among Democrats, Gallego voiced early interest in the November 2020 contest to complete McCain's Senate term. Gallego told reporters that he would have no trouble winning the Democratic nomination but conceded that Arizona's competitive general-election battleground posed challenges. The success of Kyrsten Sinema in her 2018 Senate campaign offered encouragement for Gallego's maverick style, though he faced historical barriers in Arizona as a Latino with a liberal voting record. Gallego unexpectedly stepped aside in the face of robust fundraising by early Democratic contender Mark Kelly--the husband of Giffords—and became an enthusiastic supporter of Kelly. Depending on the outcome of that contest, he might have other statewide opportunities as soon as 2022.

In March 2019, his ex-wife Kate Gallego won the special election to succeed Rep. Greg Stanton as mayor of Phoenix.

AZ-7: Central and Western Phoenix　　　　　Cook Partisan Voting Index: D+23

Population		Race and Ethnicity		Income	
Total	782,330	White	19.9%	Median Income	$39,005
Land area (sq. miles)	205	Black	9.4%	District Income Rank	422
Pop/ sq mi	3814	Latino	64.2%	Poverty Rate	31.1%
Born in State	48.3%	Asian	2.3%	With health insurance	78.1%
		Two or more races	1.7%	Cash public assistance	2.8%
Age Groups		Other	2.4%	Food stamp/SNAP	26.3%
Under 18	31%				
18-34	28.1%	**Education**		**Work**	
35-64	33.7%	H.S grad or less	59.9%	White Collar	7.2%
Over 64	7.2%	Some college	26%	Sales and Service	49.3%
		College Degree, 4 yr	9.3%	Blue Collar	29.4%
Military		Post grad	4.6%	Government	10%
Veteran/ Active Duty	4.8%				

2012 Pres. Vote	Obama	101,028	(72%)	Romney	37,353	(27%)		
2016 Pres. Vote	Clinton	117,958	(71%)	Trump	37,232	(22%)	Johnson	6,228	(4%)

Downtown Phoenix: Phoenix is a relatively new American metropolis. It has grown to a big city just in the past two generations. Yet it is also an ancient city, or built on top of one. The Arizona Canal several miles north of downtown Phoenix, runs along the route of a canal built about 600 years ago by the Hohokam aboriginal people. They distributed irrigated water diverted from the Salt River in its wet moments to farmers in what today is called the Valley of the Sun, and they made sophisticated astronomical observations from the mountains that jut up from the desert. This society disappeared for reasons unknown less than half a century before the Spaniards arrived in North America.

Half a century ago, Phoenix spread six miles north, west and east of the downtown and only a few miles south. Downtown was its only office center and its main shopping area, and people blew fans over boxes of ice to cool off. Today, the old warehouse district continues to evolve into an innovation and technology center. The view from downtown Phoenix stretches toward office towers many miles to the north, northeast and northwest. In 2017, its 66,000 new residents trailed only San Antonio as the fastest-growing city, and Phoenix overtook Philadelphia as the fifth-largest in the nation.

The city opened its first light-rail transit line in 2008, connecting residents of the Tempe and Mesa suburbs to downtown Phoenix. In 2015, the city council approved a 35-year, $32 billion transportation plan for 40 more miles of light rail across the area, plus additional bus service, with financing from a sales tax hike. A nearly six-mile extension to South Phoenix was planned for 2023. Completion was scheduled for 2019 on the South Mountain Freeway—a nearly $2 billion, 22-mile Loop 202 highway extension between downtown Phoenix and Chandler—which connects Interstate 10 on each end. The project shares financing from the sales tax. Sky Harbor airport — which had little growth in passenger traffic during the decade ending in 2017 — planned to complete by 2020 a $600 million renovation of its international terminal, which it renamed for Sen. John McCain. At Grand Canyon University in West Phoenix, on-campus enrollment was 20,000, with more than 75,000 online students.

The 7th Congressional District of Arizona is centered in downtown Phoenix. It covers the capitol, in a rundown neighborhood a couple of miles to the west, and the airport, situated in an industrial corridor several miles east. It includes most of southern Phoenix, and its boundaries follow approximately the southern and western city limits. It stretches south into Guadalupe and northwest into parts of Glendale. Geographically, the district covers most of the land between South Mountain and Camelback Mountain. The district is 64 percent Hispanic, and its median income is the lowest in the state. Most of the immigrants have been Mexican.

The local veterans' hospital became the unfortunate symbol of the failure of the Veterans Affairs Department's health system: delayed or inadequate care, fabricated records and flawed management. During a 2015 visit to the hospital, President Barack Obama said that the care was "outstanding," but that there was a need to restore "trust and confidence" in the VA. During campaign visits to Arizona, Donald Trump criticized the Phoenix hospital and promised improvements for veterans. "Nobody has been treated worse and there is no more corrupt group in terms of government than what's happening with the VA in Arizona. You're the poster child for everybody. And we're going to fix it, and we're going to take care of our vets, our greatest people," he told a June 2016 rally in Phoenix. As of October 2018, the hospital retained its one-star rating on a five-star scale.

Politically, this is the most Democratic district in the state. Hillary Clinton got 71 percent of the vote, the same as Obama in 2012.

Debbie Lesko (R)

Elected 2018, 1st full term, b. Jan 01, 1959; Sheboygan, WI; University of Wisconsin - Madison, B.B.A.; Marquette University (WI); Christian Church; Married (Joe Lesko); 3 children.

DC Office: 1113 LHOB 20515, 202-225-4576, Fax: 202-225-6328, lesko.house.gov

State Offices: Glendale, 623-776-7911.

Committees: *Homeland Security*: Border Security, Facilitation & Operations; Transportation & Maritime Security (RMM). *Judiciary*: Crime, Terrorism & Homeland Security; Immigration & Citizenship. *Rules*: Rules & Organization of the House (RMM).

Group Ratings

	ADA	ACLU	AFL-CIO	LCV	ITI	COC	HAFA	ACU	CFG	FRC
2018	-	-	-	0%	C	60%	92%	100%	85%	100%

Key Votes of the 115th Congress

1. Obama-care revision	N/A	5. Family planning regs	N/A	9. Guantanamo prisoners	N/A
2. Tax Cuts	N/A	6. Body cameras/immigration	N/A	10. Ground missiles, limit	N/A
3. Omnibus appropriations	N/A	7. Abortion ban	N/A	11. Defense Dept. spending	N/A
4. Dodd-Frank revision	Y	8. Concealed carry	N/A	12. FISA rules	N/A

Election Results

Election	Name (Party)	Vote (%)		Cand. Spent	Ind. Exp. Support	Ind. Exp. Oppose
2018 General	Debbie Lesko (R)	168,835	(55%)	$1,997,923	$1,289,971	$47,899
	Hiral Tipireni (D)	135,569	(45%)	$4,048,106	$550,679	$536,626
2018 Primary	Debbie Lesko (R)	73,778	(77%)			
	Sandra Dowling (R)	21,825	(23%)			

Republican Debbie Lesko struggled to take her seat in 2018 during a special election in April and then in November. Lesko, a fiscal conservative, faced primary opposition and well-financed Democratic challenges as she survived contests that were closer than expected in what had been a secure GOP seat. She succeeded Republican Rep. Trent Franks, a fervent social conservative who served 15 years and resigned in December 2017 following reports that he offered to pay aides to serve as a surrogate mother for his child.

Lesko grew up near Sheboygan Wisconsin and graduated from the University of Wisconsin with a bachelor's in business administration. She moved to Arizona, ran a business in construction sales and became active in civic and political activities in Glendale. She was elected to the state House in 2008 for the first of three terms, while serving as Arizona chairwoman of the American Legislative Exchange Council. During four years in the state Senate, she chaired the Appropriations Committee and served as president pro tempore.

Soon after Franks quit, Lesko resigned from the Senate to launch her campaign. She took a hard line on immigration, emphasized support for President Donald Trump and was endorsed by former Gov. Jan Brewer. The special election, which drew 12 Republican and three Democratic contenders, became unexpectedly messy. Initially, Lesko's chief challenger was Steve Montenegro, a state senator who had been endorsed by Franks and Republican Sen. Ted Cruz, Texas. He was damaged by a pre-election sex scandal, with text messages and nude photos that he exchanged with a female legislative aide. Phil Lovas, who was Arizona chairman for Trump in the 2016 campaign, charged Lesko with violating the federal campaign law by using $50,000 from her state legislative campaign account. Lesko won with 35 percent of the vote; Lovas and Montenegro each got 24 percent.

The Democratic nominee was Hiral Tipernini, a former emergency-room physician who supported expanded health-care coverage and protections for immigrants. The little-known Tipernini, who immigrated from India as a child, had virtually no national party backing. But she drew support from Emily's List and extensive grass-roots financing and significantly out-spent Lesko. During a debate, Tipernini criticized the GOP "tax cut for the rich," while Lesko praised Trump for "following through with [his] promises." Republicans sought to depict Tipernini as out of touch with the district. Following late polls showing a close contest, Trump and GOP leaders urged votes for Lesko. Her 52%-48% victory was unexpectedly close—another early signal of suburban unhappiness with Trump and congressional Republicans.

In the House, Lesko joined the conservative Freedom Caucus, where she was the only female member. The first legislation that she filed would increase state autonomy in setting education policy. "Arizonans know their schools better than any bureaucrat," she said.

The November election for a two-year term was a rematch with Tipernini. Again, the Democrat outspent Lesko, by about $2 million to $1 million, but received little national-party aid. During a meeting of the two candidates with the editorial board of the Arizona Republic, Lesko opposed expansion of federal health-care programs and said that she was open to raising the eligibility age for recipients of Social Security. Tipernini said that Medicare should be widely available as a public insurance option, with financing by federal tax increases. Lesko ran ads calling Tipernini a "phony" doctor who had not practiced for a decade.

This time, Lesko won, 55%-45%. Also on Election Day, 65 percent of Arizona voters approved a referendum that repealed an expanded school-voucher program that Lesko had helped to enact. Some conservative groups had criticized Lesko's plan as poorly organized. The election results were further marks of under-performance by Lesko in her comfortably Republican district.

AZ-8: Western Phoenix Suburbs   Cook Partisan Voting Index: R+13

Population		Race and Ethnicity		Income	
Total	761,786	White	69.5%	Median Income	$63,062
Land area (sq. miles)	540	Black	4.1%	District Income Rank	147
Pop/ sq mi	1411.6	Latino	19.4%	Poverty Rate	9.3%
Born in State	34%	Asian	3.5%	With health insurance	92.1%
		Two or more races	2.5%	Cash public assistance	1.7%
Age Groups		Other	0.9%	Food stamp/SNAP	6.8%
Under 18	22.5%				
18-34	19.4%	**Education**		**Work**	
35-64	37.2%	H.S grad or less	33.3%	White Collar	20.9%
Over 64	20.9%	Some college	37.6%	Sales and Service	45.2%
		College Degree, 4 yr	18.8%	Blue Collar	16.4%
Military		Post grad	10.3%	Government	12.6%
Veteran/ Active Duty	12.1%				

2012 Pres. Vote	Romney	179,555	(62%)	Obama	107,335	(37%)		
2016 Pres. Vote	Trump	190,163	(57%)	Clinton	120,992	(36%)	Johnson	12,712	(4%)

Glendale, Peoria: In 1938, when most of Phoenix's West Valley was barren, desert landscape, Flora Mae Statler paid 35 cents an acre to acquire land on the site of what became the city of Surprise. Statler chose the name, she later recalled, because she'd "be surprised if this town ever amounted to much." But the city got the last laugh on Statler: Over the past half-century, it has become one of the fastest-growing cities in Maricopa County. Since 2000, its population more than quadrupled.

Once a haven for retirees looking for warmer climates, Surprise and Phoenix's surrounding western suburbs have been booming, although the collapse of the housing market slowed the tempo. Astride Grand Avenue, the only diagonal street in the rigorous grid of metro Phoenix, is the suburb of Glendale, not so long ago just a crossroads but now home to 247,000 people. The city is also the home of the Phoenix Coyotes hockey arena and University of Phoenix Stadium (renamed in 2018 as the State Farm Stadium), which has a retractable roof and capacity of more than 78,000. The stadium hosted the 2015 Super Bowl, which had a local windfall of $720 million, plus the 2016 NCAA football championships and the 2017 NCAA Final Four basketball tournament; more sports extravaganzas have been scheduled. Nearby Westgate City Center is one of several edge cities in Phoenix's Valley of the Sun. Tucked between Surprise and Glendale are Peoria, as middle-American s its namesake in Illinois, and Sun City, a huge retirement community that markets its affordability. Peoria has spent close to $100 million to revive its older neighborhood as an historic area. The master-planned community of Anthem, 30 miles north of downtown, has about 22,000 residents.

All of these cities are part of the 8th Congressional District of Arizona, which covers Phoenix's West Valley. After a slow recovery from the housing bust and subsequent economic downturn in the mid-2000s, real estate values have been on the rise. The scheduled opening in 2019 of the $400 million Desert Diamond Casino West Valley north of the stadium, operated by the Tohono O'odham Nation, stirred controversy over tribal rights; initially, the facility was licensed to operate only bingo-style games. A few miles beyond Glendale is Luke Air Force Base, which has the largest fighter training wing in the Air Force and the only active duty F-16 training base in the United States. It functions as the chief operational training base for pilots of the F-35A Lightning II fighter jets, many of which have been purchased by other nations. President Donald Trump visited the base in October 2018 to discuss its weapons, technology and pilot training.

This has been conservative territory, though Republican downturns in the suburbs have been apparent here. Trump won this district, 57%-36%, compared with Mitt Romney's 62%-37% lead in the 2012 presidential election.

Greg Stanton (D)

Elected 2018, 1st term, b. Mar 08, 1970; Phoenix; Marquette University (WI), B.A., 1992; University of Michigan Law School, J.D., 1995; Catholic; Married (Nicole Stanton); 2 children.

Elected Office: Phoenix City Council, 2000-2009; AZ Deputy Attorney General 2009-2011; Phoenix Mayor, 2012-2018.

Professional Career: Attorney

DC Office: 128 CHOB 20515, 202-225-9888, stanton.house.gov

State Offices: Phoenix, 602-956-2463.

Committees: *Judiciary*: Courts, Intellectual Property & Internet. *Transportation & Infrastructure*: Aviation; Highways & Transit.

Election Results

Election	Name (Party)	Vote (%)		Cand. Spent	Ind. Exp. Support	Ind. Exp. Oppose
2018 General	Greg Stanton (D)	159,583	(61%)	$2,253,724	$7,617	$214,448
	Steve Ferrara (R)	101,662	(39%)	$1,501,611	$812,240	
2018 Primary	Greg Stanton (D)		(100%)			

Freshman Democrat Greg Stanton barely worked up a sweat in the desert as he won the seat vacated by Rep. Kyrsten Sinema when she ran successfully for the Senate. Like others among the handful of white male Democrats who won seats in Congress, he voiced standard-issue progressive views and was comfortable with party leaders. His easy victory in what was designed in the 2012 redistricting as a competitive seat is a prime example of suburbs moving toward Democrats.

Stanton, a Phoenix native, graduated from Marquette University and got his law degree from the University of Michigan. After practicing law in Phoenix for a few years, he was elected to the city council at age 30. In a review of his eight years on the council, which he departed in 2009, the Phoenix New Times concluded, "A cynical political watcher might say that Stanton often picked neighborhood interests over special interests, carefully measured each decision, and weighed its political ramification with an eye to someday making a bid for mayor."

After working two years as an Arizona deputy attorney general, Stanton in 2011 won his first term as mayor with 56 percent of the vote. A mix of Democrats and Republicans recently have held the position, which generally has operated with limited partisanship. Stanton claimed to have operated in that tradition by setting aside partisan politics.

In a profile in 2017, Governing magazine named him as one of its "public officials of the year." Under Stanton, the publication wrote, "the city has taken significant steps in the direction of sustainability," including major expansion of light rail, bus service and bike lanes. During his year as mayor, Phoenix had major economic growth, including a big increase in tech jobs.

In announcing his bid for Congress, Stanton styled himself as "a progressive who gets thing done." He criticized President Donald Trump for his reversal of President Barack Obama's policy on the Paris climate agreement, and embraced the enrollment of immigrants in the Deferred Action fo Childhood Arrivals program. "There has never been a more consequential time in the fight to protec the middle class," he said. He was unopposed in the Democratic primary and he had no apparent worry about a prospective opponent. In May 2018, he stepped down as mayor to launch his campaign.

His Republican challenger was Steve Ferrara, a surgeon who has used endovascular technique. that he developed while serving in the U.S. Navy, where he was chief medical officer. As a first-time candidate, his fundraising was competitive with Stanton. Ferrara criticized Stanton's record as mayor but he received little encouragement from national Republicans. Seth Leibsohn, a prominent forme local radio talk-show host who was a leader in the successful effort in 2016 to defeat a referendum to legalize marijuana in Arizona, drew early attention as a Republican candidate. But he failed to secure enough valid signatures for his candidacy.

Stanton's local popularity as the two-term mayor of Phoenix initially led him to consider running against Sinema for the Senate nomination. His easy election to the House could position him fo a future statewide bid. Democrats in Arizona have suffered from a limited bench of attractive candidates.

AZ-9: Central and Eastern Phoenix Suburbs   Cook Partisan Voting Index: D+

Population		Race and Ethnicity		Income	
Total	761,619	White	56.3%	Median Income	$54,210
Land area (sq. miles)	165	Black	5.5%	District Income Rank	239
Pop/ sq mi	4621.8	Latino	27.7%	Poverty Rate	17.5%
Born in State	38.5%	Asian	4.9%	With health insurance	86.7%
		Two or more races	2.7%	Cash public assistance	1.8%
Age Groups		Other	2.8%	Food stamp/SNAP	9.9%
Under 18	21.3%				
18-34	31.2%	**Education**		**Work**	
35-64	36.6%	H.S grad or less	30.1%	White Collar	10.9%
Over 64	10.9%	Some college	32.3%	Sales and Service	44.5%
		College Degree, 4 yr	23.5%	Blue Collar	14.7%
Military		Post grad	14.3%	Government	11.6%
Veteran/ Active Duty	6.8%				

2012 Pres. Vote	Obama	135,244	(51%)	Romney	123,263	(47%)		
2016 Pres. Vote	Clinton	155,158	(54%)	Trump	109,123	(38%)	Johnson	14,768	(5%)

Tempe, Western Mesa: As metropolitan Phoenix has expanded in the Valley of the Sun over the past half century, it has absorbed the crossroads towns that were once separate and distinct. One such town is Tempe, east of downtown Phoenix. It was founded in 1871 as Hayden's Ferry by the father of future Democratic Sen. Carl Hayden, who held that office from 1927 to 1969, and it was renamed in 1879 for an ancient Greek vale. Arrival of the railroad in 1887 was instrumental in that progress. The old agricultural town centered on Arizona State University, and both the town and the university have expanded greatly over the decades, while struggling to keep up with development and the financial costs of gentrification. The campus, which sits astride a rise with a fine view of much of metropolitan Phoenix, has an undergraduate enrollment of 43,000 students, plus 9,000 graduate students. The research park on the campus has 48 business tenants with 6,000 employees. In June 2018, ASU announced plans to open a new campus in downtown Mesa. In the Mayo Clinic's partnership with the university to develop the Mayo Medical School to emphasize innovative, patient-centered care the first students entered in 2017.

Tempe is relatively affluent, with 185,000 people in 2017, up from 142,000 in 1990, which is slower growth than other Phoenix suburbs. The city has nine stations along the original 20-mile light rail system from the city, with a three-mile extension from downtown to the campus scheduled to open in 2021. Its Mill Avenue district across from the ASU campus is a pedestrian-friendly downtown featuring red brick sidewalks and turn-of-the-century buildings. The day before college football's Fiesta Bowl in Glendale, Tempe hosts a parade and block party. The plans of the National Hockey

League's Arizona Coyotes to move from Glendale to a new arena in Tempe ran into roadblocks, including objections from ASU.

The 9th Congressional District of Arizona includes Tempe and parts of Scottsdale, Mesa, Chandler and Phoenix. It was drawn to be the only politically competitive district in the Phoenix area, but its demographic characteristics are favorable for Democrats. The district contains high shares of college graduates and high-income households. Hillary Clinton won the district in 2016, 54%-38%, a boost for Democrats over the 51%-47% local win by President Barack Obama in 2012. Outside of Arizona's two majority-minority districts, the 9th contains the largest concentration of Hispanics, at 29 percent, and its strongest Democratic performance.

ARKANSAS

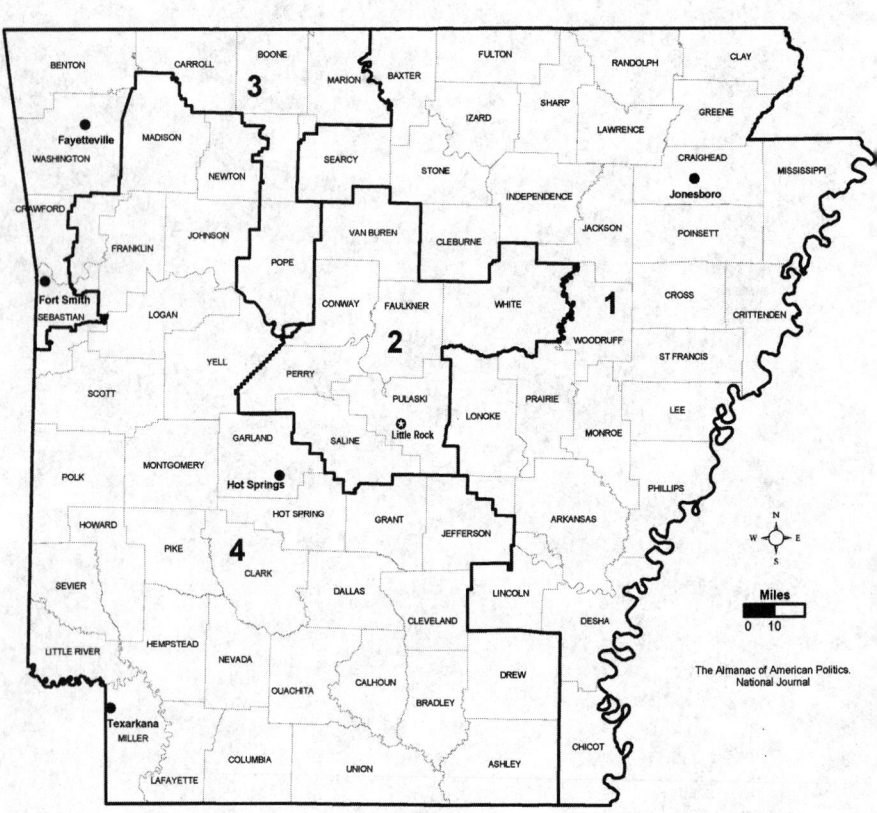

Congressional district boundaries were first effective for 2012.

Arkansas, the state that brought Bill Clinton to national prominence, has turned decisively away from the party he led. In 2008, the state's governor, both senators and three of its four House members were Democrats. Today, the GOP holds everything. And in a state that's whiter, poorer, older, more rural and with lower rates of college education than the national average – five key demographic factors in determining partisan leanings today – there's little chance that Democrats will be returning to influence in Arkansas anytime soon. In 2018, a great year nationally for the Democrats, only one of the state's four Republican House members won by fewer than 30 points.

Like Clinton, Arkansas began life without many advantages. It consists of the land left over when Louisiana and Missouri were carved out of the Louisiana Purchase and what is now Oklahoma was fenced off as Indian Territory. In area, it is the second-smallest state between the Mississippi River and the Pacific Ocean. In population, it is the smallest southern state except for Mississippi (the two are neck and neck) and, if you consider it southern, West Virginia. Arkansas was not blessed with great natural resources, with the exception of bauxite, once the main source of aluminum, and flame-retarding bromine. Its first two senators could not agree on how to pronounce the state's name, but since 1881, it has been illegal to call it ar-KAN-sas. Settled by poor farmers with large families, few slaves and little cash, Arkansas has had no major city like Atlanta, Dallas or even Memphis. Arkansas was settled more by Scots-Irish farmers than by grand plantation owners. It fought for the Confederacy, except for a few Union men in the northwest, and it followed other southern states in establishing government-enforced racial segregation. It is the birthplace of Pentecostal denominations like the Church of God in Christ, which had roots in late 1800s Little Rock, and the Assemblies of God, founded in Hot Springs in 1914 and now headquartered in Springfield Missouri.

In 1973, when Clinton was returning to the state from Yale Law School, the dominant figure in Arkansas, as far as most Americans knew, was Orval Faubus, governor from 1955 to 1967. Faubus had blocked desegregation of Little Rock's Central High School in 1957 until President Dwight Eisenhower sent in federal troops to enforce the court's order. And Arkansas was one of five states to vote for segregationist George Wallace for president in 1968. But Arkansas was evolving, culturally and economically, in ways that made Clinton's career possible. Faubus was succeeded by governors who repudiated his legacy: Republican Winthrop Rockefeller in 1966 and Democrat Dale Bumpers in 1970. Their politics made Clinton, then 28, a plausible candidate in the Republican-dominated third Congressional District in 1974. He narrowly lost to the incumbent Republican but came to the attention of leading entrepreneurs in the northwest corner of Arkansas, none of whom had quite yet achieved national fame: Sam Walton, whose first Walmart had opened only a dozen years before; Don Tyson of chicken-producing Tyson Food; and J.B. Hunt and his trucking firm. In less than two decades, Walton was America's richest man, and Clinton was president.

Arkansas still ranks low on many national indexes — its median household income is the nation's fifth-lowest, and nearly one-in-six residents (and 22 percent of children) live in poverty. Its population growth since 2010 has lagged the national average. Rates of high school degrees are only slightly lower than in the U.S. as a whole, but only 22 percent of Arkansas residents have a bachelor's degree, far below the U.S. average of 31 percent. The incarceration rate in Arkansas was the country's fourth-highest in 2016, trailing only Louisiana, Oklahoma and Alabama, according to the Sentencing Project. The state's unemployment rate after the Great Recession peaked at 8.4 percent, a full point and a half worse than the national high. By October 2016, it had fallen to 3.8 percent, a rate it remained at or below for the next two years. Arkansas continues to lead the nation in rice production while ranking No. 2 in chickens and No. 5 in cotton. Its agricultural export economy has made Arkansas vulnerable to tariffs imposed by the Trump administration; retaliatory tariffs threatened $339 million in exports, according to the U.S. Chamber of Commerce, and direct foreign investment in the state was at risk.

Little Rock has become a vibrant regional center, with exurban growth spreading out past the Pulaski County line, and it has been attracting tourists thanks to the William J. Clinton Presidential Center, the nation's largest presidential library. Northwest Arkansas has been booming even more, with Rogers, Fayetteville, Bentonville and Springdale growing by 11 percent or more between 2010 and 2017. Bentonville is where Walmart's headquarters are housed and where Sam Walton's daughter, Alice Walton, in 2011 opened the Crystal Bridges museum, with a magnificent collection of American art; Fayetteville is home to the University of Arkansas and the research and technology firms its presence has midwifed.

Left behind, however, are the aging, shrinking rural regions of the state. More than half of the state's 75 counties lost jobs between 2010 and 2015, and more than two-thirds lost population over the same period, according to economist Michael Pakko of the University of Arkansas-Little Rock. More than one-third of Arkansas' public school teachers are at retirement age. Along with the aging of the population, the state's shift from goods-producing sectors to service sectors has accelerated the shift toward metropolitan areas. The Hispanic population, at about 8 percent, is modest but growing, and since the 1980s, Arkansas has been home to the largest concentration of Marshall Islanders outside the Pacific islands, owing to historical labor ties to Tyson Foods. Still, "we need more migrants," Pam Willrodt, a demographer at UALR, told the Arkansas Democrat-Gazette. "We need more young, vibrant people who will then start having more babies."

Politically, Arkansas was long solidly Democratic, with Republican pockets in the mountains of the northwest. For years, it produced Democratic politicians who accumulated great seniority and power in Washington: longtime House Ways and Means Chairman Wilbur Mills; Sens. John McClellan and J. William Fulbright, who represented the state for a total of 65 years from the 1940s to the 1970s; and Sens. Dale Bumpers and David Pryor, who served for a total of 42 years from the 1970s to the 1990s. Republicans won some gubernatorial races — Winthrop Rockefeller in the 1960s, Frank White in 1980 (when he beat Clinton), and future presidential candidate Mike Huckabee in 1998 and 2002 — and John Paul Hammerschmidt amassed influence in the House, serving from 1967 to 1993. Still, as late as the 1990s, Arkansas remained one of the most Democratic states in the South in presidential and congressional elections.

Not so any longer. As throughout the Scots-Irish belt of America, which runs from western Pennsylvania southwest along the Appalachian chain and west to Texas, Arkansans turned sharply against Barack Obama and Hillary Clinton, who decided to run for the Senate in New York rather than returning to Arkansas after her husband vacated the White House. The Democrats' share of the Arkansas vote in the 2008, 2012 and 2016 presidential elections fell from 39 percent to 37 percent to less than 34 percent against Trump, who was extraordinarily popular in rural areas. Down ballot, the GOP has been relentlessly ascendant. Today, the governor, both chambers of the legislature, both U.S. senators, all four U.S. House seats, and every elected state-level office is held by a Republican. The legislature, with more farmers serving than lawyers, has steered to the right, voting to cut taxes and passing a raft of socially conservative legislation, including a measure declaring that life begins at conception and a ban on most abortions after 12 weeks. Arkansas became the third state to receive approval from the Trump administration to impose work requirements for Medicaid recipients and the first to enact them. State government finances have been in good shape thanks to budget reforms instituted after the state defaulted on bonds in the 1930s (its bank balance in January 1933 was supposedly $4.80).

There is a residual strain of populism in Arkansas — voters approved minimum wage hikes in 2014 and 2018. Against the wishes of GOP Gov. Asa Hutchinson, voters approved a medical marijuana initiative in 2016 (though Hutchinson and the GOP legislature have worked to slow its implementation). But, unlike other Southern states such as North Carolina and Virginia that have turned purple due to an influx of liberal-leaning outsiders, Arkansas has seen its fastest growth in the historically Republican northwest and in the GOP-leaning Little Rock exurbs. In Arkansas, Clintonism is the past, not the future.

Population		Race and Ethnicity		Income	
Total	2,977,944	White	73.0%	Median Income	$43,813
Land area (sq. miles)	52,035	Black	15.4%	State Income Rank	49
Pop/ sq mi	57.2	Latino	7.2%	Poverty Rate	18.1%
Born in state	61.3%	Asian	1.4%	With health insurance	89.4%
		Two or more races	2.1%	Cash public assistance	2.1%
Age Groups		Other	0.9%	Food stamp/SNAP	13.6%
Under 18	23.7%				
18-34	22.7%	**Education**		**Work**	
35-64	37.6%	H.S grad or less	48.7%	White Collar	33.0%
Over 64	16.0%	Some college	29.3%	Sales and Service	40.4%
		College Degree, 4 yr	14.1%	Blue Collar	26.6%
Military		Post grad	7.9%	Government	15.6%
Veteran/ Active Duty	9.3%				

Presidential Politics

2016 Primary (D)	Clinton (D)	146,057 (66%)	Sanders (D)	66,236 (30%)			
2016 Primary (R)	Trump (R)	134,744 (33%)	Cruz (R)	125,340 (31%)	Rubio (R)	101,910 (25%)	
	Carson (R)	23,521 (6%)					
2016 Pres. Vote	Trump (R)	684,872 (61%)	Clinton (D)	380,494 (34%)	Johnson (L)	29,829 (3%)	
2012 Pres. Vote	Romney (R)	647,744 (61%)	Obama (D)	394,409 (37%)			

Like most southern states, Arkansas voted more Democratic than the nation as a whole in presidential elections from Reconstruction to 1960. Since then, it has done so only when Jimmy Carter and Bill Clinton were atop the Democratic ticket. In the past five elections, it has voted 51 and 54 percent for George W. Bush, 59 percent for John McCain, and 61 percent for Mitt Romney and Donald Trump. Between the presidential elections of 2000 and 2016, only in West Virginia has the Democratic percentage declined more precipitously than in Arkansas. In 1996, Bill Clinton carried all but nine of the state's 75 counties. In 2016, his wife, Hillary Clinton, won just eight. The Democratic base in presidential contests is Pulaski County (Little Rock), where more than a third of the residents are African American. Jefferson County (Pine Bluff) also leans Democratic. Northwest Arkansas, the Ozark Mountain region, is historically Republican and home to the corporate headquarters of Walmart in Bentonville. Relatively fast growing suburban counties of Falkner and Saline around Little Rock are also GOP strongholds.

In the 2016 GOP presidential primary, Trump edged out Texas Sen. Ted Cruz, 33%-31%. Florida Sen. Marco Rubio won 25 percent. Trump's strength was in the state's rural eastern counties along the Mississippi River and in the rural Southwest. He also narrowly beat Cruz in Northwest Arkansas. Cruz prevailed in the counties around Little Rock, including Falkner and Saline; Rubio won Pulaski, where Trump finished third. In the Democratic primary, Clinton, the former first lady of the state, prevailed easily over Vermont Sen. Bernie Sanders, 66%-30%. She won 73 counties, losing only tiny Carroll and Newton counties in the northwest. But familiarity did not help Clinton in the general election: she captured only 34 percent of the vote, trailing the 37 percent Obama scored in 2012.

Congressional Districts

116th Congress Lineup	4R	**115th Congress Lineup**	4R

The rapid Republican takeover of Arkansas since 2010, when it was the last remaining southern state where Democrats still held the governorship and both houses of the legislature, has also extended to the congressional delegation. When Republicans that year flipped Democrats' usual 3-to-1 seat majority by picking up the open 1st and 2nd districts, national Democratic strategists applied pressure on their Arkansas counterparts to radically revamp the state's map by creating a solidly Democratic black-influenced district linking Little Rock with the state's Delta region.

But what party strategists in Washington wanted fell on deaf ears in Little Rock, where Democrats' first order of business was protecting sole surviving Blue Dog Democrat Mike Ross in the southern 4th District. In 2011, Gov. Mike Beebe signed off on a map that barely changed the 1st and 2nd districts but pushed the slow-growing 4th District north to take a big bite of rural Republican counties out of the 3rd District. Three months later, Ross announced his retirement, and Democrats lost the 4th District in a landslide, locking them out of the state's House delegation for the first time since Reconstruction.

Since then, Democrats have not come close to winning any seat despite bids in 2014 for open seats in the 2nd and 4th districts. With Republicans in control in Little Rock for the next redistricting, litigation appears to be the only option for Democrats to gain a district with black influence. As in the past, that likely would require an artful redrawing of the 1st and 2nd districts.

Asa Hutchinson (R)

Elected 2014, term expires 2023, 2nd term; b. Dec. 3, 1950, Bentonville; Bob Jones U., B.S. 1972; U of AR (Fayetteville), J.D. 1975; Christian; Married (Susan); 4 children.

Elected Office: Chairman, AR Republican Committee, 1990-95; U.S. House, 1996-2001.

Professional Career: Bentonville City Attorney, 1997-1978; U.S. Attorney, 1982-1985; Director, DEA, 2001-2003; Under Secretary for Border & Transportation Security, Department Homeland Security, 2003-2005.

Office: 500 Woodlane St, Little Rock, 72201; 501-682-2345; Fax: 501-682-1382; Website: governor.arkansas.gov.

Lt. Gov.: Tim Griffin (R) **Atty. Gen:** Leslie Rutledge (R) **Sec. of State:** John Thurston (R)

State Legislature: Senate: 9D, 26R **House:** 24D, 76R

Election Results

Election	Name (Party)	Vote (%)
2018 General	Asa Hutchinson (R)	582,406 (65%)
	Jared Henderson (D)	283,218 (32%)
	Mark West (Lib)	25,885 (3%)
2018 Primary	Asa Hutchinson (R)	143,648 (70%)
	Jan Morgan (R)	62,757 (30%)

Prior winning percentage: 2014 (55%), House: 2000 (unopposed); 1998 (81%); 1996 (56%)

Republican Asa Hutchinson won his second term as governor in 2018, improving from 55 percent of the vote in 2014 to 66 percent four years later – the highest percentage in Arkansas since the advent of four-year terms in 1986. He has governed as a pragmatic conservative in his solidly Republican state.

Hutchinson grew up on a farm with his brother Tim, who later became a senator. Their parents also operated a Christian radio station and school. After graduating from Bob Jones University, Asa Hutchinson attended the University of Arkansas law school at the same time Bill Clinton started teaching there. He became U.S. attorney in western Arkansas and prosecuted Clinton's half-brother, Roger, for cocaine possession. He lost a longshot 1986 bid for the Senate against Democrat Dale Bumpers, then ran for attorney general in 1990 and lost again. He spent the next five years as the state GOP chairman.

Hutchinson easily won election to the House in 1996 to succeed his brother, who moved to the Senate. He combined a conservative voting record with a pleasant demeanor to become an important player in a short time. In 1998, he served as one of the House's impeachment managers against

Clinton. When George W. Bush was elected president, he tapped Hutchinson to head the Drug Enforcement Administration, then to be undersecretary for transportation and border security in the new Homeland Security Department. Hutchinson returned to Arkansas to run for governor in 2006, but he lost. After the 2012 mass shooting in Newtown Connecticut, the National Rifle Association advocated allowing teachers and school security personnel to carry firearms and tapped Hutchinson to head a "multifaceted" education and training program "available to every school in America free of charge."

With Democratic Gov. Mike Beebe term-limited in 2014, Hutchinson prepared for a race. He faced former Rep. Mike Ross, who in 12 years in the House had been a Blue Dog Democrat with a moderate voting record, including a vote against the Affordable Care Act. Hutchinson took less ideological stands during the campaign than he had in the past. He backed a November ballot measure to increase the state minimum wage and to provide additional funding for early-childhood education, two proposals that Democrats nationally had favored. He also aired an ad targeting women that featured his school-age granddaughter, who helped him advocate a plan to put computer-science classes in every high school and to help women compete for high-tech jobs. Backed by $6.2 million from the Republican Governors Association aimed at tying Ross to President Barack Obama and other national Democrats, Hutchison prevailed, 55%-42%. Once in office — and leading the state's first unified Republican government since Reconstruction — Hutchinson succeeded in getting much of his agenda enacted, including a middle-class tax cut, scaled back from $100 million to $80 million.

A pair of legislative battles from his first two years stood out. One was the latest chapter in the fight over the state's "private option" — Beebe's creative way of getting a red state to accept Medicaid expansion under the Affordable Care Act, by applying federal funds for Medicaid-eligible residents toward securing them private health coverage. It was approved narrowly in 2013 and reauthorized even more narrowly in 2014. Facing fierce conservative opposition in the legislature, Hutchinson took a middle course, keeping the program in place through the end of 2016 and establishing a task force to draw up recommendations for a possible new direction after that. In April 2016, he used a line-item veto to keep the expansion alive.

The other conflict involved a religious freedom measure that blew up shortly after a similar bill in Indiana drew fire for allegedly enabling businesses to refuse to serve gays and lesbians. As in Indiana, disapproval from the business community, including home-state giant Walmart, was critical in forestalling the measure. Hutchinson rejected the first version he received from lawmakers. The legislature complied with his request for changes and Hutchinson signed the revised measure.

Hutchinson took a harder line on some issues – he opposed the settlement of Syrian refugees in Arkansas, and criticized an Obama administration effort to pressure public schools to allow transgender students to use bathrooms and locker rooms for their chosen gender, calling it "offensive, intrusive and totally lacking in common sense." But he also signed a bipartisan criminal justice measure and backed agricultural sales to Cuba, even visiting the island nation after the Obama administration's reopening of ties.

In 2017, Hutchinson signed a $50 million tax cut for lower-income residents as well as a bill that tied future higher education funding to performance-based metrics. He also signed a raft of bills designed to enact a voter-passed medical marijuana ballot measure that he had opposed, although some advocates criticized the implementation process as too slow. Hutchinson also signed a bipartisan measure of symbolic importance – one that separated what had been a joint holiday celebration of Martin Luther King Jr. and Confederate Gen. Robert E. Lee.

In 2018, Hutchinson leapt at the opportunity offered by the Trump administration to impose work requirements on many of the 285,000 beneficiaries of Arkansas' expanded Medicaid program. The requirements would eventually require able-bodied, childless adults between 19 and 49 to either work or perform 20 hours a week of volunteer service or vocational training. (The 645,000 beneficiaries in traditional Medicaid were not affected.) After seeing participation drop several months into the new requirements, the state scrapped its mandate that participants submit their proof of compliance online, a provision that put residents without internet access at a disadvantage. In July 2018, Hutchinson doubled down on the state's efforts to keep secret the information about companies that supply lethal-injection drugs for death row inmates. He argued that making this information public would hamper the state's ability to obtain the drugs, putting future executions at risk.

Hutchinson also grappled with the possible consequences of President Donald Trump's tariffs and aggressive trade posture. Nearly 350,000 jobs in Arkansas depend on trade, according to the World Trade Center Arkansas, and agricultural exports such as cotton, rice and soybeans were among the first to lose out in the trade skirmish. In addition, a trade war threatened to sink a big economic development project undertaken by China – a Sun Paper plant in Arkadelphia that would produce cardboard box components and employ an estimated 2,000 people during construction and 1,000 in the timber industry. On the response to tariffs, Hutchinson had to tread carefully: Trump won 61 percent of the Arkansas vote in 2016 and maintained 55 percent approval through November 2018, according to Morning Consult. "When it comes to our balance of trade, President Trump is right in putting pressure on our allies to respect the United States' interest in a more balanced and fair trading relationship," Hutchinson told Talk Business & Politics. "However, I have consistently cautioned the president to avoid a trade war that would harm Arkansas exports, including our agricultural commodities, that depend upon world markets."

In his bid for a second term, Hutchinson faced a primary challenge by television commentator Jan Morgan. Hutchinson represented the establishment wing of the GOP, while Morgan took a more Trumpist approach (though Trump himself endorsed Hutchinson shortly before the primary). Morgan charged that the incumbent hadn't cut taxes enough and that he was too soft on Second Amendment rights, but Hutchinson waved away the criticism, telling KUAR radio, "It's simply fear mongering. It's playing to the lowest and basest instincts of people that they want to believe the sky is falling." In the primary, Hutchinson defeated Morgan, 70%-30%. In the fall, he faced Democrat Jared Henderson, who had formerly headed Teach for America in Arkansas. While Henderson cut an attractive young profile, he was a political novice and, more importantly, had the wrong party affiliation for the state. In August, the governor's nephew, state Sen. Jeremy Hutchinson, was indicted on 12 charges of conspiring to steal thousands of dollars in campaign contributions and falsifying documents to cover it up. But the news didn't affect the governor's electoral chances, as Hutchinson ended up defeating Henderson, 65%-32%. Henderson won only seven counties -- down from the 23 won by Ross in 2014. After his victory, Hutchinson said he planned to pursue new income tax cuts in 2019, as well as a pay hike for teachers, government restructuring and a highway bill. n 2019, Hutchinson signed a $97 million income tax cut as well as a measure to ban abortions 18 weeks into a pregnancy, except in cases of rape, incest and medical emergencies. The state had already imposed a ban at 20 weeks.

John Boozman (R)

Elected 2010, term expires 2022, 2nd term, b. Dec 10, 1950; Shreveport, LA; University of Arkansas, O.D., 1972; Southern College of Optometry (TN), O.D., 1977; Baptist; Married (Cathy Marley Boozman); 3 children; 2 grandchildren.

Elected Office: Rogers School Board, 1994-2001; U.S. House, 2001-2011.

Professional Career: Optometrist, Boozman-Hof Regional Eye Clinic, 1977-2001.

DC Office: 141 HSOB 20510, 202-224-4843, Fax: 202-228-1371, boozman.senate.gov

State Offices: El Dorado, 870-863-4641; Fort Smith, 479-573-0189; Jonesboro, 870-268-6925; Little Rock, 501-372-7153; Lowell, 479-725-0400; Mountain Home, 870-424-0129; Stuttgart, 870-672-6941.

Committees: *Agriculture, Nutrition & Forestry:* Commodities, Risk Management & Trade (Chmn); Conservation, Forestry & Natural Resources; Nutrition, Agricultural Research & Specialty Crops. *Appropriations:* Commerce, Justice, Science & Related Agencies; Department of Defense; Financial Services & General Government; Military Construction & Veteran Affairs & Related Agencies (Chmn); State, Foreign Operations & Related Programs; Transportation, HUD & Related Agencies. *Environment & Public Works:* Clean Air & Nuclear Safety; Fisheries, Water, and Wildlife; Transportation & Infrastructure. *Veterans' Affairs.*

Group Ratings

	ADA	ACLU	AFL-CIO	LCV	ITI	COC	HAFA	ACU	CFG	FRC
2018	-	5%	-	7%	-	90%	65%	73%	47%	100%
2017	5%	C	0%	0%	C	86%	C	80%	81%	100%

Almanac Ratings 2017-18

	Economy	Social	Foreign	Composite
Liberal	0%	0%	0%	0%
Conservative	100%	100%	100%	100%

Key Votes of the 115th Congress

1. Obama-care revision	Y	5. Gun regulations	Y	9. Kavanaugh confirmation	Y
2. Tax Cuts	Y	6. Family planning regs	Y	10. Saudi arms sales	N
3. Dodd-Frank revision	Y	7. Gorsuch confirmation	Y	11. FISA rules	Y
4. Omnibus appropriations	Y	8. Immigration restrictions	Y	12. Military aid in Yemen	N

Election Results

Election	Name (Party)	Vote (%)		Cand. Spent	Ind. Exp. Support	Ind. Exp. Oppose
2016 General	John Boozman (R)	661,984	(60%)	$4,097,463	$164,806	
	Conner Eldridge (D)	400,602	(36%)	$2,227,706		$29,991
	Frank Gilbert (L)	43,866	(4%)			
2016 Primary	John Boozman (R)	298,039	(77%)			
	Curtis Coleman (R)	91,795	(24%)			

Prior winning percentages: 2010 (57%), House: 2008(79%), 2006 (62%), 2004 (59%), 2002 (99%), 2001 special (56%)

Republican John Boozman, Arkansas' senior senator, personifies his state's dramatic political shift from the last remaining Democratic stronghold in the Deep South to the bedrock base for the Republican Party. When he won a special election to the House in 2001, he was the only Republican in the state's congressional delegation, now entirely controlled by the GOP. Like the state's junior senator, Tom Cotton, Boozman ousted a two-term Democratic incumbent by a wide margin to secure his seat in the chamber. His defeat of Blanche Lincoln in 2010 made him only the second Republican to represent Arkansas in the Senate since Reconstruction. Today, he is the longest-serving member of Arkansas' six-person delegation. An amiable conservative, his main public criticism of President Donald Trump has been on trade policy; he has otherwise provided a reliable vote for Trump and the GOP. Boozman occasionally works across the aisle, as he did during his five terms in the House. He had little trouble winning re-election to a second Senate term in 2016, notwithstanding the Democrats' touting of their nominee as a leading prospect for an upset.

Born in Shreveport, Louisiana, Boozman grew up in Fort Smith, the second-largest city in Arkansas. He credits his upbringing — his father was an Air Force master sergeant and bomber during WWII — for his appreciation of issues that military families face. Boozman attended the University of Arkansas, where he was an offensive lineman on the football team. He left after completing his pre-optometry requirements and went on to graduate from the Southern College of Optometry in 1977. He opened a clinic in Rogers with his older brother, Fay Boozman, an ophthalmologist. John Boozman also raised polled Hereford cattle that were competitive in the show ring.

Boozman had his first experience in public office as a member of the Rogers Board of Education, a seat he won in 1994. Four years later, Fay Boozman— by then a member of the state Senate — unsuccessfully ran against Lincoln for an open Senate seat, as John Boozman got a taste of statewide politics working in his brother's campaign. Fay Boozman went on to serve for six years as director of the state health department under Gov. Mike Huckabee until his 2005 death in an accident on his farm. In 2001, John Boozman sought the 3rd District seat vacated by Republican Rep. Asa Hutchinson, who left to lead the Drug Enforcement Administration; Boozman had Huckabee's support in the special election. After emerging with a 57%-43% victory in the primary runoff, Boozman won the general election, 56%-42%.

He quickly aligned himself with Arkansas' rice and chicken producers and showed independence from the Bush White House by voting to end the trade embargo of Cuba — a position he still holds, although he has changed his approach by pushing more piecemeal measures. He exhibited his more conservative side in opposing Bush's immigration proposal, calling it amnesty for undocumented immigrants. A devout evangelical Christian — he co-chaired the 2017 National Prayer Breakfast in Washington — Boozman sponsored measures to display the Ten Commandments in the House and Senate chambers and sought to weaken restrictions on churches' political activities. Boozman created a dust-up in 2005 by sponsoring and then withdrawing a bill to increase the maximum workday for truckers to 16 hours. It was a move sought by Arkansas-based Walmart but lambasted by critics as a "sweatshop on wheels" that would have jeopardized safety.

In 2010, Boozman entered the Senate race against Lincoln, who was seeking a third term. The political dynamics in the state had changed markedly since his initial election to the House; GOP presidential nominee John McCain had trounced Democratic nominee Barack Obama in 2008 in the state. Boozman had some vulnerabilities in an eight-candidate primary contest: He had backed Bush's controversial 2008 legislation to bail out the nation's financial institutions in the midst of the Great Recession — an issue that tea party supporters used against some Republicans in 2010. But the endorsement of former vice presidential nominee Sarah Palin helped to inoculate Boozman. As the best-known candidate and having represented a district that was home to the largest concentration of the state's GOP voters, Boozman captured 53 percent of the primary vote, avoiding a runoff.

Meanwhile, Lincoln's re-election bid was hampered by a spirited primary challenge from the left by Democratic Lt. Gov. Bill Halter, who not only made her drain her campaign war chest but also forced her into a runoff. She narrowly won, but the battle left her weakened. Like other Republican Senate candidates in 2010, Boozman sought to exploit the state's disenchantment with Obama by seeking to tie Lincoln to the White House. Lincoln tried to distance herself from Obama and stress the importance to the state of her position as chair of the agriculture committee. Senate Republican Leader Mitch McConnell gave Boozman a boost by promising him a seat on that panel if he won. Echoing an attack line used against Boozman in his first congressional campaign, Lincoln criticized him for supporting Social Security "privatization." Boozman countered that Lincoln was taking a card out of the old Democratic playbook by trying to scare seniors.

The race was no contest: Boozman swept to a 58%-37% win as part of the national GOP tide. Boozman got his promised seat on the agriculture committee and his clout was enhanced a couple of years later when he was named to appropriations panel.

Boozman has compiled a consistently conservative record. A staunch abortion opponent, Boozman introduced a measure to require parental notification at least four days before a minor could have an abortion. He has supported efforts to withdraw federal funding to Planned Parenthood. In 2015, Boozman became chair of the Appropriations Subcommittee on Financial Services and General Government and teamed up with fellow Republicans in attacking the Consumer Financial Protection Bureau — created as part of the 2010 Dodd-Frank financial reforms. Boozman joined several Republicans in withdrawing support for legislation aimed at cracking down on the theft of internet content after critics — including websites such as Google and Wikipedia and their users — contended it would give the Justice Department the power to force internet service providers to block access to sites accused of stealing intellectual property.

On farm policy, Boozman's stances have reflected state and regional interests more than ideology. In 2012, he joined 34 colleagues in voting against the Senate version of the farm bill reauthorization; the opponents included many fellow southerners who felt it did too little for farmers in their region, particularly rice and peanut growers. A year later, Boozman switched and voted for a version of the farm bill that had been revised to the liking of southern agricultural interests.

He has been a reliable vote for his party leaders on major legislation and presidential nominations during the Trump presidency. Perhaps Boozman's biggest achievement during those first two years was progress in his long pursuit of slowly peeling back the Cold War-era trade embargo of Cuba. He and Democratic Sen. Heidi Heitkamp of North Dakota secured passage in the 2018 farm bill of their proposal to allow farmers to use Agriculture Department to promote their products in Cuba, the first measure related to Cuba to pass in almost two decades. His support for that contrasted to some conservative opposition, including from Cotton, over the lack of stricter work requirements for millions of Americans who use food stamps that were passed by House Republicans but jettisoned after Senate Democrats refused to support the measure. With the retirement of Sen. Pat Roberts of Kansas in 2020, Boozman is the Republican next in line to chair the agriculture committee.

On the environmental front, he supported Trump's decision to withdraw the U.S. from the Paris climate agreement and to kill the Obama-era plan for the Environmental Protection Agency to reduce carbon emissions at power plants — a move Boozman said would drive up costs in Arkansas. Like others in his party, he doubts the scientific consensus that humans are contributing to global warming.

While Arkansas' two senators generally vote in unison, they have taken opposite views on a few policies beyond Cuba. Boozman sided with GOP leaders and Trump on changing some federal sentencing laws through the "First Step Act," which Cotton excoriated in public and said was a "criminal leniency bill." Boozman also joined 12 Republican Senators in criticizing the Trump administration's "zero tolerance" immigration policy that led to the separation of migrant families at the southern border and sparked a national outcry.

Like many Republicans, Boozman has criticized Trump's use of tariffs. As the president challenged America's traditional allies, Boozman, a former member of the NATO Parliamentary Assembly, continued to stress the importance of the organization. He was also an original co-sponsor of the resolution put forward Sen. Bob Corker of Tennessee to explicitly hold Saudi Crown Prince Mohammed Bin Salman responsible for the death of Washington Post columnist Jamal Khashoggi.

Boozman had emergency heart surgery in April 2014 after discovery of an aortic aneurysm, but returned to Capitol Hill a couple of months later. Three years later, he underwent a successful follow-up procedure.

In 2016, at 65, he ran for a second term. His Democratic opponent, Conner Eldridge, was a quarter of a century younger and had served as U.S. attorney in Arkansas from 2010-2015 after working as a congressional aide and bank executive. Boozman criticized Eldridge as someone who would enable "a third term of Barack Obama." Eldridge distanced himself from Obama on issues like gun control, while citing his record prosecuting child abusers and pornographers as U.S. attorney.

Eldridge was banking on the anti-incumbent mood in the 2016 election. After release of the decade-old video with then-Republican presidential candidate Trump's lewd comments about women, Boozman characterized the comments as evidence that the presidential race was a "race to the bottom of humanity," adding: "As a husband, father of three daughters, and grandfather of two precious little girls, if I ever heard anyone speak this way about them, they would be shopping for a new set of teeth." But Boozman never withdrew his support of Trump. And, during a debate a week after the video surfaced, he said he supported Trump because the next president would likely nominate several Supreme Court justices. Boozman won, 60%-36%.

Tom Cotton (R)

Elected 2014, term expires 2020, 1st term, b. May 13, 1977; Dardanelle; Harvard University, A.B., 1998; Claremont Graduate University, Att., 1999; Harvard University Law School (MA), J.D., 2002; Methodist; Married (Anna Cotton); 2 children.

Military Career: U.S. Army 2004-2009 (Afghanistan & Iraq)

Elected Office: U.S. House, 2012-2014.

Professional Career: Clerk, U.S Court of Appeals, 2002-2003; Practicing attorney, 2003-2004; Management consultant, McKinsey & Co., 2010-2011.

DC Office: 326 RSOB 20510, 202-224-2353, Fax: 202-228-0908, cotton.senate.gov

State Offices: El Dorado, 870-864-8582; Jonesboro, 870-933-6223; Little Rock, 501-223-9081; Springdale, 479-751-0879.

Committees: *Armed Services*: Airland (Chmn); Seapower; Strategic Forces. *Banking, Housing & Urban Affairs*: Economic Policy (Chmn); Housing, Transportation & Community Development; Securities, Insurance & Investment. *Intelligence. Joint Economic.*

Group Ratings

	ADA	ACLU	AFL-CIO	LCV	ITI	COC	HAFA	ACU	CFG	FRC
2018	-	14%	-	0%	-	80%	78%	82%	71%	100%
2017	0%	C	0%	0%	C	86%	C	80%	80%	100%

Almanac Ratings 2017-18

	Economy	Social	Foreign	Composite
Liberal	0%	0%	0%	0%
Conservative	100%	100%	100%	100%

Key Votes of the 115th Congress

1. Obama-care revision	Y	5. Gun regulations	Y	9. Kavanaugh confirmation	Y
2. Tax Cuts	Y	6. Family planning regs	Y	10. Saudi arms sales	N
3. Dodd-Frank revision	Y	7. Gorsuch confirmation	Y	11. FISA rules	Y
4. Omnibus appropriations	N	8. Immigration restrictions	Y	12. Military aid in Yemen	N

Election Results

Election	Name (Party)	Vote (%)		Cand. Spent	Ind. Exp. Support	Ind. Exp. Oppose
2014 General	Tom Cotton (R)......	478,819	(57%)	$13,948,938	$8,004,645	$15,802,295
	Mark Pryor (D)......	334,174	(40%)	$14,578,504	$987,646	$15,005,636
	Nathan LaFrance (L)......	17,210	(2%)			
	Mark Swaney (G)......	16,797	(2%)			
2014 Primary	Tom Cotton (R)......Unopposed					

Prior winning percentages: House: 2012 (60%)

Perhaps no Republican better personifies the 2014 class that retook the Senate majority than Tom Cotton of Arkansas. Just months after being sworn in, he led an effort to undermine President Barack Obama's Iran nuclear deal. Despite being the youngest senator, he has been frequently cited as one of President Donald Trump's closest congressional allies. His populist views on immigration and his hawkish stances toward Iran and China have found a perfect partner in the president. Avowedly conservative with a prickly wit, Cotton has been unsparing in a body that values congeniality. Cotton has been undeterred and the subject of frequent reports that he might join the president's Cabinet, which underlines speculation that he might one day run for the White House himself.

A Harvard University-educated veteran of the wars in Iraq and Afghanistan, Cotton has risen to political renown meteorically: In 2014, he ousted Democratic Sen. Mark Pryor, the bearer of a well-known name in Arkansas politics, after serving just one term in the House. Hardly a natural politician, he is more the cerebral, introverted, principled conservative than a back-slapper who enjoys mixing it up on the campaign trail. Still, Cotton's tough-minded views caught the attention of national groups when he sought an open House seat in 2012, earning endorsements from the anti-tax Club for Growth and the late Sen. John McCain of Arizona, who shared his hawkish views.

A sixth-generation Arkansan, Cotton grew up on his family's cattle farm in Dardanelle. Even at a young age, he made an impression with his serious, studious demeanor. Friends remember him as a contrarian and admirer of Winston Churchill. He studied government at Harvard and later earned a degree from its law school. Cotton clerked for a federal appeals court judge and later went worked at two law firms. He has said 9/11 caused him to re-examine his life. He enlisted in the Army in December 2004 and turned down an opportunity to join the Judge Advocate General's Corps, preferring to serve in combat.

Cotton was deployed to Baghdad in May 2006 as a platoon leader in the 101st Airborne Division, leading daily patrols through the city. His ferocity came through during his deployment when he wrote a letter to The New York Times, responding to a story the newspaper broke in 2006 about the Bush administration's program tracing financial transactions of people suspected of ties to terrorist organizations. "You may think you have done a public service," he wrote, "but you have gravely endangered the lives of my soldiers and all other soldiers and innocent Iraqis here." He went on: "Next time I hear that familiar explosion—or next time I feel it—I will wonder whether we could have stopped that bomb had you not instructed terrorists how to evade our financial surveillance. By the time we return home, maybe you will be in your rightful place: not at the Pulitzer announcements, but behind bars."

Though the Times chose not to publish the letter, Cotton had copied PowerLine, a conservative blog, which did publish it. His words made a big impression on some leading conservatives. William Kristol, the editor of The Weekly Standard, befriended Cotton and became his champion. In March 2007, Cotton joined the Old Guard at Arlington National Cemetery, the regiment that guards the Tomb of the Unknown Soldier. The following year, he went to Afghanistan as an operations officer for a provincial construction team. After completing his military service, Cotton postponed pursuit of political office and joined McKinsey & Co., a high-powered management consulting firm.

When conservative Democratic Rep. Mike Ross announced in 2011 that he would not seek re-election, Republicans saw an opportunity, and Cotton decided it was the right time to take the plunge into politics. He won the GOP primary with 58 percent of the vote over Beth Anne Rankin, a onetime aide to former Gov. Mike Huckabee, and trounced Democratic state Rep. Gene Jeffress in the general election with 60 percent of the vote, becoming just the second Republican elected in the historically Democratic 4th District.

In the House, Cotton compiled a conservative record and exhibited an uncompromising streak. He opposed an initial version of the 2014 farm bill, which he scorned as a "food stamp bill." He later backed a version that didn't contain food stamp programs. He opposed disaster relief for Hurricane Sandy victims. After the April 2013 Boston Marathon bombing, he blasted the Obama administration for "failing in its mission to stop terrorism before it reaches its targets in the United States." Cotton didn't spare his party's own anti-interventionist wing and, just months later, joined with another military veteran, Rep. Mike Pompeo of Kansas — who later became the secretary of State under Trump — to write an op-ed in The Washington Post urging fellow Republicans to support Obama's call for military intervention in Syria.

Pryor held the same seat that his father, onetime Gov. David Pryor, had occupied for three terms; Republicans hadn't even bothered to field a candidate against him in 2008. But, six years later, Arkansas' increasingly rightward shift, combined with Obama's deep unpopularity there, provided an opening for the GOP. Cotton, with his military background and strong conservative credentials, was seen as the party's best prospect to unseat Pryor. Even though he was one of the most conservative Democrats in the chamber, Mark Pryor was painted by Republicans as a liberal Obama ally. The GOP hammered him for backing the Affordable Care Act and the Obama administration's $787 billion economic stimulus bill. The Democrats' strategy was to paint Cotton as an extremist, driven by ideological convictions that put him at odds with most Arkansans. They highlighted his vote against lower student loan interest rates — he was the only member of the state's delegation to oppose it — and his opposition to the farm bill. Cotton said hometown banks should finance student loans rather than the federal government. And he took aim at the food stamp component of the farm bill that lacked standards like work requirements and drug testing.

Ultimately, the Democratic tactic of depicting Cotton as too far to the right failed to make a dent, thanks to Arkansas' decade-long trend toward the GOP. Cotton won easily, 57%-40%. His victory marked a milestone for Arkansas, the first time since Reconstruction that Republicans held every seat in its congressional delegation.

Cotton made an early impression on the Armed Services Committee when he grilled an Obama Defense Department official about Guantanamo Bay. Obama had promised to close that facility, used to detain foreigners suspected of terrorism, during his 2008 campaign. But Cotton said, "The only problem with Guantanamo Bay is that there are too many empty cells."

Intended to head off what Cotton saw as the White House negotiating a bad nuclear deal with Iran, his Iran letter garnered national attention. It warned the Islamic republic's leaders that striking an agreement with Obama without congressional approval was nothing more than an executive agreement that could be short-lived — since it could be undone by a future president. While Cotton persuaded 46 of his Senate Republican colleagues — all but seven members of the GOP majority — to join him in signing the letter, White House officials were infuriated, saying it was an inappropriate interference in the conduct of foreign policy. The Senate overwhelmingly approved the plan for congressional review of an agreement with Iran, although Obama ultimately rounded up enough supporters to block a super-majority needed to disapprove the deal.

A Trump tweet praising Cotton in the run-up to the 2016 Republican Convention fueled speculation that the Arkansan was on a short list of possible nominees for vice president. He was an in-demand speaker in Cleveland, including appearances before the delegations from Iowa, New Hampshire and South Carolina — states that would be the first to select delegates in advance of the 2020 convention. When Trump's candidacy hit the rocks in the fall following the release of the "Access Hollywood" video in which he made lewd comments about women, Cotton was one of many Republicans who distanced themselves from the party's nominee. But he later walked it back, saying Trump had apologized and could "change his ways," and reaffirmed his endorsement of the soon-to-be president.

At times, Cotton's sharp tongue has made even some members of his own party uncomfortable. His support of legislation to rein in legal immigration rankled fellow Republican Sen. Lindsey Graham of South Carolina. Graham said his colleague had become "sort of the Steve King of the Senate," referring to the controversial House Republican from Iowa who would later be stripped of his committee seats after making racist comments in a New York Times interview. Cotton said, "The difference between Steve King and Lindsey Graham is that Steve King can actually win an election in Iowa. ... He didn't make it to the starting line and he didn't even make it off the kiddie table in the debates." Those comments were measured compared to Cotton's extensive criticism of criminal justice overhaul legislation. In a Wall Street Journal op-ed, Cotton wrote that criminal justice changes were a "jailbreak that would endanger communities."

Cotton's uncompromising attitude has been in evidence even when home state economic interests were involved. When Obama acted to restore diplomatic relations with Cuba in 2015, after more than a half-century, most of Arkansas' all-Republican congressional delegation — along with the state's GOP governor — welcomed the move, seeing the prospect of a new export market for the state's abundant rice crop. Cotton was the lone holdout in the delegation, joining other hard-line Republican conservatives on Capitol Hill. He was slammed by journalists back home for avoiding the home state press during the Senate's consideration of legislation to repeal the Affordable Care Act, which Cotton helped write as a member of the 13-member all-male group tasked with shaping the Senate's proposal. Despite the prominent role of senior Sen. John Boozman and the support of the rest of the delegation for the final version of 2018 farm bill, Cotton opposed it and slammed the measure, like previous efforts, for lacking stringent requirements for recipients of food stamps.

Like many Republicans, Cotton questioned Trump's decision to impose steel and aluminum tariffs, including on allies. But one would be hard pressed to find many criticisms of Trump in any interview the senator has given. He might not always agree with the commander in chief, but he articulates those disagreements in a manner far different than most other Republicans. In return, Trump has sided with Cotton over then-Secretary of State Rex Tillerson and then-Secretary of Defense Jim Mattis, who had cautioned against pulling out of the Iran nuclear agreement. Cotton also urged Trump to replace Michael Flynn as national security adviser with Army Gen. H.R. McMaster and help Marine Corps Gen. John Kelly snag a spot in the Cabinet, before Kelly became Trump's chief of staff.

But influencing Trump is a fickle business. Cotton touted in an October 2017 interview with Politico the difference in his interactions with the White House before McMaster and Kelly's appointments. He pointed to McMaster, Kelly and Tillerson's counsel to the president to stay the course in the war in Afghanistan and commit additional troops as "the way the policymaking process should work." Just over a year after the interview, Tillerson and McMaster were gone, Kelly was spending his final days in the administration and Trump had announced he was pulling troops out of Syria and reportedly ready to order a massive drawdown of troops in Afghanistan. After building a reputation as a derailer of ballyhooed bipartisan proposals, Cotton ended 2018 with a rare loss by opposing criminal justice changes. Such a position positioned him against an effort backed by Jared Kushner, a senior White House adviser and Trump's son-in-law, along with most Republicans in Congress.

Rick Crawford (R)

Elected 2010, 5th term, b. Jan 22, 1966; Homestead Air Force Base, FL; Southwest Missouri State University, Att., 1993; Arkansas State University, Jonesboro, B.S., 1996; Baptist; Married (Stacy Crawford); 2 children.

Military Career: U.S. Army 1985-1989

Professional Career: News anchor; Agri-reporter; Marketing Manager, John Deere; Owner, AgWatch Network.

DC Office: 2422 RHOB 20515, 202-225-4076, Fax: 202-225-5602; crawford.house.gov

State Offices: Cabot, 501-843-3043; Dumas, 870-377-5571; Jonesboro, 870-203-0540; Mountain Home, 870-424-2075.

Committees: *Agriculture*: Commodity Exchanges, Energy & Credit; General Farm Commodities & Risk Management. *Permanent Select on Intelligence*: Counterterrorism, Counterintelligence & Counterproliferation (RMM); Intelligence Modernization & Readiness. *Transportation & Infrastructure*: Highways & Transit; Railroads, Pipelines & Hazardous Materials (RMM).

Group Ratings

	ADA	ACLU	AFL-CIO	LCV	ITI	COC	HAFA	ACU	CFG	FRC
2018	-	4%	-	6%	-	83%	57%	79%	53%	100%
2017	0%	C	8%	0%	C	93%	C	85%	75%	100%

Almanac Ratings 2017-18

	Economy	Social	Foreign	Composite
Liberal	5%	5%	3%	4%
Conservative	95%	95%	98%	96%

Key Votes of the 115th Congress

1. Obama-care revision	Y	5. Family planning regs	Y	9. Guantanamo prisoners	N
2. Tax Cuts	Y	6. Body cameras/immigration	N	10. Ground missiles, limit	N
3. Omnibus appropriations	Y	7. Abortion ban	Y	11. Defense Dept. spending	Y
4. Dodd-Frank revision	Y	8. Concealed carry	Y	12. FISA rules	Y

Election Results

Election	Name (Party)	Vote (%)	Cand. Spent	Ind. Exp. Support	Ind. Exp. Oppose
2018 General	Rick Crawford (R)............................ 138,757	(69%)	$539,187		
	Chintan Desai (D)........................ 57,907	(29%)	$128,810		
	Elvis Presley (Lib)................................ 4,581	(2%)			
2018 Primary	Rick Crawford (R)...	(100%)			

Prior winning percentages: 2016 (76%), 2014 (63%), 2012 (56%), 2010 (52%)

First District Rep. Rick Crawford, who in 2010 became the first Republican since Reconstruction to win this eastern Arkansas district, has settled in and delivers federal payments and projects back home. Like the many Democrats who served this and similar rural southern districts in decades past, he is usually a loyalist who quietly produces farm and other legislation for party leaders. A former news anchor and owner of an agricultural broadcasting business, he keeps an eye out for the region's cotton and rice farmer. As with other areas in Arkansas, his district has become safely Republican.

Crawford was born in Florida on the former Homestead Air Force Base, where his father, a munitions expert, was stationed. Moving around a lot, he attended a dozen schools as a child. After graduating from high school in Hudson New Hampshire, he enlisted in the Army, where he trained as a bomb-disposal technician, disabling suspected live explosives. Crawford became a sergeant, did a tour of duty in Pakistan, and later served on U.S. Secret Service details for Presidents Ronald Reagan and George H.W. Bush.

When his military service ended, he enrolled at Arkansas State University in Jonesboro to study agribusiness and economics. He competed on the college rodeo circuit until injuries forced him to quit. In 1994, he declared personal bankruptcy, but eventually found full-time employment — and discovered he had some skills — in rodeo announcing. He worked some 100 shows a year before finishing his degree. Working the rodeo-broadcasting gigs helped Crawford land a news-anchor job in Jonesboro after graduation. His experience in agricultural broadcasting led to his own business called the AgWatch Network, a farm-news outlet that broadcasted on dozens of radio stations in the mid-South, as well as on television stations in Little Rock and Jonesboro.

When Crawford decided to challenge seven-term Democratic Rep. Marion Berry, national Republicans were skeptical, hoping for a more seasoned candidate. Crawford gained traction after Berry announced his retirement, making the district ripe for a GOP takeover. Crawford coasted to an easy primary victory and argued in the general election that Democrats had lost touch with the region's rural and small-town conservative voters. Democrat Chad Causey, Berry's former chief of staff, highlighted Crawford's personal bankruptcy and attacked him for not releasing his financial records. Crawford portrayed Causey as a Washington insider beholden to national Democrats. Former President Bill Clinton returned to Arkansas to help raise money for Causey, to no avail. Crawford won, 52%-44%.

In the House, Crawford sits on the Agriculture Committee, where he focuses on ways to protect farmers from overly burdensome regulations, and was a conferee for the 2018 farm bill. Crawford supported President Donald Trump's tariffs on steel and aluminum, saying fears of a "trade war" were overblown. He argued tariffs would help boost soybean exports (the Agricultural Counsel of Arkansas disagreed) along with bolstering the district's steel industry. He helped to enact crop insurance changes in the 2014 farm bill. Crawford took the lead among a bipartisan group of House members from Delta districts who opposed a move by the Obama administration to reverse a provision in the new law that shifted inspection of catfish imports from the Agriculture Department to the Food and Drug Administration. On the Transportation and Infrastructure Committee, Crawford added a provision to the 2015 highway bill that permitted farm vehicles to use a three-mile stretch of the redesignated Interstate 555 near Jonesboro. In 2017, he became a co-chair of the Congressional Steel Caucus.

His inclination to seek bipartisan consensus occasionally has caused problems for Crawford. He has urged a more flexible approach on illegal immigration, arguing that immigrants are an important economic force, and he opposed Republicans' compromise immigration bill in 2018. He still largely toes the party line though, supporting Trump nearly 98 percent of the time, per FiveThirtyEight. At first, Crawford expressed concerns about the American Health Care Act, the GOP's failed plan to replace Obamacare, citing problems with the process, but he eventually voted yes when the House passed the bill.

Crawford won his first reelection with 56 percent of the vote. In 2016, Democrats failed to run a candidate against him. Ahead of his 2018 reelection, he brought House Intelligence Committee Chairman Devin Nunes, R-Calif., to the district for a fundraiser. His Democratic opponent Chintan Desai attacked him for that and for supporting the release of the House GOP's memo on the beginnings of the Russia investigation, but Crawford took 69 percent of the vote. With a Republican-controlled legislature to protect the GOP during redistricting, Crawford appears to have become entrenched in what only a decade ago was a "Yellow Dog" Democratic district.

AR-1: Eastern Arkansas   Cook Partisan Voting Index: R+17

Population		Race and Ethnicity		Income	
Total	723,743	White	76.1%	Median Income	$39,864
Land area (sq. miles)	19,318	Black	17.8%	District Income Rank	415
Pop/ sq mi	37.5	Latino	3.2%	Poverty Rate	20%
Born in State	66.2%	Asian	0.5%	With health insurance	89.7%
		Two or more races	1.9%	Cash public assistance	1.9%
Age Groups		Other	0.5%	Food stamp/SNAP	17.3%
Under 18	23.3%				
18-34	21%	**Education**		**Work**	
35-64	38.2%	H.S grad or less	54.9%	White Collar	17.5%
Over 64	17.5%	Some college	29.2%	Sales and Service	40%
		College Degree, 4 yr	10.5%	Blue Collar	30.9%
Military		Post grad	5.5%	Government	16.2%
Veteran/ Active Duty	9.5%				

2012 Pres. Vote	Romney	154,551	(61%)	Obama	92,085	(36%)		
2016 Pres. Vote	Trump	169,438	(65%)	Clinton	78,688	(30%)	Johnson	5,489	(2%)

The Delta, Jonesboro: The Mississippi Delta, the flat, mucky, river-crossed lowland on both sides of the great river, was some of the country's first industrial farmland. Uncultivated for most of the 19th century, the Delta's big landowners eventually used machines to drain the muddy marshlands and persuaded poor blacks to move there to tend fields of cotton, rice and, later, soybeans. The results were bountiful agriculture and impoverished people. But the first minimum-wage and war-industry jobs up North drew young people out of the region, and the mechanical cotton picker idled many farm workers.

This area remains poor by national standards. Education rates are low, unemployment is high and the district is among the bottom 5 percent in the nation in median income. Opioid addiction is a growing problem, and the district ranked seventh in the country for opioid prescription rates.

Local rice farmers are among the biggest recipients of federal farm subsidies, and some have begun selling carbon credits to major companies like Microsoft. In Stuttgart, Riceland Foods is a farmer-owned agricultural marketing cooperative and the world's largest miller and marketer of rice. The local rice fields also attract ducks, making Arkansas the most productive state for mallard hunters. In the small town of Gillett, a political highlight is the annual Coon Supper, where Govs. Bill Clinton and Mike Huckabee frequently mingled with guests.

The local economy is increasingly supported by manufacturing. The Jonesboro area has become a rail-car manufacturing center with the opening of a Southwest Steel Processing Co. facility in Newport. Several big auto parts plants operate in Marion, across the Mississippi River from Memphis. In 2013, Big River Steel built a $1.1 billion flat-rolled flex mill facility in Blytheville, and in 2018 a $1.2 billion expansion doubled its capacity to produce high-grade electrical steel – increasingly in demand for hybrid and electric vehicles. Chinese-based textile company Shandong Ruyi Technology Group chose Forrest City for its first U.S. plant, investing $410 million and bringing 800 jobs to the region.

The 1st Congressional District of Arkansas includes almost all of the state's Delta lands and stretches west to the cool, green Ozarks. The largest city in the district is Jonesboro – heart of one of the fastest-growing areas in the state -- whose cheap labor and flat land have made it a hub for food-processing companies like Nestle and Frito-Lay. Jonesboro native John Grisham makes a number of references to the city in his book A Painted House.

For decades, the Delta was the most Democratic part of Arkansas. Some of the hill counties are ancestrally Republican. Craigshead County (Jonesboro) and Lonoke County near Little Rock are the largest in the district and both have become heavily Republican. Six rural counties along the Mississippi River voted for Hillary Clinton in 2016, but overall the district voted 65 percent for Donald Trump, giving him his biggest margin statewide.

French Hill (R)

Elected 2014, 3rd term, b. Dec 05, 1956; Little Rock; Vanderbilt University (TN), B.S., 1979; Roman Catholic; Married (Martha Hill); 2 children.

Professional Career: Staff, U.S. Senate Committee on Banking, Housing & Urban Affairs, 1982-1984; Deputy Assistant, U.S. Treasury, 1989-1991; Special Assistant, Economic Policy Council, 1991-1993; Sr. advisor, Gov. Huckabee, 2008; Banker, Businessman.

DC Office: 1533 LHOB 20515, 202-225-2506, Fax: 202-225-5903, hill.house.gov

State Offices: Conway, 501-358-3481; Little Rock, 501-324-5941.

Committees: *Financial Services*: Investor Protection, Entrepreneurship & Capital Markets; Nat'l Security, International Development & Monetary Policy.

Group Ratings

	ADA	ACLU	AFL-CIO	LCV	ITI	COC	HAFA	ACU	CFG	FRC
2018	-	11%	-	6%	-	92%	58%	80%	55%	100%
2017	0%	C	8%	3%	C	92%	C	88%	80%	100%

Almanac Ratings 2017-18

	Economy	Social	Foreign	Composite
Liberal	2%	7%	5%	5%
Conservative	99%	93%	95%	95%

Key Votes of the 115th Congress

1. Obama-care revision Y	5. Family planning regs Y	9. Guantanamo prisoners N
2. Tax Cuts Y	6. Body cameras/immigration N	10. Ground missiles, limit N
3. Omnibus appropriations Y	7. Abortion ban Y	11. Defense Dept. spending Y
4. Dodd-Frank revision Y	8. Concealed carry Y	12. FISA rules Y

Election Results

Election	Name (Party)	Vote (%)	Cand. Spent	Ind. Exp. Support	Ind. Exp. Oppose
2018 General	French Hill (R)	132,125 (52%)	$3,350,225	$140,000	$867,672
	Clarke Tucker (D)	116,135 (46%)	$2,346,621	$24,508	$657,293
	Joe Swfford (Lib)	5,193 (2%)			
2018 Primary	French Hill (R)	(100%)			

Prior winning percentages: 2016 (58%), 2014 (52%)

Since his first race in 2014, French Hill has won reelection relatively easily following his initial competitive campaign in this Republican-leaning district. In the House, he has been a mostly reliable

GOP vote and has focused chiefly on his work on the Financial Service Committee, where he has brought his extensive private-sector experience in banking.

A ninth-generation Arkansan, Hill's career as an investment banker linked his business and policy interests. The son and grandson of commercial and investment bankers, he earned a bachelor's degree in economics from Vanderbilt University. He worked as a banking officer and senior financial analyst for Interfirst Bank in Dallas until 1982, when he moved to Washington as a legislative aide for Texas Republican Sen. John Tower, who was a senior member of the Banking Committee. When Tower retired two years later, Hill became director of the Dallas-based Mason Best Co. After returning to Washington in 1989 as a deputy assistant Treasury secretary, he became a senior policy adviser for President George H.W. Bush and the Economic Policy Council. Hill returned to investment banking as chairman of First Commerce Trust and First Commercial Investments. In 1999, he joined with other investors to form Delta Trust & Bank in Little Rock, serving as its chairman. In 2008, Hill served as senior adviser for former Arkansas Gov. Mike Huckabee's run for the White House.

Hill sought the open House seat when Rep. Tim Griffin ran successfully for lieutenant governor. Against two credible opponents in the primary, he campaigned on a platform of fiscal conservatism that he highlighted in ads promoting "old Blue," a dusty 1998 Volvo. He took some heat for failing to mention his other cars, including a BMW and Mercedes-Benz, but easily won the primary with 55 percent of the vote. Hill pushed for a reduction in the corporate income tax while opposing efforts to hike the minimum wage — a stance he modified when voters approved an effort to put the issue on the ballot.

National Democrats were enthusiastic about former North Little Rock Mayor Patrick Henry Hays. But Hill had a heavy fundraising advantage, particularly with contributions from the securities and investment industry and won with 52 percent of the vote, slightly underperforming the district's recent GOP vote.

With his assignment to the Financial Services Committee, Hill sought changes in the 2010 Dodd-Frank banking law and worked to enhance the accountability of federal agencies that handle banking issues. He sponsored a measure to put the Federal Reserve in charge of enforcing the Volker Rule, part of Dodd-Frank that restricts a bank's ability to trade with its own money. The bill passed the House but was not taken up in the Senate, though some of the provisions he had pushed for easing regulation of community banks were included in the Economic Growth, Regulatory Relief, and Consumer Protection Act that President Donald Trump signed in May 2018. Along with Nevada Democratic Rep. Ruben Kihuen, in 2017 Hill helped lead the charge on a change to the mortgage disclosure rule on title insurance by the Consumer Financial Protection Bureau, an agency he has often criticized.

In 2016, Hill was the only House Republican from Arkansas to face a Democratic challenger, and he won 58 percent of the vote. In 2018, national Democrats initially made him a top target. State Rep. Clarke Tucker hammered Hill over his vote to repeal Obamacare, arguing that would weaken protections for people with preexisting conditions. Hill pushed back that Tucker was weak on immigration. He took the challenge seriously, bringing in Vice President Mike Pence to stump for him. The race was roiled in the final days after an out-of-state group ran an ad invoking the Supreme Court hearing for Justice Brett Kavanaugh in which two women urged people to vote for Hill because "we can't afford to let white Democrats take us back to the bad old days of race verdicts, life sentences and lynchins' when a white girl screams rape." Hill condemned the ad. He went on to win by six points, with 52 percent of the vote.

AR-2: Central Arkansas   Cook Partisan Voting Index: R+7

Population		Race and Ethnicity		Income	
Total	757,113	White	68.5%	Median Income	$49,526
Land area (sq. miles)	4,978	Black	22.2%	District Income Rank	319
Pop/ sq mi	152.1	Latino	5.1%	Poverty Rate	15.7%
Born in State	66.1%	Asian	1.5%	With health insurance	90.1%
		Two or more races	2.2%	Cash public assistance	1.9%
Age Groups		Other	0.5%	Food stamp/SNAP	11.1%
Under 18	23.5%				
18-34	24.1%	**Education**		**Work**	
35-64	37.8%	H.S grad or less	40.9%	White Collar	14.6%
Over 64	14.6%	Some college	30%	Sales and Service	42%
		College Degree, 4 yr	18.2%	Blue Collar	20.1%
Military		Post grad	11%	Government	17.6%
Veteran/ Active Duty	10%				

2012 Pres. Vote	Romney	160,140	(55%)	Obama	125,527	(43%)		
2016 Pres. Vote	Trump	160,782	(52%)	Clinton	127,883	(42%)	Johnson	8,630	(3%)

Little Rock, Pulaski: Little Rock has been the capital of Arkansas and its largest city for more than a century. The geographic center of an otherwise rural state, it is home to the presidential library of former Arkansas Gov. Bill Clinton. The city was harshly criticized for its role at the dawn of the civil rights movement. In September 1957, Democratic Gov. Orval Faubus sent in the National Guard to block a desegregation order at Central High School. President Dwight Eisenhower sent in U.S. troops and federalized the National Guard to enforce the order, and Little Rock became a synonym for bigotry around the world. Forty years later, the Little Rock Nine who integrated the high school returned for an anniversary commemoration with Clinton. "It was Little Rock that made racial equality a driving obsession in my life," Clinton said. In 2018, Pulaski County elected former Little Rock assistant police chief Eric Higgins as its first black sheriff.

On the banks of the Arkansas River in Little Rock is the Clinton Presidential Center and Park, which opened in 2004. But the political influence of the Clintons in the city they once dominated has faded. Other than biographical details that she voiced at the Democratic convention that year, Hillary Clinton largely ignored her former home during her 2016 presidential campaign.

The 2nd Congressional District of Arkansas includes Little Rock and North Little Rock, an industrial suburb across the Arkansas River known informally for years as Dog Town. The district also takes in Saline (named for its early salt works) and Faulkner (named for fiddle player Sanford C. Faulkner, the original Arkansas Traveler) counties, which have grown rapidly. In 2018, Saline was the third fastest growing county in the state. With its large shipping facilities, Little Rock is a robust market for trade and international companies. Dassault Falcon Jet is the top manufacturing employer in the region. A plant in North Little Rock employs 500 people who make cosmetics for the L'Oreal and Maybelline cosmetics brands. And Canadian-based DBG chose Conway as its U.S. headquarters to make metal products for agriculture and heavy commercial vehicles.

Welspun Corp., an India-based producer of large-diameter steel pipes for oil and gas companies, manufactured at its Little Rock plant more than 700 miles of the 36-inch-diameter steel pipe for the Keystone XL Pipeline project prior to President Barack Obama's rejection of TransCanada's proposal and further court-ordered delays. Another 350 miles of pipe remained idle awaiting a possible revival.

This is the least conservative of the state's four districts, though it has a GOP lean. Pulaski County (Little Rock) is entirely in the 2nd District and includes just over half of district voters and is comfortably Democratic. The outlying areas, led by Faulkner and Saline, have become heavily Republican and outweigh the Pulaski vote. In the 2016 presidential election, Donald Trump won 52 percent of the district vote — a dip from the 55 percent for Republican Mitt Romney in 2012. In a pattern similar to the 2014 contests for governor and senator, Hillary Clinton won 56 percent of the vote in Pulaski, but Trump's lead in Saline and Faulkner more than made up for that margin.

Steve Womack (R)

Elected 2010, 5th term, b. Feb 18, 1957; Russellville, AZ; Arkansas Tech University, B.A., 1979; Southern Baptist; Married (Terri Williams Womack); 3 children; 2 grandchildren.

Military Career: AR Army National Guard 1979-2009

Elected Office: Rogers Mayor, 1998-2010.

Professional Career: Stn. Manager, KURM Radio, 1979-1990; Rogers Cty. Council, 1983-1984, 1997-1998; Executive officer, Army ROTC, University of AR, 1990-1996; Financial consultant, Merrill Lynch, 1996.

DC Office: 2412 RHOB 20515, 202-225-4301, Fax: 202-225-5713, womack.house.gov

State Offices: Fort Smith, 479-424-1146; Harrison, 870-741-6900; Rogers, 479-464-0446.

Committees: *Appropriations*: Defense; Transportation, HUD & Related Agencies. *Budget (RMM)*.

Group Ratings

	ADA	ACLU	AFL-CIO	LCV	ITI	COC	HAFA	ACU	CFG	FRC
2018	-	4%	-	6%	-	92%	72%	76%	54%	100%
2017	0%	C	8%	0%	C	93%	C	85%	67%	100%

Almanac Ratings 2017-18

	Economy	Social	Foreign	Composite
Liberal	5%	0%	0%	2%
Conservative	95%	100%	100%	98%

Key Votes of the 115th Congress

1. Obama-care revision	Y	5. Family planning regs	Y	9. Guantanamo prisoners	N
2. Tax Cuts	Y	6. Body cameras/immigration	N	10. Ground missiles, limit	N
3. Omnibus appropriations	Y	7. Abortion ban	Y	11. Defense Dept. spending	Y
4. Dodd-Frank revision	Y	8. Concealed carry	Y	12. FISA rules	Y

Election Results

Election	Name (Party)	Vote (%)		Cand. Spent	Ind. Exp. Support	Ind. Exp. Oppose
2018 General	Steve Womack (R)............................ 148,717	(65%)	$1,093,148			
	Joshua Mahony (D)............................ 74,952	(33%)	$263,817			
	Michael Kalagias (Lib)............................ 5,899	(3%)				
2018 Primary	Steve Womack (R)............................ 47,757	(84%)				
	Robb Ryerse (R)............................ 8,988	(16%)				

Prior winning percentages: 2016 (77%), 2014 (79%), 2012 (76%), 2010 (72%)

Republican Steve Womack, first elected in 2010, has become an active Republican lawmaker with a knack for cutting deals and working across the aisle. That bipartisan approach was curtailed some once he became the Budget Committee chairman in early 2018 after Chairwoman Diane Black of Tennessee stepped down to devote time to her unsuccessful race for governor. With the GOP's loss of the House, he became the Budget ranking member.

Womack was born in Russellville Arkansas and spent a good portion of his childhood in Moberly Missouri. His father, a local radio broadcaster, introduced him to popular political figures in the region, including former Sens. Tom Eagleton and Stuart Symington and Gov. Warren Hearnes, all Missouri Democrats. "If I 'Dr. Phil' myself about what got me involved in public service, it's that I always admired political leaders," Womack said. After high school, Womack earned his bachelor's degree at Arkansas Tech. He and his father established KURM Radio, which focused on community news, weather, the county fair, high school football and Little League baseball. Womack covered local politics for the station.

In 1990, as a member of the Army National Guard, Womack served as executive officer of the Army ROTC program at the University of Arkansas. In 2002, he led a peacekeeping task force of 500 troops in the Sinai Desert in Egypt. Womack was elected mayor of Rogers in 1998 and worked to turn the city into a shopping destination. He also had a reputation for tough enforcement of immigration laws. Local Hispanic leaders were incensed when Womack claimed a majority of crimes in the city were committed by illegal immigrants. In 2007, Womack directed city officials to cooperate with raids by federal immigration agents on a Northwest Arkansas Mexican restaurant chain. After Hispanic motorists filed a lawsuit charging racial profiling by Rogers and its police department, a settlement was reached without an award of damages or an admission of guilt; Womack formed a committee to build better relations with the immigrant community.

When then-Rep. John Boozman ran for the Senate in 2010, Womack topped a crowded field of Republicans, then won in November, 72%-28%.

In the House, Womack established himself as firmly conservative and won a coveted slot on the Appropriations Committee as a freshman by arguing that being a mayor had taught him how to say "no." But he has been eager to say "yes" to local interests in their dealings with the federal government. With Rep. Jackie Speier, D-Calif., and others, he filed a bill to allow states to require Amazon and other out-of-state retailers to collect sales tax when they sell products over the internet, something that benefited brick-and-mortar retailers such as Arkansas' Walmart, which already collect state sales taxes online. He joined with Rep. Jim Costa, another California Democrat, to create the Chicken Caucus; the poultry industry maintains more than 2,000 chicken houses in Benton County.

Womack assumed the chairmanship of the Budget Committee, beating out Rob Woodall of Georgia and Bill Johnson of Ohio for the post. The position thrust him into unenviable fights over government funding and President Donald Trump's fiscal priorities. He defended Trump's budget, which included more spending on infrastructure and a border wall, while arguing that the 2017 tax cuts would boost the economy (and thus federal revenues). He also supported defense spending increases as critical to national security. The Budget Committee passed a plan in June 2018 with cuts to entitlement program such as Medicare to balance the budget in nine years, but it was never brought to vote on the House floor.

Womack co-chaired a Joint Select Committee on Budget and Appropriations Process Reform to seek bipartisan solutions to the budget process on Capitol Hill. Among the recommendations were to move from annual to biennial budgets. No major reforms came out of the committee, which disbanded amid partisan squabbling. "I am extremely disappointed in our failure and in my colleagues who lacked the 'political will' we have preached is so needed in Washington to vote out this good, bipartisan proposal," Womack said

Womack, who earlier endorsed Sen. Marco Rubio of Florida for the presidential nomination, displayed his moderate credentials prior to the 2016 Republican national convention when he advised Trump to select Ohio Gov. John Kasich as his running mate. "I think that would be the very best possible outcome for [Trump's] sake and for the sake of our party in terms of some sustainability," he said in a local newspaper interview. At the convention, his parliamentary skill led Republican officials to select him to preside during what they feared might be a contentious debate over the convention rules.

Back home, Womack avoided a Republican primary and a Democratic challenger in his reelection bids until 2018. In the GOP primary, pastor Robb Ryerse ran to his left, supporting "Medicare for all" and an increase in the minimum wage, leading Womack to question whether Ryerse was even a true Republican; Womack won 84%-16%. In the general election he faced Democrat Josh Mahony, who attacked Womack on his opposition to immigration reform, support for a border wall and brought up the immigration controversies from Womack's tenure as Rogers mayor. Womack argued that Mahony would be a lackey of Democratic leader Nancy Pelosi. The congressman won reelection 65%-33%, carrying every county in the district.

AR-3: Northwest Arkansas   Cook Partisan Voting Index: R+19

Population		Race and Ethnicity		Income	
Total	782,339	White	75.6%	Median Income	$48,058
Land area (sq. miles)	5,401	Black	2.9%	District Income Rank	338
Pop/ sq mi	144.8	Latino	14%	Poverty Rate	16.3%
Born in State	49.1%	Asian	2.9%	With health insurance	88.6%
		Two or more races	2.6%	Cash public assistance	1.5%
Age Groups		Other	2%	Food stamp/SNAP	10.4%
Under 18	25%				
18-34	24.7%	**Education**		**Work**	
35-64	36.5%	H.S grad or less	45.3%	White Collar	13.8%
Over 64	13.8%	Some college	28.2%	Sales and Service	40%
		College Degree, 4 yr	17%	Blue Collar	25.3%
Military		Post grad	9.4%	Government	11.5%
Veteran/ Active Duty	8.6%				

2012 Pres. Vote	Romney	168,703	(66%)	Obama	81,413	(32%)		
2016 Pres. Vote	Trump	180,921	(62%)	Clinton	89,081	(31%)	Johnson	10,587	(4%)

Fayetteville, Fort Smith: The northwest corner of Arkansas has become one of America's boom areas, with major corporate headquarters and dozens of small factories, tourist attractions and retirement developments in the Ozarks. The area is the fastest growing in the state, and as of 2017 was the 14th fastest growing in the country. Anchoring the local economy are three major employers: Walmart Stores, Tyson Foods, and J.B. Hunt Transport Services. The area has a rapidly growing population of Hispanics working at these companies in Springdale and Rogers. About 10,000 "climate refugees" from the Marshall Islands in the South Pacific moved here to escape the long-term risk of a rising ocean. This is also home to the University of Arkansas in Fayetteville, where young lawyers Bill Clinton and Hillary Rodham settled.

The friendly atmosphere, the prevalence of religious faith, and the natural backdrop of rounded green mountains and wide valleys in northwest Arkansas have contributed to the economic creativity. There have also been touches of genius. Sam Walton, who opened his first Walmart on the town square of Bentonville (it's now a small museum), had the inspiration to build a retail chain in tradition-minded small towns and rural areas using sophisticated computerized management. It made him the richest man in America before he died in 1992, though he still drove a pickup truck and kept the corporate headquarters in a deliberately unglitzy building in Bentonville. That will soon change though, with Walmart, by far the largest employer in this corner of the state, announcing in 2017 that it is building an updated corporate headquarters, citing a need to upgrade facilities and technology in a more modern setting. Construction will be done in five to seven years and will consolidate smaller offices across the state into one main home office.

Other firms have flocked in, especially to do business with Walmart, the world's largest food retailer. Tyson Foods in Springdale is the world's leading chicken producer and processor. The region's unemployment is low, but local leaders have moved to diversify into professional services and tourism. In Fayetteville, which U.S. News and World Report in 2016 ranked as the third best place to live in the United States, voters in 2015 approved an ordinance to ban discrimination based on gender identity or sexual orientation. In 2017, the Arkansas Supreme Court struck down the ordinance, ruling it created a protected class not covered under state law.

The 3rd Congressional District covers Northwest Arkansas, including Bentonville, Fayetteville and Springdale, plus Fort Smith on the Oklahoma line. Politically, this area has been consistently the most Republican part of Arkansas since the Civil War. John Paul Hammerschmidt was elected to the House in 1966 as one of the first Republican congressmen from the South, and the district has not elected a Democrat since. He beat 28-year-old Bill Clinton in the Democratic year of 1974, ending Clinton's first bid for public office with a loss (although he got an impressive 48 percent of the vote). Lately, Christian conservatives have entered politics, and new migrants and corporate managers have voted heavily for the GOP. In 2016, Donald Trump won 62 percent, less than the 66 percent support for Mitt Romney in 2012. As with other campus towns across the nation, Trump fared relatively poorly in Washington County (Fayetteville), the largest in the district, with 51 percent.

Bruce Westerman (R)

Elected 2014, 3rd term, b. Nov 18, 1967; Hot Springs; University of Arkansas, B.S., 1990; Yale University (CT), M.S., 2001; Southern Baptist; Married (Sharon French); 4 children.

Elected Office: AR House, 2010-2014, Minority Leader, 2012-2013, Majority Leader, 2013-2014.

Professional Career: Fountain Lake School Board, 2006-2010, President, 2009-2010; Engineer, forester, Mid-South Engineering; Deacon, Walnut Valley Baptist Church.

DC Office: 209 CHOB 20515, 202-225-3772, Fax: 202-225-1314, westerman.house.gov

State Offices: El Dorado, 870-864-8946; Hot Springs, 501-609-9796; Ozark, 479-667-0075; Pine Bluff, 870-536-8178.

Committees: *Natural Resources*: Energy & Mineral Resources; National Parks, Forests & Public Lands. *Transportation & Infrastructure*: Highways & Transit; Water Resources & Environment (RMM).

Group Ratings

	ADA	ACLU	AFL-CIO	LCV	ITI	COC	HAFA	ACU	CFG	FRC
2018	-	7%	-	0%	-	75%	82%	88%	75%	100%
2017	0%	C	8%	0%	C	93%	C	89%	85%	100%

Almanac Ratings 2017-18

	Economy	Social	Foreign	Composite
Liberal	0%	3%	0%	1%
Conservative	100%	97%	100%	99%

Key Votes of the 115th Congress

1. Obama-care revision	Y	5. Family planning regs	Y	9. Guantanamo prisoners	N
2. Tax Cuts	Y	6. Body cameras/immigration	N	10. Ground missiles, limit	N
3. Omnibus appropriations	N	7. Abortion ban	Y	11. Defense Dept. spending	Y
4. Dodd-Frank revision	Y	8. Concealed carry	Y	12. FISA rules	Y

Election Results

Election	Name (Party)	Vote (%)		Cand. Spent	Ind. Exp. Support	Ind. Exp. Oppose
2018 General	Bruce Westerman (R)	136,740	(67%)	$1,248,366		
	Hayden Shamel (D)	63,984	(31%)	$140,149		
2018 Primary	Bruce Westerman (R)	40,201	(80%)			
	Randy Caldwell (R)	10,151	(20%)			

Prior winning percentages: 2016 (75%), 2014 (55%)

Republican Bruce Westerman, with strong social conservative credentials, was elected in 2014 in the district that had been the home until 2012 of the most recent House Democrat from Arkansas. With his defeat of James Lee Witt, who was the Federal Emergency Management Agency director in the Clinton administration, the former president's legacy in the area continued to diminish. Westerman's unique background in forestry has given him opportunities to influence policy in the House.

Born in Hot Springs, Westerman earned his bachelor's degree in biological and agricultural engineering at the University of Arkansas, where he played for the Razorbacks football team. He completed his master's in forestry at Yale. He worked as a plant engineer for Riceland Foods and as an engineer and forester for Mid-South Engineering before being elected to the Arkansas House in 2010. When the GOP two years later took control of both chambers of the state legislature for the first time since Reconstruction, Westerman became House majority leader. He had a solid record as a conservative, voting to override a gubernatorial veto of a voter ID law and to approve a bill banning abortions after 20 weeks. He supported legislation expanding gun rights, setting dress codes in public schools, requiring that tests for driver's licenses be offered only in English, pushing for fiscal conservatism and opposing expansion of Medicaid under the Affordable Care Act.

The 4th District, with its strong Old South flavor, had elected just two Republicans since Reconstruction — now-Sen. Tom Cotton and Jay Dickey, a four-term congressman who lost in 2000 to Mike Ross after Dickey voted to impeach home-towner Bill Clinton, who remained popular in the district. In the 2014 primary, Westerman defeated energy businessman Tommy Moll 54%-46%. Westerman ran stronger in the southern part of the district, while Moll swept most of the northern counties. Westerman's 4,345-vote margin in Garland County accounted for his victory. Both candidates resided in Hot Springs. In the general election, Witt ran a vigorous, old-style campaign. He was one of the few prominent Democratic candidates in recent years who opposed gay marriage and abortion rights and supported gun rights. Despite a campaign visit from Clinton and outspending his opponent by $250,000, Witt could not overcome the GOP tide in the district. Westerman won easily, 54%-43%.

In the House, he joined the GOP whip team and served on the Budget Committee. On the Natural Resources Committee, Westerman used his academic background in forestry and took an interest in the 2.5 million acres of timber on public lands in his district. His Resilient Federal Forests Act, which set management policies on federally owned timber and would impose legal hurdles on litigants who seek to limit forestry plans, passed the House in both 2015 and 2017, but the Senate never considered it. Some forest management tools he pushed for were included in the 2018 farm bill, but many were ultimately stripped during conference. In the wake of devastating forest fires in California in late 2018, Westerman – the only licensed forester in Congress -- argued that the legislation was even more pressing, and he introduced legislation that would authorize more firefighting tools for at-risk communities and more help to the Forest Service.

Westerman hasn't faced a serious challenge since he was first elected. In 2018, he faced a primary challenge from Pentecostal pastor Randy Caldwell, who had recently moved back home to Arkansas, saying God had told him to run for Congress. Westerman won easily, 80%-20%. In the general election, he beat Democrat Hayden Shamel, a teacher who ran on raising the minimum wage and increased spending on education, by 67%-31%. Shamel carried Jefferson County (Pine Bluff), the lone Democratic holdout in the district.

AR-4: Western Arkansas   Cook Partisan Voting Index: R+17

Population		Race and Ethnicity		Income	
Total	714,749	White	71.8%	Median Income	$39,248
Land area (sq. miles)	22,338	Black	19.3%	District Income Rank	419
Pop/ sq mi	32	Latino	5.8%	Poverty Rate	20.8%
Born in State	64.6%	Asian	0.6%	With health insurance	89%
		Two or more races	1.7%	Cash public assistance	2.9%
Age Groups		Other	0.8%	Food stamp/SNAP	15.9%
Under 18	22.8%				
18-34	20.5%	**Education**		**Work**	
35-64	38.4%	H.S grad or less	54.4%	White Collar	18.3%
Over 64	18.3%	Some college	29.6%	Sales and Service	39.5%
		College Degree, 4 yr	10.6%	Blue Collar	31.6%
Military		Post grad	5.5%	Government	17.6%
Veteran/ Active Duty	9.2%				

2012 Pres. Vote	Romney	164,350	(62%)	Obama	95,384	(36%)
2016 Pres. Vote	Trump	173,731	(64%)	Clinton	84,842	(31%)

Hot Springs, Pine Bluff: West from the Delta flatlands along the Mississippi River, where the water-soaked fields produce America's largest rice crop, are small cities like Pine Bluff and El Dorado and the Ouachita Mountains. Southern Arkansas might well be called the northwest corner of the Deep South. It includes the state's largest African-American population in Pine Bluff, a reminder that parts of southern Arkansas near the Delta were once plantation country. There is also oil production, and the broiler-chicken industry looms large in these parts. The accent is clearly Arkansan: El Dorado, Nevada and Lafayette are all pronounced with long a's and accents on the penultimate syllable, and Ouachita, with a bow to the original French rendition of the Indian name, is WASH-i-taw.

The 4th Congressional District occupies much of the southern half of Arkansas, stretching from the eastern part of the state all the way west to Texarkana. Not far from the Texas border is the little railroad-crossing, county-seat town of Hope, where President Bill Clinton and his first White House chief of staff, Mack McLarty, were classmates in Miss Mary's kindergarten room and where former Gov. Mike Huckabee grew up a decade later. Hot Springs is the spa resort and gambling haven where Clinton's stepfather sold Buicks, his mother bet on the horses, and he excelled in high school. Established in 1832, Hot Springs National Park is the oldest federal reserve in the country, predating Yellowstone by 40 years (though Hot Springs was not declared a national park until 1921).

To the east is Pine Bluff, where a century and a half ago Union soldiers withstood a Confederate attack on the fortified courthouse square. Despite the presence of several plants for poultry giant Tyson Foods, the region has taken hits to its economy and population. The metro region has seen the biggest decrease in population in the state since 2010. Highland Pellets opened a wood pellet facility in Pine Bluff at the end of 2017 that is set to produce 600,000 metric tons annually, which will permit power plants to lower their carbon footprint. In Camden, Lockheed Martin relocated its production of the Tactical Missile System In 2018, Natural State Wellness Enterprises chose the area for its medical marijuana cultivation facility. And Weyerhaeuser completed a $190 million upgrade to its sawmill in Dierks. The area could also get a tourism boost after voters in 2018 legalized casinos in Pope and Jefferson counties and in Hot Springs, where Oaklawn Racing and Gaming announced a $100 million expansion of its famed horse track, adding a luxury hotel, event space and casino.

The 4th includes territory in the Ozark National Forest to the northwest, including Madison, Johnson and Franklin counties. The district leans substantially Republican. Jefferson County (Pine Bluff), just south of Little Rock and 55 percent African-American, was the only county in the district that voted for Hillary Clinton in 2016.

CALIFORNIA

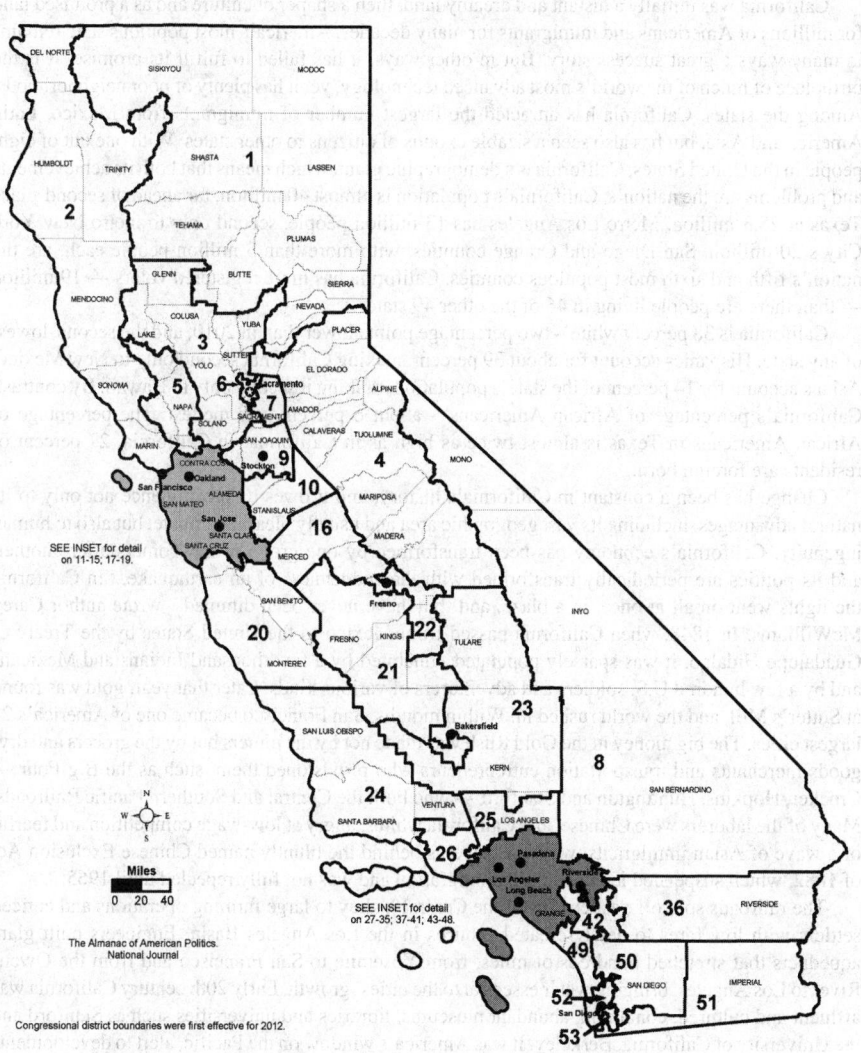

The Almanac of American Politics.
National Journal

Congressional district boundaries were first effective for 2012.

Americans have long thought of California as the Golden State, but its political hue has become ever-bluer in recent years. In 2018, Democrats capped their previous gains in the state by flipping seven Republican-held U.S. House seats, including all four GOP seats in Orange County, the onetime political base of Richard Nixon and Ronald Reagan. After the 2018 elections, the number of Republicans in California's congressional delegation was reduced to seven out of 53 seats. Likewise, former San Francisco Mayor and Lt. Gov. Gavin Newsom flipped Orange County to blue as he was elected governor with the largest percentage for a Democrat in California history.

California was initially a distant and dreamy land, then a shaper of culture and as a promised land for millions of Americans and immigrants for many decades. America's most populous state remains in many ways a great success story. But in other ways, it has failed to fulfill its promise. It is the birthplace of much of the world's most advanced technology, yet it has plenty of poor neighborhoods. Among the states, California has attracted the largest number of immigrants from Mexico, Latin America and Asia, but has also seen a sizable exodus of citizens to other states. With one out of eight people in the United States, California is a demographic giant, which means that both its achievements and problems are the nation's. California's population is almost 40 million, far ahead of second-place Texas at 28.3 million. Metro Los Angeles has 13 million people, second only to metro New York City's 20 million. San Diego and Orange counties, with more than 3 million people each, are the nation's fifth and sixth most populous counties. California has more registered voters — 19 million — than there are people living in 46 of the other 49 states.

California is 38 percent white – two percentage points lower than in 2010, and the second-lowest of any state. Hispanics account for about 39 percent, making California second only to New Mexico. Asians account for 14 percent of the state's population, ranking it second only to Hawaii. By contrast, California's percentage of African Americans – about 6 percent – is modest. The percentage of African Americans in Texas is almost twice as high as in California. In California, 27 percent of residents are foreign born.

Change has been a constant in California's history, and it owes its preeminence not only to its natural advantages, including its vast geographic area and usually pleasant climate, but also to human ingenuity. California's economy has been transformed by one group of newcomers after another, and its politics are periodically transformed with the suddenness of an earthquake. "In California the lights went on all at once, in a blaze, and they have never been dimmed," wrote author Carey McWilliams. In 1848, when California passed from Mexico to the United States by the Treaty of Guadalupe Hidalgo, it was sparsely populated, inhabited by a few thousand Indians and Mexicans and by a few hundred U.S. soldiers and adventurers of various kinds. Later that year, gold was found at Sutter's Mill, and the world rushed in. Within months, San Francisco became one of America's 25 largest cities. The big money in the Gold Rush was made not by the miners but by the grocers and dry-goods merchants and transportation entrepreneurs who provisioned them, such as the Big Four — Crocker, Hopkins, Huntington and Stanford — who built the Central and Southern Pacific Railroads. Many of the laborers were Chinese, and California whites, angry at low-wage competition and fearful of a wave of Asian immigrants, were the impetus behind the bluntly named Chinese Exclusion Act of 1882, which suspended legal Chinese immigration and was not fully repealed until 1965.

The railroads sold off vast chunks of the Central Valley to large farming operations and enticed settlers with low fares to newly created suburbs in the Los Angeles Basin. Engineers built giant aqueducts that stretched hundreds of miles, from Yosemite to San Francisco and from the Owens River to Los Angeles, bringing water essential to the cities' growth. Early 20th century California was affluent and cultured, containing abundant museums, libraries and universities such as Stanford and the University of California, Berkeley. It was America's window on the Pacific, alert to developments in China and Japan, Hawaii and the Philippines, and it was eager to extend America's economic reach and military strength -- yet as McWilliams wrote, Southern California was an "island" separated from the rest of the country. That began to change in World War II, when it became one of the great defense-industry states, building ships and airplanes by the thousands. Millions of Americans came and millions stayed. The population rose from 7 million in 1940 to 17 million in 1963, when California passed New York as the nation's most populous state.

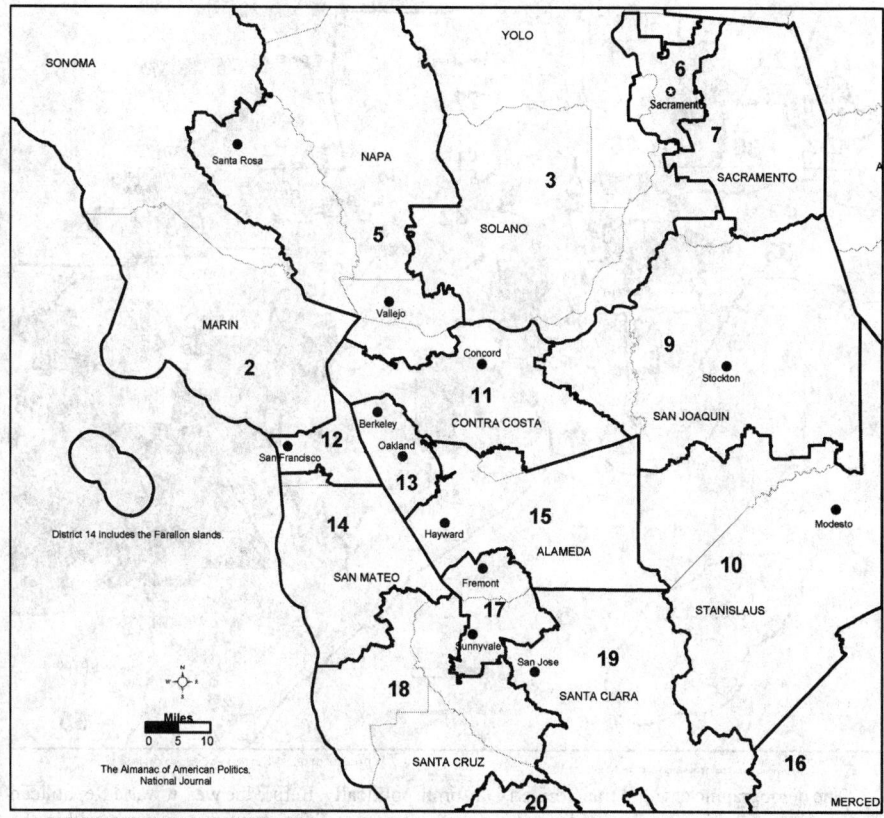

The Almanac of American Politics.
National Journal

Congressional district boundaries were first effective for 2012.

The heads of the big units of government and business planned California's future — leaders such as President Franklin D. Roosevelt and industrial mogul Henry J. Kaiser, who constructed vast shipyards and steel and aluminum factories. Republican Gov. Earl Warren husbanded tax monies after the war to build schools and the freeways that did as much as Detroit's auto factories – if not more -- to cement the automobile's place in American culture. Educators Robert Sproul and Clark Kerr transformed the University of California system into what Kerr called "the multiversity," and Democratic Gov. Pat Brown added to the vast web of canals and aqueducts that brought water from the wet north to the dry south. But the real engine of growth was the little people who took advantage of this infrastructure and built a humming economy. When California's defense plants closed down after World War II, government and civic leaders imagined that hundreds of thousands would head back east. But in those days before universal air conditioning and thermal winter clothing, people had experienced a climate in which it was comfortable to be outdoors all year. They wanted to stay, and so, as urbanologist Jane Jacobs pointed out, they created one-eighth of all the new jobs in the nation in the late 1940s in metro Los Angeles. This growth, multiplied thousands of times over, helped make California a mega-state. Meanwhile, Los Angeles County became what New York City was 100 years before: the great entry point in the United States, with some of the largest concentrations of Mexicans, Iranians, Samoans, Filipinos, Salvadorans, Armenians, Guatemalans, Koreans and Thais outside their native lands. The farmlands of the Imperial County are 83 percent Hispanic. San Francisco County is 34 percent Asian and Santa Clara County in Silicon Valley is 35 percent Asian.

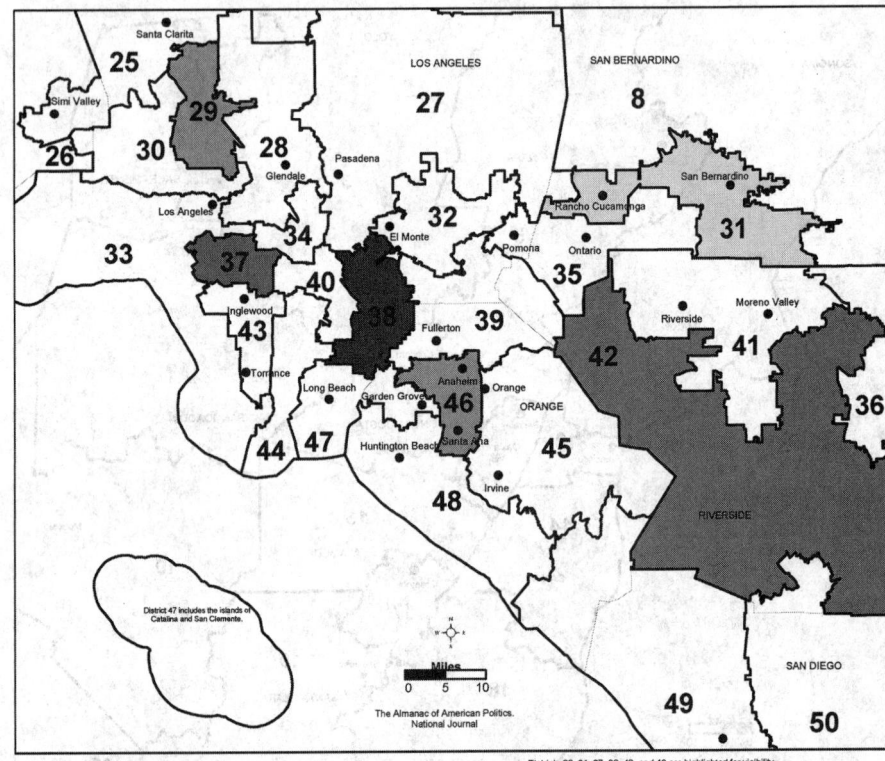

The demographic changes transformed California politically. Before the war, it was a Republican state with progressive leanings. Most of the struggles for political power took place within the Republican Party. The in-rush of the GI generation, with its allegiance to the New Deal, and the building of auto and steel factories with unionized workforces, transformed California into a two-party state. These new migrants were middle- and working-class -- family men and women enjoying a life in suburbs in the lovely California climate. Warren's progressive Republicans remained dominant through the mid-1950s, but with Brown's election as governor in 1958, a group of liberal Democrats took over. Things turned sour in the mid-1960s, when student rebellions at Berkeley and the Watts riots upset the New Deal order. Californians responded by calling in a disillusioned New Dealer espousing the cultural conservatism of the GI generation -- Ronald Reagan. Then, in 1974, California elected Pat Brown's son Jerry as governor and for a time was entranced by his fresh vision of baby boomer liberalism. California's laid-back lifestyle became a magnet for highly educated boomers, lawyers, scientists, techies and show-biz types. But it took time for them to become the dominant force in state politics. California voted Republican in every presidential election from 1968 to 1988 (Californians headed the ticket four times in that span), and Brown's administration was not wholly successful on policy, partly because he always seemed to have one eye on the presidency. In 1978, voters froze property taxes by passing Proposition 13 and ousted three of his state Supreme Court justices in 1986, after Brown had left office. Republicans followed Brown in the governorship: George Deukmejian, elected in 1982 and 1986, and Pete Wilson, elected in 1990 and 1994.

As Reagan was occupying the White House, California's defense industry boomed, and Silicon Valley began to flower south of San Francisco. Immigration continued in vast numbers, with newcomers living in the stucco bungalows and garden apartments that white, blue-collar workers left behind in neighborhoods like those south and east of downtown Los Angeles. Large swaths of the San Fernando Valley and Santa Ana in Orange County became predominantly Latino. Public policy was increasingly set by the Democratic legislature, led from 1980 to 1995 by Assembly Speaker Willie Brown. In the 1990s, disaster struck in several forms. Defense cutbacks hit the Los Angeles area hard, corporate mergers and relocations caused additional upheaval, and television screens were filled with seemingly apocalyptic news — floods, wildfires, earthquakes, riots and sensational trials. The state government responded competently to the natural disasters, but less well to those that were man-made. Lou Cannon's "Official Negligence," the definitive story of the Rodney King case, is a story of public-sector incompetence as dismaying as that spotlighted for the nation in the O.J. Simpson murder trial.

   Since the recession of the early 1990s, California has seen an outflow of people, mostly white and middle-class-to-affluent; between 2007 and 2016, 6 million people left the state, while about 5 million moved into California from elsewhere in the United States. In the meantime, from the late 1990s to the housing bust of 2007, federal policies encouraging mortgages for borrowers of more modest means produced a housing and construction boom in the Inland Empire — the sprawling San Bernardino and Riverside counties east of Los Angeles — and in the Central Valley. Latinos moved out from central Los Angeles County and bought new houses with little or no down payment and hopes of windfall profits from seemingly endless home price increases. But the market crashed in 2007, and the Inland Empire and Central Valley had some of the nation's highest foreclosure rates. For the next five years, California also had one of the nation's highest unemployment rates. California's population is up nearly 6 percent since the 2010 census, but that is actually a slowdown from the heady years of the 20th century. Part of the reason: the state's birthrate, which in 2015-2016 sank to its lowest level since the Great Depression. International migration, especially from Mexico, also declined. For the first time in its history, the 2010 reapportionment did not add any seats to California's House delegation. In 2020, the state could even lose one.

   In the decades after World War II, California was a key target in presidential elections. In Reagan's time, it went Republican in presidential elections while usually tilting Democratic in congressional and state contests. But starting in the early 1990s, it has become one of the bedrock Democratic states. The shift occurred slowly: While Bill Clinton carried California 46%-33% in 1992 and proceeded to lavish attention on the state, Republican Gov. Pete Wilson won reelection in 1994 by a 14-point margin while supporting Proposition 187, which barred state aid to illegal immigrants. But ever since, California's increasing Latino voter share has given Democrats enormous margins.

   Two other voting blocs have helped make California solidly Democratic. One group consists of affluent, highly educated whites living in lush corners of the big metropolitan areas, many with ties to the state's two resilient economic and cultural behemoths — Hollywood and Silicon Valley. (Apple recently reported revenues five times bigger than Wyoming's state GDP, and the median Facebook employee was paid $240,430 annually.) They tend to be liberal on cultural issues such as abortion rights and same-sex marriage, more moderate on fiscal issues, and hostile to the religious conservatives who hold sway within the national Republican Party. These voters have been similarly repelled by the increasingly conservative edge of the state's vestigial GOP, while adapting just fine to the increasingly left-wing tilt of the state and national Democratic Party. In the Reagan years, affluent neighborhoods, except for the heavily Jewish west side of Los Angeles, usually cast large Republican majorities; since then, they have voted increasingly Democratic. This has helped Democrats maintain large majorities in California's House delegation and in both houses of the state legislature since 1996. The second group now bolstering Democratic fortunes is Asian Americans, who are a major population group in Orange County and the San Gabriel Valley. In 1992, they favored George H.W. Bush over Clinton, but by the 2016 election, they backed Hillary Clinton over Donald Trump, 70%-17. Asian voters have become an important factor in the lopsided margins by which Democrats carry the San Francisco Bay Area and Los Angeles County.

   California's two governors from 1998 to 2010 -- Democrat Gray Davis and Republican Arnold Schwarzenegger -- tried to exert some discipline over the state's finances, with limited success. The power of public employee unions continued upward pressure on government spending, especially when California's progressive tax structure brought gushers of revenue in prosperous years. When revenues plummet, as they did after the tech boom ended in 2000 or when the housing market crashed in 2007, the pressure is then to increase taxes. Davis was unable to hold spending down and was blamed for electricity blackouts. He was recalled, 55%-45%, and on the replacement ballot, Schwarzenegger finished first with 49 percent. In office, the ex-bodybuilder/actor sought a conservative shift via ballot measures, but voters rebuffed him, and his job ratings flagged. He turned things around by backing liberal measures like carbon emissions reduction legislation and bonds for a high-speed rail line, and it was enough to easily win him reelection in 2006, although his popular support faltered as the economy turned south.

California's economy was slowing even before the housing market crashed in 2007. But the Great Recession made things far worse. One-third of California homeowners owed more on their mortgages than their houses were worth; the proportion hit 60 percent in parts of the Inland Empire. Corporate executive complained that high taxes, stringent regulations, complex land-use controls and high litigation risks hampered the economic recovery. Public employee unions' success in negotiating large pension benefits, combined with overall personnel costs and weakening economic conditions, led to some municipal bankruptcies, such as Vallejo in 2008 and Stockton and San Bernardino in 2012. Seemingly adrift, California voters turned to a familiar face — Jerry Brown. In 2010, he defeated former eBay chief executive Meg Whitman for the governorship, 54%-41%, despite her spending $141.5 million of her own money. Once mocked as the flaky "Governor Moonbeam," Brown gained ground-level experience as a two-term mayor of troubled Oakland and matured into a moderate technocrat who knew the inside game; crucially, he was at last undistracted by presidential ambitions. Task No. 1 was fixing the state's fiscal outlook; Brown made great strides, ultimately squeezing out an annual surplus that would have been unthinkable a few years earlier. While the nation's overall economic comeback helped, Brown also played a role by successfully urging passage of a 2012 ballot measure that temporarily hiked sales taxes and income taxes on higher-earners. But public pensions remained a challenge, and state employee unions retained their stranglehold on policy affecting their members.

As the decade approached its close, California had the fifth-largest economy on the planet – bigger than the United Kingdom, France and Brazil. Yet poverty persisted – almost one of every five Californians is at or below the poverty line when adjusted for the cost of living. The "savage inequality" of Los Angeles "is a crippling travesty, with tent cities as commonplace as million-dollar homes," Los Angeles Times columnist Steve Lopez wrote. "You can emerge from a restaurant that serves $80 steaks, wade through the human catastrophe of sprawling homelessness, drive home to gated glory in Tesla luxury, but get stuck in traffic so bad you'd be better off traveling by donkey." The main reason for the high cost of living is the high cost of housing. Fewer than a third of California households can afford a median-price home, according to the California Realtors Association. California ranks second to New York for homelessness per capita and first for unsheltered homelessness. California needs about 3.5 million new homes — three times its current pace of construction -- to keep up with population growth and keep housing costs down, according to McKinsey Global Institute. As housing has become more expensive, commutes have lengthened, and traffic has grown further due to a rise in car ownership, particularly among lower-income Californians newly able to buy a car. In its coastal environs, California has an increasingly two-tiered society, with not much of a middle class in between; San Francisco ranks as the second-most unequal metro area in the nation and saw the fastest growth in inequality in recent years, according to the Brookings Institution.

Once upon a time, people used to analyze California politics by distinguishing between Northern California and Southern California. Northern California — the Central Valley and the North Coast as well as the San Francisco Bay Area — tended to vote Democratic. Southern California — Los Angeles County as well as the smaller suburban and desert counties — tended to vote for Republicans. Today, the geographic divisions run on a different axis. The dichotomy is now between coastal California — all the counties that touch the ocean or San Francisco Bay — and interior California. Politically, coastal California votes Democratic and furthers liberal policies. In California's interior, the income gap is not nearly as wide, and the cost of living is lower, but private-sector job creation was not stellar before 2007 and has been dismal since. If interior California were a separate state, it would be competitive in presidential elections and would have 19 electoral votes. But coastal California, more than twice as populous as interior California, is dominant politically. For the most part, since Prop 187, the state has been out of reach for Republicans. Even in the 2014 wave year for Republicans, California's GOP candidates for statewide office secured between 41 and 47 percent of the vote, and the Democrats who coasted to victory included not just Brown but several younger politicians with bigger ambitions — Attorney General Kamala Harris, who succeeded Barbara Boxer in the Senate in 2016 and later jumped into the 2020 presidential race, and Lt. Gov. Gavin Newsom, who won the governorship in 2018. (Harris and Newsom continued the pattern of San Francisco, rather than Los Angeles, being the state's wellspring of political talent, from the elder and younger Browns to Sens. Dianne Feinstein and Boxer to House Speaker Nancy Pelosi.)

In the 2016 election, California voted for Clinton by 30 points, up from Barack Obama's 23-point margin in 2012. No Republican has won statewide office since 2006, and Republican voter registration has fallen not just below Democratic registration but also that of "no party preference" voters. One unexpected consequence of Democratic dominance has been California becoming a key ideological node for pugnacious conservatism and Trumpism. Breitbart News, and key new-right figures as different as Steve Bannon and Ben Shapiro, have worked out of Los Angeles; the Claremont Institute near Los Angeles became a crucible of pro-Trump thinking and a farm team for Trump's White House; White House immigration adviser Stephen Miller grew up in Santa Monica; and Trump supporter Peter Thiel emerged from Silicon Valley. Resistance to Trump, however, has been more broadly entrenched in the state. Attorney General Xavier Becerra sued the Trump administration on a wide range of policy issues; state Senate President Kevin de Leon helped enact sanctuary state legislation, which limits law enforcement cooperation with federal Immigration and Customs Enforcement; and Brown traveled to sign climate-change agreements with foreign countries, as both sides understood that they were more in tune with each other than they were with the Trump administration. Given California's trade ties with Asia, the state also worried about Trump's protectionist agenda.

In the latter half of the decade, California faced a different kind of reckoning, as the twin pillars of the state's economy experienced cultural crises. The #MeToo movement targeting sexual misconduct emerged in Hollywood, with a secondary appearance in Silicon Valley (as well as one among lawmakers in Sacramento). Meanwhile, the role of companies like Facebook in enabling the spread of misinformation during the 2016 presidential campaign, combined with overall angst about the impact of social media on society at large, damaged the tech sector's previously deep reservoir of goodwill. An Axios-SurveyMonkey poll found that a majority of Americans were concerned that the government won't be able to regulate tech companies effectively. California was also reminded of its vulnerability to natural disaster in November 2018 with the Camp Fire, the most destructive in the state's history; it destroyed the Sierra foothills town of Paradise, killing 86 and gutting nearly 14,000 homes. But despite the upheavals, the election of Newsom to succeed Brown in 2018 – along with a newly bolstered Democratic supermajority in the legislature – suggested that the state's leftward lurch in politics was likely to continue, not abate.

Population		Race and Ethnicity		Income	
Total	38,982,847	White	37.9%	Median Income	$67,169
Land area (sq. miles)	155,779	Black	5.5%	State Income Rank	9
Pop/ sq mi	250.2	Latino	38.8%	Poverty Rate	15.1%
Born in state	55.1%	Asian	13.9%	With health insurance	89.5%
		Two or more races	2.9%	Cash public assistance	3.6%
Age Groups		Other	1.0%	Food stamp/SNAP	9.3%
Under 18	23.4%				
18-34	25.0%	**Education**		**Work**	
35-64	38.4%	H.S grad or less	38.1%	White Collar	38.1%
Over 64	13.2%	Some college	29.3%	Sales and Service	41.8%
Military		College Degree, 4 yr	20.4%	Blue Collar	20.2%
Veteran/ Active Duty	6.0%	Post grad	12.2%	Government	13.5%

Presidential Politics

2016 Primary (D)	Clinton (D) 2,745,302 (53%)	Sanders (D) 2,381,722 (46%)			
2016 Primary (R)	Trump (R) 1,665,135 (75%)	Kasich (R) 252,544 (11%)	Cruz (R)	211,576 (9%)
2016 Pres. Vote	Clinton (D) 8,753,792 (62%)	Trump (R) 4,483,814 (32%)	Johnson (L) 478,500 (3%)
	Stein (G) 278,658 (2%)				
2012 Pres. Vote	Obama (D) 7,854,285 (60%)	Romney (R) 4,839,958 (37%)			

Since 1972, California has had substantially more electoral votes than any other state. That fact gave Republicans a near lock on the presidency in the 1970s and 1980s. Then, from 1992 to 2016, Democrats swept the state, giving them a structural advantage in the Electoral College. The state's vote for Democratic presidential candidates has grown from 46 percent in 1992 to 62 percent in 2016. Democrats are winning where the voters are: In the 10 counties that cast the most ballots in the 2016 presidential race, Hillary Clinton captured all 10, including, for the first time since 1936, Orange County, the one-time home of GOP conservatism in California. Clinton received a higher percentage of votes than any presidential candidate since FDR won 67 percent in California in 1936. Clinton won the vote in seven congressional districts represented by Republicans; Donald Trump, who captured only 32 percent of the vote, won no district represented by a Democrat.

For years, California's June primary was a kingmaker. Nelson Rockefeller's presidential hopes dissolved when he lost to Barry Goldwater in the 1964 GOP contest. In 1968; Robert Kennedy prevailed over Eugene McCarthy in the Democratic contest, but he was assassinated by Sirhan Sirhan after delivering his victory speech at the Ambassador Hotel in Los Angeles. George McGovern edged out Hubert Humphrey in the 1972 Democratic primary and the state's delegation was decided by a pivotal credentials fight at the Democratic National Convention where McGovern prevailed, assuring him the nomination. But the state lost its marquee status in four of the next five presidential elections when both parties' nominations were essentially clinched long before California voted. This irrelevance prompted Republican and Democratic state officials to move the 1996 primary from the first week in June to March 26, which was still too late in the primary calendar to make a difference. In 2000 and 2004, California jumped up to the first week of March, and in 2008, it joined 14 other states holding primaries on Feb. 5, Super Tuesday (eight other states conducted a caucus). Still, the Golden State primary never achieved the star status it once held. To save money, the legislature switched California's presidential primary back to its traditional date in early June, when state and congressional primaries are held.

As the Democratic primary approached the finish line in 2016, both Clinton and Vermont Sen. Bernie Sanders ran hard in California. Sanders camped out in the state and held dozens of events and rallies. Clinton, leaving nothing to chance, devoted the final five days before the primary campaigning in the state and dispatched her husband and other surrogates to dozens of events. While Sanders promoted his progressive agenda, Clinton argued that she would be the strongest candidate to take on Trump in the general election. The primary was a bit anti-climactic: The day before voters went to the polls, the Associated Press and CNN reported that Clinton had wrapped up enough convention delegates, including super delegates, to claim the nomination. Nonetheless, more than 5 million turned out to give Clinton a 53%-46% victory. She carried every major metropolitan area. Sanders won most of the state's counties north of Sacramento. Because Trump wrapped up the Republican nomination in May, California had little importance for Republicans. But eager to remain in the limelight, he held rallies around the state and won 75 percent of the vote.

Democrats seeking a marquee role for the 2020 nominating contest have moved the state's primary to March 3, when it likely will be clustered with several states. Will it become a kingmaker again? We've seen this maneuver before with varying degrees of success. One wild card in the primary is the role of early voting in a state where millions of voters have cast their ballots this way. In the 2016 general election, almost 8.5 million votes were cast absentee or early out of a total of almost 14.2 million.

Congressional Districts

116th Congress Lineup	46D 7R	115th Congress Lineup	39D 14R

Republicans in California are in such a deep hole that there is nothing close to a historical model for their predicament. The 46 House Democrats from their state are larger than the total delegation of any other state in the nation's history. (At its peak, in the 1940s, New York had 45 districts; now, it has 27.) Those 46 have several notable characteristics. They have ethnic and gender diversity: 18 women, 14 Hispanics, 6 Asians, 2 blacks. Geographically, they hold all of the 20 seats that include more than 10 percent of Los Angeles or Orange counties, plus all 10 seats in the Bay Area. Given that they account for 20 percent of all House Democrats, it's no surprise that they include four committee chairs and countless subcommittee chairs — plus, of course, Speaker Nancy Pelosi.

By contrast, none of the woeful total of seven Republican-held districts covers a pebble of the Pacific Coast. Three of them border most of the barren boundary with Nevada, two are at the southern end of the Central Valley and the remaining two include parts of Riverside and San Diego counties. In 2018, Democrats targeted seven Republican-held districts. They won all seven. Not coincidentally, these were the only seven Republican-held seats that Hillary Clinton won in 2016. The seven districts that Republicans continue to hold — for now, at least — were the only districts in California that Donald Trump won. Strikingly, in the other 49 states, Republicans held a 193-189 House majority in January 2019.

California has a rich tradition of partisan gerrymandering and incumbent protection: Republicans drew the lines to their advantage in the 1940s and 1950s, Democrats in the 1960s, 1970s, and 1980s. Democratic Rep. Phillip Burton, the former godfather of the process, used to defend the drawing of safe seats by deviously arguing it was inhumane to make congressmen catch red-eye flights to Washington every week. In 2001, consultant Michael Berman, the brother of then-Rep. Howard Berman, charged every incumbent Democrat $20,000 to draw a map that granted Democrats 33 and Republicans 20 safe seats.

Those customs were largely eliminated by two significant changes in the 2012 redistricting. Thanks to voter approval, 61%-39%, of a 2010 ballot proposition spearheaded by GOP Gov. Arnold Schwarzenegger, the state became a large laboratory for redistricting reform. The Democratic-dominated legislature was forced to cede power to a 14-member Citizens Redistricting Commission barred from taking into account any partisan data or where incumbents live. The other historical development was that, for the first time since it was admitted to the Union in 1850, California in 2012 did not gain House seats following the decennial census.

After months of tedious meetings and mountains of public testimony, the commission in August 2011 adopted a new map that radically -- and more logically -- rearranged the state's 53 seats. Under the 2001 map, mangled lines had produced a delegation so safe that just one House seat changed partisan hands one time in 10 years' worth of elections. Moreover, clever incumbent protection had delayed advancements in Latino representation; in 2010, Latinos were 38 percent of California's population, but held just nine of the state's 53 seats. The new map threw 27 incumbents into 13 districts and created 14 seats with no resident incumbent. It created three new or altered districts with functional majorities of Latino citizens.

The end result in 2012 was the most upheaval and loss of seniority California's delegation had ever seen. The state's new top-two jungle primary law meant that candidates of the same party advanced to the November election in eight districts. In addition to seven retirees (three Democrats, four Republicans) in 2012, several senior members lost reelection and 40-year Democratic veterans George Miller and Henry Waxman retired in 2014. What incumbents viewed as seniority, many voters saw as entrenchment. Reformers got the burst of competition and new blood they wanted.

Ironically, there was nothing "nonpartisan" about the map the commission produced, and it has turned out to be much more beneficial for Democrats than the one the Democratic legislature passed in 2001. In 2014, spurred by then-House Majority Leader Kevin McCarthy of Bakersfield, Republicans waged a half-dozen competitive challenges. But every Democrat survived — a few by narrow margins. Despite a few more close contests in 2016, including the defeat of veteran Democratic Rep. Mike Honda by another Democrat in the 17th District, another cycle passed with no changes in party control. Then, in 2018, came the Republican deluge. They lost two seats in the Central Valley, one in L.A. County, and all four that they held in substantial parts of Orange County.

What next? In 2020, no doubt, Republicans will seek to regain some of the seven seats they lost in 2018. If Donald Trump is seeking reelection and has not increased his popularity, that could be an uphill challenge. The greater risk might be that Republicans will lose some of their remaining seven districts. As for the next round of redistricting in 2022, the GOP won't be saved by clever map-drawers. They will need to find ways to appeal to more voters. Perhaps the only other option that could offer hope is some form of proportional representation statewide that would award House seats proportionally -- Democrats won 66 percent of the popular vote in California House races in

2018, but got 87 percent of the seats. That option would be a long shot. But their plight in California has become desperate.

Gavin Newsom (D)

Elected 2018, term expires 2023, 1st term; b.Oct. 10, 1967, San Francisco; Santa Clara University, B.S.,1989; Unknown; Married (Jennifer); 3 children.

Elected Office: Board Member, San Francisco Board of Supervisors, 1997-2003; Mayor, San Francisco, 2004-2010; CA Lt. Gov., 2011-2018.

Professional Career: Author; Founder, PlumpJack

Office: 1303 10th St., Suite 1173, Sacramento, 95814; 916-445-2841; Fax: 916-558-3160
Lt. Gov.: Eleni Kounalakis (D) **Atty. Gen:** Xavier Becerra (D) **Sec. of State:** Alex Padilla (D)
State Legislature: Senate: 28D, 10R, 2V **House:** 61D, 19R

Election Results

Election	Name (Party)	Vote (%)
2018 General	Gavin Newsom (D)	7,721,410 (62%)
	John H. Cox (R)	4,742,825 (38%)
2018 Primary	Gavin Newsom (D)	2,343,792 (34%)
	John H. Cox (R)	1,766,488 (25%)
	Antonio Villaraigosa (D)	926,394 (13%)
	Travis Allen (R)	658,798 (10%)
	John Chiang (D)	655,920 (9%)

In a largely suspense-free election, California voters in 2018 overwhelmingly elected Gavin Newsom to succeed four-term Democratic Gov. Jerry Brown, lowering the curtains on a decades-long Brown family dynasty and completing Newsom's charmed rise in California politics, including stints as mayor of San Francisco and as lieutenant governor under Brown. Once a pro-business moderate, at least by San Francisco standards, Newsom moved leftward as the state evolved in the Trump era, advocating a progressive wish list that included single-payer health insurance.

"With perfect hair, sparkling teeth, deep-pocketed supporters and a meteoric rise to national prominence, Newsom always seems headed for something bigger," the Associated Press wrote during the 2018 campaign. The New Yorker described him as having "the air of a man who just sauntered off a yacht." In the words of New York magazine, Newsom "looks more like a politician than any actor who's ever played one in a movie." The conservative National Review said Newsom "embodies Golden State liberalism: the perfect appearance, the bear-hug embrace of identity politics, the celebration of Silicon Valley moguls tempered by hand-wringing about income inequality, the grandiose, fanciful plans for building the state into a modern utopia."

Newsom was born into an affluent and well-connected family in California. His father, William A. Newsom III, was childhood friends with the oil heirs Gordon and Paul Getty and was later tapped to administer Getty family trusts. Another childhood friend was John Burton, a future Democratic state lawmaker and congressman. Newsom's grandfather, William A. Newsom II, served as a campaign manager for Edmund G. (Pat) Brown, Jerry Brown's father and one of his predecessors as governor; the younger Brown appointed Newsom's father to a Superior Court judgeship and then to the state Court of Appeals. Before becoming a judge, Newsom's father ran unsuccessfully for the state Senate; during the 1968 campaign, he stumped with Robert F. Kennedy just days before he was assassinated. But Newsom's parents separated when he was young, and he and his sister Hilary were mostly raised by their mother, Tessa, who sometimes held more than one job to support the family; Newsom, however, sometimes took vacations with the Gettys to exotic locales. Newsom's father died about a month after his son won the governorship. His mother died after a long bout with cancer in 2002; in 2018, the New Yorker reported that Newsom had helped her commit assisted suicide, a decision he said gave him PTSD.

Newsom has grappled with dyslexia – to this day, he uses an elaborate coping system involving handwritten notes and binders – but as a youngster he excelled at baseball and basketball. In high school, "he began applying hair gel and wearing blazers and business suits, a costume inspired by 'Remington Steele,' the TV show that starred Pierce Brosnan as a con man who assumes the identity of a glamorous private detective," according to the New Yorker. After graduating from Santa Clara University, Newsom went into business, backed by a roster of investors that included members of the Getty family. He began with a wine store on San Francisco's Fillmore Street, but his holdings eventually expanded to include some two dozen enterprises, including bars, restaurants, hotels and wineries. (His sister now handles the businesses.) Newsom crossed over into politics when San Francisco Mayor Willie Brown named him to the city's Parking and Traffic Commission, and later to a vacant seat on the city's Board of Supervisors.

In 2003, Newsom ran for mayor of San Francisco and won. Some of his ideas were quirky, such as installing turbines under the Golden Gate Bridge to harness the tides, or his decision to deliver a state of the city address in a 7-1/2 hour YouTube monologue. "We were willing to try new things," Newsom recalled to San Francisco Chronicle columnist Heather Knight. He was able to erase a $483 million deficit in 2010 without calamitous closures, but the city's homeless problem – despite his efforts to replace cash assistance with housing and other services – proved stubborn. Another issue, however, drew Newsom's national attention: His decision in 2004, years before it became mainstream, to order city clerks to approve same-sex marriages. After more than 4,000 couples took advantage of the new policy, the state Supreme Court struck it down, and many Democrats kept their distance from Newsom.

Newsom faced another challenge as mayor – his own personal life. In 2007, he admitted an affair with a staffer, Ruby Rippey-Tourk, who was married to another top Newsom staffer and friend. He went into counseling for abusing alcohol, and his marriage to Kimberly Guilfoyle, a prosecutor-turned-television personality, fell apart. (In an oddity of this political era, Guilfoyle was later romantically linked to Donald Trump Jr.; Newsom, for his part, married Jennifer Siebel in 2008, with whom he has had four children.) The affair didn't seem to hurt Newsom's political ambitions; he easily won reelection as mayor, and after an aborted gubernatorial campaign in 2010, he switched to the race for lieutenant governor and won, as Brown won his race to return to the governor's office. Newsom's eight years as lieutenant governor were largely quiet; the office's official duties are limited, and his relationship with Brown, despite the families' longstanding ties, was distant, even frosty. So it was not a surprise that Newsom began running for governor shortly after winning reelection, giving him more than three and a half years to prepare his bid to succeed Brown. In 2014, he published a book, Citizenville, in which he positioned himself as a high-tech wonk.

In California's top-two primary, Newsom faced former Los Angeles Mayor and former Assembly Speaker Antonio Villaraigosa, as well as state Treasurer John Chiang, and former Superintendent of Public Instruction Delaine Eastin, all Democrats, plus Republican John Cox. Newsom ran ads attacking Cox, which were widely interpreted as an effort to boost the Republican's standing among GOP primary voters, which in turn would increase Newsom's chances of facing a Republican in the runoff rather than another Democrat. Villaraigosa, despite strong financial support from education reform advocates, underperformed in the primary, particularly among his putative base of Hispanic voters. (Villaraigosa could have become the state's first Hispanic governor since the 19th century.) Newsom finished first with 34 percent, followed by Cox with 25 percent, Villaraigosa with 13 percent, Republican Travis Allen with 10 percent, Chiang with 9 percent, and Eastin with 3 percent. Cox – who had lost multiple races in his home state of Illinois – was hobbled by his partisan affiliation, and an endorsement by Trump amounted to a kiss of death. In a general election that never turned truly competitive, Newsom spent a substantial amount of time on the trail boosting other Democrats who were running to flip the U.S. House. In the end, Newsom defeated Cox, 62%-38%, which was the highest percentage ever for a Democrat in California. It was also the first time since 1887 that a Democratic governor succeeded a Democratic governor in California. Newsom's electoral map was largely similar to Brown's four years earlier, but Newsom, unlike Brown, won historically Republican Orange County.

As a candidate, Newsom advocated a progressive agenda: universal preschool, two years of free community-college tuition, single-payer health insurance, and support for low-income housing. Observers noted a leftward drift from his mayoral days on such issues as bail reform and immigration enforcement. Such proposals generally went further than Brown did; his predecessor put a priority on fiscal caution, which helped turn a $26.6 billion deficit at the beginning of Brown's term into a $14 billion surplus at the end, plus an $18 billion rainy day fund. Newsom, for his part, expressed weaker support for some of Brown's big projects, including high-speed rail lines and twin north-south water tunnels. Newsom also seemed to relish the chance to go toe to toe with Trump, who he'd engaged on Twitter. In his inaugural address, Newsom said, "We will prove that people of good faith and firm will can still come together to achieve big things. We will offer an alternative to the corruption and incompetence in the White House. Our government will be progressive, principled and always on the side of the people." A few weeks later, he largely abandoned the costly rail dream—with the ironic exception of a corridor in the more-Republican Central Valley.

Despite his prominence at the helm of the country's largest state – not to mention his charisma – Newsom says he currently harbors no presidential ambitions, even though he initially floated that possibility a full two decades before he won the governorship. Today, Newsom told the Associated Press, "I have no interest in anything to do with any of that. I mean, I don't know how else to say it. It's just anathema to anything I'm interested in in life."

Dianne Feinstein (D)

Elected 1992, term expires 2024, 5th full term, b. Jun 22, 1933; San Francisco; Stanford University (CA), Bach. Deg., 1955; Jewish; Married (Richard C. Blum); 1 child; 3 stepchildren.

Elected Office: San Francisco Board of Supervisors, 1970-1978, President, 1970-1971, 1974-1975, 1978; San Francisco Mayor, 1978-1988.

Professional Career: CA Women's Parole Board, 1960-1966; Director, Bank of CA, 1988-1989.

DC Office: 331 HSOB 20510, 202-224-3841, Fax: 202-228-3954, feinstein.senate.gov

State Offices: Fresno, 559-485-7430; Los Angeles, 310-914-7300; San Diego, 619-231-9712; San Francisco, 415-393-0707.

Committees: *Appropriations*: Agriculture, Rural Development, FDA & Related Agencies; Commerce, Justice, Science & Related Agencies; Department of Defense; Department of the Interior, Environment & Related Agencies; Energy & Water Development (RMM); Transportation, HUD & Related Agencies. *Intelligence. Judiciary (RMM)*: Ex Officio membership on all subcommittees. *Rules & Administration.*

Group Ratings

	ADA	ACLU	AFL-CIO	LCV	ITI	COC	HAFA	ACU	CFG	FRC
2018	-	73%	-	93%	-	40%	5%	5%	19%	0%
2017	95%	C	100%	100%	C	29%	C	0%	4%	0%

Almanac Ratings 2017-18

	Economy	Social	Foreign	Composite
Liberal	93%	93%	51%	79%
Conservative	7%	7%	49%	21%

Key Votes of the 115th Congress

1. Obama-care revision	N	5. Gun regulations	N	9. Kavanaugh confirmation	N
2. Tax Cuts	N	6. Family planning regs	N	10. Saudi arms sales	Y
3. Dodd-Frank revision	N	7. Gorsuch confirmation	N	11. FISA rules	Y
4. Omnibus appropriations	N	8. Immigration restrictions	N	12. Military aid in Yemen	Y

Election Results

Election	Name (Party)	Vote (%)	Cand. Spent	Ind. Exp. Support	Ind. Exp. Oppose
2018 General	Dianne Feinstein (D)...................... 6,019,422	(54%)	$17,612,064	$226,320	
	Kevin De Leon (D)......................... 5,093,942	(46%)	$2,457,537		$949,232
2018 Primary	Dianne Feinstein (D)...................... 2,947,035	(44%)			
	Kevin De Leon (D)........................... 805,446	(12%)			

Prior winning percentages: 2012 (63%), 2006 (59%), 2000 (56%), 1994 (47%), 1992 special (54%)

In early 2017, Dianne Feinstein, California's senior senator, became the top Democrat on the Judiciary Committee — the first woman to occupy the chairmanship or ranking member slot on that panel. It was but one in a series of firsts for Feinstein in a political career that began a half-century earlier. She became the first woman to serve on the Senate Judiciary panel after arriving in the chamber after a 1992 special election — which took place during what became known as the "Year of the Woman." The election of a record number of women to the Senate that year was attributed in part to political backlash over the handling of sexual harassment accusations against Supreme Court nominee Clarence Thomas during his 1991 confirmation hearings before the Judiciary panel. In 2018, history came full circle, with Feinstein playing a high-profile — and controversial — role when another high court nominee, Brett Kavanaugh, faced sexual assault allegations before the same committee.

The campaign that initially sent Feinstein to Capitol Hill was precedent-setting. Democrat Barbara Boxer, who served four terms as Feinstein's California colleague, was chosen the same year — marking the first time that a state had elected two female senators. The two campaigned together in 1992, with Feinstein at one point saying: "Just as Cagney had Lacey and Thelma had Louise, Dianne has Barbara and Barbara has Dianne." But Feinstein has crafted a reputation as a law-and-order liberal throughout her career. She became San Francisco's first female mayor after her predecessor was assassinated by a former public official. While Boxer retired in 2016, Feinstein — as the Senate's oldest member, at 85 — ran for re-election two years later. She won by a comfortable margin, but only after a bumpy campaign in which the centrist elements of her record collided with a Democratic Party electorate that had shifted leftward.

Feinstein has never been easy to pigeonhole: For many years, she backed the death penalty, while also being one of the Senate's most persistent advocates of gun control legislation. She has been a staunch defender of government surveillance programs and federal intelligence gathering agencies. But she rebuked the harsh interrogation techniques used on terrorism suspects after 9/11 and fought with the CIA over that issue. Born Dianne Goldman, she grew up in San Francisco's lush Presidio Heights neighborhood. Her father, a prominent physician, was Jewish, while her mother belonged to the Russian Orthodox faith. Feinstein attended San Francisco's Convent of the Sacred Heart before converting to Judaism at 20.

She hoped to follow in her father's footsteps, but in her first semester at Stanford University, got a D in genetics and decided she did not have the aptitude for medicine. However, she loved the class she took on American political thought. And she had an uncle active in local Democratic politics who is said to have fueled her interest in moving in that direction. Feinstein graduated with a degree in criminology and then, while on an internship, wrote a paper about post-conviction phases of the justice system. She sent the paper to Gov. Pat Brown, for whom her father was a personal physician. Despite her youth — she was just 27 — the governor appointed her to the California Women's Board of Terms and Parole.

In 1969, she won her first election, to the San Francisco County Board of Supervisors. However, she was defeated in bids for mayor in 1971 and 1975 and began to question her future in San Francisco's polarized politics. "I was convinced I was not electable," she said years later. One day in late November 1978, Feinstein — who had lost her second husband, neurosurgeon Bertram Feinstein, to cancer just months earlier — was talking to reporters, openly contemplating leaving politics. Hours later, as president of the Board of Supervisors, she became the city's acting mayor after Mayor George Moscone and fellow Supervisor Harvey Milk were shot to death by former Supervisor Dan White. Feinstein discovered Milk's body and had to announce to the world what had happened.

Her steadiness and sense of command calmed the city, and she went on to win full mayoral terms in 1979 and 1983. In 1984, Democratic presidential candidate Walter Mondale considered naming Feinstein as his running mate. But he passed her over for Geraldine Ferraro partly because of qualms about the business dealings of Feinstein's third husband, Richard Blum, to whom she has been married since 1980. Feinstein presided over the 1984 Democratic National Convention in San Francisco, while, ironically, Ferraro confronted questions about her husband's business dealings. Blum's extensive assets have helped make Feinstein the third wealthiest senator, according to a 2018 Roll Call compilation; they also have yielded periodic political headaches for her, in the form of conflict of interest allegations.

Ineligible for a third term as mayor, Feinstein left the city's politics in 1987 and ran for governor in 1990, buoyed by a $3 million loan she and her husband made to the effort. She won the Democratic primary 52%-41% but lost 49%-46% to Republican Pete Wilson in the general election. During that campaign, Feinstein — who had been against the death penalty as a young member of the Board of Terms and Parole — said she had changed her mind and had come to believe capital punishment was a deterrent for certain types of crimes. She was booed at the 1990 State Democratic Convention over her stance but won points for a willingness to demonstrate her independence. Nearly three decades later, facing an aggressive re-election challenge from the left, Feinstein said her position on the death penalty had changed again. "It became crystal clear to me that the risk of unequal application is high and its effect on deterrence is low," Feinstein said shortly before the 2018 Senate primary, adding that her change of heart had come "several years ago."

When Wilson appointed little-known state Sen. John Seymour to replace himself in the Senate, Feinstein announced for the 1992 special election to fill the remainder of the term. She defeated state Controller Gray Davis 58%-33% in a heated primary that soured her relationship with Davis, who went on to be elected governor in 1998. Seymour struggled throughout the campaign, shifting to support abortion rights and seeing his attacks on illegal immigration fall flat. Feinstein won 54%-38%.

Feinstein's tough-on-crime background led her to sponsor a ban on the manufacture and sale of assault weapons in the Senate in 1994, which President Bill Clinton signed into law. When Idaho Republican Larry Craig contended that her definition of assault weapons was not rigorous enough and challenged her knowledge of firearms, she stopped the argument in its tracks by reminding the Senate of the tragedy earlier in her political career. "I know something about what firearms can do," Feinstein said. She pressed unsuccessfully for reauthorization of the assault weapons ban in 2004, when Congress was under GOP control.

As the Democratic Party's support for gun control waned — some blamed the assault weapons ban for the party's loss of Congress in 1994 — Feinstein had a harder time persuading colleagues to consider gun restrictions. The public mood changed following the December 2012 mass shooting of 26 children and teachers at an elementary school in Newtown, Conn. Feinstein became the point person in the Democratic-controlled Senate for legislation even tougher than the 1994 law; it sought to ban assault weapons and high-capacity magazines. But Democratic leaders abandoned the proposal to focus on measures they hoped could draw more bipartisan support, such as expanding criminal background checks for gun purchases. After those proposals failed in the spring of 2013, Feinstein blamed the National Rifle Association for making colleagues afraid to vote on gun control legislation. In 2016, after the Orlando, Fla., nightclub shooting in which 49 people were killed, Feinstein tried again — sponsoring a measure to deny the sale of firearms to those in the federal government's terrorist screening database. The proposal was defeated on a largely party-line vote.

Feinstein became the Judiciary Committee's ranking member less than a month before President Donald Trump nominated federal appeals court Judge Neil Gorsuch to a Supreme Court seat that had been vacant for nearly a year after the death of Justice Antonin Scalia. In an interview with the San Francisco Chronicle before Gorsuch's confirmation hearings, she blasted Senate Republicans' refusal to grant appeals court Judge Merrick Garland, President Barack Obama's nominee for the vacancy, a hearing or vote throughout the last year of Obama's tenure as "appalling". "The humiliation that he went through," Feinstein said of Garland. "Asking people just to meet with him and getting turned down. ... Walking these halls day and night and getting the back of the Republican hand. Many of us haven't recovered from that."

Feinstein had opposed the two high court nominations of another Republican president, George W. Bush, a decade earlier. After an interview with Supreme Court nominee John Roberts in July 2005, she called him "very impressive" but voted against confirmation out of concern he might overturn the Roe v. Wade decision that protects women's access to abortions. She also opposed Samuel Alito's confirmation in early 2006; Bush had nominated Alito after his initial choice of White House counsel Harriet Miers ran into trouble, prompting Feinstein to say, "I don't believe they would have attacked a man the way she was attacked." As the Judiciary Committee's top Democrat, Feinstein also highlighted her concerns about Roe v. Wade's future when Gorsuch came before the panel in

March 2017. She called the 1973 decision "settled law," while noting Trump's campaign promise to appoint anti-abortion judges. Although Gorsuch had not ruled directly on abortion, "his writings do raise questions," Feinstein said.

But it was Feinstein's handling of Trump's next Supreme Court nominee, federal appeals court Judge Brett Kavanaugh, that generated rancor from the president and Senate Republican leaders — as well as some quiet grumbling among her Democratic colleagues. Shortly after Kavanaugh's nomination was announced in July 2018, Christine Blasey Ford approached her congresswoman, Democrat Anna Eshoo of California with sexual assault allegations against Kavanaugh dating back to the early 1980s. Blasey Ford initially insisted on confidentiality; her allegations were put in a letter that was forwarded to Feinstein in late July. The existence of the letter was first disclosed in mid-September by The Intercept, an online publication — shortly after Kavanaugh had testified at length during the committee's confirmation hearings. It was not until then that Feinstein provided the letter to other committee Democrats, who urged her to forward it to the FBI — which she did.

Feinstein denied she or anyone in her office had leaked the letter and defended not having brought it to light sooner. "Let me be clear: I did not hide Dr. Ford's letter. ... She asked me to keep it confidential, and I kept it confidential," she told the Judiciary Committee. She also told reporters she had been "looking for a way to get it investigated by an outside investigator" without violating Blasey Ford's confidentiality. But several of her Democratic colleagues were said to be upset at what they regarded as her clumsy handling of the matter from a political standpoint — as Republican argued the letter was an 11th-hour, desperate effort to derail Kavanaugh's nomination. "When Sen. Feinstein sat with Judge Kavanaugh for a long, long meeting, she had this letter," Trump told reporters. "Why didn't the Democrats bring it up then? Because they obstruct and because they resist." Senate Majority Leader Mitch McConnell said Feinstein "decided to spring it at the end."

The letter prompted a follow-up hearing at which Blasey Ford and Kavanaugh testified, after which Feinstein blasted Kavanaugh's "aggressive and belligerent" behavior. With several key senators undecided, Republican leaders agreed to a supplemental FBI investigation. It found no corroboration of the allegations by Blasey Ford or other women. Feinstein joined other Democrats in criticizing the scope of the FBI probe, which did not include interviews with Blasey Ford or Kavanaugh. "When he wasn't yelling and demeaning senators, he was making misleading statements that cast doubt on his overall trustworthiness," Feinstein said of Kavanaugh and his testimony at the follow-up hearing. "I don't think that would happen with FBI agents seated across the table." Kavanaugh was narrowly confirmed, with Trump using the controversy to fire up his base at rallies before the 2018 midterm elections. He targeted Feinstein, accusing her of "disgraceful behavior," as his supporters responded with chants of "lock her up" — the same war cry aimed at Hillary Clinton during Trump rallies two years earlier.

Before becoming the senior Democrat at the Judiciary panel, Feinstein chaired the Intelligence Committee from 2009 until Republicans retook the Senate in 2015. During the Bush administration, she took issue with other Democrats who claimed the USA Patriot Act — passed in the wake of 9/11 — had led to violations of civil liberties. During the second term of the Obama administration, when former National Security Agency contractor Edward Snowden leaked details of the NSA's domestic surveillance efforts, she accused Snowden of treason while taking the agency to task for being unable to prevent him from accessing so much highly classified material. She also defended the NSA's far-reaching covert collection of Americans' phone records.

The latter episode caused her approval ratings back home in California to plummet. Feinstein shrugged it off, telling the Los Angeles Times, "Numbers go down, numbers go up. I don't think people understand" the NSA's work. But in spring 2015, as debate raged over reauthorizing the Patriot Act, she backed ending the NSA's bulk collection of phone records — putting her in league with most Democrats and libertarian-leaning Republicans. She again took a hard line after the San Bernardino shooting rampage in late 2015, as the Justice Department sought access to an iPhone used by one of the shooters. She pushed a draft bill to give law enforcement a "back door" to encrypted communications, putting her at odds with technology firms and civil libertarians. With Trump in office, Feinstein was among a minority of Senate Democrats who in early 2018 joined most Republicans to support renewal of a key provision — Section 702 — of the Foreign Intelligence Surveillance Act, allowing the NSA to obtain communications of foreigners outside the United States without a warrant. Civil liberties advocates have complained it provides a loophole for warrantless surveillance of Americans.

As chairman of the Senate Rules and Administration Committee in 2009, Feinstein managed Obama's swearing-in. That was another first for a woman, as was Feinstein's assumption of the Intelligence panel chairmanship. "My view is that it's time for a new start. I want to see the Senate Intelligence Committee with much closer oversight and a much closer relationship with the intelligence community," she said. That relationship turned confrontational, as Feinstein questioned the rationale and effectiveness of waterboarding and other "enhanced interrogation techniques" on terrorist suspects following 9/11. She won nearly unanimous committee approval for an investigation into the CIA's interrogation tactics. In late 2012, it yielded a 6,700-page report. With the aim of making a 500-page "executive summary" public, the committee forwarded it to the White House for review.

To Feinstein's displeasure, the Obama White House turned the document over to the target of the probe — the CIA — for review. Tensions spilled into public view in the spring of 2014, when media reports appeared in which the CIA accused Senate staffers working on the investigation of hacking into the agency's computers. Feinstein, in a Senate floor speech, said it was the CIA that had removed classified documents from the committee staff's computers in the middle of the investigation. The CIA later apologized. In late 2014, the Intelligence Committee released the "torture report" slamming the "deeply flawed" Bush-era approach to the harsh interrogation methods used by the CIA on detainees. Vermont Sen. Patrick Leahy, who preceded Feinstein as the Judiciary panel's ranking Democrat, told Roll Call: "She was under enormous pressure to allow a cover-up. She didn't."

In March 2018, amid her latest re-election campaign, Feinstein took heat from her left when she described Deputy CIA Director Gina Haspel — Trump's then-nominee to head the agency — as a "good deputy director." Haspel had supervised a secret CIA prison in Thailand where detainees were subjected to the methods criticized in the 2014 report. As Feinstein declined to take a position on the nomination of Haspel to be the first woman to lead the CIA, her leading election opponent, former state Senate President Kevin de Leon, goaded her, telling The Hill: "Having released a torture report, Feinstein knows better than most how morally and legally wrong torture is. This should be an easy call." A week before the floor vote on Haspel, Feinstein announced she would oppose confirmation, saying, "For the Senate to confirm someone so involved with the [interrogation] program to the highest position at the CIA would in effect tell the world that we approve of what happened, and I absolutely do not."

The 2018 contest marked the first serious challenge Feinstein had confronted in a quarter of a century. Running for her first full term in the Republican-dominated year of 1994, she faced Rep. Michael Huffington, who spent $30 million of his own money. At the time, he was married to Arianna Huffington, who later founded HuffPost. Days before that election, it was revealed that Feinstein, despite earlier denials, had employed a woman whose work permit had expired. She won 47%-45%. In 2000, moderate GOP Rep. Tom Campbell challenged her. Feinstein greatly outspent him and won 56%-37%. In her 2006 and 2012, she defeated little-known opponents by margins of 59%-35% and 63%-37%, respectively.

Feinstein announced for a fifth full term in October 2017, but her political standing at home appeared tenuous. She was met with boos and audience members with signs reading "Retire Feinstein" at two town hall meetings in the spring of 2017. A month before announcing her candidacy, she encountered a firestorm of criticism after an appearance in San Francisco at which she counseled "some patience" over Trump's presidency — while expressing hope that the president would learn and change. Her comments spurred de Leon, term limited out of another run for his state Senate seat, into the race. And it set up a contest that reflected the broader debate over the direction of the Democratic Party.

"We don't owe Trump patience. We owe Californians resistance," de Leon told the Los Angeles Times. Feinstein responded, "Resistance to me means doing the best I can to serve people in the way we do. ... Now, I don't rant and rail because I've got other ways of being constructive, and I think the majority of people want me to be constructive." After the 2016 election, the California Democratic Party structure became dominated by progressives who found de Leon's definition of resistance closer to their own. At the state party's February 2018 convention, de Leon defeated Feinstein 54%-37% — albeit short of the 60 percent needed for an endorsement. But, in June's nonpartisan "blanket" primary, Feinstein finished far ahead. She took 44 percent of the vote; de Leon got 12 percent — setting up a November runoff. Four Republican candidates trailed, all polling in single digits.

Feinstein lined up endorsements from the party establishment — notably Obama, former Vice President Joe Biden and fellow San Franciscan House Democratic Leader Nancy Pelosi. Feinstein's personal wealth also came into play: She gave her campaign $3.7 million and loaned it another $8 million. She spent nearly $18 million by the time the campaign was over, seven times as much as de Leon. One-third of a century younger than Feinstein, de Leon didn't make age an issue. But he called attention to her long tenure in office, saying she was out of touch. "It's time to have a voice that's reflective of today's California, not the California of a quarter-century ago," he told Vox.

Public polls showed Feinstein with a double-digit lead and indicated much of de Leon's support came from Republicans looking to cast a vote against the incumbent. She won 54%-46%, in what likely was her final campaign. At 85, when she began her new term, she was the oldest senator.

Kamala Harris (D)

Elected 2016, term expires 2022, 1st term, b. Oct 24, 1964; Oakland; Howard University (DC), Bach. Deg.; University of California Hastings College of Law, J.D; Baptist; Married (Douglas Emhoff).

Elected Office: District Attorney, San Francisco, 2004-2011; CA Attorney General, 2011-2016

DC Office: 112 HSOB 20510, 202-224-3553, Fax: 202-224-2200, harris.senate.gov

State Offices: Fresno, 559-497-5109; Los Angeles, 213-894-5000; Sacramento, 916-448-2787; San Diego, 619-239-3884; San Francisco, 415-355-9041.

Committees: *Budget. Homeland Security & Government Affairs*: Federal Spending Oversight & Emergency Management; Investigations. *Intelligence. Judiciary*: Constitution; Subcommittee on Intellectual Property.

Group Ratings

	ADA	ACLU	AFL-CIO	LCV	ITI	COC	HAFA	ACU	CFG	FRC
2018	-	86%	-	100%	-	30%	8%	9%	19%	0%
2017	100%	C	100%	100%	C	29%	C	0%	4%	0%

Almanac Ratings 2017-18

	Economy	Social	Foreign	Composite
Liberal	91%	91%	85%	89%
Conservative	9%	9%	15%	11%

Key Votes of the 115th Congress

1. Obama-care revision	N	5. Gun regulations	N	9. Kavanaugh confirmation	N
2. Tax Cuts	N	6. Family planning regs	N	10. Saudi arms sales	Y
3. Dodd-Frank revision	N	7. Gorsuch confirmation	N	11. FISA rules	N
4. Omnibus appropriations	N	8. Immigration restrictions	N	12. Military aid in Yemen	Y

Election Results

Election	Name (Party)	Vote (%)		Cand. Spent	Ind. Exp. Support	Ind. Exp. Oppose
2016 General	Kamala Harris (D)	7,542,753	(62%)	$14,718,666	$1,512,017	$3,000
	Loretta Sanchez (D)	4,710,417	(38%)	$2,951,762	$104,488	
2016 Primary	Kamala Harris (D)	3,000,689	(40%)			
	Loretta Sanchez (D)	1,416,203	(19%)			
	Duf Sundheim (R)	584,251	(8%)			

Not long after she was first elected as San Francisco's district attorney in 2004, Kamala Harris raised money for a young Democratic state senator named Barack Obama, then embarking on a Senate campaign half a continent away in Illinois. Harris and Obama not only shared backgrounds as the children of multiracial marriages, they have shared career paths. "With an Indian mother and a Jamaican father, Harris strikes some observers as a California version of Barack Obama," the Los Angeles Times wrote in October 2004, a month before Obama was elected senator. In 2016, Harris herself won election to the Senate. And in January 2019, she announced her presidential candidacy after two high-profile, buzz-filled years on Capitol Hill — mirroring Obama's meteoric rise to the White House years earlier.

Whether or not the former California attorney general succeeds in following Obama into the nation's highest office, her election to the Senate was precedent-setting on many fronts. She became the first woman of color to be elected senator from California. Nationwide, she was the second African-American woman to serve in the Senate. And the election of Harris, who was born just months after passage of the Civil Rights Act of 1964, marked the first time three African-Americans had served simultaneously as senators. Such milestones aside, Harris — while targeting black voters, particularly the Democratic Party's key bloc of African-American women, as she announced her presidential bid — has at times expressed ambivalence about making racial issues central to her political persona. "I don't feel compelled to sing long ballads about my experiences with injustice," she told the Los Angeles Times in 2015.

But such experiences were part of Harris' upbringing, even in the left-leaning Northern California of the 1960s and 1970s. Her parents met as graduate students at the University of California, Berkeley. In the early 1970s, Harris' elementary school was only the second in Berkeley to integrate by use of busing. Her parents divorced when she was five, and Harris and her younger sister, Maya Harris, a senior policy adviser to Hillary Clinton's 2016 presidential bid and chairwoman of her sister's 2020 White House bid, visited their father, a Stanford University economics professor, on weekends. "The neighbors' kids were not allowed to play with us because we were black," Kamala Harris said years later. "In Palo Alto. The home of Google."

Harris spent her high school years in Montreal, where her mother worked as a breast cancer researcher affiliated with McGill University. She earned her undergraduate degree at Howard University in Washington, the nation's oldest historically black college, and interned in the office of California Democratic Sen. Alan Cranston. Harris returned to the Bay Area to earn a law degree at the University of California's Hastings College of Law. She took a job in the Alameda County district attorney's office, prosecuting crimes ranging from homicide and robbery to child sexual assault cases in Oakland. In 1998, she transferred to the San Francisco district attorney's office, before moving to the city attorney's office as head of its division on families and children.

Harris' 2016 Senate election was a breeze compared to her early outings in the electoral arena. In 2003, she challenged her onetime boss, San Francisco District Attorney Terence Hallinan. His office had come under criticism for low conviction rates and an outdated administrative operation. Fighting for his political life, Hallinan sought to link Harris to Willie Brown, a colorful and controversial figure then completing his final term as San Francisco's mayor. Harris dated Brown in the 1990s, when he was speaker of the California Assembly, and he had appointed her to a couple of state boards that added nearly $100,000 in annual compensation to her district attorney's office salary. Hallinan attacked Harris as part of "the old Willie Brown machine." Harris and Brown had stopped dating after he became mayor in 1996. In November 2003, Hallinan ran slightly ahead of Harris, 36%-34%, with the rest going to a third candidate. In a runoff a month later, Harris won 56%-44%.

Harris faced a political firestorm early in her first term, when, three days after the murder of a San Francisco police officer, Isaac Espinoza, she announced she would not seek the death penalty for the accused killer. At the time, Democratic Sen. Dianne Feinstein, now Harris' senior colleague, called for the death penalty in the case — and suggested she would not have backed Harris for district attorney if she had known Harris opposed capital punishment. Harris later conceded she had been "politically naive" to rule out the death penalty so soon after Espinoza's killing, but argued the killer's second-degree murder conviction and sentence of life without parole had justified her action. Republican strategists have suggested the episode would become fodder for attack ads if Harris becomes her party's 2020 presidential nominee.

After winning praise for being among the first district attorneys in the nation to emphasize alternatives to incarceration for drug-related offenses, Harris ran unopposed for a second term in 2007. However, as she prepared to run for the open state attorney general seat in 2010, Harris published a book titled "Smart On Crime" that, a decade later, attracted renewed interest — particularly from the Democratic Party's progressive wing — with her presidential bid. In the book, Harris voiced several views that broke with progressives' criminal justice reform agenda and downplayed racial bias in policing. "There is a widely held notion that poor communities, particularly poor African-American and Latino communities, consider law enforcement the enemy. ... In fact, the opposite is true. ... I can state categorically that economically poor people want and support law enforcement," she wrote in the book. She adopted a markedly different tone in her January 2019 presidential announcement speech. "Too many unarmed black men and women are killed in America," she said in the speech. "Too many black and brown Americans are being locked up. Our criminal justice system needs drastic repair."

In the attorney general contest, Harris dealt with another controversy from her tenure as district attorney: The theft of cocaine by a technician in San Francisco's police crime lab forced Harris to drop drug charges in nearly 1,300 cases, and a judge accused her office of hiding damaging information about the technician. Harris denied the charge, but her Republican opponent, Los Angeles District Attorney Steve Cooley, sought to use it against her — while going after her handling of the Espinoza-murder case. Harris criticized Cooley for saying he would go to court to defend "Proposition 8," a ban on same-sex marriage narrowly approved by voters in 2008. Final returns gave Harris a razor-thin victory, 46.1%-45.3%, making her the state's first female — and first African-American — attorney general.

One of her high-profile accomplishments was brokering a $25 billion settlement with several large mortgage institutions for improper foreclosure practices during the housing market crash — which, according to her office, yielded $18 billion in mortgage relief for California homeowners. After the settlement, Harris created a task force to prosecute mortgage and foreclosure fraud. She has since been dogged by criticism over failing to act against OneWest Bank — then headed by Steven Mnuchin, who would become Treasury secretary under President Donald Trump. The California Department of Justice found OneWest had participated in "widespread misconduct" in foreclosing on homes and recommended Harris file a civil enforcement action. In 2019, a Harris campaign spokesman told CNBC that Harris had limited authority to go after OneWest at the time. "Unfortunately, the law was squarely on their side and they were shielded from state subpoenas because they're a federal bank," the spokesman said. While Harris was the only Democratic Senate candidate to receive a donation from Mnuchin — $2,000 — during the 2016 election cycle, she later voted against his confirmation as Treasury secretary.

Harris' ties to Obama grew tighter during her tenures as district attorney and attorney general. She was the first elected official in California to endorse his candidacy in the race for the 2008 Democratic presidential nomination; as president, Obama got her a prime-time speaking role at the 2012 Democratic National Convention. He caused a stir at a 2013 San Francisco area fundraiser when he said: "She's brilliant and she's dedicated, she's tough. She also happens to be, by far, the best-looking attorney general in the country." The president later called Harris to apologize. A year later, Harris was mentioned as a possible replacement for U.S. Attorney General Eric Holder. But she was fighting a re-election campaign, which she won by a 15-point margin, and then disavowed interest in moving to the Obama administration. When Obama endorsed Harris' Senate candidacy in July 2016, her opponent, Democratic Rep. Loretta Sanchez, drew political blowback after she grumbled that Obama had backed Harris because they were both black.

Harris and Sanchez faced off in the 2016 general election thanks to California's "blanket" primary system, in which the top two vote-getters in the first round advance to a runoff, regardless of party. Harris had jumped into the Senate race after Sen. Barbara Boxer announced her retirement in January 2015 and emerged as the front-runner when two other leading Democrats — Lt. Gov. Gavin Newsom, who became governor in 2019, and former Los Angeles Mayor Antonio Villaraigosa — declined to run. Sanchez, hoping for a path to victory in a state that is nearly 40 percent Latino, entered the contest four months after Harris had. Harris won the endorsement of the California Democratic Party, and, in the June first-round primary, captured 40 percent of the vote in a 34-candidate field. Sanchez finished a distant second, taking 19 percent of the vote.

Although Sanchez started the general election against Harris lagging in both the polls and in fundraising, the matchup had several intriguing aspects. While featuring two women who were minority group members, it also marked the first high-profile contest between two candidates of the same party since the adoption of the state's blanket primary six years earlier. The candidates presented a contrast in style. Harris had been criticized as too cautious as attorney general, while Sanchez earned a shoot-from-the-hip reputation during her 20-year career in Congress.

While there was little ideological daylight between the two, Sanchez adjusted her pitch to attract Republicans and independents. She collected endorsements from GOP officeholders and went on a conservative radio talk show to tout her record against "Islamic extremists." Sanchez also tried to peel away some Democratic support by pointing to $6,000 in donations made by Trump, then the Republican presidential nominee, to Harris' 2014 attorney general re-election campaign. Harris gave the money to charity following disparaging remarks Trump made about Mexicans in 2015. When Sanchez sought to tie these donations to Harris' failure to open an investigation of Trump University after a 2010 federal class-action lawsuit against the company, Harris pointed to a $1.1 billion judgment her office had won against another large for-profit institution, Corinthian Colleges. Harris won 62%-38%.

On the Intelligence panel, Harris raised her national profile after less than six months in office. Utilizing the rapid-fire, aggressive style of questioning honed during a career as a prosecutor, she took on several high-ranking Trump administration officials who testified before the panel — most notably then-Attorney General Jeff Sessions, who was left rattled by her grilling about his dealings with Russian officials on behalf of the Trump campaign. "I am not able to be rushed this fast. It makes me nervous," Sessions told Harris during a June 2017 committee session. Amid GOP protests that Harris was interrupting Sessions and not allowing him to finish his answers, Intelligence Chairman Richard Burr intervened. "Sen. Harris, let him answer," the North Carolina Republican said. A week earlier, Burr had cut off Harris' questioning of Deputy Attorney General Rod Rosenstein, saying she was not allowing Rosenstein to finish his answers. It sparked suggestions of sexism. "Again, @SenKamalaHarris was doing her job," another Intelligence Committee member, Oregon Democratic Sen. Ron Wyden, asserted via Twitter. "She was interrupted for asking tough questions. I was not interrupted." Harris utilized the episode for fundraising purposes, telling potential donors via email: "Thank you for standing with me yesterday when the GOP tried to shut me down."

Such instances notwithstanding, Harris spent her first year in the Senate following the playbook of other recent freshman members who had been seen as presidential contenders as soon as they arrived on Capitol Hill: She turned down requests for interviews with national news media, while insisting she was focusing on the job to which she had been elected. Harris' initial votes established her as a member of what some of her colleagues referred to jokingly as the "2020 Caucus," as she was among the most aggressive senators on the Democratic side in opposing Trump administration appointments. As Senate Democrats defended more than two dozen seats in the 2018 midterm elections, she was among the hottest draws on the campaign circuit.

Harris sought to burnish her criminal justice reform credentials amid criticism from some progressives for several past positions — including sidestepping her stance on two sentencing reform ballot initiatives while she was attorney general. One, in 2012, modified California's "three strikes" law for repeat offenders in the case of nonviolent offenses; the other, in 2014, reduced certain nonviolent felonies to misdemeanors. Both were approved by wide margins; Harris said she had remained neutral because her office prepared the title and summary seen by voters, although this had not kept several of her predecessors from taking sides in similar battles. In mid-2017, she teamed up with a libertarian-leaning Republican Sen. Rand Paul of Kentucky on legislation aimed at encouraging states to replace money-based bail systems with individualized risk assessments. "A lot of what we're talking about is disparities in terms of how Americans are treated in the criminal justice system because of their wealth," Harris said of the bill. A year later, she co-sponsored a measure to legalize marijuana — another issue on which she previously had avoided a clear position.

Needled by the Los Angeles Times as "unwilling to stake out a position on controversial issues" during her tenure in state office, Harris showed little such reticence in the Senate. She was the first senator to sign on to the "Medicare for all" bill sponsored by Vermont Sen. Bernie Sanders and co-sponsored legislation for tuition-free college — another idea espoused by Sanders when he sought the party's 2016 presidential nomination. In early 2018, Harris was one of three Senate Democrats to vote against a bipartisan immigration bill. It provided a path to citizenship for immigrants brought to the country illegally as children — called "Dreamers" — but Harris objected to the $25 billion allotted for border security. According to Politico, her move angered Minority Leader Chuck Schumer and other Democrats looking to strike a long-elusive immigration deal with the White House but won her points from progressives. Harris later called for re-examining the Immigration and Custom Enforcement Agency "from the ground up" — prompting a White House twitter attack that she was giving comfort to transnational gangs. Harris shot back, accusing Trump of "ripping babies from their mothers," a reference to his policy that separated immigrant families at the southern border.

Still, Harris remained an object of suspicion among some party progressives for reasons ranging from her criminal justice record to what they considered a coziness with the party establishment — including her early endorsement of Clinton in 2016. But, as she launched her own presidential bid to generally positive reviews, polls found many Democratic voters lacked a clear view of Harris' background and for what she stood. "It's a challenge to maintain her true broader image and maintain her true broader base with the progressives," Democratic pollster Celinda Lake told the Los Angeles Times. "She has both. It's a bit of balancing act." And there is the matter of her complicated, sometimes contradictory record in public life. Democratic strategist Gillian Rosenberg Armour — a veteran of Obama's first presidential campaign — put it this way on CNBC: "How [Harris] frames her record is really going to be the deciding factor."

Doug LaMalfa (R)

Elected 2012, 4th term, b. Jul 02, 1960; Oroville; Butte College (CA), A.A., 1980; California Polytechnic State University, San Luis Obispo, B.S., 1982; Evangelical; Married (Jill LaMalfa); 4 children.

Elected Office: CA Assembly, 2002-2008; CA Senate, 2010-2012.

Professional Career: Manager family rice farm.

DC Office: 322 CHOB 20515, 202-225-3076, lamalfa.house.gov

State Offices: Auburn, 530-878-5035; Chico, 530-343-1000; Redding, 530-223-5898.

Committees: *Agriculture*: Biotechnology, Horticulture & Research; Conservation & Forestry (RMM). *Transportation & Infrastructure*: Highways & Transit; Railroads, Pipelines & Hazardous Materials; Water Resources & Environment.

Group Ratings

	ADA	ACLU	AFL-CIO	LCV	ITI	COC	HAFA	ACU	CFG	FRC
2018	-	4%	-	3%	-	75%	65%	71%	53%	100%
2017	0%	C	11%	0%	C	93%	C	85%	77%	100%

Almanac Ratings 2017-18

	Economy	Social	Foreign	Composite
Liberal	3%	6%	0%	3%
Conservative	97%	94%	100%	97%

Key Votes of the 115th Congress

1. Obama-care revision	Y	5. Family planning regs	Y	9. Guantanamo prisoners	N
2. Tax Cuts	Y	6. Body cameras/immigration	N	10. Ground missiles, limit	N
3. Omnibus appropriations	N	7. Abortion ban	Y	11. Defense Dept. spending	Y
4. Dodd-Frank revision	Y	8. Concealed carry	Y	12. FISA rules	Y

Election Results

Election	Name (Party)	Vote (%)		Cand. Spent	Ind. Exp. Support	Ind. Exp. Oppose
2018 General	Doug LaMalfa (R)	160,046	(55%)	$1,039,360	$155	$10,380
	Audry Denney (D)	131,548	(45%)	$1,084,846	$95,151	
2018 Primary	Doug LaMalfa (R)	98,354	(52%)			
	Audrey Denney (D)	34,121	(18%)			
	Jessica Holcombe (D)	22,306	(12%)			
	Marty Walters (D)	16,032	(8%)			
	Gregory Cheadle (R)	11,660	(6%)			

Prior winning percentages: 2016 (59%), 2014 (61%), 2012 (57%)

Republican Doug LaMalfa, elected in 2012 in this isolated district, has caused few ripples in Congress. His committee work has focused on local issues. With the shrinking of its Republican delegation, LaMalfa became more of a go-to resource for other rural interests in California.

LaMalfa hails from what he calls "the real California," a wide swath of rural country north of Sacramento. A fourth-generation rice farmer from Richvale in Butte County, he was born in Oroville and attended area schools. He later graduated with degrees in agriculture and business from California Polytechnic State University in San Luis Obispo. LaMalfa and his wife, Jill, operate in Richvale the farm his great-grandfather started in 1931.

He won election in 2002 to the state Assembly, where he spent six years, and was elected to the Senate in 2010. LaMalfa made his name in Sacramento by promoting agricultural interests and fighting new government spending and regulation. He sought unsuccessfully to freeze funding for the state's voter-approved high-speed rail project, citing its cost overruns. He opposed a state-level Dream Act proposal giving financial aid to children of illegal immigrants.

When he ran for Congress in 2012, LaMalfa became embroiled in controversy when it was discovered that a staffer had set up an anonymous website attacking his chief Republican rival, former state Sen. Sam Aanestad. The site, which criticized Aanestad's record in the Senate and questioned whether he was truly a dentist, was taken down. In the primary, LaMalfa came in first under California's all-party system, getting 38 percent of the vote. The second-highest vote getter was Democrat Jim Reed, an estate and tax attorney, with 25 percent. Aanestad finished third with 14 percent. LaMalfa amassed five times more money than Reed, with the largest sums coming from agricultural interests. Critics highlight the $4.7 million in federal agricultural subsidies he received for his family's rice farm. LaMalfa claimed the federal help was necessary for a small farm to comply with onerous federal regulations; rice farmers have long received sizable support. His 57%-43% win was in line with the recent presidential vote in the district. He won all 11 counties, but had only 51 percent in Butte — which had the largest turnout.

In the House, LaMalfa worked with neighboring Democratic Rep. John Garamendi to create a large new reservoir in Glenn and Colusa counties to serve northern California, paid for mostly with state funding. It would be twice as large as Folsom Lake, which has served much of the region. In November 2018, the Trump administration approved a $450 million loan for the Sites Reservoir project, which will build a tunnel to the existing reservoir. He worked on a Republican bill to assure that metropolitan water districts would receive all available water from the reservoir, but the measure was opposed by Democrats. On the farm bill that was enacted in 2018, LaMalfa took credit for provisions designed to prevent large fires in federal forests, including increased timber sales and accelerated salvage operations.

In 2014, LaMalfa was reelected 61%-39% over Heidi Hall, a conservation expert with the state's Department of Water Resources, who promised to "break through the bitter partisanship" in Washington. She spent $233,000 — not enough to be competitive in this sprawling district. LaMalfa increased his support in Butte County to 56 percent. In 2018, Democratic challenger Audrey Denney said that LaMalfa "isn't doing his job," given the high tariffs that local farmers were suffering. Denney, who taught agriculture at California State University, Chico, and was a first-time candidate, matched LaMalfa in spending, with $1.1 million each. The Chico Enterprise-Record newspaper endorsed Denney and said that LaMalfa was "a yes man for Trump." In his closest victory, LaMalfa won, 55%-45%. The challenger took the population centers of Butte and Nevada counties, with 54 and 55 percent of the vote; LaMalfa won the remaining nine counties.

Following the election, he responded to a Trump tweet that criticized forest management in California. Threats to federal funding were "not helpful," LaMalfa said.

CA-1: Northeast   Cook Partisan Voting Index: R+11

Population		Race and Ethnicity		Income	
Total	704,958	White	77.1%	Median Income	$48,524
Land area (sq. miles)	28,089	Black	1.5%	District Income Rank	333
Pop/ sq mi	25.1	Latino	13.4%	Poverty Rate	17.9%
Born in State	69.2%	Asian	2.7%	With health insurance	91.3%
		Two or more races	3.6%	Cash public assistance	3.7%
Age Groups		Other	1.7%	Food stamp/SNAP	10.5%
Under 18	20%				
18-34	22.1%	Education		Work	
35-64	37.9%	H.S grad or less	35.2%	White Collar	20%
Over 64	20%	Some college	40.8%	Sales and Service	45.2%
		College Degree, 4 yr	15.6%	Blue Collar	20.8%
Military		Post grad	8.4%	Government	18.4%
Veteran/ Active Duty	10.2%				

2012 Pres. Vote	Romney	171,902	(56%)	Obama	122,379	(40%)		
2016 Pres. Vote	Trump	176,358	(56%)	Clinton	114,727	(36%)	Johnson	14,110	(4%)
	Stein	7,501	(2%)					

Redding, Chico: Rising 14,000 feet over low foothills and the Central Valley, visible for 100 miles, is the snow-capped volcanic cone of Mount Shasta, one of a string of (supposedly) burnt-out volcanoes up and down the Pacific Coast. This is the far northern tier of California, where truck traffic on Interstate 5 is the only reminder of the choked metropolitan areas where most of the state's people live. This is lumber country mostly, where the mountains that rise on all sides — the Coast Range to the west, the Sierra Nevada to the east, the scattered mountains sealing off the Central Valley north of Redding — are thick with trees. It's rugged, flannel-shirt, two-lane-road country that was left behind economically when Los Angeles and San Francisco boomed after World War II. Since the 1980s, this northern end of California has been attracting people, mostly young families who come here to raise their children in a small-town environment, plus retirees looking for a calm atmosphere and low cost of living.

The 1st Congressional District of California is mountainous and mostly rural. It is the largest district in the state, with two major population areas. One is Redding, south of Mount Shasta, where increased high-altitude snowfall from Pacific Ocean moisture has allowed the Whitney Glacier to defy global warming trends by growing in the past century, the only glacier to do so. The second is farther south, at the edge of the Sierra foothills, around the Butte County communities of Paradise and Chico, home to a state university campus and Sierra Nevada Pale Ale, where the brewery is powered by a solar installation. Butte produces about 60 percent of the nation's almonds and 10 percent of the walnuts — a nearly $500 million business. President Barack Obama created local controversy when he issued an executive order that expanded the Cascade-Siskiyou National Monument, which is mostly across the border in Oregon. Interior Secretary Ryan Zinke reviewed options to scale back the expansion, but the Trump administration took no action before Zinke resigned in December 2018.

The area has suffered recent calamities. Following heavy rain and snow in 2017, the Oroville Dam, the tallest in the nation, developed a large hole that forced a shutdown of the spillway and resulted in $1.1 billion in repairs, including the equivalent of a new half-mile spillway. The incident resulted from poor design and maintenance; officials were hopeful about the long-term prospects for the dam. In November 2018, the area surrounding Paradise in Butte County suffered the most devastating wildfire in California history, including the loss of 86 lives and more than 14,000 homes. Officials were criticized for inadequate preparation, including the local evacuation plan. Pacific Gas and Electric was investigated for poor protection of its power equipment, which may have fueled what some called a "fire tornado."

The 1st District covers the northeast corner of California, sharing borders with Oregon and Nevada. Politically, it has a Democratic heritage but is culturally conservative and often angry at intrusions by urban environmentalists. Until 1980, the area elected rough-and-ready Democrats who pulled strings in Sacramento and Washington to build roads and dams. Since then, it has elected abstemious Republicans who have solidly conservative voting records and tend to local needs. The mountain areas have a stronger Republican lean. Butte and Nevada counties, which are on the southern border of the district, have nearly half of the population and they lean Democratic. Its 56 percent of the vote for Donald Trump in 2016 made this his second-best district in the state, behind the Bakersfield-based 23rd District.

Jared Huffman (D)

Elected 2012, 4th term, b. Feb 18, 1964; Independence, MO; University of California, Santa Barbara, B.A., 1986; Boston College Law School (MA), J.S.D., 1990; Protestant - Unspecified Christian; Married (Susan Huffman); 2 children.

Elected Office: Board member, Marin Municipal Water District, 1994- 2006; CA Assembly, 2006-2012.

Professional Career: Attorney, McCutchen, Doyle, Brown & Enersen, 1990-1992; Managing partner, Boyd, Huffman & Williams, 1992-1996; Managing partner, The Legal Solutions Group, 1996-2001; Sr. Attorney, Natural Resources Defense Cncl., 2001-2006.

DC Office: 1527 LHOB 20515, 202-225-5161, Fax: 202-225-5163, huffman.house.gov

State Offices: Eureka, 707-407-3585; Fort Bragg, 707-962-0933; Petaluma, 707-981-8967; San Rafael, 415-258-9657; Ukiah, 707-671-7449.

Committees: *Natural Resources*: Energy & Mineral Resources; National Parks, Forests & Public Lands; Water, Oceans & Wildlife (Chmn). *Select Committee on the Climate Crisis. Transportation & Infrastructure*: Highways & Transit; Water Resources & Environment.

Group Ratings

	ADA	ACLU	AFL-CIO	LCV	ITI	COC	HAFA	ACU	CFG	FRC
2018	-	93%	-	91%	-	45%	4%	8%	5%	0%
2017	100%	C	91%	100%	C	29%	C	4%	0%	0%

Almanac Ratings 2017-18

	Economy	Social	Foreign	Composite
Liberal	100%	98%	100%	99%
Conservative	0%	2%	0%	1%

Key Votes of the 115th Congress

1. Obama-care revision	N	5. Family planning regs	N	9. Guantanamo prisoners	Y
2. Tax Cuts	N	6. Body cameras/immigration	Y	10. Ground missiles, limit	Y
3. Omnibus appropriations	N	7. Abortion ban	N	11. Defense Dept. spending	N
4. Dodd-Frank revision	N	8. Concealed carry	N	12. FISA rules	N

Election Results

Election	Name (Party)	Vote (%)		Cand. Spent	Ind. Exp. Support	Ind. Exp. Oppose
2018 General	Jared Huffman (D)	243,081	(77%)	$503,441		
	Dale Mensing (R)	72,576	(23%)	$4,908		
2018 Primary	Jared Huffman (D)	144,005	(73%)			
	Dale Mensing (R)	41,607	(21%)			
	Andy Caffrey (D)	13,072	(7%)			

Prior winning percentages: 2016 (77%), 2014 (75%), 2012 (71%)

Democrat Jared Huffman, first elected in 2012, has joined activist lawmakers in the California delegation and beyond. With his deep interest and expertise on resource issues, he has taken a committee leadership position and has had policy impact with both partisan and bipartisan initiatives. With the Democratic takeover of the House, he chaired the powerful Natural Resources Subcommittee on Water, Oceans and Wildlife.

Huffman was born in former President Harry Truman's hometown of Independence Missouri. He attended the University of California, Santa Barbara, on a volleyball scholarship, later becoming a three-time NCAA All-American. Three years later, Huffman earned his law degree and went to work on antitrust litigation at a San Francisco-based firm before opening his own practice. His interest in student athletics led to his involvement in a variety of Title IX cases, including a landmark case in which California State University agreed to guarantee gender equity in its men's and women's athletic programs.

In 1994, Huffman ran for and won a position on the board of the Marin Municipal Water District, which led to a job as a senior attorney on water and fisheries issues with the Natural Resources Defense Council. In 2006, he defeated a 14-year Marin County supervisor in the primary and was elected to the state Assembly, with a focus on environmental policy. During his three terms, he helped block efforts by Republican Gov. Arnold Schwarzenegger to construct a $356 million death row complex at San Quentin.

When he ran for the House in 2012, Huffman had the support of Democratic leaders and a celebrity endorsement from Mickey Hart, former drummer for the Grateful Dead. In California's jungle primary, eight Democrats split the progressive vote. Huffman finished first with 37 percent. In the general election, he defeated Republican Daniel Roberts, 71%-29%.

Huffman quickly showed his activist stripes on the Natural Resources panel, with an initial focus on his district's diverse interests — including fishing and forestry. The House approved his bill to add Mendocino public lands to the California Coastal National Monument, and he worked with Republican Jamie Herrera Beutler of Washington on their bill to sustain Pacific coast fishing communities by reducing interest rates for groundfish fishing boats. Huffman spoke out regularly on climate change and raised options that might appeal to Republicans, such as energy efficiency and weather resiliency. With Democratic Rep. Jackie Speier, he filed disaster-relief legislation on behalf of California fishery workers and businesses.

On the Water, Power and Oceans Subcommittee, which handles local projects that are vital to many lawmakers, Huffman said he has sought to tackle "the complex natural resource issues that we face in a constructive, problem-solving manner." That included a bill he filed in July 2018 to increase protection of public lands in large parts of northwest California and assist local communities in guarding against wildfires. As vice-ranking member on Natural Resources in 2017-18, he used the position to combat "President Trump's radical agenda to expand dirty energy and undermine public health safeguards." Following the 2018 election, he promised increased oversight of the Trump administration and said that he would seek to block its program for offshore oil drilling, including areas off the California coast.

On the Transportation and Infrastructure panel, Huffman filed a bill to replace the 18.4 cents-per-gallon federal tax on gasoline with a carbon tax, which might average about 50 cents per gallon and be designed to finance highway and transit improvements. He has been active on issues outside his committee work. In 2016, the House passed his amendment to prohibit the Confederate battle flag from being flown at cemeteries run by the Veterans Affairs Department.

In November 2017, Huffman said he was a humanist and "I don't believe in God" — reportedly the second member of Congress ever to declare such a position. With Democratic Rep. Jamie Raskin of Maryland, he created the congressional Freethought Caucus. Its goals included "public policy formed on the basis of reason, science and moral values," and the promotion of the "secular character of our government by adhering to the strict constitutional principle of the separation of church and state."

He has won reelection with minimal major-party opposition. Following the 2018 election, the Marin Independent Journal wrote that Huffman plans to be a "lifer" in the House and that his ambition is to chair the Natural Resources Committee. He is well on his way.

CA-2: Coastal North   Cook Partisan Voting Index: D+22

Population		Race and Ethnicity		Income	
Total	717,270	White	71.3%	Median Income	$68,709
Land area (sq. miles)	12,952	Black	1.3%	District Income Rank	103
Pop/ sq mi	55.4	Latino	17.4%	Poverty Rate	12.7%
Born in State	59.5%	Asian	3.7%	With health insurance	91.9%
		Two or more races	3.7%	Cash public assistance	2.3%
Age Groups		Other	2.6%	Food stamp/SNAP	7.2%
Under 18	20%				
18-34	19.1%	**Education**		**Work**	
35-64	41.8%	H.S grad or less	27.8%	White Collar	19.1%
Over 64	19.1%	Some college	31.5%	Sales and Service	40.5%
		College Degree, 4 yr	24.5%	Blue Collar	16%
Military		Post grad	16.2%	Government	15.3%
Veteran/ Active Duty	7.6%				

2012 Pres. Vote	Obama	230,212	(69%)	Romney	89,908	(27%)			
2016 Pres. Vote	Clinton	238,157	(68%)	Trump	80,545	(23%)	Johnson	12,239	(4%)
	Stein	12,778	(4%)						

Marin, Sonoma: The North Coast of California is unlike any other place in America. It is the only part of the lower 48 states first settled by Russians, who built Fort Ross in 1812. They sold it in 1841 to a Swiss pioneer named John Augustus Sutter; a Sutter employee's discovery of gold near Sacramento seven years later started the Gold Rush. It is the only part of the world with large numbers of redwood trees, shooting up hundreds of feet in the drizzly air. It is wet country, and for years it was one of America's prime lumbering areas. Coastal Eureka and smaller lumber towns are filled with filigreed Victorian houses and old mills, but also art galleries, hiking trails, pubs and waterfront hotels.

Humboldt County is known for its quality marijuana fields, and the local economy relies heavily on the product. With about 35,000 pot growers along the North Coast, including 12,500 in Humboldt, the saturation of marijuana growers led to increased production and lower prices. Environmental groups have grown concerned about the impact on the region's salmon streams. Their farms consume enormous amounts of water while also spilling pesticides, fertilizers and other products into the Eel and Klamath rivers, which historically have produced large salmon harvests. The problem has been compounded by California's extended drought and wildfires, plus the influx of young people who can get good pay and are eager to join in the harvest — typically from September to November. The 2016 approval of the statewide referendum for recreational use of marijuana increased those challenges. Some experts believe that the weed industry in northern California eventually might rival the size of wine production. In Humboldt, that has moved the local industry toward "boutique" shops that cater to various tastes, but has resulted in competitive challenges from counties closer to the Bay Area that benefit from more rapid distribution, the Washington Post reported in March 2018. In Sonoma and Mendocino counties, the cannabis crop was badly damaged in 2017 by the area's massive wildfires.

The local seafood industry has suffered in recent years, due in part to warmer and more acidic ocean waters. With the decreased harvest, the price of Chinook salmon and Dungeness crab soared. Encouraged by local Democrats, President Barack Obama set aside some of these land and ocean areas in two large marine sanctuaries off the coast of Marin and Sonoma counties. That left NOAA with control of 350 miles off the California coast and the many species that thrive there. One variable for Humboldt: From 2011 until 2016, it annually had the largest earthquake in the nation. In 2017, it was overtaken by quakes in Montana and Idaho.

The 2nd Congressional District of California runs from the Oregon border in the northwest corner of the state down through Marin County to San Francisco Bay. It includes all the coastal counties of Del Norte, Humboldt, Mendocino and Marin, which are connected by Highway 101, and inland Trinity County. The North Coast lumbering area, from Mendocino north, was once filled with rough-hewn working men, and was historically Democratic. Now the focus is on sustainable forestry and the area remains heavily Democratic, but with more socially liberal views. The district takes in nearly half of Sonoma County, including Healdsburg, the Alexander Valley and Simi Winery, one of the oldest boutique wineries in the state. About 40 percent of the voters are in upscale Marin, which identifies more with the Bay Area than with the North Coast. Hillary Clinton won Marin County in 2016 with a huge 79 percent of the vote. Due to the rural vote, her overall 68%-23% was lower than her performance in several other Bay Area districts.

John Garamendi (D)

Elected 2009, 6th term, b. Jan 24, 1945; Camp Blanding, FL; University of California, Berkeley, B.A., 1966; Harvard Business School (MA), M.B.A., 1970; Christian Church; Married (Patricia Wilkinson Garamendi); 6 children; 10 grandchildren.

Elected Office: CA Assembly, 1974-1976; CA Senate, 1976-1990; CA state ins. commissioner, 1991-1994, 2002-2006; CA Lt. Governor, 2007-2009.

Professional Career: U.S. Peace Corps, Ethiopia, 1966-1968; Deputy Secretary, U.S. Department of Interior, 1995-1998.

DC Office: 2368 RHOB 20515, 202-225-1880, Fax: 202-225-5914, garamendi.house.gov

State Offices: Davis, 530-753-5301; Fairfield, 707-438-1822.

Committees: *Armed Services*: Readiness (Chmn); Strategic Forces. *Transportation & Infrastructure*: Coast Guard & Maritime Transportation; Economic Dev't, Public Buildings & Emergency Management; Highways & Transit; Water Resources & Environment.

Group Ratings

	ADA	ACLU	AFL-CIO	LCV	ITI	COC	HAFA	ACU	CFG	FRC
2018	-	75%	-	91%	-	58%	4%	9%	4%	0%
2017	90%	C	97%	94%	C	46%	C	0%	0%	0%

Almanac Ratings 2017-18

	Economy	Social	Foreign	Composite
Liberal	94%	92%	81%	89%
Conservative	6%	8%	19%	11%

Key Votes of the 115th Congress

1. Obama-care revision	N	5. Family planning regs	N	9. Guantanamo prisoners	Y
2. Tax Cuts	N	6. Body cameras/immigration	Y	10. Ground missiles, limit	Y
3. Omnibus appropriations	Y	7. Abortion ban	N	11. Defense Dept. spending	Y
4. Dodd-Frank revision	N	8. Concealed carry	N	12. FISA rules	Y

Election Results

Election	Name (Party)	Vote (%)		Cand. Spent	Ind. Exp. Support	Ind. Exp. Oppose
2018 General	John Garamendi (D)	134,875	(58%)	$819,089		
	Charlie Schaupp (R)	97,376	(42%)	$27,020		
2018 Primary	John Garamendi (D)	74,552	(54%)			
	Charlie Schaupp (R)	58,598	(42%)			

Prior winning percentages: 2016 (59%), 2014 (53%), 2012 (54%), 2010 (59%), 2009 special (53%)

John Garamendi is one of the House's most politically seasoned Democrats, with a public service career spanning more than 40 years. An active legislator, with committee interests in military and transportation issues, he has adjusted to redistricting changes in 2011 that made his district more competitive, but still safely Democratic. His experience has given him independence and an outspoken style.

Garamendi was raised on his family's cattle ranch in Calaveras County. At the University of California, Berkeley, he was an All-American offensive lineman in football and a competitive wrestler. After graduating, he joined the Peace Corps and served in Ethiopia, where his wife, Patti, also was a volunteer. The experience launched his career in public service. After returning to California, he won his first campaign in 1974 to the state Assembly. In 1976, he was elected to the state Senate, where he eventually became majority leader. During his career, he did two stints as the state's insurance commissioner and also was President Bill Clinton's deputy secretary of the Interior. He failed twice in bids to become governor of California. In the 2006 Democratic primary for lieutenant governor, Garamendi narrowly defeated Jackie Speier. He went on to beat Republican Tom McClintock in the general election. Garamendi was planning to seek an open seat for governor in 2010 when Ellen Tauscher resigned from the House in June 2009 to become President Barack Obama's undersecretary of State for arms control and international security.

In the jockeying before the special election in September, state Sen. Mark DeSaulnier was an early favorite and gained endorsements from prominent Democrats. DeSaulnier was better known locally. Garamendi, who had higher name identification from his statewide campaigns, was endorsed by Clinton and former Vice President Al Gore. In the September all-party primary, Garamendi prevailed among Democrats, with 26 percent to DeSaulnier's 18 percent. DeSaulnier later was elected to the House. In the runoff, Republican attorney David Harmer, though competitive financially, faced an uphill battle in a suburban San Francisco district that tilted Democratic. Garamendi embraced Obama's agenda while Harmer opposed the president and his bailouts of the financial and auto industries. Garamendi won 53%-43%.

In the House, Garamendi has been an ardent environmentalist. He was among the strongest critics of offshore oil drilling in the wake of the BP oil spill in the Gulf of Mexico, pressing for his proposal to bar new federal drilling leases off the coasts of California, Oregon and Washington. He was outspoken in opposing Democratic Gov. Jerry Brown's plan to build two 35-mile tunnels to pipe Sierra Nevada snowmelt to San Joaquin Valley farms and Southern California cities. He called the proposal "a boondoggle" for the benefit of wealthy farmers in the Southland and said that it "wouldn't create a drop of new water for the state and would serve only to reignite the California water wars." Brown failed to gain final state and federal approval before he retired in January 2019. Gov. Gavin Newsom has been less enthusiastic about the project.

On Transportation and Infrastructure, as the ranking minority member of the Coast Guard and Maritime Transportation Subcommittee, Garamendi sought to enhance farm and manufacturing exports. He had some Republican support for his bill to strengthen the maritime industry by requiring that a share of strategic energy exports be shipped on U.S.-flagged vessels, but the GOP-controlled House failed to act on the proposal. He helped win enactment in a broader water-resources bill of a measure to restore parts of the Lake Tahoe area. His Almanac vote ratings have placed him toward the center of the House in each of the three issue areas.

He has been a harsh critic of President Donald Trump, though they have had limited dealings. In broadcast interviews, Garamendi has said that Trump sees himself "as a dictator, as above the law," that "he has no empathy" and that his failure to respond to threats from Russia could amount to grounds for impeachment. With his increased seniority on the Armed Services Committee, where he chairs the Readiness Subcommittee, Garamendi has become more active on military issues.

California's independent redistricting commission in 2011 put Garamendi's residence in the newly redrawn 3rd District, where 77 percent of voters were new to him, making ripe for a GOP challenge in 2012. In the June primary, he got 51 percent of the vote, setting up a general election with Republican Kim Vann, a Colusa County supervisor. Vann sought to broaden her appeal by refusing to sign the Republicans' no-tax pledge and by embracing popular provisions in Obama's health care legislation. She ran a strong campaign and the U.S. Chamber of Commerce spent $600,000 on her behalf. But Garamendi won with 54 percent, precisely the district's vote for Obama.

In 2014, Garamendi faced another competitive reelection. He won the June "all-party" primary against Assemblyman Dan Logue with 53.5 percent of the vote. In the general election, Logue opposed a minimum-wage hike and comprehensive immigration reform. Garamendi supported both, plus high-speed rail for California. Garamendi had a fundraising advantage: $1.3 million to $800,000 and took got 52.7 percent of the total vote. With the weakening of Republicans in suburbs throughout California, Garamendi seems secure and likely to end his career in the House.

CA-3: North Central   **Cook Partisan Voting Index: D+5**

Population		Race and Ethnicity		Income	
Total	730,723	White	48%	Median Income	$61,268
Land area (sq. miles)	6,184	Black	5.9%	District Income Rank	164
Pop/ sq mi	118.2	Latino	29.5%	Poverty Rate	15.6%
Born in State	60.4%	Asian	11%	With health insurance	91.3%
		Two or more races	4.3%	Cash public assistance	3.8%
Age Groups		Other	1.4%	Food stamp/SNAP	10.4%
Under 18	23.7%				
18-34	26.3%	**Education**		**Work**	
35-64	36.6%	H.S grad or less	40%	White Collar	13.4%
Over 64	13.4%	Some college	35.3%	Sales and Service	41.7%
		College Degree, 4 yr	15.3%	Blue Collar	24.5%
Military		Post grad	9.4%	Government	21.4%
Veteran/ Active Duty	10.1%				

2012 Pres. Vote	Obama	131,237	(54%)	Romney	104,145	(43%)			
2016 Pres. Vote	Clinton	138,882	(52%)	Trump	105,860	(40%)	Johnson	11,300	(4%)

Western Sacramento Suburbs, Solano: In California's Central Valley, north and west of Sacramento, are the farm counties of Colusa, Sutter and Yuba. Marysville, the county seat of Yuba County, sits on the east bank of the Feather River. This heavily agricultural region includes locally cultivated rice hybrids from Colusa County, the leading rice-producing county in the nation. Sutter County is the nation's largest producer of prunes and the third-largest producer of walnuts. The local farm economy has suffered in recent years and Colusa County has lost thousands of farm jobs with scant recovery. In November 2018, its unemployment rate of 12.1 percent was second-highest in the state, behind Imperial County. Despite its high poverty rate, new residential development in Yolo made it the second (behind Merced) fastest-growing county in the state in 2017. Passage of a state water bond plus approval of a federal loan have been steps toward construction of the giant Sites Reservoir in Colusa.

Solano County, which is about midway between the Bay Area and Sacramento, has been thriving economically as an exurban commuter locale and styles itself as "a place of opportunity." The Yuba City area has one of the largest Sikh populations in the United States. In 2017, Preet Didbal became the first Sikh woman in the nation elected mayor. Davis is home to a branch of the University of

California, with an activist liberal faculty and student body. The university, with 37,000 students, has been ranked the best in the world for its veterinary and forensic science programs.

The 3rd Congressional District of California includes Republican-leaning areas like Colusa, Sutter and Yuba counties, along with a large portion of more Democratic Lake County closer to the wine country. Solano and adjacent Yolo counties, which include about 40 and 25 percent of the district respectively, are comfortably Democratic. To the west are Fairfield and Vacaville, on the outskirts of the Bay Area. Fairfield is home to Travis Air Force Base, which has more than 10,000 personnel and is home to the military's airlift and aerial refueling, including the KC-46A tanker. Politically, the rural counties have made the 3rd more competitive. In 2016, Hillary Clinton led in the district, 52%-40%.

Tom McClintock (R)

Elected 2008, 6th term, b. Jul 10, 1956; Bronxville, NY; University of California, Los Angeles, B.S., 1978; Baptist; Married (Lori McClintock); 2 children.

Elected Office: CA Assembly, 1982-1992, 1996-2000; CA Senate, 2000-2008.

Professional Career: Newspaper columnist, journalist, public policy analyst.

DC Office: 2312 RHOB 20515, 202-225-2511, Fax: 202-225-5444, mcclintock.house.gov

State Offices: Roseville, 916-786-5560.

Committees: *Judiciary*: Crime, Terrorism & Homeland Security; Immigration & Citizenship. *Natural Resources*: National Parks, Forests & Public Lands; Water, Oceans & Wildlife (RMM).

Group Ratings

	ADA	ACLU	AFL-CIO	LCV	ITI	COC	HAFA	ACU	CFG	FRC
2018	-	21%	-	6%	-	67%	96%	100%	97%	100%
2017	5%	C	8%	0%	C	93%	C	96%	83%	89%

Almanac Ratings 2017-18

	Economy	Social	Foreign	Composite
Liberal	7%	9%	9%	8%
Conservative	93%	91%	91%	92%

Key Votes of the 115th Congress

1. Obama-care revision	Y	5. Family planning regs	Y	9. Guantanamo prisoners	N
2. Tax Cuts	N	6. Body cameras/immigration	N	10. Ground missiles, limit	N
3. Omnibus appropriations	N	7. Abortion ban	Y	11. Defense Dept. spending	N
4. Dodd-Frank revision	Y	8. Concealed carry	Y	12. FISA rules	N

Election Results

Election	Name (Party)	Vote (%)		Cand. Spent	Ind. Exp. Support	Ind. Exp. Oppose
2018 General	Tom McClintock (R)	184,401	(54%)	$1,703,131	$15,000	$797,533
	Jessica Morse (D)	156,253	(46%)	$3,640,538	$160,575	
2018 Primary	Tom McClintock (R)	109,679	(52%)			
	Jessica Morse (D)	42,942	(20%)			
	Regina Bateson (D)	26,303	(12%)			
	Mitchell White (R)	14,433	(7%)			
	Roza Calderon (D)	13,621	(6%)			

Prior winning percentages: 2016 (63%), 2014 (60%), 2012 (61%), 2010 (61%), 2008 (50%)

Republican Tom McClintock, who was first elected in 2008, has been a conservative leader in California for decades, actively espousing his limited-government views in floor speeches, television interviews and op-ed columns. In contrast to tea party and other junior House Republicans, he has spent most of his career in public office and he often deliberately pursues a separate course from the self-styled outsiders. His legislative accomplishments have been limited.

McClintock spent his early childhood in White Plains New York. After graduating from the University of California, Los Angeles, he worked briefly as a political columnist and a state Senate aide before winning a seat in the California Assembly at age 26. From his earliest days in the legislature, McClintock was perhaps its most vocal, if not the most effective, budget hawk, railing against tax increases and high spending under Democratic and Republican administrations alike. Supporters saw an eloquent champion of conservative ideas, a policy wonk with a penchant for quoting Abraham Lincoln.

McClintock tested the limits of his statewide appeal in an increasingly liberal California through a relentless effort to win higher office. He ran for state controller in 1994 and again in 2002, narrowly losing each time. In 2006, he was unsuccessful as his party's nominee for lieutenant governor, even as Republican Gov. Arnold Schwarzenegger sailed to reelection. No race elevated McClintock's profile in the state as much as his quixotic campaign for governor in the 2003 recall election. As star-struck Republicans lined up behind former actor Schwarzenegger, McClintock forged ahead, presenting himself as the true Republican. He finished with 13 percent.

Opportunity struck again for McClintock in 2008. After Republican Rep. John Doolittle announced he would step down amid a federal probe of disgraced Republican lobbyist Jack Abramoff, McClintock ran in an intense primary against former Rep. Doug Ose, a Republican moderate who held the neighboring district seat from 1999 to 2005. Ose, who also lived outside the district, attacked McClintock as a career politician and carpetbagger who had represented the Thousand Oaks area in southern California during more than two decades in the Legislature. McClintock ran ads branding Ose as a liberal who had voted to raise taxes and had earmarked millions of dollars for federal projects in his district. McClintock won the primary 54%-39%. In the general election, McClintock faced Democrat Charlie Brown, a retired Air Force officer who renewed criticism of McClintock as an opportunist who didn't live in the district. In his unexpectedly close win of precisely 1,800 votes, 50.2%-49.8%, McClintock took six of the nine counties.

McClintock has been a faithful conservative vote, though an occasionally nettlesome one to House GOP leaders. He promised to eschew spending earmarks for his district and called for the earmarking process to be abolished. McClintock consistently filed amendments to slash funding, even when Republicans controlled the House. He joined Democratic Rep. Jared Huffman of California to win House passage of an amendment to strike a special-interest provision that required U.S. military bases in Europe to burn anthracite coal from Pennsylvania.

In January 2013, he was an outspoken foe of spending without offsets on disaster relief for victims in New Jersey and New York of Hurricane Sandy. In a clash with fellow conservatives in September 2015, a few days before Speaker John Boehner resigned, McClintock resigned from the House Freedom Caucus because its tactics "thwarted vital conservative policy objectives and unwittingly become Nancy Pelosi's tactical ally."

On the Natural Resources Committee, McClintock chaired the Water and Power Subcommittee for four years. He complained that about half of the state's water supply is consumed to meet various environmental regulations. In 2017, he filed a bill to streamline the process for federal approval of dams. Although the House did not act, McClintock lauded the Trump administration for its October 2018 executive action to prioritize expanded water storage in California. From 2015 to 2018, he chaired the Federal Lands Subcommittee, which has jurisdiction over national forests and parks. The House passed his bill to speed emergency timber salvage as a tool to reduce fire hazards on federal lands.

McClintock was 1 of 13 Republicans to vote against House passage of the tax-cut bill in December 2017. He reversed course on the final deal after he was satisfied with changes that expanded the availability of the deduction for state and local taxes. In May 2018, he ran for chairman of the Republican Study Committee, the longtime forum for House conservatives. He lost to first-term Rep. Mike Johnson of Louisiana.

McClintock faced an unusual election challenge in 2014, when his chief opponent was a moderate Republican who criticized McClintock as too conservative for his district. Art Moore, a West Point graduate who worked on intelligence issues as a consultant, complained about gridlock and dysfunction in Washington and said that competition was good for the GOP. McClintock dismissed Moore as a Democratic front. He outspent the challenger, $1.75 million to about $200,000. In the all-party primary, Moore trailed McClintock 56%-23%. In November, McClintock got 60 percent, nearly the same vote share as in his two previous election wins. In 2016, no Republican challenged McClintock and he breezed to reelection with his best-yet 63 percent of the vote.

In 2018, he faced his first well-financed Democratic challenger. Jessica Morse, a political newcomer and former State Department aide, called McClintock "a career politician" who followed the party line. McClintock said that Morse supported the liberal agenda, including "Medicare for all." Morse spent $3.6 million, twice as much as the incumbent. There was little outside money in the contest. McClintock won, 54%-46%, the closest victory of his career. In the population centers of Placer and El Dorado counties, he got 53 percent and 54 percent, respectively. Morse led in two small counties. The outcome suggested potential problems for McClintock, including redistricting uncertainties in the Sacramento area, which has four Democratic-held districts.

CA-4: East Central   Cook Partisan Voting Index: R+10

Population		Race and Ethnicity		Income	
Total	726,653	White	76.3%	Median Income	$72,371
Land area (sq. miles)	12,836	Black	1.2%	District Income Rank	78
Pop/ sq mi	56.6	Latino	13.2%	Poverty Rate	9.7%
Born in State	65.4%	Asian	4.9%	With health insurance	93.7%
		Two or more races	3.4%	Cash public assistance	2.4%
Age Groups		Other	1.1%	Food stamp/SNAP	6.1%
Under 18	21.1%				
18-34	17.9%	**Education**		**Work**	
35-64	41.2%	H.S grad or less	28.7%	White Collar	19.8%
Over 64	19.8%	Some college	38.6%	Sales and Service	43.3%
Military		College Degree, 4 yr	21.5%	Blue Collar	15.4%
Veteran/ Active Duty	10.1%	Post grad	11.3%	Government	16.6%

2012 Pres. Vote	Romney	195,388	(58%)	Obama	133,473	(40%)			
2016 Pres. Vote	Trump	190,924	(53%)	Clinton	138,790	(39%)	Johnson	17,650	(5%)

Northern Sacramento Suburbs, Madera: California sprang into existence with the Gold Rush of 1849. Statehood and the creation of the first 27 counties followed in 1850. The new state's first boom area was the Mother Lode Country in the foothills of the Sierra Nevada above Sacramento. Mining camps the size of Eastern cities grew up almost overnight in vacant valleys locked amid steep hills, with thousands of would-be millionaires gathered to find gold. Most of those who actually got rich did so by providing goods and services that catered to miners' needs. In Placerville, John Studebaker had a buggy shop, Philip Armour ran a butcher shop, and Mark Hopkins had a dry goods store. The biggest mine in California was in Grass Valley in 1857 and was worked for half a century. But long before that, most of the Mother Lode Country emptied out, leaving ghost towns and villages with hundreds of deserted houses, an antique vacation country left behind in time.

The area has been resurrected as a booming exurban and tourist mecca. Thousands of Californians — many of them families from smog-filled, middle-class suburbs of the Los Angeles Basin and the San Francisco Bay Area — went looking for a more pleasant, small-town, orderly environment and found it along fast-flowing creeks where the '49ers camped. Placer County, which includes Sacramento suburbs and part of the Mother Lode Country, grew 56 percent from 2000 to 2017, among the most rapid in California. It also ranks among its wealthiest counties. USA Today described the region this way: "The American River near Coloma becomes a virtual freeway of whooping rafters on summer weekends. The Mother Lode also offers modern-day prospectors an intriguing pastiche of bed-and-breakfast inns, musty antique stores and such blink-and-you'll-miss-'em outposts as Volcano, Fiddletown, and Rough and Ready."

The 4th Congressional District of California takes in the Mother Lode counties of Mariposa and Tuolumne and a large share of Yosemite National Park. The Mariposa Grove of giant sequoias reopened in June 2018 following a three-year environmentally friendly restoration project, the largest in its history. Placer County is the largest in the district. Many residents are concentrated in Sacramento suburbs like Roseville, which has grown 69 percent since 2000. Officials have approved the first phase of the plan by developers for more than 14,000 homes in Placers' Vineyards, a 5,230-acre planned community just west of Roseville, which will also include commercial centers, business parks and schools. A swath of the district also has a large elderly population. In Amador, Calaveras, and Tuolumne counties, senior citizens make up 25 percent of the population, twice the state average.

This has been the most solidly Republican district in northern California. The 4th was Mitt Romney's third-best district in California, when he won 58%-40%. In a warning for Republicans, Donald Trump slipped when he took the district, 53%-39%.

Mike Thompson (D)

Elected 1998, 11th term, b. Jan 24, 1951; St. Helena; California State University, Chico, B.A., 1982; California State University, Chico, M.A., 1996; Roman Catholic; Married (Janet Thompson); 2 children; 3 grandchildren.

Military Career: U.S. Army 1967-1973 (Vietnam)

Elected Office: CA Senate, 1990-1998.

Professional Career: Supervisor, Beringer Winery; CA Assembly fellow, 1982-1983; Chief of Staff, CA Assemblyman Lou Papan, 1984-1987; Chief of Staff, CA Assemblywoman Jackie Speier, 1987-1990; Owner, vineyard.

DC Office: 406 CHOB 20515, 202-225-3311, Fax: 202-225-4335, mikethompson.house.gov

State Offices: Napa, 707-226-9898; Santa Rosa, 707-542-7182; Vallejo, 707-645-1888.

Committees: *Ways & Means*: Health; Select Revenue Measures (Chmn).

Group Ratings

	ADA	ACLU	AFL-CIO	LCV	ITI	COC	HAFA	ACU	CFG	FRC
2018	-	75%	-	100%	-	50%	4%	4%	5%	0%
2017	90%	C	92%	94%	C	50%	C	4%	0%	0%

Almanac Ratings 2017-18

	Economy	Social	Foreign	Composite
Liberal	96%	94%	92%	94%
Conservative	4%	6%	8%	6%

Key Votes of the 115th Congress

1. Obama-care revision	N	5. Family planning regs	N
2. Tax Cuts	N	6. Body cameras/immigration	Y
3. Omnibus appropriations	N	7. Abortion ban	N
4. Dodd-Frank revision	N	8. Concealed carry	N

9. Guantanamo prisoners	Y
10. Ground missiles, limit	Y
11. Defense Dept. spending	N
12. FISA rules	Y

Election Results

Election	Name (Party)	Vote (%)	Cand. Spent	Ind. Exp. Support	Ind. Exp. Oppose
2018 General	Mike Thompson (D).......................... 205,860	(79%)	$1,564,326		
	Anthony Mills (I)............................. 55,158	(21%)			
2018 Primary	Mike Thompson (D)........................... 121,428	(79%)			
	Anthony Mills (D)............................. 13,538	(9%)			
	Nils Palsson (I).................................. 12,652	(8%)			

Prior winning percentages: 2016 (77%), 2014 (76%), 2012 (75%), 2010 (63%), 2008 (68%), 2006 (66%), 2004 (67%), 2002 (64%), 2000 (65%), 1998 (62%)

Democrat Mike Thompson, first elected in 1998, has a moderate voting record that has been among the least liberal of coastal Californians. When Democrats regained House control in 2019, he became chairman of the Ways and Means Subcommittee on Select Revenue Measures, which is the starting point for tax legislation. Thompson, who watches out for the interests of the wine industry, is a trusted ally of Speaker Nancy Pelosi and a major fundraiser for his party.

Thompson grew up in the Napa Valley town of St. Helena, dropped out of high school, served in the Army in Vietnam, and earned a Purple Heart. Later, he got a bachelor's and master's degree from what is now California State University, Chico. He owned a vineyard and worked as a maintenance supervisor for Beringer, a big winery in the valley. From 1984 to 1990, he was chief of staff to two Assembly members from the Bay Area. In 1990, he was elected to the state Senate, where he chaired the Budget Committee. In 1998, he ran for the House seat of Republican Frank Riggs, who planned to challenge Democratic Sen. Barbara Boxer that year. Thompson faced weak opposition and had support from almost every interest group that matters in the district: unions, medical providers, vintners, oil and timber interests, environmental advocates, law enforcement groups and fishermen. His issue stands — opposition to oil drilling off the California coast, support of abortion rights and the death penalty — were broadly popular. He won the primary 78%-22% and the general election 62%-33%.

As an active member of Ways and Means, he has been a proponent for the wine industry and other rural interests in California. He enacted a tax break for landowners who place their land under conservation easements, a way to preserve farmland. As co-chairman of the Congressional Wine Caucus, he has battled with allies of beer and alcohol wholesalers over a bill giving states new power to restrict sales over the internet. When a bipartisan group of lawmakers in 2011 introduced a bill to ensure state governments can continue to regulate alcohol under the 21st Amendment, Thompson warned, "the federal government has no business picking winners and losers in the wine, beer and distilled spirits industry." In 2016, he introduced a bipartisan bill to reduce the excise tax on sparkling wine to the rate charged for still wine. The Republican tax bill that was enacted in 2017, which Thompson opposed, included his provision to increase access to tax credit for large wineries, plus beer and liquor distributors. On another local farm issue, Thompson filed with neighboring Democratic Rep. Jared Huffman a bill to strengthen criminal penalties for illegal marijuana farms.

When he became chairman of the Select Revenue Measures Subcommittee, Thompson said his priorities included investigating the impact of Republican tax cuts, updating policies for infrastructure and renewable energy, and "standing up for communities devastated by disaster" -- a reference to constituents and communities in his district and elsewhere in northern California who have been devastated by wildfires.

Thompson has joined both the centrist New Democrats and the Blue Dog Coalition. He has agreed with Republicans on the need to abolish the estate tax, which he said unfairly burdens family farms. In 2016, the House passed his Small Business Health Care Relief Act to provide protections for tax benefits under health reimbursement arrangements, despite conflicts with the Affordable Care Act. The measure became part of the 21st Century Cures Act, which was enacted that year. As an advocate of the rights of airline passengers, he filed a bill that required airlines to provide basic necessities such as food, water and well-ventilated facilities when flights are delayed for long periods. The Obama administration issued a rule modeled after the legislation, and those provisions were included in a bill that reauthorized the Federal Aviation Administration.

He remains a reliable lieutenant for Pelosi. She tapped him to coordinate redistricting efforts for Democrats following the 2010 census. Following the deadly school massacre in Newtown Connecticut in December 2012, she named Thompson, a hunter and former chair of the Congressional Sportsmen's Caucus, to head a House Democratic task force to develop a response on gun issues. His proposals, which went nowhere in the Republican-controlled House, included steps to close the internet and gun-show loopholes in existing rules and expand background checks to all gun sales. On behalf of his bipartisan gun violence prevention task force in January 2019, he said that the Amerian public "demanded action to help end the tragedy of gun violence … and we will deliver." On Feb. 27, the House passed its broadest gun-control measure in a quarter-century on a largely party-line vote.

Thompson has been easily reelected and has been popular throughout the varied parts of his district. With Pelosi saying she will not serve as Speaker beyond 2022, Thompson faces a decision on whether to return with her to the West or keep his influential committee niche.

CA-5: Wine Country   Cook Partisan Voting Index: D+21

Population		Race and Ethnicity		Income	
Total	727,704	White	50%	Median Income	$71,526
Land area (sq. miles)	1,731	Black	6.1%	District Income Rank	83
Pop/ sq mi	420.4	Latino	27.9%	Poverty Rate	11.3%
Born in State	59.8%	Asian	10.8%	With health insurance	91.7%
		Two or more races	4%	Cash public assistance	2.7%
Age Groups		Other	1.2%	Food stamp/SNAP	7.6%
Under 18	20.9%				
18-34	22.7%	**Education**		**Work**	
35-64	40.1%	H.S grad or less	33.5%	White Collar	16.3%
Over 64	16.3%	Some college	35.4%	Sales and Service	44.1%
		College Degree, 4 yr	20.7%	Blue Collar	20.7%
Military		Post grad	10.3%	Government	14.1%
Veteran/ Active Duty	7.3%				

2012 Pres. Vote	Obama	199,924	(70%)	Romney	78,703	(27%)		
2016 Pres. Vote	Clinton	210,950	(68%)	Trump	74,088	(24%)	Johnson	11,171	(4%)
	Stein	7,681	(3%)					

Sonoma, Napa: In sunny valleys sealed off from the Coast Range, some of the nation's premium wine grapes are grown on ridges. Three decades ago, there were only 20 wineries in Napa Valley. Today there are several hundred, with more just west of the ridges in Sonoma County. The tourism industry in Sonoma County has had double-digit annual increases, with more marketing of the region to foreign tourists, including boutique hotels and high-end wine tastings. In Napa, the emphasis has turned from the vineyards to bottling and tourism; in 2014, more than two-thirds of the grapes used for wine were from outside the county. Olive trees are also grown here. Santa Rosa, wine country's largest city, is increasingly upscale and laborers have become hard-pressed to find housing. In October 2017, a horrendous wildfire was the most destructive ever to that time, with the loss of 3,000 homes in Santa Rosa and damage to the wineries — including from smoke.

Vallejo is named for a Mexican general and early member of the California Senate. From 1853 to 1996, the city was the site of the giant Mare Island Naval Shipyard, where 41,000 people worked during World War II. After the shipyard closed, Vallejo filed for bankruptcy in 2008, a dire turn of events also blamed on the huge public employee salaries and pensions the city was paying — 292 of 411 city workers earned more than $100,000 a year. Although it emerged from bankruptcy, the city retained huge pension costs. Since the crisis, Vallejo has become one of the hottest real-estate markets in the nation and a popular housing alternative for young professionals to the prohibitively expensive San Francisco. The Hub, a new art gallery and event space, attracts visitors. Commuters can take a one-hour ferry ride to the Embarcadero, instead of the two-hour commute during rush hour. Some of the shipyard's huge dry docks remain in operation for ship repair.

The 5th Congressional District includes all of Napa County and parts of Contra Costa, Lake, Vallejo-based Solano and Sonoma counties. Sonoma is the population center, with about 40 percent of the district, with another 20 percent each in Napa and Sonoma. All of these areas are heavily Democratic, more akin to the Bay Area than to farm country, and the district is unlikely to be competitive any time soon. Hillary Clinton in 2016 took the district, 69%-24%.

Doris Matsui (D)

Elected 2005, 7th full term, b. Sep 25, 1944; Poston, AZ; University of California, Berkeley, B.A., 1966; Methodist; Widow (Robert Matsui); 1 child ; 2 grandchildren.

Professional Career: Transition team, President-elect Bill Clinton, 1992-1993; Deputy Assistant to the President, deputy Director of public liaison, White House, 1993-1998; Lobbyist, 1998-2005.

DC Office: 2311 RHOB 20515, 202-225-7163, Fax: 202-225-0566, matsui.house.gov

State Offices: Sacramento, 916-498-5600.

Committees: *Energy & Commerce*: Communications & Technology; Consumer Protection & Commerce; Environment & Climate Change; Health.

Group Ratings

	ADA	ACLU	AFL-CIO	LCV	ITI	COC	HAFA	ACU	CFG	FRC
2018	-	89%	-	94%	-	50%	6%	4%	15%	0%
2017	90%	C	92%	100%	C	50%	C	4%	0%	0%

Almanac Ratings 2017-18

	Economy	Social	Foreign	Composite
Liberal	98%	98%	97%	98%
Conservative	2%	2%	3%	2%

Key Votes of the 115th Congress

1. Obama-care revision	N	5. Family planning regs	N	9. Guantanamo prisoners	Y
2. Tax Cuts	N	6. Body cameras/immigration	Y	10. Ground missiles, limit	Y
3. Omnibus appropriations	N	7. Abortion ban	N	11. Defense Dept. spending	N
4. Dodd-Frank revision	N	8. Concealed carry	N	12. FISA rules	N

Election Results

Election	Name (Party)	Vote (%)		Cand. Spent	Ind. Exp. Support	Ind. Exp. Oppose
2018 General	Doris Matsui (D)	162,411	(80%)	$874,719		
	Jrmar Jefferson (D)	39,528	(20%)			
2018 Primary	Doris Matsui (D)	99,789	(88%)			
	Jrmar Jefferson (D)	13,786	(12%)			

Prior winning percentages: 2016 (75%), 2014 (73%), 2012 (75%), 2010 (72%), 2008 (74%), 2006 (71%), 2005 special (68%)

Democrat Doris Matsui, after winning a special election in 2005 to replace her late husband, Robert Matsui, has matched his legislative prowess with a choice seat on the Energy and Commerce Committee, where she has had an impact on health and communications policy. Although she does not attract much attention, she has been skillful in identifying issues and building coalitions to address them.

Matsui, who was born in a Japanese internment camp in Arizona, was a well-known political figure during her husband's career in Congress. She grew up in Dinuba in Fresno County and graduated from the University of California, Berkeley. In Sacramento, she chaired the board of the local public television station and participated in many civic organizations. After working on Bill Clinton's presidential campaign, she joined his transition team and then served as deputy director of public liaison, where she worked on economic and budget issues. When she left the White House in 1998, she became a senior adviser at a Washington law firm.

Robert Matsui, who was a senior member of the Ways and Means Committee, died of complications from a rare blood disorder in January 2005, after serving 13 terms. A few days after his memorial services, Doris Matsui announced that she would run in the special election. None of Matsui's 10 opponents in the nonpartisan contest had significant political experience or name recognition. She emphasized her support for local water projects and her opposition to President George W. Bush's proposal for personal retirement accounts in Social Security. Some called the contest a "coronation," but the lack of competition surely reflected the respect the Matsuis had won over the years. She won the all-party primary with 68 percent of the vote to 9 percent for the runner-up. Since then, she has not faced a competitive major-party challenger.

With her seat on Energy and Commerce, she has taken the initiative on telecommunications and consumer issues. In 2015, she filed a bill that would ban companies from charging more for faster internet access. After Trump administration officials at the Federal Communications Commission overturned what had become "net neutrality" rules, Matsui sought to revive the earlier policy and reiterated her calls for "the free and open internet."

As co-chair of the Congressional Spectrum Caucus, Matsui has proposed steps for the next generation of broadband networks and she has enacted measures to facilitate the auction of parts of the federal spectrum. With Republican Rep. Brett Guthrie of Kentucky, who also serves on Energy and Commerce, she filed a bill in June 2018 that sets aside additional funds for agencies seeking to increase spectrum for commercial use.

She has filed legislation to remove roadblocks to health care technology. In 2016, Congress enacted legislation that she filed with Republican Rep. Mike Burgess of Texas: the Expanding Capacity for Health Outcomes (ECHO) Act, which was designed to use technology to provide expertise in community health centers and among other providers in underserved areas. Matsui has sought to expand the community-based mental health system, including her proposal for certified community behavioral health centers. With Guthrie in December 2018, she proposed more funding for awareness and early diagnosis of life-threatening sepsis.

On environmental issues, Matsui has co-chaired the Sustainable Energy and Environmental Coalition to address climate change. In response to train derailments, she urged federal regulators in 2015 to implement stronger safety rules for trains carrying oil. Matsui co-chaired the Congressional Caucus on Women's Issues, where she helped to enact the Human Trafficking Prevention, Intervention, and Recovery Act of 2015.

Matsui sometimes invokes her family's experience in internment camps to warn of potential civil liberties abuses. Following the election of Donald Trump, she criticized his call for restrictions on immigration from Muslim-majority countries. "Casting a shadow on everyone, not just individuals doing these bad things, is not the American way," she told The Sacramento Bee. "We are a nation of immigrants inviting people from all over the world." In January 2019, she called "unconscionable" a proposal from Trump to pay for the wall on the border with Mexico, in part, with funds that were set aside for flood protection in Sacramento. "These previously allocated funds should not be diverted to fulfill an unpopular campaign promise," Matsui said.

CA-6: Sacramento   Cook Partisan Voting Index: D+21

Population		Race and Ethnicity		Income	
Total	743,423	White	37.3%	Median Income	$51,479
Land area (sq. miles)	175	Black	12.2%	District Income Rank	278
Pop/ sq mi	4247.2	Latino	27.8%	Poverty Rate	21.2%
Born in State	59.8%	Asian	15.3%	With health insurance	90.3%
		Two or more races	5%	Cash public assistance	6.4%
Age Groups		Other	2.3%	Food stamp/SNAP	15.6%
Under 18	24.8%				
18-34	27.3%	**Education**		**Work**	
35-64	36.3%	H.S grad or less	39.7%	White Collar	11.6%
Over 64	11.6%	Some college	32.7%	Sales and Service	45.8%
		College Degree, 4 yr	18.1%	Blue Collar	18.5%
Military		Post grad	9.6%	Government	21.7%
Veteran/ Active Duty	6.3%				

2012 Pres. Vote	Obama	156,141	(69%)	Romney	63,862	(28%)		
2016 Pres. Vote	Clinton	168,687	(68%)	Trump	59,549	(24%)	Johnson	9,354	(4%)
	Stein	4,975	(2%)					

Sacramento: Sacramento, capital of the nation's most populous state and a vibrant metropolis with its 43-mile light-rail system, is no longer just a small city with a lot of civil servants and a vegetable-packing economy. Sacramento started as a port on the sluggish waters of the Sacramento and American rivers. It was the destination of many overland migrants, the site of Sutter's Fort, where workers for John Augustus Sutter found the gold that set off the Gold Rush of 1848, and the western terminus of the Pony Express in 1860. This was the natural choice at the time to be California's capital, halfway between San Francisco Bay and the Mother Lode Country in the foothills of the Sierras, and in the middle of California's vast valley. It has the corporate home of the world's largest almond processing plant, and agriculture continues to be important in Sacramento, or Sacto, as some locals call it. A prime local concern: The confluence of the two rivers and a growing population have made the area a major flood hazard. More than $2 billion has been spent on levees and other steps to reduce risk, though doubts remain. Next to New Orleans, Sacramento is the most vulnerable city in the nation to a catastrophic flood, The Washington Post reported in 2017.

In the old days, government was not a big business. Just a few lobbyists hung out in saloons on K or J streets, the governor's mansion was a musty antique, and the summers' 100-plus degree days emptied out what there was of the city. Air conditioning long ago replaced awnings, and freeways and shopping malls have followed the city's growth east and north toward the Sierra foothills. Platoons of lobbyists, lawyers and consultants set up permanent shop, and new hotels have been built to serve them. Today, more than 1,850 registered lobbyists prowl the halls of the capitol, transforming the once working-class bastion. In 2017, its 2.7 million people — an increase from about 800,000 in 1980 -- were about the same as metro Portland or San Antonio.

Most of the growth has been outside the city. Technology firms have moved east from Silicon Valley into the metro area, with Intel and Hewlett-Packard maintaining large campuses. Bay Area refugees have welcomed less expensive living standards. The growth has resumed in recent years, after it was temporarily slowed by housing shortages and the recession. In 2016, the 3 percent growth rate in the area was twice the national average. Local officials hope to make Sacramento the center for development of self-driving vehicles. In August 2017, they created the Autonomous Transportation Open Standards Lab, a public-private consortium.

The 6th Congressional District of California consists of the city of Sacramento, West Sacramento in Yolo County and parts of Sacramento County. The majority-minority district contains affluent neighborhoods and scattered low-income Latino and black neighborhoods, plus new condominiums north of the American River and middle-class subdivisions south of downtown. Its ethnically diverse communities include, among others, Hmong refugees from Laos, Vietnamese, Russians and Ukrainians. In contrast to the 7th District, which is a politically mixed area, this is the solidly Democratic part of greater Sacramento.

Ami Bera (D)

Elected 2012, 4th term, b. Mar 02, 1965; Los Angeles; University of California, Irvine, B.S., 1987; University of California, Irvine, M.D., 1991; Unitarian; Married (Janine Bera); 1 child.

Professional Career: Professor, University of CA Davis, 2004-2012, Association dean, 2004-2008; Chief med. officer, Sacramento County Department of Health & Human Services, 1999-2004; Med. Director, Mercy Healthcare Sacramento, 1998-1999; MedClinic Med. Group, physician, 1999, Assistant med. Director, 1997-1998, chief of internal med. Department, 1996-1997.

DC Office: 1727 LHOB 20515, 202-225-5716, Fax: 202-226-1298, bera.house.gov

State Offices: Sacramento, 916-635-0505.

Committees: *Foreign Affairs*: Asia, the Pacific & Nonproliferation; Oversight & Investigations (Chmn). *Science, Space & Technology*: Space & Aeronautics.

Group Ratings

	ADA	ACLU	AFL-CIO	LCV	ITI	COC	HAFA	ACU	CFG	FRC
2018	-	71%	-	91%	-	83%	6%	12%	13%	0%
2017	70%	C	89%	100%	C	71%	C	4%	0%	11%

Almanac Ratings 2017-18

	Economy	Social	Foreign	Composite
Liberal	83%	91%	62%	78%
Conservative	17%	9%	38%	22%

Key Votes of the 115th Congress

1. Obama-care revision	N	5. Family planning regs	N	9. Guantanamo prisoners	Y
2. Tax Cuts	N	6. Body cameras/immigration	Y	10. Ground missiles, limit	N
3. Omnibus appropriations	Y	7. Abortion ban	N	11. Defense Dept. spending	Y
4. Dodd-Frank revision	Y	8. Concealed carry	N	12. FISA rules	Y

Election Results

Election	Name (Party)	Vote (%)		Cand. Spent	Ind. Exp. Support	Ind. Exp. Oppose
2018 General	Ami Bera (D)	155,016	(55%)	$1,613,283	$10,000	
	Andrew Grant (R)	126,601	(45%)	$541,784	$11,145	$53,000
2018 Primary	Ami Bera (D)	84,776	(52%)			
	Andrew Grant (R)	51,221	(31%)			
	Yona Barash (R)	22,845	(14%)			

Prior winning percentages: 2016 (51%), 2014 (50%), 2012 (52%)

Democrat Ami Bera, after winning three consecutive tight contests since he was elected in 2012, had his first comfortable victory in 2018. A physician and medical administrator before he entered public office, he has been the rare Democrat in the large California delegation who occasionally has sought to separate himself from the party's mainstream, including the embrace of Speaker Nancy Pelosi. That may have limited his opportunities for advancement in the House.

Bera was born in Hollywood, the son of parents who emigrated from India to the United States in the 1950s to attend college. His mother studied education and became a public elementary school teacher; his father paid for his engineering degree by ushering at Los Angeles Dodgers baseball games. The younger Bera excelled in science and math, and went to the University of California, Irvine, to study biology and then earn his medical degree.

After several years practicing internal medicine, Bera became the medical director of care management for Mercy Healthcare Sacramento. There, he discovered inefficiency and set about identifying "simple solutions" to reduce waste. He became the county's chief medical officer and realized that the managers were unprepared to meet the demands of the uninsured, which became a top priority for Bera. He said that the Affordable Care Act "is not the direction I would have gone," but believes that the law offers a solid starting point to bring down spiraling costs.

In 2010, Bera challenged Rep. Dan Lungren, a Republican stalwart and former state attorney general. Bera was an impressive fundraiser, drawing donations from Indian Americans across the country. He accused Lungren of being out of touch with district voters, while the incumbent portrayed him as a rubber stamp for Pelosi's liberal agenda. Nearly $700,000 in late ads from GOP strategist Karl Rove's American Crossroads organization helped seal Lungren's win. Bera began almost immediately to make a second run in the post-redistricting district, which was three percentage points more Democratic. Bera benefited from a Sacramento Bee endorsement that said "Bera has matured, and Lungren has failed to meet local expectations." He won, 52%-48%.

Bera has been one of the California delegation's most moderate and politically attuned members. In 2014, he backed an unsuccessful version of the farm bill that cut $20 billion from the federal food stamp program. He described the vote as a signal of his willingness to compromise. Bera was one of 28 House Democrats who voted in 2015 for presidential authority to make international trade deals, which caused heartburn for many Democrats. Angry leaders of organized labor said they would not back Bera for reelection, to which he responded that he would not succumb to "bullying" tactics or "special-interest" groups. In 2017, Bera became co-chairman with Republican Rep. Tom Reed of New York of the bipartisan Problem Solvers Caucus, which he described as "a great way to get members from both sides of the aisle to focus on areas where we agree and can make progress." To reduce the complexity of Obamacare, he proposed making enrollment automatic. His Almanac vote ratings have placed Bera among the least liberal Democrats.

On the Foreign Affairs Committee, Bera worked to improve ties between India and Afghanistan. He accompanied President Barack Obama to India, where he praised the civilian nuclear agreement that was reached with Prime Minister Narenda Modi. Bera regularly spoke out against the Obama administration's contemplation of military action against Syria, preferring to let diplomacy work. In 2017, Bera became vice-ranking member of the Foreign Affairs panel. Still, he continued to buck his party, as 1 of 18 Democrats in July 2018 who voted for a proposal to support the Immigration and Customs Enforcement agency, though he said that his support was reluctant and the Republican resolution was "a partisan gimmick."

In his competitive district, Bera remained a top GOP campaign target. In 2014, he faced former Rep. Doug Ose, who served six years before abiding by his term-limits pledge to retire in 2004. This became the most expensive House campaign in the 2014 cycle. National Republican groups poured more than $6 million into the general election on Ose's behalf, while Democrats spent more than $5 million for Bera. Bera released an ad showing him with patients and touting his decision to forgo his salary during the 2013 government shutdown. In a contest that took several days to resolve, he eked out a win, 50.4%-49.6%.

In 2016, unions remained unhappy with Bera's support for Obama's Trans-Pacific Partnership trade deal, but they failed to find a primary challenger. Republicans cleared the field for Sacramento County Sheriff Scott Jones, who was attacked by Democrats over decade-old allegations that he sexually harassed a young woman who was a deputy sheriff, which he denied. Bera faced his own ethical problems after his 83-year-old father in May 2016 pleaded guilty to election fraud in the financing of his son's first two campaigns and was sentenced to a year in prison. Bera said that his father made "a grave mistake" and prosecutors said that they had no evidence that he knew of his father's actions, but Jones and other Republicans challenged those assertions. Bera out-raised Jones, $4.3 million to $1.3 million, but Republicans had the advantage in party support, roughly $5 million to $4 million. Jones conceded 10 days following Election Day, after late-counted votes gave Bera a 51.2%-48.8% win.

Bera's reelection in 2018 was comparatively easy. Against Andrew Grant, a former Marine intelligence officer, he spent three times as much money and the contest received little attention. Bera won, 55%-45%. Following the election, Bera remained non-committal on whether he would support Pelosi for Speaker and he attended meetings with House members who were her critics. With the Problems Solvers Caucus, he pushed for House rules changes. Pelosi eventually supported a modified version and Bera voted to return her as Speaker. His caution caused tension with many of his California colleagues, who have enthusiastically backed her. In the majority, Bera became chairman of the Foreign Affairs Subcommittee on Oversight and Investigations.

CA-7: Sacramento   **Cook Partisan Voting Index: D+3**

Population		Race and Ethnicity		Income	
Total	739,746	White	53.7%	Median Income	$69,964
Land area (sq. miles)	549	Black	7%	District Income Rank	95
Pop/ sq mi	1348.3	Latino	17.4%	Poverty Rate	12.2%
Born in State	60.8%	Asian	15.3%	With health insurance	93%
		Two or more races	5.3%	Cash public assistance	4.1%
Age Groups		Other	1.4%	Food stamp/SNAP	8.8%
Under 18	23.7%				
18-34	21.9%	**Education**		**Work**	
35-64	40.1%	H.S grad or less	30.5%	White Collar	14.3%
Over 64	14.3%	Some college	36.4%	Sales and Service	43%
		College Degree, 4 yr	21.9%	Blue Collar	15.3%
Military		Post grad	11.1%	Government	21.3%
Veteran/ Active Duty	8.2%				

2012 Pres. Vote	Obama	145,147	(51%)	Romney	133,888	(47%)			
2016 Pres. Vote	Clinton	159,066	(52%)	Trump	124,249	(40%)	Johnson	14,747	(5%)

Eastern Sacramento Suburbs: Until recently, Sacramento was chiefly the metropolis of a fertile valley that produced a marvelous variety of crops: rice, plums, almonds, olives, asparagus, pears, hops, beans, celery, onions and potatoes, plus caviar-yielding sturgeon in pools of filtered water. The farmlands remain, and the capital city flourished as a center of government. Greater Sacramento has been one of the fastest-growing metro areas in the country. Almost all the growth was away from the floodplain of the Sacramento River, in the higher land east of the city that eventually turns into hills rising toward the Sierra Nevada. After home sales plunged in 2007, the county's housing market has rebounded.

Still, the county has a high rate of income inequality. Across the American River in Fair Oaks, Gov. Gavin Newsom moved his family into a $3.7 million mansion after he took office. In Arden-Arcade, pockets of poverty remain; the poverty rate jumped from 20 percent in 2015 to 28 percent in 2016, the largest increase in the state. California Northstate University, a private institution, planned to open by 2024 a teaching hospital and medical center in rapidly growing Elk Grove.

The 7th Congressional District of California includes suburban Sacramento and much of Sacramento County outside the mostly urban 6th District. All of its residents are in Sacramento County. There is the old town of Folsom, where the Intel campus — the largest tech site in the area -- had about 6,000 employees in 2018. Intel calls the research lab its "nerve center," where engineers develop its core intellectual property. The company's chips once dominated the market, but the decline in the share of personal computers and laptops in the world led Intel to shift some of its production to semiconductors. With its high pay scale for engineers, the prosperous company town has moved beyond the image singer Johnny Cash created in his song, Folsom Prison Blues — though, in his honor, the city opened in 2017 the 2.5 mile Johnny Cash Trail, which runs along the prison property. The city of Sacramento historically has been Democratic. Sacramento County, with its rapid growth, has been marginal. In the 2004 presidential race, Democrat John Kerry won the county over George W. Bush by just 1,118 votes. By 2016, the Democratic advantage had grown to 59%-35% for Hillary Clinton. With the more conservative parts of the county in the 7th, Clinton took the district, 52%-40%.

Paul Cook (R)

Elected 2012, 4th term, b. Mar 03, 1943; Meriden, CT; Southern Connecticut State University, B.S., 1966; California State University, San Bernardino, M.P.A., 1996; University of California, Riverside, M.A., 2000; Roman Catholic; Married (Jeannie Cook); 2 children.

Military Career: U.S. Marine Corps 1966-1992 (Vietnam)

Elected Office: CA Assembly, 2006-2012; Yucca Valley Town Council, Yucca Valley Mayor, 1998-2006.

Professional Career: Professor, U of CA Riverside, 2002-2012; Assistant Professional, Copper Mountain College, 1998-2002; Executive Director, Yucca Valley Chamber of Commerce, 1993-1994.

DC Office: 1027 LHOB 20515, 202-225-5861, Fax: 202-225-6498, cook.house.gov

State Offices: Apple Valley, 760-247-1815; Yucaipa, 909-797-4900.

Committees: *Armed Services*: Seapower & Projection Forces; Tactical Air & Land Forces. *Natural Resources*: Indigenous Peoples of the United States (RMM); National Parks, Forests & Public Lands.

Group Ratings

	ADA	ACLU	AFL-CIO	LCV	ITI	COC	HAFA	ACU	CFG	FRC
2018	-	7%	-	0%	-	83%	43%	72%	54%	100%
2017	0%	C	32%	3%	C	93%	C	59%	48%	89%

Almanac Ratings 2017-18

	Economy	Social	Foreign	Composite
Liberal	8%	12%	5%	9%
Conservative	92%	88%	95%	91%

Key Votes of the 115th Congress

1. Obama-care revision	Y	5. Family planning regs	Y	9. Guantanamo prisoners	N
2. Tax Cuts	Y	6. Body cameras/immigration	N	10. Ground missiles, limit	N
3. Omnibus appropriations	Y	7. Abortion ban	Y	11. Defense Dept. spending	Y
4. Dodd-Frank revision	Y	8. Concealed carry	Y	12. FISA rules	Y

Election Results

Election	Name (Party)	Vote (%)		Cand. Spent	Ind. Exp. Support	Ind. Exp. Oppose
2018 General	Paul Cook (R)..................................... 102,415	(60%)		$1,390,585	$26,598	$7,500
	Tim Donnelly (R)................................. 68,370	(40%)				$8,000
2018 Primary	Paul Cook (R)..................................... 44,482	(41%)				
	Tim Donnelly (R)................................. 24,933	(23%)				
	Marjorie Marge Doyle (D)............ 23,675	(22%)				
	Rita Ramirez (D)................................. 10,990	(10%)				

Prior winning percentages: 2016 (62%), 2014 (68%), 2012 (57%)

Republican Paul Cook, a 26-year Marine Corps veteran and Vietnam-era war hero, won this seat in 2012 at the age of 69. He became a diligent and policy-focused lawmaker on national defense and natural resources, and one of the least publicity-minded in the House GOP. His military and community backgrounds make him a throwback to an era when many Republicans styled themselves as representative of Main Street and were reliable supporters of party leaders.

Cook grew up and attended school in Meriden Connecticut. He studied education at Southern Connecticut State University and joined the Marines after graduating. His first assignment sent him to Vietnam, where he served as an infantry officer and platoon commander. During the war, he received the Bronze Star and two Purple Heart citations. He returned to the United States in 1968, eventually earning a promotion to captain while training infantry in North Carolina. He rose through the ranks and, as a colonel, became the area commander for the Marine base at Camp Pendleton in California.

After he retired from the military in 1992, Cook moved to Yucca Valley and was executive director of the local Chamber of Commerce before heading back to school to earn degrees in public administration and political science. He taught political science and history at several California universities before earning tenure at Copper Mountain College, which has a close relationship with the local Marine base.

Cook won a seat on the Yucca Valley Town Council and ultimately served as the town's mayor. In 2006, he was elected to the state Assembly after defeating better-known candidates. As chairman of the Assembly's Veterans Affairs Committee (while serving in the minority party), he worked on issues related to retirement homes, child custody, higher education and other services for veterans. He also worked to protect children from sexual predators, a legislative accomplishment of which he said he is particularly proud.

In his race for Congress, Cook enjoyed the support of a host of California Republicans and the U.S. Chamber of Commerce. In a crowded field of 13 candidates, Cook trailed a tea party candidate, Gregg Imus, in the primary by just 237 votes; he was 240 votes ahead of third-place finisher Phil Liberatore, who also was a Republican. Cook picked up momentum in the general-election campaign, outspending Imus more than 5-to-1. He ran on promises not to raise taxes and to fight for veterans and military families, while distancing himself from Democrats. Under California's all-party primary system, Cook defeated his fellow Republican, 57%-43%.

With his natural base on the Armed Services Committee, he has focused on national security and has mostly been a Pentagon loyalist. In the defense spending bill that Congress enacted in 2018, he took credit for an amendment to increase domestic production of the nation's strategic and critical minerals, which are key ingredients for military technology. He added prohibitions on the acquisition of these materials by China, Russia, Iran and North Korea.

Cook has focused on overseas policies. In 2014, he wrote in a column in the San Bernardino Sun that the Obama administration had "faltered in our commitment to Iraq," and he called for military action against the Islamic State in Iraq and Syria by arming proxy groups, but not with U.S. troops. In October 2017, Cook filled the vacancy to become chairman of the Foreign Affairs Subcommittee on the Western Hemisphere. Six months later, Cook wrote in the Miami Herald that President Barack Obama had made "unwarranted concessions" to the Castro regime in Cuba and that the Cuban people had only "rubber-stamped" the Communist Party's list of candidates for the National Assembly; he called on the Trump administration to reimpose restrictions on the regime in Cuba. He added to the defense authorization bill a provision for a more strategic approach by the U.S. military in South America.

On the Natural Resources Committee, Cook won House passage in 2016 of his bill to establish the Alabama Hill National Scenic Area on the eastern slope of the Sierra Nevada in Inyo County.

In 2018, he worked on an innovative proposal to enhance conservation and off-road recreation in the California desert with the creation of six "off-highway vehicle recreation areas," which would total 300,000 acres. Cook called it "one of the most significant pieces of conservation and recreation legislation in decades." In November 2018, the House on a voice vote passed the proposal, which has attracted Democratic cosponsors from California in the House and Senate. Environmental groups objected to the amount of land set aside. In 2019, he became ranking Republican on the Subcommittee for Indigenous Peoples.

Cook twice breezed to reelection against weakly funded Democrats. In 2018, he again faced a tea party Republican in the runoff. Tim Donnelly, a former state assemblyman, said he was the candidate of Trump supporters, though President Donald Trump endorsed Cook. With $1.4 million, Cook outspent Donnelly 5-to-1; he won in November, 60%-40%.

CA-8: High Desert   Cook Partisan Voting Index: R+9

Population		Race and Ethnicity		Income	
Total	719,950	White	45.4%	Median Income	$50,051
Land area (sq. miles)	32,867	Black	7.4%	District Income Rank	312
Pop/ sq mi	21.9	Latino	40.2%	Poverty Rate	20.6%
Born in State	65.7%	Asian	3%	With health insurance	90.1%
		Two or more races	2.7%	Cash public assistance	6.4%
Age Groups		Other	1.4%	Food stamp/SNAP	18%
Under 18	27.7%				
18-34	23.5%	**Education**		**Work**	
35-64	35.9%	H.S grad or less	46.1%	White Collar	12.9%
Over 64	12.9%	Some college	37.5%	Sales and Service	45.8%
		College Degree, 4 yr	10.1%	Blue Collar	25.6%
Military		Post grad	6.3%	Government	19.8%
Veteran/ Active Duty	10.8%				

2012 Pres. Vote	Romney	118,278	(56%)	Obama	88,579	(42%)			
2016 Pres. Vote	Trump	127,471	(54%)	Clinton	92,238	(39%)	Johnson	8,210	(4%)

San Bernardino County: The eastern High Desert of California runs along the Nevada border, with a huge swath of land uninhabited for dozens of miles. In the west are the towns of Apple Valley and Victorville, a high-growth area that was once home to cowboy stars Roy Rogers and Dale Evans. Other San Bernardino County cities and towns dot the landscape: the heavily Hispanic city of Adelanto; Hesperia, a wayside on the Mormon Trail; and Needles, where the fictional Joad family stops soon after entering California in The Grapes of Wrath. To the north, off Interstate 15 heading to Las Vegas, are Barstow and the military training center at Fort Irwin. A fork splits Interstates 15 and 40, and both highways straddle the outskirts of the Mojave National Preserve before moving into Nevada. In Victorville, which is at the entrance to the desert, a fierce wind in April 2018 resulted in a destructive invasion of tumbleweed. A private company announced that it will start train service from Victorville to Las Vegas by 2022; it plans to extend that service to the Los Angeles area. San Bernardino has the most land of any county in the nation, but more than 80 percent of it is publicly owned.

The 8th Congressional District of California covers Mono and Inyo counties, as well as the rural parts of San Bernardino County; more than 90 percent of the population is in San Bernardino. The 8th does not include the city of San Bernardino, which accounts for only 10 percent of the county's 2.2 million population. Its geography is vast. It sweeps in the sleepy Mojave Desert and mountains, Death Valley (where the International Dark-Sky Association laments the visibility of lights from Las Vegas), and Owens Valley, the source of Los Angeles' water supply and the site of the California "Water Wars" that became the inspiration for the movie Chinatown. In July 2018, Death Valley reached a temperature of 127 degrees and recorded an average for the month of 108 degrees, the hottest month ever measured on the planet. The district includes Mammoth Lakes and the Mammoth ski resort area in the Inyo National Forest, where more than 40 feet of snow fell during the winter of 2016-17. Despite pockets of Democratic support, this is strong Republican territory. Donald Trump won the district, 55%-40%.

Jerry McNerney (D)

Elected 2006, 7th term, b. Jun 18, 1951; Albuquerque, NM; St. Joseph's Military Academy (KS); U.S. Military Academy (NY), Att., 1971; University of New Mexico, B.S., 1973; University of New Mexico, M.S., 1975; University of New Mexico, Ph.D., 1981; Roman Catholic; Married (Mary McNerney); 3 children.

Professional Career: National security contractor, Sandia National Labs., 1979-1985; Engineer, U.S. Windpower Kenetech, 1985-1994; Energy consultant, 1994-1999; CEO, start-up wind turbine manufacturer, 2000-2006.

DC Office: 2265 RHOB 20515, 202-225-1947, Fax: 202-225-4060, mcnerney.house.gov

State Offices: Antioch, 925-754-0716; Stockton, 209-476-8552.

Committees: *Energy & Commerce*: Communications & Technology; Consumer Protection & Commerce; Energy; Environment & Climate Change. *Science, Space & Technology*: Energy.

Group Ratings

	ADA	ACLU	AFL-CIO	LCV	ITI	COC	HAFA	ACU	CFG	FRC
2018	-	88%	-	91%	-	50%	2%	12%	5%	0%
2017	90%	C	97%	97%	C	57%	C	0%	0%	11%

Almanac Ratings 2017-18

	Economy	Social	Foreign	Composite
Liberal	94%	97%	88%	93%
Conservative	6%	4%	12%	7%

Key Votes of the 115th Congress

1. Obama-care revision	N	5. Family planning regs	N	9. Guantanamo prisoners	Y
2. Tax Cuts	N	6. Body cameras/immigration	Y	10. Ground missiles, limit	Y
3. Omnibus appropriations	N	7. Abortion ban	N	11. Defense Dept. spending	Y
4. Dodd-Frank revision	N	8. Concealed carry	N	12. FISA rules	NV

Election Results

Election	Name (Party)	Vote (%)		Cand. Spent	Ind. Exp. Support	Ind. Exp. Oppose
2018 General	Jerry McNerney (D)	113,414	(56%)	$1,100,689		
	Marla Livengood (R)	87,349	(44%)		$95,369	
2018 Primary	Jerry McNerney (D)	55,923	(53%)			
	Marla Livengood (R)	43,242	(41%)			
	Mike Tsarnas (A)	6,038	(6%)			

Prior winning percentages: 2016 (57%), 2014 (52%), 2012 (56%), 2010 (48%), 2008 (55%), 2006 (53%)

Democrat Jerry McNerney has settled into a district that is not fully hospitable to a Democrat. He has become relatively secure — with help from his collegial style and the weakness of local Republicans. In seven elections since 2007, he has never won more than 57 percent of the vote. He has been more moderate than most California Democrats and often seeks bipartisanship. Although he has usually been a party loyalist, he has not joined the northern California inner circle surrounding House Speaker Nancy Pelosi.

McNerney's father was a union organizer in the 1930s and later worked for the U.S. Geological Survey in Albuquerque, where Jerry McNerney was born. Along with his twin brother, he was sent to a military boarding school in Hays Kansas, and later won an appointment to the U.S. Military Academy. He left West Point after two years in the late 1960s because he opposed the war in Vietnam. He transferred to the University of New Mexico, where he earned his bachelor's degree and a doctorate in differential geometry. He spent several years as a contractor for Sandia National Laboratories, working on national security programs. In 1985, he moved to the private sector with U.S. Windpower and later was chief executive of a wind turbine firm. McNerney, who named his daughter Windy, claimed that his work contributed to keeping 8.3 million tons of carbon dioxide out of the atmosphere.

In 2006, McNerney was an unlikely winner against Republican Rep. Richard Pombo, a local rancher in an area that was dubbed "Pombo Country." As chairman of the House Resources Committee, Pombo was leader of the property-rights movement backed by ranchers and farmers. McNerney was endorsed by the state party and by local organized labor and easily won the primary, though the Democratic Congressional Campaign Committee favored another candidate. In the general election, Pombo outspent McNerney by nearly 2-to-1. McNerney turned the election into a referendum on Pombo, who was hated by national environmental groups, which called him an "eco-thug" and "Wildlife Enemy No. 1." Bolstered by a strong anti-Republican tide, McNerney won 53%-47%.

In the House, McNerney established a moderate voting record. On the influential Energy and Commerce Committee, he won a provision regulating carbon emissions as part of a measure to encourage electric vehicle usage. He has turned his friendship with Republican Rep. Bob Latta of Ohio, a committee member, into productive bipartisanship. According to Roll Call, their alliance began during a visit with other members to inspect the nuclear waste repository at Yucca Mountain in Nevada. In October 2018, they created a WiFi Caucus to "open a dialogue about appropriate policy solutions" related to the digital divide. In January 2019, after the House had switched party control, they collaborated to file a bill to encourage public-private partnerships to enhance security of the power grid. That led them to create the Grid Innovation Caucus. McNerney and Latta have acknowledged working with each other on multiple issues, especially on the committee.

With his background as an engineer, McNerney has worked with scientists on a bill that he filed in 2017 to request the National Academies of Science to explore technologies in the emerging study of "geoengineering," which they hope can address the challenges of climate change. He teamed up with Rep. Pete Olson of Texas, another Republican on Energy and Commerce, to co-chair the Congressional Artificial Intelligence Caucus, which was created to review related technological issues.

His history of tight reelection races has promoted his interest in issues that have been less partisan, McNerney said. "I have to be more moderate," he told The Modesto Bee in 2012. "If I alienate Republicans, I can't win. If I alienate Democrats, I can't win."

Republicans came after him in 2010. They fielded a credible challenger in David Harmer, son of John Harmer, who was Ronald Reagan's lieutenant governor. Harmer promised to shun earmarks, calling them "the gateway drug of federal spending." Democratic interest groups attacked Harmer for a 2000 op-ed column calling for the abolition of public education. The race was close and ballot-counting continued for days after the election, until McNerney prevailed with 48 percent of the vote.

In 2012, McNerney's opponent was Ricky Gill, an ambitious 25-year-old Indian American hailed as a rising GOP star. Gill raised nearly $3 million, and the National Republican Congressional Committee spent another $2.5 million on his behalf. As a Lodi native, Gill had ties to the area. Gill described himself as a "different kind of Republican," holding moderate stances on immigration and education. McNerney called Gill a novice who was propped up by his wealthy parents' business ties. McNerney also benefitted from the strong showing in California of President Barack Obama to win, 56%-44%.

The 2014 election shaped up as an easier contest. Republican challenger Tony Amador was a former police officer and U.S. marshal who had become a perennial political loser; he spent only $62,000 and had no national party assistance. But the Republican tide across the nation had some reach into the interior of California. With a boost in the vote from Contra Costa, McNerney won with 52 percent. In the Democratic year of 2018, he faced little-known Republican Marla Livengood, a former aide to Pombo who worked on local regulatory issues. McNerney outspent her by more than 10-to-1. In a measure of the limits of the local Democratic vote, he won, 56%-44%.

CA-9: Central Valley   **Cook Partisan Voting Index: D+8**

Population		Race and Ethnicity		Income	
Total	750,185	White	34.4%	Median Income	$60,717
Land area (sq. miles)	1,245	Black	8.5%	District Income Rank	171
Pop/ sq mi	602.4	Latino	38.1%	Poverty Rate	16.8%
Born in State	64%	Asian	14.2%	With health insurance	90.6%
		Two or more races	3.8%	Cash public assistance	5.1%
Age Groups		Other	0.9%	Food stamp/SNAP	13.9%
Under 18	27.3%				
18-34	23.3%	**Education**		**Work**	
35-64	37.1%	H.S grad or less	45.8%	White Collar	12.3%
Over 64	12.3%	Some college	34.4%	Sales and Service	43%
Military		College Degree, 4 yr	13.6%	Blue Collar	27.8%
Veteran/ Active Duty	6.2%	Post grad	6.2%	Government	15.4%

2012 Pres. Vote	Obama	127,418	(58%)	Romney	88,403	(40%)		
2016 Pres. Vote	Clinton	134,719	(56%)	Trump	90,484	(38%)	Johnson	8,518 (4%)

Stockton, San Joaquin: California is often defined by its cosmopolitan cities, its gorgeous Pacific coastline and its world-class vineyards. But beyond Beverly Hills and Nob Hill, there is another California that likes to get its hands dirty. This is an old part of the state, settled in the 1840s. When the Gold Rush fortune seekers departed, the land was left to a determined population of farmers. Crisscrossed with railroads and canals, the Central Valley became one of the world's greatest agricultural regions. The San Joaquin River channel was deepened to 37 feet, and Stockton today is the Central Valley's port. The rich land attracted immigrants from all over: Mexicans came up Route 99 and joined Germans from the Dakotas flocking to the town of Lodi. Italian and Yugoslavian immigrants brought their Old World crops. Yankees and Okies brought their distinct churches and beliefs. Recently, Southeast Asian refugees have crowded into the old streets of Stockton. The region endures the usual plagues of a farm economy, such as the availability of migrant workers at harvest time and chronic concerns about the water supply. With large use of chemicals and pesticides, air pollution in the San Joaquin Valley has been ranked as the worst in the nation, with high levels of cancer and asthma. A recently discovered problem has been that the valley has been sinking as the result of groundwater pumping and irrigation, according to a NASA study in 2017.

In recent decades, the Central Valley has also become a suburban zone. Because of the high cost of living in the San Francisco Bay Area, racial minorities have been moving to outlying suburbs. Workers with modest incomes bought lower-priced houses around Tracy and Stockton and commute to work on Interstate 580, past the windmills of Altamont. The population in San Joaquin County in 2017 was 42 percent Hispanic, 17 percent Asian and 8 percent black. Stockton has become a poster child for urban dysfunction. In June 2012, facing close to $1 billion in long-term debt, Stockton became the biggest city in American history to declare bankruptcy; the following year, the record went to Detroit. In October 2014, a bankruptcy judge approved the city's plan, with higher taxes and slashed payments to bondholders, but little impact on public pensions. CNBC in 2016 ranked it as the worst city in the United States in which to start a business. To address endemic poverty, Stockton officials in August 2018 launched a trial period for a universal basic income, with a $500 monthly guarantee for all residents.

The 9th Congressional District contains about two-thirds of San Joaquin County, plus an eastern slice of Contra Costa County and a southern nip of Sacramento County. It includes all of Stockton, plus Lodi, a town with a sizable Muslim community and a thriving downtown. The district takes in fast-growing Brentwood in Contra Costa County. Nearby in Antioch, city officials in 2018 hired an image consultant to address the city's brand, which had become unsafe and uninteresting. The district is not overwhelmingly Democratic and could become competitive, especially with continued economic woes. Hillary Clinton got 56 percent of the vote in 2016.

Josh Harder (D)

Elected 2018, 1st term, b. Aug 01, 1986; Turlock; Stanford University (CA), Bach. Deg., 2008; Harvard University Kennedy School of Government (MA), M.P.P., 2014; Christian Church; Married (Pamela Harder).

Professional Career: Management Consultant, Bessemer Venture Partners.

DC Office: 131 CHOB 20515, 202-225-4540, harder.house.gov

State Offices: Modesto, 209-579-5458.

Committees: *Agriculture*: Biotechnology, Horticulture & Research; Livestock & Foreign Agriculture. *Education & Labor*: Health, Employment, Labor & Pensions; Higher Education & Workforce Investment.

Election Results

Election	Name (Party)	Vote (%)		Cand. Spent	Ind. Exp. Support	Ind. Exp. Oppose
2018 General	Josh Harder (D)	115,945	(52%)	$8,355,286	$1,261,347	$6,186,024
	Jeff Denham (R)	105,955	(48%)	$4,887,068	$911,456	$7,207,789
2018 Primary	Jeff Denham (R)	45,719	(38%)			
	Josh Harder (D)	20,742	(17%)			
	Ted D. Howze (R)	17,723	(15%)			
	Michael Eggman (D)	12,446	(10%)			
	Virginia Madueño (D)	11,178	(9%)			
	Sue Zwahlen (D)	9,945	(8%)			

Freshman Democrat Josh Harder, who worked as a venture capitalist in San Francisco, was elected in a nearby district that had the lowest median income in the Bay Area. Downplaying his high-finance connections, he sought to identify with the rural communities of his youth. Harder defeated Republican Rep. Jeff Denham, an almond farmer who had gained influence among House Republicans and initially did not appear to take Harder seriously. His victory left the GOP without any of the more than a dozen districts closest to San Francisco—a significant political shift since the 1990s.

Growing up in Turlock in the Central Valley farming area, Harder interned while he was in high school for Denham, who was then a state senator. He graduated from Stanford University and got master's degrees in business administration and public policy from Harvard. After working for the Boston Consulting Group, where he advised businesses around the world, he joined the San Francisco-based Bessemer Venture Partners. He returned to the Bay Area as a vice president of the firm, where his clients were chiefly telecommunications firms.

When he launched his campaign for Congress, "Harder was reluctant to talk about his background in tech investing, taking pains to stress the more home-grown parts of his biography," according to Recode, a website that covered the high-tech industry. Denham was eager to remind voters of that background, running ads that referred to Harder as "a shady San Francisco venture capitalist." Recode reported that Harder became the only former venture capitalist serving in the House.

The all-party primary featured six Democratic candidates—including beekeeper Michael Eggman, the challenger to Denham in 2014 and 2016, when he lost 52%-48%. "[Harder's] profile just doesn't fit this district and that is why I am running again," Eggman told CNN. In addition to Denham, the other Republican candidate was Ted Howze, a conservative who styled himself as more loyal to President Donald Trump, especially on immigration issues. To the relief of House Democrats who feared that Howze would place second, which would have shut out Democrats in November, Harder got 17 percent of the total vote, trailed by Howze with 15 percent and Eggman with 10 percent. Denham led the field with 38 percent.

In the House, Denham spent much of 2018 seeking to fill the post-election opening for the top Republican post at the House Transportation and Infrastructure Committee, where he was a senior member. He was a chief advocate of an unusual House parliamentary procedure to force a vote on a bipartisan bill for immigration reform, which GOP leaders and Trump strongly opposed.

As the campaign intensified in the closing months, Denham said during a September debate that Harder was "a core of the liberal elite," whose venture capitalism cost local jobs, increased costs and sought to shift water from Central Valley farms. Harder responded that the incumbent had failed to secure "one federal dollar" for local water projects during his eight years in Congress and that Denham's criticism of his business record was "a bucket of lies."

Harder was a prolific fundraiser, garnering ample support from his Bay Area network. With his more than $8 million, he nearly doubled the spending by Denham, who benefited from more than $2 million in spending by House Republican groups. Harder won, 51%-49%, in the only northern California contest that took several days following the election to declare a winner. He led in both Stanislaus County and the less populous San Joaquin part of the district. With Howze's early interest in a 2020 challenge, Harder faced the prospect of a tough reelection campaign.

CA-10: Central Valley   Cook Partisan Voting Index: EVEN

Population		Race and Ethnicity		Income	
Total	737,719	White	43%	Median Income	$59,543
Land area (sq. miles)	1,819	Black	3%	District Income Rank	185
Pop/ sq mi	405.6	Latino	43%	Poverty Rate	15.3%
Born in State	66.2%	Asian	6.7%	With health insurance	91.4%
		Two or more races	3.2%	Cash public assistance	4.7%
Age Groups		Other	1.2%	Food stamp/SNAP	13.4%
Under 18	27.3%				
18-34	23.9%	**Education**		**Work**	
35-64	37%	H.S grad or less	49%	White Collar	11.8%
Over 64	11.8%	Some college	33.7%	Sales and Service	42.1%
		College Degree, 4 yr	12%	Blue Collar	30.3%
Military		Post grad	5.3%	Government	13.6%
Veteran/ Active Duty	5.8%				

2012 Pres. Vote	Obama	108,923	(51%)	Romney	101,160	(47%)		
2016 Pres. Vote	Clinton	116,335	(48%)	Trump	109,145	(45%)	Johnson	9,370	(4%)

Modesto, Stanislaus: The Central Valley of California is a miraculous landscape, an outdoor factory stretching as far as the eye can see. Nature created the vast flatlands, rimmed by mountains rising in the distant haze. In the 20th century, people disciplined the land with a remorseless mile-square grid of roads, the California Aqueduct, and dozens of arrow-straight canals. Pipes fitted with valves and gauges pump water, fertilizer and pesticides to the fields in measured quantities with industrial precision. The crops grow in carefully spaced rows. The rich soil and the irrigated water were too precious to waste on decorative fountains or flower gardens. Throughout history, farming here has been a business, not a way of life. In the 19th century, the U.S. government did not give the land to 160-acre homesteaders but rather sold it to large enterprises in thousands-of-acres parcels. Among the most famous local capitalists were the Gallo brothers, Ernest and Julio, who started a winery in Modesto in 1933 with virtually no money. It now covers more than 23,000 acres of vineyards, with 90 brands that produce more than 86 million cases of wine each year.

In recent years, the Central Valley has become one of California's boom areas, not just for crops, but also for people. Middle-income workers in the San Francisco Bay Area drive east at the end of the day on Interstate 580 to modestly priced homes in Modesto, the town immortalized (when it was much smaller) in the 1973 film American Graffiti. Warehouses and factories have sprung up on land that for all its farming value is cheaper than industrial land in the Bay Area. But there have been costs: Traffic is a problem, air-pollution levels on bad days can be among the worst in the nation, and the pace of life has become more hectic. The over-pumping of groundwater has caused the valley to sink a half-inch each month, the Los Angeles Times reported. Stanislaus County saw record farming revenues of $3.7 billion in 2016, with almonds the leading crop. Milk and walnuts were other profitable products. Officials in Modesto have taken steps to redevelop the former Crows Landing airfield into a business park and airport.

The 10th Congressional District of California includes all of Stanislaus County and part of San Joaquin County, including Tracy, Ripon and the almond center of Manteca. Nearly three-fourths of the voters are in Stanislaus. It takes in Modesto, Oakdale and Riverbank. The political tradition here had been Democratic. In the 1960s, Democrats in Washington and Democratic Gov. Pat Brown built the irrigation canals and authorized the water subsidies. This area produced two House Democratic whips, John McFall in the mid-1970s and Tony Coelho in the 1980s. But the Central Valley grew to be more culturally conservative than other parts of the state. In recent decades, it has trended Republican, and even the Latinos here are less solidly Democratic than those in Los Angeles. Still, with a 43 percent Hispanic population, this has become one of the few political "swing" areas in California. In each of the past three presidential elections, Democrats have won the district by about three percentage points.

Mark DeSaulnier (D)

Elected 2014, 3rd term, b. Mar 31, 1952; Lowell, MA; College of The Holy Cross (MA), B.A., 1974; Harvard University John F. Kennedy School of Government (MA), 2003; Roman Catholic; Divorced; 2 children.

Elected Office: Concord City Council, 1991-1994; Concord Mayor, 1993; Contra Costa County Board Supervisors, 1994-2006, chair, 1994; CA Assembly 2006-2008; CA Senate, 2008-2014.

Professional Career: Deputy probation officer; Warehouse worker; Hotel service; Restauranteur; Business owner; Fellow, JFK School of Gov't, Harvard University, 2003.

DC Office: 503 CHOB 20515, 202-225-2095, Fax: 202-225-5609, desaulnier.house.gov

State Offices: Richmond, 510-620-1000; Walnut Creek, 925-933-2660.

Committees: *Education & Labor:* Early Childhood, Elementary & Secondary Education; Workforce Protections. *Oversight & Reform:* National Security; Subcommittee on Economic & Consumer Policy. *Rules.* *Transportation & Infrastructure:* Highways & Transit; Railroads, Pipelines & Hazardous Materials.

Group Ratings

	ADA	ACLU	AFL-CIO	LCV	ITI	COC	HAFA	ACU	CFG	FRC
2018	-	96%	-	100%	-	55%	8%	4%	28%	0%
2017	100%	C	97%	100%	C	36%	C	0%	0%	0%

Almanac Ratings 2017-18

	Economy	Social	Foreign	Composite
Liberal	100%	100%	98%	99%
Conservative	0%	0%	2%	1%

Key Votes of the 115th Congress

1. Obama-care revision	N	5. Family planning regs	N	9. Guantanamo prisoners	Y
2. Tax Cuts	N	6. Body cameras/immigration	Y	10. Ground missiles, limit	Y
3. Omnibus appropriations	N	7. Abortion ban	N	11. Defense Dept. spending	N
4. Dodd-Frank revision	N	8. Concealed carry	N	12. FISA rules	NV

Election Results

Election	Name (Party)	Vote (%)		Cand. Spent	Ind. Exp. Support	Ind. Exp. Oppose
2018 General	Mark DeSaulnier (D)	204,369	(74%)	$333,977		
	John Fitzgerald (R)	71,312	(26%)			
2018 Primary	Mark DeSaulnier (D)	107,115	(68%)			
	John Fitzgerald (R)	36,279	(23%)			
	Dennis Lytton (D)	8,695	(6%)			

Prior winning percentages: 2016 (72%), 2014 (67%)

Democrat Mark DeSaulnier, elected to a solidly blue district in 2014, has shown his legislative experience and expertise. With particular interest in education and transportation policy, he gained new opportunities when Democrats took control of the House.

DeSaulnier is a veteran of California politics with blue-collar bona fides. He had been a trucker, probation officer and hotel worker before entering the restaurant business, eventually owning several Bay Area dining locales. A keen interest in local politics inspired him to run for Concord City Council in 1991, and he became mayor in 1993. In those early years, he was a Republican. Gov. Pete Wilson appointed him to the influential state Air Resources Board in 1997. As he saw the GOP move to the right, DeSaulnier switched parties and became a Democrat. He was elected to the state Assembly in 2006 and the state Senate in 2008. He chaired the Transportation Committee in each chamber. DeSaulnier had not always marched with his party in Sacramento. He opposed proposals to revive California's troubled high-speed rail project, and he pledged to work with business groups to amend his corporate tax bill so it had a better chance of passage.

In 2014, when 40-year veteran and influential liberal leader George Miller announced his retirement, DeSaulnier got his opening. He had lost a special election five years earlier to a better-known candidate, John Garamendi. This time, DeSaulnier made sure he was well-positioned. Armed with the biggest war chest and a slew of endorsements, DeSaulnier quickly became the frontrunner. He used his day job in the state Senate to advance liberal priorities. That included a bill to adjust the state corporate tax rate according to the wage disparity in each firm – a measure that resonated with Democrats but fell short of the required two-thirds majority to pass. He proposed another bill to set up a pilot project to reform the state's gasoline tax so that motorists pay based on mileage rather than by the gallon. That measure passed. DeSaulnier easily won election to the open seat. He took 59 percent of the vote in the first round of voting, well ahead of 28 percent for Republican Tue Phan-Quang. In the general election, he took 67 percent. This was a relatively low-cost contest, with DeSaulnier spending $540,000.

In the House, DeSaulnier continued his predecessor Miller's tenure on the (re-named) Education and Labor Committee. After three years, he enacted the first bill he introduced, which expanded the John Muir National Historic Site with 44 additional acres of donated land in Martinez. Muir, a conservationist, was the father of the national parks. He filed legislation to make the income from student Pell Grants tax-exempt for low-income recipients. In response to incidents in which law-enforcement agents had their firearms stolen from their cars, DeSaulnier proposed a bill that would require federal agents to store their guns in a locked box while they are in a car. He pursued other proposals to reduce gun violence, including the creation of an independent board to seek solutions. Following up on his call for "radical and immediate change" in Bay Area transportation, he joined with Sen. Dianne Feinstein to support a new bridge across the bay to southern San Francisco, plus an accompanying underwater rail tube.

He took several steps to call attention to the case of the Port Chicago 50, a group of African Americans who were found guilty of mutiny in 1944 when they refused to return to work following a huge munitions explosion during the loading of a ship at the Naval Magazine in Concord, which killed 320 people. The House-passed defense spending bill in May 2016 included his amendment to require that the Navy investigate their treatment at the time to determine if there was racial bias. In 2015, outgoing Navy Secretary Ray Mabus said he favored a posthumous pardon.

In 2016, DeSaulnier announced he had had months of chemotherapy treatment for a form of leukemia, which was a blood cancer that is not curable but is manageable. He created the Congressional Cancer Survivors Caucus to seek additional research funds.

CA-11: Outer East Bay

Cook Partisan Voting Index: D+21

Population		Race and Ethnicity		Income	
Total	749,531	White	46.4%	Median Income	$83,343
Land area (sq. miles)	494	Black	7.8%	District Income Rank	44
Pop/ sq mi	1518.5	Latino	26.8%	Poverty Rate	10.6%
Born in State	53.4%	Asian	13.6%	With health insurance	91.9%
		Two or more races	4.4%	Cash public assistance	2.5%
Age Groups		Other	1%	Food stamp/SNAP	6.8%
Under 18	22.4%				
18-34	21.4%	**Education**		**Work**	
35-64	40.5%	H.S grad or less	29%	White Collar	15.7%
Over 64	15.7%	Some college	28%	Sales and Service	41.2%
		College Degree, 4 yr	26.9%	Blue Collar	15.4%
Military		Post grad	16.1%	Government	12.5%
Veteran/ Active Duty	5.6%				

2012 Pres. Vote	Obama	203,699	(68%)	Romney	90,226	(30%)		
2016 Pres. Vote	Clinton	223,559	(71%)	Trump	70,869	(23%)	Johnson	10,993	(4%)

Concord, Richmond: The maritime journey inward from the Pacific Ocean to the vast flatness of California's Central Valley passes through a wondrous variety of terrain. The traveler starts at the Golden Gate Bridge, with the lush green Presidio on one side and the bluffs of mountains in Marin County on the other. The journey continues through San Francisco Bay, through the narrow Carquinez Strait to Suisun Bay, with its sloughs and marshes and ships ready for scrap, and finally past the mountains, to the flat, fertile expanse of California's great interior. This journey was a familiar route to the first Americans in California, and it passes by much of the industrial base of the Bay Area. On the east side of Suisun Bay is Richmond, developed almost instantaneously during World War II when Henry J. Kaiser built a shipyard in its deep-water port and 91,000 people from all over the country were put to work building ships for the Pacific theater. What became known as Rosie the Riveter Memorial Park is now a national historical park.

In recent years, Richmond citizens have harbored doubts about safety at a Chevron refinery plant, the scene of frequent fires and explosions. After an August 2012 fire at the plant, some residents alleged Chevron was causing high asthma rates and pollution, while business leaders defended the company as a jobs creator. The federal Chemical Safety Board issued a report in 2015 that Chevron was responsible for the fire because it failed to respond when experts warned of defects at the plant. In the 2014 election, Chevron fueled a backlash when it endorsed four candidates for the Richmond city council and spent more than $3 million on their behalf. All of them lost. A local political science professor said the result showed that "ordinary people can defeat huge corporate power." In a settlement of lawsuits, Chevron in 2018 agreed to pay $160 million for improvements at several sites nationally, including $20 million for safety projects in Richmond. In January 2019, the San Francisco Bay Ferry began service from a new terminal in Richmond to the Embarcadero across the Bay. The step was a boost for the economy in Richmond, though some community groups were fearful of gentrification. In another transportation milestone, BART in May 2018 opened a 10-mile extension of its East Bay service to Antioch. To reduce construction costs, the new line is served by diesel trains, which use advanced biofuels.

The 11th District of California is entirely in Contra Costa County, including all of Richmond and Concord, which is the largest city in the county. About 30 percent of the county's voters are in adjoining districts. Interstate 680 running north-south provides a spine for businesses and shopping centers up and down the San Ramon Valley, from burgeoning Concord to Walnut Creek. The district also takes in the "Lamorinda" area of Lafayette, Moraga and Orinda. After California State University dropped plans to build a new campus at the site of the mostly unused Concord Naval Weapons Station, the city council updated development plans that envisioned more than 12,000 housing units and 6 million square feet of commercial space; about 70 percent was expected to be used as parkland and open space, though a private group sued to offer an alternative development. The Trump administration abandoned its proposal to use part of the station for a migrant detention facility. The district is solidly Democratic, but less culturally liberal than San Francisco. Hillary Clinton got 71 percent of the vote in 2016.

Nancy Pelosi (D)

Elected 1987, 16th full term, b. Mar 26, 1940; Baltimore, MD; Trinity College (DC), A.B., 1962; Roman Catholic; Married (Paul F. Pelosi); 5 children; 9 grandchildren.

Professional Career: CA Dem. Party, Northern Chairman, 1977-81, St. Chairman, 1981-1983; DSCC finance Chairman, 1985-1986; PR Executive, Ogilvy & Mather, 1986-1987.

DC Office: 1236 LHOB 20515, 202-225-4965, Fax: 202-225-8259, pelosi.house.gov

State Offices: San Francisco, 415-556-4862.

Speaker of the House.

Group Ratings

	ADA	ACLU	AFL-CIO	LCV	ITI	COC	HAFA	ACU	CFG	FRC
2018	-	77%	-	100%	-	58%	8%	4%	12%	0%
2017	95%	C	94%	94%	C	36%	C	7%	5%	0%

Almanac Ratings 2017-18

	Economy	Social	Foreign	Composite
Liberal	95%	94%	93%	94%
Conservative	5%	6%	7%	6%

Key Votes of the 115th Congress

1. Obama-care revision	N	5. Family planning regs	N	9. Guantanamo prisoners	Y
2. Tax Cuts	N	6. Body cameras/immigration	Y	10. Ground missiles, limit	Y
3. Omnibus appropriations	Y	7. Abortion ban	N	11. Defense Dept. spending	Y
4. Dodd-Frank revision	N	8. Concealed carry	N	12. FISA rules	Y

Election Results

Election	Name (Party)	Vote (%)		Cand. Spent	Ind. Exp. Support	Ind. Exp. Oppose
2018 General	Nancy Pelosi (D)..............................	275,292	(87%)	$2,799,608		$2,482,371
	Lisa Remmer (R)..............................	41,780	(13%)	$10,282		
2018 Primary	Nancy Pelosi (D)..............................	141,365	(69%)			
	Lisa Remmer (R)..............................	18,771	(9%)			
	Shahid Buttar (D)..............................	17,597	(9%)			
	Stephen Jaffe (D)..............................	12,114	(6%)			

Prior winning percentages: 2016 (81%), 2014 (83%), 2012 (85%), 2010 (80%), 2008 (72%), 2006 (80%), 2004 (83%), 2002 (80%), 2000 (84%), 1998 (86%), 1996 (84%), 1994 (82%), 1992 (83%), 1990 (77%), 1988 (76%), 1987 special (67%)

Nancy Pelosi, who regained in January 2019 the gavel as Speaker of the House that she held from 2007 to 2011, also has served for 12 years in the far less glamorous role of minority leader. She deserved great credit for her patience and discipline in restoring Democratic control of the chamber. The only woman to serve as Speaker, her accomplishments have been among the most productive for the House in the past century. The many cycles of her command have demonstrated that she has been one of the most polarizing figures in politics, even within her own party. But, as she demonstrated in early 2019 with her initial caution in responding to allegations of wrongdoing against President Donald Trump, she has been responsive to the numerous factions within the Democratic Caucus—especially to the interests of the more than three dozen first-termers who had won Republican-held seats. Perhaps her greatest skill, which she learned as the youngest of six children of the vaunted d'Alesandro family of Baltimore, has been the care and feeding of a partisan organization, including the two-way demands of political loyalty.

Detested by Republicans for her proudly liberal views and assertive style, Pelosi has been beloved in her party — even by her internal critics -- for her legislative accomplishments as well as her fundraising and politicking, which continued unabated in her late-70s. As Trump learned quickly and painfully after she returned as Speaker, Pelosi and her persistence should never be underestimated. And yet, that made it all the more remarkable that her own party forced her to agree to a maximum of four more years as Speaker, which she had defiantly resisted before she realized that it was an offer that she could not refuse.

Elected to Congress in June 1987, she has the energy and shrewdness of one who has handled the most delicate of political chores, and the charm and unflappability of one who is the mother of five and grandmother of nine. During her most recent eight years as minority leader, Pelosi's public image receded, Republicans ran thousands of ads vilifying her in their successful campaign to retain control of the House. In 2018, voters — especially in the pivotal suburbs across the nation, no longer were swayed by the warnings of GOP strategists and candidates or presidential tweets -- that a return of Democratic control under Pelosi would be tantamount to the Apocalypse.

Democrats' dismal showings in the 2010 and 2014 midterm elections fueled speculation and some internal demands that it was time for her to step aside. But she has proven far too skilled at hauling in campaign funds. "I'm the one that brung everyone to the party by winning the House in the first place," she told The Washington Post during the 2016 cycle. "I could have walked away, but we built something and then we want to take it to the next step" — winning back control of the House. In 2018, with help from the rank and file, she delivered on her plea, "Just win, baby."

Pelosi grew up on Albemarle Street in Baltimore's Little Italy, just east of downtown. Her father, Thomas D'Alesandro Jr., served in the House from 1939 to 1947 and was mayor of Baltimore for 12 years after that. Her mother, Annunciata D'Alesandro ("Big Nancy"), was an indefatigable political organizer, and her brother, Thomas, was mayor from 1967 to 1971. Pelosi says of her parents, "What I got from them was about economic fairness. That was the difference between Democrats and Republicans all those years ago." She graduated from Trinity University in Washington D.C., where she met her husband Paul. After marrying, they moved to his hometown of San Francisco. There he became a successful real estate investor, and she raised their children and got into local Democratic politics. The couple eventually became extremely wealthy, with a home in San Francisco, a vineyard in the Napa Valley, a townhome in the Sierras, and a condominium in Washington. Their diversified investments have placed Pelosi among the five wealthiest House members.

In the 1970s, Pelosi struck rough-hewn Rep. John Burton of California as just another stylish hostess in a city that had many of them. But she soon got Burton's attention and that of his older brother, Rep. Phillip Burton, the de facto liberal leader of the House, who lost his race for majority leader to Texas Democrat Jim Wright by one vote in 1976. That year, Pelosi returned east to run the Maryland campaign of presidential candidate Jerry Brown, then and later governor of California. She was able to relate both to "Governor Moonbeam," as Brown was dubbed, and to the practical-minded politicians she had met through her parents. In 1977, she became chairwoman of the Northern California Democratic Party, and four years later, she became chairwoman of the California Democratic Party. The positions required a considerable amount of diplomacy, including dealing with fractious regional antagonisms. But Pelosi managed to remain on good terms with various warring Democrats and help the party hold majorities in the legislature.

Then in 1982, John Burton declined to run for reelection in a new Marin- and San Francisco-based district. Some Democrats sounded out Pelosi, whose Presidio Heights home was in the district, but she declined to run, and the seat went to Marin-based Democrat Barbara Boxer. Instead, Pelosi worked with Mayor Dianne Feinstein to land the 1984 Democratic National Convention for San Francisco. In 1985, she ran for Democratic National Chairman but lost to Paul Kirk. Before long, though, she had another opportunity. Phil Burton's widow, Sala Burton, was elected to succeed her husband after his death in 1983, but her health failed too. In 1987, as she was dying of cancer, she told her friends whom she wanted to succeed her: Nancy Pelosi.

This time, she ran, moving her residence from Presidio Heights to a Pacific Heights rental apartment. Her chief opponent in the Democratic primary was San Francisco Supervisor Harry Britt, who had succeeded Harvey Milk after he was assassinated. San Francisco's gay community at that time was not as mainstream as it is now, but Britt, who was gay, had a good record in office and Pelosi had to work hard to beat him, 35%-31%.

In her early days in Congress, Pelosi focused on important issues of local sensitivity. One was the Presidio. Burton had enacted a provision that transferred the Presidio from the military to the

Interior Department. The problem was that it was so expensive to maintain, it threatened to exceed the National Park Service's budget. Through several Congresses, Pelosi worked to get bipartisan support for a funding source, and in 1997 created the Presidio Trust.

Another sensitive issue was human rights, especially in China. After the Tiananmen Square massacre in 1989, Pelosi sponsored an amendment to give Chinese students the right to remain in the United States, but President George H.W. Bush vetoed it. In 1991, she became lead sponsor of the bill to make China's most-favored-nation status conditional on human rights reforms. The House overrode Bush's veto, but it was upheld in the Senate. After that, Pelosi led the annual fight against normalizing trade relations with China. She did all this at some political risk. Pelosi's position was by no means universally popular with Asian Americans in her district; many thought the United States should trade and negotiate quietly with China. Pelosi courted support from people on the opposite end of the ideological spectrum, especially religious conservatives in the Republican caucus who also wanted to remain vigilant on China's human rights record.

In addition to her seat on Appropriations, Pelosi rose to the position of senior Democrat on the Intelligence Committee. Following the September 11 attacks, she joined in the committee's conclusion that, while the intelligence community did not have specific evidence in advance, it did have information that was relevant to the attacks.

Her move into the leadership was persistent, shrewd and well-organized. In 1997, as a member of the Ethics Committee, she doggedly pursued charges against Republican Speaker Newt Gingrich and worked with Minority Whip David Bonior in using scorched-earth tactics against him. In 1999, she launched a campaign for majority whip, anticipating that Democrats would win a majority in 2000. Her opponent was Hoyer. They were old acquaintances, having served as interns for Sen. Daniel Brewster of Maryland in the 1960s, but not confreres: there were considerable stylistic and ideological differences, plus apparent deep-seated antagonisms.

But in 2000, Republicans held onto their majority, and the race for majority whip was moot. Not for long, though. Michigan's Republican legislature, in drawing new congressional districts, put Bonior in a district that he could not win, and he decided to run for governor. He resigned as minority whip, and Pelosi was off and running against Hoyer. Some supporters played up her potential to become a celebrity — "a glamorous grandmother who knocks people off their feet," as then-Rep. Neil Abercrombie of Hawaii put it. With nearly unanimous support from the 32 California Democrats and from most women in the Caucus, . Pelosi started with a strong base. In October 2001, she won by a convincing 118-95. A major stepping-stone came in the fall of 2002, when she actively encouraged opponents of the resolution authorizing the use of force in Iraq, which Minority Leader Dick Gephardt had enthusiastically endorsed. Pelosi contended that supporters had not made the case for using force and that she had seen no evidence that Iraq "poses an imminent threat to our nation." To the surprise of many, her efforts helped win 126 Democratic votes against the resolution, while 81 backed Gephardt's position. In retrospect, the split signaled a transition in the caucus. Once the disappointing 2002 election results were in and Gephardt said that he was stepping down, Pelosi had all but locked up the support of a majority of the caucus. Harold Ford of Tennessee made a belated, quixotic bid designed to appeal to a combination of blacks and New Democrats, but Pelosi won 177-29.

As the Democratic leader in the House, she brought a burst of energy — and favorable press coverage — to a party that badly needed both. She showed hands-on management in selecting members for committee vacancies and in developing a Democratic message criticizing the agenda of President George W. Bush. As Republicans pressed their agenda, Pelosi declared that Democrats would take "a party position" in opposition to the Republican Medicare prescription-drug bill. But 16 Democrats voted for the final deal in November 2003, providing the critical margin for passage. She was largely silent about the renegades, many of whom were responding to local pressures favoring the bill.

Pelosi traveled the country in 2004 raising money and boosting local candidates. If she became Speaker, Pelosi pledged, she would reform the House to give a greater voice to all members and to assure fairness. The three-seat loss in the November election that year turned out to be yet another disappointment for House Democrats. Bush's declining job approval ratings and the rising prospects of Democrats in the 2006 election helped Pelosi maintain party discipline.

For months, House Democrats worked to come up with a platform for 2006 and emerged with a "Six for '06" program, including an increase in the minimum wage and approval of the remaining recommendations of the 9/11 Commission. Pelosi campaigned tirelessly across the country and was rewarded when Democrats gained 31 seats, enough for a Democratic majority, on Election Day.

As she assumed the office that put her second in line for the presidency, Pelosi said in January 2007, "This is an historic moment, for Congress, and for the women of this country. It is a moment for which we have waited more than 200 years. For our daughters and granddaughters, today we have broken the marble ceiling. To our daughters and granddaughters, the sky is the limit."

Beneath the velvet glove, Pelosi continued to operate with an iron fist. One of her key issues was reducing carbon dioxide emissions to curb global warming. So she announced the creation of a Select Committee on Energy Independence and Global Warming, to be headed by Energy and Commerce member Edward Markey of Massachusetts, a long-time ally. Energy and Commerce Chairman John Dingell of Michigan protested that he was being sidelined, but Pelosi had her way — not for the final time.

Pelosi and her Democratic leadership ran a tight ship and were largely successful, at least in the House. The Democrats' bill to expand the Children's Health Insurance Program was passed by both chambers, but Bush vetoed it. When gasoline hit $4 a gallon and public opinion began to favor more offshore oil drilling, Pelosi refused to allow a roll call vote. "I'm trying to save the planet," she said. But Democrats too were coming under pressure to act on gas prices, and Pelosi agreed to allow a vote on a bill that gave states a role in offshore drilling decisions.

Then, crisis struck, as the financial industry teetered on the verge of collapse, with the potential to send the United States into a second Great Depression. Treasury Secretary Henry Paulson and Federal Reserve Chairman Ben Bernanke confronted the House in September 2008 with a request for $700 billion to bail out big, failing financial firms. Pelosi, with Financial Services Committee Chairman Barney Frank of Massachusetts, decided to grant the request. But a few days later, it became clear that many Democrats were unwilling to vote for it. Pelosi announced she would bring Democrats along if 100 Republicans supported it as well. When the bill came to a vote on Sept. 29, it was defeated, and Republicans blamed Pelosi for speaking harshly about Bush administration economic policies. The Senate changed some of the terms of the bill, and it passed on Oct. 1. The House took up the Senate version and, with some vote switches prompted by Pelosi, passed it two days later.

In the November 2008 election, Democrats gained 21 House seats, and Pelosi entered 2009 as the leader of 257 Democrats — the biggest majority a Speaker had enjoyed since Democrat Thomas Foley of Washington in 1993-94. Pelosi made it plain to the new Obama administration that she expected it to work through her and not make side deals with Democratic factions, much less Republicans. She presided over a record of legislative accomplishments that many consider the most impressive since the Great Society Congress of 1965-66.

The first order of business was Obama's massive economic stimulus bill. Pelosi largely delegated the specifics to Appropriations Chairman David Obey of Wisconsin. The $819 billion measure was passed without a single Republican vote. The size of the stimulus was reduced in the Senate, and Pelosi negotiated hard to get the final price tag to $787 billion.

On Iraq, Pelosi said she was unhappy with Obama's decision to leave 50,000 troops there and also with the Justice Department's decision not to prosecute Bush administration officials for approving enhanced interrogation techniques. She was embarrassed in May 2009 when the Central Intelligence Agency released documents indicating that she had been present at a September 2002 briefing where waterboarding was discussed. In a tense press conference, she said, "In that or any other briefing, we were not and, I repeat, were not told that waterboarding or any of these other enhanced interrogation techniques were used" — only that they were legal.

Pelosi again pushed hard for legislation restricting carbon emissions, her signature issue. She quietly supported California Rep. Henry Waxman's shrewdly executed campaign to replace Dingell as chairman of Energy and Commerce, with prime jurisdiction over the issue. And she worked closely with Waxman and Markey on the contents of the bill, including Waxman's concessions to win over conservative Democrats. She even met with 11 Republican moderates to get their support. In late June, the bill passed, 219-212, with eight Republicans voting yes. But the Senate did not act.

The other major initiative for Pelosi was Obama's health care overhaul. But finding agreement on complex and far-reaching changes to the medical insurance system, including a controversial proposal to let people opt into a federally sponsored plan, delayed the bill in committee for many weeks. As Pelosi had feared, opposition to the bill gained momentum at town hall meetings across the country during the August recess, including many in Democratic districts. Lawmakers were more skittish about the legislation when they returned. Pelosi agreed to changes in the controversial "public option" but refused to give in to pressure from conservative Democrats to drop it from the bill. And, in the 11th hour and to the dismay of abortion-rights supporters, she agreed to accept Michigan Rep. Bart Stupak's amendment that included vague language that some supporters – though by no means all --

said would bar coverage for abortions. The bill was passed 220-215 on Nov. 7, with 39 Democrats voting no and one Republican voting yes.

The public option proved to be an even tougher sell in the Senate, which ultimately voted on Christmas Eve for a health care overhaul minus the government insurance provision. Then on Jan. 19, 2010, Republican Scott Brown won the special Senate election in Massachusetts for the seat vacated by the death of Ted Kennedy. In his campaign, Brown had promised to be the 41st vote against the health care bill, denying Democrats the 60 votes they needed to stop a filibuster. The obstacles were great. But Pelosi characteristically braced for the fight. "We're in the majority," she told Obama. "We'll never have a better majority in your presidency in numbers than we've got right now. We can make this work."

Public opinion polls in early 2010 showed the public to be increasingly wary of the changes to the health care system. Pelosi agreed to drop a House-passed surtax on high-income earners, which was replaced by an excise tax on high-end insurance plans. She also got Stupak and other anti-abortion lawmakers to agree to changes to their provision that they had previously deemed unacceptable. On the day of the vote, March 21, Pelosi marched with fellow Democrats from their offices to the Capitol, while an angry crowd, held back by Capitol police, chanted "Kill the bill." Pelosi's attitude toward the anti-Obama health care forces was clear in a statement in January of that year: "We will go through the gate. If the gate is closed, we will go over the fence. If the fence is too high, we will pole vault in. If that doesn't work, we will parachute in. But we are going to get health care reform passed for the American people." The final roll call was 219-212, without a single Republican vote. The Senate acquiesced to the House changes and Obama signed the bill.

Its passage was the defining moment of Pelosi's initial speakership and showcased her skills at putting together complex legislation and rounding up reluctant votes, amid volatile public opinion. Polls around the country showed a large number of Democratic incumbents trailing their Republican challengers. In September, she hoped to send Democrats home to campaign on a high note by having them vote to extend the Bush-era income tax cuts except for upper income-earners of $200,000 or more. But when it became clear the votes weren't there, she moved to adjourn a week earlier than scheduled. It was acknowledgement that her ability to control a majority, after four years of doing so time and again, was in the hands of a restless electorate in November.

That fall, Pelosi campaigned for Democrats across the country, but she was more a liability than an asset in conservative-leaning districts. Democrats lost 63 seats, the most the party had lost since the 1938 election, and Republicans took majority control in January. Following the election, it was widely expected that Pelosi would relinquish her hold on her leadership position. But after two days of prayer and conversations, Pelosi announced she wanted to run for minority leader again. She could not stop North Carolina's conservative Heath Shuler from launching a quixotic challenge. Pelosi prevailed in the caucus vote 150-43. When asked to explain why she won, she said, "Because I'm an effective leader, because we got the job done on health care and Wall Street reform and consumer protection, the list goes on. Because they know that I'm the person that can attract the resources, both intellectual and otherwise, to take us to victory because I have done it before." Still, Pelosi began the 112th Congress in January 2011 with 19 Democrats voting against her — the most defections that any party leader had suffered since 1913. Most of those votes were cast by the diminished corps of moderate "Blue Dog" Democrats.

Despite her furious fundraising, Pelosi and her lieutenants struggled to craft a path to the majority that would circumvent the twin Democratic demons of redistricting and demographic shifts in many large metropolitan areas. In many parts of the nation, from Pennsylvania and Ohio to Florida and Texas, where Democrats once dominated the House delegations, her cultural liberalism and the relentless attacks of Republicans severely limited her appearances in public events on behalf of Democratic candidates or House members with whom she worked regularly at the Capitol. After two more elections, House Democrats in January 2015 held 188 seats, their smallest total since 1928.

At that point, Pelosi bowed to demands for new, younger faces in leadership. She appointed Rep. Ben Ray Luján of New Mexico, a Latino, to head the Democratic Congressional Campaign Committee. Later, she installed Eric Swalwell, a Bay Area upstart, as co-chair of the powerful Steering and Policy Committee along with longtime ally Rosa DeLauro of Connecticut. But her diminished influence was displayed in her inability to deliver the ranking member post on the Energy and Commerce Committee to her close friend and fellow Californian Anna Eshoo. New Jersey's Frank Pallone, working with Minority Whip Steny Hoyer and other allies, beat out Eshoo for the job on a secret ballot after the 2014 election.

News reports revealed growing frustration among younger rank-and-file members with what they saw as the entrenchment of longtime, and aging, figures in leadership and top committee slots —

mostly, they were Pelosi allies. The 63 votes for 43-year-old Rep. Tim Ryan of Ohio in November 2016 when he challenged Pelosi for leader were a manifestation of economic populism and the desire for change, though she remained secure with a majority of the Democratic Caucus. She responded that "our values" continued to unify Democrats but made further tinkering of leadership ranks, including the creation of a new "vice ranking member" slot for a junior Democrat at each House committee.

In the minority, Pelosi's lingering legislative influence was both positive and negative. In March 2015, she worked with Speaker John Boehner in an impressive joint show of strength to win overwhelming House passage of a "doc fix" bill that solved longstanding problems with Medicare and other health care programs. Then, she had a showdown with Obama in June 2015 when she joined with rank-and-file Democrats who mostly opposed the expedited congressional procedures on the prospective Trans-Pacific Partnership agreement that the president and his aides were negotiating with Asian allies and had become a centerpiece of his second-term agenda. In effect, Pelosi abandoned the lame-duck president for the Democrats' allies in organized labor, even though Obama made a last-minute personal plea for support at a closed-door meeting of the caucus.

In the 2016 election, Democrats regained only six seats. The bigger shock of Hillary Clinton losing to Donald Trump left House Democrats with an even weaker legislative hand. Eventually, however, the unpopularity of Trump and Democrats' rabid opposition to the Republican agenda sparked new enthusiasm among activists about their prospects for big House gains in 2018. Pelosi moved aggressively to take advantage of that opportunity — especially with fundraising and candidate recruitment. She kept a lower profile in seeking to shape the campaign message.

Democrats were disappointed by their failure to win any of the four special elections for Republican-held open seats during the first six months of 2017, including a district in the Atlanta suburbs that had record spending. Their initial breakthrough came in March 2018 when Democratic newcomer Conor Lamb won the vacant seat in the Pittsburgh suburbs and rural areas of southwest Pennsylvania — though Lamb emphasized during his campaign that he would not support Pelosi for a House leadership position. In his ads, the former Marine called it "a big lie" by Republicans that he would support Pelosi. Not least because of Lamb's success, that soon became a pattern for front-line Democratic candidates, including some in her home state. Pelosi and her allies shrugged, at least for public consumption. "I think I'm worth the trouble," she told reporters, when asked about the continuing GOP attacks on Democrats who might be supporting her.

In her efforts to assist front-line candidates across the country, Pelosi's actions fit a familiar pattern: Closed-door events with the candidate and donors; very few public sessions; and minimal contact with local news media, except for occasional interviews with friendly reporters — sometimes accompanied by other prominent Democrats. For the most part, she stayed out of Trump's line of fire. And, compared to years earlier, her comments about Democrats' legislative plans were more generic. As of mid-October 2018, as Democrats had improved their prospects for taking House control, Pelosi and Democratic colleagues had "begun mapping out their priorities," Politico reported.

Once it became clear that Democrats had regained House control, Pelosi's immediate priority was gaining assurance that she would have the requisite 218 votes to become Speaker. That became an exhausting process that took nearly a month to resolve, with various Democrats voicing differing levels of commitment and seeking favors in exchange. She finally secured the requisite support only after submitting to the demands of some Democratic reformers that she agree to limit her tenure as the top House Democrat.

Her challenge was all the more difficult because many of the Democrats least willing to support her were elected in districts most likely to have competitive contests in 2020. In the Jan. 3, 2019, selection of the new Speaker, Pelosi received 220 votes — four more than the required majority of those voting. Of the 15 Democrats who voted for another person or responded "present," 11 (including Lamb) were serving their first full term. Each of those 11 took a seat that previously was held by a Republican.

Back home, Pelosi has been overwhelmingly reelected — typically with more than 80 percent of the vote. In 2008, antiwar protester Cindy Sheehan ran against her as an independent. Pelosi refused to debate or acknowledge Sheehan, who wound up getting 16 percent of the vote, more than the Republican nominee's 10 percent. Pelosi got 72 percent.

CA-12: San Francisco   **Cook Partisan Voting Index: D+37**

Population		Race and Ethnicity		Income	
Total	752,652	White	43.1%	Median Income	$97,282
Land area (sq. miles)	39	Black	5.1%	District Income Rank	17
Pop/ sq mi	19313.6	Latino	14.9%	Poverty Rate	11.8%
Born in State	38.8%	Asian	31.8%	With health insurance	94.6%
		Two or more races	4%	Cash public assistance	2.4%
Age Groups		Other	1.1%	Food stamp/SNAP	5%
Under 18	13.1%				
18-34	30.8%	**Education**		**Work**	
35-64	41.4%	H.S grad or less	23.5%	White Collar	14.7%
Over 64	14.7%	Some college	19.2%	Sales and Service	34.8%
		College Degree, 4 yr	34.2%	Blue Collar	8.5%
Military		Post grad	23.2%	Government	10.8%
Veteran/ Active Duty	3.4%				

2012 Pres. Vote	Obama	269,461	(84%)	Romney	40,003	(13%)		
2016 Pres. Vote	Clinton	309,221	(86%)	Trump	31,158	(9%)	Stein	8,881	(3%)
	Johnson	7,949	(2%)					

San Francisco: On Feb. 20, 1915, a crowd of 150,000 gathered on the grounds of the Panama-Pacific International Exposition to see the Spanish-Italian baroque-style structure built on reclaimed land in what was to become San Francisco's Marina district. The Exposition ostensibly celebrated the completion of the Panama Canal, but it was clearly intended to show off San Francisco's recovery from the 1906 earthquake. It also spotlighted the city as the central focus of America's efforts to open an economic door to the eastern part of the world, especially in light of the acquisition of Hawaii and the Philippines and of its interest in an open-door policy with China and trade with Japan. The Exposition established the physical style of San Francisco, encouraging the use of Mediterranean color, accent and detail that characterizes many of the post-Victorian houses and commercial structures in The City, as the San Francisco Examiner called it for years. It set the tone for the picturesque Marina district, and for Fisherman's Wharf and Ghirardelli Square. On a sunny day, San Francisco can look almost tropical, with brown mountains baking in the sun and light shining off the pastel stucco buildings. When the clouds scud in from the Pacific, it can look sinister, full of dark corners where a private detective's partner might encounter unexpected temptations. The buildings can be majestic, like the monumental Beaux-Arts City Hall. The tawdry hotels of the Tenderloin District have become a gritty neighborhood with its own charms. The hills can be a grueling hike — and seem disproportionately uphill.

San Francisco grew from nothing to a major city in the single year of 1850, an instant product of the California Gold Rush. Within just a few years, culture was flourishing in the city, and San Francisco developed a parochial pride in the great writers who worked there — Jack London, Ambrose Bierce, Frank Norris — and in giving birth to the Arts and Crafts movement. Later, San Francisco newspaper scribe Herb Caen coined the term "beatnik" to describe the youthful penchant for freedom in the 1950s and wrote definitively about the hippies who thronged Haight-Ashbury a decade later. In the 1970s, the city was among the first to embrace the gay rights movement, in The Castro district. Gays lately have been moving to the suburbs and straights have been moving into the city. In 2014, a Gallup survey found that the overall metro area had the largest LGBT share of the population in the nation, at 6.2 percent, but the city itself was only 3.6 percent. Over the years, the city's booming economy — based initially on food processing, but now on finance, technology and clothing (Levi Strauss, the Gap) — attracted talented newcomers, though its population is increasingly polarized between high-income and low-income. In a growing entertainment district in Mission Bay, the NBA's Warriors planned to open in 2019 their $500 million Chase Center — replacing their longtime home across the bay at the Oracle Center, near the downscale Oakland Coliseum.

The income inequality ratio in San Francisco is especially high chiefly because the wealthy are really wealthy. Thanks to the flood of high-tech workers pouring in, many of whom commute daily to Silicon Valley on luxurious corporate buses ("Google buses"), the city's housing costs are so high that low-income persons have become virtually precluded from living in most parts of the city. In early 2018, the median home-sale price was a mind-boggling $1.6 million, which had doubled in five years. In June 2018, federal statisticians calculated the break point for low-income families in San Francisco, plus Marin and San Mateo counties, was $117,400. This hyper-gentrification has led to economic stratification and has produced growing protests of activists and low-income groups that target the tech industry and developers. San Francisco has the lowest percentage of children, 13 percent, of any major city, raising questions about its post-modern future. Although it is proudly tolerant, San Francisco is one of California's whitest cities, with only about half as many black residents as it had in 1970. The population on the west side is substantially Asian, but Asians are increasingly migrating to other parts of the Bay Area. Demographers projected that the gentrified city could regain its white-majority status. The commuter traffic, already heavy on the freeway and in rapid transit, has started to overwhelm the city's growing network of ferries.

In the past half-century, the city has elected a diverse group of mostly staunch liberal politicians, notably Mayor George Moscone and the first openly gay supervisor, Harvey Milk. Both were shot to death in 1978 by Dan White, a former city supervisor, who was found guilty of the lesser crime of voluntary manslaughter. Over the next decade, the city's cultural liberalism was tempered by Democratic Mayor Dianne Feinstein, who vetoed a domestic partnership ordinance and opposed commercial rent control. In 1995, Willie Brown, ousted after 15 years as speaker of the state Assembly, returned home and was elected mayor. Brown's political flair was always in evidence, but high taxes and an increasing homeless population drove out blue-collar families and immigrants.

As his successor, San Francisco installed Gavin Newsom, who in 2004 started issuing marriage licenses to same-sex couples, although California voters had outlawed same-sex marriage. The state Supreme Court ordered him to stop and voided the marriages. In 2008, Newsom was vindicated when the same court declared the ban on same-sex marriage unconstitutional. That action was temporarily overturned later that year by the statewide Proposition 8, in a 52%-48% vote . The U.S. Supreme Court nullified that referendum in its seminal ruling in June 2013, when it ruled that supporters of the ballot measure had no standing to defend the referendum in court. After Newsom was elected California's lieutenant governor, the Board of Supervisors appointed City Administrator Ed Lee as interim mayor. Lee, the first Asian American to serve in that office, subsequently won two four-year terms, though he died of a heart attack in December 2017. With the election of London Breed, an African American in a city with a 5 percent black population, San Francisco became the largest city in the nation with a woman serving as mayor.

The 12th Congressional District of California takes in most of the city and county of San Francisco, except the southwest corner, which is in the 14th District. It includes all of San Francisco's high-rise downtown area, the crowded and bustling Chinatown, Telegraph Hill, Nob Hill and Russian Hill, North Beach, Pacific Heights, and the Marina District (which does not have a very big marina). In the valleys are the Fillmore and Western Addition areas. The 12th also has Noe Valley; the Castro, still mainly gay; Haight-Ashbury, once the bedraggled center of hippie culture and now another gentrifying San Francisco neighborhood; and Potrero Hill, with its restored houses overlooking downtown. The Asian population of the district has grown to 32 percent, African Americans have dropped to 5 percent and Hispanics are 15 percent. Hillary Clinton won 86 percent of the vote in 2016, placing the 12th among the top 10 most Democratic districts in the nation.

Barbara Lee (D)

Elected 1998, 11th full term, b. Jul 16, 1946; El Paso, TX; Mills College (CA), B.A., 1973; University of California, Berkeley, M.S.W., 1975; Baptist; Divorced; 2 children; 5 grandchildren.

Elected Office: CA Assembly, 1991-1997; CA Senate, 1997-1998.

Professional Career: Chief of Staff, U.S. Rep. Ron Dellums, 1975-1987.

DC Office: 2470 RHOB 20515, 202-225-2661, Fax: 202-225-9817, lee.house.gov

State Offices: Oakland, 510-763-0370.

Committees: *Appropriations*: Agriculture, Rural Development, FDA & Related Agencies; Labor, Health & Human Services, Education & Related Agencies; State, Foreign Operations & Related Programs. *Budget.*

Group Ratings

	ADA	ACLU	AFL-CIO	LCV	ITI	COC	HAFA	ACU	CFG	FRC
2018	-	96%	-	100%	-	45%	9%	8%	23%	0%
2017	100%	C	100%	100%	C	38%	C	4%	5%	0%

Almanac Ratings 2017-18

	Economy	Social	Foreign	Composite
Liberal	100%	98%	100%	99%
Conservative	0%	2%	0%	1%

Key Votes of the 115th Congress

1. Obama-care revision	N	5. Family planning regs	N	9. Guantanamo prisoners	Y
2. Tax Cuts	N	6. Body cameras/immigration	Y	10. Ground missiles, limit	Y
3. Omnibus appropriations	N	7. Abortion ban	N	11. Defense Dept. spending	N
4. Dodd-Frank revision	N	8. Concealed carry	N	12. FISA rules	N

Election Results

Election	Name (Party)	Vote (%)		Cand. Spent	Ind. Exp. Support	Ind. Exp. Oppose
2018 General	Barbara Lee (D)	260,580	(88%)	$1,315,859		
	Laura Wells (G)	34,257	(12%)		$4,500	
2018 Primary	Barbara Lee (D)	159,751	(99%)			

Prior winning percentages: 2016 (91%), 2014 (89%), 2012 (87%), 2010 (84%), 2008 (86%), 2006 (86%), 2004 (85%), 2002 (81%), 2000 (85%), 1998 (83%), 1998 special (67%)

Democrat Barbara Lee, who won a special election in 1998, is one of Congress' most liberal members and a close ally of Speaker Nancy Pelosi, who represents the district across San Francisco Bay. From her seat on the Appropriations Committee, Lee has sought to help the poor while condemning U.S. military involvement overseas and seeking to broaden diplomatic relations. She narrowly lost two bids for House leadership posts to other Democrats who are racial minorities.

Lee spent her childhood in Texas and says her political thinking was shaped by her early exposure to race discrimination. While in labor with her, Lee's mother was at first denied treatment at an El Paso hospital. Lee attended a segregated school in that city until her parents sent their children to a Catholic school. In 1960, the family moved to Southern California, where Lee was the first black cheerleader in her high school, a distinction she won after enlisting the help of the local chapter of the NAACP. In 2008, Lee authored a memoir, Renegade for Peace and Justice, in which she discussed her experiences as a single welfare mother raising two children while attending college and her early days of social advocacy. "In order to go the policy front, I had to do the personal," she said. Lee graduated from Mills College in Oakland and got a degree in social work at the University of California, Berkeley. She started a community mental health center in Berkeley and worked as a staffer for 12 years for Rep. Ron Dellums, who chaired the House Armed Services Committee. She was elected to the California Assembly in 1990 and to the Senate in 1996. After Dellums announced he was resigning, he endorsed Lee as his successor, and she won the special election with 67 percent of the vote. She has not faced a serious primary or general election challenge.

Lee agitates for a reduction in the nation's weapons stockpiles and sharp cuts in Pentagon spending. She was a founder of the Out of Iraq Caucus, a group of the most vocal antiwar House members. In 2008, the House passed, 399-24, her bill to prevent permanent U.S. military bases in Iraq or U.S. control of Iraqi oil. In January 2015, after President Barack Obama announced his plan to restore diplomatic relations with Cuba, the San Francisco Chronicle reported that she had a "gentlewoman's agreement" with Obama that she would become the ambassador to Havana. Lee denied the report and full-scale diplomatic relations were not restored, but she enthusiastically backed his efforts to lift the embargo and reach out to Cuba. She visited Cuba more than two dozen times and met senior officials to facilitate relatively minor agricultural and tourist dealings and to encourage more trust. When Fidel Castro died in November 2016, she extended her "deepest condolences" — a view that was not universally shared in Congress or the country and that was criticized by many.

Lee's consistent opposition to military action occasionally has made her a lonely voice. As most Democrats voted to authorize the Clinton administration to bomb Serbia in 1999, Lee was the only House member to oppose a resolution supporting U.S. troops. In September 2001, she was the only member of Congress to vote against the resolution authorizing the use of force in response to the terrorist attacks. "If we rush to launch a counterattack, we run too great a risk that women, children and other noncombatants will be caught in the crossfire," she said. Lee received threats of violence, and the Capitol police provided her with 24-hour protection. But she had supportive rallies in her district. During the debate in October 2002 to authorize the use of force in Iraq, Lee offered an alternative calling for diplomatic action, which was defeated 355-72.

In 2017, she made another bid to remove presidential authority to use military force against the Islamic State. This time, with a Republican in the White House, some conservative Republicans joined her — citing the need to safeguard the power of Congress to declare war. To the surprise of many, Lee was successful in an Appropriations Committee vote. But Speaker Paul Ryan used his parliamentary power to remove Lee's amendment before the spending bill reached the House floor.

In 2007, House Speaker Nancy Pelosi gave Lee a seat on Appropriations. As co-chair of the Progressive Caucus, she laid out an agenda with three priorities: economic justice and security, protection of civil rights and liberties, and promotion of global peace. As Republican criticism mounted over earmarked spending, Lee remained a staunch defender of the practice. "I'll tell them to come to my community and see what we can accomplish with whatever federal dollars we can get," she said in 2009.

After the 2008 election, Lee became chairwoman of the Congressional Black Caucus. She and other caucus members lamented Obama's failure to pay more attention to minorities. Unlike many other Black Caucus members who backed Hillary Clinton in 2008, Lee was his early supporter, in large part because of Obama's opposition to the Iraq war. In 2016, she did not take sides between Clinton and Sen. Bernie Sanders.

Pursuing her longstanding ambition for a leadership post, Lee ran for vice chair of the Democratic Caucus following the 2016 election. Against Rep. Linda Sanchez from Los Angeles, Lee faced multiple obstacles: The party leadership already included Pelosi from the Bay Area and Rep. James Clyburn of South Carolina from the Black Caucus. Sanchez, at 47, was a generation younger and better connected to various Democratic factions. Sanchez won, 98-96.

Two years later, Lee ran for the vacant position of caucus chair — in the House majority, this time. Her opponent was Hakeem Jeffries of New York, a 48-year-old junior Democrat, also from the Black Caucus. She lost, 123-113, with some residue of ill will. Lee said she was the victim, at 72, of age and sex discrimination — though each of the three top Democratic leaders was older than her. "That's something that women, especially women of color, African-American women, have to face." Pelosi named Lee as the third co-chair of the Democratic Steering and Policy Committee. At Appropriations, Lee's seniority has positioned her close to a subcommittee chairmanship.

CA-13: East Bay

Cook Partisan Voting Index: D+40

Population		Race and Ethnicity		Income	
Total	750,102	White	34.2%	Median Income	$70,222
Land area (sq. miles)	97	Black	17%	District Income Rank	94
Pop/ sq mi	7749.8	Latino	21.9%	Poverty Rate	16.4%
Born in State	48.5%	Asian	20.6%	With health insurance	91.4%
		Two or more races	4.9%	Cash public assistance	3.4%
Age Groups		Other	1.3%	Food stamp/SNAP	8.5%
Under 18	18.9%				
18-34	28.5%	Education		Work	
35-64	39.3%	H.S grad or less	29.6%	White Collar	13.3%
Over 64	13.3%	Some college	23.6%	Sales and Service	36.8%
		College Degree, 4 yr	25.7%	Blue Collar	14.5%
Military		Post grad	21.1%	Government	16%
Veteran/ Active Duty	4.3%				

2012 Pres. Vote	Obama	268,093	(88%)	Romney	27,474	(9%)		
2016 Pres. Vote	Clinton	291,926	(87%)	Trump	22,743	(7%)	Stein	12,039	(4%)

Oakland, Berkeley: On the East Bay opposite San Francisco, Oakland and Berkeley stand today on one of the lushest sites in America, overlooking the San Francisco-Oakland Bay Bridge and the Golden Gate Bridge and basking in the sunshine that is more common here than across the bay. Both cities host great institutions. In different ways they became museum pieces, antiques from a moment in the 1960s when both, especially Berkeley, gained identities that became hard to shake. But Oakland, in particular, has been transformed by the wealth that has made San Francisco accessible chiefly to the top income classes.

Berkeley was founded as a university town, named after the 18th-century Irish philosopher Bishop George Berkeley for his proclamation, "Westward the course of empire takes its way." Famous for years as the home of first-rate scholarship at the University of California, Berkeley became famous politically in the 1960s as ground zero of student rebellion. In 1969, students led protests at "People's Park," a lot owned by the university, and Republican Gov. Ronald Reagan sent in the National Guard to protect state property, an episode in which both sides relished the confrontation. Berkeley gave birth to a street culture that still exists. With its view of the bay, the campus is beautiful, and old buildings like the shingled Claremont Hotel are grand. Construction of new offices and apartment buildings has created a more modern look in the past couple decades.

Oakland has a different history, centered on commerce. (Gertrude Stein was wrong: There is a there there.) It became the western terminus of the transcontinental railroad in 1870 and was connected by ferry to San Francisco. It has always had heavy industry, and its port today is the fifth-busiest in the country. The docks attracted young roustabouts like the writer Jack London, after whom a downtown square is named. With the Bay Area's largest black community, Oakland spawned the Black Panthers, a militant organization that came to define late 1960s radicalism. "The Black Panthers were mostly young activists whose personal lives and oftentimes limited professional opportunities were defined by Oakland's increasingly impoverished landscape," wrote Peniel Joseph in his history of the Black Power movement, Waiting 'Til the Midnight Hour.

In 1994, Jerry Brown arrived. Governor of California 20 years earlier, Brown irritated local factions by firing department heads and ignoring longstanding alliances, but he seemed to take seriously his mission of propelling Oakland to prominence. Crime rates dropped, and the local economy thrived, partly with the growth of middle-income refugees from the exorbitant housing costs of San Francisco. Many longtime residents, especially African Americans, complained about rising costs, and they moved to the outskirts. The city's black population fell from 47 percent in 1980 to 24 percent in 2017.

Although poverty remained prevalent, the Oakland real estate market rebounded. Population, after falling by 10,000 from 2000 to 2010, increased by 34,000 in the next seven years. Hispanics increased to 27 percent and Asians to 16 percent. The December 2016 Ghost Ship fire that killed 36 persons at a warehouse in an entertainment district was horrific, though it put a spotlight on the bustling arts scene in Oakland. The Oakland Airport completed a $200 million renovation of its main terminal. In 2017, it had its most passengers since 2007.

The local sports scene was in turmoil. After winning the NBA championship three times since 2015 at Oracle Arena in Oakland, the Golden State Warriors crossed the bay in 2019 to a new arena in San Francisco's Mission Bay. The NFL's Raiders, following the failure of lengthy discussions for a new stadium in Oakland, planned to move in 2020 to a publicly financed stadium in Las Vegas; after failing to find a temporary home elsewhere and withdrawing legal complaints against their long-time landlord, they agreed in February 2019 to stay at least one more year in Oakland. The apparent good news was that baseball's Athletics said they would build a stadium near Jack London Square and convert their home at the Oakland Coliseum into an amphitheater, with a tech center and housing.

The 13th Congressional District of California consists of Oakland and Berkeley; the suburb of San Leandro, originally settled by Portuguese immigrants; and the island city of Alameda. It's the most Democratic district in California and one of the most liberal in the nation. The 7 percent of the vote in 2016 for Donald Trump in the 13th was lower than all but two districts in New York City.

Jackie Speier (D)

Elected 2008, 6th full term, b. May 14, 1950; San Francisco County; University of California, Davis, B.A., 1972; University of California Hastings College of Law, J.D., 1976; Roman Catholic; Married (Barry Dennis); 2 children.

Elected Office: San Mateo County Board of Supervisors, 1980-1986; CA Assembly, 1986-1998; CA Senate, 1998-2006.

Professional Career: Staff aide, Rep. Leo Ryan, 1973-1978; Director, gov. affairs, Community Gatepath, 1996-1998; Director, gov. affairs, Electronic Arts, 1996-1998; Attorney, 2007-2008.

DC Office: 2465 RHOB 20515, 202-225-3531, Fax: 202-226-4183, speier.house.gov

State Offices: San Mateo, 650-342-0300.

Committees: *Armed Services*: Military Personnel (Chmn); Strategic Forces. *Oversight & Reform*: Government Operations; Subcommittee on Environment. *Permanent Select on Intelligence*: Counterterrorism, Counterintelligence & Counterproliferation; Intelligence Modernization & Readiness.

Group Ratings

	ADA	ACLU	AFL-CIO	LCV	ITI	COC	HAFA	ACU	CFG	FRC
2018	-	82%	-	-	-	60%	14%	-	35%	0%
2017	90%	C	92%	100%	C	46%	C	4%	5%	0%

Almanac Ratings 2017-18

	Economy	Social	Foreign	Composite
Liberal	94%	87%	100%	94%
Conservative	6%	13%	0%	6%

Key Votes of the 115th Congress

1. Obama-care revision	N	5. Family planning regs	N	9. Guantanamo prisoners	Y
2. Tax Cuts	N	6. Body cameras/immigration	Y	10. Ground missiles, limit	Y
3. Omnibus appropriations	N	7. Abortion ban	N	11. Defense Dept. spending	N
4. Dodd-Frank revision	NV	8. Concealed carry	N	12. FISA rules	N

Election Results

Election	Name (Party)	Vote (%)		Cand. Spent	Ind. Exp. Support	Ind. Exp. Oppose
2018 General	Jackie Speier (D)	211,384	(79%)	$678,662		
	Cristina Osmena (R)	55,439	(21%)			
2018 Primary	Jackie Speier (D)	123,900	(79%)			
	Cristina Osmena (R)	32,054	(21%)			

Prior winning percentages: 2016 (81%), 2014 (77%), 2012 (79%), 2010 (76%), 2008 (75%)

Democrat Jackie Speier, who won a special election in April 2008, has become an influential House Democrat dealing with military and intelligence issues. She has become an outspoken advocate for gender equity and has taken a special interest in accountability for rapes and sexual assaults within the military and in society as a whole. In the House, she brought with her unique experiences as a young House aide. A committed liberal, she also has focused on consumer-protection issues.

Born in San Francisco's Sunset district, Speier graduated from the University of California, Davis, and got her law degree at UC Hastings College of the Law. While an undergraduate, she interned in Sacramento for Democratic Assemblyman Leo Ryan and later joined his staff after he was elected to Congress. In November 1978, Speier accompanied third-term Rep. Ryan to Jonestown Guyana, to investigate claims that some of Ryan's constituents, who were members of a church called the Peoples Temple, were being held against their will by the Rev. Jim Jones of San Francisco. Some defectors from the church joined Ryan's entourage for the journey home, but the group made it only as far as the airport. Four assassins sent by Jones opened fire on the defenseless group. Ryan and four others, including two journalists, were killed. Speier was shot five times and left for dead on the airstrip, where she waited 15 hours before the Guyana police rescued her. In the meantime, Jones, back at his jungle camp, set in motion events that shocked the world. He forced his cult followers to commit "revolutionary suicide" by drinking poison-laced punch, which resulted in the deaths of more than 900 followers, some of them babies and children.

Once back in California, Speier underwent 10 surgeries, including skin grafts. Despite her injuries, she ran in the special election to succeed Ryan, gaining only 15 percent of the total vote and finishing third among Democrats in the primary. She then went local to build her political career, starting on the San Mateo County Board of Supervisors and serving 18 years in the state legislature. Her pinnacle achievement was legislation protecting consumers' privacy from invasive practices by banks and insurance companies. In 2006, she unsuccessfully sought the nomination for lieutenant governor.

When Democratic Rep. Tom Lantos, chairman of the House Foreign Affairs Committee and the only Holocaust survivor to serve in Congress, announced his retirement in January 2008, he endorsed Speier as his successor. He died in February of complications from cancer of the esophagus. She won the all-party special election with 75 percent of the vote against four little-known opponents.

Immediately after she took her oath of office, she caused a ruckus when she launched a sharp partisan attack on President George W. Bush's handling of the war in Iraq. "History will not judge us kindly if we sacrifice four generations of Americans because of the folly of one," she declared. Her remarks triggered a volley of boos among Republican members on the House floor. Speier responded that she had been "forthright." In 2010, Speier joined 59 other Democrats in voting for a resolution requiring the withdrawal of troops from Afghanistan.

As a member of the Armed Services Committee, Speier regularly has spoken about military men and women who have been raped or sexually assaulted, and she has taken the lead in improving delivery of benefits to Bay Area veterans. As chairwoman—and previously ranking Democrat--on the committee's personnel panel, she has advocated steps such as access to free birth control and counseling for women in the military. Her objective, Speier said, was "to ensure that our government demonstrates the same level of commitment to our military personnel that they demonstrate by putting their lives on the line to defend our country." On the House Intelligence Committee, she said in April 2017 that Rep. Devin Nunes of California, the chairman of the panel, should resign that post because he had shared sensitive information with White House officials. Nunes subsequently stepped aside as chairman for several months, pending an ethics investigation.

Speier expanded her focus on sexual assault to academia, where she has shined the spotlight on sexual harassers. She filed a bill to require universities to operate under greater transparency with respect to substantiated cases of sex discrimination. In 2014, she called on NFL Commissioner Roger

Goodell to resign because of his handling of domestic-violence cases involving several of the league's players. After Education Secretary Betsy DeVos rescinded Obama-era guidance on campus sexual assaults, citing its denial of due process, Speier filed a bill in October 2017 to codify the old guidance. As she put it, "we're not going back to a period of time when a woman who is raped is not believed or her case is swept under the rug."

When the "me too" movement gained force in 2017, Speier took the lead in calling for accountability for members of Congress accused of sexual harassment. With Republican Rep. Barbara Comstock of Virginia, she described incidents that she and other women experienced as congressional aides — including, Speier said, some who had "their private parts grabbed on the House floor." She explicitly condemned the behavior of members who subsequently resigned within weeks, including Democratic Sen. Al Franken of Minnesota, Democratic Rep. John Conyers of Michigan and Republican Rep. Blake Farenthold of Texas. In December 2018, Speier joined a bipartisan group that reached agreement to revise procedures for how sexual harassment allegations are handled in Congress, including a requirement that violators are personally liable for financial settlements. "Time is finally up for members of Congress who think that they can sexually harass and get away with it," she said.

Earlier in her career, Speier focused on more traditional consumer and fairness issues. She spent five days living on a food-stamp budget of $4.50 a day to call attention to rising poverty. During debate in 2009 on financial services regulations, Speier passed in the House an amendment requiring big banks to have at least $1 in capital for every $15 in assets. In the final bill, lawmakers eased the requirement.

Speier considered running for state attorney general in 2010 but opted to stay in the House. She has not faced a serious reelection challenge. Following the 2018 election, she published a memoir, Undaunted, including candid accounts of her personal and professional trials.

CA-14: San Francisco Peninsula   Cook Partisan Voting Index: D+27

Population		Race and Ethnicity		Income	
Total	750,274	White	34.6%	Median Income	$101,753
Land area (sq. miles)	260	Black	2.9%	District Income Rank	11
Pop/ sq mi	2891.2	Latino	23.9%	Poverty Rate	7.6%
Born in State	46.9%	Asian	33%	With health insurance	94%
Age Groups		Two or more races	3.9%	Cash public assistance	1.7%
Under 18	20%	Other	1.8%	Food stamp/SNAP	3.8%
18-34	23.3%	**Education**		**Work**	
35-64	41.5%	H.S grad or less	27.9%	White Collar	15.2%
Over 64	15.2%	Some college	26%	Sales and Service	41.2%
Military		College Degree, 4 yr	28.3%	Blue Collar	13.7%
Veteran/ Active Duty	4.2%	Post grad	17.8%	Government	12%

2012 Pres. Vote	Obama	200,343	(74%)	Romney	63,589	(24%)		
2016 Pres. Vote	Clinton	229,008	(76%)	Trump	54,229	(18%)	Johnson	8,126 (3%)

San Mateo: The city of San Francisco sits at the tip of the San Francisco Peninsula on the California coast. This is geologically interesting country. The San Andreas Fault runs just east of the Coast Range, underneath the reservoirs that store San Francisco's water supply. To the west are green mountains running down to the ocean. To the east is a zone of flat land between the mountains and San Francisco Bay, an unbroken chain of suburbs and urban settlement, with light industry and salt flats along the bay front. Daly City and Pacifica on the ocean are a kind of extension of San Francisco's old working-class districts, with boxy houses on streets looking out on the ocean or the freeway. Today, these neighborhoods are home to many of the Bay Area's Asian immigrants. Pacific Islanders are prominent, too. A large concentration of Samoans is in Daly City, and San Bruno is home to a sizable Tongan community. A strip of Highway 1 that winds along the coastal cliffs south of Pacifica has passed through an area known as "Devil's Slide" for the mudslides that often follow heavy storms. A nearly one-mile tunnel now bypasses Devil's Slide.

On the bay side is South San Francisco, where Herb Boyer and Bob Swanson sketched on a napkin their plans for the first biotechnology company, Genentech. They bought space in an old warehouse on the waterfront near a Bethlehem Steel plant. The area is now one large biotech campus overlooking the bay, with lawns, parkways and earth-toned office complexes, the center of the industry. YouTube, started in 2005, is headquartered in San Bruno. Oracle, a computer software company, is based in a cluster of gleaming glass buildings in Redwood City. The exorbitant cost of real estate has imposed a premium on large employers. On the site of the former Bay Meadows racetrack near San Mateo, developers completed in 2018 the first phase of their 83-acre master-planned community. Stanford University opened in 2019 its Redwood City campus, four building complexes that were scheduled to house 2,700 employees and provide extensive amenities on 35 acres, five miles up El Camino Real. This is the first major expansion of the university from Leland Stanford's original "farm," as many refer to the main campus.

Between the Bayshore Freeway and Interstate 280 are middle class suburbs that grew up to be cities with office complexes — Millbrae, Burlingame, San Mateo and San Carlos. The supply of new housing has not come close to keeping up with demand. From 2010 until 2015, only 3,844 new homes were built at the same time that 72,000 jobs were created, according to a report by a local business group. Given that a disproportionate share of those new homes were in the deluxe class, that helps to explain why many workers have been forced to look elsewhere for a home. In San Mateo and San Francisco, households with up to $117,000 income were classified at the poverty level, in terms of their costs. Agricultural production in San Mateo, which remains chiefly in floral and nursery crops, has dropped because of such factors as the paucity of labor, the high cost of land and the drought. The area has been the source of incredible athletic talent: Junipero Serra, an all-boys Catholic high school in San Mateo, enrolled both New England Patriots quarterback Tom Brady and former San Francisco Giants slugger Barry Bonds.

The 14th Congressional District of California consists of these northern peninsula suburbs plus the southwest corner of San Francisco, which has less than 20 percent of the district population. It takes in about 80 percent of affluent San Mateo County. The 14th is 33 percent Asian and 24 percent Hispanic. The economic orientation here was historically toward San Francisco, then later toward Silicon Valley. But now the district has its own burgeoning biotech industry, with income levels among the highest in California.

Eric Swalwell (D)

Elected 2012, 4th term, b. Nov 16, 1980; Sac City, IA; University of Maryland - College Park, B.A., 2003; University of Maryland School of Law, J.D., 2006; Christian - Non-Denominational; Married (Brittany Ann Watts); 2 children.

Elected Office: Dublin City Council, 2010-2012.

Professional Career: Deputy District Attorney, Alameda County, 2006-2012.

DC Office: 407 CHOB 20515, 202-225-5065, Fax: 202-226-3805, swalwell.house.gov

State Offices: Castro Valley, 510-370-3322.

Committees: House Democratic Steering and Policy Committee Co-Chair. *Judiciary*: Constitution, Civil Rights & Civil Liberties; Courts, Intellectual Property & Internet. *Permanent Select on Intelligence*: Intelligence Modernization & Readiness (Chmn); Strategic Technologies & Advanced Research.

Group Ratings

	ADA	ACLU	AFL-CIO	LCV	ITI	COC	HAFA	ACU	CFG	FRC
2018	-	78%	-	89%	-	50%	10%	4%	25%	0%
2017	90%	C	95%	97%	C	43%	C	4%	5%	0%

Almanac Ratings 2017-18

	Economy	Social	Foreign	Composite
Liberal	96%	90%	97%	94%
Conservative	4%	10%	3%	6%

Key Votes of the 115th Congress

1. Obama-care revision	N	5. Family planning regs	N	9. Guantanamo prisoners	Y
2. Tax Cuts	N	6. Body cameras/immigration	Y	10. Ground missiles, limit	Y
3. Omnibus appropriations	N	7. Abortion ban	N	11. Defense Dept. spending	N
4. Dodd-Frank revision	N	8. Concealed carry	N	12. FISA rules	Y

Election Results

Election	Name (Party)	Vote (%)	Cand. Spent	Ind. Exp. Support	Ind. Exp. Oppose
2018 General	Eric Swalwell (D)...............................177,989	(73%)	$1,792,682		
	Rudy Peters (R)...................................65,940	(27%)	$55,343		
2018 Primary	Eric Swalwell (D)................................90,971	(71%)			
	Rudy Peters (R)...................................33,771	(26%)			

Prior winning percentages: 2016 (74%), 2014 (70%), 2012 (52%)

Democrat Eric Swalwell, elected in 2012 when he defeated a 40-year Democratic incumbent who had been a Bay Area icon, moved quickly to mend fences with Democratic Leader Nancy Pelosi and her team. With his youth and focus on tech and intelligence issues, Swalwell has brought fresh thinking and a hyper-active media presence. He also sought to create a political presence as a 2020 presidential candidate, with his appeal to the millennial generation.

Born in Sac City Iowa, Swalwell grew up in Dublin California. He attended the University of Maryland, where he was bitten by the political bug and graduated with a bachelor's in government and politics and then a law degree. He got his start in politics as an unpaid intern on Capitol Hill, working for then-Rep. Ellen Tauscher, a Bay Area Democrat. To make ends meet, he worked two summer jobs around the Capitol, at the local gym and a restaurant, where he kept an eye out for members of Congress. After graduation, Swalwell returned to California and got a job as a prosecutor in the Alameda County district attorney's office, where he rose to the post of deputy district attorney. "I put a lot of bad guys away," he told voters on the campaign trail. In 2010, he ran successfully for city council in Dublin, an outer suburb of San Francisco.

Other prominent California Democrats had been patiently waiting for Rep. Pete Stark to retire, including former Obama administration official Ro Khanna, who raised more than $1 million for a congressional bid. But as the 2012 election approached, Khanna and others opted to let the irascible Stark — a senior Democrat on the House Ways and Means Committee -- serve another term unchallenged. Swalwell jumped the line. Much of the Democratic establishment backed Stark. Swalwell got support from a smattering of local officials, including Tauscher, his former boss, who became a State Department official in the Obama administration. Swalwell began the campaign by pointedly competing in running races across the district, a series his campaign dubbed the "race for change." The contrast between the 80-year-old incumbent and the 31-year-old challenger was hard to miss. Beyond his hustle, Swalwell's campaign was largely fueled by Stark's own missteps. During a debate, Stark made multiple mistakes for which he had to apologize.

Swalwell reached out to Republicans and independents dissatisfied with Stark's long liberal tenure. He didn't promise to vote all that differently from Stark — he describes himself as a solid Democrat, though he believes "every human problem does not need a legislative solution" — but said that he would at least listen intently as their congressman. His 52%-48% victory in the November run-off was an ironic way for Stark to exit: Four decades earlier, Stark had made much the same argument in unseating the previous octogenarian congressman. Swalwell has the time to match their mark -- but might not have the patience.

Swalwell began his campaign in 2014 with warnings from Stark and his allies that they planned to get even. His chief challenger was Democratic state Senate Majority Leader Ellen Corbett. She attacked Swalwell's inexperience and lack of Democratic credentials. Turning the tables, the incumbent claimed support from the party establishment and benefited from a huge fundraising advantage. Corbett raised only $225,000 to Swalwell's $2 million for the cycle. Surprisingly, Corbett failed to survive the all-party primary. Swalwell got 49 percent of the total vote, and Corbett ran 430 votes behind Republican candidate Hugh Bussell. The general election became an afterthought, with Swalwell winning, 70%-30%. Since then, his Republican challengers have had scant financing or prospects in this district.

Swalwell joined the Intelligence Committee and served as the ranking Democrat on its CIA Subcommittee, which oversees the agency's policy, activities and budget. The House-passed intelligence authorization bill in 2016 included his proposal to keep Congress informed about foreign fighters traveling to terrorist safe havens. In April 2017, Swalwell joined the partisan conflicts on the committee. He attacked Rep. Devin Nunes, a California Republican, for releasing a memo alleging illegal government surveillance of the Trump campaign in 2016 and said that he should step down as committee chairman. "What the Republicans did was poisonous to the investigation" of alleged Russian interference, he said. Nunes subsequently stepped aside for a few months during an Ethics Committee review. When House Republicans ended their investigation a year later, Swalwell said that they sent "a bright green light to Russia to continue its interference at America's ballot boxes."

On the Judiciary Committee, Swalwell filed with veteran Republican Rep. Jim Sensenbrenner of Wisconsin the Rapid DNA bill, which encouraged new technology for quick analysis of such evidence in police investigations. In December 2018, when Swalwell mocked the National Rifle Association with a tweet that it would lose its "war" if it fought a government attempt to confiscate guns, the NRA ran a cover story about him in its magazine, which it titled, "Gas Bag in the House." He tweeted triumphantly that he was "living in the NRA's head."

Swalwell kept busy with party-oriented work. He joined other junior House Democrats to create the Future Forum — chiefly to engage with millennials, especially on campuses. With his social-media skills, he became the Snapchat king of Congress. Pelosi gave him a political assignment to oversee Democratic outreach to young voters. She also appointed Swalwell to an insider post as co-chair of the Democratic Steering and Policy Committee. He became a frequent talking head on news broadcasts, especially to discuss issues facing the Intelligence Committee. In 2019, he became chairman of the panel's Intelligence Modernization and Readiness Subcommittee.

Swalwell made the most of these assignments and stopped regularly in Iowa and New Hampshire during his weekly cross-country trips from his district to Washington. Following the 2018 election, he grew more open about his plan to run for president and impressed some Democratic voters with his youthful enthusiasm and partisan attacks. Kicking off his presidential bid in April 2019 with a rally at the high school in Dublin where he graduated, Swalwell listed gun safety as "my top priority." He left the door open to run for reelection to the House in 2020 if his presidential campaign was not "viable." The history of House members running for president has not been encouraging.

CA-15: Southern East Bay   **Cook Partisan Voting Index: D+20**

Population		Race and Ethnicity		Income	
Total	764,963	White	33.6%	Median Income	$103,109
Land area (sq. miles)	599	Black	5.7%	District Income Rank	10
Pop/ sq mi	1276.1	Latino	22.8%	Poverty Rate	7.3%
Born in State	51.1%	Asian	32.3%	With health insurance	94.5%
		Two or more races	4.2%	Cash public assistance	3.2%
Age Groups		Other	1.5%	Food stamp/SNAP	5.4%
Under 18	23.9%				
18-34	21.6%	**Education**		**Work**	
35-64	42.1%	H.S grad or less	29.9%	White Collar	12.4%
Over 64	12.4%	Some college	26.8%	Sales and Service	36.7%
Military		College Degree, 4 yr	26.7%	Blue Collar	16.1%
Veteran/ Active Duty	4.8%	Post grad	16.6%	Government	11.6%

2012 Pres. Vote	Obama	177,243	(68%)	Romney	77,748	(30%)			
2016 Pres. Vote	Clinton	198,964	(69%)	Trump	68,808	(24%)	Johnson	10,604	(4%)

Hayward, Fremont: The East Bay is the workaday, unglamorous side of the San Francisco Bay Area — a narrow strip of land between the bay and the surprisingly high mountains that rise just to the east. The shoreline is not picturesque, with its closed-down Navy bases and its docks, airports and salt evaporators. In World War II, when the shipyards of Richmond were buzzing, the East Bay south of Oakland was still largely uninhabited farm fields. After the war, the area filled up, south along old Route 17: Hayward, with its California State University campus and seafood industry; Union

City, with its rail yards; and Newark, with dozens of industrial plants ranging from salt processing to computer network servers. Hit hard by the dot-com bust at the turn of the century, the East Bay revived with biotech, construction and health care.

The national labs are a vital presence here. At Lawrence Livermore National Laboratory, the federal government conducts nuclear-warhead and energy research. In October 2018, the lab unveiled a new supercomputer, which was the third largest in the world and will guard the nation's nuclear stockpile. Also in Livermore is a part of the Albuquerque-based Sandia National Labs, which offers scientific and technological expertise on the nation's most challenging security issues. Since the 1980s, anti-nuclear protestors have gathered at Livermore to commemorate historical events and denounce nuclear weapons.

Underneath the East Bay is the Hayward Fault, not as famous as the San Andreas, but a branch of it that is just as dangerous. An earthquake there in 1868 registered about 7.0 on the Richter scale and destroyed downtown Hayward. Another rupture is overdue, and 7 million people in the region might be shaken significantly. In January 2018, an earthquake with a 4.4 magnitude struck underneath Berkeley. It was the biggest shake from the Hayward Fault since a 4.5 tremblor hit Fremont in 1981. Another major local hazard: Coastal land has been sinking in the Hayward area at a dangerous pace and faster than elsewhere along San Francisco Bay, according to academic researchers. Rising sea levels have compounded the threat.

The 15th Congressional District of California is made up of East Bay towns in southern Alameda County and part of Castro Valley. It includes a small slice of Contra Costa County near San Ramon. The majority-minority district is racially and ethnically mixed: 32 percent Asian, 23 percent Hispanic, and 6 percent black. It includes Hayward, with its Hispanic and Asian populations that are two-thirds of the total for the city, and Union City, which has become more than 50 percent Asian. In 2016, Hillary Clinton got 69 percent of the vote, which was smaller than her vote in seven other Bay Area districts.

Jim Costa (D)

Elected 2004, 8th term, b. Apr 13, 1952; Fresno; California State University, Fresno, B.S., 1974; Roman Catholic; Single.

Elected Office: CA Assembly, 1978-1994; CA Senate, 1994-2002.

Professional Career: Consultant, 2002-2004.

DC Office: 2081 RHOB 20515, 202-225-3341, Fax: 202-225-9308, costa.house.gov

State Offices: Fresno, 559-495-1620; Merced, 209-384-1620.

Committees: *Agriculture*: Livestock & Foreign Agriculture (Chmn). *Foreign Affairs*: Europe, Eurasia, Energy & the Environment. *Natural Resources*: Water, Oceans & Wildlife.

Group Ratings

	ADA	ACLU	AFL-CIO	LCV	ITI	COC	HAFA	ACU	CFG	FRC
2018	-	60%	-	69%	-	70%	12%	27%	13%	0%
2017	60%	C	71%	31%	C	79%	C	5%	10%	0%

Almanac Ratings 2017-18

	Economy	Social	Foreign	Composite
Liberal	40%	76%	73%	63%
Conservative	60%	24%	27%	37%

Key Votes of the 115th Congress

1. Obama-care revision	N	5. Family planning regs	N	9. Guantanamo prisoners	Y
2. Tax Cuts	N	6. Body cameras/immigration	NV	10. Ground missiles, limit	Y
3. Omnibus appropriations	Y	7. Abortion ban	N	11. Defense Dept. spending	Y
4. Dodd-Frank revision	Y	8. Concealed carry	N	12. FISA rules	Y

Election Results

Election	Name (Party)	Vote (%)		Cand. Spent	Ind. Exp. Support	Ind. Exp. Oppose
2018 General	Jim Costa (D)..	82,266	(58%)	$2,322,182	$110,097	$58,486
	Elizabeth Heng (R)................................	60,693	(42%)	$1,226,518		
2018 Primary	Jim Costa (D)..	39,527	(53%)			
	Elizabeth Heng (R)................................	35,080	(47%)			

Prior winning percentages: 2016 (58%), 2014 (51%), 2012 (57%), 2010 (52%), 2008 (74%), 2006 (unopposed), 2004 (53%)

Democrat Jim Costa, elected in 2004, is a third-generation farmer who concentrates on the agricultural issues that affect his district's rural residents, often going his own way from his party. The 2018 election, in addition to giving Costa influential niches on his committees, restored Democrats to neighboring districts north and south of his seat in the Central Valley. He continues to survive competitive reelection challenges.

Born in Fresno, he was raised on his family's dairy farm. He is the grandson of Portuguese immigrants who settled in the San Joaquin Valley near the turn of the 20th century. In 1978, Costa was elected to the state Assembly, where he was known as a moderate Democrat. In 2002, after he was forced to retire at age 50 because of term limits, Costa founded a consulting firm. Two years later, when Democratic Rep. Cal Dooley retired after 14 years, Costa entered the race with solid name recognition. In the March primary, he faced a bruising challenge from Lisa Quigley, Dooley's chief of staff. Quigley grew up in the Central Valley, but she hadn't lived in the district in nearly two decades. Costa questioned her residency and her agricultural credentials. Quigley was endorsed by Dooley and national abortion rights groups, and she painted Costa as a special-interest lobbyist. In the campaign's final days, Quigley ran ads mentioning Costa's 1986 arrest for soliciting a prostitute and a 1994 incident in which police found drug paraphernalia in his home. Costa shrugged off the attacks and won the primary by an unexpectedly large 73%-27%.

In the general election, Costa began as a clear favorite in the Democratic-leaning district. But the Republican nominee, state Sen. Roy Ashburn, ran a formidable campaign. He criticized Costa for supporting tax policies that he said hurt low-income families. The National Republican Congressional Committee ran $1.5 million in ads saying, "Jim Costa — he's gonna cost ya." But Costa's lengthy legislative record didn't readily lend itself to the "liberal" label. In a relatively low turnout event, Costa won 53%-47%.

Costa sits on the Agriculture and Natural Resources committees, both important to his district. In 2019, he became chairman of the Livestock and Foreign Agriculture Subcommittee. As a member of the House-Senate conference committee that completed the 2018 farm bill, Costa claimed credit for export incentives for California-grown commodities, technical assistance for fruit and vegetable growers and increased groundwater management.

Local water supply has been a continuing preoccupation for Costa. With then-Rep. Dennis Cardoza, a fellow Blue Dog from the valley, he was among the final undecided votes in 2010 on President Barack Obama's health care overhaul. Republicans charged that they were given extra public water allocations for their region, though both denied there was any connection. Costa was one of 10 Democrats to vote for California GOP Rep. Devin Nunes' House-passed bill in 2012 to change California's system of water laws to benefit San Joaquin Valley farmers. In 2016, he helped to enact the sweeping water resources bill, with vital provisions that steered more water to the San Joaquin Delta. He cited flood planning for Merced County, steps to stretch the water supply of the San Joaquin River and expedited review of proposed water transfers. In 2018, the omnibus measure enacted for water development included Costa's bipartisan bill to increase water-storage capacity.

Costa has bucked his party on fiscal issues that bring out his conservative impulses. He was one of 22 House Democrats to support a failed proposal in 2012 to adopt the Simpson-Bowles commission's budget, which would have imposed politically painful spending reductions to balance the budget.

Costa did not face a significant reelection challenge until 2010. That year, Republican rancher Andy Vidak sought to blame Costa for the area's weak economy, running billboards depicting him as the pitchfork-holding "American Gothic" farmer with Speaker Nancy Pelosi at his side. Vidak surged in the polls, and in the closing weeks the race became a toss-up. Costa put in a month of heavy retail politicking, and he got last-minute help from the Democratic Congressional Campaign Committee. In a recount that dragged on for three weeks, Costa won 52%-48%.

The 2012 redistricting gave Costa what seemed to be the favorable 16th District, though three-fourths of it was new political territory for him. The 2014 election became a big surprise. In the first round of voting in June, Fresno County dairyman Johnny Tacherra easily led three other Republican candidates and moved into the general election with Costa. Running with no national-party assistance and one modestly paid campaign aide, Tacherra worked the grassroots to show his connection to the drought-stricken district, and he painted the incumbent as out of touch. Costa outspent the challenger by nearly 5-to-1. When the initial votes were tallied, Tacherra shockingly held a narrow lead. But Costa prevailed just before Thanksgiving. He won by 1,334 votes on the strength of taking 64 percent of the Fresno County vote. Tacherra handily won Madera and Merced counties. Following that scare, Costa sided with Republicans on multiple House votes, including support of the Keystone XL pipeline and new restrictions on Obama's regulatory authority.

Costa was better prepared when Tacherra returned for a rematch in 2016. Donald Trump, a Republican handicap in this Latino-majority district, gave Democrats an opportunity to increase turnout. The 168,000 voters were nearly twice the turnout in the 2014 mid-term, With the National Republican Congressional Committee more focused on support for two vulnerable GOP incumbents in the Central Valley, Tacherra had less opportunity to make his case. Costa won 58%-42%. Virtually all of his 27,000-vote margin came from Fresno.

In 2018, Costa faced Elizabeth Heng, the daughter of Cambodian refugees and a former aide to Republican Rep. Ed Royce of California. Heng criticized Costa as unproductive and said that it was time for a change. But it was a bad year for Republicans in California, and Costa outspent her, $2.3 million to $1.2 million. The 58%-42% outcome had a similar pattern to Costa's reelection two years earlier. Following up on the conditional support that he voiced for Nancy Pelosi during his campaign, Costa worked with other moderate Democrats to secure her backing for rules changes before agreeing to vote for her for Speaker.

In the huge California Democratic delegation, Costa is the most senior member from an inland district.

CA-16: Central Valley   Cook Partisan Voting Index: D+9

Population		Race and Ethnicity		Income	
Total	725,356	White	22.8%	Median Income	$40,689
Land area (sq. miles)	2,840	Black	5.5%	District Income Rank	409
Pop/ sq mi	255.4	Latino	60.2%	Poverty Rate	29.3%
Born in State	65%	Asian	9%	With health insurance	87.2%
		Two or more races	1.7%	Cash public assistance	10.1%
Age Groups		Other	0.8%	Food stamp/SNAP	26.3%
Under 18	30.4%				
18-34	26.6%	**Education**		**Work**	
35-64	33%	H.S grad or less	57.7%	White Collar	10%
Over 64	10%	Some college	30%	Sales and Service	43%
		College Degree, 4 yr	8.4%	Blue Collar	35.5%
Military		Post grad	3.9%	Government	15.9%
Veteran/ Active Duty	4.8%				

2012 Pres. Vote	Obama	88,973	(59%)	Romney	59,808	(39%)	
2016 Pres. Vote	Clinton	98,504	(57%)	Trump	61,813	(36%)	Johnson 5,546 (3%)

Merced, Part of Fresno: Under orders from the Spanish governor of California to explore what lay beyond the coastal mountains, army officer Gabriel Moraga became one of the first Europeans to behold the Central Valley, a fertile expanse teaming with wildlife — heron, antelope, elk and grizzly bear. He brought his soldiers through the Pacheco Pass, which would become the main route for exporting the natural riches of the valley to the port cities springing up along the coast. During his travels in the early 1800s, Moraga bestowed Spanish names on the places and rivers he encountered. So the region he was inspired to call "Blessed Sacrament" became Sacramento. After one long and dusty day, he stumbled on a much-welcomed river, which he called Merced, or, "River of Our Lady of Mercy." Like much of the rest of the valley, Merced grew to be a hub of agriculture. Located north of Fresno, its economy was long hitched to agribusiness. Harvest time attracted thousands of itinerant farmworkers from Mexico and elsewhere. Later, the region's affordable housing inspired new waves of migration. By 2017, Latinos had grown to 60 percent of the population in Merced.

The 16th District of California encompasses all of Merced County and takes in parts of Madera and Fresno counties. These parts of the San Joaquin Valley are 60 percent Hispanic and include much of the city of Fresno and its lower-income neighborhoods. The neighboring 22nd District includes more populous and suburban parts of Fresno County; much of the county's farmland is in the 21st. A bit more than a third of the population of the 16th is in Merced, where the per capita income is lower than in Fresno city and county and population growth in 2017 was the fastest in the state. Unemployment here in recent years was among the nation's highest, with Merced County's jobless rate at 20 percent in early 2012. Its 5.9 per cent unemployment rate in September 2018 was the county's lowest since 1990. Still, the 16th and the 21st Districts were tied with the highest poverty rates in the state. The University of California, Merced, the 10th university in the vast UC system, opened in 2005 and had 8,500 students in 2018, with plans for continued rapid growth. Uniquely in the UC system, a slight majority of the students are Latinos and an even larger share of them are the first in their family to attend college, though graduation rates are notably lower than elsewhere in the state. Highway 99 connects most of the key cities and towns in the district, with their common agricultural and water interests: Livingston, Atwater, Merced, Chowchilla, Madera and down to Fresno. After the drought had become a new job crippler and major cutbacks in water supply forced many farmers to reduce their expenses or abandon their fields, the increased water supply since 2016 created a sudden turnaround.

With its heavy concentration of Latinos and other immigrant groups, which respond to Voting Rights Act imperatives for fair Hispanic representation, Hillary Clinton won the 16th with 57 percent. Voter registration and turnout remain relatively low.

Ro Khanna (D)

Elected 2016, 2nd term, b. Sep 13, 1976; Philadelphia, PA; University of Chicago (IL), A.B., 1998; Yale University Law School (CT), J.D., 2001; Hinduism; Married (Ritu Ahuja); 2 children.

Professional Career: Law Professor; Author; Deputy Assistant Secretary, United States Department of Commerce.

DC Office: 221 CHOB 20515, 202-225-2631

State Offices: Santa Clara, 408-436-2720.

Committees: *Armed Services*: Intelligence, Emerging Threats & Capabilities; Strategic Forces. *Budget*. *Oversight & Reform*: Government Operations; Subcommittee on Economic & Consumer Policy.

Group Ratings

	ADA	ACLU	AFL-CIO	LCV	ITI	COC	HAFA	ACU	CFG	FRC
2018	-	93%	-	100%	-	58%	9%	4%	25%	0%
2017	100%	C	95%	97%	C	36%	C	7%	5%	0%

Almanac Ratings 2017-18

	Economy	Social	Foreign	Composite
Liberal	100%	98%	97%	99%
Conservative	0%	2%	3%	2%

Key Votes of the 115th Congress

1. Obama-care revision	N	5. Family planning regs	N	9. Guantanamo prisoners	Y
2. Tax Cuts	N	6. Body cameras/immigration	Y	10. Ground missiles, limit	Y
3. Omnibus appropriations	N	7. Abortion ban	N	11. Defense Dept. spending	N
4. Dodd-Frank revision	N	8. Concealed carry	N	12. FISA rules	N

Election Results

Election	Name (Party)	Vote (%)		Cand. Spent	Ind. Exp. Support	Ind. Exp. Oppose
2018 General	Ro Khanna (D)...............................	159,105	(75%)	$1,724,007	$1,222	
	Ron Cohen (R)...............................	52,057	(25%)	$3,034		
2018 Primary	Ro Khanna (D)...............................	72,676	(62%)			
	Ron Cohen (R)...............................	26,865	(23%)			
	Khanh Tran (D)...............................	8,455	(7%)			
	Stephen Forbes (D)...............................	6,259	(5%)			

Prior winning percentages: 2016 (61%)

Democrat Ro Khanna, elected in 2016, was a patent lawyer in Silicon Valley who was elected to the House after failing in attempts to win two other Bay Area seats. He often advocates the views of the tech industry, though he occasionally has differed with them. As a self-styled reformer, he also has been willing to go his own way among House Democrats. He won his seat against Democratic Rep. Mike Honda in a rematch of their tight contest two years earlier. Like Honda, Khanna was a first-generation Asian American, with immediate ancestors who had been victims of political prosecution.

Khanna was born in Philadelphia. Shortly before, his parents had emigrated from India to seek a better life for their children. His father was an electrical engineer and his mother was a substitute school teacher. Khanna's maternal grandfather had joined the independence movement in India led by Mahatma Gandhi and was imprisoned for several years for promoting human rights. Khanna got his bachelor's in economics from the University of Chicago and his law degree from Yale University. He was a volunteer campaigner in Barack Obama's successful bid for the state Senate in 1996.

Khanna worked for a law firm in the Silicon Valley, where he specialized in intellectual property issues and wrote the book Entrepreneurial Nation: Why Manufacturing is Still Key to America's Future. He taught economics at Stanford and law at Santa Clara University. He has shown interest in three separate Bay Area congressional districts. In 2004, he challenged Rep. Tom Lantos in the 2004 Democratic primary, with criticism for his support of the war in Iraq; Khanna got 20 percent of the vote. He was a deputy assistant secretary at the Commerce Department during Obama's first term as president. Gov. Jerry Brown appointed Khanna to the California Workforce Investment Board. He set his eyes on the seat held by Democratic Rep. Pete Stark of California in a district across the Bay from Lantos, but Eric Swalwell beat him to the punch by defeating Stark in 2012.

With a strong corps of campaign contributors, many of them Indian Americans, Khanna decided to take on Democratic Rep. Mike Honda in 2014 in an adjacent district. Honda spent 14 months as a youngster with his Japanese family in a World War II internment camp in Colorado. With help from House Speaker Nancy Pelosi, Honda got a seat on the Appropriations Committee and focused on trying to win more funding for education programs. In their initial contest, Honda led Khanna in the primary 48%-28%. Republican candidates took the remaining votes. Honda was endorsed by major Democratic leaders, including Obama and Pelosi. Khanna had endorsements from local technology leaders. Khanna styled himself as more tech-friendly and half Honda's age. Honda supporters dismissed Khanna as a "tech groupie." The November 2014 contest was much closer, with Honda prevailing 51.8%-48.2%. Khanna outspent Honda $4.4 million to $3.4 million, but learned the difficulty of ousting a generally popular incumbent.

Khanna barely stopped campaigning and expanded his message to talk about broader economic issues, including automation. Honda was hindered by an investigation by the House Ethics Committee for his failure to keep his official House staff separate from his 2014 campaign. The case resulted in loss of political support, including the endorsements of Obama and some local tech leaders. Honda's campaign ran a negative ad in which a south Asian actor depicted Khanna taking a call from "Wall Street" on his cell phone. Khanna led the 2016 primary, 39.1%-37.4%. In the general election, Khanna outraised Honda, $3.7 million to $3 million. Support for Honda collapsed, which Khanna later attributed to "a frustration with Washington." In the Asian-majority district, control switched from Japanese to Indian heritage. Khanna won, 61%-39%.

In the House, Khanna served on the Armed Services Committee, where he won approval of his amendment to the 2017 defense spending bill that required a review of Pentagon procurement practices to encourage more transparency in its commercial acquisitions. He filed a bill to end U.S. military involvement in the war in Yemen and he encouraged President Donald Trump to remove U.S. troops from Syria and Afghanistan.

In Khanna's work on tech issues, Trump signed in December 2018 a bill that he filed with Republican Rep. John Ratcliffe of Texas to modernize the technology of federal agencies, including their websites and public services. Khanna said the tech industry needs to do a better job of dispersing "the concentration of economic opportunity," especially to minority groups and rural areas. In 2019, he was vice chair of the Congressional Progressive Caucus. He and freshman Rep. Alexandria Ocasio-Cortez of New York were the only two Democrats to vote against the opening-day package of House rules changes; they objected to continuation of "pay as you go" budgeting, which Khanna tweeted was "terrible economics." He joined other party activists in challenging the decision by Democratic leaders to support all House seeking reelection. He also became a co-chairman of the presidential campaign of Sen. Bernie Sanders and emphasized the importance for Democrats to embrace all elements of their "coalition" if they hoped to defeat Trump in 2020.

In his first reelection campaign, Republican challenger Ron Cohen voiced conspiracy theories, including that the September 2001 attacks were an inside job. Khanna won, 75%-25%.

CA-17: South Bay   **Cook Partisan Voting Index: D+25**

Population		Race and Ethnicity		Income	
Total	762,175	White	24.1%	Median Income	$115,390
Land area (sq. miles)	185	Black	2.4%	District Income Rank	3
Pop/ sq mi	4123.2	Latino	16.2%	Poverty Rate	6.7%
Born in State	38.9%	Asian	53.3%	With health insurance	95.5%
		Two or more races	3.2%	Cash public assistance	2.5%
Age Groups		Other	0.8%	Food stamp/SNAP	3.3%
Under 18	21.8%				
18-34	25.7%	**Education**		**Work**	
35-64	40.7%	H.S grad or less	23.9%	White Collar	11.8%
Over 64	11.8%	Some college	20.3%	Sales and Service	28.8%
		College Degree, 4 yr	29%	Blue Collar	12.4%
Military		Post grad	26.9%	Government	7.5%
Veteran/ Active Duty	3.1%				

2012 Pres. Vote	Obama	163,862	(72%)	Romney	58,193	(26%)		
2016 Pres. Vote	Clinton	184,151	(73%)	Trump	51,079	(20%)	Johnson	8,314	(3%)

San Jose suburbs, Central San Jose: A few decades ago, the broad valley of Santa Clara County around San Jose was mostly orchards and vineyards. Sheltered by mountains from the chilly ocean fogs, with soil incredibly fertile once it was irrigated, this valley produced peaches, plums, prunes, apricots and grapes and made San Jose the nation's biggest fruit-packing center. Today, subdivisions, shopping centers, office buildings — especially large tech companies -- have replaced the orchards, and the population of the county exceeds 1.9 million. Real estate prices in Santa Clara County have been soaring. The average sales price for a single-family home, which reached $1 million in 2016, grew by another 12 percent in 2017. Nearby Fremont in Alameda County has experienced economic rejuvenation. A shuttered General Motors/Toyota plant was taken over by Tesla Motors, which has been building high-end electric cars there. With assembly line upgrades, the company produced 250,000 cars in 2018, though the federal tax credit for consumer purchases expired at the end of the year; the company envisioned production of 500,000 vehicles in 2019, with Fremont as its only fully operational plant. Fremont could become "the Detroit of the 21st century," gushed the newsletter California Planning & Development Report. Fremont is also home to the Little Kabul neighborhood, which may be the largest Afghan enclave in the western world.

The 17th Congressional District curves around the southern tip of San Francisco Bay and the Don Edwards National Wildlife Refuge — named for the long-time liberal member of the House Judiciary Committee. It consists of the city of Santa Clara and a northern wedge of Santa Clara County, the sixth biggest county in the state, with large numbers of Chinese, Vietnamese and Mexican immigrants. It is one of three districts that is based largely or entirely in Santa Clara. In 2017, the county's population was 38 percent Asian and 26 percent Hispanic. The district also takes in the northern part of San Jose, part of Fremont, Newark, Sunnyvale and Cupertino, where Steve Jobs started Apple in a garage in the 1970s and where the company is still based. Apple opened its solar-powered Apple Park "spaceship" headquarters in April 2018, a $5 billion state-of-the-art building in Cupertino that houses some 12,000 employees on a 175-acre site. The hallways in the round building exceed one mile. Technology firms are an important driver of the district's economy. LinkedIn opened its "net zero energy" campus in Sunnyvale. Other companies that plan large office space in Sunnyvale — strategically located behind San Jose and Palo Alto -- include Google, Amazon, Facebook and another corporate campus for Apple. Lockheed Martin, which shifted its Trident missile manufacturing elsewhere, retained a large presence in Sunnyvale for other missile and satellite programs. On the less successful side of the ledger is Solyndra, the Fremont-based solar energy company that received economic stimulus money from the Obama administration and then went bankrupt in 2011. SolarCity, a California-based solar power company purchased by Tesla, took over its complex in Fremont and reportedly has struggled.

Both Cupertino and Milpitas are more than 60 percent Asian, and this growing population has become a political force. The 17th District as a whole is 53 percent (and climbing) Asian American, by far the largest percentage of any district in California. Its median household income of $115,390 was third in the nation. Hillary Clinton won this district, 73%-20%.

Anna Eshoo (D)

Elected 1992, 14th term, b. Dec 13, 1942; New Britain, CT; Canada College (CA), A.A., 1975; University of San Francisco (CA), Att., 1979; Roman Catholic; Divorced; 2 children.

Elected Office: San Mateo County Board of Supervisors, 1983-1992, President, 1986.

Professional Career: San Mateo County Dem. Party, 1980-1992; Speaker pro tempore, CA assembly speaker, 1981-1982.

DC Office: 202 CHOB 20515, 202-225-8104, Fax: 202-225-8890, eshoo.house.gov

State Offices: Palo Alto, 650-323-2984.

Committees: *Energy & Commerce*: Communications & Technology; Health (Chmn).

Group Ratings

	ADA	ACLU	AFL-CIO	LCV	ITI	COC	HAFA	ACU	CFG	FRC
2018	-	86%	-	94%	-	50%	8%	4%	15%	0%
2017	95%	C	95%	100%	C	50%	C	4%	5%	0%

Almanac Ratings 2017-18

	Economy	Social	Foreign	Composite
Liberal	96%	94%	95%	95%
Conservative	5%	6%	5%	5%

Key Votes of the 115th Congress

1. Obama-care revision	N	5. Family planning regs	N	9. Guantamano prisoners	Y
2. Tax Cuts	N	6. Body cameras/immigration	Y	10. Ground missiles, limit	Y
3. Omnibus appropriations	Y	7. Abortion ban	N	11. Defense Dept. spending	N
4. Dodd-Frank revision	N	8. Concealed carry	N	12. FISA rules	N

Election Results

Election	Name (Party)	Vote (%)		Cand. Spent	Ind. Exp. Support	Ind. Exp. Oppose
2018 General	Anna Eshoo (D).....................................	225,142	(74%)	$1,020,113	$1,834	$310,703
	Christine Russell (R)........................	77,096	(26%)			
2018 Primary	Anna Eshoo (D).....................................	133,993	(73%)			
	Christine Russell (R)........................	42,692	(23%)			

Prior winning percentages: 2016 (71%), 2014 (68%), 2012 (71%), 2010 (69%), 2008 (70%), 2006 (71%), 2004 (70%), 2002 (68%), 2000 (70%), 1998 (69%), 1996 (65%), 1994 (61%), 1992 (57%)

Democrat Anna Eshoo, first elected in 1992, has had impressive accomplishments on the powerful Energy and Commerce Committee, especially on communications issues. In recent years, her career seemed to have peaked. Following the 2014 election, she sought the top Democratic slot on the committee, but lost to Frank Pallone of New Jersey. Two years later, she decided not to serve as the ranking Democrat on any of the panel's subcommittees so that junior members could have an opportunity. But with her enthusiasm revived at age 76 when Democrats regained House control, she became chairwoman of the Health Subcommittee. Not coincidentally, her close friend Nancy Pelosi returned as House Speaker. A few weeks before the 2018 election, Eshoo played an unexpected, though off-stage, role in the riveting confirmation hearing of Brett Kavanaugh to the Supreme Court.

Born in Connecticut, Eshoo is the only member of Congress of Assyrian descent. Her father, a jeweler and an FDR Democrat, sparked her interest in politics at a young age by taking her to political rallies. As a youngster, her mother briefly lived in Baghdad. The family moved to California. Eshoo married, had two children, and for a while was a stay-at-home mother working on a degree in English literature. (She later divorced.) She was active in civic groups, chaired the San Mateo County Democratic Party and in 1982 was elected to the San Mateo Board of Supervisors. In 1988, she ran for the House against Republican Rep. Tom Campbell. The two spent a total of $2.5 million, which was big bucks in those days. Campbell won 52%-46%. In 1992, Campbell gave up his seat to run for the Senate, and Eshoo again ran. In the primary, she prevailed 40%-36% against Assemblyman Ted Lempert, who had strong backing from environmentalists In what was still a swing district, she had a tough contest against Republican Tom Huening, a San Mateo supervisor who was backed by Silicon Valley business leaders. Eshoo won by a convincing 57%-39%. She has not had a serious challenge for reelection.

Eshoo's voting record has been mostly liberal, with more-moderate views on issues such as taxes that affect high-income earners in her district. She joined Republicans and high-tech interests in votes on securities litigation and normalizing trade relations with China. But she sided with most Democrats in 2015 in opposing trade promotion authority for President Barack Obama, chiefly to conclude the Trans-Pacific Partnership.

From 2011 to 2016, Eshoo was the senior Democrat on the Energy and Commerce Subcommittee on Communications and Technology — a panel with obvious importance to her district. She has been a strong supporter of net neutrality, the concept that broadband providers should be prohibited from blocking certain traffic or setting up tiered pathways for internet content. She argued in favor of ensuring that the FCC provides an adequate supply of spectrum that any company can use for free. She was the leading Democratic supporter of the permanent moratorium on internet access taxes paid by consumers, which was enacted in 2016. Following the election that year, she voluntarily gave up the subcommittee post. "Senior members like myself must consider the best interest of our party and our need to develop leaders for the future. In other words, it's time to walk my talk," Eshoo said.

That came two years after Eshoo sought unsuccessfully to replace Rep. Henry Waxman of California, when he retired as the ranking Democrat on Energy and Commerce. Even with the active support of Pelosi, for whom Eshoo had been a valuable confidant since they first met at a Democratic event in the Bay Area in the early 1970s, that proved to be a step too far. Eshoo was stymied by multiple factors: Pallone had more seniority, a point that he and his allies emphasized. The secret vote became an opportunity for some Democrats to express unhappiness with Pelosi and their deepening minority status in the House. During the next two years, Eshoo took issue with President Donald Trump and administration officials on issues such as the sale of spectrum to AT&T and Verizon, the president's refusal to release his tax returns and his incendiary rhetoric.

Eshoo returned to center stage in 2019 to fill the Democratic opening at the Health Subcommittee. "The 2018 midterm elections were won on the issue of health care and the American people now expect us to deliver," she said. She listed her priorities as strengthening of the Affordable Care Act, lower prices for prescription drugs and investments in the National Institutes of Health. Eshoo has a lengthy record on health technology issues. In 2009, she prevailed over Waxman in winning passage of a measure allowing makers of "biologic" drugs up to 12 years of protection from competition from the generic drug industry. The 21st Century Cures Act, which was enacted in 2016, had a section she prepared with Republican Rep. Susan Brooks of Indiana that strengthened the nation's biodefense to respond to public health emergencies.

Eshoo's return to center stage in the House was preceded by her cameo role in the Senate Judiciary Committee hearings on Kavanaugh in September 2018. That resulted when Christine Blasey Ford, a constituent, contacted her during the summer to discuss Kavanaugh's alleged sexual attack of her when they were high school students outside of Washington D.C. during the mid-1980s. Following a meeting in her office in Palo Alto, Eshoo suggested that Ford share the information with Sen. Dianne Feinstein of California, the senior Democrat on the Judiciary Committee. "At the end of the meeting, I told her I believed her," Eshoo said to the San Jose Mercury News. Ford sent the letter to Feinstein, who withheld the information for several weeks from other committee members and investigators, until it was leaked to reporters for The Washington Post. Republicans attacked the development, after the initial committee hearings had ended, as an 11th-hour attack on Kavanaugh for which there was scant evidence. Amid the furor, Eshoo defended Ford as "not a creature of Washington D.C." and said that Kavanaugh's response was "totally disqualifying." Eshoo did not play a formal role in the Senate proceedings.

Like her close friend Pelosi, Eshoo has stirred interest in the closing of her congressional career.

CA-18: Silicon Valley   **Cook Partisan Voting Index: D+23**

Population		Race and Ethnicity		Income	
Total	735,753	White	54.5%	Median Income	$122,124
Land area (sq. miles)	696	Black	1.8%	District Income Rank	1
Pop/ sq mi	1056.9	Latino	16.4%	Poverty Rate	6.9%
Born in State	47%	Asian	22.5%	With health insurance	95.1%
		Two or more races	4%	Cash public assistance	1.3%
Age Groups		Other	0.8%	Food stamp/SNAP	2.7%
Under 18	22.3%				
18-34	20.9%	**Education**		**Work**	
35-64	42%	H.S grad or less	17.6%	White Collar	14.8%
Over 64	14.8%	Some college	20.7%	Sales and Service	30.2%
		College Degree, 4 yr	30.1%	Blue Collar	9%
Military		Post grad	31.7%	Government	9%
Veteran/ Active Duty	4.7%				

2012 Pres. Vote	Obama	218,082	(68%)	Romney	92,457	(29%)		
2016 Pres. Vote	Clinton	246,464	(73%)	Trump	67,842	(20%) Johnson	13,894	(4%)

Western San Jose, Palo Alto: Silicon Valley is a place and a state of mind, an area that had no distinctive identity four decades ago but that people all over the world today recognize and imitate. In the 1980s and 1990s, Silicon Valley emerged as the center of America's computer industry, a place where creative minds developed products that large corporations never thought would sell. Its beginnings can be traced back to 1939, when William Hewlett and David Packard started their electronics firm in a Palo Alto garage, or perhaps even to 1891, when Stanford University was founded on the estate of a California governor and senator. Not every aspect of the computer business is centered here, as Microsoft and IBM can attest. But the compact Silicon Valley is where most of the giants and much of the creativity of the technology business — as well as many dot-coms — have been based, and where they continue to grow in their pricey surroundings and generate extraordinary wealth.

How did Silicon Valley come to be where it is? One factor is Stanford, the students it attracts and produces, and its tradition of encouraging faculty members to pursue profit-making activity. Another key component is venture capital, widely available from innovation-minded old San Francisco money. A third ingredient is the presence of smart young innovators, attracted to the valley's pleasant climate. Sheltered by hills from coastal fogs and rains, Silicon Valley boasts mostly sunny weather with perceptible but gentle seasons, perfect for year-round outdoor sports. These communities were rustic but never poor, rural but not small-minded, country-like but still easily accessible to urban luxuries. People here were ahead of the rest of the nation in fighting for the environment, in favoring natural over processed foods and in incorporating regular exercise into busy lives.

When the internet bubble burst in 2000, Silicon Valley fell on hard times. By one estimate, the area lost 220,000 jobs, nearly two-thirds of the 350,000 created during the dot-com boom. Stock prices plummeted and real estate prices did too. Billions of dollars in paper wealth disappeared, and technology exports from California fell. Since then, it has had a strong revival. In 2017, the valley exceeded 1.6 million jobs, higher than in 2000 and a robust increase from the 1.3 million jobs in 2010. Housing prices have roared back and are again among the highest in the nation. Half the employees in the valley are foreign-born.

The 18th Congressional District of California includes large portions of Silicon Valley, along with Palo Alto and Stanford University. It includes a slice of San Jose and a slice of Menlo Park to the north. Further south along El Camino Real is Mountain View, where Google plans to open by 2020 an ambitious new headquarters known as Charleston East for its more than 85,000 employees. The Fast Company business website described the design as a "titanic metal circus tent" that will be covered by solar panels. Also underway for Google in Mountain View is a massive "village" campus that will feature 8,000 homes, ample retail space and 35 acres of public areas. The lack of housing for tech workers has been so dire that many live in recreational vehicles along the streets of Mountain View. There are some ultra-wealthy enclaves here: Woodside, with its mansions in the hills, and Los Altos Hills, with its stark contemporary homes overlooking San Francisco Bay. The district takes in small San Jose-area cities such as Campbell, Los Gatos and the increasingly Asian Saratoga. To the west is a long stretch of hills and wilderness areas, and Route 1 that overlooks the Pacific Ocean. About three-fourths of the population is in Santa Clara County, with the remainder in southern San Mateo and northern Santa Cruz. The district's median household income of $122,100 ranked as the highest in the nation.

The area's political heritage is progressive, with a mix of environmental, dovish and culturally liberal. Through the 1980s, this was a center of moderate Republicanism, typified by former Reps. Pete McCloskey and Tom Campbell. But that brand has become virtually extinct here, as in most of the nation. The GOP vote in the 18th dropped from 29 percent for Mitt Romney in 2012 to 20 percent for Donald Trump in 2016.

Zoe Lofgren (D)

Elected 1994, 13th term, b. Dec 21, 1947; San Mateo; Stanford University (CA), B.A., 1970; Santa Clara University Law School (CA), J.D., 1975; Lutheran; Married (John Marshall Collins); 2 children.

Elected Office: Santa Clara Board of Supervisors, 1980-1994.

Professional Career: Staff Assistant, U.S. Rep. Don Edwards, 1970-1978; Practicing attorney, 1978-1980; Professor, University of Santa Clara School of Law, 1977-1980.

DC Office: 1401 LHOB 20515, 202-225-3072, Fax: 202-225-3336, zoelofgren.house.gov

State Offices: San Jose, 408-271-8700.

Committees: *House Administration (Chmn). Joint Library. Joint Printing. Judiciary*: Courts, Intellectual Property & Internet; Immigration & Citizenship (Chmn). *Science, Space & Technology*: Space & Aeronautics. *Select Committee on the Modernization of Congress.*

Group Ratings

	ADA	ACLU	AFL-CIO	LCV	ITI	COC	HAFA	ACU	CFG	FRC
2018	-	91%	-	97%	-	45%	10%	13%	23%	0%
2017	95%	C	92%	100%	C	57%	C	7%	5%	11%

Almanac Ratings 2017-18

	Economy	Social	Foreign	Composite
Liberal	97%	96%	99%	97%
Conservative	3%	4%	1%	3%

Key Votes of the 115th Congress

1. Obama-care revision	N	5. Family planning regs	N	9. Guantanamo prisoners	Y
2. Tax Cuts	N	6. Body cameras/immigration	Y	10. Ground missiles, limit	Y
3. Omnibus appropriations	N	7. Abortion ban	N	11. Defense Dept. spending	N
4. Dodd-Frank revision	N	8. Concealed carry	N	12. FISA rules	N

Election Results

Election	Name (Party)	Vote (%)	Cand. Spent	Ind. Exp. Support	Ind. Exp. Oppose
2018 General	Zoe Lofgren (D)............................ 162,496	(74%)	$1,239,563		
	Justin Aguilera (R)........................ 57,823	(26%)	$21,254		
2018 Primary	Zoe Lofgren (D)............................ 97,096	(99%)			

Prior winning percentages: 2016 (74%), 2014 (67%), 2012 (67%), 2010 (68%), 2008 (71%), 2006 (73%), 2004 (71%), 2002 (67%), 2000 (72%), 1998 (73%), 1996 (66%), 1994 (65%)

Zoe Lofgren, a Democrat first elected in 1994, has been an active legislator on multiple issues, and perhaps the savviest defender of high technology's interests in the House. In 2019, she became chairwoman of the House Administration Committee, whose jurisdiction includes federal election laws in addition to management of the House. A year earlier, Lofgren lost a bid to become the top Democrat on the Judiciary Committee. She remained busy on that panel, as the head of its pivotal Immigration Subcommittee. She has extensive experience in dealing with constitutional controversies related to presidents, including impeachment, and she has pointedly raised concerns about President Donald Trump.

Lofgren grew up in the Bay Area, where her father was a Teamsters truck driver and her mother worked for the Machinists Union. She graduated from Stanford University, then moved to Washington to work for Democratic Rep. Don Edwards while he was a leader on the Judiciary Committee that voted to impeach President Richard Nixon. She stayed on for eight years as an aide to Edwards. She met her husband, a lawyer, one Election Night. Lofgren returned to California to get a law degree, then specialized in immigration law. She served 14 years on the Santa Clara County Board of Supervisors. When Edwards retired, Lofgren ran for his House seat. Her chief Democratic opponent, former San Jose Mayor Tom McEnery, was better known. But Lofgren raised twice as much money, with support from liberal women's organizations and women in the California delegation. Lofgren won the primary 45%-42% and easily took the general election. She has had no trouble winning reelection.

Lofgren's voting record, while mostly liberal, includes bipartisan free-market positions that often are responsive to local businesses and law enforcement. Working with Republicans, she won expanded allotments of visas for tech-industry workers. She pushed for looser controls on encryption exports, securities litigation limitations and relaxation of trade restraints on supercomputers, all big Silicon Valley causes. When the House split 210-210 on a proposal to restrict government access to library records, Lofgren was the only House member to vote "present." She said the amendment went too far in preventing legitimate law enforcement searches. In 2015, she filed a bipartisan bill to prevent privacy intrusions by drones and other unmanned aircraft, and later formed a Fourth Amendment Caucus to protect the privacy and security of Americans in the digital age.

When Democrats won the majority in 2006, Lofgren, a trusted lieutenant of House Speaker Nancy Pelosi, became chairwoman of the Judiciary Subcommittee on Immigration and related issues. She hoped for a major overhaul of immigration policy, but the politically charged issue bogged down. When Republicans regained control of the House, Lofgren was an outspoken supporter of a bill to change the visa system to allow more highly skilled immigrants from China and India to become permanent legal residents. In 2011, the bill passed the House easily, with Lofgren joining Judiciary Chairman Lamar Smith of Texas. She was the chief sponsor of a new law to allow overseas military personnel and their spouses more time to file for permanent resident status through marriage. Other immigration proposals that Lofgren has supported would provide visas to spouses of green-card applicants and eliminate the lottery system from the visa program for skilled foreigners.

With Republican Rep. Robert Goodlatte of Virginia, the Judiciary Committee chairman, Lofgren criticized in 2015 the backlog of "green card" visa applications for talented foreign workers. In 2016, she filed with Democratic Sen. Patrick Leahy of Vermont the Refugee Protection Act, a proposal that reaffirmed the nation's commitment to refugees and strengthened safeguards for those seeking protection from persecution and violence.

Lofgren tried to get a foothold in leadership by running for vice chair of the Democratic Caucus in 2003. But Pelosi, who is also from the Bay Area, had just been elected minority leader and the Congressional Black Caucus pressed for one of its members to join the leadership. Lofgren got 53 votes to 95 for the victorious James Clyburn of South Carolina.

In 2009, Lofgren took over as chairwoman of the House Ethics Committee just as it launched a politically sensitive inquiry of House Ways and Means Chairman Charles Rangel of New York, and as questions were being raised about the connections of other senior Democrats to lobbyists. Lofgren's skills as a former staffer and law professor were tested by the politically combustible cases. She said in early 2010 that at least 36 lawmakers — around 8 percent of the House — had been subjected to scrutiny for their dealings with interest groups the previous year. Her panel subsequently found that no House members colluded with lobbyists. Rangel was afforded a trial but walked out in protest. Lofgren and the rest of the panel refused to back down, and a few days later voted 9-1 to censure him — a decision Lofgren called "quite wrenching."

Lofgren joined the dozens of House Democrats who boycotted in January 2017 the inauguration of President Donald Trump. "I acknowledge the fact that he is the incoming president, but I'm not in the mood to celebrate that fact," she told the Los Angeles Times. After he released his executive order that temporarily banned refugees and some immigrant groups, she filed a bill to prohibit the use of federal funds to enforce his action. Republicans refused her call for immediate action. Months later, she issued a statement raising the question of whether Trump suffered from early-stage dementia and she encouraged Vice President Mike Pence and members of Trump's cabinet to have the president undergo physical and mental health exams. "Has emotional disorder so impaired the president that he is unable to discharge his duties?" Lofgren asked.

When Rep. John Conyers of Michigan resigned in December 2017, following revelations of sexual misconduct with House aides, Lofgren sought to replace him as the senior Democrat on the Judiciary Committee, citing her experience with the Nixon impeachment as a staffer and with the impeachment of Bill Clinton after she was elected to the House. Rep. Jerry Nadler of New York, who has two years more seniority, also sought the position. Nadler prevailed in the secret ballot in the Democratic Caucus, reportedly on a 118-72 vote.

When Democrats regained the majority, Lofgren was routinely approved to chair the House Administration Committee — filling the top Democrat slot on the panel that was held by Rep. Robert Brady of Pennsylvania, who had retired. When she took the position, Lofgren said that her priorities for the committee included legislation "to empower the American voter, to end partisan gerrymandering and voter suppression, secure our election infrastructure from foreign interference and initiate programs to restore the integrity of Congress." Plus, she had a busy agenda as head of the Immigration Subcommittee.

CA-19: South Bay   **Cook Partisan Voting Index: D+24**

Population		Race and Ethnicity		Income	
Total	760,615	White	25.4%	Median Income	$91,357
Land area (sq. miles)	915	Black	2.7%	District Income Rank	25
Pop/ sq mi	831	Latino	40.6%	Poverty Rate	10.9%
Born in State	50.9%	Asian	27.6%	With health insurance	91.8%
Age Groups		Two or more races	2.9%	Cash public assistance	3%
Under 18	23.7%	Other	0.8%	Food stamp/SNAP	8.1%
18-34	24.7%	**Education**		**Work**	
35-64	39.8%	H.S grad or less	38.7%	White Collar	11.8%
Over 64	11.8%	Some college	27%	Sales and Service	40.9%
Military		College Degree, 4 yr	22.1%	Blue Collar	20.1%
Veteran/ Active Duty	3.8%	Post grad	12.2%	Government	11.3%

2012 Pres. Vote	Obama	165,530	(71%)	Romney	61,643	(27%)			
2016 Pres. Vote	Clinton	188,304	(72%)	Trump	55,489	(21%)	Johnson	8,620	(3%)

Southern San Jose: With more people than San Francisco, a tradition of high-tech innovation, and a professional sports team, San Jose finally has claims on national attention and respect. Yet San Jose does not register on the national consciousness as it should. At the southern end of San Francisco Bay, it remains in the shadow of the city on the Golden Gate. San Jose is quite different. It got its start as a farm-market town, with canneries and fruit-packing operations for the produce from the surrounding fertile plains. Farm labor icon Cesar Chavez settled with his family in the East San Jose barrio of Sal Si Puedes ("Get out if you can"). San Jose sits not on the bay but on the Southern Pacific rail line above the marshes and salt evaporators. Its major transportation arteries are the freeways — U.S. 101, Interstates 280, 680, and 880, California 87 — that encircle its revitalized downtown and the larger Bay Area.

Starting in the 1950s, San Jose grew in every direction, with developers hopscotching across the farmland and at times putting up subdivisions faster than the few city employees could update the street maps. Its population exceeds 1 million, not far below San Francisco and Oakland combined; it is growing faster than the other two and has more available land. Economically, San Jose has been sustained by everything from its traditional agriculture to manufacturing to the technology businesses that are centered in Silicon Valley towns just to the west and north, and are omnipresent here: an American city, 21st-century style. Santa Clara County not long ago had the highest median household income in the nation. Now, it is merely the highest in California. A Brookings Institution study of the period from 2014 to 2016 ranked San Jose as the second fastest-growing city in the world, behind Dublin Ireland. San Francisco and Los Angeles were the only other American cities in the top 20.

For many years, San Jose has been a focal point for immigration issues. It has Northern California's largest Mexican-s American community, many of them farmworkers. Recent years have brought a diverse and substantial presence from Latin America and East and South Asia. In 2017, 52 percent of Santa Clara County residents speak a language other than English at home, mostly Spanish, Vietnamese or Chinese; 39 percent are foreign born. County voters in 2016 approved a half-cent increase in the sales tax for transportation projects. BART officials, who expected to start service from Fremont to the outskirts of San Jose by the end of 2019, have announced plans for an extension to downtown San Jose (with an innovative transportation hub) and the airport.

The 19th Congressional District of California consists of substantial portions of San Jose, including much of the city's downtown area and the neighborhoods of Alum Rock and East Foothills. The district takes in eastern and southern parts of Santa Clara County, including Morgan Hill, a traditional farming town that has branched into technology. Near the southern edge of the district is Gilroy, which is 61 percent Hispanic, the garlic capital of the world and home of the huge annual garlic festival. Politically, the district is solidly Democratic. Along with the 17th and 18th Districts, this is one of three Santa Clara-based districts where Hillary Clinton got at least 72 percent of the vote in 2016.

Jimmy Panetta (D)

Elected 2016, 2nd term, b. Oct 01, 1969; Washington, DC; Monterey Peninsula College (CA), A.A., 1989; University of California, Davis, B.A., 1991; Santa Clara University (CA), J.D., 1996; Catholic; Married (Carrie Panetta); 2 children.

Military Career: U.S. Navy 2003-2011 (Afghanistan)

Elected Office: Monterey County Deputy District Attorney, 2010-2016.

Professional Career: Clerk, United States Department of State, 1992; Alameda County Deputy District Attorney, 1996-2010; Vice Chairman, Monterey Country Central Democratic Committee, 2012-2016.

DC Office: 212 CHOB 20515, 202-225-2861, Fax: 202-225-6791, panetta.house.gov
State Offices: Salinas, 831-424-2229; Santa Cruz, 831-429-1976.

Committees: *Agriculture*: Biotechnology, Horticulture & Research; Livestock & Foreign Agriculture; Nutrition, Oversight & Department Operations. *Budget*. *Ways & Means*: Trade.

Group Ratings

	ADA	ACLU	AFL-CIO	LCV	ITI	COC	HAFA	ACU	CFG	FRC
2018	-	79%	-	94%	-	50%	8%	4%	29%	0%
2017	75%	C	95%	97%	C	57%	C	0%	0%	11%

Almanac Ratings 2017-18

	Economy	Social	Foreign	Composite
Liberal	94%	94%	84%	91%
Conservative	6%	6%	16%	9%

Key Votes of the 115th Congress

1. Obama-care revision	N	5. Family planning regs	N	9. Guantanamo prisoners	Y
2. Tax Cuts	N	6. Body cameras/immigration	Y	10. Ground missiles, limit	Y
3. Omnibus appropriations	N	7. Abortion ban	N	11. Defense Dept. spending	Y
4. Dodd-Frank revision	N	8. Concealed carry	N	12. FISA rules	Y

Election Results

Election	Name (Party)	Vote (%)		Cand. Spent	Ind. Exp. Support	Ind. Exp. Oppose
2018 General	Jimmy Panetta (D)	183,677	(81%)	$543,065	$1,222	
	Ronald Paul Kabat (I)	42,044	(19%)			
2018 Primary	Jimmy Panetta (D)	102,828	(81%)			
	Ronald Paul Kabat (I)	19,657	(15%)			

Prior winning percentages: 2016 (71%)

Democrat Jimmy Panetta, easily elected to the House in 2016, developed his own profile separate from his dad, Leon Panetta, a Washington insider for four decades. He made a point of pursuing bipartisanship, as did his father early in his own House career. Jimmy Panetta's initial work in Congress focused on local issues. With a seat on the Ways and Means Committee in 2019, he gained an opportunity to enhance his legislative profile.

The youngest of three sons of former Defense Secretary and CIA Director Leon Panetta, Jimmy grew up in Carmel Valley. He got his bachelor's degree from the University of California, Davis, and his law degree from Santa Clara University. Growing up, he got up-close insight on Washington through the eyes of his father. Panetta began his legal career as a prosecutor for the Alameda County District Attorney. Later, he was appointed to the California Council on Criminal and Juvenile Justice, which provided guidance to the governor's office on criminal justice programs. In 2003, he was commissioned as an intelligence officer with the U.S. Navy Reserve. Four years later, he took a leave of absence from work and served with a special operations task force deployed to Afghanistan, as an intelligence officer with the Joint Special Operations Command. Before his election to Congress, he was the deputy district attorney in Monterey County.

Panetta worked on missile and chemical weapons nonproliferation issues for the State Department and the Monterey Institute of International Studies. He also managed his family's large walnut farm in the area. His wife, Carrie McIntyre Panetta, was a Superior Court judge in Monterey County. His father, who chaired the Panetta Institute on Public Policy, held this seat for 16 years and chaired the House Budget Committee before he took posts such as White House chief of staff and Defense secretary. "I am not afraid to pick up the phone and reach out to [my father] when necessary," Jimmy Panetta told Politico. "But he also understands that … I'm the one who has to make the decision, despite what he may advise."

After Democrat Sam Farr -- who held the seat for nearly 24 years after Leon Panetta resigned to join the Clinton White House -- announced his retirement, Jimmy Panetta was the immediate front-runner. His only major-party opponent was Republican Casey Lucius, a city councilwoman in Pacific Grove and a professor of national security at the Naval Postgraduate School. She was a strong conservative on most national security and economic issues, and had relatively liberal views on social issues. Lucius raised $420,000, compared with $1.4 million for Panetta. She probably never had a chance against the partisan lean and the iconic family name in this district. Panetta led the "top two" primary, 71%-20%, and took the general election, 71-29%.

In the House, Panetta initially positioned himself to address local issues. He proposed legislation to remove the cap on visas to victims of crime. In June 2018, he introduced a bill to reverse a Trump administration decision to roll back regulations to sustain ocean and coastal resources. Later, he filed a bill to increase funds for affordable housing for farmworkers.

Panetta made a point of working with Republicans in the House. He visited the rural district of Rep. Rodney Davis of Illinois. They discussed areas of common interest, including agricultural research. "We have to be civil to each other to get things done," Panetta said. With Rep. Matt Gaetz, a

Florida freshman, he proposed the "Warrior Act," to improve access for disabled veterans to athletic competition sponsored by the Defense Department.

With his seat on Ways and Means, Panetta took a big step toward influential deal-making in the House. He listed his priorities on the committee as "smarter trade policies that benefit our local industries, including agriculture, enacting fairer tax policies, increasing access to health care and coverage, and protecting federal programs for vulnerable children and our seniors." He said that he was committed to an "evidence-based process" for such legislation. He retained his seat on the Agriculture Committee.

In 2018, Panetta was reelected without major-party opposition.

CA-20: Central Coast   **Cook Partisan Voting Index: D+23**

Population		Race and Ethnicity		Income	
Total	734,923	White	37.1%	Median Income	$66,078
Land area (sq. miles)	4,874	Black	1.8%	District Income Rank	127
Pop/ sq mi	150.8	Latino	52.7%	Poverty Rate	14.9%
Born in State	57.5%	Asian	5.1%	With health insurance	88.2%
		Two or more races	2.6%	Cash public assistance	2.5%
Age Groups		Other	0.6%	Food stamp/SNAP	8.1%
Under 18	24.7%				
18-34	26.3%	**Education**		**Work**	
35-64	36.4%	H.S grad or less	44.1%	White Collar	12.6%
Over 64	12.6%	Some college	28.5%	Sales and Service	40.7%
		College Degree, 4 yr	16.6%	Blue Collar	27.7%
Military		Post grad	10.8%	Government	15.2%
Veteran/ Active Duty	6.3%				

2012 Pres. Vote	Obama	168,956	(71%)	Romney	62,427	(26%)		
2016 Pres. Vote	Clinton	180,499	(70%)	Trump	59,580	(23%)	Johnson	8,425	(3%)
	Stein	6,737	(3%)					

Monterey, Southern Santa Cruz: The California coast around Monterey Bay is for many a working definition of paradise. This kernel of California, site of the first state capital, still makes a fine living off the land and sea, as it has for 150 years. The inspiration for The Grapes of Wrath and many other John Steinbeck novels, the fields around Salinas provide much of the nation's lettuce and cauliflower. The area is often referred to as "the salad bowl of the world." Nearby, the farmlands around Castroville supply the country with its artichokes, and the vast greenhouses around Watsonville have been a popular supplier of roses. The fishing fleet and the 18 now-closed canneries of Monterey (the last sardines were canned in 1964) have generated a new industry. Once described by Steinbeck as "a poem, a stink, a grating noise, a quality of light, a tone, a habit, nostalgia, a dream," Cannery Row has been refurbished with upscale shops and hotels. The magnificent Monterey Bay Aquarium is one of California's top tourist destinations, and the National Marine Sanctuary holds more than 400 shipwrecks and ditched aircraft. The Monterey Bay area calls itself the world's language-learning capital, with the Defense Language Institute, Language Line Services, and Cal State Monterey Bay's School of World Languages and Cultures. This area was a magnet for the 1960s counterculture. The wealthy now entertain themselves with the annual Monterey Car Week, which sells many classic models. In 2018, a 1962 Ferrari sold for $44 million, a record for the event.

For many, the main attraction of the Monterey peninsula is the lush 17-Mile Drive along the Pacific Coast Highway, with Pebble Beach's golf courses, the Del Monte Lodge and Carmel, whose restrictive laws — no house numbers, no door-to-door mail delivery, no stoplights, no wearing of high-heeled shoes without permits —attempt to maintain the atmosphere of when it was an artists' colony. Monterey has suffered its own affordability gap. These days, top-flight buyers include many investors from China, many of whom initially spent time in the area for language training. Monterey County has been spending for its future. In 2016, voters approved — following two defeats in the previous decade — a sales tax increase to finance transportation improvements. With the hope to ease congestion on Highway 101, construction began in August 2018 on extension of Salinas Rail service to the Bay Area and Sacramento. In Santa Cruz, officials struggled to prevent erosion along the famed boardwalk. Heavy rains in early 2017, the worst in California history, caused mud slides and landslides that closed for months the Pacific Coast Highway and the Pfeiffer Canyon Bridge, which provided the only access to Big Sur.

The 20th Congressional District of California includes the entire coast of Monterey Bay and follows the stunning Big Sur coastline south along the steep slopes, taking in extensive wilderness areas and some of the most beautiful scenery in America. To the north along Monterey Bay, it runs past Watsonville to Santa Cruz. The district extends inland, into sunny valleys sheltered from ocean mists, and covers some of the nation's richest farmland. Most of the farmworkers are Latino, mainly Mexican. All of Monterey and San Benito counties are located here, and the district takes in most of Santa Cruz County and a small slice of Santa Clara. About half the population is in Monterey.

The gap between rich and poor in Monterey County is wide. It has thousands of homes valued at more than $1 million, but 12 percent of households live below the poverty line and 54 percent do not live in an English-speaking home. In March 2018, the mayor of Salinas accused Monterey of sending some of its growing homeless population to Salinas. Monterey reportedly has the highest share of non-citizens of any county in the state. A half-century ago, this was a solidly Republican area, dominated politically by the landowners in Salinas and the townspeople who sympathized with them, plus retirees. An influx of young people, attracted less by the economy than by the atmosphere, moved these counties — like most of the California coast -- nearly as far to the left as much of the Bay Area. In 2016, Hillary Clinton got 75 percent of the vote from Santa Cruz and 67 percent from Monterey. This district has climbed steadily to 53 percent Hispanic.

T.J. Cox (D)

Elected 2018, 1st term, Walnut Creek; University of Nevada, Reno, B.S.; Southern Methodist University (TX), M.B.A.; Religion unknown; Married (Kathleen Murphy); 4 children.

Professional Career: Engineer; Founder, Central Valley New Market Tax Credit Fund.

DC Office: 1728 LHOB 20515, 202-225-4695, cox.house.gov

State Offices: Bakerfield, 661-864-7736.

Committees: *Agriculture*: Biotechnology, Horticulture & Research; Livestock & Foreign Agriculture. *Natural Resources*: Oversight & Investigations (Chmn); Water, Oceans & Wildlife.

Election Results

Election	Name (Party)	Vote (%)		Cand. Spent	Ind. Exp. Support	Ind. Exp. Oppose
2018 General	T.J. Cox (D)............................	57,239	(50%)	$2,870,377	$34,422	$419,953
	David G. Valadao (R).................	56,377	(50%)	$3,242,348	$37,398	$2,123,047
2018 Primary	David G. Valadao (R).................	34,290	(63%)			
	T.J. Cox (D)............................	20,293	(37%)			

Democrat TJ (Terrance John) Cox was the final new Member who was declared the winner of a House seat in 2018—and one of the least expected. He started the campaign cycle as one of several Democratic contenders in the 10th District in the northern Central Valley. When Democrats needed a stronger candidate in the 21st, Cox made the switch. Initially, he faced an uphill challenge against Republican Rep. David Valadao, who had won three surprisingly easy terms in this heavily Hispanic, Democratic-leaning district. Showing that the party's wave extended beyond the coastal area, Cox became the seventh California Democrat to take a GOP district.

A native of Walnut Creek, California, Cox got his bachelor's degree in chemical engineering from the University of Nevada Mackay School of Mines and a master's in business administration from Southern Methodist University. As an entrepreneurial professional engineer, he launched many businesses; the first, while he was in college, was a company that installed home energy-savings devices. Cox spent a decade working on engineering and construction projects around the world. His work in Central Valley agriculture included the start-up of successful almond-processing businesses.

In a 2006 campaign for Congress in a Fresno-based district, he lost 61%-39% to veteran Republican Rep. George Radanovich.

Based on his experience as a volunteer with Habitat for Humanity, Cox founded in 2010 the Central Valley New Market Tax Credit Fund, which used federal tax credits to assist small businesses and non-profits. Its investments included the development of community health clinics, job-training facilities, clean energy plants and affordable housing. The results, he said, included 1,500 jobs plus health-care services for 40,000 persons in the Central Valley, "Showcasing that clean-energy is good business," he said that a prime success of the fund was the development of a bioenergy plant that turned dead trees from the Sierras into clean energy.

Days before the filing deadline in March 2018, Cox moved his campaign to the 21st District after Emilio Huerta abandoned his poorly-financed campaign. Huerta, the son of the iconic United Farmworkers co-founder Delores Huerta, had lost to Valadao, 57%-43%, in a 2016 challenge that disappointed House Democratic campaign leaders.

When he entered the contest, Cox said that he did not reside in the district but that he had many business interests there. While he had worked on economic development projects, Cox said, "David Valadao and his Washington friends were fighting to slash taxes for the richest corporations and rip away health care from thousands of Central Valley families," while supporting President Donald Trump.

Valadao often sought bipartisanship on agricultural and immigration issues in the House and occasionally clashed with Trump. His allies initially dismissed Cox as a "Washington insider… hand-picked" by House Democrats who "forced out" Huerta after Cox had "district-shopped" across California. Later in the campaign, The Fresno Bee reported that Cox had claimed his principal residence in Bethesda Maryland, as part of his business activities; a Cox spokesman reportedly declined to comment.

During their sole campaign debate, Valadao defended his record and said that many of Cox's charges were false. Cox responded that Valadao—and Republicans—had failed to fix local problems, including immigration and water supply. Valadao said that conservatives in the House Freedom Caucus had stymied his efforts on immigration. In its endorsement of Cox, the Bee wrote that Cox was "more focused on the needs of the district's residents," while Valadao had voted for GOP initiatives that were harmful to local interests.

Cox outspent Valadao, $3.2 million to $2.9 million, in a contest that received little national attention. In the vote count, which took more than three weeks before it was completed, Cox's victory came from his 61 percent of the vote in Kern County. Valadao took the other three counties.

CA-21: Central Valley   **Cook Partisan Voting Index: D+5**

Population		Race and Ethnicity		Income	
Total	712,221	White	16.9%	Median Income	$40,330
Land area (sq. miles)	6,730	Black	3.7%	District Income Rank	412
Pop/ sq mi	105.8	Latino	74.4%	Poverty Rate	29.3%
Born in State	62.1%	Asian	3%	With health insurance	85%
		Two or more races	1.3%	Cash public assistance	8.4%
Age Groups		Other	0.6%	Food stamp/SNAP	23.6%
Under 18	31.3%				
18-34	27.3%	**Education**		**Work**	
35-64	33.1%	H.S grad or less	67.3%	White Collar	8.3%
Over 64	8.3%	Some college	24.6%	Sales and Service	35.7%
		College Degree, 4 yr	5.9%	Blue Collar	47.2%
Military		Post grad	2.3%	Government	14.3%
Veteran/ Active Duty	5%				

2012 Pres. Vote	Obama	65,146	(55%)	Romney	51,917	(44%)		
2016 Pres. Vote	Clinton	73,773	(55%)	Trump	52,972	(39%)	Johnson	4,029	(3%)

Southern Fresno Suburbs, Eastern Bakersfield: By car, California's Central Valley is a monotonous landscape: mile after mile of farmland with mile-square grid roads, intersected by railroads and canals, with an occasional cluster town. The land is hilly and gets more water near the Sierra Nevada mountains, and this is where the larger cities are. On the other side are the Westlands, where the land is flatter and the water scarcer. Its 600,000 acres are the nation's largest irrigation district. Here the land was always developed and sold in big plots; today, it has some of the world's largest farming operations. The land produces abundantly: alfalfa, cantaloupes, cotton, grapes, lima beans, olives, peaches, plums, raisins, sugar beets, tomatoes, walnuts, wheat. The landowners are a hardy and politically independent lot, but they have been happy to receive government help over the years, with money for crop price supports (in the case of cotton), agricultural research, irrigation systems and, most important, subsidized and plentiful water.

Landowners have fought hard against liberals' efforts to change their way of life, from Democratic Gov. Jerry Brown's encouragement of Cesar Chavez's United Farm Workers in the 1970s to House Natural Resources Committee Chairman George Miller's 1992 law to divert more water to the Sacramento delta and charge higher prices for it in the valley. From the other side, they have been stymied when conservatives in Congress have deadlocked on expansion of guest-worker programs pushed by valley farmers. In September 2017, the Westlands water district voted to oppose the $17 billion plan by Gov. Jerry Brown to build two long water tunnels to supply the state; it objected to the proposed financing. This region is a major contributor to California's oil production, and Kern County has the most oil wells in the state. Census Bureau data have shown that the population growth in Kings County has been heavily Hispanic, poor and less likely to be married. Workers in the area's growing food-processing industry were often seasonal. The abundant rains in 2017 filled local reservoirs and were a huge relief. But the continuing shortfall of groundwater was a warning that a turnaround was not guaranteed.

The 21st Congressional District is rural, includes large portions of the Westlands Water District, and links communities with similar agricultural and water interests. It takes in all of heavily Hispanic Kings County and parts of Fresno and Kern counties. Fresno and Kern each have about one-third of the district's voters and Kings has one-fourth. The remainder are in a small corner of Tulare. The town of Delano is Chavez's old headquarters, and at the southeastern foot of the district is the Latino part of downtown Bakersfield. The district has increased to 74 percent Hispanic, but Hispanic voter registration and turnout typically remain low. The district leans Democratic, with 55 percent for Hillary Clinton in 2016. But a local Republican can win with the right background and political appeal.

Devin Nunes (R)

Elected 2002, 9th term, b. Oct 01, 1973; Tulare County; College of the Sequoias (CA), A.A., 1993; California State Polytechnic University, B.S., 1995; California State Polytechnic University, M.S., 1996; Roman Catholic; Married (Elizabeth Tamariz Nunes); 3 children.

Elected Office: Col. of the Sequoias Governing Board, 1996-2002.

Professional Career: Appt. Director, USDA Rural Development, 2001.

DC Office: 1013 LHOB 20515, 202-225-2523, Fax: 202-225-3404, nunes.house.gov

State Offices: Clovis, 559-323-5235; Visalia, 559-733-3861.

Committees: *Joint Taxation. Permanent Select on Intelligence (RMM). Ways & Means*: Health (RMM); Trade.

Group Ratings

	ADA	ACLU	AFL-CIO	LCV	ITI	COC	HAFA	ACU	CFG	FRC
2018	–	4%	–	3%	–	91%	45%	72%	52%	100%
2017	10%	C	17%	3%	C	92%	C	80%	55%	100%

Almanac Ratings 2017-18

	Economy	Social	Foreign	Composite
Liberal	7%	9%	0%	5%
Conservative	93%	91%	100%	95%

Key Votes of the 115th Congress

1. Obama-care revision	Y	5. Family planning regs	Y	9. Guantanamo prisoners	N
2. Tax Cuts	Y	6. Body cameras/immigration	N	10. Ground missiles, limit	N
3. Omnibus appropriations	Y	7. Abortion ban	Y	11. Defense Dept. spending	Y
4. Dodd-Frank revision	Y	8. Concealed carry	Y	12. FISA rules	Y

Election Results

Election	Name (Party)	Vote (%)	Cand. Spent	Ind. Exp. Support	Ind. Exp. Oppose
2018 General	Devin Nunes (R)............................ 117,243	(53%)	$10,543,086	$260	$927,179
	Andrew Janz (D)............................ 105,136	(47%)	$9,026,634	$180,508	$260
2018 Primary	Devin Nunes (R)............................ 70,112	(58%)			
	Andrew Janz (D)............................ 38,596	(32%)			

Prior winning percentages: 2016 (68%), 2014 (72%), 2012 (62%), 2010 (100%), 2008 (68%), 2006 (67%), 2004 (73%), 2002 (71%)

Devin Nunes, a Republican first elected in 2002 at age 29, is an influential conservative with ambitions within and beyond the House. He has briefly toyed with running for the Senate and in 2016 he joined the Trump transition discussion of selection of Cabinet members. Speaker John Boehner in 2015 tapped him to chair the House Intelligence Committee, which quickly raised his profile and plunged him into controversy — including sharp conflict with Rep. Adam Schiff of California, the panel's top Democrat. Following the election of President Donald Trump, Nunes encountered harsh criticism for his cooperation with Trump in the panel's investigation of alleged Russian influence in the 2016 presidential election. While his actions were reviewed by the House Ethics Committee for eight months, Nunes transferred control of that inquiry to other committee Republicans.

Nunes is the descendant of Portuguese immigrants from the Azores. His grandfather established the 600-acre-plus dairy farm that his parents ran when he was growing up in Tulare County. He graduated from California Polytechnic State University, San Luis Obispo, with degrees in agriculture, worked on the family farm, and married a local elementary schoolteacher whose family roots are also in Portugal. In 1998, at age 25, Nunes ran for the House in a neighboring district and finished second in the primary, 52%-48%. In 2000, he was the Tulare County campaign chairman for Republican Rep. Bill Thomas, who became the Ways and Means Committee chairman in 2001. That year, with Thomas' help, Nunes was appointed California director of rural development for the U.S. Department of Agriculture. (His immediate family sold its farm in 2006 and moved to Iowa, where they bought a dairy farm and resided, according to a profile of Nunes in Esquire in September 2018. Only his uncle Gerald retained a dairy farm in Tulare. Nunes had not publicly discussed these details and his family was reluctant to acknowledge their Iowa presence to the reporter for Esquire.)

When California's redistricting plan was unveiled in September 2001, a Fresno-area district was left without an incumbent, and Nunes moved quickly. He was supported by Thomas, whose deep-pocketed campaign contributors in the pharmaceutical and insurance industries agreed to help Nunes. At home, Nunes won the endorsement of the California Farm Bureau, the state's largest farm organization and a powerful voice in Central Valley politics. He faced serious primary challenges from Jim Patterson, Fresno's conservative former mayor, who was backed by the anti-tax group Club for Growth, and California Assembly member Mike Briggs. All three promised to seek new water sources for farmers about to lose the San Joaquin River as a primary source after environmentalists successfully lobbied to restore the river. The candidates all called for tax cuts, fewer federal regulations and expanded guest-worker programs for immigrants. Nunes won with 37 percent of the vote to 33 percent for Patterson and 26 percent for Briggs. In November, Nunes won easily, 70%-26%.

Nunes has a mostly conservative voting record. In the Almanac vote ratings, he was been near the center of House Republicans. Nunes can deliver a cutting sound bite, once comparing government spending with the actions of "a broke gambler who desperately keeps doubling down in a vain effort to break even." He said that conservative Republicans who were blamed by many for shutting down part of the government in 2013 because they opposed the Affordable Care Act were "lemmings with suicide vests."

Legislatively, Nunes has dived into his district's most pressing issue: the use of water from the San Joaquin River. He clashed with supporters of alternatives to increase water flow over the Friant Dam so salmon could be returned to the parched lower reaches of the San Joaquin. Leaders of such projects were like "communist politburo members who collect big checks and do nothing," he said.

When California's drought worsened, Nunes lashed out at the Obama administration for allying with "radical environmentalists" in preventing farmers from getting sufficient water for their crops. He got a bill through the House in 2012 to reshape California's water-rights system to deliver more San Joaquin water for farmers; Democrats condemned the move as a "water grab" and it did not move in the Senate, something Nunes attributed to California's Democratic senators for defending "their environmental wacko friends."

A member of Ways and Means, at the outset of the health care debate in 2009 Nunes joined his ally Paul Ryan in introducing a bill providing tax credits for people to buy insurance and ending the tax exemption for businesses providing workers with the benefit. Their strategy pre-empted other Republicans who preferred to take more time to craft a plan. Nunes later introduced his own bill in 2012 to create a voluntary pilot program in which Medicare and Medicaid recipients would be given a debit-style "Medi-choice" card to buy health insurance. Following the 2016 election, he joined Ryan in support of a border adjustment tax that would tax imports and invest in the domestic economy, and said that opposition from some business groups was "a little offensive," given that other nations have comparable fees. The proposal failed to achieve sufficient Republican support to become part of their 2017 tax bill.

As Intelligence Committee chairman from 2015 to 2018, Nunes revamped the panel's subcommittees, forming new ones to concentrate on scrutinizing the CIA, as well as the NSA and cybersecurity. He initially was an advocate for intelligence agencies and kept a low profile, though he traveled widely. "My goal is to make sure we are getting our members out to every corner of the world," Nunes told McClatchy Newspapers when he took over as chairman. "You cannot conduct serious oversight work without getting on the ground and actually talking to the folks that are doing the work."

That changed with the election of Trump. Nunes had served on the executive committee of his presidential transition team, which advised on the selection of Cabinet members. He was among the first to recommend the selection of James Mattis for Defense secretary. From the House, he advocated fellow Reps. Mike Pompeo for director of the CIA. He said that he had no interest of his own in those positions.

Nunes initially voiced reluctance after the election to investigate ties between Russia and the Trump campaign. But, following the inauguration, he joined ranking Democratic Rep. Adam Schiff of California in announcing that the Intelligence Committee would review Russian cyber-activity against the United States and its allies, plus the response of the intelligence community. He voiced concern about the leaking of Trump-related material to the news media. The leaking and his complaints about it led to a sharpening of partisan lines on the committee, which was a contrast to the bipartisan review of the election by the Senate Intelligence Committee.

Nunes got into trouble when he allegedly received classified information from a friendly source at the White House and then discussed the report with journalists, among others. He contended that there was surveillance of Trump and his associates at Trump Tower in New York City during the presidential transition. In March 2017, Nunes briefed Trump at the White House on his findings. When Democrats learned of his activities and voiced objections, Nunes initially apologized to the committee. Not satisfied, the committee Democrats demanded that he recuse himself from the investigation. On April 6, the House Ethics Committee announced that it would investigate Nunes for possible "unauthorized disclosures." On the same day, he said that he would transfer control of the Intelligence Committee inquiry to other members, though he retained his chairmanship of the panel.

The bipartisan leaders of the Ethics Committee announced in a one-paragraph statement on Dec. 7 that, based on the conclusions of experts on intelligence classification, "the information that Rep. Nunes disclosed was not classified;" they closed their case. Nunes said that the allegations were "obviously frivolous and were rooted in politically motivated complaints against me by left-wing activist groups." Subsequently, several House Republicans charged that law-enforcement officials violated intelligence procedures in their review of alleged Russian interference in the election. After Justice Department and FBI officials disputed those contentions, Nunes dismissed the objections as "spurious." That prompted new demands by Democrats in February 2018 for Nunes to step aside as chairman. He refused. In August, MSNBC reported that Nunes said at a closed-door GOP fundraising event that House Republicans were "the only ones" to protect Trump from the investigation by special counsel Robert Mueller.

With Nunes having become a partisan lightning rod, he faced a robust challenge to his reelection in his comfortably Republican district. Nunes had never been held below 62 percent in his campaigns. His challenger Andrew Janz, a 34-year-old Trump critic and former deputy district attorney in Fresno County, voiced a law-and-order message and called Nunes "a national security danger."

He complained that the Democratic Congressional Campaign Committee gave him no support and refused to return his phone calls. "A DCCC spokesperson basically told me to my face, 'Janz, you're on your own," he told Politico in September 2018. This became the most expensive House contest in 2018, with Nunes outspending Janz, $10.5 million to $9 million in a relatively cheap media market. After having led Janz, 58%-32% in the primary, Nunes won in November, 53%-47%.

Following the election, Nunes was relegated to ranking minority member of the Intelligence Committee. His position as the number-two Republican on the Ways and Means Committee seemed secure, assuming that he retains his House seat.

CA-22: Central Valley   Cook Partisan Voting Index: R+8

Population		Race and Ethnicity		Income	
Total	748,078	White	39.1%	Median Income	$56,097
Land area (sq. miles)	1,165	Black	2.9%	District Income Rank	213
Pop/ sq mi	642.1	Latino	47.5%	Poverty Rate	19.8%
Born in State	68.7%	Asian	7.6%	With health insurance	90.5%
		Two or more races	2.2%	Cash public assistance	6.8%
Age Groups		Other	0.8%	Food stamp/SNAP	16.7%
Under 18	28.4%				
18-34	24.9%	**Education**		**Work**	
35-64	34.7%	H.S grad or less	42.1%	White Collar	12%
Over 64	12%	Some college	33.6%	Sales and Service	41.9%
		College Degree, 4 yr	15.8%	Blue Collar	24.7%
Military		Post grad	8.4%	Government	18.9%
Veteran/ Active Duty	6.1%				

2012 Pres. Vote	Romney	125,213	(57%)	Obama	92,005	(42%)		
2016 Pres. Vote	Trump	125,089	(52%)	Clinton	102,292	(42%)	Johnson	8,628	(4%)

Eastern Fresno City and Suburbs: In California's Central Valley, between the flat Westlands and the Sierras, is Fresno, a city that is both agricultural and industrial, middle American and ethnically diverse. Although it began as a farm-market center, the city has long since grown out to the north, east and west from its downtown, and its economy has expanded to other sectors — construction, transportation and financial services. It is a creation of the Industrial Age and the Central Pacific Railroad. Historian Kevin Starr described the San Joaquin Valley, at the heart of the Central Valley, as "the most productive unnatural environment on Earth." Fresno's city fathers bred the local wine grape, developed the raisin industry and introduced the Smyrna fig. These are among the area's 300-plus crops, which include cotton, lima beans, nectarines, almonds, tomatoes, cantaloupes, plums, peaches and alfalfa.

Dairy is now the biggest commodity and Tulare County leads the nation in milk and dairy sales, with more than 600,000 cattle. Its nearly 11 billion pounds of milk production in 2017 more than doubled the total from Merced and Kings, the next two largest counties in California. In 2017, Tulare slightly trailed neighboring Kern County as the largest agricultural producer in the United States, with more than $7 billion in value.

Central Valley agriculture is industrial in its thoroughness and in its ownership by large corporations. The vineyards outside Fresno radiate in mechanical precision, with vines just 10 feet apart and exposed to the relentless summer sun: nothing romantic or quaint about it. Except for the disruption of the severe recession followed by drought, times have been good. The weak dollar boosted farm exports, large citrus groves benefited from losses in hurricane-plagued Florida and nuts found new export markets. Groundwater contamination has become a growing problem in Tulare, where it affects 99 percent of the drinking water.

Construction of the bullet train from San Francisco to Los Angeles began in the Central Valley, where the project was fiercely opposed by many local officials worried that it could attract too many people to the Fresno area, forcing residents out of single-family homes and into dense, urban communities. The original cost estimate of $6.4 billion for the 118 miles from Merced to Bakersfield proved wildly optimistic. The final tab for that portion was projected to exceed $10 billion. Speaking to the Legislature, Gov. Gavin Newsom said that he had decided to kill the project, except for the Central Valley corridor.

The 22nd District covers a bit more than half of Fresno County and most of Tulare. Route 99, the old Farm-to-Market Corridor, runs through the district and leads to the Hispanic-majority city of Tulare. In the northern part of the district is Clovis, billed as the "gateway to the Sierras." The central area takes in the smaller city of Dinuba and Visalia, which is the district's largest whole city. It is a largely agricultural district that has been safely Republican. Fresno County is one of the most conservative urban centers in the nation. As was the case throughout California, Donald Trump underperformed in 2016. In Fresno, where Mitt Romney got 51 percent in 2012, Trump got 46 percent. In Tulare, which is a bit less than one-third of the total, the Republican vote dropped from 58 percent to 53 percent.

Kevin McCarthy (R)

Elected 2006, 7th term, b. Jan 26, 1965; Bakersfield; Bakersfield College (CA), 1985; California State University, Bakersfield, B.A., 1989; University of California, Bakersfield, M.B.A., 1994; Baptist; Married (Judy McCarthy); 2 children.

Elected Office: Trustee, Kern Commissioner Col. Board, 2000-2002; CA Assembly, 2002-2007, Minority Leader, 2004-2006.

Professional Career: Owner, Kevin O's Deli, 1986-1987, Mesa Marin Batting Range, 1991-1992; Staff, U.S. Rep. Bill Thomas, 1987-2002.

DC Office: 2468 RHOB 20515, 202-225-2915, Fax: 202-225-2908, kevinmccarthy.house.gov

State Offices: Bakersfield, 661-327-3611.

House Minority Leader.

Group Ratings

	ADA	ACLU	AFL-CIO	LCV	ITI	COC	HAFA	ACU	CFG	FRC
2018	-	4%	-	3%	-	92%	41%	80%	58%	100%
2017	0%	C	16%	3%	C	93%	C	78%	64%	100%

Almanac Ratings 2017-18

	Economy	Social	Foreign	Composite
Liberal	5%	4%	0%	3%
Conservative	95%	97%	100%	97%

Key Votes of the 115th Congress

1. Obama-care revision	Y	5. Family planning regs	Y	9. Guantanamo prisoners	N
2. Tax Cuts	Y	6. Body cameras/immigration	N	10. Ground missiles, limit	N
3. Omnibus appropriations	Y	7. Abortion ban	Y	11. Defense Dept. spending	Y
4. Dodd-Frank revision	Y	8. Concealed carry	Y	12. FISA rules	Y

Election Results

Election	Name (Party)	Vote (%)		Cand. Spent	Ind. Exp. Support	Ind. Exp. Oppose
2018 General	Kevin McCarthy (R)	131,113	(64%)	$4,459,632		
	Tatiana Matta (D)	74,661	(36%)	$102,891		
2018 Primary	Kevin McCarthy (R)	81,633	(69%)			
	Tatiana Matta (D)	14,935	(13%)			
	Wendy Reed (D)	11,974	(10%)			
	Mary Helen Barro (D)	6,363	(5%)			

Prior winning percentages: 2016 (69%), 2014 (75%), 2012 (73%), 2010 (99%), 2008 (100%), 2006 (71%)

Kevin McCarthy, a gregarious former Capitol Hill staffer elected in 2006, has combined hard work, the ability to reach across party factions and some survivor skills to step up as the House GOP leader. His disappointments include that he fell short in October 2015, when John Boehner unexpectedly announced his resignation as House Speaker and McCarthy was the heir apparent. At that time, with Republicans as the House majority, he ran into numerous obstacles, including opposition from conservatives and self-induced errors. When it became clear that he could not get 218 votes in the House, he stepped aside for Paul Ryan and remained as majority leader. Ryan, who served three years as Speaker, had a less comfortable relationship with President Donald Trump than did McCarthy and seemed relieved to walk away from the ongoing chaos and their House setbacks.

In the transition from Ryan to McCarthy in 2018, Republicans lost 40 seats and relinquished House control for the first time since 2010. As is customary, the responsibility for that big midterm loss rested chiefly with the president. Trump's continuing appeal to his base of blue-collar, rural voters gave Democrats a large opening to gain seats in suburbs, especially with women candidates. They skillfully exploited those opportunities. Still, the loss of seven GOP seats from McCarthy's home state was a sharp indictment of his own limited home-state appeal and skills, especially his unwillingness to go his own way from Trump. (Since McCarthy's first election to the House, the number of Republicans from California has dropped from 19 to 7.) Although he seemed to remain on good terms with the president, the results weakened McCarthy's own base among House Republicans and shifted congressional influence to Senate Republicans. Back in the minority, his chief challenge was to find a way for the GOP to regain House control. That posed a dilemma of how closely they should cooperate with Trump.

McCarthy grew up in Bakersfield, where his blue-collar family has lived for generations and often voted Democratic. He moved in the other direction. At 19, he won $5,000 in the state lottery and invested it in a deli, which helped pay for business school at Cal State, Bakersfield. In college, he was elected chairman of the California Young Republicans and later headed the national Young Republicans organization. After he sold the deli, he got a job in the local office of Rep. Bill Thomas, who was on his way to chairing the powerful Ways and Means Committee. McCarthy eventually became Thomas' district director and protégé. In 2000, he was elected to the Kern County Community College Board, and in 2002 he was elected to the Assembly. As Republican leader, McCarthy worked with Republican Gov. Arnold Schwarzenegger on the budget, workers' compensation issues and redistricting.

When Thomas announced his retirement in March 2006, just four days before the filing deadline, McCarthy was the obvious candidate to succeed him. He faced token Republican primary opposition. In November, he won 71%-29%. During that campaign, he raised more than $1 million and traveled the country for other Republican candidates. That attracted the attention of party leaders. After the election, he was chosen the freshman representative on the Republican Steering Committee, which makes committee assignments. He chaired the Platform Committee at the 2008 Republican National Convention, winning praise for uniting conservatives and moderates.

McCarthy landed a leadership position in 2009 when Minority Whip Eric Cantor of Virginia appointed him chief deputy whip — an unusual responsibility for a House member in his second term. On the night of President Barack Obama's inauguration, he reportedly implored a gathering of leading GOP lawmakers and activists plotting strategy to be aggressive. "If you act like you're the minority, you're going to stay in the minority," McCarthy said, according to Robert Draper's 2012 book Do Not Ask What Good We Do: Inside the U.S. House of Representatives. "We've gotta challenge them on every single bill and challenge them on every single campaign." In a sign of his media savvy, McCarthy cooperated extensively with Draper.

In the next two years, McCarthy wore multiple hats. He was the head of recruiting for the National Republican Congressional Committee, in what became the highly successful 2010 election for the GOP. He traveled widely looking for candidates, identifying challengers to take on Democrats accustomed to weak opposition. Ultimately, Republicans had candidates in 430 of the 435 congressional districts, the highest number ever at that time. Even after he recruited the candidates, McCarthy kept in constant contact with the top contenders, often with quick cell phone calls while he was heading to meet other prospects. With Cantor and Ryan, he led the party's "Young Guns" program to spotlight and finance Republican challengers. Minority Leader John Boehner assigned McCarthy and Rep. Peter Roskam of Illinois to draw up a document similar to the House Republicans' 1994 Contract with America. They ultimately compiled the "Pledge to America" policy manifesto. Kept deliberately vague to deter Democratic attacks, it did not make as big an impression as the 1994 document. It sought to commit incoming and veteran Republicans to a single set of policies, such as extending the Bush-era tax cuts and repealing Obama's health care overhaul.

McCarthy was rewarded for his impressive efforts after Republicans won control of the House. He was the overwhelming choice for whip, the third-ranking position for the House majority. In his new job, McCarthy employed a nice-guy approach in building trust. He mountain-biked with Republican members in the mornings and rounded up others in the evenings for group dinners, drawing them out by asking questions such as, "What's the most embarrassing thing that happened to you at college?" He encouraged lawmakers to hang around his whip office on the first floor of the Capitol and got acquainted with their families. "A conference united around policies creates better legislation than using intimidation," McCarthy told The New York Times.

McCarthy paid particular attention to the often-rambunctious tea party freshmen elected in 2010. He offered them advice, including telling them to vote their conscience at times even if it meant disagreeing with the leadership. Sometimes the results were disastrous — especially for the whip, whose job is to assure the majority party prevails. When the leadership decided in April 2011 to back a continuing resolution to keep the federal government operating, 59 Republicans defected. And at the height of the "fiscal cliff" negotiations in December 2012, when the two parties struggled against a deadline to agree on spending and tax cuts, Boehner's "Plan B" proposal was pulled from the floor when it became clear that it lacked sufficient Republican votes.

But there was little second-guessing of McCarthy after Cantor stepped down as majority leader following his unexpected 2014 primary defeat. With the support of friendly colleagues and the GOP's establishment wing, McCarthy geared up a campaign within hours to replace his fallen friend. Early on, there were rumblings that he might face stiff competition from a seasoned House Republican. But Idaho maverick Raul Labrador became his only opponent. Labrador never stood a chance against McCarthy's formidable vote-counting operation.

In his new job, McCarthy laid out broad-based objectives that were designed to appeal across the board. When it came to specifics, he usually showed his allegiance to House conservatives. After their big election victories in 2014, he promised to overhaul how the House did its work by giving committee chairmen more autonomy, assuring that GOP leaders work more closely with their Senate counterparts, and finding issues to draw a clear contrast between the parties.

In early 2015, McCarthy helped create a working group of committee chairs to develop a Republican alternative to the Affordable Care Act. But after a month, Republicans were second-guessed for their scant workload or legislative success. They picked what many saw as an unwinnable fight with Obama over immigration policy. In another setback, the leadership jettisoned a planned vote on an anti-abortion bill after some Republican women lawmakers complained. With slight modifications, the House passed that bill a few months later.

The continuing Republican infighting that led to Boehner's September 2015 resignation as Speaker helped to stymie the move by McCarthy to take over as his successor. The conservative Freedom Caucus required that he meet a series of demands before several of its members would support him. When a partisan firestorm erupted after he claimed credit in a broadcast interview with Sean Hannity of Fox News for the hearings on the 2012 Benghazi terrorist attack, which resulted in political damage to Hillary Clinton, McCarthy was slow to respond and proved to be unprepared to fill the big shoes. Eventually, McCarthy advised Ryan that he was the best hope for House Republicans. Still, McCarthy became a key lieutenant to Ryan, his longtime ally, and remained a major GOP fundraiser and advocate.

During those three years, until he inherited the wreckage as minority leader, McCarthy faced some rocky moments in seeking to manage Republicans — and the House. In 2018, for example, a group of relatively centrist Republicans pressed to provide a pathway to some sort of legal status for immigrants who had entered the nation illegally. Ryan opened the door by telling reporters, "What we're trying to do is find where the consensus sweet spot is." McCarthy disagreed, siding with immigration hardliners who opposed any conciliatory action and believed that most grassroots Republicans would object. Even though the party centrists included some California Republicans with large Hispanic constituencies, McCarthy tweeted a few weeks before the election, "Few things are more fundamental to a nation than a protected border." The GOP inaction on immigration legislation became a factor in the defeat of some of McCarthy's California colleagues

The latent tension between Ryan and McCarthy became apparent in other ways, as when some Republicans said in early 2018 that Ryan should not wait until after the election to step down as Speaker. "Ryan is losing his grip on the feuding House Republican conference," the Washington Post reported in May. The story cited GOP members who wanted McCarthy to take control ASAP.

For that matter, some conservatives remained reluctant to support McCarthy as the successor to Ryan. That became apparent when Rep. Jim Jordan of Ohio, a founder of the Freedom Caucus, entered the contest for party leader — in part to seek concessions on how McCarthy would manage the party if he became Ryan's successor. A further wrinkle was provided by Rep. Steve Scalise of Louisiana, the Republican Whip. He told reporters that he was interested in moving up the GOP leadership but that he wouldn't challenge McCarthy. His comments seemed to leave the possibility that Scalise might run for the top party post if McCarthy had failed to secure the votes.

In addition, McCarthy was a prominent and unabashed ally when Donald Trump became a candidate and later president. He was a go-between in the more difficult relationship between Trump and Ryan. "As majority leader, my role is to keep a team together," he told The Washington Post. "I think it's been helpful." The Post described their relationship as "light on policy nitty-gritty but heavy on back-slapping, deal-making and personal rapport." During a celebratory lunch the day before his inauguration, Trump called him out, "There's my Kevin." This deference led GOP critics to describe McCarthy as a sycophant for the president, though others welcomed his role as an intermediary.

These and other variables compounded the uncertainty for McCarthy. If he became Speaker, Paul Kane wrote in The Washington Post in May 2018, McCarthy "will almost certainly be a weak Speaker worried about ideological threats within the House Republican Conference." As it turned out, the House GOP setbacks in the election meant that no Republican would take the gavel. In the selection of the new minority leader, McCarthy defeated Jordan, 159-43. Even though McCarthy seemed in control of the downsized GOP Conference, the ambitions and animosities lingered.

As minority leader, McCarthy had a limited relationship with most Democrats, including Pelosi. But over the years he occasionally has sought to reach out. Facing partisan criticism of scant Republican participation at the 50th anniversary celebration of civil rights protests in Selma Alabama in March 2015, he made a last-minute decision to join the festivities. In one of the few cases in which he engaged in bipartisan legislating, McCarthy in December 2016 worked closely with his home-state Democratic Sen. Dianne Feinstein to ease the problems caused by California's crippling drought. They agreed on a California-focused piece of the water-resources bill, including expanded reservoir storage, financing of water recycling in the cities, and desalination projects. Outgoing Democratic Sen. Barbara Boxer blasted their "poison pill," but Obama signed the measure.

At home, McCarthy had no major party opposition in his first three reelection bids. In 2018, he was elected with 64 percent of the vote, the smallest in his seven election victories, against little-known Democratic challenger Tatiana Marin. Although that contest was barely a nuisance, the outcome was symptomatic of the shellacking that House Republicans took that year in McCarthy's home state. They lost half of the 14 seats that they had held in the state delegation since 2012. Their election successes gave Democrats (and Nancy Pelosi) 46-7 control of the state delegation — an embarrassing takedown for the Republicans' new House leader. GOP problems in California resulted from numerous factors beyond his control. But their miseries were a reminder of McCarthy's limitations at home — in contrast to other GOP leaders in years past who could rely on their dominance of home-state delegations, for example, in Ohio and Texas.

CA-23: Central Valley   Cook Partisan Voting Index: R+14

Population		Race and Ethnicity		Income	
Total	738,134	White	46.5%	Median Income	$57,341
Land area (sq. miles)	9,898	Black	6.2%	District Income Rank	200
Pop/ sq mi	74.6	Latino	38.6%	Poverty Rate	19%
Born in State	69.2%	Asian	5.1%	With health insurance	91.1%
		Two or more races	2.7%	Cash public assistance	5.8%
Age Groups		Other	0.9%	Food stamp/SNAP	13.4%
Under 18	27.4%				
18-34	24.3%	**Education**		**Work**	
35-64	36.2%	H.S grad or less	45.1%	White Collar	12.1%
Over 64	12.1%	Some college	34.9%	Sales and Service	40.6%
		College Degree, 4 yr	13.1%	Blue Collar	26.2%
Military		Post grad	6.9%	Government	20.3%
Veteran/ Active Duty	8.2%				

2012 Pres. Vote	Romney	139,816	(62%)	Obama	82,119	(36%)		
2016 Pres. Vote	Trump	142,351	(58%)	Clinton	88,314	(36%)	Johnson	9,850	(4%)

Central and Western Bakersfield and Suburbs: Bakersfield, near the southern end o California's Central Valley, has been the focus of great migrations four times: in the gold rush of 1885 in the boomlet that followed the discovery of oil in 1899; in the 1930s flight of Dust Bowl refugee from Oklahoma, Kansas and Texas; and in a flood of newcomers in the past two decades, whe: Bakersfield and Kern County grew more rapidly than California's biggest metro areas. The migratio that made the deepest imprint was in the 1930s. The Okies drove across a thousand miles of brown landscape, then through the Tehachapi Pass, and found this vast green valley, with its irrigated fields and its eucalyptus-shaded towns — the richest farming country in the world. The story is told vividly in novelist John Steinbeck's The Grapes of Wrath and in Dan Morgan's Rising in the West, which explains how the Okies' descendants prospered in California. As a result, the area around Bakersfield hosts a thriving country-music scene that included the late Merle Haggard and Buck Owens.

People here are culturally conservative with little empathy for Los Angeles-style liberalism. More recently, Latinos have been coming in large numbers for farm work. The result is that the Central Valley, including Bakersfield, had both high population growth and high unemployment for a decade. Its 41 percent population increase from 2000 to 2010 placed Bakersfield among the top 10 fastest-growing cities in the nation; by 2015, it had grown by another 9 percent. The flip side was that unemployment at the end of 2018 remained at 6.6 percent — its lowest since 2006, but well above the national rate. Reduced oil prices during and following the recession, and the accompanying disincentive for drilling, became another hit to the Kern County economy, which is home to 70 percent of the oil production in California and produces more oil than any other county in the nation.

In recent years, the area has taken an "all of the above" approach to energy production. With new seismic technology, oil exploration firms have located additional oil deposits in Kern County, including in one field that has produced oil for nearly a century. Perhaps more surprising, Kern had more than 4,500 wind turbines in 2017, the highest number for any county in the nation. Aera Energy announced plans for construction in 2019 of what it contends will be the nation's largest solar-energy farm, spreading over 770 acres, which will be adjacent to the company's oil fields. The area continues to suffer from a less desirable mark: the poorest air quality of any city across the nation. More than 15 percent of the residents in the Bakersfield area suffer from asthma or some form of heart disease, a private study found.

The 23rd Congressional District includes about 80 percent of Kern County, with the remainder in rural Tulare and a northern tip of Los Angeles County. It includes much of downtown Bakersfield. The 23rd covers the southern part of the Sierras, including Sequoia National Forest and Lake Isabella. The southern end of the district in the Mojave Desert encompasses the sprawling Edwards Air Force Base, where Chuck Yeager flew the X-1 and where the Space Shuttle frequently landed. It recently has become the testing site for the B-21 Raider, the next-generation long-range strike bomber, which is scheduled for delivery in the mid-2020s. In Antelope Valley, Lancaster hopes to be the first city in the nation to rely on solar power for all of its energy demand. About 80 percent of the voters in the district are in Kern. The 23rd is 39 percent Hispanic. In 2016, as in 2012, this was the most Republican district in California. Donald Trump led Hillary Clinton, 58%-36%, a dip from 62 percent for Mitt Romney. Kern, the most populous Trump county in California, gave him 53 percent of the vote.

Salud Carbajal (D)

Elected 2016, 2nd term, b. Nov 18, 1964; Moroleon, Mexico; University of California, Santa Barbara, B.A., 1990; Fielding University (CA), Mast. Deg., 1994; Catholic; Married (Gina Carbajal); 2 children.

Military Career: U.S. Marine Corps Reserves 1984-1992

Elected Office: Staff, County Supervisor Naomi Schwartz, 1993-2004; Member, Santa Barbara County Board of Supervisors, 2004-2016.

DC Office: 1431 LHOB 20515, 202-225-3601, Fax: 202-225-5632, carbajal.house.gov

State Offices: San Luis Obispo, 805-546-8348; Santa Barbara, 805-730-1710; Santa Maria, 805-730-1710.

Committees: *Agriculture*: Biotechnology, Horticulture & Research; General Farm Commodities & Risk Management; Livestock & Foreign Agriculture. *Armed Services*: Strategic Forces; Tactical Air & Land Forces. *Transportation & Infrastructure*: Aviation; Highways & Transit; Water Resources & Environment.

Group Ratings

	ADA	ACLU	AFL-CIO	LCV	ITI	COC	HAFA	ACU	CFG	FRC
2018	-	73%	-	83%	-	73%	2%	9%	11%	0%
2017	75%	C	92%	100%	C	50%	C	0%	0%	11%

Almanac Ratings 2017-18

	Economy	Social	Foreign	Composite
Liberal	86%	91%	80%	86%
Conservative	14%	9%	20%	14%

Key Votes of the 115th Congress

1. Obama-care revision	N	5. Family planning regs	N	9. Guantanamo prisoners	Y
2. Tax Cuts	N	6. Body cameras/immigration	Y	10. Ground missiles, limit	NV
3. Omnibus appropriations	Y	7. Abortion ban	N	11. Defense Dept. spending	Y
4. Dodd-Frank revision	N	8. Concealed carry	N	12. FISA rules	NV

Election Results

Election	Name (Party)	Vote (%)		Cand. Spent	Ind. Exp. Support	Ind. Exp. Oppose
2018 General	Salud Carbajal (D)	166,550	(59%)	$2,050,874	$47,198	$72,588
	Justin Fareed (R)	117,881	(41%)	$1,494,048	$20,104	
2018 Primary	Salud Carbajal (D)	94,558	(54%)			
	Justin Fareed (R)	64,177	(36%)			
	Michael Erin Woody (R)	17,715	(10%)			

Prior winning percentages: 2016 (53%)

Democrat Salud Carbajal, elected in 2016 in a contentious contest for an open seat, easily won a rematch two years later. He offered an innovative proposal that was designed to reduce gun violence. He occasionally reached out for bipartisanship, though he usually remained a party loyalist.

Carbajal was born in Mexico, and his family moved to a small mining town in Arizona when he was five. His father worked in a copper mine until it closed. One of eight children, he was the first in his family to graduate from college. He got his bachelor's in Iberian studies from the University of California, Santa Barbara, and a master's in organizational management from Fielding University. Carbajal was a member of the U.S. Marine Corps Reserve for eight years, including two years of active stateside duty during the Gulf War. He had several jobs on the public payroll, including chief of staff to a county supervisor and program director in the Santa Barbara Public Health Department. He served for 12 years on the Santa Barbara County Board of Supervisors, where he worked to improve local schools, protect the environment and advocate sustainable, clean energy sources. Carbajal has participated in several broader public forums on environmental issues.

Carbajal was the favorite of the Democratic establishment when Rep. Lois Capps announced her retirement in 2015. Santa Barbara Mayor Helene Schneider, who spoke positively about Vermont Sen. Bernie Sanders in the presidential campaign, was another Democratic contender. Capps and Democratic Leader Nancy Pelosi were early supporters of Carbajal. On the Republican side, the chief candidates were Assemblyman Katcho Achadjian and businessman Justin Fareed. In the "top two" nonpartisan primary, Carbajal and Fareed were the frontrunners with 33 percent and 21 percent.

In the general election, Fareed, who had served a year in Washington as an aide to Republican Rep. Ed Whitfield of Kentucky, accused Carbajal of being long on "political rhetoric and not actual solutions to the problems we're facing." Carbajal described himself as a public servant who worked across party lines. In September, he apologized for what he thought was a private remark when he referred to Lompoc, a military town that includes the Vandenberg base, as the "armpit" of Santa Barbara. Carbajal raised $3.1 million to $2.3 million for Fareed. The two national parties spent total of nearly $4 million on the contest, which turned out closer than had been expected. Fareed took San Luis Obispo with 51.5 percent of the vote. But Carbajal won the more populous Santa Barbara with 57 percent, and led overall, 53%-47%.

On the Armed Services Committee, Carbajal won approval of an amendment to the defense spending bill in 2018, which directed the Pentagon to report on innovative ways to reduce water use and improve water sustainability on military bases. He advocated for a cyber security training complex at Camp San Luis Obispo. On other local issues, he filed bills to bar oil and gas drilling off California's Central Coast and to encourage renewable energy in San Luis Obispo following the closing of the Diablo Canyon nuclear power plant. His Almanac vote ratings placed him among centrist Democrats.

Following the mass shooting at the high school in Parkland Florida in February 2018, Carbajal gained attention for legislation that he earlier filed to provide funds to states that implement restraining orders designed to prevent incidents of gun violence. Supporters said the proposal might have detected in advance behavioral problems of the assailant. Carbajal said that the National Rifle Association, which opposed his bill, had become synonymous with "No Republican Action."

In his rematch with Fareed, Carbajal spent $2 million to Fareed's $1.5 million. This time, Carbajal was not on a Democratic watch list and he won, 59%-41%. Following the election, he gained seats on the Agriculture and Transportation and Infrastructure committees, in addition to Armed Services.

CA-24: Central Coast

Cook Partisan Voting Index: D+7

Population		Race and Ethnicity		Income	
Total	732,284	White	54.8%	Median Income	$67,574
Land area (sq. miles)	6,883	Black	1.7%	District Income Rank	111
Pop/ sq mi	106.4	Latino	35.9%	Poverty Rate	14.8%
Born in State	60.1%	Asian	4.5%	With health insurance	89.3%
		Two or more races	2.5%	Cash public assistance	2.1%
Age Groups		Other	0.6%	Food stamp/SNAP	6.7%
Under 18	20.7%				
18-34	28.4%	**Education**		**Work**	
35-64	35.2%	H.S grad or less	33.8%	White Collar	15.7%
Over 64	15.7%	Some college	32.6%	Sales and Service	42.6%
		College Degree, 4 yr	20.4%	Blue Collar	20.6%
Military		Post grad	13.3%	Government	17%
Veteran/ Active Duty	7.7%				

2012 Pres. Vote	Obama	158,119	(54%)	Romney	126,049	(43%)		
2016 Pres. Vote	Clinton	176,979	(56%)	Trump	113,887	(36%)	Johnson	13,426	(4%)
	Stein	6,733	(2%)					

Santa Barbara, San Luis Obispo: In a state where stunning coastal landscapes and charming small towns are a dime a dozen, Santa Barbara stands out as someplace special. It is a collection of red tile roofs and leafy live oaks, sheltered by towering mountains just above the sea. The impression is a bit misleading, for Santa Barbara has its problems. Most of its quaint white stucco buildings were put up not as part of 18th-century mission settlement, but after a 1925 earthquake leveled much of the town. The city has long been one of the nation's richest retirement communities, one comfortable with its high living costs and determined to preserve its pristine environment and serenity.

Both features came under threat spectacularly in 1969, when an underwater oil well ruptured, coating the beach with oil. Pictures of the oil slick in the channel, and of volunteers trying to wash oil off grounded birds, helped to launch the 1970s environmental movement. Almost all of the wells are closed now. The oil spill left a long-lasting residue in Santa Barbara's politics. This was once a mostly Republican community, uninterested in redistribution of wealth, but always concerned about the environment and having moderate-to-liberal impulses on cultural issues. Like most of coastal California, it has moved decisively to the left.

Much of the Santa Barbara coastline is occupied by Vandenberg Air Force Base, which was the site in December 1958 of the first U.S. test missile launch and now sends unmanned government and commercial satellites into polar orbit. In October 2018, the Space X company launched a satellite into orbit for the Argentine space agency and landed its first-stage booster at the base eight minutes later. The largest towns in northern Santa Barbara County, as well as in San Luis Obispo, are pleasant, comfortable places, as untrendy as you can find in coastal California. The cost of rental housing in both counties has become unaffordable for many local workers. Farmers in Santa Barbara recently have revived the planting of coffee beans, with expectations of quick local growth. In January 2018, the massive Thomas fire, followed by heavy rains, resulted in mud slides in Montecito that caused the worst-ever loss of lives and property from a natural disaster in the county. In San Luis Obispo, Gov.

Jerry Brown in September 2018 signed a bill that gave the county $85 million to cover local costs for the shutdown of the Diablo Canyon nuclear power plant by 2025, when permits for its reactors expire; a state commission said that PG&E ratepayers could not be charged for the costs.

The 24th Congressional District of California includes all of San Luis Obispo and Santa Barbara counties. Santa Barbara is the larger of the two, and its 46 percent Latino population is twice that of its northern neighbor. Santa Maria is the largest city in Santa Barbara County. The 24th also brings in the northwest corner of Ventura County and a separate coastal part of San Buenaventura to the south, and it encompasses much of the Los Padres National Forest. Politically, the district favors Democrats. Closer to Los Angeles, Santa Barbara leans more heavily Democratic than does SLO.

Katie Hill (D)

Elected 2018, 1st term, b. Aug 25, 1987; Aberdeen, TX; California State University Northridge, B.A., 2008; California State University Northridge, M.P.A., 2014; Married (Kenny Hill).

Professional Career: Policy Advocate & Executive Director, People Assisting The Homeless, 2010-2014.

DC Office: 1130 LHOB 20515, 202-225-1956, Fax: 202-226-0683, katiehill.house.gov

State Offices: Palmdale, 661-839-0532.

Committees: *Armed Services*: Seapower & Projection Forces; Tactical Air & Land Forces. *Oversight & Reform*: Subcommittee on Economic & Consumer Policy; Subcommittee on Environment. *Science, Space & Technology*: Space & Aeronautics.

Election Results

Election	Name (Party)	Vote (%)		Cand. Spent	Ind. Exp. Support	Ind. Exp. Oppose
2018 General	Katherine Hill (D)............................	133,209	(54%)	$8,410,151	$7,215,053	$4,674,870
	Stephen Knight (R)........................	111,813	(46%)	$2,583,074		
2018 Primary	Stephen Knight (R)........................	61,411	(52%)			
	Katherine L. Hill (D)............................	24,507	(21%)			
	Bryan Caforio (D)............................	21,821	(18%)			
	Jess Phoenix (D)....................................	7,549	(6%)			

Freshman Democrat Katie Hill, with a fresh voice for the rapidly changing demographics in the exurbs north of Los Angeles, took control of a district that had been safely Republican a few years earlier. As a rock-climbing, gun-owning and bisexual executive of a large non-profit agency that provided homes for the homeless, she captured the gestalt of what she described as "a new generation of leaders." In a documentary that Vice News produced for HBO, she called her campaign, "the most millennial ever."

Hill defeated Republican Rep. Steve Knight, a former Los Angeles police officer who entered local politics with conservative views that were widely embraced at the time in this area. Her victory switched control of the final Republican-held House district that was predominantly in Los Angeles County.

A native of rapidly growing Santa Clarita, Hill got a bachelor's degree and a master's of public administration from California State University (Northridge). Starting as a policy advocate for People Assisting the Homeless, she eventually became executive director of the statewide non-profit group. Working with health care providers, law enforcement, and employers, Hill handled hundreds of government contracts and dealt with complex social issues.

She helped to win passage of two ballot initiatives in Los Angeles County to increase funds for homeless services. "You don't need to talk about the policy details as much as you should give people a reason to trust you," she told Rolling Stone, in describing how she connected to young people. In her first bid for elected office, she conveyed an informal, down-to-earth style. "People care about whether they can like you and trust you."

Knight styled himself as tough on spending and a problem-solver during his years in local and state government. Like his predecessor, Republican Rep. Buck McKeon, who chaired the House Armed Services Committee, Knight worked on military issues, including the nearby Point Magu Naval Air Station.

In the "top two" primary to determine the general-election alternative to Knight, the other prominent Democratic candidate was trial lawyer Steve Caforio, who ran against Knight in 2016 with support from the Democratic Congressional Campaign Committee and lost, 53%-47%. This time, the DCCC—with groups of women and gay-rights advocates—rallied around Hill's outgoing persona. She led the Democratic candidates, with 21 percent of the vote to 18 percent for Caforio. Knight topped the field in the primary with 52 percent.

In the district's expensive advertising market, the candidates relied on succinct themes. Hill's people-power message highlighted that she was not beholden to party bosses or special interests. Knight pointed to the strong economy and passage of tax cuts by the Republican-controlled Congress.

With Hill's huge fundraising advantage, she outspent Knight by about 3-to-1. Each benefited from outside money. Former New York City Mayor Mike Bloomberg's Independence PAC spent more than $4 million in late ads on her behalf. Speaker Paul Ryan's Congressional Leadership Fund spent nearly $4 million, which nearly doubled Knight's own spending.

Hill won comfortably, 54%-46%. Knight got 51 percent in a sliver of Ventura County, which included about one-fifth of the voters. Republicans, seeking to regain the district, faced the imperative to adjust to its shifting voter base.

CA-25: Northern LA Exurbs   **Cook Partisan Voting Index: EVEN**

Population		Race and Ethnicity		Income	
Total	720,000	White	42.3%	Median Income	$75,860
Land area (sq. miles)	1,691	Black	7.7%	District Income Rank	70
Pop/ sq mi	425.9	Latino	38.3%	Poverty Rate	13.4%
Born in State	62.6%	Asian	8.1%	With health insurance	91.2%
		Two or more races	3%	Cash public assistance	3.3%
Age Groups		Other	0.6%	Food stamp/SNAP	7.5%
Under 18	26.6%				
18-34	22.2%	**Education**		**Work**	
35-64	40.2%	H.S grad or less	37.6%	White Collar	11%
Over 64	11%	Some college	35.1%	Sales and Service	42%
		College Degree, 4 yr	18.1%	Blue Collar	19.1%
Military		Post grad	9.2%	Government	15%
Veteran/ Active Duty	6.1%				

2012 Pres. Vote	Romney	125,258	(50%)	Obama	120,701	(48%)		
2016 Pres. Vote	Clinton	137,491	(50%)	Trump	119,249	(43%)	Johnson	9,969	(4%)

Santa Clarita, Palmdale: For decades, as the mild-temperature flatlands of the Los Angeles Basin and San Fernando Valley filled up with people, the rugged mountains and hot desert to the north in Los Angeles County remained mostly empty. In recent years, more people began moving north through Newhall pass on Interstate 5 and northeast on Route 14 to the high desert country. Immediately north of the pass is Santa Clarita, the third-largest city in the county with more than 180,000 residents, and the Six Flags Magic Mountain theme park. Northeast on Route 14, past the former gold-mining center of Acton, the mountains stop at the San Andreas Fault and the desert stretches out low and flat. This is Antelope Valley, with huge aerospace plants and military bases around Palmdale and Lancaster, where more than 400,000 people live. Not far from upscale shopping centers, there has been a resurgence of specialty farm crops such as baby carrots, organic onions and parsnips. Access to health care has been a problem in Antelope Valley and the life expectancy of African Americans here has been four years shorter than for blacks in the rest of Los Angeles County.

The Air Force Plant 42 is home to many defense contractors, with projects that include the B-2 Stealth Bomber, the F-117 Stealth Fighter, and the F-35 Joint Strike Fighter. The RQ-170 Sentinel, a next-generation drone reportedly used in CIA operations, has been developed at Lockheed Martin's Skunk Works facility in Palmdale. Northrop Grumman has a deal to build 100 of the B-21 Long-Range Strike Bombers, with close to half the work expected at Palmdale and 5,000 employees by late 2019, in a contract that could total $80 billion. In a welcome diversification, Santa Clarita has become a favorite alternative production site for Hollywood studios 30 miles to the south. In 2018, the state began to purchase land for a 63-mile high-desert freeway in the Mojave between Palmdale and Lancaster in San Bernardino County. This would become the first new freeway in the L.A. area since the Century Freeway (the 105) opened in 1993. At least some portions of the new freeway were expected to charge tolls.

The 25th Congressional District of California includes all of the Santa Clarita Valley and the high desert parts of Los Angeles County. About one-fifth of the district is in Ventura County. The district extends to most of Simi Valley in Ventura, including the Ronald Reagan Presidential Foundation and Library, which has become one of the most popular tourist attractions north of Los Angeles. Housed there are 55 million pages of presidential documents and a large piece of the Berlin Wall, which Reagan famously urged Soviet leader Mikhail Gorbachev to tear down. In October 2018, the library added a three-dimensional holographic image of Reagan, which includes his facial features. This was the first-ever such exhibit in a presidential library.

Politically, the district had been comfortably Republican. During the past decade, the influx of Latinos, which have grown to 38 percent of the 25th, and the extension of the L.A. psyche to this once-rural area have eliminated the GOP's voter-registration advantage and made this a competitive district. Hillary Clinton won comfortably in 2016, 50%-43%.

Julia Brownley (D)

Elected 2012, 4th term, b. Aug 28, 1952; Aiken, SC; Mount Vernon College, B.A., 1975; American University (DC), M.B.A., 1979; Episcopalian; Divorced; 2 children.

Elected Office: CA Assembly, 2006-2012; Santa Monica Malibu School Board, 1994-2006.

Professional Career: Product Manager, Steelcase, 1984-1992; Sales Manager, Pitney Bowes, 1981-1984; Sales Manager, Burroughs Corporation, 1976-1981.

DC Office: 2262 RHOB 20515, 202-225-5811, Fax: 202-225-1100, juliabrownley.house.gov

State Offices: Oxnard, 805-379-1779; Thousand Oaks, 805-379-1779.

Committees: *Select Committee on the Climate Crisis. Transportation & Infrastructure*: Aviation; Highways & Transit. *Veterans' Affairs*: Health (Chmn); Technology Modernization.

Group Ratings

	ADA	ACLU	AFL-CIO	LCV	ITI	COC	HAFA	ACU	CFG	FRC
2018	-	79%	-	89%	-	67%	4%	4%	20%	0%
2017	80%	C	97%	100%	C	62%	C	4%	0%	11%

Almanac Ratings 2017-18

	Economy	Social	Foreign	Composite
Liberal	84%	95%	62%	81%
Conservative	16%	5%	38%	19%

Key Votes of the 115th Congress

1. Obama-care revision	N	5. Family planning regs	N	9. Guantanamo prisoners	N
2. Tax Cuts	N	6. Body cameras/immigration	Y	10. Ground missiles, limit	Y
3. Omnibus appropriations	Y	7. Abortion ban	N	11. Defense Dept. spending	Y
4. Dodd-Frank revision	N	8. Concealed carry	NV	12. FISA rules	Y

Election Results

Election	Name (Party)	Vote (%)		Cand. Spent	Ind. Exp. Support	Ind. Exp. Oppose
2018 General	Julia Brownley (D)	158,216	(62%)	$1,434,509	$23,667	
	Antonio Sabato Jr. (R)	97,210	(38%)	$349,068		
2018 Primary	Julia Brownley (D)	72,764	(54%)			
	Antonio Sabato Jr. (R)	30,107	(22%)			
	Jeffrey Burum (R)	26,656	(20%)			

Prior winning percentages: 2016 (60%), 2014 (51%), 2012 (53%)

Democrat Julia Brownley, elected in 2012, slowly established control of the Ventura County seat that had long been held by Republicans. She has carved out a niche on veterans' health issues and on shifting gender norms and has become a senior Democrat on the Veterans' Affairs Committee.

Brownley grew up in Virginia in a Republican household. It wasn't until she went to Washington D.C.'s all-girls Mount Vernon College that she began to consider her personal politics. There, shaped by the emerging women's movement and the war in Vietnam, Brownley said she felt at home in the Democratic Party. After college, she pursued a career in marketing, earning a master's degree from American University and then working as a sales manager for several large companies. That career introduced her to her husband (they are now divorced) and brought her to California. Brownley's experiences with her children helped to push her into politics. Her daughter, Hannah, suffered from dyslexia. Working with the school system to improve Hannah's education inspired Brownley to run for the Santa Monica-Malibu school board in 1994. She stayed on the board for 12 years and served as its president. Frustrated with what she considered insufficient funding for the school district, Brownley in 2006 won a seat in the state Assembly. There, she chaired the Education Committee, advocating higher spending on the state's schools at every level.

In the contest for the open seat in the 26th District, Brownley moved up the coast from Santa Monica and faced off in the primary against Linda Parks, a Republican-turned-independent hoping to steal moderate votes from Brownley. State Sen. Tony Strickland led the all-party primary with 44 percent, to 27 percent for Brownley and 18 percent for Parks. Strickland attacked Brownley for moving to the district. Contributions to Strickland from the U.S. Chamber of Commerce and other groups led Brownley to call him a captive of "Washington special interests." The Los Angeles Times endorsed her, saying that the "ideologically rigid" Strickland lacked "real-world pragmatism." She won, 52.7%-47.3%. Strickland in 2014 ran — and lost — to a Republican in the adjacent GOP-leaning 25th District.

Brownley initially had problems finding a comfort level with her new constituency. Her official bio listed that she served on a school board for 12 years, but it did not say where. She found a niche on the Veterans' Affairs Committee, where she was ranking Democrat on the Health Subcommittee. In 2016, the House passed her bill to identify the best mental health and suicide-prevention program for at-risk women veterans. In September 2018, Brownley organized a letter in which 83 House members wrote to the Veterans Affairs Department that it had an "obligation" to include gender-reassignment surgery in its coverage for veterans, stating that denial of the procedure was "unconscionable." She estimated that there were 160,000 transgender veterans. In the majority, she became the number-two Democrat on the committee behind Mark Takano, also of California.

She pursued her interest in education issues by calling for increased funding of bilingual programs. As co-chair of the House Dyslexia Caucus, she won enactment of the Research Excellence and Advancements for Dyslexia (READ) Act to require the National Science Foundation to spend at least $2.5 million annually for dyslexia research. In January 2019, Brownley filed a bill to rewrite federal law to replace references to "husband" and "wife" with the term "spouse." Each gendered reference in the federal code "undermines and de-legitimizes same-sex couples," she said.

Brownley faced another competitive campaign in 2014. Republican Assemblyman Jeff Gorell showcased his moderate voting record in Sacramento. Brownley was far better funded, $3.4 million to $1.3 million, and benefited from more than $2 million in national party funding. She won narrowly, 51.3%-48.7%. In the next cycle, the Democratic Congressional Campaign Committee included Brownley among the first 14 members of its Frontline program of House Democrats who were expected to be vulnerable. Perhaps that scared off potential challengers. Republican challenger Rafael Dagnesses, a real estate agent, was little-known politically and raised only $184,000, including $100,000 of self-financing. Brownley won, 60%-40%.

Republican dynamics continued to deteriorate in 2018. The GOP initially talked up Antonio Sabato Jr. -- an actor who appeared on General Hospital and on reality shows and was a model for Calvin Klein underwear. On a broadcast in February 2018, he said that he had been "blacklisted" in Hollywood because he was a supporter of President Donald Trump. Earlier, he said that former President Barack Obama was "absolutely" a Muslim. That no longer was sound politics in this district. Brownley outspent Sabato, $1.4 million to $349,000, and won, 62%-38%. Like all coastal Democrats in California, she had become entrenched.

CA-26: Southern Ventura

Cook Partisan Voting Index: D+7

Population		Race and Ethnicity		Income	
Total	725,161	White	43.7%	Median Income	$80,281
Land area (sq. miles)	939	Black	1.6%	District Income Rank	52
Pop/ sq mi	772.2	Latino	45.1%	Poverty Rate	10.9%
Born in State	57.1%	Asian	6.7%	With health insurance	88.6%
		Two or more races	2.4%	Cash public assistance	2%
Age Groups		Other	0.5%	Food stamp/SNAP	7.5%
Under 18	24.2%				
18-34	23.1%	**Education**		**Work**	
35-64	38.5%	H.S grad or less	35.5%	White Collar	14.2%
Over 64	14.2%	Some college	31.6%	Sales and Service	40.3%
		College Degree, 4 yr	20.3%	Blue Collar	23%
Military		Post grad	12.5%	Government	14%
Veteran/ Active Duty	7.1%				

2012 Pres. Vote	Obama	147,753	(54%)	Romney	119,677	(44%)		
2016 Pres. Vote	Clinton	169,083	(57%)	Trump	105,259	(36%)	Johnson	11,301	(4%)

Oxnard, Thousand Oaks: For many Americans, Simi Valley remains best known as the site of the 1992 trial where four Los Angeles police officers were acquitted for the beating of taxi driver Rodney King, who famously said, "People, I just want to say, can we all get along?" Granted, the incident took place during riots in South Los Angeles. The city of Simi Valley is a very different place than South L.A. -- a product of the 1960s, the expansive postwar years when migrants from points across the United States moved west to Los Angeles and then spread beyond city and county limits to fill up the valleys between the mountains. They brought a distaste for the crime and civil strife that seemed all too common in Los Angeles during that turbulent decade in U.S. history. In the valleys of Ventura County, northwest of Los Angeles, people built communities in what had been orange and lemon groves. Like California overall, the Ventura County population has trended socially liberal and economically conservative. To the south is upscale Thousand Oaks, one of the safest large cities in the nation and the headquarters of biotechnology giant Amgen Inc. Farther west in Pleasant Valley is Camarillo, which is home to numerous technology firms.

The local economy has a strong export market, including pharmaceuticals, semiconductors and citrus fruit. A downside is that the economic growth and high cost of living have created a shortage of housing for farm workers. In December 2018, economists at California Lutheran University reported that the shortage contributed to the stagnant economy in Ventura. The once-robust local farming, especially strawberries, has been reduced — a victim of imports, labor costs and the drought. The annual strawberry festival in Oxnard, which drew more than 60,000 in May 2018, featured strawberry beer and nachos. In the inland valleys still farther west is Ojai, which remains a center for tourism. During the filming of the 1937 Frank Capra movie Lost Horizon, an aerial shot of the Ojai Valley was used to represent the mythical earthly paradise of Shangri-La. To the north in the foothills of wilderness areas here is the Santa Clara River Valley, with Fillmore, Piru and Santa Paula. The area has suffered recent disasters: In November 2018, the Woolsey fire — destroying more than 1,600 structures — was the worst ever in Ventura and L.A., where it reached to Malibu. Also that month a mass shooting at a bar in Thousand Oaks left 13 dead, including a police officer.

The 26th Congressional District covers more than 80 percent of Ventura County, including its largest city, Oxnard. The district takes in Thousand Oaks and the Santa Clara River Valley. The 26th juts into Porter Ranch, a thin slice of Los Angeles County to the north of Northridge, but with only a few thousand voters. The 26th District leans Democratic, though it is more competitive than an

Democratic-held district in L.A. County. Hillary Clinton led Donald Trump, 57%-36%. She took the county overall, 56%-38%.

Judy Chu (D)

Elected 2009, 5th full term, b. Jul 07, 1953; Los Angeles; University of California, Santa Barbara, Att., 1973; University of California, Los Angeles, B.A., 1974; California School Professional Psychology, Los Angeles, M.A., 1977; California School Professional Psychology, Los Angeles, Ph.D., 1979; Married (Michael Eng).

Elected Office: Garvey School Board, 1985-1988; Monterey Park City Council, 1988-2001; Mayor, Monterey Park; CA Assembly, 2001-2006; CA Board Of Equalization, 2006-2009, vice Chairman, 2009.

Professional Career: Professor, Los Angeles City College, Psychology Department, 1981-1988; E. Los Angeles College, Psychology Department, 1988-2001.

DC Office: 2423 RHOB 20515, 202-225-5464, Fax: 202-225-5467, chu.house.gov
State Offices: Claremont, 909-625-5394; Pasadena, 626-304-0110.

Committees: *Small Business*: Contracting & Infrastructure; Investigations, Oversight & Regulations (Chmn). *Ways & Means*: Health; Oversight; Worker & Family Support.

Group Ratings

	ADA	ACLU	AFL-CIO	LCV	ITI	COC	HAFA	ACU	CFG	FRC
2018	-	89%	-	97%	-	50%	8%	4%	15%	0%
2017	100%	C	95%	100%	C	43%	C	7%	5%	0%

Almanac Ratings 2017-18

	Economy	Social	Foreign	Composite
Liberal	100%	98%	100%	99%
Conservative	0%	2%	0%	1%

Key Votes of the 115th Congress

1. Obama-care revision	N	5. Family planning regs	N	9. Guantanamo prisoners	Y
2. Tax Cuts	N	6. Body cameras/immigration	Y	10. Ground missiles, limit	Y
3. Omnibus appropriations	N	7. Abortion ban	N	11. Defense Dept. spending	N
4. Dodd-Frank revision	N	8. Concealed carry	N	12. FISA rules	N

Election Results

Election	Name (Party)	Vote (%)		Cand. Spent	Ind. Exp. Support	Ind. Exp. Oppose
2018 General	Judy Chu (D)	160,504	(79%)	$494,890		
	Bryan Witt (D)	42,132	(21%)	$9,900		
2018 Primary	Judy Chu (D)	86,932	(84%)			
	Bryan Witt (D)	17,186	(17%)			

Prior winning percentages: 2016 (67%), 2014 (59%), 2012 (64%), 2010 (71%), 2009 special (62%)

Democrat Judy Chu, who won a 2009 special election, became the first Chinese-American woman in the House. She is a strong liberal and has been active in the Congressional Asian Pacific-American Caucus. With her seat on the Ways and Means Committee, her interests include her many constituents in the motion picture industry and other creative entrepreneurs.

Chu grew up in Los Angeles as the daughter of an electrical technician who brought his wife from China under the War Brides Act. The family moved to the Bay Area when she was in junior high school. She graduated from the University of California, Los Angeles, got a Ph.D. in psychology, then taught for 13 years at East Los Angeles Community College. She served on the Garvey School District board for three years and was mayor of Monterey Park for 12 years. In 2000, Chu was elected to the California Assembly, where she focused on criminal justice and environmental issues. As chairwoman of the Appropriations Committee, she sponsored a tax amnesty program that brought in significant sums for the state. In 2006, she was elected to the state Board of Equalization, where she worked on closing tax loopholes.

After Rep. Hilda Solis was appointed as President Barack Obama's Secretary of Labor, the contest for the Democratic nomination became a race between Chu and state Sen. Gil Cedillo, the leading Hispanic candidate. Rather than simply an ethnic showdown between an Asian and a Latino, the special election was more nuanced. Chu was endorsed by much of the Democratic establishment, including prominent Hispanics such as Los Angeles Mayor Antonio Villaraigosa and members of Solis' family. The Los Angeles County Labor Federation, which was impressed by Chu's support for farm workers, backed her, as did EMILY's List, the national advocacy group for pro-abortion rights Democratic women. Chu won the all-party primary with 32 percent, to 23 percent for Cedillo and 14 percent for Emanuel Pleitez, a 26-year-old financial analyst who had worked on Obama's presidential campaign. Because Judy Chu failed to receive a majority of the total vote, she faced a runoff with Republican Betty Chu, a Monterey Park councilwoman who was Chu's distant cousin by marriage. The Democrat won, 62%-33%.

After her nephew, a lance corporal in the Marine Corps stationed in Afghanistan, committed suicide in 2011 after being beaten up by his fellow Marines, Chu began introducing anti-hazing bills. In the fiscal 2017 defense spending bill, the House included her proposal to require the Defense Department to create a national database of military hazing incidents and submit an annual report on its efforts to end the practice. She founded and co-chaired the Creative Rights Caucus, which advocates increased copyright protections for creative artists.

As chair of the Asian Pacific-American Caucus, Chu sponsored a House-passed resolution in 2012 to have the United States apologize for the anti-immigrant Chinese Exclusion Act of 1882. Her grandfather was forced to carry a certificate of U.S. residence for about 40 years. "It is for my grandfather, and for all Chinese Americans who were told for six decades by the U.S. government that the land of the free wasn't open to them, that we must pass this resolution," she said. When President Donald Trump took office, she voiced concern that discrimination against Muslims could parallel the Japanese internment camps during World War II. She filed a bill to increase mental health awareness among Asian Americans and to overcome the stigma. In December 2017, she was arrested during a rally at the Capitol on behalf of young undocumented immigrants.

When Chu took her seat on Ways and Means in 2017, ranking Democrat Richard Neal cited her experience with tax issues on the Board of Equalization plus her commitment to tax fairness. She criticized the committee's handling of Republican efforts to repeal and revise the Affordable Care Act. "This plan was rushed to committee, there has not been time for the Congressional Budget Office to release their analysis of how much this will cost or how many Americans will be covered," Chu said. With Democrats in House control, she worked with Neal to get access to Trump's tax returns. Even with her Ph.D. in psychology, Chu tweeted, she could not "fully capture how emotionally insecure our president is."

At home, Republican Jack Orswell, a small business owner and former FBI agent, challenged Chu and got 41 percent of the vote. That was the only time Chu has been held below 60 percent in this safely Democratic district. A month after the election, the House Standards of Official Conduct (Ethics) Committee issued Chu a letter of reproval after concluding that she interfered with the panel's investigation of whether her House aides had performed campaign work. "The committee acknowledged that my intention was to ease the staff member's anxiety and that I expressed regret for this one moment of contact," Chu said. In 2018, her sole opponent was Democrat Bryan Witt, who spent only $10,000. Chu won, 79%-21%.

CA-27: San Gabriel Foothills

Cook Partisan Voting Index: D+16

Population		Race and Ethnicity		Income	
Total	719,377	White	26.4%	Median Income	$73,445
Land area (sq. miles)	700	Black	4.3%	District Income Rank	76
Pop/ sq mi	1027.8	Latino	28%	Poverty Rate	12.6%
Born in State	47.4%	Asian	38.2%	With health insurance	91.3%
		Two or more races	2.4%	Cash public assistance	2.2%
Age Groups		Other	0.6%	Food stamp/SNAP	4.2%
Under 18	19.4%				
18-34	22.1%	**Education**		**Work**	
35-64	41.5%	H.S grad or less	33%	White Collar	17%
Over 64	17%	Some college	25%	Sales and Service	41.3%
		College Degree, 4 yr	25.2%	Blue Collar	13.2%
Military		Post grad	16.8%	Government	13.9%
Veteran/ Active Duty	3.8%				

2012 Pres. Vote	Obama	161,528	(63%)	Romney	90,278	(35%)			
2016 Pres. Vote	Clinton	174,544	(66%)	Trump	74,984	(28%)	Johnson	7,862	(3%)
	Stein	5,717	(2%)						

Pasadena, Monterey Park: In the early part of the 20th century, when Los Angeles was growing rapidly and on its way to becoming one of America's major cities, its richest citizens settled not on the beach (too clammy and cold) or on the west side (too dusty and remote), but in communities they built at the base of the San Gabriel Mountains. Their snow-capped peaks, rising 10,000 feet above the city, are visible most of the year. The place to be was Pasadena, home of the Rose Bowl, Cal Tech and a baroque-domed city hall. Pasadena and South Pasadena have carefully preserved their bungalow neighborhoods, and Pasadena preserved and rebuilt the 80-year-old curving Colorado Boulevard Bridge over Arroyo Seco. With 16 percent of Pasadena living below the poverty level, city officials have sought to develop additional options for affordable housing. Nearby is luxurious San Marino, home of the Huntington Library, one of the world's great museums and scholarly institutions, with more than 150 acres of botanical gardens. Arcadia has the Santa Anita Park racetrack and the Los Angeles County Arboretum & Botanic Garden. Wealthy Chinese have invested in business opportunities in the area.

Parts of this area have significant Asian populations. Chinese and other Asians are 67 percent of the population in Monterey Park, which has been called America's first suburban Chinatown, and 61 percent in Rosemead. In 2017, Money Magazine listed Monterey Park as the third-best place to live in the United States, citing its recreational activities. Young Asian Americans produced a YouTube rap video titled "626" — the area code for much of the San Gabriel Valley — and it went viral. In 2018, the movie Crazy Rich Asians was a sensation that drew huge audiences in Asian-American neighborhoods. The Rose Bowl and the Tournament of Roses Parade annually yield spending of $38 million — a larger draw for L.A. than the Oscars.

The 27th Congressional District includes much of the Pasadena area and other portions of Los Angeles County. It takes in San Marino and the San Gabriel foothills communities of Altadena, Glendora, Sierra Madre and San Antonio Heights, where vicious cycles of drought, fire, rain and mudslides have become familiar. Proposals to designate a large part of the San Gabriel Mountains as a national monument have drawn protests, especially from bikers, hunters and other recreational users. Also in the district are San Gabriel, Temple City and Claremont, dubbed "The City of Trees and Ph.D.'s" after its Claremont Colleges -- plus the conservative-leaning Claremont Institute. The 27th has a small indentation of San Bernardino County, near Upland, which leans Republican, but it is barely 5 percent of the district. The 27th is 38 percent Asian American, the second-highest of any California district, and 28 percent Hispanic. Politically, it is solidly Democratic, though not as strongly as some other L.A.-area districts. Hillary Clinton won the district, 66%-28%.

Adam Schiff (D)

Elected 2000, 10th term, b. Jun 22, 1960; Framingham, MA; Stanford University (CA), B.A., 1982; Harvard University Law School (MA), J.D., 1985; Jewish; Married (Eve Sanderson Schiff); 2 children.

Elected Office: CA Senate, 1996-2000.

Professional Career: Prosecutor, U.S. Attorney General Office, L.A., 1987- 93; Practicing attorney, 1986-1987, 1995-1996.

DC Office: 2269 RHOB 20515, 202-225-4176, Fax: 202-225-5828, schiff.house.gov

State Offices: Burbank, 818-450-2900; Los Angeles, 323-315-5555.

Committees: *Permanent Select on Intelligence (Chmn).*

Group Ratings

	ADA	ACLU	AFL-CIO	LCV	ITI	COC	HAFA	ACU	CFG	FRC
2018	-	79%	-	97%	-	50%	6%	8%	22%	0%
2017	90%	C	97%	100%	C	43%	C	0%	0%	0%

Almanac Ratings 2017-18

	Economy	Social	Foreign	Composite
Liberal	100%	98%	89%	96%
Conservative	0%	2%	11%	4%

Key Votes of the 115th Congress

1. Obama-care revision	N	5. Family planning regs	N	9. Guantanamo prisoners	Y
2. Tax Cuts	N	6. Body cameras/immigration	Y	10. Ground missiles, limit	Y
3. Omnibus appropriations	N	7. Abortion ban	N	11. Defense Dept. spending	Y
4. Dodd-Frank revision	N	8. Concealed carry	N	12. FISA rules	Y

Election Results

Election	Name (Party)	Vote (%)		Cand. Spent	Ind. Exp. Support	Ind. Exp. Oppose
2018 General	Adam Schiff (D)	196,662	(78%)	$2,968,691		
	Johnny Nalbandian (R)	54,272	(22%)		$35,730	
2018 Primary	Adam Schiff (D)	94,249	(74%)			
	Johnny Nalbandian (R)	26,566	(21%)			
	Sal Genovese (D)	7,406	(6%)			

Prior winning percentages: 2016 (78%), 2014 (77%), 2012 (77%), 2010 (65%), 2008 (69%), 2006 (64%), 2004 (65%), 2002 (63%), 2000 (53%)

Adam Schiff, elected in 2000, is an active and ambitious Democrat who has become a powerful voice on national security — and an outspoken critic of President Donald Trump -- as chairman of the House Intelligence Committee. He has demanded answers to allegations of misbehavior, including alleged encouragement of Russian interference in the 2016 election. In his early House years, Schiff emphasized his fiscal moderation and interest in intellectual property issues that concern many of his constituents. His leadership has increased speculation about his future beyond the House, which Schiff has encouraged.

Schiff's father was a traveling salesman and later owned a lumberyard. Schiff grew up throughout the country, graduating from high school in Northern California. He went on to Stanford University and Harvard Law School. From 1987 to 1993, he worked in the U.S. attorney's office in Los Angeles. He ran for the California Assembly and lost three times. In 1996, he was elected to the state Senate. In his first two years, he enacted dozens of measures, including a bill guaranteeing up-to-date textbook in classrooms and another reforming the child support system. Schiff also taught political science a Glendale Community College.

Schiff ran for the House in the first election following the 1998 impeachment of President Bil Clinton. He challenged Republican James Rogan, who was a Judiciary Committee leader and persuasive voice for the case against Clinton, which centered on the president's lying under oath about an affair with a White House intern. Clinton pal and entertainment mogul David Geffen promised to raise millions of dollars to oppose him. The Schiff-Rogan race became a fundraising marathon, and was then the most expensive House race on record. The candidates raised more than $10 million combined, and much more was spent independently by Clinton's supporters as well as his detractors. Rogan branded his opponent as a traditional tax-and-spend liberal who would "run naked through the Treasury, spending everything he can." Schiff attacked Rogan for calling abortion a holocaust for the African-American community. Schiff won by an unexpectedly large 53%-44% vote, and has been easily reelected since.

In the House, Schiff joined the Blue Dog Coalition of moderate to conservative Democrats and has sometimes worked across party lines. Schiff served as co-chairman of the Congressional International Anti-Piracy Caucus, where he sponsored a bill to provide law enforcement and copyright holders with new tools to target websites based offshore that offer pirated music, movies and other counterfeit goods. He was instrumental in bipartisan legislation that made identity theft a crime. Schiff stirred complaints from liberal constituents when he supported the resolution approving the use of force in Iraq in 2002 and for voting for the USA Patriot Act, the anti-terrorism law that gave new powers to law enforcement.

As the years passed, his views became more conventionally liberal. After the Supreme Court in the 2012 Citizens United case overturned a Montana law barring corporate spending in state elections, he worked with Harvard law professor Laurence Tribe to introduce a constitutional amendment to allow Congress and the states to impose limitations on independent campaign expenditures. After the fatal police shooting of an unarmed black man in Ferguson Missouri in 2014, Schiff pushed Attorney General Eric Holder to help state and local law enforcement agencies acquire body-worn cameras. In the Almanac vote ratings in recent years, Schiff ranked consistently among the most liberal members of the House.

On foreign policy, Schiff has pressed for recognition of the Armenian genocide as the responsibility of the Ottoman Empire, a move Turkey adamantly opposes. His resolution was approved by the House Foreign Affairs Committee in 2007, but he agreed to postpone further action after a strong response from Turkey. Schiff has been concerned that major national security actions should not be left solely to a president's discretion. He has filed legislation to repeal the Authorization for Use of Military Force, which Congress passed after the 2001 attacks. He said it "was never intended to authorize a war without end, and it now poorly defines those who pose a threat to our country." When he offered an amendment based on the measure to the fiscal 2014 defense appropriations bill, it was defeated after Republicans said it was dangerous to set a specific timeline. Following the election of Trump in 2016, Schiff voiced new concern that the failure to limit presidential action was "very troubling."

When the Islamic State (ISIS) terrorist group began capturing large swaths of territory in the Middle East in 2014, Schiff sought to call attention to the threat of Americans and Europeans carrying out attacks at home. Later, when Obama outlined a plan to deal with ISIS, Schiff became heavily involved in unsuccessful efforts to have Congress authorize the president's actions. "It's hard to explain the relative silence of my libertarian colleagues at a time when the president is about to announce a war effort that may take years," Schiff told The Washington Post. Schiff strongly objected to the Republican push to investigate the terrorist attacks on U.S. facilities in Benghazi Libya. In 2014, he told Fox News that a select committee on the matter was "a colossal waste of time" and that his party should boycott it — something that House leaders refused to do. He subsequently served on the select committee.

Democratic Leader Nancy Pelosi gave Schiff a significant national security niche when she named him the top Democrat on the House Intelligence Committee in 2015. He brought to the table new proposals on intelligence policy. He filed legislation to require greater transparency for the U.S. military drone program. He opposed paying ransoms to free Americans held by rebel groups, such as ISIS. He also advocated major changes in the National Security Agency's phone metadata surveillance program, which would require the government to request phone company records on a case-by-case basis.

Schiff used his Intelligence Committee post to criticize the failure of the Obama administration to sanction Russia for its computer hacking that he said had been designed to influence the 2016 election, and he demanded that Congress investigate. "They didn't just steal data, they weaponized it. They dumped it during an election with the specific intent of influencing the outcomes of that election and sowing discord in the United States," he said. That led to his demands to investigate the Trump campaign's possible connection to Russian interference. Schiff voiced early warnings of

Trump's use of "alternative facts," which he said "undermines his credibility" and is "a crisis waiting to happen." In March 2017, he accused Republican Rep. Devin Nunes of California, the committee chairman, of working closely with Trump and said that Nunes should step aside "from any further involvement in the Russia investigation." A week later, the House Ethics Committee began a review of Nunes's actions and he informally recused himself from the Russia inquiry.

During the review in 2017-18 by the Republican-controlled panel, Schiff pressed for a complete investigation. When the GOP majority balked, he often sought to hold them accountable. "All this has vaulted Schiff into the unlikely role of being the Democrats' leader not just on the investigation but on all things Trump and Russia," the Los Angeles Times reported in a July 2018 profile. "He has become a fixture on cable TV and the Sunday talk shows, distilling and explaining the latest developments in the marquee saga of the Trump presidency. ... For many, he is the voice of reason, a steadying influence, the sober narrator in a time when chaos reigns."

After Nunes — who had regained his authority as chairman following the conclusion of the ethics inquiry — brought the formal investigation to what Schiff viewed as a premature conclusion in March 2018, he pursued his own review of Trump's actions. Trump tweeted that, "Sleazy Adam Schiff, the totally biased Congressman looking into 'Russia,' spends all his time on television pushing the Dem loss excuse!" Following Trump's meeting with Russian president Vladimir Putin in Helsinki in July 2018, Schiff called the president "the gravest threat to American democracy." Those counterattacks, in turn, increased his popularity among grassroots Democrats who were hostile to Trump.

After Democrats regained House control in the 2018 election, Pelosi appointed Schiff as Intelligence Committee chairman. He vowed to pursue oversight of the Trump campaign and presidency, which he said Republicans had "completely abdicated." He would seek to "restore Congress as a co-equal branch of government," he said. In April 2019, Schiff said that the report of special counsel Robert Mueller on his investigation of Russian interference in the 2016 presidential election included allegations of obstruction of justice by Trump that were "far worse than anything that Richard Nixon" and "more significant than Watergate."

Schiff thought seriously about running for the open seat after Sen. Barbara Boxer in 2015 said she would not seek reelection. When he quietly announced that he would remain in the House, he kept the door open to "other challenges in the future." In 2017, he voiced interest in succeeding Dianne Feinstein whenever she departs the Senate. That option has remained unavailable. Meanwhile, Schiff spent time in Iowa and New Hampshire as he explored a bid for the Democratic presidential nomination. "I would never say never to something," he told a Los Angeles Times reporter who asked him in October 2018 whether he might run. That prospect was daunting, not least after Sen. Kamala Harris and Rep. Eric Swalwell, both from California, became early contenders. Four months later, during a political event in New Hampshire, he said that he would not run for president in 2020. Still, that left the door open for other opportunities.

CA-28: Northern Los Angeles   Cook Partisan Voting Index: D+23

Population		Race and Ethnicity		Income	
Total	717,921	White	55.2%	Median Income	$62,319
Land area (sq. miles)	218	Black	2.7%	District Income Rank	155
Pop/ sq mi	3286.4	Latino	25.3%	Poverty Rate	15%
Born in State	37.5%	Asian	13.3%	With health insurance	88%
		Two or more races	2.9%	Cash public assistance	3.1%
Age Groups		Other	0.7%	Food stamp/SNAP	5.9%
Under 18	15.6%				
18-34	27.3%	**Education**		**Work**	
35-64	42.4%	H.S grad or less	29.6%	White Collar	14.7%
Over 64	14.7%	Some college	25.1%	Sales and Service	39.4%
		College Degree, 4 yr	30.1%	Blue Collar	11.7%
Military		Post grad	15.1%	Government	9.3%
Veteran/ Active Duty	3%				

2012 Pres. Vote	Obama	187,441	(70%)	Romney	70,757	(27%)			
2016 Pres. Vote	Clinton	208,645	(72%)	Trump	64,607	(22%)	Stein	7,433	(3%)
	Johnson	7,050	(2%)						

Westside and Hollywood: The Westside of Los Angeles is perhaps the most glamorous and flashiest concentration of affluence in the world. It is the heartland of one of America's mos productive and creative industries and one of the nation's major exports, show business. The first moviemakers came here looking for a place to shoot silent films where the sunlight was more dependable than in Astoria Queens, or Englewood New Jersey. They found it in Hollywood, a suburb just annexed by burgeoning Los Angeles when the first movie studio was built in 1911. In 1923 came the "Hollywood" sign (it said "Hollywoodland" then), overlooking the soon-famous intersection of Hollywood and Vine. By the 1930s, big studio lots were scattered around town, over the mountains in Burbank, or out toward the ocean in Westwood and Culver City. Miraculously, the studio bosses of that era — most of them Jewish immigrants with little ancestral experience of America — created a popular culture that was universally accessible and embodied the American spirit in a way that still rings true.

Beneath the Verdugo Mountains is Burbank, which Dr. David Burbank, a dentist, founded as a large ranch, on what is now a backlot of Warner Brothers. The city has become the "media capital of the world," including the headquarters for Warner Brothers, ABC Studios and Disney, plus many small entertainment and multimedia companies. The movie studios have been an integral part of the local economy. Warner Brothers remained the largest employer in Burbank, with 5,000 jobs in 2018, followed by Disney with 3,900. (NBC Studios moved to the huge Universal Studio complex in San Fernando Valley.) To reduce congestion in a residential neighborhood that has resulted from more than 3 million annual tourists, Warner Brothers said in July 2018 that it plans to build a tramway from its lot to the Hollywood sign. More middle-class is Glendale, north of downtown Los Angeles, site of Forest Lawn Cemetery and DreamWorks Animation. Glendale is a diverse city with a large concentration of Armenians, a politically influential community that has remained hostile to Turkey. In April 2018, the city council approved a plan for a private museum to celebrate the Armenian-American experience.

Following 70 percent approval of a referendum in 2016, a new 14-gate terminal is planned at the Hollywood Burbank Airport, though planners have wrestled with its estimated $1 billion cost. South of the Hollywood Hills, West Hollywood has a large gay community. It is home to the Sunset Strip, a launching pad for many rock 'n' roll acts, including The Doors, Guns N' Roses and Led Zeppelin. In 2017-18, the #MeToo movement rocked Hollywood with revelations of sexual misconduct and rampant abusive behavior by powerful men – and a few women -- at the top of studios — executives, producers, directors, actors and more. "There is fear. There is tension. And there is no end in sight," Brooks Barnes wrote in The New York Times in November 2018.

The 28th Congressional District, which is located between the San Fernando Valley and Pasadena, includes La Crescenta-Montrose and La Cañada Flintridge, home of NASA's Jet Propulsion Laboratory. The largest cities are Glendale and Burbank. This is a solidly Democratic district, with 25 percent Hispanic and 13 percent Asian population. Hillary Clinton got 72 percent of the vote in 2016.

Tony Cárdenas (D)

Elected 2012, 4th term, b. Mar 31, 1963; Pacoima; University of California, Santa Barbara, B.S., 1986; Christian Church; Married (Norma Cárdenas); 4 children.

Elected Office: Los Angeles City Council, 2004-2012; CA Assembly, 1996-2002.

Professional Career: Real-estate broker, 1987-1996; Life ins. salesman, 1986-1987; Electrical engineer, Hewlett-Packard, 1986.

DC Office: 2438 RHOB 20515, 202-225-6131, Fax: 202-225-0819, cardenas.house.gov

State Offices: Panorama City, 818-221-3718.

Committees: *Energy & Commerce*: Communications & Technology; Consumer Protection & Commerce; Health.

Group Ratings

	ADA	ACLU	AFL-CIO	LCV	ITI	COC	HAFA	ACU	CFG	FRC
2018	-	88%	-	49%	-	64%	12%	6%	27%	0%
2017	90%	C	95%	97%	C	71%	C	7%	5%	11%

Almanac Ratings 2017-18

	Economy	Social	Foreign	Composite
Liberal	96%	96%	84%	92%
Conservative	4%	4%	16%	8%

Key Votes of the 115th Congress

1. Obama-care revision	N	5. Family planning regs	N	9. Guantanamo prisoners	Y
2. Tax Cuts	N	6. Body cameras/immigration	Y	10. Ground missiles, limit	Y
3. Omnibus appropriations	N	7. Abortion ban	N	11. Defense Dept. spending	Y
4. Dodd-Frank revision	N	8. Concealed carry	N	12. FISA rules	N

Election Results

Election	Name (Party)	Vote (%)		Cand. Spent	Ind. Exp. Support	Ind. Exp. Oppose
2018 General	Tony Cardenas (D)	124,697	(81%)	$1,302,967		
	Benito Bernal (R)	29,995	(19%)	$3,537		
2018 Primary	Tony Cardenas (D)	43,579	(67%)			
	Benito Bernal (R)	11,353	(17%)			
	Joe Shammas (D)	5,278	(8%)			
	Angelica Maria Duenas (G)	4,164	(6%)			

Prior winning percentages: 2016 (75%), 2014 (75%), 2012 (74%)

Democrat Tony Cárdenas, elected in 2012, has been active on the House Energy and Commerce Committee and a leader of the Hispanic Caucus. He has been a player on issues that affect his district in the San Fernando Valley. In 2018, Cardenas became the target of a lawsuit alleging abusive behavior toward a young woman. The charges also were referred to the House Ethics Committee.

As the youngest of 11 children of Mexican immigrant parents, Cárdenas was born and raised in the Valley city of Pacoima, where his father was a self-employed gardener. He earned a bachelor's degree in electrical engineering from the University of California, Santa Barbara. He subsequently went to work for Hewlett-Packard but left just five months later. "There has to be something different for me," he remembered thinking.

He returned home to sell life insurance for a year, then sold real estate for five years before opening his own brokerage firm in the San Fernando Valley. During that time, the Valley had become more Latino — but, he observed, political representation did not mirror that change. One day, a friend suggested that he run for political office. He did, and in 1996 became the first Latino to represent the Valley in the state Assembly. Cárdenas worked to reform California's gang prevention and intervention programs. He increased funding for juvenile justice programs. Cárdenas says he became interested in gang-intervention programs after many of his childhood friends had run-ins with the law, lamenting, "They weren't exactly living a life that we had dreamed of."

In 2003, Cárdenas was elected to the Los Angeles City Council, where he continued to work on gang prevention. He sought additional opportunities for minority-owned businesses to compete for the city's bond underwriting work. He pushed for policies to fight human trafficking and prevent the mistreatment of animals.

When he decided to run for Congress in a redrawn district with no incumbent that was destined to elect a Latino, Cárdenas received 64 percent of the vote in the primary. His closest competitor was "No Party Preference" perennial candidate David Hernandez, who mocked Cárdenas for touting his Latino roots. Those attacks barely resonated in the Democratic district, and Cárdenas won in November 74%-26%.

Cardenas has worn several hats in the House. He co-chaired two bipartisan groups: the Crime Prevention and Youth Development Caucus, and the Congressional Student-Athlete Protection Caucus. With Republican Rep. Carlos Curbelo of Florida, he created the Connecting the Americas Caucus, to strengthen business opportunities between the United States and Latin American nations

In 2014, Cardenas became chairman of BOLD PAC, the fundraising arm of the Congressional Hispanic Caucus, which raised $11 million in 2017-18. Since 2014, the Hispanic Caucus has added Democratic members in several states, including four more in California. (In 2018, Curbelo was defeated by a challenger backed by BOLD PAC.) Following the 2016 election, he won a Democratic leadership position for a member who had served less than three terms. He defeated Rep. Debbie Dingell of Michigan, 91-76.

On the Energy and Commerce Committee, Cardenas was among the first House members to oppose the proposed merger of Comcast and Time Warner Cable, which he said would harm competition, raise costs and "eliminate good jobs in California." Following regulatory overview, the deal was scuttled. In 2017, he filed a bill to protect at-risk youth from termination of their Medicaid eligibility while they were prison inmates. The measure was enacted as part of the comprehensive legislation to combat opioid addiction. Cardenas had a brief, but angry, clash on the House floor in January 2019 when Republican Rep. Jason Smith of Missouri during a debate yelled in the direction of Cardenas, "Go back to Puerto Rico!" Cardenas reportedly charged across the aisle and asked who had said that. Subsequently, Smith apologized to him.

In 2016, Cardenas faced Democrat Richard Alarcon, a former member of the Los Angeles City Council who subsequently had his conviction overturned on charges that he and his wife committed perjury in misstating their home address for a political campaign. Alarcon raised only $70,000 to $1.7 million for Cardenas and was defeated, 75%-25%. He got 81 percent against a little-known Republican challenger in 2018.

Cardenas faced uncertain prospects after a woman in April 2018 filed a lawsuit against him charging him with drugging and fondling her while they were at a Los Angeles golf outing in 2007, when she was 16. A lawyer for Cardenas said that he was "sickened and distraught by these horrific allegations, which are 100 percent, categorically untrue." At the suggestion of then-Democratic Leader Nancy Pelosi, the allegations were referred to the House Ethics Committee for "a full investigation of the facts." Cardenas said that he would cooperate with the review.

CA-29: Central San Fernando Valley

Cook Partisan Voting Index: D+29

Population		Race and Ethnicity		Income	
Total	721,965	White	18.7%	Median Income	$50,823
Land area (sq. miles)	92	Black	3.6%	District Income Rank	291
Pop/ sq mi	7844.9	Latino	68.5%	Poverty Rate	19.9%
Born in State	46.7%	Asian	7.6%	With health insurance	83.4%
		Two or more races	1.1%	Cash public assistance	4.6%
Age Groups		Other	0.5%	Food stamp/SNAP	12.4%
Under 18	24.1%				
18-34	27.7%	**Education**		**Work**	
35-64	38.3%	H.S grad or less	56.3%	White Collar	9.9%
Over 64	9.9%	Some college	24.3%	Sales and Service	47.4%
		College Degree, 4 yr	14.7%	Blue Collar	27.4%
Military		Post grad	4.7%	Government	9%
Veteran/ Active Duty	2.6%				

2012 Pres. Vote	Obama	129,323	(77%)	Romney	34,454	(21%)			
2016 Pres. Vote	Clinton	152,517	(78%)	Trump	32,963	(17%)	Stein	4,863	(3%)
	Johnson	4,328	(2%)						

Van Nuys: A hiker looking north from the crest of the Santa Monica Mountains in 1912 would have seen a valley almost totally empty and barren, 20 miles long and 12 miles wide. Separated by the Cahuenga Pass from rapidly growing Los Angeles and Hollywood, the San Fernando Valley was bought up in massive tracts by civic leaders as they were urging city engineer William Mulholland to build a huge 250-mile aqueduct from the Owens Valley to bring water to Los Angeles and persuading the city in 1915 to annex 200 square miles of the Valley. In the years after World War II, this was modern suburbia, filled with Leave It to Beaver families. More recently, the San Fernando Valley has become postmodern urban. The driver topping the crest saw office towers looming out over slightly hazy air, shopping centers, occasional palm trees, stucco subdivisions, and the squat factory and warehouse buildings that once made Los Angeles County a top manufacturing locale.

Many of the big plants have closed and the Valley has changed. The 1950s white families with stay-at-home moms have been replaced by Latino families with parents juggling two jobs and trying to raise children who will have a better chance than they had. Farther south, in Van Nuys, Canoga Park and Burbank, was the industrial base — the GM plants were mostly shut down in the 1980s, and the last large factory, the Pratt and Whitney Rocketdyne plant, was sold to manufacturer GenCorp in 2012. The big factories have been supplanted by hundreds of small factories and multimedia plants. Despite soaring costs of housing, the economy in the Valley has strengthened, the Los Angeles Daily News reported in May 2018. The information and technology sector has become a "catalyst," and there has been "a relative abundance" of good jobs, according to a report by local economic researchers.

The southern rim of the Valley, around the North Hollywood area, remains heavily Jewish and is attracting new families who often send their kids to religious schools. People with money cluster near the foot of the mountains around the Valley; those less well-off settle on the flatlands beyond. The Valley has been plagued by increased crime, including gangs, which has accompanied a rise in homelessness. The L.A. Metro transit agency took steps in June 2018 toward a new light-rail line that would run for nine miles through the Valley and would open prior to the 2028 Olympics. The busy Van Nuys airport, which is used chiefly for private planes and charters, has received grants to repair its deteriorating runways and taxiways and announced plans in October 2018 for a new hangar and office building.

The 29th Congressional District of California consists of the eastern part of the San Fernando Valley in the city of Los Angeles. It includes affluent North Hollywood, as well as Van Nuys, North Hills and Panorama City. The southeast part of the district takes in the NoHo Arts District. Parts of the northern end of the Valley, including economically declining Pacoima and the small city of San Fernando, are in the district. Whiteman Airport and Los Angeles Valley College are also here. The District is 69 percent Hispanic and solidly Democratic. Hillary Clinton got 78 percent of the vote here in 2016.

Brad Sherman (D)

Elected 1996, 12th term, b. Oct 24, 1954; Los Angeles; Orange Coast University (CA), Att.; University of California, Los Angeles, B.A., 1974; Harvard University Law School (MA), J.D., 1979; Jewish; Married (Lisa Kaplan Sherman); 3 children.

Elected Office: CA Board of Equalization, 1990-1995, Chairman, 1991-1995.

Professional Career: Practicing attorney, Accountant, 1980-1990.

DC Office: 2181 RHOB 20515, 202-225-5911, Fax: 202-225-5879, sherman.house.gov

State Offices: Sherman Oaks, 818-501-9200.

Committees: *Commission Congressional Mailing Standards. Financial Services*: Housing, Community Development & Insurance; Investor Protection, Entrepreneurship & Capital Markets; Nat'l Security, International Development & Monetary Policy. *Foreign Affairs*: Asia, the Pacific & Nonproliferation (Chmn); Middle East, North Africa & International Terrorism. *Science, Space & Technology*: Research & Technology.

Group Ratings

	ADA	ACLU	AFL-CIO	LCV	ITI	COC	HAFA	ACU	CFG	FRC
2018	-	86%	-	97%	-	55%	6%	4%	12%	0%
2017	90%	C	95%	100%	C	43%	C	4%	0%	0%

Almanac Ratings 2017-18

	Economy	Social	Foreign	Composite
Liberal	98%	98%	90%	95%
Conservative	2%	2%	10%	5%

Key Votes of the 115th Congress

1. Obama-care revision	N	5. Family planning regs	N	9. Guantanamo prisoners	Y
2. Tax Cuts	N	6. Body cameras/immigration	Y	10. Ground missiles, limit	Y
3. Omnibus appropriations	Y	7. Abortion ban	N	11. Defense Dept. spending	N
4. Dodd-Frank revision	N	8. Concealed carry	N	12. FISA rules	N

Election Results

Election	Name (Party)	Vote (%)		Cand. Spent	Ind. Exp. Support	Ind. Exp. Oppose
2018 General	Brad Sherman (D)........................ 191,573	(73%)		$449,276		
	Mark Reed (R)............................... 69,420	(27%)				
2018 Primary	Brad Sherman (D)........................ 80,038	(62%)				
	Mark Reed (R)............................... 35,046	(27%)				
	Raji Rab (D)................................. 6,753	(5%)				
	Jon Pelzer (D)............................... 6,642	(5%)				

Prior winning percentages: 2016 (73%), 2014 (66%), 2012 (60%), 2010 (65%), 2008 (69%), 2006 (69%), 2004 (62%), 2002 (62%), 2000 (66%), 1998 (57%), 1996 (49%)

Brad Sherman, a Democrat first elected in 1996, has shown that he is a rough and ready political scrapper — in support of Israel and against Wall Street, for example. His reelection brawl in 2012 against more senior Democrat Howard Berman left lingering wounds within the party. Sherman remains outspoken, especially on foreign policy, and he has been an early proponent of the impeachment of President Donald Trump.

Sherman grew up in Monterey Park, in the San Gabriel Valley east of Los Angeles. He started working on Democratic campaigns at age 6, stuffing envelopes for Rep. George Brown. He set up his own stamp-wholesaling firm at age 14. He graduated with high honors from the University of California, Los Angeles, worked as an accountant, and then went to Harvard Law School. He came back to the Los Angeles area to practice tax law, and represented the Philippines in its successful effort to seize the assets of deposed President Ferdinand Marcos.

In 1990, Sherman was elected from Los Angeles County to the state Board of Equalization, which is a sort of tax court. He was known as a stickler for detail, a "tax nerd," as one former staffer said, who used the office with a keen scent for political advantage. In the 1996 contest for an open seat, Sherman and his Republican opponent, businessman Rich Sybert, were self-financers; Sherman spent $578,000 of his own money. Both stressed their ideological moderation. Sherman campaigned against then-House Speaker Newt Gingrich and the Republican Congress, though he supported the death penalty, called for phasing out racial quotas and preferences, and favored tough measures on illegal immigration. Sybert stressed his independence from Gingrich as well as his support for abortion rights and environmental protection. Sherman won 49%-44%.

In the House, his voting record has been more moderate than those of most other Los Angeles County Democrats, and he has shown occasional independence from party leaders. One of the few certified public accountants in Congress, Sherman serves on the Financial Services Committee, where he has sought to unravel corporate accounting scandals. In 2008, he was an outspoken foe of the Troubled Assets Relief Program to bail out the financial services industry, dubbing it "cash for trash." When domestic auto company executives testified in favor of a proposed bailout for that industry, Sherman got them to concede that they had all flown separately to Washington in private airplanes, a revelation that sparked a public backlash. Sherman helped form the new Consumer Financial Protection Bureau as part of the 2010 Dodd-Frank financial overhaul law. But Rep. Barney Frank of Massachusetts accused him of overstating his role after Sherman boasted that he had "more to do with Dodd-Frank than anyone except Dodd and Frank."

Sherman faced his first serious opposition when redistricting following the 2010 census resulted in a bitter contest with Berman, a 30-year House veteran who had chaired the Foreign Affairs Committee. Berman had the backing of much of the state's Democratic establishment as well as the support of Hollywood elites for his work on anti-piracy legislation. But Berman was at a serious geographic disadvantage: The new 30th District covered twice as much of Sherman's old turf as Berman's base, which was in the new 29th District.

The final tab for the race was $16.3 million. Sherman went on the attack, depicting Berman as a Washington insider who didn't understand constituents' concerns. Berman highlighted his opponent's inability to get more than a handful of bills into law, while criticizing him for loaning his campaigns money and then charging interest, an allegation that Sherman heatedly denied. The acrimony peaked at an October debate when the two loudly bickered over immigration legislation, and Sherman threw his arm around his opponent's shoulders and demanded, "You want to get into this?" A sheriff's deputy and a debate organizer stepped between them to prevent an escalation. Berman sent out a YouTube video of the incident accusing Sherman of trying to start a fight, prompting Sherman to apologize. But it was too little, too late for Berman. Sherman won easily, 60%-40%.

Sherman soon paid the price when Pelosi stymied his bid to become the senior Democrat on the Foreign Affairs Committee, where he had been next in line among Democratic members behind Berman; instead, Democrats selected Rep. Eliot Engel of New York. In his committee work, Sherman often was assertive. As the top Democrat on the Asia and the Pacific Subcommittee, he strongly opposed President Barack Obama's deal with Iran on nuclear weapons, which he described as "preposterous." But he said that Trump's efforts to decertify the deal could have dangerous consequences. When many Democrats boycotted the speech of Israeli Prime Minister Benjamin Netanyahu in 2015, Sherman said he was "honored" to serve on the escort committee that accompanied him into the House chamber. Later, Sherman demanded congressional review of a deal that Trump was discussing with Saudi Arabia for cooperation on civilian nuclear power. "Congress has an equal role in the conduct of American foreign policy," he said. In the majority, he became chairman of the renamed Asia, the Pacific and Nonproliferation Subcommittee.

In July 2017, Sherman was the first member of Congress to offer an article of impeachment against Trump — citing alleged obstruction of justice in the investigation of Russian interference in the 2016 election. He reintroduced his proposal in January 2019.

California Democratic Assemblyman Matt Dababneh resigned in December 2017 following accusations of sexual harassment, including while he was working as Sherman's district director. Although current and past aides said that he likely did not know about Dababneh's behavior, they speculated that Sherman would not have responded well to criticism of his former aide and said that Sherman was a difficult boss who often screamed at his staffers and suffered high turnover. Sherman acknowledged to McClatchy News that he was a "demanding boss."

Since 2012, Sherman has had much easier reelections. In 2018, against Republican small businessman Mark Reed, a perennial candidate who did not file a campaign-finance report, Sherman won 73%-27%. His hold on this district appears secure, though he is mindful that redistricting is unpredictable and can pose challenges.

CA-30: Southern and Western San Fernando Valley

Cook Partisan Voting Index: D+18

Population		Race and Ethnicity		Income	
Total	758,784	White	50.2%	Median Income	$76,169
Land area (sq. miles)	136	Black	4.5%	District Income Rank	66
Pop/ sq mi	5581.8	Latino	29.1%	Poverty Rate	11.5%
Born in State	45.7%	Asian	12.6%	With health insurance	89.8%
		Two or more races	3.1%	Cash public assistance	2.1%
Age Groups		Other	0.7%	Food stamp/SNAP	4.8%
Under 18	19.8%				
18-34	24.2%	**Education**		**Work**	
35-64	41.3%	H.S grad or less	29.3%	White Collar	14.7%
Over 64	14.7%	Some college	28.2%	Sales and Service	39.9%
		College Degree, 4 yr	27.8%	Blue Collar	13%
Military		Post grad	14.6%	Government	8.7%
Veteran/ Active Duty	3.9%				

2012 Pres. Vote	Obama	186,301	(65%)	Romney	91,680	(32%)		
2016 Pres. Vote	Clinton	209,149	(69%)	Trump	77,701	(26%)	Johnson	8,278	(3%)
	Stein	6,244	(2%)					

The Valley, Reseda: In the early 20th century, when the movie business was young, the San Fernando Valley was a vast expanse of empty land that had been annexed to Los Angeles in 1915. Moviemakers, looking for filming sites for a western, drove past the vacant lots of Westwood, up narrow roads through the Santa Monica Mountains, and into the vast Valley, sheltered from ocean breezes and rain-bearing clouds by the mountains. This big bowl of land was transformed, first into 1950s suburbia, and then into a postmodern city of its own, economically vital and ethnically diverse. Even in its suburban years, the San Fernando Valley was not entirely residential. Big factories provided jobs. In those years, this was fast-growing, family-friendly territory. But in a not so family-friendly development, the Valley became a hub for the adult-film industry. After Los Angeles County voters approved a measure in 2012 that required actors to wear condoms in sex scenes to control the spread of sexually transmitted disease, some adult-movie producers moved studio operations out of the region. Other porn businesses diversified to new forms of technology and paraphernalia, and their headquarters remained in the area. The defeat of a similar statewide initiative in 2016 opened the door to the return of the porn industry in the Valley, which had suffered a 95 percent drop in porn permit requests. Most of the big studios are not far away in Burbank, though Universal Studios — including NBC — comprise a motion-picture and entertainment complex and theme park in the Valley.

Parts of the Valley have been unhappy to be linked with the city of Los Angeles, whose City Council has imposed high taxes and irksome regulations. A secession movement arose, and the issue was put on the 2002 ballot. The Valley voted 51%-49% for it, with stronger support in the southern and western sections. But it failed to get the needed majority in all of Los Angeles to pass. Partly in response, the council in 2013 tightened rules on who can participate in such neighborhood elections, eliminating what had been called "Starbucks shareholders." Following the recession, the Valley's economy improved, thanks in part to a massive expansion in California's enterprise zone program. Nevertheless, many thousands of middle-class residents have relocated in recent years to less-costly places. Sales prices for housing rose 11 percent in 2018. The Valley has been selected to host several events in the 2028 Olympics, including canoe, kayak, equestrian and shooting competitions. In November 2018, the Woolsey fire — the worst ever in southern California, which destroyed more than 1,600 structures extending to Malibu -- started in the nearby mountains and spread quickly through dry brush.

The 30th Congressional District covers the western and southern parts of the San Fernando Valley within Los Angeles. Along its southern border, the 30th includes the upscale territory of Tarzana, Encino and Hidden Hills. In the center of the district are industrial Canoga Park, Winnetka and largely Hispanic Reseda. On the northern end are Granada Hills, where the San Fernando Valley's first oil well was drilled in 1916, and O'Melveny Park, one of the largest parks in Los Angeles. Also in the district is California State University, Northridge. Less than 1 percent of the 30th reaches into Ventura County. In a district that is 29 percent Hispanic and 13 percent Asian, Hillary Clinton led, 69%-26%.

Pete Aguilar (D)

Elected 2014, 3rd term, b. Jun 19, 1979; Fontana; University of Redlands, B.R.E., 2001; Roman Catholic; Married (Alisha Aguilar); 2 children.

Elected Office: Redlands City Council, 2006-2014; Mayor, Redlands, 2010-2014.

Professional Career: Business owner; Interim Director & deputy Director, Inland Empire regional office of the Gov., 2001.

DC Office: 109 CHOB 20515, 202-225-3201, Fax: 202-226-6962, aguilar.house.gov

State Offices: San Bernardino, 909-890-4445.

Committees: *Appropriations*: Defense; Homeland Security; Transportation, HUD & Related Agencies. *House Administration.*

Group Ratings

	ADA	ACLU	AFL-CIO	LCV	ITI	COC	HAFA	ACU	CFG	FRC
2018	-	75%	-	91%	-	75%	6%	8%	32%	0%
2017	75%	C	97%	100%	C	57%	C	4%	0%	11%

Almanac Ratings 2017-18

	Economy	Social	Foreign	Composite
Liberal	95%	98%	67%	87%
Conservative	5%	2%	33%	13%

Key Votes of the 115th Congress

1. Obama-care revision	N	5. Family planning regs	N	9. Guantanamo prisoners	N
2. Tax Cuts	N	6. Body cameras/immigration	Y	10. Ground missiles, limit	Y
3. Omnibus appropriations	N	7. Abortion ban	N	11. Defense Dept. spending	Y
4. Dodd-Frank revision	N	8. Concealed carry	N	12. FISA rules	Y

Election Results

Election	Name (Party)	Vote (%)		Cand. Spent	Ind. Exp. Support	Ind. Exp. Oppose
2018 General	Pete Aguilar (D)	110,143	(59%)	$2,012,285	$17,996	
	Sean Flynn (R)	77,352	(41%)	$1,212,346		
2018 Primary	Pete Aguilar (D)	41,337	(46%)			
	Sean Flynn (R)	40,622	(45%)			
	Kaisar Ahmed (D)	8,108	(9%)			

Prior winning percentages: 2016 (56%), 2014 (52%)

Democrat Pete Aguilar's 2014 win returned the 31st District seat to the Democrats, following turbulent local politics that gave the predominantly Hispanic district to Republicans in 2012. With his smooth reelection and a prominent niche on the Appropriations Committee, the youthful Aguilar seemed to restore stability at home. He lost a Democratic leadership bid, but he could have other opportunities.

Aguilar was born in Fontana and grew up in San Bernardino. He earned undergraduate degrees in government and business administration at the University of Redlands. One of his first jobs was at the San Bernardino County Courthouse cafeteria, where his blind grandfather was the operator. In 2001, Gov. Gray Davis appointed Aguilar as deputy director of the Inland Empire Regional Office of the Governor. In 2006, Aguilar was appointed to the Redlands City Council, making him the youngest-ever council member. He was elected mayor in 2010 by his fellow council members.

In 2012, he ran in this redrawn minority district. Four Democrats divided the vote in the all-party primary. Aguilar was the frontrunner among them with 23 percent of the total vote. But the two Republicans emerged at the top, with 27 and 25 percent. Rep. Gary Miller — who decided to run here for his eighth term, despite not having represented any of the district — won in November over fellow Republican Bob Dutton, 55%-45%.

Miller announced he would not seek reelection in 2014, and Aguilar again sought the seat. History almost repeated itself in the primary, as four Democrats faced off against three Republicans. GOP candidate Paul Chabot came in first with 27 percent; Aguilar had 17 percent and hung onto a 209-vote lead over Republican Leslie Gooch. This time, the four Democratic candidates in the primary got 53 percent of the total vote. Aguilar hammered Chabot for what he called his too-conservative views on education, immigration and heath care. Chabot, an Iraq war vet and Naval Reserve intelligence officer, focused on those experiences and how to combat terrorism. Aguilar won 51%-49%. Aguilar outspent Chabot, $2.2 million to $469,000, and was boosted by more than $1.5 million in national party money. Republicans seem to have missed an opportunity by steering clear of this contest, to Chabot's dismay.

In the House, Aguilar criticized President Barack Obama's executive action on immigration reform as not good enough and demanded congressional action. With Republican Rep. Will Hurd of Texas, he filed a bill in January 2018 to give a path to citizenship to students with Deferred Action for Childhood Arrivals (DACA) status. When Speaker Paul Ryan refused to schedule the bill, Aguilar and Hurd took the unusual step of seeking to force a floor vote with a discharge petition. Although all Democrats signed, they fell two signatures short of the requisite majority of members to get House action. Aguilar was successful in adding to the 2018 defense spending bill his proposal to broaden the availability of grants in the Defense Department's cyber scholarship program. The broader bill was enacted in August 2018. Aguilar got a seat on the Appropriations Committee in 2017. He also is a chief deputy whip in the Democratic Whip organization and whip for the centrist New Democrat Coalition.

Early in the 2016 campaign cycle, the National Republican Congressional Committee placed Aguilar on its "Donkeys List" of vulnerable incumbents. Chabot, who had written an e-book about his 2014 campaign experience, decided to run again. He cited Aguilar's failure to improve the continuing weak local economy. Chabot referred to his opponent as "Agu-liar" and generated controversy when he issued "terrorist hunting permits" to campaign donors. Aguilar again had a big fundraising advantage, $2 million to $1.2 million, and national Republicans spent little money to back up their attacks on Aguilar. The higher presidential-year turnout provided a boost for Aguilar, who won 56%-44%. Aguilar, like most House Democrats, had an easier time in 2018. Republican Sean Flynn, an economics professor at Claremont College and author of the book Economics for Dummies, criticized the health care policies of both parties and advocated more choices for consumers. Flynn spent $1.3 million — more than his earlier opponents — to $2.4 million for Aguilar. But it didn't seem to help. Aguilar won, 59%-41%.

In the new Congress, Aguilar ran for vice chairman of the Democratic Caucus. He said his moderate views would provide diversity of thought among party leaders. Although several Democrats had expressed an interest in the post, the only other contender was Katherine Clark of Massachusetts. The more liberal Clark won, 144-90. Aguilar got a notable consolation prize. He was named vice chairman of the Appropriations Committee, a position designated for a junior member. He also got a seat on the Defense Subcommittee, which controls the largest chunk of discretionary spending in the federal budget.

CA-31: Southwestern San Bernardino   Cook Partisan Voting Index: D+8

Population		Race and Ethnicity		Income	
Total	740,071	White	26.7%	Median Income	$58,167
Land area (sq. miles)	218	Black	10.1%	District Income Rank	192
Pop/ sq mi	3391.1	Latino	52.6%	Poverty Rate	19%
Born in State	63.9%	Asian	7.6%	With health insurance	88.7%
		Two or more races	2.3%	Cash public assistance	5.4%
Age Groups		Other	0.6%	Food stamp/SNAP	16.5%
Under 18	26.7%				
18-34	27.3%	**Education**		**Work**	
35-64	36%	H.S grad or less	44.5%	White Collar	10%
Over 64	10%	Some college	32.1%	Sales and Service	44%
		College Degree, 4 yr	14.8%	Blue Collar	24.5%
Military		Post grad	8.6%	Government	17%
Veteran/ Active Duty	5.4%				

2012 Pres. Vote	Obama	118,043	(54%)	Romney	83,822	(41%)		
2016 Pres. Vote	Clinton	131,966	(57%)	Trump	83,706	(36%)	Johnson	7,729 (3%)

Rancho Cucamonga: In the 1970s, as the coastal portions of the Los Angeles Basin became fully developed, and in the 1980s, as real estate values skyrocketed, people with modest incomes and young families increasingly moved east, from the high-cost, high-crime coast to the smoggier, hotter valleys inland. There was a lot of empty, low-priced land in what people began calling the Inland Empire, defined usually as San Bernardino and Riverside counties, and especially in the desert to the north and east of the passes through the mountains that rim the Basin. This was a high-growth area, with a population that expanded from 1.6 million in 1980 to 4.6 million in 2017, when it became Hispanic-majority. In this century's first decade, there was a boom in commercial real estate, especially warehouses to store merchandise offloaded at the port of Los Angeles-Long Beach. The uptick in construction attracted many Latinos, both citizens and immigrants. San Bernardino has become the second-largest county in the nation — behind Miami-Dade in Florida — with a population that is 53 percent Latino, an increase in Latino population from 241,000 in 1980 to 1.2 million in 2017. The city of San Bernardino is 64 percent Latino.

In 2007 the housing bubble burst. The Inland Empire had one of the nation's highest foreclosure rates and housing values fell by half. Nowhere were the problems greater than in the city of San Bernardino, which was declared one of the weakest metropolitan areas in the country for job creation. The city was criticized for carrying inflated pension costs and high government salaries, with nearly one in four city employees earning more than $100,000 a year in 2010. Facing a $45.8 million budget shortfall, San Bernardino voted to declare bankruptcy in July 2012. It emerged from bankruptcy in

June 2017, though it faced continuing budget constraints. In Rancho Cucamonga, economic growth shut down most of the orange groves. County development officials announced in 2016 that they had created more than 10,000 jobs — more than the earlier total -- at the site of Norton Air Force Base, which closed in 1994.

In December 2015, San Bernardino gained unwanted attention as it joined the international list of terrorism sites. A disgruntled five-year county employee, wearing military fatigues and firing a rifle, killed 14 and wounded 22 in a terrorist shooting at a holiday reception with many of his fellow workers. Police killed him and his wife in a shoot-out a few hours later as they were pursued in a fleeing sports utility vehicle. The Chicago-born shooter and his Pakistani-born wife, both Muslims, made a Facebook statement in support of the Islamic State terrorist organization. The event was described at the time as the deadliest terrorist act on American soil since September 2001, though that mark has been overtaken.

The 31st Congressional District is the only district that is entirely within San Bernardino County; four other districts are partly in the county. This includes the cities of Colton, Loma Linda and Redlands along I-10, Rancho Cucamonga to the west and most of downtown San Bernardino. Rialto and Upland are split between this district and the more heavily Latino 35th to the south. The 31st was designed to comply with Voting Rights Act rules against racial discrimination. The district is 53 percent Hispanic and politically leans Democratic. Hillary Clinton got 57 percent of the vote, though the area has been competitive locally.

Grace Napolitano (D)

Elected 1998, 11th term, b. Dec 04, 1936; Brownsville, TX; Texas Southmost College, Att.; Cerritos College (CA), Att.; Roman Catholic; Widow; 5 children (5 from previous marriage); 14 grandchildren; 2 great-grandchildren.

Elected Office: Norwalk City Council, 1986-1992; Norwalk Mayor, 1990- 92; CA Assembly, 1992-1998.

Professional Career: Employee, Ford Motor Co., 1970-1992.

DC Office: 1610 LHOB 20515, 202-225-5256, Fax: 202-225-0027, napolitano.house.gov

State Offices: El Monte, 626-350-0150.

Committees: *Natural Resources*: Water, Oceans & Wildlife. *Transportation & Infrastructure*: Aviation; Highways & Transit; Railroads, Pipelines & Hazardous Materials; Water Resources & Environment (Chmn).

Group Ratings

	ADA	ACLU	AFL-CIO	LCV	ITI	COC	HAFA	ACU	CFG	FRC
2018	-	86%	-	94%	-	50%	5%	4%	15%	0%
2017	75%	C	100%	77%	C	45%	C	-	0%	0%

Almanac Ratings 2017-18

	Economy	Social	Foreign	Composite
Liberal	90%	90%	57%	79%
Conservative	11%	11%	43%	21%

Key Votes of the 115th Congress

1. Obama-care revision	N	5. Family planning regs	N
2. Tax Cuts	N	6. Body cameras/immigration	Y
3. Omnibus appropriations	N	7. Abortion ban	N
4. Dodd-Frank revision	N	8. Concealed carry	N

9. Guantanamo prisoners	NV
10. Ground missiles, limit	NV
11. Defense Dept. spending	NV
12. FISA rules	N

Election Results

Election	Name (Party)	Vote (%)		Cand. Spent	Ind. Exp. Support	Ind. Exp. Oppose
2018 General	Grace Napolitano (D).......................	121,759	(69%)	$128,835		
	Joshua Scott (R).............................	55,272	(31%)	$4,931		
2018 Primary	Grace Napolitano (D)........................	56,674	(100%)			

Prior winning percentages: 2016 (62%), 2014 (60%), 2012 (66%), 2010 (74%), 2008 (82%), 2006 (75%), 2004 (100%), 2002 (71%), 2000 (71%), 1998 (68%)

Grace Napolitano, a Democrat first elected in 1998, has concentrated on issues affecting lower-income Hispanics in her Southern California district, including jobs, water scarcity and mental health. Her committee assignments and seniority have given her the most clout on pork-barrel projects, on both land and water, of any California Democrat or member of the Hispanic Caucus.

Napolitano grew up in the lower Rio Grande Valley of Texas, married at age 18, and eventually had five children. When she was 23, the family moved to California. She got a job as a secretary at Ford Motor Co. and stayed for 22 years. After her first husband died, she married Frank Napolitano, and in 1980, they started a pizzeria. She served on the Norwalk City Council from 1986 to 1992 and served one term as mayor, becoming the first Latino to hold the position. In 1992, she was elected to the California Assembly.

In 1998, she ran for Congress when 16-year Democratic Rep. Esteban Torres announced three days before the filing deadline that he was retiring. Torres' surprise move was designed to promote the election of Jamie Casso, his son-in-law and chief of staff, who immediately announced his candidacy. Napolitano was not deterred and got into the race. She criticized Casso for not living in the district, and he criticized an $180,000 loan she made to her campaign at an unusual 18 percent interest rate. Napolitano had the backing of national liberal women's organizations, including EMILY's List, plus the benefit of higher name recognition. The two candidates had few differences on major issues. Napolitano signed a pledge to serve only three terms. She won the primary by 618 votes, assuring her victory in November in the heavily Democratic district.

Napolitano, a former chairwoman of the Congressional Hispanic Caucus, has been more consensus-oriented on immigration legislation than some caucus members. She has been a longtime advocate on issues related to the mentally ill, an interest that was sparked by a report that one in three Hispanic girls contemplates suicide. "Mental health is treatable. But [the Latino community has] a stigma attached to it," Napolitano said. As chair of the Congressional Mental Health Caucus, she has written that most people who commit suicides use guns, and she advocated steps to reduce such incidents. With Republican Rep. John Katko of New York, she filed in July 2018 legislation with financial incentives to increase the number of mental-health professionals.

On the Natural Resources Committee, she chaired the panel's Water and Power Subcommittee from 2007 until 2011, with a focus on Southern California's acute need for an more water. She held hearings to examine possible solutions and said that desalination research was critical to economic growth. In 2014, she unveiled her "Water in the 21st Century" bill, which provided $2 billion in loans and grants for water recycling, stormwater capture and treatment, groundwater management and water infrastructure projects. After the 2014 election, she stepped aside for Rep. Raul Grijalva of Arizona to become senior Democrat on the full committee.

On the Transportation and Infrastructure Committee, as the ranking Democrat on the Water Resources and Environment Subcommittee, Napolitano worked to fix "our nation's crumbling water infrastructure." She encouraged regulators to find ways to recycle water for irrigation use and groundwater replenishment and to assist local water agencies to find more ways to recapture water for their reservoirs. In 2018, she was part of the bipartisan committee leadership that enacted new water-resource grants, which shifted funding to the states by requiring them to pay at least 80 percent of the costs for new projects. Taking over as chairwoman of the subcommittee in January 2019, she said, "we must increase federal investment in our water infrastructure and drought resiliency measures."

In 2003, Napolitano abandoned her earlier pledge to serve only three terms. She has not been seriously challenged for reelection. In 2012, she won with 66 percent of the vote in the redrawn 32nd District, in which more than 80 percent of voters were new to her. In 2014, she was held to 60 percent by Arturo Alas, a real estate agent who opposed the move by President Barack Obama to create a national monument in the San Gabriel Mountains. Alas was part of what Reuters described as a group of "ethnically diverse young libertarians" who have sought to revive the Republican Party in Los

Angeles. In 2016, she had an unusual campaign when Democratic Assemblyman Roger Hernandez finished second in the June all-party primary but then faced allegations of domestic violence from his ex-wife. In August, he formally ended his campaign, though he got 38 percent of the vote against Napolitano. In 2018, Republican challenger Joshua Scott, a 25-year-old political newcomer, entered the contest a month before the primary and spent about $5,000. Napolitano won, 69%-31%.

Napolitano's husband died of cancer in December 2017. She had missed about half of the House votes in the previous few months. She reportedly recovered from a stroke that she suffered in 2016. At 82, when House Democrats regained control in January 2019, she was among the four oldest members.

CA-32: Eastern L.A. Suburbs

Cook Partisan Voting Index: D+17

Population		Race and Ethnicity		Income	
Total	721,884	White	15.7%	Median Income	$64,151
Land area (sq. miles)	124	Black	2.5%	District Income Rank	143
Pop/ sq mi	5810.9	Latino	62%	Poverty Rate	13.5%
Born in State	56.3%	Asian	17.9%	With health insurance	87%
		Two or more races	1.3%	Cash public assistance	3.4%
Age Groups		Other	0.7%	Food stamp/SNAP	8.7%
Under 18	22.9%				
18-34	25.8%	**Education**		**Work**	
35-64	38.1%	H.S grad or less	51.5%	White Collar	13.2%
Over 64	13.2%	Some college	27.6%	Sales and Service	46%
		College Degree, 4 yr	15%	Blue Collar	25.9%
Military		Post grad	6%	Government	12.3%
Veteran/ Active Duty	3.7%				

2012 Pres. Vote	Obama	133,061	(65%)	Romney	66,269	(33%)			
2016 Pres. Vote	Clinton	146,459	(66%)	Trump	60,921	(28%)	Johnson	5,996	(3%)
	Stein	4,678	(2%)						

Azusa, West Covina: It was the great route west to California in the first half of the 20th century: Passengers on the Santa Fe Railroad's Super Chief or motorists on U.S. 66, after hours and days in barren desert, would descend through Cajon Pass into the Los Angeles Basin, and come upon orange groves and exotic plants thriving beneath the 10,000-foot snow-capped San Gabriel Mountains. The railroad and highway ran through a line of towns built by Midwestern Protestants as independent communities. Foothills cities such as La Verne and San Dimas have horse trails and their own rodeos.

The small city of Irwindale resolved in September 2018 its long-running legal dispute in which it had cited the Huy Fong Foods Co. as a public nuisance because of the odor from Sriracha hot sauce production. The chili sauce has a devoted following. Bon Appetit has named it one of its favorite foods. The company made a commitment to solve the problem with the smell, but it had failed to follow through with cash payments that a judge had ordered to compensate for its failure to make tax payments. In another environmental dispute, five companies that had been ruled responsible for contaminated groundwater in the San Gabriel Valley were ordered by a state water-quality agency to clean up the mess by 2027, at an estimated cost of $250 million. After L.A. Metro opened an 11-mile light-rail "foothill" extension of the Gold Line from Pasadena to Azusa, the approval of a 2016 referendum to extend a sales tax increase for transit funding led Metro to plan the next extension to LaVerne, with eventual construction to Montclair and perhaps the Ontario Airport. The rail extension was one of 28 projects that Metro planned to complete prior to the Olympic games in 2028.

The 32nd District is 62 percent Hispanic and 18 percent Asian. The western parts of the compact 32nd District — the areas closer to downtown Los Angeles — are heavily Latino: Covina, West Covina and Azusa all are Hispanic-majority cities. Nearly 40 percent of the population is foreign-born. In Baldwin Park, which is 74 percent Hispanic and 19 percent Asian, more than 80 percent of its population speaks a language other than English at home. Outlying areas to the east, such as La Verne and San Dimas, have lower poverty rates and higher household incomes. The heavily Hispanic composition of this district makes it safe Democratic territory. The demographic shifts helped to account for an increase in the Democratic margin from 62%-36% for Barack Obama in 2008 to 66%-28% for Hillary Clinton in 2016.

Ted Lieu (D)

Elected 2014, 3rd term, b. Mar 29, 1969; Taipei, Taiwan; Stanford University (CA), B.A., 1991; Stanford University (CA), B.S., 1991; Georgetown University Law Center (DC), J.D., 1994; Roman Catholic; Married (Betty Lieu); 2 children.

Military Career: U.S. Air Force 1995-1999; U.S. Air Force Reserve 2000-pres.

Elected Office: Torrance City Council, 2002-2005; CA Assembly, 2005-2010. CA Senate, 2011-2014.

Professional Career: Clerk, U.S. Court of Appeals, 9th Circuit; Practicing attorney.

DC Office: 403 CHOB 20515, 202-225-3976, Fax: 202-225-4099, lieu.house.gov

State Offices: Los Angeles, 323-651-1040; Manhattan Beach, 310-321-7664.

Committees: *Foreign Affairs*: Middle East, North Africa & International Terrorism; Oversight & Investigations. *Judiciary*: Courts, Intellectual Property & Internet; Crime, Terrorism & Homeland Security.

Group Ratings

	ADA	ACLU	AFL-CIO	LCV	ITI	COC	HAFA	ACU	CFG	FRC
2018	-	87%	-	89%	-	67%	9%	14%	24%	0%
2017	85%	C	97%	91%	C	50%	C	0%	0%	14%

Almanac Ratings 2017-18

	Economy	Social	Foreign	Composite
Liberal	93%	91%	70%	84%
Conservative	7%	9%	30%	16%

Key Votes of the 115th Congress

1. Obama-care revision	N	5. Family planning regs	N	9. Guantanamo prisoners	NV
2. Tax Cuts	N	6. Body cameras/immigration	Y	10. Ground missiles, limit	NV
3. Omnibus appropriations	N	7. Abortion ban	N	11. Defense Dept. spending	Y
4. Dodd-Frank revision	N	8. Concealed carry	N	12. FISA rules	N

Election Results

Election	Name (Party)	Vote (%)		Cand. Spent	Ind. Exp. Support	Ind. Exp. Oppose
2018 General	Ted Lieu (D)	219,091	(70%)	$709,386		
	Kenneth Wright (R)	93,769	(30%)	$159,217		
2018 Primary	Ted Lieu (D)	100,581	(62%)			
	Kenneth Wright (R)	48,985	(30%)			
	Emory Rodgers (D)	13,435	(8%)			

Prior winning percentages: 2016 (66%), 2014 (59%)

Democrat Ted Lieu, elected in 2014 in one of the nation's richest and most liberal House districts, has pursued an activist approach, with both new liberal initiatives and occasional bipartisan action. He relentlessly tweaks President Donald Trump, both in the Judiciary Committee and on his Twitter feed, where he has nearly a million followers and his bio states, "I don't take orders from Vladimir Putin." He was selected to a Democratic leadership communications position.

A Taiwanese-American whose working-class family settled in Cleveland Ohio when he was a toddler, he got his bachelor's degree from Stanford and a law degree from Georgetown University. Lieu's early career centered on law and military service. After four years of active duty in the Air Force, including a posting in the JAG Corps, he divided his time between working in the private sector and serving on the Torrance City Council. In 2005, he won a special election to serve in the state Assembly, followed by election to the state Senate in 2010. He backed a successful bill allowing undocumented immigrants to take the bar exam, and called for a statewide referendum expressing opposition to the Citizens United campaign-finance ruling. On affirmative action, he staked out a more centrist position, opposing a bill that would have overturned the affirmative action ban at California state universities. That move drew criticism from black and Latino lawmakers.

When liberal icon Henry Waxman announced his retirement in 2013 after 40 years, he set off a primary fight that attracted no fewer than 18 candidates. Along with Lieu, the best known were Republican Elan Carr, who served with the Army in Iraq and was a deputy in the L.A. District Attorney's office, former L.A. mayoral candidate Wendy Greuel, and self-help guru Marianne Williamson, an independent. Lieu leveraged his deep political ties to the district, his liberal voting record in Sacramento, and a lineup of top Democratic endorsements, including L.A. Mayor Eric Garcetti, as well as the Los Angeles Daily News. He underscored the need for more Asian-American representation in Congress. In the June primary, he came in second to Carr, 21%-19%; Greuel was third with 17 percent. That set Lieu up for an easy victory in a party stronghold, and his wealthy voters could help raise money for other Democrats. He won in November, 59%-41%.

Lieu was president of the Democrats' freshman class. He became the first House Democrat to announce opposition to the request by President Barack Obama to authorize the use of military force against the Islamic State. "I do not believe the administration has made the case that ISIL represents a direct, grave threat to our nation," he said. He joined several other junior House members in launching the bipartisan Post-9/11 Veterans Caucus. Noting that his district has one of the nation's largest populations of homeless veterans, plus a huge VA health care system, he emphasized the need for innovative solutions to the problems of returned service members. But he opposed suggestions to privatize veterans' health care services. Lieu enacted a bill in 2016 to authorize leases for the VA's campus in West Los Angeles that would construct 1,200 units for homeless vets.

Lieu has voiced many concerns with Trump. With his seats on the Foreign Affairs and Judiciary Committees, Lieu filed a bill in 2017 with Sen. Edward Markey of Massachusetts to prevent the president from authorizing a nuclear first strike without a declaration of war by Congress. In October 2018, he played an audio tape on the House floor with the voices of crying migrant children who had been separated from their undocumented families at the border with Mexico. "This looks like kidnapping," he tweeted before he spoke. The Republican presiding officer told Lieu that his recording was "a breach of decorum" of the House. After several additional minutes, he ended his exchange.

In each of his reelection campaigns, Lieu was challenged by Kenneth Wright, a pediatric eye surgeon from South Bay, who described himself as a progressive Republican and told the Santa Monica Daily Press that Lieu was "a real bought-out politician." Lieu won 66 percent in 2016 and 70 percent in 2018, when Wright was out-spent 6-to-1.

After the 2018 election, Lieu won a co-chair position on the Democratic leadership's Policy and Communications Committee. His plans, he said, were to "stop any harmful policies of the Trump administration and Republicans, work on a bipartisan basis to advance positive legislation to move our country forward, and execute our oversight responsibilities."

CA-33: Coastal and Central L.A.   Cook Partisan Voting Index: D+16

Population		Race and Ethnicity		Income	
Total	715,197	White	65%	Median Income	$103,176
Land area (sq. miles)	289	Black	2.8%	District Income Rank	9
Pop/ sq mi	2478.3	Latino	12.9%	Poverty Rate	9%
Born in State	46.4%	Asian	14.3%	With health insurance	94.8%
		Two or more races	4.2%	Cash public assistance	1.2%
Age Groups		Other	0.7%	Food stamp/SNAP	1.8%
Under 18	18.7%				
18-34	23.3%	**Education**		**Work**	
35-64	41.4%	H.S grad or less	14%	White Collar	16.6%
Over 64	16.6%	Some college	21.9%	Sales and Service	31.5%
		College Degree, 4 yr	36.4%	Blue Collar	6.5%
Military		Post grad	27.5%	Government	9.6%
Veteran/ Active Duty	4.7%				

2012 Pres. Vote	Obama	210,010	(61%)	Romney	127,421	(37%)		
2016 Pres. Vote	Clinton	239,982	(68%)	Trump	93,706	(26%)	Johnson	12,485	(4%)

Westside, Santa Monica: Showbiz still sets the tone for the Westside of Los Angeles. It remains tremendously profitable, and not just for the big conglomerate-owned studios. There are tens of thousands of entrepreneurs, actors, writers and craftsmen who are the best in the world at what they do and who tend to cluster on the Westside because so many others in the entertainment business work there. Not everyone is in show business, of course. The Westside is metro Los Angeles's biggest office center, with horrific traffic during the morning and evening rush hours. Most office workers can't afford to live in the limited and expensive neighborhoods nearby. The city's Purple Line subway is being extended to the Westside, a nine-mile extension from Wilshire/Western. Over the objections of Beverly Hills school district officials, the $5.6 billion project includes a tunnel underneath Beverly Hills High School. Construction broke ground in 2014 and its scheduled completion has been delayed to 2026. The project has been the object of endless litigation, including a January 2018 lawsuit by the school district to demand a full environmental review.

Beverly Hills and the Westside remain the locus of some of America's most expensive residential real estate, where people buy houses for millions of dollars, tear them down, and build new houses for many more millions. Rodeo Drive is one of the world's premier high-priced shopping areas. The L.A. City Council in 2015 imposed restrictions in 20 neighborhoods on what residents described as "mansionization," the building of mansion-like homes that are unusually large for their lots. The area has had a large and diverse Jewish community. Iranian Jews have poured in since 1979 and make up about one-fifth of the population of Beverly Hills. The old three-block Fairfax district has been home to many Russian Jewish immigrants and a number of corner delis, including the historic Canter's Deli that opened in 1931 and remains open 24/7. That neighborhood had seen so much gentrification that it was "virtually unrecognizable," the Los Angeles Review of Books reported in August 2018. The closing of the Santa Monica airport, which had been scheduled for 2018, has been delayed to 2028 — perhaps not coincidentally, when L.A. will host the Olympics. The horrific Woolsey fire in November 2018 destroyed entire neighborhoods in Malibu.

The 33rd Congressional District of California, the coastal district of Los Angeles, contains the upscale cities of Beverly Hills, Brentwood and parts of the Westside, which it shares with the 28th District. In the hills of Bel Air, $100 million homes have become common — and relatively modest. It takes in the campus of the University of California, Los Angeles and the J. Paul Getty Museum. Santa Monica is in the 33rd, as are the 21 miles of Malibu on the Pacific Ocean. It dips south to take in Marina del Rey and skirts along the ocean past Los Angeles International Airport to El Segundo — where the Los Angeles Times, under its new owner, relocated its downtown office in 2018 — plus Manhattan Beach and Redondo Beach. Its southernmost point is Rancho Palos Verdes, where, on cliffs overlooking the ocean, is famed architect Frank Lloyd Wright's Wayfarers Chapel, also known as "The Glass Church." With a racial composition that is almost two-thirds white, the district is less ethnically diverse than other congressional districts in greater Los Angeles. But it is solid Democratic territory, though with a loftier median household income that placed the district among the wealthiest 2 percent in the nation. Hillary Clinton in 2016 got 68 percent of the vote. Many typically Republican voters in the 33rd abandoned Donald Trump.

Jimmy Gomez (D)

Elected 2017, 1st full term, b. Nov 25, 1974; Southern California; University of California, Los Angeles, B.A.; Harvard University John F. Kennedy School of Government (MA), M.P.P.; Religion unknown; Married (Mary Hodge).

DC Office: 1530 LHOB 20515, 202-225-6235, Fax: 202-225-2202, gomez.house.gov
State Offices: Los Angeles, 213-481-1425.

Committees: *Oversight & Reform*: Subcommittee on Civil Rights & Civil Liberties; Subcommittee on Environment. *Ways & Means*: Health; Worker & Family Support.

Group Ratings

	ADA	ACLU	AFL-CIO	LCV	ITI	COC	HAFA	ACU	CFG	FRC
2018	-	93%	-	97%	-	50%	9%	4%	21%	0%
2017	55%	C	-	95%	C	40%	C	-	6%	17%

Almanac Ratings 2017-18

	Economy	Social	Foreign	Composite
Liberal	82%	70%	96%	83%
Conservative	18%	30%	4%	17%

Key Votes of the 115th Congress

1. Obama-care revision	N/A	5. Family planning regs	N/A	9. Guantanamo prisoners	Y
2. Tax Cuts	N	6. Body cameras/immigration	Y	10. Ground missiles, limit	Y
3. Omnibus appropriations	N	7. Abortion ban	N	11. Defense Dept. spending	N
4. Dodd-Frank revision	N	8. Concealed carry	N	12. FISA rules	N

Election Results

Election	Name (Party)	Vote (%)		Cand. Spent	Ind. Exp. Support	Ind. Exp. Oppose
2018 General	Jimmy Gomez (D)	110,195	(73%)	$1,429,468	$479,475	
	Kenneth Mejia (G)	41,711	(27%)	$119,695		
2018 Primary	Jimmy Gomez (D)	54,661	(79%)			
	Kenneth Mejia (G)	8,987	(13%)			
	Angela McArdle (Lib)	5,804	(8%)			

Prior winning percentages: 2017 special (60%)

Democrat Jimmy Gomez settled into this seat after winning the June 2017 special election against a leader of the local Korean-American community. He gained a seat on the Ways and Means Committee and became involved in Democratic Caucus activities.

Gomez was born and raised in southern California; his parents had immigrated from Mexico in the early 1970s. After graduating from high school, he worked 16 hours daily for several months at a fast-food restaurant and a local superstore. In search of a quality education, he enrolled in a community college and got his bachelor's degree at UCLA and then a master's in public policy from the John F. Kennedy School of Government at Harvard University.

He spent more than a decade working with local and federal officials, including former Rep. Hilda Solis, at the Democratic National Committee and labor unions — most recently as political director of the United Nurses Associations of California. In the Assembly, where he was first elected in 2012, Gomez styled himself as a progressive. He authored an expansion of California's Paid Family Leave program to cover all workers who paid into it, which was enacted.

The vacancy was created when Xavier Becerra resigned to fill the vacancy for attorney general of California, which was created when Kamala Harris was elected to the Senate. First elected to the House in 1992, he chaired the Democratic Caucus for four years, making him the most prominent Latino in the House. Becerra's resignation spurred a wide-open contest for his successor. The 24 candidates, who did not include a single Republican, featured several women candidates and supporters of presidential candidate Sen. Bernie Sanders. None of them emerged from the pack. Nine candidates raised more than $100,000. They were led by Robert Lee Ahn, an attorney who worked in his family's real estate business and had been a member of the Los Angeles Planning Commission. He self-financed nearly one-third of the total $1.7 million that he spent. Gomez was supported by much of the local Democratic establishment, including Becerra. He spent $1.1 million and got more than $300,000 in additional campaign support from organized labor and Latino groups.

In the primary, Gomez got 25 percent of the vote and Ahn had 22 percent. No other candidate got more than 10 percent. Because the election had no partisan impact in the House, it received less national attention than the four other special elections that were held during the spring of 2017. Gomez won the run-off, 60%-40%. The nearly 33,000 voters contrasted to the 260,000 voters that month in the special election in the Atlanta suburbs.

Gomez quickly delivered on his promise to confront President Donald Trump and his policies. Referring to family separations at the border with Mexico, he tweeted that Trump's idea of helping

California is "terrorizing and tearing families apart." In December 2018, he traveled to the border to investigate reports of illegal rejections of asylum seekers at ports of entry. Instead, Gomez and Rep. Nanette Barragan spent the night in what he called a "cage," which was built by border agents and also enclosed refugee children and immigration activists. That treatment, he said, showed how deeply Trump had "decayed the rule of law in a country that modeled democracy for the modern world."

When Gomez asked a Justice Department official whether personal data gathered during the census could be referred to law-enforcement agencies, a department lawyer advised in an internal email that they should not give him "too much" response, according to information revealed by a Freedom of Information Act request by The Washington Post. Gomez responded that the emails "prove that the Trump administration is using every tool at their disposal to vilify our immigrant communities."

Gomez was reelected without major-party opposition. He won, 73%-27%, against 27-year-old Green Party candidate Kenneth Mejia, a certified public accountant who ran on a progressive platform.

Following the 2018 election, Gomez was tapped for Ways and Means, which he called "the frontline in the battle to protect our social safety net system." He became vice chairman of the Future Forum, a group of young House Democrats who focused on issues facing youthful Americans.

CA-34: Los Angeles   **Cook Partisan Voting Index: D+35**

Population		Race and Ethnicity		Income	
Total	728,048	White	10.6%	Median Income	$40,215
Land area (sq. miles)	48	Black	4.1%	District Income Rank	414
Pop/ sq mi	15275.9	Latino	64%	Poverty Rate	26.3%
Born in State	42.8%	Asian	19.3%	With health insurance	78%
		Two or more races	1.4%	Cash public assistance	4.7%
Age Groups		Other	0.6%	Food stamp/SNAP	12.6%
Under 18	21.2%				
18-34	29.8%	**Education**		**Work**	
35-64	38.1%	H.S grad or less	54.7%	White Collar	10.9%
Over 64	10.9%	Some college	20.1%	Sales and Service	47.2%
		College Degree, 4 yr	18.1%	Blue Collar	24.3%
Military		Post grad	7%	Government	8.5%
Veteran/ Active Duty	2.1%				

2012 Pres. Vote	Obama	127,510	(83%)	Romney	21,739	(14%)			
2016 Pres. Vote	Clinton	154,259	(83%)	Trump	19,784	(11%)	Stein	6,129	(3%)

Downtown/Northeast L.A.: Downtown L.A. has been booming, with thousands of apartments, new hotels, shops and restaurants. Much of the financing has come from foreign investment. Although driving a few blocks can be a Manhattan-type nightmare, the area has become surprisingly pedestrian-friendly, with attractive plazas like the one around the Los Angeles Public Library. This is the heart of the nation's largest county, whose 10.2 million people are nearly twice as many as Chicago's Cook County. The New York City metro area exceeds by about 50 percent the population of the L.A. metro area (13.4 million), which includes Long Beach and Anaheim. L.A. is "a capital of commerce and high-energy cultural diversity [where] entire neighborhoods have risen from the dead," Los Angeles Times columnist Steve Lopez wrote in August 2018. But it also is a place where "savage inequality is a crippling travesty." A new landmark in the Financial District is the Wilshire Grand Center, which opened in June 2017 as the tallest building west of the Mississippi River, with 73 floors.

South of downtown is the garment district, with factories in nondescript buildings, an economically vibrant area that has helped make Los Angeles-Long Beach the largest manufacturing center in America, with 350,000 workers in 2018. The county's minimum-wage increase to $13.25 in 2018 caused some job loss in the Garment District, with factories moving across the border to Tijuana. The Los Angeles County Economic Development Corporation worried that it has become difficult to find workers with sufficient education and skill sets. As the host of the 2028 Olympics, L.A. will have new opportunities to showcase its strengths and shortcomings.

Surrounding downtown Los Angeles and largely detached from it are ethnically diverse neighborhoods, many of them built in the mid-20th century. They have changed character with every new immigration flow. To the north is Lincoln Heights, one of the oldest neighborhoods in the city and a heavily Hispanic area centered* on the busy shopping street of North Broadway. Highland Park and Eagle Rock, which were white middle-class enclaves 30 years ago, are now ethnically mixed and middle-class with large numbers of Latinos and Asians. Eagle Rock is the home of Occidental College, where former President Barack Obama attended his first two years of college and where a state highway has been named for him. West of downtown is Pico Union, an entry point for new immigrants where Greeks, Mexicans and Central Americans co-mingle. Historic Filipinotown, known locally as Hi-Fi, was settled by Filipinos in the early 1900s and in recent years has become more of a polyglot. Further west toward (but not reaching) Beverly Hills is bustling and increasingly hip Koreatown, with boutique hotels, plus clubs and restaurants for a busy night life. Beyond the commercial strips in Koreatown, the Asian community has gained a social and political identity as it has moved to the middle class.

These areas, plus Montecito Heights, Dodger Stadium and Elysian Park, are parts of California's 34th Congressional District. Just east of the Financial District, and on the other side of a maze of interstate highways, the district takes in Chinatown and Boyle Heights, once an entry neighborhood for Irish and Jewish immigrants and for the past 40 years predominantly Mexican American. The population surge of the 1980s stopped, and this became a slow-growing district, as those newcomers moved out to middle-class neighborhoods and incoming immigrants spread more evenly around the Los Angeles Basin. The district is 64 percent Hispanic and 19 percent Asian. Politically, it is in the top 5 percent of Democratic districts in the nation.

Norma Torres (D)

Elected 2014, 3rd term, b. Apr 04, 1965; Escuintla, Guatemala; Rio Hondo College, Att.; Mount San Antonio College (CA), Att., 2000; National Labor College (MD), B.A., 2012; Roman Catholic; Married (Louis Torres); 3 children.

Elected Office: Pomona City Council, 2000-2006; Pomona Mayor, 2006-2008; CA Assembly, 2008-2013; CA Senate, 2013-2014.

Professional Career: Emergency dispatcher; Sales rep..

DC Office: 2444 RHOB 20515, 202-225-6161, Fax: 202-225-8671, torres.house.gov

State Offices: Ontario, 909-481-6474.

Committees: *Appropriations:* Financial Services & General Government; State, Foreign Operations & Related Programs; Transportation, HUD & Related Agencies. *Rules:* Rules & Organization of the House (Chmn).

Group Ratings

	ADA	ACLU	AFL-CIO	LCV	ITI	COC	HAFA	ACU	CFG	FRC
2018	-	81%	-	94%	-	67%	8%	8%	26%	0%
2017	80%	C	97%	97%	C	64%	C	4%	5%	11%

Almanac Ratings 2017-18

	Economy	Social	Foreign	Composite
Liberal	94%	97%	89%	93%
Conservative	6%	3%	11%	7%

Key Votes of the 115th Congress

1. Obama-care revision	N	5. Family planning regs	N	9. Guantanamo prisoners	Y
2. Tax Cuts	N	6. Body cameras/immigration	Y	10. Ground missiles, limit	Y
3. Omnibus appropriations	N	7. Abortion ban	N	11. Defense Dept. spending	Y
4. Dodd-Frank revision	N	8. Concealed carry	N	12. FISA rules	Y

Election Results

Election	Name (Party)	Vote (%)	Cand. Spent	Ind. Exp. Support	Ind. Exp. Oppose
2018 General	Norma Torres (D)............................ 103,420	(69%)	$559,967		
	Christian Valiente (R)........................ 45,604	(31%)	$7,377		
2018 Primary	Norma Torres (D)............................... 32,474	(51%)			
	Christian Valiente (R)........................ 21,572	(34%)			
	Joe Baca (D)....................................... 9,417	(15%)			

Prior winning percentages: 2016 (72%), 2014 (64%)

Democrat Norma Torres, who won an open seat in 2014, has taken an interest in issues affecting her Central American homeland and her local ports. She has shown her cachet in the House by gaining seats on two of its prime committees: Appropriations and Rules.

Torres was born in Guatemala but entered the United States at age 5, when her parents sent her to live with relatives in Whittier California, so she would be safe from that country's bloody civil war. Her interest in community safety led to work as a 911 dispatcher in Pomona, where she soon developed a deeper interest in public service. One episode was particularly profound: In 1994, while she was handling other calls, a fellow dispatcher put a frantic Spanish-speaking woman on hold because no one else could speak with her. When Torres finally picked up, she heard a domestic dispute escalate on the other line, resulting in the shooting death of an 11-year-old. Shaken, she led a successful fight to compel the police to hire more bilingual dispatchers. At age 47, she received her bachelor's degree in labor studies from the National Labor College in Silver Spring, Maryland, where she took online courses.

Torres became involved in broader community issues, especially union organizing and immigrants' rights. She was elected to the Pomona City Council in 2000 and was elected mayor in 2006. The following year, when she returned for the first time to her hometown in Guatemala, she was treated like a celebrity. In 2008, her rise continued as she won a seat in the state Assembly. She chaired the Housing and Community Development Committee, where she helped to secure $2 billion for the "Keep Your Home" program to assist homeowners to avoid foreclosure. She wrote a law that modernized the 911 system by directing cell phone callers to their local police department during an emergency. After winning a 2013 special election to the state Senate, Torres championed a law to generate more revenue for programs that train and place doctors in medically underserved communities. To assist immigrants, she coauthored a measure that transferred $3 million to help unaccompanied minors fleeing Central America.

In 2014, Gloria Negrete McLeod decided not to seek reelection to the House and instead ran for a seat on the San Bernardino County Board of Supervisors, which she ultimately lost. In the all-party primary, Torres faced three other Democrats and a Republican. With a sizable cash advantage, name recognition and endorsements by major unions and liberal women's groups, she got 67 percent to Democrat Christina Gagnier's 15 percent. During the full campaign, she outspent Gagnier $423,000 to $84,000, and won 63%-37%.

During her first term, Torres used her seat on the Homeland Security Committee as an opportunity to oversee ports of entry in her district's Ontario International Airport and the inland port serving the maritime ports of Los Angeles and Long Beach. She told a reporter for the Inland Valley Daily Bulletin that she was surprised and dismayed by the pervasive partisanship, including in her committee work. "Homeland Security, you think 'that's life and death,'" she said. "But we're not able to work together on this issue." In 2017, she enacted a bill to strengthen sharing and coordination of cybersecurity information at the ports, following a malware attack at the Los Angeles port.

On international issues, Torres founded the bipartisan Central America Caucus to enhance understanding of the region, including immigration issues. Unlike many House Democrats, she decided to attend the inauguration of President Donald Trump. "I am the embodiment of everything Trump has demonized and demeaned," she said in a statement. "I will stand over his shoulder, just as I will during the next four years, to remind him that I and people like me deserve a seat at the table, and we will watch his every move." She showed her emotion during a House debate on restrictive immigration legislation in 2018 when she recounted her experience in crossing the border as a five-year-old. "I was welcomed here in a loving home. I was not put in a freezing cell," she said, with her voice breaking. "My parents had no choice. My mother died a couple years later. ... Let's help those who can't help themselves."

In March 2018, Democratic Leader Nancy Pelosi appointed Torres to fill a vacancy on the Rules Committee. Following the election, she was named to the Appropriations Committee, where she said that her priorities included expansion of the Gold Line light rail in her district and modernization of the Ontario airport.

Torres has been easily reelected twice against Republican challengers whom she out-spent by 100-to-1.

CA-35: Inland Empire   Cook Partisan Voting Index: D+19

Population		Race and Ethnicity		Income	
Total	735,165	White	14.3%	Median Income	$58,467
Land area (sq. miles)	169	Black	6.2%	District Income Rank	190
Pop/ sq mi	4353.2	Latino	70%	Poverty Rate	16.9%
Born in State	61.1%	Asian	6.8%	With health insurance	84.6%
		Two or more races	1.9%	Cash public assistance	4.9%
Age Groups		Other	0.7%	Food stamp/SNAP	14.8%
Under 18	26.9%				
18-34	27.6%	**Education**		**Work**	
35-64	36.8%	H.S grad or less	56.1%	White Collar	8.7%
Over 64	8.7%	Some college	28.6%	Sales and Service	44.5%
		College Degree, 4 yr	11.2%	Blue Collar	32.8%
Military		Post grad	4.1%	Government	11.8%
Veteran/ Active Duty	3.6%				

2012 Pres. Vote	Obama	108,983	(67%)	Romney	49,433	(31%)		
2016 Pres. Vote	Clinton	127,761	(67%)	Trump	50,824	(27%)	Johnson	5,069	(3%)

Fontana, Ontario: The gateway to the Los Angeles Basin for decades was San Bernardino. This was an agricultural zone until World War II, when Henry J. Kaiser built the West Coast's first major steel mill between the Santa Fe and Southern Pacific rail lines in Fontana, just west of San Bernardino. Today, these lands have largely filled up. The Inland Empire, as it is called, may be where the smog piles up against the mountains, but it also has an energetic small business economy, with lower real-estate costs than elsewhere in the Los Angeles basin. After the large Kaiser steel mill closed in Fontana in 1994, new businesses moved in to supplant it. Earlier at this site, future California Gov. Arnold Schwarzenegger had a knock-down, drag-out fight with the enemy metal alloy machine in the 1991 blockbuster Terminator 2: Judgment Day.

Business growth has been spurred by huge distribution and warehouse centers that service overseas cargo from the Long Beach port. The recession hit hard in the Inland Empire, with home foreclosures among the highest in the nation and many residents fleeing the region. Jobs returned slowly, with some help from the local California Steel plant that employed about 1,000 workers. Housing costs have increased since the recession, as the supply of affordable homes in the Inland Empire has dropped. Pomona remains the site of the county fairground and a motor speedway. Ontario arrived on the national map with a rock festival in 1978 that drew 225,000 spectators, the largest one-day paid concert. Today, it offers a fiber-optic broadband service that city official promote as one of the nation's first "giga-bit communities." Also contributing to the commercial growth is Ontario International Airport, which was transferred from control of Los Angeles International Airport in 2016 and has been listed as the fastest-growing in the nation. In June 2018, FedEx said it will spend $100 million at the airport to upgrade its ground services.

The 35th District is mostly in San Bernardino County, taking in heavily Hispanic areas in Fontana and Ontario. Ontario Mills is one of the largest shopping malls in the United States. Also here is part of Chino, a meatpacking area. This district covers Pomona Valley and the city of Pomona in Los Angeles County, though Pomona College is part of the Claremont Colleges a few miles away in the 27th District. The three largest cities — Fontana, Ontario and Pomona — are similar in size and each is about 70 percent Hispanic; the population in Fontana is a bit larger, as is household income. This is a safe Democratic district, where Hillary Clinton got 67 percent of the vote in 2016.

Raul Ruiz (D)

Elected 2012, 4th term, b. Aug 25, 1972; Zacatecas, Mexico; University of California, Los Angeles, B.S., 1994; Harvard University, M.P.P., 2001; Harvard University, M.D., 2001; Harvard University, M.PH, 2007; Seventh-Day Adventist; Married (Monica Ruiz); 2 children (twins).

Professional Career: Emergency physician, Eisenhower Med. Center, 2007-2013; Association dean, University of CA Riverside School of Med., 2011-2012.

DC Office: 2342 RHOB 20515, 202-225-5330, Fax: 202-225-1238, ruiz.house.gov

State Offices: Hemet, 951-765-2304; Palm Desert, 760-424-8888.

Committees: *Energy & Commerce*: Environment & Climate Change; Health; Oversight & Investigations.

Group Ratings

	ADA	ACLU	AFL-CIO	LCV	ITI	COC	HAFA	ACU	CFG	FRC
2018	-	71%	-	91%	-	75%	2%	4%	10%	0%
2017	75%	C	97%	100%	C	64%	C	4%	0%	11%

Almanac Ratings 2017-18

	Economy	Social	Foreign	Composite
Liberal	85%	93%	56%	78%
Conservative	15%	7%	44%	22%

Key Votes of the 115th Congress

1. Obama-care revision	N	5. Family planning regs	N	9. Guantanamo prisoners	N
2. Tax Cuts	N	6. Body cameras/immigration	Y	10. Ground missiles, limit	Y
3. Omnibus appropriations	Y	7. Abortion ban	N	11. Defense Dept. spending	Y
4. Dodd-Frank revision	N	8. Concealed carry	N	12. FISA rules	Y

Election Results

Election	Name (Party)	Vote (%)	Cand. Spent	Ind. Exp. Support	Ind. Exp. Oppose
2018 General	Raul Ruiz (D).. 122,169	(59%)	$2,444,257	$26,260	$3,450
	Kimberlin Brown Pelzer (R)................ 84,839	(41%)	$840,762	$15,000	
2018 Primary	Raul Ruiz (D).. 65,554	(55%)			
	Kimberlin Brown Pelzer (R)................ 27,648	(23%)			
	Dan Ball (R).. 9,312	(8%)			
	Douglas Hassett (R).............................. 6,001	(5%)			

Prior winning percentages: 2016 (62%), 2014 (54%), 2012 (53%)

Democrat Raul Ruiz, an emergency room doctor, has turned his district safely Democratic after narrowly defeating a veteran Republican incumbent in 2012. He has pursued health care issues on the influential Energy and Commerce Committee, and also has worked on environment and communications issues.

The son of farmworkers, Ruiz was born and raised in the Coachella Valley. He says he dreamed of being a doctor from a very young age. A family friend paid for Ruiz to apply to the University of California, Los Angeles, but he needed money for tuition. Ruiz went door-to-door in his hometown with a handmade contract, asking for contributions to his college fund in exchange for his future medical service to the community. He raised almost $2,000. After graduating from UCLA, Ruiz went to Harvard Medical School. As a student, he spent almost a year in Chiapas Mexico through a health and social justice organization, Partners in Health. "I came out of there realizing the tremendous nature of poverty and how real policies can actually affect human lives," he later told The Desert Sun newspaper. After graduating from Harvard with three degrees, including master's degrees in public policy and public health, Ruiz returned to the Coachella Valley and served in the emergency room of a nonprofit hospital.

Ruiz was Republican Rep. Mary Bono Mack's first Hispanic opponent since she won the seat of her late husband, musician Sonny Bono, who died in a skiing accident in 1998. She won the first round, 58%-42%. Ruiz got more than $1.1 million in support from the Democratic Congressional Campaign Committee. In the final weeks of the race, a local newspaper received an eight-page document from Bono Mack's campaign that outlined a Thanksgiving protest in which Ruiz was arrested and charged with two misdemeanors while attending Harvard. At issue was Ruiz's participation in the National Day of Mourning, an annual event at Plymouth Rock to publicize the suffering of Native Americans since the Pilgrims' arrival in 1620. Both charges were dropped in a deal that also discharged claims of police brutality. Bono Mack's campaign cast Ruiz's participation as anti-American and as left-wing extremism, and released a recording of a speech he gave at the protest. Ruiz characterized her efforts as desperate. Ruiz was endorsed by The Desert Sun, which said that Bono Mack had gotten too comfortable in Congress. He won, 53%-47%.

On the Veterans Affairs Committee, the former emergency room doctor took on problems with VA hospitals. He catalogued complaints of poor services and filed bills designed to reduce the claims backlog and to make it easier for veterans to use video conferencing for hearings before the Board of Veterans' Appeals. He served two years as the senior Democrat on the Natural Resources Subcommittee on Indian, Insular and Native American Affairs, where he explored ways to improve health care and economic growth for Native Americans.

With his seat on Energy and Commerce in 2017, Democratic leaders touted Ruiz for his bill to mandate essential benefits in limited-duration health insurance plans and to bar exclusion of individuals with pre-existing conditions. Republicans took no action on his measure. In April 2018, he passed a bill to create a demonstration program for increased access to treatment of opioid use; his measure was wrapped into broader bipartisan legislation that was enacted later that year. Ruiz also won enactment of his bill to expand broadband access for Native American tribes in the Coachella Valley.

Ruiz and Republican Rep. Brad Wenstrup of Ohio — another physician — formed a caucus that advocated on behalf of veterans with ailments that likely were caused by burn pits used for waste and chemical disposal in Iraq and Afghanistan. The defense spending bill that was enacted in 2018 included their amendment to end burn pits.

In 2014, Ruiz was a top target of the National Republican Congressional Committee. He benefited from unexpected events that drew extensive local media coverage, including two airplane flights during which he provided emergency service to other passengers. His opponent, Brian Nestande, a Republican Assemblyman and a former top aide to Bono Mack, proved to be a mediocre fundraiser. Ruiz outspent him $3.1 million to $1.3 million and won, 54%-46%.

Two years later, Ruiz showed interest in the open seat of retiring Democratic Sen. Barbara Boxer, but deferred to two better-known Democrats. The candidacy of Rep. Loretta Sanchez limited his opportunity to rally Latino support. Instead, he was opposed for reelection by Republican state Sen. Jeffrey Stone, who was the former mayor of Temecula. The outcome was a 62%-38% blowout for Ruiz, who raised $3.2 million and seemed to have taken control of a once-secure Republican seat. During the disastrous 2018 election for California Republicans, Kimberlin Brown Pelzer, a former television actress, criticized the House GOP's "giving structure." Ruiz outspent her 3-to-1 and won, 59%-41%.

CA-36: Eastern Riverside County   Cook Partisan Voting Index: D+2

Population		Race and Ethnicity		Income	
Total	740,835	White	41.1%	Median Income	$46,772
Land area (sq. miles)	5,913	Black	4.1%	District Income Rank	354
Pop/ sq mi	125.3	Latino	48.7%	Poverty Rate	19.8%
Born in State	55.2%	Asian	3.2%	With health insurance	86.6%
Age Groups		Two or more races	1.8%	Cash public assistance	3.9%
		Other	1%	Food stamp/SNAP	11.2%
Under 18	23.4%				
18-34	20.3%	**Education**		**Work**	
35-64	36%	H.S grad or less	47.5%	White Collar	20.3%
Over 64	20.3%	Some college	31.7%	Sales and Service	50.6%
Military		College Degree, 4 yr	12.8%	Blue Collar	23.3%
		Post grad	8%	Government	12.8%
Veteran/ Active Duty	8.2%				

2012 Pres. Vote	Obama	107,914	(51%)	Romney	101,156	(48%)		
2016 Pres. Vote	Clinton	123,795	(52%)	Trump	103,051	(43%)	Johnson 6,172	(3%)

Indio, Palm Springs: From the air a few decades ago, a night flight east from Los Angeles flew over the lights of homes of 10 million people and then into almost perfect darkness. The city then was a vast metropolis surrounded by almost uninhabited territory. Today, the sprinkled pattern of white lights has spread into the Inland Empire around Riverside and San Bernardino and has multiplied outward into the desert. Over the 10,000-foot-high San Jacinto Mountains, desert communities boomed: Palm Springs was once the lone winter resort for the stars but now is popular for its retro architecture and as a destination for gay couples. Reflecting a more youthful and open culture, including trendy hotels and clubs, it became in 2017 the first city in the nation in which all elected officials are LGBT: three gay men, a transgender woman and a bisexual woman. Palm Springs is one of a string of communities along Highway 111 and Frank Sinatra and Bob Hope drives. The clean, dry, roomy desert, where the days are almost always crystal clear and the sky usually cloudless, generated $7 billion in tourist revenue in 2017.Two presidents retired to the desert and its many golf courses here: Dwight Eisenhower wintered in Palm Desert, and Gerald Ford resided for 30 years in nearby Rancho Mirage.

The growth in the Coachella Valley has been chiefly in heavily Latino and fast-growing agricultural cities. The valley's nine cities extend from Palm Springs south and east to Coachella. Of its roughly 1 million acres, 700,000 have been designated for conservation, which keeps them mostly pristine. The area produces roughly 95 percent of the dates consumed in the U.S. The annual music and arts festival in Coachella, which began in 1999, has become the largest music festival in the world, with the most revenue. In 2018, it sold out each of its six days of performances during two weekends in April, with daily sales of 125,000. A third weekend for the Stagecoach country music festival attracted 75,000 daily. In 2018, a new hall featured 15 restaurants. The estimated impact for the local economy was $494 million. With its scenic location in the desert and a relatively short drive from Los Angeles, the events draw wide attention in the entertainment world.

The 36th District covers eastern Riverside County. Interstate 10 runs through the district, taking in Banning and Beaumont on the western side and stretching east to Blythe at the Arizona border. There are huge socio-economic contrasts: Per capita income of $39,500 in Palm Springs is more than 60 percent higher than that of Indio and nearly three times Coachella. Joshua Tree National Park, with its high-desert sands, is a popular tourist spot here. The 36th is the largest and least urban of three congressional districts that are entirely within Riverside. Its Hispanic population has grown to 49 percent. This has been a politically competitive district, though Hillary Clinton's 52%-43% win continued a trend toward Democrats.

Karen Bass (D)

Elected 2010, 5th term, b. Oct 03, 1953; Los Angeles; University of Southern California School of Medicine; San Diego State University, 1973; California State University - Dominguez Hills, B.S., 1990; Baptist; Divorced; 2 children (1 deceased); 4 stepchildren.

Elected Office: CA Assembly, 2005-2010, speaker, 2008-2010.

Professional Career: Physician's Assistant, Los Angeles County General Hosp.; Instructor, University of S. CA; Executive Director, Community Coalition, 1990-2004.

DC Office: 2059 RHOB 20515, 202-225-7084, Fax: 202-225-2422, bass.house.gov

State Offices: Los Angeles, 323-965-1422.

Committees: *Foreign Affairs*: Africa, Global Health, Global Human Rights & Internat'l Orgs (Chmn). *Judiciary*: Courts, Intellectual Property & Internet; Crime, Terrorism & Homeland Security (Chmn).

Group Ratings

	ADA	ACLU	AFL-CIO	LCV	ITI	COC	HAFA	ACU	CFG	FRC
2018	-	92%	-	66%	-	50%	9%	-	26%	0%
2017	100%	C	100%	97%	C	36%	C	4%	5%	0%

Almanac Ratings 2017-18

	Economy	Social	Foreign	Composite
Liberal	99%	97%	98%	98%
Conservative	1%	3%	3%	2%

Key Votes of the 115th Congress

1. Obama-care revision	N	5. Family planning regs	NV	9. Guantanamo prisoners	Y
2. Tax Cuts	N	6. Body cameras/immigration	Y	10. Ground missiles, limit	Y
3. Omnibus appropriations	N	7. Abortion ban	N	11. Defense Dept. spending	N
4. Dodd-Frank revision	N	8. Concealed carry	N	12. FISA rules	N

Election Results

Election	Name (Party)	Vote (%)		Cand. Spent	Ind. Exp. Support	Ind. Exp. Oppose
2018 General	Karen Bass (D)..................................210,555	(89%)		$603,238		
	Ron Bassilian (R)...............................25,823	(11%)		$8,193		
2018 Primary	Karen Bass (D)....................................99,118	(89%)				
	Ron Bassilian (R)...............................12,020	(11%)				

Prior winning percentages: 2016 (81%), 2014 (84%), 2012 (86%), 2010 (86%)

Karen Bass, elected in 2010, is a former California Assembly speaker and an influential Democrat who has drawn flattering comparisons to another speaker from California, Nancy Pelosi. With her impressive leadership skills, including on Africa-related legislation and on Democratic Party organization, Bass gained several plum assignments when Democrats regained House control.

Bass was born and raised in Los Angeles. Her father was a letter carrier and her mother was a homemaker. Her father had moved to California from Texas after World War II; her mother was a Los Angeles native who learned to speak Spanish as a child. At age 14, Bass got involved in Democratic Sen. Robert F. Kennedy's 1968 presidential campaign by signing up her mother as a precinct captain and then doing all the neighborhood canvassing herself. At her high school in West Los Angeles, Bass joined her teachers in protests against the Vietnam War. She attended San Diego State University and stayed active in community organizing. Bass received a nursing certificate from the University of Southern California and a bachelor's degree from California State University, Dominguez Hills. "School wound up being rather secondary for me," she said. Bass served on a committee that investigated accusations of police abuses in Los Angeles.

In 1990, Bass founded the Community Coalition, a nonprofit that worked with African-American and Latino communities in South Los Angeles to combat drug use and gang violence by shutting down liquor stores and motels. The group campaigned against Proposition 187, which sought to deny public services to illegal immigrants, and Proposition 209, which prohibited affirmative action admissions policies in public universities. Bass served as executive director for 14 years.

Bass won election to the state Assembly in 2004. She sponsored several bills aimed at reforming the state's foster care system and expanding health insurance programs for children. In her first term, she was the majority whip; in her second, she was majority leader; and in her third term, she became the first black female speaker in any state legislature in the United States. Trying to balance California's budget in the midst of a fiscal crisis consumed much of her tenure. She negotiated budget compromises with Gov. Arnold Schwarzenegger that included cuts to education and social spending. Bass described her two years as speaker as "painful" and said, "I ran for office because I wanted to create, build, and expand programs, not tear them apart."

In 2010, when she ran for an open seat, other prominent Democrats stayed out of the race, assuming that Bass would easily win on turf she had represented in the Assembly. She won the Democratic primary with 85 percent of the vote. In the general election, she got 86 percent. She has not faced a serious reelection challenge.

Bass has taken on leadership assignments. On Foreign Affairs, as the senior Democrat on the Subcommittee on Africa, Global Health, Global Human Rights and International Organizations, her work has included successful efforts to extend the African Growth and Opportunity Act. During the Ebola crisis in 2014, she urged President Barack Obama to send U.S. troops to care for Ebola patients in west Africa. In 2018, Congress enacted a revised version of her bill to promote democracy and economic recovery in Zimbabwe.

At the same time that she took over as Africa subcommittee chairman in 2019, Bass unexpectedly became chairwoman — in an interim status -- of the Judiciary Subcommittee on Crime, Terrorism and Homeland Security. Rep. Sheila Jackson Lee of Texas temporarily stepped aside from that post, pending an Ethics Committee investigation of her handling of sexual-abuse claims by a former aide. Bass has maintained her advocacy of the poor and disadvantaged. She created the Congressional Caucus on Foster Youth and has filed several bills to improve foster care. The comprehensive bill that was enacted in 2018 to fight opioid addiction included a Bass provision to promote health insurance for former foster youth.

Her most prominent position when Congress convened in January 2019 was as chairwoman of the Congressional Black Caucus, which grew to 55 members (including two senators) following the 2018 election. In describing her challenge, Bass said that instead of celebrating American diversity, "the reaction by some has essentially unleashed a dragon — a dragon that is unleashing its last breath and so he is dangerous as he lashes out." The dragon, she said, "is hate. The dragon is white supremacy." The CBC, she added, will have "tremendous power and influence," in party leadership and at committees, and "will exercise every ounce of our power and influence to continue the fight for justice."

Bass has pursued partisan interests. She co-chaired the Democratic Congressional Campaign Committee's Women LEAD program, charged with recruiting more female candidates. She has charged that Republican voter identification legislation was aimed at curtailing minorities' voting participation. "One of the darkest shadows of the past century is creeping into this one: one of our most basic rights — the right to vote, a right that we fought for and won — is under attack," she said.

In 2015, after an intensive review of House Democratic internal rules, Bass said that the best way to resolve internal conflicts was to elect more Democrats to the House. "The way to get more opportunities is to get the majority, not to go after each other," she told The Washington Post. After House Democrats achieved that objective in the 2018 election, some insurgents suggested Bass as an alternative choice for Speaker. Bass remained a consistent supporter of Pelosi. She could be in the mix during the next Democratic transition. If she is interested, her profile as an African-American woman from California would offer a large base in the Democratic Caucus.

CA-37: Los Angeles — Cook Partisan Voting Index: D+37

Population		Race and Ethnicity		Income	
Total	721,893	White	25.3%	Median Income	$54,063
Land area (sq. miles)	55	Black	22.4%	District Income Rank	242
Pop/ sq mi	13063.6	Latino	38.7%	Poverty Rate	20.1%
Born in State	47.1%	Asian	10.1%	With health insurance	86.2%
		Two or more races	2.7%	Cash public assistance	4.2%
Age Groups		Other	0.8%	Food stamp/SNAP	9.5%
Under 18	19.4%				
18-34	29.9%	**Education**		**Work**	
35-64	38.4%	H.S grad or less	37.2%	White Collar	12.3%
Over 64	12.3%	Some college	25%	Sales and Service	42.9%
		College Degree, 4 yr	22.5%	Blue Collar	15.1%
Military		Post grad	15.3%	Government	10.7%
Veteran/ Active Duty	3.1%				

2012 Pres. Vote	Obama	222,329	(85%)	Romney	33,307	(13%)		
2016 Pres. Vote	Clinton	236,621	(85%)	Trump	26,608	(10%)	Stein	6,355 (2%)

Western L.A./South L.A., Culver City: Since the Los Angeles riots of 1992 and 1965, the city has had to live down its reputation as being inhospitable to African Americans, a problem exacerbated by racial tensions in the city's police department. This was the epicenter of L.A.'s two postwar riots, in the Watts district in 1965 and at the corner of Florence and Normandie in 1992. But by other measures, blacks in Los Angeles have been doing better than those elsewhere in the United States.

Job opportunities — up to and including the office of mayor for 20 years — have been relatively good for blacks. The long-simmering tension between the LAPD and the African-American community has been ameliorated by the region's changing demographics, with significant reduction in reported crime. Former Los Angeles Mayor Antonio Villaraigosa proudly noted that two-thirds of the city's police officers were non-white, though the command staff remained 55 percent white. A less positive, though dramatic, side of the story has emerged. Partly due to the high cost of housing, blacks fell from 17 percent of Los Angeles in the 1980s to 9 percent (of both the city and county) in 2017. Watts has become more than 70 percent Latino. The city ranked 40th out of 52 cities in the nation in terms of housing and income for the blacks who have remained, L.A.-based urban-affairs scholar Joel Kotkin wrote.

The shortage of housing has been a spur to gentrification and rising prices. Baldwin Hills is a high-income, African-American neighborhood. Near View Park-Windsor Hills along Slauson Avenue are other comfortable black-majority neighborhoods. Crenshaw, an Art Deco neighborhood built in the 1920s and 1930s, is the birthplace of West Coast hip hop music. In one of the more rundown sections of Crenshaw, former L.A. Lakers basketball star (and current Lakers executive) Magic Johnson built his multiplex theaters. The once desolate Culver City, which features sprawling studios and media businesses, has experienced an urban renaissance and is home to trendy new restaurants and a historically restored Culver Hotel. Local accessibility will benefit from the scheduled opening in 2020 of a 8.5-mile light-rail line from Crenshaw to Los Angeles International Airport, at a $2 billion cost.

These parts of Los Angeles are the heart of the 37th Congressional District, which is bisected by the Santa Monica Freeway. The district includes the University of Southern California, a private university with more than 43,000 students, and the adjacent Los Angeles Memorial Coliseum, which has hosted two Olympics, many famous concerts and speeches, and is the home of USC football. The former St. Louis Rams, who lost the Super Bowl in 2019, returned to L.A. in 2016 and moved into the Coliseum until their new stadium in Inglewood is completed. At nearby Exposition Park, construction began in May 2018 of a $1.5 billion museum that will house the huge art collection of filmmaker George Lucas, who earlier sought to base the museum in Chicago. Among the other cultural landmarks are the California Science Center, the Natural History Museum and the California African American Museum. The Westside Pavilion, a landmark shopping center, will be converted to office space because of declining retail business, the developer said in March 2018. The District is about 39 percent Latino and 22 percent black. Even with that declining total, the 37th and the 43rd districts were tied for the highest share of black residents in all of California. It is one of the most Democratic districts in the nation. Hillary Clinton got 85 percent of the local vote.

Linda Sánchez (D)

Elected 2002, 9th term, b. Jan 28, 1969; Orange; University of California, Berkeley, B.A., 1991; University of California School of Law, Los Angeles (JD), J.D., 1995; Roman Catholic; Married (James M. Sullivan); 1 child ; 3 stepchildren.

Professional Career: Practicing attorney, 1995-1998; Executive Secretary treas. Of Orange County AFL-CIO, 2000-2002.

DC Office: 2329 RHOB 20515, 202-225-6676, Fax: 202-226-1012, lindasanchez.house.gov

State Offices: Norwalk, 562-860-5050.

Committees: *Ways & Means*: Oversight; Select Revenue Measures; Social Security.

Group Ratings

	ADA	ACLU	AFL-CIO	LCV	ITI	COC	HAFA	ACU	CFG	FRC
2018	-	89%	-	97%	-	45%	6%	4%	15%	0%
2017	95%	C	100%	100%	C	43%	C	4%	5%	11%

Almanac Ratings 2017-18

	Economy	Social	Foreign	Composite
Liberal	100%	98%	95%	98%
Conservative	0%	2%	5%	2%

Key Votes of the 115th Congress

1. Obama-care revision	N	5. Family planning regs	N	9. Guantanamo prisoners	Y
2. Tax Cuts	N	6. Body cameras/immigration	Y	10. Ground missiles, limit	Y
3. Omnibus appropriations	N	7. Abortion ban	N	11. Defense Dept. spending	N
4. Dodd-Frank revision	N	8. Concealed carry	N	12. FISA rules	N

Election Results

Election	Name (Party)	Vote (%)	Cand. Spent	Ind. Exp. Support	Ind. Exp. Oppose
2018 General	Linda Sanchez (D)..............................139,188	(69%)	$931,432	$23,667	
	Ryan Downing (R)..........................62,968	(31%)			
2018 Primary	Linda Sanchez (D)................................54,691	(63%)			
	Ryan Downing (R)..........................32,584	(37%)			

Prior winning percentages: 2016 (71%), 2014 (59%), 2012 (68%), 2010 (63%), 2008 (70%), 2006 (66%), 2004 (61%), 2002 (55%)

Linda Sánchez, first elected in 2002, provided a younger and outspoken voice in the Democratic leadership. Her hope to take a more prominent position crashed following the 2018 election when her husband, a business executive in Connecticut, was indicted for using taxpayer funds to pay for personal expenses. Her hopes already were in jeopardy because she had openly clashed with Nancy Pelosi and demanded change of top Democratic leaders. Sanchez remained a member of the Ways and Means Committee, where she has been a defender of the Affordable Care Act.

Sanchez is one of the seven children of Mexican immigrant parents Ignacio Sánchez, a machinist, and Maria Macias, a bilingual education aide in an elementary school. Her parents met while trying to organize a union at a tire shop where they worked when they were young. She earned her bachelor's degree in Spanish literature at the University of California, Berkeley, and her law degree at the University of California, Los Angeles, working her way through school with jobs as a security guard, nanny and teacher's aide. She became a civil rights lawyer and was executive secretary-treasurer of the Orange County Federation of Labor. Her sister Loretta Sánchez served 20 years in the House from an Orange County district before she ran unsuccessfully for the Senate in 2016. "She's definitely the more liberal one," Loretta said.

When the new district lines were unveiled after the 2000 census, Linda Sánchez was one of six Democrats who ran for the seat. Her most important asset was her sister's support. She tapped Loretta's extensive fundraising network, walked precincts with her, and appeared in a television commercial with her. These connections gave Linda Sánchez an advantage over her two chief opponents, who were better known when the race began: Assemblywoman Sally Havice and South Gate Councilman Hector De La Torre. The three candidates differed very little on the issues.

Sánchez's ties to labor helped her build a strong voter-turnout operation. She won the endorsement of then-House Minority Whip Nancy Pelosi of California. Her opponents charged that she was a political opportunist who abandoned her married name and residence to revive her Latina roots and run in the new district. She won the primary with 33 percent of the vote; De La Torre received 29 percent and Havice had 19 percent. In November, Republican Tim Escobar, a financial adviser and former Army helicopter pilot, called her an inexperienced liberal extremist. Sánchez won 55%-41%, and she has been reelected easily since, though not by overwhelming margins.

Sánchez has a strongly liberal voting record. In the Almanac vote ratings, her scores have ranked among the most liberal on economic issues. She has sponsored bills to end the Social Security Administration's policy of denying benefits to same-sex couples and to establish a federal definition of school bullying to protect vulnerable students, including those who have been targeted because of their sexual orientation. She can be quick to use her sharp tongue against political foes. In 2011, bloggers on the right derided her for saying on MSNBC that a potential government shutdown would hurt her financially.

When Democrats held the majority and George W. Bush was president, Sánchez chaired the Judiciary Subcommittee on Commercial and Administrative Law, where she held hearings to oversee allegations that his administration had initiated politically motivated firings of U.S. attorneys around the country. After senior White House political adviser Karl Rove refused to cooperate, Sánchez initiated a contempt of Congress action. Rove capitulated after Bush left office. As the top Democrat on the Ethics Committee, she was at the center of several thorny cases. Later, as co-founder of the House Trade Working Group, Sánchez pledged tougher review of proposed international trade deals that she feared would ship jobs overseas. She helped to lead opposition to the Trans-Pacific Partnership agreement.

Following the 2016 election, Sánchez was elected vice-chair of the Democratic Caucus. She cited her background as a working mother in the contest for with Rep. Barbara Lee, also of California, which she won 98-96. "My role in the next four years is to be as vocal an advocate as I can for what my constituents want and need, and I will put myself in Donald Trump's path at every turn to confront him about these issues," Sánchez told The Los Angeles Times.

Those plans changed significantly. Probably the most important factor was the comment by Sanchez during a C-SPAN interview in October 2017 that "it's time to pass the torch to a new generation of leaders." At that point, when Democratic prospects for regaining control of the House in the next election seemed slim, her move was bold, but she might have prevailed if Democrats had remained in the minority. That door opened a bit further when caucus chairman Joe Crowley in June unexpectedly lost renomination to his seat in New York. The landscape for House Democrats, of course, changed when they gained 40 seats and Pelosi moved to reclaim her position as Speaker. At that point, it became highly unlikely that Sanchez would remain part of a Pelosi leadership team.

Sanchez's leadership prospects were extinguished when her husband, James Sullivan, a lobbyist and former chairman of the Connecticut Municipal Electric Energy Cooperative, was indicted with other executives for diverting federal funds to cover his personal travel. Coincidentally, that criminal action was disclosed on Nov. 8, two days after the election. The indictment was all the more perilous for Sánchez because she had attended related events as Sullivan's spouse, though she said she had received advice from the Ethics Committee. That day, she withdrew from the contest for caucus chair. She joined a group of House Democratic dissidents who opposed Pelosi's bid for Speaker. When she eventually agreed to serve no more than four more years as Speaker, Sanchez agreed with others to endorse her.

Sanchez retained her seat on Ways and Means when Congress convened in 2019. But her prospects for moving up the political ladder had dimmed and her future was in question.

CA-38: Eastern L.A. suburbs   Cook Partisan Voting Index: D+17

Population		Race and Ethnicity		Income	
Total	720,150	White	16.7%	Median Income	$65,963
Land area (sq. miles)	101	Black	3.7%	District Income Rank	129
Pop/ sq mi	7097.9	Latino	62%	Poverty Rate	11.8%
Born in State	60.7%	Asian	15.2%	With health insurance	87.7%
		Two or more races	1.5%	Cash public assistance	3.5%
Age Groups		Other	0.8%	Food stamp/SNAP	7.9%
Under 18	23.1%				
18-34	24.6%	**Education**		**Work**	
35-64	38.6%	H.S grad or less	46.9%	White Collar	13.7%
Over 64	13.7%	Some college	30.6%	Sales and Service	44.7%
		College Degree, 4 yr	15.6%	Blue Collar	24%
Military		Post grad	6.9%	Government	14.3%
Veteran/ Active Duty	4.1%				

2012 Pres. Vote	Obama	149,141	(65%)	Romney	75,780	(33%)			
2016 Pres. Vote	Clinton	166,224	(67%)	Trump	68,033	(27%)	Johnson	6,730	(3%)
	Stein	5,055	(2%)						

Whittier, Norwalk: In the years just after World War II, much of southeast Los Angeles County was farmland — citrus groves and dairy farms. In the next two decades, housing subdivisions were built and new cities incorporated so that what had been a few towns separated by farmland became one continuous swath of suburbia. The towns were different in character. Whittier, founded by Midwestern Quakers, was the hometown of Richard Nixon, a young lawyer who was elected to Congress in 1946. Lakewood, just north of Long Beach, used to be an area of lima bean fields.

Developers built it up so rapidly in the 1950s that Life magazine featured it as one of the first mass-produced suburbs.

Most of these communities are known as Gateway Cities in southeast Los Angeles County: Artesia, which Dutch and Portuguese dairy experts developed into a major dairy center for Southern California; Pico Rivera, which is 89 percent Hispanic; and La Mirada, named by Rand McNally Publishing founder Andrew McNally when he purchased 2,300 acres in the area in the late 1800s. After World War II, Montebello became a center of the large community of displaced Armenians. They built a monument to the Armenian genocide martyrs. In the northern part of Montebello, a few miles from downtown Los Angeles, Southern California Gas Co. has a few dozen wells that produce oil and natural gas; as recently as the 1990s, some leaked onto nearby properties. In Norwalk, Southern California Edison in April 2017 began operation of the world's first hybrid battery and gas turbine power plants that has provided a cleaner alternative during periods of peak demand. Officials of the L.A. Metro have plans to extend their light-rail Green Line from Norwalk to connect it with the transit station at LAX Airport, which could become a commuter alternative to the crowded freeways. In October 2018, Metro took a step toward two potential extensions of the Gold Line light-rail from east L.A. to South El Monte and to Whittier.

The 38th Congressional District encompasses Whittier and some of the Gateway Cities in southeast Los Angeles County. It extends from outside of Monterey Park nearly to Long Beach. It includes Norwalk, the district's largest city, which is 70 percent Hispanic, South El Monte and Montebello. Its small northern tip of Orange County amounts to 3 percent of the district. The 38th is 62 percent Hispanic and solidly Democratic. Hillary Clinton got 67 percent of the vote in 2016.

Gil Cisneros (D)

Elected 2018, 1st term, b. Feb 12, 1971; Los Angeles; George Washington University (DC), B.A., 1994; Regis University, M.B.A., 2002; Brown University (RI), M.A., 2015; Catholic; Married (Jacki Cisneros); 2 children (twins).

Military Career: U.S. Navy 1994-2004

Professional Career: Shipping and Manufacturing Manager, Frito-Lay, 2004-2010.

DC Office: 431 CHOB 20515, 202-225-4111, cisneros.house.gov

State Offices: Fullerton, 714-329-7467.

Committees: *Armed Services*: Military Personnel; Seapower & Projection Forces. *Veterans' Affairs*: Disability Assistance & Memorial Affairs; Health; Oversight & Investigations.

Election Results

Election	Name (Party)	Vote (%)		Cand. Spent	Ind. Exp. Support	Ind. Exp. Oppose
2018 General	Gil Cisneros (D)	126,002	(52%)	$11,932,019	$1,798,112	$6,194,597
	Young Kim (R)	118,391	(48%)	$2,885,758	$685,292	$3,948,460
2018 Primary	Young Kim (R)	30,019	(21%)			
	Gil Cisneros (D)	27,469	(19%)			
	Phil Liberatore (R)	20,257	(14%)			
	Andy Thorburn (D)	12,990	(9%)			
	Shawn Nelson (R)	9,750	(7%)			
	Bob Huff (R)	8,699	(6%)			
	Sam Jammal (D)	7,613	(5%)			
	Mai-Khanh Tran (D)	7,430	(5%)			

Freshman Democrat Gil Cisneros was the first known winner of a lottery to take some of his earnings to finance election to Congress. Following a career in the military, he won a "MegaMillions" drawing, which gave him $266 million. He spent more than $8 million of his winnings on his campaign. In his first bid for political office, he ran for the seat of retiring Republican Rep. Ed

Royce, who chaired the House Foreign Affairs Committee. His contest with Young Kim, a state representative, was one of the closest in the nation.

A native of Torrance California, Cisneros graduated from George Washington University, which he attended on a Navy ROTC scholarship. He got a master's in business administration from Regis University and a master of arts in urban education policy from Brown University. He was a supply officer in the Navy, then worked as a manager at Frito Lay plants. Two weeks after he lost that job, Cisneros drew his lucky lottery ticket at a restaurant in Los Angeles. His lump-sum payment, following taxes, was $165 million. With some of the money, he set up a foundation to help needy young people prepare for college.

A former Republican, Cisneros decided to run for Congress because the Trump administration was "trying to rip health care away from people," he told the Orange County Register. The first round of voting featured seven Republicans, six Democrats and four others. Kim, the Republican frontrunner, had emigrated from Korea and was an aide to Royce; she served four years in the California Assembly.

Another leading Democratic candidate, Andy Thorburn, also became a millionaire after winning the lottery. He loaned his campaign nearly $3 million, which covered most of its spending. Democratic officials feared that a clash between their two lottery winners would poison the well and result in Republicans taking the "top two" spots for the general election. Instead, Kim led the field with 21 percent and Cisneros was runner-up with 19 percent. Politico labeled the contest "the weirdest race in the country."

The general election was mostly standard fare, though Cisneros said during the campaign that "it's time for new leadership" for House Democrats. His broader theme was that he was running to "restore sanity to Washington." He also voiced gratitude to the Navy for giving him an opportunity to "change my life," he told NBC News.

In an October debate before an audience mostly of students at California State University (Fullerton), Kim said that she would be a better representative because she had lived in the area for three decades. "I look like the district, I talk like the district and I fit the district," she said. News reports said that Kim limited her public appearances and media contacts during the campaign.

Cisneros spent a total of $12 million in the campaign. Kim spent a bit less than $3 million, though other Republicans spent a similar amount on her behalf. In an outcome that was not declared for more than a week after the election, Cisneros won, 51%-49%. He had a margin of about 8,000 votes in Los Angeles County. Kim won more narrowly in Orange and San Bernardino counties. His arrival in Congress stirred questions about his ambitions, including his willingness to spend more of his winnings.

CA-39: Northern Orange County   Cook Partisan Voting Index: EVEN

Population		Race and Ethnicity		Income	
Total	726,854	White	30.6%	Median Income	$85,147
Land area (sq. miles)	204	Black	2.3%	District Income Rank	37
Pop/ sq mi	3556	Latino	33.8%	Poverty Rate	10%
Born in State	53.8%	Asian	30.5%	With health insurance	90.9%
		Two or more races	2.3%	Cash public assistance	2.1%
Age Groups		Other	0.7%	Food stamp/SNAP	5.3%
Under 18	21.9%				
18-34	23.7%	**Education**		**Work**	
35-64	40.3%	H.S grad or less	29.4%	White Collar	14.1%
Over 64	14.1%	Some college	29.6%	Sales and Service	41.9%
		College Degree, 4 yr	27.4%	Blue Collar	15%
Military		Post grad	13.6%	Government	13.1%
Veteran/ Active Duty	4.8%				

2012 Pres. Vote	Romney	133,742	(51%)	Obama	124,108	(47%)		
2016 Pres. Vote	Clinton	140,231	(51%)	Trump	116,783	(43%)	Johnson	9,850	(4%)

Fullerton, Yorba Linda: During the Southern California land boom in the 1880s, Massachusetts grain merchants George and Edward Amerige headed west in search of new business opportunities. They went on a duck hunting trip near Anaheim and eventually opened a real estate business in the city. Through negotiations with railroad agent George Fullerton, the Ameriges eventually purchased 430 acres of land for $68,000 and allowed the railroad the right-of-way — provided, of course, that the railway's route include the new town they were developing. Local residents later voted to name the locale Fullerton, and it developed as a prime source of juicy Valencia oranges.

Today, the city is home to California State University, Fullerton, which enrolls about 40,000 students, with the largest business school in the state and a payroll of 15,000 workers. Nearby is affluent Yorba Linda, which has a median household income of $124,000 and is one of the wealthiest cities in the nation. Two Yorba Linda council members were recalled in 2016 following voter protests over a scheduled 380 percent increase in water rates over five years, which the council had approved unanimously; a third board member lost reelection, and a fourth did not seek another term. In 2018, the city elected as mayor 25-year-old Tara Campbell, who grew up locally and studied sports journalism at the University of Southern California before getting into politics. Yorba Linda is the birthplace of President Richard Nixon and the site of his presidential library. Only 40,000 people lived in Orange County in 1913 when Nixon was born; 3.2 million live there today, with a population that is 34 percent Hispanic and 21 percent Asian.

The 39th Congressional District of California is based in northern Orange County and includes the southeast corner of Los Angeles County and the southwest corner of San Bernardino County. About two-thirds of the voters are in Orange County. In San Bernardino, it includes part of Chino, which had been the site of a large youth prison. It also has large meatpacking plants, whose smell can carry across the valley on a windy day. Chino Hills, incorporated in 1991, is full of subdivisions for commuters who battle the heavy traffic on Interstate 5. In Los Angeles County, the 39th includes Diamond Bar, which is 55 percent Asian. The Orange County section takes in parts of Anaheim. Buena Park is a rapidly growing city that has become a center for Korean businesses as well as an entertainment destination — an Orange County version of Koreatown in central L.A. The district is 34 percent Hispanic and 31 percent Asian. Politically, the 39th has included some of the few remaining areas of Los Angeles County that elect Republicans. That has been changing. Hillary Clinton led Donald Trump in the district, 51%-43%, and she ran even better in the L.A. County portion.

Lucille Roybal-Allard (D)

Elected 1992, 14th term, b. Jun 12, 1941; Boyle Heights; California State University, Los Angeles, B.A., 1965; Catholic; Married (Edward T. Allard III); 2 children; 2 stepchildren; 9 grandchildren.

Elected Office: CA Assembly, 1987-1992.

Professional Career: Community relations; Nonprofit Executive.

DC Office: 2083 RHOB 20515, 202-225-1766, Fax: 202-226-0350, roybal-allard.house.gov

State Offices: Commerce, 323-721-8790.

Committees: *Appropriations*: Homeland Security (Chmn); Labor, Health & Human Services, Education & Related Agencies.

Group Ratings

	ADA	ACLU	AFL-CIO	LCV	ITI	COC	HAFA	ACU	CFG	FRC
2018	-	89%	-	100%	-	50%	6%	4%	15%	0%
2017	100%	C	97%	94%	C	38%	C	4%	5%	0%

Almanac Ratings 2017-18

	Economy	Social	Foreign	Composite
Liberal	97%	100%	92%	96%
Conservative	3%	0%	8%	4%

Key Votes of the 115th Congress

1. Obama-care revision	N	5. Family planning regs	N	9. Guantanamo prisoners	Y
2. Tax Cuts	N	6. Body cameras/immigration	Y	10. Ground missiles, limit	Y
3. Omnibus appropriations	N	7. Abortion ban	N	11. Defense Dept. spending	Y
4. Dodd-Frank revision	N	8. Concealed carry	N	12. FISA rules	N

Election Results

Election	Name (Party)	Vote (%)	Cand. Spent	Ind. Exp. Support	Ind. Exp. Oppose
2018 General	Lucille Roybal-Allard (D)............ 93,938	(77%)	$437,629		
	Rodolfo Cortes Barragan (G)........ 27,511	(23%)	$15,939		
2018 Primary	Lucille Roybal-Allard (D)........... 35,636	(80%)			
	Rodolfo Cortes Barragan (G)....... 8,741	(20%)			

Prior winning percentages: 2016 (71%), 2014 (61%), 2012 (59%), 2010 (77%), 2008 (77%), 2006 (77%), 2004 (75%), 2002 (74%), 2000 (85%), 1998 (87%), 1996 (82%), 1994 (82%), 1992 (63%)

Lucille Roybal-Allard, first elected in 1992, was the first Mexican-American woman to be elected to Congress. Immigration policy has been her continuing priority, along with social programs serving the poor. In 2019, as chairwoman of the Appropriations Subcommittee on Homeland Security, she was well-positioned to oversee that federal agency and its funding and to work on immigration issues. Although she has maintained a low profile, her policy niche and her mark as the first Latina to chair an Appropriations subcommittee have elevated her stature in Congress and in the Hispanic community.

Roybal-Allard grew up in the Los Angeles area, the daughter of longtime Democratic Rep. Edward Roybal, who was the first Latino to serve on the Los Angeles City Council and became a founder of the Congressional Hispanic Caucus. She dreamed of a show business career as a teenager and later worked as a department store clerk and for nonprofit organizations. After raising a family — two of her children are lawyers — she followed her father into politics when she was 45 years old. She was elected to the California Assembly in 1986. Six years later he retired from the House, and she ran for the seat in a district that took in much of the territory he had represented for 30 years. Roybal-Allard won easily with 75 percent of the vote in the primary and 63 percent in the general election.

Roybal-Allard has compiled a solidly liberal voting record and was among the Hispanic lawmakers pushing President Barack Obama to act boldly on immigration reform. One session between lawmakers and Obama domestic policy adviser Cecilia Munoz grew so testy that Roybal-Allard walked out, The Washington Post reported in April 2012. She called Obama's reelection a mandate to focus on a comprehensive immigration overhaul. "The truth is that the facts are on our side, the majority of Americans are on our side and the momentum is on our side," she said at the time. But the House Republican majority largely disagreed with her.

With Republican control of Congress and later the presidency, Roybal-Allard's role on immigration became increasingly defensive. When Republicans in March 2015 sought to use the Homeland Security appropriations bill to restrict Obama's executive actions, she became more visible and vocal in what was becoming a fight against increased deportations of those in the country illegally. The Trump administration's overt actions to separate families at the border with Mexico in 2018 were "heartless" policy that was "tearing children from the loving arms of their undocumented parents," she protested. At the time, she worked with other congressional Democrats on legislation to reunify parents and children. The Democratic takeover of the House that year significantly increased their leverage, though it was no guarantee of action so long as Trump retained his approach. Taking charge of her subcommittee at what she called a "deeply consequential moment," Roybal-Allard said that her priorities were to "keep fighting for humane immigration policies that secure our borders, hold our agencies accountable for mistreatment of migrants, keep families together, end child detention, reduce the number of detention beds, and create a path to citizenship."

She has a long history of advocacy for immigrants of all sorts. When Senate Finance Committee Democrats proposed restrictions on illegal immigrants participating in health care programs as part of the 2010 overhaul, she joined a group of Hispanics who succeeded in modifying the provision. She was an original cosponsor in 2001 of the DREAM Act, which now would provide a path to citizenship for college- or military-bound students and also protect that group from deportation. During Obama's final weeks in office, she requested that he issue a blanket pardon to the estimated 750,000 so-called dreamers. The official White House response was, "Only Congress can create legal status for undocumented individuals." In 2018, Roybal-Allard was unsuccessful in working with dissident Republicans to force a vote in the Republican-controlled House. Those prospects improved when Democrats won House control.

Roybal-Allard has pushed for in-state college tuition rates for illegal immigrants. She has filed legislation aimed at raising labor standards and protections for children of migrant farm workers to the same level as occupations outside of agriculture. When Obama in 2014 posthumously gave the Presidential Medal of Freedom to her father, she recalled his success in working on bipartisan terms, including with Republican presidents, on behalf of undocumented immigrants.

On the Appropriations Committee, Roybal-Allard championed a new federal courthouse in Los Angeles. In October 2016, the $350 million building officially opened with 24 courtrooms and chambers for 32 judges. She got a bill signed into law to coordinate federal programs and research on underage drinking, and to fund a media campaign on its dangers.

Roybal-Allard isn't as close to Minority Leader Nancy Pelosi and her inner circle as have been other Democratic women from California, which sometimes has limited her leverage in the House. In 2006, Roybal-Allard seconded the nomination of Steny Hoyer of Maryland for majority leader, in opposition to Pelosi's preferred candidate, John Murtha of Pennsylvania. Hoyer won the contest, so Roybal-Allard has retained a friend in high places. She served with both Hoyer and Pelosi on Appropriations.

At home in 2012, under the state's new top-two, all-party primary rules, Roybal-Allard found herself with a Democratic challenger, college instructor David Sanchez. He held her to 59 percent of the vote, her lowest ever. They faced each other again in 2014, when she won, 61%-39%. Sanchez did not report spending any campaign money in either contest. Since then, Roybal-Allard has had no major-party opposition and her victory margins have returned to the comfort zone. She will have this seat as long as she wants it. At age 77 when she gained her subcommittee chairmanship, other calculations on how long to remain may include that she is the seventh-ranked Democrat on the Appropriations Committee and that those more senior members include some who are younger, as well as women.

CA-40: Eastern Los Angeles

Cook Partisan Voting Index: D+33

Population		Race and Ethnicity		Income	
Total	714,946	White	4.5%	Median Income	$43,499
Land area (sq. miles)	58	Black	4.6%	District Income Rank	392
Pop/ sq mi	12392.9	Latino	87.6%	Poverty Rate	25.2%
Born in State	54.5%	Asian	2.4%	With health insurance	79.7%
		Two or more races	0.4%	Cash public assistance	6.6%
Age Groups		Other	0.4%	Food stamp/SNAP	18.6%
Under 18	29.3%				
18-34	27.3%	**Education**		**Work**	
35-64	35.2%	H.S grad or less	70.2%	White Collar	8.2%
Over 64	8.2%	Some college	20.3%	Sales and Service	46.5%
		College Degree, 4 yr	7%	Blue Collar	37.4%
Military		Post grad	2.5%	Government	8.8%
Veteran/ Active Duty	1.7%				

2012 Pres. Vote	Obama	115,637	(82%)	Romney	23,446	(17%)		
2016 Pres. Vote	Clinton	135,472	(82%)	Trump	21,077	(13%)	Stein	3,805	(2%)

Bell Gardens, Downey: East Los Angeles is a piece of Latin America transplanted to California. Hard-working immigrants from Mexico and Central and South America come to find affordable housing, doubling and tripling up with other families in places that are close enough to drive an old car to work in factories and warehouses south and east of downtown Los Angeles. The Gold Line extension of L.A.'s transit agency made their commutes considerably easier by bringing light rail service to the area. This part of Los Angeles includes the 1940s working-class suburb of Huntington Park, with its shopping strip on the wide Pacific Boulevard, plus Bell Gardens, Downey and Maywood, all of which are now predominantly Latino. Each calls itself a "sanctuary city" for illegal immigrants, as do both the city and county of Los Angeles.

Downey is home to Raytheon's Public Safety Regional Technology Center, which won a contract to upgrade Los Angeles County's emergency dispatch system. In the 1950s, the existence of an airplane production plant that built 13,000 airplanes for World War II led to what became the North American Rockwell company (purchased later by Boeing) and the early epicenter of space flight, including the Apollo program that sent men to the moon. In more cosmic terms, Downey is home to the world's oldest surviving McDonald's hamburgers site; it was started by Dick and Mac McDonald in 1953 and featured golden arches. Maywood, which is little more than one square mile, suffered from a municipal corruption scandal that forced it to lay off all but one of its employees in 2010 and has struggled to reorganize its governance. Somewhat more affluent Bellflower, once a prime shopping area, has made a comeback with multiple shopping centers.

These are communities in the 40th Congressional District of California, radiating south from East Los Angeles and downtown L.A. Bisecting much of the district is the concrete-lined Los Angeles River. Environmentalists have pushed the city for years to clean it up and return it to a more natural condition, with adjacent parkland and bicycle paths, while preserving its flood-control assets. In November 2016, county voters overwhelmingly approved a $1 billion plan for a restoration that was designed to dig up the cement and restore the river along a 19-mile stretch between Vernon and Long Beach, and create an urban greenway from Glendale to downtown with additional land the city had purchased. With state aid of $100 million that the legislature approved in July 2017 to initiate early improvements, local and state officials have continued to explore options.

The 40th District also takes in Paramount, where local businessmen Frank and Lawrence Zamboni invented refrigeration technology for the dairy industry and the Zamboni ice-resurfacing machine for skating rinks. With an 88 percent (and climbing) Latino population, and 41 percent foreign-born, this has become the most Hispanic district in California. Its 82 percent vote for Hillary Clinton in 2016 was only her fourth-best district in the L.A. area.

Mark Takano (D)

Elected 2012, 4th term, b. Dec 10, 1960; Riverside; Harvard College (MA), A.B., 1983; School of Education, University of California, Riverside, M.F.A., 2010; Methodist; Single.

Elected Office: Board of Trustees, Riverside Commissioner Col. District, 1990-2012, President, 1992, 1997-198, 2005-2006.

Professional Career: Teacher, Rialto Unified School District, 1988-2013; Substitute teacher, Boston, 1984-1985.

DC Office: 420 CHOB 20515, 202-225-2305, Fax: 202-225-7018, takano.house.gov

State Offices: Riverside, 951-222-0203.

Committees: *Education & Labor*: Higher Education & Workforce Investment; Workforce Protections; *Veterans' Affairs (Chmn)*.

Group Ratings

	ADA	ACLU	AFL-CIO	LCV	ITI	COC	HAFA	ACU	CFG	FRC
2018	-	93%	-	97%	-	50%	4%	4%	15%	0%
2017	100%	C	95%	100%	C	38%	C	0%	0%	0%

Almanac Ratings 2017-18

	Economy	Social	Foreign	Composite
Liberal	99%	98%	100%	99%
Conservative	1%	2%	0%	1%

Key Votes of the 115th Congress

1. Obama-care revision	N	5. Family planning regs	N	9. Guantanamo prisoners	Y
2. Tax Cuts	N	6. Body cameras/immigration	Y	10. Ground missiles, limit	Y
3. Omnibus appropriations	N	7. Abortion ban	N	11. Defense Dept. spending	N
4. Dodd-Frank revision	N	8. Concealed carry	N	12. FISA rules	N

Election Results

Election	Name (Party)	Vote (%)	Cand. Spent	Ind. Exp. Support	Ind. Exp. Oppose
2018 General	Mark Takano (D)............................... 108,227	(65%)	$731,769		
	Aja Smith (R).................................... 58,021	(35%)	$41,795		
2018 Primary	Mark Takano (D)................................. 45,585	(59%)			
	Aja Smith (R).................................... 32,360	(42%)			

Prior winning percentages: 2016 (65%), 2014 (57%), 2012 (59%)

Mark Takano, a Democrat elected in 2012 after narrowly losing an election 20 years earlier, has begun to make an impact as a committee chairman — a position he called "the honor of my lifetime" following a long and winding quest for congressional influence. In his relatively bipartisan work on veterans' issues, he has taken an interest in strengthening operations within the Veterans Affairs Department rather than pushing for more health care options outside the VA. Takano has brought his experience as an inner-city schoolteacher, and his dexterity with social media. He is the first openly gay person of a racial minority — "gaysian," as he jokingly describes himself -- to hold a seat in Congress.

Born and raised in Riverside, Takano grew up in a self-described "typical Japanese-American family" with a strong emphasis on education, self-reliance and public service. In his youth, he played junior football. He was fascinated by politics and remembers watching the televised Watergate hearings of the House Judiciary Committee, entranced by Democratic Rep. Barbara Jordan of Texas. He got his bachelor's in government from Harvard University. He was planning to go to law school but decided instead to try teaching, taking a job as a substitute teacher in the Boston area. He returned to school to get a teaching certificate and took a job as an English and social studies teacher at the Rialto Unified School District. In 1990, Takano was elected to the Riverside Community College District's Board of Trustees. He became the board's longest-serving member, with two terms as president.

Takano made a bid for an open House seat in 1992 but lost to Republican Ken Calvert in one of the closest elections in California history. In a 1994 rematch, Calvert defeated him by a double-digit margin. Takano jokingly calls the ensuing time his "wilderness years," when he traveled to foreign countries while continuing to teach. In 2012, he ran in the all-party primary in the redrawn 41st District, which leaned Democratic. Republican John Tavaglione, a veteran Riverside County supervisor, got 45 percent of the vote to 37 percent for Takano. Tavaglione had worked with Democrats in Riverside County and he took some moderate positions, declining to sign conservative activist Grover Norquist's "no new taxes" pledge. Takano ran as a populist, attacking lobbyists and oil and insurance companies. In the much higher turnout in November, Takano won 59%-41%.

Takano has cited his teaching experience in his work on the renamed Education and Labor Committee. He worked with other House Democrats to form a Public Education Caucus, which protested the lack of public school experience for Education Secretary Betsy DeVos. In the minority, Takano made creative use of social media and his communications skills to score rhetorical points and attempt to influence Washington debates. He used a red pen to grade a letter that House Republicans had privately circulated among themselves about immigration. He gave the letter an "F," scrawled multiple comments in red, advised the GOP members to "See me after work," and posted the results on his Tumblr page.

On the Veterans' Affairs Committee, Takano spent six months as the acting ranking minority member after Democratic Rep. Corrine Brown of Florida was indicted and forced to step aside in July 2016. In 2017, he yielded the position to Rep. Tim Walz of Minnesota, who was more senior in the House. When Walz was elected governor, Takano was the obvious choice for committee chairman. He pledged to retain the panel's commitment to bipartisanship, rejected "ideological agendas" and said he would give the VA "the tools needed to meet these challenges head-on," referring to the diversity and shifting demographics among veterans. In 2018, he was the lead Democratic sponsor of a bill to extend sick-leave benefits to wounded warriors working in medical positions at the VA. "A lot of what is good for veterans is a template or platform for us to solve broader social challenges" like homelessness and expanding health care access, he told the Riverside Press-Enterprise.

On other issues, Takano joined a delegation to Cuba in October 2017 that encouraged LGBT rights during meetings with officials. He criticized the decision of President Donald Trump to reinstate travel and trade restrictions on the island. "My sense is the Cubans are very much eager to cooperate in unprecedented ways," he told The Washington Blade. At home, he said that Trump's policy to separate immigrant families at the border with Mexico "echoed my family's World War II internment," which had lasting damage. He added that Trump and administration officials were "lying when they claim to be merely following the law." In 2017, he was a co-founder of the Advanced Energy Storage Caucus to promote public understanding of gaining better access to reliable and affordable electric power.

In 2014, Takano faced a competitive challenger. Steve Adams, a Republican councilman from Riverside who called himself "apolitical" and said that an increase in the minimum wage would cost jobs. Takano outspent Adams more than 5-to-1, and won 57%-43%. In his subsequent reelections, he got nearly two-thirds of the vote in perfunctory contests.

CA-41: Inland Empire   Cook Partisan Voting Index: D+12

Population		Race and Ethnicity		Income	
Total	747,233	White	23.4%	Median Income	$60,629
Land area (sq. miles)	317	Black	8.8%	District Income Rank	172
Pop/ sq mi	2360.6	Latino	59.6%	Poverty Rate	17.7%
Born in State	62.6%	Asian	5.5%	With health insurance	85.5%
		Two or more races	2%	Cash public assistance	4.5%
Age Groups		Other	0.8%	Food stamp/SNAP	13.3%
Under 18	27.3%				
18-34	28.7%	**Education**		**Work**	
35-64	34.9%	H.S grad or less	52.4%	White Collar	9.1%
Over 64	9.1%	Some college	30.7%	Sales and Service	44%
		College Degree, 4 yr	10.6%	Blue Collar	31.1%
Military		Post grad	6.3%	Government	15.2%
Veteran/ Active Duty	5.3%				

2012 Pres. Vote	Obama	114,040	(62%)	Romney	67,314	(36%)		
2016 Pres. Vote	Clinton	126,197	(61%)	Trump	68,526	(33%)	Johnson	6,847	(3%)
	Stein	4,219	(2%)					

Central and Western Riverside, Moreno Valley: Riverside was a sleepy town of 34,000 people, a couple hours' drive from Los Angeles, when Richard and Pat Nixon were married there in 1940 at the Mission Inn, built in 1876 and, with its bell towers, fountains and stained-glass windows, an inspired setting for a wedding. Riverside was not much larger, with 46,000 people, when Ronald and Nancy Reagan spent their honeymoon at the Mission Inn a dozen years later. Riverside then was a citrus center, a market town amid orange groves, where the local agricultural college developed, among other things, the navel orange. Today the Mission Inn is again doing business, after being shuttered from 1985 to 1992, but Riverside has changed completely. The city has grown to 328,000 people. Riverside County has about 2.4 million people, nearly a quadrupling of its population since 1980. This has been a boom part of California, where modest-income families with jobs in the L.A. region found new houses in inexpensive developments and small businesses found steady markets.

The Great Recession halted that progress. Since then, the local economy has begun to turn around, though the area has struggled with economic development. Riverside, the fourth-largest county in California, had the largest population gain in the state in 2018. Also that year, Ontario Ranch was the first "gigabit" community in southern California, with technologically "smart" and more affordable homes. The University of California, Riverside in 2017 graduated its first class of medical students, following a lengthy struggle to secure accreditation because of questions about the school's long-term funding. Riverside County has had a shortage of doctors. A 42-million-square-foot warehouse by World Logistics Center, which would be the largest in the nation and create perhaps 20,000 jobs, has faced legal problems in gaining approval of permits for its proposed 40 million square foot industrial center on farmland in the eastern Moreno Valley. Courts invalidated earlier development and environmental impact plans.

The 41st District includes western parts of Riverside County and all of Riverside city, and the towns of Moreno Valley and Perris. Of the three House districts in the county, this is the most urban. Politically, it leans comfortably Democratic, but less so than Los Angeles or San Francisco urban districts. In 2016, Hillary Clinton defeated Donald Trump, 61%-33%.

Ken Calvert (R)

Elected 1992, 14th term, b. Jun 08, 1953; Corona; Chaffey Community College (CA), A.A., 1973; San Diego State University, B.A., 1975; Protestant - Unspecified Christian; Divorced.

Professional Career: Restaurant owner, 1975-1980; Real estate broker, 1980-1992; Chairman, Riverside County Repub. Party, 1984-1988.

DC Office: 2205 RHOB 20515, 202-225-1986, Fax: 202-225-2004, calvert.house.gov

State Offices: Corona, 951-277-0042.

Committees: *Appropriations*: Defense (RMM); Energy & Water Development & Related Agencies.

Group Ratings

	ADA	ACLU	AFL-CIO	LCV	ITI	COC	HAFA	ACU	CFG	FRC
2018	-	4%	-	6%	-	92%	50%	76%	49%	100%
2017	0%	C	13%	6%	C	93%	C	78%	68%	100%

Almanac Ratings 2017-18

	Economy	Social	Foreign	Composite
Liberal	3%	0%	0%	1%
Conservative	97%	100%	100%	99%

Key Votes of the 115th Congress

1. Obama-care revision	Y	5. Family planning regs	Y	9. Guantanamo prisoners	N
2. Tax Cuts	Y	6. Body cameras/immigration	N	10. Ground missiles, limit	N
3. Omnibus appropriations	Y	7. Abortion ban	Y	11. Defense Dept. spending	Y
4. Dodd-Frank revision	Y	8. Concealed carry	Y	12. FISA rules	Y

Election Results

Election	Name (Party)	Vote (%)		Cand. Spent	Ind. Exp. Support	Ind. Exp. Oppose
2018 General	Ken Calvert (R)	131,040	(56%)			
	Julia Peacock (D)	100,892	(44%)	$144,244		
2018 Primary	Ken Calvert (R)	70,289	(61%)			
	Julia Peacock (D)	30,237	(26%)			
	Norman Quintero (D)	9,540	(8%)			

Prior winning percentages: 2016 (59%), 2014 (66%), 2012 (61%), 2010 (56%), 2008 (51%), 2006 (60%), 2004 (62%), 2002 (64%), 2000 (74%), 1998 (56%), 1996 (55%), 1994 (55%), 1992 (47%)

Ken Calvert, a Republican first elected in 1992, has been an ally of GOP leaders and one of the few Californians in the party with persistent influence in Congress. He holds a plum spot on the Appropriations Committee, where he chaired a subcommittee that was at the center of frequent conflicts with Democrats. In 2019, he became the ranking minority member of the Defense Subcommittee, which has a more bipartisan history.

Calvert grew up in Corona. While at San Diego State University, where he majored in economics, he was a congressional intern at the Senate Watergate hearings of 1973. Later, he ran the family restaurant back home and, in 1980, got into the commercial real estate business. In 1982, at age 29, he ran for Congress in a district that included almost all of Riverside County and lost a nine-candidate primary to Al McCandless by 868 votes. In 1992, he ran in a new district and won the GOP primary with 28 percent of the vote. His Democratic opponent was Mark Takano, a middle-school teacher who had the support of teachers' unions and Japanese Americans. Calvert beat Takano by 519 votes (Takano was elected to represent the neighboring 41st District in 2012.) Three decades after Calvert first ran, the booming Riverside County has three entire districts in Congress and a small corner of a fourth.

Soon after he was elected, Calvert ran into trouble at home when the Riverside Press-Enterprise reported that he had been stopped by police with a prostitute in his car. Calvert apologized and said that he was upset because his wife had divorced him the month before and his father had recently committed suicide. His opponents in 1994 used the incident against him. Calvert won the primary 51%-49%, with only an 884-vote margin, against business professor Joseph Khoury. Takano, running again in the general election, ran an ad that accused Calvert of "flagrant womanizing." But with the Republican tide that year, Calvert won 55%-38%.

Calvert has compiled a moderate-to-conservative voting record. He broke with most GOP colleagues in 2008 by supporting housing finance legislation, citing his district's high foreclosure rate. He has been a major backer of E-Verify, an online system he helped enact that allows employers to confirm the immigration status of new hires. Critics have faulted the system's accuracy, while farm groups have complained it has hurt their efforts to recruit workers. In 2018, he called for steps to make E-Verify mandatory for job seekers. He called for lie-detector tests for refugees attempting to enter the United States from Syria or Iraq. He has regularly filed a bill to cut off funds to local governments that style themselves as "sanctuary cities" and resist federal efforts to deport undocumented immigrants who have been jailed. Democrats, he wrote for Fox News in May 2018, "protect criminal illegal immigrants" over public safety.

After spending his early years on the Armed Services Committee, Calvert in 2007 snagged a coveted seat on Appropriations, where he aggressively sought spending earmarks for his district. He took over in 2013 the plum position as chairman of the Subcommittee on Interior and the Environment. He said he was interested in finding ways to strengthen domestic energy production on federal lands. Calvert has taken special interest in his constituents' demands for funds for wildfire fighting and prevention programs. To encourage the building of more infrastructure projects, he has backed legislation to streamline highway construction timelines. In an unusual instance of his opposing President Donald Trump, Calvert worked with Democrats in 2018 to continue support for an Interior Department program to create a smart-phone app to provide early warning of an earthquake.

In 2019, with Republicans in the minority, Calvert took the top GOP slot on the Defense Subcommittee. Promising to work closely with Democratic Rep. Pete Visclosky of Indiana, the subcommittee chairman, Calvert said that — even with the boost in Pentagon spending during the Trump's first two years in office — "we still have much more to do" to improve readiness of forces, upgrade equipment and respond to new challenges in cyber and in space. He also took a seat on the House Select Intelligence Committee.

In 2003, Calvert abandoned his 1992 pledge to serve only 12 years in Congress. He was reelected easily. Campaign opponents have called into question his ethics. In 2006, the Los Angeles Times reported that he and his real estate partner had bought a four-acre tract for $550,000, then sold it less than a year later for $985,000, after Calvert secured an $8 million spending earmark for expansion of a nearby freeway interchange. Calvert denied wrongdoing, noting that it was not illegal for a member of Congress to make personal investments.

In 2008, Calvert had a close contest against Democrat Bill Hedrick, a Corona-Norco school board member who was poorly funded and had no national party help but benefited from Calvert's ethics problems. Calvert won by a little more than 6,000 votes, 51.2%-48.8%. Hedrick returned for a rematch in 2010. This time, he got help from the Democratic Congressional Campaign Committee, which ran ads slamming Calvert for voting against the economic stimulus bill, children's health legislation and other initiatives. But they were two years late. Calvert won 56%-44, spending more than $1.5 million to Hedrick's $493,000.

He has twice been challenged by Tim Sheridan, a lawyer and official of the National Treasury Employees Union. Calvert got 66 percent in 2014 but was held to a 59%-41% win in 2016, when turnout more than doubled from two years earlier. In 2018, Calvert was challenged by Julie Peacock, a high school teacher and first-time candidate who called for more oversight of the Trump administration. She said that Calvert was out of touch and called him a "murderer" because of his opposition to gun control. Peacock spent less than one-tenth of Calvert $1.5 million, but held him to a relatively close 56%-44% win. Democrats, who gained seven House seats in California in 2018, might have missed an opportunity to give Calvert more of a scare.

CA-42: Inland Empire

Cook Partisan Voting Index: R+9

Population		Race and Ethnicity		Income	
Total	777,599	White	42.9%	Median Income	$77,297
Land area (sq. miles)	936	Black	5.2%	District Income Rank	63
Pop/ sq mi	830.8	Latino	38.5%	Poverty Rate	10.7%
Born in State	61%	Asian	9%	With health insurance	90.2%
		Two or more races	3.4%	Cash public assistance	2.7%
Age Groups		Other	0.8%	Food stamp/SNAP	7.5%
Under 18	27.2%				
18-34	22.9%	**Education**		**Work**	
35-64	38.4%	H.S grad or less	38.6%	White Collar	11.5%
Over 64	11.5%	Some college	36.3%	Sales and Service	43.9%
		College Degree, 4 yr	16.5%	Blue Collar	20.6%
Military		Post grad	8.6%	Government	15.6%
Veteran/ Active Duty	8.4%				

2012 Pres. Vote	Romney	131,438	(57%)	Obama	96,212	(41%)			
2016 Pres. Vote	Trump	143,175	(53%)	Clinton	111,103	(41%)	Johnson	9,587	(4%)

Corona, West Riverside: The fastest growth in the Los Angeles metropolitan area over the past 25 years has been in the Inland Empire, at the eastern end of the Los Angeles Basin. Mostly orange groves and dairy farms a few decades ago, this territory is now the site of personal upward mobility and ethnic and cultural diversity. The main ingredient of the growth has been small entrepreneurial businesses, many of them started by people with Asian or Latino immigrant backgrounds. One locale that has been strong is Murrieta. It doubled in population from 2000 to 2010, though growth has slowed since then. Its families are mostly young, with a 29 percent Hispanic share that is below the state average. In an example of the need for additional public services, plus the shifting political culture, voters in some of these areas — including those in Murrieta, who dedicated the revenue to fire-fighting -- approved in November 2018 a one-cent increase in the sales tax. An illustration of the increasingly high-end life style in parts of Riverside County was the ambition of developers to open in June 2019 a new set of movie theaters, which will include the largest indoor screen in California. To respond to the acute shortage of housing, the county board in December 2017 approved plans for new villages in Nuevo, with more than 8,700 homes. Environmental groups sought to half the project.

Despite occasional tensions since World War II, this area has styled itself as a welcoming destination for legal immigrants. That mindset became more complex with the illegal immigration problems on the southern border. In July 2014, local protesters surrounded and forced back three buses filled with immigration detainees who had been sent to Riverside County from Texas and were approaching a local Border Patrol station. The local mayor said the protesters were worried whether the town could safely house the detainees. Border problems continued in June 2016, when law-enforcement authorities in Corona targeted illegal drugs and firearms trafficking from a Mexican prison gang. In August 2018, the city council in Murrieta went on the record seeking repeal of the California law permitting sanctuaries to protect undocumented immigrants.

The 42nd Congressional District is based in Riverside County, which is the largest part of the Inland Empire. On the western side of Riverside, it takes in the towns of Corona, Norco, Murrieta, Lake Elsinore and the new city of Menifee. The 42nd is the largest land mass of the 21 House districts in the L.A. metro area. The district has been solidly Republican, with a 38 percent Hispanic population. Donald Trump led Hillary Clinton, 53%-41%, one of seven districts in California where he had a majority of the vote.

Maxine Waters (D)

Elected 1990, 15th term, b. Aug 15, 1938; St. Louis, MO; California State University, Los Angeles, B.A., 1970; Christian Church; Married (Amb. Sidney Williams); 2 children; 2 grandchildren.

Elected Office: CA Assembly, 1977-1991.

Professional Career: Head Start teacher, 1966; Deputy, City Councilman David Cunningham, 1973-1976.

DC Office: 2221 RHOB 20515, 202-225-2201, Fax: 202-225-7854, waters.house.gov

State Offices: Los Angeles, 323-757-8900.

Committees: *Financial Services (Chmn).*

Group Ratings

	ADA	ACLU	AFL-CIO	LCV	ITI	COC	HAFA	ACU	CFG	FRC
2018	-	89%	-	94%	-	55%	4%	4%	12%	0%
2017	100%	C	100%	94%	C	36%	C	0%	0%	0%

Almanac Ratings 2017-18

	Economy	Social	Foreign	Composite
Liberal	98%	98%	92%	96%
Conservative	2%	2%	8%	4%

Key Votes of the 115th Congress

1. Obama-care revision	N	5. Family planning regs	N	9. Guantanamo prisoners	Y
2. Tax Cuts	N	6. Body cameras/immigration	Y	10. Ground missiles, limit	Y
3. Omnibus appropriations	Y	7. Abortion ban	N	11. Defense Dept. spending	Y
4. Dodd-Frank revision	N	8. Concealed carry	N	12. FISA rules	N

Election Results

Election	Name (Party)	Vote (%)	Cand. Spent	Ind. Exp. Support	Ind. Exp. Oppose
2018 General	Maxine Waters (D)	152,272 (78%)	$1,125,096		$1,037,633
	Omar Navarro (R)	43,780 (22%)	$992,451		
2018 Primary	Maxine Waters (D)	63,908 (72%)			
	Omar Navarro (R)	12,522 (14%)			
	Frank T. DeMartini (R)	6,156 (7%)			

Prior winning percentages: 2016 (76%), 2014 (71%), 2012 (71%), 2010 (79%), 2008 (83%), 2006 (84%), 2004 (81%), 2002 (78%), 2000 (87%), 1998 (89%), 1996 (86%), 1994 (78%), 1992 (483%), 1990 (79%)

Maxine Waters, a Democrat first elected in 1990, has gained new influence as chair of the Financial Services Committee. For years, she was known chiefly for her incendiary rhetoric and a protracted ethics controversy involving her husband. That changed in 2013 when she settled into a substantive role as ranking Democrat on Financial Services, where she has been a harsh critic of big banks and sought expanded aid for low-income groups. More recently, she and President Donald Trump have directed harsh invective toward each other.

Waters grew up in St. Louis, one of 13 children. She has said, "I know all about welfare. I remember the social workers peeking in the refrigerator and under the beds." She moved to California in 1961, worked in a garment factory and raised two children. Waters got a sociology degree at California State University, Los Angeles, and became an assistant Head Start teacher after the Watts riot of 1965. She likes to call herself "The Organizer" and has shown the capacity to draw big supportive crowds to her protests over the years. From 1973 to 1976, she worked on the staff of a Los Angeles city councilman. She has held elected office since 1976, when she won a seat in the California Assembly. She helped pass legislation divesting state pension funds from apartheid South Africa, setting up a child abuse prevention training program, and prohibiting police strip searches for nonviolent offenses. When Democratic Rep. Augustus Hawkins retired in 1990 after 28 years in the House, Waters was the obvious choice for the seat and won it easily. Her husband, Sidney Williams, a former professional football player and Mercedes-Benz salesman, became President Bill Clinton's ambassador to the Bahamas.

Having grown up in poverty and under Jim Crow, Waters believes fervently in federal aid for the poor and for racial preferences to help blacks overcome the legacies of slavery, segregation and discrimination. She has favored big reductions in defense spending in favor of domestic spending. She voted against the Gulf War resolution in 1991 and was a staunch opponent a decade later of the Iraq war as well as the subsequent troop buildup in Afghanistan. She has brought an intensity bordering on fury to her work. Her anger is a political weapon she uses shrewdly to get both publicity and results. "I don't have time to be polite," Waters says.

Waters isn't afraid to step on toes. When House Appropriations Chairman David Obey of Wisconsin sought to ban spending earmarks named after members in 2009, she heatedly confronted him over his refusal to fund her request for the Maxine Waters Employment Preparation Center. Obey eventually prevailed. She pushed for federal loan guarantees to cities for economic and infrastructure development. Waters successfully sponsored an amendment to triple spending to erase the debts of poor nations, mostly in Africa. She has sponsored bills to repeal mandatory minimum sentences for drug crimes, and charges that the war on drugs has created "apartheid" in the United States.

She was an occasional thorn in the side of President Barack Obama, starting with her endorsement of Hillary Clinton during the 2008 Democratic presidential primaries. She and other Congressional Black Caucus members held up a vote on the financial services overhaul in November 2009 because they said the administration wasn't addressing the needs of segments of the black community. Waters repeatedly discussed the need to "educate" people advising Obama and she encouraged him to fight harder when negotiating with the GOP on budget matters. "The Congressional Black Caucus loves the president, too. We're supportive of the president, but we're getting tired," she said in 2011. "The unemployment is unconscionable. We don't know what the strategy is."

On the Financial Services Committee, she has a long history of working to address housing issues. When Rep. Barney Frank retired in 2012, Waters succeeded him as the ranking member, giving her a larger platform to push her pro-regulatory, pro-consumer agenda. With Democrats in the minority, she sponsored measures to overhaul discredited housing finance programs, expand affordable housing and aid local governments to rehabilitate foreclosed homes. In 2016, Congress enacted a bill that included her provision to expand the use of rental vouchers for Section 8 housing. She harshly criticized the Federal Reserve Board and big bankers for their financing practices and tight credit. During a 2016 committee hearing, she responded to admissions by Wells Fargo of its wrongdoing in creating 2 million fake accounts by urging the break-up of the bank. "It's too big to manage," she said.

Waters skillfully exploited divisions between conservative Republicans and big business, Politico reported in 2014. She had become "a sympathetic ally for corporate America" — notably on extension of the Export-Import Bank, which makes loans to businesses involved in trade. Her position has given her the opportunity to work with various interests, she said, "even if you've never worked with them before and even if you're never going to work with them again." In response to industry concerns about unintended consequences, she helped to tweak changes in flood-insurance regulations. Waters remained a regulatory stalwart, as when she filed a bill in 2015 to set limits on the Securities and Exchange Commission before it can grant waivers to those she called "bad actors" who have previously pled guilty to fraudulent activity. She also retained her focus on broader economic conflicts, including income inequality. In 2014, she returned to her home town of St. Louis for the funeral of Michael Brown, whose shooting by police sparked riots in nearby Ferguson. She joined the community in "calling for justice."

In taking the gavel at Financial Services, Waters said that she would end the rollback of banking regulations, though she said that she wanted to work with House Republicans. She said that she demanded accountability by public and private interests. "She is going to make a lot of powerful people uncomfortable," according to an analysis by the Vox website following the election. Waters planned extensive oversight, from the need for more housing to Trump's finances, including his business ties to Deutsche Bank. She was especially interested in regulatory cutbacks at the Consumer Financial Protection Bureau and what she called its "anti-consumer actions." "I am not interested in simply having a fight," she told the Los Angeles Times. "But I won't let anybody run over me."

Waters' personal finances have become the target of watchdogs. In 2005, the liberal-leaning Citizens for Responsibility and Ethics in Washington criticized the fact that members of her family had made more than $1 million in eight years doing business with companies, candidates and causes that she had helped in her official capacity. Her reply: "They do their business and I do mine." In 2009, news stories raised the issue of whether Waters had urged federal regulators to give favorable treatment to a bank in which she and her husband had a financial interest. Regulators told The New York Times that Waters in 2008 helped set up a meeting with bankers, including one whose chief executive asked them for $50 million in government bailout funds. Waters defended her actions, saying, "I have been an outspoken advocate for minority communities and businesses in California and nationally for decades."

The House Ethics Committee charged her with three counts of breaking House rules barring lawmakers from taking actions in their own financial interest. Hoping to seize political advantage, Republicans clamored to have ethics trials of Waters and Charles Rangel of New York held before the November 2010 elections. Her trial was postponed when committee leaders cited the discovery of additional evidence. Waters contended that the delay proved that the case against her was weak. "I have been denied basic due process," she said. In September 2012, the committee announced that Waters would not be charged with violating House rules.

During the ceremony to count the electoral votes for the 2016 election, she sought unsuccessfully to get a senator to join her in objecting to certification of the vote and forcing debate about the victory of Donald Trump. "I don't honor him, I don't respect him and I don't want to be involved with him," she said in explaining her decision not to attend Trump's inauguration. In her frequent objections to his policies, Waters was an early advocate of impeachment and she said that Trump should resign. On Twitter and at his political rallies, Trump responded by referring to her as "an extraordinarily low IQ person." Even some House Democrats objected when Waters urged activists, when they see administration officials, to "tell them they're not welcome anymore, anywhere."

Waters was the frequent target of angry rhetoric and threats by foes outside of Congress. Two weeks before the 2018 election, investigators uncovered bombs that had been sent to her office through the mail. "I ain't scared," she responded.

Waters has remained a force to be reckoned with in L.A. politics and she has been reelected without difficulty. The rising Hispanic percentage in her district has become the biggest threat to her career. But even with more than twice as many Hispanics than blacks, she has had no trouble keeping this seat. In 2018, she faced an unusual — though ineffectual — challenge from Omar Narvarro, a 29-year-old Republican activist and part-time salesman at a Target department store, who echoed some of Trump's rhetoric about Waters. Navarro spent an unusually large $1 million, some of which he took as salary payments. He lost, 78%-22%.

CA-43: Southern and Western L.A.   **Cook Partisan Voting Index: D+29**

Population		Race and Ethnicity		Income	
Total	726,570	White	14.4%	Median Income	$52,806
Land area (sq. miles)	72	Black	22.2%	District Income Rank	260
Pop/ sq mi	10087	Latino	47.1%	Poverty Rate	18.9%
Born in State	54.2%	Asian	12.7%	With health insurance	85.7%
		Two or more races	2.7%	Cash public assistance	4.7%
Age Groups		Other	1%	Food stamp/SNAP	11.5%
Under 18	24.1%				
18-34	25.8%	**Education**		**Work**	
35-64	38.5%	H.S grad or less	45%	White Collar	11.6%
Over 64	11.6%	Some college	29.4%	Sales and Service	48.1%
		College Degree, 4 yr	17.6%	Blue Collar	21.1%
Military		Post grad	7.9%	Government	12.6%
Veteran/ Active Duty	4.1%				

2012 Pres. Vote	Obama	173,342	(78%)	Romney	44,485	(20%)		
2016 Pres. Vote	Clinton	183,434	(78%)	Trump	39,039	(17%)	Johnson	5,546	(2%)
	Stein	4,637	(2%)					

Inglewood, Torrance: In the years just after World War II, Los Angeles was the fastest-growing metropolitan area in America. LAX, today the world's fifth-busiest airport, with eight central terminals, was then a small airfield amid open country. The mile-square grids east, north and south of the airport were just filling up with subdivisions. Inglewood, east of the airport around the Hollywood Park racetrack, attracted the young families of people who had moved to Los Angeles during the war — workers in the giant aircraft factories or in the small factories that every day were making California less dependent on goods from back East. In Hawthorne, near what has become the southeast corner of the airport, future celebrities were growing up — Sonny Bono, the Beach Boys and, during her early years, Marilyn Monroe. Gardena, east of Hawthorne, was known for its legal poker clubs and its Japanese-American residents, back from the wartime internment camps. Hawthorne had been home to a big Northrop Grumman plant. Now, Space Exploration Technologies (Space X) is based in Hawthorne and is sending cargo shipments to the International Space Station. In December 2018, Elon Musk unveiled his Boring Company's test transportation tunnel — 1.4 miles under the Space X headquarters -- which was designed as a prototype for harried L.A. freeway drivers.

The City Council in 2003 officially renamed the community South Los Angeles in an effort to rid it of the "South Central" stigma of gang wars and race riots. In the days of residential segregation, much of this area was the home of Los Angeles' black community, its numbers greatly expanded by migration from the South during and after the war. As the nation's focus on civil rights receded in the 1980s and 1990s, this part of Los Angeles continued to deal with racial tensions and chronic economic problems. An almost bankrupt Inglewood Unified School District was given $55 million as part of an emergency state takeover in 2012; six years later, the Los Angeles Times reported, the school district continued to face a budget crisis and buildings in disrepair.

Inglewood has a brighter future as the location of the lavish 300-acre stadium and shopping complex that is scheduled to open in 2020 as the home for both the former St. Louis Rams and San Diego Chargers of the National Football League. The stadium has been designated as a site for the 2028 Olympics, including the opening ceremonies, plus the 2022 Super Bowl. On what had been the home of Hollywood Park, the privately owned and multi-purpose stadium, with a price tag of perhaps $5 billion, has become a new model for NFL owners seeking to build ever-larger and more remunerative palaces. It has spurred the already-underway gentrification of Inglewood, where the median value of a home increased 37 percent between January 2016 and June 2018; that new sticker price of $542,000 still trailed the median countywide price of $609,000. The scheduled 2020 opening of the 8.5 mile Crenshaw/LAX light-rail line plus extensive residential development have added to the makeover of Inglewood, where a return of white residents has begun.

The 43rd Congressional District covers much of this section of Los Angeles County, including Gardena, and the heavily Hispanic areas of Alondra Park, Hawthorne and Lawndale. It takes in part of Torrance, which is home to large Korean and Japanese communities and to the North American headquarters of Honda. On the northern end of the district is Inglewood and to the south is West Carson. At the Los Angeles International Airport, a $4.9 billion elevated train serving the airport area is scheduled to open in 2023 and reduce one source of local congestion. This is safe Democratic territory. Hillary Clinton got 78 percent of the district vote in 2016. The current district lines are 47 percent Hispanic and 22 percent black. But the black community wields more political clout.

Nanette Barragán (D)

Elected 2016, 2nd term, b. Sep 15, 1976; San Pedro; University of California, Los Angeles, B.A., 2000; University of Southern California, J.D., 2005; Catholic; Single.

Elected Office: Hermosa Beach City Council, 2013-2015; Mayor Pro Tem, Hermosa Beach, 2015.

Professional Career: Practicing attorney.

DC Office: 1030 LHOB 20515, 202-225-8220, barragan.house.gov

State Offices: Carson, 310-831-1799; San Pedro, 310-831-1799; South Gate, 310-831-1799.

Committees: *Energy & Commerce*: Energy; Environment & Climate Change; Health. *Homeland Security*: Oversight, Management & Accountability; Transportation & Maritime Security.

Group Ratings

	ADA	ACLU	AFL-CIO	LCV	ITI	COC	HAFA	ACU	CFG	FRC
2018	-	93%	-	94%	-	58%	9%	8%	24%	0%
2017	90%	C	100%	97%	C	38%	C	4%	5%	11%

Almanac Ratings 2017-18

	Economy	Social	Foreign	Composite
Liberal	93%	98%	97%	96%
Conservative	7%	2%	3%	4%

Key Votes of the 115th Congress

1. Obama-care revision	N	5. Family planning regs	N	9. Guantanamo prisoners	Y
2. Tax Cuts	N	6. Body cameras/immigration	Y	10. Ground missiles, limit	Y
3. Omnibus appropriations	N	7. Abortion ban	N	11. Defense Dept. spending	N
4. Dodd-Frank revision	N	8. Concealed carry	N	12. FISA rules	N

Election Results

Election	Name (Party)	Vote (%)		Cand. Spent	Ind. Exp. Support	Ind. Exp. Oppose
2018 General	Nanette Barragan (D)...............................	97,944	(68%)	$856,947		
	Aja Brown (D)......................................	45,378	(32%)		$17,665	
2018 Primary	Nanette Barragan (D)........................	39,453	(66%)			
	Aja Brown (D)......................................	10,257	(17%)			
	Jazmina Saavedra (R)...........................	6,153	(10%)			
	Stacey Dash (R)....................................	4,361	(7%)			

Prior winning percentages: 2016 (52%)

Democrat Nanette Barragán, elected in 2016 in a close contest with an African-American state senator, benefited from the support of activist Democratic women and her large Hispanic community. Building on her impressive professional background, she has taken the lead among junior House Democrats on immigration and the environment. Barragan was reelected easily under unusual circumstances: Her opponent in the general election, the Democratic mayor of Compton, dropped out of the contest due to her pregnancy and spent scant funds, but her name remained on the ballot and she got nearly one-third of the vote.

Barragán was the youngest of 11 children of undocumented immigrants from Mexico. She succeeded with what the Los Angeles Times described as "an up-from-the-bootstraps story" from the hardscrabble streets of Carson to graduate from UCLA and get a law degree from the University of Southern California. In the Clinton White House she worked on African-American outreach in the Office of Public Liaison. She was an extern for a California Supreme Court justice and later worked for the Los Angeles Legal Aid Foundation and the U.S. attorney's office. As a lawyer with Latham & Watkins, a top Los Angeles firm, she handled an immigration asylum case on behalf of a mother and child from Guatemala that lasted three years.

In 2012, Barragán took a leave from her law firm to work on the reelection campaign of President Barack Obama. A year later, she was elected to the Hermosa Beach City Council. She served barely a month as mayor before stepping down to run for Congress. She gained attention for working to impose a ban on oil drilling in Santa Monica Bay, where an oil company had planned to set up rigs.

When Rep. Janice Hahn retired for a successful run for the Los Angeles County Board of Supervisors, the front-runners were Barragán and state Sen. Isadore Hall III, an African American who was endorsed by much of the California Democratic establishment, including Gov. Jerry Brown. In its editorial, the Times wrote that Hall's self-styled "moderate" appeal benefited from large campaign donations from oil companies, casinos, tobacco companies and the alcohol lobby. In the first round of voting, Hall led the 10-candidate field with 40 percent of the vote to 22 percent for Barragán. Each candidate raised about $1.9 million. Barragán got a big boost with nearly $700,000 in support from Women Vote!, a Super PAC created by EMILY'S List, the abortion-rights group. She won in November, 52%-48%, a margin of 7,835 votes.

Barragán was selected as an assistant whip and as one of three co-presidents of the Democrats' freshman class. She said that she decided to attend the inauguration of President Donald Trump, while wearing a symbolic pink fleece hat, because "I want to show Donald Trump that immigrants have always added immeasurable value to our nation and we will not go away. We are here to stay." Later, when she attended the White House's congressional ball, she showed her resistance to Trump by giving him a perfunctory hand shake and moving quickly to talk with the first lady. "I asked if I could stand in front of Melania Trump instead of him," she told Politico. "I literally just shook his hand out of courtesy."

On immigration issues, Barragan said she supported legislation to assist the so-called dreamers — undocumented immigrants who arrived in the U.S. as youth — because a young cousin of hers was worried that he faced deportation. With fellow California first-term Rep. Jimmy Gomez, she went to the southern border and stayed overnight to assist asylum seekers. During the visit, while the group was kept in a caged area by Border Patrol agents, she said that her requests for information and access were denied. "Intimidation tactics at its worst," she tweeted.

With two other freshman Democrats, Reps. Pramila Jayapal of Washington and Donald McEachin of Virginia, Barragan organized the United for Climate and Environmental Justice Task Force, whose proposals included a one-sentence constitutional amendment to affirm the right of all persons to clean air and water and the "sustainable preservation" of the environment. She chaired the environmental task forces of both the Hispanic Caucus and the Progressive Caucus. In 2019, she got a seat on the influential Energy and Commerce Committee, where she said she would be a voice for communities "on the frontlines of the negative health impacts associated with climate change and environmental injustice."

At home, Barragan initially was challenged for reelection by Compton Mayor Aja Brown and Stacey Dash, an actress who had become a commentator on Fox News. Dash dropped out of the contest a month after filing her candidacy, citing the "bitterness" in politics and "the rigors of campaigning." Brown ended her campaign a few days later with her announcement that she was pregnant. Both remained on the ballot. In the all-party primary, Barragan got 66 percent to 17 percent for Brown. In the general election, during which Brown did not campaign and was outspent by nearly 50-to-1, Barragan won, 68%-32%.

CA-44: Southern L.A.   Cook Partisan Voting Index: D+35

Population		Race and Ethnicity		Income	
Total	723,533	White	6.5%	Median Income	$49,774
Land area (sq. miles)	79	Black	15.6%	District Income Rank	315
Pop/ sq mi	9117.1	Latino	69.9%	Poverty Rate	21.7%
Born in State	57.4%	Asian	5.8%	With health insurance	83.3%
		Two or more races	1.3%	Cash public assistance	7.3%
Age Groups		Other	1%	Food stamp/SNAP	17.1%
Under 18	27.9%				
18-34	26.7%	**Education**		**Work**	
35-64	35.7%	H.S grad or less	61.6%	White Collar	9.7%
Over 64	9.7%	Some college	25.8%	Sales and Service	46.5%
		College Degree, 4 yr	9.2%	Blue Collar	34%
Military		Post grad	3.3%	Government	11.5%
Veteran/ Active Duty	3%				

2012 Pres. Vote	Obama	155,459	(85%)	Romney	24,995	(14%)			
2016 Pres. Vote	Clinton	164,251	(83%)	Trump	24,261	(12%)	Stein	4,213	(2%)

San Pedro, Compton: Just five days after President Lyndon Johnson signed the landmark Voting Rights Act into law, a police arrest gone wrong led to the explosion of the Watts riots. Six days later, 34 people were dead, more than 1,000 were injured and Los Angeles had a wound that would take years to heal. Still, the area has shown some recovery and it has retained a rich cultural heritage. In Compton, the Central Avenue entertainment district during the postwar years was filled with clubs and theaters hosting Ella Fitzgerald, Sarah Vaughan, Duke Ellington and Louis Armstrong.

Compton symbolizes many deep social problems: high crime rates, gang violence, drugs and poverty. The influential late 1980s rap group N.W.A. expressed the frustration of many city residents with the song Straight Outta Compton. That led to a full-length hit movie in 2015 with the same title, which told the story of the rappers. The Bloods and Crips street gangs have seen the rise of Hispanic counterparts. Blacks are disproportionately the victims, and they are most of the gang members. The once-dominant blacks in Compton have been overtaken by Hispanics, 65 percent to 33 percent. The Bloods and Crips eventually reached a truce, which contributed to a limited reduction in crime. At the same time, many of the Latinos have been buying homes and opening businesses. Real estate prices in Compton began to soar, spurred partly by investors speculating on the long-term prospects. But not all is well. A state audit in March 2018 found that the Compton government mismanaged taxpayer funds. In 2016, the city had the highest murder rate in California. Notable success stories: Serena and Venus Williams grew up in Compton before they became world-class tennis champions. Local gangs protected the sisters as their prominence grew. And rapper Kendrick Lamar in 2018 won a Pulitzer Prize for music.

The 44th Congressional District includes Carson, Compton, Willowbrook and Rancho Dominguez, plus the overwhelmingly Hispanic South Gate and Lynwood — 95 percent and 88 percent Latino, respectively. The district stretches south to include coastal areas, including San Pedro and some of Long Beach, which are more middle-class in character. It shares some terminals in the massive ports of Los Angles and Long Beach. Similar to other coastal parts of Los Angeles, a 44 percent plurality of San Pedro is white. Overall, the district is 70 percent Hispanic and 16 percent black. Politically, it is solidly Democratic. Hillary Clinton got 83 percent of the vote here. Until 2012, the area south and west of downtown Los Angeles selected three African-Americans to the House. The changing demographics have left barely enough blacks to influence the selection of two African-American members.

Katie Porter (D)

Elected 2018, 1st term, b. Jan 03, 1974; Des Moines, IA; Yale University (CT), B.A., 1996; Harvard University, J.D., 2001; Episcopalian; Divorced; 3 children.

Professional Career: Public Interest Attorney; Law Professor, University of California, Irvine.

DC Office: 1117 LHOB 20515, 202-225-5611, porter.house.gov

State Offices: Irvine, 949-668-6600.

Committees: *Financial Services*: Consumer Protection & Financial Institutions; Investor Protection, Entrepreneurship & Capital Markets.

Election Results

Election	Name (Party)	Vote (%)	Cand. Spent	Ind. Exp. Support	Ind. Exp. Oppose
2018 General	Katherine Porter (D)	158,906 (52%)	$6,662,223	$3,445,100	$5,539,795
	Mimi Walters (R)	146,383 (48%)	$5,003,566	$798,565	$6,802,764
2018 Primary	Mimi Walters (R)	86,764 (52%)			
	Katherine Porter (D)	34,078 (20%)			
	Dave Min (D)	29,979 (18%)			
	Brian Forde (D)	10,107 (6%)			

Freshman Democrat Katie Porter shifted her academic and advocacy interests in banking law from the classroom to Congress. Along the way, she took a crash course in the rapidly evolving politics of Orange County, which a few decades ago was the heartland of California Republicans. Porter built on her connections to prominent Democrats who shaped her interest in banking and gained influence in the party. She defeated Republican Rep. Mimi Walters, whose business and political careers were emblematic of the GOP establishment.

Porter, who grew up in a farm town in Iowa, graduated from Yale University, where her undergraduate thesis focused on the effects of corporate farming on rural America. She got her law degree from Harvard University, where she became a protégé of professor (and later Sen.) Elizabeth Warren—an expert on the consumer impact of banking practices. They co-authored a book, The Law of Debtors and Creditors.

After teaching at the University of Iowa law school, Porter shifted to California where then-Attorney General Kamala Harris appointed her to monitor the state's share of a mortgage fraud settlement. At the University of California, Irvine, Porter was a bankruptcy law professor.

Porter was the first Democrat to challenge Walters in the 2018 campaign. "I've spent my career fighting powerful interests," she told the Orange County Register. "I'm running to take that fight to Washington." In her first campaign ad, both Warren and Harris introduced and praised her." Porter's chief Democratic opponent in the all-party primary was Dave Min—another professor at the Irvine law school and a financial policy expert. Their clash became nasty and personal. Min had previously worked for Sen. Chuck Schumer of New York, a frequent defender of Wall Street and big banks. Min ran ads attacking Porter for her backing from "Washington insiders," notably EMILY's List, the group that supports Democratic women who favor abortion rights.

At the Democratic state convention, which endorsed Min by a single vote, Porter said that Democrats should be "electing a Democrat who will act like a Democrat." According to the Huffington Post, several convention delegates said that advocates of a Porter rival had spread rumors that Porter's sealed divorced records included information that might be politically damaging. That report suggested that Min was the source of the rumors. In the June primary for second place behind Walters, Porter led Min, 20%-18%.

During her two terms in the House, Walters supported cutbacks in federal regulation, including repeal of the Affordable Care Act. As the only one of the four House Republicans from Orange County who voted for the sweeping tax-cut legislation in 2017, she enthusiastically embraced the measure, which had some adverse effects on well-off taxpayers in high-tax states.

Porter sought to link Walters to President Donald Trump's actions and his administration's repeal of consumer protections. She told CNBC that Walters was "refusing to see the corruption that's right in front of her." With talking points that once would have been broadly supported in Orange County, Walters responded that Porter's "liberal policies … will not sit well in this district." As the Register described the contest, "Both sides are campaigning in terms of national, not local, politics."

The two candidates and their parties spent a total of nearly $30 million on the contest, with a nearly even split. Porter won, 52%-48%. With the slow vote count that was the case in much of California, it took more than a week before Porter's victory was official. In Washington, her past alliances—plus a seat on the Financial Services Committee--gave Porter the opportunity to shape the national debate on banking issues. Preparing for her reelection campaign also was likely to keep her busy.

CA-45: Central Orange   Cook Partisan Voting Index: R+3

Population		Race and Ethnicity		Income	
Total	762,519	White	51.4%	Median Income	$97,431
Land area (sq. miles)	330	Black	1.8%	District Income Rank	16
Pop/ sq mi	2307.9	Latino	18.7%	Poverty Rate	9.2%
Born in State	49.2%	Asian	23.8%	With health insurance	93.7%
Age Groups		Two or more races	3.7%	Cash public assistance	1.6%
Under 18	21.8%	Other	0.6%	Food stamp/SNAP	2.9%
18-34	22.7%	**Education**		**Work**	
35-64	41.3%	H.S grad or less	19.2%	White Collar	14.2%
Over 64	14.2%	Some college	26.9%	Sales and Service	37%
Military		College Degree, 4 yr	32.7%	Blue Collar	9.7%
Veteran/ Active Duty	5%	Post grad	21.1%	Government	11.1%

2012 Pres. Vote	Romney	169,489	(55%)	Obama	133,114	(43%)		
2016 Pres. Vote	Clinton	162,449	(49%)	Trump	144,713	(44%)	Johnson	13,200	(4%)

Irvine, Lake Forest: Orange County is the sixth most populous county in the United States, having grown steadily from 130,000 people in 1940 to nearly 2 million in 1980 and to 3.2 million in 2017. It narrowly trails its neighbor San Diego County. It is now a community with the patina of maturity, and in some respects, of an aging community fraying at the edges. In recent years, its economy has been constantly reshaped: Tourism remains key, but there is no single industry responsible for Orange County's prosperity. Orange County was rocked by recession in 2008, when the hyperinflation of the local housing market abruptly burst and home values slid as much as 20 percent. Rapid moves by local governments to cut costs and attract new projects, such as alternative energy jobs, helped the county recover faster than other California counties.

The third-largest city in Orange County is Irvine. Irvine Ranch was purchased by Gold Rush merchant James Irvine from the Sepulveda and Yorba families. As Orange County grew, the Irvine family was sitting on some immensely valuable territory, the last large plot of vacant land in metro Los Angeles. In 1959, the Irvines donated a site for the University of California, Irvine, which has grown to 36,000 students. In the 1970s, they sold the rest to developers. Irvine was born as a planned community, with eight-lane parkways, huge office parks, shopping malls and attractive subdivisions. It attracted high-tech and high-growth businesses, highly educated and affluent people. About 42 percent are Asian, including large numbers of Koreans and Vietnamese, and the city is home to a Chinese-language library. Diamond Jamboree, a youthful and upscale Asian-themed retail hub, in October 2018 announced plans to expand, including a Michelin-starred dim sum restaurant. "Asian and Mexican cultures are jointly transforming this once sleepy suburb," Ronald Brownstein wrote for CNN in March 2018.

Republican since 1936, Orange County became a symbol of conservatism, first in California and then nationally. This was a solid base for Ronald Reagan in his campaigns for governor and president. In 1988, the district's 317,000-vote plurality for George H.W. Bush was his largest in any county in the nation. Orange County has become more diverse. The all-white Orange County stereotype is thoroughly out of date. Nearly one-third of the county's residents were born in another country, and 46 percent speak a language other than English at home. Its majority-minority population in 2017 had grown to 34 percent Hispanic and 21 percent Asian, though only 2 percent black. The GOP advantage has vanished — and not by a small amount. Hillary Clinton led Donald Trump in Orange County, 51%-43%, a margin of 103,000 votes.

The 45th Congressional District is made up of central and south Orange County. Its population center is Irvine, and it also takes in parts of Anaheim, Orange and Mission Viejo. It is 24 percent Asian and 19 percent Hispanic. This is one of three districts that are based entirely in Orange County, while three others are partly in the county. Its once strongly Republican lean has shifted. In a district that Mitt Romney won 55%-43% in 2012, Clinton led 49%-44%, a drop of one-fifth in the Republican vote.

Lou Correa (D)

Elected 2016, 2nd term, b. Jan 24, 1958; Los Angeles; California State University (Fullerton), B.S., 1980; University of California, Los Angeles, J.D., 1985; University of California, Los Angeles, M.B.A., 1985; Catholic; Married (Esther Reynoso Correa); 4 children.

Elected Office: CA Assembly, 1998-2004; Orange County Board of Supervisors, 2005-2006; CA Senate, 2006-2014.

Professional Career: Investment banker/ real estate broker; California High Speed Rail Authority, 2015-2016.

DC Office: 1039 LHOB 20515, 202-225-2965, correa.house.gov
State Offices: Santa Ana, 714-621-0102.

Committees: *Homeland Security*: Border Security, Facilitation & Operations; Transportation & Maritime Security (Chmn). *Judiciary*: Courts, Intellectual Property & Internet; Immigration & Citizenship.

Group Ratings

	ADA	ACLU	AFL-CIO	LCV	ITI	COC	HAFA	ACU	CFG	FRC
2018	-	75%	-	91%	-	83%	9%	21%	32%	20%
2017	60%	C	84%	91%	C	79%	C	7%	5%	11%

Almanac Ratings 2017-18

	Economy	Social	Foreign	Composite
Liberal	65%	90%	54%	70%
Conservative	35%	10%	46%	30%

Key Votes of the 115th Congress

1. Obama-care revision	N	5. Family planning regs	N	9. Guantanamo prisoners	N
2. Tax Cuts	N	6. Body cameras/immigration	Y	10. Ground missiles, limit	N
3. Omnibus appropriations	N	7. Abortion ban	N	11. Defense Dept. spending	Y
4. Dodd-Frank revision	Y	8. Concealed carry	N	12. FISA rules	N

Election Results

Election	Name (Party)	Vote (%)	Cand. Spent	Ind. Exp. Support	Ind. Exp. Oppose
2018 General	Lou Correa (D)...................................... 102,278	(69%)	$513,467	$75,000	
	Russell Lambert (R)............................ 45,638	(31%)			
2018 Primary	Lou Correa (D)...................................... 43,700	(62%)			
	Russell Lambert (R)............................ 22,770	(32%)			

Prior winning percentages: 2016 (70%)

Democrat Lou Correa, elected to an open seat in 2016, has a close connection to the Mexican-American immigrant community and a grassroots political style. He has taken his deal-making approach to the handling of homeland-security issues.

He was born in East Los Angeles. His grandfather and American-born father returned to Mexico to look for work. When he was a year old, his mother died in an automobile accident in Mexico. After spending five more years in Mexico, he returned with his father plus aunts and uncles to Anaheim, where they struggled in subsistence-living in small apartments. "I had enough to eat, and I had a roof over me when I slept. That's all I really cared about," he told the Los Angeles Times. After graduating from Anaheim High School, he got his bachelor's at California State University, Fullerton, and then a law degree and MBA from UCLA. He worked as an attorney, investment banker and real estate broker.

The passage in 1994 of Proposition 187, which targeted illegal immigration, made Correa politically active. He ran for the state Assembly in 1996 and lost by 93 votes. Two years later, he easily defeated the Republican incumbent. After six years in the Assembly, he was elected to the Orange County Board of Supervisors and then eight years in the state Senate. In 2014, he narrowly lost a bid to return to the board. Correa styled himself as a political moderate, often to the annoyance of Democratic leaders. "A lot of politicians will wring their hands and put a wet finger in the air to get a feel for what he should do," former Senate Majority Leader Donn Perata told the Times. "Lou just intuitively knew." He was consistent in his advocacy of immigrants' rights and criticized President Barack Obama for his deportations.

When 10-term Democratic Rep. Loretta Sanchez decided to run for the Senate, Correa sought the open seat and was endorsed by Sanchez and many Democratic Party leaders. In the eight-candidate first round of voting, he got 42 percent. Runner-up with 15 percent was Garden Grove Mayor Bao Nguyen, who had fled Vietnam as a baby with his parents. Nguyen, a Democrat, appealed to supporters of Sen. Bernie Sanders. Correa, who was an early supporter of Hillary Clinton for president, appealed chiefly to Latinos in this heavily Hispanic district. With a fundraising advantage of $920,000 to $270,000, he had another easy win in the general election, 70%-30%.

In the House, unlike many other Democrats, Correa attended the inauguration of President Donald Trump. "I'm going to D.C. to be at the table when decisions are made that affect my constituents. Either we are at the table or we are on the menu," he said. He went to work at the Homeland Security Committee, where he won House passage of bills that revised the management of acquisition activities and imposed tighter security standards on firearms controlled by the Homeland Security Department. Following a visit to the border with Mexico in November 2018, Correa called for a "Marshall Plan" to stimulate the economies of nations in Central America and reduce the poverty and violence in the region. Current policies at the border were "not working," he said. In 2019, he became chairman of the panel's Subcommittee on Transportation and Maritime Security.

His House-passed bill to permit the burial in a veteran's cemetery of a spouse or eligible dependent of active-duty service member where the family member dies first was added to a broader veterans bill that was enacted in December 2018. With Republican Rep. Matt Gaetz of Florida, Correa introduced the "Sensible Enforcement of Cannabis Act" to prevent prosecution of persons using marijuana in states where it is permitted for legal or medical purposes. In an unusual controversy, he refused to back down when conservative critics demanded that he remove an award-winning student painting on the wall of his office, which depicted the Statue of Liberty wearing a hijab. Policing art, he told The Washington Post in August 2017, would lead to a "very dangerous slippery slope."

Correa was reelected, 69%-31%, against Republican Russell Lambert, who reported no campaign spending. In 2019, Correa became communications co-chair of the Blue Dogs, the coalition of fiscally conservative Democrats.

CA-46: Northern Orange   Cook Partisan Voting Index: D+15

Population		Race and Ethnicity		Income	
Total	730,094	White	17.7%	Median Income	$59,863
Land area (sq. miles)	72	Black	1.5%	District Income Rank	181
Pop/ sq mi	10179.8	Latino	66.3%	Poverty Rate	18.2%
Born in State	51.1%	Asian	12.8%	With health insurance	82%
		Two or more races	1.2%	Cash public assistance	3.7%
Age Groups		Other	0.4%	Food stamp/SNAP	13.7%
Under 18	26%				
18-34	28.7%	**Education**		**Work**	
35-64	36.2%	H.S grad or less	57%	White Collar	9.1%
Over 64	9.1%	Some college	24.9%	Sales and Service	48.4%
		College Degree, 4 yr	13.4%	Blue Collar	28.4%
Military		Post grad	4.6%	Government	8%
Veteran/ Active Duty	2.9%				

2012 Pres. Vote	Obama	95,479	(61%)	Romney	56,252	(36%)			
2016 Pres. Vote	Clinton	119,762	(66%)	Trump	50,403	(28%)	Johnson	5,630	(3%)
	Stein	3,711	(2%)						

Santa Ana, Central and Western Anaheim: When Walt Disney began planning Disneyland in the late 1940s, he did not have to drive far from downtown Los Angeles before finding undeveloped land. Dairy farms and orange groves covered most of southeast Los Angeles County and adjacent Orange County, which had only 216,000 people in 1950. As Disneyland opened there in 1955 and became a great success, the area around it — a mass of flatland surrounded by mountains and sea — found itself directly in the path of the most explosively growing metropolitan area in the United States. With 3.2 million people, this has become the nation's sixth-largest county.

Just as Orange County was once transformed by newcomers from Los Angeles County and the Midwest, so it is again being transformed by immigrants, from Mexico and other parts of Latin America, and from Vietnam, Taiwan, Korea and other parts of East Asia. The county seat of Santa Ana is a major arrival point for immigrants from Mexico and is 77 percent Hispanic, of whom nearly half have been counted as non-citizens. Other immigrants have moved farther out, like so many Southern Californians before them, working multiple jobs, commuting on freeways and living in stucco subdivisions. There are concentrations in various places — Latinos in Santa Ana and much of Anaheim plus Vietnamese in Garden Grove, who constitute the largest Vietnamese community in the nation. Overall, the county has the third largest Asian population in the nation, behind Los Angeles and Santa Clara counties. These demographic changes have made for some political wobble. After the 1994 approval of Proposition 187, which sought to deny most social services to illegal immigrants, many more Latinos began voting, mostly Democratic. Santa Ana, which declared its community a "sanctuary city" in 2017, joined the state of California a year later contesting a suit by the Justice Department that challenged their action; several other cities in Orange County sided with the feds.

The 46th Congressional District covers central and western areas of Orange County. It takes in parts of Santa Ana, which is the second-largest city in Orange County, and Orange. It includes a significant portion of Anaheim, Orange County's largest city and 54 percent Hispanic. Homelessness has become a major issue in Anaheim, with the city closing down several tent encampments after a large shelter was opened in December 2018. The district is the Democratic core of the county, with population that is 66 percent Hispanic and 13 percent Asian. The Democratic presidential vote increased from 58 percent in 2008 to 66 percent in 2016. Resolving an issue that had gained prominence during that campaign, Disneyland in September 2018 agreed with its hotel workers union to increase the minimum wage to $15 hourly in 2019 and $18 in 2021. The park planned to open in the summer of 2019 Star Wars Land, its largest-ever expansion, with galactic attractions and a cost of $1 billion.

Alan Lowenthal (D)

Elected 2012, 4th term, b. Mar 08, 1941; New York, NY; Hobart College (NY), B.A., 1962; Ohio State University, M.A., 1965; Ohio State University, Ph.D., 1967; Jewish; Married (Deborah Malumed); 2 children; 1 grandchild.

Elected Office: Long Beach City Council, 1992-1998; CA Assembly, 1998-2004; CA Senate, 2004-2012.

Professional Career: Professor, CA. St. University Long Beach, 1969-1998.

DC Office: 108 CHOB 20515, 202-225-7924, Fax: 202-225-7926, lowenthal.house.gov

State Offices: Garden Grove, 714-243-4088; Long Beach, 562-436-3828.

Committees: *Natural Resources*: Energy & Mineral Resources (Chmn); National Parks, Forests & Public Lands; Water, Oceans & Wildlife. *Transportation & Infrastructure*: Coast Guard & Maritime Transportation; Highways & Transit; Railroads, Pipelines & Hazardous Materials; Water Resources & Environment.

Group Ratings

	ADA	ACLU	AFL-CIO	LCV	ITI	COC	HAFA	ACU	CFG	FRC
2018	-	89%	-	94%	-	42%	6%	0%	15%	0%
2017	100%	C	97%	97%	C	36%	C	0%	0%	0%

Almanac Ratings 2017-18

	Economy	Social	Foreign	Composite
Liberal	100%	98%	100%	99%
Conservative	0%	2%	0%	1%

Key Votes of the 115th Congress

1. Obama-care revision	N	5. Family planning regs	N	9. Guantanamo prisoners	Y
2. Tax Cuts	N	6. Body cameras/immigration	Y	10. Ground missiles, limit	Y
3. Omnibus appropriations	N	7. Abortion ban	N	11. Defense Dept. spending	N
4. Dodd-Frank revision	N	8. Concealed carry	N	12. FISA rules	N

Election Results

Election	Name (Party)	Vote (%)		Cand. Spent	Ind. Exp. Support	Ind. Exp. Oppose
2018 General	Alan Lowenthal (D)	143,354	(65%)	$332,485		
	John Briscoe (R)	77,682	(35%)	$47,673		
2018 Primary	Alan Lowenthal (D)	70,539	(61%)			
	John Briscoe (R)	25,122	(22%)			
	David Clifford (R)	20,687	(18%)			

Prior winning percentages: 2016 (64%), 2014 (56%), 2012 (57%)

Alan Lowenthal, a Democrat first elected in 2012, is a rare academician seeking to bring pragmatic problem-solving to Washington. As the new chairman of a subcommittee dealing with energy and mineral resource issues, he planned to focus on sustainable and renewable energy development. His port district has made him very familiar with freight and offshore production issues. With lengthy experience at home and in Sacramento, he kept a low profile in the House minority but raised thoughtful ideas.

Lowenthal was born in New York City, grew up in Queens and went to high school on Long Island. Lowenthal studied psychology at Hobart College, where he got a bachelor's degree, and he continued his studies at Ohio State University, earning a masters and a doctorate. During his doctoral training, he had an internship in San Francisco and decided that he wanted to live in California. Lowenthal took a position at California State University, Long Beach, in 1969 as an assistant professor.

He became involved in local politics in 1989, when the misconduct of a Long Beach police officer led Lowenthal to seek reforms of the police department, including new procedures for citizen complaints. He joined Long Beach Area Citizens Involved, an umbrella group of community organizations trying to influence local government, and eventually became the group's president. In 1992, he won a seat on the Long Beach City Council. He was elected to the state Assembly in 1998, and to the state Senate six years later. In the legislature, Lowenthal focused on reducing air pollution at California ports and protecting public health. "I wanted to make sure the community was livable and the port economically viable," he said.

Long Beach Councilman Gary DeLong, Lowenthal's opponent in 2012, ran as a moderate Republican who said he would not be bound by the decisions of the House Republican leadership. In this firmly Democratic district, Lowenthal did his best to tie DeLong to the GOP establishment. He seized on a comment DeLong made at a community event in which he said he had not seen scientific evidence that confirms the existence of climate change. DeLong had the edge in spending, $1.4 million to $1.2 million. Lowenthal won 57%-43%.

Lowenthal has styled himself as a behind-the-scenes operator. "I don't scream and yell," he told the Long Beach Post in December 2018. "I just make it very clear where I am and what I am going to do." A long-time environmentalist, he has advocated upgraded technology to handle freight "in a way that reduces pollution and gets us off carbon." As the senior Democrat starting in 2015 on the Natural Resources Subcommittee on Energy and Mineral Resources, he focused on renewable energy development, especially on public lands. When he became subcommittee chairman, he introduced a package of bills that would prevent drilling in the oceans around the United States. "We must make it clear, once and for all, that our coastlines will not pay the price of oil production greed and hubris," he said. Lowenthal has occasionally sought bipartisan opportunities, including his legislation with Republican Rep. Don Young of Alaska to provide funding for conservation of threatened species and habitat.

Lowenthal has worked on foreign policy issues. With Republican Rep. Steve Chabot of Ohio, he formed and co-chaired the Congressional Cambodia Caucus. Long Beach has the largest community of Cambodians outside that nation. In 2016, the House passed his resolution condemning the government of Cambodia for its physical attacks and other persecution of the opposition. He has taken an interest in gay-rights issues, including a bill that he prepared with Democratic Sen. Ed Markey of Massachusetts that seeks to protect the rights of LGBTQ people around the world.

As a reformer, Lowenthal claimed that his work in the Assembly helped to pave the way for the public referendum creating a citizens' redistricting commission in California. With Republican Rep. Brian Fitzpatrick of Pennsylvania, he has filed a resolution that urged an end to political gerrymandering. Mindful of the political mine fields, their proposal did not offer an alternative. "You have to crawl before you walk," Lowenthal told the Long Beach Press-Telegram.

In the 2014 campaign, Republican Andy Whallon, a former aeronautical engineer, promised more job creation. Whallon spent only $60,000, and Lowenthal's 56%-44% victory was close to his initial election. In 2016, the turnout was twice as large and Lowenthal won a rematch with Whallon, 64%-36%. He had a new opponent in 2018: John Briscoe, a member of the Board of Trustees in the Ocean View school district, who called himself a "commonsense conservative." Lowenthal outspent him more than 10-to-1 and won, 65%-35%.

CA-47: Coastal L.A./Inland Orange

Cook Partisan Voting Index: D+13

Population		Race and Ethnicity		Income	
Total	717,209	White	31.5%	Median Income	$63,887
Land area (sq. miles)	216	Black	7.1%	District Income Rank	145
Pop/ sq mi	3317.2	Latino	35.3%	Poverty Rate	16.3%
Born in State	54.5%	Asian	22.2%	With health insurance	89.1%
		Two or more races	2.8%	Cash public assistance	3.3%
Age Groups		Other	1.2%	Food stamp/SNAP	9.6%
Under 18	22.5%				
18-34	25.1%	**Education**		**Work**	
35-64	39.8%	H.S grad or less	37.8%	White Collar	12.6%
Over 64	12.6%	Some college	31.2%	Sales and Service	43%
		College Degree, 4 yr	20.4%	Blue Collar	19.8%
Military		Post grad	10.7%	Government	13.1%
Veteran/ Active Duty	5.1%				

2012 Pres. Vote	Obama	147,456	(60%)	Romney	92,010	(38%)		
2016 Pres. Vote	Clinton	161,743	(62%)	Trump	80,162	(31%)	Johnson	9,260	(4%)
	Stein	5,690	(2%)					

Long Beach, Garden Grove: With 469,000 people, Long Beach would be a major metropolis almost anywhere but in Los Angeles County, where it seems just the largest of many suburbs. But it has an identity of its own. Founded as a beach resort in 1888, it soon became a port when Los Angeles civic leaders decided that if their town was to be a world-class city, it must have a world-class harbor. Since nature had not provided one, they built it where the Los Angeles River flows into the ocean at the western edge of Long Beach. By 1909, Los Angeles had annexed the harbor towns of San Pedro and Wilmington on the other side of the river. Over the next decades, the two cities persuaded the federal government to dredge channels and build a breakwater and turning basins. Long Beach was developing other businesses as well. It sprouted oil derricks in the 1920s and briefly became one of the nation's big oil producers. It was the site of major aircraft plants in the 1940s and beyond.

Since then, the Los Angeles-Long Beach port has become the nation's busiest cargo center, with huge steel-gray container ships pulling up to enormous automated loading facilities. The two ports in the complex compete with each other on business terms, but collaborate on many issues. The L.A. port is the larger, with 26 terminals and 86 cranes handling more than 25,000, 20-foot containers daily. Long Beach, with 30,000 employees and 68 gantry cranes in 2017, handles the equivalent of 18,600 containers daily docked at 10 piers and 80 berths. From there, nearly half the cargo leaves by rail in more than 40 daily trains along the high-speed, 20-mile Alameda Corridor to the large rail yards near downtown Los Angeles. Trucking accounts for a declining share of the $180 billion in annual cargo on 2,000 vessels through the port. These facilities handle 49 percent of goods imported into the nation, and a smaller share of exports. More than 90 percent of the port shipments are to or from East Asia. Even though cargo volume in 2018 was a record, the international trade policies of President Donald Trump raised concerns that a tariff war would have an adverse long-term impact on the port.

The Queen Mary, converted into a floating hotel, is a big tourist attraction in Long Beach. In 2017, the company that owns the ship unveiled plans for a $250 million renovation of the vessel, which was built in the 1930s. There are new high-rises and a huge aquarium along the beach, with more than $3 billion in projects to revive the downtown that had been deteriorating. The city, which likely will host events during the 2028 Olympics, has suffered from downsized manufacturing. Three years after shutting down production of its Globemaster III military transports, Boeing in November 2018 listed for sale the property, which is adjacent to the airport. The Long Beach plant had been the last aircraft-manufacturing facility in California. In 2017, the Long Beach council voted to prohibit city employees from collecting information on undocumented immigrants. A replacement span for the Gerald Desmond Bridge from the port to the Long Beach freeway, which will be wider and higher than the current span, was expected to be finished in late 2019.

The 47th Congressional District is centered on Long Beach, and takes in Signal Hill, where oil rigs are still pumping. Parts are in Orange County, including Los Alamitos and Cypress, which has a large Asian-American population and is the birthplace of golfing great Tiger Woods. Parts of Garden

Grove and Westminster, founded as a Presbyterian temperance colony in 1870, are shared with the 48th District. Nearly two-thirds of the total vote is in Los Angeles County. Politically, it leans strongly Democratic. In 2016, Hillary Clinton led Donald Trump, 62%-31%.

Harley Rouda (D)

Elected 2018, 1st term, b. Dec 10, 1961; Columbus, OH; University of Kentucky, Bach. Deg., 1984; Capital University School of Law, J.D., 1986; Ohio State University, M.B.A., 2002; Christian - Non-Denominational; Married (Kaira Sturdivant Rouda); 4 children.

Professional Career: Chief Executive Officer and President, Real Living, Incorporated, 2002-2009; Director, Insight Bank, 2004-2010; . Chief Executive Officer, Trident Holdings 1990-2018

DC Office: 2300 RHOB 20515, 202-225-2415, Fax: 202-225-2263, rouda.house.gov

State Offices: Newport Beach, 714-960-6483.

Committees: *Oversight & Reform*: National Security; Subcommittee on Environment (Chmn). *Transportation & Infrastructure*: Highways & Transit; Water Resources & Environment.

Election Results

Election	Name (Party)	Vote (%)		Cand. Spent	Ind. Exp. Support	Ind. Exp. Oppose
2018 General	Harley Rouda (D)............................... 157,837	(54%)	$7,655,289	$868,510	$4,037,474
	Dana Rohrabacher (R)........................ 136,899	(46%)	$2,739,630	$426,752	$11,688,424
2018 Primary	Dana Rohrabacher (R)........................ 52,737	(30%)			
	Harley Rouda (D)............................... 30,099	(17%)			
	Hans Keirstead (D)............................. 29,974	(17%)			
	Scott Baugh (R)................................. 27,514	(16%)			
	Omar Siddiqui (D)............................... 8,658	(5%)			

Freshman Democrat Harley Rouda rode the anti-Republican surf in Orange County to defeat Rep. Dana Rohrabacher, who often fueled controversy—including in his own party--during 30 years in the House. Rouda had been little-known in California politics, having resided there for only a few years. Aided by his heavily financed campaign and the local unpopularity of President Donald Trump, his victory was easier than had been expected.

A native of Columbus Ohio, Rouda graduated from the University of Kentucky. He got a master's of business administration from Ohio State University and his law degree from Columbus-based Capital University Law School. In his legal practice, he handled business-related issues. Rouda ran a successful real estate brokerage firm that his father had started in Ohio. After he sold the business in 2007, he moved his family to southern California.

Even after his move, Rouda remained a Republican. Although he had not been politically active, some Democrats voiced unhappiness during the campaign that his party switch had been recent. He decided to run for Congress, he said, because Trump had changed the nation and its politics for the worse, with Rohrabacher's consistent support.

Of the seven other Democrats running in the jungle primary, Rouda's chief opponent— Hans Keirstead—had some similarities in his profile. Each entered politics following a successful professional career and self-financed much of his campaign. Keirstead, a neuroscientist, ran into controversy following reports that a former student had filed a complaint of misconduct against him. No allegations were specified or proved. The reports might have affected the outcome of the primary, given that Rouda led Keirstead by only 125 votes. Each received 17 percent. Rohrabacher led the field with 30 percent.

In the general election, Rouda said that the district needed a representative who was "accessible and unifying," and that "Washington is in desperate need of real, meaningful, and lasting change."

With his motto of "fighting for freedom and having fun," Rohrabacher had a widespread reputation for hyperbolic rhetoric and non-conformity. His unusual causes included dismissal of claims of global warming, intervention in Afghanistan and support for Russian president Vladimir

Putin. His legislative record was skimpy and Republican leaders repeatedly denied him a committee chairmanship. With what was a safe Republican district, he rarely faced a serious election challenge.

Amid the shifting politics of his Orange County district, the drumbeat of a serious campaign challenge in 2018 barely caught his attention. Rohrabacher was slow to raise campaign funds and he continued to call himself a "political maverick ... taking on both parties." In reaching out to voters, he failed to mention his Republican affiliation in a campaign mailer, for example. Still, his vote for the House GOP bill to repeal the Affordable Care Act was a sufficient reminder for many voters.

In a campaign debate, Rohrabacher said that Rouda's willingness to provide Medicare to undocumented immigrants would "collapse that system." Rouda denied that charge, which Rohrabacher's campaign documented with a clip from Rouda's comment during a debate prior to the primary. Rouda repeated his support to give legal status to immigrants who came to the United States as children. Referring to the challenger, Rohrabacher said that local voters "don't know who he is"

Rouda's spending of more than $7 million for his entire campaign tripled what Rohrabacher spent. The two parties and other groups tossed in more than $15 million—including a late ad campaign exceeding $4 million by former New York City Mayor Michael Bloomberg's gun-control group.

The combination of factors resulted in a definitive setback for Rohrabacher, 54%-46%. Rouda's status as a lapsed Republican might be as much influence as the Orange County GOP can wield.

CA-48: Coastal Orange   Cook Partisan Voting Index: R+4

Population		Race and Ethnicity		Income	
Total	727,426	White	55.7%	Median Income	$87,413
Land area (sq. miles)	145	Black	1.1%	District Income Rank	33
Pop/ sq mi	5000.5	Latino	21.4%	Poverty Rate	10.3%
Born in State	52.3%	Asian	18%	With health insurance	91.6%
		Two or more races	3%	Cash public assistance	1.5%
Age Groups		Other	0.7%	Food stamp/SNAP	4.8%
Under 18	19.9%				
18-34	22.1%	**Education**		**Work**	
35-64	41.5%	H.S grad or less	25.6%	White Collar	16.5%
Over 64	16.5%	Some college	30%	Sales and Service	41.2%
		College Degree, 4 yr	28.3%	Blue Collar	13.3%
Military		Post grad	16.1%	Government	9.5%
Veteran/ Active Duty	5.7%				

2012 Pres. Vote	Romney	169,249	(55%)	Obama	133,103	(43%)		
2016 Pres. Vote	Clinton	152,035	(48%)	Trump	146,595	(46%) Johnson	13,127	(4%)

Huntington Beach, Costa Mesa: In the 1950s, when the Beach Boys were at Hawthorne High School in L.A., surfers would drive far down the coast to the vast expanse of Huntington Beach in Orange County to catch a wave. This was empty country then, vegetable fields and orange groves mainly, with nary a freeway or shopping center in sight. Today, the 42-mile shoreline of Orange County is pretty much filled in with pricey coastal resorts and other developments. Huntington Beach, a city of nearly 202,000, is a mixture of family subdivisions and garden apartments and home of the International Surfing Museum. Its eight miles of beach and self-depiction as Surf City make it a tourist draw in the summer. In 2018, city officials received county approval for a new use of the ocean: a desalination plant to counter the state's water crisis. But they were struggling with the estimated $2 billion cost.

To the north is Westminster, the center of a prominent Vietnamese-American community, with miles of shops in Little Saigon with Vietnamese names and its own Vietnamese-language daily newspaper. Southeast along San Diego Freeway is Fountain Valley, the central focus of many Asian-owned technology businesses. Near the coast is Costa Mesa, site of South Coast Plaza's luxury stores and a grand performing arts center. Like other California cities, it has experienced a huge influx of Hispanic immigrants, and adapting has been rocky. The city council in Costa Mesa, which is 37 percent Hispanic, shut down a day-laborer center. In May 2018, it joined other Orange County cities in opposing California's law to protest sanctuary cities. In September, a county judge ruled on behalf of Huntington Beach in a similar lawsuit.

The 48th Congressional District takes in much of coastal Orange County and is anchored by Huntington Beach. It includes the oceanside cities of Laguna Beach, with its art galleries and cute shops, and Newport Beach, one of California's richest cities, which was rated in 2016 by Coldwell Banker as the second-most expensive housing market in the country (behind Saratoga California), with an average listing of $2.1 million. Newport Beach was the setting for the popular teen drama, The O.C. With their entrepreneurial spirit, many of the Vietnamese communities compete with each other, for example, in celebrating the Lunar New Year ("Tet").

Parts of Garden Grove and Santa Ana are in the district, as are Fountain Valley, Seal Beach and Leisure World, its large gated community for seniors. Politically, this district has leaned Republican. In April 2016, Costa Mesa was the site of Donald Trump's first campaign speech in California. In the district, Mitt Romney led President Barack Obama in 2012, 55%-43%. That changed in 2016, when Hillary Clinton prevailed over Trump, 47%-46%.

Mike Levin (D)

Elected 2018, 1st term, b. Oct 20, 1978; Inglewood; Duke Law School (NC); Stanford University (CA), B.A., 2001; Catholic; Married (Chrissy Levin); 2 children.

Professional Career: Attorney.

DC Office: 1626 LHOB 20515, 202-225-3906, mikelevin.house.gov

State Offices: Dana Point, 949-281-2449; Oceanside, 760-599-5000.

Committees: *Natural Resources*: Energy & Mineral Resources; Water, Oceans & Wildlife. *Select Committee on the Climate Crisis. Veterans' Affairs*: Economic Opportunity (Chmn); Health.

Key Votes of the 115th Congress

1. Obama-care revision	N	5. Family planning regs	N	9. Guantanamo prisoners	Y
2. Tax Cuts	N	6. Body cameras/immigration	Y	10. Ground missiles, limit	Y
3. Omnibus appropriations	Y	7. Abortion ban	N	11. Defense Dept. spending	N
4. Dodd-Frank revision	N	8. Concealed carry	N	12. FISA rules	N

Election Results

Election	Name (Party)	Vote (%)		Cand. Spent	Ind. Exp. Support	Ind. Exp. Oppose
2018 General	Mike Levin (D)	166,453	(56%)	$5,381,467	$1,943,292	
	Diane Harkey (R)	128,577	(44%)	$1,608,374	$817,683	$3,262,776
2018 Primary	Diane Harkey (R)	46,468	(26%)			
	Mike Levin (D)	31,850	(18%)			
	Sara Jacobs (D)	28,778	(16%)			
	Doug Applegate (D)	23,850	(13%)			
	Kristin Gaspar (R)	15,467	(9%)			
	Rocky Chavez (R)	13,739	(8%)			

Freshman Democrat Mike Levin won his first bid for elected office. He had been active politically as the leader of the Orange County Democratic Party and as a fundraiser in 2016 for Hillary Clinton's presidential campaign. A lawyer who worked on environmental and energy policy issues, Levin also embraced other progressive initiatives. He replaced Republican Rep. Darrell Issa, former chairman of the House Oversight and Government Reform Committee, who retired after having become a prime target for Democrats.

Levin, a native of Orange County, was the son of a Mexican-American mother and a Jewish father in a family of refugees from Austria. He got his bachelor's degree from Stanford, where he was a classmate and became a friend of Chelsea Clinton, and his law degree from Duke University. After serving as executive director of Orange County Democrats, his interest in environmental law led him to join a company that developed technology to convert waste gas from landfills and wastewater plants into zero-emission electricity. He served on the board of the Center for Sustainable Energy.

Following Issa's unexpectedly narrow victory by 1,621 votes in 2016, Levin launched his candidacy in March 2017. He decided to run while returning to California from New York City, where he spent election night in 2016. "When Donald Trump became president," he told the San Diego Union-Tribune, "I started evaluating right then and there." He described himself as "a political organizer" and he was endorsed by numerous liberal groups and House Democrats from California, plus local grassroots activists who had protested Issa.

In California's nonpartisan primary, Levin faced three other well-financed Democrats who had various shortcomings. Doug Applegate, a retired Marine Corps colonel and Issa's previously unknown challenger in 2016, had been accused of threatening his ex-wife, who obtained a restraining order against him. Sarah Jacobs benefited as the only woman in the group and from $1 million in self-funding. But she received unfavorable news-media coverage for inflating her job descriptions as a State Department contractor during the Obama administration and as an aide in the 2016 Clinton campaign. Paul Kerr, a real-estate investor, contributed and loaned nearly $6 million to his campaign, but he suffered from political inexperience.

Levin led the Democrats in the primary, with 17 percent of the total vote, to 16 percent for Jacobs and 13 percent for Applegate. In his home base of Orange County, which cast only one-fifth of the vote, he led Jacobs by more than 3,000 votes. Jacobs led Levin by fewer than 400 votes in San Diego County.

Republican Diane Harkey ran first overall in the primary, with 26 percent of the total vote, though the four Democrats received 51 percent of the combined vote. Harkey was politically experienced as a member of the state Board of Equalization, which manages tax collection, and as a former Assemblywoman. She described herself as a "tax-fighter" and mostly praised the policies of President Donald Trump, though she raised concerns about some of his style and tactics. In its editorial endorsing Levin, the Union-Tribune praised him for taking on Trump and criticized Harkey as "overly defensive" and "ill-equipped" for the job.

Levin had a big financial advantage, as he more than tripled Harkey's spending during the closing months of the campaign. He was lifted by the Democratic surge throughout southern California, where he had the most comfortable victory of the seven Democratic newcomers who won House seats. In his 56%-44% victory, Levin had nearly 60 percent of the vote in San Diego portion of the district; Harkey led by about 5,000 votes in Orange County.

His lengthy experience in Democratic politics proved beneficial to Levin in his campaign and should serve him well in finding his way in the House.

CA-49: Northwest San Diego   **Cook Partisan Voting Index: R+1**

Population		Race and Ethnicity		Income	
Total	736,520	White	61%	Median Income	$82,202
Land area (sq. miles)	553	Black	2.6%	District Income Rank	46
Pop/ sq mi	1331.7	Latino	26%	Poverty Rate	9.6%
Born in State	50.4%	Asian	6.7%	With health insurance	91.4%
		Two or more races	3%	Cash public assistance	1.9%
Age Groups		Other	0.8%	Food stamp/SNAP	4%
Under 18	23%				
18-34	23.6%	**Education**		**Work**	
35-64	39.2%	H.S grad or less	25.6%	White Collar	14.2%
Over 64	14.2%	Some college	30.4%	Sales and Service	40.7%
		College Degree, 4 yr	27%	Blue Collar	14.9%
Military		Post grad	17.1%	Government	11.3%
Veteran/ Active Duty	13%				

2012 Pres. Vote	Romney	153,856	(52%)	Obama	134,447	(46%)		
2016 Pres. Vote	Clinton	159,081	(50%)	Trump	135,576	(43%)	Johnson 13,636	(4%)

Oceanside, Vista: The California coast between Los Angeles and San Diego has never entirely filled up with development — and never will as long as the Marine Corps retains custody of Camp Pendleton, the giant training base just south of the Orange-San Diego County line and the Corps' largest expeditionary training facility on the West Coast. The land along the coast and inland in northern San Diego County, usually referred to as North County, was largely empty territory a half-century ago — never fertile enough to produce a large farm community, never endowed with much manufacturing, never actively promoted as a retirement community. But North County has been growing rapidly since then. Today more than 800,000 people live here, and who can blame them? This is one of America's most beautiful and comfortable environments, with ocean and mountain scenery, sunny and warm weather, and low crime. Amid dry but not desert landscape, there are miles of rolling hills, with occasional sagebrush-like bushes. It has attracted thousands of new migrants — many, but by no means all, retirees. The commercial value of the land and buildings at Camp Pendleton, with its 17 miles along the coast, is more than $1.7 billion. The Trump administration reportedly has discussed using it to house 47,000 illegal immigrants.

Southern California Edison announced in 2013 the permanent shutdown of the San Onofre nuclear plant because of the financial costs and regulatory uncertainty of restarting a reactor following discovery of a radiation leak, plus flaws in the plant's steam generators. The company started the decommissioning in 2018, which it estimated as a 20-year, $4.4 billion project. In return, homeowners in the area expected that their properties would appreciate several billion dollars in value. In Carlsbad, a $1 billion desalination plant opened in 2015, partly in response to the California water crisis, and has been meeting about 10 percent of the region's water demands.

The 49th Congressional District covers the southernmost coastal area of Orange County, including Laguna Niguel and the heavily Republican San Clemente. Known as the "Spanish Village by the Sea," San Clemente is where Richard Nixon retired to write his memoirs after resigning the presidency. Nixon purchased his 5.5 acre estate in 1969, reportedly for a bit less than $1 million, though the financing was complicated and later controversial. He sold it in 1980. In May 2018, it was reported that the subsequent owner, the retired chief executive of Allergan pharmaceutical company, had reduced the listed price of the property to $63.5 million. Nearby, in Dana Point, a developer got county approval for a $330 million renovation of the old harbor. The district takes in parts of northern San Diego County and the North County, including Oceanside, Encinitas and Carlsbad, home of the La Costa resort and a big tourist destination. Much of the interior area is a mix of mountains and canyons, and lightly inhabited. About three-fourths of the voters in the 49th are in San Diego.

Politically, the district has leaned Republican. Hillary Clinton turned that around in 2016, when she led Donald Trump, 50%-43%.

Duncan Hunter (R)

Elected 2008, 6th term, b. Dec 07, 1976; San Diego; San Diego State University, B.A., 2001; Marine Corps Officer Candidate School (VA), 2002; Baptist; Married (Margaret Hunter); 3 children.

Military Career: U.S. Marine Corps 2002-2005; U.S. Marine Corps Reserve 2005-2017 (Afghanistan)

Professional Career: Business analyst, Cayenta Inc., 2000-2002; Residential developer, 2005-2007.

DC Office: 2429 RHOB 20515, 202-225-5672, Fax: 202-225-0235, hunter.house.gov

State Offices: El Cajon, 619-448-5201; Temecula, 951-695-5108.

Group Ratings

	ADA	ACLU	AFL-CIO	LCV	ITI	COC	HAFA	ACU	CFG	FRC
2018	-	4%	-	0%	-	73%	69%	88%	47%	100%
2017	0%	C	18%	0%	C	93%	C	81%	76%	100%

Almanac Ratings 2017-18

	Economy	Social	Foreign	Composite
Liberal	7%	3%	0%	3%
Conservative	93%	97%	100%	97%

Key Votes of the 115th Congress

1. Obama-care revision	Y	5. Family planning regs	Y	9. Guantanamo prisoners	N
2. Tax Cuts	Y	6. Body cameras/immigration	N	10. Ground missiles, limit	N
3. Omnibus appropriations	Y	7. Abortion ban	Y	11. Defense Dept. spending	Y
4. Dodd-Frank revision	Y	8. Concealed carry	Y	12. FISA rules	Y

Election Results

Election	Name (Party)	Vote (%)	Cand. Spent	Ind. Exp. Support	Ind. Exp. Oppose
2018 General	Duncan Hunter (R)............................ 134,362	(52%)	$1,851,535	$4,981	$156,559
	Ammar Campa-Najjar (D).................. 125,448	(48%)	$3,957,089	$362,300	
2018 Primary	Duncan Hunter (R)............................. 69,563	(47%)			
	Ammar Campa-Najjar (D).................... 25,799	(18%)			
	Bill Wells (R)...................................... 18,951	(13%)			
	Josh Butner (D)................................... 18,944	(13%)			
	Patrick Malloy (D)......................... 8,607	(6%)			

Prior winning percentages: 2016 (64%), 2014 (71%), 2012 (68%), 2010 (63%), 2008 (56%)

Republican Duncan D. Hunter, elected in 2008 to the seat held for 28 years by his father, Duncan Hunter, has been just as much of a defense hawk as his father, a former chairman of the House Armed Services Committee. His political career was jarred when he and his wife, Margaret, were indicted for campaign-finance violations for allegedly using campaign funds for personal expenses. In what had been a safe seat, he barely survived reelection in a bitter campaign that also saw charges of terrorism and hostility to Muslims. The trial was scheduled for September 2019.

The younger Hunter grew up in El Cajon and got a degree in business administration from San Diego State University, after having started a website design company with a friend during his sophomore year. He worked in the computer industry for several years during the technology boom of the late 1990s. The Sept. 11, 2001, terrorist attacks prompted him to rethink his career plans. The next day, Hunter quit his job and enlisted in the Marine Corps. After completing officer training, Hunter was commissioned as a lieutenant. He was deployed to Iraq in 2003, served in Baghdad after the fall of the city, and in 2004 fought in the battle of Fallujah. In 2006, he was promoted to captain and placed on reserve status. He became a major in 2012.

Though he earlier had shown little interest in following his father into politics, he said his battlefield experiences led him to reconsider public service. Shortly after announcing his candidacy in March 2007 for his retiring father's House seat, Hunter was again called to active duty, this time in Afghanistan. Hunter was prohibited from any campaign activities, including fundraising and planning, and held only one event before leaving. In his absence, the management of his nascent campaign fell to his wife. She took over all appearances and campaign duties in addition to caring for their three young children. When Hunter called home from Afghanistan, it was illegal for him even to inquire how the campaign was going. When his duty ended in December 2007, he returned to campaign full-time.

In the June primary, Hunter faced Santee Councilman Brian Jones and San Diego Board of Education President Bob Watkins. Hunter and his family surrogates effectively ran on the basis of his military credentials. He benefited from his father's political and congressional connections, raising nearly three times as much as his Republican challengers. He cruised to victory in the June primary with 72 percent of the vote. In the general election, Democrats paid little attention and Hunter prevailed, 56%-39%. He regularly won reelection with more than 60 percent.

On the Armed Services Committee, Hunter cited national security as his top priority. "I can tell you what the guys on the ground, the men and women out there fighting, actually need," Hunter said. "We have a whole lot of brass out there at the Pentagon and in the DOD who haven't left their offices in six or seven years." He has been vocal about the need for more defense spending. In 2012, he said that the shortage of amphibious ships is "one of the most glaring gaps in the Navy," he said.

Hunter has been outspoken on military personnel issues. He strongly opposed repealing the "don't ask, don't tell" policy prohibiting openly gay military personnel, telling National Public Radio that the bond between soldiers "is broken if you open up the military to transgenders, to hermaphrodites, to gays and lesbians." He opposed requiring women to register for the military draft with the Selective Service. After Navy Secretary Ray Mabus said in 2016 that he supported making women eligible for combat posts in the Marines, Hunter said that such a plan was "a greater threat to the Marine Corps than ISIS."

As chairman of the Transportation and Infrastructure Subcommittee on Coast Guard and Maritime Transportation, Hunter took the lead in the House during the 2015 enactment of a Coast Guard authorization bill, which included more authority to crack down on smuggling and funding for a polar icebreaker. Hunter's work on this legislation was useful for the San Diego region, where the Coast Guard has operated since 1937 and now patrols for illegal immigration and drug enforcement. Hunter's other interests include tougher immigration laws and finding ways to halt the outflow of jobs overseas. In 2014, he opposed the creation in Escondido of a shelter for children who had crossed the border illegally.

In February 2016, Hunter was one of the first congressional Republicans to endorse Donald Trump for president, saying that they agreed on many national security and immigration issues. During the campaign, Democratic challenger Patrick Malloy cited reports that Hunter had used campaign funds for personal purposes. Hunter largely ignored the charges, and he was reelected 63%-37%. In December 2016, the House Ethics Committee issued a statement that it was investigating the allegations.

With Trump as president, Hunter spearheaded enactment of additional maritime legislation, including new technology and equipment for the Coast Guard and the Save Our Seas Act for cleaner oceans. He backed Trump's demands for border security and urged him to use the military to build a wall at the border and "provide the full border enforcement Americans expect and deserve." Prior to Trump's rapprochement with North Korea, Hunter in September 2017 called for a U.S. pre-emptive strike against its nuclear facilities. "You could assume right now that we have a nuclear missile aimed at the United States and here in San Diego," he said in a radio interview.

His legislative activities came to a halt in August 2018, when the Justice Department indicted Hunter and his wife for using hundreds of thousands of dollars of campaign funds to pay for personal expenses, including family vacations. The charges listed more than 1,000 overdraft charges on their checking account and large credit-card debt. Hunter's lawyer said the indictment was politically motivated and that two of the prosecutors had attended a fundraiser for Hillary Clinton in 2015. Following the indictment, Speaker Paul Ryan said the charges were "deeply serious" and he stripped Hunter of his committee assignments, including the subcommittee chairmanship. Hunter otherwise continued his House duties, pending the trial. In June 2019, Hunter's legal woes deepened when his wife pleaded guilty to a single count of conspiracy.

The indictment raised the stakes and the conflicts in Hunter's reelection campaign. Democratic challenger Ammar Campa-Najjar, a 29-year-old of Palestinian and Mexican descent, called him "corrupt" and criticized his "racist" ads. Hunter said his opponent was backed by Muslim groups seeking to "infiltrate Congress." Campa-Najjar, a political newcomer, spent $4 million, with most of his contributions received after the indictment. Hunter spent $1.9 million and had limited national party assistance. Trump defended Hunter and criticized the indictment in a tweet. Hunter won 51.7%-48.3%. In the June primary, Hunter and two other Republican candidates had received a total of 62 percent of the vote. Campa-Najjar said that he will seek the seat again in 2020. Others likely will enter that contest.

CA-50: Inland San Diego   **Cook Partisan Voting Index: R+11**

Population		Race and Ethnicity		Income	
Total	744,267	White	55.6%	Median Income	$70,774
Land area (sq. miles)	2,787	Black	2.5%	District Income Rank	89
Pop/ sq mi	267	Latino	31.8%	Poverty Rate	12.2%
Born in State	55.4%	Asian	5.5%	With health insurance	89%
		Two or more races	3.3%	Cash public assistance	3%
Age Groups		Other	1.4%	Food stamp/SNAP	8%
Under 18	24.2%				
18-34	23%	**Education**		**Work**	
35-64	39.1%	H.S grad or less	37.1%	White Collar	13.7%
Over 64	13.7%	Some college	35.1%	Sales and Service	45.4%
		College Degree, 4 yr	18.5%	Blue Collar	20.5%
Military		Post grad	9.4%	Government	13.4%
Veteran/ Active Duty	10.4%				

2012 Pres. Vote	Romney	165,104	(60%)	Obama	102,649	(38%)			
2016 Pres. Vote	Trump	159,822	(54%)	Clinton	115,864	(39%)	Johnson	12,240	(4%)

Escondido, El Cajon: San Diego began as a port, but today most metropolitan-area residents live out of sight of the sea, in hilltop neighborhoods that look out over distant ridges and freeways or in warm, sunny valleys amid the mountains that become dense and taller as one travels east from the Pacific Ocean. There is a discernible difference in attitudes and values between those who have settled inland and those who live nearer the ocean, part of the split between coastal California and interior California that has been at the heart of the state's political struggles and culture wars. Outside of the city of San Diego, these groups in San Diego County have tended to identify as Republicans. Coastal residents tend to be more affluent, and those who settle inland are more likely to be culturally traditional, supportive of the military and dubious about the ability of government to help society's have-nots. Part of this can be explained by the area's large military presence. A 2018 report estimated that the Pentagon accounts for about $50 billion in annual spending in San Diego County, which is more than 20 percent of the local economy. That includes 143,000 civilians and active-duty military and 57 ships home-ported in San Diego, and two aircraft carriers based in Coronado. More than 240,000 veterans and military retirees have settled in the area.

North of San Diego on Interstate 15 is Escondido, a conservative city that is 51 percent Hispanic. Tensions between the Escondido political leadership and Latino activists have heightened in recent years, as the City Council passed several tough ordinances cracking down on illegal immigration. In November 2018, the long-running conflict clashed over the Justice Department's lawsuit against the California law supporting sanctuary cities. Mayor Sam Abed, who immigrated legally from Lebanon in the 1980s, visited the White House earlier in the year and supported its policies. With a large turnout from newly enfranchised Hispanic voters, he lost reelection to a liberal majority led by new mayor Paul McNamara, a retired Marine colonel.

The 50th Congressional District of California takes in much of the mountain and desert interior of San Diego County. The district includes a small slice of Riverside County, which is mostly in Temecula, the site of the largest wine-producing region in southern California. It touches neither the Pacific Ocean nor the border with Mexico, but it comes within a few miles of each. Eastern parts of the district are lightly inhabited. In the mountains is tiny Alpine and in the desert is the town of Borrego Springs, amid the giant Anza-Borrego Desert State Park. El Cajon has the nation's second-largest community of Chaldeans, Catholic Arabs from Iraq; some call the city, "Baghdad on the border." That Chaldean community has had conflicts with the church's international leadership over possible excommunication of local priests unless they recognized the authority in Baghdad. Politically, this district is solidly Republican. This was the strongest California district for Donald Trump south of Bakersfield. He led Hillary Clinton, 54%-39%.

Juan Vargas (D)

Elected 2012, 4th term, b. Mar 07, 1961; National City; University of San Diego, B.A., 1983; Fordham University (NY), 1987; Harvard University Law School (MA), J.D., 1991; Roman Catholic; Married (Adrienne D'Ascoli); 2 children.

Elected Office: San Diego City Council, 1993-2000; CA Assembly, 2000-2006, Assistant Majority Leader, 2000; CA Senate, 2010-2012.

Professional Career: Practicing attorney, Luce, Forward, Hamilton, & Scripps; Vice President., external affairs, Safeco Ins., 2006-2008; Vice President., corporate legal, Liberty Mutual Group, 2008-2010.

DC Office: 2244 RHOB 20515, 202-225-8045, Fax: 202-225-2772, vargas.house.gov

State Offices: Chula Vista, 619-422-5963; El Centro, 760-312-9900.

Committees: *Financial Services*: Housing, Community Development & Insurance; Investor Protection, Entrepreneurship & Capital Markets; Nat'l Security, International Development &

Monetary Policy; Oversight & Investigations. *Foreign Affairs*: Middle East, North Africa & International Terrorism; Western Hemisphere, Civilian Security, & Trade.

Group Ratings

	ADA	ACLU	AFL-CIO	LCV	ITI	COC	HAFA	ACU	CFG	FRC
2018	-	89%	-	91%	-	55%	8%	4%	24%	0%
2017	90%	C	100%	100%	C	57%	C	4%	5%	11%

Almanac Ratings 2017-18

	Economy	Social	Foreign	Composite
Liberal	96%	100%	95%	97%
Conservative	4%	0%	5%	3%

Key Votes of the 115th Congress

1. Obama-care revision	N	5. Family planning regs	N	9. Guantanamo prisoners	Y
2. Tax Cuts	N	6. Body cameras/immigration	Y	10. Ground missiles, limit	Y
3. Omnibus appropriations	N	7. Abortion ban	N	11. Defense Dept. spending	N
4. Dodd-Frank revision	N	8. Concealed carry	N	12. FISA rules	N

Election Results

Election	Name (Party)	Vote (%)		Cand. Spent	Ind. Exp. Support	Ind. Exp. Oppose
2018 General	Juan Vargas (D)	109,527	(71%)	$631,316		
	Juan Hidalgo (R)	44,301	(29%)	$58,825		
2018 Primary	Juan Vargas (D)	50,132	(64%)			
	Juan Hidalgo (R)	11,979	(15%)			
	John Renison (R)	10,972	(14%)			

Prior winning percentages: 2016 (73%), 2014 (69%), 2012 (72%)

Democrat Juan Vargas, first elected in 2012, has taken control of the district that he first sought in 1996. In this border district, he has spent much of his time on immigration. On the Financial Services Committee, where he has personal expertise, he opposed in 2018 the rollback of the Dodd-Frank banking regulatory law.

Vargas was born in National City, just south of San Diego. He is the son of braceros, who were among the millions of legal Mexican immigrants brought to the U.S. for cheap labor. He grew up on a chicken ranch in an urbanized area. He considered entering the priesthood but said he was wary of going straight into a seminary. Instead, he graduated from the University of San Diego. After college, Vargas studied with the Jesuits, working with the poor, orphans and refugees in El Salvador and elsewhere. The Jesuits sent him to Fordham University, where he studied philosophy and earned a master's degree. At Fordham, he met his future wife, Adrienne, a fellow student who worked with him at a soup kitchen in the Bronx. At Harvard, he earned a law degree alongside a student named Barack Obama.

After law school, Vargas settled in San Diego and briefly worked at a large corporate law firm. He served on the City Council for seven years, then won election to the California Assembly, where he stayed for six years. In 2010, he won election to the state Senate, where he chaired the Banking and Financial Institutions Committee and advocated government support for children and the elderly. He sponsored a bill mandating the reporting of child abuse by athletic coaches in California. Between his stints in the legislature, he was an executive with two insurance companies.

Vargas ran three unsuccessful campaigns for Congress against Rep. Bob Filner in Democratic primaries. Filner stepped down in 2012 and was elected mayor of San Diego, but quickly faced allegations of sexual harassment and resigned under pressure. Running for the open seat, Vargas and fellow Latino Democrat Denise Moreno Ducheny competed in California's all-party primary. But Vargas lavished attention on the Republican candidate, Michael Crimmins, to help him slide into second place. He refused to participate in a debate unless Crimmins was included. Meanwhile, Vargas hammered Ducheny for a previous drunken-driving arrest. Crimmins edged Ducheny 20%-15%. His defeat in the fall election was all but assured in the strongly Democratic district. It was a smart strategy. Vargas won 71%-29%. He has had no trouble with reelection.

Vargas has sought to provide a sympathetic ear to immigrants and refugees, no matter their circumstances. After protesters turned away busloads in Murrieta, he met with them the next day in El Centro in 2014. Carrying a Bible, Vargas prayed with them and told them that they would be treated "fairly and with dignity." He did not promise that they would remain in the United States. In 2016, he filed legislation that would require the military to inform recruits who are not citizens about the citizenship process while they are in training. While Donald Trump during his presidential campaign was promising to build a wall along the border with Mexico, Vargas told civic groups in his district that he wanted to build more bridges. With Republican Rep. Duncan Hunter, Vargas filed a bill to provide protection and a "safe haven" for local Chaldean Christians who had been threatened by their religious leaders in Iraq.

On the Financial Services Committee, Vargas worked with members who shared his interest in insurance issues. He cosponsored a bipartisan measure that conditioned trade agreements with the nations of the European Union on their rejection of the anti-Israel boycott, divestment and sanctions movement. That provision was enacted in 2015 as part of the measure that gave trade promotion authority to Obama. He said that the Dodd-Frank banking law "had worked well." In 2018, the House passed a Vargas bill to require that the Government Accountability Office study how online marketplaces facilitate drug and sex trafficking and offer solutions to Congress.

Vargas remained hostile to President Trump. On a June 2018 visit to an immigration detention facility with other members of Congress, including Nancy Pelosi, he said that the administration's family-separation policies at the border were "monstrous." When Trump met at the Capitol that month with House Republicans, Vargas joined four other House Democrats and shouted at Trump, "Don't you have kids, Mr. President?" Trump ignored them.

CA-51: San Diego to Nevada

Cook Partisan Voting Index: D+22

Population		Race and Ethnicity		Income	
Total	730,908	White	12.9%	Median Income	$44,759
Land area (sq. miles)	4,792	Black	6.3%	District Income Rank	378
Pop/ sq mi	152.5	Latino	70.5%	Poverty Rate	22.7%
Born in State	52.3%	Asian	8%	With health insurance	84.3%
		Two or more races	1.5%	Cash public assistance	5.3%
Age Groups		Other	0.7%	Food stamp/SNAP	18.1%
Under 18	26.3%				
18-34	28.3%	**Education**		**Work**	
35-64	34.4%	H.S grad or less	55.9%	White Collar	11%
Over 64	11%	Some college	29.9%	Sales and Service	53%
		College Degree, 4 yr	10.3%	Blue Collar	25.5%
Military		Post grad	3.9%	Government	16.2%
Veteran/ Active Duty	8.9%				

2012 Pres. Vote	Obama	115,610	(69%)	Romney	48,108	(29%)			
2016 Pres. Vote	Clinton	147,603	(71%)	Trump	46,825	(23%)	Johnson	5,714	(3%)
	Stein	4,065	(2%)						

Eastern Chula Vista, Imperial: Anchoring a corner of the continental United States, San Diego not so long ago was a small Navy town known for its good harbor and splendid weather. It is now a major metropolis of 1.4 million people and the center of a county of 3.3 million. To its occasional discomfort, it is also one of the largest cities directly on an international border, situated between countries with strikingly different economic conditions, political systems and cultural traditions. San Diego sits on the busiest border crossing in the world, and on a daily basis agents for the Border Patrol play a sometimes violent cat-and-mouse game with people trying to cross illegally. Apprehensions in the San Diego sector, which totaled 26,000 in 2015, jumped to 38,600 in 2018 — the highest since 2011. At the San Ysidro port of entry, local agents in August 2018 seized what likely was a record total of 20,000 fentanyl pills — synthetic heroin -- which had been stored inside a car panel.

Thousands of legal workers cross the border daily to reach the industrial zone on San Diego's southern edge, in Otay Mesa and San Ysidro and the industrial suburbs of Chula Vista and National City. In Chula Vista, officials plan to raise the Bayfront by eight feet to protect a planned hotel and conference center from the rising sea. Many children from Mexico cross daily to attend public and private schools. Latinos pour billions of dollars into the San Diego economy and are scattered in various parts of the city. Oddly, there is not much evidence of Mexican style in San Diego — less than in Los Angeles.

The thinly populated and agricultural Imperial County to the east has faced enormous economic adversity. Its unemployment rate, which was 18 percent in November 2018, has routinely remained the highest in California. The county is 84 percent Hispanic. Its salvation may lie in energy innovation. San Diego Gas & Electric, which has moved quickly to meet state requirements for the use of solar and wind power, might reach its goal of 50 percent renewable by 2020, which would be a decade ahead of its plan. Tesla has a large plant to draw lithium — used in electric car batteries — from the Salton Sea. A lithium geothermal power plant near the Salton Sea was expected to open in 2022. A second developer, which has purchased more than 1,300 acres, plans similar plants.

The 51st Congressional District of California covers California's entire border with Mexico, from the Arizona state line at Yuma to the southeast corner of the city of San Diego near Balboa Park, the eastern side of San Diego Bay, plus National City and Chula Vista. It includes the Salton Sea basin in the eastern desert and the Tijuana River National Estuarine Research Reserve on the western coast. About one-fourth of the vote is cast in Imperial County, with the remainder in San Diego County. The district is 71 percent Hispanic. The Democratic share of the presidential vote increased to 71 percent in 2016.

Scott Peters (D)

Elected 2012, 4th term, b. Jun 17, 1958; Springfield, OH; Duke University (NC), B.A., 1980; New York University Law School, J.D., 1984; Lutheran; Married (Lynn Gorguze); 2 children.

Elected Office: San Diego City Council, 2000-2008, President, 2006-2008.

Professional Career: Economist, U.S. Environmental Protection Agency, 1980-1981; Deputy Attorney, San Diego City, 1991-1996; Practicing attorney, 1984-1991, 1996-2000; CA Commission on Tax Policy in the New Economy, 2002-2003; CA Coastal Commission, 2002-2005; San Diego Unified Port District Commission, 2009-2012.

DC Office: 2338 RHOB 20515, 202-225-0508, scottpeters.house.gov

State Offices: San Diego, 858-455-5550.

Committees: *Budget. Energy & Commerce*: Energy; Environment & Climate Change; Oversight & Investigations.

Group Ratings

	ADA	ACLU	AFL-CIO	LCV	ITI	COC	HAFA	ACU	CFG	FRC
2018	-	71%	-	86%	-	83%	11%	20%	26%	0%
2017	75%	C	84%	97%	C	77%	C	4%	3%	0%

Almanac Ratings 2017-18

	Economy	Social	Foreign	Composite
Liberal	76%	93%	61%	77%
Conservative	24%	8%	39%	23%

Key Votes of the 115th Congress

1. Obama-care revision	N	5. Family planning regs	N	9. Guantanamo prisoners	Y
2. Tax Cuts	N	6. Body cameras/immigration	Y	10. Ground missiles, limit	N
3. Omnibus appropriations	Y	7. Abortion ban	N	11. Defense Dept. spending	Y
4. Dodd-Frank revision	Y	8. Concealed carry	N	12. FISA rules	Y

Election Results

Election	Name (Party)	Vote (%)		Cand. Spent	Ind. Exp. Support	Ind. Exp. Oppose
2018 General	Scott Peters (D)	188,992	(64%)	$1,742,477		
	Omar Qudrat (R)	107,015	(36%)	$368,025		
2018 Primary	Scott Peters (D)	98,744	(59%)			
	Omar Qudrat (R)	25,530	(15%)			
	James Veltmeyer (R)	19,040	(11%)			

Prior winning percentages: 2016 (57%), 2014 (52%), 2012 (51%)

Scott Peters, first elected in 2012, secured his seat after two costly and tight campaigns against experienced local Republicans. That success benefited from a centrist voting record and his occasional distancing from the liberal views of congressional Democrats from California.

Peters is the son of a Lutheran minister who fought against redlining in Detroit in the 1960s. A threat against his family sparked a police chief to suggest his father take them out of town for a week. At age 14, while the family was briefly living in Chicago, Peters had his first taste of politics campaigning for Democrat George McGovern's unsuccessful 1972 presidential race. He studied political science and economics at Duke, taking a low-wage job cleaning pigeon cages for the psychology department to support himself. He graduated from New York University's law school.

His wife, Lynn Gorguze, forged a successful career in private equity, and her work brought them to San Diego in 1988. She is the daughter of a wealthy La Jolla industrialist who contributed to Republicans. For 2018, Roll Call ranked Peters as the 17th wealthiest member of Congress, with a net worth of $32 million. Peters had a wide-ranging, 16-year career as a lawyer handling environmental regulation, corporate taxes and litigation; served as a deputy county counsel; and opened a private practice before being elected to the city council in 2000. During two terms — the last three years as president — Peters worked on reducing sewage spills, redeveloping neighborhoods to make them more walkable, boosting jobs with support for a downtown ballpark and creating the city's first ethics commission.

In 2012, Peters endured a bruising primary battle against Lori Saldaña, a former state Assembly member. She drew support from a left-leaning coalition, but Peters snagged many Democratic endorsements. Despite outspending Saldaña 5-to-1, Peters eked out a victory by just 700 votes. Running against three-term Republican Rep. Brian Bilbray, Peters found himself on the defensive against GOP attacks that he underfunded public-employee pensions during his tenure on the council, something that had marred his unsuccessful race for city attorney in 2009. He accused Bilbray of talking as a moderate while voting as a conservative, and he touted his own desire not to be bound by ideology. "I'm just not a purist. You set goals and you have to work with everyone to figure out how to get what you can," he said. Peters self-financed his campaign with more than $1 million and outspent the incumbent, $4.3 million to $2.8 million; he won 51%-49%.

His votes in the House, as shown by the Almanac vote ratings, have stamped him as a centrist. He tried to remain a political outsider by creating and publicizing his #FixCongressNow plan of broad changes in how Congress and elections operate, including five-day work weeks. He said Democrats "must move beyond economic fairness and now take the lead on creating an agenda for economic growth." His 2015 vote to give trade promotion authority to President Barack Obama infuriated the AFL-CIO, which denied him the support of organized labor in the 2016 campaign. Peters lined up in favor of steps to combat climate change, protect seniors on Medicare and promote immigration reform.

With his seat on the Energy and Commerce Committee, Peters pursued bipartisan collaboration and economic development. In June 2017, the House passed his bill to cut red tape in reviewing permits for hydropower projects and to give incentives for carbon-free investments. In 2017 and 2018, he led trade missions to the United Kingdom and Japan to promote San Diego. He became a vice-chair of the centrist New Democrat Coalition in 2019.

Peters faced a difficult reelection in 2014 against Republican Carl DeMaio, a former member of the city council who had narrowly lost a 2012 run for mayor of San Diego. DeMaio, who is openly gay, sought to move beyond traditional Republican support. In the first round, Peters got 42 percent of the vote with DeMaio at 36 percent, and three Republicans divided the remainder. That was a clear sign that Peters was vulnerable. DeMaio styled himself as a "next generation Republican," but Peters ran a tough ad campaign that focused on the challenger's sometimes abrasive style and hardline positions on the city council. DeMaio was put on the defensive by a former campaign aide's charges of sexual harassment and bribery. Peters outspent DeMaio, $4.5 million to $3.4 million, and the two candidates split another $7 million in national party money. Peters won 52%-48%. No charges were filed against DeMaio and the accuser later admitted that some of his charges were lies.

Since then, Peters has won easily. In 2016, Peters faced Denise Gitsham, who had worked for Karl Rove during the 2000 presidential campaign of Gov. George W. Bush and then joined Bush's White House staff. Gitsham emphasized her small-business values and raised $1.4 million. But Peters raised $3.5 million and won 57%-43%, with some likely benefit from the strong showing of Hillary Clinton in the presidential campaign. Two years later, Republican challenger Omar Qudray, a former prosecutor in the military, cited the weak business climate in San Diego and criticized Peters for a lack of transparency. Peters outspent his challenger by more than 5-to-1 and took 64 percent of the vote.

CA-52: Northern San Diego   Cook Partisan Voting Index: D+6

Population		Race and Ethnicity		Income	
Total	754,053	White	58.3%	Median Income	$89,955
Land area (sq. miles)	267	Black	2.8%	District Income Rank	31
Pop/ sq mi	2824.2	Latino	14.3%	Poverty Rate	9.5%
Born in State	42.6%	Asian	19.6%	With health insurance	93.8%
		Two or more races	4.1%	Cash public assistance	1.3%
Age Groups		Other	0.9%	Food stamp/SNAP	2.8%
Under 18	19.8%				
18-34	28.4%	**Education**		**Work**	
35-64	38.3%	H.S grad or less	16.4%	White Collar	13.5%
Over 64	13.5%	Some college	26.1%	Sales and Service	34.4%
		College Degree, 4 yr	32.7%	Blue Collar	8.8%
Military		Post grad	24.8%	Government	13.5%
Veteran/ Active Duty	12.2%				

2012 Pres. Vote	Obama	163,911	(52%)	Romney	143,726	(46%)		
2016 Pres. Vote	Clinton	191,325	(57%)	Trump	117,057	(35%)	Johnson	14,807 (4%)

La Jolla, Mission Bay: When the United States was dictating the terms of the Treaty of Guadalupe Hidalgo in 1848 after its successful war with Mexico, it made sure the southern boundary of its new California territory was just south of the port of San Diego. This is one of three splendid natural harbors on the Pacific Coast, and in 1914, the Marine Corps established a base on North Island. This was just the first of many military bases in San Diego, with its mild climate, deep harbor and plentiful land for aircraft maneuvers. Naval Base San Diego has been the major West Coast U.S. Navy base for more than 50 years, the second-largest Navy port behind Norfolk, and home to 143,000 active-duty personnel, with more than one-fourth of the nation's Marines. Also located here are about 240,000 veterans, and the retired aircraft carrier Midway.

The port and Navy base in the sheltered harbor remain the central focus of a rapidly growing metropolis that now stretches far inland and to the north. Downtown features post-modern buildings like the Horton Plaza amid a few well-preserved early-20th-century relics like the Spreckels Theatre. Across the harbor, on the sand spit that guards it against the ocean, is the white frame castle of the Hotel Del Coronado, with its dark wooden interior — the U.S.'s largest wooden structure, opened in 1888 and a favored resort of past American presidents. Work was scheduled to begin in early 2019 on a $200 million renovation of the Del, with completion in 2022. Already underway was construction of a $1.5 billion redevelopment on the city's waterfront. There was wide agreement with the airport's plan in 2018 to replace its 50-year-old terminal. But its confined location in the port area leaves scant space to expand and its plan conflicted with a host of local agencies, including transit and the port.

The coastal area is not all Navy. To the north, the Pacific waves pound against the beach beneath unique rock formations along the coast. Part of La Jolla is here, including the Scripps Institute of Oceanography. To the south are raffish Mission Beach; Ocean Beach, with its strong rip currents; and Point Loma, overlooking the entrance to the harbor. The weather — a sunny 70 degrees most of the time — lures tourists and new residents. San Diego is home to Comic-Con International, a four-day comic book and pop culture event that caps its attendance at 130,000 people annually. The 2017 move of the National Football League's San Diego Chargers up the freeway to Los Angeles was a blow to civic pride, but an acknowledgment of the smaller local market that objected to the team's demand for a new stadium.

The 52nd Congressional District includes much of the city of San Diego. It is one of two districts that are entirely within San Diego County. It runs along the west coast, taking in most of the city's Navy installations, ports and beaches. Inland and north of San Diego, it includes high-income Poway and most of La Jolla. The Asian population of the 52nd exceeds the Hispanic community, 20 percent to 14 percent — a split that has been growing. Its median income is the highest of the five San Diego-based districts. Politically, it has been a competitive congressional battleground, though it leans to Democrats in presidential contests. Hillary Clinton defeated Donald Trump, 57%-35%.

Susan Davis (D)

Elected 2000, 10th term, b. Apr 13, 1944; Cambridge, MA; University of California, Berkeley, B.S., 1965; University of North Carolina, M.A., 1968; Jewish; Married (Dr. Steve Davis); 2 children; 3 grandchildren.

Elected Office: San Diego School Board, 1983-1992, President, 1989-1992; CA Assembly, 1994-2000.

Professional Career: Devel. Association, KPBS Radio, 1980-1982.; Executive Director, Aaron Price Fellows, 1990-1994.

DC Office: 1214 LHOB 20515, 202-225-2040, Fax: 202-225-2948, susandavis.house.gov

State Offices: San Diego, 619-280-5353.

Committees: *Armed Services*: Military Personnel; Strategic Forces. *Commission Congressional Mailing Standards. Education & Labor*: Early Childhood, Elementary & Secondary Education; Higher Education & Workforce Investment (Chmn). *House Administration. Joint Printing.*

Group Ratings

	ADA	ACLU	AFL-CIO	LCV	ITI	COC	HAFA	ACU	CFG	FRC
2018	-	86%	-	94%	-	67%	8%	4%	21%	0%
2017	85%	C	92%	100%	C	54%	C	4%	0%	11%

Almanac Ratings 2017-18

	Economy	Social	Foreign	Composite
Liberal	93%	100%	92%	95%
Conservative	7%	0%	8%	5%

Key Votes of the 115th Congress

1. Obama-care revision	N	5. Family planning regs	N	9. Guantanamo prisoners	Y
2. Tax Cuts	N	6. Body cameras/immigration	Y	10. Ground missiles, limit	Y
3. Omnibus appropriations	Y	7. Abortion ban	N	11. Defense Dept. spending	Y
4. Dodd-Frank revision	N	8. Concealed carry	N	12. FISA rules	N

Election Results

Election	Name (Party)	Vote (%)		Cand. Spent	Ind. Exp. Support	Ind. Exp. Oppose
2018 General	Susan Davis (D)............................	185,667	(69%)	$281,769		
	Morgan Murtaugh (R)......................	83,127	(31%)	$94,455		
2018 Primary	Susan Davis (D)............................	93,051	(64%)			
	Morgan Murtaugh (R)......................	20,827	(14%)			
	Matt Mendoza (R)...........................	19,710	(14%)			

Prior winning percentages: 2016 (67%), 2014 (59%), 2012 (61%), 2010 (62%), 2008 (69%), 2006 (68%), 2004 (66%), 2002 (62%), 2000 (50%)

Susan Davis, a Democrat first elected in 2000, has worked quietly behind the scenes on issues that range from education and election reform to local and national military matters. In 2019, she had ambitious plans as chair of the subcommittee handling higher education issues. She is the number-two Democrat on two major House committees.

Davis grew up in Richmond California, the daughter of a pediatrician. She graduated from the University of California, Berkeley, and got a degree in social work at the University of North Carolina. After she married, she and her husband lived for a time in Japan while he served as an Air Force doctor during the Vietnam War. They moved to San Diego, where she was a producer for a local television station while also volunteering in civic groups, including as president of the local League of Women Voters. In 1983, Davis was elected to the San Diego school board. In 1994, she won the first of three terms in the California Assembly, where she chaired the Consumer Protection Committee.

Facing term limits, Davis in 2000 challenged Rep. Brian Bilbray, a Republican who had won three close elections. She portrayed him as too conservative for the district, though he took liberal and moderate positions on abortion rights and environmental protection. The AFL-CIO ran so much advertising on her behalf that Davis asked the union to stop. Davis won 50%-46%, and has been reelected without a serious challenge. Bilbray returned to Congress in 2006 when he won a special election in the neighboring district, though he lost his seat a second time in 2012.

Davis' voting record tends to be in the center of House Democrats, though more liberal on social issues, as shown by the Almanac vote ratings. On the Education and Labor Committee (previously Education and the Workforce), her priorities have included aid for school districts with a large military presence, student loans and incentives for better teachers. She angered organized labor by voting to give both Presidents George W. Bush and Barack Obama wide authority to negotiate international trade deals. San Diego is a city that has been built on trade. When organized labor rescinded its endorsement of her in 2015, she had a big drop in campaign contributions from unions, but there was no discernible electoral impact.

Her priorities as the top Democrat on the Higher Education Subcommittee have included increased federal aid for college students, equal opportunity, student safety and career and technical training – especially for women. In July 2018, she took the lead on a proposal by several House Democrats to provide debt-free college education and said that college should be "an attainable goal for all students." Davis is the number-two Democrat on the full committee behind Rep. Bobby Scott of Virginia.

On the Armed Services Committee, Davis has been active on women's health issues, including abortion services for military women. In 2009, as chairwoman of the Personnel Subcommittee, she helped secure a higher military pay raise than President Barack Obama requested. In 2016, she proposed the Military Hunger Prevention Act to make it easier for needy military families to get food stamps. She found herself in an unusual position that month when she opposed a 2.1 percent military pay hike because of the potential impact on other programs. "I am concerned that by increasing [pay] above the requested amount, we are taking funds away from other critical priorities, including readiness," she said. In 2018, after she said that President Donald Trump's ban on transgender service in the military was "discrimination," Davis was part of a bipartisan group that sought to block it. She enacted an amendment to the aviation bill in 2018 to protect emergency responders from illegal drone use during disasters; the measure was based on incidents in San Diego.

Speaker Nancy Pelosi in 2019 gave Davis a seat on the House Administration Committee, which has jurisdiction over election law. Davis has filed legislation to remove restrictions on voting by mail across the nation and to restrict partisan activities by state election officials. She was one of four House Democrats who were sued for displaying rainbow "pride" flags in their offices. After the federal appeals court in Washington D.C. dismissed the lawsuit, Davis said the result was a victory for "freedom and equality."

Davis has usually been reelected with ease. In 2014, against modest Republican opposition, Davis posted weak reelection performances. In the first round, she got 56 percent of the vote against seven other candidates, none of them a Democrat. In November against Larry Wilske, whom she outspent more than 5-to-1, Davis won with 59 percent. She has improved her performance since then.

CA-53: San Diego   **Cook Partisan Voting Index: D+14**

Population		Race and Ethnicity		Income	
Total	761,273	White	40.4%	Median Income	$68,799
Land area (sq. miles)	135	Black	7.7%	District Income Rank	102
Pop/ sq mi	5621.1	Latino	33.7%	Poverty Rate	13.1%
Born in State	50.6%	Asian	13.1%	With health insurance	89.9%
		Two or more races	4.1%	Cash public assistance	2.4%
Age Groups		Other	1%	Food stamp/SNAP	7.3%
Under 18	20.7%				
18-34	29.2%	**Education**		**Work**	
35-64	37.8%	H.S grad or less	29.5%	White Collar	12.3%
Over 64	12.3%	Some college	33.4%	Sales and Service	43.1%
		College Degree, 4 yr	23.8%	Blue Collar	13.8%
Military		Post grad	13.3%	Government	17.6%
Veteran/ Active Duty	11.8%				

2012 Pres. Vote	Obama	174,616	(61%)	Romney	103,513	(36%)		
2016 Pres. Vote	Clinton	200,237	(64%)	Trump	91,822	(29%)	Johnson	11,325	(4%)
	Stein	6,132	(2%)					

East San Diego, La Mesa: Often thought of as California's most conservative, straight-arrow city because of its long association with the U.S. Navy and the military, San Diego is now a multi-ethnic metropolis, with a population that is 30 percent Hispanic and 17 percent Asian; more than 40 percent of households speak a language other than English In a sense, the city is returning to its roots. San Diego was a part of newly independent Mexico from the 1820s and did not join the United States until after the Mexican-American War. It sits directly across the border from the Tijuana metropolitan area, and roughly 300,000 people a day cross from one city to the other, including 20,000 pedestrians. The drive across the border at the San Ysidro port of entry, the busiest entry point in the Western Hemisphere, often takes as long as two hours. Regular users can move more quickly through the Ready Lane if they have the requisite electronic documents. The completion of an expansion in 2019 was expected to result in northbound capacity to booths spread over 34 lanes, with plans to widen the southbound I-5 from five lanes to ten. When President Donald Trump closed down the port for five hours in November 2018, local shop-owners suffered a loss of $5 million.

San Diego has had a competitive and sometimes stormy political narrative. In 2012, 10-term Democratic Rep. Bob Filner was elected the city's first Democratic mayor in 20 years. But he quickly ran into ethical problems and survived only seven months before he resigned under pressure in the face of sexual harassment allegations by at least 18 women. He later pleaded guilty to a false imprisonment charge, and served three months of home confinement. Republican Kevin Faulconer, a former public relations executive, won a special election to complete Filner's term and then easily won a full term in 2016. Of all the Republican mayors in the nation, he has led the largest city. In 2017, Forbes magazine reported that San Diego could be the city that is "ground zero" and that its economy would be at risk of "a massive, sudden blow" if Trump pursued aggressive deportation of illegal immigrants. The San Diego City Council in May 2018 opposed the California law to support sanctuary cities, though the county favored it. San Diego is projected to continue its rapid growth rate, with a nearly 50 percent increase by 2050. Most of that likely will come from Hispanics.

The 53rd Congressional District is geographically the smallest San Diego-area district, taking in the eastern edge of the city and points inland to include the suburbs of Lemon Grove and Spring Valley. It includes La Mesa and La Presa, which is 50 percent Hispanic, and extends about two miles short of the border with Mexico. The district has a number of parks, lakes and open space preserves. The zoo is among the 10 largest in the world. Politically, this is a safe Democratic district. The Republican presidential vote fell from 36 percent in 2012 to 29 percent in 2016.

COLORADO

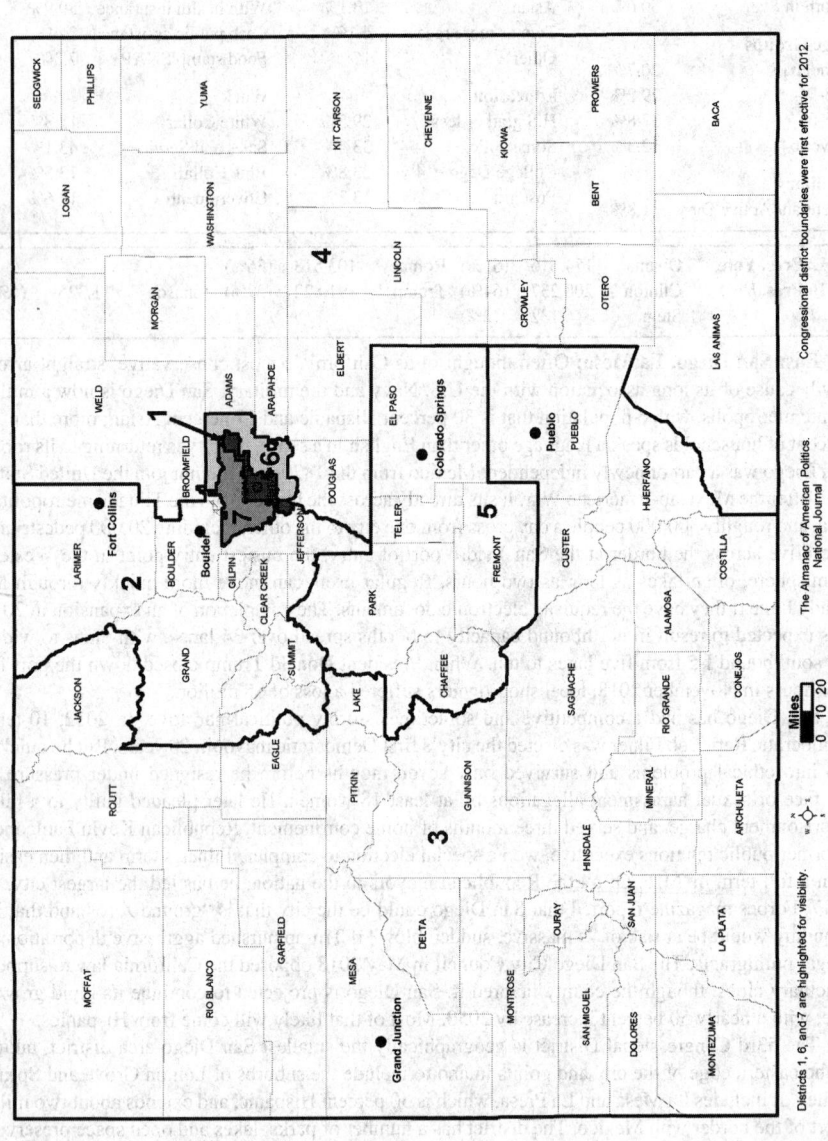

Congressional district boundaries were first effective for 2012.

The Almanac of American Politics.
National Journal

Districts 1, 6, and 7 are highlighted for visibility.

Colorado has been the kind of state Democrats point to when they dream of a future where their party is ascendant – fast-growing, well-educated, economically successful, tech-savvy, demographically diverse and beautifully situated. Increasingly, that Democratic fantasy is turning into a reality.

One summer day in 1893, Katherine Lee Bates, an English teacher at Colorado College, made her way by prairie wagon and mule up 14,114-foot Pikes Peak. Inspiration struck as she looked out over the spacious skies from the purple mountain's majesty to the amber waves of grain on the fruited plain, and she wrote the first version of America the Beautiful. Set to music, her words have resonated ever since, even though more than 90 percent of Americans up through World War II lived east of the Rockies, which rise above Denver, Boulder and Colorado Springs. As the "Centennial State" that was admitted to the Union in 1876, Colorado has been at the leading edge of the nation's economic, cultural and political evolution. For all its magnificent scenery, Colorado is demographically an urban state; just over half its 5.7 million people reside in metropolitan Denver, and four-fifths live within the urban strip paralleling the Front Range. And it is a healthy state, with the nation's lowest rates of obesity and highest rates of physical activity. You burn off more calories when you live 5,000 feet above sea level – and near alluring mountain scenery -- as most Coloradans do.

Colorado's history has been typified by occasional booms punctuated by long pauses of moderate growth. The first boom came just before the Civil War, when gold and silver were discovered in the Rockies; you can still see the grand opera houses and courthouses built in cities from that era -- Cripple Creek, Central City, Aspen and Telluride. But mining boom towns tend to go bust, and Denver, on the South Platte River just east of the mountains, soon became the region's leading city, driven by meatpacking, banking and manufacturing, as well as by state government and regional federal operations.

The state capitol, situated exactly 5,280 feet above sea level, looks north and west over Denver's busy downtown, with skyscrapers built during the energy boom of the 1970s and the telecom boom of the 1990s. Off toward the usually dry river bed are Coors Field, home of Major League Baseball's Rockies, and the Lower Downtown ("LoDo") neighborhood with its warehouses renovated into restaurants and clubs. To the east is the startling architecture of Denver International Airport on the plains, its canopy simultaneously suggesting the snow-capped Rockies, pioneers' covered wagons and Native American teepees. To the south is the sprawling Denver Tech Center, and all around are fast-growing subdivisions. Colorado has grown faster than the national average, but it has not experienced the explosive growth of Arizona and Nevada in recent decades. It has also avoided their debilitating housing bubbles, although affordable housing has become a problem in the Denver metro area; the median rent for one-bedroom apartments rose by 22.4 percent between 2014 and 2017, twice as fast as the nation as a whole, according to Apartmentlist.com

Unemployment has tracked below the national average, peaking at 8.9 percent in the fall of 2010 and typically remaining in the 3 percent range beginning in mid-2016; often, it has been even lower in the Denver-Aurora-Lakewood metropolitan area. Colorado has attracted fewer retirees and low-skill immigrants than Arizona and Nevada, and more young adults. Its attainment rates for bachelor's degrees rank among the nation's highest, and the graduates that settle in the state are eager to make a good living in what has generally been a growth economy and a place with natural and man-made amenities. Denver is famous for its parks and bike paths, and Boulder is a national center for bungee jumping, mountain biking, snowshoe running and hot-air ballooning.

The 1980s brought a bust, when an energy slump hit the state's relatively undiversified economy. But big and small tech firms boomed in the 1990s, accompanied by other types of high-salary work, including financial services, aerospace and satellites. An affluent electorate was willing to chip in to expand amenities, cultural institutions and a new rail line connecting the airport with downtown. Tourists have flocked in: In 2017, for the eighth year in a row, the state set new records for visitors. Most strikingly, Coloradans voted to make their state the first jurisdiction in the world to fully license the manufacture, cultivation and sale of marijuana. While problems emerged, such as a difficulty in regulating "edibles," local jurisdictions have been thrilled with the new revenue, and the decision has been popular. On the downside, the state has recently experienced an intense drought, harming agriculture and producing a spike in wildfires. Five of the 20 biggest wildfires in the state's history occurred in 2018, a worry for the 2.9 million people who live in Colorado's "wildland-urban interface."

Colorado has been reshaped politically by its successive waves of newcomers, who have increased the state's population from 1.7 million in 1960 to 5.7 million today. The conservative and boosterish Colorado of the 1960s was transformed in the 1970s by young liberal migrants who called for environmental protections and slow growth. Then in the 1990s, a new wave of migrants — tech-savvy, family-oriented cultural conservatives — moved Colorado's politics to the right. If the spirit of the 1970s newcomers was embodied by Boulder, with its pedestrian mall, outdoor sports shops and vegetarian restaurants, then the spirit of the 1990s was epitomized by religious conservatives in Colorado Springs, home of the Air Force Academy and Dr. James Dobson's Focus on the Family. Today, some of the state's fastest-growing areas are on the northern edge of the Front Range; Loveland and Fort Collins, less than 20 miles from Wyoming, have each grown by 15 percent since the 2010 Census and are turning bluer, matching the state. If current population trends continue, the state is in line to gain a congressional seat after the 2020 census.

For decades, Colorado has been governed by a series of temporarily dominant party coalitions. But that may be ending, as Democrats consolidate their demographic gains. Colorado's Latino population now stands at 21 percent, the seventh-highest percentage of any state. The state also has one of the nation's youngest populations, with many millennials living in university enclaves. Denver and Boulder attract young professionals imbued with progressive values, while the ski resorts — Telluride, Aspen, Vail, Crested Butte, Steamboat Springs — are inhabited by the wealthy and the people who wait on them in boutiques and restaurants, both demographics that lean Democratic.

In 2006, Democrats won the first of four consecutive gubernatorial races, and in 2008 the party held its national convention in Denver, foreshadowing a win in the fall that helped send Barack Obama to the White House. As that was happening, Republicans remained competitive in contests for statewide offices, U.S. House seats and the state legislature, sometimes aided by Democratic overreach, including a stretch in 2013 and 2014 when the newly Democratic-controlled legislature enacted a gun control measure in the wake of a massacre at a movie theater in suburban Aurora. This prompted a Republican backlash in the 2014 midterms, with the GOP flipping the state Senate, falling just short in the state House, and winning an upset Senate race as GOP Rep. Cory Gardner defeated incumbent Democratic Sen. Mark Udall. The Republican revival proved to be short-lived: In 2016, Hillary Clinton beat Donald Trump by nearly five points, as the pro-Democratic tilt of suburban areas outweighed the migration of blue-collar areas toward Trump.

Democrats expanded their dominance during the 2018 midterms. Rep. Jared Polis, a liberal Democrat, won the gubernatorial race, 53%-43% -- more than three times bigger than the winning margin that his predecessor, Democratic Gov. John Hickenlooper, had put together four years earlier. Even more impressively, Democrats in 2018 flipped the attorney general, treasurer and secretary of state seats, as well as control of the state Senate and the 6th Congressional District. The one notable failure for liberals was the defeat of a ballot measure that would have imposed strict setback limits on oil and gas drilling; amid a doubling of oil production since 2013, the measure secured only 44 percent of the vote. Not surprisingly, one of the Democrats' biggest Senate targets in 2020 will be Gardner, the last Republican with a major statewide perch.

Population		Race and Ethnicity		Income	
Total	5,436,519	White	68.6%	Median Income	$65,458
Land area (sq. miles)	103,642	Black	3.9%	State Income Rank	12
Pop/ sq mi	52.5	Latino	21.3%	Poverty Rate	11.5%
Born in state	42.7%	Asian	3.0%	With health insurance	90.6%
		Two or more races	2.4%	Cash public assistance	2.1%
Age Groups		Other	0.8%	Food stamp/SNAP	8.2%
Under 18	23.0%				
18-34	24.7%	Education		Work	
35-64	39.3%	H.S grad or less	30.4%	White Collar	41.2%
Over 64	13.0%	Some college	30.2%	Sales and Service	40.4%
		College Degree, 4 yr	24.8%	Blue Collar	18.4%
Military		Post grad	14.6%	Government	13.4%
Veteran/ Active Duty	9.9%				

Presidential Politics

2016 Caucus (D)   Sanders (D)   72,846 (59%)   Clinton (D)   49,789 (40%)
2016 Pres. Vote   Clinton (D) 1,338,870 (48%)   Trump (R)   1,202,484 (43%)   Johnson (L)   144,121   (5%)
2012 Pres. Vote   Obama (D) 1,323,102 (51%)   Romney (R)1,185,243 (46%)

Colorado, once a Republican state in presidential elections, has cast its ballots in three consecutive elections for Democrats. Hillary Clinton defeated Donald Trump 48%-43%, on the strength of support from Hispanics and college-educated white voters. That kind of backing has made the greater Denver area a Democratic stronghold. In 2016, nearly half of the state's presidential vote came from Denver, its three major suburban counties — Adams, Arapahoe and Jefferson — and adjacent Boulder County, home to the University of Colorado. This area gave Clinton almost three-out-of-five votes cast for president. Nearby Douglas County, which includes some Denver exurbs, remained a Republican bastion and Trump won it handily, along with other more urban counties on the southern Front Range like El Paso (Colorado Springs) and, narrowly, Pueblo. Voters in this manufacturing community behaved like their brethren in the Midwestern Rust Belt, favoring Trump, who became the first GOP presidential nominee to carry Pueblo County since Richard Nixon in 1972. Incumbent Democratic Sen. Michael Bennett, who was up for reelection in 2016, carried the county by nine percentage points. The old coal mining counties of Las Animas and Huerfano also switched to Trump after having backed Obama in 2012.

Between LBJ in 1964 and Barack Obama in 2008, the only Democrat to carry Colorado was Bill Clinton in 1992, and it's likely that independent candidate Ross Perot siphoned off enough GOP voters from George H.W. Bush to produce that outcome. But Democrats had Colorado in their sights when they selected Denver for their 2008 national convention site. Obama formally accepted the nomination in Mile High Stadium.

Colorado held an early March presidential primary from 1992 until 2000, which never attracted much national attention. In 2003, to save money, the legislature voted to eliminate the presidential primary and let the parties hold caucuses. The 2016 Republican and Democratic versions were both notable. Colorado GOP officials opted not to hold a typical presidential preference poll at their local caucuses, with the aim of sending uncommitted delegates to the party confab in Cleveland. But Texas Sen. Ted Cruz skillfully organized the subsequent congressional district conventions and the state convention and packed the delegation with his supporters, prompting Trump to complain that the Colorado GOP caucuses were "rigged." Vermont Sen. Bernie Sanders swamped Clinton in the March 1 Democratic caucuses, 59%-40%. The turnout of more than 122,000 exceeded the roughly 120,000 who participated in the party caucuses eight years earlier when Obama defeated Clinton 67%-32%, and was one of the few contests where Democratic turnout was up from 2008.

Congressional Districts

116th Congress Lineup	4D 3R	115th Congress Lineup	3D 4R

After the 2010 census, the two parties had a lengthy and bitter stalemate in the state legislature that forced the federal courts to intervene. A Denver district judge chose a Democratic plan for the sake of making the Republican-held 6th District south of Denver more "competitive." That map's biggest shift was to remove nearly all of heavily Republican Douglas County from the 6th District and replace it with increasingly Hispanic Aurora to the north, making the seat of GOP Rep. Mike Coffman seven percentage points less Republican. After three failed challenges in competitive contests, Democrats in 2018 finally defeated Coffman. That has left the state with four Democratic-held seats in the Denver metro area, including Boulder, and three Republican-held seats in outlying districts to the east, south and west.

The state is projected to gain an additional House seat after the 2020 census. With Democrats winning control in 2018 of the governor's office and the legislature, they seem likely to draw the new district, with a Democratic lean, in the metro area. That might require the shift of some Democratic voters from the Denver-based 1st and artful drawing of the three other Democratic-held districts, where the party has gained increasing — but not solid -- control. Democratic map-drawers likely will pull some left-leaning bastions from the three Republican-held districts.

Jared Polis (D)

Elected 2018, term expires 2023, 1st term; b. May 12, 1975, Boulder; Princeton University, B.A., 1996; Jewish; Married (Marlon Reis); 2 children.

Elected Office: Member, CO Board of Education, 2000-2007, Chair, 2004-2005; US House, 2009-2018.

Professional Career: Co-Founder, American Information Systems; Entrepreneur; Philanthropist.

Office: 200 E. Colfax Ave., Room 136, Denver, 80203-1792; 303-866-2471; Fax: 303-866-2003; Website: colorado.gov

Lt. Gov.: Dianne Primavera (D) **Atty. Gen:** Phil Weiser (D) **Sec. of State:** Jena Griswold (D)

State Legislature: Senate: 19D, 16R   **House:** 40D, 24R, 1I

Election Results

Election	Name (Party)	Vote (%)
2018 General	Jared Polis (D)	1,348,888 (53%)
	Walker Stapleton (R)	1,080,801 (43%)
	Scott Helker (Lib)	69,519 (3%)
2018 Primary	Jared Polis (D)	283,340 (45%)
	Cary Kennedy (D)	157,396 (25%)
	Michael Johnston (D)	149,884 (24%)
	Donna Lynne (D)	46,382 (7%)

Jared Polis, a Democrat first elected to the House in 2008, won the Colorado governorship in 2018, becoming the first openly gay man to be elected to either office. He won the governorship easily, 53%-43% -- a margin more than three times bigger than the one his predecessor, Democrat John Hickenlooper, had put together four years earlier.

Polis was born in Boulder but grew up in the San Diego suburb of La Jolla, with frequent vacations back in Colorado. His mother, a poet, and his father, an artist, were both politically active during the anti-war movement of the late 1960s. As a fifth-grader, and on his own volition, he addressed the La Jolla City Council to stop development in an urban canyon near his home; the mayor told the local paper that his argument swayed the vote to no. Initially preferring to go into politics immediately without attending college, Polis agreed with his parents to simply speed up the process: He graduated from high school in three years and applied successfully to Princeton at age 16, where he would earn a political science degree. As a student government official, Polis ran what he billed as the world's first fully online election (it was 1995) and joined with two sophomore friends to launch American Information Systems, an internet service provider. It was the first of 20 companies that Polis founded or co-founded. "He's a preternaturally ambitious person who's always had an eye on his next move, and who's always had the money to help himself get there," the Colorado Independent wrote in an extensive, four-part profile.

Soon afterward, Polis turned his parents' small greeting-card company, Blue Mountain Arts, into a website that at its height was the eighth most popular on the internet. He sold it for $780 million, then built Proflowers.com, which enabled customers to order fresh flowers directly from growers. In 2006, the flower service sold for $477 million. Along the way, at 25, he changed his name from Jared Polis Schutz to Jared Schutz Polis to honor his grandmother.

Financial security allowed Polis to focus on his political passions. In 2000, four years out of college, he was elected to the Colorado State Board of Education; he challenged an appointed incumbent, drove all over the state in a school bus, and spent $1.2 million, all of which broke the mold for the low-profile position. Polis won by 90 votes, outspending his opponent by more than 100 to 1. He served one six-year term and chaired the board for one year. Polis was most proud of his advancement of school choice through charter schools and his work improving accountability standards for schools. In part with his own money, he founded two innovative charter schools in Colorado, which helped new immigrants assimilate, especially with flexible day or evening programs, and teachers trained to help students learn English.

Political observers fully expected Polis to raise his political profile further, and he did. He became part of a "Gang of Four" consisting of Colorado multimillionaires, including QuarkXPress founder Tim Gill, medical device heiress Patricia Stryker and geophysicist and MicroMAX software creator Rutt Bridges. The group nurtured a web of liberal activist organizations and shrewdly framed and targeted issues such as same-sex marriage, ultimately reshaping the political landscape, including taking control of both legislative chambers in 2004.

When a House seat opened in 2008, he decided to run. In the Democratic primary, he faced former state Senate President Joan Fitz-Gerald and conservationist Will Shafroth. Most of the state's Democratic establishment backed Fitz-Gerald. Pouring in his own money, Polis outspent his opponents 4-to-1. He got 42 percent of the vote, followed by Fitz-Gerald with 38 percent and Shafroth with 20 percent. At age 33, he breezed through the general election, 63%-34%. In the entire campaign, he spent $7 million, of which $6 million was his own. After that, he was not seriously challenged for the House seat, either in a primary or a general election. The Center for Responsive Politics ranked Polis in 2015 as the second-richest member of the House, pegging his net worth at $388 million. It was during his initial House campaign that Polis came out as gay.

In Washington, Democratic leaders gave Polis a seat on the Rules Committee, a tool of the majority leadership that controls the terms of debate for major bills on the House floor; despite the minority's institutional weakness, Polis was considered effective at getting floor consideration of Democratic amendments. He has taken many progressive positions, including a role as chief House sponsor of the Employee Non-Discrimination Act and promoting a bill that would legalize marijuana as a controlled substance and tax it, initially at 10 percent. But he has also defied the "Boulder liberal" stereotype at times. In 2009, Polis jumped into the health care debate, successfully torpedoing a proposal by his own party that would have paid for elements of the overhauled system with a tax on the highest-earning Americans. He was one of 22 Democrats in 2012 who voted for a plan that was based on the recommendations of President Barack Obama's Simpson-Bowles deficit-reduction commission. In 2015, he was one of 28 House Democrats who voted to give trade promotion authority to Obama, and he backed the Trans-Pacific Partnership.

In 2018, Hickenlooper was term-limited out following eight years of generally centrist leadership. Polis' path to the gubernatorial nomination involved some sharp elbows. By the time he joined the Democratic primary field, it already included fellow Rep. Ed Perlmutter as well as several candidates with statewide experience. Within weeks of Polis' entry and the specter of a heavily self-funding primary opponent, Perlmutter dropped out. Former state treasurer Cary Kennedy, backed by teachers' unions, initially gained establishment support, but an ad sponsored by an independent teachers' PAC that targeted Polis and former state Sen. Mike Johnston prompted a backlash against Kennedy. In the end, Polis, backed by $10 million of his own money, received 44 percent, Kennedy got 25 percent, Johnston got 24 percent, and Lt. Gov. Donna Lynne won 7 percent. On the GOP side, two-term state treasurer and Bush family member Walker Stapleton won the nomination 48%-30% over self-funding challenger Victor Mitchell.

In the general election, Polis proposed taxpayer-funded universal pre-kindergarten; increased spending for teacher salaries and smaller class sizes; single-payer health care; an end to $1.6 billion in excise and corporate tax breaks; a phase-out of private prisons; an expansion of rural broadband; and 100 percent renewable energy by 2040. "Climate change is a blinking red light, and we have to act now or our children will end up suffering the consequences of inaction," Polis told the Denver Post. Stapleton countered that Polis' goals were unreasonably expensive -- "free is really expensive," Stapleton said at one debate – while adding that any shift away from oil and gas would imperil hundreds of thousands of jobs in the state. But Polis had actually moved some distance toward the oil and gas industry over the previous few years. In 2014, he pushed for a pair of ballot measures that would have made it more difficult to undertake fracking projects. The measures never made it to the ballot when Gov. John Hickenlooper agreed to review alternative policy options. Four years later, during his run for governor, Polis opposed a similar ballot measure that would have hampered fracking. Polis also softened his views on gun control, this time to the left. Meanwhile, Polis broke new tactical ground in targeting marijuana users and people who work in the cannabis industry, using a mix of text messages and voter registration drives at dispensaries, the Colorado Sun reported. His campaign spent more than $22 million, blowing away state records.

Polis ended up winning 10,000 more votes statewide than Hillary Clinton had during the presidential year of 2016. In Denver and three neighboring counties – Adams, Arapahoe and Jefferson – Democrats collected 35 percent more raw votes with Polis than they had with Hickenlooper four years earlier, and they expanded the party's winning gubernatorial margin in each of those counties by between six and 10 points. Polis won by 13 points in Larimer County (which includes fast-growing Fort Collins and Loveland), an improvement on Hickenlooper's five-point win there. He was also able to shave the GOP's winning margin in El Paso County (traditionally conservative Colorado Springs) from 27 points to 16.

Michael Bennet (D)

Elected 2009, term expires 2022, 3rd term, b. Nov 28, 1964; New Delhi, India; Wesleyan University (CT), B.A., 1987; Yale University Law School (CT), J.D., 1993; Religion not stated; Married (Susan Daggett Bennet); 3 children.

Professional Career: Counsel to Deputy Attorney General, U.S Department of Justice, 1995-1997; Managing Director, Anschutz Investment Co., 1997-2003; Chief of staff, Denver Mayor John Hickenlooper, 2003-2005; Superintendent, Denver Public Schools, 2005-2009.

DC Office: 261 RSOB 20510, 202-224-5852, Fax: 202-228-5097, bennet.senate.gov

State Offices: Alamosa, 719-587-0096; Colorado Springs, 719-328-1100; Denver, 303-455-7600; Durango, 970-259-1710; Fort Collins, 970-224-2200; Grand Junction, 970-241-6631; Pueblo, 719-542-7550.

Committees: *Agriculture, Nutrition & Forestry*: Commodities, Risk Management & Trade; Conservation, Forestry & Natural Resources (RMM); Rural Development & Energy. *Finance*: Energy, Natural Resources & Infrastructure (RMM); Social Security, Pensions & Family Policy; Taxation & IRS Oversight. *Intelligence*.

Group Ratings

	ADA	ACLU	AFL-CIO	LCV	ITI	COC	HAFA	ACU	CFG	FRC
2018	-	71%	-	100%	-	60%	8%	14%	15%	8%
2017	90%	C	100%	84%	C	29%	C	0%	4%	8%

Almanac Ratings 2017-18

	Economy	Social	Foreign	Composite
Liberal	89%	89%	68%	82%
Conservative	11%	11%	32%	18%

Key Votes of the 115th Congress

1. Obama-care revision	N	5. Gun regulations	N	9. Kavanaugh confirmation	N
2. Tax Cuts	N	6. Family planning regs	N	10. Saudi arms sales	Y
3. Dodd-Frank revision	Y	7. Gorsuch confirmation	N	11. FISA rules	N
4. Omnibus appropriations	Y	8. Immigration restrictions	N	12. Military aid in Yemen	Y

Election Results

Election	Name (Party)	Vote (%)	Cand. Spent	Ind. Exp. Support	Ind. Exp. Oppose
2016 General	Michael Bennet (D) 1,370,710	(50%)	$24,460,995	$1,277,047	$705,306
	Darryl Glenn (R) 1,215,318	(44%)	$4,955,031	$2,987,974	$90,511
	Lily Tang Williams (L) 99,277	(4%)	$6,810		
2016 Primary	Michael Bennet (D) .... Unopposed				

Prior winning percentages: 2010 (48%)

The route by which Democrat Michael Bennet, Colorado's senior senator, reached Capitol Hill was an unusual one, notwithstanding his upbringing in the Washington establishment. Bennet's pre-Senate resume is among the more eclectic of members of that chamber. He moved from law and politics to finance, where he became a multimillionaire, and then to education, where he was superintendent of a large urban school district, before returning to politics in his current role. He was a surprise choice in 2009 — appointed over several better-known contenders – for a vacant seat in the Senate, where he has gained a reputation as an affable legislator and quick study.

But if Bennet's path to the Senate was improbable, his course since joining it often has been unpredictable: He has crafted a reputation as a centrist ready to reach across party lines to achieve legislative progress. In this regard, Bennet has not been unlike other Democrats to win statewide in Colorado – a purple state with an increasingly blue hue – in recent decades. To keep his seat, Bennet, at 54, has faced a couple of bruising campaigns where he was relentlessly attacked for supporting most major initiatives of President Barack Obama, who took office the month Bennet arrived on Capitol Hill. But Bennet also has pursued an independent course on several high-profile issues during and after the Obama administration, sometimes to the displeasure of his party's increasingly vocal progressive wing. While Bennet has signaled his ambitions don't stop at the Senate -- he announced a longshot presidential bid in the spring of 2019 after months of hinting at a run -- his aspirations will likely be complicated by his status as a party moderate.

Bennet's lineage is impressive and intriguing: His father's family dates back to the arrival of the Mayflower, while his mother was born in the Jewish ghetto of Warsaw, Poland, immigrating to the United States after being hidden from the Nazis during World War II. Bennet was born in New Delhi, India, in 1964, where his father, Douglas Bennet, was an aide to Ambassador Chester Bowles. The elder Bennet, after working for such leading Democratic senators as Hubert Humphrey, Edmund Muskie and Thomas Eagleton, went on to become a top State Department official in the Carter and Clinton administrations as well as president of NPR. One of three children, Michael Bennet grew up and attended private schools in Washington, D.C., and was a Senate page in high school. A younger brother, James, is the editorial page editor of The New York Times.

Bennet is a third-generation graduate of Wesleyan University; his father later served as president of the school. After school, Bennet worked for Democratic Ohio Gov. Richard Celeste, a family friend. Later, at Yale Law School, he was editor-in-chief of the Yale Law Journal. He was an associate in Lloyd Cutler's influential law firm in Washington before being named counsel to Deputy Attorney General Jamie Gorelick in the Clinton administration; he wrote speeches for Attorney General Janet Reno. Bennet's move west came in 1997 when his wife, Susan Daggett, a natural resources lawyer, accepted a job with the Earthjustice Legal Defense Fund in Denver. Bennet went to work for an investment company headed by billionaire Philip Anschutz, a political conservative. While Bennet had never read a balance sheet, Anschutz was impressed by Bennet and hired him — while ordering Bennet to attend accounting school at night at his own expense.

Bennet landed such assignments as overseeing the consolidation of three theater chains into Regal Entertainment Group, one of the country's largest movie theater chains. . After six years with Anschutz, during which he accumulated $12 million, Bennet returned to the public sector when a fellow Wesleyan alumnus, John Hickenlooper, was elected Denver mayor and asked him to be his chief of staff. Bennet said he gave up millions in stock options to accept "an opportunity that wouldn't come around again." His accomplishments included a plan to balance the city's budget by cutting 10 percent — without laying off any workers. "I have referred to him as the second mayor, the hidden mayor," Hickenlooper, who later served two terms as governor, told The Denver Post. Bennet's late entry into the 2020 presidential contest put him on a collision course with his one-time boss: Hickenlooper announced his own White House bid two months earlier.

In 2005, the position of Denver Public Schools superintendent came open, and Bennet was among the top candidates — even though he had no experience in education, had attended private schools, and was sending his daughter to a private kindergarten. The board picked him to head a system of 73,000 students, three-quarters of whom were Latino or African-American. He quickly triggered controversy by moving to close a problem-plagued high school in the city's African-American community and disperse its students to other schools. But he instituted a plan to boost performance standards in the schools while creating workshops to teach principals how to lead schools to reform. Proficiency in reading and math rose by 6 percent during Bennet's four-year tenure, according to the Washington-based Council of Great City Schools.

After Obama was elected, Bennet was on the short list to head the. Department of Education. But Bennet was not even regarded as a long shot for the Senate when Obama picked Colorado Sen. Ken Salazar to be his Interior secretary. Bennet had limited national political experience, consisting mainly of a 2004 speech he gave to a group of business leaders denouncing the Iraq war and President George W. Bush. But Democratic Gov. Bill Ritter astonished just about everyone by naming Bennet to fill the remaining two years of Salazar's term. Ritter said he was impressed with Bennet's record of bringing diverse interests together to solve problems and his pragmatic approach to turning around troubled public and private enterprises. Some leading Democrats were not happy. The Washington Post later recounted how now-Senate Minority Leader Chuck Schumer of New York called Ritter at the time — and sarcastically thanked him for throwing away a Democratic seat on an unknown politician who could not win re-election.

Once sworn in, Bennet dug into legislating with gusto. On the Health, Education, Labor, and Pensions Committee, he introduced a bill to strengthen the Food and Drug Administration's ability to prevent tainted drugs from reaching consumers. In a rare example of bipartisan cooperation following the 2010 election, Bennet's proposal became law in 2012. Drawing on his experience with Denver's schools, he added more than half a dozen proposals as the Obama administration sought to replace the No Child Left Behind education law, such as tying new teacher licensing to performance and increasing the flexibility of school districts in spending federal money. His colleagues credited Bennet with moving both parties to the middle in that debate, finally leading to passage of a new law, the Every Student Succeeds Act, in late 2015. "He bridged the gap with the Republicans," the HELP panel's ranking Democrat, Sen. Patty Murray of Washington, said.

As he prepared to seek election in 2010, Bennet drew a fierce primary challenge from former state House Speaker Andrew Romanoff – one of the better known names passed over for the Senate appointment a year earlier. Romanoff portrayed himself as an outsider, and, drawing on Bennet's work for Anschutz, attacked the incumbent as a tool of Wall Street. While Romanoff surged in the closing days of the primary in a year that was tough for incumbents, Bennet hung on to win, 54%-46%. In November, Bennet faced another tough contest against Weld County District Attorney Ken Buck, who had won the GOP nomination over the establishment candidate, former Lt. Gov. Jane Norton, with the backing of tea party activists. Buck portrayed Bennet as part of the problem in big-spending Washington, and attacked his vote for Obama's Affordable Care Act. But Buck proved to be gaffe-prone during the campaign, and Bennet made an issue of his 2005 decision as district attorney not to prosecute an accused rapist; Buck said at the time that a jury would likely conclude that the victim's complaint was a case of "buyer's remorse."

Bennet proved to be a strong fundraiser, and, with $11.5 million in campaign funds, saturated the airwaves portraying Buck as too extreme for Colorado's independent-minded voters; Buck had called for dismantling the Department of Education and opposed abortion in all circumstances. Buck raised $5 million of his own and had help from the American Crossroads super PAC, which invested another $5 million in ads attacking Bennet. But Bennet held the upper hand despite voting for major elements of Obama's agenda. "To a very large extent, Bennet made the issue not about the national economy, but about the characteristics of Ken Buck," Colorado College political scientist Bob Loevy told

The Denver Post. Bennet won 48%-46%. Four years later, Buck won a House seat from Colorado's predominantly Republican 4th District.

Returning to Capitol Hill, where the House had flipped to Republican control and the Senate had a decreased Democratic majority, Bennet looked for additional opportunities to reach across the aisle. He became part of a bipartisan "Gang of Eight" seeking ways to avoid the "fiscal cliff" looming at the end of 2012. A leader of that group was Bennet's close friend, Virginia Sen. Mark Warner, a fellow centrist Democrat. However, the "fiscal cliff" solution ultimately adopted at the end of 2012 was largely the result of negotiations between the Obama White House and Senate Republican leaders; Bennet was one of three Senate Democrats to oppose it. He said it "does not put in place a real process to reduce the debt down the road." Bennet's focus on this issue has persisted: In November 2018, he unveiled a plan to replace the House and Senate budget committees with a "Joint Select Committee on Fiscal Responsibility," charged with reducing the national debt by an amount equal to at least 5 percent of the gross domestic product over a decade. "I say this as a Democrat: I don't think there's anything progressive about having $19 trillion in debt on the balance sheet of this country," he said during his 2016 re-election bid.

Shortly after the 2012 elections, then-Senate Majority Leader Harry Reid offered Bennet the chairmanship of the Democratic Senatorial Campaign Committee. It took Bennet three weeks to accept it; he was concerned it would interfere with efforts to work across the aisle. For accepting the two-year post, Bennet was awarded a seat on the powerful Finance Committee. It turned out to be a disastrous election cycle for Democrats, who lost nine seats and control of the Senate. Despite the dismal showing, Bennet escaped the second-guessing that inevitably follows such failures, as many in the party quietly blamed the Obama White House. Among the political casualties was Bennet's Colorado colleague, Sen. Mark Udall, who ran a race similar to Bennet's in 2010 by stressing his opponent's "extreme" positions. In turn, Udall's Republican opponent, now-Sen. Cory Gardner — upset about DSCC ads aimed at him — skewered Bennet as "the chief partisan of the United States Senate."

Notwithstanding this introduction, Bennet and Gardner developed a bipartisan bromance. Shortly after arriving in the Senate, Gardner met with Bennet, and both stressed a desire to work together. Gardner invited Bennet on a tour of Colorado's Eastern Plains, where he grew up, with Bennet following by hosting a tour of his former domain, the Denver school system. During their first two years serving together, Bennett and Gardner co-authored more than a dozen pieces of legislation – several specific to Colorado, but others national in scope. They found common ground on energy issues, agreeing on an "all of the above" approach favoring renewable sources while vowing to protect Colorado's liquid natural gas industry. They also were in accord on the Keystone XL pipeline: In early 2015, Bennet was among just eight Democrats to join all Senate Republicans in an unsuccessful effort to override Obama's veto of the controversial project connecting Canada's oil sands fields with Gulf Coast refineries. The pipeline got the green light after the President Donald Trump took office two years later.

Another notable Bennet-Gardner collaboration came in the first year of the Trump administration, when they joined a bipartisan group of a half-dozen senators working on immigration reform – a response to Trump's September 2017 announcement that he planned to cancel the Deferred Action for Childhood Arrivals program initiated by Obama. After several months, the six senators agreed on a legislative package that included legal status for the children of undocumented immigrants covered by DACA along with enhanced border security. But the effort died after Trump declined to sign on. It was a follow-on to Bennet's participation in another "Gang of Eight" effort several years earlier. That resulted in a bipartisan immigration reform proposal that passed the Senate in 2013 but died after the House refused to take it up.

Bipartisan friendships aside, Gardner's upset victory over Udall emboldened national Republicans — who targeted Bennet as the one incumbent Democrat they had a chance of ousting in 2016. However, problems on the GOP side provided Bennet with a series of breaks. First, the Republicans failed to attract a top-tier candidate. Those declining included a member of Congress, the state attorney general, and a district attorney who had gained statewide attention for prosecuting the 2012 Aurora movie theater shooting in which 12 died. As five lesser known Republicans sought the party's nomination, former state Rep. Jon Keyser emerged as the choice of the GOP establishment. But barely two months before the June primary, Keyser was removed from the ballot after a number of the signatures on his nominating petition were deemed invalid. He was subsequently reinstated, but had to fight a lawsuit seeking to have him removed again. He finished a distant fourth, with the nomination going to El Paso County Supervisor Darryl Glenn.

Glenn, an African-American and Air Force veteran who served in Iraq and Afghanistan, was boosted by endorsements from such conservative luminaries as Texas Sen. Ted Cruz and former Alaska Gov. Sarah Palin. But Glenn ended up being outspent 4-1 by Bennet, who hammered away at a remark Glenn made during a primary debate; "it's not about reaching across the aisle" to compromise, Glenn had said. As he had six years earlier, Bennet suggested his opponent was too extreme for Colorado. Polls three weeks from the general election showed Bennet with a double-digit lead. It ended up being closer, with Bennet winning 50%-44%, his victory largely tracking Democratic presidential candidate Hillary Clinton's 48%-43% win in the state on a county-by-county basis.

With the Democrats out of power at both ends of Pennsylvania Avenue, Bennet found himself squeezed between home-state and national party pressures when Trump, in January 2017, nominated Denver-born federal judge Neil Gorsuch to the Supreme Court. Even some leading Democrats in Colorado pressed Bennet to back Gorsuch, while nationally, many Democrats remained enraged over the Republican-controlled Senate's refusal to consider Obama's nomination of another federal judge, Merrick Garland, for the vacancy – and were pushing for a filibuster. Bennet lobbied fellow Democrats to head off a filibuster fight, according to Politico. He argued to Schumer that, since Gorsuch would succeed the late conservative Justice Antonin Scalia, it wouldn't alter the balance of the court – and it was the next vacancy that would really matter. But the Democratic leadership opted to filibuster, and Majority Leader Mitch McConnell invoked the "nuclear option" effectively changing the rules to do away with filibusters for Supreme Court nominations.

Bennet sought to steer a middle course. As one of Gorsuch's home-state senators, he observed tradition and introduced the nominee to the Judiciary Committee, while voting to allow Gorsuch's nomination to go to the Senate floor – one of just four Democrats to do so. But, on the final vote, he opposed Gorsuch's confirmation. A visibly exasperated Bennet took a harder line 18 months later with the Supreme Court nomination of federal Judge Brett Kavanaugh, taking to the Senate floor to castigate McConnell for how the process had been handled. Earlier, Bennet helped a Colorado woman, Debbie Ramirez, enlist the help of a prominent Denver law firm after Ramirez became the second individual to accuse Kavanaugh of sexual misconduct – dating back to when she and Kavanaugh were Yale University undergraduates.

Thanks in part to his status as a swing-state senator, there was continuing speculation about Bennet as a presidential aspirant. Following the 2018 election, Bennet's limited profile outside of his home state received a boost when he shed his generally calm demeanor to deliver an emotional floor speech aimed at Texas Republican Ted Cruz, a hardline conservative, amid a 34-day government shutdown. When Cruz sought to blame the Democrats for the shutdown, Bennet -- in a response that went viral on social media -- pointed to Cruz's role in a 2013 shutdown during the Obama administration. "These crocodile tears that the senator from Texas is crying for the first responders are too hard for me to take," Bennet declared. After undergoing successful surgery for prostate cancer, Bennet became the second Colorado centrist in the contest.

In a March 2018 Washington Post op-ed explaining his latest difference with a majority of his Democratic Senate colleagues – his vote for legislation rolling back rules imposed on smaller banks by the 2010 Dodd-Frank financial regulatory overhaul – Bennet concluded with a broader defense of his approach to governance. "On issue after issue, voices on the left and right routinely decry modest concessions as a betrayal of principle. More often than not, that principle turns out to be little more than a tactic to garner media attention by casting small differences on policy as cataclysmic. Until this changes, we will struggle to make progress as both parties retreat to their corners instead of doing the unglamorous, vital work of governing," Bennet wrote, in a preview of his 2020 campaign pitch.

Cory Gardner (R)

Elected 2014, term expires 2020, 1st term, b. Aug 22, 1974; Yuma; Colorado State University, B.A., 1997; University of Colorado School of Law, J.D., 2001; Lutheran; Married (Jamie Gardner); 2 children.

Elected Office: CO House, 2005-2010; U.S. House, 2011-2015.

Professional Career: Communications Director, National Corn Growers Assn., 2001-2002; Staffer, Sen. Wayne Allard, 2002-2005; Owner, Farmers Implement dealership.

DC Office: 354 RSOB 20510, 202-224-5941, Fax: 202-224-6524, gardner.senate.gov

State Offices: Colorado Springs, 719-632-6706; Denver, 303-391-5777; Durango, 970-259-1231; Fort Collins, 970-484-3502; Grand Junction, 970-245-9553; Greeley, 970-352-5546; Pueblo, 719-543-1324; Yuma, 970-848-3095.

Committees: *Commerce, Science & Transportation*: Communications, Technology, Innovation & the Internet; Subcommittee on Aviation & Space; Subcommittee on Science, Oceans, Fisheries & Weather (Chmn); Subcommittee on Transportation & Safety. *Energy & Natural Resources*: Energy; National Parks; Public Lands, Forests & Mining; Water & Power. *Foreign Relations*: East Asia, the Pacific & International Cybersecurity Policy (Chmn); Near East, South Asia, Central Asia & Counterterrorism; West Hem Crime Civ Sec Dem Rights & Women's Issues.

Group Ratings

	ADA	ACLU	AFL-CIO	LCV	ITI	COC	HAFA	ACU	CFG	FRC
2018	-	29%	-	7%	-	90%	62%	86%	62%	100%
2017	0%	C	0%	0%	C	86%	C	76%	73%	100%

Almanac Ratings 2017-18

	Economy	Social	Foreign	Composite
Liberal	6%	6%	8%	7%
Conservative	94%	94%	92%	93%

Key Votes of the 115th Congress

1. Obama-care revision	Y	5. Gun regulations	Y	9. Kavanaugh confirmation	Y
2. Tax Cuts	Y	6. Family planning regs	Y	10. Saudi arms sales	N
3. Dodd-Frank revision	Y	7. Gorsuch confirmation	Y	11. FISA rules	N
4. Omnibus appropriations	N	8. Immigration restrictions	Y	12. Military aid in Yemen	N

Election Results

Election	Name (Party)	Vote (%)		Cand. Spent	Ind. Exp. Support	Ind. Exp. Oppose
2014 General	Cory Gardner (R)	983,891	(48%)	$12,490,384	$9,012,838	$30,646,858
	Mark Udall (D)	944,203	(46%)	$20,463,869	$6,684,190	$23,665,575
	Gaylon Kent (L)	52,876	(3%)			
2014 Primary	Cory Gardner (R)	338,324	(100%)			

Prior winning percentages: House: 2012 (58%), 2010 (52%)

When Cory Gardner, became chairman of the National Republican Senatorial Committee at the end of 2016 at 42, he was the youngest lawmaker in a generation to take over a position that often has led to higher rungs in the Senate GOP leadership. But Colorado's junior senator's two-year stint in the NRSC post — which ended shortly after Election Day 2018 — could turn out to be very much of a double-edged sword as he seeks a second term. Even as the Republicans were ousting Democratic senators in several red states under Gardner's watch, a blue wave was inundating his home state: Democrats won all statewide offices, recaptured the state Senate and gained ground in Colorado's U.S. House delegation. And, in 2020, Gardner's name will appear on the ballot just beneath that of President Donald Trump, who polls showed to be less popular in Colorado in mid- to late 2018 than when he lost the state by 5 points to Democrat Hillary Clinton in 2016. Such back-home political realities have placed Gardner — one of only two sitting Republican senators from states that Clinton carried — atop national Democratic target lists in the forthcoming election cycle.

In fact, Gardner did not vote for the Trump in 2016; he wrote in the name of now-Vice President Mike Pence after first calling on the then-candidate Trump to step aside following the emergence of the "Access Hollywood" video showing Trump making lewd comments about women. But, during the first half of the Trump presidency, potential opponents have pointed to Gardner's voting record of siding with Trump more than 91 percent of the time, according to ratings compiled by FiveThirtyEight. Meanwhile, Gardner's stint as head of the NRSC often put him in close proximity to the president. "He's tremendous and done so much," Trump said of Gardner at a campaign rally in West Virginia in August 2018, after the two men were photographed stepping off Air Force One together. "Clearly that night was a night that Cory Gardner would like to soon forget and a ride on Air Force One he wishes he didn't take," Denver political analyst Eric Sondermann told Colorado-based Westword, alluding to the fact that two Trump associates, Michael Cohen and Paul Manafort, had been convicted in federal court earlier the same day.

But Gardner also has been adept at putting distance between himself and Trump on issues such as immigration and marijuana legalization when opinion in his home state has collided with the current administration's. And nine months before the ride on Air Force One, Gardner split from Trump in a special Senate election in Alabama — withdrawing NRSC support for GOP nominee Roy Moore following reports he had initiated sexual contact with teenage girls when he was in his 30s. "If he refuses to withdraw and wins, the Senate should vote to expel him," Gardner said of Moore, adding that the women accusing Moore "spoke with courage and truth" — even as Trump was endorsing the nominee. Earlier, Gardner had criticized Trump when the president equivocated in his condemnation of white nationalists, after one person was killed and nearly three-dozen more injured at a white supremacist rally in Charlottesville Virginia. "Mr. President — we must call evil its name," Gardner tweeted. "These were white supremacists and this was domestic terrorism."

Such stances underscore that Gardner — known for being upbeat and optimistic — is not going to let Democrats pigeonhole him in a state where he is the only Republican to win a U.S. Senate or gubernatorial race in the past decade and a half. "He won by calling himself 'a new kind of Republican,' and so be it if that means being outspoken when he disagrees with the president," Steve Gordon, an operative who worked on Gardner's 2014 Senate campaign, told Roll Call. "That's just who he is, and fortunately for him, it's also good politics at home."

A fifth-generation Coloradan, Gardner grew up in Yuma, a tiny farming and ranching town 150 miles east of Denver. After graduating from Colorado State University, Gardner returned to Yuma in pursuit of an agrarian lifestyle. But his father urged him to consider a profession less closely tied to the vagaries of rural Colorado. Gardner earned a law degree from the University of Colorado and took a job as communications director for the National Corn Growers Association. The following year, he became an aide to Republican Sen. Wayne Allard, whose former seat Gardner now occupies. In the summer of 2005, Gardner was appointed to fill a vacancy in the Colorado House, and a year later he won election to a full term.

Believing one-term Democratic Rep. Betsy Markey to be vulnerable in early 2010 in a district that had previously been held by Republicans since 1973, the state GOP coalesced around Gardner: They emphasized his deep roots in the 4th District's heavily Republican Eastern Plains. Gardner pounded Markey for supporting President Barack Obama's spending policies while skirting the social issues that could have alienated voters in some of the district's suburban areas. His strategy worked, and, at 36, Gardner was elected to Congress with 52 percent of the vote. On Capitol Hill, where Republicans had just recaptured the House, Gardner was one of his freshman class's most faithful followers of the GOP leadership. He befriended future House Speaker Paul Ryan of Wisconsin, often joining Ryan on the campaign trail during the latter's vice presidential candidacy in 2012. Gardner received a seat on the influential Energy and Commerce Committee and frequently assisted in House Republican messaging on energy matters. He authored bills to open parts of Alaska to oil drilling and to require the president to promote a policy aimed at lowering gas prices by tapping the Strategic Petroleum Reserves. Both passed the House, but went nowhere in a Senate then under Democratic control.

After easily winning re-election in 2012, Gardner rejected the idea of running for the Senate against Democratic incumbent Mark Udall, a top target of national Republicans. But Gardner changed his mind after other potential top-tier candidates — including three House members, a former member and the state's attorney general —said no. He secured the GOP nomination in April 2014. An independent poll that month showed Gardner, despite never having run statewide and only entering the race weeks earlier, in a dead heat with Udall, who was saddled with Obama's plummeting approval ratings. Gardner ran as a political outsider, while portraying Udall — who had spent a decade in the House prior to winning the Senate seat opened up in 2008 by Allard's retirement — as a rubberstamp for Senate Democratic leaders and a captive of Washington. He also hammered away at Udall's support for the Affordable Care Act. Udall responded by painting Gardner as extreme on social issues and ran ads attacking him on birth control and abortion. His charges that Gardner held positions that were hostile to women, reinforced by outside groups that spent lavishly, saturated the airwaves.

But Udall's campaign strategy backfired. In a major blow to Udall, The Denver Post, the state's largest newspaper that typically backs Democrats, endorsed Gardner. "Udall is trying to frighten voters rather than inspire them. His obnoxious one-issue campaign is an insult to those he seeks to convince," the endorsement said, adding, "In every position [Gardner] has held over the years— from the state legislature to U.S. House of Representatives — he has quickly become someone to be reckoned with and whose words carry weight." Gardner defended himself against Udall's attacks by saying that he had listened to voters and changed his stance on a "personhood" bill that could have resulted in a ban on certain forms of birth control. He went so far as to write an op-ed demanding birth control pills be available over the counter. On another major issue in a state that is more than 20 percent Hispanic-American, Gardner relaxed his earlier hard-line stance on immigration. In 2013, he had backed an unsuccessful House effort to block the Obama administration's Deferred Action for Childhood Arrivals program intended to protect the children of undocumented immigrants. But, running statewide, he supported giving immigrants who serve in the armed forces a path to citizenship.

Such moves appeared to reassure voters that Gardner was not the inflexible ideologue that Democrats charged him of being, and on Election Day, he scored a 48%-46% win over Udall. The contest coincided with the 2013-2015 tenure of Colorado's other senator, Michael Bennet, as chairman of the Democratic Senatorial Campaign Committee. In that role, Bennet sought to stave off Udall's defeat with tactics that prompted Gardner to criticize his future in-state colleague as "the chief partisan of the United States Senate." But Gardner sought to mend fences after the campaign, and the two men have since found common ground on both national and Colorado-centric issues. Notably, in September 2017, Gardner's shift on immigration policy continued as he joined Bennet as a co-sponsor of the so-called DREAM Act, which would have shielded immigrants brought to the country illegally as children from deportation and given then a pathway to citizenship. Gardner's decision to sponsor the measure came just after Trump announced plans to cancel the DACA program initiated by Obama. Gardner and Bennet were part of a bipartisan group of a half-dozen senators who in early 2018 agreed on a legislative package pairing legal status for those covered by the DACA program and other immigration changes with enhanced border security. But the effort was stymied after Trump told two members of the group he was not ready to embrace the proposal.

In another collaboration, Gardner and Bennet joined Oregon's senators on a bill to legalize banking for recreational-marijuana companies; Colorado and Oregon were the first states to legalize recreational marijuana. In June 2018, Gardner teamed up with one of the Senate's leading progressives, Democratic Sen. Elizabeth Warren of Massachusetts, on a bill to protect the rights of states that have legalized pot, including Massachusetts. Six months earlier, Gardner had threatened to block the Trump administration's nominations for Justice Department positions after then-Attorney General Jeff Sessions revoked the Obama administration's "Cole memo." The letter discouraged prosecutors from enforcing federal marijuana prohibition in states that had legalized pot. After a months-long standoff in which Gardner held up confirmation of about 20 nominees, he relented when Trump assured him that Sessions' action would not affect Colorado. Later, introducing the bill he co-authored with Warren, Gardner complained that the federal government "is closing its eyes and plugging its ears" at a time when many states had OK'd recreational marijuana. He said the legislation would ensure that Washington respects "the will of the voters — whether that is legalization or prohibition — and not interfere in any states' legal marijuana industry."

But Gardner largely adhered to the party line on another high-profile, hot-button issue: health care. Caught between a conservative base in rural Colorado whose support he needs in a re-election fight and Democrats and independents — among whom the Affordable Care Act has become increasingly popular, according to in-state polling — Gardner spent much of the first year of the Trump administration trying to sidestep the issue. Dealing with it was further complicated by his post in the GOP Senate Republican leadership and his 2014 campaign vow to support a repeal of "Obamacare." While other members of the Senate Republican leadership pressed for repeal of "Obamacare" in media briefings during the first part of 2017, Gardner sought to change the subject when his turn came to speak. But he ultimately supported all of the major Republican proposals to undo the Affordable Cart Act, an effort that was blocked in July 2017 when a handful of Republicans joined Senate Democrats in opposing the move. "I am committed to reforming our nation's broken health care system, and I'll continue to work to bring relief to Coloradans being hurt by the negative impacts of Obamacare," Gardner said afterward.

One of Gardner's more significant legislative accomplishments was a measure he co-sponsored with Democratic Sen. Gary Peters of Michigan. It resolved a three-year battle between House Republican leaders and the scientific community over how the National Science Foundation should operate. While the House had passed a series of proposals along partisan lines, Gardner and Peters — working together as members of the Commerce, Science and Transportation Committee — crafted a bipartisan measure that scientists saw as much more supportive of the NSF. Legislation signed into law by Obama in late 2016 reflected the Gardner-Peters approach.

With his re-election bid looming, Gardner in early 2019 sought to thread the political needle between his largely pro-Trump Republican base and the broader Colorado electorate. It did not end up happily for him, as the Denver Post -- in a blistering editorial -- expressed regret for having endorsed Gardner in 2014. When Trump, responding to Congress' refusal to appropriate $5.7 billion for a southern border wall, announced he would declare a national emergency to obtain the money, Congress approved a resolution disapproving of the president's action. Initially, Gardner told Colorado Public Radio he opposed Trump's move and that he had personally told the president so. But Gardner ultimately voted against the resolution, which a dozen of his Republican colleagues joined Senate Democrats in supporting. Calling Gardner's position "completely inconsistent with every stance he has taken on Trump's presidency," the Denver Post editorialized: "We no longer know what principles guide the senator and regret giving him our support in a close race against Mark Udall."

With Gardner atop the national Democrats' target list, by mid-2019, a dozen Democrats had announced their candidacies, including ex-House Speaker Andrew Romanoff, who lost a competitive primary challenge to Sen. Michael Bennet in 2010. Two others who were first elected in 2018 were reportedly considering a campaign: Secretary of State Jena Griswold and Rep. Joseph Neguse. But Senate Democratic Leader Chuck Schumer's top prospect to take on Gardner, former Gov. John Hickenlooper, opted to run for the party's presidential nomination. For Gardner, an upside was that his NRSC stint gave him easy entrée to a national GOP fundraising base. He "should have no problem having all of the resources necessary to fend off whoever it might be," Justin Prendergast, a GOP political consultant told The Denver Post, adding, "It's probably going to be the most expensive Senate race in the nation."

Diana DeGette (D)

Elected 1996, 12th term, b. Jul 29, 1957; Tachikawa, Japan; Colorado College, B.A., 1979; New York University Law School, J.D., 1982; Presbyterian; Married (Lino Lipinsky); 2 children.

Elected Office: CO House, 1992-1996, Assistant Minority Leader, 1994-1995.

Professional Career: Practicing attorney, 1982-1996.

DC Office: 2111 RHOB 20515, 202-225-4431, Fax: 202-225-5657, degette.house.gov

State Offices: Denver, 303-844-4988.

Committees: *Energy & Commerce*: Communications & Technology; Environment & Climate Change; Oversight & Investigations (Chmn). *Natural Resources*: Energy & Mineral Resources; National Parks, Forests & Public Lands.

Group Ratings

	ADA	ACLU	AFL-CIO	LCV	ITI	COC	HAFA	ACU	CFG	FRC
2018	-	92%	-	91%	-	55%	9%	4%	21%	0%
2017	90%	C	91%	89%	C	50%	C	9%	7%	11%

Almanac Ratings 2017-18

	Economy	Social	Foreign	Composite
Liberal	95%	94%	100%	96%
Conservative	5%	6%	0%	4%

Key Votes of the 115th Congress

1. Obama-care revision	N	5. Family planning regs	N	9. Guantanamo prisoners	Y
2. Tax Cuts	N	6. Body cameras/immigration	NV	10. Ground missiles, limit	Y
3. Omnibus appropriations	N	7. Abortion ban	N	11. Defense Dept. spending	N
4. Dodd-Frank revision	N	8. Concealed carry	N	12. FISA rules	N

Election Results

Election	Name (Party)	Vote (%)	Cand. Spent	Ind. Exp. Support	Ind. Exp. Oppose
2018 General	Diana DeGette (D)............................ 272,886	(74%)	$851,868		
	Casper Stockham (R)....................... 85,207	(23%)	$621		
	Raymon Doane (Lib)........................ 11,600	(3%)			
2018 Primary	Diana DeGette (D)............................ 91,102	(68%)			
	Saira Rao (D).................................. 42,398	(32%)			

Prior winning percentages: 2016 (68%), 2014 (66%), 2012 (68%), 2010 (67%), 2008 (72%), 2006 (80%), 2004 (74%), 2002 (66%), 2000 (69%), 1998 (67%), 1996 (57%)

Diana DeGette, first elected in 1996, is an energetic liberal and a chief deputy whip who has been among the House Democrats anxiously awaiting the chance to succeed the party's older, entrenched leaders. Taking over in January 2019 as chair of the Energy and Commerce Oversight Subcommittee, DeGette pursued numerous inquiries of the Trump administration. With her occasional success in the past with bipartisan legislation, DeGette insisted that Congress could "walk and chew gum" — enacting policy while investigating the president.

DeGette is a fourth-generation resident of Denver, though she was born on a military base in Japan. She says that she was inspired at age 13 by the television show Storefront Lawyers to "crusade for justice," and decided she would be a public interest lawyer. She attended New York University's law school on a full scholarship, then returned to Denver to practice employment law. In 1992, at age 35, DeGette was elected to the Colorado House. Her signature accomplishment was the Bubble Bill, which was aimed at protecting women at abortion clinics by making it illegal for protesters to come within eight feet of a person entering or leaving a health care facility. The U.S. Supreme Court upheld the constitutionality of the law in a 6-3 decision. In 1995, when Rep. Patricia Schroeder, a pioneer of the feminist left, announced she was retiring, DeGette ran for the seat. Organizationally adept, legislatively creative and politically progressive, she proved a worthy successor to Schroeder.

In both the minority and the majority, she has achieved legislative successes. On Energy and Commerce she has focused on health care issues. She teamed with Republican Rep. Mike Castle of Delaware to expand funding for stem cell research. President George W. Bush opposed using federal tax money for such research, and in 2006 vetoed their bill. In 2009, President Barack Obama, using his executive powers, removed most federal restrictions on stem cell research. She wrote a book on the topic called Sex, Science, and Stem Cells.

On other health issues, she cosponsored in 2009 the Food Safety Enhancement Act. She secured two key provisions giving the Food and Drug Administration the power to mandate product recalls and authorizing the FDA to establish a food-tracking system. Mandatory recall authority for the FDA became law in the Food Safety Modernization Act in 2011. During the health care overhaul debate in 2009 and 2010, DeGette helped to shape the final abortion provisions in the legislation. With Republican Energy and Commerce Chairman Fred Upton of Michigan, she launched an initiative in 2015 to reduce the time for getting "breakthrough drugs" into the hands of needy patients. Their 21st Century Cures bill was one of the few major bipartisan measures enacted during Obama's final two years as president. DeGette called the legislation "a watershed moment in this country for biomedical research." In November 2018, DeGette and Republican Rep. Tom Reed of New York issued a report on the rising price of insulin.

DeGette has been active on other issues affecting Colorado and the West. After Colorado and Washington state in 2012 passed laws legalizing marijuana, she filed legislation that barred the federal government from pre-empting such state laws. On Energy and Commerce, she has pushed to address climate change, including U.S.-led international funding of renewable energy production. She has pushed for legislation to expand federal wilderness areas in Colorado.

DeGette has been active in House leadership politics, but has had setbacks. In 2001, she supported Maryland's Steny Hoyer in his unsuccessful bid for Democratic whip against California's Nancy Pelosi, who went on to become House Speaker. When Hoyer got the job as party whip in 2002, DeGette moved into the role of party strategist. When Democrats gained control of the House in 2007, she seriously considered running for whip against South Carolina's James Clyburn. She said she ultimately decided that it would have been disruptive to have another internal struggle. Clyburn made DeGette his chief deputy whip. A few days after the 2018 election, when Democrats regained the House majority, she declared her candidacy for whip. But history repeated itself, and DeGette backed down when Clyburn reclaimed his post. With each of the top three Democratic leaders about to become octogenarians, DeGette warned, "We need to have some transition planning."

As a hefty consolation prize, she took over the Oversight Subcommittee, which has long been a prime investigative niche in Congress. Her targets for review included the Environmental Protection Agency, prescription drug prices and family unification at the border.

DeGette has had limited campaign opposition. In 2002, Ramona Martinez, a 15-year member of the Denver City Council and a Democratic National Committeewoman, criticized her for having lost touch with the district. DeGette returned her family to Denver from the Maryland suburbs in 2001 and won impressively, 73%-27%.

Sixteen years later, she received a similar challenge. Saira Rao, a first-generation Indian-American who had practiced law on Wall Street before settling in Denver and publishing children's books, said that DeGette was not sufficiently active in her district and that it was time for a change. DeGette defended her record and said her seniority would benefit the district, especially if Democrats regained House control. Both candidates were well-funded. DeGette won, 68%-32%. "It really didn't turn out to be a very strong challenge, did it?" DeGette said to a reporter on primary night. Rao responded with Twitter attacks on journalists and other Democrats.

CO-1: Denver Metro   Cook Partisan Voting Index: D+21

Population		Race and Ethnicity		Income	
Total	802,167	White	57.7%	Median Income	$62,195
Land area (sq. miles)	190	Black	8%	District Income Rank	156
Pop/ sq mi	4230.4	Latino	27.8%	Poverty Rate	14%
Born in State	41.5%	Asian	3.4%	With health insurance	89.2%
		Two or more races	2.3%	Cash public assistance	2.3%
Age Groups		Other	0.8%	Food stamp/SNAP	8.9%
Under 18	20.5%				
18-34	29.6%	Education		Work	
35-64	38.4%	H.S grad or less	29.9%	White Collar	11.5%
Over 64	11.5%	Some college	23.8%	Sales and Service	38.5%
		College Degree, 4 yr	28.5%	Blue Collar	15.5%
Military		Post grad	17.7%	Government	11%
Veteran/ Active Duty	6%				

2012 Pres. Vote	Obama	254,400	(69%)	Romney	106,334	(29%)			
2016 Pres. Vote	Clinton	277,790	(69%)	Trump	93,486	(23%)	Johnson	18,996	(5%)

Denver: Denver is serious about being the Mile High City: There are three markers on the granite steps of the gold-domed capitol that proclaim the elevation of 5,280 feet. Denver is situated a few miles from where the High Plains yield to the sharp peaks of the Front Range of the Rockies. With 704,000 people in 2017, a 17 percent increase since 2010, the city for a century has been the economic and cultural capital of the Rocky Mountain region. On top of its western heritage and early-20th-century elegance, Denver has developed an exuberant postmodern style. The National Western Stock Show held here every year and the LoDo entertainment district along the South Platte River evoke the Old West. The capitol, the spacious parks and the aspens that line the streets give the city a lush, burnished air, in contrast to the dry plains and stark peaks.

Amid its downtown grid are the skyscrapers of the 1970s energy boom and the 1990s tech boom, plus Coors Field, where Major League Baseball's Colorado Rockies play, the Elitch Gardens Theme and Water Park, and the Denver Museum of Nature & Science. Barack Obama claimed the Democratic presidential nomination at Mile High Stadium in 2008, with grand theatrics and expectations. Most of its neighborhoods have strong housing demand, including the African-American neighborhoods of northeastern Denver, filled with neat 1950s bungalows, and the Hispanic quarter northwest of downtown. To the south, Westwood has become a Mexican cultural district. More than three-quarters of the metro area's people now live in the suburbs, and Denver has disproportionate numbers of singles and cultural liberals who value an urban and physically active lifestyle in the gentrified areas near the capitol.

In early 2015, a local bakery that had prepared many cakes for gay-themed events generated national attention when it refused to prepare a cake for a gay wedding ceremony. In a clash with the Colorado Civil Rights Commission, the state's civil rights division ruled that the baker did not discriminate for refusing to include biblical phrases on the cakes. In June 2018, the Supreme Court supported the baker in a 7-2 ruling that was narrowly written and addressed procedural rather than substantive issues. Responding to the city's large Latino community, Denver Mayor Michael Hancock said following the 2016 election that the city's police officers would not cooperate with enforcement of federal immigration laws. In January 2018, he refused to meet with President Donald Trump to discuss the status of the sanctuary city. "Denver doesn't violate federal law, and we won't be intimidated," Hancock tweeted.

Denver is the progressive heart of Colorado. The city has elected Hispanic and black mayors and is 32 percent Latino. In the early 1970s, Denver liberals were hostile to growth and boosterism. Since then, city leaders have argued that growth can produce more of the distinctiveness that people here appreciate. But gentrification, with soaring increases in housing costs, has become divisive. When an upscale coffee shop moved into a historically black neighborhood north of the capitol and its owner jokingly posted a sign, "Happily gentrifying the neighborhood since 2014," many residents were outraged. Hancock called the sign "disrespectful" and the owner apologized.

The 1st Congressional District covers all of Denver and stretches northeast to include Denver International Airport. The district drops southwest to include suburban parts of Jefferson County, where Columbine High School was the location in 1999 of a mass shooting, when two teenage boys killed 13 people. More than 80 percent live in Denver County. The 1st, which last elected a Republican in 1970, is the most solid Democratic district in the state.

Joe Neguse (D)

Elected 2018, 1st term, b. May 13, 1984; Bakersfield; University of Colorado, Boulder, Bach. Deg., 2005; University of Colorado, Boulder, J.D., 2009; Christian Church; Married (Andrea Neguse); 1 child.

Professional Career: Founder, New Era Colorado; Staff Assistant, CO Rep. Andrew Romanoff; Attorney, Snell and Wilner, 2009-2015; Executive Director , CO Department of Regulatory Agencies, 2015-2017

DC Office: 1419 LHOB 20515, 202-225-2161, neguse.house.gov

State Offices: Boulder, 303-335-1045; Fort Collins, 970-372-3971.

Committees: *Judiciary*: Antitrust, Commercial & Administrative Law; Immigration & Citizenship. *Natural Resources*: National Parks, Forests & Public Lands; Water, Oceans & Wildlife. *Select Committee on the Climate Crisis.*

Election Results

Election	Name (Party)	Vote (%)		Cand. Spent	Ind. Exp. Support	Ind. Exp. Oppose
2018 General	Joseph Neguse (D)............................	259,608	(60%)	$1,049,367	$1,953	
	Peter Yu (R)...................................	144,901	(34%)	$61,745		
	Nick Thomas (I)...............................	16,356	(4%)			
	Roger Barris (Lib)............................	9,749	(2%)	$32,641		
2018 Primary	Joseph D. Neguse (D)......................	76,829	(66%)			
	Mark Williams (D)...........................	40,044	(34%)			

Democrat Joe Neguse easily won his first term from Colorado and took office as the state's first African-American elected to Congress. His victory marked the rapid political rise of the son of Eritrean refugees who were granted asylum in the United States after fleeing the East African nation. Neguse's youthful advance ironically became something of an American success story in which he found himself under attack for working too closely with establishment figures in the Denver area. He replaced Democrat Jared Polis, who was elected governor.

Neguse's parents separately fled Eritrea in 1980 and settled in Bakersfield California, where they were introduced to each other by mutual friends. When Joe was six, his family moved to Denver, where his parents worked in accounting and banking. He got his undergraduate and law degrees from the University of Colorado and was elected by voters to the university's board of regents.

After working for Colorado House Speaker Andrew Romanoff, Neguse co-founded New Era Colorado, a youth voter registration and mobilization non-profit. He ran for Secretary of State in 2014 and lost to Republican Wayne Williams, 47%-45%. Gov. John Hickenlooper appointed Neguse as director of the Colorado Department of Regulatory Agencies, the state's consumer protection agency. He later joined Snell and Wilner, a Denver law firm.

Following Polis's long-expected decision to run for governor, Neguse was the Democratic frontrunner to succeed him. He took progressive views on issues such as single-payer health care and environmental protection. An outspoken critic of President Donald Trump and his immigration policies, Neguse cited his parents' experiences in seeking asylum in the United States from their war-torn nation. Contending that "the American dream" was under assault by Trump, he told the Coloradoan, "I think about my parents who immigrated to this county 35 years ago and how different their lives would be and my life would be if they tried to immigrate today."

He faced competition in the primary from Mark Williams, a former Air Force pilot who became a tech-industry executive. Neguse had a nearly 10-to-1 fundraising advantage over Williams. He was supported in the primary by many Democratic leaders, including former Vice President Joseph Biden and House Minority Whip Steny Hoyer, plus several labor unions and the liberal-advocacy group Democracy for America.

Williams, a former chairman of Boulder County Democrats, embraced "citizen" campaigns and criticized Neguse's approach from "the world of old politics." When he announced his candidacy months after Neguse already had been running, Williams told a candidate forum in Boulder, "the knives came out pretty quick" from what he called the Democratic "old-boy network" in the Denver area.

Neguse won the primary, 66%-34%, and led comfortably in each of the 10 counties. Boulder cast nearly half the total vote. In November, he easily defeated Republican Peter Yu, a local businessman. His narrow setback in his earlier bid for statewide office suggested that Neguse will remain upwardly mobile.

CO-2: Northern Front Range   **Cook Partisan Voting Index: D+9**

Population		Race and Ethnicity		Income	
Total	782,425	White	82.7%	Median Income	$75,021
Land area (sq. miles)	7,535	Black	0.9%	District Income Rank	71
Pop/ sq mi	103.8	Latino	10.6%	Poverty Rate	10.9%
Born in State	35.6%	Asian	3.1%	With health insurance	92.9%
		Two or more races	2.1%	Cash public assistance	1.5%
Age Groups		Other	0.7%	Food stamp/SNAP	4.7%
Under 18	19.7%				
18-34	27%	**Education**		**Work**	
35-64	39.8%	H.S grad or less	19.6%	White Collar	13.5%
Over 64	13.5%	Some college	26.4%	Sales and Service	37.6%
		College Degree, 4 yr	31.6%	Blue Collar	14.4%
Military		Post grad	22.3%	Government	14.5%
Veteran/ Active Duty	7.4%				

2012 Pres. Vote	Obama	255,208	(58%)	Romney	174,028	(40%)		
2016 Pres. Vote	Clinton	264,966	(56%)	Trump	164,769	(35%)	Johnson	24,820	(5%)

Fort Collins, Boulder: Nestled against the Front Range of the Rocky Mountains is Boulder, home of the 30,000-student University of Colorado, once billed by the city as "a combination of Lycra-clad athletes, New Age artists, and thoughtful intellectuals sipping cappuccinos." Boulder is one of the nation's leading centers for bungee jumping, mountain biking, snowshoeing, rock and ice climbing, downhill skiing, land surfing and hot-air ballooning. It has been called the nation's No. 1 town for outdoor sports by Outdoor magazine, and in 2016 ranked fifth among mid-sized metropolitan areas with the best quality of life. Marathoners from around the world train in several camps here. All have come because of the setting. The streets of Boulder look up at craggy peaks rising to 14,000 feet from a mile-high plain stretching farther east than the eye can see.

The economics also have been appealing. Boulder has become a magnet for technology firms dissatisfied with the more congested Silicon Valley. In 2017, National Geographic rated Boulder the "happiest" city in the United States. Perhaps not coincidentally, USA Today in May 2018 reported that Census Bureau data ranked Boulder the 17th wealthiest; 61 percent of the adult population in the city are college graduates, the highest share in the nation. The Fort Collins-Loveland area north of Boulder ranked fourth in the National Geographic index, which included such metrics as healthy eating, civic engagement and vacation time. Fort Collins has faced some challenges. Demographic changes have widened the local income gap. Grassroots groups were displeased when the state Supreme Court in 2016 unanimously ruled that the Fort Collins moratorium on hydraulic fracking violated the state's authority to regulate oil and gas. In the immediate aftermath of the ruling, local drilling was scant.

The 2nd Congressional District is centered in Boulder. Interstate 70 charts a scenically awesome course through the mountains as it takes in Rocky Mountain acreage, and it is often congested with cars loaded with skis and snowboards. The district includes the old coal mining town of Central City, which describes itself as "the richest square mile on earth" and is home to multiple casinos. The lodges and resorts of Vail are farther west on Interstate 70. Once dependent on mining and agriculture, Vail evolved into an international resort city after the 10th Mountain Division ski troops were introduced to the Eagle River Valley in the 1940s. After World War II, a group of Army buddies returned and developed a ski resort, which has become a lush vacation destination. Boulder County is a partisan hub for Democrats, but the rest of the district is relatively balanced politically. Larimer County, with Fort Collins and Loveland, is the largest county with more than 40 percent of the voters in the district. Boulder has about 30 percent. Except for Vail-based Summit County, the rural counties to the west are more Republican; they have few voters.

Scott Tipton (R)

Elected 2010, 5th term, b. Nov 09, 1956; Espanola, NM; Fort Lewis
College (CO), B.A., 1978; Anglican; Married (Jean Tipton); 2 children.

Elected Office: CO House, 2009-2011.

Professional Career: Owner, CEO, Mesa Verde Pottery.

DC Office: 218 CHOB 20515, 202-225-4761, Fax: 202-226-9669,
tipton.house.gov

State Offices: Alamosa, 719-587-5105; Durango, 970-259-1490;
Grand Junction, 970-241-2499; Pueblo, 719-542-1073.

Committees: *Financial Services*: Consumer Protection & Financial Institutions; Housing,
Community Development & Insurance.

Group Ratings

	ADA	ACLU	AFL-CIO	LCV	ITI	COC	HAFA	ACU	CFG	FRC
2018	-	7%	-	9%	-	83%	56%	76%	51%	100%
2017	0%	C	8%	6%	C	93%	C	81%	67%	100%

Almanac Ratings 2017-18

	Economy	Social	Foreign	Composite
Liberal	1%	7%	0%	3%
Conservative	99%	93%	100%	97%

Key Votes of the 115th Congress

1. Obama-care revision	Y	5. Family planning regs	Y	9. Guantanamo prisoners	N
2. Tax Cuts	Y	6. Body cameras/immigration	N	10. Ground missiles, limit	N
3. Omnibus appropriations	Y	7. Abortion ban	Y	11. Defense Dept. spending	Y
4. Dodd-Frank revision	Y	8. Concealed carry	Y	12. FISA rules	Y

Election Results

Election	Name (Party)	Vote (%)		Cand. Spent	Ind. Exp. Support	Ind. Exp. Oppose
2018 General	Scott Tipton (R).....................................	173,205	(52%)	$1,653,106		
	Diane Mitsch Bush (D).......................	146,426	(44%)	$1,820,482	$16,072	
	Mary Malarsie (I)...............................	10,831	(3%)	$103,979		
2018 Primary	Scott Tipton (R).....................................	(100%)				

Prior winning percentages: 2016 (55%), 2014 (58%), 2012 (53%), 2010 (50%)

Scott Tipton, a conservative Republican elected in 2010, has been known to buck his party's
leadership and show occasional bipartisanship in dealing with local resource issues. In 2016 and
2018, he easily survived well-financed Democratic challenges from the liberal base of his district.

Tipton was born in Española New Mexico. His family moved to Cortez Colorado three months
after he was born. His father was a construction worker for a Denver-based company. When Tipton
enrolled in Fort Lewis College in Durango, he became the first member of his family to go beyond
high school. Tipton returned to his hometown to establish a production facility for Native American
pottery and jewelry, employing childhood friends who belonged to the Ute and Navajo tribes. When
his fledgling business was encumbered by onerous and redundant government paperwork, he said
that the experience made him a critic of government interference with small businesses.

In 2006, he mounted his first political campaign against Democrat John Salazar, then a freshman
in the 3rd District. Salazar won 62%-37% in a Democratic year, but Tipton increased his visibility.
Two years later, he won a seat in the Colorado House. As a Republican legislator, Tipton said he
sometimes felt marginalized by the Democratic Party's hegemony in the state capital.

In a 2010 rematch, Tipton portrayed Salazar as too deferential to the Democratic leadership,
slamming the incumbent for his votes in favor of President Barack Obama's $787 billion economic
stimulus bill and the Affordable Care Act. Salazar also was perceived as having close ties to

Obama, who had tapped his younger brother, Ken Salazar, as Interior secretary. John Salazar deemphasized his party label, calling himself "An Independent Voice for Rural Colorado." The district's conservative voters were energized and Tipton prevailed, 50%-46%.

Early in 2011 Tipton voted against a major spending bill because he favored steeper cuts. He joined other conservatives in opposing House Speaker John Boehner's deal with the White House to raise the debt limit that year. On the Financial Services Committee, Tipton has been a leader in Republican efforts to reduce regulations imposed by the 2010 Dodd-Frank banking law.

Tipton has been more centrist on resource issues. The Denver Post pointed out that he favored government funding for a local bicycle trail, a popular position in an environmentally conscious district. He supported funding to preserve groundwater in the San Luis Valley. He criticized the slow response and "poor communication" by the Environmental Protection Agency after the blowout at the King Gold Mine in 2016 deluged the Durango area and contaminated the Animas River with wastewater. In 2015, he proposed a 30-year plan for American energy that would rely on all sources.

In March 2018, Tipton combined two of his prime local interests with a proposal to increase revenues from energy development on federal lands and spend some of the funds to maintain national parks. Three months later, the Natural Resources Committee — on which Tipton serves — approved his Education and Energy Act, which would take energy royalties from public lands and return them to the states to pay for public education. He called the proposal "a win-win," especially for Colorado, with its huge federal acreage.

Democrats targeted Tipton in 2012, backing the challenge of state Rep. Sal Pace, who attacked Tipton's vote for Rep. Paul Ryan's Medicare reform plan. "If you dare put an idea on the table, you get demonized," Tipton complained during a debate. Tipton outspent Pace, $2.2 million to $1.9 million, and won, 53%-41%. After he won an uncompetitive reelection in 2014, Tipton voiced interest in challenging Democratic Sen. Michael Bennet in 2016, with the potential to emulate the 2014 success of then-Rep. Cory Gardner over Sen. Mark Udall in another matchup of a rural Republican and a metro Democrat. But Tipton turned down what would have been an uphill challenge.

Instead, he again found himself a reelection target of national Democrats. This time, his opponent was Gail Schwartz, a former state senator from Crested Butte, who attacked Tipton for circulating draft legislation that had been prepared with assistance from an energy company that was a large campaign contributor to him. Tipton said that Schwartz's support for higher renewable energy standards had cost the area hundreds of energy-related jobs, especially in the coal industry. Schwartz received large support from national liberal groups, including $2.9 million from the House Majority PAC. Tipton prevailed by an impressive 55%-40%, with 66 percent in Mesa (Grand Junction) and 53 percent in Pueblo — the two largest counties. Schwartz led in 13 of the 29 counties, especially in the high-mountain resort areas.

In 2018, Tipton faced another competitive challenge: Diane Bush, a former state representative and social science professor, advocated a single-payer system for health care. She refused to take a position on the proposed Jordan Cove pipeline to send natural gas to a liquefication terminal on the Oregon coast. Tipton criticized the cost of her health care plan and said she was too liberal for the district. Bush outspent Tipton, $1.8 million to $1.7 million, and had support from national environmental and progressive groups. In a Democratic year, Tipton's victory was a bit closer than two years earlier, 52%-44%. He again scored big in Mesa County and won narrowly in Pueblo.

CO-3: Western Slope   **Cook Partisan Voting Index: R+6**

Population		Race and Ethnicity		Income	
Total	731,888	White	71%	Median Income	$51,456
Land area (sq. miles)	49,732	Black	0.8%	District Income Rank	279
Pop/ sq mi	14.7	Latino	24.4%	Poverty Rate	15.2%
Born in State	49.4%	Asian	0.7%	With health insurance	87.7%
		Two or more races	1.5%	Cash public assistance	2.8%
Age Groups		Other	1.6%	Food stamp/SNAP	11.7%
Under 18	22%				
18-34	21.7%	**Education**		**Work**	
35-64	39.5%	H.S grad or less	37%	White Collar	16.8%
Over 64	16.8%	Some college	32.7%	Sales and Service	43%
		College Degree, 4 yr	20.1%	Blue Collar	23.4%
Military		Post grad	10.2%	Government	15.4%
Veteran/ Active Duty	9.6%				

2012 Pres. Vote	Romney	185,459	(52%)	Obama	163,885	(46%)			
2016 Pres. Vote	Trump	195,966	(52%)	Clinton	151,057	(40%)	Johnson	17,687	(5%)

Grand Junction, Pueblo: On a clear night from the air, they look like tiny mottled veins, thickest near Denver. These are the lights of the civilization Americans have built on the Western Slope of the Rockies in Colorado. The lights follow the trails of valley roads and mountainside switchbacks. The nodes mark the dozens of little towns built during mining boom years: the Gold Rush of the 1870s, the uranium boom of the 1950s, and the oil-shale boomlet of the 1970s. The Western Slope — everything west of the Front Range, with dozens of peaks over 14,000 feet — has always been an impediment to east-west movement. The miners who tracked gold and silver and lead ores also built Victorian towns with opera houses and gingerbread storefronts in Aspen and Telluride, in valleys and defiles scarcely accessible to the outside world. Many of these towns have been restored by ski resort operators and joined by dozens of new condominiums and shopping malls. Cries of overdevelopment have followed.

Amid the tourism, development continued of gas deposits trapped beneath the Roan Plateau. In 2016, the U.S. Geological Survey increased by 40 times its estimate of natural gas reserves in the area's Piceance Basin, which would be the second largest in the nation behind the Marcellus Shale centered in Pennsylvania. A large share of the western Colorado reserves are on federal lands, where drilling companies planned to use hydraulic fracturing. In 2017, several counties in this area reported the largest number of new permits for drilling in the past decade.

The political map of the Western Slope is as diverse as its history. Typically, the high-income areas, with lots of residents opposed to new oil and gas drilling, are the most Democratic, while more modest-income, working-class towns are the most Republican. A ribbon of counties along the Wasatch Range, from Wyoming on the northern border to New Mexico on the southern border, votes mostly Democratic. They include Aspen and the former coal mining centers of Crested Butte and Steamboat Springs, once Republican, today sporting ski lodges. Durango, an old frontier town, has moved in the same direction. Some areas are still heavily Republican and hostile to environmentalists and liberals generally: the rough-handed mining area around Grand Junction, the population center of the district, where piles of tailings still crackle with radioactivity; and the northwest corner of the state, where people remember the oil shale boom with nostalgia. In other ways, Colorado has moved toward less dependence on fossil fuel. In August 2018, the Public Utilities Commission approved a plan to shut down two coal-fired plants in Pueblo and replace them with renewable energy, with the goal of 2026 for renewables to account for more than half of the state's power.

The 3rd Congressional District of Colorado includes most of the Western Slope and occupies nearly half of Colorado. It extends east of the Front Range to include the industrial city of Pueblo. There, on the banks of the Arkansas River, the Rockefellers built large steel factories before World War I to make barbed wire and rails. In 2016, the Army began to operate a $4.5 billion plant at the Pueblo Chemical Depot to destroy the largest remaining stockpile of chemical weapons: more than 780,000 shells with 2,600 tons of a mustard gas agent. The target date for completion of 2020 was in jeopardy when the Army reported in March 2018 that the plant had met setbacks in its costs and schedule due to concerns about worker safety; officials were exploring other options for disposal. Pueblo County is the second-largest in the district and has been comfortably Democratic, with a 43 percent Hispanic population. In 2016, Donald Trump won by 390 votes, with his blue-collar and rural appeal. The 3rd has the lowest median income and education levels in the state. With the chief exception of the resort counties, the district has leaned increasingly Republican. After John McCain won here 50%-49% in 2008, Trump increased the Republican spread to 52%-40%.

Kenneth Buck (R)

Elected 2014, 3rd term, b. Feb 16, 1959; Ossining, NY; Princeton University (NJ), A.B., 1981; University of Wyoming (WY), J.D., 1985; Wesleyan; Married (Perry Lynn); 2 children (2 from previous marriage).

Elected Office: Weld County, CO, DA 2005-2014.

Professional Career: Practicing attorney, 1987-2002; Staff, U.S. Committee to Investigate Cover Arms Transactions with Iran, 1986-1987.

DC Office: 2455 RHOB 20515, 202-225-4676, buck.house.gov

State Offices: Castle Rock, 720-639-9165; Greeley, 970-702-2136.

Committees: *Foreign Affairs*: Oversight & Investigations; Western Hemisphere, Civilian Security, & Trade. *Judiciary*: Antitrust, Commercial & Administrative Law; Immigration & Citizenship (RMM).

Group Ratings

	ADA	ACLU	AFL-CIO	LCV	ITI	COC	HAFA	ACU	CFG	FRC
2018	-	9%	-	6%	-	67%	98%	95%	97%	100%
2017	5%	C	5%	6%	C	93%	C	96%	96%	100%

Almanac Ratings 2017-18

	Economy	Social	Foreign	Composite
Liberal	8%	12%	3%	8%
Conservative	92%	88%	97%	92%

Key Votes of the 115th Congress

1. Obama-care revision	Y	5. Family planning regs	Y	9. Guantanamo prisoners	N
2. Tax Cuts	Y	6. Body cameras/immigration	N	10. Ground missiles, limit	N
3. Omnibus appropriations	N	7. Abortion ban	Y	11. Defense Dept. spending	Y
4. Dodd-Frank revision	Y	8. Concealed carry	N	12. FISA rules	N

Election Results

Election	Name (Party)	Vote (%)		Cand. Spent	Ind. Exp. Support	Ind. Exp. Oppose
2018 General	Ken Buck (R)................................	224,038	(61%)	$607,493		
	Karen McCormick (D).................	145,544	(39%)	$872,528	$37,034	
2018 Primary	Ken Buck (R)...		(100%)			

Prior winning percentages: 2016 (64%), 2014 (65%)

Republican Ken Buck, with his political revival in 2014, has become a Freedom Caucus member and an outspoken conservative critic of what he calls the Republican Party's loss of principles. He won the House seat after narrowly losing four years earlier a Senate contest to Democrat Michael Bennet that many expected Buck would win.

Buck cultivated his political chops early in his career. Fresh out of the University of Wyoming law school, he worked for then-Rep. Dick Cheney on the House's 1986-87 probe into the Iran-Contra scandal and later served as a trial attorney in the Justice Department. He returned to Colorado in the 1990s as chief of the Criminal Division in the U.S. Attorney's Office. In 2005, he successfully ran for Weld County district attorney and was reelected twice. But his political hopes crashed in 2010. In the GOP primary for a Senate seat, he attracted national attention by commenting that he would make a better candidate than his opponent, Lt. Gov. Jane Norton, because he didn't "wear heels." Buck won the primary, 52%-48%. Further damage was done when he compared homosexuality to alcoholism on Meet the Press. He lost to Bennet by less than 2 percentage points, prompting many Republicans to view Colorado, along with Delaware and Nevada, as Senate pickup opportunities that the party squandered with weak candidates.

Sporting a more professional image and emphasizing his career in law enforcement, Buck launched another shot at the Senate in 2014 against first-term Democratic Sen. Mark Udall. But when Rep. Cory Gardner threw his hat in the ring, Buck decided to step aside to compete instead for Gardner's open 4th District, where the turf is friendly for Republicans. GOP strategists were grateful to get a stronger Senate challenger. The softer-edged Gardner was relieved to avoid a competitive primary. In the primary for Gardner's House seat, Buck's name recognition and conservative reputation gave him a big edge over three GOP opponents. He steered away from making controversial comments. Instead, he highlighted issues such as energy independence, touting his support for the Keystone XL pipeline. Boosted by endorsements from Gardner and other top Republicans, as well as the local newspaper, The Greeley Tribune, Buck topped the primary field with 44 percent. In the general election, Buck easily beat Vic Meyers, 65%-29%. In this district, he seems secure.

He was elected president of the Republican freshman class and said he would focus on problem-solving, not partisanship. But Buck maintained his blunt-spoken style. Criticizing President Barack Obama for abusing his executive authority, he said, "No more acting like King Barack." Buck was quick to stir his own controversy. Three months after he took office, he brought an AR-15 rifle to his office on Capitol Hill. The weapon is illegal in the District of Columbia. Buck said the rifle was not loaded and that he had received approval from the Capitol Police

Buck faced the threat of insurrection from his freshman class after he was one of 34 Republicans who failed to support party leadership on a procedural vote on legislation to provide trade promotion authority to Obama. In June 2015, freshman Republican Carlos Curbelo of Florida told The Hill newspaper, "We haven't met enough, we haven't gotten to know each other enough, we're not communicating enough. ... [Buck] listened to everyone, and he acknowledged everyone's concerns."

In July 2018, the House passed Buck's bill to permit non-profit status for mutual irrigation and ditch companies that reinvest revenue earned from non-member sources. A member of the Judiciary Committee, he filed a bill with Sen. Ron Johnson of Wisconsin to permit states to provide temporary work visas to foreign workers, instead of relying on the federal government. .

Buck continued to go his own way. He wrote a book, Drain the Swamp, in which he criticized the "bullying" tactics of House GOP leaders, including their fundraising obsession and "war on conservatives." In a July 2017 opinion column for The Denver Post headlined "The Republican Party is dead," Buck wrote that the GOP "no longer has a vision for a better America."

At home, Buck considered a bid for attorney general in 2018 to succeed Cynthia Coffman, who ran unsuccessfully for governor. Instead, he told a radio talk show, he decided to continue with "the job that I enjoy doing here in D.C." He has easily won reelection. In 2018, Democrats nominated Karen McCormick, a veterinarian and political newcomer, who described herself as a problem-solver. She supported steps to permit individuals younger than 65 to buy into Medicare coverage. McCormick's nearly $1 million outspent the $600,000 by Buck. He won, 61%-39%, and led in every county except for the small piece of Boulder.

CO-4: Eastern Colorado

Cook Partisan Voting Index: R+13

Population		Race and Ethnicity		Income	
Total	780,344	White	72.5%	Median Income	$71,357
Land area (sq. miles)	38,103	Black	1.2%	District Income Rank	84
Pop/ sq mi	20.5	Latino	21.9%	Poverty Rate	9.7%
Born in State	48.3%	Asian	1.9%	With health insurance	92.3%
		Two or more races	1.9%	Cash public assistance	2.1%
Age Groups		Other	0.6%	Food stamp/SNAP	8%
Under 18	25.7%				
18-34	21.7%	**Education**		**Work**	
35-64	39.9%	H.S grad or less	33.2%	White Collar	12.7%
Over 64	12.7%	Some college	32.3%	Sales and Service	38.8%
		College Degree, 4 yr	22.9%	Blue Collar	21.6%
Military		Post grad	11.6%	Government	13.7%
Veteran/ Active Duty	8.5%				

2012 Pres. Vote	Romney	210,019	(59%)	Obama	140,855	(39%)		
2016 Pres. Vote	Trump	230,945	(57%)	Clinton	137,784	(34%)	Johnson	20,104	(5%)

Weld, Douglas: The High Plains of eastern Colorado are dusty brown, gently rolling up toward the Rocky Mountains. The land is fertile, but dry. Rainfall is rare, the rivers are just a trickle most of the year, and in many places, groundwater is scarce. It is fine wheat country when irrigated, and one of the foremost beef cattle regions. But it has been squeezed in recent decades by declining prices for wheat, declining demand for beef and increased prices for water because of the high demand in Denver and along the Front Range. Bitter confrontations have erupted over who gets access to the South Platte River, leading to limitations on pumping from the basin. Local farmers have found that the value of their water rights to metro Denver far exceeds what they could hope to earn by farming. Their neighbors have condemned them for selling out and betraying a way of life. The free market that once made the High Plains the scene of farm protests has caused some of it to empty out and revert to untamed land, ready again for increasingly numerous buffalo, elk, deer and bighorn sheep. In another revenue source for open land, a wind farm with 300 turbines on 100,000 acres in five counties opened in September 2018 and produced enough energy to power more than 300,000 homes.

This area stretches into the Denver suburbs, which have continued their rapid population growth. Until the 1970s, Douglas County was a sparsely populated patch of the High Plains just east of the Front Range and south of Denver. From 2000 to 2010, with a surge of telecom and aerospace companies, it grew 62 percent, making it the fastest-growing county in the state. In 2017, the county was the fifth wealthiest in the nation with a median income of $109,926. Activists have pressed for a more free-enterprise approach to governance. This is Patio Land, as writer David Brooks has described it: an area with a high-tech economy, highly educated families with relatively conservative cultural values and looking for a safe environment for children, with the serenity — if not the close personal ties — of a small town and the creativity of a metropolis.

The 4th Congressional District covers much of the Eastern Plains and nearly the entire eastern half of the state. It includes all of Weld County and two-thirds of Douglas. Each county includes about one-third of the district's population. Its large share of the land in Adams and Arapahoe counties is sparsely populated and stops short of the Denver exurbs. A small slice of Boulder County is a Democratic outlier, with only about 10 percent of the district. Due chiefly to its influx of oil and gas workers, Weld County was the fourth fastest-growing metro area in the nation during the 12 months ending June 2016. The pumping of wells has caused problems for farmers because of rising groundwater. The 4th is a solidly Republican district.

Doug Lamborn (R)

Elected 2006, 7th term, b. May 24, 1954; Leavenworth, KS; University of Kansas School of Journalism, B.S., 1978; University of Kansas School of Law, J.D., 1985; Christian Church; Married (Jeanie Lamborn); 5 children.

Elected Office: CO House, 1995-1999; CO Senate, 1998-2006.

Professional Career: Practicing attorney, 1987-2007.

DC Office: 2371 RHOB 20515, 202-225-4422, Fax: 202-226-2638, lamborn.house.gov

State Offices: Buena Vista, 719-520-0055; Colorado Springs, 719-520-0055.

Committees: *Armed Services*: Readiness (RMM); Tactical Air & Land Forces. *Natural Resources*: Energy & Mineral Resources; Water, Oceans & Wildlife.

Group Ratings

	ADA	ACLU	AFL-CIO	LCV	ITI	COC	HAFA	ACU	CFG	FRC
2018	-	11%	-	0%	-	83%	92%	92%	78%	100%
2017	0%	C	5%	0%	C	93%	C	96%	95%	100%

Almanac Ratings 2017-18

	Economy	Social	Foreign	Composite
Liberal	0%	11%	3%	5%
Conservative	100%	89%	97%	96%

Key Votes of the 115th Congress

1. Obama-care revision	Y	5. Family planning regs	Y	9. Guantanamo prisoners	N
2. Tax Cuts	Y	6. Body cameras/immigration	N	10. Ground missiles, limit	N
3. Omnibus appropriations	Y	7. Abortion ban	Y	11. Defense Dept. spending	Y
4. Dodd-Frank revision	Y	8. Concealed carry	Y	12. FISA rules	Y

Election Results

Election	Name (Party)	Vote (%)		Cand. Spent	Ind. Exp. Support	Ind. Exp. Oppose
2018 General	Doug Lamborn (R)	184,002	(57%)	$777,024		$57,885
	Stephany Rose Spaulding (D)	126,848	(39%)	$307,853	$20,305	
	Douglas Randall (Lib)	11,795	(4%)	$0		
2018 Primary	Doug Lamborn (R)	54,974	(52%)			
	Darryl Glenn (R)	21,479	(20%)			
	Owen Hill (R)	19,141	(18%)			
	Bill Rhea (R)	6,167	(6%)			

Prior winning percentages: 2016 (62%), 2014 (60%), 2012 (65%), 2010 (66%), 2008 (60%), 2006 (60%)

Doug Lamborn, a conservative Republican first elected in 2006 and a fierce partisan, has been slow to shut down competitive challenges from either party. An occasional maverick, he has been bypassed for prime posts despite his seniority, including his unsuccessful bid in 2016 to take over as chairman of the Veterans Affairs Committee.

The son of a prison guard, Lamborn was born in Leavenworth Kansas. He studied journalism and earned a law degree at the University of Kansas. He said he voted for Jimmy Carter in 1976, but was then drawn to the Republican politics of Ronald Reagan in the 1980s. In 1987, Lamborn moved his family to Colorado Springs, where he practiced business and real estate law and became an avid mountain climber. In 1994, he was elected to the state House, and he was appointed in 1998 to a Senate seat. During 12 years in the legislature, Lamborn compiled a firmly conservative record on social and fiscal issues.

When Republican Joel Hefley retired and created an open seat in 2006, he endorsed Jeff Crank, a former aide. Lamborn won the backing of the anti-tax Club for Growth and the Colorado Christian Coalition. Crank won the delegate vote at the GOP convention, but Lamborn secured a place on the primary ballot and vowed never to raise taxes. The Christian Coalition sent a mailer suggesting Crank backed the "radical homosexual lobby." In the primary, absentee ballots flipped the results and Lamborn won by 892 votes, 27%-25%.

In November, Hefley accused Lamborn of running a "sleazy" primary and refused to endorse him. Democrat Jay Fawcett, an Air Force Academy graduate, purchased a newspaper ad featuring three dozen prominent local Republicans who declined to endorse their party's nominee. Despite October polls showing a dead heat, Lamborn won, 60%-40%.

In the House, Lamborn became one of his party's most conservative members. During the 2011 debt and budget talks, he bucked House Speaker John Boehner because he wanted President Barack Obama to agree to deeper cuts. During the 2013 budget debate, Lamborn helped to prepare the budget plan of the Republican Study Committee, which made further large cuts in domestic programs. Later, he called for cuts in Social Security, Medicare and farm programs to pay for increased defense spending. He voiced concern that military cutbacks would affect personnel and missile programs in the Colorado Springs area.

His bid for the Veterans Affairs Committee chairmanship fell short in the leadership-controlled Republican Steering Committee. Lamborn, who was the most senior GOP member of the committee, was defeated by Phil Roe of Tennessee. As chairman of the Natural Resources Subcommittee on Energy and Mineral Resources, Lamborn supported more development of all forms of energy.

On the Armed Services Committee, Lamborn in 2019 became ranking Republican on the Readiness subcommittee. He has been an outspoken supporter of a Space Force and said that Colorado Springs should be "the epicenter of national security space." As a co-founder of the Missile Defense Caucus, he has advocated the development of new technology.

Back home, he has faced continuing problems. Lingering resentment over the 2006 primary led to a rematch with Crank in 2008. This time, Lamborn won 44%-30%. In 2014, he barely won the GOP primary, 53%-47%, over Bentley Rayburn, a retired Air Force general who complained that Lamborn was "out of touch" with local concerns about possible military base closings in the area. Similar criticisms were raised in the general election by Democratic foe Irving Halter, also a retired Air Force general. Halter raised $834,000 compared with only $490,000 for Lamborn, an unusual contrast for a veteran incumbent. Lamborn won 60%-40%, which signaled his weakness in a Republican year.

His 2016 campaign suffered a self-imposed wound when he failed to take his opponent seriously. Calandra Vargas, a political neophyte, challenged Lamborn at the Republican convention. In a rousing speech that Vargas called "a statement on behalf of my generation," she "brought some of the crowd to its feet," the Colorado Springs Gazette reported. Vargas got 58 percent of the vote — just short of the 60 percent required to prevent a primary challenge. Lamborn won the primary, 68%-32%. In November, Lamborn won 62%-31% against Misty Plowright, a trans-gender Democrat who said that her campaign was inspired by Bernie Sanders.

Lamborn suffered from more self-inflicted wounds in 2018 when the state Supreme Court threw him off the ballot because he violated a state law that required state residents to collect signatures for his candidacy. A federal judge overturned the ruling and held that the residency requirement was "likely unconstitutional." In the primary, he faced two local officials: state Sen. Owen Hill and El Paso County Commissioner Darryl Glenn. Hill described his two opponents as "counterfeit conservatives" and "swamp things." Glenn, a retired Air Force lieutenant colonel, challenged Sen. Michael Bennet in 2016 and lost 50%-44%. Lamborn won the primary with 52 percent; Glenn and Hill split the opposition vote with 20 and 18 percent, respectively. Against Democrat Stephany Spaulding, a professor of women's and ethnic studies at the University of Colorado and a political newcomer, Lamborn won, 57%-39%, his lowest share of the vote in seven campaigns.

CO-5: Central Colorado   Cook Partisan Voting Index: R+14

Population		Race and Ethnicity		Income	
Total	772,116	White	71.7%	Median Income	$61,391
Land area (sq. miles)	7,266	Black	5.4%	District Income Rank	160
Pop/ sq mi	106.3	Latino	15.7%	Poverty Rate	11.2%
Born in State	33.1%	Asian	2.5%	With health insurance	91.8%
		Two or more races	3.8%	Cash public assistance	2.7%
Age Groups		Other	0.9%	Food stamp/SNAP	10%
Under 18	23.8%				
18-34	25.4%	**Education**		**Work**	
35-64	37.9%	H.S grad or less	28.6%	White Collar	12.9%
Over 64	12.9%	Some college	36%	Sales and Service	42.6%
		College Degree, 4 yr	21.6%	Blue Collar	17.2%
Military		Post grad	13.8%	Government	17%
Veteran/ Active Duty	21.9%				

2012 Pres. Vote	Romney	200,558	(59%)	Obama	129,904	(38%)		
2016 Pres. Vote	Trump	212,558	(57%)	Clinton	123,537	(33%)	Johnson 22,195	(6%)

Colorado Springs: In the center of Colorado, Pikes Peak, espied by Zebulon Pike in 1806, and Colorado Springs, with the Garden of the Gods and the Broadmoor hotel, have been tourist attractions for more than 100 years. In the second half of the 20th century, Colorado Springs, safe in the vastness of North America, became a great American military fortress. During the 1960s, the Pentagon constructed the North American Aerospace Defense Command more than 1,000 feet below Cheyenne Mountain, a fortified bunker theoretically able to survive a nuclear strike from a Soviet missile. The Pentagon, in part because of local traffic congestion, moved NORAD's surveillance operations to nearby Peterson Air Force Base, site of space-based defense research, with the option of a rapid return to secure Cheyenne Mountain in an emergency. Other military installations dominate the landscape as well: the Army installation at Fort Carson; the Air Force Academy; and Schriever Air Force Base, named for Gen. Bernard A. Schriever, a pioneer in the development of ballistic missile programs. By some measures, this area has the biggest military footprint in the nation, with 40,000 active-duty troops and another 60,000 civilian jobs.

Colorado Springs has built a high-tech, innovative economy. State officials project that, by 2021, El Paso County will surpass Denver County as Colorado's largest. One downside locally: The area must contend with occasional out-of-control fires that have become the bane of the West. Paradoxically perhaps, above-average precipitation has increased the growth of grasses, which can be a fuel for the fires. Several locales have transplanted healthy trees in an attempt to reduce the risk of further conflagrations.

Led by the arrival of James Dobson's Focus on the Family in 1994, Colorado Springs has been a center of conservative Christianity, the home of Colorado's young conservatism and the counterpoint to Denver's liberalism. This was the birthplace of Colorado's anti-tax initiatives and of Amendment 2, which in 1992 repealed the city's gay rights ordinances only to be later overturned by the U.S. Supreme Court. It is one of America's most Republican metropolitan areas. Following Dobson's exit in 2010, his organization reduced its payroll by nearly half from its peak employment of 1,400 workers, though it remained a powerful force in Colorado and beyond.

The 5th Congressional District takes in Colorado Springs and all of El Paso County. It includes all or part of four rural counties: Park, Teller, Fremont and Chaffee. More than 85 percent of the district's voters are in El Paso. Along with the 4th District, it has been the strongest Republican district in Colorado. Still, its 57 percent for Donald Trump in 2016 had less impact than did the 69 percent vote for Hillary Clinton in the 1st District (Denver), when Clinton won statewide 48%-43%.

Jason Crow (D)

Elected 2018, 1st term, b. Mar 15, 1979; Beaver Dam, WI; University of Wisconsin - Madison, B.A., 2002; University of Denver (CO), J.D., 2009; Christian - Non-Denominational; Married (Deserai Crow); 2 children.

Military Career: U.S. Army 2002-2006; CO Army National Guard 2006-2007 (Afghanistan & Iraq)

Professional Career: Holland and Hart, LLP, 2009-2018.

DC Office: 1229 LHOB 20515, 202-225-7882, crow.house.gov

State Offices: Aurora, 720-748-7514.

Committees: *Armed Services*: Intelligence, Emerging Threats & Capabilities; Readiness. *Small Business*: Economic Growth, Tax & Capital Access; Innovation & Workforce Development (Chmn); Rural Development, Agriculture, Trade & Entrepreneurship.

Election Results

Election	Name (Party)	Vote (%)		Cand. Spent	Ind. Exp. Support	Ind. Exp. Oppose
2018 General	Jason Crow (D)	187,639	(54%)	$5,624,004	$2,960,040	$4,563,150
	Mike Coffman (R)	148,685	(43%)	$3,689,459	$1,187,095	$8,238,393
2018 Primary	Jason Crow (D)	49,851	(66%)			
	Levi Tillemann (D)	25,757	(34%)			

Freshman Jason Crow defeated Republican Rep. Mike Coffman in a district that had become a prime Democratic target. Crow, who served as an Army Ranger in Iraq and Afghanistan, was a close adviser to Democratic leaders in Colorado. Coffman had become more politically independent as he faced strong challengers in each election since 2012, when redistricting made his district more competitive. Unlike earlier opponents, Crow was making his first bid for elected office and he gave Coffman less of a target to attack.

Crow, a native of Wisconsin, graduated from the University of Wisconsin and got his law degree from the University of Denver. As an infantry officer with the Army's 82nd Airborne Division, he led a platoon of paratroopers during the invasion of Iraq and received a Bronze Star. After attaining the rank of captain, he was assistant chief of staff with the Colorado Army National Guard.

Crow was a partner in the large Denver-based law firm of Holland and Hart, where his profile said that he "conducted internal investigations nationwide, responded to emergency events, and handled a wide-range of government inquiries." In political activities, he co-chaired the veterans affairs transition committee for Colorado Gov. John Hickenlooper and co-chaired Veterans for Mark Udall in his Senate campaign.

In the Democratic primary, Crow faced Levi Tillerman, a technology adviser who was endorsed by Progressive Democrats of America and called for the impeachment of President Donald Trump.

After House Democratic leaders endorsed Crow before the primary and urged Tillerman to withdraw, Tillerman released a recorded conversation and objected to the outside influence. Crow responded that he learned, including in the Army, "that it's better and more enduring to build than to tear down," the Denver Post reported; he added that President George W. Bush made a mistake in going to war in Iraq. Crow spent $1 million in the primary, to $350,000 for Tillerman, and he won with 66 percent of the vote.

Coffman, who was a Marine Corps officer in both Iraq wars, was Colorado Secretary of State and he succeeded conservative GOP Rep. Tom Tancredo in 2008. He was an active member of the Armed Services Committee, where he chaired the Personnel Subcommittee, and the Veterans' Affairs Committee, where he pursued investigations of huge cost overruns at the VA hospital under construction in Aurora. As his district shifted to a large Hispanic population, Coffman learned Spanish and spent time in immigrant neighborhoods. His three most recent reelection campaigns were costly contests against prominent Democratic state legislators.

In the general election, Coffman distanced himself from President Donald Trump and cited his work in the House with bipartisan groups. On immigration, he backed a path to citizenship for children who entered the United States illegally and he objected on Twitter to what he called Trump's call to "rewrite immigration law by executive fiat." Crow criticized his lack of leadership on immigration, among other issues. He called Coffman a career politician "who has taken millions of dollars from corporate PACs and these special interests, and it dictates how he votes." Crow noted in particular the National Rifle Association's support for Coffman.

In the costly contest, the candidates and their party allies spent more than $25 million. Coffman suffered a major blow in late September when Speaker Paul Ryan's Congressional Leadership Fund canceled plans for advertisements on behalf of Coffman, amid polls that showed Crow leading.

Following the election, which he won 54%-43%, Crow got a seat on the Armed Services Committee and he joined the growing cadre of military veterans in both parties who have encouraged bipartisanship.

CO-6: Eastern and Southern Denver Suburbs   Cook Partisan Voting Index: D+2

Population		Race and Ethnicity		Income	
Total	792,196	White	61.5%	Median Income	$75,962
Land area (sq. miles)	475	Black	8.9%	District Income Rank	69
Pop/ sq mi	1669	Latino	20%	Poverty Rate	9.2%
Born in State	41.2%	Asian	5.9%	With health insurance	90.5%
Age Groups		Two or more races	2.9%	Cash public assistance	1.7%
Under 18	25.9%	Other	0.8%	Food stamp/SNAP	6.7%
18-34	22.3%	**Education**		**Work**	
35-64	40.6%	H.S grad or less	28.4%	White Collar	11.2%
Over 64	11.2%	Some college	29.7%	Sales and Service	41.1%
Military		College Degree, 4 yr	27.2%	Blue Collar	16.9%
Veteran/ Active Duty	8.4%	Post grad	14.8%	Government	11.4%

2012 Pres. Vote	Obama	182,464	(52%)	Romney	164,398	(47%)			
2016 Pres. Vote	Clinton	191,099	(50%)	Trump	157,115	(41%)	Johnson	19,727	(5%)

Arapahoe County, Aurora: Two generations ago, most people in metropolitan Denver lived in the city itself. At the city limits, the tree-shaded sidewalks gave way to the empty High Plains. Today, more than three-quarters of metro Denver residents live outside the city, some in long-settled suburbs, some in large new subdivisions on rolling land with magnificent views of the Rocky Mountains. Littleton, originally a small, long-settled suburb just south of Denver, now extends to vast new tracts. Other areas that surround Denver were once quite rural but have grown into modern suburbs. To the east of the now-closed Stapleton Airport is Aurora; the area has developed as a hub for alternative energy firms, where new technologies can be studied for their commercial value. Just south of Littleton is fast-growing Douglas County and Highlands Ranch, whose 100,000 residents form one of the largest unincorporated communities in the nation.

Much of the growth in Arapahoe County, which includes many of the suburbs south and east of downtown Denver, has resulted from a large number of immigrants to the area. One in five are foreign-born, and 160 languages are spoken in the Aurora public schools. Solidly Republican until a few years ago, the county has become a hard-fought political battleground in one of the most competitive states. Its population increased 12 percent between 2010 and 2017. Hispanics make up 19 percent of the population, with 11 percent black and 6 percent Asian. Those increases have led to social tensions in what had been mostly working-class white communities. The immigration policies of President Donald Trump have raised concerns. In 2018, the Aurora City Council objected to including a citizenship question on the 2020 census form, though it earlier opposed calls to declare itself a sanctuary city.

Aurora, which is the largest city in Arapahoe, has been the site not only of innovation but also of unspeakable tragedy. At a July 2012 midnight showing of the movie The Dark Knight Rises, a mentally unstable gunman shot and killed 12 people and injured 58 others, an event that sparked an outpouring of public outrage and sympathy. In 2015, James Holmes was found guilty of the murders. That pain was compounded because nearby Littleton was the location of Columbine High School, which suffered in 1999 what had been the nation's worst school massacre when two teenagers killed 13 people and themselves. In 2018, a new VA hospital opened in Aurora following five years of delay and $1 billion in cost overruns.

The 6th Congressional District covers Aurora, Littleton and other south Denver suburbs. About two-thirds of the district is in Arapahoe County, with the remainder in Adams and Douglas counties. Hillary Clinton led Donald Trump, 50%-41%, in the district and had a slightly larger lead in the Arapahoe vote.

Ed Perlmutter (D)

Elected 2006, 7th term, b. May 01, 1953; Denver; University of Colorado, Boulder, B.A., 1975; University of Colorado School of Law, J.D., 1978; Protestant - Unspecified Christian; Married (Deana M. Perlmutter); 3 children.

Elected Office: CO Senate, 1995-2003.

Professional Career: Practicing attorney, 1979-2006.

DC Office: 1226 LHOB 20515, 202-225-2645, Fax: 202-225-5278, perlmutter.house.gov

State Offices: Lakewood, 303-274-7944.

Committees: *Financial Services*: Nat'l Security, International Development & Monetary Policy; Oversight & Investigations. *Rules:* Rules & Organization of the House. *Science, Space & Technology*: Space & Aeronautics.

Group Ratings

	ADA	ACLU	AFL-CIO	LCV	ITI	COC	HAFA	ACU	CFG	FRC
2018	-	75%	-	89%	-	55%	8%	8%	17%	0%
2017	90%	C	95%	100%	C	38%	C	7%	5%	0%

Almanac Ratings 2017-18

	Economy	Social	Foreign	Composite
Liberal	92%	94%	84%	90%
Conservative	8%	6%	16%	10%

Key Votes of the 115th Congress

1. Obama-care revision	N	5. Family planning regs	N	9. Guantanamo prisoners	Y
2. Tax Cuts	N	6. Body cameras/immigration	Y	10. Ground missiles, limit	Y
3. Omnibus appropriations	Y	7. Abortion ban	N	11. Defense Dept. spending	Y
4. Dodd-Frank revision	N	8. Concealed carry	N	12. FISA rules	Y

Election Results

Election	Name (Party)	Vote (%)	Cand. Spent	Ind. Exp. Support	Ind. Exp. Oppose
2018 General	Ed Perlmutter (D) 204,260	(60%)	$1,457,685		
	Mark Barrington (R) 119,734	(35%)	$52,108		
	Jennifer Nackerud (Lib) 14,012	(4%)			
2018 Primary	Ed Perlmutter (D)	(100%)			

Prior winning percentages: 2016 (55%), 2014 (55%), 2012 (54%), 2010 (53%), 2008 (64%), 2006 (55%)

Ed Perlmutter, first elected in 2006, has been the most centrist member of Colorado's congressional delegation and a self-described "business-oriented Democrat." He usually backs his party on major issues, but has sought out Republicans to work on financial, homeland security and energy matters. As was the case following the 2018 election in discussions among House Democrats about the future of Nancy Pelosi, he has skillfully turned apparent personal setbacks into opportunities to influence the Democratic mainstream.

Perlmutter grew up in Jefferson County, walking precincts with his father on Democratic campaigns. His family owned a concrete business. He attended the University of Colorado and earned a law degree in 1978, then went into private practice. In 1994, Perlmutter won election to the state Senate from a northern Jefferson County district that had not elected a Democrat in nearly 30 years. In the legislature, he gained a reputation as a mediator and served two years as Senate president pro tem. As chairman of the renewable energy caucus, he worked on legislation protecting consumer rights and promoting responsible growth.

In 2002, Perlmutter was considered the early frontrunner for the new 7th District seat. But he opted not to run, citing the time it would take away from his three daughters. The district elected Republican Bob Beauprez by just 121 votes. When Beauprez ran unsuccessfully for governor in 2006, Perlmutter entered the race. Against Peggy Lamm, a former state representative who had been the sister-in-law of former Democratic Gov. Richard Lamm, he won the primary 53%-38%. In the general, Republican Rick O'Donnell argued that Perlmutter's marriage to a Denver lobbyist for a D.C.-based lobbying firm would lead to conflicts of interest. (They later divorced and he remarried to a school teacher.) Beauprez's poor showing in the governor's race, and President George W. Bush's unpopularity worked against O'Donnell. Perlmutter won, 55%-42%.

In the House, Perlmutter has been a fairly consistent but not automatic Democratic vote. He chaired the centrist New Democrat Coalition's energy task force. In sync with local interests, he promoted an all-of-the-above energy policy, including incentives to lenders who create a market for energy-efficient buildings. He got a provision in the House-passed climate change bill in 2009 to benefit environmentally conscious banks, drawing criticism from Republicans when it was revealed that he was an investor in one of them. In 2015, he stuck with most House Democrats and opposed trade promotion authority for President Barack Obama.

He split with Colorado Democrats and immigration groups in 2011 in supporting Secure Communities, a federal program to speed up deportations of illegal immigrants convicted of crimes. But he criticized as "disgraceful" President Donald Trump's decision in September 2017 to end the Deferred Action for Childhood Arrivals (DACA) program for young immigrants.

On the Financial Services Committee, Perlmutter joined Republicans in adding protections for taxpayers to the government rescue of financial markets in 2008. With Republican Rep. Steve Pearce of New Mexico, he won House passage in September 2018 of a bill to expand the Financial Crimes Enforcement Network to include terrorism. When centrist Democrats earlier that year joined House Republicans on a bill to loosen some restrictions in the 2010 Dodd-Frank law, Perlmutter surprisingly was not among them. Although he backed its regulatory relief for small banks and credit unions, he voted against the measure because, he said, "We must continue to hold big banks accountable and protect consumers from another financial crisis."

In 2010, Perlmutter decided against running for governor. His reelection in that big Republican year was tougher than his initial contest. Aurora GOP Councilman Ryan Frazier, an African-American Navy veteran, attacked him for contributing to government overspending. Frazier got considerable help from national Republicans groups, but he couldn't keep pace financially with Perlmutter, who spent nearly $3 million and won with 53 percent of the vote. Perlmutter drew another formidable challenger two years later in Joe Coors, a wealthy heir to his family's brewing empire.

Coors sought to make an issue of Perlmutter's ex-wife's work as a lobbyist for California solar manufacturer Solyndra, which failed after getting significant federal help. Perlmutter fired back by accusing Coors of outsourcing jobs, which Coors denied. Perlmutter prevailed 53%-41%.

Following the 2016 election, he showed his independence with public support for Rep. Tim Ryan of Ohio in his unsuccessful challenge to Minority Leader Nancy Pelosi. "We need a change," he said. In April 2017, Perlmutter announced his candidacy to succeed term-limited Gov. John Hickenlooper in 2018, with a call for Colorado to "keep moving forward." Three months later, he unexpectedly dropped out of the contest. "I love this state," he told reporters. "But it takes time, it takes money, it takes energy, and putting all those together, I found looking deep down, it was going to be difficult." He acknowledged that he faced fundraising challenges against Jared Polis, his self-financing House Democratic colleague who won the contest.

In August 2017, Perlmutter reversed himself again when he decided to seek another term in the House. He easily won reelection against a poorly financed Republican challenger. Four Democrats who had been running for his seat stepped aside. They included Daniel Baer, an openly gay foreign policy expert who was a human-rights official at the State Department during the Obama administration.

In the months leading to the 2018 election and in the days immediately following the Democratic takeover, Perlmutter remained a leading proponent of an overhaul of party leadership. When House Democrats met in late November to routinely select Pelosi as their choice for Speaker, he was among 32 caucus members who opposed her. He continued to work with renegades on an alternative, though none emerged.

Meanwhile, as Politico later reported, "Pelosi reached out privately to Perlmutter over the Thanksgiving break to kick-start talks, and the two decided to see if they could work out an agreement." Two weeks later, they reached a deal in which Pelosi agreed to serve no more than four additional years as party leader. "I am now convinced that generational change has started and will continue to accelerate," Perlmutter said. He added that Pelosi was "the best person to lead a very diverse and ambitious caucus."

For a Democrat who had decided in 2017 to quit elected office, his skills as a deal-maker positioned Perlmutter as a key player among party factions.

CO-7: Western and Northern Denver Suburbs   Cook Partisan Voting Index: D+6

Population		Race and Ethnicity		Income	
Total	775,383	White	64%	Median Income	$65,880
Land area (sq. miles)	342	Black	1.5%	District Income Rank	130
Pop/ sq mi	2266.5	Latino	28.7%	Poverty Rate	10.5%
Born in State	50.6%	Asian	3.2%	With health insurance	89.6%
		Two or more races	1.9%	Cash public assistance	1.7%
Age Groups		Other	0.8%	Food stamp/SNAP	7.9%
Under 18	23.5%				
18-34	24.8%	**Education**		**Work**	
35-64	39%	H.S grad or less	36.6%	White Collar	12.7%
Over 64	12.7%	Some college	31%	Sales and Service	41.8%
		College Degree, 4 yr	21%	Blue Collar	20.9%
Military		Post grad	11.3%	Government	12.3%
Veteran/ Active Duty	8%				

2012 Pres. Vote	Obama	196,386	(56%)	Romney	144,446	(42%)		
2016 Pres. Vote	Clinton	192,637	(51%)	Trump	147,645	(39%)	Johnson 20,592	(6%)

Jefferson County: West of Denver, on broad avenues running toward the mountains, the inner circle of suburbs comprise Jefferson County. Affluent in the south and more marginal near the Denver city limits, its population is nearly as large as Denver. In contrast to the Mile High City, the politics of Jeffco has made it one of the nation's most competitive battlegrounds. Its voters backed George W. Bush in 2000 and 2004, then supported Barack Obama in 2008 and 2012. National political campaigns battle-test their message here, and many political reporters have flocked to the county in an attempt to get their fingers on the pulse of the nation. Jefferson is "one of the most important counties in the nation and symbolic in every way of the battle for the soul of the middle class," a local political observer told Governing.

To the west of the city is the town of Golden, with the old Colorado School of Mines and the Coors brewery. To the northwest are Arvada and Wheat Ridge, middle-income suburbs with an increasing number of Latinos. Farther north along Interstate 25 are rapidly growing Federal Heights, Thornton and Northglenn. In 2017, officials began to issue permits for a 10-mile toll road between Golden and Bloomfield that was designed to connect highways around the metro area. Commerce City, with its large oil refinery, nearly tripled its population from 2000 to 2017. In September 2018, adjacent to Commerce City, the Interior Department opened the Rocky Mountain Arsenal National Wildlife Refuge. Federal judges continued to review the safety of the refuge at what had been the site of a nuclear weapons plant, which shut down in 1989 and was cleaned up at a cost of $7 billion.

The 7th Congressional District covers the suburbs north and west of Denver, sweeping in Arvada, Lakewood, Thornton and Westminster, which are the district's largest cities. Golden is the western edge of the district. Within a few miles of downtown Denver, it takes in parks, lakes and recreational spots. Nearly two-thirds of the district is in Jefferson County, with southern and western slices of the county in the 1st and 2nd Congressional Districts. The remainder of the district population is in the western end of Adams County, extending just north of the airport.

In 2016, the county and state were out of sync with the nation, with Hillary Clinton leading Donald Trump in Jeffco, 49%-42%. Still, the county leaned to Republicans in other contests that year. With Clinton having an overall margin of 51%-39%, the district was a tad more Democratic than Jeffco. Still to be determined is whether the county regains its status as a political bellwether or instead becomes a symbol of the suburban shifts across the nation.

CONNECTICUT

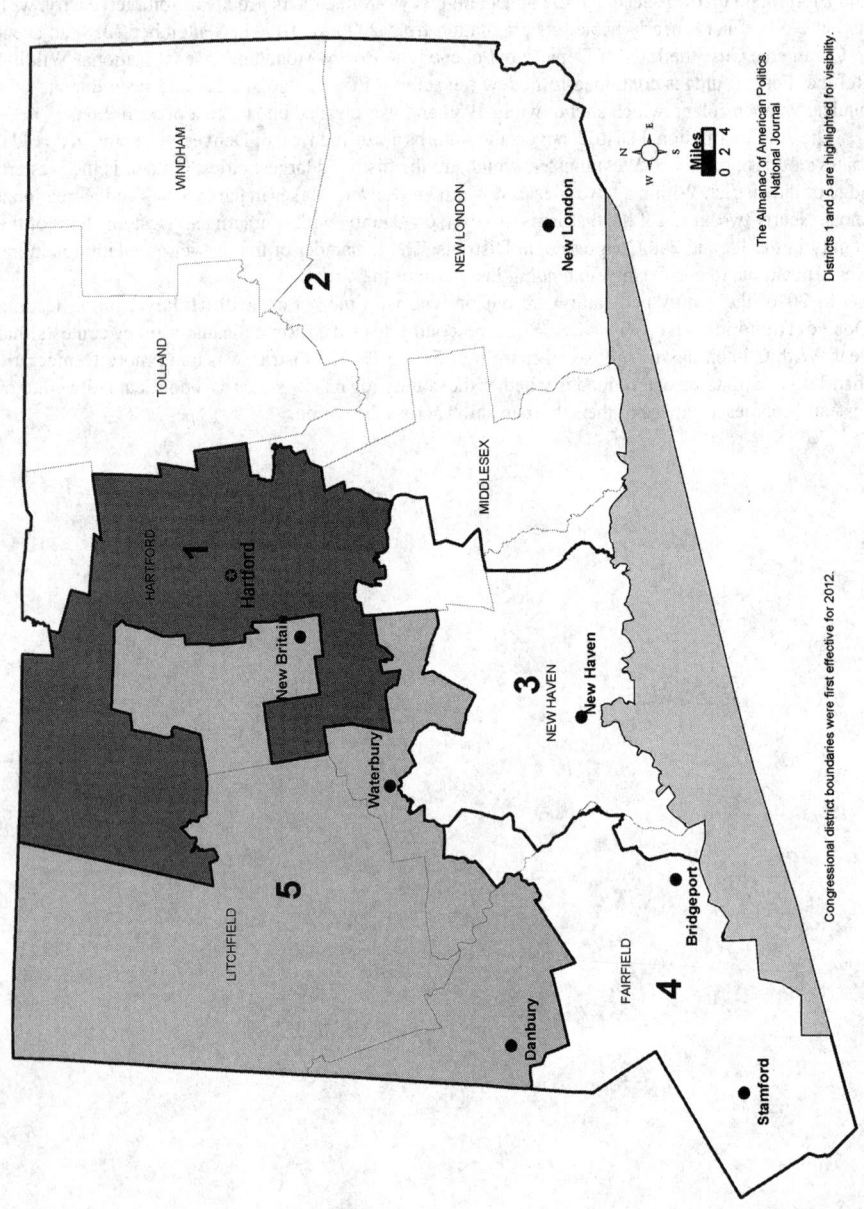

The Almanac of American Politics.
National Journal

Districts 1 and 5 are highlighted for visibility.

Congressional district boundaries were first effective for 2012.

Connecticut is in some respects America's highest achieving state, with one of the highest rates of bachelor's degrees, one of the top median incomes, and great accumulations of wealth — but it is also a state with a yawning gap between the rich and poor, visible in the contrast between hedge fund managers' estates in Greenwich and the slums of Bridgeport not all that far away. The home of Yale University is in the upper tier of states competitive in the global knowledge economy, yet it has grown achingly slowly. Adjusted for inflation, Connecticut's gross domestic product in 2017 was 8.5 percent lower than a decade earlier, and by late 2018 the state had an unemployment rate about half a percentage point higher than the nation as a whole. The state's population has treaded water in recent years, and economic stagnation has created budgetary pressures that put the dominant Democratic Party on the defensive.

Connecticut was founded by Puritans who considered Massachusetts too lenient, though they were also open to certain reforms. In 1784, Connecticut voted for gradual emancipation of the state's slaves, one of the first societies anywhere to do so. Across the state, 11 percent of residents are black, 15 percent Hispanic, and 4 percent are Asian-American, while the city's capital and largest city, Hartford, is 28 percent foreign-born, peopled by immigrants from Cape Verde, the Middle East, Asia and the Caribbean. Native Americans have built a gaming empire – the Foxwoods Resort Casino, opened in 1992 and owned by the 900-member Mashantucket Pequot tribe, and its big competitor, the Mohegan Sun, owned by the 1,700-member Mohegans – but profits have slumped with added competition, including an MGM casino in Springfield Massachusetts that opened in 2018.

Connecticut's accumulated affluence came not from any jackpot invention but from a knack for tinkering and making productive use of savings. Connecticut made clocks, hats, combs, cigars, silk thread, pins, matches, brass and furniture. The companies that invented Pez candy, Nivea skin cream and the Wiffle ball are still headquartered in Orange, Norwalk, and Shelton, respectively. The quintessential Connecticut Yankee, Eli Whitney, was the inventor not only of the cotton gin but also of rifles with interchangeable parts, and Samuel Colt won a War Department contract to manufacture guns for the Mexican-American War. (The state's longstanding gun connections caused tension following the 2012 massacre at Sandy Hook Elementary School in Newtown.)

During the defense buildup of the 1980s, Connecticut produced Air Force jets and Army helicopters and, in the Electric Boat Shipyard in New London, most of the Navy's nuclear submarines, continuing a long seafaring tradition memorialized at Mystic Seaport. The current buildup looks promising for Connecticut's defense sector: Pratt & Whitney makes engines for F-35 fighters, while Sikorsky, a subsidiary of Lockheed Martin, and Electric Boat, now a subsidiary of General Dynamics, can look forward to billions of dollars in contracts. Pratt & Whitney also makes engines for the commercial Airbus A320. These companies plan to expand by thousands of workers and create business for local subcontractors in the coming years – so much business that the state has scrambled to boost its workforce's waning base of manufacturing skills.

In recent decades, Connecticut has focused more attention on white-collar skills. It has long been home to several of the nation's great insurance companies -- its laws are unusually friendly to creditors and harsh on debtors – and hedge funds have sprouted in suburbs like Greenwich on the fringes of New York City. This was not a recipe for job creation: Bridgewater, a $150 billion hedge fund, employs only about 1,400 (very well-compensated) people. By contrast, the state's modestly sized central cities — New Haven, Hartford and Bridgeport — have been plagued by crime, depopulation and corruption. In March 2018, the state said it would pay off Hartford's debt so the city could avoid bankruptcy, a $550 million commitment over 20 years. "Get out of Greenwich, in other words, and you encounter lovely but stagnant suburbs — grist for so many ennui-afflicted short stories — studded with the occasional pocket of urban poverty," Annie Lowrey wrote in New York magazine.

Writing in The Atlantic in 2017, Derek Thompson dubbed Connecticut the Rorschach State. "Conservatives look at Connecticut and see a liberal dystopia, where high taxes have ruined the economy. Liberals, on the other hand, see a capitalist horror show, where the rich dwell in gilded mansions, ensconced in sylvan culs-de-sac, while nearby towns face rising poverty and bankruptcy." There's evidence to support both critiques. The state has the second-highest tax burden in the country, and the pension burden is set to grow from $2.9 billion in 2018 to $5 billion in 2026. But a bigger problem may be who pays those taxes. Connecticut's heavy dependence on the finance sector to fill state coffers leaves it hostage to the whims of Wall Street. In the meantime, Connecticut was an unintended casualty of the comeback of America's big cities, Thompson argued: Big companies once fled dysfunctional megacities in the 1970s for leafy environs like Connecticut, but today, they're moving in the other direction.

Indeed, Connecticut has experienced a run of high-profile corporate departures. In 2016, General Electric said it would quit its 70-acre, 800-job headquarters in Fairfield, where it had been based since 1974, for Boston. The following year, Alexion Pharmaceuticals left its longtime corporate home in New Haven and moved to Boston, although the company said it would maintain a reduced presence in New Haven. Meanwhile, the state dodged a bullet when Aetna – founded and headquartered in Hartford since 1853 – announced it was being sold to CVS Health Corp. As part of the deal, the company's planned move to Manhattan was shelved for 10 years, with a promise to keep employment stable for four.

For much of the 20th century, Connecticut politics was an ethnic struggle between Yankee Republicans and Catholic Democrats. Slowly, as Catholic birthrates exceeded those of Protestants, Democrats gained ground. For a long historical moment, the central cities and Catholic suburbs voted Democratic and the WASP-y suburbs and rural towns voted Republican. But those days are gone. In 2004, 2008 and 2012, white Protestants and Catholics voted Republican; secular whites, blacks and Latinos went heavily Democratic. Cultural issues have played a role. The state's ban on contraceptives produced the U.S. Supreme Court's Griswold decision in 1965, the precursor of Roe v. Wade, and abortion rights now command high levels of support. In 2005, the legislature legalized civil unions for same-sex couples, and in 2008, the state Supreme Court converted all these into same-sex marriages. Connecticut legislators have also voted for in-state college tuition for children of illegal immigrants, for public financing of state legislative races, and for strict carbon emission reductions.

In congressional races, Connecticut has become solidly Democratic. As recently as 2006, Republicans (albeit moderate ones) held a majority of the state's five-member U.S. House delegation. Since 2009, all five seats have been Democratic. The 2018 election of progressive Democrat Jahana Hayes to represent the 5th District – which had been represented by three Republicans and one Democrat between 1985 and 2007 – is symbolic of the state party's leftward drift. No Republican has won a Senate seat in Connecticut since maverick Lowell Weicker in 1982. Oddly, Connecticut did not have a Democratic governor for two decades, but that changed in 2010 with the election of Dannel Malloy, the longtime mayor of Stamford who won two close races. However, economic stagnation, fiscal challenges and worries about the state's pension burden sank Malloy's approval ratings, enabling Republicans in 2016 to gain enough seats to tie the state Senate and shave the Democratic edge in the state House to just a couple seats.

But Republican hopes of additional gains ran into the broad unpopularity of Donald Trump. Already in the 2016 presidential race, affluent, historically Republican towns that felt warmly toward Mitt Romney in 2012 swung heavily toward Hillary Clinton: Darien swung by 53 points toward the Democrats compared with 2012, New Canaan swung by 50 points, and Greenwich swung by 29 points. In 2017 local elections, Democrats made broad gains in such affluent suburbs as Farmington, Glastonbury and Southington. Then, in 2018, Democrats swept every major office including the governorship, while also gaining significant ground in both chambers of the legislature. Distaste for Trump, apparently, mattered more to the state's voters than concerns about Democratic management back home.

Population		Race and Ethnicity		Income	
Total	3,594,478	White	68.1%	Median Income	$73,781
Land area (sq. miles)	4,842	Black	9.8%	State Income Rank	6
Pop/ sq mi	742.3	Latino	15.4%	Poverty Rate	10.1%
Born in state	55.0%	Asian	4.3%	With health insurance	93.6%
		Two or more races	2.0%	Cash public assistance	3.7%
Age Groups		Other	0.4%	Food stamp/SNAP	12.4%
Under 18	21.2%				
18-34	22.0%	Education		Work	
35-64	40.8%	H.S grad or less	37.0%	White Collar	42.5%
Over 64	16.0%	Some college	24.6%	Sales and Service	40.7%
		College Degree, 4 yr	21.5%	Blue Collar	16.8%
Military		Post grad	17.0%	Government	13.0%
Veteran/ Active Duty	6.7%				

Presidential Politics

2016 Primary (D)	Clinton (D)	170,045 (52%)	Sanders (D)	152,379 (46%)			
2016 Primary (R)	Trump (R)	123,523 (58%)	Kasich (R)	60,522 (28%)	Cruz (R)	24,987 (12%)	
2016 Pres. Vote	Clinton (D)	897,572 (55%)	Trump (R)	673,215 (41%)	Johnson (L)	48,676 (3%)	
2012 Pres. Vote	Obama (D)	905,083 (58%)	Romney (R)	634,892 (41%)			

Hillary Clinton favored higher taxes on the highest earners while billionaire Donald Trump winced at that idea. But the Democrat nonetheless defeated Trump 55%-41% in one of the nation's highest-income states, where many corporate executives who work in New York live to avoid relatively high Empire State taxes. What gives? Liberal stands on cultural issues have trumped economic concerns among affluent Connecticut voters and many of the state's white ethnics still adhere to their Democratic roots of generations past. The wealthy "gold coast" towns of Darien, Greenwich, New Canaan and Westport in Fairfield County, home to hedge fund investors and old WASP money, once a Republican bastion in the state, have been alienated by the influence of Christian evangelicals in the GOP. Nor did Trump's brand of populism play well among these voters: those four towns saw double-digit percentage increases in the vote for Clinton over the Obama vote four years earlier.

The GOP primary was held April 26, and Trump rolled to victory, 58%-28%, over Ohio Gov. John Kasich, who had hoped that the state's more moderate electorate might embrace his brand of centrism. But the Connecticut GOP primary was limited to registered Republicans and they delivered all of the state's convention delegates to Trump. The Democratic primary was much more spirited. Barack Obama had beaten Clinton in the primary eight years earlier, 51%-47%, giving Vermont Sen. Bernie Sanders some hope for success, but his past support for limiting the liability of gun manufacturers was a handicap in a state that saw 20 children and six adults murdered at the Sandy Hook Elementary School mass shooting in Newtown in 2012. Gov. Dannel Malloy, a top Clinton surrogate and gun-control advocate made sure to remind his fellow Democrats of Sanders' past liability position. Clinton won the New York City suburbs and the Gold Coast, where Sanders' hostility toward Wall Street was not welcomed. She also captured the state's major cities, including New Haven. Sanders prevailed in western Connecticut and in the eastern portion of the state, which has a number of rural townships, more conservative communities like Groton and New London, both of which Sanders carried, and the University of Connecticut at Storrs. It was a hard-fought primary, but Clinton won 52%-46%. Despite the closeness of the contest, all 15 of the superdelegates from Connecticut backed Clinton, a prime example of what the Sanders camp felt was unfair about this class of Democratic convention delegates made up of elected and party officials.

It's easy to forget that from 1972 to 1988, Republican presidential candidates won the Nutmeg State. In 1988, Democratic nominee Michael Dukakis won only one of the state's eight counties, Hartford. In 2016, Clinton won six, losing only Litchfield and Windham. Democrats were not always the liberal party on social issues in Connecticut. Culturally conservative working-class Irish, Italian and Polish Catholics in Hartford, New Britain, New Haven, Bridgeport and New London were once the backbone of the party.

Congressional Districts

116th Congress Lineup	5D	115th Congress Lineup	5D

Connecticut has a bipartisan redistricting process. Two Republicans and two Democrats from each chamber of the legislature meet to draw the lines. If their map is approved by a two-thirds vote in both chambers, it becomes law. Otherwise, a ninth member is chosen by the other eight, and they try to reach consensus. The customary collaboration didn't work in 2011, when Democrats controlled all five House seats. Republicans wanted to remove the heavily Democratic cities of Bridgeport and New Britain from the 4th and 5th districts, respectively, to make both seats' boundaries smoother and more competitive. When the commission failed to meet its Supreme Court-extended deadline, the court stepped in and appointed Columbia Law Professor Nathaniel Persily as special redistricting master. With instructions from the court to make minimal changes, Persily shifted only 28,975 residents between districts. Since then, Democrats have retained their firm hold on all five districts.

Despite some doubts prior to the 2018 election, Democrats are in complete control in Hartford. Redistricting outcomes in 2021 likely will be similar to a decade earlier. The longtime Republican success in western Connecticut districts has been relegated to the distant past. As recently as 2006, the GOP had three of the five seats in the House delegation.

Ned Lamont (D)

Elected 2018, term expires 2023, 1st term; b. Jan. 3, 1954, Washington, DC; Harvard University, B.A., 1976; Yale University, M.B.A, 1980; Unknown; Married (Annie); 3 children.

Elected Office: Member, Greenwich Board of Selectmen, 1987-1989.

Professional Career: Managing Editor, Black River Tribune, 1976-1978; Teacher, 2004-2006; Founder & CEO, Lamont Digital; Professor, Connecticut State University, 2008-2018.

Office: 210 Capitol Ave., Hartford, 06106; 860-566-4840; Fax: 860-524-7395; Website: ct.gov
Lt. Gov.: Susan Bysiewicz (D) **Atty. Gen:** William Tong (D) **Sec. of State:** Denise Merrill (D)
State Legislature: Senate: 22D, 14R **House:** 90D, 60R, 1I

Election Results

Election	Name (Party)	Vote (%)
2018 General	Ned Lamont (D)	694,510 (49%)
	Bob Stefanowski (R)	650,138 (46%)
	Oz Griebel (I)	54,741 (4%)
2018 Primary	Ned Lamont (D)	172,567 (81%)
	Joe Ganim (D)	39,976 (19%)

After two unsuccessful runs for statewide office, Democrat Ned Lamont won the Connecticut governorship in 2018, buoyed by voter dissatisfaction with President Donald Trump. It was the third consecutive time a Democrat had won the governorship by a narrow margin, and the first time since 1924 that an open seat was won by the party of the outgoing governor.

Lamont was a child of privilege -- his great-grandfather, Thomas W. Lamont, was chairman of J.P. Morgan – but he later amassed his own fortune as an entrepreneur. Lamont attended Phillips Exeter Academy, earned his bachelor's degree from Harvard, and received an MBA from the Yale School of Management. After college, he founded a newspaper and eventually Lamont Digital

Systems, a cable TV firm that, after rebranding as Campus Televideo, grew to serve 1 million college students nationally; he sold it in 2015. Lamont took some early steps toward public service, including a stint on the Greenwich board of selectmen in the 1980s.

In 2006, he ran for the U.S. Senate, challenging incumbent Democrat Joe Lieberman in the primary; Lamont ran from the left and took aim at Lieberman's support for the Iraq War, inspiring a wave of liberal activists in the process. Lamont won the primary, but the incumbent ran as an independent in the general election and prevailed in the three-way contest. In 2010, Lamont ran in the gubernatorial primary against former Stamford Mayor Dannel Malloy. Lamont led in early polls, but Malloy won the primary, 57%-43%. Malloy went on to serve two terms as governor, but his tenure in office was hampered by a weak state economy, interminable budget battles and groaning pension burdens. At one point in 2017, the biennial budget deficit exceeded $5 billion, and a standoff between Malloy and legislative Republicans lasted for months. In April 2017, to the relief of many Democrats, Malloy announced that he would not seek a third term.

Lamont's early interest and his deep pockets kept most credible Democratic candidates out of the race, and he ended up facing only Bridgeport Mayor Joe Ganim, who had served seven years in federal prison after being convicted in a kickback scheme. Lamont won 81%-19%, prevailing everywhere except for Ganim's hometown. Meanwhile, the Republican primary was a five-way bruiser that included Danbury Mayor Mark Boughton, former UBS chief financial officer Bob Stefanowski, former hedge fund chief David Stemerman, former Trumbull selectman Tim Herbst, and tech entrepreneur Steve Obsitnik. Stefanowski, advocating a phase-out of the state's personal and corporate income taxes, finished first with 29 percent, followed by Boughton with 21 percent, Stemerman with 18 percent, Herbst with 18 percent and Obsitnik with 13 percent. In an election cycle in which the Democrats were mostly playing offense nationally, Connecticut was one state where Republicans had hopes of flipping a gubernatorial seat. But every GOP primary candidate ran a strongly conservative campaign and touted their support for Trump – a sound strategy in a base-dominated primary, but a gift to Lamont, who successfully leveraged this rhetoric against Stefanowski in the general election.

Lamont attacked Stefanowski's tax and spending platform as fiscally reckless, promising instead not to raise the state income or sales tax. He also said he favored a cut in property taxes, though he was vague about how to pay for it. He said that legalizing sports betting and recreational marijuana would raise some money, as would tolls on out-of-state trucks, though critics said that limiting tolls that way might run into legal challenges. (Stefanowski, for his part, ruled out tolls entirely.) Lamont, unlike Stefanowski, pledged not to draw down the state's $1.2 billion reserve fund. Meanwhile, Lamont -- who had also secured the ballot line of the progressive Working Families Party -- backed an eventual $15 per hour minimum wage as well as mandatory paid family and medical leave. Oz Griebel, a former Republican lawyer and business figure, ran as an independent, but, despite some debate exposure, faded in the stretch.

Lamont defeated Stefanowski, 49%-46%, with Griebel taking 4%. The contest was close enough that Stefanowski was ahead until late votes from the Democratic strongholds of New Haven and Hartford were counted. Beyond those cities and their nearby suburbs, a key to Lamont's win was likely the New York City suburbs of Fairfield County, which Malloy had won by a hair's breadth in 2014 but which Lamont took by eight points. While Stefanowski increased the number of GOP votes in Fairfield County by 26 percent over 2014, Lamont increased his raw votes in Fairfield by a striking 46 percent.

As he prepared to take office, Lamont faced deficit projections of 10 percent for 2019 and 12 percent in 2020. He also prepared to grapple with state employee unions, a key constituency in the battle over pension obligations. Lamont had their backing during the campaign, but after his election, he was expected to seek some pension clawbacks and an end to "double-dipping" by pension recipients who still held public-sector jobs.

Richard Blumenthal (D)

Elected 2010, term expires 2022, 2nd term, b. Feb 13, 1946; Brooklyn, NY; Harvard College (MA), A.B., 1967; Cambridge University (England), Att., 1968; Yale University Law School (CT), J.D., 1973; Jewish; Married (Cynthia Allison Malkin); 4 children.

Military Career: U.S. Marine Corps Reserve 1970-1975

Elected Office: CT House, 1984-1987; CT Senate, 1987-1990; CT Attorney General, 1991-2010.

Professional Career: Teacher, Washington D.C. Public Schools, 1968- 1969; Staff Assistant, White House Office of Economic Opportunity, 1969-1970; Clerk, Supreme Court Justice Harry Blackmun, 1974-1975; Administrative Assistant, Sen. Abraham Ribicoff, 1975-1976; U.S Attorney CT, 1977-1981; Practicing Attorney, 1981-1990.

DC Office: 706 HSOB 20510, 202-224-2823, Fax: 202-224-9673, blumenthal.senate.gov
State Offices: Bridgeport, 203-330-0598; Hartford, 860-258-6940.

Committees: *Aging. Armed Services*: Airland; Cybersecurity; Seapower. *Commerce, Science & Transportation*: Communications, Technology, Innovation & the Internet; Manufacturing, Trade & Consumer Protection (RMM); Subcommittee on Science, Oceans, Fisheries & Weather; Subcommittee on Security; Subcommittee on Transportation & Safety. *Judiciary*: Antitrust, Competition Policy & Consumer Rights; Border Security & Immigration; Oversight, Agency Action, Federal Rights & Federal Courts (RMM); Subcommittee on Intellectual Property. *Veterans' Affairs.*

Group Ratings

	ADA	ACLU	AFL-CIO	LCV	ITI	COC	HAFA	ACU	CFG	FRC
2018	-	73%	-	100%	-	50%	3%	9%	5%	0%
2017	100%	C	100%	100%	C	29%	C	0%	4%	0%

Almanac Ratings 2017-18

	Economy	Social	Foreign	Composite
Liberal	97%	97%	96%	96%
Conservative	3%	3%	5%	4%

Key Votes of the 115th Congress

1. Obama-care revision	N	5. Gun regulations	N	9. Kavanaugh confirmation	N
2. Tax Cuts	N	6. Family planning regs	N	10. Saudi arms sales	Y
3. Dodd-Frank revision	N	7. Gorsuch confirmation	N	11. FISA rules	N
4. Omnibus appropriations	Y	8. Immigration restrictions	N	12. Military aid in Yemen	Y

Election Results

Election	Name (Party)	Vote (%)		Cand. Spent	Ind. Exp. Support	Ind. Exp. Oppose
2016 General	Richard Blumenthal (D)................. 1,008,714	(63%)	$6,794,120			
	Dan Carter (R).................................. 552,621	(35%)	$244,556			
2016 Primary	Richard Blumenthal (D)................ unopposed					

Prior winning percentages: 2010 (54%)

For two decades, Democrat Richard Blumenthal was Connecticut's aggressive, media-savvy attorney general, focusing on one consumer protection issue after another and becoming the state's most popular elected official in the process. Blumenthal's modus operandi changed little during his first term in the Senate: His focus remained on acting as a consumer advocate in high-profile controversies ranging from transportation safety to TV blackouts by professional sports leagues. It was a winning formula back home — Blumenthal was re-elected in 2016 by a margin of nearly 30 points — even if it didn't yield much visibility in the nation's capital.

But Blumenthal's inside-the-Beltway profile has spiked since he returned to Capitol Hill for a second term and Donald Trump moved in to the other end of Pennsylvania Avenue. As a member of the Senate Judiciary Committee, Blumenthal repeatedly challenged White House actions on constitutional grounds, sometimes taking the administration to court. The president responded with a continuing series of barbs, usually via Twitter, targeting Connecticut's senior senator for a controversy that has dogged Blumenthal since his first Senate run: comments earlier in his career suggesting that he had served in the Vietnam War when he had not. "We call him Da Nang Richard," Trump gibed in October 2018 — a reference to where U.S. combat troops first landed in Vietnam — after Blumenthal had questioned the credibility of Supreme Court nominee Brett Kavanaugh.

The sniping involved two natives of New York's outer boroughs — Blumenthal was born in Brooklyn, Trump in Queens — with ties to rival camps in the often-cutthroat battles over Manhattan real estate. According to a 2016 Roll Call analysis of available data, Blumenthal, with a minimum net worth of $70 million, is among the 10 wealthiest members of Congress — largely by dint of marriage. Blumenthal's wife, Cynthia, is the daughter of real estate magnate Peter Malkin. Trump also made his name in New York real estate, often in competition with Malkin. The two had a feud involving the complex ownership structure of the Empire State Building. Blumenthal's father, Martin, fled Nazi Germany in 1935 — 11 years before his son's birth — and became wealthy by trading commodities in his adopted country.

After graduating Harvard University with a degree in political science, Richard Blumenthal moved on to Yale Law School, where he edited the Yale Law Journal. His post-college list of employers reads like a "Who's Who" of the Washington elite in the 1970s. They included longtime Washington Post publisher Katharine Graham; future New York Sen. Daniel Patrick Moynihan, then a top adviser in the Nixon White House; and Supreme Court Justice William Brennan — for whom Blumenthal clerked.

After a stint as a top aide to Sen. Abraham Ribicoff — who then held the seat Blumenthal now occupies — President Jimmy Carter in 1977 appointed the 31-year-old Blumenthal as U.S. attorney for Connecticut. His career in elected office started with the Connecticut Assembly in 1984; he moved to the state Senate in 1987 before his successful run for attorney general in 1990. Blumenthal used the latter position to pursue lawsuits against health insurers and polluters as well as Big Tobacco and some of the nation's leading banks. Detractors derided him as "Sue 'Em All Blumenthal." Voters elected him to five terms, never with less than 59 percent of the vote. Although unhesitant to take on powerful corporate targets, Blumenthal earned a reputation for caution when it came to his own political future. He resisted repeated entreaties from Democrats to run for governor, a post occupied by Republicans during much of his tenure as the state's top lawyer.

Just as Blumenthal finally seemed ready to take the plunge for higher office — eyeing a 2012 challenge to Democratic-turned-independent Sen. Joe Lieberman — an unexpected opening occurred. Veteran Democratic Sen. Chris Dodd, embattled at home over allegations that he had accepted political favors, retired at the beginning of 2010. Blumenthal switched from seeking re-election as attorney general to run for Dodd's seat. At first, Blumenthal's Senate race looked to be an electoral stroll in the park, given his popularity in a onetime swing state that had turned blue. But it was also the year that the tea party took flight, and the Republican nominee, Linda McMahon — who, with her husband, Vince McMahon, started World Wrestling Entertainment — harnessed an upswing in GOP voter energy to make it a real contest.

The first sign things were not going to be easy for Blumenthal was a New York Times report on the exaggeration of his military service. A member of the Marine Corps Reserve from 1970 to 1975, Blumenthal claimed on several occasions to have served in Vietnam, though he never had been deployed. According to the Times, Blumenthal, after a series of deferments had run out, joined a reserve unit in Washington that conducted drills and focused on local projects such as fixing a campground and organizing a Toys for Tots drive. The McMahon campaign attacked him for distorting his record, putting a chink in his best asset: his image as a selfless crusader. Blumenthal apologized, but his wide lead in the polls was gone. Blumenthal's camp went after McMahon over sexism and use of steroids in professional wrestling, where McMahon had earned a fortune as WWE president. By the end of the campaign, she had spent more than $50 million — almost six times as much as Blumenthal — with most of it coming from her own pocket. But she "had persistent trouble winning over women voters, despite the fact she would have become the first female senator in the state's history," the Hartford Courant reported. "Some women were turned off by some of the racier images of WWE." Blumenthal scored a comfortable, if not overwhelming, 55%-43% win.

In a touch of irony, Blumenthal found himself the ranking Democrat on the Veterans' Affairs Committee four years after arriving in the Senate. His son Matthew was an officer in the Marine Corps

Reserve and served in Afghanistan; son Michael entered the Navy midway through Blumenthal's first Senate term. Blumenthal teamed up with the Veterans' Affairs panel chairman, Republican Johnny Isakson of Georgia, to sponsor a bill to overhaul the troubled Veterans Affairs Department — including provisions to facilitate the firing of problem employees while protecting whistleblowers and to expand mental health programs for veterans. A stripped-down version of the bill was adopted during the lame-duck session in December 2016. Sen. Jon Tester of Montana, who outranked Blumenthal in seniority, opted to take over as ranking Democrat in advance of a tough 2018 re-election. "The position or the title is less important than the work," Blumenthal said, vowing to "work with even greater determination to improve services for our veterans."

Blumenthal's consumer advocacy efforts during his first Senate term were aimed largely at transportation safety. As a member of the Commerce, Science and Transportation Committee, he called for General Motors to create a compensation fund for victims of defective ignition switches in the company's automobiles. After the company announced it was setting up such a fund in mid-2014, Blumenthal joined Democratic Sen. Edward Markey of Massachusetts in keeping up the pressure on GM. A year later, Blumenthal called on Takata to establish a similar fund for victims of its ruptured air bags. Company officials rejected Blumenthal's request, but later agreed to set up such a fund in early 2017 as part of a $1 billion settlement with the Justice Department. If Blumenthal's frequent jawboning didn't often translate into enacted legislation, he contended it nonetheless helped prod the targeted industries to do the right thing. And, appearing to address critics who have accused him of being more interested in attention than results, Blumenthal]told The Connecticut Mirror: "One lesson to me is that legislation is only one lever to fight for benefits for the people of Connecticut. I can use my position to shine a light on problems."

Blumenthal has continued to team up with Markey on consumer issues: In the spring of 2018, the two stalled legislation that would have removed regulatory obstacles to driverless-car development. The move came a month after a driverless vehicle killed a pedestrian in Arizona; Blumenthal insisted that any legislation include the ability to manually override self-driving cars. Around the same time, Blumenthal and Markey introduced a "privacy bill of rights," to be enforced by the Federal Trade Commission, for users of such platforms as Facebook and Google. Their legislation followed revelations that Cambridge Analytica, a consulting firm with ties to the 2016 Trump campaign, had obtained data on as many as 87 million Facebook users without permission. The bill was introduced just before an appearance before the Commerce Committee by CEO Mark Zuckerberg, during which Blumenthal suggested the Cambridge Analytica episode had violated a 2011 consent decree between Facebook and the FTC. "What happened here was, in effect, willful blindness," Blumenthal told Zuckerberg. "It was heedless and reckless."

Throughout his first term, Blumenthal had few disagreements with a White House controlled by his own party. A notable example occurred a month before the 2016 elections, when he was at the forefront of the successful effort to override President Barack Obama's veto of a bill allowing families of 9/11 victims to sue the Saudi Arabian government in U.S. courts. "I stood up to the president," Blumenthal said afterward. "Trust me, there was a lot of pressure to back down."

Immediately following Trump's swearing-in, Blumenthal found himself standing up to the president on multiple fronts: He was sharply critical of several nominees for top executive branch positions and helped lead congressional opposition to Trump's early efforts to ban travelers from predominantly Muslim nations. Five months into the new administration, he led nearly 200 congressional Democrats in a lawsuit charging that Trump, by retaining his global business empire, was in violation of the emoluments clause of the Constitution, which restricts federal officials from accepting of payments or gifts from foreign states.

Trump aimed tweets at Blumenthal just weeks into his presidency after the senator, following a meeting with Supreme Court nominee Neil Gorsuch, told to reporters that Gorsuch had characterized Trump's frequent criticisms of federal judges as "disheartening" and "demoralizing." Gorsuch later publicly acknowledged that Blumenthal — who joined most Senate Democrats in voting against Gorsuch's confirmation — had quoted him correctly. But it was after Blumenthal characterized Trump's May 2017 firing of FBI Director James Comey as "a looming constitutional crisis" that could ultimately lead to impeachment that the president unleashed a tweetstorm. Deriding Blumenthal as "Richie" — a nickname by which Blumenthal has never been known — Trump wrote: "Watching Senator Richard Blumenthal speak of Comey is a joke. 'Richie' devised one of the greatest military frauds in U.S. history." Employing a few exaggerations of his own, Trump continued: "For ... years, as a pol in Connecticut, Blumenthal would talk of his great bravery and conquests in Vietnam — except he was never there. When ... caught, he cried like a baby and begged for forgiveness ... and now he is judge & jury. He should be the one who is investigated for his acts."

Blumenthal kept a stiff upper lip. "Our national security and the rule of law are at stake. I am not going to be distracted or bullied by these slurs," he said in August 2017, after his comments during an appearance on CNN triggered another Trump tweet labeling him a "phony Vietnam con artist!" The rhetorical siege escalated a year later when another Trump Supreme Court nominee, Kavanaugh, faced confirmation hearings. Blumenthal asked if Kavanaugh was familiar with "Falsus in uno, falsus in omnibus" — a legal dictum that suggests jurors can deem a witness to lack credibility on all matters if he or she says one thing that is not true. "The core of why we're here, really, is credibility," Blumenthal declared in the wake of sexual assault allegations against Kavanaugh by Christine Blasey Ford. Trump, joined by allies on Capitol Hill, counterattacked. "@SenBlumenthal lied for years about serving in Vietnam, which is all you need to know about his courage & honesty," Sen. Tom Cotton, R-Ark., tweeted while Blumenthal was questioning Kavanaugh. "Maybe he should reconsider before questioning Judge Kavanaugh's credibility."

Blumenthal's 2016 re-election bid might have provided a colorful preview of this war of words — had Larry Kudlow, who later became Trump's chief economic adviser, carried through on a threat to challenge the incumbent. In 2015, Blumenthal came under heavy lobbying pressure as one of the last Democratic holdouts on taking a position on the Obama administration's nuclear agreement with Iran. Kudlow vowed to challenge Blumenthal if he voted for the deal, which Blumenthal ultimately agreed to support. But, after seven months of talking about taking on Blumenthal, Kudlow decided against running, which would have forced him to give up his platform as a conservative commentator for CNBC. However, he served notice that he was planning to make an issue of Blumenthal's entire public career. "All these anti-business lawsuits never went anywhere," Kudlow told the Hartford Courant, referring to Blumenthal's tenure as attorney general. "It was death by 1,000 press releases.'" In a preemptive strike, Blumenthal sent out mailings calling Kudlow "anti-Main Street" and seeking to tie him to Trump, then a contender for the Republican presidential nomination. "He called the recession 'therapeutic' and workers laid off in 2008 'whiners,'" one Blumenthal fundraising letter said of Kudlow.

Kudlow's withdrawal left Connecticut Republicans scrambling for an alternative. A month before the state GOP nominating convention, conservative state Rep. Dan Carter entered the race, and was overwhelmingly chosen by delegates. But Carter was virtually unknown statewide, and Blumenthal outspent him 20-1, cruising to a 63%-35% victory — twice the margin by which Democratic presidential nominee Hillary Clinton, once Blumenthal's classmate at Yale Law School, carried Connecticut.

Chris Murphy (D)

Elected 2012, term expires 2024, 2nd term, b. Aug 03, 1973; White Plains, NY; Oxford University Exeter College (England), Att., 1995; Williams College, B.A., 1996; University of Connecticut School of Law, J.D., 2002; Protestant - Unspecified Christian; Married (Catherine Holahan Murphy); 2 children.

Elected Office: CT House, 1999-2003; CT Senate, 2003-2006; U.S. House, 2007-2013.

Professional Career: Southington CT Planning & Zoning Commission, 1997-1999; Practicing attorney, 2002-2006.

DC Office: 136 HSOB 20510, 202-224-4041, Fax: 202-224-9750, murphy.senate.gov

State Offices: Hartford, 860-549-8463.

Committees: *Appropriations*: DOL, HHS & Education & Related Agencies; Legislative Branch (RMM); Military Construction & Veteran Affairs & Related Agencies; State, Foreign Operations & Related Programs; Transportation, HUD & Related Agencies. *Foreign Relations*: Africa & Global Health Policy; Europe & Regional Security Cooperation; Near East, South Asia, Central Asia & Counterterrorism (RMM). *Health, Education, Labor & Pensions*: Children & Families; Primary Health & Retirement Security.

Group Ratings

	ADA	ACLU	AFL-CIO	LCV	ITI	COC	HAFA	ACU	CFG	FRC
2018	-	71%	-	100%	-	50%	3%	9%	5%	0%
2017	95%	C	100%	95%	C	29%	C	0%	4%	0%

Almanac Ratings 2017-18

	Economy	Social	Foreign	Composite
Liberal	97%	97%	69%	87%
Conservative	3%	3%	31%	13%

Key Votes of the 115th Congress

1. Obama-care revision	N	5. Gun regulations	N	9. Kavanaugh confirmation	N
2. Tax Cuts	N	6. Family planning regs	N	10. Saudi arms sales	Y
3. Dodd-Frank revision	N	7. Gorsuch confirmation	N	11. FISA rules	N
4. Omnibus appropriations	Y	8. Immigration restrictions	N	12. Military aid in Yemen	Y

Election Results

Election	Name (Party)	Vote (%)		Cand. Spent	Ind. Exp. Support	Ind. Exp. Oppose
2018 General	Chris Murphy (D)	825,579	(60%)	$7,487,098	$5,513	
	Matthew Corey (R)	545,717	(39%)	$185,883		
2018 Primary	Chris Murphy (D)		(100%)			

Prior winning percentages: 2012 (55%); House: 2010 (54%), 2008 (59%), 2006 (56%)

By his own admission, Democrat Chris Murphy, Connecticut's junior senator, was first elected to that chamber in 2012 without a passionate purpose for being there. That changed just five weeks after Election Day, when a mass shooting took place at Sandy Hook Elementary School in Newtown, in the House district that Murphy had represented for three terms. He rushed to the school and remained with grieving parents until all the fatalities — 20 children and six teachers and aides — were carried out. "There wasn't one issue that was driving me to get up every day and go to work. There is today," Murphy later told Politico. "This was something different ... in part because my son just graduated from first grade. I'm the same age as all of these parents. I walked out of that tragedy feeling like I had just been handed my mission in public service."

Those comments came shortly after Murphy sought move the needle on gun control with a Senate filibuster following the Orlando, Florida nightclub shooting, in which 49 were killed, in June 2016. Murphy held the floor for nearly 15 hours and won concessions from the GOP to hold votes on several gun control measures. But the result was the same as what had followed other episodes of gun violence in recent years: Proposals to expand background checks to cover gun shows and sales over the internet and to bar sale of guns to those on terrorist watch lists fell short. "I'm embarrassed that it's taken this long to pass a law," an exasperated Murphy told survivors of another mass shooting — at Marjory Stoneman Douglas High School in Parkland Florida, in early 2018, during which 17 died — when they visited Newtown later that year.

While he has yet to achieve a major expansion in federal gun control statutes, Murphy has gained a political opportunity: During the past two election cycles, he has raised money and campaigned for candidates across the country who share his views. Combined with initiatives to recast Democratic Party messaging on issues ranging from military intervention abroad to health care policy at home, Murphy was widely viewed as a potential 2020 presidential candidate. A self-described progressive Democrat who bankrolled a grassroots effort called Fight Back Connecticut to rally voters against the policies of President Donald Trump, Murphy has demonstrated a pragmatic side by reaching out to Republicans — and even the Trump administration on some issues. "Murphy, I think, is a top-tier candidate if he wants to run" for president, former Democratic National Chairman Howard Dean told the Hartford Courant. "He's the perfect Democrat to respond to Trump." For his part, Murphy continually brushed aside suggestions that he consider a run against Trump, even as he was easily winning a second Senate term. "I've been pretty clear but I'm sure people are going to continue asking me about running," he told Connecticut Magazine just before his 2018 re-election.

As one of the Senate's youngest members, who will be just 47 on Election Day 2020, he can afford to wait. With an aggressive presence on TV and social media, Murphy's aspirations don't appear to stop at Capitol Hill. During what has become an annual walk across his home state, Murphy told The Washington Post in 2016 that he is a "big ball of political ambition." He continued: "Everyone doing this job is fooling themselves if they don't admit that we are attracted to the show business element of it. We are all doing this in part because we enjoy being in front of the cameras."

Raised in the Hartford suburb of Wethersfield, Murphy has been in politics virtually his entire adult life. After graduating from Williams College in 1996, he signed on as campaign manager for Democrat Charlotte Koskoff, who came within 1,600 votes of toppling then-Rep. Nancy Johnson. Two years later, Murphy ran for office himself, winning a seat in the state House when he was 25; He moved on to the state Senate in 2002 — while juggling his state legislative duties with earning a law degree.

In early 2005, Murphy announced plans to challenge Johnson. Besides the war in Iraq, which Murphy opposed, the debate focused on the Medicare prescription drug benefit that Johnson had helped design in 2003 as chairman of the House Ways and Means Health Subcommittee. Murphy contended that the program's enrollment deadlines penalized seniors and spotlighted drug industry contributions to Johnson. Johnson, who had served for nearly a quarter-century, outspent Murphy by 2-1. But, as the Democrats rode a national wave to retake the House majority, Murphy won 56%-44%.

In the House, Murphy was a loyal Democrat, although he boasted of his role in Center Aisle Caucus, which he described as "one of the few places in the House where Republicans and Democrats are ... getting together to try and talk about the importance of civility." While his district was home to many insurance industry employees, he backed a government-run public option to compete with private insurers during the 2009-10 debate over the Affordable Care Act. It is an issue in which Murphy remained involved: In late 2018, he floated a proposal to give individuals and businesses the option of buying into Medicare under the exchanges established by the Affordable Care Act, an alternative to the "Medicare for all" approach pushed by Vermont Sen. Bernie Sanders and others in the Democrats' progressive wing. "We're not going to pass a single-payer health care bill any time in the next few years. And so we need to have a conversation about how we get there," Murphy told Politico.

Beginning with his House tenure, Murphy has been an ardent advocate for "Buy America" requirements, introducing bills to require federal contracting officials to solicit information from businesses regarding how many U.S. jobs would be retained or created if their bid were chosen. A decade later, Murphy lauded the Trump administration for helping to build support for Senate legislation he authored to allow businesses and the public to examine the waivers federal agencies use to avoid Buy America requirements. Murphy introduced the bill in January 2018 with Republican Sens. Lindsey Graham of South Carolina and Rob Portman of Ohio. While it did not move out of committee, Murphy told the Connecticut Post that year "Trump is stronger on 'Buy America' than [President Barack] Obama. I wish that were not the case, but it's true. I disagree with 90 percent of what he says, but I give him credit where credit is due."

Murphy announced his bid for the Senate in 2012 when four-term Sen. Joe Lieberman said he would not run again. Murphy faced a primary against former Connecticut Secretary of State Susan Bysiewicz, now the state's lieutenant governor. She ran a controversial TV ad seeking to link Murphy to Wall Street in the wake of the 2008 financial meltdown; it cited more than $700,000 in contributions to Murphy from Wall Street sources over a six-year period. But Bysiewicz found herself on the defensive after having to acknowledge the ad had overstated donations Murphy received from hedge funds. Murphy won the primary by 2-1.

The general election turned out to be déjà vu. Linda McMahon, the former professional wrestling magnate who had lost the 2010 Senate race to Democratic Sen. Richard Blumenthal, was again the Republican nominee. And, like Blumenthal two years earlier, Murphy struggled in the general election despite being an odds-on favorite at the start of the campaign. While Blumenthal had stumbled due to inflated claims on his military record, Murphy was tripped up over revelations that he missed mortgage payments and had been sued over failure to pay rent. Murphy blamed a busy schedule for the missed payments. As she had in 2010, McMahon tapped into her personal wealth, burning through nearly $50 million. Murphy targeted McMahon — later appointed by Trump to head the Small Business Administration — on issues affecting seniors, contending she would pose a threat to Social Security and Medicare. On Election Day, McMahon lost by the same 55%-43% margin by which she had come up short to Blumenthal.

On domestic policy, Almanac vote rankings show Murphy to be among the most liberal senators in the chamber. As a member of the Health, Education, Labor and Pensions Committee, he has been an outspoken defender of the Affordable Care Act and led Senate Democrats defense of Obamacare from Republican attacks during his first term. His willingness to perform this politically onerous task served him well with Democratic leaders: Murphy was given a coveted seat on the Appropriations Committee — the first Connecticut senator in almost 30 years to sit on that influential panel. Perhaps Murphy's major legislative achievement to date was a mental health bill, co-authored with Republican Sen. Bill Cassidy of Louisiana, which was signed into law by Obama at the end of 2016. Hailed as the first major piece of mental health legislation in a decade, it was designed to strengthen insurance coverage for mental health treatment while providing grants to increase the number of psychiatrists and psychologists nationwide. A state report following the Sandy Hook school shooting found that the gunman, Adam Lanza, had gone untreated for both psychiatric and physical disorders.

In contrast to Lieberman, Murphy emerged as one of the Senate's most outspoken doves on U.S. involvement in the Middle East. He gained widespread attention in 2013 when he told Obama — who had called Murphy at home — that he could not support the administration's plan to take military action against Syria. "I can't say that it was a comfortable position to be in, having a public dispute with the president so early in my freshman term," Murphy told the Connecticut Mirror. A year later, he came out against the Obama administration's efforts to train and arm Syrian rebels to fight ISIS.

Murphy said he became wary of U.S. military involvements because of what he saw as the failures of the wars in Afghanistan and Iraq. "I want ISIS defeated in Syria," he said. "But too much can go wrong, for not enough possible gain, for the U.S. to increase our involvement in the Syrian civil war." When at the end of 2018, Trump ordered the withdrawal of 2,000 troops from Syria — a move widely criticized by both congressional Democrats and Republicans — Murphy charged in a floor speech that Trump's action "was done in a ham-handed manner that makes us weaker in the world." But Murphy slammed the initial move to involve the U.S. military in Syria. "I thought this was a bad idea from the start," he said. "We should admit we have just prolonged [the war] instead of trying to end it."

Less than a week before Trump ordered the troop withdrawal from Syria, Murphy — a strong critic of the administration's close relationship with Saudi Arabia — joined with Sanders and conservative Republican Sen. Mike Lee of Utah to spearhead passage of a resolution withdrawing U.S. support for Saudi-backed forces at war in Yemen. It was a bipartisan rebuke to Trump — and marked the first time that the Senate, under the terms of the War Powers Act, had supported withdrawing forces from a war that Congress had not voted to approve. While skeptical of overseas military involvement, Murphy, as a member of the Foreign Relations Committee, has proposed sharply increasing foreign aid, including a new Marshall Plan to combat the rise of political extremism overseas. "The amateurism of Trump's foreign policy is absolutely stunning," Murphy told HuffPost in 2017. "He has zero interest in learning about the world."

Connecticut Republicans failed to recruit a top-tier challenger to take on Murphy in 2018. The Republican nomination went to Matthew Corey, a pro-Trump small-businessman who had lost three previous bids for the House of Representatives; Corey won the primary by a 3-1 margin over his only challenger. Murphy spent a significant amount of time campaigning for Democratic candidates elsewhere. Murphy spent $7.5 million—compared to Corey's $186,000—and won by a 60%-39% margin.

Several months before his re-election, Murphy scored a small victory on his signature legislative issue when Trump, in March 2018, signed an appropriations measure containing the "Fix NICS" bill. That legislation, which Murphy co-authored with Texas Republican John Cornyn, was designed to increase the frequency with which state and federal agencies report offenses to the National Instant Criminal Background Check System that would bar people from legally buying firearms. Cornyn and several other Texas legislators got behind the plan after a gunman who had escaped from a mental health facility killed 26 people at a Baptist church in rural Texas. The gunman should have been on the NICS database checked by federally licensed gun dealers but wasn't.

The Fix NICS measure was a rare instance of the National Rifle Association supporting gun restrictions. At the same time, Trump backed away from several other gun control measures — such as universal background checks — that he had seemed to embrace at a White House meeting several weeks earlier attended by Murphy. Reacting to Trump's signing of the bill, Murphy said: "The small steps forward on gun safety … are good news. But let's be honest — the [National Rifle Association] still has veto power over the Republican-led Congress. Republicans still won't schedule a debate on guns in the Senate, and if the small provisions in the budget are all that they are willing to do, that would be a tragic insult to all the kids who are rising up across the country demanding that Congress end the gun violence epidemic." That statement echoed his earlier vow to a Connecticut Post reporter. "I'm young," Murphy said, "but I'm planning to be around the Senate long enough to beat the gun lobby."

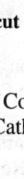

John Larson (D)

Elected 1998, 11th term, b. Jul 22, 1948; Hartford; Trinity College (CT); Central Connecticut State University (CT), B.S., 1971; Catholic; Married (Leslie Best Larson); 3 children.

Elected Office: E. Hartford Board of Education, 1977-1979; E. Hartford Town Council, 1979-1983; CT Senate, 1986-1998, President pro-tem, 1990-1998.

Professional Career: H.S. teacher, 1972-1977; Ins. broker, 1977-1998; Sr. fellow, Yale Bush Center, 1995-1998.

DC Office: 1501 LHOB 20515, 202-225-2265, Fax: 202-225-1031, larson.house.gov

State Offices: Hartford, 860-278-8888.

Committees: *Ways & Means*: Select Revenue Measures; Social Security (Chmn).

Group Ratings

	ADA	ACLU	AFL-CIO	LCV	ITI	COC	HAFA	ACU	CFG	FRC
2018	-	80%	-	94%	-	58%	4%	8%	3%	0%
2017	80%	C	95%	97%	C	57%	C	4%	5%	14%

Almanac Ratings 2017-18

	Economy	Social	Foreign	Composite
Liberal	95%	83%	95%	91%
Conservative	5%	17%	5%	9%

Key Votes of the 115th Congress

1. Obama-care revision	N	5. Family planning regs	N	9. Guantanamo prisoners	Y
2. Tax Cuts	N	6. Body cameras/immigration	Y	10. Ground missiles, limit	Y
3. Omnibus appropriations	Y	7. Abortion ban	N	11. Defense Dept. spending	Y
4. Dodd-Frank revision	N	8. Concealed carry	N	12. FISA rules	N

Election Results

Election	Name (Party)	Vote (%)	Cand. Spent	Ind. Exp. Support	Ind. Exp. Oppose
2018 General	John Larson (D)	175,087 (64%)	$1,185,082		
	Jennifer Nye (R)	96,024 (35%)			

Prior winning percentages: 2016 (64%), 2014 (62%), 2012 (70%), 2010 (60%), 2008 (72%), 2006 (74%), 2004 (73%), 2002 (67%), 2000 (72%), 1998 (58%)

Democrat John Larson, first elected in 1998, has been an influential figure among House Democrats and popular with colleagues. As a senior member of the tax-writing Ways and Means Committee and chairman of its Social Security Subcommittee, he pursued his expertise in the program. Once a leadership lieutenant of Speaker Nancy Pelosi, Larson had become a cautious critic during the Democrats' long struggle in the minority.

One of eight children, Larson grew up in the Mayberry Village public-housing project in East Hartford, and is fond of saying that he is a "product of public housing, public education and public service." His father was a fireman at Pratt & Whitney. His mother had a job at the state capitol and served on the town council. Speaking at the 2012 Democratic National Convention, he said that his mother had dementia and required round-the-clock care, paid for in part through her Social Security benefits. "Don't ever tell me or any American that's a handout," he said. "It's the insurance they paid for."

After graduating from Central Connecticut State University, Larson taught high school and coached athletics. In 1982, he was elected to the state Senate. Four years later, he became Senate president. He sponsored one of the nation's first family and medical leave laws, a prototype for the federal bill signed by President Bill Clinton in 1993.

Larson seemed headed for the governorship. But Comptroller Bill Curry in 1994 built an organization of union members and liberal activists and beat him 55%-45% in the primary. When Democratic Rep. Barbara Kennelly ran for governor in 1998, Larson ran for her seat. In the primary, he won 46%-43% over Secretary of State Miles Rapoport. In the general election, he competed against Kevin O'Connor, a 31-year-old lawyer. Larson won 58%-41% and has not been seriously challenged since.

Larson's voting record places him near the center of his party. In the House minority, he worked with Republicans on legislation, especially Ways and Means Chairman Kevin Brady on a measure to make permanent a research and development tax credit. He has been co-chairman of the bipartisan Congressional Joint Strike Fighter Caucus, which backs the F-35, whose engines are made by Pratt & Whitney.

In 2003, Pelosi tapped Larson as senior Democrat on the House Administration Committee, the congressional housekeeping panel that handles office budgets and other perks of interest to colleagues. Among his legislative interests at the committee was campaign finance reform, including a proposal to allow the federal government to match funds raised by a candidate who agrees to accept only contributions of $100 or less. In 2006, he was elected Democratic Caucus vice chairman. His competitors were Jan Schakowsky of Illinois and Joseph Crowley of New York. With Schakowsky's supporters, Larson prevailed on the second ballot 116-87 over Crowley. When Rahm Emanuel quit the House to become chief of staff to President Barack Obama, Pelosi cleared the field for Larson to become caucus chairman.

Larson took on a number of leadership assignments, including dealing with party dissidents who complained that Pelosi's Iraq strategy was too accommodating to President George W. Bush and later coordinating the Democrats' strategy on energy policy. Some Democrats privately derided him as Pelosi's cheerleader, but he shrugged off such comments, saying that his "bottom-up, member's member" approach differed from the imperious style of Emanuel, but was no less effective. After meeting the four-year limit in that post, Larson served as a mentor to younger members. He said he would welcome a return to party leadership, but that time may have passed. His voice grew more independent following the 2016 election when he joined critics of Pelosi. The Democratic Caucus needed "a frank discussion about what happened," he said.

Coincidentally, in 2017, Larson's close friend Rep. Richard Neal of Massachusetts — who had also shown independence from Pelosi — became the top Democrat at the Ways and Means Committee. Larson took the initiative within the party by launching a bicameral Expand Social Security Caucus, with Bernie Sanders and Elizabeth Warren as co-chairs in the Senate. He filed the Social Security 2100 Act, which he said was designed to assure the long-term solvency of the program, with increased support for low-income beneficiaries and tax increases on higher earners. "I am committed to taking commonsense steps to expand benefits and to make the system solvent for the next 75 years and beyond," Larson said. The Congressional Progressive Caucus endorsed the proposal.

Larson was an outspoken foe of the tax cuts that Republicans enacted in December 2017. He criticized the legislation for adding to the deficit. He also complained about tax cuts for high earners while contradictorily bemoaning the adverse effects on high-income states such as Connecticut. "I don't know how they look at themselves in the mirror," he said. He called the bill's elimination of the deduction for medical expenses "a direct assault on the elderly."

At home, Larson talked up his proposal for a massive "big dig" tunnel project that would replace the two interstate highways that bisect downtown Hartford and East Hartford, and likely would take decades to build. "It's time for the Hartford region to think big again," he wrote. He said that the project was about "economic vitality, growth for the region and creating livable communities." He called for a tax on carbon emissions to finance national transportation improvements.

"The choice is simple," Larson said about his proposed tunnels. "Think big again and make this happen." That approach defined his broader objectives.

CT-1: North-central Connecticut   **Cook Partisan Voting Index: D+12**

Population		Race and Ethnicity		Income	
Total	715,329	White	61.8%	Median Income	$69,910
Land area (sq. miles)	675	Black	14.3%	District Income Rank	96
Pop/ sq mi	1059	Latino	16.4%	Poverty Rate	11.1%
Born in State	58.3%	Asian	5%	With health insurance	94.7%
Age Groups		Two or more races	2%	Cash public assistance	5.1%
Under 18	21.2%	Other	0.4%	Food stamp/SNAP	15.1%
18-34	22%	**Education**		**Work**	
35-64	40.2%	H.S grad or less	37.6%	White Collar	16.6%
Over 64	16.6%	Some college	25.5%	Sales and Service	40.6%
Military		College Degree, 4 yr	21.1%	Blue Collar	16.1%
Veteran/ Active Duty	6.2%	Post grad	15.8%	Government	14.2%

2012 Pres. Vote	Obama	200,910	(63%)	Romney	112,962	(36%)		
2016 Pres. Vote	Clinton	195,305	(59%)	Trump	119,395	(36%)	Johnson	9,468	(3%)

Hartford: The Puritans who founded Hartford certainly never expected, or even hoped, that Connecticut's Yankees would turn out to be shrewd businessmen. Yet this is exactly what happened. Mark Twain moved to Hartford in 1871 to become director of an insurance company, and in time became the Connecticut capital's most famous citizen. Some have departed, but Connecticut retains one of the largest concentrations of financial and insurance firms in the nation, mostly in the Hartford area. Its merchants wrote fire insurance, using the capital they had accumulated in the Napoleonic Wars to finance their ventures. Samuel Colt was instrumental in developing the state's armaments base; he conceived of the revolving-barrel pistol after watching the wheel of a ship spin while at sea. His gun factory, just south of downtown Hartford, became one of the nation's great arms plants. Thanks to the broad Connecticut River, Hartford became an inland seaport.

Despite their downsizing, insurance and armaments remain economic mainstays of Hartford,. But many employers have moved out of Hartford itself, hastening the decline of this once rich city. Insurance industry employment dropped to 47,000 statewide in 2014, though it rebounded to 60,000 in 2018. Some recent good news was that Aetna, after abandoning plans to move to New York City, was purchased in 2018 by CVS, which agreed to keep the insurance business in Hartford. Since the 1980s, the central core has been filled with bedraggled, high-crime neighborhoods littered with abandoned buildings Where 177,000 people lived in 1950, there were about 123,400 residents in 2018. The population is 39 percent African American and 43 percent Hispanic — mostly Puerto Rican. There have been signs of recovery. The University of Connecticut opened in 2017 a large downtown campus, inter-city train service has expanded, and new housing and retail facilities are under construction. A baseball stadium just north of downtown opened belatedly in 2017, though the city held nearly $70 million in bond debt on it. Luke Bronin, a former Rhodes Scholar who served with the Navy in Afghanistan, has brought a youthful urgency as mayor. After Donald Trump was elected president, Bronin said that Hartford would remain a "sanctuary city" that would protect illegal immigrants. "We're not going to let our police force be commandeered by the federal government to target families that aren't posing any threat to anyone," he said in March 2018. Also that month, Hartford avoided bankruptcy when the state took responsibility for payment of $755 million of city bonds.

Across the river is the Pratt & Whitney jet engine plant in East Hartford, cornerstone of Connecticut-based United Technologies. Though its operations have been shrunk by Pentagon spending cutbacks and its local workforce is less than one-fourth its size in 1980, it builds engines for more than 600 customers around the world. The areas west of Hartford are affluent suburbs and faring much better.

The 1st Congressional District of Connecticut is centered on Hartford. West Hartford has the most voters, though its population is only half the size of Hartford. The district is shaped like a lobster claw. The top half passes through Windsor. The claw then swings west across the northern border of the state, taking in small towns and part of Torrington. The bottom half of the district includes

Bristol, site of the sprawling headquarters of ESPN, the multimedia network that has cut back from its peak in 2017 of 4,000 local workers (of nearly 8,000 worldwide). Although ESPN shifted some of its operations to New York City, executives said that company headquarters would remain in Bristol. The Hartford area has long been more Democratic than the rest of Connecticut. The 2016 election produced a twist, when Hillary Clinton dropped below 60 percent and got a slightly larger vote in the upscale 4th District.

Joe Courtney (D)

Elected 2006, 7th term, b. Apr 06, 1953; West Hartford; Tufts University (MA), B.A., 1975; University of Connecticut School of Law, J.D., 1978; Roman Catholic; Married (Audrey Courtney); 2 children.

Elected Office: CT House, 1987-1994.

Professional Career: Practicing attorney, 1978-2006; CT coordinator, John Edwards President campaign, 2004.

DC Office: 2332 RHOB 20515, 202-225-2076, Fax: 202-225-4977, courtney.house.gov

State Offices: Enfield, 860-741-6011; Norwich, 860-886-0139.

Committees: *Armed Services*: Seapower & Projection Forces (Chmn); Tactical Air & Land Forces. *Education & Labor*: Health, Employment, Labor & Pensions; Higher Education & Workforce Investment

Group Ratings

	ADA	ACLU	AFL-CIO	LCV	ITI	COC	HAFA	ACU	CFG	FRC
2018	-	78%	-	91%	-	64%	4%	4%	2%	0%
2017	90%	C	95%	97%	C	64%	C	4%	5%	11%

Almanac Ratings 2017-18

	Economy	Social	Foreign	Composite
Liberal	94%	87%	89%	90%
Conservative	6%	13%	11%	10%

Key Votes of the 115th Congress

1. Obama-care revision	N	5. Family planning regs	N	9. Guantanamo prisoners	Y
2. Tax Cuts	N	6. Body cameras/immigration	Y	10. Ground missiles, limit	Y
3. Omnibus appropriations	Y	7. Abortion ban	N	11. Defense Dept. spending	Y
4. Dodd-Frank revision	N	8. Concealed carry	N	12. FISA rules	N

Election Results

Election	Name (Party)	Vote (%)		Cand. Spent	Ind. Exp. Support	Ind. Exp. Oppose
2018 General	Joe Courtney (D)	179,731	(62%)	$864,929		
	Dan Postemski (R)	102,483	(35%)			

Prior winning percentages: 2016 (63%), 2014 (62%), 2012 (68%), 2010 (59%), 2008 (66%), 2006 (50%)

Democrat Joe Courtney, elected in 2006, has tirelessly promoted issues that are important to him, chiefly defense and education. With his influence on the Armed Services Subcommittee on Seapower and Projection Forces, he has delivered huge local benefits as a guardian of General Dynamics' Electric Boat plant and the New London Naval Submarine Base.

Courtney was raised in West Hartford. He studied at Tufts University, graduated from the University of Connecticut law school and went into private practice. In 1986, he won the first of four terms in the state House, where he served as chairman of the public health and human services committees. He ran unsuccessfully for lieutenant governor in 1998, then unsuccessfully in 2002 against Republican Rep. Rob Simmons, who won 54%-46%. Courtney returned for a rematch in 2006. Democrats worked diligently to nationalize the race by exploiting voter anger over the Iraq war and

GOP ethics scandals in Congress. Simmons touted his independence from the Bush administration on partial-birth abortion and same-sex marriage votes. He also highlighted his successful lobbying to keep the submarine base off the 2005 base-closing list. Courtney prevailed in the closest House race of the 2006 election, with a winning margin of 83 votes out of the more than 242,000 cast.

In the House, Courtney got a seat on Armed Services, where he effectively lobbied for the Navy's shipbuilding program at Groton. He worked with other Connecticut and Rhode Island lawmakers in 2007 to secure an extra $588 million in the defense appropriations bill for submarines, paving the way for the Navy to double its submarine production from one to two a year. That led to his nickname from colleagues: "Two Sub Joe." He has told the Hartford Courant that he faithfully studied Electric Boat employment listings like baseball box scores, looking for signs of anxiety because of the threat of defense cuts.

Courtney took over as co-chair of the Congressional Shipbuilding Caucus and worked to prevent a one-year cut in submarine production in 2014 while protecting the appropriation for a "stretched" version of a Virginia-class sub with cruise-missile tubes, which was designed at the Electric Boat yard. He successfully lobbied the Pentagon to include in its Quadrennial Defense Review the need for a future fleet of as many as 55 submarines, up from the 48 called for in 2006. In the 2014 defense spending bill, he secured as much as $3.5 billion for a "National Sea-Based Deterrence Fund" that would allow the Pentagon to finance a new class of submarines to be built in Groton. In 2015, as the senior Democrat on the Seapower Subcommittee, he worked closely with Armed Services Committee Republicans to defeat an attempt by members of the House Appropriations Committee to restore annual funding for the new submarines. "We haven't seen this much work [at Electric Boat] since the late '80s and early '90s," Courtney told the Courant in 2016.

In June 2018, Courtney sought to accelerate a $1 billion down payment for the submarines, which he said would be more cost-effective. But the Appropriations Committee did not include the money in its defense spending bill. A Defense Department official said that Courtney's proposal would "disrupt" military spending. He subsequently complained about the lack of a shipbuilding strategy that would permit Congress to "look at maritime issues in a logical way." As chairman of the Seapower Subcommittee in 2019, he was positioned to demand a response. On another military issue with a local connection for Courtney, he asked the Coast Guard in June 2018 to investigate reports of discrimination and harassment at its academy in New London.

Courtney has generally been a loyal Democrat. Representing a district that includes the University of Connecticut, Courtney has been the leading champion of below-market interest rates on federally backed college loans. With Sen. Elizabeth Warren of Massachusetts, he filed a bill in 2015 that would save the average student borrower $2,000. During the 2009 health care debate, he led House Democratic opposition to a proposed "Cadillac tax" on high-cost health insurance plans, which he said would harm millions in the middle class. He helped change it to a 3.8 percent tax on non-wage income, shifting much of the cost from union members to investors.

Unlike most Democrats elected in 2006, Courtney has had a much easier time keeping his office than he did in winning it, never receiving less than 60 percent in his next six campaigns. In 2018, he had a peculiar experience: Republican challenger Dan Postemski, an Iraq war veteran and perennial candidate, complained that the state and national GOP was giving him insufficient support and he shut down his campaign with a blunt "the hell with them" dismissal. "They were trying to make me a politician," he posted on Facebook. "They abandoned me, so I abandoned them." Postemski conceded the obvious: "No one's going to beat Joe Courtney."

CT-2: Eastern Connecticut   Cook Partisan Voting Index: D+3

Population		Race and Ethnicity		Income	
Total	708,127	White	82%	Median Income	$74,427
Land area (sq. miles)	1,988	Black	3.6%	District Income Rank	73
Pop/ sq mi	356.3	Latino	8.1%	Poverty Rate	8.4%
Born in State	56.7%	Asian	3.3%	With health insurance	95.6%
		Two or more races	2.6%	Cash public assistance	3.9%
Age Groups		Other	0.4%	Food stamp/SNAP	10.3%
Under 18	19.6%				
18-34	23%	**Education**		**Work**	
35-64	40.9%	H.S grad or less	37%	White Collar	16.5%
Over 64	16.5%	Some college	28.2%	Sales and Service	40.9%
		College Degree, 4 yr	19.6%	Blue Collar	18.3%
Military		Post grad	15.1%	Government	16%
Veteran/ Active Duty	10.4%				

2012 Pres. Vote	Obama	177,522	(56%)	Romney	135,212	(43%)	
2016 Pres. Vote	Clinton	165,799	(49%)	Trump	155,975	(46%)	Johnson 13,080 (4%)

New London, Norwich: When Puritans from Massachusetts and England arrived in eastern Connecticut, the flinty hills were the home of small Indian tribes, whose numbers had been decimated by warfare and even more by disease. Factories quickly developed around mills in little villages on the fast-flowing Quinebaug and Shetucket rivers. Soon, New London and Norwich were among the 13 colonies' leading workshops and ports. The infamous plot of Connecticut native Benedict Arnold to deliver West Point in New York to the British was uncovered during the American Revolution, but his company did succeed in burning New London to the ground in 1781 and sacking Fort Griswold. The region's deep vein of human industriousness sustained it into the 20th century, when new technology took over in shaping the area. Four nuclear power plants were built here, more than in any other place in the nation. In Groton, the "Submarine Capital of the World" situated across the Thames River from New London, General Dynamics' Electric Boat company built its first submarines in 1915 and, later, nuclear subs.

The reductions in military spending following the end of the Cold War were painful for the region and the long-term survival of the port was in doubt. But Congress provided a jolt of additional spending and the Navy chose Electric Boat to be the prime contractor for a new class of 12 ballistic-missile submarines, with an ultimate price tag of perhaps $100 billion. That increased the payroll at Groton to 16,000 in 2017, with thousands more planned. The shipyard, which is undergoing a nearly $1 billion expansion, also helps to build two attack submarines annually. Construction has begun on a $100 million national Coast Guard museum on the New London downtown waterfront.

The area's economic base has relied heavily on entertainment, specifically gambling. The Foxwoods Resort Casino, built by the 650-member Mashantucket Pequot tribe, once was the largest casino in the Western Hemisphere. But its number of employees dropped from 10,500 to 6,500 in 2017. In nearby Uncasville is the site of the Mohegan Sun casino, with a slightly smaller payroll. Competition from nearby states and the slow national economy stunted the growth of gaming in the area. Foxwoods struggled to restructure billions of dollars in debt. Concerned about competition from a new MGM casino in Springfield Massachusetts, the two tribes pursued plans for a casino across the border in Connecticut. In October 2018, a federal judge ruled that the tribes lacked standing to compel the Interior Department to override the objections of MGM and accept revisions to the state's gambling agreement.

The 2nd Congressional District includes most of the eastern half of the state, centering on the small cities of New London and Norwich and including mill towns and the University of Connecticut in Storrs. The district stretches west to the outskirts of Hartford and to antique-filled small towns like Essex and Old Lyme on Long Island Sound. For many years, this was a politically marginal district, with close battles between Yankee Republicans and Catholic Democrats. Although it recently trended comfortably Democratic, the 49%-46% margin for Hillary Clinton in 2016 was 10 points less than Barack Obama's 56%-43% local win in 2012.

Rosa DeLauro (D)

Elected 1990, 15th term, b. Mar 02, 1943; New Haven ; Queen Mary College - London School of Economics (England), 1963; Marymount College (NY), B.A., 1964; Columbia University (NY), M.A., 1966; Roman Catholic; Married (Stanley Greenberg); 3 children; 4 grandchildren.

Professional Career: Executive Assistant, New Haven Mayor Frank Logue, 1976-1977; Executive Assistant & develop. admin., City of New Haven, 1977-1979; Chief of Staff, U.S. Sen. Christopher Dodd, 1981-1987; Executive Director, Countdown '87, 1987-1988; Executive Director, EMILY's List, 1989-1990.

DC Office: 2413 RHOB 20515, 202-225-3661, Fax: 202-225-4890, delauro.house.gov

State Offices: Derby, 203-735-5005; Naugatuck, 203-729-0204; New Haven, 203-562-3718.

Committees: House Democratic Steering and Policy Committee Co-Chair. *Appropriations*: Agriculture, Rural Development, FDA & Related Agencies; Labor, Health & Human Services, Education & Related Agencies (Chmn). *Budget*.

Group Ratings

	ADA	ACLU	AFL-CIO	LCV	ITI	COC	HAFA	ACU	CFG	FRC
2018	-	79%	-	91%	-	58%	4%	4%	2%	0%
2017	95%	C	97%	77%	C	36%	C	4%	6%	0%

Almanac Ratings 2017-18

	Economy	Social	Foreign	Composite
Liberal	96%	87%	95%	93%
Conservative	4%	13%	5%	8%

Key Votes of the 115th Congress

1. Obama-care revision	N	5. Family planning regs	N	9. Guantanamo prisoners	Y
2. Tax Cuts	N	6. Body cameras/immigration	Y	10. Ground missiles, limit	Y
3. Omnibus appropriations	Y	7. Abortion ban	N	11. Defense Dept. spending	Y
4. Dodd-Frank revision	N	8. Concealed carry	N	12. FISA rules	N

Election Results

Election	Name (Party)		Vote (%)	Cand. Spent	Ind. Exp. Support	Ind. Exp. Oppose
2018 General	Rosa DeLauro (D)	144,452	(94%)	$804,734	$1,321	
	Angel Cadena (R)	9,825	(6%)			

Prior winning percentages: 2016 (69%), 2014 (67%), 2012 (75%), 2010 (64%), 2008 (77%), 2006 (76%), 2004 (72%), 2002 (66%), 2000 (72%), 1998 (71%), 1996 (71%), 1994 (68%), 1992 (57%), 1990 (52%)

Rosa DeLauro, a Democrat first elected in 1990, is an outspoken liberal and a party leader on health and food safety issues. As chair of the House Appropriations subcommittee on health and education funding, and a confidant of Speaker Nancy Pelosi, DeLauro has a prime seat at the Democratic leadership table.

DeLauro grew up in New Haven's Wooster Square and has been well-connected politically. Both of her parents were New Haven aldermen. Her mother, Luisa DeLauro, served 35 years, the longest tenure in New Haven history. In Wooster Square Park, a granite monument of a table, bench and two chairs honors the family's home as a social services center. Rosa DeLauro's husband, Stanley Greenberg, was Bill Clinton's chief pollster from 1991 to 1994 and worked for Al Gore's presidential campaign in 2000 and John Kerry's in 2004. As Obama's White House chief of staff, Rahm Emanuel, a family friend who lived for a while in the basement of DeLauro's Capitol Hill home, officiated at the wedding of Greenberg's daughter Anna, a partner in their political consulting firm.

DeLauro has been in politics nearly all her life. She was a development administrator in New Haven in the 1970s, chief of staff to Democratic Sen. Christopher Dodd from 1980 to 1987, then spent a year working to stop U.S. military aid to Nicaraguan contras before she became director of EMILY's List, the women's campaign fundraising group that supports abortion rights. When the 3rd District seat opened in 1990, DeLauro prevailed 52%-48% over anti-tax and anti-abortion Republican state Sen. Tom Scott. She has not faced serious competition since 1992, when she won a rematch against Scott, 66%-34%.

DeLauro is one of the Democratic leadership's most vocal champions in debate. Pelosi in 2011 admiringly described her as "a force of nature." She is an active and ardent supporter of feminist causes. A cancer survivor, she sponsored the law to require that patients and doctors, not insurance companies, decide on 48-hour hospital stays for mastectomies. She lobbied for insurance coverage of early-detection tests for cervical cancer, and helped to enact "Johanna's Law" to increase awareness of gynecological cancers. In 2009, the House passed her bill, the Lilly Ledbetter Fair Pay Act, which extended the statute of limitations for women alleging wage discrimination, reversing a Supreme Court decision. In the House minority for eight subsequent years, DeLauro was less prolific as a legislator.

When Democrats regained House control, DeLauro took charge of the Appropriations Subcommittee on Labor, Health and Human Services and Education — a position, she said, that was "a dream come true." Serving as the House's chief spender on those programs was "my heart and soul," she told The Connecticut Post. She has been outspoken in opposing cuts in education programs that were proposed by President Donald Trump. At a May 2017 hearing, DeLauro said that Education Secretary Betsy DeVos was "heartless ... millions of kids around this country are going to suffer." Also that year, DeLauro authored a book about her experiences in seeking to preserve the social safety net for the poor -- The Least Among Us: Waging the Battle for the Vulnerable.

As a former chair of the Appropriations Subcommittee on Agriculture, Rural Development, Food and Drug Administration, DeLauro has retained a keen interest in food safety, which she said should have the same priority as prescription drug and medical device safety. She said that the FDA was "badly broken" and faulted the Obama administration for not doing enough to address the problems. At a 2016 event with Sen. Richard Blumenthal of Connecticut, she said food companies are "preying on consumers' good intentions" by putting artificial ingredients in "natural" products, given the lack of any prohibition. In 2018, she called for an investigation of the regulation of laboratory-grown meats.

In an often testy clash with President Barack Obama during his final two years in office, DeLauro was a leader among House Democrats in siding with unions to oppose the proposed Trans-Pacific Partnership trade agreement that the United States was negotiating with 11 nations. Despite the prospect of lower tariffs, her greater concern was that the deal would kill good-paying jobs. It was vital, she said, that "everyone who works hard and plays by the rules has a chance to succeed." When Trump took office and withdrew the United States from the deal, and subsequently moved to revise the North American Free Trade Agreement — which had long stirred attacks from DeLauro — she found herself in an unusual alliance. "It really is the best opportunity that we have," she said.

As co-chair of the Steering and Policy Committee, DeLauro has been instrumental in advising on committee assignments for House Democrats, which are especially vital for the party in the majority. She has "an encyclopedic knowledge of members' committee aspirations," Pelosi said. In return, DeLauro has remained an avid booster of Pelosi's continuation as the top House Democrat, despite growing restiveness in the Democratic Caucus. "You want the attributes of intellectual capacity, strategic acumen, compassion and core values. Add to that a spine of steel," DeLauro told The Connecticut Post.

DeLauro has run twice for chairwoman of the Democratic Caucus and suffered two painfully close setbacks. In 1998, she lost 108-97 to Martin Frost of Texas; Minority Leader Richard Gephardt then named her an assistant leader in charge of the party's message. In 2002, she lost 104-103 to Robert Menendez of New Jersey after an intense year-long contest. In 2004, DeLauro led the drafting of the Democratic platform when John Kerry was nominated for president. She has remained an influential voice on platform fights and other policy conflicts among Democrats, with her skillful blend of policy and politics. Following the House upheaval in the 2018 election, she gained another opportunity to demonstrate her legislative skills.

CT-3: South Central Connecticut   **Cook Partisan Voting Index: D+9**

Population		Race and Ethnicity		Income	
Total	717,162	White	65.1%	Median Income	$66,465
Land area (sq. miles)	470	Black	13.1%	District Income Rank	123
Pop/ sq mi	1524.8	Latino	15.1%	Poverty Rate	11.3%
Born in State	62.1%	Asian	4.3%	With health insurance	94.3%
		Two or more races	2.1%	Cash public assistance	3.6%
Age Groups		Other	0.3%	Food stamp/SNAP	12.8%
Under 18	20%				
18-34	24.7%	**Education**		**Work**	
35-64	39.2%	H.S grad or less	39.5%	White Collar	16.1%
Over 64	16.1%	Some college	24.5%	Sales and Service	41.5%
		College Degree, 4 yr	19.2%	Blue Collar	16.6%
Military		Post grad	16.8%	Government	12.8%
Veteran/ Active Duty	6.1%				

2012 Pres. Vote	Obama	191,197	(63%)	Romney	110,867	(36%)		
2016 Pres. Vote	Clinton	179,832	(56%)	Trump	129,968	(40%)	Johnson	7,628 (2%)

New Haven: The New Haven Colony was founded in 1637 by a group of Puritan settlers who opted to bypass the Massachusetts Bay Colony after concluding the religious practices near Boston weren't strict enough. Their new colony was successful and grew rapidly. More than 150 years later, a young Yale graduate named Eli Whitney won an order from the young U.S. government to produce 10,000 muskets at $13.40 each. Whitney had invented the cotton gin six years earlier, which had embroiled him in a lengthy patent suit. He was determined to make a quick profit on the musket contract, so he set up a system of interchangeable parts and invented a milling machine and gauges: the birth of standardized American manufacturing. For the next 150 years or so, New Haven mass-produced rifles, clocks, locks, hardware and toys — anything its tinkerers and entrepreneurs could fashion. Today, few factories remain in New Haven. The factory that produced Winchester rifles and guns for 140 years closed in 2006. Southern Connecticut around New Haven discovered a new source of prosperity in scores of small technology and biomedical firms. Although the area's defense contracts are modest compared with those of the city's heyday, Stratford-based Sikorsky Aircraft envisioned 8,000 employees and a doubling of its spending by 2032, chiefly on the King Stallion heavy-lift cargo helicopter for the Marine Corps. In 2017, the company won a $3.8 billion contract to manufacture Black Hawk helicopters for Saudi Arabia.

With significant crime rates and many neighborhoods scarred by abandoned homes, New Haven has shrunk in population. In 2017, it had 131,000 people, down from 164,000 in 1950 but little-changed in the past 40 years. The city has roughly equal shares of blacks, whites and Hispanics. Yale University, with its Gothic spires and red-brick halls, has always been the visual focus of New Haven and is now its largest employer. From 2014 to 2017, Yale provided 60 percent of the city's economic development. With two new residential colleges opened in 2017, the university planned a 15 percent increase in undergraduate enrollment. A year later, Yale expanded the campus of its elite law school. Local revival was sparked by a state development program that turned old retail and office buildings into residences and by $1 billion in investments by biotech firms. Racial minorities and immigrants have had an influential voice in New Haven.

The 3rd Congressional District covers the New Haven metropolitan area and extends to the outskirts of the former industrial cities of Bridgeport, Waterbury and Meriden. The metro area has long since spread beyond the narrow city limits into what were once Yankee villages and countryside. The suburb of Hamden has made it onto the CNNMoney list of the 100 best places to live. Politically, the 3rd was once a marginal district, regularly changing partisan hands in the 1980s. It has become strongly Democratic, though with a recent twist. President Barack Obama got 63 percent of the vote in each of his campaigns. But Hillary Clinton got only 56 percent in 2016, while the Democratic presidential vote in the adjacent 4th District, which is more upscale, rose from 55 percent to 60 percent.

Jim Himes (D)

Elected 2008, 6th term, b. Jul 05, 1966; Lima, Peru; Harvard University, B.A., 1988; Oxford University (England), M.Phil, 1990; Presbyterian; Married (Mary Himes); 2 children.

Elected Office: Greenwich Board of Estimate & Taxation, 2006-2007.

Professional Career: Financial analyst & Vice President., Goldman Sachs, 1990-2002; Chairman, Greenwich Housing Authority, 2003-2006; Vice President., Enterprise Community Partners, 2004-2008.

DC Office: 1227 LHOB 20515, 202-225-5541, Fax: 202-225-9629, himes.house.gov

State Offices: Bridgeport, 866-453-0028; Stamford, 203-353-9400.

Committees: *Financial Services*: Investor Protection, Entrepreneurship & Capital Markets; Nat'l Security, International Development & Monetary Policy. *Permanent Select on Intelligence*: Defense Intelligence & Warfighter Support; Strategic Technologies & Advanced Research (Chmn).

Group Ratings

	ADA	ACLU	AFL-CIO	LCV	ITI	COC	HAFA	ACU	CFG	FRC
2018	-	79%	-	91%	-	67%	10%	20%	10%	0%
2017	90%	C	92%	100%	C	57%	C	4%	3%	0%

Almanac Ratings 2017-18

	Economy	Social	Foreign	Composite
Liberal	80%	94%	89%	87%
Conservative	20%	7%	11%	13%

Key Votes of the 115th Congress

1. Obama-care revision	N	5. Family planning regs	N	9. Guantanamo prisoners	Y
2. Tax Cuts	N	6. Body cameras/immigration	Y	10. Ground missiles, limit	Y
3. Omnibus appropriations	Y	7. Abortion ban	NV	11. Defense Dept. spending	Y
4. Dodd-Frank revision	Y	8. Concealed carry	N	12. FISA rules	Y

Election Results

Election	Name (Party)	Vote (%)		Cand. Spent	Ind. Exp. Support	Ind. Exp. Oppose
2018 General	Jim Himes (D)..	168,726	(61%)	$802,588		
	Harry Arora (R).....................................	106,921	(39%)	$707,741		

Prior winning percentages: 2016 (60%), 2014 (54%), 2012 (60%), 2010 (52%), 2008 (50%)

Jim Himes, a Democrat elected in 2008, is a former investment banker who puts his understanding of Wall Street to use at the Financial Services Committee and in conversations with colleagues. Given the growing hostility of many Democrats to deep-pocket financiers, — especially hedge funds, which are based predominantly in his district — his influence in the Democratic Caucus has faced some limitations. But he has found ways to asserted himself on other issues, such as guns and national security. And the 2018 election brought the arrival of numerous like-minded colleagues. as a business-friendly Democrat, a dwindling cohort that likely needs to expand for the party to regain House control.

Though he represents one of the wealthiest areas of the country, Himes grew up in different surroundings. Born in Lima, Peru, he spent his early years in Peru and Colombia, where his father worked for the Ford Foundation. Around the time of his 10th birthday, after his parents divorced, he came to the United States with his mother and two sisters and settled in Pennington, New Jersey. He speaks fluent Spanish and maintains a deep interest in Latin America. Himes earned his undergraduate degree from Harvard University and was a Rhodes Scholar at Oxford. When he returned to the United States, he worked Working for Goldman Sachs as a financial analyst. On Sept. 11, 2001, he was at his office in Lower Manhattan and did volunteer work with ambulance crews. After 12 years with, he left the investment house in 2002 as a vice president. The following year, he joined Enterprise

Community Partners, a Columbia, Maryland-based nonprofit dedicated to alleviating urban poverty. Beginning in 2004, he managed its offices in the Northeast.

Like many other Wall Street executives, Himes raised a family with his wife, Mary, living in the affluent suburb of Greenwich. Himes became active in chaired the town Democratic committee, and served as chairman from 2003 to 2007. He was a campaign volunteer in 2006 for Democrat Diane Farrell, who finished about 7,000 votes behind Rep. Christopher Shays, a moderate Republican who had withstood repeated Democratic campaign assaults. The following April, Himes announced his own challenge against Shays. Himes set a torrid fundraising pace, aided in large measure by his Wall Street connections. The Democratic Congressional Campaign Committee made him a top prospect. After easily dispatching a minor challenger in the primary, Himes focused on Shays and the George W. Bush administration and attempted to link the two over the Iraq war. Himes embraced the national Democratic establishment, frequently reminding voters that he was running with presidential nominee Barack Obama. In the past, Shays' moderate record and Capitol Hill seniority helped him weather political storms. But in 2008, the enthusiasm for Barack Obama provided a powerful final push that gave Himes a 51%-48% win. He comfortably took the district's urban centers and managed to stay competitive in the affluent suburbs that tend to break Republican.

Himes has taken a centrist approach in Congress, supporting Obama's major Democratic priorities but also asserting his independence on behalf of his district. He riled some Democratic leaders when he joined several other junior lawmakers in 2010 to form a working group to propose large spending cuts in defense, energy, housing and agriculture. In March 2012, he was one of 22 Democrats who supported a failed amendment to implement the recommendations of the Simpson-Bowles deficit reduction commission.

On the Financial Services Committee, he has engaged on district-related issues. When the committee took up what became the sweeping Dodd-Frank financial overhaul bill, he helped craft a provision regulating the complex financial instruments known as derivatives. Consumer advocates criticized Himes and other centrist Democrats, accusing them of watering down derivatives controls passed by the Senate in an effort to appease Wall Street. Himes argued that the bill took significant steps to crack down on abuses at investment firms. During the furor in 2009 over bonuses paid to executives at AIG International and other firms receiving federal rescue money, he cosponsored a measure requiring all future compensation to be performance-based; it passed the House but stalled in the Senate. He routinely speaks with colleagues about the industry. "He can explain things like derivatives and credit default swaps in plain English so [members] can have some degree of fluency in this, which is extremely helpful," fellow Connecticut Democrat Joe Courtney told the Connecticut Post.

Following the 2014 election, he failed in his bid to be Nancy Pelosi's choice to chair the Democratic Congressional Campaign Committee. She gave the post to Rep. Ben Ray Lujan of New Mexico, who was more junior and represented a much lower income district than Himes, who had been the DCCC's finance chairman. An anti-Wall Street activist praised Pelosi for "rejecting the Wall Street wing of the Democratic Party."

Himes has worked on national-security issues as a member of the Select Intelligence Committee, and filed a bill that states that only Congress has the power to declare and wage war. Under Republican control, he said that the panel had become "not functional," in its failure to adequately investigate Russian interference in the 2016 election. In January 2018, Himes was 1 of 65 Democrats who voted for House passage of a bill to allow the National Security Agency to intercept without warrants calls or emails from suspected foreign terrorists. When Democrats won House control, he voiced interest in chairing the Intelligence panel. But Rep. Adam Schiff of California had locked up that assignment. Instead, following a reorganization of the committee, Himes became chairman of the Strategic Technologies and Advanced Research Subcommittee, which oversaw new tools for intelligence collection.

After the 2016 election, he became chairman of the House's New Democrat Coalition, a self-described "fiscally responsible, moderate bloc of lawmakers." He said that he would defend and support Americans "who get left behind." He urged Democrats to remain mindful of the centrist voters whose support they would need to win House control. Liberal Democrats who have called for abolishing the Immigration and Customs Enforcement (ICE) agency, for example, have "made life harder for the 60 or 70 Democrats fighting in districts where we need to win," Himes told a conference of centrist Democrats in July 2018, Time magazine reported.

He has occasionally voiced his frustration with Congress, including its failure to deal with gun violence. In an October 2017 op-ed in The Washington Post following the mass shooting in Las Vegas, Himes wrote that Congress ought to "make incremental reform year by year in the areas that have vast public support." Instead, he wrote, "an impotent Congress will hold a moment of silence, and an uninterested president will order flags flown at half-mast and make a show of a somber visit to the scene of the latest crime."

Republicans hoped to unseat Himes has become entrenched in what had been a solidly Republican seat. In 2010, against state Sen. Dan Debicella, Himes portrayed him as an extremist and won 53%-47%. Debicella tried again in 2014, and the outcome was similar. Himes won 54%-46%. He got 71 percent in Bridgeport and Norwalk, which cast 21 percent of the total vote. Debicella won seven of the other nine communities and hill towns, but that upscale vote was not enough to overcome the urban support for Himes.

CT-4: Southwest Connecticut   Cook Partisan Voting Index: D+7

Population		Race and Ethnicity		Income	
Total	738,259	White	61.7%	Median Income	$92,799
Land area (sq. miles)	461	Black	11.6%	District Income Rank	24
Pop/ sq mi	1602.4	Latino	19.1%	Poverty Rate	9%
Born in State	42.4%	Asian	5.2%	With health insurance	90.2%
		Two or more races	1.9%	Cash public assistance	1.9%
Age Groups		Other	0.4%	Food stamp/SNAP	9.6%
Under 18	23.7%				
18-34	20.4%	**Education**		**Work**	
35-64	41.3%	H.S grad or less	31.1%	White Collar	14.6%
Over 64	14.6%	Some college	20.2%	Sales and Service	40.5%
		College Degree, 4 yr	26.7%	Blue Collar	13.6%
Military		Post grad	22%	Government	9.4%
Veteran/ Active Duty	4.4%				

2012 Pres. Vote	Obama	170,827	(55%)	Romney	136,527	(44%)		
2016 Pres. Vote	Clinton	195,494	(60%)	Trump	119,976	(37%)	Johnson	9,144	(3%)

Bridgeport, Stamford: No one in colonial America imagined that southern Connecticut would someday lodge one of the largest concentrations of wealth in the world. The soil was stony, the terrain unaccommodating and the harbors not as convenient as those in New York, Rhode Island and Massachusetts. For 200 years, this was the home of unnoticed Yankee farmers, sailors and tinkerers. After rich New Yorkers began taking the train north to country houses in Connecticut, in the 20th century Greenwich and other Yankee villages clustered around commuter railroad stations became the home of New York's elite.

Starting in the 1950s, New York City-based executives, eager to minimize their commutes and avoid New York's income taxes, moved their headquarters to Greenwich and farther into Fairfield County. Greenwich, sometimes referred to as "Wall Street by the Sea" for its proliferation of hedge fund offices and financial firms, is closest to New York and commands the highest commercial rents of all these places. But not all is well in the corporate suites: General Electric, which has been headquartered in Fairfield and has had its own problems, has begun its relocation to Boston — in part, to escape high taxes.

The 4th Congressional District is the wealthiest district in the nation's wealthiest state. The district covers most of the southwest corner of Connecticut along Long Island Sound, from industrial Bridgeport, now the state's largest city, to affluent Greenwich. The district's waterfront towns include bustling and pricey Stamford, woodsy Darien, modest Norwalk, artsy-craftsy Westport, and Fairfield. In low-income Bridgeport, some downtown revitalization accompanied the state-financed Harbor Yard sports complex. This social disparity within Fairfield County has ranked the 4th District among the highest in the nation in income inequality. In an attempt to adjust the balance, local developers have sought to encourage more millennials to move into the area. Local officials have had second thoughts about the cost increase—to $1 billion—and the inconvenience of a scheduled project in Norwalk to replace the swing Walk Bridge, which was built in the 19th century. The Norwalk bridge is one of four movable bridges on the main line to New Haven, all in need of major repair. In Stamford, a $500 million plan to upgrade and expand the train station was abandoned in 2016 after state officials said the real estate and construction team failed to meet requirements.

For many years, the heavily affluent suburbs outvoted Bridgeport and elected moderate-to-liberal Republicans such as Clare Boothe Luce, Lowell Weicker and Chris Shays to Congress. But the influence of Christian conservatives in the national GOP repelled local Episcopalians and other mainline Protestants, and they have been increasingly voting Democratic. At the same time, the district has been diversifying. It is now only 62 percent non-Hispanic white, the lowest percentage in the state, with the largest share of Latinos. Hillary Clinton in 2016 got 60 percent of the vote. For now, this socially liberal and economically flush district remains comfortably Democratic — and largely hostile to President Donald Trump.

Jahana Hayes (D)

Elected 2018, 1st term, b. Mar 08, 1973; Waterbury; Naugatuck Valley Community College (CT); Southern Connecticut State University, B.S., 2005; University of Saint Joseph (CT), M.A., 2012; Methodist; Married (Milford Hayes); 4 children.

Professional Career: High School History Teacher, 2004-2018.

DC Office: 1415 LHOB 20515, 202-225-4476

State Offices: Waterbury, 860-223-8412.

Committees: *Agriculture*: Livestock & Foreign Agriculture; Subcommittee Nutrition, Oversight & Department Operations. *Education & Labor*: Civil Rights & Human Services; Early Childhood, Elementary & Secondary Education.

Election Results

Election	Name (Party)	Vote (%)		Cand. Spent	Ind. Exp. Support	Ind. Exp. Oppose
2018 General	Jahana Hayes (D)............................	151,225	(56%)	$1,283,152	$88,901	
	Manny Santos (R)..........................	119,426	(44%)	$71,924		
2018 Primary	Jahana Hayes (D)............................	24,693	(62%)			
	Mary Glassman (D).............................	14,964	(38%)			

Democrat Jahana Hayes scored one of the big upsets of 2018 when she took this Democratic-leaning seat, chiefly by winning the primary against an opponent backed by the party establishment. Hayes, a first-time candidate, had been best-known for winning the national Teacher of the Year award in 2016. Embracing the policy goals of national progressive activists, she became the first African-American Democrat to win a congressional seat in Connecticut. Hayes replaced three-term Democratic Rep. Elizabeth Esty, who decided not to seek reelection following criticism of her handling of sexual-abuse charges against the top aide in her congressional office.

Hayes, a native of Waterbury, grew up in public housing. "Her family struggled with addiction, relied on public assistance and at one point lost their apartment," according to her campaign bio. For Hayes, the cycle of poverty intensified when she was pregnant at age 17 and became a single mother. With encouragement from friends, she enrolled in a local community college, got her bachelor's degree at Southern Connecticut State University, plus graduate degrees from the University of Saint Joseph and University of Bridgeport. She won plaudits as a social studies teacher at a high school in Waterbury. Meanwhile, she married a local police detective and became the mother of four children.

At the White House ceremony where she received her national award, Hayes was so enthusiastic that she continued clapping while President Barack Obama voiced his tribute to her. "You can't be great if you're not enthusiastic," Obama cheerfully ad libbed.

Esty decided in April 2018 not to seek another term, following news reports of the allegations against her chief of staff. Local Democratic leaders rallied around Mary Glassman, a former town official. When Hayes expressed interest in running, they told her she had no chance of winning. Glassman narrowly got the endorsement of the Democratic convention, which was controlled by those leaders.

"People told me I had no chance and I had no business trying to do this," Hayes later said. She pressed ahead to the primary, with backing from national progressive groups, including teachers unions and supporters of Sen. Bernie Sanders's 2016 presidential campaign. Sen. Chris Murphy, who earlier held the House seat, privately encouraged Hayes.

With campaign funds nearly equal to the amount raised by Glassman, Hayes ran ads in the relatively inexpensive market featuring Obama and her high school students. Her personal appeal clicked with the voters, as Hayes won the primary, 62%-38%. She ran strongly in the old urban areas of the district, with 80 percent of the vote in Waterbury, and at least 60 percent in each of the other cities: New Britain, Meriden and Danbury. Perhaps surprisingly, she also won many of the aristocratic country towns in Litchfield County. Glassman won her suburban home town of Simsbury.

In November, Hayes faced Manny Santos, who won the Republican primary with 52 percent of the vote against two opponents. A native of Portugal, Santos had a potentially appealing story as an immigrant, a Marine veteran and the former mayor of Meriden. But he had scant financing and received little attention from the national GOP in what has occasionally been a battleground district. Rep. Gary Franks, an African-American Republican and also a Waterbury native, served three terms from the area in the 1990s.

Hayes was one of three racial-minority women from the Northeast who in 2018 won House districts that had been held by white Democrats. The other two—Alexandria Ocasio-Cortez of New York and Ayanna Pressley of Massachusetts—defeated veteran incumbents in Democratic primaries. Running in more media-centered urban districts, they received far more publicity than did Hayes. The former school teacher initially was more of a team player for House Democrats.

CT-5: Western and Central Connecticut   Cook Partisan Voting Index: D+2

Population		Race and Ethnicity		Income	
Total	715,601	White	70%	Median Income	$71,132
Land area (sq. miles)	1,248	Black	6.1%	District Income Rank	87
Pop/ sq mi	573.3	Latino	17.8%	Poverty Rate	10.6%
Born in State	55.8%	Asian	3.8%	With health insurance	93.3%
		Two or more races	1.6%	Cash public assistance	3.8%
Age Groups		Other	0.7%	Food stamp/SNAP	14.1%
Under 18	21.5%				
18-34	20%	**Education**		**Work**	
35-64	42.1%	H.S grad or less	39.4%	White Collar	16.4%
Over 64	16.4%	Some college	24.7%	Sales and Service	40%
		College Degree, 4 yr	20.6%	Blue Collar	19.1%
Military		Post grad	15.2%	Government	12.7%
Veteran/Active Duty	6.3%				

2012 Pres. Vote	Obama	164,627	(54%)	Romney	139,324	(45%)		
2016 Pres. Vote	Clinton	161,142	(50%)	Trump	147,901	(46%)	Johnson	9,356 (3%)

Waterbury, Danbury, New Britain: Over the years, Connecticut's stony soil has become home to some of the most affluent people in the world. This is true in the hills of northwest Connecticut, distant from the interstates and from Connecticut's small urban capital of Hartford. In Litchfield County are exquisite Yankee towns like Washington and Kent, where Connecticut's ship owners once invested their accumulated capital in factories and mills. They now are considered the "anti-Hamptons," a weekend country-home mecca for ultra-rich New Yorkers seeking to avoid the glitz of Southampton and East Hampton. In towns that feature new money, Avon and Simsbury have become comfortable bedroom communities to Hartford.

Not far away are grittier parts, small industrial cities such as New Britain, America's ball-bearing capital for years and the hometown of Paul Manafort, the 2016 campaign manager for President Donald Trump; Meriden, which turned from making ivory combs, clocks and cutlery to producing electrical signaling equipment, biotech filters and nuclear instruments; and Waterbury, once the nation's largest producer of brass. Like many manufacturing centers, these towns have fallen on hard times, though there have been recovery efforts. Danbury, once the nation's leading producer of hats, has become a center for clean energy technology. Danbury-based FuelCell Energy — which manufactures and serves technology for clean power plants — announced plans to double its production.

East of Danbury is the small town of Newtown, where gunman Adam Lanza shocked the nation and ignited debates — but little action — over gun control, care for the mentally ill and the marketing of violence to the young when he killed 26 people, 20 of them children, at Sandy Hook Elementary School, in 2012. The old building was demolished out of respect for the victims, and a new school opened in 2016.

The 5th Congressional District of Connecticut covers much of the northwestern corner of the state, including the northern towns of Fairfield County. It has two arms that reach into the hills of central Connecticut — one to Democratic Meriden and the other to the affluent and Republican-leaning Farmington Valley suburbs of Hartford. It has been a Democratic-leaning district, but Republicans have become competitive here. Barack Obama won it by 14 points in 2008. Hillary Clinton's margin fell to 50%-46%. She won the four old industrial cities, but Donald Trump took most of the towns west of Avon and Farmington and from Litchfield to the east.

DELAWARE

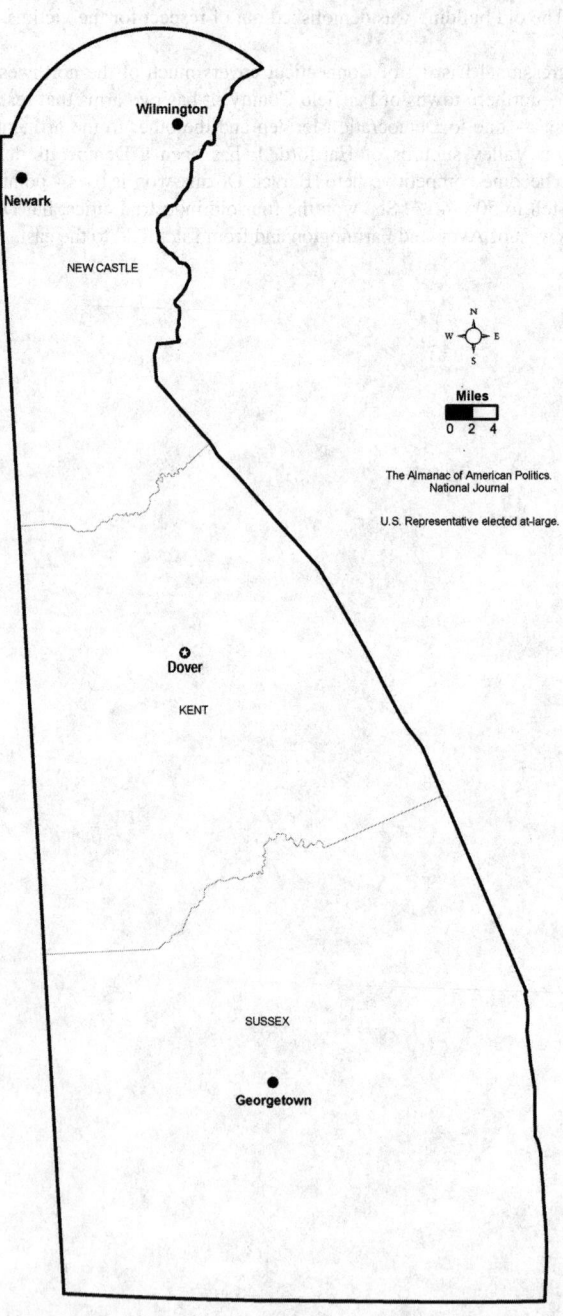

Wilmington

Newark

NEW CASTLE

N
W   E
S

Miles
0   2   4

The Almanac of American Politics.
National Journal

U.S. Representative elected at-large.

Dover

KENT

SUSSEX

Georgetown

There was a time not long ago when Delaware politics was competitive, pitting middle-of-the-road Democrats and Republicans against each other for control of state and federal offices. But as the national GOP has moved to the right and Democrats to the left, Democrats have become dominant in Delaware – a reality underlined in the 2018 midterm elections, when Democrats flipped the last GOP-held statewide offices and enabled Democrats to claim all nine of them -- the first time either party had managed that feat in Delaware in almost five decades.

On Dec. 7, 1787, 30 Delawareans met at the Golden Fleece Tavern in Dover and voted unanimously to ratify the Constitution. And thus, the second smallest state in area became, as it likes to boast, the First State. This small corner of America has a long history. The mouth of the Delaware River was explored by Henry Hudson, and the Dutch and Swedes built settlements on the west bank in the 1630s. But the three counties of Delaware owe their separate existence to the politics of the proprietors of William Penn's colony to the north and to Delawareans' determination -- even before July 4, 1776 -- to declare independence not only from Britain but also from Pennsylvania.

Throughout most of its history, Delaware has been unusually affluent. Its income levels during the early 20th century were the nation's highest, and they remain close to the top today – Democratic dominance in the state is another indication that the Democratic Party is becoming the party of affluent suburbanites. The many members of the du Pont family maintain beautiful cobblestone mansions in its chateau country, and the charming Brandywine Valley, which spills across the 12-mile semicircular border with Pennsylvania, includes a trove of refined tourist attractions. The Mason-Dixon Line forms Delaware's western border with Maryland, and the state has both Northern and Southern heritages. It was still a slave state when the Civil War broke out, but 92 percent of its blacks were free. Today, its population is 22 percent black, well above the national average; in 2016, Lisa Blunt Rochester became the first African American (and first woman) to represent Delaware in Congress. On his train ride to Washington in January 2009, newly elected President Barack Obama, joined by native son Joe Biden, paid tribute to Delaware's Underground Railroad and diplomatically did not mention that Abraham Lincoln, during his 1861 train ride to Washington, decided not to risk a stop in slaveholding Delaware.

The state's population grew by 18 percent in the 1990s, 15 percent from 2000 to 2010, and has risen by 7 percent so far this decade. One reason has been a flow of retirees from Pennsylvania, Maryland and New Jersey; Delaware's percentage of senior citizens is tied for sixth in the nation. The state today has immigrant communities in the Wilmington area, and it has Southern-accented farmers in Kent and Sussex counties, plus Latino migrants working in its chicken plants (chickens outnumber people by 300 to 1 and produce tons of processed chicken dung known as "broiler litter," suspected of polluting water downstate near Millsboro) as well as in its beach-tourism industry (residents of the Washington D.C. area flock to such Atlantic Ocean resorts as Rehoboth Beach and Bethany Beach during the summer). The state is 9 percent Hispanic, two points higher than neighboring Pennsylvania, and 4 percent Asian. Newark has grown from a country crossroads to a small city as the University of Delaware has expanded. Well-preserved 18th century buildings line the streets of New Castle, the capital from 1704 to 1777; it is the home of the First State National Historical Park, a collection of vintage buildings dedicated by Obama in 2013, making Delaware the final state to secure a National Park Service unit.

For much of the last two centuries, the central focus of Delaware's economy was the business started by Éleuthère Irénée du Pont, the practical-minded son of a dreamy, idealistic French immigrant. He built a gunpowder mill on the banks of Brandywine Creek in 1802 — the first enterprise of the du Pont family. Over time it became one of America's great munitions and chemical companies. It switched from gunpowder to dynamite in the 1880s, and the company grew especially rapidly during World War I, generating so much capital that it bought a large share of General Motors stock in 1914 and for 30 years controlled GM, which was for much of that time the nation's largest corporation. DuPont capital also financed what was arguably the world's finest research and development program. In the years on either side of World War II, DuPont prospered by bringing to the consumer and industrial markets new synthetics and plastics such as rayon, nylon, synthetic dyes, cellophane, Lucite, Teflon and Dacron: "Better Living Through Chemistry." After several rounds of belt-tightening in the state, the company completed a mega-merger with Dow Chemical from 2015 to 2017 and become DowDuPont, though it will eventually be split into three new companies.

Delaware has had an outsized impact on national policy. In the late 19th century, the state passed pioneering laws of incorporation, giving more flexibility and power to managers and owners. Most of the companies in the Fortune 500 and on the New York Stock Exchange and Nasdaq are incorporated in Delaware. Their legal births take place in a federal-style building near the capitol in Dover, which means that much of the nation's corporate law, especially on mergers and acquisitions, is made in Delaware's Chancery Court. And one of their primary residences is 1209 North Orange St. in Wilmington, a "non-descript, two-story office building" just north of the city's downtown, as The Guardian has described it. In that unassuming locale, the newspaper reported, 285,000 companies are domiciled – "more than any other known address in the world" – including Apple, American Airlines, Coca-Cola and Walmart, as well as companies started by both Hillary Clinton and Donald Trump. "We have 378 entities registered in the state of Delaware, meaning I pay you a lot of money, folks," Trump said at a campaign rally in Delaware. "I don't feel at all guilty, OK?"

Delaware also helped foster a new industry: credit cards. In 1981, Republican Gov. Pete du Pont pushed through a law abolishing Delaware's usury laws and lowering its bank franchise tax. Inflation was high, and banks were looking for a state with no limit on interest rates to locate their credit card operations. MBNA Corp. moved there from Maryland in 1982, invented the affinity card in 1983, and became the nation's largest credit card issuer. Bank of America acquired MBNA in 2005. Two years later, the financial crisis hit the credit card business hard, helping send Delaware into recession. Even after the economy recovered, consolidation and retrenchment produced job losses in the state's financial sector. While Wilmington's downtown and waterfront are experiencing something of a revival, affluence hasn't reached everywhere: Hispanic poverty levels in Delaware are more than twice the rate for whites, and in some census tracts in Wilmington the poverty rate for African Americans runs as high as 69 percent.

Delaware's state budget relies heavily on unconventional revenue streams that focus on out-of-state sources. Repossession of unclaimed property accounts for 15 percent of the state's revenue – a cash stream so alluring that 23 states went to court to claw it back. The state also gets 3 percent of its budget from turnpike tolls ($4 for just 11 miles on heavily trafficked I-95), 22 percent from corporate and franchise taxes and 7 percent from the lottery and slot machines. Exporting taxes has allowed Delaware to be one of the five states with no sales tax, and its property taxes are among the nation's lowest. A bipartisan mix of governors has lowered the income tax several times in recent years. The state leaped at a new opportunity in 2018, when the U.S. Supreme Court allowed states to legalize sports betting. Delaware became the first state to allow it, with Gov. John Carney placing the first bet -- $10 on the Philadelphia Phillies to beat the Chicago Cubs – although it was unclear how lucrative the market would remain once other states followed suit.

Delaware elections are not usually bitter. Thanks to the state's small size, politics remain intimate. Historically, "the Delaware Way" prevails -- a habit of party establishments exerting tight control and minimizing ideological and personal conflicts. There's even a unique custom, dating back to 1792, of "Return Day." On the Thursday after an election, winning and losing candidates go to the Sussex County seat of Georgetown and ride together in carriages to receive the bipartisan cheers of the voters and, literally, bury a hatchet in a box of Lewes Beach sand.

Since the 1990s, Delaware has trended Democratic; it hasn't elected a Republican governor since 1988. From 1972 to 2000, Delaware had a bipartisan presence in the Senate, with Republican William Roth, first elected in 1970, getting along well with Democrat Biden, first elected in 1972 at age 29 (he turned the constitutional age of 30 before the term started). But Roth, at 79, was defeated in 2000 by then Gov. Tom Carper. Carper won reelection twice easily, then, in 2018, he faced a primary challenge by Kerri Evelyn Harris, a biracial, lesbian Air Force veteran and auto mechanic who backed a strongly progressive agenda and charged that with Carper, "nice isn't getting the job done." But Democratic voters stuck with the more pragmatic Carper, 65%-35%.

After Biden won the vice presidency in 2008, his seat went to Democrat Chris Coons. The state House turned Democratic in 2008, joining the state Senate and the governorship for unified control. During this period, the state pursued generally liberal policies. Delaware's Supreme Court abolished the death penalty, the state approved same-sex marriage and transgender rights, and Gov. Jack Markell signed a marijuana decriminalization bill.

The 2016 election provided some notes of caution for Democrats. Hillary Clinton won the state, but her margin was 11 points, well short of Barack Obama's 19 in 2012. Donald Trump won two of the state's three counties, albeit the smallest and most rural -- Kent, which had backed Obama in 2012, and Sussex. But 2016 appears to have been a blip. The state GOP turned away from centrism and toward Trump – "We are going to, as a party, support the Trump movement and see what we can do to help it here in Delaware," said Michael Harrington, the state chairman elected in 2017. It appears to have been a miscalculation. In a closely watched state Senate special election, the nation's first after Trump was inaugurated, the Democrats easily won, 58%-41%. Then, in the 2018 midterm elections, Democrats strengthened their edge in both legislative chambers, including significant increases in non-white and female legislators, reversing previous declines. They also ousted Republican state treasurer Ken Simpler, who had been considered a rare GOP rising star, and won the open, GOP-held auditor seat that Democrats hadn't won in three decades. Until further notice, the "Delaware Way" seemed Democratic.

Cook Partisan Voting Index: D+6

Population		Race and Ethnicity		Income	
Total	943,732	White	63.0%	Median Income	$63,036
Land area (sq. miles)	1,949	Black	21.3%	State Income Rank	14
Pop/ sq mi	484.3	Latino	9.0%	Poverty Rate	12.1%
Born in state	45.1%	Asian	3.8%	With health insurance	93.3%
		Two or more races	2.3%	Cash public assistance	2.3%
Age Groups		Other	0.5%	Food stamp/SNAP	12.1%
Under 18	21.6%				
18-34	22.6%	**Education**		**Work**	
35-64	38.8%	H.S grad or less	41.9%	White Collar	39.8%
Over 64	17.0%	Some college	27.1%	Sales and Service	41.3%
		College Degree, 4 yr	18.0%	Blue Collar	18.9%
Military		Post grad	12.9%	Government	14.2%
Veteran/ Active Duty	9.5%				

Presidential Politics

2016 Primary (D)	Clinton (D)	55,954 (60%)	Sanders (D)	36,662 (39%)			
2016 Primary (R)	Trump (R)	42,472 (61%)	Kasich (R)	14,225 (20%)	Cruz (R)	11,110 (16%)	
2016 Pres. Vote	Clinton (D)	235,603 (53%)	Trump (R)	185,127 (42%)	Johnson (L)	14,757 (3%)	
2012 Pres. Vote	Obama (D)	242,584 (59%)	Romney (R)	165,484 (40%)			

Delaware used to be a presidential bellwether: It mimicked the popular vote winner of every presidential election from 1952 to 2000, the longest winning streak of any state. But starting with the disputed election of 2000, this relatively wealthy state began to vote significantly more Democratic than the national average. While Al Gore won the 2000 popular vote by about half a percentage point nationwide, he carried Delaware by 13 points. Lately, that Democratic margin has dropped from a high of 25 points in 2008 to roughly 11 in 2016 when Hillary Clinton defeated Donald Trump 53%-42%. In a sense, tiny Delaware is two states: New Castle County and its suburbs dominate the state and nearly three out of five presidential votes are cast there. Like affluent parts of other major metropolitan areas, New Castle, which includes the state's largest city, Wilmington, and its majority African-American population, began tilting toward Democrats in the mid-1990s. It voted 2-to-1 or more for Obama in 2008 and 2012. In 2016, New Castle voted for Clinton, 62%-33%. Lower Delaware, the other part of the state, is made up of more rural Kent and Sussex counties, the latter of which is also home to the state's popular beach towns. That area votes Republican and it backed Trump over Clinton, 55%-40%. Four years earlier it had sided with Mitt Romney 52%-47% over Barack Obama. Most Delaware voters still see plenty of ads, because in the past three elections, all candidates have targeted Pennsylvania, and New Castle and Kent are in the Philadelphia media market. (Sussex is in the Salisbury Maryland market.)

In 2016, Delaware held its primary on April 26 along with four other states and was overshadowed by the more pivotal contest in next-door Pennsylvania. Trump defeated Ohio Gov. John Kasich

61%-20%, winning New Castle 51%-27% and lower Delaware by a whopping 69%-14%. More than 65,000 votes were cast in the GOP primary, more than double the total in 2012. The Democratic contest was a bit more competitive: Clinton dispatched Vermont Sen. Bernie Sanders 60%-39%, winning each section of the state by roughly the same margin. Democratic turnout was more than 92,000 votes, only 4,000 less than the mark set in 2008 when Obama defeated Clinton 53%-42%.

Congressional Districts

116th Congress Lineup	1D	115th Congress Lineup	1D

John Carney (D)

Elected 2016, term expires 2021, 1st term; b. May. 20, 1956, Wilmington; Dartmouth College, BA 1978; Univ. Del. MPA 1987; Roman Catholic; Married (Tracey); 2 children.

Elected Office: DE Finance Secretary, 1997-2000; DE Lt. Governor, 2001-2009; US House, 2011-2017.

Office: 150 Martin Luther King Jr Blvd, Dover, 19901; 302-744-4101; Fax: 302-739-2775; Website: delaware.gov.

Lt. Gov.: Bethany Hall-Long (D) **Atty. Gen:** Kathy Jennings (D)

State Legislature: Senate: 12D, 9R **House:** 26D, 15R

Election Results

Election	Name (Party)	Vote (%)
2016 General	John Carney (D)..	248,404 (58%)
	Colin Bonini (R)...	166,852 (39%)
2016 Primary	John Carney (D)..	unopposed (100%)

Prior winning percentage: House: 2014 (64%), 2012 (59%), 2010 (57%)

John Carney, a former congressman elected to the governorship in 2016, is the second of nine children born to two teachers and has lived in Wilmington for most of his life. He has been careful to stress his humble upbringing and the fact that he, his wife and their two children lived in a modest row house before the governor's mansion. Carney has spent nearly his entire adult life in public office, except for brief stints as president and chief operating officer of Transformative Technologies, a Delaware technology firm, and as executive vice president of a wind farm start-up called DelaWind. After earning an English degree at Dartmouth College and a master's from the University of Delaware, Carney served as an aide to Joe Biden, the state's longtime Democratic senator. In the 1990s, he became a top aide to then-Gov. Thomas Carper, also a Delaware senator. Carney was the state secretary of finance under Carper from 1997 to 2000. That year, he won the first of two terms as lieutenant governor. Then in 2008, he lost a high-profile gubernatorial primary against Jack Markell, a former telecommunications executive and self-described "card-carrying capitalist."

Carney began the 2008 race as the favorite of party officials who, hoping to avoid a primary, urged Markell to run for lieutenant governor instead. But Markell was steadfast about wanting the top job. Deprived of his anticipated coronation, Carney lined up support from much of the party establishment, including outgoing Gov. Ruth Ann Minner, state legislators and unions. But Markell campaigned tirelessly across the state and raised more than $4 million, including $725,000 of his own money, a record fundraising haul in a Delaware governor's race. As Minner's popularity flagged after two terms in office, Carney subtly distanced himself from her by campaigning on a theme of change. Still, Markell's victory in the September primary was a stunner. He took 51 percent to Carney's 49 percent, a margin of about 1,700 votes.

Carney regrouped for 2010 and ran for the state's at-large House seat, which was vacated by moderate Republican Michael Castle, who was running (unsuccessfully as it turned out) for the Senate. Carney faced largely self-funding Republican Glen Urquhart, a Rehoboth Beach developer. Carney ran on his support for renewable energy technology and jobs as well as his opposition to oil drilling off the Delaware shoreline. Urquhart also called attention to Carney's attempt to lobby the state for assistance in 2009, when he worked for DelaWind. But liberal-leaning Delawareans were skittish about Urquhart's conservative positions, which included repeal of the Affordable Care Act and abolition of the departments of Energy and Education. Carney won, 57%-41%, a rare instance of a Democratic takeover of a seat in that GOP-friendly year.

In the House, Carney followed the example of his predecessor Castle, a nine-term centrist Republican. Not long after taking office, Carney was assigned to the Financial Services Committee and struck up a friendship with fellow freshman Jim Renacci, a Republican from Ohio, in whom he saw a common approach to problems. They started a breakfast group that eventually grew to 14 lawmakers. "If our group can sit down, hear each other out, and come up with solutions we all agree on, that says something," Carney said in September 2011. Carney became the first freshman Democrat to pass an amendment in the House when he added a provision to a bill making rail security a priority for U.S. intelligence agencies. Carney joined another Republican, Stephen Fincher of Tennessee, in drafting legislation to make it easier for small and medium-sized companies to undertake an initial public offering. Their measure passed the Financial Services Committee on a 54-1 vote in February 2012 and became law two months later after House Republicans included it in their job-creation agenda. Carney showed a more partisan edge when he joined a June 2016 sit-in on the House floor over expanding gun background checks.

Carney still harbored gubernatorial ambitions, and he would have set them aside, at least temporarily, had Biden's son Beau – a rising star and the odds-on favorite to win the governorship had he run in 2016 -- not died of brain cancer in 2015. After the younger Biden's death, all attention turned to Carney. His prominence in the state and Delaware's weak Republican bench combined to make the 2016 gubernatorial contest arguably the least competitive in the nation. After some uncertainty about who the GOP would field as a candidate, state Sen. Colin Bonini jumped in. But Carney's fundraising edge was on the order of 20 to 1 and Markell's two terms hadn't inspired the sort of fatigue that would have given the Republican an opening, especially in a presidential election year when Hillary Clinton was almost certain to win the state. Carney ended up losing Republican-leaning Sussex County by eight points and narrowly won Kent County, but he crushed Bonini in the most populous county by far, New Castle, by a roughly 2-to-1 margin.

Carney entered office with the prospect of a $385.6 million deficit, and he called for "shared sacrifice." It took five months of negotiations that stretched into overtime before the governor and legislators agreed on a budget in July 2017. A large part of the delay came from disagreements over changing the prevailing wage for state construction projects (a move sought by Republicans) and a hike in income taxes (which was sought by Democrats). Ultimately, the two sides agreed to set these issues aside and instead enacted a bill that raised $66 million in alcohol, tobacco and home sales taxes and increased funding for the Vaughn Correctional Center in Smyrna, the site of a siege in February 2017 in which a correctional officer was killed. In his January 2018 state of the state speech, Carney said that the budget deal reached in 2017 "closed a $400 million budget shortfall, but we did not go far enough, unfortunately, and as a result, our long-term budget problems continue to linger."

In 2018, after failing to win agreement in the legislature to double the state's budget stabilization account, Carney signed an executive order that took a partial step toward that goal. Carney signed a compromise bill to raise the minimum wage – eventually rising to $9.25, with some carveouts for younger and less-experienced workers, short of the $10.25 sought by many Democrats. Approval of the minimum wage bill enabled passage of an $816.3 million bond bill for transportation and school and university construction, an amount 40 percent higher than the previous year.

It was a busy legislative session on other issues. Delaware became the first state to ban all marriages for minors. It also banned gay-conversion therapy. Carney also signed a bill to guarantee state workers 12 weeks of paid family leave. On gun rights, Carney was unable to win passage of measures to ban certain classes of semi-automatic weapons and high-capacity magazines, but he was able to sign a ban on bump stocks, which are designed to speed up firing of semi-automatic weapons; a measure curbing gun rights for individuals with mental illness; and a crackdown on straw purchasers of guns. Meanwhile, a bill to legalize recreational marijuana – which Carney had opposed – fizzled. All told, Carney remained popular; on the eve of the 2018 midterms, a University of Delaware poll had Carney's approval rating north of 60 percent.

Tom Carper (D)

Elected 2000, term expires 2024, 4th term, b. Jan 23, 1947; Beckley, WV; Ohio State University, B.A., 1968; University of Delaware, Newark, M.B.A., 1975; Presbyterian; Married (Martha Ann Stacy Carper); 2 children.

Military Career: U.S. Navy 1968-1973; U.S. Naval Reserve 1973-1992 (Vietnam)

Elected Office: DE Treasurer, 1976-1983; U.S. House, 1983-1993; DE Governor, 1993-2001.

Professional Career: Industrial devel. specialist, DE Div. of Econ. Devel., 1975-1976; Chmn, National Governors Association, 1998-1999.

DC Office: 513 HSOB 20510, 202-224-2441, Fax: 202-228-2190, carper.senate.gov

State Offices: Dover, 302-674-3308; Georgetown, 302-856-7690; Wilmington, 302-573-6291.

Committees: *Environment & Public Works (RMM)*. *Finance*: Energy, Natural Resources & Infrastructure; Health Care; Taxation & IRS Oversight. *Homeland Security & Government Affairs*: Investigations (RMM); Regulatory Affairs & Federal Management.

Group Ratings

	ADA	ACLU	AFL-CIO	LCV	ITI	COC	HAFA	ACU	CFG	FRC
2018	-	62%	-	100%	-	60%	5%	9%	5%	0%
2017	80%	C	100%	95%	C	29%	C	4%	4%	0%

Almanac Ratings 2017-18

	Economy	Social	Foreign	Composite
Liberal	90%	90%	60%	80%
Conservative	10%	10%	40%	20%

Key Votes of the 115th Congress

1. Obama-care revision	N	5. Gun regulations	N
2. Tax Cuts	N	6. Family planning regs	N
3. Dodd-Frank revision	Y	7. Gorsuch confirmation	N
4. Omnibus appropriations	Y	8. Immigration restrictions	N

9. Kavanaugh confirmation	N
10. Saudi arms sales	Y
11. FISA rules	Y
12. Military aid in Yemen	Y

Election Results

Election	Name (Party)	Vote (%)		Cand. Spent	Ind. Exp. Support	Ind. Exp. Oppose
2018 General	Tom Carper (D)..................................	217,385	(60%)	$2,798,144	$765,450	$1,230,346
	Robert Arlett (R)............................	137,127	(38%)	$238,002		
2018 Primary	Tom Carper (D)..................................	53,635	(65%)			
	Kerri Evelyn Harris (D).......................	29,407	(35%)			

Prior winning percentages: 2012 (66%), 2006 (70%), 2000 (56%); Governor: 1996 (70%), 1992 (65%); House: 1990 (66%), 1988 (68%), 1986 (66%), 1984 (59%), 1982 (52%)

Democrat Tom Carper, Delaware's senior senator, is arguably the most successful politician in state history. He has won 14 statewide elections — most recently a 2018 contest for a fourth Senate term — and, when that term ends, will have held public office for 48 years without losing a race. Serving as state treasurer, at-large House member and governor before arriving in the Senate, Carper has earned a reputation as a centrist consensus-builder that has made him well-liked on both sides of the aisle on Capitol Hill. At home, he fits into what insiders refer to as the "Delaware Way." That's the low-key, pragmatic manner of shaping public policies long practiced in a pocket-sized state that has the feel of an extended town — in which most of the key players know each other well and voters are accustomed to a retail politics that make for first-name relationships with top elected officials. But, in 2018, the Delaware Way collided with the sharp-edged tactics of the Democratic Party's ascendant progressive wing. The 71-year-old Carper, hinting this was likely to be his last campaign, survived the first serious primary challenge of his long career, telling The New York Times, "What we have now are a lot of forces from outside the state who don't think there's room for a centrist anymore."

Nearly two years earlier, Carper received progressive blowback from inside the Beltway — when he leveraged his seniority to take over as ranking Democrat on the Environment and Public Works Committee, succeeding retiring California Sen. Barbara Boxer. The moderate Carper was a pronounced contrast to the liberal Boxer, and environmentalists were less than overjoyed — given Carper's status as one of only eight Senate Democrats to vote to override President Barack Obama's veto of the controversial Keystone XL pipeline project in 2015. Consistent with his consensus-oriented style, Carper had complained that the pipeline — which President Donald Trump later greenlighted — "impeded our ability to work together and make progress even on issues that we're in agreement on. We need to address this issue and we need to move on."

However, once the ranking member on Environment and Public Works, Carper moved to underscore his pro-environment credentials, joining widespread Democratic criticism of Scott Pruitt, Trump's first choice to head the Environmental Protection Agency. During Pruitt's 17-month tenure, Carper spearheaded Democratic criticism of the EPA administrator for rolling back Obama era regulations and his lavish spending of public funds for personal amenities — the issue that forced Pruitt's resignation. Carper's recent focus on environmental issues followed his longtime leading role on the Homeland Security and Governmental Affairs Committee, including his two years as chairman. His work there underscored his image as a results-oriented legislator focused on important issues outside of the political limelight — notably, his persistent efforts to put the Postal Service on a sound financial footing.

Carper grew up in Southside Virginia and attended Ohio State University on a Navy ROTC scholarship; he arrived in Delaware as a Navy ensign. After serving in Southeast Asia during the Vietnam War, in which he piloted submarine-hunting planes, Carper returned to earn his MBA at the University of Delaware. More than four decades later, Carper traveled to Vietnam with Obama to strengthen ties with that nation. In 1976, at 29, Carper was elected as Delaware's state treasurer. Six years later, leading state Democrats — including then-Sen. Joe Biden — prodded Carper to leave his politically secure post to challenge Republican incumbent Thomas Evans for the state's at-large House seat. The ensuing race marked a rare detour from the Delaware Way; the New York Post labeled it "the nation's dirtiest campaign" that year. Evans had been politically damaged by an "association" with a young female lobbyist named Paula Parkinson, and Carper's marriage was dragged into the campaign. Carper won with 52 percent of the vote. Carper, who divorced and remarried not long after the 1982 campaign, denied charges of spousal abuse at the time. But, in an interview a decade and a half later, he admitted to having "slapped" his first wife once; the issue would resurface years later in the 2018 Senate contest.

After a decade in the House accumulating a moderate voting record — his strong support of a constitutional amendment requiring a balanced budget set him apart from many fellow Democrats — Carper in 1992 was party to what is still referred to as "The Swap" by Delaware insiders. Carper and Republican Gov. Michael Castle were friends who, despite differing partisan affiliations, were considered ideological twins. Castle was term-limited and ran for the House, while Carper ran to succeed Castle as governor and won with nearly two-thirds of the vote. As governor, he pursued an agenda that was more conservative than liberal: He reduced income tax rates by about 10 percent and signed a bill authorizing charter schools.

Barred from seeking a third term in 2000, Carper faced a possible interruption in a nearly quarter century of unbroken electoral success. Some thought five-term GOP Sen. William Roth would retire and Castle would run to succeed him; Carper went so far as to say publicly that he would bow out of politics, at least temporarily, rather than run against his Republican friend. But Roth sought re-election and Castle shied away from a primary challenge to the incumbent. So Carper ran for Senate. Both Carper and Roth had high approval ratings and were familiar figures to voters. Roth had a legislative record that benefited many Delaware residents; as chairman of the Senate Finance Committee, he engineered the eponymous Roth IRA. His main problem was that he was 79 years old. Carper, then 53, was careful not to campaign negatively, but his slogan, "A Senator for Our Future," spotlighted the age gap. Roth stayed in Washington and made only a few appearances in the state. In October, he fainted twice on the campaign trail, once in full view of cameras. On Election Day, Carper won 56%-44%.

As he had in the House, Carper has amassed a middle-of-the-road voting record in the Senate; in 2017, Almanac ratings scored him as the eighth least liberal Democrat. During the Affordable Care Act debate early in the Obama administration, Carper bucked party liberals by opposing a government-run plan for those who could not afford private insurance. However, rather than attack the public option idea, he tried to broker a compromise he and other centrist Democrats could support. The public option was dropped from the final legislation, but Carper first sought to advance an alternative plan that would have allowed individual states to decide whether to offer a public option to compete with private insurers. More recently, his opposition to the Democratic progressive wing's "Medicare for all" proposal was an issue during his 2018 primary campaign. Besides seeking to shape health policy, Carper has utilized his seat on the influential Finance Committee to back free trade: In 2015, when many left-leaning Democrats were distancing themselves from Obama on a free trade pact with 12 nations with borders on the Pacific Ocean, Carper was joined by only a dozen fellow Democrats in the final vote that granted Obama special negotiating authority for the deal — from which Trump withdrew after taking office.

On the Homeland Security and Governmental Affairs Committee, Carper enacted legislation beefing up protections against government payments to ineligible claimants of retiree or disability benefits and requiring audits to identify billions lost through waste and fraudulent claims. He also shepherded bills beefing up the government's cybersecurity. He has been in the forefront of flagging potential conflicts of interest posed by Trump's business interests. When the director of the Office of Government Ethics came under fire for suggesting that Trump should divest himself of his holdings while responding to a letter from Carper in early 2017, Carper issued a strongly worded defense of the director, Walter Shaub. "We as members of Congress should be focused on how our president-elect has no plan to resolve his massive conflicts of interest before assuming the highest office in our country," Carper said. Once Trump took office, Carper requested the federal Office of Special Counsel investigate members of the administration for allegedly violating the Hatch Act, which restricts some political activities by federal employees.

But the issue within the committee's jurisdiction with which Carper has been most identified is the so-far unsuccessful effort to rescue the ailing Postal Service. He worked with a fellow centrist, Republican Susan Collins of Maine, in 2006 to pass the first major revision of Postal Service operations since 1970. Delaware is a major center of the credit card industry, which accounts for about one-quarter of mail sent through the Postal Service. As the service ran large deficits, Carper in 2012 — with the Senate in Democratic control — engineered bipartisan passage of legislation with buyout and early retirement incentives and the option of reducing delivery to five days to save costs. But the bill stalled in the Republican-controlled House, leaving Carper so frustrated that he created a Facebook page complaining about the lack of action. Carper has kept pushing biennially for reform: In 2018, he sought to attach his latest Postal Service modernization bill to annual spending legislation, but the move was blocked by Senate GOP leaders. He also blasted a Trump administration proposal to privatize the Postal Service.

As a former chairman of the Environment and Public Works' subcommittee on clean air, Carper has focused on legislation to reduce air pollution and halt climate change, while again reaching across the political aisle. With Republican Lamar Alexander of Tennessee, he co-authored legislation a decade ago that would have limited emissions of sulfur dioxide, nitrous oxide, mercury and carbon dioxide; the pair also pushed for a bill to slash emissions from power plants. Such efforts made little headway, and Carper later was supportive of Obama administration efforts to accomplish similar aims through EPA regulations. When Pruitt appeared before the Environment and Public Works panel in early 2018, Carper lit into him over his attacks on Obama era actions. "I don't say this lightly: You repeatedly misrepresent the truth about Mr. Obama's record," Carper told Pruitt. "Stop doing it."

At of the end of 2017, Carper ranked sixth from the bottom among Senate Democrats on the lifetime voting scorecard compiled by the League of Conservation Voters. But the group nevertheless endorsed him as he faced Kerri Evelyn Harris, a 38-year-old Air Force veteran and community organizer making her first run for public office, in the 2018 Democratic primary. Largely bereft of funds — Carper outspent her 20-1 — Harris was seen as little threat to the incumbent. But then, in late June, the party's progressive wing scored a stunning upset when now-Rep. Alexandria Ocasio-Cortez ousted Joe Crowley, the chairman of the House Democratic Caucus, in a New York district. Operatives from the Ocasio-Cortez campaign and successful progressive candidates elsewhere descended on Delaware to aid Harris, and the New York-based Working Families Party mounted an independent expenditure campaign on her behalf. Contending Carper's consensus-oriented politics were no longer relevant in the polarized Trump era, Harris told The New York Times: "A warm smile, a firm handshake and a witty comment isn't doing it. Nice isn't getting the job done." Notwithstanding the reliance of the Delaware economy on the financial services industry — which employs about 10 percent of the state's workforce — Harris went after Carper for a history of votes favored by the banking sector. Most recently, Carper and his Delaware colleague, Chris Coons, split from a majority of Senate Democrats in 2018 to vote for a rollback of portions of the 2010 Dodd-Frank financial reforms. Remembering recent political history — Castle's upset in the 2010 Republican Senate primary by a lightly regarded tea party challenger — Carper left little to chance. He advertised heavily, and to assuage the party's left, he emphasized support for a $15 per hour minimum wage and decriminalization of marijuana. And, after being one of just four Senate Democrats to support Brett Kavanaugh's confirmation to the federal appeals court in 2006, he came out against Kavanaugh's 2018 nomination to the Supreme Court, terming the nominee a "profound disappointment" in his years on the bench.

"My gut tells me that they believe that Kerri is the next Alexandria Ocasio-Cortez and they believe that I'm somehow the next Joe Crowley," Carper told CNN before the primary. "They think that Delaware is New York City. And I think they're mistaken on all three counts." His assessment was on target. While Crowley had been accused of increasing absenteeism from his district, Carper rode Amtrak home to Wilmington most evenings after congressional sessions. And while Crowley's district had become a magnet for millennials who supported his challenger, Delaware lacked a similar demographic. Harris, who is biracial, was running in a state only 23 percent African-American. While giving Carper his toughest race since his initial election to the Senate, she lost, 65%-35%.

Harris stuck to policy differences, but in late September, the president's son, Donald Trump Jr., via Twitter brought up the decades-old episode in which Carper had admitted to slapping his then-wife. The tweet was in apparent retaliation for a Carper tweet about the Office of Special Counsel citing first lady Melania Trump's spokeswoman for a Hatch Act violation. Carper's Republican opponent, Sussex County Councilman Rob Arlett — who had chaired the Trump Delaware campaign — then raised the matter in a debate. He accused Carper of having lied "for 19 years about that. There was a big cover-up. There was big collusion." Carper responded: "40 years ago, I made a mistake. I owned it. I didn't hide it. It was public knowledge." He told Arlett: "Every other year for 40 years, people like you, my friend, try to dredge this up, to make mischief, political mischief, for me. It doesn't work. ... And you know what? It's not going to work this time either." In November, Carper defeated Arlett 60%-38%.

Carper — who will be 77 when his term ends — hinted that the 2018 election would be his last, as he quoted lyrics from the 1965 Rolling Stones hit "The Last Time." If the bare-knuckled nature of this last campaign suggested that Delaware's longtime political modus operandi may be on its way out as well, the irony is that Carper's influence and effect within what has become a blue state have perhaps never been greater: At the outset of 2019, the First State's governor, at-large House member, chief justice and secretary of state were all onetime Carper aides.

Chris Coons (D)

Elected 2010, term expires 2020, 1st full term, b. Sep 09, 1963; Greenwich, CT; University of Nairobi (Kenya); Tower Hill School (DE); Amherst College (MA), B.A., 1985; Yale University Law School (CT), J.D., 1992; Yale University Divinity School (CT), Mast. Deg., 1992; Presbyterian; Married (Annie Lingenfelter); 3 children.

Elected Office: President, New Castle County Council, 2001-2005; New Castle County Executive, 2005-2010.

Professional Career: Practicing attorney, W.L. Gore & Associates, 1996-2004.

DC Office: 218 RSOB 20510, 202-224-5042, Fax: 202-228-3075, coons.senate.gov

State Offices: Dover, 302-736-5601; Wilmington, 302-573-6345.

Committees: *Appropriations*: Commerce, Justice, Science & Related Agencies; Energy & Water Development; Financial Services & General Government (RMM); State, Foreign Operations & Related Programs; Transportation, HUD & Related Agencies. *Ethics (RMM)*. *Foreign Relations*: Africa & Global Health Policy; East Asia, the Pacific & International Cybersecurity Policy; Europe

& Regional Security Cooperation. *Judiciary*: Border Security & Immigration; Constitution; Crime & Terrorism; Subcommittee on Intellectual Property (RMM). *Small Business & Entrepreneurship.*

Group Ratings

	ADA	ACLU	AFL-CIO	LCV	ITI	COC	HAFA	ACU	CFG	FRC
2018	-	77%	-	100%	-	60%	5%	9%	5%	0%
2017	90%	C	100%	89%	C	29%	C	4%	4%	0%

Almanac Ratings 2017-18

	Economy	Social	Foreign	Composite
Liberal	94%	94%	77%	88%
Conservative	6%	6%	23%	12%

Key Votes of the 115th Congress

1. Obama-care revision	N	5. Gun regulations	N	9. Kavanaugh confirmation	N
2. Tax Cuts	N	6. Family planning regs	N	10. Saudi arms sales	Y
3. Dodd-Frank revision	Y	7. Gorsuch confirmation	N	11. FISA rules	N
4. Omnibus appropriations	Y	8. Immigration restrictions	N	12. Military aid in Yemen	Y

Election Results

Election	Name (Party)	Vote (%)		Cand. Spent	Ind. Exp. Support	Ind. Exp. Oppose
2014 General	Chris Coons (D)............................	130,655	(56%)	$8,958,014	$57,744	
	Kevin Wade (R)............................	98,823	(42%)	$111,823	$72,702	
2014 Primary	Chris Coons (D)............................	Unopposed				

Prior winning percentages: 2010 special (57%)

In April 2018, as the Foreign Relations Committee was voting on whether to send the nomination of Mike Pompeo to be secretary of State to the Senate floor, Delaware's junior senator, Democrat Chris Coons, changed his vote from "no" to "present." Coons' action had no effect on the outcome but avoided the need for Coons' friend, Republican Johnny Isakson of Georgia, to rush back to Washington from a funeral in Atlanta. Such demonstrations of comity, once common in the Senate, have been rare in the current hyperpartisan environment — so much so that the now-retired chairman of the Foreign Relations panel, Tennessee Republican Bob Corker, became teary-eyed while talking to reporters about Coons' gesture. It also was illustrative of Coons' impetus to work across party lines since coming to the Senate nearly a decade ago — an effort which he has accelerated in recent years, even as tone of Donald Trump's presidency has pushed many of his Democratic colleagues in other directions.

Coons believes his stance has paid off in the Republican-controlled Senate, even if the dividends appear limited. The same month he voted "present" on the Foreign Relations Committee, he worked with two other Republicans, Lindsey Graham of South Carolina and Thom Tillis of North Carolina, to gain Judiciary Committee approval of a bill that would have protected special counsel Robert Mueller from being fired by Trump before completing an investigation of Russian interference in the 2016 elections. The measure was later stymied on the Senate floor by Majority Leader Mitch McConnell. In another high-profile bipartisan initiative within the Judiciary panel, Coons and then-Sen. Jeff Flake of Arizona delayed a vote on Supreme Court nominee Brett Kavanaugh in late 2018 while the FBI looked into sexual assault allegations against him. The most recent "bipartisan index" compiled by The Lugar Center deemed Coons the third-most bipartisan Senate Democrat. Coons acknowledges such outreach could generate a left-wing primary challenge when he runs for re-election in 2020, like his in-state colleague, Thomas Carper, faced in 2018. "It could happen to me," Coons told Politico. "I'm just not worried about it."

Coons' stoicism might reflect that few expected him to end up in the Senate in the first place. "Chris Coons may turn out to be the luckiest politician in America this year," CNN said in the fall of 2010. When Coons entered the Senate race months earlier, he was a distinct underdog for the seat held for nearly four decades by Vice President Joe Biden. But in mid-September of that year, after the biggest upset of the 2010 Republican primary season, Coons transformed into the overwhelming favorite to win the final four years of Biden's term.

Coons' family moved to Delaware during his childhood; bankruptcy wiped out much of his father's business success, and his parents divorced. His mother, Sally, a schoolteacher, remarried: Coons' stepfather, Robert Gore, played a key role in the founding of a highly successful family enterprise, Newark, Del.-based W.L. Gore and Associates. Holder of the patent for water-resistant Gore-Tex fabric, the firm is among the Top 200 privately held companies in the United States. As a student at Wilmington's elite Tower Hill School, Coons considered himself a Republican and volunteered for Ronald Reagan's 1980 presidential campaign. He converted to the Democratic Party as a student at Amherst College. Studying in Kenya for a semester, Coons said that observing his host family changed the way he thought about poverty and free markets. It led him to write a tongue-in-cheek column for the college newspaper titled, "Chris Coons: The Making of a Bearded Marxist," which would later surface as an issue in his initial Senate race.

After graduating from Amherst with a dual major in chemistry and political science, Coons did relief work with a church group in South Africa before attending Yale Law School. He also enrolled in Yale's Divinity School, graduating in 1992 with a law degree and a Master of Arts in religion. Coons co-chaired the 2019 National Prayer Breakfast with Republican Sen. James Lankford of Oklahoma, another frequent collaborator of Coons'. After Yale, Coons worked with low-income students in New York and then returned to Delaware in 1996 after marrying and worked as an attorney for W.L. Gore, of which his stepfather was then president. Coons' first foray into politics came in 2000, when he was elected president of the New Castle County Council. Four years later, he was elected county executive on an anti-corruption platform; his predecessor had been dogged by scandal.

When Biden was elected vice president in 2008 — winning re-election to the Senate at the same time — the assumption was that his son, Delaware Attorney General Beau Biden, would run in the special election to succeed him. But Beau Biden, who died in May 2015, decided against it — preoccupied with a major controversy affecting the attorney general's office, and perhaps influenced by the widespread appraisal that the general election would be an uphill battle against moderate-to-liberal Republican Rep. Michael Castle. Elected statewide 12 times, Castle, a former governor, was a heavy favorite despite Delaware's increasingly Democratic tilt. But, in a year in which the tea party emerged as a major force, Castle lost the primary in a stunning upset to Christine O'Donnell, a conservative consultant who had been defeated by Joe Biden two years earlier.

With Castle gone, Coons catapulted to a double-digit lead in the polls. O'Donnell was put on the defensive by decade-old TV footage — in which she claimed to have dabbled in witchcraft on Bill Maher's talk show "Politically Incorrect." Her attempt at damage control resulted in a widely ridiculed campaign ad in which she assured voters: "I am not a witch. I'm nothing you've heard. I am you." O'Donnell sought to shift the focus to Coons' record of raising taxes as county executive — but neither that nor attempts to target his "Bearded Marxist" essay gained much traction. "I am a clean-shaven capitalist," Coons wisecracked. He won in a 57%-40% landslide, with exit polls showing him taking many Republican votes. In style, the low-key Coons was a marked contrast to his voluble Senate predecessor. But, in terms of cross-party relationships, Coons emulated Biden — known during the Obama administration as the "McConnell whisperer" for his ability to negotiate with the often prickly Senate GOP leader. "Look, I'd be thrilled if at some point ... people saw me as having the same level of passion and commitment to my core principles, yet the ability to have and sustain meaningful friendships across the aisle," Coon said of Biden in an interview years later.

Early in his first term, Coons, as a member of the Energy and Natural Resources Committee, worked with Oklahoma Republican Jim Inhofe to scrutinize the renewable fuels standard, earlier mandated by Congress to increase production of biofuels. His lauded gesture during the Pompeo nomination vote had its roots in the period immediately following the 2010 elections: With the Senate in Democratic control, Coons was given the chairmanship of the Foreign Relations' Africa subcommittee in recognition of the time he spent on that continent. He struck up a friendship with Isakson, then the subcommittee's ranking Republican. In 2017, Coons was named the ranking Democrat on the Senate Ethics Committee — once again pairing him with Isakson, who had become the Ethics panel's chairman when the Republicans regained control of the Senate in 2015. In between, Coons and Isakson teamed up to start the Senate Chicken Caucus, in recognition of the importance of the poultry industry to their home states.

But perhaps Coons' most prominent bipartisan bromance involved Flake, a persistent Trump critic. "We have opposed each other on nearly every vote for as long as we've served in the Senate," Coons wrote in a New York Times op-ed piece in fall 2017 about Flake's retirement. "I may disagree with Mr. Flake on policy, but I consider him an honorable man, a loyal friend and a valued colleague. His retirement is deeply troubling to me because he represents a principled and patriotic Republican Party, one that has long championed strong American leadership around the world, and one I now fear is falling apart. That should scare all Americans. It sure scares me." The two senators, as Foreign Relations Committee colleagues, had forged a friendship during travel abroad. And, serving together on the Judiciary Committee, Flake and Coons were allies to force a vote on the committee-passed legislation protecting Mueller. But it was a Judiciary Committee session in late September 2018, as the panel was preparing to vote on the Kavanaugh nomination, that produced high drama: While the committee marked time, attention was focused on private negotiations between Coons and Flake in an adjacent anteroom.

Flake earlier in the day had said he would vote for Kavanaugh but wavered after being confronted in an elevator by survivors of sexual abuse. The Coons-Flake private discussion began after Coons, in an impassioned public plea, said, "I, for one, will not countenance the refrain said by too many in response to these allegations that it happened too long ago and that in our nation, boys will be boys." What emerged from the talk was a gentleman's agreement under which Flake would vote to approve the nomination in committee, but not on the Senate floor without a delay for an FBI investigation into the allegations against Kavanaugh. Republican leaders, still struggling to round up the votes needed to confirm Kavanaugh, had no choice but to accede a weeklong delay. Coons' effort delayed the nomination but did not derail it: Kavanaugh was narrowly confirmed with Flake voting yes and Coons joining all but one of his Democratic colleagues in voting no. Coons criticized the FBI's handling of the investigation he had triggered, telling ABC News the day of the vote: "I was disappointed in the scope of the interviews and I was disappointed in the scope of the materials. ...You can't find what you don't look for."

Coons has also worked on drier subjects within the Judiciary Committee's jurisdiction — notably, the perennial issue of curbing patent abuses. A patent overhaul bill Coons introduced early in 2015 was praised by the biotechnology and pharmaceutical industries. However, it was criticized by the consumer electronics sector as doing little to restrain "patent trolls" — firms that purchase patents largely to seek financial settlements for infringement from other firms. In 2017, Coons tried again, introducing legislation his office characterized as an improvement on the previous bill designed to "make it easier and less costly for patent holders to enforce their patents." Co-sponsors included Democrat Dick Durbin of Illinois and Republican Tom Cotton of Arkansas. The measure won praise from conservative groups and a coalition of technology firms but failed to advance.

Coons had no trouble winning a full term in 2014, defeating his Republican opponent, Kevin Wade — who unsuccessfully ran against Carper two years earlier — by 13 points in a difficult year for Democrats. He emerged with what he described as a rekindled appetite for campaigning, along with an interest in one of the Senate's most partisan posts — chairman of the Democratic Senatorial Campaign Committee — as the party began its quest to regain the Senate majority lost in the 2014 elections. But Coons withdrew from consideration, citing three teenagers at home and the travel demanded of the DSCC chairperson. Like Carper and, earlier, Biden, had Coons commuted from Wilmington to Washington when Congress was in session. "He's also inherently a pretty bipartisan guy and was concerned it would be harder to make real progress on some of his legislative priorities while running the DSCC," a Coons spokesman said. Senate Democratic leaders again eyed Coons for the post after the 2016 elections, when there was a paucity of takers in an election cycle in which the Democrats would be defending more than three times as many seats as the GOP. Again, Coons pleaded family considerations in taking a pass.

The 2016 campaign took a toll on Coons' bipartisan mien: In the fall of 2015, he lambasted Trump as "a thin-skinned reality-TV star" and "a Cheeto-faced short-fingered vulgarian" during a Democratic rally in Delaware. A year later, it fell to the Yale Divinity School graduate to journey to New York and invite Trump to the January 2017 National Prayer Breakfast, of which he was co-chair. Coons avoided partisan issues during his 20-minute meeting at Trump Tower with the president-elect and focused on his own experiences attending weekly prayer breakfasts with other senators; his campaign remarks did not come up, Coons said. He also expressed remorse to the Wilmington News Journal about the insults hurled at Trump a year earlier, saying he regretted "that one incident of my not keeping a measured tone in the campaign." If Coons has since refrained from insults at Trump's appearance, he has shown little quarter regarding the president's claims. When former Trump attorney Michael Cohen, in a November 2018 guilty plea in conjunction with Mueller's investigation, said that talks about construction of a Trump Tower in Moscow had continued well into the 2016 campaign, Coons told CNN, "That makes it clear that now-President Trump was flat-out lying as candidate Trump when he said, and tweeted repeatedly, 'I have no business interests in Russia.'"

At the same time, Coons has not hesitated to direct tough comments at his own party's left wing. "Yes, he has taken progressive votes, but he has also taken some bad votes and led the charge on some compromises that have not fit the moment," Angel Padilla, policy director at the liberal activist group Indivisible, told Politico. As they did with Carper in 2018, progressives have taken Coons to task for what they believe to be his coziness with the financial services industry, which has a large presence in Delaware. Coons joined Carper — and 14 other Democrats — in voting for a Trump-supported bill rolling back some provisions of the 2010 Dodd-Frank financial reforms.

For his part, Coons has criticized the party's progressive wing for "engaging in a relentless race to the left, with more and more outrageous proposals." He has suggested positions taken by progressives, from abolishing the Immigration and Customs Enforcement agency to attacking energy companies, hampered opportunities for the Democrats to win back voters who sent to Trump to the White House. "Forty percent of voters self-identify as pragmatic or moderate. We cannot abandon them," he said. Alluding to the MSNBC liberal talk show host, Coons added, "Instead of having something that makes a Twitter hashtag and gets you on Rachel Maddow and fires people up, we need to have something that fires people up and is a policy position we can actually defend."

Lisa Blunt Rochester (D)

Elected 2016, 2nd term, b. Feb 10, 1962; Philadelphia, PA; Padua Academy (DE), 1980; Fairleigh Dickinson University, Bach. Deg., 1985; University of Delaware, M.A., 2003; Christian Church; Widow; 2 children.

Elected Office: Delaware Secretary of Labor, 1998-2001.

Professional Career: Deputy Secretary, Delaware Department of Health and Social Services; Personnel Director, Delaware Office of Management and Budget, 2001-2004; Chief Executive, Metropolitan Wilmington Urban League, 2004-2007.

DC Office: 1519 LHOB 20515, 202-225-4165, bluntrochester.house.gov

State Offices: Georgetown, 302-858-4773; Wilmington, 302-830-2330.

Committees: *Energy & Commerce*: Consumer Protection & Commerce; Energy; Environment & Climate Change; Health.

Group Ratings

	ADA	ACLU	AFL-CIO	LCV	ITI	COC	HAFA	ACU	CFG	FRC
2018	-	79%	-	94%	-	64%	8%	8%	8%	0%
2017	90%	C	97%	97%	C	57%	C	4%	5%	11%

Almanac Ratings 2017-18

	Economy	Social	Foreign	Composite
Liberal	89%	98%	89%	92%
Conservative	12%	2%	11%	8%

Key Votes of the 115th Congress

1. Obama-care revision	N	5. Family planning regs	N	9. Guantanamo prisoners	Y
2. Tax Cuts	N	6. Body cameras/immigration	Y	10. Ground missiles, limit	Y
3. Omnibus appropriations	Y	7. Abortion ban	N	11. Defense Dept. spending	Y
4. Dodd-Frank revision	Y	8. Concealed carry	N	12. FISA rules	Y

Election Results

Election	Name (Party)	Vote (%)		Cand. Spent	Ind. Exp. Support	Ind. Exp. Oppose
2018 General	Lisa Rochester (D)	227,353	(65%)	$977,079		
	Scott Walker (R)	125,384	(35%)			
2018 Primary	Lisa Rochester (D)		(100%)			

Prior winning percentages: 2016 (56%)

Lisa Blunt Rochester, elected in 2016, is a Democrat who had a relatively quiet first two years in elected office. She spent more time than did most freshmen working to foster bipartisanship, which is valued in her home state. The first woman and person of color to represent Delaware in Congress, she seemed to limit her activities as a member of the Congressional Black Caucus. Her actions encouraged speculation that her political ambitions extend beyond the House.

Blunt Rochester was born in Philadelphia and moved with her family to Wilmington when she was a child. She has a political pedigree as a Democrat. Her father was president of the Wilmington City Council. Her sister was an aide to Joe Biden in his Senate office, and state director for the Obama-Biden campaign. Blunt Rochester got her bachelor's in international relations from Fairleigh Dickinson University, and received a master's degree in urban affairs and public policy from the University of Delaware. In 1987, she began her political career as an intern for then-Rep. Tom Carper, and recalls her experience as a case-worker dealing with constituent issues. She continued with Carper when he was elected governor in 1992. She initially was a policy adviser and eventually served three years as secretary of labor in the governor's cabinet, where she focused on connecting employers to resources and jobseekers.

When Carper was elected to the Senate in 2000, Blunt Rochester joined the cabinet of new Democratic Gov. Ruth Ann Minner as personnel director. In that job her responsibilities included an investigation of the Delaware State Police for racial and sexual discrimination. She moved to the private sector as chief executive officer of the Metropolitan Wilmington Urban League, a public policy think tank. There, she met her future husband, Charles Rochester, an engineer working in China. She moved to Shanghai after they married in 2006, writing a book, Thrive, that profiled women who reinvented themselves while living in a foreign country. She decided to write the book after nothing fell into place during her job search in China until she attended a 10-day meditation retreat in Hong Kong that helped her to clarify what she wanted from life. She wrote the book with two co-authors — women from Mexico and Kenya who also had accompanied their husbands to Shanghai. Blunt Rochester moved back to the United States when her husband was transferred to Boston. He died suddenly in 2014 after rupturing his Achilles tendon, and she returned to Delaware.

When John Carney ran for governor, Blunt Rochester was an early frontrunner to take the House seat. In the competitive six-candidate Democratic primary, she won with 44 percent of the vote. The runners-up were state Sen. Bryan Townsend and Iraq War veteran Sean Barney, who got 25 and 20 percent respectively. Blunt Rochester loaned her campaign an additional $400,000 for the primary. Her net worth exceeded $5 million. In the general election against Republican Hans Reigle, Blunt Rochester criticized Donald Trump for supporting "hateful, racist and discriminatory" policies. Reigle, who had been mayor of the small town of Wyoming, called for more steps to prevent illegal immigration. Blunt Rochester won 56%-41%. She took 64 percent in New Castle County. Reigle won the two smaller counties.

With seats on the Agriculture and Education and the Workforce committees, Blunt Rochester worked with Republicans and sometimes voted for their bills. With Rep. Glenn Thompson of Pennsylvania, she wrote an op-ed calling for extension of the Family Violence Prevention and Services Act. She was one of eight House Democrats who voted to re-open the government in February 2018 following a brief shutdown and was the only Democratic cosponsor of a House-passed bill to extend disaster aid to homeowners in coastal areas.

Blunt Rochester was less favorably disposed to President Donald Trump. After visiting a detention facility for immigrant children in New York City, she described the experience as "painful and traumatic." She criticized as "deeply troubling" and "dangerous" reports in May 2017 that Trump had shared with the Russian government highly classified information about terrorist threats.

Blunt Rochester was reelected, 60%-38%, against Scott Walker, who spent little money and discussed his addiction to alcohol. She seemed politically secure in incumbent-friendly Delaware.

DISTRICT OF COLUMBIA

The capital of the most powerful and affluent nation in history, Washington is a physically beautiful city of great achievements and astonishing contrasts that go back more than 200 years. In 1787, the Constitution's framers, familiar with contemporary London and Paris mobs and remembering how unruly crowds had threatened the Continental Congress in Philadelphia, gave the new federal government control over the 10-mile-square that came to be called the District of Columbia. The Residence Act of 1790 located the District on the Potomac River along the borders of Maryland and Virginia, though in 1848 the portion west of the Potomac was retroceded to Virginia on the grounds that the federal government would never need it. Over the years, Congress kept control of the District for its own advantage and, at times, out of distrust of the city's large African-American population. In the late 18th century, African Americans made up one-quarter of Washington's residents. The city was a refuge for free blacks before the Civil War and right after emancipation. Radical Republicans gave the District self-government in 1871, but the experiment ended three years later after Gov. Alexander Shepherd spent the city into bankruptcy. In the 20th century, Washington's growth spurts, starting with the New Deal and World War II, resulted in the development of large, mostly white suburbs in Virginia and Maryland. It was at this time that African Americans became a larger percentage of the city's population, reaching a majority in the 1960 census.

With the civil rights movement, the way that many District residents viewed their lack of voting rights began to change. In 1961, Congress amended the Constitution to give District residents the right to vote for president; in 1968, residents began voting for the school board; in 1971, they received a non-voting delegate in Congress; and in 1973, the District of Columbia Home Rule Act allowed the city to elect a mayor and a city council, though Congress retained control over the District's budget and the ability to review its legislation. For some time, self-government worked no better than it did in the 1870s. The Alexander Shepherd of modern times was the late Marion Barry, who held office for 16 of 20 years between 1978 and 1998. Under Barry, the District struggled. Neighborhoods fell into disarray and violent crime rates increased. Meanwhile, the size of local government soared to 51,000 employees. Barry nonetheless regularly won re-election. In January 1990, District police arrested him at a D.C. hotel for cocaine possession. After a six-month stint in prison, he returned to city government. Barry was elected to the city council in 1992 and won a fourth term as mayor in 1994.

At that time, the District was experiencing a dire fiscal crisis, and Congress stepped in. Republican House Speaker Newt Gingrich tasked Rep. Tom Davis, a Republican from Northern Virginia, with the job of stabilizing the District's finances. Working closely with the District's elected delegate, Democrat Eleanor Holmes Norton, Davis set up a financial control board whose head, Anthony Williams, hacked away at the payroll and reformed management practices. In 1998, Barry chose not to run for a fifth term. Williams won the Democratic primary and general election. The financial control board immediately relinquished power to the new mayor, and in 2000, a court returned control of most District departments to the city.

Beginning with William's tenure, the District's population started rising, from 572,000 in 2000 to 694,000 in 2017, with a substantial portion of this increase coming from well-educated, unmarried young people: almost 57 percent of the D.C. adult population has at least a bachelor's degree—one of the highest percentages in the country—while it is estimated that 71 percent are unmarried (a decline from 76 percent in 2011). Approximately 35 percent can be categorized as millennials, and the median age is 34.

With youth and population growth have come gentrification and an exceptionally high cost of living. A March 2016 study found the D.C. rental market was the sixth most expensive in the country, with median rent for a one-bedroom apartment at $2,200. The rental market has sprouted new bars and restaurants, rental bikes and bike lanes, food trucks and cupcake stores, dog parks and streetcar tracks. In southeast D.C., Nationals Park and other new developments are transforming neighborhoods along the Anacostia River, sometimes at the expense of longtime community members. Incomes and property values in the area doubled in the last decade, but the number of black residents, many who were born in the District, fell 25 percent from 2000 to 2016. The announcement that Amazon would locate its second headquarters, and 25,000 high-paying jobs, in Crystal City, Virginia, stoked fears of further displacement and inequality in the D.C. area.

The city's black population has dropped since its peak of 71 percent in 1970, as low-income black neighborhoods emptied out and middle-income blacks moved to majority-black suburbs. 2011 marked the first year in almost a half century that African Americans were not the majority in the District. As of July 2017, 47.7 percent of the city was African American. The city's white population grew from 30 percent in 2000 to 41 percent in 2017. The west side of the District and the neighborhoods surrounding Capitol Hill are mostly white. African Americans are the majority in eastern D.C. neighborhoods like Anacostia.

Adrian Fenty succeeded Anthony Williams as mayor in 2007. Fenty's biggest initiative was improving the floundering public schools. At Fenty's behest, the city council transferred control of the schools from an independent board of education to the mayor's office. Fenty's superintendent, Michelle Rhee, closed non-performing and underused schools and negotiated a contract with the union that gave teachers the option of earning merit pay and Rhee the power to dismiss low-performing teachers. Rhee also encouraged the charter school movement. Charter school enrollments in the District rose from 25 percent in 2006 to 47 percent in 2018, among the highest in the country.

In 2010, Council President Vincent Gray harnessed African-American discontent with gentrification to defeat Fenty for the Democratic nomination. Gray soon found his administration derailed by a series of scandals and a federal investigation, which set the stage for a grueling primary in 2014. Gray lost, 44%-32%, to Muriel Bowser, a councilwoman with close ties to Fenty. Bowser defeated David Catania, a Republican-turned-Independent councilman, in a contentious general election, 54%-34%. Bowser did not face serious opposition in 2018 and won re-election with 76 percent of the vote.

Bowser has taken some risks as mayor, especially when it comes to the matter of District autonomy. In 2015, she defied the Republican-controlled Congress by allowing a voter-approved ballot measure that effectively legalized marijuana to take effect. In 2018, Bowser said she supported legalizing marijuana sales in the District, although the decision is ultimately up to Congress. Bowser also supported the Budget Autonomy Act, which passed by a citywide referendum in 2013. After a 2016 legal ruling in favor of the act, some conservative House Republicans vowed to assert their oversight powers and repeal it. In October 2018, Bowser angered liberals by signing legislation to repeal a June voter initiative that replaced the tipped minimum wage for restaurant workers with a universal wage.

Bowser is a vocal proponent of D.C. statehood. She has said that the success of the statehood movement (which enjoys widespread support in the District) depends on Democratic victories at the federal level. After Democrats took back the House in 2018, Speaker Nancy Pelosi and other Democratic leaders endorsed statehood. However, the Republican-controlled Senate will likely stymie any legislation granting statehood in the near future.

The federal government is the city's chief employer, and roughly 15 percent of the federal workforce is based in the metro area. President Donald Trump campaigned on the motto "drain the swamp" and has advocated for a smaller federal workforce. The District's hospitality and tourism industries have prospered in recent years. A record-setting 20.8 million Americans visited the capital in 2017, spending $7.5 billion on local transportation, hotels and restaurants.

Politically, the District is liberal and has shown a distaste for Trump. In the 2016 election, he received only 4% of the vote. Trump's presence in the city is accentuated by the luxury hotel he owns on Pennsylvania Avenue. The hotel, which opened in September 2016, has become a meeting center for prominent GOP officials, conservative groups and donors, and, occasionally, foreign dignitaries. The hotel is at the center of a lawsuit filed by the Maryland and D.C. attorneys general alleging Trump has violated the Constitution's emoluments clause by accepting gifts from foreign officials and benefits from state governments. After Trump became involved in a decision to keep the FBI headquarters in downtown D.C. instead of moving it to the suburbs, there was speculation that he was attempting to limit potential competitors from moving into the area and threatening his nearby hotel's business.

Population		Race and Ethnicity		Income	
Total	672,391	White	36.0%	Median Income	$77,649
Land area (sq. miles)	61	Black	46.9%	Poverty Rate	17.4%
Pop/ sq mi	11,013.8	Latino	10.7%	With health insurance	95.3%
Born in state	36.8%	Asian	3.7%	Cash public assistance	3.7%
		Two or more races	2.2%	Food stamp/SNAP	14.4%
Age Groups		Other	0.5%		
Under 18	17.6%			**Work**	
18-34	34.6%	**Education**		White Collar	61.7%
35-64	35.9%	H.S grad or less	27.4%	Sales and Service	32.0%
Over 64	11.9%	Some college	16.1%	Blue Collar	6.3%
		College Degree, 4 yr	23.8%	Government	24.6%
Military		Post grad	32.8%		
Veteran/ Active Duty	5.6%				

Presidential Politics

2016 Conv. (R)	Rubio (R)	1,059 (37%)	Kasich (R)	1,009 (36%)	Trump (R)	391 (14%)	
	Cruz (R)	351 (12%)					
2016 Primary (D)	Clinton (D)	76,704 (78%)	Sanders (D)	20,361 (21%)			
2016 Pres. Vote	Clinton (D)	282,830 (91%)	Trump (R)	12,723 (4%)			
2012 Pres. Vote	Obama (D)	267,070 (91%)	Romney (R)	21,381 (7%)			

Eleanor Holmes Norton (D)

Elected 1990, 15th term, b. Jun 13, 1937; Washington; Antioch College (OH), B.A., 1960; Yale University (CT), M.A., 1963; Yale University Law School (CT), J.D., 1964; Episcopalian; Divorced; 2 children.

Professional Career: Clerk, Judge A. Leon Higginbotham, 1964-1965; Assistant legal Director, ACLU, 1965-1970; Adjunct Assistant Professional, NY University Law School, 1970-1971; Staff, NY mayor, 1971-1974; Chair, NYC Human Rights Comm., 1970-1977; Chair, US Equal Empl. Oppor. Comm., 1977-1981; Sr. fellow, Urban Inst., 1981-1982; Professor, Georgetown University Law Center, 1982-1990.

DC Office: 2136 RHOB 20515, 202-225-8050, Fax: 202-225-3002, norton.house.gov

State Offices: Washington, 202-408-9041; Washington, 202-678-8900.

Committees: *Oversight & Reform*: Government Operations; Subcommittee on Civil Rights & Civil Liberties. *Transportation & Infrastructure*: Aviation; Economic Dev't, Public Buildings & Emergency Management; Highways & Transit (Chmn); Railroads, Pipelines & Hazardous Materials.

Election Results

Election	Name (Party)	Vote (%)		Cand. Spent	Ind. Exp. Support	Ind. Exp. Oppose
2018 General	Eleanor Holmes Norton (D)	199,124	(87%)			
	Nelson Rimensnyder (R)	9,700	(4%)			
	Natale Stracuzzi (G)	8,636	(4%)			
2018 Primary	Eleanor Holmes Norton (D)	60,842	(77%)			
	Kim Ford (D)	18,713	(23%)			

Prior winning percentages: 2016 (89%), 2014 (97%), 2012 (89%), 2010 (89%), 2008 (92%), 2006 (100%), 2004 (91%), 2002 (93%), 2000 (90%), 1998 (90%), 1996 (90%), 1994 (89%), 1992 (85%), 1990 (62%)

Eleanor Holmes Norton is a Democrat who was elected delegate from the District of Columbia in 1990. The daughter of a District government employee and a school teacher, Norton graduated from Antioch College and got a law degree at Yale. She volunteered for the Student Nonviolent Coordinating Committee and traveled to Mississippi in 1963 to help register African-American voters. On June 11, she met with civil-rights activist Medgar Evers, who tried to convince her to moveto Jackson and work as a civil rights lawyer. Just hours after Evers dropped her off at a bus station, a white supremacist shot and killed him in his driveway. Norton worked for the American Civil Liberties Union and the New York City Commission on Human Rights, and was head of the Equal Employment Opportunity Commission in the Carter administration. Afterward, she taught law at Georgetown University. When the delegate seat came open in 1990, she edged past Council Member Betty Anne Kane, 39%-33%, in the primary. Norton has been re-elected easily since; in 2018, she won 87% of the vote.

Her relationship with congressional Republicans active on District matters has been mixed. She worked closely with former Republican Rep. Tom Davis of Virginia on several issues. In 1995, she collaborated with Davis and Speaker Newt Gingrich to create the fiscal control board that oversaw the District's financial recovery. In 1999, she and Davis worked together to pass a law providing in-state tuition for District students at colleges and universities in any state. But Norton has clashed with Republicans seeking to impose restrictions on District policies. When Republican Rep. Andy Harris of Maryland announced his intentions to challenge a voter-approved ballot measure decriminalizing marijuana in 2014, Norton stated, "D.C. residents can rest assured that when a mandate comes directly from the people, they haven't seen a fight like the fight I'm preparing to make against Rep. Andy Harris and any other member of Congress who attempts to undo our democratic process."

She has clashed with presidents in recent years. Norton was frustrated by President Barack Obama's 2011 budget deal with House Republicans because it kept a school voucher program in the District's budget. She also disagreed with Obama's opposition to a 2013 House bill to allow the District to tap local revenues for government operations. She has been a vocal opponent of President Donald Trump. She has continued her opposition to school voucher programs under the Trump administration, which supported expanding the program, and slammed a push by Sen. Ted Cruz of Texas and Rep. Mark Meadows of North Carolina, both Republicans, to give any D.C. resident a voucher to attend private school.

Norton has been frustrated in her attempts to secure full voting rights for D.C. in the House. During the 2000s, she came just short of securing D.C. a voting representative in Congress, with the agreement that the state that just missed out on an additional House seat in Congress would get one more district. That passed the House in 2007 but fell just short in the Senate; in 2009, it passed the Senate, but with a poison-pill amendment that would eliminate the district's strict gun control laws. In 2015, she introduced the New Columbia Admission Act, proposing to carve out a 51st state around the White House, Capitol, Supreme Court and National Mall. Norton rejected an idea floated by then-House Oversight Committee Chairman Jason Chaffetz of Utah to make the District a part of Maryland, saying residents of both jurisdictions didn't want that.

When Democrats took over the House in 2019, Norton's hand was strengthened. She regained her right to vote on House floor amendments, something Republicans had long denied her and territorial delegates. Democratic leaders also supported D.C. statehood. That fight has become a cause celebre in liberal circles. If Democrats take control of the White House and Senate in the coming years, there's a real chance Norton's decades-long push could finally succeed.

Norton has had a number of successes on local issues, including the Southeast Federal Center Public-Private Development Act, which promoted development around the Washington Navy Yard, and the decision to place the Coast Guard headquarters on the grounds of the old St. Elizabeth's Hospital. She sponsored a financial transparency act for D.C. judges that Obama signed into law in 2016. With little apparent success, she sent a letter to Trump, requesting that he consult her on nominations for federal judicial and law enforcement positions in the District. Norton's legislative agenda is not solely local. As the chair of the Transportation and Infrastructure Highways and Transit Subcommittee, she has advocated increased funding for roads and mass transit projects. She has introduced or co-sponsored a bill to dismantle the U.S. nuclear weapons program.

FLORIDA

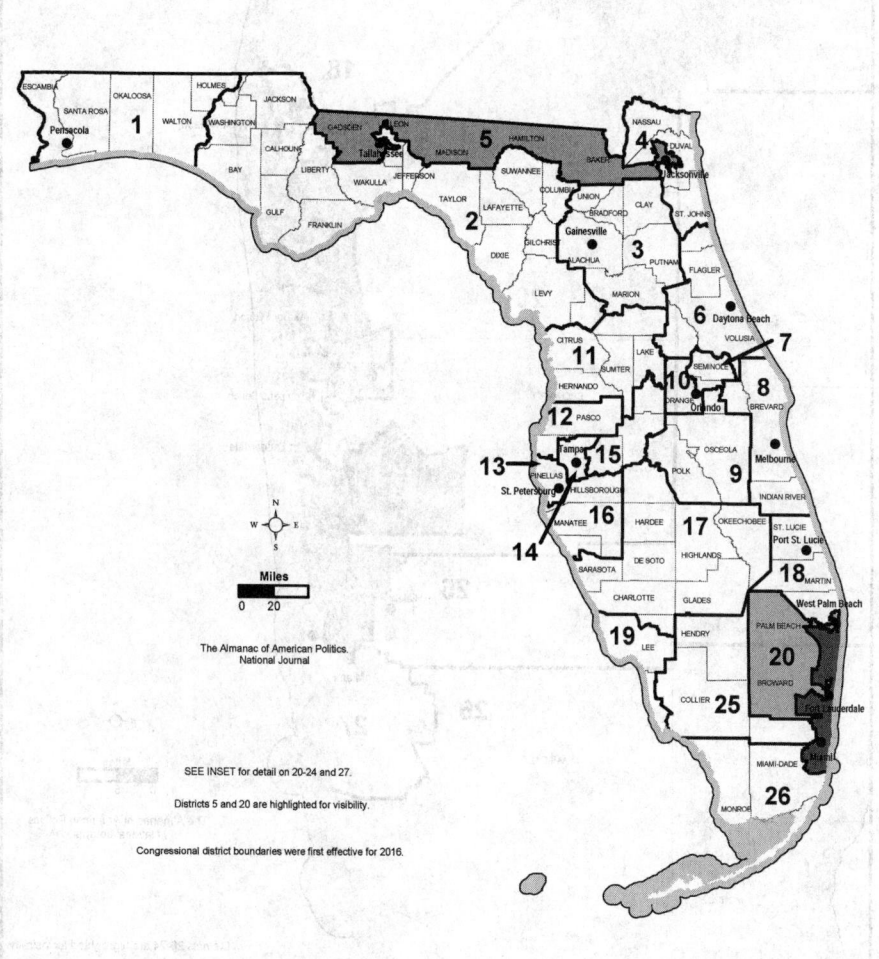

The Almanac of American Politics.
National Journal

Miles
0   20

SEE INSET for detail on 20-24 and 27.

Districts 5 and 20 are highlighted for visibility.

Congressional district boundaries were first effective for 2016.

Ever since election night 2000, Florida has played host to some of the closest – and most closely watched – elections in the nation. The presidential races of 2012 and 2016, the gubernatorial races of 2010, 2014 and 2018, and the Senate race of 2018 were all decided by less than 1.2 percentage points. In each of these races, save the 2012 presidential race, the Republican candidate won – illustrative of how the Florida electorate, despite the state's near-constant demographic swirl, has consistently come up red, albeit by the narrowest of margins.

Inset for Greater Miami

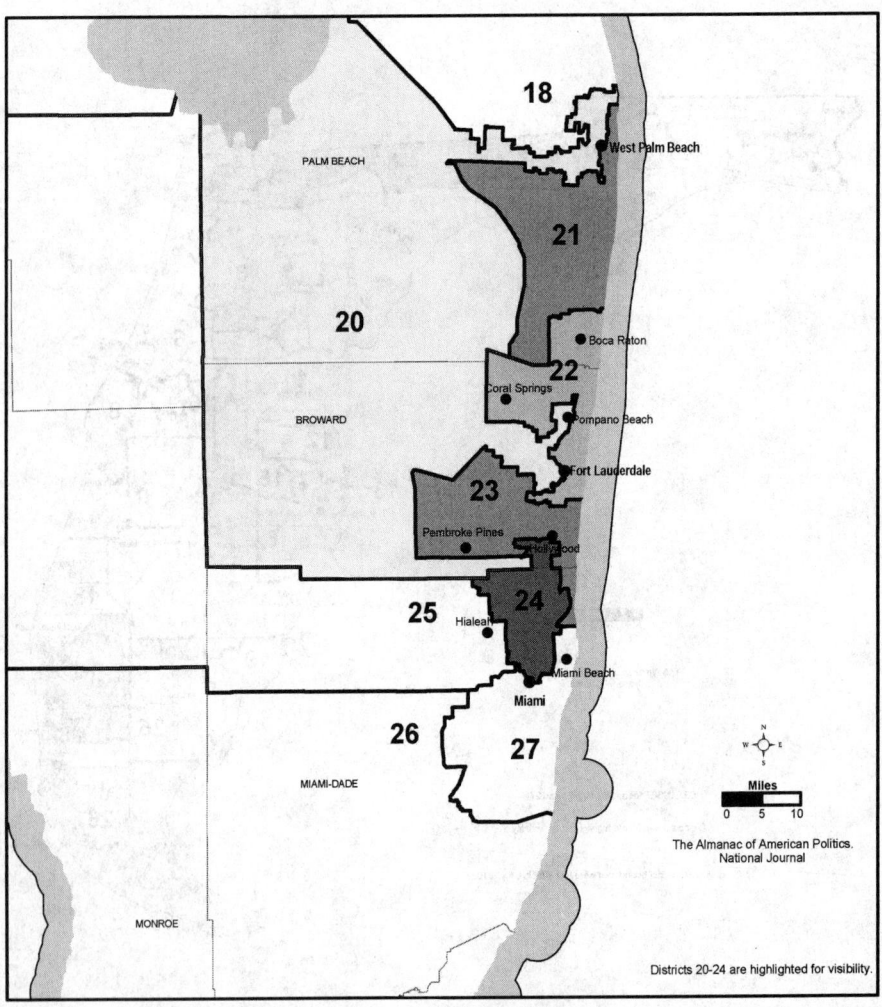

The Almanac of American Politics.
National Journal

Districts 20-24 are highlighted for visibility.

Congressional district boundaries were first effective for 2016.

More than 500 years ago, in March 1513, the Spanish conquistador Juan Ponce de León spied the coast of Florida. For the next 400 years, anyone sailing along Florida's 1,197 miles of coastline and 663 miles of beach would not have seen anything much different from what Ponce de Leon saw. But within the past century the state has been transformed, from a swampy, under-settled, mostly rural state of 1.5 million people (the smallest population in the South), to a metropolitan powerhouse of almost 21 million people that overtook New York as the third most populous state in 2014. The result is a heterogeneous nation-state, historically Southern, demographically Northeastern and Midwestern, and culturally, at least partly, Latin American. It has been economically vibrant for most of the past century, but vulnerable to sudden contractions, as in the mid-1920s when a hurricane abruptly ended the Miami real estate boom, and later during the Great Recession. But Florida has bounced back before, and it is growing again – a population spike of more than 11 percent since 2010 alone.

Florida is the only Atlantic Coast state that was not part of the colonial United States. In 1819, it was acquired from Spain, through the exertions of John Quincy Adams and Andrew Jackson. Adams thought that in foreign hands Florida could block the Gulf of Mexico and the Mississippi Valley, while Jackson saw it as a haven for runaway slaves and a launching pad for Indians to raid the farmers and planters of what was then the American Southwest. Florida was a minor agricultural state until the early 20th century, when its sunshine economy based on citrus production and tourism took hold. Florida's balmy winter climate inspired railroad barons Henry Flagler and Henry Plant to build grand resort hotels and accompanying rail lines (Flagler on the Atlantic coast and Plant on the Gulf), which not only brought vacationers to Florida but also helped transport Florida oranges north to urban markets. Later, auto entrepreneur Carl Fisher promoted tourism to Florida and construction of the Dixie Highway, which in the 1920s helped millions of visitors travel to the state, many of whom decided to stay. Miami, founded in 1896, boomed until the hurricane hit in 1926; in the 1930s, New Yorkers started retiring to art deco apartments in Miami Beach.

By the 1960s, retirees from further north were flocking to the state looking for year-round sunshine – driving down I-95 from the northeast and ending up on the Atlantic coast, or down I-75 from the Midwest to reach the Gulf coast. Retirees joined agriculture and tourism as Florida's main economic drivers, but new industries, many related to the space program, also migrated to the state. In the 1980s and 1990s, the percentage of families with children as a share of Florida's population grew rapidly, lured by jobs and opportunities in communities that hadn't existed a generation earlier. The state's tourism sector, no longer dependent solely on beautiful beaches, was transformed as Orlando became the "Theme Park Capital of the World," starting, but hardly ending, with the Disney empire. The cruise business exploded; Port Miami was the global leader for cruise travel, but Port Canaveral, about an hour's drive east from Orlando, and Port Everglades, outside of Fort Lauderdale, operate huge terminals as well. If normalization with Cuba isn't reversed, it could eventually spur even more embarkations. All told, the state economy now tops $1 trillion, which would rank as the world's 17th-largest economy.

Florida is also an aerospace industry hub. Brevard County's Cape Canaveral Spaceport complex has launch pads operated not just by NASA but also the state, SpaceX and United Launch Alliance, a military contractor; two-thirds of the 58 commercial launches licensed by the federal government since 2015 have occurred in Florida. Brazilian manufacturer Embraer assembles executive jets in Melbourne, and it recently added a new maintenance facility to its North American headquarters complex in Fort Lauderdale. European turboprop maker ATR relocated its North American operations to Miami Springs, and aerospace giant Northrop Grumman has invested heavily in its operations in Melbourne. The Florida Panhandle is home to several military installations, including Pensacola Naval Air Station and Eglin Air Force Base, which helped attract defense contractors, commercial aviation companies and industrial airparks to the region. Central Florida, meanwhile, is developing a high-tech corridor that runs from Tampa (home of the University of South Florida) through Orlando (the University of Central Florida) to the Space Coast and reaches up to Gainesville (the University of Florida).

But like other fast-growing states, Florida's economy has also been built on construction and real estate, which makes it subject to sudden downturns. As real estate values plummeted during the Great Recession, the foreclosure crisis hit few states as hard as Florida. Many banks there compounded the problem by their inability to process the glut of distressed properties though the state's court system, and fraud was not uncommon. Local tax receipts, heavily dependent on property values and the construction industry, slumped. Unemployment rose from 3.5 percent in January 2007 to a peak of 11.2 percent in January 2010, and more people left Florida than moved there for the first time since post-World War II demobilization. The recession lasted longer in Florida than it did most other states, with the economy not really picking up until 2012. By late 2018, Florida had an unemployment rate of 3.3 percent, slightly better than the national average, but median incomes were stuck roughly $8,000 below the national average.

One of the state's original economic pillars, the citrus industry, has been crippled by citrus greening disease, which cut employment by almost a third between 2012 and 2015. Then, in 2017, Hurricane Irma felled between 50 and 90 percent of the crop in some areas, producing the worst economic year for the industry since the end of World War II, while also bringing a new biological invader, a bacterium known as canker. Much of the rest of Florida's agriculture sector has either remained stagnant or contracted; agriculture currently accounts for less than 1 percent of state economic output. No wonder, then, that developers have purchased 1 million acres of farmland over the last decade. One potential growth area related to agriculture: medical marijuana, approved in a ballot measure on its second try in 2016.

The state had been forced to grapple with other natural threats. One is climate change, which is projected by some to raise the sea level by one to four feet over the next century. After a relatively quiet period for hurricanes, Florida was hit by two $10 billion-plus storms -- Irma in 2017 and Michael the following year. Then, in 2018, the state was hit by an unusually wide-ranging plague of Karenia brevis – a single-celled algae that causes red tide, killing sea life, fouling beaches and causing human respiratory problems. A separate toxic blue-green algae bloom on Lake Okeechobee and other fresh water bodies only made matters worse.

Retirees continue to flock to Florida; one-fifth percent of the population is 65 or older, the nation's highest percentage. The fastest-growing retirement locale is The Villages in Sumter County, northwest of Orlando; it has grown by one-third since 2010, and for four years in the past decade, it grew faster than any metro area in the country. Michael Grunwald, writing in Politico, called The Villages "a 40-square-mile cruise ship" inhabited by active seniors partial to the paddle-tennis-like game of pickleball. "The Villages represents the traditionalist side of a cultural and political war that began in the '60s and never really ended, an us-against-them battle over values between conservative Red America and progressive Blue America," Grunwald wrote, adding that when Donald Trump "vows to make America great again, they sense that he means more like The Villages." Sumter County produced the highest rate of voter turnout of any Florida county in 2018. And it's not the only reason for Republican optimism: Of the 25 fastest-growing metro areas in the country, 10 were in Florida, and nine of them backed Trump in 2016.

But Florida is also increasingly diverse. A quarter of the population is Latino, up from 22 percent since 2010. For refugees from Cuba and Haiti and for immigrants from the Caribbean and Latin America, Florida has been a land of freedom from authoritarian and turbulent lands. Its population has been continually replenished with people from other states, foreign countries and the U.S. territory of Puerto Rico. Today, a little more than one-third of Florida residents are natives. Miami has long been the economic and commercial capital of Latin America: You can fly nonstop from Miami to just about any major city in Latin America, and both English and Spanish are common and Portuguese not unknown. Spurred by a weak economy and a debt crisis – and then by Hurricane Maria in 2017 -- large numbers of Puerto Ricans have been moving to Orlando and Osceola County, as have Venezuelans, Colombians and Dominicans; Mexicans are more prevalent in the state's verdant southwestern farmlands (Hendry, Collier and Hardee Counties). While Cubans still dominate Miami-Dade, they make up less than a third of the state's overall Hispanic population. Along the Gulf Coast are a necklace of affluent communities. The Panhandle, the so-called Redneck Riviera around Pensacola and Panama City, is culturally Southern. State government is headquartered in Tallahassee, chosen because it was midway between the population centers of Jacksonville and Pensacola at a time when almost no one lived on the peninsula; Tallahassee and the university town of Gainesville are liberal bastions in a sea of conservatism.

Florida has a fragile civil society, and it can be chaotic and disorderly at times; the state has often ranked in the top 10 in violent crime. Most people do not have deep roots in the state — most communities sprang into existence within living memory — and if Florida gives people more freedom and options than elsewhere, it also gives them more disruption than many anticipated. (Aggregating stories of weird crimes in Florida has become a cottage industry, with no signs of slowing.) Florida has more gun permits than any other state, and it pioneered the right for citizens to carry concealed weapons in 1987. The state's "stand-your-ground" law, which allows Floridians to use deadly force when they believe their lives are threatened, became a focal point in the tragic 2012 shooting death of an unarmed black teenager, Trayvon Martin, in Sanford. Guns came to the fore again with the terrorism-inspired incident at the Pulse nightclub in Orlando in June 2016 – at the time, the deadliest mass shooting in modern U.S. history, with 49 killed and 53 injured. Then, in February 2018, a teenaged former student went on a shooting rampage at Marjory Stoneman Douglas High School in Parkland that killed 17 and injured 17 others. The school-age survivors touched off a national movement for gun control that bore partial fruit in Tallahassee, as Republican Gov. Rick Scott within weeks signed a law that raised the age to buy rifles and shotguns from 18 to 21, applied a three-day waiting period to long guns, and banned "bump stocks," which enable rapid firing.

The nation's other three largest states are one-sided politically, with California and New York heavily Democratic and Texas heavily Republican. Florida, by contrast, remains closely divided, though Republicans have held the upper hand since the 1990s, holding the governorship and the legislature since then. Trump and Hillary Clinton, like other recent presidential candidates, devoted significant attention to Florida in 2016, with Trump winning by fewer than 120,000 votes, or just over 1 percent of the nearly 9.4 million cast. (The 2012 margin for Obama had been fewer than 75,000 votes.) Clinton, targeting minority voters, won Hispanics, 62%-35%, and secured roughly 250,000 more votes than Obama had in 2012, including six-digit increases in the Democratic bastions of Miami-Dade, Broward (Fort Lauderdale), Palm Beach and Orange counties. But the first female presidential nominee did three points worse among women than Obama had, and Trump benefited from a white surge. Running strongly in the I-4 corridor, the Republican nominee won 442,000 more votes than Mitt Romney had in 2012.

Florida was a marquee state in the 2018 midterm elections, with high-profile races for governor and senator. Scott, the deep-pocketed two-term governor, challenged incumbent Democratic Sen. Bill Nelson, while two candidates who began the primary season as underdogs – Trump-aligned Rep. Ron DeSantis and progressive Tallahassee Mayor Andrew Gillum – faced off for governor. In a year shaped by a national Democratic wave and youth energy sparked by the Parkland shootings, Nelson and Gillum managed to secure about 90 percent of the raw votes Clinton had won in a presidential year, and they made gains in several urban-suburban counties compared to 2016, running particularly strong among college-educated white women, who were alienated by Trump and his allies DeSantis and Scott. Nelson and Gillum flipped Duval (Jacksonville), Pinellas (St. Petersburg), Seminole (suburban Orlando) and St. Lucie (Fort Pierce), and Nelson also flipped Monroe (the Keys). This is what enabled Democrats to keep the two races close, and also made possible the election of a Democratic state agriculture commissioner and the flipping of two House seats.

Yet Republicans claimed the biggest prizes, as Scott and DeSantis won their races by 10,000 and 32,000 votes, respectively, out of more than 8 million cast. How did they do it? First, Trump wasn't as unpopular in Florida as he was in other states. Second, both Republican candidates overperformed in Miami-Dade County, where both Democratic nominees received about 140,000 fewer votes than Clinton had – a bigger drop-off than in the neighboring Democratic strongholds of Broward and Palm Beach. Scott and DeSantis assiduously courted Hispanic voters – not just Cuban-Americans but also Venezuelans and Central Americans who responded to the Republicans' labeling of Gillum as a socialist. Third, while Florida is slowly growing less white, the Republicans continued to benefit from strong turnout and support from rural and working-class whites, as well as from retirees in places like Sumter County, where Scott and DeSantis got roughly the same number of raw votes – and slightly higher percentages -- as Trump did in 2016. As long as retirees keep flocking to the state, Republicans have a shot at maintaining their upper hand in the Sunshine State.

Population		Race and Ethnicity		Income	
Total	20,278,447	White	54.9%	Median Income	$50,883
Land area (sq. miles)	53,625	Black	15.4%	State Income Rank	38
Pop/ sq mi	378.2	Latino	24.7%	Poverty Rate	15.5%
Born in state	35.9%	Asian	2.6%	With health insurance	85.1%
		Two or more races	1.8%	Cash public assistance	2.1%
Age Groups		Other	0.6%	Food stamp/SNAP	14.4%
Under 18	20.3%				
18-34	21.4%	Education		Work	
35-64	38.9%	H.S grad or less	41.4%	White Collar	34.6%
Over 64	19.4%	Some college	30.2%	Sales and Service	47.0%
		College Degree, 4 yr	18.2%	Blue Collar	18.4%
Military		Post grad	10.3%	Government	11.9%
Veteran/ Active Duty	9.3%				

Presidential Politics

2016 Primary (D)	Clinton (D)	1,101,414 (64%)	Sanders (D)	568,839 (33%)			
2016 Primary (R)	Trump (R)	1,079,870 (46%)	Rubio (R)	638,661 (27%)	Cruz (R)		404,891 (17%)
	Kasich (R)	159,976 (7%)					
2016 Pres. Vote	Trump (R)	4,617,886 (49%)	Clinton (D)	4,504,975 (47%)	Johnson (L)	207,043	(2%)
2012 Pres. Vote	Obama (D)	4,237,756 (50%)	Romney (R)	4,163,447 (49%)			

Florida continues to be the largest and one of the most competitive battleground states in the country. With 29 electoral votes, the same number as New York, only California and Texas have more. Florida Democratic strategist Steven Schale, one of the state's savviest political observers, notes that since 1992, when the Sunshine State became a White House battleground, more than 50 million votes have been cast in seven presidential elections and the two parties are separated by a miniscule 0.02 percent: Republican candidates having received a net 12,000 votes more than Democrats. Donald Trump defeated Hillary Clinton in 2016 by nearly 113,000 votes, 49%-48%. But the outcome was hardly a foregone conclusion. Just over 69 percent of Florida's voters cast their ballots before Election Day and daily pre-election data from state and local election officials indicated that Clinton was leading in the early vote. Indeed, among all ballots cast before Election Day, Clinton garnered an advantage of roughly 247,000. But among those who voted on Election Day, Trump prevailed by some 360,000, tipping the state into his column. Both Trump and Clinton turned out their respective partisan bases in the state: Republicans in the Panhandle and the northern tier of the state, as well as those in the Fort Myers media market, voted solidly for Trump; voters in Tallahassee (the state capital and home of Florida State University) and Gainesville (the University of Florida) and the Democratic bastion of Miami-Dade and Broward counties went decisively for Clinton. In the third county on the so-called "Gold Coast," Palm Beach, the Democratic vote lagged, but Clinton still prevailed. Comparing the vote in the base regions of the two parties, Clinton came out ahead by about 140,000 votes, a margin slightly higher than Obama's advantage over Mitt Romney in 2012.

The election was decided in the state's famed I-4 corridor, which stretches from Daytona on the Atlantic Coast, through the burgeoning Orlando area, to the Tampa-St. Petersburg metro on the Gulf Coast. The early vote from the I-4 corridor gave Trump a scant 11,000-vote lead, but on Election Day, Trump voters surged to the polls and his lead along I-4 swelled to more than 250,000, securing the state for the GOP standard-bearer. According to a post-election analysis by Schale, Trump's victory in the I-4 corridor was fueled largely by his strength in the region's suburbs and exurbs. While Clinton outpolled Trump in the more urban turf — Orange, Osceola and Seminole counties around Orlando, as well as Tampa-St. Petersburg — by about 200,000 votes, Trump won 15 other counties near and along I-4 by a whopping 450,000. In just three — Hernando and Pasco north of Tampa-St. Pete and Volusia (Daytona Beach) — Romney's margin over Obama was some 24,000 votes in 2012. Trump's advantage over Clinton in these three counties was more than 112,000. That difference alone would have been more than enough to wipe out Obama's statewide victory margin of 74,309 in 2012. Floridians got to know the candidates well during the campaign. According to an analysis by Kantar Media, both pumped more advertising dollars into Florida than any other state. An ABC News report just prior to Election Day found that in the last month of the general election campaign, Trump and Clinton spent more days in Florida — Trump, 10; Clinton, 8 —than any other state. And the voters responded: 9.4 million Floridians cast ballots in the presidential election, up from 8.5 million in 2012.

Florida's presidential primary had not been crucial in determining a nomination between 1976, when Democrat Jimmy Carter defeated George Wallace and ended Wallace's career in national politics, and 2008, when Arizona Sen. John McCain defeated Romney, a victory that propelled him to success one week later in the more than 20 states that held primaries or caucuses on Super Tuesday. In 2016, Trump dispatched one of his chief rivals, Florida Sen. Marco Rubio, from the Republican nominating contest. By the time of the Florida primary on March 15 Rubio could not rally his home-state voters and former Florida Gov. Jeb Bush, who had pulled out of the GOP nominating contest earlier, declined Rubio's overtures to his former mentor to endorse him. Trump breezed to a victory over Rubio 46%-27%, and Texas Sen. Ted Cruz finished third. Rubio won only one of the state's 67 counties, Miami-Dade, with its sizable Cuban-American electorate. Trump swept the rest of the state and Florida's winner-take-all primary netted him the state's 99 GOP convention delegates, a huge haul that helped him solidify his grip on the Republican nomination. The Democratic race was less critical to Clinton. In a primary where roughly half the voters were non-white, Clinton rallied African Americans and Hispanics to defeat Vermont Sen. Bernie Sanders 64%-33%. Sanders carried just nine rural counties in the Panhandle and northern rim of the state.

Congressional Districts

116th Congress Lineup	13D 14R	115th Congress Lineup	11D 16R

Florida has gained congressional districts after every census since 1930, when it elected four House members. Its 15-seat gain since 1960 is more than any other state, including Texas, during that half-century. Following the 2010 census, Florida increased from 25 to 27, leaving it with a delegation the same size as New York's. Republican Gov. Rick Scott's narrow victory and big GOP margins in the legislature after 2010 meant that Republicans controlled the redistricting process. But they have consistently lost seats since then. Their growth opportunities have been limited by two factors: Republicans' already robust 19-6 edge in the delegation following a banner year, and a voter-approved referendum in 2010 seeking to rein in the kind of gerrymandering that had created one of the strangest patchworks of districts in the country.

Democrats have made the most of their opportunities. The delegation has shifted to 14 Republicans and 13 Democrats — the best showing by Democrats since 1990. There has been a logic to their pick-ups since 2010. All of them have been in metropolitan areas — including three in Orlando, one in Tampa-St. Petersburg and three in South Florida. The Democratic delegation includes four African Americans, two Latinos and one Asian American; eight of the 13 are women. Of the 14 Republicans, all but one are white males. The exception, Mario Diaz-Balart, is the most senior of the GOP group and the only surviving Latino from what had been three. (The delegation has seen frequent change. Diaz-Balart and Democrat Debbie Wasserman Schultz, who were elected in 2002 and 2004, are its senior members.)

As the political insiders and outsiders prepare for redistricting, they faced the prospect that Republicans will retain partisan control in Tallahassee and that the state will gain two new seats. Although the GOP might be tempted to force one or two of the Democratic incumbents into a competitive reelection — perhaps in Orlando and Miami, though each of those areas has experienced in the past decade a large influx of Democratic-leaning Hispanics — their safest course might be to concede the 13 Democratic seats and stake their claim to the two additional districts, perhaps by drawing them in Republican-leaning suburbs and growing exurbs. Those could be in the center of the state and along the Treasure Coast north of Palm Beach County.

Looming over the planning by the two parties are the activist reformers — with their continuing threat of voter initiatives and court review. Their Fair District movement has had a significant impact in the past decade, starting with the passage of a referendum in 2010 that limited the use of political gerrymanders. That action required legislators to draw compact districts conforming to county and city boundaries and prohibited them from taking into account partisan data or incumbent residences.

The delayed impact resulted in a court-drawn map for the 2016 election that helped Democrats gain two seats in the Orlando area and one in St. Petersburg, though they lost a swing district on the Treasure Coast. In 2018, the redistricting changes plus broader demographic shifts led to the Democratic pick-up of two Hispanic-majority seats in Miami-Dade County.

The recent history of redistricting suggests that neither party in Florida has been inclined to take the course of least resistance, and that citizens groups will assert their prerogatives. It's a safe bet that the state and federal courts will have additional opportunities for influence.

Ron DeSantis (R)

Elected 2018, term expires 2023, 1st term; b. Sept. 14, 1978, Jacksonville; Yale University, B.A., 2001; Harvard Law School, J.D., 2005; Catholic; Married (Casey); 2 children.

Military Career: US Navy, 2004-2010 (Iraq); US Navy Reserves, 2010-pres.

Elected Office: US House, 2013-2018.

Professional Career: Federal prosecutor.

Office: 400 S. Monroe St., Tallahassee, 32399-0001; 850-488-7146; Fax: 850-487-0801

Lt. Gov.: Jeanette Núñez (R) **Atty. Gen:** Ashley Moody (R)

State Legislature: Senate: 17D, 23R **House:** 46D, 71R, 3I

Election Results

Election	Name (Party)	Vote (%)
2018 General	Ron DeSantis (R)...	4,076,186 (50%)
	Andrew Gillum (D)...	4,043,723 (49%)
2018 Primary	Ron DeSantis (R)...	916,298 (57%)
	Adam Putnam (R)..	592,518 (37%)

Prior winning percentage: House: 2016 (59%), 2014 (63%), 2012 (57%)

With the strong support of President Donald Trump, Republican Rep. Ron DeSantis won the Florida governorship in 2018, edging out Tallahassee Mayor Andrew Gillum by just 32,000 votes out of more than 8 million cast. The victory rocketed DeSantis to national prominence just months after turning 40.

DeSantis grew up in northeast Florida, where his father installed television ratings devices for Nielsen. A talented baseball player, DeSantis played on a team from Dunedin that made the final four of the 1991 Little League World Series. He went on to captain the squad at Yale, where he majored in history. To help pay for his studies, he held a variety of jobs, including collecting trash, moving furniture and coaching baseball clinics. He earned his law degree at Harvard and became a judge advocate general in the Navy, earning a Bronze Star and serving at Guantanamo Bay and in Iraq. His military service helped shape his views on national security, including his skepticism of nation-building. While there are a lot of "good people" in Iraq, he added that "getting involved in guerilla war doesn't play to our strengths." He remained a lieutenant commander in the Navy Reserve.

DeSantis ran for office when the new 6th District unexpectedly had no incumbent following the 2012 redistricting. He had written a book, "Dreams From Our Founding Fathers," a play off President Barack Obama's book, "Dreams From My Father." In it, he argued that Obama and like-minded Democrats "have charted a course that is alien to our Republic's philosophical foundations." Touting his military experience and strong conservative views, DeSantis easily defeated six rivals in the primary, winning 39 percent of the vote. He won endorsements from such tea party favorites as former U.N. Ambassador (and later National Security Advisor) John Bolton and Sen. Mike Lee of Utah, and he amassed a pronounced fundraising advantage. In the general election, he faced Democrat Heather Beaven, a fellow Navy veteran, but in the heavily Republican district DeSantis won, 57%-43%.

In the House, DeSantis forged ties to conservative Republicans, but also built bridges to the party's establishment. Unlike several other junior Republicans from Florida, he voted in January 2015 to give John Boehner another term as Speaker, despite pressure from constituents to oppose him; this helped enable DeSantis to secure the chairmanship of the Oversight and Government Reform Subcommittee on National Security. But DeSantis helped found the Freedom Caucus, which would go on to cause headaches for Boehner and his team. Facing pressure from Majority Whip Steve Scalise to toe the party line, DeSantis quit his post on the Republican whip team.

After Sen. Marco Rubio said that he would run for president and forgo reelection to the Senate in 2016, DeSantis entered the race. His plan was to run as the conservative alternative, with extensive support from national advocacy groups such as the Club for Growth and Senate Conservatives Fund. But he faced steep challenges in gaining traction in the wide-open GOP primary, including low name ID outside of his district and the greater diversity among Florida Republicans than within his constituency. As DeSantis was struggling, Rubio responded to pleas from party leaders to reclaim his seat days before the June filing deadline, and after Rubio jumped back in, DeSantis quit the Senate race. State Rep. Fred Costello, the leading Republican candidate for his House seat and the second-place finisher in the 2012 primary DeSantis had won, declined to leave the race. But DeSantis, with a large war chest, won the primary in a blow-out, 61%-25%. In November, he coasted to a 59%-41% victory.

Two years later, DeSantis sought higher office again -- this time the governorship, which was coming open with the impending departure of term-limited Republican Gov. Rick Scott. Initially, the frontrunner for the GOP nomination was Adam Putnam, a former state legislator and congressman and, most recently, the twice-elected state agriculture secretary. Putnam, a familiar figure in the state who came from a prominent citrus family, had locked up most of the GOP establishment support and amassed a significant campaign treasury. But Putnam took heat for his ties to sugar interests and for his office's improper handling of concealed weapons permits, which resulted in almost 300 such licenses being improperly issued.

DeSantis gained ground on Putnam for one reason above all: Trump, who on Twitter and eventually in person made clear that DeSantis was his favorite in the race. (Ironically, DeSantis hadn't endorsed Trump in the 2016 Republican primary.) Trump's backing was amplified by Trump-aligned conservative media voices such as Sean Hannity and Mark Levin, and he won the support of donors such as Sheldon Adelson. DeSantis focused his pitch on national issues, spurning Putnam's more traditional approach of running a Florida-focused campaign. "DeSantis made 121 appearances on Fox and Fox Business — his campaign estimates it would have cost his campaign $9.3 million to purchase all that airtime," veteran Florida political reporter Marc Caputo wrote. DeSantis even aired a commercial in which he taught one of his children to build Trump's border wall using blocks and read "The Art of the Deal" to his infant. Despite being mocked outside of pro-Trump circles, the ad – and DeSantis' overall strategy – proved immensely powerful in a primary that would be decided by the party's base voters. In the end, the race wasn't close: DeSantis defeated Putnam, 57%-37%.

The Democratic primary was at least as interesting, with an equally unexpected result. The frontrunner for the nomination was former Rep. Gwen Graham, a moderate and the daughter of popular former Gov. and Sen. Bob Graham. Other candidates included former Miami Beach Mayor Philip Levine and a pair of deep-pocketed businessmen, Chris King and Jeff Greene. Gillum, despite his evident charisma and oratorical skills, attracted relatively little attention at first.

Gillum – like DeSantis, 39 years old at the time of his nomination -- was the fifth of seven children born to a bus driver and a construction laborer. At Florida A&M University, where he became the first in his family to earn a college degree, Gillum became a leader in student government and drove opposition to then-Gov. Jeb Bush's education policies. Gillum was elected to the Tallahassee City Commission at 23 and became mayor for four years, forging strong ties with his working-class constituents and focusing on criminal justice and education. Gillum took heat for the city's high crime rate and for his handling of power outages after Hurricane Hermine in 2016. Meanwhile, an ongoing FBI investigation into allegations of corruption in city government cast a shadow over Gillum's campaign.

However, Gillum found success with a staunchly progressive agenda that was in tune with the Democrats most likely to vote in the primary. He called out Florida's "stand your ground" law, but also ventured into federal policy that is not the purview of a governor, calling for abolishing Immigration and Customs Enforcement "in its current form" and arguing in favor of a national single-payer health care system. Support from liberal billionaires George Soros and Tom Steyer helped

Gillum close the gap, while Greene targeted Graham and Levine in an advertising blitz, leaving Gillum relatively unscathed. Gillum took 34 percent to Graham's 31 percent, Levine's 20 percent, and Greene and King far behind. Spurning a progressive-moderate alliance with Graham, Gillum chose King as his running mate. The twin victories by DeSantis and Gillum amounted to a rejection of centrism in the nation's most populous swing state.

DeSantis got off to a troubled start in the general election. In a television interview shortly after his victory, DeSantis attacked Gillum by saying, "The last thing we need to do is to monkey this up by trying to embrace a socialist agenda with huge tax increases and bankrupting the state." Critics saw his phrasing as racially tinged. Then the Washington Post reported that DeSantis on four occasions had addressed a conference run by activist David Horowitz, who had said that America's "only serious race war" is against whites. DeSantis flatly rejected charges that he was racist, but at the very least, the episodes proved to be distractions. "A month after winning the nomination, the DeSantis campaign looks strikingly wobbly compared to the juggernaut Republican gubernatorial campaigns we've seen from Jeb Bush, Charlie Crist and Rick Scott," the Tampa Bay Times' Adam Smith wrote in September.

On the issues, DeSantis reaffirmed his conservative agenda. He advocated tax cuts and repeal of the Affordable Care Act, and said that he would not have signed the gun control bill signed by Scott after the mass shooting at Marjory Stoneman Douglas High School in Parkland. He took a more moderate approach on the environment, at least on the suspected water-quality causes of the large and worrisome red tide outbreak – a position in line with DeSantis' longstanding criticism of the sugar industry's environmental practices. (DeSantis' stance on the environment had limits; he expressed uncertainty about climate change and humans' role in it.) Gillum stuck with his progressive agenda – so much so that Democratic Sen. Bill Nelson, a moderate engaged in an intense reelection battle against Scott, distanced himself from Gillum's policy agenda. Nelson made clear that he opposed abolishing ICE and did not favor single-payer health care; he also expressed skepticism about setting the minimum wage as high as $15.

On balance, Gillum maintained a modest but consistent lead in the polls. The debates between DeSantis and Gillum were packed with tension. DeSantis scorched Gillum over the FBI investigation, while Gillum attacked DeSantis over race. "How the hell am I supposed to know every single statement somebody makes?" DeSantis said. "I am not going to bow down to the altar of political correctness." Gillum responded, "I'm not calling Mr. DeSantis a racist. I'm simply saying the racists believe he's a racist." DeSantis put together a narrow victory – so close that it was a week and a half before Gillum conceded.

The handover between Scott and DeSantis proved awkward. Shortly before leaving office, Scott announced appointments for some 84 positions, prompting DeSantis to say he would "definitely rescind" some of them. Despite their shared partisan ties, David Smiley of the Miami Herald wrote, DeSantis seemed to be taking a different approach than his predecessor. "He's forged closer relationships with Republican leaders, shown greater deference to his own top lieutenants and even given some Democrats hope for compromise by awarding senior posts to members of the other party." Scott and DeSantis may be sparring some more as the next Republican presidential contest approaches.

Marco Rubio (R)

Elected 2010, term expires 2022, 2nd term, b. May 28, 1971; Miami; Tarkio College (MO), Att., 1990; Santa Fe College (NM), Att., 1991; University of Florida, B.S., 1993; University of Miami (FL), J.D., 1996; Roman Catholic; Married (Jeanette Dousdebes); 4 children.

Elected Office: West Miami City Commissioner, 1998-2000; FL House, 2000-2008, Speaker, 2006-2008.

Professional Career: Practicing attorney, 1997-2010; Professor, FL Intl. University, 2009-2010.

DC Office: 284 RSOB 20510, 202-224-3041, Fax: 202-228-0285, rubio.senate.gov

State Offices: Jacksonville, 904-354-4300; Miami, 305-596-4224; Orlando, 407-254-2573; Palm Beach Gardens, 561-775-3360; Pensacola, 850-433-2603; Tallahassee, 850-599-9100; Tampa, 813-853-1099.

Committees: *Aging. Appropriations*: Commerce, Justice, Science & Related Agencies; Department of the Interior, Environment & Related Agencies; DOL, HHS & Education & Related Agencies; Military Construction & Veteran Affairs & Related Agencies; State, Foreign Operations & Related Programs. *Foreign Relations*: East Asia, the Pacific & International Cybersecurity Policy; State Dept & USAID Mngmnt, Internat'l Ops & Internat'l Dev; West Hem Crime Civ Sec Dem Rights & Women's Issues (Chmn). *Intelligence. Small Business & Entrepreneurship (Chmn)*.

Group Ratings

	ADA	ACLU	AFL-CIO	LCV	ITI	COC	HAFA	ACU	CFG	FRC
2018	-	5%	-	0%	-	89%	77%	86%	67%	100%
2017	0%	C	0%	0%	C	83%	C	84%	90%	100%

Almanac Ratings 2017-18

	Economy	Social	Foreign	Composite
Liberal	0%	0%	0%	0%
Conservative	100%	100%	100%	100%

Key Votes of the 115th Congress

1. Obama-care revision	Y	5. Gun regulations	Y	9. Kavanaugh confirmation	Y
2. Tax Cuts	Y	6. Family planning regs	Y	10. Saudi arms sales	N
3. Dodd-Frank revision	Y	7. Gorsuch confirmation	Y	11. FISA rules	Y
4. Omnibus appropriations	Y	8. Immigration restrictions	Y	12. Military aid in Yemen	N

Election Results

Election	Name (Party)	Vote (%)		Cand. Spent	Ind. Exp. Support	Ind. Exp. Oppose
2016 General	Marco Rubio (R)............................	4,835,191	(52%)	$21,152,492	$6,102,547	$6,894,783
	Patrick Murphy (D)........................	4,122,088	(44%)	$8,684,853	$5,145,141	$28,326,406
	Paul Stanton (L).............................	196,956	(2%)	$19,601		
2016 Primary	Marco Rubio (R)............................	1,029,830	(72%)			
	Carlos Beruff (R)..............................	264,427	(19%)			

Prior winning percentages: 2010 (49%)

Marco Rubio, Florida's senior senator, has gone through a remarkable number of political transformations in his still-young political career. He had been: A conservative institutionalist in the Florida legislature, a tea party darling in 2010, a rising national star promoted by establishment-minded party elders in the Senate, a key player on immigration reform efforts in 2013, a top-tier presidential candidate in 2015 and one of many candidates vanquished in embarrassing fashion by Donald Trump in that campaign. In Rubio's second term in the Senate, he has mostly been a party-line vote for his onetime primary rival, though he's held fast on the foreign policy issues closest to his heart.

Born in Miami, Rubio grew up in a working-class neighborhood near the city's Little Havana neighborhood. He was the third child of emigrants who left Cuba in 1956, before Fidel Castro came to power. Rubio has often described himself as the "son of exiles" who were forced out by Castro's regime, though he used that characterization less after facing media scrutiny over whether he had embellished the story. His father worked long days as a hotel bartender after immigrating to Miami, and his mother was a hotel maid with a second job at Kmart. The family moved to follow work; Rubio spent six years in Las Vegas while his parents worked in the hotels before returning to Miami for high school. At the encouragement of an aunt, he was baptized as a Mormon along with his mother and sister, only to convert back to Catholicism as a teenager.

Rubio initially was a Democrat, inspired by Massachusetts Sen. Ted Kennedy's famous "the dream shall never die" speech at the 1980 Democratic National Convention. But he soon joined his grandfather in becoming a staunch Ronald Reagan supporter. Rubio played football in high school, and despite his small stature, earned a football scholarship to Tarkio College in Missouri. He returned to Florida after the school went bankrupt, spent a year at a junior college and then earned his bachelor's degree at the University of Florida. As an undergraduate, he worked for a couple of leading Cuban-American GOP politicians from the Miami area, interning for Rep. Ileana Ros-Lehtinen and volunteering on Rep. Lincoln Diaz-Balart's first campaign.

In his last year at the University of Miami Law School, Rubio ran the Dade County operation for Republican Sen. Bob Dole's presidential campaign in 1996. There, he met future Florida Gov. Jeb Bush, who served as a mentor and ally until their relationship soured when both ran for president in 2016.

At 26, Rubio ousted a city commissioner in West Miami, a small, heavily Cuban town just south of Miami International Airport. He still lives there with his wife Jeanette, a onetime Miami Dolphins cheerleader, and their four children. Rubio had been on the city commission only a year before running for the Statehouse. Rubio rose through the ranks in Tallahassee, becoming Florida House speaker in 2005 at 34 and the youngest person and the first Hispanic-American to achieve that position. At a ceremony, Bush presented him with a sword, a symbolic passing of the conservative torch in the state. Rubio toured Florida, holding "idea-raisers" to find budget-neutral ideas to improve the state. The 100 ideas he liked best were bundled into a book, and many of the more incremental proposals passed easily. His favorite, replacing the state property tax on primary residences with a sales tax increase, stalled but earned him praise from fiscal conservatives.

Forced out of the state House by term limits, Rubio caught the tea party movement's lightning in its nascent days and used it to power his upstart Senate primary campaign against then-popular Republican Gov. Charlie Crist. The governor had been urged by leading national Republicans to run for the Senate, and he had a huge cash and name recognition advantages. Rubio initially seemed ready to defer to Crist, telling the Tampa Bay Times in early 2009 that Crist was the "best candidate" for the job. But conservatives never trusted Crist, who is now a House Democratic member. His embrace of President Barack Obama's $787 billion economic stimulus bill — and his literal embrace of the president at a public event — infuriated many. Rubio announced his bid in May 2009 and received early support from then-Sen. Jim DeMint of South Carolina, a conservative stalwart who was backing insurgent GOP candidates, as well as quiet support from Bush and his allies. By the time Crist realized the conservative base was slipping away, it was too late. On the verge of losing the primary in the spring of 2010, Crist quit the Republican Party to run as an independent.

In the general election, Rubio faced Crist and the Democratic nominee, Rep. Kendrick Meek. Crist started off with an early lead in the polls, but his support plummeted as he got caught in the crossfire from Rubio on the right and Meek on the left, both of whom painted Crist as an opportunist. Crist tried to become the de facto Democratic candidate, but Meek refused to drop out, denying Crist a one-on-one matchup with Rubio. Tea party activists embraced Rubio's campaign and slogan "Reclaim America," but Rubio was careful not to come off as a firebrand, like some of the movement's other stars. He stressed fiscal responsibility, opposed abortion rights and took a more conservative position than Crist on immigration, supporting Arizona's crackdown on undocumented immigrants. Rubio won the race with 49 percent of the vote; Crist took 30 percent and Meek 20 percent.

In the Senate, Rubio's voting pattern initially kept the tea party happy. He was one of just eight senators to oppose the New Year's Day 2013 fiscal cliff deal.

At party elders' urging, Rubio sought to offer his party a lifeline on immigration to bolster its low standing among Hispanic-Americans. He attempted to craft a compromise to the stalled DREAM Act aimed at helping undocumented immigrants brought to the U.S. as children. His alternative called for extending legal residency to immigrants bound for college or the military. The proposal came under sharp attack from the right, and he sought to characterize it as being less about immigration and more about humanitarian relief for a group facing deportation. But Rubio's political momentum ended in 2011 when Obama used his executive powers to put into place the major elements of Rubio's bill, leaving the senator grumbling that he deserved some of the credit.

With the 2012 presidential campaign looming, Rubio — after vowing to remain neutral during the primary season — endorsed former Massachusetts Gov. Mitt Romney and came to Romney's aid on immigration. Romney had Rubio on his running-mate shortlist before picking Wisconsin Rep. Paul Ryan. The speculation benefited the senator, elevating his national profile while leaving him a safe political distance from a candidate many conservatives considered inauthentic. Rubio introduced Romney at the Republican National Convention in Tampa. His speech drew widespread praise, with some pundits deeming it the best of the convention.

Buzz about a 2016 Rubio presidential run began after Obama's re-election. He did little to tamp it down, giving several policy-oriented speeches, including one in which he mentioned the phrase "middleclass" nearly three dozen times while discussing the need to close "the opportunity gap." As income inequality became an increasingly prominent issue, Rubio worked to come up with a conservative answer, focusing on college affordability. He was chosen to give the Republican response to Obama's State of the Union address. That didn't go well, as Rubio's dry-mouthed struggle through the first half of the speech and a frantic dive for a water bottle drew more attention than anything he said.

After hesitating, Rubio joined what became known as the "Gang of Eight" negotiations on immigration. The group produced a comprehensive bipartisan bill to tighten border security while creating an eventual path to citizenship for many undocumented immigrants. The legislation passed the Senate by a wide margin in 2013, but House GOP leaders refused to take it up. Rubio got some praise from donors and establishment figures, but faced severe blowback from his former tea party allies. Right-wing radio turned on its onetime hero, and Rubio, who had been leading some early 2016 presidential polls, saw his stock plummet. He retreated to his original stance on immigration, telling a crowd at the 2015 Conservative Political Action Conference that he had learned voters would not approve a pathway to citizenship until it's "proven to them that future illegal immigration will be controlled" — and that immigration reform should be done in a piecemeal fashion, with border security first.

Rubio's impatience with the Senate became visible. "I don't know that 'hate' is the right word," Rubio told The Washington Post about the chamber in 2015. "I'm frustrated."

Rubio announced his presidential bid in April 2015, seeking to draw a contrast with both Bush and former Secretary of State Hillary Clinton, the Democratic front-runner. "This election is a generational choice about what kind of country we will be," Rubio said in his announcement speech. As the campaign heated up, he sought to further distance himself from his past immigration work, accusing one rival, Texas Sen. Ted Cruz, of being weak on immigration. But Rubio's attack backfired: The target was a Cruz amendment that had been a ploy to sink the bill by taking a pathway to citizenship off the table. Even critics of Cruz suggested that Rubio's attacks were disingenuous.

Rubio finished third in the first-in-the-nation Iowa caucuses in early February 2016, and rolled into New Hampshire with a head of steam. But his campaign came apart on the debate stage a few days later and he never recovered. As New Jersey Gov. Chris Christie badgered him for repeating a "memorized 25-second speech," Rubio lost his usual oratorical command, proving Christie's point by repeating talking points over and over. Rubio finished fifth in New Hampshire. He was more steady in later debates and finished second in two other early primary states, South Carolina and Nevada. But Rubio still trailed Trump and knew he needed to shake things up to prevail in his must-win home state primary. Rubio tried to match insults with the front-running Trump, a move he later said he regretted. After mocking Trump's appearance, orange skin and small hands, he moved to another body part: "You know what they say about guys with small hands," Rubio snickered. Trump, master of the snide nickname, later derided Rubio as "Little Marco" in a debate 10 days before their showdown in Florida.

Trump won that primary by a landslide, 46%-27%, carrying 66 of 67 counties. Some suggested the loss, which forced Rubio's withdrawal from the presidential race, was a byproduct of Rubio burning too many bridges at home. "He is extremely skilled and ambitious. He is also extremely not loyal," Tony DiMatteo, a Tampa area GOP leader who helped Rubio launch his 2010 Senate bid, told the Tampa Bay Times. Others attributed Rubio's demise to failing to build on the optimistic, forward-looking persona that had gotten him elected to the Senate six years earlier. Rubio himself argued his downfall came from factors outside of his control — an upbeat message at odds with the angry mood of many in the electorate. "America is in the middle of a real political storm, a real tsunami, and we should have seen this coming," Rubio told Real Clear Politics. "Look, people are angry, and people are very frustrated." But Rubio's series of strategic missteps, particularly on immigration, and his inability to go toe-to-toe with Christie, much less Trump, also were key factors in his loss.

Rubio swore time and again that he was done with the Senate even if his presidential campaign came up short: "I have only said like 10,000 times I will be a private citizen in January," he said in a May 2016 tweet. But by the end of June, he was a candidate for re-election — prodded both by fears among Republican leaders that the seat was in jeopardy without him in the race and his own hope of remaining relevant on the national political scene. He promised to be a check on Trump should they both win: "We will need senators willing to encourage him in the right direction, and if necessary, stand up to him. I've proven a willingness to do both," he said as he announced his Senate run. Florida's lieutenant governor and two members of Congress bowed out of the GOP Senate race, and Rubio won the August primary with 72 percent of the vote.

A victory in November wasn't a sure bet in a state where Clinton was ahead in many polls and national Democratic leaders had lined up behind two-term Rep. Patrick Murphy. Murphy, borrowing a page from some of Rubio's presidential rivals, raised the issue of the incumbent's high Senate absenteeism rate. The Democrat also sought to tie Rubio to Trump at every turn. But the 33-year-old Murphy was hit with media reports showing that he had overstated his resume. Rubio had a big edge in campaign spending: In the closing weeks of the campaign, as they concluded that Murphy had no path to victory, national Democratic groups pulled back on Florida ad buys to concentrate on less expensive media markets in other states. Rubio won 52%-44%, as Trump bested Clinton in the state 49%-48%. Exit polls showed Rubio, who had tepidly endorsed Trump just before the Republican convention in July, running several points ahead of Trump among women and independent voters, while outdistancing Trump by double digits among Latinos.

Returning to Washington, Rubio refocused on the Foreign Relations Committee. With Trump entering the White House, Rubio signaled that he would continue calling for a more muscular, interventionist America. He teamed with Democratic Sen. Ed Markey of Massachusetts to urge the new president to strengthen the system of longstanding U.S. strategic alliances — notably NATO, the subject of several skeptical comments by Trump. "I'm prepared to be a senator that will encourage him to make the right decisions, but also stand up to the bad decisions and the bad policies if he's elected president," Rubio said of Trump.

For a time, it appeared Rubio might be derail the confirmation of Trump's first secretary of State, Rex Tillerson — the former Exxon Mobil chief executive known for his close relationship with Russian President Vladimir Putin. Rubio, who had characterized Putin as a "gangster" and "thug" during the presidential campaign, expressed "serious concerns" about Tillerson and grilled the nominee during hearings. Hours before the committee vote, Rubio backed away from a confrontation with his erstwhile rival for the White House and announced he'd back Tillerson.

That was not the only time Rubio threatened to take on Trump before backing down. He warned he might oppose Trump's pick to head NASA, Oklahoma Rep. Jim Bridenstine, because he wanted a nonpolitician to lead a program that is a major job creator in Florida's Space Coast region. Rubio relented after Bridenstine promised he'd run the agency in a nonpolitical way, casting the deciding vote for confirmation.

Rubio also backed Trump's trade war with China, after earlier criticizing Trump for not being aggressive enough. — a newly aggressive stance for Rubio towards the country, and one that largely comports with Trump's views. In doing so, he took a Trumpian tone on Twitter: "Sadly #China is out-negotiating the administration & winning the trade talks right now," he tweeted in May 2018. "This is #NotWinning."

But Rubio remained consistent on some key foreign policy priorities that have long driven his worldview, refusing to join other Republican lawmakers who defended Trump at all costs. Rubio, a member of the Senate Intelligence Committee, defended special counsel Robert Mueller's investigation into whether Russia had colluded with Trump's presidential campaign. Rubio's campaign had been targeted by Russian agents during the 2016 primary, according to Mueller's probe. He's repeatedly voted for sanctions on Russia and introduced legislation that would automatically trigger sanctions on countries that the director of national intelligence determined had attempted to interfere in elections. In early 2019, Rubio was one of 11 GOP senators to break with Trump and vote with Democrats in an unsuccessful push to keep sanctions in place on an influential Russian oligarch with close ties to Putin.

Rubio sought to co-opt some of Trump's rhetoric, calling for a "new nationalism" in a 2018 speech. And he continued to look for new GOP-friendly policies to help low-income Americans and address his longtime concerns with income inequality. He worked with Ivanka Trump to develop paid family-leave legislation. He pushed Republicans to increase the expanded child tax credits for the working poor in the GOP's tax overhaul, threatening to vote against the bill if the credits weren't increased. He voted for the final package that included large tax cuts for corporations and wealthy Americans after GOP leaders increased the tax credit to $1,400 from a proposed $1,100 per family.

Rubio said the balancing act between party loyalty and standing up to Trump when necessary could be difficult, but said it was necessary for him to be an effective legislator.

"Yes, there are issues that will cross the line, and you've got to speak out. But you've also got a job to do on a regular basis, and it's just that if we spend all day just responding to the daily outrage cycle, we don't have time to do the rest of our job. And so, everyone's found a different way forward. I found, if there are lines that are crossed, I'm going to speak out strongly," he told The New Yorker in 2018.

His cautious approach toward Trump has occasionally paid off. Rubio persuaded him to reverse Obama-era policies opening up trade and travel with Cuba and played a role in pushing Trump toward more hard-line policies toward Venezuela.

Rick Scott (R)

Elected 2018, term expires 2024, 1st term, b. Dec 01, 1952; Bloomington, IL; University of Missouri, B.S., 1975; Southern Methodist University Law School (TX), J.D., 1978; Christian Church; Married (Ann Scott); 2 children; 6 grandchildren.

Military Career: U.S. Navy 1970-1972

Elected Office: FL Governor, 2011-2018.

Professional Career: Columbia Hospital Corporation of America, Co-Founder, Chief Executive Officer, and President 1987-1997; Attorney.

DC Office: 716 HSOB 20510, 202-224-5274, rickscott.senate.gov

State Offices: Tallahassee, 850-942-8415; Tampa, 813-225-7040.

Committees: *Aging. Armed Services*: Airland; Cybersecurity; Personnel. *Budget. Commerce, Science & Transportation*: Communications, Technology, Innovation & the Internet; Subcommittee on Science, Oceans, Fisheries & Weather; Subcommittee on Security; Subcommittee on Transportation & Safety. *Homeland Security & Government Affairs*: Federal Spending Oversight & Emergency Management; Regulatory Affairs & Federal Management.

Election Results

Election	Name (Party)	Vote (%)	Cand. Spent	Ind. Exp. Support	Ind. Exp. Oppose
2018 General	Rick Scott (R)................................. 4,099,505	(50%)	$83,029,150	$554,877	$35,696,033
	Bill Nelson (D).............................. 4,089,472	(50%)	$29,774,682	$19,150,229	$31,760,801
2018 Primary	Rick Scott (R)................................. 1,456,187	(89%)			
	Roque De La Fuente (R)............. 187,209	(11%)			

Prior winning percentages: Governor: 2014 (48%), 2010 (49%)

Republican Rick Scott, a conservative former health care CEO, has used his huge personal fortune and hard-driving personality to win three close statewide races, proving to be a tough and resilient politician in America's ultimate swing state, even as his aloof style has made him enemies in both parties. The former Florida governor moved to the Senate in 2019 by grinding out a close victory, his third straight win with less than 51 percent of the vote.

Scott grew up in Kansas City, Mo., the son of a truck driver and a JCPenney clerk. He enlisted in the Navy after one year of community college. After his military service, Scott enrolled in the University of Missouri-Kansas City and, displaying an early entrepreneurial streak, financed his education by buying two doughnut shops and hiring his mother to manage them. After graduating, he earned a law degree from Southern Methodist University and joined a large firm, where he specialized in health care mergers and acquisitions.

In 1987, Scott put together a $6 billion bid to purchase HCA, a hospital company founded by the father and brother of former Tennessee GOP Sen. Bill Frist. When that offer was rejected, he and Texas billionaire Richard Rainwater launched their own hospital company, Columbia, in 1988. That company expanded, buying dozens of hospitals in the next decade, and in 1994 Scott bought HCA on his second attempt.

By 1997, Columbia/HCA was the nation's largest health care company and its seventh largest employer, with 340 hospitals, $20 billion in revenue and 285,000 employees. But the FBI began investigating whether Columbia/HCA had overbilled Medicare and Medicaid, twice raiding the firm's hospitals. The board of directors ousted Scott, who wanted to fight the FBI's accusations rather than settling, shortly after the second raid. The firm pleaded guilty to several federal fraud charges in 2000 and 2002 settlements and paid $1.7 billion in fines — at the time, the largest health care fraud fine in U.S. history. Scott invoked his Fifth Amendment right against self-incrimination 75 times rather than answer questions during a related deposition — a spectacle that came to haunt his future campaigns. His business associates told The New York Times at the time that Scott was a brilliant and incisive businessman who was undone by his fatal flaws, including arrogance and aggressiveness that had permeated the company. Scott would later display both those traits in his political career.

Scott left Columbia/HCA with $10 million in cash and $300 million in stock and options. In rehabilitating his image, Scott maintained that he was never charged with wrongdoing. "I learned very hard lessons from what happened, and those lessons have helped me become a better businessman and leader," he said. Scott later bought control of America's Health Network cable channel and in 2001 co-founded Solantic, which operates walk-in urgent care centers throughout Florida and specializes in patients without insurance. He moved to Naples in 2003.

As the national political conversation turned to health care during the early Obama years, Scott showed an increased interest in politics. In early 2009, he spent $5 million on TV ads attacking Democrats' health insurance reform proposals, particularly a provision creating a government-financed insurance option. A month after the Affordable Care Act became law in 2010, Scott launched his campaign for governor, immediately dropping another $5 million on ads.

The early GOP front-runner and establishment favorite was Attorney General Bill McCollum, a former House member and the 2000 GOP Senate nominee. Scott unveiled a catchy economic plan with seven steps to create 700,000 jobs in seven years, by cutting corporate and property taxes, reducing public payroll and streamlining government agencies. The two engaged in an intense TV ad war, with Scott painting McCollum as a tax-and-spend career politician and McCollum highlighting Columbia/HCA's Medicare fraud settlements. Scott spent nearly $50 million of his own money on the primary, edging McCollum, 46%-44%.

Scott's opponent in the general election was Florida Chief Financial Officer Alex Sink, a moderate former banker. The general election continued in an acrimonious vein, as Democratic ads revived the Columbia/HCA case and Republican ads painted Sink as a "Tallahassee insider" and a supporter of President Barack Obama, who was toxic in that year's midterm elections. Scott prevailed, 49%-48%, boosted by his huge campaign spending: $83 million, $73 million of which came from his own pocket. He carried Hispanics by a narrow margin and had a big lead among Cuban voters, according to exit polls.

Scott took an conservative approach, cutting the state budget by $1.3 billion and vetoing bills totaling a record $615 million, moves that thrilled tea partiers but enraged some of the GOP lawmakers whose earmarks for local projects were axed. Scott took on teachers unions, signing education bills that expanded school voucher funding and increased charter school enrollment. He rejected $2.4 billion in federal transportation funds for a high-speed train line between Tampa and Orlando, claiming Florida taxpayers would have to pay for part of the project. The project had been in the works for years, and legislators from both parties criticized Scott's decision.

Scott enraged Democrats by requiring welfare recipients to take drug tests. The law proved popular with conservatives in other states, but was struck down by a federal judge. Scott signed a bill cracking down on companies dealing with Cuba and Syria, but infuriated many in the Cuban-American community by issuing a statement complaining that the law was unenforceable without support from the federal government. That earned a rebuke from Sen. Marco Rubio, who said Scott had undermined the new policy — one of many disputes between the two Florida Republicans over the years.

Scott shifted to the center as he prepared for re-election, looking to shed his tea party image and recast himself as an education champion. In 2014, he signed a record $77 billion budget that increased funding for public schools, universities, child protection services and the environment. After vetoing a bill in 2013 that would have allowed undocumented Florida residents to apply for a temporary driver's licenses, he signed legislation providing in-state college tuition to them in 2014, angering immigration hard-liners.

Scott's brash manner, combined with a sluggish economic recovery, kept his poll numbers low. The governor's vulnerability inspired former Republican Gov. Charlie Crist to make a comeback, this time as a Democrat. Crist scolded Scott for cutting education and restricting abortion and vowed to raise the minimum wage. Scott promised to pump money into education, environmental protection, airports and seaport infrastructure and to cut taxes by up to $1 billion while maintaining his focus on creating jobs. In one bizarre episode, Scott refused to go on stage at a televised debate because Crist had a portable fan beneath his podium, arguing it violated debate rules. He relented only after several minutes of live TV with only Crist onstage, a moment that turned into fodder for late-night comedians.

Scott defeated Crist, 48%-47%, bolstered by another GOP midterm wave. Scott once again spent a fortune, including more than $12 million in the race's closing days. Crist was better-funded than Sink but was still badly outspent. Scott didn't perform as strongly with Hispanic voters as he had before, losing the statewide Hispanic vote by a wide margin and narrowly losing the Cuban vote. But he spurred huge turnout in GOP-heavy communities.

Scott began his second term with a $1 billion state surplus, which he planned to use on increased education spending and tax cuts. But he committed some self-inflicted wounds. Scott forced out the widely respected commissioner of the Florida Department of Law Enforcement, Gerald Bailey, and had to backtrack from a claim that Bailey had resigned on his own. Bailey accused Scott's office of frequently meddling in the department's work, including requests to run interference in a federal money laundering probe of a GOP donor and falsely implicate an Orange County clerk in an investigation of a prison release scandal. Scott denied Bailey's allegations.

Scott was criticized from all sides for waffling on Medicaid expansion. The governor had long opposed it, arguing the state would have to pick up more of the costs once the federal government reduced its subsidies. But he reversed course after Obama won the state a second time in 2012, saying his change of heart had come after his mother died in an intensive care unit in late 2012, calling it a "compassionate, common-sense step forward." But he didn't push the idea aggressively in the face of a hostile Republican-controlled Legislature. He reversed himself again in 2015. A Centers for Medicare and Medicaid Services decision not to renew a Medicaid waiver spurred state Senate Republicans to embrace Medicaid expansion, but the more conservative Florida House refused, leading to a intraparty budget impasse. Scott, after failing to persuade federal officials to extend the state's Medicaid waiver, announced he couldn't support Medicaid expansion. Republicans of all stripes criticized his handling of the budget impasse, while Democrats howled that he'd once again deprived 660,000 Floridians of health insurance.

Disasters, both natural and man-made, made their mark in 2016. Florida grappled with the threat of Zika virus. Scott declared a state of emergency, called for more federal assistance and offered free testing for pregnant women, who were at highest risk. Little noticed: Five years earlier, Scott and lawmakers had slashed the state's mosquito-control budget. In June, an ISIS-inspired gunman killed 49 and injured 53 at Pulse, a LGBTQ nightclub in Orlando. That October, Hurricane Matthew wracked the Atlantic Coast, ending a decade without a significant hurricane in the state. Scott was praised for his response, though the courts rebuked him for refusing to extend the state's voter-registration deadline because of the storm. Ultimately, an estimated 100,000 more voters registered for the general election, thanks to the court-ordered extension.

The other big story of 2016, of course, was Donald Trump. Scott was officially neutral during the Florida primary, but he wrote an op-ed favorable to Trump in USA Today in early January — long before it was clear Trump would be the nominee. The move was a slight to Rubio, the latest escalation in their tensions. After Trump won the Florida primary, Scott endorsed him. He was named national chairman of the pro-Trump Rebuilding America Now super PAC and worked hard to elect his fellow billionaire businessman. Trump carried Florida by a narrow margin.

Scott began the Trump presidency with close ties to the White House and a goal to stay in national politics by running against longtime Democratic Sen. Bill Nelson. The race would prove to be Scott's most challenging. Unlike in his first two victories, he ran with the wind in his face. He also faced a more popular opponent than his previous two: Nelson's sunny personality contrasted with Scott's lack of charisma, though Nelson's popularity would prove relatively shallow as the campaign wore on. Throughout the campaign, Trump made moves that alienated key voting blocs in the state while infuriating Democrats.

Scott had a few advantages, as well. One was obvious: His immense wealth allowed him to deluge the airwaves throughout the race. Scott's campaign apparatus was in top shape from the start, partly from the huge amount of money he had spent on field efforts over the years. Scott also began the race with much higher name recognition than Nelson, and with the highest approval ratings of his career. The month Scott launched his campaign, a Morning Consult poll said he had a 55 percent approval rating.

Scott knew he was in for a tough fight from the beginning, while Nelson seemed much slower on the uptake. Nelson hadn't faced a tough election fight since his first Senate win in 2000, and never fully seemed to grasp the workings of a modern campaign. He didn't hire a campaign manager until March 2018, months after Scott had put his team in place, and throughout the campaign seemed reluctant to go on the attack, to the chagrin of his Democratic allies.

As often happens in Florida, natural disasters played a major role in the campaign. Scott initially got positive headlines for his handling of Hurricane Irma, a major storm that hit the state in 2017. But he later faced questions on why he had not responded to pleas for help from a Hollywood Hills nursing home where 12 people died of heat-related causes and whether he had wasted taxpayers' money with unnecessary emergency contracts.

Scott's handling of a major outbreak of a "red tide" algae bloom on both the Atlantic and Gulf coasts and other toxic algae blooms around the state in late 2018 didn't go well. The outbreaks killed wildlife and closed beaches up and down the coasts. Nelson's allies dubbed him "Red Tide Rick" in a series of attacks, blaming his moves to cut various environmental regulations for the severity of the outbreak.

The storm that may have had the biggest political effect hit hundreds of miles off Florida's coast. Hurricane Maria devastated Puerto Rico in late 2017, killing roughly 3,000 people and forcing hundreds of thousands to flee the island, many resettling in Florida. Scott reached out to welcome the new residents and prove he was responding well to the crisis, even as the Trump administration bungled its response. He visited Puerto Rico eight times after the hurricane, courted Puerto Rican voters living in the state and rejected Trump's claim that the death count had been inflated by Democrats and local officials to make the president look bad.

That fit the pattern of Scott's hard work with various Hispanic communities. He took Spanish lessons as governor and was a regular at various Cuban, Colombian, Venezuelan, Dominican and Puerto Rican events across Florida. Nelson put in nowhere near that effort. That may have been the difference, as exit polls showed Scott won about 45 percent of the Hispanic vote, an increase over his 2014 performance and especially impressive considering how Trump had alienated those communities.

Gun violence pushed its way into the campaign. A shooting at a Parkland high school in February 2018 left 17 students dead and had become the deadliest school shooting in U.S. history and the third mass shooting in Florida in as many years, after massacres at the Orlando nightclub and Ford Lauderdale airport. The rampage triggered massive protests and put huge pressure on the pro-gun Scott. It gave Nelson a chance to hammer Scott. At a CNN town hall shortly after the shooting, Nelson attacked the governor for refusing to act on the issue and contrasted Scott's refusal to attend an event with students with Rubio's attendance. The two senators had a strong bipartisan friendship, and Rubio seemed happy to let Nelson draw that contrast. Scott responded by backing legislation that increased from 18 to 21 the minimum age at which one can buy a rifle and created three-day waiting periods for long-gun purchases. The law was the first new gun control measure in the state in two decades and gave Scott bipartisan credibility on the issue even as it angered some in his base. That was not Scott's only pivot to the center during the campaign: Reversing his former position, he split with Trump to oppose offshore drilling along Florida's coast. Until late in the campaign, he declined to appear with the president when Trump campaigned in the state.

Scott spent tens of millions on TV ads over the spring and summer — while Nelson was silent — and built a small but steady lead in public polling. National Democratic groups responded in midsummer and Nelson went on the air not long after that, and by mid-September appeared to have reversed the tide of the race, pulling into a small lead in most public polls that held through Election Day.

Scott's campaign howled that the public polls were wrong. Election night proved them right. Scott emerged with a narrow win. But the contest ended in uncertainty as lawyers rushed in for a statewide recount. Just like in the 2000 presidential recount, legal fights centered around ballot-design problems in Democratic-heavy Broward County. Because of a flaw, the Senate race was not listed prominently on ballots. There was a significantly larger drop in Senate votes in Broward than anywhere else in the state, likely enough to have cost Nelson his seat. Nelson's attorneys subsequently battled the Broward result in the courts, but ran out of options after 12 days, and Nelson conceded.

Scott spent almost $64 million of his own money on the race and his campaign outspent Nelson by 3 to 1, though national Democratic groups tightened that gap. More than $200 million was spent, making it the most expensive Senate campaign in history.

Scott's final margin of victory was just over 10,000 votes out of more than 8 million cast. He was the only GOP Senate candidate in a state Trump won by less than 18 percentage points to defeat a Democratic incumbent. His margin of victory was about 1 percentage point below Trump's, making him the only Republican Senate candidate in a competitive race who came close to Trump's 2016 percentage and showing that Florida remains deeply — if closely — divided along partisan lines.

Scott was sworn in to the Senate a few days after the rest of his colleagues. He made 70 last-minute appointments in a move that infuriated his successor, Republican Ron DeSantis. Scott, never short on ambition, is viewed as a potential 2024 presidential candidate.

Matt Gaetz (R)

Elected 2016, 2nd term, b. May 07, 1982; Hollywood; Florida State University, B.S., 2003; College of William and Mary - Marshall-Wythe Law School (VA), J.D., 2007; Baptist.

Elected Office: FL Senate, 2010-2016.

Professional Career: Practicing attorney.

DC Office: 1721 LHOB 20515, 202-225-4136, Fax: 202-225-3414, gaetz.house.gov

State Offices: Fort Walton Beach, 850-479-1183; Pensacola, 850-479-1183.

Committees: *Armed Services*: Military Personnel; Tactical Air & Land Forces. *Judiciary*: Antitrust, Commercial & Administrative Law; Courts, Intellectual Property & Internet.

Group Ratings

	ADA	ACLU	AFL-CIO	LCV	ITI	COC	HAFA	ACU	CFG	FRC
2018	-	9%	-	9%	-	70%	76%	89%	80%	100%
2017	5%	C	13%	6%	C	93%	C	93%	90%	100%

Almanac Ratings 2017-18

	Economy	Social	Foreign	Composite
Liberal	10%	7%	0%	6%
Conservative	90%	94%	100%	94%

Key Votes of the 115th Congress

1. Obama-care revision	Y	5. Family planning regs	Y	9. Guantanamo prisoners	N
2. Tax Cuts	Y	6. Body cameras/immigration	N	10. Ground missiles, limit	N
3. Omnibus appropriations	N	7. Abortion ban	Y	11. Defense Dept. spending	Y
4. Dodd-Frank revision	Y	8. Concealed carry	Y	12. FISA rules	Y

Election Results

Election	Name (Party)	Vote (%)		Cand. Spent	Ind. Exp. Support	Ind. Exp. Oppose
2018 General	Matt Gaetz (R)	216,189	(67%)	$1,041,625	$44,700	$7,500
	Jennifer Zimmerman (D)	106,199	(33%)	$49,943		
2018 Primary	Matt Gaetz (R)	65,169	(65%)			
	Cris Dosev (R)	30,433	(30%)			
	John Mills (R)	4,992	(5%)			

Prior winning percentages: 2016 (69%)

Republican Matt Gaetz was elected in 2016 to a solidly Republican open seat with superior fundraising and his conservative appeal. He focused on the military interests of his district. His House career took an unexpected turn when he became an outspoken public defender of President Donald Trump and a critic of his accusers, making frequent television appearances.

A Florida native, Gaetz graduated from Florida State University and got his law degree from the College of William and Mary in Virginia. After briefly practicing law with a firm in Fort Walton Beach, he ran in 2010 for an open seat in the state House. He was unopposed that year and in his two reelections. He chaired the House Finance and Tax Committee, where he was an enthusiastic supporter of tax cuts. As a social conservative, he sought to expand the pro-gun "Stand Your Ground" law. The American Conservative Union gave him its "Defender of Liberty" award.

Before Rep. Jeff Miller announced his retirement, Gaetz had been planning to run for the seat in the state Senate that had been held by his influential father, Senate President Don Gaetz, who was retiring. After the two had a heart-to-heart talk, his father told the Pensacola News Journal, "Matt said he didn't like anything that was happening in Washington, and I said, 'Well, Matt, maybe you should go there and do something about it.'" His son was the first to enter the contest.

In the Republican primary, Sen. Greg Evers led in an early poll and had higher favorability scores than Gaetz. Evers gained national attention when he raffled off a semi-automatic rifle among people in the district who "liked" his Facebook page. He explained that he was trying to highlight the importance of the right to bear arms during a time of rising terrorism. Gaetz drew attention when he said that the Black Lives Matter group was "a terrorist organization," and he criticized Evers for voting to expand Medicaid. Gaetz opposed cuts in the military, which were detrimental to the district. "When the Pentagon gets a cold, we get the flu," he said. Gaetz's advertising called him "the most conservative" candidate. A late-filing candidate was Cris Dosev, a self-financing Pensacola businessman and political newcomer. Gaetz spent $1.1 million, which exceeded the total for his opponents. Gaetz won the seven-candidate primary with 36 percent of the vote to 22 percent for Evers and 21 percent for Dosev. In the general election, Steven Specht, an Air Force veteran, spent $54,000 and attracted scant public attention. Gaetz won, 69%-31%. .

In the House, he got useful assignments on the Armed Services and Judiciary committees. With Democratic Rep. Seth Moulton of Massachusetts, Gaetz filed legislation to modify medical marijuana practices of the Veterans Affairs Department so that cannabis would be a more realistic treatment option for veterans, as an alternative to opioids and other addictive painkillers. The action was supported by the American Legion.

By the end of 2017, Gaetz had become a tireless defender of Trump. His efforts began that November when he filed a House resolution to force special counsel Robert Mueller to resign because of his alleged conflicts of interest. By January, Gaetz sought to declassify a House Republican memo alleging investigative abuses by the FBI. That led Trump to make regular phone calls to Gaetz. "I think it's because I defend him on television," Gaetz told BuzzFeed. Asked by a reporter whether he might be gaining notoriety rather than star power, he responded, "What's the difference?" He added in the interview, "I was tired of the Democrats being the only team playing offense."

The reaction was not entirely positive, even among Republicans. GOP political strategist Rick Wilson, a critic of Trump, wrote that Gaetz and his allies had worked Trump, "playing to his vanity, giving Fox News the kind of talking head action money can't buy." Salon, a liberal website, depicted Gaetz as "Fox's answer to Joe Scarborough," the liberal commentator on MSNBC who, ironically, held Gaetz's House seat as a Republican in the 1990s.

At home, Gaetz faced another GOP primary challenge from Dosev. Trump tweeted his endorsement of Gaetz as "one of the finest and most talented people in Congress." He again won easily, 65%-30%; in November, he won, 67%-33%. Following the election, Gaetz was one of four co-chairs of the transition committee for Gov. Ron DeSantis. In April 2019, he dismissed on-line speculation that he was contemplating an unusual move to run for a Senate seat across the state line in Alabama, though he conceded that he "may have mentioned" the possibility to others.

FL-1: Western Panhandle   Cook Partisan Voting Index: R+22

Population		Race and Ethnicity		Income	
Total	748,579	White	73.5%	Median Income	$53,480
Land area (sq. miles)	4,016	Black	13.2%	District Income Rank	246
Pop/ sq mi	186.4	Latino	6.3%	Poverty Rate	13.3%
Born in State	39.2%	Asian	2.5%	With health insurance	87.6%
		Two or more races	3.9%	Cash public assistance	1.8%
Age Groups		Other	0.7%	Food stamp/SNAP	12.5%
Under 18	21.6%				
18-34	24.5%	**Education**		**Work**	
35-64	38.1%	H.S grad or less	36.6%	White Collar	15.8%
Over 64	15.8%	Some college	36.2%	Sales and Service	46.7%
		College Degree, 4 yr	17.6%	Blue Collar	18.7%
Military		Post grad	9.4%	Government	16.7%
Veteran/ Active Duty	20.7%				

2012 Pres. Vote	Romney	242,942	(69%)	Obama	106,810	(30%)		
2016 Pres. Vote	Trump	256,609	(67%)	Clinton	107,063	(28%)	Johnson	12,770	(3%)

Pensacola, Fort Walton: The "Redneck Riviera" is the affectionate local name for the Gulf Coast beaches of Florida's Emerald Coast, stretching from Pensacola east to Destin. This has been military country since John Quincy Adams persuaded Spain to sell Florida to the United States in 1819, with the goal of gaining control of the port of Pensacola on the Gulf of Mexico. In October

1861, the Union defeated the Confederates in a battle to control Santa Rosa Island, the outermost spit of land protecting Pensacola Bay. In the 20th century, the Pensacola Naval Air Station was turned into the nation's first naval-aviation training base, giving birth to carrier aviation. About 17,000 people — close to half of them active-duty military — are employed at Eglin Air Force Base, which spreads over three counties. With approximately 100,000 square miles of airspace stretching over the Gulf to the Florida Keys, Eglin is considered the largest air base in the free world. It has been the Air Force center for the development, acquisition, testing, deployment and sustainment of all air-delivered weapons, including the F-35 Joint Strike Fighter.

The western panhandle of Florida is culturally part of Dixie and lies closer to Houston than to Miami. A columnist for the Pensacola News Journal once recommended the creation of an independent commonwealth of West Florida. "We don't have much in common with the people inhabiting what I call peninsular Florida," wrote Jerry Maygarden. "I'm convinced that the further south you drive, the further north you get." Until recently, the panhandle was heavily dependent on the military and had little of its own economy. But as the South has become more prosperous, the shore has attracted vacationing and retiring southerners to its vast, fine-grained, white sand beaches and its pleasant, inlet-dotted bays. It has become a leading spring break destination for sometimes-rowdy college students and the site of a large annual gay Memorial Day weekend party.

The economy in the Pensacola area has been strong. In August 2017, the Gulf Power utility completed work on a giant solar project at Eglin and two other military facilities on the panhandle, with 120 megawatts that could power 18,000 homes. In June 2018, a $46 million aerospace facility to maintain, repair and overhaul aircraft from around the world began operations at Pensacola Airport. A month later, the airport authority agreed to expand that operation, which could yield an additional 1,700 jobs.

The 1st Congressional District of Florida runs from Pensacola, adjoining the Alabama border, through Fort Walton Beach and Destin to Santa Rosa Beach. It is so far west it is in the Central time zone. Inland, the 1st takes in rural Walton and Holmes counties. With 41 percent in Pensacola-based Escambia County, the district population has grown steadily. Young civilians, as well as military retirees, have settled here and raised education and quality-of-life issues. The region has long been culturally and economically conservative, with a strong pro-military bent. Donald Trump had his best Florida showing in the district, with a 68%-28% win.

Neal Dunn (R)

Elected 2016, 2nd term, b. Feb 16, 1953; New Haven, CT; Washington and Lee University (VA), Bach. Deg.; George Washington University Medical School (DC), M.D.; Catholic; Married (Leah Dunn); 3 children; 3 grandchildren.

Military Career: U.S. Army 1989-2001

Professional Career: Urologist; Banker.

DC Office: 316 CHOB 20515, 202-225-5235, Fax: 202-225-5615, dunn.house.gov

State Offices: Panama City, 850-785-0812; Tallahassee, 850-891-8610.

Committees: *Agriculture*: Biotechnology, Horticulture & Research (RMM); Commodity Exchanges, Energy & Credit. *Veterans' Affairs*: Health (RMM).

Group Ratings

	ADA	ACLU	AFL-CIO	LCV	ITI	COC	HAFA	ACU	CFG	FRC
2018	-	4%	-	0%	-	92%	71%	80%	54%	100%
2017	0%	C	11%	3%	C	93%	C	84%	82%	100%

Almanac Ratings 2017-18

	Economy	Social	Foreign	Composite
Liberal	2%	0%	0%	1%
Conservative	98%	100%	100%	99%

Key Votes of the 115th Congress

1. Obama-care revision	Y	5. Family planning regs	Y	9. Guantanamo prisoners	N
2. Tax Cuts	Y	6. Body cameras/immigration	N	10. Ground missiles, limit	N
3. Omnibus appropriations	Y	7. Abortion ban	Y	11. Defense Dept. spending	Y
4. Dodd-Frank revision	Y	8. Concealed carry	Y	12. FISA rules	Y

Election Results

Election	Name (Party)	Vote (%)	Cand. Spent	Ind. Exp. Support	Ind. Exp. Oppose
2018 General	Neal Dunn (R)................................... 199,335	(67%)	$843,766		
	Bob Rackleff (D)................................ 96,233	(33%)	$256,061		
2018 Primary	Neal Dunn (R).....................................	(100%)			

Prior winning percentages: 2016 (67%)

Neal Dunn, elected in 2016, is one of several House Republicans who have been physicians. He also served in the military — a combination that left him well-suited to chair the Veterans' Affairs Subcommittee on Health for a few months, until the GOP lost House control.

Dunn was born in Boston to a military family. Growing up, he was an Eagle Scout and active in rifle competitions. He received an Army ROTC scholarship at Washington & Lee University, where he got his bachelor's degree before earning his medical degree from George Washington University. He completed his residency at Walter Reed Army Medical Center and served as an attending urologist in the Army for 11 years, before moving to Panama City, where he had his medical practice for 25 years. Dunn became the chief medical officer for the Advanced Urology Institute in North Florida. In 2014, Senate President Don Gaetz (the father of Dunn's colleague Don Gaetz in the adjacent 1st District) appointed him to the Enterprise Florida Board of Directors. Dunn was founding chairman of Summit Bank in Panama City.

When first-term Democratic Rep. Gwen Graham decided after redistricting not to seek reelection in 2016 and to focus on her run for governor in 2018, the district became a strong Republican pick-up opportunity. The two chief GOP contenders were Dunn and Mary Thomas, a Tallahassee attorney. Because Panama City-based Bay County had 50 percent more Republicans than did the parts of Tallahassee-based Leon County in the district, that gave Dunn an advantage. Former U.S. Attorney Ken Sukhia, a third GOP candidate, also was from Leon. Dunn ran as an "unapologetic conservative Republican" whose top priority was to repeal the Affordable Care Act. That objective required, he said, lawmakers "who have represented patients, not bureaucrats."

Some conservatives criticized Dunn for having made campaign contributions to Florida Democratic Senator Bill Nelson and to former Gov. Charlie Crist, who was elected to the House in 2016 as a Democrat. Thomas was backed by the conservative Club for Growth, which spent $584,000 on her behalf and called Dunn "a liberal lobbyist." Dunn spent $2 million for her his campaign, with Thomas and Sukhia spending $1.1 million and $207,000 respectively. Dunn defeated Thomas 41%-39%, a margin of 1,711 votes. Sukhia got 19 Percent. Thomas won 11 of the 19 counties. Dunn won easily in Bay County and oddly took Leon County, which the three candidates split almost evenly. In the general election, Dunn faced Walt Dartland, a former Marine Corps major and state deputy attorney general, who called himself "pretty conservative in terms of fiscal policy." Dartland spent $130,000 and was competitive only in Leon County. Dunn won, 67%-30%.

In the House, Dunn's chief legislative work was on the Veterans' Affairs Committee. President Donald Trump signed a bill with two provisions proposed by Dunn. His Veterans Increased Choice for Transplanted Organs and Recovery (Victor) measure gave veterans more choices for organ transplants. His other provision, the Veterans Opioid Abuse Prevention Act, connected VA health care providers to a national network of state-based prescription drug monitoring programs. "As a doctor and a veteran, I have met heroes who need help, but aren't finding it at the VA. We can change that," Dunn said. Following a shuffling of committee assignments in May 2018, Dunn became chairman of the panel's Health Subcommittee. He promised to assist veterans who "return from war only to find they have to fight government bureaucracy." But he lost his gavel following the elections six months later.

In October 2018, Dunn took on a new workload after Hurricane Michael devastated parts of his district. He filed bills to assure education and retirement benefits for storm victims. And he sought to expedite repairs at Tyndall Air Force Base. Following the election, he said that recovery activities would remain a priority.

Dunn had an easy reelection. He won GOP renomination without opposition and defeated Democrat Bob Rackleff, 67%-33%. A former Leon County commissioner, Rackleff took 54 percent in Leon, which cast nearly one-fourth of the total vote. Dunn won the remaining counties.

FL-2: Central Panhandle   **Cook Partisan Voting Index: R+18**

Population		Race and Ethnicity		Income	
Total	712,695	White	76.8%	Median Income	$47,146
Land area (sq. miles)	11,002	Black	12.7%	District Income Rank	350
Pop/ sq mi	64.8	Latino	6.2%	Poverty Rate	16.4%
Born in State	52.1%	Asian	1.7%	With health insurance	87.1%
		Two or more races	2%	Cash public assistance	2%
Age Groups		Other	0.6%	Food stamp/SNAP	14.7%
Under 18	20.1%				
18-34	22.1%	**Education**		**Work**	
35-64	39%	H.S grad or less	46.1%	White Collar	18.8%
Over 64	18.8%	Some college	30.6%	Sales and Service	44.7%
Military		College Degree, 4 yr	14.1%	Blue Collar	20.5%
Veteran/ Active Duty	12.8%	Post grad	9.2%	Government	23%

2012 Pres. Vote	Romney	217,045	(65%)	Obama	114,693	(34%)			
2016 Pres. Vote	Trump	234,990	(66%)	Clinton	108,636	(30%)	Johnson	8,400	(2%)

Panama City, Parts of Tallahassee: Much of northern Florida is swampy lowlands. Along the 355-mile route across the northern tier of the state from Jacksonville on the Atlantic Coast to Pensacola on the Gulf of Mexico, there are occasional small towns — some of them from the 19th century — and lots of empty land. To outsiders, this is mostly fly-over or drive-through Florida. In a few decades, perhaps this area will become a modern version of central Florida from Orlando to Tampa, or south Florida from Palm Beach to Miami.

For now, there are only two urban centers along the northern tier. By Florida standards, each is small. Tallahassee, inland from the Gulf and relatively isolated, became the state capital when Florida's then-modest population lived mostly along the state's northern tier, placing it, more or less, at its center of gravity. Ralph Waldo Emerson, visiting Tallahassee at the time, called it a "grotesque place, rapidly settled by public officers, land speculators, and desperadoes." Until fairly recently, it remained little more than a Spanish-mossed county seat with a pair of universities and a handsome Creole capitol, which was built in 1845 and preserved opposite its 1977 skyscraper replacement. Since the 1980s, it has spread out and become a middling-sized city, with a sometimes fractious political and legal elite, bringing a taste of urbanized Florida to the state's north. In 2015, the University of Toronto's Martin Prosperity Institute released a study that found Tallahassee the most segregated city in the United States in terms of economics, education and occupation. Tallahassee has not yet attained the critical mass of Sacramento, Austin or Albany — the capitals of the other largest states in the nation. But, with increased development, perhaps it is on its way. There is certainly plenty of room for physical growth.

Panama City is a very different place. What was a popular spring break destination along the state's pretty and underappreciated northwest beaches has become a growing retirement and resort area. This area had retained one of the highest percentages of native Floridians. But that is changing. The opening of an airport in 2010 near Panama City spurred development. The area has suffered several blows in recent years. In 2015, Panama City officials voted to ban alcohol on the beach during each March. In March 2016, that resulted in a 41 percent decline in the city's revenue and a $40 million hit to its economy. Local officials had some success as they sought to increase revenues from family-oriented summer vacationers. Devastation struck in October 2018 when the area was walloped by Hurricane Michael, the strongest storm ever to hit the Panhandle. In Panama City, 60 percent of the homes were destroyed — due partly to lax building codes. At Tyndall Air Force Base, 95 percent of the buildings no longer functioned. The base continued to operate, though many of those living there were in tents. Another local crisis was an opioid epidemic. In May 2018, officials in surrounding Bay County sued pharmaceutical manufacturers, with a claim of negligence — one of many such suits across the nation.

The 2nd District of Florida, the largest in the state, is an amorphous area based in Panama City plus the parts of the Tallahassee area that are not in the 5th District. The drive from Panama City at the northwest tip to Inglis in the southeast is a Texas-sized 251 miles. Redistricting changes dropped the black population in the new 2nd to 13 percent and created a solidly Republican district. As the Tallahassee Democrat newspaper aptly described in July 2016, the odd configurations of the new district lines in that city lack "common sense." Gone are the Democratic parts of Tallahassee, though the state capital remained. In their place are seven mostly rural and white counties that curve along the bend of the Gulf with mostly undeveloped beaches and move inland to the outskirts of Ocala and Gainesville. Donald Trump won this district, 66%-30%.

Ted Yoho (R)

Elected 2012, 4th term, b. Apr 13, 1955; Minneapolis, MN; Florence State University (University of North Alabama), Att.; Broward Community College (FL), A.A., 1977; University of Florida, B.S., 1979; University of Florida Veterinary College, D.V.M., 1983; Roman Catholic; Married (Carolyn Yoho); 3 children.

Professional Career: Veterinarian, 1983-present.

DC Office: 1730 LHOB 20515, 202-225-5744, Fax: 202-225-3973, yoho.house.gov

State Offices: Gainesville, 352-505-0838; Ocala, 352-390-6413; Orange Park, 904-276-9626; Palatka, 386-326-7221.

Committees: *Agriculture*: Biotechnology, Horticulture & Research; Subcommittee Nutrition, Oversight & Department Operations. *Foreign Affairs*: Asia, the Pacific & Nonproliferation (RMM); Western Hemisphere, Civilian Security, & Trade.

Group Ratings

	ADA	ACLU	AFL-CIO	LCV	ITI	COC	HAFA	ACU	CFG	FRC
2018	-	15%	-	0%	-	75%	78%	88%	82%	100%
2017	5%	C	3%	3%	C	93%	C	96%	92%	100%

Almanac Ratings 2017-18

	Economy	Social	Foreign	Composite
Liberal	2%	9%	3%	5%
Conservative	98%	91%	97%	95%

Key Votes of the 115th Congress

1. Obama-care revision	Y	5. Family planning regs	Y	9. Guantanamo prisoners	N
2. Tax Cuts	Y	6. Body cameras/immigration	N	10. Ground missiles, limit	N
3. Omnibus appropriations	N	7. Abortion ban	Y	11. Defense Dept. spending	Y
4. Dodd-Frank revision	Y	8. Concealed carry	Y	12. FISA rules	N

Election Results

Election	Name (Party)	Vote (%)		Cand. Spent	Ind. Exp. Support	Ind. Exp. Oppose
2018 General	Ted Yoho (R)	176,616	(58%)	$671,941		$10,750
	Yvonne Hayes Hinson (D)	129,880	(42%)	$55,075	$10,662	
2018 Primary	Ted Yoho (R)	54,828	(76%)			
	Judson Sapp (R)	17,059	(24%)			

Prior winning percentages: 2016 (57%), 2014 (65%), 2012 (65%)

Republican Ted Yoho, unexpectedly elected to the House in 2012 as an outsider candidate, became an active player on foreign policy issues, especially in Asia. He has participated in conservative groups among House Republicans. He said that he does not plan to seek reelection in 2020.

Yoho was born in Minneapolis, the fifth of six sons, and moved with his family at age 11 to South Florida. After a short stint at Florence State University (now the University of North Alabama) on a football scholarship, he soon returned to Florida. He married his high school sweetheart, Carolyn, and decided to become a veterinarian. The couple moved to Gainesville, where he got a bachelor's degree in animal science at the University of Florida, then graduated from its veterinary college. Yoho built a successful large-animal practice.

Over time, he got fed up with politicians who either couldn't or wouldn't fix "the mess" in Washington that many of them helped to create. He sold his veterinary practice and launched his campaign for Congress in 2012. "One political consultant told us this race would be a good 'practice run,'" he recalled. In the Republican primary, Yoho was not nearly as well-known as 12-term Rep. Cliff Stearns and state Sen. Steve Oelrich of Gainesville. Stearns had a huge cash advantage. He committed a few errors, including focusing his attention on Oelrich.

With just one paid employee, Yoho ran aggressively as a Christian (Roman Catholic) and a conservative. He emphasized his experience in running a successful small business, where he was on the receiving end of regulations and "garbage legislation" from Washington. He opposed raising taxes, but refused to sign conservative activist Grover Norquist's no-tax pledge on the grounds that a war or other events might leave few alternatives. He said he would serve no more than eight years in the House. Yoho ran a campaign ad showing suited "politicians" feeding from a pig trough. Using $50,000 of his own money, he edged out Stearns by just 875 votes, with 34 percent; Oelrich trailed with 19 percent. He had no trouble in the general election, taking 65 percent of the vote.

On his first day in office in January 2013, Yoho joined a protest by a small group of conservatives who refused to back a second term as House Speaker for John Boehner of Ohio. Instead, Yoho cast his vote for Majority Leader Eric Cantor of Virginia. During his first term, he styled himself as a tea party leader who was eager to stand up to the political establishment. He advocated the impeachment of President Barack Obama and said that voting rights should be limited to property owners. When Obama issued his executive order on immigration in 2014, Yoho introduced a bill to rescind the president's authority to stop deportations; the president's action, he later said, would open the door to chain migration into the United States.

When a floating group of House conservatives, spurred by outside groups, said they would not vote to give Boehner a third term as Speaker in 2015, Yoho was the first to volunteer as a candidate. He issued a statement, "Enough of career politicians, enough of political gamesmanship, and enough of the lack of leadership in Washington." But he failed to galvanize the opposition. Rep. Daniel Webster, another Florida Republican, later emerged and attracted 12 votes as the leading GOP alternative to Boehner. In addition to his own vote, the other Yoho supporter was Rep. Thomas Massie of Kentucky. Yoho became a founding member of the Freedom Caucus and the Second Amendment Caucus. GQ magazine ranked him among "America's 20 craziest politicians" – on a highly partisan list that included only three Democrats. Tea party advocates continued to embrace him.

In 2017, with a president of his own party, Yoho became more productive — chiefly from his perch as chairman of the Foreign Affairs Subcommittee on Asia and the Pacific. In July 2018, with Democratic Rep. Brad Sherman of California, he enacted a bill to demand accountability on human rights by North Korea. They discussed steps to strengthen sanctions against Pyongyang, but the Trump administration said that such steps were not needed. He also called for sanctions against Cambodia for its actions "undermining democracy." In October 2018, Trump signed Yoho's bill that reformed how the executive branch manages international development finances — streamlining several programs into a single finance corporation.

In 2016, Yoho was challenged by Democrat Ken McGurn, a local developer. Their spending figures were relatively close: almost $800,000 for Yoho to $600,000 for McGurn, who self-financed about half his contest. This was Yoho's most competitive campaign. He won 57%-40% and took five of the six counties. In Alachua, the largest county, McGurn led, 56%-41%. Two years later, his Democratic challenger was Yvonne Haynes Hinson, a former Gainesville city commissioner. She spent less than one-tenth of Yoho's total, and lost 58%-42%, while winning Alachua.

Prior to the 2018 election, Yoho reaffirmed his self-imposed limitation of four terms.

FL-3: North Florida   **Cook Partisan Voting Index: R+9**

Population		Race and Ethnicity		Income	
Total	720,286	White	68.6%	Median Income	$47,047
Land area (sq. miles)	3,560	Black	15.8%	District Income Rank	352
Pop/ sq mi	202.3	Latino	9.3%	Poverty Rate	19.1%
Born in State	49.9%	Asian	3.4%	With health insurance	87.7%
		Two or more races	2.5%	Cash public assistance	2%
Age Groups		Other	0.5%	Food stamp/SNAP	14.1%
Under 18	20.8%				
18-34	26.5%	**Education**		**Work**	
35-64	37%	H.S grad or less	42.7%	White Collar	15.7%
Over 64	15.7%	Some college	31%	Sales and Service	44.9%
		College Degree, 4 yr	15.4%	Blue Collar	17.9%
Military		Post grad	10.9%	Government	19.3%
Veteran/ Active Duty	11.9%				

2012 Pres. Vote	Romney	185,688	(58%)	Obama	137,401	(43%)		
2016 Pres. Vote	Trump	197,478	(56%)	Clinton	141,362	(40%)	Johnson	9,138	(3%)

Jacksonville Suburbs, Gainesville: The flat grasslands of central Florida, once bypassed by southbound tourists heading for the coastal resorts and cities, have become a prime growth area in this high-growth state. Central Florida's economy once depended on farming, on tourists getting off the interstate and on state institutions, most notably the University of Florida in Gainesville. Then retirees began settling in places like the bluegrass country around Ocala, one of America's prime horse-breeding grounds, and the area began to share the development boom, growing 19 percent from 2000 to 2007. But then the recession hit the region hard, with home foreclosures reaching record levels.

By 2014, Ocala-based Marion County led the state in economic growth. Ocala has become a distribution center in the heart of Florida, including a FedEx hub. In October 2017, Forbes magazine ranked the Ocala area eighth in the nation for projected job growth. In addition to the university, the Gainesville area has added hundreds of manufacturing jobs since 2010. Gainesville has styled itself as "a new American city," which has addressed numerous social problems. In north-central Florida, including the rapidly growing outskirts of Jacksonville, voting patterns have solidified for the Republicans and have partly offset the movement toward Democrats in South Florida.

The 3rd Congressional District of Florida is a compact core of north Florida, with 82 percent of its population in three counties: all of Alachua, which includes Gainesville; all of Clay, which is chiefly Orange Park, Middleburg and other suburbs southwest of Jacksonville; and nearly half of Marion, which includes Ocala. With the exception of firmly Democratic Gainesville and its large campus, these areas are comfortably Republican.

What had been the third strongest Republican district in Florida before redistricting in 2016 slipped to 8th. Donald Trump won 56%-40%.

John Rutherford (R)

Elected 2016, 2nd term, b. Sep 02, 1952; Omaha, NE; Florida Junior College, A.A., 1972; Florida State University, B.S., 1974; Catholic; Married (Patricia Rutherford); 2 children; 6 grandchildren.

Elected Office: Sheriff, City of Jacksonville, 2003-2015.

DC Office: 1711 LHOB 20515, 202-225-2501, Fax: 202-225-2504, rutherford.house.gov

State Offices: Jacksonville, 904-831-5205.

Committees: *Appropriations*: Homeland Security; Military Construction, Veterans Affairs & Related Agencies; Transportation, HUD & Related Agencies.

Group Ratings

	ADA	ACLU	AFL-CIO	LCV	ITI	COC	HAFA	ACU	CFG	FRC
2018	-	3%	-	6%	-	92%	44%	68%	49%	100%
2017	0%	C	19%	3%	C	92%	C	76%	57%	100%

Almanac Ratings 2017-18

	Economy	Social	Foreign	Composite
Liberal	10%	6%	3%	6%
Conservative	90%	94%	98%	94%

Key Votes of the 115th Congress

1. Obama-care revision	Y	5. Family planning regs	Y	9. Guantanamo prisoners	N
2. Tax Cuts	Y	6. Body cameras/immigration	N	10. Ground missiles, limit	N
3. Omnibus appropriations	Y	7. Abortion ban	Y	11. Defense Dept. spending	Y
4. Dodd-Frank revision	Y	8. Concealed carry	Y	12. FISA rules	Y

Election Results

Election	Name (Party)	Vote (%)	Cand. Spent	Ind. Exp. Support	Ind. Exp. Oppose
2018 General	John Rutherford (R)...... 248,420	(65%)	$362,514	$10,000	
	Ges Selmont (D)...... 123,351	(32%)	$105,086		
2018 Primary	John Rutherford (R)......	(100%)			

Prior winning percentages: 2016 (70%)

Republican John Rutherford, who was elected in 2016, has followed the mold of his predecessor, Republican Ander Crenshaw, a quiet insider who served on the Appropriations Committee. He joined the committee midway through his first term. Of the three incoming Republicans from north Florida that year, Rutherford operated most closely as a leadership ally. Well-known locally as the sheriff of Jacksonville, he handily won election.

Rutherford, who has lived in Jacksonville since he was six, earned an associate's degree in police administration from Florida Junior College and a bachelor's degree in criminology from Florida State University. He began his police career as a patrolman in 1974 and was the Jacksonville police department's director of corrections from 1995 until 2003. He was elected sheriff of Jacksonville in 2003 and stepped down 12 years later because of term limits.

As sheriff, Rutherford introduced several initiatives to reduce crime. In addition to greater community engagement, he focused on better treatment of the mentally ill to reduce their recidivism rate. By the end of his tenure, Jacksonville's violent crime rate was at a 40-year low. He also served as chairman of the Florida Sheriff's Association, where he advocated state legislation that would reduce crime.

After Crenshaw announced his retirement, seven Republicans competed in the primary. In addition to Rutherford, the best-known were state Rep. Lake Ray and Hans Tanzler, son of a former Jacksonville mayor. Tanzler challenged Rutherford's conservative credentials, including the former sheriff's opposition to the death penalty, and his support for higher taxes and for protecting illegal immigrants in Jacksonville. Rutherford charged that Tanzler was a "political insider" who had backed former Republican Gov. Charlie Crist, which resulted in Tanzler getting the position of executive director of the St. Johns River Water Management District board.

Rutherford spent $833,000 for his campaign. Tanzler reported $814,000, half of which was self-financed. The quieter Ray spent $242,000. Rutherford won 39 percent of the primary vote to 20 percent for Ray and 19 percent for Tanzler; the vote was split evenly across the three counties. The general election was an afterthought. Democrat David Bruderly, who said he welcomed the label of "perennial candidate," spent $50,000. Rutherford won, 70%-28%. With its current boundaries, he is secure in this district.

In the House, Rutherford went to work on the Homeland Security Committee. The House passed his bill consolidating the more than $2 billion in leases and real-estate costs of the more than 20 components of the Homeland Security Department. With Rep. Michael McCaul of Texas, the chairman of the committee, Rutherford filed a bill to improve the efficiency of the department's acquisition programs. The House passed that bill in 2017, plus another Rutherford bill to permit the department to work on overseas counterterrorism task forces. On the Veterans' Affairs Committee, he sponsored a bill that created a scholarship program to recruit medical students to work at VA hospitals. That provision was rolled into a more comprehensive veterans' measure that Congress approved.

In May 2018, Republican leaders selected Rutherford to fill a vacancy on the Appropriations Committee. That seat positioned him to look after the interests of Jacksonville's large Navy bases. Later in the year, he took credit for congressional approval of purchasing three additional littoral combat ships from the shipbuilding yard at Mayport.

Politically, Rutherford sought to strike a balance between serving as a GOP team player and limiting partisanship. In an August 2017 interview with the Florida Times-Union, he responded to a question about the Twitter habits of President Donald Trump: "I don't think it's as great a medium as he thinks it is."

FL-4: Jacksonville area   **Cook Partisan Voting Index: R+17**

Population		Race and Ethnicity		Income	
Total	763,855	White	75.7%	Median Income	$66,753
Land area (sq. miles)	1,569	Black	9%	District Income Rank	121
Pop/ sq mi	486.8	Latino	7.9%	Poverty Rate	9.7%
Born in State	40.6%	Asian	4.5%	With health insurance	89.5%
		Two or more races	2.5%	Cash public assistance	1.6%
Age Groups		Other	0.5%	Food stamp/SNAP	7.7%
Under 18	21.1%				
18-34	23.1%	**Education**		**Work**	
35-64	40.3%	H.S grad or less	30.4%	White Collar	15.5%
Over 64	15.5%	Some college	30.9%	Sales and Service	41.1%
		College Degree, 4 yr	25.2%	Blue Collar	14.8%
Military		Post grad	13.5%	Government	11.6%
Veteran/ Active Duty	13.5%				

2012 Pres. Vote	Romney	248,603	(66%)	Obama	124,086	(33%)		
2016 Pres. Vote	Trump	261,828	(62%)	Clinton	143,674	(34%)	Johnson	12,473	(3%)

Parts of Jacksonville and Suburbs: With a metropolitan area of 1.6 million people, and continuing to grow, Jacksonville has overcome its reputation as Florida's overlooked city. Not long ago, it was considered a backwater, dominated by insurance companies and smelly paper mills. Jacksonville is now the largest city by land area in the contiguous 48 states, boasting a National Football League franchise and bold skyscrapers looming above the St. Johns River. Wide freeways sidestep primeval wetlands on their way to huge beachfront subdivisions.

Jacksonville's harbor has grown as a destination for cargo and cruise-line operations, with a total annual economic impact of more than $27 billion. With Naval Station Mayport and Naval Air Station Jacksonville — two of the three largest metro-area employers — the city has a significant military employment base. Shipbuilding and repair provide more than 10,000 jobs in the area. The city is the headquarters of railway giant CSX and hosts major operations such as UPS and Bank of America.

Business leaders have made the area into the "Silicon Valley of Logistics" — building on its land, air and sea transportation facilities. In 2018, the Port Authority began to dredge 11 miles of the river from 40 feet to 47 feet. Jacksonville is the busiest container port in Florida, though both Savannah and Charleston annually handle several times as many units. In 2018, Amazon opened a fulfillment center, with 2,000 employees. UPS plans to complete in 2019 a $196 million expansion of its ground hub, which could handle more than 80,000 packages per hour. The Navy designated Mayport and San Diego as the bases for its new class of 52 littoral combat ships, which are faster and carry more weapons but with a smaller crew. Starting in 2018, Navy pilots were flying overseas unmanned Triton drone systems from their computers at the naval air station. Mayport was selected by the Navy as the East Coast headquarters of its Triton drone operations. Earlier, Mayport lost out to Norfolk Virginia in seeking to become a home to aircraft carriers.

The 4th District of Florida is centered in Jacksonville-based Duval County, with a smaller piece of the county in the 5th District. It also is home to most of St. Johns County, which has become the third-fastest growing and the wealthiest county in the state. Amid the new construction in much of St. Johns is the well-restored St. Augustine, founded by Spanish colonists as the oldest permanent European settlement in North America — 42 years older than Jamestown Virginia. To the north is rapidly growing Nassau County, including a massive planned community in Yulee. The boosterish Jacksonville civic culture and significant military presence make the 4th a pro-business, pro-military and pro-Republican district. With the redistricting changes, Mitt Romney in 2012 would have retained his 66 percent of the vote, his second best in Florida. In 2016, local support for Donald Trump dropped to 62 percent, another example of reduced support for Trump from affluent GOP voters.

Al Lawson (D)

Elected 2016, 2nd term, b. Sep 23, 1948; Midway; University of Florida, B.S., 1970; Florida State University, M.S., 1973; Episcopalian; Married (Delores J. Brooks Lawson); 2 children; 2 grandchildren.

Elected Office: FL House, 1982-2000; FL Senate, 2000-2010, Minority Leader, 2008-2010.

Professional Career: Prof. Basketball player & coach, Florida State Univ.; President, Lawson & Assoc. Inc. .

DC Office: 1406 LHOB 20515, 202-225-0123, Fax: 202-225-2256, lawson.house.gov

State Offices: Jacksonville, 904-354-1652; Tallahassee, 850-558-9450.

Committees: *Agriculture*: Biotechnology, Horticulture & Research; General Farm Commodities & Risk Management; Subcommittee Nutrition, Oversight & Department Operations. *Financial Services*: Consumer Protection & Financial Institutions; Housing, Community Development & Insurance; Subcommittee on Diversity & Inclusion.

Group Ratings

	ADA	ACLU	AFL-CIO	LCV	ITI	COC	HAFA	ACU	CFG	FRC
2018	-	67%	-	89%	-	75%	6%	12%	8%	0%
2017	80%	C	94%	69%	C	54%	C	8%	0%	0%

Almanac Ratings 2017-18

	Economy	Social	Foreign	Composite
Liberal	75%	87%	60%	74%
Conservative	25%	13%	40%	26%

Key Votes of the 115th Congress

1. Obama-care revision	N	5. Family planning regs	N	9. Guantanamo prisoners	N
2. Tax Cuts	N	6. Body cameras/immigration	Y	10. Ground missiles, limit	Y
3. Omnibus appropriations	Y	7. Abortion ban	N	11. Defense Dept. spending	Y
4. Dodd-Frank revision	Y	8. Concealed carry	N	12. FISA rules	Y

Election Results

Election	Name (Party)	Vote (%)		Cand. Spent	Ind. Exp. Support	Ind. Exp. Oppose
2018 General	Al Lawson (D)	180,527	(67%)	$632,570		
	Virginia Fuller (R)	89,799	(33%)	$56,899		
2018 Primary	Al Lawson (D)	53,990	(60%)			
	Alvin Brown (D)	35,584	(40%)			

Prior winning percentages: 2016 (64%)

Democrat Al Lawson, elected in 2016 under unusual circumstances in a district that had been radically altered in a mid-decade redistricting that benefited him, faced continuing campaign challenges. His legislative activities initially focused on agriculture and support of small business.

Lawson, a fourth-generation Floridian, was born in Midway. He worked his first job in the Gadsden Community tobacco fields at the age of 8. In high school, he was an accomplished athlete and went on to play basketball at Florida Agricultural and Mechanical University, where he was a team leader. He received his bachelor's degree in political science, then earned a master's in public administration from Florida State University. He had a brief career in professional basketball. Lawson was elected to the Florida House in 1982 and served for 18 years before winning election in 2000 to the state Senate, where he served for another 10 years. He chaired the House Natural Resources Committee, authoring the Preservation 2000 environmental law, which created the largest state-funded land acquisition program in the country.

Following his departure from the legislature, he became a lobbyist and insurance agent. Lawson had twice run for Congress. In 2010, he sought the Democratic nomination in the Tallahassee-based 2nd District, losing narrowly in the primary to seven-term Rep. Allen Boyd. Then he lost in the 2012 general to Republican Rep. Steve Southerland, who had defeated Boyd two years earlier.

In the 2016 primary, Lawson took on yet another incumbent. This time, it was the Democratic primary against Rep. Corinne Brown, a 12-term incumbent who had overcome numerous obstacles during her career, but couldn't survive the combination of adverse redistricting and a criminal indictment for corruption. They were running in a radically redrawn district that had two geographic poles: Brown's hometown of Jacksonville and Lawson's long-time base in Tallahassee and Gadsden.

Brown, first elected in 1992, focused on constituents in her House work and used the slogan "Corrine Delivers" in her reelection campaigns. Her ability to provide money and other help to her financially ailing district kept her in office, despite a string of controversial comments and ethics issues. In a major development eight weeks before the primary, a federal grand jury issued a 22-count indictment of Brown following a lengthy investigation into what prosecutors termed a phony educational charity that she and her chief of staff turned into a personal slush fund with $800,000 in solicitations. Brown pleaded not guilty.

Lawson won the primary, 48%-39%, with LaShonda Holloway getting 13 percent. Both Lawson and Brown ran well in their home areas, but Lawson did better even though his base had a smaller turnout. In Tallahassee-based Leon County plus adjoining Gadsden, Lawson won 76 percent of the 31,491 votes. In Jacksonville-based Duval County, Brown won 62 percent of the 39,888 votes cast. Those three counties, separated by 160 miles, cast 86 percent of the total votes. Brown, a veteran incumbent, spent only $572,000, including a $100,000 personal loan. Lawson spent $356,000 for his campaign. He easily won the general election. In 2017, Brown was convicted on 18 felony counts and began to serve a five-year sentence.

In the House, Lawson was a member of the House-Senate conference committee that approved the final version of the 2018 farm bill. It included his legislation to increase federal support for historically black colleges and universities, with steps such as development of an agricultural work force and food security. The defense-spending bill that Congress enacted in 2018 included a Lawson-sponsored provision that assists small startup businesses to commercialize their products.

Lawson attracted attention during President Donald Trump's State of the Union message to Congress in January 2018, when he appeared to be the only member of the Congressional Black Caucus who applauded the president's approval of lower unemployment rates for blacks. After Trump later told another audience that he would send a "thank you" note to whoever was applauding, Lawson said that he didn't need a letter and he told a reporter, "Don't judge me on my clapping."

At home, Lawson was challenged in the August 2018 Democratic primary by Alvin Brown, the former mayor of Jacksonville. Brown criticized Lawson for his approval of Trump and for his support of Florida's "stand your ground" law that protects gun owners. "There's nothing wrong with being a moderate," Lawson responded. Each spent about $500,000. In a pattern similar to Lawson's victory in the 2016 primary, he trailed in Duval County, which had a larger turnout, but had a 5-to-1 lead in Leon and Gadsden counties. Lawson won, 60%-40%.

FL-5: Northern Florida metro areas   **Cook Partisan Voting Index: D+12**

Population		Race and Ethnicity		Income	
Total	722,646	White	40%	Median Income	$39,667
Land area (sq. miles)	3,817	Black	46.9%	District Income Rank	416
Pop/ sq mi	189.3	Latino	7.8%	Poverty Rate	24.3%
Born in State	60.4%	Asian	2.6%	With health insurance	85.9%
		Two or more races	2.1%	Cash public assistance	3.5%
Age Groups		Other	0.5%	Food stamp/SNAP	23.2%
Under 18	23%				
18-34	29%	**Education**		**Work**	
35-64	36%	H.S grad or less	47.3%	White Collar	12%
Over 64	12%	Some college	32.5%	Sales and Service	49.8%
		College Degree, 4 yr	13.6%	Blue Collar	20%
Military		Post grad	6.5%	Government	19.4%
Veteran/ Active Duty	10.5%				

2012 Pres. Vote	Obama	197,194	(64%)	Romney	109,822	(35%)		
2016 Pres. Vote	Clinton	191,195	(61%)	Trump	111,891	(36%)	Johnson	5,997	(2%)

Downtown Jacksonville and Parts of Tallahassee: Before the Civil War, most of Florida was still an uncharted watery wilderness, festooned with exotic greenery, inhabited by unusual animals, a part of the United States so far out of the experience of most Americans as to seem foreign. As late as 1940, Florida had the smallest population of any Southern state, and most of the people here lived in classic Dixie rural counties with small courthouse towns. Civic affairs were run by the richest white men, and African Americans lived in poorly constructed, unpainted shotgun shacks propped up on blocks, with little money and no vote. This was a land of swamps, lakes and orange groves. The broad St. Johns River, one of the few North American rivers that flows (if only sluggishly) north, meanders through orange-grove country to the port of Jacksonville.

The city's planners have been eager to revitalize the downtown area, which is dominated by shipyards, warehouses and some office buildings. In 2018, Shad Khan, the billionaire businessman owner of the Jacksonville Jaguars football franchise, made sweeping development proposals for both the riverfront and the downtown area around the stadium. It was unclear whether he might proceed with both options. In September 2018, the Mayo Clinic announced plans for a new medical building on its 400-acre local campus. Especially with the major hurricane damage elsewhere in the state in recent years, officials have voiced growing concern about the threat of destruction if a major storm hits the extensive low-lying areas of the city.

Tallahassee, the seat of state government with many public-sector jobs, has been a source of discomfort for the state's Republican rulers. Its African-American population grew from about 25 percent in the 1990s to 35 percent in 2018. The city's liberal bent is fueled by its two big universities in the downtown area, Florida State and Florida A&M. This remains a government town, as promises from state leaders of a "new economy" have been mostly unfulfilled. Local leaders took offense when President Donald Trump in an October 2018 campaign event in Florida derided Mayor Andrew Gillum, the unsuccessful Democratic nominee for governor, for the "worst statistics" of his city — including its crime and corruption. Nearby Gadsden County, the state's only black-majority county, is rural and heavily Democratic. The countryside around Tallahassee is distinctly Dixie and is more reminiscent of southern Georgia than of southern Florida. The landscape is marked by cotton fields, soft pine stands, catfish farms and small towns with big churches.

The 5th Congressional District is like a barbell that extends more than 160 miles from Jacksonville to Tallahassee. But the barbell is unequal. The Jacksonville-based Duval County territory has 403,000 residents, while the western end in Leon and Gadsden Counties has 206,000 persons. The Jacksonville section of the district includes much of downtown and the large port, though it stops a few miles short of the Atlantic. The larger share of Duval County is the core of the solidly Republican 4th District. On the western end, the 5th includes close to 60 percent of Leon; the more Republican section is in the 2nd District. The Leon County portion can show its weight in elections because its many government employees are more politically connected. Between the two ends of the barbell are five rural Republican counties, each with a population of less than 30,000.

The new 5th, like the old one, is the only Democratic district north of Orlando. Hillary Clinton won in 2016, 61%-36%. Its population is 47 percent African American and 8 percent Hispanic. It trails only two south Florida districts in its black population.

Michael Waltz (R)

Elected 2018, 1st term, b. Jan 31, 1974; Boynton Beach; Virginia Military Institute, B.A., 1996; Christian Church; Divorced; 1 child.

Military Career: U.S. Navy and Reserve 1996-2007 (Afghanistan)

Professional Career: U.S. Department of Defense, Program Manager, 2004-2007, Afghanistan Country Director, 2006-2007; Special Advisor to the Vice President for South Asia and Counterterrorism, 2007-2009; Fox News Contributor, 2016-2018; Chief Executive Officer, METIS Solutions, 2010-2018.

DC Office: 216 CHOB 20515, 202-225-2706, waltz.house.gov

State Offices: Deland, 386-279-0707; Palm Coast, 386-302-0442; Port Orange, 386-238-9711.

Committees: *Armed Services*: Intelligence, Emerging Threats & Capabilities; Seapower & Projection Forces. *Science, Space & Technology*: Investigations & Oversight; Space & Aeronautics.

Election Results

Election	Name (Party)	Vote (%)	Cand. Spent	Ind. Exp. Support	Ind. Exp. Oppose
2018 General	Michael G. Waltz (R)........................ 187,891	(56%)	$1,979,069	$2,546,699	$630,785
	Nancy Soderberg (D)..................... 145,758	(44%)	$3,176,921	$1,674,902	$572,499
2018 Primary	Michael G. Waltz (R)........................ 32,916	(42%)			
	John Ward (R).................................. 23,593	(30%)			
	Fred Costello (R).............................. 21,074	(27%)			

Freshman Republican Michael Waltz won competitive primary and general-election contests for his GOP-leaning seat. He had extensive experience with military and national security issues as a Green Beret in the Army, where he had combat tours in Afghanistan, and as a top policy aide at the Pentagon and White House during the presidency of George W. Bush. Later, he built his own business that advised the Defense Department and private-sector companies on topics such as terrorism and training. In his first political bid, he succeeded Republican Ron DeSantis, who ran successfully for Florida governor.

Waltz, a Florida native, graduated from the Virginia Military Institute. He commanded an Army Special Forces unit that had multiple deployments to Afghanistan and the Middle East, and joined with other Special Forces units in four provinces along the border with Pakistan. On one of those tours, he led the search for Bowe Bergdahl, an Army soldier who had deserted his unit and was held captive for five years by the Taliban. While in the military, Waltz was director for Afghanistan policy at the Pentagon and, as an adviser to Vice President Dick Cheney, he served as policy director for counterterrorism in the Bush White House. He retired as a lieutenant colonel.

In the private sector, Waltz was president of Metis Solutions, a defense and intelligence contracting firm. He also was a cofounder and partner of Askari Associates, an international consulting firm that provided strategic advice to foreign governments and businesses. Based in Washington during most of that time, he was a senior fellow at the Foundation for Defense of Democracies and a fellow with the International Security program of the New America Foundation; he was a commentator on military issues for several news organizations.

When DeSantis decided to run for governor, Waltz made his move into politics. "I will fight for you in Congress like I fought for you in combat," he said. Also seeking the Republican nomination were John Ward, a retired Navy intelligence officer, and former state representative Fred Costello. Waltz and Ward each spent more than $1 million in the primary—much of it self-financed in each case—and had additional support from outside groups. Waltz called for expansion of the commercial space industry into Volusia County and reform of the Veterans Affairs Department. Ward, a business investor, emphasized changes in domestic programs and rollbacks of federal regulations. Waltz took the primary with 42 percent of the vote to 30 percent for Ward and 27 percent for Costello.

In the general election, Waltz faced Nancy Soderberg, who had a lengthy career in Washington as a foreign policy aide. With President Bill Clinton, she was a top aide to the National Security Council and she held the rank of Ambassador to the United Nations. President Barack Obama tapped her to chair the Public Interest Declassification Board, an advisory committee created by Congress. Subsequently, Soderberg directed the public service leadership program at the University of North Florida in Jacksonville. The Orlando Sentinel reported that each candidate had thin ties to the district and was accused of "carpetbagging" by opponents.

Soderberg focused on the need for improved health care services and criticized Republican-enacted tax cuts. Like many House Democratic candidates in 2018, she outspent her opponent. Waltz discussed national security concerns and his experiences as a small business owner. He said that the outcome of the primaries showed that voters had little concern about where the candidates resided. "I wish I'd been here," Waltz told the Sentinel. "I'd been running around getting shot at the last few years."

With his victory, Waltz joined a growing number of Afghanistan and Iraq war veterans from both parties in the House, who occasionally have pressed for bipartisanship on national security issues.

FL-6: Northeast Florida   **Cook Partisan Voting Index: R+7**

Population		Race and Ethnicity		Income	
Total	740,950	White	74.1%	Median Income	$45,873
Land area (sq. miles)	2,171	Black	10%	District Income Rank	365
Pop/ sq mi	341.3	Latino	11.9%	Poverty Rate	15.3%
Born in State	34.8%	Asian	1.8%	With health insurance	86.1%
		Two or more races	1.7%	Cash public assistance	2%
Age Groups		Other	0.5%	Food stamp/SNAP	13.4%
Under 18	18.1%				
18-34	18.7%	**Education**		**Work**	
35-64	38.7%	H.S grad or less	43%	White Collar	24.5%
Over 64	24.5%	Some college	33.9%	Sales and Service	48.1%
		College Degree, 4 yr	14.8%	Blue Collar	20.5%
Military		Post grad	8.3%	Government	11.7%
Veteran/ Active Duty	12.2%				

2012 Pres. Vote	Romney	178,105	(53%)	Obama	158,779	(47%)		
2016 Pres. Vote	Trump	215,940	(56%)	Clinton	151,453	(40%)	Johnson	8,694	(2%)

Daytona Beach: In 1513, Spanish explorer Juan Ponce de León headed to the New World, hoping to discover the Fountain of Youth. Instead, he found Ponte Vedra Beach, located just south of modern day Jacksonville. A few decades later, Spanish colonists founded St. Augustine, the oldest permanent European settlement in North America. Less well-known is New Smyrna Beach. Another 75 miles down the Atlantic Coast, it was established in 1768 in an attempt by the British to colonize Florida with Greek settlers, whom they believed to be ideally suited to the warm climate. They were not, however, well suited for the brutal wilderness conditions. By 1777, many had abandoned the colony, walking and swimming back to St. Augustine. The area was a popular hideout for rum-runners during Prohibition, and today has become a popular vacation spot and quieter in many ways than nearby and better-known Daytona Beach.

The beaches in Daytona have been attracting sun-seekers for decades, although the city is best known for the Daytona 500 held each February at Daytona International Speedway. Further inland, northeast Florida still retains a taste of "Old Florida." DeLand has a small-town atmosphere centered on Stetson University. In tiny Pierson, known as the "Fern Capital of the World," 54 percent of the population was Latino, according to the 2010 census; many perform the labor-intensive work of trimming the fern fronds. These other parts of Volusia County have managed to avoid the familiar pattern in Florida of miles of high-rise condominiums.

Flagler and St. Johns, the two coastal counties between Jacksonville and Daytona Beach, were filled with cattle ranches a few decades ago. Between 2000 and 2010, the population in Flagler nearly doubled and St. Johns increased by more than half. These growth rates slowed dramatically during the recession. Since then, tourists have returned to the beaches and housing permits picked up, especially with retirees. A $200 million hotel and convention center in Daytona Beach, which will be the largest development along the beach, was scheduled for completion in 2020.

The 6th District covers the Atlantic coast for nearly 90 miles, more than any other district in Florida, from just south of St. Augustine to the Canaveral National Seashore, which has offered splendid views of NASA lift-offs from the John F. Kennedy Space Center. Other Florida districts along the Gulf or in the Keys offer longer stretches of beachfront, but with fewer towns or people.

About 70 percent of the population is concentrated in Volusia County, 20 percent in the northern beachfront counties, with the balance in rural Lake County. Donald Trump did well in the many blue-collar communities of Volusia and got 55 percent of the county vote, compared with only 50 percent for Mitt Romney in 2012.

Stephanie Murphy (D)

Elected 2016, 2nd term, b. Sep 16, 1978; Ho Chi Minh City, Vietnam; College of William and Mary (VA), B.A., 2000; Georgetown University (DC), M.S., 2004; Christian Church; Married (Sean Murphy); 2 children.

Professional Career: Foreign Affairs Specialist, U.S Dept. of Defense, 2004-2008; Businesswoman; Faculty/Instructor, Rollins College, 2014-2016.

DC Office: 1710 LHOB 20515, 202-225-4035, Fax: 202-226-0821, stephaniemurphy.house.gov

State Offices: Orlando, 888-205-5421; Sanford, 888-205-5421.

Committees: *Ways & Means*: Trade; Worker & Family Support.

Group Ratings

	ADA	ACLU	AFL-CIO	LCV	ITI	COC	HAFA	ACU	CFG	FRC
2018	-	64%	-	83%	-	75%	6%	12%	22%	20%
2017	65%	C	79%	91%	C	71%	C	0%	3%	11%

Almanac Ratings 2017-18

	Economy	Social	Foreign	Composite
Liberal	62%	81%	67%	70%
Conservative	38%	19%	33%	30%

Key Votes of the 115th Congress

1. Obama-care revision	N	5. Family planning regs	N	9. Guantanamo prisoners	Y
2. Tax Cuts	N	6. Body cameras/immigration	Y	10. Ground missiles, limit	Y
3. Omnibus appropriations	Y	7. Abortion ban	N	11. Defense Dept. spending	Y
4. Dodd-Frank revision	Y	8. Concealed carry	N	12. FISA rules	Y

Election Results

Election	Name (Party)	Vote (%)		Cand. Spent	Ind. Exp. Support	Ind. Exp. Oppose
2018 General	Stephanie Murphy (D)........................ 183,113	(58%)	$3,080,677	$344,870	$67,879
	Mike Miller (R)................................... 134,285	(42%)	$1,086,118		$806,399
2018 Primary	Stephanie Murphy (D).......................... 49,060	(86%)			
	Chardo Richardson (D)................ 7,846	(14%)			

Prior winning percentages: 2016 (52%)

Democrat Stephanie Murphy, elected in 2016 when she narrowly defeated influential House Republican Rep. John Mica, worked with centrist Democrats and across the political aisle. She has impressed many with her personal story as a refugee from Vietnam with a remarkably self-made life story in the American immigrant tradition. In the House, she became a leader of the junior Democrats.

At six months, Stephanie Dang fled Vietnam on a refugee boat with her family. After the small craft ran out of fuel and went adrift in the South China Sea, the group was rescued by the U.S.

Navy, which provided supplies that aided in the boat reaching Malaysia and a refugee camp. The Lutheran Church helped the family to the United States, and they eventually settled in Virginia. She graduated in 2000 from the College of William and Mary. On Sept. 11, 2001, she was working at Deloitte Consulting in Washington. Motivated by a desire for public service, she quit that job to attend graduate school at the Georgetown University School of Foreign Service, where she got a master's degree.

She then served as a national security specialist for the secretary of Defense. She helped to organize the rescue effort for victims of a 2004 tsunami in South Asia. Her work as chief of staff to a global strategic guidance planning effort won her a Defense Department Medal for Exceptional Civilian Service. Later, she was an executive at Sungate Capital, advising on investment decisions and implementing government affairs initiatives. After marrying Sean Murphy, whom she had met while working at Deloitte, they settled in Winter Park, Florida, where his family had been politically active. She taught business and social entrepreneurship at Rollins College. As an advocate of LGBT rights, she was a prominent voice in support of that community following the June 2016 terrorist attack at Pulse Nightclub in Orlando, which killed 49.

Murphy got her start in politics in early 2016 when she was advising the Democratic Congressional Campaign Committee, which was looking for a challenger to Mica who had chaired the House Transportation and Infrastructure Committee. After other possible contenders declined or were not credible candidates, the DCCC recruited Murphy to run, She was mentored by several prominent Democratic women, including Nancy Pelosi. Murphy spent $1.1 million to $1.8 million for Mica, who had not faced a serious Democratic opponent since 2002 and was slow to take her candidacy seriously. She received $4.7 million in support from the DCCC and other party affiliates, and at least $3 million more from liberal groups. The National Republican Congressional Committee spent $1.7 million for Mica.

Murphy said that Mica was out of touch with the district, and she criticized his views on gun control, gay rights and women's issues. "He is a career politician who has been part of the problem," she said. Mica highlighted the many benefits, including significant transportation projects that he had delivered to the district. Donald Trump became an issue in the campaign after Mica gave Trump and his business legislative assistance in securing a $3 million annual lease at the Old Post Office Building on Pennsylvania Avenue in Washington as the site for his lavish new Trump International Hotel. Mica had proudly acknowledged his role. Two weeks before the election, the DCCC issued a statement that, "Mica has not only helped Trump line his own pockets, he's stood by Trump every step of the way, even after he was caught bragging about sexual assault."

Murphy became the giant killer, 51.5%-48.5%. Mica got 53 percent of the vote in Seminole County. But Murphy prevailed with 58 percent of the vote in Orange County.

In the House, Murphy filed a bill to end the 22-year ban on the use of federal funds to conduct research to promote gun control, often mischaracterized as a federal ban on gun-violence research. Subsequently, her measure was enacted as part of a spending bill. In October 2018, Time magazine placed her photo on the cover of a story about the gun debate. She became a leader of the bipartisan Problem Solvers Caucus, which prepared recommendations to change House procedures to encourage more open debate. Following the 2018 election, Pelosi agreed to some of those changes to secure support from Murphy and several other moderate Democrats in her campaign for House Speaker.

In 2019, Murphy became chair of two groups of House Democrats: the centrist Blue Dog Coalition and the Future Forum of young party members. "In this new era of divided government, we Democrats must introduce bold ideas and fight for our shared values, and we must also seek bipartisan cooperation," she said. She also got a seat on the powerful Ways and Means Committee.

As expected, Murphy faced a competitive challenge for reelection from Mike Miller, a state representative. Miller called for lower taxes and a balanced budget. Murphy criticized the tax cuts enacted by Republicans in 2017, which she claimed "disproportionately benefitted the wealthiest among us." Murphy outspent Miller, $3.1 million to $1.1 million, and won 58%-42%, with 54 percent of the vote in Seminole. At least until the next round of redistricting, she secured what had been a Republican district.

FL-7: Northern Orlando Suburbs

Cook Partisan Voting Index: EVEN

Population		Race and Ethnicity		Income	
Total	748,154	White	58.9%	Median Income	$56,681
Land area (sq. miles)	393	Black	9.8%	District Income Rank	206
Pop/ sq mi	1905.3	Latino	24.2%	Poverty Rate	14.4%
Born in State	39.1%	Asian	4.3%	With health insurance	87.3%
		Two or more races	2.2%	Cash public assistance	1.8%
Age Groups		Other	0.5%	Food stamp/SNAP	10.2%
Under 18	20%				
18-34	27.9%	**Education**		**Work**	
35-64	38.6%	H.S grad or less	28.9%	White Collar	13.5%
Over 64	13.5%	Some college	32.9%	Sales and Service	43.4%
		College Degree, 4 yr	25.3%	Blue Collar	13.1%
Military		Post grad	12.8%	Government	10.8%
Veteran/ Active Duty	7.2%				

2012 Pres. Vote	Obama	164,728	(50%)	Romney	163,723	(50%)		
2016 Pres. Vote	Clinton	186,658	(51%)	Trump	160,178	(44%)	Johnson	11,551 (3%)

Seminole, Orange: For much of the 19th century, central Florida was a sparsely populated region at the southern frontier of the state. The native Timucua tribe had been driven to extinction by war and disease, and only a few towns of any size dotted the state's interior. Steamboats traveled up and down the St. Johns River to supply small trading centers that sprang up at the end of the navigable portions of that waterway on Lake Monroe and Lake Jesup (known for its many alligators) in what is now Seminole County. This state of affairs largely persisted until 1971, when Disney World opened in neighboring Orange County, setting off startling growth and development in the region. Tourism flourished and Seminole County became one of the primary beneficiaries of that explosive development. Its population shot up from 55,000 in 1960 to 463,000 in 2017. The once-quiet county became a collection of largely high-end suburbs with a median income of $60,739, the third-highest in the state. The area was hit hard by the housing collapse and recession, but has been rebounding. The $2.3 billion reconstruction of a 21-mile stretch of Interstate 4 in Seminole and Orange counties will add express lanes through Orlando.

The 7th Congressional District of Florida includes all of Seminole County, which supplies 60 percent of the population, and about one-fourth of Orange County. Seminole has been a key battleground county in one of the nation's key battleground states, and it could become a new bellwether. In June 2018, The New York Times described Seminole as "a modern microcosm whose population most closely matches the nation's current mix." It has become a brighter spot for Democrats in Florida. The 49%-47% win for Donald Trump in Seminole was notably closer than the 53%-46% county lead for Mitt Romney when he lost the state in 2012. As more apartment complexes have been built, Seminole has become younger and more urban. From 2010 to 2017, the Hispanic population grew from 17 percent to 21 percent. In 2018, Democrats Bill Nelson and Andrew Gillum each had a two-point lead in Seminole, even though they lost statewide in their contests for the Senate and governor.

Redistricting in 2016 added the eastern side of Orlando, which had a significant Hispanic population. The district overall became 24 percent Hispanic and 10 percent black. As a result of these changes, the district in 2012 became a virtual tie between President Barack Obama and Mitt Romney. In 2016, Hillary Clinton took the 7th, 51%-44%, a notable improvement for Democrats.

Bill Posey (R)

Elected 2008, 6th term, b. Dec 18, 1947; Washington, DC; Brevard Community College (FL), A.A., 1969; Stetson University (FL), Att., 1978; Methodist; Married (Katie Ingram Posey); 2 children; 3 grandchildren.

Elected Office: Rockledge City Council, 1976-1986; FL House, 1992-2000; FL Senate, 2000-2008.

Professional Career: McDonnell Douglas Astronautics Co., 1966-1969; Crawford & Co./Gay & Taylor, 1970-1974; Founder, Posey & Co. Realtors, 1974-present.

DC Office: 2150 RHOB 20515, 202-225-3671, Fax: 202-225-3516, posey.house.gov

State Offices: Melbourne, 321-632-1776.

Committees: *Financial Services*: Consumer Protection & Financial Institutions; Oversight & Investigations. *Science, Space & Technology*: Space & Aeronautics.

Group Ratings

	ADA	ACLU	AFL-CIO	LCV	ITI	COC	HAFA	ACU	CFG	FRC
2018	-	17%	-	0%	-	73%	84%	88%	82%	100%
2017	0%	C	9%	0%	C	93%	C	88%	84%	100%

Almanac Ratings 2017-18

	Economy	Social	Foreign	Composite
Liberal	6%	16%	0%	7%
Conservative	94%	84%	100%	93%

Key Votes of the 115th Congress

1. Obama-care revision	Y	5. Family planning regs	Y	9. Guantanamo prisoners	N
2. Tax Cuts	Y	6. Body cameras/immigration	NV	10. Ground missiles, limit	N
3. Omnibus appropriations	N	7. Abortion ban	Y	11. Defense Dept. spending	Y
4. Dodd-Frank revision	Y	8. Concealed carry	Y	12. FISA rules	Y

Election Results

Election	Name (Party)	Vote (%)		Cand. Spent	Ind. Exp. Support	Ind. Exp. Oppose
2018 General	Bill Posey (R)......................................	218,112	(60%)	$1,013,614		
	Sanjay Patel (D)........................	142,415	(40%)	$330,899		
2018 Primary	Bill Posey (R)..	(100%)				

Prior winning percentages: 2016 (63%), 2014 (66%), 2012 (59%), 2010 (65%), 2008 (53%)

Bill Posey, a Republican first elected in 2008, has pursued his personal interest in finance issues and his district's interest in space issues, with high seniority in his committee assignments. He combines extensive experience in business and local government, with a penchant to shake up business-as-usual and an occasionally maverick approach.

Posey was born in Washington, D.C. and moved several times because of his father's work in the aircraft business. His family landed in Brevard County in 1956. After graduating from high school, Posey took a job with McDonnell Douglas Astronautics at the Kennedy Space Center. He worked on the Apollo 11 Launch Team that in 1969 sent the first men to the moon, and he attended Brevard Community College at night. After Apollo 11, Posey was laid off and went into real estate as founder of Posey & Co. Realtors. Until an accident at an Orlando speedway in 2004 left him with spinal fractures, Posey had been an accomplished stock car racer. As the first member of his family to register as a Republican, Posey was elected to the Rockledge City Council in 1976 and served a decade. Later, he served eight years each in the state House and Senate. He authored legislation that set new standards for state government accountability.

In 2008, he ran for an open seat. Other Republicans who had been interested in running fell in line. Democrats were unable to find a strong candidate. Posey faced Democrat Stephen

Blythe, a Melbourne family physician, and made government accountability and immigration reform the central themes of his campaign. It was an amiable contest. The candidates expressed mutual admiration and said they would vote for each other if they could not vote for themselves. Posey outspent Blythe by almost 9-to-1 and won 53%-42% in a Democratic year.

Once in Washington, Posey voted with Democrats to extend unemployment benefits and joined a bipartisan bill to double the one-year waiting period before lawmakers who leave their seats can lobby ex-colleagues. His skepticism about the war in Afghanistan made him practically a centrist on foreign policy: In 2011, he was among 16 House Republicans to vote in support of a phased withdrawal of troops. On the Financial Services Committee, he got the results of every committee vote posted on its website within two days. He pushed a measure to require state governments to submit fiscal accounting reports as a condition of getting federal money. In July 2018, he won enactment of his legislation to expand protections, including compensation, for American victims of international terrorism.

On the Space, Science and Technology Committee, Posey has worked on behalf of the Kennedy Space Center and the Space Coast to find ways to live with NASA cutbacks. He won praise from the local Sunshine State News for using that seat "as a bully pulpit to push private space flight and jab the Obama administration for retreating from space exploration." In March 2018, he spearheaded a letter of congressional support for a new mobile launcher that NASA was seeking.

His maverick instincts have extended to House leadership contests. In 2015, Posey voted for fellow Florida Rep. Daniel Webster for Speaker, instead of John Boehner. That October, he again joined the dissidents, as one of nine Republicans who voted for Webster when Paul Ryan was elected to succeed Boehner.

At home, he has not faced a serious reelection threat. In 2018, his Democratic challenger was Sanjay Patel, a former technology consultant and Bernie Sanders delegate at the 2016 Democratic convention who said that the district needed "real representation." Posey won, 60%-40%.

FL-8: Space Coast/Northern Treasure Coast   **Cook Partisan Voting Index: R+11**

Population		Race and Ethnicity		Income	
Total	730,040	White	75.3%	Median Income	$50,998
Land area (sq. miles)	1,752	Black	9.5%	District Income Rank	287
Pop/ sq mi	416.7	Latino	10.3%	Poverty Rate	13.3%
Born in State	33.1%	Asian	2.1%	With health insurance	87.6%
		Two or more races	2.2%	Cash public assistance	2%
Age Groups		Other	0.6%	Food stamp/SNAP	11.2%
Under 18	18.4%				
18-34	18%	**Education**		**Work**	
35-64	39.4%	H.S grad or less	38.1%	White Collar	24.2%
Over 64	24.2%	Some college	33.7%	Sales and Service	44.6%
		College Degree, 4 yr	17.3%	Blue Collar	18.3%
Military		Post grad	10.9%	Government	12.8%
Veteran/ Active Duty	13.9%				

2012 Pres. Vote	Romney	206,074	(57%)	Obama	153,138	(42%)	
2016 Pres. Vote	Trump	234,648	(58%)	Clinton	151,412	(37%)	Johnson	11,387	(3%)

Melbourne: When Cape Canaveral was chosen in the 1940s as the nation's rocket testing site, only 20,000 people lived in all of Brevard County, which stretches along 63 miles of the coast north and south of the cape. It was a quiet, winter-vacation spot that relied on fishing and citrus and its location on the sunny Atlantic Coast. Rockets could be launched eastward so that spent parts fell into the ocean. In 2018, Brevard had 590,000 people, and its metropolitan area had the fastest-growing economy in the state. The county is mostly coastal communities and has no major city center. But it has a white-collar, service economy, knitted together by interest in the space program. The Kennedy Space Center attracts 1.7 million visitors annually, which is fewer than in the days when space flights captured the public's imagination. When the Florida Public Service Commission announced in 1998 that the region needed a new area code, a space enthusiast suggested 321. The North American agency that assigns area codes agreed.

Local uncertainty grew following the retirement of the space shuttle fleet, a move that slashed thousands of aerospace jobs. Officials have sought alternatives. The large share of individuals affiliated with the space program led to a spurt in technological entrepreneurship in sectors as varied as aviation, synthetic materials and clean energy. Harris Corp. — a Fortune 500 defense contractor based in Brevard — has 6,600 employees locally. Elon Musk's SpaceX company, which operates launch pads at Cape Canaveral Air Force Station and Kennedy Space Center, and a rocket refurbishing facility in Port Canaveral, had its maiden launch in 2018.

Proximity to Disney World and Orlando spawned growth in the cruise-line business, which has soared beyond expectations. Port Canaveral in 2018 was the second-largest passenger port in the world, with its 4.5 million annual cruisers, trailing only Miami. A third terminal for the port was planned by Carnival for a 2020 opening to accommodate a new and even-larger ship. Eco-tourism is another promising avenue for growth. The Merritt Island National Wildlife Refuge and Canaveral National Seashore draw wildlife aficionados to view their vast array of flora and fauna.

The 8th Congressional District of Florida encompasses all of Brevard and Indian River counties, and makes a nip in the eastern end of Orange County. About 80 percent of the population resides in Brevard. Among the bigger towns are Cocoa Beach, Melbourne, Palm Bay and Vero Beach. The district has become safely Republican. Donald Trump captured 58 percent of the vote here. This was a rare district in Florida that had no change in the 2016 redistricting.

Darren Soto (D)

Elected 2016, 2nd term, b. Feb 25, 1978; Ringwood, NJ; Rutgers University (NJ), B.A., 2000; George Washington University School of Law (DC), J.D., 2004; Catholic; Married (Amanda Soto).

Elected Office: FL House, 2007-2012; FL Senate, 2012-2016, Deputy Minority Whip, 2012-2014.

DC Office: 1507 LHOB 20515, 202-225-9889, Fax: 202-225-9742, soto.house.gov

State Offices: Haines City, 202-600-0843; Kissimmee, 407-452-1171; Lake Wales, 202-600-0843; Orlando, 202-332-4476; Winter Haven, 202-615-1308.

Committees: *Energy & Commerce*: Communications & Technology; Consumer Protection & Commerce; Environment & Climate Change. *Natural Resources*: Indigenous Peoples of the United States.

Group Ratings

	ADA	ACLU	AFL-CIO	LCV	ITI	COC	HAFA	ACU	CFG	FRC
2018	-	86%	-	100%	-	50%	2%	4%	5%	0%
2017	85%	C	97%	100%	C	64%	C	0%	0%	11%

Almanac Ratings 2017-18

	Economy	Social	Foreign	Composite
Liberal	94%	100%	87%	94%
Conservative	6%	0%	14%	6%

Key Votes of the 115th Congress

1. Obama-care revision	N	5. Family planning regs	N	9. Guantanamo prisoners	Y
2. Tax Cuts	N	6. Body cameras/immigration	Y	10. Ground missiles, limit	Y
3. Omnibus appropriations	N	7. Abortion ban	N	11. Defense Dept. spending	Y
4. Dodd-Frank revision	N	8. Concealed carry	N	12. FISA rules	N

Election Results

Election	Name (Party)	Vote (%)	Cand. Spent	Ind. Exp. Support	Ind. Exp. Oppose
2018 General	Darren Soto (D)................................. 172,172	(58%)	$1,387,535	$974,830	$15,000
	Wayne Liebnitzky (R)....................... 124,565	(42%)	$59,182	$11,563	
2018 Primary	Darren Soto (D)................................. 36,586	(66%)			
	Alan Grayson (D)............................... 18,528	(34%)			

Prior winning percentages: 2016 (58%)

Darren Soto, elected in 2016 as the first Puerto Rican elected to Congress from Florida, remains the state's only Hispanic Democrat. He has prevailed in competitive primaries against his predecessor and his predecessor's wife As was the case when he was a state legislator, Soto has styled himself as a coalition-builder.

Soto was born in New Jersey to a Puerto Rican father and an Italian-American mother. He worked in finance for Prudential Insurance while he attended Rutgers University, where he graduated with a bachelor's in economics, and got his law degree from George Washington University. Soto practiced as a commercial and civil rights attorney in central Florida. He joined the Young Democrats club in Orlando, where friends encouraged him to run for the state House. He was successful at age 28 and served there for six years, and then another four years in the Senate. He passed legislation making it easier for immigrant children with deferred-action status to acquire a driver's license. Gov. Rick Scott vetoed the measure, sparking widespread protests. Soto helped to enact a bill that reduced from five years to one year the statute of limitations for banks to collect foreclosure debt. In 2014, he passed legislation giving the Florida Supreme Court authority to admit immigrant lawyers into the Florida Bar.

Soto sought the House seat when Rep. Alan Grayson ran for the Senate. A leading opponent in the primary was Dena Grayson, a biochemist who had a medical residency and a doctorate in molecular cell biology. She married Grayson three months before the primary. Susanna Randolph, the wife of Orange County Tax Collector Scott Randolph, spent hundreds of thousands of dollars for negative ads against Soto. As the frontrunner, Soto discussed the need for better-paying local jobs. He highlighted his efforts in Tallahassee to deliver tens of millions to fight citrus disease in Polk County orchards. He spent $1.2 million for the campaign, compared with $730,000 for Randolph and $620,000 for Grayson.

Soto won the primary with 36 percent of the vote; Randolph and Grayson each got 28 percent. In Osceola, which cast the most votes, Soto took 44 percent. He ran third with 26 percent in Polk, which had the smallest share of Hispanics. In the general, Soto faced Wayne Liebnitzky, a businessman and retired Navy aviation electrician. The challenger raised $32,000. Soto won, 57%-43%, which was nearly the same as the presidential vote in the district.

On the House Agriculture Committee, Soto worked on the farm bill and claimed credit for five provisions that were in the final deal in December 2018. They included farm-related technology to assist veterans with disabilities, the removal of algae from the list of excluded materials for biomass crop research, more emphasis on specialty crop research on sensor and image technology in farming, and codification of a research and development farm program between Israel and the United States. In 2017, he enacted a separate bill to improve the conservation of sharks by limiting the sale of billfish caught by U.S. fishing vessels.

In December 2017, Soto traveled to Puerto Rico to organize a task force to advise local residents who were moving to central Florida. He was a member of the bipartisan Problem Solvers Caucus that prepared revisions in House procedures and got Nancy Pelosi to agree to some of the changes when she was seeking support from Democrats to become Speaker. "Our proposal is a progressive one, that each member should have reasonable input in Congress on behalf of their constituents," he told the Orlando Sentinel.

In the Democratic primary for reelection, he faced his predecessor, Alan Grayson, though the district lines had changed since Grayson gave up the seat in his unsuccessful bid for the Senate. During a debate, Grayson criticized Soto's support for conservative legislation while he served in the legislature, plus his belated endorsement of progressive legislation in Congress. Soto responded, according to a report in Politico, that he would "give the district the dignity and respect it deserves." He was endorsed by Pelosi and former Vice President Joe Biden. Soto spent more than $1 million in the primary. Grayson spent $600,000 and — notably — left nearly $1 million in his account. Soto won, 66%-34%, and took more than two-thirds of the vote in both Osceola and Orange counties. In a rerun of his general election two years earlier against Liebnitzky, Soto won, 58%-42%. In 2019, he got a plum assignment to the Energy and Commerce Committee.

FL-9: Central Florida   Cook Partisan Voting Index: D+5

Population		Race and Ethnicity		Income	
Total	810,034	White	42.7%	Median Income	$48,016
Land area (sq. miles)	2,313	Black	12%	District Income Rank	340
Pop/ sq mi	350.2	Latino	40%	Poverty Rate	17.3%
Born in State	30.7%	Asian	2.8%	With health insurance	83.1%
Age Groups		Two or more races	1.9%	Cash public assistance	2.5%
Under 18	24.1%	Other	0.6%	Food stamp/SNAP	18.3%
18-34	22.6%	**Education**		**Work**	
35-64	38%	H.S grad or less	45.3%	White Collar	15.3%
Over 64	15.3%	Some college	32%	Sales and Service	49.6%
Military		College Degree, 4 yr	15.3%	Blue Collar	20.7%
Veteran/ Active Duty	7.8%	Post grad	7.4%	Government	10.4%

2012 Pres. Vote	Obama	159,113	(56%)	Romney	124,120	(44%)		
2016 Pres. Vote	Clinton	195,368	(54%)	Trump	149,352	(42%)	Johnson 7,899	(2%)

Orlando, Kissimmee: Orlando has become the area with the fastest-growing Puerto Rican population in the United States. Places like Azalea Park in Orange County, as well as Buenaventura Lakes (known as "BVL" to the locals) in neighboring Osceola County, have Puerto Rican- majority populations. One local real estate agent who specializes in the Puerto Rican homes market called BVL "a Puerto Rican Levittown," referring to the developments that sprung up after World War II , where the children of turn-of-the-century immigrants made their first moves into suburban life and the American middle class. Businesses increasingly cater to this emerging "Little Puerto Rico." Goya foods located its central Florida distribution center in nearby Meadow Woods. Non-Hispanic companies such as the supermarket chain Publix have sought to adapt, opening Sabor (Spanish for "taste") stores here, for example. Countless small businesses appealing to the burgeoning Hispanic population line streets.

Central Florida is home to what has become the fast-growing center of the Puerto Rican community. In 2017, 54 percent of the 352,000 residents in the relatively empty and cheaper spaces of Osceola were Hispanic. At the same time, 31 percent of the 1.35 million in Orange were Hispanic. The population of those two counties in 1960 was 19,000 and 263,000, respectively. The recent increase in Puerto Ricans has been driven, in part, by islanders escaping the economic collapse in their commonwealth as a result of its severe public debt.

The devastating blow that Hurricane Maria in September 2017 struck to the island, where many communities were without electricity for months — and rivaled Katrina (2005, Louisiana and Mississippi) and Harvey (2017, Texas) in its intensity and costs -- added tens of thousands more to the exodus. In response, Florida declared its own state of emergency and created disaster relief centers in Orlando and Miami. Islanders settled with family and friends, and had no plans to return to Puerto Rico. With the help of a strong local economy, many were able to find jobs. But the social dislocation was extensive, including for long-term housing and local schools. In the two months following Maria, "more than 2,500 Puerto Rican students have enrolled in Orange and Osceola county schools," the Orlando Sentinel reported. Even before this disruption, the Census Bureau reported, the share of English-speaking households in Osceola dropped to 51 percent.

Lake Nona — a master-designed community south of the airport with more than 12,000 residents -- has been among the booming areas for local development. It includes the world's largest tennis facility, a huge new training campus for KPMG and an Amazon fulfillment center. The airport, which is divided between the 9th and 10th districts and passed Miami in 2017 with the largest passenger load in Florida, plans to open a new terminal in 2021.

The 9th District of Florida represented a bow by both political and judicial voices in redistricting to the emerging political realities of central Florida. The Hispanic share of its population is 40 percent, and growing. Many black neighborhoods in Orlando were shifted to the adjoining 10th District, which is based entirely in Orange County and is also heavily Democratic; blacks are only 12 percent of the new 9th. In exchange, the district gained a large slice of eastern Polk County, which leans Republican. The district retains all of Osceola.

Politically, there is an important caveat to those numbers: According to official Florida election data, only 40 percent of Hispanics in the 9th have been eligible to vote. Many are too young, others choose not to register and some are not legally in the United States. (Puerto Ricans are immediately eligible to vote on the mainland). Consequently, it will take time for their political power to catch up to their demographic influence. Plus, Puerto Rican voters in Florida are not a unified voting bloc. That became apparent in the 2018 Senate election when Republican Rick Scott outworked Democratic Sen. Bill Nelson among Puerto Ricans and added tens of thousands more GOP votes in central Florida than Donald Trump received in 2016. That had a huge impact in an election that Scott won by about 10,000 votes.

Val Demings (D)

Elected 2016, 2nd term, b. Mar 12, 1957; Jacksonville; Webster University (MO), M.P.A.; Southern Police Institute; Florida State University, B.S., 1979; African Methodist Episcopal; Married (Jerry L. Demings); 3 children; 5 grandchildren.

Professional Career: Social worker; Police officer; Commander of Special Operation, FLPD, 2003-2006; Police Chief, FLPD, 2007-2012.

DC Office: 217 CHOB 20515, 202-225-2176, Fax: 202-226-6559, demings.house.gov

State Offices: Orlando, 321-388-9808.

Committees: *Homeland Security*: Transportation & Maritime Security. *Judiciary*: Antitrust, Commercial & Administrative Law; Crime, Terrorism & Homeland Security. *Permanent Select on Intelligence*: Defense Intelligence & Warfighter Support; Intelligence Modernization & Readiness.

Group Ratings

	ADA	ACLU	AFL-CIO	LCV	ITI	COC	HAFA	ACU	CFG	FRC
2018	-	69%	-	94%	-	58%	6%	4%	18%	0%
2017	90%	C	95%	97%	C	57%	C	0%	0%	11%

Almanac Ratings 2017-18

	Economy	Social	Foreign	Composite
Liberal	100%	93%	89%	94%
Conservative	0%	8%	11%	6%

Key Votes of the 115th Congress

1. Obama-care revision	N	5. Family planning regs	N	9. Guantanamo prisoners	Y
2. Tax Cuts	N	6. Body cameras/immigration	Y	10. Ground missiles, limit	Y
3. Omnibus appropriations	Y	7. Abortion ban	N	11. Defense Dept. spending	Y
4. Dodd-Frank revision	N	8. Concealed carry	N	12. FISA rules	Y

Election Results

Election	Name (Party)	Vote (%)	Cand. Spent	Ind. Exp. Support	Ind. Exp. Oppose
2018 General	Val Demings (D)...	(100%)	$481,689	$10,000	
2018 Primary	Val Demings (D).................................... 73,601	(75%)			
	Wade Darius (D).................................. 24,534	(25%)			

Prior winning percentages: 2016 (65%)

Val Demings was one of three newly elected Orlando-area Democrats in 2016: an African-American woman, a Latino man and a Vietnamese-American woman. Their districts cover 99 percent of Orange County, plus large parts of three surrounding counties in this rapidly growing metropolitan area. Demings, who was the most experienced of the three, had a background in police work that made her a prime recruit for House Democrats. She likes to call herself a unifier. Her husband, Jerry Demings, took office in December 2018 as Orange County mayor, the first African American to hold that position.

Demings was born in Jacksonville, the youngest of seven children. Her mother was a maid and her father was a janitor. She got a bachelor's degree in criminology from Florida State University, the first in her family to graduate from college. She started as a social worker in Jacksonville, but set her sights on becoming a police officer. After moving to Orlando and enrolling in the police academy, where she was the class president, Demings served with the police department for 27 years, including four years as chief of police. She placed a priority on community engagement to address some of the root causes of violent crime. In 2012, Demings ran in the old 10th District against first-term Republican Rep. Daniel Webster. With the narrow GOP leaning of the district at the time, she lost a close contest, 52%-48%. In that campaign, she was aided by more than $2 million from the political committee that then-New York City Mayor Michael Bloomberg created to support gun control.

Following the major changes in the 2016 redistricting, Webster wisely concluded that he could not win the revamped district and ran in an open seat in the 11th District to the west; the GOP largely conceded his old seat. Demings was elected in two relatively easy contests. In the four-candidate Democratic primary, she won 57 percent of the vote against credible opponents. State Sen. Geraldine Thompson, who was runner-up with 20 percent, criticized the national party for giving Demings a speaking slot at the Democratic national convention a month earlier. Bob Poe, the former state Democratic chairman, self-financed his campaign with $2 million; he got 17 percent. In one ad, he said that Demings had condoned police brutality. Demings spent $1.5 million, and benefited from another $538,000 spent on her behalf by a Bloomberg Super PAC. In November, Demings defeated little-known Republican Thuy Lowe, 65%-35%.

On the Homeland Security Committee, Demings persuaded officials of the Homeland Security Department to revise their criteria so that Orlando became eligible for anti-terrorism grants. After gaining a seat on the Judiciary Committee in December 2017, she joined Jerry Nadler, the panel's ranking Democrat, on a resolution that proposed the censure of President Donald Trump after he referred to immigrants arriving in the United States from "shithole" countries. "We cannot allow racism and prejudice to become the basis for federal policy," Demings said. In 2019, Speaker Nancy Pelosi gave her a much-sought seat on the Intelligence Committee.

In the 2018 election, she had a primary challenge from Wade Darius. He spent $42,000 – about 10 percent of the total spending by Demings. She won, 75%-25% and had no opposition in November. Demings and her husband, who was Orlando police chief (the same position that his wife later held) and served three terms as sheriff of Orange County before he was elected mayor, have been married since 1988.

FL-10: Central Florida

Cook Partisan Voting Index: D+11

Population		Race and Ethnicity		Income	
Total	787,875	White	37.5%	Median Income	$50,380
Land area (sq. miles)	436	Black	27.2%	District Income Rank	302
Pop/ sq mi	1805.2	Latino	26.7%	Poverty Rate	16.6%
Born in State	36.7%	Asian	5.2%	With health insurance	82.7%
		Two or more races	2.3%	Cash public assistance	2.3%
Age Groups		Other	1.1%	Food stamp/SNAP	18%
Under 18	24.1%				
18-34	25.9%	**Education**		**Work**	
35-64	39.1%	H.S grad or less	39.9%	White Collar	10.9%
Over 64	10.9%	Some college	30.5%	Sales and Service	49%
		College Degree, 4 yr	20.4%	Blue Collar	17.4%
Military		Post grad	9.3%	Government	8%
Veteran/ Active Duty	6%				

2012 Pres. Vote	Obama	164,590	(61%)	Romney	104,367	(39%)			
2016 Pres. Vote	Clinton	194,934	(61%)	Trump	110,062	(35%)	Johnson	7,205	(2%)

Downtown Orlando: Who would have supposed 50 years ago that the most popular tourist destination in the world would rise amid the swamps and orange groves of central Florida? The answer: Walt Disney, and just about no one else. In the mid-1960s, Disney looked at the map and decided that the intersection of Interstate 4 and Florida's Turnpike, the "crossroads of Florida," just a few miles southwest of Orlando, was the perfect place for the vast theme park he was planning. The spirit of the place was established by a man who never lived there but created something now taken for granted. Disney conceived the first theme park in Orange County California in 1955, but he perfected it in the 17,000 acres of Florida swamp that his associates stealthily snapped up and where Walt Disney World opened in 1971. With the invention of the theme park, Disney also pioneered sophisticated communications, utility and waste-disposal methods — all out of sight and underground. Disney World is not just an engineering marvel. It required more than 60,000 "cast members" (employees) with know-how and earnest cheerfulness to entertain its 20.5 million visitors in 2017. The number of workers is the largest in the world for a company at a single site.

Disney is hardly the only site that has made Orlando one of the world's great tourist destinations. Other popular theme parks here include Sea World and Universal Studios. Cape Canaveral is less than 40 miles away. The technology economy also has moved into Greater Orlando. Defense contractor Lockheed Martin planned to open in 2019 a new building at its "mission system and training" facility southwest of the city, with several thousand employees. In downtown, the University of Central Florida planned to open in the autumn of 2019 a new campus, with 7,700 students; its main campus is 13 miles east of downtown. Downtown Orlando was the site of the horrific terrorist attack that killed 49 persons at the Pulse nightclub in 2016, which renewed calls for gun control. Continuing growth — of the downtown skyline and in the expanding metropolitan region — has spurred what may be uphill efforts to control the sprawl and congestion in one of the nation's booming areas. Privately financed passenger train service to Tampa was scheduled to start in 2021.

The new 10th Congressional District of Florida is entirely in Orange County, including the western portion of Orlando, with the enormous Disney complex near its southern border. Redistricting increased both its black and Hispanic shares to 27 percent. Many of those minority voters had been in the old 5th District, which ran from Jacksonville to Orlando. The population gains, on top of devastating frosts downsized the acreage for the eponymous citrus that gave the county its name by 50 percent from 2005 to 2015, and by more than 95 percent during the past half-century. The district has small black rural settlements, such as lettuce-producing Zellwood and Eatonville, a town depicted in the stories of Zora Neale Hurston, a preeminent novelist and folklorist. In 2016, Hillary Clinton won, 62%-35%.

Daniel Webster (R)

Elected 2010, 5th term, b. Apr 27, 1949; Charleston, WV; Georgia Institute of Technology, B.E.E., 1971; Baptist; Married (Sandy Jordan); 6 children; 14 grandchildren.

Elected Office: FL House, 1980-1998, speaker, 1996-1998; FL Senate, 1998-2008.

Professional Career: Owner, Webster Air Conditioning & Heating.

DC Office: 1210 LHOB 20515, 202-225-1002, Fax: 202-226-6559, webster.house.gov

State Offices: Brooksville, 352-241-9230; Inverness, 352-241-9204; Leesburg, 352-241-9220; The Villages, 352-383-3552.

Committees: *Natural Resources*: National Parks, Forests & Public Lands; Water, Oceans & Wildlife. *Transportation & Infrastructure*: Aviation; Highways & Transit; Water Resources & Environment.

Group Ratings

	ADA	ACLU	AFL-CIO	LCV	ITI	COC	HAFA	ACU	CFG	FRC
2018	-	15%	-	0%	-	73%	87%	92%	81%	100%
2017	10%	C	3%	3%	C	93%	C	96%	86%	100%

Almanac Ratings 2017-18

	Economy	Social	Foreign	Composite
Liberal	4%	6%	3%	5%
Conservative	96%	94%	97%	95%

Key Votes of the 115th Congress

1. Obama-care revision	Y	5. Family planning regs	Y	9. Guantanamo prisoners	N
2. Tax Cuts	Y	6. Body cameras/immigration	NV	10. Ground missiles, limit	N
3. Omnibus appropriations	N	7. Abortion ban	Y	11. Defense Dept. spending	Y
4. Dodd-Frank revision	Y	8. Concealed carry	Y	12. FISA rules	N

Election Results

Election	Name (Party)	Vote (%)		Cand. Spent	Ind. Exp. Support	Ind. Exp. Oppose
2018 General	Daniel Webster (R)............................	239,395	(65%)	$395,002		
	Dana Cottrell (D)...............................	128,053	(35%)	$73,882		
2018 Primary	Daniel Webster (R)............................		(100%)			

Prior winning percentages: 2016 (65%), 2014 (62%), 2012 (52%), 2010 (56%)

Republican Daniel Webster, a staunch and often activist conservative, prevailed in contentious elections in 2010 and 2012. He settled into the House with an insider's demeanor, but then unexpectedly became the chief GOP challenger to Speaker John Boehner and, later, Paul Ryan in futile bids by conservatives to register their unhappiness. Webster subsequently was stripped of his prime committee assignment, though he outlasted both Speakers and gained a niche among conservatives for his willingness to challenge GOP leaders. Further demonstrating his survival skills, he switched districts following the 2016 redistricting.

Webster was born in Charleston West Virginia and is distantly related to his 19th century namesake, considered one of the greatest senators and orators in history. His family moved to Florida when he was 7 years old because a doctor told them the climate would help cure young Daniel's sinus problems. He graduated from the Georgia Institute of Technology in 1971 with a degree in electrical engineering and eventually took over his family's heating and air conditioning business in Orlando. He became politically active in 1979, when he led his church's effort to turn a house into a Sunday school, only to be refused a zoning exemption by the county commission.

Webster won a seat in the state House in 1980 and later became the first Republican speaker of the Florida House in 122 years. He sponsored a bill to ban nude performances in bars and another that would have required the legislature to study the impact of proposed laws on families. In 1998, Webster moved to the state Senate, where he pushed to ease gun regulations and restrict abortion rights, including his bill requiring women to get an ultrasound test and view the results before getting an abortion. He led legislative efforts to prolong the life of Terri Schiavo, a woman in a persistent vegetative state who became a national cause for conservatives.

With the backing of national Republicans, he challenged controversial Democratic Rep. Alan Grayson in 2010. Grayson had become a lightning rod for conservatives because of his harsh rhetoric. Webster and Republicans believed that Grayson was a poor fit for the more tempered politics of the swing Orlando-based district. Webster refused to debate Grayson, or to return his attacks in kind, saying, "We're taking the high road. I'm not getting down in the dirt with him." He focused his campaign on the size of the federal government and the passage of President Barack Obama's health care law. Grayson's strategy energized liberals nationally, and he raked in $6 million for his campaign. The voters turned him out decisively, 56%-38%.

In the newly Republican-controlled House, Webster won a seat on the Rules Committee, a coveted position usually reserved for members whom leaders can trust to hew to the party line. As a measure of his initial status as a House insider, he became the first GOP freshman to get a substantive bill through the House, with a measure aimed at limiting executive bonuses at companies that received financial industry bailout funds. Webster voiced conditional support for a comprehensive reform plan that would give illegal immigrants a pathway to citizenship.

In 2012, Grayson talked about a rematch with Webster, but instead ran for — and won – the seat in the new solidly Democratic 9th District. Webster was initially considered a reelection shoo-in in his 10th District against Val Demings, the former Orlando police chief, but she outworked and outraised the congressman. The Democrat accused Webster of using taxpayer money to create a "lobbyists' lounge" when he served in the legislature, a reference to his decision to spend about $100,000 for renovations to the speaker's office suite. He adamantly denied that the remodeling was done to serve lobbyists. The GOP tilt of the district proved decisive and Webster won 52%-48%.

As Congress prepared to convene in January 2015, Webster surprised many on Capitol Hill by speaking out against Speaker John Boehner and Republican management of the House. In previous weeks, he had quietly circulated to other Republicans a white paper that was titled "Widgets, Principles and Republicans." It concluded that "Congress is broken, the Republican brand is in trouble, and nothing can change unless congressional processes become less power- and self-preservation driven, and more open to rank-and-file members," the Orlando Sentinel reported. "A lot of people liked it," Webster later said. Webster agreed to enter his name for Speaker two hours before the vote. He was supported by 12 Republican lawmakers, which was fewer than the number who had told him they would support him, he said. Boehner won a bare majority and avoided what could have been a catastrophic second ballot.

With Boehner's allies outraged by his candidacy and urging retribution, Webster was stripped of his seat on the Rules Committee. He issued a conciliatory statement that "my candidacy and vote was not a vote against personalities, policies or even John Boehner." But Boehner was feeling more pressure from conservatives. At the end of September, he had had enough of the internal sniping and he announced that he would step down as Speaker. Webster announced his candidacy to replace Boehner. He attracted little support, even when Majority Leader Kevin McCarthy abandoned his bid to move up. After most House Republicans rallied behind Ryan, Webster got the votes of nine Republicans.

Webster regained status as a rank-and-file member. In August 2018, he won enactment of a bill to aid small businesses with cybersecurity. He cited his own experience in business, plus the security challenges in the modern world. The following month, Congress passed his bipartisan bill to strengthen disaster preparedness for hospitals and long-term care facilities.

At home, Webster encountered stormy waves in 2015 when the court's plan for redistricting turned his district into one that he said would be "impossible" for him to win. He intervened before the state Supreme Court to seek a reversal, but made no progress. Unexpectedly, he was rescued when neighboring Rep. Rick Nugent announced that he would retire from his solidly Republican 11th District. But there was a catch: Nugent's chief of staff, Justin Grabelle, said he was running for his boss' seat, with the support of Nugent. Webster had little familiarity with the new district. But he had one big advantage: He was an incumbent and Grabelle was a first-time candidate. Webster raised more than twice as much money: $1 million to $360,000. He won, 60%-40%, including all five counties. In this Republican district, Webster breezed to victory in November with 65 percent of the vote.

In the run-up to the 2018 election, Grayson explored another congressional run, with Webster as a possible foe. Instead, Grayson sought a return to the 9th District. But Rep. Darren Soto defeated him by a 2-to-1 margin in the Democratic primary. Webster was easily reelected. Even with his new experience in the minority party, he has become a more conventional House member.

FL-11: Gulf Coast, Central Florida   **Cook Partisan Voting Index: R+15**

Population		Race and Ethnicity		Income	
Total	738,652	White	79.5%	Median Income	$45,051
Land area (sq. miles)	2,386	Black	6.9%	District Income Rank	371
Pop/ sq mi	309.6	Latino	10.1%	Poverty Rate	14.1%
Born in State	29.5%	Asian	1.2%	With health insurance	88.7%
		Two or more races	1.6%	Cash public assistance	1.8%
Age Groups		Other	0.7%	Food stamp/SNAP	12.6%
Under 18	15.8%				
18-34	14.4%	**Education**		**Work**	
35-64	34.3%	H.S grad or less	47.4%	White Collar	35.5%
Over 64	35.5%	Some college	32.1%	Sales and Service	50.8%
		College Degree, 4 yr	13.2%	Blue Collar	21%
Military		Post grad	7.4%	Government	12.1%
Veteran/ Active Duty	14.9%				

2012 Pres. Vote	Romney	216,349	(59%)	Obama	145,565	(40%)		
2016 Pres. Vote	Trump	266,257	(64%)	Clinton	133,448	(32%)	Johnson	7,953	(2%)

Ocala, Tampa suburbs: Over the past quarter-century, Florida's urban areas have grown in almost every direction, occupying the high ground between the swamps that still take up much of the state's peninsula. The pattern of development is evident in counties to the north and east of St. Petersburg and Tampa, where subdivisions, trailer parks and Winn-Dixie supermarkets sprang up in what had been farms and sleepy little towns, with low brick buildings baking in the Florida sun. Drawn by the many inland lakes, greenery and the pleasant climate, retirees from the Midwest flocked here by traveling south on Interstate 75 — a pattern distinct from the retirees who drove Interstate 95 from the Boston-Washington corridor to south Florida. The development here has been nothing short of astonishing; the population of Hernando County increased tenfold since 1970, while Citrus County increased nearly that much, though each county has slowed since 2010. The rapid development has created an uneasy tension with environmental concerns. The federal government declared the Crystal River National Wildlife Refuge a restricted manatee refuge after tourists were observed chasing, riding and poking the gentle sea cows.

The 11th Congressional District of Florida covers much of this rapidly growing area. It includes all of coastal Citrus and Hernando counties, where the beach areas are largely undeveloped, plus Sumter County, which contain large tracts of open land. The numbers here offer insight into changing retirement patterns. Sumter County's population is growing rapidly — by 34 percent from 2010 to 2017 — mostly a result of the massive retirement community known as The Villages, with more than 100 miles of golf cart paths and a population that reached 125,000 in 2017. Jobs in construction and health care have been soaring. After having been the fastest growing metro area in the nation from 2013 to 2015, it slipped to tenth, though The Villages has begun to expand into neighboring locales in Lake County. The median age in Sumter is 66.4 years, which makes it the only county in the nation that exceeds 65; of the total population, 57 percent are at least 65. The residents are 90 percent white and they vote more than 2-to-1 for Republicans. The community is "the most significant source of Republican optimism for many years to come," Politico wrote in June 2018.

The remaining 40 percent of the district is inland in Lake and Marion Counties, in places like Inverness, Spring Hill and Brooksville. This was once politically marginal territory, but it has become reliably Republican. Donald Trump took the district, 65%-32%.

Gus Bilirakis (R)

Elected 2006, 7th term, b. Feb 08, 1963; Gainesville; St. Petersburg Junior College (FL), 1983; University of Florida, B.S., 1986; Stetson University College of Law (FL), J.D., 1989; Greek Orthodox; Married (Eva Lialios Bilirakis); 4 children.

Elected Office: FL House, 1998-2006.

Professional Career: Intern, U.S. President Ronald Reagan, 1983; Intern, NRCC, 1984; Aide, U.S. Rep. Don Sundquist, 1985; Teacher, St. Petersburg College, 1997-2001; Practicing attorney, 1989-2006.

DC Office: 2227 RHOB 20515, 202-225-5755, Fax: 202-225-4085, bilirakis.house.gov

State Offices: New Port Richey, 727-232-2921; Tarpon Springs, 727-940-5860; Wesley Chapel, 813-501-4942.

Committees: *Energy & Commerce*: Communications & Technology; Health. *Veterans' Affairs*: Disability Assistance & Memorial Affairs; Economic Opportunity (RMM).

Group Ratings

	ADA	ACLU	AFL-CIO	LCV	ITI	COC	HAFA	ACU	CFG	FRC
2018	-	4%	-	6%	-	91%	65%	80%	53%	100%
2017	0%	C	5%	0%	C	93%	C	88%	77%	100%

Almanac Ratings 2017-18

	Economy	Social	Foreign	Composite
Liberal	5%	4%	7%	5%
Conservative	95%	97%	93%	95%

Key Votes of the 115th Congress

1. Obama-care revision	Y	5. Family planning regs	Y	9. Guantanamo prisoners	N
2. Tax Cuts	Y	6. Body cameras/immigration	N	10. Ground missiles, limit	N
3. Omnibus appropriations	Y	7. Abortion ban	Y	11. Defense Dept. spending	NV
4. Dodd-Frank revision	Y	8. Concealed carry	Y	12. FISA rules	Y

Election Results

Election	Name (Party)	Vote (%)		Cand. Spent	Ind. Exp. Support	Ind. Exp. Oppose
2018 General	Gus Bilirakis (R)............................	194,564	(58%)	$2,020,031		
	Chris Hunter (D)..........................	132,844	(40%)	$761,296		$25,829
	Angelika Purkis (I)............................	7,510	(2%)	$17,593		
2018 Primary	Gus Bilirakis (R).......................	(100%)				

Prior winning percentages: 2016 (69%), 2014 (100%), 2012 (64%), 2010 (71%), 2008 (63%), 2006 (56%)

Gus Bilirakis, a Republican first elected in 2006, came into office distancing himself from partisan fights and focusing on his legislative agenda. While gaining seniority, he has sharpened his rhetorical edge. But he was unsuccessful in seeking to chair the House Veterans' Affairs Committee. His work on health care issues has played well at home.

Bilirakis remembers stuffing envelopes at age 7 for Republican Louis "Skip" Bafalis, who lost his 1970 bid for governor but was elected to five terms in Congress. As an undergraduate at the University of Florida, Bilirakis interned in the Reagan White House and went on to earn a law degree from Stetson University. He later was a probate lawyer and estate planner. In 1998, he was elected to the first of four terms in the Florida House. Bilirakis' career was closely tied to his father's. When 12-term Republican Rep. Michael Bilirakis decided to retire, his son drew nominal opposition for the GOP nomination. Gus Bilirakis was not shy about running on the family name and his Greek heritage. He appeared on the ballot as Gus Michael Bilirakis and raised money from many political action committees that supported his father, who served on the Energy and Commerce Committee.

Democrats recruited Phyllis Busansky, a former member of the Hillsborough County Commission and the first executive director of the state's welfare-to-work program. Both candidates were responsive to the district's many senior citizens. Bilirakis pointed to his credentials as a lawyer who specialized in elder law. HIs soft-spoken style contrasted with Busansky's assertive personality. She ran television ads portraying Bilirakis as a follower who relied on his father's reputation. President George W. Bush, Vice President Dick Cheney and Speaker Dennis Hastert all stumped for Bilirakis and helped him raise money. In a strongly Democratic year, he outspent Busansky $2.6 million to $1.4 million, and won 56%-44%.

In the House, Bilirakis has shown centrism. In 2008, he worked with Rep. Lloyd Doggett, a Texas Democrat, to win House passage of a "silver alert" bill to assist states in finding senior citizens who disappear. He was one of 10 Republicans in 2009 to support a bill to limit executive bonuses in financial companies receiving government bailout money. On other issues he was a more conventional Republican. In 2010, he took the House floor on several occasions to denounce the Democrats' health care overhaul as a "government takeover." On the Foreign Affairs Committee, he followed his father's footsteps in standing up for Greek causes.

After the 2012 election, Bilirakis got a seat on Energy and Commerce, where left-leaning groups attacked him for earlier signing a pledge that he "opposes any legislation relating to climate change that includes a net increase in government revenue." When he worked with Democrats in 2014 to oppose soaring premium hikes for flood insurance coverage, Majority Whip Kevin McCarthy bounced him from his whip team. "I have no hard feelings at all, but I had to do what I had to do," Bilirakis told the Tampa Bay Times. In 2014, President Barack Obama signed his bill to promote travel by reauthorizing Brand USA, a public-private partnership that encourages tourists to visit the United States. Some conservatives had opposed the bill as excessive spending. As vice chairman of the Veterans' Affairs Committee, he worked on the 2014 law to overhaul the VA hospital system. That resulted, he said, in the opening of an out-patient clinic in New Port Richey. He enacted bills to offer alternative therapies to veterans. Following the 2016 election, Bilirakis failed in his bid for chairman of the committee. Party leaders gave the post to the less-senior but more-outgoing Phil Roe of Tennessee.

In 2017-18, he played up his bipartisan initiatives. On the spending bill that was enacted in February 2018, he and Democratic Rep. Kathy Castor of his neighboring district — a colleague on Energy and Commerce — won approval of their measure for increased penalties for Medicare fraud. He also took charge of a provision to extend for two years the program for community health centers. Bilirakis co-chaired the International Religious Freedom Caucus. And he had a centrist ranking among Republicans in the Almanac vote ratings for 2017-18.

In a district that leans Republican, Bilirakis has not faced a serious reelection challenge. In 2018, he had his smallest victory margin since he was first elected, 58%-40%, against Democrat Chris Hunter, who spent $761,000 to the $2 million for Bilirakis. Hunter was a former FBI agent and a federal prosecutor who pursued international fugitives until he quit his job with the Justice Department in December 2017. "We're a better country than this," he told voters, in referring to the Trump administration. Hunter was endorsed by national environmental groups, but Democrats found superior opportunities elsewhere in Florida. The outcome might encourage the party to wage a better-funded challenge to Bilirakis.

FL-12: Northern Tampa Suburbs   **Cook Partisan Voting Index: R+8**

Population		Race and Ethnicity		Income	
Total	743,356	White	78.5%	Median Income	$50,542
Land area (sq. miles)	859	Black	4.4%	District Income Rank	298
Pop/ sq mi	865.8	Latino	12.3%	Poverty Rate	12%
Born in State	31.1%	Asian	2.6%	With health insurance	88.1%
		Two or more races	1.7%	Cash public assistance	2.5%
Age Groups		Other	0.6%	Food stamp/SNAP	11.8%
Under 18	19.3%				
18-34	17.2%	**Education**		**Work**	
35-64	39.8%	H.S grad or less	40.6%	White Collar	23.7%
Over 64	23.7%	Some college	32.6%	Sales and Service	45.8%
		College Degree, 4 yr	17.8%	Blue Collar	15.9%
Military		Post grad	9.1%	Government	11.7%
Veteran/ Active Duty	11.7%				

2012 Pres. Vote	Romney	182,794	(53%)	Obama	156,722	(46%)		
2016 Pres. Vote	Trump	218,488	(57%)	Clinton	147,759	(39%)	Johnson 9,918	(3%)

Pasco, Pinellas: In 1873, turtle hunters discovered a large sponge bed off the coast of the Pinellas Peninsula. Soon, boats from Key West began harvesting the sponges, and shortly thereafter, trading outposts were set up at sites that grew into Tarpon Springs and Anclote. Anclote is now just a speck on the map, but Tarpon Springs is a busy city of 25,000. With more than 10 percent of the population, it boasts the highest share of Greek Americans of any place in the United States — descendants of the Greek sponge fishermen who began arriving in the early 1900s. Over the years, Pasco County has become a classic bedroom community as development has moved up the once-empty coast. But population density remains low compared with other parts of Florida.

There were plans to change this. Two big financial companies — St. Petersburg's Raymond James Financial and Baltimore's T. Rowe Price —purchased land in Pasco County and each planned to build large campuses for thousands of employees. But each abandoned its plans and built elsewhere. More positively, developers in December 2018 opened a 16 million gallon clearwater lagoon in Wesley Chapel, with more than 2,000 homes. Meddler Toledo, an international supplier of precision equipment closed its facility in Hillsborough and opened a new manufacturing plant in Pasco, with 600 employees. Medical tourism has become a growing industry for patients who travel for treatment they cannot receive in their home states or other nations.

The 12th Congressional District covers an area north and east of Tampa and St. Petersburg. In Pinellas County, that includes Tarpon Springs, Palm Harbor and Dunedin. Two-thirds of the district includes all of Pasco County. This area was largely undeveloped until the 1950s, but now hosts a string of towns along the Gulf of Mexico. Further inland, the district covers older settlements like Land O'Lakes, Dade City and Zephyrhills, established in 1911 as a retirement center for veterans of the Union Army in an area that remains on the edge of huge swamps.

As Florida retirements became more feasible for people with modest incomes in the 1970s and 1980s, the partisan balance locally shifted toward Democrats. In the 1990s, young arrivals with professional and technical backgrounds and partisan independence turned this into a politically marginal area. Republican-drawn redistricting and the modest minority populations have given the 12th District a secure Republican lean.

Charlie Crist (D)

Elected 2016, 2nd term, b. Jul 24, 1956; Altoona, PA; Wake Forest University (NC), Att.; Florida State University, B.S., 1978; Cumberland School of Law, Stamford University (AL), J.D., 1981; Methodist; Married (Carole Rome Crist); 2 stepchildren.

Elected Office: FL Senate, 1993-1999; FL Education Commissioner, 2001-2003; FL Attorney General, 2003-2007; FL Governor, 2007-2011.

Professional Career: Staff, United States Senator Connie Mack, 1988-1989; FL Deputy Secretary of Business and Prof. Reg., 1999-2001.

DC Office: 215 CHOB 20515, 202-225-5961, Fax: 202-225-9764, crist.house.gov

State Offices: Seminole, 727-318-6770; St. Petersburg, 727-318-6770; St. Petersburg, 727-318-6770.

Committees: *Appropriations*: Commerce, Justice, Science & Related Agencies; Defense; Financial Services & General Government. *Science, Space & Technology*: Environment; Space & Aeronautics.

Group Ratings

	ADA	ACLU	AFL-CIO	LCV	ITI	COC	HAFA	ACU	CFG	FRC
2018	-	69%	-	94%	-	67%	2%	8%	10%	0%
2017	75%	C	92%	83%	C	64%	C	4%	0%	14%

Almanac Ratings 2017-18

	Economy	Social	Foreign	Composite
Liberal	74%	79%	52%	68%
Conservative	26%	21%	48%	32%

Key Votes of the 115th Congress

1. Obama-care revision	N	5. Family planning regs	N	9. Guantanamo prisoners	N
2. Tax Cuts	N	6. Body cameras/immigration	NV	10. Ground missiles, limit	Y
3. Omnibus appropriations	Y	7. Abortion ban	N	11. Defense Dept. spending	Y
4. Dodd-Frank revision	N	8. Concealed carry	N	12. FISA rules	Y

Election Results

Election	Name (Party)	Vote (%)		Cand. Spent	Ind. Exp. Support	Ind. Exp. Oppose
2018 General	Charlie Crist (D)..............................	182,717	(58%)	$1,313,724	$461	
	George Buck (R)...........................	134,254	(42%)	$33,221		
2018 Primary	Charlie Crist (D)..	(100%)				

Prior winning percentages: Governor: 2006 (52%)

Democrat Charlie Crist was elected in 2016 to what had been a Republican-held seat, with a boost from the state's new redistricting plan. His win marked his first victory in a decade-long political odyssey in which he evolved from Republican to independent to Democrat, and that resulted in two statewide defeats after he had served four years as governor. As a House freshman, he was active on national and local issues.

Crist was born in Altoona Pennsylvania, where his grandfather, a Greek immigrant from Cyprus who arrived in America in 1912, ran a shoe-shine parlor. His family moved to Atlanta before his first birthday, when his father, who shortened the family name from Christodoulos to Crist, was accepted to medical school at Emory University. In 1960, the Crists settled in St. Petersburg. A nearby Greek community and a rising population of retirees made the location a nice fit for a young doctor hoping to build a practice. By the time Charlie was 10, he was campaigning for his father who sought — and won — a seat on the Pinellas County School Board. In high school, Charlie was the starting quarterback and class president. He was a walk-on player at Wake Forest University, which he attended for two years. He transferred to Florida State, where he was student body vice president and homecoming king. He earned his law degree at Cumberland School of Law in Alabama, then worked as general counsel for the minor league division of Major League Baseball.

After an unsuccessful run for the state Senate in 1986, Crist served as state director for Republican Sen. Connie Mack. He ran again for the state Senate and won, serving six years. In the legislature, he gained the nickname of "Chain Gang Charlie" for taking touch stances on crime. He gained a reputation as an ambitious, media-savvy pol, always sporting a healthy tan and blessed with retail campaigning skills. He was on the state ballot six times between 1998 and 2014, with three victories. In 1998, he challenged Democratic Sen. Bob Graham but lost, 62%-38%. In the next six years, he was elected state education commissioner, attorney general and then governor in 2006, when he succeeded term-limited Jeb Bush.

Crist brought to the governorship a folksy style and a bipartisan perspective that contrasted with the more cerebral and ideological approach of Bush. The first issue he tackled was insurance. Seven hurricanes had slammed Florida in 2004 and 2005, and property-insurance rates had skyrocketed. Crist denounced insurance companies for being stingy about paying claims, and he expanded the state-owned Citizens Property Insurance until it became the largest wind insurer in Florida. Fiscally, Crist proved to be as conservative as Bush had been. His policies seemed to appeal to both conservatives and liberals.

His job ratings were extraordinarily high, including among Democrats and independents. But Republicans didn't rate him as high as Bush. When a Senate seat opened in 2010, Crist said he would seek the GOP nomination. The National Republican Senatorial Committee immediately endorsed him over former Florida House Speaker Marco Rubio. But the conservative Rubio received support from local and national activists. Crist deepened the hostility of Republicans when he endorsed President Barack Obama's $787 billion economic stimulus bill. By the time Crist realized the conservative base was slipping away, it was too late. On the verge of losing the primary, Crist quit the Republican Party and ran as an independent against Rubio and Democratic Rep. Kendrick Meek. He got caught in the crossfire between Rubio and Meek, both of whom painted Crist as a political opportunist. Crist tried to appeal as the de facto Democratic candidate, but Meek refused to bow out. Rubio won with 49 percent of the vote to 30 percent for Crist and 20 percent for Meek.

Crist returned to the campaign trail in 2014 in another bid for governor — this time as a Democrat and with the enthusiastic support of Obama. Running against Gov. Rick Scott, Crist adopted the Democratic playbook and criticized Scott for cutting education and restricting abortion; he vowed to raise the minimum wage. Scott blamed Crist for leaving the state in poor economic shape, and he took credit for the subsequent economic turnaround. In a Republican year, Crist lost 48%-47%, a margin of 64,000 votes.

With two statewide losses, most politicians would have called it quits. But Crist gained a new opportunity when redistricting made the 13th District, with his home base of St. Petersburg, an inviting target. Crist secured the support of the Democratic Congressional Campaign Committee. He appeared to lock up the seat after Republican Rep. David Jolly, a former congressional aide and lobbyist who won his House seat in a special election in March 2014, said it would be "impossible" for a Republican to win the new seat. Jolly decided to run instead for the Senate after Rubio decided to run for president and not seek a second term in the Senate.

That game plan changed in June 2016, a few days before the filing deadline, when Rubio opted to reclaim his Senate seat. Jolly tried to salvage his situation by stepping back to seek reelection to his House seat. He had made his bid even more uphill, with his poor-mouthing of campaign fundraising generally and the National Republican Congressional Committee specifically. The NRCC denied financial support to Jolly. With money that he had raised for his Senate campaign, Jolly had a fundraising advantage, $3.9 million to $2 million. But Crist was bolstered by $2.6 million in support from the DCCC and other party adjuncts.

The contest turned out closer than most — including Jolly — had expected. Democrats sought to tie Donald Trump around Jolly's neck. Jolly described Crist as an "untrustworthy political opportunist." Crist won, 52%-48%. Without redistricting, he almost certainly would have lost.

As a freshman, Crist served on the Financial Services Committee and joined Democrats who sought to prevent a loosening of the 2010 Dodd-Frank banking regulations. "With this bill, members are being asked to again trust the very people who brought us to this financial crisis," he told the House. Crist was more successful with his initiatives. In July 2018, the House passed a bill that he sponsored with Republican Rep. Jeff Denham of California to install on-site medical waste treatment systems at VA facilities. He wrote an op-ed column for USA Today that called for restoration of voting rights to ex-felons in Florida. Voters approved that step in a November 2018 referendum. In January 2019, Crist got a seat on the Appropriations Committee.

In 2018, Crist had an easy reelection, 58%-42%, against Republican George Buck, a poorly funded consultant on emergency management. He ended the campaign with $1.7 million in his account. Given his electoral history and the unpredictability of Florida politics, another statewide bid for Crist in 2022 was not out of the question.

FL-13: St. Petersburg, Clearwater   **Cook Partisan Voting Index: D+2**

Population		Race and Ethnicity		Income	
Total	717,518	White	71.8%	Median Income	$47,370
Land area (sq. miles)	182	Black	12.2%	District Income Rank	346
Pop/ sq mi	3948.1	Latino	9.5%	Poverty Rate	15.2%
Born in State	34.2%	Asian	3.4%	With health insurance	86.6%
		Two or more races	2.4%	Cash public assistance	2.8%
Age Groups		Other	0.6%	Food stamp/SNAP	12.9%
Under 18	17.1%				
18-34	19.6%	**Education**		**Work**	
35-64	41.2%	H.S grad or less	39.2%	White Collar	22.1%
Over 64	22.1%	Some college	32.1%	Sales and Service	46.8%
		College Degree, 4 yr	18.5%	Blue Collar	16.8%
Military		Post grad	10.2%	Government	10.7%
Veteran/ Active Duty	11.1%				

2012 Pres. Vote	Obama	183,112	(55%)	Romney	147,251	(44%)		
2016 Pres. Vote	Clinton	178,892	(49%)	Trump	167,348	(46%)	Johnson	10,022	(3%)

Pinellas County: When Spanish explorers arrived in what is now St. Petersburg some 500 years ago, they discovered an area covered by a primeval pine forest and teeming with bears, panthers, turkeys and bald eagles. They named the area "Punta Pinal" ("point of pines"), a name that has since been Anglicized into the Pinellas Peninsula. The area remained under-populated — only 50 families lived here when the Civil War broke out — until two events accelerated its development. First, the Orange Belt Railway connected the region to national markets in the 1880s. Second, Dr. W.C. Van Bibber, addressing the American Medical Society convention in 1885, named the peninsula the healthiest place on earth, setting off a stampede of interest. By 1897, the Belleview Hotel was built in Clearwater, and the area began its transition to a major tourist destination — and, later, a retirement community. In the 21st century, St. Petersburg has become a progressive community. The city plans to be the first in Florida to rely 100 percent on renewable energy. Construction of a 26-acre Pier District, with a marine education center, in downtown St. Petersburg was scheduled for completion in late 2019.An additional eight-lane span across the Bay to Tampa was planned for 2024, which will replace one of the two current sections of the Howard Frankland Bridge. The Tampa-St. Pete area in 2017 dropped from 7th to 10th among the nation's largest-gaining metro areas.

The population of Pinellas County more than doubled in the 1920s, and did so once more in the 1950s. Mostly from the North and modestly affluent, the newcomers adapted easily to a place whose civic tone was set by the St. Petersburg Times (now the Tampa Bay Times) and its longtime owners, Nelson and Henrietta Poynter: sober, good-humored and supportive of clean government and civil rights. They brought Republican voting habits, and presaged the political revolution that would take place in Florida. Democrats had a 56-point registration edge over Republicans here in 1940. By 1950, that edge was only six. In 1954, Pinellas County Republicans elected William Cramer to Congress, the first Republican from Florida since 1882. The Republican tilt faded and Pinellas County is now a swing area. Until 2016, the House seat remained consistently in GOP hands.

The 13th Congressional District is located entirely within Pinellas County. But redistricting in 2016 made a major shift. It added about 100,000 people in the heavily African-American and Democratic precincts in south St. Petersburg that had been part of the Tampa-based 14th District. In return, the district lost parts of northern Pinellas, including the area surrounding Dunedin. The district retained the remainder of St. Petersburg plus Clearwater, where resorts have grown more upscale. It includes many of the beach communities on the barrier islands facing the Gulf of Mexico, including Belleair Beach down to Treasure Island. Inland, it incorporates the new subdivisions of Largo in the center of the peninsula. The redistricting shifts had a significant political impact. In the old 13th, President Barack Obama in 2012 led by about 5,000 votes. With the new lines, Obama's lead would have been, 55%-44%. Hillary Clinton won here in 2016 by a narrower 50%-46%.

Kathy Castor (D)

Elected 2006, 7th term, b. Aug 20, 1966; Miami; Emory University - Atlanta (GA), B.A., 1988; Florida State University School of Law, J.D., 1991; Presbyterian; Married (Bill Lewis); 2 children.

Elected Office: Hillsborough County Commissioner, 2002-2006.

Professional Career: Assistant General counsel, FL Department of Community Affairs, 1991-1994; Practicing attorney, 1994-2000.

DC Office: 2052 RHOB 20515, 202-225-3376, Fax: 202-225-5652, castor.house.gov

State Offices: Tampa, 813-871-2817.

Committees: *Energy & Commerce*: Consumer Protection & Commerce; Health; Oversight & Investigations. *Select Committee on the Climate Crisis (Chmn).*

Group Ratings

	ADA	ACLU	AFL-CIO	LCV	ITI	COC	HAFA	ACU	CFG	FRC
2018	-	75%	-	91%	-	58%	6%	4%	2%	0%
2017	95%	C	92%	86%	C	43%	C	8%	3%	0%

Almanac Ratings 2017-18

	Economy	Social	Foreign	Composite
Liberal	94%	97%	89%	93%
Conservative	7%	4%	11%	7%

Key Votes of the 115th Congress

1. Obama-care revision	N	5. Family planning regs	N	9. Guantanamo prisoners	Y
2. Tax Cuts	N	6. Body cameras/immigration	Y	10. Ground missiles, limit	Y
3. Omnibus appropriations	Y	7. Abortion ban	N	11. Defense Dept. spending	Y
4. Dodd-Frank revision	N	8. Concealed carry	N	12. FISA rules	Y

Election Results

Election	Name (Party)	Vote (%)	Cand. Spent	Ind. Exp. Support	Ind. Exp. Oppose
2018 General	Kathy Castor (D)...	(100%)	$407,136		
2018 Primary	Kathy Castor (D)...	(100%)			

Prior winning percentages: 2016 (62%), 2014 (unopposed), 2012 (70%), 2010 (60%), 2008 (72%), 2006 (70%)

Kathy Castor, a Democrat first elected in 2006, has used her background as an environmental lawyer on behalf of local interests and has staunchly upheld Democratic positions in energy debates. She has worked closely with Republicans to protect her district's sprawling MacDill Air Force Base. In January 2019, Speaker Nancy Pelosi gave Castor a plum assignment as chair of the Select Committee on the Climate Crisis, although the panel had no legislative authority. Castor continued to serve on the Energy and Commerce Committee, which has jurisdiction on the issue.

Castor studied political science at Emory University, earned her law degree from Florida State University, and worked as a land-use attorney. Her parents were heavily involved in public service. Her father, Don Castor, sat on the Hillsborough County Court for two decades. Her mother, Betty

Castor, served in the state Senate, as state education commissioner and as president of the University of South Florida. In 2004, Betty Castor was the Democratic nominee for Senate, but lost 49%-48% to Republican Mel Martinez. Kathy Castor ran unsuccessfully for the state Senate in 2000, but two years later won a four-year term on the Hillsborough County Commission.

In 2006, Kathy Castor ran for the open House seat, benefiting from the family name ID. In a district with a nearly 2-to-1 Democratic advantage, she faced four opponents in the primary. The most formidable was state Senate Minority Leader Les Miller, a veteran African-American legislator. With the support of EMILY's List, Castor raised nearly $1 million before the primary and outspent Miller 3-to-1. She won 54%-34%. In the general election, Castor campaigned for expanded health care for low-income families, stronger ethics and lobbying rules, and a rapid withdrawal of U.S. troops from Iraq. She won, 70%-30%.

Castor served on the House Ethics Committee, and chaired the subcommittee looking into California Democratic Rep. Maxine Waters' alleged efforts to help get federal bailout money for a bank in which her husband owned stock. Waters was cleared of wrongdoing in 2012. As a reward for her service on the Ethics panel, considered an undesirable posting, Castor got the seat on Energy and Commerce.

In 2009 Castor joined a group of liberals on the panel who insisted that any savings from a government-run insurance option in the Democrats' proposed health care overhaul should be used to increase subsidies for low-income persons. Also that year, she added an amendment to the climate-change bill to allow states to set rates for electricity generated from renewable energy under state incentive programs. In the Almanac's vote ratings, she has ranked among the liberal half of House Democrats.

Castor was a major player on offshore drilling following the 2010 BP oil spill in the Gulf of Mexico, prodding the company and the Obama administration for more research on the spill's impact. In 2012, she worked to add a provision to a transportation bill directing that most fines collected under the Clean Water Act should go for Gulf clean-up instead of to the Treasury. In September 2017, she won House passage of her bill with Republican Rep. Dennis Ross of Florida to encourage private flood insurance policies in high-risk areas. The bill died in the Senate. Castor has avidly looked out for MacDill, headquarters of the U.S. Central Command and Special Operations Command. When the Air Force in 2016 narrowed the list of bases to host the Air Force's KC-46 next-generation aerial refueling jet, she pushed MacDill but was unsuccessful.

Castor, whose district has the third-highest number of Cuban Americans in the nation, embraced increased trade and travel to Cuba and was the first House member from Florida to support lifting travel restrictions. She praised President Barack Obama's decision to reopen diplomatic relations with Cuba. In March 2016, she accompanied him when he became the first president to visit the island since 1928. When local officials in Miami objected to suggestions that they could host a Cuban chancery, Castor repeatedly volunteered Tampa as the site. When the Trump administration tightened restrictions on Americans traveling to Cuba, and prohibited dealings with some state-owned entities, she objected that the "backward policy" marked a "return to failed Cold War isolationist policies toward Cuba and the Cuban people."

When Democrats regained House control following the 2018 election, Pelosi tapped Castor to chair the updated version of the climate-change panel that worked with Energy and Commerce in 2009 to win House approval of major legislation. At the insistence of Energy and Commerce Chairman Frank Pallone of New Jersey, Castor's select committee was limited to studying the issues and making recommendations. It was not given subpoena or legislative authority.

Castor welcomed the opportunity. "We're going to press for dramatic carbon pollution reduction, she told USA Today. "We want to win the clean energy future to defend the American way of life and avoid catastrophic and costly weather events that have dire impacts." Castor said that the select committee would have a "collaborative" relationship with Energy and Commerce to address the "dire crisis." Some progressive activists complained that Pelosi failed to create a more independent panel.

At home, Castor faced a tough re-election challenge in the Republican year of 2010 from Republican Mike Prendergast, a retired Army colonel. She narrowly outspent him and won with 60 percent of the vote, the lowest of her career. In 2016, the additional Republican voters from redistricting left her with a victory margin of 62%-38% in what continued to be an uncompetitive district. In 2018, she was unopposed in both the primary and general election.

FL-14: Tampa   **Cook Partisan Voting Index: D+7**

Population		Race and Ethnicity		Income	
Total	750,173	White	46.2%	Median Income	$50,891
Land area (sq. miles)	276	Black	17.2%	District Income Rank	289
Pop/ sq mi	2720.5	Latino	29.5%	Poverty Rate	17.6%
Born in State	39.5%	Asian	4.4%	With health insurance	85.8%
		Two or more races	2.1%	Cash public assistance	3.2%
Age Groups		Other	0.6%	Food stamp/SNAP	17.4%
Under 18	21.5%				
18-34	26.5%	**Education**		**Work**	
35-64	39.3%	H.S grad or less	37.9%	White Collar	12.7%
Over 64	12.7%	Some college	27.1%	Sales and Service	45%
		College Degree, 4 yr	21.9%	Blue Collar	15.2%
Military		Post grad	13.1%	Government	11.3%
Veteran/ Active Duty	7.7%				

2012 Pres. Vote	Obama	178,860	(58%)	Romney	128,066	(41%)		
2016 Pres. Vote	Clinton	188,870	(57%)	Trump	128,796	(39%)	Johnson	8,719	(3%)

Hillsborough County: Tampa's history goes back not much more than a century. Its industrial past can be traced to 1886, when Cuban cigar-makers from Key West settled in the city's Latin Quarter, called Ybor City. The city developed along the waterfront, with distinctive architectural touches like the 13 minarets on the Arabian-style Tampa Bay Hotel, built by railroad and real estate tycoon Henry B. Plant in the 1890s and now part of the University of Tampa. For a time, Tampa was Florida's only true industrial city, with a working-class, white population base. Today it has a diverse economy: a service sector, two universities and tourism, led by the Busch Gardens theme park. Tampa's subdivisions, condominiums, office towers and low-rise commercial buildings have spread inland across swamps and lowlands. After a slow recovery from the recession, business activity has picked up. In 2018, ground was broken for Water Street Tampa -- the $3 billion, 16-block mega-development, which will include a College of Medicine and Heart Institute. In 2017, there was a 55 percent increase in container shipments at the Port of Tampa, which already handled the most cargo of any Florida port. The airport completed a $1 billion upgrade in 2018, including a 1.4 mile people-mover rail, and plans to open a new terminal in 2023. Also in 2018, Major League Baseball's Tampa Bay Rays abandoned plans for a new stadium in Ybor City to replace their domed facility in St. Petersburg.

Through its history, Tampa has remained a city of families and young people. Senior citizens account for only about 12 percent of the residents here, an unusually low percentage for Florida. It has been an important military center for much of its existence. During the Spanish-American War, when railroads were making their way down Florida's Atlantic Coast, Tampa was a major embarkation point for U.S. troops. MacDill Air Force Base, on the south side of the city and jutting into Tampa Bay, is the vital headquarters of Central Command, which ran the Persian Gulf War and the campaigns in Afghanistan and Iraq. It is also headquarters for Special Operations Command, and the coordinating center for international special operations forces.

The 14th Congressional District is centered on Tampa. With 57 percent of Hillsborough County, it includes most of the city of Tampa and its close-in suburbs, such as Town 'n' Country. The county population, which grew by 15 percent from 2010 to 2017, has increased by at least 30 percent in nearly every decade since 1950; it is the fourth largest in Florida. In the 2016 redistricting, the 14th lost the heavily African-American and lower-income neighborhoods in St. Petersburg and gained a new areas of northern Hillsborough. Those changes increased the Republican vote in the district by about seven percentage points, though it remained safely Democratic. The new 14th gave Hillary Clinton a 57%-39% win.

Ross Spano (R)

Elected 2018, 1st term, b. Jul 16, 1966; Brandon; University of South Florida, B.A., 1994; Florida State University School of Law, J.D., 1998; Baptist; Married (Amie Spano); 4 children.

Elected Office: FL State House, 2012-2018.

Professional Career: Attorney.

DC Office: 224 CHOB 20515, 202-225-1252, spano.house.gov

State Offices: Lakeland, 863-644-8215.

Committees: *Small Business*: Economic Growth, Tax & Capital Access; Investigations, Oversight & Regulations (RMM). *Transportation & Infrastructure*: Highways & Transit; Railroads, Pipelines & Hazardous Materials; Aviation.

Election Results

Election	Name (Party)	Vote (%)		Cand. Spent	Ind. Exp. Support	Ind. Exp. Oppose
2018 General	Ross Spano (R).. 151,380	(53%)		$913,838	$132,113	$1,220,235
	Kristen Carlson (D)............................. 134,132	(47%)		$2,058,671	$119,263	$2,391,338
2018 Primary	Ross Spano (R)...................................... 26,904	(44%)				
	Neil Combee (R)..................................... 20,590	(34%)				
	Sean Harper (R)....................................... 6,018	(10%)				
	Danny Kushmer (R)................................. 4,067	(7%)				
	Ed Shoemaker (R)..................................... 3,379	(6%)				

Republican Ross Spano was elected to an open seat in Florida in a contest that received relatively little attention—and spending—compared to other contests in the state. He highlighted his conservative views and record as a state representative. With the unexpected retirement of Republican Rep. Dennis Ross late in the campaign cycle, Democrats faced problems in recruiting an experienced candidate. The outcome was relatively tight, which fueled post-election speculation that Democrats and their allies might have missed an opportunity to pick off the seat.

Spano, a native of Hillsborough County, graduated from the University of South Florida and got his law degree from Florida State University. He was a partner in a small Tampa-based firm that handled business law and estate cases. He served six years in the state House from a district in Hillsborough. During his first term, he won enactment of his bipartisan bill to assist victims of human trafficking in avoiding public taint. "What could be more horrible than that, to be victimized once but to have that victimization continue to follow you the rest of your life?" he told the Tampa Bay Times.

Following the retirement of Ross—who had served quietly for four terms as a frequent ally of GOP leaders—the chief Republican candidates were Spano and former state Rep. Neil Combee, a Polk County farmer who the Trump administration tapped as a Florida official at the Agriculture Department. Each accused the other of making hostile comments about Donald Trump during the 2016 presidential campaign. Spano was endorsed by Florida Sen. Marco Rubio.

In what became a battle of political bases, Spano won the five-candidate primary with 44 percent of the vote to 34 percent for Combee. Spano had a nearly 3-to-1 lead in Hillsborough, which cast about 29,000 votes; Combee led 2-to-1 among the 25,000 voters in Polk.

Democratic nominee Kristen Carlson was executive director of the Florida Citrus Processors Association. A first-time candidate, she had been a prosecutor in Pasco County and an attorney with two state agencies, including the Citrus Department, where she worked on new labeling requirements for orange juice. She styled herself as a problem-solver who put politics aside. Carlson was endorsed by EMILY's List, which supports Democratic women who favor abortion rights. She had a relatively easy time in the Democratic primary, winning 54 percent of the vote against two other candidates.

In the general election, the contest showed up on the political radar screen in mid-October. Republican strategists "sounded the alarm" and complained that Spano had not "raised enough money to define himself" following the release of two public polls showing that the contest was tied, according to the Cook Political Report. Carlson spent a bit more than $2 million in the campaign—

much less than many House Democratic candidates in battleground districts, but twice as much as Spano. In the final two weeks of the campaign, Speaker Paul Ryan's Congressional Leadership Fund spent $500,000 on Spano's behalf.

Spano crossed the finish line with a 53%-47% win. He led narrowly in Hillsborough, which cast half of the total vote, and in Lake County. Despite Carlson's connections to the citrus industry, most of Spano's victory margin came in rural Polk County. In the House, he likely will be checked regularly by the Republican campaign team to assure that he is prepared for his reelection campaign.

FL-15: Central Florida

Cook Partisan Voting Index: R+6

Population		Race and Ethnicity		Income	
Total	761,327	White	58.7%	Median Income	$52,460
Land area (sq. miles)	1,087	Black	13.8%	District Income Rank	264
Pop/ sq mi	700.2	Latino	21.8%	Poverty Rate	14.7%
Born in State	42.9%	Asian	3%	With health insurance	86.7%
		Two or more races	2.1%	Cash public assistance	2.4%
Age Groups		Other	0.7%	Food stamp/SNAP	14.1%
Under 18	23.3%				
18-34	22.5%	**Education**		**Work**	
35-64	38.8%	H.S grad or less	44.3%	White Collar	15.4%
Over 64	15.4%	Some college	31%	Sales and Service	45.4%
		College Degree, 4 yr	16.7%	Blue Collar	20.5%
Military		Post grad	8.1%	Government	11.7%
Veteran/ Active Duty	10%				

2012 Pres. Vote	Romney	156,847	(52%)	Obama	139,537	(46%)			
2016 Pres. Vote	Trump	177,634	(53%)	Clinton	144,226	(43%)	Johnson	8,906	(3%)

Tampa Suburbs, Lakeland: The heart of central Florida is Polk County, filled with lakes and small-to-medium-sized cities. Lakeland, with a population of 108,000, is the biggest city here and home to the corporate headquarters of the Publix chain of grocery stores, the largest employee-owned supermarket chain in the nation. With 8,200 employees in the area and a plan to add 700 more and to more than double the size of its headquarters facility by 2020, Publix is the largest employer in the county. Lakeland-area home prices historically made it one of the most affordable areas in the Sunshine State. In 2018, local real estate agents reported double-digit annual increases in sales, including a median sales price of $161,000. U.S. News and World Report rated the Lakeland area 9th on its list of "Best Places People Are Moving to in the U.S. in 2018."

This is the part of Florida that has been most dependent on agriculture. Strawberries, cattle and citrus are economic mainstays, although periodic freezes in recent years have persuaded some orange growers to move south or to switch to tomatoes. Polk has had a double-digit percentage drop in the number of farms and acreage in the past decade. In 2016, for the first time in 21 years, Polk no longer produced the most citrus in Florida. Due chiefly to the lingering effects of frost and a citrus bacterial disease, the county in 2017 lost 6,500 grove acres, nearly 10 percent of its total. Compounding the problem that year, Hurricane Irma in September destroyed more than half the citrus crop. DeSoto has become the number-one county for oranges. Farmers fear the long-term loss of the state's nearly $1 billion annual strawberry harvest, due chiefly to labor costs and competition from Mexico. Proportionately, there have been more manufacturing jobs here than almost anywhere else in Florida (though still not very many). Some new businesses, including distribution centers, have taken advantage of cheap property values to build new plants in Lakeland. In Hillsborough, the Plant City area produces close to 90 percent of Florida's strawberry yield. At its annual Strawberry Festival in March, hundreds of thousands of patrons consume at least as many shortcakes. One of the few remnants of old Florida, this area has not become a major retiree haven.

The 15th Congressional District is a rural and suburban combo. About 35 percent of the district's population lives in agricultural Polk County, and 50 percent in the rapidly growing suburbs in Hillsborough County east of Tampa. Redistricting in 2016 had scant partisan impact. Overall, the district remains reliably Republican. Donald Trump won 53%-43%.

Vern Buchanan (R)

Elected 2006, 7th term, b. May 08, 1951; Detroit, MI; Cleary University (MI), B.B.A., 1975; University of Detroit (MI), M.B.A., 1986; Baptist; Married (Sandy Harris Buchanan); 2 children.

Military Career: MI Air National Guard 1970-1976

Professional Career: Taekwondo instructor, 1971-1974; Marketing rep., Burroughs Corporation, 1975-1976; Founder, Vern Buchanan & Association, 1976-1978; Founder & CEO, American Speedy Printing Centers, 1976-1992; Founder & Chairman, Buchanan Automotive Group, 1992-2007; Founder & Chairman, Buchanan Enterprises, 1992-2007.

DC Office: 2427 RHOB 20515, 202-225-5015, Fax: 202-226-0828, buchanan.house.gov

State Offices: Bradenton, 941-747-9081; Sarasota, 941-951-6643.

Committees: *Ways & Means*: Health; Trade (RMM).

Group Ratings

	ADA	ACLU	AFL-CIO	LCV	ITI	COC	HAFA	ACU	CFG	FRC
2018	-	7%	-	40%	-	82%	41%	58%	46%	100%
2017	0%	C	14%	9%	C	93%	C	72%	61%	100%

Almanac Ratings 2017-18

	Economy	Social	Foreign	Composite
Liberal	9%	7%	13%	9%
Conservative	91%	94%	87%	91%

Key Votes of the 115th Congress

1. Obama-care revision	Y	5. Family planning regs	Y	9. Guantanamo prisoners	N
2. Tax Cuts	Y	6. Body cameras/immigration	N	10. Ground missiles, limit	N
3. Omnibus appropriations	Y	7. Abortion ban	Y	11. Defense Dept. spending	Y
4. Dodd-Frank revision	Y	8. Concealed carry	Y	12. FISA rules	Y

Election Results

Election	Name (Party)	Vote (%)	Cand. Spent	Ind. Exp. Support	Ind. Exp. Oppose
2018 General	Vern Buchanan (R)............................ 197,483	(55%)	$4,361,570	$117,528	$1,057,306
	David Shapiro (D)............................ 164,463	(45%)	$2,563,528	$182,750	$61,706
2018 Primary	Vern Buchanan (R)...	(100%)			

Prior winning percentages: 2016 (60%), 2014 (62%), 2012 (54%), 2010 (69%), 2008 (56%), 2006 50%)

Vern Buchanan, a Republican first elected in 2006, initially had tough election campaigns. Much of the pain was self-inflicted, with questionable business dealings and campaign finances. Buchanan has become a senior member of the powerful Ways and Means Committee, though his work in 2017 on the GOP's big tax cuts exposed him to new political attacks. In the minority, he became ranking Republican on the Trade Subcommittee.

Buchanan grew up outside of Detroit, the eldest of six children and the son of a factory foreman. He joined the Michigan Air National Guard and worked his way through college as a tae kwon do instructor. He earned a business degree at Cleary University and later an MBA at the University of Detroit. Buchanan founded American Speedy Printing Centers and made his fortune by selling 700 quick-printing franchises before his 40th birthday. In 1990, he moved his family to Florida, where he found new success as an automobile dealer with franchises throughout the Southeast. Buchanan has been among the wealthiest members of Congress. In 2018, his estimated net worth of $74 million placed him eighth on the list, Roll Call reported.

Buchanan became active in Republican politics, serving as a top fundraiser for Gov. Jeb Bush and Sen. Mel Martinez. In 2002, he wanted to run for the House seat, but stepped aside for Secretary of State Katherine Harris, who had become a national figure for her role in the 2000 presidential vote recount. Buchanan got his chance in 2006, when Harris ran for the Senate. His party connections and personal wealth made him the frontrunner. In the primary, he stressed his conservative credentials while challenging his chief rival's, and spent more than $2 million of his own money. Buchanan won 32 percent of the vote in the five-way primary.

Democratic nominee Christine Jennings, who like Buchanan was a transplanted Midwesterner and a self-made business success, was a bank owner. National Democrats pummeled Buchanan for his business dealings. Buchanan characterized Jennings as a pro-tax liberal. Despite the Republican advantage in the district, Buchanan was hurt by the attacks and the poor political environment for the GOP. This was the most expensive House race in 2006. Buchanan spent more than $8 million, including $5.5 million of his own money. Jennings spent $3 million, with about $2 million from her own pocket. After a recount, Republican election officials certified Buchanan the winner by 369 votes. Jennings alleged voting machine malfunction, but several rounds of testing were inconclusive.

Entering the House, Buchanan softened his ideological positions. He was one of 19 Republicans who supported most of the Democrats' early legislative agenda when they took control in 2007. "I ran as a conservative, but I also ran as someone who is going to be independent," Buchanan told the Sarasota Herald-Tribune. On Ways and Means, he joined the bipartisan deal in 2015 to adjust Medicare payments to doctors and extend the Children's Health Insurance Program. Following the BP oil spill in 2010, he pushed for a moratorium on all deep-water drilling permits in the Gulf of Mexico. When the Trump administration in 2018 proposed to weaken off-shore drilling regulations, Buchanan called the move "reckless and unacceptable."

He took stances to the right on immigration and terrorism, calling for an English official-language law and using military tribunals instead of civilian courts to try terrorist suspects. The former car dealer voted against the bailout of Detroit automakers in 2008 because, he said, the companies "failed to develop viable restructuring proposals."

In 2011, Buchanan attracted unwanted attention. The Sarasota Herald-Tribune reported that during the past year he had spent almost $1 million in campaign contributions on himself, companies he owned, or family members. Most of the money reportedly was used to repay campaign checks he wrote to himself in 2006. He steadfastly denied any wrongdoing, and maintained that the Federal Election Commission had exonerated him. But in December 2011, the Herald-Tribune unearthed FEC documents saying that attorneys investigating the matter found Buchanan to be "less than forthright and at times unbelievable."

With ethics questions swirling in 2012, his House seat looked to be in jeopardy. Democrat Keith Fitzgerald made Buchanan's integrity the main focus of his campaign and launched a website called the Buchanan Files, with links to news stories on the investigations. Then, over the summer, the Ethics Committee said it had ended its probe of Buchanan; in September his office announced that the Justice Department had concluded its investigation without charging him. Buchanan outspent Fitzgerald, $2.7 million to $1.4 million and prevailed, 54%-46%.

Buchanan has eyed other political opportunities, especially after Sen. Marco Rubio said in 2015 that he would not seek reelection. But he has grown more comfortable in the House as he has gained seniority. He moved into the elite ranks as a subcommittee chairman on Ways and Means. Starting in late 2015, he chaired three panels in three years: Human Resources, Oversight and Tax Policy.

He was an enthusiastic proponent of the tax cuts enacted by Republicans in December 2017, which he billed as "a little something extra in your paycheck." Those tax cuts became a source of embarrassment for Buchanan when his annual financial disclosure report to the House subsequently revealed that he purchased a yacht on the same day he voted for House passage of the legislation. Earlier, the Associated Press reported that the measure was "a potential windfall" for him. A spokesman refused to discuss the personal impact for Buchanan, but said, "This isn't about Vern, it's about the tens of thousands of small businesses that have been unfairly penalized by high taxes."

Democrats pounced on his finances. David Shapiro, his challenger in November, ran an ad claiming the tax law gave Buchanan "a tax handout of up to $2 million." Shapiro, a partner in a Sarasota law firm, loaned $200,000 to his own campaign. Buchanan won, 55%-45% -- comparable to his earlier victory margins.

FL-16: Central Gulf Coast   Cook Partisan Voting Index: R+7

Population		Race and Ethnicity		Income	
Total	782,096	White	70.8%	Median Income	$56,355
Land area (sq. miles)	1,293	Black	8.1%	District Income Rank	210
Pop/ sq mi	604.8	Latino	17.1%	Poverty Rate	12.1%
Born in State	31%	Asian	2%	With health insurance	86.6%
		Two or more races	1.4%	Cash public assistance	1.9%
Age Groups		Other	0.5%	Food stamp/SNAP	9.7%
Under 18	19.8%				
18-34	17%	**Education**		**Work**	
35-64	37.5%	H.S grad or less	38.7%	White Collar	25.7%
Over 64	25.7%	Some college	29.6%	Sales and Service	45.6%
		College Degree, 4 yr	19.2%	Blue Collar	19.2%
Military		Post grad	12.5%	Government	10.7%
Veteran/ Active Duty	11.4%				

2012 Pres. Vote	Romney	185,357	(54%)	Obama	155,694	(45%)		
2016 Pres. Vote	Trump	213,271	(53%)	Clinton	170,442	(43%)	Johnson	9,302 (2%)

Bradenton, North Sarasota: When the Ringling Brothers made a success of the circus they founded in the 1880s, they needed a place for performers and animals to rest during the winter months. They settled on Sarasota: just far enough north to be reachable by railroad and just far enough south to be semitropical so the elephants would stay healthy. John Ringling established the Ringling Museum of Art and a huge sculpture garden, and built his own Venetian palace, the Ca' d'Zan. Next door, his brother, Charles, built a pair of neoclassical revival mansions in pink Georgia marble, which are now part of New College of Florida. But this was still a sparsely populated area until just after World War II, when the balmy Gulf Coast attracted new settlers — affluent, well-educated Republicans from upper-crust suburbs in the North. The population exploded. Manatee and Sarasota counties grew from a combined 64,000 people in 1950 to 805,000 in 2017.

In May 2017, alas, the final curtain came down on the Ringling Brothers Circus (in a New York City performance) due to several factors, including a drop in ticket sales and protests by animal-rights groups. Otherwise, the post-recession recovery has been strong, including the Sarasota opening of the luxury indoor Mall at University. The bayfront area along the Intracoastal Waterway is lined with high-rises and is often clogged with traffic from Bradenton to Sarasota. In May 2018, the groundbreaking for the $1 billion Quay waterfront district, including a new performing arts center, was a major step for downtown. Though some technology firms diversify the economy, the district as a whole remains reliant on tourists and well-off retirees: People 65 and older are 40 percent of the population in Sarasota, and one-third in Manatee. Now a center for sports tourism, Bradenton has a rowing facility that was a model for the 2020 Olympic Games in Tokyo. The 2017 World Rowing Championships and the 2018 World Sailing annual conference were both held in Sarasota. Reality check: Bradenton has become the opioid overdose capital of Florida, especially with fentanyl analogs. The area also suffered from an invasion of red tide algae on the beaches, which resulted in a 20 percent drop in tourist revenue in late 2018.

The 16th Congressional District of Florida remains based in Manatee and Sarasota, though it includes barely half of Sarasota. The district continues to include the pricey Longboat Key and Lido Key and the more casual Siesta Key. Besides all of Bradenton-based Manatee, the district swings north along the east coast of Tampa Bay to include the southern edge of Hillsborough. In both Sarasota and southern Hillsborough, Interstate 75 comes within a few miles of the Gulf of Mexico. West of 75, these areas are close to fully developed. East of 75, the lands had been mostly undeveloped until recent years. Some lower-cost subdivisions have opened in those areas.

For many years, the 16th District was heavily Republican, though voting results have grown closer. In 2016, Donald Trump won the district, 54%-43%.

Greg Steube (R)

Elected 2018, 1st term, b. May 19, 1978; Bradenton; University of Florida, B.S., 2001; University of Florida Levin College of Law, J.D., 2003; Methodist; Married (Jennifer Mary Retzer); 1 child.

Military Career: U.S. Army 2004-2008 (Iraq)

Elected Office: FL House, 2010-2018.

Professional Career: Attorney, Becker & Poliakoff.

DC Office: 521 CHOB 20515, 202-225-5792, Fax: 202-225-3132, steube.house.gov

State Offices: Okeechobee, 941-575-9101; Punta Gorda, 941-575-9101.

Committees: *Judiciary*: Antitrust, Commercial & Administrative Law; Immigration & Citizenship; Crime, Terrorism & Homeland Security. *Oversight & Reform*: Government Operations. *Veterans' Affairs*: Disability Assistance & Memorial Affairs; Health.

Election Results

Election	Name (Party)	Vote (%)		Cand. Spent	Ind. Exp. Support	Ind. Exp. Oppose
2018 General	Greg Steube (R)	193,326	(62%)	$664,529	$961,380	$200,000
	Allen Ellison (D)	117,194	(38%)	$2,500		
2018 Primary	Greg Steube (R)	48,983	(62%)			
	Bill Akins (R)	15,142	(19%)			
	Julio Gonzalez (R)	14,409	(18%)			

Freshman Republican Greg Steube had easy victories in both the primary and general elections to win what has been a safely Republican seat. With service in the military, agriculture and the Florida Legislature, he had the background to become an active player in Congress. His victory in November had an unusual feature when his initial Democratic opponent died suddenly of a heart attack. Steube replaced five-term GOP Rep. Tom Rooney, a lawmaker who retired at age 48 after voicing unhappiness with how Republicans were running Washington.

Steube grew up in rural Manatee County, where he had an early interest in ranching. His father, Brad Steube, was sheriff of Manatee County, which is in the adjacent 16th District. He got his bachelor's and law degrees from the University of Florida; as an undergraduate, he majored in beef cattle sciences. After enlisting in the Army following the September 2001 attacks, he served in the Judge Advocate General's Corps and was an infantry captain in Operation Iraqi Freedom. From 2011 to 2017, Steube was affiliated with Becker and Poliakoff, a large Florida-based law firm that has lobbied actively in Tallahassee.

In 2010, Steube cited his experience in agriculture and law to win a seat in the state House. He took credit for placing two constitutional amendments on Florida ballots in 2012, which provided tax breaks for low-income seniors and the surviving spouses of military veterans; each was approved by the voters. Term-limited in 2016, he won a seat in the state Senate, where he chaired the Judiciary Committee. He claimed to sponsor more pro-gun bills than any other member of the Legislature.

When Rooney stepped down, Steube was the early frontrunner to succeed him. He was endorsed by the state's largest organization of citrus growers, a large industry in the district, plus several national conservative groups, including the House Freedom Caucus. The Club for Growth spent nearly $800,000 on his behalf. Also running in the primary were Bill Akins, a businessman and Vietnam veteran, and state Rep. Julio Gonzalez, a surgeon who was endorsed by the U.S. Chamber of Commerce. In the Legislature, both Steube and Gonzalez "have advanced conservative legislation, largely without success," the Sarasota Herald-Tribune reported.

Steube criticized Gonzalez for having endorsed Florida Sen. Marco Rubio against Donald Trump in the 2016 Republican presidential campaign. Gonzalez criticized Steube for exaggerating his military record and for running in a district in which he had not been a resident. Each spent a bit more than $500,000 in the primary; Akins spent less than one-tenth of that. Steube won with 62 percent of the vote, to 19 percent for Akins and 18 percent for Gonzalez.

Democrats nominated April Freeman, a film and television producer who had been the Democratic nominee in two earlier House campaigns. When she died four weeks after the primary,

Democrats designated Allen Ellison, an adviser on economic development, to run in her place, though state law required that Freeman's name remain on the ballot. In this district, no Democratic candidate had much chance of winning.

Steube emphasized commitment to his conservative views. "The Tallahassee establishment was surprised when I actually followed up on my conservative campaign promises. I don't think the D.C. swamp will like it either," he said.

FL-17: South Central Florida   **Cook Partisan Voting Index: R+13**

Population		Race and Ethnicity		Income	
Total	743,040	White	74.8%	Median Income	$46,034
Land area (sq. miles)	5,572	Black	7.4%	District Income Rank	363
Pop/ sq mi	133.4	Latino	14.6%	Poverty Rate	15.3%
Born in State	32.5%	Asian	1.3%	With health insurance	86%
		Two or more races	1.4%	Cash public assistance	1.8%
Age Groups		Other	0.4%	Food stamp/SNAP	11.4%
Under 18	17.1%				
18-34	16.1%	**Education**		**Work**	
35-64	35.9%	H.S grad or less	49.9%	White Collar	30.9%
Over 64	30.9%	Some college	29.1%	Sales and Service	48.1%
		College Degree, 4 yr	13.4%	Blue Collar	23.8%
Military		Post grad	7.7%	Government	12.9%
Veteran/ Active Duty	12.7%				

2012 Pres. Vote	Romney	179367	(58%)	Obama	128,684	(41%)
2016 Pres. Vote	Trump	220,156	(62%)	Clinton	123,919	(35%)

Charlotte, South Sarasota, Okeechobee: The population of Charlotte County didn't reach 10,000 until the 1950s. But local histories assure us that the region was anything but quiet before then. In 1886, when railroads reached the convergence of the Peace River and Charlotte Harbor, the area was home to a small fishing center, a port that mostly shipped phosphate, and a few cattle ranches. But the exotic locale, pleasant climate and emerging sport of tarpon fishing encouraged developers to turn it into a destination for the wealthy. Elizabeth Colt, widow of gun-manufacturer Samuel Colt; John Wanamaker, of the eponymous Philadelphia department store; and other wealthy individuals began annual sojourns to winter in the semitropical paradise. But these riches existed uneasily alongside what remained of a frontier-like culture.

Today, Charlotte County is a very different place. The invention of air conditioning, advances in transportation and the surge of financially secure retirees conspired to drive rapid growth. The county's population roughly doubled each decade from the 1950s to the 1980s. Since then, the gains have slowed. From 2010 to 2017, the population grew from 160,000 to 182,000; Port Charlotte, developed in the 1950s, has become the most populous locale. Punta Gorda maintains a small-town and small-business feel and has been regularly rated among the best places to retire by seniors groups. Of its population, 55 percent are 65 or older and 95 percent are white. Inland is Babcock Ranch, the nation's first town that is entirely solar-powered—with 343,000 solar panels over 440 acres in a Florida Power & Light facility. The master-planned development gained its first residents in January 2018 and expects that it will grow to 50,000.

The 17th Congressional District of Florida has been based in Charlotte County, with lots of additional pieces. The district stretches from Sarasota and Charlotte counties on the Gulf coast north through the Big Cypress Swamp to Bartow in Polk County. The remainder of the population sprawls over five lightly populated and mostly rural counties, and includes Lake Okeechobee. The landscape, largely overlooked by most Floridians, remains dominated by cattle farms and others that produce citrus, tomatoes and vegetables. In 2017, DeSoto County narrowly edged Polk County in production of oranges, with 11.7 million boxes. Hurricane Irma devastated much of the crop the following year. Charlotte and Sarasota each have a bit more than one-fourth of the population. The 62 percent for Donald Trump in 2016 was his best Florida district south of Orlando.

Brian Mast (R)

Elected 2016, 2nd term, b. Jul 10, 1980; Grand Rapids, MI; Palm Beach Atlantic University, Att., 2002; American Military University, 2010; Harvard University, Bach. Deg., 2016; Christian Church; Married (Brianna Mast); 3 children.

Military Career: U.S. Army 2000-2012 (Afghanistan, WIA)

Professional Career: Analyst, National Nuclear Security Admin., 2011-2012; Explosive Specialist, U.S Dept. of Homeland Security, 2012-2015.

DC Office: 2182 RHOB 20515, 202-225-3026, Fax: 202-225-8398, mast.house.gov

State Offices: North Palm Beach, 561-530-7778; Port St Lucie, 772-336-2877; Stuart, 772-403-0900.

Committees: *Foreign Affairs*: Asia, the Pacific & Nonproliferation; Middle East, North Africa & International Terrorism. *Transportation & Infrastructure*: Aviation; Coast Guard & Maritime Transportation; Water Resources & Environment.

Group Ratings

	ADA	ACLU	AFL-CIO	LCV	ITI	COC	HAFA	ACU	CFG	FRC
2018	-	14%	-	29%	-	83%	45%	52%	48%	100%
2017	5%	C	21%	23%	C	93%	C	63%	62%	89%

Almanac Ratings 2017-18

	Economy	Social	Foreign	Composite
Liberal	22%	6%	10%	13%
Conservative	78%	95%	90%	87%

Key Votes of the 115th Congress

1. Obama-care revision	Y	5. Family planning regs	Y	9. Guantanamo prisoners	N
2. Tax Cuts	Y	6. Body cameras/immigration	N	10. Ground missiles, limit	N
3. Omnibus appropriations	N	7. Abortion ban	Y	11. Defense Dept. spending	Y
4. Dodd-Frank revision	Y	8. Concealed carry	Y	12. FISA rules	Y

Election Results

Election	Name (Party)	Vote (%)	Cand. Spent	Ind. Exp. Support	Ind. Exp. Oppose
2018 General	Brian Mast (R)................................ 185,905	(54%)	$5,850,842	$1,149,815	$1,333,957
	Lauren Baer (D)................................ 156,454	(46%)	$4,521,008	$364,148	$1,324,599
2018 Primary	Brian Mast (R)..................................... 55,527	(78%)			
	Mark Freeman (R)................................. 8,096	(11%)			
	Dave Cummings (R)............................... 7,888	(11%)			

Prior winning percentages: 2016 (54%)

Republican Brian Mast, elected to an open seat in 2016, took an interest in environmental issues that sometimes separated him from other Republicans. An Army veteran who lost both legs while serving in Afghanistan, Mast quickly gained a cachet on veterans' issues in Congress and was considered as a possible head of the Veterans Affairs Department in the Trump administration. His district remained a competitive swing seat.

Brian Mast was born in Grand Rapids, Michigan. After graduating from high school there, he followed in his father's footsteps and enlisted in the Army. He served under the elite Joint Special Operations Command as a bomb disposal expert. This meant, he wrote in his campaign bio, "that life was always dangerous and very often deadly." His task was to detect and destroy improvised explosive devices. The final one that he found along a roadside in Kandahar, Afghanistan caused catastrophic injuries, including the loss of his legs below the knees, a portion of his forearm and a finger. He received numerous military honors.

As part of his recovery, Mast shared his expertise with the National Nuclear Security Administration's Office of Emergency Operations and the Bureau of Alcohol, Tobacco, Firearms and Explosives. Following his retirement from the Army, he worked in counter-terrorism and national defense as an explosives specialist for the Transportation Security Administration. He served as a volunteer for the Israel Defense Forces. In 2016, Mast graduated with a degree in economics from Harvard University's online program. Another distinctive characteristic is that he always wears shorts, he said, because his prosthetics legs rip through his pants.

While recovering from his injuries, Mast vowed to serve in Congress. His opportunity came with the House seat in a swing district, when Democrat Patrick Murphy ran for the Senate. He won the six-candidate Republican primary with 38 percent of the vote. The runner-up with 26 percent was Roberta Negron. As the wife of Senate president Joe Negron, she had the support of many Florida Republican leaders and raised $948,000.

The general election was another steep challenge for Mast. Democratic nominee Randy Perkins, who founded a lucrative debris-removal company in Florida following the devastation of Hurricane Andrew in 1992, self-financed $10.1 million of his $10.8 million campaign. In a campaign debate, Perkins showed little subtlety. He asked Mast about the health insurance coverage he receives as a veteran, and why "the sacrifices and service you provided for this country make you capable of solving issues" facing Congress. Mast raised $2.8 million for his campaign and received more than $3.5 million in support from the Congressional Leadership Fund. He won in November, 54%-43%. Mast won by fewer than 1,000 votes in St. Lucie County, but nearly doubled the vote for Perkins in Martin County.

On the Transportation and Infrastructure Committee, Mast sought improvements in the water systems serving Lake Okeechobee, to prevent what he called a potential environmental disaster, especially from toxic algae. He pressed for expedited review of regulation of Lake Okeechobee and for the development of large-scale water filtration technology. His provision was included in the water resources bill that Congress enacted in December 2018. Mast refused to endorse Florida Gov. Rick. Scott in his Senate bid that year until he endorsed his proposal. "I'm not going to support anyone who doesn't support our water," he said. Following the election that November of Ron DeSantis as governor, Mast chaired his transition advisory committee on environmental policy, including water issues.

In September 2017, President Donald Trump signed Mast's bill to extend various veterans programs, mostly on a routine basis. The following spring, White House officials said that Mast was among those considered to serve as head of the VA. One strike against him with conservatives may have been his support for a ban on some semi-automatic weapons, following the shootings in February at the high school in Parkland Florida, where Mast grew up.

Mast had a competitive challenge for reelection from Lauren Baer, a former foreign policy adviser to President Barack Obama, who criticized Mast for his support of Trump administration policies. Each candidate spent several million dollars and had extensive party support. Mast won, 54%-46%. He got 53 percent in Palm Beach County, which cast nearly half the vote, and led by by nearly 2-to-1 in Martin; Baer took St. Lucie by a few hundred votes.

FL-18: Palm Beach, Treasure Coast — Cook Partisan Voting Index: R+5

Population		Race and Ethnicity		Income	
Total	744,294	White	67.7%	Median Income	$56,264
Land area (sq. miles)	1,513	Black	12.5%	District Income Rank	212
Pop/ sq mi	492	Latino	15.8%	Poverty Rate	12.3%
Born in State	32.1%	Asian	2.2%	With health insurance	87%
		Two or more races	1.5%	Cash public assistance	1.7%
Age Groups		Other	0.5%	Food stamp/SNAP	8.6%
Under 18	18.8%				
18-34	17.5%	**Education**		**Work**	
35-64	39.2%	H.S grad or less	38.6%	White Collar	24.5%
Over 64	24.5%	Some college	31.1%	Sales and Service	47%
		College Degree, 4 yr	19.3%	Blue Collar	17.5%
Military		Post grad	11%	Government	11.4%
Veteran/ Active Duty	10.1%				

2012 Pres. Vote	Romney	175,755	(51%)	Obama	162,984	(48%)	
2016 Pres. Vote	Trump	203,771	(53%)	Clinton	168,558	(44%)	

Palm Beach Gardens, St. Lucie: Urban Florida has fanned far across the swamplands from its original nuclei in beachfront resort communities. Once, metro Palm Beach was a narrow stretch along Lake Worth; now it runs inland almost halfway to Lake Okeechobee, spreading out from its original locus around the posh Breakers Hotel. Old beach towns such as Hobe Sound have become the hub of affluent developments that extend north to Stuart in Martin County. Farther north, near the old town of Fort Pierce, are larger but more modest developments like Port St. Lucie, which had a population of only 330 in 1970. In 2018, it became the eighth largest city in Florida, with a population of 189,000, topping Fort Lauderdale. Of the 314,000 in St. Lucie County, the Hispanic share has grown to 19 percent. Farther south, northern Palm Beach County is changing as well. The county, along with the state of Florida, subsidized the Scripps Research Institute's new center in Jupiter. That attracted several other biotechnology businesses to Jupiter. Mayor Todd Wodraska called the city "a biotechnology hub where important scientific advances are realized."

The 18th Congressional District includes all of Martin County, with its affluent towns of Stuart and Hobe Sound, as well as all of more modest St. Lucie County. To the south, about 40 percent of the district's population resides in the northern precincts of Palm Beach County, including Palm Beach Gardens, an area filled with gated communities and home to the Professional Golfers' Association of America. A few miles east of the PGA's official home is Jupiter, where the largest concentration of PGA golfers reside amid lush greenery and plush mansions. At least 35 members of the PGA Tour, plus many retired stars, live in a 20-mile stretch along the Atlantic Ocean, just north of Palm Beach. Nearby, the $150 million Harbourside Place entertainment complex includes the Woods Jupiter restaurant owned by Tiger Woods. In December 2018, the PGA announced plans for a new headquarters in Frisco Texas, north of Plano.

The 2016 presidential election gave a big boost to the Republican ticket. And that's not because Donald Trump sent his guests and employees to the voting precincts from his Mar-a-Lago estate, which is a few miles down Route 1 —and in the 21st Congressional District. Trump won the 18th, 53%-44%, compared with Mitt Romney's 52%-48% local win over President Barack Obama in 2012. A notable feature of those numbers was the county breakdown: The Republican performance had a 10-point increase from 2012 to 2016 in its margin in the more-populous St. Lucie County, which more than doubled the change in Martin and the Palm Beach parts of the district.

Francis Rooney (R)

Elected 2016, 2nd term, b. Dec 04, 1953; Muskogee, OK; Georgetown Preparatory School, North Bethesda (MD), 1971; Georgetown University (DC), Bach. Deg., 1975; Georgetown University Law Center (DC), J.D., 1978; Roman Catholic; Married (Kathleen Rooney); 3 children; 2 grandchildren.

Elected Office: U.S Ambassador to the Holy See, 2005-2008.

Professional Career: Owner, Rooney Holdings, Inc.

DC Office: 120 CHOB 20515, 202-225-2536, Fax: 202-226-3547, francisrooney.house.gov

State Offices: Cape Coral, 239-599-6033; Naples, 239-252-6225.

Committees: *Education & Labor*: Health, Employment, Labor & Pensions; Workforce Protections. *Foreign Affairs*: Europe, Eurasia, Energy & the Environment; Western Hemisphere, Civilian Security, & Trade (RMM).

Group Ratings

	ADA	ACLU	AFL-CIO	LCV	ITI	COC	HAFA	ACU	CFG	FRC
2018	-	4%	-	20%	-	91%	81%	96%	79%	100%
2017	5%	C	6%	0%	C	93%	C	96%	82%	100%

Almanac Ratings 2017-18

	Economy	Social	Foreign	Composite
Liberal	8%	6%	0%	4%
Conservative	92%	94%	100%	96%

Key Votes of the 115th Congress

1. Obama-care revision	Y	5. Family planning regs	Y	9. Guantanamo prisoners	N
2. Tax Cuts	Y	6. Body cameras/immigration	N	10. Ground missiles, limit	N
3. Omnibus appropriations	Y	7. Abortion ban	Y	11. Defense Dept. spending	Y
4. Dodd-Frank revision	Y	8. Concealed carry	Y	12. FISA rules	Y

Election Results

Election	Name (Party)	Vote (%)	Cand. Spent	Ind. Exp. Support	Ind. Exp. Oppose
2018 General	Francis Rooney (R)...................... 211,465	(62%)	$921,175	$308,735	
	David Holden (D)............................... 128,106	(38%)	$546,355		
2018 Primary	Francis Rooney (R).....................	(100%)			

Prior winning percentages: 2016 (66%)

Republican Francis Rooney, whose personal wealth has driven away serious competition, has pressed bipartisan initiatives, especially on the environment. After his success in building his own construction companies, and as a deep-pocket political contributor with high-level connections and assignments, he was elected in 2016.

Born in Oklahoma, Rooney earned his bachelor's and law degrees from Georgetown University. He spent more than three decades in business, serving as founder and chairman of Rooney Holdings Inc. and, after 2008, as chief executive officer of the family-owned Manhattan Construction Group, which is a subsidiary of Rooney Holdings. His many construction projects include the soon-to-be replaced Texas Rangers Stadium with his friend George W. Bush, who was then the managing partner of the team; the presidential libraries in Texas for both Presidents Bush; the underground Capitol Visitors Center on the Capitol grounds, and the International Terminal at Hartsfield-Jackson Airport in Atlanta. He was a contributor to prominent Republican candidates, including seven-figure donations to Bush and Mitt Romney, and has been an active participant in GOP politics. He served three years as U.S. ambassador to the Vatican.

Before deciding to seek the open House seat, Rooney seriously considered in 2016 a bid for the Senate seat that had been opened by Marco Rubio's retirement. "It's very difficult in Florida to win a general Senate election in a presidential year without some coattails from a presidential nominee," he told Politico in explaining why he decided not to seek the seat. "And a rational businessman might not want to take that bet."

The House seat unexpectedly was opened when Republican Curt Clawson decided not to seek a second term. Rooney's opponents in the primary had political experience: Sanibel councilman Chauncey Goss, whose father Porter Goss had held this House seat, and former Secret Service agent Dan Bongino, who had run for office in Maryland. Rooney took 53 percent of the vote to 30 percent and 17 percent, respectively, for Goss and Bongino. Rooney raised about $3.9 million for the primary, of which $3.2 million was self-financed. The two other contenders raised about $300,000 each. In the general, Rooney defeated Robert Neeld, 66%-34%. He contributed another $1 million from his pocket to that campaign, while Neeld raised $14,000.

In the House, Rooney joined the Climate Solutions Caucus, a bipartisan group seeking to address climate change. In 2017-18, he was one of two House Republicans to call for a carbon tax; the other was Carlos Curbelo, also of Florida, who was defeated for reelection. "Sea level rise is existential for southwest Florida," Rooney told the Washington Times. He also filed a resolution stating that the issue requires immediate action and he called for a ban on oil drilling in the eastern Gulf of Mexico.

In April 2017, President Donald Trump signed Rooney's bill to repeal an Obama administration regulation that restricted certain savings programs run by state or local agencies for non-government employees.

Rooney had occasional partisan moments. In a December 2017 interview, he called for a "purge" of FBI agents who were biased against Trump and he said that the "deep state" controlled Robert Mueller's investigation of alleged Russian interference in the 2016 election. He was easily re-elected, 62%-38%, against David Holden, a Wells Fargo financial analyst.

FL-19: Southern Gulf Coast   **Cook Partisan Voting Index: R+13**

Population		Race and Ethnicity		Income	
Total	777,171	White	69.9%	Median Income	$54,971
Land area (sq. miles)	750	Black	7.6%	District Income Rank	228
Pop/ sq mi	1035.7	Latino	19.6%	Poverty Rate	13.6%
Born in State	23.7%	Asian	1.5%	With health insurance	85.3%
		Two or more races	1.1%	Cash public assistance	1.4%
Age Groups		Other	0.3%	Food stamp/SNAP	9.3%
Under 18	17.2%				
18-34	16.9%	**Education**		**Work**	
35-64	36.1%	H.S grad or less	39.6%	White Collar	29.8%
Over 64	29.8%	Some college	28.5%	Sales and Service	49.4%
		College Degree, 4 yr	19.6%	Blue Collar	18.7%
Military		Post grad	12.3%	Government	9.7%
Veteran/ Active Duty	10.4%				

2012 Pres. Vote	Romney	195,186	(61%)	Obama	124,771	(39%)		
2016 Pres. Vote	Trump	227,096	(59%)	Clinton	143,001	(37%)	Johnson	8,014	(2%)

Fort Myers, Naples: Florida's Gulf Coast is at the edge of the tropics, a physical environment once teeming with disease and inhospitable to advanced civilization, but now evolved into a model for retirement living. One of the earliest white settlements here was Fort Myers, built in 1850 as an Army post to pursue the Seminole Indians; in 1858, the last of the Seminole were driven out. For a century after that, this corner of Florida was mostly deserted, save for some small resort communities developed around wide, white-sand beaches with gentle breakers. The inlets and broad estuaries are perfect for boating, and the wetlands are graced with exotic birds. Thomas Edison had his winter home in Fort Myers, Henry Ford used to visit here, and tourists were drawn to beaches thick with seashells on nearby Sanibel and Captiva islands. But the local economy could not support many permanent residents. At the beginning of World War II, there were only 68,000 people living on the Gulf Coast from Bradenton south to Naples.

The climate and environment, and the fact that Florida has no state income or inheritance tax, attracted waves of affluent postwar suburbanites from the Midwest and Northeast. Developers such as Barron Collier, who financed the building of the Tamiami Trail across the soggy Everglades and designed Naples with the wealthy in mind, were determined to avoid the high-rise canyons that line the Atlantic from Palm Beach to Miami. Their alternative was to construct low-rise, city-style developments.

When the recession hit in 2008, this area had the nation's largest number of housing foreclosures, accounting for nearly half of the home sales. Local officials' predictions of a slow recovery initially were borne out: The Cape Coral-Fort Myers area lost more jobs than any other metropolitan area in the state in 2012. Since then, business conditions improved notably. From 2010 to 2017, the population of Lee County increased by 20 percent. In October 2018, US News ranked Fort Myers as the second-best place in the nation to retire. In a cautionary note, the Washington-based Economic Policy Institute in 2018 ranked the area from Naples to Marco Island as second in the nation for income inequality. Hurricane Irma in September 2017 caused more than $700 million in losses in Lee County.

The 19th Congressional District occupies the southern half of the habitable Gulf Coast below Tampa Bay. Nearly 30 percent of the residents here are over 65. The 19th includes almost all of Lee County and about half of the population of Collier County, including Naples and Marco Island. Over three-quarters of the district's residents live in Fort Myers, Cape Coral and Bonita Springs, and on Sanibel and Captiva. In a state where Republican registration rates often understate GOP voting strength, just 27 percent were registered Democrats, the lowest share of any Florida congressional district. The minor downside for Republicans: Donald Trump won 59 percent of the vote here, a smaller share than he received in five other Florida districts in 2016.

Alcee Hastings (D)

Elected 1992, 14th term, b. Sep 05, 1936; Altamonte Springs; Crooms Academy (FL), 1954; Fisk University (TN), B.A., 1958; Howard University (DC), Att., 1960; Florida Agricultural and Mechanical University College of Law, J.D., 1963; African Methodist Episcopal; Divorced; 3 children.

Elected Office: Broward County Circuit Court judge, 1977-1979.

Professional Career: Practicing attorney, 1964-1977, 1989-1992; Federal judge, U.S. District Court, 1979-1989.

DC Office: 2353 RHOB 20515, 202-225-1313, Fax: 202-225-1171, alceehastings.house.gov

State Offices: Tamarac, 954-733-2800; West Palm Beach, 561-461-6767.

Committees: *Rules*: Legislative & Budget Process.

Group Ratings

	ADA	ACLU	AFL-CIO	LCV	ITI	COC	HAFA	ACU	CFG	FRC
2018	-	92%	-	94%	-	67%	6%	4%	12%	0%
2017	95%	C	100%	94%	C	38%	C	0%	0%	0%

Almanac Ratings 2017-18

	Economy	Social	Foreign	Composite
Liberal	95%	97%	92%	95%
Conservative	5%	3%	8%	5%

Key Votes of the 115th Congress

1. Obama-care revision	N	5. Family planning regs	N	9. Guantanamo prisoners	Y
2. Tax Cuts	N	6. Body cameras/immigration	Y	10. Ground missiles, limit	Y
3. Omnibus appropriations	Y	7. Abortion ban	N	11. Defense Dept. spending	Y
4. Dodd-Frank revision	Y	8. Concealed carry	N	12. FISA rules	N

Election Results

Election	Name (Party)	Vote (%)	Cand. Spent	Ind. Exp. Support	Ind. Exp. Oppose
2018 General	Alcee Hastings (D)............................ 202,659	(100%)	$687,735	$536	
2018 Primary	Alcee Hastings (D).............................. 52,628	(74%)			
	Sheila Cherfilus-McCormick (D).. 18,697	(26%)			

Prior winning percentages: 2016 (80%), 2014 (82%), 2012 (88%), 2010 (79%), 2008 (82%), 2006 (100%), 2004 (100%), 2002 (77%), 2000 (76%), 1998 (100%), 1996 (73%), 1994 (100%), 1992 (59%)

Alcee Hastings, a Democrat first elected in 1992, has shrugged off an assortment of scandals, including his impeachment for bribery and perjury when he was a federal judge in the 1980s. Today he remains a friendly and often candid figure with Democratic colleagues in the House and South Florida constituents. With the Democrats' return to the House majority and at age 82, he regained a well-placed committee niche, after having mulled retirement while in the minority.

Hastings had a wide-ranging upbringing in the segregated America of the post-World War II decades. He grew up in a black suburb of Orlando and moved as a child to Jersey City and New York, where his parents worked as domestic servants for a rich Jewish family. He attended a Rosenwald school in Altamonte Springs, one of hundreds established for Southern blacks by Sears executive Julius Rosenwald. He graduated from Fisk University in Nashville and from Florida A&M law school in Tallahassee. From those beginnings, he made a rapid ascent, practicing law in Fort Lauderdale and finishing fourth in the five-candidate Democratic primary when he ran for the U.S. Senate in 1970, at age 34. He became a state judge in Broward County in 1977 and was confirmed as a federal judge in 1979.

Then his career took a sharp turn downward. He was charged with conspiring with a friend to take a $150,000 bribe and give two convicted swindlers light sentences. A Miami jury acquitted Hastings in 1983, but the friend was convicted. The U.S. Court of Appeals for the 11th Circuit called for impeachment in 1987 and referred the case to Congress. Hastings was impeached by the House on a vote of 413-3 and convicted by the Senate, 69-26. In the House, Democratic Rep. John Conyers of Michigan, a senior member of the Congressional Black Caucus, made the case for impeachment. As a footnote, during a 1997 investigation into the Federal Bureau of Investigation crime lab, the Department of Justice found that an agent falsely testified against Hastings.

After his removal from the bench, Hastings in 1990 ran an abortive campaign for governor, then lost in a primary for secretary of state. When the 23rd District was created in 1992, he led in the primary 28%-27%. In the October runoff, he faced Palm Beach County legislator Lois Frankel, who blasted Hastings for his record. He responded, "The bitch is a racist." Hastings was helped by a ruling from federal Judge Stanley Sporkin that his removal from office was invalid because the full Senate did not hear the charges; a subsequent supreme court ruling in a separate case nullified Sporkin's ruling, but that became a moot point. He won the runoff 58%-42%, with voting closely following racial lines. He won the general election 59%-31%. (Twenty years later, when Frankel ran successfully in an adjacent district, Hastings endorsed her and offered praise.) Since his first win, he has not had a serious primary or general election challenge.

In the House, Hastings' voting record has been mostly liberal, and his rhetoric has been proudly so. His Almanac vote ratings ranked him among the more liberal half of House Democrats. Pro-Israel groups are among his most active campaign contributors, and he has been a strong supporter of the Jewish state. In contrast to many House Democrats who boycotted the March 2015 appearance before Congress of Israeli Prime Minister Benjamin Netanyahu, Hastings said he agreed with Netanyahu that Europe had become increasingly dangerous for Jews.

In 2004, with the support of Republican Speaker Dennis Hastert, Hastings was elected president of the Organization for Security and Cooperation in the pan-European Parliamentary Assembly and served two one-year terms. In 2006, the House passed his resolution condemning Iran for hosting a conference on Holocaust denial. However, he drew the attention of ethics investigators in 2010 over whether he exceeded foreign travel stipends. He told the Wall Street Journal that he was generous in giving money to people he encountered and said: "You are all concerned about nickels and dimes, and I'm not. You know, in a taxicab in Kazakhstan, I don't have time to get a receipt — I don't speak Kazakh." The investigation was dropped in 2011. In 2018, Newsweek listed Hastings as the second poorest member of Congress. His negative net worth of more than $2 million included many unpaid bills from his impeachment expenses.

Hastings is the number-two Democrat on the Rules Committee, an influential post that gives him a hand in discussing the terms for bringing bills to the floor. Although he has more seniority in the House and on the committee than does Jim McGovern of Massachusetts, the latter became Rules chairman in January 2019 due to a long-ago deal between then-Rep. Joe Moakley of Massachusetts — who had been McGovern's mentor — and Democratic Leader Dick Gephardt. Hastings has been adept in the often arcane politics of the committee. He irked conservatives in 2010 for his defense of a controversial "deem and pass" strategy for the health care overhaul that was briefly considered. He paraphrased an expression of Thomas Edison's: "There ain't no rule around here; we're trying to accomplish something." Taking an original stand, Hastings has called for a commission to consider expanding the size of the House beyond 435 members. He said there were too many constituents in each district for lawmakers to serve them adequately. In a perhaps less original stand, he noted during a Rules Committee hearing in 2015 that Texas was "a crazy state to begin with." When the Texas Republican delegation demanded an apology, he refused.

Hastings has continued to draw — and survive — attention for issues apart from legislating. In 2014, the House Ethics Committee dismissed charges of sexual harassment against him that had been brought by a Republican congressional aide, but added that his behavior had been "less than professional." In December 2017, Roll Call reported that the federal Treasury paid $220,000 to the aide as part of that settlement. Hastings said that he had not been aware of the settlement and was "outraged that any taxpayer dollars were needlessly paid." Hastings has opened the door to retirement. Following his reelection in 2014, he said that he would assess the prospects for Democrats regaining control of the House. Whenever he exits, he likely won't go quietly. At an August 2018 political rally in south Florida, The Florida Sun Sentinel reported, Hastings said that a "crisis" would be if President Donald Trump fell into the Potomac River, but a "catastrophe" would be "if anybody saves his ass." In January 2019. Hastings said that he was being treated for pancreatic cancer.

FL-20: Western Broward and Palm Beach   Cook Partisan Voting Index: D+31

Population		Race and Ethnicity		Income	
Total	765,067	White	18.3%	Median Income	$43,648
Land area (sq. miles)	2,161	Black	52.6%	District Income Rank	390
Pop/ sq mi	354.1	Latino	24.1%	Poverty Rate	20.4%
Born in State	41.9%	Asian	2.6%	With health insurance	80.1%
		Two or more races	1.8%	Cash public assistance	3.2%
Age Groups		Other	0.6%	Food stamp/SNAP	22.7%
Under 18	24.3%				
18-34	24.3%	**Education**		**Work**	
35-64	38.5%	H.S grad or less	49.9%	White Collar	12.9%
Over 64	12.9%	Some college	29%	Sales and Service	52.1%
		College Degree, 4 yr	13.8%	Blue Collar	20.9%
Military		Post grad	7.2%	Government	11.2%
Veteran/ Active Duty	4.4%				

2012 Pres. Vote	Obama	219,939	(82%)	Romney	45,701	(17%)
2016 Pres. Vote	Clinton	231,595	(80%)	Trump	52,250	(18%)

Parts of Fort Lauderdale and West Palm Beach: In the morning shadow of the high-rise condominiums that line the Atlantic Ocean, beyond the quiet waters that separate the barrier islands from the mainland, and a few blocks off old U.S. 1, are the African-American neighborhoods of South Florida's Gold Coast. They are clusters of older stucco homes and commercial storefronts, ranging from upper-middle-class enclaves to rundown slums. These neighborhoods, largely populated by the working poor and with relatively few seniors, are bypassed by most tourists.

To the west is a land of swamps and drainage canals, with some farms and citrus groves. Some people live in migrant worker camps, while others live in small towns around Lake Okeechobee. The water quality in the lake has raised alarms on both the southeast and southwest coasts of Florida. Sugar is a big industry throughout this part of Florida. But in 2008, the South Florida Water Management District approved Gov. Charlie Crist's proposal to buy much of the land owned by U.S. Sugar Corp. around Lake Okeechobee for $1.35 billion, with most farming originally scheduled for phase-out within seven years. That would allow water to pass over land from the lake, through the Everglades, to the Gulf of Mexico.

The recession forced the plan to be delayed and scaled back. Sugar farmers continued to battle against it, while environmentalists sought its revival. In 2018, the state approved a $1.6 billion plan for a reservoir that will eventually cover 16,000 acres and will reduce discharges and toxic algae blooms. Construction began in November 2018, though environmentalists objected that sugar companies retained control of extensive lands for at least two more years. Meanwhile, sugar production has been booming. In 2017, sugar cane growers in Palm Beach County reported the largest crop in their history — 12.2 million tons. The sugar industry in Florida employs more than 14,000 workers, and sugar cane has remained the most valuable field crop in the state. The Port of Palm Beach has become the fourth-largest container port in Florida. Much of the cargo is sugar-related, and the commerce is largely with Caribbean islands.

The 20th Congressional District of Florida gathers together many of South Florida's black neighborhoods in a geographically contrived, but demographically coherent, constituency. The body of the district is in the Everglades. The bulk of the district's population resides in the two arms that extend east from the Everglades, with one going into West Palm Beach and the other into Fort Lauderdale. These arms surround most of the 21st and 22nd Congressional Districts.

The top arm moves through northern Palm Beach County, past high-income Wellington and into West Palm Beach and Palm Beach Lakes. The lower arm of the district reaches into Broward County to take in African-American areas in Fort Lauderdale, Lauderhill, North Lauderdale and Pompano Beach. The population in Broward is about twice that in Palm Beach County. In 2018, Brightline express train service began between West Palm Beach and Miami, with a one-hour travel time, in place of about twice that for drivers on high-traffic days on I-95.

Overall, the population is 53 percent black and 24 percent Hispanic, and surpassed the Dade County-based 24th District for the largest black population, though the 24th had a larger minority population, including Hispanics. Hillary Clinton led here, 80%-18%, her second-best in the state behind the 24th.

Lois Frankel (D)

Elected 2012, 4th term, b. May 16, 1948; New York (Manhattan), NY; Boston University (MA), B.A., 1970; Georgetown University Law Center (DC), J.D., 1973; Jewish; Divorced; 1 child.

Elected Office: FL House, 1986-1992, 1994-2002; Mayor, West Palm Beach, 2003-2011.

Professional Career: Law clerk, Hon. Judge David Norman, 1973-1974; Assistant public defender, West Palm Beach, 1974-1978; Practicing lawyer, 1978-2003.

DC Office: 2305 RHOB 20515, 202-225-9890, Fax: 202-225-1224, frankel.house.gov

State Offices: Boca Raton, 561-998-9045.

Committees: *Appropriations*: Energy & Water Development & Related Agencies; Labor, Health & Human Services, Education & Related Agencies; State, Foreign Operations & Related Programs. *Joint Economic.*

Group Ratings

	ADA	ACLU	AFL-CIO	LCV	ITI	COC	HAFA	ACU	CFG	FRC
2018	-	83%	-	100%	-	55%	4%	4%	12%	0%
2017	80%	C	97%	94%	C	46%	C	0%	0%	14%

Almanac Ratings 2017-18

	Economy	Social	Foreign	Composite
Liberal	94%	90%	81%	88%
Conservative	6%	10%	20%	12%

Key Votes of the 115th Congress

1. Obama-care revision	N	5. Family planning regs	N	9. Guantanamo prisoners	Y
2. Tax Cuts	N	6. Body cameras/immigration	Y	10. Ground missiles, limit	Y
3. Omnibus appropriations	Y	7. Abortion ban	N	11. Defense Dept. spending	Y
4. Dodd-Frank revision	N	8. Concealed carry	N	12. FISA rules	Y

Election Results

Election	Name (Party)	Vote (%)	Cand. Spent	Ind. Exp. Support	Ind. Exp. Oppose
2018 General	Lois Frankel (D)..	(100%)	$458,200		
2018 Primary	Lois Frankel (D)..	(100%)			

Prior winning percentages: 2016 (63%), 2014 (58%), 2012 (55%)

Democrat Lois Frankel, elected in 2012 after decades in public office, has shown her legislative and political expertise, including occasional interest in reaching across the aisle. Even while she was serving in the minority party, Frankel scored some achievements on urban problems and women's issues.

Frankel was born in New York City and raised in Great Neck on Long Island. Her father was in manufacturing and her mother was a homemaker. Frankel studied psychology at Boston University with the intent of becoming a psychiatrist, but her career plans changed when she became involved in the social movements of the late 1960s. "I was a student activist, and I was involved in antiwar protesting and the women's liberation movement," Frankel told National Journal. "There were so many movements ... it was all bubbling." She has joked that she "majored in protests."

Frankel got her law degree from Georgetown University and spent a year as a law clerk before moving to West Palm Beach. She became a public defender and advocate for numerous social causes. Frankel won an open state House seat in 1986 and quickly rose to become the first woman minority leader in Florida. She wrote the state's first AIDS law, which ensured confidentiality in testing.

She ran unsuccessfully against Alcee Hastings for a new House seat in 1992, losing the Democratic primary in a runoff, 58%-42%.

After term limits forced Frankel to leave the Florida House, she thought about challenging Gov. Jeb Bush in 2002, but withdrew before the primary. After she was elected mayor of West Palm Beach in 2003, she compiled what the South Florida Sun-Sentinel described as an "impressive" record, though she angered several labor unions when the city laid off workers.

In 2012, Frankel challenged freshman Republican firebrand Allen West. When West announced that he would run in the neighboring Treasure Coast district, made more GOP-friendly by redistricting, Frankel faced a primary with Broward County Commissioner Kristin Jacobs. They had nearly identical stances on issues, but Frankel had the backing of party leaders. She was endorsed by Hastings and got a rare visit from House Minority Leader Nancy Pelosi eight days before the primary. She coasted to a 61%-39% win.

In the general, Frankel attacked Republican nominee Adam Hasner for his support of Wisconsin Rep. Paul Ryan's budget plan, which would have introduced vouchers into the Medicare program, and for his stance against abortion rights. As each candidate tried to avoid sounding extreme, the Sun-Sentinel remarked that they had "shed their past personas like pythons in the Everglades." The Miami Herald endorsed Frankel, citing her "longer familiarity" with the district. Its Democratic lean helped her pull out a 55%-45% win. Each candidate spent $3.4 million.

Arriving in the House minority, Frankel made alliances with conservative Republicans. On the Transportation and Infrastructure Committee, she served in 2014 on the House-Senate conference committee that reached a final agreement on a water resources bill; it included additional dredging for expansion of Port Everglades plus water conservation and supply in the Everglades swamps. She joined another public works deal in 2016 on a water resources bill that delivered $2 billion for restoration of the Everglades.

Frankel joined two South Florida colleagues among the 25 House Democrats who voted to disapprove of the Obama administration's agreement with Iran on its nuclear program. "It legitimizes Iran's nuclear program after 15 years and gives Iran access to billions of dollars without a commitment to cease its terrorist activity," she said. But, once the deal had been implemented, she opposed the move by President Donald Trump to withdraw. She said that such a step would "destabilize the region, isolate the U.S. from our European allies and undermine American credibility around the world."

In 2017-18, Frankel co-chaired the bipartisan Congressional Women's Caucus with Republican Rep. Susan Brooks of Indiana. To dramatize the revelations of sexual harassment and other misconduct by powerful men in both the public and private sectors, she led an initiative for Democratic women to wear black at Trump's State of the Union address in January 2018. Given their inability to "shout back at the president" at such an event, she said, they agreed on the need for "a message of solidarity." On a partisan basis, Frankel chaired a new political action committee that aided women candidates running in 2018. Following the election, as Democratic factions clashed over the party's takeover of the House, Frankel warned that they "would turn us into the Republicans," referring to recent GOP internal schisms. She gained a seat on the Appropriations Committee.

When the state Supreme Court redistricting order in August 2015 threw Frankel into the same district with Democratic Rep. Ted Deutch, the two of them pledged to avoid a showdown. Frankel made the logical choice to run in the Palm Beach County-based 21st District. That forced Deutch to run in the Broward-based 22nd District, which was a bit less Democratic but included his home in Boca Raton. Each easily won reelection against an under-financed Republican challenger.

FL-21: Southern Palm Beach County   **Cook Partisan Voting Index: D+9**

Population		Race and Ethnicity		Income	
Total	754,832	White	57.1%	Median Income	$55,616
Land area (sq. miles)	257	Black	15.2%	District Income Rank	221
Pop/ sq mi	2938.8	Latino	23.2%	Poverty Rate	13.2%
Born in State	26.4%	Asian	2.6%	With health insurance	84.5%
		Two or more races	1.4%	Cash public assistance	2.1%
Age Groups		Other	0.5%	Food stamp/SNAP	10%
Under 18	18.9%				
18-34	18.8%	**Education**		**Work**	
35-64	36.9%	H.S grad or less	37.4%	White Collar	25.4%
Over 64	25.4%	Some college	28.7%	Sales and Service	48.9%
		College Degree, 4 yr	21.3%	Blue Collar	16.2%
Military		Post grad	12.7%	Government	9.5%
Veteran/ Active Duty	7.7%				

2012 Pres. Vote	Obama	192,282	(60%)	Romney	123,820	(39%)
2016 Pres. Vote	Clinton	206,239	(58%)	Trump	137,490	(39%)

Palm Beach, Lake Worth: When the first millionaires came to Palm Beach in the 1920s to winter in their new mansions, there was virtually nothing man-made between Palm Beach and Miami. In 1920, Dade, Broward and Palm Beach counties boasted a mere 66,000 residents. By 1950, the combined population of the three counties had jumped to almost 700,000, and the beachfront areas had largely been incorporated and developed. But the interior regions of the counties, near where Florida's turnpike would soon be laid out, remained marshy, sparsely inhabited and ripe for development. As the coastal areas were filling up, the inland swamps were being drained, abetted by a sequence of canals and levees built by the state in response to flooding from a series of hurricanes in 1947.

More than 3.4 million people inhabited Broward and Palm Beach counties in 2017, an increase from 3.1 million in 2010. Palm Beach has 1.5 million. The Palm Beach area remains, as it has been since the 1920s, the precinct of the very rich. The top Rolls Royce dealer in the world is in Palm Beach. Wellington is an international site for equestrian events, including polo. High-speed train service from West Palm Beach to Miami began service in May 2018. In 2018, work began on $145 million of waterfront development in downtown West Palm Beach -- including apartment buildings, retail space and a hotel.

The 21st District is entirely in Palm Beach County. Its ocean-front communities start at the north with Palm Beach, which includes President Donald Trump's Mar-a-Lago club hotel. As the new winter White House, the town received a tourist boost, though there were the inevitable inconveniences, especially in a densely populated area. The county's law-enforcement agencies were reimbursed $3 million for their costs in 2017, which was less than half of the additional expenses they claimed. The private airport in nearby Lantana was occasionally closed during peak hours. Although revenue at Mar-a-Lago decreased during Trump's first year as president, the value of the property increased from $150 million to $160 million, according to Forbes magazine. Palm Beach is separate from the mainland and accessible on two bridges or by continuing to the south on South Ocean Boulevard. To the south, Lake Worth, Boynton Beach and Delray Beach include narrow ocean-front locales; each of these cities sprawl several miles to the west. Delray Beach, the site in 1956 of a civil rights showdown over access to the beaches, now hosts international tennis events and has a large Haitian community. The district winds through a series of largely unincorporated residential communities to the west. Subdivisions extend far beyond the Florida Turnpike.

With the new lines, President Barack Obama in 2012 would have won, 60%-39%. Hillary Clinton took the district, 59%-39%. Her vote became a problem for Democrats because they increasingly need to roll up their vote in south Florida to balance setbacks elsewhere in the state.

Ted Deutch (D)

Elected 2010, 5th term, b. May 07, 1966; Bethlehem, PA; University of Michigan, B.A., 1988; University of Michigan Law School, J.D., 1990; Jewish; Married (Jill Deutch); 3 children (twins).

Elected Office: FL Senate, 2006-2010.

Professional Career: Practicing attorney, 1991-2010.

DC Office: 2447 RHOB 20515, 202-225-3001, Fax: 202-225-5974, teddeutch.house.gov

State Offices: Boca Raton, 561-470-5440; Coral Springs, 954-255-8336; Margate, 954-972-6454.

Committees: *Ethics (Chmn). Foreign Affairs*: Europe, Eurasia, Energy & the Environment; Middle East, North Africa & International Terrorism (Chmn). *Judiciary*: Courts, Intellectual Property & Internet; Crime, Terrorism & Homeland Security.

Group Ratings

	ADA	ACLU	AFL-CIO	LCV	ITI	COC	HAFA	ACU	CFG	FRC
2018	-	77%	-	94%	-	73%	4%	4%	2%	0%
2017	85%	C	94%	89%	C	33%	C	4%	0%	0%

Almanac Ratings 2017-18

	Economy	Social	Foreign	Composite
Liberal	95%	93%	83%	90%
Conservative	5%	7%	17%	10%

Key Votes of the 115th Congress

1. Obama-care revision	N	5. Family planning regs	N
2. Tax Cuts	N	6. Body cameras/immigration	NV
3. Omnibus appropriations	Y	7. Abortion ban	N
4. Dodd-Frank revision	N	8. Concealed carry	N

9. Guantanamo prisoners	Y
10. Ground missiles, limit	Y
11. Defense Dept. spending	Y
12. FISA rules	Y

Election Results

Election	Name (Party)	Vote (%)		Cand. Spent	Ind. Exp. Support	Ind. Exp. Oppose
2018 General	Ted Deutch (D)............................	184,634	(62%)	$954,920	$536	
	Nicolas Kimaz (R)............................	113,049	(38%)	$201,129		
2018 Primary	Ted Deutch (D)............................	54,236	(87%)			
	Jeff Fandle (D)............................	8,441	(14%)			

Prior winning percentages: 2016 (59%), 2014 (100%), 2012 (78%), 2010 (63%)

Democrat Ted Deutch, who won a special election in 2010, has become an active legislator, with a knack for making bipartisan deals. His appointment as chairman of the House Ethics Committee showed that he had gained cachet with Democratic leaders. He gained a different kind of renown in February 2018, when he joined the group of lawmakers who have been forced to react and explain their community following a nightmarish event — the mass shooting at the high school in Parkland.

Deutch has working-class roots in Bethlehem Pennsylvania, where his father ran a small painter contracting company and his mother kept the books. His parents did not go to college and were determined that their five children would. He excelled in high school and was class president for four years. During that period, heart disease forced his father into early retirement and he spent a lot of time watching CNN. Deutch said that sitting next to his dad discussing what was unfolding on the news channel fueled his budding interest in current events. At the University of Michigan, Deutch got his bachelor's in political science and a law degree. He volunteered in political campaigns, including for Democratic presidential candidate Joe Biden in 1987. He caught the eye of an academic adviser who encouraged him to apply for a Harry S Truman Scholarship, which recognizes students with potential for public service careers.

After law school, Deutch specialized in real estate law. That provided his initial entry to Washington, at a firm hired to sell off government assets from the savings and loan crisis. With his wife and their children, they moved to Boca Raton, where Ted's older brother, also a lawyer, hired him to handle his law firm's real estate business. Deutch got active in Florida politics. He worked on issues and raised money for Bill Clinton's two presidential campaigns. He also lobbied for pro-Israel causes. In 2006, he was elected to the Florida Senate. During three years in Tallahassee, he authored two signature measures: a bill putting a surcharge on tobacco products to help pay for smoking prevention programs and cancer research, and a bill barring the state from investing pension funds in any enterprise that aided Iran's effort to attain nuclear weapons or that abetted genocide in the Darfur region of Sudan.

When Democratic Rep. Robert Wexler resigned to head a Middle East think tank, Deutch announced for the seat. His liberal, pro-Israel politics appealed to the area's many Jewish retirees, and his state Senate seat filled half of the congressional district. Deutch faced minimal opposition in the Democratic primary, which was tantamount to election in a district where Democrats outnumbered Republicans 2-to-1. In the general election, Republican Ed Lynch tried to make the election a referendum on the Obama administration and its health care bill. Lynch joined national Republican leaders in calling for repeal. Deutch maintained that the changes would improve access to health care for people without insurance and for seniors. Deutch won 62%-35%, outspending his opponent $1.7 million to $117,000.

With seats on the Foreign Affairs and Judiciary committees, he displayed a savvy legislative instinct, even when Republicans had House control. In 2017, he organized with Republican Rep. Carlos Curbelo of Florida the bipartisan Climate Solutions Caucus; Deutch said that the caucus was, in part, a reaction to the decision by President Donald Trump to withdraw the United States from the Paris climate agreement that was reached in 2015. Later, Deutch signed onto a bipartisan proposal to create a carbon tax. The legislation enacted in October 2018 to respond to the opioid crisis included provisions cosponsored by Deutch to assist local communities and to crack down on individuals who receive kickbacks for improper patient referrals. He has drawn attention for campaign-finance reform proposals. One was a constitutional amendment to ban all corporate money in politics. That later evolved into his Democracy for All Amendment, which would overturn recent Supreme Court rulings that reduced restrictions on money in politics.

Deutch has been persistent on foreign policy conflicts. He got a provision in the 2012 Iran sanctions law that required companies to disclose to the Securities and Exchange Commission their business dealings with Iran. As ranking Democrat on the Middle East and North Africa Subcommittee, he became a go-to guy for his many Jewish constituents and the broader pro-Israel lobby in Washington. In 2014, he helped to write the Iran Threat Reduction Act, which imposed additional transparency and human rights requirements on Iran. He was outspoken after Secretary of State John Kerry concluded the agreement because, Deutch said, it failed to address "too many issues I have long raised as essential to any nuclear deal with Iran." Later, he filed a bill that made it easier to impose sanctions on Iran for violations of the agreement. In 2018, Congress approved final action on a bill that he filed with Republican Rep. Ileana Ros-Lehtinen that codified and implemented a memorandum of understanding for $38 billion over 10 years in military assistance to Israel.

In 2019, Deutch became chairman of the House Ethics Committee. As the senior Democrat on that panel the two previous years, he worked closely with the then-chair, Republican Rep. Susan Brooks of Indiana. They joined together on more than 50 actions, including statements, by the committee.

Following the February 2018 shootings at Marjory Stoneman Douglas High School in his district, Deutch became an outspoken advocate for action on gun control. "It is not too soon. It is too late for the 17 lives that were lost," he said in a CNN town hall a few days later. Following the 2018 election, he said that he would push for congressional action on two measures: universal background checks and a ban of "bump stocks," a firearm attachment that allows a gun to fire at a near-automatic rate, neither of which were relevant to the Parkland shooting.

Republicans have not seriously challenged Deutch since he was first elected.

FL-22: Northern Broward, Boca Raton   Cook Partisan Voting Index: D+6

Population		Race and Ethnicity		Income	
Total	742,818	White	58.5%	Median Income	$59,830
Land area (sq. miles)	167	Black	14.6%	District Income Rank	182
Pop/ sq mi	4439.8	Latino	21.1%	Poverty Rate	11.8%
Born in State	27.9%	Asian	3.2%	With health insurance	85.2%
		Two or more races	1.9%	Cash public assistance	1.2%
Age Groups		Other	0.6%	Food stamp/SNAP	8.6%
Under 18	18.8%				
18-34	19.7%	**Education**		**Work**	
35-64	41.6%	H.S grad or less	33.2%	White Collar	19.9%
Over 64	19.9%	Some college	28.8%	Sales and Service	45.3%
		College Degree, 4 yr	24%	Blue Collar	15.3%
Military		Post grad	14%	Government	9.1%
Veteran/ Active Duty	7%				

2012 Pres. Vote	Obama	182,437	(56%)	Romney	139,387	(43%)
2016 Pres. Vote	Clinton	202,357	(56%)	Trump	146,229	(41%)

Fort Lauderdale: The Marjory Stoneman Douglas High School in Parkland was added to the list of sites across the nation that have dealt with the excruciating experience of a mass shooting, with the accompanying horror and heartbreaking scenes. In February 2018, a teenage gunman who had attended the school, killed 17 persons with a semi-automatic rifle and was arrested nearby after a brief chase. The community — students, family, teachers and local officials — responded with demands for gun control and organized the March for Our Lives, a rally in Washington the following month that attracted several hundred thousand participants. Their demands for a political movement shaped "a new kind of debate about gun violence," The Atlantic wrote. The school attracted students from across Broward County to Parkland, a wealthy and growing community near Coral Springs and the Everglades. (Stoneman Douglas was a conservationist who helped to preserve the Everglades.)

The towns and cities that now populate the western portions of Broward County were generally incorporated during the late 1950s and early 1960s. This helped fuel yet another boom in Florida real estate, as people flocked to the new developments. It wasn't just retirees and developers who took an interest in the region. Westinghouse Electric Corp. initially invested in Coral Springs in the 1960s as a sort of "urban laboratory" for products such as central air conditioning, motion detecting lights, security systems and fully electric kitchens. In 1981, IBM developed its first personal computer at a lab in Boca Raton.

Downtown Fort Lauderdale, separated from the beach by miles of canals, is the site of the Museum of Art Fort Lauderdale, the Broward Center for the Performing Arts and the International Swimming Hall of Fame. Along with neighboring Wilton Manors, it became the home of choice for many gay people. In 2016, the Census Bureau reported that Fort Lauderdale had the highest percentage of same-sex couple households of any mid-sized or large city in the nation; Wilton Manors in November 2018 became the second locality in the nation — after Palm Springs California — to elect an all-LGBTQ local government. In 2016, Port Everglades was the third-busiest port in the world for the number of passengers, behind Miami and Port Canaveral. Its plans to deepen and expand its channel to accommodate larger ships, including container vessels, were delayed to limit the impact on nearby coral reef; it opened a new $120 million terminal in November 2018.

The 22nd Congressional District includes the southeast corner of Palm Beach, chiefly Boca Raton, where the azure fountains and red-tiled roofs of the Boca Raton Resort & Club, which was opened in 1926, bespeak a vision of a holiday Florida. After moving through coastal parts of Pompano Beach and Fort Lauderdale, the district includes parts of upscale Plantation but loops around African-American precincts, placed in the 20th District. What was a Republican enclave until the 1990s has become a reliably Democratic district. Hillary Clinton took the new 22nd, 56%-41%, two points lower than her vote in the 21st to the north.

Debbie Wasserman Schultz (D)

Elected 2004, 8th term, b. Sep 27, 1966; Forest Hills (Queens), NY; University of Florida, B.A., 1988; University of Florida, M.A., 1990; Jewish; Married (Steve Schultz); 3 children.

Elected Office: FL House, 1992-2000, Minority Leader pro tem., 1999-2000; FL Senate, 2000-2004.

Professional Career: Legislative aide, 1989-1992.

DC Office: 1114 LHOB 20515, 202-225-7931, Fax: 202-226-2052, wassermanschultz.house.gov

State Offices: Aventura, 305-936-5724; Sunrise, 954-845-1179.

Committees: *Appropriations*: Energy & Water Development & Related Agencies; Homeland Security; Military Construction, Veterans Affairs & Related Agencies (Chmn). *Oversight & Reform*: National Security; Subcommittee on Civil Rights & Civil Liberties.

Group Ratings

	ADA	ACLU	AFL-CIO	LCV	ITI	COC	HAFA	ACU	CFG	FRC
2018	-	77%	-	100%	-	64%	6%	4%	12%	0%
2017	95%	C	97%	86%	C	43%	C	5%	0%	0%

Almanac Ratings 2017-18

	Economy	Social	Foreign	Composite
Liberal	94%	94%	89%	92%
Conservative	6%	6%	11%	8%

Key Votes of the 115th Congress

1. Obama-care revision	N	5. Family planning regs	N	9. Guantanamo prisoners	Y
2. Tax Cuts	N	6. Body cameras/immigration	NV	10. Ground missiles, limit	Y
3. Omnibus appropriations	Y	7. Abortion ban	N	11. Defense Dept. spending	Y
4. Dodd-Frank revision	N	8. Concealed carry	N	12. FISA rules	Y

Election Results

Election	Name (Party)	Vote (%)		Cand. Spent	Ind. Exp. Support	Ind. Exp. Oppose
2018 General	Debbie Wasserman Schultz (D)	161,611	(58%)	$1,691,322		
	Joe Kaufman (R)	99,446	(36%)	$485,618		
	Tim Canova (I)	13,697	(5%)	$581,732	$33,234	
2018 Primary	Debbie Wasserman Schultz (D)		(100%)			

Prior winning percentages: 2016 (57%), 2014 (63%), 2012 (63%), 2010 (60%), 2008 (77%), 2006 (100%), 2004 (70%)

Debbie Wasserman Schultz, a hard-charging Democrat elected in 2004, returned to a lower-profile role in the House following a tumultuous 2016. After she was forced out as chair of the Democratic National Committee as the party convention convened in Philadelphia, she then endured her toughest political challenge in the Democratic primary for her seat, which became an extension of the presidential-primary conflict between Hillary Clinton and Bernie Sanders. That led her to abandon her interest in a top leadership post in the House and to burrow into her work at the Appropriations Committee and with the Democratic whip team.

Like many of her constituents, Wasserman Schultz was born in Queens. She grew up on Long Island, where she ran for student council every year and always lost. She got bachelor's and master's degrees from the University of Florida. State Rep. Peter Deutsch, a Democrat and former New Yorker from Broward County, gave her a summer job and then appointed her as his legislative aide. In 1992, he ran for the House and urged Wasserman Schultz to run for his seat in the legislature. She did, knocking on doors for six months and finishing far ahead of four opponents in the Democratic primary. At age 26, she became the youngest woman elected to the state House. She served eight years there, including two as minority leader, followed by four in the state Senate. She called herself "a pragmatic liberal," and she sponsored a controversial law to require an equal number of men and women on state boards and a bill that failed to pass requiring dry cleaners and some other businesses to charge the same prices for women as for men.

When Deutsch ran in 2004 for the Democratic nomination for an open Senate seat, Wasserman Schultz again moved to replace him. She collected more than $1 million for what turned out to be a non-contest in the decisive Democratic primary, since no one else filed to run. Against a Republican who attacked the "homosexual agenda" in the public schools, she won 70%-30%. For the next decade, she did not face a serious challenge, allowing her to channel campaign contributions to her colleagues from a wide spectrum of Democratic interests.

In the House, Wasserman Schultz has had a mostly liberal voting record, although she has been more centrist on foreign policy. She has been one of the Florida delegation's most ardent opponents of offshore oil drilling, declaring after the 2010 BP oil spill in the Gulf of Mexico that "our country needs to run on something other than oil."

Her blazing ascension up the leadership ladder began in 2006 when she was appointed co-chairwoman of the Democratic Congressional Campaign Committee's "Red to Blue" program. Working closely with chairman Rahm Emanuel, she became a party spokeswoman and a mentor to Democratic recruits. When Democrats won House control that year, Majority Whip James Clyburn tapped her as a chief deputy whip. She snagged a seat on the Appropriations Committee and chaired the Legislative Branch Subcommittee. She took charge of the Capitol Visitors Center project, which was plagued by cost overruns, and extracted commitments on costs and completion dates.

Her success seemed all the more impressive when she announced in 2009 that for much of the previous year she had been battling breast cancer. Although her tumor was in the early stages, which would typically require only surgery and radiation, she said that she elected to have a double mastectomy after learning that as an Ashkenazi Jew, she had a greater predisposition to recurrence. The mother of three school-aged children, Wasserman Schultz was diagnosed just after turning 40. "I didn't want it to define me," she told The New York Times of her illness.

The foreign policy pursuits of President Barack Obama forced Wasserman Schultz to navigate tricky terrain. As a long-time critic of the Cuban regime, she offered only limited and murky support when the president in December 2014 announced breakthrough initiatives to Cuba. When many House Democrats, including some Jewish members, protested the March 2015 speech to Congress by Israeli Prime Minister Benjamin Netanyahu, she carefully said, "Israel is an issue that should not be made partisan." In what became for many a test of party loyalty in September 2015, her decision to support Obama's nuclear deal with Iran led to strong objections from her many Jewish constituents and party contributors.

In 2011, Wasserman Schultz beat out former Ohio Gov. Ted Strickland to take the helm of the DNC, with Vice President Joe Biden citing "her tenacity, her strength, her fighting spirit, and her ability to overcome adversity." Vowing that the party would be "laser-focused on the economy" as it sought to reelect Obama, she was a ferocious Republican critic. She blasted House Budget Committee Chairman Paul Ryan's budget blueprint because it would "allow insurance companies to deny you coverage and drop you for pre-existing conditions" — a claim that the fact-checking website PolitiFact judged to be false.

Wasserman Schultz was frequently deployed in 2012 as a campaign surrogate for Obama, attending hundreds of events across the nation. But she developed a strained relationship with Obama campaign officials, who privately accused her of coming across as too partisan on television. Election Night's results served as her vindication: Not only did Obama win with substantial support from women and Jewish voters, two constituencies that Wasserman Schultz cultivated, but he captured Florida, a state where Republican Mitt Romney enjoyed a sizable lead in pre-election polls.

The most severe test of her mettle came during the 2016 Democratic presidential campaign showdown between Clinton and Sanders. She consistently denied criticisms that her actions as DNC chair had favored Clinton, whom Wasserman Schultz had strongly backed in the 2008 campaign. "I will be frank with you — if I was trying to rig the outcome of the primary, trust me, I could have," she told VICE News following the election. "There are so many things that we — not I — we could have done to enhance the campaign of one candidate over another." But amid the tensions at the July convention in Philadelphia, the demands by combative Sanders allies for a scalp — what she called a scapegoat for their own mistakes -- left her and the Clinton forces little option if they wanted to have a harmonious week. Even after she resigned the day before the convention opened, she played a behind-the-scenes role in managing the proceedings that she had organized during the past two years.

Controversy continued to tarnish that experience. In a book about the Democratic debacle in 2016, Donna Brazile, who became interim chair of the DNC in the months prior to the election, wrote that "Debbie was not a good manager" and that she — with Obama and Clinton -- had left the party deeply in debt. Wasserman Schultz also faced inquiries from Justice Department and congressional investigators seeking details of DNC opposition research on Donald Trump plus alleged Russian hacking of DNC computers during the campaign.

Following the convention, Wasserman Schultz turned her attention to a vigorous primary challenge from local law professor Tim Canova. As a Sanders backer, he had been criticizing her for months as insufficiently progressive in Congress and too responsive to special interests. He called her a "corporate stooge" and sought to exploit the unhappiness of the Sanders forces at the convention. Sanders endorsed Canova and signed a fundraising letter on his behalf, but failed to make a personal appearance as had been expected. Wasserman Schultz had several factors going her way: Canova's political inexperience; her lengthy and close relationship with constituents; persistence and energy; ample fundraising; and support from many party leaders, including Obama and Clinton. Each candidate had plenty of money: $4 million for Wasserman Schultz to $3.8 million for Canova. She won the primary, 57%-43%. In the general election that was routine, Wasserman Schultz won, 57%-40%, against Republican Joseph Kaufman, a writer who had made two earlier challenges. In 2018, she faced both opponents again. This time, Canova ran as an independent in November and got 5 percent of vote. She defeated Kaufman, 58%-36%.

The political options for Wasserman Schultz have long been a topic of intrigue. In March 2015, she ruled out a race for Marco Rubio's Senate seat, which might have been a missed opportunity given what turned out to be a weak Democratic field. That decision seemed to confirm that her political future was in the House. She moved up in seniority on the Appropriations Committee, where she became top Democrat on the Financial Services subcommittee and then on the panel in charge of military construction and veterans affairs. When Democrats regained House control, she regained her post as an Appropriations "cardinal," this time with the military construction panel

The lingering question of her leadership ambition seemed to be resolved after the 2018 election, when Wasserman Schultz remained on the sidelines as several relatively junior House Democrats won low-level party posts. Whether she was damaged by the controversies linked to her support for Clinton or had simply become another victim of the decade-long logjam among Democratic leaders remained unclear. At age 52, she retained options in the House and at home.

FL-23: Southern Broward, Coastal Dade   **Cook Partisan Voting Index: D+11**

Population		Race and Ethnicity		Income	
Total	751,320	White	43.3%	Median Income	$62,823
Land area (sq. miles)	190	Black	13.2%	District Income Rank	150
Pop/ sq mi	3948.9	Latino	36.8%	Poverty Rate	11%
Born in State	32%	Asian	4%	With health insurance	86.9%
		Two or more races	1.8%	Cash public assistance	1.5%
Age Groups		Other	0.8%	Food stamp/SNAP	9.6%
Under 18	21%				
18-34	20.7%	**Education**		**Work**	
35-64	41.8%	H.S grad or less	31%	White Collar	16.5%
Over 64	16.5%	Some college	30.2%	Sales and Service	44.6%
		College Degree, 4 yr	23.9%	Blue Collar	13.7%
Military		Post grad	14.8%	Government	10.9%
Veteran/ Active Duty	4.9%				

2012 Pres. Vote	Obama	187,346	(61%)	Romney	115,878	(38%)	
2016 Pres. Vote	Clinton	209,078	(62%)	Trump	120,967	(36%)	

Hollywood: When Broward County was created in 1915, its name was to be "Everglades County," reflecting its largely agricultural character, save for a few fledgling beachfront communities like Fort Lauderdale. Development proceeded slowly. Instead, it was named for Napoleon Bonaparte Broward, a roguish riverboat captain who served as Florida governor early in the 20th century. Joseph Wesley Young dreamed of building a resort community by the sea and founded Hollywood in 1925. But a hurricane the following year devastated the infant town, people fled in droves, and Young's holdings were eventually auctioned off in 1930. But this prime beachfront real estate could not remain undeveloped for long, and by 1980, the population was exploding. Over time, these new South Florida residents increasingly came from the Northeast, and brought those Democratic politics. They were instrumental in transforming the state's Democratic Party from a rural, Southern party run by the so-called "Pork Chop Gang" of conservative senators into one more closely resembling its Northern counterparts, and eventually helped turn Florida into a swing state.

Today, Broward County is in the midst of another transformation. It is now a minority-majority county, the third largest in the nation (behind Riverside in California and Clark in Nevada), with the non-Hispanic white share of the 1.9 million population dropping to 36 percent in 2018. Blacks and Latinos are both 30 percent; each is a big increase since 2000. The most common countries of origin for these newcomers are Haiti, Jamaica and Colombia; one in three residents are foreign-born, but many of them are undocumented. While Broward gave Richard Nixon 72 percent of the vote in 1972, 44 years later it was Hillary Clinton's second-strongest county in the state, giving her two-thirds of the vote. The Fort Lauderdale Airport, once a sleepy facility, is the third-busiest in Florida and has moved closer to Miami in its passenger load. It has pursued $3.2 billion of improvements — including new gates and parking, and a runway over Federal Highway. With its growth, some problems have remained with local governance. They included, as the slow results from the 2018 election reminded, a cumbersome vote-counting process. Its lack of serious partisan competition, Politico wrote in November 2018, "has led to bad incentives and bad habits for county leaders."

The 23rd District of Florida includes much of southern Broward County. The district is anchored by coastal Hollywood, where huge high-rises house large numbers of retirees from the Northeast and new resorts attract vacationers. From there, the district moves inland, with a slight northwestern trajectory. It includes Davie, a former ranching town where the businesses lining downtown all have an "Old Western" motif. The western end of the district is new-growth suburbs, such as Southwest Ranches and Weston, which has many lakes and inlets and a large concentration of Venezuelan Americans. About 90 percent of the district's residents live in Broward, with the remainder occupying a string of barrier islands in northern Miami-Dade County, in North Miami just to the north of Miami Beach. Located here are some of the high-rises along Collins Avenue facing the ocean and Latino neighborhoods north of 88th Street.

The district leans substantially Democratic. In the past two presidential elections, the vote for Barack Obama and Hillary Clinton held steady at 62 percent.

Frederica Wilson (D)

Elected 2010, 5th term, b. Nov 05, 1942; Miami; Fisk University (TN), B.S., 1963; University of Miami (FL), M.Ed., 1972; Episcopalian; Widow; 3 children; 5 grandchildren.

Elected Office: FL House, 1998-2002; FL Senate, 2002-2010.

Professional Career: Teacher; principal; Assistant principal.

DC Office: 2445 RHOB 20515, 202-225-4506, Fax: 202-226-0777, wilson.house.gov

State Offices: Hollywood, 954-921-3682; Miami Gardens, 305-690-5905; West Park, 954-989-2688.

Committees: *Education & Labor*: Early Childhood, Elementary & Secondary Education; Health, Employment, Labor & Pensions (Chmn). *Transportation & Infrastructure*: Highways & Transit; Railroads, Pipelines & Hazardous Materials; Water Resources & Environment.

Group Ratings

	ADA	ACLU	AFL-CIO	LCV	ITI	COC	HAFA	ACU	CFG	FRC
2018	-	88%	-	97%	-	50%	4%	4%	13%	0%
2017	90%	C	100%	86%	C	50%	C	0%	0%	0%

Almanac Ratings 2017-18

	Economy	Social	Foreign	Composite
Liberal	94%	98%	88%	93%
Conservative	6%	2%	12%	7%

Key Votes of the 115th Congress

1. Obama-care revision	N	5. Family planning regs	N	9. Guantanamo prisoners	Y
2. Tax Cuts	NV	6. Body cameras/immigration	Y	10. Ground missiles, limit	Y
3. Omnibus appropriations	Y	7. Abortion ban	N	11. Defense Dept. spending	Y
4. Dodd-Frank revision	N	8. Concealed carry	N	12. FISA rules	NV

Election Results

Election	Name (Party)	Vote (%)	Cand. Spent	Ind. Exp. Support	Ind. Exp. Oppose
2018 General	Frederica Wilson (D)...	(100%)	$382,147		
2018 Primary	Frederica Wilson (D)............................ 66,202	(84%)			
	Ricardo de le Fuente (D)................... 12,924	(16%)			

Prior winning percentages: 2016 (100%), 2014 (86%), 2012 (86%), 2010 (86%)

Democrat Frederica Wilson, elected in 2010, has compiled a solidly liberal voting record while speaking out on behalf of her low-income constituents, particularly Haitian Americans. She calls herself "a voice for the voiceless" and has engaged in unusually harsh exchanges with President Donald Trump and his top aides about some of her constituents.

Wilson's politics were inspired by her father, Thirlee Smith, a native of Timpson Texas, a town that in his day had an active chapter of the Ku Klux Klan. "He would sit me on his knee and tell me stories of what happened to him in Texas and how people were lynched," she recalled. In Miami, Smith ran a restaurant and a billiard hall, and became active in the civil rights movement, registering voters and pushing for sanitation workers' rights. The couple's three children were sensitized to acts of injustice at a young age. Once, in high school, Wilson spied a new kid in school being teased for wearing torn clothes. Wilson, who weighed about 70 pounds at the time, stepped into the circle of bullies and ordered them to leave the boy alone. She pursued a career in education and eventually politics.

Wilson graduated from Fisk University with a bachelor's degree in elementary education, and got her master's from the University of Miami. She worked as a teacher and then became an assistant educational coordinator for a Head Start program and later became principal. She served on the Miami-Dade County School Board. In 1984, she joined a campaign to lobby Congress to remove Haitian refugees from a local detention center. The Haitian women in particular, she said, "had no privacy at all, from guards, from visitors, from INS, from no one. When they would take a shower, they had no curtains. They were treating them like animals." The women were eventually released and allowed to remain in Miami.

Wilson was elected to the Florida House in 1998. After four years, she won a seat in the state Senate. In each chamber, she served as minority whip. In 2004, she led a sometimes bitter fight against Gov. Jeb Bush to scale back the use of standardized testing in schools, which she said had a negative impact on children. Wilson was known in the legislature for her trademark headgear of brightly colored, often rhinestone-studded hats, which were inspired by her grandmother, who wore similar hats as a cultural tradition in her native Bahamas.

When Democrat Kendrick Meek ran unsuccessfully for the Senate, Wilson ran for his House seat. In the nine-candidate Democratic primary, she won with 35 percent of the vote, helped by four candidates splitting Haitian voter support. In the fall, she won with 86 percent against an independent.

In the House, Wilson delivered a series of impassioned speeches following the death of black teenager Trayvon Martin, who in 2012 was shot in Sanford Florida by neighborhood watch volunteer George Zimmerman. Wilson said she was "tired of burying young black boys." Wilson founded the 5000 Role Models of Excellence Project, a local version of My Brother's Keeper, to assist at-risk young males. "There is this tension that never goes away between the police and especially black boys," she said. President Barack Obama praised her efforts during a White House event in 2014. After several violent hazing incidents at colleges, Wilson proposed denying federal aid to students who are punished by colleges or convicted for hazing. In the majority in 2019, she became chairwoman of the Education and Labor Subcommittee on Health, Employment, Labor and Pensions, where she promised reforms to "restore fairness to our economy."

In 2014, the Obama administration adopted Wilson's proposal for a family reunification program for Haitian immigrants. The action was part of the U.S. response to a devastating earthquake in Haiti in 2010 that left 1.5 million homeless. Wilson became the most visible advocate for the nearly 300 school girls in Nigeria who had been kidnapped in 2014 by the Boko Haram terrorist group. She traveled to Nigeria to meet on their behalf with Nigerian officials.

Wilson's conflicts with the Trump White House stemmed from her criticism of the president's brief comments in a phone call with a widow prior to a ceremony at the Miami airport to receive the body of her husband, an Army sergeant from her district who had been killed on duty in Niger. When Trump's comments indicated, "I guess he knew what he was signing up for," the sergeant's pregnant widow "was rolled up almost in a fetal position, crying," Wilson recounted, adding to reporters, Trump "doesn't know how to be president." Subsequently, presidential chief of staff John Kelly publicly criticized Wilson for grandstanding and an example of "empty barrels making the most noise." Three months later, after Trump included Haiti as one of the places he referred to as "shithole countries," Wilson boycotted his State of the Union address, which she said was filled with "lies and innuendoes."

At home, Rudy Moise, a Haitian-American lawyer and doctor who finished second in the 2010 primary, returned for a rematch in 2012, and this time snagged a rare endorsement from a foreign leader, Haitian President Michel Martelly. Wilson countered with one from Obama and won with 66 percent.

In 2016, her primary challenge came from Randal "The Thrill" Hill, who was a local celebrity as a former football star for the University of Miami and the NFL's Miami Dolphins and became a special agent for the Department of Homeland Security. He criticized Wilson as a career politician who failed to solve problems. "Given her years of leadership, Wilson still deserves to be in the starting lineup," the Sun Sentinel wrote in its endorsement. She won the primary, 78%-22%. In 2018, she got 84 percent of the vote in the primary against a fringe challenger who had run in a special election for a congressional vacancy in California in 2017.

FL-24: Northern Dade, Southern Broward   Cook Partisan Voting Index: D+34

Population		Race and Ethnicity		Income	
Total	741,759	White	11.9%	Median Income	$37,821
Land area (sq. miles)	102	Black	47.4%	District Income Rank	424
Pop/ sq mi	7248.7	Latino	38.2%	Poverty Rate	24.1%
Born in State	42.4%	Asian	1.2%	With health insurance	75%
		Two or more races	0.8%	Cash public assistance	3.7%
Age Groups		Other	0.5%	Food stamp/SNAP	29.5%
Under 18	22.3%				
18-34	24.9%	**Education**		**Work**	
35-64	39.7%	H.S grad or less	53.8%	White Collar	13.1%
Over 64	13.1%	Some college	26.9%	Sales and Service	53.1%
		College Degree, 4 yr	12.8%	Blue Collar	21.5%
Military		Post grad	6.5%	Government	11.9%
Veteran/ Active Duty	2.8%				

2012 Pres. Vote	Obama	217,431	(86%)	Romney	35,148	(14%)	
2016 Pres. Vote	Clinton	219,784	(82%)	Trump	40,817	(15%)	

Liberty City, Miami Gardens: North from downtown, alongside Interstate 95, Miami's main north-south artery, is the largest African-American community in Florida. It stretches from the American Airlines Arena northwest to Overtown — originally called "Colored Town" — where racially restrictive covenants in the rest of Miami forced the city's original African-American laborers to reside. From there the community has spread through Allapattah and Liberty City to the brightly painted minarets and Moorish arches of the city of Opa-Locka, whose name is a shortened version of the Seminole name for the area. This has been a kind of frontierland in Miami, where hostilities between the city's blacks and its Cuban-American majority have played out. Many of Miami's African Americans have resented the economic upward mobility and political strength of the Cubans.

There is also tension between Cubans and Haitians in Little Haiti, exacerbated by federal policies that give refugee status to Cubans who reach U.S. shores, while Haitians are treated as any other immigrant group with potential for deportation. President Donald Trump has increased that tension with his hostility toward Haitian immigrants and their homeland. During a January 2018 meeting on immigration at the White House, he reportedly said, "Why do we need more Haitians? Take them out," and referred to "all these people from shithole countries." This animosity is reflected in partisan politics. Cuban Americans have been solidly Republican over the years, though somewhat less so recently. South Florida African Americans have remained largely Democratic, as has the growing Haitian-American community.

The 24th Congressional District covers the historic heart of Miami's black community. Located here are much of northeast Miami-Dade County, including Liberty City, which has suffered extensive crime and gun violence, Overtown and Opa-Locka. Miami Gardens, the third-largest city in Miami-Dade (after Miami and Hialeah), has suffered numerous incidents of alleged police abuses, especially against blacks. Allapattah reportedly has been in the throes of gentrification. In November 2018, Miami-Dade voters narrowly rejected approval of the county's 35th city, near Aventura. The county has explored a new elevated rail line through African-American neighborhoods along 27th Street. To the north are heavily Haitian-American towns like Golden Glades, El Portal, Ives Estates and North Miami Beach.

On the other side of the Broward County line, about 12 percent of the district resides in fast-growing Pembroke Pines. Redistricting dropped the district's black population to 47 percent, while Hispanics increased to 38 percent, though actual Hispanic voter registration and turnout is closer to 25 percent. The 24th has been among the top 10 most Democrats districts in the nation and the highest in the South. President Barack Obama in 2012 won 88 percent of the vote with the old lines. Hillary Clinton got 83 percent of the new district.

Mario Diaz-Balart (R)

Elected 2002, 9th term, b. Sep 25, 1961; Fort Lauderdale; University of South Florida, Att., 1982; Roman Catholic; Married (Tia Diaz-Balart); 1 child.

Elected Office: FL House, 1988-1992, 2000-2002; FL Senate, 1992-2000.

Professional Career: A.A., Miami Mayor Xavier Suarez, 1985-1988; Public relations executive.

DC Office: 404 CHOB 20515, 202-225-4211, Fax: 202-225-8576, mariodiazbalart.house.gov

State Offices: Doral, 305-470-8555; Naples, 239-348-1620.

Committees: *Appropriations*: Defense; Transportation, HUD & Related Agencies (RMM).

Group Ratings

	ADA	ACLU	AFL-CIO	LCV	ITI	COC	HAFA	ACU	CFG	FRC
2018	-	13%	-	17%	-	92%	38%	46%	38%	100%
2017	10%	C	36%	6%	C	93%	C	63%	51%	100%

Almanac Ratings 2017-18

	Economy	Social	Foreign	Composite
Liberal	16%	18%	5%	13%
Conservative	84%	82%	95%	87%

Key Votes of the 115th Congress

1. Obama-care revision	Y	5. Family planning regs	Y	9. Guantanamo prisoners	N
2. Tax Cuts	Y	6. Body cameras/immigration	NV	10. Ground missiles, limit	N
3. Omnibus appropriations	Y	7. Abortion ban	Y	11. Defense Dept. spending	Y
4. Dodd-Frank revision	Y	8. Concealed carry	Y	12. FISA rules	Y

Election Results

Election	Name (Party)	Vote (%)		Cand. Spent	Ind. Exp. Support	Ind. Exp. Oppose
2018 General	Mario Diaz-Balart (R).....................	128,672	(60%)	$2,584,001		$338,777
	Mary Barzee Flores (D)........................	84,173	(40%)	$2,156,689	$18,607	
2018 Primary	Mario Diaz-Balart (R)...............	(100%)				

Prior winning percentages: 2016 (62%), 2014 (100%), 2012 (76%), 2010 (67%), 2008 (72%), 2006 (80%), 2004 (73%), 2002 (66%)

Mario Diaz-Balart, a Republican first elected in 2002, has been a pragmatic legislator who has been among the handful of GOP Latinos seeking to nudge their party closer to the political middle on immigration issues. As chairman of an Appropriations subcommittee, he delivered large sums to projects back home. Election setbacks for the GOP in 2018 left Diaz-Balart as the last Republican and unswerving hardliner against Cuba's regime from south Florida.

The Diaz-Balart family history was intertwined with that of Fidel Castro and the rise of communism on the island nation of Cuba. Mario's father, Rafael Lincoln Diaz-Balart, was the majority leader in pre-revolution Cuba's House of Representatives. His uncle and grandfather also served in the Cuban House. The Diaz-Balarts fled Cuba in 1959, shortly after Castro took over and after their house was looted and burned while they were vacationing in Paris. His aunt was briefly Castro's wife and was the mother of the dictator's only recognized child. One of Mario's three older brothers is Lincoln Diaz-Balart, who served in the House from 1992 to 2010, then set up a consulting firm. Another brother, Jose, is an anchorman with Spanish-language Telemundo and an occasional anchor with NBC News, and Rafa is an international banker based in Miami.

Mario Diaz-Balart was born in the United States after the family had resettled. He dropped out of the University of South Florida at age 24 to work for former Miami Mayor Xavier Suarez, a Republican. In 1988, he was elected to the Florida House; four years later, at age 31, he became the youngest person elected to the state Senate. Diaz-Balart was chairman of the Senate Ways and Means Committee, where he was a budget hawk. His 1995 call for state agencies to cut spending by 25 percent earned him the nickname "The Slasher" — a moniker he wore with pride.

The eight-year term limit forced him from the Senate in 2000, so he again ran for the Florida House and was elected. No ordinary freshman, Diaz-Balart requested and received the chairmanship of the congressional redistricting committee. The resulting plan included a western Miami-Dade district that he tailored for himself. He coasted to victory over Democratic state Rep. Annie Betancourt, a former social worker and the widow of a Bay of Pigs veteran. With support from teachers and other unions, Diaz-Balart won 65%-35%.

In the House, Diaz-Balart's voting record has moved from what initially was mostly conservative. His Almanac vote ratings have ranked him near the center of the House for each of the three issue areas. With Republican leaders eager to diversify their caucus, he got a coveted seat on the Appropriations Committee. As chairman of the Subcommittee on Transportation, Housing and Urban Development, he worked with the Trump administration in 2017-18 to deliver $20 million to Miami International Airport and more than $70 million for other local transportation projects. In the minority, Diaz-Balart became ranking Republican on the transportation subcommittee. He has used his Appropriations seat to secure funding for the Everglades and consistently has opposed oil drilling off Florida's coast in the Gulf of Mexico.

Diaz-Balart organized the Congressional Hispanic Conference, a Republican alternative to the Democrats' Congressional Hispanic Caucus, and he has often engaged on immigration issues. With GOP Rep. Ileana Ros-Lehtinen, who retired in 2018, he supported a bill to allow children of illegal immigrants to qualify for college aid. After Republican Mitt Romney overwhelmingly lost the Hispanic vote to President Barack Obama in 2012, Diaz-Balart was among those urging support for a broad immigration reform bill, which he has called the "800-pound gorilla." Republicans "cannot pretend there are not millions of people in an underground society," he told the Orlando Sentinel. "We can no longer pretend that it's not affecting our ability to be competitive."

He participated in private discussions with many members of each party in an effort to find common ground on immigration. When House Republican leaders in 2014 declared the issue dead at the time, Diaz-Balart called the result "disappointing and highly unfortunate" and said it was "highly irresponsible not to deal with the issue." In 2018, he spearheaded an initiative by dissident Republicans to sign a discharge petition to force House votes on legislation to give legal status to undocumented immigrants; they fell short.

Diaz-Balart adamantly opposed the push by President Barack Obama to resume diplomatic relations with Cuba, and he has continued to resist tourist travel as an important revenue source for the Castro government. Diaz-Balart said that Cuba had not met the terms set by Congress before the embargo could be lifted. When trade restrictions have been relaxed, he added, "the oppression worsens." With Sen. Marco Rubio of Florida, he pressed President Donald Trump to continue the crackdown and was mostly pleased with the results.

In 2008, Diaz-Balart faced a serious challenge from Joe Garcia, the Miami-Dade County Democratic chairman and former executive director of the Cuban American National Foundation. Garcia opposed the restrictions on Cuba and criticized the incumbent for focusing on Cuba rather than on gas prices and the crisis in housing foreclosures. Diaz-Balart won by a narrow 53%-47%. (Four years later, Garcia was elected in the 26th District, then lost his seat in 2014 after one term.)

After his close call, Diaz-Balart in 2010 sought and won his brother Lincoln's seat in a more Republican district when Lincoln retired from the House. With redistricting since then, he has returned to the new 25th district that extended across the Everglades and has been easily reelected. That didn't stop him, though, from joining Democratic Rep. Corrine Brown in a lawsuit challenging their state's Fair Districts reforms; they claimed the anti-gerrymandering law unfairly hurt minority voters. Following the failure of their courtroom challenges, Brown lost her seat in 2016.

Diaz-Balart has remained in good shape politically. In 2016, he faced his first major-party opponent since 2008. Little-known Democratic challenger Alina Valdes, a Cuban-born immigrant who became a physician and supported a single-payer health care system, had scant financing of $37,000 and was defeated, 62%-38%. In 2018, Democratic challenger Mary Barzee Flores, a former local judge, spent more than $2 million and received extensive support from liberal groups. But Diaz-Balart had another easy victory, 60%-40%.

In 2016, Diaz-Balart kept his distance from the Trump campaign. With Trump in office, he largely sought to avoid public conflicts. "I literally do not read tweets," Diaz-Balart told the Miami Herald in October 2018. "My job is to get things done."

FL-25: Southern Florida

Cook Partisan Voting Index: R+4

Population		Race and Ethnicity		Income	
Total	756,894	White	18.7%	Median Income	$46,827
Land area (sq. miles)	3,501	Black	3.6%	District Income Rank	353
Pop/ sq mi	216.2	Latino	76%	Poverty Rate	18.9%
Born in State	25.8%	Asian	1.1%	With health insurance	77.7%
		Two or more races	0.3%	Cash public assistance	2%
Age Groups		Other	0.3%	Food stamp/SNAP	26.7%
Under 18	20.1%				
18-34	21.3%	**Education**		**Work**	
35-64	40.5%	H.S grad or less	53%	White Collar	18.1%
Over 64	18.1%	Some college	23.9%	Sales and Service	47.3%
		College Degree, 4 yr	15.5%	Blue Collar	26.7%
Military		Post grad	7.6%	Government	7.6%
Veteran/ Active Duty	3.3%				

2012 Pres. Vote	Romney	121,350	(54%)	Obama	100,519	(45%)
2016 Pres. Vote	Trump	131,320	(49%)	Clinton	126,668	(48%)

Hialeah, Other Miami Suburbs: Cuban Americans have proved to be one of America's most dynamic immigrant groups over the past half-century, growing from 50,000 in 1960, the year after Fidel Castro took over Cuba, to well over 1 million today. They almost singlehandedly transformed Dade County from a place that John Kennedy won by 15 percent in 1960 to one that George H.W. Bush won by 11 percent in 1988. Over time, the Cuban-American neighborhoods centered along S.W. 8th Street — Calle Ocho — expanded west to the Florida Turnpike Extension in Fountainebleau and Sweetwater, and northwest to Hialeah. Starting in the 1980s, there was an influx of other Latinos, from Nicaragua, El Salvador, Venezuela and Colombia. In the process, new communities were built and old ones transformed.

The 25th Congressional District extends nearly across Florida but remains very much a creature of Miami-Dade, where nearly two-thirds of its residents live. It includes many of the heavily Cuban neighborhoods west and northwest of Miami. To the west in the county, it takes in Doral, home to one of the nation's highest concentration of Venezuelan Americans. In the July 2017 referendum to change the Venezuela constitution, more than 100 residents of south Florida voted. Some refer to Doral and its rapidly growing business center just beyond the Miami International Airport as "Doralzuela." In 2017, Venezuelans accounted for 17 percent of the residential real estate purchases in south Florida by foreign buyers. Farther north, it includes parts of raffish Hialeah and nearby Miami Lakes, a planned town developed in the 1960s. With 96 percent of the residents Hispanic and 92 percent Spanish-speaking, Hialeah has the largest such concentration in the nation, and the smallest share of English-speaking residents; about 73 percent were foreign-born. In May 2018, the county approved plans by developers for a massive $4 billion American Dream Miami mega-mall that would pave over as many as 197 acres of wetlands between Interstate 75 and the Florida Turnpike. Environmentalists continued their challenges.

The district continues west and north to Hendry County, one of Florida's largest producers of oranges. The farm town of Clewiston has made plans to upgrade its AirGlades Airport to a huge two-way commercial cargo center for both perishable and manufactured goods, with a new 11,000-foot runway. The facility, which opened in 1942 as part of the domestic military response to World War II, would not have commercial service. In early 2018, the Federal Aviation Administration said that the project met environmental standards. The district sprawls across the Everglades to the edge of fast-growing Naples in Collier County. Residents of Collier County comprise nearly one-third of the district's population; most live in heavily Republican suburbs and exurbs of Naples a few miles from the Gulf of Mexico. The Big Cypress National Preserve, a huge swamp in the Everglades, was created by preservationists and established in 1974 as the first such preserve created in the United States. In April 2017, a federal judge approved testing for oil and gas in the swamps.

Of the three Republican-held districts based in Miami-Dade, the 25th has the most Hispanic voters and it votes the most Republican, but not overwhelmingly so, according to Florida election data. The district's population is 76 percent Hispanic, 37 percent of whom report Cuban origins. Half the population is foreign-born. In a district that Mitt Romney took four years earlier, 51%-49%, Donald Trump won, 50%-48%.

Debbie Mucarsel-Powell (D)

Elected 2018, 1st term, b. Jan 18, 1971; Ecuador; Pitzer University, B.S., 1992; Claremont Graduate University, Mast. Deg., 1996; Catholic; Married (Robert Powell); 3 children.

Professional Career: Director of Development, Florida International University, 2003-2007; Associate Vice President for Advancement, Herbert Wertheim College of Medicine, 2007-2011; President, DMP Associates, 2006-2018.

DC Office: 114 CHOB 20515, 202-225-2778, mucarsel-powell.house.gov

State Offices: Key West, 305-292-4485; Miami, 305-222-0160.

Committees: *Judiciary*: Crime, Terrorism & Homeland Security; Immigration & Citizenship. *Transportation & Infrastructure*: Economic Dev't, Public Buildings & Emergency Management; Water Resources & Environment.

Election Results

Election	Name (Party)	Vote (%)	Cand. Spent	Ind. Exp. Support	Ind. Exp. Oppose
2018 General	Debbie Mucarsel-Powell (D)............... 119,797	(51%)	$4,567,911	$7,917,929	$5,814,052
	Carlos Curbelo (R).......................... 115,678	(49%)	$4,896,739	$2,205,017	$3,457,197
2018 Primary	Debbie Mucarsel-Powell (D)................ 21,002	(64%)			
	Demetries Grimes (D)...................... 12,098	(37%)			

Democrat Debbie Mucarsel-Powell, elected in 2018, emphasized her immigrant roots in winning her first elected office. She worked in several jobs that served low-income communities in the Miami area. She won election against Republican Rep. Carlos Curbelo, who secured prime assignments from House GOP leaders—though he often clashed with President Donald Trump. With millions of dollars in outside funds from both parties, the campaign became a clash of messages, especially on health care. In this district, that benefited the challenger.

Mucarsel-Powell, who emigrated with her mother from Ecuador at age 14 and initially settled in southern California, graduated from Pitzer College and got her master's degree in international political economy from Claremont University. Her father was killed by gun fire in Ecuador.

She worked for several non-profit groups, including the Miami Zoo and the Coral Restoration Foundation. Mucarsel-Powell spent 14 years working on neighborhood programs at Florida International University, including its medical college, where she was an associate dean. She became active as a volunteer in Democratic politics and was narrowly defeated when she ran for the state Senate in 2016.

After escaping the poverty of her childhood and embracing middle-class life in south Florida, Mucarsel-Powell said that she launched her campaign for Congress with concern that the opportunities that were available to her family "are disappearing for too many of our neighbors today." Her work in the health care sector, she said, made it "inconceivable that politicians in D.C. would consider ripping away health care access from our families." That was a reference to the House-passed legislation, supported by Curbelo, to overhaul the Affordable Care Act. She easily won the Democratic nomination with 63 percent of the vote against Demetrius Grimes, a retired Navy officer.

Her image of the "American Dream" resonated in the Latino community, in contrast to the anti-immigrant rhetoric and actions of the Trump administration. Curbelo, who said in 2016 that he voted against Trump and disavowed his "very ugly campaign," sought with other House Republicans to push their own program on issues such as immigration and climate change. Mucarsel-Powell said that the GOP's legislative inaction showed Curbelo's constituents "what it feels like to be let down by Washington politicians," NBC News reported in Miami.

Curbelo's campaign, backed by Republicans ads, cited a news article in the Daily Beast claiming that Robert Powell, a lawyer for international businesses and Mucarsel-Powell's husband, had earlier represented an oligarch from Ukraine who had questionable financial dealings and allegedly committed contract killings. Her campaign spokesman responded that Mucarsel-Powell had nothing to do with her husband's business dealings.

Mucarsel-Powell was among the few successful House Democratic challengers in 2018 who were outspent by the GOP incumbent. Still, she and Curbelo each spent more than $4 million. In addition, the two national parties spent nearly $20 million on the contest. Mucarsel-Powell won, 51%-49%. Curbelo became a victim of the "anti-Trump surge," the Miami Herald reported in a post-election analysis. Given widespread opposition to the president in that district, it seemed ironic that on the day after Curbelo's election defeat, Trump cited him among other House Republicans who lost reelection because they had decided to "stay away," rather than embrace the administration.

Mucarsel-Powell and Donna Shalala in the adjacent district were the only Democratic newcomers in the Florida delegation. Shalala brought far more policy experience and national leadership to the job. But her stronger community ties positioned Mucarsel-Powell to be more adept with her political connection at home.

FL-26: Southern Florida   **Cook Partisan Voting Index: D+6**

Population		Race and Ethnicity		Income	
Total	772,867	White	16.9%	Median Income	$53,318
Land area (sq. miles)	2,185	Black	10.7%	District Income Rank	249
Pop/ sq mi	353.8	Latino	69.7%	Poverty Rate	17.1%
Born in State	35%	Asian	1.8%	With health insurance	80.3%
		Two or more races	0.7%	Cash public assistance	2.2%
Age Groups		Other	0.3%	Food stamp/SNAP	23.3%
Under 18	22%				
18-34	23.6%	**Education**		**Work**	
35-64	40.7%	H.S grad or less	46.7%	White Collar	13.7%
Over 64	13.7%	Some college	27.6%	Sales and Service	49.7%
		College Degree, 4 yr	18%	Blue Collar	19.9%
Military		Post grad	7.8%	Government	11.3%
Veteran/ Active Duty	3.7%				

2012 Pres. Vote	Obama	136,753	(55%)	Romney	108,375	(44%)	
2016 Pres. Vote	Clinton	164,252	(56%)	Trump	117,205	(40%)	

Inland Dade, the Keys: At the tip of the Florida Keys, a string of islands connected to each other and to mainland Florida by U.S. 1, is Key West, the southernmost city in the continental United States. Over the years, Key West has attracted famous residents — Ernest Hemingway, Tennessee Williams, Jimmy Buffett — and a large gay population, many living in quaint clapboard bungalows called "conch houses." Along the way, U.S. 1 stretches 100 miles through small town, parklands and beaches from Key Largo to Key West on a mostly two-lane highway, with several long causeways. With only a 21 percent Hispanic population, the Keys are a stark contrast to most of southern Florida. In September 2017, Hurricane Irma scored a direct hit on the Keys. Many homes were not rebuilt. Jobs and tourist dollars suffered double-digit percentage drops a year later. Long-term environmental threats from rising seas have led state officials to raise the height of some bridges on the Keys.

On the mainland, an influx of immigrants, first from Cuba and then from other Caribbean nations as well as Central and South America, has filled in the landscape of southern Miami-Dade County. This immigration surge has created a multicultural pastiche of ethnicities. Tamiami is majority Cuban, but now boasts sizable Nicaraguan, Colombian, Dominican and Venezuelan communities. Homestead, which was leveled by Hurricane Andrew in 1992 but has since been redeveloped, and neighboring Florida City have sizable African-American populations. In 2018, Homestead had a 34 percent poverty rate and received unfavorable publicity as the location of a detention center for more than 1,000 undocumented immigrant children.

The 26th Congressional District combines Monroe County (whose residents are mostly on the Keys) with much of southern Miami-Dade County. The large majority of the residents live in mostly Hispanic neighborhoods on the western and southern edges of metropolitan Miami, close to the swamps. Here one can drive out on roads past the subdivisions and find strawberry, tomato and citrus farms. The trees thin out, and then the road just ends at the Everglades — an interconnected sea of wetlands that once covered 8.9 million acres of southern Florida. Then, it was a coherent ecosystem, a "river of grass" in which water moved slowly down a gentle slope to the ocean. But the state's white settlers were intent on making the swampland more useful, and in 1948 Congress approved the construction of 1,720 miles of canals and levees to channel and drain the Everglades, making it possible to use the land for agriculture and housing.

Floridians have had second thoughts about taming the Everglades. Since 2000, Congress has approved billions of dollars for restoration. In 2008, the state proposed buying much of the land owned by U.S. Sugar Corp. around Lake Okeechobee for $1.35 billion, with farming to be phased out in seven years. The recession forced Gov. Charlie Crist to scale back the project by more than half. Timetables have been delayed by several years, though most state officials say they are committed to the broad objectives. When Congress enacted a water resources bill in 2016, it included $1.9 billion for Everglades restoration. In 2017, the state approved $1.6 billion for a reservoir as part of the cleanup.

The district is 70 percent Hispanic, including 41 percent Cuban American. This is marginal political territory. In 2012, President Barack Obama carried the district 53%-46%. Hillary Clinton in 2016 increased the Democrats' advantage to 57%-41%, though Donald Trump flipped Monroe County to the GOP.

Donna Shalala (D)

Elected 2018, 1st term, b. Feb 14, 1941; Cleveland, OH; Western College for Women (OH), B.A., 1962; Syracuse University (NY), Ph.D., 1970; Catholic; Single.

Elected Office: U.S. Department of Health and Human Services Secretary, 1993-2001.

Professional Career: Assistant Secretary for Policy Development and Research, U.S. Department of Housing and Urban Development, 1977-1980; President, Hunter College of the City University of New York, 1980-1987; Chancellor, University of Wisconsin, Madison, 1987-1993; President, University of Miami, 2001-2015; President, The Clinton Foundation, 2015-2017.

DC Office: 1320 LHOB 20515, 202-225-3931, shalala.house.gov

State Offices: Miami, 305-668-2285.

Committees: *Education & Labor:* Early Childhood, Elementary & Secondary Education; Health, Employment, Labor & Pensions. *Rules:* Legislative & Budget Process.

Election Results

Election	Name (Party)	Vote (%)		Cand. Spent	Ind. Exp. Support	Ind. Exp. Oppose
2018 General	Donna E. Shalala (D)......................	130,743	(52%)	$3,915,356	$382,528	$1,998,408
	Maria Elvira Salazar (R)..............	115,588	(46%)	$2,036,219	$115,533	$2,053,359
	Mayra Joli (I).............................	6,255	(2%)	$75,729		
2018 Primary	Donna E. Shalala (D)......................	14,158	(32%)			
	David Richardson (D).....................	12,192	(28%)			
	Kristen Rosen-Gonzalez (D).........	7,783	(18%)			
	Matt Haggman (D).........................	7,511	(17%)			
	Michael Hepburn (D).....................	2,723	(6%)			

Democrat Donna Shalala arrived in Congress with several distinctions. She had a lengthy record in public service, close connections to Bill and Hillary Clinton, prominence as a health policymaker and the mark as one of the oldest freshmen ever elected. In her first bid for elected office, Shalala struggled unexpectedly, in both the primary and general election. She required extra attention from party officials in what they envisioned as a slam-dunk takeover of the Miami-Dade County district.

Shalala succeeded Republican Rep. Ileana Ros-Lehtinen, who had chaired the Foreign Affairs Committee and retired after nearly 30 years in the House. In this heavily Hispanic district, Ros-Lehtinen and candidates in both parties objected strenuously to the immigration policies of President Donald Trump.

Shalala was born in Cleveland Ohio and has Lebanese ancestry. She got her bachelor's degree from Western College for Women in Oxford Ohio and her doctorate from the Maxwell School of Citizenship and Public Affairs at Syracuse University. She started her career as a political science professor at City University of New York and later at Columbia University. During the Carter administration, Shalala was an assistant secretary at the Department of Housing and Urban Development. She returned to academia as president of Hunter University and chancellor at the Madison campus of the University of Wisconsin.

As Secretary of Health and Human Services throughout the Clinton presidency, she worked closely with the President and first lady on what became their failed health care initiative. She retained a close relationship with the Clintons and later became chief executive officer of the Clinton Foundation. For 14 years, she was president of the University of Miami, where she had a high public profile—both locally and nationally.

After Ros-Lehtinen announced her retirement amid her continuing criticism of Trump, Democrats with community ties entered the contest months before Shalala. She was less familiar in the city's neighborhoods and her failure to speak Spanish became a notable shortcoming. To her benefit, Shalala was well-known among business and political leaders of Miami. Some opponents and other critics said "she has proved to be an overly cautious, instinctively moderate politician who compromises her principles and sometimes her own integrity," Huffington Post reported.

Other Democratic candidates had been local officials and spoke Spanish. Most prominent were state Rep. David Richardson and Kristen Gonzalez, a member of the Miami Commission. Richardson ran on a progressive agenda, including "Medicare for All," and he criticized Shalala's past contributions to Republican candidates. Each raised more than $2 million for the primary. Shalala won the primary over Richardson, 32%-27%; Gonzalez was third with 18%.

Republican nominee Maria Salazar, who was well-known locally as a Spanish-language television news reporter, described Shalala as "not from here." Salazar said that it was offensive that Shalala's campaign announced a visit by Rep. Barbara Lee of California, who was friendly with the Castro regime in Cuba. Shalala said she was unaware of the schedule, and Lee's appearance was canceled. During campaign debates, which were conducted in Spanish, Shalala wore an ear-piece that translated the dialogue to English. She was knowledgeable on federal issues and routinely attacked Trump, including his cozy dealings with Russian president Vladimir Putin.

In the closing weeks of the campaign, House Democrats and their allies spent more than $500,000 for Shalala. With polls showing a tight contest, Republicans reportedly spent $1.5 million for Salazar. With help from progressive white voters in Miami Beach, Shalala won, 52%-46%. Following her "lackluster campaign," the Miami Herald reported, "Shalala has Trump to thank for her new seat in Congress." When she took office, the only older freshman in congressional annals was 78-year-old Rep. James Bowler of Illinois, who was elected in 1953 and died in office after serving four years.

FL-27: Miami   **Cook Partisan Voting Index: D+5**

Population		Race and Ethnicity		Income	
Total	750,149	White	21.3%	Median Income	$52,353
Land area (sq. miles)	113	Black	4%	District Income Rank	266
Pop/ sq mi	6637.3	Latino	71.7%	Poverty Rate	15.4%
Born in State	28.9%	Asian	1.9%	With health insurance	82.6%
		Two or more races	0.7%	Cash public assistance	1.6%
Age Groups		Other	0.4%	Food stamp/SNAP	19.9%
Under 18	18.1%				
18-34	22.8%	**Education**		**Work**	
35-64	41.7%	H.S grad or less	39.4%	White Collar	17.4%
Over 64	17.4%	Some college	22.6%	Sales and Service	44.6%
		College Degree, 4 yr	21.8%	Blue Collar	15.6%
Military		Post grad	16.2%	Government	8.4%
Veteran/ Active Duty	2.6%				

2012 Pres. Vote	Obama	144,588	(53%)	Romney	126,327	(46%)
2016 Pres. Vote	Clinton	174,132	(58%)	Trump	115,815	(39%)

Coral Gables, Miami Beach: A century ago, Miami was a tiny tropical village where the Miami River empties into Biscayne Bay. Today, it is a world-class city. The surrealistic high-rises of Brickell Boulevard, the winding lanes of Coral Gables and the shimmer of orange and pink neon signs in the hot night air: This is Miami. It lives on the cusp of two civilizations, North America and Latin America, with different traditions, styles and sensibilities converging in this one place, with the strengths of each despite some frictions. In Miami, where it is easy to fly directly to any part of Latin America, top business and banking services are available to a sophisticated Spanish-speaking, and usually also English-speaking, clientele. With 5.6 million (and rapidly growing) cruise passengers in 2018, the port was the busiest in the world.

Miami for decades has also been the locus of Cuban America, ever since the first refugees fled Fidel Castro in 1959. Increasing numbers of Cuban immigrants, implacably opposed to the totalitarian Castro, entered the voting stream as Republicans. Now, they are a dominant voice in a Latino majority in Miami-Dade County (as Dade County was renamed in 1997). But the Latino population has grown more diverse: Little Havana, centered on Calle Ocho (S.W. 8th Street), is home to many Nicaraguans, Hondurans and Peruvians.

The 27th Congressional District of Florida is one of Miami-Dade's three Hispanic-majority districts. It is 72 percent Hispanic, including 43 percent Cuban, and 4 percent non-Hispanic black. The district follows Calle Ocho from Little Havana west to heavily Hispanic West Miami and Westchester. North of Miami International Airport, the district includes Miami Springs and parts of Hialeah. At the southern end of the district are low-income areas along U.S. 1, like Naranja and Homestead, which was leveled by Hurricane Andrew in 1992 but has since been redeveloped.

To the east, the district sweeps up many of metro Miami's high-income residential areas: Coral Gables, with luxurious streets laid out in the 1920s; and Cocoplum, a gated community of huge houses and boat docks for rich Cuban Americans. Off-shore and connected by causeways is Key Biscayne, with its high-rise apartments owned mostly by Latino immigrants and their second-generation offspring. On the southern tip of Miami Beach is its world-famous South Beach, where luxurious art-deco hotels attract the glitziest celebrities of North America, Latin America and Europe. One topic of concern: With rising tides and less available space, the natural sand on the beaches has been disappearing. Some of it has been replaced by the Army Corps of Engineers, which uses scoops or hoses to move sand from the sea floor and pipe it back to the eroding beach. This is called "renourishment," though the substitute sand is not unlimited.

For years, the district voted Republican, but there have been shifts here. Obama carried the district 53%-47% in 2012. Hillary Clinton's 58%-39% win over Donald Trump was boosted, in part, by redistricting in 2016. Still, Democrats cannot take for granted their local strength. In Miami-Dade, Clinton won by 29 percentage points in 2016; two years later, Democratic Sen. Bill Nelson took the county by 21 points in his narrow statewide defeat.

GEORGIA

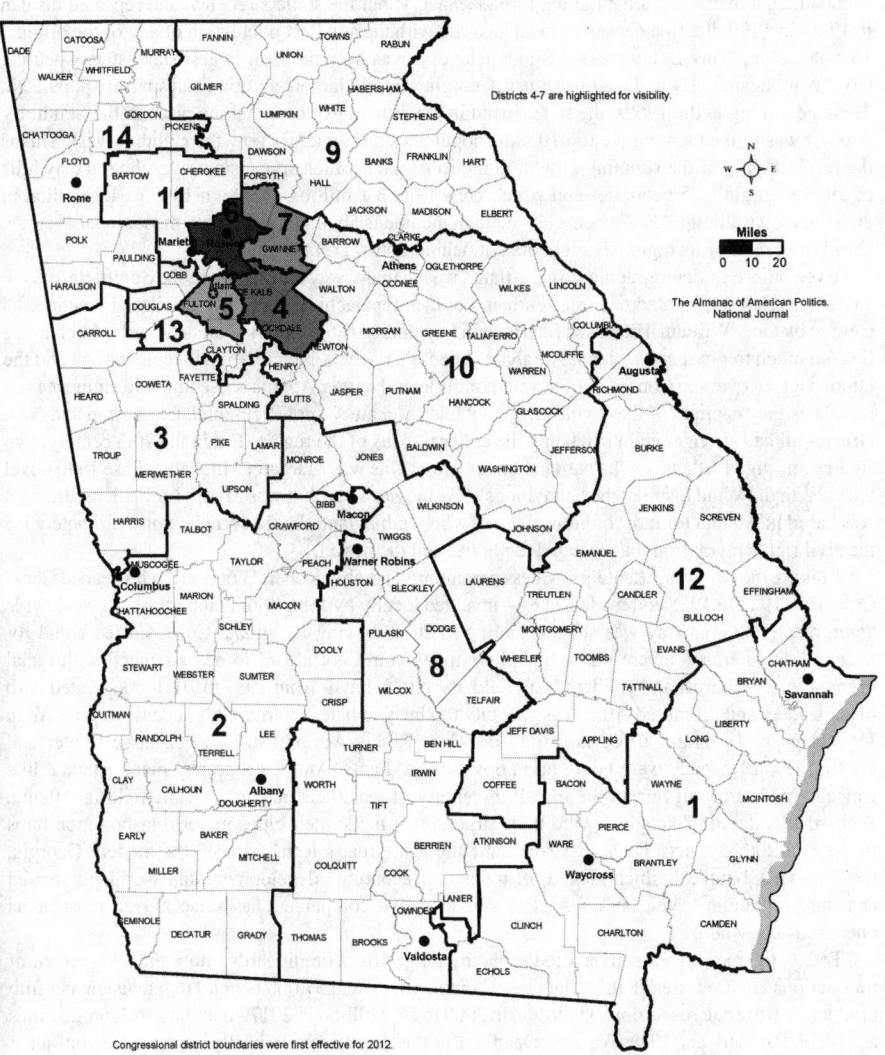

Districts 4-7 are highlighted for visibility.

Miles
0   10   20

The Almanac of American Politics.
National Journal

Congressional district boundaries were first effective for 2012.

Georgia, once a Democratic bastion like the rest of the South, went heavily for Republicans over the past two decades in both federal and state races. But changing demographics have given Democrats hope that they can become competitive in the state – and in 2016 and 2018 the party made impressive progress peeling away suburban Republicans, even if it wasn't enough to win key statewide races, thanks to residual GOP support in rural areas.

Georgia was the last of the 13 colonies to be founded -- by British soldier and politician James Oglethorpe in 1733 as an "asylum of the unfortunate," reserved for debtors and other outcasts from England. Oglethorpe, a humanitarian, forbade slavery, but the settlers rebelled and repealed his ban in 1750. In 1790, the first census showed Georgia with the smallest population of any of the original 13 states except tiny Delaware and Rhode Island. It was only the fifth largest slave state when the Civil War began. Early in the 20th century, Georgia was still largely agrarian and sparsely populated. Then, beginning in the 1960s, the state shared in the growth explosion taking place in the South. By 2000, it was ranked among the top 10 most populous states, and it's now the eighth largest. This is the result mainly of the stunning growth in metro Atlanta, which spreads out over the red clay hills of 29 of Georgia's 159 counties and which grew from 3.1 million people in 1990 to 4.2 million in 2000 and 5.9 million in 2017. Georgia's median income is about $6,000 below the national average, ahead of several of its regional neighbors but behind both Carolinas.

Even before its demographic surge, Atlanta was in many ways the center of the South. Before the Civil War, Atlanta, located near the south end of the Appalachian chain, was a railroad junction. Its capture by Gen. William Tecumseh Sherman in September 1864 and his scorched-earth March to the Sea did much to produce President Abraham Lincoln's reelection victory in November 1864 and the Union victory over the Confederacy seven months later. Neither Atlanta's rise to world eminence nor its role as the "capital" of the South was inevitable. A century ago, Richmond, Charleston and New Orleans all had stronger claims to being the cultural focus of the region. But in the 20th century, two figures imprinted Atlanta on the national imagination. One was Margaret Mitchell, whose 1936 novel Gone With the Wind inspired the eponymous 1939 movie. The other was Martin Luther King Jr., who was based in Atlanta for most of his career and who, with Atlanta-based organizations, ultimately led the civil rights revolution that changed the South and the nation.

Linking the two was Atlanta's business community, notably Robert Woodruff, who headed Coca-Cola from 1923 to 1955 and made Coke — invented locally by John Stith Pemberton — a worldwide enterprise. (The company was still expanding in 2018, buying the global Costa Coffee brand for $5.1 billion.) Perhaps aware that a global company could not afford to be associated with racial segregation, Woodruff and William Hartsfield, the city's mayor from 1937 to 1961, cooperated with black leaders and promoted Atlanta as "the city too busy to hate." Hartsfield's successor, Ivan Allen Jr., elected in 1961 and 1965, supported the Civil Rights Act of 1964, as Peachtree Center and the first Hyatt Regency were going up in downtown Atlanta. And if geography made Atlanta, like Chicago, a natural rail hub in the mid-19th century, it was their mayors — Hartsfield in Atlanta, Richard J. Daley in Chicago — who built airports that made their cities major transportation hubs in the mid-20th century. Then, in 1996, came the last, great jolt that created the modern Georgia, the summer Olympics, which kicked off a wave of economic development and worldwide media exposure (although CNN, one of Atlanta's great native companies, has since moved most of its operations elsewhere).

Today, the metro area's diversified economy ranges from credit cards (more than 70 percent of transactions are processed in the Atlanta area, employing some 37,000 people) to television and film production (revenue rose from $93 million in 2008 to $2.7 billion in 2017, including such productions as "Black Panther" and "The Walking Dead"). But the state has periodically experienced conflict at the intersection of business and social policy. When Delta, which employs 33,000 people in Georgia, responded to the 2018 high school shootings in Parkland Florida by canceling a standing discount for National Rifle Association members, Republicans in the legislature threatened to end a $50 million sales tax exemption on jet fuel. In the end, lawmakers backed off, but the episode highlighted ongoing strains within the GOP.

Today, Georgia is 31 percent black, 9 percent Hispanic and 4 percent Asian. That's the third-highest African-American percentage in the country (behind Mississippi and Louisiana) and the second-lowest percentage of whites east of the Mississippi River (after Maryland). The state has seen faster Hispanic population growth than any of the 10 states with the largest Hispanic populations. Nearly 1 of every 10 Georgians is foreign-born, up from 2.7 percent in 1990, and one-third of the foreign-born residents of Atlanta are undocumented, on the higher end of the major metro areas, according to Pew.

Metro Atlanta's population features wide pockets of prosperity, along with top-flight cultural institutions, a large millennial population and a vibrant LGBT community. African Americans have been moving to middle-class, suburban counties west and southeast of the city, while Hispanics have been clustering along Interstate 85 in Gwinnett County and Interstate 75 in Cobb County to the north. Gwinnett is home to clusters of Koreans, Cubans, Indians, Vietnamese and Mexicans; non-white children account for three of every four students in the school system, up from one in five two decades ago, according to the Washington Post. The FX television show Atlanta, a popular and critical hit, has given the diverse region some national cultural cred.

As this new Atlanta grew up, Georgia's rural outstate regions have struggled. According to the FCC, 29.1 percent of Georgia's rural population has no broadband, a rate almost 10 times as high as the state's urban population. Among the states that didn't expand Medicaid under the Affordable Care Act, Georgia has one of the highest rates of uninsured low-income adults; this in turn has led to a rash of rural hospital closures. Georgia agriculture ranks high in the production of broilers, peanuts, pecans and cotton, but many farmers were hit hard by Hurricanes Irma in 2017 and Michael in 2018.

Georgia cast the second-highest Democratic percentage for president in 1960, but in the next two elections, Georgia voters swung sharply, backing Barry Goldwater in 1964 and George Wallace in 1968. Statewide election contests were typically fought out in Democratic primaries that pitted Atlanta-supported moderates against rural-supported segregationists or conservatives, and the latter usually won. Then came change, in the person of Jimmy Carter, a former two-term state senator who was elected governor in 1970 with a rural base. After taking office, Carter proclaimed racial reconciliation and installed a portrait of King in the state capitol. Carter thus became one of the first politicians from the rural South to celebrate and honor the civil rights movement, and in the process, set himself on the road to being elected president in 1976. Carter was followed by a series of Democratic governors with connections to rural parts of the state — George Busbee, Joe Frank Harris, Zell Miller and Roy Barnes.

But countervailing political trends transformed Georgia into a mostly Republican state. Affluent voters in metro Atlanta became generally Republican, while white voters outside metro Atlanta became Republican stalwarts; for years, Georgia's most prominent politician nationally was Republican Rep. Newt Gingrich. George W. Bush carried the state 55%-42% in 2000 and Republican presidential nominees have carried it with between 51 percent and 58 percent of the vote ever since. With help from party switchers, Republicans captured the state Senate in 2002 and the state House in 2004 and have kept large majorities in both chambers. And the GOP has dominated statewide and federal races for the better part of two decades.

Changing demographics in the Atlanta area have given Democrats hope of gaining ground. Barack Obama carried metro Atlanta narrowly in the presidential elections of 2008 and 2012. However, he lost Georgia outside metro Atlanta by a 3-to-2 margin, underlining a widening urban-rural (and black-white) divide. In 2014, Republican consolidation of the rural vote helped GOP candidates defeat highly touted Democrats up and down the ballot by larger-than-predicted margins. But in 2016 and 2018, Democrats made real progress in the state, even if it wasn't enough to win.

In 2016, Donald Trump won the state, but three metro counties that had supported Mitt Romney in 2012 shifted to Hillary Clinton – Gwinnett, with a 15-point swing, Cobb, with a 14-point swing, and Henry, with a seven-point swing. Clinton carried several other metro counties -- including Fulton, Douglas, Rockdale and DeKalb -- by margins that were 8 to 13 points higher than Obama had managed four years earlier.

Then, in the 2018 midterms, Georgia was one of the nation's marquee battlegrounds, thanks to its gubernatorial race. Republicans nominated Brian Kemp, who ran as a Trump acolyte and aired an ad pledging to personally round up "criminal illegals" in his pickup truck. Democrats picked the more liberal of two primary contenders -- Stacey Abrams, an African-American former state House minority leader. After gubernatorial elections in 2010 and 2014 with largely static turnout, the two nominees whipped their bases into gear in 2018: Kemp increased Republican gubernatorial votes by

47 percent over 2014, while Abrams increased Democratic votes by a startling 68 percent and won almost 46,000 more votes than Clinton had in a presidential year.

It wasn't enough to deliver Abrams a win, but the GOP's gubernatorial margin continued to shrink -- from 10 points in 2010 to eight points in 2014 to 1.4 points, or less than 55,000 votes, in 2018. Kemp cleaned up in rural areas, but Abrams trounced Kemp in once-Republican Atlanta suburbs, winning Cobb with 54 percent, Gwinnett with 57 percent and Henry with 57 percent. Democrats also ousted GOP Rep. Karen Handel, who held Gingrich's old seat; nearly upset another House Republican, Rob Woodall; and gained seats in the state legislature. While the GOP still won every key statewide office in 2018, Georgia seemed on the verge of becoming a genuinely competitive presidential state in 2020. "Nervous Republicans acknowledge they can't win future statewide contests by tanking in the fast-growing suburbs, where Trump's middling approval ratings and a more diverse electorate is reshaping political debate," wrote the Atlanta Journal-Constitution's Greg Bluestein.

Population		Race and Ethnicity		Income	
Total	10,201,635	White	53.6%	Median Income	$52,977
Land area (sq. miles)	57,513	Black	30.9%	State Income Rank	32
Pop/ sq mi	177.4	Latino	9.3%	Poverty Rate	16.9%
Born in state	55.0%	Asian	3.8%	With health insurance	85.2%
		Two or more races	1.9%	Cash public assistance	1.8%
Age Groups		Other	0.5%	Food stamp/SNAP	14.5%
Under 18	24.5%				
18-34	23.7%	**Education**		**Work**	
35-64	39.1%	H.S grad or less	41.7%	White Collar	36.6%
Over 64	12.7%	Some college	28.3%	Sales and Service	41.0%
		College Degree, 4 yr	18.6%	Blue Collar	22.4%
Military		Post grad	11.4%	Government	14.7%
Veteran/ Active Duty	9.0%				

Presidential Politics

2016 Primary (D)	Clinton (D)	545,674 (71%)	Sanders (D)	215,797 (28%)			
2016 Primary (R)	Trump (R)	502,994 (39%)	Cruz (R)	305,847 (24%)	Rubio (R)	316,836 (24%)	
	Carson (R)	80,723 (6%)	Kasich (R)	72,508 (6%)			
2016 Pres. Vote	Trump (R)	2,089,104 (51%)	Clinton (D)	1,877,963 (46%)	Johnson (L)	125,306 (3%)	
2012 Pres. Vote	Romney (R)	2,078,688 (53%)	Obama (D)	1,773,827 (45%)			

Georgia has recently been a reliable Republican state in presidential elections. The GOP nominee has carried the state in every election since 1984 except for 1992, when Bill Clinton won the Peach State. But some surveys into the fall of 2016 suggested that Hillary Clinton might have a shot at repeating her husband's accomplishment. Georgia once was part of the Solid South for Democrats and in 1976 native son Jimmy Carter carried all 159 of its counties. Carter won all but 13 in 1980, when Ronald Reagan won a national landslide. Donald Trump kept Georgia in the Republican ranks, defeating Clinton by 51%-46%, not far from the comfortable 53%-45% victory Mitt Romney posted over Barack Obama in 2012. But there were notable differences in the results around Atlanta: Clinton was the first Democrat to carry the two largest suburban counties, Cobb and Gwinnett, since Carter in 1976. Gwinnett, formerly a Republican stronghold, has seen its GOP margins decline as its population became more diverse, especially with an increase in Hispanics. Cobb, once the political base of former Republican House Speaker Newt Gingrich, has an adult population in which 44 percent of adults have a bachelor's degree or higher. Those factors gave Clinton a boost in these traditional GOP suburbs, where Trump's populism and brash style turned off some establishment voters. Overall, Clinton slashed the Republican margin in eight suburban counties that ring Atlanta — Cherokee, Cobb, Douglas, Fayette, Forsyth, Henry, Gwinnett and Walton — from 18 points in 2012 to six points in 2016. Still, that GOP edge, combined with the Republican advantage in the rest of the state, gave Trump his victory. For Democrats, the challenge is how to build on their base in urban Atlanta, Savannah, Augusta, Columbus and Macon, and in the declining rural counties in central Georgia that were once home to cotton plantations. One glaring weakness for Clinton was with Georgia's white population: according to the television network exit poll, she received only 21 percent of their votes. Georgians like their primary to play an important role in presidential politics. In 1992, Democratic Gov. Zell Miller scheduled it one week before Super Tuesday to help Democratic nominee Bill Clinton, and it did: The Dixie victory gave him critical momentum going into the large batch of southern primaries one week later. Clinton swept those contests, and Miller was rewarded with a keynoter slot at the Democratic convention in New York's Madison Square Garden. (Miller would gain notoriety 12 years later in the same spot delivering the keynote address to the Republican convention, eviscerating Democratic standard-bearer John Kerry.) Georgia Secretary of State Brian Kemp was a leader in 2016 in organizing a so-called "SEC primary," named after the South's college football powerhouse Southeastern Conference. Six other southern states — Alabama, Arkansas, Oklahoma, Tennessee, Texas and Virginia — held presidential primaries on March 1. Initially, many observers thought this would give an advantage to Texas Sen. Ted Cruz, but Trump ended up being the main beneficiary as he won five of those states, losing only in Oklahoma and Texas. In Georgia, Trump defeated Florida Sen. Marco Rubio, 39%-24%, with Cruz finishing a close third. Trump won 155 of the state's counties, losing only four to Rubio: Fulton, DeKalb and Cobb in the Atlanta metro, and Clarke, home of the University of Georgia. The Democratic primary was an afterthought. Clinton crushed Vermont Sen. Bernie Sanders, 71%-28%. Clinton won better than four-fifths of those African-American ballots. Democrats saw their presidential primary turnout decline by about 300,000 votes from the record they set in 2008. Republicans set a new record, exceeding the previous high-water mark in 2008 by more than 300,000 votes.

Congressional Districts

116th Congress Lineup	5D 9R	115th Congress Lineup	4D 10R

Republicans have gained firm control of redistricting, with boundaries that appear relatively clean while concentrating minority voters. The results in the 2014 and 2016 elections, not entirely accidental: 10 Republicans, all of them white and all of them first elected since 2010; 4 Democrats, all of them African-American and all serving since at least 2006. But Democrats in 2018 scored a major gain with the 6th District, a suburban Atlanta district that is 60 percent white and which Republicans had comfortably held since it was created in 1992. Regardless of the election outcome in 2020, this switch seems certain to have a significant impact on redistricting. Even though Republicans will retain control of the map-drawing, they will be hard-pressed to retain what had been 10 secure seats in what is expected to remain a 14-seat delegation in a state that has edged toward a 50-50 partisan balance. Their problem is that they have lost large numbers of voters not only in the 6th in the northern suburbs, but also in the 7th District, which is in neighboring Gwinnett County. Perhaps their best option will be to try to secure one of those seats for the next decade—with some voters from the three GOP-heavy districts north of the metro area -- and abandon the other.

The legislature in 2012 achieved the GOP goals with a few partisan tweaks. First, Republicans added the state's new 14th seat thanks to rapid growth along north Georgia's I-85 corridor. Second, they shored up south Georgia's 8th District by switching downtown Macon to the adjacent 2nd District, which gained an African-American majority. Third, they targeted Democratic Rep. John Barrow, the only remaining white Democrat from the Deep South, by cutting Savannah's black neighborhoods out of his 12th District. Republicans needed a second election cycle before they succeeded on the last count.

In retrospect, Republicans were pressing their luck with their 10-4 advantage in the delegation — a dramatic shift from the Democrats' 9-1 control during most of the 1980s, when backbench Republican Newt Gingrich was plotting historic shifts. In reality, the true partisan balance in Georgia has been shown to be somewhere between those two ratios. With the prospect that Republicans will retain control of redistricting, they are almost certain to invite legal challenges even if they concede a fifth seat to Democrats. Also of interest will be how the new lines are drawn in metro Atlanta. A new Democratic-leaning district could have black control, it could have the racial mix that has taken control in majority-minority Gwinnett or it could be closer to its current upscale suburban model —

the type of district where House Democrats scored major gains across the nation in 2018. The three other Democratic-held seats in the metro area likely will retain their current base in Atlanta, plus DeKalb and Clayton counties.

Brian Kemp (R)

Elected 2018, term expires 2023, 1st term; b. Nov. 2, 1963, Athens; University of Georgia, B.S.; Christian; Married (Marty); 3 children.

Elected Office: GA Senate, 2003-2007; GA Secretary of State, 2010-2018.

Office: 203 Capitol Pl SW, Atlanta, 30334; 404-656-1776; Fax: 404-657-7332; Website: georgia.gov
Lt. Gov.: Geoff Duncan (R) **Atty. Gen:** Chris Carr (R) **Sec. of State:** Brad Raffensperger (R)
State Legislature: Senate: 21D, 35R **House:** 75D, 105R

Election Results

Election	Name (Party)	Vote (%)
2018 General	Brian Kemp (R)	1,978,408 (50%)
	Stacey Abrams (D)	1,923,685 (49%)
2018 Primary runoff	Brian Kemp (R)	406,703 (69%)
	Casey Cagle (R)	178,893 (31%)
2018 Primary	Casey Cagle (R)	236,987 (39%)
	Brian Kemp (R)	155,189 (26%)
	Hunter Hill (R)	111,464 (18%)
	Clay Tippins (R)	74,182 (12%)

Brian Kemp, a Donald Trump-aligned Republican who had served as Georgia's secretary of state, narrowly defeated Democrat Stacey Abrams in an ideologically polarizing gubernatorial race in 2018. Abrams, who was seeking to become the first African-American woman to win a governorship, energized minority turnout and made significant inroads in previously Republican suburbs of Atlanta. But Kemp's support from the state's rural areas was just enough to enable him to avoid a general-election runoff.

Growing up, Kemp worked on a farm near Athens. His ancestors include a Revolutionary War major, George Washington's postmaster general, and several state legislators. He graduated from the University of Georgia – the fourth generation in his family to do so – earning a bachelor's degree in agriculture. Kemp found financial success in homebuilding and real estate, although some of his ancillary investments in agriculture struggled. Frustrated in his interactions with local zoning rules, Kemp ran for the state Senate in 2002 and won in a strong Republican year. In 2006, he ran unsuccessfully for agriculture commissioner, but four years later, Gov. Sonny Perdue appointed him to the vacant secretary of state post. In that position, Kemp enacted a voter registration system that allowed voters to register online and by a mobile app. But critics accused him of overzealously purging voters from the rolls. Kemp was also in office during a data breach of private information, including Social Security numbers, that affected more than 6 million voters.

In 2017, Kemp became the first major Republican to announce a bid for governor, in anticipation of an open seat vacated by two-term Republican Gov. Nathan Deal. Of the candidates seeking the nomination, Lt. Gov. Casey Cagle had the most establishment support, although several other candidates ran as well – former state Sen. Hunter Hill, consulting firm executive Clay Tippins, and state Sen. Michael Williams. Each aggressively courted the Republican base, but Kemp was perhaps the most uncompromising in doing so. In one ad, he pointed a shotgun at a "young man" who was "interested in" one of his daughters. In another, he promised to personally "round up illegal criminals" using his pickup truck. He painted Cagle as "a puppet" who was "not fighting for us. He's fighting for those with deep pockets whose interests are not ours." Stylistically, Cagle adopted a calmer, more optimistic tone and took positions that, while still conservative, were somewhat closer to the middle. Late in the primary campaign, Cagle miscalculated by attacking Hill in the hope of facing Kemp in the runoff; his camp saw Kemp as a candidate who would be easier to beat in a one-on-one race. Cagle got what he wanted – he finished first in the primary with 39 percent, while Kemp finished second with 26 percent -- but the two-man runoff only emphasized the base-vs.-establishment dynamic, and that ended up boosting Kemp. Things worsened for Cagle when Tippins released a secretly recorded conversation he'd made in which Cagle expressed frustration with the primary having been a fight "over who could be the craziest." Then, in a coup de grace, Trump tweeted an endorsement of Kemp. He ended up winning, 69%-31%.

The Democratic primary was no less dramatic, pitting the "two Staceys." Stacey Abrams was born poor, but in a family with a strong educational drive. Abrams was "born in Wisconsin while her mother was in graduate school, but spent most of her childhood in Gulfport Mississippi, where (her mother) Carolyn's advanced degree was good for a job as a librarian, earning less than the school janitor," Molly Ball wrote in Time magazine. The family later moved to Atlanta to pursue work in the Methodist ministry. Abrams earned degrees from Spelman College, the University of Texas and Yale Law School, and she developed an interest in both politics and business. In 1992, she challenged then-Mayor Maynard Jackson over some of his policies at a town hall event; Jackson proceeded to hire her to work in the city's youth services office. Then, Abrams served as deputy city attorney. She also started a company that sold bottled water for babies, and then another that handled payments for small businesses. In her spare time, Abrams wrote romance novels under a pen name.

In 2006, Abrams won a seat in the state House; four years later, she was elected minority leader, the first woman to be chosen to lead a caucus in either chamber. Considered brainy, strategic, and charismatic, Abrams took charge of the shrunken Democratic ranks, at times shrewdly cooperating with the Republican majority, hammering out deals on criminal justice reform, transportation spending and educational scholarships, among other issues. The legislative sparring over the state's HOPE educational scholarships became a focal point of Abrams' primary battle against the second Stacey. Stacey Evans, who is white, grew up poor, raised by a single mother who moved the family in and around northern Georgia 16 times. Evans, who owed her educational start to the scholarship, accused Abrams of weakening the HOPE program in collaboration with Georgia Republicans.

The battle of the Staceys divided the political establishment, but not always in consistent ways; some leading African-American political figures backed Evans, for instance. Both candidates could make credible arguments that they were liberal – more so than any previous Democratic gubernatorial candidate in Georgia -- but they could also show patterns of pragmatism. A key divergence came in their broader political strategy. Evans sought to recreate the old Georgia Democratic model of courting enough white moderates to put the party over the top. By contrast, Abrams -- who had spearheaded a voter-mobilization group called the New Georgia Project -- sought to energize less-frequent voters, many of them non-white. Ultimately, Democratic primary voters went hard for Abrams' approach; she defeated Evans, 76%-24%.

Despite some feints toward the center, the general election developed as a battle between two clashing ideologies. "Georgians are going to have the clearest choice that they've probably ever had in a general election for the office of governor," state House Speaker David Ralston told the New York Times. The candidates divided sharply over expanding Medicaid, abortion, immigration, gun policy and marijuana legalization. Trump actively supported Kemp, including a rally in Macon days before the election.

The closing weeks of the campaign were dominated by allegations about voter fraud – an issue of special sensitivity to Kemp because he refused to step down as secretary of state, and critics said he was essentially overseeing his own election, although all vote-counting operations were conducted at the local level. On top of years of purges of inactive voters, Democrats decried the state law that required an "exact match" in information on voting applications and other government databases. An estimated 53,000 voters had their ability to vote placed in "purgatory" because of a failure to meet the match requirements, which could be as minor as missing a hyphen. While such voters could still cast a provisional ballot, an Associated Press analysis found these voters to be disproportionately black, injecting race into an already racially charged contest. Then, two days before the election, Kemp opened a probe of whether the state Democratic Party had hacked into the voter registration system – a charge that was immediately dismissed by Democrats.

When the votes were counted, the margin was close enough that Abrams did not immediately concede. The final tally showed that Kemp won by 55,000 votes out of 3.9 million cast, and he had only an 18,000-vote cushion above the threshold he needed to avoid a runoff. Abrams made significant gains in once-Republican suburbs of Atlanta, but Kemp dominated in rural areas, enabling his victory. While Kemp had demonstrated Republicans' continued ability to win statewide races in Georgia, Abrams came out of the election poised to be a continuing force in state – if not national – politics. Three months later, she gave the Democratic response to Trump's State of the Union message to Congress.

In May 2019, Kemp signed a "heartbeat" bill that bans abortion once a fetal heartbeat can be detected, possibly six weeks into pregnancy. Critics said that can be before a woman knows she's pregnant.

Johnny Isakson (R)

Elected 2004, term expires 2022, 3rd term, b. Dec 28, 1944; Atlanta; University of Georgia, B.B.A., 1966; Methodist; Married (Diane Davison Isakson); 3 children; 9 grandchildren.

Military Career: U.S. Air Force Reserve 1966-1967; GA Air National Guard 1966-1972

Elected Office: GA House, 1976-1990, Republican Leader, 1983-1990; GA Senate, 1993-1996; U.S. House, 1999-2004.

Professional Career: Northside Realty, 1967-1999, President, 1979-1999; Cochair, Dole GA presidential campaign, 1988, 1996; Chairman, GA Board Of Ed., 1996-1997.

DC Office: 131 RSOB 20510, 202-224-3643, Fax: 202-228-0724, isakson.senate.gov

State Offices: Atlanta, 770-661-0999.

Committees: *Ethics (Chmn). Finance*: Health Care; International Trade, Customs & Global Competitiveness; Taxation & IRS Oversight. *Foreign Relations*: Africa & Global Health Policy; East Asia, the Pacific & International Cybersecurity Policy; State Dept & USAID Mngmnt, Internat'l Ops & Internat'l Dev (Chmn). *Health, Education, Labor & Pensions*: Employment & Workplace Safety (Chmn). *Veterans' Affairs (Chmn).*

Group Ratings

	ADA	ACLU	AFL-CIO	LCV	ITI	COC	HAFA	ACU	CFG	FRC
2018	-	6%	-	7%	-	100%	60%	77%	53%	100%
2017	0%	C	0%	0%	C	100%	C	77%	73%	100%

Almanac Ratings 2017-18

	Economy	Social	Foreign	Composite
Liberal	30%	30%	3%	21%
Conservative	70%	70%	97%	79%

Key Votes of the 115th Congress

1. Obama-care revision	Y	5. Gun regulations	Y	9. Kavanaugh confirmation	Y
2. Tax Cuts	Y	6. Family planning regs	Y	10. Saudi arms sales	N
3. Dodd-Frank revision	Y	7. Gorsuch confirmation	NV	11. FISA rules	Y
4. Omnibus appropriations	Y	8. Immigration restrictions	Y	12. Military aid in Yemen	N

Election Results

Election	Name (Party)	Vote (%)	Cand. Spent	Ind. Exp. Support	Ind. Exp. Oppose
2016 General	Johnny Isakson (R).......................... 2,135,806	(55%)	$8,866,720	$1,588,675	
	Jim Barksdale (D).......................... 1,599,726	(41%)	$5,036,206	$4,001	
	Allen Buckly (L)................................ 162,260	(4%)			
2016 Primary	Johnny Isakson (R)............................ 447,661	(78%)			
	Derrick Grayson (R)............................ 69,101	(12%)			
	Mary Kay Bacallao (R)......................... 60,898	(11%)			

Prior winning percentages: 2010 (59%), 2004 (58%); House: 2002 (80%), 2000 (75%), 1999 special (65%)

Johnny Isakson, Georgia's senior senator, is reliably conservative. But his folksy demeanor and willingness to work the across the aisle have made him an occasional deal-maker, particularly when it comes veterans issues. Even though he shared a ballot with Donald Trump, he has not shied away from criticizing the president, a stark contrast to his colleague, Sen. David Perdue, who became one of Trump's closest allies.

Several of Isakson's bipartisan efforts have been on the Senate Veterans' Affairs Committee, which Isakson — who spent six years in the Air National Guard after he graduated from college — has chaired since Republicans regained Senate control in 2015. Most notably, he spearheaded a 2017 expansion of the GI Bill that made it easier to fire employees inside the Department of Veterans Affairs after a series of scandals sparked outrage over how the VA cared for roughly 21 million veterans. Isakson also has chaired the Ethics Committee, making him the only senator to chair two committees simultaneously.

Isakson credits his pre-politics career for teaching him the virtues of negotiation and compromise. "If you want to ever learn how to accept rejection, sell real estate for a few years," he told the Associated Press in 2010. Isakson grew up outside Atlanta in south Fulton County. His father, Ed Isakson, drove a Greyhound bus and his parents bought, renovated and sold old houses for profit; Johnny Isakson has said his family lived in eight houses by the time he was 6. Ed Isakson ultimately helped found Northside Realty, and Johnny Isakson, after graduating from the University of Georgia, went to work for the firm in 1967. He became its president in 1979 and, before relinquishing that position two decades later, built the enterprise into the largest independent real estate brokerage in the Southeastern United States. Roll Call ranked Isakson 47th among the wealthiest members of Congress, based on 2016 filings.

In 1974, Isakson made his first bid for elective office, losing a race for the Georgia House. Two years later, he ran again and won, becoming one of just 19 Republicans in that body; there were 161 Democrats at the time. "Custer had better odds that we had," Isakson told Atlanta magazine in early 2016, referring to Lt. Col. George Custer who famously lost and died in the Battle of Little Bighorn. In 1983, Isakson began an eight-year stint as House minority leader. He ran for governor in 1990, losing 53%-45% to Democrat Zell Miller — whom he would later succeed in the Senate. Elected to the state Senate in 1992, Isakson made a second run for statewide office in 1996; he lost the Republican nomination for Senate to wealthy businessman Guy Millner in a runoff. Millner narrowly lost to Democrat Max Cleland in the general election that year, and, a month later, Gov. Miller appointed Isakson head of the state board of education.

Just as Isakson's partisan political career seemed over, it was revived by two timely retirements. In November 1998, Newt Gingrich said he would step down as speaker of the House and not take his seat in the next Congress. That opened a vacancy in the 6th District, which included much of Atlanta's northern suburbs and, at the time, was heavily Republican. Isakson was by far the best-known of the six candidates in a February 1999 nonpartisan election. He spent $500,000 of his own money and won the seat with 65 percent of the vote. In the House, he took a leading role in negotiations on President George W. Bush's signature education law, the No Child Left Behind Act, which tied federal funds for schools to test performances. He added a provision requiring that 25 percent of technology funds be used for teacher classroom training.

The second retirement came in 2004 when Miller stepped down after one term as governor. Isakson had two serious competitors in the Republican primary: Herman Cain, who grew up in Atlanta and owned Omaha, Neb.,-based Godfather's Pizza and later ran for president; and Rep. Mac Collins, whose district included the southern edge of metro Atlanta. Cain and Collins were both conservatives who opposed abortion rights. Isakson was opposed to abortion, too, but had voted against a law preventing the use of foreign aid to fund abortions overseas and had voted to allow servicewomen to have abortions at their own expense in military hospitals. Collins called him "a certified moderate."

Isakson won the primary with 53 percent of the vote. In the general election campaign, he faced one-term Rep. Denise Majette. Isakson attacked Majette's liberal voting record, including her vote against an $87 billion spending bill for the war in Iraq. Majette, at the time seeking to become only the second African-American woman ever elected to the Senate, criticized Isakson for seeking to undercut Bush's education reforms by not voting to fully fund them. Isakson won 58%-40%, almost the same margin by which Bush had beaten Democratic presidential nominee John Kerry in the state.

Isakson has shown a willingness to compromise in high-stakes fiscal battles during his Senate tenure. The former real estate broker voted for the Troubled Asset Relief Program during the 2008 financial crisis. During negotiations over the "fiscal cliff" — when a combination of tax increases and spending cuts were scheduled in January 2013 — Isakson pushed Senate leaders to broker a deal with the White House and keep Bush-era tax cuts for all but the wealthiest Americans. In 2013, he was one of only nine Senate Republicans to vote for a bipartisan budget deal to mitigate some spending cuts and raise some fees.

On another highly charged issue on Capitol Hill in recent years, immigration, Isakson's record of working across the aisle has been mixed. In 2007, he and his Senate colleague, Republican Saxby Chambliss — who retired in 2014 — worked with a bipartisan group of senators on a bill that included a path to legalization for undocumented workers, a guest worker program and tougher enforcement. He and Chambliss took heat back home: They were booed by hard-liners at the 2007 Georgia Republican Convention. A month later, when Senate Democratic leaders brought the bill to the floor, Isakson and Chambliss said they would vote against it unless border security funding was also raised. Isakson similarly voted against a 2013 bipartisan immigration bill.

Isakson took on President Barack Obama over a couple of key domestic issues. The Republican senator became entangled in a controversy during the 2009 health care debate when conservatives seized on end-of-life counseling provisions, which former GOP vice presidential nominee Sarah Palin derided as "death panels." Obama responded that one of the leading sponsors of the effort was Isakson, a longtime advocate for end-of-life counseling and assistance in drafting living wills. But Isakson rebutted Obama, contending that he backed a much different policy; the provisions ultimately were dropped from the bill. Near the end of Obama's presidency, in 2016, Isakson led a Senate effort to nullify the so-called fiduciary rule, a Labor Department regulation requiring financial advisers to act in the best interests of their clients regarding retirement accounts. Obama vetoed a resolution passed by the Republican-controlled Congress to vacate the rule, which opponents said was too complex and would increase the cost of investment advice. After Trump took office, a legal challenge to the rule killed it for good.

As chairman of the Veterans' Affairs panel, Isakson was among the first legislators to sound alarms about veterans' treatment by the VA, holding a hearing at Atlanta's VA Medical Center in August 2013. In the spring of 2016, he teamed with the committee's then-ranking Democrat, Sen. Richard Blumenthal of Connecticut, to overhaul practices at the troubled Department of Veterans Affairs. But amid an intraparty squabble over the legislation, the proposal to make it easier to fire troublesome VA employees was shelved until 2017 when Isakson and the panel's new ranking Democratic member, Sen. Jon Tester of Montana, included it in their expansion of the GI Bill, to Trump's delight. The law, which sailed through Congress, increased veterans benefits by more than $3 billion over the next decade and removed a 15-year cap on GI bill benefits for new enlistees. Isakson later backed Tester after the president was infuriated over his role in sinking White House physician Ronny Jackson's nomination to be VA secretary.

Before assuming the Ethics Committee chairmanship in 2015, Isakson had a solid working relationship with the panel's top Democrat, then-Sen. Barbara Boxer of California. The pair took the rare step of announcing in May 2011 that the committee had uncovered evidence that Sen. John Ensign had broken the law and referred the matter to the Justice Department, even after the Nevada Republican had resigned. Boxer and Isakson took heat from watchdog groups, which noted that the panel dismissed every case that came before it in 2012 and 2013. They issued a statement at the end of 2014, saying the panel "has significantly increased its efforts to educate and train the Senate community to prevent misconduct and ensure that senators and staff live up to the highest ethical standards."

In 2017, Sen. Christopher Coons of Delaware took over as the top Democrat on the Ethics panel. Isakson and Coons, who have collaborated on several fronts, both represent states where poultry is a major industry. In April 2018, the committee wrote a letter "severely admonishing" Democratic

Sen. Robert Menendez of New Jersey, after the panel investigated allegations that he had improperly weighed in on behalf of South Florida eye doctor Salomon Melgen, after receiving gifts and travel on Melgen's private jet. The panel had paused its investigation into Menendez after he was charged by the Justice Department, a case that eventually resulted in a mistrial.

The Ethics panel has traditionally been highly secretive, but that could change as the committee grapples with new issues. In a rare public statement, the panel confirmed that it was looking into sexual assault allegations against Sen. Al Franken, shortly before the Minnesota Democrat resigned. Some Republicans promised that if Alabama Judge Roy Moore won a special election in 2017, the Ethics Committee would investigate allegations that Moore had sexually assaulted young girls nearly four decades earlier, charges that rocked the election campaign. Isakson followed the lead of Senate Majority Leader Mitch McConnell and called on Moore to drop out of the race. Moore stayed in the race and lost narrowly to Democrat Doug Jones.

Isakson has remained lukewarm on Trump, matching some of his criticisms with proposals on the Senate floor. Notably, he was a co-sponsor of two bills that would have reined in the administration's national security rationale for many of its tariffs and prevented the Department of Commerce from imposing tariffs on automobiles and automotive parts without an International Trade Commission study of the industry, a move Isakson said was rooted in the industry's footprint in Georgia. He blasted Trump after the president equivocated in denouncing neo-Nazis and other hate groups after a protest in Charlottesville, Virginia turned deadly.

Isakson announced in June 2015 that he had been diagnosed with Parkinson's disease. He insisted it would have no effect on his ability to carry out his Senate duties or to seek a third term, while later acknowledging that he had not revealed his condition to anyone other than his wife for the first two years. Isakson's health issue was never directly raised during the 2016 campaign, although there were occasional veiled references.

After top Democrats declined to challenge him, the party's Senate nomination went to little-known Atlanta investment manager Jim Barksdale. While he spent more than $4.9 million — including $4.4 million from his own pocket — Barksdale was plagued by turnover in his campaign staff and questions about why he had borrowed themes from left-leaning Democratic presidential contender Bernie Sanders for a campaign in a state that titled to the GOP. Isakson was never at serious risk and went on to win 55%-41%.

His health became the focus again in 2017, when Senate Republicans were forced to a keep open a vote for a full hour, so that Isakson, recovering from back surgery and in a wheelchair, could arrive from the airport and cast the tie-breaking vote on a measure to repeal an Obama-era regulation that prevented states from denying certain funding to health care providers, like Planned Parenthood, that provide abortions. Then recovering from back surgery and in a wheel chair, Isakson's vote broke the tie.

David Perdue (R)

Elected 2014, term expires 2020, 1st term, b. Dec 10, 1949; Macon; Georgia Institute of Technology, B.S., 1972; Georgia Institute of Technology, Mast. Deg., 1975; Methodist; Married (Bonnie Dunn); 2 children.

Professional Career: Management consultant, Kurt Salmon Associates; Sr. Vice President of Asia operations, Sara Lee; President & CEO, Reebok; Chairman & CEO, Dollar General; Co-founder, Perdue Partners.

DC Office: 455 RSOB 20510, 202-224-3521, Fax: 202-228-1031, perdue.senate.gov

State Offices: Atlanta, 404-865-0087.

Committees: *Agriculture, Nutrition & Forestry:* Commodities, Risk Management & Trade; Conservation, Forestry & Natural Resources; Livestock, Marketing & Agriculture Security. *Armed Services:* Cybersecurity; Readiness & Management Support; Seapower (Chmn). *Banking, Housing & Urban Affairs:* Economic Policy; Housing, Transportation & Community Development (Chmn); Securities, Insurance & Investment. *Budget.*

Group Ratings

	ADA	ACLU	AFL-CIO	LCV	ITI	COC	HAFA	ACU	CFG	FRC
2018	-	14%	-	7%	-	70%	82%	82%	68%	100%
2017	0%	C	0%	0%	C	86%	C	88%	87%	100%

Almanac Ratings 2017-18

	Economy	Social	Foreign	Composite
Liberal	0%	0%	2%	1%
Conservative	100%	100%	98%	99%

Key Votes of the 115th Congress

1. Obama-care revision	Y	5. Gun regulations	Y	9. Kavanaugh confirmation	Y
2. Tax Cuts	Y	6. Family planning regs	Y	10. Saudi arms sales	N
3. Dodd-Frank revision	Y	7. Gorsuch confirmation	Y	11. FISA rules	Y
4. Omnibus appropriations	N	8. Immigration restrictions	Y	12. Military aid in Yemen	N

Election Results

Election	Name (Party)	Vote (%)	Cand. Spent	Ind. Exp. Support	Ind. Exp. Oppose
2014 General	David Perdue (R)	1,358,088 (53%)	$13,796,681	$3,875,475	$5,137,744
	Michelle Nunn (D)	1,160,811 (45%)	$16,063,248	$2,000,453	$12,871,729
2014 Primary Run Off	David Perdue (R)	245,725 (51%)			
	Jack Kingston (R)	237,193 (49%)			
2014 Primary	David Perdue (R)	185,466 (31%)			
	Jack Kingston (R)	156,157 (26%)			
	Karen Handel (R)	132,944 (22%)			
	Phil Gingrey (R)	60,735 (10%)			
	Paul Broun (R)	58,297 (10%)			

When President Donald Trump met with Republican congressional leaders shortly after his inauguration, there were the usual suspects: Senate Majority Leader Mitch McConnell and Speaker Paul Ryan flanked him on either side and across the table was Mike Pence. But the man to the vice president's right was not a top party leader or White House official. In fact, he was 85th in Senate seniority. But the presence of Georgia's Republican Sen. David Perdue, elected in 2014, was the clearest signal on just how much the former Fortune 500 CEO's profile was rising.

Perdue has found a kinship with Trump and often been depicted as the West Wing's bridge to Senate Republicans. A political outsider, Perdue arrived in Washington in 2015 having bested three sitting congressmen and the daughter of Peach State political royalty. Add to that Perdue's talent on the golf course and it is easy to see why the president reportedly calls the senator at all hours. Their partnership has not resulted in the passage of major legislation. But he and Arkansas Sen. Tom Cotton are the Senate Republicans most likely to echo the White House's economic populism. It also helps that while many of his colleagues react to the Trump news du jour, Perdue almost always defers to him. One resulting question has been how Perdue can win re-election in 2020 — possibly against a top Democratic recruit — in a state that is expected to be a toss-up at the top of the ballot.

Perdue spent most of his professional career in the business world — as a management consultant and later as an executive at several of the country's major corporations. He is the only former CEO of a Fortune 500 company in Congress, by dint of having run Dollar General for four years. In the Senate, he has been the staunchly conservative legislator that he promised to be on the campaign trail.

In 2014, Perdue sank more than $4.3 million of his personal fortune (in 2016, Roll Call ranked him 31st among the wealthiest members of Congress) into winning a crowded GOP primary. Although Perdue had the advantage of a familiar surname in Georgia politics, he won the general election over a Democrat with an even bigger political name: Michelle Nunn. Along the way, Perdue found that his reputation as a turnaround expert for troubled companies was a double-edged sword.

Perdue was born in Macon and raised in Warner Robins; his parents were teachers. After earning a bachelor's degree in industrial engineering and a master's in operations research from Georgia Tech, he launched a career in management consulting. He served as a senior vice president at three companies with familiar brand names: Sara Lee, Haggar, and Reebok. At Reebok, he became president and CEO of the company's athletic brands and was credited with reviving the Reebok sneaker line. His tenure was far rockier at Pillowtex, a North Carolina-based textile giant where he was hired in 2002 as chairman and CEO to guide a firm that had recently emerged from Chapter 11 bankruptcy. Perdue was gone after nine months — and four months after his departure, the firm went under, with a nationwide loss of 7,600 jobs. A legal deposition that surfaced during the campaign, in which Perdue acknowledged that he had "spent most of my career" at Pillowtex outsourcing jobs, provided ammunition for his foes. Perdue's defenders said he was hamstrung by a $50 million pension liability that did not surface until after he had arrived at the firm. That discovery prompted the banks that owned Pillowtex to seek to sell the company rather than further invest in it.

Soon after leaving Pillowtex in 2003, Perdue became CEO of another company, Dollar General, that had been through a troubled period. He streamlined operations, and, while he was forced to close several hundred stores because of competition and changing demographics, the company's stock price doubled and 2,600 new stores were opened during his four-year tenure. Perdue left in 2007, when Dollar General was sold to a private equity firm. His time there made him a multimillionaire, as he received a reported $42 million between 2007 and 2008. He began to contemplate seeking public office during his Dollar General tenure. Perdue launched his Senate candidacy in 2013, after Republican Sen. Saxby Chambliss announced his retirement. He hoped for a boost from his family name: His first cousin, Sonny Perdue, was elected governor in 2002 and served two terms. (Sonny Perdue, with whom David Perdue formed a global trading firm in 2011, became secretary of Agriculture in the Trump administration.)

Other Republicans quickly jumped into the Senate primary, all but guaranteeing a runoff — since no candidate was likely to get to the 50 percent threshold during the first round of voting. Perdue and Rep. Jack Kingston appeared to be the two early favorites — with Reps. Paul Broun and Phil Gingrey and former Georgia Secretary of State Karen Handel also in the race. Perdue had the advantages of personal wealth and a well-known name. Kingston had the support of much of the Washington establishment, including the U.S. Chamber of Commerce. Perdue spent heavily from his own pocket in the first round of the primary, running ads painting himself as the only political outsider in the race and depicting his opponents as literal crybabies. Gingrey and Broun ran weak campaigns and finished a distant fourth and fifth, respectively. Despite abysmal fundraising, Handel caught fire in the closing weeks of the campaign after a video emerged of Perdue mocking her for not having a college degree. She was boosted by a late endorsement from former vice presidential nominee Sarah Palin, a tea party favorite.

Perdue and Kingston won runoff slots with 31 percent and 26 percent, respectively; Handel was third with 22 percent. Kingston led in early polling heading into the six-week runoff period, and he quickly locked in endorsements from both establishment and tea party leaders — including Handel and Gingrey, former House Speaker Newt Gingrich, and RedState.com's Erick Erickson, a leading tea party voice in the state. Kingston hammered Perdue on his business career, slamming him for ties to a national group that supported amnesty for undocumented immigrants and for outsourcing at Sara Lee and Haggar. He also took aim at Perdue's experience at Pillowtex. Perdue spent heavily on ads portraying Kingston as a Washington insider and playing up his own independence; he pulled off a 51%-49% win, buoyed by a strong performance in the greater Atlanta media market.

Perdue faced Democrat Nunn, daughter of former Sen. Sam Nunn, who was as popular at home as he was influential during four terms in the Senate. Michelle Nunn was CEO of the Points of Light Foundation, a well-known Atlanta-based charity found by the Republican president George H.W. Bush. Democrats were bullish about her chances despite what was shaping up to be a rough year for the party nationally. While the state had taken a turn to the right in the prior two decades, it was seen increasingly in play for Democrats thanks to changing demographics — a sharp increase in its Latino residents, on top of greater voter turnout among the 30 percent of its population that is African-American. Nunn hammered Perdue on his business career, portraying him as a heartless corporate raider. For a time, she led in the polls, and it appeared the race was headed to a runoff — with a Libertarian candidate siphoning enough of the vote to keep Perdue and Nunn under the required 50 percent. But Perdue dipped into his fortune once again to run ads tying Nunn to President Barack Obama, who was deeply unpopular in the state. On Election Day, he won 53%-45%.

Arriving on Capitol Hill, Perdue often followed a hard-line conservative path that set him apart from many of his Republican colleagues. When a bipartisan deal was reached in early 2015 on long-term legislation to avoid the annual "doc fix" — which had caused Congress to scramble each year to come up with the money to avoid cutting Medicare reimbursement rates to physicians — it passed the Senate by 92-8. Perdue was among the handful of opponents, saying the measure would add to the federal debt. As a member of the Judiciary Committee, he joined a core of conservatives who resisted a bipartisan criminal justice overhaul bill. In December 2018, he voted for the final version that was signed into law by Trump.

Perdue also sits on the Budget Committee. After six months of surveying his Senate colleagues, he unveiled in late 2016 an ambitious plan to fix the dysfunctional budget process, arguing that such a move was essential to restraining growth of the federal debt. The proposal, which would have effectively merged Congress's authorizing and appropriations panels, encountered significant blowback — particularly a provision that would have cut the salaries of legislators and their aides if they failed to meet the requirements of the budget process. Perdue responded that his proposal was not final and that his goal was to prompt a discussion about what could be done to improve the process. He served on a joint select panel in 2018 to improve the budget process and later bemoaned a leadership failure on both sides of the aisle in the Senate and House that stymied the group, which overwhelmingly rejected its own proposals.

Like many of his colleagues, Perdue was incensed that Republicans' eight-year effort to repeal the Affordable Care Act was killed on the Senate floor by a single vote. Unlike his colleagues, Perdue made his grievances public. He made it known that he did not understand why Sens. Lisa Murkowski, Susan Collins and John McCain were able to keep their gavels after dooming their party's health care plan.

Perdue's work with Cotton on changing the nation's legal immigration laws may remain his biggest legacy from the first two years of the Trump presidency. In August 2017, the pair unveiled at the White House a modified version of their bill that would cut legal immigration levels in half over a decade and move the nation toward a "merit-based" immigration system, similar to Canada's, by judging applicants on employment-based criteria, such as job skills, English proficiency and education level. Some of their colleagues chided the pair that their proposal was red meat for Trump's base. The announcement was overshadowed by reports that Trump called Haiti and African countries "shitholes" during a meeting on immigration policy. Democratic Whip Dick Durbin said that Trump used such language. Perdue and Cotton, who were also at the meeting, said he did not. The story dominated national headlines for days.

Perdue endorsed Trump a month before the Republican Convention in July 2016, and played a leading role in the Georgia campaign that fall. That gave him the ultimate card with the GOP base heading into a fraught general election in 2020. After close races at the top of the ballot in 2018, Georgia was expected to be a presidential toss-up. Moreover, Perdue could find himself confronting a top Democratic challenger, perhaps Stacey Abrams, the former state House minority leader who narrowly lost to Republican Gov. Brian Kemp in 2018. Columbus Mayor Teresa Tomlinson also considered a run for the Senate.

For his part, Perdue proved in his 2014 campaign that he is more than willing to spend his own money. He will need to work out some rough edges on the campaign trail, as when he snatched the phone of a Georgia Tech student. Perdue said it was a misunderstanding and that he thought the student wanted a selfie. But the incident went viral. In any case, Perdue may not be in Washington for long. He promised in 2014 that he would only serve two terms in Senate.

Buddy Carter (R)

Elected 2014, 3rd term, b. Sep 06, 1957; Port Wentworth; Young Harris College, A.S., 1977; University of Georgia School of Pharmacy (GA), B.S., 1980; Methodist; Married (Amy Coppage); 3 children; 3 grandchildren.

Elected Office: Pooler City Council, 1994-1995; Pooler Mayor, 1996-2004; GA House, 2005-2009; GA Senate, 2009-2014.

Professional Career: Pharmacist; Owner, Carter's Pharmacy Inc.

DC Office: 2432 RHOB 20515, 202-225-5831, Fax: 202-226-2269, buddycarter.house.gov

State Offices: Brunswick, 912-265-9010; Savannah, 912-352-0101.

Committees: *Energy & Commerce*: Consumer Protection & Commerce; Environment & Climate Change; Health. *Select Committee on the Climate Crisis*.

Group Ratings

	ADA	ACLU	AFL-CIO	LCV	ITI	COC	HAFA	ACU	CFG	FRC
2018	-	4%	-	0%	-	82%	77%	88%	68%	100%
2017	0%	C	5%	0%	C	93%	C	93%	85%	100%

Almanac Ratings 2017-18

	Economy	Social	Foreign	Composite
Liberal	6%	12%	0%	6%
Conservative	94%	88%	100%	94%

Key Votes of the 115th Congress

1. Obama-care revision	Y	5. Family planning regs	Y	9. Guantanamo prisoners	N
2. Tax Cuts	Y	6. Body cameras/immigration	N	10. Ground missiles, limit	N
3. Omnibus appropriations	Y	7. Abortion ban	Y	11. Defense Dept. spending	Y
4. Dodd-Frank revision	NV	8. Concealed carry	Y	12. FISA rules	Y

Election Results

Election	Name (Party)	Vote (%)		Cand. Spent	Ind. Exp. Support	Ind. Exp. Oppose
2018 General	Buddy Carter (R)............................. 144,741	(58%)	$958,046			
	Lisa Ring (D)................................. 105,942	(42%)	$191,728			
2018 Primary	Buddy Carter (R)..	(100%)				

Prior winning percentages: 2016 (100%), 2014 (61%)

First elected in 2014, Republican Earl "Buddy" Carter fits comfortably in the Main Street wing of the GOP. He has used his seat on the influential Energy and Commerce Committee to collaborate with President Donald Trump on occasionally controversial health care and prescription-drug issues, with which he had extensive private-sector experience. He won his seat after surviving a fierce primary battle with a tea-party candidate.

A successful pharmacy owner, his campaign photo featured him behind the counter of his small-town drug store. Carter was spurred by his interest in local business issues to run for mayor of Pooler in 1996; he served eight years. He then won election to the state House in 2004 and moved to the state Senate in 2008, securing seats on the appropriations and health panels and eventually rising to deputy whip. The House seat opened when Rep. Jack Kingston made an unsuccessful Senate bid.

The 1st District is solidly Republican, but not as deep-red as other parts of Georgia, thanks in part to northern transplants who have settled there. That may have helped Carter in 2014, when he faced off in the primary against a well-funded challenger, surgeon Bob Johnson, who tried to outgun Carter from the right. Carter underscored his legislative and private-sector record, highlighting endorsements from the Chamber of Commerce and local business groups while diving into the wonky details of issues such as flood insurance and port dredging.

Johnson blasted Carter as a political insider and took aim at his ties to pharmacy groups, implying that Carter deliberately delayed the reporting of Medicaid reimbursements to his pharmacies. These positions helped Johnson win the backing of the Club for Growth. In the July runoff, Carter tied himself closely to Kingston, who also was on the runoff ballot, and he took aim at inflammatory comments by Johnson. The Club for Growth spent nearly $400,000 against Carter. He prevailed, 54%-46%. Carter took about 60 percent in Savannah-based Chatham County. Democratic nominee Brian Reese did not seriously challenge him. Carter won 61%-39%.

Carter's selection to Energy and Commerce in 2017 gave him an opportunity to apply his drugstore knowledge to health care issues. As co-chair of the House Community Pharmacy Caucus, he called for lifting the exclusion in federal law that prevents many state and private health care plans from compensating pharmacists for patient-care services. More broadly, he emphasized his efforts to repeal the Affordable Care Act and replace it with market-oriented solutions. He defended Trump's efforts and said that Republican senators who voted against the GOP initiative had "a knot in their ass" and that the deadlock was "extremely frustrating for those of us who have put so much into this effort."

At a White House ceremony in October 2018, Trump signed his bipartisan legislation that Carter said would reduce prescription costs by repealing the "gag clause" that permitted pharmacy benefit managers to bar pharmacists from informing customers about lower-priced options. Carter called it "a great day for patients." Also that month, Trump signed legislation designed to reduce opioid addiction, which included Carter's provisions to empower pharmacists with authority to reduce excessive prescription sales from so-called pill mills.

The Atlanta Journal-Constitution reported that some interest groups had raised concerns that a former pharmacist would face conflicts in handling the committee's agenda. Carter said he had checked carefully with the House Standards of Official Conduct (Ethics) Committee to avoid problems. "I think it would be irresponsible of me not to use my expertise from years in health care to participate in the discussion of health care," he added. Carter had previously transferred ownership of his businesses to his wife, who then sold two of the pharmacies.

On an issue that has caused local divisions, Carter said he was "very adamant" in his support for off-shore oil exploration and drilling. In January 2018, he applauded an initiative by the Trump administration to expand access to federal waters, though he cautioned that "any energy exploration must be done in a way that does not harm our beautiful coastline."

In the 2018 campaign, Democratic challenger Lisa Ring attacked Carter's position on off-shore drilling and said that her view was, "No drilling. Period." In a debate, Carter said that climate change was real, but that it should be addressed "in such a way that we won't cause undue financial stress on people." He outspent Ring by more than 6-to-1 and was reelected 58%-42%. The turnout was more than 50 percent greater than his mid-term victory in 2014.

GA-1: Southeast Georgia   Cook Partisan Voting Index: R+9

Population			Race and Ethnicity		Income	
Total	727,997		White	59.3%	Median Income	$49,245
Land area (sq. miles)	7,983		Black	29.3%	District Income Rank	323
Pop/ sq mi	91.2		Latino	6.7%	Poverty Rate	17.9%
Born in State	56%		Asian	1.7%	With health insurance	84.7%
Age Groups			Two or more races	2.3%	Cash public assistance	1.4%
Under 18	24%		Other	0.6%	Food stamp/SNAP	15.2%
18-34	25.5%		**Education**		**Work**	
35-64	36.8%		H.S grad or less	42.4%	White Collar	13.7%
Over 64	13.7%		Some college	32.2%	Sales and Service	42.7%
Military			College Degree, 4 yr	15.7%	Blue Collar	24.2%
Veteran/ Active Duty	15.1%		Post grad	9.7%	Government	18.4%

2012 Pres. Vote	Romney	145,525	(56%)	Obama	111,903	(43%)		
2016 Pres. Vote	Trump	151,996	(56%)	Clinton	110,190	(41%)	Johnson	7,382	(3%)

Savannah, Brunswick: In Georgia, the focus is usually on Atlanta, but the state also has some urbane smaller cities with deep roots in the past. One is Savannah, the state's first capital, which by the 1830s was one of America's booming cotton ports. It languished after the Civil War and lived off paper mills and chemical plants for much of the 20th century, while impoverished blacks on the islands a few miles offshore still spoke Gullah dialects. In the past few decades, houses and churches have been restored on a street grid laid out more than 200 years before.

Today, Savannah is one of the most graciously preserved cities in the country and a prime destination for tourists, who have bolstered the local economy by $2.7 billion annually. The population of the city is 55 percent African American. The region has become a vibrant center for overseas trade. State and local officials have been deepening the port of Savannah to 47 feet and extending the channel of the Savannah River by seven miles, at a cost of nearly $1 billion, to attract the next generation of large container ships, which carry more cargo through the widened Panama Canal; completion was scheduled for 2022. While dredging was still underway, the port was attracting larger ships and cargos. The city actively competes with neighboring and equally well-preserved Charleston South Carolina, not only for tourists but for shipping. Savannah is the fourth-busiest port in the nation and it has the busiest single terminal for container cargo in North America, which expedites fast distribution to customers. Preservationists have complained that the commercial boom has jeopardized the urban plan that was designed by Gov. James Oglethorpe in the 1730s. Local groups have sought to change the name of the Eugene Talmadge Bridge across the Savannah River; the former governor was an ardent segregationist.

The 1st Congressional District of Georgia covers the state's entire Atlantic coast, including all of Savannah. Also in the 1st are the Sea Islands, with a prospering resort economy and efforts to preserve the African-American Gullah culture and its eponymous West African-originated Creole language. Along the coast south of Savannah is the tiny, historic black settlement of Pin Point. Its citizens are mostly descendants of the first slaves in the area, and its most famous son is Supreme Court Justice Clarence Thomas. The Pin Point Heritage Museum and the restoration of a seafood factory where his mother once worked were a tribute to him.

The district has small cities, including Brunswick, a World War II shipbuilding center that has been revitalized as the gateway to the Sea Islands, and isolated Waycross, a railroad junction and gateway to the Okefenokee Swamp, the largest swamp in North America. Many popular films about the South have been produced in the region, including Glory and Forrest Gump. A private group has gained initial federal approval for a commercial spaceport at an abandoned industrial site in Camden County, near the Florida border, with its first launch planned in 2020. Residents of nearby Cumberland Island and environmentalists objected, citing potential hazards.

This was Democratic country for a century after Gen. William Tecumseh Sherman's troops marched through Georgia. Today it has become more firmly Republican, with the exception of Savannah-based Chatham County, which is the population center. The district's 29 percent African-American population also keeps down the GOP vote. Mitt Romney and Donald Trump each won 56 percent.

Sanford Bishop (D)

Elected 1992, 14th term, b. Feb 04, 1947; Mobile, AL; Morehouse College (GA), B.A., 1968; Emory University Law School (GA), J.D., 1971; Baptist; Married (Vivian Creighton Bishop); 1 child; 1 grandchild.

Military Career: U.S. Army Reserve 1969-1971

Elected Office: GA House, 1977-1990; GA Senate, 1991-1992.

Professional Career: Primary partner Attorney, Bishop & Buckner, P.C., 1972-1992.

DC Office: 2407 RHOB 20515, 202-225-3631, Fax: 202-225-2203, bishop.house.gov

State Offices: Albany, 229-439-8067; Columbus, 706-320-9477; Macon, 478-803-2631.

Committees: *Appropriations*: Agriculture, Rural Development, FDA & Related Agencies (Chmn); Financial Services & General Government; Military Construction, Veterans Affairs & Related Agencies.

Group Ratings

	ADA	ACLU	AFL-CIO	LCV	ITI	COC	HAFA	ACU	CFG	FRC
2018	-	77%	-	63%	-	82%	10%	21%	16%	20%
2017	65%	C	92%	69%	C	71%	C	4%	0%	13%

Almanac Ratings 2017-18

	Economy	Social	Foreign	Composite
Liberal	74%	73%	80%	76%
Conservative	26%	27%	20%	24%

Key Votes of the 115th Congress

1. Obama-care revision	N	5. Family planning regs	NV	9. Guantanamo prisoners	Y
2. Tax Cuts	N	6. Body cameras/immigration	Y	10. Ground missiles, limit	Y
3. Omnibus appropriations	Y	7. Abortion ban	N	11. Defense Dept. spending	Y
4. Dodd-Frank revision	Y	8. Concealed carry	Y	12. FISA rules	Y

Election Results

Election	Name (Party)	Vote (%)		Cand. Spent	Ind. Exp. Support	Ind. Exp. Oppose
2018 General	Sanford Bishop (D)....................... 136,699	(60%)	$1,177,938			
	Herman West Jr. (R).................... 92,472	(40%)	$15,777			
2018 Primary	Sanford Bishop (D).....................	(100%)				

Prior winning percentages: 2016 (61%), 2014 (60%), 2012 (64%), 2010 (51%), 2008 (69%), 2006 (68%), 2004 (67%), 2000 (54%), 1998 (57%), 1996 (54%), 1994 (66%), 1992 (64%)

Sanford Bishop, first elected in 1992, has been among the most conservative members of the Congressional Black Caucus — and among House Democrats generally. As a rural southerner, he has touted his A+ score from the National Rifle Association and his support for tobacco interests. On the Appropriations Committee, he has been an advocate for his district's interests in military and farm programs. With the Democratic takeover of the House, he became a subcommittee "cardinal" and a powerful lawmaker on agriculture spending.

Bishop grew up in Mobile Alabama, where his father was a college president. He went to Morehouse College in Atlanta, where he was student body president in 1968 and sang at Martin Luther King Jr.'s funeral. "I resolved, after his death, that I would try to follow in his footsteps," he told the Columbus Ledger-Enquirer years later. He went to Emory Law School, then served in the Army. After a year in New York, he settled in Columbus to practice law. He was elected to the state House in 1976 at age 29. He served there until 1990, when he was elected to the Georgia Senate. In 1992, he ran for the House against Democratic Rep. Charles Hatcher, who, with more than 800 check overdrafts, was damaged by the House bank scandal that year; in addition, redistricting changes increased the African-American population of the district. Bishop defeated Hatcher in the runoff, 53%-47%, and won the general election 64%-36%.

Bishop joined the conservative Blue Dog Democrats and over the years supported a balanced budget, school prayer, a ban on flag burning and a proposed constitutional amendment to prohibit same-sex marriage. He unsuccessfully sought the chairmanship of the Intelligence Committee after the 2006 election. He strongly backed the Affordable Care Act, describing it as "a piece of legislation whose time has come. People should not have to choose between going to the grocery store and getting their medicine." Bishop joined the "Problem Solvers" coalition of lawmakers who promote bipartisanship.

With a seat on Appropriations, Bishop has worked to safeguard and deliver funds to an array of local interests. For four years, he was ranking Democrat on the Military Construction, Veterans Affairs and Related Agencies Subcommittee, where he advocated the interests of his district's expansive military facilities. He worked with the Obama administration to strengthen the VA Department. Throughout his career, Bishop has looked out for Georgia's peanut farmers. He worked with Republicans on the Freedom to Farm Act to fashion a "market-oriented, no-net cost" program for peanuts. On the 2008 farm bill, he helped design the peanut-rotation program, which he said encouraged "a cleaner, greener method of planting while ensuring an affordable and accessible supply to the markets that rely on U.S.-grown peanuts."

His clout on farm issues was enhanced when he switched in 2017 to ranking Democrat on the Agriculture Subcommittee. With his takeover as chairman in 2019, Bishop was well-positioned to deal with Agriculture Secretary Sonny Perdue, the former Georgia governor with whom Bishop decades earlier served in the state Senate. In an October 2018 interview with the Atlanta Journal-Constitution, Bishop said he was pleased with Perdue's work in the Trump administration. "He knows the area, he knows the needs of agriculture firsthand, and I think he brings a great deal to that position," Bishop said.

He has been up-front in separating himself from mainstream Democratic views. He was among the handful of Democrats who did not support the June 2016 House sit-in that protested inaction on gun-control legislation. In December 2017, he was one of only six Democrats to vote for the House-passed bill that provided reciprocity between states for carrying a concealed handgun. Earlier that year, he joined Republicans on the Appropriations Committee who supported a provision to exempt electronic cigarettes from regulation by the Food and Drug Administration. His objective, he said, was "to help people ... cycle off of cigarettes." In July 2018, he was one of seven Democrats to vote for a House-passed resolution to oppose a tax on emissions of carbon dioxide. Bishop's Almanac vote ratings have ranked him among conservative House Democrats.

Bishop faced serious reelection competition in 2000 from Republican Dylan Glenn. The contest between two African Americans in a rural, then majority-white district was unprecedented, but race was not an issue in the campaign. Bishop largely ignored the challenger and ran on his record, while Glenn offered the perspective of a new generation focusing on economic growth. Bishop won 54%-46%.

In 2010, Republicans targeted him for what they called excessive fealty to Speaker Nancy Pelosi. His opponent was Mike Keown, a white state representative who highlighted Bishop's support of the Democrats' health care overhaul. He attacked Keown for lacking much of a political record and got a break when a strategist for Keown was indicted in a vote-buying case in Alabama. Bishop prevailed 51%-49%. Republican-led redistricting in 2012 strengthened Bishop and turned his seat into an African-American majority district, while reinforcing neighboring GOP Rep. Austin Scott. Since then, Bishop has not faced a serious challenge. In 2018, running against Republican challenger Herman West Jr., whom he outspent by nearly 70-to-1, Bishop took more than 70 percent of the vote in each of the three urban-based counties: Bibb, Dougherty and Muscogee. That exceeded his overall 44,000-vote margin, as West took 12 of the smaller rural counties.

After Democrats lost the House in 2010, Bishop refused to back Pelosi for minority leader. He warned that her leadership would make it difficult to recruit candidates in the South and Republican-leaning states. When they regained control in 2018, he moved quickly to support her for Speaker — and assure his own cachet in the new majority.

GA-2: Southwest Georgia   Cook Partisan Voting Index: D+6

Population		Race and Ethnicity		Income	
Total	680,145	White	40.1%	Median Income	$36,332
Land area (sq. miles)	9,626	Black	51.7%	District Income Rank	428
Pop/ sq mi	70.7	Latino	5%	Poverty Rate	26.8%
Born in State	72%	Asian	1.1%	With health insurance	83.8%
		Two or more races	1.7%	Cash public assistance	1.9%
Age Groups		Other	0.5%	Food stamp/SNAP	24.4%
Under 18	24.1%				
18-34	24.5%	**Education**		**Work**	
35-64	37%	H.S grad or less	52%	White Collar	14.4%
Over 64	14.4%	Some college	30.3%	Sales and Service	44.3%
		College Degree, 4 yr	10.7%	Blue Collar	26.6%
Military		Post grad	6.9%	Government	20.6%
Veteran/ Active Duty	11.7%				

2012 Pres. Vote	Obama	153,998	(59%)	Romney	107,242	(41%)
2016 Pres. Vote	Clinton	136,456	(55%)	Trump	107,361	(43%)

Columbus, Macon: The hub of central Georgia, Macon is a city proud of its restored houses and its Japanese cherry trees, which it shows off during its annual International Cherry Blossom Festival. It has been the home of music legends Otis Redding, James Brown, Little Richard and the Allman Brothers, and of the Harriet Tubman African-American Museum.

The long shadow of history is felt here. Before the Civil War, the southwest corner of Georgia was mostly plantation country. This is where the Confederate Army ran the Andersonville military prison. About 13,000 of the 45,000 Union soldiers confined there died, and they are remembered at the National Prisoner of War Museum at Andersonville. Today, the U.S. military is a strong presence. Fort Benning, which spreads into Alabama, is the nation's fifth-largest military installation, home of the Army Infantry School and of the Army Armor School. Benning can now train as many as 17,000 at a time. In recent years, nearly $7 billion has been spent on improvements at the post. In 2015, the base suffered a cutback of about 1,000 troops following force realignments. It retained about 11,000 military personnel and nearly as many civilians. In October 2018, the Columbus Ledger-Enquirer reported that overseas threats left Benning "positioned well to remain a major military player."

Much of the rest of this region is farmland. Cotton and peanuts are major crops, and pecans are also grown here. Near the Florida border is Cairo, birthplace of black baseball pioneer Jackie Robinson. Albany, with several factories, also has a civil rights museum and was the site of some of Martin Luther King Jr.'s protests in the 1960s. Not far from Albany, between upland pine stands and bottomland habitats, is the Chickasawhatchee Swamp, one of the Southeast's largest freshwater swamps. Plains is the childhood home of President Jimmy Carter, who remained active and has said he wants to be buried in his front yard. He attended the Macon funeral of Gregg Allman in 2017 and joined Stacey Abrams in her campaign for governor the next year. The closing of several rural polling places in 2018 raised objections from Abrams and civil-rights groups. In Decatur County, local officials have encouraged the development of solar-energy farms, though the tariff hikes of President Donald Trump posed problems. Hurricane Michael — a Category Three storm in October 2018 and the worst hurricane to hit the area in more than a century -- caused "catastrophic" damage in rural areas, including for pecan farmers.

The 2nd Congressional District of Georgia covers the southwestern part of the state. It includes the cities of Columbus, Macon and Albany, as well as Grady and Decatur counties on the Florida border and the counties along the Chattahoochee River border with Alabama. The 2nd District is the slowest-growing district in the state. It is barely a black-majority district and has a Democratic lean, though not nearly as strong as the three black-majority districts in the Atlanta area. Of those four districts, the 2nd was the only one where the Democratic share of the presidential vote fell in 2016. Hillary Clinton won the district 55%-43%. Of the 29 counties, she led in 11 — including the three chief population centers. Donald Trump ran strongly in the rural parts of the district.

Drew Ferguson (R)

Elected 2016, 2nd term, b. Nov 15, 1967; West Point, AL; University of Georgia, Bach. Deg., 1988; Medical College of Georgia, D.M.D., 1992; Catholic; Married (Elizabeth Ferguson); 4 children.

Elected Office: Mayor of West Point, GA, 2008-2016.

Professional Career: Practicing dentist, Medical College of GA, 1998-2016.

DC Office: 1032 LHOB 20515, 202-225-5901, Fax: 202-225-2515, ferguson.house.gov

State Offices: Newnan, 770-683-2033.

Committees: Republican Chief Deputy Whip. *Ways & Means*: Select Revenue Measures; Social Security.

Group Ratings

	ADA	ACLU	AFL-CIO	LCV	ITI	COC	HAFA	ACU	CFG	FRC
2018	-	4%	-	6%	-	92%	70%	84%	56%	100%
2017	0%	C	5%	0%	C	93%	C	93%	81%	100%

Almanac Ratings 2017-18

	Economy	Social	Foreign	Composite
Liberal	2%	9%	0%	3%
Conservative	99%	91%	100%	97%

Key Votes of the 115th Congress

1. Obama-care revision	Y	5. Family planning regs	Y	9. Guantanamo prisoners	N
2. Tax Cuts	Y	6. Body cameras/immigration	Y	10. Ground missiles, limit	N
3. Omnibus appropriations	Y	7. Abortion ban	Y	11. Defense Dept. spending	Y
4. Dodd-Frank revision	Y	8. Concealed carry	Y	12. FISA rules	Y

Election Results

Election	Name (Party)	Vote (%)		Cand. Spent	Ind. Exp. Support	Ind. Exp. Oppose
2018 General	Drew Ferguson (R)............................ 191,996	(66%)	$1,009,017			
	Chuck Enderlin (D)......................... 101,010	(34%)	$52,617			
2018 Primary	Drew Ferguson (R).............................43,381	(74%)				
	Philip Singleton (R)............................ 14,948	(26%)				

Prior winning percentages: 2016 (68%)

Republican Drew Ferguson moved quickly into House leadership as the GOP's chief deputy whip following the 2018 election. That positioned him as a leading critic of the new Democratic majority and a strategist for Republican efforts to regain House control. Ferguson, who was a dentist and the mayor of West Point, won his seat in 2016 following a contentious primary runoff, with support from the business community.

A native of West Point, Ferguson earned his bachelor's degree from the University of Georgia and his doctorate in dental medicine from the Medical College of Georgia. He established a family dental practice and joined the Medical College faculty. Meanwhile, his concern about the loss of local industrial jobs led him to participate actively in the civic and business life of West Point, which has a population of 4,000. In 2008, Ferguson was elected mayor, with priorities to lower barriers for local businesses.

The open House seat in 2016 resulted in a seven-candidate Republican primary. The best-known contender was state Sen. Mike Crane, who was viewed as the most conservative candidate, especially on social issues; he identified himself as close to Texas Sen. Ted Cruz, who made a campaign appearance. The Club for Growth endorsed Crane and spent more than $800,000 on his behalf. Ferguson highlighted his record as mayor of West Point, including the economic impact of its Kia auto plant. He won the endorsement of retiring Rep. Lynn Westmoreland, who said Ferguson was "a strong, conservative voice for hard-working Georgians" who could build political relationships. Ferguson led Crane in the May primary, 27%-26%, a margin of 93 votes.

In the runoff nine weeks later, Crane said he was "standing for liberty and freedom" against "a bunch of big government, big business, crony-capitalist types masquerading as true conservatives and now they have all lumped themselves together into one group." Ferguson responded that government requires coalition-building, rather than "going up there with a stick of dynamite and blowing it all up." The U.S. Chamber of Commerce spent more than $650,000 on his behalf. Crane's campaign spent about $500,000, almost half of Ferguson's fundraising. Ferguson prevailed 54%-46%. Of the 13 counties, he won 11 — all except Coweta and Fayette, in the exurbs of Atlanta. In the general election against Angela Pendley, a political neophyte, Ferguson won easily, 68%-32%. He took every county except Henry.

In the House, Ferguson showed independence from President Donald Trump by opposing his tariffs on automobiles and parts. He led an initiative by Georgia Republicans in June 2018 to send a letter to Commerce Secretary Wilbur Ross with their objections. Voicing concern about the threat to Kia workers, Ferguson told the Atlanta Journal-Constitution, "I have a commitment to fight for the good guys." Referring to the earlier closing of textile mills in his home town, he added, "I've watched bureaucrats and policymakers here in D.C. destroy my hometown once. I'll do everything to make sure they don't do it again."

With a boost from Westmoreland, who was an ally of House leaders, Ferguson quickly became a party insider. They identified him as one of several mainstream newcomers who defeated party outsiders in heavily GOP districts. Republican Leader Kevin McCarthy toured the Kia plant with him in October 2018.

Following the election, after Rep. Patrick McHenry stepped down as chief deputy whip to seek the ranking Republican slot on the Financial Services Committee, GOP Whip Steve Scalise named Ferguson as his successor. "Drew is respected and well liked and has built relationships across the entire spectrum of our conference," said Scalise, who appeared at a local event on behalf of Ferguson earlier in the year. That position has become a stepping-stone to additional influence for other senior House Republicans. Ferguson also gained a seat on the powerful Ways and Means Committee.

GA-3: Southern Atlanta Exurbs   Cook Partisan Voting Index: R+18

Population		Race and Ethnicity		Income	
Total	721,355	White	66%	Median Income	$55,443
Land area (sq. miles)	3,838	Black	23.7%	District Income Rank	224
Pop/ sq mi	187.9	Latino	5.6%	Poverty Rate	14.9%
Born in State	61.9%	Asian	1.9%	With health insurance	87.9%
		Two or more races	2.2%	Cash public assistance	1.6%
Age Groups		Other	0.5%	Food stamp/SNAP	13.5%
Under 18	24.6%				
18-34	22%	**Education**		**Work**	
35-64	39.2%	H.S grad or less	44.2%	White Collar	14.2%
Over 64	14.2%	Some college	29.8%	Sales and Service	40.1%
		College Degree, 4 yr	16.7%	Blue Collar	26.6%
Military		Post grad	9.4%	Government	15.9%
Veteran/ Active Duty	10.3%				

2012 Pres. Vote	Romney	195,075	(66%)	Obama	97,748	(33%)			
2016 Pres. Vote	Trump	200,624	(64%)	Clinton	102,155	(33%)	Johnson	9,085	(3%)

Newnan, Carrollton: South of Atlanta, Henry County has been among the fastest growing areas in the United States, with a leap in population of 71 percent from 2000 to 2010, though the pace slowed to a 10 percent increase in the next seven years. The county's flourishing residential, commercial and industrial development, which has become part of Atlanta's exurbs, took root near its Interstate 75 interchanges. West of Henry County is the old courthouse town of Fayetteville, whose Holliday-Dorsey-Fife House is thought to have inspired the columned architecture of Tara in author Margaret Mitchell's classic Gone With the Wind. The surrounding area in Fayette County is engulfed by subdivisions spreading out from Atlanta. Sprawl has reached Newnan and Carrollton in Coweta and Carroll counties and spreads farther south to Thomaston.

In the old textile town of West Point in Troup County, along the Alabama border, South Korean automaker Kia invested more than $1 billion for a local plant, its first North American facility, which opened in 2009. With its suppliers, the company said it brought more than 15,000 jobs to the region. By 2016, Kia reported that it had produced 2 million vehicles at the facility, with the popular Optima and Sorento SUV models; the assembly line had three full shifts during the week. Kia executives worried about the impact of tariffs imposed by President Donald Trump, especially with the company's extensive imports of parts.

Much of this territory is in the 3rd Congressional District of Georgia. It takes in part of the Atlanta metro area, including southwest and central Henry County and Peachtree City, where many airline pilots live and use the city's famous golf cart paths that connect homes to businesses and shopping areas. Newnan is home of the African-American Museum and the adjacent Farmer Street Cemetery, believed to be the largest slave cemetery in the South. The district stretches south to include LaGrange and part of Columbus. LaGrange, where the police chief in 2017 publicly apologized for a lynching that took place in 1940, was ranked by WalletHub among the best small cities in which to start a business. Nearby is Warm Springs, where Franklin D. Roosevelt received extensive physical rehabilitation as president. Coweta is the population center of the district, followed by Fayette and Carroll counties. This is conservative country, with a large share of military and tradition-minded families. The ancestral politics of this area was Democratic, but that is as much a part of history now as Tara. The 3rd is a solidly Republican district. After Mitt Romney got 66 percent of the vote in 2012, the vote for Donald Trump dipped to 64 percent — a minor reflection of the more widespread disenchantment with Trump in metro Atlanta Republican districts.

Hank Johnson (D)

Elected 2006, 7th term, b. Oct 02, 1954; Washington, DC; Clark College (GA), B.A., 1976; Texas Southern University, Thurgood Marshall School of Law, J.D., 1979; Buddhism; Married (Mereda Davis Johnson); 2 children.

Elected Office: DeKalb County comm., 2001-2006.

Professional Career: Practicing attorney, 1980-2006; Association judge, DeKalb County magistrate court, 1989-2001.

DC Office: 2240 RHOB 20515, 202-225-1605, Fax: 202-226-0691, hankjohnson.house.gov

State Offices: Decatur, 770-987-2291.

Committees: *Judiciary:* Antitrust, Commercial & Administrative Law; Courts, Intellectual Property & Internet (Chmn). *Transportation & Infrastructure:* Aviation; Economic Dev't, Public Buildings & Emergency Management; Highways & Transit.

Group Ratings

	ADA	ACLU	AFL-CIO	LCV	ITI	COC	HAFA	ACU	CFG	FRC
2018	-	82%	-	100%	-	50%	8%	4%	15%	0%
2017	95%	C	95%	97%	C	46%	C	7%	5%	11%

Almanac Ratings 2017-18

	Economy	Social	Foreign	Composite
Liberal	98%	93%	98%	96%
Conservative	2%	7%	3%	4%

Key Votes of the 115th Congress

1. Obama-care revision	N	5. Family planning regs	N	9. Guantanamo prisoners	Y
2. Tax Cuts	N	6. Body cameras/immigration	Y	10. Ground missiles, limit	Y
3. Omnibus appropriations	N	7. Abortion ban	N	11. Defense Dept. spending	N
4. Dodd-Frank revision	N	8. Concealed carry	N	12. FISA rules	N

Election Results

Election	Name (Party)	Vote (%)		Cand. Spent	Ind. Exp. Support	Ind. Exp. Oppose
2018 General	Hank Johnson (D)	227,717	(79%)	$383,043		
	Joe Profit (R)	61,092	(21%)	$79,051		
2018 Primary	Hank Johnson (D)	55,060	(80%)			
	Juan Parks (D)	13,966	(20%)			

Prior winning percentages: 2016 (76%), 2014 (100%), 2012 (74%), 2010 (75%), 2008 (100%), 2006 (75%)

Hank Johnson, a Democrat who won the seat in 2006, has a solidly liberal voting record and has sought to broaden debate on legal rights. On the Judiciary Committee, where he has been a harsh critic of President Donald Trump, he pursued wide-ranging interests -- including internet access — as chairman of a subcommittee. At home, following competitive Democratic primary challenges, he has become secure.

Johnson was born in Washington D.C., where his father was director of classifications and paroles for the Bureau of Prisons and his mother was a schoolteacher. He practiced law as a civil and criminal litigator and served 12 years as a magistrate judge in DeKalb County and then five years on the DeKalb County Commission. Although his immediate family members are Presbyterians, he has been a Buddhist since the 1970s; he and Democratic Sen. Mazie Hirono of Hawaii, are the first practicing Buddhists in Congress. "If you could say what drives me, it's the middle ground, the middle way," he told The Atlanta Journal-Constitution in 2009, invoking a Buddhist principle.

In 2006, Johnson ousted Democratic Rep. Cynthia McKinney in the primary. McKinney was a controversial incumbent whose own party lost patience with her. After McKinney led Johnson, 47%-44%, in the July primary, his fundraising suddenly picked up for the runoff, as donors, including former Democratic Gov. Roy Barnes, weighed in against McKinney. She responded by criticizing Johnson's past financial troubles, which included declaring bankruptcy in the late 1980s. In the runoff, turnout was up and Johnson easily won, 59%-41%. He breezed to victory in the general election.

In the House, Johnson has made eyebrow-raising statements that have landed him atop liberal as well as conservative blogs. After South Carolina Republican Rep. Joe Wilson shouted, "You lie!" at President Barack Obama in 2009 when he unveiled his health care plan to Congress, Johnson suggested that if the House took no disciplinary action against Wilson, "We'll have folks putting on white hoods and white uniforms again." Amid a series of incidents during 2015 in which African Americans had been shot by police, Johnson said, "It feels like open season on black men in America."

With Democratic takeover of the House, Johnson became chairman of the Judiciary Subcommittee on Courts, Intellectual Property and the Internet. He said that the committee might investigate numerous issues related to Trump. Following the Senate's confirmation of Supreme Court Justice Brett Kavanagh, he raised the possibility of further review of allegations against Kavanaugh. Johnson filed a bill to restrict such ousters in the future after Trump fired FBI Director James Comey.

Johnson has sparked discussion of an array of topics in the legal system. His law enforcement proposals made scant progress in the Republican-controlled Congress, but they have become part of broader national debates. In 2015, his Arbitration Fairness Act, to increase consumer protections in arbitration cases, raised issues about practices that favor business, especially in mandatory arbitration cases without judicial oversight. He introduced bills to increase data privacy and protect consumers from identity theft, and he criticized Atlanta-based Equifax following reports of a huge data breach by the credit-rating agency. In response to urban crime problems, he has filed bipartisan legislation to restrict free Defense Department transfers of surplus military equipment to state and local law enforcement agencies. "Militarizing America's main streets won't make us any safer, just more fearful and more reticent," Johnson said. In response to police malpractice, he introduced a bill to reform grand jury procedures, including the appointment of special prosecutors in the investigations of police officers for the killing of civilians. That bill would apply to local law enforcement agencies that receive federal funding. In 2019, Johnson was selected as secretary of the Congressional Black Caucus.

In 2009, Johnson announced that he had battled hepatitis C, an incurable blood-borne liver disease, for more than a decade. Two Democrats lined up to challenge him in the 2010 primary. Johnson insisted his health was fine and unveiled an endorsement from President Barack Obama, who said the congressman "has done an outstanding job." He won the primary with 55 percent to 26 percent for former DeKalb County CEO Vernon Jones and 18 percent for former DeKalb County Commissioner Connie Stokes. Johnson was challenged in 2014 by well-known DeKalb County Sheriff Tom Brown, who criticized Johnson's lack of accomplishments and mocked his 2010 comment that the island of Guam "will become so overly populated that it will tip over and capsize." With another Obama endorsement, Johnson won 55%-45%. Since then, he has easily defeated weak challengers, including 80 percent in the Democratic primary in 2018 against Juan Parks, a high school instructor. In the neighboring 6th District, his former aide Jonathan Ossoff spent more than $30 million in the special election in June 2017. Following the narrow loss by Ossoff, Johnson voiced his "suspicion" that "the election was stolen from him." No action was taken.

GA-4: Eastern Atlanta Suburbs   Cook Partisan Voting Index: D+24

Population		Race and Ethnicity		Income	
Total	739,094	White	24.2%	Median Income	$52,414
Land area (sq. miles)	497	Black	58.7%	District Income Rank	265
Pop/ sq mi	1488.3	Latino	9.3%	Poverty Rate	17.8%
Born in State	47%	Asian	5.1%	With health insurance	83%
		Two or more races	2%	Cash public assistance	1.9%
Age Groups		Other	0.7%	Food stamp/SNAP	17.3%
Under 18	25.7%				
18-34	23.3%	**Education**		**Work**	
35-64	40.4%	H.S grad or less	38.7%	White Collar	10.6%
Over 64	10.6%	Some college	31.1%	Sales and Service	43.6%
		College Degree, 4 yr	18.8%	Blue Collar	21.8%
Military		Post grad	11.4%	Government	14.8%
Veteran/ Active Duty	7.9%				

2012 Pres. Vote	Obama	218,428	(74%)	Romney	76,016	(26%)		
2016 Pres. Vote	Clinton	224,907	(75%)	Trump	66,433	(22%)	Johnson	7,323	(2%)

DeKalb: In 1920, when Gutzon Borglum began sculpting Jefferson Davis, Robert E. Lee and Stonewall Jackson into the side of Stone Mountain — the largest single piece of sculpture in the world — the huge outcropping of granite was a day's drive into the country east of central Atlanta. Even when the memorial was completed in 1972, suburban development barely reached that far. But today, after some of the most explosive metropolitan growth in the country, DeKalb (pronounced duh-KAB by locals) County is at the heart of the Atlanta metropolitan area. And this monument to the Confederate heroes — located along the Stone Mountain Freeway a few miles from the Interstate 285 Perimeter surrounding Atlanta — incongruously sits amid one of the most cosmopolitan and liberal constituencies in the South.

In 1962, the most recent attempt at a cross-burning by the Ku Klux Klan resulted in an armed clash with state police and later agreement on a small, non-violent "religious ceremony" at the top of the mountain. In a sign of the times, most of the current visitors to Stone Mountain are African Americans, with many ignoring the Confederate history and enjoying the parkland as a recreational area. The local community has discussed adding to the mountain a monument to Martin Luther King Jr., including a narrative history of Georgia. When she ran for governor in 2018, Democrat Stacey Abrams said that the carving of the three generals "remains a blight on our state and should be removed."

South DeKalb County has been transformed from mostly rural territory in the 1970s into one of the nation's largest collections of middle-class African-American neighborhoods, rivaled only by Prince George's County Maryland. DeKalb's population grew by 22 percent in the 1990s. Since 2010, it has resumed its growth, with an increase of 8 percent by 2018. It is now about 59 percent African American and 9 percent Latino. The county is culturally diverse, with more than 64 languages spoken.

The demographic changes have moved its politics to the left. DeKalb was a Republican county in the 1960s. Now, it is the most heavily Democratic major county in Georgia. Hillary Clinton led 81%-16% in 2016. As the county has evolved, south DeKalb has become much more African American and its property values have declined compared with north DeKalb. To attract more business, the county has offered tax breaks. Motion-picture companies and other entertainment industries have spent $2 billion annually in DeKalb. Calls for increased local autonomy in several areas of Georgia have increased support for the "cityhood" movement, including in black-majority and economically struggling Stonecrest, in southern DeKalb. In March 2017, the Trump administration objected after the DeKalb sheriff's office said it would not comply with federal orders to deport illegal immigrants.

The 4th Congressional District includes about half of DeKalb County, with northern and western parts of DeKalb spilling into the neighboring 5th and 6th districts. The district takes in several communities in Gwinnett County to the north, all of Rockdale County, and close to half of more-rural Newton County. Slightly more than half the voters are in DeKalb, and 20 percent are in Gwinnett. The 4th is a black-majority district and heavily Democratic, though the neighboring 5th District is more urban and even more Democratic.

John Lewis (D)

Elected 1986, 17th term, b. Feb 21, 1940; Troy, AL; Western Washington University, Att., 2000; Pike County Training School (AL), 1957; American Baptist Theological Seminary (TN), B.A., 1961; Fisk University (TN), B.A., 1963; Protestant - Unspecified Christian; Widower (Lillian Miles Lewis); 1 child.

Elected Office: Atlanta City Council, 1982-1986.

Professional Career: Chairman, Student Nonviolent Coord. Committee, 1963-1966; Field Foundation, 1966-1967; Community org. Director, Southern Regional Cncl., 1967-1970; Executive Director, Voter Ed. Project, 1970-1976; Director, ACTION, 1977-1980; Community affairs Director, National Consumer Coop. Bank, 1980-1986.

DC Office: 300 CHOB 20515, 202-225-3801, Fax: 202-225-0351, johnlewis.house.gov

State Offices: Atlanta, 404-659-0116.

Committees: *Joint Taxation. Ways & Means:* Oversight (Chmn).

Group Ratings

	ADA	ACLU	AFL-CIO	LCV	ITI	COC	HAFA	ACU	CFG	FRC
2018	-	89%	-	97%	-	45%	8%	4%	17%	0%
2017	100%	C	97%	100%	C	36%	C	7%	5%	0%

Almanac Ratings 2017-18

	Economy	Social	Foreign	Composite
Liberal	100%	95%	100%	98%
Conservative	0%	5%	0%	2%

Key Votes of the 115th Congress

1. Obama-care revision	N	5. Family planning regs	N	9. Guantanamo prisoners	Y
2. Tax Cuts	N	6. Body cameras/immigration	Y	10. Ground missiles, limit	Y
3. Omnibus appropriations	N	7. Abortion ban	N	11. Defense Dept. spending	N
4. Dodd-Frank revision	N	8. Concealed carry	N	12. FISA rules	N

Election Results

Election	Name (Party)	Vote (%)	Cand. Spent	Ind. Exp. Support	Ind. Exp. Oppose
2018 General	John Lewis (D).....................................	275,406 (100%)	$1,410,548		
2018 Primary	John Lewis (D)...	(100%)			

Prior winning percentages: 2016 (84%), 2014 (100%), 2012 (84%), 2010 (74%), 2008 (100%), 2006 (100%), 2004 (100%), 2002 (100%), 2000 (77%), 1998 (79%), 1996 (100%), 1994 (69%), 1992 (72%), 1990 (76%), 1988 (78%), 1986 (75%)

John Lewis, a Democrat first elected in 1986, made history a half-century ago as a leader of the civil rights movement. That experience has informed his work as a legislator on voting rights and poverty, and made him an iconic figure in American politics. Especially in the House, he carries great moral authority, though he has had modest legislative influence. With Democrats' return to the majority, he was positioned to serve as a rallying force with his party's base, especially with his strong opposition to President Donald Trump.

A sharecropper's son from Troy Alabama, Lewis was seized by religious fervor as a child, preaching in the barnyard, determined to be a minister. Lewis was the first in his family to finish high school. He wrote to Rev. Ralph Abernathy for help in suing for the right to enter Troy State College, and he met Rev. Martin Luther King Jr. when he was 18. In 1959, he helped organize the first lunch counter sit-in, which was received with open hostility. In 1960, the day after John F. Kennedy was elected president, Lewis sat in the Krystal Diner in Nashville, where a waitress poured cleansing powder down his back and water over his food to get him to leave. The restaurant manager then turned a fumigating machine on him.

In May 1961, he was on the first of the Freedom Rides, in which protesters rode buses through the South to challenge segregation and were attacked as they went. Lewis was viciously beaten in Rock Hill South Carolina and Montgomery Alabama. He spoke at the 1963 March on Washington, criticizing Kennedy liberals for inaction on civil rights and calling for massive help for the poor. In 1964, he helped coordinate the Mississippi Freedom Project. And in March 1965, he led the Selma-to-Montgomery march to petition for voting rights. During that historic event, he was beaten by policemen, who fractured his skull. Quietly maintaining his poise and sound judgment under harsh circumstances, Lewis was one of the people who risked their lives to make the civil rights revolution happen. He worked for Robert Kennedy's campaign for president in 1968 and was with him in Indianapolis when they heard King had been shot. He recounted his experiences in memoirs: his 1998 autobiography, Walking with the Wind; a 2012 book, Across That Bridge: Life Lessons and a Vision for Change, in which he describes what he learned in his early years; and March, a graphic trilogy that described his life in the civil rights movement and won the 2016 National Book Award.

In Lewis' first foray into electoral politics in 1977, he was defeated by Democrat Wyche Fowler in a special election to succeed Democratic Rep. Andrew Young. After winning a seat on the Atlanta City Council in 1981, Lewis ran again for Congress in 1986. He trailed Julian Bond 47%-35% in the primary, but Lewis won the runoff by assembling a coalition of poor blacks and nearly 90 percent of the whites. "Vote for the tugboat, not the showboat" was his slogan, stressing his work on local issues. He has been reelected easily ever since.

Lewis has been a strong partisan, with a staunchly liberal voting record. Usually quiet, he can speak in the forceful cadences reminiscent of black civil rights-era preachers. At the dramatic finale of the health care legislation in 2010, Lewis linked arms with House Speaker Nancy Pelosi and walked to the Capitol through a gauntlet of taunting anti-health care reform protesters. In 2001, when Pelosi became Democratic whip, Lewis initially challenged her, then switched his support to Steny Hoyer of Maryland. Lewis is the senior chief deputy whip in the Democratic leadership. On the Ways and Means Committee, where he chairs the Oversight Subcommittee, he has not been strongly identified with any tax or spending issues. Only occasionally does he defect from his party, as when he opposed the 1994 crime bill because of his disapproval of capital punishment.

Lewis has worked to commemorate the civil rights revolution in which he played such a large part. He got a federal building in Atlanta named for King and won historic trail designation for the demonstrators' route from Selma to Montgomery. Since 1998, he has led members of Congress on pilgrimages to civil rights sites. Lewis has stoutly defended racial quotas and preferences. He strongly championed reauthorization of the Voting Rights Act in 2006 when Republicans were the House majority, and his support helped ensure it carried by a large majority over the objections of critics who claimed it was no longer necessary. After the Supreme Court in 2013 limited Justice Department review of voting-law changes in the South, he built bipartisan support to reverse that ruling. But he failed to make legislative progress in the following years.

The 2008 presidential campaign was a difficult experience for Lewis. Following extensive pleas from various camps, he endorsed Hillary Clinton in 2007 as "a strong leader," and he defended her from attacks by other civil rights leaders. When Barack Obama won the Georgia primary, Lewis came under local and national pressure to switch to his camp. In late February, he endorsed Obama "following a long, hard, difficult struggle" and spoke of Obama's candidacy as a transformational moment. "Something's happening in America, something some of us did not see coming," Lewis said. "It's a movement. It's a spiritual event."

Obama welcomed the switch, and Lewis became an outspoken advocate, perhaps excessively so, as in an October statement when he compared the campaign rhetoric of Republican nominee John McCain to that of former segregationist presidential candidate George Wallace of Alabama. McCain, who referred to Lewis as "an American hero whom I admire," called the comparison "beyond the pale." He actively supported Hillary Clinton in the 2016 campaign, while downplaying in the Democratic primaries the civil-rights record of Bernie Sanders, to the dismay of Sanders supporters. "If there is one person ready to be president Day One, [it's] this woman," he told a Las Vegas rally in February.

In a dramatic epilogue in February 2009, Elwin Wilson of Rock Hill apologized on national television for slugging Lewis in the Freedom Ride attack, saying, "I am ashamed." Seated next to him, Lewis embraced the 68-year-old man, and said, "I forgive you." Lewis called the apology "amazing, unreal, unbelievable" and said that it showed the "power of reconciliation."

Lewis took his protest tactics in a new direction and to a new cause when he organized a sit-in on the House floor in June 2016 for Democrats to object to Republicans' inaction on gun control, following the terrorist attack that killed 49 at the Pulse nightclub in Orlando Florida. In an extraordinary scene, which ran counter to the rules and precedents of the House, dozens of members initially yelled objections and held protest signs. Following the adjournment that day, they sat on the House floor — many of them surrounding Lewis — to demand that the House vote. The sit-in continued for more than 24 hours and attracted national attention, especially on social media, as House Democrats used their cell phones to send personalized video messages. Lewis initially conceived the tactics with Rep. John Larson of Connecticut. Republicans were unmoved, beyond their displeasure over the violation of House decorum. They revised House rules in 2017 to raise the option, perhaps unenforceable, of fines or other penalties in an attempt to prevent a recurrence.

A few days before the inauguration of Donald Trump in January 2017, Lewis sparked another informal challenge to House traditions when he told a television interviewer that he did not accept the "legitimacy" of Trump's November election. When Trump Tweeted in response that "Congressman John Lewis should spend more time on fixing and helping his district … rather than falsely complaining about the election results," and that the protests were "All talk, talk, talk – no action or results," several dozen House Democrats responded by boycotting the Inaugural ceremony at the Capitol. That response grew to a crescendo, with the Democrats' 40-seat House gain in 2018. In an unusual twist in that campaign, Lewis backed the nominations of two white Democrats -- Rep. Mike

Capuano of Massachusetts and former Rep. Gwen Graham of Florida, who campaigned for governor — against younger, black challengers. Ayanna Pressley and Andrew Gillum both prevailed in their primaries.

Lewis continued to boycott official events with Trump. In the majority, he was among the most outspoken congressional advocates of impeachment. He pressed for investigations of Trump, including his tax returns, and a legislative review of Republican-enacted tax cuts. And he continued his call for gun control.

GA-5: Atlanta Metro   Cook Partisan Voting Index: D+34

Population		Race and Ethnicity		Income	
Total	751,264	White	28.4%	Median Income	$47,961
Land area (sq. miles)	265	Black	57.9%	District Income Rank	342
Pop/ sq mi	2835.9	Latino	6.9%	Poverty Rate	22.2%
Born in State	53.4%	Asian	4.3%	With health insurance	84.6%
		Two or more races	2%	Cash public assistance	2.2%
Age Groups		Other	0.5%	Food stamp/SNAP	18.3%
Under 18	20.9%				
18-34	31.8%	**Education**		**Work**	
35-64	36.5%	H.S grad or less	35%	White Collar	10.8%
Over 64	10.8%	Some college	24.4%	Sales and Service	40.1%
		College Degree, 4 yr	23.1%	Blue Collar	15%
Military		Post grad	17.5%	Government	13.7%
Veteran/ Active Duty	6.1%				

2012 Pres. Vote	Obama	241,280	(83%)	Romney	45,828	(16%)		
2016 Pres. Vote	Clinton	259,807	(85%)	Trump	36,384	(12%)	Johnson	9,564	(3%)

Atlanta: Venture out of the quiet of the Ebenezer Baptist Church or the shade of the Rev. Martin Luther King Jr.'s boyhood home two blocks away and into the steamy heat of the Georgia sun, and one can see, a mile away, downtown Atlanta's atrium skyscrapers. They are evidence of the wealth and vibrant growth of the commercial capital of the South, the metropolis that has grown up where there was little more than a railroad junction at the time of the Civil War. But the human achievement that is downtown Atlanta is overshadowed by the revolution started in large part by a man who grew up on Auburn Avenue. Atlanta's white establishment during King's time, led by Mayors William Hartsfield and Ivan Allen and Coca-Cola's Robert Woodruff, deserve credit for abandoning segregation, but it was King and other civil rights leaders who took the risks that led them to do so. Atlanta's city fathers acted out of goodwill, but also with an eye for the economic growth of the city, having seen the damage that resulted in other southern cities harmed by violent resistance—notably, Birmingham.

Today, Atlanta is the center of the nation's ninth-largest metropolitan area. From Auburn Avenue, it spreads into two dozen counties of northern Georgia. Its Hartsfield-Jackson Atlanta International Airport is the busiest in the world, with 104 million passengers in 2017. That was a big lead over Chicago's O'Hare, which was the U.S. runner-up with 70 million. Internationally, the runner-up with passengers was Beijing, though the new airport in Istanbul was expected to surpass each. Business conventions and the airport helped bolster the city's $12 billion hospitality industry. The new three-mile electric streetcar route is part of a broader plan for light rail lines. In 2016, voters approved a five-year increase in the sales tax to finance new projects for the region's rapid transit system. Planners project a population increase of 2.5 million in the region by 2040.

Atlanta has vibrant office centers, in downtown, Midtown and Buckhead to the north. Modern sports facilities were built for the 1996 Summer Olympics. The Georgia Dome had a lifespan of barely 20 years before being demolished and replaced by the palatial Mercedes Benz Stadium on an adjacent lot of the Georgia World Congress Center Authority, plus a luxury hotel and additional open space. Coca-Cola's skyscraper headquarters stands as a symbol of Atlanta's most successful worldwide business. The company donated a $10 million parcel of land near Centennial Olympic Park for a $100 million civil rights museum to house King's papers. Planning has continued on the Atlanta BeltLine, which Citylab has described as an ambitious urban-redevelopment project, with a "22-mile multi-use path connecting 45 neighborhoods;" affordable housing has faced obstacles.

The election of Keisha Lance Bottoms as mayor in November 2017 — and the stark racial voting patterns in her narrow victory over Mary Norwood -- revealed "a city whose political divide is still largely centered around race," according to an analysis by Governing. Atlanta has the highest income-inequality rates in the nation, and many neighborhoods have objected to gentrification.

The 5th Congressional District of Georgia includes much of the city of Atlanta, Forest Park and the smaller communities of Lake City and Morrow in Clayton County. It includes most of posh and Republican Buckhead, where the influence of the small population is chiefly financial.

This area unexpectedly drew national attention a week before Inauguration Day 2017 when Donald Trump — angered by criticism of him by longtime Democratic Rep. John Lewis — tweeted that the 5th District "is in horrible shape and falling apart (not to mention crime infested) …" Even in the self-styled "city too busy to hate," his reference to local crime had some factual basis. As the Trump transition team noted, Atlanta had the 14th-highest violent crime rate among the nation's cities, though the rate had decreased during the previous decade. But based on an array of measures, Trump's criticism fell short, as a fact-check by PolitiFact concluded: "While [the 5th District] has higher unemployment and poverty rates than the national average, it still has a thriving economic hub in Atlanta and higher educational attainment."

Lucy McBath (D)

Elected 2018, 1st term, b. Jun 01, 1960; Joliet, IL; Virginia State University, B.A., 1982; Christian Church; Married (Curtis McBath); 2 children (2 deceased).

Professional Career: Flight Attendant, Delta Airlines 1984-2014

DC Office: 1513 LHOB 20515, 202-225-4501, mcbath.house.gov

State Offices: Atlanta, 470-773-6330.

Committees: *Education & Labor*: Health, Employment, Labor & Pensions; Workforce Protections. *Judiciary*: Antitrust, Commercial & Administrative Law; Crime, Terrorism & Homeland Security.

Election Results

Election	Name (Party)	Vote (%)		Cand. Spent	Ind. Exp. Support	Ind. Exp. Oppose
2018 General	Lucy McBath (D)	160,139	(51%)	$2,455,546	$4,995,100	$1,601,172
	Karen Handel (R)	156,875	(49%)	$8,145,213	$2,335,905	$6,669,081
2018 Primary	Lucy McBath (D)	14,285	(54%)			
	Kevin Abel (D)	12,303	(46%)			

Freshman Democrat Lucy McBath, an election newcomer, won in a district that had been the site in 2017 of an epic special election. She had become politically active as a gun-control advocate following the death of her son in a shooting. McBath defeated Republican Rep. Karen Handel, who won the earlier contest that was the most costly House election in history. She spent a tiny fraction of what the Democrat spent in losing that early contest. Her victory highlighted the revival of Democrats in suburban districts, including in the South.

McBath grew up in Joliet Illinois. Her father, a dentist, was president of the state chapter of the NAACP. She graduated from Virginia State University. For nearly 30 years, she was a flight attendant for Delta Airlines. In 2012, her son, Jordan Davis, was killed by a man who complained about the music on his car radio while at a gas station in Florida. The assailant was convicted of first-degree murder. McBath became a national spokeswoman for two political advocacy groups: Everytown for Gun Safety and Moms Demand Action for Gun Sense in America. In 2016, she spoke to the Democratic convention about gun violence.

Having planned to run for the Legislature in Georgia, McBath decided to run for Congress following the killing of 17 persons at the high school in Parkland Florida in February 2018. "Championing for them in Washington is still championing for my child," she told The Washington

Post. In the Democratic primary, McBath faced Kevin Abel in the runoff. He was a businessman who depicted McBath as a single-issue candidate working with national groups. Abel outspent her, but McBath was aided by gun-control groups. She won the run-off, 54%-46%.

Handel, a long-time local Republican official, was vastly outspent in the 2017 special election by Democrat Jon Ossoff, who spent a record $31 million for his campaign, chiefly small donations from across the nation. With a boost from House Speaker Paul Ryan's Congressional Leadership Fund, Handel won, 52%-48%. The outcome was a dispiriting setback for Democrats.

In her bid for a full term, Handel was far better-known than her challenger. She initially seemed safe and paid little attention to McBath. In addition to the personal story about her son, McBath cited her battle with breast cancer to argue for improved health care services, including expansion of Medicaid.

Several factors gave her a late burst of momentum during the final days of the campaign. Former New York City Mayor Michael Bloomberg, chief patron of the gun-control groups with which McBath was affiliated, spent $4 million on ads; that nearly doubled McBath's total spending. The Democratic Congressional Campaign Committee ran extensive ads on her behalf in the closing days, as did Democratic women's groups.

Stacey Abrams, the Democratic candidate for governor, ran an energetic campaign in the metro Atlanta area, which included a closing rally with President Barack Obama. By contrast, Brian Kemp, the Republican candidate for governor, focused his campaign on rural and exurban parts of the state, which were not part of this contest.

With a huge turnout that came close to the total vote in the district in the 2016 presidential contest, McBath won, 51%-49%. Handel led in Fulton and Cobb counties. McBath's victory margin came with her 60 percent of the vote in DeKalb County, the Democratic core of the district; the DeKalb turnout was the smallest of the three counties. She was the first Democrat to win the district since the 1992 redistricting, when it was substantially redrawn. Even with the Democratic gains in the district, she was likely to face a serious challenge for reelection.

GA-6: Northern Atlanta Suburbs　　　　　　　　**Cook Partisan Voting Index: R+8**

Population		Race and Ethnicity		Income	
Total	742,017	White	60.1%	Median Income	$86,295
Land area (sq. miles)	299	Black	13.1%	District Income Rank	35
Pop/ sq mi	2483.7	Latino	12.8%	Poverty Rate	8.9%
Born in State	33%	Asian	11%	With health insurance	88.7%
		Two or more races	2.2%	Cash public assistance	0.8%
Age Groups		Other	0.8%	Food stamp/SNAP	4.8%
Under 18	24.7%				
18-34	20.8%	**Education**		**Work**	
35-64	42.8%	H.S grad or less	19.8%	White Collar	11.7%
Over 64	11.7%	Some college	20.5%	Sales and Service	35.7%
		College Degree, 4 yr	36.8%	Blue Collar	10%
Military		Post grad	23%	Government	7.7%
Veteran/ Active Duty	5.8%				

2012 Pres. Vote	Romney	186,998	(61%)	Obama	114,796	(37%)		
2016 Pres. Vote	Trump	160,029	(48%)	Clinton	155,087	(47%)	Johnson	16,148　(5%)

Fulton, Cobb: In the red clay north of Atlanta, an almost wholly new metropolitan quarter has grown up over the past four decades. Affluent Atlanta has spread out past the Perimeter, the local name for Interstate 285, into territory that was once farms, small towns and modest factory cities. Where there were perhaps 100,000 people in the 1950s, there are more than 1 million today. No longer is downtown Atlanta the only focus. The edge city of Perimeter Center is not just for shopping: It is a major office center, exceeding downtown Atlanta in square footage. Along the usually jammed Georgia 400 highway, in the fast-growing northern part of Fulton County, are the affluent suburbs of Sandy Springs, Roswell and Alpharetta.

Home Depot, the nation's second-largest retailer, is based in Sandy Springs. That city has been an innovator in outsourcing basic government services to private industry. In 2016, it imposed what it said would be a temporary three-year halt to its contract procedures to encourage local stability and because city leaders feared disruption during a planning and development boom. In the interim, no-bid contracts were permitted and several contractors were added to the organization chart for Sandy Springs. Mercedes-Benz USA had groundbreaking in September 2016 for its new corporate headquarters, which are being moved to Sandy Springs from New Jersey. Alpharetta, the self-styled "Technology City of the South," has been rated by NerdWallet as the best small city in the nation to start a business. More than 640 tech companies do business locally. In Brookhaven, which has prided itself on its multi-cultural diversity, the preparation of its bid to be the second headquarters of Amazon caused some complaints about the potential threat to immigrant-owned businesses, including many Asian and African-style restaurants. City leaders defended their planning and said that the gentrification was underway, in any case.

The 6th Congressional District is based in the northern Atlanta suburbs. It includes the northern sections of DeKalb and Fulton counties and the eastern part of Cobb County. Nearly half the population is in Fulton. The New York Times listed the district as one of 15 in the nation where a majority of the adult residents have a college degree.

The district had been safely Republican. Mitt Romney and John McCain got 61 percent and 59 percent of the vote, respectively. That changed radically when Donald Trump won, 48%-47%, one of several upscale suburban districts in the South where the GOP vote dropped precipitously in 2016. The lasting significance of that vote grew more apparent in subsequent contests. The political and demographic shifts in the districts raised the prospect of significant changes in the redistricting following the 2020 census.

Rob Woodall (R)

Elected 2010, 5th term, b. Feb 11, 1970; Athens; Furman University (SC), B.A., 1992; University of Georgia, J.D., 1998; Methodist; Single.

Professional Career: Clerk, private firm, 1993-1994; Chief of Staff, Legislative aide, Rep. John Linder, 1994-2010.

DC Office: 1724 LHOB 20515, 202-225-4272, Fax: 202-225-4696, woodall.house.gov

State Offices: Lawrenceville, 770-232-3005.

Committees: *Budget. Rules:* Legislative & Budget Process (RMM); Rules & Organization of the House. *Select Committee on the Modernization of Congress. Transportation & Infrastructure:* Aviation; Highways & Transit; Water Resources & Environment.

Group Ratings

	ADA	ACLU	AFL-CIO	LCV	ITI	COC	HAFA	ACU	CFG	FRC
2018	-	7%	-	3%	-	92%	66%	96%	61%	100%
2017	0%	C	5%	3%	C	93%	C	96%	88%	100%

Almanac Ratings 2017-18

	Economy	Social	Foreign	Composite
Liberal	3%	6%	0%	3%
Conservative	97%	94%	100%	97%

Key Votes of the 115th Congress

1. Obama-care revision	Y	5. Family planning regs	Y	9. Guantanamo prisoners	N
2. Tax Cuts	Y	6. Body cameras/immigration	Y	10. Ground missiles, limit	N
3. Omnibus appropriations	Y	7. Abortion ban	Y	11. Defense Dept. spending	Y
4. Dodd-Frank revision	Y	8. Concealed carry	Y	12. FISA rules	Y

Election Results

Election	Name (Party)	Vote (%)	Cand. Spent	Ind. Exp. Support	Ind. Exp. Oppose
2018 General	Rob Woodall (R)............................ 140,443	(50%)	$1,368,295		
	Carolyn Bourdeaux (D)................... 140,010	(50%)	$2,702,965	$1,154,003	
2018 Primary	Rob Woodall (R)............................... 30,450	(72%)			
	Shane Hazel (R)............................... 11,883	(28%)			

Prior winning percentages: 2016 (60%), 2014 (659%), 2012 (62%), 2010 (67%)

Republican Rob Woodall, elected in 2010, joined the House with Capitol Hill experience that made him more savvy about how Congress works and less inclined to bash government than other GOP colleagues who entered with him. He matched their activism and fiscal conservatism, but fell short in efforts to gain several party posts. At home, his record of safe elections came to a shocking close in 2018, when he was unprepared and nearly lost his seat. In February 2019, he announced that he would not seek reelection.

Woodall was born in Athens, where his parents were finishing their studies at the University of Georgia. The family was of modest means, shopped at Goodwill stores and drove used cars. Woodall went to college on an ROTC scholarship and had a summer job on the assembly line at an RC Cola bottling plant. While in law school, he worked for a firm in Washington. He loved being on the frontlines of national policymaking and worked out a deal with the dean of the University of Georgia School of Law to finish his degree in Washington. In 1994, Woodall took a 50 percent pay cut to start work as a legislative aide to Republican Rep. John Linder. He worked more than 15 years for Linder and became his chief of staff.

He ran for the House after Linder announced his retirement. Eight candidates entered the GOP primary. Woodall and radio talk-show host Jody Hice led the first round of voting. Hice self-funded his runoff campaign and outspent Woodall. Both candidates courted support from tea party groups. Woodall embraced their principles of limited government, strict constitutional construction and fiscal responsibility. Yet, most local groups backed Hice, especially after he bought billboards sporting a Soviet-era hammer and sickle and depicting Obama as a socialist. Woodall, endorsed by Linder, won the August runoff, 56%-44% and easily won the general election. In 2014, Hice was elected to the neighboring 10th District seat.

Woodall defined his main issue as the federal tax code, which he calls "a monstrosity" that should be replaced with a national sales tax. He says the tax code punishes productivity and encourages debt, and that a national sales tax would boost the rate of personal savings. He has regularly filed a Fair Tax bill. By 2016, he had 73 cosponsors, though the tax-writing committees took no action. Woodall and his allies had little impact on the sweeping tax cuts and other changes that were enacted in December 2017.

Woodall has shown occasional independence. On the typically Democratic issue of campaign finance reform, he introduced a bill to bar incumbents from holding onto their campaign money between elections. In 2011, he was one of seven Republicans who opposed a measure allowing permit holders to carry concealed weapons across state lines. In 2015, he was one of 19 House Republicans who voted for a proposal to remove U.S. troops from fighting the Islamic State until Congress formally authorized such hostilities.

Woodall became chairman of the Republican Study Committee's budget and spending task force. When Louisiana's Steve Scalise stepped down as RSC chairman to become majority whip in June 2014, Woodall was appointed interim chairman. He suffered a series of setbacks as he sought to move up the leadership ladder. After the 2014 election, he ran for chairman of the Republican Policy Committee, but finished third. In late 2017, when Rep. Diane Black of Tennessee stepped down as chair of the House Budget Committee, Woodall sought to succeed her and called for reform of the budget process. He lost to Steve Womack of Arkansas, who was more of a party loyalist. In 2019, Woodall failed to win the top GOP spot on the Rules Committee, where he had served since entering the House.

In the 2016 presidential campaign, Woodall initially supported Sen. Marco Rubio for president and later joined what he called the "angst brigade" when Donald Trump became the frontrunner for the Republican nomination. He finally endorsed Trump at the GOP convention in July, and said that he saw a Trump presidency as an opportunity for Congress to assert itself.

Woodall faced double-barreled opposition in 2018. He was challenged in the Republican primary by Shane Hazel, a former Marine with no political experience, who criticized Woodall for his "F" rating from conservative groups and asked him at a debate, "Why don't you run as a Democrat?" Woodall won, 72%-28%. The more serious threat came from Democrat Carolyn Bourdeaux, who taught at Georgia State University. She said that Trump was "corrupt" and the health care system was "badly broken." Woodall ran his first-ever campaign ad, which the Atlanta Journal-Constitution described as a "cheerful spot" about the district's diversity that didn't mention "his party, his opponent, President Donald Trump or even the policy issues." Bourdeaux out-spent him by nearly 2-to-1. Some Republican strategists expected a close outcome, though probably not as close as the final result: a 433-vote win for Woodall. He took 68 percent in Forsyth. Bourdeaux got 55 percent in Gwinnett, which cast more than three-fourths of the vote. Following Woodall's retirement announcement, Bourdeaux said that she would run again in 2020 in what shaped up as wide-open primaries and a competitive contest between the two parties.

GA-7: Northeastern Atlanta Suburbs   Cook Partisan Voting Index: R+9

Population		Race and Ethnicity		Income	
Total	778,970	White	45.8%	Median Income	$70,486
Land area (sq. miles)	393	Black	19%	District Income Rank	92
Pop/ sq mi	1984.1	Latino	19.3%	Poverty Rate	10.5%
Born in State	35.5%	Asian	13.1%	With health insurance	83.6%
		Two or more races	2.2%	Cash public assistance	1.4%
Age Groups		Other	0.6%	Food stamp/SNAP	8.2%
Under 18	27.6%				
18-34	21.2%	Education		Work	
35-64	42%	H.S grad or less	32.4%	White Collar	9.2%
Over 64	9.2%	Some college	27.5%	Sales and Service	40.4%
		College Degree, 4 yr	26.7%	Blue Collar	18.2%
Military		Post grad	13.5%	Government	9.5%
Veteran/ Active Duty	5.9%				

2012 Pres. Vote	Romney	158,741	(60%)	Obama	101,169	(38%)			
2016 Pres. Vote	Trump	150,845	(51%)	Clinton	132,012	(44%)	Johnson	12,115	(4%)

Gwinnett, Forsyth: In the past two decades, greater Atlanta has grown out in every direction: south past the airport, west over the Chattahoochee River, north past Perimeter Center, and east and northeast past Stone Mountain. The outer suburbs north of Atlanta have grown — and changed -- fastest of all. Gwinnett County combines mature neighborhoods of affluent professionals and entrepreneurs with closer-in communities near Interstate 85 that have been attracting Georgia's largest concentration of Hispanics along with middle-class blacks. The county's rapidly growing school system boasts that its students speak more than 100 languages. Farther out in Lawrenceville, Duluth and Buford, downtown Atlanta seems very far away, both physically — it is 20 to 40 miles, and more than an hour of clogged rush-hour driving, to Peachtree Street — and in state of mind. For many, Atlanta is something off the highway on the way to Hartsfield-Jackson Atlanta International Airport.

The growth and its diversity here are hard to overstate. Gwinnett County's population grew 37 percent from 2000 to 2010, to more than 805,000. In the next seven years, it grew to 920,000, despite the slowdown during the recession. Like other metro Atlanta counties, the non-Hispanic white population has been dropping in Gwinnett schools, while the overall student numbers soar. The share of the county population who are immigrants increased from 6 percent in 1990 to 32 percent in 2014. In 2015, the Washington-based Migration Policy Institute estimated that 71,000 immigrants were living illegally in Gwinnett. Overall, the minority population in the county has grown to 28 percent African American, 21 percent Hispanic and 12 percent Asian. Population projections for 2040 include close to 1.4 million, with less than 30 percent white. The demographic changes in Gwinnett have brought political change (the first Democrats and racial minorities were elected to the county commission in 2018) and social upheaval (including increased homelessness and demands by local activists for voting rights). To the north, Forsyth has been the fastest growing and wealthiest county in

Georgia. In a once-rural area where blacks were terrorized and forced out in 1912, suburban housing and business development have been booming.

The 7th Congressional District of Georgia comprises about 70 percent of Gwinnett County and 70 percent of Forsyth County. In each county, Donald Trump fared relatively poorly in the 2016 election. Gwinnett, which voted 54%-45% for Mitt Romney over President Barack Obama in 2012, backed Hillary Clinton over Trump, 51%-45% -- the first presidential election since 1976 in which the county has voted Democratic. In Forsyth, the 81%-18% vote for Romney dropped to 71%-24% for Trump. Overall, the Republican vote in the district fell to 51%-44% in 2016 from the previous 60%-38%.

Austin Scott (R)

Elected 2010, 5th term, b. Dec 10, 1969; Augusta; Tiftarea Academy, Chula, GA, 1987; University of Georgia Terry College of Business, B.B.A., 1993; American College (PA), 1995; Baptist; Married (Vivien Scott); 2 children.

Elected Office: GA House, 1997-2010.

Professional Career: Owner, Southern Group; Agent, Principal Financial Group, 1993-2010.

DC Office: 2417 RHOB 20515, 202-225-6531, Fax: 202-225-3013, austinscott.house.gov

State Offices: Tifton, 229-396-5175; Warner Robins, 478-971-1776.

Committees: *Agriculture:* Commodity Exchanges, Energy & Credit (RMM); General Farm Commodities & Risk Management. *Armed Services:* Intelligence, Emerging Threats & Capabilities; Readiness.

Group Ratings

	ADA	ACLU	AFL-CIO	LCV	ITI	COC	HAFA	ACU	CFG	FRC
2018	-	4%	-	3%	-	92%	62%	76%	53%	100%
2017	0%	C	21%	0%	C	93%	C	81%	75%	100%

Almanac Ratings 2017-18

	Economy	Social	Foreign	Composite
Liberal	6%	0%	0%	2%
Conservative	94%	100%	100%	98%

Key Votes of the 115th Congress

1. Obama-care revision	Y	5. Family planning regs	Y	9. Guantanamo prisoners	N
2. Tax Cuts	Y	6. Body cameras/immigration	N	10. Ground missiles, limit	N
3. Omnibus appropriations	Y	7. Abortion ban	Y	11. Defense Dept. spending	Y
4. Dodd-Frank revision	Y	8. Concealed carry	Y	12. FISA rules	Y

Election Results

Election	Name (Party)	Vote (%)	Cand. Spent	Ind. Exp. Support	Ind. Exp. Oppose
2018 General	Austin Scott (R).................................	198,152 (100%)	$428,034		
2018 Primary	Austin Scott (R)...	(100%)			

Prior winning percentages: 2016 (68%), 2014 (unopposed), 2012 (unopposed), 2010 (53%)

Republican Austin Scott, in the rural southern tradition, has been an active lawmaker on military and agriculture issues who usually operates behind the scenes and doesn't seek attention. After defeating a Democratic incumbent in 2010 and then becoming politically secure at home, he has occasionally been blunt in criticizing various Republican factions or former allies.

Born in Augusta, Scott's father was an orthopedic surgeon and his mother was a teacher. He graduated from the University of Georgia with a degree in risk management and insurance. After college, he opened an insurance brokerage firm, which he operated for 17 years. Scott was elected to the state House at 26. He sponsored a bill to provide more funding for the state's trauma-care system, championed the expansion of charter schools and supported the right of students to express their religious beliefs in schools. In January 2009, he announced his candidacy for governor. But his campaign failed to gain traction, and he decided to challenge four-term Democratic Rep. Jim Marshall.

Marshall styled himself as a conservative Democrat and voted against President Barack Obama's health care law. But he was vulnerable in 2010 simply because he was a Democrat. Scott promised to reduce the deficit, and he attacked the incumbent for voting for Obama's $787 billion economic stimulus bill. Marshall, unlike most Democrats, was endorsed by the U.S. Chamber of Commerce and the National Rifle Association. Still, Scott won the seat, 53%-47%. In all but one election since, he ran without major-party opposition. In 2016, he faced Democrat James Harris, who did not file a campaign spending report and was defeated, 68%-32%.

In the House, Scott was elected freshman class president and was regularly asked to explain his boisterous classmates' actions to the news media. They never intended to speak with a single voice, he replied in November 2011: "I think of us as a group of independent thinkers." A year later, he said that their main job was "to play defense against what [President Barack Obama] was going to do. I think we were pretty effective at doing that." By 2018, he downplayed their influence. "We didn't come to take over the country," he said.

As a member of the Armed Services Committee, unlike many of the military's boosters on the panel, he has maintained that defense spending must be examined for budget cuts. But he has advocated aggressively on behalf of his district. In 2015, Scott collaborated with neighboring Republican Rep. Buddy Carter to preserve the A10-C Warthog, which provides support for larger aircraft in low-visibility and low-altitude combat and has two squadrons at Moody Air Force Base in Valdosta. He opposed the Obama administration's request for another round of base closings, which could jeopardize Moody and Robins Air Force Base to the north in Warner Robins. In December 2016, he claimed credit for an amendment to the annual defense spending bill that removed proposed language that might have led to the shift of work from Air Force depots, including Robins.

In 2018, Scott voiced serious concerns about the Trump administration's plan for a new Advanced Battle Management System that would replace the Joint Surveillance Target Attack Radar System (JSTARS), which has been based at Robins. That resulted in his unusual clash with Georgia Republican Sen. David Perdue, who advocated the proposal as a member of the Senate Armed Services Committee. After Congress rejected a plan backed by Scott for additional planes at Robins, Scott placed responsibility on Perdue. "If David said yes, it would have happened," he told the Macon Telegraph. He warned of potential dire consequences for Robins. "I do not believe you want to be an Air Force base without a flying mission when you go into a round of" base-closings.

On the Agriculture Committee, as chairman of the Commodity Exchanges, Energy, and Credit Subcommittee, Scott took on the financially complex and often risky derivatives markets and sought a bipartisan solution that struck a balance between market integrity and market access. In 2015, the House passed his bill to renew the Commodity Futures Trading Commission. In 2018, he was unsuccessful in pushing for more controls on recipients of food stamps. He supported the final deal, he said, because it "delivers the necessary policy our farmers desperately need," including support for peanut producers.

Scott criticized Republican factions for placing obstacles in front of other legislation in 2017-18. When Rep. Mark Meadows and other conservatives in the House Freedom Caucus stymied action to repeal the Affordable Care Act, Scott tweeted, "Mark Meadows betrayed Trump and America." Later, when GOP moderates — over the objections of party leaders -- pushed a proposal to normalize the status of young illegal immigrants, Scott complained, "There ought to be discipline" for the mavericks.

Scott was a grudging supporter of Donald Trump in the 2016 presidential campaign. He initially endorsed Sen. Marco Rubio and called Trump "a con man." In September, he issued a statement concluding, "I am committed to defeating Hillary Clinton this November," which failed to mention Trump's name.

GA-8: South-Central Georgia   Cook Partisan Voting Index: R+15

Population		Race and Ethnicity		Income	
Total	703,499	White	59.9%	Median Income	$43,142
Land area (sq. miles)	8,712	Black	30.2%	District Income Rank	394
Pop/ sq mi	80.8	Latino	6.3%	Poverty Rate	21.3%
Born in State	69%	Asian	1.5%	With health insurance	83.8%
		Two or more races	1.6%	Cash public assistance	1.7%
Age Groups		Other	0.4%	Food stamp/SNAP	17.3%
Under 18	23.9%				
18-34	23.8%	Education		Work	
35-64	37.9%	H.S grad or less	50.5%	White Collar	14.4%
Over 64	14.4%	Some college	28.9%	Sales and Service	41.8%
		College Degree, 4 yr	12%	Blue Collar	25.9%
Military		Post grad	8.7%	Government	21.4%
Veteran/ Active Duty	10.9%				

2012 Pres. Vote	Romney	163,908	(62%)	Obama	99,676	(38%)		
2016 Pres. Vote	Trump	168,193	(63%)	Clinton	91,360	(34%)	Johnson	5,961 (2%)

Warner Robins, Valdosta: South-central Georgia is a region of farm and forest lands and a collection of small, and some tiny, towns. Twiggs and Wilkinson counties have been among the world's major sources of kaolin, a clay used for china and ceramics. In Juliette, an old mill town that's too small for most maps, scenes from Fried Green Tomatoes were filmed; a former hardware store there became the film's Whistle Stop Café.

With its Air Logistics Center and testing and repair site for the F-22 Raptor, Robins Air Force Base and the surrounding city of Warner Robins have become a major presence. The sprawling base employed 22,000 people and had an economic impact of $2.9 billion in 2018. In June 2018, the Air Force announced its long-term plan to replace the Joint Surveillance Target Attack Radar System (JSTARS) at Robins with the Advanced Battle Management System, a new global air space intelligence, surveillance and reconnaissance information system that the Trump administration embraced. The following month, House-Senate negotiators on the annual defense-spending bill killed plans to purchase additional aircraft for the JSTARS program. The eventual impact for Robins remained to be seen. In adjacent Twiggs County, Georgia Power planned to start operation in late 2019 of the largest solar-power plant in the Southeast.

In Pulaski County is Hawkinsville, founded on the banks of the Ocmulgee River and a winter home for harness horse training. Nearby is Tifton, home to the Georgia Museum of Agriculture. Farther south along Interstate 75 is Valdosta, a racially split city of 56,100 that has the most successful high school football program in the country. No team in the nation has won more games than the Valdosta High School Wildcats, who have a won-loss record of 911-227-34 since 1913; in 2016, the team won its 24th state championship. Valdosta is also where Doc Holliday, made famous by the gunfight at the O.K. Corral, spent much of his youth.

The 8th Congressional District includes Monroe and Jones counties north of Macon in central Georgia and stretches all the way south to the Florida border; most of Macon is in the Democratic-leaning 2nd District. The 8th covers Berrien County, known for its turpentine and bell peppers, and it takes in most of Lowndes County, where Valdosta is located. The district is solidly Republican. Donald Trump won 63 percent of the vote here in 2016.

Doug Collins (R)

Elected 2012, 4th term, b. Aug 16, 1966; Gainesville; North Georgia College and State University (Military College of Georgia) Foundation Inc., B.A., 1988; New Orleans Baptist Theological Seminary (LA), M.Div., 1996; John Marshall University Law School (Atlanta), J.D., 2008; Baptist; Married (Lisa Jordan); 3 children.

Military Career: U.S. Air Force Reserve 2002-pres. (Iraq)

Elected Office: GA House, 2007-2012.

Professional Career: Practicing attorney, 2008-2012; Pastor, Chicopee Baptist Church, 1994-2005.

DC Office: 1504 LHOB 20515, 202-225-9893, Fax: 202-226-1224, dougcollins.house.gov

State Offices: Gainesville, 770-297-3388.

Committees: *Judiciary (RMM)*.

Group Ratings

	ADA	ACLU	AFL-CIO	LCV	ITI	COC	HAFA	ACU	CFG	FRC
2018	-	3%	-	3%	-	92%	75%	80%	57%	100%
2017	0%	C	5%	0%	C	93%	C	93%	88%	100%

Almanac Ratings 2017-18

	Economy	Social	Foreign	Composite
Liberal	2%	0%	0%	1%
Conservative	99%	100%	100%	100%

Key Votes of the 115th Congress

1. Obama-care revision	Y	5. Family planning regs	Y	9. Guantanamo prisoners	N
2. Tax Cuts	Y	6. Body cameras/immigration	N	10. Ground missiles, limit	N
3. Omnibus appropriations	Y	7. Abortion ban	Y	11. Defense Dept. spending	Y
4. Dodd-Frank revision	Y	8. Concealed carry	Y	12. FISA rules	Y

Election Results

Election	Name (Party)	Vote (%)	Cand. Spent	Ind. Exp. Support	Ind. Exp. Oppose
2018 General	Doug Collins (R)............................224,661	(80%)	$676,175		
	Josh McCall (D)...............................57,912	(20%)	$82,751		
2018 Primary	Doug Collins (R)..	(100%)			

Prior winning percentages: 2016 (100%), 2014 (81%), 2012 (76%)

Republican Doug Collins, elected to a newly drawn seat in 2012, quickly gained influence in the House. In 2019, he became the top Republican on the Judiciary Committee — a vital post for defending President Donald Trump. Earlier, he showed his legislative chops and held a GOP leadership post. He has background in both divinity and the law.

Collins was born in Gainesville and grew up in Hall County. His father was a state trooper, and his mother worked a variety of jobs in town. In 1988, Collins graduated from North Georgia College and State University, where he studied political science and business. The same year, he met his wife, Lisa, at church. He worked in several jobs in the hazardous-materials industry, but then felt a calling to the ministry. After spending time volunteering as a youth minister, he entered the New Orleans Baptist Theological Seminary. He returned to Gainesville, serving as pastor of Chicopee Baptist Church. In 2002, Collins joined the Air Force Reserve and, in 2008, did a tour in Iraq as a chaplain, an experience that he says gave him "a whole different perspective of what freedom is like and what the lack of it is like." He got a law degree in Atlanta and opened his own practice in Gainesville. He served six years in the state House, including one term as floor leader during the term of Republican Gov. Nathan Deal, whom he had known since high school.

When Georgia got a 14th district following the 2010 reapportionment, Republicans drew the new 9th District without an incumbent. When Collins decided to run, his chief primary opponent was

Gainesville talk-show host Martha Zoller, a tea party favorite. She criticized Collins' role in devising the referendum to raise the sales tax by a penny to address traffic congestion, which was widely rejected in most of the state. Collins touted his experience crafting budgets and his service in Iraq. He hammered Zoller for having stated that President Barack Obama was "a nice guy." The two fought to a near-draw in July's primary, with Collins on top by 734 votes. In the runoff, Zoller was endorsed by former Alaska Gov. Sarah Palin and 2012 presidential candidates Herman Cain, Newt Gingrich and Rick Santorum. Deal recorded a robo-call for Collins, who played on the local roots of his major endorsers with the slogan, "We are the 9th District." Collins outspent Zoller 3-to-2 and prevailed, 55%-45%, then coasted to victory in November.

In the House, Collins was assigned to the Judiciary Committee — a good post for a lawyerly mind. In 2015, the committee approved his proposal to give more authority to state and local governments to enforce national immigration laws. Obama signed into law in 2016 a Collins bill to guarantee a federal law enforcement officer the right to carry a firearm during a covered furlough from the job. Collins broke a two-decade deadlock in his district by adding a provision to the defense spending bill in 2013 that transferred 282 acres of local land from the Forest Service to the Army, which has used the area for training Rangers. The location in Lumpkin County is near the Military College of Georgia.

Collins moved into House leadership following the 2016 election when he defeated Bill Flores of Texas for vice chairman of the House Republican Conference, 170-61. With his seat on the Rules Committee, which acts as an arm of the House leadership, Collins had an additional niche as a legislative insider. He visited other districts across the nation on behalf of GOP colleagues in competitive campaigns.

He had a busy two years of legislating. In January 2017, the House passed his bill to give Congress the right to review major new federal regulations before they took effect. "It's time Congress reasserts its constitutional authority to legislate, rather than letting unelected bureaucrats institute rules that impact the economy to the tune of hundreds of millions of dollars," he said. This opened the door for Republicans to work with President Donald Trump in overturning dozens of Obama-era regulations.

Collins worked with Democrats to enact in 2018 his Music Modernization Act, which protected the royalty rights of songwriters from online streaming sites. "Music providers should be able to compensate creators with transparency in a way that makes sense for the 21st century," he and Rep. Judy Chu, D-Calif., wrote in an op-ed for Variety. Also that year, he was instrumental in House passage of criminal-justice reform legislation, including the reduction of mandatory-minimum sentences.

Those successes positioned Collins for his successful bid to become ranking Republican at the Judiciary Committee. His chief opponent, Rep. Jim Jordan of Ohio, was more senior and backed by Trump. Collins benefited from his superior legislative accomplishments and his party-building. He warned Democrats on Judiciary against pursuing "political vendettas."

At home, Collins was reelected easily. He faced an unusual challenge in the 2016 primary. Former Rep. Paul Broun, who for nearly eight years had represented the adjacent 10th District and then ran a distant fifth in the 2014 GOP primary for an open Senate seat, ran a quixotic challenge. Collins outspent Broun nearly 10-to-1 and won 61%-22%. In 2018, he had no primary opposition. In November, he took 80 percent of the vote against Josh McCall, a teacher with a Bernie Sanders-style agenda.

GA-9: Northeast Georgia   **Cook Partisan Voting Index: R+31**

Population		Race and Ethnicity		Income	
Total	725,451	White	77.6%	Median Income	$50,214
Land area (sq. miles)	5,211	Black	6.7%	District Income Rank	310
Pop/ sq mi	139.2	Latino	12.8%	Poverty Rate	16.3%
Born in State	60.9%	Asian	1.2%	With health insurance	84.1%
		Two or more races	1.3%	Cash public assistance	2.3%
Age Groups		Other	0.4%	Food stamp/SNAP	13.4%
Under 18	23.3%				
18-34	20.2%	**Education**		**Work**	
35-64	39.1%	H.S grad or less	50.2%	White Collar	17.4%
Over 64	17.4%	Some college	27.8%	Sales and Service	40.1%
		College Degree, 4 yr	13.7%	Blue Collar	29.4%
Military		Post grad	8.4%	Government	13.2%
Veteran/ Active Duty	8.6%				

2012 Pres. Vote	Romney	207,581	(78%)	Obama	54,310	(21%)		
2016 Pres. Vote	Trump	231,194	(77%)	Clinton	57,468	(19%)	Johnson	8,553	(3%)

Gainesville: Northeast Georgia is a land where the coastal plains and cotton fields yield to gently rolling hills and, near the North Carolina border, to the Appalachian Mountains. For most of its history, this was quiet, rural country, with courthouse towns and a few small cities, mostly forgotten by national elites, bypassed even by Union soldiers on their march to the sea. These largely rural areas have been an occasional source of derision and curiosity. James Dickey's 1970 novel Deliverance is a thinly disguised portrait of life along the Coosawattee River in Gilmer and Murray counties (although the movie was filmed on the Chattooga River in Rabun County).

Though the area was traditionally agrarian, the northern part of Georgia has undergone a rush of change over two decades. Interstate highways have brought it within easy range of Atlanta. Vacation and retirement communities have sprung up in the mountains and around the lakes. The area around Lake Sidney Lanier, named for the 19th century poet who wrote "The Song of the Chattahoochee," is filled with vacation houses and second homes. The popular Appalachian Trail starts (or ends) at Springer Mountain — a nearly 2,200-mile hike to (or from) Mount Katahdin in Maine. Baseball great Ty Cobb, nicknamed "The Georgia Peach," was born in tiny Narrows in Banks County and played semi-pro ball in Royston, which now houses the Ty Cobb Museum. Agribusiness remains important, with huge poultry processors in Hall County around Gainesville. In December 2018, state officials announced plans to build a $90 million inland port in Gainesville, which will connect by rail to the harbor in Savannah. Thousands of Latinos from Mexico and other countries have come to the Gainesville area to snap up jobs. Workplace enforcement of undocumented immigrants has increased since President Donald Trump took office and local poultry farms have had difficulty finding enough workers, the Gainesville Times reported in January 2018.

The 9th Congressional District of Georgia covers the northeast corner of the state. Rural and mostly white, the district is anchored by Gainesville's Hall County, and includes the northern slice of fast-growing Forsyth and a small part of Athens-based Clarke County. It is the most Republican district in the state and was the third most Republican in the nation following the 2012 and 2016 elections, according to The Cook Political Report, when it was surpassed only by two districts in west Texas. Donald Trump also took 77 percent in 2016.

Jody Hice (R)

Elected 2014, 3rd term, b. Apr 22, 1960; Atlanta; Asbury College (KY), B.A., 1982; Southwestern Baptist Theological Seminary (TX), M.Div., 1986; Luther Rice Seminary and University (GA), B.A., 1988; Southern Baptist; Married (Dee Hice); 2 children; 4 grandchildren.

Professional Career: Adjunct faculty, Luther Rice University; Pastor; Talk radio host, The Jody Hice Show.

DC Office: 409 CHOB 20515, 202-225-4101, hice.house.gov

State Offices: Milledgeville, 478-457-0007; Monroe, 770-207-1776; Thomson, 770-207-1776.

Committees: *Natural Resources:* National Parks, Forests & Public Lands; Water, Oceans & Wildlife. *Oversight & Reform:* Government Operations; National Security (RMM); Subcommittee on Civil Rights & Civil Liberties.

Group Ratings

	ADA	ACLU	AFL-CIO	LCV	ITI	COC	HAFA	ACU	CFG	FRC
2018	-	11%	-	0%	-	75%	90%	100%	93%	100%
2017	5%	C	5%	0%	C	93%	C	96%	98%	100%

Almanac Ratings 2017-18

	Economy	Social	Foreign	Composite
Liberal	0%	3%	0%	1%
Conservative	100%	97%	100%	99%

Key Votes of the 115th Congress

1. Obama-care revision	Y	5. Family planning regs	Y	9. Guantanamo prisoners	N
2. Tax Cuts	Y	6. Body cameras/immigration	N	10. Ground missiles, limit	N
3. Omnibus appropriations	N	7. Abortion ban	Y	11. Defense Dept. spending	Y
4. Dodd-Frank revision	Y	8. Concealed carry	Y	12. FISA rules	Y

Election Results

Election	Name (Party)	Vote (%)		Cand. Spent	Ind. Exp. Support	Ind. Exp. Oppose
2018 General	Jody Hice (R)	190,396	(63%)	$570,539		
	Tabitha Johnson-Green (D)	112,339	(37%)	$12,382		
2018 Primary	Jody Hice (R)	42,960	(79%)			
	Bradley Griffin (R)	5,846	(11%)			
	Joe Hunt (R)	5,644	(10%)			

Prior winning percentages: 2016 (100%), 2014 (67%)

Republican Jody Hice, who was elected in 2014 in his second bid for an open seat, became a leader of the small-government conservative activists in the House Freedom Caucus. He occasionally created problems for Republican leaders, though he was enough of a team player to gain a seat on the Armed Services Committee.

Hice was born in Atlanta and grew up in Tucker Georgia. He graduated from Asbury College, earned his master's degree from Southwestern Seminary and his doctorate from Luther Rice University, a Christian college and seminary in Lithonia. He founded The Culture and Values Network and hosted The Jody Hice Show, a conservative talk radio program.

A Baptist minister who served several churches in the metro Atlanta area, he argued in his 2012 book, It's Now or Never: A Call to Reclaim America, that supporters of abortion rights are worse than Adolf Hitler and that homosexuality causes shorter life spans as well as depression. He got his first taste of political battle in 2003 when he helped lead a campaign against a lawsuit by the American Civil Liberties Union seeking to remove a Ten Commandments display at the Barrow County courthouse. Five years later, he waged a successful effort against the Internal Revenue Service over whether politically active clergy can keep their tax-exempt status. In 2010, Hice was the close runner-up to Rob Woodall in the Republican primary for the neighboring 7th District.

When the seat opened in the 10th, Hice jumped in and was among the best-known names in the GOP primary field of seven. The initial favorite was trucking company executive Mike Collins, who played up the achievements of his father, former Republican Rep. Mac Collins. Hice slammed Collins as an insider who was too close to Washington because of his father, whom he attacked as well. Collins struck back, painting Hice as an extremist. He cited passages from Hice's book that argued against First Amendment protections for Muslims. Collins created his own vulnerability when he equivocated on whether Congress should raise the debt ceiling.

Hice led the May primary by a hair, at 34 percent. In the July runoff, Hice had the advantage because he could unify the conservative vote and he defeated Collins, 54%-46%. He easily won in November. Immediately after the election, the liberal website Salon declared Hice "America's worst new congressman."

During his 2014 campaign, Hice had said that he would support "new leadership with a backbone." After John Boehner in September 2015 announced that he would step down as Speaker, Hice was among a group of renegades who backed Rep. Daniel Webster of Florida as his successor. When it became clear that Rep. Paul Ryan had broad support among Republicans, Hice received a minor concession from Ryan and then agreed to support him.

Hice joined the Freedom Caucus of conservatives who often went their own way from Republican leaders. Much of his focus was on social issues, including his pledge to oppose any bill that funded Planned Parenthood. He filed the Nuclear Family Priority Act, which addressed what he called the problem of chain migration, by limiting the assurance that legal status will be granted to extended family members of legal immigrants. Hice also was a founding member of the Second Amendment

Caucus. In 2017, he initially opposed the Republican measure to repeal the Affordable Care Act because he argued that the alternative was not sufficiently conservative. He went along following a late change that permitted states to opt out of the basic coverage requirements if they got a waiver.

In 2016, Hice made a belated and unenthusiastic endorsement of Donald Trump a month before the November election. "If you are struggling with who to vote for, just remember the platforms the parties are running on," he said. Once Trump became president, Hice joined other conservatives who sought to limit investigations of his alleged wrongdoing. He apparently had found a balance between his conservative advocacy and working with Republican leaders. He has been reelected easily.

GA-10: East-Central Georgia

Cook Partisan Voting Index: R+15

Population		Race and Ethnicity		Income	
Total	728,072	White	65.2%	Median Income	$51,042
Land area (sq. miles)	7,096	Black	25.2%	District Income Rank	286
Pop/ sq mi	102.6	Latino	5.4%	Poverty Rate	17.8%
Born in State	64.9%	Asian	2.1%	With health insurance	87.4%
		Two or more races	1.7%	Cash public assistance	1.6%
Age Groups		Other	0.4%	Food stamp/SNAP	13.9%
Under 18	23.6%				
18-34	24.4%	**Education**		**Work**	
35-64	38.1%	H.S grad or less	47.4%	White Collar	13.9%
Over 64	13.9%	Some college	27.4%	Sales and Service	41.5%
Military		College Degree, 4 yr	14.9%	Blue Collar	24.6%
Veteran/ Active Duty	7.9%	Post grad	10.3%	Government	18.4%

2012 Pres. Vote	Romney	184,162	(63%)	Obama	107,040	(36%)			
2016 Pres. Vote	Trump	193,029	(61%)	Clinton	112,691	(36%)	Johnson	9,353	(3%)

Athens, Eastern Atlanta Exurbs: The north and south wings of Gen. William Tecumseh Sherman's Union Army converged at Milledgeville, wrote author E.L. Doctorow in his novel The March: "And then the town of Milledgeville, empty and quiet, sat in its dishevelment, gusts of wind flying paper and brush against the sides of buildings and the leavings of coal fires scuttering in the street." The ghosts of the Civil War never left this region. Baldwin County's Milledgeville was the capital of Georgia from 1804 to 1868, and it is where Georgia legislators decided in 1861 to secede from the Union. Sherman's Army occupied the town and burned the state penitentiary, and the state capital was eventually moved to Atlanta.

It's no wonder that central Georgia and its tragedies have served as inspiration for several great Southern writers. Alice Walker, author of The Color Purple, was born in Eatonton, and her writing draws on family oral histories of life in rural Georgia. Also from Eatonton was Joel Chandler Harris, a freed slave who used the character "Uncle Remus" to write old southern stories with authentic folklore. Erskine Caldwell's scandalous best-seller, Tobacco Road, about an illiterate, Depression-racked farm family, was said to be influenced by his time living in the small town of Wrens in Jefferson County. Monroe was the site in 1946 of what may have been the last mob lynching in the nation; the crime was never prosecuted.

Today, the region's economy is dominated by small, high-tech manufacturing, Atlanta's urban sprawl, and the long reach of the University of Georgia in Athens, a campus filled with graceful Greek Revival mansions, boxwood gardens and magnolias. In Walton County, a locally based business powered up a one-megawatt community solar electricity generation farm. Baxalta, a global biotech firm, opened in 2018 a $1.2 billion plasma products manufacturing facility near Covington, creating about 1,500 jobs.

The 10th Congressional District runs from Barrow, Oglethorpe and Wilkes counties in the north to Baldwin, Washington and Jefferson counties in the south. Rapidly growing and affluent Columbia County — outside of Augusta -- is divided between this district and the 12th. The district takes in toward Atlanta Republican portions of fast-growing Gwinnett and Henry counties, and the well-to-do county of Oconee. With more than 300 miles of shoreline, the Lake Oconee area has gated communities and golf courses that beckon second-home buyers and retirees. Despite the overall economic growth in Georgia, some of the rural counties have been lagging. As the home of the state university, Clarke is the largest county in the district and its liberal base, with local debates about poverty and racism. Otherwise, this district is solidly Republican. Donald Trump's 61 percent of the vote in 2016 was similar to recent GOP presidential performances.

Barry Loudermilk (R)

Elected 2014, 3rd term, b. Dec 22, 1963; Riverdale; Community College of the Air Force (AL), A.A.S., 1987; Wayland Baptist University (TX), B.S., 1992; Baptist; Married (Desiree Loudermilk); 3 children; 2 grandchildren.

Military Career: U.S. Air Force 1984-1992 (Operation Desert Storm)

Elected Office: GA House, 2005-2010; GA Senate, 2011-2013.

Professional Career: Chairman, GA Republican party, 2001-2004; Business owner.

DC Office: 422 CHOB 20515, 202-225-2931, Fax: 202-225-2944, loudermilk.house.gov

State Offices: Atlanta, 770-429-1776; Cartersville, 770-429-1776; Woodstock, 770-429-1776.

Committees: *Financial Services*: Consumer Protection & Financial Institutions; Oversight & Investigations. *House Administration. Joint Library. Joint Printing.*

Group Ratings

	ADA	ACLU	AFL-CIO	LCV	ITI	COC	HAFA	ACU	CFG	FRC
2018	-	22%	-	0%	-	75%	89%	96%	78%	100%
2017	0%	C	6%	0%	C	92%	C	96%	96%	100%

Almanac Ratings 2017-18

	Economy	Social	Foreign	Composite
Liberal	4%	16%	3%	8%
Conservative	97%	84%	97%	92%

Key Votes of the 115th Congress

1. Obama-care revision	Y	5. Family planning regs	Y	9. Guantanamo prisoners	N
2. Tax Cuts	Y	6. Body cameras/immigration	N	10. Ground missiles, limit	N
3. Omnibus appropriations	N	7. Abortion ban	NV	11. Defense Dept. spending	Y
4. Dodd-Frank revision	Y	8. Concealed carry	Y	12. FISA rules	N

Election Results

Election	Name (Party)		Vote (%)		Cand. Spent	Ind. Exp. Support	Ind. Exp. Oppose
2018 General	Barry Loudermilk (R)		191,887	(62%)	$610,592		
	Flynn Broady Jr. (D)		118,653	(38%)	$23,432		
2018 Primary	Barry Loudermilk (R)			(100%)			

Prior winning percentages: 2016 (67%), 2014 (100%)

Republican Barry Loudermilk was elected in 2014 with the support of tea party groups in a lively primary. Following several legislative battles and personal traumas, his rhetoric softened and he increased his search for political common ground.

Loudermilk was born in Riverdale and got an associate degree in telecommunications technology from Air Force Community College and a bachelor of science in occupational education and information systems technology from Wayland Baptist University. After serving in the Air Force plus a stint in the cybersecurity business, he turned to politics. He chaired the Georgia Republican Party for four years. His decade as a state legislator included four years in the Senate, where he chaired the science and technology panel. He authored a book, And Then They Prayed, which features inspirational stories from American history.

The GOP primary in 2014 drew six candidates. Loudermilk and former Republican Rep. Bob Barr were the top two vote-getters in the primary, with 37 percent and 26 percent. In the runoff,. Barr, a former federal prosecutor, four-term House member, civil libertarian and Libertarian presidential candidate in 2008, played up his conservative bona fides, including his role in the 1998 impeachment proceedings against President Bill Clinton. Loudermilk, taking a sharp anti-establishment turn, cited Barr's Washington experience as a liability. He called Barr too soft on immigration and criticized him for backing Attorney General Eric Holder's nomination in 2009. Loudermilk trounced Barr in the runoff, 66%-34%. Loudermilk won without opposition in November — which once was rare for a freshman.

When the House Republican Conference met in November to organize for the new Congress, Loudermilk was one of three members who cast what he called a "principled vote" against John Boehner for another term as Speaker. He told the Cherokee Tribune that he was "probably punished" with his failure to get the committee assignment he had sought. By 2017, he had paid his penance and got seats on Financial Services and House Administration, two committees where House leaders have interests.

Loudermilk later took some heat from the right, after Boehner stepped down in October and he voted for Paul Ryan as the next Speaker. When Conservative radio host Glenn Beck challenged him for supporting a "Mitt Romney guy," Loudermilk said that Ryan would assert the congressional power of the purse with President Barack Obama. Following the 2016 election, Loudermilk called for an investigation of alleged Russian interference. Citing his background in cybersecurity, he told a reporter, "Whether it's the Russians, the Chinese or an ally of ours ... you have to have an investigation. It's not an indictment; it's a gathering of facts." In 2017, he dropped his membership in the Freedom Caucus, saying he did not have enough time, while increasing his activity with the more leadership-oriented Republican Study Committee.

Loudermilk survived an unusual array of life-threatening incidents: the May 2017 shooting at a congressional Republican baseball practice in Alexandria Virginia, an apparently random shooting in March 2018 while he and his wife were driving through the north Georgia mountains, plus train and car accidents that resulted in fatalities. Subsequently, he told the Atlanta Journal-Constitution, he sought a more civil approach to politics. He reached out for more bipartisanship on budget and banking issues. With Rep. Gerry Connolly, D-Va., he filed a bill to set customer-service standards for federal agencies.

In 2018, Loudermilk was easily reelected against Democrat Flynn Broady, a prosecutor in the Cobb County Solicitor General's Office and a former Army infantry sergeant in Iraq. A first-time candidate, Broady received scant party or fundraising backing.

GA-11: Northwestern Atlanta Suburbs   Cook Partisan Voting Index: R+17

Population		Race and Ethnicity		Income	
Total	744,447	White	67.1%	Median Income	$69,534
Land area (sq. miles)	1,071	Black	15.9%	District Income Rank	97
Pop/ sq mi	694.9	Latino	11.1%	Poverty Rate	10.8%
Born in State	44.5%	Asian	3.4%	With health insurance	86.4%
		Two or more races	2%	Cash public assistance	1.7%
Age Groups		Other	0.4%	Food stamp/SNAP	8.2%
Under 18	24.1%				
18-34	24.2%	**Education**		**Work**	
35-64	40.4%	H.S grad or less	31.7%	White Collar	11.3%
Over 64	11.3%	Some college	28%	Sales and Service	40.3%
		College Degree, 4 yr	26.4%	Blue Collar	16.9%
Military		Post grad	13.9%	Government	10.6%
Veteran/ Active Duty	7.8%				

2012 Pres. Vote	Romney	200,863	(67%)	Obama	94,634	(32%)			
2016 Pres. Vote	Trump	198,877	(60%)	Clinton	116,575	(35%)	Johnson	14,355	(4%)

Cherokee, Cobb: Marietta is one of Atlanta's largest suburbs. Its economic mainstay for many years was defense contractor Lockheed Martin, which built the F-22 jet fighter and the C-130 cargo plane. When the F-22 in 2009 became the first casualty of the Obama administration's decision to cut what it considered unnecessary weapons programs, that assembly line shut down in 2011. But layoffs at the Marietta plant were limited, chiefly because the Pentagon had ordered additional F-35 fighter jets, parts of which are built there. Prospects for Lockheed Martin and Marietta brightened in 2016, when the company won a contract for the C-130 Super Hercules airlift plane, which employs about 5,000 workers at its local plant. Nearby Dobbins Air Force Base, which had been confined to use by the military and Lockheed, has expanded its operations to include cargo flights. Aerospace is the largest manufacturing industry in Georgia. The WellStar Kennestone Regional Medical Center, a sprawling, 57-acre campus, is another major employer in Marietta.

The city retains far more racial and ethnic diversity than nearby counties: 32 percent of Marietta is African American, and 21 percent is Hispanic. The Atlanta Braves in 2017 moved from downtown to their new Sun Trust Park baseball stadium in close-in Cobb County, a short distance from the busy interchange of Interstates 75 and 285. Revenues from the stadium, plus nearby newly constructed commercial buildings, have boosted county finances by about $20 million annually. Cherokee is the fastest-growing county in metro Atlanta, with a 19 percent increase from 2010 to 2018. Bartow County, to the northwest of Marietta, grew 32 percent from 2000 to 2010, though the growth slowed to 5 percent in the next seven years and it remains largely a bedroom community. The county seat of Cartersville hosts the Smithsonian-affiliated Booth Western Art Museum, which has a large collection of Western American and Civil War-era art.

The 11th Congressional District of Georgia is anchored by Marietta, which is the county seat and the largest city in Cobb, and takes in all of Bartow and Cherokee counties. Cobb is the final remaining majority-white county in metro Atlanta, though for only a few more years: whites dropped to 52 percent in 2017 while blacks increased to 29 percent. Its once solidly Republican vote has shifted — like many suburbs across the nation. The northern tip of Fulton County, includes part of Buckhead, with the governor's mansion. The district's 67 percent vote for Mitt Romney in 2012 slipped to 60 percent for Donald Trump in 2016. In Bartow and Cherokee combined, Trump drew 74 percent support. In the parts of Cobb and Fulton in the 11th, he got about 50 percent.

Rick Allen (R)

Elected 2014, 3rd term, b. Nov 07, 1951; Augusta; Auburn University School of Architecture and Fine Arts (GA), B.S., 1973; Methodist; Married (Robin Reeve); 4 children; 12 grandchildren.

Professional Career: Founder, R.W. Allen & Associates, 1976.

DC Office: 2400 RHOB 20515, 202-225-2823, Fax: 202-225-3377, allen.house.gov

State Offices: Augusta, 706-228-1980; Dublin, 478-272-4030; Statesboro, 912-243-9452; Vidalia, 912-403-3311.

Committees: *Agriculture*: Conservation & Forestry; General Farm Commodities & Risk Management. *Education & Labor*: Early Childhood, Elementary & Secondary Education (RMM); Health, Employment, Labor & Pensions.

Group Ratings

	ADA	ACLU	AFL-CIO	LCV	ITI	COC	HAFA	ACU	CFG	FRC
2018	-	7%	-	0%	-	75%	68%	84%	62%	100%
2017	0%	C	5%	0%	C	93%	C	93%	85%	100%

Almanac Ratings 2017-18

	Economy	Social	Foreign	Composite
Liberal	3%	3%	0%	2%
Conservative	97%	97%	100%	98%

Key Votes of the 115th Congress

1. Obama-care revision	Y	5. Family planning regs	Y	9. Guantanamo prisoners	N
2. Tax Cuts	Y	6. Body cameras/immigration	N	10. Ground missiles, limit	N
3. Omnibus appropriations	N	7. Abortion ban	Y	11. Defense Dept. spending	Y
4. Dodd-Frank revision	Y	8. Concealed carry	Y	12. FISA rules	Y

Election Results

Election	Name (Party)	Vote (%)	Cand. Spent	Ind. Exp. Support	Ind. Exp. Oppose
2018 General	Rick Allen (R)................................. 148,986	(59%)	$1,066,182		
	Francys Johnson (D)........................... 101,503	(41%)	$254,040		
2018 Primary	Rick Allen (R)..................................... 37,776	(46%)			
	Francys Johnson (D)............................ 16,991	(21%)			
	Eugene Yu (R)............................ 11,938	(15%)			
	Robert Ingham (D)........................... ... 10,011	(12%)			
	Trent Nesmith (D)............................ 5,139	(6%)			

Prior winning percentages: 2016 (62%), 2014 (55%)

Republican Rick Allen, elected in 2014 when he defeated Georgia's only remaining white Democrat in the House, focused on agricultural and education issues in his committee work. He was typically a leadership loyalist and made few waves.

A native of Augusta, Allen graduated from Auburn University with a bachelor of science degree in building construction. After spending three years as a project manager with a local builder, he founded R.W. Allen & Associates, a construction company he has operated since 1976 in the Augusta and Athens areas. His experience as a small business owner and job creator, plus his inexperience in government office, formed the centerpiece of his congressional campaign.

Allen had sought the Republican nomination in 2012, but finished second in the primary. Two years later, he spent nearly a million dollars of his own money and won the five-way primary with 54 percent of the vote. In the general election, Allen criticized Rep. John Barrow — one of the few remaining fiscally conservative Blue Dog Democrats in the House — for hewing too closely to President Barack Obama's agenda, while touting his own conservative credentials. Allen also highlighted his support for the Second Amendment, though Barrow boasted an A+ rating and endorsement from the National Rifle Association. With little daylight between the candidates on many issues, the Republican strategy focused on the national Democratic Party. Barrow outspent Allen $3.5 million to $2.5 million, but the nearly $4 million in national GOP assistance more than made up the difference. Allen won handily, 55%-45%. Barrow won Richmond (Augusta), the largest county, with 66 percent of the vote. Allen took 71 percent in Columbia, the next-largest county, and all but two of the remaining 17 counties.

Allen entered the House with more mainstream Republican views and style than other GOP newcomers. In 2016, the House passed his bill to prevent the Internal Revenue Service from targeting citizens who exercise their First Amendment rights. Allen cited recent cases in which tea party and other conservative groups were singled out when they applied for tax-exempt status.

On the Agriculture Committee, Allen claimed credit for winning support of a cost-sharing program for cotton ginning. In 2018, he was a member of the House-Senate conference committee that resolved final details of the farm bill. He sought unsuccessfully to increase work requirements for food-stamp recipients, but cited provisions that strengthened risk-protection for producers. On the Education and the Workforce Committee, he contributed job-promoting provisions to the Career-Technical Education bill, which also was enacted that year. The increased cyber activity at Fort Gordon, he said, will create "the Silicon Valley of the South."

Allen faced a political balancing act. From the left, he was condemned by gay-rights advocates for delivering at a closed-door meeting of the House Republican Conference an opening prayer that referred harshly to homosexuals. With his Main Street business views, Allen supported extension of the Export-Import Bank. That led to attack ads against him from Americans for Prosperity, an arm of the conservative Koch brothers. But tea party groups have failed to wage a significant primary challenge against him.

Democratic challenger Patricia Carpenter McCracken made no "known appearances" to oppose Allen during the 2016 campaign, The Augusta Chronicle reported. Allen was reelected, 62%-38%. In 2018, Democrat Francis Johnson, former president of the Georgia NAACP, ran a more vigorous campaign and said that he would seek to improve the quality of life in rural Georgia. Johnson said Republicans "promised the world," but failed to deliver improved health care. Allen won, 59%-41%, and took every county except for Richmond, which he lost 2-to-1.

GA-12: East Georgia   Cook Partisan Voting Index: R+9

Population		Race and Ethnicity		Income	
Total	713,701	White	55.4%	Median Income	$42,825
Land area (sq. miles)	8,185	Black	34.7%	District Income Rank	395
Pop/ sq mi	87.2	Latino	5.9%	Poverty Rate	22.1%
Born in State	67.1%	Asian	1.7%	With health insurance	85.6%
		Two or more races	1.7%	Cash public assistance	1.9%
Age Groups		Other	0.6%	Food stamp/SNAP	18.2%
Under 18	23.9%				
18-34	25.8%	**Education**		**Work**	
35-64	37%	H.S grad or less	50%	White Collar	13.3%
Over 64	13.3%	Some college	29.2%	Sales and Service	42.2%
		College Degree, 4 yr	12.6%	Blue Collar	25.6%
Military		Post grad	8.2%	Government	20.6%
Veteran/ Active Duty	12.4%				

2012 Pres. Vote	Romney	148,622	(55%)	Obama	117,131	(44%)			
2016 Pres. Vote	Trump	152,204	(57%)	Clinton	108,937	(41%)	Johnson	6,534	(2%)

Augusta: Upriver from Savannah is the city of Augusta. Founded in 1735 as a fur-trading post, it has been home since 1835 to the Medical College of Georgia, now part of Georgia Regents University, a public academic health center. It has become a manufacturing hub for big companies like Procter & Gamble, International Paper and Dart Container and has gained prominence for military cyber operations.

Many know the city best as the site of Augusta National Golf Club, a private club where the Masters Tournament is held every April, amid azaleas in bloom, reverence for its traditions by both players and spectators, and an annual economic impact in the tens of millions of dollars. Some of that beauty has come at a price. Since about 2000, the club has spent more than $40 million to bulldoze modest homes in an adjacent neighborhood into a parking lot. The exceptions remain two stubborn families, who are lonely for 51 weeks a year, like the location and haven't succumbed to the offers for their modest bungalows. When they or their heirs agree to the inevitable deal, they will pocket several times the price received by the homebuyers who sold early.

The 12th Congressional District takes in Augusta's Richmond County and part of neighboring Columbia County. They include half the total population for the district. Richmond is 57 percent African American, while Columbia is 18 percent. From 2010 to 2015, Columbia grew from 124,000 to 152,000; Richmond had virtually no change at 202,000. In Augusta, the Fort Gordon Army base is home to 12,000 troops, 4,600 civilians and the Army Signal Corps. The base is the headquarters for the cyber command of the Army, plus a National Security Agency facility. They are designed to work with other federal agencies to develop and field cyberspace capabilities, modernize networks and improve sensors and tools for defensive operations. In 2018, the Georgia Technology Authority opened a cyber center to promote collaboration with the military and others. In Waynesboro, Georgia Power continued construction on its much-delayed Vogtle plant, the last nuclear power plant under construction in the nation. The district includes Vidalia, home of the famous sweet onion, a state-owned brand harvested in only 20 counties, with help from guest workers. Its 35 percent black population is the largest of any of the 10 Republican-held districts in Georgia.

In 2016, Donald Trump won the presidential vote, 57%-41%, a slight increase in the Republican vote from previous presidential elections. The two largest counties in the 12th went in very different directions. Hillary Clinton won Richmond, the Democratic core, 65%-32%. Trump won Columbia, 67%-29%. He won all but one of the other 17 counties in the 12th.

David Scott (D)

Elected 2002, 9th term, b. Jun 27, 1945; Aynor, SC; University of Florida, B.A., 1967; University of Pennsylvania Wharton School of Business Aresty Institute, M.B.A., 1969; Baptist; Married (Alfredia Aaron Scott); 2 children; 2 grandchildren.

Elected Office: GA House, 1975-1982; GA Senate, 1983-2002.

Professional Career: Founder & President, Dayn-Mark Advertising, 1979-2002.

DC Office: 225 CHOB 20515, 202-225-2939, Fax: 202-225-4628, davidscott.house.gov

State Offices: Jonesboro, 770-210-5073; Smyrna, 770-432-5405.

Committees: *Agriculture*: Commodity Exchanges, Energy & Credit (Chmn); General Farm Commodities & Risk Management. *Financial Services*: Consumer Protection & Financial Institutions; Investor Protection, Entrepreneurship & Capital Markets.

Group Ratings

	ADA	ACLU	AFL-CIO	LCV	ITI	COC	HAFA	ACU	CFG	FRC
2018	-	82%	-	86%	-	82%	8%	13%	16%	0%
2017	85%	C	97%	89%	C	62%	C	4%	0%	0%

Almanac Ratings 2017-18

	Economy	Social	Foreign	Composite
Liberal	77%	97%	73%	82%
Conservative	23%	4%	28%	18%

Key Votes of the 115th Congress

1. Obama-care revision	N	5. Family planning regs	N	9. Guantanamo prisoners	N
2. Tax Cuts	N	6. Body cameras/immigration	Y	10. Ground missiles, limit	Y
3. Omnibus appropriations	Y	7. Abortion ban	N	11. Defense Dept. spending	Y
4. Dodd-Frank revision	Y	8. Concealed carry	N	12. FISA rules	Y

Election Results

Election	Name (Party)	Vote (%)		Cand. Spent	Ind. Exp. Support	Ind. Exp. Oppose
2018 General	David Scott (D)	223,157	(76%)	$1,050,481		
	David Callahan (R)	69,760	(24%)	$24,672		
2018 Primary	David Scott (D)		(100%)			

Prior winning percentages: 2016 (100%), 2014 (100%), 2012 (72%), 2010 (69%), 2008 (69%), 2006 (69%), 2004 (100%), 2002 (60%)

Democrat David Scott, first elected in 2002, is distinctly more of a centrist than most other members of the Congressional Black Caucus. He gets along well with many Republican colleagues and has been a force for bipartisanship. Scott often works on issues that go beyond race — chiefly, agriculture and banking.

Born in rural South Carolina, Scott is the son of a minister and grandson of a deacon. During his middle school years, his family moved to tony Scarsdale New York, where his parents took jobs as a chauffeur and housekeeper for a wealthy family. Scott was the only African American in his otherwise all-white school. He graduated from Florida A&M University, then did an internship at the Labor Department in Washington. There he met George Taylor, an authority in labor-management relations who encouraged the bright young man to apply to the prestigious Wharton School at the University of Pennsylvania, where Scott earned his MBA. He moved to Atlanta and in 1974 was elected to the Georgia House. In 1982, he won election to the state Senate, where he served for 20 years and chaired the Rules Committee. From 1979 to 2002, he owned Dayn-Mark Advertising, which creates and places radio, television and print ads. The firm has been operated by his wife and two daughters.

In 2002, Scott ran for the newly created 13th District, which was heavily Democratic. Four other Democrats ran, the best known of whom was former state party Chairman David Worley, who nearly defeated Republican Rep. Newt Gingrich in 1990. If voters didn't know Scott as a state legislator, most knew of his campaign co-chairman: Henry Aaron, the Hall of Fame slugger and Atlanta-area icon, who is Scott's brother-in-law. Scott brought his advertising expertise, plastering the interstate highways with eye-catching billboards. His chief competitors, Worley and state Sen. Greg Hecht, both white, ran ads attacking each other. Scott won the primary with 54 percent of the vote. He won the general election, 60%-40%.

As a freshman, Scott was one of seven Democrats to vote for final passage of President George W. Bush's tax cut, and one of 16 to vote for the prescription drug benefit under Medicare. He split with most of his party by voting for a constitutional amendment to ban same-sex marriage. In recent years, Scott has become a more reliable party vote, but he has had no reluctance to go his own way. In 2016, he urged President Barack Obama to "stop pussyfooting around, get a sense of urgency and declare war" on Islamic terrorism. "What the hell does it make sense for us to have the most powerful military in the world and we don't use it to protect the American people?" he asked.

On the Financial Services Committee, Scott initially opposed the bailout of the financial markets. After Chairman Barney Frank promised to address the Black Caucus' call for additional protections for homeowners facing foreclosure, Scott switched his vote to support the revised version in 2010. In 2018, he was part of the bipartisan coalition that enacted an easing of the regulations in the 2010 law.

On the Agriculture Committee, he is the second-ranking Democrat on the panel and has been the top Democrat on multiple subcommittees. At the Senate confirmation hearings for Agriculture Secretary Sonny Perdue — with whom he served in the state Senate — Scott lavished praise on him for his role, as governor, in changing the state flag. With the Democratic takeover in 2019, Scott became chairman of the Commodity Exchanges, Energy and Credit Subcommittee, which had been chaired by fellow Georgia Rep. Austin Scott, a Republican. On the farm bill that was enacted in 2018, he secured agriculture scholarships for historically black colleges and universities. Scott led the successful opposition to work requirements for food-stamp recipients, which he said were "racist" and "mean-spirited."

Scott has been an active presence in his district, sponsoring health and job fairs as well as "help for homeowners" events giving constituents the ability to ask questions of federal housing officials. He has been the subject of several unflattering stories about back taxes he owed on his home and business. He attracted both primary and general election challenges in 2008 and 2010. But none of his opponents held Scott below 60 percent of the vote. In 2018, he easily defeated his first Republican challenger since 2012.

He attracted attention at home in 2016 when he endorsed the reelection of Republican Sen. Johnny Isakson. "He's my friend. He's my partner," Scott said in a radio interview. They have known each other since they were junior members in the state House. Rejecting the calls of some Georgia Democrats to eliminate the Confederate statues on Stone Mountain, Scott advocated new sculptures that explained slavery and the root causes of the Civil War. "Tell the black man's struggle, how he overcame," he told The Atlanta Journal-Constitution. "We can't do that if we obliterate the Confederacy or the Civil War as if it didn't exist. It's a part of our history."

GA-13: Southwestern Atlanta Exurbs   **Cook Partisan Voting Index: D+20**

Population		Race and Ethnicity		Income	
Total	740,677	White	26.6%	Median Income	$55,060
Land area (sq. miles)	715	Black	58%	District Income Rank	227
Pop/ sq mi	1036	Latino	10.7%	Poverty Rate	16.1%
Born in State	50.7%	Asian	2.6%	With health insurance	84.1%
		Two or more races	1.8%	Cash public assistance	1.8%
Age Groups		Other	0.3%	Food stamp/SNAP	16.8%
Under 18	27.2%				
18-34	22.3%	**Education**		**Work**	
35-64	40.4%	H.S grad or less	40.7%	White Collar	10.1%
Over 64	10.1%	Some college	31.1%	Sales and Service	42.8%
		College Degree, 4 yr	17.7%	Blue Collar	23.9%
Military		Post grad	10.5%	Government	14.9%
Veteran/ Active Duty	9.4%				

2012 Pres. Vote	Obama	202,828	(69%)	Romney	87,742	(30%)		
2016 Pres. Vote	Clinton	213,805	(71%)	Trump	80,086	(27%)	Johnson	7,136	(2%)

Clayton, Cobb: In the 1960s, Atlanta's blacks were clustered in ghetto neighborhoods on the south and west sides of the city. The north side and the suburbs in every direction were heavily white. The great landmarks of the civil rights movement, and the headquarters of many of its leading organizations, were in the central city. Today, metro Atlanta's thriving black middle class has moved outward in almost every direction in one of the nation's fastest-growing metro areas — to DeKalb County to the east, to Clayton directly south of the city, to southwest Fulton, to Cobb and Douglas counties to the north and west.

These substantial population shifts, however, have not broken longstanding patterns in housing and education. "Despite blacks' substantial inroads into suburban areas further from the central city, trends among non-Hispanic white households muted the impact of this suburbanization on region-wide segregation levels," Karen Pooley wrote in a 2105 study on "Segregation's New Geography," in the journal Southern Spaces. For the metro Atlanta area, "nearly all of the counties adding non-Hispanic black households between 2000 and 2010 lost non-Hispanic whites. ... As a result, although metro Atlanta's blacks 'are less geographically concentrated, less confined to areas near the urban core, and scattered more widely around the metropolitan area,' they remain highly segregated."

The Hartsfield-Jackson Atlanta International Airport is the busiest in the world, with 104 million passengers arriving and departing in 2017. (Not all of them are on Friday afternoons.) It also has become a huge revenue source for the area, with its many suppliers. Local interests laid out a blueprint to turn the area surrounding the airport into an "aerotropolis," with an "airport city" that would include a corporate center, autonomous rapid-transit systems and a corridor of green trails. Planners envision the area as a central business district, which covers 165 square miles and has 300,000 residents. The transformation could take decades, but "significant change" is expected in the next 20 years. One of their objectives is to create the kind of development south of Atlanta that has taken place elsewhere in the metro area and surrounding large airports elsewhere in the nation. Warehousing is a rapidly growing industry surrounding the airport.

The 13th Congressional District of Georgia is a collection of suburban areas that have attracted Atlanta's African-American middle class. It includes most of Clayton County, which is 72 percent African American and 13 percent Latino. It takes in all of Douglas County, and parts of Cobb, Fulton, Fayette and Henry counties. Clayton, Cobb, Douglas and Fulton each have similar shares of the voters in the 13th. The airport is just across the district line in the 5th. In 2017, Six Flags theme parks in Cobb generated more than $372 million economic impact in the district. In Fayetteville, Pinewood Studios — with 18 sound stages on 700 acres, and growing — is one of the largest film and entertainment studios outside of California. The 13th is a black-majority district and solidly Democratic. In 2016, Hillary Clinton won the district, 71%-26%.

Tom Graves (R)

Elected 2010, 5th full term, b. Feb 03, 1970; St. Petersburg, FL; University of Georgia, B.B.A., 1993; Baptist; Married (Julie Howard Graves); 3 children.

Elected Office: GA House, 2003-2010.

Professional Career: Founder, Tough Turf Land Sculpting; Owner, Southern Vision; Real estate developer.

DC Office: 2078 RHOB 20515, 202-225-5211, Fax: 202-225-8272, tomgraves.house.gov

State Offices: Dalton, 706-226-5320; Rome, 706-290-1776.

Committees: *Appropriations:* Commerce, Justice, Science & Related Agencies; Financial Services & General Government (RMM); Labor, Health & Human Services, Education & Related Agencies. *Select Committee on the Modernization of Congress (RMM).*

Group Ratings

	ADA	ACLU	AFL-CIO	LCV	ITI	COC	HAFA	ACU	CFG	FRC
2018	-	7%	-	0%	-	83%	87%	96%	62%	100%
2017	0%	C	3%	3%	C	93%	C	96%	90%	100%

Almanac Ratings 2017-18

	Economy	Social	Foreign	Composite
Liberal	3%	7%	0%	3%
Conservative	97%	93%	100%	97%

Key Votes of the 115th Congress

1. Obama-care revision	Y	5. Family planning regs	Y	9. Guantanamo prisoners	N
2. Tax Cuts	Y	6. Body cameras/immigration	N	10. Ground missiles, limit	N
3. Omnibus appropriations	Y	7. Abortion ban	Y	11. Defense Dept. spending	Y
4. Dodd-Frank revision	Y	8. Concealed carry	Y	12. FISA rules	Y

Election Results

Election	Name (Party)	Vote (%)	Cand. Spent	Ind. Exp. Support	Ind. Exp. Oppose
2018 General	Tom Graves (R)................................. 175,743	(77%)			
	Steven Foster (D)........................ 53,981	(23%)		$6,965	
2018 Primary	Tom Graves (R)...	(100%)			

Prior winning percentages: 2016 (100%), 2014 (100%), 2012 (73%), 2010 (100%), 2010 special (56%)

Republican Tom Graves, who won a special election in 2010, transitioned from a maverick who was a periodic annoyance to House GOP leaders to an inside player as chairman of an Appropriations subcommittee. Following the 2018 election, he fell short — for now, at least -- in his audacious bid to wield more clout over federal spending as the senior Republican on Appropriations. He remained well-positioned as a leader of House conservatives.

Graves is from the small town of Ranger, with fewer than 100 people, where he still resides with his wife, Julie Graves, and their three children on a farm. Growing up, he lived in a single-wide trailer on a tar and gravel road, the son of a Georgia Power laborer who told him to "dream big and then work hard." Graves took out loans and worked to pay for college, becoming the first in his family to earn a degree, in business administration from the University of Georgia. After graduation, Graves worked for Federated Department Stores, now Macy's, as an asset recovery specialist. He saved his money and, in 1995, bought a small landscaping business. Graves eventually sold off portions of the company to begin investing in real estate.

He met his future wife at Roswell Street Baptist Church, and she was instrumental in getting him involved in the anti-abortion movement. He has said he opposes abortion "without exception," including cases in which the mother's life is at stake. In 2001, he and Julie, the founding president of the Gordon County Right to Life chapter, successfully opposed the construction of an abortion clinic in the area. The campaign propelled Graves to a seat on the county board and later in the Georgia House, where he served more than seven years. Of his political philosophy, he says, "there is a spectrum of conservatism from fiscal to social ... and I'm a conservative all the way across the board."

In the special election to succeed Nathan Deal, who resigned to run for governor, Graves bested Republican state Sen. Lee Hawkins, 56%-44%, in a June 2010 runoff for the remainder of Deal's term. The two clashed again in the primary for a full term. Graves supported constitutional amendments to balance the budget and to give the president line-item veto power over spending bills. Hawkins cast Graves as "out of touch" and attacked him for a bank loan that had gone into default. But he could not overcome Graves' backing by national Republican organizations, House Minority Leader John Boehner and local tea party groups. Graves won the August runoff, 55%-45%, earning a full term without Democratic opposition.

In Washington, Graves joined the Tea Party Caucus and got a slot on Appropriations — two steps not always viewed as consistent with each other. In his early years, Graves consistently voted to buck the leadership on spending bills. Senior House Republicans, including some in leadership, reportedly sought to single out Graves for punishment by stripping his Appropriations seat.

In 2013, Graves led a rebellion against Boehner's strategy over a bill to fund government operations. With the clock ticking toward an Oct. 1 deadline to pass the measure, Graves proposed an amendment to stop funding for the Affordable Care Act. Boehner and other GOP leaders opposed tying the two into one take-it-or-leave-it bill, but Graves drummed up support from 60 fellow conservatives. Under pressure, Boehner backed down. As expected, the Democratic-controlled Senate voted 54-44 to strip the health care provision from the government funding bill. The subsequent stalemate led to the first partial government shutdown in 17 years. Graves said that his constituents supported him, and that the Obama administration botched implementation of the new law.

Meanwhile, he sought to head the Republican Study Committee and won the endorsement of the conservative group's founders, normally considered key to getting the nod. But the more senior Steve Scalise of Louisiana also sought the job, citing his ability to work with the leadership and his success in passing bills. Scalise petitioned for a vote of the full membership and pulled off an upset. For Scalise, that was a big step in his move to become a GOP leader.

In 2015, Graves gained a different sort of insider position: chairman of the Legislative Branch Subcommittee on Appropriations. On accepting the position, he pledged to use it as "a prime opportunity to walk the conservative talk." He successfully opposed an amendment to increase public accessibility to reports of the Congressional Research Service.

In 2017, Graves took over as chairman of the Financial Services Subcommittee, where the portfolio included implementation of the Dodd-Frank financial services law. He worked with Republican leaders on alternatives to combine all spending into a single bill to show their commitment to fiscal discipline. His proposal was quietly abandoned following uncertainty over whether it could pass. Graves griped that the House was continuing the status quo.

In 2018, he made a point of cutting $585 million from the funds that had been allotted to his subcommittee. He said that the savings in the bill, which the House passed in July, would be deposited in a "fund for America's kids and grandkids" and would be spent only when the federal deficit was eliminated. (The deficit for fiscal 2018 was $779 billion.). His subcommittee bill, combined with other spending measures, was delayed by deadlock over other issues, notably funding of President Donald Trump's proposed border wall with Mexico. Early that year, Graves showed his displeasure by urging that Republicans replace Speaker Paul Ryan, who had announced his plan to retire. That idea, too, went nowhere.

Graves took his unhappiness with the appropriations deadlock into his bid to succeed committee Chairman Rodney Frelinghuysen of New Jersey, who had announced his retirement early in 2018. That was a bold move for a relatively junior member, who was the 11th in seniority among committee Republicans, with four senior members seeking the top post. His active campaigning, including efforts to curry favor with Republican Leader Kevin McCarthy, stirred resentment. "Senior appropriators suspicious of Graves say that's simply not the way it's done on a committee long governed by seniority and experience," Politico reported.

When Republicans assembled following the election, with their loss of the House majority downgrading the appropriations post to ranking minority member, they selected Rep. Kay Granger of Texas. She had several advantages, including seniority, gender and her larger home-state delegation.

Graves has drawn some negative headlines at home. He was accused of hypocrisy in 2012 when The Atlanta Journal-Constitution reported that the Federal Deposit Insurance Corporation bailed out Graves and Georgia Senate Majority Leader Chip Rogers for about half of a $2.3 million loan the two men had received five years earlier to rehabilitate a North Georgia hotel. The dispute was settled out of court.

In 2018, he was reelected, 77%-23%, against Democrat Steven Foster. The challenger, who was serving a prison sentence on Election Day following his conviction for drunk driving, reportedly had been the owner of an "adults-only, clothing-optional lifestyle retreat" in north Georgia. For Graves, that background for his opponent might have reinforced his reluctant status in the political establishment.

GA-14: Northwest Georgia   Cook Partisan Voting Index: R+27

Population		Race and Ethnicity		Income	
Total	704,946	White	77.1%	Median Income	$48,731
Land area (sq. miles)	3,623	Black	8.7%	District Income Rank	330
Pop/ sq mi	194.6	Latino	11.3%	Poverty Rate	15.8%
Born in State	59%	Asian	1%	With health insurance	85.1%
		Two or more races	1.5%	Cash public assistance	3%
Age Groups		Other	0.3%	Food stamp/SNAP	14.1%
Under 18	25.1%				
18-34	21.5%	**Education**		**Work**	
35-64	39.4%	H.S grad or less	53.8%	White Collar	14%
Over 64	14%	Some college	28.8%	Sales and Service	39.6%
		College Degree, 4 yr	11%	Blue Collar	32.7%
Military		Post grad	6.4%	Government	12.5%
Veteran/ Active Duty	7.9%				

2012 Pres. Vote	Romney	170,385	(73%)	Obama	58,886	(25%)			
2016 Pres. Vote	Trump	191,849	(75%)	Clinton	56,513	(22%)	Johnson	7,510	(3%)

Rome, Dalton: Northwest Georgia was the home of the Cherokee Nation before the tribe was sent west in the 1830s on the Trail of Tears. It has been manufacturing country for the past century. Hundreds of textile mills and dozens of carpet mills once clustered near the supply of natural cotton and along the railroad lines heading southwest at the base of the southern Appalachian chain. The late 19th-century boosters of the New South hailed factories as the vanguard of technological progress. The plants produced a higher standard of living than did the farms on this stubborn land. But the mills put scant premium on education or the cultivation of civic virtues and did little to bring in higher-skilled work. All-white hiring practices maintained racial segregation in mostly white north Georgia.

Today, this area has developed a different kind of economy, as metro Atlanta has spread out along highways to the north and west. There are sprawling subdivisions in what once were mill towns. Floyd County is home to an auto parts manufacturing cluster. To the north in Dalton, the traditional craft of tufted bedspread handiwork was transformed into a carpet industry so large that at the turn of the 21st century, four Georgia companies — three of them in Dalton -- produced most of the nation's tufted carpet. The shortage of workers resulted in the arrival of many Hispanics, many of them illegal immigrants. In recent years, recession and automation have reduced the workforce in the carpet industry. But the industry continues to employ more than 50,000 workers in Georgia.

The immigration debate has moved front and center in Dalton. The stricter enforcement and tough rhetoric of President Donald Trump raised local concerns over the shortage of workers, even though most employees had legal status and many had lived in the area for decades; a recent state law required employers to use an online system to verify that workers were legal. Business leaders who had opposed the policies of President Barack Obama nonetheless welcomed the illegal immigrants who had been brought to town. In early 2018, NPR reported, the carpet companies had "too many open jobs, and not enough applicants to fill them." Hispanics remain almost half the population of Dalton; they include several thousand so-called DACA immigrants, who are undocumented children. At Dalton State University, Hispanics were 25 percent of the student body in 2016.

The 14th Congressional District covers the northwest corner of Georgia, including Dalton-based Whitfield County. Chattanooga Tennessee's metro area has expanded across the state line into places like Chickamauga and LaFayette in Walker and Catoosa counties. It takes in Floyd County and its largest city, Rome, as well as Paulding County, which extends beyond Cobb County in exurban Atlanta. Fast-growing Paulding is the population center with about one-fourth of the voters, followed by Floyd and Whitfield. Politically, the 14th is among the safest Republican districts in the nation. In 2016, Donald Trump won 75 percent of the vote.

HAWAII

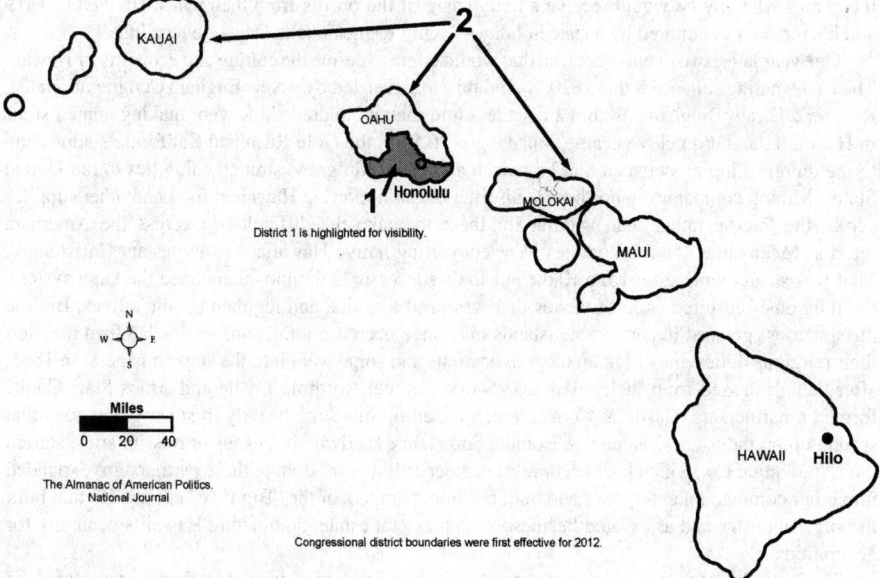

KAUAI

2

OAHU

1 Honolulu

District 1 is highlighted for visibility.

MOLOKAI

MAUI

N
W E
S

Miles
0   20   40

The Almanac of American Politics.
National Journal

HAWAII   Hilo

Congressional district boundaries were first effective for 2012.

America's state in the middle of the Pacific is geographically the most remote archipelago in the world, but it is hardly isolated. It has long been a crossroads of trade between the Asian and American continents, and it has been a vital military base for the United States since before the attack on Pearl Harbor in 1941. More recently, it produced a president, Barack Obama.

Thrust up from the ocean by volcanoes, Hawaii is geologically some of the youngest land on earth, and it continues to undergo transformations. Polynesians sailing double-hulled canoes from the Marquesas Islands nearly 2,000 miles away were the first humans to inhabit Hawaii roughly 1,600 years ago. Over time, several small kingdoms developed across the islands, each ruled by an ali'i nui (a grand or great chief). The islands' insulation from the Western world ended when British Captain James Cook, on an exploration to find the Northwest Passage, landed on Kauai in 1778. He would also die in Hawaii on a return visit a year later after a confrontation with natives. Toward the end of the century the most powerful ali'i nui, Kamehameha, began a campaign of conquest, and by 1810, all the islands were united into one kingdom under his rule. With unification came foreign trade: Pacific fur traders who stopped off recognized that Hawaiian sandalwood would be popular in the markets of the Far East where it was prized for ornamental use and burning as incense. As king, Kamehameha controlled the harvesting of sandalwood, and by 1811 he was reaching deals with Boston maritime merchants whereby he would receive a hefty share of the profits from their sales. He died in 1819 and his memory is honored by a state holiday — King Kamehameha Day — every June 11.

One year later, two events occurred that would come to define the culture and economy of Hawaii. The first whaling ship arrived in 1820. So did missionaries, led by a New England Congregationalist, Reverend Hiram Bingham. Within a decade, more than a hundred ships were making annual stops in Honolulu, and it quickly became a thriving port. With the Gold Rush and California's admission to the union, shipping between San Francisco and Honolulu grew, strengthening ties to the United States. Mining companies in northern California began importing Hawaiian food and other supplies across the Pacific rather than waiting for them to make the difficult trip across the American interior. Meanwhile, the missionaries were converting native Hawaiians to Protestant Christianity. That was steady work after King Kamehameha's successor, Liholiho, abandoned the kapu system, the religiously inspired code of taboos that was used to guide and regulate people's lives. But the missionaries' greatest impact on the islands may have been economic, not spiritual. When they left their religious duties, they took up other avocations and some went into the sugar business. In 1851, after being released from their missionary work, Samuel Northrup Castle and Amos Starr Cooke formed a partnership, Castle & Cooke, which ended up investing heavily in sugar plantations that sprung up on the islands. Samuel Alexander and Henry Baldwin, both sons of missionaries, started the Haiku Sugar Co., which later become Alexander & Baldwin. Both of these partnerships expanded into other commercial enterprises and both became members of the "Big Five" companies that built the sugar industry and associated businesses such as real estate, dominating Hawaii's economy for generations.

The boom in sugar required the importation of labor, because a series of epidemics devastated the native population as it came into increasing contact with Westerners. Soon, contract workers from China and Japan were coming to Hawaii. American sugar interests helped elect King Kalakaua to the Hawaiian throne over the British-leaning Queen Emma in 1874. Kalakaua returned the favor and sought a trade agreement with the United States in 1876 that allowed the duty-free sale of Hawaiian sugar in the states. But American planters and businessmen eventually tired of the caprices of the royal family and in January 1893, with the help of the Marines, ousted Queen Liliuokalani from the Iolani Palace and called on the United States to annex Hawaii. President Grover Cleveland demurred, and Hawaii for five years was a republic until President William McKinley annexed it. This history is a source of regret for some. An Onipa'a ceremony remembering Liliuokalani's overthrow was staged by John Waihee, the first governor of Native Hawaiian descent, in January 1993, with the American flag conspicuously absent. Later that year, Congress passed and President Bill Clinton signed an apology for the overthrow of Liliuokalani 100 years before. In 2009, Hawaii staged a commemoration, not a celebration, of the 50th anniversary of statehood.

The Japanese attack on Pearl Harbor led the United States to enter World War II, which brought a massive influx of U.S. armed forces to Hawaii. Military construction boomed. The overall population of the islands doubled to 858,000 by 1944, spurring greater demand for retail services and consumer products. After the war, the economy cooled as the nation demobilized, but with the Korean conflict in the early 1950s, there was another military build-up. The many sailors and troops who transited Hawaii on their way to the front lines, or who were stationed there, invariably shared its charms with family and friends when they returned home. By the 1960s, tourism had displaced sugar, pineapples and other agricultural products as Hawaii's leading industry. From statehood in 1959 to 1990, Hawaii's economic engine roared.

Then Hawaii's economy stumbled. The end of the Cold War brought a decline in military spending, and work at the shipyard at Pearl Harbor slowed significantly. In Japan, a "lost decade" led vacationers to cut back their trips to Hawaii, as Japanese real estate investors stopped bidding up and buying up properties in Oahu.

Hawaii also saw the demise of its plantation agriculture. Once, one-fifth of the sugar consumed in the United States came from Hawaii, but competition from lower-cost international producers and occasional environmental concerns closer to home changed all that. In 2016, the Hawaiian Commercial and Sugar Co. closed its doors after 180 years, laying off all 675 workers at its 36,000-acre plantation on Maui and marking a definitive end to the local sugar industry. By then, Del Monte had already picked its last pineapples on the islands. By 2015, a disused Dole cannery was being prepared for a new, more boutique existence as a 2,000-square-foot factory for processing Waialua-grown cacao, part of a boomlet of artisanal chocolate in the state; only Hawaii among the 50 states has the right climate conditions for growing cacao. If such ventures succeed, they will join such specialty crops as papayas, macadamia nuts, Kona coffee and genetically engineered seeds in a vastly reduced agriculture sector that today contributes only about one-half of 1 percent to the state GDP.

During the Great Recession, real estate in Hawaii experienced an even worse downturn than in the country as a whole. Tourism slumped, though it eventually recovered. Japan continues to account for about one-fifth of the state's tourists and, with nearly 1.6 million coming in 2017, is by far the biggest source of visitors from any country other than the U.S. itself. Hawaii's unemployment peaked at only 7.3 percent during the Great Recession and was 2.4 percent in November 2018 – tied with Iowa for the lowest in the nation.

Hawaii, so far removed from any other land, has a particularly fragile ecology, with a profusion of bird and plant species that are vulnerable to invasive predators. Airliners' wheel housings are routinely inspected for the brown tree snakes that have killed off most of the birds in Guam. The oceans around the islands are vulnerable, too. In 2006, President George W. Bush issued an order dedicating the Northwestern Hawaiian Islands Marine National Monument. The area contains 70 percent of the nation's tropical, shallow-water coral reefs, some 7,000 marine species (one-quarter found nowhere else), the endangered Hawaiian monk seal population and threatened species of predatory fish (sharks, groupers and jacks), as well as what remains of the USS Yorktown, which sank during the Battle of Midway in 1942. In 2016, Obama, who spent much of his youth in Hawaii, became the seventh president to preserve the area to one degree or another, expanding the protected area fourfold to more than half a million square miles, including barring commercial fishing and other resource extraction but allowing recreational fishing, scientific study and traditional Hawaiian cultural practices. Mauna Loa volcano is so forbidding that NASA has been using its environs to isolate researchers for months at a time in preparation for the long journey to Mars. But Hawaii is losing much of its famed beachfront. The U.S. Geological Survey has estimated that chronic erosion is affecting 70 percent of the beaches on Oahu, Kauai and Maui, and parts of Waikiki Beach -- the birthplace of modern surfing, where legendary Olympic athlete Duke Kahanamoku introduced the longboard more than a century ago -- are barely ribbons of carbonate sand today. Spooked by the web of changes, Hawaii became the first state to pass legislation that implemented parts of the Paris climate accord.

Fair-weather Hawaii has one of the lowest energy usage rates per capita of any state, but because it has traditionally had to import petroleum, its energy costs are well above the national average. To reverse this pattern, the state has encouraged offshore wind and geothermal power, which have been controversial, as well as solar, which has been popular.

Nature was unusually troublesome in 2018. The Kilauea volcano on the Big Island, which had begun to erupt virtually without pause in 1983, spewed forth one of its most disruptive lava flows in recent memory between May and September, covering thousands of acres in the Leilani Estates and

Kapoho neighborhoods, shooting plumes 330 feet into the air, destroying more than 700 buildings, shuttering a geothermal plant that provided almost 30 percent of the island's power, and blanketing the island with potentially hazardous "vog," or sulfur-dioxide-infused volcanic fog. The volcano then paused for three months – an unprecedented stretch of quiet since 1983, suggesting to scientists that the volcano's 35-year run may be at an end, at least in its current location. Lava wasn't the only hazard in 2018 – rain was, too. In April, 50 inches of rain fell in a single day on Kauai, breaking a national record. Then a rare hurricane, Lane, threatened the island, soaking parts of the Big Island with nearly 20 inches of rain and sending residents in other parts of the archipelago scrambling to shelters. All told, the year of disasters was estimated to cost the state $1 billion, not counting lost tourism revenue.

Less than 4 percent of Hawaii residents lack health insurance, just 1 percentage point off the national low, and the state leads the nation in life expectancy at 81.3 years. In 2015, Hawaii became the first state to raise the legal age of smoking to 21. But while wellness is not a big problem, homelessness has been. Driven by an expensive housing market, the number of homeless people grew by 36 percent between 2010 and 2016, the nation's third-biggest increase. However, progress was made in 2017 and 2018.

Asian migrant laborers had long practiced traditions of hard work, family loyalty and group solidarity that found expression most vividly in the performance of the 442nd "Go for Broke" Regimental Combat Team, which was made up mostly of sons of Japanese immigrants and became the most decorated unit in U.S. military history. Once discriminated against, Japanese Americans today have the state's highest annual household incomes. Meanwhile, the Yankee spirit has been evident in Hawaii's commercial success and in its attachment to the rule of Anglo-American law. The Hawaiian spirit is apparent in the vitality of the aloha ambience, the welcoming of others despite their differences, and a willingness to absorb the teachings of others while maintaining a certain Polynesian attitude toward life.

When Hawaii entered the union, it had a Republican territorial governor, and Democrat John F. Kennedy carried the state in the 1960 presidential election by just 115 votes. From 1962 to 2002, Hawaii's politics were dominated by a Democratic machine that had its beginning in the 1950s, when World War II veterans such as Daniel Inouye, Spark Matsunaga and George Ariyoshi joined forces with former mainlander John Burns, who as a police officer during the war helped prevent persecution of Japanese Americans. They allied themselves with the then-powerful International Longshoremen's and Warehousemen's Union, which represented sugar and pineapple plantation hands as well as dockworkers, cementing the allegiance of Japanese-American voters. The Burns-Inouye alliance built on the grievances against the haole (the Hawaiian word for white) owners of the big companies, and triumphed.

Voting in Hawaii has tended to follow ethnic lines. Japanese Americans were the heart of the Democratic Party, along with Native Hawaiians; whites, with relatively high incomes, leaned Republican. Lower-income Filipinos were heavily Democratic, with Chinese somewhat less so. Over the years this machine built a large government: About one-fifth of Hawaii's workers are government employees. Some suggest that this arrangement has favored seniority over competence, resulting in a lack of accountability. This came into sharp relief in 2018, when a state official mistakenly sent a text alert saying the state was under nuclear attack; reviews of the incident found that the employee had a history of performance problems that were never addressed, despite concerns among his co-workers. Gene Park, a former Hawaii government employee turned journalist, later wrote that "the sad part is that the worker's ineptitude and the chaos he caused have exposed to the world old, ugly tropes about Hawaiian accountability and competence that residents would love nothing more than to shake off."

Hawaii's political playing field has become particularly lopsided since former two-term Gov. Linda Lingle, a Republican, left office in 2010 and lost a seemingly competitive Senate race in 2012 by a 2-to-1 margin. In 2008, Hawaii gave native son Obama 72 percent of its presidential vote, and in 2012, he got 70 percent. Hillary Clinton did marginally worse in 2016, but she still coasted, 62%-30% -- her widest winning margin in any state. Meanwhile, Democrats have controlled the state House since statehood, and in 2016 the party won every seat in the state Senate, before slipping back to a 24-1 margin in 2018. During the tenure of President Donald Trump, the state has hewed to its history of diversity and acceptance, taking a leading role in challenging his immigration travel bans in court.

Population		Race and Ethnicity		Income	
Total	1,421,658	White	22.2%	Median Income	$74,923
Land area (sq. miles)	6,423	Black	1.7%	State Income Rank	4
Pop/ sq mi	221.4	Latino	10.2%	Poverty Rate	10.3%
Born in state	53.7%	Asian	37.0%	With health insurance	95.4%
Age Groups		Two or more races	19.4%	Cash public assistance	3.4%
Under 18	21.6%	Other	9.4%	Food stamp/SNAP	11.4%
18-34	23.7%	Education		Work	
35-64	38.0%	H.S grad or less	36.2%	White Collar	34.2%
Over 64	16.7%	Some college	31.9%	Sales and Service	47.8%
Military		College Degree, 4 yr	21.2%	Blue Collar	18.0%
Veteran/ Active Duty	13.4%	Post grad	10.8%	Government	20.3%

Presidential Politics

2016 Caucus (D)	Sanders (D)	23,521 (70%)	Clinton (D)	10,126 (30%)		
2016 Caucus (R)	Trump (R)	6,805 (43%)	Cruz (R)	5,063 (32%)	Rubio (R)	2,068 (13%)
	Kasich (R)	1,566 (10%)				
2016 Pres. Vote	Clinton (D)	266,891 (62%)	Trump (R)	128,847 (30%)	Johnson (L)	15,954 (4%)
	Stein (G)	12,737 (3%)				
2012 Pres. Vote	Obama (D)	306,658 (71%)	Romney (R)	121,015 (28%)		

Hawaii's voters have historically supported Democrats for the White House. Since the state began casting presidential ballots in 1960, the only two Republican victories came in reelection landslides: Ronald Reagan's in 1984 and Richard Nixon's in 1972. Almost 70 percent of Hawaii's votes come from Oahu; the other islands are even more Democratic-leaning than the most urban island in the archipelago. In 2016, Hillary Clinton defeated Donald Trump 62%-30%. In 2008 and 2012, Hawaiians embraced their native son, Barack Obama, and he won each election with more than 70 percent of the vote.

Hawaii chooses presidential delegates by caucus. Efforts to switch to a primary died in the state legislature in 2018, but there could be another push to change in 2019. In a state where whites make up less than a quarter of the population, Hawaii's diversity was no barrier to Trump in the GOP caucuses on March 8: he defeated Texas Sen. Ted Cruz, 43%-32%. Florida Sen. Marco Rubio finished a distant third. None of the GOP candidates campaigned in the state. On the Democratic side, both Democratic senators backed Clinton, but Rep. Tulsi Gabbard resigned her position as vice chair of the Democratic National Committee to support Sen. Bernie Sanders. More than 33,000 attended the Democratic caucuses and gave the Vermonter a 70%-30% victory. Sanders's wife, Jane, made a campaign stop before the March 26 caucuses.

Congressional Districts

116th Congress Lineup	2D	115th Congress Lineup	2D

Hawaii has two congressional districts: The 1st includes urban Honolulu and extends westward to Pearl Harbor and the rural area beyond. The 2nd includes the rest of Oahu and the Neighbor Islands. The 1st District, the most heavily Asian district in the country, is the slightly less Democratic of the two and elected a Republican in 1986, 1988 and briefly in 2010, when Honolulu Councilman Charles Djou won an unusual special election against split Democratic opposition. In 2018, Djou renounced his membership in the Republican Party because of disagreements with President Donald Trump. The lower-income 2nd District has elected only Democrats since it was created in 1971.

Timing and ambition tend to overstep boundaries in Hawaii: In 2010, Democrat Colleen Hanabusa unseated Djou in the 1st District although she lived in the 2nd. In 2012, both major candidates for the open 2nd District lived in the 1st. When the 1st became open again in 2018, Ed Case was elected. A decade earlier, he served two terms in the 2nd District. Given the recent volatility, more changes in the House delegation seem possible. But it remains a heavy lift for Republicans to win a seat here. With virtually equal population in the two districts, shifts of the boundaries likely will be minimal.

David Ige (D)

Elected 2014, term expires 2022, 2nd term; b. Jan. 15, 1957, Honolulu; U of HI –Manoa, B.A., 1979; M.A., 1985; Buddhist; Married (Dawn); 3 children.

Elected Office: HI Senate 1994-2014; U.S. House, appointed 1985.

Professional Career: Electronics engineer, Pacific Analysis Corp.; Senior Administrator, General Telephone & Electronics Hawaiian Telephone, 1981-1999; Project Manager, Pihana Pacific, LLC., 1999-2001; Vice President of Engineering for Net Enterprise, Inc., 2001-2002; Project Manager, R.A. Ige and Associates, Inc., 2003.

Office: 415 S Beretania St #5, Honolulu, 96813; 808-586-0034; Fax: 808-586-0006; Website: governor.hawaii.gov.

Lt. Gov.: Josh Green (D)

State Legislature: Senate: 24D, 1R **House:** 46D, 5R

Election Results

Election	Name (Party)	Vote (%)
2018 General	David Ige (D)	244,934 (63%)
	Andria Tupola (R)	131,719 (34%)
	Jim Brewer (G)	10,123 (3%)
2018 Primary	David Ige (D)	124,572 (51%)
	Colleen Hanabusa (D)	107,631 (44%)

Democrat David Ige, Hawaii's second Japanese-American governor, was reelected in 2018 after a strong primary challenge from Rep. Colleen Hanabusa. Once considered a lost cause for a second term, Ige benefited from a strong response to natural disasters and an underperformance by Hanabusa.

Ige serves in the 21st century, but his family history embodies a major story line of 20th century Hawaii. Born and raised in Pearl City, he was the fifth of six boys of Japanese-American parents who had settled in Hawaii a generation earlier, at a time when those of Japanese ancestry were widely discriminated against. His father, Tokio, won a Purple Heart and a Bronze Star serving in the famous 100th Battalion, 442nd Regimental Combat Team of the U.S. Army during World War II, which was made up mostly of sons of Japanese immigrants. Hawaii's longtime protector in the Senate, Dan Inouye, was also a member. The veterans cultivated the educational institutions that trained the next generation of leaders, including Ige.

After studying engineering and business, Ige launched a successful career as an electrical engineer and project manager, working on information technology and telecommunications. Ige wasn't even planning to enter politics in 1985, when Democratic Gov. George Ariyoshi, who was looking for smart young professionals to appoint to vacant seats in the legislature, tapped Ige, who had been recommended by local activists in Pearl City. Ige wasn't a member of the Democratic Party when Ariyoshi reached out to him. He went on to win reelection four times before advancing to the state Senate in 1994, all while continuing his regular employment.

He brought a novice's sensitivities to his new job and recoiled when he quickly came to understand that the legislative process is often an inside game where knowledge is not always shared and the public is often excluded from decision making. That led to Ige's focus on improving communication with voters (and among his own colleagues) and their access to information. Drawing on his experience in the private sector, he often applied technology to the tasks of meeting his goals, posting draft legislation, hearing notices and budget documents online and setting up an electronic network to involve hundreds of high school students in the legislative process through a primitive form of videoconferencing. Ige built a reputation as a well-studied policy expert, working on issues ranging from education reform to auto insurance to land conservation. His years of committee work paid off when he rose to chair the state Senate Ways and Means Committee in 2009.

When Ige announced his gubernatorial bid in 2013, it was widely seen as a David-and-Goliath contest. Incumbent Democrat Neil Abercrombie outspent Ige by more than 10-to-1, and President Barack Obama, along with most other prominent Hawaii Democrats, endorsed him. What Abercrombie didn't expect was the voters' pushback against his personal style, which was widely viewed as confrontational. Many Asian Americans were unhappy with his decision to appoint Lt. Gov. Brian Schatz, rather than Rep. Colleen Hanabusa, to fill Inouye's seat after his death in 2012. He also pursued policies that alienated Hawaii's powerful public-sector unions. The Hawaii State Teachers Association, which had backed Abercrombie in his primary in 2010, decided to endorse Ige in 2014. Putting forth an image of quiet competence, Ige won a shocker, defeating Abercrombie in the August primary by a staggering 35 percentage points — the first time that a sitting Hawaii governor had lost a primary since 1962. Ige's challenge in the general against former Lt. Gov. "Duke" Aiona was making sure that independent Mufi Hannemann didn't draw away too many centrist voters who would otherwise vote Democratic. By the closing weeks of the campaign, Ige had consolidated his lead and ended up beating Aiona by about a dozen percentage points.

In office, Ige broke with the tendency of most of his predecessors to govern as the ali'i nui (the term for a great or grand chief from Hawaii's early days) and began meeting every other week with the leaders of the state House of Representatives and Senate. But lawmakers questioned his nomination of Carleton Ching to lead the Department of Land and Natural Resources, the state agency charged with protecting Hawaii's delicate habitat. Ching had spent 12 prior years as the chief lobbyist for Castle & Cooke, one of the state's biggest developers. Ige pulled the nomination and the Senate confirmed Suzanne Case, who had been executive director of the Nature Conservancy.

During the biennial budget process, Ige and legislative leaders decided with little fanfare or public discussion to allow the temporary hike in the state's top income tax rate to expire. The most far-reaching measure he approved early in his first term was legislation that sets the most ambitious clean energy goal in the country: to make Hawaii self-sufficient in energy and meet 100 percent of its needs with renewable sources.

Ige signed three bills restricting gun rights. One prevents those charged with stalking or sexual assault from possessing a firearm. Another allows law enforcement to seize guns and ammunition from those disqualified by mental health concerns, while a third requires the entry of Hawaii gun owners' names into a national FBI database. Ige also grappled with the state's continuing challenges of homelessness, issuing an emergency proclamation to extend outreach efforts and urging greater investment in affordable housing. Ige achieved some success in economic development, working to extend international flights to Kona on the Big Island, rather than just Honolulu International Airport on Oahu, which had been the state's only international commercial airport since 2010.

Ige's trickiest challenge was handling a heated and long-running controversy over the $2 billion Thirty Meter Telescope project on the Big Island, which would build the world's largest telescope on Mauna Kea, a 14,000-foot mountain that is perhaps the best place in the world to study the skies. However, it would be located on land that some Native Hawaiians consider sacred. Its construction inspired demonstrations that led to arrests. After a protracted court battle, the state Supreme Court approved a building permit in 2018.

Also in 2018, Ige signed bills to make the state carbon-neutral by 2045, to permit physician-assisted suicide, and to ban gay conversion therapy, while vetoing a bill that would have allowed the use of medical marijuana for treating substance abuse. He signed the world's first ban on oxybenzone and octinoxate, two chemicals in sunscreen that have been blamed for harming coral. Ige applauded efforts by the state attorney general's office to counter policies of the Trump administration, saying in his state of the state address that "we are doing more than any other state to stand up for what is right – such as DACA and the Paris Climate Accord – and stop what is wrong, such as the travel ban and stopping transgender members of the military from defending our flag and our freedoms."

Just as Ige challenged Abercrombie in the 2014 Democratic primary, Ige himself received a primary challenge in 2018, from Hanabusa. Hanabusa is a Yonsei, a fourth-generation American of Japanese ancestry. Each of her grandfathers was among the more than 100,000 Japanese Americans forcibly relocated and interned after Japan's attack on Pearl Harbor during World War II. She was raised on a sugar plantation by her maternal grandmother while her parents worked long hours running a gas station in Waianae. In addition to two tours of duty in the U.S. House, Hanabusa had spent 12 years in the state Senate, including a four-year run as state Senate president – the first woman to lead either chamber of the state legislature. She narrowly lost a primary against Schatz in 2014.

Hanabusa sought to portray Ige as an ineffectual leader, and fate initially intervened to make her case. In January 2018, a state employee mistakenly sent out a text alert that the state was under nuclear attack. It proved to be due to human error, but the mistake was not fully corrected for 38 minutes, and questions swirled around Ige's handling of the incident, including why he didn't act immediately after learning about it two minutes into the crisis. The incident undercut Ige's reputation for cool competence. "When you hear the stories about what people did in 38 minutes, it gives you a clear sense that it truly affected so many people," Hanabusa charged during a debate. By March, Hanabusa was leading in a Honolulu Star-Advertiser poll, 47%-27%, and she was racking up endorsements.

But fate intervened once again with a succession of natural disasters – flooding on Kauai and Oahu, and volcanic eruptions on the Big Island -- that Ige was credited with handling much more effectively. Ige ended up defeating Hanabusa by seven points. Hanabusa's failure to articulate a compelling message also mattered, Colin Moore, director of the University of Hawaii's Public Policy Center, told Honolulu Civil Beat. "There was a window for her to really mount a strong campaign and really make a strong case for her candidacy and she missed it," Moore said. After the hard-fought primary, the 2018 general election was anticlimactic, as Ige defeated Republican Andria Tupola in the heavily Democratic state, 63%-34%. But relations remained raw between the governor and state legislators, many of whom had backed Hanabusa. Ige acknowledged this in his inauguration address, saying, "I am not asking for anyone's blind support, but a willingness to keep an open mind, to leave personal agendas outside the door, and to commit to an unyielding determination to work together."

Brian Schatz (D)

Appointed 2012, term expires 2022, 1st full term, b. Oct 20, 1972; Ann Arbor, MI; School for International Training (Kenya), 1992; Pomona College, B.A., 1994; Jewish; Married (Linda Kwok Kai Yun); 2 children.

Elected Office: HI House, 1998-2006; HI Lt. Governor, 2010-2012.

Professional Career: CEO, Helping Hands HI, 2004-2010; Chairman, HI Democratic Party, 2008-2010.

DC Office: 722 HSOB 20510, 202-224-3934, Fax: 202-228-1153, schatz.senate.gov

State Offices: Honolulu, 808-523-2061.

Committees: *Appropriations*: Commerce, Justice, Science & Related Agencies; Department of Defense; DOL, HHS & Education & Related Agencies; Military Construction & Veteran Affairs & Related Agencies (RMM); Transportation, HUD & Related Agencies. *Banking, Housing & Urban Affairs*: Financial Institutions & Consumer Protection; National Security & International Trade & Finance. *Commerce, Science & Transportation*: Communications, Technology, Innovation & the Internet (RMM); Manufacturing, Trade & Consumer Protection; Subcommittee on Aviation & Space; Subcommittee on Science, Oceans, Fisheries & Weather; Subcommittee on Security. *Ethics. Indian Affairs.*

Group Ratings

	ADA	ACLU	AFL-CIO	LCV	ITI	COC	HAFA	ACU	CFG	FRC
2018	-	75%	-	100%	-	50%	3%	14%	5%	0%
2017	95%	C	100%	100%	C	29%	C	0%	4%	0%

Almanac Ratings 2017-18

	Economy	Social	Foreign	Composite
Liberal	97%	97%	78%	90%
Conservative	3%	3%	22%	10%

Key Votes of the 115th Congress

1. Obama-care revision	N	5. Gun regulations	N	9. Kavanaugh confirmation	N
2. Tax Cuts	N	6. Family planning regs	N	10. Saudi arms sales	Y
3. Dodd-Frank revision	N	7. Gorsuch confirmation	N	11. FISA rules	N
4. Omnibus appropriations	Y	8. Immigration restrictions	N	12. Military aid in Yemen	Y

Election Results

Election	Name (Party)	Vote (%)	Cand. Spent	Ind. Exp. Support	Ind. Exp. Oppose
2016 General	Brian Schatz (D)............................... 306,604	(74%)	$1,932,020		
	John Carroll (R).................................... 92,653	(22%)	$54,517		
	Joy Allison (C)....................................... 9,103	(2%)			
2016 Primary	Brian Schatz (D)................................ 162,905	(86%)			
	Makani Christensen (D)................. 11,899	(6%)			

Prior winning percentages: 2014 special (67%)

Democrat Brian Schatz's appointment to the Senate at the end of 2012 was at odds with the deathbed wishes of his predecessor, Daniel Inouye — long the state's most powerful and beloved political figure. In a letter to Gov. Neil Abercrombie before he died, Inouye — who had occupied the Senate seat for nearly a half-century — asked that Rep. Colleen Hanabusa be named his successor. But Abercrombie named Schatz, his lieutenant governor and running mate. A former state legislator and state Democratic chair, Schatz was sworn in 10 days after Inouye's death — and, in 2014, narrowly held off Hanabusa in a primary battle over filling the remainder of Inouye's term. Since then, Schatz has been elected to a full six-year term and emerged as an outspoken, liberal member of the Senate Democratic Caucus who crafts comprehensive legislative proposals on high-profile issues — part of a quest to achieve consensus across disparate elements of his party as it sought to reclaim the White House in 2020.

"I want Democrats in the Senate, Democrats running for Congress, to rally around an aggressive, progressive agenda," Schatz told New York magazine. "And it's not a gotcha, litmus test-style agenda, but one that, if we enact it, would be on a scale that is equal to the problems and has the ability to actually motivate voters." Unlike numerous like-minded Senate Democrats of similar age, the 46-year-old Schatz has renounced any designs on his party's 2020 presidential nomination. But he has persuaded a half-dozen of his Senate Democratic colleagues either running for or eyeing the White House to co-sponsor his legislative initiatives to expand health care coverage and make college more affordable. "He's well-liked within the caucus; he's someone folks listen to," Democratic strategist Jim Manley, a longtime Senate leadership aide, told New York magazine. "If given a chance, he has an opportunity to be a significant player in the Senate."

Schatz was born one of two identical twins in Ann Arbor, Mich., to cardiologist Irwin Schatz. His twin brother, Stephen, runs a statewide partnership between the Hawaii Department of Education and the University of Hawaii aimed at achieving an increase in the number of college degrees. In the mid-1960s, while working in Detroit, Irwin Schatz became aware of a decades-long study being conducted by the U.S. Public Health Service in Tuskegee, Ala., in which poor black sharecroppers with syphilis were left untreated so researchers could study the effects. A letter of protest he wrote to health officials helped trigger a public debate that led to new standards governing research on human subjects. When Brian Schatz was 2, his father accepted a job at the University of Hawaii. After graduating from the prestigious Punahou School — which Barack Obama also attended — Schatz went to Pomona College in California, studying abroad in Kenya before receiving his degree. He returned to Hawaii and worked as a community organizer, including heading a beach preservation group and later running a social services agency.

In 1998, Schatz, then 26, was elected to represent an urban Honolulu district in the Hawaii Legislature, where he served for eight years. In 2006, he was one of 10 candidates in the Democratic primary for an open congressional seat. Schatz finished sixth — losing to former Lt. Gov. Mazie Hirono, now Schatz's Senate colleague. The same year, Schatz founded a group urging Obama to run for president; he served as spokesman for the Hawaii Obama campaign before being elected state Democratic Party chairman in the spring of 2008. Two years later, he resigned and announced his candidacy for lieutenant governor. He ran with Abercrombie, a longtime member of Congress; they won by 17 percentage points in November. In office, Schatz worked on energy and climate issues and helped pass same-sex civil unions in the state. When the 88-year-old Inouye died six weeks after the November 2012 election, the state Democratic Party — as required by law — sent Abercrombie three names from whom he would choose a replacement: Hanabusa, former congressional candidate Esther Kia'aina and Schatz. While Hanabusa was Inouye's choice, Abercrombie, who had a well-publicized rift with Inouye and much of the state's Democratic establishment, chose his ally, Schatz.

Schatz flew to Washington on Air Force One with President Obama, who had been spending Christmas in Hawaii, and was sworn in as the Senate faced crucial end-of-year votes, particularly on the "fiscal cliff" created by a combination of automatic tax increases and spending cuts. The timing made Schatz the state's senior senator by days. Hirono, elected in November 2012 to replace retiring Democratic Sen. Daniel Akaka, was to be sworn in until Jan. 3.

Hanabusa, after deciding to run in the 2014 Democratic primary for the remaining two years of Inouye's term, sought to depict Schatz — 40 at the time of his appointment — as inexperienced. Abercrombie was said to have privately cited the 20-year age gap between Schatz and Hanabusa in making his choice, arguing that Schatz was in a position to serve longer and accumulate more seniority. Hanabusa was backed by the political networks of Inouye and Akaka and had financial support from EMILY's List, a national political action committee that backs Democratic women who favor abortion rights. Schatz lined up support from the national Democratic establishment, including Obama, then-Senate Majority Leader Harry Reid and progressive and environmental groups.

The contest broke along ethnic lines, as Hawaii's primaries often do, with Schatz winning among liberal white voters and Hanabusa, who is Japanese-American, performing well with Native Hawaiians and Asian-Americans. The initial results of the Aug. 9 primary, on the heels of a tropical storm that damaged parts of Hawaii and prevented two precincts from voting, gave Schatz a 1,635-vote lead. State election officials said a makeup election would be held in areas affected by the storm the following Friday; Hanabusa unsuccessfully filed a legal challenge, contending those sections were insufficiently recovered to have voters cast ballots. After those precincts had voted, Schatz's lead stood at 1,769 votes out of a statewide total of more than 237,000 cast. He won 49%-48%. Schatz's victory in November was a cakewalk; so was his election to a full term in 2016. In both cases, he took 70 percent of the vote. Meanwhile, Schatz's onetime running mate, Abercrombie, lost a 2014 bid for renomination by a 66%-30% margin. His loss was fueled in part by having ignored the dying wishes of Inouye.

On Capitol Hill, Schatz maintained the abiding interest in environmental issues, particularly climate change, that he demonstrated in state office. In 2015, his amendment to the Keystone XL pipeline bill put lawmakers on record on whether they believe "climate change is real and human activity significantly contributes" to it. The amendment, the first Senate vote on climate change in eight years, got 50 votes in favor, including five from Republicans. Schatz and Democratic Sen. Sheldon Whitehouse of Rhode Island introduced a proposed tax on carbon emissions they said would yield $2 trillion in revenue over 10 years.

They tried again in 2017, going so far as to appear before a conservative think tank, the American Enterprise Institute, to garner Republican support for their idea. "The idea is quite simple: Unleash markets to tackle climate change," Schatz said. "It establishes incentives that allow capital to flow and businesses to thrive when they can use clean energy, letting the free market compete and innovate and make profits." The AEI event was part of an effort to attract at least one Republican senator to co-sponsor the bill. But the legislation again died, with no GOP backers — and with Schatz shifting to attack mode. "The Republican Party is the only major political party on the planet that is explicitly dedicated to making climate change worse," he tweeted in spring 2018. Schatz's proclivity for sharp-tongued tweets also was on display several months earlier, when President Donald Trump made controversial comments in which he equivocated in condemning white nationalist groups who organized a Charlottesville, Va., rally that turned violent. "As a Jew, as an American, as a human, words cannot express my disgust and disappointment," Schatz tweeted. "This is not my President."

Schatz's appointment in 2012 coincided with the election of another progressive Democrat: Chris Murphy of Connecticut. As the two youngest senators at the time, Schatz and Murphy sponsored legislation aimed at college affordability by providing incentives to school administrators to lower costs. In 2018, Schatz unveiled a more ambitious plan. With a $95 billion price, it proposed matching grants to states that committed to providing debt-free education — covering tuition and all other expenses — for public university students. The measure was a follow-on to Vermont Sen. Bernie Sanders' call for free tuition at public colleges during his 2016 presidential bid. Schatz's proposal attracted the co-sponsorship of numerous Senate progressive Democrats eyeing the 2020 Democratic nomination. "It's essential that we have a plan for when we take power back," Schatz said. "We don't know when that will be, but we need to be ready to roll legislatively, and it's just a fact that campaigns are not equipped to prepare the kind of public policy that can be enacted."

A similar motivation was behind legislation Schatz rolled out in 2017 that would have enabled states to set up a "public option" for health insurance by expanding Medicaid and allowing any individual to buy in to it instead of purchasing private insurance. Schatz's plan was intended as a progressive, more incremental alternative to Sanders' "Medicare for all" proposal, which would give all Americans a government-operated insurance plan. Several of the Democratic presidential contenders who had sponsored Sanders' plan signed on to Schatz's bill as well. "With health care, somebody at some point decided that there was a bright line and that you had to pick sides," Schatz told the Atlantic. "Well, I reject that view. I think we should respect each other as colleagues, respect each other as progressives, enough to take all of these bills, and have hearings, and subject them to scrutiny."

Amid his increasing focus on high-profile national issues, Schatz has spent a great deal of time on issues related to Hawaii. He often reached across the political aisle to senators representing rural states with similar issues. In 2016, Schatz and Utah Republican Sen. Orrin Hatch passed a "telehealth" bill, intended to spur the use of videoconferencing to link teams of specialists to primary care providers in rural and underserved areas. Obama signed legislation by Schatz and Republican Sen. John Thune of South Dakota that was aimed at fostering greater federal involvement in tourism efforts by Native Hawaiian, Alaska Native and Indian communities. In December 2018, Schatz and Thune teamed up to pass a bill to improve the system for incoming missile alerts. It followed an incident during which, amid rising tensions with North Korea, an alert was mistakenly sent out in Hawaii — causing widespread panic before it was corrected after more than half an hour.

Perhaps Schatz's biggest local impact has come not through legislation, but in an executive order from his fellow Punahou School alumnus Obama. In late spring of 2016, Schatz wrote to Obama, asking that the Papahanaumokuakea Marine National Monument, which surrounds the uninhabited Northwestern Hawaiian Islands, be quadrupled in size. The marine reserve, created by President George W. Bush, is home to 7,000 marine and terrestrial species, a quarter of which are found nowhere else on earth. Schatz asked Obama to increase the size of the protected area to nearly 583,000 square miles — an area greater than Alaska. Obama utilized his power under the 1906 Antiquities Act to make it the largest protected land or ocean conservation area on Earth.

Given his youth and base in a blue state, Schatz could be around Capitol Hill for a long time. In 2017, he was named one of three chief deputy whips. His recent fundraising activities won praise from Minority Leader Chuck Schumer. If Schatz doesn't end up as a Senate Democratic leader, he could eventually chair the Appropriations panel — the same gavel once wielded by Inouye, the man whose deathbed wish sought to detour Schatz from Capitol Hill.

Mazie Hirono (D)

Elected 2012, term expires 2024, 2nd term, b. Nov 03, 1947; Fukushima, Japan; University of Hawaii, Manoa, B.A., 1970; Georgetown University Law Center (DC), J.D., 1978; Buddhism; Married (Leighton Kim Oshima); 1 stepchild.

Elected Office: U.S. House, 2006-2012; HI Lt. Governor, 1994-2002; HI House, 1980-1994.

Professional Career: Deputy HI Attorney General, 1978-1980; Practicing lawyer, 1984-1988.

DC Office: 713 HSOB 20510, 202-224-6361, Fax: 202-224-2126, hirono.senate.gov

State Offices: Honolulu, 808-522-8970.

Committees: *Armed Services*: Emerging Threats & Capabilities; Readiness & Management Support; Seapower (RMM). *Energy & Natural Resources*: Energy; National Parks; Public Lands, Forests & Mining. *Judiciary*: Border Security & Immigration; Constitution (RMM); Oversight, Agency Action, Federal Rights & Federal Courts; Subcommittee on Intellectual Property. *Small Business & Entrepreneurship. Veterans' Affairs.*

Group Ratings

	ADA	ACLU	AFL-CIO	LCV	ITI	COC	HAFA	ACU	CFG	FRC
2018	-	77%	-	100%	-	50%	5%	10%	15%	0%
2017	100%	C	100%	100%	C	29%	C	0%	4%	0%

Almanac Ratings 2017-18

	Economy	Social	Foreign	Composite
Liberal	100%	100%	86%	95%
Conservative	0%	0%	15%	5%

Key Votes of the 115th Congress

1. Obama-care revision	N	5. Gun regulations	N	9. Kavanaugh confirmation	N
2. Tax Cuts	N	6. Family planning regs	N	10. Saudi arms sales	Y
3. Dodd-Frank revision	N	7. Gorsuch confirmation	N	11. FISA rules	N
4. Omnibus appropriations	Y	8. Immigration restrictions	N	12. Military aid in Yemen	Y

Election Results

Election	Name (Party)	Vote (%)	Cand. Spent	Ind. Exp. Support	Ind. Exp. Oppose
2018 General	Mazie K. Hirono (D)......................... 276,316	(71%)	$2,518,141	$2,997	
	Ron Curtis (R)................................. 112,035	(29%)			
2018 Primary	Mazie K. Hirono (D)......................... 201,604	(100%)			

Prior winning percentages: 2012 (63%); House: 2010 (72%), 2008 (76%), 2006 (61%)

In her initial decade on Capitol Hill — first in the House and later in the Senate — Democrat Mazie Hirono, Hawaii's junior senator, was a low-profile legislator focused on matters of direct interest to her island state. That changed with Donald Trump. As the Senate's sole immigrant member, Hirono in 2016 rebuked the immigration policies of the Republican presidential nominee. Following Trump's surprise win, as many of her stunned Democratic colleagues opted for conciliatory statements, Hirono came out swinging — later telling Time magazine: "I didn't feel like making a 'Let's give the man a chance' speech. His entire campaign was so negative and antithetical to everything I believe." In the ensuing two years, Hirono would describe the president as xenophobic and regularly call him a liar. But it was in Judiciary Committee hearings for Supreme Court nominee Brett Kavanaugh that she ingratiated herself with the left — as she took on both Kavanaugh and the Republicans pushing his confirmation in blunt, unvarnished terms.

Hirono startled in a September 2018 news conference when, amid allegations of sexual assault against Kavanaugh, she took aim at the broader issue of sexual misconduct. "Guess who is perpetuating all of these kinds of actions? It's the men in this country," she said. "And I just want to say to the men in this country: Just shut up and step up. Do the right thing for a change." A day later, she called for Senate Majority Leader Mitch McConnell to "do the right thing." Asked how the often-inscrutable McConnell had reacted, Hirono told The Washington Post, "It's kind of hard to read him." But, in the same interview, she didn't mince words when asked about Senate Republicans' treatment of Christine Blasey Ford, who had first raised sexual assault allegations against Kavanaugh. "They've extended a finger," Hirono said of the GOP, adding that she was being "very graphic in what I say," partly because of her advocacy for sexual assault victims early in her career. "I've been fighting these fights for a —" Hirono said, pausing a moment. "I was going to say a f---ing long time."

Hirono has held state or federal office for almost four decades. Elected to the Senate in 2012, she became the first Asian-American woman to serve there and only its second nonwhite woman. Hirono is also the first senator born in Japan; she immigrated to Hawaii before her eighth birthday with her mother, Laura, who fled an abusive husband who drank and gambled frequently. As a child, she shared a bed in a boarding house with her mother and older brother, and at age 10 she went to work to help support the family. A sister died of pneumonia in Japan at 2 because they did not have access to a hospital. It's an episode Hirono, choking back tears, recalled in a July 2017 floor speech during debate on repealing the Affordable Care Act. Laura Hirono found work as a typesetter for a Japanese-language newspaper — minimum wage, no health insurance. "Growing up as a young girl in Hawaii, my greatest fear was that my mother would get sick. And, if she got sick, how were we going to pay for her care?" Mazie Hirono said during that speech. "And, if she didn't go to work, there would be no pay. I know what it's like to run out of money at the end of the month. That was my life as an immigrant here."

Speaking only Japanese when she arrived, Hirono mastered English in public school and became a naturalized citizen in 1959, the year Hawaii became a state. As a college student, she worked in 1968 with at-risk youths; it transformed her into a political activist. After graduating from the University of Hawaii, Hirono was a staffer in the Hawaii Legislature and for several political campaigns before decamping for Washington. She earned a law degree from Georgetown University and returned to Honolulu to work for the Hawaii attorney general's office. She was elected to the state House in 1980 and served until 1994, when she was elected lieutenant governor. Hobbled by a bumpy relationship with her running mate, Gov. Ben Cayetano, Hirono barely won her party's nomination for governor in 2002, edging out then-state House Majority Leader Ed Case 41%-40%. Her general election campaign was undermined by Democratic Party scandals involving illegal campaign contributions. Despite the state's strongly Democratic tilt, Hirono lost to Republican Linda Lingle 52%-47%.

Hirono formed a political action committee to assist Democratic women who backed abortion rights. Hirono got her chance to return to elected office in 2006, when Case — then in his first stint in the U.S. House — unsuccessfully challenged veteran Sen. Daniel Akaka in the Democratic primary. Hirono ran for Case's open House seat and emerged atop a 10-candidate primary field. Brian Schatz, now Hawaii's senior senator, finished sixth. Hirono easily won the general election.

In yet another first, Hirono and Rep. Hank Johnson of Georgia became the first Buddhists to serve in Congress. She amassed a liberal voting record in the House; her enthusiastic support of the Democratic agenda led the Hawaii Tribune-Herald to say, in endorsing her in 2008, "We wish she'd be a little more independent and less partisan." She was a staunch earmarker of funds for Hawaii; in fiscal 2010, she ranked third among House members in accumulating special-request spending items, according to the nonprofit Taxpayers for Common Sense. Earmarking has since been curtailed.

When Akaka announced his retirement in 2012, Hirono was the early Democratic favorite for the Senate, although she faced a primary challenge from Case, a party moderate. Meanwhile, Republicans landed their best possible candidate when Lingle agreed to run. In an unusual development, veteran Republican Rep. Don Young of Alaska, who served on the Transportation and Infrastructure Committee with Hirono, endorsed her in the Democratic primary. "While Mazie and I don't see eye to eye on everything, we've done something too many people in Washington refuse to cross the aisle and do: We've worked together," Young said, referring to their cooperation to preserve native Hawaiian and Native Alaskan education programs. Hirono defeated Case 57%-40%, setting up a rematch of their contest a decade earlier.

Lingle campaigned on her record as a moderate governor and vowed not to be beholden to Senate GOP leaders. She ran an ad criticizing Hirono for not getting any of her own bills signed into law. Democrats eviscerated Lingle for her praise of Sarah Palin during a speech introducing Palin as the party's vice presidential nominee at the 2008 Republican Convention. Lingle said she would vote for 2012 GOP presidential nominee Mitt Romney, which didn't play well in the home state of President Barack Obama. Hirono argued that a vote for Lingle could put Republicans back in the Senate majority — threatening the influence of Sen. Daniel Inouye, the Appropriations Committee's top Democrat and an iconic figure in Hawaii. She defeated Lingle in a landslide, 63%-37%.

Inouye died six weeks after Election Day; then-Gov. Neil Abercrombie appointed Schatz, his lieutenant governor, as Inouye's replacement. Schatz started his Senate service in late December of that year, and so Hirono became the state's junior senator by only days. Hirono was said to be unhappy at being leapfrogged by Schatz, and her allies sought to delay Schatz's swearing-in. But they were overruled by then-Majority Leader Harry Reid, who did not want a seat left vacant as a showdown on the "fiscal cliff" of expiring tax cuts and spending reductions was coming to a head. Initially maintaining her usual low profile, Hirono devoted significant effort to immigration issues. Reflecting the emergence of Filipino-Americans as her state's largest ethnic minority, Hirono worked to allow surviving Filipino veterans of World War II living in the United States to be joined by their children.

On the Judiciary Committee, Hirono played an active role in the panel's debate of immigration legislation in 2013. While most of her amendments dealt with issues specific to Hawaii, she championed a provision touching on what would later become a matter of intense controversy during the Trump administration: the separation of families seeking asylum along the U.S.-Mexico border. Her language — which cleared the panel on a party-line vote — required border agents to ask apprehended individuals whether they were traveling with spouses or children. The intent, Hirono said, was to ensure that families were not separated during the interrogation process, thereby making migrants "more vulnerable by returning them to dangerous places without their family members." The immigration bill passed the Senate with bipartisan support, but was not taken up in the House.

In May 2017, Hirono disclosed she had been diagnosed with late-stage kidney cancer. Her right kidney was removed, along with five inches of a rib to which the cancer had spread. She opted to undergo immunotherapy, requiring infusions every three weeks. Her emboldened rhetoric was on display during the Affordable Care Act debate two months later, when most Senate Republicans backed an unsuccessful effort to repeal Obamacare. Noting that, in the aftermath of her cancer diagnosis, she had heard from many GOP colleagues "who wrote me wonderful notes, sharing with me their own experience with major illness in their families or loved ones," Hirono — pounding her hand on her desk on the Senate floor — asked: "You showed me your care. You showed me your compassion. Where is that tonight?"

In 2018, Hirono began posing two questions to Trump administration nominees: "Since you became a legal adult, have you ever made any unwanted requests for sexual favors or committed any verbal or physical harassment or assault of a sexual nature?" and "Have you ever faced discipline or entered into a settlement related to this kind of conduct?" Hirono told Newsweek: "I want nominees who come before me … to know that these questions are about to become normal. We all have a responsibility to take action to stop sexual harassment and assault, and create lasting cultural change." She was saltier in off-air comments to NPR, while denying her line of questioning was rooted in partisanship. It was intended to vet judges on whether they "care about individual and civil rights," Hirono said. "If that's considered liberal, as opposed to what I call justice and fairness, as I am wont to say, f--- them!"

Kavanaugh answered "no" to both of Hirono's standing questions before the Judiciary Committee. Hirono later said she was unaware at the time that Blasey Ford had written a confidential letter to the ranking Democrat on the committee, California Sen. Dianne Feinstein, containing allegations of sexual assault by Kavanaugh while they were both in high school. When the letter surfaced, Republican leaders initially resisted Democratic demands for an FBI investigation — prompting Hirono to say Republicans were rushing to confirm Kavanaugh because the high court's "session is going to start in October and the president wants his guy there to, he hopes, help him evade criminal or civil proceedings." When then-Judiciary Chairman Chuck Grassley said he was doing everything possible to facilitate an appearance by Blasey Ford, Hirono — on ABC's "World News Tonight" — retorted, "That's such bullshit. I can hardly stand it." ABC News bleeped out Hirono's profanity.

A month after Kavanaugh was confirmed, Hirono easily won reelection 71%-29% against Ron Curtis, a retired systems engineer. Rep. Tulsi Gabbard disavowed interest in an insurgent Democratic primary bid, telling the Honolulu Star-Advertiser that Hirono was "doing a good job."

In a rare public spat within the state's all-Democratic delegation, Gabbard swiped at Hirono in early 2019 over the what she said was Hirono's aggressive vetting of judicial nominees. In an op-ed in The Hill newspaper, Gabbard alleged "religious bigotry" in the questioning of Brian Buescher of Nebraska, a Trump judgeship nominee. Gabbard did not mention names, but it was clearly a shot at Judiciary Committee questioning of Buescher by California Sen. Kamala Harris and Hirono. While saying she opposed Buescher's confirmation, Gabbard added, "I stand strongly against those who are fomenting religious bigotry, citing as disqualifiers Buescher's Catholicism and his affiliation with the Knights of Columbus," a Catholic fraternal society. Hirono said her concerns involved Buescher's public statements, not his religion. Hirono's office issued a further response, "It is unfortunate that Congresswoman Gabbard based her misguided opinion on the far-right wing manipulation of these straightforward questions."

Ed Case (D)

Elected 2018, 3rd full term, b. Sep 27, 1952; Hilo; Hawaii Preparatory School, 1970; Williams College, B.A., 1975; University of California Hastings College of Law, J.D., 1981; Protestant - Unspecified Christian; Married (Audrey Nakamura); 4 children.

Elected Office: HI House, 1994-2002, Majority Leader 1999-2001; U.S. House, 2002-2007.

Professional Career: Legislative Assistant, U.S. Rep. Spark Matsunaga; Partner and Attorney, Carlsmith Ball Law Firm.

DC Office: 2443 RHOB 20515, 202-225-2726, case.house.gov

State Offices: Honolulu, 808-650-6688.

Committees: *Appropriations*: Commerce, Justice, Science & Related Agencies; Legislative Branch; Military Construction, Veterans Affairs & Related Agencies. *Natural Resources*: Indigenous Peoples of the United States; National Parks, Forests & Public Lands; Water, Oceans & Wildlife.

Election Results

Election	Name (Party)		Vote (%)	Cand. Spent	Ind. Exp. Support	Ind. Exp. Oppose
2018 General	Ed Case (D)	134,650	(73%)	$481,141		
	Cam Cavasso (R)	42,498	(23%)	$150,889		
2018 Primary	Ed Case (D)	47,482	(40%)			
	Doug Chin (D)	30,283	(26%)			
	Donna Kim (D)	21,554	(18%)			
	Kaniela Ing (D)	7,531	(6%)			
	Beth Fukumoto (D)	7,473	(6%)			

Prior winning percentages: 2004 (63%), 2002 special (51%)

Democrat Ed Case returned to the House where he had previously served. He departed in 2006, when he waged an unsuccessful primary challenge to Democratic Sen. Daniel Akaka. In Hawaiian politics, where candidates often go back and forth in the offices they seek, Case has the unusual distinction of returning to the House in a different district than he initially served. His political career has been marked by constant clashes with the Democratic machine that was led for decades by Sen. Daniel Inouye, though it has weakened since his death in 2012. Case replaced Colleen Hanabusa, who lost the Democratic primary for governor.

A fourth-generation Hawaiian, Case graduated from Williams College and Hastings Law School in San Francisco. He spent three years on Capitol Hill as an aide to Sen. Spark Matsunaga. He returned home to join a Honolulu law firm, where he specialized in land and commercial law. After earlier defeats, he was elected to the state House in 1994, where he was majority leader in 1999 and 2000.

In 2002, he narrowly lost the primary for governor to then-Lt. Gov. Mazie Hirono, who subsequently lost to Republican Laura Lingle. Unexpectedly, Case ran for the House later that year after longtime Democratic Rep. Patsy Mink died in September. Case won a special election with 44 candidates in a winner-take-all contest. In 2004, he defeated Republican challenger Mike Gabbard, the father of current Democratic Rep. Tulsi Gabbard. During four years in the House, he had a centrist voting record, which was a bit more conservative on foreign issues.

In his controversial challenge in 2006 to the 82-year-old Akaka, who was strongly backed by Inouye, Case argued that Hawaii, with two octogenarian Senators, needed to prepare for the inevitable transition by electing a more youthful Democrat who could begin accumulating seniority. Akaka had a limited legislative record, but he was revered in Hawaii for his gentleness and modesty. He won, 55%-45%. "The machine won," said Case. He returned to the Islands to practice law, though he lost bids for open seats in the House in 2010 and the Senate in 2012. In 2013, he became senior vice president of a group of Hawaiian hotels and said that he likely had ended his political career.

In 2018, he entered the House race on the final day before the filing deadline. Case's policy priorities included ending partisan gridlock and maintaining the U.S.-Asia relationship. "I'm running again because we must do better, and I want to be part of the solution," Case said. This time, he cited his experience, in both Washington and the private sector. "I'm also running because our Hawaii needs proven effective leadership in Congress."

Two Democrats who were well-known locally got a head start in campaigning and fundraising: Lt. Gov. Doug Chin, who had been appointed the state's attorney general by Gov. David Ige, and state Sen. Donna Kim, who had been Senate president. Each of them outspent Case, who self-financed almost half the roughly $350,000 he spent on the primary. Case benefited from his more extensive political experience and name recognition. He won with 39 percent of the vote to 25 percent for Chin and 18 percent for Kim. The general election here was an afterthought.

Given the rapid turnover—and internal challenges—among Hawaii's top leaders in recent years, it might be premature to conclude that Case's return to the House will be the last stop in his political odyssey.

HI-1: Honolulu Metro

Cook Partisan Voting Index: D+17

Population		Race and Ethnicity		Income	
Total	711,225	White	16%	Median Income	$78,813
Land area (sq. miles)	209	Black	1.9%	District Income Rank	58
Pop/ sq mi	3399.4	Latino	8.5%	Poverty Rate	8.7%
Born in State	52.9%	Asian	49%	With health insurance	96%
		Two or more races	16.9%	Cash public assistance	3.1%
Age Groups		Other	7.7%	Food stamp/SNAP	9.2%
Under 18	20.2%				
18-34	24.1%	**Education**		**Work**	
35-64	38.2%	H.S grad or less	34%	White Collar	17.5%
Over 64	17.5%	Some college	30.9%	Sales and Service	47.2%
		College Degree, 4 yr	23.1%	Blue Collar	16.7%
Military		Post grad	12%	Government	21.4%
Veteran/ Active Duty	13.7%				

2012 Pres. Vote	Obama	151,023	(70%)	Romney	62,875	(29%)			
2016 Pres. Vote	Clinton	132,009	(63%)	Trump	63,916	(31%)	Johnson	7,195	(3%)
	Stein	4,431	(2%)						

Honolulu: The landmarks for visitors to Honolulu are the Joint Base Pearl Harbor-Hickam military facility, the USS Arizona monument in Pearl Harbor, the downtown area, with its wondrously Victorian Iolani Palace, and, of course, Waikiki, with its 40-story hotels rising within a few feet of each other. This part of Hawaii is tightly packed with people living between the 3,000-foot Koolau Range and the beaches and harbor, where tropical bungalows and garden apartments house Hawaiians of all incomes. Behind New York, San Francisco and Los Angeles, Honolulu is the densest metropolitan area in the nation. Hawaii's largest shopping centers and its state university are located here.

Hawaii's topography jams cars onto just a few freeways and avenues, where traffic slows during rush hour and the aloha spirit is sorely tested. But hope has been (slowly) on the way for relief of traffic congestion. The Honolulu Authority for Rapid Transportation is working on a 20-mile elevated rail line that will serve downtown and outlying communities, the largest public-works project in state history. By 2018, costs had increased to $9.5 billion from the $5.2 billion projection in 2012. Added costs are being financed by a surcharge on the excise tax and additional hotel taxes. The completion date has been delayed until at least 2025. The four-car trains will include racks for bicycles and surfboards.

The military remains an important presence on Oahu, even as the Naval Base at Pearl Harbor and Hickam Air Force Base merged into a joint base. The base still operates Boeing's C-17 Globemaster III cargo jet. Honolulu is key to the roaring tourism industry. In 2017, Hawaii attracted a record 9.4 million visitors. Hawaiian Airlines has non-stop flights from Honolulu to several cities on the mainland. In another significant step, a local business plans a delayed completion in 2021 of the Seawater Air Conditioning project, which is designed to produce enough chilled fresh water to supply all of Honolulu's cooling needs by 2045.

The 1st Congressional District of Hawaii is entirely in Honolulu, on Oahu. With little land left to develop on the southern part of the island, it is growing less rapidly than the rest of the state. Politically, the neighborhoods around Honolulu's downtown and the university campus are middle and lower-income and usually vote Democratic. To the west, around the harbor, are many military families in modest neighborhoods who vote for candidates from both parties. To the east, around Diamond Head and the Kahala and Koko Head beach areas, is higher-income territory that has voted Republican. Developers have explored plans to combat beach erosion at Waikiki, which is mostly man-made and has exceeded two feet from the public-access staircase to the beach. Asians are 49 percent of the population in the 1st and 23 percent were foreign-born. In 2016, Hillary Clinton won 63 percent of the vote.

Tulsi Gabbard (D)

Elected 2012, 4th term, b. Apr 12, 1981; Leloaloa, AS; Alabama Military Academy, Accelerated Officer Candidate School, 2007; Hawaii Pacific University, B.S., 2009; Hinduism; Married (Abraham Williams).

Military Career: HI Army National Guard 2003-pres. (Iraq)

Elected Office: HI House, 2002-2004; Honolulu City Council, 2010-2012.

Professional Career: Founder, Kanu Productions, 2011-present; Co-founder, Healthy Hawaii Coalition, 2000-present; Legislative aide, Sen. Daniel Akaka, 2006-2007.

DC Office: 1433 LHOB 20515, 202-225-4906, Fax: 202-225-4987, gabbard.house.gov

State Offices: Honolulu, 808-541-1986.

Committees: *Armed Services*: Intelligence, Emerging Threats & Capabilities; Readiness. *Financial Services*: Nat'l Security, International Development & Monetary Policy; Subcommittee on Diversity & Inclusion.

Group Ratings

	ADA	ACLU	AFL-CIO	LCV	ITI	COC	HAFA	ACU	CFG	FRC
2018	-	88%	-	94%	-	73%	6%	8%	16%	0%
2017	95%	C	92%	91%	C	46%	C	4%	3%	13%

Almanac Ratings 2017-18

	Economy	Social	Foreign	Composite
Liberal	95%	90%	95%	93%
Conservative	5%	10%	5%	7%

Key Votes of the 115th Congress

1. Obama-care revision	N	5. Family planning regs	N	9. Guantanamo prisoners	Y
2. Tax Cuts	N	6. Body cameras/immigration	Y	10. Ground missiles, limit	Y
3. Omnibus appropriations	Y	7. Abortion ban	N	11. Defense Dept. spending	N
4. Dodd-Frank revision	N	8. Concealed carry	N	12. FISA rules	N

Election Results

Election	Name (Party)	Vote (%)		Cand. Spent	Ind. Exp. Support	Ind. Exp. Oppose
2018 General	Tulsi Gabbard (D)............................	153,271	(77%)	$1,368,225		
	Brian Evans (R).....................................	44,850	(23%)			
2018 Primary	Tulsi Gabbard (D)...........................	94,629	(84%)			
	Sherry Alu Campagna (D)....................	13,947	(12%)			

Prior winning percentages: 2016 (81%), 2014 (76%), 2012 (77%)

Democrat Tulsi Gabbard, first elected in 2012, was one of the first two female combat veterans and the first Hindu in Congress. At home and in Washington, she has been outspoken and independent. Her occasional freelancing on national security issues has generated bipartisan criticism. As a prominent supporter of Bernie Sanders in the 2016 campaign, she clashed with some leading Democratic officials. As one of the first Democrats to declare their candidacy for president in 2020, she had a rocky start.

The fourth of five children, Gabbard was born in American Samoa and moved with her family to Hawaii at a young age. Her father, Mike Gabbard, serves in the Hawaii Senate, where he chaired the Agriculture and Environment Committee; he switched parties in 2007 because, he said, he thought he would have more influence as a Democrat. Her mother, Carol Gabbard, formerly served on the state Board of Education. Both made names in Hawaii politics as strong opponents of gay marriage, an issue that resulted in controversy for their daughter. Gabbard was homeschooled, and with her brothers and sister helped run a family restaurant. She graduated from Hawaii Pacific University with a degree in business administration.

At age 19, Gabbard and her father cofounded the Healthy Hawaii Coalition, an environmental-education nonprofit that teaches elementary students about the ways humans can positively and negatively affect the environment. In 2002, she won a seat representing West Oahu in the state House. At 21, she was the youngest woman ever elected to a state legislature. "A lot of people told me I was crazy and too young, but I really felt the need and passion to do more with my life and be able to make a positive impact for others," she told National Journal.

While serving in the legislature, she enlisted in the Hawaii Army National Guard as a private. In 2004, her unit was activated for Iraq, but Gabbard was not given orders to deploy. Declaring, "No way would I stay home and watch 3,000 of my brothers and sisters deploy without me," she withdrew from the campaign and voluntarily deployed with the medical unit for 18 months. At Fort McClellan's Officer Candidate School in Alabama, she was the first woman to graduate at the top of her class. She deployed again in 2008, to Kuwait as a military police platoon leader training counterterrorism units. In between tours of duty, she worked as a legislative aide to Democratic Sen. Daniel Akaka. Elected to the Honolulu City Council in 2010, she said her proudest accomplishments included helping to legalize food trucks and organizing an environmental cleanup following a landfill overflow. She started her own film production company, Kanu Productions.

Gabbard was the first of six Democrats to jump into the race for an open House seat, touting herself as a fresh voice for Washington. Her chief primary opponent, who led for most of the race, was former Honolulu Mayor Mufi Hannemann. She called for subsidizing alternative energy projects to diversify Hawaii's tourism-dependent economy, as well as making the state's energy supply more secure. Her 55%-34% victory over the experienced Hannemann surprised observers. She easily won the general.

In the House, she has shown independence on the Armed Services Committee, a useful assignment for a lawmaker from Hawaii. She often collaborated with Republicans and grew critical of President Barack Obama's foreign policy. One of her chief priorities has been to bring all troops home from Afghanistan. In 2014, she said that it "makes no sense" to pursue military action against the Islamic State, and she added that summer that the mission was "lost." She criticized the Obama administration for failing to "recognize that this is about radical Islam." She was one of 22 House Democrats who voted with all Republicans to condemn the Obama administration for failing to notify Congress of the exchange for Army Sgt. Bowe Bergdahl, who had abandoned his unit in Afghanistan.

With Republican Rep. Martha Roby of Alabama, Gabbard warned in a letter to other House members in 2015 that Pentagon spending cuts scheduled to take effect later that year would "undermin[e] our national security, local economies, and the livelihoods of military families." She was a co-founder of a bipartisan House caucus to assist veterans' transition to civilian life. In October 2015, Gabbard was promoted to major in the National Guard.

Gabbard praised the election in 2014 of Prime Minister Narenda Modi of India, and met personally with Modi in New York and then in New Delhi. On the House Foreign Affairs Committee, she worked with Republicans in 2015 on legislation to toughen economic sanctions against North Korea. In 2016, she was one of three House members who voted against a resolution that condemned the Syrian government for war crimes, on the ground that it could result in U.S. military action. On domestic issues, Gabbard joined a bipartisan "No Labels" group of about 70 House members seeking common ground on fiscal policies. "Millennials care less about party labels and blind partisanship, and care more about getting things done," she said. Gabbard also gained attention for joining some Republicans in the House gym for regular sessions of "CrossFit" and circuit training.

In February 2016, Gabbard resigned as a vice chair of the Democratic National Committee and endorsed Sanders. She praised him for understanding "how and when we use our military power — and just as importantly, when we don't use that military power." Earlier, she criticized the DNC's scheduling of presidential debates for favoring Hillary Clinton. At home, Gabbard has coasted to reelection.

Gabbard's dealings with President Donald Trump have run the gamut. During his post-election transition, she met with him at his New York headquarters, reportedly to discuss serving as the U.S. representative to the United Nations. They discussed their common ground on the Islamic threat and the need to revamp military interventions overseas. In January 2017, on a fact-finding mission to Syria, she unexpectedly met with President Bashar al-Assad. She was widely criticized by members of both parties for giving credibility to a leader whose forces have killed hundreds of thousands of Syrians and caused millions of refugees. Gabbard responded that the United States should focus on the more immediate threat from the Islamic State and end its talk of "regime change" in Syria, which she said could lead to conflict with Russia. Later, she said she was "skeptical" that Assad had launched chemical weapons on the Syrian people and she criticized Trump's limited military response, which resulted in more second-guessing from Democrats. Her hostility toward Trump grew when she said in April 2017 that she was "doing my homework" on impeachment.

Her political independence led some political observers to conclude that Gabbard appealed to Trump voters, plus those who supported Sanders. "Never before have we seen a Democrat who has managed to receive praise from Bernie Sanders and Steve Bannon at the same time," Democratic contributor Michael Starr Hopkins wrote for The Hill newspaper in November 2017. "Gabbard has made clear that she is indebted to no one and unwilling to be just another Democrat." In signs that she was exploring a run for president, she spoke at a Democratic fundraising event in Iowa in October 2017, visited political organizers in New Hampshire in September 2018 and worked on a book for publication in 2019.

In January 2019, Gabbard said in an interview with CNN, "I have decided to run." At that time, she had unusual conflicts with other Democrats. In an op-ed for The Hill, she criticized politicians who have "weaponized religion for their own selfish gain, fomenting bigotry, fears and suspicions based on the faith, religion or spiritual practices of their political opponents." Without naming them, she referred implicitly to two Democratic senators — Kamala Harris of California and her home-state colleague Mazie Hirono — who had raised questions about a judicial nominee membership in the Knights of Columbus, a Catholic service organization. When other Democrats attacked her earlier comments that were critical of gay rights, Gabbard said that her views had changed and she apologized for having "said and believed things that were wrong, and worse, they were very hurtful to people in the L.G.B.T.Q. community." A lengthy profile in the New Yorker in November 2017 wrote that she had a "stubbornly personal approach" to politics.

Some Hawaii Democrats seized on her national ambitions to step up interest in her House seat. State Sen. Kai Kahele announced his candidacy in January 2019. According to the Hawaii elections office, Gabbard could simultaneously run for president and for her seat in Congress. Reality might force her to choose.

HI-2: Outer Oahu   Cook Partisan Voting Index: D+19

Population		Race and Ethnicity		Income	
Total	710,433	White	28.4%	Median Income	$71,289
Land area (sq. miles)	6,213	Black	1.4%	District Income Rank	85
Pop/ sq mi	114.3	Latino	11.9%	Poverty Rate	12%
Born in State	54.4%	Asian	25%	With health insurance	94.8%
		Two or more races	21.8%	Cash public assistance	3.7%
Age Groups		Other	11.3%	Food stamp/SNAP	13.8%
Under 18	23.1%				
18-34	23%	**Education**		**Work**	
35-64	37.9%	H.S grad or less	38.2%	White Collar	16%
Over 64	16%	Some college	32.8%	Sales and Service	48.5%
		College Degree, 4 yr	19.3%	Blue Collar	19.5%
Military		Post grad	9.6%	Government	19.3%
Veteran/ Active Duty	13.2%				

2012 Pres. Vote	Obama	155,635	(71%)	Romney	58,140	(27%)		
2016 Pres. Vote	Clinton	134,882	(61%)	Trump	64,931	(30%)	Johnson	8,759 (4%)
	Stein	8,306	(4%)					

Other Islands: The 2nd Congressional District encompasses each island in the Hawaii archipelago, including most of Oahu's acreage beyond the city of Honolulu. It takes in Wheeler Army Airfield and some farmlands north of Pearl Harbor, between two jagged chains of mountains that lift the island out of the sea. Over the mountains to the west on Oahu is the Leeward Coast — calm, sultry and lightly populated. Over the mountains to the northeast is the Windward Coast, with many prosperous subdivisions in and around Kaneohe and Kailua.

The 137 islands have distinct personalities. Hawaii, the Big Island, is the size of Connecticut and boasts huge cattle ranches; the active volcano Kilauea, which started erupting in 1983 and has not stopped since; and Mauna Kea, the highest mountain in the world if the count begins at its base far under the ocean. In an isolated dome on Mauna Loa, NASA scientists have studied behavior of humans when they have been isolated. On the north shore, with heavy rainfall and tropical foliage, is the old port of Hilo and Hawaii's macadamia nut industry; this is a blue-collar Democratic area in a natural wonderland. On the Kona Coast, where there is little rainfall and the landscape is dominated by lava flows, there are retirement condominiums and a higher-income population. In 2017, this island had the largest increase in airline passengers in the state. Months of new eruptions in 2018, with dramatic flows of lava and ash, closed a small corner of Kilauea.

Maui, favored more by North American than Asian tourists, has dozens of upscale resorts and idyllic beaches. In 2017, the first dispensary to sell marijuana in Hawaii opened on Maui. Kauai, much of which was devastated by Hurricane Iniki in 1992, is the least developed and most agricultural of the main islands. Parts of it have the nation's highest rainfall, while others seldom get wet. In 2016, Obama used his executive authority to create south and west of Hawaii the world's largest protected marine sanctuary, quadrupling the size of the existing refuge.

A fact that has been little-noted by mainlanders: Production of sugar and pineapples has virtually disappeared in Hawaii, chiefly a result of land costs and a higher return for other uses. In 2016, the Hawaiian Commercial and Sugar Co. on Maui ended its harvest as the remaining sugar mill in Hawaii and laid off what remained of 650 employees. At one time, the state produced 20 percent of the sugar consumed in the United States. The largest pineapple plantation shut down in 2009. Overall, the district is solidly Democratic. Hillary Clinton won, 61%-30%, slightly below her performance in the 1st District.

IDAHO

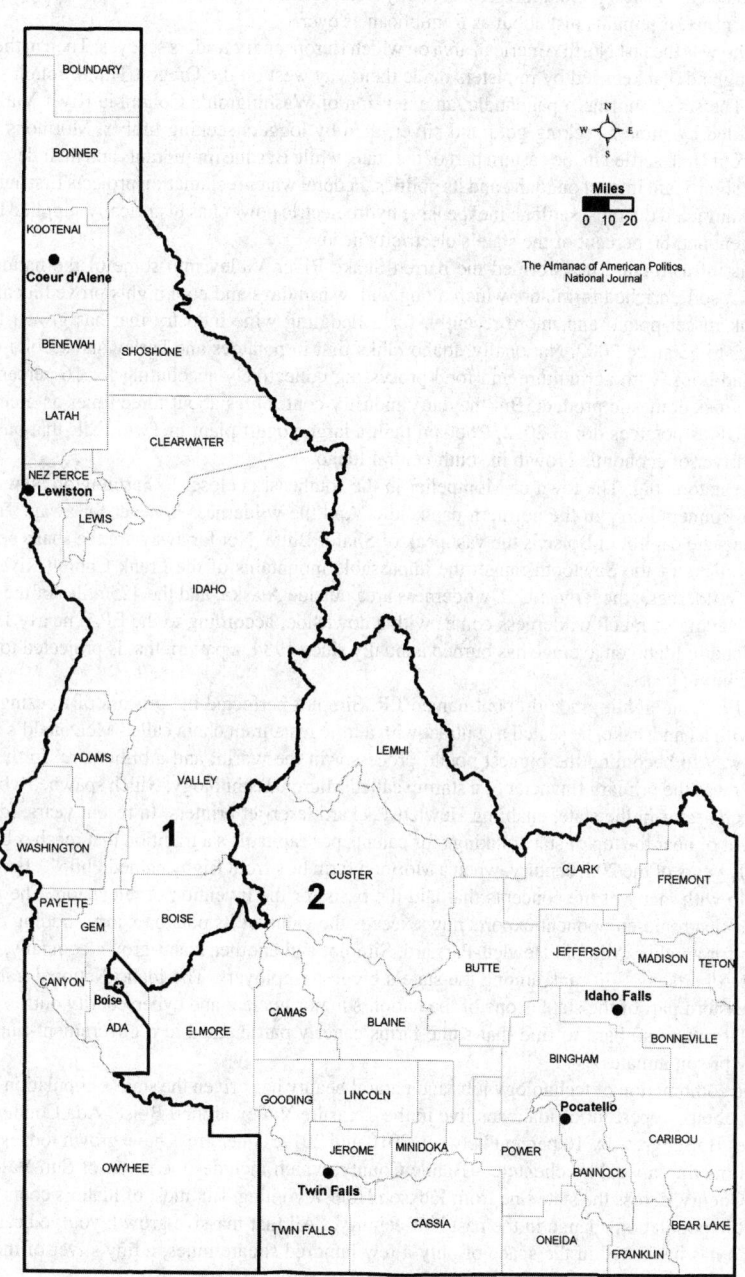

BOUNDARY

BONNER

KOOTENAI

● Coeur d'Alene

BENEWAH

SHOSHONE

LATAH

CLEARWATER

NEZ PERCE
● Lewiston

LEWIS

IDAHO

ADAMS

VALLEY

LEMHI

WASHINGTON

PAYETTE

GEM

BOISE

CANYON

Boise

ADA

ELMORE

CAMAS

BLAINE

CUSTER

BUTTE

CLARK

FREMONT

JEFFERSON

MADISON

TETON

● Idaho Falls

BONNEVILLE

BINGHAM

GOODING

LINCOLN

OWYHEE

JEROME

MINIDOKA

POWER

● Pocatello

CARIBOU

BANNOCK

● Twin Falls

TWIN FALLS

CASSIA

ONEIDA

FRANKLIN

BEAR LAKE

1

2

N
W—E
S

Miles
0 10 20

The Almanac of American Politics.
National Journal

Congressional district boundaries were first effective for 2012.

Tucked near the northwest edge of the continental United States, far from any major metro area, Idaho has seen its population grow by more than two-thirds since 1990 and, along with Nevada, experienced the fastest population growth of any state from 2017 to 2018. Despite (or maybe because of) this influx, it remains just about as Republican as ever.

Idaho was the last North American area on which European fur traders set eyes. Then in the 1840s, New England Yankees led by ministers made their way west on the Oregon Trail through southern Idaho. The state's northern panhandle, an extension of Washington's Columbia River Valley, was first settled by miners seeking gold and silver, then by loggers seeking timber. Mormons moving north from Utah settled in the eastern part of the state, while Basque immigrants and their descendants made a significant impact on Idaho and its politics. Federal water reclamation projects first authorized in 1894 attracted the most settlers; inexpensive hydroelectric power has historically supplied between 60 percent and 80 percent of the state's electricity needs.

This infrastructure transformed the barren Snake River Valley into some of the nation's best volcanic, soil-enriched farmland, which along with warm days and cool nights proved ideal for the Burbank russet potato and, more recently, for a fledgling wine industry that has grown from 11 wineries to 53 since 2002. Nationally, Idaho ranks first in potatoes and barley and second in sugar beets and hops, with agriculture and food processing collectively accounting for 16 percent of the state's gross domestic product. But the dairy industry contributes about three times as much to the state GDP as potatoes do; in 2012, Chobani built a large yogurt plant in Twin Falls that has been a major driver of economic growth in south-central Idaho.

The state is big: The town of Montpelier in the southeast is closer to Farmington New Mexico than to Bonners Ferry in the northern panhandle. And the wilderness is never far away. Towering over the state capitol in Boise is the vast peak of Shafer Butte. Not far away are the sharp peaks and broad valleys of the Sawtooth range; the impassable mountains of the Frank Church-River of No Return Wilderness, the largest U.S. wilderness area outside Alaska; and the 425 miles of the Salmon River. Having so much wilderness comes with a downside; according to the EPA, nearly 1 percent of the land in Idaho on average has burned annually since 1984, a pattern that is projected to worsen in the coming years.

In 1953, an eighth-grade dropout named J.R. Simplot perfected the process of freezing French fries; with a handshake, he sealed a contract with a little restaurant chain called McDonald's and was on his way to becoming the biggest potato processor in the world, and a billionaire. In the 1970s, Simplot was the primary financier of a startup called Micron Technology, which spawned a booming high-tech sector in the state, enabling Hewlett-Packard laser-jet printers. In recent years, Idaho has ranked at or near the top of state rankings for patents per capita. It's a tradition that reaches back into the early years of the 20th century, when a Mormon farm boy from Rigby named Philo T. Farnsworth came up with many of the concepts that laid the basis for the invention of television. The value of Idaho's electronic-component exports now exceeds the value of its potato exports, trading one type of chip for another. Micron, Hewlett-Packard, Simplot and another Idaho-grown company, grocery retailer Albertsons, still rank among the state's biggest employers. The Idaho National Laboratory in the eastern part of the state is one of the nation's major nuclear and cybersecurity outfits. By late 2018, labor was so hard to find that some farms eagerly participated in a government-run plan to employ prison inmates.

The combination of technology jobs and natural beauty has driven the state's population growth. Today, about 40 percent of Idahoans live in the Treasure Valley around Boise; Ada County, which includes Boise, grew by 16 percent between 2010 and 2017. Other areas have grown too, especially those attracting a wealthy clientele – Blaine County, which includes the resort of Sun Valley, and Teton County, across the state line from Jackson Hole Wyoming. But most of Idaho's counties have seen little population change in the past half-century. "All that massive growth you've heard about in Idaho has happened in the space of only a few hundred square miles, a tiny sliver of the state," longtime political observer Randy Stapilushas noted.

Hispanic residents doubled between 2000 and 2017 and account for more than 12 percent of Idaho residents. Idaho has welcomed not only Americans from other states but those from abroad, including refugees. The state has absorbed more than 20,000 refugees since the 1970s, mostly in Boise and Twin Falls -- first Vietnamese and Cambodians, then Bosnians, and more recently refugees from Iraq, Afghanistan, Sudan, Congo, Eritrea, Nepal and Iran. In Twin Falls, just 17 miles from a World War II internment camp for Japanese Americans, this has periodically spawned controversy. But an anti-refugee ballot measure proposal in 2016 failed to secure enough signatures, despite fake Russian-controlled Facebook accounts trying to stir up an anti-refugee rally. The Mormon population may be a reason for the state's tolerant streak, due to its international missionary outreach: Idaho has the second highest percentage of Mormons of any state.

In its early years as a silver-producing state, Idaho backed populism and opposed the gold standard; from 1900 to 1960, it was politically marginal. It elected prominent national Democrats such as Sen. Frank Church, an intelligence watchdog and 1976 presidential candidate, and Gov. Cecil Andrus, Jimmy Carter's Interior secretary. But Idaho has become staunchly Republican. Since 1964, no Democratic presidential nominee has won more than 37 percent of the vote here. Idahoans tend to see themselves as pioneering entrepreneurs who, rather than seek federal help, want to get a bloated, bossy federal government off their backs. The U.S. government owns 63 percent of Idaho's land, and most Idahoans strongly oppose federal policies that block road-building on one-third of national forestland, limit grazing on public lands, and breach Snake River dams to protect salmon (in the process, depriving potato farmers of water). Idaho has elected only Republicans to the governorship since 1994 and to the Senate since 1978. The GOP has won every election in Idaho's two House seats since 1994, except in 2008, when Democrat Walt Minnick beat a fiery freshman in the western 1st District. Minnick was ousted two years later.

Democratic dreams of making inroads in Idaho have regularly been dashed. Gains of upscale professionals and minorities have been balanced out, if not exceeded, by the influx of conservative-leaning engineers and entrepreneurs who have come from California and all over for a fresh environment and a fresh start — and fewer cumbersome or expensive regulations. "People keep thinking, 'Oh, you've got all these people moving in, it's going to kind of moderate and you're going to get a two-party system,'" Gary Moncrief, a retired professor at Boise State University, told the New York Times. "People have been talking about that now for 30 years and it just hasn't happened, and part of that is because of the nature of the people that are moving here."

In 2016, Donald Trump fared a few percentage points worse in the state than Mitt Romney had in 2012, mirroring Trump's relatively weak performance among Mormon Republicans. Much of Trump's shortfall flowed to Evan McMullin, a Mormon and an independent Republican who won almost 7 percent of the vote. As was the case in 2012, only two Idaho counties – Latah, which includes the university town of Moscow, and ski-resort-dotted Blaine – voted Democratic in the presidential race. In 2018, the Democratic wave barely reached Idaho. In the gubernatorial race, Democrats nominated an unusually liberal candidate, Paulette Jordan, who lost, 60%-38%, and the GOP won all statewide races. But Democrats won a few legislative races in typically Republican territory just beyond the borders of Boise. And the brightest ray of hope for Democrats was a ballot measure to expand Medicaid under the Affordable Care Act which, with the late backing of outgoing Republican Gov. Butch Otter, passed with more than 60 percent of the vote. The Medicaid expansion was signed into law, after a compromise was struck over adding work requirements to the measure.

Population		Race and Ethnicity		Income	
Total	1,657,375	White	82.5%	Median Income	$50,985
Land area (sq. miles)	82,643	Black	0.6%	State Income Rank	37
Pop/ sq mi	20.1	Latino	12.2%	Poverty Rate	14.5%
Born in state	47.7%	Asian	1.3%	With health insurance	87.9%
		Two or more races	2.0%	Cash public assistance	3.2%
Age Groups		Other	1.3%	Food stamp/SNAP	11.3%
Under 18	26.2%				
18-34	22.6%	Education		Work	
35-64	36.6%	H.S grad or less	37.2%	White Collar	34.3%
Over 64	14.6%	Some college	36.1%	Sales and Service	41.4%
		College Degree, 4 yr	18.2%	Blue Collar	24.4%
Military		Post grad	8.5%	Government	15.1%
Veteran/ Active Duty	9.8%				

Presidential Politics

2016 Caucus (D)	Sanders (D)	18,640 (78%)	Clinton (D)	5,065 (21%)			
2016 Primary (R)	Cruz (R)	100,889 (45%)	Trump (R)	62,413 (28%)	Rubio (R)	35,290 (16%)	
	Kasich (R)	16,514 (7%)					
2016 Pres. Vote	Trump (R)	409,055 (59%)	Clinton (D)	189,765 (27%)	McMullin (I)	46,476 (7%)	
	Johnson (L)	28,331 (4%)					
2012 Pres. Vote	Romney (R)	420,911 (65%)	Obama (D)	212,787 (33%)			

Idaho is one of the most Republican states in presidential politics. No Democratic nominee has come close to carrying it since the 1964 LBJ landslide, when the incumbent Democratic president managed to defeat Barry Goldwater, 51%-49%. Donald Trump handily beat Hillary Clinton, 59%-28%, with six third-party and independent candidates garnering 13 percent. More than 690,000 Idahoans cast presidential ballots, a record, representing 74 percent of registered voters. Trump was the first GOP nominee not to break 60 percent since Bob Dole won the state in 1996 with 52 percent of the vote. The only pocket of Democratic strength is Ada County, home to the state capital and Idaho's largest city, Boise. But even in Ada, Democrats regularly get defeated. The remainder of the state, from the panhandle in the north to the industrial farms and ski resorts in the south, is Republican territory.

Idaho held a GOP presidential primary on March 8. Texas Sen. Ted Cruz defeated Trump 45%-28%, followed by Florida Sen. Marco Rubio with 16 percent. Ohio Gov. John Kasich, who had the endorsement of GOP Gov. Butch Otter, finished fourth with 7 percent. Democrats held a caucus on March 22 and Vermont Sen. Bernie Sanders dominated the local party gatherings, defeating Clinton 78%-21%. Actress Susan Sarandon stumped for Sanders in the state, and he carried every county except tiny Lewis in the panhandle, which he lost by one vote. In 2018, the Idaho Democratic State Central Committee decided to switch from a caucus to a primary for 2020.

Congressional Districts

116th Congress Lineup	2R	**115th Congress Lineup**	2R

Idaho has two congressional districts, which split Boise between them. It also has a six-member bipartisan reapportionment commission, which probably gives Democrats more of a role in the process than they deserve in a state where roughly four-fifths of state legislators are Republicans. Still, drawing a seat friendly to Democrats is a near-impossible task in Idaho and the commission's tradition has been to simply shift the Boise dividing line between the 1st and 2nd districts slightly west every 10 years to accommodate the 1st District's stronger growth. In 2011, robust growth in northern Idaho and Boise's western suburbs forced the 1st District to shed about 58,000 residents. After a three-month stalemate, one Democratic commissioner folded and agreed to merely move the boundary three miles west. The shift subtly made the 1st District about a point more Republican, perhaps giving 2nd District Republican Mike Simpson a few more moderate primary voters. Simpson easily survived a conservative challenge in the 2014 primary.

The latest Census Bureau data on Idaho shows that population growth has been strong across the state, though the 1st District would have to shift about 20,000 of its residents to the 2nd District to achieve a new balance in 2022. Perhaps more significantly, continued growth could position Idaho for the first time in its history to gain a third seat, perhaps in the following decade. That would generate significant jousting, including whether Boise should get its own seat or continue to influence two— or possibly all three—seats, with the other seats based in the north and the east.

Brad Little (R)

Elected 2018, term expires 2023, 1st term; b. Feb. 15, 1954, Emmett; University of Idaho, B.S., 1976; Episcopalian Married (Teresa); 2 children.

Elected Office: ID Senate, 2001-2009, President, 2009-2019; ID Lt. Gov., 2009-2019.

Professional Career: Owner and Partner, Little Land and Livestock Company.

Office: 700 W Jefferson St #228, Boise, 83720; 208-334-2100; Fax: 208-334-3454; Website: gov.idaho.gov

Lt. Gov.: Janice McGeachin (R) **Atty. Gen:** Lawrence Wasden (R) **Sec. of State:** Lawerence Denney (R)

State Legislature: Senate: 7D, 28R **House:** 14D, 56R

Election Results

Election	Name (Party)	Vote (%)
2018 General	Brad Little (R)	361,661 (60%)
	Paulette Jordan (D)	231,081 (38%)
2018 Primary	Brad Little (R)	72,548 (38%)
	Raul Labrador (R)	63,478 (33%)
	Tommy Ahlquist (R)	51,008 (27%)

Idaho voters in 2018 chose Brad Little, the state's Republican lieutenant governor, to be the state's next governor, opting for continuity with the tenure of three-term Republican Gov. C.L. "Butch" Otter. Little, the low-key establishment candidate, won a tough Republican primary. In November, he easily defeated a progressive Democrat, Paulette Jordan, who was running to become the nation's first Native American governor.

Little is a third-generation Idahoan whose grandfather emigrated from Scotland in 1894 and established a sheep operation that spanned across much of southwest Idaho; he became "Idaho's Sheep King," and it wasn't an exaggeration. His son carried on the business, and his grandson worked on the ranch while growing up and after graduating from the University of Idaho in 1977. Little served as president of the Idaho Wool Growers Association, chaired two committees of the American Sheep Industry Association, and chaired the Idaho Association of Commerce and Industry. But the family eventually sold the sheep operation and moved into the cattle business. They also opened some of their land for use as an off-road vehicle park.

The family's second business was politics. Little's father served in the state legislature and was a Republican National Committee member; as a youngster, Little helped his father campaign for Barry Goldwater in 1964. Four years later, he sat next to Ronald Reagan at the Republican National Convention, and in 1972, Little became a delegate himself. In 2001, GOP Gov. Dirk Kempthorne appointed Little to a vacant state Senate seat, and he proceeded to win election four times. Then, in 2009, Little was appointed to the vacant lieutenant governorship and won the seat on his own in 2010 and 2014. When Otter announced he would not be seeking a fourth term, Little jumped in and received Otter's endorsement.

Little was the establishment favorite, focusing on traditional Republican priorities such as low taxes and low spending, but he faced two other major candidates in the free-spending, attack-ad-saturated 2018 primary. Both Rep. Raul Labrador, a member of the House Freedom Caucus, and Tommy Ahlquist, a developer running as an outsider, challenged Little from the right. Ben Ysursa, a former Republican secretary of state, told the Idaho Press-Tribune, "I've been around elections for 45 years, and this is the most negative gubernatorial primary I've ever seen." Little got 38 percent, followed by Labrador with 33 percent and Ahlquist with 27 percent. Little's strongest region was the farmland in the western part of the state, while Ahlquist ran stronger in heavily Mormon eastern Idaho (Ahlquist is Mormon, as is Labrador) and Labrador ran well in the northern part of the state, which he represented in Congress, and among evangelical voters.

Meanwhile, Idaho Democrats had a competitive primary between Jordan, a former state House member and former Coeur d'Alene Tribal Council official, and A.J. Balukoff, a businessman, Boise school board member and former gubernatorial candidate. In a contest that echoed the Hillary Clinton-Bernie Sanders split two years earlier, most Democratic officials backed Balukoff, a moderate. But Jordan, 38 years old, ran an insurgent campaign that attracted attention and small-dollar donations from across the country. Jordan offered a more progressive agenda than Idaho has typically seen, even from its Democrats. She supported LGBTQ rights, federal funding for Planned Parenthood, marijuana decriminalization, Medicaid expansion and clean energy subsidies, while opposing stand-your-ground gun laws. Some precincts in and around Boise ran out of ballots due to unexpectedly high turnout driven by interest in her candidacy. When the dust settled, Jordan defeated Balukoff, 58%-40%.

Despite the energy behind Jordan's gubernatorial bid, the general election wasn't close, as has been the pattern in Idaho in recent years. Little ran a largely orthodox Republican campaign, though he supported teacher pay raises and Idaho's version of the Common Core curriculum, while opposing efforts to implement school choice. While Little previously was critical of the Affordable Care Act, he said during the campaign that he would respect the results of a ballot measure to implement Medicaid expansion under that law. After the ballot measure passed with greater than 60 percent of the vote, Little reiterated his pledge (and after taking office, he eventually signed the expansion into law, with work requirements added). He defeated Jordan, 60%-38%. Jordan fared about as well statewide as Balukoff had four years earlier, although she won Ada County by a noticeably narrower margin. Compared to 2014, the Democrats increased their raw vote haul in the gubernatorial race by 36 percent -- but the Republicans increased theirs by an even more impressive 54 percent. For Democratic candidates, success in Idaho remains on the distant horizon.

Mike Crapo (R)

Elected 1998, term expires 2022, 4th term, b. May 20, 1951; Idaho Falls; Brigham Young University (UT), B.A., 1973; Harvard University Law School (MA), J.D., 1977; Mormon; Married (Susan Diane Hasleton Crapo); 5 children; 8 grandchildren.

Elected Office: ID Senate, 1985-1992, Leader, 1988-1992; U.S. House, 1993-1998.

Professional Career: Clerk, Judge James M. Carter, 1977-1978; Vice Chairman, Bonneville County Republican Comm., 1979-1981; Vice Chairman, ID district 29 Republican Comm., 1982-1984; Practicing attorney, 1978-1992.

DC Office: 239 DSOB 20510, 202-224-6142, Fax: 202-228-1375, crapo.senate.gov

State Offices: Boise, 208-334-1776; Coeur D'Alene, 208-664-5490; Idaho Falls, 208-522-9779; Lewiston, 208-743-1492; Pocatello, 208-236-6775; Twin Falls, 208-734-2515.

Committees: *Banking, Housing & Urban Affairs (Chmn)*: Ex Officio membership on all subcommittees. *Budget. Finance*: Energy, Natural Resources & Infrastructure; International Trade, Customs & Global Competitiveness; Taxation & IRS Oversight. *Joint Taxation. Judiciary*: Antitrust, Competition Policy & Consumer Rights; Constitution; Oversight, Agency Action, Federal Rights & Federal Courts; Subcommittee on Intellectual Property.

Group Ratings

	ADA	ACLU	AFL-CIO	LCV	ITI	COC	HAFA	ACU	CFG	FRC
2018	-	18%	-	7%	-	70%	70%	82%	77%	100%
2017	0%	C	0%	0%	C	86%	C	84%	90%	100%

Almanac Ratings 2017-18

	Economy	Social	Foreign	Composite
Liberal	0%	0%	0%	0%
Conservative	100%	100%	100%	100%

Key Votes of the 115th Congress

1. Obama-care revision	Y	5. Gun regulations	Y	9. Kavanaugh confirmation	Y
2. Tax Cuts	Y	6. Family planning regs	Y	10. Saudi arms sales	N
3. Dodd-Frank revision	Y	7. Gorsuch confirmation	Y	11. FISA rules	Y
4. Omnibus appropriations	N	8. Immigration restrictions	Y	12. Military aid in Yemen	N

Election Results

Election	Name (Party)	Vote (%)	Cand. Spent	Ind. Exp. Support	Ind. Exp. Oppose
2016 General	Mike Crapo (R)	449,017 (66%)	$6,461,442		
	Jerry Sturgill (D)	188,249 (28%)	$709,348		
	Ray Writz (C)	41,677 (6%)	$2,925		
2016 Primary	Mike Crapo (R)	Unopposed			

Prior winning percentages: 2010 (71%), 2004 (99%), 1998 (70%); House: 1996 (69%), 1994 (75%), 1992 (61%)

After a quarter of a century on Capitol Hill, Republican Mike Crapo, Idaho's senior senator, has wielded influence as chairman of the Banking, Housing and Urban Affairs Committee. In 2018, he led a bipartisan coalition in the Senate that pared back the Dodd-Frank financial reforms and persuaded House Republicans and other critics of the law to agree to a less sweeping rewrite than many of them had sought. Crapo continued in the Senate leadership role of chief deputy majority whip and was next in line among Republicans to chair the powerful Finance Committee.

Representing a state that has long been a GOP bastion, the mild-mannered Crapo has a lengthy record of reaching across the political aisle to seek consensus. Notably, he served in 2011-2012 as a member of the "Gang of Six" — a bipartisan group of senators who came up with a plan to reduce the federal deficit by $3.7 trillion over a decade, though they achieved scant success. More than a quarter of the deficit savings would have come from increased tax revenues, a move that was anathema to many conservatives. "Mike's one of those guys that is a realist and understands that in legislation you don't get everything you want, but the good outweighs the bad," Sen. Jon Tester of Montana, a Democrat on the Banking, Housing, and Urban Affairs Committee who has negotiated with Crapo, told The Wall Street Journal in 2016. A decade earlier, then-Senate Democratic Leader Harry Reid singled out Crapo as one of three GOP senators who would make an "outstanding" Supreme Court justice.

His powerful Senate niche has represented a comeback from adversity. After a battle with cancer early in his Senate tenure, he was arrested in 2012 for drunken driving in suburban Virginia in an incident that drew national attention. The consumption of alcohol represented a violation of Crapo's Mormon faith, and Idahoans — nearly 25 percent of whom are Mormon — were bewildered. The Lewiston Morning Tribune ran an editorial headlined, "Is This Mike Crapo the Same Guy We Knew?" Crapo apologized, pleaded guilty to a misdemeanor, and, over a two-year period, held town halls in all of Idaho's 200 incorporated cities. That resulted in his political rehabilitation.

A fourth-generation Idahoan, Crapo was born and raised in Idaho Falls. His father ran the local post office, and his mother stayed home to care for the family's six children. The couple farmed 200 acres, growing potatoes and grain. After earning an undergraduate degree from Brigham Young University, Crapo graduated from Harvard Law School. In 1984, he was elected to the Idaho Senate at 33. Two years earlier, leukemia took the life of his older brother, Terry, who had been the state House majority leader and a rising star in Idaho politics. The brothers were close, and Mike Crapo followed his brother's path to the Legislature. He became Senate president pro tem in 1988.

Crapo ran for an open seat in Congress in 1992 on a platform of spending cuts, a balanced-budget amendment and the line-item veto. He won the primary by a margin better than 2-1. In the general election, "Cowboy Democrat" J.D. Williams, the state controller, ran on a "Put America First" platform on industrial policy and trade. Crapo won 61%-35%. Crapo became a Republican freshman class leader and championed institutional reforms, advocating for more power for rank-

and-file members to bring bills to the floor. Like many Republicans at that time, he favored strict budget rules to force tough decisions. He supported across-the-board discretionary spending cuts, excluding Social Security. Crapo opposed the North American Free Trade Agreement in 1993, but later supported normalizing trade relations with China and Cuba.

Crapo faced a career choice in 1997. Republican Gov. Phil Batt retired, and GOP Sen. Dirk Kempthorne said he would run for governor. Crapo ran for Kempthorne's Senate seat the following year and was unopposed in the Republican primary. His opponent in the fall was trial lawyer Bill Mauk, a former Democratic state chairman. Despite its large Mormon population, Idaho had never elected a Mormon to the Senate — until Crapo. He won 70%-28%, carrying every county. He has been easily reelected ever since.

In the wake of the 2008 financial industry meltdown, Crapo worked on the Dodd-Frank financial reforms but was disappointed with the result. He expressed frustration that the bill did not revamp troubled mortgage giants Fannie Mae and Freddie Mac. He opposed the reform's creation of a Consumer Financial Protection Bureau and its requirement for commercial banks to spin off most of their derivatives-trading operations. At the same time, Crapo praised provisions in the 2010 law that required banks to hold more capital in reserve, saying this had helped "create a more stable protection against the need for taxpayer bailouts."

When President Barack Obama's re-election in 2012 dashed Republican hopes that Dodd-Frank could be repealed, Crapo sought to reshape parts of it. He took aim at what he considered overly broad regulation of derivatives trading. In 2014, as the panel's ranking Republican, Crapo teamed with then-Banking Chairman Tim Johnson, a South Dakota Democrat, on a plan to dismantle government-sponsored enterprises Fannie Mae and Freddie Mac, while shifting more of the risks of mortgage lending to the private sector. Other Democrats in the Senate and Obama administration objected.

On some high-profile issues, Crapo has sided with the most conservative corners of the Senate. At the height of the 2008 recession, he was among a dozen Senate Republicans who voted against a Bush administration request to create the $700 billion Troubled Asset Relief Program aimed at shoring up troubled financial institutions. In 2013, he opposed the bipartisan immigration overhaul bill that cleared the Senate by a wide margin.

On other issues, Crapo has not allowed ideology to interfere with the search for consensus. Serving on the bipartisan Simpson-Bowles debt reduction commission in 2010, he endorsed the commission's plan, which called for tax increases, spending cuts and changes in entitlement programs. That put him at odds with House Republicans on the panel, including then-Budget Chairman Paul Ryan of Wisconsin. While calling the plan "flawed and incomplete," he joined a statement saying "the time for action is now." Crapo worked over the next two years as a member of the bipartisan "Gang of Six" to forge a budget compromise. He voted in favor of the New Year's Day 2013 budget deal aimed at averting the so-called fiscal cliff of automatic tax increases and spending cuts. But he characterized it as a "missed opportunity to comprehensively address our nation's economic crisis."

In 2015 and 2016, Crapo counted seven bipartisan measures he sponsored that Obama signed into law. One of those had a personal dimension for him as a cancer survivor: He had his prostate removed in 2000 and underwent radiation treatment when the cancer recurred five years later. In 2016, Crapo attended a White House ceremony at which Obama signed a reauthorization of the Toxic Substances Control Act, which contained a provision known as "Trevor's Law." The bill— named for Trevor Schaefer of Boise, who survived a diagnosis of brain cancer at 13 — required the tracking of childhood and adult cancer clusters around the nation. Crapo, who has been cancer-free for more than a decade, said his own diagnosis had "accelerated and intensified" his interest in biomedical research, telling the Idaho Statesman, "Certainly, I believe when one gets the diagnosis that they have cancer, it's a gut-wrencher, and it's an attitude-changer in a lot of ways."

Meanwhile, Democratic challenger Jerry Sturgill was seeking to make a campaign issue in 2016 of Crapo's arrest for driving under the influence four years earlier. On Dec. 23, 2012, Crapo left his Capitol Hill apartment and drove across the Potomac River to Alexandria, Va., where he scored a 0.11 blood-alcohol level on a breathalyzer test after running a red light. The legal limit for driving in Virginia was .08. Crapo admitted to having had several shots of vodka, according to the police report. Two weeks later, Crapo pleaded guilty to a misdemeanor and received a $250 fine and 12-month suspension of his driver's license. "It was a poor choice to use alcohol to relieve stress — and one at odds with my personally held religious beliefs," he said after the episode. "The DUI revealed a long cover-up of personal behavior inconsistent with how Sen. Crapo had presented himself as a tee-totaling member of our church, one who had held high office," said Sturgill, a fellow Mormon — alluding to the fact that Crapo had become a bishop in the church when he was 31.

In an interview with the Idaho Statesman shortly before the 2016 election, Crapo said he had not had a drink since the episode, adding, "I do apologize again for that conduct, one of the worst times of my life, in terms of frankly being disappointed in myself and realizing that I disappointed my constituents." He said that he had worked "really hard" to recommit to his work and earn the support of his constituents, adding, "I think that I have made a strong case for that." The voters appeared to agree. Crapo defeated Sturgill 66%-28%. Later, the Federal Election Commission investigated alleged violations in the handling of Crapo's campaign account, including payments to his wife, Susan.

In the presidential campaign, Crapo initially endorsed GOP nominee Donald Trump. He became one of the first Republicans to withdraw his endorsement after release of the decade-old tape on which Trump could be heard boasting about sexually assaulting women. Crapo said Trump's "disrespectful, profane and demeaning" comments made him unfit for the presidency and suggested Trump be replaced with vice presidential nominee Mike Pence. Two weeks before the election, Crapo acknowledged that was not going to happen and restored his endorsement of Trump — citing the stakes in the coming election, particularly the prospect that the next president could have an opportunity to nominate several Supreme Court justices.

After Trump took office, Crapo's public comments were positive. "I've spent the last 14 months fighting for things that I think are good for the country," he said in a speech to the Legislature in Boise in February 2018. He cautioned that opponents of Trump in the Senate were seeking to stop his administration "from even standing full up, let alone achieving its agenda." He praised the effects of the tax cuts enacted in December 2017. "The economy has been growing at about 3.2 percent," Crapo told an Idaho reporter in July 2018. "We now have more jobs available than people seeking jobs."

On the banking committee, the term-limited Sen. Richard Shelby of Alabama in 2017 was forced to cede the gavel to Crapo — to the barely concealed delight of committee Democrats, who were on scratchy terms with Shelby. "We have a working relationship," the committee's senior Democrat, Sherrod Brown of Ohio, said of Crapo. "He's way more conservative than I am, but he's straightforward and honorable." Crapo sought common ground with Brown on cutbacks of Dodd-Frank banking regulations.

Those talks failed. But Crapo had success with a group of four relatively centrist Democrats on his committee — three of whom happened to be seeking reelection in 2018 in states that Trump had easily won in 2016. After extensive negotiations, they agreed on an extensive package reducing the number of banks subject to the increased scrutiny of the law and exempted smaller banks from some of the Dodd-Frank requirements. In March 2018, the Senate passed the bill, 67-31, with 16 Democrats joining Crapo. That agreement largely pre-empted more sweeping changes sought by House Republicans. "It is a bipartisan compromise, the changes are commonsense, and it will allow financial institutions to better serve their customers and communities, while maintaining safety and soundness and important consumer protections," he said after Trump signed the bill.

On the Finance Committee, Crapo advocated for international trade deals. Although he supported a renegotiation of NAFTA with Canada and Mexico, he cautioned Trump to keep the existing deal in place in the meantime — not least because of his home state's extensive commercial dealings with Canada. Crapo criticized Trump's extensive use of tariffs and he sought to narrow presidential discretion in trade negotiations.

Following the 2018 elections, Crapo faced the possibility that he could move up to chair the Finance Committee. But Chuck Grassley of Iowa asserted his seniority to reclaim that position and defer Crapo's switch, at least for two years. Crapo showed that he remained in the good graces of Majority Leader Mitch McConnell, who tapped him to manage committee assignments for Republican senators at the start of the new Congress for the eighth consecutive time.

Jim Risch (R)

Elected 2008, term expires 2020, 2nd term, b. May 03, 1943; Milwaukee, WI; University of Wisconsin, Milwaukee, Att., 1963; University of Idaho, B.S., 1965; University of Idaho, Law School, J.D., 1968; Roman Catholic; Married (Vicki L. Choborda); 3 children; 7 grandchildren.

Elected Office: Ada County Prosecuting Attorney, 1970-1974; ID Senate, 1974-1989, 1995-2003, Majority Leader, 1976-1982, pres. pro temp., 1982-1989; ID Lt. Governor, 2003-2006, 2007-2009; ID Governor, 2006-2008.

Professional Career: Rancher; Sr. partner, Risch Goss Insinger Gustavel, 1975-2008.

DC Office: 483 RSOB 20510, 202-224-2752, Fax: 202-224-2573, risch.senate.gov

State Offices: Boise, 208-342-7985; Coeur d'Alene, 208-667-6130; Idaho Falls, 208-523-5541; Lewiston, 208-743-0792; Pocatello, 208-236-6817; Twin Falls, 208-734-6780.

Committees: *Energy & Natural Resources*: Energy; Public Lands, Forests & Mining; Water & Power. *Ethics. Foreign Relations (Chmn). Intelligence. Small Business & Entrepreneurship.*

Group Ratings

	ADA	ACLU	AFL-CIO	LCV	ITI	COC	HAFA	ACU	CFG	FRC
2018	-	14%	-	7%	-	70%	81%	82%	75%	100%
2017	0%	C	0%	0%	C	86%	C	84%	96%	100%

Almanac Ratings 2017-18

	Economy	Social	Foreign	Composite
Liberal	0%	0%	0%	0%
Conservative	100%	100%	100%	100%

Key Votes of the 115th Congress

1. Obama-care revision	Y	5. Gun regulations	Y	9. Kavanaugh confirmation	Y
2. Tax Cuts	Y	6. Family planning regs	Y	10. Saudi arms sales	N
3. Dodd-Frank revision	Y	7. Gorsuch confirmation	Y	11. FISA rules	Y
4. Omnibus appropriations	N	8. Immigration restrictions	Y	12. Military aid in Yemen	N

Election Results

Election	Name (Party)	Vote (%)		Cand. Spent	Ind. Exp. Support	Ind. Exp. Oppose
2014 General	Jim Risch (R)	285,596	(65%)	$1,761,223		
	Nels Mitchell (D)	151,574	(35%)	$357,052		
2014 Primary	Jim Risch (R)	119,209	(80%)			
	Jeremy Anderson (R)	29,939	(20%)			

Prior winning percentages: 2008 (58%)

Republican James Risch became chairman of the Foreign Relations Committee, a prominent position in the Senate, in 2019. During his career, Risch has combined aggression with blunt-spoken critiques of foreign policy, though he has been far more circumspect with President Donald Trump than he was with President Barack Obama.

As he replaced retired Republican Bob Corker of Tennessee, who had been an irritant to Trump and once referred to the White House as an "adult day care center" as chairman, Risch took a different approach. When he was selected as chairman, he issued a brief statement that focused on "giving Idaho a voice on the world stage" and assuring that the concerns of the state were addressed. He made clear that he would remain supportive of the president and be unlikely to challenge him, even when they disagreed. Risch pursued oversight of Trump with "less zeal" than Corker did, The Washington Post reported.

Risch has a record of public service in Idaho that spanned more than three decades. Beginning as a local prosecutor, he went on to become a leader in the state Senate and lieutenant governor — and served a seven-month stint as the state's governor before his election to the Senate in 2008. Born in Milwaukee, he attended the University of Wisconsin at Milwaukee before transferring to the University of Idaho, where he earned a bachelor's degree in forestry. He became a successful rancher outside Boise and earned his law degree from the state university.

In 1970, when he was 27, Risch was elected Ada County prosecutor, a high-profile position in the state's capital and largest city, Boise. He went after the illicit drug trade so aggressively that his enemies tried to plant a bomb in his car. After that incident, Risch and his wife and political confidant, Vicki, put tape on the hood of their car every night so they could detect any tampering in the morning.

Risch has been a successful businessman and ranked high on lists of the Senate's wealthiest members. His business interests have included a property management firm and joint ownership of 250 acres in the Boise area. A Newsweek report in March 2018 of the richest members of Congress pegged him as 32nd, with a net worth of at least $15.6 million.

In 1974, Risch was elected to the Idaho Senate, where he would serve longer than anyone else in state history. He always carried an index card in his back pocket, one side listing bills that he wanted to pass and the other listing bills he was determined to kill. He became majority leader after the 1976 election by defeating colleague Larry Craig — whom Risch would succeed in the U.S. Senate three decades later. After six years as majority leader, he spent another six years as Senate president pro tem.

Risch's political career hit a rough patch after he was defeated by a Democratic challenger in 1988. He ran again for the state Senate in 1994, but lost in the GOP primary. A year later, he returned to that chamber when he was appointed to fill a vacancy. Less confrontational this time around, Risch moved back into the ranks of leadership as assistant Republican floor leader. In 2001, he had his eye on the vacant lieutenant governor's job when C.L. "Butch" Otter resigned after winning a seat in Congress. Gov. Dirk Kempthorne passed over Risch to appoint state Sen. Jack Riggs to the post. Risch defeated Riggs in the 2002 GOP primary 35%-28%; the rest of the vote was split among four other candidates.

After three years in the shadow of Kempthorne, Risch assumed the top job when President George W. Bush tapped Kempthorne to be Interior secretary. Risch had just over half a year to serve in what he considered his dream job and was determined to make the most of it. Within two weeks of taking office, he ordered a reorganization of Idaho's Health and Welfare Department. He created the position of state drug czar to combat the spread of meth in the state. Displeased that the Legislature failed to provide property tax relief during its regular session, Risch called the first special session in 14 years. The heavily Republican body passed bills cutting local property taxes by $260 million, raising the sales tax from 5 percent to 6 percent, and cutting state spending by $50 million. Voters approved the tax changes by a nearly 3-1 margin.

In an odd twist, Risch returned to his previous post after his stint as governor, because then-Rep. Otter had gotten a head start on the 2006 gubernatorial campaign before Kempthorne's elevation to the president's Cabinet. In November, Risch defeated former Democratic Rep. Larry LaRocco 58%-39% to become lieutenant governor. But another office soon became available: the Senate seat won by Craig, Risch's old rival, in 1990. Craig was arrested in a Minneapolis airport men's room in 2007 for soliciting sex from an undercover police officer and pleaded guilty to disorderly conduct. He resisted immense pressure from his Senate colleagues to resign, instead deciding against seeking re-election in 2008. Risch had little competition for the Republican nomination. His Democratic opponent was, once again, LaRocco. Risch raised more than twice as much money as his opponent and cruised to victory by a margin of nearly 25 percentage points.

"I'm reputedly the most conservative member of the Senate," Risch told the Boise Metro Chamber of Commerce in 2016. Statistics back him up: Almanac ratings showed that his voting scores have been among the most conservative in the Senate. "I ran for this office as a deficit hawk, and now that I am here, I have moved even further in that direction," Risch told the Idaho Statesman. Risch's aggressive style has at times been a contrast to his more mild-mannered senior colleague, Republican Sen. Mike Crapo, although the two have similar voting records. "Crapo and I are very, very close — we're like brothers," Risch told the Idaho Statesman. "I mean, nobody votes the same more than we do: 99.9 percent of the time."

Risch made his initial imprint in the Senate as a critic of Obama's foreign policy. When the Foreign Relations panel sought to take up the New START arms control treaty with Russia in 2010, Risch tried to stop the vote: He cited new intelligence that he said he couldn't reveal in open session but which had led him to question Russia's intentions. And when the then-Democratic majority Senate approved the pact, Risch unsuccessfully demanded a delay, noting that Russian troops reportedly had stolen five U.S. Humvees used in military exercises. He said in 2012 that the Law of the Sea treaty defining nations' ocean usage and another administration-backed effort to conclude a United Nations treaty on reducing firearms "would push the U.S. away from our constitutional foundations and supplement its authority with judgments from international courts and UN bureaucracies."

After the Russian military supported rebels in eastern Ukraine in 2014, Risch urged the U.S. to provide weapons to the Ukrainian government. During testimony that year by Secretary of State John Kerry, Risch scolded the onetime Foreign Relations chairman. "I tell you, you can't help but get the impression our foreign policy is just spinning out of control. And we are losing control in virtually every area we are trying to do something in," Risch said. In 2015, when Risch was one of 47 Senate Republicans to sign a letter to Iranian leaders warning that striking a nuclear agreement with the Obama White House without congressional approval could be short-lived, Kerry blasted the move as ignoring "200 years" of precedent in the conduct of foreign policy. Risch called Kerry's statement "absolute nonsense." He argued that senators had the right and responsibility to communicate with foreign officials. Such blunt talk has made Risch a frequent talking head. "He knocks out the television interviews. Risch is knowledgeable, engaging, quick on his feet and easy to understand," Idaho journalist Chuck Malloy said.

Like other congressional Republicans, Risch worked to define his relationship with Trump. Following the 2016 elections, his statement omitted mention of the winner. "Americans have clearly expressed their desire to move in the direction of our founders' vision of freedom from government intrusion and the opportunity for personal success," he said. After watching Trump in office and speaking with him, Risch did not always agree with him. But he preferred to avoid public confrontation. "Whether you like or dislike President Trump, he is a person of strong will," Risch said in a March 2018 interview with Politico, during which he avoided specific issues. "He is a person who, when he makes up his mind and is determined to do something, he will do it."

Risch made headlines the previous month when he warned during a conference in Germany that a war "of biblical proportions" could break out with North Korea and would leave "mass casualties the likes of which the planet has never seen." He later clarified that North Korea, not the United States, would cause such a conflict with its nuclear arsenal to which Trump would be forced to respond. As it turned out, Trump and North Korean dictator Kim Jong Un met in Singapore in June 2018 and Kim said he would stop testing missiles and nuclear weapons.

When Trump's July 2018 meeting with Russian President Vladimir Putin in Helsinki resulted in widespread criticism by members of Congress in both parties that Trump had been too deferential, Risch defended him. Although he voiced concern with some of Trump's rhetoric during a joint appearance with Putin, Risch told PBS "NewsHour," "Even the president's enemies and his critics acknowledge that he has been tougher [with Russia] than anybody else." Risch said that Russia sought to influence the 2016 election, but that there was "no evidence of collusion" with Trump.

In a December 2018 interview with the Idaho Falls Post-Register, Risch refused to say whether Saudi Arabian leaders were responsible for the slaying of journalist Jamal Khashoggi in the Saudi Embassy in Istanbul. He continued to oppose placing sanctions on the Saudis. That position placed Risch at odds with Corker and several other GOP Senators.

On the domestic front, Risch has pushed to rein in the power of the Environmental Protection Agency, telling the Twin Falls Times-News in 2011 that he thought it was possible to have clean air and water "without sending out the Gestapo to enforce the thing." He has reached across the aisle to increase the roles of alternative energy sources, such as biomass and geothermal. He and Crapo joined with Democrats Ron Wyden and Jeff Merkley of Oregon to pass legislation that would have opened public lands to development of geothermal energy. The measure was part of a broader bipartisan energy bill that the Senate passed in 2016. In a long-running dispute over the local policies of Cecil Andrus — the most recent Democratic governor of Idaho, who also served as Interior secretary during the Carter administration — Risch temporarily blocked in March 2018 a provision in a spending bill to name an Idaho forest for Andrus, who had died a few months earlier. Risch refused to explain his objections to reporters.

In 2014, Risch won a second term in the Senate by a nearly 2-1 margin. Facing re-election in 2020, Risch— who turns 77 that year — seemed safe for another six years. His high-profile chairmanship likely would continue to shape his Senate role.

Russ Fulcher (R)

Elected 2018, 1st term, b. Mar 09, 1962; Meridian; Micron University; Boise State University, B.B.A., 1984; Boise State University, M.B.A., 1988; Protestant - Unspecified Christian; Married (Kara Fulcher); 3 children.

Elected Office: ID Senate, 2005-2014.

Professional Career: Adjunct Professor, Boise State University, 2002-2003; Vice President, Preco Electronics.

DC Office: 1520 LHOB 20515, 202-225-6611, fulcher.house.gov

State Offices: Coeur d'Alene, 208-667-0127; Lewiston, 208-743-1388; Meridian, 208-888-3188.

Committees: *Education & Labor:* Health, Employment, Labor & Pensions; Higher Education & Workforce Investment. *Natural Resources:* National Parks, Forests & Public Lands; Water, Oceans & Wildlife.

Election Results

Election	Name (Party)	Vote (%)		Cand. Spent	Ind. Exp. Support	Ind. Exp. Oppose
2018 General	Russell Fulcher (R)......	197,719	(63%)	$853,395	$560,155	
	Christina McNeil (D)......	96,922	(31%)			
2018 Primary	Russell Fulcher (R)......	42,790	(43%)			
	David Leroy (R)......	15,414	(16%)			
	Luke Malek (R)......	14,152	(14%)			
	Christy Perry (R)......	11,108	(11%)			
	Michael Snyder (R)......	10,288	(10%)			

Republican freshman Russ Fulcher, an outspoken conservative, easily won the seat that was opened by Rep. Raul Labrador, who ran unsuccessfully in the GOP primary for Idaho governor. His victory revived his political career following Fulcher's loss to Gov. Butch Otter in the 2014 GOP primary. Fulcher's narrow defeat to Otter, who served three terms as governor, positioned him as the frontrunner after Labrador sought to move up the political ladder. Fulcher, like Labrador during his four terms in the House, was strongly supported by national conservative groups.

Fulcher grew up on a dairy farm in Meridian, and received his bachelor's degree and a master's in business administration from Boise State University. He was a marketing executive and later handled international sales for Boise-based technology companies, Micron Technology and Preco Electronics. Fulcher also was a commercial real estate broker, and he gained expertise in electrical engineering and energy policy.

He served 10 years in the state Senate, where he was chairman of the Republican Caucus. During that time, he criticized Otter for cooperating with the Obama administration to set up a health insurance exchange in Idaho as part of the Affordable Care Act. "Idaho became the administrator for a federal health care law that Idahoans do not want and cannot afford," said Fulcher, who joined other Republicans in the Legislature to oppose the proposal. Fulcher lost the primary to Otter, 51%-44%. Later, Fulcher said the action resulted in a huge increase in the state's health insurance costs.

Running for Congress, Fulcher was endorsed by numerous conservative activists and interest groups, including the Club for Growth, which described Fulcher as "the only conservative" in the contest. Also endorsing him was Labrador, who earlier backed Fulcher's challenge to Otter and said that Fulcher would continue his "fight for liberty" in Washington. (Fulcher had launched a second bid for governor, but switched his plans when Labrador decided to seek the office.) His chief opponent was 70-year-old trial lawyer David Leroy, who was the state's attorney general and lieutenant governor more than 30 years and lost a Republican primary for Congress in 1994.

With his stronger campaign, Fulcher easily led the primary with 43 percent of the vote to 16 percent for Leroy and 14 percent for state Rep. Luke Malek, who said that he voted for Independent Evan McMullin in the 2016 presidential election. Fulcher won each of the 19 counties in the district. About 28 percent of the total vote was cast in Ada County and another 20 percent in adjacent Canyon County. Fulcher raised more than $500,000 for the primary, in addition to a similar amount the Club for Growth spent on his behalf. Leroy led the other candidates in fundraising, with about $362,000.

In this heavily Republican state, Fulcher's success in November over Democrat Christina McNeil, a real estate agent and an advocate for immigrants, was never in doubt. A few days after the primary, Fulcher added some excitement to the contest when he suffered broken ribs following a spill while riding a motorcycle. His victory seemed to leave him well-positioned to seek a Senate seat when one of Idaho's veteran senators steps down.

ID-1: Western Idaho

Cook Partisan Voting Index: R+21

Population		Race and Ethnicity		Income	
Total	849,292	White	84.2%	Median Income	$51,632
Land area (sq. miles)	39,418	Black	0.5%	District Income Rank	276
Pop/ sq mi	21.6	Latino	10.6%	Poverty Rate	14%
Born in State	43.7%	Asian	1.2%	With health insurance	87.9%
		Two or more races	2.1%	Cash public assistance	3.2%
Age Groups		Other	1.3%	Food stamp/SNAP	11.4%
Under 18	25.5%				
18-34	20.8%	**Education**		**Work**	
35-64	38%	H.S grad or less	38.2%	White Collar	15.7%
Over 64	15.7%	Some college	36.7%	Sales and Service	42.3%
		College Degree, 4 yr	17.3%	Blue Collar	24.4%
Military		Post grad	7.8%	Government	15.1%
Veteran/ Active Duty	10.3%				

2012 Pres. Vote	Romney	213,080	(65%)	Obama	105,645	(32%)			
2016 Pres. Vote	Trump	229,034	(64%)	Clinton	91,284	(25%)	McMullin	16,087	(5%)
	Johnson	14,916	(4%)						

Western Boise, Coeur D'Alene: The 1st Congressional District of Idaho stretches 479 miles from the Nevada border to Canada and includes the outskirts of Boise and all of the panhandle. It encompasses two high-growth areas: the western suburbs of Boise and the Coeur d'Alene area in Kootenai County. Coeur d'Alene, which is in the mountains, is about 30 miles east of Spokane Washington. With 2,000 employees, its largest employer is the family-owned Hagadone Corp. Headquartered in an 18-story resort hotel on Lake Coeur d'Alene, the company publishes more than 20 newspapers, has its own advertising agency, and offers hospitality and real estate services.

To the south outside of Boise, commercial developers took over land in Nampa that not long ago grew wheat and alfalfa. The population nearly doubled in the 1990s, and it became Idaho's second-largest city. Since 2010, the boom in subdivisions has switched to nearby Meridian, which grew 40 percent from 2010 to 2018 and became the fastest-growing city in the state; with population exceeding 106,000, it surpassed Nampa and was the tenth fastest-growing city in the nation in 2017. "We all anticipated that Meridian would grow fast, but Meridian is fast even by Meridian standards," a local demographics planner told the Idaho Statesman in 2018. Closer-in Meridian is part of Boise-based Ada County, which is split between the state's two districts, with most of the city in the 2nd and the suburbs in the 1st. In 2018, Nampa was rated the best-run city in America by WalletHub, a personal finance website. In Coeur d'Alene, much of the population growth has resulted from wealthy retirees from California.

The growth in these once-rural areas has reinforced, rather than altered, the political landscape. Newcomers routinely say they moved to conservative Idaho to escape from city life, although some old-timers still worry that their communities may become new versions of San Jose or Orange County. Politically, the 1st District of Idaho is overwhelmingly Republican. Kootenai County, once a Democratic stronghold, now leans Republican as much as conservative Canyon County in Boise's suburbs. Northern mining counties were once the district's Democratic base; now that base is the university town of Moscow in Latah County. In 2016, as in 2012, Latah was one of only two counties to vote for the Democratic presidential nominee. Overall, the biggest change in the district vote was the drop on the Democratic side from 32 percent in the 2012 presidential election to 25 percent in 2016.

Mike Simpson (R)

Elected 1998, 11th term, b. Sep 08, 1950; Burley; Utah State University, Att., 1972; Washington University School of Dental Medicine (MO), D.D.S., 1977; Utah State University, B.S., 2002; Mormon; Married (Kathy Johnson Simpson).

Elected Office: Blackfoot City Council, 1980-1984; ID House, 1984-1998, speaker, 1993-1998.

Professional Career: Practicing dentist, 1977-1998.

DC Office: 2084 RHOB 20515, 202-225-5531, Fax: 202-225-8216, simpson.house.gov

State Offices: Boise, 208-334-1953; Idaho Falls, 208-523-6701; Twin Falls, 208-734-7219.

Committees: *Appropriations:* Energy & Water Development & Related Agencies (RMM); Interior, Environment & Related Agencies.

Group Ratings

	ADA	ACLU	AFL-CIO	LCV	ITI	COC	HAFA	ACU	CFG	FRC
2018	-	4%	-	14%	-	100%	40%	60%	51%	100%
2017	5%	C	30%	9%	C	92%	C	65%	43%	100%

Almanac Ratings 2017-18

	Economy	Social	Foreign	Composite
Liberal	12%	6%	5%	8%
Conservative	88%	94%	95%	92%

Key Votes of the 115th Congress

1. Obama-care revision	Y	5. Family planning regs	Y	9. Guantanamo prisoners	N
2. Tax Cuts	Y	6. Body cameras/immigration	N	10. Ground missiles, limit	N
3. Omnibus appropriations	Y	7. Abortion ban	Y	11. Defense Dept. spending	Y
4. Dodd-Frank revision	Y	8. Concealed carry	Y	12. FISA rules	Y

Election Results

Election	Name (Party)	Vote (%)	Cand. Spent	Ind. Exp. Support	Ind. Exp. Oppose
2018 General	Mike Simpson (R)............................ 170,274	(61%)	$580,770		
	Aaron Swisher (D)....................... 110,381	(39%)	$115,782		
2018 Primary	Mike Simpson (R)...	(100%)			

Prior winning percentages: 2016 (63%), 2014 (61%), 2012 (65%), 2010 (69%), 2008 (71%), 2006 (62%), 2004 (71%), 2002 (68%), 2000 (71%), 1998 (53%)

Mike Simpson, an independent-minded and hard-working Republican first elected in 1998, has been an influential lawmaker regardless of which party controls the House. He has used his post on the Appropriations Committee to deliver huge federal benefits to his district and to enact sweeping federal lands measures. He often reaches out to Democrats on economic and social issues. He easily defeated a primary challenge from the right in 2014.

Simpson grew up in Blackfoot, became a dentist, and joined his father's dental practice. He was elected to the city council in 1980 and to the state House in 1984. In 1993, he became speaker of the Idaho House while he maintained his dental practice. In the legislature, he was known as a moderate in a conservative chamber, affable and able to get differing sides together. When Republican Gov. Phil Batt announced he would retire in 1998, Simpson wanted to run, but GOP Sen. Dirk Kempthorne's decision to seek the office closed that option. Instead, he ran for the House when GOP Rep. Mike Crapo went for Kempthorne's Senate seat.

The election was hotly contested. In the Republican primary, state Rep. Mark Stubbs opposed nuclear programs at the Idaho National Laboratory, while Simpson wanted more work at the facility. Simpson refused to take a pledge to serve only three terms; the other candidates agreed to it. Term-limit advocates spent heavily against Simpson. Simpson ran ads against "out-of-state folk" interfering with Idaho's elections. He beat Stubbs 47%-41%. The Democratic nominee was Richard Stallings, who served four terms in the House and lost to Kempthorne for the Senate in 1992. Stallings emphasized his conservative voting record in the House and said he would act to boost falling farm commodity prices. Simpson won 53%-45%, losing Pocatello, Sun Valley and Boise, but winning just about everywhere else.

Simpson's open-mindedness led Esquire magazine in 2008 to call him one of the 10 best members of Congress, saying he "lives by the philosophy that democratic representation is a matter of finding not advantageous positions but common ground." He was one of just 16 House Republicans in March 2012 to back a budget plan along the lines of the bipartisan commission chaired by Alan Simpson (not related) and Erskine Bowles, and he led a bipartisan group of legislators urging budget negotiators to "go big" and look at raising taxes as well as cutting spending.

Simpson has wielded his influence on the Appropriations Committee to secure funding for the Bureau of Reclamation, the Army Corps of Engineers and the Idaho National Laboratory in his district. As a leading defender of appropriations earmarks, he disagreed when his friend Speaker John Boehner eliminated them, though Simpson supported greater transparency in the process. As chairman of the Energy and Water Development Subcommittee from 2013 to 2018, he promoted the Idaho Lab and other efforts to spur energy independence for the United States. In 2015, he played a key parliamentary role in breaking the deadlock on funding the Homeland Security Department, even though he did not serve on the subcommittee responsible for that bill. In September 2018, his energy and water bill was one of the appropriations measures enacted prior to the new fiscal year. It included hundreds of millions of dollars of additional spending for the Idaho Lab

In 2015, Simpson gained a legacy victory when Obama signed the Sawtooth National Recreation Area and Jerry Peak Wilderness Additions Act, which included the Boulder-White Cloud Management Area designating 276,000 acres in central Idaho as wilderness, prohibiting development. He spent more than a decade negotiating the plan with numerous constituencies ranging from mountain bikers to environmentalists, only to run into opposition from fellow Idaho Republicans. Having earlier warned that he would "die trying" to make a deal, Simpson had filed a scaled-down version to find common ground and to pre-empt potential unilateral action by Obama to declare the area a national monument. "The threat of a national monument, I think, convinced a lot of people it was better to have an Idaho solution than one imposed by Washington D.C.," Simpson said.

After easily winning reelection, he encountered problems in 2010, when his support for the rescue of the financial markets and other independent stances drew two primary opponents. They held Simpson to 58 percent, his worst primary showing since 1998. By 2014, Simpson's legislative rating from the conservative group Heritage Action was 45 percent. The anti-tax group Club for Growth spent more than $500,000 on behalf of Bryan Smith, who sought to portray Simpson as a Washington insider who was a captive of special interests. The U.S. Chamber of Commerce, the National Rifle Association, the National Association of Realtors and other groups responded by pouring in about $4 million on Simpson's behalf; Mitt Romney, a fellow Mormon, appeared in a Simpson ad. Smith ran ads criticizing Simpson as a "supporter of earmarks" and complaining that he "supports a scheme to give amnesty to illegal aliens." In the primary, Simpson coasted to an easy 62%-38% victory. In November, Stallings made another attempt to return to office and lost 61%-39%.

Despite his idiosyncratic style and the internal Republican schisms, Simpson appeared to be more influential and outspoken than ever. A month before the 2016 election, he stated that Donald Trump was "unfit to be president" and reiterated that he had never endorsed him. That view drew some support for Simpson at home. With Trump as president, Simpson remained an occasionally harsh critic. When Trump in the Oval Office publicly referred to "shithole" countries in the developing world, Simpson called his comment "stupid and irresponsible and childish." In June 2018, he told reporters that Trump's view "changes so frequently that anybody who depends on that, I think, is in trouble." But Simpson told the editorial board of the Idaho State Journal prior to the 2018 election that he was "pleasantly surprised" by Trump's record and that it was "hard to argue with success," especially on the economy. In a pre-election editorial endorsement, the Idaho Statesman praised Simpson for having "understood better than most how to become an effective congressman."

Following the 2018 election, Simpson supported Kay Granger of Texas — who out-ranked him in seniority -- as the new senior Republican on Appropriations. If she had been defeated, he said earlier, he would have run for the position. He became ranking Republican on the Energy and Water Development Subcommittee at Appropriations.

ID-2: Eastern Idaho

Cook Partisan Voting Index: R+17

Population		Race and Ethnicity		Income	
Total	808,083	White	80.8%	Median Income	$50,222
Land area (sq. miles)	43,225	Black	0.8%	District Income Rank	309
Pop/ sq mi	18.7	Latino	13.8%	Poverty Rate	15%
Born in State	51.8%	Asian	1.4%	With health insurance	87.9%
		Two or more races	2%	Cash public assistance	3.1%
Age Groups		Other	1.2%	Food stamp/SNAP	11.2%
Under 18	27%				
18-34	24.3%	Education		Work	
35-64	35.2%	H.S grad or less	36%	White Collar	13.5%
Over 64	13.5%	Some college	35.4%	Sales and Service	40.3%
Military		College Degree, 4 yr	19.2%	Blue Collar	24.5%
Veteran/ Active Duty	9.1%	Post grad	9.4%	Government	15.1%

2012 Pres. Vote	Romney	207,831	(64%)	Obama	107,142	(33%)			
2016 Pres. Vote	Trump	180,021	(54%)	Clinton	98,481	(30%)	McMullin	30,389	(9%)
	Johnson	13,415	(4%)						

Eastern Boise, Idaho Falls: The 2nd District of Idaho, from Boise east to the Wyoming border, is one of America's most picturesque, with thick forests, mountain ranges, broad river valleys and vacant expanses. It was settled from the east by overland pioneers who stopped in Idaho to establish farms, and from the south by Mormons moving up from Utah to Franklin, Bear Lake and Caribou counties. It has one of the largest concentrations of Mormons among congressional districts.

On Interstate 15, Idaho Falls serves as the modern metropolis for a vast region stretching from West Yellowstone Montana to the Salmon River Mountains. Near Idaho Falls, on a windswept, desolate range is Idaho National Laboratory, known locally as "The Site." The Energy Department's leading laboratory for civilian nuclear energy research, development and demonstration, the facility covers 890 square miles and employs 4,400 workers in Boise and many more elsewhere in the state. It has kept the area's economy fairly stable, thanks in part to its work cleaning up Cold War-era nuclear plants. The Naval Nuclear Propulsion Program has launched a $1.6 billion facility at the lab to handle spent fuel. The lab planned to open in late 2019 a new cybersecurity research center. Utah Associated Municipal Power Systems has begun work on a commercial nuclear reactor plant, with 12 reactors. In Twin Falls, Greek yogurt maker Chobani operates one of the largest yogurt-processing plants in the world and employs about 1,000 people. Pocatello is an old railroad town with unionized railroad workers. The city is home to Idaho State University.

To the west, amid the mountains, are Sun Valley and the nearby town of Ketchum. Sun Valley was established as a ski resort in 1936 by business mogul Averell Harriman before he began his political career. Ketchum attracted writer Ernest Hemingway in 1939, and various movie stars followed. In recent years, Blaine County, which includes Sun Valley and Ketchum, has attracted rich expatriates from the East and West coasts, who have made it the most Democratic county in Idaho. In 2016, Blaine — by 59%-31% -- was one of only two counties in the state to vote for Hillary Clinton. The Idaho Falls area and the farmland along the Snake River have been among the most Republican areas in the nation.

The 2nd District of Idaho includes most of Boise, where high-tech businesses and tourism have fueled the economy. Boise is home to Micron Technology, which is a leading patent holder for digital memory and employs 6,800 people. The Hewlett-Packard campus also is in the district. The city has been among the fastest-growing in the nation. From 2000 to 2017, it grew by 22 percent. Forbes ranked it number-two as the favorite location for young professionals in 2017. Donald Trump fared poorly with many of the local Mormons. His 54 percent was 10 points below the vote for Mitt Romney in 2012. Otherwise, the district, like the state as a whole, is solidly Republican.

ILLINOIS

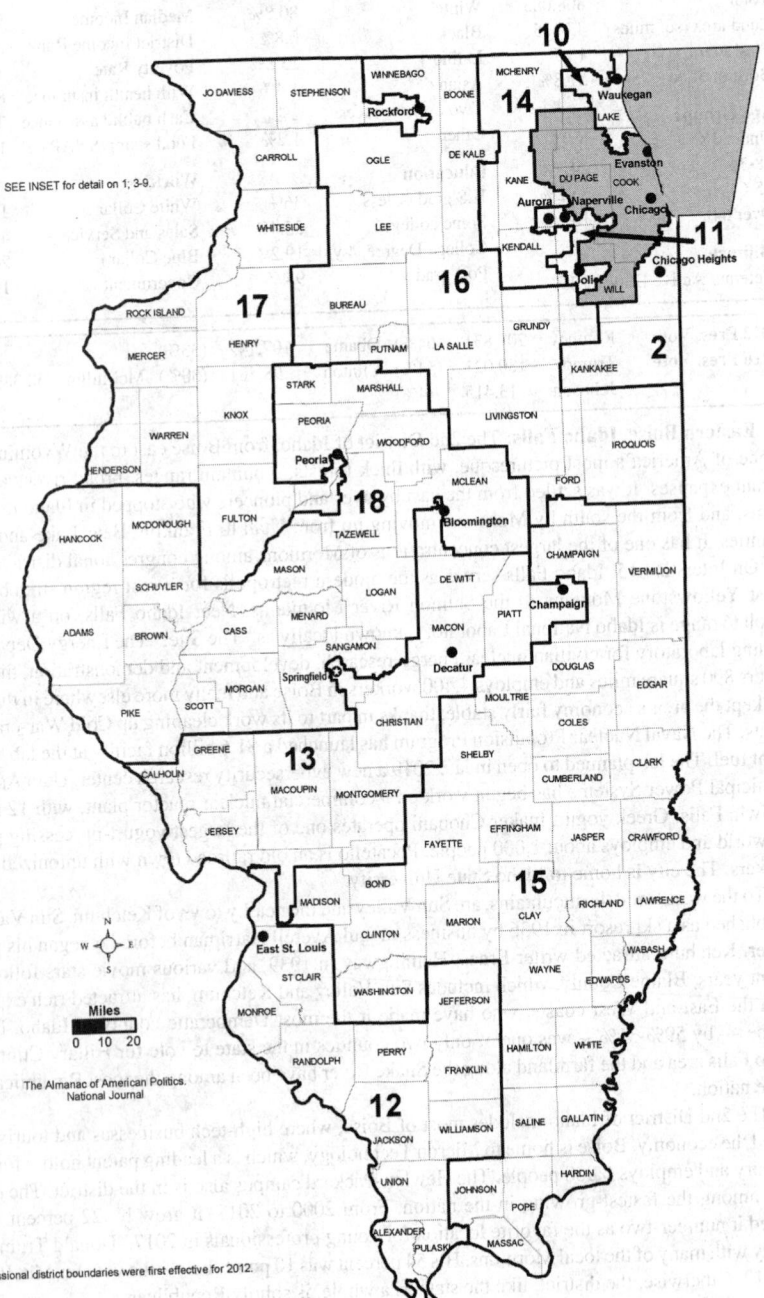

SEE INSET for detail on 1; 3-9.

Congressional district boundaries were first effective for 2012.

The Almanac of American Politics.
National Journal

Miles
0 10 20

Over the past decade, Illinois and the giant city that dominates it, Chicago, have experienced the best and the worst of times. On Election Night 2008, a million people thronged to Chicago's lakefront Grant Park to cheer Barack Obama, one of their own. Then, only a month later, the public had a chance to listen to recordings of Gov. Rod Blagojevich demanding recompense for nominating Obama's successor as senator, for which he would be impeached and removed from office, and later convicted and imprisoned. Later, for more than two years, the state was mired in a budget stalemate between a Republican governor and a Democratic legislature, leaving programs unfunded for months and bills piling up. Chicago's deadly crime wave surged as the city saw more murders than New York and Los Angeles combined. A parade of Illinois political notables followed Blagojevich's lead into ethical and legal ignominy, and native daughter Hillary Clinton lost the presidential race in stunning fashion. The only reason for cheer, it seemed, came in the fall of 2016, when the Chicago Cubs won their first World Series in more than a century, prompting 5 million people – half the population of metropolitan Chicago – to attend a celebratory parade.

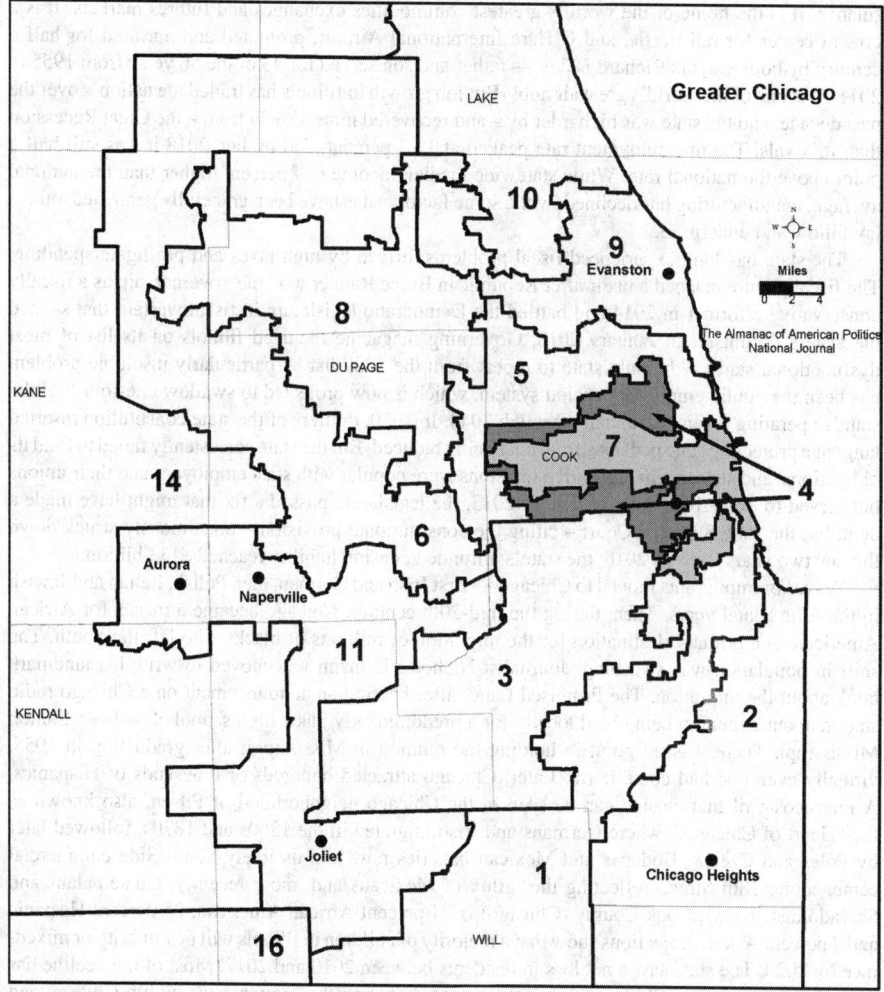

Congressional district boundaries were first effective for 2012.   Districts 4 and 7 are highlighted for visibility.

Though it dips within about 50 miles of the Confederacy, Illinois entered the Union as a free state, and early leaders made a point of promoting Chicago as a destination for westward-heading Yankee migrants. Illinois has come a long way since May 1860, when Abraham Lincoln was nominated at the Republican National Convention in the 10,000-seat Wigwam convention center in Chicago, less than a mile from Grant Park. That year, Chicago was the nation's ninth largest city, with 112,000 people. Over the next three decades, it grew so rapidly that it became the country's second largest city, with 1.4 million people by the time it hosted the Columbian Exposition in 1893. "Make no little plans," Chicago architect Daniel Burnham exhorted. And the city made enormous plans, building grand parks on the lakefront, erecting America's first downtown of skyscrapers, lining its boulevards with retail palaces, creating a great university from scratch on the Exposition's Midway Plaisance, and hosting union agitators as well as corporate leaders. Chicago started with the advantage of a great location, where the Great Lakes meet the prairies of the vast Mississippi Valley, and the city's entrepreneurs made it the hub of the nation's railroad network and the center of trade in lumber, grain and meat.

Today, Chicago is the nation's third-largest metropolis, a creative, world-class city, the center of a metropolitan area of 9.5 million people with highly educated workers, top-flight higher education and ample private capital. In commerce, Chicago has been a prime producer and processor of food products, a major manufacturing center and the strongest service economy between the coasts. In finance, it is the home of the world's greatest commodities exchanges and futures markets. It is a crucial center for rail traffic, and O'Hare International Airport, promoted and nurtured for half a century by both Mayors Richard Daley — father and son served for 43 of the 56 years from 1955 to 2011 — is one of the world's great air hubs. But job growth in Illinois has trailed the nation's over the past decade, and the state was hit harder by – and recovered more slowly from – the Great Recession than its rivals. The unemployment rate peaked at 11.2 percent, and by late 2018 it was still half a point above the national rate. While statewide median income is 4 percent higher than the national average, manufacturing has declined; while some factory sites have been gracefully gentrified, others lay fallow and underused.

The state has long experienced fiscal problems, driven by high taxes and profligate spending. The fiscal picture reached a nadir after Republican Bruce Rauner won the governorship as a fiscally conservative reformer in 2014 and battled the Democratic legislature in fiscal warfare that sapped the state's optimism. In January 2018, Governing magazine included Illinois on its list of most dysfunctional states – the only state to repeat from the 2009 list. A particularly insoluble problem has been the public-employee pension system, which is now projected to swallow one-fourth of the state's operating revenues annually through 2044. In 1970, drafters of the state constitution inserted language protecting state pensions from ever being reduced. But the state consistently failed to fund its obligations, and subsequent legislative revisions were popular with state employees and their unions but served to exacerbate the problem. In 2013, the legislature passed a fix that might have made a dent, but the state Supreme Court – citing the constitutional provision – unanimously struck down the law two years later. In 2018, the state's unfunded pension liability reached $133 billion.

Waves of immigrants moved to Chicago — first Irish and German, then Polish, Italian and Jewish in the Ellis Island years. Then, during the mid-20th century, Chicago became a mecca for African Americans – a primary destination for the migration of millions of blacks who left the South. The shift in population was sweeping: Journalist Nicholas Lemann was moved to write his landmark book about the migration, The Promised Land, after hearing an announcement on a Chicago radio station about a reunion being held locally for a predominantly black high school class from Canton Mississippi. There was no point in holding the reunion in Mississippi; after graduating in 1955, virtually everyone had come north. Later, Chicago attracted hundreds of thousands of Hispanics. A microcosm of that change can be seen in the Chicago neighborhood of Pilsen, also known as the "Heart of Chicago," where Germans and Irish migrated in the 1860s and 1870s, followed later by Poles and Czechs. Bodegas and Mexican bakeries now line its lively South Side commercial center along 18th Street, reflecting the influx of Mexicans and, more recently, Guatemalans and Salvadorans. Today, Cook County (Chicago) is 24 percent African American, 25 percent Hispanic and 7 percent Asian. Projections show that a majority of children in Illinois will be minority or mixed-race by 2020. The state saw a net loss in residents between 2010 and 2017. Most of the decline has come from outside the Chicago metropolitan area, but even the growth rates within Chicagoland during that period were modest, typically below 2 percent.

Chicago has struggled with revenue shortfalls, insolvent pensions, recalcitrant public employee unions and an underperforming school system, but Chicago's biggest problem in recent years has been a spiral of violence. In 2016, the city had 771 homicides, the most in two decades, as well as more than 3,500 shootings -- an increase of more than 1,000 over the previous year. The violence was most heavily concentrated in five of Chicago's 22 police districts – heavily black, low-income neighborhoods with a significant gang presence – and it did not help that distrust between the police and residents was at a low ebb following the November 2015 release of video showing Laquan McDonald, a 17-year-old African American, being shot 16 times by a white police officer. Protests ensued, and Chicago Police Superintendent Garry McCarthy lost his job. It led the Department of Justice to issue a report on the history of excessive use of force by Chicago police. While Democratic Mayor Rahm Emanuel took steps to ease the crisis and improve prospects within the affected neighborhoods, the rise in crime came to define the city nationally. As president, Donald Trump seized on Chicago as a poster child for his (often inaccurate) claims that homicides were soaring nationally. The number of murders dropped by 16 percent in 2017 from the previous year, and shooting incidents and shooting victims fell as well. But spasms of violence would sometimes occur, such as the weekend in August 2018 when 75 people were shot and 12 were killed. Despite this, the city center has remained healthy, with such corporations as Motorola and McDonald's returning from the suburbs and the city's school system, despite stresses, showing signs of improvement.

On the surface, Illinois tracks many of the nation's demographics closely, but the divide between Chicagoland and the rest of the state ("downstate," regardless of precise location) has intensified. Look no further than guns: Even as Chicago leaders wished for tougher gun laws, some downstate counties were voting themselves "gun sanctuaries" where the Second Amendment was sacrosanct. "Downstaters have always thought of Chicago as a black hole of street violence and political corruption, sucking up tax dollars generated by honest, hard-working farmers," wrote the Chicago Reader. By contrast, Chicagoans (who tend to self-identify by their city, not their state) "have always thought of downstate — when they've thought of it at all — as an irrelevant agricultural appendage full of Baptists and gun owners who'd just love to turn Illinois into North Kentucky." Decades of deindustrialization and political polarization have now widened those gaps. "Chicago and downstate are like conjoined twins, one of whom has a weak heart and is being kept alive at the expense of his stronger sibling," wrote James Krohe Jr., the author of "Corn Kings and One-Horse Thieves: A Plain-Spoken History of Mid-Illinois."

Obama and Emanuel – who decided not to seek another term in 2019 and was succeeded by Lori Lightfoot, the first African American and lesbian mayor of Chicago -- are just the most recent Illinois politicians to stand astride the national scene. Perhaps biggest of all was Richard J. Daley, the mayor of Chicago from 1955 until his death in 1976 and a player in national politics. His eldest son, Richard M. Daley, was elected mayor in 1989 and was popular with the city's business elite, ethnic whites and affluent suburbanites (who were not so fond of his father), while also keeping good ties to blacks and Hispanics.

But Illinois political history is rife with machine politics and cronyism. Even Lincoln was no stranger to the Republican machine of his day, which rallied thousands of partisans to cheer him at his debates with Stephen Douglas in 1858 and packed the Wigwam for him in 1860. Machine politics continued in the 20th century, as politicians in a closely divided state competed for public jobs and as politicians of both parties courted the immigrants streaming into Chicago. "We do not have a few 'rotten apples,'" wrote former Chicago alderman Dick Simpson and freelance writer Thomas J. Gradel in the book Corrupt Illinois. "We have a rotten apple barrel and a pervasive culture of corruption." With four Illinois governors in the past 50 years having gone to the pokey (including Blagojevich, who's due to be released in 2024), it's hard to argue with them. The ethical swamp has recently extended beyond Cook County: Former Republican House Speaker Dennis Hastert was sentenced to 15 months in a blackmail case that revealed his past sexual abuse of young boys as a wrestling coach, and Republican Aaron Schock from Peoria was forced from the House and indicted on federal charges after remodeling his congressional office as if it were Downton Abbey.

Politically, Illinois emerged from the Civil War as a solidly Republican state, with fast-growing Chicago and the northern counties settled by Yankees decisively outvoting the southern folk from Springfield south to Cairo (pronounced Kay-roe), which is closer to Mississippi than to Chicago. During the Depression, Chicago became reliably Democratic. In the decades that followed, the suburbs, wary of Chicago, became Republican (and developed machines of their own). For generations, downstate politicians offered an attractive balance to Chicago dominance – Democratic

Sens. Alan Dixon and Paul Simon, and Republican Govs. Jim Edgar and George Ryan. But since 2002, suburban Cook has moved from purple to blue, the collar counties have shifted from red to purple, and downstate has moved from purple to red. These changes have been fueled largely by the growth of Hispanic and Asian populations in the suburbs and by the loss of population and jobs -- mining, manufacturing, and farming -- downstate. On balance, the state as a whole has moved from purple to blue.

The 2016 election showed how the state's politics had changed. A moderate Republican from the Chicago suburbs, Mark Kirk, was unable to keep Democrat Tammy Duckworth from flipping his Senate seat. In the presidential race, Clinton improved on Obama's 2012 showing, thanks to a sharp move toward Clinton in Chicagoland, mirroring what happened in urban areas nationally. Trump, as he did elsewhere nationally, ran strongly in rural areas; the GOP's vote margin outside of Cook and the collar counties was more than three times higher in 2016 than 2012, and Clinton's vote total in those areas cratered by 20 percent compared with Obama's. All told, 75 percent of the Democratic presidential votes in 2016 came from Cook and the collar counties, up from 69 percent four years earlier – a trend line that seems likely to continue. "It's not unheard of in the last 20 years for a statewide Republican candidate to carry every county but one or two and still lose his race, so long as Cook County is one of the counties he loses," National Review's Andrew Ferguson has written. In 2018, Democrats won all of Illinois' statewide offices along with historic majorities in the legislature.

Population		Race and Ethnicity		Income	
Total	12,854,526	White	61.9%	Median Income	$61,229
Land area (sq. miles)	55,519	Black	14.1%	State Income Rank	17
Pop/ sq mi	231.5	Latino	16.8%	Poverty Rate	13.5%
Born in state	67.2%	Asian	5.2%	With health insurance	91.5%
		Two or more races	1.8%	Cash public assistance	2.5%
Age Groups		Other	0.2%	Food stamp/SNAP	13.3%
Under 18	23.0%				
18-34	23.4%	Education		Work	
35-64	39.2%	H.S grad or less	37.8%	White Collar	37.6%
Over 64	14.4%	Some college	28.8%	Sales and Service	41.3%
		College Degree, 4 yr	20.5%	Blue Collar	21.2%
Military		Post grad	13.0%	Government	11.9%
Veteran/ Active Duty	6.4%				

Presidential Politics

2016 Primary (D)	Clinton (D)	1,039,555 (51%)	Sanders (D)	999,494 (49%)			
2016 Primary (R)	Trump (R)	562,464 (39%)	Cruz (R)	438,235 (30%)	Kasich (R)	286,118 (20%)	
	Rubio (R)	126,681 (9%)					
2016 Pres. Vote	Clinton (D)	3,090,729 (55%)	Trump (R)	2,146,015 (38%)	Johnson (L)	209,596 (4%)	
2012 Pres. Vote	Obama (D)	3,019,512 (58%)	Romney (R)	2,135,216 (41%)			

For a century, Illinois was a political bellwether, voting only twice for losing presidential candidates between 1896 and 1996 — in 1916 and 1976, when it went Republican while the nation went Democratic. It even sided with Dwight Eisenhower in 1952 and 1956, against native son Adlai Stevenson. But starting in the 1990s, Illinois has become significantly more Democratic than the nation. It voted 55 percent for Al Gore and John Kerry in 2000 and 2004 and gave home-stater Barack Obama 62 percent in 2008 and 58 percent in 2012. Hillary Clinton, who was born in Chicago, saw the Democratic percentage dip in 2016 when she bested Donald Trump in the state, 55%-38%. But the Democrat's margin of victory over the Republican nominee actually increased two-tenths of a percentage point over 2012, as the GOP vote in the Chicago collar counties of DuPage, Kane and Lake fell off. Clinton won all three of those, plus Will. That mirrored a national trend where suburban counties of major metropolitan areas leaned more Democratic in 2016. Cook County, home to Chicago and 41 percent of the state's population, was very good to Clinton: more than half of her 2.9 million votes statewide came from the city and its close-in suburban townships. Across the state, rural counties in the upper Mississippi River basin that had traditionally voted Democratic sided with Trump. In 2012, 10 such counties backed Obama. In 2016, only Rock Island remained in the Democratic column. Knox County, home to Galesburg, an old railroad center, went from voting for Obama 58%-41% in 2012 to 48-45% for Trump.

The Illinois primary was once a pivotal moment in presidential nominating contests. But as more states have moved their primaries to earlier dates, Illinois has not played a key role in deciding a nomination. That changed in 2016, when the state gave important boosts to both of the major parties' eventual standard-bearers. The Democratic contest was particularly close: Clinton edged Vermont Sen. Bernie Sanders, 51%-49%. After suffering an upset loss in the Michigan primary one week earlier, it was vital for Clinton to shut down Sanders' momentum in the industrial Midwest. Cook County and Chicago delivered again for Clinton, giving her more than 60 percent of her statewide primary total. She had the backing of Chicago Democratic ward bosses who passed out palm cards with Clinton's name on them. Sanders carried all but one (Lake) of Chicago's collar counties and most of rural Illinois. On the Republican side, Trump defeated Texas Sen. Ted Cruz 39%-30%. Ohio Gov. John Kasich finished third with 20 percent and came in second in Cook County. But he failed to win over Republicans in the Chicago suburbs and exurbs, which signaled that his candidacy was unlikely to gain traction. While the GOP turnout in the five suburban collar counties was up by some 135,000 votes over 2012 levels, it exceeded Democratic turnout only by about 27,000. In Lake and Will counties, more voters participated in the Democratic primary than the Republican contest.

Congressional Districts

116th Congress Lineup	13D 5R	115th Congress Lineup	11D 7R

Illinois, with its sluggish population growth, has lost at least one seat in all but one reapportionment since 1930, when it had 27 seats. That pattern will continue in 2022, when it almost certainly will drop to 17, though it likely will avoid the loss of a second seat. For now, Democrats in Illinois have a strong hand — including firm control of the legislature and governorship, plus a 13-5 hold on the House delegation. No doubt, they will be eager to eliminate a Republican seat. But that might be easier said than done, given the current political dynamics.

The essential tension is relatively straightforward: The most obvious option is to eliminate a seat in Chicagoland — either a minority-held district in the city, or one of the gerrymandered districts in the collar counties. The good news/bad news for Democrats is that, with their pick-up of three of those suburban seats in the 2016 and 2018 elections, they hold all 12 of the region's seats. So, assuming no partisan changes in the 2020 election, erasing a Chicago-area seat would result in one of those Democrats getting the short straw. (The fact that those three pick-ups were in adjacent seats in the suburbs north and west of Chicago — the 6th, 10th and 14th districts -- points to one option for extensive boundary shifts.)

Creative Democratic map-drawers might find a way to pin the loss on a Republican-held seat — perhaps by weakening the neighboring 12th or 13th districts in southern Illinois. Even in such a scenario, they would face significant challenges in protecting each of the three African-American districts in the city, given that there might not be a sufficient number of black residents for districts that will be required to gain population. Each of those three seats has been roughly 50 percent African American in recent population counts. (A similar scenario in Los Angeles during recent redistricting has resulted in the loss of African American seats in that city.)

Another urban complication is that Latinos might have a strong case to gain a second district in Cook County. A potential solution to that dilemma could result in the creation of a district where Latinos gain significant influence. But the likely consequence of such a scenario is that another Chicago-area Democrat likely would be placed in jeopardy.

Another potentially uncomfortable feature for local Democrats is that Illinois has been the site of their most creative gerrymandering in the nation during recent redistricting. Depending on the dynamics among redistricting reformers or in the federal courts, that could create discomfort if Chicago pols engage in customary political chicanery.

That was the outcome in 2011 when, under pressure from party leaders desperate to offset Republican gains in other states, Illinois Democrats released a map designed to eliminate up to six Republican seats. The state's Republican delegation issued a joint statement aptly calling it "little more than an attempt to undo the results of the elections held just six months ago." Following extensive litigation, a three-judge panel upheld the congressional map. In the 2012 election, Democrats swept four of five targets for a 12-6 edge from what had been 11-8 Republican control. The GOP subsequently gained two seats in 2014 before losing three more since then.

J.B. Pritzker (R)

Elected 2018, term expires 2023, 1st term; b. Jan. 19, 1965, Atherton, CA; Duke University, B.A.; Northwestern University, J.D., 1993; Jewish; Married (M.K. Muenster); 2 children.

Professional Career: Co-Founder & Managing Partner, Pritzker Group.

Office: 207 State House, Springfield, 62706; 217-782-0244; Fax: 217-524-4049

Lt. Gov.: Juliana Stratton (D) **Atty. Gen:** Kwame Raoul (D) **Sec. of State:** Jesse White (D)

State Legislature: Senate: 40D, 19R **House:** 74D, 44R

Election Results

Election	Name (Party)	Vote (%)
2018 General	J.B. Pritzker (D)	2,479,746 (54%)
	Bruce Rauner (R)	1,765,751 (39%)
	William McCann (C)	192,527 (4%)
	Grayson Jackson (Lib)	109,518 (2%)
2018 Primary	J.B. Pritzker (D)	597,756 (45%)
	Daniel K. Biss (D)	353,625 (27%)
	Chris Kennedy (D)	322,730 (24%)

Democratic venture capitalist J.B. Pritzker won the Illinois governorship in 2018 after spending a record $171.5 million from his own pocket to oust Republican Bruce Rauner, himself a wealthy venture capitalist. Rauner had run four years earlier as an outsider who would fix the state's fiscal mess. But Pritzker was able to leverage voters' weariness with a lengthy budget stalemate between Rauner and the Democratic legislature that resulted in delayed payments and canceled services.

Pritzker's family is one of America's wealthiest, estimated to be worth a collective $33.5 billion, stemming from a variety of holdings, including Hyatt hotels. The fortune was divided, at times acrimoniously, among various descendants beginning in the late 1990s. The share held by the governor's immediate family is now estimated to be $3.2 billion, enough to edge out President Donald Trump as the country's richest current elected official; Pritzker is the second-richest elected official ever, after Michael Bloomberg. (As it happens, the Trump and Pritzker families engaged in a legal battle over New York real estate in the 1970s.)

Pritzker grew up in the Bay Area of California. His father, Donald, had moved to California to enter the hotel business with his brother Jay. One of his earliest memories was of door-knocking for Democratic candidates with his mother, Sue. "I grew up with parents who were very dedicated to social justice," he told the Chicago Jewish News during his run for governor. While the family found financial success, it also experienced tragedy: His father died at 39, when J.B. was 7, and his mother struggled with alcoholism until her death at 49, when J.B. was 17. In the decade between their deaths, family life was difficult, Pritzker has said.

Pritzker earned his undergraduate degree from Duke University and received a law degree from Northwestern University. He worked for a time in Washington for Democratic Sens. Terry Sanford of North Carolina and Alan Dixon of Illinois, meeting his wife M.K. during this period; she was an aide to Sen. Tom Daschle of South Dakota. In 1990, they settled in Chicago, which was the extended family's longtime home. With his brother Anthony, Pritzker founded a private equity firm, the Pritzker Group, that among other things held a stake in SpaceX, the aerospace company founded by entrepreneur Elon Musk. (His third sibling, Penny, served as Commerce secretary in the Obama administration.) Pritzker also founded a digital incubator called 1871, named for the year of the great fire in Chicago. He chaired the Illinois Human Rights Commission and helped establish Northwestern's Center on Wrongful Convictions. In the political realm, he ran third in a House primary to Democrat Jan Schakowsky in 1998 and became a major Democratic donor. His biggest leap into politics came when he challenged Rauner for governor.

Rauner had won in 2014 as a first-time candidate, touting a platform of economic reform and challenging what he deemed the hidebound political culture of the state dominated by Chicago Democrats. "To the people of Illinois, and the people outside our state who have been reluctant to invest in Illinois because of the insider deals and cronyism," Rauner vowed in his inaugural address, "I say this; I'm nobody that nobody sent, and I've come to work for you." It was a clever play off the famous political phrase uttered by a Chicago Ward boss, "We don't want nobody that nobody sent," to a young Abner Mikva— later a Chicago-area congressman and federal judge — who had just moved to the city and wanted to volunteer in the 1948 campaign. Rauner introduced a "turnaround agenda" that included term limits, overhauls of workers' compensation and education funding, a property tax freeze, and pension system changes. More than anything, Rauner sought to limit the power of private-sector unions and undercut public-sector collective bargaining, much the same agenda that Republican Gov. Scott Walker had pursued with such success in Wisconsin a few years earlier.

But the irresistible force met the immovable object in Democratic House Speaker Mike Madigan, an old-style machine pol who had survived six governors with his immense powers intact -- "the single most powerful state legislator in the country," Christopher Z. Mooney, a University of Illinois-Chicago political scientist, has called him. Madigan, a protégé of the late Chicago Mayor Richard J. Daley who got his first politically connected job as a young man operating a garbage truck, served as state Democratic Party chair, a committeeman for Chicago's 13th Ward, and the longest-tenured speaker in any state in two centuries. Madigan and Senate President John Cullerton had the votes to block the Rauner initiatives they opposed, so Rauner tried to leverage the state budget -- minus K-12 funding, which continued to be passed separately -- to force the Democrats in the legislature to pass his agenda. The Democrats were unmoved. For two years, a standoff between Rauner and the legislature turned Illinois into a fiscal laughingstock, unable to pay its bills and slapped with near-junk-level credit ratings.

It took until mid-2016 for the two sides to cut a deal for a six-month stopgap plan that enabled schools, universities and social services to continue, but that did little to pay down a backlog of some $13 billion in bills or to solve the state's $130 billion-plus unfunded public pension liability. In 2016, Rauner dipped into his personal fortune to try to mold a more amenable legislature, but his investment of $50 million produced gains of only four seats in the House and two in the Senate. Finally, in the summer of 2017, the legislature managed to enact a budget, after a narrow override of Rauner's veto.

Amid plunging approval ratings and the certainty of a tough reelection battle in a blue state, Rauner enacted some bills in collaboration with Democrats. He signed a law to keep law enforcement from detaining people based only on their immigration status. Another required the state to pay for abortions for poor women; Rauner had initially said he would veto it. He also signed an education bill that provided state money to bolster poorer districts, and he signed another to allow patients who had been prescribed an opioid painkiller to switch to medical cannabis instead. Rauner even signed off on an annual state commemorative day for Barack Obama, on his Aug. 4 birthday. (Government offices would remain open, however.) He also enacted a budget in May 2018 – for the first time, without rancor. Rauner also made some moves more popular with his Republican base.

Among conservative Republicans, Rauner's bipartisan efforts – especially the abortion bill – were considered a betrayal. State Rep. Jeanne Ives ran an insurgent campaign to deny him renomination. In an ad criticized by much of the GOP establishment, a purportedly transgender actor mockingly thanked Rauner for "signing legislation that lets me use the girl's bathroom," while a young woman in a pussy hat said, "Thank you for making all Illinois families pay for my abortions." Rauner barely won the GOP primary, 51.5%-48.5%. Meanwhile, in the Democratic primary, Pritzker took 45 percent, over suburban Chicago state Sen. Daniel Biss, with 27 percent, and Chris Kennedy, a son of Robert F. Kennedy, with 24 percent.

The well-heeled candidates sparred over taxes. Pritzker proposed replacing the state's flat income tax with a progressive tax system. Rauner countered that Pritzker's changes would mean higher taxes. Pritzker promised that most residents would come out ahead in the switch, though he was vague on the details, effectively undermining his promise. Pritzker endorsed the $15 minimum wage that Rauner had vetoed, along with other progressive priorities; his website gave prominent placement to a section titled "Resisting Trump," in which he said he was "ready to fight every day to make sure Illinois is a firewall against Donald Trump's destructive agenda and hateful rhetoric." Pritzker dealt with a series of embarrassments – secret recordings of conversations with then-Gov. Rod Blagojevich about his possible interest in being appointed state treasurer or attorney general, and revelations about a $330,000 property tax break he secured by removing toilets from a mansion he owned, an action the Cook County inspector general called a "scheme to defraud." But none fundamentally altered the arc of the race; Pritzker led Rauner from start to finish, and for the last few months of the race, handicappers no longer considered the contest competitive. Pritzker won 54%-39%, with candidates from the Conservative and Libertarian parties who collectively took 7 percent.

In February 2019, Pritzker signed a bill to raise the state minimum wage in steps to $15 by 2025.

Dick Durbin (D)

Elected 1996, term expires 2020, 4th term, b. Nov 21, 1944; East St. Louis; Georgetown University (DC), B.S., 1966; Georgetown University Law Center (DC), J.D., 1969; Roman Catholic; Married (Loretta Schaefer Durbin); 3 children (1 deceased); 3 grandchildren.

Elected Office: U.S. House, 1983-1997.

Professional Career: Staff, Lt. Gov. Paul Simon, 1969-1972; Legal counsel, IL Sen. Judiciary Committee, 1972-1982; Professor, S. IL School of Med., 1978-1982.

DC Office: 711 HSOB 20510, 202-224-2152, Fax: 202-228-0400, durbin.senate.gov

State Offices: Carbondale, 618-351-1122; Chicago, 312-353-4952; Rock Island, 309-786-5173; Springfield, 217-492-4062.

Committees: Senate Minority Whip. *Agriculture, Nutrition & Forestry*: Commodities, Risk Management & Trade; Conservation, Forestry & Natural Resources; Rural Development & Energy. *Appropriations*: Department of Defense (RMM); DOL, HHS & Education & Related Agencies; Energy & Water Development; Financial Services & General Government; State, Foreign Operations & Related Programs; Transportation, HUD & Related Agencies. *Judiciary*: Border Security & Immigration (RMM); Constitution; Crime & Terrorism; Subcommittee on Intellectual Property. *Rules & Administration*.

Group Ratings

	ADA	ACLU	AFL-CIO	LCV	ITI	COC	HAFA	ACU	CFG	FRC
2018	-	82%	-	100%	-	50%	3%	9%	5%	0%
2017	95%	C	100%	100%	C	29%	C	0%	4%	0%

Almanac Ratings 2017-18

	Economy	Social	Foreign	Composite
Liberal	97%	97%	89%	94%
Conservative	3%	3%	11%	6%

Key Votes of the 115th Congress

1. Obama-care revision	N	5. Gun regulations	N	9. Kavanaugh confirmation	N
2. Tax Cuts	N	6. Family planning regs	N	10. Saudi arms sales	Y
3. Dodd-Frank revision	N	7. Gorsuch confirmation	N	11. FISA rules	N
4. Omnibus appropriations	Y	8. Immigration restrictions	N	12. Military aid in Yemen	Y

Election Results

Election	Name (Party)	Vote (%)		Cand. Spent	Ind. Exp. Support	Ind. Exp. Oppose
2014 General	Dick Durbin (D)	1,929,637	(54%)	$12,614,224	$22,998	$717,746
	Jim Oberweis (R)	1,538,522	(43%)	$2,416,926	$5,353	$690,250
	Sharon Hansen (L)	135,316	(4%)	$2,367		
2014 Primary	Dick Durbin (D)	Unopposed				

Prior winning percentages: 2008 (68%), 2002 (60%), 1996 (54%); House: 1994 (55%), 1992 (57%),1990 (66%), 1988 (69%), 1986 (68%), 1984 (61%), 1982 (50%

Democrat Dick Durbin, Illinois' senior senator, has spent nearly four decades on Capitol Hill as a key player — in both the House and Senate. For the past decade and a half, Durbin, as party whip, has been the No. 2 Senate Democrat. But in early 2015, when Democratic Leader Harry Reid retired, he endorsed Chuck Schumer — a hard-charging New Yorker who was No. 3 in the leadership structure — to leapfrog over the more diplomatic Durbin as his successor. Durbin opted not to challenge Schumer — with whom he shared a Capitol Hill townhouse for more than two decades — and, while he retained the whip's post without opposition, the turn of events ended his hope of climbing the leadership ladder any farther. However, he has continued to round up votes for his party's positions and maintained his status as a major player on bipartisan initiatives. And Durbin, whose congressional tenure has spanned six presidents, could be around for more: He has served notice he plans to seek a fifth term in 2020.

Durbin grew up in modest circumstances in East St. Louis. His father, a railroad night watchman, died of lung cancer when Durbin was 14 — an event that later prompted him to push for what became one of his leading legislative achievements. He graduated from Georgetown University and its law school while working as an intern for Illinois Democratic Sen. Paul Douglas, who held the seat Durbin now occupies. Durbin returned home to join future-Sen. Paul Simon's staff when Simon was lieutenant governor. He was a state Senate staff member for much of the 1970s, even serving as that chamber's parliamentarian — valuable training for someone who would later gain a reputation as an expert in Senate procedures. Durbin's first two tries for elected office, including a 1978 bid as Democrats' nominee for lieutenant governor, were unsuccessful. But in 1982, he won the nomination to oppose Republican Rep. Paul Findley, who was among the few members of Congress to call for a more even-handed policy toward Palestinians. Durbin had no trouble raising money from well-heeled Israel supporters and narrowly ousted Findley from a central Illinois district.

In the House, Durbin won a seat on the Appropriations Committee, eventually becoming a member of that panel's "college of cardinals." In 1993, Durbin became chairman of the subcommittee with jurisdiction over agriculture programs and the Food and Drug Administration. Years later, in the Senate, he enacted major reforms in the FDA's food safety inspection powers; President Barack Obama, in 2011, signed a Durbin-crafted bill allowing the FDA to issue mandatory recalls of food products. His centerpiece legislative accomplishment in the House was the ban on smoking on domestic airline flights, enacted in 1988 and inspired by the death of his chain-smoking father. At the time, Durbin had little idea of its long-term societal effect. "I didn't realize it would make a difference in terms of whether you could smoke on a train, on a bus, in a building, in a restaurant, in a hospital," he said in a 2015 interview. He later pushed to limit tobacco subsidies and give the FDA authority to regulate tobacco as a health hazard — both accomplished after years of effort. In 2018, he and Republican Sen. Lisa Murkowski of Alaska introduced a bill imposing restrictions on e-cigarettes. "I am convinced that e-cigarettes represent the 're-invention of smoking' cooked up by Big Tobacco to hook a new generation," Durbin said.

As a member of the House, Durbin rented a room in a Capitol Hill home owned by California Democratic Rep. George Miller; Schumer, then also a House member, was already a tenant. The Durbin-Schumer weekday roommate relationship continued after both had moved on to the Senate and become rivals for the leadership. The arrangement ended in 2014, when Miller retired from Congress and sold the townhouse — but not before inspiring a TV sitcom: "Alpha House."

Finding himself in the minority party in the House after the 1994 elections, Durbin announced he would seek the Senate seat being relinquished in 1996 by Simon, his former boss and mentor. Durbin defeated former state treasurer and future governor Pat Quinn by a margin better than 2-1 in the primary and comfortably won the general election with 56 percent of the vote. He won reelection in 2002 and 2008 by 60 percent or more. While held to 54 percent during a difficult year for Democrats in 2014, he still defeated his Republican opponent by double digits.

Durbin has compiled a voting record that places him in the Senate's left wing: In 2015, the Almanac's annual vote rankings put him in a tie for the third most liberal score among Democrats. "He's able to pull off the style of sounding like a moderate or compromiser when he often doesn't act like one," University of Illinois political scientist Brian Gaines said. But Durbin has cautioned the Democrats' progressive wing about pushing the party too far to the left. "We have to really appeal to that sensible center," Durbin said in a 2017 interview with a Chicago radio station. "It's a thin stripe now. It used to be a lot wider stripe, but it's an important and determining factor in most elections." He has not hesitated on several occasions to take on liberal orthodoxy; during negotiations on taxes and spending aimed at averting the "fiscal cliff" in late 2012, Durbin exhorted Democrats to support a deal that included cuts to entitlement programs. "My liberal friends who say, 'Don't touch it (Medicare),' they're crazy," Durbin said at the time. Earlier, he served on the bipartisan Simpson-Bowles deficit reduction commission that recommended raising the Medicare eligibility age.

On social issues, Durbin, a Catholic, favored restrictions on abortion while in the House but has opposed most such restrictions in the Senate — a shift that reportedly occurred after he met with victims of rape and incest. In 2004, the priest at his home church in Springfield said he wouldn't give Durbin communion as a consequence of his position. "Is that all this church is about, is one issue?" Durbin responded. "For bishops to announce that they are going to penalize Catholics on certain votes I think is … reaching too far." In February 2018, the bishop of Springfield reaffirmed the church's stance after Durbin voted against a Senate bill prohibiting abortion starting at 20 weeks after fertilization. "The determination continues that Sen. Durbin is not to be admitted to Holy Communion until he repents of this sin," the bishop, Thomas Paprocki, said in a statement. Durbin's position on another social issue shifted: Initially a death penalty supporter, he told the Springfield-based State Journal Register in 2011 that the death penalty should be abolished except for "compelling exceptions" such as "terrorism and crimes of that nature."

Durbin's ascent in the Senate leadership ranks began in 2001, when he was named assistant floor leader. After Democratic Leader Tom Daschle lost his 2004 re-election bid in South Dakota, Reid succeeded him, and Durbin moved to secure election to Reid's old job as minority whip. Durbin won by acclamation after one potential opponent counted heads and decided not to challenge him. His new position was but one significant development for him arising out of the 2004 election. He acquired a new junior colleague from Illinois: Obama. In an institution of sizable egos, many senators have had tense relationships with home-state colleagues —particularly when the two belong to the same party. But, rather than chafing at Obama's quick rise and celebrity, Durbin urged him to run for president and later introduced the presidential nominee at the 2008 Democratic National Convention. Durbin did not join Obama at the massive 2008 election night celebration in Chicago's Grant Park because his 40-year-old daughter had died three days earlier, but he again introduced Obama at the 2012 convention.

Often described as the president's closest friend in the Senate during Obama's eight years in office, Durbin frequently appeared on talk shows to defend Obama's major legislative achievement: the Affordable Care Act. In 2015, it was left to Durbin to lead the campaign to line up Senate support for the Obama administration's nuclear agreement with Iran — a pact from which President Donald Trump later withdrew — after other members of the Democratic leadership came out against the deal or were slow to embrace it. His efforts helped ensure there were enough votes to block a resolution of disapproval pushed by the Senate GOP majority. The same year, Durbin exhibited his tough-talking side when Obama's nomination of Loretta Lynch for attorney general faced a protracted delay by Senate Republicans. Durbin said Republican leaders were putting Lynch at the "back of the bus," an allusion to civil rights icon Rosa Parks. Arizona Republican Sen. John McCain demanded an apology for what he said was Durbin's effort to "suggest that racist tactics are being employed." Durbin refused to back down, saying he had thought "long and hard" before making his remarks.

Before Obama became president, Durbin was chief sponsor of the DREAM Act, a bill providing a path to citizenship for children brought to the country illegally as children through college or military service. He praised Obama in 2012 for issuing an executive order — called Deferred Action for Childhood Arrivals — to protect nearly 750,000 young immigrants when it became clear Congress would not act. When Trump announced plans to cancel Obama's DACA order in the fall of 2017, Durbin was part of a bipartisan group of a half-dozen senators who reached agreement on a legislative package pairing legal status for those covered by DACA program with other immigration reforms and enhanced border security.

But the effort was stymied after Durbin and Republican Sen. Lindsey Graham of South Carolina were told by Trump during a White House meeting that the president was not prepared to embrace the proposal. The aftermath of the meeting produced a series of charges and countercharges. Durbin told CNN that the bipartisan group had been "sandbagged" after Trump had earlier agreed to move ahead with comprehensive immigration reform that included DACA. He also confirmed published reports that the president had referred to several African nations as "s---hole countries" — a remark that created a diplomatic firestorm. Trump, in a Reuters interview, declined "to get into what I said," adding, "I've lost all trust in Durbin." The president doubled down, tweeting "Senator Dicky Durbin totally misrepresented what was said at the DACA meeting. ... Durbin blew DACA and is hurting our Military."

Durbin and Trump were on the same page when Congress, at the end of 2018, overwhelmingly passed a criminal justice reform bill — an effort on which Durbin and Iowa Republican Chuck Grassley, then chairman of the Judiciary Committee, had teamed up several years earlier. Their initiative fell short in 2016 amid resistance from hard-line GOP conservatives, but they vowed to try again. The measure signed by Trump boosted efforts at prisoner rehabilitation at federal facilities, while granting judges more discretion in sentencing those convicted of drug-related offenses. "A breakthrough I'd never expect — the election of Donald Trump as president," Durbin told NBC News while discussing how the bill passed. "What does that have to do with this? He brought his son-in-law to town." While an unusual coalition of liberal and conservative groups had pushed for a broader bill, Trump's son-in-law and adviser, Jared Kushner, initially committed the White House to a narrower proposal focused on prison reform. But Durbin and Grassley argued that an earlier version of the bill passed by the House didn't go far enough and ultimately reached a deal with the White House to include sentencing reforms in the final measure.

A Durbin-Grassley collaboration on drug prices was also in accord with an initiative supported by Trump. The two senators in August 2018 won Senate approval of funding to study and implement ads that would disclose the price of pharmaceuticals; it was like part of a plan advocated by Trump to lower drug prices. "More information …will help give American consumers a break and start to slow down the skyrocketing cost of prescription drugs," Durbin said after he and Grassley attached an amendment to a version of the annual spending bill for the Department of Health and Human Services. But the amendment was removed during a House-Senate conference committee. Durbin blamed House Republicans for capitulating to lobbying by the Pharmaceutical Research and Manufacturers of America. "We need transparency & it's time to put consumers ahead of Big Pharma," Durbin tweeted.

Despite a pro-union voting record, Durbin split with organized labor early in his congressional career to support the North American Free Trade Agreement and normal trade relations with China during the Clinton administration. In part, his stance reflected Illinois' status as a major exporter. But Durbin later said he felt betrayed by the results of NAFTA and has opposed more recent trade agreements. In 2015, he joined most Democratic senators in opposing Obama's request for expedited authority to negotiate a major trade agreement with Asia — a deal that Trump renounced after taking office. Durbin was critical of Trump when the president announced a sweeping series of tariffs on imported steel in early 2018, likening it to "dropping a bomb on a flea." "Launching an all-out trade war will alienate the allies we need to actually solve the problem of steel dumping, and could have huge unintended consequences for American manufacturers who depend on imported materials," he said.

Perhaps Durbin's most high-profile legislative achievement of his Senate tenure came in conjunction with passage of the 2010 Dodd-Frank financial reforms. As part of Dodd-Frank, he engineered passage of what is widely referred to as the "Durbin amendment," giving the Federal Reserve authority to reduce the "swipe fees" that banks charge merchants for processing debit card transactions. It made Durbin a scourge of the nation's banking industry, which mounted an extensive lobbying effort to get rid of the Durbin amendment. When legislation to repeal some provisions of Dodd-Frank — later signed by Trump — began moving through Congress in mid-2017, Republican leaders of the House Financial Services Committee planned to include repeal of the Durbin amendment. But they backed off after counting votes, leaving Durbin's legislative handiwork in place. If leading banks are no fan of Durbin's, neither are groups pushing for tort reform. They have long accused him of defending the interests of the nation's trial lawyers and point to nearly $4.5 million in contributions, according to the Center for Responsive Politics, that Durbin received from lawyers and law firms in his three bids for re-election.

Closer to home, Durbin has not been hesitant to use his clout as a member of the Appropriations Committee to keep an eye out for another major player in the nation's financial marketplace: the

Chicago-based commodities exchanges. He has opposed new fees on the exchanges and, at one point, worked behind the scenes to soften the effects of proposed controls on speculators in the oil futures market while gas prices soared. It is emblematic of how Durbin has utilized his leadership position to protect the interests of Illinois. In late 2012, he helped prod the Justice Department to assist the state's financially strapped government by buying a former prison, over objections from Republicans who feared it would be used to house inmates from Guantanamo Bay. In January 2013, Durbin became chairman of Appropriations' Defense Subcommittee, and its ranking Democrat two years later. He has used the position to fund production of electronic warplanes for the Navy manufactured at Boeing's St. Louis plant, just across the Mississippi River from Illinois.

Durbin became majority whip in 2007 following the Democrats' capture of the Senate and returned as minority whip in 2015 when the GOP regained control — shortly before Reid anointed Schumer as the new Democratic leader. For much of 2015 and 2016, Durbin claimed enough support to remain whip, even as Sen. Patty Murray of Washington declined to rule out a challenge to him. Schumer declined to take sides in the matter, further straining what had once been a close relationship between the two former roommates. Meanwhile, as some Illinois Democrats suggested that Durbin would be their strongest candidate to retake the governorship in 2018, Durbin declined to take the option of returning to Springfield off the table. The turmoil within the Senate Democratic leadership ranks was resolved a week after Election Day 2016: Durbin was unanimously re-elected as whip, as Schumer crafted a new job — assistant Democratic leader — for Murray. In the wake of Trump's surprise election, Durbin declined to run for governor, telling the Chicago Tribune he had been approached by many Illinois constituents saying: "Stay in the Senate. We need you."

Durbin will turn 76 after Election Day 2020, but he sought to put a damper on retirement speculation in January 2019 as he was elected to yet another two-year term as whip. He told CNN that he would seek re-election, while cautioning, "I haven't made a formal announcement. ... Don't take that as a formal announcement." Durbin, who in 2017 underwent a procedure to correct an abnormal heart rhythm, added: "I'm raising money and trying to lose a few pounds. And that's a good indicator that I'm looking forward to 2020." He also joined the Agriculture, Nutrition and Forestry Committee — a panel with jurisdiction of political importance to Illinois' downstate region.

Tammy Duckworth (D)

Elected 2016, term expires 2022, 1st term, b. Mar 12, 1968; Bangkok, Thailand; University of Hawaii, B.A., 1989; George Washington University Elliot School of International Affairs (DC), M.A., 1992; Northern Illinois University, Att., 2001;Capella University (MN), Ph.D.; Religion not stated; Married (Bryan Bowlsbey); 2 children.

Military Career: U.S. Army Reserve 1991-1996; IL Army National Guard 1996-2004 (Iraq, WIA)

Professional Career: Assistant Secretary, U.S Veterans Affairs Department, 2009-2011; Director, IL Veterans Affairs Department, 2006-2009; Mngr., Rotary Intl., 2003-2004.

DC Office: 524 HSOB 20510, 202-224-2854, Fax: 202-228-0618

State Offices: Belleville, 618-722-7070; Carbondale, 618-677-7000; Chicago, 312-886-3506; Rock Island, 309-606-7060; Springfield, 217-528-6124.

Committees: *Armed Services*: Airland; Personnel; Readiness & Management Support. *Commerce, Science & Transportation*: Communications, Technology, Innovation & the Internet; Subcommittee on Aviation & Space; Subcommittee on Security; Subcommittee on Transportation & Safety (RMM). *Environment & Public Works*: Clean Air & Nuclear Safety; Fisheries, Water, and Wildlife (RMM). *Small Business & Entrepreneurship*.

Group Ratings

	ADA	ACLU	AFL-CIO	LCV	ITI	COC	HAFA	ACU	CFG	FRC
2018	-	62%	-	86%	-	56%	3%	6%	6%	0%
2017	100%	C	100%	100%	C	29%	C	0%	4%	0%

Almanac Ratings 2017-18

	Economy	Social	Foreign	Composite
Liberal	97%	97%	76%	90%
Conservative	3%	3%	24%	10%

Key Votes of the 115th Congress

1. Obama-care revision	N	5. Gun regulations	N	9. Kavanaugh confirmation	N
2. Tax Cuts	N	6. Family planning regs	N	10. Saudi arms sales	Y
3. Dodd-Frank revision	N	7. Gorsuch confirmation	N	11. FISA rules	Y
4. Omnibus appropriations	Y	8. Immigration restrictions	N	12. Military aid in Yemen	Y

Election Results

Election	Name (Party)	Vote (%)		Cand. Spent	Ind. Exp. Support	Ind. Exp. Oppose
2016 General	Tammy Duckworth (D)	3,012,940	(55%)	$9,000,361	$683,882	$2,061,868
	Mark Kirk (R)	2,184,692	(40%)	$10,513,124	$727,085	$62,499
	Kent McMillen (L)	175,988	(3%)			
	Scott Summers (G)	117,619	(2%)			
2016 Primary	Tammy Duckworth (D)	1,220,128	(64%)			
	Andrea Zopp (D)	455,729	(24%)			
	Napoleon Harris (D)	219,286	(12%)			

Prior winning percentages: House: 2014 (56%); 2012 (55%)

The 2016 election of Democrat Tammy Duckworth marked a couple of racial and ethnic milestones in Senate history. The daughter of an American father and a Thai mother, Duckworth is the first Thai-American senator, while she and Democrat Kamala Harris of California — elected on the same day — became only the second and third Asian-American women to serve in that chamber. Duckworth set another marker in April 2018 when she became the first sitting senator to give birth. Perhaps an equally precedent-setting aspect of Duckworth's election was the campaign that preceded it: More than a quarter-century after the passage of the Americans With Disabilities Act, the contest between Duckworth and her opponent, Republican incumbent Mark Kirk, was the first Senate campaign in which both candidates used wheelchairs.

In 2004, during the Iraq War, a rocket-propelled grenade struck the Army helicopter that Duckworth was piloting, taking both of her legs; she has used a wheelchair or prosthetic legs ever since. Kirk had a severe stroke in 2012 that kept him away from Capitol Hill for a year; it left him partly paralyzed, forcing him to use either a wheelchair or a cane to get around. Politically, the fact that both candidates had a disability was an equalizer of sorts: Each was freed to unleash rhetorical attacks without the risk of being seen as taking advantage of the other's vulnerability. Likewise, once in office, Duckworth found her disability — and the way she had acquired it — appeared to have a liberating effect on both the tone and substance of her comments. At the outset of 2018, when President Donald Trump blamed Democrats for a government shutdown he said harmed the military, Duckworth lit into the president as "Cadet Bone Spurs" — a reference to the medical diagnosis that had enabled Trump to avoid military service during the Vietnam War. "I will not be lectured about what our military needs by a five-deferment draft dodger," Duckworth said on the Senate floor.

Ladda Tammy Duckworth was born in Bangkok and spent much of her early life abroad because her father, a Vietnam veteran, worked for the United Nations and at several international firms. The family lived in Singapore and Indonesia before settling in Hawaii when Duckworth was 16. Her father had difficulty finding work, and she took a series of low-paying jobs to help pay the bills. "Thank God for the food stamps, public education and Pell Grants that helped me finish high school and college," Duckworth said during a speech at the 2012 Democratic National Convention. She studied marine biology at the University of Hawaii and later earned a master's degree in international affairs at George Washington University. Her interest in Southeast Asian history, culture and politics led to doctoral work at Northern Illinois University.

In 1990, Duckworth — whose family has a record of military service dating back to the American Revolution — joined the Army ROTC at George Washington University. During her training, she met her future husband, Bryan Bowlsbey, who became a major in the Illinois Army National Guard — the same unit from which Duckworth retired as a lieutenant colonel in 2014. Although she later said she had opposed President George W. Bush's decision to invade Iraq, she felt it was her duty to complete her military service. Duckworth became one of the first women to fly combat missions in Iraq. The rocket-propelled grenade that hit her Black Hawk helicopter on Nov. 12, 2004, nearly killed her. After her co-pilot landed the craft, a second helicopter crew, after evacuating the wounded, returned to retrieve what they thought was her corpse. "I am no hero," she said in a 2018 Vogue magazine interview. "The guy who carried me out of there? He's the hero." Duckworth's right arm was badly wounded and she lost her legs. She underwent numerous surgeries, and while recovering at Walter Reed National Military Medical Center, she met Sen. Barack Obama of Illinois, a member of the Veterans' Affairs Committee — who later called on her to testify.

Illinois' other senator, Democratic Whip Richard Durbin, invited her to the 2005 State of the Union address and later urged her to run for a seat in Chicago's western suburbs being relinquished by longtime GOP Rep. Henry Hyde in 2006. But local Democrats lined up behind the party's 2004 nominee against Hyde, leading to a competitive primary that Duckworth won 44%-40%. In November, she lost to Republican Peter Roskam, 51%-49%. It was two years after the helicopter attack, and Duckworth later said she hadn't yet fully recovered from her wounds. Weeks after her defeat, she was named director of the Illinois Veterans Affairs Department. It was at times a bumpy experience, including a lawsuit that two employees filed against her, alleging workplace retaliation. The suit was settled out of court several months before the 2016 Senate election; while a Duckworth spokesman dismissed it as frivolous, the suit provided fodder for early attacks by Kirk.

Duckworth received a prominent speaking spot at the 2008 convention — at which the party nominated Obama to be president — and in early 2009 she was named as the Veterans Affairs Department's assistant secretary for public and intergovernmental affairs in the Obama administration. Two years later, Duckworth left the VA to launch a second run for Congress. The 8th District, in Chicago's northwestern suburbs, had been redrawn to be more favorable to Democrats. With another endorsement from Durbin, she easily won the March primary, and again received prime-time exposure at the party's 2012 National Convention. Her general election opponent was GOP Rep. Joe Walsh, elected in 2010 amid the national tea party wave. He had a reputation for outspokenness but also for damaging political moments, such as missing child support payments and exploding at a constituent meeting. Redistricting left Walsh with only a small piece of his old district, and Duckworth won with 55 percent.

In the House, Duckworth joined the Armed Services Committee, where she filed a bill to extend maternity leave for servicewomen. Duckworth became a mother for the first time two weeks after being re-elected by a 12-point margin in 2014. In early 2015, she scored a legislative victory when Obama signed the Clay Hunt Suicide Prevention for American Veterans Act — to improve mental health services for veterans — at a White House ceremony. Duckworth announced her challenge to Kirk in March 2015, saying, "I view my time now as a bonus, and that has allowed me to speak up without fear." Several other Democrats in the Illinois House delegation took a pass on the Senate race, and Duckworth easily won the March 2016 primary with 64 percent against two opponents.

Kirk had made clear that his near-fatal stroke would not deter him from seeking a second term. But he began the 2016 election cycle as the most endangered Senate incumbent in the nation. He had narrowly won Obama's former Senate seat in 2010 over a Democratic opponent with political baggage. In seeking re-election, he had to run during a presidential year in a state that had not cast its Electoral College votes for a Republican in nearly three decades. On Capitol Hill, Kirk had crafted a record as a fiscal conservative and foreign policy hawk but was to his party's left on social issues. That served him well during the decade he represented a congressional district in Chicago's suburbs, but alienated a significant number of Republicans statewide without attracting much Democratic support. A poll taken in mid-2015 showed Kirk's disapproval rating outweighing his approval score.

Kirk struggled to raise money — Duckworth outraised him 2-1 — and a series of oral gaffes raised quiet questions about whether the stroke had affected his behavior. In October, Illinois' largest newspaper, the Chicago Tribune, endorsed Duckworth, saying, "Our reluctant judgment is that, due to forces beyond his control, Kirk no longer can perform to the fullest the job of a U.S. senator." Less than two weeks before Election Day, Kirk placed the final nail in his candidacy with another gaffe: During a debate, Duckworth pointed to her family's history of military service dating to the Revolutionary War. Kirk gibed, "I'd forgotten your parents came all the way from Thailand to serve George Washington." Democrats blasted the remark as racist, and Kirk's campaign initially declined to offer an apology. On Election Day, Duckworth won 55%-40%, a similar margin to Hillary Clinton's 56%-39% victory over Trump in the state. As she had in the House, Duckworth focused on veterans issues. A Duckworth-authored bill that became law at the end of 2018 added veterans to the list of small-business owners eligible to obtain federal surplus personal property at no cost.

She also introduced legislation aimed at halting deportation of veterans, while making it easier for soldiers who are not U.S. citizens to achieve such status.

Duckworth drew on her veteran's experience and perspective to repeatedly lambaste Trump. When the president asked the Pentagon to draw up plans for a military parade in Washington, she said: "If he wants to spend that kind of money — it will be hundreds of thousands, if not millions of dollars — then let's send that to the troops or send it to their family members. Let's not blow it on a parade for Trump's ego." Duckworth said Trump's desire to ban transgender troops from serving was "sickening" in view of his effort to avoid military service. "When I was bleeding to death in my Black Hawk helicopter after I was shot down, I didn't care if the American troops risking their lives to help save me were gay, straight, transgender, black, white or brown. All that mattered was they didn't leave me behind," she said. And in mid-2018, when the NFL moved to bar players from kneeling during the national anthem — an action Trump endorsed — Duckworth tweeted a photo of her prosthetic legs and wrote, "I will always stand on these legs for the flag and anthem, but it was ALSO my honor to defend people's right to free speech including those who choose to #TakeAKnee to express outrage at the glaring disparity in how Americans of different races are treated."

Duckworth's Almanac voting score placed her among the dozen most liberal senators in 2017. But she has sought distance herself from the party's progressive wing. "I think that you can't win the White House without the Midwest," Duckworth told CNN. "And I don't think you can go too far to the left and still win the Midwest." She disagreed with other Democrats, including her California classmate Harris, who wanted to abolish Immigration and Customs Enforcement. "If you abolish ICE now, you still have the same president with the same failed policies," she said. Of the "Medicare for all" legislation pushed by another progressive, Vermont Sen. Bernie Sanders, Duckworth told the St. Louis Post-Dispatch, "I just don't think the Sanders proposal is achievable. ... For me, it is about realistically implementing something."

Duckworth made Senate history with the birth of her second daughter, and her appearance on Capitol Hill 10 days later with the baby amid bipartisan fussing provided an upbeat interlude in the increasingly polarized chamber. The birth, which came nearly a month after Duckworth turned 50, was made possible by in vitro fertilization. Senate rules had barred children from the floor of the chamber, but senators voted unanimously to allow both male and female members to bring infants onto the floor. Two months later, mother and baby appeared together at a Capitol Hill demonstration criticizing the Trump administration policy — later reversed — of separating migrant families at the U.S.-Mexico border. After giving a speech holding her infant daughter, Duckworth told CNN, "I could only imagine what it would be like to have my daughter — my breastfeeding child — ripped away from me the way some of these other moms' babies have been."

Bobby Rush (D)

Elected 1992, 14th term, b. Nov 23, 1946; Albany, GA; Roosevelt University (IL), B.A., 1973; University of Illinois, Chicago, Att., 1977; University of Illinois, Chicago, M.A., 1994; McCormick Theological Seminary (IL), M.Th., 1998; Baptist; Married (Paulette Holloway); 7 children (1 deceased).

Military Career: U.S. Army 1963-1968

Elected Office: Chicago city alderman, 1983-1992; 2nd ward committeeman, 1984.

Professional Career: Member, Student Non-Violent Coord. Committee, 1966-1968; Co-founder, IL Black Panther Party, 1968; Med. clinic Director, 1970-1973; Ins. agent, 1978-1983.

DC Office: 2188 RHOB 20515, 202-225-4372, Fax: 202-226-0333, rush.house.gov

State Offices: Chicago, 773-779-2400.

Committees: *Energy & Commerce*: Consumer Protection & Commerce; Energy (Chmn); Health.

Group Ratings

	ADA	ACLU	AFL-CIO	LCV	ITI	COC	HAFA	ACU	CFG	FRC
2018	-	90%	-	91%	-	55%	11%	8%	20%	0%
2017	90%	C	86%	69%	C	50%	C	10%	6%	14%

Almanac Ratings 2017-18

	Economy	Social	Foreign	Composite
Liberal	81%	84%	91%	85%
Conservative	19%	16%	9%	15%

Key Votes of the 115th Congress

1. Obama-care revision	N	5. Family planning regs	NV	9. Guantanamo prisoners	Y
2. Tax Cuts	N	6. Body cameras/immigration	Y	10. Ground missiles, limit	Y
3. Omnibus appropriations	N	7. Abortion ban	N	11. Defense Dept. spending	Y
4. Dodd-Frank revision	N	8. Concealed carry	N	12. FISA rules	N

Election Results

Election	Name (Party)	Vote (%)	Cand. Spent	Ind. Exp. Support	Ind. Exp. Oppose
2018 General	Bobby Rush (D).............................. 189,560	(74%)	$285,759		
	Jimmy Lee Tillman II (R).............. 50,960	(20%)			
	Thomas Rudbeck (I)............................17,365	(7%)	$217,353		
2018 Primary	Bobby Rush (D).......................	(100%)			

Prior winning percentages: 2016 (74%), 2014 (73%), 2012 (74%), 2010 (80%), 2008 (86%), 2006 (84%), 2004 (85%), 2002 (83%), 2000 (88%), 1998 (89%), 1996 (87%), 1994 (76%), 1992 (83%)

Once a Black Panther and prison inmate, Democrat Bobby Rush was elected in 1992 and has become an elder liberal statesman of Congress and Chicago's sharp-edged political scene. He will go down in history as the only politician ever to beat Barack Obama in an election. His legislative legacy, though less formidable, gained new opportunity in 2019 when he took over as chairman of the Energy and Commerce Energy Subcommittee.

Rush grew up on the North Side, a Boy Scout whose mother was a Republican precinct captain. While in the Army, he became involved in the Student Nonviolent Coordinating Committee in the South, then became disillusioned with the military and went AWOL in 1968. That year, he founded the Illinois Black Panthers, with its "Power to the People" slogan, and recruited Fred Hampton, who became chairman of the organization but was later killed by police in a 1969 raid. The next day, police raided Rush's family's apartment, but he wasn't there. Rush served six months in prison for illegal possession of firearms. During his time with the Black Panthers, he ran a program providing free breakfasts to children and a medical clinic that developed the nation's first mass sickle cell anemia testing program. "I don't repudiate any of my involvement in the Panther party. It was part of my maturing," Rush later said.

In 1983, he was elected the 2nd Ward alderman on the Chicago City Council and was a strong supporter of Harold Washington, who became the city's first black mayor. Rush earned master's degrees in political science and theological studies. Ordained as a Baptist minister, Rush founded a church in 2002 in the depressed Englewood community, but it struggled financially and closed. In 2017, a Cook County judge ordered him to pay $1.1 million on a delinquent bank loan and later arranged for garnishment of a share of Rush's congressional salary.

In 1992, Rush challenged Democratic Rep. Charles Hayes, an older-generation politician with a union background. Just before the primary, it was revealed that Hayes had 716 overdrafts at the House bank, a practice among lawmakers that blossomed into a national scandal. Rush won 42%-39%.

In the House, Rush has a liberal voting record. His rhetoric has softened over the years, and his more deliberate style contrasts sharply with his days as a Panther, though he sometimes chafes at legislative compromises. He backed the 2010 health care overhaul law, but only after sending mixed signals because of his unhappiness over the removal of a provision to reimburse hospitals for indigent care. He claimed credit for provisions in the law that dealt with women's health and postpartum depression.

He has devoted much of his time to the Energy and Commerce Committee, where he chaired the Commerce, Trade and Consumer Protection Subcommittee. In the minority, he was the ranking Democrat for eight years on the Energy Subcommittee. He sought increased job opportunities for minorities throughout the energy industry. As chairman of the Energy Subcommittee in 2019, he pledged to "protect consumers, address climate change and ensure that we are investing in infrastructure and our energy workforce."

Rush waged a quixotic campaign in 1999 against Richard M. Daley's iron grip on the mayor's office. He was a frequent Daley critic, and during the campaign he attacked the mayor for tolerating police brutality, inadequate mass transit service, and cronyism in city government. Only three of the 50 aldermen endorsed him. Rush tried to build a multiracial coalition, but his only chance was with black voters. Daley was popular, and his financial advantage overwhelming. The incumbent won the primary 72%-28%, with nearly 45 percent of the African-American vote and the support of many prominent black ministers.

After that pounding, Rush found himself challenged in his own primary in 2000 by two state senators — Donne Trotter and the then little-known Barack Obama. Obama waged an aggressive campaign, saying at the time that Rush "exemplifies a politics that is reactive, that waits for crises to happen, then holds a press conference, and hasn't been particularly effective at building broad-based coalitions." Obama came under attack for being absent from the state legislature for two months and missing a vote on a gun control bill while on a family trip to Hawaii, where he was raised. "It was a race in which everything that could go wrong did go wrong," Obama later wrote in his book, The Audacity of Hope. Rush was helped by an endorsement from President Bill Clinton. He beat Obama 61%-30%.

During Obama's pitched battle with Hillary Clinton in the 2008 presidential primary, Rush endorsed Obama, calling it "one of the most difficult decisions I've had to make in politics." In 2019, he filed legislation to name Interstate 57—which has its northern terminus in the 1st District—as the Barack Obama Highway. That designation would offer daily reminders of Obama in his home town, where other expressways are named for Kennedy, Eisenhower, Stevenson and local stalwarts.

His political career has taken some odd twists. In the 2015 mayoral election, Rush unexpectedly endorsed the reelection of Rahm Emanuel, and criticized challenger Chuy Garcia for having "cheapened" the legacy of Harold Washington with his claims of building a Latino-black coalition. Rush had a primary challenge in 2016 from veteran South Side Alderman Howard Brookins, who raised $200,000 and had the support of Mike Madigan, the powerful Illinois House speaker and state party chairman. Rush received financial and other help from Emanuel. Of the $586,000 that Rush raised during the cycle, he paid more than $100,000 to family members — in the Chicago tradition. In 2018, he had no primary opposition and defeated Republican challenger Jimmy Tillman, 74%-20%. In Will County, which cast only 15 percent of the vote, Tillman led, 53%-37%. Those numbers were a warning that steep population loss on the South Side could jeopardize one of the three African-American districts in Chicago in the 2022 redistricting.

Rush had a brush with cancer in 2008. He spent much of the year recovering from salivary gland cancer and surgery to remove a tumor near his jaw. Doctors later declared him cancer-free. Following the death of his wife, Carolyn, in 2017, he married Paulette Holloway, a minister who has traveled the world as a missionary. Rush's health appeared to have improved. His financial woes continued. In 2018, the House Ethics Committee sanctioned him with a reapproval for having failed to pay rent on his campaign office for more than 24 years, which the panel ruled was a violation of the House's gift rules.

IL-1: Chicago

Cook Partisan Voting Index: D+27

Population		Race and Ethnicity		Income	
Total	712,456	White	35.3%	Median Income	$50,666
Land area (sq. miles)	258	Black	50.9%	District Income Rank	297
Pop/ sq mi	2757.4	Latino	10.1%	Poverty Rate	18.9%
Born in State	76.7%	Asian	1.9%	With health insurance	91.4%
		Two or more races	1.6%	Cash public assistance	3.7%
Age Groups		Other	0.3%	Food stamp/SNAP	21.1%
Under 18	22.9%				
18-34	23%	**Education**		**Work**	
35-64	39%	H.S grad or less	38.8%	White Collar	15.1%
Over 64	15.1%	Some college	33.5%	Sales and Service	46.5%
		College Degree, 4 yr	16.5%	Blue Collar	19.6%
Military		Post grad	11.2%	Government	16.4%
Veteran/ Active Duty	5.9%				

2012 Pres. Vote	Obama	262,936	(79%)	Romney	67,557	(20%)
2016 Pres. Vote	Clinton	245,945	(75%)	Trump	69,913	(21%)

South Side, Southwest Suburbs: The South Side of Chicago has been home to a large urban black community for nearly a century, which is one of the reasons why the metro area has the third largest African-American population in the nation, after New York and Atlanta. A hundred years ago, there were just a few blocks where black families from the South could settle. But the ghetto grew rapidly with the first influx of blacks from the Mississippi Delta in the 1910s. By the 1920s, the South Side was well established as a center of black-owned businesses and of music, from blues to jazz. Politically, the South Side was heavily Republican throughout those years. The comfortable, white Protestants who settled in solid brick houses here believed in the party of Yankee propriety, while the African Americans had faith in the party of Lincoln. This Republican heartland was represented in the House in the 1920s by Appropriations Chairman Martin Madden. After he died in the Appropriations Committee room in 1928, the 1st District elected Republican Oscar De Priest, the first African American elected to the House in the 20th century.

The New Deal attracted blacks to the Democratic Party, and black Democrat Arthur Mitchell defeated De Priest in 1934. The South Side has been Democratic ever since. For 40 years, it was a cooperative part of Chicago's Democratic machine. Then, after the death of longtime Rep. William Dawson, it rebelled against Mayor Richard J. Daley. The South Side seemed to take over the city when Rep. Harold Washington, who had been elected twice in this district, was elected mayor in 1983 and 1987. After he died in November 1987, other black South Side politicians bogged down in infighting.

The 1st Congressional District of Illinois includes about half of Chicago's African-American community on the South Side. It also takes in several black Cook County suburbs and extends about 40 miles into conservative-leaning rural parts of Will County, which cover about 15 percent of the district. Overall, its gerrymandered voting population is 51 percent black and 10 percent Hispanic. The 1st has a northern salient that extends to South 26th Street and includes the Gothic spires of the University of Chicago and the mansions of Kenwood, now an eclectic and racially integrated mix of well-to-do inhabitants. Kenwood, considered part of the greater Hyde Park community, was home to Barack Obama before he ran for president. After a lengthy review, the leaders of his $500 million presidential library decided on a location in Jackson Park, which is on Lake Shore Drive a few blocks east of the university and is scheduled to open in 2021. Local residents voiced concern that the gentrification might force them out of the area.

The Woodlawn neighborhood served as the setting for Lorraine Hansberry's 1959 play A Raisin in the Sun chronicling a black family's challenges moving into what was then a largely white neighborhood. In Englewood, thousands of homes have been built with federal support in recent years in hopes of creating a new black middle-class community. Despite the persistent poverty in Englewood, a new shopping complex with a Whole Foods has opened. A new high school was scheduled to open in 2019, which would be the first new school building since the 1970s. Still, the broader picture for the South Side has remained grim. Even as the population for the entire city increased by 42,000 from 2010 to 2015, the population on the Far South Side away from the lake dropped by 50,000, a loss of 10 percent, according to Crain's Chicago Business.

Chicago in recent years has experienced a gang-fueled crime wave. Murders peaked at 762 in 2016, which exceeded the combined total in the larger cities of New York and Los Angeles. Since then, murders have declined but remained high. In 2018, the city deployed more than 400 additional police officers on the streets on the South and West sides.

The 1st District is overwhelmingly Democratic. Hillary Clinton prevailed against Donald Trump, 75%-21% -- only the fourth-best Democratic performance in Illinois.

Robin Kelly (D)

Elected 2013, 3rd full term, b. Apr 30, 1956; New York, NY; Bradley University, B.A., 1977; Bradley University, M.A., 1982; Northern Illinois University, Ph.D., 2004; Christian - Non-Denominational; Married (Nathaniel Horn); 2 children.

Elected Office: IL House, 2002-2007.

Professional Career: Director, minority student services and professional counselor, Bradley University, 1990-1992; Director, community affairs, Village of Matteson, IL, 1992-2006; Chief of Staff, IL Treas., 2007-2010; Chief admin. officer, Cook County Board President, 2010-2012.

DC Office: 2416 RHOB 20515, 202-225-0773, Fax: 202-225-4583, robinkelly.house.gov

State Offices: Chicago, 773-321-2001; Kankakee, 708-679-0078; Matteson, 708-679-0078.

Committees: *Energy & Commerce*: Consumer Protection & Commerce; Energy; Health. *Oversight & Reform*: National Security; Subcommittee on Civil Rights & Civil Liberties.

Group Ratings

	ADA	ACLU	AFL-CIO	LCV	ITI	COC	HAFA	ACU	CFG	FRC
2018	-	86%	-	97%	-	58%	8%	4%	12%	0%
2017	100%	C	97%	100%	C	46%	C	7%	5%	0%

Almanac Ratings 2017-18

	Economy	Social	Foreign	Composite
Liberal	96%	100%	98%	98%
Conservative	4%	0%	2%	2%

Key Votes of the 115th Congress

1. Obama-care revision	N	5. Family planning regs	N	9. Guantanamo prisoners	Y
2. Tax Cuts	N	6. Body cameras/immigration	Y	10. Ground missiles, limit	Y
3. Omnibus appropriations	Y	7. Abortion ban	N	11. Defense Dept. spending	N
4. Dodd-Frank revision	N	8. Concealed carry	N	12. FISA rules	N

Election Results

Election	Name (Party)	Vote (%)		Cand. Spent	Ind. Exp. Support	Ind. Exp. Oppose
2018 General	Robin Kelly (D)	183,816	(81%)	$696,196		
	David Merkle (R)	43,875	(19%)			
2018 Primary	Robin Kelly (D)	80,659	(82%)			
	Marcus Lewis (D)	17,640	(18%)			

Prior winning percentages: 2016 (80%), 2014 (79%), 2013 special (71%)

Democrat Robin Kelly, who won a special election in 2013, has impressed Democrats with her clean-government appeal and ardent support for stronger gun-control laws. She developed a bipartisan partnership on information-technology issues. In the majority, she gained a seat on the Energy and Commerce Committee.

Kelly grew up in New York and moved to Illinois to attend Bradley University in Peoria, where she graduated with a bachelor's degree in psychology and a master's degree in counseling and human development services. She earned a Ph.D. in political science from Northern Illinois University. After working at a youth shelter and a counseling center, she returned to Bradley to become director of minority student services. She then spent 14 years as director of community affairs in Matteson, a village on Chicago's South Side.

In 2002, Kelly won a seat in the Illinois House, where she served three terms. She resigned her seat in 2007 to become chief of staff to state Treasurer Alexi Giannoulias, who ran unsuccessfully in 2010 for the Senate. Also that year, she ran to replace Giannoulias as treasurer, but lost to GOP state Sen. Dan Rutherford, 50%-45%. She became chief administrative officer to Cook County Board President Toni Preckwinkle.

The House seat became vacant when Rep. Jesse Jackson Jr. resigned amid a criminal investigation and later served nearly two years in prison for his conversion of campaign contributions to personal use. Jackson, the son of civil rights leader Jesse Jackson, had easily won reelection in 2012, but submitted his resignation two weeks later, citing mental and physical health problems. Three months later, he pleaded guilty to wire and mail fraud after prosecutors said he used about $750,000 in campaign money for personal expenses.

Kelly stepped forward for the special election, and won the backing of local Democratic power brokers. "She is not a showboat," the Chicago Tribune said in supporting her candidacy. "She won't dazzle you with ebullience. She doesn't grandstand. She just works hard." Kelly was endorsed by New York City Mayor Michael Bloomberg, who created a super PAC to support politicians advocating tougher gun laws. His PAC broadcast ads lauding Kelly for backing universal background checks and a ban on some types of semi-automatic weapons, while criticizing former Democratic Rep. Debbie Halvorson, who had the National Rifle Association's endorsement when she represented a suburban district based in Will County. Kelly won the primary, 50%-24%, over Halvorson. "We not only won an election," Kelly said in her victory speech. "We took on the NRA, we gave a voice to the voiceless, and we put our communities on a brand new path to a brighter day."

Kelly served as senior Democrat on the Oversight and Government Reform Subcommittee on Information Technology. Her interests have included improving cybersecurity, strengthening computer infrastructure and encouraging new technologies. With Republican Rep. Will Hurd of Texas, chairman of the subcommittee, Kelly issued a report in September 2018 calling for increased federal funding for research and development of artificial intelligence. "The government is already using AI," she told reporters. "We just need to focus on increasing effectiveness and efficiency." She and Hurd "work really well together," she said.

She has retained her focus on tighter gun control. Her several bills included a requirement that the surgeon general issue an annual report on the effects of gun violence on public health, and a grant of authority to the Consumer Product Safety Commission to regulate pistols, revolvers and other firearms as consumer products. When the NRA attacked her as "Assault Gun Kelly," she responded that she was not "anti-gun," but that she favored "commonsense" gun reform that respected "the right of every American to live free from the threat of gun violence." In October 2017, she rejected criticism by President Donald Trump that Chicago had high rates of gun violence despite its strict gun-control laws. "More than ½ of (Chicago's) crime guns come from outside IL," she tweeted.

Following her defeat in 2010, Kelly sought other opportunities to run statewide. She gave serious consideration to challenging the 2016 reelection of Republican Sen. Mark Kirk, who had narrowly defeated Giannoulias in 2010. Before she could challenge Kirk, she faced the prospect of a difficult Democratic primary. Rep. Tammy Duckworth received the early endorsement of EMILY's List, which supports Democratic women candidates who favor abortion rights. Kelly said that she had deeper experience. Democratic officials leaned toward Duckworth, with her fresher appeal and political base in the suburbs. She voiced early interest in challenging Republican Gov. Bruce Rauner in 2018. But that Democratic primary was dominated by deep-pocket self-financers.

IL-2: Chicago   **Cook Partisan Voting Index: D+29**

Population		Race and Ethnicity		Income	
Total	704,321	White	27.8%	Median Income	$47,510
Land area (sq. miles)	1,081	Black	56.4%	District Income Rank	345
Pop/ sq mi	651.7	Latino	13.6%	Poverty Rate	20.3%
Born in State	75.4%	Asian	0.7%	With health insurance	90.2%
		Two or more races	1.2%	Cash public assistance	4.3%
Age Groups		Other	0.2%	Food stamp/SNAP	23%
Under 18	24.4%				
18-34	21.7%	**Education**		**Work**	
35-64	39.2%	H.S grad or less	41.8%	White Collar	14.7%
Over 64	14.7%	Some college	35.7%	Sales and Service	46%
		College Degree, 4 yr	14.1%	Blue Collar	24.1%
Military		Post grad	8.4%	Government	15.6%
Veteran/ Active Duty	6.9%				

2012 Pres. Vote	Obama	250,777	(81%)	Romney	57,692	(19%)
2016 Pres. Vote	Clinton	236,740	(77%)	Trump	58,026	(19%)

Southeast Chicago, Kankakee: Chicago is a great center of both commerce and industry. If the city's white-collar offices are heavily concentrated in the Loop, its blue-collar heavy industries are most visible on the far South Side. This part of Chicago, diminished in economic importance today, is historically significant. The remnants of its great hulking factories around Lake Calumet and the nearby rail yards have an undeniable majesty. Thomas Geoghegan wrote in his book, Which Side Are You On?, of the fights to win benefits for the workers of shuttered steel mills and of the decline of the labor movement in a place where it got much of its inspiration. This is where the Pullman strike of 1894 was broken by federal troops and where policemen killed 10 union supporters in the Little Steel strike of 1937.

For decades, those workplaces have been mostly empty buildings that suburbanites speed past on the Calumet and Dan Ryan expressways. There have been rumblings of a limited revival. In 2018, developers announced plans for an industrial complex on the site of a former Republic Steel mill. Ford Motor Co. plans to build pickup trucks and SUVs at its assembly plant in Hegewisch, where it already has more than 5,200 workers who had been producing Taurus and Explorer vehicles. But a plan to develop a neighborhood with as many as 20,000 homes was abandoned because of soil contamination on the site — another former steel mill.

The 2nd Congressional District of Illinois is a mix of the urban, majority African-American landscape of Chicago's old South Side industrial area and several Cook County suburbs to the south. In the city, the district includes Jackson Park on the lakeshore just to the south of the Museum of Science and Industry, where the Columbian Exposition of 1893 was held and where the Obama presidential library will be built, as part of the lakefront; perhaps coincidentally, a Tiger Woods company in 2016 unveiled plans to create a nearby championship golf course, which will merge and restore two existing courses. To the south are South Shore, a once heavily Jewish neighborhood and now home to middle-class blacks, and the old industrial area around Lake Calumet.

From its northern tip, the 2nd District extends more than 60 miles through eastern Will County and all of Kankakee County; combined, those two counties comprise about 24 percent of the district population. The district is one of the most Democratic in the nation. The Chicago portion of the 2nd is overwhelmingly black, though many African Americans, especially young parents fleeing Chicago public schools and crime, are moving into suburbs directly to the south — Harvey, Dolton, Markham, Hazel Crest and Lynwood. Farther south are economically revitalized Homewood and Flossmoor; high-income Olympia Fields; and the still vibrant Park Forest, the post-war planned town where William H. Whyte's The Organization Man was set.

Daniel Lipinski (D)

Elected 2004, 8th term, b. Jul 15, 1966; Chicago; Northwestern University, B.S., 1988; Stanford University (CA), M.S., 1989; Duke University (NC), Ph.D., 1998; Catholic; Married (Judy Berkebile Lipinski).

Professional Career: Assistant Professional, University of TN, 2001-2004.

DC Office: 2346 RHOB 20515, 202-225-5701, Fax: 202-225-1012, lipinski.house.gov

State Offices: Chicago, 773-948-6223; Lockport, 815-838-1990; Oak Lawn, 708-424-0853; Orland Park, 708-403-4379.

Committees: *Science, Space & Technology*: Energy; Research & Technology. *Transportation & Infrastructure*: Aviation; Highways & Transit; Railroads, Pipelines & Hazardous Materials (Chmn).

Group Ratings

	ADA	ACLU	AFL-CIO	LCV	ITI	COC	HAFA	ACU	CFG	FRC
2018	-	46%	-	91%	-	67%	17%	13%	28%	60%
2017	75%	C	89%	100%	C	57%	C	19%	0%	44%

Key Votes of the 115th Congress

1. Obama-care revision	N	5. Family planning regs	Y	9. Guantanamo prisoners	N
2. Tax Cuts	N	6. Body cameras/immigration	Y	10. Ground missiles, limit	Y
3. Omnibus appropriations	Y	7. Abortion ban	Y	11. Defense Dept. spending	Y
4. Dodd-Frank revision	N	8. Concealed carry	N	12. FISA rules	Y

Election Results

Election	Name (Party)	Vote (%)	Cand. Spent	Ind. Exp. Support	Ind. Exp. Oppose
2018 General	Daniel Lipinski (D)........................ 163,053	(73%)	$1,906,895	$188,110	$1,726,572
	Arthur Jones (R)............................... 57,885	(26%)			
2018 Primary	Daniel Lipinski (D)........................ 48,675	(51%)			
	Marie Newman (D)........................ 46,530	(49%)			

Prior winning percentages: 2016 (100%), 2014 (65%), 2012 (69%), 2010 (70%), 2008 (73%), 2006 (77%), 2004 (73%)

Democrat Daniel Lipinski, who was first elected in 2004, goes his own way from party leaders. He has put his engineering background to work on infrastructure, technology and constituent service. With his conservative voting record on social issues, Lipinski has become a prime target of liberal activists -- and some House colleagues. After barely surviving a primary challenge in 2018, his future seemed in jeopardy.

Daniel Lipinski grew up in Chicago, in the city's 23rd Ward, and first served as a campaign volunteer for his father, Bill Lipinski, who represented the district for 22 years. He got engineering degrees from Northwestern and Stanford universities before switching to political science for his doctorate at Duke. He worked as an aide to four House Democrats from Illinois, though not in his father's office, and was an American Political Science Association congressional fellow for the House Democratic Policy Committee. He wrote his doctoral thesis on the topic of congressional newsletters (Congressional Communication, published by the University of Michigan Press). At the beginning of 2004, he was an assistant professor of political science at the University of Tennessee in Knoxville.

Lipinski's nomination to run for his father's seat is a case study in Chicago's still-thriving backroom politics. In summer 2004, Bill Lipinski denied widespread rumors that he would give up his seat. Then on Aug. 13, he abruptly announced he would not seek re-election in November because he wanted to return to Chicago and "spend more time with my wife." A meeting was scheduled for Aug. 17 for the 19 ward and township Democratic committeemen in the 3rd District, including Bill Lipinski, the 23rd Ward committeeman. At the meeting, he proposed the most qualified person he could think of, his son, Daniel, who was nominated without opposition. That support was tantamount to election in the 3rd District, and he sailed to victory in November.

In the House, Daniel Lipinski has kept his pledge to be "not really that different from my father," who was the most conservative Democrat in the Illinois delegation. He has opposed same-sex marriage and abortion except when the mother's life is at stake. Showing his continued independence while his party was in the minority, Lipinski was among the House Democrats who declined to vote for Nancy Pelosi as their party's leader. "The Democratic Caucus needs to take an honest look at the last few elections and recognize that the party's brand does not play well in the House districts we need to pick up to gain the majority," he said following the 2016 election. He declined to support the Affordable Care Act in 2010, saying that its provision banning federal funds for abortions wasn't strong enough. Of the 34 House Democrats who voted against Obamacare, he is one of only three who remain in the House. The others are Stephen Lynch of Massachusetts and Collin Peterson of Minnesota.

As a member of the Science, Space, and Technology Committee, where he was senior Democrat on the Research and Technology Subcommittee, Lipinski worked with Republican Michael McCaul of Texas to win House passage of cybersecurity legislation. In 2013-14, he took credit for bipartisan enactment of two bills designed to boost the economy: The American Manufacturing Competitiveness Act, which requires a National Strategic Plan for Manufacturing every four years; and the Cybersecurity Enhancement Act, to protect Americans from cybercrimes.

Lipinski always has an eye on Midway International Airport, which generates the most jobs of any employer in the district. He devotes attention to rail infrastructure and has been a vocal advocate for CREATE, a public-private partnership to improve the Chicago area's passenger and freight rail. On the Public Works and Transportation Committee, Lipinski claimed credit for additional funds for Great Lakes clean-up and harbor improvement, plus "buy American" requirements, in the water resources bill that was enacted in 2016 In October 2018, he unveiled a proposal to end the dumping of raw sewage into the Great Lakes, with federal funds to assist local agencies. In the majority, he gained a plum assignment—given his interests—as chairman of the Railroads, Pipelines and Hazardous Materials Subcommittee.

He has continued to show independence on other issues. In 2015, he was the only Democrat to join 171 House Republicans in sponsoring the First Amendment Defense Act, which barred the federal government from acting against a business or person who refuses to provide a service for same-sex married couples based on religious or moral objections. The Almanac vote ratings have ranked Lipinski among the most conservative Democrats, especially on social issues.

At home, Lipinski occasionally has drawn significant primary opposition. In 2006, John Sullivan, an assistant Cook County state's attorney, made an issue of Lipinski getting the seat in "a backroom deal." Financial planner John Kelly used "no tricks, no fix" as a campaign slogan. Lipinski won with 54 percent, to 26 percent for Kelly and 20 percent for Sullivan. In the 2008 primary, he faced Cook County Assistant State's Attorney Mark Pera, an abortion rights supporter who questioned his campaign payments to his father. Liberal interest groups, local reformers, and others contributed to Pera, who spent $770,000. Lipinski prevailed, 54%-25%. For the next four cycles, he easily won reelection against underfunded GOP challengers and little Democratic opposition.

That changed in 2018. Lipinski faced a well-organized primary challenge from Maria Newman, a former marketing consultant who attacked him for voting against his district. Newman was backed by veteran Chicago-area Democratic Reps. Jan Schakowsky and Luis Gutierrez, plus progressive and women's groups. The support for Newman from Schakowsky, a close ally of Pelosi, threw into question the customary support for incumbents by the Democratic Congressional Campaign Committee. After pressure from centrist House Blue Dogs, the DCCC endorsed Lipinski barely a week before the primary, as did Pelosi and other Democratic leaders. Newman spent $1.5 million on her campaign and received a similar amount of support from allied groups. Lipinski spent less than $2 million and was backed by most large labor unions. Lipinski won, 51%-49%. Newman took 59 percent of the vote in suburban Will County, but it cast only 12 percent of the total.

In November, Republican nominee Arthur Jones was a Holocaust-denier and a former leader of the American Nazi Party. A frequent candidate who won the primary without opposition, Jones was disavowed by national GOP groups. In a district where Republican prospects are nil in any case, Lipinski won, 74%-26%.In early 2019, Newman said that she will run again in the Democratic primary. That revived divisions among House Democrats when Rep. Cheri Bustos of Illinois, who chaired the Democratic Congressional Campaign Committee, said that she would support all incumbents in 2020, including Lipinski.

Even if he survives reelection in 2020, Lipinski faced the threat of steady growth of Hispanics in his district and the prospect that Illinois will lose at least one seat in the 2022 redistricting. One potential source of protection: Illinois House Speaker Mike Madigan, who was part of the cabal that gave Lipinski his seat in 2004, retained an interest in protecting his local domain.

Following the 2018 election, Lipinski joined the bipartisan Problem Solvers Caucus in demanding changes in House rules in exchange for supporting Pelosi for Speaker. Not coincidentally, Pelosi agreed to the proposal by Lipinski and Republican Rep. Darin LaHood of Illinois for a select House committee to modernize the legislative process and other congressional operations.

IL-3: Chicago   Cook Partisan Voting Index: D+6

Population		Race and Ethnicity		Income	
Total	724,628	White	58%	Median Income	$64,489
Land area (sq. miles)	237	Black	4.7%	District Income Rank	141
Pop/ sq mi	3055.2	Latino	31.8%	Poverty Rate	11.1%
Born in State	70.3%	Asian	4.3%	With health insurance	89.8%
		Two or more races	1%	Cash public assistance	2.3%
Age Groups		Other	0.2%	Food stamp/SNAP	11.8%
Under 18	24.5%				
18-34	22.1%	**Education**		**Work**	
35-64	39.6%	H.S grad or less	45.1%	White Collar	13.8%
Over 64	13.8%	Some college	27.7%	Sales and Service	42.7%
		College Degree, 4 yr	17.3%	Blue Collar	25.1%
Military		Post grad	10%	Government	12.1%
Veteran/ Active Duty	5%				

2012 Pres. Vote	Obama	143,910	(56%)	Romney	109,212	(43%)		
2016 Pres. Vote	Clinton	157,273	(55%)	Trump	113,874	(40%)	Johnson	9,177	(3%)

Southwest Side, West Suburbs: A century ago, humorist Finley Peter Dunne's fictional Mr. Dooley pontificated on matters political in a saloon on Archery Road. This was Archer Avenue on the South Side of Chicago, one of the radial streets that cut across what was once open prairie near the Loop and along the Chicago River. Archer Avenue was one of the paths of outward migration and upward mobility for the children and grandchildren of Chicago's ethnic and cultural groups, and still is. Italians from the river wards along the Chicago Sanitary and Ship Canal moved west, the South Side Irish moved west and south along Cicero Avenue toward Oak Lawn, and the Bohemians (as they were called then; now Czechs) were heavily concentrated in the neat bungalows of industrial suburbs like Berwyn. Today, Latinos are driving these same avenues, up before dawn to arrive at factory jobs, or taking Chicago Transit Authority "El" trains to the Loop or to "edge city" jobs along the expressways. Another transportation center is Midway International Airport, Chicago's main airport from 1927 until O'Hare International Airport opened in 1955, and now a busy discount hub. It has renovated and expanded its congested terminals and parking lots, all squeezed into the heart of a busy commercial area on the Southwest Side. The facility has undergone a $323 million redevelopment, including a new and faster security pavilion.

The 3rd Congressional District of Illinois consists of much of this territory, crisscrossed by grid-pattern streets, the canal, the railroad lines and the switching yards so common in this, the center of the nation's rail network. It is part of Chicago's bungalow belt, where Poles cling to their heritage, with many weekend schools teaching Polish to local kids and adults. A narrow corridor on the near South Side extends to the Bridgeport neighborhood, the lifetime home of the late Mayor Richard J. Daley and the storied Irish stronghold that produced four other Chicago mayors. In recent years, Bridgeport has diversified, as Hispanics and Asians have moved in along with artists taking studio space in old warehouses. The neighborhood also has reinvented itself as a commercial and entertainment destination, with a new maritime museum along the Chicago River In 2019, officials unveiled a $75 million "advanced manufacturing center" at Richard J. Daley College, a two-year community college, with the hope that it will lead to the creation of 14,000 manufacturing jobs within a decade.

The 3rd includes the far southwest edge of Chicago, with its early 20th century, prairie-style houses in villages such as the mostly white ethnic Oak Lawn; a few older, affluent suburbs like Western Springs; and middle-income towns like Palos Hills. An eastern slice of Will County includes the towns of Orland Park, Lockport and Lemont, home to the large campus of Argonne National Laboratory. The lab conducts basic and applied research in high energy physics and other disciplines, and has become a research hub for batteries and energy storage, nicknamed "Lithium Valley" by its director.

The Hispanic population has grown to about 32 percent, the second largest Hispanic constituency in the state. African Americans are only 5 percent. The district has become decidedly more suburban than urban: In 2018, the vote was 30 percent city and nearly 60 percent in the Cook suburbs. Politically, this area is ancestrally Democratic, culturally conservative, multiethnic and viscerally patriotic. Of the seven congressional districts that include parts of Chicago, the 3rd has cast the highest percentages for Republican presidential candidates. It remains solidly Democratic, but it faces the risk of major shifts following redistricting in 2022. Hillary Clinton got 55 percent of the vote in 2016.

Jesús Garcia (D)

Elected 2018, 1st term, b. Apr 12, 1956; Durango, Mexico; University of Illinois, Chicago, B.A., 1999; University of Illinois, Chicago, M.A., 2002; Catholic; Married (Evelyn Garcia); 3 children.

Elected Office: Chicago City Council, 1986-1993; IL Senate, 1993-1998; Cook County Board of Commissioners, 2010-2018.

DC Office: 530 CHOB 20515, 202-225-8203, chuygarcia.house.gov

State Offices: Chicago, 773-342-0774.

Committees: *Financial Services*: Nat'l Security, International Development & Monetary Policy. *Transportation & Infrastructure*: Aviation; Highways & Transit; Railroads, Pipelines & Hazardous Materials.

Election Results

Election	Name (Party)	Vote (%)		Cand. Spent	Ind. Exp. Support	Ind. Exp. Oppose
2018 General	Jesus Garcia (D)	143,895	(87%)	$650,215	$13,750	
	Mark Wayne Lorch (R)	22,294	(13%)	$7,290		
2018 Primary	Jesus Garcia (D)	49,631	(66%)			
	Sol Flores (D)	16,398	(22%)			
	Richard Gonzalez (D)	8,921	(12%)			

Freshman Democrat Jesus "Chuy" Garcia took his House seat after a long career in Chicago politics, where he has been a leader of the increasingly influential Latino community. He was best-known nationally for forcing Chicago Mayor Rahm Emanuel to a competitive runoff in his 2015 reelection. Garcia replaced veteran Rep. Luis Gutierrez, who retired after 26 years. Garcia brought a more progressive pedigree than Gutierrez, an ally of Emanuel. Rather than challenge his popularity, both Emanuel and Gutierrez supported Garcia in his easy primary victory in the heavily Democratic district.

Garcia was born in Mexico and his father was a farmworker in several parts of the United States. Following his arrival in Chicago with his family as a 10-year-old, he graduated from the University of Illinois, Chicago, where he later received his master's degree in urban planning. His early activity in Chicago politics was with the successful 1983 mayoral campaign of Harold Washington, who tapped Garcia as his deputy water commissioner. He served six years as an alderman on the Chicago City Council (where he was a Washington ally in the fierce Council Wars), six years in the state Senate and seven years on the Cook County Board of Commissioners. In the latter position, he passed a measure ending the county's cooperation with the Immigration and Customs Enforcement agency.

Following his 1998 Senate reelection loss to an ally of then-Mayor Richard M. Daley, Garcia founded and became executive director of the community development organization Enlace Chicago, and he chaired the board of the Latino Policy forum. Garcia remained an ally of local political reformers and supported Sen. Bernie Sanders for the 2016 Democratic presidential nomination; Gutierrez backed Hillary Clinton.

In his challenge to Emanuel in 2015, Garcia gained support from many African-American leaders who were unhappy with some of the mayor's policies, including his management of police and education. Backed by the large teachers' union, Garcia attacked Emanuel as "insensitive" in closing nearly 50 local schools. Gutierrez joined most of the city's political establishment, including Latino leaders, in support of the mayor, citing his positive actions on immigration issues. Emanuel's 56%-44% victory in the runoff, the first in the city's history, sparked dissension in the local Hispanic community.

Gutierrez, who had often talked about quitting Congress because of his frustration with inaction on federal immigration legislation, announced his retirement in November 2017 on the eve of the filing deadline. Some Chicago political insiders speculated that Emanuel encouraged the move to short-circuit another potentially risky challenge to the mayor in his 2019 reelection, which he ultimately abandoned.

Emanuel's endorsement of Garcia largely cleared the field for his nomination, including several aldermen who had voiced interest in running; the primary became a formality. The runner-up in the 66%-22% contest was Sol Flores, a community activist who founded an advocacy group for housing and domestic assistance. In the Chicago tradition, Garcia gained added influence on the same day by helping to elect several of his allies from the city's Southwest Side to key local and county positions.

Mexican-American Garcia is the first member of Congress from that largest demographic in Chicago's Hispanic community. Gutierrez was born in Puerto Rico and often worked on issues that were vital to the island. "The Southwest Side was ripe for change," Garcia told The Huffington Post following the primary. "The aspirations of the Mexican community for greater political empowerment would be an important ingredient in this election cycle." In the large freshman class of House Democrats, he was among the most experienced office-holders.

IL-4: Chicago   Cook Partisan Voting Index: D+33

Population		Race and Ethnicity		Income	
Total	703,303	White	21.5%	Median Income	$49,321
Land area (sq. miles)	52	Black	3.7%	District Income Rank	321
Pop/ sq mi	13409	Latino	70%	Poverty Rate	19.6%
Born in State	53.3%	Asian	3.5%	With health insurance	80.1%
		Two or more races	1%	Cash public assistance	3.4%
Age Groups		Other	0.3%	Food stamp/SNAP	20.4%
Under 18	26.1%				
18-34	28.4%	**Education**		**Work**	
35-64	36.6%	H.S grad or less	55.9%	White Collar	8.9%
Over 64	8.9%	Some college	21.2%	Sales and Service	44%
		College Degree, 4 yr	15.5%	Blue Collar	30.1%
Military		Post grad	7.5%	Government	7.9%
Veteran/ Active Duty	2.4%				

2012 Pres. Vote	Obama	137,326	(81%)	Romney	28,955	(17%)		
2016 Pres. Vote	Clinton	172,367	(81%)	Trump	27,808	(13%)	Johnson	4,892	(2%)
	Stein	4,852	(2%)					

Parts of North and Southwest Sides: Just west of the Loop, the Chicago River splits into the North and South branches, both penetrating the heart of old neighborhoods where immigrants got their start. The South Branch is the guts of Chicago, the site of one of Western civilization's astonishing engineering feats. In 1900, the course of the river was reversed so that sewage flowed downstate through a canal rather than out into Lake Michigan. Just blocks away was Maxwell Street, then thronged with market stalls and long the arrival point for Chicago-bound Jews. Not far away in an Italian American neighborhood on Halsted Street was Jane Addams' Hull House, the original settlement house, where social workers instructed new immigrants on adapting to American life. To the south were Pilsen, arrival neighborhood for the Bohemians (Czechs), and the Irish neighborhoods along Archer Avenue. To the north was Milwaukee Avenue, the main street of Polish Americans and Ukrainian Americans.

Today, many of these places are arrival neighborhoods again, mostly for Chicago's wide variety of Hispanic immigrants. On the South Side, in the old river wards, is Chicago's Mexican-American community, extending west into Pilsen and into the once Bohemian suburb of Cicero, famous as a haven for Al Capone's mobsters in the 1920s. Times have changed: Beginning in the 1980s, Cicero became a transit point for Mexican immigrants, many of whom then made their permanent residences elsewhere in Chicago. Its official census population is 84,000, of whom 89 percent are Hispanic. But town officials believe the actual number is significantly higher because of the influx of undocumented residents. Chicago has by far the largest Latino concentration north of Texas and Florida and between the two coasts.

The 4th Congressional District of Illinois remains the only majority-Hispanic district in the Midwest. With the South Side Mexican-American areas and the smaller North Side Puerto Rican communities separated by the West Side black ghetto, the solution was the creation of one of the most bizarrely designed congressional districts in the country, shaped like a pair of earmuffs. Essentially these two Latino communities, defined by careful boundaries to maximize the district's Hispanic percentage, are connected by a thin line of territory stretching around the black-majority 7th District at the Cook-DuPage County line. Of the 70 percent of residents who are Hispanic, four-fifths are Mexican-American. The district is entirely in Cook County, with close to 75 percent of the votes cast in Chicago or Cicero.

On both the south and north sides, economic changes have led to social tensions. Pilsen, which is across the Chicago River from Bridgeport, has become "ground zero for gentrification," the Chicago Tribune wrote in April 2018. Although the effect can be disruptive, the editorial added, "There is indeed room for balance between economic growth and preservation of neighborhood character and affordability." The district contains the rapidly gentrifying neighborhoods of Logan Square, famous for its boulevards and spacious mansions surrounding Milwaukee Avenue, and Humboldt Park, which includes the nation's only museum that focuses on Puerto Rican arts and culture. There, young professionals are moving in, with trendy restaurants, new condominiums and boutique shops locating alongside traditional Latin American taquerias and Hispanic churches. The Chicago Advocate referred to the area as the "Hipster Mecca of the Midwest." The chief downside is for the tenants — many of them Hispanic -- who have been forced out by housing costs that have surged, including a 19 percent spike in the price of homes sold in 2018. Between 2000 and 2017, more than 20,000 Hispanics moved out of the Logan Square neighborhood and 12,000 whites moved in. The area regained its white plurality.

Mike Quigley (D)

Elected 2009, 5th full term, b. Oct 17, 1958; Indianapolis, IN; Roosevelt University (IL), B.A., 1981; University of Chicago (IL), M.P.P., 1985; Loyola University Law School (IL), J.D., 1989; Christian - Non-Denominational; Married (Barbara Quigley); 2 children.

Elected Office: Cook County commissioner, 1998-2009.

Professional Career: Cook County aldermanic aide, 1983-1989; Adjunct Professional, Roosevelt University, 2006-2007; Adjunct Professional in political science, Loyola University Chicago, 2002-2009; Practicing attorney, 1990-present.

DC Office: 2458 RHOB 20515, 202-225-4061, Fax: 202-225-5603, quigley.house.gov

State Offices: Chicago, 773-267-5926; Chicago, 773-267-5926.

Committees: *Appropriations:* Financial Services & General Government (Chmn); Interior, Environment & Related Agencies; Transportation, HUD & Related Agencies. *Permanent Select on Intelligence:* Counterterrorism, Counterintelligence & Counterproliferation; Strategic Technologies & Advanced Research.

Group Ratings

	ADA	ACLU	AFL-CIO	LCV	ITI	COC	HAFA	ACU	CFG	FRC
2018	-	75%	-	97%	-	58%	11%	8%	20%	0%
2017	80%	C	95%	97%	C	43%	C	7%	5%	0%

Almanac Ratings 2017-18

	Economy	Social	Foreign	Composite
Liberal	92%	97%	89%	93%
Conservative	8%	3%	11%	7%

Key Votes of the 115th Congress

1. Obama-care revision	N	5. Family planning regs	N	9. Guantanamo prisoners	Y
2. Tax Cuts	N	6. Body cameras/immigration	Y	10. Ground missiles, limit	Y
3. Omnibus appropriations	Y	7. Abortion ban	N	11. Defense Dept. spending	Y
4. Dodd-Frank revision	N	8. Concealed carry	N	12. FISA rules	Y

Election Results

Election	Name (Party)	Vote (%)		Cand. Spent	Ind. Exp. Support	Ind. Exp. Oppose
2018 General	Mike Quigley (D)..............................	213,992	(77%)	$1,094,820		
	Tom Hanson (R).................................	65,134	(23%)			
2018 Primary	Mike Quigley (D)..............................	66,254	(63%)			
	Sameena Mustafa (D)........................	25,591	(24%)			
	Benjamin Wolf (D)............................	10,032	(10%)			

Prior winning percentages: 2016 (68%), 2014 (63%), 2012 (66%), 2010 (71%), 2009 special (69%)

Mike Quigley is a reform-minded Democrat who won a special election in 2009 and has built legislative influence in the district that had been held by Rahm Emanuel. He is both an avid hockey player — he has had more than 300 stitches to prove it — and an ex-political science professor whom The New York Times once called "the king of Chicago's public-policy nerds." In the House, he has become a force on the Appropriations and Intelligence committees.

Quigley grew up in the working-class suburb of Carol Stream in DuPage County. He graduated from Roosevelt University, got a master's in public policy at the University of Chicago and his law degree from Loyola University in Chicago. He practiced criminal law and taught political science part-time at Loyola. He started his career in politics as an aide to Alderman Bernard Hansen and got involved in a community battle to stop the addition of lights for night games at Wrigley Field, which is in the heart of an old, gentrified neighborhood. He lost that fight, but the Cubs mostly remained a good neighbor.

In 1998, Quigley was elected to the Cook County Board of Commissioners, where he became an independent voice and a frequent nemesis of board President John Stroger. He pushed reforms such as ending patronage jobs at the Cook County Forest Preserve District, promoted environmental action, and sponsored a proposal to allow gay couples to register as domestic partners. In 2005, Quigley decided to challenge Stroger for board president, but later dropped out and backed Forrest Claypool, who lost to Stroger.

After President Barack Obama plucked Emanuel from the House to serve as his chief of staff, many candidates jumped into the wide-open Democratic primary. State Rep. Sara Feigenholtz was endorsed by EMILY's List, which supports abortion rights. Alderman Patrick O'Connor and state Rep. John Fritchey had local party machine support. Quigley ran a late ad comparing Feigenholtz to President Richard Nixon, saying she had resorted to unfair campaign charges. That may have extinguished any lingering friendship between Quigley and Feigenholtz, who had dated briefly years earlier. Quigley received key newspaper endorsements from the Chicago Sun-Times and the Chicago Tribune, the latter praising him for an "outstanding record of independent, reform-minded performance in office." In a low-turnout event, Quigley won the primary with 20 percent of the vote to 17 percent for Fritchey and 15 percent for Feigenholtz. Quigley breezed to victory in the general election.

In the House, Quigley has been a consistent Democratic vote but one who is unafraid to ruffle feathers. He was among the first Democrats in 2010 to call on Rep. Charles Rangel of New York to give up his Ways and Means Committee chairmanship while battling ethics problems. He cofounded the Congressional Transparency Caucus and introduced legislation requiring lobbyists to disclose the name of each executive branch official and each member of Congress and staffer with whom they meet.

He ran a persistent campaign to require Congressional Research Service reports to be made public. "Taxpayers have a stake in these reports, providing more than $100 million annually to support the work of the Congressional Research Service," he wrote in Time. "Unfortunately, these reports are often made available to just a select few inside the Beltway, leaving everyday citizens out in the dark." Opponents objected that public disclosure would infringe on the information needs of lawmakers, though many of the reports were commercially available for those who could pay for them and quite a few are available for free online. He largely prevailed in the fiscal 2018 omnibus spending bill, which required that CRS publish on its website all non-confidential reports. In a bit of legislative arcana, CRS made available its in-depth research reports, but not its executive-level briefing documents, Roll Call reported.

Quigley moved into the House hierarchy with a seat on the Appropriations Committee, where he was the only Illinois member from either party. In 2019, he became chairman of its Financial Services Subcommittee, whose spending domain includes White House operations. He objected strongly to the partial government shutdown in January 2019, which resulted from the clash over a wall on the border with Mexico. He cited how the shutdown was affecting various agencies on which the public relies. "It's never appropriate to hold paychecks and vital government services hostage as a deal-making tactic," he told the House. During his two previous years as the panel's top Democrat in the minority, Quigley objected to numerous Republican-sponsored policy riders, including restrictions on the Internal Revenue Service and the needle-exchange program of the District of Columbia.

On the Intelligence Committee, Quigley joined other Democrats in objecting to how Republicans ran the panel when they were in the majority. In February 2018, he urged Speaker Paul Ryan to remove Chairman Devin Nunes. He called them "co-conspirators" in protecting President Donald Trump, who was "freaked out" by the investigation of Russian involvement in the 2016 election.

He has been active in calling for tighter gun control laws. On two other issues of importance to his constituents, he has pushed for an extension of the visa waiver program to Poland, and for review by the Food and Drug Administration of its policy that bans gay and bisexual men from donating blood. He has been a leader of the LGBT Equality Caucus.

Quigley has coasted to reelection. In 2018, as was the case eight years earlier, he toyed with the idea of running for an open seat for mayor, but decided not to join the crowded field in each case. That decision, Crain's Chicago Business wrote, resulted from "a mix of seniority and opportunity" — namely, the Democrats' takeover of the House and his Appropriations subcommittee chairmanship.

IL-5: Chicago

Cook Partisan Voting Index: D+20

Population		Race and Ethnicity		Income	
Total	737,064	White	68.3%	Median Income	$78,227
Land area (sq. miles)	96	Black	2.7%	District Income Rank	59
Pop/ sq mi	7701	Latino	19.6%	Poverty Rate	9.3%
Born in State	55.4%	Asian	7%	With health insurance	91.6%
		Two or more races	2.2%	Cash public assistance	1.6%
Age Groups		Other	0.2%	Food stamp/SNAP	6.5%
Under 18	18.6%				
18-34	31.4%	**Education**		**Work**	
35-64	37.6%	H.S grad or less	26.3%	White Collar	12.4%
Over 64	12.4%	Some college	20.4%	Sales and Service	36.8%
Military		College Degree, 4 yr	32.5%	Blue Collar	13.1%
Veteran/ Active Duty	3.5%	Post grad	20.9%	Government	9.5%

2012 Pres. Vote	Obama	188,166	(66%)	Romney	90,715	(32%)			
2016 Pres. Vote	Clinton	229,944	(70%)	Trump	78,074	(24%)	Johnson	12,645	(4%)

North Side, Cook Suburbs: Few places in America today have more ethnic and cultural variety than the North Side of Chicago. This has been the destination of one immigrant group after another. Its neighborhoods harbor all manner of successful, middle-class people. Wooden workingmen's cottages from the late 19th century give way to sturdy brick houses from the early 1900s, and then to the prairie bungalows of the 1920s and the white-shuttered, orange-brick colonials of the 1950s. Chicago was America's top immigrant destination for Poles, Lithuanians, Czechs, Slovaks, Ukrainians and Romanians. Something about the heavy, dull clouds of the long winters, the short, hot summers, and a climate suited to potatoes and cabbage and other hardy vegetables may have reminded them of Central and Eastern Europe, with the addition of the bustling Loop. In the 1980s, upwardly mobile immigrants from Mexico and Guatemala, Korea and the Philippines, were moving in.

Family ties, webs of acquaintances that reach back to ancestral villages, have made the North Side of Chicago a natural port of entry for Eastern bloc migrants, even as other newcomers arrive with relationships extending to Latin America and Southeast Asia. The collapse of the Soviet Union encouraged new rounds of immigrants in the 1990s from Poland and Ukraine, joined by those from Pakistan, India and Bosnia. A couple of blocks from the Chicago River and the Kennedy Expressway is the grand old St. Stanislaus Kostka Church, an iconic center of the Polish community since the 19th century that now conducts masses in Spanish.

The 5th Congressional District covers an oddly shaped swath across Chicago's North Side and the city's western suburbs, running from the lakefront to, and including, O'Hare International Airport on the northwest side of the city, and dipping into western suburbs such as Elmhurst and affluent Hinsdale. It takes in the old Polish-American and Ukrainian-American neighborhoods and shops around Milwaukee Avenue, and the Italian neighborhoods running west on Grand Avenue. It also includes the gentrified Chicago neighborhoods of Old Town, where old houses and factories are being converted into upscale condominiums, often over the objections of preservationists. Nearby Lincoln Park is the second-*richest neighborhood in Chicago (after the Gold Coast); it abounds with boutiques, clubs and restaurants and contains DePaul University, the nation's largest Roman Catholic university. Those commercial activities have substantially reduced the residential population. In trendy Ravenswood, with large Victorian homes on tree-lined streets, the friendly business climate has created a craft brewing and distilling hub.

The district is home to baseball's famed Wrigley Field, which opened in 1914 and is a protected landmark that has defied the teardown trend in ballparks. The Friendly Confines finally rewarded the century-long heartbreak of its fans when the Cubs won the World Series in 2016, while in the midst of a $750 million renovation and update of the iconic edifice; the delayed completion is scheduled during the 2019 season. Just east of Wrigleyville is Boystown, the epicenter of Chicago's gay community; rainbow flags are present on most businesses in the neighborhood. At ever-growing O'Hare, four airlines announced plans to spend $8 billion by 2026 to modernize and expand the terminals, with a 25 percent increase in passenger gates and expectations of increased overseas flights. McDonald's abandoned its corporate headquarters in Oak Brook, including renowned Hamburger University, for a new site in Chicago's West Loop area, which is in the 7th District. The 5th District contains the largest white population of the seven districts based in Chicago: The Hispanic share has increased modestly to 20 percent. A scant 3 percent is African-American. While the 5th now has some Republican-leaning western suburbs, it remains a solidly Democratic district. In 2016, Hillary Clinton won, 70%-24%.

Sean Casten (D)

Elected 2018, 1st term, b. Nov 23, 1971; Dublin, Ireland; Middlebury College (VT), B.A., 1993; Dartmouth College, Hanover (NH), M.S., 1998; Married (Kara Casten); 2 children.

Professional Career: President and Chief Executive Officer, Turbosteam Corporation, 2000-2007; Co-Founder, Recycled Energy Development LLC.

DC Office: 429 CHOB 20515, 202-225-4561, casten.house.gov

State Offices: West Chicago, 630-520-9450.

Committees: *Financial Services*: Investor Protection, Entrepreneurship & Capital Markets; Oversight & Investigations. *Science, Space & Technology*: Energy; Environment. *Select Committee on the Climate Crisis.*

Election Results

Election	Name (Party)	Vote (%)		Cand. Spent	Ind. Exp. Support	Ind. Exp. Oppose
2018 General	Sean Casten (D)	169,001	(54%)	$6,165,646	$277,762	$3,398,677
	Peter J. Roskam (R)	146,445	(46%)	$7,064,428	$771,526	$6,490,845
2018 Primary	Sean Casten (D)	19,774	(30%)			
	Kelly Mazeski (D)	17,984	(27%)			
	Carole Cheney (D)	11,663	(17%)			
	Amanda Howland (D)	8,483	(13%)			
	Becky Anderson Wilkins (D)	4,001	(6%)			

Freshman Democrat Sean Casten, a political newcomer, was elected in a suburban district that Democratic redistricters designed as a Republican seat. A scientist and entrepreneur, he worked on clean-energy projects. Casten defeated Rep. Peter Roskam, who had been a House Republican leader and was a senior member of the Ways and Means Committee, where he had a prominent role in crafting the 2017 tax cuts. That legislation was not the political bonanza that the GOP had expected. Roskam was the most senior of four Ways and Means Republicans who were defeated for reelection in 2018.

A native of Ireland, Casten majored in molecular biology at Middlebury College and got master's degrees in biochemical engineering and engineering management from Thayer School of Engineering at Dartmouth College. During his career working on clean-energy technologies, he was president of Massachusetts-based Turbostream Corp., which used energy-recycling techniques to reduce greenhouse gasses. With his father, Casten founded Illinois-based Recycled Energy Development, which sought ways to capture waste heat to generate electricity; the company was sold in 2016. He chaired the U.S. Combined Heat and Power Association and he worked with states in the Northeast on a plan that became the Regional Greenhouse Gas Initiative.

Following his initial House election in 2006, when he narrowly defeated now-Sen. Tammy Duckworth, Roskam became politically entrenched. In 2014, he lost to Rep. Steve Scalise of Louisiana in a House Republican contest for Majority Whip. Hillary Clinton's 49%-42% win in his district in 2016 was Roskam's initial signal of political problems at home. With Donald Trump as president, he remained a team player for the GOP on legislation, including taxes and health care.

In challenging Roskam, Casten cited his "immoral tax plan that is saddling our country with crippling debt and could force cuts to Social Security and Medicare." If elected, he told the Chicago Sun-Times, he would make climate change and the growth of "green business" his chief focus. He criticized Roskam as a career politician and for his failure to "hold [Trump] accountable for his actions."

In the Democratic primary, the initial frontrunner was Kelly Mazeski, a commissioner in Barrington Hills and breast-cancer survivor who had the support of prominent Illinois Democrats and EMILY'S List, which backs Democratic women who favor abortion rights. She was handicapped by four other women running in the primary. Casten prevailed, 30%-27%, over Mazeski. Republicans subsequently raised questions about whether a Super PAC—to which Casten's father was a large contributor—violated restrictions on coordination with the candidate in its negative ads against Mazeski.

Roskam outspent Casten, $7.1 million to $6.2 million in the campaign. Including outside groups, total spending exceeded $24 million.Roskam conceded "there's a lot to criticize" with Trump and sought to turn against Casten the local unpopularity of the president. In criticizing Casten's "politics of ridicule," Roskam said that he was ironically copying Trump's approach. That rhetorical twist may have served chiefly to reinforce that Trump had become a major drag on Roskam and other local Republicans.

In his 54%-46% victory, Casten won four of the five counties. Roskam took Lake County, which cast less than 10 percent of the vote. Slightly more than half of the votes were cast in DuPage County, where Casten got 54 percent. Perhaps the biggest threat to Casten's reelection would be an attempt by the once-solidly Republican base in DuPage to coalesce behind a challenger.

IL-6: West-Central Chicagoland

Cook Partisan Voting Index: R+2

Population		Race and Ethnicity		Income	
Total	725,875	White	76.4%	Median Income	$96,460
Land area (sq. miles)	379	Black	2.5%	District Income Rank	18
Pop/ sq mi	1916.3	Latino	10.2%	Poverty Rate	5.3%
Born in State	65.5%	Asian	9.1%	With health insurance	95%
		Two or more races	1.7%	Cash public assistance	1.2%
Age Groups		Other	0.1%	Food stamp/SNAP	4.5%
Under 18	23.7%				
18-34	19.2%	**Education**		**Work**	
35-64	42.8%	H.S grad or less	22.5%	White Collar	14.3%
Over 64	14.3%	Some college	26.1%	Sales and Service	38%
		College Degree, 4 yr	31.1%	Blue Collar	13.4%
Military		Post grad	20.4%	Government	9.7%
Veteran/ Active Duty	5.2%				

2012 Pres. Vote	Romney	179,607	(53%)	Obama	151,760	(45%)			
2016 Pres. Vote	Clinton	177,549	(49%)	Trump	152,935	(42%)	Johnson	18,336	(5%)

DuPage, Kane: Most residents of Chicagoland now live in the suburbs, and increasingly in the collar counties surrounding Cook County. DuPage County, straight west of Chicago, had 103,000 residents in 1940; in 2017, there were 930,000, with new subdivisions still springing up at the western edges. This is no longer a one-trick county of bedroom suburbs. It has become an engine of economic growth, containing the Illinois Technology and Research Corridor, one of suburban Chicago's biggest employment hubs.

Nearby are graceful, old railroad-commuter towns like Hinsdale and Downers Grove, plus Barrington Hills, known for its country manors and large open areas protected by preservationists. Naperville, once a country village, is now an edge city, with a school district that is top-ranked in science. Wheaton is home to the Illinois landmark Cantigny, a 500-acre public park and recreation area that was once the estate of Col. Robert McCormick, longtime publisher of the Chicago Tribune. Wheaton College, known as the "evangelical Harvard," boasts Reverend Billy Graham among its alumni.

Politically, these suburbs were once rock-ribbed Republican, convinced that civic virtues could best be realized by opposing the party of City Hall in Chicago. In the 1990s, they became less Republican, as voters recoiled from the national party's cultural conservatism. After voting for Republicans in every presidential election in the 20th century, DuPage County twice voted for President Barack Obama, though narrowly. Hillary Clinton in 2016 increased the Democratic advantage to a more pronounced 54%-40%. In 2018, Republicans in DuPage had additional setbacks in state and local elections — "a political tsunami that both carried and lifted Democrats -- all women — to unprecedented heights in county government," the Daily Herald reported. The once rural county has become more diverse; foreign-born residents now make up 19 percent of the county-wide population. This increase is part of the broader racial shifts across Chicagoland, which is moving soon to majority-minority status.

The 6th Congressional District of Illinois forms a large C that encompasses a small wedge of Cook County and parts of the collar counties of Kane, McHenry and Lake; a bit more than half the population lives in DuPage, smaller parts of which have been grafted onto five other districts. It takes in towns including Barrington, Wheaton, Winfield, Downers Grove and parts of Naperville. The 6th was designed during the 2012 redistricting as a Republican bastion, with the solidly GOP Palatine in Cook, St. Charles in Kane, and Crystal Lake in McHenry. Despite those intentions, the Republican vote here slipped markedly in 2016. What had been a 53%-45% lead for Mitt Romney in 2012 became a 49%-42% lead for Hillary Clinton. Even with that weak performance, this was the best district for Trump in Chicagoland, though the worst vote of the seven districts in Illinois that were Republican-held at the time.

Danny Davis (D)

Elected 1996, 12th term, b. Sep 06, 1941; Parkdale, AR; Arkansas Agricultural and Mechanical College, B.A., 1961; Chicago State University (IL), M.A., 1968; Union Institute and University, Ph.D., 1977; Baptist; Married (Vera G. Davis); 2 children (1 deceased); 4 grandchildren (1 deceased).

Elected Office: Chicago city alderman, 1979-1990; Cook County commissioner, 1990-1996.

Professional Career: Teacher, Chicago Public Schls., 1962-1969; Health care planner, 1969-1979.

DC Office: 2159 RHOB 20515, 202-225-5006, Fax: 202-225-5641, davis.house.gov

State Offices: Chicago, 773-533-7520.

Committees: *Ways & Means*: Trade; Worker & Family Support (Chmn).

Group Ratings

	ADA	ACLU	AFL-CIO	LCV	ITI	COC	HAFA	ACU	CFG	FRC
2018	-	88%	-	97%	-	64%	11%	9%	14%	0%
2017	100%	C	97%	94%	C	38%	C	4%	5%	0%

Almanac Ratings 2017-18

	Economy	Social	Foreign	Composite
Liberal	95%	97%	92%	95%
Conservative	6%	3%	8%	5%

Key Votes of the 115th Congress

1. Obama-care revision	N	5. Family planning regs	N	9. Guantanamo prisoners	Y
2. Tax Cuts	N	6. Body cameras/immigration	Y	10. Ground missiles, limit	Y
3. Omnibus appropriations	NV	7. Abortion ban	N	11. Defense Dept. spending	Y
4. Dodd-Frank revision	Y	8. Concealed carry	N	12. FISA rules	N

Election Results

Election	Name (Party)	Vote (%)		Cand. Spent	Ind. Exp. Support	Ind. Exp. Oppose
2018 General	Danny Davis (D)	215,746	(88%)	$428,147		
	Craig Cameron (R)	30,497	(12%)			
2018 Primary	Danny Davis (D)	81,570	(74%)			
	Anthony Clark (D)	28,867	(26%)			

Prior winning percentages: 2016 (84%), 2014 (85%), 2012 (85%), 2010 (82%), 2008 (85%), 2006 (87%), 2004 (86%), 2002 (83%), 2000 (86%), 1998 (93%), 1996 (83%)

Danny Davis, a Democrat first elected in 1996 at age 55, is a liberal who has been eager for political advancement. He waged two unsuccessful campaigns for Chicago mayor and twice flirted with running for president of the Cook County Board of Commissioners. His opportunities to seek other office likely have ended, but he has become a senior statesman in the Congressional Black Caucus and a subcommittee chairman at House Ways and Means.

Davis grew up on a cotton farm in Arkansas, graduated from college in that state, then moved to Chicago and worked as a teacher, assistant principal, and guidance counselor in Chicago public schools. For 10 years, he ran a community health project on the West Side. He was elected alderman in the 29th Ward in 1979, and supported Mayor Harold Washington, the city's first black mayor, in his notorious 1980s battles with white machine aldermen dubbed the "Council Wars." In 1990, Davis was elected a Cook County commissioner.

In 1996, Davis ran for an open seat. His major opponents were 3rd Ward Alderman Dorothy Tillman, an ally of Chicago Mayor Richard M. Daley, and 28th Ward Alderman Ed Smith. Davis campaigned as a big-government liberal, calling for a $7.60 minimum wage, affirmative action programs and a nationalized health care plan. He won with 33 percent and has not faced a serious challenge since. In 2000, he lost his 29th Ward committeeman post to a Daley-backed challenger — a political hat that many Chicago elected officials find at least as vital as their government hats.

In the House, Davis has a liberal voting record. He has pushed for tax incentives for businesses that create jobs in inner-city communities and distressed rural areas. He was a champion of organized labor as he worked with a bipartisan coalition that in 2006 enacted big changes in the Postal Service. Since then, congressional agreement on postal overhaul has remained elusive.

His devotion to issues affecting the poor has won him respect even among Republicans. With his wife, Vera, Davis in the mid-2000s supported a local program to increase the low share of black home ownership in his district by offering credit counseling and innovative forms of mortgage financing. With the view that everybody deserves a second chance, Davis has taken a deep interest in the problems of former convicts seeking to transition to the mainstream. He teamed on a bipartisan bill creating tax credits to encourage transitional housing and job training for former prisoners. It evolved into his Second Chance Act, which President George W. Bush signed into law in 2008. Davis has filed legislation to make available educational Pell Grants to prisoners. That option was eliminated when the Democratic-controlled Congress enacted the 1994 crime bill.

On the Ways and Means Committee, Davis was an outspoken defender of the committee's chairman, New York Democrat Charles B. Rangel, during his ethics scandal in 2010, and called enactment that year of the Affordable Care Act "good for black America." With Democrats in the House minority, he was the ranking member of the Human Resources Subcommittee. He became chairman in 2019 of the renamed Worker and Family Support panel.

In 2006, Davis sought to become Cook County Board president after incumbent John Stroger suffered a serious stroke. But Democratic committeemen overwhelmingly supported Stroger's son,

Todd, for the nomination. After the 2008 election, Davis campaigned publicly for the support of Democratic Gov. Rod Blagojevich to fill Obama's Senate seat. Blagojevich called Davis his top choice, but Davis turned down what was bound to be a tainted appointment after Blagojevich was criminally charged and then convicted for trying to gain personally from his power to make the appointment.

After Daley announced in 2010 he would not seek reelection as mayor, Davis jumped into the race, collecting endorsements from 15 African-American aldermen. But with pressure mounting to settle on a single black candidate, he endorsed former Sen. Carol Moseley Braun, who had stressed her fundraising advantage over Davis. She lost to Rahm Emanuel.

Following the election of Donald Trump as president, Davis said that he was "not a happy camper." He added, "I think we will struggle for the next four years, but we'll never give up." A week later, the 15-year-old grandson of Davis was shot to death in a dispute over the possession of gym shoes. He called for the declaration of a "state of emergency" in high-crime areas of Chicago to address crime, violence, education, economic development and related problems. In 2018, he filed a bill to reduce gun sales by placing national excise taxes on firearms and ammunition. Cook County has a similar tax.

IL-7: Chicago

Cook Partisan Voting Index: D+38

Population		Race and Ethnicity		Income	
Total	725,329	White	28.2%	Median Income	$54,112
Land area (sq. miles)	63	Black	47.9%	District Income Rank	241
Pop/ sq mi	11601.5	Latino	14.9%	Poverty Rate	23.5%
Born in State	62.8%	Asian	7%	With health insurance	89.3%
		Two or more races	1.6%	Cash public assistance	3.9%
Age Groups		Other	0.3%	Food stamp/SNAP	22.4%
Under 18	20.8%				
18-34	30.9%	**Education**		**Work**	
35-64	36.1%	H.S grad or less	36.4%	White Collar	12.2%
Over 64	12.2%	Some college	22.9%	Sales and Service	40.5%
		College Degree, 4 yr	21.8%	Blue Collar	13.8%
Military		Post grad	19%	Government	11.7%
Veteran/ Active Duty	3.8%				

2012 Pres. Vote	Obama	263,928	(87%)	Romney	35,595	(12%)			
2016 Pres. Vote	Clinton	271,156	(87%)	Trump	28,523	(9%)	Johnson	6,759	(2%)

Downtown, West Side: An airplane passenger on a cloudless day can get a clear view of the biggest man-made cityscape between the Atlantic and Pacific oceans: Chicago's Loop. Its high rises and parks along Lake Michigan were built a century ago, and the downtown district was named in 1897 for the quadrilateral shape the elevated train forms around the city's center. International School modernists built their most impressive collection of buildings here and along Lake Shore Drive in the years after World War II. The Loop now spreads beyond the elevated train, or the "El" as it's known locally. It reaches west beyond the financial exchanges to the 110-story Willis (formerly Sears) Tower — once the world's tallest building, now seventeenth and second in the United States behind One World Trade Center in New York — situated near the Chicago River. The Loop reaches north and stops at the Gold Coast, the wondrous shopping district along North Michigan Avenue. After the sale in 2017 of Tribune Tower, one of the most distinctive buildings on Michigan Avenue, the Chicago Tribune moved its offices a few blocks south to Prudential Plaza, which overlooks Millennium Park. West of the Gold Coast is the River North neighborhood, which has become one of the city's most vibrant. In the South Loop, plans were underway for "The 78," a huge riverfront campus, with plans for 10,000 residential units; the site name alludes to the fact that the city already had 77 official community areas.

This is the face Chicago likes to present to the world: giant structures rising where the prairies meet the great lake, a vast concentration of brains and muscle, the nerve center of the nation's commodities markets, and, most recently, a hive of political activity. President Barack Obama's high-rise headquarters in 2012 filled a 50,000-square foot floor at One Prudential Plaza. South of the Loop sits McCormick Place, the largest convention center in North America; Obama celebrated his reelection victory here in November 2012. At Grant Park, the president delivered his historic 2008 victory speech in front of 240,000 onlookers cheering the election of the nation's first African-American president. The 319-acre park includes several of the city's civic treasures, including the Art Institute, Millennium Park and Buckingham Fountain.

Not far west of the luxurious lakefront neighborhoods are the muscle and sinew, gristle and fat of the city. The West Side of Chicago, the vast acres directly west of the Loop, for years was a grimy and dangerous slum, with some areas almost completely abandoned. Many factories that made Chicago the chocolate and candy center of the nation were shuttered, and production went mostly overseas. The West Side began to revive in the 1990s. The United Center attracted commercial development, lower crime rates and higher land values. Former meatpacking buildings have been turned into art galleries. To the relief of local sweet tooths, more than 60 food or beverage companies expanded in or moved to Chicago from 2011 to 2018. A massive new downtown dormitory houses students from nearby DePaul University, Roosevelt University and Columbia College.

The 7th Congressional District of Illinois contains the Loop, most of the North Michigan corridor, the Near North Side, and a few South Side neighborhoods. Its heart, demographically and spiritually, is the predominantly African-American West Side, parts of which remain more depopulated and socially disorganized than the predominantly black South Side. Like other minority neighborhoods in Chicago, the West Side has suffered from the recent surge in murders and other violence. A few blocks west of McCormick Place on the South Side is Chinatown, which has retained its ethnic quality while it has grown and avoided gentrification. Lori Lightfoot, who was elected mayor of Chicago in April 2009, had success in bridging the local political divides. As the successor to Rahm Emanuel, she faced continuing challenges, including education, crime and the city's financial woes.

Just outside the city limits to the west, but in the district, is Oak Park, the boyhood home of writer Ernest Hemingway and the location of architect Frank Lloyd Wright's home and museum and many of his prairie-style houses. Farther out the Eisenhower Expressway are well-heeled River Forest; more modest Maywood, which is a black-majority suburb; Broadview; and Hillside. African Americans now make up 48 percent of the district, with 15 percent Hispanic. It is the most heavily Democratic district in the state. Hillary Clinton got 87 percent of the vote here in 2016.

Raja Krishnamoorthi (D)

Elected 2016, 2nd term, b. Jul 19, 1973; New Delhi, IN; Princeton University (NJ), B.A., 1995; Harvard University, J.D., 2000; Hinduism; Married (Priya Krishnamoorthi); 2 children.

Professional Career: Clerk, U.S District Court N. IL, 2000-2002; Staff, Illinois Housing Development Auth., 2005-2007; IL Special Asst. Attorney General, 2006-2007; Deputy State Treasurer of IL, 2008-2009.

DC Office: 115 CHOB 20515, 202-225-3711, Fax: 202-225-7830
State Offices: Schaumburg, 847-413-1959.

Committees: *Oversight & Reform*: Subcommittee on Economic & Consumer Policy (Chmn); Subcommittee on Environment. *Permanent Select on Intelligence*: Intelligence Modernization & Readiness; Strategic Technologies & Advanced Research.

Group Ratings

	ADA	ACLU	AFL-CIO	LCV	ITI	COC	HAFA	ACU	CFG	FRC
2018	-	79%	-	94%	-	67%	6%	4%	20%	0%
2017	85%	C	95%	100%	C	64%	C	4%	0%	11%

Almanac Ratings 2017-18

	Economy	Social	Foreign	Composite
Liberal	94%	98%	89%	94%
Conservative	6%	2%	11%	6%

Key Votes of the 115th Congress

1. Obama-care revision	N	5. Family planning regs	N	9. Guantanamo prisoners	Y	
2. Tax Cuts	N	6. Body cameras/immigration	Y	10. Ground missiles, limit	Y	
3. Omnibus appropriations	Y	7. Abortion ban	N	11. Defense Dept. spending	Y	
4. Dodd-Frank revision	N	8. Concealed carry	N	12. FISA rules	Y	

Election Results

Election	Name (Party)	Vote (%)		Cand. Spent	Ind. Exp. Support	Ind. Exp. Oppose
2018 General	Raja Krishnamoorthi (D)..................... 130,054	(66%)		$1,839,327		
	Jitendra Diganvker (R)....................... 67,073	(34%)				$49,760
2018 Primary	Raja Krishnamoorthi (D)................................	(100%)				

Prior winning percentages: 2016 (58%)

Raja Krishnamoorthi, elected on a second try in 2016, brought bipartisanship and a positive attitude to his work in the House. His domestic interests included education and solar energy. He embraced his family ancestry in India and sought steps to facilitate visas for workers in the United States. Following his loss in 2012 to more politically experienced Democrat Tammy Duckworth, who was then elected to the Senate, he has had no trouble securing his suburban seat.

Krishnamoorthi was born in India, came to the United States when he was three months old and was raised in Peoria, where his father was a professor of engineering at Bradley University. He earned a bachelor's degree in mechanical engineering from Princeton University and got a law degree from Harvard. Following law school, Krishnamoorthi clerked for a federal judge in Chicago and later became a partner in the law firm of Kirkland & Ellis. In 2004, he served as issues director for the Senate campaign of Barack Obama; the two had met at a Chicago reception for lawyers interested in civil rights, prior to Obama's unsuccessful campaign in 2000 for a House seat. In 2008, he was an adviser to Obama's presidential campaign. While practicing law, Krishnamoorthi served as a special assistant attorney general in the state's Public Integrity Unit. He was a member of the Illinois Housing Development Authority and the Illinois deputy treasurer, where he helped to manage the state's technology venture capital fund.

In the private sector, Krishnamoorthi was president of Sivananthan Labs and Episolar Inc., a group of small businesses that developed and sold national security and renewable energy products. He was co-founder of InSPIRE, a non-profit organization that provides training in solar technology to inner-city students and veterans, and a former vice chairman of the Illinois Innovation Council. He sought the Democratic nomination for state comptroller in 2010, but lost narrowly. When he first ran for the House two years later, Duckworth was actively supported by Democratic Sen. Richard Durbin and much of the state party establishment — though she too had lost a previous campaign. Duckworth won the primary, 66%-34%.

In 2016, Krishnamoorthi had the easy win. In the Democratic primary, he benefited from a big fundraising advantage and his campaign experience, plus the large Asian — including Indian-American -- population in the district. "Instead of buildings walls, we should be building bridges," an explicit contrast to Republican presidential nominee Donald Trump, was a campaign theme. With help from the active nationwide community of Democrats with an Indian heritage, Krishnamoorthi spent $2.6 million. The other two candidates were state Sen. Michael Noland, who cited his support for a single-payer health care system, and Villa Park Village president Deborah Bullwinkel. The Daily Herald endorsed Krishnamoorthi, writing that "he approaches all political issues pragmatically and with an openness that can make him both cooperative and persuasive in conducting the business of a congressman." He won the primary with 57 percent of the vote to 29 percent for Noland and 14 percent for Bullwinkel.

In the general, Republican Pete DiCianni, a member of the DuPage County Board and former mayor of Elmhurst, cited the "disappointing" loss of nearly $100 million in mutual funds from the state's college savings program while Krishnamoorthi was deputy treasurer. Krishnamoorthi won, 58%-42%, including 54 percent of the vote in DuPage. In 2018, he faced a token challenger for reelection and got 66 percent of the vote.

He got to work quickly on the Education and the Workforce Committee, where he filed with Rep. Glenn Thompson of Pennsylvania, a senior Republican on the panel, a bill to expand career and technical education programs and respond to changing labor markets. The House passed the bill unanimously in June 2017 and a modified version was enacted in July 2018, with Krishnamoorthi standing directly behind President Donald Trump at the White House signing ceremony. "We desperately need some bipartisan victories right now," Krishnamoorthi told the Daily Herald.

Many of his views have been conventionally liberal, though Krishnamoorthi has added his background as a business entrepreneur and his bipartisan approach. With Republican Rep. Ralph Norman of South Carolina, he created the Congressional Solar Caucus to encourage grassroots support for new technologies. Among his objectives, he said, was educating other lawmakers about the availability and low cost of solar energy, plus the need for additional federal research and development. With Rep. Mike Gallagher of Wisconsin, another freshman Republican who entered the House with him, Krishnamoorthi formed the bipartisan Middle-Class Jobs Caucus. "There are 6 million unfilled jobs because employers can't locate the skills and knowledge they need," he told the Princeton Alumni Weekly. The two lawmakers initially bonded as fellow Princeton grads.

On international issues, Krishnamoorthi joined other Indian-American members of Congress in an informal "Samosa Caucus," a reference to an Indian snack. They encouraged Trump's efforts to collaborate with India. He also filed with Republican Rep. Mike Coffman of Colorado legislation to give more flexibility to holders of B-1 visas to switch jobs and gain exemptions. One goal, he said, was to ensure that "immigration laws match our country's high-tech workforce requirements."

A veteran Washington journalist was impressed by Krishnamoorthi's activities. "A conversation with him can leave you feeling hopeful, even at this often unhopeful time, about the future of our democracy," Fred Hiatt, editorial page editor of The Washington Post, wrote in a December 2017 column.

IL-8: Chicago's Northwest Suburbs

Cook Partisan Voting Index: D+8

Population		Race and Ethnicity		Income	
Total	716,738	White	52%	Median Income	$68,211
Land area (sq. miles)	206	Black	4.5%	District Income Rank	106
Pop/ sq mi	3487.4	Latino	28.1%	Poverty Rate	9.8%
Born in State	58.7%	Asian	13.2%	With health insurance	89.1%
		Two or more races	1.8%	Cash public assistance	2%
Age Groups		Other	0.4%	Food stamp/SNAP	9.9%
Under 18	23.8%				
18-34	23.5%	**Education**		**Work**	
35-64	40.3%	H.S grad or less	38.7%	White Collar	12.4%
Over 64	12.4%	Some college	28.2%	Sales and Service	42.2%
Military		College Degree, 4 yr	22.2%	Blue Collar	23.6%
Veteran/ Active Duty	4.4%	Post grad	11%	Government	7.9%

2012 Pres. Vote	Obama	133,208	(58%)	Romney	94,944	(41%)			
2016 Pres. Vote	Clinton	148,277	(58%)	Trump	92,892	(36%)	Johnson	9,851	(4%)

DuPage: Schaumburg has a long tradition as one of America's major corporate headquarters cities. Sixty years ago, this suburb northwest of Chicago was farmland. Since then, Schaumburg — near the intersection of the Northwest Tollway and Interstate 290, and a few miles beyond O'Hare International Airport — became the headquarters of large companies such as Motorola, AT&T and Sears. But those companies, and others, have relocated or downsized. Some of their abandoned suburban campuses have plans for redevelopment. In addition to subdivisions as far as the eye can see, Schaumburg has other attractions, including a performing arts center, an orchestra for young people and a traditional downtown district that it built from scratch.

Despite those attractions, the area recently has faced challenges. Some large companies have abandoned their suburban mindset, finding that large, isolated corporate campuses breed insularity and make it harder to recruit talent. Chicago Mayor Rahm Emanuel lured suburban businesses to relocate downtown with financial incentives. Motorola's mobile handset division, after being bought by Google, moved to Chicago's Merchandise Mart. AT&T decided to leave its suburban Hoffman Estates office, and moved 500 employees to downtown Chicago. Financially beleaguered Sears stayed in Hoffman Estates, but its problems extend far beyond its corporate location. From 2006 through 2016, its annual revenues dropped by about half. In October 2018, Sears filed for bankruptcy.

Since 2007, more than 50 companies have moved from these suburbs to downtown Chicago. Still, some of the Schaumberg facilities continue to prosper. Zurich North America, an insurance company, houses nearly 3,000. Sunstar, an oral-health care company, has a new corporate presence, with 400 employees. Still, in late 2018, the vacancy rate for suburban Chicago offices had increased to 23.7 percent, the highest level since 2014.

The 8th Congressional District of Illinois is made up of Schaumburg and the more Democratic communities in Chicago's northwest suburbs, including Carol Stream in DuPage County and nearly majority Hispanic Elgin and Carpentersville in Kane County. About half the population of the 8th resides in the northwest corner of Cook County; most of the remainder are within jagged lines of northern DuPage, plus a few are in a small slice of Kane. It is one of the most Asian-American districts in the Midwest, at 13 percent of the population. Schaumburg has one of the nation's largest concentrations of Indian Americans, at 11 percent. Once-homogeneous DuPage County has seen an influx of immigrants, and more than a quarter of its residents now speak a first language other than English at home. The area lacks a regional identity, other than the "Northwest Suburbs."

In the past decade, like other parts of the Chicago suburbs, this area has moved toward the Democrats. Hillary Clinton carried the district with 57 percent in 2016. But it retains its suburban sensibilities. A moderate Republican could be competitive here.

Jan Schakowsky (D)

Elected 1998, 11th term, b. May 26, 1944; Chicago; University of Illinois, B.A., 1965; Jewish; Married (Robert Creamer); 3 children; 6 grandchildren.

Elected Office: IL House, 1990-1998.

Professional Career: Founder, National Consumers Unite, 1969-1973; Prog. Director, IL Public Action, 1976-1985; Executive Director, IL St. Cncl. of Sr. Citizens, 1985-1990.

DC Office: 2367 RHOB 20515, 202-225-2111, Fax: 202-226-6890, schakowsky.house.gov

State Offices: Chicago, 773-506-7100; Evanston, 847-328-3409; Glenview, 847-328-3409.

Committees: *Budget.* *Energy & Commerce*: Consumer Protection & Commerce (Chmn); Environment & Climate Change; Oversight & Investigations.

Group Ratings

	ADA	ACLU	AFL-CIO	LCV	ITI	COC	HAFA	ACU	CFG	FRC
2018	-	89%	-	100%	-	50%	9%	4%	18%	0%
2017	100%	C	95%	100%	C	38%	C	7%	5%	0%

Almanac Ratings 2017-18

	Economy	Social	Foreign	Composite
Liberal	100%	100%	100%	100%
Conservative	0%	0%	0%	0%

Key Votes of the 115th Congress

1. Obama-care revision	N	5. Family planning regs	N	9. Guantanamo prisoners	Y
2. Tax Cuts	N	6. Body cameras/immigration	Y	10. Ground missiles, limit	Y
3. Omnibus appropriations	N	7. Abortion ban	N	11. Defense Dept. spending	N
4. Dodd-Frank revision	N	8. Concealed carry	N	12. FISA rules	N

Election Results

Election	Name (Party)	Vote (%)		Cand. Spent	Ind. Exp. Support	Ind. Exp. Oppose
2018 General	Jan Schakowsky (D)	213,368	(73%)	$1,161,606		
	John Elleson (R)	76,983	(27%)	$72,875		
2018 Primary	Jan Schakowsky (D)		(100%)			

Prior winning percentages: 2016 (67%), 2014 (66%), 2012 (66%), 2010 (66%), 2008 (75%), 2006 (75%), 2004 (76%), 2002 (70%), 2000 (76%), 1998 (75%)

Jan Schakowsky, a Democrat elected in 1998, is an outspoken progressive. She blends deep policy background with lengthy organizational experience, and has been a stalwart on Nancy Pelosi's Democratic leadership team. As a senior member of the Energy and Commerce Committee, and chair of its Consumer Protection and Commerce Subcommittee, she has been instrumental in setting the party's agenda on health and consumer issues.

Schakowsky grew up in Rogers Park and worked for two years as a teacher. In 1969, she formed National Consumers Unite to fight for date-of-freshness labels on dairy products and other food. Later she joined Illinois Public Action, a consumer group. In 1985, she became executive director of the Illinois State Council of Senior Citizens, where she organized the pivotal 1989 protest of Democratic Ways and Means Chairman Dan Rostenkowski's Medicare catastrophic health care law for seniors. Television news images of the powerful Rostenkowski fleeing an angry crowd of old people led Congress to repeal the benefit, which many said did not provide adequate coverage. In 1990, Schakowsky was elected to the state House from Evanston and Skokie, and later became Democratic floor leader.

With an open seat in 1998, her strategy was to run from the left — "I don't think I can be defined as too far left in a district like this," she said — and to build a volunteer organization. With ads in college papers, she hired young field organizers to identify Schakowsky voters. She raised $1.4 million, with help from the abortion-rights group EMILY's List. Her opponent was state Sen. Howard Carroll, who had the support of most Democratic ward committeemen and attacked Schakowsky for her opposition to the death penalty. Schakowsky's 1,500 workers, 250 of them from labor unions, helped her to a 45%-34% win. She easily won the general election and has been reelected without difficulty.

Her Almanac vote ratings have consistently been among the most liberal in the House. A close ally of Pelosi, Schakowsky has worked with Democratic leaders on electoral strategy, including leading a training program for political organizers and encouraging participation by women. She was an early supporter when Pelosi got her start in leadership, and was rewarded with a chief deputy whip post. As a major party fundraiser, she has drawn heavily from the traditional Democratic constituencies of lawyers, liberal women's interest groups and unions.

In early 2006, she ran for vice chair of the Democratic Caucus. With support from Pelosi, Schakowsky was the early front-runner. But on the first ballot, she finished third. With Schakowsky's former supporters on board, Connecticut's John Larson prevailed. The contest occurred soon after her husband, Robert Creamer, the longtime head of Illinois Public Action Fund, pleaded guilty to bank fraud in a check-kiting scheme. Schakowsky said her husband had "made mistakes," but that she was unaware of his financial problems and that she stood by him.

Schakowsky briefly considered a run for the Senate in 2004 but decided against it. In 2008, she voiced interest in appointment to the remainder of President-elect Barack Obama's Senate term. She was an early backer of Obama for president, giving cover to other prominent Democratic women who may have wanted to back him but felt obliged to support New York Sen. Hillary Clinton.

On the Intelligence Committee in 2009, Schakowsky backed Pelosi's claim that she had not been informed of the use by U.S. interrogators of water boarding. She was the only committee member in 2011 to oppose cybersecurity legislation, saying that the measure didn't do enough to safeguard civil liberties. In what she called an "anguished" decision, she boycotted the 2015 speech to Congress by Israeli Prime Minister Benjamin Netanyahu on the grounds that his actions might jeopardize both nuclear talks with Iran and bipartisan support for Israel.

Her legislative work has centered on the Energy and Commerce Committee. Schakowsky helped to enact in 2008 the child product safety bill, which increased regulations, and she has remained active on consumer issues. In 2009, she was a strong supporter of creating a federally run insurance option in the Democrats' health care bill. The public option provision ultimately was dropped because of opposition from party moderates. Pelosi appointed Schakowsky to the Simpson-Bowles commission on the national debt in 2010, where she opposed ending federal economic stimulus funds and argued that safety-net spending should be exempt from budget cuts. She argued that debt reduction options should include income distribution tables to show who would be hit hardest. She remained outspoken as a critic of income inequality.

She filed in 2016 the Medicare Fair Drug Pricing Act, which advanced her longstanding demand for transparency and accountability in prescription drug pricing, plus negotiation for the price of certain drugs covered by Medicare.

In 2018, Schakowsky stirred controversy among House Democrats when she actively backed Maria Newman in her Democratic primary challenge to Chicago-area Rep. Daniel Lipinski — an unusual step, especially with Schakowsky's leadership ties. "This is not personal," she told reporters. It's "based on issues" — including their splits on abortion, gay rights and immigration. Centrist Democrats successfully urged Pelosi to support Lipinski in what became his narrow victory. Following the November election, Schakowsky told The Hill, "I'm furious, I'm just furious" with dissident House Democrats who initially held back their support for Pelosi's return as Speaker.

As subcommittee chairman, she said that the central issues facing the panel were product safety, data privacy and security, and auto safety.

IL-9: Chicago

Cook Partisan Voting Index: D+18

Population		Race and Ethnicity		Income	
Total	723,142	White	64%	Median Income	$68,686
Land area (sq. miles)	105	Black	8.7%	District Income Rank	104
Pop/ sq mi	6864.2	Latino	11.6%	Poverty Rate	12%
Born in State	53.2%	Asian	12.7%	With health insurance	91.8%
		Two or more races	2.5%	Cash public assistance	2.4%
Age Groups		Other	0.4%	Food stamp/SNAP	9.5%
Under 18	20.4%				
18-34	22.4%	**Education**		**Work**	
35-64	40.4%	H.S grad or less	25.9%	White Collar	16.8%
Over 64	16.8%	Some college	21.3%	Sales and Service	37.7%
		College Degree, 4 yr	30.3%	Blue Collar	13%
Military		Post grad	22.4%	Government	9.3%
Veteran/ Active Duty	4%				

2012 Pres. Vote	Obama	200,686	(65%)	Romney	102,728	(33%)		
2016 Pres. Vote	Clinton	237,984	(69%)	Trump	84,527	(25%)	Johnson 11,494	(3%)

North Side, Northern Cook: "Make no little plans," architect Daniel Burnham once said, and he made no little plans for the Chicago lakefront. The glorious parks he designed are among America's urban jewels, and the row of high-rise apartment buildings — some austere works of masters of the International style, some in traditional styles evocative of some other place and time, some sleek Art Deco works of the 1920s and 1930s — is a splendid accompaniment. Beyond the lakefront is all the diversity of Chicago. In sturdy brick houses, with scarcely a shoehorn's space between them, or in stubby apartment buildings, are ethnic and racial groups of every sort, from Argentinians to Slavs, from Poles to Plains Indians. In the 1970s, the neighborhoods behind the lakefront seemed to be getting seedier. Since then, they have been gentrifying, as young couples and gays, professionals and entrepreneurs renovate old houses and open new businesses. Today, this part of Chicago has as much urban energy and lively diversity as any place in America. In what it describes as the largest capital improvement project in its history, the Chicago Transit Authority planned to start construction in 2019 on rebuilding the Red Line, its busiest route, and modernizing the Purple Line from the North Side to Wilmette.

The lakefront has long been the most heavily Jewish part of Chicago. The local Jewish community, prominent for more than a century, has never been as much of a political force as it is in New York, or connected to a glamorous industry as in Los Angeles. Yet these voters' liberal impulses have been strong: the 19th century impulse to resist state authority and the imposition of cultural uniformity, and the 20th century impulse to strive for social justice. Chicago's North Side Jews have been a solidly Democratic voting bloc, involved with — but mostly keeping at arm's length — the old Democratic machine. They supported for mayor one of their own, Rahm Emanuel, but were disappointed when he fell short as a reformer.

The 9th Congressional District of Illinois covers the north end of Chicago's lakefront, from just north of Diversey Harbor and the Lincoln Park Zoo past the thriving Asian and Jewish communities in West Rogers Park and on to the suburb of Evanston, founded by Methodists to promote temperance (a cause that never prospered in Chicago). Evanston, where the local History Center is in the former home of Charles Dawes, who was vice president for four years with Calvin Coolidge, has moved from Yankee Republicanism to postgraduate Democratic. From Evanston and upscale Wilmette, where the only Baha'i Temple in the country — and one of only eight worldwide -- often clogs local streets, the 9th presses inland through Skokie to Morton Grove and Niles, which unveiled plans in February 2018 to build an $80 million entertainment district. Skokie made national headlines when

Nazi sympathizers got court permission to march there in 1977. Skokie's residents settled the score with the opening in 2009 of the Illinois Holocaust Museum and Education Center. Farther out in Des Plaines, the McDonald's museum, a replica of the franchise's first restaurant, was demolished in August 2018. The company gave the land to the city, though officials had no immediate plans.

The district, which is entirely in Cook County though two-thirds of its voters are outside of Chicago, reaches west to incorporate once rock-solid Republican territory — Park Ridge, where Hillary Rodham in 1964 got her first taste of politics in high school as a "Goldwater girl"; the cluster of office buildings and interchanges in Rosemont, next to O'Hare International Airport; and parts of Arlington Heights, developed in the 1950s and 1960s on the Chicago & Northwestern commuter rail line. The 9th's population is 9 percent black, 12 percent Hispanic, and 13 percent Asian, and is solidly Democratic, though less so than most of the districts based in Chicago. As one of at least four hometowns for Clinton, the district gave her 69 percent of the vote in 2016.

Brad Schneider (D)

Elected 2016, 3rd term, b. Aug 20, 1961; Denver, CO; Northwestern University, B.S., 1983; Kellogg Graduate School of Management, Northwestern University (IL), M.B.A., 1988; Jewish; Married (Julie Dann); 2 children.

Elected Office: U.S House, 2013-2015.

Professional Career: Strategic Mgmt Consultant & Founder, Cadence Consulting Group.

DC Office: 1432 LHOB 20515, 202-225-4835, Fax: 202-225-0837, schneider.house.gov

State Offices: Lincolnshire, 847-383-4870.

Committees: *Small Business*: Economic Growth, Tax & Capital Access. *Ways & Means*: Health; Social Security.

Group Ratings

	ADA	ACLU	AFL-CIO	LCV	ITI	COC	HAFA	ACU	CFG	FRC
2018	-	77%	-	91%	-	73%	8%	17%	17%	0%
2017	75%	C	95%	100%	C	64%	C	0%	0%	11%

Almanac Ratings 2017-18

	Economy	Social	Foreign	Composite
Liberal	73%	100%	67%	80%
Conservative	27%	0%	33%	20%

Key Votes of the 115th Congress

1. Obama-care revision	N	5. Family planning regs	N	9. Guantanamo prisoners	Y
2. Tax Cuts	N	6. Body cameras/immigration	Y	10. Ground missiles, limit	Y
3. Omnibus appropriations	Y	7. Abortion ban	N	11. Defense Dept. spending	Y
4. Dodd-Frank revision	Y	8. Concealed carry	N	12. FISA rules	Y

Election Results

Election	Name (Party)	Vote (%)	Cand. Spent	Ind. Exp. Support	Ind. Exp. Oppose
2018 General	Brad Schneider (D)............................. 151,860	(66%)	$2,573,209		
	Doug Bennett (R)............................ 80,361	(34%)	$286,570		
2018 Primary	Brad Schneider (D)...	(100%)			

Prior winning percentages: 2016 (53%), 2012 (51%)

Democrat Brad Schneider, a business consultant who made a late career move to politics, won his reelection in 2018 after having regained his House seat two years earlier. He and Republican Robert Dold had an unusual dance in which Dold won two off-year elections and Schneider won the two presidential cycles. Each brought a message of centrist bipartisanship — along with escalating campaign finances. With the GOP's decline in many suburbs, Schneider seemed to have locked down the district — for now, at least.

Schneider was born and raised in Denver, where his parents were active Democrats. As a kid, he joined them to canvass for Hubert Humphrey's presidential campaign in 1968. Schneider went to Northwestern University, where he received a bachelor's degree in industrial engineering and a master's from the Kellogg Graduate School of Management. After spending a year in Israel working on a kibbutz, he returned to Chicago to take a corporate consulting job. Eventually, he became a consultant, working with small and mid-sized businesses. He worked for the Jewish United Fund and served as director of the Business and Professional People for the Business Interest, a local social-justice organization.

Dold, the owner of a pest-control company, eked out a victory in 2010 for the seat of Republican Mark Kirk, who was elected to the Senate that year. As part of their post-census redistricting, Democrats in Springfield removed several of Dold's best precincts in the high-income towns of Palatine, Northbrook and Winnetka. In the process, they remade the 10th into the most Democratic district represented by a Republican in the House.

In the four-way Democratic primary in 2012, Schneider's chief opponent was Ilya Sheyman, a 25-year-old former community organizer who drew staunch support from liberal groups such as MoveOn.org, which launched a "Republicans for Schneider" website to highlight his past support for Kirk and other Republicans. Schneider got the backing of the Democratic establishment and won the primary 47%-39%. In the general, Schneider accused Dold of voting in lockstep with GOP leaders on major issues, including women's health and abortion rights. Dold called the charge misleading and cited his dissent from the leadership on such issues as the environment, education and gun control. But the Democratic tide in Illinois proved too much for him to overcome, and he lost 50.6%-49.4%.

Without President Barack Obama on the ticket in 2014, Republicans were enthusiastic about Dold's prospects. He stressed his moderate credentials while depicting Schneider as ineffective. This was one of the most expensive campaigns in the nation in 2014. Schneider outspent Dold $4.8 million to $3.6 million, while national parties and outside groups spent a total of roughly $10 million more in the contest. This time, Dold won 51.3%-48.7%.

In 2016, Schneider was undaunted. Joining him in the primary was Highland Park Mayor Nancy Rotering, an attorney who had the support of EMILY's List, the political action committee that funds Democratic women who support abortion rights. As was the case in the 2012 primary, liberal activists griped about Schneider. But he prevailed 54%-46%, not all that impressive for a former House member. Dold moved quickly to disavow Donald Trump. The National Republican Congressional Committee ran an ad that praised Dold for his independence from Trump. Once again, both sides spent lavishly: Dold led $5.6 million to $4.9 million. And he had the advantage with outside money on his behalf, about $6 million to $3 million. Schneider regained the seat by the relatively comfortable 52.4%-47.6%, with similar results in Lake and Cook counties.

As a House Foreign Affairs Committee member, Schneider filed a bipartisan bill to impose additional sanctions on Russia if it interfered with the 2018 election. With the centrist Blue Dogs, he worked on a strategy for Democrats to raise concerns about Russian interference in the 2016 election without tying the inquiry directly to Trump. "We all want to know that the integrity of our vote is going to be protected," he told Politico. Schneider said that Trump was "shameful" during his press conference in Helsinki Finland with Russian president Vladimir Putin when he "chose to side with a foreign dictator over our own intelligence and law enforcement agencies" in reviewing the 2016 election.

With the bipartisan Problem Solvers Caucus, he enacted a school safety measure and amendments to the defense spending bill that encouraged tech transfer for federally funded research and required a report from the Pentagon on Iran's proxy support in Syria and Lebanon. He filed legislation to provide federal funding for communities — such as Zion, in his district — that store nuclear waste.

His reelection in 2018 was the first routine contest in a decade. Schneider won, 66%-34%, against Douglas Bennett, a business consultant and Republican activist. Schneider outspent his challenger, $3.4 million to $278,000; both national parties focused instead on nearby contests northwest of Chicago.

In January 2019, Schneider won a seat on the Ways and Means Committee. He set a priority of removing restrictions on the state and local deduction for taxpayers, which were imposed in the 2017 tax cuts and have been loudly opposed by high-income, high-tax suburbanites such as those in Schneider's district.

IL-10: Northern Chicagoland

Cook Partisan Voting Index: D+10

Population		Race and Ethnicity		Income	
Total	715,072	White	58.1%	Median Income	$77,213
Land area (sq. miles)	300	Black	6.6%	District Income Rank	64
Pop/ sq mi	2385.3	Latino	22.7%	Poverty Rate	9.2%
Born in State	56.2%	Asian	10.3%	With health insurance	90.7%
		Two or more races	1.9%	Cash public assistance	2.1%
Age Groups		Other	0.3%	Food stamp/SNAP	9.7%
Under 18	24.6%				
18-34	21.7%	**Education**		**Work**	
35-64	39.7%	H.S grad or less	32%	White Collar	14%
Over 64	14%	Some college	23.8%	Sales and Service	40%
		College Degree, 4 yr	25.5%	Blue Collar	18.1%
Military		Post grad	18.7%	Government	8.9%
Veteran/ Active Duty	7.3%				

2012 Pres. Vote	Obama	157,400	(58%)	Romney	112,552	(41%)			
2016 Pres. Vote	Clinton	178,872	(61%)	Trump	94,103	(32%)	Johnson	11,681	(4%)

Lake, Northern Cook: Since 1855, when the Chicago & North Western opened the railroad line from downtown Chicago north along the lakeshore, the North Shore suburbs along Lake Michigan have been home to Chicago's elite. The North Shore starts in Evanston, goes north through Wilmette, Winnetka and Glencoe, and then leaves Cook County and crosses into the eastern Lake County towns of Highland Park and Lake Forest. Each burg has a slightly different personality, each is long established and mightily prosperous, and each exudes a patina of age. These are communities of affluent, well-educated people living in an environment whose natural beauty — the vistas over Lake Michigan, the gentle rolling terrain, and the old trees — is carefully disciplined. Corporate headquarters fit comfortably here, including Baxter Healthcare, Abbott Laboratories and Allstate Insurance. In January 2018, Caterpillar moved its corporate home to Deerfield from its long-time site in Peoria. Later that year, Takeda Pharmaceutical closed its local headquarters and moved to Boston. The population of Lake County barely changed between 2010 and 2018, which was better than many other parts of Illinois.

The exceptions to the atmosphere of gracious high living are Waukegan and the nearby area around the Great Lakes Naval Training Center, where the median income is dramatically lower. The award-winning "Years of Living Dangerously" documentary on the National Geographic Channel in 2016 described the struggle in Waukegan as the area moved to clean up its coal-fueled power plant. In 2017, the WalletHub website ranked Waukegan last among 505 cities nationwide in the decrease in its local poverty rate. Farther north along the lake, the small community of Zion has struggled to recover from the shutdown in 1998 of the local nuclear power plant, which was caused by an operational error. Local leaders, unhappy that the radioactive spent fuel has not been removed, have sought federal aid in removing or storing the nuclear waste.

The 10th Congressional District of Illinois is the North Shore district. The district starts on the lakefront in Glencoe and runs north in a thin strip all the way to the blue-collar, majority-Hispanic city of Waukegan and on to the Wisconsin border. It moves inland to include most of Lake County and some Cook County suburbs west to Wheeling and parts of Mount Prospect. The district includes upscale Northbrook and Deerfield, plus Libertyville, near where the Adlai Stevensons, the governor and two-time presidential nominee and his son the former senator, owned a farm. After the family home on the property was donated to Lake County, it was restored in 2008 as the Adlai Stevenson Center on Democracy. Three-fourths of the district is in Lake, with the 6th and 14th Districts in the more Republican western corners of the county. Politically, the 10th leans sufficiently Democratic that Hillary Clinton won 61%-32%. In non-presidential elections, the area has been competitive locally. But the Republican Party has lost favor with this longtime elite business district. In 2018, Democrats won control of the county board for the first time in Lake's history.

Bill Foster (D)

Elected 2012, 5th full term, b. Oct 07, 1955; Madison, WI; University of Wisconsin, B.A., 1976; Harvard University, Ph.D., 1983; Married (Aesook Byon); 2 children.

Elected Office: U.S. House, 2008-2010.

Professional Career: Scientist, Fermi National Accelerator Lab., 1990- 2006; Co-founder, Electronic Theatre Controls, 1975-2007.

DC Office: 2366 RHOB 20515, 202-225-3515, Fax: 202-225-9420, foster.house.gov

State Offices: Aurora, 630-585-7672; Joliet, 815-280-5876.

Committees: *Financial Services*: Consumer Protection & Financial Institutions; Investor Protection, Entrepreneurship & Capital Markets. *Science, Space & Technology*: Energy; Research & Technology.

Group Ratings

	ADA	ACLU	AFL-CIO	LCV	ITI	COC	HAFA	ACU	CFG	FRC
2018	-	82%	-	94%	-	75%	12%	16%	23%	0%
2017	95%	C	92%	100%	C	50%	C	4%	0%	0%

Almanac Ratings 2017-18

	Economy	Social	Foreign	Composite
Liberal	86%	100%	92%	92%
Conservative	14%	0%	8%	8%

Key Votes of the 115th Congress

1. Obama-care revision	N	5. Family planning regs	N	9. Guantanamo prisoners	Y
2. Tax Cuts	N	6. Body cameras/immigration	Y	10. Ground missiles, limit	Y
3. Omnibus appropriations	Y	7. Abortion ban	N	11. Defense Dept. spending	Y
4. Dodd-Frank revision	Y	8. Concealed carry	N	12. FISA rules	Y

Election Results

Election	Name (Party)	Vote (%)		Cand. Spent	Ind. Exp. Support	Ind. Exp. Oppose
2018 General	Bill Foster (D)	145,407	(64%)	$1,141,627		
	Nick Stella (R)	82,358	(36%)	$270,585		
2018 Primary	Bill Foster (D)		(100%)			

Prior winning percentages: 2016 (60%), 2014 (53%), 2012 (59%), 2008 (58%), 2008 special (53%)

Democrat Bill Foster returned to the House in 2012, with a big boost from redistricting. Foster, a physicist, initially won a special election following the resignation of former House Speaker Dennis Hastert, only to lose in 2010. His new district is a more natural fit in both partisan and professional terms for Foster, who proudly styles himself as the only scientist in Congress with a Ph.D. He showed his occasional independence following the 2018 election when he joined the small group of Democrats who forced concessions from Nancy Pelosi on the terms of her future as House Speaker.

Foster began life as a Washington insider. His parents met on Capitol Hill, where each worked for a senator. His father became a law professor at the University of Wisconsin, and Foster grew up in Madison, graduated from the university, and got his Ph.D. in physics from Harvard University. He was a physicist for 16 years at Fermilab, where he pursued groundbreaking research in elementary particle physics. Foster also ran a theater-lighting business with his younger brother that made each a multimillionaire.

He had not sought public office before volunteering in the 2006 campaign of Patrick Murphy, a Pennsylvania Democrat who ousted a House Republican incumbent. At age 51, Foster then spent five months working on Murphy's Capitol Hill staff. After Hastert resigned in 2007, Foster ran in the Democratic primary against the more liberal Jonathan Laesch, who had lost to Hastert in 2006.

Foster won, 50%-43%. Against Republican Jim Oberweis, a successful dairy owner who had lost numerous statewide campaigns, Foster was boosted by a 30-second endorsement from the Barack Obama presidential campaign. He won, 53%-47%. Foster was the first Democrat to represent the north-central Illinois district since the Great Depression.

In the House, Foster served on the Financial Services Committee, where he supported the bailout of the financial markets. He voted for the $787 billion economic stimulus legislation and the 2010 health care overhaul. He helped to restore $62.5 million in funding for Fermilab. In the 2010 election, Foster did not mention his party affiliation and outspent Republican Randy Hultgren, $3.7 million to $1.6 million. But Hultgren won, 51%-45% -- one of five Republicans that year who took a Democratic seat in Obama's home state.

Foster soon got another chance. During 2011 redistricting, Democrats carved out a new, Democratic-leaning district that shifted closer to Chicagoland. Foster faced veteran Rep. Judy Biggert, a moderate Republican. At a face-to-face meeting with the Chicago Tribune editorial board, he tried to tie her to President George W. Bush's economic policies that "eviscerated U.S. manufacturing." Biggert snapped back, "You Democrats have never talked about anything that you're going to do. It's always what we did wrong." The race wasn't pretty, and Foster won convincingly with 59 percent.

Foster regained his seat on the Financial Services Committee, though he was now in the minority. He warned that Republican bills to strip regulatory authority from the Securities and Exchange Commission would weaken investor protections. On the Science, Space and Technology Committee he said that he wanted to counter the "attacks" on science, including the National Science Foundation. He cited his background as a scientist when he voted for a chief priority for Obama: the deal with Iran to limit that nation's access to nuclear material that could be used for a weapon. "My support of this agreement is informed not just by trust but by science," said Foster, who added that he had attended 15 technical briefings.

The scientific standards flipped when President Donald Trump said in a 2018 broadcast interview that climate-change scientists "have a very big political agenda." Foster responded that the comment was "an unfortunate example of the president's inability to understand the importance of science," especially when it's not "politically convenient."

Following the 2018 election, Foster said he would not support Pelosi for Speaker unless she agreed to a transition plan to allow a new generation of leadership. "The top three positions in [House Democratic] leadership being stagnant for 16 years is simply an unfortunate situation for our party and our country," he told the Daily Herald. Initially, he set a limit of two years before Pelosi and other party leaders stepped down. Foster teamed with Reps. Ed Perlmutter of Colorado and Linda Sanchez of California to negotiate the deal in which Pelosi agreed to a maximum of four more years. The term limit, he said, was "the heart of the negotiation."

Back home, Foster faced competitive contests in his Democratic-friendly district. In 2014, he was a national Republican target when he was challenged by state Rep. Darlene Senger, whom he outspent by more than 2-to-1. The Republican had small leads in DuPage and Cook counties, but Foster rolled up big margins in Will and Kane counties and won 53 percent of the vote. In 2016, DuPage County Board member Tonia Khouri won a three-way Republican primary by 370 votes. Her under-performance in the primary led national Republicans to cut back support . Khouri distanced herself from the calls by Republican presidential candidate Donald Trump to deport illegal immigrants. Foster won, 60%-40%.

By 2018, national Republicans had given up on this district. Foster won, 64%-36%, over Nick Stella, a cardiologist with no political background, whom Foster outspent by more than 5-to-1. He had led the way in a decade-long battle in which control of five House seats in the suburbs west and north of Chicago eventually switched from Republicans to Democrats.

IL-11: Southwestern Chicagoland

Cook Partisan Voting Index: D+9

Population		Race and Ethnicity		Income	
Total	723,626	White	51.9%	Median Income	$72,108
Land area (sq. miles)	281	Black	11%	District Income Rank	80
Pop/ sq mi	2575.6	Latino	27.1%	Poverty Rate	9.9%
Born in State	65.2%	Asian	7.6%	With health insurance	90.7%
		Two or more races	2.2%	Cash public assistance	1.6%
Age Groups		Other	0.3%	Food stamp/SNAP	11.4%
Under 18	26.2%				
18-34	22.8%	**Education**		**Work**	
35-64	39.7%	H.S grad or less	36.8%	White Collar	11.3%
Over 64	11.3%	Some college	28.2%	Sales and Service	41.1%
		College Degree, 4 yr	22%	Blue Collar	22.9%
Military		Post grad	13.1%	Government	9.5%
Veteran/ Active Duty	5.3%				

2012 Pres. Vote	Obama	151,825	(58%)	Romney	106,532	(41%)		
2016 Pres. Vote	Clinton	164,664	(58%)	Trump	99,087	(35%)	Johnson	11,728	(4%)

Aurora, Joliet: Joliet, known as the city of steel and stone, got its start in the mid-19th century as a melting pot of Irish, German, Slovakian, Slovenian, Polish, Croatian and Hungarian immigrants who built the canals and railroads that connected the city with the rest of the state, from the Great Lakes to the Mississippi River. It emerged as the state's largest transportation hub outside Chicago. Workers labored in the stone quarries and steel mill, which by the turn of the century became the economic engine of the manufacturing city. The rails remain relevant to daily life, with officials working to upgrade the safety of the several trains that pass through Aurora each day with freight cars filled with crude oil from North Dakota. The nickname for Aurora is the "city of lights." It was the first in the nation to use electricity to light an entire city.

Business developments in the area have been mixed. Caterpillar, which had downsized its local plant and shifted jobs to Mexico in recent years, laid off another 800 workers in 2018. Butterball shut down its meatpacking plant, with a loss of 600 jobs. Both plants were in Montgomery, which is across the Fox River from Aurora. More encouraging has been Amazon's large fulfillment centers in Aurora and Joliet. Those sites confirm the prime transportation facilities of the Chicagoland area, plus the plentiful supply of low-cost and less-skilled workers. State officials earlier gave tax credits to Amazon in exchange for a guarantee of additional jobs.

The 11th Congressional District includes Joliet in Will County, parts of Naperville in southern DuPage County, and Aurora in Kane County. About 27 percent of the district is Hispanic, with 11 percent black and 8 percent Asian. Will County has nearly one-half of the district vote. It is the fastest-growing of the large suburban Chicago counties, jumping from a population of 502,000 in 2000 to 693,000 in 2017, as the number of Hispanic residents more than doubled and the number of Asian Americans nearly tripled. Aurora, the state's second most populous city with a long history of manufacturing, saw its population grow 41 percent from 2000 to 2017, also thanks to a near doubling of Hispanics, who have become nearly half of the total. The district's jigsaw-like boundaries run along the technology corridor in DuPage County, and straddle some large engineering facilities. The Argonne National Laboratory and Fermilab, another national laboratory, are just outside the district lines.

In 2016, Hillary Clinton won this safely Democratic district, 58%-35%. With the growing Hispanic population here and in the adjacent 3rd District, the Democratic dominance likely will strengthen in what had been part of the Republican heartland not many years ago.

Mike Bost (R)

Elected 2014, 3rd term, b. Dec 30, 1960; Murphysboro; University of Illinois; University of Illinois, 1993; Southern Baptist; Married (Tracy Stanton Bost); 3 children; 11 grandchildren.

Military Career: U.S. Marine Corps, Electronic Specialist, Radar Repairman 1979-1982

Elected Office: IL House 1995-2015; Trustee, Murphysboro Township, 1993-1995; Treasurer, Murphysboro Township, 1989-1992; Jackson County Board, 1984-1988.

Professional Career: Cert., Firefighter II Academy, University, of IL, 1993.

DC Office: 1440 LHOB 20515, 202-225-5661, Fax: 202-225-0285, bost.house.gov

State Offices: Alton, 618-622-0766; Carbondale, 618-457-5787; Granite City, 618-622-0766; Mt. Vernon, 618-513-5294; O'Fallon, 618-622-0766.

Committees: *Agriculture*: Biotechnology, Horticulture & Research; Commodity Exchanges, Energy & Credit. *Transportation & Infrastructure*: Highways & Transit; Railroads, Pipelines & Hazardous Materials; Water Resources & Environment. *Veterans' Affairs*: Disability Assistance & Memorial Affairs (RMM); Oversight & Investigations.

Group Ratings

	ADA	ACLU	AFL-CIO	LCV	ITI	COC	HAFA	ACU	CFG	FRC
2018	-	7%	-	3%	-	83%	40%	64%	45%	100%
2017	0%	C	32%	6%	C	93%	C	63%	43%	100%

Almanac Ratings 2017-18

	Economy	Social	Foreign	Composite
Liberal	8%	4%	0%	4%
Conservative	92%	97%	100%	96%

Key Votes of the 115th Congress

1. Obama-care revision	Y	5. Family planning regs	Y	9. Guantanamo prisoners	N
2. Tax Cuts	Y	6. Body cameras/immigration	N	10. Ground missiles, limit	N
3. Omnibus appropriations	Y	7. Abortion ban	Y	11. Defense Dept. spending	Y
4. Dodd-Frank revision	Y	8. Concealed carry	Y	12. FISA rules	Y

Election Results

Election	Name (Party)		Vote (%)		Cand. Spent	Ind. Exp. Support	Ind. Exp. Oppose
2018 General	Mike Bost (R)	134,884	(52%)	$2,777,027	$70,903	$2,333,388
	Brendan Kelly (D)	118,724	(45%)	$3,866,644	$557,734	$3,599,437
	Randy Auxier (G)	7,935	(3%)	$14,572		
2018 Primary	Mike Bost (R)	31,658	(84%)			
	Preston Nelson (R)	6,258	(17%)			

Prior winning percentages: 2016 (54%), 2014 (52%)

Republican Mike Bost, after settling into what had been a safe Democratic seat for decades, turned back a serious reelection challenge in 2018. At a time when the GOP has been wiped out in the suburbs, including in Illinois, his success in rural America has shown one way for the party to rebuild — though it's not sufficient on its own.

Bost was born and raised in Murphysboro and enlisted in the Marine Corps upon graduating from high school. Following his service, he became a firefighter while working in the family trucking business. In 1989, he and his wife opened a beauty shop, the White House Salon, which they have continued to run. In his advocacy of smaller government and lower taxes, Bost often has cited his small business ownership as the formative experience that drove him into politics.

After several stints in local office, Bost was elected to the Illinois House in 1994, and later became Republican Caucus chairman. His work focused on sectors important to the region — especially coal and agriculture — and he became known for tangling with Democrats, who have controlled that chamber since 1996. He won national attention with an outburst on the House floor in 2012 as he protested the rules for a pension bill. After he tossed papers into the air and punched them, he cried out, "Let my people go!" Video of his tirade wound up on YouTube and went viral, attracting more than 430,000 views.

Armed with name recognition — "Meltdown Mike" — that he tried to spin to his advantage, Bost in 2014 challenged first-term Democratic Rep. Bill Enyart, a retired two-star general. The district's growing divide over coal politics made it a top pick-up priority for the GOP. Bost tried to make the best of his outspoken reputation. "If you want a person who goes and sits and does nothing and not argue on your behalf, then I'm not your guy," he told voters. The contest escalated into one of the most expensive House races in the country. Each party spent more than $4 million, an extraordinary amount. Bost won by a surprisingly comfortable 52%-42%, the first Republican to represent St. Clair County since 1942. Enyart took the two largest counties, St. Clair and nearby Madison, but by relatively small margins. Bost won nine of the remaining 10 counties.

He made increasing local jobs his chief priority. In response to the temporary closing of the local U.S. Steel plant, he urged the Obama administration to enforce international trade laws against unfair practices of other nations. He worked on legislation to protect American companies from trade "dumping" by foreign competitors. As chairman of the Veterans' Affairs Subcommittee on Disability Assistance and Memorial Affairs in 2017, he won enactment of a bipartisan bill designed to reduce the time for appeals of veterans claims.

With several other House Republicans, Bost sought to change House rules to permit a return of spending earmarks, but was stymied by the opposition of Speaker Paul Ryan. In an interview with a St. Louis radio station, Bost objected to House Republicans who "would rather shut down government than govern."

Democrats have listed Bost as one of their top campaign targets. In 2016, after they failed to recruit a well-known challenger, Democrats rallied behind C.J. Baricevic, a 31-year-old lawyer and first-time candidate. Baricevic spent $1 million, to $2.3 million for Bost, whose 54%-40% victory margin was similar to 2014.

Two years later, Bost faced another serious challenger: Brendan Kelly, the prosecutor in St. Clair County and a former Navy officer with blue-collar roots. As Kelly cited his common ground with Trump on immigration and trade issues, Democrats pitched his appeal to Trump voters. At a rally for Bost in Carbondale a week before the election, Trump called Bost "a warrior" who has frequently sought his assistance. The St. Louis Post-Dispatch, which had previously endorsed Bost, backed Kelly — in part, for his willingness to criticize his own party. Kelly outspent Bost $4.1 million to $2.9 million and the national parties spent an additional $6 million on the contest. Bost won more narrowly, but still comfortably, 52%-45%, with strength outside the population centers.

IL-12: Southwest Illinois   **Cook Partisan Voting Index: R+5**

Population		Race and Ethnicity		Income	
Total	700,568	White	76.3%	Median Income	$47,214
Land area (sq. miles)	5,008	Black	16.7%	District Income Rank	349
Pop/ sq mi	139.9	Latino	3.4%	Poverty Rate	17.8%
Born in State	69.1%	Asian	1.2%	With health insurance	92.8%
		Two or more races	2.1%	Cash public assistance	3.1%
Age Groups		Other	0.3%	Food stamp/SNAP	16.9%
Under 18	22.3%				
18-34	22.5%	**Education**		**Work**	
35-64	39.2%	H.S grad or less	42.2%	White Collar	16%
Over 64	16%	Some college	35.4%	Sales and Service	43.8%
		College Degree, 4 yr	13.4%	Blue Collar	24.6%
Military		Post grad	9%	Government	16.2%
Veteran/ Active Duty	11.4%				

2012 Pres. Vote	Obama	153,718	(50%)	Romney	149,165	(48%)		
2016 Pres. Vote	Trump	173,692	(54%)	Clinton	126,818	(40%)	Johnson	11,115	(4%)

East St. Louis, Carbondale: Their waters roiling together, the nation's two mightiest rivers, the Mississippi and Missouri, join just a few miles below Alton Illinois. Its 19th-century buildings recall its turbulent history, when it was the home of antislavery agitator Elijah Lovejoy, who was murdered by a mob. Nearby in Hartford, explorers Lewis and Clark spent five months preparing their team and collecting supplies for their journey westward. Farther south along the Mississippi is East St. Louis, situated on the Illinois side of the river, with a view of the Gateway Arch in the larger St. Louis on the Missouri side. It is a terminus for dozens of rail lines and highways that funnel into bridges over the river. Once a rail and stockyard center second only to Chicago, East St. Louis is now one of America's poorest and most troubled cities, a half-abandoned slum with one of the nation's highest crime rates and a rapidly declining tax base. Violent-crime data regularly showed that this was the most dangerous city in the United States, with an increase in crime that rivaled lawless third-world countries; in 2018, those figures turned down, with assistance from a federal "Project Safe Neighborhood" crime-fighting program. After peaking at 82,000 in 1960, its population is now below 27,000 and 96 percent African American, with 43 percent living in poverty.

South of East St. Louis and the industrial area around Belleville, the river counties are lightly inhabited. This was the site of the French Kaskaskia settlement that became Illinois's first capital in 1818, but repeated flooding turned it into an island and reduced its population to nine people and many more egrets. Farther south, the river abuts coal country and is not far from Carbondale, once a coal center but now, as the home of Southern Illinois University, bustling with students.

The southern end of Illinois is sometimes known as Little Egypt, where the Ohio River meets the Mississippi: flat, fertile farmland, protected by giant constructed levees because it is susceptible to yearly floods. The marshy landscape has created the Sinkhole Plain, with more than 10,000 sinkholes. There is more than a touch of Dixie here: The unofficial capital of Little Egypt, Cairo (pronounced KAY-roh), is a declining town closer to Memphis than to Chicago. A more enticing locale is the Shawnee National Forest, which has preserved Native American sites that are 10,000 years old.

The 12th District of Illinois covers all this Mississippi riverfront from Alton south to Cairo, with some inland territory as well. Slightly more than half its population is in the Metro East area in St. Clair and Madison counties. Combined, those two counties dipped from 539,000 in 2010 to 528,000 in 2017. Many of those departees have moved across the river to Missouri, with its lower taxes. The largest employer in Southern Illinois is Scott Air Force Base near Belleville, which has a workforce of 12,500 and is home of the U.S. Transportation Command, which directs troops and supply movements around the world.

The bright spot in the local economy has been the turnaround in steel. With a boost from hefty tariffs on steel imports, this district led the nation in its increase of steel-related jobs since President Donald Trump took office. At Granite City's US Steel plant, the company said in July 2018 that 800 workers would be hired. In 2015, 2,000 workers had been laid off by the temporary closing of the plant. The district has suffered a steep drop in Democratic support. In 2008, Barack Obama defeated John McCain, 55%-44%. Eight years later, Donald Trump won the district, 54%-40%.

Rodney Davis (R)

Elected 2012, 4th term, b. Jan 05, 1970; Des Moines, IA; Millikin University (IL), B.A., 1992; Roman Catholic; Married (Shannon Davis); 3 children.

Professional Career: Staff assistant, IL Secretary of State, 1992-1996; Projects Director, Rep. John Shimkus, 1997-2012; Executive Director, IL Republican Party, 2011.

DC Office: 1740 LHOB 20515, 202-225-2371, Fax: 202-226-0791, rodneydavis.house.gov

State Offices: Champaign, 217-403-4690; Decatur, 217-791-6224; Maryville, 618-205-8660; Normal, 309-252-8834; Springfield, 217-791-6224; Taylorville, 217-824-5117.

Committees: *Agriculture*: Biotechnology, Horticulture & Research; Subcommittee Nutrition, Oversight & Department Operations. *Commission Congressional Mailing Standards (RMM). House Administration (RMM). Joint Library. Joint Printing. Select Committee on the Modernization of*

Congress. Transportation & Infrastructure: Highways & Transit (RMM); Railroads, Pipelines & Hazardous Materials.

Group Ratings

	ADA	ACLU	AFL-CIO	LCV	ITI	COC	HAFA	ACU	CFG	FRC
2018	-	7%	-	6%	-	83%	42%	56%	46%	100%
2017	0%	C	28%	9%	C	93%	C	61%	44%	100%

Almanac Ratings 2017-18

	Economy	Social	Foreign	Composite
Liberal	8%	6%	28%	14%
Conservative	92%	94%	72%	86%

Key Votes of the 115th Congress

1. Obama-care revision	Y	5. Family planning regs	Y	9. Guantanamo prisoners	NV
2. Tax Cuts	Y	6. Body cameras/immigration	N	10. Ground missiles, limit	NV
3. Omnibus appropriations	Y	7. Abortion ban	Y	11. Defense Dept. spending	Y
4. Dodd-Frank revision	Y	8. Concealed carry	Y	12. FISA rules	Y

Election Results

Election	Name (Party)	Vote (%)	Cand. Spent	Ind. Exp. Support	Ind. Exp. Oppose
2018 General	Rodney Davis (R)................................	136,516 (50%)	$3,804,097	$52,252	$2,986,067
	Betsy Londrigan (D)............................	134,458 (50%)	$4,212,426	$417,000	$1,897,699
2018 Primary	Rodney Davis (R)..	(100%)			

Prior winning percentages: 2016 (60%), 2014 (59%), 2012 (47%)

Republican Rodney Davis was first elected in a tight 2012 contest and had become entrenched in this seat — to the surprise of Democrats, including redistricters in Illinois. He has been an active and often bipartisan legislator. Davis, an occasional critic of President Donald Trump and GOP policies, barely survived reelection in 2018 in what has become a swing seat. He seemed a likely Democratic target in 2020.

Davis was born in Des Moines Iowa but moved to Taylorville Illinois when he was 7 years old, and has never left the area. His parents opened a McDonald's franchise, where Davis pitched in to work before going to college. His political science courses at Millikin University spurred an interest in holding public office. After graduation, Davis joined the staff of Illinois Secretary of State George Ryan. At the time, Ryan's office was engaged in what was later exposed as massive fraud, illegally selling government licenses. Davis was not implicated in the scheme.

He got his first campaign experience at 25, running for the Illinois legislature in 1996. He lost, but then managed Rep. John Shimkus' first reelection bid. With time off to run unsuccessfully for mayor of his hometown in 2000, Davis spent more than a decade on Shimkus' district office staff. During those years, he was the lawmaker's project coordinator, securing local, federal and private funding for public works projects.

When Rep. Tim Johnson announced he was retiring from Congress shortly after winning his primary in 2012 in his redistricted seat, a small group of Illinois GOP leaders chose Davis to replace him on the ballot. In the general election, Davis faced Democrat David Gill, an emergency room physician and perennial candidate. Davis stressed the need to repeal President Barack Obama's health care reform law and to cut government spending, though he made an exception for federal Pell Grants (the district has several colleges and universities). Both candidates launched fierce negative attacks over the airwaves, prompting Johnson at one point to tell both of them to stop it. Davis eked out a victory by a margin of 1,002 votes -- 46.5%-46.2%. The national parties spent more than $6 million on the contest.

Davis has been busy on two committees: Agriculture, and Transportation and Infrastructure. Unusual for a freshman, he helped to shape in 2014 two major pieces of legislation. On that farm bill, he added requirements that the Environmental Protection Administration give farmers a seat at the table when the agency considered new regulations that affect their industry. On the water resources bill, he helped craft language that permits the Army Corps of Engineers to cooperate with private businesses to complete projects needed to improve the nation's waterways.

When Congress passed a five-year highway funding bill in 2015, Davis took credit for provisions on behalf of pipeline welders and freight auto-haulers and for a provision for new tools to identify underlying causes for drunk driving. In 2019, he became the senior Republican on the influential Highways and Transit Subcommittee. Davis has shown occasional independence, as when he was one of 30 House Republicans who voted in 2016 to give illegal immigrant "dreamers" the right to join the military. His Almanac vote ratings have placed him near the center of the House

In 2014, Davis survived two significant challenges. In the Republican primary, his challenger was Erika Harold, a Harvard Law School graduate and 2003 Miss America, who had tea party support. In her campaign, she said that she represented "the next generation of Republican leadership," and that the GOP needed to reach out to a broader constituency. But Davis, who largely focused on his record as a freshman, won, 55%-41%.

Democratic challenger Ann Callis, a former chief justice of the Madison County court, took relatively conservative views for a Democrat, including her description of the Affordable Care Act as "a disaster." She won the support of the Sierra Club, while Davis was backed by the United Mine Workers and the coal industry, which objected to the Obama administration's hostility to coal. Callis spent $1.9 million, to $3.4 million for Davis. Davis won by a robust 59%-41% and took 13 of 14 counties, losing only Champaign. In 2016, Democrats passed on a major challenge to Davis.

Davis distanced himself from Trump during the campaign, withdrawing his support following the release of a recording of Trump making lewd comments about women. Davis called the behavior "inexcusable." Following the election, Davis maintained his independence. There was "absolutely no doubt," he said, that the Russians "meddled" in the 2016 election. He criticized the tariffs that Trump imposed on imports as "devastating to our agricultural sector." He said that the Trump administration should "absolutely not" separate children from their parents at the border. On the 2018 farm bill, Davis cited his support for provisions that protected crop insurance and organic products. But he voiced disappointment that the final version did not strengthen job training and other requirements for food stamp beneficiaries.

That independence hardly discouraged a strong challenge in 2018. In contrast to Callis in 2014, Democrat Betsy Dirksen Londrigan said that Davis' support for repeal of the Affordable Care Act spurred her decision to run, and it became the focal point of the campaign. In this swing district, both candidates kept their distance from Trump. Londrigan outspent Davis, $4.2 million to $3.8 million, and the parties added more than $5 million to the contest. Davis won, 50.4%-49.6%, a margin of 2,058 votes. Londrigan won her home county of Sangamon, plus the university counties of McLean and Champaign; the latter had the largest turnout and gave her 69 per cent of the vote. Davis won the other 11 counties, including Decatur-based McLean. He had the closest win of the five remaining House Republicans from Illinois.

IL-13: West-Central Illinois

Cook Partisan Voting Index: R+3

Population		Race and Ethnicity		Income	
Total	706,023	White	78.5%	Median Income	$50,373
Land area (sq. miles)	5,794	Black	11.3%	District Income Rank	303
Pop/ sq mi	121.9	Latino	3.3%	Poverty Rate	18.5%
Born in State	74.8%	Asian	3.8%	With health insurance	94.1%
		Two or more races	2.7%	Cash public assistance	2.2%
Age Groups		Other	0.4%	Food stamp/SNAP	13.5%
Under 18	20.4%				
18-34	28.4%	**Education**		**Work**	
35-64	36.1%	H.S grad or less	38.7%	White Collar	15.1%
Over 64	15.1%	Some college	30.9%	Sales and Service	42.3%
		College Degree, 4 yr	18%	Blue Collar	19.6%
Military		Post grad	12.4%	Government	18.6%
Veteran/ Active Duty	8.3%				

2012 Pres. Vote	Romney	147,104	(49%)	Obama	146,732	(49%)			
2016 Pres. Vote	Trump	159,013	(49%)	Clinton	141,540	(44%)	Johnson	14,681	(5%)

St. Louis exurbs, Champaign: Springfield, the capital of Illinois, has changed rather little since its great moment in history — when it was home to Abraham Lincoln, railroad lawyer, elected to the House as a Whig opponent of the Mexican War and later, the 16th president of the United States. Today, beyond the suburban fringe, the prairie countryside outside Springfield is still mostly farmland with few towns, filled with large industrial farms producing soybeans and corn. Farming technology has changed vastly, but the patterns of cultivation, the contours of the land, even the shape of the ribbons of back country roads, cannot be entirely different from what Lincoln saw as a lawyer making his way from one county seat to another on the circuit.

Nor has downtown Springfield changed all that much, at least compared with booming Midwestern capitals like Columbus, Indianapolis or even Des Moines. Lincoln's clapboard house is preserved in Springfield, and so is the courtroom where he argued cases before federal judges. The downtown block where Lincoln and his partner William Herndon kept their law offices is open for inspection, as is the state capitol built here in 1839. The governor's mansion downtown, built in 1855, is the third oldest continuously occupied residence in the country. Today, Springfield is known more for its dysfunction: a continuing loss of public jobs under governors of both parties; the dispiriting paralysis and debt of state government; and the corruption resulting in four of the state's past 10 governors being sentenced to jail time.

The 13th Congressional District contains prairie lands from Collinsville, just outside St. Louis, to Champaign-Urbana, a three-hour drive northeast. It includes much of Bloomington, birthplace of Vice President Adlai Stevenson, who served under Democrat Grover Cleveland, and the hometown of his grandson, Gov Adlai Stevenson II, nominated by Democrats for president in 1952 and 1956. The largest of the towns in the district are anchored by the state's universities: The University of Illinois in Champaign-Urbana, Illinois State University in Bloomington-Normal, and Illinois Wesleyan University, also in Bloomington. Decatur is home to politically influential Archer Daniels Midland, one of the world's largest agricultural processors and a major champion of ethanol. Amid its employment cuts elsewhere in Illinois, Caterpillar moved 500 manufacturing jobs to Decatur in 2018. Except for youthful Champaign, downstate has been suffering population losses — part of the pattern statewide.

Politically, the district has been closely divided, with the cultural conservatism of the prairie meshing with the liberal academic population centers and government capital in Springfield. In 2016, when Donald Trump won 49%-44%, the result revealed the diminished enthusiasm for Democrats in rural areas plus Trump's working-class appeal. There was a different story two years later: J.B. Pritzker was the first Democratic candidate for governor to win in Champaign County since 1936.

Lauren Underwood (D)

Elected 2018, 1st term, b. Oct 04, 1986; Mayfield Heights, OH; University of Michigan, B.S., 2008; Johns Hopkins University, M.S.N., 2009; Johns Hopkins University, M.PH, 2009; Johns Hopkins University, M.PH, 2009; Christian Church; Single.

Professional Career: Government Affairs Fellow, American Association of Colleges of Nursing, 2009-2009; National Institutes of Health Fellow, 2008-2009; Research Nurse, Johns Hopkins University, 2009-2010; , U.S. Department of Health and Human Services, Policy Coordinator, 2010-2014, Senior Advisor 2014-2017; Adjunct Professor, Georgetown University School of Nursing & Health Studies, 2013-2018.

DC Office: 1118 LHOB 20515, 202-225-2976, underwood.house.gov

State Offices: West Chicago, 630-549-2190.

Committees: *Education & Labor*: Health, Employment, Labor & Pensions. *Homeland Security*: Cybersecurity, Infrastructure Protection & Innovation; Emergency Preparedness, Response & Recovery. *Veterans' Affairs*: Disability Assistance & Memorial Affairs.

Election Results

Election	Name (Party)	Vote (%)		Cand. Spent	Ind. Exp. Support	Ind. Exp. Oppose
2018 General	Lauren Underwood (D)................ 156,035	(53%)		$4,621,549	$2,385,139	$921,639
	Randy Hultgren (R)............................ 141,164	(47%)		$2,332,074	$29,480	$2,646,953
2018 Primary	Lauren Underwood (D)................ 29,391	(57%)				
	Matt Brolley (D).................................... 6,845	(13%)				
	Jim Walz (D).. 5,100	(10%)				
	Victor Swanson (D)............................... 3,597	(7%)				
	John Hosta (D)..................................... 2,578	(5%)				
	George Weber (D)................................. 2,570	(5%)				

Democrat Lauren Underwood won election in 2018 in the most Republican-leaning district in the Chicago suburbs. A registered nurse who became an expert on health care policy, she has built on her experiences in the Obama administration. Underlying the significance of Underwood's initial election campaign was that African-Americans typically don't have great success when they run in a district that is 3 percent black and among the wealthiest 10 percent in the nation. Underwood's gender and her health-policy expertise were more influential in the election outcome. One of several African-American Democrats who were elected in largely white districts, she defeated Republican Rep. Randy Hultgren, who had not faced a serious reelection challenge in his four terms.

Underwood was a native of Naperville, which is a few miles outside the 14th District. She graduated from the University of Michigan with a bachelor's of science in nursing, and got master's degrees in nursing and public health from Johns Hopkins University. As a special assistant to President Barack Obama, she advised communities on how to respond to disaster and public-health emergencies. In 2016, Obama appointed her as a senior adviser at the Health and Human Services Department, where she earlier worked on implementation of the Affordable Care Act. She advised local governments on steps to maximize cost-efficient care and taught nurses at Georgetown University.

With her pre-existing heart condition, Underwood said that Hultgren's vote to repeal the Affordable Care Act spurred her to run for Congress. "The country needs new leaders who can put partisanship aside and make progress on the issues that matter to our community," she told the Chicago Sun-Times. She called Hultgren "a career politician with little to show for it."

In the Democratic primary, Underwood faced six other candidates—all of them white men. Her chief opponent was Matt Brolley, a civil engineer and president of Montgomery Village who cited his experience in working with others in local government. The Daily Herald reported that Underwood "stood out as much for her detailed positions" as for her race or gender. She won the primary with 57%-13% over Brolley.

Hultgren challenged Underwood's views on health policy. The biggest difference between the two of them, he told the Sun-Times, was that she "helped engineer a federal takeover of the health care system in this country that left [residents of the 14th District] with higher health care costs, limited choice in their health care options and less control over their own health care." He cited his own efforts to encourage bipartisanship in Congress.

Underwood's more than $5 million for the campaign doubled the spending by Hultgren. House Democrats and their allies, including women's groups, spent more than $2 million on her behalf. In her 53%-47% victory, Underwood remarkably won all seven counties. Her largest margin came from Kane, which cast one-fourth of the vote. The poor reelection support in these counties for Republican Gov. Bruce Rauner was a partisan drag on Hultgren.

The victories of Underwood and Sean Casten in the adjoining 6th District gave Democrats a clean sweep of the 12 districts in Chicagoland—a pattern that resulted in several large metro areas across the nation in 2018, with the erosion of Republican support in suburbia. Those are the types of districts that will be paramount in the GOP attempt to regain House control.

IL-14: Northwestern Chicagoland

Cook Partisan Voting Index: R+5

Population		Race and Ethnicity		Income	
Total	730,782	White	79%	Median Income	$90,082
Land area (sq. miles)	1,598	Black	2.9%	District Income Rank	29
Pop/ sq mi	457.4	Latino	11.9%	Poverty Rate	6.1%
Born in State	71%	Asian	4.4%	With health insurance	95%
		Two or more races	1.6%	Cash public assistance	1.3%
Age Groups		Other	0.2%	Food stamp/SNAP	6.1%
Under 18	26.1%				
18-34	18.7%	**Education**		**Work**	
35-64	42.5%	H.S grad or less	29.5%	White Collar	12.7%
Over 64	12.7%	Some college	30.5%	Sales and Service	40.1%
		College Degree, 4 yr	25.3%	Blue Collar	18.8%
Military		Post grad	14.7%	Government	11.5%
Veteran/ Active Duty	6.3%				

2012 Pres. Vote	Romney	172,162	(54%)	Obama	140,495	(44%)			
2016 Pres. Vote	Trump	167,327	(48%)	Clinton	154,058	(44%)	Johnson	17,259	(5%)

McHenry, Kane: In the exurbs west of Chicago, the decade since the recession has seen an economic slowdown. At the peak of the housing boom, Kendall County looked like the city's new suburban frontier. It was rated the fastest-growing large county in the nation by the Census Bureau in 2010. Its population more than doubled in the decade after 2000, as urban flight brought in families attracted by its affordable housing, good schools and low crime rates, all located near job centers in suburban DuPage and Kane counties. Farmland quickly transformed into new housing subdivisions. In effect, Kendall became a suburb of the suburbs. But the downside of the rapid growth became evident during the collapse of the housing finance market, when Kendall posted the highest foreclosure rate in the state. Several new developments in towns like Yorkville became ghost towns after a sudden halt to building. Kendall County grew only 3.6 percent from 2010 to 2013, barely above the national average; the next four years produced modest 6 percent growth.

The experience was similar elsewhere: McHenry County grew by 300 people from 2010 to 2017, after the population had boomed by 19 percent in the previous decade. Those numbers should produce "alarm bells," the Northwest Herald reported in April 2017. The most common explanation is a combination of high taxes and fewer jobs. In McHenry, two-thirds of working residents commute to jobs in other counties. Young people have been leaving at a disproportionate rate. These problems have resulted partly from dysfunctional state governance, which has had the highest unfunded pension liability and the worst credit rating in the nation.

The 14th District of Illinois arcs through seven of the Chicago collar counties, including most of what have been solidly Republican Kendall and McHenry and also Republican-leaning chunks of Kane and western Lake County, where little lake communities are surrounded by new suburbs like Wauconda, Deer Park and Volo. About 55 percent of the voting population resides in McHenry and Kane. Of all the Chicagoland districts, the 14th is the least ethnically diverse, with a 79 percent white population. Huntley is the site of Del Webb's Sun City; with about 9,000 residents, it claims to be largest retirement community in the Midwest. It also contains smaller parts of Will, DeKalb and DuPage counties. Batavia-based Fermilab, which describes itself as America's particle physics and accelerator laboratory and has 1,750 employees, received approval in July 2018 from the Energy Department to proceed with the design of a project that will generate an unprecedented stream of neutrinos, which are subatomic particles.

This is the most Republican district in the suburbs, though much of "downstate" has become notably more Republican than the 14th. Still, Democrats can run competitively here. Barack Obama narrowly carried it, under the present lines, with 50 percent of the vote in 2008. Donald Trump won here 48%-44% in 2016.

John Shimkus (R)

Elected 1996, 12th term, b. Feb 21, 1958; Collinsville; Christ College (CA), 1989; U.S. Military Academy (NY), B.S., 1990; Southern Illinois University, M.A., 1997; Lutheran; Married (Karen Muth Shimkus); 3 children.

Military Career: U.S. Army 1980-1986; U.S. Army Reserve 1985-pres.

Elected Office: Collinsville Township trustee, 1989-1993; Madison County Treasurer, 1990-1996.

Professional Career: H.S. teacher, 1986-1990.

DC Office: 2217 RHOB 20515, 202-225-5271, Fax: 202-225-5880, shimkus.house.gov

State Offices: Danville, 217-446-0664; Effingham, 217-347-7947; Harrisburg, 618-252-8271; Maryville, 618-288-7190.

Committees: *Energy & Commerce*: Communications & Technology; Environment & Climate Change (RMM); Health.

Group Ratings

	ADA	ACLU	AFL-CIO	LCV	ITI	COC	HAFA	ACU	CFG	FRC
2018	-	4%	-	6%	-	92%	40%	67%	44%	100%
2017	0%	C	29%	6%	C	93%	C	70%	51%	100%

Almanac Ratings 2017-18

	Economy	Social	Foreign	Composite
Liberal	6%	4%	0%	3%
Conservative	94%	97%	100%	97%

Key Votes of the 115th Congress

1. Obama-care revision	Y	5. Family planning regs	Y	9. Guantanamo prisoners	N
2. Tax Cuts	Y	6. Body cameras/immigration	N	10. Ground missiles, limit	N
3. Omnibus appropriations	Y	7. Abortion ban	Y	11. Defense Dept. spending	Y
4. Dodd-Frank revision	Y	8. Concealed carry	Y	12. FISA rules	Y

Election Results

Election	Name (Party)	Vote (%)	Cand. Spent	Ind. Exp. Support	Ind. Exp. Oppose
2018 General	John Shimkus (R)............................... 181,294	(71%)	$1,232,686		
	Kevin Gaither (D)......................... 74,309	(29%)	$47,787		
2018 Primary	John Shimkus (R)..	(100%)			

Prior winning percentages: 2016 (100%), 2014 (75%), 2012 (69%), 2010 (71%), 2008 (64%), 2006 (64%), 2004 (69%), 2002 (55%), 2000 (63%), 1998 (61%), 1996 (50%)

John Shimkus, a Republican first elected in 1996, has been an aggressive supporter of business and a fierce critic of regulations he considers overly burdensome. As a senior member of the Energy and Commerce Committee, he has failed in efforts to repeal the Affordable Care Act and to pass legislation to dispose of nuclear waste at the Yucca Mountain site in Nevada.

Shimkus grew up in Collinsville, in Madison County. His father was an installer for Illinois Bell, and his mother a township trustee. Shimkus graduated from West Point, trained in the Army as a Ranger and paratrooper, then taught high school in Collinsville. In 1988, he ran for the Madison County Board and lost. The next year, he was elected a Collinsville Township trustee. In 1990, he was elected Madison County treasurer. He challenged then-Rep. Dick Durbin in 1992 and lost 57%-43%, a closer margin than in Durbin's previous campaigns.

In 1996, when Durbin ran for the Senate, Shimkus easily won the Republican primary, with 51 percent against seven other candidates. In the general election, he faced state Rep. Jay Hoffman. Both were anti-abortion, pro-gun, and in favor of a balanced budget constitutional amendment. Hoffman raised more money and had the support of the AFL-CIO, but Shimkus won, 50.3%-49.7%.

In the House, Shimkus' voting record is generally conservative, with an occasional centrist streak. He was one of 16 House Republicans in 2012 to back a budget plan along the lines of the bipartisan Simpson-Bowles commission.

On the Energy and Commerce Committee, Shimkus' ardor has sometimes triggered criticism of what the left describes as hyperbole. When Democrats issued a draft plan to regulate greenhouse gas emissions in 2009, he called it the "largest assault on democracy and freedom in this country that I've ever witnessed." Shimkus has been especially vocal about energy production: supporting nuclear power, extending tax credits for ethanol, and giving incentives to coal-to-liquid refineries to help coal-producing areas. In 2005, he helped pass the law that gasoline must contain a minimum volume of renewable fuels, such as biodiesel and ethanol; that has resulted in what has become known as the Renewable Fuel Standard. In November 2018, he released with GOP Rep. Bill Flores of Texas a draft proposal to revise the RFS to provide "more value to consumers and more certainty to industry," including encouragement of higher-octane fuels.

Shimkus has lost two bids to become Energy and Commerce chairman, though in each case he walked away with a significant consolation prize. In 2010, he lost out to the more senior Fred Upton of Michigan. Shimkus was named chairman of the new Environment and the Economy Subcommittee. After several years of painstaking effort and bipartisan compromise, he scored a legislative coup in 2016 when Obama signed the Chemical Safety for the 21st Century Act, which was an update of the Toxic Substances Control Act.

Following the 2016 election, when Upton was term-limited, Shimkus ran again for committee chairman and was challenged by Greg Walden of Oregon. Shimkus this time had the benefit of seniority. But Walden had gained chits as successful chairman of the National Republican Congressional Committee. Speaker Paul Ryan reportedly endorsed Walden — a decisive factor. Instead, Shimkus remained chairman of the Environment Subcommittee. In 2018, the House overwhelmingly approved his amendment to an appropriations bill to store waste from commercial nuclear power plants at Yucca Mountain. As in the past, the senators from Nevada stymied further action. Shimkus criticized Ryan and other House GOP leaders for failing to "stand strong" on the House's position. (In the minority in 2019, he became ranking Republican on the renamed Enviornment and Climate Change Subcommittee.)

Shimkus clashed with Ryan in seeking to end the House ban on spending earmarks. Previous Speaker John Boehner had imposed the ban to satisfy critics of excessive federal spending and to avoid occasional abuses. Shimkus decried the abandonment of congressional prerogatives. "All appropriations begin in the House, per the Constitution. So, we've turned over our power of the purse to the executive branch, which can then make their own decisions based on their political whims," he said. Ryan refused to include the reversal with other House rules changes in 2017.

As a former high school teacher, Shimkus earlier took what seemed to be a routine assignment as chairman of the House page board. But five weeks before the 2006 election, revelations that Republican Rep. Mark Foley had sent inappropriate and sexually explicit emails to former male pages was a political bombshell, including for Shimkus and then-GOP Speaker Dennis Hastert. Both men had known of questionable contacts Foley had with pages and failed to investigate. The House Ethics Committee later found that Shimkus should have shared the information with other House members on the page board, but did not call for sanctions.

In 2002, Shimkus had a redistricting-forced contest against Rep. David Phelps, a conservative Democrat. After a spirited contest, in which organized labor spent more than $1.5 million against him, Shimkus won 55%-45%. When he first ran, Shimkus said he would limit himself to six terms. But in 2005, he called his pledge "a mistake," and said, "unless everyone plays by the same rules, term limits don't make sense." He has not faced a serious challenge since then. He might seek another opportunity to take the top GOP post on Energy and Commerce.

IL-15: Eastern South-Central Illinois   **Cook Partisan Voting Index: R+21**

Population		Race and Ethnicity		Income	
Total	701,048	White	90.8%	Median Income	$50,821
Land area (sq. miles)	14,696	Black	4.1%	District Income Rank	292
Pop/ sq mi	47.7	Latino	2.8%	Poverty Rate	14.4%
Born in State	75.7%	Asian	0.7%	With health insurance	93.2%
		Two or more races	1.3%	Cash public assistance	2.6%
Age Groups		Other	0.3%	Food stamp/SNAP	14%
Under 18	22.4%				
18-34	20.8%	**Education**		**Work**	
35-64	39%	H.S grad or less	45.8%	White Collar	17.8%
Over 64	17.8%	Some college	34.9%	Sales and Service	40%
		College Degree, 4 yr	12.8%	Blue Collar	30%
Military		Post grad	6.4%	Government	13.9%
Veteran/ Active Duty	9.2%				

2012 Pres. Vote	Romney	197,262	(64%)	Obama	105,015	(34%)		
2016 Pres. Vote	Trump	226,606	(70%)	Clinton	78,573	(24%)	Johnson	12,468	(4%)

Metro St. Louis, Champaign County: Much of Southern Illinois is a land of prairies, of flat, treeless stretches sloping imperceptibly down to the Ohio and Mississippi rivers. It was settled almost entirely from the south by farmers coming overland from Kentucky, such as Abraham Lincoln's ancestors, who settled in what was then the state capital of Vandalia. Just beyond the Ohio River, they found hilly terrain, some of which turned out to have vast coal deposits. As they traveled farther north, they must have been astonished, after miles of thick forest, to see the great American prairie stretch before them, a vast sea of empty land extending past the horizon. The black soil proved wondrously rich and the land was soon crisscrossed by rail lines taking their produce away and bringing in industrial products from St. Louis, Chicago and points east. This was the home turf of John L. Lewis, the imperious leader of the United Mine Workers who during the middle of the 20th century was one of the most powerful and eloquent figures in American public life.

The local mining industry in recent years has become a shadow of itself. In 1990, Illinois produced 62 million tons of coal and employed 10,000 workers in mining; by 2014, 4,500 workers produced 58 million tons. Employers and workers drew some hope — and a few jobs -- from the campaign promises of Donald Trump to revive the production and burning of coal; in 2017, mining increased by 10 percent, though jobs fell by 3 percent. In Mattoon, General Electric shut down in 2017 its Lamp Plant facility, which once produced flash cubes for camera and employed 1,800 workers.

The 15th Congressional District of Illinois, the largest geographically in the state, extends more than 250 miles up and down the Indiana border, and 150 miles across. Vermilion County and northern Champaign County are on the northern border of the district, which extends west to a few miles from East St. Louis and the Mississippi River. It covers all or part of 33 counties in the rich heartland of Southern Illinois. The old National Road (paralleled by Interstate 70), the traditional boundary between the part of downstate Illinois settled by southerners and the part settled by Yankees, traverses the district. Effingham, which straddles that line, is where corn and soybean fields give way to hills and valleys with orchards and woodlands. Racial diversity is limited here; in 2017, the district was 91 percent white.

The biggest voting blocs in the 15th are in Madison and Clinton counties (parts of the St. Louis metropolitan area), Coles County (home to Eastern Illinois University), plus Champaign and Vermilion County. Politically, these prairie lands were the home of former House Speaker Joseph (Uncle Joe) Cannon, a Republican from the manufacturing city of Danville (population, 32,977), which is the largest in the district. Traditional Democrats have become hard to find here. In 2016, Trump won 70 percent of the vote and each county except for university-based Champaign. This is the most Republican district in Illinois — increasingly so since 2008, when John McCain got 55 percent.

Adam Kinzinger (R)

Elected 2010, 5th term, b. Feb 27, 1978; Kankakee; Illinois State University, B.A., 2000; Illinois State University, B.A., 2000; Christian Church; Single.

Military Career: U.S. Air Force 2003-2009; IL Air National Guard 29-pres. (Iraq)

Elected Office: McLean County Board, 1998-2003.

Professional Career: Partner, sales rep., STL Technology, 2000-2003.

DC Office: 2245 RHOB 20515, 202-225-3635, Fax: 202-225-3521, kinzinger.house.gov

State Offices: Ottawa, 815-431-9271; Rockford, 815-708-8032; Watseka, 815-432-0580.

Committees: *Energy & Commerce*: Communications & Technology; Energy. *Foreign Affairs*: Europe, Eurasia, Energy & the Environment (RMM); Middle East, North Africa & International Terrorism.

Group Ratings

	ADA	ACLU	AFL-CIO	LCV	ITI	COC	HAFA	ACU	CFG	FRC
2018	-	4%	-	3%	-	83%	41%	64%	45%	100%
2017	0%	C	32%	6%	C	93%	C	63%	45%	100%

Almanac Ratings 2017-18

	Economy	Social	Foreign	Composite
Liberal	8%	4%	5%	5%
Conservative	92%	97%	95%	95%

Key Votes of the 115th Congress

1. Obama-care revision	Y	5. Family planning regs	Y
2. Tax Cuts	Y	6. Body cameras/immigration	N
3. Omnibus appropriations	Y	7. Abortion ban	Y
4. Dodd-Frank revision	Y	8. Concealed carry	Y

9. Guantanamo prisoners	N
10. Ground missiles, limit	N
11. Defense Dept. spending	Y
12. FISA rules	Y

Election Results

Election	Name (Party)	Vote (%)		Cand. Spent	Ind. Exp. Support	Ind. Exp. Oppose
2018 General	Adam Kinzinger (R)	151,254	(59%)	$2,009,505	$64,145	
	Sara Dady (D)	104,569	(41%)	$389,416		
2018 Primary	Adam Kinzinger (R)	44,878	(68%)			
	James Marter (R)	21,242	(32%)			

Prior winning percentages: 2016 (100%), 2014 (71%), 2012 (62%), 2010 (65%)

Republican Adam Kinzinger, elected in 2010, is a telegenic conservative who has racked up considerable experience in the military and political worlds. A former Air Force pilot, he has been a foreign policy wonk and a harsh critic of President Donald Trump.

Kinzinger was born in Kankakee, but spent the majority of his life in Bloomington. He attributed his interest in public service to his father, who ran a nonprofit homeless shelter, and his mother, a public school teacher. Wanting to stay near home, he got a bachelor's degree in political science from Illinois State University. In 1998, as a sophomore, he took seriously a joking suggestion that he run for the McLean County Board. He did, defeating an incumbent, and served five years. With the September 11 terrorist attacks, "that's when I basically woke up," he recalled. A month later, he joined the Air Force. He served three tours in Iraq and one in Afghanistan.

In 2009, following his final tour in Iraq, Kinzinger campaigned for the district based in Will County. Touting his military service, he had important backing from local tea party activists and defeated four opponents in the Republican primary, with 64 percent of the vote. In the fall, he faced first-term Rep. Debbie Halvorson, who had racked up an impressive 58 percent of the vote in 2008. Halvorson attacked Kinzinger's stance on free trade and depicted him as inexperienced. She ran a campaign ad with a senior citizen scolding, "Young man, you have no idea what you're doing." Kinzinger countered with endorsements from Mitt Romney and Sarah Palin. He picked up an endorsement from the Chicago Sun-Times, which often backs Democrats. Halvorson outspent him $2.5 million to $1.8 million, but Kinzinger won convincingly, 57%-43%.

He became a favorite of GOP leaders, who put him on the whip team and gave him a choice seat on the Energy and Commerce Committee, where he has generally upheld business' interests. The House in 2012 passed his bill aimed at helping states streamline certification requirements for veterans with emergency medical technician training who want to continue as civilian EMTs. Time named him one of its "40 Under 40" young leaders.

Kinzinger has focused on multiple energy sources of interest to his constituents. As he noted on his congressional website, the 16th District "is home to four nuclear power plants, miles of windmills, hydropower plants, and ethanol and biodiesel plants." He has been a major booster of nuclear energy that, he said, "will sustain our economic expansion and keep the lights on while we work to catch up with our international competition." In an August 2017 op-ed column for the Chicago Sun-Times, he wrote, "Our nation could continue to lead the world in this technology, or we can cede this role to Russia and China." In December 2018, he enacted a bill with Democratic Rep. Mike Doyle of Pennsylvania to improve the "transparency, predictability and fairness" of the fee structure for nuclear regulation.

Politically entrenched and with growing seniority, Kinzinger became more activist in the GOP's establishment wing, especially on national security issues. In 2014, he criticized the Pentagon budget-cutting plan of Kentucky Sen. Rand Paul as "devastating for our party." In 2015, he filed a resolution that would grant the president full authority to wage war against the threat posed by the Islamic State. Following the 2016 Republican convention, he cited Trump's criticism of NATO and attacks on Muslims in his decision not to endorse his campaign for president. "Donald Trump is beginning to cross a lot of red lines of the unforgivable in politics. I'm not going to support Hillary, but in America we have the right to skip somebody," Kinzinger said on CNN.

Following the election, he said that it was vital for the United States to call Russia to account for its actions to "mess around" with our election systems, and that the response by Trump "to disparage the intel-gathering mechanisms that we have here is not the right answer." Kinzinger — who has continued to serve in the Air National Guard, as a major -- used his seat on the House Foreign Affairs Committee to harshly criticize Russia at a time when Trump and some of his congressional allies had softened their attacks. During a June 2017 interview with Politico, in which he referred to Putin as someone "who kills his enemies," Kinzinger added, "It shows how much people need leadership on foreign policy."

Kinzinger continued his regular attacks on Trump's actions overseas, calling the December 2018 announcement to remove U.S. troops from Syria "a really bad decision." He was among the first congressional Republicans to call for an independent counsel to investigate allegations of ties between Trump's campaign and Russia. Following Trump's disparagement of House Republicans who lost reelection in 2018, Kinzinger said he was "very disgusted." In 2019, he became ranking Republican on the Europe, Eurasia, Energy and the Environment Subcommittee.

At home, Democratic-engineered redistricting in 2012 put Kinzinger in the same district as 10-term Republican Rep. Don Manzullo, who was twice his age. The race upended the traditional rules of seniority: Kinzinger won the endorsement of top House GOP leaders, while Manzullo played up his tea party support. Kinzinger touted his combat tours and hit Manzullo for voting to raise the debt limit 12 times in his career. Primary voters decided to go with youth and the future over experience and the past, and Kinzinger won 54%-46%. He has not faced serious opposition since.

IL-16: North-Central Illinois   Cook Partisan Voting Index: R+8

Population		Race and Ethnicity		Income	
Total	698,425	White	83.7%	Median Income	$58,129
Land area (sq. miles)	7,917	Black	3.7%	District Income Rank	193
Pop/ sq mi	88.2	Latino	9.3%	Poverty Rate	12.2%
Born in State	76.7%	Asian	1.4%	With health insurance	93.9%
		Two or more races	1.6%	Cash public assistance	2.1%
Age Groups		Other	0.2%	Food stamp/SNAP	11.9%
Under 18	22.4%				
18-34	21.3%	Education		Work	
35-64	39.5%	H.S grad or less	43.8%	White Collar	16.8%
Over 64	16.8%	Some college	34.3%	Sales and Service	40.9%
		College Degree, 4 yr	13.9%	Blue Collar	28%
Military		Post grad	8%	Government	12.7%
Veteran/ Active Duty	8.6%				

2012 Pres. Vote	Romney	160,435	(53%)	Obama	137,749	(45%)		
2016 Pres. Vote	Trump	173,068	(55%)	Clinton	119,529	(38%)	Johnson	15,073	(5%)

Rockford, Ottawa: The third largest city in Illinois is Rockford, on the Rock River, settled by Swedes as well as Yankees, and once a leading furniture and machine tool manufacturer. Rockford's manufacturing base steadily declined after World War II, and by the 1980s, it had a serious unemployment problem. Growth also has become stagnant in DeKalb County, which had been booming with relatively cheap housing before the 2008 recession. In neighboring Boone County, the farming village of Poplar Grove saw its population triple between 2000 and 2010, but growth went flat and thousands of undeveloped lots were left barren.

The area's economic revival has become a matter of back to the future. The Obama administration's auto bailout gave a jump start to the area's economy. The workforce at the big Chrysler plant on 280 acres a few miles east of Rockford in Belvidere, which had dropped to 200 in 200, rebounded to employ more than 4,000 workers on three shifts, with additional workers at nearby suppliers. The factory and its workers got more good news when Chrysler decided to shift production of its Jeep Cherokee from Toledo Ohio to Belvidere, which had manufactured other Jeep models. With completion of the $350 million project, Belvidere produced more than 400,000 vehicles annually, compared with the 220,000 at the shuttered Toledo plant. The Belvidere plant grew to 5,400 workers, plus more than 2,000 new jobs for local suppliers. The Jeep Cherokee has the most American-made parts of any vehicle manufactured in the United States

The 16th Congressional District is where downstate Illinois begins, at least where it begins west of Chicago. The elongated district forms a crescent surrounding the exurbs of Chicago as it makes a long hook from the Wisconsin border on the north to the Indiana border on the east. It includes parts of Rockford, the population base of the district. Farther south, on bluffs above the Illinois River, are the factory towns of Ottawa, LaSalle, and Streator. On the eastern side of the district is DeKalb County, long the world's leading manufacturer of barbed wire. Dixon, to the west, is where Ronald Reagan grew up.

These mostly small towns traditionally were some of the most heavily Republican territory in the country, but they have become more competitive. Barack Obama carried the district with 50 percent in 2008, but Donald Trump scored a big turnaround win in 2016, 55%-38%.

Cheri Bustos (D)

Elected 2012, 4th term, b. Oct 17, 1961; Springfield; Illinois College - Jacksonville, Att., 1981; University of Maryland - College Park, B.A., 1983; University of Illinois - Springfield, M.A., 1985; Roman Catholic; Married (Gerry Bustos); 3 children; 2 grandchildren.

Elected Office: East Moline City Council, 2007-2011.

Professional Career: Vice President., Iowa Health Systems, 2008-2012; Sr. Director, Trinity Regional Health System, 2002-2008; Reporter, Quad-City Times, 1985-2002.

DC Office: 1233 LHOB 20515, 202-225-5905, Fax: 202-225-5396, bustos.house.gov

State Offices: Peoria, 309-966-1813; Rock Island, 309-786-3406; Rockford, 815-968-8011.

Committees: Democratic Congressional Campaign Committee chairman. *Agriculture*: Livestock & Foreign Agriculture. *Appropriations*: Defense; Labor, Health & Human Services, Education & Related Agencies; Military Construction, Veterans Affairs & Related Agencies.

Group Ratings

	ADA	ACLU	AFL-CIO	LCV	ITI	COC	HAFA	ACU	CFG	FRC
2018	-	75%	-	91%	-	67%	4%	8%	15%	0%
2017	80%	C	97%	94%	C	57%	C	0%	0%	11%

Almanac Ratings 2017-18

	Economy	Social	Foreign	Composite
Liberal	81%	97%	81%	86%
Conservative	19%	4%	19%	14%

Key Votes of the 115th Congress

1. Obama-care revision	N	5. Family planning regs	N	9. Guantanamo prisoners	Y
2. Tax Cuts	N	6. Body cameras/immigration	Y	10. Ground missiles, limit	Y
3. Omnibus appropriations	Y	7. Abortion ban	N	11. Defense Dept. spending	Y
4. Dodd-Frank revision	N	8. Concealed carry	N	12. FISA rules	Y

Election Results

Election	Name (Party)	Vote (%)	Cand. Spent	Ind. Exp. Support	Ind. Exp. Oppose
2018 General	Cheri Bustos (D)	142,659 (62%)	$2,126,875		
	Bill Fawell (R)	87,090 (38%)	$53,198		
2018 Primary	Cheri Bustos (D)	(100%)			

Prior winning percentages: 2016 (60%), 2014 (56%), 2012 (53%)

Democrat Cheri Bustos, first elected in 2012, took advantage of her roots in Illinois politics — her father was a chief of staff for the late Democratic Sen. Alan Dixon — and the district's Democratic leanings. She has joined her party's leadership team to assert influence as one of the few remaining House Democrats who represent large rural areas.

Bustos grew up in the state capital of Springfield. Her mother was a social worker and preschool teacher, and her father was a journalist before entering government. Her first paid job was selling tacos and lemonade at the Illinois State Fair. As a 10-year-old, she met future Democratic Sens. Paul Simon and Dick Durbin, who at the time was a staffer for then-Lt. Gov. Simon. After attending Illinois College, where she excelled at basketball and volleyball, Bustos graduated from the University of Maryland with a bachelor's degree in political science and history. She earned a master's degree in journalism at the University of Illinois and became a reporter for the Quad-City Times, where she covered city government, corruption, crime, health care and other issues over a 17-year career. Her husband, Gerry, is the Rock Island County sheriff.

After leaving journalism, Bustos went into public relations for regional health care providers, including as vice president of public relations and communications for Iowa Health System. Health-related issues are a key concern for her: She lost her uninsured sister-in-law to cancer a few years earlier, and her brother to cancer months later, after his insurance refused to cover the medication he needed. President Barack Obama's Affordable Care Act, she said, was "at least in the right direction." But Bustos insisted that more was needed to improve what she calls a "broken" system.

She was elected to the City Council in East Moline, and served from 2007 to 2011. Emphasizing economic development, she founded and chaired the East Moline Downtown Revitalization Committee. Democrats in Springfield had used redistricting to make the House district more Democratic for a challenge to freshman Republican Rep. Bobby Schilling, a former pizzeria owner. When Bustos entered the race, her friendship with Durbin paid off. He provided a rare primary endorsement and urged other Democrats to exit the race. She won the primary over two other candidates with 54 percent of the vote.

Her race in the fall against Schilling attracted more than $3 million each from Democratic and Republican party groups, in addition to the more than $2 million that each candidate raised. Bustos received an early endorsement from the abortion rights group EMILY's List and was backed by several labor unions. She won, 53%-47%.

Bustos concentrated, at first, on her committee work on agriculture and transportation issues. She leaned on her collegiate sports background to emerge as a star shortstop on the congressional women's softball team.

In 2014, her rematch against Schilling proved less competitive than their initial contest. This time, she outspent her opponent $3.1 million to $1.1 million, and Schilling had scant GOP financial support. In an otherwise Republican year in Illinois and elsewhere, Bustos rolled to a 55%-45% win, with 2-to-1 leads in Peoria and Rockford, and 54 percent of the vote in Rock Island County. In 2016, Bustos won her first easy election: 60-40 percent against Patrick Harlan, a truck driver and local tea party leader.

Following the 2016 election, House Democrats chose Bustos as one of three co-chairs of the Democratic Communications and Policy Committee. She spent much of the 2018 cycle mentoring and campaigning with Rust Belt Democratic candidates. That successful effort paid off. In December 2018, House Democrats chose her to chair the Democratic Congressional Campaign Committee. Previously, the Democratic leader had filled the position. She was on a roll. Ironically, one of her first internal conflicts was in her home state, when she was announced as the host of a fundraiser for Illinois Democrat Rep. Dan Lipinski, who has faced contentious primary challenges from the Left. Protests from abortion-rights groups and other progressive activists led Bustos to withdraw from the event, though she maintained her support of Lipinski—and all other Democratic incumbents.

Bustos had gained frequent mentions as a statewide contender, either for the Senate or governor. Now, her future in the House has become wide open. She could be a contender to move up in leadership, and might be in the mix for an opening as the Democratic leader.

IL-17: Northwest Illinois   **Cook Partisan Voting Index: D+2**

Population		Race and Ethnicity		Income	
Total	694,242	White	75.8%	Median Income	$46,751
Land area (sq. miles)	6,933	Black	11.4%	District Income Rank	355
Pop/ sq mi	100.1	Latino	9.1%	Poverty Rate	17.2%
Born in State	72%	Asian	1.4%	With health insurance	92.8%
		Two or more races	2%	Cash public assistance	3%
Age Groups		Other	0.2%	Food stamp/SNAP	17.7%
Under 18	22.7%				
18-34	21.6%	**Education**		**Work**	
35-64	38.2%	H.S grad or less	47.2%	White Collar	17.5%
Over 64	17.5%	Some college	33.9%	Sales and Service	43.1%
		College Degree, 4 yr	12.7%	Blue Collar	29%
Military		Post grad	6.3%	Government	11.5%
Veteran/ Active Duty	8.7%				

2012 Pres. Vote	Obama	168,796	(57%)	Romney	119,789	(41%)		
2016 Pres. Vote	Trump	136,017	(47%)	Clinton	133,999	(46%)	Johnson	13,457	(5%)

Moline, Rock Island: Illinois' western prairies are some of America's richest agricultural land. They were first settled by Yankees coming overland from northern Indiana and Ohio and upstate New York. After 1848, Germans left their homeland in search of better opportunities and settled in a place that in many ways resembled the flat, orderly plains of northern Germany. These migrants farmed quarter-sections and built small towns, with banks and stores, community churches and libraries. As farming expanded, so did the need for agricultural equipment. Entrepreneurs and investors built farm-machinery factories, and the Quad Cities of the Mississippi — Davenport and Bettendorf in Iowa, Rock Island and Moline in Illinois — became one of the nation's biggest agricultural equipment-manufacturing centers. John Deere, a blacksmith from Vermont, set up a "self-polishing plow" shop in 1837 in the small Rock River town of Grand Detour Illinois. His company, now headquartered in Moline, ranked 102nd on the 2018 Fortune 500 list of largest American corporations From 2010 to 2016, the population in the Illinois parts of the Quad Cities dropped by 4 percent; tellingly, the population on the Iowa side of the river grew 4 percent during that period. The good news on both sides: Construction of a new, higher-capacity bridge across the river is scheduled for completion in 2021.

Caterpillar, which fell from 42nd in 2014 on the Fortune 500 list to 65th in 2018, has been an iconic Peoria brand that operates around the world. Its local payroll has shrunk to 12,000 from 35,000 jobs in the 1970s. With a worldwide drop in farm-commodity prices plus a weakening economy in some of those emerging-growth markets, overall sales of farm equipment plummeted. From 2012 to 2016, Cat's annual revenues dropped from $66 billion to $37 billion, though it bounced back to $45.5 billion in 2017. Adding to the local pain, the company announced in 2017 the move of its corporate headquarters from Peoria to the Chicago area. "Speed and agility for our senior leadership team to be able to travel around the globe is very important," the company's CEO said. Implicit in his explanation: For many of these top executives, plus their corporate advisers, the location of O'Hare International Airport was only part of the reality that fast-paced Chicago had more appeal than life in Peoria. The overall local impact has been devastating. In the early 1990s, nearly one in four Peoria jobs was in manufacturing; by 2016, that had dropped to one in eight.

The 17th Congressional District links the Illinois portion of the Quad Cities with arms extending to the Democratic-leaning parts of Peoria to the east and Rockford to the north. It takes in the hilly, almost mountainous country in the northwest corner of the state. The district is steeped in political history: Some 30 miles west of Rockford is Freeport, whose town square hosted 15,000 people coming to hear Abraham Lincoln and Stephen Douglas in one of their seven debates in 1858. Not far away, on a little river once navigable by Mississippi River steamboats, is Galena, the home of Ulysses S. Grant.

The district contains some of the few parts of rural America carried by Barack Obama, who took the district 57%-41% in 2012. Four years later, Democratic performance in the 17th was as bad as job numbers in Peoria. Donald Trump led Hillary Clinton 47-46%, a rare bright spot for Republicans in Illinois.

Darin LaHood (R)

Elected 2015, 2nd full term, b. Jul 05, 1968; Peoria; Loras College, B.A., 1990; John Marshall Law School, J.D., 1997; Catholic; Married (Kristen LaHood); 3 children.

Elected Office: IL Senate, 2011-2015.

Professional Career: Staff, U.S Rep. Charles Jeremy Lewis, 1990-1994; Cook County Prosecutor, 1997-1999; Tazewell County Prosecutor, 1999-2001; Prosecutor, NV U.S Attorney, 2001-2005; Adjunct Professor, University of Nevada- Las Vegas, 2003-2005.

DC Office: 1424 LHOB 20515, 202-225-6201, Fax: 202-225-9249, lahood.house.gov

State Offices: Bloomington, 309-205-9556; Jacksonville, 217-245-1431; Peoria, 309-671-7027; Springfield, 217-670-1653.

Committees: *Joint Economic*. *Ways & Means*: Oversight; Select Revenue Measures.

Group Ratings

	ADA	ACLU	AFL-CIO	LCV	ITI	COC	HAFA	ACU	CFG	FRC
2018	–	7%	–	0%	–	75%	75%	76%	55%	100%
2017	0%	C	21%	0%	C	93%	C	85%	74%	100%

Almanac Ratings 2017-18

	Economy	Social	Foreign	Composite
Liberal	3%	3%	0%	2%
Conservative	97%	97%	100%	98%

Key Votes of the 115th Congress

1. Obama-care revision	Y	5. Family planning regs	Y	9. Guantanamo prisoners	N
2. Tax Cuts	Y	6. Body cameras/immigration	N	10. Ground missiles, limit	N
3. Omnibus appropriations	N	7. Abortion ban	Y	11. Defense Dept. spending	Y
4. Dodd-Frank revision	Y	8. Concealed carry	Y	12. FISA rules	Y

Election Results

Election	Name (Party)	Vote (%)	Cand. Spent	Ind. Exp. Support	Ind. Exp. Oppose
2018 General	Darin LaHood (R)............................	195,927 (67%)	$922,073		
	Junius Rodriguez (D).....................	95,486 (33%)	$68,826		
2018 Primary	Darin LaHood (R)............................	61,722 (79%)			
	Donald Rients (R)...........................	16,535 (21%)			

Prior winning percentages: 2016 (72%), 2015 special (69%)

Republican Darin LaHood, who won a special election in September 2015, has faced minimal competition in his campaigns. With his seat on the powerful House Ways and Means Committee, he has restored stability to this traditionally GOP district.

LaHood, who had been a conservative state senator, is the son of former GOP Rep. Ray LaHood, who served seven terms before he retired and became secretary of Transportation under President Barack Obama. Ray LaHood earlier was an aide to Robert Michel, the longtime House minority leader. Darin LaHood, a Peoria native, earned his bachelor's from Loras College and a law degree from John Marshall Law School. He spent nine years as a state and federal prosecutor, including with the U.S. attorney's office in Las Vegas Nevada, where he was recognized for his "outstanding work in fighting terrorism." He returned home to join a law firm in Peoria and was elected to the state Senate in 2010. National Journal profiled him as "a media-shy, ethics-focused political scion," a welcome antithesis to his immediate predecessor, Republican Aaron Schock.

Elected to four terms, Schock drew more notice for his youth and buff physique until the focus shifted to his office-decorating tastes and lifestyle. An accumulation of well-publicized controversies involving his use of taxpayer money led him to announce his resignation in March 2015. Most notable was a Washington Post article about the lavish redecoration of his House office in the style of the popular television series Downton Abbey. He was indicted in 2016 on 24 counts, including wire fraud, false filings of tax returns and Federal Election Commission reports, and theft of government funds. His trial was set for June 2019.

After the seat became vacant, several prominent local Republicans stepped aside, in apparent recognition of LaHood's strength and the desire of local Republicans to avoid more controversy. His sole primary opponent was little-known Mike Flynn, a libertarian Republican political operative and a former editor of the Breitbart News conservative website. He criticized the LaHoods as career politicians out of touch with the real world. LaHood won the Republican primary, 69%-28%. Democrat Rob Mellon, a high school history teacher and captain in the Army Reserve, raised little money or attention. LaHood won the general, 71%-29%.

LaHood settled into the House with serious purpose and little attention. He helped to enact two bills during his first term: support for federal computer networking and information technology research; and a provision for fish and wildlife restoration in the Great Lakes that was part of a broader water-resources bill. In January 2018, he made a major career move when he won the seat on the Ways and Means Committee that had been left vacant by the resignation of Republican Rep. Pat Tiberi of Ohio. The committee had completed its chief work on health and tax legislation in 2017, though LaHood joined the panel's approval prior to the 2018 election of a bill to make the recent tax cuts permanent. He urged the Trump administration to reach agreement on trade deals with China and Mexico, as urged by farmers and manufacturers in his district.

With Democratic Rep. Dan Lipinski of Illinois (who served with the elder LaHood, as did his father, Rep. Bill Lipinski) he filed a resolution calling for a Joint Committee on the Organization of Congress to consider possible reforms. "Every generation or so, Congress has had to reevaluate itself and make big changes in order to be effective and responsive to the American people," LaHood said. Republican leaders ignored the proposal. But Nancy Pelosi agreed to create a select committee in exchange for the votes of several Democrats in her bid for House Speaker following the 2018 election.

LaHood has been easily reelected, and was in position to serve a lengthy career in the House. In 2016, he distanced himself from some of Donald Trump's controversial comments, though he supported Trump as preferable to Hillary Clinton.

IL-18: West-Central Illinois   **Cook Partisan Voting Index: R+15**

Population		Race and Ethnicity		Income	
Total	711,884	White	89%	Median Income	$62,337
Land area (sq. miles)	10,516	Black	3.7%	District Income Rank	154
Pop/ sq mi	67.7	Latino	2.7%	Poverty Rate	9.8%
Born in State	78%	Asian	2.7%	With health insurance	95.5%
		Two or more races	1.6%	Cash public assistance	1.5%
Age Groups		Other	0.4%	Food stamp/SNAP	9%
Under 18	22.3%				
18-34	21%	**Education**		**Work**	
35-64	39.4%	H.S grad or less	36.8%	White Collar	17.3%
Over 64	17.3%	Some college	31%	Sales and Service	39.9%
		College Degree, 4 yr	20.9%	Blue Collar	20.5%
Military		Post grad	11.3%	Government	14.6%
Veteran/ Active Duty	8.9%				

2012 Pres. Vote	Romney	203,198	(61%)	Obama	125,079	(37%)			
2016 Pres. Vote	Trump	210,530	(60%)	Clinton	115,441	(33%)	Johnson	17,058	(5%)

Parts of Peoria and Springfield: Old vaudeville bookers, presented with a new act, used to ask, "Will it play in Peoria?" The implication was that if an act went over in this small city on the bluffs above the Illinois River, 154 miles from Chicago and 171 miles from St. Louis, it would go over just about anywhere. In the first half of the 20th century, Peoria seemed pretty typical of America. If its citizens were mostly of British or German descent, with a small percentage of African Americans, that was the image of ordinary America that prevailed into the 1960s. But Peoria's economy has changed, much as America's has changed. This has been a heavy manufacturing town, dominated by big plants that produce farm machinery and earth-moving equipment. Its biggest employer has been Caterpillar, which was founded in 1910 with 12 employees; a century later, it is the world's leading producer of earth-moving and construction equipment, and one of America's major exporters.

But the blue-collar workers now are not so numerous and the unions have weakened. The Peoria area suffered terribly in the 1980s, as big farm-machinery plants laid off workers and some closed down. President Barack Obama came to Peoria to stump for his economic stimulus bill, which he said offered hope of a rebound for the manufacturing giant. But the revival of Caterpillar, a company that proudly operates around the world, proved of less benefit to Peoria: 95 percent of its potential customers live outside the United States, and the company feels a need to manufacture where it sells.

The 18th Congressional District of Illinois, variously configured, has been the Peoria district since the 1940s, and now includes nearly two-thirds of the city and its suburbs. Much of the downtown area and the Caterpillar campus in East Peoria, with six factory buildings along the Illinois River, are in the 17th District to the northwest. With all or parts of 10 counties, the 18th begins at Quincy along the Mississippi River and runs east through rich farmland to the suburbs of Peoria, Bloomington and Springfield. In addition to President Abraham Lincoln, who served one term in Congress, 1847-49, the 18th has been represented by two national Republican leaders: Everett McKinley Dirksen, who was the Senate Republican leader from 1959-69, and Robert Michel, House Republican leader from

1981-95. Democratic redistricters drew this as a heavily Republican district; the 60 percent for Donald Trump in 2016 was his second-best in the state.

INDIANA

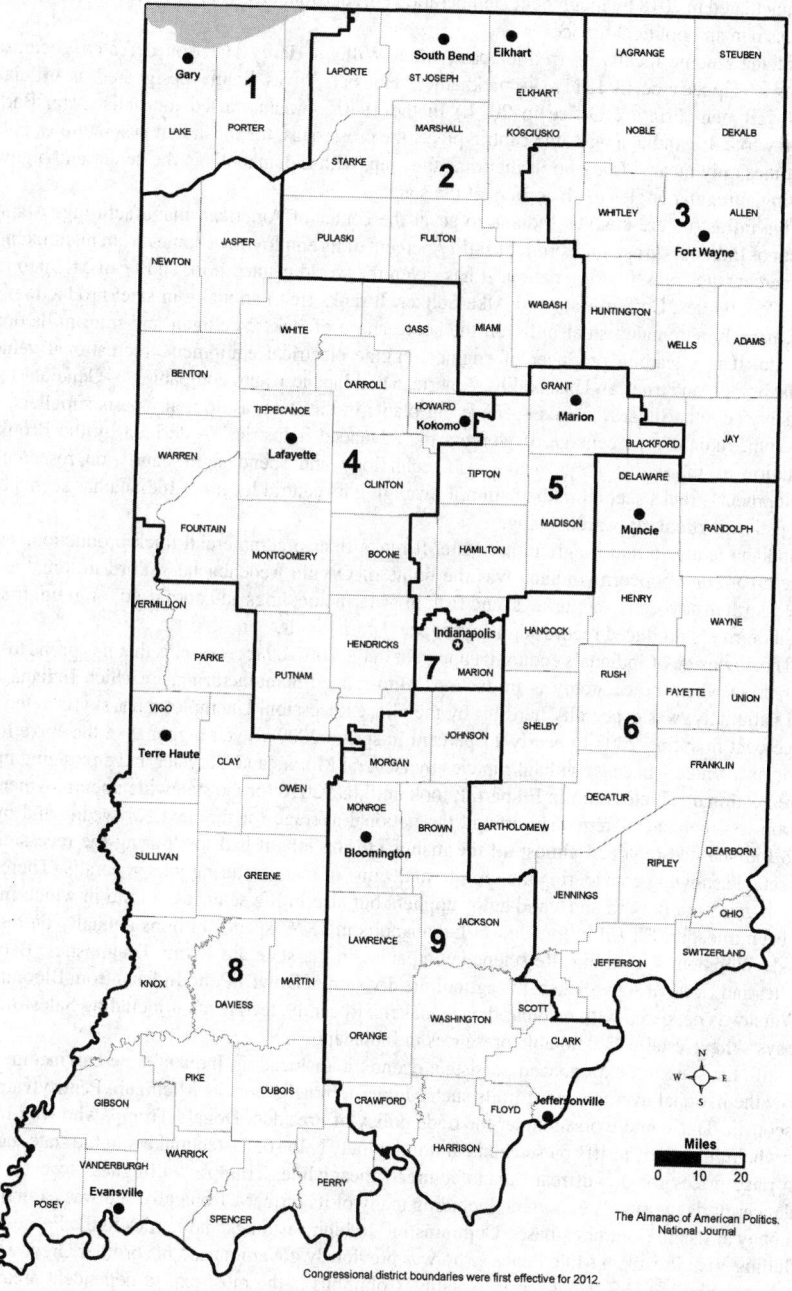

The Almanac of American Politics.
National Journal

Congressional district boundaries were first effective for 2012.

Indiana, a key manufacturing hub of the industrial Midwest and a major farm state, voted for Barack Obama in 2008 during a tough recession. But as the economy has recovered, the state has returned to its Republican roots. The Democrats' almost total wipeout in federal and statewide races was punctuated in 2018 by incumbent Democratic Sen. Joe Donnelly's six-point loss to a Republican businessman and political novice.

Indiana's name recalls its frontier past, when William Henry Harrison defeated Tecumseh's Indians at Tippecanoe in 1811. (Its nickname, "Hoosiers," was finally designated as official by the Government Printing Office in 2017.) In the 1940s, Indiana-raised journalist John Bartlow Martin wrote that Indiana was "the central place, the crossroads, the mean that is sometimes golden, sometimes only mean." Look no further than the map, with Indianapolis in the center and highways radiating at regular angles to all corners of the state.

This infrastructure enables Indiana to sit at the center of American manufacturing. About 29 percent of Indiana's gross state product and 17 percent of its employment comes from manufacturing; both percentages rank first the nation. It has given the world canned pork and beans, tomato juice, Coca-Cola bottles, Coffee-Mate and Alka-Seltzer. It ranks first nationally in steel production, with giant, heavily automated steel mills on the south shore of Lake Michigan and mini-mills dotting the state. It is a leading producer of engines, engine electrical equipment, recreational vehicles, mobile homes, and truck and bus bodies. American and Japanese auto companies — General Motors, Chrysler, Toyota, Subaru, Honda — have big plants in the state, as do many parts suppliers, such as Delphi. Indiana's percentage of workers in "advanced industries" – defined by the Brookings Institution as those that focus heavily on technology and spend significantly on research and development – ranks second in the nation. Leveraging its central location, Indiana has seen a boom in logistics, particularly warehousing.

Indiana is also a major agriculture state. It ranks first in commercial duck production, second in ice cream and popcorn (Indiana was the home of Orville Redenbacher), third in tomatoes and eggs, fourth in soybeans and turkeys, and fifth in watermelon, hogs and corn used for grain. In 2018, Indiana farmers produced record-high soybean and corn yields.

The downside of Indiana's economy, apparent in the 2007-09 recession, is that it is prone to sharp contraction when the economy is in decline. Auto-related manufacturing, in which Indiana ranks third nationally, was especially hard-hit by the Great Recession. Unemployment skyrocketed from 4.5 percent in spring 2007 to nearly 11 percent in spring 2009 – even higher than the spike for the nation as a whole – because of bankruptcies by General Motors and Chrysler and a plunging market for recreational vehicles built in Elkhart. It took until late 2016 for the statewide unemployment rate to drop to 4 percent. It remained around the national average for the next two years, and by late 2018 Indiana had regained almost all the manufacturing jobs it had lost during the recession -- a respectable showing considering the long-term decline of manufacturing jobs generally. There were big job gains not only in autos and auto suppliers but also in life sciences, a field in which Indiana has been a leader. Eli Lilly, founded in Indianapolis in 1876, spends billions annually on research and development. Other big life-science companies in the state are Roche Diagnostics, Beckman Coulter and Corteva Agriscience, the agriculture division of DowDuPont. Indiana from Bloomington to Warsaw is peppered with medical-device makers. Recently, tech firms -- including Salesforce and Infosys -- have established notable presences in Indianapolis.

Still, the state has experienced persistent economic dislocation: Indiana's median income ranks below the national average and it trails such Midwestern neighbors as Michigan, Pennsylvania and Wisconsin. This could worsen under the trade policy of President Donald Trump, who won Indiana overwhelmingly. His tariffs on steel and aluminum may help some steelmakers in the state, but they also raise prices for downstream manufacturers; meanwhile, Trump's willingness to enter into a trade war hurts the state's exporters, including many of its farmers. Ironically, a prime example of a company at risk is Columbus-based Cummins Inc., which has longstanding ties to the Pence family, including Vice President Mike Pence (who was previously governor) and his brother Greg, who just won a neighboring U.S. House seat. Notably, Columbus is the most export-dependent area in the country, according to Brookings. "I'm very worried," Cummins Chairman and CEO Tom Linebarger told The Washington Post.

One increasing source of economic activity in Indiana has been sports. Indiana's most famous venue opened in 1909 — the Indianapolis Motor Speedway, where the Indy 500 is still held every Memorial Day weekend. (The original bricks have been replaced by asphalt, except for one yard at the start/finish line.) Today, Indianapolis —capital of the state that gave America such basketball icons as Larry Bird, Bobby Knight and the movie "Hoosiers" — has refashioned itself as a national sports center, with the NFL's Colts at Lucas Oil Stadium, the NBA's Pacers at Bankers Life Fieldhouse, a Triple-A baseball team that is regularly one of the top-drawing minor-league clubs, NCAA headquarters in Indianapolis, and a guarantee of hosting Final Four basketball every few years.

Culturally, Indiana is a lot like an earlier America. Its one major hub, Indianapolis, is only the nation's 34th largest metro area, and 70 percent of the state's population resides elsewhere. The small-town ethos seeps into the songs of John Mellencamp, who is from Seymour. Except for the steel area around Gary — really a part of Chicagoland — Indiana has relatively few descendants from the 1840-1924 wave of immigration. Overall, its population is 10 percent black, 7 percent Hispanic and 2 percent Asian. It does have religious diversity, with 109 denominations; according to the Glenmary Research Center, only six states have more. In early 2015, Indiana played host to a high-profile, if brief, national battle between two big, longstanding constituencies within the state — its Christian conservatives and its pragmatic business class. These two camps battled over a religious-freedom law that critics said would make it possible for businesses to discriminate against gays and lesbians. After Pence signed the law, it drew fire not only from liberals but also from much of the state's business establishment, including such athletic mainstays as NASCAR, the NCAA and the NBA. The backlash pushed Pence and legislative leaders to scale back the measure, which in turn led to criticism from religious conservatives.

Indiana's politics have traditionally been shaped by a divide between Yankees from Ohio and New England, and "Butternuts," as they were called in the Civil War years, from Kentucky and the South. Most Yankees became Republicans, and most Butternuts became Democrats, a split that persisted for generations. Indiana was a crucial political target from the Civil War to the New Deal, a big reason why there were Hoosiers on 11 Republican and Democratic national tickets in the 16 elections between 1868 and 1928 — more than any other state except New York. Ancestral partisan ties enabled Democrats to hold the governorship from 1988 to 2004 and to be competitive in state legislative elections. At the presidential level, however, Indiana's cultural conservatism and lack of a dovish tradition generally kept it in the Republican column. It voted 56%-43% for Lyndon Johnson in 1964, but over the next 10 elections, it was so resolutely Republican that it was never even targeted by Democrats, and only one Hoosier, Dan Quayle, was placed on a national ticket. One reason for the Republican lean was that Indianapolis and the smaller factory towns were not as heavily Democratic as Chicago, Detroit or Cleveland, a trend reinforced by the 1970 consolidation of the city of Indianapolis and Marion County, which brought urban and suburban areas under the same jurisdictional umbrella.

For Democrats, 2008 was a high-water mark, when Barack Obama won the state at a time of economic distress. Since then, Democratic prospects in the more culturally conservative Butternut regions have cratered, hampering the party's statewide hopes; moderate Democrats like former Gov. and Sen. Evan Bayh (and his liberal father, Sen. Birch Bayh) have left less of a political and policy legacy than pragmatic Republicans such as long-serving Sen. Richard Lugar and two-term Gov. Mitch Daniels. The senior Bayh and Lugar both died within weeks of each other in early 2019.

In 2016, the Trump-Pence ticket ran strong in Indiana. Trump focused relentlessly on working-class white voters and the Midwestern manufacturing industry, underlined by his post-victory trip to the state to announce that some of Carrier's jobs would remain in the state rather than head to Mexico. (The company made the last of its 600 agreed-upon layoffs in January 2018; 1,100 jobs remain in Indianapolis.) Trump -- channeling the bristling charisma of basketball icon Knight, who endorsed him days before the primary -- defeated Hillary Clinton by 19 points, almost twice Mitt Romney's margin in 2012. While Obama won 15 counties in 2008 and nine in 2012, Clinton managed to win only four in 2016, and she came within 10 percentage points in only three others.

Democrats fared little better in 2018, when the big contest was over the seat held by Democratic Sen. Joe Donnelly. He had nabbed an open Senate seat in 2012 after Republican state Treasurer Richard Mourdock disastrously opined that pregnancy resulting from rape is part of God's plan.

In 2018, Donnelly faced businessman Mike Braun, who emerged from a vicious GOP primary and received strong backing from Trump, including a November rally in Fort Wayne. Donnelly stressed his bipartisan credentials and drew contrasts with his party's "radical left," but it wasn't enough; Braun prevailed, 51%-45. Donnelly won more than twice as many counties as Clinton and ran well in affluent Hamilton County, outpacing Clinton's vote totals by 4,000 even though Donnelly was running in a midterm rather than a presidential election year. He also won Vigo County (Terre Haute), in line with its somewhat mysterious pattern of following the national electoral tides; the county has voted for the losing presidential candidate only twice since the 1890s. But Donnelly was hammered in the state's rural areas, falling 20 percent short of his own vote totals from 2012. The Democrats did no better in House races: No election for a GOP-held seat was decided by less than 10 points.

Population		Race and Ethnicity		Income	
Total	6,614,418	White	79.8%	Median Income	$52,182
Land area (sq. miles)	35,826	Black	9.1%	State Income Rank	35
Pop/ sq mi	184.6	Latino	6.7%	Poverty Rate	14.6%
Born in state	68.3%	Asian	2.1%	With health insurance	89.7%
		Two or more races	1.9%	Cash public assistance	1.8%
Age Groups		Other	0.3%	Food stamp/SNAP	11.5%
Under 18	23.9%				
18-34	22.9%	Education		Work	
35-64	38.6%	H.S grad or less	45.5%	White Collar	33.2%
Over 64	14.6%	Some college	29.2%	Sales and Service	39.4%
		College Degree, 4 yr	16.1%	Blue Collar	27.4%
Military		Post grad	9.2%	Government	10.7%
Veteran/ Active Duty	8.0%				

Presidential Politics

2016 Primary (D) Sanders (D)	335,074 (52%)	Clinton (D)	303,705 (48%)		
2016 Primary (R) Trump (R)	591,514 (53%)	Cruz (R)	406,783 (37%)	Kasich (R)	84,111 (8%)
2016 Pres. Vote Trump (R)	1,557,286 (56%)	Clinton (D)	1,033,126 (37%)	Johnson (L)	133,993 (5%)
2012 Pres. Vote Romney (R)	1,420,543 (54%)	Obama (D)	1,152,887 (44%)		

Indiana rarely generates much drama in the race for the White House. In 1968, Robert F. Kennedy upset Eugene McCarthy and Lyndon Johnson's stand-in, Gov. Roger Branigin, in the Democratic primary. In 2008, Barack Obama contested the primary and general election. After organizing for the primary, which Obama narrowly lost to Clinton, his campaign set up 44 offices around the state for the general election and mobilized 80,000 volunteers. Obama carried only 15 of Indiana's 92 counties in the fall, but he got a big vote out of Gary and Indianapolis, cut into traditional GOP margins in the Indianapolis suburbs and exurbs, won blue-collar counties such as Delaware (Muncie) and Madison (Anderson) and swept college towns to post a 50%-49% win over Arizona Republican Sen. John McCain. Four years later the Obama campaign wrote off the state and Mitt Romney captured it easily, 54%-44%. In 2016, Donald Trump tapped Hoosier GOP Gov. Mike Pence as his running mate, and he increased the Republican margin in the state, defeating Hillary Clinton in November, 57%-38%. Trump's vow to restore manufacturing jobs resonated in the state's blue-collar communities and he won all but four counties: Lake (Gary), Marion (Indianapolis), Monroe (Bloomington and Indiana University) and St. Joseph (South Bend and the University of Notre Dame).

In the May 3 primaries, Indiana served up plenty of excitement. Texas Sen. Ted Cruz said that winning Indiana was critical to the success of his GOP nomination bid. He got a reasonably clear shot at Trump after Ohio Gov. John Kasich stopped campaigning in the state. Pence endorsed the Texan. And Cruz announced that former Republican White House hopeful Carly Fiorina would be his running mate should he capture the nomination. Cruz dropped his gloves and called Trump a "pathological liar" and an unparalleled "narcissist." Trump took up the challenge and waged a vigorous fight. His efforts were rewarded with a 53%-37% victory over Cruz, who won only five counties and announced the suspension of his campaign in his concession speech. The decisive win prompted Republican National Committee Chairman Reince Priebus to take to Twitter that night and declare that Trump was the party's "presumptive nominee." The next day, Kasich withdrew.

The outcome of the Democratic primary was less consequential, but it did sustain Vermont Sen. Bernie Sanders's bid. After losing four East Coast primaries a week earlier, Sanders desperately needed a win to slow Clinton's momentum. The Vermonter campaigned heavily in the state. Clinton nursed her lead and campaign resources, and decided not to spend any money on TV advertising before the primary. Sanders won 52%-48%. Clinton won Marion and Lake counties with their relatively high share of African-American voters, and 17 largely rural counties along the state's southern tier. Indiana has no party registration and it's likely that many voters felt the Republican primary was more pivotal, and engrossing, than the Democratic contest.

Congressional Districts

116th Congress Lineup	2D 7R	115th Congress Lineup	2D 7R

Indiana law provides that if the state House and Senate cannot agree on congressional redistricting, the decision goes to a five-member commission, with the tie-breaking member appointed by the governor. In 2011, Republicans had control of the process. They weakened the 2nd District for the Democrats. When Democratic Rep. Joe Donnelly in 2012 ran for the Senate, Republican Jackie Walorski took his House seat. That gave the GOP a 7-2 majority in the delegation, with Democrats retaining the 1st and 7th districts centered on Gary and Indianapolis. A look at the map shows that the nine districts seem to have been drawn logically and without many jagged lines.

If anything, the partisan patterns have become more entrenched. Since 2012, no House Republican has been seriously threatened. Four of the seven are serving their first or second term. Each of their predecessors ran for the Senate. In six of the seven GOP-held districts, Donald Trump ran better than Mitt Romney four years earlier. The exception was the 5th District in suburban Indianapolis, which had by far the highest median income in the state. Notably, the Democratic presidential vote slipped in the two Democratic-held districts.

Partisan control of the redistricting map has not always assured success. The 2nd, 8th and 9th districts recently have been the most competitive, with the greatest likelihood of party switches. Given the overwhelming Republican control of the legislature, Democrats must either find a way to win the governor's office in 2020 or run more competitive candidates for Congress. Another option would be to disperse some Democratic voters in the 1st and 7th districts into the outlying districts and make all of them more competitive. That option seems unlikely to draw much support in Indianapolis.

Eric Holcomb (R)

Elected 2016, term expires 2021, 1st term; b. May. 2, 1968, Indianapolis; Hanover College, BA; First Church of God; Married (Janet).

Military Career: U.S Navy, 1990-1996.

Elected Office: IN Lt. Governor 2016-2017; Chair, IN Republican Party, 2010-2013.

Professional Career: Staff, U.S Rep. John Holstettler 1997-2000; Chief of Staff, U.S Sen. Dan Coats 2013-2015.

Office: 200 W Washington St, Indianapolis, 46204; 317-232-4567; Fax: 317-232-3443; Website: in.gov/gov.

Lt. Gov.: Suzanne Crouch (R) **Atty. Gen:** Curtis Hill (R) **Sec. of State:** Connie Lawson (R)

State Legislature: Senate: 10D, 40R **House:** 33D, 67R

Election Results

Election	Name (Party)	Vote (%)
2016 General	Eric Holcomb (R)..	977,362 (53%)
	John Gregg (D)...	844,343 (46%)

Eric Holcomb was elected governor of Indiana in 2016, even though he entered the race less than four months before Election Day. On July 26, Holcomb -- who had become lieutenant governor only five months earlier -- became the Republican Party's choice to be its gubernatorial nominee, filling the void left when Donald Trump tapped GOP Gov. Mike Pence as his running mate. Holcomb faced a competitive general-election contest but won by a wider-than-expected margin amid a pro-Trump wave in the state. He has governed in the pragmatic mold of his former boss, Republican Gov. Mitch Daniels, rather than following Pence's more ideologically charged approach.

Holcomb grew up in Indianapolis and earned a degree in American history from Hanover College, the same school Pence had graduated from nine years earlier. (The two governors belonged to the same fraternity but didn't overlap.) Holcomb served a six-year stint in the Navy in Jacksonville Florida and Lisbon Portugal, then got involved in Republican politics in Indiana. He lost a race for state representative, served as campaign manager and district director for Rep. John Hostettler, and worked in several positions, including deputy chief of staff, for Daniels between 2003 and 2011. He was also the director of Daniels' Aiming Higher PAC, which proved critical in electing a long-lasting Republican legislative supermajority. After working for Daniels, Holcomb served for two years as chairman of the Indiana Republican Party. Later, he served as chief of staff to the state's Republican senator, Dan Coats, before resigning in 2015 to run for the seat Coats was vacating. But with weak polling, Holcomb exited that race. Then Lt. Gov. Sue Ellspermann resigned and Pence nominated him as her successor. The legislature approved the appointment in March 2016.

Pence was set to run for a second term as governor in 2016 against Democrat John Gregg, the moderate former state House Speaker he had defeated narrowly in 2012. Then, in July, Trump tapped Pence as his running mate, and the gubernatorial contest was thrown into flux. Pence was already the official nominee for governor and, under party rules, it was up to the state party to choose a new nominee. Several well-known Republicans sought the nod, including Reps. Susan Brooks and Todd Rokita. Of these, Holcomb was the only one who had never won an election (though he has shot a basketball in a high school gym in all 92 counties in the state). On July 26, the party formally tapped Holcomb, following the lead of Pence, who had endorsed his No. 2.

The two campaigns had enough money to compete – Holcomb was bolstered by generous funding from the Republican Governors Association, while Gregg got a boost from Democratic spending intended primarily to help elect former Sen. Evan Bayh to Coats' Senate seat – but Gregg seemed to have the edge, with the Democrat up in polls by between four and 12 points as late as October. On Election Day, however, the Trump-led tide in the state was too much for Gregg to overcome. Holcomb won by a narrower margin than Trump's 19-point victory, but it was enough -- 51%-45%, close to Pence's winning margin in 2012.

Aided by a Republican-dominated legislature, Holcomb enacted many of his campaign proposals. In 2017, he expanded a pre-kindergarten pilot program to cover 20 counties; he signed a bill to make the state education superintendent an appointed post rather than an elected position beginning in 2024; he lowered reimbursement levels for electricity ratepayers who install solar or wind capacity; and he released a five-year, $4.7 billion road maintenance and construction plan that included the completion of Interstate 69 as well as maintenance, resurfacing or replacement of thousands of miles of roads and bridges. The funds will come from a 10-cent-a-gallon gas tax hike that is expected to collect $1.2 billion per year by 2025. Holcomb also signed a bill that allowed counties to establish needle exchanges, rather than having to wait for state approval. Needle exchanges were initially encouraged following some debate after a major HIV outbreak in Scott County in 2015. The need has only intensified with the spread of opioid addiction; overdose deaths in Indiana set a record in 2017, costing the state economy an estimated $4.3 billion, according to Indiana University's Kelley School of Business.

In 2018, Holcomb pleased conservatives by signing a law that would require medical providers to report detailed information to the state if they treat women who experience complications from abortion. He made liberals and moderates happy when he signed a law ending occupational licensing restrictions on "dreamers," or immigrants who had been brought illegally into the United States when they were children. Meanwhile, Holcomb struck a deal with the operator of the Indiana Toll Road, a 156-mile long throughway that stretches from Illinois to Ohio, that allowed the operator to hike truck tolls by 35 percent in exchange for transferring $1 billion to the state for road work. About 80 percent of the proceeds were earmarked for expanding I-65 and I-70 by 2024, while much of the remainder was allocated to improving U.S. highways in the northern part of the state.

Holcomb did have a couple of headaches in 2018. He failed to convince the Indiana Republican Party to strike its four-year-old platform language defining its preferred family structure as marriage "between a man and a woman." Holcomb had urged language that rhetorically supported all adults who had children. He urged Republican Attorney General Curtis Hill to resign following allegations that he had groped several women at a legislative celebration in March. However, neither the calls by Holcomb nor by fellow Republicans Brian Bosma, the House speaker, and David Long, the Senate president pro tem, succeeded in pushing Hill from office. Holcomb has also struggled with a long-running problem in the state – overseeing the Indiana Department of Child Services.

The biggest threat to the state, however, came from Trump's trade policy, which helped some steelmakers but hurt a much broader group of downstream manufacturers and exporters, including farmers. Holcomb straddled the divide, saying he appreciated Trump's desire to punish "those who do not play by the rules," but adding that he wanted "exemptions that protect Indiana's trading partners." All told, Holcomb has had a relatively low profile in office and has shied away from bold initiatives, but he has been steady and personable, and has received high marks from the voters who are aware of him.

Todd Young (R)

Elected 2016, term expires 2022, 1st term, b. Aug 24, 1972; Lancaster, PA; U.S. Naval Academy (MD), B.S., 1995; University of Chicago's Graduate School of Business, M.B.A., 2000; University of London's Institute of U.S. Studies, M.A., 2001; Leipzig Graduate School of Management, 2001; Indiana University Law School, J.D., 2006; Christian Church; Married (Jennifer T. Young); 4 children.

Military Career: U.S. Navy 1990-1991; U.S. Marine Corps 1995-2000.

Elected Office: US House, 2011-2017.

Professional Career: Staff, Heritage Foundation, 2001; Legislative Assistant, Sen. Richard Lugar, 2001-2003; Adviser, Governor Mitch Daniels, 2004; Management consultant, 2004-2006; Deputy prosecutor, Orange County, 2007-2010.

DC Office: 185 DSOB 20510, 202-224-5623, young.senate.gov
State Offices: Evansville, 812-350-8956; Fort Wayne, 260-422-7397; Indianapolis, 812-288-3999; New Albany, 812-336-3000.

Committees: National Republican Senatorial Committee Chairman. *Commerce, Science & Transportation*: Communications, Technology, Innovation & the Internet; Manufacturing, Trade & Consumer Protection; Subcommittee on Security; Subcommittee on Transportation & Safety. *Finance*: Health Care; International Trade, Customs & Global Competitiveness; Social Security, Pensions & Family Policy. *Foreign Relations*: East Asia, the Pacific & International Cybersecurity Policy; Internat'l Dev Instit & Internat'l Econ, Energy & Environ Policy (Chmn); State Dept & USAID Mngmnt, Internat'l Ops & Internat'l Dev. *Small Business & Entrepreneurship*.

Group Ratings

	ADA	ACLU	AFL-CIO	LCV	ITI	COC	HAFA	ACU	CFG	FRC
2018	-	5%	-	7%	-	90%	68%	91%	59%	100%
2017	0%	C	0%	0%	C	86%	C	80%	81%	100%

Almanac Ratings 2017-18

	Economy	Social	Foreign	Composite
Liberal	0%	0%	20%	7%
Conservative	100%	100%	81%	94%

Key Votes of the 115th Congress

1. Obama-care revision	Y	5. Gun regulations	Y	9. Kavanaugh confirmation	Y
2. Tax Cuts	Y	6. Family planning regs	Y	10. Saudi arms sales	Y
3. Dodd-Frank revision	Y	7. Gorsuch confirmation	Y	11. FISA rules	Y
4. Omnibus appropriations	Y	8. Immigration restrictions	Y	12. Military aid in Yemen	Y

Election Results

Election	Name (Party)	Vote (%)	Cand. Spent	Ind. Exp. Support	Ind. Exp. Oppose
2016 General	Todd Young (R)............................. 1,423,991	(52%)	$15,194,428	$3,591,044	$16,862,554
	Evan Bayh (D)............................. 1,158,947	(42%)	$10,886,830	$388,888	$23,884,578
	Lucy Brenton (L)................................ 149,481	(6%)	$483		
2016 Primary	Todd Young (R)............................. 661,136	(67%)			
	Marlin Stutzman (R)........................... 324,429	(33%)			

Prior winning percentages: House: 2014 (62%); 2012 (55%); 2010 (52%)

Todd Young, Indiana's senior senator, was one of just two new Republicans elected to that body in 2016, concurrent with Donald Trump's surprise White House win. But if Young was generally a loyal supporter of Trump during his first two years in the Senate — ratings by FiveThirtyEight showed Young voting in favor of the president's position nearly 93 percent of the time — his style has been more akin to former Indiana GOP Sen. Richard Lugar, for whom Young once worked. In a third of a century on Capitol Hill, Lugar established a reputation as a pragmatic conservative who frequently reached across the political aisle. Likewise, Young described himself as an "independent-minded, center-right conservative Republican" in a 2018 interview with the South Bend Tribune. "But I went to Washington to get things done. Typically, that requires developing strong relationships with your Democratic colleagues." In fact, a think tank established by Lugar ranked Young among its Top 10 senators in its 2017 "Bipartisan Index," which measures sponsorship of legislation with members of the other party. But Young may be faced with a political balancing act when he chairs the National Republican Senatorial Committee during the 2020 cycle — a job in which he will be tasked with preserving the Senate GOP majority.

For much of the latter part of the 20th century, the Senate seat Young holds was occupied by two men: Democrat Birch Bayh and Republican Dan Quayle, both of whom went on to achieve national prominence. After that, control of the seat for nearly three decades shifted between two Hoosiers with close ties to either Bayh or Quayle: Dan Coats, who got his political start as a Quayle aide, and Evan Bayh, Birch Bayh's son and a former governor. Young falls within this tradition: His wife is a niece of Marilyn Quayle, who is married to former Vice President Dan Quayle. And Young won in 2016 by thwarting Evan Bayh's comeback bid in one of that year's marquee Senate contests.

While Young was born in Lancaster, Pa., and spent his first 13 years outside Indiana, his family has ties to the Hoosier State stretching back five generations. His father owns a small heating and air-conditioning equipment business; his mother is a registered nurse. Young went to high school in Hamilton County, a well-to-do suburb of Indianapolis, where his prowess as a soccer player helped his school's team win a state championship. He enlisted in the Navy after high school, and, a year later, received an appointment to the U.S. Naval Academy, where he also played on the soccer team. Upon graduation, he opted for service in the Marine Corps, where he worked with drones doing reconnaissance work — including a stint fighting narcotics trafficking in the Caribbean.

Transferred to Chicago to oversee Marine recruiting, Young attended the University of Chicago's business school at night, earning an M.B.A. while becoming a fan of free-market economist Friedrich von Hayek. Young went on to the University of London's Institute for the Study of the Americas, where he received a second master's degree and wrote a thesis on the economic history of Midwestern agriculture. Moving to Washington, he worked at the conservative Heritage Foundation and as a legislative assistant to Lugar. In 2004, Young returned to Indiana to work on the gubernatorial campaign of Republican Mitch Daniels.

While attending Indiana University's law school at night, he met his wife, Jennifer Tucker Young. After Young earned his law degree in 2006, he and his wife went to work at a law firm established by her great-grandfather in the southern Indiana town of Paoli, commuting from nearby Bloomington. Now the parents of four children, they continue to reside in Bloomington — home of Indiana University's main campus and an island of liberalism in a red state that has voted Democratic in only one presidential election in the past 50 years. "I'm a Bloomington conservative. My wife and I call it missionary work," Young has joked on occasion.

In January 2009, Young announced plans to run for the House of Representatives seat held by Democrat Baron Hill, who was first elected in 1998. Young narrowly won a three-way primary that included former Rep. Mike Sodrel — who had ousted Hill in 2004, only to see Hill regain the seat two years later. In the 2010 fall campaign, Young attacked Hill as a rubber stamp for the Obama administration. Hill, a former high school basketball star in a hoops-crazy state, emphasized his Hoosier roots and characterized Young as an out-of-touch lawyer who had spent much of his career outside Indiana. In a year in which House Democrats lost more than 60 seats nationwide, Young ousted Hill 52%-42%.

Having cultivated ties to House leaders, Young was awarded a prized seat on the Ways and Means Committee at the beginning of his second term in 2013. The same year, he took over as lead sponsor of a key legislative initiative for Republican conservatives: the REINS Act, which would have given Congress oversight of federal regulations with economic effects exceeding $100 million. Unlike some of his more hard-line Class of 2010 colleagues, he supported the 2011 compromise to raise the debt limit, saying he wanted deeper spending cuts but that the measure "moves us in the right direction." But, despite his desire to work with Democrats, Young at times utilized sharp rhetoric, once calling Senate Democratic Leader Harry Reid "useless" and Reid's House counterpart, Nancy Pelosi, "an irrelevant cheerleader for lost-cause liberalism." He had a competitive re-election fight in 2012, defeating his Democratic opponent, Shelli Yoder, a former Miss Indiana who called for turning the region into a leader in clean energy, 55%-45%, but had little trouble winning a third term in 2014.

After the second of two separate stints in the Senate, Coats — who would go on to become the director of national intelligence in the Trump administration — announced his retirement in March 2015. Young, then 42, announced his bid to succeed Coats in July of that year. The state GOP establishment rallied around Young, and several other House Republicans opted to run for re-election after having eyed the Senate seat. But Rep. Marlin Stutzman, who had mounted a tea party-infused insurgency in the primary against Coats six years earlier, ran again. He charged that the "D.C. establishment" had selected Young "to play as their puppet." Initially, it appeared Young's prospects were complicated by the presence of another party establishment candidate: former state GOP Chairman Eric Holcomb. But Holcomb withdrew just days after the filing deadline, opting to become the running mate of then-Gov. Mike Pence.

Young's next hurdle was an effort by Indiana Democrats to have him thrown off the primary ballot for not having filed enough petition signatures in one congressional district. The national GOP came to Young's aid, and the state election commission rejected the ballot challenge. In the May primary, Young overwhelmed Stutzman, 67%-33%, and seemed poised to cruise to victory against the Democrats' candidate: Hill, his 2010 opponent. However, in July 2016, Evan Bayh — who earlier had turned aside entreaties to run again for the seat that he held from 1998 to 2010 — was persuaded to change his mind, and Hill stepped aside. Early public opinion polls showed Bayh with a 20-point lead, and national Democrats saw him as a shoo-in. But it didn't take long for problems to surface for Bayh.

Unlike his father — author of the 25th and 26th amendments to the U.S. Constitution — the younger Bayh never appeared fully comfortable in the Senate. After forgoing re-election in 2010, he said he was fed up with congressional gridlock in an op-ed for The New York Times. Bayh said it was time for him to "contribute to society in another way." By the end of the campaign, Young — aided by nearly $29 million from independent groups — had succeeded in reframing Bayh's desire to contribute to society into a question of how much society had contributed to Bayh. The Democrat's net worth had increased six fold after he left the Senate, and he was put on the defensive by an Associated Press report disclosing he had had numerous conversations with headhunters and future corporate employers during his last year on Capitol Hill. The report noted Bayh was among a small group of Democrats who helped kill a tax increase on private equity gains. The increase was opposed by Apollo Global Management, with whom Bayh had met — and for whom he later went to work. Compounding the controversy was that, prior to publication of the AP report, Bayh told The Indianapolis Star he had not met with Apollo Global during that period.

Bayh's ties to the state since leaving the Senate also came into question. His voter status had been classified as inactive. And, while asserting that he remained an Indiana resident, he was found to have rarely spent time at an Indianapolis condominium he owned — during a local television interview, he couldn't recall the correct address of the residence. Such stumbles were symptomatic of Bayh's apparent expectation that he could return to his old seat without major effort; he was unprepared for the rigors of a competitive campaign. By mid-October, some polls were showing the race had become a dead heat. Independent expenditure groups poured in $18 million in an effort to prop up his struggling candidacy. It wasn't enough: The final returns gave Young a 52%-42% win.

Like his onetime boss Lugar, who took on Republican and Democratic presidents on foreign policy, Young has challenged the White House on that front — particularly on the war in Yemen. In December 2018, he was among just seven Republicans to join with all Senate Democrats to support a resolution withdrawing U.S. support for Saudi-backed forces in Yemen. Young, a member of the Foreign Relations Committee, also authored legislation with the panel's ranking Democrat, Robert Menendez of New Jersey, to suspend U.S. arms sales to Saudi Arabia because of that country's efforts to prevent food and medical supplies from entering Yemen. Earlier, Young had put a hold on Senate confirmation of Trump's choice for State Department legal adviser, which he lifted after Trump agreed to press the Saudis to lift their blockade of Yemeni ports — a tactic that had triggered concerns of widespread famine. "It offends my sensibilities — and I know it offends the sensibilities of all Americans — that there are countries in this day and age that are using food as a weapon of war," Young told USA Today in late 2018. "And it further offends my sensibilities ... that the United States has partnered with these countries."

On domestic issues, perhaps Young's most notable bipartisan legislative effort has been a bill authored with Sen. Elizabeth Warren of Massachusetts. The measure, which cleared the House and Senate at the end of 2018, requires federal agencies to report in their budget requests whether they acted on recommendations by federal auditors and inspectors for cost reductions and program improvements. Young contended that $90 billion in savings could result if such recommendations were followed. "Let's face it: She's sort of emblematic of the left," Young told the South Bend Tribune: "I candidly wanted to send a message. I can work with anyone, anyone who wants to advance a good government agenda."

Notwithstanding such bipartisan efforts, Young sought the highly partisan task of heading the NRSC for the 2020 election cycle and was chosen by the Senate GOP Caucus without opposition. "I'm really excited about the opportunity. ... The committee did a lot to help my campaign back in 2016, and I think I can do a lot to make sure we defend and strengthen the Republican majority," Young told the AP. He will face the challenging task of defending 22 Republican-held seats as the Democrats defends just 12 — with Trump on top of the ballot. In 2017, Young exhibited his independent streak when — in a move that put him at odds with Trump — he joined then-NRSC Chairman Cory Gardner of Colorado in calling on Roy Moore to step aside as the Republican Senate nominee in Alabama. It followed revelations of sexual advances toward teenage girls by Moore while in his 30s. "After giving Roy Moore ample time to unequivocally deny the disturbing allegations against him, those allegations remain far more persuasive than the denials," Young tweeted. "The appearance of grossly reprehensible behavior disqualifies him from service in the United States Senate. If he does not step aside, we need to act to protect the integrity of the Senate."

Mike Braun (R)

Elected 2018, term expires 2024, 1st term, b. Mar 24, 1954; Jasper; Wabash College (IN), B.A., 1976; Harvard University, M.B.A., 1978; Catholic; Married (Maureen Braun); 4 children.

Elected Office: IN House, 2014-2017.

Professional Career: Owner, Meyer Distributing.

DC Office: 374 RSOB 20510, 202-224-4814, braun.senate.gov

State Offices: Evansville, 317-822-8240; Fort Wayne, 260-427-2164; Hammond, 219-937-9650; Indianapolis, 317-822-8240; South Bend, 574-288-6302.

Committees: *Aging. Agriculture, Nutrition & Forestry*: Conservation, Forestry & Natural Resources (Chmn); Livestock, Marketing & Agriculture Security; Rural Development & Energy. *Budget. Environment & Public Works*: Clean Air & Nuclear Safety (Chmn); Fisheries, Water, and Wildlife; Transportation & Infrastructure. *Health, Education, Labor & Pensions*: Employment & Workplace Safety; Primary Health & Retirement Security.

Election Results

Election	Name (Party)	Vote (%)	Cand. Spent	Ind. Exp. Support	Ind. Exp. Oppose
2018 General	Mike Braun (R)............................ 1,158,000	(51%)	$19,149,604	$3,437,301	$30,910,945
	Joe Donnelly (D)............................ 1,023,553	(45%)	$15,686,770	$10,720,943	$24,767,726
	Lucy Brenton (Lib)........................ 100,942	(4%)			
2018 Primary	Mike Braun (R)............................ 208,602	(41%)			
	Todd Rokita (R)............................ 151,967	(30%)			
	Luke Messer (R)............................ 146,131	(29%)			

One of the most talked-about — and arguably successful — TV ads of the 2018 midterm elections depicted Republican Mike Braun, now Indiana's junior senator, toting life-size cardboard cutouts of his two GOP Senate primary opponents, Reps. Luke Messer and Todd Rokita. In the cutouts, both House members are wearing navy suits, white shirts and red ties: It's what they wore during the first televised debate of the campaign, at which Braun appeared in a blue shirt wearing neither coat nor tie. In the ad, several voters say they can't tell Messer and Rokita apart and Braun, posing with the two cardboard candidates, asks the television audience, "Can you pick out the businessman in this lineup?" In a primary in which all three contenders ran as avid supporters of President Donald Trump, the ploy underscored Braun's contention that he most closely reflected the outsider profile of the businessman in the White House.

Braun won the nomination and, in November, ousted one-term Democratic Sen. Joe Donnelly in a traditionally Republican state trending increasingly red — as he derided the low-profile incumbent with Trumpian nicknames like "Sleepin' Joe" and "Mexico Joe." The latter was a reference to Donnelly having invested in a company run by his brother that created jobs in Mexico. Like Trump, Braun is not only a businessman, but a wealthy one: His holdings, pegged at between $35 million and $96 million in a disclosure form, place him among the five wealthiest senators. Most of Braun's wealth is from an auto-parts distribution firm he expanded over three decades. But, with 6,000 acres of land — mostly timber stands — spread over nine Indiana counties, Braun is among the state's largest private landowners. And, also like Trump, Braun didn't hesitate to fund his own campaign. He poured nearly $11.6 million in personal loans into his campaign, more than half of that during the primary — which was key to his overtaking the House members initially considered the front-runners.

But unlike Trump, Braun is considered frugal by family and friends; he scoffs at companies that operate with "extreme overhead and Taj Mahal corporate headquarters." He worked out of a trailer for years even after his business had become successful. He didn't buy a new vehicle until he was in his 50s. While Trump has faced multiple bankruptcies, Braun credits thriftiness with helping his business survive two recessions that killed off many competitors. "You live like you are going out of business every day and it makes you healthy," he told The Indianapolis Star. "He is the most conservative, tightest guy I know," his wife of 40 years, Maureen Braun, said.

Braun, 65, grew up in the Southern Indiana town of Jasper, where he still lives. After earning his undergraduate degree from Wabash College in Crawfordsville, Ind., he left the state to earn an MBA from Harvard Business School. Returning to Jasper, he sold kitchen cabinets for three years and co-founded Crystal Farms Inc. — now one of the largest turkey operations in the Midwest — before joining his father's business manufacturing truck bodies for farmers. The enterprise almost failed during the farm crisis of the early 1980s. Braun responded by redirecting the business toward selling truck accessories, later expanding it to include warehousing and shipping. Today, the firm, Meyer Distributing, employs more than 900 workers in 35 states. Before he joined the Senate, Braun's political experience comprised 10 years on the Jasper School Board and a three-year stint in the Indiana House of Representatives that began in 2015. His interest in the latter post appears to have been piqued by his younger brother, Steve Braun, winning a state legislative seat two years earlier from the Indianapolis suburbs.

Re-elected to the Indiana House in 2016, Mike Braun resigned in November 2017 to focus on his Senate bid. It was several months after Messer and Rokita entered the contest, which would come to be described as one of the nastiest contests of the 2018 midterm elections. Messer and Rokita overlapped at Wabash College and, in the quarter of a century that followed, had seen each other as rivals as they climbed the political ladder: Rokita as Indiana secretary of state before election to Congress and Messer as a member of the state Legislature before moving to Washington, where he became a member of the congressional leadership as chairman of the House Republican Policy

Committee. Their entry into the Senate race was preceded by months of jockeying in the competition to take on Donnelly — elected six years earlier largely because of self-inflicted wounds by his Republican opponent and viewed by many GOP strategists as the most vulnerable Senate Democrat up for election in 2018.

In the end, Braun's primary victory was attributable to both his wealth, which allowed him to air TV ads before Messer and Rokita did, and the common political dynamic of front-running candidates damaging each other so badly that a third contender wins. Rokita made issues of Messer moving his family out of Indiana and to a home in the Washington suburbs and a $240,000 annual contract for part-time legal work paid to Messer's wife by an Indianapolis suburb. Messer accused Rokita of "spreading lies and half-truths," prompting a memo from the Rokita camp labeling Messer "unhinged" and a "ticking time bomb." They tried to outdo each other in fealty to Trump: A Rokita TV ad showed him in a "Make America Great Again" hat, while Messer trumpeted efforts to nominate the president for a Nobel Peace Prize for having brought North Korea to the negotiating table. But Rokita was quick to point to 2016 comments by Messer suggesting Trump was not up to the job of being president, while Messer's camp highlighted Rokita calling Trump "vulgar if not profane" in a published interview at the time.

Messer and Rokita focused on attacking each other even as Braun gained ground, albeit Braun had found himself criticized for voting in Democratic primaries until 2012 — two years before his election to the Indiana House as a Republican. Braun defended himself as a lifelong Republican while saying that, given longtime Democratic dominance in some Southern Indiana counties, he and other conservatives had little choice but to vote in Democratic primaries if they wanted a say in local government. For his part, Braun criticized Messer and Rokita as "career politicians" and lawyers "who never really practiced." In his final TV ad before the May primary, Braun sought to reinforce his shared background with Trump as businessman and political outsider, saying he was running because "President Trump paved the way." Braun won the primary with 41 percent of the vote, while Rokita and Messer finished with 30 percent and 29 percent, respectively.

In Donnelly, Braun faced a general election opponent widely labeled an "accidental senator." A New York native who earned undergraduate and law degrees from the University of Notre Dame in South Bend, Donnelly was elected in 2006 to represent a House district including that area. In 2011, after the district was redrawn, Donnelly ran for the Senate. He started out as a long shot, but the seat became in play after tea party-backed state Treasurer Richard Mourdock toppled six-term Sen. Richard Lugar in the Republican primary. While the then-80-year-old Lugar's primary defeat was attributed to having lost touch with GOP voters, Mourdock did himself in during the general election with incendiary comments. Asked about abortions in cases of rape, Mourdock said: "Life is that gift from God. And I think even when life begins in that horrible situation of rape, that it is something that God intended to happen." Donnelly — an abortion rights opponent who said the procedure should be permitted in cases of rape and incest — capitalized on Mourdock's missteps, winning by 50%-44%.

In the Senate, Donnelly kept a low profile, crafting a centrist voting record and focusing on issues — like improving care for veterans and combating opioid addiction — that didn't invite sharp partisan divisions. Halfway through his term, the Lugar Center — a Washington-based think tank founded by Lugar — issued a "bipartisan index" that found Donnelly to be fourth-most bipartisan senator to serve during the previous two decades. But, unlike several of his Democratic colleagues from red states — who had developed distinct resumes and personas to transcend partisan disadvantages — Donnelly's efforts at bipartisanship placed him on a political tightrope.

Donnelly was among only three Senate Democrats who, early in the Trump administration, voted to confirm Supreme Court nominee Neil Gorsuch — angering his base. Later in 2017, when he came under intense pressure to support Republicans' tax cut bill, there were suggestions he could invite a primary challenge by doing so. Donnelly ultimately voted against the measure, calling it a "giveaway to Wall Street and other big money interests." His decision triggered attacks from Trump. Donnelly — whose pro-Trump voting score was the third highest among Senate Democrats, according to ratings by FiveThirtyEight — sought to inoculate himself from Republican voters' anger by emphasizing areas where he agreed with the president. In one ad, he highlighted his support of Trump's proposed southern border wall. Another ad showed the president praising Donnelly during a bill signing ceremony for "right to try" legislation he had sponsored that enabled patients with terminal illnesses to obtain unapproved drugs that might save their lives.

For a time, it appeared Donnelly might pull off this delicate balancing act: Polls at the outset of the fall election season showed him a few points ahead of Braun. And some within the GOP fretted about the tempo of the Braun campaign as Donnelly campaigned hard throughout the state.

But Braun kept pumping in his own money — $2.7 million in loans just in the final month of the campaign — as he campaigned on a platform in lockstep with Trump, including support of the border wall and repeal of the Affordable Care Act, which Donnelly supported. On international trade — of key significance in a state in which both agriculture and nonfarm manufacturing play leading economic roles — Braun had expressed opposition to tariffs during the primary campaign. But he later modified his position to put himself more in line with Trump's aggressive use of tariffs, calling concerns about them overdramatized — as Donnelly decried their negative effects on the state's economy. Responding to the "Mexico Joe" taunts, a Donnelly ad went after Braun's business for selling Chinese-made auto parts. "I voted against every bad trade deal that hurts Hoosiers," Donnelly was quoted as saying by Bloomberg News. "Mike Braun has used those same trade deals to outsource Hoosier jobs to China."

Braun steered clear of the media after debates, and, in contrast to Mourdock six years earlier, avoided mistakes. But it was the furor over Brett Kavanaugh's confirmation to the Supreme Court in the closing weeks of the campaign that may have sealed the outcome. As the nomination was headed to the Senate floor, Donnelly was among the last senators to tip his hand — saying he had "deep reservations" about putting Trump's nominee on the high court, following allegations by Christine Blasey Ford that Kavanaugh had sexually assaulted her when they both were in high school. In the view of independent observers, it energized the Republican base while nationalizing the Senate contest in a state Trump had carried by 19 points. Braun appeared to share this view, telling The New York Times, "The thing that took the whole energy level up was Judge Kavanaugh ... It boosted all races across the country and especially here, measurably so."

Trump visited the state three times during the final two weeks of the campaign, and, by the end, the contest ranked third among 2018 Senate races in independent expenditure funding — with $41 million going to prop up Donnelly and $28 million to boost Braun. On Election Day, Braun won, 51%-45%; Donnelly captured just eight counties, compared to 27 in 2012. And he appeared to have been whipsawed between Republicans unhappy over his opposition to Kavanaugh and Democrats turned off by his efforts to woo Trump voters. "It looks like Joe Donnelly's attempt to run to the middle turned off his base in a way that was detrimental to him," Andy Downs, director of the Mike Downs Center for Indiana Politics, told The Indianapolis Star. "Donnelly beat up on the far left quite a bit, and there were voters across the state who were turned off by that and did not want to hold their noses and go out and vote for him."

Braun pledged during the campaign to refuse a pension and serve no more than two terms before returning to the woods around Jasper — where he likes to hunt rabbits, doves and quail. His passion is said to be an annual quest for valuable morel mushrooms, which appear briefly each spring. As for his willingness to dig deep into his pocket in his hunt for a Senate seat — despite his frugal nature — Braun told the Star, "That's how big a deal I think it is that if guys like me don't step in, across the spectrum, that we're going to keep going down the trail where we were headed before Trump came along."

Pete Visclosky (D)

Elected 1984, 18th term, b. Aug 13, 1949; Gary; Indiana University Northwest, B.S., 1970; University of Notre Dame Law School (IN), J.D., 1973; Georgetown University Law Center (DC), LL.M., 1982; Roman Catholic; Married (Ms. Joanne Royce); 2 children.

Professional Career: Practicing attorney, 1973-1976, 1983-1984; Aide, U.S. Rep. Adam Benjamin, 1977-1982.

DC Office: 2328 RHOB 20515, 202-225-2461, Fax: 202-225-2493, visclosky.house.gov

State Offices: Merrillville, 219-795-1844.

Committees: *Appropriations*: Defense (Chmn); Energy & Water Development & Related Agencies.

Group Ratings

	ADA	ACLU	AFL-CIO	LCV	ITI	COC	HAFA	ACU	CFG	FRC
2018	-	86%	-	94%	-	58%	6%	8%	4%	0%
2017	90%	C	95%	100%	C	36%	C	4%	0%	0%

Almanac Ratings 2017-18

	Economy	Social	Foreign	Composite
Liberal	94%	97%	97%	96%
Conservative	6%	4%	3%	4%

Key Votes of the 115th Congress

1. Obama-care revision	N	5. Family planning regs	N	9. Guantanamo prisoners	Y
2. Tax Cuts	N	6. Body cameras/immigration	Y	10. Ground missiles, limit	Y
3. Omnibus appropriations	Y	7. Abortion ban	N	11. Defense Dept. spending	N
4. Dodd-Frank revision	N	8. Concealed carry	N	12. FISA rules	N

Election Results

Election	Name (Party)	Vote (%)		Cand. Spent	Ind. Exp. Support	Ind. Exp. Oppose
2018 General	Pete Visclosky (D)	159,611	(65%)	$818,787		
	Mark Leyva (R)	85,594	(35%)			
2018 Primary	Pete Visclosky (D)	42,269	(81%)			
	Antonio Daggett Sr. (D)	5,813	(11%)			
	Larry Chubb (D)	4,406	(8%)			

Prior winning percentages: 2016 (82%), 2014 (61%), 2012 (67%), 2010 (59%), 2008 (71%), 2006 (70%), 2004 (68%), 2002 (67%), 2000 (72%), 1998 (73%), 1996 (69%), 1994 (57%), 1992 (70%), 1990 (66%), 1988 (77%), 1986 (73%), 1984 (71%)

Peter Visclosky, a Democrat first elected in 1984, took over 34 years later one of the most powerful niches in the House: chairman of the Appropriations Subcommittee on Defense. "I'm an appropriator," he once said. "Money makes policy." Visclosky has kept a low public profile throughout a career that has faced limits, due partly to ethics charges. He ranked as the third most-senior Democrat in the House and he broke the record for the longest tenure of any House Member from Indiana.

Visclosky grew up in Lake County. His father was mayor of Gary in the early 1960s, and Visclosky went to Indiana University Northwest there and to law school at the University of Notre Dame. He practiced law and then worked for six years in Washington for local Rep. Adam Benjamin, a Democrat. Benjamin died of a heart ailment in 1982, and Visclosky returned to Indiana.

In 1984, at age 34, he ran in the Democratic primary against Katie Hall, a black state senator who had been given the 1982 nomination — and thus the election, in this Democratic district — by Gary Mayor Richard Hatcher, who was also the district's party chairman. In their contest, Visclosky pulled out all the stops to reach voters since he couldn't rely on the local Democratic establishment. He called himself the "Slovak Kid" to connect with the district's many European ethnic groups, and he held hot dog dinners to attract young people and others not usually involved in local politics. Visclosky narrowly prevailed over Hall with 34 percent of the vote to her 33 percent. He won the general election with 71 percent of the vote.

Visclosky has concentrated much of his effort on projects to help the local economy, especially the steel industry. He has a solidly pro-union voting record. He is a leader of the Congressional Steel Caucus and has been vigilant in monitoring surges in steel imports. He has urged the International Trade Commission to maintain trade protections and has repeatedly introduced bills requiring that federally funded projects use only American-made steel. In 2018, Visclosky said that the tariffs that President Donald Trump imposed on steel imports were "necessary because the American manufacturing industry has been decimated for years by illegal trade."

Visclosky has trended moderate on social and foreign policy in his voting record, and he occasionally has shown independence. He opposed the House-passed bill in 2009 establishing a cap-and-trade system to curb greenhouse gas emissions because it "leaves no margin of error as it relates to jobs in the domestic steel industry." In 2008, he opposed creation of the Troubled Asset Relief

Plan for the ailing financial services industry, although he did back a subsequent proposal to bail out major automakers.

When Democrats earlier were in the majority, he chaired the Energy and Water Development Subcommittee, making him one of the powerful "cardinals" of the House. He was forced to step aside temporarily in June 2009 after he was subpoenaed in a grand jury investigation of possible corruption. In 2007, The Indianapolis Star reported that Visclosky had steered more than $12 million to out-of-state defense companies that contributed to his campaign. Much of that money had been secured through the efforts of a now-defunct lobbying firm, PMA Group, that hired a former top Visclosky aide, Richard Kaelin, the newspaper reported. The House Ethics Committee formally cleared Visclosky and six other Appropriations members in 2010. In 2013, he did not challenge the decision of Democratic leaders to name Nita Lowey of New York — an ally of Nancy Pelosi — as the top Democrat on the full committee, even though she had less seniority than Visclosky. Bloomberg News, noting that he subsequently shunned national media attention, in 2018 described him as "a friend of the defense industry."

In 2013, he became ranking Democrat on the Defense Appropriations Subcommittee, which has a history of bipartisanship. He took issue with the contention by Trump, after he became president, that the nation's nuclear arsenal needed modernization. "The president's loose and imprecise language is in stark contrast to the consummate professionalism of the men and women of our nuclear forces," Visclosky said. With House Armed Services Committee Chairman Adam Smith, D-Wash., he called for a new round of military-base closings.

Visclosky had been adept at securing federal funding for projects in his district and at doling out such projects to other lawmakers, though those so-called earmarks have been prohibited since 2011. He called for increased federal spending on infrastructure, especially for mass transit, which he said would help revitalize his district's economy. "I am very big on transformational projects," he has said.

At home, Visclosky was secure politically until he became a target in the corruption probe. Even then, Republicans had trouble finding a candidate who could compete in the costly Chicago media market. Against weak and poorly financed challengers, Visclosky since 1994 has not dropped below 59 percent in his share of the vote. In November 2018, he won 65%-35%, against Republican Mark Leyva, a carpenter who has run seven unsuccessful contests against Visclosky.

IN-1: Northwest Indiana

Cook Partisan Voting Index: D+8

Population		Race and Ethnicity		Income	
Total	716,518	White	62.9%	Median Income	$54,925
Land area (sq. miles)	1,157	Black	18.6%	District Income Rank	229
Pop/ sq mi	619.3	Latino	15.2%	Poverty Rate	15.6%
Born in State	59%	Asian	1.3%	With health insurance	90.5%
		Two or more races	1.6%	Cash public assistance	1.8%
Age Groups		Other	0.3%	Food stamp/SNAP	13.2%
Under 18	23.5%				
18-34	21.5%	**Education**		**Work**	
35-64	39.9%	H.S grad or less	46%	White Collar	15.1%
Over 64	15.1%	Some college	31.4%	Sales and Service	41.5%
Military		College Degree, 4 yr	14.8%	Blue Collar	27.3%
Veteran/ Active Duty	7.8%	Post grad	7.7%	Government	10.6%

2012 Pres. Vote	Obama	182,021	(61%)	Romney	111,217	(37%)			
2016 Pres. Vote	Clinton	162,358	(53%)	Trump	124,638	(41%)	Johnson	13,287	(4%)

Gary, Hammond: At the southernmost shore of Lake Michigan is a part of America made by steel. In the northwest corner of Indiana, where the water highway of the Great Lakes comes closest to the rail highway of the transcontinental railroads, America's leading capitalists of a century ago identified an ideal site for manufacturing steel. On empty sand dunes, United States Steel, then the nation's largest corporation, founded the city of Gary in 1906 and named it for the company's chairman, Chicago Judge Elbert Gary. For nearly 70 years, the steel mills attracted a diverse and middle-class workforce, more like Chicago than the rest of Indiana: Irish, Poles, Czechs, Ukrainians and blacks from the South.

Politics here has always been turbulent, from the long and unsuccessful steel strike of 1919 to the racially polarized politics of the 1960s and 1970s. The tone of public life — the clash between union stewards and management foremen, between African Americans and Eastern European ethnics, between the stalwarts of different factions vying for control of Gary's massive City Hall — was a clash of steel on steel. Steel brought sudden growth and sudden depression to northwest Indiana. The massive storefronts built on Gary's aptly named Broadway bear witness to the confidence and exuberance of the 1920s. The steel mills went cold during the Depression but were again thronged with workers during World War II. In the years afterward, their massiveness helped create the illusion that a robust economic life in the steel towns of Gary, Hammond and East Chicago would last forever.

The oil crunch of 1979 was the catalyst for change, reducing the demand for large-sized autos, the biggest customer for steel. Steel, which employed 70,000 workers in northwest Indiana in 1979, dropped to 18,000 in 2016, though it remained the No. 1 steel-producing state, as it has been since 1980. Obsolete mills were closed, old mills modernized and new ones built that cut the number of man hours needed by two-thirds. Just-in-time methods were introduced, and management and highly skilled workers cooperated to engineer higher-quality, less-expensive steel to meet market demands. The result has been a modest, though confidence-building, turnaround: In 2018, steel-industry jobs in Indiana had increased to more than 24,000, of which 18,000 were in the northwest corner. U.S. Steel, which in 2016 settled a Justice Department lawsuit on clean-air violations and agreed to remove and repair aging machinery in Gary, announced in August 2018 a $750 million revitalization of its Gary plant. President Donald Trump, who a few months earlier imposed a 25 percent tariff on steel imports, touted the revival of domestic production.

The increased production has been a boost for Gary, which in recent years has been largely in ruins. A 2012 Federal Reserve Bank of Chicago study categorized Gary as "overwhelmed" by the decline of manufacturing. From 2014 to 2017, Lake County was the second fastest-growing county in the state. Contending that its residents were "resilient, eager to work," Mayor Karen Freeman-Wilson urged Amazon to consider Gary for its second headquarters; the city failed to make the list of 20 finalists. The continuing reality was that white flight to the suburbs reduced the city's population from a peak of 178,000 in 1960 to 80,000 in 2018, of whom 84 percent are African American. More than one-third of them lived in poverty.

Indiana's 1st Congressional District stretches from Gary and Hammond along the Lake Michigan shoreline east to Michigan City. In majority-white Hammond, the population loss has not been as dramatic as in Gary, and it has had an influx of Hispanic immigrants. In July 2018, British Petroleum said it planned to spend $300 million to expand its refinery in Hammond. The 1st includes all of Lake and Porter counties. Valparaiso, which is notable for its annual Popcorn Festival honoring Orville Redenbacher, opened in 2016 a $260 million paper recycling mill. About two-thirds of the vote in the 1st is in Lake County. In 2016, Donald Trump's appeal to blue-collar workers and his promise to reduce subsidized imports struck a local chord. He cut in half the 24-point victory of President Barack Obama in 2012. Lake County was one of only four counties that backed Hillary Clinton, albeit with a lower raw vote and percentage than in Indianapolis-based Marion County.

Jackie Walorski (R)

Elected 2012, 4th term, b. Aug 17, 1963; South Bend; Liberty Baptist College (VA), Att., 1983; Taylor University (IN), B.A., 1985; Assembly of God; Married (Dean Swihart).

Elected Office: IN House, 2004-2010.

Professional Career: TV reporter, WSBT-TV, 1985-1989; Executive Director, St. Joseph County Humane Society, 1989-1991; Director of institutional advancement, Ancilla College, 1991-1996; Director of annual giving, IN University, 1997-1998; Founder, Impact Intl., 1999-2003.

DC Office: 419 CHOB 20515, 202-225-3915, Fax: 202-225-6798, walorski.house.gov

State Offices: Mishawaka, 574-204-2645; Rochester, 574-223-4373.

Committees: *Ethics. Ways & Means*: Oversight; Worker & Family Support (RMM).

Group Ratings

	ADA	ACLU	AFL-CIO	LCV	ITI	COC	HAFA	ACU	CFG	FRC
2018	-	4%	-	3%	-	92%	62%	76%	54%	100%
2017	0%	C	5%	0%	C	93%	C	93%	90%	100%

Almanac Ratings 2017-18

	Economy	Social	Foreign	Composite
Liberal	2%	4%	0%	2%
Conservative	99%	97%	100%	98%

Key Votes of the 115th Congress

1. Obama-care revision	Y	5. Family planning regs	Y	9. Guantanamo prisoners	N
2. Tax Cuts	Y	6. Body cameras/immigration	N	10. Ground missiles, limit	N
3. Omnibus appropriations	Y	7. Abortion ban	Y	11. Defense Dept. spending	Y
4. Dodd-Frank revision	Y	8. Concealed carry	Y	12. FISA rules	Y

Election Results

Election	Name (Party)	Vote (%)		Cand. Spent	Ind. Exp. Support	Ind. Exp. Oppose
2018 General	Jackie Walorski (R)	125,499	(55%)	$2,771,313	$20,210	$59,982
	Mel Hall (D)	103,363	(45%)	$3,851,381	$1,036	$950
2018 Primary	Jackie Walorski (R)	43,016	(79%)			
	Mark Summe (R)	11,684	(21%)			

Prior winning percentages: 2016 (59%), 2014 (59%), 2012 (49%)

Republican Jackie Walorski was first elected in 2012 to what had been a political swing seat. After two close campaigns — one defeat and one victory -- she solidified her political position and staked out her legislative niche with mainstream Republican views on most issues, with occasional bipartisanship on military and veterans issues. As one of the dwindling number of Republican women and with a seat on the Ways and Means Committee, she sought opportunities to assert influence in the House.

Walorski grew up in a working-class family in South Bend, the granddaughter of Polish and German immigrants. Her father was a firefighter, and her mother worked at a hospital. She was the first in her family to attend college, graduating from Taylor University with a bachelor's degree in communications. She didn't become passionate about politics until she heard presidential candidate Ronald Reagan speak, recalling that he said Republicans "believed in smaller government and the power of individuals controlling their own destiny."

Walorski spent her first few years out of college working as a television reporter, and then became an administrator for Ancilla College and Indiana University. In 1999, Walorski and her husband, Dean Swihart, volunteered as Christian missionaries in Romania. They were in Romania at the time of the Sept. 11, 2001, terrorist attacks, an experience that she said was life-changing. "We really did not know if we'd ever see our country or family again," she said. When the couple returned to Indiana, Walorski won a seat in the state House, where she served six years. She cosponsored the state's voter identification law, which withstood a challenge in the Supreme Court, and worked to establish the Indiana Economic Development Corporation as a public and private cooperative venture.

Walorski campaigned in tight races. In her 2010 challenge to Democratic Rep. Joe Donnelly, Walorski got more than $1 million in national party aid. Donnelly outspent her, $2 million to $1.3 million, and she lost 48%-47%, a margin of 2,538 votes. When Donnelly ran successfully for the Senate, Walorski faced off against Democrat Brendan Mullen, an Army veteran of the Iraq war who campaigned as a pro-gun, anti-abortion rights moderate. The redrawn district's Republican tilt was instrumental in her close win, 49%-48%, a margin this time of 3,920 votes. Walorski was boosted by Mitt Romney's presidential bid and by Mike Pence's campaign for governor.

In the House, Walorski focused on local issues and avoided the leadership and electoral ambitions of other junior Republicans from Indiana. As chair of the Nutrition Subcommittee of the Agriculture Committee, she held hearings on the food stamp program, including possible steps to better serve families and taxpayers. On the Armed Services and Veterans' Affairs committees, she worked with veterans' groups to encourage local business opportunities. In 2013, she enacted her proposal for whistleblower protections for victims of sexual assault in the military and a safe environment to report attacks.

With a seat on Ways and Means in 2017, Walorski voiced concern over the impact of tariffs on auto parts. Though careful not to criticize directly President Donald Trump, she cited her "eyeball to eyeball" exchanges with Commerce Secretary Wilbur Ross. The sweeping legislation that Congress enacted in 2018 to reduce opioid addiction included her proposal to improve access to non-opioid pain treatments. Walorski voiced concern that family separations at the border with Mexico "failed to live up to our American ideals;" she urged a solution for children with illegal status.

Politically, Walorski grew more secure. Her challenger in 2014 was Joe Bock, a global health professor at Notre Dame. Walorski attacked him for votes to increase his own pay as a member of the Missouri legislature in the 1980s and suggested that he was a carpetbagger. In a bad year for Democrats, the incumbent won 59%-38%. In 2016, Walorski distanced herself from some of Trump's actions. "I don't think anybody supports everything they've seen in a president," she said. "My job is to represent this district no matter who is in the White House."

Democrat Mel Hall, who had been a senior adviser to a large Washington-based law firm, spent nearly $4 million against Walorski in 2018. He called her a "career politician" who refused to hold town meetings with constituents. Walorski's victory margin was reduced to 55%-45%. She led in all counties except for South Bend-based St. Joseph, where Hall got 57 percent of the vote. The result was "an impressive win at a time of a serious challenge," according to the post-election analysis of the South Bend Tribune.

IN-2: North-Central Indiana

Cook Partisan Voting Index: R+11

Population		Race and Ethnicity		Income	
Total	722,649	White	80.1%	Median Income	$50,295
Land area (sq. miles)	3,959	Black	6.8%	District Income Rank	307
Pop/ sq mi	182.6	Latino	9.4%	Poverty Rate	15%
Born in State	68.9%	Asian	1.2%	With health insurance	87.7%
		Two or more races	2%	Cash public assistance	1.9%
Age Groups		Other	0.5%	Food stamp/SNAP	11.5%
Under 18	25%				
18-34	21.9%	**Education**		**Work**	
35-64	37.8%	H.S grad or less	50.4%	White Collar	15.3%
Over 64	15.3%	Some college	28.2%	Sales and Service	38.2%
		College Degree, 4 yr	13.4%	Blue Collar	32.6%
Military		Post grad	7.9%	Government	9%
Veteran/ Active Duty	7.6%				

2012 Pres. Vote	Romney	154,837	(56%)	Obama	116,320	(42%)			
2016 Pres. Vote	Trump	163,539	(58%)	Clinton	99,496	(36%)	Johnson	12,905	(5%)

South Bend, Elkhart: When the University of Notre Dame was founded in 1842, Catholics were still a rarity in most of America and certainly rare on the limestone-bottomed prairie of northern Indiana. This was still farm country and South Bend no more than a crossroads on the banks of the St. Joseph River. But by the 1920s, both the school and the town had grown. Notre Dame, thanks to its football team, the Fighting Irish, was the most famous Catholic university in the land, and South Bend was a significant industrial city, home of Studebaker, Bendix and dozens of other factories. In the past 50 years, Notre Dame has grown in size and reputation, but South Bend, like many Rust Belt cities, diminished in size and reputation. In the 1960s, Studebaker went out of business. In the early 1980s, there were massive factory layoffs.

But these high-profile job losses were accompanied by the much less visible creation of jobs in small factories throughout the region. The work in those facilities required more skill than did the old assembly lines, and the products had to be more responsive to just-in-time prime contractors or computer-inventory retailers. In recent years, many employers have had trouble filling job openings, and the economic base is more secure than when it depended on the fate of two or three big companies. Meanwhile, Notre Dame has led another transition, to a more technology-focused economy. After acquiring the Midwest Institute for Nanoelectronics Discovery, it created research centers for new processes and techniques. A priority of the university's roughly $100 million in research projects has been its Environmental Change Initiative, which has explored the related problems of invasive species, land use and climate change, and their synergistic impact on water resources.

Elkhart County is a manufacturing hub, with creative ways to turn a profit and phenomenal employment increases. Local companies there make everything from pharmaceuticals to musical instruments. The county is best known as the manufacturing center for most of the nation's recreational vehicles. The local economy made an impressive turnaround, as joblessness in Elkhart dropped in a decade from nearly 20 percent to 2.4 percent in 2018. RV shipments from Elkhart were 321,000 in 2013, nearly double the total in 2009; by 2017, sales spiked again to 504,000. Despite concerns about the impact of tariffs imposed on steel and aluminum by President Donald Trump, which added more than $2,000 to the cost of the average RV, manufacturing employment in Elkhart in 2018 had doubled to 72,000 from 37,000 a decade earlier. With a reported 10,000 job openings in the area at the end of 2017, the RV industry planned to build a tech institute to train more workers in Elkhart. Other parts of the local auto business have diversified. In Mishawaka, the plant that had manufactured Hummer military vehicles until it shut down in 2009 shifted in 2015 to production of Mercedes sports utility vehicles; in 2018, the same assembly plant transitioned to a Chinese-owned company that produced electric vehicles.

The 2nd Congressional District of Indiana is centered on South Bend. This is a blue-collar and ethnic city, with a politically ambitious Democratic mayor, Pete Buttigeig. It has one of the nation's largest percentage of Hungarian Americans, plus a growing community of Mexican Americans. The Republican base of the district has been secured. The shifts in what had been the swing 2nd have resulted from broader politics that go beyond redistricting. Democrats got little credit for the local economic gains during the Obama presidency. Within boundaries that Barack Obama in 2008 took by 699 votes, Donald Trump won the working-class district, 58%-36%.

Jim Banks (R)

Elected 2016, 2nd term, b. Jul 16, 1979; Columbia City; Indiana University, Bloomington, Bach. Deg., 2004; Grace College, M.B.A., 2013; Evangelical; Married (Amanda Banks); 3 children.

Military Career: U.S. Navy Reserve 2012-pres. (Afghanistan)

Elected Office: IN Senate, 2010-2016.

DC Office: 1713 LHOB 20515, 202-225-4436, Fax: 202-226-9870, banks.house.gov

State Offices: Fort Wayne, 260-702-4750.

Committees: *Armed Services*: Intelligence, Emerging Threats & Capabilities; Tactical Air & Land Forces. *Education & Labor*: Health, Employment, Labor & Pensions; Higher Education & Workforce Investment. *Veterans' Affairs*: Economic Opportunity; Technology Modernization (RMM).

Group Ratings

	ADA	ACLU	AFL-CIO	LCV	ITI	COC	HAFA	ACU	CFG	FRC
2018	-	7%	-	0%	-	83%	92%	92%	75%	100%
2017	0%	C	5%	0%	C	93%	C	93%	98%	100%

Almanac Ratings 2017-18

	Economy	Social	Foreign	Composite
Liberal	0%	7%	0%	2%
Conservative	100%	93%	100%	98%

Key Votes of the 115th Congress

1. Obama-care revision	Y	5. Family planning regs	Y	9. Guantanamo prisoners	N
2. Tax Cuts	Y	6. Body cameras/immigration	N	10. Ground missiles, limit	N
3. Omnibus appropriations	Y	7. Abortion ban	Y	11. Defense Dept. spending	Y
4. Dodd-Frank revision	Y	8. Concealed carry	Y	12. FISA rules	Y

Election Results

Election	Name (Party)	Vote (%)	Cand. Spent	Ind. Exp. Support	Ind. Exp. Oppose
2018 General	Jim Banks (R)..................................... 158,927	(65%)	$1,055,165	$16,249	
	Courtney Tritch (D)............................. 86,610	(35%)	$838,738		
2018 Primary	Jim Banks (R)...	(100%)			

Prior winning percentages: 2016 (70%)

Jim Banks was elected to an open seat following a competitive primary contest. He brought extensive experience in the Navy Reserve plus support from national conservative groups, and focused chiefly on national security issues.

Banks was born and continued to reside in Columbia City, not far from Fort Wayne. He graduated from Indiana University, where he was president of College Republicans, and got an MBA at Grace College and Seminary. He worked as a real estate broker with the Bradley Co. in Fort Wayne. Elected to the state Senate in 2010, where he claimed the most conservative record, he chaired the Veterans Affairs and the Military Committee. He invoked a state law to take a leave of absence in 2014, while he served for eight months at NATO headquarters in Afghanistan, where he assisted with equipment for the Afghans. He received the Defense Meritorious Service Medal for his military leadership. During that time, his wife, Amanda Banks, was appointed acting state senator.

When Rep. Marlin Stutzman announced that he was running for the open Senate seat in 2016, Banks staked out ground among conservative advocacy groups. His political consultant told Banks that he needed to become "less wonky" during the campaign, according to a story in GQ. "You don't need to impress people with your intellect," the consultant told him. Affiliates of the Club for Growth and the Senate Conservatives Fund spent more than $700,000 on his behalf. Brown raised $1.1 million for the primary, compared with $992,000 for farmer Kip Tom, and $338,000 for Elizabeth Brown, a veteran Fort Wayne elected official. He won the primary with 34 percent to 32 percent for Tom and 25 percent for Brown. David McIntosh, the head of the Club for Growth who during the 1990s served in an earlier version of this district, made the election of Banks a top priority and took credit for playing a "pivotal role" in the victory. In the general, Banks defeated Tommy Schrader, a perennial Democratic candidate, 70%-23%.

On the Armed Services Committee, Banks said that his objective was to "ensure our men and women in uniform receive the resources they need to protect our nation." In 2017, he filed a bill to authorize the use of force against the Islamic State in Iraq and Syria (ISIS). "The Constitution grants Congress the power of declaring war, and we need to take that obligation seriously," Banks said. "Rather than continuing to fight ISIS under an authorization passed by Congress in 2001 to fight al-Qaeda, it is time to pass a new authorization for the use of military force against ISIS." Sen. Todd Young of Indiana filed a companion measure in the Senate, though Congress took no action.

Banks made other attempts to call for discipline in the nation's foreign policy. Following the friendly meeting in Helsinki in July 2018 between President Donald Trump and Russian President Vladimir Putin, he warned, "Russia is not our friend." Banks unsuccessfully urged Treasury Secretary Steve Mnuchin to cancel a visit to Saudi Arabia that October "until the world receives answers" about the apparent murder of journalist and activist Jamal Khashoggi at the Saudi embassy in Istanbul. As the top Republican on the Veterans Affairs Subcommittee on Technology Modernization, he reviewed the costly upgrade of VA medical records.

The political challenge for Banks eased when he won reelection in 2018 without a Republican primary. Democrat Courtney Tritch, who ran a marketing firm, spent nearly as much as the $1.1 million by Banks. The incumbent took all 12 counties and won, 65%-35%, including 56 percent of the vote in the population center of Allen County.

IN-3: Northeast Indiana

Cook Partisan Voting Index: R+18

Population		Race and Ethnicity		Income	
Total	736,567	White	83.7%	Median Income	$51,784
Land area (sq. miles)	4,180	Black	5.9%	District Income Rank	273
Pop/ sq mi	176.2	Latino	6%	Poverty Rate	13.2%
Born in State	72.2%	Asian	2.1%	With health insurance	87.7%
		Two or more races	2.1%	Cash public assistance	1.8%
Age Groups		Other	0.2%	Food stamp/SNAP	10.7%
Under 18	25.8%				
18-34	21.6%	**Education**		**Work**	
35-64	38%	H.S grad or less	46.8%	White Collar	14.6%
Over 64	14.6%	Some college	30.8%	Sales and Service	37.7%
Military		College Degree, 4 yr	14.7%	Blue Collar	32.4%
Veteran/ Active Duty	7.7%	Post grad	7.7%	Government	8.3%

2012 Pres. Vote	Romney	179,629	(63%)	Obama	102,536	(36%)			
2016 Pres. Vote	Trump	189,587	(64%)	Clinton	87,699	(30%)	Johnson	13,903	(5%)

Fort Wayne: The northeast corner of Indiana was first settled by people of New England Yankee stock, establishing orderly communities with public schools and even colleges. They were joined by German immigrants, who built tidy farms and their own civic institutions. In the northern part of the state, there are hills, lakes and the strange swamp that is the central focus of Gene Stratton-Porter's children's classic, A Girl of the Limberlost. The one large city here, Fort Wayne, was built on the flat terrain along the Maumee River that flows to Toledo Ohio. It grew as a factory town, surging ahead and then falling back as large factories, often tied to the auto industry, opened and downsized over the years.

Manufacturing jobs in the Fort Wayne area dropped significantly in the 2000s. The local economy started to revive after a $150 million biodiesel complex opened in Claypool, with the largest soybean processing plant in the United States, which can produce 88 million gallons of fuel annually. In May 2015, General Motors announced that it planned a $1.2 billion expansion of its plant for full-size pickup trucks, which employed 3,800 workers. Kosciusko County, named for the Polish general who served during the Revolutionary War, is renowned for medical supplies. In the town of Warsaw (yes, named for the Polish capital), residents have been making orthopedic devices for more than a century, and the demand keeps growing as baby boomers age. The head of the local Chamber of Commerce expects a big increase in demand for artificial knees: good news for Warsaw, bad news for seniors.

The 3rd Congressional District covers the northeastern part of the state and is centered on Fort Wayne. It is a surprisingly diverse area, with a mix that includes a concentration of Amish, plus Central Americans, Bosnians, Somalis and the nation's largest number of Burmese refugees. In the metro area, only 6 percent of the total population is Hispanic, but the Hispanic share of the population under 18 is much higher. This part of Indiana has been heavily Republican since the Civil War, though it has sometimes veered Democratic in times of economic distress.

The seat sometimes sends its representatives on to higher positions: Dan Quayle, elected here in 1976, was later a senator and vice president. Dan Coats, who succeeded Quayle in the Senate, was ambassador to Germany before winning a second term in the Senate in 2010 and then became Director of National Intelligence with President Donald Trump. In 2016, Rep. Marlin Stutzman tried, but failed, to continue that pattern. He trailed badly in the GOP primary to replace the retiring Coats. In the 2008 and 2012 presidential elections, the 3rd was the most Republican district in Indiana. Donald Trump improved the GOP vote to 64 percent, but that was only his second-highest in the state behind the 6th District.

Jim Baird (R)

Elected 2018, 1st term, b. Jun 04, 1945; Covington; Purdue University (IN), B.S., 1967; Purdue University (IN), M.S., 1969; Purdue University (IN), M.S., 1969; University of Kentucky, Ph.D., 1975; Methodist; Married (Denise Baird); 3 children.

Military Career: US Army 1969-1971 (Vietnam)

Elected Office: Putnam County Board of Commissioners, 2006-2010; IN House, 2010-2018.

DC Office: 532 CHOB 20515, 202-225-5037, Fax: 202-226-0544, baird.house.gov

State Offices: Danville, 317-563-5567.

Committees: *Agriculture*: Biotechnology, Horticulture & Research; Commodity Exchanges, Energy & Credit. *Science, Space & Technology*: Environment; Research & Technology (RMM).

Election Results

Election	Name (Party)	Vote (%)		Cand. Spent	Ind. Exp. Support	Ind. Exp. Oppose
2018 General	Jim Baird (R)	156,539	(64%)	$380,790	$9,139	$18,679
	Tobi Beck (D)	87,824	(36%)	$111,428		
2018 Primary	Jim Baird (R)	29,319	(37%)			
	Steve Braun (R)	23,602	(30%)			
	Diego Morales (R)	11,997	(15%)			
	Jared Thomas (R)	8,435	(11%)			

Republican freshman Jim Baird brought a combination of academic, business and political experience in the Indiana farm community to his surprising victory in an open district. Although he trailed significantly in fundraising, his chief opponent's support from outside political action committees may have backfired in the GOP primary. Baird succeeded Todd Rokita, who lost the GOP Senate primary to Mike Braun—the older brother of Steve Braun, who had been expected to defeat Baird.

Baird got his undergraduate and master's degrees in animal science from Purdue University and his Ph.D. from the University of Kentucky, where he specialized in nutrition for pigs. He served as a first lieutenant in the Army during the Vietnam War, where he lost an arm during combat and received numerous honors. A life-long resident of the district, he owned several businesses, including a family farm and a home health care agency. He was a livestock specialist with Purdue University's Cooperative Extension Service.

Following his service as a Putnam County commissioner, he was elected to the Indiana House for eight years. He worked on agriculture and veterans issues, and chaired the Health and Medicaid Subcommittee of House Ways and Means. He received an award for civility among the legislators.

In the contest to replace Rokita in the heavily Republican district, Steve Braun was well-connected, including his stint as head of the Workforce Development Department under then-Gov. Mike Pence. Braun was endorsed by the state Chamber of Commerce and the Farm Bureau. Diego Morales, another GOP candidate, also had been an aide to Pence in Indianapolis. Even with his lengthy time in office, Baird ran as an outsider, with his attacks on "career politicians" and calls for "a commonsense approach to fix the broken system in Washington." Compared to the $1.2 million that Braun raised, Baird raised little more than $200,000 for the primary—most of which was from a personal loan. But he displayed a superior grassroots appeal.

The closing days of the campaign were marked by negative advertising from several outside political action committees. One of those late mailers criticized Baird's vote to increase the state's gasoline tax and said that he had cost Hoosiers "an arm and a leg." Given his war injuries, that attack generated a sympathetic response for Baird from voters. "Disrespecting our wounded combat veterans crosses a line that Hoosiers will not tolerate," responded Baird, who earned a Bronze Star and two Purple Hearts in Vietnam.

Baird won the primary with 37 percent of the vote to 30 percent for Braun and 15 percent for Morales. The turnout of 80,000 voters, which likely was driven by local support for Rokita, was the largest of any district in Indiana in the primary. In this heavily Republican district, Baird easily defeated Democrat Tobi Beck, a woman Army veteran. At 73 when he took office, he was among the oldest first-termers ever to arrive in Congress, which seemed likely to limit his tenure.

IN-4: West-Central Indiana

Cook Partisan Voting Index: R+17

Population		Race and Ethnicity		Income	
Total	745,099	White	85.6%	Median Income	$55,420
Land area (sq. miles)	6,353	Black	3.6%	District Income Rank	225
Pop/ sq mi	117.3	Latino	6%	Poverty Rate	12.9%
Born in State	70.1%	Asian	2.9%	With health insurance	90.8%
		Two or more races	1.6%	Cash public assistance	1.4%
Age Groups		Other	0.3%	Food stamp/SNAP	9.2%
Under 18	23.1%				
18-34	24.8%	**Education**		**Work**	
35-64	37.6%	H.S grad or less	44.8%	White Collar	14.5%
Over 64	14.5%	Some college	29.7%	Sales and Service	37.6%
		College Degree, 4 yr	16.1%	Blue Collar	29.3%
Military		Post grad	9.4%	Government	12.5%
Veteran/ Active Duty	8%				

2012 Pres. Vote	Romney	170,244	(61%)	Obama	103,103	(37%)			
2016 Pres. Vote	Trump	194,403	(64%)	Clinton	91,265	(30%)	Johnson	16,704	(6%)

Indianapolis Suburbs, Lafayette: The landscape of central and western Indiana is some of the most prosaic in the United States. It is mostly flat, with neat farms and towns of frame bungalows, looking mostly unchanged from many years ago. Across this landscape have run some of the nation's chief transportation arteries. The earliest was the old National Road, from Baltimore to St. Louis, which was paralleled by U.S. 40 in the 1930s. The region was also crisscrossed by the great east-west rail lines carrying famed passenger trains like the Wabash Cannonball. There is no Cannonball today. People bounce around the Midwest on commuter airlines from small city to hub, and while U.S. 40 is still there, it has been superseded by Interstate 70. The landscape still looks rural, and there are some large farms, with more than 80 percent of agricultural income from corn and soybeans, and a small slice from hogs. The economy is more industrial, with small factories in crossroads and courthouse towns. President Donald Trump's trade war with China brought big cuts in soybeans exports and prices.

Tippecanoe County's Lafayette, where the main employer is Purdue University, has been growing and prosperous. It has benefited from a partnership between Toyota and longtime local auto manufacturer Subaru that helped the Lafayette plant's workforce grow to 5,800 people, making it the largest private employer in Tippecanoe. After spending $1.3 billion to expand the facility, Subaru has added production of its Impreza and Ascent models, with about 400,000 vehicles annually. Kokomo, which suffered from the collapse of local auto manufacturing, has ranked third in the nation in its economic recovery since the Great Recession, according to a Bloomberg News study. Fiat-Chrysler has a large local plant. In Whitestown, the fastest-growing town in Indiana, the population more than doubled between 2010 and 2017. More than 40 companies have grown or moved to surrounding Boone County during that time.

Purdue Research Foundation and Browning Investments created the Purdue Research Foundation, with expected investment of more than $1 billion in West Lafayette. In October 2018, it began construction of a Convergence Center for Innovation and Collaboration. Manufacturing in West Lafayette has increased to roughly 19,000 workers. The recent spurt in research has led to a boost in the Asian population, with 22 percent in West Lafayette.

The 4th Congressional District covers much of west-central Indiana, including western parts of suburban Indianapolis. Each of the 16 counties usually votes Republican. Only Tippecanoe, which is the largest and has about 20 percent of the voters, is competitive. Hendricks County in the Indianapolis suburbs is heavily Republican. In 2016, Donald Trump won 64 percent of the district vote.

Susan Brooks (R)

Elected 2012, 4th term, b. Aug 25, 1960; Ft. Wayne; Miami University of Ohio, B.A., 1982; Indiana University Law School, Indianapolis, J.D., 1985; Roman Catholic; Married (David M. Brooks); 2 children.

Professional Career: Deputy mayor of Indianapolis, 1998-1999; Practicing attorney, 2000-2001; U.S. Attorney, S. District of IN, 2001-2007; Sr. Vice President., General counsel, Ivy Tech Comm. College, 2007-2012.

DC Office: 2211 RHOB 20515, 202-225-2276, Fax: 202-225-0016, susanwbrooks.house.gov

State Offices: Anderson, 765-640-5115; Carmel, 317-848-0201.

Committees: *Energy & Commerce*: Communications & Technology; Health; Oversight & Investigations. *Select Committee on the Modernization of Congress.*

Group Ratings

	ADA	ACLU	AFL-CIO	LCV	ITI	COC	HAFA	ACU	CFG	FRC
2018	-	4%	-	6%	-	91%	55%	72%	55%	100%
2017	0%	C	11%	9%	C	93%	C	78%	61%	100%

Almanac Ratings 2017-18

	Economy	Social	Foreign	Composite
Liberal	5%	4%	0%	3%
Conservative	95%	97%	100%	97%

Key Votes of the 115th Congress

1. Obama-care revision	Y	5. Family planning regs	Y	9. Guantanamo prisoners	N
2. Tax Cuts	Y	6. Body cameras/immigration	N	10. Ground missiles, limit	N
3. Omnibus appropriations	Y	7. Abortion ban	Y	11. Defense Dept. spending	Y
4. Dodd-Frank revision	Y	8. Concealed carry	Y	12. FISA rules	Y

Election Results

Election	Name (Party)	Vote (%)	Cand. Spent	Ind. Exp. Support	Ind. Exp. Oppose
2018 General	Susan Brooks (R)............................	180,035 (57%)	$1,392,361		
	Dee Thornton (D)...............................	137,142 (43%)	$150,902		
2018 Primary	Susan Brooks (R)..	(100%)			

Prior winning percentages: 2016 (62%), 2014 (65%), 2012 (73%)

Republican Susan Brooks, first elected in 2012, built quickly on her impressive experience in policy and law enforcement. For two years, she chaired the Ethics Committee. On the Energy and Commerce Committee, she has channeled the interests and understated conservatism of the Indianapolis business establishment. Even with the House Republicans' loss of the majority, her star continued to rise. At home, she has been unsuccessful in seeking statewide office.

Brooks was born in Auburn Indiana and raised in Fort Wayne. At Homestead High School, she played basketball, volleyball, and tennis — and was a member of the cheerleading squad. She attended Miami University in Oxford Ohio, where she pursued a joint degree in political science and sociology and was president of her sorority. She earned a law degree from Indiana University and joined an Indianapolis-based criminal defense practice. That exposed her to what she called the "root causes" of crime, such as domestic strife and mental health problems.

In 1998, as deputy mayor of Indianapolis, Brooks established the Violence Reduction Partnership, a multiagency collaboration designed to curb homicide, gun assaults and armed robberies. In 2001, she was appointed U.S. attorney for the Southern District of Indiana by President George W. Bush. Over the next six years, she prosecuted drug kingpins, helped consolidate the office's counter-terrorism apparatus, and drew attention to human trafficking, "something we really weren't talking about in Indianapolis," she said. In 2007, Brooks became senior vice president and general counsel for Ivy Tech Community College, a statewide institution.

In 2012, Brooks and her chief GOP rival, former Rep. David McIntosh, entered the House contest before veteran Rep. Dan Burton announced his retirement, which may have contributed to his decision to endorse another candidate, Marion Mayor Wayne Seybold. McIntosh, who served in the House from 1995 to 2001, received endorsements from Republican power brokers, including former Vice President Dan Quayle and the National Rifle Association.

McIntosh's campaign was undone by questions about his residential status. After leaving Congress to run for governor of Indiana, he settled in Washington as a lobbyist in a large law firm. But he continued to vote in Indiana, renting area properties to maintain his residency. McIntosh was later absolved of any wrongdoing by a local election board, but not before he had lost the Republican primary. Brooks prevailed with 30 percent of the vote to 29 percent for McIntosh, a difference of 1,010 votes. Seybold finished fourth with 11 percent. In the general, against Democrat Scott Reske, a state legislator and former Marine Corps officer, Brooks won 58%-38%.

In the House, Brooks co-chaired the Congressional High-Tech Women's Caucus, with an objective to encourage more women to enter the tech industry. She was one of 87 Republicans who voted to end the partial government shutdown in 2013, which she termed "very much a low point in governing for me." On the Select Committee to Investigate Benghazi, she defended the panel from charges that its investigation was designed to embarrass Democratic presidential candidate Hillary Clinton. She responded that the panel's review had been "very fact-centric."

With her seat on the influential Energy and Commerce Committee, Brooks set as a top priority repeal of the medical device tax in the Affordable Care Act — a priority for many businesses in the Indianapolis area. She was part of a bipartisan House group in 2015 that enacted an extension of the Children's Health Insurance Program, along with changes in Medicare payments to doctors. Also on the committee, she cited her work on the Twenty First Century Cures Act. As chairman of the Ethics Committee in 2017-18, Brooks dealt with sexual-harassment and related charges against multiple House members. She said that it was "very shocking" to learn that lawmakers had used $17 million in public funds to settle charges that had been filed against them. She told the Indianapolis Star that the Ethics Committee wanted to "create a positive work environment" in the House and she called for the creation of a victim's advocate office where aides could seek counsel in the future.

Brooks was embroiled in a controversial effort by other House Republicans to make the investigations of the largely autonomous Office of Congressional Ethics more subservient to the Ethics Committee. Collaborating with Brooks, Speaker Paul Ryan had opposed that internal change on the eve of the new Congress in January 2017. Following an overnight uproar inside and outside the House, Republican renegades agreed to abandon the change. In 2019, she stepped down as the top Republican on the Ethics panel.

Also in 2017-18, as co-chair of the bipartisan Congressional Caucus on Women's Issues, Brooks joined Rep. Lois Frankel, D-Fla., to call for increased funding for the Violence Against Women Act. Brooks kept her distance from President Donald Trump on some of his hard-edged policies. When he ordered a travel ban on people entering the United States from a group of mostly majority-Muslim countries, she said she opposed a religious test for immigrants or refugees.

When Mike Pence accepted the vice presidential nomination in July 2016, Brooks was one of three candidates in the 10-day campaign for the decision by the 22-member state Republican Central Committee to replace him as the nominee for governor. Brooks reportedly received significant support in the back-room discussions. But Pence's support of Eric Holcomb, whom he had earlier selected as his lieutenant governor, would have made it embarrassing for the state party to defy his wishes after Trump had selected Pence as his running mate. In 2015, she thought about running for an open Senate seat, but concluded that she could have more impact for Indiana by staying in the House.

In 2018, Democrat Dee Thornton, a business executive and political newcomer, criticized "the lack of moral courage" by political leaders and the lack of accessibility by Brooks to her constituents. Though not seriously threatened, Brooks won her narrowest election victory, 57%-43%. She took Hamilton County with 61 percent of the vote; Thornton led only in Marion County, with 59 percent. In June 2019, Brooks announced that she will not seek reelection, creating what likely will be a competitive open-seat contest in 2020.

IN-5: Northern Indianapolis Metro   Cook Partisan Voting Index: R+9

Population		Race and Ethnicity		Income	
Total	757,787	White	81.8%	Median Income	$67,341
Land area (sq. miles)	1,925	Black	7.9%	District Income Rank	115
Pop/ sq mi	393.7	Latino	4.2%	Poverty Rate	9.5%
Born in State	65.3%	Asian	3.4%	With health insurance	92.5%
		Two or more races	2.2%	Cash public assistance	1.7%
Age Groups		Other	0.3%	Food stamp/SNAP	7.5%
Under 18	24.4%				
18-34	21.4%	**Education**		**Work**	
35-64	40.3%	H.S grad or less	29.5%	White Collar	13.9%
Over 64	13.9%	Some college	25.8%	Sales and Service	37.6%
		College Degree, 4 yr	28.1%	Blue Collar	15.6%
Military		Post grad	16.7%	Government	10.1%
Veteran/ Active Duty	7.2%				

2012 Pres. Vote	Romney	196,743	(58%)	Obama	139,300	(41%)			
2016 Pres. Vote	Trump	193,018	(52%)	Clinton	150,083	(41%)	Johnson	20,505	(6%)

Hamilton County: Indiana's most rapid growth has taken place in the suburban ring counties around Indianapolis, especially in Hamilton County, directly north of the city. This is affluent suburbia, with subdivisions full of spacious houses, shopping centers and office developments in what not too long ago were farm fields. Hamilton County's population increased from 82,000 in 1980 to 182,000 in 2000 and to 275,000 in 2010 — a 50 percent jump in a decade, making it one of the fastest growing counties in the Midwest. The growth continued, and reached 324,000 in 2017. A group of business and civic leaders has developed a mass transit plan that could spur even greater growth.

Hamilton County has drawn many wealthy people from Indianapolis, where they had been concentrated on the north side of the city. Now, they're more likely to be in the former farm communities of Carmel, Fishers and Noblesville. Since the creation of its Midtown development in 2014, wealthy Carmel has attracted new businesses and condominiums. The Roche Diagnostics medical-services company has completed the first phase of a $300 million expansion on its 159-acre campus in Fishers. Hamilton has the highest median household income in Indiana and is the 35th richest county in the nation, with a population that is nearly 90 percent white. Hamilton is the most Republican of the large counties in Indiana and has been one of the most Republican in the nation. It voted 66%-32% for Mitt Romney in 2012. But the county's support for Donald Trump in 2016 dropped to 57%-37%, a common trend in high-income areas across the nation. In 2018, county Democrats ran — and sometimes won — in precincts where they have barely been a presence in recent years.

The 5th Congressional District is located in the center of the state and includes the northern Indianapolis suburbs. In addition to Hamilton County, which has exceeded 40 percent of the population, the 5th takes in all or part of seven other counties. Some, such as Grant and Tipton, are Republican-leaning. The mostly upscale northern slice of Indianapolis's Marion County is the second largest part of the district and has become Democratic-leaning; the remaining 70 percent of Marion is in the heavily Democratic 7th District. The district also includes the politically mixed Madison County, with its county seat in Anderson, a manufacturing town. The overall makeup of this district is Republican. But the reduced support for Trump in Hamilton trimmed the Republican presidential vote in the district from 58 percent in 2012 to 53 percent in 2016, ranking as the lowest of the state's seven Republican-held districts.

Greg Pence (R)

Elected 2018, 1st term, b. Nov 04, 1956; Columbus; Loyola University Chicago (IL), Bach. Deg., 1981; Loyola University Chicago (IL), M.B.A., 1986; Catholic; Married (Denice Pence); 4 children; 5 grandchildren.

Military Career: U.S. Marine Corps 1979-1984

Professional Career: President, Kiel Brothers Oil Company,1988-2004; Antique Mall owner.

DC Office: 222 CHOB 20515, 202-225-3021, pence.house.gov

State Offices: Columbus, 812-799-5230.

Committees: *Foreign Affairs*: Europe, Eurasia, Energy & the Environment. *Transportation & Infrastructure*: Economic Dev't, Public Buildings & Emergency Management; Highways & Transit; Railroads, Pipelines & Hazardous Materials.

Election Results

Election	Name (Party)	Vote (%)		Cand. Spent	Ind. Exp. Support	Ind. Exp. Oppose
2018 General	Greg Pence (R)..................................... 154,260		(64%)	$2,520,083	$4,086	
	Jeannine Lee Lake (D).................. 79,430		(33%)			
	Tom Ferkinhoff (Lib)............................ 8,030		(3%)			
2018 Primary	Greg Pence (R)............................... 47,962		(65%)			
	Jonathan Lamb (R)............................ 17,526		(24%)			

Freshman Republican Greg Pence rode his familiar name to an easy victory in a district that his younger brother, Vice President Mike Pence, held for 12 years before he was elected Indiana governor in 2012. With his minimal engagement at campaign events or with the news media, Greg Pence— in the first political campaign of his own--used his close connections to influential political players to raise robust campaign funds and gain prominent endorsements. They included House Republican leaders, the political action committee of President Donald Trump, and his predecessor Rep. Luke Messer, who ran unsuccessfully in the GOP Senate primary. Pence largely ignored his opponents, including a self-funding Republican businessman who accused Pence of "running on nepotism."

After graduating from Loyola University of Chicago, where he later received a master's degree in business administration, Pence served as a lieutenant in the Marine Corps. He had a prominent business career in the Columbus Indiana area that took a separate route from his politically adept brother. Those marketplace experiences had a mixed record that left millions of dollars in fines and debt.

Following his father's path, Pence became president of the Kiel Brothers Oil Company, a local oil-supply business that developed a chain of more than 200 convenience stores in Indiana and surrounding areas. But the company faced financial difficulties after the state assessed an $8.4 million penalty for causing environmental damage with leaky storage tanks. Additional problems ensued when the price of oil collapsed in the years after Pence took control.

In 2004, "the chain announced it was filing for bankruptcy. Pence resigned that same day," the Indianapolis Star reported in a campaign profile of Pence. According to The New York Times, a Columbus bank—on which Pence had served as a director—later sued him for $3.8 million in debts that he had guaranteed; Pence agreed "to settle for pennies on the dollar." A Pence campaign aide said that the business problems resulted from major changes in the oil industry beyond his control.

When Republican Gov. Mitch Daniels took office in 2005, he gave Pence the number-two position with the Indiana Department of Environmental Management, the same agency that had fined his oil business for its spills and for failure to comply with safety regulations. Pence left that position after less than three months, "saying his work was finished," the Star reported. In recent years, Pence and his wife Denise owned two antique malls in southern Indiana.

In Pence's low-profile campaign, he raised more than $1.2 million prior to the primary. His chief opponent in that contest was Jonathan Lamb, a former commodities trader who became a successful local businessman and mostly self-financed his campaign with $450,000 in personal loans. Lamb, who said that Pence was "unwilling to be transparent and upfront with the voters about his failure and share his business resume," also criticized his opponent's scant campaign appearances. "How can we educate the voters on what the true issues are if the perceived heir-apparent to the seat won't talk and grant interviews?" Lamb told the Star.

Like his brother Mike, Pence emphasized his conservative views on social issues. Even with his deep Washington connections, his campaign slogan was, "Greg Pence will fight for Hoosier values, not D.C. values." His campaign website did not directly refer to the vice president, beyond the candidate's staunch support of "the Trump-Pence agenda."

Pence defeated Lamb, 64%-24%. In November, he gave little attention to lightly funded Democrat Jeannine Lee Lake.

IN-6: Southeast Indiana   Cook Partisan Voting Index: R+18

Population		Race and Ethnicity		Income	
Total	718,307	White	91.6%	Median Income	$50,994
Land area (sq. miles)	6,207	Black	2.6%	District Income Rank	288
Pop/ sq mi	115.7	Latino	2.7%	Poverty Rate	14.2%
Born in State	70.9%	Asian	1.4%	With health insurance	90.1%
		Two or more races	1.4%	Cash public assistance	2.1%
Age Groups		Other	0.2%	Food stamp/SNAP	11.6%
Under 18	22.5%				
18-34	21.5%	**Education**		**Work**	
35-64	39.5%	H.S grad or less	50.7%	White Collar	16.5%
Over 64	16.5%	Some college	28.4%	Sales and Service	38.8%
		College Degree, 4 yr	13.1%	Blue Collar	30%
Military		Post grad	7.8%	Government	11.3%
Veteran/ Active Duty	8.7%				

2012 Pres. Vote	Romney	172,452	(60%)	Obama	106,365	(37%)		
2016 Pres. Vote	Trump	204,129	(67%)	Clinton	82,498	(27%)	Johnson	14,897 (5%)

Muncie: Muncie became famous as the "Middletown" where sociologists Robert and Helen Lynd lived and did research for their landmark report in 1924 and 1925. The Lynds were attracted to Muncie because it was typical of "every small city from Maine to California," as Life magazine put it. But it wasn't exactly. Muncie was a factory town in a country still almost 50 percent rural in the 1920s, and it was almost entirely Protestant and Northern in a country that was one-fifth Catholic and one-third Southern. Muncie was more typical in that it was culturally homogeneous but economically riven. In the 1920s, when General Motors opened a plant in Muncie, the city celebrated its common values and was loath to admit its economic disparities. In the 1930s, those differences were exposed when Muncie, like much of the industrial Midwest, was unionized, a process that sometimes led to violent clashes. Workers who were joining CIO unions and voting for Democrats fiercely opposed the business elite — local bankers, merchants, GM executives and the Ball family's glass company.

Today, the region has remained a story of both sides of the American economic coin. "Local auto parts plants were in many ways the engine that drove the Muncie economy. At its peak in the 1950s, Warner Gear (later BorgWarner Automotive) employed more than 5,000 workers," the Muncie Star-Press wrote in a profile of its hometown in 2015. The BorgWarner plant closed in 2009. Earlier, the city was devastated in 2006 by the loss of a General Motors manual transmission plant. In 2018, the two largest employers in Muncie were Ball State University and the Indiana University hospital.

The area regained some of its manufacturing heft with the arrival of a foreign-owned automaker: The Honda plant in Greensburg employed 2,500 non-union workers who annually manufacture 250,000 cars, including the introduction in 2018 of the Insight, a gas-electric hybrid. The international trade policies of President Donald Trump became a big concern in this trade-dependent area. Columbus, the hometown of Vice President Mike Pence, has more than 40 overseas companies with local operations, with nearly 10,000 employees.

There is one constant in these environs: basketball. It is the civic religion here. Most of the nation's largest high school gyms are in Indiana. The Fieldhouse, in New Castle, near the Indiana Basketball Hall of Fame, is the largest of them all. Tiny Milan High School's 1954 state championship victory over Muncie Central was the basis for the 1986 movie Hoosiers.

The 6th Congressional District of Indiana covers most of the east-central and southeast parts of the state. It includes Muncie in the north as well as Richmond, founded by a major branch of American Quakers and home to their Earlham College. Batesville, to the south, is the site of the Batesville Casket Co., which makes the coffins for U.S. military personnel who die in the line of duty. In 2016, the Republican presidential ticket got 68 percent of the district vote, its best showing in the state. The fact that Pence represented the 6th from 2001 until 2013 was a local boost for Trump.

Andre Carson (D)

Elected 2008, 6th full term, b. Oct 16, 1974; Indianapolis; Concordia University, B.S., 2003; Indiana Wesleyan University, M.A., 2005; Islam (Muslim); Married (Mariama Carson); 1 child.

Elected Office: Indianapolis/Marion City-County Council, 2007-2008.

Professional Career: Investigator, IN State Excise Police, 1996-2005; Investigator, IN Department of Homeland Security, 2006-2008.

DC Office: 2135 RHOB 20515, 202-225-4011, Fax: 202-225-5633, carson.house.gov

State Offices: Indianapolis, 317-283-6516.

Committees: *Permanent Select on Intelligence*: Counterterrorism, Counterintelligence & Counterproliferation (Chmn); Strategic Technologies & Advanced Research. *Transportation & Infrastructure*: Aviation; Railroads, Pipelines & Hazardous Materials.

Group Ratings

	ADA	ACLU	AFL-CIO	LCV	ITI	COC	HAFA	ACU	CFG	FRC
2018	-	83%	-	94%	-	67%	9%	17%	13%	0%
2017	100%	C	97%	91%	C	36%	C	8%	5%	0%

Almanac Ratings 2017-18

	Economy	Social	Foreign	Composite
Liberal	84%	100%	91%	92%
Conservative	16%	0%	9%	8%

Key Votes of the 115th Congress

1. Obama-care revision	N	5. Family planning regs	N	9. Guantanamo prisoners	Y
2. Tax Cuts	N	6. Body cameras/immigration	Y	10. Ground missiles, limit	Y
3. Omnibus appropriations	Y	7. Abortion ban	N	11. Defense Dept. spending	N
4. Dodd-Frank revision	Y	8. Concealed carry	N	12. FISA rules	Y

Election Results

Election	Name (Party)	Vote (%)		Cand. Spent	Ind. Exp. Support	Ind. Exp. Oppose
2018 General	Andre Carson (D)	141,139	(65%)	$824,921		
	Wayne Harmon (R)	76,457	(35%)			
2018 Primary	Andre Carson (D)	37,662	(88%)			
	Sue Spicer (D)	3,499	(8%)			

Prior winning percentages: 2016 (60%), 2014 (55%), 2012 (63%), 2010 (59%), 2008 (65%), 2008 special (54%)

Democrat André Carson won his seat in a 2008 special election to succeed his grandmother, Julia Carson, who died in office. An occasionally outspoken progressive and active in the Congressional Black Caucus, he has pursued national security issues at the Intelligence Committee. As a Muslim, he has been a sharp critic of the travel ban that President Donald Trump imposed on several majority-Muslim nations.

Originally interested in the priesthood, Carson converted to Islam and became the second Muslim elected to Congress. Carson also had an artistic side. He wrote poetry as a young man and performed as a rap artist under the name "Juggernaut." With a career in law enforcement in mind, he got a bachelor's degree in criminal justice management from Concordia University and a master's degree in business management from Indiana Wesleyan. Carson spent nine years as a plainclothes officer of the Indiana Excise Police, which enforces alcohol and tobacco laws. "I loved law enforcement," he told Esquire magazine in 2010. "But this job sure beats sitting and waiting for something bad to go down at three in the morning."

He recalled that his political interest began in 1984, at age 10, when he attended the Democratic convention in San Francisco and heard civil rights leader Jesse Jackson speak. Carson said his thinking was transformed by reading The Autobiography of Malcolm X, and he attended Nation of Islam leader Louis Farrakhan's Million Man March in 1995. In 2007, at age 32, he won a seat on the Indianapolis City-County Council, his first elected office.

After Julia Carson died in December 2007, her grandson faced significant opposition for the Democratic nomination in the special election to fill the remainder of her term. At the January 2008 Democratic caucus, he won a bare majority with 223 of the 439 votes. State Rep. David Orentlicher, a lawyer and doctor, got 123 votes, and Marion County Treasurer Michael Rodman came in third with 27 votes. Against Republican state Rep. Jon Elrod, a lawyer, Carson received extensive assistance from the Democratic Congressional Campaign Committee. He called for withdrawing U.S. troops from Iraq, endorsed tax cuts for working families, and said companies should have incentives to keep them from sending jobs overseas. He won, 54%-43%. Carson has faced minimal opposition since, though his vote percentage in the general election has been relatively small compared with most other Black Caucus members.

In the House, his voting record has been mostly liberal. He placed near the center of House Democrats in the Almanac vote ratings for 2017. He initially opposed the $700 billion bailout of financial markets in 2008, but switched his position after Barack Obama, then the Democratic presidential nominee, urged him to support it. Carson has been a senior whip on Minority Whip Steny Hoyer's team. Before the final vote on the health care overhaul in 2010, he claimed that angry protesters outside the Capitol hurled racial epithets at him and civil-rights icon Rep. John Lewis of Georgia.

As the first Muslim to get a seat on the Intelligence Committee, Carson's selection produced protests from some conservative activists. He has won committee approval of his amendments to increase the transparency of government efforts to counter violent extremism at home and abroad, calling it "critical that we maintain strong oversight of these programs to protect American privacy and civil rights." In May 2018, the House passed Carson's amendment to the defense-spending bill to require mental health assessments for service members who have been deployed.

As ranking Democrat on the panel's Emerging Threats Subcommittee in 2018 when the GOP controlled the House, Carson criticized committee Republicans for shutting down the investigation of Russian interference in the 2016 election; he said they were "putting our country's national security interests and democracy at risk." He said Trump's decision to withdraw the United States from the nuclear deal with Iran was "illogical, shortsighted and extremely dangerous."

His biting rhetoric has sometimes gotten Carson in trouble. At a town hall meeting in 2011, Carson said that some members of the tea party movement in Congress would love to see blacks "hanging on a tree." In March 2018, Indianapolis Star columnist Tim Swarens attacked Carson for failing to criticize Farrakhan for anti-Semitic comments in a speech. "How much hatred must Farrakhan spread before Carson and other prominent Democrats disavow and distance themselves from him?" Swarens wrote, adding that Carson said he opposed anti-Semitism but that he failed to include any mention of Farrakhan.

During the 2016 campaign, Carson voiced concern about what he called Trump's anti-Muslim rhetoric. "That saying about 'Make America Great Again' is a form of meta-messaging to a certain segment, we're talking about our white brothers and sisters, largely blue collar," he said. When the Supreme Court in June 2018 upheld a modified version of the travel ban in a 5-4 decision, Carson called it "a shameful sanctioning of discrimination."

IN-7: Indianapolis

Cook Partisan Voting Index: D+11

Population		Race and Ethnicity		Income	
Total	753,500	White	53.4%	Median Income	$41,211
Land area (sq. miles)	304	Black	29.5%	District Income Rank	405
Pop/ sq mi	2479.9	Latino	11.1%	Poverty Rate	22.4%
Born in State	67.8%	Asian	2.9%	With health insurance	86.3%
		Two or more races	2.6%	Cash public assistance	2.2%
Age Groups		Other	0.5%	Food stamp/SNAP	19%
Under 18	25.9%				
18-34	26.3%	**Education**		**Work**	
35-64	36.8%	H.S grad or less	48.5%	White Collar	11%
Over 64	11%	Some college	28.8%	Sales and Service	44.7%
		College Degree, 4 yr	15.2%	Blue Collar	25.5%
Military		Post grad	7.6%	Government	9.9%
Veteran/ Active Duty	7.4%				

2012 Pres. Vote	Obama	164,902	(63%)	Romney	92,674	(35%)			
2016 Pres. Vote	Clinton	156,046	(58%)	Trump	95,656	(36%)	Johnson	12,689	(5%)

Indianapolis: Indianapolis, radiating outward from the soldiers and sailors statue in Monument Circle, is precisely at the center of Indiana and is the largest and most dominant city in the state. What residents once disparaged as "Nap Town" has become a thriving metropolis, including downtown. The city is the political and governmental capital, industrial and financial hub, and the intellectual center of Indiana as well. It is symmetrically laid out: Just to the west of the circle is the state capitol, to the north is the American Legion headquarters, to the east is the City-County building, and to the south are the Circle Centre mall, Lucas Oil Stadium, home of the NFL's Indianapolis Colts, and the headquarters of the National Collegiate Athletic Association. Indianapolis has fostered its niche as the nation's amateur sports capital, especially for basketball. It also is a popular place for religious conventions. Home to the iconic Indianapolis 500, the motorsports industry is a prominent business for the state.

Many large companies are based in Indianapolis. Pharmaceutical giant Eli Lilly & Co. spent $400 million to expand its insulin manufacturing operations, including two insulin cartridge filling lines. In 2018, Verizon made Indianapolis one of four cities where it was testing its new 5G broadband service. FedEx has its second-largest airport hub here, where it can sort 2 million packages each day. State officials — including then-Gov. Mike Pence -- have promoted the city as a high-tech jobs center, which some have dubbed "Silicon Prairie." Less certain is the fate of old-line manufacturer Carrier. Shortly before he took office, President Donald Trump visited the Indianapolis plant to claim credit for a deal in which the company cut back its plan to send jobs to Mexico. But by early 2018, Carrier had imposed new layoffs. Workers had growing fears of automation, in addition to the threat of cheap foreign labor.

Indiana's 7th Congressional District takes in most of Indianapolis. The more prosperous northern edge of the city is in the 5th District. In decades past, Indianapolis had robust political competition in local and national races. More recently, affluent young people have been moving to counties farther out. The median income has dropped in Marion County, especially in the 7th. It has become solidly Democratic. In 2016, Hillary Clinton won the District, 58%-36%, a dip from 2012, when Barack Obama took the 7th, 63%-35%. The District has the largest minority population in the state, though it remains 53 percent white. It is one of only two Democratic districts in the state; the other is the Gary-based 1st.

Larry Bucshon (R)

Elected 2010, 5th term, b. May 31, 1962; Taylorsville, IL; University of Illinois - Urbana, B.S., 1984; University of Illinois Medical School - Chicago, M.D., 1988; Lutheran; Married (Kathryn Bucshon); 4 children.

Military Career: U.S. Navy Reserve 1989-1998

Professional Career: Practicing cardiothoracic surgeon, 1995-1998; Ohio Valley HeartCare, 1998-2010, President, 2003-2010; Chief & Medical Director, St. Mary's Hospital.

DC Office: 2313 RHOB 20515, 202-225-4636, Fax: 202-225-3284, bucshon.house.gov

State Offices: Evansville, 812-465-6484; Jasper, 812-482-4255; Terre Haute, 812-232-0523; Vincennes, 855-519-1629.

Committees: *Energy & Commerce*: Consumer Protection & Commerce; Energy; Health.

Group Ratings

	ADA	ACLU	AFL-CIO	LCV	ITI	COC	HAFA	ACU	CFG	FRC
2018	-	4%	-	3%	-	92%	56%	72%	51%	100%
2017	0%	C	24%	6%	C	93%	C	74%	64%	100%

Almanac Ratings 2017-18

	Economy	Social	Foreign	Composite
Liberal	6%	4%	0%	3%
Conservative	94%	97%	100%	97%

Key Votes of the 115th Congress

1. Obama-care revision	Y	5. Family planning regs	Y	9. Guantanamo prisoners	N
2. Tax Cuts	Y	6. Body cameras/immigration	N	10. Ground missiles, limit	N
3. Omnibus appropriations	Y	7. Abortion ban	Y	11. Defense Dept. spending	Y
4. Dodd-Frank revision	Y	8. Concealed carry	Y	12. FISA rules	Y

Election Results

Election	Name (Party)	Vote (%)		Cand. Spent	Ind. Exp. Support	Ind. Exp. Oppose
2018 General	Larry Bucshon (R)............................ 157,396	(64%)		$832,362	$11,023	
	William Tanoos (D)...................... 86,895	(36%)		$226,574		
2018 Primary	Larry Bucshon (R)............................... 34,516	(63%)				
	Richard Moss (R)........................... 13,831	(25%)				
	Rachel Convington (R).......................... 6,451	(12%)				

Prior winning percentages: 2016 (64%), 2014 (60%), 2012 (53%), 2010 (58%)

Republican Larry Bucshon, elected in 2010, is among the physicians from his party who have been outspoken critics of Democrats on the Affordable Care Act. On the Energy and Commerce Committee, he has sought opportunities for bipartisan consensus, including on energy and communications issues and occasionally health care reforms.

Bucshon was raised in the rural town of Kincaid Illinois. As an undergraduate at the University of Illinois, his rightward shift solidified when he became enamored of President Ronald Reagan. In high school, Bucshon decided on a career in medicine, inspired by the surgeons he met at the hospital where his mother was a nurse. He got his medical degree at the University of Illinois at Chicago and completed a residency at the Medical College of Wisconsin, where he specialized in cardiothoracic surgery. Bucshon enlisted in the Naval Reserve, serving for nearly a decade. After three years in private practice in Wichita Kansas, he joined Ohio Valley HeartCare, a large cardiology and cardiovascular surgery practice in Evansville. In 2003, he became its president.

Bucshon ran when Democratic Rep. Brad Ellsworth sought a Senate seat in 2010. Helped by the National Republican Congressional Committee, Bucshon prevailed over seven other candidates in the GOP primary, edging out tea party-backed Kristi Risk, 33%-29%. In the general, he faced state

Rep. Trent Van Haaften, who fit the centrist mold of Ellsworth. Van Haaften was a prosecutor in rural Posey County who emphasized his law-and-order background, while Bucshon campaigned on curbing spending and repeal of the Democrats' health care overhaul. Bucshon raised and spent $1.1 million, compared with $762,000 for Van Haaften. He won 57%-38%.

Bucshon actively opposed the excise tax on medical device equipment, as well as a Medicare cost-control board included in the health care law. "I have been a practicing physician for over 15 years, and I don't think I have seen anything potentially more detrimental to seniors' health care than the Independent Payment Advisory Board," he said. But conservatives criticized his backing of the August 2011 increase in the debt limit, unlike other Indiana GOP freshmen.

In a lengthy profile in October 2018, the Evansville Courier-Press described Bucshon as "a serious, sober minded – if unspectacular – legislator" who was in the middle of the House. A colleague said he was "a work horse, not a show horse." On Energy and Commerce, he joined in bipartisan support for the 2015 law establishing a permanent fix in Medicare reimbursement of doctor fees. Bucshon cited his cooperation with another doctor, Democratic Rep. Ami Bera of California, on repeal of a complex billing procedure imposed by Medicare officials. With committee Democrats Frank Pallone of New Jersey and Joe Kennedy of Massachusetts, Bucshon filed a bipartisan bill to encourage monitoring programs for prescription drug addiction. In 2016, He worked with Republican leaders on their priority legislation to treat opioid addiction. He criticized in November 2018 a proposal by President Donald Trump to limit prescription-drug prices; Bucshon called it a step toward "government price-fixing."

Also on Energy and Commerce, Bucshon worked on energy legislation to promote his district's large coal resources, and telecommunications priorities such as expanded broadband access. In March 2018, he was the lead sponsor of a bill to increase tax credits for coal-powered utility plants; the measure went nowhere.

In 2012, tea party candidate Risk mounted another primary challenge to Bucshon but could not come close to competing financially, and the incumbent won 58%-42%. His Democratic challenger in the general election was broadcaster and former state Rep. Dave Crooks, who sought to portray Bucshon as out of touch with regular voters and touted his own culturally and fiscally conservative views. Bucshon got help from conservative super PACs that ran ads on his behalf in the campaign's closing weeks, notching a hardly overwhelming 53%-43% victory. Since then, Bucshon has become entrenched in a district with a long history of electing Democrats. In the 2018 Republican primary, challenger Richard Moss criticized him as "liberal Larry." Bucshon won, 63%-25%.

In the House minority for the first time following the 2018 election, Bucshon faced the challenge of seeking bipartisan opportunities while remaining a loyal Republican.

IN-8: Southwest Indiana

Cook Partisan Voting Index: R+15

Population		Race and Ethnicity		Income	
Total	720,806	White	90.4%	Median Income	$49,193
Land area (sq. miles)	7,255	Black	4.1%	District Income Rank	325
Pop/ sq mi	99.3	Latino	2.4%	Poverty Rate	14.6%
Born in State	75.6%	Asian	1%	With health insurance	90.5%
Age Groups		Two or more races	1.8%	Cash public assistance	2%
Under 18	22.5%	Other	0.4%	Food stamp/SNAP	11.6%
18-34	22.2%	**Education**		**Work**	
35-64	39%	H.S grad or less	48.3%	White Collar	16.3%
Over 64	16.3%	Some college	31%	Sales and Service	38.9%
Military		College Degree, 4 yr	13.2%	Blue Collar	30.2%
Veteran/ Active Duty	8.7%	Post grad	7.4%	Government	11.4%

2012 Pres. Vote	Romney	169,317	(58%)	Obama	114,907	(40%)		
2016 Pres. Vote	Trump	194,208	(64%)	Clinton	92,844	(31%)	Johnson	13,569 (5%)

Evansville, Terre Haute: "Evansville," wrote John Bartlow Martin in 1947, "is the capital of a tri-state area comprising the neglected tag ends of Indiana, Kentucky and Illinois." It was a factory town then, making car parts and refrigerators, drawing workers from Kentucky, Tennessee and the picturesque but not very fertile hills of Southern Indiana.

Evansville has become a headquarters for midsized companies that offer good-paying, skilled jobs. Car parts still get made here, though it is auto assembly that helps anchor the local manufacturing economy. Toyota in 1998 opened a plant in nearby Princeton that builds SUVs and minivans. With an expansion scheduled for 2019 to build more SUVs, the plant employed more than 5,100 workers. The recovery of the auto industry helped Evansville weather the recession. But the local Whirlpool refrigerator production plant closed in 2010, followed by the shuttering of its refrigeration product design center. In 2017, Alcoa reopened its aluminum smelter, increasing its workforce to 1,500 jobs.

In Vanderburgh County, Evansville is one of two major population centers of the 8th Congressional District, which covers Southwest Indiana. The other, in Vigo County, is Terre Haute, an old manufacturing town and the boyhood home of socialist Eugene Debs. It hosts a maximum-security penitentiary, which includes the only federal death chamber; an arrival in 2001 was Dylann Roof, who was convicted in the 2015 church shootings in Charleston South Carolina. In 2018, a Facebook post declared that Evansville had the unwanted distinction of "meth capital of the world;" local police responded that the information was five years old. The district takes in Vincennes, a small town on the banks of the Wabash River and the original capital of Indiana. Downstream is New Harmony, an early utopian community established by Welsh philanthropist and visionary Robert Owen.

Southern Indiana is ancestrally Democratic, just as northern Indiana is ancestrally Republican. The southern counties were hostile to the Union during the Civil War, and then in New Deal times workers in Evansville moved toward the Democrats. Vigo remains a swing county, which has voted for the winning presidential candidate in all but two elections since the 19th century. For decades, the result was a very close political balance, and this district was known as the "Bloody 8th" for its tight congressional races. At one point in the 1970s, it sent four different members to the House in four successive elections. In 1984, the state certified the Republican the winner by exactly 34 votes. The Democratic majority in the House investigated and overturned the result in a fight that left many Republican bitter. As with other rural and blue-collar areas, the trend in presidential politics has been away from Democrats. In 2008, John McCain led Barack Obama, 51%-48%. In 2016, Donald Trump swept Hillary Clinton, 64%-31%. Before the May primary, Trump had a rally in Evansville that drew 12,000 supporters, an early demonstration of the challenge facing national Democrats.

Trey Hollingsworth (R)

Elected 2016, 2nd term, b. Sep 12, 1983; Clinton, TN; Webb School (TN); University of Pennsylvania, B.S.E., 2004; Georgetown University (DC), M.P.P., 2014; Christian Church; Married (Kelly Hollingsworth); 1 child.

Professional Career: Small Business Owner.

DC Office: 1641 LHOB 20515, 202-225-5315, Fax: 202-226-6866, hollingsworth.house.gov

State Offices: Franklin, 317-851-8710; Jeffersonville, 812-288-3999.

Committees: *Financial Services*: Investor Protection, Entrepreneurship & Capital Markets; Subcommittee on Diversity & Inclusion.

Group Ratings

	ADA	ACLU	AFL-CIO	LCV	ITI	COC	HAFA	ACU	CFG	FRC
2018	-	7%	-	11%	-	75%	74%	76%	78%	100%
2017	0%	C	3%	6%	C	93%	C	88%	88%	100%

Almanac Ratings 2017-18

	Economy	Social	Foreign	Composite
Liberal	6%	3%	13%	8%
Conservative	94%	97%	87%	92%

Key Votes of the 115th Congress

1. Obama-care revision	Y	5. Family planning regs	Y	9. Guantanamo prisoners	N		
2. Tax Cuts	Y	6. Body cameras/immigration	N	10. Ground missiles, limit	N		
3. Omnibus appropriations	N	7. Abortion ban	Y	11. Defense Dept. spending	Y		
4. Dodd-Frank revision	Y	8. Concealed carry	Y	12. FISA rules	Y		

Election Results

Election	Name (Party)	Vote (%)		Cand. Spent	Ind. Exp. Support	Ind. Exp. Oppose
2018 General	Trey Hollingsworth (R)......................	153,271	(56%)	$1,473,320	$6,096	$157,740
	Liz Watson (D)...................................	118,090	(44%)	$2,468,055	$93,198	
2018 Primary	Trey Hollingsworth (R)......................	46,892	(78%)			
	James Alspach (R)...............................	13,449	(22%)			

Prior winning percentages: 2016 (54%)

Republican Trey Hollingsworth, elected in 2016 with no political experience and a limited connection to the 9th District, remained the target of critics who said that he had used ample self-financing to buy his seat. In his reelection campaign, he faced another candidate from the Democratic part of the district who failed to move beyond her home base. In the House, Hollingsworth worked to cut back banking regulation as a member of the Financial Services Committee.

Hollingsworth was raised in Clinton Tennessee, a small city near Knoxville, which is about 230 miles from Indiana. He graduated from the University of Pennsylvania, with a degree in real estate, and later got a master's degree in public policy from Georgetown University. In the meantime, Hollingsworth became a managing partner and majority owner of his family's fast-growing Hollingsworth Capital Partners, which refurbished vacant factories — including some in Indiana. In 2008, he and a group of partners opened Alexin, an aluminum casting plant in Indiana. According to the Indianapolis Star, his company had filed legal papers in five other states that obligated him to live outside of Indiana to represent his business interests.

In September 2015, after then-Rep. Todd Young announced his campaign for the Senate, Hollingsworth moved from Tennessee to Jeffersonville Indiana. A month later, he announced his campaign for the open seat. In the hotly contested five-candidate primary, he spent heavily on campaign ads that touted his business acumen and outsider status. His challengers included Indiana Attorney General Greg Zoeller and state Sens. Erin Houchin and Brent Waltz. "Mr. Hollingsworth just moved here from Tennessee in the fall of last year trying to buy a congressional seat," Houchin said. Zoeller, who started the contest as the best-known candidate, called Hollingsworth a "political scam artist." Hollingsworth won the primary with 35 percent of the vote, to 25 percent for Houchin and 22 percent for Zoeller.

Democratic nominee Shelli Yoder was an Indiana native and a former Miss Indiana, who coincidentally lived in Tennessee for 10 years. In 2012, she challenged Young and lost, 55%-45%. According to the Indianapolis Star, which described her as "the quintessential Hoosier," Yoder attacked Hollingsworth for trying to buy the seat with "generic GOP talking points rather than an understanding of Southern Indiana." Hollingsworth attacked Yoder for supporting Hillary Clinton and her policies.

Hollingsworth spent nearly $3.6 million for his campaign, of which $3.1 million was self-financed. His campaign report disclosed that his net worth exceeded $50 million. He had more than $2.5 million in support from national Republican committees and a Super PAC. Yoder spent $1.4 million and had $1 million support from the Democratic Congressional Campaign Committee. Hollingsworth prevailed, 54%-41%, with his anti-establishment message and business credentials. He won each of the 13 counties except for Monroe, which was Yoder's base and the Democratic stronghold.

Hollingsworth made few waves in the House. Fulfilling a campaign promise, his first legislation was a constitutional amendment to limit senators to two six-year terms and House members to four two-year terms. On the Financial Services Committee, he worked with other Republicans to ease some of the regulatory provisions of the Dodd-Frank financial services law, which was enacted in 2010 to address the banking crisis. That law's biggest failure, he said, was that "it institutionalized 'too big to fail,' instead of ending it." In July 2018, Hollingsworth showed independence when he was one of six Republicans to vote against a House-passed resolution opposing a carbon tax.

At home, Hollingsworth was attacked for failing to hold town-hall meetings and largely avoiding Monroe County, the population center and Democratic bastion. According to critics, "He's unavailable back home [and] … unaccountable out in Washington, with a voting record that indicates he's more responsive to his donors than to his constituents," according to a pre-election report in Indianapolis Monthly, a city-based magazine. The report cited supporters of Hollingsworth who credited him with "a more personal, individualized approach to connecting with constituents," especially in friendly territory.

In his reelection bid, Hollingsworth won the Republican primary, 78%-22% against James Dean Alspach, a political maverick who did not report spending any money on his campaign and promised that, if successful, he would run for president. He faced a more credible Democratic challenger: Liz Watson, an attorney from Bloomington and former labor-policy aide for Democrats at the House Education and the Workforce Committee, who was running her first campaign. She attacked Hollingsworth's out-of-state roots and his refusal to participate in campaign debates. With support from progressive and anti-gun groups, Watson outspent the incumbent, $2.5 million to $1.5 million. The outcome was similar to 2016: Watson took 69 percent in Monroe County, which had the largest turnout. Hollingsworth won the remaining 12 counties and prevailed, 56%-44%.

The most likely threat to Hollingsworth would be if a prominent local Republican consolidated local opposition to him — perhaps with a boost from a 2021 redistricting that changes the boundaries of the district.

IN-9: South-Central Indiana   Cook Partisan Voting Index: R+13

Population		Race and Ethnicity		Income	
Total	743,185	White	89.5%	Median Income	$53,862
Land area (sq. miles)	4,487	Black	2.8%	District Income Rank	244
Pop/ sq mi	165.6	Latino	3.3%	Poverty Rate	13.7%
Born in State	64.9%	Asian	2.3%	With health insurance	91.2%
		Two or more races	1.9%	Cash public assistance	1.4%
Age Groups		Other	0.3%	Food stamp/SNAP	9.1%
Under 18	22%				
18-34	24.7%	**Education**		**Work**	
35-64	38.5%	H.S grad or less	44.8%	White Collar	14.8%
Over 64	14.8%	Some college	29.2%	Sales and Service	40.1%
		College Degree, 4 yr	15.9%	Blue Collar	25%
Military		Post grad	10%	Government	13%
Veteran/ Active Duty	8.5%				

2012 Pres. Vote	Romney	173,433	(57%)	Obama	123,436	(41%)		
2016 Pres. Vote	Trump	198,108	(60%)	Clinton	110,837	(34%)	Johnson	15,534	(5%)

Bloomington, Indianapolis Suburbs, Louisville Suburbs: The immense Ohio River is the largest tributary of the Mississippi. In Southern Indiana, it runs along the Indiana-Kentucky border and is an artery of commerce. Utilitarian barges have replaced the old steamers, except for riverboat casinos. Along the river are towns like Corydon, which was the state capital from 1816 to 1825. Salem was the home of John Milton Hay, personal secretary to President Abraham Lincoln and later secretary of State in the William McKinley and Theodore Roosevelt administrations.

In 2016, the new Lewis and Clark Bridge opened on the Ohio River between Jeffersonville and Prospect Kentucky. In a less auspicious note for the river, Jeffersonville-based Jeffboat in 2018 shut down its barge-manufacturing operations. The company, which had employed more than 1,000, cited oversupply and a "very poor" outlook for new construction. The local shipyard opened in 1834. An affiliated company had nearly 4,000 employees in its barge-freight business.

In Indiana's 9th Congressional District, the largest city is Bloomington, where Indiana University and its 48,000 students are based. The university planned to open in 2020 a new health campus, hospital and regional academic health center. Bloomington, which has been rated second in the Milken Institute's index of best-performing cities for high-tech employment, has developed a technology park near the IU campus. Monroe County-based Bloomington is a Democratic stronghold. But its vote usually is overwhelmed — especially by nearby Johnson and Morgan counties, which are growing Republican bastions in the suburbs of Indianapolis. The Louisville Kentucky suburbs in Clark and Floyd counties have trended Republican.

IOWA

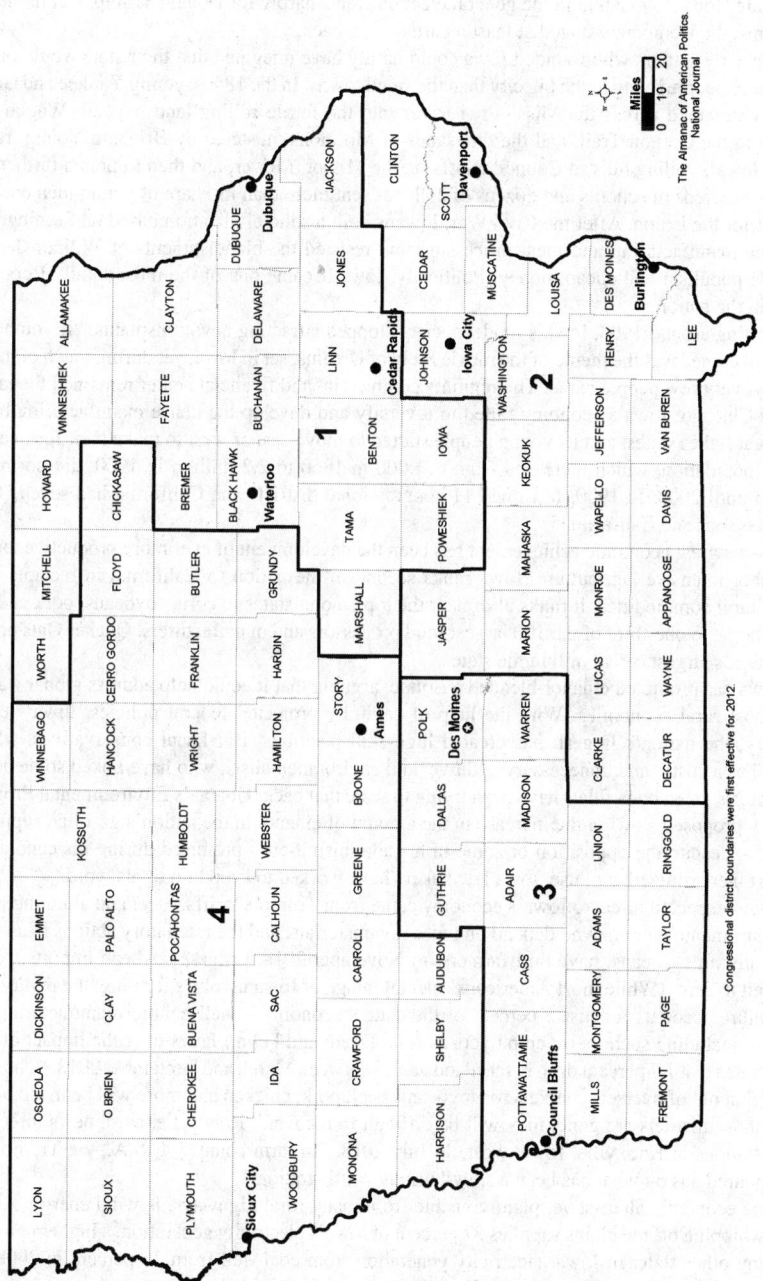

Congressional district boundaries were first effective for 2012

Iowa holds a special place in American politics thanks to its presidential caucuses, preceded by months of retail politicking on the snowy prairie. In recent decades, the state has been hotly contested between the two parties. In 2016, it was transformed from the state that launched Barack Obama into the White House to one that in the general election went sharply for Donald Trump. But in the 2018 midterms, the Democrats staged at least a partial comeback.

The early settlers who founded Iowa could hardly have imagined that their state would one day have more people living in the big city than the small towns. In the 1840s, young Yankee and German farmers streamed across the Mississippi River into the fertile rolling land beyond. Wagon trains headed to the Oregon Trail, and the thousands of Mormons mustered by Brigham Young traveled across Iowa's rolling hills to Council Bluffs on the Missouri River, and then to points further west. Iowa's hundreds of schools and dozens of colleges sent more than its share of young men back East to fight for the Union. After the Civil War, Iowans built a solid civilization based on farming, farm-machine manufacturing and meat processing that resisted the blandishments of William Jennings Bryan's populism and cheap money. Politically, Iowa became one of the most solidly Republican states in the nation.

Starting around 1900, Iowa's model society stopped attracting new transplants. "If you build it, they will come" was the theme of the movie Field of Dreams, set in Iowa, yet during much of the 20th century, very few people came. The region's commercial and financial center remained the railroad hub of Chicago; Iowa's economy failed to diversify and develop the dense manufacturing base of the Great Lakes states, and its young people started to move east or west to make their fortunes. The state's population, which increased from 674,000 in 1860 to 2.2 million in 1900, did not reach 3 million until 2008. In 1900, Iowa had 11 congressional districts and California had seven. Today, Iowa has four and California 53.

Iowa's great economic achievement has been the development of ever more productive, but also less labor-intensive, agriculture. Iowa ranks second in the nation to California in receipts for all agricultural commodities. It ranks at or near the top among states in corn, soybeans, pork and eggs, and is home to one-third of the 100 largest food processors and manufacturers. Quaker Oats operates the nation's largest cereal mill in the state.

Iowa has promoted ethanol-blended gasoline, arguing that it could help address global warming and boost rural economies. With the help of carefully protected federal policies, Iowa's ethanol industry, the nation's largest, has created high-skill positions. But fiscal conservatives, who see ethanol as a costly and unnecessary additive, and environmentalists, who have poked some holes in the sector's green bona fides, have been trying to scale that back. Obama's Environmental Protection Agency proposed slowing the increase in the amount of ethanol in the nation's gasoline supply, but Trump – despite the opposition of some in his administration – promised during his candidacy to support increasing ethanol use. Iowa lawmakers have worked to keep him to his word.

An unexpected threat to Iowa's economy came from Trump's tariffs. Steel and aluminum tariffs have hurt manufacturers who depend on those raw materials, and the retaliatory actions from China, especially on soybeans, have hurt farmers; in November 2018, Chinese soybean imports from the U.S. fell to zero. (While most Americans' mental image of Iowa involves farming, the reality is that agriculture accounts for just 5 percent of the state's economy – well behind manufacturing at 18 percent, including such major employers as John Deere and Pella.) Fears over the impact of tariffs contributed to a 1.7 percent drop in farmland values between March and September 2018. "The cost of being shut out of overseas markets for soybeans, beef, pork, chicken and more will be in the billions. Once those markets are gone, they will be difficult to recover," Robert Leonard, news director for radio stations in Knoxville, Iowa, wrote in July 2018. "In farm country, U.S.A., the Trump tariffs have poured gas on what has been a slow-burning conflagration."

One economic alternative, plainly visible from many rural highways, is wind energy. Already, wind whipping off the plains supplies 37 percent of Iowa's electricity generation, a higher percentage than any other state. In Iowa, electricity generation from coal fell from 76 percent in 2008 to 45 percent in 2017. Mega-rich investor Warren Buffett's Berkshire Hathaway has spent billions on renewable energy in the state since 2004, and he promised to double that investment in the coming years – dependent, like ethanol, on continuing federal subsidies. The growth in wind energy has, in turn, helped lure data centers that need cheap electricity, including facilities for Apple, Facebook,

Google and Microsoft. It has also spawned detractors who point out that the turbines are noisy and dangerous to wildlife, although when Trump criticized wind power at a rally in Cedar Rapids, reaction within the state was largely negative.

After a stretch of population shrinkage due to farmland woes in the 1980s, there has been a modest rebound. Iowa has grown by about 3 percent since 2010, the longest run of population growth in the state since 1900. Those gains have occurred almost entirely in metropolitan areas; more than half of Iowa's population today is concentrated in just 10 of the state's 99 counties. That change is evident around Des Moines, where cornfields have given way to exurban development. West of the capital city, Clive, Johnston, Waukee and West Des Moines have seen double-digit population growth since 2010. To the north, Ankeny, Altoona and Bondurant have been booming. The state's two major college towns, Iowa City (University of Iowa) and Ames (Iowa State) are also seeing significant population gains.

Mexican immigrants have been moving to smaller cities with meatpacking plants; the state's population is now 6 percent Hispanic. Jobs and small-town life attracted Bosnians and Liberians as well as Congolese, Sudanese and Somali refugees. But Iowa is still a mostly white state, with a population that's only 5 percent black and 3 percent Asian. Iowa lost far fewer jobs in the 2007-09 recession than in the 1980s. Unemployment reached just 6.6 percent in mid-2009 – well below the 10 percent national peak -- and the state was tied for the lowest unemployment rate in the nation by late 2018 at 2.4 percent.

Iowa has its distinctive political rituals, none more famous than its first-in-the-nation presidential caucuses. One, two, even three years beforehand, White House hopefuls journey to the Iowa State Fair, held every August on the east side of Des Moines, to shake hands, eat a pork chop on a stick, and marvel at the famed butter cow sculpted out of 600 pounds of churned whole milk. Voter turnout has been among the nation's highest.

For much of the 20th century, Iowa was a culturally and politically counter-cyclical state, headed in the opposite direction of the rest of the nation. In the industrial New Deal era, it stayed mostly agricultural and Republican, even as Davenport and Des Moines radio announcer Ronald Reagan became an enthusiastic Roosevelt Democrat before heading to Hollywood. In the 1980s, when Reagan, by then a conservative Republican, was president and Iowa's economy was hit hard, anxiety became the dominant note of Iowa's politics, as voters sought protection from the vagaries of the market. In the 1988 caucuses, Iowa Republicans voted against Reagan's vice president, George H.W. Bush (despite Bush's victory over Reagan in the caucuses eight years earlier), while Iowa Democrats backed the somewhat populist Dick Gephardt. That fall, Iowa gave Democratic presidential nominee Michael Dukakis his second highest vote percentage of any state.

Iowa's political leanings can confound national expectations. To a greater degree than other states, Iowa has a dovish streak on foreign policy, leavened by a desire for international trade. The Iowa delegation voted for the 1993 North American Free Trade Agreement, the 1999 normalization of trade relations with China (Mexicans eat lots of corn and the Chinese like pork), and the 2015 measure to give trade promotion authority to Obama. In April 2009, well before same-sex marriage became more mainstream, the state Supreme Court unanimously ruled that Iowa's limitation of marriage to opposite-sex couples violated the state constitution. The state's high court took another liberal stand in 2015, unanimously striking down a rule by the Iowa Board of Medicine that would have prohibited Iowa doctors from using telemedicine to prescribe abortion-inducing drugs to rural women. But in 2017, Planned Parenthood closed four clinics after the GOP legislature redirected Medicaid family planning funding away from providers that offer abortion. And the state passed a "fetal heartbeat" law that would be among the toughest in the nation if courts allow it to go into effect.

Iowa voted twice for Democrat Bill Clinton, for Democrat Al Gore by just 4,144 votes in 2000, and for Republican George W. Bush by 10,059 votes in 2004. Iowa gave Obama a critical boost in its 2008 caucuses and then gave him its Electoral College votes in 2008 and 2012, before handing them to Trump in 2016. That year, the state received dwindling attention from the presidential candidates once it became clear that Trump – on his way to outperforming past Republican nominees among older, white, rural voters – would do well in Iowa. In the end, a state that backed Obama by six points in 2012 went for Trump by 10. No fewer than 31 counties -- almost one of every three -- shifted from Obama to Trump. The GOP also took control of the state Senate; this allowed the GOP to pass a raft of long-blocked conservative legislation in 2017. Few Democrats represent predominantly rural districts in the legislature any more.

But just as Iowa seemed to be moving out of reach for Democrats, the party partially rebounded in the 2018 midterms. The GOP retained the governorship, but only by 50%-48%. Republican votes for governor didn't grow appreciably from 2014 to 2018, but the Democratic vote total grew by almost 50 percent; the Democratic candidate, Fred Hubbell, won 11 counties, compared to just one for the party's 2014 nominee. More strikingly, Democrats Cindy Axne and Abby Finkenauer flipped two of Iowa's three GOP-held House seats, and a fourth Democrat held controversial Rep. Steve King to 50 percent of the vote. A Democrat also ousted the incumbent Republican state auditor. Democrats might contest the state more seriously in the next general election than anyone would have guessed in 2016.

Population		Race and Ethnicity		Income	
Total	3,118,102	White	86.5%	Median Income	$56,570
Land area (sq. miles)	55,857	Black	3.3%	State Income Rank	25
Pop/ sq mi	55.8	Latino	5.7%	Poverty Rate	12.0%
Born in state	70.8%	Asian	2.3%	With health insurance	94.4%
		Two or more races	1.7%	Cash public assistance	2.2%
Age Groups		Other	0.5%	Food stamp/SNAP	11.2%
Under 18	23.4%				
18-34	22.8%	**Education**		**Work**	
35-64	37.7%	H.S grad or less	39.7%	White Collar	35.3%
Over 64	16.1%	Some college	32.6%	Sales and Service	39.2%
		College Degree, 4 yr	18.7%	Blue Collar	25.6%
Military		Post grad	9.0%	Government	13.3%
Veteran/ Active Duty	8.2%				

Presidential Politics

2016 Caucus (D)	Clinton (D)	70,047 (50%)	Sanders (D)	69,692 (50%)			
2016 Caucus (R)	Cruz (R)	51,666 (28%)	Trump (R)	45,429 (24%)	Rubio (R)	43,228 (23%)	
	Carson (R)	17,394 (9%)					
2016 Pres. Vote	Trump (R)	800,983 (51%)	Clinton (D)	653,669 (42%)	Johnson (L)	59,186 (4%)	
	Bush (R)	(3%)					
2012 Pres. Vote	Obama (D)	822,544 (52%)	Romney (R)	730,617 (46%)			

Every four years, in the dead of winter, tens of thousands of Iowans troop to caucuses in nearly 2,000 precincts to begin the formal process of electing a president. The caucuses were scheduled early in the 1972 cycle by liberal Democrats who wanted more leverage for their views, and that year they started George McGovern on his way to the Democratic nomination. The caucuses have had other, unanticipated consequences. In 1976, Jimmy Carter's chief strategist, Hamilton Jordan, determined that an intensive campaign and a surprise victory could transform a little-known candidate into a national contender. About 50,000 Iowa Democrats caucused and Carter got the boost Jordan anticipated, finishing second to an "uncommitted" slate but winning more votes than any other actual candidate, almost 28 percent. With momentum from Iowa, Carter won the subsequent New Hampshire primary and was on his way to the Democratic nomination. Without the caucuses, Carter might well have just been another former Georgia governor.

Over the next 20 years, the Iowa caucuses were less decisive, but they almost always drew a crowd. In 2000, the Iowa caucuses became crucial again for both parties. George W. Bush won the 25,000-strong August 1999 Republican straw poll at Ames, after which Dan Quayle, Lamar Alexander and Elizabeth Dole dropped out, unable to win enough GOP donors who had flocked to Bush. John McCain skipped the straw poll and the caucuses, and staked his candidacy on winning the New Hampshire primary. Bush continued to build his organizational strength and defeated Steve Forbes, 41%-31%. On the Democratic side, the race was between Al Gore and Bill Bradley. In his first White House run in 1988, Gore skipped what he called the "madness" in "the small state of Iowa." But a decade later, he declared, "I love Iowa." With the help of organized labor, he defeated Bradley 63%-37%.

In 2008, both parties had candidates competing in the Iowa caucuses, but the Democratic contest was more vigorous. Hillary Clinton led in initial polls, but her vote for the 2002 Iraq war resolution and her refusal to apologize for it (as John Edwards had in 2005) hurt her with dovish Iowa Democrats. Republican candidates attracted less attention. Mitt Romney outspent all the other Republicans combined and had the most staffers. But Mike Huckabee quietly built a network of evangelical Christians and home-school parents, and the former Baptist minister's folksy manner was appealing. With some 239,000 participants in the Democratic caucuses, a record, Obama won 38 percent of their "delegate strength," a clear victory. His success in a state with a 3 percent black population was pivotal. Clinton's victory in the New Hampshire primary five days portended a long, close race. In retrospect, it's hard to see how Obama could have become president without winning Iowa. The result on the Republican side was also important. Three out of five caucus attendees were evangelical or born-again Christians; and nearly half of them voted for Huckabee, who beat Romney, 34%-25%. Romney's defeat eroded his support in New Hampshire and enabled McCain to revive his candidacy. The Arizonan was the first Republican presidential nominee to have finished lower than third in Iowa.

In 2012, only Republicans had a contest. Romney eschewed extensive campaigning and didn't participate in the Ames straw poll. Tim Pawlenty, from neighboring Minnesota, regarded Iowa as a must-win state and worked to bring supporters to Ames. Michele Bachmann, also from Minnesota, was a favorite of tea party Republicans. Also campaigning hard, and with determined supporters, was libertarian Ron Paul. Bachmann won the straw poll with 29 percent, with Paul second at 28 percent. Pawlenty, running third with 14 percent, withdrew the next morning. In the final weeks before the GOP caucuses, Romney stepped up his efforts and Rick Santorum surged. Turnout was 121,000, a bit higher than in 2008. Romney and Santorum each won 25 percent of the vote, with Paul coming in third at 21 percent. Bachmann finished sixth, with 6,046 votes, not much more than the 4,823 she had won at the straw poll, and she dropped out the next day. But there was ambiguity about who actually won. The counting is done by the Iowa GOP, not state election officials, and initial reports showed Romney ahead of Santorum by a handful of votes; 16 days later, Santorum was declared the winner by 34 votes, though results from eight precincts were still missing. Some Republicans argued for removing the Iowa caucuses as the first nominating contest, to no avail. To help fend off that criticism, the 16-member central committee of the Iowa GOP voted unanimously in June 2015 to cancel its straw poll, which had begun in 1979.

The 2016 caucuses set records for both parties. The Republican side marked the electoral debut of Donald Trump. The New York billionaire developer eschewed the painstaking retail organizing of Iowans in favor of large, raucous rallies. While his chief rival, Ted Cruz, cultivated local evangelical leaders, Trump imported national evangelical figures such as Jerry Falwell Jr. to campaign with him in the run-up to caucus night. Many of the state's religious conservatives viewed Trump with skepticism from the moment he told the Family Leadership Summit in Ames, "Why do I have to repent or ask for forgiveness, if I am not making mistakes?" Cruz's investment in organization helped the Texan claim a narrow 28%-24% victory over Trump. Florida Sen. Marco Rubio surged at the end of the campaign and finished a close third with 23 percent. None of the other candidates gained any traction and the winnowing process began as Kentucky Sen. Rand Paul and former winners Huckabee and Santorum promptly withdrew. After Cruz's victory, Trump charged the Texan "stole" the caucuses and committed "voter fraud" with a supposedly misleading direct mail piece. One thing that all Republicans cheered was the record GOP caucus turnout of 186,874.

Clinton began her Iowa campaign with a huge lead in the polls over Vermont Sen. Bernie Sanders. But as the race wore on, Sanders gained ground, capitalizing on the traditional dovish views and liberal sentiments of Iowa Democrats. In the closing days of the campaign she received the endorsement of the state's leading newspaper, The Des Moines Register, and had Democratic Sens. Tim Kaine of Virginia, Cory Booker of New Jersey and Kristen Gillibrand of New York stumping Iowa on her behalf. The Democratic caucus was the closest on record, in either party: Clinton edged Sanders in "delegate equivalents" by a razor-thin 49.84%-49.59% margin. Iowa Democrats announced that 171,517 participated in their caucuses. The television network news survey of Democratic caucus-goers found that Sanders won millennial voters by a ratio of six-to-one over Clinton.

The general election in Iowa was also bracing. In a state with a relatively small share of minority voters and college graduates, Trump bested Clinton, 51%-42%. The shift toward Republicans since 2012, when Obama beat Romney 52%-46%, was the largest Democratic drop-off in any battleground state.

Iowa's caucuses have come under repeated attack, but they have survived efforts in both parties to end the state's kick-off role in the presidential nominating contests. As David Yepsen, the longtime dean of Iowa political reporters, wrote in 2008, "Defending the caucuses is a never-ending battle and a never-ending responsibility of political leaders in both parties in Iowa." Critics of the Iowa caucuses will continue to complain that the process is arcane and, like New Hampshire, the state lacks diversity. But the candidates made a quick start to grab the leadoff spot in 2020.

Congressional Districts

116th Congress Lineup	3D 1R	115th Congress Lineup	1D 3R

Iowa's congressional district lines are drawn by the nonpartisan Legislative Services Bureau and then approved by the governor and legislature. But the process has not been entirely apolitical. The bureau is not supposed to take past voting patterns or a legislator's place of residence into account, and it has been even-handed in good Iowa fashion. But the governor and legislators can and do. As a result of the 2018 election, those influencers have remained chiefly Republican. And, in the often-competitive Iowa districts, the House delegation that year shifted from 3-to-1 Republican control to 3-to-1 Democratic control. In the current map, each of the four districts is based in one of the state's corners. That likely will continue to be a starting point, though such an approach offers plenty of opportunity for new options and partisan balances — including parochial questions such as which district would be the best fit for locales such as Cedar Rapids, Ames and Council Bluffs. In any case, the delegation almost certainly will continue to have four seats. That stability has often not been the case in the past. In the six reapportionments between 1960 and 2010, Iowa lost a district four times — downsizing from eight seats to the current four.

With the one-seat loss following the 2010 census, the even-handed plan that was announced in March 2011 resulted in a competitive contest in a Des Moines-based district between two incumbents: Republican Tom Latham and Democrat Leonard Boswell. Latham won, then retired in 2014. That year, Republicans won two open-seat contests, which shifted back in 2018. In the past, the one Iowa district that has been viewed as secure has been GOP control of the northwest 4th District, which has been held by Rep. Steve King. But the controversial King could put that seat in play — during redistricting, or otherwise.

Kim Reynolds (R)

Assumed office in 2017, term expires 2023, 1st full term; b. Aug. 4, 1959, St. Charles; Northwest Missouri State University, att. 1977-1980; Southeastern Community College, att.; Southwestern Community College, att. 1992-1995; Iowa State Univ., BA 2016.; United Methodist; Married (Kevin); 3 children.

Elected Office: IA Senate 2009-2011; IA Lt. Governor, 2011-2017.

Professional Career: Pharmacist assistant; Staff, Clarke County Treasurer.

Office: Iowa State Capitol, 1007 E. Grand Ave., Des Moines, 50319; 515-281-5211; Fax: 515-725-3527; Website: iowa.gov.

Lt. Gov.: Adam Gregg (R) **Atty. Gen:** Tom Miller (D) **Sec. of State:** Paul Pate (R)

State Legislature: Senate: 18D, 32R **House:** 47D, 53R

Election Results

Election	Name (Party)	Vote (%)
2018 General	Kim Reynolds (R)..	667,275 (50%)
	Fred Hubbell (D)...	630,986 (48%)
2018 Primary	Kim Reynolds (R)...	94,118 (100%)

Iowa Gov. Kim Reynolds, a Republican, was elevated from lieutenant governor in May 2017 after long-serving Gov. Terry Branstad was confirmed as ambassador to China. Then, the following year, Reynolds won a term of her own, defeating Democrat Fred Hubbell, 50%-48% -- the narrowest victory for an Iowa governor since 1956.

Reynolds hails from rural Iowa; she was born in Truro and raised in St. Charles. Her father worked at a John Deere factory, as did her grandfather and several other family members. Reynolds' father, unlike other family members, did not become a union member; he also farmed on the side. Reynolds attended Northwest Missouri State University, Southeastern Community College, and Southwestern Community College, but had not accumulated enough credits to graduate. She finally rectified that during her tenure as lieutenant governor, when she received a bachelor of liberal studies degree from Iowa State University. The speaker at the commencement ceremony was Sen. Joni Ernst, a longtime political ally of Reynolds.

While raising her young children, Reynolds worked as a part-time supermarket checker at a Hy-Vee. She also worked as a pharmacist's assistant and later as a motor vehicles clerk in the Clarke County treasurer's office. When the incumbent county treasurer declined to seek a new term, Reynolds won the seat and was re-elected three times. In 1998, she sought the GOP nomination for a state Senate special election. Despite securing the support of Branstad, she lost. Reynolds faced a personal crisis during this period when she was arrested in 1999 and 2000 for drunk driving. "Sitting in a jail cell that night, 'scared to death' because of alcoholism's grip on her psyche, Reynolds says she prayed, 'I can't do this on my own anymore. I need help,'" she told Politico's Tim Alberta. Reynolds reached 17 years of sobriety as she was running for governor.

In 2008, Reynolds won a seat in the state Senate, and two years later, Branstad tapped her as his running mate. Having just survived a tough primary against Bob Vander Plaats, a strong social conservative, Branstad faced pressure to consolidate his party's support by choosing a running mate in Vander Plaats' mold. Instead, he settled on Reynolds, a more conventional economic conservative.

As lieutenant governor, Reynolds co-chaired the state advisory council on STEM education (science, technology, engineering and math). She also worked on trade promotion, making trips to China, South Korea, Germany, Brazil, Vietnam, the Philippines and Thailand. She considered but eventually declined a chance to run for the seat vacated by longtime Democratic Sen. Tom Harkin in 2014. Instead, it was Donald Trump who charted the course for Reynolds' political future when he tapped Branstad as ambassador to China. Branstad's nomination took longer than expected to surface in the Senate, so while Reynolds was widely seen as the governor-in-waiting, it was Branstad who presided over a landmark legislative session in early 2017. The previous fall, as Trump was winning the state, voters had also thrown out the Democratic majority in the state Senate, effectively removing the party's last defense against a conservative agenda. That enabled Branstad to sign a rollback of public-employee collective-bargaining, rewrite workers' compensation laws, restrain medical malpractice awards and lawsuits against livestock producers, enact a stand-your-ground law, weaken local jurisdictions' rights to establish gun-free zones, allow teens age 14 and older to use handguns with adult supervision, put in place a strict voter-ID law, cut the number of days for early voting, ban abortion after 20 weeks and require a 72-hour waiting period in cases where it remains legal.

After Branstad won confirmation as ambassador to China, Reynolds became the first woman to serve as Iowa's governor. Soon after taking office, she tapped former Branstad adviser and public defender Adam Gregg to fill the vacant position of lieutenant governor, on the condition that he not be in the line of succession, a caveat that avoided a possible legal challenge to an unelected lieutenant governor. Later that year, Reynolds' administration blocked a proposed rule to regulate guns in child-care facilities; she said the proposal needed more discussion. Reynolds also grappled with Branstad's decision to have private companies run the state's Medicaid program, which serves more than 600,000 residents. Following the switch, an ombudsman detailed hundreds of complaints about service under the new system; in the meantime, estimates of monetary savings shrank significantly.

On the political front, Reynolds caught a break when an expected primary opponent, former Cedar Rapids Mayor Ron Corbett, fell short of enough signatures to qualify for the ballot. The Democrats saw their primary turn into a rout, as businessman Fred Hubbell won 56 percent in a six-way race. Hubbell had name recognition in the state; his great-great-grandfather had co-founded the life insurance company Equitable of Iowa in 1867, and the candidate chaired the family-owned department store chain, Younkers, before taking the reins of Equitable in 1987. He also survived a 13-day hijacking in Pakistan and Afghanistan in 1981. "When your life is threatened every day, you see somebody shot and killed a few feet away from you, you really start to think, 'What am I going to do differently?'" he told the Atlantic. Hubbell later served as acting director of the state's economic development department in 2009.

During the campaign, Reynolds touted the state's strong economy and fiscal situation, as well as a $2 billion cut in individual and corporate taxes that she had signed. Hubbell, who spent millions of his own dollars on his candidacy, focused on health care, including Reynolds' handling of Medicaid, mental-health funding, and taxes, which he said the highest earners didn't pay enough of. The candidates diverged on public funding for private education (Reynolds favored it, Hubbell didn't) and abortion (Reynolds signed a measure that could outlaw most abortions after detection of a fetal heartbeat, while Hubbell called himself "an unabashed supporter of Roe v. Wade"). Reynolds fired Iowa Finance Authority Director Dave Jamison when a history of sexual harassment came to light. In October, she called sexual harassment "not a partisan issue." The incumbent also attacked Hubbell for not releasing his full tax returns.

But another inescapable factor hovered over the race: Trump, whose approval rating in the state was under water just two years after his easy victory there. A particularly difficult moment came in August 2018, when officials announced charges against an undocumented immigrant for abducting and killing college student Mollie Tibbetts. The case became a cause celebre for illegal-immigration hardliners, and Trump gave it a national platform, saying at a rally, "You heard about today with the illegal alien coming in, very sadly, from Mexico and you saw what happened to that incredible, beautiful young woman. Should've never happened." Reynolds, for her part, said, "As Iowans, we are heartbroken, and we are angry. We are angry that a broken immigration system allowed a predator like this to live in our community, and we will do all we can [to] bring justice to Mollie's killer."

Reynolds pulled out a victory, 50%-48%, even as several other midwestern states run by Republican governors -- including Illinois, Kansas, Michigan, and Wisconsin -- saw their governorships fall to the Democrats. Hubbell ran a strong race, increasing the number of Democratic gubernatorial votes by between 45 percent and 73 percent above the party's 2014 level in such populous counties as Polk (Des Moines), Story (Ames), Johnson (Iowa City), Dubuque, Scott (Davenport), and Linn (Cedar Rapids). Reynolds owed her victory to strong support in rural areas. "The redder areas are getting redder," Republican strategist Matt Strawn told the Des Moines Register. "You're seeing the bluer urban centers get bluer. And it looks like the suburbs are going to be caught in the middle." In some areas of the state, a significant number of voters backed a Democrat for Congress yet stuck with Reynolds for governor; according to calculations by the Register, those Democrats fared better than Hubbell did in 85 of the state's 99 counties.

Chuck Grassley (R)

Elected 1980, term expires 2022, 7th term, b. Sep 17, 1933; New Hartford; University of Northern Iowa, B.A., 1955; University of Northern Iowa, M.A., 1956; University of Iowa, 1958; Baptist; Married (Barbara Ann Speicher Grassley); 5 children.

Elected Office: IA House, 1959-1974; U.S. House, 1975-1981.

Professional Career: Farmer; Sheet metal shearer, 1959-1961; Assembly line worker, 1961-1971.

DC Office: 135 HSOB 20510, 202-224-3744, Fax: 202-224-6020, grassley.senate.gov

State Offices: Cedar Rapids, 319-363-6832; Council Bluffs, 712-322-7103; Davenport, 563-322-4331; Des Moines, 515-288-1145; Sioux City, 712-233-1860; Waterloo, 319-232-6657.

Committees: Senate President Pro Tempore. *Agriculture, Nutrition & Forestry*: Commodities, Risk Management & Trade; Conservation, Forestry & Natural Resources; Livestock, Marketing & Agriculture Security. *Budget*. *Finance (Chmn)*: Ex Officio membership on all subcommittees. *Joint Taxation*. *Judiciary*: Antitrust, Competition Policy & Consumer Rights; Border Security & Immigration; Oversight, Agency Action, Federal Rights & Federal Courts; Subcommittee on Intellectual Property.

Group Ratings

	ADA	ACLU	AFL-CIO	LCV	ITI	COC	HAFA	ACU	CFG	FRC
2018	-	18%	-	0%	-	80%	72%	82%	84%	100%
2017	5%	C	0%	0%	C	86%	C	80%	81%	100%

Almanac Ratings 2017-18

	Economy	Social	Foreign	Composite
Liberal	6%	6%	0%	4%
Conservative	94%	94%	100%	96%

Key Votes of the 115th Congress

1. Obama-care revision	Y	5. Gun regulations	Y
2. Tax Cuts	Y	6. Family planning regs	Y
3. Dodd-Frank revision	Y	7. Gorsuch confirmation	Y
4. Omnibus appropriations	N	8. Immigration restrictions	Y

9. Kavanaugh confirmation	Y
10. Saudi arms sales	N
11. FISA rules	Y
12. Military aid in Yemen	N

Election Results

Election	Name (Party)	Vote (%)		Cand. Spent	Ind. Exp. Support	Ind. Exp. Oppose
2016 General	Chuck Grassley (R)......................... 926,007	(60%)	$10,306,743	$284,077	$37,897
	Patty Judge (D)................................... 549,460	(36%)	$2,189,617	$22,035	$80,410
	John Heiderscheit (L)........................... 41,794	(3%)			
2016 Primary	Chuck Grassley (R)....................... . Unopposed				

Prior winning percentages: 2010 (64%), 2004 (70%), 1998 (68%), 1992 (70%), 1986 (66%), 1980 (54%); House: 1978 (75%), 1976 (57%), 1974 (51%)

One of the longest ever serving senators, Charles Grassley is equal parts cankerous and approachable. The conservative Iowan was responsible as Judiciary chairman for confirming the most federal judges ever in a two-year period, including two Supreme Court justices, and reorienting the third branch of government.

Iowa's senior senator shares the legacy of how that was achieved: supporting Senate Majority Leader Mitch McConnell's decision to block President Barack Obama's nomination of Merrick Garland to the Supreme Court and curtailing the traditional deference to senators on lower court nominees. But Grassley has said the same panel that "reached the height of discord" during Brett Kavanaugh's confirmation to the Supreme Court also passed legislation responding to the opioid crisis, addressing elder abuse and reforming the juvenile justice system. And in major bipartisan victory, Grassley teamed up with Sens. Dick Durbin and Mike Lee to pass the biggest changes to federal sentencing laws in a generation. The First Step Act addressed what are now acknowledged as missteps in tough-on-crime legislation that disproportionately affected communities of color. Summing up this legacy, Grassley tweeted at end of 2018: "To all the ppl who always disagree w my tweets bc I'm a Republican-what do u think of us passing bipartisan criminal justice reform that I've worked on for yrs???"

Perceptions of Grassley on Capitol Hill, where he is the Senate's second oldest member at 85 — California Democrat Dianne Feinstein three months his senior — have evolved since his arrival in the chamber in 1980. His first election was facilitated by the Reagan presidential landslide, which brought a wave of reliable, often hard-line conservatives into that chamber. But virtually all of the Senate Republican Class of 1980 was gone within a term or two. Grassley not only survived but thrived. He transcended an initial image as a one-dimensional conservative and has been a dogged overseer of federal agencies and a hero to government whistleblowers, as well as an independent-minded deal-maker.

Grassley grew up on a farm in New Hartford. His parents were Democrats who switched to the Republican Party when Franklin D. Roosevelt ran for a third term in 1940. Grassley received his bachelor's degree from the University of Northern Iowa and, while still in graduate school, ran for the Iowa House in 1956, losing by only 70-some votes. Two years later, he ran again and won at 25. While in the state Legislature, he worked as a sheet-metal shearer and on an assembly line. He won an open House seat in 1974, the hugely successful post-Watergate year for Democrats; he squeaked in with 51 percent of the vote. Six years later, he garnered 54 percent while ousting Democratic Sen. John Culver. A classmate of Massachusetts Sen. Ted Kennedy at Harvard University, Culver was among a group of influential liberals — notably George McGovern of South Dakota, Birch Bayh of Indiana and Frank Church of Idaho — that dominated the Senate during the 1960s and 1970s but was swept out of office in the 1980 wave.

Grassley has always been a committed fiscal conservative; he was among just eight senators to oppose the 2013 deal aimed at averting the so-called fiscal cliff because, he said, "Washington has a spending problem, not a taxing problem, and this deal doesn't do anything about the spending problem." He also is a steady conservative on social issues: He opposes abortion rights and most gun control initiatives. In 2013, he voted to block a compromise measure to expand background checks for gun owners after the mass shooting at Sandy Hook Elementary School in Connecticut, in which 28 were killed.

But he is a populist in the Midwestern agrarian tradition, suspicious of concentrations of both public and private power. He has made oversight of bloated, indifferent or corrupt government agencies a focal point of his Senate career. In the mid-1980s, his first major legislative achievement was passing the Federal False Claims Act, which imposed legal liability on those defrauding the government; he has said it has returned more than $59 billion to the federal Treasury. In 2015, Grassley blasted the Justice Department over its administration of civil asset forfeiture laws, a position that allied him with the American Civil Liberties Union.

Grassley also has shown an inclination to challenge Wall Street. He attacked the Securities and Exchange Commission in 2011 for failing to detail how it handled nearly 20 referrals of suspicious trading at a major hedge fund. A year earlier, he was one of only four Republicans who voted for the Senate version of the Dodd-Frank financial reforms, although he voted against the final version of the bills. The same year, he was the only Republican to vote with Democrats on the Senate Agriculture Committee for sweeping reform of the derivatives market. He supported the government rescue of the financial industry in 2008, a vote for which he faced criticism from Iowa conservatives.

In February 2016, after the death of Justice Antonin Scalia gave Obama an opportunity to nominate a replacement for his Supreme Court seat, the Republican-controlled Senate took no action to fill the vacancy until after the presidential election. Although it was apparent that McConnell was the driving force, Democrats aimed the bulk of their rhetorical fire at the often independent-minded Grassley — hoping to force him to hold hearings on Obama's choice, Garland, a federal appeals court judge. But Grassley held firm.

Soon after, President Donald Trump took office and nominated another appeals court judge, Neil Gorsuch, for the opening. Republicans needed to "go nuclear" to confirm Gorsuch, removing the 60-vote threshold to OK Supreme Court nominees. Opposition to Gorsuch paled in comparison to the hostility aimed at Trump's next nominee, Brett Kavanaugh, who replaced retired Justice Anthony Kennedy, widely viewed as having been the court's swing vote. After Christine Blasey Ford, a professor at Palo Alto University, went public with allegations that Kavanaugh had sexually assaulted her at a party more than three decades earlier, when they were both in high school. Kavanaugh denied the charges. Democrats pushed for the FBI to investigate the matter, but Grassley denied that the bureau had any role to play and said committee staff were pursuing every lead that had been reported. Kavanaugh responded to Ford's claims in a raw, emotional manner, at times sneering at Democrats on the Judiciary panel. Sen. Lindsey Graham also started an oral slugfest against Democrats and their handling of the allegations. After the hearings, Grassley pressed for an immediate vote in committee, but it was unclear if Kavanaugh would get a favorable report. A last-minute deal hatched by Republican Jeff Flake and Democrat Chris Coons led to a favorable, party-line recommendation, but with the agreement that the FBI would conduct a limited investigation into some of the allegations against the nominee. Senators on the fence said the new probe did not change their minds about what they perceived to be a lack of evidence backing up Ford's claims, and Kavanaugh was confirmed on 50-48 vote.

For all the partisan rancor on the panel, Grassley refused to give up on a long-sought bipartisan agreement. In 2015, Grassley became interested in the public push for criminal justice reform, then being led by Durbin and Lee, and was ready to cash in any favor or good will to ensure passage. While the First Step Act was narrowed from the original Obama-era proposal, two persistent detractors impeded final passage: Jeff Sessions, who remained outspoken despite having left the Senate to become attorney general, and Sen. Tom Cotton of Arkansas. Trump fired Sessions soon after the 2018 midterms. But Grassley was unable to woo Cotton and therefore McConnell was uneasy about bringing a bill to the floor that might divide the GOP. Teaming up with presidential son-in-law Jared Kushner and Trump, Grassley successfully turned the screws on McConnell. The legislation sailed through on 87-12 vote.

Grassley has been among the Senate's sharpest critics of the so-called H-1B visa program, which enables the U.S. technology industry to bring in highly skilled workers from overseas. He had teamed with Durbin to curb the program—which Grassley has said has been used to replace U.S. workers and reduce wages.

Protecting government whistleblowers has been a passion for Grassley. "Whistleblowers are often treated like skunks at a picnic. It takes guts to put your career on the line to expose waste and fraud, and whistleblowers need senators who will listen and advocate for them," Grassley said in 2014. The announcement came on the 25th anniversary of passage of the 1989 Whistleblower Protection Act—which he co-authored. He also helped pass, in late 2012, an update of the whistleblower law that, among other things, created ombudsmen to educate federal agency managers about whistleblower rights.

In Iowa, Grassley inherited an 80-acre farm in 1960 and has added to it over the years. It became a 750-acre estate that produced corn and soybeans and is managed by the senator's son Robin. In Washington, Grassley has exhibited a populist skepticism in debates over farm subsidies. He has argued that high payments to individual farmers put the entire agriculture program in political jeopardy. He was one of only 13 senators to vote against the 2018 farm bill. Grassley said the final legislation was too kind to wealthy farmers and offered subsidies to too many people who might not work directly on a farm.

In January 2019, Grassley gave up his Judiciary Committee gavel and began chairing the Finance Committee. The move placed him squarely in the debate of fraught issues for his party. Grassley has been critical of Trump's use of tariffs and the Iowa Republican signaled that he would review the law that president has used to claim a national security threat to impose tariffs. In another potential blockbuster fight, Grassley said he would like to learn more about the law that would allow his panel access to Trump's tax returns, which the president has refused to release. Grassley has used the committee to look out for the interests of his home state. Corn-based ethanol is an important product of Iowa's agribusiness, and Grassley has used his influence to win advantageous tax treatment of ethanol and wind energy, another major industry in the state. Grassley previously agreed to phase out a key tax credit for the wind industry that was set to end in 2020. In an area of possible bipartisan cooperation, he has been viewed as more open to addressing prescription drug prices than Orrin Hatch of Utah, the previous chairman, was.

Grassley enjoyed a warm relationship with Montana Democratic Sen. Max Baucus when the two men took turns chairing the Finance Committee. Baucus helped Grassley round up bipartisan support for President George W. Bush's income tax cuts early on and later supported the Republican-sponsored Medicare prescription drug program legislation that Grassley was a leader in crafting. By the same token, when Obama became president in 2009 and proposed what would become his signature health care law, Grassley was one of the senators negotiating a deal, despite pressure from within his party. In the end, Grassley voted against the Affordable Care Act, saying it would cut funding for Medicare and fail to hold down taxes or contain costs. After Baucus resigned to become ambassador to China, Sen. Ron Wyden of Oregon, with whom Grassley had teamed up on drug pricing legislation, became the top Democrat on the panel.

In November 2018, Grassley set the record for the longest stretch in the Senate without missing a roll call vote, a record that went back more than a quarter-century to July 1993 when he was touring flood damage along the Mississippi River. While some have cited concerns over his age, Grassley still runs four times a week, starting at 4:15 a.m. and going for about 3 miles. Outside of politics, he is known for his colorful use of Twitter and Instagram. A notable target of his is the History Channel, which Grassley harangues on social media for programming he has said doesn't live up to the network's name.

In 2016, Grassley appeared to be cruising to re-election until controversy over the Garland nomination erupted: Believing that his handling of that issue had created a political opening, national Democrats coaxed former Iowa Lt. Gov. Patty Judge — previously the state's first female agriculture commissioner — into the race. Touting herself as "one Judge" that Grassley could not ignore, she sought to use the Garland incident as evidence that Grassley had grown out of step with Iowa voters.

Judge garnered the backing of the DSCC and EMILY's List. But Grassley defeated Judge, 60%-36%. She carried only one of the state's 99 counties: Johnson County, home to the University of Iowa. While he has insisted that retirement is far away, watchers of Iowa politics have speculated that he might retire soon. In the meantime, Grassley in early 2019 condemned Rep. Steve King, the next-senior member of the Iowa congressional delegation, following a litany of racist comments. But like other Iowa Republicans, Grassley had endorsed King in 2018, when King was narrowly re-elected.

Joni Ernst (R)

Elected 2014, term expires 2020, 1st term, b. Jul 01, 1970; Red Oak; Iowa State University (IA), B.S., 1992; Columbus College (IA), M.P.A., 1995; Lutheran; Divorced; 1 child ; 2 stepchildren.

Military Career: U.S. Army Reserves 1992-2001; Iowa Army National Guard 2001-20015 (Iraq)

Elected Office: IA Senate, 2011-2014.

Professional Career: Auditor, Montgomery County IA, 2005-2011.

DC Office: 730 HSOB 20510, 202-224-3254, Fax: 202-224-9369, ernst.senate.gov

State Offices: Cedar Rapids, 319-365-4504; Council Bluffs, 712-352-1167; Davenport, 563-322-0677; Des Moines, 515-284-4574; Sioux City, 712-252-1550.

Committees: Senate Republican Conference Vice Chairman. *Agriculture, Nutrition & Forestry*: Livestock, Marketing & Agriculture Security; Nutrition, Agricultural Research & Specialty Crops; Rural Development & Energy (Chmn). *Armed Services*: Emerging Threats & Capabilities (Chmn); Readiness & Management Support; Seapower. *Environment & Public Works*: Clean Air & Nuclear Safety; Superfund, Waste Management, & Regulatory Oversight. *Judiciary*: Border Security & Immigration; Crime & Terrorism; Oversight, Agency Action, Federal Rights & Federal Courts. *Small Business & Entrepreneurship*.

Group Ratings

	ADA	ACLU	AFL-CIO	LCV	ITI	COC	HAFA	ACU	CFG	FRC
2018	-	10%	-	7%	-	80%	75%	86%	72%	100%
2017	0%	C	0%	0%	C	86%	C	80%	77%	100%

Almanac Ratings 2017-18

	Economy	Social	Foreign	Composite
Liberal	6%	6%	0%	4%
Conservative	94%	94%	100%	96%

Key Votes of the 115th Congress

1. Obama-care revision	Y	5. Gun regulations	Y	9. Kavanaugh confirmation	Y
2. Tax Cuts	Y	6. Family planning regs	Y	10. Saudi arms sales	N
3. Dodd-Frank revision	Y	7. Gorsuch confirmation	Y	11. FISA rules	Y
4. Omnibus appropriations	N	8. Immigration restrictions	Y	12. Military aid in Yemen	N

Election Results

Election	Name (Party)	Vote (%)		Cand. Spent	Ind. Exp. Support	Ind. Exp. Oppose
2014 General	Joni Ernst (R)	588,575	(52%)	$11,913,212	$12,247,026	$25,196,618
	Bruce Braley (D)	494,370	(44%)	$12,068,095	$4,225,010	$18,841,528
	Douglas Butzier (L)	26,815	(2%)			
2014 Primary	Joni Ernst (R)	88,535	(56%)			
	Sam Clovis (R)	28,418	(18%)			
	Mark Jacobs (R)	26,523	(17%)			
	Matt Whitaker (R)	11,884	(8%)			

Joni Ernst's rise to prominence in national politics has been swift. Victory in a five-way Senate primary, triumph over a widely favored congressman and succeeding a liberal lion in the Senate catapulted Iowa's junior senator as high as a shortlist for vice president. She became the first woman to serve in the Senate Republican leadership in a decade, and with her resumé and residency in a key state for presidential elections, she was poised to keep flourishing — if she can survive what was expected to be a tough re-election campaign.

Propelled by her surprise victory, Iowa's junior senator earned high-profile exposure during her initial years on Capitol Hill. Less than a month after being sworn in to the Senate, Republican leaders tapped her to give the GOP response to President Barack Obama's State of the Union address in 2015. She had a prominent speaking role at the 2016 Republican National Convention in Cleveland, where she also was in high demand as a surrogate before state delegations. However, in the mold of past senators who have arrived on Capitol Hill with a measure of celebrity but who strived to demonstrate a serious purpose, Ernst said her top priorities were representing her home state and acquiring legislative expertise. After meeting with Donald Trump in July 2016, amid speculation that she was under consideration to be his running mate, Ernst told Politico: "I made that very clear to him that I'm focused on Iowa. I feel that I have a lot more to do in the United States Senate. ... I'm just getting started here."

As an Iraq War veteran, Ernst has been a sought-after voice on veterans issues and has advocated a forceful foreign policy in line with the late Sen. John McCain, who campaigned extensively for her. While mostly restrained in her criticism of Trump, she has been critical of the president's trade policy and his decision to ban transgender people from serving in the military and, unlike many other Republicans, she has pushed Trump to release his tax returns.

Born and raised on a farm in rural Montgomery County in southwest Iowa, Ernst won scholarships to attend Iowa State University, where she majored in psychology; she later earned a master's degree in public administration from Georgia's Columbus State University. She joined the National Guard in 1993 and was deployed to Kuwait during the Iraq War a decade later; she highlighted her status as a veteran and her rank as a lieutenant colonel throughout the 2014 campaign, during which national security was high on voters' list of concerns. At the end of 2015, Ernst retired as a lieutenant colonel after 23 years in the Iowa National Guard, citing her Senate duties and family obligations. Earlier in the year, the left-leaning HuffPost had questioned her claim to be the first female combat veteran elected to serve in the Senate — pointing out that she had commanded a transportation company that never came under fire during her service in Iraq. "It was only by luck and the blessings of God that my soldiers did not encounter an assault," Ernst shot back.

Ernst was elected Montgomery County auditor in 2004, serving two terms before winning election to the state Senate in 2010, taking the seat left vacant by now-Gov. Kim Reynolds. When better-known Republicans wooed by the party strategists — notably then-Rep. Tom Latham — opted against running for Tom Harkin's Senate seat, Ernst became part of a five-way primary to replace the retiring five-term Democrat. Some establishment Republicans stood behind wealthy businessman Mark Jacobs after he indicated a willingness to pump several million dollars of his personal fortune into the race. But the "squeal" ad pushed Ernst to front of the pack. "I grew up castrating hogs on an Iowa farm. So, when I get to Washington, I'll know how to cut pork. ... Washington's full of big spenders, let's make them squeal," she said in a spot that went viral, placed her on the front pages of major newspapers and was the talk of cable TV. Buoyed by her newly found name recognition, she won the primary with 56 percent of the vote. Her success was also rooted in her knack for appealing to both the tea party and establishment wings of the GOP — best summarized by her dueling endorsements by 2008 Republican vice presidential nominee Sarah Palin and 2012 presidential nominee Mitt Romney.

While Ernst waded through a GOP primary, Rep. Bruce Braley, a former trial lawyer first elected to the House in 2006, glided through his, as the Democratic Party ensured that the field was clear for the man expected to carry on the tradition of Iowa splitting its Senate delegation. But in a testament to Braley's hubris and the power of opposition research, Braley's effort was plagued by gaffes and missteps to such a degree that several political publications and handicappers later anointed his as the worst campaign of 2014. The most notable of those gaffes occurred at a private fundraiser of trial lawyers in Texas, where he was caught on tape deriding the prospect of veteran Sen. Chuck Grassley chairing the Judiciary Committee if the Republicans regained a Senate majority — characterizing Grassley as "a farmer from Iowa who never went to law school, never practiced law." Republican PAC America Rising recorded the clip and weaponized it in an ad campaign that blanketed the state.

The comments were widely reported by local and national journalists and fueled the perception that Braley was an out-of-touch elitist, compared to Ernst's folksy image as a small-town Iowan.

Democrats counterattacked by portraying Ernst as a tea party member in the mold of Palin and former Minnesota Rep. Michele Bachmann. Then-Democratic National Committee Chairwoman Debbie Wasserman Schultz called Ernst "an onion of crazy." Braley and his allies hammered away at Ernst's calls to abolish the Education Department and the Environmental Protection Agency and her opposition to federal minimum wage laws and her support for a "personhood" constitutional amendment to ban all abortions. Democrats griped about Ernst being the Teflon candidate of 2014, and she triumphed 52%-44%.

On both the Armed Services and Homeland Security committees, Ernst focused on fighting terrorism and improving care for veterans. In June 2015, an Ernst amendment to the defense spending bill, which would have allowed the Obama administration to sidestep the Iraqi government and directly arm Kurdish forces fighting the Islamic State, was defeated 54-45. A handful of leading Democrats sided with Ernst, while a few fellow GOP conservatives voted against her. She joined a push by several senators from both parties for a new authorization for the use of military force against ISIS. Ernst took a more partisan tack in her speech to the Republican convention, blasting Obama's response to ISIS as "pathetic" and citing FBI reports of an ISIS presence in all 50 states. That speech, focused on military issues, was something of a contrast to her response to Obama's State of the Union address in early 2015, which was heavy on personal retrospective.

She authored a handful of bills that were signed into law by Obama. The Female Veterans Suicide Prevention Act authorized additional studies and treatment programs. Another allowed the ashes of women who served in World War II to be buried in Arlington National Cemetery for the first time.

During the Trump presidency, Ernst mostly followed the well-worn path of politely criticizing the president and only on major Republican policies like support for free trade and a more robust foreign policy. She joined a handful of her colleagues in expressing concern over Trump's proposal to withdraw troops from Syria and further questioned the president over his decision to suspend military exercises with South Korea, while he pursued a broader deal with North Korean leader Kim Jong Un. Like others in the Iowa delegation, she pushed back on Environmental Protection Agency Administrator Scott Pruitt's efforts to undermine the Renewable Fuel Standard, a key policy for the powerful biofuels lobby in the state. Attacking the EPA was a major selling point for Ernst on the campaign trail and she wasted little time by leading the GOP's charge against the 2014 Clean Water Act but Obama vetoed the GOP-led efforts to gut his administration's plan. The rule was later stayed in federal court and the Trump administration sought a replacement. In a nod to her campaign appeal to make Washington "squeal," Ernst sponsored bills aimed at gutting the federal bureaucracy and burnishing herself an image as a Washington outsider. Those proposals included cutting taxpayer money given to former presidents, nixing a tax write-off that members of Congress use for their time in Washington and even moving federal agencies from Washington.

Ernst was positioned to play a key role on Supreme Court confirmations and the debate over immigration policy after she and Tennessee Republican Sen. Marsha Blackburn became the first Republican women to serve on the Senate Judiciary Committee. The pair were added after top Senate Republicans were chastised for the lack of women on the panel during Brett Kavanaugh's fierce Supreme Court confirmation hearings.

The first woman from Iowa elected to Congress, Ernst is widely considered a top target in 2020. While she will not face the gaffe-prone Braley again, she will be able to tout her success on key local items, like delivering funds for Cedar Rapids' flood wall after the city was devastated by a 2008 flood. Democrats ran into early recruitment problems in finding a top-flight challenger—which was a sign of Ernst's local appeal. Former Gov. Tom Vilsack was early in turning down the opportunity. Freshman Rep. Cindy Axne followed him. In June 2009, urban planner Theresa Greenfield announced her challenge to Ernst and rallied support from Democrats.

Abby Finkenauer (D)

Elected 2018, 1st term, b. Dec 27, 1988; Dubuque; Drake University (IA), Bach. Deg., 2013; Catholic; Single.

Elected Office: IA House, 2014-2018.

Professional Career: Congressional Page, U.S. Rep. Jim Nussle; Legislative Assistant, IA State Rep. Todd Taylor.

DC Office: 124 CHOB 20515, 202-225-2911, finkenauer.house.gov

State Offices: Cedar Rapids, 319-364-2288.

Committees: *Small Business*: Innovation & Workforce Development; Rural Development, Agriculture, Trade & Entrepreneurship (Chmn). *Transportation & Infrastructure*: Highways & Transit; Water Resources & Environment.

Election Results

Election	Name (Party)	Vote (%)		Cand. Spent	Ind. Exp. Support	Ind. Exp. Oppose
2018 General	Abby Finkenauer (D)	170,342	(51%)	$4,554,485	$484,854	$957,907
	Rod Blum (R)	153,442	(46%)	$2,048,383	$400,133	$1,994,336
	Troy Hagemen (Lib)	10,285	(3%)			
2018 Primary	Abby Finkenauer (D)	29,745	(67%)			
	Thomas Heckroth (D)	8,516	(19%)			
	Courtney Rowe (D)	3,381	(8%)			
	George Ramsey (D)	2,837	(6%)			

Democrat Abby Finkenauer, first elected in 2018, defeated two-term Republican Rep. Rod Blum in a district that has regularly switched parties. Finkenauer emphasized her working-class background and her support for organized labor during her four years as a state representative. Blum remained loyal to President Donald Trump, even in the face of increased tariffs on imports that had raised alarms among Iowa farmers. With Rep. Alexandria Ocasio-Cortez of New York, another first-term Democrat, Finkenauer became one of two women ever elected to Congress before age 30.

Finkenauer grew up in the rural town of Sherrill, a few miles from Dubuque. Her father was an iron welder and her mother worked in the Dubuque schools. She graduated from Drake University with a bachelor's degree in public relations, then worked for a community foundation in Dubuque. In 2014, Finkenauer was elected to the state House, where she styled herself as a defender of working families and a vocal advocate for women.

When the Republican-controlled Legislature voted in 2017 to limit collective-bargaining rights, she condemned the legislation. "You had a lot of union guys who had voted Republican who just saw their rights gutted," Finkenauer later told The Atlantic. Many of them were early supporters when she decided to run for Congress, she added.

Finkenauer, an early challenger to Blum, became a robust fundraiser—with help from EMILY's List, the abortion-rights group that supports Democratic women candidates. The other Democratic contenders included Thomas Heckroth, who had been an aide to former Sen. Tom Harkin, an Iowa Democrat. Heckroth criticized Finkenauer for failing to report outside income she received while serving in the Legislature; her spokesman dismissed the allegation. Finkenauer more than doubled the combined spending of her three opponents and won the primary with 67 percent of the vote.

In the general election, Finkenauer criticized Blum for his support of Republican legislation to cut taxes and repeal the Affordable Care Act. She told voters that the issues that mattered were "so dang personal," including workers' rights, student loan debt and health care costs, the Des Moines Register reported. Her campaign, including its large fundraising, reflected "a larger wave of young, female Democrats seeking higher office," according to the Register.

Blum's campaign prospects were dampened when the House Ethics Committee announced in September that it was investigating whether he had violated House rules for failing to disclose that he had founded an internet marketing company while serving in Congress. In response, Blum apologized for what he called a "minor error" and blamed his opponents for "a crusade of personal destruction on me."

Trump made a campaign appearance in the Dubuque area during the summer, and praised Blum for securing funding for flood control in Cedar Rapids. But news stories several weeks before the election reported that national Republican groups were pessimistic about Blum's campaign and were withdrawing their support. When polls reportedly showed that the contest had tightened during the closing days of the campaign, then-Speaker Paul Ryan's Congressional Leadership Fund reversed course and spent more than $400,000 for television advertising on Blum's behalf.

In her 51%-46% victory, Finkenauer won the three largest counties: Linn, Black Hawk and Dubuque. Blum took all but one of the other 17 mostly rural counties.

IA-1: Northeast Iowa

Cook Partisan Voting Index: D+1

Population		Race and Ethnicity		Income	
Total	770,452	White	88.7%	Median Income	$57,084
Land area (sq. miles)	12,049	Black	3.7%	District Income Rank	202
Pop/ sq mi	63.9	Latino	3.9%	Poverty Rate	11.1%
Born in State	75.6%	Asian	1.6%	With health insurance	94.8%
		Two or more races	1.7%	Cash public assistance	2.3%
Age Groups		Other	0.5%	Food stamp/SNAP	10.5%
Under 18	23%				
18-34	22.5%	**Education**		**Work**	
35-64	37.7%	H.S grad or less	41%	White Collar	16.8%
Over 64	16.8%	Some college	32.9%	Sales and Service	39.4%
		College Degree, 4 yr	17.8%	Blue Collar	26.7%
Military		Post grad	8.3%	Government	11.2%
Veteran/ Active Duty	8.4%				

2012 Pres. Vote	Obama	225,585	(56%)	Romney	170,753	(42%)		
2016 Pres. Vote	Trump	190,410	(48%)	Clinton	176,535	(45%)	Johnson 15,661	(4%)

Cedar Rapids, Dubuque, Waterloo: Northeast Iowa, along the Mississippi River and westward, has some of the loveliest landscape in America. Here the Mississippi flows past green bluffs, then broadens out in great quiet pools alongside picturesque towns. A century and a half ago, as settlers surged west of the Mississippi, Germans stopped at the river bluffs reminiscent of their native land and built neat farmhouses and substantial towns. Inland, on the rolling hills portrayed with surprisingly little exaggeration in the paintings of Iowa's Grant Wood, and in the more open territory to the west, New England Yankees and midwesterners built their characteristic farmhouses, barns, town halls, church spires and small colleges. Railroad companies, headquartered in Chicago, extended their networks of steel rails over the plains and rivers. Dubuque is a self-styled green city that has some large factories but is also proud of its waterfront-generated tourism. The city received All America City awards in 2012 and 2013. Local leaders cite their vision of a "Sustainable Dubuque," which allowed them to transform a rusting city in the 1980s into a successful place that rejuvenated urban life. Among the longstanding employers is John Deere, which employs about 2,600 people locally and has boosted its output of crawler products, a large and powerful tractor.

Southwest of Dubuque is Cedar Rapids, Iowa's second-largest city. It sports high-tech employers and contemporary office buildings. Unlike most of Iowa, its population boomed in the past two decades, and its per capita income rose. Both Cedar Rapids and Waterloo "built an internet infrastructure in the mid-1990s to draw technology companies to the area," then nurtured small technology companies, the Des Moines Register reported. The production of ethanol and other biofuels in Cedar Rapids contributed to its economic health. Although ethanol production slumped in recent years with the decline in demand for gasoline blends, C.R. continued to produce more ethanol than any other city in the world. It remains the number-one corn-processing city in the world. Traditional industries remain a mainstay: Go down by the river, and you can't miss the smell of cooking oats coming from the Quaker Oats and General Mills factories. In Waterloo, John Deere employed 5,000.

The 1st Congressional District covers much of northeast Iowa, including the Mississippi riverfront and Cedar Rapids, Dubuque and Waterloo. Politically, this area has leaned Democratic.

Dubuque, heavily German Catholic, for years has been Iowa's most Democratic city, unless abortion rights are the issue. But the district had a remarkable swing in 2016. Donald Trump won the 1st, 49%-45%. He led in 18 of the 20 counties, losing only Cedar Rapids-based Linn and Waterloo-based Black Hawk; he won Dubuque by 610 votes. In 2012, President Barack Obama won 56%-42% and took 17 counties. Nearly 40 percent of the residents are not affiliated with a party.

Dave Loebsack (D)

Elected 2006, 7th term, b. Dec 23, 1952; Sioux City; Iowa State University (IA), B.S., 1974; Iowa State University (IA), M.A., 1976; University of California, Ph.D., 1985; Methodist; Married (Teresa Loebsack); 2 children (2 from previous marriage); 2 stepchildren; 3 grandchildren.

Professional Career: Professor, Cornell College, 1982-2006.

DC Office: 1211 LHOB 20515, 202-225-6576, Fax: 202-226-0757, loebsack.house.gov

State Offices: Davenport, 563-323-5988; Iowa City, 319-351-0789.

Committees: *Energy & Commerce*: Communications & Technology; Energy.

Group Ratings

	ADA	ACLU	AFL-CIO	LCV	ITI	COC	HAFA	ACU	CFG	FRC
2018	-	79%	-	94%	-	67%	2%	8%	10%	0%
2017	90%	C	95%	94%	C	57%	C	0%	0%	0%

Almanac Ratings 2017-18

	Economy	Social	Foreign	Composite
Liberal	78%	98%	76%	84%
Conservative	22%	2%	24%	16%

Key Votes of the 115th Congress

1. Obama-care revision	N	5. Family planning regs	N	9. Guantanamo prisoners	Y
2. Tax Cuts	N	6. Body cameras/immigration	Y	10. Ground missiles, limit	Y
3. Omnibus appropriations	Y	7. Abortion ban	N	11. Defense Dept. spending	Y
4. Dodd-Frank revision	N	8. Concealed carry	N	12. FISA rules	Y

Election Results

Election	Name (Party)	Vote (%)		Cand. Spent	Ind. Exp. Support	Ind. Exp. Oppose
2018 General	Dave Loebsack (D)	171,446	(55%)	$1,890,219	$2,863	
	Chris Peters (R)	133,287	(43%)	$395,179		
2018 Primary	Dave Loebsack (D)		(100%)			

Prior winning percentages: 2016 (54%), 2014 (53%), 2012 (56%), 2010 (51%), 2008 (57%), 2006 (51%)

Democrat Dave Loebsack, elected in 2006, is a retired college professor who offsets his liberal leanings by seeking out similarly pragmatic Republicans. He has worked to connect with the rural voters in his district. In April 2019, he announced that he will retire after seven terms.

A native of Sioux City, Loebsack lived in poverty as a child with his mother, grandmother and three siblings in a two-bedroom house. He worked as a high school janitor to pay for college. He got a master's degree at Iowa State University and went on to the University of California, Davis, to earn a Ph.D. in political science. From 1982 until his election to Congress, he was a professor of international relations at Cornell College in Mount Vernon, a few miles from Cedar Rapids. He had been active in local politics for several years, including a stint as fundraising chairman for Linn County Democrats.

When Loebsack decided to challenge Republican Rep. Jim Leach in 2006, he insisted that his campaign was not an attack on the moderate, popular Leach's three decades in Congress but rather on the GOP leadership. The war in Iraq was a pivotal issue then. Leach was the only member of the Iowa delegation to oppose the war, but Loebsack sought to tie him to President George W. Bush's Defense secretary, Donald Rumsfeld, nonetheless. Leach had been an aide to Rumsfeld when he was a House member from Illinois in the late 1960s, Leach refused to disparage his former boss,

Loebsack raised only $522,000, and he had little support from the Democratic Congressional Campaign Committee. But Leach unwittingly helped Loebsack overcome those obstacles by eschewing negative campaigning and vigorous fundraising. He refused to accept contributions from political action committees or from sources outside the district and raised only $491,000. Leach was endorsed by the district's major newspapers, but voters chose Loebsack, 51%-49%.

Although he initially compiled a liberal voting record, Loebsack moved steadily to the center when Republicans controlled the House. He has been among the Democrats joining Republicans in calling for the comptroller general to audit the Federal Reserve, and he joined GOP lawmakers in supporting an end to public subsidies of the national party conventions. He joined the Center Aisle Caucus, an informal group of about 40 House members seeking to establish greater civility between the parties. Loebsack has opposed efforts to impeach President Donald Trump. As a Democrat in a district that Trump won, he has argued the Russia investigation should be allowed to play out, drawing the ire of some progressives.

On the Armed Services Committee, Loebsack added a provision to the 2012 defense authorization bill to have behavioral health specialists embedded with National Guard and Reserve units during training. He drew praise at home for protecting the Rock Island Arsenal from cutbacks. In 2015, he made an unusual mid-career switch of committee assignments to Energy and Commerce. On that panel, he pushed for legislation to assist rural areas, including encouragement of regulatory action to promote more broadband in underserved places. And he's pushed to establish a National Flood Center in the mold of the Iowa Flood Center.

Loebsack has occasionally shown traces of his earlier activism. In 2017, he banded with Democrats in opposing the GOP tax plan, claiming it was too slanted toward high earners. In June 2016, he joined the Democrats' sit-in on the House floor to demand votes on gun legislation. "This isn't a stunt," he said in response to criticism from Speaker Paul Ryan. "We're serious about this." After the October 2017 massacre in Las Vegas that killed 58 people, Loebsack said "it is past time we act" and that "words alone are not enough."

Still, Loebsack has voiced criticism for how national Democrats have failed to reach rural voters. After the 2016, he told the Quad City Times that "Iowa could have been taken a little more seriously" by Hillary Clinton's campaign. At the Iowa State Fair in 2018, he told the Des Moines Register that "The best thing the Democratic Party can do going forward is recognize that the Midwest isn't San Francisco, it's not Long Island or Queens. It's completely different." Loebsack explained his own approach – including his focus on expanding broadband access -- to the Wall Street Journal: "I go to where people, work, live and play. I'll go out to a farm and we may not agree on all the issues, but I'll go there and hear them out."

Loebsack has faced competitive campaigns. He won a comfortable reelection, 57%-39%, in 2008 against political neophyte Mariannette Miller-Meeks, a Republican ophthalmologist. She returned for a rematch in 2010, hoping the national political climate favoring her party would give her a boost. She criticized Loebsack's support for the health care overhaul. His work on behalf of flood-stricken communities in the district helped offset his support of Obama's policies, and he won, 51%-46%. When redistricting in 2012 left Loebsack with a constituency nearly half new, GOP strategists hoped his professorial style might alienate some rural voters and they put up John Archer, a conservative attorney for John Deere. Loebsack spent plenty of time back home and won handily, 56%-43%.

In 2014, Miller-Meeks ran a third time against Loebsack, spending $1 million from her own campaign and another million from the NRCC. He spent $1.7 million, and survived the Iowa Democratic massacre that year, with 52.6 percent of the vote. Loebsack's 19,600-vote margin in Johnson County exceeded his 14,000-vote overall lead in the district; he also won the other relatively urban counties, but trailed badly in rural areas. In 2016, he had an easier campaign when his opponent, Christopher Peters, raised only $212,000. Loebsack won, 54%-46, even as Trump carried the district narrowly. Peters ran again in 2018, but Loebsack improved his margin, winning 55%-43%. With Loebsack's retirement, the presidential-year turnout likely will produce a competitive contest to select his successor. The early frontrunner for the Democratic nomination was former state Sen. Rita Hart, who ran unsuccessfully for lieutenant governor in 2018.

IA-2: Southeast Iowa

Cook Partisan Voting Index: D+1

Population		Race and Ethnicity		Income	
Total	777,339	White	85.8%	Median Income	$53,724
Land area (sq. miles)	12,262	Black	4.1%	District Income Rank	245
Pop/ sq mi	63.4	Latino	5.5%	Poverty Rate	13.5%
Born in State	67.9%	Asian	2.3%	With health insurance	94%
		Two or more races	1.8%	Cash public assistance	2.1%
Age Groups		Other	0.3%	Food stamp/SNAP	11.7%
Under 18	22.8%				
18-34	23.5%	**Education**		**Work**	
35-64	37.7%	H.S grad or less	40.2%	White Collar	16%
Over 64	16%	Some college	31.7%	Sales and Service	38.8%
		College Degree, 4 yr	17.7%	Blue Collar	26.3%
Military		Post grad	10.4%	Government	15.4%
Veteran/ Active Duty	8.3%				

2012 Pres. Vote	Obama	219,946	(56%)	Romney	168,534	(43%)			
2016 Pres. Vote	Trump	186,384	(49%)	Clinton	170,796	(44%)	Johnson	13,719	(4%)

Davenport, Iowa City: Southeast Iowa is a land of rolling hills and deep river valleys, of undulant farm fields and big skies, of prosperous small towns and grain elevators and factories. In the southeastern part of the state, one can find Iowa's contributions to the Quad Cities along the Mississippi River and the Illinois border. Bettendorf is where riverboat gambling was launched in the U.S. in 1991. Davenport, on the hills over the Mississippi, still has the look of the city where Ronald Reagan got his first radio job. Now, its largest employers are John Deere and the Rock Island Arsenal. Other manufacturers in the area have had ups and downs -- Procter & Gamble announced in 2018 it was cutting 500 jobs from its Iowa City plant, moving its hair care and body wash sections to West Virginia. But Sterilite Corp. opened a new plastic housewares plant, bringing 500 jobs to Davenport.

West of Davenport is Iowa City, a university town dotted with trendy bookstores and vegetarian eateries, that has been ranked among America's most gay-friendly cities, Muscatine County, near the Mississippi River, had the first two towns in Iowa with a Hispanic majority, a legacy of abundant farm work in the area and, more recently, jobs at the Tyson Foods pork processing plant in nearby Columbus Junction. Hundreds of workers who perform grueling jobs at the plant have been Burmese refugees. Muscatine also has a special relationship with the Chinese government, including a sister city, but that bond was strained amid the country's retaliatory tariffs on soybeans.

Since a 2008 raid of an Iowa slaughterhouse, where nearly 400 immigrants were arrested, companies report that they have become more careful about hiring only employees with legal papers. By 2016, more than 1,000 refugees from Congo recently had settled in Johnson County. Iowa City voted in 2017 to become a "sanctuary city," saying it largely wouldn't take steps to enforce federal immigration law. The Davenport City Council also voted to observe Indigenous Peoples Day instead of Columbus Day.

The 2nd Congressional District covers the southeast quadrant of the state, with regularly shaped lines. Its population centers are Davenport and Iowa City. Maharishi Vedic City in Jefferson County is where followers of the Maharishi Mahesh Yogi built Maharishi University in 1973 and made the town a magnet for practitioners of transcendental meditation. Politically, the district is more progressive, thanks in large part to big Democratic majorities in Iowa City. But 2016 brought an unexpected shift: Donald Trump won 49%-45% (the same outcome as in the neighboring 1st District) and he won every county except for Iowa City-based Johnson and Davenport-based Scott, which are the two largest counties in the 2nd.

Cindy Axne (D)

Elected 2018, 1st term, b. Apr 20, 1965; Des Moines; Drake University (IA); University of Iowa, B.A., 1987; Northwestern University, M.B.A., 2002; Catholic; Married (John Axne); 2 children.

Professional Career: Chicago Tribune Media Group, 2000-2003; Administrator, IA Department of Administrative Services, 2005-2007, IA Department of Management, 2007-2010, IA Department of Natural Resources, 2010-2014; Principal, Axne Consulting Group, 2014-2016.

DC Office: 330 CHOB 20515, 202-225-5476, axne.house.gov

State Offices: Council Bluffs, 712-890-3117; Creston, 202-225-5476; Des Moines, 515-400-8180.

Committees: *Agriculture*: Commodity Exchanges, Energy & Credit; Conservation & Forestry. *Financial Services*: Housing, Community Development & Insurance; Investor Protection, Entrepreneurship & Capital Markets.

Election Results

Election	Name (Party)	Vote (%)		Cand. Spent	Ind. Exp. Support	Ind. Exp. Oppose
2018 General	Cindy Axne (D)	175,642	(49%)	$5,160,139	$754,501	$3,558,481
	David Young (R)	167,933	(47%)	$2,792,231	$623,353	$4,726,924
	Bryan Holder (Lib)	7,267	(2%)			
2018 Primary	Cindy Axne (D)	32,910	(58%)			
	Eddie Mauro (D)	15,006	(26%)			
	Pete D'Alessandro (D)	8,874	(16%)			

Freshman Democrat Cindy Axne won her first election with a well-organized campaign. She won the Democratic nomination over two well-financed primary opponents after the apparent frontrunner unexpectedly dropped out following discovery that her ballot petitions had been forged. Axne had experience with local and state government. She defeated Republican Rep. David Young, who served two terms and found himself in a political vise as the result of tariffs imposed by President Donald Trump. With Rep. Abby Finkenauer, she is one of the first two women from Iowa elected to the House.

Axne grew up in Des Moines and graduated from the University of Iowa with a degree in journalism. She got a master's in business administration from the Kellogg School at Northwestern University. She worked on strategic planning for the Tribune Company in Chicago and started a digital-design business with her husband, John.

When their first son started kindergarten in Des Moines, Axne was outraged to learn that some local children did not have access to a full-day program. Complaining about the inequality, she organized an advocacy group and negotiated for nearly a year with school officials before gaining their agreement to make full-day kindergarten available to all local students. Later, she worked for nearly a decade with more than 20 Iowa state agencies under governors from both parties to assist in improving the delivery of their services.

Axne's campaign got a boost when Theresa Greenfield, a business executive, learned at the March 2018 filing deadline that her advisor had forged signatures that were required for all candidates. That left two other contenders in the Democratic primary: Pete D'Alessandro, who was campaign coordinator for Sen. Bernie Sanders in 2016, and Eddie Mauro, president of an insurance company and leader of a social justice advocacy group. Axne styled herself as a problem-solver. She easily won the primary over runner-up Mauro, 58%-26%.

In a district where the farm economy is vital, even in urban areas, Young found himself at odds with Trump over his trade war with China and the resulting tariffs on many crops. "I don't like tariffs, I think tariffs are a tax on consumers, employers, and employees," he told the Daily Iowan, a campus newspaper. Still, Trump remained popular in many rural communities, including places where farmers were losing business. The president favorably called out Young during an October campaign rally in Council Bluffs. A former chief of staff to Iowa Sen. Chuck Grassley, Young had shown his political skills by gaining a seat on the House Appropriations Committee.

Like other successful House Democratic challengers in 2018, Axne was a strong fundraiser. She spent more than $5 million, which nearly doubled the spending by Young. House Democrats and their party allies dropped more than $2 million on her behalf.

In her close victory, Axne got 56 percent in Polk County, which cast a bit more than one-half of the total vote. Remarkably, Young took the remaining 15 counties—with over 60 percent of the vote in all but three of them: two counties in the Des Moines suburbs and Council Bluffs-based Pottawattamie County. Like much of Iowa, this district likely will remain a political battleground.

In early 2019, Axne explored a potential challenge in 2020 to Sen. Joni Ernst and she received encouragement from Senate Democrats. But she decided to seek reelection and faced the prospect of a rematch with Young, who said that he would seek his former seat.

IA-3: Southwest Iowa

Cook Partisan Voting Index: R+1

Population		Race and Ethnicity		Income	
Total	811,951	White	83.8%	Median Income	$62,390
Land area (sq. miles)	8,790	Black	4%	District Income Rank	153
Pop/ sq mi	92.4	Latino	6.7%	Poverty Rate	10.7%
Born in State	67.6%	Asian	3.1%	With health insurance	94.5%
		Two or more races	2%	Cash public assistance	2.3%
Age Groups		Other	0.4%	Food stamp/SNAP	12.2%
Under 18	25%				
18-34	22.5%	**Education**		**Work**	
35-64	38.6%	H.S grad or less	35.8%	White Collar	13.9%
Over 64	13.9%	Some college	31.8%	Sales and Service	40.7%
		College Degree, 4 yr	22.5%	Blue Collar	20.8%
Military		Post grad	9.7%	Government	12.2%
Veteran/ Active Duty	7.7%				

2012 Pres. Vote	Obama	203,622	(51%)	Romney	186,645	(47%)		
2016 Pres. Vote	Trump	192,960	(48%)	Clinton	178,937	(45%)	Johnson	16,693 (4%)

Des Moines, Council Bluffs: Iowa, which today seems very much in the middle of the country, was once part of the West. It was not only the home of sober farmers and pious burghers, but also the eastern terminus of the first transcontinental railroad, a way station for people in a hurry to get across the Great Plains to the Rockies and the Pacific Northwest. Those who stayed behind used the wealth accumulated by methodical husbandry of their fertile farmlands to implant firmly the glories of Western Civilization. One can feel that impulse today in Des Moines, looking across the river from downtown to the Victorian capitol, its gold dome above a Corinthian pediment. Terrace Hill, the beautifully restored governor's mansion, sits atop a rise overlooking the Raccoon River.

The city of Des Moines remains classically Middle American, even as it gains a livelier downtown and spreads into the countryside. The area has become a sanctuary for people looking for a family-friendly urban lifestyle. Insurance, agricultural supply, printing and financial service businesses have expanded in office centers downtown and at freeway interchanges. Principal Financial Group employs more than 6,400 people in the area. Kemin Industries, which makes nutritional ingredients, completed the initial step of a multi-phase expansion of its headquarters. More than 12,000 Bosnians have settled in Des Moines, many of whom work at meatpacking.

Des Moines and the southwest corner of Iowa make up the 3rd Congressional District. The second-most populous city here is Council Bluffs, home to the mansion of Gen. Grenville Dodge, who in 1859 lobbied Illinois lawyer Abraham Lincoln on the need for a transcontinental railroad. Lincoln got it through Congress in 1862, Dodge became its chief engineer, and Council Bluffs became its eastern terminus when it was completed in 1869. Surrounded by beef-grazing territory, Council Bluffs looks west across the Missouri River to Omaha, taking on the culturally more conservative tone of Nebraska. The area has developed an economically hip side with seven data centers owned by Microsoft, Amazon and Google, plus four by Facebook, at a total cost of more than $10 billion. Iowa has become an attractive place for these facilities because of its tax incentives, plenty of cheap land and access to high-speed fiber optics.

The small rural towns, where businesses have been struggling, were fertile ground for Donald Trump's campaign. Aside from Des Moines and Polk County, he took the other 15 counties in the

3rd, with an overall win of 48%-45%. In October 2018, politics in the district shifted again. For the first time since 2012, registered Democrats outnumbered registered Republicans.

Steve King (R)

Elected 2002, 9th term, b. May 28, 1949; Storm Lake; Northwest Missouri State University, Att., 1970; Roman Catholic; Married (Marilyn King); 3 children; 7 grandchildren.

Elected Office: IA Senate, 1996-2002.

Professional Career: Owner, King Construction Co., 1975-2002.

DC Office: 2210 RHOB 20515, 202-225-4426, Fax: 202-225-3193, steveking.house.gov

State Offices: Ames, 515-232-2885; Fort Dodge, 515-573-2738; Mason City, 641-201-1624; Sioux City, 712-224-4692; Spencer, 712-580-7754.

Group Ratings

	ADA	ACLU	AFL-CIO	LCV	ITI	COC	HAFA	ACU	CFG	FRC
2018	-	9%	-	9%	-	83%	73%	76%	74%	80%
2017	0%	C	8%	0%	C	93%	C	81%	74%	100%

Almanac Ratings 2017-18

	Economy	Social	Foreign	Composite
Liberal	4%	3%	6%	4%
Conservative	96%	97%	94%	96%

Key Votes of the 115th Congress

1. Obama-care revision	Y	5. Family planning regs	Y	9. Guantanamo prisoners	N
2. Tax Cuts	Y	6. Body cameras/immigration	N	10. Ground missiles, limit	N
3. Omnibus appropriations	N	7. Abortion ban	Y	11. Defense Dept. spending	Y
4. Dodd-Frank revision	Y	8. Concealed carry	Y	12. FISA rules	Y

Election Results

Election	Name (Party)	Vote (%)		Cand. Spent	Ind. Exp. Support	Ind. Exp. Oppose
2018 General	Steve King (R)	157,676	(50%)	$965,614	$5,291	$509,458
	J.D. Scholten (D)	147,246	(47%)	$3,192,434	$125,313	$2,500
2018 Primary	Steve King (R)	28,053	(75%)			
	Cyndi Hanson (R)	9,437	(25%)			

Prior winning percentages: 2016 (54%), 2014 (62%), 2012 (53%), 2010 (66%), 2008 (60%), 2006 (59%), 2004 (63%), 2002 (62%)

Republican Steve King, who first won his seat in 2002, practices a brand of in-your-face conservatism that has devolved into support for white nationalist and white supremacist ideology, provoking the condemnation of Republican leadership. The immigration hardliner was threatened with congressional censure for incendiary comments made in January 2019. But he could face a much more fraught electoral threat, drawing for the first time a credible primary challenger after winning his narrowest re-election victory yet in 2018.

King was born in Storm Lake and attended Northwest Missouri State University, though he didn't graduate. In 1975, he founded the King Construction Co. After building up his business, he launched his political career in 1996, with his election to the state Senate, where he quickly gained a reputation as a strong conservative. He opposed abortion rights, affirmative action and same-sex marriage. He sponsored Iowa's "God and Country" bill, which required Iowa schools to recognize that the United States "has derived its strength from biblical values," and he was a driving force behind the state's English-only law. On economic matters, King supported repeal of the state's inheritance tax, and backed a 15 percent state income tax cut and a right-to-work law.

When the House seat came open in 2002, King was the only rural candidate among the four chief contenders. He led in the June primary with 30 percent of the vote. Because no candidate received the required 35 percent, the nomination was determined by a special party convention three weeks later. The 533 voting delegates needed three ballots to select a winner. King led on each ballot and defeated House Speaker Brent Siegrist of Council Bluffs, 272-253, in the final round. The general election outcome was never in doubt.

In the House, King has not been shy about sharing his hyper-partisan views, and he has received national press coverage for controversial remarks. During the 2015 State of the Union message, he complained on Twitter that an undocumented immigrant seated with first lady Michelle Obama was "deportable." After King filed a bill that intended to keep the courts from ruling on gay-marriage cases, then-Democratic Rep. Jared Polis of Colorado joked in April 2015 that he planned to file the "Restrain Steve King from Legislating Act." A Carroll, Iowa, Daily Times Herald columnist who assembled some of King's quotes into a book, King Kong Krazy, called him "maniacally nationalistic."

In recent years, King's focus on white identity politics has become more emboldened following the election of President Donald Trump, who shares his penchant for inflammatory language and strict immigration policies. King wasn't an initial backer of Trump, though, having been the national co-chairman of Texas Sen. Ted Cruz's campaign and helping him win the Iowa caucuses in 2016. Even after Trump became the nominee, King remained somewhat skeptical, voicing concern that Trump was "softening" his view on enforcement of immigration laws. He blasted Trump for considering a deal to fund a border wall in exchange for a path to legalization for children in the Deferred Action for Childhood Arrivals program. When Trump came under attack for separating children from their parents at the border and holding them in detention center, King came to his defense. "These are children that are cared for with better care than they get in their home country," he told TMZ.

King advocates English as the official language of the United States. In 2008, an Iowa district court judge ruled in favor of King's challenge to state officials who had placed bilingual voting forms on state websites. In 2007, as the ranking Republican on the Judiciary Immigration Subcommittee, King built a model fence on the House floor to show how simple it would be to construct a 2,000-mile fence on the border with Mexico. In a 2013 interview, he said that many illegal immigrants "weigh 130 pounds and they've got calves the size of cantaloupes because they're hauling 75 pounds of marijuana across the desert." By that time, GOP leaders had denied him the top subcommittee post.

When Republicans won control of the House in 2011, King introduced a bill to end birthright citizenship, an idea that has gained currency in some circles but generates strong opposition among Hispanics. "Steve King is positioning our party for disaster," the Latino group Somos Republicans said in a statement. The measure went nowhere, but gained attention again in 2018 when Trump took up the mantle. In 2018, he introduced a bill that would allow for the arrest of people in sanctuary cities who help illegal immigrants.

King had reelection troubles in 2012. His Democratic opponent was Christie Vilsack; her husband, Tom Vilsack, had been Iowa governor and then served as President Barack Obama's secretary of Agriculture. With help from popular Gov. Terry Branstad, he escaped with a 53%-45% victory. In 2014, a good year for Republicans, King breezed with 62 percent of the vote against Jim Mowrer, an Iraq war veteran, who outspent King $2.2 million to $2 million. Democrats turned their attention elsewhere in 2016, and King coasted to reelection.

But in 2018, as Democrats were seeing momentum nationally and in Iowa, King faced a tougher-than-expected challenge from Democrat J.D. Scholten, a former professional baseball player who toured the district in a Winnebago named "Sioux City Sue," after the Gene Autry song. Scholten ran a populist campaign and criticized King's racist comments.

After 11 people were killed at a Pittsburgh synagogue just before Election Day, more of King's alliances and social media postings – including retweeting a Nazi sympathizer -- came under scrutiny. The anti-Semitic shooter had made posts saying that "invaders" were responsible for his "people" being "slaughtered" – rhetoric that echoed language King has long used. King became incensed at the comparisons, but he was already getting heat after traveling to Austria to meet with officials of a far-right political party. And he had recently endorsed a Toronto mayoral candidate with white nationalist ties who had appeared on a neo-Nazi podcast.

Scholten brought in $3.2 million (including almost $1 million during the final week of the campaign) to King's $966,000. In addition, the National Republican Congressional Committee signaled that it wouldn't send King any help. Companies such as Intel Corp., Land O'Lakes, and AT&T said they would no longer donate to King. But King eked out a 50%-47% win.

Shortly after that result, state Sen. Randy Feenstra announced he would challenge King in the 2020 GOP primary and Iowa Gov. Kim Reynolds said she would stay neutral in the race, a blow to King.

King responded that he would hold town halls in all of the district's 39 counties; previously he had quit doing so, claiming they were simply attractions for paid protesters. But it became clear that King's incendiary language and racist comments wouldn't cease. In an interview with the New York Times, King waxed: "White nationalist, white supremacist, Western civilization — how did that language become offensive? Why did I sit in classes teaching me about the merits of our history and our civilization?" In response to the Democrats' most diverse freshman class ever, he remarked, "You could look over there and think the Democratic Party is no country for white men." King tried to backtrack following the interview, saying he was a "nationalist" and a supporter of "western civilization's values," not that he supported "white nationalism and white supremacy."

South Carolina Sen. Tim Scott, the only African-American Republican in the Senate, wrote in a Washington Post op-ed, "Some in our party wonder why Republicans are constantly accused of racism — it is because of our silence when things like this are said." Democrats floated the idea of a congressional censure. Maybe most consequentially, Iowa's two Republican senators condemned his remarks. Sen. Joni Ernst said King's comments were "offensive and racist — and not representative of our state of Iowa." And Sen. Chuck Grassley – who endorsed King in 2018 even as the NRCC dropped him – told Axios, "I find it offensive to claim white supremacy. I will condemn it."

House Minority Leader Kevin McCarthy responded by stripping King of his committee assignments—both Agriculture and Judiciary—which seemed a firm repudiation.

As pressure from national Republicans continued to mount, retirement was not out of the question for King.

IA-4: Northwest and Central Iowa   Cook Partisan Voting Index: R+11

Population		Race and Ethnicity		Income	
Total	758,360	White	87.9%	Median Income	$52,799
Land area (sq. miles)	22,757	Black	1.5%	District Income Rank	261
Pop/ sq mi	33.3	Latino	6.7%	Poverty Rate	12.7%
Born in State	72.1%	Asian	2%	With health insurance	94.3%
		Two or more races	1.4%	Cash public assistance	2.2%
Age Groups		Other	0.5%	Food stamp/SNAP	10.4%
Under 18	22.6%				
18-34	22.9%	**Education**		**Work**	
35-64	36.8%	H.S grad or less	41.8%	White Collar	17.7%
Over 64	17.7%	Some college	34.2%	Sales and Service	37.6%
		College Degree, 4 yr	16.6%	Blue Collar	28.7%
Military		Post grad	7.4%	Government	14.5%
Veteran/ Active Duty	8.4%				

2012 Pres. Vote	Romney	204,685	(53%)	Obama	173,391	(45%)		
2016 Pres. Vote	Trump	231,229	(60%)	Clinton	127,401	(33%)	Johnson 13,113	(3%)

Sioux City, Ames: Sioux City, one of the oldest market towns on the Great Plains, is nestled in the Loess Bluffs above the Missouri River. Sioux City has not grown much in the past half century. Its original economic base has become obsolete: The waterfront, once raucous with boatmen and stockyard workers, is now quiet. The stockyards, which employed thousands of people and slaughtered millions of hogs during their peak years in the 1920s, are shuttered. Downtown stores have been replaced by shopping malls at the edge of town, where people spend a day doing a season's shopping and then drive for hours to return to farm communities in one of four nearby states.

There are still plenty of hogs in western Iowa. Instead of meeting sellers in the markets in Sioux City, packers now contract directly with large farms and have built modern slaughterhouses nearby. Tyson Foods has facilities in Buena Vista and Crawford counties; it closed a plant in Cherokee County in 2014, though it refused to lease the empty plant. Iowa Food Group LLC has occupied the vacant space. Storm Lake, in Buena Vista County, is more than half non-white, attracting immigrants and refugees from Mexico and Central America, Asia and Africa to work in its factories with wages that have remained low and stagnant. In 2015, 31 percent of Iowa's energy was based on wind farming. It is second only to Texas in the amount of electricity generated by wind, despite objections from some farmers to the noise and the hazard to birds. Mid-America, which is owned by Warren Buffett's Berkshire Hathaway, built the state's largest wind farm, with 218 turbines, near Primghar, helping O'Brien County top the state in wind production.

Western Iowa is small-town territory. It has some of the world's most productive soil and some of its most creative agricultural scientists and farmers. Ames, in Story County, is home to Iowa State University and was the host of the Iowa Republican presidential straw poll, which launched several nomination contests until GOP leaders decided in 2015 to cancel it. Ames is part of the growth zone around Des Moines and its annual unemployment rate has been among the lowest in the country— though the cost of living has increased faster than wages. In Winnebago County near the Minnesota border is Winnebago Industries, which manufactures motor homes and recreational vehicles on computer-controlled assembly lines with robotic equipment. The company has bounced back since the Great Recession by shifting its appeal from retirees to younger consumers, who often prefer less-gaudy vehicles. From its headquarters in Forest City, the company employs more than 3,000 employees.

The 4th Congressional District is Iowa's largest geographically, stretching from South Dakota nearly to Illinois. Donald Trump won this 90 percent white district with 61 percent of the vote — his best in the state, by far.

KANSAS

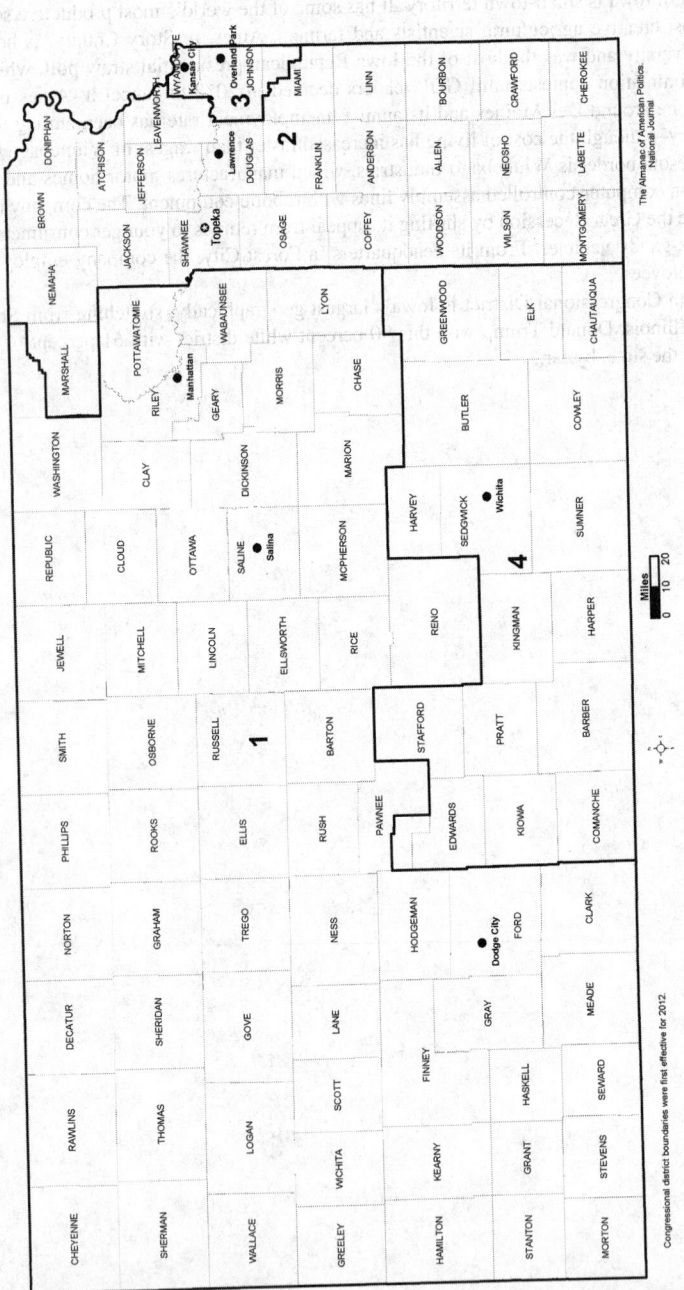

Miles
0 10 20

Congressional district boundaries were first effective for 2012.

Kansas is usually depicted as flat, average and uninteresting. It's not really, and in recent years its politics have been anything but. Conservatives have tried to turn the state into a small-government model for the nation and a place that pushed the envelope on policies on illegal immigration and voter fraud. Moderate Republicans made gains in 2016 legislative elections, followed two years later by notable Democratic victories.

The political upheaval of recent years is a reminder that Kansas' history has been punctuated by episodes of anger and rage, sweeping through the tall sheaves like the tornado in the Wizard of Oz. The state was born in a moment of violence: the Bleeding Kansas of the 1850s that led proximately to the Civil War. The trigger was the Kansas-Nebraska Act of 1854, which left to local settlers the question of whether the new Kansas Territory would be a free or slave state. Pro-slavery "bushwhackers" rode over the line from Missouri, stealing elections and writing a pro-slavery constitution. But larger numbers of free-soil "jayhawkers," from New England and the Yankee-settled Great Lakes states, put down roots and, despite the massacres perpetrated by abolitionist John Brown, prevailed and established their own law and order. This was a civil war before the Civil War. Later, Kansas became the birthplace of the Buffalo Soldiers, the African-American units that fought in the Indian Wars; their home base, Fort Leavenworth, is the oldest continuously active military reservation west of the Mississippi River and remains a key facility today.

Calmer times followed the war: The antislavery majority bent the soil to the plow and built small towns with sturdy networks of schools, churches and colleges. But the rebellious impulse did not entirely die out. Kansans' livelihoods were always at risk: Hailstorms, grasshopper invasions, dry seasons or a drop in world farm prices could mean disaster for thousands of families. The high rainfall of the 1880s attracted hundreds of thousands of new settlers. The low rainfall of the 1890s produced a bust and a populist rebellion; others followed in the 1930s, 1950s and 1970s. But afterwards, the state always returned to jayhawker Republicanism.

Owing to its geography, Kansas was, and remains, a farm state. It is flatter than an IHOP pancake, reported some geographers in 2003, though that flatness is not unrelieved. The Flint Hills between Kansas City and Wichita are irregular uplands, with the Tallgrass Prairie National Preserve hosting bus trips where bison still range. The imaginary tornado that swept Dorothy and Toto out of Kansas was echoed by a very real, 205-mile-per-hour tornado in 2007 that destroyed the town of Greensburg. Drought has been common; one in 2011, the worst since the dust storms of the 1930s, lowered the water table, killed livestock and wildlife, and forced the draining of reservoirs to keep Missouri River barges afloat. In 2018, all of Kansas was considered to be in drought, with the most extreme conditions in the southwestern part of the state. The Ogallala Aquifer — the Great Plains' vast underground reservoir, stretching across 174,000 square miles -- shrank twice as quickly between 2011 and 2017 as it had over the previous six decades, according to the Denver Post.

Almost 70 percent of Kansas residents live in metropolitan areas, Wichita State University calculations show. The state's five biggest counties – Johnson (suburbs of Kansas City), Sedgwick (Wichita), Shawnee (Topeka), Wyandotte (Kansas City proper) and Douglas (Lawrence) – accounted for 54 percent of the state's population in 2017; Johnson County saw an 8.3 percent gain between 2010 and 2017, while Douglas County saw an 8.6 percent bump. These counties accounted for essentially all of the state's population growth during that period, with the decline in rural areas putting a new spin on the phrase, "Get the hell out of Dodge." (The phrase refers to the frontier town Dodge City in rural, southwestern Kansas.)

Metropolitan Kansas City is the nation's second largest railroad hub, with a diverse economy that is by no means dependent on farming (though it does produce some of the nation's best barbecue). Wichita is the home base of Koch Industries, a conglomerate that started as an oil refining company and which recently has become a major force in politics; it has spent lavishly to promote the free-market credo of its owners, Charles and David Koch, an agenda that was historically in tune with the GOP but increasingly hasn't been in the era of Donald Trump, from whom the brothers distanced themselves. Wichita has also been a leader in general aviation; Beechcraft, Cessna, Lear and Spirit have plants there, though the region was hit hard when Boeing left its 97-building operation in 2014 after more than eight decades. Oil and gas have a foothold in the state as well.

Today, Kansas is 85 percent white (a figure that includes both non-Hispanics and Hispanics). But the Kansas Health Institute projects that the state is on track to become a majority-minority state in 2066. Hispanics today account for 11.5 percent of the population, with large and increasing populations in the state's meatpacking belt -- Dodge City, Garden City and the inaptly named Liberal, where Trump more than doubled Hillary Clinton's vote in 2016.

Kansas has been reliably Republican in presidential elections and in most congressional contests for years; it has not elected a Democrat to the Senate since 1932. But state politics was dominated for 40 years by a coalition of Democrats and moderate Republicans, according to University of Kansas political scientist Burdett Loomis. That was the case under Republican Gov. Bill Graves, elected in 1994 and 1998, and Democratic Gov. Kathleen Sebelius, elected in 2002 and 2006. When she resigned to become President Barack Obama's secretary of Health and Human Services, she was succeeded by her lieutenant governor, Mark Parkinson, a former Republican state chairman who switched parties because of the rightward drift of the state GOP. Today, heirs of Alf Landon, Dwight Eisenhower (whose presidential library is in his hometown of Abilene) and longtime Sens. Bob Dole and Nancy Landon Kassebaum have been eclipsed by Republicans with harder-edged conservative views on fiscal and social issues.

In 2010, Sam Brownback, after 14 years in the Senate, was elected governor. Brownback and the legislature trimmed pending a bit, abolished three state agencies, closed welfare offices and eliminated arts funding. In 2011, the legislature passed four bills limiting abortion and Brownback set up programs to encourage faith-based counseling on marriage and fatherhood. With Secretary of State Kris Kobach, he enacted a requirement that voters show photo identification and proof of citizenship. Brownback's signature initiative, signed in mid-2012, was a tax cut that removed 330,000 businesses off the tax rolls. Within months, he and the Koch-backed Americans for Prosperity targeted nine lawmakers for defeat in the August 2012 Republican primary; their candidates won, giving both chambers an even more solid conservative majority. The economic returns from the tax cuts were less than predicted, in part because spending continued to increase, and Standard & Poor's and Moody's slashed the state's credit rating. Throughout 2014, Brownback's approval ratings lagged. But in a solidly Republican year, Brownback beat the odds, winning by four points.

As Brownback's second term wore on, his approval ratings were among the worst of any governor in the nation. In the 2016 primaries, Brownback-aligned candidates lost a net of two dozen state House and Senate primaries to challengers backed by teachers' unions, roadbuilders and hospitals. In November, Kansas voted for Trump, 57%-36%, but Democrats gained seats in both state legislative chambers -- a bad omen for Brownback. In 2017, bipartisan majorities voted to expand Medicaid under the Affordable Care Act, but legislators fell short of overriding Brownback's veto. The legislature did override Browback's veto of a bill to undo $1.2 billion of his signature tax cuts.

In the 2018 Republican primary, Kobach defeated the establishment choice, Jeff Colyer, who had been serving as governor since Brownback took a Trump administration post. The prospect of facing the polarizing Kobach energized Democrats. State Sen. Laura Kelly defeated Kobach, 48%-43%. Kelly increased the Democratic raw vote by 26 percent over the party's 2014 gubernatorial nominee and by 19 percent over Hillary Clinton's showing in the 2016 presidential race. (After the election, three moderate Republicans in the legislature switched parties; all were women from Johnson County.) But Republicans didn't crater; they won a competitive race to succeed Kobach as secretary of state. Indeed, in a sign of Kelly's future challenges, conservatives clawed back some of the seats they'd lost in the legislature, weakening the Democrats' alliance with moderate Republicans.

Population		Race and Ethnicity		Income	
Total	2,903,820	White	76.5%	Median Income	$55,477
Land area (sq. miles)	81,759	Black	5.6%	State Income Rank	27
Pop/ sq mi	35.5	Latino	11.5%	Poverty Rate	12.8%
Born in state	59.0%	Asian	2.8%	With health insurance	90.4%
		Two or more races	2.8%	Cash public assistance	1.8%
Age Groups		Other	0.9%	Food stamp/SNAP	8.6%
Under 18	24.7%				
18-34	23.6%	Education		Work	
35-64	37.0%	H.S grad or less	35.7%	White Collar	37.9%
Over 64	14.7%	Some college	31.9%	Sales and Service	38.9%
Military		College Degree, 4 yr	20.6%	Blue Collar	23.2%
Veteran/ Active Duty	9.4%	Post grad	11.7%	Government	15.5%

Presidential Politics

2016 Caucus (D)	Sanders (D)	26,429 (68%)	Clinton (D)	12,593 (32%)			
2016 Caucus (R)	Cruz (R)	37,512 (47%)	Trump (R)	18,443 (23%)	Rubio (R)	13,295 (17%)	
	Kasich (R)	8,741 (11%)					
2016 Pres. Vote	Trump (R)	671,018 (57%)	Clinton (D)	427,005 (36%)	Johnson (L)	55,406 (5%)	
	Stein (G)	23,506 (2%)					
2012 Pres. Vote	Romney (R)	692,634 (60%)	Obama (D)	440,726 (38%)			

Except for 1964, when it narrowly favored Lyndon Johnson over Barry Goldwater, Kansas has voted Republican for president for three-fourths of a century. In the 105 counties, George W. Bush, Mitt Romney and Donald Trump each lost only two: Wyandotte, which includes Kansas City and has a majority-minority population; and Douglas, which is home to the University of Kansas in Lawrence. John McCain in 2008 lost one more, by just over 200 votes, Crawford County, home to Pittsburg State University. In 1996, the state legislature voted to cancel the April presidential primary and both parties have held caucuses since. Texas Sen. Ted Cruz handily beat Trump in the 2016 GOP contest, 48%-23%. More than 78,000 attended, compared with 30,377 in 2012. In the Democratic caucuses, Vermont Sen. Bernie Sanders defeated Hillary Clinton 68%-32%. More than 39,000 participated in the Democratic contest, up slightly from the 37,089 in 2008, when Barack Obama overwhelmed Clinton by a nearly 3-1 margin.

Congressional Districts

116th Congress Lineup	1D 3R	115th Congress Lineup	4R

The 2018 election results added new dynamics to the redistricting outlook in Kansas, with the election of a Democratic governor and one Democratic member in what had been an all-Republican House delegation since the 2012 redistricting. In addition, the occasionally influential coalition of Democrats and moderate Republicans in the capitol could provide additional protection for at least one district where congressional Democrats retain leverage. Ambitious Democrats also are mindful that the districts based in Topeka and Wichita have had competitive contests recently, though the GOP base seems firm in each. Still, there are caveats that should limit Democratic exuberance, including the prospect that freshman Democratic Rep. Sharice Davids will face a competitive contest to retain her Kansas City-area seat in 2020 and that Republicans hold more than 2-to-1 majorities in both the state Senate and House.

The outcome of the most recent redistricting may be instructive. In spring 2012, a coalition of Democrats and moderate Republicans in the state Senate passed one redistricting plan and the conservative-dominated House passed another; they adjourned in May without reaching agreement. A federal court took the case, and a three-judge panel approved a map that moved Lawrence to the 2nd District and put Manhattan, home of Kansas State University, and Fort Riley into the western and central 1st district. Those new boundaries were relevant at least as much for regional and business interests as for their partisan implications.

Laura Kelly (D)

Elected 2018, term expires 2023, 1st term; b. Jan. 24, 1950, New York, NY; Bradley University, B.S.; Indiana University, Bloomington, M.S.; Catholic; Married (Ted Daughety); 2 children.

Elected Office: KS Senate, 2005-2018.

Professional Career: Executive Director, Kansas Recreation and Park Association, 1988-2004; Recreation Therapist, Rockland Children's Psychiatric Center; Director, Recreation Therapy/Physical Education, National Jewish Hospital for Respiratory and Immune Diseases.

Office: 300 S.W. Tenth Ave., Suite 241-S, Topeka, 66612; 785-296-3232; Fax: 785-296-7973; Website: governor.kansas.gov

Lt. Gov.: Lynn Rogers (D) **Atty. Gen:** Derek Schmidt (R) **Sec. of State:** Scott Schwab (R)

State Legislature: Senate: 11D, 28R, 1I **House:** 41D, 84R

Election Results

Election	Name (Party)	Vote (%)
2018 General	Laura Kelly (D)	506,509 (48%)
	Kris Kobach (R)	453,030 (43%)
	Greg Orman (I)	68,498 (6%)
2018 Primary	Laura Kelly (D)	80,377 (51%)
	Carl Brewer (D)	31,493 (20%)
	Joshua Svaty (D)	27,292 (18%)
	Arden Andersen (D)	13,161 (8%)

Laura Kelly was elected governor of Kansas in 2018, amid fatigue with the policies of the conservative Republicans who dominated state politics for the better part of a decade. A longtime state legislator, Kelly reached beyond the Democratic base and won support from moderate Republicans who preferred her pragmatic approach to that of the GOP nominee, conservative Secretary of State Kris Kobach.

Kelly was born in New York City but moved often as a child. Her family settled in Salina Kansas in the mid-1980s, then moved to Topeka. Kelly worked as an advocate for mental health services and patient care. For 19 years, she ran the Kansas Recreation and Park Association. Kathleen Sebelius, the future Democratic governor, tried to recruit her as a candidate in 1994; while Kelly turned her down, the two became longstanding allies. Initially an independent, Kelly became a Democrat. "It just became clear to me that the ideological arm of the Republican Party was really inflaming the culture wars, and I felt very uncomfortable with that, so I thought I needed to get off the fence and make a declaration," Kelly told the Wichita Eagle. She narrowly won a state Senate seat in 2004.

In the Senate, Kelly served for more than a decade in top committee positions overseeing health, budget and social-services policy. That gave her a front-row seat for some of the biggest battles during the governorship of Republican Sam Brownback. He pursued an ambitious conservative agenda, the centerpiece of which was the largest tax cut in Kansas history, trimming more than $1 billion in state revenue. This, coupled with continued increases in spending, produced a large and persistent budget gap that critics said hampered the state's economic growth. In 2017, President Donald Trump offered Brownback the post of ambassador-at-large for international religious freedom. For much of that year, Brownback awaited confirmation, producing an awkward situation in Topeka, as Lt. Gov. Jeff Colyer served as the heir apparent, but without the powers of the governorship.

Colyer, who had been educated at Georgetown University and Cambridge University, practiced as a plastic surgeon in suburban Kansas City. He took several trips to treat patients in combat zones in Iraq, Afghanistan, Rwanda and Sierra Leone. The differences between Brownback and Colyer – who were elected as a ticket in 2010 -- were often more stylistic than substantive. While Colyer was considered less confrontational, both shared an opposition to abortion and expansive government, and the two were aligned on overhauling the state's Medicaid program. After the Senate confirmed Brownback in January 2018, Colyer was sworn in as governor – and immediately prepared his campaign.

While the GOP officially controlled both chambers, Colyer often faced off against an alliance of Democrats and moderate Republicans that had expanded its influence in the 2016 election. The House rejected a tax cut that would have shielded multinational companies from taxes on repatriated assets for one year. Republicans also got bad news when the state Supreme Court ruled against a school funding plan passed by the legislature.

Colyer faced a primary challenge from Kobach, the two-term secretary of state who received national attention for his tough approach to illegal immigration. His intense focus on voter fraud led to his appointment as vice chair of a panel created by Trump to study the issue. While Colyer won most of the GOP establishment's support, Kobach parlayed Trump's backing in a late tweet into a victory, though his win was so narrow it took more than a week to officially call the race. Moderate Jim Barnett received almost 9 percent of the vote.

The results of the GOP primary buoyed Democrats, who were more eager to face Kobach than Colyer. The Democratic primary included three major candidates. In addition to Kelly – who Sebelius had encouraged to run – the field included former Wichita Mayor Carl Brewer and former state lawmaker and onetime agriculture secretary Josh Svaty. The candidates generally agreed on taxes, health care and education, but Svaty criticized some of Kelly's past votes as pro-gun. Kelly joined Brewer in criticizing some of Svaty's past anti-abortion votes. Kelly, the only woman in the race, pulled ahead by stressing Medicaid expansion – which Brownback, Colyer and Kobach had all opposed -- and by advocating a steady-as-she-goes approach that she billed as an antidote to Brownback. "I don't think this is time for another experiment," she said. Kelly got 51 percent, ahead of Brewer with 20 percent and Svaty with 18 percent.

In the general election, Kobach grappled with an embarrassing episode in court, when a judge overseeing a voter-identification case struck down the law Kobach was defending, held him in contempt and ordered him to take remedial legal education. Kobach tried to distance himself from the still-unpopular Brownback, but he maintained his loyalty to Trump, which alienated moderate Republicans. Two former Republican governors, Mike Hayden and Bill Graves, endorsed Kelly, as did former GOP Sens. Nancy Landon Kassebaum and Sheila Frahm, along with dozens of former and current GOP state lawmakers. Third-party candidate Greg Orman, a self-styled centrist who had run a strong challenge to Sen. Pat Roberts in 2014, initially seemed poised to play a spoiler role, pulling about 10 percent in polls and leaving Kobach and Kelly deadlocked. But Kelly won with 48 percent, to 43 percent for Kobach and 7 percent for Orman. Kelly's victory was driven by heavily suburban counties. Brownback had won both Johnson and Sedgwick narrowly in 2014, but Kelly took Johnson by 17 points and Sedgwick by six. "There will be a lot of talk around America about the blue wave, but I don't believe that's what's happened here in Kansas," Kelly said in her victory speech. "What happened in Kansas was a wave of common sense, a wave of bipartisanship."

Kelly started her term with a significantly improved state budget picture thanks to a growing economy inherited from her predecessor, and she planned to pursue an expansion of Medicaid under the Affordable Care Act – a move long blocked by Republicans – as well as increased school funding along the lines of what the state Supreme Court has sought. Despite her own victory, Kelly faced challenges in the legislature after gains by conservatives at the expense of moderates in 2018.

Pat Roberts (R)

Elected 1996, term expires 2020, 4th term, b. Apr 20, 1936; Topeka; Kansas State University, B.A., 1958; Arizona State University, 1964; Methodist; Married (Frankie Fann Roberts); 3 children; 5 grandchildren.

Military Career: U.S. Marine Corps 1958-1962

Elected Office: U.S. House, 1981-1997.

Professional Career: Co-owner & editor, The Westsider, 1962-1967; A.A., U.S Sen. Frank Carlson, 1967-1968; A.A., U.S Rep. Keith Sebelius, 1968-1980.

DC Office: 109 HSOB 20510, 202-224-4774, Fax: 202-224-3514, roberts.senate.gov

State Offices: Dodge City, 620-227-2244; Overland Park, 913-451-9343; Topeka, 785-295-2745; Wichita, 316-263-0416.

Committees: *Agriculture, Nutrition & Forestry (Chmn)*: Ex Officio membership on all subcommittees. *Ethics.* *Finance*: Energy, Natural Resources & Infrastructure; Health Care; International Trade, Customs & Global Competitiveness. *Health, Education, Labor & Pensions*: Children & Families; Primary Health & Retirement Security. *Rules & Administration.*

Group Ratings

	ADA	ACLU	AFL-CIO	LCV	ITI	COC	HAFA	ACU	CFG	FRC
2018	-	5%	-	7%	-	90%	65%	73%	47%	100%
2017	0%	C	0%	0%	C	86%	C	80%	81%	100%

Almanac Ratings 2017-18

	Economy	Social	Foreign	Composite
Liberal	6%	6%	0%	4%
Conservative	94%	94%	100%	96%

Key Votes of the 115th Congress

1. Obama-care revision	Y	5. Gun regulations	Y	9. Kavanaugh confirmation	Y
2. Tax Cuts	Y	6. Family planning regs	Y	10. Saudi arms sales	N
3. Dodd-Frank revision	Y	7. Gorsuch confirmation	Y	11. FISA rules	Y
4. Omnibus appropriations	Y	8. Immigration restrictions	Y	12. Military aid in Yemen	N

Election Results

Election	Name (Party)	Vote (%)		Cand. Spent	Ind. Exp. Support	Ind. Exp. Oppose
2014 General	Pat Roberts (R)	460,350	(53%)	$8,113,419	$3,380,996	$5,794,771
	Greg Orman (I)	368,372	(43%)	$5,702,323	$1,016,961	$7,230,146
	Randall Batson (L)	37,469	(4%)			
2014 Primary	Pat Roberts (R)	127,089	(48%)			
	Milton Wolf (R)	107,799	(41%)			
	D.J. Smith (R)	15,288	(6%)			
	Alvin Zahnter (R)	14,164	(5%)			

Prior winning percentages: 2008 (60%), 2002 (86%), 1996 (62%), House: 1994 (77%), 1992 (68%), 1990 (63%), 1988 (100%), 1986 (75%), 1984 (76%), 1982 (68%), 1980 (62%)(62%)

Republican Pat Roberts, Kansas' senior senator, announced in January 2019 that he will not seek re-election. That will end 40 years of service in Congress that had notable similarities and contrasts to the career of Bob Dole, the most prominent Kansas politician of recent decades, who resigned from the Senate to run for president — and lost. Stylistically, Roberts has been Dole's political heir: Each started his career in rural Kansas and gained a reputation on Capitol Hill for direct talk and acerbic wit. But while Dole moved toward the political center as he ascended through the Senate leadership, Roberts — with the exception of farm programs — shifted rightward in the twilight of his career, in apparent response to a changing political landscape in his home state. And, unlike Dole, Roberts shunned the leadership ranks to make his mark on agricultural and national security issues. He has the distinction of having chaired the agriculture committee in both the House and Senate.

Besides a sharp tongue, Dole and Roberts share a history as natives of a rural state in the nation's geographical center who spent most of their adult years working and living in the nation's capital. For Roberts, a perception among many home state voters that he had become more a creature of Washington than of Kansas came close to ending his Senate career in 2014, when he was 78.

His abolitionist great-grandfather, Roberts likes to say, "arrived in Kansas with a flat-bed press, a six-gun and a Bible" and founded the state's second-oldest newspaper, the Oskaloosa Independent. His father was Republican National Committee chairman during the years when one of Kansas' most famous sons, Dwight Eisenhower, was president. Roberts has chaired the commission leading the effort to erect a memorial to Eisenhower across Independence Avenue from the National Mall. Construction began in November 2017 and was scheduled for completion in May 2020. Born in Topeka, Roberts graduated from Kansas State University with a journalism degree. He served four years in the Marine Corps and then spent five years running a weekly newspaper in the suburbs of Phoenix. In 1967, Roberts arrived on Capitol Hill as an aide to Kansas Republican Sen. Frank Carlson. He served for 12 years as chief aide to Republican Keith Sebelius, who represented Kansas' 1st District and was the father-in-law of future Democratic Gov. Kathleen Sebelius. The relationship between Roberts and Kathleen Sebelius, once friendly, strained amid partisan warfare over President Barack Obama's signature health insurance overhaul.

Keith Sebelius succeeded Dole in the 1st District in 1968 when the latter was elected to the Senate. After Sebelius retired in 1980, Roberts won the GOP primary with 56 percent of the vote in a three-way contest and then won the general election. Roberts concentrated on farm issues, learning their intricacies and minutiae while traveling in a van to keep in touch with constituents in the sprawling "Big First." His voting record was regarded as moderate. In 1996, when Republican Sen. Nancy Landon Kassebaum retired, Roberts ran for her seat, easily defeating his Democratic opponent 62%-34%.

"When you're from Kansas, you're not appointed to [the Agriculture Committee], you're sentenced to it," Roberts once quipped. Since 2015, Roberts has been chairman of the Senate Agriculture Committee. In 2018, he was instrumental in crafting a farm bill, the omnibus measure that authorizes federal agricultural and nutrition programs. From the start, he pursued bipartisanship, in contrast to the partisan approach of the Republican-controlled House. He largely prevailed. That legislation became a capstone to his decades of work on farm legislation, which has seen a notable evolution of his views.

In 1995, after Republicans won majority control of Congress for the first time in 40 years, Roberts became chairman of the House Agriculture Committee. He had long believed that the huge subsidies of the early 1980s would never return. Faced with tight budget parameters, Roberts drafted the "Freedom to Farm" bill to phase out subsidies over seven years. In September 1995, his bill failed in committee when Southern Republicans, eager to protect cotton, rice and peanut subsidies, opposed it. Two months later, Roberts persuaded Agriculture conferees to include most of his proposal in the 1996 budget reconciliation bill, which President Bill Clinton vetoed. To attract more support, Roberts agreed to changes, including maintaining cotton and rice marketing loans. His legislation, the biggest change in agriculture policy since the New Deal, became law in April 1996 — just months before Roberts was elected to the Senate.

The Freedom to Farm Act worked well in 1997, and farmers seemed to do fine with a diminished government role. But in 1998, crop prices plunged and some farmers demanded a return to the old system. From his new seat in the Senate, Roberts resisted. Instead, bills were passed to accelerate payments and give farmers an extra $4 billion in disaster aid. Roberts argued limiting production would not raise prices because the United States accounts for less than one-fifth of world agricultural production. Freedom to Farm came up for reauthorization in 2002, when Democrats were in control of the Senate. Roberts acknowledged the law "didn't work out as anybody would have hoped" and pushed for farm savings accounts. Democrats rejected the proposal in favor of reviving countercyclical subsidies when crop prices are low and creating a larger Conservation Reserve Program, which paid farmers to let land fallow to protect environmentally sensitive areas. Roberts argued the legislation that ultimately passed would provide no aid when production was low and crop prices rose, which is what happened when drought struck the Great Plains in the summer of 2002.

Roberts' experience with the 2012 farm bill in some ways was reminiscent of that earlier battle. Roberts was the ranking Republican on the Senate Agriculture Committee while Democrats were in the majority. The 2012 Senate-passed version of the farm bill bore Roberts' handiwork that called for ending a system of target prices as part of a shift from fixed prices and payments for farmers.

Roberts joined Democrats, and many Northern Republicans, in arguing that the farm bill shouldn't be about making sure certain groups get the same amount of federal aid they had received in the past. But House Republicans and many Southern growers fought the idea: Those farmers said the private crop insurance called for in the Senate proposal did not work for crops like rice and peanuts. As 2012 ended, Senate Republican Leader Mitch McConnell of Kentucky negotiated a nine-month farm bill extension as part of the New Year's Day 2013 deal aimed at averting the "fiscal cliff." The broad principles of that bill were enacted in 2014.

As Agriculture chairman, Roberts worked with Michigan Sen. Debbie Stabenow, the panel's ranking Democrat, to pass a measure requiring the labeling of genetically modified. Roberts hailed it as the most important farm legislation in 20 years. Roberts and Stabenow also crafted a compromise on reauthorization of the school meals program, which largely maintained the child-nutrition standards that first lady Michelle Obama had adopted as a signature issue. It cleared their committee, but efforts to enact a bill into law fell short at the end of 2016.

In 2017, despite having a Republican president and GOP-controlled House, Roberts insisted on bipartisan cooperation. "This is not the time for a revolutionary farm bill," he said. That meant he opposed most efforts by House Republicans to reduce or place restrictions — including work requirements — on food stamp assistance and other nutrition aid for low-income beneficiaries. He said the partisan process in the House was "very unfortunate." The bill he had crafted with Stabenow, which the Senate passed 86 to 11 in June 2018, preserved the extensive conservation program, expanded crop insurance and reduced farm-support payments, especially to landowners not actively managing their farms. Roberts' bill also increased support for organic and local foods. The decline in commodity prices in recent years put pressure on Congress to extend the expiring farm programs. Both the Senate and House overwhelmingly passed the final agreement in December 2018.

Roberts has encouraged farm exports: He was a lead sponsor of a 2000 law that relaxed the embargo on exports of food and medicine to Cuba. Roberts was joined by his House successor and now-Senate colleague, Republican Jerry Moran, in contending such a move would benefit Kansas farmers, even though many of their Republican colleagues fought moves to normalize relations with Cuba. As a senior member of the Finance Committee, Roberts usually advocated expansion of international trade.

His other major sphere of influence has been national security. In 1999, as chairman of the Emerging Threats and Capabilities Subcommittee of Armed Services, he held hearings probing the nation's vulnerability to terrorists and — two years before 9/11 — argued targets would be "selected for their symbolic value, like the World Trade Center in the heart of Manhattan." He became immersed in the issue of intelligence gathering while chairing the Intelligence Committee from 2003 to 2007. In the summer of 2004, committee members led by Roberts blasted intelligence-gathering practices leading up to the 2003 invasion of Iraq and concluded the CIA had not seriously considered the possibility that Iraqi leader Saddam Hussein had no weapons of mass destruction. Roberts proposed that the Intelligence panel take over from the Armed Services Committee oversight of Defense Department's intelligence operations, but the proposal met with predictable resistance on turf-conscious Capitol Hill.

Roberts rotated off the Intelligence Committee in 2007. After Obama took office, Roberts staunchly opposed shifting detainees from Guantanamo Bay in Cuba to Fort Leavenworth in Kansas. "Not in our backyard," he said. "Not in Kansas. Not on my watch." Throughout the Obama era, he delayed the confirmations of executive branch nominees to the Defense and Justice departments to pressure the Pentagon to block such transfers. In May 2016, a top Defense official assured Roberts that the clock had run out on any effort to bring Guantanamo detainees to Kansas.

Roberts had no Democratic challenger in 2002 when he sought a second Senate term. In 2008, former Rep. Jim Slattery, who had been working in Washington as a lawyer and lobbyist since losing a race for governor in 1994, returned to the state to challenge him. Slattery ran a vigorous campaign, but Roberts, who routinely visited all 105 Kansas counties, spent nearly $7 million and won 60%-36%.

Six years later, the tables turned. Roberts had to defend himself against portrayals of him as a captive of the Capital Beltway. Initially, Roberts was considered a safe bet for a fourth term, especially with his home-state colleague Moran running the Senate GOP campaign committee. But Roberts almost fell victim to anti-incumbency sentiment and a first-time candidate in Milton Wolf, a radiologist who had the strong support of tea party groups ascendant in Kansas Republican politics.

Wolf — a second cousin to Obama — frequently noted that Roberts had been in Washington as either an aide or legislator for half a century. He based his campaign around his opposition to his cousin's Affordable Care Act. Roberts was not a fan of the law. When his old friend Health and Human Services Secretary Kathleen Sebelius said she would have "zero tolerance" for insurers claiming costs were increased by the bill, Roberts was livid. "She is threatening to shut down private companies for exercising their First Amendment right to free speech," he said. In October 2013, Roberts went so far as to call for Sebelius' resignation, accusing her of "gross incompetence" in conjunction with the problem-plagued rollout of the website for enrolling in "Obamacare." Roberts call for Sebelius' resignation came three days after Wolf announced his primary challenge.

Wolf gained traction in February 2014 after news outlets reported Roberts did not have a home in Kansas and listed as his voting address a Dodge City home belonging to longtime supporters. Roberts, seeking to defuse the controversy, did himself little good when he told a local radio station, "Every time I get an opponent — I mean, every time I get a chance, I'm home." Wolf had to deal with a controversy of his own: He was discovered to have posted patients' X-rays on his Facebook page, accompanying some of them with jokes that many found distasteful. Roberts managed a 48%-41% primary win.

Roberts' troubles didn't end there. His Democratic opponent dropped out of the race in September, a move that increased the prospects of Greg Orman, a well-funded independent candidate. Republicans blasted Orman's past support for Obama and his positions on abortion and immigration. Polls late in the race showed it to be a toss-up. It didn't help when media outlets reported in October that Roberts had missed two-thirds of the Agriculture Committee's meetings since 2000, feeding critics' arguments that he was out of touch. National Republicans poured more than $10 million into a race they had thought was over once the primary ended. Roberts ended up beating Orman by nearly 11 points.

While still conservative, his voting record showed signs of moderating: In September 2015, he was the only one of the six-member, all-Republican Kansas congressional delegation to support a stopgap spending bill to avoid a government shutdown. After a third of a century on Capitol Hill, "I'm done voting to shut down the government. I'm just done," Roberts told The Topeka Capital-Journal. "I've been through three shutdowns. Every time it was so terribly counter-productive. Then to get back up and running, it costs even more money."

Roberts has had his disagreements with President Donald Trump, though he has mostly kept them quiet. "I don't think you get anywhere criticizing the president," he told Politico. Still, he said that many Kansans were "not going to be happy" about Trump waging a trade war with China. When Trump proposed offering aid to farmers who were hurt by his tariffs, Roberts called the response, "problematic, to say the least." He supported the Republican plan to replace the Affordable Care Act, though he said he was unhappy with parts of it, including its effect on rural hospitals and home health programs.

In announcing his retirement as the longest-serving member of Congress from Kansas, Roberts cited his undefeated record of 24-0 as a candidate. It was unclear whether he would have faced — or survived — a Republican primary if he had run again in 2020. The recent history of Kansas politics suggests a wide-open contest for the GOP nomination. Among the Republicans who received early attention were former Gov. Jeff Colyer; former state Secretary of State Kris Kobach, who lost a bid for governor in 2018; Rep. Roger Marshall; former Rep. Kevin Yoder; state Senate President Susan Wagle and U.S. Secretary of State Mike Pompeo, who served three House terms from Kansas. Despite recent Democratic successes in Kansas, the state has not elected a Democrat to the Senate since 1932, a record that seemed likely to continue.

Jerry Moran (R)

Elected 2010, term expires 2022, 2nd term, b. May 29, 1954; Great Bend; Fort Hays State University (KS), 1973; University of Kansas, B.S., 1976; University of Kansas, J.D., 1981; Methodist; Married (Robba Addison Moran); 2 children.

Elected Office: KS Senate, 1989-1997, Majority Leader, 1995-1996; U.S. House, 1997-2011.

Professional Career: Operations officer, Consolidated State Bank, 1975-1977; Mgr., Farmers State Bank & Trust Co., 1977-1978; Practicing attorney, 1981-1996; Instructor, Ft. Hays St. University, 1986.

DC Office: 521 DSOB 20510, 202-224-6521, Fax: 202-228-6966

State Offices: Hays, 785-628-6401; Manhattan, 785-539-8973; Olathe, 913-393-0711; Pittsburg, 620-232-2286; Wichita, 316-269-9257.

Committees: *Appropriations*: Agriculture, Rural Development, FDA & Related Agencies; Commerce, Justice, Science & Related Agencies (Chmn); Department of Defense; DOL, HHS & Education & Related Agencies; Financial Services & General Government; State, Foreign Operations & Related Programs. *Banking, Housing & Urban Affairs*: Financial Institutions & Consumer Protection; Housing, Transportation & Community Development; National Security & International Trade & Finance. *Commerce, Science & Transportation*: Communications, Technology, Innovation & the Internet; Manufacturing, Trade & Consumer Protection (Chmn); Subcommittee on Aviation & Space; Subcommittee on Transportation & Safety. *Indian Affairs. Veterans' Affairs.*

Group Ratings

	ADA	ACLU	AFL-CIO	LCV	ITI	COC	HAFA	ACU	CFG	FRC
2018	-	19%	-	14%	-	90%	67%	77%	59%	100%
2017	0%	C	0%	0%	C	86%	C	84%	88%	100%

Almanac Ratings 2017-18

	Economy	Social	Foreign	Composite
Liberal	11%	11%	23%	15%
Conservative	89%	89%	77%	85%

Key Votes of the 115th Congress

1. Obama-care revision	Y	5. Gun regulations	Y	9. Kavanaugh confirmation	Y
2. Tax Cuts	Y	6. Family planning regs	Y	10. Saudi arms sales	N
3. Dodd-Frank revision	Y	7. Gorsuch confirmation	Y	11. FISA rules	N
4. Omnibus appropriations	Y	8. Immigration restrictions	N	12. Military aid in Yemen	Y

Election Results

Election	Name (Party)	Vote (%)		Cand. Spent	Ind. Exp. Support	Ind. Exp. Oppose
2016 General	Jerry Moran (R)	732,376	(62%)	$4,227,284		$529
	Patrick Wiesner (D)	379,740	(32%)	$34,939		
	Robert Garrard (L)	65,760	(6%)			
2016 Primary	Jerry Moran (R)	230,907	(79%)			
	D.J. Smith (R)	61,056	(21%)			

Prior winning percentages: 2010 (70%); House: 2008 (82%), 2006 (79%), 2004 (91%), 2002 (91%), 2000 (89%), 1998 (81%), 1996 (73%)

Kansas' junior senator, Jerry Moran, has quietly shown his independence of Republican objectives and President Donald Trump — in contrast to more outspoken critics within the Senate GOP ranks. He voiced reservations in some of those cases, including the hard-line position of most of his colleagues on nominations to the Supreme Court and repeal of the Affordable Care Act. His proclivity for middle ground in the Senate has been striking, given the ideological wars among Kansas Republicans, which he has largely avoided. The willingness of Moran to go his own way stands in contrast to the partisan influence that he wielded as chairman of the National Republican Senate Committee during the 2014 election cycle, when Republicans flipped nine seats and regained the Senate majority — a party goal that had proved elusive.

While accumulating a conservative voting record, Moran demonstrated an independent streak during his more than two decades in Congress. Success in chairing a party's in-house campaign committee has frequently translated into ascending the leadership ladder. Moran, once majority leader of the Kansas Senate, has downplayed any such aspirations on Capitol Hill. "I like my independence. The more that you are part of the leadership, the less flexibility you sometimes have in the positions you take," he told the Eagle. At the same time, in what has been something of a limitation, Moran has acquired a reputation for political caution. Some years ago, Moran's home state colleague, Pat Roberts — known for his pointed wit — stood before a gathering of Kansas Republicans and joked that he had been invited only because pop stars were unavailable. "Actually, both Jerry Moran and I received invitations, but he couldn't decide," Roberts was reported to have wisecracked.

Moran grew up the son of an oil-field worker in the tiny town of Plainville in the western plains of Kansas. In college, he interned for GOP Rep. Keith Sebelius, the father-in-law of future Democratic

Gov. Kathleen Sebelius. The job gave Moran a close-up view of the 1974 impeachment hearings of President Richard Nixon. After graduating with a degree in economics from the University of Kansas, Moran worked as a banker before earning a law degree. In 1988, he won election to the state Senate, becoming majority leader in his last term. When Roberts ran for the Senate in 1996, Moran sought the open House seat. He won the primary with 76 percent of the vote, tantamount to election in a sprawling rural district as big as Illinois. Moran won re-election a half-dozen times in the "Big First," where he annually held town halls in each of the district's 69 counties.

Moran's independence — and caution — showed up occasionally during his House tenure. To the dismay of Speaker Dennis Hastert, Moran was one of 25 House Republicans who opposed the 2003 Republican-sponsored Medicare prescription drug bill. In a memoir, Hastert did not call out Moran by name, but left little doubt about whom he was talking. "Some members had assured me that they would be with us, but when the crunch time came, they weren't," Hastert wrote. "One prairie state member, a fourth-term representative from a solidly Republican district, voted no, then ran and hid. I sent people to find him, they couldn't." Afterward, Moran said the bill did not do enough to lower prescription drug prices, adding that he favored a Democratic proposal to give federal officials negotiating authority to lower drug costs.

Moran ran for the Senate in 2010 when Republican Sam Brownback announced he would step aside to run for governor after Kathleen Sebelius resigned to become secretary of Health and Human Services in the Obama administration. Moran first had to get by fellow GOP Rep. Todd Tiahrt. The two waged a nasty and expensive primary race, costing nearly $7 million combined. Tiahrt sought to turn the contest into a referendum on who was more conservative, and the candidates battled over endorsements. Former Alaska Gov. Sarah Palin and former Pennsylvania Sen. Rick Santorum were in Tiahrt's camp, while Moran secured the backing of two outspoken Senate conservatives: Tom Coburn of Oklahoma and Jim DeMint of South Carolina. With the endorsement of most of the state's leading newspapers, Moran won 50%-45%, prevailing on the strength of his base in the state's most Republican district. He won the general election with 70 percent of the vote.

Moran was given a seat on the Appropriations Committee after he entered the Senate, while committing to efforts to ban "earmarks" — funds directed to a legislator's pet projects. Moran sought earmarked funding while in the House and took heat for it during the primary against Tiahrt. He defended himself by noting he also had sought earmark restrictions while in the House. That disinclination to spending restraints was at odds with his position as one of 26 senators in 2011 to oppose a bipartisan deal to raise the nation's debt limit, noting that the $21 billion in deficit reduction over the first year of the agreement would cover less than a week's worth of borrowing.

In 2012, Moran found himself in an awkward situation when a frail 89-year-old former GOP Sen. Bob Dole — who for three decades had occupied the seat Moran now holds — showed up on the Senate floor in a wheelchair. Dole, who has had limited use of his right arm since being wounded in World War II, engineered passage of the Americans with Disabilities Act in 1990; he returned to the Senate to lobby for an international treaty designed to encourage other nations to meet similar objectives. Moran, after having declared he supported the treaty and would be "standing up for the rights of those with disabilities," cast a key vote to block treaty ratification. He later said "foreign officials should not be put in a position to interfere with U.S. policymaking." The statement embraced an argument made by hard-line conservatives but disputed by the treaty's proponents.

Moran has cited Kansas farmers in pushing to reopen trade with Cuba, another position that put him at odds with many in his party. In 2007, he won House approval of an amendment to ease restrictions on shipments of food and medicine to the island nation, only to see it removed from the legislation to avoid a veto by President George W. Bush. In the Senate, Moran inserted a provision into a 2012 appropriations bill to ease agricultural trade by allowing direct cash payments from Cuban buyers to U.S. institutions. It also was stripped out. In 2015, after President Barack Obama moved to normalize relations with Cuba, Moran said, "What we have been doing has not worked. ... because it's a unilateral sanction. When wheat, for example, is not sold to Cuba, it's not that they're not buying wheat, it's that wheat's being purchased from some other place: our competitors."

As chairman of the NRSC during the 2014 election cycle, Moran worked to avoid mistakes that had tripped up his party in the prior two cycles — nomination of poorly vetted, ideologically rigid candidates whose missteps had allowed several imperiled Democrats to survive. "We tried to get all aspects of our party — from tea party to the Chamber of Commerce — to sit in a room and decide on a candidate they could all agree on," he said. Moran reached out to Sen. Rob Portman of Ohio, a member of the GOP's establishment wing who agreed to serve as the NRSC's vice chairman for finance, and Sen. Ted Cruz of Texas, who was appointed vice chairman for grassroots and political outreach.

Despite his success in regaining the Senate majority, Moran faced the ire of conservative activists upset by his efforts to help Roberts withstand a primary challenge from Milton Wolf, a tea party-backed physician; they looked for a candidate to take on Moran in 2016. In the face of this threat, Moran appeared to tack right. Almanac vote ratings pegged him as the fifth most conservative member of the Senate in 2015. He was among a handful of conservatives who voted against Every Student Succeeds Act; the Senate adopted it on an 85-12 vote in late 2015.

Still, Moran has leaned to the center. Two days after the death of Supreme Court Justice Antonin Scalia in February 2016, as Senate Republican leaders made clear their opposition to replacing Scalia until after the presidential election, Moran said the Senate had an obligation to consider a nominee put forth by Obama, telling The Topeka Capital-Journal, "The Republican-led Senate, which I worked hard to secure, has a constitutional responsibility in the process of determining Supreme Court justices." Moran repeated his stance the following month in a meeting with 10 people in the town of Cimarron — after Obama had nominated Judge Merrick Garland. "I can't imagine the president has or will nominate somebody that meets my criteria, but I have my job to do," Moran said, according to the Garden City Telegram. He added, "I think the process ought to go forward."

Moran found himself under sharp attack from conservative groups. Then-Rep. Mike Pompeo suggested he might enter the race. A week after his comments at the town hall meeting, Moran retreated, saying through an aide that he "didn't need hearings to conclude" Garland had been rendered "unacceptable to serve on the Supreme Court" because of his judicial philosophy. Pompeo — who became CIA director and then secretary of State in the Trump administration — announced several weeks later he would not run for Senate, citing the limited time before the primary. But he issued a parting shot at Moran, telling Politico, "Filling this vacancy on the U.S. Supreme Court is the transgenerational issue of our time. ... The Senate cannot fold again on this one. As I watched this waffling up close, I began to contemplate a Senate run." A year later, during his Senate confirmation hearings to head the CIA, Pompeo was accompanied by Roberts, but not Moran.

Wolf did not file, leaving D.J. Smith, who took 6 percent against Roberts and Wolf in the 2014 Senate primary, as Moran's only intraparty challenger. Moran won the primary by a 4-1 margin, and, in November, was re-elected to a second term 62%-32% in a state that has not elected a Democrat to the Senate since 1932.

Following Trump's election, as congressional Republicans set repeal and replacement of "Obamacare" as their top legislative priority, Moran was not convinced. "The Senate health care bill missed the mark for Kansas and therefore did not have my support," he tweeted in late June, which was a factor in the Senate's delay in taking up the bill. His chief concern, he said, was the need to protect people with pre-existing conditions. He was responding to objections from constituents and Kansas hospitals. During a town hall meeting in early July in the small town of Palco, not far from his hometown, Moran lamented the failure of the two major parties to seek consensus. "Not one inch are we giving," The New York Times reported him as saying.

When he returned to the Capitol for additional back-room negotiations with Senate Republicans, led by Majority Leader Mitch McConnell, Moran remained steadfast, saying the proposal failed to address rising health care costs. After another week, Moran agreed to support a procedural vote to start debate of what he called "the full legislative process," though he continued to oppose the McConnell-led initiative as "bad policy." As it turned out, Sen. John McCain returned from his treatment for cancer and became the third Republican to object to the procedural step, killing the measure and taking the public heat for its demise. "Trying to do something with one party alone is a mistake," Moran said in a Kansas radio interview. Local health care advocates praised his responsiveness to their concerns.

Moran also showed his independence in voicing concern over Trump's tariffs, especially their adverse effects on Kansas farmers. "China is a problem," he told a meeting of farmers outside of Manhattan in May 2018, the High Plains Journal reported. "They cheat. They misbehave. They don't follow the rules. But the solution is not a broad tariff battle. ... Don't isolate us and keep us out of the markets." He criticized Trump after the president met with Russian President Vladimir Putin in Helsinki in July 2018, saying he had missed an opportunity to "publicly condemn Russia for election interference or offer strong support for the NATO alliance."

In the 2018 election for Kansas governor, Moran remained "the quiet observer" about Kris Kobach, the conservative Republican nominee, the Salina Journal reported. Moran might have to account to other Republicans for his caution if he seeks a third term in 2022.

Roger Marshall (R)

Elected 2016, 2nd term, b. Aug 09, 1960; El Dorado; Butler Community College, A.S., 1980; Kansas State University, Bach. Deg., 1982; University of Kansas, M.D., 1987; Christian Church; Married (Laina Marshall); 4 children; 1 grandchild.

Military Career: U.S. Army Reserve 1984-1991

Professional Career: Physician.

DC Office: 312 CHOB 20515, 202-225-2715, marshall.house.gov

State Offices: Garden City, 620-765-7800; Salina, 785-829-9000.

Committees: *Agriculture*: Commodity Exchanges, Energy & Credit; Livestock & Foreign Agriculture. *Science, Space & Technology*: Environment (RMM); Research & Technology.

Group Ratings

	ADA	ACLU	AFL-CIO	LCV	ITI	COC	HAFA	ACU	CFG	FRC
2018	-	4%	-	6%	-	92%	53%	68%	47%	100%
2017	0%	C	8%	0%	C	93%	C	78%	74%	100%

Almanac Ratings 2017-18

	Economy	Social	Foreign	Composite
Liberal	4%	0%	0%	1%
Conservative	96%	100%	100%	99%

Key Votes of the 115th Congress

1. Obama-care revision	Y	5. Family planning regs	Y	9. Guantanamo prisoners	N
2. Tax Cuts	Y	6. Body cameras/immigration	N	10. Ground missiles, limit	N
3. Omnibus appropriations	Y	7. Abortion ban	Y	11. Defense Dept. spending	Y
4. Dodd-Frank revision	Y	8. Concealed carry	Y	12. FISA rules	Y

Election Results

Election	Name (Party)	Vote (%)		Cand. Spent	Ind. Exp. Support	Ind. Exp. Oppose
2018 General	Roger Marshall (R)	153,082	(68%)	$568,535		$238,722
	Alan LaPolice (D)	71,558	(32%)	$200,565		
2018 Primary	Roger Marshall (R)	64,843	(79%)			
	Nick Reinecker (R)	17,593	(21%)			

Prior winning percentages: 2016 (66%)

Republican Roger Marshall was elected in 2016 after defeating Rep. Tim Huelskamp in the GOP primary. The contest attracted national attention and financing as a conflict over the party's direction. Marshall delivered on his promise to get a seat on the Agriculture Committee, where he worked on the 2018 farm bill and pursued new ambitions.

Born in El Dorado Kansas, Marshall worked on the family farm. He got his bachelor's degree in biochemistry from Kansas State University and his medical degree from the University of Kansas. As an obstetrician-gynecologist in Great Bend, he delivered more than 5,000 babies and was chairman of the board of Great Bend Regional Hospital. He served seven years in the Army Reserve, where he was a captain and trained a mobile hospital support unit.

Huelskamp's no-holds-barred conservatism had made him a leader of the House Freedom Caucus and an outspoken internal critic of Republican leadership during his three terms. Even after he was stripped of his chief committee assignments in 2012, which reportedly was the first time in more than a century that the local representative did not have a seat on the Agriculture panel, he continued to go his own way. Marshall saw his opening.

With the district's many farmers actively engaged in the contest, endorsements had an impact. Perhaps the most significant was the support for Marshall by the Kansas Farm Bureau, which for the first time opposed an incumbent. The bureau's voice had an impact in this district, which is among the leading livestock producers in the nation. Long-ago local hero Bob Dole, at age 92, tweeted his endorsement of Marshall. The U.S. Chamber of Commerce endorsed Marshall and spent about $400,000 on his behalf. The state chamber backed Huelskamp, who also benefited from more than $400,000 the Club for Growth spent on his behalf. Marshall's $1.5 million in fundraising was competitive; $300,000 was self-financed. Perhaps the most significant endorsement was one that Huelskamp failed to get — from House Speaker Paul Ryan, who remained neutral and refused the incumbent's request to promise him a return to the Agriculture Committee. Marshall won the August primary by an unexpectedly large margin, 57%-43%.

Following his personal request to Ryan, Marshall got a seat on the Agriculture Committee, as well as the Science, Space and Technology Committee, where he advocated on behalf of the National Bio and Agro-Defense Facility in Manhattan. He was a member of the House-Senate conference committee on the farm bill in 2018, where he pushed for stricter requirements for food stamp recipients, although they weren't included in the final version. He secured an amendment helping wildfire victims in his district. Marshall joined the House Republicans' "Doc Caucus" and pushed for repeal of the Affordable Care Act. During debate in 2017, he got backlash after telling the health care site STAT that, "Just like Jesus said, 'The poor will always be with us.' There is a group of people that just don't want health care and aren't going to take care of themselves." He later tried to clarify, saying in a statement he was trying to explain that "we cannot build a national health care policy around any one segment of the population." He voiced opposition to President Donald Trump's tariffs, citing harm to the farm and dairy industries in the district. Marshall told Breitbart News he supported a path to legalization for young immigrants, saying that "these kids are the American Dream, and they are conservatives."

At home, Marshall was reelected easily after Huelskamp decided not to seek a rematch. Initially, the Kansas Farm Bureau hesitated to endorse Marshall after he reportedly was seeking a seat on the Ways and Means Committee in lieu of the Agriculture Committee. Such an idea gave its members "heartburn," the Farm Bureau said; eventually, Marshall chose to retain his assignment. After Sen. Pat Roberts in January 2019 announced his retirement, Marshall—after two years, the most senior member of the House delegation--thought about entering the wide-open contest to succeed him. He was the early leader in fundraising among the potential candidates. In addition to Roberts, other members from the "Big First" have used it as a stepping stone to the Senate, including Dole and Sen. Jerry Moran.

KS-1: Central and Western Kansas   Cook Partisan Voting Index: R+24

Population		Race and Ethnicity		Income	
Total	712,978	White	77%	Median Income	$49,608
Land area (sq. miles)	52,543	Black	2.9%	District Income Rank	316
Pop/ sq mi	13.6	Latino	15.7%	Poverty Rate	14%
Born in State	63.2%	Asian	1.6%	With health insurance	90.4%
		Two or more races	2.2%	Cash public assistance	1.5%
Age Groups		Other	0.6%	Food stamp/SNAP	8.1%
Under 18	24.2%				
18-34	25.6%	**Education**		**Work**	
35-64	34.6%	H.S grad or less	40.9%	White Collar	15.6%
Over 64	15.6%	Some college	34.7%	Sales and Service	38.5%
		College Degree, 4 yr	16.1%	Blue Collar	28.5%
Military		Post grad	8.2%	Government	18.6%
Veteran/ Active Duty	11.1%				

2012 Pres. Vote	Romney	184,232	(70%)	Obama	72,668	(28%)		
2016 Pres. Vote	Trump	183,446	(69%)	Clinton	64,388	(24%)	Johnson	11,976	(5%)

Manhattan, Dodge City: "A prairie is not any old piece of flatland in the Midwest," wrote Kansas-born reporter Dennis Farney. "No, a prairie is wine-colored grass, dancing in the wind. A prairie is a sun-splashed hillside, bright with wild flowers. A prairie is a fleeting cloud shadow, the song of the meadowlark. It is the wild land that has never felt the slash of the plow." The prairie Farney described once covered almost all of Kansas and dipped into Oklahoma. Now only a little virgin prairie can still be found, in the Flint Hills region west and south of Topeka. At the Tallgrass National Prairie Preserve, you can see 30 miles on a clear day and a waist-deep sea of grass waves in the wind as it did when traders and pioneers on the Santa Fe Trail passed through some 175 years ago.

Farther west, near the 100th meridian, begins a region where the Rocky Mountains block moisture from reaching the land, and the prairie gives way to plains. Much of this western area was grazing land, first for buffalo, and then for the cattle driven to Kansas railheads like Abilene and Dodge City in the 1870s and 1880s.

Today, the area's farm-dependent economy is changing the district overall. Agricultural towns have seen a steep decline in population, while big meatpacking plants in Dodge City, Garden City and Liberal (the "Golden Triangle of meatpacking") have attracted large numbers of Hispanic immigrants, bringing with them a population boom. That evolution has even given way to a new "Latino-English" accent in the area, which Kansas State University linguists called the "Liberal sound" for the city whose Hispanic population has grown from 20 percent a few decades ago to nearly 60 percent. Nearby Fort Dodge schools reported a spike to 79 percent. Many of the new arrivals are non-English speaking, even in high school. There are growing pockets of Burmese, Vietnamese and northern African immigrants in places like Garden City, where only about 40 percent of residents are now white, making it one of the most diverse communities in Kansas. Some immigrants say they have been welcomed and have assimilated well. But there have been backlashes. In 2018, three members of a Kansas militia were convicted of plotting to bomb an apartment complex with Somali refugees in Wright, near Dodge City.

The dairy industry has made a comeback, enticed by inexpensive land and labor and abundant feed stocks. Farmers here faced a long-term crisis: Their water is drying up. In 2018, the area suffered one of the worst droughts in 150 years. Still, the area has been one of the fastest-growing dairy producers in the nation. In Manhattan, the National Bio and Agro-Defense Facility has been a boost to Kansas State University and the local economy.

The 1st Congressional District covers all of western and north-central Kansas. It extends more than 300 miles from the Colorado border to the outskirts of Topeka. While the area today is solidly Republican, it was not always so. Farmer uprisings handed the area to the Populists for much of the late 1800s, a Democrat represented southwest Kansas during the Great Depression and again in the late 1950s. Republican Bob Dole represented western Kansas from 1961 to 1969. The district takes in almost everything west of the Flint Hills and Abilene, the boyhood home of President Dwight Eisenhower. Just south of Salina, near the center of the state, is Lindsborg, which has one of the highest concentrations of Swedish Americans in the country. It also includes Emporia, where progressive newspaper editor William Allen White published the once-famous Emporia Gazette; the paper is still run by the White family.

The district contains 61 full counties and parts of two others. Only Nebraska's 3rd District and South Dakota's at-large seat have more counties. Their average population is about 12,000. By square miles, the district is the 13th largest in the nation. The 1st is in the top 5 percent of the most Republican districts nationwide. Donald Trump won 69 percent of the vote here in 2016.

Steve Watkins (R)

Elected 2018, 1st term, b. Sep 18, 1976; Lackland Air Force Base, TX; U.S. Military Academy - West Point (NY), B.S., 1999; Massachusetts Institute of Technology, M.R.P., 2010; Harvard University, M.P.A., 2017; Methodist; Married.

Military Career: U.S. Army 1999-2005
Professional Career: Defense contractor.
DC Office: 1205 LHOB 20515, 202-225-6601, watkins.house.gov
State Offices: Pittsburg, 620-231-5966; Topeka, 785-234-5966.

Committees: *Education & Labor*: Health, Employment, Labor & Pensions; Higher Education & Workforce Investment. *Foreign Affairs*: Middle East, North Africa & International Terrorism. *Veterans' Affairs*: Disability Assistance & Memorial Affairs; Technology Modernization.

Election Results

Election	Name (Party)	Vote (%)	Cand. Spent	Ind. Exp. Support	Ind. Exp. Oppose
2018 General	Steve Watkins (R)	126,098 (48%)	$1,184,652	$2,361,868	$4,152,622
	Paul Davis (D)	123,859 (47%)	$3,932,965	$1,427,884	$5,030,157
	Kelly Standley (Lib)	14,731 (6%)			
2018 Primary	Steve Watkins (R)	20,052 (27%)			
	Caryn Tyson (R)	17,749 (24%)			
	Kevin Jones (R)	11,201 (15%)			
	Steve Fitzgerald (R)	9,227 (12%)			
	Dennis Pyle (R)	9,126 (12%)			
	Doug Mays (R)	6,221 (8%)			

Freshman Republican Steve Watkins narrowly won a Republican-leaning district, in a contest that was in doubt until the end. He struggled with multiple problems, including questions about his connections to his home state, party affiliation and fundraising. As a retired Army captain and defense contractor, Watkins had an extensive national security background. He replaced retiring Rep. Lynn Jenkins, a Republican moderate who served five terms and earlier held a House leadership post. He faced a continuing challenge to entrench himself at home.

Watkins, a native of Topeka, got a bachelor's degree in engineering from the U.S. Military Academy and a master's from the Massachusetts Institute of Technology. As an Army captain, he led combat patrols on Afghanistan's border with Pakistan. He remained in Central Asia for nearly a decade as an independent contractor, working chiefly for the Defense Department, with expertise in engineering and economic development. He was part of an expedition that attempted to climb Mount Everest, though the expedition was cut short by a deadly earthquake. And he competed in the Iditarod Sled Dog Race in Alaska, when he was stationed there with the military.

After Watkins declared his candidacy, questions were raised about his absence from Kansas for more than two decades and his inquiries about running as a Democrat. Three Kansas Democrats said that they met with Watkins before he decided which party primary to enter, the Kansas City Star reported. Watkins acknowledged the meeting, but said that he never considered running as a Democrat. Another Republican candidate called him "a charlatan, a fraud and an opportunist." Watkins said that Kansas "was always home in my heart," and that, with his international experience, "I'm not seeing any candidate in the race that knows what I'm talking about."

The Republican primary included seven candidates, including several current or former state legislators. Three of them raised about a half-million dollars—including Watkins, who loaned his campaign a large share of its funds for the primary. Despite the controversies, many Republicans viewed Watkins as the "best-funded and least ideological" candidate, according to the Cook Political Report. He won the primary 27%-23% over the runner-up, state Sen. Caryn Tyson.

Democrat Paul Davis, who won the nomination without opposition, was well-known as the former state House minority leader. He challenged Gov. Sam Brownback in 2014, and lost 50%-46%. In a debate, Davis accused Watkins of "dishonesty" about his personal life. Watkins dismissed the "character attacks," emphasized that he was a Republican and "political outsider," and contrasted himself to the progressive views of Davis. During an early October rally in Topeka, President Donald Trump supported Watkins and said that a vote for Davis was "a vote for "the radical agenda" of Nancy Pelosi.

The Star endorsed Davis as the "easy and clear" choice, and said that Watkins was "deeply flawed," with false claims and "no experience in politics." Davis, who was endorsed by many local Republicans, was well-financed with nearly $4 million for his campaign, and another $5 million in support from national Democrats. Watkins's total spending was about $1.2 million but he had more national party support than Davis. Campaign-finance questions were raised about a super PAC that supported Watkins, which received $100,000 from his father.

Watkins won, 48%-47%. Davis had big leads in Topeka-based Shawnee and Lawrence-based Douglas, the two largest counties in the district. Running strongly in the rural parts of the district, Watkins took the remaining 23 counties. Prior to his election, McClatchy News reported, some local Republicans said that they would vote for Watkins and could "replace him in two years" if he failed to clarify allegations against him.

KS-2: Eastern Kansas   **Cook Partisan Voting Index: R+10**

Population		Race and Ethnicity		Income	
Total	714,182	White	82.8%	Median Income	$52,031
Land area (sq. miles)	14,143	Black	4.4%	District Income Rank	270
Pop/ sq mi	50.5	Latino	6.5%	Poverty Rate	14.5%
Born in State	64%	Asian	1.5%	With health insurance	91.1%
		Two or more races	3.4%	Cash public assistance	2.1%
Age Groups		Other	1.3%	Food stamp/SNAP	9.7%
Under 18	23.1%				
18-34	23.8%	**Education**		**Work**	
35-64	37.1%	H.S grad or less	38.8%	White Collar	16%
Over 64	16%	Some college	32.8%	Sales and Service	39.9%
		College Degree, 4 yr	17.3%	Blue Collar	23.9%
Military		Post grad	11.1%	Government	19.6%
Veteran/ Active Duty	10%				

2012 Pres. Vote	Romney	163,138	(55%)	Obama	124,401	(42%)			
2016 Pres. Vote	Trump	165,002	(56%)	Clinton	110,597	(37%)	Johnson	13,250	(5%)
	Stein	6,811	(2%)						

Topeka, Kansas City Suburbs: The green plains of eastern Kansas have seen more than their share of American history. In 1827, on bluffs above the Missouri River, the Army built Fort Leavenworth, famous in later years for its war college and military prison and now the oldest U.S. fort west of the Mississippi River. In the 1850s, newly founded towns along the Kansas River and along the Missouri border were the centers of Bleeding Kansas, the name the state took after pro-slavery bushwhackers set up a state capital in tiny Lecompton and antislavery New Englanders established their stronghold down the river at Lawrence. These tensions bled into the Civil War; William Quantrill's infamous nighttime raid on pro-Union Lawrence in 1863 resulted in the burning to the ground of all but two businesses and the death of around 200 inhabitants.

Topeka, the antislavery and modern capital, today sits on a low bluff above the Kansas River. The city's system of legal segregation prompted the 1954 landmark case, Brown v. Board of Education, which unanimously concluded "separate but equal" is not equal. In November 2017, the city elected as its mayor Michelle de la Isla, a Latina and native of Puerto Rico. Topeka has had some success attracting corporate headquarters, including Hill's Pet Nutrition. There are more than 300 animal health companies in the corridor between Manhattan and Columbia Missouri. The population of Topeka declined each year from 2012 to 2017, though its loss has not been as large as in western Kansas. Leavenworth became a controversial national site when President Barack Obama and others considered it as an alternative to house terrorism detainees held at the Guantanamo Bay facility in Cuba. Chelsea Manning was a prisoner at the fort after she was convicted of disclosing classified military information to Wikileaks. Obama commuted her term. In 2018, she trailed badly in the Democratic primary for the Senate in Maryland.

The area around Lawrence, where the University of Kansas is based, has grown steadily. Its economy has out-performed most of the state. Farther south of the cities, on the Missouri border, are the hills called "the Balkans," where Eastern European coal miners settled in towns such as Pittsburg and Girard. This area was once a center of American socialism: Clarence Darrow and Upton Sinclair made pilgrimages, and the local paper, Appeal to Reason, had a national circulation of 750,000.

These disparate areas, Topeka and Lawrence, Fort Leavenworth, the wheat-growing counties, and the Balkans — most of eastern Kansas except the Kansas City metropolitan area — make up the 2nd Congressional District. Topeka-based Shawnee County and Lawrence-based Douglas account for close to half the population. In recent decades, Democrats have been competitive in state races here. For 20 of the years from 1970 to 1994, Democrats held the 2nd District seat. Republicans have held it for all but two years since. Like Mitt Romney in 2012, Donald Trump won 56 percent of the vote in this district.

Sharice Davids (D)

Elected 2018, 1st term, b. May 22, 1980; Frankfurt, Germany; Haskell Indian Nations University Board of Regents, Att.; Haskell Indian Nations University Board of Regents, Att.; Haskell Indian Nations University Board of Regents, Att.; University of Kansas, Att.; University of Missouri, B.A., 2007; Cornell University Law School (NY), J.D., 2010; Single.

Professional Career: Mixed Martial Artist; Attorney, SNR Dentons, 2010-2012; Director, Community and Economic Development, Pine Ridge Indian Reservation; White House Fellow, 2016-2017

DC Office: 1541 LHOB 20515, 202-225-2865, davids.house.gov

State Offices: Overland Park, 913-621-0832.

Committees: *Small Business*: Economic Growth, Tax & Capital Access; Innovation & Workforce Development. *Transportation & Infrastructure*: Aviation; Economic Dev't, Public Buildings & Emergency Management; Highways & Transit.

Election Results

Election	Name (Party)	Vote (%)		Cand. Spent	Ind. Exp. Support	Ind. Exp. Oppose
2018 General	Sharice Davids (D)............................ 170,518	(54%)		$4,762,853	$1,957,705	$2,438,957
	Kevin Yoder (R)................................ 139,762	(44%)		$4,883,339	$522,138	$3,008,513
	Chris Clemmons (Lib)............................ 8,021	(3%)				
2018 Primary	Sharice Davids (D)............................ 23,379	(37%)				
	Brent Welder (D)................................ 21,190	(34%)				
	Tom Niermann (D)................................ 8,939	(14%)				
	Mike McCamon (D)................................ 4,354	(7%)				

Democrat Sharice Davids, elected in 2018, won her first campaign with a profile that once would have been considered exotic in Kansas: a lesbian Native American who had competed professionally in mixed martial arts. She defeated Rep. Kevin Yoder, who had gained influence among House Republicans as an Appropriations subcommittee chairman. Yoder struggled with the deep hostility to President Donald Trump among his suburban constituents in the wealthiest House district in Kansas. In an unusual twist for a challenger, Davids responded cautiously to demands from Yoder for campaign debates.

Davids, a native of Leavenworth, graduated from the University of Missouri-Kansas City and got her law degree from Cornell University. She joined SNR Denton, an international law firm. A member of the Ho-Chunk Nation, a Native American tribe in Wisconsin, she worked with tribes on economic-development opportunities. On a reservation in South Dakota, she opened a coffee shop, which ultimately failed and resulted in a $20,000 court judgment against her.

In late 2016, during the final months of the Obama administration, Davids became a White House Fellow with the hope to remain if Hillary Clinton was elected president. Instead, she worked on the transition at the Transportation Department during the early days of the Trump administration. The anti-Trump anger that resulted, she said, gave her the incentive to run for Congress. "It's about people wanting to see change," she told the Kansas City Star.

The wide-open Democratic primary attracted six candidates. In addition to Davids, the other leading contender was Brent Welder, who worked for Sen. Bernie Sanders in the 2016 Democratic presidential campaign. Sanders appeared at a rally in Kansas City on behalf of Welder, who also was endorsed by the Congressional Progressive Caucus.

Davids positioned herself as the centrist in the primary and benefited from nearly $400,000 in advertising on her behalf from EMILY's List, which backs Democratic women supporting abortion rights. That amount doubled what she raised for the primary. Davids pointed to her background as "very out of the ordinary for the people who represent us in Congress." She was endorsed by the Star, which cited her "unique array of life experiences" and willingness to seek compromise. Davids defeated Welder, 37%-33%.

Yoder criticized Davids for her vague responses to policy questions. "She tries to play coy on these issues," such as immigration and health care, he said during their sole debate, which was a week before the election. Davids often responded broadly that she would "stand up for Kansas values, not for Donald Trump's values." Yoder sought to distance himself from Trump. He did not attend a Trump campaign rally in Kansas. Instead, he cited his friendship with Democratic Rep. Emanuel Cleaver in the neighboring Missouri district and used a brief image of the two of them in a campaign ad.

Each candidate spent about $5 million in the contest. Including outside spending, the total was about $18 million, though Republicans canceled more than $1 million of scheduling advertising a month before the election.

The unpopularity of Trump and Kris Kobach, the unsuccessful GOP nominee for governor, was too much for Yoder to overcome. As earlier polls had predicted, Davids won easily, 54%-44%. She took 52 percent of the vote in traditionally Republican Johnson County, which cast four-fifths of the total. She more than doubled the vote for Yoder in Kansas City-based Wyandotte County, while Yoder took the smaller vote in more rural Miami County. For Davids, her reelection prospects will depend, in part, on whether Kansas Republicans can repair their internal divisions.

KS-3: Kansas City Metro
Cook Partisan Voting Index: R+4

Population		Race and Ethnicity		Income	
Total	754,183	White	72.3%	Median Income	$71,268
Land area (sq. miles)	757	Black	8.4%	District Income Rank	86
Pop/ sq mi	996	Latino	11.8%	Poverty Rate	9%
Born in State	43.8%	Asian	4.5%	With health insurance	90.8%
		Two or more races	2.6%	Cash public assistance	1.1%
Age Groups		Other	0.4%	Food stamp/SNAP	6.2%
Under 18	25.8%				
18-34	22%	**Education**		**Work**	
35-64	39.4%	H.S grad or less	26.4%	White Collar	12.8%
Over 64	12.8%	Some college	27.2%	Sales and Service	38.1%
		College Degree, 4 yr	29.2%	Blue Collar	16.1%
Military		Post grad	17.3%	Government	10.8%
Veteran/ Active Duty	7.1%				

2012 Pres. Vote	Romney	177,886	(54%)	Obama	146,406	(44%)		
2016 Pres. Vote	Clinton	161,479	(47%)	Trump	157,304	(46%)	Johnson	17,127	(5%)

Johnson County: Though its central core is in Missouri, about 40 percent of metropolitan Kansas City's residents live west of the state line in Kansas. Some are in Kansas City Kansas, or KCK as it is sometimes called, where the low-lying land near the Missouri River used to house one of the nation's largest stockyards. This is still a working-class town with lots of modest frame houses, new Latino neighborhoods that have surpassed in size the African-American community, and a Catholic ethnic neighborhood. Kansas City's Wyandotte County has lost 21,000 people since the 1970s, and is now majority-minority: 29 percent Hispanic and 23 percent black. It is one of only four such counties in the state; the other three are in the southwestern corner, where farms and meatpacking plants have attracted immigrants from Mexico.

South of Kansas City and Wyandotte County is Johnson County, which has nearly tripled since 1970. It is more affluent and close to four times the size of Wyandotte. The newer neighborhoods are arrayed along the interstates, as subdivisions have replaced croplands. They have grown to the point that Overland Park, Olathe, Shawnee and Lenexa are among the largest cities in the state; Overland Park is the second-largest behind Wichita. Between 2013 and 2018, 7,200 apartments were built in the county. These towns became more than just residential neighborhoods over the past few decades. Sprint Nextel, which has been headquartered in Overland Park, in April 2018 merged with T-Mobile, the new majority owner. After Applebee's left Lenexa to cross the river in 2011, city officials responded by persuading SelectQuote Senior Insurance Services to move from the Missouri side two years later. This swap is emblematic of a major problem for the region: Tax incentives are used by states to lure businesses across the tight state borders, producing a net wash in job creation, but a decrease in overall revenues. The local Hall Family Foundation concluded in a 2016 report that the corporate welfare competition during the previous five years had cost the two states more than $200 million in tax revenues, for a net gain of just 414 jobs for Kansas.

Johnson County, like Wyandotte (and the Missouri suburbs, too), has been diversifying demographically. In 1980, the county was 97 percent white. But the share of non-Hispanic whites dropped to 80 percent of the population in 2017. Wyandotte has an old Democratic machine style of politics, though its influence has been tempered by the consolidation of city and county governments. Johnson, by contrast, has long been heavily Republican, but with plenty of moderate and even liberal voters on cultural issues. It has been a battleground for the fierce fights between moderate and conservative wings of the Kansas Republican Party, which sometimes benefit Democrats.

The 3rd Congressional District consists of all of Johnson and Wyandotte counties, and a corner of rural Miami County. In a notable turnaround, Hillary Clinton led Donald Trump, 47%-46%, in this district, which Mitt Romney won, 54%-44% in 2012. Clinton took Wyandotte, 62%-33%. Trump won Johnson County, but only by 48%-45%, in contrast to Romney's 58%-40% advantage.

Ron Estes (R)

Elected 2017, 1st full term, b. Jul 19, 1956; Topeka; Tennessee Technological University, B.S.; Tennessee Technological University, M.B.A.; Lutheran; Married (Susan Oliver); 3 children.

Elected Office: Sedgwick County Treasurer, 2004-2010; KS Treasurer, 2010-2017.

Professional Career: Businessman; Farmer.

DC Office: 1524 LHOB 20515, 202-225-6216, Fax: 202-225-3489, estes.house.gov

State Offices: Wichita, 316-262-8992.

Committees: *Ways & Means*: Social Security; Worker & Family Support.

Group Ratings

	ADA	ACLU	AFL-CIO	LCV	ITI	COC	HAFA	ACU	CFG	FRC
2018	-	0%	-	0%	-	82%	78%	84%	61%	100%
2017	0%	C	-	0%	C	100%	C	81%	76%	100%

Almanac Ratings 2017-18

	Economy	Social	Foreign	Composite
Liberal	12%	21%	4%	12%
Conservative	88%	80%	96%	88%

Key Votes of the 115th Congress

1. Obama-care revision	Y	5. Family planning regs	N/A	9. Guantanamo prisoners	N
2. Tax Cuts	Y	6. Body cameras/immigration	N	10. Ground missiles, limit	N
3. Omnibus appropriations	Y	7. Abortion ban	Y	11. Defense Dept. spending	Y
4. Dodd-Frank revision	Y	8. Concealed carry	Y	12. FISA rules	Y

Election Results

Election	Name (Party)	Vote (%)		Cand. Spent	Ind. Exp. Support	Ind. Exp. Oppose
2018 General	Ron Estes (R)	144,248	(59%)	$1,544,411	$92,000	
	James Thompson (D)	98,445	(41%)	$1,290,889	$13,894	$90,000
2018 Primary	Ron Estes (R)	57,522	(81%)			
	Ron M. Estes (R)	13,159	(19%)			

Prior winning percentages: 2017 special (53%)

Republican Ron Estes was elected in April 2017 to the seat vacated by Mike Pompeo, who became director of the Central Intelligence Agency and later secretary of State under President Donald Trump. Estes was a longtime businessman and elected official who ran a lackluster campaign in the special election. His victory was narrower than has been customary in this district for Republicans, who scrambled to avoid potential embarrassment during the final days before the vote. His 2018 re-election rematch win was much more comfortable.

Estes was born in Topeka, a fifth-generation Kansan. He got a bachelor's in civil engineering and then an MBA, both from Tennessee Technological University. He was a consultant and had management roles in several different industries, including aerospace, automotive, and oil and gas, where he implemented improved efficiencies with financial and other computer systems. He won his first elected office in 2004, as treasurer of Sedgwick County. In 2010, he was elected Kansas treasurer. In each position, he focused on improving efficiency, customer service and saving tax money. He became active in national associations for state treasurers and held several positions in the Republican Party, serving as the Kansas vice chairman.

After Pompeo resigned, each party selected its candidate at a small nominating convention. That limited time and financial costs, but it also meant that the candidates had to persuade only a small number of party activists. The chief competitor to Estes was Alan Cobb, a coalitions director for Trump's national campaign and onetime aide to former Sen. Bob Dole. Estes won on the second ballot. At the Democratic selection meeting two days later, civil rights attorney James Thompson also won on the second ballot and quickly tried to cast the contest in national terms.

But the contest was slow to attract either local or national media attention. In the closing days, Republicans worried about the outcome. Trump and Vice President Mike Pence recorded robocalls urging Republicans to vote, and Texas Sen. Ted Cruz held an election eve rally. Democrats benefited from the hostility toward Trump among their supporters. In the early vote of more than 23,000 in Sedgwick County, Thompson got 61 percent. He raised $340,000, which was competitive with Estes' $400,000. In a district where Trump five months earlier led 60%-33%, Estes won 52%-46%. He narrowed the gap in Sedgwick so that he lost by only about 1,900 votes, which showed that Republicans were successful with Election Day turnout. The closer-than-usual outcome was a harbinger of eventual Democratic success elsewhere in the state in 2018. Retrospectively, liberal activists second-guessed a possible missed opportunity.

In the House, Estes has been a reliable Republican vote. He expressed concern about Trump's tariffs on China, fearing they could hurt local business and farmers. "While I support President Trump's desire to negotiate a level playing field with our trade partners, we need a targeted approach that embraces free and fair trade over tariffs and protectionism," he said. Estes voiced support for the conservative Wichita-based Koch brothers after Trump attacked them on Twitter for not falling in line behind him. Estes said that Koch Industries was vital to the district and that the brothers were important "in promoting free and fair trade, limited government and personal liberties."

Thompson ran again in 2018. This time, Estes prevailed, 59%-41% -- a more traditional Republican showing in the district. Unlike other Democrats who were successful in Kansas, Thompson ran a more ideological campaign, supporting Medicare for all and a $15 minimum wage. In July, he bought in Sen. Bernie Sanders and rising progressive star Alexandria Ocasio-Cortez. Estes allied himself with Trump and his policies, including support for the GOP tax cuts and a wall along the Mexican border. The more noteworthy part of his reelection may have been the GOP primary, where Estes faced a candidate named … Ron M. Estes. The other Estes, an aerospace engineer who had worked on the International Space Station, described himself as more fiscally moderate and socially progressive; he opposed the Republican tax overhaul and supported the Affordable Care Act. The incumbent – who said the "M" in his opponent's name stood for "misleading" -- claimed the other Ron Estes was an "imposter" and a case of "Democrat dirty tricks." The incumbent prevailed, 81%-19%. The challenger spent less than $3,000.

KS-4: South Central Kansas   Cook Partisan Voting Index: R+15

Population		Race and Ethnicity		Income	
Total	722,477	White	74%	Median Income	$52,955
Land area (sq. miles)	14,316	Black	6.7%	District Income Rank	255
Pop/ sq mi	50.5	Latino	12.1%	Poverty Rate	14%
Born in State	65.7%	Asian	3.3%	With health insurance	89.1%
		Two or more races	3%	Cash public assistance	2.4%
Age Groups		Other	0.8%	Food stamp/SNAP	10.6%
Under 18	25.8%				
18-34	22.6%	**Education**		**Work**	
35-64	37.1%	H.S grad or less	37.6%	White Collar	14.5%
Over 64	14.5%	Some college	33.6%	Sales and Service	39.3%
		College Degree, 4 yr	19.1%	Blue Collar	25.1%
Military		Post grad	9.8%	Government	13.7%
Veteran/ Active Duty	9.3%				

2012 Pres. Vote	Romney	164,553	(62%)	Obama	96,433	(36%)
2016 Pres. Vote	Trump	165,266	(60%)	Clinton	90,541	(33%)

Wichita: With about 390,000 people, Wichita has been a Great Plains metropolis. It is still growing, but it has fallen behind the size of Omaha and Tulsa. It began as a farm market town and grew with local oil and gas discoveries in the 1920s. The aircraft business began in 1911 when Clyde Cessna first flew his plane from a farm in Kingman County, and five years later, moved his operations to north Wichita. The real impetus for the industry came during World War II and the years just afterward, when aircraft factories sprouted up on the Kansas prairie. Wichita suddenly became the nation's major producer of small aircraft. Workers poured in, many from neighboring Arkansas and Oklahoma, giving the city a taste of southern culture.

The September 11 attacks were a severe blow to the overall airline industry, with the loss of some 15,000 local jobs, from which the area has not fully recovered. The Navy gave the area a boost in 2004 with a contract for 100 modified 737s to be used to hunt submarines. Then, the 2007-09 recession sparked another wave of layoffs, with Cessna idling more than 1,000 workers; Hawker Beechcraft filed for bankruptcy in 2012. Boeing, once the area's largest employer, shut down its local facilities in 2014; company officials cited cuts in the Pentagon budget and high overhead costs. In 2017, there were signs of a rebound when Spirit AeroSystems announced a $1 billion factory bringing 1,000 jobs to build fuselages, plus engine and wing parts for Boeing 737s – the biggest local jobs announcement since 2009. Still, some companies struggled to find qualified workers after many had left the area following the layoffs and closures. Wichita has tried to revitalize its downtown area, hoping to make the city more attractive and to train workers with tuition-free programs. The Kansas Health Institute forecasts population growth in the Wichita metro area, with minorities making up more than half the total population by 2066.

Cargill Inc., the largest privately held corporation in the United States, is based in Wichita and includes 75 businesses. In 2018, it opened a new $60 million headquarters for Cargill Protein, with 800 local workers. Cargill began construction in 2017 of a $90 million biodiesel plant in north Wichita. Koch Industries, owned by the politically active and conservative Koch brothers, which has been second only to Cargill as the nation's largest privately held company, employs about 60,000 in the United States and has revenues of about $100 billion, much of it in agriculture and technology. At a time when the Kochs were battered politically for their well-financed conservative activism and shifting to a softer edge, their company was beloved at home as an employer and philanthropist. David Koch retired from the family business in 2018 due to health reasons, and his older brother Charles continued to distance their political network from the influence of President Donald Trump, doubling down on their free-market principles.

Kansas' 4th Congressional District covers wheat-growing areas to the east and west, but 70 percent of its people are in Wichita and Sedgwick County. It occasionally votes Democratic in local and state contests, including for its first African-American mayor, Carl Brewer. He served two terms and was hailed as a consensus-builder when he stepped down in 2015; he was succeeded by Jeff

Longwell, a Republican. The 4th has been solidly Republican in federal elections. Donald Trump got 60 percent of the vote.

KENTUCKY

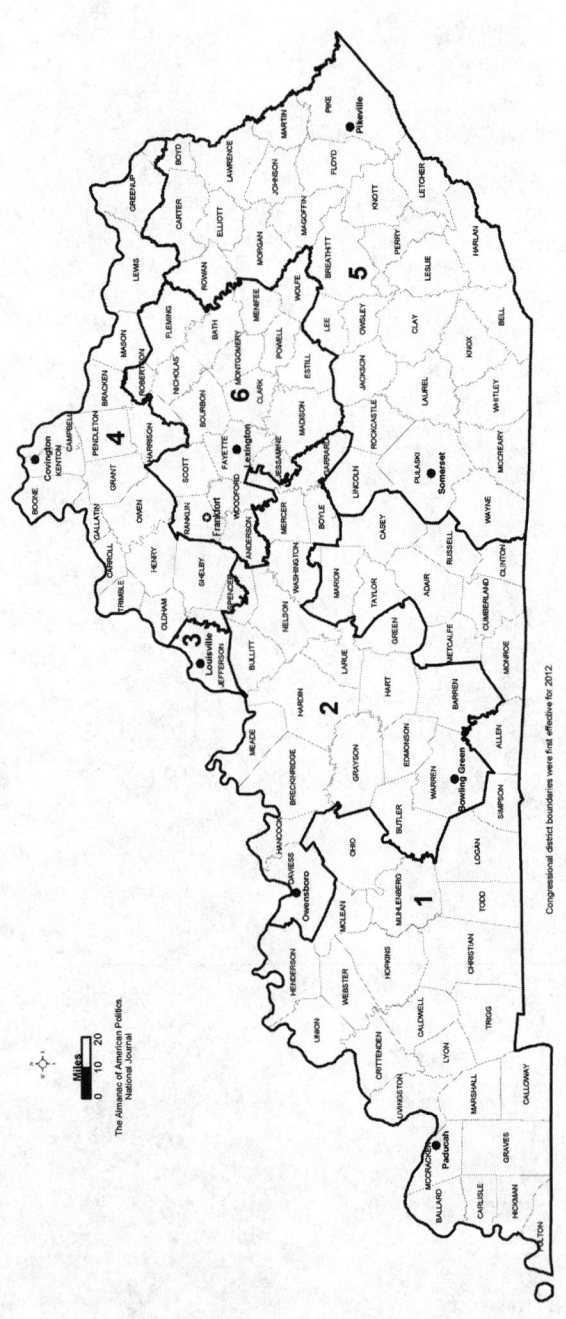

Congressional district boundaries were first effective for 2012

The Almanac of American Politics,
National Journal

Miles
0   10   20

It built slowly and steadily, but starting in 2015 Kentucky completed its transition from Democratic to Republican, a shift supercharged by opposition to President Barack Obama and the decline of one of the state's signature industries, coal.

Kentucky was once part of Virginia. When it was split off and admitted to the union in 1792, it became the first state west of the Appalachian chain. In 1798, Thomas Jefferson, aroused by the Federalists' Alien and Sedition acts, ghostwrote the Kentucky Resolutions, a defense of self-governance (and proto-nullification) by the states. Kentucky's largest county is named for Jefferson, and its largest city for the monarch to whom he was credentialed as ambassador to France, Louis XVI. Kentucky has a constitution informed by a Jeffersonian suspicion of concentrating power. Its one-term limit on governors was raised to two only in 1992, and until 2001 it limited its state legislature to one 60-day session every two years, with much important business handled in special sessions. The state has 120 counties – the third most of any state, after the much more populous Texas and Georgia.

Kentucky -- home to the Cumberland Gap, the pass through the Appalachian Mountains where Virginia meets Kentucky and Tennessee – remains a logistical hub. The state is within a day's drive of more than half the U.S. population, and its large air-freight shipping terminals at the Louisville and Cincinnati-Northern Kentucky airports offer access to customers around the world. That was a big reason why UPS located in Louisville and Amazon, the nation's largest online retailer, has 11 fulfillment, return and customer service centers in the state, employing some 10,000 full-time workers. Amazon Prime announced in 2017 an air-hub expansion at the Cincinnati-Northern Kentucky airport, which was poised to become the largest investment ever by a company in northern Kentucky.

The automobile industry has sought some of the same logistical advantages, as well as a business-friendly environment. Kentucky is at the center of "auto alley," which runs from the Great Lakes to the Gulf of Mexico. Kentucky is home to four car and truck assembly lines: two Ford plants in Louisville, General Motors' Corvette factory in Bowling Green (also home to the National Corvette Museum), and a Toyota plant in Georgetown – the company's largest anywhere, currently undergoing a $1.3 billion upgrade. Three of the state's auto plants -- the two in Louisville and the one in Georgetown, just north of Lexington -- are located in the portion of Kentucky known as the "Golden Triangle," the most productive and populous part of the state. The Golden Triangle extends from Jefferson County (Louisville) east to Fayette County (Lexington) and then north to Boone and Kenton Counties (suburban Cincinnati) -- the state's four largest counties by population. They are faster growing and have higher median household incomes than Kentucky as a whole, and several of their adjacent counties are wealthier still and have seen even faster population growth. Scott County, near Lexington, grew 16 percent between 2010 and 2017, a rate almost seven times higher than the state as a whole. Oldham County, next door to Louisville, grew by almost 10 percent over the same period, and it has a median household income of more than $92,000, roughly twice the state average.

The Golden Triangle is home to much of Kentucky's prized thoroughbred industry, including the Kentucky Derby, which has been run since 1875 on the first Saturday in May. By itself, the Derby has an estimated $400 million economic impact in the state, and the industry as a whole packs a $4 billion punch, employing more than 55,000 Kentuckians. The hottest sector these days has been the state's $8.5 billion distillery industry and its fast-growing bourbon-tourism business. The Golden Triangle, with some nearby counties, is the home of global bourbon production: 95 percent of the liquor is produced in Kentucky, due to a combination of calcium-and-magnesium-producing blue limestone, big swings in temperature, and soil favorable to corn production. The state has more than 50 distilleries, triple the number in 2009, thanks to rising interest and investment in small-batch bourbon; from 2012 to 2017, bourbon sales increased by more than 50 percent. Riding this growth, the industry spent or prepared to spend in excess of $1 billion on capital projects, including restaurants and hotels to attract tourists to what is branded as the Kentucky Bourbon Trail. More than 1 million people visited in 2016 and 2017; in 2018, Lonely Planet put Kentucky's bourbon region on its list of top 10 U.S. travel destinations. The main worry facing the industry is retaliatory tariffs imposed by the European Union and several other countries, to counter actions by President Donald Trump and possibly designed to trouble Kentuckian Mitch McConnell, the Senate majority leader.

Outside the Triangle -- and the small metro areas of Owensboro and Bowling Green -- Kentucky is not doing so well. Nationally, Kentucky's median income ranks near the bottom. The state's 17.2

percent poverty rate in 2017 was the fifth-worst rate in the country. The state's small non-white communities fare even worse: a 25.7 percent poverty rate for African Americans and 25.8 percent for Latinos. In late 2018, its unemployment rate ranked among the top 10 states. With higher-education attainment in Kentucky below the national average, companies in the state see a mismatch between workforce skills and job openings. In most places beyond the Golden Triangle, population has been stagnant or falling. The University of Louisville projected that two-thirds of the state's counties will lose population between 2015 and 2040.

One reason has been the decline of coal. In eastern Kentucky, once the state's leading coal region, industry employment has dropped from roughly 15,000 in mid-2009 to a little over 4,000 in 2017. "It's essentially trying to recover from an economic atomic bomb," Harlan County Judge-Executive Dan Mosley told the Lexington Herald-Leader. The reasons are numerous. The increasing popularity of hydraulic fracturing for low-cost natural gas has contributed significantly to the national slowdown in coal demand. Tougher federal regulations to protect water quality around mines, federal encouragement to shift away from coal, and greater industry sensitivity to the fuels used to generate electricity have exacerbated the downturn. And many coal seams in eastern Kentucky have been stripped of their most accessible product, raising the cost of extraction. In western Kentucky, production has not been nearly as hard hit; the higher sulfur content of its coal once had difficulty coping with clean-air rules, but the installation of scrubbers at many power plants helped sustain the region's mines.

Another declining product has been tobacco. For most of the last century, many Kentucky farmers grew at least a small crop of tobacco. But health concerns and evolving social mores gradually took their toll. (A quarter of Kentuckians smoke, more than any other state but West Virginia, and the state leads the nation in lung cancer.) Cash payments to farmers who had owned tobacco quotas ended in 2014, a decade after Congress abolished quotas and price supports. Leading politicians from both parties have eagerly endorsed efforts to expand hemp cultivation, which was legalized by the 2018 farm bill. In a sign of the times, the GOP-led state government in 2018 signed off on a 50-cent-per-pack cigarette tax hike to fund education and other programs.

As in other parts of Appalachia, addiction has spread. Kentucky ranks in the top five states for opioid death rates, and legislative efforts to curb the tide have proven ineffective. "We are in a crisis state," said Gov. Matt Bevin, a Republican. Kentucky's Democratic attorney general, Andy Beshear, has filed several opioid-related lawsuits against companies such as Walgreens and Johnson & Johnson, though the Kentucky Senate rejected a state House-passed measure that could have been the first prescription-opioid tax in any state. Meanwhile, 54 Kentucky counties are among the 220 in the U.S. that have been cited by the Centers for Disease Control and Prevention as being most at risk of a major HIV outbreak – a consequence of the rise in injected drugs. Kentucky also ranked high in new, acute hepatitis C cases. When the state, under Democratic Gov. Steve Beshear, took advantage of health insurance expansion under the Affordable Care Act, the response was more enthusiastic than in almost any other state, as Kentucky's uninsured rate fell by more than half. The state's Medicaid expansion has survived criticism by Bevin and the Republican legislature, though the governor sought to impose work requirements for able-bodied, childless adults who sign up for the Medicaid expansion.

Kentucky long favored the Democratic Party, which can trace its ancestry at least tenuously back to Jefferson. The Bluegrass region and the western end of the state were slaveholding territory and voted Democratic. Louisville, with many German immigrants, was an anti-slavery town, and for years flirted with Republicans, but in the past century, the city and surrounding Jefferson County has been conspicuously more Democratic than the state as a whole. The eastern mountains were pro-Union and remain Republican, except for a few counties where the United Mine Workers organized coal miners in the 1930s. But the national Democratic Party has moved to the left on social issues, while Kentucky has been home to Kim Davis, the elected Rowan County clerk who refused to sign same-sex marriage licenses, and a $100 million Noah's Ark tourist attraction and Creation Museum built by Biblical literalists in Williamstown, between Cincinnati and Lexington; more than 1 million visited in its first year. Kentucky has gone solidly Republican in the past five presidential elections.

For a while, state-level Democrats held on, thanks to incumbency. But the party's registration edge has eroded, and in the 2015 election, Democrats lost the governorship to tea party-aligned

Republican Matt Bevin. Republicans also flipped the offices of state auditor and state treasurer, and the GOP barely fell short of seizing the attorney general's office; Jenean Hampton, Bevin's running mate, became the first African American to be elected statewide. In 2016, the GOP won control of the state House for the first time since 1920, joining the state Senate, which had been in Republican hands since 2000.

Kentucky's demographics have been a good fit for Donald Trump's strengths. Kentucky is the seventh-whitest state in the country at 85 percent, and only three states (Maine, Vermont and West Virginia) have a smaller Hispanic percentage. It's also among the top 10 rural states. In 2016, Trump won by 33 points. The fact that Hillary Clinton had said "we're going to put a lot of coal miners and coal companies out of business" did not help her cause.

The new GOP majority enacted a number of state policies that conservatives had long awaited, including a right-to-work law, an end to prevailing wages on public construction jobs, and establishment of charter schools. But Kentucky Republicans also faced turbulence. In 2018, House Speaker Jeff Hoover resigned his leadership post after settling allegations that he had sexually harassed a female staff member. Teachers rallied at the capitol to protest Bevin's attempts to overhaul the state's pension system. The legislature passed a watered-down bill, but not before Bevin harshly criticized teacher's unions. Amid flagging approval ratings for Bevin, Democrats – including a wave of teachers running for office – expressed optimism that they would make gains in the 2018 election. But about three-quarters of the teachers who challenged incumbents or sought open seats lost, and the GOP dominance in Frankfort remained essentially unchanged. One silver lining for Democrats was their defeat of Davis, the county clerk. After the election, a special session that Bevin called to address the pension issue quickly collapsed.

Population		Race and Ethnicity		Income	
Total	4,424,376	White	85.1%	Median Income	$46,535
Land area (sq. miles)	39,486	Black	7.9%	State Income Rank	46
Pop/ sq mi	112.0	Latino	3.4%	Poverty Rate	18.3%
Born in state	69.5%	Asian	1.3%	With health insurance	92.1%
		Two or more races	1.9%	Cash public assistance	2.1%
Age Groups		Other	0.3%	Food stamp/SNAP	16.1%
Under 18	22.9%				
18-34	22.5%	Education		Work	
35-64	39.4%	H.S grad or less	47.9%	White Collar	33.3%
Over 64	15.2%	Some college	28.9%	Sales and Service	40.3%
		College Degree, 4 yr	13.6%	Blue Collar	26.4%
Military		Post grad	9.6%	Government	14.4%
Veteran/ Active Duty	8.6%				

Presidential Politics

2016 Caucus (R)	Trump (R)	82,493 (36%)	Cruz (R)	72,503 (32%)	Rubio (R)	37,579 (16%)
	Kasich (R)	33,134 (14%)				
2016 Primary (D)	Clinton (D)	212,534 (47%)	Sanders (D)	210,623 (46%)		
2016 Pres. Vote	Trump (R)	1,202,971 (63%)	Clinton (D)	628,854 (33%)	Johnson (L)	53,752 (3%)
2012 Pres. Vote	Romney (R)	1,087,190 (60%)	Obama (D)	679,370 (38%)		

It has been 20 years since Democrats won Kentucky in a presidential election. With two Southerners on their ticket, they carried the state in 1992 and 1996. In 2000, Al Gore from neighboring Tennessee was hobbled by stands hostile to tobacco, coal and guns, all staples of Kentucky culture. George W. Bush carried the state 57%-41% that year, and Republicans have won by growing margins ever since. In 2012, Barack Obama carried only four of Kentucky's 120 counties, including those containing the state's two largest cities, Louisville and Lexington, and the state capital of Frankfort. He carried only one historically Democratic county in the eastern mountains. Even when losing by landslide margins, George McGovern carried seven mountain counties in 1972 and Walter Mondale carried 12 mountain counties in 1984. Obama's tougher regulations on coal extraction and use and a decline in energy markets antagonized Kentuckians, and Donald Trump defeated Hillary Clinton

63%-33%. The Democratic nominee carried just two counties, Jefferson (Louisville) and Fayette (Lexington and the University of Kentucky). Clinton didn't do herself any favors when she told a CNN town hall in February in next-door Ohio, "We're going to put a lot of coal miners and coal companies out of business," in describing her proposals for moving the country toward cleaner energy sources. Democratic Rep. John Yarmouth, a Clinton booster who represents Louisville, told WHAS-11 News, "The first time I heard it, I said, 'Oh my God, that's deadly.'"

Despite that miscue, Clinton managed to eke out a victory over Vermont Sen. Bernie Sanders in the Democratic primary on May 17. One reason for her victory was her decision to shift the discussion to cars and trucks that are produced at four plants around the state, which is also home to many auto parts suppliers. She criticized Sanders for voting against the release of funds from the Troubled Asset Relief Program, a measure primarily designed to benefit Wall Street, but which also included money for the auto bailout. Clinton revved up her television advertising in the state and added stops to her campaign schedule. Every effort was needed — she prevailed by fewer than 2,000 votes. Kentucky Republicans opted to hold a caucus on March 5, at the behest of home-state Sen. Rand Paul, who was seeking the GOP presidential nomination. That allowed Paul to get around a state law that forbids a candidate from appearing on two ballots at the same time. Paul was up for reelection in 2016, and he would have had to choose between the presidential primary and the Senate primary. Paul contributed $250,000 to the state GOP to help defray the costs of conducting the caucus. But a poor showing in the Iowa caucuses caused Paul to exit the presidential race before it got to Kentucky. Trump defeated Texas Sen. Ted Cruz, 36%-32%, followed by Florida Sen. Marco Rubio and Ohio Gov. John Kasich, both well back. More than 228,000 attended the caucuses, exceeding the number who voted in either of the previous two GOP presidential primaries.

Congressional Districts

116th Congress Lineup	1D 5R	115th Congress Lineup	1D 5R

After the 2010 census, the two parties agreed to a compromise that made few shifts in congressional district lines. The result has been a six-member delegation in which Republicans have consistently controlled each district except for the Democratic-held 3rd District in Louisville's Jefferson County. Since then, Republicans have taken control of the state House and the governor's office; the executive office is up for grabs in November 2019. For more than a decade, the political geography of Kentucky has been that the 6th District — the only one that does not border another state -- is the only seat that has shifted party control or had competitive contests. The redrawing of that district could attract extensive attention, though Republicans likely will retain the upper hand — in that district and statewide.

Matt Bevin (R)

Elected 2015, term expires 2019, 1st term; b. Jan. 9, 1967, Denver, CO; Washington and Lee University, BA 1989; Southern Baptist; Married (Glenna); 10 children (4 adopted, 1 deceased).

Military Career: U.S Army, 1989-1993.

Professional Career: Financial Consultant, SEI Investments Company; Vice President, Putnam Investments; President, Bevin Brothers Manufacturing Company.

Office: 700 Capitol Ave., Suite 100, Frankfort, 40601; 502-564-2611; Fax: 502-564-0437; Website: kentucky.gov.

Lt. Gov.: Jenean Hampton (R) **Atty. Gen:** Andy Beshear (D) **Sec. of State:** Alison Lundergan Grimes (D)

State Legislature: Senate: 9D, 29R **House:** 39D, 61R

Election Results

Election	Name (Party)	Vote (%)
2015 General	Matt Bevin (R)..	511,771 (53%)
	Jack Conway (D)...	426,827 (44%)
	Drew Curtis (I)..	35,627 (4%)
2015 Primary	Matt Bevin (R)..	70,479 (33%)
	James Comer Jr. (R)...	70,396 (33%)
	Hal Heiner (R)..	57,948 (27%)
	Will T. Scott (R)..	15,364 (7%)

Just a year after unsuccessfully challenging Mitch McConnell, the Senate's top Republican, in a GOP primary, Matt Bevin won the governorship in 2015. In office, he signed a number of bills that enacted long-sought policies for conservatives. But his aggressively outsider approach soured relations with Democrats, the news media and some fellow Republicans.

Bevin grew up in Shelburne New Hampshire, the second of six children in a family of modest means that lived on their livestock and produce from their garden. He has told audiences that he shared a bedroom with his three brothers in a house without central heat. "It's those stories and the family's history of self-reliance that he says helped form his view that government should just get out of people's way," wrote Joseph Gerth in the Louisville Courier Journal. Bevin attended the Gould Academy, a boarding school in Bethel Maine, and Washington & Lee University, where he majored in East Asian studies and took part in ROTC. Bevin rose to captain, serving four years of active duty with the 5th Mechanized Infantry Division. After the Army, Bevin went into the financial industry and other entrepreneurial ventures, amassing between $13.4 million and $54.9 million in net worth, according to ethics filings. He and his wife, Glenna, have nine children, four of them adopted from Ethiopia.

In 2014, Bevin challenged McConnell – not only the Senate's leading Republican, but also the state's political powerhouse – from the right in the GOP primary. Two national conservative groups with deep pockets took an interest in Bevin's candidacy: the Madison Project, which had helped Republican Ted Cruz's successful insurgent Senate bid in Texas, and the Senate Conservatives Fund, a political action committee allied with former South Carolina Sen. Jim DeMint, then-president of the Heritage Foundation and a leader of the party's conservative wing. McConnell didn't take his opponent lightly; he ran ads calling Bevin an "East Coast Con Man" and "Bailout Bevin." Bevin returned fire, tagging McConnell as a career politician. But Bevin was an inexperienced candidate who made numerous errors — he attended a cock-fighting rally and claimed it was a "state's rights" event — and McConnell crushed him, 60%-35%. After the primary, Bevin refused to endorse McConnell, saying, "You can't punch people in the face, punch people in the face, punch people in the face, and ask them to have tea and crumpets with you and think it's all good."

The election was barely in the rear-view mirror when Bevin decided to run for governor. Democrat Steve Beshear, whose most prominent achievement was adding more than 400,000 able-bodied, childless Kentuckians to the Medicaid rolls under the Affordable Care Act, was term-limited. In the primary, Bevin faced three major candidates – then-Agriculture Commissioner James Comer, Louisville businessman Hal Heiner and former state Supreme Court Justice Will T. Scott. The primary was nasty, including allegations by Comer's ex-girlfriend that he had abused her emotionally and physically when they were both in college. The airing of the allegations were linked to the husband of Heiner's running mate, so he faced some backlash from the episode. Bevin ran an ad showing two kids in a food fight, representing Heiner and Comer. Somewhat unexpectedly, Bevin came out on top on Election Day – by 83 votes. Bevin and Comer each took 33 percent, with Heiner at 27 percent and Scott at 7 percent.

Heading into the general election, Bevin sought to repair ties with McConnell, deleting past tweets critical of his former opponent and making a self-deprecating video about their animosity. McConnell endorsed Bevin, but didn't go out of his way to offer tangible support. Bevin ran on ending the Common Core educational curriculum, implementing drug testing for recipients of public assistance, enacting a right-to-work law and, most notable in policy terms, dismantling Kynect, the state's Obamacare health insurance exchange. Attorney General Jack Conway, the Democratic nominee, had a mixed record in past elections, notably a loss to Rand Paul in the 2010 Senate race. But most pre-election surveys gave Conway a modest lead. As it turned out, the polls were wrong: Bevin won with relative ease, 53%-44%. He also had coattails, helping oust state auditor Adam Edelen, who was considered a rising Democratic star.

Once in office, Bevin tapped Heiner, one of his primary rivals, as his secretary of education and workforce. The new governor signed a bill mandating that women seeking an abortion receive a face-to-face consultation 24 hours before the procedure, and he tackled the state's pension underfunding problems, which were among the nation's worst. As promised, he sought a federal waiver to change the benefit structure for those that had been added to the Medicaid rolls. Beshear's son Andy – narrowly elected attorney general on the same day Bevin won the governorship – clashed with his father's successor on cuts to higher education (the courts sided with Beshear), a reorganization of the state pension board, and Bevin's replacement of the University of Louisville board of trustees. Bevin's first year ended well, as he, McConnell and Donald Trump helped flip the state House to GOP control for the first time since 1920, joining the state Senate, which had been in Republican hands since 2000.

The legislative realignment gave Bevin a stronger hand in policy. He signed a pair of abortion bills, including one to ban the procedure after 20 weeks, and another to require a fetal ultrasound to be played audibly for, and in view of, the mother. Bevin carried through on his campaign promise to sign a right-to-work law (Kentucky was the last state in the South to enact one) and he signed a measure allowing charter schools, which had long been blocked by the House. Citing civil-liberties concerns, Bevin vetoed a bill passed by near-unanimous margins that would have empowered judges to order outpatient treatment for some people who are unable to recognize their own mental illnesses. The legislature overrode him.

In 2018, Kentucky politics was dominated by two issues. One was Bevin's effort to enact work requirements for Medicaid recipients, a policy the Trump administration had allowed states to pursue. Bevin's initial plan was scrapped by a federal judge in June 2018, but state officials put together an alternate policy, and it received approval from the Trump administration in late 2018. The policy required most adults covered by the Medicaid expansion who were between 19 and 64 to spend 80 hours a month either working in a job, looking for a job, receiving job training, attending school or volunteering.

Meanwhile, Bevin's efforts to address the state's pension problems kicked off a bitter fight with teachers. He pursued a plan that would have reduced guaranteed retirement benefits for teachers, as well as other government employees, to better reflect changes in most private retirement systems. Educators angrily protested: More than two dozen school districts closed due to sickouts, and districts across the state shut down a few days later as teachers rallied at the state capitol. Bevin, angered by the revolt, set off a bipartisan firestorm when he told reporters, "I guarantee you somewhere in Kentucky today a child was sexually assaulted that was left at home because there was nobody there to watch them. I guarantee you somewhere today, a child was physically harmed or ingested poison because they were home alone because a single parent didn't have any money to take care of them." He later apologized. The enacted bill offered a hybrid plan for new teachers that included some aspects of a 401(k) plan.

The pension law had been attached to a wastewater bill and passed both chambers the day it was introduced. However, this lightning-quick process became the measure's undoing in December 2018 when the state Supreme Court struck down the law, saying lawmakers did not follow the required legislative process. Calling this "a sad day for Kentucky," Bevin called a special session to try to pass a new pension bill. But it dissolved a day later without new legislation, leaving the issue in limbo.

Bevin didn't skirmish only with teachers; he also squabbled with his own party. The GOP-controlled legislature overrode vetoes of tax and spending bills, and the governor feuded with House Speaker Jeff Hoover. Hoover criticized Bevin's comments critical of teachers, while Bevin called on Hoover to resign after allegations of sexual harassment. (Hoover initially resisted but eventually resigned from his leadership post.) Bevin's aggressive style has drawn comparisons with Trump: He blasted a Kentucky state judge, saying he was a "political hack," and didn't hesitate to block people on social media. Bevin's relationship with the press was frosty at best, and at times he targeted top media outlets in personal terms. Bevin attacked Courier Journal reporter Tom Loftus as "Peeping Tom" and "sick" for investigating where the governor was residing. Bevin also posted a video accusing Bill Lamb, general manager of a Louisville TV station, of lying. "He can't take criticism at all, of any kind," Lamb responded.

In 2019, Bevin signed a tax cut that is expected to reach $107 million a year, but the state's Medicaid work requirements suffered a setback in the courts, as did a 2018 law banning abortions using the dilation and evacuation method. Bevin's approval rating was only 30 percent on the eve of the 2018 elections, leading three of the state's top Democrats -- Andy Beshear, Edelen and House Democratic Floor Leader Rocky Adkins -- to run for governor. Beshear won the Democratic primary with 39 percent, while Bevin notched an unimpressive 52 percent in a primary that included freshman state Rep. Robert Goforth and two minor candidates. The Bevin-Beshear matchup in November promised to be unusually competitive for a gubernatorial race in such a solidly red state.

Mitch McConnell (R)

Elected 1984, term expires 2020, 6th term, b. Feb 20, 1942; Tuscumbia, AL; University of Louisville (KY), B.A., 1964; University of Kentucky Law School, J.D., 1967; Baptist; Married (Elaine Chao); 3 children from previous marriage.

Elected Office: Jefferson County Judge Executive., 1978-1985.

Professional Career: Chief Legislative Assistant, U.S Sen. Marlow Cook, 1968-1970; Deputy Assistant U.S Attorney General, 1974-1975.

DC Office: 317 RSOB 20510, 202-224-2541, Fax: 202-224-2499, mcconnell.senate.gov

State Offices: Bowling Green, 270-781-1673; Fort Wright, 859-578-0188; Lexington, 859-224-8286; London, 606-864-2026; Louisville, 502-582-6304; Paducah, 270-442-4554.

Committees: Senate Majority Leader. *Agriculture, Nutrition & Forestry*: Commodities, Risk Management & Trade; Nutrition, Agricultural Research & Specialty Crops; Rural Development & Energy. *Appropriations*: Agriculture, Rural Development, FDA & Related Agencies; Department of Defense; Department of the Interior, Environment & Related Agencies; Energy & Water Development; Military Construction & Veteran Affairs & Related Agencies; State, Foreign Operations & Related Programs. *Rules & Administration*.

Group Ratings

	ADA	ACLU	AFL-CIO	LCV	ITI	COC	HAFA	ACU	CFG	FRC
2018	-	5%	-	14%	-	90%	65%	82%	53%	100%
2017	0%	C	0%	0%	C	86%	C	80%	81%	100%

Almanac Ratings 2017-18

	Economy	Social	Foreign	Composite
Liberal	7%	7%	0%	5%
Conservative	93%	93%	100%	95%

Key Votes of the 115th Congress

1. Obama-care revision	Y	5. Gun regulations	Y	9. Kavanaugh confirmation	Y
2. Tax Cuts	Y	6. Family planning regs	Y	10. Saudi arms sales	N
3. Dodd-Frank revision	Y	7. Gorsuch confirmation	Y	11. FISA rules	Y
4. Omnibus appropriations	Y	8. Immigration restrictions	Y	12. Military aid in Yemen	N

Election Results

Election	Name (Party)	Vote (%)		Cand. Spent	Ind. Exp. Support	Ind. Exp. Oppose
2014 General	Mitch McConnell (R)	806,787	(56%)	$30,435,557	$5,855,598	$10,552,995
	Alison Lundergan Grimes (D)	584,698	(41%)	$18,829,908	$1,481,186	$17,092,419
	David Patterson (L)	44,240	(3%)			
2014 Primary	Mitch McConnell (R)	213,753	(60%)			
	Matt Bevin (R)	125,787	(35%)			

Prior winning percentages: 2008 (53%), 2002 (65%), 1996 (56%), 1990 (52%), 1984 (50%)

If many politicians look in the mirror and see a president, Republican Mitch McConnell sees a Senate majority leader. And, in mid-2018, Kentucky's senior senator became the longest serving Republican leader in the chamber's history and third overall for a party leader, behind record holder Democrat Mike Mansfield, who served throughout the 1960s and 1970s. McConnell often has pointed to Mansfield as a role model, and there are parallels: McConnell is a restrained personality most comfortable operating outside of the spotlight, with his power derived from mastery of the Senate's arcane procedures and close-to-the vest strategizing. In the age of mass media, McConnell is a dour presence on TV news shows; New York Times columnist Gail Collins once said he has "the natural charisma of an oyster." But McConnell navigates a modern-day Senate that, with its deep ideological and partisan divisions, bears scant resemblance to the more collegial chamber of Mansfield's time. And, since his party regained the Senate majority in 2015, he has shown little hesitancy to dispense with tradition to advance his party's agenda — even at the cost of widespread enmity on and off Capitol Hill.

While Mansfield's party held the majority throughout his time as leader — which coincided with passage of the landmark laws of the civil rights era and President Lyndon Johnson's "Great Society" — McConnell spent his first eight years as leader in the minority. He remains identified more with his ability to erect procedural hurdles during the administration of President Barack Obama — whom McConnell once described as "the most left-wing president since Woodrow Wilson" — than his record of enacting major legislation since his party regained the White House with the election of President Donald Trump. But focusing on McConnell's limited record of legislative accomplishment overlooks his use of the Senate confirmation process to transform the federal judiciary, most notably by holding open a Supreme Court seat for the last 10 months of Obama's presidency. A year after refusing to vote on — or even grant a hearing to — an Obama Supreme Court nominee, McConnell used the "nuclear option" to change Senate rules to thwart a Democratic filibuster of a Trump nominee to the high court. That action expanded a precedent that Senate Democrats created in 2013 for lower-court nominees.

In an interview published by The New York Times in early 2019, McConnell called his thwarting of Obama's effort to appoint Merrick Garland to fill the vacancy left by the death of Justice Antonin Scalia "the most consequential thing I've ever done." It not only let Trump fill the seat with conservative Neil Gorsuch, it let McConnell and Trump appoint a steady flow federal judges at all levels, shifting the judicial branch rightward for a generation. Even as Senate Democrats accused him of damaging institutional norms with his tactics, McConnell has remained a subject of suspicion on the right; conservative populists see him as a Washington establishment figure who has pursued their policy agenda, notably repeal of "Obamacare," with insufficient fervor. Such outsiders form the core of the political base of Trump, with whom McConnell has had a sometimes bumpy relationship — perhaps inevitable given their "very different" personalities, as McConnell has put it. In contrast to Trump's no-holds-barred blasts on Twitter, McConnell chooses his words with care and calculation. "The idea of an off-the-cuff comment is anathema to him," then-Louisville Courier-Journal columnist John David Dyche wrote in a 2009 biography.

The disciplined and determined Republican partisan who runs the Senate began his career on the left wing of his party. Another biographer, former New Republic writer Alec MacGillis, noted in his 2014 book that McConnell supported abortion rights and labor unions — favoring collective bargaining for public employees — in the years before his election to the Senate, and moved rightward with his party. Addison Mitchell McConnell grew up in Alabama, where he overcame polio. The family moved to Louisville, Ky., when McConnell was 13; he has been in politics for all of his adult life. In between college at the University of Louisville and law school at the University of Kentucky, he was an intern for Kentucky Republican Sen. John Sherman Cooper, then a friend of Mansfield and a member of what has become a critically endangered bloc in the Senate: moderate Republicans. McConnell later said he admired Cooper for carrying out "his best judgment instead of pandering to the popular view." The young McConnell watched as Cooper helped round up votes to break a filibuster of the 1964 Civil Rights Act and accompanied Cooper to the White House when Johnson signed the measure.

After graduating from law school, McConnell became chief legislative assistant to Kentucky Sen. Marlow Cook and served in the Justice Department during the Ford administration. After moving back to Louisville, McConnell in 1977 was elected Jefferson County judge-executive. He was re-elected in 1981, and, in 1984, took on Democratic Sen. Walter "Dee" Huddleston. McConnell ran an ad that has become a classic in political advertising circles. It showed bloodhounds sniffing for Huddleston in vacation locales where the incumbent had collected speaking fees while the Senate was in session. McConnell won by about 5,000 votes out of 1.2 million cast. He emerged during his first term as an outspoken foe of campaign finance reform, with his stance a mix of principle — he argued that money represented a form of free speech — and expediency. "I never would have been able to win my race," he later wrote of his first Senate election, "if there had been a limit on the amount of money I could raise and spend."

In 1990, after winning a second term, McConnell tried to get on the leadership ladder by running for the chairmanship of the National Republican Senatorial Committee, the Senate GOP's campaign arm. He lost, but tried again in 1996 and won, serving in the post for the 1998 and 2000 election cycles. McConnell's acumen as a political strategist has been on display since. He has often shaped the party's message, repeating poll-tested phrases intended to sway public opinion. And while one longtime aide characterized McConnell as "the principal enabler of the Trump agenda" in a 2019 New York Times Magazine profile, the Republican leader — in the same article — voiced skepticism about the viability of Trump's base as the long-term future of the Republican Party. "The party has to be bigger than white men who didn't graduate from college," McConnell said after the 2018 elections. "And you look at what happened to the House of Representatives. Look at the suburbs. … We were losing women. And that's not a sustainable position, politically, if you want to be a competitive party."

McConnell became Senate Republican whip after his third re-election victory in 2002. He campaigned for months among his colleagues when the job opened, and his only opponent dropped out several days before the contest. Then, in December 2002, Republican Leader Trent Lott of Mississippi came under a storm of criticism when he spoke favorably of Strom Thurmond's segregationist campaign for president in 1948 at an event honoring Thurmond's 100th birthday. McConnell was Lott's strongest public defender, threatening retaliation against Democrats if they moved to censure him. But, as the controversy showed no sign of abating, he privately recommended to Lott that he "step down as soon as possible." Ordinarily, McConnell might have been in line for the leader's position, but he did not challenge Tennessee's Bill Frist when — urged on by the Bush White House — Frist ran for Lott's post. Frist became Senate majority leader and McConnell majority whip and a key adviser to Frist, who was relatively unversed in Senate procedure. Frist retired in 2006 and Republicans lost their Senate majority that year. McConnell became minority leader.

McConnell stressed the importance of discipline to his GOP colleagues, preaching about how sticking together and playing "team ball" would give them greater leverage. Republicans learned that they crossed McConnell at their own peril. "There are few things more daunting in politics than the determined opposition of McConnell," late Arizona GOP Sen. John McCain once said, perhaps recalling McConnell's ongoing efforts to derail the 2002 McCain-Feingold campaign reform law. In his first two years as minority leader, which intersected with the end of George W. Bush's presidency, McConnell held 41 or more Republicans together to get his Democratic counterpart, Majority Leader Harry Reid, to meet his demands. In the process, the Republicans conducted a record number of filibusters: The number of cloture motions filed during McConnell's first Congress as GOP leader was almost twice the previous high mark. It nearly doubled again in 2013-2014, just before Republicans retook the Senate majority.

For more than six years before becoming leader, McConnell occupied the Senate floor desk at which Kentucky's most famous political figure, Henry Clay — "the Great Compromiser" — once sat. "Clay did not compromise in the sense of forsaking his principles," McConnell said in a floor speech in late 2006. "Rather, his skill was to bring together disparate ideas and forge a consensus among his colleagues. That is a skill we could certainly use more of now." But it was comments made four years later, just before the 2010 midterm election, that exemplified the impede-at-all-costs philosophy critics saw as McConnell's true colors. "The single most important thing we want to achieve is for President Obama to be a one-term president," he said in an interview with National Journal — two years before Obama was due to run for a second term. McConnell complained that another part of the interview had been overlooked, in which he had said of incumbent president, "If he's willing to meet us halfway on some of the biggest issues, it's not inappropriate for us to do business with him." But McConnell was less conciliatory a couple of months earlier when, after having his first one-on-one meeting with Obama, he expressed limited interest in finding common ground. Asked whether there were too much obstruction in the Senate, McConnell replied, "I think the Senate is operating largely like our founding fathers anticipated it would."

McConnell struck a couple budget deals with the Obama White House after the 2010 elections — in which the Republicans gained six Senate seats, leaving Democrats far short of a filibuster-proof majority. In 2011, negotiations stalled in a drawn-out duel over raising the federal debt ceiling, raising fears of a default with broad international consequences. McConnell met with his former Senate colleague, Vice President Joe Biden — known in the White House as "the McConnell Whisperer," according to Bob Woodward's book, "The Price of Politics" — to strike a deal. The agreement denied Obama any increases in taxes or revenue and foisted the hard budget choices on a bipartisan "super committee." The protracted process over increasing the debt limit, a move made necessary by earlier spending decisions by Congress, disturbed many on and off Capitol Hill, but McConnell said the debt ceiling had become a useful GOP bargaining chip. "It's a hostage that's worth ransoming," he told The Washington Post.

The debt ceiling talks served as a prelude to the "fiscal cliff" negotiations in late 2012, which were aimed at averting automatic budget cuts and tax hikes that could impair the nation's economic recovery. By then, the super committee had become gridlocked, Obama had won a second term and Senate Democrats had added a couple seats to their majority. Talks between Obama and congressional Republicans proved fruitless. McConnell reached out to Biden, setting in motion more than a dozen conversations that culminated in a New Year's Day 2013 agreement. McConnell called the deal "an imperfect solution," but said it was preferable to the large spending cuts that would have kicked in — while vowing not to accept any tax hikes in future dealings with Democrats. Still, activists on the right were outraged that it gave Obama his long-desired tax increase on the wealthy. Foreshadowing the attacks from the right to which McConnell would be subjected early in the Trump presidency, ForAmerica Chairman Brent Bozell said in an ad: "His role as President Obama's bag man in the latest fiscal cliff disaster clearly demonstrates that Sen. McConnell is more interested in the art of the bad deal than standing up and fighting for conservative principles."

In early part of the 2016 campaign, McConnell kept his distance from Trump. In May, he issued a perfunctory endorsement after it became clear Trump was on his way to the presidential nomination — but a month later, voiced concerns in a CNN interview that Trump's comments about Hispanic-Americans could hurt efforts to expand the GOP base, much as presidential candidate Barry Goldwater's vote against the 1964 Civil Right Act had alienated African-Americans a half-century earlier. And when the "Access Hollywood" tape, on which Trump can be heard boasting about sexually assaulting women, emerged, McConnell termed the comments "repugnant, and unacceptable in any circumstance." Asked about these criticisms after Trump's election, McConnell offered a less-than-ringing endorsement. "I am not going to relitigate the events of the past," he told reporters. "We have a new president. I would like to see him get off on a positive start." McConnell was more upbeat a month into Trump's presidency. "Back during the campaign, there were a lot of questions: 'Is Trump really a conservative?' … But if you look at the steps that have been taken so far, looks good to me," he said. By that time, McConnell's wife, Elaine Chao, whom he married in 1993, had been named Trump's Transportation secretary; she had been Labor secretary under President George W. Bush.

McConnell took a harder line on Russia than Trump, calling Russian President Vladimir Putin a "thug," although he turned aside calls from McCain and others to create a special Senate committee to look into Russian interference in the 2016 elections. Likewise, in late fall of 2018, McConnell refused to take up legislation — approved by the Judiciary Committee with bipartisan support — to protect special counsel Robert Mueller from firing by Trump. Mueller was investigating whether there had been any collusion between Russia and the Trump campaign. And in early 2019, McConnell stood to the side and publicly deferred to Trump's decision to force a shutdown of the federal government after the new House Democratic majority refused to give the president funding for a wall along the southern border — even as McConnell privately told a luncheon of senators that the shutdown was not working. "There is no education in the second kick of a mule," McConnell said, using a favorite expression, according to The Hill.

Several months earlier, in an apparent high point in their relationship, the president called McConnell "the greatest leader, in my opinion, in history" at a Kentucky rally. It was a major turnaround from July 2017, when Republican efforts to repeal the Affordable Care Act collapsed in the Senate. "Mitch, get back to work," Trump tweeted. McConnell, speaking to a Rotary Club in his home state a month later, said: "Our new president, of course, has not been in this line of work before. I think he had excessive expectations about how quickly things happen in the democratic process." McConnell also said he was "not a fan of tweeting, and I've said that to him privately." That didn't stop Trump from responding with a tweet: "Can you believe that Mitch McConnell, who has screamed Repeal & Replace for 7 years, couldn't get it done." Asked by reporters whether McConnell should step down, Trump said, "If he doesn't get repeal and replace done, and if he doesn't get taxes done, meaning cuts and reform, and if he doesn't get a very easy one to get done, infrastructure … then you can ask me that question."

McConnell got the $1.5 trillion tax bill passed at the end of 2017, after a last-ditch effort to repeal the Affordable Care Act collapsed. McConnell started the Trump presidency with a Republican caucus of 52, two fewer than the previous Congress. He faced a new Democratic counterpart, Minority

Leader Chuck Schumer — who, taking a page from McConnell's playbook, held his caucus together in the face of efforts to do away with "Obamacare." And, after seven years repeating "repeal and replace," Republicans still had no consensus on what to replace the health care law with. Three repeal options — crafted in closed, Republican-only sessions directed by McConnell's office — died on the Senate floor in July 2017; 13 Republicans voted against at least one of the three options, enough to sink all of them in the face of solid Democratic resistance. A fourth option, which would have replaced the Affordable Care Act with block grants, died three months later.

McConnell opted for a more open and inclusive process with the tax cut and reform bill — although Democrats charged that the modus operandi fell far short of "regular order." Unlike with the health care legislation, McConnell saw to it there was a committee markup. "We had endless meetings getting everybody comfortable with the substance," McConnell told The New York Times afterward. "That was a stark contrast with a lot of the meetings we had on health care." The final bill was approved 51-48, with all Republicans on board. It included repeal of the mandate on individuals to purchase health care — which, as McConnell noted, "takes a big chunk" out of the Affordable Care Act.

"I love the tax bill and a lot of the other things we did. But I think lifetime appointments — not only to the Supreme Court but to the circuit courts — are the way you have the longest lasting impact on the country," McConnell told Politico in October 2018, shortly after the rancorous debate over Trump's nomination of federal appeals court Judge Brett Kavanaugh to the Supreme Court. "The president and his team have sent up, in my view, excellent judges, and we've had the unity we've needed … to get them confirmed." In a speech to the conservative Heritage Foundation the same month, McConnell boasted of confirming 29 circuit court judges since Trump took office — 16 percent of all appeals court jurists. He touted this as a record pace "in any administration in history." Republicans confirmed 83 judges at the circuit and district court levels during the first two years of the Trump administration. According to Politico, that was 20 more judges than were approved during the first two years of the Obama administration, when Democrats controlled the Senate.

Kavanaugh's nomination was the one of the fiercest battles in a war over judicial appointments in a decade. The war escalated early in the Obama administration when Republicans, under McConnell's leadership, insisted on confirming district court nominees individually — departing from the tradition of approving them in groups. McConnell slowed the judicial nomination process further after becoming majority leader toward the end of Obama's tenure in 2015 — after Reid, two years earlier, had first invoked the " nuclear option " amid delays in confirming presidential appointments. The move changed Senate rules to prevent filibusters of executive branch appointments and judicial nominations below the Supreme Court level. McConnell all but telegraphed his future intentions that day in 2013. "You will regret this, and you may regret it a lot sooner than you think," he told Reid. By most accounts, McConnell and Reid — another low-key figure who preferred operating behind the scenes — had perhaps the worst relationship of any two Senate leaders since such posts were formalized in the early 1900s.

Determined to prevent Obama from altering the ideological makeup of the court less than a year before he was due to leave office, McConnell refused to hold confirmation hearings or a vote on a replacement for Scalia until the next president was sworn in. "This nomination will be determined by whoever wins the presidency in the polls," McConnell said, urging Obama to reconsider even submitting a nominee — more than three weeks before the president nominated Garland, a federal appeals court judge. Most Republicans refused to even meet with Garland, widely seen as a moderate. McConnell's move was unprecedented. "What is remarkable is the opposition is not to a particular candidate or even to the notion Obama will only nominate someone too extreme, but that he should not have any right to have a nomination considered," Julian Zelizer, a professor of history and public affairs at Princeton University, told The New York Times. McConnell's gamble paid off; Trump won the presidency and nominated another federal appeals court judge, Gorsuch, less than two weeks after taking office.

Schumer, as leader of a 48-member minority in which many remained angry over the treatment of Garland, urged a filibuster of the Gorsuch nomination. According to The Wall Street Journal, some Democrats — to avert extending the "nuclear option" to Supreme Court nominations — discussed providing enough votes to confirm Gorsuch in return for a commitment not to change the 60-vote supermajority threshold for future nominees. But such a deal never materialized. On April 6, all but three Democrats voted against ending debate on the nomination, leaving it five votes short. Then, on a 52-48 party-line vote, the Senate changed its rules and dropped the 60-vote threshold — clearing the way for Gorsuch's confirmation on a 54-45 vote.

The rules change affected only presidential nominations, not legislation, and McConnell — who frequently used legislative filibusters while in the minority — said there were no plans to change that. "Who would be the biggest beneficiary of that right now? It would be the majority, right?" McConnell told reporters. "There's not a single senator in the majority who thinks we ought to change the legislative filibuster. Not one." Later that year, the issue played into the tensions between McConnell and Trump, as the president demanded — as usual, via Twitter — that Senate Republicans, amid the failure of the Obamacare repeal, scrap the 60-vote threshold in legislative debates. McConnell replied that, even if he wanted to make the change, the support was lacking among Senate Republicans. "The votes are simply not there," he said. In the spring of 2019, McConnell escalate the partisan parliamentary warfare when he engineered a rules change for debate on the confirmation on sub-Cabinet officials and district court judges—reducing the time allowed from 30 hours to just two hours once cloture was invoked. It was designed to limit the Democrats' use of delaying tactics similar to those that McConnell used during the Obama administration.

Meanwhile, there were signs of an improving relationship between McConnell and Schumer. In early 2018, they negotiated a deal to raise the debt ceiling while providing an additional $300 billon over two years for defense and domestic programs. The same month, Schumer appeared at a lecture series at the McConnell Center at the University of Louisville, and gave a warm introduction to his Republican counterpart. "Actually, the Senate is a pretty collegial place. We don't dislike each other. We have to work together," McConnell was quoted as saying by The Washington Post, in an apparent response to those who suggested such collegiality had eroded on his watch. Any collegiality was tested later in the year after the retirement of Supreme Court Justice Anthony Kennedy, which allowed Trump to make his second Supreme Court appointment in less than two years. Despite widespread Democratic opposition, the nomination of Kavanaugh appeared to be on track for approval — until sexual assault allegations dating to his high school days surfaced.

With control of the Senate at stake in the coming midterm elections, McConnell sought to keep the nomination on track for approval before Election Day — while resisting calls for an FBI investigation into the allegations against Kavanaugh from Christine Blasey Ford. "Give the American people one good reason why we shouldn't ask the FBI to investigate," Schumer told McConnell on the Senate floor, adding of his rival: "He slowed down a nomination to the Supreme Court for a year — and now a few days is too much. Give me a break." He later accused McConnell of telling "blatant falsehoods … day after day on this floor." Scrambling to line up the votes needed for confirmation, McConnell agreed to an FBI investigation — and a weeklong delay in the process — after Arizona Republican Jeff Flake said he would not consider voting for Kavanaugh without a probe. The FBI failed to corroborate allegations by Blasey Ford and other accusers, and, on Oct. 6, Kavanaugh was confirmed on a 50-48 party-line vote. The furor over Kavanaugh created a backlash among grassroots conservatives, leading to the defeat of Democrats in three red states in November and the growth of Republican's Senate majority to 53.

Eleventh-hour campaigning by Trump was a major factor in the outcome in those races, underscoring the political logic of the strange alliance between McConnell and the president. But, a year earlier, the two men had gone in different directions as Republicans lost a Senate seat in deep-red Alabama in a December 2017 special election, trimming their advantage to 51-49. When longtime Republican Sen. Jeff Sessions was named Trump's attorney general in early 2017, Alabama's attorney general, Luther Strange, was appointed to the seat. Roy Moore, the controversial former chief justice of the state Supreme Court, jumped into the election to fill the final three years of Sessions' term — while seeking to tie Strange, a onetime Washington lobbyist, to McConnell. Like Moore, Rep. Mo Brooks positioned himself as an outsider in the Republican primary; he even campaigned from a bus featuring a "Ditch Mitch" sign. Moore finished first, and he and Strange advanced to a runoff. A McConnell-affiliated super PAC spent more than $4 million on behalf of Strange, but Moore won the late September runoff 55%-45%. McConnell issued an endorsement saying that Moore "ran a spirited campaign centered around a dissatisfaction with the progress made in Washington. I share that frustration and believe that enacting the agenda the American people voted for last November requires us all to work together."

But, in early November, four women — speaking on the record to The Washington Post — described sexual advances Moore had made on them nearly 40 years earlier when they were in their teens and he was in his 30s; one was 14 at the time. Publicly, McConnell called for Moore to step aside, and the National Republican Senate Committee cut off support to the Moore campaign. He also hinted that Moore could be expelled from the Senate if he won, saying in an appearance on ABC's "This Week" that the Ethics Committee would "have to consider the matters that have been litigated in the campaign." Privately, fearing that fallout from the controversy could endanger the

GOP Senate majority the following year, McConnell urged Trump to keep his distance from Moore. He also was reported to have commissioned a memo by election lawyers with several scenarios for heading off Moore: One called for Strange to resign and a new senator appointed, who would then run as an independent after the governor delayed the special election. But Trump, who had taken heat from his political base for endorsing Strange over Moore in the runoff, not only brushed aside McConnell's advice, he sought to rescue Moore's candidacy with a strong endorsement in the closing week — he even appeared at a rally for Moore miles from the Alabama border. But it was not enough to overcome Moore's political baggage, and Democrat Doug Jones won 50%-48%.

In Kentucky, which has trended increasingly red, McConnell has long been the de facto boss of the state Republican Party. But his grip has been challenged in recent years with the rise of the party's tea party wing. After helping Republican Jim Bunning win a Senate seat in 1998, McConnell lost faith in Bunning's political skills — and, going into the 2010 election, made clear he felt that Bunning should not run again. Bunning was livid, but bowed out, and McConnell's choice to replace him was Kentucky Secretary of State Trey Grayson. Also running was Rand Paul, son of Texas Rep. Ron Paul — a onetime Libertarian Party presidential candidate. In the primary, Rand Paul, with tea party support, trounced Grayson, and went on to win in November. Confronted with a difficult bid for another term in 2014, McConnell reached out to Paul — endorsing Paul's unsuccessful bid for the 2016 Republican presidential nomination.

McConnell took the challenge in his fifth re-election race seriously, given his low approval ratings in state polling; by the fall of 2013, he had raised more than $13 million. He faced a serious threat in the GOP primary from Matt Bevin, a wealthy businessman favored by tea party forces. But Bevin was an inexperienced candidate who made numerous errors, and McConnell crushed him 60%-35%. Bitter from the loss, Bevin declined to endorse McConnell in that year's general election, and, a year later, launched a campaign for governor. After coming out on the losing side in the 2010 primary that Paul had won, McConnell stayed out of the 2015 gubernatorial primary. Bevin won narrowly — and, in a reversal, wooed McConnell's support, while excising a large number of anti-McConnell posts from his Twitter account. It worked. "I think we need to let bygones be bygones and get together and try to change Kentucky," McConnell told the Lexington-Herald Leader. In November, Bevin was elected to succeed term-limited Democratic Gov. Steve Beshear.

In the 2014 general election, McConnell faced Democrat Alison Lundergan Grimes, Kentucky's 34-year-old secretary of state. She was seen as a credible opponent, but committed several errors, notably refusing to answer a question about whether she had voted for Obama in 2012. It was widely viewed as an opportunistic effort to keep the president, highly unpopular in Kentucky, at a distance. Democrats thought the race would be about which candidate voters liked better, a fight they thought they could win given McConnell's weak approval numbers. Instead, the contest became about who voters trusted, and McConnell relentlessly tied Lundergan Grimes to Obama at every turn. McConnell won with 56 percent of the vote.

McConnell has seldom had it easy at re-election time. He had spirited competition from former Louisville Mayor Harvey Sloane in 1990, future Gov. Beshear in 1996, and Lois Combs Weinberg, daughter of a former governor, in 2002. Sloane and Beshear held McConnell to 52 percent and 55 percent, respectively. McConnell did better against Weinberg, winning with 65 percent. In 2008, Democrats recruited Bruce Lunsford, a multimillionaire hospital and nursing home operator. Lunsford spent nearly $11 million, more than $7 million of it his own money, and ran a string of negative ads against McConnell — one a takeoff on McConnell's bloodhound ad of a quarter of a century earlier. McConnell won with 53 percent, making him the longest serving senator in Kentucky history.

McConnell has signaled that he plans to seek a seventh term in 2020, and, once again, could face a competitive race. Several polls in late 2017 and 2018 found his approval rating to be around 30 percent. Efforts were said to be underway to recruit a tea party-aligned challenger in the GOP primary, even though Bevin said that he would "of course" support McConnell this time around. On the Democratic side, Schumer reportedly was encouraging Amy McGrath – the former Marine combat pilot who narrowly lost a 2018 House challenge in the 6th District – to take on McConnell. In addition, Matt Jones, host of the state's most popular radio show, Kentucky Sports Radio, said he was considering a run. If McConnell wins re-election, he would be on track in early 2023 to surpass his role model, Mansfield, as the longest serving Senate leader.

Rand Paul (R)

Elected 2010, term expires 2022, 2nd term, b. Jan 07, 1963; Pittsburgh, PA; Baylor University (TX), 1984; Duke University (NC), M.D., 1988; Presbyterian; Married (Kelley Paul); 3 children.

Professional Career: Ophthalmologist, 1993-2010; Founder, S. KY Lions Eye Clinic, 1995.

DC Office: 167 RSOB 20510, 202-224-4343, Fax: 202-228-6917, paul.senate.gov

State Offices: Bowling Green, 270-782-8303; Louisville, 502-582-5341.

Committees: *Foreign Relations*: Europe & Regional Security Cooperation; Internat'l Dev Instit & Internat'l Econ, Energy & Environ Policy; Near East, South Asia, Central Asia & Counterterrorism; State Dept & USAID Mngmnt, Internat'l Ops & Internat'l Dev. *Health, Education, Labor & Pensions*: Children & Families (Chmn); Employment & Workplace Safety. *Homeland Security & Government Affairs*: Federal Spending Oversight & Emergency Management (Chmn); Investigations. *Small Business & Entrepreneurship*.

Group Ratings

	ADA	ACLU	AFL-CIO	LCV	ITI	COC	HAFA	ACU	CFG	FRC
2018	-	45%	-	7%	-	80%	88%	100%	100%	100%
2017	10%	C	14%	5%	C	71%	C	100%	93%	100%

Almanac Ratings 2017-18

	Economy	Social	Foreign	Composite
Liberal	19%	19%	56%	31%
Conservative	82%	82%	44%	69%

Key Votes of the 115th Congress

1. Obama-care revision	Y	5. Gun regulations	Y	9. Kavanaugh confirmation	Y
2. Tax Cuts	Y	6. Family planning regs	Y	10. Saudi arms sales	Y
3. Dodd-Frank revision	Y	7. Gorsuch confirmation	Y	11. FISA rules	N
4. Omnibus appropriations	N	8. Immigration restrictions	N	12. Military aid in Yemen	Y

Election Results

Election	Name (Party)	Vote (%)		Cand. Spent	Ind. Exp. Support	Ind. Exp. Oppose
2016 General	Rand Paul (R)	1,090,177	(57%)	$5,994,444	$83,795	
	Jim Gray (D)	813,246	(43%)	$4,665,712	$337,895	$563,868
2016 Primary	Rand Paul (R)	169,180	(85%)			
	James Gould (R)	16,611	(8%)			
	Stephen Slaughter (R)	13,728	(7%)			

Prior winning percentages: 2010 (56%)

Rand Paul benefitted from propitious political timing when he launched his first run for elected office a decade ago. He gained political experience working on his father's 2008 bid to be the GOP's presidential nominee, but was still just an ophthalmologist with a limited statewide profile when he announced a Senate bid in 2009. When a friend asked what his chances of success were, Paul chuckled: "Oh, I guess probably in the 5 percent range." But Paul waded in just in time to catch the rising tide of the tea party movement, enabling him to upset the Kentucky GOP establishment and win election as the state's junior senator. Less than four years later, some polls showed him leading the crowded field of prospects for the GOP presidential nomination, with a Time magazine cover anointing him "The Most Interesting Man in Politics." However, by the time the first delegates to party's nominating convention had been chosen in early 2016, Paul's bid for the presidency had come crashing down.

Paul shared much of the ideology of his father, who had left the GOP to run as the Libertarian Party's White House candidate in 1988 and returned to bid for the Republican presidential nominations in 2008 and 2012. But the appeal of Paul's noninterventionist — critics would say neo-isolationist — foreign policy views fell flat in the 2016 election cycle, amid the rise of the Islamic State terrorist group and escalating terror attacks abroad. And, despite his status as a political outsider — often reinforced via his tactics on Capitol Hill — Paul found himself eclipsed by an outsider with more celebrity: Donald Trump. Salvaging re-election to a second Senate term, Paul returned to Capitol Hill in early 2017 for a surprising third act in his political career: occasional golfing partner and frequent defender of Trump, whom Paul had derided as a "delusional narcissist and an orange-faced windbag" during their presidential campaign rivalry. In mid-2018, as Trump's conciliatory stance toward Russian President Vladimir Putin generated bipartisan criticism in Congress, Paul stood alone in supporting the president's posture toward a nation widely blamed for meddling in the 2016 presidential election.

Born in Pittsburgh, Paul was raised in Lake Jackson, Texas, where his father, former Rep. Ron Paul, set up an obstetrics practice. Rand Paul and his father have denied reports that he was named after author Ayn Rand, whose advocacy of laissez-faire capitalism made her highly popular in libertarian circles. Named Randal at birth, Paul was known as Randy growing up and switched to Rand as an adult. Paul followed his father's footsteps and became a physician. He attended Baylor University but did not earn an undergraduate degree. He received a high score on the entrance exam to Duke University School of Medicine and was admitted. After graduating, Paul moved to Bowling Green, Ky., near his wife's hometown, and opened an ophthalmology practice and a clinic to treat low-income patients. Foreshadowing his political career, Paul took an outsider stance in medicine: Unhappy with the American Board of Ophthalmology, which had long certified practitioners of that specialty, he mounted an unsuccessful effort to create a rival certification board.

While helping his father's campaigns, he mulled running for office himself; when he gave a speech on April 15, 2009 — Tax Day — to a tea party group, the energy of the crowd convinced him "something enormous was going on," he later told the Bowling Green Daily News. Two months later, Republican Sen. Jim Bunning announced his retirement and Paul declared his candidacy. The favorite for the nomination was Kentucky Secretary of State Trey Grayson, who won the backing of Senate Republican Leader Mitch McConnell, de facto boss of the Kentucky GOP. But Paul had access to his father's devoted network of contributors. Backers embraced his outspoken views that the government should stick to the functions outlined in the Constitution — that agencies such as the Environmental Protection Agency and the Education Department should be abolished and the powers of the Federal Reserve curbed. Foreshadowing criticism that would later confront his presidential bid, Paul faced ads saying he was weak on national security. But Paul, boosted by the accelerating tea party movement, won the primary 59%-35% — a rout. McConnell made a point of appearing at a victory rally for Paul, who voted for McConnell for Senate GOP leader after declining to say whether he would do so.

State Attorney General Jack Conway narrowly defeated Lt. Gov. Dan Mongiardo for the Democratic nomination. Conway hammered Paul for having voiced opposition in principle to — but not outright repeal of —the 1964 Civil Rights Act as government interference with private business. Conway also seized on Paul's support for raising the Social Security retirement age and opposing federal involvement in drug enforcement. In contrast to the anti-abortion Paul, Conway supported abortion rights and the Affordable Care Act, which Democrats had passed earlier in 2010. But Conway hurt himself with an ad that political insiders considered over the top. In it, the narrator asks, "Why was Rand Paul a member of a secret society that called the Holy Bible a 'hoax'? ... Why did Rand Paul once tie a woman up, tell her to bow down before a false idol and say ... 'God was Aqua Buddha'?" The charges referred to pranks during Paul's college years. GQ magazine had reported Paul once belonged to a secret society that often taunted the school's administration; he and a friend were once accused of blindfolding a female acquaintance and trying to get her to smoke marijuana. Paul defeated Conway 56%-44%.

Upon arriving in the Senate, he established a Tea Party Caucus and sought to block anything he viewed as government overreach. It highlighted the philosophical chasm that has separated Paul from many other Republicans, particularly concerning U.S. foreign policy and the use of surveillance to fight terrorism. Just months after taking office, Paul tried to block extension of the USA Patriot Act, which was passed in response to 9/11. And, in 2013, he filibustered for nearly 13 hours to protest the Obama administration's use of lethal drone strikes; the move delayed John Brennan's confirmation as CIA director. It was not the last time Paul would make life difficult for Brennan, who, after Trump took office, emerged an outspoken White House critic. Trump retaliated in August

2018 by stripping Brennan of his national security clearance — a move that, according to The New York Times, occurred shortly after Paul suggested it to the president.

In January 2012, Paul made national news when he refused a pat-down from the Transportation Security Administration at a Tennessee airport. And on Capitol Hill, he unsuccessfully tried to dilute federal gun restrictions. But Paul found common ground with Democrats on other issues related to the criminal justice system. In 2013, he teamed on legislation with Democratic Sen. Patrick Leahy of Vermont, then Judiciary Committee chairman, to give federal judges greater flexibility on imposing mandatory minimum sentences.

As the 2016 campaign approached, Paul used the Senate chamber to promote his presidential aspirations. In May 2015, he conducted an 11-hour filibuster to delay another reauthorization of the Patriot Act, objecting to the government's bulk collection of phone records. His tactics not only led to a brief lapse in some government surveillance powers granted under the law, they forced Senate Majority Leader McConnell to swallow House-passed changes in the statute that he opposed. McConnell, who had built a relationship with Paul — going so far as to embrace his presidential bid — was irritated. In comments aimed at Paul, McConnell blasted those who he said were spreading disinformation about the Patriot Act. And the party's 2008 presidential nominee, Arizona Sen. John McCain — who two years earlier had labeled Paul a "wacko bird" — suggested the Kentucky senator was putting his political ambitions above national security; Paul's campaign website contained pitches like, "Get your Rand Paul filibuster starter pack!"

Paul was unapologetic. "The people who argue that the world will end and we will be overrun by jihadists are trying to use fear," Paul said. "Little by little, we've allowed our freedom to slip away." Several days earlier, he blamed other Republicans for the growth of ISIS. "ISIS exists and grew stronger because of the hawks in our party who gave arms indiscriminately, and most of those arms were snatched up by ISIS," he said on MSNBC. Paul took some steps to assuage his party's interventionist wing before his presidential campaign: While opposing the arming of rebel forces in Syria's civil war, he expressed support for limited air strikes against ISIS.

Such attempts at political balancing acts were indicative of a broader problem for Paul's presidential hopes: In the view of insiders, he muddled his message, alienating portions of his libertarian base without bringing in a lot of new support. "He wanted to win more than he wanted to support the principles," Frayda Levin, a libertarian-leaning GOP donor, told Politico. Seeking to make peace with the party establishment, Paul appeared in ads underwritten by the U.S. Chamber of Commerce during the 2014 midterm elections; back in Kentucky, he endorsed McConnell over tea party challenger Matt Bevin. But such efforts complicated Paul's fundraising: By the beginning of 2016, his presidential campaign was effectively broke, and Paul had sunk low enough in the polls that he failed to qualify for a January candidates' debate during prime time. In February 2016, Paul dropped out of the race, days after the first-in-the-nation Iowa caucuses. He finished fifth with 5 percent of the vote — less than a quarter of his father's 21.5 percent showing in Iowa four years earlier.

While pursuing his party's presidential nomination, Paul stayed on the ballot for reelection to the Senate. He took some political heat for his two-track candidacy, but also faced a legal obstacle: Kentucky law prohibits candidates from appearing on the ballot for two offices in the same election. To get around this, the Republican Party of Kentucky held a presidential caucus in March 2016 separate from the state's May primary. Paul agreed to provide $250,000 to help cover the increased cost. Democrats found a candidate in Lexington Mayor Jim Gray, who brought personal money and a business background to the race. Gray had been elected twice as an openly gay candidate in a state where, several months earlier, a county clerk garnered international attention for going to jail rather than issuing marriage licenses to same-sex couples. But Gray's sexuality was not his biggest political obstacle, according to his backers. "There are [poll] numbers that suggest that being allied in any way to President Barack Obama is much more damaging than being gay," former Rep. Ben Chandler told Roll Call. Gray acknowledged he had voted for Obama, and Paul hammered him for support of Obama's choice for a successor: Hillary Clinton. Paul won 57%-43%, as Trump defeated Clinton 63%-33% in the state.

Returning to Capitol Hill, Paul's hard-line philosophical stance complicated efforts by Republican leaders to repeal the Affordable Care Act. After three GOP-crafted options to jettison "Obamacare" failed to attract enough votes to pass the Senate in July 2017, Republican leaders tried again a couple of months later — with a plan to replace the Affordable Care Act with block grants to states. However, the effort was abandoned when it became clear a handful of Republicans would not vote for it — Paul among them. While the other dissenters felt the bill had not been thoroughly considered or went too far, Paul contended it did not go far enough in getting the government out of the private insurance market. While the final alternative — sponsored by Sens. Bill Cassidy of Louisiana and Lindsey Graham of South Carolina — would have allowed states to apply for waivers to get rid of most aspects of Obamacare, Paul didn't trust the federal government to grant such waivers.

"I've already spent the better part of the year arguing with an army of bureaucrats and lawyers in the administration trying to get them to do something President Trump and I AGREE should be done — loosening up the rules on joining group plans," Paul wrote in an op-ed for Fox News in September 2017. The following month, Trump issued an executive order — on which he and Paul had collaborated — to expand availability of less expensive insurance across state lines; Paul hailed Trump's move as "the biggest free-market reform of health care in a generation." Earlier, the president had unsuccessfully sought to prod Paul — gently, by Trump standards — to back the Graham-Cassidy legislation. "Rand Paul is a friend of mine but he is such a negative force when it comes to fixing healthcare. Graham-Cassidy Bill is GREAT! Ends Ocare!" Trump tweeted.

It was a far cry from three years earlier, when Paul asserted that "a speck of dirt is way more qualified to be president" than Trump and Trump had tweeted that Paul "reminds me of a spoiled brat without a properly functioning brain." Differences remained between the two — particularly on foreign policy. But on most high-profile votes, Paul lined up behind the president.

In July 2018, Paul threatened to block the nomination of Brett Kavanaugh to the Supreme Court over a ruling that Kavanaugh — as a federal appeals court judge — had made in favor of the bulk collection of phone records; it was the same issue that prompted Paul to filibuster the 2015 Patriot Act reauthorization. "This is a big deal," Paul told Politico. "Kavanaugh's position is basically that national security trumps privacy. And he said it very strongly and explicitly." But after meeting with Kavanaugh, Paul said he would vote for him — because no one will "ever completely agree with a nominee" and nominees "must be judged on the totality of their views, character, and opinions." A similar scenario had played out when Trump nominated Mike Pompeo to be secretary of State. Paul vowed to do "whatever it takes" to block the nomination, citing Pompeo's support for military intervention in Iraq, Iran, Syria and Afghanistan. But Paul, a member of the Foreign Relations Committee, changed his mind just before the panel voted — saying Trump had assured him Pompeo believed the Iraq War had been a mistake and that it was time for U.S. troops to leave Afghanistan. "I want Trump to be Trump," Paul told The Associated Press. "Rand Paul is a very special guy," Trump told reporters. "He's never let me down."

Such episodes highlighted a suspicion the men share a similar view of the Washington establishment in general and the intelligence community in particular. Paul voted against Trump's nomination of Gina Haspel to succeed Pompeo as CIA director, describing her as the "head cheerleader for waterboarding" — a reference to her role in "enhanced interrogation techniques" during the George W. Bush administration. Paul, echoing the president's calls for an end to the investigation into the Trump campaign's possible ties to Russia, told a conservative gathering that his stance "fits with what I've been saying for a decade now," according to The New York Times. "We've allowed too much power to gravitate to these intelligence agencies," Paul said. When Trump, in Helsinki, appeared to believe Putin's account over that of U.S. intelligence agencies about Russian election interference, Paul defended the president. "The hatred for the president is so intense that partisans would rather risk war than give diplomacy a chance," Paul said in a floor speech, describing Trump's critics as "unhinged" and "crazy." A month later, Paul flew to Moscow to meet with Russian legislators.

Nearly 10 months earlier, in November 2017, Paul made national headlines after a bizarre episode at his Kentucky home. He was on a riding lawn mower when he was tackled by his neighbor — a fellow physician named Rene Boucher. Paul broke ribs and bruised lungs; Boucher pleaded guilty to felony assault and got 30 days in jail. Boucher attacked Paul because the senator had been stacking yard trimmings along their shared property line, according to Boucher's attorney. There was an element of mystery surrounding the altercation: After initially saying Paul was fine, his office told the AP two days later that he had suffered five broken ribs. Paul later put the physical damage at six broken ribs and a pleural effusion — excess fluid around the lungs. Boucher's attorney denied suggestions that the attack had been politically motivated. "It was a very regrettable dispute between two neighbors over a matter that most people would regard as trivial," the attorney said.

After a couple of weeks of recuperation, Paul — who later was awarded more than $580,000 by a Kentucky jury in a lawsuit against Boucher — returned to Capitol Hill. In early 2018, he delayed passage for several hours of a bipartisan agreement providing an additional $300 billon over two years for defense and domestic programs. "We have Republicans hand-in-hand with Democrats offering us trillion-dollar deficits," Paul told the Senate. "I want people to feel uncomfortable." Indeed, several of Paul's colleagues appeared exasperated by early morning House and Senate sessions made necessary by Paul's ephemeral protest. Pennsylvania Republican Rep. Charlie Dent said, "When Rand Paul pulls a stunt like this, it [is] easy to understand why it's difficult to be Rand Paul's next-door neighbor."

James Comer (R)

Elected 2016, 2nd term, b. Aug 19, 1972; Carthage, TN; Western Kentucky University, B.S., 1993; Baptist; Married (Tamera Jo); 3 children.

Elected Office: Chairman, Monroe County Republican Party, 1993-1995; Delegate, Republican National Convention, 1996; KY House, 2001-2012; Commissioner, KY Department of Agriculture, 2012-2015.

Professional Career: Businessman; Farmer.

DC Office: 1037 LHOB 20515, 202-225-3115, Fax: 202-225-3547

State Offices: Madisonville, 270-487-9509; Paducah, 270-408-1865; Tompkinsville, 270-487-9509.

Committees: *Agriculture*: Biotechnology, Horticulture & Research; Livestock & Foreign Agriculture. *Education & Labor*: Civil Rights & Human Services (RMM); Higher Education & Workforce Investment. *Oversight & Reform*: Government Operations; Subcommittee on Economic & Consumer Policy; Subcommittee on Environment (RMM).

Group Ratings

	ADA	ACLU	AFL-CIO	LCV	ITI	COC	HAFA	ACU	CFG	FRC
2018	-	14%	-	0%	-	75%	86%	88%	74%	100%
2017	0%	C	5%	6%	C	93%	C	96%	92%	100%

Almanac Ratings 2017-18

	Economy	Social	Foreign	Composite
Liberal	2%	7%	0%	3%
Conservative	98%	93%	100%	97%

Key Votes of the 115th Congress

1. Obama-care revision	Y	5. Family planning regs	Y	9. Guantanamo prisoners	N
2. Tax Cuts	Y	6. Body cameras/immigration	N	10. Ground missiles, limit	N
3. Omnibus appropriations	N	7. Abortion ban	Y	11. Defense Dept. spending	Y
4. Dodd-Frank revision	Y	8. Concealed carry	Y	12. FISA rules	Y

Election Results

Election	Name (Party)	Vote (%)		Cand. Spent	Ind. Exp. Support	Ind. Exp. Oppose
2018 General	James Comer (R)	172,167	(69%)	$570,861		
	Paul Walker (D)	78,849	(31%)	$47,548	$1,048	
2018 Primary	James Comer (R)	(100%)				

Prior winning percentages: 2016 (73%)

Republican James Comer breezed to election in 2016 in what was a consolation prize of sorts, following his 83-vote loss to Matt Bevin in the Republican primary for governor the year before. He has positioned himself for another statewide run. Meanwhile, he established himself as a House ally of Senate Majority Leader Mitch McConnell and scored a big win for Kentucky farmers.

Comer grew up in rural Monroe County. He had dreamed of becoming a farmer. After graduating from Western Kentucky University, he borrowed $120,000 from a community bank to purchase his first farm and began his business. It became one of the largest farming operations in south central Kentucky. He had other interests in insurance and restaurant businesses. Comer also started young in politics, winning his first election to the state House at age 28. He served 11 years in what was then the Democratic-controlled House, where he claimed good bipartisan relationships and kept his distance from Republican "party bosses."

In 2011, Comer was elected to a four-year term as Kentucky commissioner of agriculture, the only Republican who won statewide that year. He supported legalizing the production of industrial hemp as a potential cash crop for Kentucky farmers. In his 2015 face-off for governor, Comer ran against the more outspoken conservative Bevin, who had taken on veteran Sen. McConnell in the Republican primary in 2014. "I've fought corruption. I've made government more efficient. I've focused on trying to recruit new industries and good-paying jobs to this state. I've passed legislation," Comer said in a pre-primary interview with the Lexington Herald-Leader. The official recanvass of the primary for governor showed Bevin prevailing by 83 votes.

When 11-term Republican Rep. Ed Whitfield announced his retirement, Comer was the early frontrunner and was not seriously threatened. His chief GOP challenger was Mike Pape, who gained local political connections during his many years as district director for Whitfield. Pape raised $420,000 to the $1 million that Comer raised for the campaign. The U.S. Chamber of Commerce spent another $100,000 on behalf of Comer. He won the four-candidate primary with 61 percent of the vote to 23 percent for Pape. After more experienced Democrats decided not to run, challenger Samuel Gaskins had a minimal presence. Comer won the general election, 73%-27%.

In the House, his chief committee assignment was Agriculture, where he brought extensive first-hand experience. The first bill he filed would loosen regulations on industrial hemp by reclassifying it from a controlled substance to an agricultural crop. Democrats, including Reps. Jared Polis of Colorado and Earl Blumenauer of Oregon, joined Comer in holding press conferences and other events on his proposal. "We've proven it's not a drug," Comer said. He told the Lexington Herald-Leader that the support of McConnell, who had kept in touch with the positive response of Kentucky farmers, was persuasive with "the handful of members who still cringe when I come up to talk to them about hemp." McConnell had added to the 2014 farm bill a state-based pilot program for research of industrial hemp. The House did not include his proposal to legalize hemp in its version of the 2018 farm bill. But with Comer serving on the House-Senate conference committee that crafted the final deal on the bill, it included the provision, which he called "a significant win."

On the Small Business Committee, Comer won House passage in January 2019 of his bill to clarify that the advocacy office of the Small Business Administration had the authority to research relevant issues in international economics.

In November 2018, Comer won all 35 counties and was reelected, 69%-31%, against Democrat Paul Walker, an English professor at Murray State University. He had no primary opposition. Prior to Bevin's announcement in January 2019 that he would seek reelection, Comer said that he would have run if there was a vacancy but that he had "no interest" in making another run against Bevin. Comer, who occasionally second-guessed Bevin's actions as governor, told a reporter that the two of them had not spoken during the three years since he was elected. At age 46, Comer should have plenty of other opportunities to run statewide.

KY-1: Western Kentucky

Cook Partisan Voting Index: R+23

Population		Race and Ethnicity		Income	
Total	721,011	White	87.5%	Median Income	$40,902
Land area (sq. miles)	12,080	Black	6.9%	District Income Rank	408
Pop/ sq mi	59.7	Latino	3%	Poverty Rate	19.3%
Born in State	69.4%	Asian	0.6%	With health insurance	91%
		Two or more races	1.7%	Cash public assistance	1.8%
Age Groups		Other	0.4%	Food stamp/SNAP	15.9%
Under 18	22.9%				
18-34	21.7%	Education		Work	
35-64	38.2%	H.S grad or less	54.4%	White Collar	17.2%
Over 64	17.2%	Some college	29.4%	Sales and Service	39.3%
		College Degree, 4 yr	9.3%	Blue Collar	32.5%
Military		Post grad	6.9%	Government	15.5%
Veteran/ Active Duty	9.9%				

2012 Pres. Vote	Romney	197,074	(66%)	Obama	95,273	(32%)			
2016 Pres. Vote	Trump	224,657	(72%)	Clinton	74,179	(24%)	Johnson	6,920	(2%)

Paducah: The point where the Ohio River flows into the Mississippi — the intersection Huckleberry Finn and Jim missed in the fog — must have struck early settlers as a site for a great city. But no Pittsburgh or St. Louis grew up on the fertile black soil. Instead, the Kentucky land west of the dammed-up Tennessee and Cumberland rivers, bought from the Chickasaw Indians by Gen. Andrew Jackson and Gov. Isaac Shelby in 1818 — the Jackson Purchase — was settled by farmers, mostly from the South. This was one area of Kentucky where public sentiment clearly favored the Confederacy during the Civil War. A group of delegates from western Kentucky and western Tennessee gathered in Mayfield in 1861 and are believed to have voted to join together into a single state in the Confederacy (most of the papers have been destroyed and the record is unclear). The movement was stopped by Tennessee's eventual decision to secede from the Union. To the east of the Jackson Purchase are the dwindling coalfields and the Pennyrile (after pennyroyal, a common variety of local wild mint), a land of low hills and small farms.

The 1st Congressional District of Kentucky is made up of the Jackson Purchase and much of the Pennyrile. There is a distinctive Southern atmosphere here — in the crops that are grown, in the historically low wages, and in the fact that the big city with the most influence locally is Nashville, not Louisville. The 240 miles from Paducah to the state capital in Frankfort has created more than a physical separation. That's especially true for the four counties that border the Mississippi River, where St. Louis and New Orleans are their frame of reference. Paducah, on the Ohio River, has reinvented a large area with an artist relocation program that has boosted development in the Lowertown Arts District. The sprawling Army base at Fort Campbell is home to the 101st Airborne Division, which deployed multiple times during the Iraq and Afghanistan conflicts. Including its facilities in Tennessee, the base had 26,500 troops in 2017 — a drop of about 9,000 in five years, but not as deep a cut as at other large Army facilities. Industrial hemp, which is used as a fuel and fiber, has gained a foothold in the Paducah area. In some areas, it has replaced tobacco as a better investment. Some call Kentucky the "hemp capital of the world."

The Jackson Purchase and the Pennyrile are ancestrally Democratic. Paducah produced one of the most enduring Democratic politicians of the 20th century: Alben Barkley, who was the Senate majority leader for 10 years and Harry Truman's vice president. This part of the state never elected a Republican to Congress until 1994. But the Republican voting pattern has become firmly established in national elections. The 62%-37% win for John McCain over Barack Obama in 2008 grew to a 72%-24% win for Donald Trump over Hillary Clinton. The two strongest Republican districts in Kentucky are the 1st and the 5th, which are the two most rural in Kentucky and are among the lowest 10 percent of districts nationwide in their median income.

Brett Guthrie (R)

Elected 2008, 6th term, b. Feb 18, 1964; Florence, AL; U.S. Military Academy (NY), B.S., 1987; Yale University (CT), M.P.A., 1997; Church of Christ; Married (Elizabeth Clemons); 3 children.

Military Career: U.S. Army 1987-1990; U.S. Army Reserve 199-22

Elected Office: KY Senate, 1998-2008.

Professional Career: Vice President., Trace Die Cast, 2001-2008.

DC Office: 2434 RHOB 20515, 202-225-3501, Fax: 202-226-2019, guthrie.house.gov

State Offices: Bowling Green, 270-842-9896; Owensboro, 270-842-9896; Radcliff, 270-842-9896.

Committees: *Education & Labor*: Higher Education & Workforce Investment. *Energy & Commerce*: Health; Oversight & Investigations (RMM); Consumer Protection & Commerce.

Group Ratings

	ADA	ACLU	AFL-CIO	LCV	ITI	COC	HAFA	ACU	CFG	FRC
2018	-	4%	-	0%	-	92%	65%	88%	59%	100%
2017	0%	C	8%	0%	C	93%	C	93%	82%	100%

Almanac Ratings 2017-18

	Economy	Social	Foreign	Composite
Liberal	3%	4%	0%	2%
Conservative	97%	97%	100%	98%

Key Votes of the 115th Congress

1. Obama-care revision	Y	5. Family planning regs	Y	9. Guantanamo prisoners	N
2. Tax Cuts	Y	6. Body cameras/immigration	N	10. Ground missiles, limit	N
3. Omnibus appropriations	Y	7. Abortion ban	Y	11. Defense Dept. spending	Y
4. Dodd-Frank revision	Y	8. Concealed carry	Y	12. FISA rules	Y

Election Results

Election	Name (Party)	Vote (%)		Cand. Spent	Ind. Exp. Support	Ind. Exp. Oppose
2018 General	Brett Guthrie (R)	171,700	(67%)	$1,293,764		
	Hank Linderman (D)	79,964	(31%)		$153,977	
	Thomas Loecken (I)	5,681	(2%)			
2018 Primary	Brett Guthrie (R)		(100%)			

Prior winning percentages: 2016 (100%), 2014 (69%), 2012 (64%), 2010 (68%), 2008 (53%)

Republican Brett Guthrie, elected in 2008, has a military and business background that plays well with constituents, plus a reputation as a loyal party vote that endears him to GOP leaders. He holds a plum seat on the Energy and Commerce Committee, where he has enacted numerous health care bills and sought to protect the state's coal and oil industries.

A graduate of West Point, Guthrie served 14 years in the Army, first in the Reserve, then as a field artillery officer with the 101st Airborne Division at Fort Campbell. After his discharge, Guthrie joined the family business in Bowling Green, Trace Die Cast Inc., a leading supplier of aluminum castings for the automobile industry. His father started the business with five employees in the 1980s. In 1998, he was elected to the state Senate, where he became chairman of the Transportation Committee, helping the state develop its highway budget. Republicans expected him to join their leadership, but Guthrie set his sights on Congress.

When the seat was open in 2008, Guthrie had no opposition for the Republican nomination. The Democratic nominee was state Sen. David Boswell, a 30-year veteran of Kentucky politics. He ran as a conservative Democrat, and the two contenders were virtually indistinguishable on the issues. Both opposed abortion rights and supported gun ownership, and both spoke out against the massive bailout for the financial industry that Congress passed that fall. Guthrie ran ads tying Boswell to liberal Democrats and their opposition to offshore drilling. He emphasized his military background to the district's large active and retired military population. The Democratic Congressional Campaign Committee ran an ad claiming that Trace Die Cast had sent jobs to Mexico, and former President Bill Clinton stumped for Boswell. Guthrie had a war chest of nearly $1.3 million compared with Boswell's $917,000. He won 53%-47%. Since then, he usually has been reelected with at least two-thirds of the vote.

In the House, Guthrie has been a dependable Republican. He took a softer line in criticizing the Environmental Protection Agency than other Republicans on Energy and Commerce, telling the Owensboro Messenger-Inquirer that the agency needed to strike a better balance between regulation and the economy. "I've been to Mexico City and Beijing," he said. "I don't want to have to wear a mask when I go outside. But I want regulations that don't put companies out of business and cost my district $60,000-a-year jobs." In 2016, the House passed the bill that he authored with Energy and Commerce Democratic Rep. Kathy Castor of Florida to give companies in the concrete masonry industry more flexibility to research and promote their products.

Guthrie has had responsibilities at two key House subcommittees. As vice chairman of the Health Subcommittee, when the GOP was in the majority, he focused on steps to replace Obamacare with "patient-centered health care solutions" and to make the Medicaid program more effective. He failed to achieve those big goals but he has taken several incremental steps. In 2018, he enacted bills to update the Missing Children's Assistance Act, facilitate in-home health services for Medicaid beneficiaries, provide legal protections for sports medicine professionals who cross state lines and create a public health infrastructure to aide patients with Alzheimer's disease and related dementia. On the Education and the Workforce Committee, Guthrie chaired the Higher Education and the

Workforce Subcommittee. In September 2018, the House passed a bill that he filed with Democratic Rep. Suzanne Bonamici of Oregon to expand financial-aid counseling, especially for student-loan recipients.

Guthrie, who during the 2016 campaign urged Donald Trump to work with Congress "in a positive way," said following a June 2018 meeting at the White House to discuss concerns about family separation of immigrants at the southern border, "we cannot continue to allow this to happen."

KY-2: Central Kentucky   Cook Partisan Voting Index: R+19

Population		Race and Ethnicity		Income	
Total	747,700	White	87.4%	Median Income	$48,902
Land area (sq. miles)	7,177	Black	5.4%	District Income Rank	328
Pop/ sq mi	104.2	Latino	3.3%	Poverty Rate	16.2%
Born in State	71%	Asian	1.3%	With health insurance	92.9%
		Two or more races	2.1%	Cash public assistance	1.9%
Age Groups		Other	0.4%	Food stamp/SNAP	14%
Under 18	23.4%				
18-34	22.5%	**Education**		**Work**	
35-64	39.2%	H.S grad or less	49.7%	White Collar	14.9%
Over 64	14.9%	Some college	30.3%	Sales and Service	39.6%
		College Degree, 4 yr	11.7%	Blue Collar	30.6%
Military		Post grad	8.2%	Government	14.2%
Veteran/ Active Duty	10.7%				

2012 Pres. Vote	Romney	186,231	(63%)	Obama	103,410	(35%)			
2016 Pres. Vote	Trump	219,152	(68%)	Clinton	89,563	(28%)	Johnson	9,269	(3%)

Louisville Suburbs, Bowling Green, Elizabethtown: In the 1770s and 1780s, Americans began settling the limestone-soil country of central Kentucky, staking out towns like Bardstown and Elizabethtown and starting academies and colleges. They were well-settled when Stephen Foster wrote "My Old Kentucky Home" just before the Civil War. The war tore deeply here. This part of Kentucky gave birth to Abraham Lincoln, and during the conflict it lost thousands of soldiers, both Union and Confederate. The Lincoln family was not immune to this division; Mary Todd Lincoln's brother-in-law, Benjamin Hardin Helm, fought on the side of the Confederacy and rose to the rank of general before dying at the Battle of Chickamauga. Lincoln himself was never particularly popular here prior to his death. Kentucky's most famous son won only 1 percent of the vote in the state in 1860; his home county gave him just three votes. Today, the area hosts several Kentucky landmarks — Fort Knox, the nation's gold depository; some of the nation's largest bourbon distilleries; and Mammoth Cave, the world's largest accessible cavern, which is near Bowling Green. In the small town of Bardstown, site of My Old Kentucky Home State Park, the annual Kentucky Bourbon Festival draws more than 50,000 visitors to the weeklong event. In August 2018, Jim Beam, which has operated in Kentucky since 1795, announced that it would spend $165 million to expand its distilleries in Bullitt and Nelson counties.

The 2nd Congressional District of Kentucky consists of much of the territory south and southwest of Louisville, starting with Spencer County and heading south to Bowling Green, where Rand Paul had his eye clinic before he entered politics. That city is the headquarters of apparel giant Fruit of the Loom, and it has a bustling General Motors Corvette assembly plant, the only place in the world where the sleek sports cars have been produced since 1981. In 2017, GM spent $430 million to upgrade the Bowling Green assembly plant, which produced 40,689 cars during the 2016 model year — more than triple production in 2010. The National Corvette Museum is across the street from the plant. The district jogs west along the Ohio River to Owensboro, a port with warehouses that receive aluminum alloys to make lightweight engine parts. The aluminum industry in 2018 had 20,000 workers in Kentucky, which led the nation. Also in Owensboro, the Bluegrass Music Hall of Fame opened that year. The city has successfully courted new economic development, including the headquarters of U.S. Bank, the fifth-largest commercial bank in the United States, with close to 2,000 employees locally. Owensboro still tries to preserve the feeling of "Old Kentucky," and hosts an annual international barbecue festival where mutton, a throwback to Welsh shepherds who settled in western Kentucky, remains a favorite.

Much of the district is rural and small-town country. For many years, it favored Democrats, but in the 1990s voters moved to the Republican Party, which better matched their conservative cultural leanings. Donald Trump got 68 percent of the vote in 2016.

John Yarmuth (D)

Elected 2006, 7th term, b. Nov 04, 1947; Louisville; Yale University (CT), B.A., 1969; Georgetown University Law Center (DC), Att., 1972; Jewish; Married (Catherine Yarmuth); 1 child.

Professional Career: Stockbroker, 1969-1971; Sr. aide, U.S. Sen. Marlow Cook, 1971-1975; Publisher, Louisville Today magazine, 1976-1982; Assistant Vice President. of university relations, University of Louisville, 1983-1986; Vice President., Caretenders, 1986-1990; Owner, columnist, & Executive editor, Louisville Eccentric Observer, 1990-2002; Co-host, Yarmuth & Ziegler, 2003; Commentator, Hot Button, 2004-2005.

DC Office: 402 CHOB 20515, 202-225-5401, Fax: 202-225-5776, yarmuth.house.gov

State Offices: Louisville, 502-582-5129; Louisville, 502-933-5863.

Committees: *Budget (Chmn).*

Group Ratings

	ADA	ACLU	AFL-CIO	LCV	ITI	COC	HAFA	ACU	CFG	FRC
2018	-	89%	-	91%	-	50%	4%	4%	5%	0%
2017	100%	C	97%	100%	C	43%	C	4%	5%	0%

Almanac Ratings 2017-18

	Economy	Social	Foreign	Composite
Liberal	97%	97%	100%	98%
Conservative	3%	4%	0%	2%

Key Votes of the 115th Congress

1. Obama-care revision	N	5. Family planning regs	N	9. Guantanamo prisoners	Y
2. Tax Cuts	N	6. Body cameras/immigration	Y	10. Ground missiles, limit	Y
3. Omnibus appropriations	N	7. Abortion ban	N	11. Defense Dept. spending	N
4. Dodd-Frank revision	N	8. Concealed carry	N	12. FISA rules	N

Election Results

Election	Name (Party)	Vote (%)		Cand. Spent	Ind. Exp. Support	Ind. Exp. Oppose
2018 General	John Yarmuth (D)	173,002	(62%)	$882,292		
	Vickie Yates Glisson (R)	101,930	(37%)	$709,053		
2018 Primary	John Yarmuth (D)		(100%)			

Prior winning percentages: 2016 (64%), 2014 (64%), 2012 (64%), 2010 (55%), 2008 (59%), 2006 (51%)

Democrat John Yarmuth, who was first elected in 2006, is a former journalist who has enjoyed rebuking Republicans, especially home-state colleague Mitch McConnell, the Senate majority leader. In 2019, Yarmuth took over as chairman of the House Budget Committee, which positioned him as a top party spokesman.

Yarmuth hails from a wealthy Louisville family. His father, Stanley Yarmuth, founded National Industries, a conglomerate that started as a used car business; his maternal grandfather, Samuel Klein, ran the Bank of Louisville. After graduating from Yale University, he worked briefly as a stockbroker and then as an aide to Republican Sen. Marlow Cook. Yarmuth attended two years of law school but didn't finish his degree.

He founded Louisville Today magazine and served as publisher from 1976 until 1982. He ran unsuccessfully for Louisville alderman in 1975, and for county commissioner in 1981. He worked in public relations from 1983 to 1990 for the University of Louisville and for a health care company.

Unhappy with the policies of President Ronald Reagan, Yarmuth switched his party affiliation to Democrat in 1985. In 1990, Yarmuth founded the Louisville Eccentric Observer, a free newsweekly popularly known as LEO, and for the next 15 years penned a column called "Hot Coals" that promoted his mostly liberal views. He also did televised political commentary.

In 2006, five-term Republican Rep. Anne Northup was vulnerable in the district. The Democratic Congressional Campaign Committee touted attorney Andrew Horne, an Iraq war veteran and first-time candidate. But Yarmuth raised more money and proved a more formidable candidate than Horne, winning the four-way primary 54%-32%. He called for an immediate pullout of troops from Iraq and referred to Northup as a "rubberstamp" for President George W. Bush. Northup campaigned on Republican tax cuts and her work for the district. She unleashed an advertising offensive that blasted Yarmuth for his liberal writings, saying he supported removing the phrase "under God" from the Pledge of Allegiance and legalizing marijuana. Northup raised $3.4 million to Yarmuth's $2.3 million, which included $700,000 of his own money. Northup could not overcome the national tide against Republicans that year. Yarmuth won, 51%-48%.

In 2008, Northup returned for a rematch, after losing a primary contest for governor. She criticized Yarmuth for supporting the $700 billion bailout for the financial markets and attacked his "present" vote on a resolution honoring Christmas, asserting he had lost touch with his constituents. Even though Northup raised more money, Yarmuth won more easily, 59%-41%. He has become entrenched in his seat.

Yarmuth told Esquire magazine in 2010 that he had trouble adjusting to elected office: "I never had to compromise on my opinion in the column. Suddenly you have to swallow all sorts of compromises, and that's not easy at all." With his journalism background, he joined a "messaging" group that advised Speaker Nancy Pelosi and other Democratic leaders on media strategy. He snared a seat on the Ways and Means Committee, but lost it after Republicans regained control of the House in 2011. His "Keeping Our Campaigns Honest Act" would require disclosure of the donors behind super PACs and tax-exempt organizations.

He has frequently jabbed at McConnell, with whom he has clashed since the 1970s. "Mitch McConnell will always do what's in Mitch McConnell's best interest," he has said. Yarmuth goes places rhetorically where most Democrats won't venture. After the House passed the fiscal-cliff budget compromise, he praised House Speaker John Boehner for being "courageous" in sending the Senate-passed deal to the House floor. He told Roll Call that the health care law was the right thing to do policy-wise, but "big picture, politically, it probably wasn't worth it." He told a Louisville radio station after the Senate made changes to the bill, "We couldn't really go to the average American citizen and say, 'Here's what it means to you.'"

In naming Yarmuth as the top Democrat on the Budget Committee after the 2016 election, Pelosi said he "will represent our values in the budget debate, is a master at communicating to the public and has been a leader in advocating the use of social media." Yarmuth described his role: "Budgets are statements of our values, and the Budget Committee provides us the opportunity to show the American people the sharp contrasts between Democratic values and those of Republicans in the House and White House." As committee chairman following the 2018 election, he told the Louisville Courier Journal, he planned to turn the panel into a national forum for taxpayers on a host of causes. Unusually for a Budget chairman, when he asked the Congressional Budget Office for a report on the "design and policy considerations" of a single-payer health plan, he asked that a cost estimate not be included. But in his first few months as chairman, Yarmuth did not start work on the panel's prime legislative responsibility: a budget plan for the next fiscal year, which would be a framework for total spending and revenue. He cited the major policy differences among House Democrats.

Yarmuth has captained the Democrats in the annual congressional golf tournament. A highlight of his career was when he joined two other House Democrats in a 2015 round of golf with President Barack Obama at Joint Base Andrews. For several years, he has owned a home at the Trump golf club in Ireland. Asked by Roll Call in October 2017 whether he would like to play a round of golf with President Donald Trump, Yarmuth said, "That'd be a very tough call for me. ... I so cherish my one presidential golf experience. I don't want to necessarily tarnish it. I'd like to keep it as my only presidential golf memory because it was so good." Perhaps not coincidentally, the following month, he was one of six Democrats who filed articles of impeachment against Trump.

KY-3: Louisville Metro

Cook Partisan Voting Index: D+6

Population		Race and Ethnicity		Income	
Total	742,664	White	68%	Median Income	$51,316
Land area (sq. miles)	319	Black	21.5%	District Income Rank	280
Pop/ sq mi	2325.6	Latino	5.1%	Poverty Rate	15.3%
Born in State	68.6%	Asian	2.6%	With health insurance	92.7%
		Two or more races	2.5%	Cash public assistance	2.4%
Age Groups		Other	0.3%	Food stamp/SNAP	13.5%
Under 18	22.5%				
18-34	23.5%	**Education**		**Work**	
35-64	39.1%	H.S grad or less	38.1%	White Collar	14.9%
Over 64	14.9%	Some college	30.6%	Sales and Service	40.9%
Military		College Degree, 4 yr	18.3%	Blue Collar	22.9%
Veteran/ Active Duty	8.2%	Post grad	13.1%	Government	10.9%

2012 Pres. Vote	Obama	183,015	(56%)	Romney	140,539	(43%)		
2016 Pres. Vote	Clinton	186,549	(55%)	Trump	135,714	(40%)	Johnson	9,854 (3%)

Louisville: At the falls of the Ohio River, George Rogers Clark founded one of America's first inland metropolises in 1778: the river port and industrial city of Louisville. It is heavily influenced by the Cavalier culture that the second sons of big landowners from England brought to Virginia in the 17th century — and their heirs brought over the Appalachians to the valleys of Kentucky in the 18th century. When Kentucky decided not to secede from the union in 1861, the decision was not unanimous. The culture of tidewater Virginia is still evident in the Louisville lawn party. Mint juleps are served on the verandas of mansions, especially (but not only) during Kentucky Derby week in May; horse racing is a preoccupation throughout the year.

With 621,000 residents in 2017, Louisville is Kentucky's largest city. Another 150,000 reside in the remaining parts of Jefferson County. Forbes magazine rated local manufacturing the strongest in the nation in 2017. Its economy is in many ways "pre-postindustrial:" It produces cigarettes and whiskey, GE appliances and Ford automobiles. Louisville is the headquarters of Humana health services; the long-term health care facility operator Signature HealthCARE; and several fast food companies, including Yum! Brands, which owns KFC, Pizza Hut and Taco Bell; Papa John's pizza; and A Great American Brand, which operates Long John Silver's. In 2015, the local Hillerich and Bradsby company sold its Louisville Slugger baseball bat to Chicago-based Wilson Sporting Goods. But the bats continued to be manufactured at the plant in downtown Louisville. Muhammad Ali, born in Louisville as Cassius Marcellus Clay, has been memorialized by the Muhammad Ali Center, with its interactive exhibits. The Derby has an annual economic impact of $400 million. In 2018, Churchill Downs completed $70 million in improvements for parking and seats, including suites that cost $65,000 on Derby day.

The 3rd Congressional District of Kentucky includes all but a handful of precincts in Jefferson County. The large African-American population, which is 21 percent of the overall district, resides chiefly in the West End of Louisville. A low-income white population is along the strip highway that leads to Fort Knox. West Buechel, southeast of the city, has one of the highest concentrations of Yugoslavian Americans in the United States, many of whom were Bosnian refugees relocated by the government. The suburbs to the east tend to be affluent. Small, elite neighborhoods — Mockingbird Valley, Glenview and Ten Broeck — are nestled in the hills above the Ohio River.

The district, like Louisville, has long been an odd duck in Kentucky politics. If its elite were Virginia Cavaliers, many of its burghers were Germans and Pennsylvanians who made the river town a Republican and anti-slavery island in a secessionist and pro-slavery sea. That tradition helps explain how Republican Mitch McConnell won election as Jefferson County judge-executive in 1977 and 1981, when the state was electing Democrats to most other offices. Since the 1990s, Louisville has trended toward Democrats, even as the rest of Kentucky trended Republican. Jefferson was one of only two counties in 2016 to vote for Hillary Clinton — 54%-41%. In 2018, county Democrats made gains in state and local elections.

Thomas Massie (R)

Elected 2012, 4th term, b. Jan 13, 1971; Huntington, WV; Massachusetts Institute of Technology, B.S., 1993; Massachusetts Institute of Technology, M.M.E., 1996; Methodist; Married (Rhonda Massie); 4 children.

Professional Career: Founder, Chairman, & chief tech. officer, SensAble Technologies, 1993-2003; Judge Executive, Lewis County KY, 2010-2012; Farmer, 2003-present.

DC Office: 2453 RHOB 20515, 202-225-3465, Fax: 202-225-0003, massie.house.gov

State Offices: Ashland, 606-324-9898; Crescent Springs, 859-426-0080; LaGrange, 502-265-9119.

Committees: *Oversight & Reform*: Government Operations; Subcommittee on Civil Rights & Civil Liberties. *Transportation & Infrastructure*: Aviation; Highways & Transit; Water Resources & Environment.

Group Ratings

	ADA	ACLU	AFL-CIO	LCV	ITI	COC	HAFA	ACU	CFG	FRC
2018	-	36%	-	17%	-	83%	71%	92%	92%	100%
2017	35%	C	18%	17%	C	93%	C	85%	98%	89%

Almanac Ratings 2017-18

	Economy	Social	Foreign	Composite
Liberal	25%	13%	39%	26%
Conservative	75%	87%	61%	74%

Key Votes of the 115th Congress

1. Obama-care revision	N	5. Family planning regs	Y	9. Guantanamo prisoners	N
2. Tax Cuts	Y	6. Body cameras/immigration	N	10. Ground missiles, limit	N
3. Omnibus appropriations	N	7. Abortion ban	Y	11. Defense Dept. spending	N
4. Dodd-Frank revision	Y	8. Concealed carry	N	12. FISA rules	N

Election Results

Election	Name (Party)	Vote (%)	Cand. Spent	Ind. Exp. Support	Ind. Exp. Oppose
2018 General	Thomas Massie (R)...... 162,946	(62%)	$364,388		
	Seth Hall (D)............... 90,536	(35%)	$35,244		
	Mike Moffett (I)............. 8,318	(3%)			
2018 Primary	Thomas Massie (R)...........	(100%)			

Prior winning percentages: 2016 (71%), 2014 (68%), 2012 (62%)

Republican Thomas Massie, first elected in 2012 as a political outsider, has remained an iconoclast. He has been a constant thorn to Republican leaders, who have bypassed him for subcommittee chairmanships, and a free spirit who often goes his own way in House votes. He has been instrumental in starting up and leading groups of conservative activists in the House, including the Second Amendment Caucus.

Massie has an impressive scientific background. He was raised in Vanceburg Kentucky and got his bachelor's degree and master's in engineering at the Massachusetts Institute of Technology. While at MIT, Massie was part of a group that invented the Phantom, a device enabling users to interact with objects in cyberspace through touch. To market the product, he and his wife, Rhonda (his high school sweetheart and also an MIT student), started the firm SensAble Technologies, which raised more than $32 million of venture capital, created 70 jobs, and obtained 29 patents. Massie left SensAble Technologies in 2003 and returned to Kentucky with his family to run a farm, where he built a timber-frame house that runs on solar energy and is powered by a used Tesla car battery. He got interested in politics after learning about a proposed new tax in rural Lewis County. In 2010, he entered politics by winning a campaign for Lewis County judge-executive.

When he ran for an open seat in 2012, Massie described himself as a "conservative with conviction and common sense." He campaigned on his business background and won the all-important support of tea party activists. He had backed tea party favorite Rand Paul in his 2010 Senate race. Paul appeared in a TV ad for Massie. Massie won the primary handily, with 45 percent of the vote. His two chief opponents split the establishment vote. In this solidly Republican district, Massie easily won in November. He has not faced a primary challenge since.

He showed his rebellious streak on his first House vote in 2013, when he opposed John Boehner for a new term as House Speaker. Massie occasionally crossed the aisle to work with Democrats, especially on civil liberties issues where the wings of both parties came together in opposition to Big Government. In 2015, the House passed a bill that he cosponsored with Democratic Rep. Zoe Lofgren of California to require that the National Security Agency seek a judicial warrant before it could spy on U.S. citizens in its online surveillance. In 2016, the House narrowly defeated a similar amendment days after a suspected Islamic State supporter gunned down 49 persons at a gay club in Orlando Florida. Massie insisted that the proposal "does not take any tools away from those that want to investigate what happened in Orlando."

With Democratic Rep. Marc Pocan of Wisconsin, he filed a bill to repeal the Patriot Act, the post-9/11 law that has provided broad authority to security agencies. Buzzfeed profiled Massie as "Democrats' new go-to Republican." "Here's the difference between a partisan and an ideologue: An ideologue reads the bill, every word, period and section; a partisan reads the whip recommendation," he told Buzzfeed. (He's proudly the former.) His Almanac vote ratings have placed him near the center of the House, especially on economic and foreign policy issues. On most social issues, he remained a solid conservative vote.

Massie has worked with other conservatives to channel their opposition to GOP leaders. The House leadership, he said, had become "a significant source of the dysfunction" in the chamber. He has been consistent, and increasingly lonely, in his independence. After Boehner resigned, Massie was one of nine Republicans who voted against Paul Ryan as the new Speaker in October 2015. In January 2017, he was the only Republican to vote against Ryan. "I'm very concerned about the combination of Donald Trump and Paul Ryan and the implications for our national debt," he told Reason, a libertarian magazine. In 2019, he was one of six Republicans to vote against GOP Leader Kevin McCarthy in the vote for Speaker. Party leaders have responded accordingly. During his first term, Massie chaired the Technology Subcommittee, a logical assignment for his background. Since then, he has no longer been the senior Republican on that subcommittee, or any other.

Massie worked with other members to organize the conservative Freedom Caucus as a way to strengthen their legislative leverage. In 2016, he revived the Second Amendment Caucus and became its chairman. During the next two years, he filed bills to reduce from 21 to 18 the minimum age for handgun sales, allow persons with concealed-carry permits in their home state to carry in Washington D.C., and repeal gun-free zones on school grounds. The solution to school shootings, he said, was to add more armed guards or allow teachers to be armed. None of the proposals was considered by the Republican-controlled House. In 2017, he was one of three House members to vote against relief for victims of Hurricane Harvey and one of two who voted against additional economic sanctions on North Korea.

In 2016, he faced Democratic challenger Calvin Sidle, who had twice lost bids for local office in the neighboring 5th District. "Whereas he (Massie) is essentially for non-spending, I am for big spending," said Sidle, who was an Uber driver at night. Massie won, 71%-29%. During the transition to President Donald Trump, Massie made known his interest in serving as a White House science-policy adviser. There was no public indication that he was seriously considered. Sidle challenged him again in 2018. This time, Massie won, 62%-35%. In suburban Campbell and Kenton counties, his vote share slipped below 60 percent.

KY-4: Northern Kentucky   Cook Partisan Voting Index: R+18

Population		Race and Ethnicity		Income	
Total	749,054	White	90.1%	Median Income	$59,478
Land area (sq. miles)	4,382	Black	3.3%	District Income Rank	186
Pop/ sq mi	170.9	Latino	3.2%	Poverty Rate	13%
Born in State	61.7%	Asian	1.2%	With health insurance	93.1%
		Two or more races	2%	Cash public assistance	2.2%
Age Groups		Other	0.2%	Food stamp/SNAP	11.7%
Under 18	24.2%				
18-34	20.8%	Education		Work	
35-64	40.8%	H.S grad or less	42.7%	White Collar	14.2%
Over 64	14.2%	Some college	30.1%	Sales and Service	40%
		College Degree, 4 yr	16.9%	Blue Collar	23.5%
Military		Post grad	10.3%	Government	11.7%
Veteran/ Active Duty	8.7%				

2012 Pres. Vote	Romney	197,098	(63%)	Obama	108,348	(35%)		
2016 Pres. Vote	Trump	219,749	(65%)	Clinton	98,664	(29%)	Johnson	11,693	(4%)

Cincinnati and Louisville Suburbs: Along the Ohio River are some very different parts of Kentucky. Ashland, near the West Virginia border, is industrial, the former home of Ashland Inc.; the river here is bound in by tight hills that hold smoke and soot in the air. Farther down the river, the country is more bucolic. This is where Eliza fled across the ice floes in Harriet Beecher Stowe's Uncle Tom's Cabin. Farther west, between Cincinnati and Louisville, are counties that look like they're still in the 19th century. But metropolitan growth obtrudes. Oldham County, just upriver from Louisville, has some of Kentucky's oldest homes, and is by far the most affluent county in the state. In rural Williamstown, a group of Christian fundamentalists in August 2016 opened Ark Encounter, a $100 million replica of Noah's Ark, including life-like models of some of the animal creatures. Ken Ham, the project's founder, said the purpose of the ark is to send a warning of the peril awaiting society because of its errant behavior.

The three Northern Kentucky counties across the river from Cincinnati — Campbell, Kenton and Boone — are urban and suburban. Overlooking the suspension bridge built by John Roebling are new buildings on the Covington waterfront. New subdivisions are rising on the hills in Boone County, above the river, near the Cincinnati/Northern Kentucky International Airport. Newport, with its panoramic view of the Cincinnati skyline plus its nightlife, has become a regional hot spot. The airport, with its 16 percent increase in passengers in the first quarter of 2018, was the fastest-growing major airport in the nation; cargo volume increased 41 percent. In competition with FedEx and the United Parcel Service, Amazon planned to build a $1.5 billion international hub at the airport. It expected to hire more than 2,000 workers and operate more than 100 planes, starting in 2021.

The 4th Congressional District of Kentucky is the northernmost district in the state. It covers 12 counties and 280 miles along the Ohio River and also lightly populated counties just inland. Economically, it runs the gamut from coal mining towns to rich suburbs. In the low-income area surrounding Ashland, investors in 2018 explored the possibility of building a $1.7 billion aluminum rolling mill. The region's clout in state government has been understated because the political focus is more on Cincinnati than on Louisville or Lexington. The three northern Kentucky counties across the river from Cincinnati, which cast nearly half the district's votes, are heavily Republican. This is a solidly Republican district, though the 65%-29% support for Trump ranked only fourth among the five Republican-held districts in Kentucky.

Hal Rogers (R)

Elected 1980, 20th term, b. Dec 31, 1937; Barrier; Western Kentucky University, Att., 1957; University of Kentucky, Bach. Deg., 1962; University of Kentucky College of Law, J.D., 1964; Baptist; Married (Cynthia Doyle Rogers); 3 children (from a previous marriage).

Military Career: U.S. Army National Guard 1956-1963

Professional Career: Practicing attorney, 1964-1969; Pulaski-Rockcastle Commonwealth's Attorney, 1969-1980.

DC Office: 2406 RHOB 20515, 202-225-4601, Fax: 202-225-0940, halrogers.house.gov

State Offices: Hazard, 606-439-0794; Prestonsburg, 606-886-0844; Somerset, 800-632-8588.

Committees: *Appropriations*: Defense; State, Foreign Operations & Related Programs (RMM).

Group Ratings

	ADA	ACLU	AFL-CIO	LCV	ITI	COC	HAFA	ACU	CFG	FRC
2018	-	4%		6%	-	89%	42%	72%	45%	100%
2017	0%	C	16%	6%	C	93%	C	70%	51%	100%

Almanac Ratings 2017-18

	Economy	Social	Foreign	Composite
Liberal	10%	0%	0%	3%
Conservative	90%	100%	100%	97%

Key Votes of the 115th Congress

1. Obama-care revision	Y	5. Family planning regs	Y	9. Guantanamo prisoners	N
2. Tax Cuts	Y	6. Body cameras/immigration	N	10. Ground missiles, limit	N
3. Omnibus appropriations	Y	7. Abortion ban	Y	11. Defense Dept. spending	Y
4. Dodd-Frank revision	NV	8. Concealed carry	Y	12. FISA rules	Y

Election Results

Election	Name (Party)	Vote (%)		Cand. Spent	Ind. Exp. Support	Ind. Exp. Oppose
2018 General	Hal Rogers (R)	172,093	(79%)	$685,865		
	Kenneth Stepp (D)	45,890	(21%)	$643		
2018 Primary	Hal Rogers (R)	75,601	(84%)			
	Gerardo Serrno (R)	14,216	(16%)			

Prior winning percentages: 2016 (100%), 2014 (78%), 2012 (78%), 2010 (77%), 2008 (84%), 2006 (74%), 2002 (78%), 2000 (74%), 1998 (78%), 1994 (79%), 1992 (55%), 1988 (100%), 1986 (100%), 1984 (76%), 1982 (65%), 1980 (68%)

Harold Rogers, a Republican first elected in 1980, served six years as chairman of the House Appropriations Committee until he was term-limited in 2016. As the third most-senior member of the House, he chaired several subcommittees and has been an old-school deal-maker. In the days before the ban on earmarks, he not only defended them but boasted about the prodigious sums he steered back home. In the minority in 2019, he became ranking member of the State and Foreign Operations Subcommittee. He is beloved in his rural district: He regularly is reelected with more than 75 percent of the vote.

Rogers grew up in Wayne County, graduated from the University of Kentucky, served in the National Guard, then practiced law in Somerset before buying the Citizens National Bank in Somerset. In 1969, at age 34, he was elected Pulaski-Rockcastle commonwealth attorney. In 1979, he was the unsuccessful Republican nominee for lieutenant governor. The following year, when there was an open House seat, Rogers was one of 11 Republicans in the primary. He got the nomination with 23 percent of the vote and easily won in November.

His toughest race came in 1992, when redistricting combined two districts in eastern Kentucky. At first, his likely opponent was Rep. Chris Perkins, a Democrat and the son of Rep. Carl Perkins, who had chaired the Education and Labor Committee. Together, they had held the seat for 44 years. But Perkins suddenly retired, just before it was revealed that he had 514 overdrafts at the House bank. Rogers instead faced state Sen. John Doug Hays of Pike County. Rogers won with 55 percent.

His voting record is mostly, but not always, conservative. His district has long been hungry for federal aid, and Rogers often has found it difficult to maintain a conservative record on spending issues. He has argued that the federal-state partnership helped to close the gap between the impoverished area and the rest of the country.

During Republicans' initial 12 years in the House majority, Rogers chaired the Commerce, Justice, State Subcommittee starting in 1995, took over the Transportation Subcommittee in 2001, and became chairman in 2003 of the newly created Homeland Security Subcommittee. He helped to increase Kentucky to the fourth-highest state in transportation funding per capita. "The rate of return on highway spending far exceeds most other investments and is a proven engine," Rogers once wrote when he was criticized for his earmarked spending. The Hal Rogers Parkway crosses the Daniel Boone National Forest from London to Hazard.

Rogers over the years has focused on homeland security. After Congress voted to federalize airport screeners, he kept a close watch on the new agency. In 2010, he challenged the Obama administration's proposals for airport body scanners because he doubted that such a costly and manpower-intensive approach would get results. The Obama administration, he complained, had practically given up deporting illegal immigrants arrested at worksites in favor of what he derisively called "virtual amnesty."

Rogers rose to chairman of Appropriations in 2011. He took over just as most House Republicans, especially the 87 freshmen elected in 2010, were determined to end earmarking. Despite his work over the years funding projects at home, he succumbed to the moratorium on earmarks that Speaker John Boehner decreed. In 2012, Rogers touted his success as a born-again foe of wasteful spending. "We've cut the spending Congress does for three years now, which has not happened since World War II," he said.

Part of the reason for Rogers' continuing clout is his ability to work with Democrats. "He's very approachable," committee Democrat Marcy Kaptur of Ohio said. "He's a matter-of-fact sort of gentleman — I mean, he doesn't spend a lot of time on wasted words, he's terse — but I think very effective." Another source of his influence has been the inability of recent congressional majorities to pass individual appropriations bills. That led to massive omnibus spending bills, something that enabled Republicans to make policy via "riders" on the omnibus legislation.

When President Barack Obama in November 2014 issued an executive order protecting some illegal immigrants, many conservatives vowed to overturn it. But Rogers warned against using the issue to provoke another spending-bill confrontation. "I just don't think it's very smart, wise or prudent to talk about a shutdown scenario," he said. That enraged conservative activists. National Review Online ran an article headlined "Hal Rogers, Obama Republican."

In his final year as committee chairman, Rogers sought to deliver a parting gift to his constituents: Legislation to provide $1 billion for mine reclamation projects to revitalize coal communities in his district and nearby areas. The tight budget plus limited congressional action during the presidential year thwarted that goal and resulted in a status quo extension of federal spending.

In 2017, Rogers became chairman of the State and Foreign Operations Subcommittee at Appropriations. That was an unusual rebuke of an influential and senior House Republican. As McClatchy News earlier reported, Rogers wanted to chair the Defense Subcommittee. Instead, that position went to Kay Granger of Texas, who had been an expert on national security issues for many years. Two years later, Granger unexpectedly became the senior Republican on the full committee. That gave Rogers a new opportunity at the Defense Subcommittee, with the GOP in the minority. Instead, he retained the top post on the Foreign Operations Subcommittee and Ken Calvert of California took the defense slot.

KY-5: Eastern Kentucky   **Cook Partisan Voting Index: R+31**

Population		Race and Ethnicity		Income	
Total	706,248	White	95.8%	Median Income	$31,899
Land area (sq. miles)	11,235	Black	1.4%	District Income Rank	434
Pop/ sq mi	62.9	Latino	1.3%	Poverty Rate	28.3%
Born in State	78.5%	Asian	0.4%	With health insurance	91.4%
		Two or more races	0.9%	Cash public assistance	2.6%
Age Groups		Other	0.2%	Food stamp/SNAP	27.2%
Under 18	22.2%				
18-34	20.8%	**Education**		**Work**	
35-64	40.7%	H.S grad or less	62.1%	White Collar	16.3%
Over 64	16.3%	Some college	25%	Sales and Service	42.4%
		College Degree, 4 yr	6.9%	Blue Collar	28.7%
Military		Post grad	6%	Government	19%
Veteran/ Active Duty	6.7%				

2012 Pres. Vote	Romney	196,192	(75%)	Obama	60,760	(23%)
2016 Pres. Vote	Trump	221,558	(80%)	Clinton	48,628	(18%)

Somerset, Pikesville: Mountainous eastern Kentucky has been a unique place since Daniel Boone came through the Cumberland Gap in 1775. Scots-Irish pioneers soon followed him, bringing their assertive egalitarianism, loyalty to family and community, and passionate willingness to defend honor by feuds or violence. Most inhabitants of the mountains today are descendants of the Ulster Protestant and Border Scot families who settled there in the two or three generations after Boone. In the 2010 census, 0 percent of the population of Elliott, Magoffin and Menifee counties reported being foreign-born. This was never slave territory — hardly any blacks have ever lived in these mountains, and even today Leslie County is the whitest in the state. The settlers had little use for the party of slavery, and still don't. Today, the counties around Somerset and Corbin in south-central Kentucky cast some of the highest Republican percentages in the nation, election after election. The local economic populism is well-suited to Donald Trump. Social conservatism remains vocal in many of these places. In 2015, Rowan County clerk Kim Davis received national attention when she was jailed for refusing to issue marriage licenses to same-sex couples.

Early in the 20th century, vast seams of coal were discovered under the Kentucky mountains and a new economy sprang up, bringing a new politics. Coal mining was harsh and deadly work. Mine accidents, black lung disease and simple exhaustion killed tens of thousands of miners, while low wages and company stores kept them poor. Then, John L. Lewis' United Mine Workers came in, and open warfare followed, with both mine operators and union organizers willing to use violence. The union mostly won in eastern Kentucky. In his War on Poverty, President Lyndon Johnson brought attention to this and other parts of Appalachia. He launched his "war" in the town of Inez in these mountains. But his crusade has yielded mixed results at best. A half-century later, high-school graduation rates and life expectancy remained low.

Some of these areas have some of the harshest working conditions in the nation. The number of miners in eastern Kentucky fell from 14,000 in 2009 to below 4,000 in 2016. The strong rhetorical support from President Donald Trump, along with more favorable regulations, gave hope to many in the coal fields for the first time in decades. Jobs in the mines grew by 6 percent in 2017. Still, the federal Energy Information Administration projected that coal production in eastern Kentucky would decline by 70 percent between 2012 and 2020. In a September 2018 report, the Kentucky Chamber of Commerce reported that the "mountain" region of the state continued to lose population in 2017, though wages rose a bit. A research report in 2018 found that this district had the nation's second-highest opioid-prescription rate, according to the Harvard School of Public Health. Some hope came from new employment prospects. In 2018, the Justice Department said that it planned to build in Letcher County a $450 million prison, with more than 300 jobs. A lithium battery maker said its new factory in Pikeville will create 900 jobs.

The 5th Congressional District of Kentucky includes much of the territory east of the Pottsville Escarpment, which separates the Cumberland Plateau and most of the eastern mountains from the rest of the state. It includes a few counties in the eastern Pennyrile region: small towns like Somerset,

Monticello and Mount Vernon. And it takes in the mountains to the east, including Corbin, where Colonel Harland Sanders first served his fried chicken with 11 herbs and spices, birthing fast-food franchise KFC. The northeast section of the district is coal country. Few highways go through the mountains; only a handful of towns have a population over 10,000. Overall this district is heavily Republican, among the top 1 percent in the nation: The 80 percent of the vote for Trump was tied with two other districts — in Alabama and Texas — for his best performance in the nation in 2016.

Andy Barr (R)

Elected 2012, 4th term, b. Jul 24, 1973; Lexington; University of Virginia, B.A., 1996; University of Kentucky College of Law, J.D., 2001; Episcopalian; Married (Eleanor Carol Leavell); 2 children.

Professional Career: Legislative Assistant, U.S. Rep. Jim Talent, 1996-1998; Instructor, Morehead St. University; Attorney, KY gov.'s office, 2004-2007; Practicing attorney, 2008-2012.

DC Office: 2430 RHOB 20515, 202-225-4706, Fax: 202-225-2122, barr.house.gov

State Offices: Lexington, 859-219-1366.

Committees: *Financial Services*: Consumer Protection & Financial Institutions; Oversight & Investigations (RMM). *Veterans' Affairs*: Economic Opportunity; Health.

Group Ratings

	ADA	ACLU	AFL-CIO	LCV	ITI	COC	HAFA	ACU	CFG	FRC
2018	-	4%	-	0%	-	92%	71%	88%	57%	100%
2017	0%	C	5%	0%	C	93%	C	93%	85%	100%

Almanac Ratings 2017-18

	Economy	Social	Foreign	Composite
Liberal	2%	4%	0%	2%
Conservative	99%	97%	100%	98%

Key Votes of the 115th Congress

1. Obama-care revision	Y	5. Family planning regs	Y	9. Guantanamo prisoners	N
2. Tax Cuts	Y	6. Body cameras/immigration	N	10. Ground missiles, limit	N
3. Omnibus appropriations	Y	7. Abortion ban	Y	11. Defense Dept. spending	Y
4. Dodd-Frank revision	Y	8. Concealed carry	Y	12. FISA rules	Y

Election Results

Election	Name (Party)	Vote (%)	Cand. Spent	Ind. Exp. Support	Ind. Exp. Oppose
2018 General	Andy Barr (R)............................... 154,468	(51%)	$5,561,315	$1,298,655	$1,938,955
	Amy McGrath (D)............................ 144,736	(48%)	$7,564,748	$1,611,458	$3,510,801
2018 Primary	Andy Barr (R)................................ 40,514	(84%)			
	Chuck Eddy (R).................................... 7,858	(16%)			

Prior winning percentages: 2016 (61%), 2014 (60%), 2012 (51%)

After defeating Democratic Rep. Ben Chandler in their 2012 rematch, Republican attorney Andy Barr has secured this seat against competitive challengers. In 2018, he was among the few House Republicans to survive a prominent, well-financed contest. The youthful Barr seems well-placed for further political influence, in his House committee work and perhaps an eventual statewide bid.

Barr grew up in Lexington and graduated from the University of Virginia with a bachelor's degree in government and philosophy. After two years as a legislative assistant for Republican Rep. Jim Talent of Missouri, Barr returned home to earn a law degree from the University of Kentucky. He practiced law and taught constitutional and administrative law as a part-time instructor at Morehead State University. Barr served as a deputy general counsel to former Kentucky Gov. Ernie Fletcher.

In his 2010 challenge to Chandler, Barr distanced himself from Fletcher, whose tenure was marred by scandal over political hiring of state employees. Chandler won by 647 votes. Barr decided against a recount and conceded 10 days after the election. Barr got an earlier start in his 2012 rematch, though Chandler got help from redistricting. Barr attacked the policies of President Barack Obama — especially on coal, an important issue to the district — and used a picture of his own baby daughter on a campaign mailer that called Chandler a "pro-abortion extremist." Chandler brought up Barr's guilty plea to possession of a fake ID when he was 19. Barr responded with an ad calling the incident a "dumb mistake" by a teenager and blasting his rival as a "desperate politician scared of losing." He got fundraising help from outside Republican groups that helped put him over the top. He won, 51%-47%.

Barr has been active on the Financial Services Committee. In 2015, he filed legislation that would streamline financial regulations, especially affecting community banks and credit unions, which often are important in rural communities. In 2017, with support from President Donald Trump, Barr joined other committee Republicans in enacting a partial rollback of the 2010 Dodd-Frank banking regulations. The law, he said, had been bad for Kentucky, with the closing of credit unions and small banks and the opening of few new banks. "Dodd-Frank regulations clogged the plumbing of our economy, especially in rural and underserved communities," he told the Banking Committee of the state House. Barr chaired the Subcommittee on Monetary Policy and Trade, where he conducted oversight of the Federal Reserve System to encourage a stable monetary policy. He filed a bill to require "greater transparency and accountability" by the Fed in setting monetary policy.

With the encouragement of Speaker Paul Ryan, Barr in 2016 joined a House Republican task force that proposed changes in federal anti-poverty policy. Citing what he described as the positive results after the food stamp program allowed more state management of the reorganized Temporary Assistance for Needy Families program, Barr called for increased work requirements in anti-poverty programs. "Work is not a punishment; work is a blessing. It's a ticket to upward mobility," he told the Lexington Herald-Leader. "And we think poor people are not liabilities to be managed by some distant welfare bureaucracy in Washington."

Barr's initial two reelection campaign had similar patterns. In 2014, he faced Elizabeth Jensen, an education advocate and Democratic activist, whom he outspent $2.2 million to nearly $900,000. He coasted to victory with 60 percent of the vote and won all 19 counties. In 2016, Nancy Jo Kemper, former executive director of the Kentucky Council of Churches, advocated a minimum wage increase and campaign-finance reform and said she was "excited to be a Democrat." Barr outraised Kemper, $2.5 million to $454,000. This time, Barr won 61%-39%. He had a slim lead in Fayette County, 51%-49%, but rolled up big margins elsewhere in the district.

In 2018, he had a high-profile showdown with Naval Academy graduate Amy McGrath, the first female Marine to pilot an F-18 fighter in Afghanistan and a political newcomer. In the Democratic primary, she defeated Lexington Mayor Jim Gray, 49%-41%, despite the support he received from the Democratic Congressional Campaign Committee. McGrath emphasized her military service, said that it was time for a new political voice and took positions on gun control, for example, that were more progressive than customary in the district. Barr tied himself closely to Trump and Senate Majority Leader Mitch McConnell, though he disagreed with the president's call to end "birthright" citizenship for children born in the United States to non-citizens. This was one of the most expensive campaigns in the nation, with McGrath outspending Barr, $7.6 million to $5.6 million and the national parties spending another $8 million. Barr won 51%-48%, a margin of nearly 10,000 votes. McGrath won Fayette County by 25,000 votes and Frankfort-based Franklin County by less than 2,000 votes; Barr took the other 17 counties.

In 2019, Barr joined the Veterans' Affairs Committee — an attempt, perhaps, to reinforce his support with veterans and the military community.

KY-6: Bluegrass Country

Cook Partisan Voting Index: R+9

Population		Race and Ethnicity		Income	
Total	757,699	White	82.3%	Median Income	$50,452
Land area (sq. miles)	4,293	Black	8.5%	District Income Rank	299
Pop/ sq mi	176.5	Latino	4.6%	Poverty Rate	18.2%
Born in State	68.2%	Asian	1.9%	With health insurance	91.7%
		Two or more races	2.2%	Cash public assistance	1.9%
Age Groups		Other	0.4%	Food stamp/SNAP	14.6%
Under 18	22.2%				
18-34	25.4%	**Education**		**Work**	
35-64	38.6%	H.S grad or less	41.2%	White Collar	13.8%
Over 64	13.8%	Some college	28%	Sales and Service	40%
		College Degree, 4 yr	18.2%	Blue Collar	22.7%
Military		Post grad	12.6%	Government	16.9%
Veteran/ Active Duty	7.6%				

2012 Pres. Vote	Romney	170,056	(56%)	Obama	128,564	(42%)			
2016 Pres. Vote	Trump	182,141	(55%)	Clinton	131,271	(39%)	Johnson	11,074	(3%)

Lexington: With its white picket fences, horse farms and small towns, the rolling plateau of bluegrass in central Kentucky is the part of interior America longest settled by English speakers: Lexington was founded in 1775. Tobacco farming started here in the 1770s, horse racing in 1787, and the Reverend Elijah Craig is often credited with inventing bourbon distilling in 1789 (though many rivals have also affixed stakes to that claim). Tobacco, whiskey and racehorses remained the staples of the economy for six generations, until 1956, when IBM built its typewriter plant in Lexington. The personal computer eventually outclassed the typewriter, and the big employer here became Lexmark International, an IBM spinoff. In 2018, it had 2,300 local employees — now under the control of a Chinese consortium. Another mainstay is the Toyota plant in Georgetown, a town with early-19th-century houses and lush countryside just one county north of the city. This is the largest Toyota plant in the nation, with 8,200 workers. In 2017 they produced 550,000 vehicles, including the company's top-selling Camry and its new Lexus ES 350 model. In 2017, the company unveiled a $1.3 billion update of the plant to streamline production and build a new paint shop.

Lexington, which includes all of Fayette County, grew by 23 percent between 2000 and 2017, as its well-educated, young populace continued to attract business. Another 30 percent increase is projected by 2040, while two-thirds of the counties in Kentucky are projected to lose population. Jim Gray, an openly gay construction executive, served two terms as mayor before stepping down in 2018. He unsuccessfully challenged Sen. Rand Paul in 2016, then lost the Democratic primary for a House seat. His sexual orientation was not an issue in his campaigns. Also here is the University of Kentucky, where basketball mania is featured at Rupp Arena. This is the second-largest metropolitan area in the state, after Louisville-Jefferson County. Fayette was the only other county in Kentucky that Hillary Clinton won in 2016.

The 6th Congressional District of Kentucky includes Lexington and the surrounding counties. Lexington casts about 40 percent of its votes. It is the only district in Kentucky that does not border another state. To the northwest is the state capital of Frankfort, platted during the War for Independence by Gen. James Wilkinson, who was also secretly a paid agent of the Spanish Crown and who worked to cede various portions of the United States, including Kentucky, to Spain. This was traditionally a swing area of the state. Donald Trump carried the district with 55 percent of the vote.

LOUISIANA

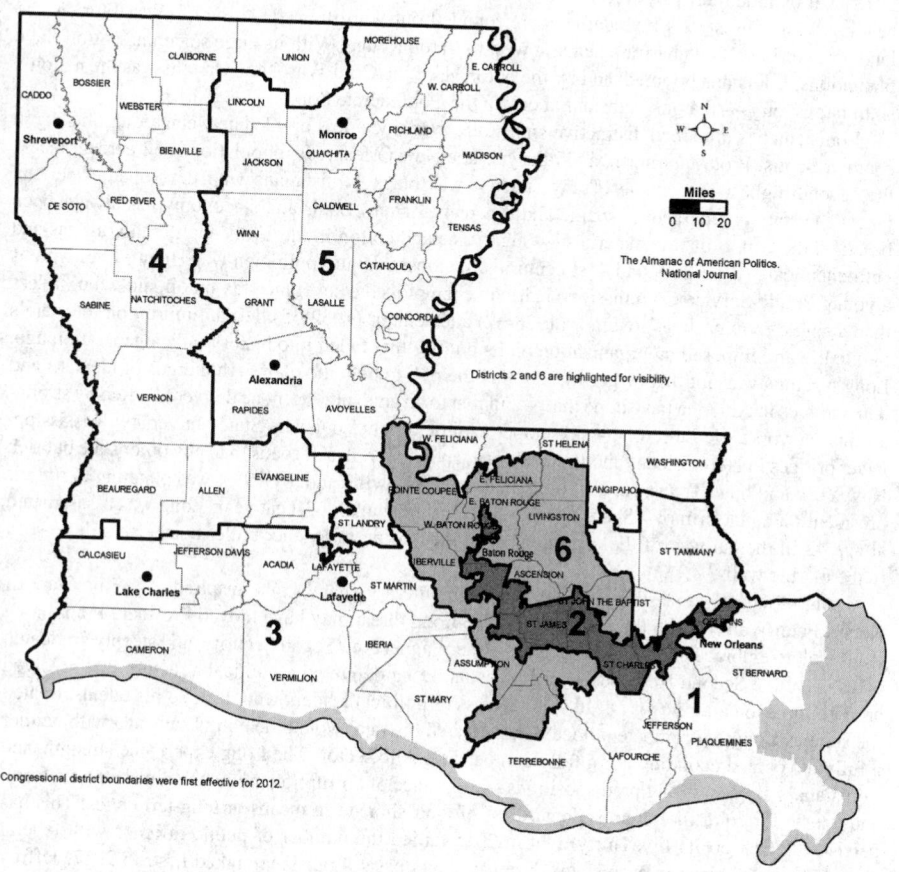

The Almanac of American Politics.
National Journal

Miles
0   10   20

Districts 2 and 6 are highlighted for visibility.

Congressional district boundaries were first effective for 2012.

In the decade between 2000 and 2010, Louisiana – ravaged repeatedly by hurricanes – ranked third to last of any state in population growth. But since 2010, Louisiana's population has increased by 3 percent, and by a striking 13 percent in Orleans Parish – Louisiana's singular, and singularly resilient, urban gem, New Orleans. The comeback hasn't been perfect, but at least it's a comeback.

In 1718, the French founded New Orleans on a ridge formed by deposits of silt and declared the Mississippi Valley the colony of Louisiana. It was transferred to Spain in 1763, and after France took possession again, Jefferson sought to buy the city in 1802. When Napoleon offered to sell the entire Louisiana Territory, Jefferson's envoys quickly and eagerly agreed to purchase it — almost doubling the land area of the young republic. Its large French and small Spanish population had been ruled under European civil law rather than English common law. When Louisiana was admitted as a state in 1812, it included territory well to the north of the city that would soon be overrun by Americans heading west. The state's boundaries were rounded out with the acquisition of West Florida, the land north of Lake Pontchartrain heading west to Baton Rouge. With its large sugar and cotton slave plantations, Louisiana boomed, and by the outbreak of the Civil War, New Orleans was the nation's sixth largest city — the only substantial city in the Confederate South.

Louisiana has remained distinctive and exotic ever since. It is divided between a Catholic Cajun south, a Baptist Protestant north, and idiosyncratic New Orleans. Its population is 32 percent black, the second-highest percentage of any state; it was black Louisianans who developed American jazz. (The state is 5 percent Hispanic and 2 percent Asian.) Louisiana's economy has always been based on the export of raw materials — sugar, rice and cotton in the 19th century, and oil, gas and petrochemicals in the 20th and 21st centuries. Its most talented politician was Huey Long, who as a young Public Service Commission chairman championed a severance tax on oil, and who, in less than a single term each as governor (1928-32) and senator (1932-35), left an imprint on the state's public life and imposed an organization on its politics that faded into history only a generation ago. Long's genius was not that he promised to tax the rich to help the poor — hundreds of idealists and demagogues in America have done that — but that to an amazing extent he delivered, often by strong-arming or worse. He built a new skyscraper capitol, a new Louisiana State University, Mississippi River bridges in New Orleans and Baton Rouge, and more miles of roads than any other state but rich New York and huge Texas. He also built a national following and, by 1935, was planning to run for president on a platform of "Share the wealth, every man a king." That year, Long was assassinated at age 42 in the hallway of the capitol he built. According to legend, bullet holes can still be seen in the marble walls.

Long's impact was lasting, and not just in the literary character he inspired — Willie Stark of Robert Penn Warren's All the King's Men. The Long threat may have moved President Franklin D. Roosevelt to embrace the liberal programs — the Wagner Act, Social Security, and steeply graduated taxes — of the Second New Deal. For Louisiana, Long delivered a political structure that revolved around him even after he was dead—and a class of political leaders who, lacking his talents, treated the state as Long's incompetent doctors had treated his fatal wound, leaving Louisiana with neither a fully developed economy nor a fully competent public sector. The Long experience strengthened Louisiana's already strong predispositions — tolerance of corruption, no interest in abstract reform, and a taste for colorful extremists regardless of their short-term means or long-term ends. This has persisted. The website FiveThirtyEight in 2015 tallied the number of public officials with federal corruption convictions in each state. On a per capita basis, Louisiana ranked first. In 2017, Jeffrey Sallet, the outgoing head of the FBI's New Orleans Division, told the Times-Picayune that "the corruption in this state is at an extremely unacceptable level."

This has not helped to create a vibrant economy. Louisiana has chronically suffered low incomes, low workforce participation, and low levels of education, with income disparities greater than almost anywhere else in the United States. In 2018, Louisiana was tied for the second-highest poverty rate in the country at nearly 20 percent, and the rate for children was 28 percent. Median family income ranked second from the bottom, exceeding only neighbor Mississippi. The United Health Foundation ranked Louisiana the nation's unhealthiest state, driven by an adult obesity rate of 36 percent, an adult smoking rate of 23 percent, and a nearly 11 percent rate of low birth-weight babies. Louisiana had the nation's highest incarceration rate until 2018, when Oklahoma leapfrogged it, and the Violence Policy

Center determined that Louisiana ranked second nationally for the frequency of men murdering women. Meanwhile, Moody's Analytics named Louisiana as the state worst prepared for a recession.

Louisiana momentarily prospered when oil prices spiked upward in 1973 and 1979, but then jobs and people flowed out in the 1980s as it failed to develop a diverse economy similar to that of its similarly oil-rich neighbor, Texas. This has made a huge difference over time. Metro New Orleans in 1940 had a population of 564,000; it was about the same size then as metro Houston (610,000) and metro Dallas (624,000). But in 2004, just before Hurricane Katrina struck, metro Houston had 5.1 million people, metro Dallas 5.8 million, and New Orleans just 1.3 million. By 2017, metro Houston had 6.9 million and metro Dallas had 7.4 million, while metro New Orleans was stuck at 1.3 million.

Hurricane Katrina, by far the costliest on record, slammed the Gulf Coast on August 29, 2005, and for several weeks, New Orleans and Louisiana dominated the national spotlight. More than 80 percent of the city was flooded after the federally built floodwalls failed, and hundreds of thousands of residents abandoned their homes for higher ground. All told, Katrina was responsible for some 1,800 deaths and at least $108 billion in property damage, including $10 billion for damage to energy infrastructure. New Orleans mostly withstood the initial winds and storm surge. But then the levees broke, submerging much of the city. The 17th Street Canal sprang a 200-foot gash through which much of the water flowed. Levees along the Industrial Canal, in the poverty-stricken 9th Ward, likewise failed to hold back water driven by a wave surge that reached over 20 feet. More than half of the 270 miles of levees and flood walls in Louisiana were breached or heavily damaged by winds and flood waters. Katrina (with another powerful storm, Rita, less than a month later) also laid bare the state's political and economic frailties. Gov. Kathleen Blanco and Mayor Ray Nagin (who was convicted of bribery charges in 2014) seemed incapable of coping with the disaster.

By July 2006, Louisiana's population declined by 250,000 (mostly in the New Orleans area), although many people eventually returned, as did tourists. In April 2010, disaster struck Louisiana again when BP's Deepwater Horizon oil rig exploded, killing 11 workers and spewing an estimated 4 million barrels of oil into the Gulf of Mexico. The oil slick that spread from the drilling site southeast of the mouth of the Mississippi River to the Mississippi River Delta threatened the state's oyster beds and shrimp fisheries. Five years later, an estimated 20 species continued to struggle. The federal government imposed a six-month moratorium on offshore drilling, a serious economic setback for the state. In the first five years after the spill, BP spent $27 billion on the recovery, economic claims and fines. Meanwhile, a second, much slower leak known as the Taylor oil spill has dumped tens of thousands of gallons a day since 2004, with no sign of slowing.

Despite its risks, offshore drilling has been a major element of Louisiana's economy since the 1940s. The state has 125,000 miles of pipeline, said to be enough to encircle the planet five times. The resumption of offshore drilling in 2011 and the increasing use of fracking — the extraction of natural gas by hydraulic fracturing — in the Haynesville shale in northwest Louisiana touched off a recovery, with billion-dollar investments in refineries, gas-to-liquid facilities, and liquefied natural gas export terminals. The oil-price slump that began around 2014 only hastened the shift of the industry's center of gravity, as companies such as ConnocoPhillips and Marathon moved their focus away from oil-drilling platforms in the gulf toward the state's shale resources further north. In 2018, BP spent $10.5 billion for 470,000 acres of shale properties in Texas and Louisiana. The chemical business, closely related to the petroleum industry, continued to show life: Formosa Petrochemical Corp. has bought a 2,400-acre site on the Mississippi River in St. James Parish for a planned $9.4 billion chemical complex.

Unemployment in Louisiana followed an unusual track, peaking at only 8.3 percent in the fall of 2010, but since then improving more slowly than the national average. By late 2018, unemployment was more than a point above the national average, exceeded by only two other resource-dependent states – Alaska and West Virginia. Employment in the state was hurt by the closure of Avondale Shipyard in Avondale and the loss of an International Paper mill in Bastrop. In January 2019, Georgia-Pacific said the digital era is leading it to abandon the office-paper business, resulting in 650 employees being laid off at its mill in Port Hudson.

In 2016, Baton Rouge experienced severe flooding that the region hasn't fully recovered from. The following year, parts of Louisiana, along with much of southeastern Texas, was soaked by Hurricane Harvey, which dumped as much as 22 inches of rain. The slow-moving storm shuttered almost a quarter of the nation's refining capacity; it became the nation's second-most expensive storm after Katrina. It was a reminder of Louisiana's mounting environmental challenges. Low-lying Louisiana is uniquely at risk from rising sea levels. Brett Anderson of the New Orleans Times-Picayune has written that if maps of the state rendered wetlands as water and counted only solid "walkable" ground as land, then the very shape of Louisiana—its iconic "boot"—would appear "as if it came out on the wrong side of a battle with a lawnmower's blades." In 2017, Gov. John Bel Edwards declared a state of emergency over coastal erosion and urged completion of a 50-year, $50 billion master plan drawn up by a state panel, largely funded by BP settlement money. Failing to curb the loss of land and wetlands could cost $11.2 billion in direct costs, lost wages, consumer spending and supply-chain disruptions over the next five decades -- not including damage caused by hurricanes, according to the Louisiana State University Economics & Policy Research Group.

For more than a century after the Civil War, Louisiana was solidly Democratic, with political divides expressed in Democratic primaries. There were splits between the Cajun Catholic parishes, which cast about 30 percent of the state's votes, and Protestant parishes north of Baton Rouge, which cast about 45 percent. Another division was by income. Low-income voters of both races tended to support Huey Long and his populist successors; higher-income voters often opposed them. So for a long time, Louisiana politics were a struggle between reformist and conservative forces on one side and roguish populists on the other, a struggle waged in lavishly financed campaigns with grandiloquent rhetoric. For more than two decades the lead role in state politics was played by Edwin Edwards, a colorful Cajun populist who was elected governor in 1972 and 1975, sat out 1979 because he was ineligible to run, and then in 1983 won a third term. While in office, he faced corruption charges and was acquitted by a jury in 1986. He lost a bid for reelection in 1987 but ran again in 1991. In Louisiana's all-party system, he won 34 percent of the vote to 32 percent for David Duke, a white supremacist who had won a special election to the legislature as a Republican in 1989 and was repudiated by most in his party. Bumper stickers read, "Vote for the crook — it's important," and a majority of voters listened; Edwards won the runoff, 61%-39%. He was convicted on corruption charges in May 2000 and went to prison. (After his release, he lost a comeback race for a U.S. House seat in 2014.)

Louisiana voted for Bill Clinton in 1992 and 1996 – the only state in the Deep South to do so – but has since voted increasingly Republican. Republican Bobby Jindal, defeated for governor 52%-48% by Democrat Blanco in 2003, came back in 2007 and won the multiparty primary with 54 percent of the vote. The congressional delegation now has five Republicans, including House Minority Whip Steve Scalise, and one Democrat; the legislature, Democratic since Reconstruction, changed hands as party switchers brought about Republican majorities in the state House in 2010 and the state Senate in 2011. Jindal, a political wunderkind, came into the governorship as a policy wonk, and governed more as ideologue than pragmatist. Louisiana on his watch was hammered by lower oil prices, which, combined with past tax cuts and little spending restraint meant that Jindal left office with a $943 million budget deficit for his final fiscal year and a projected $2 billion shortfall for 2016-2017. His approval ratings sank to the high 20s -- below even Obama's in the state – and he dropped out of the presidential race several weeks before the Iowa Caucuses.

Jindal's rocky tenure enabled a relatively obscure Democrat, West Point graduate John Bel Edwards, to succeed him. Edwards defeated Republican Sen. David Vitter for the governorship by a 56%-44% margin, amid fatigue over Jindal and a relitigation of Vitter's past scandals. In office, Edwards signed up 480,000 people for Medicaid expansion under the Affordable Care Act, something Jindal had refused to do. In addition, a criminal-justice overhaul pushed by a bipartisan coalition in the legislature and signed by Edwards in 2017 reduced the number of people imprisoned for non-violent crimes by 20 percent, and cut the number sent to prison for drug possession by 42 percent.

In 2016, Donald Trump expanded on Mitt Romney's 2012 victory in the state, widening the GOP margin from 18 points to 20, thanks to strong backing in rural areas. The other notable electoral result from 2016: Duke, the white supremacist, garnered only 3 percent of the primary vote for Vitter's open Senate seat, nowhere near enough to make the runoff. The 2018 midterms were relatively quiet, but Louisiana voters did take an important step on criminal justice, passing a ballot measure to require unanimous jury verdicts by a 64%-36% margin. The state had previously allowed guilty verdicts if

10 of 12 jurors agreed. This less-than-unanimous standard was a legacy of a 1898 state constitution that had been drafted "to establish the supremacy of the white race in the state."

Population		Race and Ethnicity		Income	
Total	4,663,461	White	59.0%	Median Income	$46,710
Land area (sq. miles)	43,204	Black	32.0%	State Income Rank	45
Pop/ sq mi	107.9	Latino	5.0%	Poverty Rate	19.6%
Born in state	78.0%	Asian	1.7%	With health insurance	87.6%
		Two or more races	1.6%	Cash public assistance	1.6%
Age Groups		Other	0.7%	Food stamp/SNAP	16.0%
Under 18	23.9%				
18-34	24.1%	**Education**		**Work**	
35-64	37.9%	H.S grad or less	49.5%	White Collar	33.1%
Over 64	14.1%	Some college	27.1%	Sales and Service	42.9%
Military		College Degree, 4 yr	15.3%	Blue Collar	24.0%
Veteran/ Active Duty	7.6%	Post grad	8.1%	Government	14.9%

Presidential Politics

2016 Primary (D)	Clinton (D)	221,733 (71%)	Sanders (D)	72,276 (23%)			
2016 Primary (R)	Trump (R)	124,854 (41%)	Cruz (R)	113,968 (38%)	Rubio (R)		33,813 (11%)
	Kasich (R)	19,359 (6%)					
2016 Pres. Vote	Trump (R)	1,178,638 (58%)	Clinton (D)	780,154 (38%)			
2012 Pres. Vote	Romney (R)	1,152,262 (58%)	Obama (D)	809,141 (41%)			

Not many general election presidential campaign ads are going to be taped in Cajun any time soon. In the past four races, Louisiana voted for the Republican nominees by 57 percent, 59 percent, 58 percent and 58 percent. The vote in Donald Trump's victory over Hillary Clinton, who received 38 percent, was remarkably similar to the regional results in the state four years earlier: Clinton and Barack Obama both won Orleans Parish with about 80 percent; the Democratic and Republican tickets were essentially tied in the Baton Rouge area, and the GOP nominee won the rest of the state with more than 62 percent of the vote.

Louisiana has rarely played a significant role in presidential primaries and caucuses, with one odd exception. That was 1996, when GOP allies of candidate Phil Gramm of Texas set up a pre-Iowa caucus in Louisiana on Feb. 6. The aim was to jumpstart Gramm's campaign. Instead, the caucuses killed it. Only 65,000 Republicans showed up at 42 voting sites and conservative commentator Pat Buchanan bested Gramm winning 13 of the 21 delegates. Gramm never recovered. In 2016, Trump narrowly defeated Ted Cruz 41%-38% on March 5, but Cruz managed to wrangle 10 additional delegates in the post-primary selection process. Trump threatened a lawsuit but never followed through. In the Democratic primary, Clinton trounced Vermont Sen. Bernie Sanders, 71%-23%. She carried 62 of the state's 64 parishes. Like many states in the south, Clinton's overwhelming support from African Americans gave her an advantage in Louisiana, where a majority of registered Democrats are black.

Congressional Districts

116th Congress Lineup	1D 5R	**115th Congress Lineup**	1D 5R

Following the 2002 redistricting in Louisiana, five of the seven districts elected House members from each party at some point in the elections from 2002 to 2010. Those politics have changed. The exodus from Louisiana after Hurricane Katrina led to the drop to six House seats after the 2010 census. As recently as 1980, the state had eight seats. Demographically, the 2nd District, centered in New Orleans, suffered the greatest population loss by far. Its black-majority district now extends to parts of Baton Rouge. The latest round of redistricting eliminated a district in Cajun country. With Republican population centers in the New Orleans suburbs, Baton Rouge, the Bayous, Shreveport and the northeast corner, creating a second Democratic or black-majority district would require creative gerrymandering, though breaking up the 2nd could ben option. The adjacent 4th and 5th Districts in northern Louisiana have 34 percent and 36 percent black population, respectively, which are widely dispersed in small cities and rural areas. With a Democratic governor, those dynamics could create opportunities.

John Bel Edwards (D)

Elected 2015, term expires 2020, 1st term; b. Sep. 16, 1966, Amite; United States Military Academy, B.S 1988; Louisiana State University Law School, J.D 1999; Roman Catholic; Married (Donna); 3 children.

Military Career: U.S Army, 1988-1996.

Elected Office: LA House, 2007-2015.

Professional Career: Attorney, Edwards & Associates.

Office: PO Box 94004, Baton Rouge, 70804-9004; 225-342-7015; Fax: 225-342-7099; Website: gov.louisiana.gov.

Lt. Gov.: Billy Nungesser (R) **Atty. Gen:** Jeff Landry (R) **Sec. of State:** Kyle Ardoin (R)

State Legislature: Senate: 14D, 25R **House:** 39D, 62R, 4I

Election Results

Election	Name (Party)	Vote (%)
2015 Primary	John Bel Edwards (D)	444,061 (40%)
	David Vitter (R)	256,105 (23%)
	Scott Angelle (R)	214,907 (19%)
	Jay Dardenne (R)	166,553 (15%)
2015 Run off	John Bel Edwards (D)	646,860 (56%)
	David Vitter (R)	505,929 (44%)

John Bel Edwards, the scion of a law-enforcement and political family, leveraged dissatisfaction with outgoing Republican Gov. Bobby Jindal and his scandal-tarred Republican opponent, then-Sen. David Vitter, to win an upset victory in Louisiana's 2015 gubernatorial race. That enabled Edwards, a Democrat, to become the only member of his party to serve in statewide office in Louisiana, which in recent years has voted heavily Republican. In office, he enacted an eclectic mix of measures, ranging from an expansion of Medicaid under the Affordable Care Act to one of the nation's most restrictive abortion laws.

Edwards was one of eight children who grew up in Amite, a town of roughly 4,000 residents 48 miles northeast of Baton Rouge in Tangipahoa Parish. His great-grandfather was the parish sheriff, and his grandfather, Frank Edwards, was a state legislator. His father, Frank Edwards Jr., also served as sheriff, as well as an appointee of then-Gov. Edwin Edwards (no relation). Edwards Jr. was succeeded as sheriff by his son -- Edwards' brother, Daniel Edwards. Another brother, Frank Edwards III, serves as police chief of nearby Independence. The family had such deep political roots that it was inducted collectively into the Louisiana Political Hall of Fame. ("Bel" is his middle name – a family name going back generations – and he is often called "John Bel.")

In high school, Edwards captained the football team and was named valedictorian. He attended West Point, graduating with a bachelor's degree in engineering, then served for eight years as an airborne ranger. He later earned his law degree from Louisiana State University and became an attorney in private practice in Amite, eschewing criminal cases because of his brother's service as sheriff. In 2007, Edwards was elected to the state House and became a member of its leadership; he served in the chamber until he was elected governor. In the House, Edwards served on the Education Committee, criticizing Jindal's emphasis on charter schools and Republican attacks on teacher tenure.

When Edwards decided to run for governor, he was far from well-known around the state – and he was a Democrat, a toxic label for recent statewide candidates in Louisiana. He gained some traction, though, by running against Jindal's record in office, including a projected $1.4 billion budget deficit and a seeming indifference to state issues while seeking the Republican presidential nomination. Edwards also pledged to raise the minimum wage and expand Medicaid, which Jindal had steadfastly refused to do. At the same time, Edwards blurred distinctions with Republicans on social issues, supporting gun rights and opposing abortion. A Catholic, Edwards ran an ad spotlighting how his family had ruled out an abortion after learning that their unborn daughter had spina bifida. She thrived and was married during Edwards' first year as governor. "I don't like being pigeonholed," he later told the Catholic magazine America. "There are people who say, 'You're pro-life on abortion, so that makes you conservative, but you're for the Medicaid expansion. That makes you liberal.' But it's the exact same Catholic Christian faith, at least as I understand it, that pushes me into both of those positions."

In Louisiana's all-party primary, Edwards faced three prominent Republicans: Public Service Commissioner Scott Angelle; Lt. Gov. Jay Dardenne; and Vitter. Most observers had assumed that Vitter's 2007 prostitution scandal was settled business following his easy reelection to the Senate in 2010, but Dardenne and Angelle raised the issue, and it gained traction. On Election Day, Edwards, facing minimal Democratic opposition, took 40 percent of the vote, as Vitter barely qualified for the Nov. 21 runoff with 23 percent. Angelle and Dardenne split the Republican anti-Vitter vote with 19 percent and 15 percent, respectively.

Edwards and his allies kept up the drumbeat on Vitter's past behavior – one ad bluntly compared "John Bel Edwards, who answered our country's call and served as a Ranger" to Vitter, "who answered a prostitute's call." Dardenne endorsed Edwards after the primary rather than back his fellow Republican. (After his victory, Edwards tapped Dardenne for a senior post in his administration.) Edwards won the runoff, 56%-44% -- the biggest Democratic gubernatorial victory in the state since 1991's "Vote for the crook, it's important" race between the ethically challenged Edwin Edwards and white supremacist David Duke.

Once in office, Edwards quickly fulfilled his promise to expand Medicaid. "With the stroke of a pen, Edwards brought one of the poorest states into the fold of the largest expansion of the welfare state since the 1960s," wrote the Texas Observer. But Edwards faced setbacks, too. By tradition, Louisiana's governor had long played a decisive role in the selection of a House speaker, but in Edwards' case, most House Republicans, joined by one Democrat, rejected his pick for the post, Democrat Walt Leger, and instead chose a Republican, Taylor Barras – a sign, many observers said, that the state's once quirky political alignments were becoming increasingly polarized along national party lines. The vote for speaker foreshadowed future sparring between the governor and the legislature over the budget, which was headed toward a $943 million deficit for fiscal 2016 and $2 billion for fiscal 2017, stemming partly from a slump in petroleum prices.

In February 2016, Edwards took the unusual step of making a televised budget address, warning of cuts to health care and higher education. He proposed hiking the state sales and cigarette taxes; reallocating some of the BP oil spill settlement money; and drawing down the rainy day fund. A 2016 special session fell short of revenue targets, but did accomplish a fair amount, including a temporary sales tax through 2018, a cigarette tax hike and corporate income tax changes.

Edwards won plaudits for his handling of two crises. One was the racial strife in Baton Rouge, which was sparked by the police killing of Alton Sterling, an African-American man, it continued with days of protests, and culminated almost two weeks later with the ambush murders of three law enforcement officers. (A few months earlier, Edwards had signed the nation's first "Blue Lives Matter" law, making the killings of police a hate crime.) Louisiana also suffered two rounds of floods – in the northern part of the state in March, and in the southern tier in August, the latter causing an estimated $8.7 billion in damage. In his handling of both episodes, Edwards "was a voice of calm and confidence," Louisiana State University professor and liberal newspaper columnist Robert Mann wrote.

Edwards faced other challenges. After issuing an executive order protecting LGBT state employees, Edwards sparred with Republican Attorney General Jeff Landry over its implementation. Landry refused to sign dozens of legal contracts for the state as long as they contained the protections. In December 2016, Edwards' order was overturned in court. The two continued to spar as Edwards' term progressed – over an Edwards-supported delay in executions due to a lack of lethal injection chemicals, and over Landry's decision to join a lawsuit seeking to overturn the Affordable Care Act. (Landry announced that he would not challenge Edwards in 2019.)

Edwards pleased social conservatives by signing several bills on abortion, including one in 2018 that banned abortions after 15 weeks, punishable by prison for the medical practitioner – the most stringent law in the nation, along with one enacted in neighboring Mississippi. But the laws were blocked in the courts. On criminal justice, Edwards in 2017 signed a package of 10 bills that curbed mandatory minimum sentences, overhauled drug sentencing, expanded alternatives to incarceration, and limited the most serious sentences for juveniles. The changes made an impact in their first year, as Louisiana fell from the top ranking in incarceration rate for the first time in years. Meanwhile, working with the legislature, Edwards managed to avoid a "fiscal cliff" that threatened funding for a wide range of popular programs; it stemmed from $1.4 billion in expiring tax changes that was set to hit on July 1, 2018. After multiple special sessions, the governor and the legislature finally reached an agreement in June 2018, just days before the cliff was to hit, that extended part of the sales tax hike through 2025.

A side effect of Edwards' efforts on criminal justice was to bring Edwards closer to the Trump administration, which had pursued a national criminal-justice overhaul that was eventually enacted in late 2018. Edwards joined a criminal justice summit at Trump's golf club in Bedminster New Jersey, and he became the only Democratic elected official to attend a White House state dinner with French President Emmanuel Macron. Edwards returned the favor by inviting Trump to visit the state penitentiary at Angola to see the laws' impact in person. Such connections to the White House could pay dividends for a Democrat seeking reelection in a state where Trump won overwhelmingly and remained popular. "It's not that I don't ever disagree" with Trump, Edwards told America magazine. "I just don't go out in public and blast the president, because I don't think it would be helpful."

As he looked ahead to his 2019 reelection campaign, Edwards maintained strong approval ratings. He spoke of making a teacher pay raise a top priority for his next term – a natural issue for a longtime ally of teachers' unions. Edwards signed a "fetal heartbeat" bill supported by social conservatives; while national democrats decried his position, it took a potent issue off the table back home. Perhaps his strongest potential Republican challenger, Sen. John Kennedy, opted against a run, but at least two Republicans jumped in the race: Rep. Ralph Abraham and deep-pocketed construction magnate Eddie Rispone.

Bill Cassidy (R)

Elected 2014, term expires 2020, 1st term, b. Sep 28, 1957; Highland Park, IL; Louisiana State University, B.S., 1979; Louisiana State University Medical School, M.D., 1983; Christian - Non-Denominational; Married (Laura Layden Cassidy); 3 children.

Elected Office: LA Senate, 2006-2008; U.S. House, 2009-2015.

Professional Career: Physician; Co-founder, Greater Baton Rouge Community Clinic; Association Professor, LSU Medical School, 1990-present.

DC Office: 520 HSOB 20510, 202-224-5824, Fax: 202-224-9735, cassidy.senate.gov

State Offices: Alexandria, 318-448-7176; Baton Rouge, 225-929-7711; Lafayette, 337-261-1400; Lake Charles, 337-493-5398; Metairie, 504-838-0130; Monroe, 318-324-2111; Shreveport, 318-798-3215.

Committees: *Energy & Natural Resources*: Energy (Chmn); Public Lands, Forests & Mining; Water & Power. *Finance*: Fiscal Responsibility & Economic Growth (Chmn); Health Care; International Trade, Customs & Global Competitiveness; Social Security, Pensions & Family Policy. *Health, Education, Labor & Pensions*: Children & Families; Employment & Workplace Safety; Primary Health & Retirement Security. *Joint Economic*. *Veterans' Affairs*.

Group Ratings

	ADA	ACLU	AFL-CIO	LCV	ITI	COC	HAFA	ACU	CFG	FRC
2018	-	14%	-	7%	-	80%	59%	86%	71%	88%
2017	0%	C	0%	0%	C	86%	C	80%	72%	100%

Almanac Ratings 2017-18

	Economy	Social	Foreign	Composite
Liberal	0%	0%	0%	0%
Conservative	100%	100%	100%	100%

Key Votes of the 115th Congress

1. Obama-care revision	Y	5. Gun regulations	Y	9. Kavanaugh confirmation	Y
2. Tax Cuts	Y	6. Family planning regs	Y	10. Saudi arms sales	N
3. Dodd-Frank revision	Y	7. Gorsuch confirmation	Y	11. FISA rules	Y
4. Omnibus appropriations	N	8. Immigration restrictions	Y	12. Military aid in Yemen	N

Election Results

Election	Name (Party)	Vote (%)		Cand. Spent	Ind. Exp. Support	Ind. Exp. Oppose
2014 General	Bill Cassidy (R)	712,379	(56%)	$14,655,887	$2,345,107	$11,190,682
	Mary Landrieu (D)	561,210	(44%)	$19,969,352	$824,174	$12,479,854
2014 Primary	Mary Landrieu (D)	619,402	(42%)			
	Bill Cassidy (R)	603,084	(41%)			
	Rob Maness (R)	202,556	(14%)			

Prior winning percentages: House: 2012 (79%), 2010 (66%), 2008 (48%)

Bill Cassidy lacked a calling card, but as Louisiana's senior senator, he has emerged as a sought-after voice in his party on health care, a role that brought him national attention during the Republican controlled Congress' 2017 efforts to repeal the Affordable Care Act. Cassidy, who despite being a former physician was initially shut out of the Senate Republicans' efforts to craft their own bill, found an audience by tying his repeal goals to the promise that it would fulfill the "Jimmy Kimmel test," named after the late-night comedian's emotional plea to preserve the ACA's provisions protecting people with pre-existing conditions. One of four former physicians in the Senate, all of whom are Republicans, Cassidy had been critical of the House's repeal efforts and defended the Congressional Budget Office against attacks that it was unrealistically estimating how many people would lose insurance. In turn, he floated a policy that would allow states to decide what to do about keeping Obamacare, a move that conservatives balked at and Democratic members thought was still too conservative.

Kimmel, in an emotional monologue days before the House repeal plan passed, spoke of his son who was born with a potentially fatal congenital heart disease, concluding in a plea that went viral that no parents should worry about being unable to afford care for their child. Cassidy was soon swarmed by reporters and even lauded by some liberal pundits. After speculation that he might break with the party on how to repeal Obamacare, Cassidy voted for all three of the plans put forward for a vote, including the last-ditch "skinny repeal" proposal that failed in dramatic fashion when Sen. John McCain joined fellow GOP Sens. Susan Collins and Lisa Murkowski in opposition. Despite the high-profile failure, Cassidy was adamant his party not give up and crafted a proposal with South Carolina Sen. Lindsey Graham. The plan was far more conservative than Cassidy's earlier proposal and Kimmel lit into the former physician by arguing that his plan did not pass Cassidy's own and now-famous test. McCain, Collins and Murkowski refused to budge, and the plan failed, like the others before it.

A three-term House member, Cassidy ousted three-term Democratic incumbent Mary Landrieu in 2014. William Morgan Cassidy was born in Highland Park, Ill., but grew up in Baton Rouge, La., the son of a life insurance salesman. He attended Louisiana State University as an undergraduate and earned a degree from LSU's medical school. During a medical residency in Los Angeles, Cassidy met his wife, Laura, also a physician. The New Orleans Times-Picayune has described Laura Cassidy as his "most trusted political adviser." She founded Louisiana Key Academy, a public charter school specializing in children with dyslexic symptoms, after one of their daughters was diagnosed with dyslexia.

In 1990, Bill Cassidy, a gastroenterologist, returned to Baton Rouge and joined the faculty of the LSU's medical school. He also began a nearly 25-year stint treating patients at LSU's Earl K. Long Hospital, part of Louisiana's charity hospital system devoted caring for uninsured patients. His wife eventually became chief of surgery at Earl K. Long. He continued working there on a part-time basis after his election to the House in 2008, until the hospital closed in 2013. He co-founded the Greater Baton Rouge Community Clinic, which provides free dental and health care to the working uninsured. He invoked his experience repeatedly during the ACA repeal fight, telling The New York Times, "There's a widespread recognition that the federal government, Congress, has created the right for every American to have health care. If you want to be fiscally responsible, then coverage is better than no coverage."

In a Times-Picayune profile, Cassidy said his family struggled financially at times when he was growing up, citing that as a major reason he had focused caring for needier people rather than working in a more traditional private practice. Several former colleagues at Earl K. Long expressed surprise at his strong opposition to Obamacare and wondered privately if his opposition was motivated by politics. Cassidy brushed aside such suggestions, saying that after witnessing government-run health care up close, he had concluded that the private insurance market is better equipped to provide medical coverage. "I believe my hospital system was one in which the government had all the power, not the patient," he said of his experience at Earl K. Long.

Cassidy had a defining moment when Hurricane Katrina hit in 2005. He created a makeshift field hospital in an abandoned Kmart store with the help of several other physicians. In a PBS documentary, he recalled entering the store after the storm to discover grease covering the floor, no electricity and no working phone lines. In two days, he and the others transformed the space to be ready to receive patients. He later said the experience played a major role in his decision to run for office.

In December 2006, Cassidy won a special election to the state Senate as a Republican. Earlier, he had contributed financially to Landrieu's first re-election in 2002. Cassidy is one of many Louisiana officeholders — including his junior colleague, Sen. John Kennedy — who have switched parties as the once solidly Democratic state transformed into a Republican stronghold.

When GOP Rep. Richard Baker resigned, Cassidy passed up the opportunity to compete in the 2008 special election. After Democratic state Rep. Don Cazayoux narrowly defeated GOP social conservative Woody Jenkins, Cassidy vowed to retake the 6th District for the Republicans. In that campaign, Cassidy described himself as a "pro-life, pro-gun rights" social conservative, while highlighting his state Senate record of voting against spending bills and cutting taxes for businesses and parents with children in private schools. Cazayoux ran an ad criticizing Cassidy for supporting creation of private savings accounts in Social Security. Democratic state Rep. Michael Jackson, who is African-American, ran as an independent, partly because of unhappiness over national Democrats' early support for Cazayoux.

Cassidy defeated Cazayoux 48%-40%, with the rest going to Jackson. He twice coasted to re-election. In the House, Cassidy had a plum seat on the Energy and Commerce Committee, which has significant jurisdiction over health care, and was called upon to publicly criticize the Obama administration on that issue. Saying that the government needed to get out of the way of patients, he supported providing incentives for preventive care along with creating health savings accounts. While a reliably conservative voter, Cassidy parted ways with his party on a few issues. In 2010, when Democrats controlled the House, Cassidy was one of four Republicans on the Agriculture Committee to vote to end the ban on U.S. travel to Cuba and ease regulations on sale of agricultural exports to the island. He backed Democratic bills to extend unemployment benefits and praised the Teach for America program that established a post-Katrina presence in Louisiana.

Cassidy's record led Louisiana Republicans to deem him the most formidable potential challenger to Landrieu, the last Senate Democrat from the Deep South at the time. Landrieu had been elected in 1996 by a mere 5,000 votes out of more than 1.7 million cast and survived re-election in 2002 and 2008 with just 52 percent each time. Over the course of Landrieu's career, Louisiana slipped politically and demographically away from the Democrats, accelerated by the departure of an estimated 125,000 Democratic voters after Katrina.

Given aspects of Cassidy's political past, his candidacy initially aroused suspicions among conservative groups about whether he was truly one of them; the Senate Conservatives Fund endorsed tea party-aligned Rob Maness, a retired Air Force colonel. Cassidy responded by making some moves to the right. He repudiated earlier support of the Troubled Asset Relief Program created to prop up financial institutions in 2008 and accepted the backing of Americans for Prosperity, the conservative group affiliated with the Koch brothers, which spent more than $3 million on ads attacking Landrieu. Cassidy also disputed whether climate change was occurring, claiming during one debate — inaccurately — that "global temperatures have not risen in 15 years." Still, Landrieu drew just 42 percent of the vote in an eight-candidate first-round election in November. Cassidy was just behind with 41 percent; Maness ran a distant third at 14 percent.

With the GOP having won enough seats in November to take over the Senate, the national import of the Landrieu-Cassidy December runoff was diminished. But with the chance to expand the new GOP majority, conservative groups spent an estimated $5.65 million in ads on his behalf. With President Barack Obama's approval rating in the state at just 39 percent, TV ads backing Cassidy "came down to four words: Mary Landrieu, Barack Obama," as Jason Berry, a New Orleans writer, put it. Cassidy rolled to an easy victory, 56%-44%, with exit polls showing only 18 percent of white voters backing Landrieu. His victory left Louisiana without a Democrat elected statewide for the first time since 1876. That changed the next year when Democrats recaptured the governorship.

As promised during the campaign, he was seated on the Energy and Natural Resources panel, a politically vital panel for his state's energy resources that Landrieu had chaired before her loss. He serves as chairman of the Energy and Natural Resources subcommittee on energy.

In early 2017, Cassidy partnered with Graham to offer a health care repeal plan that allowed states three options, including to continue running Obamacare as is. Their bill garnered little support as it came at a time when Republicans had decided to use reconciliation to ram through a repeal without the need of a single Democratic vote. But the Louisianan's legislation sparked the interest of many of his colleagues. Graham-Cassidy, as it became known, would have converted much of Obamacare's funding to block grants for states to set up their own programs along with fundamentally changing Medicaid by establishing a cap per enrollee. Most controversially, the block grant approach would have allowed states to vary premiums for people with pre-existing conditions. Cassidy defended the proposal, but the pre-existing conditions part of the bill led to the same public outcry that doomed the other proposals.

Even after repeal efforts failed, Cassidy returned to health care in 2018 by proposing eight ideas to reduce the cost of care. Perhaps his greatest legislative achievements have been health care-related. To address the opioid crisis, Trump signed bipartisan legislation with several provisions Cassidy had authored in 2018. Cassidy also partnered with Democratic Sen. Chris Murphy of Connecticut to strengthen laws requiring parity for mental and physical health care while providing grants to increase the limited supply of psychologists and psychiatrists across the country. Obama signed that measure as part of the 21st Century Cures Act.

Like the rest of his state's delegation, Cassidy had been an ardent advocate for the oil and gas industry. Both he and the rest of the Republicans in the delegation backed the Trump administration's proposal in early 2018 to open both coasts to more offshore drilling. Cassidy worked with Louisiana Rep. Steve Scalise to give more revenue from offshore drilling to Gulf Coast states as part of the tax bill that Republicans enacted in 2017.

Unlike other Republicans from Louisiana, Cassidy announced his public support for a 2018 ballot initiative to amend the state's Constitution to require unanimous jury verdicts in criminal cases. The amendment, which was backed by Democratic Rep. Cedric Richmond, passed overwhelmingly. According to the Times-Picayune, Louisiana had been the only state in which a 12-person jury verdict of 11-1 or 10-2 could result in a life sentence in prison without the possibility of parole, a 120-year-old practice that undermined the presence of African-American jurors.

As Cassidy prepared for re-election in 2020, it was unclear who would challenge him. Some Louisiana pundits have predicted Gov. John Bel Edwards could do so, if he wins re-election in 2019. If not, Maness or former secretary of state candidate Chris Tyson could run. Another big name would be former New Orleans Mayor Mitch Landrieu, the brother of the former senator. Although Cassidy seemed the strong favorite, Democrats in Louisiana have shown that they can win under limited circumstances.

John Kennedy (R)

Elected 2016, term expires 2022, 1st term, b. Nov 21, 1951; Centreville, MS; Vanderbilt University (TN), B.A., 1973; University of Virginia School of Law, J.D., 1977; Oxford University (England), B.CL, 1979; Methodist; Married (Rebecca Stulb Kennedy); 1 child.

Elected Office: Secretary, LA Department of Revenue, 1996-1999; LA Treasurer, 1999-2016

Professional Career: Special Counsel and Cabinet Secretary, Governor Buddy Roemer, 1988-1992; Practicing attorney; Adjunct Professor, Louisiana State University.

DC Office: 416 RSOB 20510, 202-224-4623, Fax: 202-228-0447, kennedy.senate.gov

State Offices: Baton Rouge, 225-926-8033; Lafayette, 337-269-5980; Monroe, 318-361-1489; New Orleans, 504-581-6190; Shreveport, 318-670-5192.

Committees: *Appropriations*: Agriculture, Rural Development, FDA & Related Agencies; Commerce, Justice, Science & Related Agencies; Department of Homeland Security; DOL, HHS & Education & Related Agencies; Energy & Water Development; Financial Services & General Government (Chmn). *Banking, Housing & Urban Affairs*: Economic Policy; Financial Institutions & Consumer Protection; Securities, Insurance & Investment. *Budget. Judiciary*: Border Security & Immigration; Crime & Terrorism; Oversight, Agency Action, Federal Rights & Federal Courts. *Small Business & Entrepreneurship.*

Group Ratings

	ADA	ACLU	AFL-CIO	LCV	ITI	COC	HAFA	ACU	CFG	FRC
2018	-	27%	-	7%	-	70%	67%	77%	90%	100%
2017	10%	C	7%	0%	C	71%	C	80%	86%	100%

Key Votes of the 115th Congress

1. Obama-care revision	Y	5. Gun regulations	Y	9. Kavanaugh confirmation	Y
2. Tax Cuts	Y	6. Family planning regs	Y	10. Saudi arms sales	N
3. Dodd-Frank revision	Y	7. Gorsuch confirmation	Y	11. FISA rules	Y
4. Omnibus appropriations	N	8. Immigration restrictions	N	12. Military aid in Yemen	N

Election Results

Election	Name (Party)	Vote (%)		Cand. Spent	Ind. Exp. Support	Ind. Exp. Oppose
2016 General	John Kennedy (R)	536,191	(61%)	$8,886,736	$744,378	$733,207
	Foster Campbell (D)	347,816	(39%)	$8,258,670	$313,915	$978,864
2016 Primary	John Kennedy (R)	482,591	(25%)			
	Foster Campbell (D)	337,833	(18%)			
	Charles Boustany (R)	298,008	(15%)			
	Caroline Fayard (D)	240,917	(13%)			
	John Fleming (R)	204,026	(11%)			

John Kennedy entered the Senate, after two failed tries in 12 years, often forcing double takes and hurried queries to confirm he was not a northeast Kennedy. Soon, Louisiana's junior senator was holding court with a throng of journalists or on television, as he quipped in his Southern drawl about just about everything. He called Sen. John McCain "tough as a boiled owl," mused that President Donald Trump's judicial picks don't belong on the bench just because they watched "My Cousin Vinny," suggested that if Trump tweeted a little less it would "not cause brain damage" and declared a White House meeting successful "because no one called anybody an ignorant slut or anything."

Kennedy's folksy fashion found a receptive audience in a town dominated by spin. His approach belied that he is one of the most educated members in the Senate, boasting five degrees, including a triple major as an undergraduate at Vanderbilt University and a pair of law degrees — from the University of Virginia and Oxford University. His legal expertise was on full display when he flummoxed a Trump judicial pick nominee, a showing that went viral and led to the nominee's withdrawal.

Kennedy has a reliably conservative voting record, going so far as to join 12 of his colleagues who voted against the bipartisan criminal justice overhaul in 2018. He has occasionally been critical of the president, especially on Russia-related issues.

Back home, Kennedy has been widely viewed as a potential candidate for governor. But in December 2018, he opted against challenging Democratic Gov. John Bel Edwards, telling Politico the Senate is "where I think I can do the most good."

Born in Centreville, Mississippi he grew up in Zachary in Louisiana's East Baton Rouge Parish. He later taught as an adjunct professor at Louisiana State University's law school.

Kennedy worked for a New Orleans law firm until he was named as special counsel to Gov. Buddy Roemer, a former member of Congress elected as a reformer. Kennedy remained with Roemer throughout his four years and helped win legislative approval of the state's first significant campaign finance regulations.

As Roemer's attorney, Kennedy defended the veto of a restrictive abortion bill that would have made the procedure illegal in cases of rape or incest. He has campaigned as an opponent of Roe v. Wade and has said that becoming a father influenced his thinking. Such shifts on policy, as well as his 2007 party switch, have provided fodder for opponents — notwithstanding that many influential Louisiana politicians have changed parties, as the onetime Democratic stronghold became a reliably red state.

After losing his first election — a race for state attorney general in 1991 — Kennedy returned to private law practice until he was named secretary of the Louisiana Department of Revenue in 1996 by Gov. Mike Foster, a Republican. Kennedy remained a Democrat and in 1999 made the first of five successful runs for state treasurer. He was re-elected as a Democrat in 2003 with no opposition but switched to the GOP in 2007 before winning a third term, again with no opponent. As treasurer, he was a bipartisan gadfly, criticizing the budget practices of the state's past three governors — two Democrats and a Republican.

Kennedy's first ran for Senate in 2004 as a Democrat. On economic issues, he positioned himself to the left of his chief Democratic rival, Rep. Chris John, in the state's "jungle" primary. Kennedy criticized the tax cuts enacted by President George W. Bush and supported increasing the minimum wage. He took conservative positions supporting gun rights and opposing same-sex marriage and abortion. In the November vote, Rep. David Vitter won 51 percent of the vote, avoiding a runoff and becoming Louisiana's first Republican senator in 120 years. John was second with 29 percent; Kennedy trailed with 15 percent. For Kennedy's next Senate bid in 2008, he was a Republican. His 2007 switch followed a political courtship by Vitter, aided by Bush's chief political strategist, Karl Rove.

Sen. Mary Landrieu was regarded as the most vulnerable Senate Democrat up for re-election in 2008. Kennedy was not the first choice of national GOP strategists, but he emerged after Rep. Richard Baker and Secretary of State Jay Dardenne declined to run. Landrieu outspent Kennedy by more than 2-1, while characterizing him as a "confused politician" who had mismanaged the Treasurer's Office. Kennedy stumbled by praising Oklahoma GOP Rep. Tom Coburn for blocking a farm disaster relief bill that Landrieu had pushed after hurricanes Gustav and Ike hit the state in 2008. Landrieu picked up endorsements from GOP officials in the New Orleans area as well as former GOP Gov. David Treen and defeated Kennedy 52%-46%.

Kennedy remained secure as treasurer, winning a fourth term in 2011 with no opposition and a fifth in 2015. With Vitter running for governor that year, Kennedy set himself up for a 2016 Senate race — spending heavily on TV commercials in his re-election campaign for treasurer, despite the absence of serious opposition. After his upset loss to Edwards in the governor's race, Vitter announced he would not seek re-election to the Senate. Twenty-four candidates filed for the open seat, with the leading Republican contenders including Kennedy and Reps. Charles Boustany and John Fleming. The latter, a founding member of the tea party-aligned House Freedom Caucus, had the backing of the Senate Conservatives Fund and the Club for Growth.

In a year in which Trump and Democratic Sen. Bernie Sanders shocked the political establishment with their outsider campaigns for president, Kennedy found success in his populist appeal too. While hailing Trump as a "change agent," Kennedy said in one ad, "You can't fix stupid, but you can vote it out." He echoed Trump's hard line on international trade agreements and President Barack Obama's signature health care law, beginning one commercial by saying, "I mean no disrespect, but Obamacare sucks."

The contest received limited national attention until August — when one candidate, former Ku Klux Klan leader David Duke, said he was "100 percent" behind Trump's agenda. As Trump bobbled a question about whether he disavowed Duke's support, Kennedy used the final televised debate before the first round of voting in November to condemn Duke as "a convicted liar and convicted felon," alluding to Duke's 2002 conviction on tax fraud. Kennedy focused most of his attention on keeping Boustany and Fleming out of the runoff. Barred by law from transferring money raised for his state treasurer campaigns into his Senate campaign account, Kennedy donated $2.4 million to the ESAFund, a super PAC that spent nearly $2 million on ads attacking those two House members.

In the first round, Kennedy finished first with 25 percent of the vote. Democrat Foster Campbell, a longtime member of the state's elected Public Service Commission supported by Edwards, finished second with 18 percent. Boustany was third with 15 percent, followed by Democrat Caroline Fayard — a New Orleans attorney supported by Landrieu — with 13 percent, and Fleming with 11 percent. Duke finished a distant seventh at 3 percent. Given Trump's 20 percentage point win in Louisiana and the state's increasingly Republican complexion, Kennedy entered the second round as a clear favorite. But in the month before the Dec. 10 runoff, Campbell outraised him, $2.5 million to $1.6 million — fueled by Democrats around the country stunned by Trump's upset victory.

As Campbell benefited from donations outside the state, he emphasized his anti-abortion stance, attacking Kennedy for supporting abortion rights while a Democrat. But Kennedy overwhelmed him, 61%-39%.

Kennedy has compiled a mostly conservative voting record with a few twists. He and Lindsey Graham of South Carolina were the only Republicans to side with Democrats to save a landmark regulation that restricted banks and credit card companies from imposing mandatory arbitration on their customers; Vice President Mike Pence broke the tie and the rule was repealed.

Steve Scalise (R)

Elected 2008, 6th full term, b. Oct 06, 1965; New Orleans; Louisiana State University, B.S., 1989; Louisiana State University, B.S., 1989; Catholic; Married (Jennifer Letulle Scalise); 2 children.

Elected Office: LA House, 1996-2007, LA Senate, 2008.

Professional Career: Systems engineer, Diamond Data Systems, eVenture Technologies.

DC Office: 2049 RHOB 20515, 202-225-3015, Fax: 202-226-0386, scalise.house.gov

State Offices: Hammond, 985-340-2185; Houma, 985-879-2300; Mandeville, 985-893-9064; Metairie, 504-837-1259.

Committees: House Minority Whip. *Energy & Commerce*: Communications & Technology.

Group Ratings

	ADA	ACLU	AFL-CIO	LCV	ITI	COC	HAFA	ACU	CFG	FRC
2018	-	6%	-	0%	-	90%	58%	90%	60%	100%
2017	15%	C	5%	-	C	90%	C	-	81%	100%

Almanac Ratings 2017-18

	Economy	Social	Foreign	Composite
Liberal	19%	19%	42%	27%
Conservative	81%	81%	58%	73%

Key Votes of the 115th Congress

1. Obama-care revision	Y	5. Family planning regs	Y	9. Guantanamo prisoners	NV
2. Tax Cuts	Y	6. Body cameras/immigration	NV	10. Ground missiles, limit	NV
3. Omnibus appropriations	Y	7. Abortion ban	Y	11. Defense Dept. spending	NV
4. Dodd-Frank revision	Y	8. Concealed carry	Y	12. FISA rules	NV

Election Results

Election	Name (Party)	Vote (%)		Cand. Spent	Ind. Exp. Support	Ind. Exp. Oppose
2018 Primary	Steve Scalise (R)............................. 192,555	(72%)		$10,366,310	$75,285	
	Tammy Savoie (D)............................. 44,273	(16%)		$255,267		
	Lee Ann Dugas (D)............................ 18,560	(7%)				

Prior winning percentages: 2016 (75%), 2014 (78%), 2012 (67%), 2010 (79%), 2008 (66%), 2008 special (75%)

Republican Steve Scalise, who won a special election in 2008, vaulted to House majority whip six years later through a blend of staunch conservatism, Cajun charm and unexpected opportunity. Now the second-ranking House Republican leader, and the top Southerner, he has been at the center of conflicts and tensions within the GOP. He has gained public attention, chiefly as the survivor of grievous gunshot windows that he suffered in 2017 at an early-morning practice session of the congressional Republican baseball team.

A native of New Orleans, Scalise grew up in Metairie. When his parents gave their son a battery-powered microphone, he played town crier on his neighborhood street, decorating his bicycle in red, white and blue and calling people to the polls — the start of a political career. He majored in computer science at Louisiana State University, where he was twice elected speaker of the student assembly. After college, he settled in Jefferson Parish as a systems engineer. In 1995, at age 30, he was elected to the state House, where he served 12 years before winning a state Senate seat in 2007. He pushed legislation to give incentives to the motion picture industry to produce films in Louisiana, and he helped pass a bill that made it the first state to bar cities from suing gun manufacturers for the actions of criminals. Scalise had considered running for the open seat in the 1st District in 1999 and 2004 but deferred to David Vitter and then to Bobby Jindal; those two were elected to statewide office and then departed public life, leaving Scalise as the last man standing.

In the special election to replace Jindal, the key contest was the Republican runoff between Scalise and state Rep. Tim Burns of St. Tammany. Burns cited Scalise's opposition to a bill banning smoking in restaurants and tried to tie him to special interests. Scalise called for limits on "out-of-control spending" and said he had "the experience to hit the ground running from Day One." Scalise won 58%-42%, capturing 83 percent of the Jefferson Parish vote. The final contest against Democrat Gilda Reed, a college instructor and political neophyte, was never in doubt in this lopsidedly Republican district. Scalise won 75%-23%.

When Scalise ran the following November for his first full term, he faced a bigger challenge. Democrat Jim Harlan, a venture capitalist, sank $1.8 million of his own money into the race and was not shy about throwing mud. In one television ad, he tried to tie Scalise to a local scandal involving a federal investigation of the abuse of tax credits by the Louisiana Institute of Film Technology; Scalise had sponsored the tax credit program in the legislature. Scalise cited his opponent's support of presidential candidate Barack Obama as evidence that Harlan was too liberal for the district. Scalise rolled to a 66%-34% win. Since then, he has coasted to reelection.

Scalise is an ardent Republican with a sharp rhetorical edge. He railed against what he called Obama's "radical agenda." On the Energy and Commerce Committee, he called for more energy production, including offshore drilling. After the massive BP oil spill in the Gulf of Mexico in 2010, he shepherded colleagues to the region to see the disaster for themselves and was incensed by Obama's moratorium on offshore drilling, calling it "reckless." He later guided through the House and into law the 2012 RESTORE Act, which called for at least 80 percent of fines collected from BP and other parties to be sent directly to areas affected by the disaster.

Before joining the leadership, Scalise showed an occasional willingness to cross it. But he also paid his dues as a rank-and-file member. He opposed the 2011 compromise on raising the debt limit, and he joined most other Louisiana Republicans in refusing to support a relief bill for Hurricane Sandy in January 2013 because it didn't have offsetting cuts in spending. After joining like-minded conservatives in the 62 efforts to repeal or defund the Affordable Care Act, he was instrumental in passage of the January 2016 bill to eliminate the health care law and end government funding for Planned Parenthood. That bill was sent to Obama, who quickly vetoed it. Scalise earned some leadership chits as chief recruiter for the National Republican Congressional Committee for the 2012 election.

Scalise has been known for his sense of humor and he is friendly with many Democrats. They include 2nd District Democrat Cedric Richmond, an old friend from their days in Baton Rouge. They have worked closely to assure coastal restoration funds for Louisiana. "Steve is an example of how things used to work in Congress," Republican Rep. Patrick McHenry of North Carolina, a close Scalise ally, told The Times-Picayune. "You'd battle it out and afterwards you can sit down and be friendly with one another."

When Ohio Republican Jim Jordan stepped down as chairman of the Republican Study Committee following the 2012 election, Georgia Republican Tom Graves won the endorsement of the group's founders and past chairmen and was set to take his place. But Scalise, who had been managing communications for the group, jumped in and demanded a more democratic method to choose the leader. "From the beginning, I felt like this ought to be a member-driven organization, and the members should decide who's the next chairman," he told National Journal. Scalise said he won the secret ballot "with votes to spare." That was a vital step in his move up the House GOP leadership ladder.

His next big step came in June 2014. Within hours of Virginia Republican Eric Cantor's shocking primary defeat, Scalise mobilized his bid to join the leadership. Kevin McCarthy of California, who had been whip, faced token opposition to replacing Cantor as majority leader. It helped that as RSC chairman, Scalise had a built-in base of support; it also helped that many Southern Republicans were anxious to see one of their own in a high-ranking post. Another benefit is that he and McCarthy had been friends since long before either was elected to Congress; that stemmed from McCarthy's national leadership of Young Republicans. Scalise left nothing to chance, lobbying many colleagues personally to eventually beat Illinois' Peter Roskam and Indiana's Marlin Stutzman for the job. "He's ... open and direct and he likes it when you're open and direct back to him," Rep. Kevin Brady of Texas, who chaired the House Ways and Means Committee, told The Times-Picayune.

Scalise can be hard-nosed, on occasion. He clashed with House Financial Services Committee Chairman Jeb Hensarling of Texas, who repeatedly balked at passing flood insurance legislation. An undaunted Scalise engineered enough GOP support to continue the program on a bipartisan basis. "We had to build a coalition, and we had to overcome a lot of obstacles," he told The Advocate of Baton Rouge. When Hensarling told the House in 2017, "At some point, God's telling [flood victims] to move," Scalise responded, "God doesn't wish ill on people whose homes represent their slice of the American dream." Hensarling retired in 2018. For Scalise, it helped that he was well-versed on the program, which is vital to his district.

Scalise faced an unexpected challenge in December 2014 when a Louisiana liberal blogger reported that Scalise had spoken to a group of white supremacists and neo-Nazis in 2002, six years before he was elected to Congress. After the story first broke and a storm of criticism, he expressed his regrets about the appearance and said he had been there to seek support for a tax proposal. He distanced himself from the local group, saying he "wholeheartedly condemned" its views; House GOP leaders as well as other Republicans backed him. A key — and credible — defender was his friend Richmond, his Democratic colleague from New Orleans.

As part of a damage-control effort, Scalise then spent months meeting with the Congressional Black Caucus and civil rights leaders. Other liberal groups seized on the opportunity to try to depict Republicans as racists. Scalise later called it "a painful time" and "the ugly side of politics," and told Politico that he would be "forever grateful" to Richmond for coming to his defense. Not everyone welcomed Scalise's denials of decade-old connections to the supremacist group. Former Ku Klux Klan leader David Duke, who ran for the 1st District seat in 1999, called Scalise a "sell-out." Duke threatened to challenge him in the 2016 election, but backed off.

The House Republican leadership team remained rocky, notably when Boehner resigned under pressure in October 2015. After McCarthy became the early frontrunner to move up, Scalise quickly showed his intentions with a letter to House Republicans that he would seek to replace McCarthy. As it turned out, McCarthy lacked sufficient support to become Speaker, and Republicans eventually turned to Rep. Paul Ryan. That left McCarthy in place, with no opportunity for Scalise to move up the ladder.

More than other congressional Republican leaders, Scalise was a consistent supporter of the presidential campaign of Donald Trump. After Trump took office and posed new challenges for congressional Republicans, Scalise's skills as whip would be crucial to the fate of the Republican program in the early months of 2017.

Scalise's future was placed in serious question in early June 2017 when he was shot and severely wounded during early-morning practice for the congressional baseball game by a Democratic partisan from Belleville Illinois who had posted social-media attacks on Trump and congressional Republicans. Scalise was rushed to a Washington hospital with internal wounds that his surgeon later said had left him at "imminent risk of death." Following multiple surgeries, Scalise's condition slowly improved. He walked onto the House floor in late September, leaning heavily on two canes, and to resounding cheers. "The last three and a half months have been a pretty challenging time for me and my family," he told the House. The overwhelming support has "given us the strength to get through all of this." Following months more of intensive medical treatment and physical therapy, in which he essentially learned to walk again, Scalise settled back into his leadership responsibilities — including extensive travel.

The health of House Republicans was less robust, as grew more apparent with the onset of the 2018 election season. In addition to their efforts to salvage the GOP majority, Scalise and McCarthy found themselves in a struggle — between themselves and with other House Republicans — for the succession to Speaker Paul Ryan, who announced in April 2018 that he would not seek reelection. Scalise said that he supported McCarthy for Speaker and hoped to replace him as Majority Leader. But that raised various questions, including the depth of GOP support for McCarthy, Scalise's ultimate intentions, the election outcome and what became the new dynamics for the Republican minority. As it turned out, Republicans selected McCarthy over Jim Jordan of Ohio for minority leader, and Scalise became minority whip without opposition.

Those selections did little to resolve the House GOP's seemingly endless internal conflicts. If recent history is any guide, Scalise before long will have an opportunity for a top leadership post — either in the majority or minority. His more enthusiastic following, especially among conservatives, could serve him well.

LA-1: New Orleans Suburbs, Southeast Louisiana

Cook Partisan Voting Index: R+24

Population		Race and Ethnicity		Income	
Total	798,345	White	72.3%	Median Income	$57,771
Land area (sq. miles)	4,030	Black	13.5%	District Income Rank	197
Pop/ sq mi	198.1	Latino	8.9%	Poverty Rate	14.2%
Born in State	73.8%	Asian	2.2%	With health insurance	88.4%
		Two or more races	1.7%	Cash public assistance	1%
Age Groups		Other	1.3%	Food stamp/SNAP	10.7%
Under 18	23%				
18-34	23%	**Education**		**Work**	
35-64	39.1%	H.S grad or less	42.7%	White Collar	14.9%
Over 64	14.9%	Some college	27.6%	Sales and Service	41.8%
Military		College Degree, 4 yr	19.1%	Blue Collar	21.6%
Veteran/ Active Duty	7.3%	Post grad	10.6%	Government	12.3%

2012 Pres. Vote	Romney	235,799	(71%)	Obama	89,430	(27%)		
2016 Pres. Vote	Trump	244,906	(69%)	Clinton	95,170	(27%)	Johnson 9,742	(3%)

St. Tammany Parish: Founded in 1718 and the nation's sixth-largest city at the outbreak of the Civil War, New Orleans is ancient for an American metropolis. It is still closely girded by the peculiar wilderness of the mushy Delta lands of the sluggish Mississippi River. For decades, you could climb a levee overlooking the Mississippi and see an expanse of water with untidy clumps of trees and disorganized-looking, seemingly abandoned docks — what Mark Twain had in his mind's eye while writing Life on the Mississippi in the 1870s. For decades, the river funneled the products of half a continent down to a single port with an international heritage and flair. The New Orleans metropolitan area has lived off that geography and history, with an inward-looking elite preoccupied with who is in which Mardi Gras krewe and interested more in the genealogy of old families than in the geography of the Oil Patch.

That mighty river and its Delta deepened the catastrophe after Hurricane Katrina struck with Category 3 force on Aug. 29, 2005, and devastated many of the area's subdivisions and streetscapes. The city's population plummeted, housing stock was destroyed, some levees were breached, and others were no longer reliable. The last act of nature to have wreaked so much damage on an American city was the San Francisco earthquake of 1906. In Plaquemines and St. Bernard parishes, many people fled the high winds and floodwaters. Some have returned. By 2017, the recovery of St. Bernard's population of 46,000 yielded an increase of about 10,000 since 2010, but the total was still down 30 percent since 2000.

Louisiana's southern coast experienced yet more turmoil with the man-made disaster known as the BP Deepwater Horizon oil spill. The rig exploded on April 20, 2010, and spewed more than 200 million gallons of crude oil into the Gulf of Mexico over three months. Once the flow was finally stemmed in July, the hardest part was yet to come: cleaning up from the largest marine oil spill in U.S. history, one that caused extensive damage to wildlife and habitats, not to mention Louisiana's coastal economy. About 600 miles of shoreline were affected.

The Katrina and BP nightmares exacerbated an ongoing disaster in the Mississippi River Delta. Coastal erosion in the bayous has caused continuing losses in the wetlands, which some experts estimate is the size of a football field for every hour. For many in this swamp land, the ominous future may have been set by the small Native American community on the Isle de Jean Charles, where 98 percent of the land has disappeared since 1955 due to erosion and sediment mismanagement; the federal Department of Housing and Urban Development spent $48 million in 2016 to move the survivors to a new community on higher ground. By 2018, more than one-fourth of the state's wetlands reportedly have been lost, with acceleration from the melting of glacial ice caps over which Louisiana has no control. In 2017, the Legislature took a significant step when it ratified a state agency's coastal master plan, which envisioned a massive restoration. The plan included 124 projects to protect or restore up to 800 square miles of new land, will build and raise levee systems across the state, and raise or relocate homes and businesses that remain threatened by storm surges and the rise in sea level. The projected 50-year cost could exceed $50 billion, though it was expected to add 10,000 jobs. Some of that money will come from the $9 billion the state received from the BP litigation. The oil industry, whose royalties will finance some of the state improvements, has been forced to prepare its own response. The rising coastline has placed at risk the huge and complex infrastructure of pipelines, refineries, tank farms and ports.

The 1st Congressional District of Louisiana stretches from suburban St. Tammany Parish north of New Orleans to Houma in Terrebonne Parish. The district takes in the vast suburb of Metairie in Jefferson Parish as well as part of western New Orleans. Metairie has remained an attractive place for new businesses, though it faced uncertainties from the unique mix of the local economy with its new and younger citizenry, plus depopulation. Most people in the 1st District live in Jefferson and St. Tammany parishes. Jefferson, of which about 60 percent is in the 1st, had 439,000 residents in 2017 — down 16,000 from 2000. In St. Tammany, which was spared from the worst effects, the population has increased from 191,000 to 256,000 during that time.

The 14 percent African-American population in the 1st is the lowest of any Louisiana district, and the 9 percent Hispanic is the highest in the state. Even with its setbacks, this is a comfortable, well-educated and heavily Republican district. Donald Trump won 69 percent of the vote, his best district in the state.

Cedric Richmond (D)

Elected 2010, 5th term, b. Sep 13, 1973; New Orleans; Harvard University John F. Kennedy School of Government (MA), Att.; Morehouse College (GA), B.A., 1995; Tulane University (LA), J.D., 1998; Baptist; Married (Raquel Greenup); 1 child.

Elected Office: LA House, 2000-2008.

Professional Career: Practicing attorney, 1998-2010.

DC Office: 506 CHOB 20515, 202-225-6636, Fax: 202-225-1988, richmond.house.gov

State Offices: Baton Rouge, 225-636-5600; Gretna, 504-365-0390; New Orleans, 504-288-3777.

Committees: *Homeland Security*: Cybersecurity, Infrastructure Protection & Innovation (Chmn); Emergency Preparedness, Response & Recovery. *Judiciary*: Courts, Intellectual Property & Internet; Crime, Terrorism & Homeland Security.

Group Ratings

	ADA	ACLU	AFL-CIO	LCV	ITI	COC	HAFA	ACU	CFG	FRC
2018	-	85%	-	46%	-	58%	7%	6%	13%	0%
2017	85%	C	97%	86%	C	54%	C	9%	5%	13%

Almanac Ratings 2017-18

	Economy	Social	Foreign	Composite
Liberal	92%	93%	95%	93%
Conservative	8%	7%	5%	7%

Key Votes of the 115th Congress

1. Obama-care revision	N	5. Family planning regs	NV	9. Guantanamo prisoners	Y
2. Tax Cuts	N	6. Body cameras/immigration	Y	10. Ground missiles, limit	Y
3. Omnibus appropriations	Y	7. Abortion ban	N	11. Defense Dept. spending	N
4. Dodd-Frank revision	N	8. Concealed carry	N	12. FISA rules	N

Election Results

Election	Name (Party)	Vote (%)		Cand. Spent	Ind. Exp. Support	Ind. Exp. Oppose
2018 Primary	Cedric Richmond (D)	190,182	(81%)	$1,563,015		
	Jesse Schmidt (I)	20,465	(9%)	$11,311		
	Belden Batiste (I)	17,260	(7%)			

Prior winning percentages: 2016 (70%), 2014 (69%), 2012 (55%), 2010 (65%)

Democrat Cedric Richmond, elected in 2010, has formed tight alliances with key lawmakers on both sides of the aisle, especially Republican Whip Steve Scalise. As chairman of the Congressional Black Caucus in 2017-18, he gained his own platform and he enhanced the group's influence. He has continued to assert his independence and to pursue opportunities for leadership within the House.

Richmond grew up in eastern New Orleans. His father died when he was 7 years old, and he was raised by his mother, a public school teacher. In his youth, life revolved around an urban park where he loved to play sports and later, while in high school, coached teams of younger boys. He graduated from Atlanta's Morehouse College, the nation's only all-male historically black college, and returned to his hometown to earn a law degree from Tulane University.

Richmond was elected in 2000 at age 26 as the youngest member of the state House. He pushed initiatives such as a redevelopment tax credit for weather-damaged areas, funding for playgrounds, and a ban on certain types of semi-automatic rifles. Richmond ran for the New Orleans City Council in 2005, but was ejected from the race when a judge ruled that he falsified his qualifying papers by failing to meet the residency requirement.

He ran for Congress in 2008, following the indictment on corruption charges of scandal-plagued Democratic Rep. William Jefferson. The six Democrats in the contest split the anti-Jefferson vote, with Richmond finishing third in the first round. Republican Anh "Joseph" Cao then eked out a 50%-47% victory in the runoff over Jefferson, who subsequently was convicted for bribery and served in prison until 2017. Two years later, Cao was extremely vulnerable given the heavily Democratic makeup of the district. Richmond took 61 percent in the primary over three other Democrats. His central message was that he would be a more reliable supporter than Cao of President Barack Obama's agenda. Cao outspent him, $2.1 million to $1.1 million. But Richmond won easily, 65%-33%.

In the House, Richmond has been a mostly loyal Democrat, occasionally departing from the party line in deference to his state's needs. He joined the business-friendly New Democrat Coalition. He has worked extensively on curbing youth violence and has seats on the Judiciary and Homeland Security committees. In 2016, Richmond filed with Republican Rep. Garrett Graves, whose district also includes parts of Baton Rouge, a bill to give additional tools to law enforcement in response to the racial conflicts that the city faced.

Richmond gained prominence from his friendship with Republican colleague Steve Scalise, with whom he has worked on obtaining more disaster-recovery money and other issues. Scalise, now minority whip, said he would be "forever grateful" to Richmond for coming to his defense in December 2014 when a website raised questions about a speech that Scalise had given to a group of white supremacists in 2002. "I don't think Steve Scalise has a racist bone in his body," Richmond said.

As chairman of the Congressional Black Caucus for two years, Richmond spoke out forcefully against President Donald Trump, the New Orleans Advocate reported in October 2018. He derided Trump as "racially challenged" and said that he had taken the nation "to a dangerous place, especially for African-Americans." To an unusual extent, Richmond used his CBC post to enhance the influence within the House of the group's members, including himself. He has been close to two senior black Democrats: James Clyburn of South Carolina, the majority whip, and Bennie Thompson of Mississippi, chairman of the Homeland Security Committee. Richmond, who worked with Clyburn on voter-mobilization responsibilities for House Democrats, publicly urged him in 2018 to run for Speaker if Democrats won the majority. When Clyburn following the election decided to support Nancy Pelosi, Richmond criticized her tentative plans to impose term limits on House committee chairmen and he encouraged other CBC members, including Rep. Marcia Fudge of Ohio, to challenge her. "I'm not anti-Pelosi, but whatever Marcia does, I'm very pro-Marcia," he told Politico. Fudge reached a deal with Pelosi and did not challenge her.

Once the leadership team was settled, Clyburn named Richmond as assistant to the whip — in effect, his "second in command," Richmond said. Serving on Thompson's panel, Richmond in 2019 became chairman of the Cybersecurity, Infrastructure Protection and Innovation Subcommittee. In May, he gained a prominent and influential new assignment as a co-chairman of Joe Biden's presidential campaign, where he expected to be a leading adviser and strategist.

At home, Richmond has entrenched himself. He had what initially seemed a competitive challenge for reelection in 2016 from East Baton Rouge Mayor Kip Holden, who had served 12 years and was term-limited. But Holden spent little money and failed to run an active campaign. Richmond won handily, 70%-20%. He took nine of the 10 parishes, with 80 percent in Orleans and 75 percent in Holden's base of East Baton Rouge. In 2018, Richmond got 81 percent of the vote against three opponents without major-party affiliation.

LA-2: New Orleans Metro, Parts of Baton Rouge

Cook Partisan Voting Index: D+25

Population		Race and Ethnicity		Income	
Total	790,128	White	28.1%	Median Income	$38,507
Land area (sq. miles)	1,268	Black	61.4%	District Income Rank	423
Pop/ sq mi	622.9	Latino	6.1%	Poverty Rate	25%
Born in State	78.4%	Asian	2.7%	With health insurance	86%
		Two or more races	1.3%	Cash public assistance	1.7%
Age Groups		Other	0.4%	Food stamp/SNAP	22.1%
Under 18	22.9%				
18-34	25.9%	**Education**		**Work**	
35-64	38.4%	H.S grad or less	49.7%	White Collar	12.8%
Over 64	12.8%	Some college	27.5%	Sales and Service	46%
		College Degree, 4 yr	14.3%	Blue Collar	23.2%
Military		Post grad	8.5%	Government	14.2%
Veteran/ Active Duty	5.9%				

2012 Pres. Vote	Obama	248,947	(76%)	Romney	74,987	(23%)
2016 Pres. Vote	Clinton	247,491	(75%)	Trump	73,779	(22%)

Orleans Parish: Established by the French and ruled by the Spanish from 1763 for almost 40 years, New Orleans was a Creole city — part French, a bit Spanish, more than a touch Caribbean — when the American flag was raised over what is now Jackson Square in 1803. The statue of Andrew Jackson still seems an intrusion in a square set off by the French Market, the Cabildo, the Presbytere, the Pontalba apartments, and St. Louis Cathedral. New Orleans was one of the six largest American cities from 1820 until the Civil War and the only sizable city in the South. It was urbanized, yet poor, with yellow fever epidemics late in the 19th century, even as it was installing electric lights. It had a riot in which Italian immigrants were massacred, even as it was laying streetcar tracks and telephone lines. It also was one of the most corrupt American cities during Reconstruction and the Gilded Age, when its votes were regularly bid for and bought. Like other Southern cities, it became rigidly segregated after 1890.

For a time during the 1970s oil boom, New Orleans seemed to be a fast-growing Sun Belt city. It suffered economically through the 1980s, when it lost substantial port business — oil to Houston and

Latin American trade to Miami. By the 1990s, New Orleans was humming again. Crime rates fell and no longer depressed tourism. Incomes went up, and home ownership increased, among African Americans as well as whites. The downtown Superdome was the friendly host of the August 1988 Republican convention.

Then, Hurricane Katrina made landfall early on a Monday morning, Aug. 29, 2005. A nightmarish scene unfolded at the Superdome, the shelter of last resort for more than 20,000 people, many of whom had fled the rising water without food, drinking water or medicine. Conditions worsened when the storm ripped two holes in the roof. A few days later, city officials began to load people on buses for transport to cities better positioned to provide services. The breach of the city's levees led to a surge that churned through the low-income 9th Ward, while the French Quarter, on higher ground, was largely untouched by the floodwaters. Still, 80 percent of New Orleans flooded.

New Orleans was in for a very long recovery. Thousands of government trailers became semi-permanent homes. City residents who had fled the floodwaters only slowly trickled back. It took years to restore regular utility service. Expectations repeatedly were downsized. In 2008, the last government trailer parks closed, and the restaurants in the French Quarter were back in business. By 2017, the city's population was 393,000, 15 percent less than in 2000, but more than 80 percent larger than in 2006, indicating an impressive recovery from the storm in many — but not all — parts of the city. Post-recession wages and median household income in the city and suburbs were also on the rise. Still, those increases have slowed. New Orleans was a relatively poor city before the hurricane and remains so.

The city's post-hurricane recovery and transition suffered when a second disaster struck in April 2010. BP's Deepwater Horizon offshore rig exploded and spewed oil into the Gulf of Mexico at an estimated rate of 60,000 barrels a day. A federally mandated moratorium on offshore drilling was lifted in October 2010 under pressure from local and state officials and the congressional delegation. The fragile regional economy took another serious blow when the 5,000 jobs at the Avondale shipyard in 2010 were all but eliminated.

With its unique character and characters, New Orleans remains a popular tourist destination. In the French Quarter — the Vieux Carré as it was originally called — are the 19th-century row houses decked out in their island pastels and ornate wrought-iron railings. At street level are restaurants, art galleries, and jazz and blues clubs, and the narrow sidewalks fill up nightly with diners, revelers, and patrons of the tiny voodoo establishments found only in New Orleans. Its storied restaurants serve a cuisine all New Orleans' own — spicy, rich and unaffected by trends in low-fat food.

Upriver from the Quarter is the Central Business District, with its skyscrapers and the Superdome, and the Garden District, with the graceful intact homes of the rich early American settlers lining St. Charles Avenue. A total of 10.5 million tourists visited New Orleans in 2016 — breaking the pre-Katrina record set in 2004 -- and they spent a record-breaking $7.4 billion. Positive business reports in 2018 included: the purchase of Avondale by two industrial-development firms that projected 2,000 transportation-related jobs, approval of a master plan for the port with perhaps $2 billion in new projects, and new petrochemical and chemical manufacturing plants outside of the city with more than 2,500 jobs.

Much to the relief of locals, the city's revamped $14.5 billion flood control system worked. In the Ninth Ward, the large influx of Vietnamese immigrants, many of whom work at sea, offered a sense of community—albeit, with continuation of the stark economic inequality in that area. Still, amid the optimism, few would guarantee that the improvements across the city would survive the next disaster. In August 2017, City Lab reported, many New Orleans neighborhoods "suffered Katrina-level floods … from a basic rainstorm." Other elements of the pre-Katrina reality remained: In 2017, 25 percent of the city lived in poverty and the city had the third-worst inequality in the nation.

The 2nd Congressional District of Louisiana includes much of the city of New Orleans. It contains nearly half of Jefferson Parish, most of Orleans Parish, and all or part of eight other parishes between New Orleans and Baton Rouge. More than 100,000 residents in largely black neighborhoods on Baton Rouge's north side were added in the 2012 redistricting to make up for the downsizing in New Orleans. By including most of the heavily black precincts in south Louisiana, the 2nd is 61 percent African American and one of the most Democratic districts in the South.

Clay Higgins (R)

Elected 2016, 2nd term, b. Aug 24, 1961; New Orleans; Louisiana State University, Att., 1983; Louisiana State University, Att., 1990; Christian - Non-Denominational; Married (Becca Higgins); 4 children (1 deceased).

Military Career: U.S. Army 1979-1985; LA National Guard 1979-1985

Elected Office: Sheriff, St. Landry Parish, 2008-2016.

DC Office: 424 CHOB 20515, 202-225-2031, Fax: 202-225-5724, clayhiggins.house.gov

State Offices: Lafayette, 337-703-6105; Lake Charles, 337-656-2833.

Committees: *Homeland Security*: Border Security, Facilitation & Operations (RMM); Oversight, Management & Accountability. *Oversight & Reform*: Subcommittee on Environment.

Group Ratings

	ADA	ACLU	AFL-CIO	LCV	ITI	COC	HAFA	ACU	CFG	FRC
2018	-	7%	-	0%	-	82%	64%	79%	67%	100%
2017	0%	C	5%	0%	C	93%	C	93%	85%	100%

Almanac Ratings 2017-18

	Economy	Social	Foreign	Composite
Liberal	5%	0%	0%	2%
Conservative	95%	100%	100%	98%

Key Votes of the 115th Congress

1. Obama-care revision	Y	5. Family planning regs	Y	9. Guantanamo prisoners	N
2. Tax Cuts	Y	6. Body cameras/immigration	N	10. Ground missiles, limit	N
3. Omnibus appropriations	N	7. Abortion ban	Y	11. Defense Dept. spending	Y
4. Dodd-Frank revision	NV	8. Concealed carry	Y	12. FISA rules	Y

Election Results

Election	Name (Party)	Vote (%)		Cand. Spent	Ind. Exp. Support	Ind. Exp. Oppose
2018 Primary	Clay Higgins (R)	136,876	(56%)	$972,918		
	Mimi Methvin (D)	43,729	(18%)	$249,446		
	Josh Guillory (R)	31,387	(13%)	$251,176		
	Rob Anderson (D)	13,477	(6%)	$12,533		

Prior winning percentages: 2016 (56%)

Republican Clay Higgins, who unexpectedly won the open seat in 2016 against a veteran state elected official, has displayed elements of President Donald Trump's outsider and outspoken appeal. Higgins, a former captain and spokesman for the St. Landry Parish sheriff's office and political newcomer, has had some eccentric moments in the House. A peculiar feature of his first term came when Rudy Giuliani, Trump's legal adviser, endorsed a GOP challenger to Higgins in his reelection bid. The president weighed in on behalf of the incumbent, who easily prevailed.

Higgins attended Louisiana State University and had several jobs, including as a police officer and manager of an automobile dealership. His personal life had some sketchy details, including an ex-wife claiming that Higgins owed more than $100,000 in child support. Before his run for Congress, he had gained local attention with "Crime Stopper" videos that he narrated. In a 2015 profile, The Washington Post described him as a "muscled Army veteran and hardened street cop who rarely cracks a smile [who might be] the most irresistibly intimidating man in America." Known as the "Cajun John Wayne," his authentic style with a touch of empathy gained something of a cult following in the bayous and on YouTube. Many of the suspects, he later said, turned themselves in in response to the message of redemption from "Uncle Clay." Higgins resigned from the sheriff's office in February 2016, citing an unspecified "matter of principle" that apparently related to an order that he was unwilling to follow. That led to calls for him to run for Congress.

When six-term Rep. Charles Boustany gave up this seat to run unsuccessfully for the Senate, the 12 candidates in the wide-open field included eight Republicans and two Democrats. The best-known Republican was Scott Angelle, the chairman of the state Public Service Commission. Angelle had switched parties after he discovered the challenge of running statewide as a Democrat in Louisiana. In 2015, he finished third in the nine-candidate contest for governor, and ran especially well in Cajun country, where he was a native. But Angelle alienated many Republicans in that bitter contest when he refused to endorse Republican Sen. David Vitter, who lost to Democrat John Bel Edwards in the runoff.

In the all-party House election in November, Angelle led Higgins, 29%-27%. Angelle had a big lead in St. Charles, Higgins's tea-party style ran well in the rural areas, and they split Lafayette. In the December runoff, Angelle highlighted his endorsement by the National Rifle Association and the Louisiana Sheriffs Association. A super PAC organized by friends of Higgins used the Trump-like slogan, "Make Louisiana Great Again." That group aired an ad that attacked Angelle as a Democrat and a crook; it was produced by a consulting firm that had worked for Vitter. Angelle denied the charges. But with Higgins' background in "reality TV," the facts occasionally were muddled. Angelle spent $1.8 million to $380,000 for Higgins. Outside groups spent about $500,000 on the contest. Higgins won the runoff, 56%-44%, with a geographic split that was similar to the first round of voting.

In the House, Higgins described his agenda in standard Republican terms of "smaller government, less bureaucracy, free markets, a strong national defense and securing America's sovereign borders." He focused his work on the Homeland Security Committee, where he said that every border is "a sacred gateway we must protect." That approach became relevant in 2019, when he became ranking Republican on the panel's Border Security Subcommittee. "Our primary focus will be providing front-line defenders with the resources that they need and that they have requested," he said.

The Louisiana-based Advocate newspaper reported that Higgins had become "a reliable vote for the party's leadership," with a mostly low-key profile. His unguarded style resulted in occasional headlines. When he joined a congressional delegation to the site of the Auschwitz death camp in Poland, he prepared a five-minute video — taken, in part, inside a gas chamber -- during which he argued that the military must be "invincible." Subsequently, the Auschwitz Memorial site responded to his film with a tweet, "There should be mournful silence. It's not a stage." A Higgins spokesman had no comment, the New Orleans Times-Picayune reported.

Following a terrorist attack at the London Bridge in England, Higgins wrote a Facebook post that the world was at war with "Islamic horror" and that the response ought to be, "Kill them all." The New Republic, a liberal publication, responded that the Higgins comment was a reminder that Trump was "the figurehead of a Republican Party that is increasingly xenophobic, authoritarian and incompetent." Higgins filed legislation calling for a random drug test every two years for all members of Congress.

In his reelection, Higgins faced six challengers, including Republican Josh Guillory, a local attorney. In June 2018, Giuliani endorsed Guillory and planned a local event. Guillory had hired as his fundraiser Jennifer LeBlanc — the "new girlfriend" of the former New York City mayor, who months earlier had worked for Higgins — Politico reported. National and state GOP officials reportedly were surprised and unhappy. Days later, Trump met with Higgins and endorsed him. Higgins spent nearly $1 million in his campaign to $250,000 for Guillory. He won with 56 percent of the vote. Guillory finished third with 13 percent.

LA-3: Southwest Louisiana

Cook Partisan Voting Index: R+20

Population		Race and Ethnicity		Income	
Total	780,962	White	67.8%	Median Income	$48,130
Land area (sq. miles)	6,983	Black	24.3%	District Income Rank	337
Pop/ sq mi	111.8	Latino	3.8%	Poverty Rate	17.8%
Born in State	83.2%	Asian	1.5%	With health insurance	87.3%
		Two or more races	2%	Cash public assistance	1.2%
Age Groups		Other	0.4%	Food stamp/SNAP	15%
Under 18	25%				
18-34	23.8%	**Education**		**Work**	
35-64	37.8%	H.S grad or less	53.2%	White Collar	13.4%
Over 64	13.4%	Some college	25.9%	Sales and Service	43%
Military		College Degree, 4 yr	14.5%	Blue Collar	26.6%
Veteran/ Active Duty	7.1%	Post grad	6.4%	Government	12.6%

2012 Pres. Vote	Romney	220,490	(66%)	Obama	107,613	(32%)
2016 Pres. Vote	Trump	231,017	(67%)	Clinton	100,241	(29%)

Lafayette, Lake Charles: More than 200 years ago, French-speaking settlers in Canada were forced to leave their land of Acadie, which the British had taken over and renamed Nova Scotia. They made their way to the wetlands of southern Louisiana, called Acadiana. Here, without much notice, they built steep-roofed houses to slough off nonexistent snow and adapted French cuisine to the crawfish and muskrats they found in abundance in the pelican-tended swamps. They are the Cajuns, and the heart of their adopted homeland is around Lafayette, just west of the Atchafalaya Basin, where Mississippi River waters pour through bayous and canals. Cajun country has thrived, thanks to the oil and gas that are plentiful on land and just offshore in the Gulf of Mexico. Oil rigs are common, and every once in a while, the swampy foliage parts to reveal a giant refinery or petrochemical plant. Cajun French has survived decades of efforts to eliminate it. Cajun music — and its black-influenced variant, zydeco — are popular here and nationally; spicy Cajun cooking attracts food lovers, who learn its secrets and then carry them home, in understated form. Mardi Gras is not just a great party but great for local business — it contributes an estimated $110 million annually to the economy in Lafayette Parish.

West of Lafayette, the economy in Lake Charles has been booming, with petrochemicals and engineering, plus construction jobs related to the natural-gas boom. The robust 28 percent job growth in the area between 2013 and 2018 was the strongest in the nation. Business conditions in Lafayette, by contrast, have depended more on the oil market. Cajun country has thrived over the decades, thanks to the oil and gas that are plentiful on land and just offshore in the Gulf of Mexico. But the occasionally low price of oil in recent years has caused a loss of jobs. In 2016, the 11.5 percent reduction in the area's economy was the third worst in the nation that year — and a notable contrast to fast-growing Lake Charles, only 70 miles to the west. Lafayette also has styled itself as a center for high-tech companies. But the state-funded Louisiana Immersive Technologies Enterprise struggled financially. In 2016, the University of Louisiana, Lafayette, took over the $27 million center and subsequently provided little information about the facility.

The 3rd Congressional District, following the 2011 redistricting, absorbed much of what had been a second district in the bayous. It covers the southern coast from the Texas border east to St. Mary County, plus much of Cajun country. The population centers are Lafayette Parish and Lake Charles-based Calcasieu Parish, which have about 30 percent and 25 percent of the district's population, respectively. The 3rd District remains very conservative. Donald Trump won 67 percent of the vote.

Mike Johnson (R)

Elected 2016, 2nd term, b. Jan 30, 1972; Shreveport; Louisiana State University, B.S., 1995; Louisiana State University Law School, J.D., 1998; Southern Baptist; Married (Kelly Lary Johnson); 4 children.

Elected Office: LA House, 2015-2016.

Professional Career: Practicing attorney; Talk radio host/columnist.

DC Office: 418 CHOB 20515, 202-225-2777, Fax: 202-225-8039, mikejohnson.house.gov

State Offices: Bossier City, 318-840-0309; Leesville, 337-423-4232; Natchitoches, 318-951-4316.

Committees: *Judiciary*: Constitution, Civil Rights & Civil Liberties (RMM); Courts, Intellectual Property & Internet. *Natural Resources*: Oversight & Investigations; Water, Oceans & Wildlife.

Group Ratings

	ADA	ACLU	AFL-CIO	LCV	ITI	COC	HAFA	ACU	CFG	FRC
2018	-	9%	-	6%	-	73%	84%	84%	79%	100%
2017	0%	C	-	0%	C	93%	C	93%	85%	100%

Almanac Ratings 2017-18

	Economy	Social	Foreign	Composite
Liberal	7%	3%	0%	3%
Conservative	93%	97%	100%	97%

Key Votes of the 115th Congress

1. Obama-care revision	Y	5. Family planning regs	Y	9. Guantanamo prisoners	N
2. Tax Cuts	Y	6. Body cameras/immigration	N	10. Ground missiles, limit	N
3. Omnibus appropriations	N	7. Abortion ban	Y	11. Defense Dept. spending	Y
4. Dodd-Frank revision	Y	8. Concealed carry	Y	12. FISA rules	Y

Election Results

Election	Name (Party)	Vote (%)		Cand. Spent	Ind. Exp. Support	Ind. Exp. Oppose
2018 Primary	Mike Johnson (R)..............................	139,326	(64%)	$867,441	$4,034	
	Ryan Trundle (D).............................	72,934	(34%)	$20,347		
	Mark David Halverson (I)...................	4,612	(2%)			

Prior winning percentages: 2016 (65%)

Republican Mike Johnson, elected in 2016 to an open seat, quickly made his mark with his ardent social conservatism and his skill at working with a cross-section of House Republicans. Following his selection as chairman of the Republican Study Committee, he moved into a position that his predecessors — including fellow Louisianan Steve Scalise — have used as a springboard into the GOP leadership. Johnson has shown a willingness to disagree with President Donald Trump, a step that some other conservatives have been reluctant to take.

Johnson is a native of Shreveport. His father, a local firefighter, was critically burned and disabled in the line of duty. Johnson got his bachelor's in business administration and a law degree at Louisiana State University. In his private practice, he advocated conservative constitutional principles. He was elected to the state House in 2015, where he had a record as a strong social and economic conservative, including support for school prayer and opposition to gay marriage. He enacted a bill that prohibited a "dismemberment" procedure for second-trimester abortions.

In the state House, Johnson stirred controversy as the chief sponsor of a religious freedom proposal that would have prohibited local governments from imposing fines or revoking tax benefits from a business based on its owner's views on marriage His measure was supported by the conservative Family Research Council, but opposed by business groups. In April 2015, a House committee defeated Johnson's bill. But Gov. Bobby Jindal then issued an executive order with similar provisions. Following that legislative session, Johnson was named an "MVP for Business" by the Louisiana Association of Business and Industry, and "Outstanding Family Advocate" by the Louisiana Family Forum

When Republican Rep. John Fleming ran unsuccessfully for the Senate, the contest for his House seat was wide-open among Republicans. Other leading contenders were Shreveport cardiologist Trey Baucum and Shreveport City Council member Oliver Jenkins. An Associated Press report described the contest as "something of an anomaly, a race that's almost downright genteel." In the first round of voting, Johnson got 25 percent of the vote; Bracum and Jenkins trailed with 18 and 16 percent. Johnson led the Republican field in 11 of the 15 parishes, including the population centers of Shreveport-based Caddo and Bossier.

Democrat Marshall Jones was the frontrunner with 28 percent. In the relatively amiable runoff, Johnson consolidated the Republican vote, while Jones had little upside. Johnson won, 65%-35%. Each candidate was pro-gun and anti-abortion. The only parish that was close was Caddo, where Johnson took 52 percent of the vote. Johnson $1 million in spending doubled the total for Jones. "I guess I wasn't able to distinguish myself from the national Democratic party," Jones said following his defeat.

In the House, Johnson won passage in May 2017 of his bill that he said was designed to close a loophole in pornography laws by protecting children from the use of sexual images. The strict penalties would include a mandatory minimum prison sentence of 15 years. Johnson called the bill "a commonsense approach to better protect children from depraved sexual predators." Some liberals criticized the measure as overly broad and warned that it would criminalize routine "sexting" on phones, especially among teenagers. The House passed the legislation, 368-51.

In an unusual collaboration, Johnson worked with Louisiana Attorney General Jeff Landry on guidelines to clarify and promote religious expression in that state's public schools. The measure was designed to protect the rights of students to "live out their faith on campus," Johnson said. Following a heated debate, including opposition by law professors and civil libertarians, the legislature passed in June 2018 a bill based on Johnson's proposal.

Johnson raised questions about Trump's policy of separating children from their families when they are detained at the border after illegally entering the country. "We must secure our borders, uphold our laws and keep families together — and we can," he said in a June 2018 statement. "Our legal system and our immigration policies always seek a proper balance between justice and compassion." While supporting Trump's efforts to "end hostile trade practices by China," Johnson warned, "we must be wary of the potential impacts American consumers could face if we spark a trade war with our allies." He advocated requiring congressional approval of trade actions by the executive branch.

Following the 2018 election, Johnson made a bid to chair the Republican Study Committee, a group that promotes conservative views and includes a majority of House GOP members. He said he would use his platform for "moving our cause forward ... [and] helping shape the future of the conservative movement." He defeated six-term Rep. Tom McClintock of California, a long-time conservative leader. According to a report in the Daily Beast, Johnson envisioned that his new position would combine forces with the Freedom Caucus as the chief forum for House conservatives. "My driving force is to get Republicans to work together, to bring the family together, so to speak," he told Daily Beast. He gained another useful post as the ranking Republican on the Judiciary Subcommittee on the Constitution, Civil Rights and Civil Liberties.

LA-4: Northwest Louisiana

Cook Partisan Voting Index: R+13

Population		Race and Ethnicity		Income	
Total	758,769	White	58.5%	Median Income	$41,017
Land area (sq. miles)	12,435	Black	33.8%	District Income Rank	407
Pop/ sq mi	61	Latino	3.9%	Poverty Rate	22%
Born in State	74.1%	Asian	0.9%	With health insurance	87.7%
		Two or more races	1.8%	Cash public assistance	3%
Age Groups		Other	1.1%	Food stamp/SNAP	17.1%
Under 18	24.4%				
18-34	23.6%	**Education**		**Work**	
35-64	36.8%	H.S grad or less	51.2%	White Collar	15.2%
Over 64	15.2%	Some college	28.9%	Sales and Service	42.6%
		College Degree, 4 yr	13%	Blue Collar	25.8%
Military		Post grad	6.9%	Government	17.2%
Veteran/ Active Duty	11.6%				

2012 Pres. Vote	Romney	191,417	(59%)	Obama	128,659	(40%)
2016 Pres. Vote	Trump	192,977	(61%)	Clinton	116,599	(37%)

Shreveport, Bossier City: Northwestern Louisiana, south of Little Rock and east of Dallas, is part of the Deep South. Unlike in New Orleans, most people here are Protestants, not Catholics. They are often tradition-minded, with names that are English or Scottish, not French. The tone is set not by wide-open Bourbon Street but by smaller Shreveport, which could be just another East Texas oil-patch town, albeit one that has its own, comparatively sedate, Mardi Gras. The countryside is agricultural, though there are some vestiges of large riverfront plantations. Roots here go back a long way. Natchitoches is the oldest town in Louisiana, founded by Louis Antoine Juchereau de St. Denis in 1714, and Shreveport was founded in the 1830s.

Oil fueled much of the region's economic growth in the 20th century. Natural gas, which took off in the 21st, was discovered in 1870. The nation's first gas pipeline was built from Caddo Field to Shreveport in 1908. However, it wasn't economical to drill until gas prices soared in 2000. Fracking at the Haynesville shale formation, which extends to east Texas, accounts for nearly 10 percent of the nation's natural gas production. That is the second-largest in the nation behind the Marcellus formation in Pennsylvania, where the deposits are shallower and thus cheaper to access. Riverboat gambling and the Port of Caddo-Bossier supplement the local economy. Benteler Steel and Tube, which operates a billion-dollar steel mill at the port, produces steel pipes for transporting oil and gas.

Shreveport officials pursued options for their downtown Cross Bayou, including a possible sports complex. Local planners continued to advocate the long-discussed Interstate 69, which might pass through Shreveport en route from south Texas to Michigan. Barksdale Air Force Base in Bossier City is home of the Global Strike Command, which combined the nation's land-based nuclear missiles and long-range nuclear bombers under single leadership. The base has planned a new entrance to facilitate access — a signal of its ongoing presence.

Since 2010, the area has become a tale of two cities. Shreveport has been among the slowest-growing mid-sized cities in the nation -- hovering around 200,000, as it has since 1990. Bossier City has grown by 11 percent to 68,600 during the past decade. The black population of Shreveport is 57 percent, compared with 26 percent in Bossier City, which has a lower poverty rate.

The 4th Congressional District of Louisiana drops down the western side of the state to the bayous. Nearly half the population is in Caddo Parish and suburban Bossier Parish around Shreveport. The rest is scattered in rural areas. The district overall is 34 percent African American and it has had the lowest Republican support in the past three presidential elections of the five Republican-held districts in Louisiana. Hillary Clinton in 2016 won Caddo with 51 percent of the vote. But Donald Trump took 71 percent in Bossier and 61 percent overall, showing that the 4th is solidly Republican.

Ralph Abraham (R)

Elected 2014, 3rd term, b. Sep 16, 1954; Alto; Louisiana State University, Bach. Deg., 1978; Louisiana State University School of Veterinary Medicine, D.V.M., 1980; Louisiana State University School of Medicine, M.D., 1994; Baptist; Married (Dianne Abraham); 3 children.

Military Career: MS National Guard Special Forces 1986-1989

Professional Career: Flight instructor; General family practitioner; Aviation medical examiner.

DC Office: 417 CHOB 20515, 202-225-8490, Fax: 202-225-5639, abraham.house.gov

State Offices: Alexandria, 318-445-0818; Monroe, 318-322-3500; St. Francisville, 985-516-5858.

Committees: *Agriculture*: Conservation & Forestry; General Farm Commodities & Risk Management. *Armed Services*: Intelligence, Emerging Threats & Capabilities; Military Personnel.

Group Ratings

	ADA	ACLU	AFL-CIO	LCV	ITI	COC	HAFA	ACU	CFG	FRC
2018	-	7%	-	0%	-	75%	67%	80%	69%	100%
2017	0%	C	13%	0%	C	93%	C	81%	75%	100%

Almanac Ratings 2017-18

	Economy	Social	Foreign	Composite
Liberal	5%	3%	0%	3%
Conservative	96%	97%	100%	97%

Key Votes of the 115th Congress

1. Obama-care revision	Y	5. Family planning regs	Y	9. Guantanamo prisoners	N
2. Tax Cuts	Y	6. Body cameras/immigration	N	10. Ground missiles, limit	N
3. Omnibus appropriations	N	7. Abortion ban	Y	11. Defense Dept. spending	Y
4. Dodd-Frank revision	Y	8. Concealed carry	Y	12. FISA rules	Y

Election Results

Election	Name (Party)	Vote (%)		Cand. Spent	Ind. Exp. Support	Ind. Exp. Oppose
2018 Primary	Ralph Abraham (R)	149,018	(67%)	$921,947		
	Jessee Carlton Fleenor (D)	67,118	(30%)	$23,763		
	Billy Burkette (I)	4,799	(2%)			

Prior winning percentages: 2016 (82%), 2014 (64%)

Republican Ralph Abraham, who was elected in 2014 after his career as a rural doctor and humanitarian pilot, initially kept to his committee work and had some legislative success. In 2019, he traveled across Louisiana as an early challenger to Democratic Gov. John Bel Edwards, who faced reelection in November in this Republican-leaning state.

Abraham grew up in rural Richland Parish, which remained his home. He trained to be a veterinarian at the LSU School of Veterinary Medicine and practiced for 10 years. In his late 30s, he changed careers and earned his medical degree at the LSU School of Medicine in Shreveport. He likes to boast he "can treat anything that walks on two or four legs." He was a 1st lieutenant in the Army and continued to serve as an aircraft commander in the Coast Guard Auxiliary. He was a volunteer pilot with Pilots for Patients, a Monroe group that provides free air transportation to people who need medical assistance and live far from hospitals or doctors.

Abraham was the third Republican elected to this seat in two years. After Rodney Alexander resigned in August 2013 to become head of the Louisiana Department of Veterans Affairs, the winner of the special election was tea-party candidate Vince McAllister, who benefited from his outsider status and his endorsement by the reality television show family in Duck Dynasty. McAllister had a brief and rocky tenure. In April 2014, a local newspaper published a surveillance video showing the married congressman passionately kissing his office's scheduler. Following the widespread airing of the videotaped embrace with an aide that led him to be dubbed "the Kissing Congressman," McAllister issued a statement saying he had "fallen short," and asked for forgiveness.

Abraham, who had never held political office, said he had been considering a run for Congress for several years and felt that the time was ripe. "It's not the America in which we grew up," he told Gannett Newspapers. "Somebody has to step up and change it." He played up his 39-year marriage, pilot experiences and "family values." Also running was Zach Dasher, nephew of TV's Duck Dynasty star Phil Robertson. The conservative Club for Growth political action committee backed Dasher with $250,000 in advertising that attacked McAllister for his personal issues.

In the November all-party election, Abraham finished first among Republicans with 23 percent of the vote, just 1,861 votes ahead of Dasher's 22 percent and well ahead of McAllister's 11 percent. Abraham had a runoff with the leading vote-getter in the nine-candidate race — Democrat Jamie Mayo, the mayor of Monroe. That proved to be a no-contest. Abraham outspent Mayo 4-to-1 for the entire campaign, and easily won the runoff, 64%-36%.

In the House, Abraham fit comfortably in the GOP establishment wing. On the Veterans' Affairs Committee, he chaired the Subcommittee on Disability Assistance and Memorial Affairs — one of the few freshmen to get a gavel. He complained when VA officials said they wanted to take money from the 2014 law designed to improve benefits and use it to cover nearly $1 billion in cost overruns at their Denver medical center. "That money was designated for those veterans," Abraham told the Monroe News-Star. In July 2016, he enacted a bill to give benefit increases to disabled veterans.

On the Agriculture Committee, Abraham pressed for normalization of trade relations with Cuba, which has been eager to get access to rice from Louisiana. He served on the House-Senate conference committee on the 2018 farm bill and supported the final agreement. Although he — and House Republicans, generally — failed in their efforts to tighten work requirements for food-stamp recipients, Abraham said that he welcomed preservation of crop insurance and greater flexibility for farmers. The final deal "is a good bill that gives our farmers and ranchers the security they need," he said.

Following the election, Abraham announced that he was running for governor in the November 2019 contest. He told the News-Star that Edwards was "focused on raising taxes" and that businesses were leaving the state. During his uncompetitive House reelection campaign in 2018, Abraham ran statewide ads that introduced himself to voters. His announcement came four days after Republican Sen. John Kennedy unexpectedly said that he would not challenge Edwards. Other better-known GOP prospects also decided not to enter the contest.

LA-5: Northeast Louisiana

Cook Partisan Voting Index: R+15

Population		Race and Ethnicity		Income	
Total	749,991	White	60%	Median Income	$36,731
Land area (sq. miles)	14,453	Black	35.4%	District Income Rank	427
Pop/ sq mi	51.9	Latino	2.4%	Poverty Rate	25%
Born in State	81%	Asian	0.7%	With health insurance	85.8%
		Two or more races	1.1%	Cash public assistance	1.7%
Age Groups		Other	0.5%	Food stamp/SNAP	19.7%
Under 18	23.9%				
18-34	23.6%	**Education**		**Work**	
35-64	37.3%	H.S grad or less	57.6%	White Collar	15.2%
Over 64	15.2%	Some college	24.8%	Sales and Service	44.9%
Military		College Degree, 4 yr	11.7%	Blue Collar	24.9%
Veteran/ Active Duty	7.7%	Post grad	5.8%	Government	18.5%

2012 Pres. Vote	Romney	201,058	(61%)	Obama	124,054	(38%)
2016 Pres. Vote	Trump	205,258	(64%)	Clinton	110,259	(34%)

Monroe, Alexandria: Northeast Louisiana is perhaps the least known part of the state. Along the Mississippi River and the Red River and their dozens of tributaries, it was plantation country before the Civil War, and there are African-American majorities today in many parishes. Away from the rivers, in the hill country, small farmers scratched out a living on land connected to parish courthouses by dusty lanes. Such was Winn Parish, where Huey P. Long, the transformative figure in modern Louisiana politics, was born in 1893 and from which he began his meteoric political career. Elected governor in 1928 and senator in 1930, he was a national figure when he was assassinated in 1935 in the new high-rise capitol he had built in Baton Rouge.

The 5th Congressional District of Louisiana contains much of this country, from the hills of Winn Parish to the several small black-majority parishes along the Mississippi. About 35 percent of the population is African American. In this largely rural district, poverty is rampant. Along the river, the health of residents in Concordia is ranked among the "sickest" in the nation. The median income is in the bottom 3 percent of the nation. The biggest urban areas here are Monroe in the north and Alexandria to the south; each has slightly less than 50,000 people and is majority-black. Monroe, in Ouachita Parish, is heavily Protestant. Alexandria, in Rapides Parish, sits at the northern extension of Cajun, Catholic Louisiana. The district also includes a few parishes east of the Mississippi River and on the outskirts of Baton Rouge.

This is one of the largest row-crop farming districts in the nation, including cotton, rice, corn and soybeans. In 2018, local farmers were battered by poor weather and President Donald Trump's trade war, which stopped soybean sales in China, creating what one producer termed "the worst agricultural crisis to hit Louisiana" in a half-century. The area is a prime source of pine timber. After the federal government stunned local officials in 2010 by determining that the Red River's levees were no longer certified, officials in Rapides Parish used federal disaster relief funds and completed the repairs in 2017. Consistent with his strong showing in other rural districts across the nation, Donald Trump won here, 64%-34%.

Garret Graves (R)

Elected 2014, 3rd term, b. Jan 31, 1972; Baton Rouge; Alabama University; Louisiana Tech University, Att., 1995; American University (DC), Att., 1996; Roman Catholic; Married (Carissa Graves); 3 children.

Professional Career: Staff, U.S. Sen. John Breaux; Staff, U.S. Rep. Billy Tauzin; Staff, U.S. Sen. David Vitter; Chairman, Coastal Protection & Restoration Authority of LA; Vice Chairman, Gulf Coast Ecosystem Restoration Task Force, U.S. EPA.

DC Office: 2402 RHOB 20515, 202-225-3901, Fax: 202-225-7313, garretgraves.house.gov

State Offices: Baton Rouge, 225-442-1731; Livingston, 225-686-4413; Thibodaux, 985-448-4103.

Committees: *Natural Resources*: Energy & Mineral Resources; Water, Oceans & Wildlife. *Select Committee on the Climate Crisis (RMM)*. *Transportation & Infrastructure*: Aviation (RMM); Water Resources & Environment.

Group Ratings

	ADA	ACLU	AFL-CIO	LCV	ITI	COC	HAFA	ACU	CFG	FRC
2018	-	18%	-	0%	-	75%	74%	92%	71%	100%
2017	0%	C	5%	3%	C	93%	C	89%	80%	100%

Almanac Ratings 2017-18

	Economy	Social	Foreign	Composite
Liberal	6%	9%	8%	8%
Conservative	94%	91%	92%	92%

Key Votes of the 115th Congress

1. Obama-care revision	Y	5. Family planning regs	Y	9. Guantanamo prisoners	N
2. Tax Cuts	Y	6. Body cameras/immigration	N	10. Ground missiles, limit	N
3. Omnibus appropriations	N	7. Abortion ban	Y	11. Defense Dept. spending	Y
4. Dodd-Frank revision	Y	8. Concealed carry	Y	12. FISA rules	N

Election Results

Election	Name (Party)	Vote (%)		Cand. Spent	Ind. Exp. Support	Ind. Exp. Oppose
2018 Primary	Garret Graves (R)	186,553	(70%)	$1,907,440		
	Justin DeWitt (D)	55,089	(21%)	$28,684		
	Andie Saizan (D)	21,627	(8%)	$11,611		

Prior winning percentages: 2016 (63%), 2014 (62%)

Republican Garret Graves, who was elected in a 2014 runoff against the celebrated 87-year-old former governor and ex-federal convict Edwin Edwards, quickly became a player and made an impact in the House, especially on energy and environment issues. His substantial background on resource issues and as a Capitol Hill aide have given him influence as a junior lawmaker. Graves has signaled his interest in a possible statewide office.

Graves, a native of Baton Rouge, is an experienced politician and policy wonk, even though he is serving in his first elected office. He left home for Washington in his early 20s and began his political career as an intern for Democratic Sen. John Breaux. After a couple of months, he joined the office of GOP Rep. Billy Tauzin and worked his way up the ladder. He also worked for the House Energy and Commerce Committee, which Tauzin chaired, and later for Sen. David Vitter. All represented Louisiana.

In 2008, newly elected Gov. Bobby Jindal selected Graves to chair the Louisiana Coastal Protection and Restoration Authority and serve as his coastal adviser. Graves won praise for a $50 billion, 50-year master plan to promote coastal restoration and improve hurricane protection, as well as for coordinating the state's response to the 2010 Deepwater Horizon oil spill in the Gulf of Mexico. He was Jindal's point man in a Southeast Louisiana Flood Protection Authority-East lawsuit against more than 100 oil and gas companies, which alleged that decades of drilling and extraction had contributed to wetlands destruction. He said that he was responsible for $18 billion in projects to improve the economic, environmental and community resilience of the state.

After Republican Rep. Bill Cassidy challenged Democratic Sen. Mary Landrieu, Graves stepped down from his state job and dove into the open-seat contest. In the all-party primary, he faced 11 other candidates, including eight Republicans. His best-known opponent was Democrat Edwards, who had been governor for 16 years and served eight years in federal prison on corruption charges. In the first round of voting in November, Edwards took 30 percent of the vote and Graves had 27 percent.

The colorful past exploits of Edwards vastly increased national attention on the contest, though he had been out of public office since 1996. He ran as a self-described New Deal Democrat and "old relic" who unabashedly favored government spending to help the district. Graves supported free-market principles and reduced government, and called for a halt to welfare in favor of incentivized hard work. He worked to convince voters that his familiarity with Washington would be a benefit but that he was not a "Washington insider." He outspent Edwards, $1.5 million to $400,000. No surprise, in this overwhelmingly Republican district, Graves won the runoff, 62%-38%.

With seats on the Natural Resources, and Transportation and Infrastructure committees, both of which are important to his district, Graves brought unusually broad experience in dealing with resource issues. His willingness to address climate change and its potential problems quickly gave him opportunities among House Republicans.

On the Water Resources and Environment Subcommittee, which he chaired in 2017-18, Graves was instrumental in the enactment of legislation in 2018 to authorize new water projects. The measure included $500 million in credit to Louisiana for coastal restoration and other water-related projects. "We've got to stop the stupidity of spending billions of dollars after disasters instead of millions before," Graves said. To combat coastal erosion, he pressed vigorously to maintain the revenue-sharing arrangement that Louisiana has with oil and gas companies. He also has "close allies with environmental groups," Politico reported in 2017.

In 2016, Graves passed amendments to accelerate $150 million in projects in Louisiana, especially in areas that had suffered extensive flood damage a few months earlier. "We've been waiting decades for the Corps to build projects designed to fix [the Louisiana coast], but all we get is lip service about how it's 'still being considered.' Meanwhile, the coast continues to disappear and our communities become increasingly vulnerable," he said. He criticized Gov. John Bel Edwards for failing to deliver aid to flood victims — many of whom were constituents of Graves.

Climbing the ladder of influence on the Transportation panel, Graves switched in 2019 to top Republican on the Aviation Subcommittee. "I am excited about the opportunity to be on the front lines helping to modernize our technology and aviation system," he said, though he added — a bit defensively — "we are not backing off" interest in water priorities for Louisiana and the nation.

In far less dramatic campaigns than his first contest, Graves has easily won reelection. Stating that he had no interest in running for governor in 2019, Graves "was thought to be looking beyond 2019 for a possible gubernatorial run," WWL-TV of New Orleans reported in December 2018. In endorsing Graves for reelection in 2018, the New Orleans Times-Picayune editorialized that he had "shown leadership" on local issues.

LA-6: Baton Rouge area

Cook Partisan Voting Index: R+19

Population		Race and Ethnicity		Income	
Total	785,266	White	67.5%	Median Income	$61,097
Land area (sq. miles)	4,034	Black	23.6%	District Income Rank	165
Pop/ sq mi	194.7	Latino	4.4%	Poverty Rate	14.1%
Born in State	77.6%	Asian	2.2%	With health insurance	90.1%
		Two or more races	1.7%	Cash public assistance	0.9%
Age Groups		Other	0.5%	Food stamp/SNAP	12%
Under 18	24%				
18-34	25.5%	**Education**		**Work**	
35-64	37.6%	H.S grad or less	43.6%	White Collar	12.9%
Over 64	12.9%	Some college	27.4%	Sales and Service	39.9%
		College Degree, 4 yr	19%	Blue Collar	22.7%
Military		Post grad	9.9%	Government	15.6%
Veteran/ Active Duty	6.7%				

2012 Pres. Vote	Romney	228,507	(66%)	Obama	110,430	(32%)			
2016 Pres. Vote	Trump	230,701	(65%)	Clinton	110,394	(31%)	Johnson	8,531	(2%)

Baton Rouge: Baton Rouge sits on a cultural fault line in Louisiana, the boundary between the French-speaking, Catholic Cajun country and the heavily Baptist region to the north. Historically, it was part of the Florida Parishes, the territory east of the Mississippi River and north of Lake Pontchartrain that was not included in the Louisiana Purchase in 1803. It still belonged to Spain, until the locals rebelled and declared their own Republic of West Florida in 1810. Then it quickly became part of Louisiana and the United States.

Today, Baton Rouge is the center of a metropolitan area of about 800,000 people. It sits on the east bank of the Mississippi and is the largest inland deep-water port located on the river. Local features are the old Gothic-style capitol, where Huey Long took office, and the three-story Art Deco capitol, which he had built and where he died at the hands of an assassin in 1935. Also here is Louisiana State University, another Long legacy. The region benefits from the research productivity of LSU's main campus and has been called the "Creative Capital of the South," because of its success in creating public-private partnerships in high-growth sectors.

The area has suffered recent problems. In July 2016, two police officers in Baton Rouge responding to an incident at a convenience store fatally shot Alton Sterling, an African American. That led to nearly two weeks of street protests, which culminated in an ambush of law-enforcement officers, three of whom were killed. State Attorney General Jeff Landry announced in March 2018 that there was not sufficient evidence to bring charges in the death of Sterling; his advocates disagreed. In August, devastating floods hit the Baton Rouge area; more than 20 inches fell in two days in some areas. This was the heaviest rain storm in the history of Louisiana and left more than $10 billion in damages, though it was not a customary hurricane.

The 6th Congressional District of Louisiana includes the majority of residents in East and West Baton Rouge parishes. A group of mostly white citizens seeking to improve their schools has advocated the creation of a new city, St. George, that would be removed from East Baton Rouge and would have a population that exceeds 80,000. The 6th district extends south to Thibodeaux and parts of the Bayous. Researchers revealed in October 2018 that they had discovered the site of a mass grave in Thibodeaux, which likely resulted from a racial massacre in 1887 when a mob of white men killed at least 30 blacks who worked at a sugar plantation. The burial site was not recorded at the time, though the researchers benefited from more than a century of informal oral histories. In 2016, writer John DeSantis published a book, Thibodeaux Massacre, with an account of the incident. Now that Baton Rouge's black neighborhoods are in the New Orleans-based 2nd District, the 6th's black population is 24 percent, which places the district solidly in the GOP camp.

MAINE

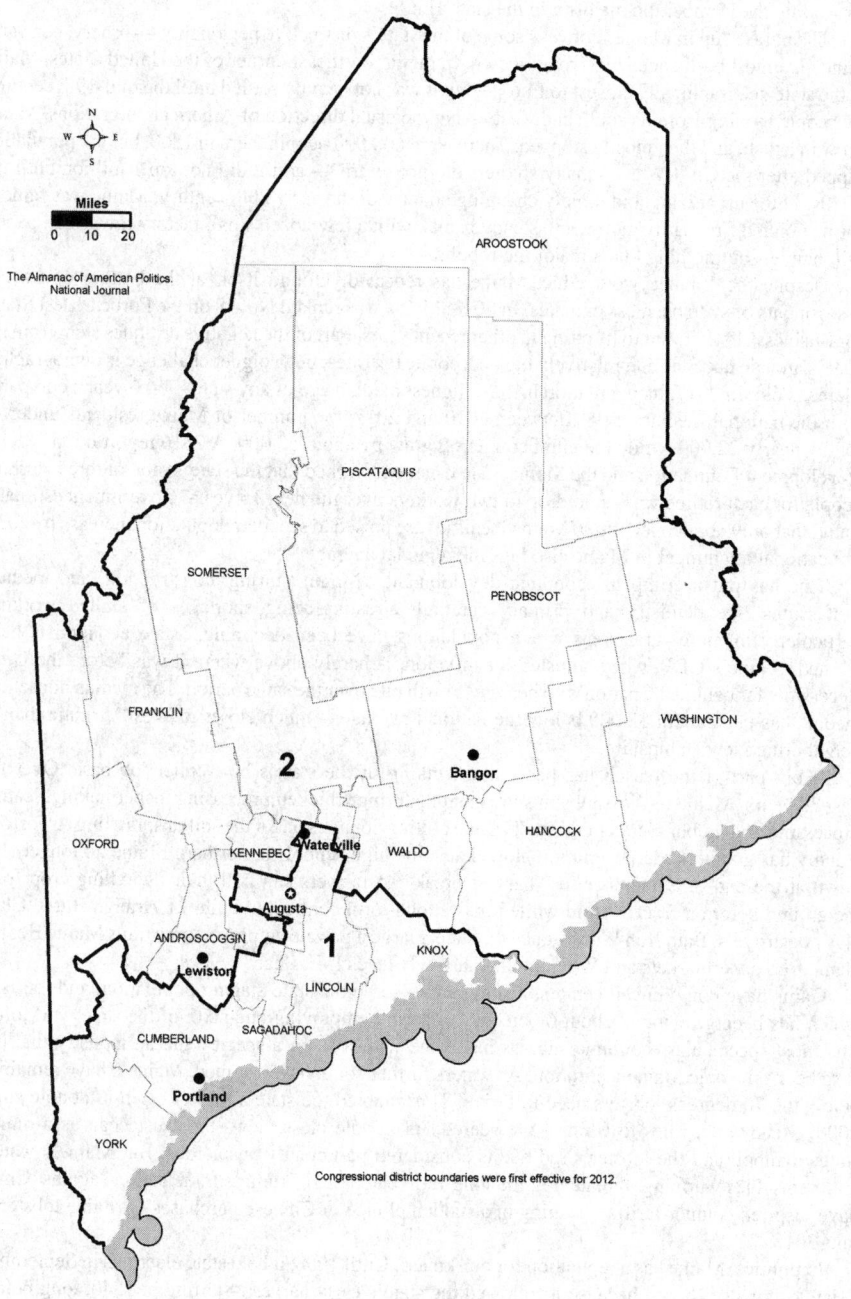

Congressional district boundaries were first effective for 2012.

Following eight years under a polarizing Republican governor and two years after giving Donald Trump a strong showing, voters in Maine swung back to the Democrats in 2018, electing a Democratic governor, ousting a Republican congressman, overturning GOP control of the state Senate, and expanding the Democratic majority in the state House.

The phrase "up in Maine" conveys some of the state's distinctive personality — ornery, contrary-minded, almost bullheaded, and rough-hewn. In the far northeast corner of the United States, Maine is the state geographically closest to Europe, but it was not heavily settled until the mid-19th century, by people moving from its south and west — not the usual direction of American migrations. Maine grew in a rush, and then mostly stopped. There were 600,000 people there in 1860, but the population dipped after the Civil War — many soldiers did not return — and it did not top 1 million until the 1970s. In the urbanizing and rapidly changing country of the early 20th century, Maine was famous for its pointed firs, hardy moose and steady habits, with a few dozen small factory towns and paper-mill hamlets but nothing like a major metropolis.

Despite the Yankee work ethic, Maine has repeatedly found itself at the bottom of various assessments of state business climates. In 2018, Maine was ranked No. 48 on the Forbes "Best States for Business" list, similar to its rating in other recent years. Part of the negative critiques stem from the state's archaic tax code and relatively high corporate tax rates, but a bigger challenge is demographic: Maine is old. In 2017, its population had the highest median age of any state -- 44.6 years, compared with the national median of 38. Between 2010 and 2017, the number of Maine residents under 18 fell by nearly 22,000, while the number over 65 grew by about 55,000. A 2016 report by the Maine Development Foundation and the Maine State Chamber warned that the state's ratio of three working people for each retiree was set to drop to two workers over the next 15 years. Government estimates found that only about one-fifth of Maine localities are poised to see their population increase by 2034. Educational attainment in Maine also lags the regional average.

This has put a crimp in economic development. "Manufacturing, construction, and medical professions like dentistry and primary care are already facing shortages of skilled workers, particularly in more rural areas where populations have been declining," state economists have warned. Maine's GDP, when adjusted for inflation, is barely above where it was before the Great Recession, far behind the nation's 16 percent growth rate over the same period. The median household income has been about $8,000 below the national average -- much closer to West Virginia than to neighboring New Hampshire.

A big part of the reason has been the shrinking of the state's blue-collar job base. Over the past 30 years, Maine has lost jobs in shoe manufacturing, chicken processing, papermaking, leather processing and timber. Scratching small Maine boiling potatoes out of the soil of sprawling Aroostook County has gotten harder, even more now that some high schools in northern Maine no longer shut down at the end of September for "harvest break" so farmers can pull their dwindling crop from the ground before it freezes. And while it has a long-term contract to build 21 Arleigh Burke Class Navy destroyers, Bath Iron Works, once the state's largest private employer, now trails Maine Health, Hannaford supermarkets and Walmart and narrowly leads L.L. Bean.

Gains have come in call centers, health care to serve the state's aging population, and tourism, which has been growing at about 6 percent a year and employing one-sixth of the state workforce. The most spectacular economic success has come with lobster, a species and an industry that has long been an iconic Maine institution. As waters further south have warmed, Maine's have remained below the 70 degrees lobsters need to thrive. This enabled the state's lobster catch to double since 2000. Meanwhile, sales to China have soared; its middle class views the crustacean as a dining status symbol, and the lobster's red hue is considered particularly auspicious. But Maine's waters are themselves warming, threatening the long-term catch, and Trump's trade actions against China have inspired counter-tariffs, resulting in a sudden plunge of Chinese purchases of Maine lobster in mid-2018.

In politics, Maine has a reputation for quirkiness. Until 1958, it held state elections in September, a date originally chosen because it followed the state's early harvest. Starting in 1840, long before the advent of public opinion polls, the election results were taken as a gauge of national sentiment — hence the saying, "As Maine goes, so goes the nation." Actually, Maine didn't vote like the rest of the country most of the time. In 1936, only Maine and Vermont voted for Republican Alf Landon over

Democrat Franklin D. Roosevelt, prompting Roosevelt's campaign manager to wisecrack, "As Maine goes, so goes Vermont." Maine was known for its flinty Yankee Republicanism and for Prohibition; it banned liquor in 1851, after which other states enacted "Maine laws." Since voting four times against FDR, it has given its statewide electoral votes to the loser in the close presidential elections of 1948, 1960, 1968, 1976, 2000, 2004 and 2016 — a record equaled by no other state.

Maine cast the nation's highest percentages for third-party presidential candidate Ross Perot — 30 percent in 1992 and 14 percent in 1996. In 1974, it elected independent James Longley, a former Republican, as governor; in 1994 and 1998, it elected independent Angus King, a former Democrat, as governor. In 2010, it came close to electing independent Eliot Cutler as governor. The winner was Republican Paul LePage, an outspoken conservative who eked out a victory with 38 percent to Cutler's 36 percent. Perhaps tiring of seeing officials elected by pluralities, voters in 2016 approved via ballot measure a system of ranked-choice voting, in which last-place finishers' second-choice votes are reallocated to the remaining candidates until one candidate reaches 50 percent. Republicans fought the system, but the courts upheld it, and ranked-choice voting was used in party primaries and in federal elections for the first time in 2018. (Existing constitutional language has kept ranked-choice voting from being used in state-level general elections.)

The 2016 election was dramatic. The state's allocation of electoral votes by congressional district made Maine aggressively contested terrain, with both Trump and Hillary Clinton stumping in the state's rural 2nd congressional district. Trump in particular saw promise in the state's heavily white, blue-collar voters; Maine is the nation's whitest state, and the 2nd district in particular had lost jobs to foreign competition for many years and tended to see the government as a distant, even malevolent force. On Election Day, the 2nd district swung heavily toward Trump. He won nine counties in the state, eight more than Mitt Romney had won in 2012, and it was enough to secure the 2nd District's electoral vote.

But in the 2018 midterms, Maine shifted back, a combination of the pro-Democratic national political environment and fatigue with LePage's cantankerous tenure. In the gubernatorial race, Democratic Attorney General Janet Mills, urging enactment of a Medicaid expansion that LePage had steadily blocked, defeated Republican businessman Shawn Moody, 51%-43%. The other closely watched race in 2018 was the 2nd District House seat that had swung so hard for Trump two years earlier. There, Democrat Jared Golden defeated incumbent Rep. Bruce Poliquin. While Poliquin led on Election Day by 2,000 votes, he failed to achieve a majority, and ranked-choice votes put Golden over the top. Poliquin challenged the result, but it was upheld in court. Time will tell whether Democrats, now back in charge, will be able to maintain their position in a state where the demographics are favorable to the Trump-era GOP.

Population		Race and Ethnicity		Income	
Total	1,330,158	White	93.6%	Median Income	$53,024
Land area (sq. miles)	30,843	Black	1.2%	State Income Rank	31
Pop/ sq mi	43.1	Latino	1.5%	Poverty Rate	12.9%
Born in state	63.3%	Asian	1.1%	With health insurance	91.0%
		Two or more races	1.9%	Cash public assistance	3.5%
Age Groups		Other	0.7%	Food stamp/SNAP	15.3%
Under 18	19.3%				
18-34	20.0%	**Education**		**Work**	
35-64	41.9%	H.S grad or less	40.2%	White Collar	36.6%
Over 64	18.8%	Some college	29.5%	Sales and Service	41.5%
		College Degree, 4 yr	19.3%	Blue Collar	21.9%
Military		Post grad	10.9%	Government	13.6%
Veteran/ Active Duty	10.5%				

Presidential Politics

2016 Caucus (D)	Sanders (D)	2,231 (64%)	Clinton (D)	1,232 (36%)		
2016 Caucus (R)	Cruz (R)	8,550 (46%)	Trump (R)	6,070 (33%)	Kasich (R)	2,270 (12%)
	Rubio (R)	1,492 (8%)				
2016 Pres. Vote	Clinton (D)	357,735 (48%)	Trump (R)	335,593 (45%)	Johnson (L)	38,105 (5%)
	Stein (G)	14,251 (2%)				
2012 Pres. Vote	Obama (D)	401,306 (56%)	Romney (R)	292,276 (41%)		

Maine is one of only two states that voted against Franklin Roosevelt in all four of his elections (Vermont was the other). However, since 1992, Maine has voted for a Democratic presidential candidate seven straight times. In 2016 Hillary Clinton defeated Donald Trump 48%-45%, but the Republican still managed to win one of the state's four Electoral College votes. That's because Maine, like Nebraska, allocates one electoral vote to the winner of each of its two congressional districts. The statewide winner receives the other two. The 1st District, which includes Portland and Augusta, is the more liberal of the two. Clinton took the 1st District with 54 percent. The 2nd District is home to old mill towns, covers the vast rural interior of the state and includes Bangor and Lewiston. The voters of this economically depressed region were drawn to Trump, just like they were to the blunt and combative GOP Gov. Paul LePage. In Rumford, known for the old Oxford Paper mill on the upper Androscoggin River, voters went from backing Obama 61%-34% in 2012 to siding with Trump 50%-41%. Overall, Trump carried the 2nd District 51%-41%. For the first time since 1972, when Maine's law to divide electoral votes by district went into effect, it split.

Maine held its first-ever presidential primary in March 1996, hoping to attract the candidates' early attention. That tactic didn't work, and the state abolished its presidential primary for 2004. In 2016, Republicans held their caucus on March 5, a Saturday, and the Democrats caucused the next day. Maine Republicans said their caucus turnout hit 18,650, more than triple from 2012's level, and Texas Sen. Ted Cruz bested Trump, 46%-33%, even though LePage had endorsed the New Yorker. Ohio Gov. John Kasich finished third with 12 percent. Vermont Sen. Bernie Sanders defeated Clinton 64%-36% in state delegates allocated by the caucuses. Maine Democrats said 46,000 participated in their caucus. Voters in both parties encountered logistical problems in conducting their caucuses and Maine's legislature enacted a March presidential primary for 2020.

Congressional Districts

116th Congress Lineup	2D	**115th Congress Lineup**	1D 1R

Maine has a bipartisan advisory commission that draws up a redistricting plan, which the legislature and governor can consider, but a state statute has stipulated that redistricting must be approved by a two-thirds vote in the legislature and delayed until the third year after the census. In practice, this has not made much difference. Since Maine lost its third congressional district following the 1960 census, the lines between the largely rural northern district and the Portland-based southern district have shifted only slightly.

In March 2011, two citizens brought a lawsuit in federal court arguing that the timetable violated the Constitution because it left in place for one election districts that were not of equal population. Although the census showed the two districts' populations differed by only 8,669 people, the court in June ruled for the plaintiffs and ordered a new plan be adopted by January 2012. The advisory commission voted 8-15 to submit the Democratic plan with minimal shifts. Harsh words were exchanged, but when the legislature met, it adopted the Democratic plan with only three dissenting votes and Gov. Paul LePage signed it into law. Then the 2nd District in 2014 elected the state's first Republican to the House in 20 years.

Now Democrats control both House seats, plus the state legislature and the governor's office. A shift of perhaps 10,000 persons from the 1st to the 2nd will make them equal in size. It's possible that Democrats will want to strengthen the Democratic base in the 2nd, by shifting a Democratic town or two from what has become their secure 1st, especially with the increased national stakes in redistricting.

Janet Mills (D)

Elected 2018, term expires 2023, 1st term; b. Dec. 30, 1947, Farmington; Colby College, Att.; University of Massachusetts, B.A.; University of Maine, J.D.; Unknown; Widow; 5 stepchildren.

Elected Office: ME House, 2002-2008; ME Attorney General, 2009-2011, 2013-2018.

Professional Career: District Attorney, Franklin & Oxford Counties, 1980-1995; Attorney.

Office: 210 State St, Augusta, 04333-0001; 207-287-3531; Fax: 207-287-1034; Website: maine.gov/governor

State Legislature: Senate: 21D, 14R   **House:** 88D, 56R, 5I, 1O, 1V

Election Results

Election	Name (Party)	Vote (%)
2018 General	Janet Mills (D)..	320,962 (51%)
	Shawn Moody (R)...	272,311 (43%)
	Teresea Hayes (I)...	37,268 (6%)
2018 Primary	Janet Mills (D)..	63,384 (54%)
	Adam Cote (D)..	53,866 (46%)

Maine voters in 2018 chose Democrat Janet Mills, a long-serving attorney general and state legislator, to move past the eight-year tenure of Republican Gov. Paul LePage, who was known for his consistent conservatism and, perhaps even more so, for his irascible statements.

Mills grew up in rural Aroostook County, the granddaughter of farmers who grew the region's signature crop – potatoes. Her political roots run deep. Mills' grandfather served two terms in the state Senate and her father, S. Peter Mills Jr., was the Republican floor leader in the state House and later served as a U.S. attorney. Her father supported Rep. Margaret Chase Smith's run for the Senate, forging lifelong bonds between the two families. One day during her 1948 Senate campaign, Smith stopped by the Mills house and held the future governor, then just six months old, on her lap, reporter Colin Woodard wrote. Smith "was a woman of both grit and integrity who held high public office with grace and vision," Mills said in 2009. "She held her ground and didn't take any grief from anyone, even from presidents and foreign leaders." Smith served in the Senate from 1949 to 1973, becoming the first woman to serve in both chambers. Mills emulated Smith's trailblazing accomplishments, becoming the state's first woman to serve as a criminal prosecutor, a district attorney, attorney general, and now as governor. She co-founded the Maine Women's Lobby, which advocated on behalf of battered women.

At 14, Mills underwent surgery for scoliosis that kept her in a body cast for most of the year. She received her bachelor's degree from the University of Massachusetts-Boston and her law degree from the University of Maine. During her university years, she told Woodard, she was shaped by the broader cultural tumult, which "encouraged my somewhat rebellious nature" and pushed her to become a Democrat. She spent the Watergate summer of 1974 interning in the American Civil Liberties Union's Washington office, and then at the Center for Law and Social Policy the following summer. Mills prosecuted criminal cases, including murders, for the attorney general's office, then was appointed – and was later reelected four times – to the post of district attorney for Androscoggin, Franklin and Oxford counties. Mills survived allegations of drug use and abuse of office; they were never substantiated and she called them politically motivated. In 1994 Mills lost a primary for the 2nd Congressional District (she lost to future Democratic Gov. John Baldacci) but in 2002 won a state House seat formerly held by her father. In 2008, the legislature named her attorney general -- Maine's system for filling this post is unique – and she remained in the job until she won the governorship, except for 2011 and 2012, when the GOP controlled the levers of appointment.

In this position, Mills had regular run-ins with LePage, a larger-than-life character in a small state. LePage was the oldest son of 18 children in a poverty-stricken, dysfunctional family; at times he slept in hallways, cars and even a strip joint. He became general manager of Marden's Surplus and Salvage, a Maine-based discount store chain, in 1996, then served as a city council member and mayor of Waterville. When LePage entered the 2010 governor's race, he led a seven-candidate Republican field with 37 percent and eked out a victory in the three-way general election with 38 percent; he would win a second term in 2014 by a more comfortable 48%-43% margin. In office, LePage pursued both fiscally and socially conservative policies, but he had a knack for irritating residents with his off-the-cuff remarks, often in a racial context. In his second term, LePage revealed that he'd been keeping a three-ring binder with mug shots of drug dealers, 90 percent of whom, he said, were black or Hispanic, something official statistics called into question.

Mills refused to represent LePage's position several times, including when he sought to appeal a ruling on cuts to Medicaid benefits, in a case involving aid to asylum seekers, and a case about the closure of a Washington County correctional facility. Such refusals led the governor to sue Mills for abuse of power. "You are clearly not doing the job as attorney general for the people of Maine ... and it appears you are using your office as a campaign headquarters," he wrote Mills during the 2018 campaign. Mills made enemies among the Penobscot Nation when she defended a federal suit over the tribe's rights to the Penobscot River and another suit over water quality standards on the river.

Sensing opportunity, Maine Democrats flocked to the gubernatorial primary. They included veteran and attorney Adam Cote, activist and attorney Betsy Sweet, and former House speaker and family therapist Mark Eves. Mills and Cote were considered the more moderate candidates in the field. Generally, though, the candidates overlapped on many issues. Mills backed increased use of renewable energy, higher starting pay for teachers, the expansion of Medicaid through the Affordable Care Act, and bans of high-capacity gun magazines and bump stocks; she was vague about whether she planned to raise taxes. The primary was decided using the ranked-choice voting system that residents had implemented through a ballot measure. In the initial voting, Mills got 33 percent, followed by Cote with 28 percent, Sweet with 16 percent, and Eves with 14 percent. After the lower-finishing candidates' votes were reassigned to the voter's second-choice candidates, Mills crossed the 50 percent threshold and was declared the winner eight days after the election.

On the Republican side, businessman Shawn Moody won with an outright majority in the initial vote, defeating Senate Majority Leader Garrett Mason with 23 percent, former Maine commissioner of Health and Human Services Mary Mayhew with 15 percent, and House Republican Leader Kenneth Fredette with 6 percent.

Moody, an independent until 2017, was an entrepreneur who built a chain of collision-repair centers. Like LePage, Moody had a challenging childhood. His parents divorced when he was a year old, and his mother was institutionalized at times. Moody's skill for repairing cars became clear in his early teens. Cobbling together his savings, Moody opened a car-repair garage on a portion of a junkyard by the time he was 18. A few years later, he bought out the whole junkyard and turned it into an advanced automobile recycling center that he sold for millions of dollars in 1999. Then, two years later, he opened Moody's Collision Centers, which expanded to 11 locations.

In 2010, without any formal political experience, Moody ran for governor as an independent, taking 5 percent of the vote in the five-way general-election that LePage narrowly won. In 2014, LePage appointed Moody to the boards of the University of Maine and the community college system. When he was ready to run again in 2018, Moody styled himself a candidate who would carry on LePage's policies in a less-confrontational style. The outgoing governor's daughter and close aides joined his campaign. Mills benefited from an energized Democratic electorate, and she leveraged her ongoing battles with LePage to draw a clear contrast, including on the expansion of Medicaid, which she promised to accomplish immediately after taking office. Mills and Moody also faced state Treasurer Teresa Hayes, who was running as an independent. On Election Day, Mills received 51 percent, defeating Moody with 43 percent and Hayes with 6 percent. She won nine counties for the Democrats, up from just two in 2014.

"For so long Maine has been known as a place of political civility, and LePage broke from that," Colby College political science professor Sandy Maisel told the Boston Globe. "The question has always been whether he changed it forever, but this election may have proved he was an aberration."

Susan Collins (R)

Elected 1996, term expires 2020, 4th term, b. Dec 07, 1952; Caribou; St. Lawrence University (NY), B.A., 1975; Roman Catholic; Married (Thomas Daffron).

Professional Career: Legislative aide, U.S Sen. Bill Cohen, 1975-1987, Staff Director, Oversight of Gov. Management SubCommittee, 1981-1987; Professional & Financial Regulation Comm., 1987-1992; New England regional Director, U.S Small Business Admin., 1992; ME deputy treas., 1993; Executive Director, Center for Family Business, Husson College, 1994-1996.

DC Office: 413 DSOB 20510, 202-224-2523, Fax: 202-224-2693, collins.senate.gov

State Offices: Augusta, 207-622-8414; Bangor, 207-945-0417; Biddeford, 207-283-1101; Caribou, 207-493-7873; Lewiston, 207-784-6969; Portland, 207-780-3575.

Committees: *Aging (Chmn). Appropriations*: Agriculture, Rural Development, FDA & Related Agencies; Commerce, Justice, Science & Related Agencies; Department of Defense; Energy & Water Development; Military Construction & Veteran Affairs & Related Agencies; Transportation, HUD & Related Agencies (Chmn). *Health, Education, Labor & Pensions*: Primary Health & Retirement Security. *Intelligence.*

Group Ratings

	ADA	ACLU	AFL-CIO	LCV	ITI	COC	HAFA	ACU	CFG	FRC
2018	-	43%	-	21%	-	80%	28%	41%	22%	63%
2017	30%	C	13%	32%	C	57%	C	48%	42%	42%

Almanac Ratings 2017-18

	Economy	Social	Foreign	Composite
Liberal	34%	34%	9%	26%
Conservative	66%	66%	91%	75%

Key Votes of the 115th Congress

1. Obama-care revision	N	5. Gun regulations	Y	9. Kavanaugh confirmation	Y
2. Tax Cuts	Y	6. Family planning regs	N	10. Saudi arms sales	N
3. Dodd-Frank revision	Y	7. Gorsuch confirmation	Y	11. FISA rules	Y
4. Omnibus appropriations	Y	8. Immigration restrictions	N	12. Military aid in Yemen	Y

Election Results

Election	Name (Party)	Vote (%)		Cand. Spent	Ind. Exp. Support	Ind. Exp. Oppose
2014 General	Susan Collins (R)	413,505	(67%)	$5,563,101	$1,157,937	$51,797
	Shenna Bellows (D)	190,254	(31%)	$2,335,587	$180,057	
2014 Primary	Susan Collins (R)	Unopposed				

Prior winning percentages: 2008(61%), 2002 (58%), 1996 (49%)

After more than two decades in the Senate, Republican Susan Collins contemplated capping her political career with a run for governor in 2018. But after months of toying with the idea, Maine's senior senator decided to remain on Capitol Hill. "I feel, as many of my colleagues told me, that I'm often a bridge between the two sides of the aisle and there have been times when I have been able to make a difference," she told reporters. "I like playing that role, and there seem to be fewer and fewer senators who enjoy playing that role." Indeed, Collins is among the last vestiges of a political breed with which Capitol Hill was once teeming: the moderate Republican. It has made her a key swing vote in a polarized, narrowly divided Senate. Such circumstances have given Collins outsize influence over the content and, frequently, the fate of key legislation and major appointments.

In 2017 and 2018, this role repeatedly put her in the spotlight — sometimes uncomfortably so. In July 2017, she was among a handful of Republicans who joined Senate Democrats to block efforts by President Donald Trump and other GOP leaders to repeal the Affordable Care Act. While Collins was literally greeted with applause at the Bangor, Maine, airport after that vote, she took heat from GOP's right wing — already angered by her public refusal to vote for Trump in 2016 (she wrote in House Speaker Paul Ryan's name instead). As she weighed a run for governor several months later, a key question was whether she could win a Republican primary for that post. But a year after her decision to stay in the Senate, Collins faced a firestorm from the left when her vote for Brett Kavanaugh, Trump's controversial Supreme Court nominee, sealed his confirmation by the narrowest of margins. The political fallout all but ensured that Collins, who previously has had little trouble winning re-election in a state with a clear Democratic lean, would face a stiff challenge for a fifth Senate term in 2020.

Notwithstanding that she is the only remaining Republican in Congress from New England, Collins insisted in a 2012 interview with Boston University Washington News Service that she "would never be anything but a Republican." Chuckling, she added: "It's in my DNA. It really is. I come from a part of the country where you're expected to apply independent judgment and that's what I've always tried to do." She sounded markedly less fervent in late 2018, amid the blowback from her Kavanaugh vote, when asked by a New York Times reporter why she remained a Republican. "I haven't given it a lot of thought, to tell you the truth," she replied. Collins grew up in Caribou, about as far northeast as you can get in the United States — and closer to the capitals of the Canadian provinces of New Brunswick and Quebec than to the Maine's capital, Augusta. Her family has been in the lumber business since 1844 and has long involved in state politics: Her father was a state senator; her mother was mayor of Caribou and chaired the board of trustees of the University of Maine System.

Collins' got her first taste of Washington as a high school senior, when she visited the capital as part of a Senate youth program. Sen. Margaret Chase Smith, then the chamber's only woman, spent nearly two hours talking with her. Collins today occupies the seat Smith once held and sits at the Senate floor desk that Smith used. Another role model was Republican Rep. William Cohen, her predecessor in the Senate and her boss for more than a decade. The lesson that both Cohen and Smith gave her, Collins said, was "do what you think is right, no matter the consequences." She interned for Cohen during the summer of 1974, when, as a freshman member of the House Judiciary Committee, he and several other Republicans voted to impeach President Richard Nixon. Cohen hired Collins a year later when she graduated from St. Lawrence University. She remained on his staff for 12 years. Cohen moved to the Senate in 1978, and Collins spent six years as staff director of a Governmental Affairs Committee subpanel that Cohen chaired. Two decades later, Collins would find herself chairing the full committee.

In 1986, Collins returned to Maine to run the state's Department of Professional and Financial Regulation, and later served as regional administrator of the federal Small Business Administration. In 1994, after winning the Republican nomination for governor, she ran third in a three-way general election contest won by independent Angus King — now her Senate colleague. Two years later, Cohen announced his retirement. Collins played up her similarities to fellow GOP moderates Cohen and Olympia Snowe. While calling for a balanced budget amendment and a line item veto, Collins pledged to serve no more than two terms — a promise she broke when she successfully sought a third term in 2008.

Collins was opposed by former Democratic Gov. Joseph Brennan. He criticized Collins for supporting repeal of the 1994 assault weapons ban. At the time, there were more gun owners per capita in Maine than any state except Alaska, and gun control was anathema in much of the state's rural areas, where Collins had grown up. But restrictions on firearms were more popular in the state's urban areas, which Brennan had represented. Brennan cut into Collins' lead with his attacks on her gun stance — but she outraised him significantly won 49%-44%.

Years later, in 2013, Collins voted against an assault weapons ban proposed in the Senate. At the same time, she became one of only four Republicans to break with her party and support a measure to expand background checks on firearms purchases, following the Newtown, Conn., school shooting in which 26 died. After that proposal and similar ones failed to gain passage, Collins in mid-2016 — following the Orlando, Fla., nightclub shooting in which 49 were killed by a lone gunman — sought to broker a compromise that would succeed. Her plan would have barred sales of guns to terrorism suspects on the government's no-fly or "selectee" list; it was designed to appeal to wavering Republicans by applying the ban to a much smaller group than a rival Democratic proposal would have. Her bill received solid Democratic support and peeled off seven of her GOP colleagues. But while it survived a procedural vote, it failed to advance.

The gun control issue was emblematic of a broader evolution for Collins: While a committed centrist throughout her Senate career, she was at first more conservative than her Maine colleague, Snowe. But she eventually eclipsed Snowe in the frequency with which she broke with her party.

In 2017, Almanac rankings put Collins with the third least conservative voting record in the GOP caucus; for the same period, FiveThirtyEight vote ratings pegged her as the second least supportive Republican of Trump.

During the Obama administration, Collins often found herself aligned with Senate Democrats. Early in President Barack Obama's first term, she provided a crucial vote to pass a $787 billion economic stimulus package — after using her leverage to insist that more than $100 billion be shaved from the original price tag. In 2010, she supported another law enacted in response to the 2008 financial crisis — the Dodd-Frank financial reforms — opposed by most Republicans. At the end of Obama's first term, in the debate over extending middle-income tax cuts passed early in George W. Bush's presidency, Collins was the only Senate Republican to support a surtax on millionaires. "They can afford to pay more to help with our deficit, and that's an area where I differ with many in our party," she said. On social issues, she was the only Republican on the Armed Services Committee to vote to repeal the ban on openly gay troops in the military in 2010.

But Obama's attempts to win Collins' support for the 2010 Affordable Care Act proved fruitless despite months of wooing. She expressed disdain for what she saw as a token effort to include a few Republican ideas in a largely Democratic-written measure. While she voted for GOP-sponsored efforts to repeal the ACA that were doomed to failure while Obama was in office, Collins opposed all three repeal options offered in the Trump era that had a chance of passing — notably the "skinny repeal," which failed when Collins joined two other Republicans and all Democrats in opposing it. While criticizing aspects of the law, she said: "These problems require a bipartisan solution. The Democrats made a big mistake when they passed the ACA without a single Republican vote. I don't want to see Republicans make the same mistake."

Collins got in line behind the $1.5 trillion GOP tax law that was enacted at the end of 2017 along party lines. It repealed a key ACA provision mandating that individuals carry health insurance or pay a penalty. Collins, while never particularly supportive of the individual mandate, was nonetheless concerned about the repeal's effects on the cost and availability of insurance. She received public assurances from Majority Leader Mitch McConnell that he would support passage of a couple of bills before the end of 2017 to mitigate any damage. But McConnell couldn't assure passage in the House — where Ryan, under conservative pressure, signaled he was not a party to the deal. While Collins voted for the final version of the tax measure, the bills to ease the impact of the individual mandate repeal were not passed by year's end.

Collins faced criticism from many who had praised her stance on the ACA months earlier; they said she had been duped. In response, she lashed out at media coverage of the episode as "unbelievably sexist," according to Bloomberg News, complaining that key provisions she had won with her leverage — such as increased medical deductions and deductibility for some state and local taxes — had been largely ignored. "I think I got more in this tax bill than any other member of the Senate," she said. Passage of the bills designed to ease health care premiums fell short again in early 2018.

Collins' role as consensus seeker and deal-maker was on display in early 2018, when a dispute over immigration policy resulted in a weekend government shutdown. A bipartisan group of nearly two dozen organized by Collins — and frustrated by a partisan standoff between McConnell and Minority Leader Chuck Schumer — began meeting in her office to find a solution. "Twenty-five senators is a quarter of the Senate, so that's a pretty powerful number of people who are able to make a difference with their votes and their voices," Collins told The New York Times. She met with McConnell and urged him to strengthen earlier statements about moving an immigration reform bill, clearing the way for Democratic support of a funding bill that reopened the government. The shutdown was brought on by House conservatives, who demanded rollbacks in the ACA in return for funding government operations. Collins tried to forge a compromise but failed. Her efforts were praised for defusing some of the partisan tensions that had prevented earlier progress.

During the early days of the Trump administration, Collins voted against the confirmation of a couple of the White House's most controversial nominees — while coming to the defense of embattled Alabama Sen. Jeff Sessions, who was nominated to be attorney general. While Sessions' nomination for a federal judgeship had been derailed three decades earlier amid reports of racist remarks, Collins — elected to the Senate the same year as Sessions — said, "I don't know the dynamics of what happened then, but I can speak to Jeff's character in the 20 years that I've known him." However, Collins was the lone Republican "no" vote on the nomination of Scott Pruitt, who rejected mainstream climate science, to head the Environmental Protection Agency.

Collins was one of two Republicans to vote against school choice advocate Betsy DeVos' nomination to be Education secretary. The defections of Collins and Alaska Sen. Lisa Murkowski forced Vice President Mike Pence to break a 50-50 tie to rescue DeVos. According to Politico, Collins held off announcing her opposition until Republicans had lined up enough votes to allow DeVos to squeak by. That was in line with longtime grumbling among Democrats that Collins only bolts from the GOP fold when the outcome is already decided.

But Senate Republican leaders were uncertain how Collins would come down on Kavanaugh's nomination until she gave a 45-minute floor speech on Oct. 5, 2018, explaining why she had decided to support him. Her support ensured Kavanaugh's confirmation the next day on a 50-48 vote. Collins, who had supported an FBI investigation into allegations of sexual assault against Kavanaugh by Christine Blasey Ford, said after reviewing the FBI's findings that Ford's claims could not be corroborated. Collins said that a two-hour meeting with Kavanaugh, along with a follow-up phone call and review of his opinions, had convinced her that he would not overturn Roe v. Wade. "Protecting this right [to abortion] is important to me," Collins said. "His views on honoring precedent would preclude attempts to do by stealth that which one has committed not to do overtly." According to The New York Times, Collins was said to be privately concerned that if Kavanaugh's nomination failed, the next person selected by Trump would be more conservative and could pose a clear danger to upholding Roe v. Wade.

Coming amid the #MeToo movement, Collins' decision triggered a furious reaction among abortion rights advocates and liberal groups — which had spent hundreds of thousands of dollars on Maine TV ads to push Collins to oppose Kavanaugh. Within days, a crowdfunding effort raised more than $3.5 million toward an effort to oust her in 2020. And several potential Democratic challengers emerged. Sara Gideon, speaker of the Maine House of Representatives, said she was thinking about running. So did former United Nations Ambassador Susan Rice who, while not a Maine resident, had a summer home and family ties there. After mulling a run for six months, Rice announced in April 2019 that she would not run -- saying the timing was not right to move her family to Maine. Collins said on NBC's "Meet the Press" in early 2019 that she is "getting ready to run," but added she would "make a final decision towards the end of this year." Meanwhile, she sought to distance herself from Trump, telling CNN she saw "nothing wrong" with other Republicans challenging him in 2020. And she pointedly declined to say whether she would endorse his re-election efforts.

In deciding against a run for governor in 2018, Collins cited seniority: She has joined the ranks of the most senior senators and could chair the powerful Appropriations Committee if she is re-elected in 2020. She now chairs the Special Committee on Aging, and, before stepping down in 2013 because of internal Senate Republican term limits, Collins was for a decade chairwoman or ranking member on the Homeland Security and Governmental Affairs Committee — where she had once been a staffer. There, she closely worked with Connecticut Sen. Joe Lieberman. After 9/11, they collaborated on a reorganization of the intelligence community, creating the Office of the Director of National Intelligence and a counterterrorism center.

During her first re-election bid in 2002, Collins was challenged by former state Senate Majority Leader Chellie Pingree. Collins won with 58 percent of the vote. Both Pingree and her daughter, former Maine House Speaker Hannah Pingree, were among potential challengers to Collins in 2020. Chellie Pingree has represented Maine's 1st District since 2008, when Democratic Rep. Tom Allen vacated that seat to oppose Collins. Allen made the Iraq War a central issue; Collins voted for the 2002 resolution authorizing the war and later opposed a Democratic attempt to set a timetable for troop withdrawal. But Collins won with 61 percent of the vote. Collins won re-election in 2014 with 68 percent of the vote against her underfunded Democratic opponent, Shenna Bellows, a former director of the Maine chapter of the American Civil Liberties Union.

In 2012, Collins married government consulting executive Thomas Daffron, who, like Collins, was once a staffer to William Cohen and was a chief operating officer of the Baltimore Orioles. Three years later, in September 2015, Collins observed a political milestone: 6,000 consecutive floor votes, a streak dating to her arrival in the Senate. As of January 2019, Collins' streak had reached 6,847 votes — despite a 2007 ankle fracture she suffered while racing to the Senate floor and a second broken ankle she got from a fall on ice in 2016. Collins has said the streak was inspired by Sen. Margaret Chase Smith, who maintained a similar streak for 13 years until surgery forced her to end it.

Angus King (I)

Elected 2012, term expires 2024, 2nd term, b. Mar 31, 1944; Alexandria, VA; Dartmouth College, A.B., 1966; University of Virginia Law School, J.D., 1969; Episcopalian; Married (Mary J. Herman); 5 children; 5 grandchildren.

Elected Office: ME Governor, 1995-2003.

Professional Career: Practicing attorney, 1969-1983, 2003-present; Chief counsel, Sen. William Hathaway, U.S Senate Subcommittee on Alcoholism & Narcotics, 1972-1975; Host, ME Public Television's MaineWatch, 1975-1993; Vice President., General counsel, Swift River/Hafslund, 1983-1989; Founder, President, Northeast Energy Management, 1989-1994; Partner, Independence Wind, 2007-2012.

DC Office: 133 HSOB 20510, 202-224-5344, Fax: 202-224-1946, king.senate.gov

State Offices: Augusta, 207-622-8292; Bangor, 207-945-8000; Presque Isle, 207-764-5124; Scarborough, 207-883-1588.

Committees: *Armed Services:* Airland (RMM); Seapower; Strategic Forces. *Energy & Natural Resources:* Energy; National Parks (RMM); Public Lands, Forests & Mining. *Intelligence. Rules & Administration.*

Group Ratings

	ADA	ACLU	AFL-CIO	LCV	ITI	COC	HAFA	ACU	CFG	FRC
2018	-	67%	-	93%	-	70%	8%	9%	5%	13%
2017	80%	C	100%	74%	C	29%	C	0%	0%	0%

Almanac Ratings 2017-18

	Economy	Social	Foreign	Composite
Liberal	76%	76%	30%	61%
Conservative	24%	24%	70%	39%

Key Votes of the 115th Congress

1. Obama-care revision	N	5. Gun regulations	Y	9. Kavanaugh confirmation	N	
2. Tax Cuts	N	6. Family planning regs	N	10. Saudi arms sales	Y	
3. Dodd-Frank revision	Y	7. Gorsuch confirmation	N	11. FISA rules	Y	
4. Omnibus appropriations	Y	8. Immigration restrictions	N	12. Military aid in Yemen	Y	

Election Results

Election	Name (Party)	Vote (%)		Cand. Spent	Ind. Exp. Support	Ind. Exp. Oppose
2018 General	Angus King (I).............................	344,575	(54%)	$4,908,730		$963,993
	Eric Brakey (R)...........................	223,502	(35%)	$1,171,899	$834,317	
	Zak Ringelstein (D).....................	66,268	(10%)	$373,232		

Prior winning percentages: 2012 (53%), Governor: 1998 (59%), 1994 (35%)

Residents of this state in the nation's northeastern tip, with its rocky and sometimes remote terrain, have often demonstrated an independent streak — and, when it comes to politics, Angus King, Maine's junior senator, is Exhibit No. 1. Originally a Democrat, King came to believe that "sometimes the best thing the government can do is get out of the way." He entered the 1994 governor's race as an independent and blasted the government for what he said was meddling in business. After two terms as Maine's chief executive, King left politics for a decade — only to emerge as a candidate for an open Senate seat in 2012, decrying the legislative gridlock in Congress. He again ran as independent, refusing to say with which party he would caucus if elected. When he won, King announced he would join the Democratic Caucus, a choice that did not surprise those who had watched his political progression in recent years. He easily won a second Senate term in 2018 with the de facto support of Maine's Democratic Party.

Between elections, King's Capitol Hill affiliation with Democrats at times appeared tenuous. In spring 2014, when Republicans had a good chance to retake the Senate majority, King created a stir when he said he might caucus with the GOP if he felt the interests of his constituents would be served. But, after the Republicans regained Senate control that November, King stuck with the Democrats. Independents are compelled to join one of the two caucuses to sit on Senate committees. "I think it is in Maine's interest to have a senator in each camp," he said, alluding to his senior colleague, Republican Susan Collins. While recent vote rankings have pegged King as more conservative than all but a handful his colleagues in the Democratic Caucus, he has opposed President Donald Trump's leading policy initiatives and several of his high-profile appointments, notably Supreme Court nominees Neil Gorsuch and Brett Kavanaugh.

King was raised in the Washington suburb Alexandria Virginia, but has spent most of his adult life "Down East." After attending Dartmouth College and University of Virginia Law School, he moved to Maine to work for a legal assistance organization and then became an aide to Maine Sen. William Hathaway, a Democrat. When King was 29, physicians discovered he had an aggressive form of skin cancer during a routine checkup, which he said he would not have scheduled if it weren't free through his insurance. Years later, he reacted angrily to a report that opponents of the Obama administration's health insurance overhaul were urging college students not to sign up for insurance under the Affordable Care Act, suggesting those dispensing such advice were "guilty of murder." King told the Bangor Daily News: "The reason I feel so strongly about this is that if someone had given me that advice when I was 25, I wouldn't be here. I'd be dead." In the Senate, he has repeatedly voted to block Republican efforts to repeal Obamacare.

After leaving Hathaway's office, King returned to Maine to practice law and start an energy conservation business. He sold the latter for $20 million in 1994, just before running for governor — a race in which he invested $750,000 of his own money. For nearly two decades, he hosted a Maine public television program, making him a well-known figure statewide. He blasted high taxes during the campaign and edged out former Democratic Gov. Joseph Brennan 35%-34%. Running a distant third was the Republican nominee, now-Sen. Collins. As governor, King cut the state budget and its workforce. He shortened waiting periods for environmental permits and opposed a ban on timber clear-cutting. But he signed a bill imposing tight controls on paper mills' dioxin discharges into waterways — and celebrated by jumping fully clothed into the Kennebec River. Re-elected in 1998 with 59 percent of the vote, he signed legislation to use state financial leverage to negotiate lower prescription drug prices for Mainers without Medicaid or private insurance. Perhaps his best-known initiative was to provide middle school students with laptops — a precedent-setting idea.

Barred from seeking a third term in 2002, there was speculation King would challenge Collins for her Senate seat, but he left politics. He embarked on a six-month, 15,000-mile road trip through 33 states, as he, his wife and two children lived in a 40-foot recreational vehicle. It produced a book: "Governor's Travels: How I Left Politics, Learned to Back Up a Bus, and Found America." He published another book, "A Senator's Eye: Celebrating Maine, Washington, and the Joys of Scraping the Windshield," in 2018. It was a collection of photos King had taken and published via Instagram during his first term.

For nearly a decade, King practiced law and worked for a mergers-and-acquisitions advisory firm while forming a wind-energy company. His re-entry into politics was almost by accident. Republican Olympia Snowe, a leading Senate moderate, had expected to seek a fourth term; but, in February 2012, she announced her retirement, decrying a partisan climate that made passing legislation daunting. King stepped in, vowing to continue where Snowe had left off. "I can be a broker for commonsense. I can speak from the middle," he said. His campaign headquarters prominently featured two photographs side by side: one of Ronald Reagan and the other of Robert Kennedy. However, the widespread speculation was that King was aligned with Democrats, having revealed he would support President Barack Obama for re-election. As governor, he endorsed Republican George W. Bush in 2000, but has since only backed Democratic presidential nominees — including Hillary Clinton in 2016.

National Democrats did little to support their 2012 Senate nominee, state Sen. Cynthia Dill, figuring that King would win and end up in their camp. A super PAC with Republican ties ran ads to boost Dill, hoping to siphon enough votes from King to allow the GOP nominee, Maine Secretary of State Charlie Summers, to win. The National Republican Senatorial Committee broadcast a spot accusing King of using political connections to win a "sketchy" federal loan guarantee for his wind-energy firm — of which he divested himself before the election — to build an industrial wind farm. While the ad barrage caused some tightening of the race, King won, capturing 53 percent of the vote to Summers' 31 percent and Dill's 13 percent.

King was supportive of Obama's second-term agenda. He voted to sustain Obama's veto of the controversial Keystone XL pipeline and helped provide the votes needed to derail a Republican-sponsored resolution to block the Iran nuclear agreement. According to his Almanac vote rankings, King has joined members of the Democrats' moderate wing, which is significantly to the left of the GOP's most centrist members, including Collins. King has argued it is not he, but rather the political landscape, that has shifted. "I've agreed more with the Democrats in part because the Republican Party has moved so far to the right," King said during an interview in late 2013. "When I was an independent in Maine 20 years ago as governor, the Republican Party was a different party."

Others contended King's floor votes told only part of the story. "If you look at who is working behind the scenes trying to find compromise, I think he is much more in that bipartisan school than are most of the Democrats and the Republicans," said Colby College government professor Sandy Maisel. Announcing for re-election in 2018, King told reporters: "I had to choose which side to caucus with, but caucusing doesn't mean I've joined the Democratic Party. ... Almost every bill that I work on is bipartisan because that's the only way things are going to get done." Three months earlier, King teamed with South Dakota Republican Sen. Mike Rounds — a fellow former governor — to achieve a long-elusive legislative consensus on immigration overhaul. Their bill — containing a path to citizenship for the children of undocumented immigrants, while providing the Trump administration with $25 billion for border security — won the support of all but three Democrats, but only eight Republicans. It fell a half-dozen votes short of the 60-vote supermajority needed to advance the measure.

At the end of 2017, King lashed out at Senate Republicans for the tightly controlled process they used to consider their tax bill that Trump later hailed as one of his signature achievements. "There were at least 15 or 20 Democrats that were anxious to do tax reform ... and there was never a chance," King told CNN. He was blunter on the Senate floor: "It's the worst process I think I have ever seen in a public body. The Bangor City Council would not amend the leash law using this process. We are talking about one of the most important bills any of us will ever vote on that has had zero hearings before the United States Senate." At one point, it appeared King's motion to send the bill back to committee, with instructions to make it deficit-neutral, might succeed: To exert leverage on their deficit-reduction alternative, three GOP senators considered voting for King's motion, and he thought he was close to corralling their support. But the Republican skeptics backed down after the Senate parliamentarian determined the trigger mechanism would run afoul of Senate rules. It made for some tense moments on the floor, as Texas Sen. John Cornyn, the Republican whip, was heard loudly telling King that his motion — which failed on a 52-48 vote — was "designed to kill the bill."

King has utilized his Armed Services Committee seat to look out for the interests of his defense industry-reliant state: The Portsmouth Naval Shipyard and Bath Iron Works are major employers in southern Maine. On the Energy and Natural Resources Committee, he teamed with the chairwoman, Alaska Republican Lisa Murkowski, to establish the Senate Arctic Caucus. On the Armed Services panel, he advocated for more icebreaking vessels and an increase in joint military operations in that region with U.S. allies. Such advocacy has reflected Maine's interest in becoming a gateway to the Northwest Passage — increasingly navigable due to climate change — and reaping economic benefits from trade and shipping. Pointing a finger at legislative dysfunction as a roadblock to U.S. Arctic policy, King lamented Senate failure to ratify the Law of the Sea Treaty, which established principles and limits on the ocean area that nations may claim. "There's an attitude in the Senate among some people that treaties are an abrogation of U.S. sovereignty," he told the Bangor Daily News. "I'm puzzled by that. It puts us on the sidelines."

Such comments bespoke a broader frustration. More than halfway into his first term, he complained during an NPR interview: "About... two-thirds of the senators have been here eight years or less. Most of us have never seen the place work. We're like a football team that's lost every game for the past five years. We don't know how to win. ... On the big issues, the controversial issues, we're just stymied." But two years later, in declaring for re-election, King sounded a note of guarded optimism. He spoke of building relationships on both sides of the aisle, saying the Capitol Hill environment was not as bleak as it might appear. "It's not back to what it was in the '70s, it's not what it should be," King told the Portland Press Herald. "But I can tell you there are little, tender shoots of bipartisan cooperation, and that is what we are trying to encourage."

King disclosed in June 2015 that he had been diagnosed with early-stage prostate cancer, but said it would not affect his re-election plans. Then-Maine Gov. Paul LePage, a conservative Republican ineligible to seek re-election, suggested on a radio show in early 2015 that he might challenge King. He finally announced in May 2017 he would not run. Trump — to whom LePage was often likened in both style and substance — later sought to coax LePage into the race, according to The

Washington Post. But LePage endorsed state Sen. Eric Brakey, a libertarian-leaning Republican who had spearheaded a successful push in Maine to allow carrying of concealed firearms without a permit. Zak Ringelstein, founder of an education technology startup, was unopposed for the Democratic nomination. Endorsed by the Democratic Socialists of America, he said state Democratic Party officials had discouraged him from running.

"I am being criticized by one of my opponents for voting with President Trump too much, and the other one for not voting with him enough, so maybe I am in the right spot," King told Maine Public Radio. On Election Day, the results were similar to six years earlier: King took 54 percent of the vote; Brakey got 35 percent and Ringelstein took 10 percent. Asked before the vote whether this would be his last campaign, the 74-year-old King replied, "I suspect so."

Chellie Pingree (D)

Elected 2008, 6th term, b. Apr 02, 1955; Minneapolis, MN; University of Southern Maine, Att., 1973; College of the Atlantic (ME), B.A., 1979; Lutheran; Divorced; 3 children; 2 grandchildren.

Elected Office: ME Senate, 1992-2000, Majority Leader, 1996-2000.

Professional Career: Farmer, 1977-1980; Founder & President, N. Island Designs Co., 1981-1992; President & CEO, Common Cause, 2003-2007.

DC Office: 2162 RHOB 20515, 202-225-6116, Fax: 202-225-5590, pingree.house.gov

State Offices: Portland, 207-774-5019; Waterville, 207-873-5713.

Committees: *Agriculture*: Biotechnology, Horticulture & Research; Conservation & Forestry. *Appropriations*: Agriculture, Rural Development, FDA & Related Agencies; Interior, Environment & Related Agencies; Military Construction, Veterans Affairs & Related Agencies.

Group Ratings

	ADA	ACLU	AFL-CIO	LCV	ITI	COC	HAFA	ACU	CFG	FRC
2018	-	92%	-	94%	-	55%	6%	8%	20%	0%
2017	100%	C	97%	100%	C	43%	C	4%	5%	0%

Almanac Ratings 2017-18

	Economy	Social	Foreign	Composite
Liberal	98%	95%	95%	96%
Conservative	2%	5%	5%	4%

Key Votes of the 115th Congress

1. Obama-care revision	N	5. Family planning regs	N	9. Guantanamo prisoners	Y
2. Tax Cuts	N	6. Body cameras/immigration	Y	10. Ground missiles, limit	Y
3. Omnibus appropriations	NV	7. Abortion ban	N	11. Defense Dept. spending	Y
4. Dodd-Frank revision	N	8. Concealed carry	N	12. FISA rules	N

Election Results

Election	Name (Party)	Vote (%)		Cand. Spent	Ind. Exp. Support	Ind. Exp. Oppose
2018 General	Chellie Pingree (D).....................	201,195	(59%)	$931,571	$61,000	
	Mark Holbrok (R).....................	111,188	(33%)	$91,527	$1,401	
	Martin Grohman (I).............................	29,670	(9%)	$361,954		
2018 Primary	Chellie Pingree (D).....................	(100%)				

Prior winning percentages: 2016 (58%), 2014 (58%), 2012 (62%), 2010 (57%), 2008 (55%)

Chellie Pingree, elected in 2008, is a blunt-talking staunch liberal with a long career in public service. Pingree has paid close attention to state issues, from ships to seafood and farming. Her decision to turn down opportunities for statewide bids indicates that she is comfortable with her influence on the House Appropriations Committee, where her seniority has placed her close to a subcommittee chairmanship.

Pingree grew up in Minnesota, the granddaughter of Scandinavian immigrants who worked as dairy farmers. Her parents moved to Minneapolis, where her father was an accountant and her mother a nurse. The city's anti-war activism during the Vietnam era had a profound influence on Pingree, and she left high school early for alternative education programs on the East Coast. At one program in Worcester Massachusetts, she met her future husband and followed him to Maine, where they settled on remote North Haven Island in Penobscot Bay. As disciples of the "back to the land" movement, they lived for years in a cabin without running water or electricity and made their living as organic farmers. Although the couple later divorced, Pingree thrived on the island. She started her own business selling knitting kits. At its peak, her North Island Designs Co. distributed 100,000 mail-order catalogs. She started her political career in local offices on the island, including serving as tax assessor.

In 1991, Pingree ran for an open seat in the state Senate. She went door-to-door in the traditionally Republican district in Knox County and won. Pingree rose to majority leader in 1996. As leader, she fought reluctant colleagues and a challenge from pharmaceutical companies and passed a law for Maine to negotiate prescription drug prices, the first such law in the country.

In 2002, Pingree challenged Republican Sen. Susan Collins, who won 58%-42%. Shortly after her loss, she became president of Common Cause, the government and campaign watchdog group. She took the reins just after the successful push to overhaul the nation's campaign finance law, though much of her time was spent in defending the new rules against constitutional challenges that ultimately threw out some of the reforms. Pingree also led Common Cause in opposing media consolidation in the hands of a few companies.

She left Common Cause in 2007 to run for the House seat that Democrat Tom Allen gave up to run another sacrificial campaign against Collins. Although she had complained for years about the influence of money in politics, Pingree had no trouble raising far more of it than any of her five Democratic rivals. She mostly eschewed money from political action committees but enjoyed the backing of EMILY's List, which funds women candidates who support abortion rights. Pingree won the primary with 44 percent of the vote. In the general election, she more than tripled the fundraising of state Sen. Charles Summers and won 55%-45%.

In the House, Pingree has been a loyal and usually liberal Democrat. She has used her seat on Appropriations to look after her region's defense interests. In 2019, she added to her portfolio a seat on the Military Construction Subcommittee, which should enhance that leverage. She has taken a strong interest in environmental issues, helping to form the House Sustainable Energy and Environmental Coalition and introducing a bill to force BP to pay royalties on the oil from its massive spill in the Gulf of Mexico in 2010.

With her continuing interest in agriculture, Pingree joined other Democrats in opposing the initial version of the 2018 farm bill that Republicans had crafted as a party-line measure. But she took credit for provisions in the final version of the measure that doubled research funds for organic farming and created a national pilot program to increase access to healthy foods for low-income families. She also helped to write a section in the bill that created a new office at the Agriculture Department to reduce food loss and waste. Pingree has been a vocal supporter of the "Green New Deal" on the progressive agenda.

She faced a competitive reelection campaign in 2010 against alternative energy company owner Dean Scontras, who got support from tea party activists. The Maine Republican Party ran ads accusing Pingree of taking trips on the corporate jet of her fiancée, hedge-fund billionaire Donald Sussman. She had a relatively easy 57%-43% win. Her subsequent marriage to Sussman, a major donor to Democratic super PACs, increased Pingree's access to big political contributors plus her own donations to other Democrats. It created some controversy when he bought a controlling interest in newspapers in Portland and Augusta. Those questions disappeared in 2015 when they filed for divorce.

Pingree often clashed with Republican Gov. Paul LePage on his call for cuts in Medicaid spending and she thought seriously about running to succeed him in 2018, when he was term-limited. She decided not to run, she said, because she had "so much more work to be done" in Congress — and perhaps mindful of the risk of another statewide loss. As it turned out, Democrats that year scored big gains in both Augusta and the House.

ME-1: Southern Maine

Population		Race and Ethnicity		Income	
Total	675,074	White	93%	Median Income	$60,757
Land area (sq. miles)	3,286	Black	1.7%	District Income Rank	170
Pop/ sq mi	205.5	Latino	1.7%	Poverty Rate	10.6%
Born in State	56.9%	Asian	1.5%	With health insurance	92%
		Two or more races	1.7%	Cash public assistance	2.9%
Age Groups		Other	0.4%	Food stamp/SNAP	12%
Under 18	19.2%				
18-34	20.2%	Education		Work	
35-64	42.1%	H.S grad or less	34.5%	White Collar	18.5%
Over 64	18.5%	Some college	28.6%	Sales and Service	41%
		College Degree, 4 yr	23.3%	Blue Collar	19.1%
Military		Post grad	13.6%	Government	12.9%
Veteran/ Active Duty	9.9%				

2012 Pres. Vote	Obama	223,040	(59%)	Romney	143,024	(38%)		
2016 Pres. Vote	Clinton	212,860	(54%)	Trump	154,399	(39%)	Johnson	18,593	(5%)

Portland: The 1st District of Maine stretches from southernmost Kittery and nearby Kennebunkport to the craggy-shored, ancestrally Republican counties to the east. It extends halfway up the Atlantic coast to Canada. The historic center is Portland, Maine's largest city, home to the yuppies and lawyers who have revived and renovated its downtown landmarks. Portland's antique charm, mostly booming economy, and tolerant lifestyle have made it a haven for singles and gays. The more than 100-year-old L.L. Bean is not far away in Freeport. Old mill towns like Biddeford and Sanford have been redeveloped.

The area has a strong defense presence. Base-closing rounds have spared the Portsmouth Naval Shipyard at Kittery, the nation's oldest continually operating naval shipyard. With a younger workforce that has grown above 6,000, the future of the yard has improved with billions of dollars in long-term federal contracts to repair and upgrade nuclear-powered submarines. Even though it is the largest such facility on the East Coast and the Navy delivered in 2016 a contract to expand the docks to permit work on the larger Virginia-class submarine, the shipyard's future has always been a topic of worried discussion for locals. Up the coast at Bath Iron Works, with 5,500 workers, job cutbacks once loomed because of downsizing of the fleet and competition with the lower-cost shipyard in Pascagoula Mississippi. Management at Bath has sought more efficiencies. In September 2018, the Navy gave Bath a $3.9 billion contract to build four destroyers, while Pascagoula got $5.1 billion to build six. The Brunswick Naval Air Station closed in 2011, with a big hit to the local economy. In its place, more than 80 businesses and 800 jobs have moved into industrial and commercial space at the overhauled Brunswick Landing.

Portland and several other coastal towns in southern Maine are in the 1st Congressional District. The district includes the five coastal counties from York to Knox, and most of inland Augusta-based Kennebec. About 40 percent of the population is in Portland-based Cumberland. The 1st also takes in several remote islands off the coast, where people enjoy a lifestyle more reminiscent of the Alaska wilderness, shuttling to the mainland on ferries and Cessna aircraft. Lobsters are more than a tradition here; they're an economic necessity. In 2016, the 5,900 licensed lobstermen and women in the state hauled in an estimated 131 million pounds, with a seventh-consecutive record harvest and a recovery from what had been virtually giveaway prices. But the haul in 2017 dropped to 110 million pounds — the smallest since 2011 and a warning that climate change and warmer temperatures in the Gulf of Maine have reduced the lobster population. The fisherman with the biggest catch reportedly spent more time than usual at sea, as the crustaceans have moved north and to deeper waters. Scallop hauls, which had been severely depleted a decade earlier, have bounced back.

Politically, the 1st District votes like the state as a whole: often ballot-splitting or voting for independents. While most attention in 2016 focused on the battle for the electoral vote in the 2nd District, Hillary Clinton easily won the 1st, 54%-39%, carrying every county except Kennebec.

Jared Golden (D)

Elected 2018, 1st term, b. Jul 25, 1982; Leed; University of Maine (Farmington), Att., 2002; Bates College (ME), B.A., 2011; Married (Isobel Golden).

Military Career: US Marine Corps 2002-2006; US Marine Corps Reserves 2008-2009 (Afghanistan & Iraq)

Elected Office: ME House, 2014-2018.

Professional Career: Professional Staff Member, U.S. Senate Committee on Homeland Security and Governmental Affairs, 2011-2013; Legislative Assistant, U.S. Sen. Susan M. Collins, 2013-2013.

DC Office: 1223 LHOB 20515, 202-225-6306, Fax: 202-225-2943, golden.house.gov

State Offices: Bangor, 207-249-7400; Caribou, 207-492-6009; Lewiston, 207-241-6767.

Committees: *Armed Services*: Seapower & Projection Forces; Tactical Air & Land Forces. *Small Business*: Contracting & Infrastructure (Chmn); Rural Development, Agriculture, Trade & Entrepreneurship.

Election Results

Election	Name (Party)	Vote (%)		Cand. Spent	Ind. Exp. Support	Ind. Exp. Oppose
2018 General	Jared F. Golden (D)	142,440	(51%)	$5,591,329	$831,432	$5,207,735
	Bruce Poliquin (R)	138,931	(49%)	$4,041,031	$458,581	$8,342,303
2018 Primary	Jared F. Golden (D)	23,611	(54%)			
	Lucas St. Clair (D)	19,853	(46%)			

Democrat Jared Golden made history in the 2018 election when he became the first candidate elected to Congress as the result of "ranked choice" voting, which voters approved for state and federal elections in a referendum in 2016. That procedure gave him his victory even though he trailed in the initial tabulation of the vote. Not surprisingly, Republican Rep. Bruce Poliquin—the loser in that contest—challenged the outcome to political and judicial audiences. But his gripes following the election had less impact than they might have had prior to the outcome.

Golden, a native of Lewiston, grew up on a golf course owned by his parents. He enlisted in the Marine Corps months after the September 2001 attacks and served in Afghanistan and Iraq. He was part of the failed attempt in 2004 to capture Osama bin Laden near the border of Pakistan. Following the end of his active duty, Golden was diagnosed with post-traumatic stress syndrome.

Returning to Maine, Golden worked in several short-term jobs and got his bachelor's degree in politics at Bates University. He joined the staff of Maine Republican Sen. Susan Collins at the Homeland Security and Government Affairs Committee. After taking a job as an aide to Democrats at the state House in Augusta, Golden was elected to the House in 2014. He worked on veterans' issues during his two terms and was the Democratic Whip.

When he announced his challenge to Poliquin, Golden said that Washington D.C. was "rigged" and that the political status quo demanded change. As the only Republican from the six states of New England during his two terms in the House, Poliquin struggled to define his role. He was widely criticized at home when he voted for the GOP bill to repeal the Affordable Care Act.

Poliquin's vulnerability drew four Democratic candidates in the Democratic primary. The biggest spender was Lucas St. Clair, a conservationist. In the initial vote count, Golden led St. Clair, 46%-39%. Once the votes for the two trailing candidates were reallocated to attain the requisite majority, Golden won 54%-46%.

Golden invoked many of the standard national Democratic themes against Poliquin. "I know we can fix our expensive healthcare system, take power back from the special interests, create middle-class jobs that pay respectable wages with real benefits, and build a better future for Maine," he said, following his victory in the primary. Poliquin, who distanced himself from President Donald Trump, characterized Golden as too liberal for the district.

In their first debate, which was filled with harsh exchanges, Golden accused Poliquin of an "astounding" number of lies and said that he had placed a priority on "taking away people's health care." Poliquin's mantra was that Golden "is a young radical who embraces a socialist agenda." Their second debate ended with Golden dismissively refusing to shake Poliquin's hand.

Golden spent $5.6 million to $4 million for Poliquin—huge sums in this rural, low-cost district. The national parties and other outside groups spent another $15 million, split between the two candidates. The Lewiston Sun Journal reported that the campaign featured the second-highest number of ads of any campaign in the nation.

Following the ranked-choice calculations, Golden won, 50.5%-49.5%, a margin of about 3,000 votes. He won the two largest locales—55% in Lewiston and 57% in Bangor. Golden's incumbency might give him some advantage: Prior to Poliquin's setback, no incumbent had lost this district in 100 years.

Republicans complained bitterly about the ranked-choice outcome. Outgoing Gov Paul LePage wrote "stolen election" on the official certificate of Golden's election. It remained to be determined whether "ranked choice" made a sufficiently positive impression in other states beyond the proudly independent (or eccentric, perhaps) Mainers.

ME-2: Northern and Central Maine

Cook Partisan Voting Index: R+2

Population		Race and Ethnicity		Income	
Total	655,084	White	94.2%	Median Income	$46,534
Land area (sq. miles)	27,557	Black	0.7%	District Income Rank	359
Pop/ sq mi	23.8	Latino	1.4%	Poverty Rate	15.2%
Born in State	70%	Asian	0.7%	With health insurance	89.9%
		Two or more races	2.1%	Cash public assistance	4.1%
Age Groups		Other	0.8%	Food stamp/SNAP	18.8%
Under 18	19.4%				
18-34	19.8%	**Education**		**Work**	
35-64	41.7%	H.S grad or less	46.1%	White Collar	19.1%
Over 64	19.1%	Some college	30.4%	Sales and Service	42.1%
		College Degree, 4 yr	15.2%	Blue Collar	25.1%
Military		Post grad	8.2%	Government	14.4%
Veteran/ Active Duty	11%				

2012 Pres. Vote	Obama	178,266	(53%)	Romney	149,252	(44%)			
2016 Pres. Vote	Trump	181,194	(51%)	Clinton	144,875	(41%)	Johnson	19,512	(6%)

Lewiston, Bangor: The 2nd District of Maine is heavily forested, rough-hewn and enormous. Covering more than 85 percent of the state, it is larger than the states of New Hampshire, Vermont and Massachusetts combined. The population is not evenly distributed. There are several different Maines represented here: The bays of coastal Maine, with their small fishing towns; the potato fields of far northern Aroostook County; and the mill towns on the fast-running rivers and streams of western Maine. Some valleys have more moose than people. The district includes the heavily Democratic mill town of Lewiston and also Eastport. At Belfast on Penobscot Bay, art galleries and boutiques have replaced fish-processing plants. This was one of America's frontiers in the 1850s, when Bangor, on the Penobscot River, was the lumber capital of the world. Lewiston, the largest city in the district, has become home to more than 7,000 refugees from Somalia and elsewhere in east Africa.

These parts of Maine have had economic troubles, losing 22,000 jobs to neighboring Canada and other foreign markets with the free-trade agreements in the 1990s. Logging, long the largest industry in Maine, has suffered job cutbacks as big paper companies sell off acreage and shut down mills. A once-thriving sardine-canning industry ended with the closing of the last cannery in 2010. There have been signs of economic life. Washington County's sandy soil produces more than 90 percent of the nation's wild blueberry crop. Although potato production is less than half what it was in 1960, some encouraging developments have included the creation of the new high-yield Caribou Russet brand and state regulatory approval in 2017 of three new genetically engineered potatoes that initially were produced in Idaho. In the North Woods, fishing for wild and native brook trout (in waters that have never been stocked) has become a $300 million annual business. Politically, the district is iconoclastic and permanently enamored of neither major political party. Donald Trump made multiple appearances here during his 2016 campaign, with appeals to its blue-collar and trade-protectionist voters, and handily won its electoral vote, 51%-41%. That was the first time the state's two districts have split in a presidential election.

MARYLAND

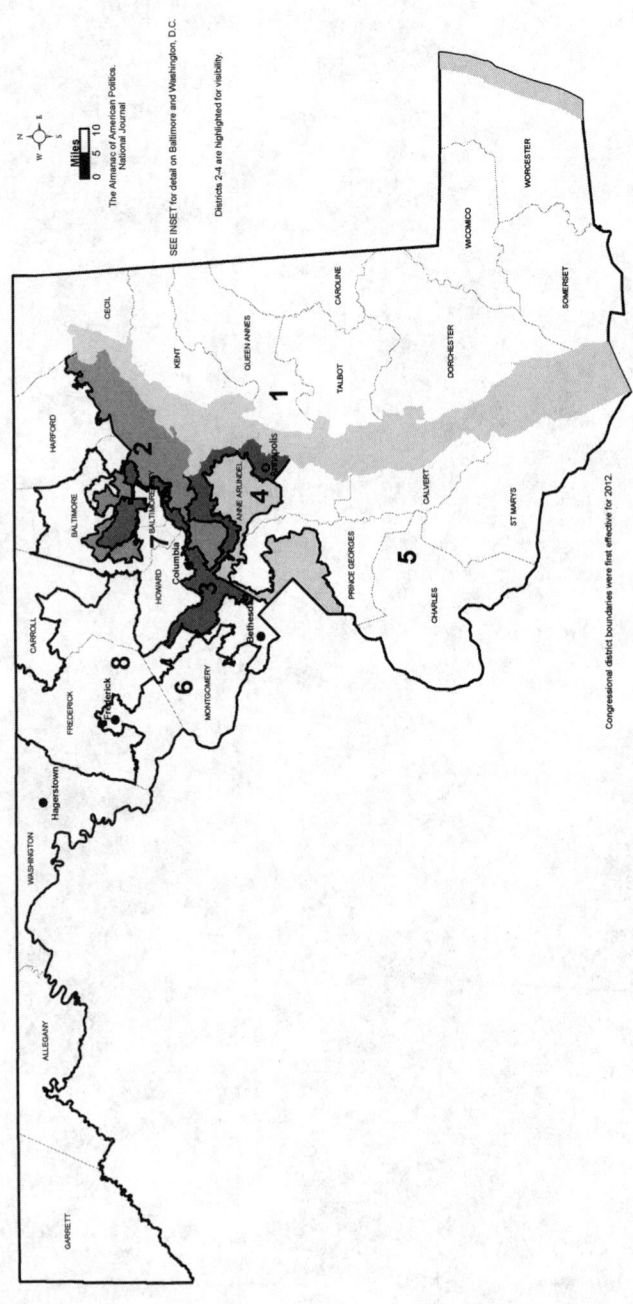

Maryland, one of the nation's most Democratic states, serves as a microcosm of the trends shaping today's Democratic Party: continuing lopsided support in ethnically and racially diverse urban areas, increasing Democratic success among affluent, suburban voters and government employees, and a waning of the party's influence in rural areas. The 2018 election produced a second term for Republican Gov. Larry Hogan – thanks in part to his aggressive distancing from President Donald Trump – but further down the ballot, Democrats routed his fellow Republicans.

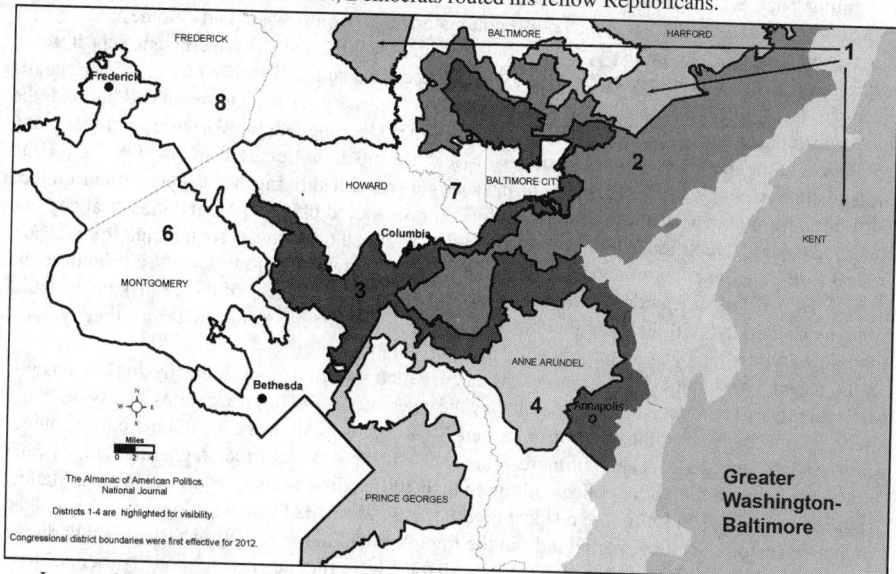

Just south of the Mason-Dixon line and north of the Union-Confederate lines during most of the Civil War (and the scene of its bloodiest one-day battle, Antietam), Maryland is a crossroads state, with both Northern and Southern influences and with both industrial and rural economies. This was the only one of the 13 colonies founded by Roman Catholics — the Calvert family — and its embrace of religious tolerance came less from high-minded ideals than from the Calverts' desire to protect their property from religious attacks. Similarly, although hot-blooded Baltimoreans wanted to secede from the Union in 1861 (the state song, "Maryland, My Maryland," is based on a poem condemning Abraham Lincoln's suppression of pro-Confederate rioters), cooler heads prevailed.

The Puritan impulse was never lively here. Prohibition was enforced only laxly in Baltimore, to the delight of its great journalist-cum-lexicographer H.L. Mencken. Slot machines were legal for years in the rural counties of the Eastern Shore, and, after years of controversy and over the pleas of racetrack owners, were legalized statewide in 2007; voters approved table games in 2012. In some corners of the state, segregation was evident well into the 1960s, and longstanding efforts to remedy segregation within the state's university system are still the subject of years-long litigation. Much of Maryland's political history reads like a chronicle of rogues (notably Spiro Agnew, who was Maryland's governor when Richard Nixon tapped him for his 1968 ticket and then resigned as vice president in October 1973 when he was charged with income tax evasion). Maryland's genial tolerance may have given it a little too savory a history, but this state cherishes its uniqueness.

Chesapeake Bay is the nation's largest estuary, with water saltier than a river but fresher than the ocean, and with unique shellfish and watermen. Pollution and years of overharvesting drastically reduced its yield, and the terrapin and Chesapeake oyster are rare today. But an ongoing statewide Save-the-Bay movement is having an impact. The estimated number of crabs nearly doubled over two years, according to a January 2017 report from the Chesapeake Bay Foundation, and the oozing of sediment on the Conowingo Dam that feeds the bay has lessened, though the foundation's 2019 report found some backsliding, amid record rainfall that pushed more pollution into the watershed.

Maryland has reason to be proud of the economy, or economies, it has built over the years. During and after World War II, half the state's population lived in the city of Baltimore. Then — in a pattern documented in Barry Levinson's Baltimore movie trilogy of Diner, Tin Men and Avalon — the proportion cratered. Now, just 10 percent of Maryland residents live in the city of Baltimore, falling from 1 million in the early 1950s to 612,000 in 2017. With its large suburban population thick with federal employees and contractors, Maryland leads the United States in median household income, 37 percent above the national average. The Census Bureau defines Washington-Baltimore as a combined statistical area that stretches to Pennsylvania and West Virginia; it's the nation's sixth largest, with 6.2 million people. But Baltimore and Washington are not fraternal twins like Dallas and Fort Worth or Minneapolis and St. Paul; they have different histories, economic bases and attitudes.

Washington is a one-industry, white-collar, capital city; the federal government kept it going while the rest of the country endured the Great Recession and a sluggish recovery. Maryland's unemployment rate peaked at only 7.8 percent in February 2010 and remained around the national average by late 2018. Maryland's roughly 145,000-strong federal workforce includes many employees at the massive National Institutes of Health complex in Bethesda and the Food and Drug Administration in Rockville; these, in turn, have generated a thriving health-related and biotech corridor in Montgomery County. Baltimore, by contrast, started off as a port and industrial city and managed to stay diversified and largely successful as it spread out into the countryside from its new central core at the Inner Harbor and the solidly built edifices of its downtown streets. It is home to the popular Oriole Park at Camden Yards (the first of the new-old ballparks of the 1990s) and to Johns Hopkins University, with its Georgian buildings along the affluent corridor that runs directly north from downtown all the way to the edge city of Hunt Valley.

In recent years, though, Baltimore has been better known for its more dystopic elements, painstakingly (and prophetically) chronicled by the celebrated HBO dramatic series The Wire. Amid a scourge of drugs and crime, relations between African-American residents and the police soured; between 2011 and 2014, The Baltimore Sun revealed, the city paid the staggering sum of $5.7 million for harms inflicted by police with more than 100 victims winning court judgments. Matters exploded in 2015, when Baltimore resident Freddie Gray, 25, died of spinal injuries after being taken into police custody. Rioting, particularly in the impoverished Sandtown-Winchester neighborhood, ensued. A curfew was imposed, and eventually charges were filed against six police officers. None were convicted. While race was a major factor, the reality was more nuanced; the "mayor, city council president, police chief, top prosecutor, and many other city leaders are black, as is half of Baltimore's 3,000-person police force," noted journalist Michael A. Fletcher in the Washington Post. In August 2016, the Department of Justice released a report critical of the city's aggressive policing strategy against quality-of-life crimes. The so-called "zero tolerance" policy helped torpedo the 2016 presidential candidacy of Martin O'Malley, who had served as mayor when the policing strategy was first carried out, and the crime wave continued in 2018, when Baltimore had more than 300 homicides for the fourth year in a row. It was a far higher per-capita murder rate than other big cities.

For years, most of Maryland's successful statewide politicians came from Baltimore, including two mayors who won the governorship, William Donald Schaefer and O'Malley. For three decades, Maryland's senators lived in Baltimore and commuted to Washington. Baltimore has a long Democratic tradition and most of its voters are registered Democrats. Until 2014, Democrats had yielded the governorship only once since 1966 — from 2002 to 2006, with Republican Bob Ehrlich. O'Malley ousted him in 2006. Democrats outnumber Republicans 7-to-1 in the state's House delegation, an even more extreme discrepancy than voting patterns would suggest, thanks to a redistricting map so aggressively gerrymandered that it has become subject to a Supreme Court challenge.

Maryland's strong Democratic preferences have enabled its members of Congress to wield influence, though that power is often quietly exercised. Paul Sarbanes retired in 2006 after six years in the House and 30 years in the Senate; he was the chief sponsor and shaper of the 2002 Sarbanes-Oxley Act, the far-reaching crackdown on corporate accounting abuses. Sen. Barbara Mikulski, who retired in 2016, was elected to the House in 1976 and to the Senate in 1986; she was the longest-serving woman ever in Congress and chaired the Appropriations Committee. She was succeeded by Chris Van Hollen, who headed the House Democrats' campaign committee in 2008 and 2010; despite being a newcomer to the chamber, he was tapped to head the Democratic Senatorial Campaign Committee's efforts in 2018, a cycle that presented Democrats with a uniquely difficult mix of seats to defend. Maryland's other senator, Ben Cardin, served 20 years in the House before winning a

Senate seat. In the House, Steny Hoyer serves as the No. 2 in the new Democratic majority under San Francisco's Nancy Pelosi, whose father, Thomas D'Alesandro, was a congressman from, and mayor of, Baltimore; the rivalry between Pelosi and Hoyer began when they were interns in the office of Sen. Daniel Brewster of Maryland.

In national politics, Maryland for many years was a marginal state. It voted Republican for president as recently as 1988. But demographic and geographic shifts have made it solidly Democratic. Maryland's African-American population is the fifth-highest of any state, at 30 percent; many blacks in Maryland, especially in Prince George's County, are college-educated and economically upscale. At the same time, the Hispanic and Asian populations have seen statewide growth rates of 33 percent and 22 percent, respectively, since 2010, especially in inner-ring suburbs like Montgomery County, which is now 19 percent Hispanic and 15 percent Asian. The percentage of foreign-born residents in Maryland trailed the national average until around 2005; it now surpasses the nation as a whole, at 15 percent. All told, a state that was 80 percent white in 1970 is now essentially a 50-50 split between white and minority residents, making it the sixth least-white state in the country.

Maryland's Democratic gains owe much to the Democratic shift in Montgomery and Prince George's counties, the two collar counties of Washington. In 2016, these counties cast 31 percent of the two-party presidential vote in the state -- well above the duo of Baltimore city and county, which had 22 percent. (Another 16 percent was cast in the Baltimore satellite counties of Anne Arundel and Howard, while 31 percent was cast elsewhere in the state.) In the 1980s, Montgomery and Prince George's weren't more Democratic than the rest of the state and were sometimes less so. But during a generation in which Republicans have backed smaller government and taken conservative cultural stands, and in which the racial and ethnic diversity of the Washington suburbs has grown, Montgomery and Prince George's have become overwhelmingly Democratic. In recent years, minority families have moved further south into once-rural and predominantly white Charles County; it is now Democratic, as well.

Such transformations have helped push Maryland to the left. In 2012, Maryland voters approved in-state college tuition for children of illegal immigrants and measures in favor of same-sex marriage. But in 2014, voters fired a warning shot at Democratic complacency, electing a little-known Republican activist, Larry Hogan, as governor over Democratic Lt. Gov. Anthony Brown, who never attracted much affection statewide and who Hogan succeeded in tying to the less popular aspects of O'Malley's tenure – a series of tax increases. Hogan won amid a strong GOP performance in swingy suburban Baltimore County and weak turnout in traditionally Democratic areas. The GOP also gained seats in the legislature, though the party remained a distinct minority.

The 2016 presidential contest in the state was never in doubt, and the topline results didn't differ much from 2012: Hillary Clinton defeated Donald Trump, 61%-35%. The election widened the state's rural-urban chasm, though one signature employer in the heavily Trump Eastern Shore, the crab industry, received unwelcome news when the new administration changed the foreign-worker visa system, effectively blocking access to many longtime Mexican workers.

As governor, Hogan worked relatively comfortably with Democratic legislators, working to protect the state's Affordable Care Act insurance exchange and seeking to ease the hit from the Trump-backed tax bill, which was structured in a way that would limit some deductions for affluent taxpayers in higher-tax states like Maryland. Even more important for his reelection prospects, Hogan regularly took issue with Trump policies and statements. His approach produced strong approval ratings in a state where 42 percent of voters considered themselves moderate in an October 2018 Washington Post-University of Maryland poll.

In their 2018 gubernatorial primary, Democrats took a contrary approach, spurning the establishment candidate, Prince George's County Executive Rushern Baker, in favor of former NAACP chief Ben Jealous, who was running as a progressive insurgent. Hogan, bolstered by a sizable fundraising edge, won, 55%-44%, a margin four percentage points wider than his race in 2014; he became the first GOP governor in Maryland to win reelection in more than six decades. Hogan made inroads in Montgomery, Prince Georges and Charles counties and poached an estimated one-third of Democrats statewide. In essentially every other 2018 race, however, Democrats surged. They flipped the county executive seats in populous Howard and Anne Arundel counties and won a competitive executive race in Baltimore County. Despite Hogan's efforts to gain ground for the GOP in the legislature, the Democrats maintained their supermajority in the Senate and actually added to their supermajority in the House.

Meanwhile, Democrat Brian Frosh easily won another term as attorney general, lending voter validation to his aggressive legal attacks on the Trump administration. Frosh's lawsuits dovetail with those of another Marylander, Baltimore-based Rep. Elijah Cummings, who was tasked with overseeing Trump and his administration as the chair of the House Oversight and Reform Committee. Hogan, too, got into the anti-Trump act, mulling a possible primary challenge to the president.

Population		Race and Ethnicity		Income	
Total	5,996,079	White	51.9%	Median Income	$78,916
Land area (sq. miles)	9,707	Black	29.3%	State Income Rank	1
Pop/ sq mi	617.7	Latino	9.6%	Poverty Rate	9.7%
Born in state	47.4%	Asian	6.2%	With health insurance	92.7%
		Two or more races	2.6%	Cash public assistance	2.4%
Age Groups		Other	0.5%	Food stamp/SNAP	10.9%
Under 18	22.5%				
18-34	23.0%	Education		Work	
35-64	40.3%	H.S grad or less	35.3%	White Collar	45.3%
Over 64	14.2%	Some college	25.7%	Sales and Service	39.0%
		College Degree, 4 yr	21.0%	Blue Collar	15.8%
Military		Post grad	18.0%	Government	21.9%
Veteran/ Active Duty	8.8%				

Presidential Politics

2016 Primary (D)	Clinton (D)	573,242 (63%)	Sanders (D)	309,990 (34%)			
2016 Primary (R)	Trump (R)	248,343 (54%)	Kasich (R)	106,614 (23%)	Cruz (R)	87,093 (19%)	
2016 Pres. Vote	Clinton (D)	1,677,928 (60%)	Trump (R)	943,169 (34%)	Johnson (L)	79,605 (3%)	
2012 Pres. Vote	Obama (D)	1,677,844 (62%)	Romney (R)	971,869 (36%)			

In the seven presidential elections since 1992, Maryland's Democratic percentages consistently ranked high among the states — second in 1992, sixth in 1996, fourth in 2000 and 2004, fifth in 2008 and 2012 and third in 2016. Only California and Hawaii gave a higher percentage to Hillary Clinton. Two regions drove Clinton's success: the close-in suburbs of Washington D.C., and Baltimore. Combined, Montgomery and Prince George's counties, which run the spectrum of wealthy white suburbs to working-class African-American communities, gave more than 80 percent of their vote to Clinton. In Baltimore city, Clinton won about 85 percent. The suburbs of Baltimore County went for Clinton, 56%-38%. In the state's rural eastern and western regions, Trump won a solid majority.

In 2016, the Maryland primary was held on April 26 with four other states and drew little attention. Trump demolished Ohio Gov. John Kasich, 54%-23%, and swept the state's 38 GOP convention delegates. Clinton defeated Vermont Sen. Bernie Sanders 63%-34%. According to the network television exit poll, African Americans made up a plurality, 46 percent, of Democratic primary voters; 43 percent were white. The former voted by a 3-to-1 margin for Clinton.

Congressional Districts

116th Congress Lineup	7D 1R	115th Congress Lineup	7D 1R

The long-running Maryland redistricting saga became the focus of Supreme Court review — more than seven years after the state approved the congressional map. The Justices heard oral arguments on March 26, 2019, and were expected to issue their ruling before the end of the court's term in June. The Court hearing, one of several redistricting claims that has drawn its attention in recent years, resulted from a ruling by a three-judge court in November 2018 that held unconstitutional the drawing of the 6th District in the western part of the state. That court had ordered a new map to be drawn for the 2020 election. Regardless of how the Supreme Court rules, a new map will be required for the 2022 redistricting. The demand by Republican Gov. Larry Hogan for changes in the state's handling of redistricting makes it likely that the new map — in 2020 and/or 2022 — will revise the lines not only for the 6th, but also for the more blatant gerrymander of several districts in the Baltimore area.

Since 2000, Democrats have used their power to control Maryland redistricting to maximum advantage. Going into the 2002 election, the delegation was divided 4-4 between the two parties. After the boundaries were changed, the suburban Baltimore 2nd District became inhospitable for Republicans as did the Montgomery County-centered 8th district. That left only two Republican districts, the 1st and the 6th. In 2011, Gov. Martin O'Malley and Democratic legislators decided to finish one of them off. They made the 1st District more Republican by adding GOP precincts in suburban Baltimore and heavily Republican areas in Carroll County, which had been in the 6th. Republican Andy Harris ended up with a very safe seat, which covered the Eastern Shore and areas north of Baltimore. At the same time, they made the 6th District in western Maryland far less Republican, chiefly by adding a large chunk of heavily Democratic Montgomery County and subtracting much of Frederick County. These moves made the adjacent 8th District less Democratic, but not enough to put their party in peril. As intended, Republican Rep. Roscoe Bartlett lost in the newly drawn 6th. To maintain two black-majority districts — the 4th in metro Washington and the 7th in metro Baltimore — the redistricters drew convoluted lines that have been featured among the nation's most gerrymandered districts.

Hogan used the opportunity to decry the partisanship and created an independent redistricting commission. The Democratic-controlled legislature responded with an alternative that was more form than substance, including a requirement that five neighboring states revise their redistricting procedures; Hogan, whose approach has received broad public approval, vetoed the plan in May 2017 as "phony." With his reelection in 2018, Hogan has leverage to force some changes. That could enhance GOP prospects for one or perhaps two additional seats that will be competitive, at least, including the western Maryland district.

Larry Hogan (R)

Elected 2014, term expires 2023, 2nd term; b. May. 25, 1956, Landover; FL St. U., B.A. 1978; Catholic; Married (Yumi); 3 children.

Professional Career: Founder & President, Hogan Companies, 1985-present; Realtor, Murphy Hogan Commercial Real Estate Services, 1999-2003; MD Secretary of Appointments, Office of Governor, 2003-2007; Founder & Chairman, Change Maryland, 2011-present.

Office: 100 State Circle, Annapolis, 21401; 410-974-3901; Fax: 401-974-3275; Website: maryland.gov.

Lt. Gov.: Boyd Rutherford (R) **Atty. Gen:** Brian Frosh (D)
State Legislature: Senate: 32D, 15R **House:** 99D, 42R

Election Results

Election	Name (Party)	Vote (%)
2018 General	Larry Hogan (R)...	1,275,644 (55%)
	Ben Jealous (D)...	1,002,639 (44%)
2018 Primary	Larry Hogan (R)...	210,935 (100%)

Prior winning percentage: 2014 (51%)

In June 2015, after barely five months in office, Republican Gov. Larry Hogan called a press conference on a hot summer afternoon to share the news that he had just been diagnosed with "a very advanced and very aggressive" form of cancer: non-Hodgkin's lymphoma. It had been discovered in late stage 3, when survival rates for that type of cancer are normally in the 50 to 70 percent range. Seeking to lighten the mood in the room, the affable Hogan wisecracked, "The best news is that my odds of getting through this and beating this are much, much better than the odds I had of beating Anthony Brown." The quip underscored that Hogan's surprise victory in deep-blue Maryland over Brown — lieutenant governor under Hogan's Democratic predecessor, Martin O'Malley — ranked as one of the major upsets nationwide in 2014.

Hogan went on to beat cancer – and, since then, his political as well as physical health has been little short of excellent: He has defied political gravity in a state where Democrats enjoy a 2-1 registration edge. The humor and candor he exhibited during 18 weeks of enervating chemotherapy treatments helped to define him to his constituents, establishing an upbeat relationship with voters that persisted throughout his first term: Polling regularly put his approval ratings at or above 70 percent. It culminated with Hogan being reelected in 2018 by a double-digit margin over former NAACP national president Ben Jealous, making him the first Maryland Republican governor since Theodore Francis McKeldin in the 1950s to win a second term. In the wake of his reelection victory, there was widespread buzz about Hogan as a possible 2020 primary challenger to President Donald Trump – which the governor did little to discourage. But, following more than six months of speculation, he opted against an insurgent presidential bid.

Notwithstanding periodic demonstrations of petulance toward opponents – some critics have likened Hogan to belligerent ex-New Jersey Gov. Chris Christie, an early mentor -- the current occupant of Government House in Annapolis generally exudes the conciliatory mien of the proverbial nice guy next door. Hogan's policy agenda has remained tightly focused on pocketbook issues. After blasting O'Malley for "40 consecutive tax increases" over eight years, Hogan boasts of holding the line on further hikes -- even as many of his tax cut proposals have gone nowhere in the Democratic-dominated General Assembly. At the same time, he has studiously avoided riling Democratic and independent voters by steering clear of efforts to roll back or dilute liberal social policy initiatives enacted on his predecessor's watch.

Hogan is the first Maryland governor in the modern political era without prior experience in elected office, buttressing his claims to not being a career politician. Such self-depictions by Hogan, a successful real estate broker, underplay the degree to which he grew up immersed in politics. As a teenager in the Washington D.C. suburb of Prince George's County, Hogan spent weekends on Capitol Hill where his father, Larry Hogan Sr., served in the House. The elder Hogan achieved national attention in 1974 as the only Republican on the House Judiciary Committee to vote for all three articles of impeachment against President Richard Nixon. In 2016, after announcing he would neither endorse nor vote for Trump, the governor said he wrote in his father's name on his presidential ballot, six months before the elder Hogan's death at 88.

By the time of the Nixon impeachment proceedings, the younger Hogan was in Florida, where he had moved with his mother following his parents' divorce. He graduated from Florida State University before returning to the Washington area to work briefly as a congressional staffer, and then for his father: The elder Hogan was elected Prince George's County executive in 1978, and the younger Hogan served as his intergovernmental liaison aide. He took time out to run in a 1981 special election when his father's former congressional seat came open, finishing second in a 12-way Republican primary for the seat ultimately won by Democrat Steny Hoyer, now House majority whip. In 1992, Hogan made a second bid for Congress, challenging Hoyer after the latter's district was significantly redrawn. Hoyer was reelected, but by the narrowest margin of his career, 53%-44%.

Hogan's real estate firm foundered in the wake of a series of bank failures in the early 1990s. After declaring personal bankruptcy in 1994, he rebuilt the Annapolis-based business. In 2002, he helped Rep. Robert Ehrlich, whom he had known for more than two decades, become the first Republican elected governor since Spiro Agnew in 1966. Hogan took a leave from his business to serve as Ehrlich's secretary of appointments. Ehrlich was ousted by O'Malley in 2006, and Hogan contemplated running in 2010 before stepping aside for an unsuccessful comeback bid by Ehrlich. A year later, Hogan began laying the foundation for a 2014 run by founding Change Maryland, an anti-tax group. He won a four-way Republican primary with 43 percent.

Hogan started the general election behind in the polls by double digits. Brown's collapse was largely attributed to what was seen in Democratic Party circles as one of the most poorly run campaigns in recent state history. A former Army officer ill at ease on the stump, Brown confidently assumed the huge Democratic edge in voter registration would sweep him into office. But, in a difficult year for Democrats nationwide, tepid turnout in Democratic bastions such as the city of Baltimore and suburban Montgomery County proved insufficient to make up for landslide Hogan margins elsewhere. Hogan won, 51%-47%. (Brown staged a comeback in 2016 by winning a seat in Congress.)

Economically troubled Baltimore, the state's largest city, yielded Hogan's first major crisis when, in April 2015, rioting broke out following the death of a black man, Freddie Gray, while in police custody. Hogan later complained that Baltimore Mayor Stephanie Rawlings-Blake, a Democrat, failed to return his phone calls for two hours as the rioting spread. When he did reach her, Hogan -- according to an interview with Washingtonian magazine two years later -- gave Rawlings-Blake an ultimatum. He told her he had two draft executive orders in front of him – one saying he was declaring a state of emergency and deploying the National Guard "at the request of the mayor of Baltimore," the other that he was doing so on his own authority. "But either way, we're coming in," Hogan recalled telling Rawlings-Blake, adding, "She calls back in 14 minutes and she says, 'Since you have a gun to my head and since you are going to do it anyway, I guess I'll ask you to come in.'"

Hogan faced some trying times in dealing with the Democratic-controlled legislature, with Democrats complaining that Hogan's first "State of the State" — normally a blueprint for governing in the year ahead — sounded much like a stump speech from the 2014 campaign. During his second year in office, Hogan labeled leaders of the state teachers' union "thugs" for criticizing a decision on school funding, and compared state legislators pushing bills to limit his powers to college students on spring break.

But several leading Democrats said Hogan became more conciliatory during the second half of his first term – whether to strike a contrast to the new presidential administration 35 miles down the road, or to defuse criticism as he geared up to run for a second term. To be sure, Hogan has still been combative at times. In early 2019, as the Democratic supermajorities in both houses of the legislature were balking at moving on a couple of Hogan's crime-related bills, the governor snapped, "This seems to be like the most pro-criminal group of legislators I've ever seen." But, after finding his vetoes overridden on a number of major pieces of legislation early on -- ranging from the restoration of voting rights for felons on parole or probation to a requirement that utility companies rely more on renewable energy sources -- Hogan increasingly sought to compromise or pre-empt Democratic moves on high-profile issues. Throughout his first term, he faced off against a couple of savvy, strong-willed legislative leaders in long-serving Senate President Mike Miller and House of Delegates Speaker Michael Busch. However, the death of Busch -- the longest-serving House speaker in Maryland history -- at the end of the 2019 legislative session, coupled with Miller's uncertain future following disclosure of his metastasized prostate cancer, could strengthen Hogan as he pursues his second-term agenda.

During the 2014 campaign, Hogan favored hydraulic fracturing, or "fracking," to tap into natural gas reserves in western Maryland; he said the state was "sitting on an economic gold mine." In 2015, he reluctantly allowed a two-year moratorium on fracking to become law without his signature. In 2017, he announced he would support a permanent ban even before legislation reached his desk -- making Maryland the third state, after New York and Vermont, to prohibit the practice. After initially opposing a 2018 ballot question on a constitutional amendment requiring the state to spend tax revenue from casinos for education, he shifted to support of the measure.

In 2014, Hogan was endorsed by the National Rifle Association and received an A- rating, with the group citing his "support and commitment to the Second Amendment." But four years later, he joined legislative Democrats to support three gun-control measures -- including a ban on bump stocks, which enhance the firing capacity of semi-automatic weapons. And, in response to a verbal challenge from Democratic gubernatorial nominee Jealous, Hogan said he had no plans to accept donations from the NRA or fill out the group's election year questionnaire. Jealous -- fueled by support from several large labor unions and the Democrats' energized progressive wing – won an eight-way race for his party's nomination with nearly 41 percent, placing 10 points ahead of Prince George's County Executive Rushern Baker, who was the choice of much of the state party establishment but suffered from mediocre fundraising and an inability to energize the rank-and-file electorate.

Jealous emerged from the Democratic primary with his campaign treasury drained while Hogan – unchallenged for renomination – started the general election flush with cash, ultimately outspending Jealous by 3-1. In addition, the Republican Governors Association spent $3 million on a TV ad campaign that started soon after the primary. Jealous was a supporter of Vermont Sen. Bernie Sanders' left-wing challenge for the 2016 Democratic presidential nomination, and, in his bid for governor, espoused statewide versions of such Sanders proposals as "Medicare for All" and debt-free college tuition. Making his first run for elected office, Jealous soon exhibited his inexperience. He cursed at a reporter who asked a question at a news conference, and made little apparent effort to expand his base beyond party progressives.

Hogan won, 55%-44%. While Jealous, vying to be the state's first African-American governor, won the black-majority jurisdictions of Baltimore city and Prince George's County, pre-election surveys showed Hogan pulling one-third of the African-American vote -- double his showing four years earlier.

Amid heightened attention from national media outlets, Hogan – a month after winning reelection – spoke before a Washington right-of-center think tank critical of Trump, declaring, "compromise and moderation should not be considered dirty words." The program for his January 2019 inauguration was seen as a shot across Trump's bow: Former Gov. Jeb Bush, who had opposed Trump for the 2016 Republican nomination, spoke, and Hogan's speech was prepared with assistance from Mark Salter, a long-time aide to the late Arizona Sen. John McCain. Hogan also made a March 2019 trip to Iowa, where the first delegates to the 2020 Republican National Convention will be chosen – ostensibly in his capacity as incoming chairman of the National Governors Association. After initially saying that "it makes no sense" to challenge Trump unless the president was significantly weakened within his own party, Hogan -- on a visit to New Hampshire in March -- said he was seriously considering a primary challenge, and announced plans to travel to 16 other states. However, in early June 2019, Hogan announced he would not run for the 2020 presidential nomination -- while announcing formation of a national advocacy group "in order to continue to be a leader in the national conversation about where our nation needs to be headed," according to a statement from the organization, An America United. He did not rule out a White House bid in 2024, telling the Washington Post, "I believe there's going to be a future in the Republican Party beyond President Trump."

Ben Cardin (D)

Elected 2006, term expires 2024, 3rd term, b. Oct 05, 1943; Baltimore; Baltimore City College (MD), 1961; Baltimore City Public Schools, 1961; University of Pittsburgh (PA), B.A., 1964; University of Maryland School of Law, J.D., 1967; Villa Julie College (MD), LL.D., 2007; Jewish; Married (Myrna Edelman Cardin); 2 children (1 deceased); 2 grandchildren.

Elected Office: MD House, 1966-1986, Speaker, 1979-1986; U.S. House, 1987-2006.

Professional Career: Practicing attorney, 1967-1986; Ways & Means Committee, MD, 1974-1979; Chairman, MD Legal Services Corporation, 1988-1995.

DC Office: 509 HSOB 20510, 202-224-4524, Fax: 202-224-1651, cardin.senate.gov
State Offices: Baltimore, 410-962-4436; Bowie, 301-860-0414; Cumberland, 301-777-2957; Rockville, 301-762-2974; Salisbury, 410-546-4250.

Committees: *Environment & Public Works*: Clean Air & Nuclear Safety; Fisheries, Water, and Wildlife; Transportation & Infrastructure (RMM). *Finance*: Health Care; International Trade, Customs & Global Competitiveness; Taxation & IRS Oversight. *Foreign Relations*: Europe & Regional Security Cooperation; Near East, South Asia, Central Asia & Counterterrorism; West Hem Crime Civ Sec Dem Rights & Women's Issues (RMM). *Small Business & Entrepreneurship (RMM)*.

Group Ratings

	ADA	ACLU	AFL-CIO	LCV	ITI	COC	HAFA	ACU	CFG	FRC
2018	-	71%	-	100%	-	50%	3%	9%	5%	0%
2017	100%	C	100%	100%	C	29%	C	0%	4%	0%

Almanac Ratings 2017-18

	Economy	Social	Foreign	Composite
Liberal	97%	97%	77%	90%
Conservative	3%	3%	23%	10%

Key Votes of the 115th Congress

1. Obama-care revision	N	5. Gun regulations	N	9. Kavanaugh confirmation	N
2. Tax Cuts	N	6. Family planning regs	N	10. Saudi arms sales	Y
3. Dodd-Frank revision	N	7. Gorsuch confirmation	N	11. FISA rules	N
4. Omnibus appropriations	Y	8. Immigration restrictions	N	12. Military aid in Yemen	Y

Election Results

Election	Name (Party)	Vote (%)		Cand. Spent	Ind. Exp. Support	Ind. Exp. Oppose
2018 General	Ben Cardin (D)	1,491,614	(65%)	$3,433,679	$3,763	$29,650
	Tony Campbell (R)	697,017	(30%)	$215,795		
	Neal Simon (I)	85,964	(4%)	$2,059,835	$341,008	
2018 Primary	Ben Cardin (D)	477,441	(80%)			
	Chelsea Manning (D)	34,611	(6%)			

Prior winning percentages: 2012 (56%), 2006 (55%); House: 2004 (63%), 2002 (66%), 2000 (76%), 1998 (78%), 1996 (67%), 1994 (71%), 1992 (74%), 1990 (70%), 1988 (73%), 1986 (79%)

Throughout his career, Democrat Ben Cardin, Maryland's senior senator, has been an unabashed policy wonk with a low-key, agreeable personality — able to work effectively with Republicans because he has shunned partisan sound bites and demonstrated an interest in the nitty-gritty of crafting legislation. But a sharp-tongued Cardin has emerged with President Donald Trump in office. A senior Democrat on the Foreign Relations Committee, he has repeatedly taken on the administration on foreign policy.

When Trump's first budget proposed deep cuts in diplomatic and foreign aid programs, Cardin blasted it as "catastrophic," writing in Time magazine: "The president does not often talk about reaffirming, promoting or funding the American values that have defined our nation since its founding nearly 250 years ago. He does however talk about 'America first' and demonizing immigrants and refugees, and one could surmise that this budget is a reflection of his own personal values." After Trump, in a Fox News interview, appeared to put abuses by Russian President Vladimir Putin on the same plane as some past actions by the United States, Cardin said, "Equating our country with an authoritarian, murderous regime is outrageous and reprehensible, even for Mr. Trump."

Amid the tough rhetoric, Cardin has sought bipartisanship, sponsoring a bill with five Republican and four Democratic colleagues to sanction Russia over its alleged interference in the 2016 elections. The legislation was signed into law in August 2017, six months before Cardin was forced to cede his high-profile position as the Foreign Relations panel's ranking member — a perch he had acquired in early 2015 when New Jersey Democrat Bob Menendez stepped down after being indicted on corruption charges. (Menendez's reinstatement as ranking Democrat came after his trial ended in a hung jury, and the Justice Department opted not to retry the case.) Notwithstanding his diminished role on the committee, Cardin kept up the heat on the Trump administration over its implementation of Russia sanctions — while speaking out on several other foreign policy fronts — throughout 2018. At the end of the year, he was overwhelmingly re-elected to a third term in the Senate, continuing a career in elected office that began more than 50 years earlier.

Although 63 years old when he first entered the Senate, Cardin was once a boy wonder of Maryland politics. Elected to the state's House of Delegates at 23 — in 1966, six months before finishing law school — he was House speaker by the time he was 35. Just as he later operated in Washington, Cardin gained a reputation in Annapolis as a consensus-builder who reached across the political aisle. The son and nephew of state legislators, Cardin grew up in the Jewish neighborhoods of northwest Baltimore: The area and era of his youth were depicted in Barry Levinson's 1982 movie "Diner." After achieving the top job in the House of Delegates, Cardin seemed to want to move from the first floor of the State House to the second — where the governor's office is. But when Democrat Barbara Mikulski left her House seat to run for the Senate in 1986, Cardin jumped into the congressional race and was easily elected.

Cardin obtained a seat on the tax-writing Ways and Means Committee, where he was a productive legislator even after the Democrats were relegated to the minority after the 1994 elections. Along with Republican Rep. Rob Portman of Ohio — who has remained a frequent legislative collaborator of Cardin's since moving to the Senate — Cardin co-sponsored the 1998 Internal Revenue Service reform law and 2000 legislation to expand 401(k) savings and other retirement plans. In 2001, when Congress enacted the Bush administration's tax cut, it included Cardin's provision to increase the limits for IRA and 401(k) contributions. Cardin continued to eye the governorship and twice considered giving up his House seat to run for it. But Senate seats don't often open in Maryland — and so when Democrat Paul Sarbanes decided to retire in 2006 after three decades in office, Cardin didn't hesitate. He began as the front-runner, even if his earnest, somewhat bland demeanor raised questions about his viability as a statewide candidate.

Cardin's leading primary opponent was former Democratic Rep. Kweisi Mfume, a charismatic figure who had left the House a decade earlier to head the national NAACP. While Mfume and Cardin were friends, Mfume and other black leaders warned that the state Democratic establishment's support for Cardin could breed resentment among African-American voters, who constitute an estimated 40 percent of registered Maryland Democrats. Cardin heavily outspent Mfume and won 44%-41%, with the vote breaking down largely along racial lines. The Republican nominee was Lt. Gov. Michael Steele, Maryland's first African-American statewide officeholder and later the first black chairman of the Republican National Committee. Democrats, including Mfume, coalesced around Cardin, who, in a tough year for Republicans nationwide, won 54%-44%.

Cardin's 2015 elevation to ranking member on Foreign Relations gave that job to a Democrat more supportive of the overseas initiatives of President Barack Obama than Menendez had been. Menendez, a Cuban-American, was resistant to engaging with Cuba; Cardin supported Obama's 2014 move to restore diplomatic ties with the island nation. Like Menendez, Cardin opposed the Iran nuclear agreement the Obama administration negotiated in 2015. In a Washington Post op-ed, Cardin wrote: "After 10 to 15 years, it would leave Iran with the option to produce enough enriched fuel for a nuclear weapon in a short time. The [agreement] would provide this legal path to a country that remains a rogue state and has violated its international nonproliferation obligations for years."

But Cardin gave Obama a quiet boost by not announcing his opposition until it had become clear the White House had sufficient votes to block a Senate resolution disapproving the deal. When Trump announced in mid-2018 he was withdrawing from the deal, Cardin — despite his original position — emerged as a critic of the move. "By breaking the deal, President Trump has breathed air into Tehran's inevitable argument to the international community: We kept our end of the deal, but America is not good for its word and cannot be trusted," he told Vanity Fair.

As a former co-chair of the U.S. arm of the Commission on Security and Cooperation in Europe, which monitors international human rights issues, Cardin has long focused on such matters. His outspoken concern about the Trump administration being overly cozy with the repressive Putin regime was not the first time he had taken on Russia. "My name is well-known in Russia, some places better than in Maryland," Cardin once said. One of Cardin's major legislative successes came with the 2012 passage of a bill that normalized trade relations with Russia after nearly 40 years — but which also required the United States to freeze the assets of, and deny visas to, Russians implicated in human rights abuses. It was titled the Magnitsky Act for a lawyer who died while in the custody of Russian authorities; the roster of sanctioned people it authorized became known in some quarters as the "Cardin List." The provision so angered Putin that he retaliated by moving to end U.S. adoptions of Russian children, a response Cardin called "embarrassing."

Just before leaving office, Obama signed legislation that contained a related measure: the Global Magnitsky Act, co-authored by Cardin and the late Arizona Republican John McCain. It gave the president authority to apply sanctions to human rights transgressions by nations other than Russia. In late 2018, Cardin — along with Menendez and then-Foreign Relations Chairman Bob Corker of Tennessee — requested that Trump determine and sanction those responsible for the slaying of Washington Post columnist Jamal Khashoggi, who was murdered inside the Saudi consulate in Istanbul. When the Trump administration responded by indicating it would decline to make such a determination, Cardin reacted with outrage. Noting that the law required the president to make a determination of responsibility within 120 days after the chairman and ranking member of the Senate Foreign Relations Committee filed a request, Cardin said, "President Trump's flagrant willingness to brush aside American rule of law to protect those in Saudi Arabia responsible for the brutal death of … Khashoggi is astounding."

The legislation introduced by Cardin at the outset of 2017 expanded the original Magnitsky Act. The bill included new mandatory sanctions against Russia, while making it difficult for Trump to reverse existing sanctions via executive action. The Cardin plan was wrapped into broader legislation that passed Congress by a veto-proof majority. Trump signed it but called some provisions "clearly unconstitutional" and served notice he chose not to enforce them. In January 2018, the Trump administration published a lengthy list containing leading Russian business and political figures but stopped short of imposing sanctions — contending the legislation was already accomplishing its aim.

Under pressure from Capitol Hill, the administration unveiled sanctions against Russia a couple of months later. It did little to mollify Cardin, who complained the new sanctions were "incomplete and overlap with some steps taken by the Obama administration." He charged, "Despite strong bipartisan congressional action, the almost purposeful foot-dragging by the Trump administration has sent a clear signal to Vladimir Putin that he can continue his destabilizing behavior against the United States."

At the same time, Cardin joined Georgia Republican David Perdue, a leading Trump ally, to sponsor global anti-corruption legislation requiring the State Department to compile an annual report rating countries worldwide on their efforts to combat corruption. The department has prepared a similar report on human trafficking. The bill, which failed to move out of committee, was introduced a couple of months after a previous Cardin international anti-corruption initiative had been stymied. In 2010, Cardin teamed with Indiana Republican Richard Lugar to attach an amendment to the Dodd-Frank financial reforms law. The amendment required U.S. oil, gas and mining firms to disclose how much they pay to foreign governments — to discourage foreign leaders from skimming payments. In early 2017, Congress, with Trump's support, killed the Obama administration regulation implementing Cardin-Lugar. The oil industry lobbied for the move, arguing the rule put its members at a disadvantage over foreign competitors. Cardin and Lugar responded in an op-ed in The Hill: "Besides Big Oil, those most eager to repeal Cardin-Lugar are the autocrats, in places like Russia, Iran or Venezuela … who want to keep the money secret from their citizens. Why do their bidding?"

While Almanac vote ratings for both 2015 and 2017 put Cardin firmly on the liberal end of the Senate Democratic Caucus, he took heat from some progressive elements of the party — as well as civil liberties advocates — for another foreign policy proposal introduced in 2017 that targeted the Boycott, Divestment, Sanctions movement. The legislation by Cardin, a staunch supporter of Israel, was aimed at barring Americans from supporting requests by foreign nations to boycott a country friendly to the United States. Advocates of the bill said it was intended only to protect U.S. companies facing pressure from interests abroad to boycott Israel over its treatment of Palestinians — but critics blasted the proposal as an unconstitutional restriction on free speech.

Cardin revised a section of the original bill that authorized penalties for companies that joined in boycotts of Israel, but the American Civil Liberties Union argued it still allowed for criminal financial penalties that violated First Amendment rights. Behind-the-scenes lobbying by Cardin to attach the measure to a spending bill at the end of 2018 fell short as Congress adjourned. A related measure — authored by Florida Republican Marco Rubio and co-sponsored by Cardin — giving state and local governments legal authority to refuse to do business with any U.S. company participating in a boycott of Israel passed the Senate in early 2019.

On the domestic front, Cardin serves on the Finance Committee, whose jurisdiction includes health care. After passage of the Affordable Care Act, Senate Democratic leaders put Cardin and Ohio's Sherrod Brown in charge of an effort to shape the party's message on the law. But Cardin successfully sponsored a 2011 bill with the Finance Committee's chairman at the time, Montana Democrat Max Baucus, to repeal a much-criticized provision of Obamacare that called for businesses to submit forms to the IRS for all purchases above $600. Before joining the committee, Cardin led the fight to include pediatric dental care as an essential benefit under the ACA — an effort prompted by the death of a 12-year-old Maryland boy who had a brain infection that started as untreated tooth decay. It was the basis of a campaign ad that ran in the weeks leading up to the April 2012 primary as Cardin was seeking a second term. In it, a young girl recounts the episode and praises Cardin, ending with the tag line, "He's my friend Ben — I hope he's your friend, too."

Other ads in the much-noticed "My Friend Ben" series showed the incumbent helping load bags onto an airplane and hauling in oysters with Maryland watermen as narrators highlighted his efforts to land funds for expansion of Baltimore-Washington International Airport and restoration of the Chesapeake Bay. The ads were an effort to compensate for Cardin's low-key modus operandi, which appeared to have left many Maryland voters with a hazy image of what he had accomplished in his first term. As it turned out, Cardin had little to worry about: He turned back a primary challenge from an African-American state senator by nearly 5-1, and, in the general election won with 56 percent of the vote, with the opposition split between the Republican nominee and a wealthy businessman running as a self-financed independent.

The "My Friend Ben" ad effort was revived in 2018: One spot showed the senator helping utility workers in a manhole, as the narrator noted efforts by Cardin — also a member of the Environment and Public Works Committee — to increase investment in drinking-water infrastructure. The race briefly received national notice when Chelsea Manning announced a Democratic primary bid. Formerly known as Bradley Manning, she had been court-martialed and imprisoned for providing classified information to WikiLeaks. Manning ran a left-wing, low-profile challenge: She received 6 percent of the vote in the June primary; Cardin was nominated with 80 percent. In the general election, the Republican nominee was Tony Campbell, a political science teacher who ran a thinly funded campaign supportive of Trump — who polls showed to be highly unpopular in Maryland. The more visible challenge came from independent candidate Neal Simon, a wealthy investment firm executive who spent $2.1 million—more than $1.1 million from his own pocket—and advertised extensively on TV.

Simon differed little from Cardin on major policy issues, but derided the incumbent as "part of the problem" of increasing gridlock on Capitol Hill. "He follows party leaders who are contributing to the partisan brawl that we're all so tired of watching," Simon said. Cardin responded by reiterating his efforts to work across the aisle, citing collaboration with Environment and Public Works Chairman John Barrasso, a Wyoming Republican, to ensure Chesapeake Bay cleanup funding as well as his coordination with McCain on issues abroad. Simon ended up realizing a tiny return on his investment: He got 4 percent of the vote. Campbell took 30 percent, and Cardin captured 65 percent and won reelection a month after his 75th birthday.

Chris Van Hollen (D)

Elected 2016, term expires 2022, 1st term, b. Jan 10, 1959; Karachi, Pakistan; Swarthmore College (PA), B.A., 1982; John F. Kennedy School of Government, Harvard University, M.P.P., 1985; Georgetown University (DC), J.D., 1990; Episcopalian; Married (Katherine Wilkens Van Hollen); 3 children.

Elected Office: MD House, 1991-1995; MD Senate, 1995-2003; U.S House, 2003-2017.

Professional Career: Practicing attorney; Legislative Assistant, U.S Sen. Charles Mathias, 1985-1987; Staff, U.S Senate Foreign Relations Commission, 1987-1989; Sr. Legislative advisor, Governor William Donald Schaefer, 1989-1991.

DC Office: 110 HSOB 20510, 202-224-4654, Fax: 202-228-0629, vanhollen.senate.gov
State Offices: Annapolis, 410-263-1325; Baltimore, 667-212-4610; Cambridge, 410-221-2074; Hagerstown, 301-797-2826; Largo, 301-322-6560; Rockville, 301-545-1500.

Committees: *Appropriations*: Commerce, Justice, Science & Related Agencies; Department of the Interior, Environment & Related Agencies; Financial Services & General Government; Legislative Branch; State, Foreign Operations & Related Programs. *Banking, Housing & Urban Affairs*: Financial Institutions & Consumer Protection; National Security & International Trade & Finance; Securities, Insurance & Investment (RMM). *Budget*. *Environment & Public Works*: Fisheries, Water, and Wildlife; Transportation & Infrastructure.

Group Ratings

	ADA	ACLU	AFL-CIO	LCV	ITI	COC	HAFA	ACU	CFG	FRC
2018	-	76%	-	100%	-	50%	3%	9%	5%	0%
2017	100%	C	100%	100%	C	29%	C	0%	4%	0%

Almanac Ratings 2017-18

	Economy	Social	Foreign	Composite
Liberal	100%	100%	89%	96%
Conservative	0%	0%	11%	4%

Key Votes of the 115th Congress

1. Obama-care revision	N	5. Gun regulations	N	9. Kavanaugh confirmation	N
2. Tax Cuts	N	6. Family planning regs	N	10. Saudi arms sales	Y
3. Dodd-Frank revision	N	7. Gorsuch confirmation	N	11. FISA rules	N
4. Omnibus appropriations	Y	8. Immigration restrictions	N	12. Military aid in Yemen	Y

Election Results

Election	Name (Party)	Vote (%)	Cand. Spent	Ind. Exp. Support	Ind. Exp. Oppose
2016 General	Chris Van Hollen (D)..................... 1,659,907	(61%)	$32,177,603	$1,758,111	
	Kathy Szeliga (R)............................. 972,557	(36%)	$1,510,202	$462,219	
	Margaret Flowers (G)........................ 89,970	(3%)	$90,437		
2016 Primary	Chris Van Hollen (D)........................ 470,320	(53%)			
	Donna Edwards (D)........................... 343,620	(39%)			

Prior winning percentages: House: 2014 (60%); 2012 (63%); 2010 (73%); 2008 (75%); 2006(77%); 2004 (75%); 2002 (52%)

Beneath an exterior of Boy Scout-like politeness, Democrat Chris Van Hollen is widely credited with possessing both the intellectual curiosity of a policy wonk and the savvy of a master political strategist. The latter attribute was front and center in late 2016 when Van Hollen was tapped to chair the Democratic Senatorial Campaign Committee — a full six weeks before he was sworn in as Maryland's new junior senator. Van Hollen had headed the House Democrats' campaign arm a decade earlier, and Senate Minority Leader Chuck Schumer was looking for an experienced hand to run the DSCC during an election cycle in which Senate Democrats would be defending three times as many seats as their Republican counterparts. Consequently, Schumer was not finding a lot of takers for the assignment among veteran members of his caucus; Van Hollen accepted the job, vowing "to hold the blue line." In the end, he accomplished just that. Democrats occupied 47 Senate seats as Congress convened in 2019, down only one from the beginning of the prior Congress — and after confronting what Van Hollen had described as the "toughest political map any one party has faced in 60 years."

Van Hollen's performance won praise from his colleagues; Senate Democrats had retained six of the 10 seats they held in states that had voted for President Donald Trump in 2016, while gaining a seat in another state — Arizona — that Trump had carried. But, immediately after the 2018 elections, Van Hollen made clear he was not interested in reprising his role at the DSCC: It was time to refocus on policy. "I did not want to sign up for another round, and I actually made that clear when I took the [DSCC] position originally," he told Bethesda Magazine in early 2019. "There are lots of [policy] issues … that I really want to focus on and turn my attention to in an even bigger way." He soon followed up with comprehensive legislation — on topics ranging from creating jobs for the long-term unemployed to improving worker compensation to combating climate change — that he hoped would influence the Democratic policy debate heading into the 2020 presidential election. At the same time, Van Hollen's turn at the DSCC bequeathed him with an informal role in the Senate Democratic leadership and a seat at the table at weekly strategy sessions.

It was the latest example of Van Hollen— whose nearly three decades in elected office include the Maryland General Assembly and both houses of Congress — quickly getting on the leadership ladder. Elected to the state Senate in 1994 by ousting an incumbent well-liked by Annapolis insiders, he moved to mend fences with the Senate president and found himself as vice chairman of an influential committee. Arriving in the House after the 2002 elections, he was chairman of the Democratic Congressional Campaign Committee by the beginning of his third term and assistant to House Speaker Nancy Pelosi by the start of his fourth. In fact, some thought Van Hollen might be on track to one day succeed Pelosi — until he announced in early 2015 he would run for the Senate seat being vacated by Democrat Barbara Mikulski.

Throughout his career in elected office, Van Hollen has taken calculated risks to move up — and seen them pay off. "Chris has an exquisite sense of timing and opportunity," said Virginia Democratic Rep. Gerry Connolly, who has known Van Hollen since they were young Senate aides. "Even when conventional wisdom told him not to, his instincts were better, his timing was superior." A penchant for risk-taking was evident in Van Hollen when he was young, when his father served as ambassador to Sri Lanka. Family members tell stories of a teenage Van Hollen who insisted on riding atop jeeps during excursions into the jungle, only to have to scramble inside on occasions when the vehicle was charged by elephants. Van Hollen was born in Pakistan while his father was a Foreign Service officer there; his mother later served as chief of the South Asia division of the State Department's Bureau of Intelligence and Research. While his father's family roots were in Baltimore, Van Hollen largely grew up abroad before returning to the United States to attend boarding school and then Swarthmore

College. He earned a master's degree in public policy from Harvard University's John F. Kennedy School of Government and a law degree from Georgetown University.

Van Hollen went to work in 1985 for Maryland Sen. Charles Mathias, a liberal Republican who held the seat Van Hollen now occupies. He soon moved to work for the Senate Foreign Relations Committee; after a hazardous trip along the Turkish-Iraqi border, he co-authored a report confirming Iraq's use of chemical weapons against its Kurdish minority. Van Hollen seemed headed for a career in the family business of diplomacy but left the committee in 1989 for a job in Maryland's federal affairs office — a move clearly aimed at positioning himself to run for office. In 1990, he was elected to the state House of Delegates on a candidate slate pledged to work to codify the Supreme Court's Roe v. Wade decision. In 1994, Van Hollen mounted a primary challenge against the state senator on whose slate he had been elected just four years earlier. His move created some blowback in local political circles, but it paid off: Van Hollen won the primary by a 3-1 margin, thanks to a well-executed campaign and missteps by the incumbent.

In 2002, Van Hollen gambled again — giving up a safe state Senate seat for an uphill run for Congress. Initially, the odds-on favorite for the Democratic nomination in Maryland's 8th District was a scion of the Kennedy dynasty: state Del. Mark Shriver, son of Sargent and Eunice Kennedy Shriver. But Van Hollen— bolstered by grassroots progressive groups with whom he had been allied on environmental and gun control issues and the endorsement of The Washington Post — defeated Shriver in the primary 44%-41%. Van Hollen then had only eight weeks to campaign against eight-term Rep. Connie Morella, a liberal Republican. The congenial Morella ran negative ads for the first time, but Van Hollen chose not to directly aim his fire at the popular incumbent. Instead, he argued that Morella's vote with the GOP to organize the House kept in power a conservative majority out of sync with most district voters. Helped by a recent redistricting plan that had made the 8th more favorable to Democrats, Van Hollen won 52%-47%. He was never seriously challenged in six re-election bids.

Notwithstanding his avowed liberalism and his leadership role at the DCCC, Van Hollen has a genial personality that let him work across the aisle on House legislation. At the outset of his second term, he was selected by Illinois Rep. Rahm Emanuel, then chairman of the DCCC, to manage candidate recruitment. When the Democrats captured the House majority in 2006 and Emanuel moved up to chair the Democratic Caucus, newly installed Speaker Pelosi exhibited her confidence in Van Hollen by naming him to head the DCCC. House Democrats gained 21 seats in November 2008, many in traditionally Republican areas, and Van Hollen and the DCCC got much of the credit — although he was undoubtedly aided by the unpopularity of outgoing President George W. Bush and a cratering economy. After Van Hollen's 2008 success, Pelosi persuaded him to stay on for a second term as DCCC chairman and sweetened the offer by giving him a leadership post: assistant to the speaker. In that post and from a perch on the powerful Ways and Means Committee, he remained active on policy issues amid his DCCC responsibilities.

In April 2009, Van Hollen introduced a cap-and-dividend bill on climate change, as an alternative to the Democrats' cap-and-trade legislation. A decade later, Van Hollen has doggedly continued to push this approach in the Senate, reintroducing in 2018 a similar cap-and-dividend legislation that would have put a carbon tax on coal, oil and gas producers and distributed the money to citizens. He has contended that, by returning the revenues derived from controlling climate change to households, "it addresses the major concern of the critics of doing something — which is that the cost will go up to the American consumer." His plan has picked up some bipartisan support, even as congressional Republicans have resisted action on the issue. In 2009, a cap-and-trade bill passed the House but died in the Senate. Donning his political strategy cap, Van Hollen at the time privately urged that action be postponed on climate change — presciently fearing that tackling it on the heels of health care reform would create a backlash among many voters. During debate on the Affordable Care Act, Van Hollen co-sponsored a successful amendment allowing dependents up to age 26 to stay on their parents' health insurance — a major talking point for Democrats defending the bill in 2010.

Early in 2009, Van Hollen sensed the national mood turning against incumbents and cautioned there would be no "third wave" in 2010. When poll results showed many Democratic incumbents trailing little-known challengers, he warned in August 2010 that Democrats were in for "a very tough campaign season." He later acknowledged cutting off DCCC funds to nine incumbents who could not be saved, while sending $12 million into districts where Democrats might win in the final days. Even so, Democrats lost 63 seats amid the nationwide tea party revolt — the largest loss either party had experienced in the House since 1948. Van Hollen's own fortunes were not adversely affected: In 2011, he gained the plum assignment as ranking Democrat on the Budget Committee, even though he had not previously served on that panel. He established a cordial working relationship with the panel's chairman, Wisconsin Republican Paul Ryan, another policy wonk who later became House speaker — notwithstanding that Van Hollen was a highly vocal critic of Ryan's conservative policy proposals.

Van Hollen's interest in the Senate predated his rise in the House leadership. When Sen. Paul Sarbanes announced his retirement in early 2005, Van Hollen seriously thought about running. He backed down when it became clear that party leaders were coalescing around Van Hollen's now-senior colleague, Ben Cardin. In March 2015, when Mikulski decided to retire after 30 years in the Senate, Van Hollen entered the contest within days and picked up the support of much of the state Democratic leadership. Coincidentally, Mikulski's announcement came just as Van Hollen was quietly discussing with fellow House Democrats a succession plan for when Pelosi and then-Minority Whip Steny Hoyer, both then in their mid-70s, left the House. "He could have been speaker of the House, if he stuck around," Van Hollen's former Republican colleague, Virginia Rep. Tom Davis, told The Washington Post. But, at the time, it was anything but clear when the leadership slots would open — or when the Democrats might regain the majority and give Van Hollen, then 57, a shot at speaker.

For perhaps the first time in his career, Van Hollen began a race for higher office as the front-runner, but his path was not without obstacles. Baltimore-based Rep. Elijah Cummings continued to contemplate running, and some polls showed him leading Van Hollen and the other major primary contender, Rep. Donna Edwards. After nearly 11 months of declining to rule out a Senate bid, Cummings filed for re-election to the House. In the early going, Van Hollen was a heavy favorite over Edwards, who suffered from a rocky relationship with the state party establishment and many of her colleagues in the Congressional Black Caucus. She struggled to raise money; Van Hollen reported a 12-1 financial advantage at the end of 2015. But Maryland is called "America in miniature" thanks to its varied geography and its 2016 Senate Democratic primary became a microcosm of the Hillary Clinton vs. Bernie Sanders presidential battle. As Sanders surged in a year of anti-incumbent sentiment, so did Edwards: She was viewed as the outsider and Van Hollen perceived as an insider, even if there were few policy differences between the two.

Cummings' decision left Edwards as the only African-American in the contest, and polls showed her with a large lead among black voters in a primary electorate estimated to be 40 percent African-American. (A post-2016 election book, "Shattered: Inside Hillary Clinton's Doomed Campaign," reported that Clinton was enraged upon hearing the Van Hollen campaign had urged union allies not to be aggressive in getting African-American voters to the polls. Both Van Hollen aides and a union that supported him have denied any effort to suppress the black vote.) Edwards' fundraising disadvantage was offset by nearly $3 million spent on her behalf by a super PAC tied to EMILY's List — an investment fueled by the fact that, with Mikulski retiring, a loss by Edwards threatened to leave the Maryland congressional delegation without a woman for the first time in four decades.

Two weeks before the April 26 primary, polls showed the race to be tight. Momentum shifted to Van Hollen when Edwards overplayed her hand with a late line of attack. It went back to 2010 legislation — the DISCLOSE Act — that Van Hollen had authored to mitigate the Supreme Court's Citizens United v. FEC ruling overturning restrictions on corporate involvement in campaign advertising. Edwards criticized Van Hollen for exempting the National Rifle Association from the legislation — to suggest he was soft on the NRA. Van Hollen, citing his advocacy of gun control dating back to his days as a state legislator, reacted angrily. "People should not be misled on the issue," he said during the campaign's final debate. To facilitate passage of the DISCLOSE Act in the House (it later failed to clear the Senate), several large membership-based organizations — including the Sierra Club, labor unions and the NRA — had been exempted; President Barack Obama backed that move at the time. The controversy escalated when a pro-Edwards super PAC echoed her criticism of Van Hollen in an ad that contained footage of Obama. The White House publicly called the ad misleading, putting Edwards on the defensive. A late poll showed Van Hollen opening a double-digit lead.

Van Hollen won 53%-39%. Edwards carried the black-majority jurisdictions of Baltimore and Prince George's County, her home base. Van Hollen won 21 of the state's 22 remaining counties. Republicans nominated Kathy Szeliga, minority whip of the House of Delegates. She characterized Van Hollen as a career politician while tying herself to the state's popular Republican governor, Larry Hogan — and seeking to downplay her conservative voting record in a blue state. Van Hollen he came out on top, 61%-36%, reflecting Clinton's 60%-34% margin over Trump in Maryland.

Van Hollen accepted the DSCC job shortly after his win, but only after leveraging it into appointment to the only Democratic vacancy on the powerful Appropriations Committee — the seat that had been held by Mikulski. It helped Van Hollen pay close attention to Maryland's needs, even as he traversed the country to bolster many of his politically vulnerable colleagues. "I thought it was very important to Maryland to fight to get on there," he said of the Appropriations panel in an interview looking back on his first two years in the Senate. The committee plays a key role in determining annual funding for several agencies headquartered or with large presences in Maryland, including the FDA, NASA and the National Institutes of Health. The state is home to nearly 150,000 federal civilian employees, the fourth most in the nation.

Besides Appropriations panel, Van Hollen was assigned to three other committees, including Agriculture. In keeping with his role at the DSCC, he gave up his slot on the Agriculture panel in early 2018 to newly appointed Minnesota Sen. Tina Smith, who filled the vacancy left by the resignation of Al Franken. Smith was facing a special election later in the year, and the Agriculture assignment was seen as boosting her prospects. Van Hollen then joined the Environment and Public Works Committee, where he teamed up with his senior in-state colleague, Cardin, to block efforts by the Trump administration to eliminate a program coordinating Chesapeake Bay restoration efforts. During the 35-day federal government shutdown in late 2018 and early 2019, Van Hollen and Cardin pushed through legislation ensuring that furloughed federal government workers would receive back pay. Meanwhile, Van Hollen mobilized colleagues to stall debate on the Senate floor — an effort to ramp up pressure on GOP leadership to bring up a funding bill to end the shutdown.

Farther from home, Van Hollen was active on several national security fronts. He and Schumer joined Arkansas Republican Tom Cotton, an outspoken conservative, to place an amendment into a defense authorization bill to limit goods and services federal agencies could obtain from two large Chinese tech firms: Huawei and ZTE. The amendment was adopted after the Commerce Department reached a deal to lift restrictions on ZTE that were imposed after the company violated sanctions against North Korea and Iran. The deal was widely criticized by members of Congress from both parties, who regarded the firms as a security threat given their ties to the Chinese government. And following on to a bill Cardin guided to passage in 2017 that was aimed at penalizing Russia for interfering in the 2016 elections, Van Hollen and Florida Republican Marco Rubio introduced legislation in early 2018 that would have required sanctions be imposed if the director of national intelligence determined within a month of an election that there had been foreign interference. The bill picked up co-sponsorship from 16 other senators but failed to advance.

Van Hollen's voting record in his first year in the Senate put him among the 10 most liberal senators, according to Almanac rankings. But he treaded carefully on some of the proposals put forth by the Democrats' emboldened progressive wing — such as the "Green New Deal," a nonbinding resolution introduced in early 2019 that called for "achieving net-zero greenhouse gas emissions." While the handful of Democratic senators who were announced presidential aspirants immediately signed on, Van Hollen displayed pragmatism, telling Bethesda Magazine: "I think it's a bold vision, and I'm certainly not opposed to it. I may at some point join it. But even if we pass that legislation with ambitious goals, it doesn't do anything to actually reduce carbon pollution."

Van Hollen ultimately signed on as a cosponsor of the Green New Deal about two months after it was introduced. But he also contended: "It's really important to have a real proposal that people can pick up and run with as soon as we have the votes to pass it. Because otherwise, what happens is that you get into the majority and all of a sudden you go, 'Oh, we have to come up with a plan.' ... It's much better to lay the groundwork in advance to have a plan."

Andy Harris (R)

Elected 2010, 5th term, b. Jan 25, 1957; Brooklyn, NY; University of Pennsylvania, Att., 1975; Johns Hopkins University, B.S., 1977; Johns Hopkins University, M.D., 1980; Johns Hopkins University Bloomburg School of Hygiene and Public Health (MD), M.H.S., 1995; Roman Catholic; Married (Sylvia Harris); 5 children; 6 grandchildren.

Military Career: U.S. Naval Reserve Medical Corps 1988-2001 (Operation Desert Storm)

Elected Office: MD Senate, 1998-2010, Minority whip.

Professional Career: Anesthesiologist, Johns Hopkins Hosp., 1980- 2010; Association Professional, Johns Hopkins Med. School, 1984-2010.

DC Office: 2334 RHOB 20515, 202-225-5311, harris.house.gov
State Offices: Bel Air, 410-588-5670; Chester, 410-643-5425; Salisbury, 443-944-8624.

Committees: *Appropriations*: Agriculture, Rural Development, FDA & Related Agencies; Labor, Health & Human Services, Education & Related Agencies.

Group Ratings

	ADA	ACLU	AFL-CIO	LCV	ITI	COC	HAFA	ACU	CFG	FRC
2018	-	14%	-	3%	-	75%	96%	96%	92%	100%
2017	5%	C	3%	6%	C	93%	C	100%	98%	100%

Almanac Ratings 2017-18

	Economy	Social	Foreign	Composite
Liberal	5%	7%	6%	6%
Conservative	95%	94%	94%	94%

Key Votes of the 115th Congress

1. Obama-care revision	Y	5. Family planning regs	Y	9. Guantanamo prisoners	N
2. Tax Cuts	Y	6. Body cameras/immigration	N	10. Ground missiles, limit	N
3. Omnibus appropriations	N	7. Abortion ban	Y	11. Defense Dept. spending	N
4. Dodd-Frank revision	Y	8. Concealed carry	Y	12. FISA rules	N

Election Results

Election	Name (Party)	Vote (%)		Cand. Spent	Ind. Exp. Support	Ind. Exp. Oppose
2018 General	Andy Harris (R)	183,662	(60%)	$1,462,190	$1,000	
	Jesse Colvin (D)	116,631	(38%)	$1,779,212		$49,827
2018 Primary	Andy Harris (R)	48,944	(86%)			
	Martin Elborn (R)	5,606	(10%)			

Prior winning percentages: 2016 (67%), 2014 (71%), 2012 (63%), 2010 (54%)

Andy Harris, elected in 2010, is the lone Republican in Maryland's congressional delegation. He juggles working with his Terrapin State colleagues on local matters with his fervently conservative views and support for President Donald Trump. He has considered running statewide and other possible routes to greater influence. At least until the next redistricting, he has no reason to worry about reelection.

Harris, a Johns Hopkins University anesthesiologist and professor, was born in Brooklyn New York to immigrants from Eastern Europe. His father, a Hungarian anti-communist activist, had been jailed in a Siberian gulag for more than a year for his political views before meeting Harris' mother, who had fled Ukraine, at a displaced persons camp in Austria. Harris credits his parents' escape from communism and the spirited dinner-table conversations they encouraged among their four sons with fostering his fiercely held beliefs in the ills of big government and the sanctity of the private sector. After Harris completed his medical studies at Johns Hopkins, he began to practice and teach there.

Harris was elected to the state Senate to represent Baltimore County in 1998. In Annapolis, he was one of the most conservative members, and he served as Senate minority whip. In 2008, he challenged Rep. Wayne Gilchrest, a moderate Republican, in a bloody primary. When Harris defeated him, Gilchrest refused to concede and then endorsed Frank Kratovil, the Democratic nominee. Kratovil continued Gilchrest's strategy of portraying Harris as too far right for the district and won by fewer than 3,000 votes.

In a rematch in 2010, Harris cast Kratovil as a puppet of President Barack Obama in a year when anti-incumbent feeling was rampant. After his first bid, Harris began to practice medicine a few days a week on the Eastern Shore, which helped deflect the criticism that he was running in an area where he had spent little time. Kratovil attacked Harris for his support of a conservative proposal to replace the income tax with a national sales tax. The first-termer was swept away by the Republican tide, 54%-42%.

Harris said the "proudest moment" of his first few months in office was voting for the House-passed omnibus spending bill that cut $61 billion for fiscal 2011. In 2013, he infuriated Maryland Democrats by joining 66 Republicans in voting against $9.7 billion in relief from Hurricane Sandy, which had battered parts of the Eastern Shore. He explained he wanted the bill to strengthen the National Flood Insurance Program instead of writing "another blank check." Although he voted for John Boehner for Speaker in January 2015, Harris demanded that Boehner deliver on his promises to conservatives. Following the 2016 election, Harris was defeated by Rep. Mark Walker of North Carolina for chairman of the Republican Study Committee, which Harris described as "a powerful vehicle for change in Congress." He had the support of conservative activists in the House Freedom Caucus.

At home, Harris sought to help the Eastern Shore by introducing a bill in 2011 authorizing federal money to study oxygen-starved "dead zones" in the Chesapeake Bay and the Gulf of Mexico that drive away fish. Harris has gone his own way on other regional issues. He infuriated residents of the District of Columbia when he sought to use congressional authority to stifle Washington's 2014 referendum legalizing sales of marijuana. On the Appropriations Committee, he has sought to roll back D.C. policies on needle-exchange programs, assisted suicide and waste. Some of his opponents have suggested a boycott of the Eastern Shore. "The fact is the Constitution gives Congress the ultimate oversight about what happens in the federal district," Harris responded. He has opposed wind energy projects off the Eastern Shore, voicing concern about the impact for boaters and fishermen. In 2018, he was one of 47 House members to vote against final passage of the farm bill.

Despite the hostility toward Trump by most Maryland politicians, including Republican Gov. Larry Hogan, Harris has remained supportive. Responding to criticism of Trump following his July 2018 meeting in Helsinki with Russian president Vladimir Putin, Harris said, "I disregard and discount anything that involves the mainstream media press."

In this district that became solidly Republican after the 2012 redistricting, he has not faced a serious reelection challenge. In 2014, Harris got 70 percent against Democrat Bill Tilghman, a retired lawyer from a longtime Eastern Shore family. In 2015, Harris voiced interest in running for the Senate seat of retiring Democrat Barbara Mikulski. The Democratic lean of the state and his Appropriations Committee membership mitigated against the uphill challenge. Instead, he had three opponents in the Republican primary, including former state delegate Michael Smigiel, a libertarian who had support from groups unhappy with Harris on marijuana in D.C. Harris won the primary with an impressive 78 percent to 11 percent for Smigiel. In 2018, Democrat Jesse Colvin, a small business owner and former Army ranger, ran against Trump and said that "Congress is broken." He spent $1.8 million, slightly exceeding the incumbent. Harris won 60%-38% and took 10 of the 12 counties.

MD-1: Eastern Maryland

Cook Partisan Voting Index: R+14

Population		Race and Ethnicity		Income	
Total	729,888	White	79.9%	Median Income	$71,900
Land area (sq. miles)	3,977	Black	11.9%	District Income Rank	82
Pop/ sq mi	183.5	Latino	3.8%	Poverty Rate	9.6%
Born in State	62.1%	Asian	2.1%	With health insurance	94.5%
		Two or more races	2%	Cash public assistance	2.1%
Age Groups		Other	0.3%	Food stamp/SNAP	10.6%
Under 18	21.5%				
18-34	20.2%	Education		Work	
35-64	40.7%	H.S grad or less	41.3%	White Collar	17.6%
Over 64	17.6%	Some college	27.8%	Sales and Service	40.8%
		College Degree, 4 yr	18.4%	Blue Collar	20.1%
Military		Post grad	12.6%	Government	18.4%
Veteran/ Active Duty	9.2%				

2012 Pres. Vote	Romney	214,988	(61%)	Obama	132,286	(37%)		
2016 Pres. Vote	Trump	225,249	(61%)	Clinton	121,840	(33%)	Johnson	12,919	(4%)

Eastern Shore: Chesapeake Bay is technically not a bay but an estuary. It was the central focus of the most thickly settled of the 13 colonies and today remains a central focus for much of modern Maryland. The first British here were amazed at the Chesapeake's oysters, terrapins, crabs and rockfish. This was an estuary civilization in colonial days, with every little hamlet tied together by the highways of bays and creeks and inlets off the Chesapeake. The streets and docks of Chestertown, Oxford, St. Michaels and Cambridge still look something like they did when George Washington slept there. In post-colonial times, when most Americans were caught up in the romance of westward movement, these estuaries and peninsulas were mostly forgotten, located too far off the main lines of railroads and highways. In the 160 years between 1790 and 1950, the Eastern Shore counties of Maryland only doubled in population.

Since then, much of the Chesapeake has changed beyond recognition. The area has grown vigorously, with second-home buyers, retirees and commuters crossing the Chesapeake Bay Bridge. Now, this is a land of genteel estates fronting the water and of Frank Perdue's thriving chicken empire around Salisbury. The 4.2 billion (with a b) pounds of chicken meat produced in 2017 on the peninsula doubled the total in 1987; the $3.4 billion value tripled during that time. With limited federal or state regulations, one result has been an increase in the stench from air pollution. Some local farmers have found that they can get a better return by leasing their land to solar-power companies.

Easton has a Waterfowl Festival and quaint St. Michaels has an OysterFest, as do other towns on that part of the three-state DelMarVa peninsula. The Assateague Island National Seashore, with its famous wild ponies, annually attracts more than 2 million visitors and supports a $100 million tourism business. That is separate from the crowded beaches and boardwalks up the coast in Ocean City. Away from the shore, in Harford County, where the population more than tripled since 1960 and the supply of farm land has been cut sharply, demands for new housing and school rooms again accelerated in 2017 after having flattened earlier in the decade.

Even more threatening is pollution. In 2010, the Chesapeake Bay Foundation settled a lawsuit against the Environmental Protection Agency to enforce limits on pollution entering the bay, especially with regulations on developers and farmers. In a January 2019 report, the Foundation gave a D- grade to the health of the bay, a downgrade from the C- two years earlier, which resulted chiefly from the Trump administration's rollback of environmental regulations plus increased storm runoff. The significant increase in the harvest of blue crabs has been reversed by the administration's change in how temporary-worker visas are distributed, which sharply reduced the supply of foreign workers for crab houses. The health of the bay's oysters resulted in the largest harvest in 30 years. Local producers in 2018 reported an increase in aquaculture growing of oysters in nets.

The 1st Congressional District of Maryland includes all nine counties of the Eastern Shore. At the top of the bay, it takes in parts of the northern Baltimore suburbs of Harford, Baltimore and Carroll counties. Nearly half the votes are cast on the west side of the bay and to the north along the Susquehanna River, chiefly in the solidly Republican suburbs of Harford. The Republican precincts in these outer Baltimore suburbs maximize Democratic performance in neighboring districts. This is the only district in Maryland where Republicans hold a voter registration edge, and the only one that presidential nominee Donald Trump carried in 2016 — with 61 percent of the vote.

Dutch Ruppersberger (D)

Elected 2002, 9th term, b. Jan 31, 1946; Baltimore; Baltimore City College (MD); University of Maryland - College Park, B.A., 1967; University of Baltimore School of Law (MD), J.D., 1970; Methodist; Married (Kay Murphy Ruppersberger); 2 children; 3 grandchildren.

Elected Office: Baltimore County Council, 1986-1994; Baltimore County Executive, 1994-2002.

Professional Career: Clerk, Judge Kenneth C. Proctor, 1970-1972; Assistant state Attorney, Baltimore County, 1972-1980; Partner, Ruppersberger, Clark & Mister, 1980-1994.

DC Office: 2206 RHOB 20515, 202-225-3061, Fax: 202-225-3094, ruppersberger.house.gov

State Offices: Timonium, 410-628-2701.

Committees: *Appropriations*: Defense; Homeland Security; Legislative Branch.

Group Ratings

	ADA	ACLU	AFL-CIO	LCV	ITI	COC	HAFA	ACU	CFG	FRC
2018	-	71%	-	94%	-	55%	8%	8%	10%	0%
2017	75%	C	92%	100%	C	50%	C	7%	0%	11%

Almanac Ratings 2017-18

	Economy	Social	Foreign	Composite
Liberal	89%	89%	63%	80%
Conservative	11%	11%	37%	20%

Key Votes of the 115th Congress

1. Obama-care revision	N	5. Family planning regs	N	9. Guantanamo prisoners	N
2. Tax Cuts	N	6. Body cameras/immigration	Y	10. Ground missiles, limit	Y
3. Omnibus appropriations	Y	7. Abortion ban	N	11. Defense Dept. spending	Y
4. Dodd-Frank revision	N	8. Concealed carry	N	12. FISA rules	Y

Election Results

Election	Name (Party)	Vote (%)		Cand. Spent	Ind. Exp. Support	Ind. Exp. Oppose
2018 General	Dutch Ruppersberger (D)	167,201	(66%)	$693,099		
	Liz Matory (R)	77,782	(31%)	$29,091		
	Michael Carney (Lib)	5,215	(2%)			
2018 Primary	Dutch Ruppersberger (D)	47,776	(78%)			
	Jake Pretot (D)	13,405	(22%)			

Prior winning percentages: 2016 (62%), 2014 (61%), 2012 (66%), 2010 (64%), 2008 (72%), 2006(69%), 2004 (67%), 2002 (54%)

Dutch Ruppersberger, elected in 2002, has retained his focus on national security issues. With his base at the Appropriations Committee, where his seniority places him close to a subcommittee chairmanship, he seeks a bipartisan approach on behalf of a district that he calls "the cybersecurity capital of the world." His district lines, which were largely drawn for him, have been at risk during the Supreme Court review of Maryland redistricting.

Charles Albert Ruppersberger grew up in Baltimore, attended the University of Maryland and graduated from the University of Baltimore School of Law. Working as a Baltimore County assistant state's attorney, Ruppersberger had a near-fatal car accident in 1975 while investigating a drug-trafficking case. When he asked his doctors at the University of Maryland's Shock Trauma Center how he could thank them, he said, they urged him to run for office so he could fund their facility. In 1986, he won a seat on the Baltimore County Council and made good on his promise to help the hospital. In 1994, he was elected Baltimore County executive.

Barred from seeking a third term in 2002, Ruppersberger seriously considered running for governor. But he was dissuaded by state party leaders who felt he was politically vulnerable following a controversy over county redevelopment. Instead, he took advantage of a favorable House district when Democrats redrew the congressional map. Against investment banker Osman Bengur, who spent more than $500,000 of his own money. Ruppersberger won the primary, 50%-36%. In the fall, he faced Helen Delich Bentley, who served in the House for a decade until she ran, unsuccessfully, for governor in 1994. Both candidates supported additional dredging of shipping channels in Chesapeake Bay and increased port security. Ruppersberger won, 54%-46%. His popular-vote margin was largely in the small part of the district in Baltimore city.

In the House, his Almanac vote ratings have been the least liberal among Maryland Democrats. With the help of Baltimore native Nancy Pelosi, he was appointed to the Intelligence Committee, where he called for expanded oversight of intelligence agencies and for shifting resources from the Iraq war to terrorist "safe havens" in Afghanistan. Working with Chairman Mike Rogers, a Michigan Republican and former FBI agent, Ruppersberger sought to repair the panel's reputation for partisan infighting. "We both focus more on the teamwork," Ruppersberger told The Washington Post. The two men traveled together to foreign hot spots and sat together at classified White House briefings.

Ruppersberger did not hesitate to criticize President Barack Obama and his administration. In 2009, he said that he had not been adequately consulted on the White House's plan to buy and launch spy satellites. With Rogers, Ruppersberger signed a report that defended the Pentagon and the Central Intelligence Agency for their handling of the attacks in 2012 on the U.S. diplomatic compound in Benghazi Libya. Even after he left the committee, he remained an advocate of the intelligence legislation enacted in 2015 to end the National Security Agency's bulk collection of telephone and email data. The House-passed defense spending bill in 2016 included his provision to create a unified command for cyber operations, based at Fort Meade.

After leaving the Intelligence Committee in 2015, Ruppersberger retained his interest in steps to strengthen cybersecurity, an area that he said had been neglected under Obama. Prompted by concern about the potential sale of shipping operations at the Port of Baltimore to the United Arab Emirates, Ruppersberger helped to enact port-security legislation.

Returning to the Appropriations Committee, where he focused on national security funding, he raised concerns about the Trump administration's handling of the issue. In May 2018, the committee approved his amendment to enforce sanctions on the Chinese telecommunications firm ZTE; the Trump administration later lifted the ban. In June, he wrote an op-ed with Republican Rep. Mike McCaul, plus Sens. Chris Coons and Marco Rubio, urging that national security policies "transcend party lines" and that the administration learn from past examples of government working in unison to "form a coherent national security strategy." In December, Ruppersberger was one of five House Democrats who voted for a procedural rule that, in effect, rejected an initiative to end U.S. participation in the war in Yemen. Progressive activists complained that Democratic leaders failed to enforce party discipline. He said that he had "nightmares" after Defense Secretary James Mattis resigned later that month. In January 2019, he wrote that President Donald Trump needed to "stop tweeting and start leading."

With his interest in local governance, he launched the Municipal Finance Caucus to assist the financing of infrastructure. In 2018, he filed a bill to restore a tax break for refunding of municipal debt, which had been eliminated by the Republican-passed tax bill.

Ruppersberger has been reelected easily. His early statewide ambitions dimmed when he passed up opportunities for vacant seats for governor and the Senate, which were won by other Democrats. Whether the next Maryland redistricting is in 2020 (if ordered by the Supreme Court) or in 2022, the changes might pose enough of a reelection challenge to encourage him to retire.

MD-2: Baltimore Metro

Cook Partisan Voting Index: D+11

Population		Race and Ethnicity		Income	
Total	757,951	White	50.6%	Median Income	$66,387
Land area (sq. miles)	349	Black	33.5%	District Income Rank	124
Pop/ sq mi	2172.5	Latino	6.9%	Poverty Rate	11.4%
Born in State	61.8%	Asian	5.4%	With health insurance	92.6%
		Two or more races	2.9%	Cash public assistance	2.8%
Age Groups		Other	0.5%	Food stamp/SNAP	13.7%
Under 18	23.1%				
18-34	24.9%	**Education**		**Work**	
35-64	39.3%	H.S grad or less	40.4%	White Collar	12.7%
Over 64	12.7%	Some college	28%	Sales and Service	42.2%
		College Degree, 4 yr	18.9%	Blue Collar	17.6%
Military		Post grad	12.6%	Government	19.6%
Veteran/ Active Duty	9.6%				

2012 Pres. Vote	Obama	193,834	(63%)	Romney	107,890	(35%)			
2016 Pres. Vote	Clinton	193,237	(59%)	Trump	114,460	(35%)	Johnson	8,990	(3%)

Parts of Baltimore County: The spokes of Baltimore's avenues spread out in all directions from the Inner Harbor, connecting the central city with the suburbs, where most residents of metropolitan Baltimore live. The streets reach east to Dundalk and Essex, industrial suburbs where the tone of life was set for years by the giant Sparrows Point steel mill, long the biggest in the country, but which was shuttered in 2012. Northeastward, they extend to charming Havre de Grace and the oldest lighthouse in continuous use on the East Coast, as well as to modest working-class suburbs in Harford County. In an arc north of downtown are middle-income towns from Randallstown to Owings Mills. A couple of miles northwest of the Baltimore County seat of Towson is Timonium, the site of the annual Maryland State Fair.

The 2nd Congressional District of Maryland is an irregularly shaped hodgepodge that includes much of this territory. Most of the district is not far from Chesapeake Bay, including the terminal for the huge Port of Baltimore, which has been rated as the most efficient container port in the nation. In 2017, it employed more than 13,000 workers and moved 807,000 automobiles — the most in the nation. With the widening of the Panama Canal, Baltimore and Norfolk Virginia were the only East Coast ports wide and deep enough for post-Panamax cargo ships. A huge redevelopment has been underway to revive Sparrows Point as the renamed Tradepoint Atlantic industrial park and international trade hub, with many commercial distribution centers, including Amazon, FedEx and Under Armour.

With its short distance from Washington D.C., the Baltimore area has become a convenient locale for military work. The Aberdeen Proving Ground tests a wide variety of military weapons. The Baltimore Sun has described it as the local "economic lifeblood," with more than 20,000 government and contractor jobs. Down the Baltimore-Washington Parkway is Fort Meade, the sprawling Army post that houses the National Security Agency and supports more than 125,000 jobs in 1,500 buildings. It has evolved from an army base to a cybersecurity center, which houses more than 100 federal agencies, including the nation's cyber defense operations and the Defense Information Systems Agency.

Like the arms of a Maryland crab, the district angles inland to include some Baltimore County suburbs, residential neighborhoods in northeast Baltimore, an industrial pocket in far southeast Baltimore and a dip south of Baltimore along Interstate 95 to include the NSA headquarters. At that point, the district crosses the Harbor Tunnel to capture the row houses of Brooklyn and Curtis Bay, whose residents are mainly descendants of German and East European immigrants who moved there to work on the docks and in the factories along the Patapsco River and the harbor. About 60 percent of the district's population is in Baltimore County, where Vice President Spiro Agnew got his start as a Democrat before he became county executive and then governor; a bit less than 10 percent is in Baltimore city, and much of the remainder in Harford County. About one-third of its population is African American. This is a comfortably Democratic district, with some Republican enclaves. In 2016, working-class Dundalk, which has shifted to Republican in recent years, gave 62 percent of its vote to Donald Trump in the general election. Overall in the district, Hillary Clinton got 59 percent.

John Sarbanes (D)

Elected 2006, 7th term, b. May 22, 1962; Baltimore; Princeton University Woodrow Wilson School of Public and International Affairs (NJ), B.A., 1984; Harvard University, J.D., 1988; Greek Orthodox; Married (Dina Sarbanes); 3 children.

Professional Career: Clerk, Judge Fred Motz, 1988-1989; Practicing attorney, Venable LLP, 1989-2006; Special Assistant MD Schls. Superintendent, 1998-2005.

DC Office: 2370 RHOB 20515, 202-225-4016, Fax: 202-225-9219, sarbanes.house.gov

State Offices: Annapolis, 410-295-1679; Towson, 410-832-8890.

Committees: *Energy & Commerce*: Energy; Health; Oversight & Investigations. *Oversight & Reform*: Government Operations.

Group Ratings

	ADA	ACLU	AFL-CIO	LCV	ITI	COC	HAFA	ACU	CFG	FRC
2018	-	86%	-	94%	-	58%	10%	4%	18%	0%
2017	100%	C	92%	100%	C	36%	C	8%	6%	0%

Almanac Ratings 2017-18

	Economy	Social	Foreign	Composite
Liberal	97%	100%	92%	96%
Conservative	3%	0%	8%	4%

Key Votes of the 115th Congress

1. Obama-care revision	N	5. Family planning regs	N	9. Guantanamo prisoners	Y
2. Tax Cuts	N	6. Body cameras/immigration	Y	10. Ground missiles, limit	Y
3. Omnibus appropriations	Y	7. Abortion ban	N	11. Defense Dept. spending	Y
4. Dodd-Frank revision	N	8. Concealed carry	N	12. FISA rules	N

Election Results

Election	Name (Party)	Vote (%)		Cand. Spent	Ind. Exp. Support	Ind. Exp. Oppose
2018 General	John Sarbanes (D)................................	202,407	(69%)	$400,640		
	Charles Anthony (R).............................	82,774	(28%)			
	David Lashar (Lib)...............................	7,476	(3%)	$26,452		
2018 Primary	John Sarbanes (D)................................	64,567	(82%)			
	Adam DeMarco (D)...............................	6,778	(9%)			
	Eduardo Rosas (D)...............................	4,847	(6%)			

Prior winning percentages: 2016 (63%), 2014 (60%), 2012 (67%), 2010 (61%), 2008 (70%), 2006 (64%)

Democrat John Sarbanes, elected in 2006, has been a prominent advocate of Democratic government-oversight proposals and has been an ally of Nancy Pelosi, the former Baltimorean. On the Energy and Commerce Committee, he has worked on issues ranging from health care to campaign finance reform. He remains young enough to fulfill his ambition to follow his father's path from the House to the Senate, where he served five terms and chaired the Banking Committee.

Sarbanes graduated from Princeton University and Harvard Law School, following the academic route taken by his dad, Paul Sarbanes, who retired in 2006 after 36 years in Congress. The younger Sarbanes returned to Baltimore to clerk for a federal District Court judge, then joined the Venable law firm, where he chaired the health care practice and represented nonprofit hospitals and senior-living providers. He spent seven years as special assistant to the Maryland superintendent of schools, serving as liaison to Baltimore schools.

In his 2006 campaign, Sarbanes enjoyed a considerable advantage because of his name recognition. But the primary race was no cakewalk. When Democratic Rep. Ben Cardin gave up his seat to run for the Senate seat of the senior Sarbanes, eight candidates filed for the primary. Contenders included veteran state Sen. Paula Hollinger and former Baltimore Health Commissioner Peter Beilenson. Sarbanes issued lengthy, detailed proposals on health care and education, which he called his top two legislative priorities. Beilenson emphasized his experience managing a large government budget. Hollinger was endorsed by the teachers union, and had been an active state lawmaker. Sarbanes, who had a small fundraising advantage, won the Democratic primary with 32 percent to 25 percent for Beilenson and 21 percent for Hollinger. In the general election, Republican John White got little attention in a Democratic year. Sarbanes won, 64%-34%.

In the House, Sarbanes has a staunchly liberal voting record. In 2010, he got a provision in an auto safety bill to fund research into new technologies to prevent drunk-driving accidents. He urged the Federal Trade Commission in 2011 to take action against Pfizer for what he described as its attempts to keep consumers away from generic versions of its successful anti-cholesterol drug Lipitor. On Energy and Commerce, he called for the regulation of Facebook because of its failure to protect personal data. "They have a tremendous amount of power," he said in April 2018. "It's one of the largest data brokerage firms in the world, vacuuming up data on two billion people every single day."

In 2016, Sarbanes took the lead on legislation that sought to address opioid addiction, which had become a major problem in Baltimore. The House passed his bill to train doctors to prescribe overdose-reversal drugs when they prescribe pain medication and other opiates. His approach, he said, was to bring together medical professionals, behavioral health experts and law enforcement with local, state and federal officials to improve addiction treatment and expand prevention services. Serving on the House-Senate conference committee that crafted the final details of the 21st Century Cures Act, which was one of the few major bills enacted that year, Sarbanes pushed for the $1 billion that was approved to expand treatment programs. In June 2018, the House passed a bill that he cosponsored to permit the forgiveness of student loans for recipients who become professionals dealing with substance abuse.

Like his father, Sarbanes has been an outspoken advocate of Greece and its Hellenic values. In 2018, he added a provision to the annual defense spending bill that prevented the U.S. transfer of F-35 fighter jets to Turkey, pending a report by the Pentagon to Congress. He has advocated legislative solutions to clean up pollution in Chesapeake Bay. When House Republicans shot down his proposal to create a national climate change service, he attacked them for their "reckless political stunt of climate change denial."

Sarbanes has promoted a 'Government by the People" campaign finance plan that would give contributors tax credits for donations and create a fund to match small donations to "grassroots" candidates who refuse political action committee money. The plan would reinvigorate democracy, he wrote, by "empowering a more diverse pool of candidates who would have the resources to run, compete and win." In 2019, that proposal evolved into H.R. 1, the For the People Act, a "drain the swamp" package that became the initial prominent legislation offered by House Democrats. As chairman of the House Democracy Reform Task Force, Sarbanes worked closely with Speaker Nancy Pelosi to add voting rights, ethics reforms, donor disclosures and restrictions on gerrymandering. The House passed the measure in March, on a party-line vote of 234-193.

Sarbanes has been reelected easily. He says that he drives home to Towson every night. When Sen. Barbara Mikulski announced her retirement in March 2015, Sarbanes initially kept his cards close to his vest. But he soon ruled out a bid for her seat. Perhaps he will seek to succeed Ben Cardin in the Senate, just as he did in the House — though Cardin, who will be 81 when his term expires in 2024, has shown no signs of retiring.

MD-3: Baltimore Metro

Cook Partisan Voting Index: D+13

Population		Race and Ethnicity		Income	
Total	752,897	White	58.9%	Median Income	$84,243
Land area (sq. miles)	304	Black	21.5%	District Income Rank	40
Pop/ sq mi	2475.5	Latino	8.9%	Poverty Rate	8.1%
Born in State	48.6%	Asian	7.2%	With health insurance	93.1%
		Two or more races	2.9%	Cash public assistance	2.1%
Age Groups		Other	0.7%	Food stamp/SNAP	8.9%
Under 18	21.1%			**Work**	
18-34	25.7%	**Education**		White Collar	14.4%
35-64	38.8%	H.S grad or less	29.4%	Sales and Service	36.1%
Over 64	14.4%	Some college	23.3%	Blue Collar	12.5%
		College Degree, 4 yr	24.9%	Government	20%
Military		Post grad	22.4%		
Veteran/ Active Duty	9.3%				

2012 Pres. Vote	Obama	205,929	(61%)	Romney	122,604	(37%)		
2016 Pres. Vote	Clinton	221,842	(62%)	Trump	113,318	(32%)	Johnson	12,324	(3%)

Annapolis: Downtown Baltimore, one of America's major urban centers since the Revolution, has been viewed as one of America's star cities. Its Inner Harbor redevelopment, with a spectacular, multilevel aquarium on the water, and its ballpark at Camden Yards are national models. The local cuisine — crab cakes and steamed crabs spiced a certain way — is known well beyond the Chesapeake Bay watershed. In 2009, about half the city became a National Heritage Area, a designation that boosted tourism and economic development. The minority neighborhoods of Baltimore have had terrible urban problems — high crime, controversial policing, abandoned neighborhoods, poor schools — but the greater Baltimore area that has grown far beyond the city and county lines has fared better and retains a distinctive character. In Annapolis, the marble-halled Statehouse, built in 1772, is where the Continental Congress ratified the Treaty of Paris that ended the Revolutionary War and is the oldest state capitol in continuous use. In August 2017, workers quietly removed from the Statehouse lawn the statue of Maryland native Chief Justice Roger Taney, who wrote the pro-slavery Dred Scott decision. The home of the U.S. Naval Academy, including the cemetery where Sen. John McCain was buried in September 2018, Annapolis is both a waterman's and yachter's port.

The 3rd District of Maryland consists of three oddly disjointed pieces of geography that extend from the Inner Harbor area. As it scoops up parts of Baltimore City, Baltimore County, Anne Arundel County, Howard County and a small slice of Montgomery County, the 3rd has been a prime contender for the most-gerrymandered district in the nation. According to The Washington Post's Wonkblog, this is the "Praying Mantis" district. From a distance, it seems like an ink spot. But there is a rationale to what some might consider its absurdity. Its boundaries were designed by Democrats with politics in mind: The 3rd borders the majority-black 7th District on three sides. One spoke extends northeast and takes in black city neighborhoods; another extends north and west from the city to the Baltimore County seat of Towson and the suburbs of Pikesville and Owings Mills. The last crooked spoke extends south to Glen Burnie and the Baltimore-Washington International Thurgood Marshall Airport, where it splits into two tangents: one goes south to Anne Arundel County and all of Annapolis, and the other heads west to Columbia in Howard County, plus rural Olney and Calverton in Montgomery County. About a third of the district's population resides in Anne Arundel, which is the least Democratic portion, and another quarter is in Baltimore city.

In Baltimore's revived Locust Point industrial neighborhood on the waterfront is the iconic orange Domino Sugars sign glowing from the refinery plant's rooftop — now powered by solar panels. The plant has continued to refine 6.6 million pounds of raw sugar a day, but other industrial land along the water is being redeveloped into upscale residential and commercial properties. The district includes the fabled restaurants and bars of Little Italy and Fell's Point. A water wheel, with solar and water power, periodically removes tons of trash and debris from the Inner Harbor. These neighborhoods have achieved a "critical mass," even as the overall city has continued to lose population, The Baltimore Sun reported in 2017. Port Covington, waterfront property in south Baltimore, is the site of a new development of apartments and offices, including the headquarters for Under Armour and its more than 10,000 employees, that is scheduled to open by 2021. In July 2018, the city of Baltimore sued more than two dozen fossil fuel companies for allegedly causing climate change and the rising seas that threaten these urban areas. "Baltimore's residents, workers and businesses shouldn't have to pay for the damage knowingly caused by these companies," the city's attorney said. The solidly Democratic 3rd voted for Hillary Clinton, 63%-32%.

Anthony Brown (D)

Elected 2016, 2nd term, b. Nov 21, 1961; Huntington, NY; U.S. Military Academy at West Point, Att.; Harvard College (MA), B.A., 1984; Harvard University Law School (MA), J.D., 1992; Roman Catholic; Married (Karmen Bailey Walker Brown); 2 children; 1 stepchild.

Military Career: U.S. Army 1984-1989; U.S. Army Reserves 1989-2014 (Iraq)

Elected Office: Maryland Assembly, 1999-2007; Lt. Governor, 2007-2015.

Professional Career: Mbr., Board of Governors; Council of State Gov't Toll Fellow; Mbr., MD House of Delegates; MD House Majority Whip

DC Office: 1323 LHOB 20515, 202-225-8699, anthonybrown.house.gov

State Offices: Annapolis, 410-266-3249; Largo, 301-458-2600.

Committees: *Armed Services*: Intelligence, Emerging Threats & Capabilities; Tactical Air & Land Forces. *Ethics. Natural Resources*: Energy & Mineral Resources; Water, Oceans & Wildlife. *Transportation & Infrastructure*: Aviation; Coast Guard & Maritime Transportation; Economic Dev't, Public Buildings & Emergency Management; Highways & Transit.

Group Ratings

	ADA	ACLU	AFL-CIO	LCV	ITI	COC	HAFA	ACU	CFG	FRC
2018	-	81%	-	83%	-	58%	9%	10%	12%	0%
2017	95%	C	97%	100%	C	57%	C	7%	5%	0%

Almanac Ratings 2017-18

	Economy	Social	Foreign	Composite
Liberal	95%	100%	89%	95%
Conservative	5%	0%	11%	6%

Key Votes of the 115th Congress

1. Obama-care revision	N	5. Family planning regs	N	9. Guantanamo prisoners	Y	
2. Tax Cuts	N	6. Body cameras/immigration	Y	10. Ground missiles, limit	Y	
3. Omnibus appropriations	Y	7. Abortion ban	N	11. Defense Dept. spending	Y	
4. Dodd-Frank revision	N	8. Concealed carry	N	12. FISA rules	Y	

Election Results

Election	Name (Party)	Vote (%)	Cand. Spent	Ind. Exp. Support	Ind. Exp. Oppose
2018 General	Anthony Brown (D)...................... 209,642	(78%)	$321,364		
	George McDermott (R)................. 53,327	(20%)			
2018 Primary	Anthony Brown (D)....................	(100%)			

Prior winning percentages: 2016 (74%)

Anthony Brown of Maryland, elected to the House in 2016, settled into his seat on the Armed Services Committee, where he brought his extensive military background and worked on issues affecting his many constituents who are active-duty or veterans, plus others who work for Pentagon contractors. Brown also got a seat on the Ethics Committee and was assigned to panels to review charges brought against other House members. His move to the House was a career transition after lengthy service in Annapolis and his unsuccessful bid for governor in 2014.

Brown is a native of Huntington New York, where his father was a native of Jamaica and worked as a physician on Long Island. He got his bachelor's and law degrees from Harvard University. He joined the Army ROTC program and was commissioned after college as a second lieutenant and served as a helicopter pilot and aviation officer in Germany. Later, in the Army Reserve, he was a lieutenant colonel in the Judge Advocate General's Corps. Following law school, where he was a classmate of Barack Obama, Brown moved to Maryland and clerked for the chief judge of the U.S. Court of Appeals for the Armed Forces. He remained a colonel in the Reserve.

In 1998, he was elected to the first of four terms in the Maryland House of Delegates and served as majority whip. In 2004, he was deployed to Iraq, where he was a senior consultant to the Iraqi Ministry of Displacement and Migration and worked on refugee problems; he earned the Bronze Star. He was elected lieutenant governor in 2006 as the running mate of Martin O'Malley and served two terms in that office. He won the Democratic nomination to run for governor in overwhelmingly Democratic Maryland in 2014, but lost to Republican Larry Hogan, 51%-47% after what many considered a lackluster campaign. He would be one of six defeated gubernatorial candidates who became members of his freshman class.

When Rep. Donna Edwards ran for the Senate, Brown was the early favorite to succeed her and won endorsements from key local Democratic officials. He ran on a campaign of "redemption" following his setback in 2014, and described himself as a "workhorse, not a show horse." His chief opponent was Glenn Ivey, a former prosecutor in Prince George's County and a partner in a Washington D.C. law firm. His wife, Jolene Ivey, a former state delegate, ran for lieutenant governor on the ticket opposing Brown in the close Democratic primary for governor in 2014. Ivey ran more outspoken advertising, pledging to "take on Republicans for all of us."

Brown, who loaned himself nearly $400,000 shortly before the primary, had a fundraising advantage over Ivey of $1.4 million to $1 million, and won the April primary, 42%-34%. State Del. Joseline Pena-Melnuk, who ran as the "progressive fighter" and raised $900,000, was third with 19 percent. In the general election that was a foregone conclusion in this district, Brown defeated businessman George McDermott, 74%-21%.

On the Armed Services Committee, Brown organized a defense and aerospace consortium of local businesses, plus academicians, with an interest in military policy to advise him on national security issues, including the aging workforce. "There has to be a public-private partnership," he told Defense News in January 2019. The consortium could also be useful in organizing data security workshops for small businesses struggling to meet government requirements, Brown said. Earlier, he filed legislation, which he called the National Security Workforce Act, to provide incentives for businesses that include workforce development in their bids for defense programs. The proposals were designed to encourage the private sector to offer the "education and training necessary to ensure that we have a competent, skilled, capable workforce," Brown said. During committee debate on the military spending bill in 2018, he offered a proposal to retain the Defense Information Systems

Agency. The legislation planned to eliminate the agency as part of its reorganization of the Pentagon. His proposal was defeated on a party-line vote.

Serving on the Ethics panel, Brown was assigned to a subcommittee to investigate the indictment on insider-trading charges that was filed in August 2018 against Republican Rep. Chris Collins of New York. Receiving such an assignment was a mark of confidence for a first-term member to deal with often dicey internal problems.

In May 2018, Brown suffered what he said was a minor stroke, which kept him away from the Capitol for more than a week.

MD-4: Eastern D.C. Suburbs   Cook Partisan Voting Index: D+28

Population		Race and Ethnicity		Income	
Total	747,699	White	26.4%	Median Income	$79,163
Land area (sq. miles)	298	Black	51.9%	District Income Rank	57
Pop/ sq mi	2510.7	Latino	16.1%	Poverty Rate	8.7%
Born in State	30.4%	Asian	3%	With health insurance	88.8%
Age Groups		Two or more races	2.1%	Cash public assistance	1.8%
Under 18	23.6%	Other	0.5%	Food stamp/SNAP	10.2%
18-34	23.4%	**Education**		**Work**	
35-64	40.5%	H.S grad or less	39.1%	White Collar	12.5%
Over 64	12.5%	Some college	28.1%	Sales and Service	42.5%
Military		College Degree, 4 yr	19%	Blue Collar	18.3%
Veteran/ Active Duty	9%	Post grad	13.8%	Government	23.9%

2012 Pres. Vote	Obama	255,226	(78%)	Romney	69,323	(21%)	
2016 Pres. Vote	Clinton	256,575	(77%)	Trump	63,390	(19%)	

Prince George's County: In 1696, the proprietors of the colony of Maryland created a new county between the Potomac and Patuxent rivers and named it after the husband of the heir to the throne, Prince George of Denmark. During its 300 years, Prince George's County has not often won national fame, though it might now. With a population that is nearly two-thirds African American, Prince George's is the home of America's largest black middle class. It is the wealthiest county with a majority black population, and continues fast-growing with an increase in total population from 802,000 in 2000 to 913,000 in 2017.

Historically, Prince George's was tobacco country, dotted by slave plantations and pretty much controlled by its white property owners. A hundred years after the Civil War, the population grew as middle-class blacks moved out of neighboring Washington D.C. into modest suburbs at the county's edge and affluent subdivisions farther to the east. Its African-American population increased from 14 percent in 1970, to 37 percent in 1980, to 65 percent in 2017. The county continues to grow, with working-class black and Hispanic residents leaving gentrified Washington for more affordable housing and better schools across the border. More than 100,000 are current or former federal employees. As the Hispanic population has climbed above 18 percent, there has been some pushback from black groups over jobs, plus new schools and public facilities in immigrant neighborhoods, including Largo and Langley Park.

With office and shopping mall development, Prince George's County has become commercially vibrant. On the edge of the Potomac River is the National Harbor development area, where the MGM casino opened in 2016; two years later, it had 4,200 employees and accounted for nearly half of the state's casino revenues. The Washington Redskins play at FedEx Field in nearby Landover, with tentative plans to move to a more luxurious stadium elsewhere in the region. Although a Supreme Court ruling in 2017 protected its nickname, local governments remained hostile, though some were willing to discuss growth options.

Prince George's County is affluent by national standards. Its median household income of $78,607 easily tops the national median of about $57,652 and is nearly double the national median for black households. Nearly 32 percent of the county population over 25 holds an undergraduate degree, which is slightly higher than the national average. Housing finance continues to plague Prince

George's. In September 2016, 26 percent of the homes in the county were underwater, compared with 18 percent in all of Maryland.

The 4th Congressional District of Maryland includes most of Prince George's County inside the Capital Beltway that rings Washington, and a GOP-leaning eastern salient into relatively rural central Anne Arundel County, including Severna Park. This is still a safely Democratic seat; Hillary Clinton carried Prince George's by an extraordinary 89%-8% in 2016. On certain social issues, however, the district is more conservative: While a 2012 referendum legalizing same-sex marriage in Maryland passed statewide with 52 percent of the vote, it narrowly failed in Prince George's County. The district's biggest employer is the federal government. Suitland, just across the D.C. border, is the home of the Census Bureau, and local and state officials have tried to lure the FBI, which plans to move from its longtime downtown Washington headquarters.

Steny Hoyer (D)

Elected 1981, 19th full term, b. Jun 14, 1939; New York, NY; University of Maryland - College Park, B.S., 1963; Georgetown University Law Center (DC), J.D., 1966; Baptist; Widower (Judith Pickett); 3 children; 3 grandchildren; 2 great-grandchildren.

Elected Office: MD Senate, 1966-1979, President, 1975-1978.

Professional Career: Practicing attorney, 1966-1980; MD Board of Higher Ed., 1978-1981.

DC Office: 1705 LHOB 20515, 202-225-4131, Fax: 202-225-4300, hoyer.house.gov

State Offices: Greenbelt, 301-474-0119; White Plains, 301-843-1577.

Committees: House Majority Leader.

Group Ratings

	ADA	ACLU	AFL-CIO	LCV	ITI	COC	HAFA	ACU	CFG	FRC
2018	-	82%	-	63%	-	50%	6%	5%	20%	0%
2017	90%	C	100%	97%	C	43%	C	4%	5%	0%

Almanac Ratings 2017-18

	Economy	Social	Foreign	Composite
Liberal	98%	100%	89%	96%
Conservative	2%	0%	11%	4%

Key Votes of the 115th Congress

1. Obama-care revision	N	5. Family planning regs	N	9. Guantanamo prisoners	Y
2. Tax Cuts	N	6. Body cameras/immigration	Y	10. Ground missiles, limit	Y
3. Omnibus appropriations	N	7. Abortion ban	N	11. Defense Dept. spending	Y
4. Dodd-Frank revision	N	8. Concealed carry	N	12. FISA rules	Y

Election Results

Election	Name (Party)	Vote (%)		Cand. Spent	Ind. Exp. Support	Ind. Exp. Oppose
2018 General	Steny Hoyer (D)............................... 213,796	(70%)		$1,708,457		
	William Devine III (R)........................ 82,361	(27%)				
2018 Primary	Steny Hoyer (D)............................... 72,493	(84%)				
	Dennis Fritz (D)............................... 13,681	(16%)				

Prior winning percentages: 2016 (67%), 2014 (64%), 2012 (69%), 2010 (64%), 2008 (74%), 2006 (83%), 2004 (69%), 2002(69%), 2000 (65%), 1998 (65%), 1996 (56.9%), 1994 (58.8%), 1992 (53%), 1990 (81%), 1988 (79%), 1986 (81.9%), 1984 (72%), 1982 (80%); 1981 special (56%)

Democrat Steny Hoyer, elected in 1981, is the longest-serving Democrat in the House. He is the majority leader and de facto leader of his party's moderate wing in the House, and he is at heart a bipartisan deal-cutter despite his role as a public critic of Republicans. He has remained part of the aging and entrenched Democratic leadership that regained House control in 2018, despite growing calls for generational transition.

Hoyer is of Danish descent. His first name, he says, was his parents' adaptation of the Danish name Steen. He grew up in New York City, but moved from place to place with his mother and stepfather, who was in the Air Force and, when Steny was in high school, was transferred from Florida to Andrews Air Force Base in Maryland. Hoyer graduated from the University of Maryland, where in 1959 he listened to Democratic presidential candidate John F. Kennedy deliver a campaign speech that inspired him to switch his major from public relations to political science. While working on his law degree at Georgetown University, Hoyer interned one summer with Maryland Sen. Daniel Brewster. Another intern in Brewster's office that summer was Nancy D'Alesandro, daughter of the former mayor of Baltimore and now House Speaker Nancy Pelosi.

In 1966, just after graduating from law school, Hoyer was elected to the Maryland Senate at age 27. He was Senate president from 1975 to 1978, the youngest person to hold that post in Maryland history. In 1978, he ran for lieutenant governor on a losing ticket. In 1981, after Rep. Gladys Spellman was incapacitated by a heart attack, the 5th District seat was declared vacant. Hoyer won the special election, edging out Spellman's husband and several other Democrats in the primary and beating a well-financed Republican in the general. Only three Republican members have more seniority in the House. Sen. Patrick Leahy of Vermont is the only congressional Democrat who has served longer.

Hoyer was also a fast riser in Congress. He excelled at constituent service and won a seat on the Appropriations Committee, where he worked with Republicans and became a champion for the Washington metro area. He has been an advocate of more spending for education and other social programs, and better pay and benefits for federal workers. He was the chief House sponsor of the Americans with Disabilities Act of 1990, which outlawed discrimination against people with disabilities. He counts that as his greatest legislative achievement, along with the 2002 federal election reform known as the Help America Vote Act. On Sept. 11, 2001, it was Hoyer's idea to have lawmakers gather in front of the Capitol in a show of unity. The group spontaneously sang "God Bless America," an image captured vividly on television on a dark day in U.S. history.

His voting record is relatively moderate among Democrats. He broke with the party by supporting the balanced budget amendment in 1995. He has backed many of the free-trade initiatives that organized labor opposed, including the North American Free Trade Agreement, though in 2015 he voted against expedited action on the Trans-Pacific Partnership. In 2002, he voted to authorize military action in Iraq and later complained that President George W. Bush "under-resourced" the war. He is a former chairman of the Helsinki Commission, and has remained a champion of human rights around the world.

Hoyer was selected in 1989 as chairman of the Democratic Caucus. When he tried to move up to the job of majority whip in 1991, he lost, 160-109, to David Bonior of Michigan. In 2001, Bonior, faced with unfavorable redistricting changes at home, decided to run for governor. Both Hoyer and Pelosi sought to replace him as minority whip. Hoyer argued that he had greater experience in leadership positions and could do a better job of unifying the caucus. With her stronger base among women and in her adopted state of California, Pelosi won 118-95.

When Pelosi ran to succeed Dick Gephardt as minority leader in 2002, Hoyer ran to succeed her as minority whip. He collected commitments for months and was elected unanimously. In that position, it was his job to be partisan, and he often was. As Hoyer conceded in 2010, as he was being criticized by Republicans, "I think both parties have acted defensively in some respects when they were in the majority." In the pivotal 2006 campaign, Hoyer worked closely with Illinois Rep. Rahm Emanuel, who chaired the committee to elect a Democratic majority. Many of the freshmen subsequently credited the help that Hoyer provided, especially those from swing districts where liberal Democratic leaders were not always welcome.

When it came time to elect leaders to the new Democratic-controlled House, Hoyer had to fight for majority leader against Pennsylvania Rep. John Murtha, who was a close ally of incoming Speaker Pelosi. In spite of their years working together, Pelosi and Hoyer still viewed each other with suspicion. Hoyer had little choice but to speak positively about his longstanding relationship with her — he called her a "favorite daughter" of Maryland — and their success in largely unifying an often-unruly party. But he left no doubt about his dismay over her arm-twisting for Murtha. Hoyer prevailed 149-86, a powerful endorsement of him for majority leader and a restraint on Pelosi. Hoyer won the support of many California Democrats who had been unified behind Pelosi and of numerous prospective committee chairmen who doubted Murtha's ability to do the job.

As majority leader, Hoyer assumed responsibility for determining the floor schedule, helping guide Democratic initiatives to passage, and holding weekly press briefings. He described his recipe for holding together what had historically been a fractious caucus this way: "First of all, work very hard on communications, find out what people can do and can't do. Secondly, put together a consensus that, while it may not be the first choice of everybody, it is a choice they can live with." And for the most part, the record justified his boast that House Democrats during their four years in the majority were "the most unified the Democratic Party has been in over half a century."

He actively pushed a "Make It in America" package of Democratic bills to boost U.S. manufacturers, with several becoming law. In early 2009, working with Pelosi, Hoyer steered to passage the $787 billion economic stimulus legislation, the first major initiative of the Obama administration. Only 11 House Democrats voted against it, and every Republican opposed it. He had a hand in the Democrats' successful efforts to increase the hourly minimum wage and in the adoption of most of the 9/11 commission's homeland security and intelligence-reform recommendations. When Democrats lost their majority in 2010, Pelosi returned to minority leader and Hoyer to whip. Hoyer came out in favor of same-sex marriage in 2012, shortly before his daughter, Stefany Hoyer Hemmer, announced publicly that she is a lesbian.

More inclined to defer to committee chairs and hew to regular order than Pelosi, he supported doing away with term limits for committee leaders, which the Republicans imposed when they were in the majority. At his urging, Pelosi agreed to their repeal in late 2008. "I am not for term limits for chairmen," Hoyer said. "It puts intellect on hold."

Hoyer has fine political instincts, works hard and can speak in an old-fashioned, patriotic style that can be genuinely moving. With Democrats returned to the minority, he drew criticism from some conservatives for his rhetoric on the GOP's hardline stance on "fiscal cliff" budget negotiations shortly after the December 2012 school massacre in Newtown Connecticut. "It's somewhat like taking your child hostage and saying to somebody else, 'I'm going to shoot my child if you don't do what I want done,'" Hoyer said of Republicans. When John Boehner stepped down as Speaker in 2015, Hoyer called it "a bad day for the House" and praised him as a "positive legislator."

Over the years, Hoyer has remained unable to edge out Pelosi in the leadership. As Democrats' prospects to regain majority control dimmed, speculation occasionally swirled that Pelosi would give up her party post and Hoyer would become her successor. But she continued to stay on. Some Democrats believe that one reason Pelosi did not walk away is that she did not want Hoyer to take the top spot. Their lengthy reign has frustrated the ambitions of junior House Democrats.

Hoyer got the better of Pelosi in November 2014 in the internal jockeying among House Democrats to succeed California's Henry Waxman as ranking member on the Energy and Commerce Committee. Pelosi lobbied on behalf of her close friend, fellow Californian Anna Eshoo, while Hoyer backed New Jersey's Frank Pallone. Hoyer's ability to count votes is "unmatched," a grateful Pallone said. "Hoyer, he's a shark who never sleeps. ... He's a shark with a killer disposition," Missouri Democrat Emanuel Cleaver, a senior Black Caucus member, told Politico.

A month later, Hoyer worked across the aisle to help President Barack Obama get a massive spending bill into law. Pelosi and other liberals objected to the measure, dubbed a "cromnibus," in large part because it loosened regulations on Wall Street banks. Occasionally, he parted company with Obama, including the "sequestration" of defense spending, which he called "totally unacceptable and irresponsible."

Hoyer played an active role in the 2018 campaign, which resulted in the Democrats' return to House control. As a candidate recruiter, he worked with national and local party groups to identify preferred candidates in battleground districts. That led to complaints by some contenders, as when Hoyer was recorded on tape urging Levi Tillerman of Colorado to step aside for Jason Crow, an Army veteran and the favorite of the party establishment, who ultimately defeated Tillerman and Republican Rep. Mike Coffman. For Democrats, Hoyer told reporters, the objective was "making sure that we have a Democrat that can win in districts that are tough."

With Democratic candidates often distancing themselves from Pelosi during the 2018 campaign, Hoyer took the opportunity to advise many of them and appear at campaign events. He revived his "Make It in America" theme and cited the success of centrist Democratic Rep. Conor Lamb, the special election winner in a Pennsylvania district that Donald Trump won in 2016. Hoyer sometimes was more open than was Pelosi to negotiating with Trump, as with the dispute over the border wall with Mexico. On occasion, he could be a harsh critic of Trump. He attacked some of his language as "racist" and said that Trump's July 2018 meeting in Helsinki with Russian president Vladimir Putin was "treasonous."

Once again, Democratic victory created tension for Hoyer with Pelosi following the 2018 election. When she agreed to term limits for Democratic leaders in order to secure the final votes that she needed to assure that she would become Speaker, Hoyer objected to formalizing the agreement or to extending it beyond Pelosi. "She's not negotiating for me," Hoyer told reporters. Implicitly, at least, he had made himself available if Pelosi failed to secure sufficient support or stepped aside. He also found himself in something of a squeeze when Rep. James Clyburn of South Carolina, the third-ranking Democratic leader, suggested that he was considering a move up the leadership ladder. In any case, the top three leaders regained the leadership positions that they had held in the majority a decade earlier, with all three preparing to turn 80 before the 2020 election.

In his district, Hoyer has pushed for funding Chesapeake Bay cleanup. He has worked shrewdly to maintain and increase jobs at the Goddard Space Flight Center in Greenbelt, at Naval Air Station Patuxent River, and at the Naval Surface Warfare Center at Indian Head. He sponsored bills allowing more federal employees to work four-day weeks, granting eight weeks of paid parental leave, and raising the government contribution to its employees' health care premiums. He kept his hand in other Maryland political campaigns, and usually but not always prevailed.

The last time Hoyer had serious competition in a general election was 1992, the first election after his district was reconfigured to extend beyond Prince George's County. He has won easily since then, and he has gained the loyalty of African-American voters in Democratic primaries. That could offer him security in the Maryland redistricting wars. Still, the endgame for his leadership ambitions and tenure in the House remained to be determined.

MD-5: Southern Maryland

Cook Partisan Voting Index: D+16

Population		Race and Ethnicity		Income	
Total	759,228	White	45.8%	Median Income	$95,144
Land area (sq. miles)	1,481	Black	37.7%	District Income Rank	21
Pop/ sq mi	512.6	Latino	8.4%	Poverty Rate	7.3%
Born in State	38.5%	Asian	4.2%	With health insurance	93.4%
		Two or more races	3.3%	Cash public assistance	2%
Age Groups		Other	0.5%	Food stamp/SNAP	7.9%
Under 18	22.8%				
18-34	23%	**Education**		**Work**	
35-64	41.7%	H.S grad or less	35.7%	White Collar	12.5%
Over 64	12.5%	Some college	29.8%	Sales and Service	39.3%
Military		College Degree, 4 yr	19.7%	Blue Collar	16.8%
Veteran/ Active Duty	12.2%	Post grad	14.8%	Government	29.7%

2012 Pres. Vote	Obama	234,859	(66%)	Romney	114,536	(32%)		
2016 Pres. Vote	Clinton	225,989	(63%)	Trump	115,869	(32%)	Johnson 9,375	(3%)

Prince George's County: Southern Maryland was established as a colony of the British Lords Baltimore, who were seeking a refuge for English Catholics in the New World. The Lords Baltimore, first George and then Cecil Calvert, founded St. Mary's in 1634, not long after the founding of Jamestown and Plymouth. Maryland became one of the two great Chesapeake tobacco colonies, with plantation houses on every inlet off the broad Potomac and Patuxent rivers. For years, the towns of southern Maryland grew slowly, and even today, many of their residents are directly descended from the old families. The region was never Puritan country. Liquor flowed even during Prohibition, and for years, Maryland law specifically allowed slot machines. But tobacco farming is nearing an end.

The area's economic base has owed much to government installations: the Civil War Point Lookout prisoner-of-war camp; the Navy's Patuxent River complex, which started as a center for aircraft testing and where many astronauts began their training; and the Naval Air Warfare Center. Metro Washington and Baltimore have been spreading into southern Maryland. The 2010 census showed rapid growth in Calvert, Charles and St. Mary's counties. Charles County has become the new home of many African-American families fleeing crime and troubled schools in Prince George's County. Today, most of Charles County's schoolchildren are black. Its median household income rose to $94,000 in 2017, thanks in part to many two-government-employee families. The economy in St. Mary's has been bolstered by about 22,000 employees at the Patuxent River facility. District-wide, more than 62,000 residents are federal employees. Chesapeake Bay is vital to the local economy. St.

Mary's has become a site for restoration of oyster beds, with increased use of aquaculture along the inlets. The cultivation helps to clean the bay.

The 5th Congressional District of Maryland comprises all of Calvert, Charles and St. Mary's counties, plus most of Prince George's County outside the Capital Beltway and a small part of southern Anne Arundel County. Prince George's, with about 40 percent of the population, and Charles, with 20 percent, are the largest and most Democratic counties in the district. The three smaller ones lean Republican. The district takes in College Park, home of the University of Maryland, and nearby Hyattsville, Greenbelt, Beltsville and Bowie. On the bay, it stops just short of Annapolis. Whites in the rural areas have trended Republican, but African Americans — both new suburbanites and descendants of old southern Maryland families — make up 38 percent of the district's population. The district has been a Democratic stronghold for decades.

David Trone (D)

Elected 2018, 1st term, b. Sep 21, 1955; Cheverly; Furman University (SC), B.A., 1977; University of Pennsylvania Wharton School of Business (PA), M.B.A., 1985; Lutheran; Married (June Trone); 4 children.

Professional Career: Founder & Owner, Total Wine & More.

DC Office: 1213 LHOB 20515, 202-225-2721, trone.house.gov

State Offices: Gaithersburg, 301-926-0300.

Committees: *Education & Labor:* Civil Rights & Human Services; Higher Education & Workforce Investment. *Foreign Affairs:* Europe, Eurasia, Energy & the Environment; Middle East, North Africa & International Terrorism. *Joint Economic.*

Election Results

Election	Name (Party)	Vote (%)		Cand. Spent	Ind. Exp. Support	Ind. Exp. Oppose
2018 General	David Trone (D)................................	163,346	(59%)	$18,770,743		
	Amie Hoeber (R)................................	105,209	(38%)		$898,951	$1,237,808
2018 Primary	David Trone (D)................................	24,103	(40%)			
	Aruna Miller (D)................................	18,524	(31%)			
	Nadia Hashimi (D)................................	6,304	(11%)			
	Roger Manno (D)................................	6,257	(10%)			

Democrat David Trone spent a record amount — mostly his own money — to win his House seat. For the co-owner of a large chain of wine and beverage stores, the victory marked his first success in campaign politics. In 2016, he spent nearly as much of his own money to seek the open seat in an adjacent Maryland district. That initial appeal as a political outsider fell short in the Democratic primary to Jamie Raskin. With his victory on his second attempt, he replaced Rep. John Delaney, another wealthy financier from the Washington suburbs, who retired to seek the Democratic presidential nomination in 2020.

Trone grew up on a farm in Pennsylvania. He graduated from Furman University and got his master's in business administration from the Wharton School at the University of Pennsylvania. His father lost the family farm to financial difficulties. But Trone went into business at a soda and beer store that his mother took over after his parents separated. In 1984, he converted that store into Beer World, a large retail shop. That was the start of a multi-state beverage empire that Trone developed with his brother Robert, and eventually rebranded as Total Wine and More. As co-owners of the largest private wine retailer in the nation, with nearly 200 stores, they became very wealthy.

In 2016, Trone sought the Democratic nomination in the heavily Democratic 8th District, when Chris Van Hollen gave up the seat in his successful run for the Senate. His opponents were Raskin, a law professor and state legislator, and Kathleen Matthews, who spent many years as a broadcast-news reporter and anchor. Spending more than $13 million of his own money to craft his outsider appeal,

Trone's self-financing became a major controversy in the campaign. Raskin won the primary with 34 percent of the vote to 27 percent for Trone and 24 percent for Matthews; he breezed to election in November.

When Delaney decided to retire, Trone's second try had several similarities—including his self-financing, a leading opponent who served in the Legislature and a district that was nearly as Democratic. This time, Trone was well-known in the urban core of the district, though he needed to get acquainted in the more-sprawling rural areas. His campaign message was familiar. In addition to his opposition to the Trump administration, he called for increased funding for the National Institutes of Health and local transportation projects.

In the eight-candidate Democratic primary, Trone's chief opponent was state Delegate Aruna Miller, an immigrant from India as a child. With her progressive agenda, she focused on expanded health care services. She criticized Trone for living in the adjacent district, in addition to his self-financing. With nearly $1.5 million that she raised, plus the support of some unions and environmental groups, Miller had the resources to be competitive. Trone raised $12 million for the primary -- $11.5 million from his own pocket.

Compared to Raskin in 2016, Miller's legislative record and her political appeal were more limited. In the primary results, Miller led Trone by 1,126 votes in Montgomery County, which cast nearly two-thirds of the total vote. But Trone swept nearly half the total vote in the four outlying counties, where he had a lead of more than 6,700 votes over Miller. That gave Trone a 40%-31% victory.

In November, Trone faced Amie Hoeber, onetime head of Army research and development at the Pentagon. Hoeber also self-financed, though with far less money than Trone. Hoeber was not positioned to seriously threaten in this Democratic district. During the fall campaign, Trone was sidelined by kidney surgery, which resulted in a loss of weight and hair. Several million more dollars of largely self-financed advertising—more than $18 million for the cycle-helped him to maintain an active campaign.

MD-6: Western Maryland

Cook Partisan Voting Index: D+6

Population		Race and Ethnicity		Income	
Total	762,155	White	59.1%	Median Income	$77,595
Land area (sq. miles)	1,950	Black	13.1%	District Income Rank	61
Pop/ sq mi	390.8	Latino	13.4%	Poverty Rate	9.4%
Born in State	43.8%	Asian	11%	With health insurance	92.7%
		Two or more races	3%	Cash public assistance	2.5%
Age Groups		Other	0.4%	Food stamp/SNAP	10.7%
Under 18	23.4%				
18-34	21.9%	**Education**		**Work**	
35-64	41.1%	H.S grad or less	33.7%	White Collar	13.6%
Over 64	13.6%	Some college	24.4%	Sales and Service	37.7%
		College Degree, 4 yr	21.7%	Blue Collar	15.5%
Military		Post grad	20.2%	Government	19.9%
Veteran/ Active Duty	7.5%				

2012 Pres. Vote	Obama	176,364	(55%)	Romney	138,539	(43%)			
2016 Pres. Vote	Clinton	189,512	(55%)	Trump	134,827	(39%)	Johnson	10,691	(3%)

D.C. Exurbs: One of America's first frontiers was western Maryland, where the Appalachian ridges that cross the state diagonally from northeast to southwest cut through long sloping fields. The land was settled by Pennsylvania Dutch and Scots-Irish hill people, not Chesapeake Bay tobacco growers. Maryland is where the 19th century's great paths to the interior were staked out: The National Road; the nation's first combined freight and passenger railroad, the Baltimore & Ohio, which crossed the wide valleys of bounteous farms and climbed over the Catoctin Mountains; and the Chesapeake and Ohio Canal, which began operating in 1828, primarily to haul coal from western Maryland to the port of Georgetown in Washington. Towns grew up with narrow streets of row houses amid cornfields, pastureland and ancient mountains.

Across this placid land moved vast armies during the Civil War. In Frederick, city officials paid the Confederates $200,000 not to burn the town, and near Sharpsburg, blue- and-gray-clad soldiers fought the Battle of Antietam on the bloodiest day in American military history. The battle is now commemorated with an annual illumination of 23,000 candles on the battlefield. A century later, without munitions, President Lyndon Johnson unveiled a different kind of War -- on Poverty -- on the steps of City Hall in Cumberland, near the coal-laced hills of Appalachia. Poverty fell here in the 1970s, but conditions worsened in the 1980s with the closure of several large factories. Frederick and Washington counties have seen large increases in Hispanics since 2000. The quickly diversifying population has created tensions: Frederick in 2010 became the first county in Maryland to declare English its official language, as county officials struggled to deal with a rise in illegal immigration. But the growing political influence of the Hispanic migrants, plus farm operators who needed the workers, won a repeal of the language measure in 2015. Montgomery County officials, by contrast, said that they will not honor federal requests to detain immigrants. In far western Garrett County, the adverse impact of hydraulic fracking on local tourism led local groups to urge Gov. Larry Hogan to issue a fracking ban, which he did in March 2018. That area is on the edge of the Marcellus Shale formation.

The 6th Congressional District stretches nearly 200 miles from Republican-leaning western Maryland along the West Virginia border to the Washington D.C. suburbs. Instead of crossing Republican pockets east to Harford County as in the past, Democratic redistricters in 2011 dropped the district south from Frederick into Montgomery County. There, it scoops up heavily Democratic Washington suburbs, including most of affluent Potomac, multicultural Gaithersburg and fast-growing Germantown. Half the district's population lives in suburban Washington. Montgomery County has added diversity: The district has the highest concentration of Asian Americans in the state (11 percent); Hispanics make up 13 percent of its population. With the district transformed into a Democratic-leaning bellwether, Hillary Clinton carried it 55%-39% in 2016. In March 2019, the Supreme Court heard arguments on a lower-court ruling that the district was an unconstitutional partisan gerrymander.

Elijah Cummings (D)

Elected 1996, 12th term, b. Jan 18, 1951; Baltimore; Howard University (DC), B.S., 1973; University of Maryland School of Law, J.D., 1976; Baptist; Married (Maya Rockeymoore); 1 child (1 from previous marriage).

Elected Office: MD House, 1983-1996, speaker pro tem, 1995-1996.

Professional Career: Practicing attorney, 1976-1996; Chief judge, MD Moot Court Board.

DC Office: 2163 RHOB 20515, 202-225-4741, Fax: 202-225-3178, cummings.house.gov

State Offices: Baltimore, 410-685-9199; Catonsville, 410-719-8777; Ellicott City, 410-465-8259.

Committees: *Oversight & Reform (Chmn). Transportation & Infrastructure*: Coast Guard & Maritime Transportation; Railroads, Pipelines & Hazardous Materials.

Group Ratings

	ADA	ACLU	AFL-CIO	LCV	ITI	COC	HAFA	ACU	CFG	FRC
2018	-	88%	-	89%	-	57%	8%	5%	10%	0%
2017	75%	C	96%	63%	C	36%	C	-	9%	0%

Almanac Ratings 2017-18

	Economy	Social	Foreign	Composite
Liberal	85%	84%	50%	73%
Conservative	15%	16%	50%	27%

Key Votes of the 115th Congress

1. Obama-care revision	N	5. Family planning regs	N
2. Tax Cuts	N	6. Body cameras/immigration	NV
3. Omnibus appropriations	NV	7. Abortion ban	N
4. Dodd-Frank revision	N	8. Concealed carry	N

9. Guantanamo prisoners	NV
10. Ground missiles, limit	NV
11. Defense Dept. spending	NV
12. FISA rules	NV

Election Results

Election	Name (Party)	Vote (%)	Cand. Spent	Ind. Exp. Support	Ind. Exp. Oppose
2018 General	Elijah Cummings (D)..................... 202,345	(76%)	$684,174		
	Richmond Davis (R)............................ 56,266	(21%)	$14,856		
	David Griggs (Lib)................................ 5,827	(2%)			
2018 Primary	Elijah Cummings (D)..................... 81,679	(92%)			

Prior winning percentages: 2016 (75%), 2014 (70%), 2012 (77%), 2010 (75%), 2008 (80%), 2006 (98%), 2004 (73%), 2002 (74%), 2000 (87%), 1998 (86%), 1996 (84%)

Democrat Elijah Cummings, who came to Congress in a 1996 special election, is a liberal who can be blunt in dealing with all sides. As chairman of the Oversight and Reform Committee, he faced daunting challenges in managing the investigations of President Donald Trump. Earlier, he parried with Republicans on investigations of the Obama administration that Cummings regularly dismissed as "witch hunts." He occasionally has had a positive relationship with Republican leaders of the committee.

"I'm not trying to do anything extraordinary. I'm trying to do what the Constitution says I'm supposed to do," Cummings told The New York Times in 2018 before taking the gavel and referring to his prospective investigations of Trump. "My saddest thought is that there will be damage done which will not be corrected during my lifetime and perhaps for a long time."

Cummings is the son of sharecroppers from South Carolina who moved north for a better life for their seven children. He grew up in Baltimore, where as an 11-year-old he was one of the first children to integrate a park's swimming pool. "People were throwing bottles, rocks, and screaming, calling us everything but a child of God," he recalled to Baltimore magazine. He graduated Phi Beta Kappa from Howard University, and got a law degree from the University of Maryland. He practiced law in Baltimore, and then in 1982, at age 31, he ran successfully for the House of Delegates, where he served 14 years and rose through the ranks to become speaker pro tem.

He ran for the House after Kweisi Mfume resigned to become president of the NAACP. Cummings' main competition was the Rev. Frank Reid III, stepbrother of Baltimore Mayor Kurt Schmoke, who raised $255,000. Cummings had support from local businesses and community-development organizations, and raised $450,000. He won with 37 percent of the vote to 24 percent for Reid. He has not been seriously challenged in a primary or general election since.

Cummings lives in troubled west Baltimore, and he is a crusader against drug abuse, for stricter gun control, and for help for low-income homeowners. From 2007 to 2010, he chaired the Coast Guard and Maritime Transportation Subcommittee at Transportation and Infrastructure, a useful niche for his port-dependent district. The House unanimously passed his bill in 2009 to reform Coast Guard acquisition practices, and a year later he helped get an authorization bill for the agency into law that included acquisition reforms.

In the 2010 campaign, when some Democrats were de-emphasizing their support of President Barack Obama's health care overhaul, Cummings was doing just the opposite. "I know the media wants us to apologize for being Democrats," he said at one rally. "They want us to apologize for health care. Why? Because the Democratic Party is the humane party."

Cummings became the top Democrat on Oversight after Republicans gained control of the House in 2011. Working alongside the energetic and partisan chairman, Californian Darrell Issa, Cummings pushed back against the GOP on subpoena powers, Democrats' access to records and numerous other matters. But he won respect from Republicans. "It's not about politics to him; he says what he believes," South Carolina Rep. Trey Gowdy told The Hill newspaper. "With Mr. Cummings, it's coming from his soul." In 2017-18, under GOP control of the panel, Cummings got their approval of 64 joint subpoenas.

Cummings did not spare President Barack Obama in his committee work. He took part in several bipartisan investigations in which he rebuked the administration for management deficiencies. He publicly battled with Edward DeMarco, overseer of government-backed mortgage giants Fannie Mae and Freddie Mac, over debt reduction for homeowners struggling to pay mortgages.

GOP lawmakers voted in 2012 to hold Attorney General Eric Holder in contempt of Congress for refusing to provide information relating to "Operation Fast and Furious," a botched effort to trace guns to drug cartels and smugglers that instead allowed firearms to cross the border into their hands. Cummings was among Holder's chief defenders, saying the attorney general "acted honorably." Cummings wrote Issa an angry letter saying that he was "more interested in perpetuating your partisan political feud in the press than in obtaining any specific substantive information." When Republicans subsequently went after the Internal Revenue Service for targeting conservative groups and Cummings began to speak at a hearing, Issa abruptly adjourned the session, ordering staffers to cut off the Democrat's microphone. The Congressional Black Caucus rose to Cummings' defense to demand that Issa be stripped of his chairmanship and publicly apologize. Issa apologized to Cummings.

When Rep. Jason Chaffetz of Utah took over as committee chairman in January 2015, he promised that he would work more cooperatively with Democrats. Chaffetz earlier spent a day with Cummings in his Baltimore district to get to know him better. "Chaffetz is a good guy," he told local residents. But at the panel's first meeting, Chaffetz pushed through a rules package that Cummings complained was "worse than the rules we had under Chairman Issa." Cummings and other Democrats tried and failed to roll back the chairman's unilateral authority to subpoena witnesses or documents.

For all of his partisan rhetoric, Cummings occasionally has shown a pragmatic streak in building bipartisan coalitions on legislation. He helped secure enactment in 2014 of the DATA Act, which requires federal agencies to publish spending information online in a searchable format. In 2016, he was chief sponsor of a bill to grant whistleblower protections for federal contractors.

The April 2015 death of Freddie Gray and subsequent riots in his hometown increased pressure on Cummings to help resolve conflicts, both immediate and more deep-seated. He joined marches and engaged with protesters, many of whom were his neighbors. "I am telling you we will not rest until we address this and see that justice is done," he said during an emotional speech at Gray's funeral.

Cummings usually wins reelection by landslide margins. In 2016, he was viewed as having considerable influence in the Democratic primary to succeed the retiring Sen. Barbara Mikulski, either as a potential candidate or as a king-maker. Instead, he remained neutral, which many viewed as a boost for Rep. Chris Van Hollen, who ultimately defeated African-American Rep. Donna Edwards. He also turned down the opportunity to run for mayor of Baltimore.

In national politics, Cummings in 2016 chaired the drafting committee for the Democratic platform, where he had the dicey responsibility of mediating between Hillary Clinton, whom he had supported during the campaign, and Sen. Bernie Sanders. With the platform, he continued his role that the Baltimore Sun described as "a kind of defense attorney for the Obama administration." The final platform was largely embraced by most Democrats, though the party faced other problems in the election.

Cummings found numerous opportunities to challenge Trump. After the director of the Office of Government Ethics in January 2017 raised questions about the president-elect's compliance with federal ethics requirements, Cummings called for a public hearing and attacked Republicans for calling the director to account while failing to investigate any of Trump's "massive global entanglements." With Democratic Sen. Ben Cardin of Maryland, he urged the creation of an independent commission to review charges of Russian hacking of computer systems during the election.

As he took the gavel to chair the committee, Cummings served notice that his interests were wide-ranging. In an initial set of letters to Trump administration officials, he requested information on topics such as family separation of migrants at the border, the handling of hurricane storm damage and the White House decision to revoke the security clearances of high-ranking former officials who became Trump critics. In May 2019, Cummings said that Trump's defiance of House Democratic demands for information in numerous inquiries had led to a "constitutional crisis." A federal judge that month rejected a challenge by the president's lawyers to a subpoena from Cummings's committee that called for Trump's accounting firm to deliver eight years of his pre-presidential financial records. In June, his committee voted to hold in contempt Attorney General William Barr and Commerce Secretary Wilbur Ross for their failure to respond to a subpoena calling for documents related to the 2020 Census. But Cummings seemed to embrace the caution of Speaker Nancy Pelosi in seeking specific steps against Trump.

Some Democrats have viewed the combative Cummings as a potential contender for a House leadership slot whenever the party's aging leaders step down. Aside from the fact that the current House Speaker is a native of Baltimore and the majority leader is from southern Maryland, potential leadership opportunities for Cummings have been limited by serious knee and heart ailments that kept him away from the Capitol for several months in 2017-18. Whatever his title, Cummings has served notice that he will demand attention.

MD-7: Baltimore Metro

Cook Partisan Voting Index: D+26

Population		Race and Ethnicity		Income	
Total	726,536	White	33.3%	Median Income	$60,903
Land area (sq. miles)	488	Black	53.3%	District Income Rank	169
Pop/ sq mi	1488.7	Latino	3.7%	Poverty Rate	16.6%
Born in State	62%	Asian	7.1%	With health insurance	93.5%
Age Groups		Two or more races	2.1%	Cash public assistance	4.2%
Under 18	21.6%	Other	0.5%	Food stamp/SNAP	19.3%
18-34	24.6%	**Education**		**Work**	
35-64	39.2%	H.S grad or less	37.7%	White Collar	14.6%
Over 64	14.6%	Some college	24.6%	Sales and Service	40.4%
Military		College Degree, 4 yr	19.9%	Blue Collar	13.4%
Veteran/ Active Duty	6.8%	Post grad	17.7%	Government	21%

2012 Pres. Vote	Obama	257,222	(76%)	Romney	76,446	(23%)		
2016 Pres. Vote	Clinton	233,796	(74%)	Trump	63,444	(20%)	Johnson	7,795 (3%)

Western and Northern Baltimore: At the junction of North and South, Baltimore is a product of both European immigration and the migration of African Americans from the South. Its black community has a rich history. The Afro-American newspaper has been published there for more than 100 years, and there was once a black symphony orchestra. Eubie Blake, one of the founders of ragtime music, grew up in Baltimore and has a museum in his honor on Charles Street. Jazz great Billie Holiday; Cab Calloway, the 1930s and 1940s big band leader; and Thurgood Marshall, the country's first African-American Supreme Court justice, all had roots in Baltimore. Near downtown on the west side is the childhood home of slugger Babe Ruth and the home of writer H.L. Mencken. For decades, this side of town had a biracial, bipartisan politics in which Democrats like Gov. Albert Ritchie and Republicans like Gov. Theodore McKeldin competed zestfully for black and white votes. Baltimore has been a black majority city since the late 1970s.

In the 1990s, the city was hit by a crime wave, with open drug markets on both the west and east sides. The city's gritty side was vividly depicted in HBO's acclaimed crime drama The Wire. In a 2016 report, the Baltimore City Paper found that 85 percent of the more than 2,500 murder victims in Baltimore during the previous decade were African-American males, and 87 percent of them were killed by people using firearms. The homicide rate in 2017 remained the worst in the nation, though local leaders projected a decline in 2018. The city has lost 6 percent of its population since 2000, and is down more than a third from its peak in 1950.

Community anger exploded in April 2015 following the death of Freddie Gray, a young black man who had suffered serious injuries in a police wagon after he had been arrested. The initial response was a series of marches and peaceful protests throughout the west side of the city, especially the Sandtown-Winchester neighborhood. The response turned violent as demonstrators smashed storefront windows, threw rocks at police and damaged their cruisers as officers made dozens of arrests. Mayor Stephanie Rawlings-Blake was slow to increase security before she imposed a curfew for several nights. Gov. Larry Hogan declared a state of emergency and sent in 3,000 National Guard troops following a request from the mayor. Their presence generally restored order. Subsequently, six Baltimore police officers were indicted for their role in the death of Gray. The first trial resulted in a hung jury and the next three trials produced acquittals of three police officers. State prosecutor Marilyn Mosby dropped the remaining charges. "For those that believe I'm anti-police, it's simply not the case. I'm anti-police brutality," she said.

In the local aftermath, Hogan and Rawlings-Blake unveiled a plan to demolish about 4,000 abandoned properties and make available $600 million, mostly state-financed, to encourage redevelopment in the Sandtown-Winchester area. In August 2016, Washington Post columnist Courtland Milloy visited the area and wrote "of a neighborhood being transformed, a sense of community beginning to be reborn despite the social and economic problems that linger." In January 2018, Mayor Catherine Pugh complained that crime remained too high and she fired the police commissioner. But the successor lasted only four months and he pleaded guilty in December for failing to file federal income taxes for three years. In May 2019, Pugh resigned after facing problems with her health plus ethics allegations about her hefty income from book sales. Pugh resigned on May 2.

Maryland's 7th Congressional District includes most of Baltimore's west side, plus the heavily African-American suburbs west of the city and extending to Catonsville along the old Baltimore National Pike. It includes much of suburban Howard County. About 40 percent of the district's votes are cast in Baltimore city's precincts, largely north of Pratt Street and including Charles Village, which is home to Johns Hopkins University. Baltimore County and Howard County each cast about 30 percent. Howard County is quite a different area. It grew 32 percent in the 1990s, and another 29 percent since then. Its largest community, Columbia, is a planned town that attracts a culturally liberal population that tends to vote Democratic. In July 2016, Ellicott City was devastated by a "1,000-year flood" that ravaged much of its historic downtown. In a tragic repetition, the city was rocked by flooding in May 2018 that caused further destruction. State and local officials explored alternatives for rebuilding. Preservationists opposed the tear-down of 10 vulnerable buildings.

Jamie Raskin (D)

Elected 2016, 2nd term, b. Dec 13, 1962; Washington, D.C., DC; Harvard College (MA), B.A., 1983; Harvard University Law School (MA), J.D., 1987; Married (Sarah Raskin); 3 children.

Elected Office: MD Senate, 2007-2016, Majority Whip, 2012-2016; MA Assistant Attorney General, 1987-1989.

Professional Career: Law Professor, American University, 1990-2017.

DC Office: 412 CHOB 20515, 202-225-5341, raskin.house.gov

State Offices: Rockville, 301-354-1000.

Committees: *House Administration. Joint Printing. Judiciary*: Antitrust, Commercial & Administrative Law; Constitution, Civil Rights & Civil Liberties. *Oversight & Reform*: Government Operations; Subcommittee on Civil Rights & Civil Liberties (Chmn). *Rules*.

Group Ratings

	ADA	ACLU	AFL-CIO	LCV	ITI	COC	HAFA	ACU	CFG	FRC
2018	-	91%	-	97%	-	50%	9%	8%	17%	0%
2017	100%	C	97%	100%	C	36%	C	7%	5%	0%

Almanac Ratings 2017-18

	Economy	Social	Foreign	Composite
Liberal	100%	100%	97%	99%
Conservative	0%	0%	3%	1%

Key Votes of the 115th Congress

1. Obama-care revision	N	5. Family planning regs	N	9. Guantanamo prisoners	Y
2. Tax Cuts	N	6. Body cameras/immigration	Y	10. Ground missiles, limit	Y
3. Omnibus appropriations	N	7. Abortion ban	N	11. Defense Dept. spending	N
4. Dodd-Frank revision	N	8. Concealed carry	N	12. FISA rules	N

Election Results

Election	Name (Party)	Vote (%)		Cand. Spent	Ind. Exp. Support	Ind. Exp. Oppose
2018 General	Jamie Raskin (D)............................ 217,679	(68%)		$609,975		
	John Walsh (R).................................. 96,525	(30%)				
2018 Primary	Jamie Raskin (D)................................ 81,071	(91%)				
	Summer Spring (D)............................... 5,239	(6%)				

Prior winning percentages: 2016 (61%)

Democrat Jamie Raskin was elected in 2016. In a district that is several miles from the Capitol, he has been familiar with Congress as a law professor and one-time House staffer, and as a veteran Maryland state legislator. His impressive collection of assignments for a second-termer positioned him at the center of the House's potential challenges to Donald Trump — in terms of the president's governance, plus his compliance with constitutional and statutory requirements. Raskin has demonstrable expertise in those areas.

A native of Washington D.C., Raskin got his bachelor's and law degrees from Harvard University, where he was editor of the law review. During college, he was an intern for the House Judiciary Committee. He joined American University's Washington College of Law as a faculty member, specializing in constitutional law. He has written widely about legal topics, including Overruling Democracy: The Supreme Court versus the American People and We the Students: Supreme Court Cases For and About America's Students. From 2001 to 2005, he chaired the Maryland Higher Education Labor Relations Board. In 2006, he ran for the state Senate and defeated the 32-year incumbent in the Democratic primary. He served as majority whip and spent much of his time building legislative coalitions, which passed proposals such as mandatory minimums for drug sentencing, strict gun control with background checks, and environmental standards for state agencies and institutions to follow in their purchasing and other operations. His wife, Sarah Bloom Raskin, was deputy secretary of the Treasury during the Obama administration.

After Democratic Rep. Chris Van Hollen decided to run for the Senate, Raskin was the early frontrunner for the seat. But the Democratic primary became unexpectedly competitive and very expensive. Raskin ran as the progressive candidate with a grassroots network among the many liberal activists in the Washington suburbs.

His two chief opponents were both political neophytes in the district, though each had a well-known profile. Kathleen Matthews spent many years as a broadcast-news reporter and anchor, and before that with Marriott as a public-relations executive. David Trone launched the Total Wine and More retail stores as a family business, which made him very wealthy. Matthews used her close connections to the Democratic establishment — abetted by her husband Chris Matthews, the veteran broadcast pundit and writer — to become a prolific fundraiser. She raised $2.7 million, including $600,000 in self-financing. Trone raised a record sum for a congressional primary: $13.4 million, all but $7,000 of which came from his own pocket. Raskin raised $2.5 million.

Raskin won the April primary, with 34 percent of the vote to 27 percent for Trone and 24 percent for Matthews. The general election gained scant attention, with little-known Republican Dan Cox raising $73,000, and losing 61%-34%. (Trone self-financed a similar sum in 2018 to win election to an open seat in the adjacent 6th District.)

With limited legislative opportunities in the minority, Raskin spent much of his first two years supporting Democratic candidates seeking House seats in 2018. His Democracy Summer project sent student interns to work for challengers in battleground districts. Following that election, he won a Democratic Caucus leadership post representing recently elected lawmakers and giving them more input with leadership. Raskin organized monthly meetings of that group.

In the majority, Raskin gained four committee assignments — an unusually large total under House rules. He circumvented the limitations with selections by Speaker Nancy Pelosi to the Rules and House Administration committees, both of which are "arms of the leadership." He remained a member of the Judiciary and Oversight and Reform committees. On the latter, he became chairman of the newly created Civil Rights and Civil Liberties Subcommittee, where he planned oversight of constitutional issues, he said, "at a time when our most precious values are under attack." At Judiciary, he became vice chairman of the Constitution, Civil Rights and Civil Liberties Subcommittee, whose similar domain has more of a legislative focus.

Raskin's multiple assignments had common threads: committee work to which he brought his expertise in constitutional law, plus leadership assignments that emphasized his partisan activism and insider knowledge. That unusual combination of skills and interests gave Raskin a wide-ranging presence. Although he cautioned that impeachment resolutions from other House Democrats were premature, Raskin told an interviewer even before Trump took office that the president's personal finances — specifically, a gift or payment from a foreign government — could become an impeachable offense.

Among the bills that Raskin has filed are a ban on federal officials from staying at properties owned by Trump's business and creation of a congressional commission of physicians and psychiatrists to conduct a complete medical exam to determine the president's fitness for the job — subject to the 25th Amendment to the Constitution, which provides for presidential succession.

With his focus on constitutional challenges, Raskin hoped to resume his classroom teaching. But, he said in a November 2018 interview with Bethesda Magazine, "I don't think it would be responsible for me to be teaching — even though it is acceptable within the rules of Congress — as long as Donald Trump is president. Once we get through the continuing crisis of the republic we're living through now, then I could contemplate it." He added that such an opportunity was at least a couple of years away.

MD-8: Northern D.C. Suburbs   **Cook Partisan Voting Index: D+14**

Population		Race and Ethnicity		Income	
Total	759,725	White	60.7%	Median Income	$100,728
Land area (sq. miles)	860	Black	11.9%	District Income Rank	13
Pop/ sq mi	883.6	Latino	14.8%	Poverty Rate	6.8%
Born in State	33%	Asian	9.2%	With health insurance	92.7%
		Two or more races	2.7%	Cash public assistance	1.3%
Age Groups		Other	0.7%	Food stamp/SNAP	5.7%
Under 18	22.6%				
18-34	20.5%	**Education**		**Work**	
35-64	41.4%	H.S grad or less	25.7%	White Collar	15.5%
Over 64	15.5%	Some college	20%	Sales and Service	33.5%
		College Degree, 4 yr	25.1%	Blue Collar	11.9%
Military		Post grad	29.2%	Government	21.8%
Veteran/ Active Duty	6.8%				

2012 Pres. Vote	Obama	222,125	(62%)	Romney	127,542	(36%)		
2016 Pres. Vote	Clinton	235,137	(63%)	Trump	112,612	(30%)	Johnson	11,143	(3%)

Montgomery County, Frederick: Colonial farmers once rolled barrels of tobacco to the port of Georgetown in Maryland, along an old road that is today the commercial spine of one of America's most affluent and best-educated areas. Wisconsin Avenue begins at the Potomac River in Washington D.C., traverses the city, and then becomes Rockville Pike after it passes over the Capital Beltway in Montgomery County. The foundation of the economy here is the federal government, with its huge facilities and ongoing construction projects — Walter Reed National Military Medical Center (which merged with Bethesda Naval Hospital), the National Institutes of Health and the Food and Drug Administration. Montgomery is a center of America's biotech industry, the home of firms such as Human Genome Sciences which, with the Human Genome Project, pioneered the study of the human genetic code. Defense contractor Lockheed Martin, with 4,700 employees, is the only manufacturing company among the county's top 10 employers. Marriott International, which has scheduled completion for 2022 of its corporate headquarters a few miles south to downtown Bethesda, employs 5,500.

From the 1960s through the 1980s, Montgomery County ranked at or near the top among counties nationwide in income and education. Downtown Bethesda remains a glitzy and popular entertainment and dining destination with expanding high-rise apartment buildings. Its increased urban development and taller office building have diminished the suburban or small-town ambiance. The county gradually became a magnet for legal immigrants attracted by the region's strong and stable economy. Today, Montgomery has a diverse population and has been overtaken in affluence regionally by other suburban counties in the metropolitan area. Along with its very upscale neighborhoods, Montgomery now has large Latino communities in areas from Wheaton northwest to Rockville. The county's population in 2017, which had grown 9 percent since 2010 and surpassed 1 million, was 20 percent African American, 20 percent Hispanic and 16 percent Asian. Even with those shifts, the median population has aged from 34 to 39 and real estate prices have soared 40 percent beyond inflation since the 1990s.

Still, the county has the nation's second-highest percentage of adults with graduate degrees, and it is thoroughly liberal on cultural issues and loyal to the Democratic Party. Montgomery County provided the margin of victory for the 2012 referendum legalizing same-sex marriage in Maryland. In 2014, the county passed legislation creating partial public financing of local elections. Perhaps its most unique precinct is Leisure World in Silver Spring, with its 8,500-plus senior citizens and an extraordinarily high voter-turnout rate, mostly Democrats.

The 8th Congressional District of Maryland includes much of the heavily populated parts of Montgomery County (Bethesda, Rockville, Silver Spring and pricey Potomac). Two-thirds of the voters reside in Montgomery, with the remainder split nearly evenly between Frederick and Carroll counties. To assist Democrats in the 6th District, which now includes 40 percent of Montgomery, it now extends beyond the Washington suburbs to include rural Republican precincts from Frederick and Carroll counties. The presidential retreat of Camp David, where Jimmy Carter brokered the Israeli-Egyptian peace accords, is outside the small town of Thurmont, though Presidents Barack Obama and Donald Trump each had less interest in the quiet, rural facility than their recent predecessors. The district is reliably Democratic but it's not as overwhelmingly liberal as it was during the previous decade. Hillary Clinton in 2016 won here 64%-31%.

MASSACHUSETTS

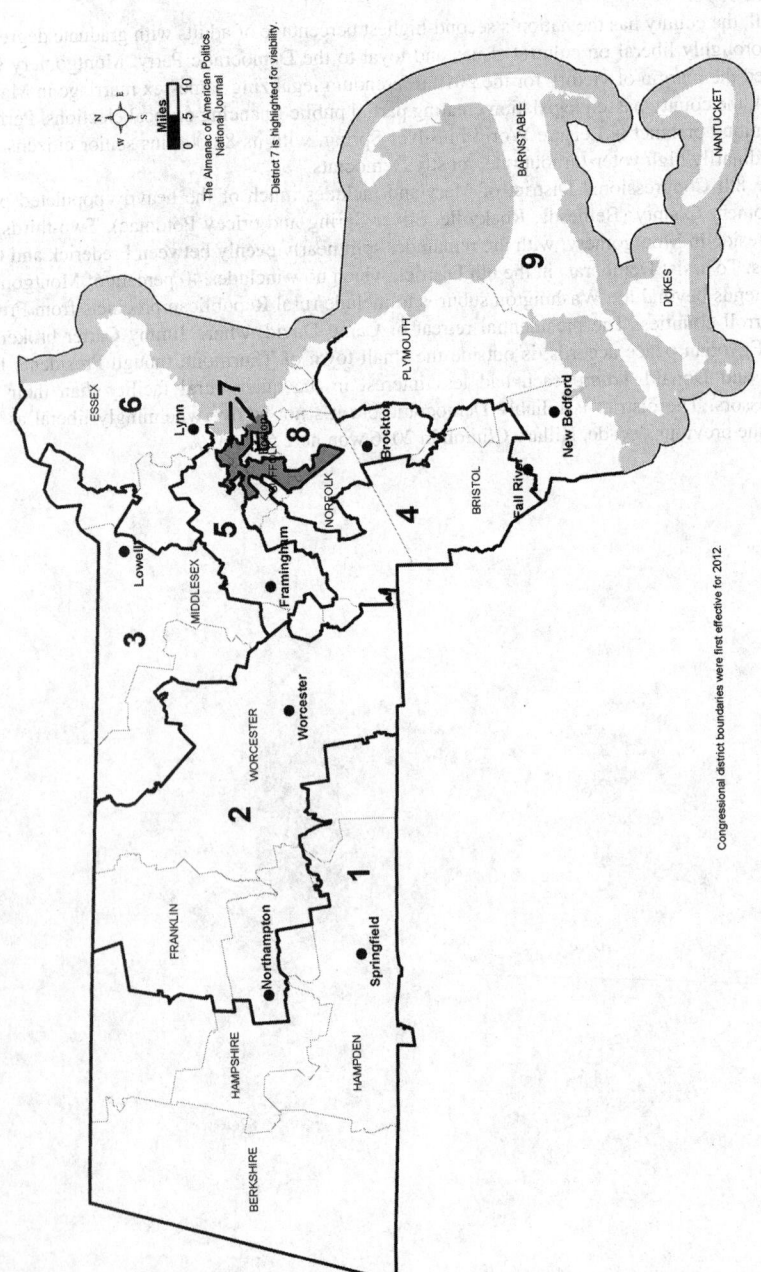

The Almanac of American Politics.
National Journal

District 7 is highlighted for visibility.

Miles
0 5 10

Congressional district boundaries were first effective for 2012.

Massachusetts, an affluent, highly educated state at the top of its economic game, is one of the nation's bluest states, but it defies pigeonholing. In 2016, the Bay State voted for Hillary Clinton by a 27-point margin – yet many of the same voters remained perfectly happy with their Republican governor, Charlie Baker, who won election two years later, 67%-33%.

The Puritan leader John Winthrop wrote that Massachusetts would be a city upon a hill -- an example to the entire world. For 150 years, New England was partial to learning, but the Puritans' austere creed was also insular and hostile to outsiders, sending merchants and fishing boats out to sea but keeping the world at bay. After the American Revolution, the wars between royal Britain and revolutionary and Napoleonic France enabled New England ship owners to cross enemy lines to become the world's leading merchants. They made vast profits and invested the money in textile mills, then railroads, then coal mines and steel mills, providing much of the capital that made industrial America.

Massachusetts remade the country in other ways. Intellectually, New England flowered in the 19th century, more than 200 years after Plymouth Rock. Writers from Boston and Cambridge, Concord and Salem — Ralph Waldo Emerson, Henry Wadsworth Longfellow, Henry David Thoreau, John Greenleaf Whittier and Nathaniel Hawthorne — created an American literature and popularized an American philosophy. There was a surge of New England Yankee influence across the continent, and beyond. By the 1820s, Boston whaling merchants and New England missionaries were planting their flag in the Sandwich Islands (Hawaii). By the 1850s, Yankees were in Iowa, Kansas and Oregon's Willamette Valley, and by the 1870s, in Los Angeles. They helped found the Republican Party and did much to start — and win — the Civil War. They planted their economic system and their values, articulated in the McGuffey Readers, across the continent.

In the meantime, Massachusetts itself and Boston, the "Hub of the Universe," were being remade. The Irish potato famine of the 1840s sent Catholic immigrants across the Atlantic, and many came to Boston, looking for work in the mills, docks and factories. Yankee Protestants had seen Catholics as their great political and cultural enemy since the 17th century and many felt that their commonwealth was under siege. As Catholics became a majority, first in Boston and then statewide, Protestants feared that the Irish would use their political clout to ladle out government jobs and benefits to their own — and the Irish had a much better flair for politics than instinct for commerce. But they encountered such bigotry and rejection by the Yankees that even as successful an Irish Catholic as Joseph Kennedy abandoned Boston for New York in 1927. Politics in Massachusetts for years was a kind of culture war between Yankee Republicans and Irish Democrats, an argument not so much over the distribution of income or the provision of services as over whose vision of Massachusetts should be honored, and whose version of history should be taught.

Sometimes the stakes were concrete — control of patronage, command of the Boston Police Department — but more often they were symbolic. Yankee Republicans tended to back activist government programs: public works and protective tariffs to help business; the Civil War and Reconstruction; uplifting (and productivity-enhancing) social movements such as temperance. The Irish found the 19th-century Democratic Party and its philosophy of laissez-faire more congenial. The Irish had come from a place where the government was the enemy, and they didn't want government spending money to help the rich or to stimulate commerce. They also didn't want government to restrict immigration, to advance blacks (potential competitors in the labor market), or to ban alcohol.

Massachusetts' Irish and Catholic percentages rose slowly over the years. Yankees had smaller families, moved west, intermarried with people of immigrant stock and lost their Yankee identity. The Irish were likelier to stay put, raise large families and maintain their identity. Slowly but surely, Massachusetts moved from being one of the most Republican states to one of the most Democratic. The predominance of the textile mills meant that for a century beginning in the 1820s, Massachusetts imported low-skill labor and exported high-skill people. As textile mills started moving south in the 1920s, Massachusetts started exporting low-skill people as well.

The Kennedys occupied a unique place in Massachusetts politics. Rose Kennedy was the daughter of John "Honey Fitz" Fitzgerald, who was elected to Congress at age 32 and served as mayor of Boston in 1906-07 and 1910-14. Her husband, Joseph Kennedy, was chairman of the Securities and Exchange Commission in the 1930s and ambassador to the Court of St. James's from 1937 to 1940. Catholic and uncommonly rich, he was a shrewd and ruthless political operator. Their only residence in Massachusetts after 1927 was their summer home in Hyannis Port. In 1946, Joseph Kennedy moved his oldest surviving son, John, to Boston, and helped steer his election to the House that year, to the Senate in 1952, and to the presidency in 1960. With their elegant manners and charm, the Kennedys were like royalty to the Irish Catholics of Massachusetts. And Catholics across the country, 78 percent of whom voted for John Kennedy, greeted the Democrat's election in 1960 with great pride. Joseph and John Kennedy were, on many issues, conservative or skeptical of liberal government intervention. But JFK's administration was increasingly identified, even before its tragic end in Dallas, as liberal. His example and that of his brother, Edward Kennedy, who was elected to the Senate in 1962 at age 30 and served 46 years, moved Massachusetts Catholics to the left. At the same time, the leftward direction of the state's elite campuses in the 1960s influenced Massachusetts Protestants.

In the 1970s and 1980s, Massachusetts had the most liberal governance and outlook on national politics of any state in the country. It was the only state to vote for George McGovern in 1972, although it voted twice for Ronald Reagan, the son of an Irish Catholic. The state elected liberal governors such as Republican Francis Sargent and Democrat Michael Dukakis. Then in the early 1990s, the 1980s "Massachusetts Miracle" turned into a curse; the state's tech, real estate and defense economy sagged, and the state government essentially went bankrupt. In 1990, when Dukakis retired as governor, voters embraced tax cuts and elected patrician Republican William Weld in his place. Four different Republicans, fiscally conservative and socially moderate, would hold the governorship for the next 16 years. The last of those four, Mitt Romney, provided the biggest policy innovation -- the health care plan passed by the legislature in 2006 that required all residents to buy health insurance, levied taxes on employers who did not provide it, and subsidized policies for low-wage earners. Romney's plan became the model for the national health care legislation passed by Congress and signed by President Barack Obama in 2010. But as he prepared to run for the GOP presidential nomination in 2008 (the first of his two presidential bids) Romney turned rightward, alienating voters back home. Democrat Deval Patrick succeeded him, becoming the state's first African-American governor in 2006. But the old model succeeded once again for Republicans in 2014 as Baker -- the cabinet secretary for governors Weld and Paul Cellucci – won the governorship. Baker's pragmatic approach has been a hit with voters even as more liberal candidates have won other offices.

Massachusetts' population has grown by 4.4 percent since 2010, and the Boston metro area has increased by 6.2 percent over the same period, enabling the Hub to keep its spot as the 10th largest metro area in the country. The statewide population is 7 percent black, 11 percent Hispanic and 6 percent Asian, with significant immigration, some from Ireland but also from Brazil and elsewhere. The state's median income ranks fifth in the country, 22 percent higher than the U.S. average – and that surely had something to do with the state's No. 1 national rankings in bachelor's and advanced degrees. Calculations by Governing magazine rated the state's economy the best-performing in the nation in 2016, and the Boston Globe noted that if it were a country, Massachusetts would rank among the richest nations in the world.

Manufacturing jobs have been replaced, and then some, by those in technology, health sciences, health care and financial services: CompTIA, a tech-industry association, reported in 2018 that Massachusetts, of all the states, had the highest concentration of tech workers relative to its overall employment base. Boston has recently become a center for technological innovations aimed at the nation's aging population, and after initial not-in-my-backyard concerns, work was underway on an 800-megawatt wind farm located 15 miles off the coast of Martha's Vineyard that would be operated from the old "Moby-Dick" whaling town of New Bedford. Tech-related sectors are growing so quickly that by 2025, the state's colleges and universities may not be able to churn out enough qualified workers, according to the Massachusetts Department of Higher Education.

With its educated electorate, Democratic leanings and mostly moderate Republican governors, cultural liberalism gradually prevailed over conservative Catholic social views in the state. Weld was one of America's first politicians to endorse gay rights, and after the legislature declined to endorse same-sex marriage, the courts in 2004 declared that same-sex couples had the right to marry; within a decade, this policy was replicated nationwide. In 2016, the legislature passed, and Baker signed into law, a measure to expand existing protections for transgender people to include public bathrooms, locker rooms and showers. After critics put the issue on the 2018 ballot, the voters upheld the protections overwhelmingly, 68%-32%. In November 2016, voters opted to legalize marijuana for recreational use, despite opposition from Baker, Boston Mayor Marty Walsh and Cardinal Sean O'Malley; two years later, cannabis shops opened in Leicester and Northampton, becoming the first recreational stores on the East Coast. At the same time, the advent of the #MeToo movement peeled back a stark hypocrisy – a legislature dominated by progressives, yet with a retrograde culture toward women. In 2017, aides, lobbyists, activists and legislators told the Boston Globe about "situations where they were propositioned by men, including lawmakers, who could make or break their careers; where those men pressed up against them, touched their legs, massaged their shoulders, tried to kiss them, grabbed their behinds, chased them around offices, or demanded sex."

At the ballot box, though, the state's leftward leanings were clear. Amid record statewide turnout in 2016, Clinton beat Donald Trump in Massachusetts by 27 points, a margin four points wider than Obama's in 2012. In a sign of the state's growing diversity, Ayanna Pressley in 2018 became the first black woman from Massachusetts elected to the House, after defeating 10-term Rep. Michael Capuano in the Democratic primary in the state's first minority-majority district. Meanwhile, Sen. Elizabeth Warren was the latest in a long line of liberal Massachusetts senators to run for president.

Population		Race and Ethnicity		Income	
Total	6,789,319	White	72.9%	Median Income	$74,167
Land area (sq. miles)	7,800	Black	6.7%	State Income Rank	5
Pop/ sq mi	870.4	Latino	11.2%	Poverty Rate	11.1%
Born in state	61.2%	Asian	6.2%	With health insurance	97.0%
		Two or more races	2.1%	Cash public assistance	2.8%
Age Groups		Other	0.8%	Food stamp/SNAP	12.3%
Under 18	20.4%				
18-34	24.2%	**Education**		**Work**	
35-64	39.9%	H.S grad or less	34.4%	White Collar	45.3%
Over 64	15.5%	Some college	23.5%	Sales and Service	39.3%
		College Degree, 4 yr	23.4%	Blue Collar	15.4%
Military		Post grad	18.7%	Government	12.1%
Veteran/ Active Duty	6.1%				

Presidential Politics

2016 Primary (D)	Clinton (D)	606,822 (50%)	Sanders (D)	589,803 (49%)			
2016 Primary (R)	Trump (R)	312,425 (49%)	Kasich (R)	114,434 (18%)	Rubio (R)	113,170 (18%)	
	Cruz (R)	60,592 (10%)					
2016 Pres. Vote	Clinton (D)	1,995,196 (60%)	Trump (R)	1,090,893 (33%)	Johnson (L)	138,018 (4%)	
2012 Pres. Vote	Obama (D)	1,921,290 (61%)	Romney (R)	1,188,314 (38%)			

Massachusetts has been a solidly Democratic state in the past eight presidential elections. Hillary Clinton defeated Donald Trump in the 2016 race, 60%-33%. What is striking about Massachusetts is how many serious presidential candidates it has produced over the past four decades: Edward Kennedy in 1980, Michael Dukakis in 1988, Paul Tsongas in 1992, John Kerry in 2004 and Mitt Romney in 2008 and 2012. Sen. Elizabeth Warren tossed her hat in the ring for 2020. Only California and Texas, with much larger populations, have produced more serious candidates over that period. Bay State hopefuls benefit from the first-in-the-nation primary status of New Hampshire, where most of the residents receive Boston television newscasts influenced by the hyper-political culture of that city.

The Massachusetts primary in 2016 was held on March 1, the same day as voters in seven Southern states cast ballots. The results gave important previews of how both parties' nominating contests were going to unfold. On the Democratic side, Clinton's narrow 50%-49% win over Vermont Sen. Bernie Sanders showed there were limits to the insurgent's appeal. In western Massachusetts, occasionally referred to as the Granola Belt for the fondness that aging hippies have shown the region, Sanders won about 56 percent of the vote. On the South Shore and the old mill towns and manufacturing centers around Route 495, Clinton and Sanders battled to a draw. Clinton pulled out her victory in Boston and upscale Democratic strongholds like Newton, Brookline and Cambridge.

According to the television network exit polls, she beat Sanders among voters with family incomes of $100,000 or more, 59%-39%. Sanders carried voters who earned less, 55%-45%.

On the Republican side, Trump won a near landslide victory, capturing 49 percent of the vote, a higher percentage than he won in conservative states like Alabama and Arkansas on the same day. Of the 351 towns and cities in Massachusetts, Trump carried all but about 20. Demonstrating strong appeal to northern blue-collar working class voters, he won almost two-thirds of the white, non-college GOP primary voters. Ohio Gov. John Kasich finished second with 18 percent, about 1,000 votes ahead of Texas Sen. Ted Cruz. Kasich's inability to rally moderate suburban Republicans and independents confirmed that he lacked a base to pose a serious challenge to Trump.

Congressional Districts

116th Congress Lineup	9D	115th Congress Lineup	9D

For many years, Massachusetts — the home of the original gerrymander -- had some of the most convoluted congressional district boundaries in the nation. It also had a habit of electing moderate Republicans from suburban enclaves. Both practices have largely disappeared. When the number of House seats fell from 14 in 1960 to 10 by 2000 and then to nine following the 2010 census, that required the loss of a seat and gave the state legislature a chance to smooth the lines. Because all the seats had been held by Democrats, it meant a Democratic loss. With the retirement of the 1st District's John Olver, the elimination of the western-most district resulted in shifts to the west for two Democrats who subsequently have become House committee chairmen: Springfield-based Richard Neal absorbed the heavily Democratic Berkshires, and Worcester-based Jim McGovern no longer extended east to Fall River. Since then, Republicans have had one opportunity: They lost a close challenge in 2012 in the 6th District against an ethically scarred incumbent. That has continued the state's streak of not having elected a Republican to the House since 1994.

For 2022, with no change in the total of nine, districts in the Boston area will need to shed modest numbers of residents to outlying districts. Republican opportunities are limited and they have no leverage in the legislature. Republican Gov. Charlie Baker could seek to enhance GOP prospects in the 6th and 9th, in the northeast and southeast corners.

Charlie Baker (R)

Elected 2014, term expires 2023, 2nd term; b. Nov. 13, 1956, Elmira, NY; Harvard U., B.A. 1979; Northwestern U., M.B.A. 1986; Protestant; Married (Lauren); 3 children.

Elected Office: MA Secretary of Health & Human Services, 1992-1994; Swampscott Board of Selectmen, 2004-2009.

Professional Career: Founder, Pioneer Institute for Public Policy Research, 1988-1991; State Health Undersecretary, 1991-1992; State Administrations & Finance Secretary, 1994-1998; CEO, Harvard Vanguard Medical Associates, 1998-1999; Entrepreneur, 2011-2014.

Office: Massachusetts State House, Room 280, Boston, 02133; 617-725-4005; Fax: 617-727-9725; **Website:** mass.gov.

Lt. Gov.: Karyn Polito (R) **Atty. Gen:** Maura Healey (D) **Sec. of State:** William F. Galvin (D)
State Legislature: Senate: 34D, 6R **House:** 127D, 32R, 1I

Election Results

Election	Name (Party)	Vote (%)
2018 General	Charlie Baker (R)...	1,781,341 (67%)
	Jay Gonzalez (D)...	885,770 (33%)
2018 Primary	Charlie Baker (R)...	174,126 (64%)
	Scott Lively (R)...	98,421 (36%)

Prior winning percentage: House: 2000 (unopposed); 1998 (81%); 1996 (56%)

Charlie Baker was easily reelected to the Massachusetts governorship in 2018. He's a moderate, pragmatic Republican in a blue state with a history of electing socially liberal, fiscally conservative Republicans to the governors' mansion. "Baker is likely the truest avatar of liberal Republicanism still standing," the Atlantic has written. Baker has frequently rated in surveys the most popular governor in the nation. "In this era of snapchats, tweets, Facebook and Instagram posts, putdowns and smack-downs, I'd ask you all to remember that good public policy is about perseverance and collaboration," Baker said during his second inaugural speech.

Baker was born in Elmira New York, to a family steeped in politics and public service. His great-grandfather was a federal prosecutor and state assemblyman; his grandfather was a prominent Newburyport politician; his father Charles was a well-connected conservative Republican who had worked for Republican presidents Richard Nixon and Ronald Reagan. His mother was a liberal Democrat, leading to political arguments at the dinner table in Needham, where Baker mostly grew up and went to public schools. "The Baker boys — and their guests — were expected to come ready to tangle intellectually, to take positions, to listen well, and to know facts," the Boston Globe has written. Baker earned a bachelor's degree in English from Harvard University, riding the bench for the basketball team (he's six-foot-six). He then received an MBA from the Kellogg Graduate School of Management at Northwestern University. (In the interim, Baker worked on the unsuccessful 1980 presidential campaign of former Texas Gov. John Connally.) He married the daughter of a Fortune 500 CEO and delved into policy work as the first executive director of the Pioneer Institute, a conservative think tank in Boston, created in part by Baker's father.

In 1992, at 36, Baker began his career in public service, when GOP Gov. William Weld appointed him secretary of Health and Human Services, heading up the largest department in state government. Baker, showing efficiency and diligence, was elevated in 1994 to be secretary of Administration and Finance, putting him in charge of the state's budget. Weld's successor, Paul Cellucci, kept Baker in that post, where, among other things, he was the original architect of the financial plan for the Big Dig, the Boston tunnel project plagued by delays and cost overruns. When Baker left government, he became CEO of Harvard Pilgrim Health Care, a nonprofit health benefits organization, from 1999 to 2009. In 2004, Baker was elected to the Board of Selectmen in his home town of Swampscott, an old fishing town on the North Shore of Boston, where the city skyline can be seen in the distance.

In his first run for governor in 2010, Baker took on Gov. Deval Patrick, who was seeking a second term. Baker promised no new taxes, and he was agnostic on human-caused climate change, a view that offended many environmentalists. Baker came off to some as distant, and he expressed some views that put him at odds with the state's Democratic-leaning electorate. He came to understand too late in the campaign that Massachusetts is "not an angry state," Baker later acknowledged to the Globe. Baker's task in the election was complicated by the presence of a third candidate, former state Treasurer Tim Cahill, who left the Democratic Party to run as an independent. This effectively split the base of the state's fiscally conservative and moderate voters that Baker needed to rally to have any hopes of winning. On Election Day, Patrick defeated Baker, 48%-42% with Cahill capturing 8%.

When he mounted a second campaign for governor in 2014, Baker had morphed into a more genial — and female-voter-friendly — contender. Facing Democratic nominee Martha Coakley, Baker cast himself as a fiscally responsible businessman, able to use his private-sector fiscal skills to heal what he called a poorly run Democratic administration. He emphasized his liberal take on social issues such as abortion and gay marriage. After stumbling with female voters in 2010, Baker chose a woman, Karyn Polito, as his running mate. The new Baker tweeted out messages on Twitter from Red Sox games and spoke easily about his openly gay brother. While Coakley accused Baker of being weak on gender issues, the strategy did not stick. CommonWealth magazine declared, "This is the new Charlie Baker. He's relaxed, he's likable, he's fun to drink beer with."

On Election Day, Coakley swept deeply Democratic Suffolk County (Boston) and Berkshire, Hampshire and Franklin counties in western Massachusetts, with college towns and resort communities full of liberal artists and former hippies. She also carried Middlesex County, with its mix of wealthy Boston suburbs like Cambridge, Belmont and Newton, heavily ethnic, heavily blue collar towns like Malden and Watertown, and Boston's I-495 exurban ring. But she did so by a narrow 50%-46% margin. Baker won the rest of the state, including Worcester County, with its classic New England small towns; Essex County, with its Merrimack Valley mill towns and North Shore affluent Boston exurbs; and Norfolk County, with its mix of upper-income Boston exurbs and coastal towns of the South Shore populated by upper-middle-class Irish Catholics.

Baker chose an eclectic cabinet – traditional pro-business Republicans and a few Democrats, even some who disagreed with positions he had taken during the campaign. True to his roots as a budgeter, Baker signed a plan in early 2015 that offered early retirement to state employees in order to reduce the workforce by up to 5,000 jobs. The Massachusetts General Court approved the proposal, a down payment on Baker's efforts to close the budget deficit.

At times Baker took right-of-center stances, as when he joined with more conservative Republican governors in 2015 to urge caution about resettling any more Syrian refugees; this drew criticism from several Democratic members of the congressional delegation. Baker also defied teachers' unions by pushing for a ballot measure to expand charter schools; in 2016, voters rejected it by a wide margin. He opposed a 2016 ballot measure to legalize marijuana; voters disagreed and passed it, and Baker signed implementing legislation. And initially at least, Baker was noncommittal about a bill to protect transgender rights, prompting a pro-LGBT audience to boo him off a stage. But three months later, in July 2016, he switched and signed the transgender law (though critics of the law worked to place a repeal measure on the 2018 ballot, which failed). Baker signed a law aimed at achieving equal pay for women by barring employers from requiring applicants to provide their salary history. He helped engineer a deal to bring General Electric's headquarters from Connecticut to Boston, though GE later downsized its presence. And he kept his promise to sign a bill combating opioid addiction; it restricted most initial prescriptions to seven days, required emergency-room evaluations within 24 hours; and mandated that doctors check a state patient database before prescribing opioids. Baker invested significant political capital in opioids, making it something of a signature issue; opioid-related overdoses in Massachusetts fell slightly from 2017 to 2018, though growing use of fentanyl remained a problem.

In November 2017, Baker signed a law that made Massachusetts the first state to ban the firearm attachments known as bump stocks following the mass-shooting in Las Vegas that utilized the devices to deadly effect. The following year, he signed a law overturning an archaic 1845 law banning abortion, safeguarding abortion rights in the event the U.S. Supreme Court were to overturn Roe v. Wade. Baker also signed legislation to enact automatic voter registration, to raise the minimum wage to $15 by 2023, to implement paid leave, to allow judges to order gun confiscation if an individual is deemed a danger to themselves or others, and to expand access to medication-based treatment for opioid addicts in jails and emergency rooms. Perhaps more popular than Baker's policies, however, was his low-key, bipartisan approach – welcome in an increasingly polarized political sphere – and his decision not to vote for his party's presidential nominee, Donald Trump. While Baker occasionally cooperated with the Trump White House, such as on opioid policy, he frequently criticized the president's comments and his policies on health care and immigration. In June 2018, he backed off sending National Guard troops to the U.S.-Mexico border to protest the administration's policy of separating minors from their migrant parents.

In the 2018 GOP primary, Baker faced Scott Lively, a Trump-aligned pastor with a record of preaching against LGBT rights. Though Lively was vastly underfunded and got little attention, he secured 36 percent of the primary vote. With Baker's popularity among the broader electorate. sky high, every prominent Democratic official took a pass on the race, leaving a final Democratic primary matchup between Jay Gonzalez, who had served as budget chief for Gov. Deval Patrick, and environmentalist Robert K. Massie. Gonzalez won the nomination and proceeded to advocate a 4 percent surtax on income over $1 million and the taxation of university endowments. But the general election was never competitive, as voters seemed satisfied with the economy, with Baker's efforts to distance himself from Trump, and with his ability to check any excesses from a legislature dominated by Democrats. Baker won every county – even Suffolk, narrowly – as he prevailed by a 67%-33% margin. Baker is eligible to run for a third term, though by 2022, the Democratic bench – including Attorney General Maura Healey and Congressman Joseph P. Kennedy III – will be large and restless.

Elizabeth Warren (D)

Elected 2012, term expires 2024, 2nd term, b. Jun 22, 1949; Oklahoma City, OK; George Washington University (DC), Att., 1968; University of Houston (TX), B.A., 1970; Rutgers University (NJ), J.D., 1976; Methodist; Married (Bruce H. Mann); 2 children; 3 grandchildren.

Professional Career: Professor, University of TX, 1981-1987; Professor, University of PA Law School, 1987-1995; Professor, Harvard Law School, 1992-2013; Chair, Congressional Oversight Panel for the Troubled Asset Relief Program, 2008-2010; Assistant to the President & Special Advisor to Treasury Secretary, 2010-2011.

DC Office: 309 HSOB 20510, 202-224-4543, Fax: 202-228-2072, warren.senate.gov

State Offices: Boston, 617-565-3170; Springfield, 413-788-2690.

Committees: Senate Democratic Conference Vice Chairman. *Aging. Armed Services:* Airland; Personnel; Strategic Forces. *Banking, Housing & Urban Affairs:* Financial Institutions & Consumer Protection (RMM); Housing, Transportation & Community Development; Securities, Insurance & Investment. *Health, Education, Labor & Pensions:* Employment & Workplace Safety; Primary Health & Retirement Security.

Group Ratings

	ADA	ACLU	AFL-CIO	LCV	ITI	COC	HAFA	ACU	CFG	FRC
2018	-	86%	-	100%	-	40%	5%	9%	19%	0%
2017	100%	C	100%	100%	C	29%	C	0%	4%	0%

Almanac Ratings 2017-18

	Economy	Social	Foreign	Composite
Liberal	97%	97%	100%	98%
Conservative	3%	3%	0%	2%

Key Votes of the 115th Congress

1. Obama-care revision	N	5. Gun regulations	N	9. Kavanaugh confirmation	N
2. Tax Cuts	N	6. Family planning regs	N	10. Saudi arms sales	Y
3. Dodd-Frank revision	N	7. Gorsuch confirmation	N	11. FISA rules	N
4. Omnibus appropriations	N	8. Immigration restrictions	N	12. Military aid in Yemen	Y

Election Results

Election	Name (Party)	Vote (%)		Cand. Spent	Ind. Exp. Support	Ind. Exp. Oppose
2018 General	Elizabeth Warren (D).....................	1,633,371	(60%)	$17,185,436	$91	$1,281,120
	Geoff Diehl (R)..............................	979,210	(36%)	$4,314,231		
	Shiva Ayyadurai (I).............................	91,710	(3%)	$5,014,779		
2018 Primary	Elizabeth Warren (D).....................	591,038	(100%)			

Prior winning percentages: 2012 (54%)

Democrat Elizabeth Warren, Massachusetts' senior senator, occupies the seat held for nearly half a century by the late Sen. Ted Kennedy. Just as the traditional liberal wing of the Democratic Party long looked to Kennedy for leadership and inspiration, progressive activists working to push the party to the left now look to Warren. In one term in the Senate, the former Harvard Law School professor has emerged as one of the most influential figures on Capitol Hill and in the Democratic Party at large — aided by a sharp tongue, deft use of social media and a large fundraising base. "She has been a lot more effective than most in communicating an anti-Wall Street message that has been part of the Democratic Party for 80 years," Charles Geisst, a Manhattan College professor who specializes in Wall Street history, told Politico. Warren has relied on that message to propel her to the higher office: Just two months after being easily reelected to a second Senate term in November 2018, she became the first of a half-dozen Democratic senators to announce a 2020 White House bid.

A Warren vs. Donald Trump matchup would be a clash of disparate brands of populism practiced by opposite ends of the political spectrum. Trump "said one thing that was right — because I've said it, too: The system is rigged. But let's be clear: It is rigged in favor of billionaires like Donald Trump," Warren said shortly after Trump's surprise victory in 2016. Warren was one of Democratic presidential nominee Hillary Clinton's most effective surrogates that year, demonstrating an ability to match insults with Trump and get under his skin. Warren derided Trump as a "small, insecure money grubber" on the stump and a "thin-skinned bully who thinks humiliating women at 3 a.m. qualifies him to be president" via Twitter; Trump responded by calling Warren "Pocahontas," a reference to a controversy over her claim of Cherokee ancestry. Warren's efforts to put that controversy to rest as she entered the 2020 race — even taking a DNA test on Trump's dare — left her with dealing with unwelcome political fallout.

Soon after Warren first arrived on Capitol Hill in 2012, progressive groups began a "draft Warren" effort to entice her into the 2016 Democratic presidential primary. In ruling herself out, she opened the way for the insurgent progressive candidacy of Vermont Sen. Bernie Sanders. Sanders fell short of victory, but he redefined the Democratic Party's platform and left Warren somewhat in his shadow and some wondering whether she had missed her moment. With both Warren and Sanders in the 2020 race and competing for an overlapping base of voters, another challenge she has faced is to distinguish herself from her fellow progressive. Sanders is a lifelong democratic socialist who at times has decried capitalism, but Warren has cast herself as focused on reforming the economic status quo. "I am a capitalist," she told CNBC in mid-2018. "I believe in markets. What I don't believe in is theft; what I don't believe in is cheating."

Like Kennedy in his day, Warren has become a bete noire to national Republican strategists — who regularly utilize her image to mobilize their base in red states. But on Capitol Hill, Warren — while hardly the deal-maker that Kennedy became during his nearly five-decade career — has shown an ability to work across the aisle on issues ranging from government efficiency to marijuana regulation to predatory lending. Warren ranked 64th for bipartisanship in 2017 according to Senate ratings by the Washington-based Lugar Center, but she scored higher than four of her six colleagues who are also announced Democratic presidential contenders. At the same time, Warren has shown little hesitancy to engage in public policy brawls with her own party. She was a thorn in President Barack Obama's side for much of second term even after he had helped launch her political career by naming her a Treasury Department special adviser in 2010. In 2018, she warred with members of her party's moderate wing over a bill easing regulation of the financial industry.

While such combativeness could be a political asset in a race against Trump, it also has raised questions about Warren's ability to unite the Democratic Party's wings. Three weeks before she entered the 2020 race, her hometown newspaper, The Boston Globe — which had urged her to get into the 2016 presidential contest — suggested she stay out this time around. "While Warren is an effective and impactful senator with an important voice nationally, she has become a divisive figure," the paper's editorial board wrote. "A unifying voice is what the country needs now after the polarizing politics of Donald Trump." But Warren appears to see her role more in terms of her previous life as a consumer advocate and outspoken reformer. "I'll always be an outsider," Warren told The Washington Post in 2015. "That's how I understand the world."

She credits her hardscrabble origins and academic research for her political convictions. Born Elizabeth Herring, she grew up in Oklahoma City where her teenage years were marred by her father's heart attack. His lost pay as a maintenance worker and medical bills imperiled the family; Warren and her mother went to work; Warren, then 13, waited tables at her aunt's Mexican restaurant. She also became a champion high school debater, and her skills enabled her to win a scholarship to The George Washington University; she completed a bachelor's degree at the University of Houston.

She married her high school sweetheart, Jim Warren, at 19 and then had two children, taught elementary school, earned a law degree from Rutgers University and went through a divorce — earning an appreciation for working mothers. She developed a specialty in bankruptcy law as a member of the law faculty at three universities before arriving at Harvard in the mid-1990s. Along the way, she married Bruce Mann, a fellow law professor. As recently as 1996, Warren was a Republican. But she said the families she met during her research into bankruptcy changed her views. "These were hard-working middle-class families who by and large had lost jobs, gotten sick, had family breakups, and that's what was driving them over the edge financially. It changed my vision," Warren said during a 2007 speech. Shortly after announcing her presidential candidacy, she told FiveThirtyEight, "I've been working on one central question for 30 years: 'What's going wrong with working families across this country, why is America's middle class getting hollowed out?'"

Warren used her academic expertise and ability to communicate complicated policy issues to frame the broader political debate and emerged as a leading advocate for consumer interests. In 1995, she became chief adviser to the National Bankruptcy Review Commission and led the unsuccessful fight against legislation that made it harder for consumers to file for bankruptcy. She appeared on the TV talk show circuit and, with her daughter, Amelia Warren Tyagi, co-authored a couple general audience books on consumer finance. The second, "All Your Worth: The Ultimate Lifetime Money Plan," made the New York Times best-seller list in 2005. In 2008, then-Senate Majority Leader Harry Reid named Warren to chair the congressional oversight panel for the $700 billion Troubled Asset Relief Program enacted after the financial crash.

A year earlier, Warren had written an article in which she proposed a "Financial Product Safety Commission" modeled on the Consumer Product Safety Commission created in the early 1970s. Her idea was incorporated into the 2010 Dodd-Frank financial reform law as an agency within the Treasury Department, and Warren was hired by the Obama White House to design and launch the Consumer Financial Protection Bureau. But her barbed criticisms over the years made her persona non grata to much of the nation's financial industry. With Senate Republicans vowing to block her appointment, Obama instead nominated former Ohio Attorney General Richard Cordray as the bureau's first director.

During the debate on Dodd-Frank, Warren successfully pushed to insulate the CFPB from congressional pressures; it got funding from the Federal Reserve and its director appointed to five-year terms. "My second choice is no agency at all and plenty of blood and teeth left on the floor," she told the HuffPost at the time. The structure rendered Republicans largely powerless to dilute the agency's influence during the Obama administration — but the CFPB's structure came back to haunt Warren with Trump in office. When Cordray left before his statutory term was up, Trump in late 2017 named Office of Management and Budget Director Mick Mulvaney as acting CFPB director. The CFPB's aggressive filing of enforcement actions against financial institutions all but disappeared. Lacking congressional leverage over the agency, Warren could do little but write pointed letters questioning Mulvaney's decisions — which Mulvaney largely ignored save for taking equally pointed counterswipes at Warren. Conservatives were gleeful: "Elizabeth Warren's Boomerang" was the headline of a Wall Street Journal editorial.

While Warren didn't get to be the CFPB's first director, her visibility during her year in the Obama administration prompted Massachusetts Democrats to encourage her to challenge Republican Sen. Scott Brown. Not long after leaving her advisory post at the Treasury Department in late 2011, Warren announced her candidacy. She became a national sensation after a speech she gave, in which she exhorted wealthy Americans to recognize the debt they owe to the community and "pay forward for the next kid who comes along," went viral. Warren became a "Doonesbury" cartoon heroine and got a prime-time speaking slot at the 2012 Democratic National Convention.

Brown had shocked Democrats by winning the January 2010 special election to succeed Kennedy. He received substantial support from the tea party but compiled a centrist voting record. He possessed an Everyman persona and pointedly referred to his opponent as "Professor Warren" to drive a wedge between her and everyday voters. However, in the last months of the campaign, she frequently asserted a vote for Brown was a vote for a GOP Senate majority, a sentiment that resonated with the blue state's electorate. Warren won 54%-46% to become the first woman to represent Massachusetts in the Senate — but not until Brown had repeatedly attacked her for claiming Cherokee ancestry. It was an issue that would dog her for years to come. Brown's backers said her claim was a ruse to exploit affirmative action plans at schools at which Warren had been hired, an allegation she denied. In late 2018, shortly before Warren easily won re-election against state Rep. Geoff Diehl, who had co-chaired Trump's campaign in the state, a Boston Globe investigation found no evidence that her claims of a Native American background had played a role in her hiring at four law schools, including Harvard's.

Warren was hardly the most liberal member of the Senate in her first year. She placed 31st, with a composite liberal score of 73.2 in National Journal rankings — although she shot up to second in 2015 Almanac rankings. In 2017, she was one of just two senators to score a perfect 100 liberal score. Before being sworn-in, Warren sought a seat on the Senate Banking, Housing and Urban Affairs Committee. Financial industry executives openly crusaded against the idea, but her liberal allies pushed back and she was named to the panel. At her first hearing in early 2013, she pressured federal regulators to take legal action against more of the nation's largest financial institutions. "They can break the law and drag in billions in profits and then turn around and settle, paying out of those profits," she said. She later pressed the Securities and Exchange Commission to seek admission of guilt from corporations found to have violated the law rather than allowing them to pay a fine without admitting guilt — and claimed part of the credit when the policy was changed to do so. Her pointed grilling of top federal officials won her more admiration from the left; The New Republic dubbed her a "Regulatory Rock Star."

Strains between Warren and the Obama White House were evident in early 2015 when Antonio Weiss, nominated to be Treasury undersecretary for domestic finance, withdrew his name. He had drawn Warren's fierce opposition: She felt his role as a Wall Street investment banker made him unsuited for a post that involved implementing the Dodd-Frank law. That episode turned out to be a relative skirmish in advance of the battle over Obama's pursuit of the Trans-Pacific Partnership. Once again, the issue was Dodd-Frank. Just as the Senate was about to vote on a bill giving Obama "fast-track" authority to expedite negotiation of the 12-nation trade accord, Warren warned that, if Democrats lost the White House in 2016, "a Republican president could easily use a future trade deal to override our domestic financial rules. A six-year fast-track bill is the missing link they need to make that happen." In an interview with Yahoo News, Obama called Warren "absolutely wrong" and appeared to question her motives. "The truth of the matter is that Elizabeth is, you know, a politician like everybody else," he said. The fast-track bill passed, but Trump withdrew the U.S. from the Trans-Pacific Partnership after taking office.

Four months after Obama left office, Warren criticized him for being out of touch with average voters, telling The Guardian: "President Obama, like many others in both parties, talks about a set of big national statistics that look shiny and great but increasingly have giant blind spots. ... The Republicans have clearly thrown their lot in with the rich and the powerful, but so have a lot of Democrats." Such statements reflected the view from the Democratic Party's left wing that Obama had spent insufficient capital on income equality issues. Those tensions also nourished early Warren-for-president talk.

At the liberal Netroots Nation conference in summer 2014, she brought the crowd to its feet with angry denunciations of big business. A draft-Warren movement ramped up; by January 2015, MoveOn.org and Democracy for America had collected nearly 250,000 signatures in an online petition urging her to run. After months of batting away questions in less than definitive terms, Warren in March 2015 said, "I am not running, and I am not going to run." By summer, the draft-Warren group announced it was folding. But Warren had succeeded in defining the battle lines of the 2016 Democratic contest — perhaps as much, if not more so, than if she had run. Clinton, preparing to launch her second presidential bid, privately solicited ideas from Warren in late 2014 — and her rhetoric on the campaign trail often sounded much like Warren's.

There was widespread speculation about a possible Clinton-Warren ticket, as Reid — reduced to Senate minority leader after the 2014 midterm elections — reportedly pushed the idea in the belief it would help pick up Senate seats in 2016. Warren had stayed out of the primary battle, endorsing Clinton only after Sanders was preparing to drop out. Her failure to endorse Sanders apparently strained relations between the party's two most visible progressives and angered several Sanders' backers — potentially complicating Warren's 2020 run. As Warren addressed the 2016 Democratic National Convention, Sanders supporters chanted, "We trusted you! We trusted you!" In what was an olive branch to the Sanders camp, Warren in a series of TV interviews in late 2017, agreed that the nominating process a year earlier had been "rigged" in favor of Clinton — a charge leveled by Sanders supporters during the campaign.

Warren's rising influence in the party had been formally recognized in late 2014 when Reid named her to the Senate Democratic leadership. In her newly created post, strategic policy adviser to the Democratic Policy and Communications Committee, she was charged with being an envoy to liberal groups and helping shape the party's message. She was elevated to vice chairwoman of the Senate Democratic Caucus in 2016 by Reid's successor as leader, New York Sen. Chuck Schumer. Warren's leadership role did not keep her from publicly chastising 16 Democrats — one-third of the Senate Democratic Caucus, some of whom were in tough reelection battles — who in March 2018 voted to support legislation authored by Senate Republicans to roll back some of the Dodd-Frank reforms. A Warren fundraising email criticizing the 16 Democrats, most of them moderates, led to a rancorous Democratic Caucus meeting. Efforts by Schumer afterward did little to persuade Warren to lower the temperature. "This is what I said I was going to do," Warren told Schumer, according to Politico. "This is why I ran for the Senate."

Warren told the Congressional Progressive Caucus that watching a handful of Democrats vote for the rollback "felt like a stab in the heart — not for me, but for all the homeowners who were cheated and the taxpayers who bailed out those banks." While Warren contended the bill would weaken regulation on many of the nation's largest banks, proponents argued the measure was largely regulatory relief for community banks and credit unions. One moderate Democrat who supported the bill, North Dakota Sen. Heidi Heitkamp, told The Atlantic that Warren had misled the public about its scope. Another, Missouri Sen. Claire McCaskill, pointed a finger at Warren when asked to identify the "crazy Democrats" she had referred to in a radio ad — from whom McCaskill was trying to separate herself. "I would not call my colleagues crazy, but Elizabeth Warren sure went after me when I advocated tooling back some of the regulations for small banks and credit unions," McCaskill told Fox News. Warren's political action committee had donated $10,000 to the McCaskill campaign and $60,000 to the Missouri Democratic Party, part of $8 million Warren raised for or donated to Democrats nationwide in the 2018 cycle.

At the outset of 2017, Warren took a seat on the Armed Services Committee. In late 2018, she delivered a speech questioning "unsustainable and ill-advised military commitments" around the globe. On the domestic front, Warren unveiled a series of detailed proposals to define the "policy primary" in 2020 — ranging from having the government manufacture generic drugs to providing universal child care. To pay for the latter, she proposed an annual 2 percent tax on household wealth of more than $50 million and 3 percent on billionaires' wealth. And, in a challenge to Trump, Warren put 10 years worth of her tax returns online — while introducing legislation requiring presidential candidates to release their tax returns and presidents to put assets that could present a conflict of interest into a blind trust and sell them off.

But Warren's acceptance of a challenge from Trump — who said he would pay $1 million to her a charity of her choice if a DNA test proved her to be Native American — backfired as she prepared to roll out her presidential candidacy. When the issue initially arose during her 2012 Senate race, Warren said she always had closely identified with her mother's side of the family — which, according to family lore, had ancestors from Cherokee and Delaware tribes. According to The Washington Post, she listed her race as "American Indian" as early as the mid-1980s when, as a University of Texas law professor, she filled out a form for the state bar. The results of the DNA test, released in October 2018, found "strong evidence" that Warren likely had a Native American ancestor 6 to 10 generations in the past, The Boston Globe reported.

Seizing on the worst case scenario, Republicans noted a native ancestor 10 generations back would make her as little as 1/1024 American Indian. Trump, brushing aside his promised charitable donation, continued to mock Warren. Some Democrats questioned her judgment in taking his bait, while Obama's former campaign manager criticized her release of the test three weeks before the midterm elections — complaining it had stepped on the party's message with majorities in Congress at stake. Meanwhile, Warren found herself caught in a revival of the sensitive debate over racial science and the extent to which DNA should govern racial and ethnic identity. And she was sharply criticized by Native American leaders, with the secretary of the Cherokee Nation saying she had made "a mockery out of DNA tests" while "dishonoring legitimate tribal governments and their citizens, whose ancestors are well documented and whose heritage is proven." Warren apologized to the principal chief of the Cherokee Nation and told The Washington Post: "I can't go back. But I am sorry for furthering confusion on tribal sovereignty and tribal citizenship and the harm that resulted."

Warren's future political aspirations received a boost from another controversy in early 2017 when Senate Majority Leader Mitch McConnell — invoking a little-used Senate rule — successfully barred her from participating further in the debate over the nomination of Alabama Sen. Jeff Sessions as Trump's first attorney general. Warren triggered McConnell's ire by reading from a letter Coretta Scott King wrote more than three decades earlier in opposition to Sessions' nomination to the federal bench at the time. The rule invoked by McConnell, instituted in 1902 after a physical fight between two senators, says "no senator in debate shall, directly or indirectly, by any form of words impute to another senator or to other senators any conduct or motive unworthy or unbecoming of a senator."

"She was warned. She was given an explanation. Nevertheless, she persisted," McConnell said on the Senate floor. The quote went viral. Warren left the Senate chamber to finish reading King's letter on Facebook and received 7 million views. McConnell — who apparently had hoped to energize the GOP base by targeting Warren — unwittingly provided her supporters and the feminist movement at large with a new rallying cry: "Persist."

Ed Markey (D)

Elected 2013, term expires 2020, 1st full term, b. Jul 11, 1946; Malden; Boston College (MA), B.A., 1968; Boston College Law School (MA), J.D., 1972; Roman Catholic; Married (Susan Blumenthal).

Military Career: U.S. Army Reserve 1968-1973

Elected Office: MA House, 1973-1976; U.S. House, 1976-2013.

Professional Career: Representative

DC Office: 255 DSOB 20510, 202-224-2742, Fax: 202-224-8525, markey.senate.gov

State Offices: Boston, 617-565-8519; Fall River, 508-677-0523; Springfield, 413-785-4610.

Committees: *Commerce, Science & Transportation*: Communications, Technology, Innovation & the Internet; Manufacturing, Trade & Consumer Protection; Subcommittee on Security (RMM); Subcommittee on Transportation & Safety. *Environment & Public Works*: Clean Air & Nuclear Safety; Superfund, Waste Management, & Regulatory Oversight; Transportation & Infrastructure. *Foreign Relations*: East Asia, the Pacific & International Cybersecurity Policy (RMM); Internat'l Dev Instit & Internat'l Econ, Energy & Environ Policy; State Dept & USAID Mngmnt, Internat'l Ops & Internat'l Dev. *Small Business & Entrepreneurship.*

Group Ratings

	ADA	ACLU	AFL-CIO	LCV	ITI	COC	HAFA	ACU	CFG	FRC
2018	-	81%	-	100%	-	40%	5%	5%	19%	0%
2017	95%	C	100%	95%	C	29%	C	0%	4%	0%

Almanac Ratings 2017-18

	Economy	Social	Foreign	Composite
Liberal	100%	100%	96%	99%
Conservative	0%	0%	4%	1%

Key Votes of the 115th Congress

1. Obama-care revision	N	5. Gun regulations	N	9. Kavanaugh confirmation	N
2. Tax Cuts	N	6. Family planning regs	N	10. Saudi arms sales	Y
3. Dodd-Frank revision	N	7. Gorsuch confirmation	N	11. FISA rules	N
4. Omnibus appropriations	N	8. Immigration restrictions	N	12. Military aid in Yemen	Y

Election Results

Election	Name (Party)	Vote (%)		Cand. Spent	Ind. Exp. Support	Ind. Exp. Oppose
2014 General	Ed Markey (D)	1,289,944	(59%)	$17,857,729	$3,214,292	
	Brian Herr (R)	791,950	(36%)	$118,532		
2014 Primary	Ed Markey (D)	Unopposed				

Prior winning percentages: 2013 special (55%), House: 2012(71%), 2010 (66%), 2008 (71%), 2006 (100%), 2004 (74%), 2002 (100%), 2000 (100%), 1998 (71%), 1996 (70%), 1994 (64%), 1992 (62%), 1990 (100%), 1988 (100%), 1986 (100%), 1984 (71%), 1982 (78%), 1980 (100%), 1978 (85%), 1976 (77%)

When Democrat Ed Markey, Massachusetts' junior senator, arrived in the chamber after winning a June 2013 special election, it was the culmination of a nearly 30-year wait. In 1984, Markey, then a four-term House member, jumped into the Democratic primary for an opening created by the retirement of Sen. Paul Tsongas. But, amid a bumpy reception, Markey reassessed his position, withdrew from the Senate contest and was reelected to the House. The winner of the Senate seat that year was then-Lt. Gov. John Kerry, who held on to it until President Barack Obama nominated him to be secretary of State at the end of 2012. However, even as Markey accumulated seniority and influence in the House, he continued to eye the Senate seat—hoping it might come open in 2004 if

Kerry, then the Democratic presidential nominee, won the White House. Finally, with Kerry poised to move to the Cabinet, Markey, at 66, saw his opportunity and grabbed it.

Just a few years earlier, when, in September 2009, the death of Sen. Ted Kennedy opened that seat after five decades, Markey passed on the special election to succeed him. The Democrats then had the House majority, and Markey, besides being third in line for the powerful chairmanship of the Energy and Commerce Committee, was also chairing a special panel tasked with laying the groundwork for legislation to curb global warming. But that soon changed: House Democrats lost their majority in the 2010 elections, with no clear prospect of regaining it anytime soon, and a highly visible Senate slot became significantly more appealing. At the time, Markey had little way of foreseeing the election of President Donald Trump and the resulting backlash that would return House Democrats to the majority in 2019. If he had chosen to remain put, Markey would almost certainly today be chairing the Energy and Commerce panel. Instead, with Senate Democrats in the minority since the 2014 elections, he has operated at the margins in that chamber — in the shadow of his state's senior senator, Democrat Elizabeth Warren, a leader of the party's progressive wing and a presidential contender.

Notwithstanding such political happenstances, what made Markey's move from one side of the Capitol to the other extraordinary is that never had a House member with Markey's seniority—nearly 37 years—opted to trade that in to become a freshman senator. Markey was only 30 when first elected to the House in 1976, and, over the years, became a key player on environmental and telecommunication issues. He has continued to focus on these areas in the Senate, still displaying the barbed rhetoric that has long endeared him to consumer advocates and environmentalists — even if his propensity for sardonic acronyms (he has gibed that GOP stands for "Gutting Our Privacy" and FDA for "Fostering Drug Addiction") often elicits groans from political insiders and the media. However, as was the case during his House tenure, Markey's hail-fellow-well-met persona has enabled him to work across the political aisle on legislation in recent years — notably with GOP Sen. Jim Inhofe of Oklahoma, an outspoken climate change skeptic.

Markey grew up in the Boston suburb of Malden, where his father was a milkman. He graduated from Boston College and was elected to the state House at 26, soon after earning a degree from Boston College's law school. He moved to an open congressional seat four years later, winning a 12-candidate primary with 22 percent of the vote — succeeding a congressional crony of John F. Kennedy. Markey broke out of the crowded field with a TV ad that remains a classic in political circles: It played off an episode in which state House leaders removed the furniture from Markey's office to retaliate for a court reform bill he had pushed over their objections. The ad shows a desk in the hallway of the Statehouse, as Markey says, "The bosses may tell me where to sit; nobody tells me where to stand."

Throughout most of his career, Markey has ranked among the most liberal members of Congress. But, in winning in 1976, Markey favored school prayer and advocated constitutional amendments to end school busing and ban abortion—positions geared to a socially conservative Catholic population in his district. He disavowed these positions before his brief 1984 Senate bid, but the timing of those reversals became a liability during that short-lived campaign. In recent decades, he has sidestepped questions about his change of position, telling The Boston Globe in 2013: "For 30 years, I have taken the progressive position, the liberal position, on each and every issue. I just evolved."

In the 2013 special Senate election primary, Markey was the establishment favorite and the more traditional liberal against Rep. Stephen Lynch, whose district includes working-class neighborhoods in and around South Boston. As a onetime iron worker, Lynch enjoyed substantial labor union support. But Markey's 3-1 cash advantage helped him prevail 57%-43%. Markey had expected his fiercest competition to come in the special general election — from former Republican Sen. Scott Brown, who had lost the state's other seat to Warren in one of the nation's highest profile Senate contests of 2012. But Brown opted instead to mount a competitive but unsuccessful Senate bid in neighboring New Hampshire in 2014.

Markey's GOP opponent in the special general election was businessman Gabriel Gomez, a former Navy SEAL and bilingual son of Colombian immigrants. Markey attacked Gomez on his gun control stance, while Gomez campaigned as a political outsider, declaring in one TV ad: "Markey is everything that's wrong with Congress: 37 years of pay raises, bounced checks, taking millions from people he regulates." But Markey's campaign treasury again gave him an advantage: He outspent Gomez by nearly 4-1, and he won 55%-45%. Markey was easily re-elected to a full six-year term in the 2014 general election, defeating his little-known opponent 59%-36%.

Markey's arrival in the Senate was not the most auspicious: Two months after his swearing-in, when the Foreign Relations Committee voted to authorize Obama's use of force against Syria, Markey voted "present" while most other committee Democrats voted in support. Markey said he was concerned about the "unintended consequences" of a U.S. military attack, which never occurred — but critics saw it as an attempt to sidestep a tough issue. Boston magazine afterward captured the widespread reaction with a headline: "Ed Markey Annoys Literally Everyone by Voting 'Present' on Syrian Resolution." Markey's decision to straddle the issue may have been related to his House vote a decade earlier in favor of the 2002 resolution authorizing the war in Iraq, a decision about which he later expressed strong regret.

Markey has comfortably fit in with the Senate's other left-leaning members from the Northeast. For 2017, Almanac vote rankings rated him as the seventh most liberal senator. Markey's score placed him just behind Connecticut Democrat Richard Blumenthal — who, like Markey, is a media-savvy political veteran who arrived in the Senate late in his career. As members of the Commerce, Science and Transportation Committee, Markey and Blumenthal have teamed up on consumer issues — including several initiatives tied to Markey's longtime legislative focus on information technology. On the heels of a June 2015 report by Markey's office titled "Tracking & Hacking: Security & Privacy Gaps Put American Drivers at Risk," the two senators authored a bill requiring automakers to come up with security standards to prevent hacking of vehicles' increasingly computerized systems. In 2018, they utilized procedural maneuvers to block passage of legislation to remove regulatory obstacles to development of self-driving cars — citing safety concerns. Their move came shortly after a driverless vehicle killed a pedestrian in Arizona.

Markey and Blumenthal also combined forces on another high-profile consumer issue in 2018 — introducing a "privacy bill of rights" for users of such platforms as Facebook and Google. Their legislation, which failed to move out of committee, followed revelations that Cambridge Analytica, a consulting firm with ties to Trump's 2016 presidential campaign, had obtained data on as many as 87 million Facebook users without permission. The bill was introduced just before Facebook CEO Mark Zuckerberg appeared before the Commerce Committee. During the hearing, Markey — who earlier had accused Facebook of "privacy malpractice" — aggressively questioned the billionaire tech executive, seeking a commitment from Zuckerberg to back legislation requiring "opt-in" consent from customers for use of their personal data.

In the House, Markey left his most lasting effect on telecommunications and IT policy — often working with Republicans to come up with innovative initiatives. His proposals were frequently inclined toward deregulation, but consumer advocates regarded him as a friend — blaming the skyrocketing cable TV bills of recent years not on Markey's legislation, but on the failure of the industry to produce the level of competition originally promised. When his Massachusetts colleague House Speaker Tip O'Neill first assigned him a coveted seat on the Energy and Commerce Committee, Markey — impressed by the high-tech boom around suburban Boston's Route 128 — joined the panel's Telecommunications Subcommittee. In early 1987, Markey became chairman of the subcommittee. It was a couple of years after a court ordered the breakup of the old "Ma Bell" monopoly, setting in motion a transformation of the nation's telecommunications industry.

In 1992, Markey crafted a cable TV regulation bill with enough support to override President George H.W. Bush's veto. The measure helped establish today's satellite TV industry. Markey lost the gavel of the Telecommunications Subcommittee when Republicans captured the House majority in 1994 but continued to exert influence as its ranking Democrat. He was a major player in passage of the landmark Telecommunications Act of 1996. The law, co-authored with Texas Republican Rep. Jack Fields, helped prod cable firms to build the broadband networks integral to the flow of information and images over today's internet. "Google, Hulu, YouTube — none of it was possible before the 1996 Telecom Act," Markey told the Globe years later. "It required broadband in order to make the business models possible."

Fast forward more than two decades, and a high point of Markey's Senate tenure came in May 2018 when — in what he trumpeted as "the most important vote we're going to have in this generation on the internet" — he led a successful effort to reverse the Trump administration's repeal of "net neutrality" rules. During the Obama administration, the Federal Communications Commission adopted rules intended to ensure that internet service providers gave equal treatment and access to all traffic on the internet; the FCC under Trump voted to repeal those regulations. Markey persuaded three Senate Republicans to join Democrats in a 52-47 vote to reinstate the 2015 regulations. His measure died in the House, but, when Democrats regained that chamber after the 2018 elections, Markey vowed to try again — as House Democratic leaders mobilized support to do so.

Markey's other major legislative interest — energy and environment — became his priority after Democrats regained the House after the 2006 elections. Speaker Nancy Pelosi chose Markey to chair a Select Committee on Energy Independence and Global Warming. It was an attempt to get around Michigan Rep. John Dingell, who as chairman of the Energy and Commerce Committee and a representative of an auto manufacturing-dependent district, had resisted efforts to toughen motor vehicle emission standards. When Dingell objected to the select committee, Pelosi announced it would not have authority to propose legislation — but she gave Markey free rein to hold hearings and make the case for a far-reaching bill to curb climate change.

After the 2008 elections, Dingell was ousted as head of the Energy and Commerce Committee, and Markey became chairman of the panel's Energy and Environment Subcommittee while retaining the select committee gavel. It gave Pelosi the players she needed to pass legislation to achieve Democrats' goal of an 85 percent cut in greenhouse gas emissions by 2050, along with a cap-and-trade program to compel companies to buy and sell credits to reduce emissions. Markey worked with the energy and manufacturing industries to gain support — or at least to reduce their opposition. After intense negotiations, the bill passed the House 219-212 in June 2009. But the Senate never took up the bill, and the issue has since made little headway on Capitol Hill. Markey told Boston magazine the bill's failure to become law was the "top" disappointment of his career.

A decade later, in early 2019, Markey again captured headlines as lead Senate sponsor of a nonbinding resolution for a "Green New Deal" pushed by the Democrats' newly emboldened progressive wing. The resolution, which urged a "10-year national mobilization effort" to achieve "net-zero greenhouse gas emissions," was co-sponsored by six Senate Democrats seeking the party's presidential nomination, including Warren. But its aspirations not only were criticized by conservatives as extreme, some liberals contended the inclusion of other sweeping goals, such as "to create millions of good, high-wage jobs and ensure prosperity and economic security," diminished emphasis on climate change. In an interview with Yale Environment 360, Markey said: "This resolution has generated more debate about climate change in three weeks than we've had in the last nine years. And that's a good thing." Included in the resolution was the goal of cleaning up hazardous waste and abandoned industrial sites: Bipartisan legislation introduced in early 2017 by Markey and Inhofe sought to encourage cleanup and reuse of "brownfields."

In the first bill introduced after his 2013 election to the Senate, Markey took aim at electric utilities — proposing a requirement that 25 percent of the power they distribute come from renewable energy sources by 2025; he noted 30 states had taken similar steps on their own. It bespoke Markey's lifelong opposition to nuclear power — which he has argued is linked inextricably to the spread of nuclear weapons. As a junior House member, Markey in 1979 pushed for a temporary ban on nuclear power plant construction. A year later, at the Democratic National Convention in New York, anti-nuclear activists threatened to collect enough signatures to put Markey up for the vice presidential nomination if convention organizers didn't grant him a prime-time speaking slot. The ploy gave the 34-year-old Markey 10 minutes to make the case to a national audience to shut down nuclear reactors and increase solar energy.

Almost four decades later, Markey is a gray-haired, veteran deal-maker — but one who has not strayed too far in tone from his rebellious youth. When Obama, during a visit to Hiroshima, Japan, in May 2016, called for a "moral awakening" and reiterated his hope for a future free of nuclear weapons, Markey took a swipe at the president for what he characterized as a "Faustian bargain" in a 2010 arms treaty with Russia — which allowed a nuclear weapons modernization plan that Markey said would cost $1 trillion over 30 years. Following the 2016 elections, amid statements from Trump indicating a willingness to engage in a renewed arms race, Markey introduced legislation to prohibit the president from launching a nuclear first strike without a declaration of war by Congress. "Donald Trump can launch nuclear codes just as easily as he can use his Twitter account," Markey said during a Foreign Relations Committee hearing.

Markey plans to seek reelection in 2020, when he will be 74. There has been widespread speculation about a possible Democratic primary challenge from among a younger generation of officeholders. But Reps. Seth Moulton -- who later announced his candidacy for the 2020 presidential nomination -- and Joe Kennedy at the end of 2018 disavowed any plans to take on Markey. In May 2019, Shannon Liss-Riordan, a Boston-based labor attorney who has been involved in several high-profile cases, announced for the Democratic nomination -- calling herself an "outsider." Speculation about Markey's future has been fueled by the 2018 primary defeat of home-state Rep. Michael Capuano. Like Markey, Capuano was a long-serving, reliably liberal legislator. But, also like Markey, Capuano — 66 at the time of his defeat — was an older white man at a time when the Democratic Party electorate showed a desire for greater diversity among its nominees.

Richard Neal (D)

Elected 1988, 16th term, b. Feb 14, 1949; Worcester; American International College (MA), B.A., 1972; University of Hartford Barney School of Business (CT), M.P.A., 1976; University of Massachusetts, Att., 1982; Roman Catholic; Married (Maureen Conway Neal); 4 children.

Elected Office: Springfield City Council, 1978-1983; Springfield Mayor, 1984-1988.

Professional Career: Staff Assistant, Springfield Mayor William C. Sullivan, 1973-1978; H.S. & college teacher, 1978-1983.

DC Office: 2309 RHOB 20515, 202-225-5601, Fax: 202-225-8112, neal.house.gov

State Offices: Pittsfield, 413-442-0946; Springfield, 413-785-0325.

Committees: *Joint Taxation (Chmn). Ways & Means (Chmn).*

Group Ratings

	ADA	ACLU	AFL-CIO	LCV	ITI	COC	HAFA	ACU	CFG	FRC
2018	-	82%	-	89%	-	58%	6%	4%	12%	0%
2017	90%	C	97%	100%	C	36%	C	4%	5%	0%

Almanac Ratings 2017-18

	Economy	Social	Foreign	Composite
Liberal	100%	94%	95%	96%
Conservative	0%	6%	5%	4%

Key Votes of the 115th Congress

1. Obama-care revision	N	5. Family planning regs	N	9. Guantanamo prisoners	Y
2. Tax Cuts	N	6. Body cameras/immigration	Y	10. Ground missiles, limit	Y
3. Omnibus appropriations	Y	7. Abortion ban	N	11. Defense Dept. spending	N
4. Dodd-Frank revision	N	8. Concealed carry	N	12. FISA rules	N

Election Results

Election	Name (Party)	Vote (%)	Cand. Spent	Ind. Exp. Support	Ind. Exp. Oppose
2018 General	Richard Neal (D)............................. 211,790	(98%)	$2,366,616	$5,580	
2018 Primary	Richard Neal (D)............................... 49,696	(71%)			
	Tahirah Amatul-Wadud (D)........... 20,565	(29%)			

Prior winning percentages: 2016 (73%), 2014 (74%), 2012 (78%), 2010 (57%), 2008 (76%), 2006(77%), 2004 (77%), 2002 (77%), 2000 (95%), 1998 (99%), 1996 (72%), 1994 (59%), 1992 (53%), 1990 (68%), 1988 (80%).

Democrat Richard Neal, first elected in 1988, stepped up 30 years later to become chairman of the tax-writing Ways and Means Committee. Asserting himself as one of his party's leaders on economic policy, he promised an active policy agenda, including on health care and retirement security. Although he has a history of finding common ground with Republicans, immediate prospects for bipartisanship seemed limited. Neal also staked his authority to review the tax returns of President Donald Trump. The Boston Globe profiled him as "the insider's insider, a veteran relationship-builder on Capitol Hill, a quiet dealmaker."

Neal grew up in Springfield amid the racial tensions of the 1960s. His parents died when he was a teenager, and Neal and his younger sisters received monthly Social Security survivor benefits while being raised by their grandmother and aunt. He graduated from American International College and earned a master's degree in public administration from the University of Hartford. In Springfield, he worked for the mayor; in 1978, while teaching high school and college history, he was elected to the City Council. As mayor from 1984 to 1988, Neal worked to rehabilitate the downtown area and revitalize neighborhoods.

His congressional predecessor, 36-year incumbent Edward Boland, chairman of the House Intelligence Committee and a longtime pal of Democratic Speaker Tip O'Neill, essentially bequeathed him the House seat. Boland announced his retirement just before the filing deadline — and after Neal had traveled the district for a year. Unopposed in the Democratic primary, Neal won the general election with 80 percent of the vote.

Neal has a generally liberal voting record, but has favored enough moderate initiatives to separate himself from more-liberal Massachusetts colleagues. He voted for the 1996 welfare overhaul and supported both the North American Free Trade Agreement and normalization of trade relations with China, although organized labor opposed the pacts. In 2015, he opposed trade promotion authority for the president — a virtually mandatory position for a senior Democrat in the House.

At Ways & Means, he had a longstanding interest in retirement security, especially for the middle class, and has filed a bipartisan bill that set guidelines for insurance companies and other investment firms to advise their account-holders. He worked with the Obama administration on a bill to require employers who do not sponsor retirement plans for their workers to automatically enroll them in individual retirement accounts funded by payroll deductions, unless an employee opts out. In his first major initiative as chairman, he proposed an innovative plan to create a Treasury Department office that would issue bonds to finance loans to pension plans in a "critical and declining" status. He has sought to reform the tax code, which he has said is "creaking under its own weight;" as chairman, he began by reviewing the Republican-passed tax cuts of 2017. He took the lead for House Democrats on a popular proposal to clamp down on companies that incorporate in Bermuda and other offshore havens to avoid U.S. taxes. Neal crusaded for repeal of the alternative minimum tax, which had increasingly ensnared middle-income taxpayers. Republicans included the repeal in their tax bill, but Neal voted against it anyway. On health care, he moved quickly for House action to assure that pre-existing conditions were covered under Obamacare.

As Ways and Means chairman, he shared with the chairman of the Senate Finance Committee the unique authority to review the returns of all taxpayers, as described by the tax law. In April 2019, he formally requested that the Internal Revenue Service provide him the tax filings of President Donald Trump during the past six years. Unlike previous presidents, Trump has consistently objected to such review. A courtroom showdown grew likely.

Neal brings an old-style interest in bipartisanship that may be unfamiliar to many junior Democrats in the House. "I think of him as someone who remembers he's a Democrat but harkens back to the old days where we were able to work across the aisle together," Janice Mays, a former Democratic staff director at Ways and Means, told the Globe. His move to the top post was a long grind. When Charles Rangel of New York was forced to step down as committee chairman in 2010 while battling ethics problems, Neal vigorously pushed for the job, arguing that the party needed to shelve its seniority tradition in favor of having a better spokesman in the role. He contended he would be a more business-friendly alternative to Sander Levin of Michigan and could work more closely with Republicans to get bills passed. He won a 23-22 vote of the Democratic Steering Committee. But he lost to Levin in the full caucus, 109-78. Following the 2016 election, the 85-year-old Levin cut back his responsibilities. Rep. Xavier Becerra of California quickly voiced interest in replacing Levin. The following day, Becerra unexpectedly accepted an offer by Gov. Jerry Brown to fill the vacancy as attorney general of California. Neal fulfilled his ambition without a challenge from another Democrat.

On local issues, Neal has focused on the economic problems of Springfield. He has secured funds for renovation of its Union Station, and more than $100 million for high-speed rail service in the region. With the large number of former Puerto Ricans living in his district, he took a special interest in the slow recovery from the devastation of the island that resulted from Hurricane Maria in September 2017. In May 2018, he demanded that the Trump administration assure funds for "infrastructure that supports utility services critical to health care delivery."

Neal had serious primary challenges in 1990 and 1992, but won reelection by healthy margins. He faced a challenge in 2010 from Republican business executive Thomas Wesley, who spent only $144,000 to $2.2 million for the incumbent. Neal campaigned aggressively, but was held to 57 percent of the vote. In 2018, he faced a primary challenge from Tahirah Amatul-Wadud, a lawyer and political newcomer who was hoping to join the Democratic insurgency that year against veteran incumbents. Amatul-Wadud spent $150,000 — 5 percent of Neal's total for the cycle — and lost, 71%-29%; she took 12 of the small hill towns in the sprawling district, but got only 24 percent in Springfield.

Following the 2016 election, Neal joined the House Democratic advocates of internal change. "It's time for the Democratic Party to start thinking about a reset," Neal said. "I've been arguing about this for years. That in many ways, the people who voted for Donald Trump, they used to be our people." Even with his independent streak, he remained loyal to Democratic Leader Nancy Pelosi when Rep. Tim Ryan of Ohio challenged her — a shrewd move, given his own influential niche. Two years later, he worked the phones on behalf of Pelosi for Speaker — at a time when other colleagues from Massachusetts were hostile or lukewarm toward her. "We're working hard to bring them into the tent," Neal told a business group in Boston before the outcome was resolved, the Springfield Republican reported. "There'll be a reconciliation." At age 69, he settled in for what he hoped would be a long and productive tenure at Ways and Means. In his first months as chairman, Neal took the lead on behalf of House Democrats in demanding that the Treasury Department give him access to Trump's tax records. When Treasury Secretary Steven Mnuchin refused, Neal planned for action in the federal courts.

MA-1: Western Massachusetts   **Cook Partisan Voting Index: D+12**

Population		Race and Ethnicity		Income	
Total	731,327	White	72.9%	Median Income	$55,577
Land area (sq. miles)	2,350	Black	5.7%	District Income Rank	223
Pop/ sq mi	311.2	Latino	17.4%	Poverty Rate	14.7%
Born in State	66.2%	Asian	2%	With health insurance	96.9%
		Two or more races	1.7%	Cash public assistance	3.9%
Age Groups		Other	0.3%	Food stamp/SNAP	18.7%
Under 18	20.8%				
18-34	22.4%	**Education**		**Work**	
35-64	39.8%	H.S grad or less	42.3%	White Collar	17%
Over 64	17%	Some college	28.5%	Sales and Service	43.7%
		College Degree, 4 yr	17%	Blue Collar	19.9%
Military		Post grad	12.1%	Government	14.4%
Veteran/ Active Duty	8.1%				

2012 Pres. Vote	Obama	213,423	(64%)	Romney	114,339	(34%)			
2016 Pres. Vote	Clinton	194,036	(56%)	Trump	123,953	(36%)	Johnson	14,550	(4%)

Springfield, Pittsfield: The stony hills and green mountains of western Massachusetts, which so inspired Henry David Thoreau in the 1840s, look a lot like they did 300 years ago. This was the frontier in the 17th century, where Puritan preachers founded towns in the wilderness, farmed the rocky soil and preached against declension. It remained Yankee New England's western frontier for nearly 200 years. In the 19th century, the area was the home of writers and artists. Edith Wharton lived grandly on her estate in Lenox. Herman Melville struck up a friendship with Nathaniel Hawthorne after purchasing a farm near Hawthorne's Pittsfield home, not far from where the Boston Symphony plays at the Tanglewood Festival each summer. As the 20th century progressed, much of western Massachusetts returned to its bucolic state. Few giant factories remain along the wide Connecticut River or the country streams. An exception is the Crane & Co. paper mill along the Housatonic River in Dalton, which since 1879 has been the only company to print money for the U.S. Treasury. The currency-production part of the company, which is the benchmark for producing currency and preventing counterfeiting, was sold in 2017 to the Connecticut-based Crane Co.—a different family. In 2018, Crane's stationery operations were purchased by a New York-based paper company. In each case, production remained at the Dalton plant. Tourism and vacation homes have been bustling in the Berkshires, but the day-to-day economy has not recovered from factory shutdowns. Even the dairy farms have shrunk, due to lower demand and economies of scale.

Springfield is the largest city in western Massachusetts and the fourth-largest in New England, far from Boston in mindset and distance but with its own historical cachet. It is the site of the armory where unhappy farmers mounted Shays' Rebellion in 1786-87. It is where basketball was invented and where the Webster's unabridged dictionaries were edited and published. Founded by Puritans in the 17th century, Springfield has become home to immigrants from a dozen countries who have worked their way up here. Hispanics and African Americans, respectively, account for 44 percent and 21 percent of the population; the poverty rate of 29 percent contrasts with 10 percent statewide.

Springfield's downtown has emptied and its tax base has shrunk in recent decades. Business leaders have tried to revive it, in part with the expansion of the Basketball Hall of Fame. The firearms manufacturer Smith & Wesson and MassMutual insurance are headquartered in Springfield. But the once-robust city has suffered from corruption and serious crime, and in 2004 was forced to submit to state control in a financial bailout. Other than tourism and academia, the economy in much of the area has remained stagnant. The August 2018 opening of the MGM casino on 14 acres in what had been the down-and-out South End of Springfield has created rare hope; success was not a sure bet, especially with competition from two long-standing tribal casinos in Connecticut. Springfield has shown other signs of life, including a $95 million rehab of the downtown train station, which reopened in 2017 with expanded service to New Haven. A $100 million factory in East Springfield started by building rail cars for the Boston-area transit system, and added Philadelphia and Los Angeles.

For many years, western Massachusetts was a heartland of the Republican Party — flinty, thrifty and chilly, just like the area's most famous politician, Calvin Coolidge. Frederick Gillett overlapped with President Coolidge for part of his six years as Speaker of the House. The area now contains some of the most liberal precincts of the United States. Progressive MSNBC host Rachel Maddow began as a broadcaster here and still has a home with her partner, Susan Mikula. "We kind of forget we're gay," Mikula told New York magazine. "We live in western Mass and New York, and it's very accommodating." Alice's Restaurant in Great Barrington was immortalized by folk singer Arlo Guthrie in his anti-war song of the same name.

The 1st District in western Massachusetts includes Springfield and the old mill towns Chicopee and Holyoke along the river, plus Dalton and once-industrial Pittsfield in the Berkshires. As recently as 1991, liberal Republican Silvio Conte represented much of this area in Congress. Not anymore. The district votes consistently Democratic, though the local orneriness reduced the presidential vote margin to 56%-36% in 2016.

Jim McGovern (D)

Elected 1996, 12th term, b. Nov 20, 1959; Worcester; American University (DC), B.A., 1981; American University (DC), M.P.A., 1984; Roman Catholic; Married (Lisa Murray McGovern); 2 children.

Professional Career: Aide, U.S. Sen. George McGovern, 1981-1984; Sr. aide, U.S. Rep. Joseph Moakley, 1982-1996.

DC Office: 408 CHOB 20515, 202-225-6101, Fax: 202-225-5759, mcgovern.house.gov

State Offices: Leominster, 978-466-3552; Northampton, 413-341-8700; Worcester, 508-831-7356.

Committees: *Agriculture*: Subcommittee Nutrition, Oversight & Department Operations. *Rules (Chmn)*; Legislative & Budget Process; Rules & Organization of the House.

Group Ratings

	ADA	ACLU	AFL-CIO	LCV	ITI	COC	HAFA	ACU	CFG	FRC
2018	-	89%	-	100%	-	50%	8%	4%	15%	0%
2017	100%	C	95%	100%	C	36%	C	7%	5%	0%

Almanac Ratings 2017-18

	Economy	Social	Foreign	Composite
Liberal	100%	100%	99%	100%
Conservative	0%	0%	1%	0%

Key Votes of the 115th Congress

1. Obama-care revision	N	5. Family planning regs	N	9. Guantanamo prisoners	Y
2. Tax Cuts	N	6. Body cameras/immigration	Y	10. Ground missiles, limit	Y
3. Omnibus appropriations	N	7. Abortion ban	N	11. Defense Dept. spending	N
4. Dodd-Frank revision	N	8. Concealed carry	N	12. FISA rules	N

Election Results

Election	Name (Party)	Vote (%)	Cand. Spent	Ind. Exp. Support	Ind. Exp. Oppose
2018 General	Jim McGovern (D).......................... 191,332	(67%)	$881,072		
	Tracy Lovvorn (R)............................ 93,391	(33%)	$34,934		
2018 Primary	Jim McGovern (D).......................................	(100%)			

Prior winning percentages: 2016 (98%), 2014 (72%), 2012 (76%), 2010 (57%), 2008 (75%), 2006(78%), 2004 (67%), 2002 (77%), 2000 (77%), 1998 (57%), 1996 (53%)

Jim McGovern, a liberal Democrat first elected in 1996, has been a savvy insider and active progressive on such causes as international human rights and ending hunger. In 2019, he became chairman of the House Rules Committee, a prime position that gives him influence on virtually all issues and access to other power centers. With his long apprenticeship and his parliamentary skills, McGovern had an opportunity for a long reign — assuming that he and others can satisfy the often-conflicting demands of Democratic factions.

McGovern grew up in Worcester, where his parents owned a liquor store. He attended American University in Washington and, while in graduate school, worked in South Dakota Sen. George McGovern's office. He ran McGovern's quixotic 1984 campaign in the Massachusetts presidential primary, where the senator finished third with 21 percent of the vote, and nominated him that year at the Democratic convention in San Francisco. Although not related by blood, Jim McGovern called George "my inspiration, my mentor, my dearest friend." He was an aide in Boston-area Rep. Joe Moakley's office and became chief of staff just as Moakley ascended to chairman of the Rules Committee. McGovern was the chief investigator in a 1989 review of the murders of six Jesuits and two lay women in El Salvador, which led to a cutoff of U.S. aid to the country.

In 1994, McGovern ran for the House and lost in the Democratic primary, 38%-30%. In 1996, he ran again, this time with no primary opposition. In the general election, Republican Rep. Peter Blute stressed his independence from then-Speaker Newt Gingrich and attacked McGovern for liberal stands on abortion rights and Cuba. McGovern ran a humorous spot that asked, "If you wouldn't vote for Newt, why would you ever vote for Blute?" At age 36, McGovern won, 53%-45%.

With deft maneuvers reflecting his Capitol Hill experience, McGovern positioned himself as a power broker in the Democratic caucus. In 2001, the dying Moakley asked Democratic Leader Dick Gephardt to help McGovern get a seat on Rules, which schedules most legislation for the House floor. McGovern got a commitment for the next available Democratic seat, with added seniority benefits. Moakley, who owed his Rules Committee seat to Speaker Tip O'Neill more than two decades earlier, showed how powerful players can retain influence in the House long after they have died.

On Rules, McGovern started with the advantage of being well-versed in House procedures. With the GOP in the majority, he showed a sharp partisan edge as he pursued parliamentary maneuvers that led to cries of outrage from House Republicans. When Louise Slaughter of New York died in March 2018, McGovern replaced her in the top Democratic post on Rules. His longstanding goals for House operations, he said, were increased public confidence in the House and more open debate, though he opposed Republican use of what he called "gotcha" amendments.

His foreign policy interests have been far-ranging. For years, McGovern was a party leader on Iraq war policy, though his influence has been more rhetorical than in changing policy. He sponsored an unsuccessful 2007 bill to withdraw U.S. troops from Iraq in six months. He turned his attention to Afghanistan, and in 2011 nearly succeeded in getting the House to pass a resolution aimed at accelerating troop withdrawals. McGovern was the House sponsor of a measure signed into law in 2012 that imposed a visa ban and asset freeze on suspected Russian human rights abusers. Russian President Vladimir Putin protested it was an intrusion into his country's affairs and retaliated by halting U.S. adoptions of Russian children, prompting McGovern to call Putin a "bully." On the Cuba Working Group, McGovern welcomed the 2014 announcement by President Barack Obama to open the diplomatic door to Cuba as "a historic, long-overdue day." When he joined the congressional delegation that accompanied Obama to Cuba in March 2016, it was at least his sixteenth visit since he was a college student in 1979. During a February 2017 visit with a congressional delegation to Cuba, he "explored new partnerships between our countries," including some on behalf of Massachusetts interests. Following the apparent murder in October 2018 of Saudi journalist Jamal Khashoggi, he sponsored a bipartisan bill to halt military sales and aid to Saudi Arabia. In December 2018, President

Donald Trump signed McGovern's bill to require that the State Department punish Chinese officials who interfere with the rights of Americans seeking access to Tibet.

McGovern pushed for a government-run public option in the 2010 health care overhaul bill, though it was dropped under pressure from Democratic moderates. Since the Supreme Court's 2010 Citizens United decision, he has introduced bills aimed at diminishing the influence of money in politics. His Almanac vote ratings have shown consistently high liberal scores. During the official counting of the electoral votes for the 2016 election, he cited reports of Russian interference in the election in his unsuccessful challenge to the proceeding. He refused "to sit quietly when our democratic institutions are under attack," he tweeted.

As chairman of the Congressional Hunger Center, McGovern has pushed for more spending on international nutrition and for less support of biofuels, which he says have driven up food costs. He has scheduled regular events to publicize his cause, sometimes with Republican allies, including "End Hunger Now" speeches. As ranking Democrat on the House Agriculture Subcommittee on Nutrition, he branded GOP efforts to cut domestic funding for food stamps "unconscionable" and "immoral." He says, "We know how to end hunger. It's not that hard."

Although Republicans held this seat not long ago, they have all but given up on it. McGovern has run unopposed in 7 of the past 10 elections, though he was held to 57 percent in the anti-Democratic environment of 2010. Like other old-school Democrats, he has been comfortable in setting long-term strategies and pressing until their time returns.

As he prepared to take over as committee chairman, McGovern recounted to the Springfield Republican newspaper that Moakley decades earlier counseled him, "Learn the names of every member of the House and be patient because some day you can be chairman of the Rules Committee." Moakley, in particular, urged him not to "do anything stupid like run for the Senate" and to remember, "Good waiters get good tips." With Rep. Richard Neal of the adjacent district as chairman of the Ways and Means Committee, western Massachusetts had prime influence.

MA-2: West Central Massachusetts

Cook Partisan Voting Index: D+9

Population		Race and Ethnicity		Income	
Total	744,002	White	78.1%	Median Income	$66,319
Land area (sq. miles)	1,628	Black	4.7%	District Income Rank	125
Pop/ sq mi	457	Latino	9.3%	Poverty Rate	12.2%
Born in State	65.1%	Asian	5.5%	With health insurance	97.3%
		Two or more races	2%	Cash public assistance	3%
Age Groups		Other	0.4%	Food stamp/SNAP	12.3%
Under 18	20.2%				
18-34	25.1%	Education		Work	
35-64	40%	H.S grad or less	36.7%	White Collar	14.7%
Over 64	14.7%	Some college	25.4%	Sales and Service	39.9%
		College Degree, 4 yr	21.7%	Blue Collar	17.2%
Military		Post grad	16.2%	Government	14.9%
Veteran/ Active Duty	6.8%				

2012 Pres. Vote	Obama	199,549	(59%)	Romney	133,195	(39%)		
2016 Pres. Vote	Clinton	197,492	(55%)	Trump	129,437	(36%)	Johnson 17,743	(5%)

Worcester: For more than 200 years, Worcester has been one of the nation's centers of tinkering, contriving and inventing, even though it is one of the few active industrial cities not located on a river, lake or seacoast. In the past, its biggest industries were valentine-making, wire-making, textiles, grinding wheels and envelopes. It is where the birth control pill was invented and where Worcester native and Clark University professor Robert Goddard shot off experimental rockets before relieved locals saw him off to New Mexico.

In the 1970s and 1980s, electronics and computer firms sprouted along Interstate 495 — the circumferential highway 20 miles east of Worcester — just as they had earlier around Route 128, closer to Boston. The high-tech boom brought prosperity, labor shortages, new residents and higher housing prices to central Massachusetts. Since then, Worcester's ingenious entrepreneurs and skilled labor force hustled. Local leaders set up a Biotechnology Research Institute to draw on the city's nine colleges and institutions of higher learning to steer the city back on course. "Worcester is booming," as a secondary market to crowded and expensive Boston, National Public Radio reported in October

2018. The area has gained the accoutrements of urban modernity, including service by major airlines and relocation of the top minor league franchise of the Boston Red Sox — for which Worcester has agreed to build in 2021 a new $90 million stadium, a deal that the team's landlord in Pawtucket, Rhode Island was not willing to provide. Worcester led Massachusetts in the number of applications for recreational marijuana licenses.

Just as Worcester's economy has changed, so has its face, with big increases in Asians and Hispanics, mainly from Puerto Rico. The area has also attracted Hmong, Vietnamese, Albanians and Africans, many of whom fled the civil war in Liberia. The second-largest city in New England, Worcester's population has increased 7 percent since 2000. The city population is 69 percent white, though the non-whites are younger and their numbers are growing faster than the whites.

The concentration of colleges and universities in the area west of Worcester brings together a critical mass of scholars and graduate students. The University of Massachusetts in Amherst is the largest, as it has expanded on former farmland. Also nearby are Amherst College and Smith College in Northampton, though the financial future of avant garde Hampshire College was in doubt in early 2019. Noted abolitionist Thomas Wentworth Higginson was the pastor of the Free Church in Worcester during the 1850s. He also became a literary mentor to a young Emily Dickinson, who lived quietly most of her life in Amherst.

The 2nd Congressional District includes Worcester and part of the Pioneer Valley. The population includes 10 percent Hispanics, and 5 percent each of Asians and blacks. To the north, it takes in Connecticut River towns such as Deerfield to the Vermont border. To the west is socially leftist Northampton. The district extends east to Leominster, a western outpost of the Boston suburbs, plus the intersection of 495 and the Massachusetts Turnpike that takes commuters into Boston. Many of the small rural towns west of Worcester vote Republican. But the district overall is firmly Democratic.

Lori Trahan (D)

Elected 2018, 1st term, b. Oct 27, 1973; Lowell; Georgetown University (DC), B.S., 1995; Catholic; Married (David Trahan); 2 children; 3 stepchildren.

Professional Career: Chief of Staff, U.S. Rep. Marty Meehan, 1995-2005; ChoiceStream, 2005-2011.

DC Office: 1616 LHOB 20515, 202-225-3411, trahan.house.gov

State Offices: Lowell, 978-459-0101.

Committees: *Armed Services*: Intelligence, Emerging Threats & Capabilities; Military Personnel. *Education & Labor*: Health, Employment, Labor & Pensions; Higher Education & Workforce Investment.

Election Results

Election	Name (Party)	Vote (%)		Cand. Spent	Ind. Exp. Support	Ind. Exp. Oppose
2018 General	Lori Trahan (D)	173,175	(62%)	$2,417,514		
	Rick Green (R)	93,445	(33%)	$921,406		
	Mike Mullen (I)	12,572	(5%)	$17,606		
2018 Primary	Lori Trahan (D)	18,580	(22%)			
	Dan Koh (D)	18,435	(22%)			
	Barbara L'Italien (D)	13,018	(15%)			
	Juana Matias (D)	12,993	(15%)			
	Rufus Gifford (D)	12,873	(15%)			
	Alexandra Chandler (D)	4,846	(6%)			

Freshman Democrat Lori Trahan narrowly won her competitive primary after a recount that lasted nearly two weeks. She breezed to victory in November in a district that has not elected a Republican since the 1970s. The campaign was her first bid for elected office. But she had long experience in local and congressional politics, including serving as a top aide in Washington for a Member who held the same seat. Trahan succeeded Niki Tsongas, who became a political force in her own right in a seat that was once held by her husband Paul Tsongas, who later sought the Democratic presidential nomination.

Trahan -- who grew up in what she called a "hard scrabble, working-class" neighborhood in Lowell — graduated from Georgetown University, where she majored in international relations and was a leader of the volleyball team; she later attended Harvard Business School. She worked nearly a decade as an aide to Democratic Rep. Marty Meehan and served as his chief of staff; Meehan, who resigned in 2007, became president of the University of Massachusetts. She served two years as deputy treasurer of Massachusetts. In the private sector, she worked for a Boston-area advertising firm and was chief executive for five years of the Concire Leadership Institute, which provides strategic consulting to businesses.

After Tsongas announced her retirement, the Democratic primary to succeed her became a wide-open contest. Trahan emphasized her local roots and the need for more women in Washington. "Better decisions are made when women are at the table," she told the Lowell Sun. The early frontrunner and best-financed candidate was Daniel Koh, who was chief of staff to Boston Mayor Marty Walsh; although the district is well outside his city, Walsh campaigned actively on behalf of Koh, whose parents were Lebanese and Korean. Other leading candidates included Rufus Gifford, a former ambassador to Denmark who had been finance director for President Barack Obama's 2012 reelection campaign, plus state lawmakers Barbara L'Italien and Juana Matias.

With the large field, the 10 Democratic candidates had little opportunity to engage with each other at local forums. During an event in June, each candidate had time to respond to only two questions. In its endorsement of Trahan, The Boston Globe cited her "granular understanding of what she hopes to accomplish in Washington."

In the unusually tight outcome, Trahan had 22 percent of the vote, with a 145-vote lead over Koh. L'Italien, Matias and Gifford trailed the leaders, with 15 percent each. Trahan's narrow lead in the election-night results had minor changes in the recount, which was supervised by the Secretary of State's office. Of the district's 37 cities and towns, Koh and Trahan led in 13 and 12, respectively. Trahan took 34 percent in Lowell and also led in several nearby towns. Koh -- who spent $3.1 million, more than twice what Trahan spent in the primary -- lacked a sizable local base.

Matias, a state representative who was born in the Dominican Republic, took 70 per cent of the vote in Lawrence, the second-largest city in the district, but that was the only place in which she ran first. L'Italien, who served 12 years in the Legislature and was endorsed by teachers unions, ran relatively well across the district but failed to capture a single town. Gifford took upscale Concord and benefited from nearly $160,000 in spending by gay-rights groups.

In November, Trahan defeated Rick Green, the wealthy owner of an online auto parts business. He ran unsuccessfully for state Republican chairman in 2013 and founded the Massachusetts Fiscal Alliance, a conservative group that published scorecards on state legislators.

With the splintered vote in her successful primary, Trahan's greatest political risk might be a single Democratic challenger who has a strong local or ideological base.

MA-3: North Central Massachusetts

Cook Partisan Voting Index: D+9

Population		Race and Ethnicity		Income	
Total	760,993	White	68%	Median Income	$74,586
Land area (sq. miles)	758	Black	2.9%	District Income Rank	72
Pop/ sq mi	1004.1	Latino	19.1%	Poverty Rate	11.7%
Born in State	61.2%	Asian	7.7%	With health insurance	96.6%
		Two or more races	1.8%	Cash public assistance	3.4%
Age Groups		Other	0.4%	Food stamp/SNAP	14.1%
Under 18	23%				
18-34	21.9%	**Education**		**Work**	
35-64	41.6%	H.S grad or less	38.3%	White Collar	13.5%
Over 64	13.5%	Some college	24.2%	Sales and Service	38.6%
		College Degree, 4 yr	21.1%	Blue Collar	18.7%
Military		Post grad	16.4%	Government	11.8%
Veteran/ Active Duty	6.1%				

2012 Pres. Vote	Obama	189,461	(57%)	Romney	137,869	(41%)			
2016 Pres. Vote	Clinton	202,952	(57%)	Trump	123,347	(35%)	Johnson	17,580	(5%)

Lowell, Lawrence: When Massachusetts was a kind of maritime republic in the 19th century, with its farmers struggling to scratch out a living from the stony soil, a few clever Yankees used their profits from the sea trade to try to tame the rapidly flowing Merrimack River and build cotton-spinning mills. Creating the cities of Lowell and Lawrence, they built model dormitories and recreation programs for their female workers. This was the center of America's textile industry for more than a century, long after the maritime industry faded. But in the 1920s, the price of labor rose and newly built mills in the Carolinas, much closer to the cotton supply, decimated the local industry that Lawrence and Lowell built. Many residents waited forlornly for an upturn in the local economy.

It came eventually, from an unexpected source. The high-tech industry drove the growth, beginning in the 1960s around the Massachusetts Institute of Technology, then moving out to the Route 128 ring road and eventually to Interstate 495, which passes through once-distant Lowell and Lawrence. Wang, headquartered in Lowell, grew spectacularly, and Democratic Sen. Paul Tsongas — the local kid who made it big before his early death to cancer — spearheaded a historic restoration of the old mill area. This was the Massachusetts miracle of the 1980s. Then came the bust: Sales of Wang's word processors and minicomputers slumped as businesses purchased personal computers and linked them together in networks.

But Lowell revived again. New immigrants provided vitality and entrepreneurial creativity. Cambodians owned many small businesses and are more than 30,000 of the local population, making Lowell second only to Long Beach California as a U.S. home for transplanted Cambodians, who fled their homeland following the brutal "killing fields" of the 1970s. Their experience in Lowell has helped to preserve Cambodian heritage and culture. Some monks conceived a Khmer monument on the Merrimack River to honor local Cambodians; unveiled in August 2017, the seven-foot stone structure featured a mother with her three young children. The former Wang buildings have been replaced with health care, banking, telecommunications and internet companies, plus fledgling renewable energy firms. Old mills have been converted to artists' lofts and upscale condos. Lawrence, which is 79 percent Hispanic and 39 percent foreign-born, became a prime target of the Trump administration as a sanctuary city. In a March 2018 speech across the state line in Manchester, President Donald Trump singled out Lawrence as a cause for the opioid crisis in New Hampshire, though local officials disagreed. In a December 2018 ranking, Lawrence was replaced by Springfield and Holyoke as the poorest city in the state.

The 3rd Congressional District of Massachusetts includes Lowell, Lawrence and the high-tech corridor along 1-495. The district includes tony suburbs near the Revolutionary War battleground of Concord, where the Minutemen stood their ground in 1775; rural and old mill towns that never revived in hills along the New Hampshire state line; and small towns west of Lowell. Except for Lowell and Lawrence, the district is ancestrally Yankee Republican. It is culturally liberal, with pockets of big wealth as well as new office parks where young families sought to live the American dream; it trended Democratic in the early 1970s. Back then, this area produced two Democratic candidates who would later run for president after having succeeded each other in the Senate: Tsongas and John Kerry. Although it went Republican in national and some statewide elections in the 1980s, the district as a whole leans to the Democrats.

Joe Kennedy (D)

Elected 2012, 4th term, b. Oct 04, 1980; Brighton; Buckingham Browne & Nichols School (MA); Stanford University (CA), B.S., 2003; Harvard University Law School (MA), J.D., 2009; Roman Catholic; Married (Lauren Birchfield); 2 children.

Professional Career: Peace Corps, 2004-2006; Assistant District Attorney, Cape & Islands, 2009-2011; Assistant District Attorney, Middlesex County, 2011-2012.

DC Office: 304 CHOB 20515, 202-225-5931, Fax: 202-225-0182, kennedy.house.gov

State Offices: Attleboro, 508-431-1110; Newton, 617-332-3333.

Committees: *Energy & Commerce*: Energy; Health; Oversight & Investigations.

Group Ratings

	ADA	ACLU	AFL-CIO	LCV	ITI	COC	HAFA	ACU	CFG	FRC
2018	-	89%	-	91%	-	50%	6%	4%	15%	0%
2017	85%	C	94%	94%	C	45%	C	4%	0%	0%

Almanac Ratings 2017-18

	Economy	Social	Foreign	Composite
Liberal	98%	95%	94%	96%
Conservative	2%	5%	6%	4%

Key Votes of the 115th Congress

1. Obama-care revision	N	5. Family planning regs	N	9. Guantanamo prisoners	Y
2. Tax Cuts	N	6. Body cameras/immigration	Y	10. Ground missiles, limit	Y
3. Omnibus appropriations	N	7. Abortion ban	N	11. Defense Dept. spending	N
4. Dodd-Frank revision	N	8. Concealed carry	NV	12. FISA rules	N

Election Results

Election	Name (Party)	Vote (%)	Cand. Spent	Ind. Exp. Support	Ind. Exp. Oppose
2018 General	Joe Kennedy (D)	245,289 (98%)	$2,980,968		
2018 Primary	Joe Kennedy (D)	60,214 (93%)			
	Gary Rucinski (D)	4,240 (7%)			

Prior winning percentages: 2016 (70%), 2014 (72%), 2012 (59%)

The election to the House in 2012 of Democrat Joseph (Joe) Kennedy III, grandson of the late Sen. Robert F. Kennedy, marked the arrival of the third generation of Kennedys to elected office. After an early period of keeping a low profile as he learned his way, he has become an informal leader of junior Democrats and comfortable in pushing his policy agenda. He has handled a Kennedy-size share of national attention. At his age, his grandfather and his great-uncles Jack and Ted already had been elected to the Senate, with varying apprenticeships.

The son of former Rep. Joe Kennedy II, who represented the Cambridge-based district from 1987 to 1999, Kennedy was born in Brighton, attended the elite Buckingham, Browne and Nichols School and shuffled between his divorced parents' homes in Cambridge and Brighton with his fraternal twin, Matt. Both majored in management science and engineering at Stanford University, where Kennedy was also a starting lacrosse goalie and team co-captain with his brother. His teammates knew him as a committed teetotaler, reportedly ordering milk when they went to bars and nicknaming him "Milkman." After graduating in 2003, Kennedy embarked on wo years in the Peace Corps. In the Dominican Republic, he helped to implement an economic development project.

Kennedy helped Matt manage Ted Kennedy's 2006 Senate reelection campaign, and he went on to study law at Harvard, where he was active in the Legal Aid Bureau, working as an advocate for tenants facing eviction from foreclosed properties. He worked on the Human Rights Journal and started an after-school program for at-risk youth in Boston. After graduating, Kennedy moved up to assistant district attorney in Middlesex County in 2011.

When Democratic Rep. Barney Frank decided to retire, Kennedy moved to Brookline to run for the seat. The AFL-CIO quickly endorsed him, and other potential candidates decided not to challenge the family name and money. He made economic fairness the central theme of his campaign, talking often about the need to create equal opportunity for education and jobs. Kennedy got help from his family, with grandmother Ethel Kennedy and both of his parents standing on street corners for him. Matt remained his most trusted confidant. Kennedy won the September primary with 90 percent of the vote.

Kennedy's Republican opponent, Marine reservist Sean Bielat, argued that Kennedy was running on his name. Kennedy characterized Bielat as a rubber stamp for Republican budget proposals, including a plan to introduce vouchers into the Medicare program. Kennedy outspent Bielat, $3.9 million to $1.1 million and won the seat, 61%-36%.

Kennedy identified his chief priority as boosting economic opportunities in his district through improved education and job training. He was one of several chief sponsors of the Revitalize American Manufacturing Act, which called for a national manufacturing strategic plan and was enacted in 2014. On the Energy and Commerce Committee, his priorities have included combating drug abuse and reducing energy prices. In 2018, he won enactment of bipartisan proposals to assure access to mental health services for children and increased availability of hearing aids to consumers.

Even with his liberal voting record, he has styled himself as bipartisan. He worked with Republican Rep. Susan Brooks of Indiana to solicit support for their bill to encourage education for opioid addiction prevention. Kennedy participates in an intense early-morning fitness program led by Republican Rep. Markwayne Mullin of Oklahoma, with whom he serves on Energy and Commerce.

While emphasizing that he was building his own record and not relying on his famous name, he knows that it is unlikely he would have made it to Congress at his age without those connections. Nancy Pelosi considered Kennedy for chairman of the Democratic Congressional Campaign Committee before selecting Ben Ray Lujan of New Mexico. He has taken advantage of his opportunities, including impressive fundraising skills. He raised a total of $14 million by 2018, and began the next cycle with a $4.2 million surplus.

He welcomed opportunities to move into the national spotlight. Speaking at a Texas rally in June 2018 with his friend Rep. Beto O'Rourke, Kennedy described the challenges that his ancestors faced as immigrants and he assailed President Donald Trump for his "betrayal of American values" by separating migrant children from their families at the border. In November 2018, he called for the national legalization of marijuana, adding that federal policy on marijuana was "badly broken." In a speech that month to a business group, he called for new economic policies that embrace what he called "moral capitalism" and offer an alternative vision to Trump.

In what seemed a revealing acknowledgment, Kennedy said he would "take a look" at a vacant Senate seat if home-state Sen. Elizabeth Warren had been elected vice president in 2016. At the Democratic National Convention that year, he introduced Warren — his former law professor — as "the toughest teacher on campus, but the wait list for her class was a mile long." With both Massachusetts senators eligible for Social Security, it's reasonable to view the latest Kennedy as near the front of that wait list -- though Rep. Seth Moulton and perhaps others likely would assure that Kennedy would not be granted a free ride. His selection to deliver the response to Trump's State of the Union message in 2018 confirmed his status as a rising star.

MA-4: Western Boston Suburbs   Cook Partisan Voting Index: D+9

Population		Race and Ethnicity		Income	
Total	751,263	White	84%	Median Income	$95,353
Land area (sq. miles)	668	Black	2.8%	District Income Rank	20
Pop/ sq mi	1124.2	Latino	4.6%	Poverty Rate	6.8%
Born in State	60.2%	Asian	5.9%	With health insurance	97.9%
		Two or more races	2.1%	Cash public assistance	1.9%
Age Groups		Other	0.5%	Food stamp/SNAP	7.6%
Under 18	22.6%				
18-34	20.5%	Education		Work	
35-64	41.8%	H.S grad or less	27.3%	White Collar	15.1%
Over 64	15.1%	Some college	22.5%	Sales and Service	35.2%
		College Degree, 4 yr	25.9%	Blue Collar	13.5%
Military		Post grad	24.4%	Government	11.3%
Veteran/ Active Duty	5.9%				

2012 Pres. Vote	Obama	211,423	(57%)	Romney	152,699	(41%)		
2016 Pres. Vote	Clinton	225,976	(58%)	Trump	133,705	(34%)	Johnson	17,360	(5%)

Brookline, Bristol County: The political transformation of Massachusetts is nowhere better illustrated than in the Boston suburbs of Newton and Brookline. These were Yankee enclaves a century ago, with avenues built to resemble the sweep of Haussmann's Grand Boulevards in Paris. Brookline was where the country club (the very first one) was established in 1882, and where Joseph Kennedy, an Irish Catholic 20-something banker seeking respectability moved his family in 1914. Brookline and Newton then were solidly Republican, the base of such leading politicians as Christian Herter, the governor of Massachusetts and U.S. secretary of State in the 1950s. As late as 1960, Brookline, Newton and adjacent wards of Boston were electing a Republican to Congress.

Then came the transformation, personified by the election in 1962 of Michael Dukakis at age 29 to the General Court (the legislature). As Massachusetts' university-educated classes became more liberal, as Jewish populations of Brookline and Newton grew, and as young, liberal-minded families refurbished the graceful old houses, these towns became Democratic bastions. The towns continue to diversify. Brookline is now 16 percent Asian, and nearly half of its school students are non-white. A local public school teaches Mandarin in kindergarten. In 2016, Newton was 31st when *Money* magazine ranked the "Best Places to Live in America." With a median price of $1.6 million, Brookline had the most expensive homes in the state. Not far behind is Newton, at $1.5 million. In a sign of the business development in these suburbs, NBC Universal planned to open in late 2019 a $125 million media center, with six televisions studios and easy access across the region.

The 4th Congressional District of Massachusetts starts with Brookline and Newton at its northern tip. Anchoring the district, they account for about a fifth of its population. About 40 miles away at the southern end of this district are the Bristol County cities of Freetown, Somerset and part of Fall River. Much of the port in Fall River has been rebuilt, chiefly for non-commercial purposes, including Heritage State Park and the boardwalk along the water. The northern and southern ends of the districts are very different sociologically and economically — affluent Boston suburbs suffered relatively little in the recession, the old textile-mill town of Fall River quite a lot. Connecting them is a corridor with a variety of towns — Foxborough with its Patriots football stadium; Sharon with its Orthodox Jews; Dover, the home of some old-time Boston Brahmins; and Wellesley with its college and high-income residents. Hopkinton is 26 miles, 385 yards from downtown Boston. Politically, these areas historically were mostly Republican but in recent decades they have been, like most of middle-income Massachusetts, Democratic.

Katherine Clark (D)

Elected 2013, 3rd full term, b. Jul 17, 1963; New Haven, CT; Saint Lawrence University, B.A., 1985; Cornell University Law School (NY), J.D., 1989; Harvard University John F. Kennedy School of Government (MA), M.P.A., 1997; Protestant - Unspecified Christian; Married (Rodney Dowell); 3 children.

Elected Office: MA House, 2008-2011; MA Senate, 2011-2013.

Professional Career: Clerk, Hon. Alfred Arraj, 1990-1991; Prosecutor, Colorado Attorney General office, 1991-1993; General counsel, MA Office of Child Care Svcs.; Policy Division Chief, MA Attorney General.

DC Office: 2448 RHOB 20515, 202-225-2836, Fax: 202-226-0092, katherineclark.house.gov

State Offices: Framingham, 508-319-9757; Malden, 617-354-0292.

Committees: House Democratic Caucus Vice Chairman. *Appropriations*: Labor, Health & Human Services, Education & Related Agencies; Legislative Branch; Transportation, HUD & Related Agencies.

Group Ratings

	ADA	ACLU	AFL-CIO	LCV	ITI	COC	HAFA	ACU	CFG	FRC
2018	-	92%	-	94%	-	58%	6%	4%	18%	0%
2017	100%	C	97%	89%	C	38%	C	4%	5%	0%

Almanac Ratings 2017-18

	Economy	Social	Foreign	Composite
Liberal	97%	95%	100%	97%
Conservative	4%	5%	0%	3%

Key Votes of the 115th Congress

1. Obama-care revision	N	5. Family planning regs	N	9. Guantanamo prisoners	Y
2. Tax Cuts	N	6. Body cameras/immigration	Y	10. Ground missiles, limit	Y
3. Omnibus appropriations	N	7. Abortion ban	N	11. Defense Dept. spending	N
4. Dodd-Frank revision	N	8. Concealed carry	N	12. FISA rules	N

Election Results

Election	Name (Party)	Vote (%)	Cand. Spent	Ind. Exp. Support	Ind. Exp. Oppose
2018 General	Katherine Clark (D).............................236,243	(76%)	$1,011,344		
	John Hugo (R)...74,856	(24%)			
2018 Primary	Katherine Clark (D)..	(100%)			

Prior winning percentages: 2016 (99%), 2014 (71%), 2013 special (66%)

Democrat Katherine Clark won a 2013 special election that resulted when previous Rep. Edward Markey, in turn, won a special election six months earlier to fill the Senate seat of John Kerry, who had become secretary of State. With her policymaking experience in state government and legislative savvy, plus her eagerness to work with more senior Democrats on the party's message, she is a fast-rising members of the Democratic Caucus.

Clark was born and raised in New Haven Connecticut, and graduated from St. Lawrence University, where she majored in history. She got her law degree at Cornell University before moving to Chicago and California to practice law. In 1995, Clark relocated to Massachusetts to earn a master's in public administration from Harvard's Kennedy School of Government. She then worked as general counsel for the Massachusetts Office of Child Care Services and as policy chief for Attorney General Martha Coakley. She was elected to the state House in 2008 and two years later to the state Senate, where she chaired the Judiciary Committee.

Markey had represented the 5th District since 1976, and his promotion set off a scramble for the safe Democratic seat among party members with years of pent-up political ambition. In the Democratic primary, Clark competed against six candidates, including Middlesex County Sheriff Peter Koutoujin, and three other state lawmakers. Her early start gave her an edge financially and in the polls. Clark focused her campaign on issues that appealed to her party's base, including equal pay for women and abortion rights.

Clark wove the stories of her grandmother, a machinist during World War II, and her mother, who was discouraged from pursuing engineering as a young girl, into her TV ads. And she discussed her husband and three young sons to repeatedly make the point that "women's issues are family issues." Clark received a fundraising boost from the abortion-rights group EMILY's List, which proved a boon in a race where progressive and labor endorsements were fractured. She prevailed in the primary with 32 percent of the vote, to 22 percent for Koutoujin. Only Clark showed strength across the district. She won easily in the December general election, with 66 percent of the vote.

Clark became the sixth-ranking member of Democratic leadership in her role as caucus vice chair. She easily won her leadership race in November 2018, thanks in part due to loyalties that she built as the 2018 recruitment vice chair of the Democratic Congressional Campaign Committee, amid its enormously successful midterms. Clark was often among the first House members that the then-candidates met during their successful campaigns.

Clark made her first splash when she played a crucial role in organizing what became an unprecedented sit-in on the House floor in June 2016 by Democrats angered by inaction on gun-control legislation, especially following the terrorist shooting attack at Pulse night club in Orlando

Florida. As she described to Time, Clark told Rep. John Lewis of Georgia that the typical moment of silence in the House was not a sufficient response. "I wanted to do something to keep gun violence in the forefront of not only the American people but, more specifically, members of Congress and [Lewis] suggested, in his words, that we do something dramatic, and he suggested having a sit-in, and it really went from there," recalled Clark, who had tried civil rights cases in private practice. "When you have John Lewis, such an icon of the civil rights fight for justice, you know that good things are going to happen." Lewis told Time that Clark should be credited for the sit-in idea.

The House sit-in, which was designed to force the hand of Speaker Paul Ryan, had little immediate impact. It brought Capitol Hill to a pause for two days, but yielded no legislative action.

In 2017, she gained additional influence with a seat on the House Appropriations Committee. Clark is a member of a tight-knit clique of Democratic women who took office in 2013. Known as "the Pink Ladies," the up-and-coming lot also includes DCCC Chairwoman Cheri Bustos of Illinois, Julia Brownley of California, Lois Frankel of Florida, Annie Kuster of New Hampshire and Grace Meng of New York.

At home, Clark has been reelected three times without opposition and seems entrenched.

MA-5: Northern and Western Boston Suburbs   Cook Partisan Voting Index: D+18

Population		Race and Ethnicity		Income	
Total	760,616	White	72.2%	Median Income	$90,564
Land area (sq. miles)	265	Black	4.7%	District Income Rank	27
Pop/ sq mi	2869.4	Latino	8.8%	Poverty Rate	8.1%
Born in State	52.6%	Asian	11.2%	With health insurance	97.1%
Age Groups		Two or more races	2.3%	Cash public assistance	1.6%
Under 18	19.8%	Other	0.8%	Food stamp/SNAP	6.8%
18-34	25%	**Education**		**Work**	
35-64	40%	H.S grad or less	26.4%	White Collar	15.2%
Over 64	15.2%	Some college	17.6%	Sales and Service	34.6%
Military		College Degree, 4 yr	27.2%	Blue Collar	10.4%
Veteran/ Active Duty	4.7%	Post grad	28.8%	Government	10.3%

2012 Pres. Vote	Obama	235,984	(65%)	Romney	119,934	(33%)		
2016 Pres. Vote	Clinton	258,908	(68%)	Trump	95,922	(25%)	Johnson	13,712 (4%)

Northern and Western Suburbs: The Yankee Protestants and Irish Catholics who settled Massachusetts arrived by boat, the Yankees to a cold, stony land with a few Indians, the Irish to a crowded city with Yankees who seemed no more welcoming. The Yankees whose ancestors once farmed the soil had, by the early 20th century, founded suburbs filled with solid brick and white frame houses. As the years went on, their local public schools emptied as young people with children moved out, and attendance at mainline Protestant churches fell. The Irish, for decades heavily concentrated in the crowded wards of Boston, started moving out to the suburbs after World War II. There were other ethnic groups here and there (Jews, Italians, French Canadians), but the major conflict — fought out in neighborhood playgrounds, in school committee meetings, and not least in political campaigns — was between Protestant Yankee Republicans and Catholic Irish Democrats. These days, much of the local conflict is among the university towns — Cambridge as the epicenter of Harvard University; Medford, home of Tufts University; and Waltham, home of Brandeis University.

The 5th Congressional District of Massachusetts is made up of northern and western Boston suburbs, where vestiges of the cultural conflict can still be seen. Geographically, the district forms an arc around Boston, starting with the clapboard beach towns of Winthrop and Revere just beyond Logan Airport, going north as far as working-class Woburn (where Charles Goodyear developed the art of vulcanizing rubber) and encompassing Natick and Framingham, the headquarters town of Staples and TJX (T.J. Maxx, Marshalls, HomeGoods). Framingham has become diverse culturally, with 67 languages spoken in the public schools. MassBay Community College selected a site in downtown Framingham for its new $60 million campus, including a health science center. This strong economy translated to high housing costs. The long-delayed and over-budget Green Line rapid-transit extension to Medford was scheduled for completion in 2021.

The 5th extends south to take in Ashland, Holliston and Sherborn, and west to take in most of Sudbury and Wayland. Sudbury is home to the historic Longfellow's Wayside Inn, which was renamed after Henry Wadsworth Longfellow's 1863 book Tales of a Wayside Inn made it a sight-seeing attraction. In Lexington, minutemen fired the shots heard 'round the world in 1775. The district reaches into Cambridge to include the Harvard campus north of the Charles River, but Massachusetts Institute of Technology is across the line in the 7th District. With the universities' presence, high technology and biotechnology have become driving forces of economic growth in the area.

Politically, the district is solidly Democratic. In the 2016 presidential campaign, this was the second strongest Democratic-performing district in Massachusetts, behind only the 7th District. Hillary Clinton led, 68%-25%.

Seth Moulton (D)

Elected 2014, 3rd term, b. Oct 24, 1978; Salem; Phillips Academy, (MA), M.P.A., 1997; Harvard University, B.S., 2001; Harvard Business School (MA), M.B.A., 2011; Harvard University John F. Kennedy School of Government (MA), M.P.A., 2011; Christian - Non-Denominational; Married (Liz Boardman); 1 child.

Military Career: U.S. Marine Corps 2002-2008 (Iraq)

Professional Career: Railway managing director, 2011-2012; Health care company president, 2012-2013.

DC Office: 1127 LHOB 20515, 202-225-8020, Fax: 202-225-5915, moulton.house.gov

State Offices: Salem, 978-531-1669.

Committees: *Armed Services*: Seapower & Projection Forces; Strategic Forces. *Budget.*

Group Ratings

	ADA	ACLU	AFL-CIO	LCV	ITI	COC	HAFA	ACU	CFG	FRC
2018	-	82%	-	89%	-	67%	12%	8%	24%	0%
2017	80%	C	95%	100%	C	57%	C	7%	5%	11%

Almanac Ratings 2017-18

	Economy	Social	Foreign	Composite
Liberal	93%	100%	78%	90%
Conservative	7%	0%	22%	10%

Key Votes of the 115th Congress

1. Obama-care revision	N	5. Family planning regs	N	9. Guantanamo prisoners	Y
2. Tax Cuts	N	6. Body cameras/immigration	Y	10. Ground missiles, limit	Y
3. Omnibus appropriations	Y	7. Abortion ban	N	11. Defense Dept. spending	Y
4. Dodd-Frank revision	N	8. Concealed carry	N	12. FISA rules	Y

Election Results

Election	Name (Party)	Vote (%)		Cand. Spent	Ind. Exp. Support	Ind. Exp. Oppose
2018 General	Seth Moulton (D)	217,703	(65%)	$2,372,635		
	Joseph Schneider (R)	104,798	(31%)	$258,087		
	Mary Jean Charbonneau (I)	11,309	(3%)	$125		
2018 Primary	Seth Moulton (D)		(100%)			

Prior winning percentages: 2016 (98%), 2014 (54%)

Democrat Seth Moulton, a former Marine Corps captain and Iraq War veteran, was elected in 2014. With unusual candor, he was outspoken in demanding accountability and change among House Democrats. His actions placed him at the forefront of Democrats seeking a post-Nancy Pelosi generation of leadership — an objective he continued to pursue even after Pelosi prevailed over her critics following the 2018 election. He has brought a similar bluntness to his legislative focus, chiefly on military issues. In 2019, he used that platform to launch a long-shot bid for president.

Moulton was born in Salem and grew up in Marblehead, the eldest of three siblings. He attended Phillips Academy Andover, an elite boarding school. He got his bachelor's degree in physics from Harvard University, delivering the Undergraduate English Oration at his commencement in which he focused on the importance of service. He joined the Marine Corps, graduated from Officer Candidate School as a 2nd lieutenant and was among the first soldiers to enter Baghdad at the beginning of the Iraq War. He served four tours of duty from 2004 to 2008, and in 2008, at age 29, he was a special liaison with tribal leaders in southern Iraq at the request of Gen. David Petraeus. He left the Marines with the rank of captain. He later earned his MBA and master's in public policy from Harvard.

He decided to get involved in politics while still in the Marines. "I actually remember the moment," he told The Atlantic. "It was after a difficult day in Najaf in 2004. A young marine in my platoon said, 'Sir, you should run for Congress someday. So this s— doesn't happen again.'" He considered running as an independent candidate in 2012 against embattled Democratic Rep. John Tierney, but decided against it. A close ally of Pelosi, Tierney was under fire because his wife, Patrice, had pleaded guilty to helping her brother file false tax returns. He eked out a 48%-47% victory against Richard Tisei, whose résumé — he is gay and a fiscal conservative who vocally opposed the social policy of his party — made him an ideal challenger. Tisei ran again in 2014 and appeared well-positioned to take Tierney out.

Republican plans were foiled when Moulton challenged Tierney in the Democratic primary, secured The Boston Globe's endorsement, and won the nomination 51%-41%. Without the baggage of Tierney, Moulton ran as a progressive Democrat and cast Tisei, who was first elected to the state legislature in 1984, as a political insider. Moulton won endorsements from Petraeus, retired Army Gen. Stanley McChrystal and former New York City Mayor Michael Bloomberg. He outspent Tisei $3.3 million to $2 million and won 55%-41%. Each candidate was aided by millions of dollars from national parties and outside groups.

Moulton immediately began drawing attention for his unusual-for-a-Democrat resume. He vowed not to be a typical congressman, saying he told his former Marine buddies to watch him closely. "I've asked a few guys in particular to in fact speak up and call me out if I become quote-unquote 'one of them,'" he told Politico.

Following a bumpy transition to the House when Tierney refused to talk to him, Moulton got a seat on the Armed Services Committee. He made multiple trips to the Middle East, to visit with troops and understand the fight against the Islamic State. He has been outspoken on the need to have a plan to win the peace in Iraq and the Middle East. In May 2016, he criticized the Obama administration's overall approach, as well as President Barack Obama's refusal to say that American troops deployed to Iraq were on a combat mission. "The bottom line is that we have a military strategy to defeat ISIS, but we don't have any long-term political strategy to ensure the peace." He focused on improving veterans' health care. Obama signed his Faster Care for Veterans Act, which enabled vets to use their phones or computers to schedule medical appointments. With Republican Rep. Matt Gaetz of Florida in 2018, he filed a bill to make it easier for the Veterans Department to offer marijuana as a medical treatment. Moulton kept up the criticism with President Donald Trump and his advisers who "use lies to manipulate what Americans think, to pit us against one another, and to pervert our democracy to attain power," he wrote in an op-ed two weeks after Trump took office. Concerned about Trump's early refugee and immigration bans, he joined a bipartisan group of House members who were military veterans to urge exceptions for people who risked their lives to aid U.S. forces.

Following the 2016 election, he demanded with other junior House Democrats a deeper review of the party's failures and discussion of new directions. In a post-election Tweet, Moulton wrote, "In the Marines, my job was clear: 'You are responsible for everything your platoon does or fails to do.' We need that in Congress." He was an early supporter of Rep. Tim Ryan of Ohio in his challenge to Pelosi for minority leader. The lengthy discussions within the Democratic Caucus resulted in some sharing of authority with the rank-and-file, though no changes in specific leadership posts. He became vice chairman of the informal Bipartisan Working Group.

As the 2018 election approached — and the prospects of Democratic control of the House brightened — Moulton continued his public and private drumbeat for what he described as "a new generation of leadership." Many Democrats agreed with him, as they revealed in their earlier vote for Ryan. Likewise, some of the incoming freshmen — mostly, military veterans -- whom Moulton had financed with his political action committee and personally supported during their campaigns had pledged that they would not support Pelosi. But the efforts by Moulton and others suffered from their failure to find a challenger — a problem that was abetted by the accommodations that Pelosi and her supporters made to some of the critics. She extinguished the lingering opposition by agreeing to limit herself to four more years as party leader — a commitment that she had initially resisted.

"We're all united behind her, but we're a stronger party because of these reforms," Moulton told The Boston Globe.

When Democrats reorganized the Armed Services Committee in 2019, they eliminated the Oversight and Investigation Subcommittee, on which Moulton had been the top Democrat. They cited a House rule limiting the number of subcommittees, though that might have been a convenient way for Pelosi to send him a message.

At home, Moulton was reelected, 65%-31% over Republican Joseph Schneider — a sign that he had become entrenched. Still, his longstanding clashes with Pelosi led some Democrats to consider a primary challenge to him in 2020. Moulton seemed to be juggling several political balls, including continuing talk of an eventual Senate campaign, though he said in December 2018 that he had no plans to challenge Sen. Edward Markey in 2020. When he plunged into the presidential campaign in April 2019, he offered "a new generation of leadership" and his focus on national-security and patriotism. At home, past and current Democratic office-holders eyed his House seat. Even if he decides to seek reelection to the House, his opposition to Pelosi stirred local talk of a primary challenge.

MA-6: North Shore

Cook Partisan Voting Index: D+6

Population		Race and Ethnicity		Income	
Total	762,560	White	81.9%	Median Income	$84,446
Land area (sq. miles)	527	Black	3.1%	District Income Rank	39
Pop/ sq mi	1447.6	Latino	8.8%	Poverty Rate	7.7%
Born in State	69.4%	Asian	4.2%	With health insurance	97.5%
		Two or more races	1.7%	Cash public assistance	2.5%
Age Groups		Other	0.4%	Food stamp/SNAP	9.4%
Under 18	20.8%				
18-34	20.3%	**Education**		**Work**	
35-64	41.7%	H.S grad or less	31.9%	White Collar	17.2%
Over 64	17.2%	Some college	24.5%	Sales and Service	39.1%
		College Degree, 4 yr	26%	Blue Collar	15%
Military		Post grad	17.6%	Government	12.4%
Veteran/ Active Duty	6.5%				

2012 Pres. Vote	Obama	212,003	(55%)	Romney	169,966	(44%)			
2016 Pres. Vote	Clinton	224,858	(55%)	Trump	153,244	(38%)	Johnson	18,124	(4%)

Lynn, Salem: The North Shore of Massachusetts Bay has often been at the leading edge of the nation's economy. In 1640, the Saugus Iron Works was built here — the beginning of American heavy industry. When Europe's great powers were convulsed in international war from 1792 to 1815, American ship owners suddenly became the richest in the world, and traders from Boston and Salem accumulated the capital needed to build textile mills and railroads and to finance much of the American Industrial Revolution. From the small port of Salem, ships left for China, bringing back porcelain and artifacts. Salem had the nation's first millionaire, Elias Hasket Derby. In 1900, it was the richest city per capita in the nation.

Today, the North Shore is less robust economically and more competitive politically than elsewhere in Massachusetts. From Boston Harbor north to the mouth of the Merrimack River, it is a collection of ethnic factory towns from Lynn to Peabody (once one of the world's great leather producers, with more than 100 tanneries) to the former shipbuilding Newburyport. There are a few high-income enclaves, such as Marblehead with its yachts. Coastal towns include artsy Rockport and the fishing center of Gloucester. In Salem, the witch trials are the town's most famous legacy, and local officials have capitalized with Halloween festivities that contribute to Salem's $100 million annual tourism industry.

The 6th Congressional District includes the North Shore from Saugus and Lynn northward to the New Hampshire line, plus towns and cities inland west to Tewksbury and Bedford. The district is mostly based in Essex County, but includes part of Middlesex County. The General Electric jet engine plant, the largest employer in Lynn, has seen its payroll drop from a peak of 13,000 in 1985 to 2,500 jobs in January 2019, though the company has been hiring machinists. It produces helicopter engines for the Black Hawk troop transport and jet engines for the F-18 Super Hornet fighter. Following an extensive review by a task force created by Republican Gov. Charlie Baker of options for development in Lynn, where the poverty rate remains nearly twice as high as in the state overall, construction began in early 2019 of $90 million in waterfront apartments. Revival of the port, with residential housing, has been a priority. In 2018, the state ended its subsidy for a seasonal commuter ferry from Lynn to Boston, which had struggled financially. Private entrepreneurs hustled for alternatives, as they prepared for the arrival in 2020 of luxury-yacht stops by Ritz Carlton, which plans to call at the Salem port.

While the district is the site of the original gerrymander — named after Elbridge Gerry, who served two terms as governor before winning election as vice president with President James Madison — the current boundaries are hardly grotesque by contemporary standards. The district's high-income Yankee towns historically were liberal Republican, while the old mill towns of Lynn, Salem, Peabody and Merrimac were Irish working-class Democratic. The 6th has leaned Democratic since the 1960s, although it twice elected a Republican in the 1990s. Hillary Clinton led 55%-38%, which was her second-poorest in the state, behind the 9th District.

Ayanna Pressley (D)

Elected 2018, 1st term, b. Feb 03, 1974; Cincinnati, OH; Boston University (MA), Att., 1994; Baptist; Married (Conan Harris Pressley); 1 stepchild.

Elected Office: Boston City Counsel, 2010-2018

Professional Career: Political Director & Scheduler, U.S. Sen. John F. Kerry; Social Security Liaison, U.S. Rep. Joseph P. Kennedy.

DC Office: 1108 LHOB 20515, 202-225-5111, pressley.house.gov

State Offices: Boston, 617-850-0040.

Committees: *Financial Services*: Consumer Protection & Financial Institutions; Subcommittee on Diversity & Inclusion. *Oversight & Reform*: Subcommittee on Civil Rights & Civil Liberties; Subcommittee on Economic & Consumer Policy.

Election Results

Election	Name (Party)	Vote (%)		Cand. Spent	Ind. Exp. Support	Ind. Exp. Oppose
2018 General	Ayanna Pressley (D)............................	216,559	(98%)	$1,386,656	$43,303	
2018 Primary	Ayanna Pressley (D).............................	60,046	(59%)			
	Michael Capuano (D)...........................	42,430	(41%)			

Ayanna Pressley became the first African American elected to the House from Massachusetts, as the result of her victory in the Democratic primary over 10-term Rep. Michael Capuano. Pressley, who served nine years on the Boston City Council, successfully shaped the contest as a battle of generations and ethnicity in the rapidly changing Boston area. Capuano, who was a loyal foot soldier for Democratic Leader Nancy Pelosi during his early years in the House and later was an unsuccessful candidate for a Senate vacancy, argued that his seniority on two House committees was a major selling point. Pressley's 58%-41% victory in the primary showed that voters agreed with her that "change can't wait."

With Rep. Joe Crowley of New York, Capuano was the only Democratic incumbent who lost a primary in 2018. (Two House Republicans were also defeated in party challenges.) In contrast to Crowley, who did not take challenger Alexandria Ocasio-Cortez seriously until the closing days of their campaign, Pressley and Capuano battled openly for months and both spent most of the money they had raised. The turnout of more than 102,000 voters was more than three times the total in the New York contest.

Pressley, a native of Chicago, attended Boston University but did not graduate — in part, because she needed to work to support her mother. She was a Boston-based aide to Rep. Joe Kennedy II (who held the House seat prior to Capuano) and had several positions, including political director, with Sen. John Kerry. In 2009, she was elected as one of four at-large members of the Boston City Council. In each of her three victories, she got the most votes of the city-wide councilors.

On the council, she took credit for the establishment of the Committee on Healthy Women, Families and Communities, which took up her interest in issues that especially affect women and girls. Pressley pressed successfully to create 75 new liquor licenses, which she said created hundreds of new jobs, especially in lower-income parts of Boston.

Against Capuano, who had not been seriously challenged since he was first elected, Pressley argued for a more assertive Democratic agenda—including the abolition of the Immigration and Customs Enforcement agency and more aggressive congressional action to limit or remove President Donald Trump. The Boston Globe, which endorsed her in an editorial, reported that her work with Kerry spurred Pressley's ambition for a seat in Congress.

Capuano styled himself as a strong liberal on most issues, including his support for a single-payer health care system and broad immigration reform. He received more endorsements than Pressley. Among them were Boston Mayor Marty Walsh and many congressional Democrats, including members of the Congressional Black Caucus. Rep. John Lewis, the Georgia Democrat and civil rights hero, made a local appearance for Capuano and praised his ability to get things done. Massachusetts Attorney General Maura Healey endorsed Pressley. Capuano spent $2.6 million on the contest, to $1.4 million for Pressley.

Pressley's victory was based entirely on her support in Boston, which cast 62 percent of the total vote and gave her a 17,700 vote lead. District-wide, she led by about 17,600 votes. Pressley also had a big edge in Cambridge, which cast 10 percent of the vote. Capuano led in his home town of Somerville and nearby Chelsea by slim margins. He doubled Pressley's vote in Everett, which cast only 5 percent of the vote. After the outcome was clear, Capuano told supporters, "Ayanna Pressley is going to be a good congresswoman." The only other African American from Massachusetts to serve in Congress was Edward W. Brooke, a Republican, who served 12 years in the Senate.

Pressley faced no opposition in November and made campaign appearances on behalf of House Democrats elsewhere in the nation — evidence of her earlier experience as a congressional aide.

MA-7: Boston area   **Cook Partisan Voting Index: D+34**

Population		Race and Ethnicity		Income	
Total	781,304	White	41.1%	Median Income	$59,649
Land area (sq. miles)	63	Black	23.4%	District Income Rank	184
Pop/ sq mi	12467	Latino	21.5%	Poverty Rate	20%
Born in State	42%	Asian	9.9%	With health insurance	95.7%
		Two or more races	2.7%	Cash public assistance	3.7%
Age Groups		Other	1.3%	Food stamp/SNAP	19.8%
Under 18	17.1%				
18-34	38.7%	**Education**		**Work**	
35-64	33.5%	H.S grad or less	38.5%	White Collar	10.7%
Over 64	10.7%	Some college	18.3%	Sales and Service	41.7%
		College Degree, 4 yr	23%	Blue Collar	12.2%
Military		Post grad	20%	Government	9.7%
Veteran/ Active Duty	2.7%				

2012 Pres. Vote	Obama	233,382	(82%)	Romney	44,275	(16%)		
2016 Pres. Vote	Clinton	254,037	(83%)	Trump	36,018	(12%)	Johnson	7,045	(2%)

Somerville, Cambridge: Boston, the most political of cities, has often been the focal point of essential moments in American history. On its streets, originally laid out as narrow 17th century cowpaths with many that still survive, Samuel Adams and Paul Revere plotted revolution, the abolitionist movement helped ignite the Civil War, and various Kennedys opened their campaign headquarters. Today's Boston is different from the Boston of John F. Kennedy's era. Then it was a gray city with no new buildings and dust on every windowsill. The sky was dark with pollution, and the air was thick with ancient Yankee and Irish animosity. The old office buildings were full of Brahmins seeking safe investments for their antique family fortunes. The government was full of Irishmen, scampering after good patronage jobs and regaling one another with political war stories. These days, that Boston is mostly gone — and memories are fading.

The new skyscrapers are full of well-educated venture capitalists, lawyers and management consultants, many working for high-tech and bio-tech companies radiating from Cambridge out into the countryside. Greater Boston may well have a larger concentration of graduate students and postgraduate hangers-on than any other major American city, and this graduate student community's world is centered in Cambridge, home of Harvard University. Boston's neighborhoods, full of large Irish families — and 95 percent white — when the city reached its peak population of 801,000 in 1950, are now different, with young singles in rowhouse apartments, professionals in waterfront apartment towers and African Americans in old triple-deckers. Most of those real-estate costs have soared. Boston has had a growth spurt to 685,000 people, and it is 25 percent African American and 19 percent Hispanic.

One of its premier civic events, the fabled Boston Marathon, was the scene of a national tragedy in April 2013 when terrorists detonated two bombs that exploded 12 seconds apart near the finish line, killing three people and injuring more than 170 others. The May 2015 jury verdict that convicted killer Dzhokhar Tsarnaev and gave him the death penalty riveted the city. The local civic spirit suffered an embarrassing setback when the U.S. Olympic Committee in January 2015 unexpectedly selected Boston to bid for the 2024 Olympic site, but reversed itself in July amid doubts by some in the business community and grassroots opposition. Still, local pride has been bolstered by the dozen championships in this millennium by the city's four chief professional sports teams — each of which has been celebrated by a "duck boat" parade through downtown Boston.

The 7th Congressional District includes most of Boston, although the State House and many of the historic sites in the North End are in the neighboring 8th District. Harvard Square and much of Cambridge are in the 5th District. But the Massachusetts Institute of Technology is in the 7th, as is the expanding Harvard campus across the Charles River in Allston, helping to make it an important — and commercially booming -- technology center. A $2.6 billion casino on the Mystic River in Everett has overcome extensive opposition and was scheduled to open in June 2019 — the largest private-sector development ever in the Boston area — though it faced late challenges to its license after Steve Wynn was removed as majority owner of the hotel owner. At Logan Airport, across the harbor, a $1 billion upgrade of the international terminal and the nearby roadways was scheduled for completion in 2022.

The 7th takes in Somerville, economically revived Chelsea and many Boston neighborhoods — newly upscale and diverse East Boston around Logan Airport, Brighton and the Back Bay, Fenway, Mattapan, Mission Hill and the South End. It also includes Randolph, where minorities are a majority; and Dorchester, a neighborhood with large numbers of working-class black, Latino, Caribbean Americans and Asian Americans. The Rev. Martin Luther King Jr. lived in Dorchester while he was earning his doctorate at Boston University. As the state's first minority-majority district, it has grown to 23 percent black, 22 percent Hispanic and 10 percent Asian. The 7th is among the most Democratic districts in the nation. Hillary Clinton won here with 83 percent of the vote. Tip O'Neill, who ably meshed Town and Gown and was the most recent Speaker to leave the powerful position on his own terms and with a secure majority, represented a version of this district from 1953 to 1987.

Stephen Lynch (D)

Elected 2001, 9th full term, b. Mar 31, 1955; Boston; Wentworth Institute of Technology (MA), B.S., 1988; Boston College Law School (MA), J.D., 1991; Harvard University John F. Kennedy School of Government (MA), M.P.A., 1999; Roman Catholic; Married (Margaret Shaughnessy Lynch); 1 child.

Elected Office: MA House, 1995-1996; MA Senate, 1997-2001.

Professional Career: Structural ironworker, 1973-1991; Practicing attorney, 1991-2001.

DC Office: 2109 RHOB 20515, 202-225-8273, Fax: 202-225-3984, lynch.house.gov

State Offices: Boston, 617-428-2000; Brockton, 508-586-5555; Quincy, 617-657-6305.

Committees: *Financial Services*: Nat'l Security, International Development & Monetary Policy; Oversight & Investigations. *Oversight & Reform*: Government Operations; National Security (Chmn). *Transportation & Infrastructure*: Aviation; Railroads, Pipelines & Hazardous Materials; Water Resources & Environment.

Group Ratings

	ADA	ACLU	AFL-CIO	LCV	ITI	COC	HAFA	ACU	CFG	FRC
2018	-	78%	-	86%	-	64%	4%	8%	10%	0%
2017	80%	C	97%	100%	C	46%	C	4%	5%	11%

Almanac Ratings 2017-18

	Economy	Social	Foreign	Composite
Liberal	94%	84%	97%	92%
Conservative	6%	16%	3%	8%

Key Votes of the 115th Congress

1. Obama-care revision	N	5. Family planning regs	N	9. Guantanamo prisoners	Y
2. Tax Cuts	N	6. Body cameras/immigration	Y	10. Ground missiles, limit	Y
3. Omnibus appropriations	Y	7. Abortion ban	N	11. Defense Dept. spending	Y
4. Dodd-Frank revision	N	8. Concealed carry	N	12. FISA rules	N

Election Results

Election	Name (Party)	Vote (%)	Cand. Spent	Ind. Exp. Support	Ind. Exp. Oppose
2018 General	Stephen Lynch (D)........................ 259,159	(98%)	$489,357		
2018 Primary	Stephen Lynch (D)........................ 52,269	(71%)			
	Brianna Wu (D).................................... 16,878	(23%)			
	Christopher Voehl (D)........................... 4,435	(6%)			

Prior winning percentages: 2016 (72%), 2014 (77%), 2012 (71%), 2010 (68%), 2008 (76%), 2006 (72%), 2004 (73%), 2002 (71%), 2001 special (65%)

Democrat Stephen Lynch, who won a special election in 2001 to succeed the late Joe Moakley, is an ironworker-turned-lawyer who is less liberal than his Massachusetts Democratic colleagues, but no less ambitious. He fell short in the 2013 special election for the Senate seat vacated by John Kerry's confirmation as secretary of State. Lynch marches to his own drummer in the House, with occasional bipartisanship and distancing from Democratic leaders.

Lynch grew up in Boston's housing projects and took pride in making good by following the old ethnic precepts of hard work, family loyalty and personal determination. After graduating from South Boston High School, he joined his father as a full-time ironworker while attending the Wentworth Institute of Technology, where he got a bachelor's degree in construction management. He became the youngest president of the 2,000-member Local 7 of the International Association of Iron Workers. He worked at several large plants that he later said suffered job losses as a result of unfair foreign trade practices. After a fall on the job cut short that career, he graduated from Boston College Law School and opened a legal practice representing working people. In 1994, he was elected to the state House. Fourteen months later, he won a special election for a seat in the state Senate.

Lynch built a political base in South Boston and had strong union ties, advantages when he pursued the seat after Moakley died. Max Kennedy, son of Robert and Ethel Kennedy, expressed interest in the race but his campaign never gained traction. Lynch became the frontrunner. He stumbled after The Boston Globe revealed his student loan defaults years earlier, plus a tax lien that was resolved in 1998. Three other state senators opposed Lynch. The strongest among them was Cheryl Jacques, who was openly gay and had support from EMILY's List and other national feminist groups that criticized Lynch's opposition to abortion rights. Lynch bested Jacques, 39%-29%. In the anti-climactic general election, he defeated another state senator, Jo Ann Sprague, 66%-33%.

In the House, Lynch's views have been right of center in the Democratic Caucus, and he has had the most conservative voting record in the Massachusetts delegation, especially on cultural issues. "That's like being called the slowest of the Kenyans in the marathon," he quipped to the Boston Herald. He was one of three Massachusetts House members to vote for the Iraq war resolution. He moderated his stance on abortion in 2013, saying he believes it is a constitutionally protected right and that as a senator he would oppose anti-abortion Supreme Court nominees. He became a supporter of gay rights causes, developing a political alliance with home-state colleague Barney Frank, an openly gay Democrat.

On the Oversight and Government Reform Committee, Lynch has taken an interest in helping the financially strapped Postal Service, where his mother was a clerk. An opponent of privatization, he filed a bipartisan resolution in 2018 with 200 cosponsors supporting the Postal Service as an independent federal agency. On the Subcommittee on National Security, which he now chairs, he traveled frequently to Afghanistan and Iraq and said his priority was "defending against threats to America." As chairman, he promised active oversight of the "ill-defined" defense strategy of President Donald Trump. On behalf of the families of the 9/11 victims, he was a leading proponent of releasing the secret 28 pages from an official report on the role of Saudi Arabia in the attacks. "It may help us at last hold those who are responsible accountable," Lynch said when the document was released in 2016. On the Financial Services Committee, he worked in 2018 with Republican Rep. Ted Budd to gain House passage of a bill to stop the illicit use of new financial technologies, including crypto-currencies.

His occasional departures from the party line have mostly been tolerated by the leadership, but Lynch went too far for them in opposing the final health care overhaul bill in 2010. He cited the Senate's decision to strip an antitrust exemption for insurance companies and the elimination of the government-run public option to compete with private insurers. "In the end, we allowed the insurance companies to prevail," he said. In July 2017, he said that the law was "unsustainable." During a 2015 broadcast interview in Boston, he said that Nancy Pelosi should step aside as House Democratic leader. "Nancy Pelosi is not going to lead the Democrats back into the majority," he said. Following the 2016 election, which he called "an epic failure and another lost opportunity," he backed Rep. Tim Ryan of Ohio against Pelosi as more in touch with "lunch-bucket Democrats" rather than the elites. Despite continuing call for change, he signed on to support Pelosi for Speaker following the 2018 election after they had "several days of productive conversation," including her "reassurances" of support for working-class priorities.

Lynch has been reelected without great difficulty. His opposition to the health care bill prompted a primary challenge from the left in 2010 from Mac D'Alessandro, a former regional political director for the Service Employees International Union. D'Alessandro drew support from MoveOn.org and other progressive groups. Lynch stressed his independence, outraised his opponent by more than 2-to-1, and won handily, 66%-34%. In the 2013 contest for Kerry's seat, running against Democratic Rep. Ed Markey, Lynch said, "I think what the Senate could use — it's such an elite club — is someone to bring the concerns of the average American people to the U.S. Senate, so they're not so insulated." Markey won the primary, 57%-42%. Lynch led with 56 percent in Norfolk County and 62 percent in Plymouth County, both part of his district. In the 2018 primary for his House seat, Lynch got 71 percent against two challengers. Brianna Wu, co-founder of a video-game company and supporter of single-payer health care, finished second and said she would run again in 2020.

MA-8: Southern Boston suburbs

Cook Partisan Voting Index: D+10

Population		Race and Ethnicity		Income	
Total	761,328	White	73.5%	Median Income	$83,928
Land area (sq. miles)	326	Black	9.4%	District Income Rank	41
Pop/ sq mi	2332.7	Latino	5.6%	Poverty Rate	9.1%
Born in State	64.9%	Asian	7.9%	With health insurance	97.5%
		Two or more races	2%	Cash public assistance	2.4%
Age Groups		Other	1.6%	Food stamp/SNAP	10.3%
Under 18	19.9%				
18-34	24.5%	**Education**		**Work**	
35-64	40.2%	H.S grad or less	31.2%	White Collar	15.4%
Over 64	15.4%	Some college	22.9%	Sales and Service	38.6%
		College Degree, 4 yr	27.3%	Blue Collar	13.2%
Military		Post grad	18.7%	Government	12.3%
Veteran/ Active Duty	6.1%				

2012 Pres. Vote	Obama	213,364	(58%)	Romney	150,825	(41%)		
2016 Pres. Vote	Clinton	231,356	(60%)	Trump	131,624	(34%)	Johnson	15,395	(4%)

Downtown Boston, Quincy, Brockton: The Irish remain the dominant political tribe here, even as parts of South Boston, long the center of Irish Boston, have gentrified. Southie's influence endures in the memory of two Irish Democrats who represented the area for all but two years from the Great Depression to the start of the 21st century. The first was John McCormack, an old-style, backroom deal-maker who served as House Speaker during the 1960s. The second was Joe Moakley, a close pal of Speaker Tip O'Neill, who chaired the influential Rules Committee before Democrats lost the House majority in 1994.

The 8th Congressional District of Massachusetts has been the most blue-collar district in the Boston area. It takes in South Boston as well as Beacon Hill, the Massachusetts State House, and is a living museum with many of the historic sites in Boston. They include the Paul Revere House; Faneuil Hall and a statue of revolutionary patriot Samuel Adams; the Old State House and the site of the Boston Massacre; the John F. Kennedy Presidential Library and Museum, plus the Edward M. Kennedy Institute for the United States Senate at Columbia Point.

Completion of the high-dollar Big Dig highway project, with a tunnel under Boston Harbor, spurred economic development in the Financial District and along the waterfront in the port, including office buildings, hotels, condominiums, the John Joseph Moakley Courthouse and a huge convention center. The booming Seaport area in the once deteriorating docks continued to transform the city, with new homes for companies ranging from Amazon to Mass Mutual insurance company, and the port has thrived with commuter ferries and mega-cruise ships. In a back-to-the-future note, seafood processing thrived because of shipments from nearby Logan Airport. But the Seaport has created new complications. Planners worried that climate change increased the long-term hazard of flooding and they explored a sea wall to protect the city. Multibillion dollar options for a mile-long rail connection between North Station and South Station remained under discussion. General Electric Co., which earlier moved its corporate headquarters from Connecticut and unveiled plans for a three-building $200 million campus along the Fort Point Channel in Southie, reversed itself in February 2019 as it downsized and returned $87 million in incentives to the state; the company planned smaller office space in the area. The urban changes have reduced some of the parochialism but have priced many of the working class from their old neighborhoods. Residents of East Boston resisted the gentrification that has overtaken South Boston. The annual St. Patrick's Day parade in Southie preceded by a rowdy political breakfast and roast remains a must-attend for state politicians.

On the South Shore, the district takes in Brockton, a once-bustling shoe manufacturing town that has suffered from extensive gun violence and has become minority-majority. Also in the district is Braintree, where a 1920 armed robbery and slaying of a shoe factory paymaster and his guard led to the trial and execution of two Italian immigrants blamed for the killings, Nicola Sacco and Bartolomeo Vanzetti, which became one of the most controversial legal disputes in American history. The 8th remains heavily Democratic. Hillary Clinton won 60%-34%.

Bill Keating (D)

Elected 2010, 5th term, b. Sep 06, 1952; Norwood; Boston College (MA), B.A., 1974; Boston College (MA), M.B.A., 1982; Suffolk University School of Law (MA), J.D., 1985; Roman Catholic; Married (Tevis Keating); 2 children.

Elected Office: MA House, 1977-1984; MA Senate, 1985-1998; Norfolk County District Attorney, 1999-2010.

Professional Career: Practicing attorney, 1999-2010.

DC Office: 2351 RHOB 20515, 202-225-3111, Fax: 202-225-5658, keating.house.gov

State Offices: Hyannis, 508-771-6868; New Bedford, 508-999-6462; Plymouth, 508-746-9000.

Committees: *Armed Services*: Intelligence, Emerging Threats & Capabilities; Strategic Forces. *Foreign Affairs*: Europe, Eurasia, Energy & the Environment (Chmn); Middle East, North Africa & International Terrorism.

Group Ratings

	ADA	ACLU	AFL-CIO	LCV	ITI	COC	HAFA	ACU	CFG	FRC
2018	-	75%	-	89%	-	67%	4%	0%	5%	0%
2017	85%	C	95%	100%	C	50%	C	4%	5%	11%

Key Votes of the 115th Congress

1. Obama-care revision	N	5. Family planning regs	N	9. Guantanamo prisoners	Y		
2. Tax Cuts	N	6. Body cameras/immigration	Y	10. Ground missiles, limit	Y		
3. Omnibus appropriations	Y	7. Abortion ban	N	11. Defense Dept. spending	Y		
4. Dodd-Frank revision	N	8. Concealed carry	N	12. FISA rules	Y		

Election Results

Election	Name (Party)	Vote (%)		Cand. Spent	Ind. Exp. Support	Ind. Exp. Oppose
2018 General	William Keating (D)	192,347	(59%)	$541,255		
	Peter Tedeschi (R)	131,463	(41%)	$850,590		
2018 Primary	William Keating (D)	50,113	(85%)			
	Bill Cimbrelo (D)	8,571	(15%)			

Prior winning percentages: 2016 (56%), 2014 (53%), 2012 (55%), 2010 (47%)

Democrat William Keating, elected in 2010, is a former prosecutor who has put his experience to work on terrorism and overseas issues — often in bipartisan ways. He also has sought to resolve maritime conflicts in Massachusetts' coastal areas.

A Massachusetts native and life-long public official, Keating followed the path of his father, a police officer and later a veterans' services agent. Keating put himself through Boston College by working at a post office. In 1977, at the age of 24, he was elected to the Massachusetts House. In 1985, Keating was elected to the state Senate, eventually becoming chairman of the Judiciary Committee and then the Committee on Taxation. He got his law degree from Suffolk University while serving in the legislature. As district attorney for Norfolk County, he became the first in the state to win a murder conviction in the absence of a victim's body by using DNA evidence He set up facilities for veterans suffering from post-traumatic stress disorder. And he helped create the Norfolk Advocates for Children, an organization for children who have been victimized by sexual assault.

Keating ran for an open seat in a district that had been in Democratic hands for nearly a half-century, though it is relatively marginal for Massachusetts. It gave Republican Scott Brown 60 percent of the vote in the 2010 special election to fill the seat of the late Democratic Sen. Edward Kennedy. Tea party-backed Republican Jeff Perry, a member of the state House, campaigned for smaller government and less spending. Keating sought to paint Perry, a police officer, as having a "troubled relationship with the truth," pointing to a case in the 1990s in which an officer under Perry's command was involved in illegal strip searches of teenage girls. Perry said he did not know about the searches at the time. Keating had a slight edge in candidate spending, $1.5 million to $1.2 million, and in spending by outside groups. In a rare, though unimpressive, triumph on an otherwise dismal election for Democrats in 2010, he won 46%-41%.

In the House, Keating became a persistent inquisitor of Homeland Security Department officials, with an interest in failings in perimeter safety at airports. He challenged the Transportation Security Administration on its overly aggressive searches of passengers, and said the agency's approach was like "locking all the doors on your house but leaving the windows open." In 2016 and again in 2017, the House passed his bill to force TSA to enhance how it protects airport access points and the perimeters of the nation's airports, and to update its risk assessment for aviation security. The Senate did not act on the measure.

On the Foreign Affairs Committee Keating sought bipartisanship in dealing with the world's trouble spots. With other senior members of the panel, Keating filed in 2015 a bipartisan anti-terrorism bill to coordinate U.S. efforts to protect historic sites around the world from attacks by the Islamic State and others, and to restrict imports of cultural property illegally trafficked from Syria. Following a 2016 congressional delegation visit to Asia, he warned that Donald Trump's comments were making American diplomacy in the Pacific more difficult. Following the apparent murder in October 2018 of Saudi journalist Jamal Khashoggi at the Saudi embassy in Turkey, Keating called for a halt of arms sales to Saudi Arabia — a step that would affect defense contractors in Massachusetts. "We're not a country founded on arms sales," he said. In 2019, he took over as chairman of the reorganized Subcommittee on Europe, Eurasia, Energy and the Environment. He said that he would seek to strengthen the alliance with Europe — "rather than threaten it as the Trump administration seems intent on doing" -- and defend against threats posed by Russia and China.

Long before the Nuclear Regulatory Commission decided in 2015 to shut down the Pilgrim nuclear power plant in Plymouth, Keating had raised concerns about its licensing. He has filed a bill to ease longstanding friction between federal and local officials in the management of the ocean area in the Monomoy Refuge off Nantucket. After complaints by local officials about congressional inaction and that Keating was too responsive to environmental critics of the proposal, Keating in May 2018 blamed House Republican leaders for failing to schedule the committee-approved bill.

At home, Keating has faced more competition for reelection than has any other current representative from Massachusetts. He had a big financial advantage over his two rivals in 2012 and won comfortably with 59 percent of the vote. His 2014 contest was tighter. GOP attorney John Chapman, a first-time candidate, raised $1 million, to $1.4 million for the incumbent. Keating won 55%-45%, with the benefit of big margins in New Bedford and Fall River. In 2018, he faced Peter Tedeschi, whose family had owned a chain of 200 local food stores. Tedeschi outspent Keating, $851,000 to $541,000, and said that he would limit himself to three terms — in contrast to the "career politician." Keating emphasized the need for oversight of the Trump administration. In a bad year for Republicans in the Northeast, he won, 60%-40%; Tedeschi took seven of the 46 cities and towns.

MA-9: Southeast Massachusetts   **Cook Partisan Voting Index: D+4**

Population		Race and Ethnicity		Income	
Total	735,926	White	86.5%	Median Income	$67,064
Land area (sq. miles)	1,215	Black	2.7%	District Income Rank	118
Pop/ sq mi	605.8	Latino	5.2%	Poverty Rate	9.9%
Born in State	70.4%	Asian	1.4%	With health insurance	96.7%
		Two or more races	2.3%	Cash public assistance	2.9%
Age Groups		Other	1.9%	Food stamp/SNAP	11.5%
Under 18	19.3%				
18-34	18.9%	**Education**		**Work**	
35-64	40.9%	H.S grad or less	37.9%	White Collar	20.9%
Over 64	20.9%	Some college	27.6%	Sales and Service	42.9%
		College Degree, 4 yr	20.8%	Blue Collar	20.1%
Military		Post grad	13.5%	Government	12.9%
Veteran/ Active Duty	8.5%				

2012 Pres. Vote	Obama	212,701	(55%)	Romney	165,212	(43%)		
2016 Pres. Vote	Clinton	205,581	(52%)	Trump	163,643	(41%)	Johnson	16,509 (4%)

Cape Cod, Fall River: The South Shore of Massachusetts Bay, from Boston southward to Plymouth and then down Cape Cod (there is a lot of dispute about which way is up and down on the Cape), is Massachusetts's oldest settled territory. The Pilgrims landed here at Plymouth Rock in 1620. This stony land was farmed by John Adams' father. Daniel Webster lived in the South Shore town of Marshfield, today a high-income suburb of Boston far out on the usually clogged Southeast Expressway.

The Kennedys spent their summers at Hyannis Port on the Cape. As a senator in the 1950s, John F. Kennedy left a lasting legacy by helping to create the 40-mile Cape Cod National Seashore, which preserved much of the beauty, including large sand dunes. Provincetown, at the tip of the Cape, is still a fishing port and also one of the major gay vacation areas in the country. Famed writers Norman Mailer, Eugene O'Neill and Tennessee Williams all spent time in Provincetown. The islands of Martha's Vineyard and Nantucket, rich whaling ports in the early 19th century, are favored summer resorts for the liberal rich of Boston, New York and Washington. The Cape has filled with year-round retirees who enjoy the beauty and quiet pace. Cape Cod Bay supports cranberry growers, who annually produce more than $100 million from more than 13,000 acres of bogs. Growers have coped with over-supply and in 2018 requested that the Agriculture Department authorize destruction of a large share of their crop. The trade dispute with China, which had become a market, worsened the problem. With the warming of ocean waters, lobsters have moved north and the local harvest of crustaceans has been decimated — reductions of as much as 90 percent since the late 1990s. Cape Cod businesses serving tourists scrambled with labor shortages after the Trump administration changed the way visas for summer workers were distributed.

The 9th Congressional District of Massachusetts follows the South Shore from Rockland to the Cape and extends west to the famous whaling seaport of New Bedford and to parts of coastal Fall River, both of which have large Hispanic populations. It includes the two tony islands, where the glitterati have generated a "not in my backyard" fury to proposed windmill farms in the nearby channel waters. After the lease for the Cape Wind site in Nantucket Sound expired in 2018, Vineyard Wind made plans for a new farm with 100 turbines 15 miles south of the Vineyard. Subject to negotiations with local fishermen, this would be the largest off-shore wind-power project in the nation and could power one-third of all residences in Massachusetts. Safety fears and financial factors led to the planned May 2019 closing of the Pilgrim nuclear power plant in Plymouth. Dismantling the reactor and cleaning up the site could take decades. The wind terminals could offer a long-term energy solution.

Politically, the South Shore and the Cape were Republican decades ago. But they have shifted and this district leans Democratic. But it is the most competitive in Massachusetts. Hillary Clinton led Donald Trump in the district, 52%-41%.

MICHIGAN

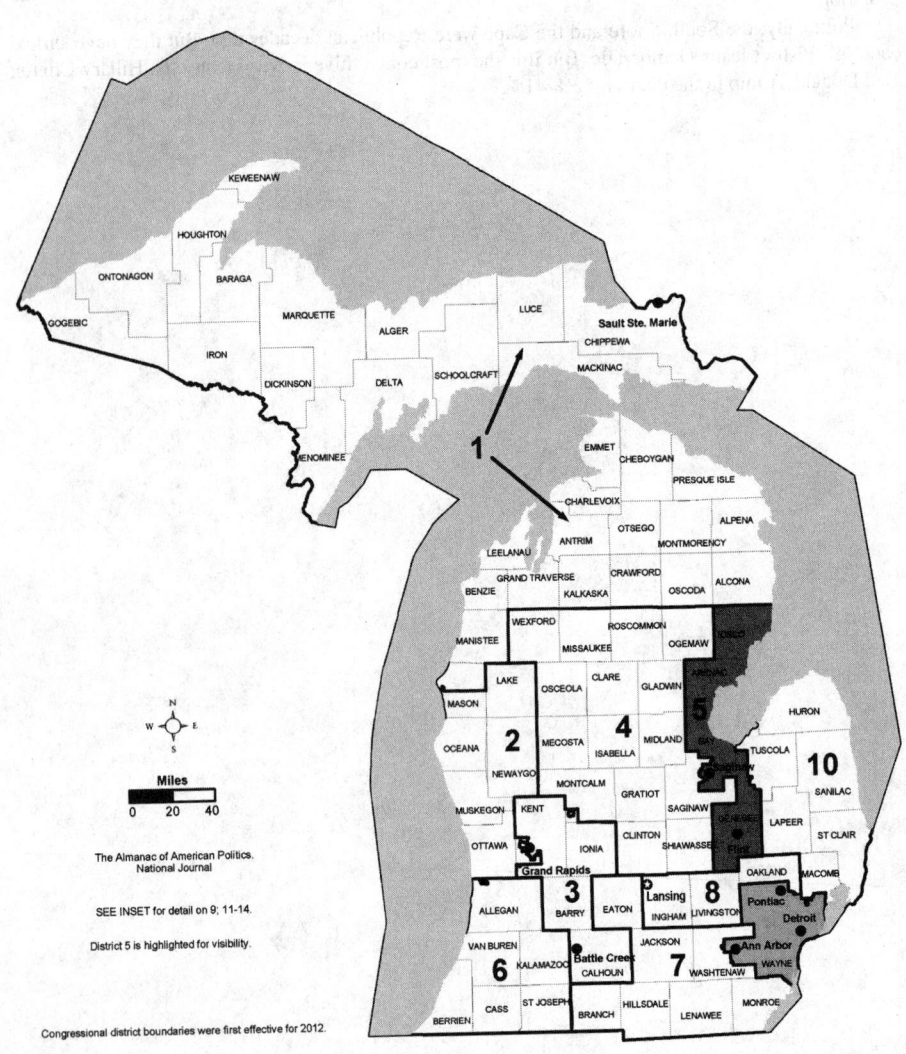

The Almanac of American Politics.
National Journal

SEE INSET for detail on 9; 11-14.

District 5 is highlighted for visibility.

Congressional district boundaries were first effective for 2012.

Michigan, though politically competitive in state-level races, hadn't voted Republican for president since 1988 – until 2016, when Donald Trump won it by three-tenths of 1 percent. It was one of the three states, along with Pennsylvania and Wisconsin, that enabled him to win the presidency by a healthy Electoral College margin, buoyed by a surge in blue-collar voters in declining industrial areas and apparent indifference from the Hillary Clinton campaign. But the state swung back in the 2018 midterm elections, flipping the governorship, the attorney general and the secretary of state – a shift that underlined how crucial the state will be in the 2020 presidential election.

Nearly 200 years ago, when the French aristocrat Alexis de Tocqueville wanted to visit the American frontier, he boarded a boat and steamed across Lake Erie to visit the Michigan Territory. Tocqueville was not the first Frenchman to travel there. In the 17th century, French explorers and missionaries sailed the Great Lakes and slapped their version of Indian names on the landscape, which is why Michigan's ch is pronounced like sh and why Mackinac is pronounced with a silent final c. (But Michiganders don't carry it to extremes: Detroit ends with a robust English oit.) Michigan was not effectively occupied by the United States until 1796 and was bypassed in the initial westward rush into Ohio, Indiana and Illinois. In 1831, Tocqueville was still able to travel through virgin woods occupied by Indian tribes. But later in that decade, Michigan was settled in a rush by Yankee migrants from upstate New York and New England, who cut down trees and built farms and orderly towns complete with schools and colleges. Politically, Michigan was full of Yankee reformers who hated slavery, manned the Underground Railroad, promoted temperance and in 1855 gave Michigan a constitution that banned (as its successors have done to this day) capital punishment. Michigan was one of the birthplaces of the Republican Party, which held its first official meeting in Jackson in 1854, and up through the 1920s, Michigan was one of the most Republican states in the nation.

After the Civil War, Michigan developed an industrial economy. Its Lower Peninsula was mostly covered with trees, and lumber was the first boom industry on which Michigan relied too much. (Even today, half the state's land area remains forested, supporting a popular hunting culture, though one that's declining as baby boomers age.) Forests were clear-cut or swept by blazes such as the 1881 fire that burned out half of Michigan's "Thumb." In the late 1800s, huge copper deposits were discovered on the Keweenaw Peninsula, which juts from the Upper Peninsula into icy Lake Superior. (The state includes 40,000 square miles of the Great Lakes, making almost half of Michigan water.) Immigrants from Italy and Finland, Cornwall and Croatia found work in the mines. Then came the auto industry. A combination of accident and shrewdness — the prickly genius of Henry Ford and the willingness of local bankers to finance auto startups — ensured that America's fastest-growing industry for the first 30 years of the 20th century was centered in Michigan. Detroit became a boomtown -- the nation's fastest-growing major metropolitan area after Los Angeles, which was then much smaller. The three-county Detroit metro area zoomed from a population of 426,000 in 1900 to 2.2 million in 1930, more than half the 4.3 million it has today. The auto industry drew labor from outside Michigan, from southern Ontario, and from the farms of Ohio and Indiana. It attracted Poles and Italians, Hungarians and Belgians, Greeks and Jews. During World War II and the two following decades, it attracted whites from the Kentucky and Tennessee mountains and blacks from the cotton country of Alabama and Mississippi.

This influx of a polyglot proletariat eventually changed Michigan's politics. The catalyst was the Great Depression of the 1930s and company managers' desire to use machines efficiently, treating employees as extensions of machines and with great distrust. That culminated in the 1937 sit-down strikes organized by the new United Auto Workers. Management and labor fought, sometimes literally, for pieces of what both sides feared was a shrinking pie. The UAW won and organized most of the companies after Democratic Gov. Frank Murphy refused to send in troops to break the illegal strikes. In the years that followed, autoworkers became more militant, and more militantly Democratic. Michigan politics became a kind of class warfare, conducted with a bitterness that split families and neighbors. The unions mostly won, because demographics benefited the Democrats: Autoworkers and post-1900 immigrants were larger in number and produced more children than did outstate Yankees or management. After Walter Reuther's election as UAW president in 1946, voters elected young, liberal G. Mennen Williams as governor in 1948. By 1954, Democrats, closely tied to the UAW, seemed to have become the natural majority in the state.

As growth continued, economic issues turned less bitter. By the early 1960s, class warfare had dissipated; in 1964, Henry Ford II joined Reuther in backing Democrat Lyndon Johnson for president. Republican George Romney, the former American Motors president elected governor in 1962, and his successor, William Milliken, accepted the social welfare policies endorsed by the UAW leadership and the Democrats. The state government was one of the nation's most vigorous, and not just for the poor and the unemployed. It supported one of the nation's most distinguished and extensive higher-education systems, built state parks and recreation areas, and pioneered efforts to end racial discrimination.

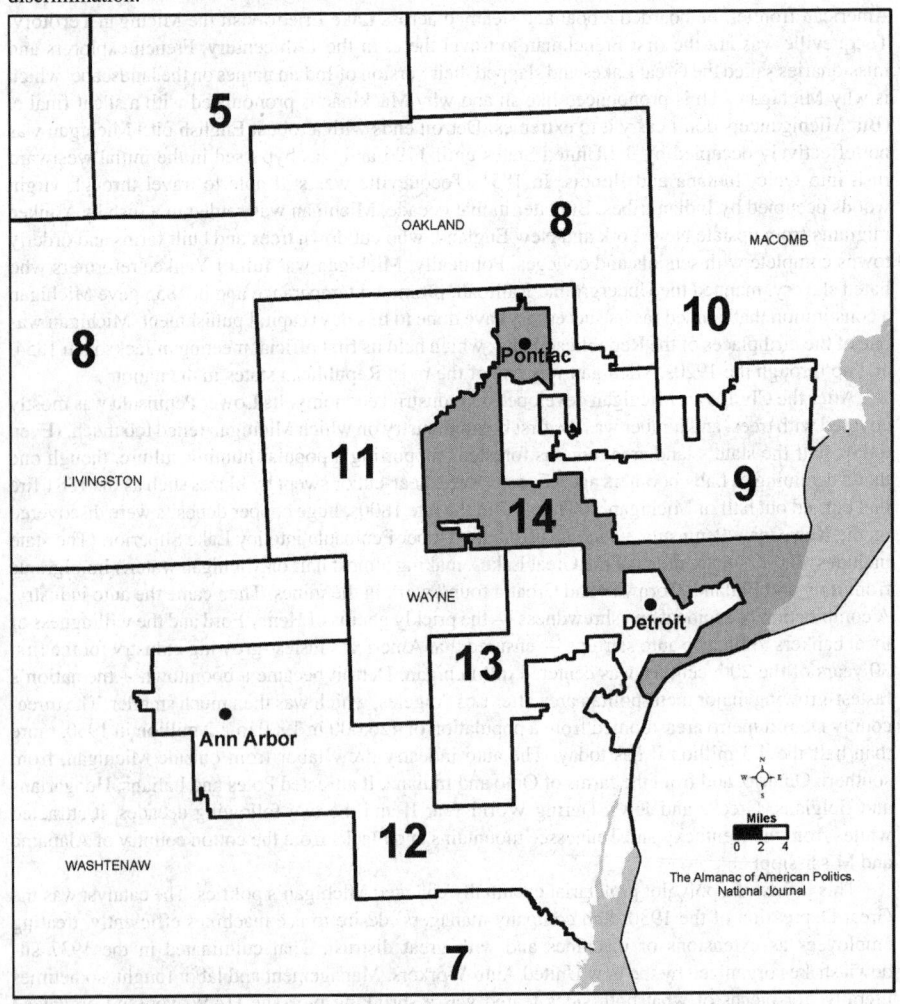

Congressional district boundaries were first effective for 2012.   District 14 is highlighted for visibility.

Michigan grew faster than the nation as a whole from 1910 to 1970, and successive censuses and reapportionments increased its House delegation from 12 to 19. But in the four decades from 1970 to 2010, Michigan grew less than one-quarter as fast as the nation, and its House delegation fell back to 14 in 2012, with a decline of one more seat projected after 2022. Since 2010, the state's population has grown by only 1.2 percent. A key turning point may have been the changes in the domestic auto industry. After the UAW's strike against General Motors in 1970, the union won its central demand: "30 and out," retirement after 30 years on the assembly line. That, in turn, led to demands for costlier retiree health benefits on top of those negotiated for active workers. The assumption was that the Big Three — General Motors, Ford, and Chrysler — would continue to dominate the U.S. auto market as they had for decades and would be able to afford top-shelf benefits. The reality turned out to be different. Foreign competitors began producing better and cheaper cars that were more responsive to changes in gas prices and consumer preferences, first in Europe and Japan and then in nonunion plants in the United States. Auto sales plummeted during the oil shock and recession of 1979-82, and Chrysler was saved from bankruptcy by a federal bailout, while GM and Ford foundered.

The auto industry became more high-tech, with fewer unionized workers and higher skill requirements. Just-in-time production methods encouraged subcontractors to stay in Michigan near big assembly plants, and the state boasted the nation's highest per capita concentration of engineers. Grand Rapids, Traverse City, and the northern and western Detroit suburbs fared well. The great exception was the city of Detroit, whose population fell from 1.8 million in 1950 to 713,000 in 2010. Starting with the 1967 rioting, crime rates in Detroit remained intolerably high for 25 years, and much of the city simply vanished — houses were abandoned or burned down, commercial frontage had nearly 100 percent vacancy rates, and the downtown was a beleaguered fortress surrounded by vacant square miles. Detroit's crumbling architecture helped give birth to a subgenre of photography called "ruin porn."

Detroit began rebounding in the 1990s. Crime and welfare rolls were down, new sports stadiums and even some new housing were built downtown, and old theaters were refurbished. But the decade that began in 2000 halted Michigan's economic progress. The Big Three, desperate to generate cash to pay huge costs for workers' and retirees' benefits, squeezed their subcontractors into bankruptcy, and GM and Chrysler followed in 2009; Ford managed to stay afloat only by mortgaging almost all its assets in 2007. Gov. Jennifer Granholm, a Democrat elected in 2002 and 2006, encouraged redevelopment, arranged for tax breaks for new facilities for the automakers and provided tax breaks to filmmakers.

While Detroit and Flint remained two of the nation's most impoverished cities – the latter afflicted with a manmade water-contamination problem – Michigan did recover along with the rest of the nation. The Big Three resumed making profits, and GM and Chrysler began buying back government-owned stock. Detroit spent several years in the biggest municipal bankruptcy in the history of North America, but in April 2018 – following a "grand bargain" with the state's GOP leadership and several years of budget surpluses -- the final financial restrictions were lifted, leaving the city entirely free of such oversight for the first time since the 1970s. In 2017, the Detroit area welcomed its first new vehicle assembly plant in a quarter century, to build off-road vehicles for the Indian company Mahindra Group; this followed local automotive-sector investments by other Indian and Chinese companies. Western Michigan, meanwhile, has been experiencing a quiet prosperity, with Grand Rapids, Kalamazoo and Muskegon increasing their economic output past pre-recession levels, thanks to a more diversified manufacturing base and lower wages.

Still, the scars on the manufacturing industry were lasting: Although the state's manufacturing workforce rose by 44 percent between the depths of the recession and late 2018, it still ended up at only 70 percent of the level it was in 2000, due in part to robotics. Other worries on the horizon include Trump administration tariffs, which raised the price of steel, and innovations such as hybrid cars and autonomous vehicles, which Michigan's automotive sector has been slow to embrace.

Michigan's population would be smaller without a steady influx of immigrants; the foreign-born now constitute nearly 7 percent of the population, more than half of whom are citizens eligible to vote. Michigan leads the nation in residents with Arab ancestry, thanks to a nearly continuous influx since the late 1800s. Arabs now account for an estimated 2 percent of Michigan's population, centered on Dearborn and other neighborhoods in the Detroit metro area; the Lebanese, Iraqi, Palestinian and Yemeni communities are well-established. In 2018, Rashida Tlaib, a Palestinian, was elected to a Detroit-based House seat. Michigan has historically ranked high nationally in refugee resettlements, although the number plunged after Trump became president, mirroring the trend in other states.

Politically, Michigan was heavily Republican from the 1850s through the 1920s, then developed a partisan equipoise during the 1930s and has mostly maintained it since. A typical result in the class-warfare era was John F. Kennedy's 51%-49% victory in 1960 — Kennedy carried metro Detroit, 62%-38%, while Richard Nixon carried outstate Michigan, 60%-39%. The Grand Rapids area, with its large Dutch-American population and many Christian conservatives, is usually the most Republican part of the state, though the city of Grand Rapids is more liberal; the area is home to the DeVos family, which founded the multi-level marketing behemoth Amway, became major Republican donors and promoted conservative policies, notably school choice, the signature issue of Trump's education secretary, Betsy DeVos. Industrial Flint, Saginaw and the Bay City corridor, with their blue-collar heritage and recent economic struggles, have generally voted heavily Democratic, as have the more highly educated areas around Lansing, the state capital, and Ann Arbor, home of the University of Michigan. The Upper Peninsula, historically Democratic, followed the patterns of rural America, turning increasingly red.

In the relatively prosperous 1990s, Michigan leaned toward Republicans in statewide contests; in the tougher 2000s, the state moved toward the Democrats. In 2010 and 2014, Republican businessman Rick Snyder won the governorship as a self-styled "one tough nerd." Just four years after Obama won the state by nine points, Trump won by less than 11,000 votes out of the almost 4.8 million cast. Gary Johnson and Jill Stein each won more votes than the difference between Trump and Clinton – 173,000 for Johnson and almost 51,000 for Stein. The most crucial shift was in Macomb County, the ancestral home of "Reagan Democrats," which Obama had won by four points but which Trump won by 11; Trump's margin of victory in Macomb was north of 48,000 votes.

Then, in 2018, the state that sealed Trump's victory snapped back. Democrat Gretchen Whitmer won the gubernatorial race by nine percentage points, winning roughly twice as many counties as Clinton had. Whitmer built on Clinton's vote share in traditionally Democratic counties, while also flipping Kent County (Grand Rapids), Eaton County (suburban Lansing), Bay County (Bay City), Saginaw County (Saginaw) and, perhaps most importantly, Macomb, by three points. Whitmer nearly matched Clinton's statewide vote total, while her Republican opponent, outgoing Attorney General Bill Schuette, underperformed Trump by 420,000. The Democrats swept the key statewide offices and seized two congressional seats, though the party's gains in the state House and Senate weren't enough to flip the heavily gerrymandered legislature – a result that might be affected by the easy passage of a redistricting reform ballot measure.

Population		Race and Ethnicity		Income	
Total	9,925,568	White	75.5%	Median Income	$52,668
Land area (sq. miles)	56,539	Black	13.7%	State Income Rank	33
Pop/ sq mi	175.6	Latino	4.9%	Poverty Rate	15.6%
Born in state	76.6%	Asian	2.9%	With health insurance	92.8%
		Two or more races	2.4%	Cash public assistance	2.8%
Age Groups		Other	0.5%	Food stamp/SNAP	14.9%
Under 18	22.3%				
18-34	22.2%	Education		Work	
35-64	39.6%	H.S grad or less	39.0%	White Collar	35.6%
Over 64	15.9%	Some college	32.9%	Sales and Service	40.8%
		College Degree, 4 yr	17.1%	Blue Collar	23.7%
Military		Post grad	11.0%	Government	10.5%
Veteran/ Active Duty	7.5%				

Presidential Politics

2016 Primary (D)	Sanders (D)	598,943 (50%)	Clinton (D)	581,775 (48%)	
2016 Primary (R)	Trump (R)	483,753 (36%)	Cruz (R)	329,617 (25%)	Kasich (R) 321,115 (24%)
	Rubio (R)	123,587 (9%)			
2016 Pres. Vote	Clinton (D) 2,268,839 (47%)		Trump (R) 2,279,543 (47%)	Johnson (L) 172,136 (4%)	
2012 Pres. Vote	Obama (D) 2,564,569 (54%)		Romney (R)2,115,256 (45%)		

Starting in 1992, Michigan voted for the Democratic presidential nominee in six consecutive elections and became a cornerstone in the so-called "blue wall" that gave Democrats accumulating 270 Electoral College votes. By 2008, Michigan gave Barack Obama a 16-percentage point margin of victory over John McCain, more than double the Democrat's national advantage. In affluent suburban Oakland County, where whites once voted Republican, voters shifted to Democrats on cultural issues in 1996 and haven't deviated from that course since. When Donald Trump smashed through the blue wall in Michigan and defeated Hillary Clinton by 10,704 votes out of 4.8 million cast — an upset that pre-election state polls didn't forecast and very few observers predicted — he did so, in part, by winning blue-collar counties that had eluded Republicans.

Exhibit "A" in that regard was Trump's victory in Macomb County, home to the Reagan Democrats. In 2012, Obama won Macomb by 16,103 votes. Trump defeated Clinton in Macomb by 48,348. Trump also won Saginaw, Bay and Monroe, and came within 1,200 votes of winning Muskegon, all blue-collar counties. Clinton carried white-collar Oakland by a margin of some 1,000 votes more than Obama did in 2012. But in Wayne County, with heavily Democratic Detroit, Clinton's vote trailed Obama's by some 76,000, suggesting an enthusiasm gap in African-American precincts. Meanwhile, Trump picked up about 15,000 votes more than Mitt Romney garnered in 2012, mostly in the western Wayne suburbs of Detroit. With such a narrow defeat, many factors could have caused Clinton's loss. Some Democrats have blamed unions for not getting out their Democratic vote. Others blamed Clinton's national team for poor organization. Michigan Democratic Rep. Debbie Dingell, whose district extends from the University of Michigan in Ann Arbor to auto plants in Dearborn and Flat Rock, wrote in a post-election piece in The Washington Post that while Obama may have helped save the auto industry, many of its workers "don't feel better off."

Earlier, the Democratic primary on March 8 was a rude awakening for Clinton and an embarrassment for the handful of pre-primary polls that showed her with a comfortable double-digit lead over Vermont Sen. Bernie Sanders, who vigorously stumped the state and highlighted his opposition to trade deals like the North American Free Trade Agreement that Clinton had once advocated. Clinton campaigned lightly during the primary, seldom outside the Detroit metro area. She carried Wayne, Macomb and Oakland counties, but lost most of the rest of the state giving Sanders a stunning 50%-48% victory. Trump's anti-trade rhetoric played well among the GOP Michigan primary electorate and he defeated Texas Sen. Ted Cruz 37%-25%. Ohio Gov. John Kasich was a close third taking 24 percent, but he carried only two of the state's 83 counties: Kalamazoo, home to Western Michigan University, and Washtenaw, home to the University of Michigan. Cruz carried only eight counties, most of those around Grand Rapids, where many voters are evangelicals.

The election in Michigan did not end on Election Day. Jill Stein, the Green Party presidential nominee, called for a recount in the state, as well as in Pennsylvania and Wisconsin. Ultimately, a federal judge in Detroit stopped the recount in Michigan, ruling that Stein's allegations of voter fraud lacked evidence. But tentative recount efforts uncovered problems with the Michigan vote, most notably in Detroit, where the Wayne County clerk discovered that in 37 percent of the city's precincts the number of ballots cast differed from the number of voters at the polls. A Michigan Bureau of Elections audit found that the discrepancies were due to human error, not illegality.

Congressional Districts

116th Congress Lineup	7D 7R	115th Congress Lineup	5D 9R

For the fifth consecutive decade, Michigan will lose at least one House seat. A total of five states share that distinction, though the total population in Michigan is smaller than in the other four. In 1950, Detroit had five entire congressional districts; today, it has barely enough population for one. But the loss of clout isn't exclusive to that city. In 1960, the Upper Peninsula had sufficient residents for 74 percent of a district; that has dropped to less than half a district. In contrast to the redistricting in 2011, when Republicans had complete control in Lansing, Democrats now have a stake — with Gov. Gretchen Whitmer — though Republicans retain both chambers of the legislature. More significantly, voters in 2018 approved a referendum that placed congressional redistricting under the control of a nominally nonpartisan commission — subject to possible court challenges.

Regardless of the procedures, the numbers remain relevant — as typically is the case with redistricting. Following their gain of two seats in 2018, Democrats control seven districts — six in the metro Detroit area and the other based in Flint and Saginaw. Republicans hold seven seats — all of them outside the metro area, though one includes a large part of Macomb County. With the population change in Detroit continuing to lag behind the increases in Grand Rapids and elsewhere outside of the metro area, the seven current Democratic-held districts (assuming that the incumbents retain control in 2020) would need to pick up Republican-leaning areas. That begs additional questions of whether Detroit will retain its two districts with African-American majorities, extending farther into the suburbs; alternatively, Detroit could have one super-district and it would take the short straw for the state's loss of a district. If the commission acts on a truly nonpartisan basis, one option could be the creation of a "fair fight," which would match one incumbent from each party. A new complication was the unanimous ruling in April 2019 by a three-judge federal court that large parts of the Michigan map were an unconstitutional "partisan gerrymander" and must be redrawn for the 2020 election. But the Supreme Court, which has never identified such a practice as an appropriate issue for judicial review, delayed subsequent action—at least until the Court's expected rulings in gerrymandering cases in Maryland and North Carolina.

Whatever the choices, the Michigan delegation — which had become stable during the past two decades -- likely is facing additional change and unpredictability.

Gretchen Whitmer (D)

Elected 2018, term expires 2023, 1st term; b. Aug. 23, 1971, Lansing; Michigan State University, B.A., 1998, J.D., 1993; Christian; Married (Marc Mallory) 2 children.

Elected Office: MI House, 2001-2006; MI Senate, 2006-2015, Minority Leader, 2011-2015; Ingham County Prosecutor, 2016.

Office: PO Box 30013, Lansing, 48909; 517-373-3400; Fax: 517-335-6863; Website: michigan.gov
Lt. Gov.: Garlin Gilchrist (D) **Atty. Gen:** Dana Nessel (D) **Sec. of State:** Jocelyn Benson (D)
State Legislature: Senate: 16D, 22R **House:** 52D, 58R

Election Results

Election	Name (Party)	Vote (%)
2018 General	Gretchen Whitmer (D)	2,266,193 (53%)
	Bill Schuette (R)	1,859,534 (44%)
2018 Primary	Gretchen Whitmer (D)	588,436 (52%)
	Abdul El-Sayed (D)	342,179 (30%)
	Shri Thanedar (D)	200,645 (18%)

Democrat Gretchen Whitmer, riding a blue wave of dissatisfaction with President Donald Trump and with outgoing GOP Gov. Rick Snyder, won the Michigan governorship in 2018. Whitmer, a veteran legislator, won a tough Democratic primary by defeating a liberal insurgency, then defeated Republican Attorney General Bill Schuette by a 9-point margin.

Whitmer was raised as one of three children in Grand Rapids and East Lansing. Her father served as chief of the state Commerce Department in a Republican administration and later as CEO of Blue Cross Blue Shield; her mother, a Democrat, was a senior lawyer in the state attorney general's office. She earned a bachelor's degree from Michigan State University and has spoken of her early desire to become a television sports correspondent. But after taking a political internship in Lansing, she changed her career focus and enrolled in law school at Michigan State. Less than three years after earning her law degree, Whitmer won a state House seat. She served six years in the House, then won a state Senate seat, rising to become the chamber's minority leader for her final four years – the first woman to lead a Senate party caucus.

In the legislature, Whitmer was a strong critic of policies passed by the GOP-controlled legislature and signed by Snyder, such as right-to-work legislation. "Gretchen is like a football team that just runs the ball and runs the ball and runs the ball," Mark Bernstein, an influential Michigan Democrat, told The New York Times. Whitmer's opposition to a religious exemption in a 2011 anti-bullying measure helped get the provision excised from the final bill. In 2013, Whitmer attracted national attention when she announced in an emotional floor speech that she had been raped in college. She told her story during debate over legislation to require abortion insurance to be purchased separately from private health plans. The bill, she said, "tells women who were raped ... that they should have thought ahead and planned for it." Only four of 48 senators at the time were women, and Whitmer decided that someone had to make a compelling case against the measure. "I think you need to see the face of the women that you are impacting by this vote today," she said. "I think you need to think of the girls that we're raising and what kind of a state we want to be where you would put your approval on something this extreme."

Whitmer had considered a run for attorney general in 2010, but decided against it. Four years later, facing Senate term limits, she considered a gubernatorial bid, but once again she opted against a run. Whitmer saw her opening in 2018, when Snyder was term-limited. She became the first Democrat to announce a candidacy, a tactic observers later credited with keeping a number of major Michigan Democrats out of the primary, including Sen. Gary Peters and Rep. Dan Kildee. From the start, Michigan Democrats were optimistic about their chances: In addition to the burst of Democratic enthusiasm in the Trump era, they expected to ride a backlash against Snyder. He had won in 2010 on his first foray into electoral politics, styling himself as "one tough nerd" – a pragmatist who was able to rise above political gridlock. But his second term was overwhelmed by a drinking-water crisis in Flint.

In the Democratic primary, Whitmer was the establishment candidate as well as the only woman in the race, although her roots outside of Detroit meant that political bigwigs from the state's biggest metro area took longer to come to her side. Whitmer had vastly more political experience than either of her challengers -- Abdul El-Sayed, a 33-year-old former city of Detroit health director, and Shri Thanedar, a deep-pocketed entrepreneur from Ann Arbor. Both positioned themselves as insurgents and attacked from her left. While Whitmer had assembled a record as a staunch defender of the Affordable Care Act, El-Sayed criticized her for not backing the single-payer Medicare for All health insurance plan; her ties to the health insurance industry came up, including her father's history with Blue Cross. Late in the primary campaign, Sen. Bernie Sanders and future Rep. Alexandria Ocasio-Cortez, two of the party's biggest names on the left, came to the state to campaign for El-Sayed. But primary voters concluded that Whitmer was plenty progressive – she supported a $15 minimum wage, legalized marijuana, and universal preschool -- and they liked her focus on nuts-and-bolts issues such as highway funding. (Her campaign bus was decorated with the motto, "Fix The Damn Roads.") On Election Day, Whitmer won 52 percent, El-Sayed took 30 percent, and Thanedar took 18 percent. To ease any residual friction with progressives and Democrats from the Detroit region, Whitmer tapped as her running mate Garlin Gilchrist, an African American who had served as director of innovation and emerging technology for the city of Detroit and who had nearly unseated an entrenched incumbent in the 2017 city clerk's race.

The Republicans also had a competitive primary, with two main contenders: Schuette, who had served two terms as attorney general, and before that as an appeals court judge, a state senator, state agriculture secretary and congressman, and outgoing Lt. Gov. Brian Calley. Snyder, who had clashed with Schuette over prosecutions in the Flint crisis, backed Calley. But Trump backed Schuette and recorded a robocall on his behalf. Schuette took 51 percent, Calley got 25 percent, state Sen. Patrick Colbeck got 13 percent and obstetrician Jim Hines won 11 percent.

The strains between Snyder and Schuette continued into the general election, with Snyder all but ignoring Schuette and several other Republican officials going so far as to endorse Whitmer. Schuette attacked Whitmer over her handling of early complaints about sexual misconduct by Larry Nassar, the gymnastics doctor at Michigan State University who would subsequently be convicted of serial sexual molestation and child pornography. She had been appointed interim prosecutor for Ingham County, which includes East Lansing, to fill a vacancy for six months. Schuette charged that Whitmer did not prosecute Nassar for sexual assault; Whitmer countered that the information given to her office was initially piecemeal, and that it spanned more than one county, making Schuette's office a more appropriate destination. In the end, the overall political environment drowned out other concerns. Whitmer won, 53%-44%.

After the loss, Republicans – who remained in control in both legislative chambers – sought to handcuff Whitmer and other incoming Democrats. They considered, then dropped, an idea to strip authority from the newly Democratic secretary of state. But they sent to Snyder one measure that would shield donors to politically active nonprofits from public disclosure and another that would curtail the attorney general's ability to pursue certain kinds of litigation opposed by lawmakers. After a national backlash against efforts to curb the powers of newly elected Democrats, Snyder vetoed the measures. Whitmer set out an agenda that included a $2 billion infrastructure bank, spending increases for preschool and K-12 education, and scholarships for higher education, though each had uncertain funding sources. She also said she would seek to free inmates and expunge criminal records for marijuana offenses, and that she would reinstate a program ended by Snyder that offered bottled water to qualifying Flint residents.

Debbie Stabenow (D)

Elected 2000, term expires 2024, 4th term, b. Apr 29, 1950; Gladwin; Michigan State University, B.A., 1972; Michigan State University, M.S.W., 1975; Methodist; Divorced; 2 children; 4 grandchildren.

Elected Office: Ingham County Commissioner, 1975-1978, Chair, 1976-1978; MI House, 1979-1991; MI Senate, 1991-1994; U.S. House, 1997-2001.

Professional Career: Social worker; Consultant & co-founder, MI Leadership Inst., 1995-1996.

DC Office: 731 HSOB 20510, 202-224-4822, Fax: 202-228-0325, stabenow.senate.gov

State Offices: Detroit, 313-961-4330; East Lansing, 517-203-1760; Flint, 810-720-4172; Grand Rapids, 616-975-0052; Marquette, 906-228-8756; Traverse City, 231-929-1031.

Committees: Senate Democratic Policy and Communications Center Chairman. *Agriculture, Nutrition & Forestry (RMM)*: Ex Officio membership on all subcommittees. *Budget. Energy & Natural Resources*: Energy; National Parks; Public Lands, Forests & Mining. *Finance*: Health Care (RMM); International Trade, Customs & Global Competitiveness. *Joint Taxation*.

Group Ratings

	ADA	ACLU	AFL-CIO	LCV	ITI	COC	HAFA	ACU	CFG	FRC
2018	-	62%	-	100%	-	60%	5%	14%	5%	0%
2017	90%	C	100%	95%	C	29%	C	0%	0%	0%

Almanac Ratings 2017-18

	Economy	Social	Foreign	Composite
Liberal	100%	100%	88%	96%
Conservative	0%	0%	12%	4%

Key Votes of the 115th Congress

1. Obama-care revision	N	5. Gun regulations	N
2. Tax Cuts	N	6. Family planning regs	N
3. Dodd-Frank revision	Y	7. Gorsuch confirmation	N
4. Omnibus appropriations	Y	8. Immigration restrictions	N

9. Kavanaugh confirmation	N
10. Saudi arms sales	Y
11. FISA rules	N
12. Military aid in Yemen	Y

Election Results

Election	Name (Party)	Vote (%)		Cand. Spent	Ind. Exp. Support	Ind. Exp. Oppose
2018 General	Debbie Stabenow (D)	2,214,478	(52%)	$14,614,819	$642,212	$642,910
	John James (R)	1,938,818	(46%)	$11,426,822	$3,682,335	
2018 Primary	Debbie Stabenow (D)	1,045,450	(100%)			

Prior winning percentages: 2012 (59%), 2006 (57%), 2000 (49%); House: 1998 (57%), 1996 (54%)

Democrat Debbie Stabenow, Michigan's senior senator, has been one of the more enduring figures in her state's politics throughout more than 40 years in elected office: She has a warm, personable demeanor that often causes opponents to underestimate her political toughness. "For nearly four decades, Republicans have sneered at Debbie Stabenow ... then she beats them, every time," then-Detroit Metro Times columnist Jack Lessenberry wrote in 2012 — when Stabenow captured 61 of the state's 83 counties to win her third Senate term by 20 percentage points. But once reliably blue Michigan has turned purple; in 2016, Donald Trump became the first Republican presidential nominee to win the state in nearly three decades. Two years later, Stabenow found herself in a re-election battle more competitive than first expected — holding on to win by about 6 percentage points over a political novice embraced by Trump.

Stabenow is the No. 4 Senate Democrat. But she is also known for reaching across the political aisle — particularly on the Agriculture Committee, which she chaired for four years before becoming its ranking Democrat in 2015. She has developed a collegial relationship with her Republican committee counterpart, Pat Roberts of Kansas — another veteran of 40 years in elected office. As debate began in 2017 on the latest five-year reauthorization of federal agricultural and nutrition programs, Stabenow and Roberts agreed to partner on the "farm bill." The upshot was that the $867 billion measure signed by Trump at the end of 2018 not only cleared the Senate on an overwhelmingly bipartisan vote, their alliance enabled Stabenow and Roberts to prevail over their House counterparts during protracted conference committee deliberations. "It goes to the question of, 'Do you want to govern?'" Stabenow told McClatchy's D.C. bureau. "Do you want to solve problems and get things done?"

Born Deborah Ann Greer, she grew up in the small northern Michigan town of Clare — where her family ran an Oldsmobile dealership. But her political base has long been the state capital, Lansing, and surrounding Ingham County, where Michigan State University is. She holds a bachelor and master's degree in social work from the latter. At first, she counseled students in public schools and made extra money singing folk songs in coffeehouses while volunteering for George McGovern's anti-Vietnam War presidential bid in 1972. Stabenow was first elected to office at 24. Angered when the Ingham County Board of Commissioners closed a nursing home, she ran for the board in 1974 and beat an incumbent who had referred to her as "that young broad." Stabenow was elected to the Michigan House four years later and to the state Senate in 1990. She ran for governor in 1994, but the state Democratic establishment lined up behind former Rep. Howard Wolpe, who won the primary with 35 percent of the vote; Stabenow placed second with 30 percent. She became Wolpe's running mate, but the ticket lost in November by a 3 to 2 margin.

Undaunted, Stabenow quickly began running for Congress in a district that included Democratic Ingham County and heavily Republican Livingston County. She won 54 percent of the vote in 1996 to oust freshman Republican Rep. Dick Chrysler. In 2000, she challenged first-term Republican Sen. Spencer Abraham in what turned out to be one of that year's critical Senate races. Abraham used his money advantage to run ads attacking Stabenow as a free-spending liberal favoring increased bureaucracy and higher taxes. Stabenow hoarded her money for an October ad buy, which turned out to be a wise strategy. She was down by 17 percentage points in polls in mid-October but answered Abraham's charges by citing her House votes for a balanced budget and ending the marriage penalty in the tax code — while attacking the incumbent as beholden to corporations and special interests. Stabenow won 49%-48%, helping Democrats gain a 50-50 split of the Senate — and becoming the first woman to represent Michigan in that chamber.

Soon after Stabenow was sworn in, Senate Democrats moved to strengthen her grip on the seat: Capitalizing on a central issue of her election campaign, they named Stabenow head of a task force on prescription drugs. She organized bus trips of seniors to Canada and pressed for measures allowing reimportation of U.S. drugs from that country. Stabenow has remained active on this issue: In late 2018, Trump signed Stabenow-authored legislation prohibiting Medicare drug plans from including "gag clauses" in their contracts with pharmacies. Such clauses had been used to bar pharmacists from telling patients that, in some instances, they could purchase a drug at a price lower than the co-pay required by insurance.

Stabenow has been among the most loyal Democrats, particularly on economic and social issues. But she joined other Rust Belt Democrats in challenging the international trade agenda put forth by President Barack Obama and his Republican predecessor, George W. Bush. In 2015, when Obama sought expedited authority to negotiate a 12-nation Pacific trade deal, Stabenow not only voted against it: she joined Ohio Republican Rob Portman to propose an amendment requiring the administration to seek enforceable currency manipulation standards in such a deal. The amendment, which did not pass, was supported by the Michigan-based Big Three automakers.

Stabenow sought to bait Trump, soon after he was elected president with the mantra "America First," into embracing legislation she has introduced perennially since 2012 — to provide tax incentives to companies that return jobs to the United States while eliminating tax breaks to those firms shifting jobs overseas. "Unfortunately, in previous years, Republican colleagues have filibustered it," Stabenow said in early 2017. While many of her congressional colleagues were critical a year later when Trump — after slapping tariffs on steel and aluminum imports — threatened to impose tariffs on autos, Stabenow was at first supportive. But in a September 2018 radio interview, she complained the administration was "just basically shooting in all directions and creating instability in terms of decisions that need to be made." A month later, she was more upbeat when Trump announced the U.S. Mexico-Canada Agreement to supplant the NAFTA. "I've said from the beginning that, given NAFTA's importance to our economy in Michigan, a modernization is long overdue," she said. "I'm encouraged that there have been positive steps forward."

When Stabenow found herself in line to chair the Agriculture Committee in 2011 the farm industry's alarm bells went off. Many of the industry's leaders viewed her as an urban liberal interested mainly in two of her state's best-known products: automobiles and cherries. By the time a new farm bill was passed in early 2014, much of the agriculture industry had taken a political U-turn — and Stabenow was praised for balancing competing interests in what is one of the most lobbied pieces of legislation on Capitol Hill. "Past farm bills pit regions against regions. I said that we were going to support all of agriculture," Stabenow told The New York Times after the bill's passage.

Traditionally, farm bills favored crops like corn and wheat that receive large subsidies. While such crops continued to benefit heavily in the 2014 rewrite overseen by Stabenow, subsidies for these commodities were cut by about 30 percent over 10 years. Although still a relatively small part of the overall bill, funding for specialty crops like fruits, vegetables and nuts — apples, blueberries and cherries are mainstays of Michigan agriculture — increased sharply. "This is not your father's farm bill," Stabenow said, pointing to savings — notably the elimination of a $5 billion-a-year, much-criticized subsidy that paid farmers whether or not they grew crops. The legislation took nearly three years to pull off, as she had to navigate regional differences. Stabenow was credited with dealing with such conflicts without allowing them to spill into public view The House-Senate conference report on the bill contained some concessions to Southern growers from the House version, but most provisions originated in the Senate, making it very much Stabenow's handiwork.

Roberts, who had been ranking member on the Agriculture Committee, became chairman in 2015. With Stabenow in the ranking member slot, they worked together to forge a compromise to require labeling of genetically modified food; it was signed into law by Obama. Several consumer groups were unhappy the bill mandated labeling be done through scannable codes rather than text or symbols. At the same time, Roberts was forced to retreat from earlier legislation he favored that would have prohibited states from requiring GMO labels — as Vermont had done in passing its own labeling law. Roberts and Stabenow also crafted a compromise on reauthorization of the school meals program, including largely maintaining the child nutrition standards first lady Michelle Obama had adopted as a signature issue. It cleared their committee unanimously but failed to become law. Early in the Trump administration, the Agriculture Department moved to give schools more flexibility in meeting federal nutrition standards for lunches.

Facing a Senate with a narrow 52-48 GOP majority at the beginning of 2017, Roberts and Stabenow opted for a farm bill draft that did not depart dramatically from the 2014 law. Their gambit worked, and the Senate passed the bill easily in June 2018. The House version squeaked through by two votes, with no Democrats voting for it. Resolving House-Senate differences in a timely manner was a major priority for the country's agricultural regions, where farmers had been hurt by a slump in commodity prices and retaliation to Trump's tariff policies. House and Senate negotiators clashed over some of the same regional issues as during the previous bill: Stabenow told The Detroit News she and Roberts had resisted House efforts to "skew" subsidies toward Southern crops like cotton and peanuts at the expense of major Midwestern crops like corn. For Michigan, Stabenow came away with expanded crop insurance for fruits, vegetables, hops and barley; greater supports for dairy, the state's agricultural mainstay; and a federal office to advocate for urban farms in cities like Detroit.

The biggest dispute involved the $70 billion annual Supplemental Nutrition Assistance Program, formerly known as food stamps, which helps more than 40 million people buy groceries. The House bill sought to expand work requirements for recipients with children older than 6; such a move would cause 1.2 million people each month to lose eligibility, according to congressional estimates. The Senate version did not contain such changes, with Roberts and Stabenow instead proposing rules to combat fraud. In the final deal on the bill, which was reached in late November 2018, the Senate view prevailed, but not until Trump — via Twitter — had accused Stabenow and other Democrats of holding up the farm bill. "Work requirements are an imperative and the Dems are a NO. Not good!" the president wrote, overlooking the fact that 20 Senate Republicans had joined the Democrats in rejecting a provision like what House conferees were seeking.

During her first term, Stabenow was selected as secretary of the Democratic Caucus. It gave Stabenow a voice at leadership meetings, though her impact was limited. Some senior Democrats quietly discussed replacing her after the 2006 elections . After her re-election, a deal was reached in which Stabenow got a seat on the influential Finance Committee and became chairwoman of the Democratic Steering and Outreach Committee while being replaced as caucus secretary. In 2011, she became vice chairwoman of what is now the Democratic Policy and Communications Committee. She was elevated to its chairmanship in 2017, when Sen. Chuck Schumer became minority leader.

Seeking a third term in 2012 against former Rep. Pete Hoekstra, Stabenow was targeted by what was arguably the most controversial TV ad of that election cycle: It featured an Asian woman bicycling through a rice paddy and thanking "Sen. Debbie Spend-It-Now" in broken English for sending U.S. jobs to China. Republicans and Democrats alike attacked Hoekstra for playing on racial stereotypes. He never recovered, and Stabenow bettered her 2006 performance, winning with 59 percent of the vote.

As the 2018 election cycle got underway, an unconventional prospect emerged: singer Kid Rock, a native of Detroit's suburbs. After starting a Kid Rock for Senate website and selling campaign-themed merchandise — and prompting several independent polls of a matchup against Stabenow — the musician said during a radio show interview in late 2017 that it had all been a joke. Sandy Pensler, a private investor and financial adviser to several large corporations, and John James, a West Point graduate and Iraq War veteran, dueled for the GOP Senate nomination. Pensler and James battled over who had the most conservative credentials. James won 55%-45%, 10 days after Trump issued an endorsement via Twitter. Trump called James "SPECTACULAR!" adding, "Rarely have I seen a candidate with such great potential. West Point graduate, successful businessman and a African American leader."

James — head of a family-run business who described himself as a "pro-life, pro-Second Amendment, pro-business conservative" — was largely unknown before the contest. . He repeatedly attacked Stabenow as out of touch and ineffective, saying, "You aren't going to get results from a 43-year career politician." Stabenow had a substantial financial edge, which allowed her to buy TV ads first. James' TV effort got off to a bumpy start; his first ad, which showed him in a school setting, had a bulletin board in the background containing an image that appeared to be a swastika. James said it was unintentional and apologized.

James' paid TV ads never mentioned he was the Republican nominee, although one spot appealed to African-American voters to leave the Democratic Party and "have a seat at both tables." That appeal had limited effect, as Stabenow garnered more than 95 percent of the black vote on Election Day, according to the Detroit News. Trump kept up a steady stream of tweets attacking Stabenow as an "automatic far left vote" and a "Schumer Puppet." While James at times tried to put some distance between himself and Trump — who had a favorability rating of 37 percent statewide in a September Detroit News poll — he asked the president to visit the state to campaign for him a week before the election on Fox News

Trump, who won Michigan by less than half a percentage point in 2016, didn't visit; Stabenow won 52%-46%. She captured only 15 of 83 counties. She took a bare majority in Macomb County, often seen as a bellwether of white, working-class America, and which had gone heavily for Trump two years earlier.

Gary Peters (D)

Elected 2014, term expires 2020, 1st term, b. Dec 01, 1958; Pontiac; Alma College (MI), B.A., 1980; University of Detroit (MI), M.B.A., 1984; Wayne State University Law School (MI), J.D., 1989; Michigan State University, M.A., 2007; Episcopalian; Married (Colleen Ochoa); 3 children.

Military Career: U.S. Navy Reserve 1993-2000 (Iraq); 2001-2005

Elected Office: Rochester Hills City Council, 1991-1993; MI Senate, 1995-2002; U.S. House, 2009-2015.

Professional Career: Assistant Vice President., Merrill Lynch, 1980-1989; Vice President., UBS/ Paine Webber, 1989-2003; Chief admin. officer, MI bureau of investments, 2003; Commissioner, MI Lottery Bureau, 2003-2007; Professor, Central MI University, 2007-2008.

DC Office: 724 HSOB 20510, 202-224-6221, Fax: 202-224-7387, peters.senate.gov

State Offices: Detroit, 313-226-6020; Grand Rapids, 616-233-9150; Lansing, 517-377-1508; Marquette, 906-226-4554; Rochester, 248-608-8040; Saginaw, 989-754-0112; Traverse City, 231-947-7773.

Committees: *Armed Services*: Airland; Emerging Threats & Capabilities (RMM). *Commerce, Science & Transportation*: Communications, Technology, Innovation & the Internet; Subcommittee on Aviation & Space; Subcommittee on Science, Oceans, Fisheries & Weather; Subcommittee on Transportation & Safety. *Homeland Security & Government Affairs (RMM)*: Ex Officio membership on all subcommittees. *Joint Economic*.

Group Ratings

	ADA	ACLU	AFL-CIO	LCV	ITI	COC	HAFA	ACU	CFG	FRC
2018	-	62%	-	100%	-	60%	5%	9%	5%	0%
2017	95%	C	100%	100%	C	29%	C	4%	0%	0%

Almanac Ratings 2017-18

	Economy	Social	Foreign	Composite
Liberal	94%	94%	80%	89%
Conservative	6%	6%	20%	11%

Key Votes of the 115th Congress

1. Obama-care revision	N	5. Gun regulations	N	9. Kavanaugh confirmation	N
2. Tax Cuts	N	6. Family planning regs	N	10. Saudi arms sales	Y
3. Dodd-Frank revision	Y	7. Gorsuch confirmation	N	11. FISA rules	Y
4. Omnibus appropriations	Y	8. Immigration restrictions	N	12. Military aid in Yemen	Y

Election Results

Election	Name (Party)	Vote (%)	Cand. Spent	Ind. Exp. Support	Ind. Exp. Oppose
2014 General	Gary Peters (D)........................... 1,704,936	(55%)	$10,289,555	$5,970,696	$8,040,765
	Terri Lynn Land (R)........................ 1,290,199	(41%)	$12,270,048	$1,960,159	$14,712,548
	Jim Fulner (L)............................ 62,897	(2%)			
2014 Primary	Gary Peters (D)........................... Unopposed				

Prior winning percentages: House: 2012 (82%), 2010 (50%), 2008 (52%)

Michigan's junior senator, Gary Peters, is the Democratic freshman class of 2014 — the sole Democrat to win an open Senate seat in an election cycle that had few bright spots for his party. While he travels around the Wolverine State on a Harley-Davidson Dyna Super Glide, Peters is referred to as wonkish. He has earned degrees from four colleges and universities in his home state. And, in the Senate, he often has focused on issues that can only be described as, well, wonkish. Peters has reached across the political aisle to co-author legislation dealing with the inner workings of government. In short, it's not the type of stuff that captures a lot of headlines back home: In January 2019, a poll conducted by a Michigan-based survey firm found that 36 percent of likely voters had never heard of Peters. "Many in Washington probably couldn't even pick him out of a lineup," Politico wrote of the freshman senator in a story published a year earlier.

But Peters was poised to raise his low profile. In 2019, Peters became the ranking Democrat on the Homeland Security and Governmental Affairs Committee — a position deftly utilized by his predecessor, former Missouri Sen. Claire McCaskill, to highlight shortcomings in the federal government. His bid for a second term is certain to draw national attention: He will be one of only two Democratic incumbents running in states that President Donald Trump captured in 2016.

While Peters could face a tough re-election battle in a once-blue state shaded purple, his electoral success extends nearly three decades — including three tough races for the House before he moved to the Senate. His family's roots in suburban Oakland County go back five generations; Peters grew up in Pontiac, the son of a public school teacher and a nursing-home aide. After graduating from Alma College in central Michigan, he spent more than two decades working as a financial adviser for large investment firms. During that time, he earned an MBA from the University of Detroit Mercy and a law degree from Wayne State University in Detroit. He enlisted in the U.S. Navy Reserve, becoming a lieutenant commander and serving in the Persian Gulf as part of the operation enforcing a no-fly zone after the 1991 Gulf War. He left the Navy Reserve in 2000, but re-enlisted after 9/11 and served for another four years. In 2017, Peters got a seat on the Armed Services Committee.

Peters' political career began with his election to the Rochester Hills City Council in 1991; he followed that by winning a seat in the Michigan Senate in 1994. There, he led an effort to ban oil drilling in the Great Lakes. Forced by term limits to give up his Senate seat, Peters mounted a short-lived candidacy for governor before running for state attorney general. He lost the 2002 election — his only electoral defeat. He then spent nearly five years as the state's lottery commissioner, earning another degree on the side at Michigan State University — a master's in philosophy with a focus on the ethics of development. In 2008, Peters challenged veteran Republican Rep. Joe Knollenberg; he won with 52 percent of the vote.

Peters has described himself as a centrist who is pro-business and socially liberal. Almanac vote rankings put him squarely in the middle of the Senate Democratic Caucus. In the House — and later in the Senate — Peters backed his party on most major votes but showed independence at times. In his freshman House term, he was put on the 2010 conference committee that drafted the final version of the landmark Dodd-Frank law on financial reforms; Peters added a provision boosting the financing businesses of the nation's automakers.

Nearly a decade later, Peters split from a majority of Senate Democrats to support Republican-sponsored legislation — signed by Trump — to roll back some provisions of the Dodd-Frank Act. Peters cited the regulatory relief that the bill provided for credit unions as a major reason for his vote; he and 16 other Democratic supporters of the bill took heat from the party's progressive wing anyway. In response, Peters noted the bill did not alter the reserve requirements and restrictions placed on the nation's largest banks, telling the Detroit Free Press, "I would never vote for anything to weaken what my friend [former Rep.] Barney Frank and I worked on in that conference committee." He also cited a provision he had attached to the rollback bill making it easier for young workers who had defaulted on student loans to work out restructured payment plans and repair negative credit reports.

In 2012, Michigan lost a congressional seat and the new map carved up Peters' district. He faced a tough choice: challenge longtime Democratic Rep. Sander Levin in another Detroit suburban district or go up against freshman Rep. Hansen Clarke, an African-American in a majority-black district. Peters had ties to the latter district from his state Senate days, and he courted labor unions and church leaders. He won the primary 47%-35%; another African-American candidate, Southfield Mayor Brenda Lawrence, who captured the seat in 2014, got 13 percent. Peters prevailed in the general election.

Peters benefited from political serendipity in 2014: In a year in which little went wrong for Senate Republicans in most battleground races, little went right for them in Michigan. Sen. Carl Levin announced his retirement in March 2013, and Peters had the Democratic Senate nomination all but locked up in weeks, as other potential contenders took themselves out of the running. When the eventual Republican nominee, former Michigan Secretary of State Terri Lynn Land, announced in late spring, her candidacy was met with something short of enthusiasm among party leaders, who had spent months trying to recruit another candidate. Peters sought to emphasize job creation and other middle-class concerns and was aided by a humorous TV ad that highlighted his everyman persona. "I wouldn't call him cheap, but our washing machine is older than the kids," his wife, Colleen Ochoa Peters, said during the 30-second spot. "It still works," he responds, as his daughter holds up a ragged sweatshirt and shoes with holes he wore frequently. The ad ends with Gary Peters, sporting the worn attire, saying, "I approved this message because my family did this ad for free."

In contrast, Land launched her TV effort with what may have been the oddest ad of the 2014 election cycle. In it, she said: "Congressman Gary Peters and his buddies want you to believe I'm waging a war on women. Really? Think about that for a moment." In the rest of the 12 seconds of the ad, Land silently sips coffee, shakes her head and looks at her watch. Several weeks later, Land put on a lackluster performance before the Detroit Regional Chamber of Commerce and all but froze when questioned by journalists. "I can't do this," she said, as she pushed away a cluster of microphones and left. The gaffe was compounded by her efforts to avoid the media for much of the rest of the campaign. The National Republican Senatorial Committee canceled a $1 million TV ad buy in the closing weeks. . Peters won 55%-41%.

Three days before Election Day, Peters became the only 2014 Senate candidate for whom President Barack Obama campaigned in person. When Obama appeared at a rally in Detroit, Peters stressed the president's bailout of the auto industry several years earlier. A little more than two years later, on Obama's final day in office, he left Peters with a farewell present: The site of a former General Motors plant in Ypsilanti was designated as a proving ground for driverless-car development, one of 10 such sites nationwide. Peters, one of the project's leading advocates, was elated, saying:

"We cannot lose being at the center of this activity for the auto industry. This is critical for our long-term future."

Peters has persisted on this issue — arguing not just Michigan's economy, but America's leadership in technology is at stake. "A lot of people see self-driving cars as the moonshot for artificial intelligence. So this is of critical economic importance to the United States," Peters told the Washington Examiner in 2018. As a member of the Commerce, Science and Transportation Committee, Peters teamed with Republican Sen. John Thune, then committee chairman, on a bill establishing federal standards for self-driving cars. The measure gradually waived traditional standards, such as steering wheels and brake pedals, for up to 80,000 vehicles per manufacturer. But several Democrats, citing safety concerns, objected to action by the Senate in 2018.

Peters has forged alliances with several GOP freshmen elected with him — largely on issues dealing with government management. With Oklahoma Republican James Lankford, Peters introduced legislation requiring federal agencies to encourage use of remanufactured parts in federal vehicle repairs. The law, enacted in 2015, was spurred by a Government Accountability Office study Peters had requested. Several months later, Obama signed another Peters-authored bill, this one with a mouthful of a name: "Making Electronic Government Accountable by Yielding Tangible Efficiencies Act" — or the MEGABYTE Act. Co-sponsored with Louisiana Republican Bill Cassidy, it sought to reduce government waste by improving management of federal software licenses. And Peters collaborated with Colorado Republican Cory Gardner to resolve a three-year battle between House Republican leaders and the scientific community over how the National Science Foundation should operate. Peters and Gardner crafted a bill that scientists saw as more supportive of the NSF. Legislation Obama signed in late 2016 reflected the Gardner-Peters approach.

Reflecting an interest in environmental issues going back to his days in the Michigan Legislature, Peters fought a yearlong battle for federal aid to deal with lead-tainted drinking water in the poor, majority-black city of Flint. As a spending bill to keep the federal government operating came up just before the 2016 pre-election recess, Peters and his Michigan colleague, Democrat Debbie Stabenow, used their leverage to block its passage — conceding only after the House agreed to attach $170 million in aid to Flint to another bill.

In early 2018, Detroit Mayor Mike Duggan and several union leaders led a quiet effort to coax Peters to run for governor, according to Bridge magazine. The move was prompted by concern over the prospects of the leading Democratic contender, Gretchen Whitmer. Peters declined to run for the job, which Whitmer won. Her victory, along with Democrats' gain of two U.S. House seats, were seen as a boost to Peters' 2020 re-election prospects in a state Trump carried by less than half a percentage point in 2016.

There has been speculation Peters could face a left-wing primary challenge from Abdul El-Sayed, a former Detroit health commissioner who sought the 2018 Democratic gubernatorial nomination. But El-Sayed told the Atlantic in early 2019, "I'm not intending to primary Gary." In June 2019, Republican businessman and Iraq war veteran John James, who ran better than expected against Stabenow in 2018, announced his challenge to Peters. Stabenow defeated James by just over 6 percentage points. Looking ahead to 2020, Peters told Roll Call, "I would expect that Michigan will be hotly contested in the presidential race — that's why the Senate race will also be a very high-profile national one."

John Bergman (R)

Elected 2016, 2nd term, b. Feb 02, 1947; Shakopee, MN; Gustavus Adolphus College (MN); University of West Florida, M.B.A., 1975; Lutheran; Married (Cindy Bergman); 5 children; 8 grandchildren.

Military Career: U.S. Marine Corps 1969-1975; RI National Guard 1975-1978; U.S. Marine Corps Reserve 1978-2003; U.S. Marine Corps 2003-2009 (Vietnam)

Professional Career: Commercial pilot; Business owner.

DC Office: 414 CHOB 20515, 202-225-4735, Fax: 202-225-4710, bergman.house.gov

State Offices: Marquette, 906-273-2227; Traverse City, 231-944-7633.

Committees: *Armed Services*: Military Personnel; Readiness; Seapower & Projection Forces. *Veterans' Affairs*: Economic Opportunity; Oversight & Investigations (RMM).

Group Ratings

	ADA	ACLU	AFL-CIO	LCV	ITI	COC	HAFA	ACU	CFG	FRC
2018	-	11%	-	9%	-	83%	51%	68%	52%	100%
2017	0%	C	11%	6%	C	93%	C	85%	75%	89%

Almanac Ratings 2017-18

	Economy	Social	Foreign	Composite
Liberal	3%	9%	0%	4%
Conservative	97%	91%	100%	96%

Key Votes of the 115th Congress

1. Obama-care revision	Y	5. Family planning regs	Y	9. Guantanamo prisoners	N
2. Tax Cuts	Y	6. Body cameras/immigration	N	10. Ground missiles, limit	N
3. Omnibus appropriations	N	7. Abortion ban	Y	11. Defense Dept. spending	Y
4. Dodd-Frank revision	Y	8. Concealed carry	Y	12. FISA rules	Y

Election Results

Election	Name (Party)	Vote (%)		Cand. Spent	Ind. Exp. Support	Ind. Exp. Oppose
2018 General	Jack Bergman (R)	187,251	(56%)	$1,417,128	$59,289	$108,600
	Matthew Morgan (D)	145,246	(44%)	$1,340,110		
2018 Primary	Jack Bergman (R)		(100%)			

Prior winning percentages: 2016 (55%)

Republican Jack Bergman, first elected in 2016, has twice won by double-digit margins against well-financed opponents in what Democrats had considered an opportunity. A retired three-star Marine Corps lieutenant general, Bergman benefited from his party label in what recently had been a swing district.

A native of Minnesota, Bergman said his ancestors worked in the iron mines of the Upper Peninsula as far back as the 1800s. He got his bachelor's from Gustavus Adolphus College in St. Peter Minnesota, and an MBA from the University of West Florida. During more than 25 years in the military, he served as commanding general of the Marine Forces Reserve in Louisiana. He retired as a lieutenant general in 2009. Bergman also was a pilot for Northwest Airlines and built a business that sold surgical equipment. Although he had no previous experience as a political candidate, he had served on the advisory council for Louisiana Republican Gov. Bobby Jindal. He resided in Watersmeet, a small town in the Ottawa National Forest, at the far western end of the U.P. He ran for a seat in the Michigan state House in 2012, but narrowly lost in the Republican primary.

When Republican Rep. Dan Benishek retired in 2016, Bergman ran as the outsider candidate in the Republican primary against two local political figures: state Sen. Tom Casperson from the U.P., who was a vocal advocate of more wolf hunting, and former state Sen. Jason Allen of Traverse City, who had been an official of the Michigan Veterans Affairs Agency. Bergman benefited from spending more than $270,000 of his own money in the primary campaign. He won with 39 percent of the vote to 32 percent for Casperson and 29 percent for Allen. Lon Johnson, who had chaired the Michigan Democratic Party, easily won the Democratic nomination.

The general election was well-financed, with each nominee getting more than $2 million of support from national party groups. Johnson emphasized his status as a political outsider against party official Johnson, whose wife Julianna Smoot was national deputy campaign manager for President Barack Obama in 2012. With neither candidate especially well-known in this sprawling district, the unexpectedly large 21-point victory for Donald Trump in the presidential contest likely provided coattails for Bergman. He took the House contest, 55%-40%.

In the House, Bergman made progress on a local priority by including authorization to replace the 50-year-old lock at Sault Ste. Marie among the water projects that Congress approved and President Donald Trump signed in October 2018. Bergman called the new lock the number-one issue of his first term. On the Veterans' Affairs Committee, he was a leading proponent of a bill to expedite medical coverage for veterans from private doctors and hospitals; Trump signed in June 2018 this overhaul of the Veterans Choice Program. In 2019, he became ranking Republican on the Oversight and Investigations Subcommittee of the veterans panel. He also got a seat on the Armed Services Committee — appropriate, he said, for the highest-ranking combat veteran ever elected to Congress.

In 2018, Bergman faced Democratic challenger Matt Morgan, who became the nominee by securing more than 30,000 write-in votes in the August primary after he had been denied ballot access because of a filing problem. Morgan, who styled himself as a progressive Marine veteran, had campaign help from filmmaker Michael Moore, a progressive icon in Michigan. Morgan, who complained that he received scant support from national Democrats, called for expanded Medicare coverage and repeal of the 2001 authorization for the use of military force as a justification for continued military engagements. Bergman outspent Davidson, $1.4 million to $1.2 million. Bergman won, 56%-44%, and took all but two of the 32 counties.

MI-1: Northern Michigan

Cook Partisan Voting Index: R+9

Population		Race and Ethnicity		Income	
Total	700,228	White	91.1%	Median Income	$46,722
Land area (sq. miles)	25,028	Black	1.5%	District Income Rank	357
Pop/ sq mi	28	Latino	1.9%	Poverty Rate	14.4%
Born in State	79.4%	Asian	0.7%	With health insurance	91.9%
		Two or more races	2.5%	Cash public assistance	2.6%
Age Groups		Other	2.4%	Food stamp/SNAP	12.8%
Under 18	18.9%				
18-34	19.3%	**Education**		**Work**	
35-64	40.2%	H.S grad or less	41.8%	White Collar	21.6%
Over 64	21.6%	Some college	33.5%	Sales and Service	44.4%
		College Degree, 4 yr	15.6%	Blue Collar	24.5%
Military		Post grad	9%	Government	13.6%
Veteran/ Active Duty	11%				

2012 Pres. Vote	Romney	189,387	(54%)	Obama	160,231	(45%)			
2016 Pres. Vote	Trump	210,816	(58%)	Clinton	133,239	(36%)	Johnson	13,785	(4%)

Upper Peninsula: Michigan's Upper Peninsula, commonly known as the U.P., is a land apart. Surrounded on three sides by frigid Lakes Superior, Huron and Michigan, there are places here that have some of the coldest climates in settled parts of North America. These storms can be cruel. The "gales of November" have caught hundreds of vessels by surprise and sent them to the bottom of the lake, including the SS Edmund Fitzgerald, whose loss was memorialized in a Gordon Lightfoot ballad.

With ground too frozen and stony and a growing season too short for most crops, the peninsula was considered a poor consolation prize when much of it was appended to the Michigan Territory in 1836 in exchange for the incipient state giving up its claim to Toledo and its surrounding areas. The mineral veins of the Keweenaw Peninsula eventually produced more than 13 billion pounds of copper, while the Marquette, Menominee and Gogebic iron ranges produced more than 1 billion tons of iron ore. Immigrants flocked here to work the mines. A plurality of residents were Finns, who must have found this cold land with its lakes and hills much like home. By the early 1900s, the U.P. had become a northern industrial belt with a workforce disposed to radical ideas and union movements.

A major strike in 1913-14 and falling ore prices after World War I accelerated the copper decline. The Empire Mine in Marquette County closed in 2016 because of limited supply and demand. Other industries have taken root. The region's natural beauty — 90 percent of the U.P. is forested — has made tourism a leading economic driver in all seasons. Skiers can take advantage of the average 200 inches of annual snowfall at several mountain resorts. In summer, there are abundant outdoor opportunities, including mountain biking and surfing. Population of the U.P. peaked at 332,000 in 1920. In 201, there were 311,000 "Yoopers," as the locals call themselves, many of whom harbor a strong sense of place. From 2010 to 2016, 14 of the 15 counties lost population. During a local political rally in April 2018, President Donald Trump endorsed the proposed 1,200-foot Soo Locks Modernization Project in the St. Lawrence Seaway. "The Soo Locks are going to hell," he said. "And we're going to get them fixed up."

The 1st Congressional District of Michigan includes the Upper Peninsula and 16 1/2 northern counties in the Lower Peninsula. Almost half the people live in the U.P. Marquette, with 21,300 people, is the largest city in the district. There has been a push to reopen mines for gold and zinc, though Native Americans and environmentalists have objected. Mackinac Island, home to a resort area where almost all cars are banned (even UPS delivers packages by bicycle), lies just east of the breathtaking Mackinac Bridge, which connects the two peninsulas. On the Lower Peninsula, along Lake Michigan, are affluent resort areas around Petoskey and Charlevoix, long summer places for people from Chicago (this is Ernest Hemingway's "Up in Michigan"). There is some agriculture on the district's southern end; the Traverse City area accounts for more than 70 percent of tart cherry production in the United States and the weeklong cherry festival attracts hundreds of thousands of visitors each summer. In a twist of President Donald Trump's policies, the area is a foreign trade zone with no tariffs on imports or exports.

Politically, the U.P. has a lengthy Democratic tradition, but it has moved toward Republicans in recent years. This is one part of Michigan that has opposed many Democratic environmental and gun-control stands. When Donald Trump took the mostly blue-collar and low-income district, 58%-36%, it became clear that the partisan shifts were more deep-seated.

Bill Huizenga (R)

Elected 2010, 5th term, b. Jan 31, 1969; Zeeland; Calvin College (MI), B.A., 1991; Christian Reformed Church; Married (Natalie Huizenga); 5 children.

Elected Office: MI House, 2003-2008.

Professional Career: Realtor, 1991-1996; Aide, Rep. Pete Hoekstra, 1997-2002; Admin., Zeeland Christian Schls., 2009-2010; Co-owner, Huizenga Gravel, 1999-present.

DC Office: 2232 RHOB 20515, 202-225-4401, Fax: 202-226-0779, huizenga.house.gov

State Offices: Grand Haven, 616-414-5516; Grandville, 616-570-0917.

Committees: *Financial Services*: Housing, Community Development & Insurance; Investor Protection, Entrepreneurship & Capital Markets (RMM).

Group Ratings

	ADA	ACLU	AFL-CIO	LCV	ITI	COC	HAFA	ACU	CFG	FRC
2018	-	4%	-	0%	-	92%	62%	96%	59%	100%
2017	0%	C	3%	0%	C	93%	C	93%	88%	100%

Almanac Ratings 2017-18

	Economy	Social	Foreign	Composite
Liberal	3%	4%	0%	2%
Conservative	97%	97%	100%	98%

Key Votes of the 115th Congress

1. Obama-care revision	Y	5. Family planning regs	Y	9. Guantanamo prisoners	N
2. Tax Cuts	Y	6. Body cameras/immigration	N	10. Ground missiles, limit	N
3. Omnibus appropriations	Y	7. Abortion ban	Y	11. Defense Dept. spending	Y
4. Dodd-Frank revision	Y	8. Concealed carry	Y	12. FISA rules	Y

Election Results

Election	Name (Party)	Vote (%)	Cand. Spent	Ind. Exp. Support	Ind. Exp. Oppose
2018 General	Bill Huizenga (R)............................ 168,970	(55%)	$1,470,207,581	$899	$861
	Rob Davidson (D)........................... 131,254	(43%)	$1,194,054		
2018 Primary	Bill Huizenga (R).......................................	(100%)			

Prior winning percentages: 2016 (63%), 2014 (64%), 2012 (61%), 2010 (65%)

Republican Bill Huizenga, elected in 2010, has upheld the rock-solid conservatism of his western Michigan district. When Republicans controlled the House, he was a key player in the overhaul of federal regulation of banks and other financial service firms. Following the 2018 election, he failed in his bid to become the top Republican on the Financial Services Committee.

Huizenga grew up in Zeeland. His grandparents were farmers who started a gravel business by selling the leftover sand and stone that was lying around the farm. In high school, Huizenga was an inattentive student who ultimately transferred to vocational school. His instructors told him he had academic potential and advised him to go to college. Between his freshman and sophomore years, he made his first real estate investment: With money saved from working in his father's gravel pit, he became the junior stakeholder in a 19-unit housing development.

After college, he worked for a local real estate firm and took over as co-owner in the family business, Huizenga Gravel. As a business owner, he says, he gained a firm understanding of the regulatory, tax and compliance issues that small businesses face. His friend, Republican Rep. Pete Hoekstra, offered him a job in his district office. After serving as Hoekstra's director of public policy, Huizenga won a seat in the Michigan House, where he was chairman of the Commerce Committee.

When Hoekstra ran unsuccessfully for Michigan governor, the real contest for his heavily Republican district was the GOP primary. In the seven-way race, Huizenga touted his conservative credentials, including his support for replacing the income tax with a 23 percent sales tax and creating private Social Security accounts. Jay Riemersma, also of Zeeland, the former regional director for the Family Research Council, ran as an anti-abortion and fiscal conservative. He attacked Huizenga for voting for a state business tax in 2007. Huizenga eked out a victory with a better campaign organization, built largely on the many contacts that he made with local political and business leaders. He prevailed by just 663 votes out of about 106,000 cast. In the general election, he faced nominal Democratic opposition.

Huizenga won quick notice for his facility with the inner workings of Congress. He enacted a bill in 2012 giving taxpayers and businesses who submit information to the Consumer Financial Protection Bureau the same confidentiality protection that other financial regulators are required to provide. For two years, Huizenga chaired the Financial Services Subcommittee on Monetary Policy and Trade, where he used his oversight of the Federal Reserve Board to promote more transparent discussion of monetary policy. In 2015, the House passed his Mortgage Choice Act, which he said was designed to remove "technicalities" in qualification requirements for lower and middle-income homeowners. With other House conservatives, he raised questions about the organization of the Export-Import Bank and prevented it from conducting business for several months. With strong support for the bank in the business community, Huizenga and its other opponents ultimately lost their battle.

In 2017-18, Huizenga was chairman of the Capital Markets, Securities and Investment Subcommittee, where he intensified his campaign to cut back the Dodd-Frank financial regulation law and reduce its impact on businesses. He spearheaded several House-passed bills during those two years to loosen the Dodd-Frank regimen, though he voiced disappointment that the House mostly deferred to the more limited Senate-passed versions. In February 2017, he enacted his bill that repealed regulations by the Securities and Exchange Commission that required mining and oil and gas companies to disclose payments they make to foreign governments. That was the third bill that President Donald Trump signed into law.

Huizenga has not always agreed with Trump. He opposed splitting immigrant families at the border with Mexico and joined Democrats at a press conference to describe his objections, including the denial of his attempt to visit a detention center in western Michigan. In June 2018, he said that Trump's tariffs on steel and aluminum failed to achieve "the desired outcome" and that the imports did not pose the claimed risk to the United States. Early that year, he took issue with Trump's proposal for deep cuts in the Great Lakes Restoration Initiative and said that Congress ultimately would decide on that funding.

Huizenga, who had consistently won reelection with more than 60 percent of the vote, was held to a 55%-43% reelection in 2018 by Democratic challenger Rob Davidson, an emergency-room doctor who favored the Medicare for All proposal and objected to Huizenga's vote to repeal the Affordable Care Act. In a debate, Huizenga distanced himself from Trump's proposal for a wall at the border, which he called "not practical." He outspent Davidson, $2.2 million to $1.3 million. Davidson took 53 percent of the vote in Muskegon and the vote was virtually even in Kent, the second and third-largest counties. Huizenga took 62 percent and led by 32,000 votes in Ottawa, the largest county, which accounted for nearly his entire victory margin.

Following the election, Huizenga competed for the open Republican position atop the Financial Services Committee. He was defeated by Rep. Patrick McHenry of North Carolina, who had more seniority plus experience in GOP leadership. Huizenga retained the top GOP slot on the re-named Investor Protection, Entrepreneurship and Capital Markets Subcommittee. At age 49, at the start of 2019, he likely will have other opportunities to assert his influence.

MI-2: West-Central Michigan   **Cook Partisan Voting Index: R+9**

Population		Race and Ethnicity		Income	
Total	729,695	White	79.1%	Median Income	$52,919
Land area (sq. miles)	3,281	Black	6.1%	District Income Rank	257
Pop/ sq mi	222.4	Latino	9.4%	Poverty Rate	13.8%
Born in State	78.9%	Asian	2.3%	With health insurance	93.4%
		Two or more races	2.6%	Cash public assistance	3%
Age Groups		Other	0.5%	Food stamp/SNAP	13.6%
Under 18	24%				
18-34	23.9%	**Education**		**Work**	
35-64	37.4%	H.S grad or less	41.8%	White Collar	14.7%
Over 64	14.7%	Some college	32.8%	Sales and Service	39.4%
		College Degree, 4 yr	17.3%	Blue Collar	29.5%
Military		Post grad	8.1%	Government	8.8%
Veteran/ Active Duty	7.6%				

2012 Pres. Vote	Romney	184,732	(56%)	Obama	142,077	(43%)			
2016 Pres. Vote	Trump	193,201	(55%)	Clinton	132,467	(38%)	Johnson	15,127	(4%)

Holland, Muskegon: When the glaciers receded from Michigan some 16,000 years ago, they left behind piles of boulders, sand and clay. Over time, the lake winds eroded the boulders, while waves ground up glacial drift deposited in the lake and washed it ashore. The end result is a lakeshore that today is home to the largest collection of freshwater dunes in the world, located in several parks along the western rim of the state.

In the late 19th century, the river ports on this shoreline were choked with logs and full of lumbermen from Norway and Sweden, Ireland and Scotland, Quebec and New England. During the timber boom, the shoreline was the locus of the country's largest migration from the Netherlands and today still has the nation's largest concentration of Dutch-Americans. Although wooden shoes are now seen only at the Tulip Festival in the town of Holland, conscientious Dutch work habits have produced many highly skilled workers. This is a busy manufacturing area, with products ranging from baby food at Gerber in Fremont to office furniture at Herman Miller in Zeeland and Haworth in Holland. In 2018, like 2017, Wallet Hub cited Holland as the best small city in America to start a small business, based on factors such as local costs and services. Away from the shore is fruit-growing country, with some of the nation's largest cherry orchards to the north and blueberry patches to the south. Since 2014, blueberry production has slowed, due to high costs.

The 2nd Congressional District of Michigan occupies four counties on the Lake Michigan shoreline, plus a tier of inland counties. It stretches from the old lumber port of Ludington south to Holland. About a fifth of the district's residents live in an arc of suburbs surrounding Grand Rapids in Kent County. The economy in western Michigan has diversified and has had the strongest growth in the state. Holland-based Ottawa, the most populous county in the district, grew by 20 percent from 2000 to 2017. The more industrial Muskegon grew by only 2 percent during that period. In 2017, Muskegon showed hopes of a business renaissance, which local leaders described as a "post-industrial revival," led by young entrepreneurs who welcome the relatively cheap land and lower labor costs.

For years, Dutch-American voters have been strongly Republican and fast-growing. The chief exception to Republican voting patterns comes from the old industrial centers in Muskegon County. In 2008 and 2012, the 2nd was the most Republican district in the state. Trump's lead of 55%-38% in 2016 ranked only fourth highest.

Justin Amash (R)

Elected 2010, 5th term, b. Apr 18, 1980; Grand Rapids; Grand Rapids Christian H.S.; University of Michigan, B.A., 2002; University of Michigan Law School, J.D., 2005; Eastern Orthodox; Married (Kara Amash); 3 children.

Elected Office: MI House, 2008-2010.

Professional Career: Practicing attorney, 2006-2007; Consultant, MI Industrial Tools, 2005-2010.

DC Office: 106 CHOB 20515, 202-225-3831, Fax: 202-225-5144, amash.house.gov

State Offices: Battle Creek, 269-205-3823; Grand Rapids, 616-451-8383.

Committees: *Oversight & Reform*: National Security; Subcommittee on Civil Rights & Civil Liberties.

Group Ratings

	ADA	ACLU	AFL-CIO	LCV	ITI	COC	HAFA	ACU	CFG	FRC
2018	-	54%	-	37%	-	58%	74%	88%	100%	80%
2017	30%	C	21%	23%	C	93%	C	78%	98%	89%

Almanac Ratings 2017-18

	Economy	Social	Foreign	Composite
Liberal	20%	50%	78%	50%
Conservative	80%	50%	22%	50%

Key Votes of the 115th Congress

1. Obama-care revision	Y	5. Family planning regs	Y	9. Guantanamo prisoners	Y
2. Tax Cuts	Y	6. Body cameras/immigration	N	10. Ground missiles, limit	Y
3. Omnibus appropriations	N	7. Abortion ban	Y	11. Defense Dept. spending	N
4. Dodd-Frank revision	Y	8. Concealed carry	N	12. FISA rules	N

Election Results

Election	Name (Party)	Vote (%)		Cand. Spent	Ind. Exp. Support	Ind. Exp. Oppose
2018 General	Justin Amash (R)............................. 169,107	(54%)		$755,093		
	Cathy Albro (D)............................ 134,185	(43%)		$138,197		
2018 Primary	Justin Amash (R)..	(100%)				

Prior winning percentages: 2016 (60%), 2014 (58%), 2012 (53%), 2010 (60%)

Justin Amash, a Republican elected in 2010, has been one of the most iconoclastic members of the House. With his libertarian views, he has been a persistent thorn in the side of GOP leaders. More than any other House Republican, Amash has maintained his independence of party leaders, including President Donald Trump. He has paid a price in terms of his influence in the House.

Amash was born in Grand Rapids, the son of a wealthy Palestinian tool importer who immigrated to the United States with the sponsorship of a Christian church. He began high school at the time of the Republican tidal wave of 1994 and graduated as class valedictorian. He majored in economics and graduated magna cum laude at the University of Michigan, then earned a degree from its law school. He counts himself as an admirer of both the 19th-century author Frederic Bastiat, who argued against taxing people to pay for schools or roads, and the 20th-century writer Friedrich Hayek, a favorite of the tea party movement who strongly opposed government intervention in the economy. Amash kept Hayek's portrait on the wall of his congressional campaign offices.

He was a consultant to his family's tool-import business and served as a corporate lawyer for a year before he was elected to the Michigan House in 2008. He fought to eliminate state taxes on businesses. The Grand Rapids Press reported in 2010 that Amash was the only "no" vote on 59 bills in his first term.

Amash entered the 3rd District race, he said, because he was fed up with the moderate voting record of eight-term GOP incumbent Vern Ehlers. When Ehlers announced his retirement, that opened the door for other Republican candidates, including former Kent County Commissioner Steve Heacock, whom Ehlers personally asked to run. In the primary race, Amash outraised both Heacock and state Sen. Bill Hardiman, and he was endorsed by the anti-tax group Club for Growth. He won the primary with 40 percent to Heacock's 26 percent and Hardiman's 24 percent. In the general election, Democratic lawyer Pat Miles accused Amash of exporting jobs to China through his ownership of Dynamic Source International, a Chinese company that supplied industrial tools to his father's tool-import business. Amash accused Miles of supporting taxpayer-funded abortions because he backed the Democrats' health care overhaul. He won, 60%-37%.

Amash immediately displayed his independence by refusing to vote in favor of House legislation he believed was unconstitutional or that he was not given adequate time to consider, voting "present" on numerous bills. He explained to The New York Times how he votes: "I follow a set of principles, I follow the Constitution. And that's what I base my votes on. Limited government, economic freedom and individual liberty." He deployed his Facebook page to detail his reasons for all of his actions.

In 2012, Democrats thought they had a chance to defeat Amash by drawing alienated GOP moderates from him. They nominated Steve Pestka, a former state representative, prosecutor and judge. He criticized Amash for his contrarian votes and began climbing in the polls after loaning his campaign more than $1 million. Amash beat Pestka by a not overwhelming 53%-44%.

Returning to Washington for a lame-duck session, Amash learned that the Speaker John Boehner-controlled Republican Steering Committee had taken him off the Budget Committee, making him one of four Republicans to receive such punishment. He called it "a slap in the face" to the GOP's expanding libertarian faction. He was a central figure in an unsuccessful attempt to persuade fellow Republicans to vote against Boehner for Speaker in January 2013.

Establishment Republicans challenged Amash in the 2014 primary. Their candidate was Brian Ellis, who served on the East Grand Rapids school board and drew support from local and national Chamber of Commerce-types. Ellis criticized what he called Amash's "bizarre" voting record. Amash's allies in the Club for Growth ran ads bashing Ellis for "leaving massive deficits" on the school board. Amash and his allies cried foul at an attack ad calling the congressman "al-Qaida's best friend in Congress." Citing his Palestinian-American heritage, Amash called the ad "disgusting." He prevailed in the August primary, 57%-43%.

Amash defended former National Security Agency contractor Edward Snowden after Snowden leaked details of the agency's domestic surveillance efforts. He managed to unite the Republican leadership and the Obama White House against himself when he proposed an amendment to strip funding for an NSA phone-surveillance program; it fell short by just 12 votes. In 2015, when the House overwhelmingly voted to end the meta-data phone collection program, he voted against the bill because, he said, "it actually expands the statutory basis for the large-scale collection of most data." In 2016, he helped to defeat a House bill to strengthen the terrorism-fighting Patriot Act by encouraging banks to alert federal authorities about possible illicit financing. Amash helped to form the Freedom Caucus, a group of libertarian-minded conservatives who have sought to reduce the power of Republican leaders. Following the 2016 election, he was a leader in creating the Second Amendment Caucus on behalf of pro-gun legislation.

In the 2016 presidential campaign, Amash supported Rand Paul and then Ted Cruz for the Republican nomination; he said that he would not support Donald Trump. After the election, Amash voiced concern about Trump's expansion of presidential powers and federal spending. "He may even go beyond what President Obama did in terms of violating our rights." He criticized what he viewed as the excesses in Trump's executive orders to limit immigrants and refugees.

Amash emerged as "the only consistent representative of a wing of libertarianism that remains alienated by Trump — advocates of a government shrunk down to a pre-New Deal size and advocates of freer trade and immigration policies," David Weigel wrote in The Washington Post in July 2018. After Trump in May 2017 fired James Comey as FBI director, Amash said the action could be grounds for impeachment and that he trusted Comey more than Trump. He called Trump's tariffs "among the most egregious of taxes." When Trump nominated Brett Kavanaugh to the Supreme Court, Amash took only a few days to voice his opposition (although he didn't have a vote), citing his objections to the judge's views on the Fourth Amendment bar on "unreasonable searches and seizures."

In January 2019, Amash was one of six House Republicans to support somebody other than Kevin McCarthy as the GOP candidate for Speaker. He voted for Rep. Thomas Massie of Kentucky; the other five voted for Rep. Jim Jordan of Ohio. He seemed comfortable and consistent in independence. One unusual consequence for a five-term House member: Amash's only committee assignment was on Oversight and Reform. Even with his senior status on that low-level panel, he was not given the perk of a ranking position on a subcommittee.

In May 2019, Amash said that the report by special counsel Robert Mueller on Russian interference in the 2016 presidential election "reveals that President Trump engaged in specific actions and a pattern of behavior that meet the threshold for impeachment." Amash, who revealed his conclusion in a tweetstorm of 13 messages, added that the report listed "multiple examples of conduct satisfying all the elements of obstruction of justice" and that, "undoubtedly any person who is not the president of the United States would be indicted based on such evidence." Initially, Amash deliberately avoided a national platform for his views. Not surprisingly, many Democrats welcomed his comments and he was widely attacked by Republicans. At home, Republican state Rep. Jim Lower responded by announcing that he would challenge Amash in the 2020 GOP primary and describing himself as "pro-Trump." With support from the president, Lower took an early lead over Amash in a poll of local Republicans.

MI-3: West-Central Michigan   **Cook Partisan Voting Index: R+6**

Population		Race and Ethnicity		Income	
Total	731,521	White	79.6%	Median Income	$56,063
Land area (sq. miles)	2,629	Black	8.4%	District Income Rank	214
Pop/ sq mi	278.3	Latino	7.2%	Poverty Rate	13.8%
Born in State	78.4%	Asian	1.9%	With health insurance	93.2%
		Two or more races	2.5%	Cash public assistance	3.1%
Age Groups		Other	0.4%	Food stamp/SNAP	13.3%
Under 18	24.4%				
18-34	23%	**Education**		**Work**	
35-64	38.7%	H.S grad or less	37.6%	White Collar	13.9%
Over 64	13.9%	Some college	31.7%	Sales and Service	39.6%
		College Degree, 4 yr	20%	Blue Collar	25.3%
Military		Post grad	10.7%	Government	9.1%
Veteran/ Active Duty	7.5%				

2012 Pres. Vote	Romney	177,772	(53%)	Obama	153,052	(46%)		
2016 Pres. Vote	Trump	180,341	(51%)	Clinton	147,335	(42%)	Johnson 15,803	(5%)

Grand Rapids Metro: Grand Rapids is Michigan's second-largest city and the center of its most prosperous metropolitan area. It grew as a center for turning the hardwood forests of northern Michigan into furniture. By the early 20th century, Grand Rapids was the leading furniture manufacturer in the nation. The Great Depression knocked the bottom out of the residential furniture market, and many manufacturers moved to North Carolina, where labor was cheaper. So Grand Rapids reinvented itself. It went into office furniture, and today three of the nation's largest office furniture manufacturers — Steelcase, Haworth and Herman Miller — are in its metropolitan area. Of the area jobs, 20 percent were in manufacturing — the largest share for any major Midwest metro, City Journal wrote in its spring 2018 magazine.

It also capitalized on a knack for sales. Rich DeVos and Jay Van Andel started Amway, the direct sales empire, which has had about 90 percent of its sales abroad. With nearly $10 billion in revenues in 2016, Amway was the largest direct-selling company in the world; China has been its largest market. DeVos's son Dick later ran the business and was the unsuccessful Republican nominee for governor of Michigan in 2006. Dick's wife, Betsy DeVos, became active in state and national Republican politics and the charter-school movement before she became Education secretary for President Donald Trump. The family members have been major charitable donors and Republican contributors for decades. Rich DeVos died in September 2018. The Grand Rapids area has been a center for machine tools, Hush Puppies shoes, and Bissell carpet sweepers. Today, while Detroit struggles to stay afloat, more diversified Grand Rapids chugs along. The metropolitan area was the nation's fastest-growing job market 2016, according to an economic-data firm.

Politically, the Grand Rapids area has been the center of Michigan Republicanism for much of the last century; cultural conservatism and a belief in market economics run deep among the descendants of the pious Dutch immigrants who settled in western Michigan in the 1870s. It has also produced national Republican leaders. The conversion of Sen. Arthur Vandenberg from isolationism to internationalism during World War II provided key support for the foreign policies of Franklin D. Roosevelt and Harry Truman; he chaired the Senate Foreign Relations Committee in 1947-48. Another was Gerald Ford, who rose to House Republican leader in 1965, vice president in 1973, and then president after Richard Nixon resigned in 1974.

The 3rd Congressional District of Michigan has three distinct parts. The first is the city of Grand Rapids itself, which constitutes about 25 percent of the population and has become heavily Democratic. The second includes most of the remainder of Kent, Ionia and Barry counties, and a small portion of Montcalm County. This part of the district, which includes a majority of its residents, is heavily Republican. The third part of the district is Calhoun County, which tends to vote close to the national average and is centered on Battle Creek, where sanitarium operator W.K. Kellogg invented corn flakes as a health food and where the local economy is weaker than in Grand Rapids and the school system suffers from structural inequities, according to studies. The net result is a district that leans Republican; Donald Trump won 51%-42% in 2016. He had his final rally of the campaign in Grand Rapids, after midnight on Election Day.

John Moolenaar (R)

Elected 2014, 3rd term, b. May 08, 1961; Midland; Hope College (MI), B.S., 1983; Harvard University, M.P.A., 1989; Christian - Non-Denominational; Married (Amy Moolenaar); 6 children.

Elected Office: Midland MI City Council, 1997-2000; MI House, 2003-2008; MI Senate, 2011-2014.

Professional Career: Chemist, Dow Chemical; Director, Middle MI Development Corporation Small Business Cntr.; School admin., Midland Academy of Advanced & Creative Studies.

DC Office: 117 CHOB 20515, 202-225-3561, Fax: 202-225-9679, moolenaar.house.gov

State Offices: Cadillac, 231-942-5070; Midland, 989-631-2552.

Committees: *Appropriations*: Agriculture, Rural Development, FDA & Related Agencies; Labor, Health & Human Services, Education & Related Agencies.

Group Ratings

	ADA	ACLU	AFL-CIO	LCV	ITI	COC	HAFA	ACU	CFG	FRC
2018	-	4%	-	6%	-	92%	58%	68%	50%	100%
2017	0%	C	18%	6%	C	93%	C	74%	61%	100%

Almanac Ratings 2017-18

	Economy	Social	Foreign	Composite
Liberal	3%	4%	0%	2%
Conservative	97%	97%	100%	98%

Key Votes of the 115th Congress

1. Obama-care revision	Y	5. Family planning regs	Y	9. Guantanamo prisoners	N
2. Tax Cuts	Y	6. Body cameras/immigration	N	10. Ground missiles, limit	N
3. Omnibus appropriations	Y	7. Abortion ban	Y	11. Defense Dept. spending	Y
4. Dodd-Frank revision	Y	8. Concealed carry	Y	12. FISA rules	Y

Election Results

Election	Name (Party)	Vote (%)		Cand. Spent	Ind. Exp. Support	Ind. Exp. Oppose
2018 General	John Moolenaar (R)	178,510	(63%)	$1,001,260	$351	
	Jerry Hilliard (D)	106,540	(37%)			
2018 Primary	John Moolenaar (R)		(100%)			

Prior winning percentages: 2016 (62%), 2014 (57%)

Republican John Moolenaar was elected in 2014, with a boost from his conservative credentials and endorsements. With his seat on the Appropriations Committee, he has focused on funding for Michigan.

Born in Midland, Moolenaar earned his bachelor's in chemistry from Hope College in Holland Michigan. He got his master's in public administration from Harvard. He was a chemist and director of business development for MITECH+ and Dow Chemical, where he helped develop new product markets. He was an administrator at the Midland Academy of Advanced and Creative Studies. In 2002, Moolenaar was elected to the state House. Later in the Senate, he chaired the Veterans, Military Affairs and Homeland Security Committee, and was vice chair of the Appropriations Committee. A Democratic foe sought to recall Moolenaar in 2011 because he voted for a bill allowing taxation of public employee pensions, but the petition did not attract enough signatures.

The retirement of Rep. Dave Camp, who chaired the House Ways and Means Committee, led to a battle among three GOP primary contenders: Moolenaar, businessman Paul Mitchell, and software consultant Peter Konetchy. Mitchell vastly outspent his opponents, dumping $3.6 million of his own money — several times what Moolenaar and Konetchy had raised, combined — into his campaign to finance an aggressive TV ad blitz. He attacked Moolenaar as insufficiently conservative, accusing the state lawmaker in an ad of enabling the Affordable Care Act by voting to expand Medicaid. Moolenaar, who signed a pledge to repeal the health care law, had voted for an overall state health agency budget that included federal dollars for Medicaid expansion.

Moolenaar turned Mitchell's campaign cash advantage against him, saying in a GOP primary debate that "quite frankly, I don't think this seat is up for sale." He had key Republican endorsements, including from Camp. Moolenaar questioned Mitchell's conservative credentials, including his contribution to the 2006 campaign of Democratic Sen. Debbie Stabenow. Moolenaar won the nomination with 52 percent of the vote, to 36 percent for Mitchell and 11 percent for Konetchy. He scored especially well in his base of Midland, where he got 67 percent. In the general, Moolenaar's more conservative views played far better in the GOP-friendly district. He defeated Democrat John Holmes, 57%-39%, and led in 14 of the 15 counties. In 2016, Mitchell was elected in an open-seat contest in the nearby 10th District in Michigan's "thumb.")

During his first term, Moolenaar won House passage of his bill to designate the National Institute of Standards and Technology in the Commerce Department to serve as the president's principal adviser on standards for technological competitiveness and innovation ability. The effect of the legislation, he said, was to "provide small manufacturers like those here in Michigan with the expertise and advice they need when investing in new technologies." He worked with Democratic Rep. Dan Kildee in 2016 to provide $170 million to fix the badly contaminated drinking water system in Flint

As a new member of Appropriations in 2017, Moolenaar worked to deliver for his home state — even if that meant challenging the Trump administration. When President Donald Trump proposed in his first budget to slash funds for clean-up of the Great Lakes, Moolenar pushed for a cut-free $300 million during committee debate. He emphasized the importance of environmental assistance, especially for local tourism. He worked with others in the Michigan delegation for replacement of the Soo Locks at Sault Ste. Marie and to deliver $97 million to Michigan State University for its Facility for Rare Isotope Beams, which assembled the most powerful radioactive beam facility in the world.

He has been reelected easily, without opposition in the GOP primary.

MI-4: Central Michigan   **Cook Partisan Voting Index: R+10**

Population		Race and Ethnicity		Income	
Total	700,749	White	91.6%	Median Income	$47,910
Land area (sq. miles)	8,458	Black	1.8%	District Income Rank	343
Pop/ sq mi	82.8	Latino	3.1%	Poverty Rate	16.3%
Born in State	85.7%	Asian	1%	With health insurance	92.4%
		Two or more races	1.8%	Cash public assistance	2.6%
Age Groups		Other	0.7%	Food stamp/SNAP	14.1%
Under 18	20.9%				
18-34	22.4%	**Education**		**Work**	
35-64	38.9%	H.S grad or less	44.6%	White Collar	17.8%
Over 64	17.8%	Some college	34%	Sales and Service	41.3%
		College Degree, 4 yr	13.5%	Blue Collar	27.2%
Military		Post grad	7.9%	Government	12.4%
Veteran/ Active Duty	8.6%				

2012 Pres. Vote	Romney	171,862	(53%)	Obama	146,088	(45%)			
2016 Pres. Vote	Trump	195,303	(59%)	Clinton	113,817	(35%)	Johnson	14,062	(4%)

Midland: Flat and treeless for miles, the central reaches of Michigan's Lower Peninsula are farm country, exposed to bitter winds and snowdrifts in winter and shining sun for precious weeks in summer. Like the steppes of Eastern Europe, these are farmlands that produce hearty crops: potatoes, navy beans, sugar beets. The cities here are often small factory towns, with neat, tree-lined streets that end at bare fields. Midland in 1891 was a declining lumber town when Herbert Dow perfected an electrolytic process to extract chemicals from northern Michigan's extensive brine wells. That was the start of Dow Chemical, still headquartered in this now upscale town and today a large producer of pesticides and agricultural biotech products. In 2015, Dow merged with another chemical giant; the resulting DowDuPont company retained a major local presence. Also that year, Dow completed its acquisition of Corning, a silicon-based materials company. With a cutback of about 700 jobs in the latter transaction, the company retained more than 5,000 jobs in the Midland area. Worries about local employment have continued. "Employees are concerned" about the prospects of creating three separate unnamed companies from the new business, the president of the United Steelworkers local told The Detroit News reported in September 2017. Some worried whether the Midland area had enough skilled workers. Poverty has increased and population has decreased in many rural parts of Michigan. Local officials launched an effort to bring more young workers and entrepreneurs to Midland.

Owosso was the birthplace of Thomas E. Dewey, later New York governor and Republican nominee for president in 1944 and 1948. It was also the home of novelist James Oliver Curwood and the location of his Curwood Castle writing studio. Mount Pleasant, to the north, is the home of Central Michigan University, the third largest public university in the state.

The 4th Congressional District of Michigan, geographically the state's second-largest, includes much of this territory north of Lansing and Grand Rapids and west of Flint and Saginaw. Two-thirds of its populace lives in rural areas. It stretches north up the highways, barely venturing outside U.S. 131 to the west and Interstate 75 to the east. The rolling country around Houghton Lake was once lumber country and is now a retirement and resort area, with condominiums and knotty-pine cottages clustered around icy green lakes. This is historically Republican territory, having sent only one Democrat to Congress since it was created in 1912. Donald Trump in 2016 won, 59%-34%. When Trump spoke in Grand Rapids in December 2016, Dow announced that it was adding 200 research and development jobs at an innovation center in Midland.

Dan Kildee (D)

Elected 2012, 4th term, b. Aug 11, 1958; Flint; Central Michigan University, B.S.; University of Michigan, Flint, Att., 1982; Roman Catholic; Married (Jennifer Kildee); 3 children; 2 grandchildren.

Elected Office: Flint MI Board of Education, 1977-1985; Genesee County Board of Commissioners, 1985-1997; Genesee County Treasurer, 1997-2009.

Professional Career: Youth specialist, Whaley Children's Center, 1976-1985; Founder, Genesee County Land Bank; Co-founder & CEO, Center For Comm. Progress, 2009-2012.

DC Office: 203 CHOB 20515, 202-225-3611, Fax: 202-225-6393, dankildee.house.gov

State Offices: Flint, 810-238-8627.

Committees: *Budget. Ways & Means*; Social Security; Trade.

Group Ratings

	ADA	ACLU	AFL-CIO	LCV	ITI	COC	HAFA	ACU	CFG	FRC
2018	-	86%	-	94%	-	67%	8%	4%	12%	0%
2017	100%	C	95%	94%	C	25%	C	7%	5%	0%

Almanac Ratings 2017-18

	Economy	Social	Foreign	Composite
Liberal	98%	98%	100%	99%
Conservative	2%	2%	0%	1%

Key Votes of the 115th Congress

1. Obama-care revision	N	5. Family planning regs	N	9. Guantanamo prisoners	Y
2. Tax Cuts	N	6. Body cameras/immigration	Y	10. Ground missiles, limit	Y
3. Omnibus appropriations	Y	7. Abortion ban	N	11. Defense Dept. spending	N
4. Dodd-Frank revision	N	8. Concealed carry	N	12. FISA rules	N

Election Results

Election	Name (Party)	Vote (%)	Cand. Spent	Ind. Exp. Support	Ind. Exp. Oppose
2018 General	Dan Kildee (D)	164,502 (60%)	$672,377		
	Travis Wines (R)	99,265 (36%)			
2018 Primary	Dan Kildee (D)	(100%)			

Prior winning percentages: 2016 (61%), 2014 (57%), 2012 (55%)

Democrat Dan Kildee, elected in 2012, initially was a quiet and usually reliable party loyalist, who focused chiefly on local issues. He took the lead in securing a congressional response to the contaminated water crisis in his district. With his new seat on the House Ways and Means Committee, he gained a broader audience for his working-class style.

Kildee grew up in a close-knit neighborhood in Flint. There were six children in his family, and so many in the neighborhood that they formed their own football team, the Genesee Jets. He carried that athleticism into high school and became captain of the hockey team. But his real interest was in hanging out at Democratic headquarters. He worked on his uncle Dale's campaigns for the state legislature and for Congress, distributing yard signs and doing other tasks.

After high school, Kildee enrolled at the University of Michigan's Flint campus and worked part-time at a treatment facility for emotionally disturbed children. That job became full-time and Kildee dropped out of college, although decades later, he earned a bachelor's degree in administration at Central Michigan University. At age 19, Kildee was elected to the Flint Board of Education. "I'd go to visit the schools and I'd quite literally get asked for a hall pass," he said. Kildee was a commissioner in Genesee County for 12 years before becoming county treasurer for another 12 years, during which time he founded a local land bank. His method for tackling abandoned properties — getting rid of them — brought him national attention. Though he took "a commonsense approach to urban planning in an age of decline," others viewed it as "a radically un-American idea that embraces defeat and limited horizons," according to a 2010 profile of Kildee in Slate. On a much larger scale, officials in Detroit have recently used a version of Kildee's land bank to assist with their huge surplus of properties.

When Dale Kildee announced his retirement after 36 years in the House, his nephew was instantly a strong contender, given his family name and his years of public service. Kildee won the primary unopposed. He had little trouble dispatching Republican former state Rep. Jim Slezak in the general, 65%-31%.

On the Financial Services Committee, Kildee focused on cleaning up blight in Flint. He eventually got $100 million in federal funds for local demolition. With a bipartisan group of House members, he filed a resolution seeking to prevent any threat to the Great Lakes from a proposed Canadian nuclear waste site. When it became clear that the Flint water crisis would require a congressional response, the Senate took the lead and overwhelmingly approved emergency assistance. In the House, Republican leaders deferred action to await broader legislation on water projects, partly due to fear that many conservatives would object to the Flint aid. Kildee complained about the delay but he didn't burn bridges. Teaming with Republican Rep. John Moolenaar of the neighboring district, they put together with Speaker Paul Ryan and other House leaders a bipartisan back-room deal for $170 million.

That success opened other doors for Kildee, who has been a vice chair of the LGBT Equality Caucus. He made known his interest in running in 2018 for the open seat for governor, though he was reluctant to join a Democratic primary contest. In May 2017, he said that he would run for reelection and focus on the challenges posed by Republicans. Following the election, he got a seat on the tax-writing Ways and Means Committee, where his chief priorities were fair international trade deals and strengthening Social Security. After having earlier voiced interest in competing for an elected leadership position, he was tapped as a chief deputy whip for the Democratic leadership.

Kildee has been reelected easily. But he has voiced ongoing worries about the perception of Democrats in middle America. With Democratic Reps. Tim Ryan of Ohio and John Yarmuth of Kentucky, he helped to form in 2017 the People's House Project, a progressive group that operated separately from the party's coastal elites. "This has to be a movement with a lot of hands rolling in the same direction," he told Vox, adding that the group would go "straight into the heartland with an economic message."

During the 2017-18 campaign cycle, he co-chaired a task force of the Democratic Congressional Campaign Committee designed to encourage participation of other members in campaign activities. Even with Democrats' success in the election, Kildee's district seemed less than secure in the long term, especially with its population downsizing and the continuing exodus of blue-collar white voters to the Republican Party.

MI-5: East-Central Michigan   **Cook Partisan Voting Index: D+5**

Population		Race and Ethnicity		Income	
Total	682,884	White	74%	Median Income	$43,583
Land area (sq. miles)	2,349	Black	17%	District Income Rank	391
Pop/ sq mi	290.8	Latino	4.9%	Poverty Rate	19.9%
Born in State	84.1%	Asian	0.9%	With health insurance	93.1%
		Two or more races	2.7%	Cash public assistance	4.1%
Age Groups		Other	0.5%	Food stamp/SNAP	21%
Under 18	22.4%				
18-34	20.7%	**Education**		**Work**	
35-64	39.6%	H.S grad or less	44.2%	White Collar	17.3%
Over 64	17.3%	Some college	36.4%	Sales and Service	45%
		College Degree, 4 yr	12.3%	Blue Collar	25.3%
Military		Post grad	7%	Government	10.3%
Veteran/ Active Duty	8.4%				

2012 Pres. Vote	Obama	205,804	(61%)	Romney	129,896	(38%)			
2016 Pres. Vote	Clinton	162,982	(49%)	Trump	148,953	(45%)	Johnson	10,880	(3%)

Flint, Bay City: The flat plains south of Saginaw Bay, the inlet of Lake Huron that separates Michigan's Thumb (people really call it that) from the mitten of the Lower Peninsula, was once one of America's top industrial areas. Some 130 years ago, it was the nation's premier lumber country, with huge stands of virgin trees feeding 36 sawmills in Bay City. When the trees were gone, farmers took over, and the land was sown with beans and sugar beets. Then, a century ago, came the automobile. Flint, a small town on a minor branch of the Saginaw River, was the home base of W.C. Durant, the investor who merged several young auto firms to form General Motors in 1908. GM put its Chevrolet and Buick factories in Flint and its power steering facility in Saginaw, chosen because it was already a center of precision machinery manufacturing.

From 1910 through the 1950s, Flint grew lustily as it built Chevys and Buicks. Miners from the east Kentucky coal fields, mountain folk from eastern Tennessee and farmers from the Black Belt of Alabama found their way to Flint. Before long, southern accents were common in an area settled by New England Yankees. Labor strife followed industrialization. In January 1937, Flint was the scene of the great sit-down strike that began when workers noticed GM preparing to move the dies that were used to stamp cars out of its plant — a potential prelude to a move to the South — and ended with GM recognizing the United Auto Workers as the bargaining agent for its workers.

Economic disaster struck with the energy crisis of the 1970s. Imports, especially from Japan, that were higher quality and lower price than American cars, took an increasing share of the market. In 1979, GM employed more than 70,000 workers in its Flint plants, a huge share of the labor force in a metropolitan area of 430,000 people. Eventually, GM closed 13 of its 15 factories, and by the late 2000s, the GM payroll had fallen below 12,000. By 2010, more than 40 percent of Flint households were in poverty, and many skilled workers had fled what Forbes magazine called one of "America's fastest-dying cities." Michael Moore, the left-wing filmmaker, has used his hometown of Flint as the locale for much of his work about rust-belt hardships.

There have been some flickering signs of hope: Since General Motors emerged from bankruptcy in 2010, it has kept open a Flint engine plant and added a third shift at its truck assembly facility, which is the oldest GM factory in the nation. In 2018, GM turned its old Chevrolet plant, where Chevrolet Avenue crosses the Flint River, into an automotive research facility with the local Kettering University. The company expected to open in 2019 a new body shop to improve the efficiency between its local assembly plant and its metal center. Still, business conditions in the Flint area remained dismal. The departure of wealth and capital resulted in deep-seated poverty and economic decline that made Flint the third-worst city in the nation (behind Detroit and Birmingham Alabama) to live in, a Wall Street data service concluded in 2017. The economic dynamism of Michigan moved west to Grand Rapids.

In 2015, a new crisis hit Flint: the belated discovery of lead contamination in its drinking water system. In a city that was 57 percent African-American and with a median household income one-half the average for the total state, the local government had turned to the Flint River as its water source while it was building a new pipeline to Lake Huron. Despite a state-ordered cleanup of the river's watershed, a lawsuit revealed that the Environmental Quality Department had failed to treat the river with an anti-corrosive agent, which resulted in severe health risks. According to the inspector general at the Environmental Protection Agency, that federal agency also was slow to respond. In his 2016 state of the state address, Snyder accepted part of the blame. "I'm sorry, and I will fix it," he said. "Government failed you at the federal, state and local level. We need to make sure this never happens again in any Michigan city." By 2018, a degree of normalcy had returned. Lead levels in the water had declined and the distribution of free water bottles ended. Criminal charges of manslaughter were brought against five state officials and a federal judge ordered the state to pay $87 million to localities to replace water lines.

The 5th Congressional District includes Flint and surrounding Genesee County — which are about 60 percent of the district — Saginaw and eastern Saginaw County, Bay City and most of Bay County, rural Arenac and Iosco counties along Lake Huron, and a strip of rural Tuscola County. Flint, evenly divided between the parties during the sit-down strikes, is now heavily Democratic, Saginaw and Bay City somewhat less so. This is the only Democratic district in the state that is not located at least partly in Wayne or Oakland counties. Hillary Clinton fared poorly in this low-income, 74 percent white district. Her lead of 49%-45% in 2016 was a big drop from 2012, when President Barack Obama won 62%-38%. That was one of many factors in her narrow loss of Michigan.

Fred Upton (R)

Elected 1986, 17th term, b. Apr 23, 1953; St. Joseph; Shatluck School (MN), 1971; University of Michigan, B.A., 1975; Congregationalist; Married (Amey Rulon-Miller Upton); 2 children.

Professional Career: Project Coordinator, U.S. Rep. David Stockman, 1975-1980; Legislative affairs, O.M.B., 1981-1983, Director, 1984-1985.

DC Office: 2183 RHOB 20515, 202-225-3761, Fax: 202-225-4986, upton.house.gov

State Offices: Kalamazoo, 269-385-0039; St. Joseph, 269-982-1986.

Committees: *Energy & Commerce*: Consumer Protection & Commerce; Energy (RMM); Health.

Group Ratings

	ADA	ACLU	AFL-CIO	LCV	ITI	COC	HAFA	ACU	CFG	FRC
2018	-	7%	-	40%	-	100%	38%	60%	45%	100%
2017	0%	C	30%	14%	C	92%	C	70%	54%	100%

Almanac Ratings 2017-18

	Economy	Social	Foreign	Composite
Liberal	8%	4%	10%	7%
Conservative	92%	97%	90%	93%

Key Votes of the 115th Congress

1. Obama-care revision	Y	5. Family planning regs	Y	9. Guantanamo prisoners	N
2. Tax Cuts	Y	6. Body cameras/immigration	N	10. Ground missiles, limit	N
3. Omnibus appropriations	Y	7. Abortion ban	Y	11. Defense Dept. spending	Y
4. Dodd-Frank revision	Y	8. Concealed carry	Y	12. FISA rules	Y

Election Results

Election	Name (Party)	Vote (%)	Cand. Spent	Ind. Exp. Support	Ind. Exp. Oppose
2018 General	Fred Upton (R)............................... 147,436	(50%)	$3,547,351	$878,729	$1,890,651
	Matt Longjohn (D)......................... 134,082	(46%)	$1,440,088	$254,245	$492,882
2018 Primary	Fred Upton (R)..	(100%)			

Prior winning percentages: 2016 (59%), 2014 (56%), 2012 (55%), 2010 (62%), 2008 (59%), 2006 (61%), 2004 (65%), 2002 (69%), 2000 (67.9%), 1998 (70%), 1996 (68%), 1994 (74%), 1992 (62%), 1990 (58%), 1988 (71%), 1986 (62%)

Fred Upton, an affable Republican first elected in 1986, chaired the House Energy and Commerce Committee for six years. Term-limited at that post in 2016, he took over as chairman of the Energy Subcommittee. He also sought to create a nonpartisan niche, which former Vice President Joe Biden embraced — to the dismay of some Democrats. Upton's voting record has been unusually moderate for a senior House Republican, though he has regularly aligned with business.

The grandson of one of the founders of Whirlpool, Upton grew up in St. Joseph. He attended the University of Michigan and worked for David Stockman -- then a brash conservative icon -- first on Stockman's congressional staff, then at the White House in the Office of Management and Budget from 1981 to 1985. Upton returned home and ran in the 1986 Republican primary against Rep. Mark Siljander, a conservative and evangelical Christian, and won 55%-45%, going on to win the seat handily in the general election.

Upton's family fortune puts him in the upper echelon among members of Congress in wealth, but he has a regular-guy image. He is well known for insisting that everyone, from reporters to staffers to fellow lawmakers, call him "Fred," and says he personally reads and signs all of his legislative mail. He is a devoted Chicago Cubs fan, rarely missing an Opening Day at Wrigley Field, and has a bat from ex-Cubs slugger Sammy Sosa in his office.

Early in his House career, Upton was a leader of the moderate Republicans' Tuesday Group, where he was outspoken about the need to find middle ground. He freely exercised his independence when his party controlled the House from 1995 to 2006, and he occasionally caused heartburn for GOP leaders. He sought, with limited success, to reduce the tax cuts of the Bush era. He backed increases in the minimum wage, and increased funding for Amtrak and Democratic measures to expand government medical insurance for poor children.

In his committee work, Upton has been more of a party regular. When he chaired the Telecommunications Subcommittee, he supported a bill to allow regional telephone companies to provide broadband service more easily, and he pushed for larger fines against broadcasters for indecent programming. President George W. Bush signed his bill to create a "safe playground for kids" on the internet, free of pornography and other inappropriate material.

Taking the helm of Energy and Commerce in 2011, he confidently predicted that "a significant number of Democrats" would join his party's efforts to overturn President Barack Obama's 2010 health care law, which he dismissed as "a massive new government program that does real and lasting damage to our current system and all those covered under it." It turned out, though, that the repeated repeal votes never drew more than a handful of Democrats in support.

Many of Upton's other initiatives as chairman got through the House on largely party-line votes and were left for dead in the Democratic-controlled Senate. They included legislation to overturn the Environmental Protection Agency's authority to regulate greenhouse gas emissions blamed for global warming. Another bill overturned the Federal Communications Commission's net neutrality rules designed to prevent internet providers from creating tiered pricing structures. He and other

Republicans, with support from the cable television industry, said net neutrality rules were enacted without the proper authority. On the investigative front, his panel dug into the Obama administration's loan guarantees to the failed solar company Solyndra Corp.

Upton's efforts delighted fellow Republicans. But the Sierra Club and other environmental groups began running ads against him at home. And some Michiganders wondered what had happened to the politician who had championed a bill to ban incandescent light bulbs as part of the 2007 energy bill, and then voted four years later to undo the measure.

With Republicans in control of the Senate in 2015, Upton expressed hope that some of his efforts to block federal environmental regulations could at least clear Congress, if not get signed into law. But the Senate failed to act on most of those initiatives. Instead, he had an unexpectedly productive two years in enacting major bipartisan legislation. He worked with Democratic Rep. Diana DeGette of Colorado to accelerate innovative medical treatments and devices. Their 21st Century Cures Act easily passed the House. It picked up additional health-policy initiatives in the Senate — including funds to fight opioid addiction and to research cures for cancer — and was enacted after the 2016 election. Upton worked with Rep. Frank Pallone of New Jersey, the senior Democrat on Energy and Commerce, to overhaul the outdated chemical safety law. That measure, too, had overwhelming bipartisan support.

Upton has been an election target from both the left and right. In 2010, former state Rep. Jack Hoogendyk ran against him in the GOP primary, criticizing Upton for voting for the bailout of the financial industry. Upton vastly outspent Hoogendyk and won 57%-43%, not a robust outcome for a longtime incumbent. Hoogendyk came back for another challenge in 2012. Upton took him more seriously this time, conducting outreach to tea party groups and winning with ease, 67%-33%. His Democratic opponent that year was Mike O'Brien, a former Marine and office furniture company manager making his first run for elective office, who blasted Upton's support for the Republican spending plan. The $294,000 that O'Brien raised was no match for Upton's $4.7 million. Upton won, 55%-43%.

In 2014, Upton drew a better-funded Democratic challenger — Paul Clements, a Western Michigan University political scientist who was dismayed by Upton's reversal on climate change. Clements received help from Harvard law professor Lawrence Lessig's Mayday political action committee, which spent more than $2 million to portray Upton as a captive of oil and drug companies. Upton denied the allegations and responded that he continued to work on a bipartisan basis to steer clear of the Washington dysfunction. Upton spent $3.9 million to $800,000 for Clements and won, 56%-40%. Clements ran again in 2016, with help from Lessig's network, but his appeal faded. Upton won more comfortably, 59%-36%.

During the 2016 campaign, Upton remained neutral on Donald Trump and the presidential campaign. Upton said that Trump should consider "stepping away from the ticket" following the early October release of the 2005 video with Trump's lewd comments about women. "It's a new low. It's outrageous. ... I urge him to think about our country over his own candidacy." After Trump was elected and issued executive orders with travel bans for refugees and immigrants, Upton criticized the plan for creating "real confusion for travelers and those who enforce the laws. When House Republicans took up their bill to revise the Affordable Care Act, he objected that the proposal did not guarantee continued coverage of pre-existing conditions. In negotiations with House GOP leaders and later with Trump, he agreed to join the party ranks after they added funding designed to assure such coverage. That deal was essential in securing a bare majority for House passage of the bill.

After being term-limited at Energy and Commerce, Upton settled in at the Energy Subcommittee as chairman and, in 2019, as the ranking Republican. He promoted bipartisan "all of the above" strategies. As a member of the bipartisan Climate Solutions Caucus, he urged "an economically realistic and pragmatic approach" to addressing climate change. He said that Trump's decision to withdraw from the 2015 Paris climate agreement was "a mistake." Upton pressed other bipartisan initiatives, including a reform of House rules prepared by the Problem Solvers Caucus, which was designed to encourage more open debate. He opposed the farm bill in 2018 because of work requirements that other Republicans imposed on food-stamp recipients.

At home, Upton openly discussed a challenge in 2018 to Democratic Sen. Debbie Stabenow. In addition to the daunting prospects that he faced in a hostile partisan climate, he feared that he might not win the GOP nomination. Those challenges became apparent that year in his reelection, which he won by the narrowest margin of his career, 50%-46%. Democratic nominee Matthew Longjohn, the former national health officer for the YMCA, sought to hold Upton accountable for supporting House repeal of the Affordable Care Act. Republican research uncovered that Longjohn, who had a medical degree, was not licensed to practice medicine. Upton outspent Longjohn, $3.5 million to

$1.4 million, and won five of the six counties — though he lost Kalamazoo, 55%-42%, which might be a bad omen for Upton.

In an unexpected twist, Democrats following the election criticized Biden for praising Upton as "one of the finest guys I've ever worked with," as he cited his work on medical research during an October event sponsored by local business groups. Biden said that his speech — for which he received a $200,000 payment — had nothing to do with Upton's reelection bid. Local Democrats complained about the timing, including GOP ads that excerpted his praise. Biden subsequently dismissed the attack on his bipartisanship: "Forgive me, Father, for I have sinned," he said to a Washington audience.

MI-6: Southwest Michigan   Cook Partisan Voting Index: R+4

Population		Race and Ethnicity		Income	
Total	713,718	White	80.9%	Median Income	$51,189
Land area (sq. miles)	3,547	Black	8.1%	District Income Rank	283
Pop/ sq mi	201.2	Latino	6%	Poverty Rate	15.4%
Born in State	70.1%	Asian	1.5%	With health insurance	92.2%
Age Groups		Two or more races	3%	Cash public assistance	2.4%
Under 18	22.9%	Other	0.4%	Food stamp/SNAP	13.6%
18-34	22.9%	**Education**		**Work**	
35-64	38.3%	H.S grad or less	39.2%	White Collar	15.9%
Over 64	15.9%	Some college	33.4%	Sales and Service	39.2%
Military		College Degree, 4 yr	16.7%	Blue Collar	26.9%
Veteran/ Active Duty	7.9%	Post grad	10.6%	Government	9.7%

2012 Pres. Vote	Romney	163,306	(50%)	Obama	158,963	(49%)		
2016 Pres. Vote	Trump	170,320	(51%)	Clinton	142,293	(43%)	Johnson	14,034 (4%)

Kalamazoo: The southwest corner of Michigan was settled by New England Yankees and Upstate New Yorkers in the 1830s and 1840s. They built small towns with schools, churches and colleges; supported temperance; and opposed capital punishment. And in 1854, they joined the newly formed Republican Party. There are towns in southwest Michigan that still recall proudly their past as termini of the Underground Railroad, and there are black families whose ancestors made their way north out of slavery to freedom. Later, big industries transformed some of the small towns into significant cities. Kalamazoo, started by Dutch Americans who introduced celery to this country, became the home of Upjohn pharmaceuticals, which is now part of Pfizer. In July 2018, Pfizer announced plans for a sterile drug manufacturing facility in Portage, which will start production by 2024.

Predominantly black and struggling Benton Harbor and predominantly white and prosperous St. Joseph are small towns that sit across from each other where the St. Joseph River empties into Lake Michigan. In April 2015, a columnist for the local newspaper described the contrasts in their school systems as a "sad tale of educational apartheid." Benton Harbor had been known as the headquarters for Whirlpool. But Whirlpool closed its plant in 2010, and many other local companies and famous industrial names such as Gibson Guitars have moved out of the area, taking their thousands of jobs. Entergy Corp. in 2018 sold its nuclear power plant in Covert Township to the owner of another nuclear plant; the facility remained on schedule for shutdown in 2022. Covert has become the site of additional controversy, with many Hispanic migrants who arrive for seasonal work on blueberry farms.

Kalamazoo, plus Grand Rapids and Muskegon, were the first parts of Michigan to recover to pre-recession economic strength. In August 2017, the Kalamazoo City Commission created a $500 million "foundation for excellence" that will encourage nonprofit groups to support local development and permit a commensurate cut in local taxes plus an increase in spending to fight poverty. Michigan's southwest corner is heavily influenced by Chicago, which is much closer than is Detroit; people here watch Chicago television and root for the Cubs or White Sox rather than the Detroit Tigers.

The 6th Congressional District occupies the southwest corner of Michigan. It takes in five counties and most of a sixth. Kalamazoo is the largest, with nearly 40 percent of the population. The counties in the far southwest of the state — Cass, Berrien and Van Buren — are part of the so-called "cabinet counties," named, respectively, for Andrew Jackson's secretary of War, attorney general, and vice president. For many decades, this was arch-Republican territory. Since the 1990s, while continuing with Republican representation, the district, in particular Kalamazoo, has trended toward the Democrats. Barack Obama took 53 percent in 2008. Hillary Clinton slipped in 2016, trailing Donald Trump 51%-43%.

Tim Walberg (R)

Elected 2010, 5th term, b. Apr 12, 1951; Chicago, IL; Western Illinois University, Att.; Taylor University (IN), B.S.; Wheaton College (IL), M.A.; Moody Bible Institute (IL), Att.; Fort Wayne Bible College, B.R.E., 1975; Protestant - Unspecified Christian; Married (Susan Walberg); 3 children; 2 grandchildren.

Elected Office: MI House, 1983-1998; U.S. House, 2007-2009.

Professional Career: Minister, 1973-1982; President, Warren Reuther Center, 1999-2000; Div. Manager, Moody Bible Inst., 2000-2005.

DC Office: 2266 RHOB 20515, 202-225-6276, Fax: 202-225-6281, walberg.house.gov

State Offices: Jackson, 517-780-9075.

Committees: *Education & Labor*: Health, Employment, Labor & Pensions (RMM). *Energy & Commerce*: Communications & Technology; Energy.

Group Ratings

	ADA	ACLU	AFL-CIO	LCV	ITI	COC	HAFA	ACU	CFG	FRC
2018	-	4%	-	0%	-	92%	58%	92%	61%	100%
2017	0%	C	8%	0%	C	93%	C	85%	80%	100%

Almanac Ratings 2017-18

	Economy	Social	Foreign	Composite
Liberal	3%	4%	0%	2%
Conservative	97%	97%	100%	98%

Key Votes of the 115th Congress

1. Obama-care revision	Y	5. Family planning regs	Y	9. Guantanamo prisoners	N
2. Tax Cuts	Y	6. Body cameras/immigration	N	10. Ground missiles, limit	N
3. Omnibus appropriations	Y	7. Abortion ban	Y	11. Defense Dept. spending	Y
4. Dodd-Frank revision	Y	8. Concealed carry	Y	12. FISA rules	Y

Election Results

Election	Name (Party)	Vote (%)		Cand. Spent	Ind. Exp. Support	Ind. Exp. Oppose
2018 General	Tim Walberg (R)............................ 158,730	(54%)	$2,254,515	$12,410	
	Gretchen Driskell (D)...................... 136,330	(46%)	$2,517,522	$84,875	$11,886
2018 Primary	Tim Walberg (R)..	(100%)			

Prior winning percentages: 2016 (55%), 2014 (54%), 2012 (53%), 2010 (50%), 2006 (50%)

Republican Tim Walberg, first elected in 2006, is an ardent social and fiscal conservative who has become a political survivor occasionally willing to seek the political center. After having narrowly lost his first reelection bid and then reclaimed the seat in 2010 in another close election, he relied on his conservative base to become entrenched with a small, but apparently sufficient, electoral majority. Following Republican losses elsewhere in 2018, his Republican-held district survived as the nearest to the outskirts of Metro Detroit.

Walberg was born in Chicago, growing up on the city's South Side. He worked in a steel mill to get through college and got his bachelor's degree from Fort Wayne Bible College and a master's from Wheaton College. He was a minister for 10 years before running for office in 1982, when he won a seat in the Michigan House by beating a moderate GOP incumbent. In his 16 years as a state legislator, Walberg had a reputation as a tireless advocate for gun rights and an opponent of abortion rights. He belonged to a group dubbed the "No" caucus for its unflinching opposition to tax hikes and increased spending. When term limits ended his tenure in 1998, he became president of a conservative education foundation and a division manager for the Moody Bible Institute of Chicago.

Walberg ran for this seat in 2004, when it was open. He placed third in a GOP primary field crowded with other conservatives; moderate Joe Schwarz won the primary with 28 percent of the vote and went on to win the general election. Two years later, Walberg tried again. He ran on a record of having never once voted for a tax increase in the legislature. The well-funded anti-tax Club for Growth poured $500,000 into television ads attacking Schwarz. The national GOP backed the incumbent, and Schwarz had a spending advantage of 2-to-1. Walberg prevailed 53%-47%, and went on to defeat a weak Democratic opponent, 50%-46%.

In 2008, Democrats nominated Mark Schauer, the Michigan Senate's minority leader and a former community organizer. Schauer focused on the economy and secured an endorsement from Republican Schwarz. The Club for Growth again spent heavily for Walberg, but Schauer had strong union support and won narrowly in a Democratic year, 49%-46%.

Walberg came back for a rematch in 2010 in a much more favorable climate for his party. In August, he won a three-way Republican primary with 57 percent of the vote. In the general election, Walberg and his allies attacked Schauer for his vote for Obama's $787 billion economic stimulus, saying that he was part of the problem of deficit spending in Washington. Schauer and his backers portrayed Walberg as too far right for the district, highlighting his support for creating private accounts in Social Security. They spotlighted a September radio interview in which Walberg said he didn't know whether Obama is an American citizen. "We don't have enough information about this president," he said. By day's end, he reversed course and acknowledged that Obama is "certainly an American citizen." Outside groups and national parties showered more than $7 million on the race. Walberg regained the seat, 50%-45%.

Walberg has had a solidly conservative voting record. As chairman of the Education and the Workforce Subcommittee on Workforce Protections, he argued that the Obama administration's proposal giving home-care workers minimum wage and overtime protections would result in reduced hours for workers and higher costs for taxpayers. He later helped block a Labor Department proposal to ban youths younger than 16 from working on family farms. In 2014, the House passed Walberg's Senior Executive Service Accountability Act, which made it easier for federal agencies to suspend or fire their top managers for sufficient cause.

In 2017, he took over as chairman of the Health, Education, Labor and Pensions Subcommittee at Education and the Workforce. He gained a seat on the Energy and Commerce Committee, which gave him an additional niche to restore what he called "patient-centered health care." He contributed to the crafting of the House-passed bill to repeal and replace Obamacare, but it died in the Senate. On other issues, Walberg collaborated with Democratic Rep. Debbie Dingell, who represented a neighboring district and served with him on Energy and Commerce, to enact a bill that clarified the review standard at the Federal Energy Regulatory Commission for energy-related mergers. He and Dingell also filed two provisions that became part of the comprehensive opioid-fighting measure that was enacted in 2018. He filed with Sen Rand Paul of Kentucky a bill to overhaul federal civil-forfeiture laws, but it made little legislative progress.

In the strong Republican year of 2014, against Democrat Pam Byrnes who spent $1.4 million but had little outside assistance, Walberg won 54%-41%. In 2016, he faced Gretchen Driskell, who was mayor of Saline for 14 years and then served in the state House. In her broadcast ads, she labelled Walberg as "Trade Deal Tim" because of his support for international trade agreements; Walberg responded that he was "a free and fair trader" and that he opposed the Trans-Pacific Partnership. Driskell evidently was hoping to benefit from coattails in the presidential campaign. But it turned out that Hillary Clinton performed poorly in this district and elsewhere in Michigan; Driskell lost badly, 55%-40%.

Driskell ran again in 2018, a more favorable climate for Democrats. She made an interesting twist by appealing to supporters of President Donald Trump with her claim that she was, like him, "a vote for change." She outspent Walberg, $2.5 million to $2.3 million. Outside groups for both parties had higher priorities elsewhere in the Detroit area and spent modestly here. Walberg won surprisingly easily, 54%-46%, and took every county except Washtenaw and Eaton.

MI-7: Southern Michigan   Cook Partisan Voting Index: R+7

Population		Race and Ethnicity		Income	
Total	703,759	White	88%	Median Income	$56,536
Land area (sq. miles)	4,228	Black	4.2%	District Income Rank	208
Pop/ sq mi	166.5	Latino	4.3%	Poverty Rate	12.2%
Born in State	74.4%	Asian	0.9%	With health insurance	93.3%
		Two or more races	2%	Cash public assistance	2.7%
Age Groups		Other	0.4%	Food stamp/SNAP	11.8%
Under 18	22.3%				
18-34	19.9%	**Education**		**Work**	
35-64	41.2%	H.S grad or less	41.3%	White Collar	16.6%
Over 64	16.6%	Some college	34.9%	Sales and Service	39.6%
		College Degree, 4 yr	15.1%	Blue Collar	27.6%
Military		Post grad	8.7%	Government	12%
Veteran/ Active Duty	8.6%				

2012 Pres. Vote	Romney	169,310	(51%)	Obama	158,963	(48%)			
2016 Pres. Vote	Trump	189,677	(55%)	Clinton	131,552	(38%)	Johnson	14,136	(4%)

Jackson, Monroe: The small cities and towns nestled in and around southern Michigan's Irish Hills, near where the major glaciers stopped their southward crawl in the last ice age, have been incubators of innovation since they were settled by Yankees from New England close to two centuries ago. Hillsdale, a picture-book old town south of Jackson, is home to Hillsdale College, founded a decade before the Republican Party by abolitionists and other likeminded people. Numerous mid-level officials in the Trump administration have been Hillsdale graduates. For their part, Senate Democrats in December 2017 blocked a provision of the Republicans' tax bill that they complained would benefit only Hillsdale. Southern Michigan mostly rejected New Deal tinkering and was hostile to the United Auto Workers union. But the people here were receptive to moral claims made by later 20th-century reformers challenging racial segregation, the Vietnam War and the Watergate cover-up. In the past 100 years, the congressional district for the region has tended to elect Democrats only in presidential wave years: in 1912, 1932, 1964 and 2008.

Jackson, an old industrial town named for a founder of the Democratic Party and site of Michigan's first prison, is one of five towns that claim to have been the birthplace of the Republican Party in 1854. Today, Jackson is a city in decline, with population loss and the highest poverty rate in Michigan. The area has had some positive developments. General Motors completed in 2016 a $583 million retooling and expansion project at its Lansing Delta Township assembly plant. That assembly plant, which has been described as a technological pioneer, had about 2,400 workers. Clemens Food Group opened in 2017 a $255 million pork processing plant in Branch County, which employed more than 800. Extended court challenges have been litigated following approval by the Nuclear Regulatory Commission of a construction license for the Fermi 3 nuclear reactor near Monroe. In April 2018, the Supreme Court dismissed an appeal by an anti-nuclear group.

The 7th Congressional District takes in six counties in southern Michigan plus parts of another. The district includes three of the so-called "cabinet counties," named for members of President Andrew Jackson's administration (Jackson presided over Michigan's admission to the Union): Branch County, named for Jackson's secretary of the Navy; Eaton County, for his first secretary of War; and Jackson County, for the president himself. The district includes the outer townships of Washtenaw County, which lean Republican; more than two-thirds of Washtenaw is in the Democratic 12th District. The 7th has leaned Republican, though not overwhelmingly so. As with other Republican-held districts in Michigan, it had a big boost in Republican presidential support in 2016. Donald Trump won, 55%-38%, compared with the 51%-48% edge for Mitt Romney in 2012.

Elissa Slotkin (D)

Elected 2018, 1st term, b. Jul 10, 1976; Holly; Columbia University School of International and Public Affairs, Mast. Deg.; Cornell University (NY), B.A., 1998; Jewish; Married (Dave Slotkin); 2 stepchildren.

Professional Career: Central Intelligence Agency, Political Analyst, 2003-2004, Intelligence Briefer, 2004-2005; Special Assistant, Office of the Director of National Intelligence, 2005-2006; Director for Iraq Policy, National Security Council, 2007-2009; Senior Advisor on Iraq Policy, U.S. Department of State, 2009-2011; Assistant Secretary of Defense for International Security Affairs, 2014-2017.

DC Office: 1531 LHOB 20515, 202-225-4872, slotkin.house.gov

State Offices: Lansing, 517-993-0510.

Committees: *Armed Services:* Intelligence, Emerging Threats & Capabilities; Readiness. *Homeland Security:* Cybersecurity, Infrastructure Protection & Innovation; Intelligence & Counterterrorism.

Election Results

Election	Name (Party)	Vote (%)		Cand. Spent	Ind. Exp. Support	Ind. Exp. Oppose
2018 General	Elissa Slotkin (D)............................	172,880	(51%)	$7,370,107	$5,613,324	$6,231,435
	Mike Bishop (R)................................	159,782	(47%)	$3,302,291	$937,833	$4,668,885
2018 Primary	Elissa Slotkin (D)............................	57,819	(71%)			
	Chris Smith (D)................................	23,966	(29%)			

Democrat Elissa Slotkin, elected in 2018, brought an impressive intelligence and national security portfolio during both Democratic and Republican administrations. Her extended assignments in Iraq were followed by policy positions at the White House and Pentagon. She defeated Republican Rep. Mike Bishop, a veteran Michigan official. In her first bid for elected office, Slotkin's campaign combined robust fundraising with strong support from voters in the university core of a district that otherwise leaned Republican. She was one of four freshman Democrats from Michigan.

Slotkin grew up in Michigan but resided elsewhere after she left for college until shortly before her campaign for Congress. She graduated from Cornell University and got a master's degree from the School of International and Public Affairs at Columbia University.

In her first week as a student in New York City amid the devastating attacks a few miles away in September 2001, Slotkin later said, "That terrible day changed the trajectory of my life. I decided that after graduate school, I would join the intelligence community and work to prevent future terrorist attacks." She joined the Central Intelligence Agency as a Middle East analyst and was deployed to Iraq for three tours over five years. During that period, Slotkin had national security and intelligence assignments at the Bush White House and State Department.

After Barack Obama was elected president, Slotkin had several senior posts at the Defense Department. They included principal adviser to the undersecretary of Defense on security strategy and policy issues, plus acting assistant secretary for international security affairs. She worked on international negotiations in the fight against ISIS and the response to aggression by Russia.

In early 2017, Slotkin said, she decided to run for Congress in a way that would set aside politics "and put our country and our community ahead of everything else." Her decision was spurred, she later said, when she saw a televised report of Bishop smiling at a White House ceremony that celebrated the House Republican repeal of the Affordable Care Act, without offering an alternative. This will not stand, she decided. "In the military, this is called dereliction of duty," she told a local reporter. "We decided to fire him that day." In the Democratic primary, she got 71 percent of the vote against Chris Smith, a criminal justice professor at Michigan State University, who ran as the more progressive candidate but raised far less campaign funds than did Slotkin.

Slotkin spent almost $8 million, which more than doubled the spending by Bishop. Including funds from the two national parties, spending on the contest exceeded $25 million. Her extended campaign allowed Slotkin to define the terms of the debate and overcome what David Wasserman of the Cook Political Report described as her most glaring vulnerability: the "carpetbagging elitist" label. Predictably, Bishop defined her as an outsider. In response, The Detroit News concluded in describing Slotkin's victory, she "seized on the issue of health care to make headway" in advocating change.

Slotkin rolled up more than a 2-to-1 margin in Ingham County, with its many university and state employees. Even though that county vote was barely one-third of the district total and Bishop easily carried the two other suburban counties, her overwhelming support in Ingham gave Slotkin a comfortable 51%-47% victory. "This didn't work out the way I anticipated," Bishop told reporters after his defeat.

She was the first Democrat elected in this district since Debbie Stabenow gave up the seat when she successfully ran for the Senate in 2000. She got seats on the Armed Services and Homeland Security committees. Slotkin's reelection campaign loomed as a pivotal test of the popularity of the Democratic takeover of the House and the new Democratic control in Michigan.

MI-8: South-Central Michigan   **Cook Partisan Voting Index: R+4**

Population		Race and Ethnicity		Income	
Total	728,626	White	82.2%	Median Income	$67,499
Land area (sq. miles)	1,503	Black	5.2%	District Income Rank	112
Pop/ sq mi	484.7	Latino	5%	Poverty Rate	11.7%
Born in State	74.9%	Asian	4.3%	With health insurance	94.5%
		Two or more races	2.9%	Cash public assistance	1.8%
Age Groups		Other	0.3%	Food stamp/SNAP	9%
Under 18	22.1%				
18-34	24.1%	**Education**		**Work**	
35-64	39.9%	H.S grad or less	27.3%	White Collar	13.9%
Over 64	13.9%	Some college	32.4%	Sales and Service	39.1%
		College Degree, 4 yr	23.5%	Blue Collar	17.1%
Military		Post grad	16.7%	Government	13.3%
Veteran/ Active Duty	6.7%				

2012 Pres. Vote	Romney	183,510	(51%)	Obama	172,131	(48%)		
2016 Pres. Vote	Trump	189,891	(50%)	Clinton	164,436	(44%)	Johnson	15,205	(4%)

Detroit Exurbs, Lansing: Lansing is Michigan's state capital, chosen in 1847 because of its geographic position halfway between Lake Huron and Lake Michigan — and away from the border with Canada and the threat of invasion by British forces. It is a tidy and pleasant city with more than its share of amenities. It has a beautifully restored capitol, a fine state history museum, and is neighbor to Michigan State University in East Lansing, founded in 1855 as America's first land grant college.

Its Oldsmobile plant stimulated growth in the first half of the 20th century, and state government did the same in the second half. Two GM assembly plants have operated in the Lansing area. At the Grand River plant, which has suffered cutbacks, GM said in August 2018 that it would spend $175 million to prepare for production of two new models. The Lansing Delta Township plant was not affected. As public employee unions have grown in membership and strength, Lansing, like other state capitals, has become heavily Democratic, as are East Lansing and surrounding Ingham County. In 2016, East Lansing voters approved the legalization of marijuana — for the possession, use or transfer of up to one ounce for people over 21 on private property, but not on the Michigan State campus. The university was wracked by controversy over its officials' mishandling of sexual-abuse charges against Larry Nassar, the longtime physician for its gymnastics team and in the Olympics, who pleaded guilty in November 2017. Otherwise, the university continued to grow and the Lansing area diversified, with about 10,000 employees working at several large insurance companies.

Just east of Ingham is quite another part of Michigan, Livingston County. Forty years ago, Livingston County was mostly rural, known mainly for its many lakes. Then, subdivisions, schools and shopping malls sprouted up. Most of these people are conservatives, happy to leave behind the urban problems of Detroit, unhappy about high taxes, and hewing to traditional religious faiths. They have made Livingston one of Michigan's fastest-growing counties — its population rose 20 percent from 2000 to 2017 — and one of its most Republican.

The 8th Congressional District of Michigan includes exurban Ingham and Livingston counties and the northern, more rural parts of Oakland County north of Detroit, which has slightly more than one-third of the district vote. In recent years, the two outlying counties more-or-less canceled each other out politically, with Oakland casting the tie-breaker. In 2016, Donald Trump took the district, 50%-43%. But the heavily Democratic trend and turnout by state workers and on the campuses in Ingham can make a difference.

Andy Levin (D)

Elected 2018, 1st term, b. Aug 10, 1960; Berkley; Williams College, B.A., 1983; University of Michigan, M.A., 1990; Harvard University Law School (MA), J.D., 1994; Jewish; Married (Mary Freeman); 4 children.

Professional Career: Staff Attorney, Commission on the Future of Worker-Management Relations, 1994-1995; Chief Workforce Officer, State of Michigan, 2007-2010; Deputy Director, MI Department of Energy, Labor & Economic Growth, 2007-2011; Founder & Managing Partner, Levin Energy Partners, 2011-2018.

DC Office: 228 CHOB 20515, 202-225-4961, andylevin.house.gov

State Offices: Warren, 586-498-7122.

Committees: *Education & Labor*: Health, Employment, Labor & Pensions; Higher Education & Workforce Investment. *Foreign Affairs*: Asia, the Pacific & Nonproliferation; Western Hemisphere, Civilian Security, & Trade.

Election Results

Election	Name (Party)	Vote (%)		Cand. Spent	Ind. Exp. Support	Ind. Exp. Oppose
2018 General	Andy Levin (D)	181,734	(60%)	$1,328,834	$509,955	
	Candius Stearns (R)	112,123	(37%)	$139,960		
2018 Primary	Andy Levin (D)	49,612	(52%)			
	Ellen Lipton (D)	40,174	(42%)			
	Martin Brook (D)	4,865	(5%)			

Freshman Democrat Andy Levin had a mostly smooth ride as he succeeded his father, Sander Levin, who retired after holding the seat for 36 years. Carl Levin, his uncle, served 36 years as a senator from Michigan. The heir — who was not shy about reminding voters of his family connections —had spent much of his career dealing with public policy, both within and outside government. His election to the House was his first successful political bid.

Although he styled himself as a conventional Democrat, Levin occasionally straddled his approach. "Andy is hard to pigeonhole. He is a successful entrepreneur, but also an equally successful union organizer," according to his campaign bio. "He has been at the forefront of progressive causes for decades – while also building highly effective programs within government." That might reflect the political shifts among some of his Macomb County constituents, who occasionally have been described as "Reagan Democrats."

Levin's family roots in the Detroit area date to the 1890s, though his father's career also gave him a presence in Washington. After graduating from Williams College and getting a master's from the University of Michigan and his law degree from Harvard University, Levin spent his early professional years as an activist on environmental issues and international human rights in places ranging from China to Haiti. He was an assistant director of organizing for the national AFL-CIO and a staff attorney for the Commission on the Future of Worker-Management Relations during the Clinton administration.

After an unsuccessful campaign for the Michigan Senate in 2006, Levin worked for Democratic Gov. Jennifer Granholm as deputy director of the state's Department of Energy Labor and Economic Growth. In 2011, he created a Detroit-based business, Levin Energy Partners, which developed public-private partnerships to achieve clean-energy solutions.

Days after his father announced his retirement, Levin launched his candidacy for Congress. Democrats needed to refocus with "a new approach to politics," he said. "More progressive. More practical. Less partisan." The election of President Donald Trump in 2016, including his narrow victory in Michigan, was "the culmination of 40 years of trickle-down economics facilitated by 60 years of divide and conquer politics." He called for building "a movement for economic and social justice."

In the Democratic primary, Levin's chief challenger was Ellen Lipton, who served six years as a state representative before she was term-limited. Lipton, who lost a bid for the state Senate in 2014, told The Detroit Free Press that she approached politics with her training as a mediator in mind: "to do more listening than talking." Levin appealed to progressive voters with his embrace of "Medicare for all" and an expansion of Social Security. The Detroit News, in endorsing Lipton, cited her work in Lansing on issues such as stem cell research and criminal justice reform. Both Levin and Lipton spent a bit more than $1 million in the primary.

Levin led the primary with 52 percent of the vote to 42 percent for Lipton; Martin Brook, who had served as president of the Bloomfield Hills School Board of Education, got 5 percent. In Macomb County, which cast nearly three-fifths of the vote, Levin took 56 percent. Lipton led Levin by a few hundred votes in Oakland County.

In November, Levin defeated political newcomer Candius Stearns -- a health care insurance agent who criticized the "outrageous" cost to consumers of the Affordable Care Act. His 60%-37% victory continued a tradition among Michigan Democrats of keeping House seats within their family for many decades: Reps. Debbie Dingell and Dan Kildee succeeded their husband and uncle, respectively.

MI-9: Northern Detroit Suburbs   **Cook Partisan Voting Index: D+4**

Population		Race and Ethnicity		Income	
Total	717,306	White	77.6%	Median Income	$55,369
Land area (sq. miles)	184	Black	13%	District Income Rank	226
Pop/ sq mi	3907.1	Latino	2.3%	Poverty Rate	13.5%
Born in State	76.2%	Asian	4.2%	With health insurance	93%
		Two or more races	2.3%	Cash public assistance	2.4%
Age Groups		Other	0.6%	Food stamp/SNAP	13.9%
Under 18	20.4%				
18-34	22.9%	**Education**		**Work**	
35-64	40.5%	H.S grad or less	38.1%	White Collar	16.2%
Over 64	16.2%	Some college	32.1%	Sales and Service	41.1%
		College Degree, 4 yr	18.3%	Blue Collar	21.1%
Military		Post grad	11.4%	Government	8.4%
Veteran/ Active Duty	6.9%				

2012 Pres. Vote	Obama	199,625	(57%)	Romney	146,185	(42%)			
2016 Pres. Vote	Clinton	183,085	(51%)	Trump	155,597	(44%)	Johnson	12,101	(3%)

Southern Macomb, Eastern Oakland: The flat expanse of land just north of Eight Mile Road, Detroit's northern city limit, was mostly vacant in the years just after World War II. A string of suburbs in Oakland County ran along Woodward Avenue from the Detroit city limits to the National Shrine of the Little Flower Catholic Church in Royal Oak, where Father Charles Coughlin in the 1930s made his radio broadcasts opposing Franklin D. Roosevelt and denouncing bankers and Jews. In the 1950s and 1960s, Woodward was one of America's greatest cruising highways, where teenagers drove big Detroit cars up and down the eight lanes and where the lights were timed at 42 miles per hour. Since 1994, the annual Woodward Dream Cruise of old cars has commemorated that era with a celebration drawing more than 1 million spectators. To the east, in Macomb County, was some industrial development along rail lines, but this too was mostly empty land in the 1950s.

Then, Polish Americans began migrating out Van Dyke Avenue from Hamtramck to Warren. Italian Americans headed out Gratiot Avenue from Detroit's east side to Roseville and Clinton Township. Belgian Americans from the Mack corridor moved out farther to St. Clair Shores. Today, half of metro Detroit's population is north of Eight Mile, as African Americans and other minorities have joined whites in moving to the suburbs. In 2017, 14 percent of Oakland County residents and 12 percent of Macomb County residents were black.

The 9th Congressional District covers this suburban territory, with about two-thirds of its population in Macomb County. On the Oakland County side are Royal Oak and Ferndale, which have been economically revitalized, attracting singles and gays as well as traditional families. The Macomb side includes the more Democratic neighborhoods in the southern part of the county: Warren and much of Sterling Heights, site of the General Motors Technical Center, a big Fiat Chrysler plant, and the M-1 tank plant, which helps make metro Detroit a major defense manufacturer. As part of its corporate cost-cutting, GM in late 2018 delayed the final steps of the $1 billion expansion and renovation of its Tech Center, with about 20,000 employees and contractors. The good news for Warren was that GM said it will spend $28 million at its local battery lab as the company increases its production of electric vehicles. Chrysler has spent a billion dollars at its Warren plant to upgrade manufacturing of Ram trucks and Wagoneer SUVs.

Farther east are the blue-collar communities of Macomb: Eastpointe (formerly known as East Detroit, it voted to change its name to make it sound less like Detroit and more like tony Grosse Pointe); Roseville; St. Clair Shores; Clinton Township; and Mount Clemens. Overall, the district is Democratic, although not overwhelmingly so. Between 2007 and 2016, more than 20,000 refugees from Iraq and Syria settled in this area. Those numbers dropped sharply at the start of the Trump administration. A Muslim group won its fight to build a mosque in Sterling Heights. In 2016, Hillary Clinton won the district by seven points. Donald Trump took Macomb, 54%-42%.

Paul Mitchell (R)

Elected 2016, 2nd term, b. May 08, 1961; Boston, MA; Michigan State University, B.A., 1978; Protestant - Unspecified Christian; Married (Sherry Mitchell); 6 children.

Elected Office: St. Clair City Council.

Professional Career: Businessman.

DC Office: 211 CHOB 20515, 202-225-2106, Fax: 202-226-1169, mitchell.house.gov

State Offices: Shelby Township, 586-997-5010.

Committees: *Armed Services*: Military Personnel; Tactical Air & Land Forces. *Transportation & Infrastructure*: Aviation; Highways & Transit; Railroads, Pipelines & Hazardous Materials.

Group Ratings

	ADA	ACLU	AFL-CIO	LCV	ITI	COC	HAFA	ACU	CFG	FRC
2018	-	7%	-	3%	-	92%	53%	76%	53%	100%
2017	5%	C	11%	3%	C	93%	C	81%	71%	100%

Almanac Ratings 2017-18

	Economy	Social	Foreign	Composite
Liberal	3%	4%	0%	2%
Conservative	97%	97%	100%	98%

Key Votes of the 115th Congress

1. Obama-care revision	Y	5. Family planning regs	Y	9. Guantanamo prisoners	N
2. Tax Cuts	Y	6. Body cameras/immigration	N	10. Ground missiles, limit	N
3. Omnibus appropriations	Y	7. Abortion ban	Y	11. Defense Dept. spending	Y
4. Dodd-Frank revision	Y	8. Concealed carry	Y	12. FISA rules	Y

Election Results

Election	Name (Party)	Vote (%)		Cand. Spent	Ind. Exp. Support	Ind. Exp. Oppose
2018 General	Paul Mitchell (R)................................ 182,808	(60%)		$684,750	$365	
	Kimberly Bizon (D)....................... 106,061	(35%)		$49,183		
	Jeremy Peruski (I)........................... 11,344	(4%)		$204,185		
2018 Primary	Paul Mitchell (R)..	(100%)				

Prior winning percentages: 2016 (63%)

Republican Paul Mitchell, elected in 2016, settled into his seat after spending millions of dollars of his own money in close primaries for open seats in separate Republican-leaning districts in two consecutive elections. He had a successful career in business before he became active in conservative causes, including as chairman of the Faith and Freedom Coalition of Michigan. He is high on the list of the wealthiest members of Congress.

Mitchell grew up in Oakland County and graduated from Michigan State University. Much of his business career was with Ross Education, where he was in charge of educational programs that aided welfare recipients and eventually became its chief executive officer. His contracts included the welfare-to-work program in Detroit. He said that his business trained 6,000 persons annually for health care jobs, WDET radio reported. Mitchell served as a commissioner with the Accrediting Bureau of Health Education Schools and as a board member of the Michigan Association of Career Colleges and Schools. In its 2018 rankings, Roll Call listed his net worth as $38 million, the 15th highest in Congress.

His 2014 House bid was for an open seat in the 4th District in the center of the state, where he got 36 percent of the vote in the Republican primary to 52 percent for John Moolenaar. In that contest, Mitchell self-financed $3.6 million. During a debate in the primary, Moolenaar said, "quite frankly, I don't think this seat is up for sale." He questioned Mitchell's conservative credentials, including his contribution to the 2006 campaign of Sen. Debbie Stabenow. The following year, Mitchell got involved in state politics when he led the fight to defeat the Proposal 1 increases in the sales and gas taxes. The ballot initiative, which was opposed by 80 percent of the voters, was initiated by highway construction and contracting companies and backed by Republican Gov. Rick Snyder and state legislative leaders.

Mitchell's run for the 10th District opened when Republican Rep. Candice Miller announced her retirement. (She was subsequently elected public works commissioner in Macomb County.) His chief opponents were state Sen. Phil Pavlov and former state Rep. Alan Sanborn. During a campaign debate, Mitchell compared himself to Donald Trump in that he "stood up to the club, funded his own primary and he kicked their backside," the MLive website reported. "It is my money to do as I wish with." Mitchell won the primary with 38 percent of the vote to 28 percent for Pavlov and 16 percent for Sanborn. In contrast to Mitchell's $4 million, they spent about $410,000 and $60,000, respectively.

In the general election, Mitchell faced former Democratic state Rep. Frank Accavitti, who had served as mayor of Eastpointe and as a Macomb County commissioner. Accavitti spent $47,000 and did not pose a serious challenge in this Republican-leaning district. Mitchell won, 63%-32%, including 61 percent in Macomb. The outcome was virtually the same as the presidential vote in the district that year.

In the House, Mitchell made few waves. He focused initially on getting federal funds to his district. On the Transportation and Infrastructure Committee, he successfully opposed President Trump's budget cuts for the Great Lakes Restoration Initiative. Mitchell worked with others in the Michigan delegation to win Trump's approval for replacement of an aging lock on the Soo Canal, which bypasses the rapids on the waterway between Lake Superior and Lake Huron — for vessels that carry, among other goods, iron ore from Minnesota. If the existing lock closed, Mitchell said, "The disruption would cause an almost complete shutdown of Great Lakes steel production."

Mitchell got a seat on the Armed Services Committee, where he worked to protect Selfridge Air National Guard Base. The facility, which has been operating since 1917, houses the A-10 Thunderbolt and the KC-135 Stratotanker.

He easily won reelection — with no Republican primary and a more than 13-to-1 spending advantage over Democrat Kimberly Bizon, an environmental activist. Mitchell led comfortably in all six counties and prevailed, 60%-35%.

MI-10: Detroit Northern Exurbs, "The Thumb"

Cook Partisan Voting Index: R+13

Population		Race and Ethnicity		Income	
Total	713,551	White	90.3%	Median Income	$61,055
Land area (sq. miles)	4,140	Black	2.7%	District Income Rank	166
Pop/ sq mi	172.3	Latino	3.1%	Poverty Rate	10%
Born in State	83.6%	Asian	1.7%	With health insurance	93.5%
		Two or more races	1.9%	Cash public assistance	2.5%
Age Groups		Other	0.3%	Food stamp/SNAP	10.9%
Under 18	22.1%				
18-34	18.8%	**Education**		**Work**	
35-64	42.4%	H.S grad or less	41.4%	White Collar	16.7%
Over 64	16.7%	Some college	35.5%	Sales and Service	39.3%
		College Degree, 4 yr	14.7%	Blue Collar	26.6%
Military		Post grad	8.4%	Government	10.2%
Veteran/ Active Duty	8.4%				

2012 Pres. Vote	Romney	187,660	(55%)	Obama	148,425	(44%)			
2016 Pres. Vote	Trump	228,190	(64%)	Clinton	113,045	(32%)	Johnson	11,997	(3%)

Macomb, St. Clair: Macomb County, just northeast of Detroit, has been one of the nation's most closely watched political battlegrounds, a place where it once seemed the electoral fate of Michigan and even the entire country might be determined. It owes much of that to its reputation as blue-collar suburbia. These suburbanites were often from the east side of Detroit and were typically Catholic, at least modestly well-off, and ancestrally Democratic. They accepted the New Deal as part of their natural heritage. In 1960, Macomb County was the most Democratic major suburban county in the nation, voting 63 percent for the first Catholic president, John F. Kennedy. But these Democrats resented the efforts of Detroit politicians to tax them to pay for welfare programs and were fearful of the city's crime problem.

From 1980 to 1992, no Democratic presidential candidate got more than 40 percent of the vote in Macomb. In 1996, after great effort and with the advice of pollster Stan Greenberg, who had studied Macomb closely, Bill Clinton carried the county by a solid 50%-39%. The 54 percent vote for Donald Trump in 2016 suggested that Macomb has gone back to the future — though farmers' unhappiness with Trump's tariffs may have limited the increase in his popularity. The setback for Hillary Clinton in Macomb was further evidence of the unpopularity of her husband's trade deals. The two victories for Barack Obama may have been exceptions, perhaps due to his more skillful political team.

"There are, in a sense, two Macombs," Zack Stanton wrote in Politico in 2017. "The county is bisected at the waist by M-59 (roughly speaking, 20 Mile Road). To the north are the traditionally Republican areas of the county ('the sticks,' as Kid Rock called it in 'Trucker Anthem'), a largely rural area dotted with small towns, which has undergone massive growth under the last two decades thanks to an influx of sprawling upper middle-class subdivisions. The southern half of the county is its traditionally Democratic portion — denser, poorer, working-class, and, by and large, built in the mid-20th century and heavily reliant on manufacturing."

Lately, central and northern Macomb County have been filling up with fast-growing and expensive subdivisions that are not as culturally liberal as the affluent parts of Oakland County. More people hold white-collar jobs than blue-collar jobs these days, and there is far less work in auto plants than during earlier generations. But the recovery has been relatively strong. In 2017, Macomb had 871,000 people, compared with 185,000 residents in 1950. It continues to grow, as farms convert to subdivisions. Those seeking optimism about the future of Macomb can point to Ford and Fiat Chrysler each spending more than $1 billion on their assembly plants at Sterling Heights. Macomb Township is the fastest-growing community in the state. St. Clair County, which has become busy with commercial development, styles itself as the gateway to Lake Huron. The tip of the Thumb has more than 20 wind farms — the most in Michigan.

The 10th Congressional District of Michigan centers on the northern tier of Macomb, and encompasses nearly half of the county's population. It includes Lapeer County and most of Michigan's "Thumb," which probably was created by geological formations several hundred thousand years ago and where population declined over the past decade. The second-largest county is St. Clair, with Port Huron and its Blue Water Bridge to Canada; Students for a Democratic Society drafted its famous Port Huron Statement just north of here in Lakeport in 1962, setting the stage for the counterculture movement. Northern Macomb has become increasingly Republican, Lapeer and St. Clair have leaned Republican, and the Thumb has long been very Republican. Half the voters are in Macomb. In 2016, Trump increased GOP support to 64%-32%, which made the 10th the most Republican district in the state. That margin was a remarkable shift in eight years from John McCain's 50%-48% tight lead over Obama.

Haley Stevens (D)

Elected 2018, 1st term, b. Jun 24, 1983; Oakland County; American University (DC), Bach. Deg., 2005; American University (DC), M.A., 2007; Christian Church; Single.

Professional Career: Chief of Staff, Presidential Task Force on the Auto Industry.

DC Office: 227 CHOB 20515, 202-225-8171, stevens.house.gov

State Offices: Livonia, 734-853-3040.

Committees: *Education & Labor*: Health, Employment, Labor & Pensions; Workforce Protections. *Science, Space & Technology*: Energy; Research & Technology (Chmn).

Election Results

Election	Name (Party)	Vote (%)		Cand. Spent	Ind. Exp. Support	Ind. Exp. Oppose
2018 General	Haley Stevens (D)	181,912	(52%)	$4,142,060	$4,247,758	$891,260
	Lena Epstein (R)	158,463	(45%)	$2,627,999	$520,619	$2,592,615
2018 Primary	Haley Stevens (D)	24,309	(27%)			
	Tim Greimel (D)	19,673	(22%)			
	Suneel Gupta (D)	19,250	(21%)			
	Fayrouz Saad (D)	17,499	(19%)			
	Nancy Skinner (D)	9,407	(10%)			

Freshman Democrat Haley Stevens took control of a suburban seat that Republicans had held for decades. She was boosted by the Democrats' strong performance statewide and the retirement of two-term Republican Rep. David Trott. Stevens — who had scant professional time in Michigan after leaving for college — emphasized her work during the Obama administration in helping to rescue the auto industry, plus her private-sector experience in promoting the tech economy. She defeated a Republican who — like Stevens — was a first-time candidate. Stevens was one of three Democratic newcomers to the House from the Detroit metropolitan area and one of five Democratic women in the Michigan delegation.

Stevens, a native of Oakland County, got her bachelor's degree in political science and a master's degree in social policy and philosophy, both from American University in Washington D.C. After working for Hillary Clinton and then for Barack Obama in the 2008 presidential campaign, she joined the new Obama administration as chief of staff for the White House auto task force that oversaw the bailout of General Motors and Chrysler, which she said resulted in the rescue of 200,000 Michigan jobs. Later, she was a policy adviser on advanced manufacturing at the Economic Development Administration.

Outside of government, Stevens developed an export-assistance program for Bloomberg Philanthropies in Louisville Kentucky. With the Chicago-based Digital Manufacturing and Design Innovation Institute, she helped to create an online certification program for digital manufacturing.

Stevens returned home in early 2017 and launched her campaign prior to Trott's decision to retire. She said that her objective was to promote Michigan's tech economy and "world-class" workforce. "I have inarguably one of the most profound backgrounds in manufacturing of anyone running for Congress in the country," she told Crain's Detroit Business. Trott, a successful foreclosure lawyer, had restored some stability to the seat after his two GOP predecessors had become cartoonish characters: Thaddeus McCotter, who ran a baffling presidential campaign in 2008, and part-time reindeer rancher Kerry Bentivolio.

Other contenders in the wide-open Democratic primary included Tim Greimel, the former state House Democratic leader; Suneel Gupta, a technology entrepreneur; and Fayrouz Saad, who was a Homeland Security Department official during the Obama administration and was backed by national progressive groups. Greimel was endorsed by the United Auto Workers and prominent Democratic officials; he was the only Democratic candidate who had held elected office. With contributions from other entrepreneurs across the nation, Gupta spent the most money in the primary. Saad, who had worked on immigration issues for Detroit Mayor Mike Duggan, highlighted her background as a Muslim woman.

Many Democrats believed that Stevens would be their strongest candidate in the general election, David Wasserman of the Cook Political Report wrote prior to the primary. "But she's' struggled to break out because the presence of another female candidate ... has kept EMILY's List on the sidelines" — a reference to the pro-abortion rights group that supports Democratic women. Stevens won the primary with 27 percent of the vote. Her three chief opponents each got about 20 percent.

Lena Epstein, the Republican nominee, was co-owner of a family business that produced automotive and industrial lubricants. In 2016, she co-chaired Donald Trump's successful presidential campaign in Michigan. In its editorial endorsing Stevens, The Detroit Free Press praised her "encyclopedic" knowledge of manufacturing issues in Michigan and criticized Epstein as "ill-prepared for elective office." Stevens outspent Epstein by a wide margin and received more than $1 million in support from House Democratic groups.

As Stevens benefited from the Democratic wave in upscale suburbs in 2018, her reelection prospects likely will be influenced by the national political climate in 2020.

MI-11: Central Detroit Suburbs   Cook Partisan Voting Index: R+4

Population		Race and Ethnicity		Income	
Total	721,434	White	79.4%	Median Income	$79,781
Land area (sq. miles)	419	Black	5.2%	District Income Rank	54
Pop/ sq mi	1720.7	Latino	3.2%	Poverty Rate	6.2%
Born in State	70.5%	Asian	9.8%	With health insurance	95%
		Two or more races	2%	Cash public assistance	1.2%
Age Groups		Other	0.4%	Food stamp/SNAP	5.6%
Under 18	22.1%				
18-34	19.8%	**Education**		**Work**	
35-64	42.7%	H.S grad or less	24.6%	White Collar	15.4%
Over 64	15.4%	Some college	28.7%	Sales and Service	35.8%
		College Degree, 4 yr	27.1%	Blue Collar	14.3%
Military		Post grad	19.6%	Government	8.4%
Veteran/ Active Duty	6.2%				

2012 Pres. Vote	Romney	199,308	(52%)	Obama	178,768	(47%)		
2016 Pres. Vote	Trump	194,245	(49%)	Clinton	177,143	(45%)	Johnson	14,960 (4%)

Southern Oakland, Western Wayne: While Detroit has struggled with seemingly endemic urban decay, many of its suburbs have shown more resilience than the city that spawned them — and a more youthful adaptability to economic change. Sixty years ago, Livonia had 18,000 people. By 2017, it had 94,000. Ford planned to spend $350 million by 2019 and add 800 jobs to its transmission plant for its F-150 pick-up trucks, with a total workforce of 2,600 in a United Auto Workers union shop. Battery maker A123 Systems had a large lithium ion factory in Livonia, though it relocated to Novi in 2017.

Novi, in Oakland County, is a high-income suburb that grew 26 percent between 2000 and 2017. Its Asian-American population was 22 percent in 2017, and it has been nicknamed "Little Tokyo." Novi had plans for a $50 million, mixed-use Asian village that would feature the first local dedicated retail, restaurant and entertainment area, Crain's Detroit Business reported in May 2018. Many of these newcomers have work visas and participate in research and development, as Japanese automotive suppliers increasingly build their products in the United States; the city has adapted by offering multilingual instruction in its hospitals, workplaces and schools. President Donald Trump's trade war has raised concerns about the local ramifications.

General Motors in recent years has sold more cars in China than in the United States. Oakland has ranked third among all counties in the nation in its total jobs that depend on Chinese investment. In partnership with Fiat-Chrysler, Google has built Waymo -- a self-drive development center in Novi. Uber also has a research and testing facility. The county has styled itself as the center for autonomous vehicles.

The 11th Congressional District of Michigan covers several suburbs west and northwest of Detroit. About three-fifths of the district is in southern Oakland County, including Troy, Birmingham and Novi, plus Bloomfield Hills and Waterford to the north; the remainder is in western Wayne County, with Northville and Plymouth plus Livonia. The district is 10 percent Asian, which is the largest minority group in the 80 percent white district. Livonia had been closely divided between the two major parties. An influx of affluent residents into this part of Wayne County made it more Republican — though not so much as the Oakland County portion. In contrast to other Republican-held districts in Michigan, the upscale 11th had little change in the 2016 presidential contest. Donald Trump won 49%-45%.

Debbie Dingell (D)

Elected 2014, 3rd term, b. Nov 23, 1953; Detroit; Convent of the Sacred Heart, Grosse Pointe, MI; Georgetown University (DC), B.S., 1975; Georgetown University (DC), M.S., 1996; Roman Catholic; Widow; 4 children.

Elected Office: Wayne State U. Board of Governors, 2007-2014.

Professional Career: President, sr. Executive public affairs, GM Foundation; Founder, Chairman, Nat'l Women's Health Resource Cntr. & the Children's Inn, Nat'l Inst. of Health; Co-host, Detroit public TV show "Am I Right."

DC Office: 116 CHOB 20515, 202-225-4071, Fax: 202-226-0371, debbiedingell.house.gov

State Offices: Dearborn, 313-278-2936; Ypsilanti, 734-481-1100.

Committees: *Energy & Commerce*: Communications & Technology; Consumer Protection & Commerce; Environment & Climate Change; Health. *Natural Resources*: National Parks, Forests & Public Lands; Oversight & Investigations.

Group Ratings

	ADA	ACLU	AFL-CIO	LCV	ITI	COC	HAFA	ACU	CFG	FRC
2018	-	86%	-	94%	-	67%	6%	4%	15%	0%
2017	100%	C	97%	100%	C	38%	C	4%	5%	0%

Almanac Ratings 2017-18

	Economy	Social	Foreign	Composite
Liberal	99%	98%	95%	97%
Conservative	1%	2%	5%	3%

Key Votes of the 115th Congress

1. Obama-care revision	N	5. Family planning regs	N	9. Guantanamo prisoners	Y
2. Tax Cuts	N	6. Body cameras/immigration	Y	10. Ground missiles, limit	Y
3. Omnibus appropriations	Y	7. Abortion ban	N	11. Defense Dept. spending	Y
4. Dodd-Frank revision	N	8. Concealed carry	N	12. FISA rules	N

Election Results

Election	Name (Party)	Vote (%)	Cand. Spent	Ind. Exp. Support	Ind. Exp. Oppose
2018 General	Debbie Dingell (D)............................. 200,588	(68%)	$855,852		
	Jeff Jones (R)................................. 85,115	(29%)			
	Gary Walkowicz (Working Class) 6,712	(2%)			
2018 Primary	Debbie Dingell (D)..	(100%)			

Prior winning percentages: 2016 (64%), 2014 (65%)

Democrat Debbie Dingell, elected in 2014, has been a longtime power player and the wife of former Rep. John Dingell, the Dean of the House who retired after 59 years and died in February 2019 after several illnesses. Her victory constituted a historic level of political continuity and she became the first wife to immediately succeed a surviving spouse. She created her own niche: less cantankerous and more of a team player than her husband, but willing to hold Democrats accountable. After the 2018 election, she became one of three co-chairs of the Democrats' policy and communications arm.

During the long era that her husband was a powerful member of Congress, Debbie Dingell was a well-known figure in her own right following their marriage in 1981, the year he became chairman of the Energy and Commerce Committee. She grew up in a family with close ties to General Motors. Her grandfather cofounded Fisher Body, an early and important GM acquisition. After completing college at Georgetown, she joined GM as a lobbyist in 1977. That year, she met her future husband. After they married, she gave up her lobbying but remained a senior executive of GM until 2009, managing its public affairs operation and heading the GM Foundation.

As an influential operative, Dingell developed an extensive network with a hand in high-stakes political activities. A member of the Democratic National Committee, she ran Al Gore's Michigan campaign in 2000 and took on the same role for John Kerry four years later. She promoted women's health issues and Michigan economic development through her work with foundations.

Dingell considered a run for the Senate when Democratic Sen. Carl Levin announced he would retire in 2014. She decided against it and Rep. Gary Peters ran instead. When her husband said that he would retire as Congress' longest-serving member, she became his likely successor. Not only is the district solidly blue, but it's a place where close ties to GM help rather than hurt. Remarkably, with her husband and his father John Dingell Sr., a Dingell family member has represented the Detroit area in the House non-stop since 1933.

Dingell faced token opposition in the August primary, which she won with 78 percent of the vote. Against Republican Terry Bowman, a Ford autoworker whom she outspent 38-to-1, Dingell coasted to a 65%-31% victory in November. After her win, she said, "I am more interested in finding solutions than looking for fights."

As a junior member in the minority party, Dingell wielded tools of influence that often were rhetorical or political. She was named a senior whip, vice-chair of the seniors' task force for the Democratic Caucus, and co-chair of a Democratic Congressional Campaign Committee project to recruit more women candidates. A few days before the 2016 election, she said that one of the "worst things" with the Affordable Care Act is that Democrats passed it without any Republican votes. She added that the two parties should cooperate to fix it — a clear rebuke to President Barack Obama and once-and-future House Speaker Nancy Pelosi.

Two days after the election, she wrote in an op-ed in The Washington Post that she had repeatedly warned campaign officials for Hillary Clinton that they were taking her state for granted. "I was the crazy one. I predicted that Hillary Clinton was in trouble in Michigan during the Democratic primary. I observed that Donald Trump could win the Republican nomination for president. And ... I noted that we could see a Trump presidency."

Dingell has set some distinctive policy viewpoints, occasionally with a personal nuance. She criticized GM when it announced in late 2018 its plan to cut more than 14,000 jobs, and she warned that she would oppose international trade modifications favored by the company if GM shifted more jobs overseas. "They'll never, ever get my support on anything," she said on CNN. With her seat on Energy and Commerce, where she has deep familiarity with its history, practices and tensions, Dingell has been a prime sponsor of legislation to speed the development of self-driving vehicles. Across the board, she emphasized the need for bipartisanship and compromise.

She was a founder and co-chair of the Medicare for All Caucus. (John Dingell Sr. filed the original bill that eventually led to the creation of Medicare.), During the 2016 House sit-in when Democrats demanded action on gun control, Dingell recounted her experience growing up with a risk of gun violence. She filed bipartisan bills to restrict access to firearms by domestic abusers and stalkers.

Following the 2018 election, the Democratic Caucus chose Dingell as a co-chair of the leadership's Democratic Policy and Communications Committee. "We have to listen to the working men and women and show them we are going to deliver on issues that matter to them," she said following her selection.

MI-12: Southern Detroit Suburbs   Cook Partisan Voting Index: D+14

Population		Race and Ethnicity		Income	
Total	708,323	White	75.1%	Median Income	$56,293
Land area (sq. miles)	403	Black	10.5%	District Income Rank	211
Pop/ sq mi	1756.7	Latino	5.6%	Poverty Rate	16.8%
Born in State	68.3%	Asian	5.3%	With health insurance	94.1%
		Two or more races	3%	Cash public assistance	2.5%
Age Groups		Other	0.4%	Food stamp/SNAP	13.1%
Under 18	21.3%				
18-34	27.7%	**Education**		**Work**	
35-64	37.4%	H.S grad or less	35.7%	White Collar	13.6%
Over 64	13.6%	Some college	30.4%	Sales and Service	39%
		College Degree, 4 yr	17.7%	Blue Collar	20.6%
Military		Post grad	16.3%	Government	13.4%
Veteran/ Active Duty	6.1%				

2012 Pres. Vote	Obama	217,542	(66%)	Romney	107,632	(33%)			
2016 Pres. Vote	Clinton	205,953	(60%)	Trump	116,719	(34%)	Johnson	10,293	(3%)

Ann Arbor: The American-made automobile may be a vanishing breed elsewhere, but it still reigns supreme in Dearborn, the home of Ford Motor Co.'s headquarters. At the far eastern edge of Dearborn is Ford's famous River Rouge complex, which initially produced anti-submarine ships for use in World War I and which at one point contained almost all the equipment needed to manufacture an automobile from raw materials through finished product.

The 12th District of Michigan covers southern and central Wayne County and is a predominantly white, blue-collar district centered on Dearborn. South of Dearborn, the district swings around heavily African-American Romulus and Inkster (which are in the 13th District), taking in several working-class Detroit suburbs known collectively as the "Downriver" area: Taylor; Southgate; Woodhaven, the site of another big Ford plant; and Flat Rock, home to a joint Ford-Mazda facility and one of the few Japanese auto plants in Michigan. When Ford in 2017 announced its plan to spend $200 million at its manufacturing and innovation center in Flat Rock, its initial focus was on electric cars. That later shifted to autonomous vehicles, including an entirely new model; work on the cheaper electrics shifted to Mexico.

Ford has made long-term commitments to Dearborn, with an upgrade of its headquarters campus plus large office space on the west side of town. In 2018, it announced plans to move up to 5,000 of its workers to a new campus in Detroit's Corktown neighborhood, which includes that city's long-abandoned train station. Also in Dearborn is the Arab American Museum, which provides an overview of Detroit's large and diverse Arab population. The district takes in Ypsilanti, where the Transportation Department established the American Center for Mobility, a driverless car testing facility at GM's abandoned Willow Run plant.

Also in the 12th is two-thirds of Washtenaw County, which centers on the University of Michigan and Ann Arbor, one of the nation's largest university towns. It is oriented to the university but also is home to auto executives and young families who like a town with plenty of bookstores, coffeehouses and liberal neighbors. The university has created a large pharmaceutical research center — with 2,200 employees -- on a campus that it purchased from Pfizer in 2007. Ann Arbor has become a rapidly growing business center that has been ranked among the most innovative cities in the nation. In 2017, Google's AdWords unit, which operates the company's "pay-per-click" advertising method, its main revenue source, opened its long-delayed corporate campus near the university, with 450 employees. A downside is that Washtenaw has become economically and racially segregated with rampant inequality across the county, according to a study by a national network of local governments.

The district is Democratic territory. In 2016, Hillary Clinton won 60 percent of the vote. The Washtenaw County portion includes about 40 percent of the district and is its center of Democratic activism. The remainder is in Wayne County.

Rashida Tlaib (D)

Elected 2018, 1st term, b. Jul 24, 1976; Detroit; Wayne State University (MI), B.A., 1998; Western Michigan University, J.D., 2004; Muslim; Married (Fayez Tlaib); 2 children.

Elected Office: MI House, 2008-2015.

Professional Career: Assistant, MI State Rep. Steve Tobocman; Social Worker

DC Office: 1628 LHOB 20515, 202-225-5126, tlaib.house.gov

State Offices: River Rouge, 313-203-7540.

Committees: *Financial Services*: Consumer Protection & Financial Institutions; Housing, Community Development & Insurance. *Oversight & Reform*: Subcommittee on Economic & Consumer Policy; Subcommittee on Environment.

Election Results

Election	Name (Party)	Vote (%)		Cand. Spent	Ind. Exp. Support	Ind. Exp. Oppose
2018 General	Rashida Tlaib (D)	165,355	(84%)	$1,542,043	$67,115	
	Sam Johnson (Working Class)	22,186	(11%)			
	D. Etta Wilcoxon (G)	7,980	(4%)			
2018 Primary	Rashida Tlaib (D)	27,841	(31%)			
	Brenda Jones (D)	26,941	(30%)			
	Bill Wild (D)	12,613	(14%)			
	Coleman Young II (D)	11,172	(13%)			
	Ian Conyers (D)	5,861	(7%)			
	Shanelle Jackson (D)	4,853	(5%)			

Freshman Democrat Rashida Tlaib was one of the first two Muslim women and the second Palestinian-American elected to the House. She narrowly won the Democratic primary and had no Republican opponent in November. Tlaib brought a distinctive voice on Arab causes in the Middle East and backed a strongly progressive agenda on domestic issues. She succeeded John Conyers, the former House Judiciary Committee chairman, who resigned at age 88 under pressure from other Democrats following charges of sexual harassment of congressional aides.

Tlaib was born in Detroit to parents who had lived in the Middle East prior to their emigration. Her father was born in a Palestinian neighborhood of Jerusalem and worked on a Ford assembly line in Detroit; her mother had resided near Ramallah in the West Bank. Tlaib got a bachelor's degree from Wayne State University and law degree from the Thomas Cooley Law School of Western Michigan University. She served six years as a state representative before she was term-limited in 2014; that year, she lost a Democratic primary for the state Senate.

In the Legislature, where she was the senior Democrat on the Appropriations Committee, she focused on environmental and public-health concerns, plus funding for education. She "demonstrated a propensity for crossing establishment forces on both sides," The Detroit Free Press reported. Subsequently, she served as an advocate and community organizer with the Sugar Law Center for Economic and Social Justice, where she worked on local and national issues, including bigotry against Muslims. She protested a speech by Donald Trump in Detroit during the 2016 campaign and was removed from the site.

When Conyers announced his resignation in December 2017, attention immediately focused on his great nephew, state Sen. Ian Conyers. The former Congressman later endorsed his son, John Conyers III, though he failed to get enough signatures to qualify for the ballot. Conyers served nearly 53 years and was one of four members who served at least a half-century in the House.

During the campaign, Tlaib styled herself as a fighter "who will stand up to the billionaires and corporations taking advantage of our communities and hijacking our government." She emphasized her heritage to protest harsh treatment of immigrants and to demand justice for Palestinians in the Middle East, including support for a "one-state solution" with Israel. Her chief opponent was Brenda Jones, president of the Detroit City Council, with a long history as a community activist. Jones was backed by the United Auto Workers and other unions and Detroit Mayor Mike Duggan.

Tlaib won the Democratic primary with 31 percent to 30 percent for Jones and 14 percent for Bill Wild, the Westland mayor. Three other candidates split the remainder of the nearly 90,000 votes. Tlaib spent a bit more than $1 million in the primary, which was roughly the total of the remaining Democratic candidates. In the Michigan delegation, she joined Republican Justin Amash, who has Palestinian ancestry. She quickly bonded with Ilhan Omar of Minnesota as the initial Muslim women elected to the House.

Tlaib's victory was accompanied by a concurrent special election for the remaining two months of Conyers' final term, following the November election. That contest had an unusual outcome, largely because two candidates for the two-year term did not file for the special election. Most of their support shifted to Jones, who converted her 900-vote loss to Tlaib in the Democratic primary for the main contest to a 1,648-vote victory in the primary for the special election. Making the dual contests even more unusual, Jones had second thoughts about taking office in the House because of concern that she would be required to step down from the city council. But she reached an understanding with House officials that permitted her to serve a month in Congress without losing her post in the city. Her limited success might open the door to a reelection challenge to Tlaib.

In the House, Tlaib was in the vanguard of liberal activists in the freshman class. On the day that she took her House oath, she gained wide attention for her profane reference to President Donald Trump and call for his impeachment at a partisan gathering. Tlaib occasionally voiced unhappiness with the caution by many Democrats and the limited steps by party leaders. "They put us in photos when they want to show our party is diverse. However, when we ask to be at the table, or speak up about issues that impact who we are, what we fight for & why we ran in the first place, we are ignored," she tweeted in April.

MI-13: Detroit Metro   **Cook Partisan Voting Index: D+32**

Population		Race and Ethnicity		Income	
Total	681,222	White	33.7%	Median Income	$33,455
Land area (sq. miles)	185	Black	54.8%	District Income Rank	433
Pop/ sq mi	3685.3	Latino	7.4%	Poverty Rate	31.5%
Born in State	76.2%	Asian	1.3%	With health insurance	89.3%
		Two or more races	2%	Cash public assistance	4.6%
Age Groups		Other	0.8%	Food stamp/SNAP	33.2%
Under 18	24.6%				
18-34	24.1%	**Education**		**Work**	
35-64	37.9%	H.S grad or less	51.4%	White Collar	13.4%
Over 64	13.4%	Some college	33.6%	Sales and Service	47.6%
		College Degree, 4 yr	9.6%	Blue Collar	27.9%
Military		Post grad	5.4%	Government	8.7%
Veteran/ Active Duty	6.3%				

2012 Pres. Vote	Obama	249,656	(85%)	Romney	41,911	(14%)
2016 Pres. Vote	Clinton	209,105	(78%)	Trump	48,111	(18%)

West areas: Detroit's early auto factories — Packard, Hudson, Ford Highland Park, Dodge Main, Briggs, Ford River Rouge, Cadillac, Kelsey-Hayes, Chrysler, Plymouth, DeSoto — were built between 1905 and 1925 about five miles from the city's center and at what was then the edge of urban development. Almost instantly, the flat farmlands all around were platted in streets arranged in a grid and built up with wooden bungalows and brick prairie-style houses. Detroit's neighborhoods filled up with factory workers and civil servants, professionals and maintenance men, corner-store owners and management personnel, Catholics and Protestants and Jews: a middle-class melting pot. With one exception: Detroit in those days had few blacks. They did not begin in earnest their great migration here from the South until around 1940, when defense plants began hiring African Americans in large numbers. In 1910, blacks made up 1 percent of Detroit's population; in 1970, the share had risen to 44 percent. Today, Detroit is 83 percent black.

The history of the city is one of conflict and uplift, inspiration and tragedy. The wartime mixture of Appalachian whites and Deep South blacks proved volatile. During the war years, blacks were pent up in a few severely overcrowded neighborhoods like the Black Bottom, most of it now covered by the Chrysler Freeway; whites opposed any attempt to expand black neighborhoods, sometimes with violent measures. This tinderbox erupted in June 1943 after a fight started on a beach on Belle Isle. Rumors spread among blacks that a white man had thrown a black woman and her baby off a bridge, while a competing rumor spread among whites that a white woman had been raped and murdered on the bridge. The ensuing race riot lasted three days and resulted in 34 deaths. After 1945, when African Americans began moving outward, real estate agents played on racial fears.

In the 1950s, whole square miles of Detroit changed racial composition in a matter of months. The 1960s started with hope that the civil rights movement, encouraged by Walter Reuther's United Auto Workers union, would improve matters. In fact, many black Detroiters found good jobs and made good incomes. Then came the riots of July 1967, followed by extensive white flight and steep increases in crime. Detroit's first African-American mayor, Democrat Coleman Young, elected in 1973, pressured major employers like the Big Three auto companies to build facilities in Detroit and raised taxes to expand city services. But economic conditions continued to deteriorate and violent crime became a part of everyday life. Detroit took on a garrison atmosphere. Crime reduced the value of much residential real estate to near zero, and the city's population fell from 1.7 million in 1960 to a still-declining 673,000 in 2017.

The auto industry's fortunes have brightened since the government takeover of General Motors and Chrysler in 2009. Despite some salutary trends, the city remained largely blighted. In March 2013, Republican Gov. Rick Snyder declared the city in a state of financial emergency, and he appointed an emergency manager to try to steer it to fiscal stability. In December 2014, Detroit emerged from bankruptcy. But that transition marked only the start of the long-term revival of the city under Mayor Mike Duggan (who was elected as the city's first white mayor in a half-century) and a rapidly changed population. All financial controls ended in April 2018. Poverty in Metro Detroit remained the worst in the nation.

The 13th Congressional District of Michigan covers much of the western half of the city. Republican redistricters had dual objectives: Maintain two black majority districts even though there are barely enough blacks to achieve those numbers and there are not enough residents in Detroit for one district, and maximize Republican strength in the neighboring suburban districts. The 13th, based entirely in Wayne County, covers an area stretching from Highland Park to the east side of downtown Detroit. New housing and some gentrification in downtown have attracted professionals, and more is on the way. Still, deep-seated poverty remains. Highland Park is the poorest community in Michigan.

One salient to the southwest takes in parts of "Mexicantown," with its growing Hispanic population, as well as the cities of Ecorse, River Rouge and Melvindale. Another swings south through white-majority neighborhoods, such as Dearborn Heights, Garden City and Westland. It takes in heavily African-American Inkster and Romulus, which is the home of Detroit's Metro Airport. Overall, the district is about 55 percent African American and one of the most strongly Democratic in the country. Hillary Clinton got 78 percent in 2016, a slight dip from the vote for President Barack Obama in 2012s. In a state that Donald Trump won by barely 10,000 votes, each dent in the Democratic turnout made a big difference in the outcome.

Brenda Lawrence (D)

Elected 2014, 3rd term, b. Oct 18, 1954; Detroit; University of Detroit Mercy, Att., 1972; Central Michigan University, Bach. Deg., 2005; Christian - Non-Denominational; Married (McArthur Lawrence); 2 children; 1 grandchild.

Elected Office: Southfield Board of Education, 1992-1996; Southfield City Council, 1997-2001, President, 1999; Southfield Mayor, 2002-2015.

Professional Career: Manager, USPS.

DC Office: 2463 RHOB 20515, 202-225-5802, Fax: 202-226-2356, lawrence.house.gov

State Offices: Southfield, 248-356-2052.

Committees: *Appropriations*: Commerce, Justice, Science & Related Agencies; Interior, Environment & Related Agencies; Transportation, HUD & Related Agencies. *Oversight & Reform*: Government Operations; National Security.

Group Ratings

	ADA	ACLU	AFL-CIO	LCV	ITI	COC	HAFA	ACU	CFG	FRC
2018	-	86%	-	94%	-	58%	8%	4%	5%	0%
2017	95%	C	95%	100%	C	45%	C	7%	5%	11%

Almanac Ratings 2017-18

	Economy	Social	Foreign	Composite
Liberal	98%	98%	92%	96%
Conservative	2%	2%	8%	4%

Key Votes of the 115th Congress

1. Obama-care revision	N	5. Family planning regs	N	9. Guantanamo prisoners	Y
2. Tax Cuts	N	6. Body cameras/immigration	Y	10. Ground missiles, limit	Y
3. Omnibus appropriations	Y	7. Abortion ban	N	11. Defense Dept. spending	N
4. Dodd-Frank revision	N	8. Concealed carry	N	12. FISA rules	N

Election Results

Election	Name (Party)	Vote (%)		Cand. Spent	Ind. Exp. Support	Ind. Exp. Oppose
2018 General	Brenda Lawrence (D).......................... 214,334	(81%)		$380,897		
	Marc Herschfus (R).............................. 45,899	(17%)				
2018 Primary	Brenda Lawrence (D)..	(100%)				

Prior winning percentages: 2016 (79%), 2014 (78%)

Democrat Brenda Lawrence was elected in 2014, with lengthy political experience. In 2019, she achieved two notable objectives: a seat on the Appropriations Committee and the co-chairmanship of the Congressional Women's Caucus. Both assignments, and the Democrats' return to House control, fit well with Lawrence's insider skills.

Lawrence was born and raised in Detroit, earned a bachelor's degree in public administration from Central Michigan University, and started her career in the U.S. Postal Service, where she was a manager and worked for more than 30 years. As her children went through the public school system in Southfield, she was drawn to education issues and was elected to the school board. Later, she won a seat on the City Council and was elected mayor in 2001. As the city's first African American or woman to hold that post, she was reelected three times. She underscored Southfield's resilience as a corporate hub that held up well despite the economic collapse of Detroit.

Lawrence's long tenure as mayor was slow to translate to other political victories. She fell short in her run for Oakland County executive in 2008, and then for lieutenant governor in 2010 with gubernatorial candidate Virg Bernero. In 2012, she made her first bid for the House, running against two sitting House Democrats: Reps. Gary Peters and Hansen Clarke. That primary became a contentious debate over race. Clarke, a biracial candidate, came under criticism amid questions over whether he was truly "black." That skirmishing gave Peters a chance to stay above the fray, and he won the primary handily, with 47 percent of the vote to 35 percent for Clarke and 13 percent for Lawrence.

Lawrence got another chance in 2014 when Peters ran successfully for the Senate. State Rep. Rudy Hobbs, who was endorsed by Detroit Mayor Mike Duggan, was the early Democratic frontrunner. Lawrence gained an edge with endorsements from unions and local business groups. Lawrence made the best of her ground operation and won the primary by 2,391 votes. This time, she got 36 percent to 32 percent for Hobbs and 31 percent for Clarke, who sought a comeback. In the general election in the heavily Democratic district, she won 77 percent of the vote.

In the House, Lawrence styled herself as a strong advocate for improved roads, bridges and regional transit. "My goal is to help make 8 Mile a major thoroughfare that is the 50-yard line of the congressional district that I represent, not a line that demarcates the haves and the have-nots," she wrote in The Detroit Free-Press. On the Oversight and Government Reform Committee, Lawrence doggedly pursued more details of the Flint water crisis. In 2018, she worked with a bipartisan group of House members that urged the Environmental Protection Agency to lower the acceptable levels of toxins in the local water. She pursued her longtime interest in solving the Postal Service's financial problems. In December 2018, she lambasted a Trump administration task force for recommendations that were "not a serious effort to help the Postal Service address its long-term future."

With her work in the women's caucus, she sought to move into the leadership of that group, which has gained influence with its growing size. With the vital support of Nancy Pelosi, Lawrence was elected co-chair following the 2018 election. The alliance between Lawrence and Pelosi -- and the latter's desire to assert control through her allies -- caused some internal friction, Politico reported in September 2018. "All I've heard so far is that Brenda is interested in this job," said Democratic Rep. Lois Frankel of Florida, who was the group's co-chair. "What is she going to do with it." Without offering specifics, Lawrence said following her selection, "I am committed to continue to collaborate in creating legislation that supports the needed and necessary goals of this caucus."

At the Appropriations Committee, Lawrence was assigned to three subcommittees that handle pieces of domestic spending. "I look forward to helping to put the spotlight on the needs of the American people and finding robust solutions to some of our most challenging concerns," she said about her assignments.

Lawrence's reelections have been uneventful, with no Democratic primary opposition and Republican challengers who did not report any campaign finances. Although she likely will survive redistricting in 2022, a combination of factors could pose complications — including Michigan's expected loss of a House seat, the stagnant population in her district, and the newly elected Democrats seeking to entrench themselves in suburban districts.

MI-14: Detroit Metro   **Cook Partisan Voting Index: D+30**

Population		Race and Ethnicity		Income	
Total	692,552	White	31.3%	Median Income	$44,197
Land area (sq. miles)	186	Black	56.5%	District Income Rank	386
Pop/ sq mi	3728.8	Latino	4.7%	Poverty Rate	23.7%
Born in State	71.5%	Asian	4.5%	With health insurance	90.5%
		Two or more races	2.6%	Cash public assistance	3.5%
Age Groups		Other	0.4%	Food stamp/SNAP	24.4%
Under 18	23.2%				
18-34	22.9%	**Education**		**Work**	
35-64	38.5%	H.S grad or less	38.8%	White Collar	15.4%
Over 64	15.4%	Some college	31%	Sales and Service	43.8%
		College Degree, 4 yr	16.6%	Blue Collar	19.3%
Military		Post grad	13.7%	Government	9.6%
Veteran/ Active Duty	5.6%				

2012 Pres. Vote	Obama	273,273	(81%)	Romney	62,794	(19%)
2016 Pres. Vote	Clinton	252,387	(79%)	Trump	58,179	(18%)

North and East areas: Few central cities in America were as vibrant in the 20th century as Detroit, the nation's fourth-largest city during the middle decades, then in a class shared or surpassed only by New York, Chicago, Philadelphia and Los Angeles. Few have been as diminished as Detroit, which now stands as the nation's 23rd-largest city, behind El Paso and just ahead of Nashville, both of which continue to grow. This was America's first automobile city, not just because it manufactured so many cars but also because it was built to automobile scale. Detroit started the 20th century about the size of Milwaukee, with fewer than half a million people and extending no farther than four or five miles from the site where the French built Fort Pontchartrain on the Detroit River in 1701. As the Motor City boomed, it grew outward along wide avenues and, starting in the 1950s, along freeways. Metro Detroit eventually expanded to 4 million people, each generation moving out in all directions, leaving behind the previous generation's neighborhoods and civic institutions.

Today, large parts of Detroit are literally empty. Formerly iconic buildings in the downtown area have been demolished, and others are all but vacant, while officials struggle to create new population centers and reestablish a business district. On the positive side, GM bought, for $72 million, the 70-story Renaissance Center, built in the 1970s for $350 million, and the company moved several thousand employees there. Quicken moved more than 10,000 employees from the suburbs to downtown and restored some of the landmark buildings in the city. At the site of the former J.L. Hudson department store, in a development spearheaded by Quicken founder Dan Gilbert, developers planned a $1 billion skyscraper, which they term "a city within a city." Ford has plans to open an innovation campus -- with 5,000 employees -- at the once-grand but long-shuttered train station. But beyond these well-policed enclaves lie acres of vacant lots and half-empty blocks where there were once five-story apartment buildings and brick houses.

Some critics worried that the focus on a relatively small area of downtown ignored large parts of Detroit that remained poor and neglected. In 2017, the violent crime rate of the city ranked second-highest in the nation. In his "one Detroit" campaign, Mayor Mike Duggan was reelected that year with 72 percent of the vote over state Sen. Coleman Young II, son of the former four-term mayor. He had legitimate claims for having promoted the turnaround, but the city still struggled to provide routine services such as trash pick-up. Duggan would be the first mayor since Dennis Archer in the 1990s to serve two full terms. Both the city and its nearby suburbs, plus state officials in Lansing, faced continuing crises about the direction of the metropolitan area.

The 14th Congressional District of Michigan is an amalgamation of heavily minority areas in metro Detroit. Its serpentine shape shows the difficulty of maintaining majority-minority districts as African Americans increasingly move out of compact neighborhoods in inner cities. The district takes in Hamtramck and the Grosse Pointes, both white majority areas, and also the northern neighborhoods of Wayne County, which became heavily African American following the flight of whites in the 1970s and 1980s. It includes the newest frontiers in African-American migration in southern Oakland County; Southfield was 0.1 percent black in the 1970 census and 70 percent black in 2010, while Oak Park went from being 0.2 percent black to 58 percent in the same period.

To the north and east, the district takes in majority-black Pontiac, which has removed most of the blight from its downtown and made an impressive comeback, with billions of dollars of investments expected in its new economic hub. GM, which has been vital to the turnaround in Pontiac, set off alarms when it announced in November 2018 that it was moving 3,000 workers from its global propulsion center in Pontiac to its technical center in Warren, where it focuses on autonomous cars. Also that month, GM dealt a devastating blow to Hamtramck with the closure of its assembly plant, which had 1,500 workers. The district is 56 percent African American and is overwhelmingly Democratic. It is split almost evenly between Wayne and Oakland counties, with their separate political networks. Hillary Clinton got 79 percent, virtually the same as in the neighboring 13th District.

MINNESOTA

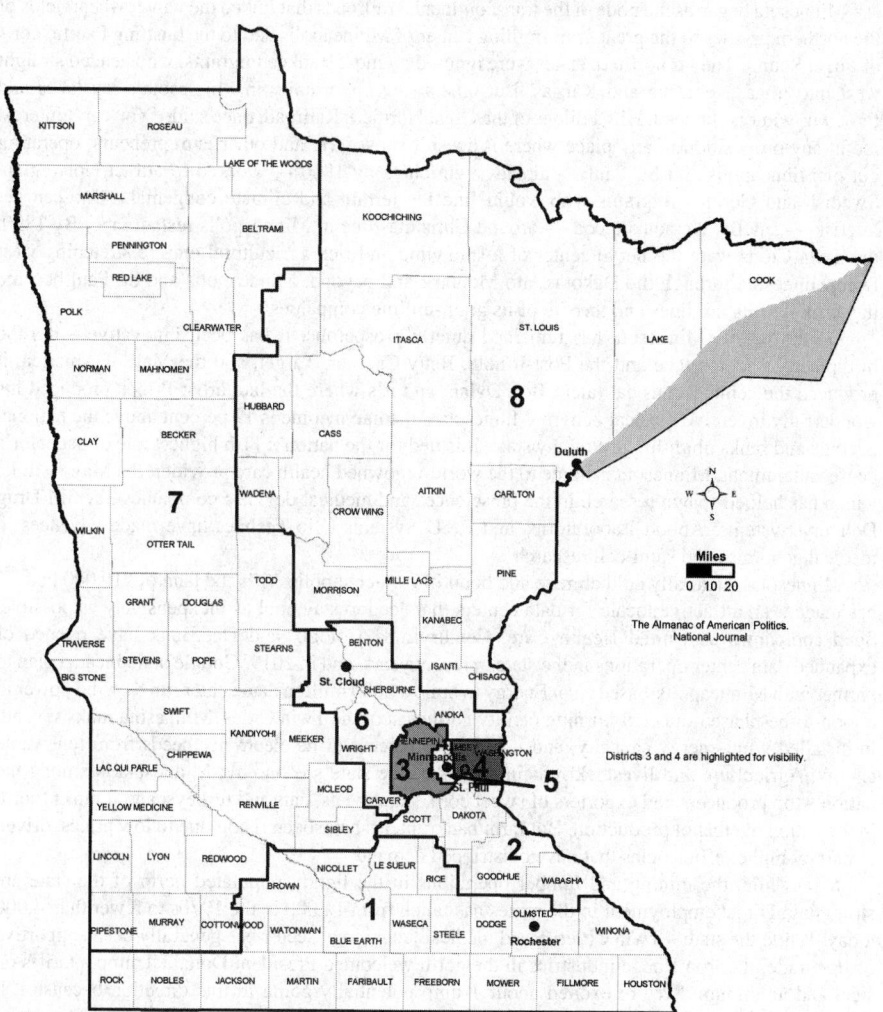

KITTSON

ROSEAU

LAKE OF THE WOODS

MARSHALL

KOOCHICHING

BELTRAMI

PENNINGTON

RED LAKE

COOK

POLK

CLEARWATER

ST. LOUIS

ITASCA

LAKE

NORMAN MAHNOMEN

HUBBARD

CLAY BECKER CASS

Duluth

7 WADENA

AITKIN CARLTON

8

WILKIN

OTTER TAIL

CROW WING

Miles
0 10 20

GRANT DOUGLAS

TODD

MORRISON

MILLE LACS

PINE

KANABEC

The Almanac of American Politics.
National Journal

TRAVERSE

STEVENS POPE

STEARNS

BENTON

ISANTI CHISAGO

BIG STONE

St. Cloud

SHERBURNE

SWIFT

ANOKA

KANDIYOHI MEEKER

6

LAC QUI PARLE

CHIPPEWA

WRIGHT

HENNEPIN
Minneapolis

WASHINGTON

Districts 3 and 4 are highlighted for visibility.

3 **4**

St. Paul

5

MCLEOD

YELLOW MEDICINE RENVILLE

CARVER

SCOTT

DAKOTA

SIBLEY

2

LINCOLN LYON REDWOOD

NICOLLET LE SUEUR

RICE

GOODHUE

WABASHA

BROWN

1

OLMSTED

PIPESTONE MURRAY COTTONWOOD WATONWAN

WASECA STEELE DODGE

Rochester

WINONA

BLUE EARTH

ROCK NOBLES JACKSON MARTIN FARIBAULT FREEBORN MOWER FILLMORE HOUSTON

Congressional district boundaries were first effective for 2012.

Minnesota hasn't voted Republican for president since Richard Nixon's landslide in 1972. (The quirk of having native son Walter Mondale on the ballot against Ronald Reagan in 1984 kept it from going Republican that year.) In 2016, the state's Democratic-Farmer-Labor Party got a wake-up call -- Minnesota was the state Hillary Clinton won with the narrowest margin save New Hampshire – but two years later, Democrats roared back, retaining the governorship, two Senate seats and all the key statewide offices, although the results underlined a widening gulf between the affluent Twin Cities region and the state's struggling, resource-dependent rural areas.

Minnesota began as the node of the transcontinental railroads that linked the winter wheat fields of the northern prairies to the great grain-milling center of Minneapolis and to the bustling Pacific ports of Puget Sound. The far northern states were ignored by most Yankee migrants, who headed straight west into Iowa, Nebraska and Kansas. But others saw opportunity in Minnesota's icy lakes and ferocious winters. James J. Hill, builder of the Great Northern Railroad, once said, "You can't interest me in any proposition in any place where it doesn't snow." He and other entrepreneurs, operating out of Minneapolis and St. Paul — already twin cities by 1860 — worked to attract Norwegian, Swedish and German migrants who would find the terrain and climate congenial. (One can get lutefisk — smelly, lye-soaked cod — around Christmastime in Minneapolis restaurants.) By 1890, the Twin Cities were the nerve center of a sprawling and rich agricultural empire stretching west from Minnesota through the Dakotas into Montana and beyond. Minneapolis and St. Paul became the termini of its rail lines and the site of its grain-milling companies

On the whole, Minnesota has remained quietly prosperous. It has been innovative – it's the birthplace of Scotch tape and the Post-It note, Betty Crocker, Target, and the Mall of America; it produced the seminal musical talent Bob Dylan; and it's where the late artist Prince produced his wonderfully inventive musical oeuvre. Minnesota's median income is 19 percent above the national average and ranks ninth-highest of any state; it is tied for the nation's 11th highest rate of bachelor's degree attainment. Minnesota is home to the world-renowned health care provider, the Mayo Clinic, which has helped spawn research in the biosciences and medical devices; companies like 3M Drug Delivery Systems, Abbott Laboratories and R&D Systems (Bio-Techne) have made advances in medical genomics and stem-cell research.

Minnesota's naturally cold climate and bountiful water supplies (it's the land of "10,000 lakes") has made it an attractive locale for data centers that need to stay cool as inexpensively as possible. Such companies as United Health Care, CenturyLink, Cologix and DataBank have opened or expanded data center operations in the state in recent years, and in 2019, Google announced a plan to partner with Minneapolis-based Xcel Energy to build a $600 million data center run by wind power in a soon-to-be-phased-out coal-burning facility northwest of the Twin Cities. Minnesota ranks seventh in installed wind-energy capacity, and it meets 27 percent of its electricity needs from renewable energy. Agriculture and livestock remain staples of the state's economy; Minnesota is among the nation's top producers and exporters of sweet corn, sugar beets, oats and turkeys, and it ranks fourth in the nation in ethanol production. But farm bankruptcies have been rising due to low prices, driven in part by higher efficiencies that have outstripped demand.

Meanwhile, the mining and lumber operations in the lightly populated north of the state are struggling. Direct employment in the mines has fallen from 14,000 in the 1970s to fewer than 4,000 today. While the state's Twin Cities-based medical technology sector has generally been supportive of free trade, the Iron Range industries in the north welcomed President Donald Trump's tariffs on steel and aluminum. "We're excited about Trump potentially going in this direction because it'll help us have a better foothold and a level playing field," Kelsey Johnson, president of the Minnesota Iron Mining Association, told the Minnesota Post in 2018. But the flow of trade is complicated: Much of the state's iron ore is exported, particularly to Canada, so retaliation is a risk. Meanwhile, pressure to revive resource extraction through new projects has become a wedge issue for the state's Democratic-Farmer-Labor Party, pitting rural hardhats against urban environmentalists. "Democrats have lost focus on kitchen-table issues in general, and blue-collar jobs in particular," Jason George of the International Union of Operating Engineers told The Hill's Reid Wilson. "The far left is trying to stop those jobs. You can't tell people you're for them when your party is trying to take away jobs." In June 2018, Trump held a rally in Duluth in which he backed an expansion of mining in the region. That fall, Republicans flipped two Democratic-held open House seats, one in the north that includes the Iron Range and the other a heavily rural district along the state's southern tier; these gains were evened out by two Twin Cities seats that flipped to the Democrats.

Minnesota has more social connectedness than any other large state, political scientist Robert Putnam noted in Bowling Alone, and this spirit of civic participation is echoed in everything from hockey to the party precinct caucuses and conventions. The Twin Cities boast of having more museums than any other city but Chicago and Washington; the Minnesota Historical Society was founded in 1849, nine years before statehood. Beyond the Twin Cities, you can visit the Spam Museum in Austin, the Judy Garland Museum in Grand Rapids, and the Laura Ingalls Wilder Museum in Walnut Grove, near the banks of Plum Creek.

Today, Minnesota is 84 percent white, making it among the whitest states in the Midwest. But minority populations have been growing from a small base, at rates between 20 and 30 percent since the 2010 census. Today, Minnesota is 6 percent black, 5 percent Hispanic and 6 percent Asian. Overall, though, the state's population has grown only modestly -- 5 percent since 2010- and that has left the state at risk of losing a seat during the 2020 congressional reapportionment. The increases have come almost exclusively from the Twin Cities metro area, with each of the most populous metro counties increasing by between 5 percent and 9 percent since 2010. The population is aging, too, leaving the minority and foreign-born share of Minnesota's population increasingly important for the state's economic future. Minnesota has the largest Somali population on the continent (Ilhan Omar became the first Somali member of the House in 2018, representing the Minneapolis-based district) and the state has large Hmong and Vietnamese communities. More than 8 percent of Minnesota residents are immigrants, and about 7 percent are U.S.-born citizens with at least one immigrant parent. This has created some tensions, and in 2010 the Justice Department indicted Somali immigrants in Minneapolis for allegedly raising money for the Islamist militant group Al-Shabaab. After Trump issued an executive order tightening immigration, Minnesota became one of the first states to sue. Trump's restrictive immigration policies also produced smaller refugee resettlement in the state than at any point in a decade, although the administration did renew temporary protected status for Somalis.

As in Wisconsin and North Dakota, a strong third-political party developed in Minnesota in the years after the Populist era. Alarmed by the concentration of economic power and wealth in the hands of a few identifiable millionaires who lived on St. Paul's Summit Avenue or on the hill above Minneapolis's Hennepin Avenue, the immigrants from Scandinavia drew on their native traditions of cooperative activity and bureaucratic socialism. The Farmer-Labor Party elected senators in the 1920s and came to dominate state politics. Gov. Floyd B. Olson secured a lengthy list of reforms that would become the foundation for modern and progressive Minnesota, including the state's first income tax, municipally owned liquor stores, large appropriations for relief, a two-year moratorium on farm foreclosures, a ban on injunctions in labor disputes, and a limit on hours worked by women in industrial jobs to 54 per week. Hurt by ties to communists, the Farmer-Laborites lost to Gov. Harold Stassen's Republicans in 1938. But this was still a New Deal state, and by 1944 the bedraggled local Democrats merged with the anti-communist faction of Farmer-Laborites to form the Democratic-Farmer-Labor Party, a name that remains to this day. Hubert Humphrey, the mayor of Minneapolis in 1945 and the key advocate of a civil rights plank at the 1948 Democratic National Convention, played a major role in this progression. Humphrey's DFL — civic-minded, closely tied to labor unions, backed by many farmers and shorn of communists — attracted dozens of talented politicians, including Eugene McCarthy, Orville Freeman and Mondale.

For a long historical moment, Minnesota's Republican Party was barely an afterthought and was practically wiped out in the post-Watergate elections of 1974. As part of its rehabilitation effort, the Republican Party of Minnesota renamed itself the Independent-Republican Party, a moniker that lasted until 1995, by which time a more conservative wing had taken over. By this time, the DFL had slowly begun to weaken as well. In 1998, three contenders in the Democratic "my three sons" gubernatorial primary were Hubert Humphrey III, Mike Freeman and Ted Mondale. "Skip" Humphrey won the divisive primary and faced St. Paul GOP Mayor Norm Coleman, but former professional wrestler and suburban mayor Jesse Ventura ran as an independent and won with a plurality. Ventura's tenure initially seemed promising -- his selections for a multi-partisan cabinet were widely admired -- but he became isolated from lawmakers, picked fights with the media and succumbed to celebrity distractions. In 2002, he decided not to run again, and the Twin Cities exurbs — the area just outside the Hennepin (Minneapolis) and Ramsey (St. Paul) core — went heavily Republican, helping Tim Pawlenty win the governorship in another three-way race. Eventually, though, the DFL regained the upper hand, as Amy Klobuchar and Al Franken won Senate seats in 2006 and 2008; while the legislature seesawed back and forth, every partisan, statewide elected post has been in DFL hands since the 2010 election, aided by the loss of major-party status and public funding for Ventura's old Independence Party after 2014. (Klobuchar would go on to run for president, while Franken resigned amid allegations of groping.)

In 2016, it looked like Minnesota was once again poised to turn toward the GOP, as Hillary Clinton won the state by only 1.5 percentage points, falling short of Barack Obama's 2012 total by more than 178,000 votes. Many of the counties that shifted from blue to red were small, but the shifts were often massive: A half-dozen predominantly rural counties saw their margins of victory shift toward Trump by between 20 and 36 percentage points. Clinton's salvation was her continued edge in the more populous Twin Cities region. Indeed, the election showed how dependent on the Twin Cities the DFL had become – whereas 57 percent of Democratic presidential votes in 2012 came from the Twin Cities, that figure rose to 63 percent in 2016.

The 2018 midterms demonstrated that obituaries of the DFL were premature. Bolstered by a projected $1.5 billion budget surplus and a pro-Democratic national wave, Rep. Tim Walz won the gubernatorial race by a 12 percentage-point margin. Meanwhile, Klobuchar and Tina Smith, the appointed successor to Franken, won their Senate races by margins of 24 and 11 percentage points, respectively, and even Rep. Keith Ellison, who was damaged by allegations of domestic abuse, won the open-seat attorney general race by four percentage points. Minnesota still has the potential to be a swing state, but as long as Trumpism defines the Republican Party, the GOP will likely face an uphill climb.

Population		Race and Ethnicity		Income	
Total	5,490,726	White	80.8%	Median Income	$65,699
Land area (sq. miles)	79,627	Black	5.9%	State Income Rank	11
Pop/ sq mi	69.0	Latino	5.2%	Poverty Rate	10.5%
Born in state	67.8%	Asian	4.6%	With health insurance	94.6%
		Two or more races	2.5%	Cash public assistance	3.4%
Age Groups		Other	1.0%	Food stamp/SNAP	8.6%
Under 18	23.4%				
18-34	23.0%	Education		Work	
35-64	39.0%	H.S grad or less	32.6%	White Collar	40.1%
Over 64	14.6%	Some college	32.6%	Sales and Service	39.1%
		College Degree, 4 yr	23.0%	Blue Collar	20.9%
Military		Post grad	11.8%	Government	11.7%
Veteran/ Active Duty	7.6%				

Presidential Politics

2016 Caucus (D)	Sanders (D)	126,229 (61%)	Clinton (D)	78,381 (38%)		
2016 Caucus (R)	Rubio (R)	41,397 (36%)	Cruz (R)	33,181 (29%)	Trump (R)	24,473 (21%)
	Carson (R)	8,422 (7%)	Kasich (R)	6,565 (6%)		
2016 Pres. Vote	Clinton (D) 1,367,825 (46%)	Trump (R) 1,323,232 (45%)	Johnson (L)	112,984 (4%)		
2012 Pres. Vote	Obama (D) 1,546,167 (53%)	Romney (R)1,320,225 (45%)				

Minnesota has the longest consecutive streak of voting Democratic for president of any state, but that run was tested in 2016. The last time Minnesota voted for the Republican nominee was in 1972, and even then it gave Richard Nixon his lowest winning percentage margin over George McGovern. Before 1932 and the New Deal, the state voted Republican in every presidential race except 1912, when it supported Republican-turned-Bull Moose candidate Teddy Roosevelt. Barack Obama won the state handily in 2008 and 2012, and few thought it would be a battleground in 2016. But with few minority voters and large swaths of rural territory, the Democratic bastion was a competitive contest and Hillary Clinton defeated Donald Trump just 46%-45%. Trump won the three most rural congressional districts in the state, the 1st, 7th and 8th, which re-elected Democratic House Members. Meanwhile, Clinton captured the 3rd District, which encompasses the southern suburbs of the Twin Cities and contains no rural population. In that district, GOP Rep. Erik Paulsen was reelected. So, in half of the state's districts, Minnesota voters split their tickets between president and Congress, the highest percentage of split-ticket districts of any state in the country.

Clinton won just nine of the state's 87 counties: the two largest vote producers, Hennepin and Ramsey, home to Minneapolis and St. Paul, respectively; Dakota and Washington, two Democratic suburban counties outside the Twin Cities; four counties on the Iron Range; and Olmsted County, home to the Mayo Clinic and the University of Minnesota at Rochester. The Democratic-Farmer-Labor Party base, formerly prairie populists, Scandinavian farmers and blue-collar workers from industrial communities, is now more likely to be the cultural liberals who cluster in comfortable neighborhoods in Minneapolis and St. Paul. Some 33 counties that voted for Obama in either 2008 or 2012 voted for Trump in 2016, many in rural areas.

In the March 1 GOP caucuses, Florida Sen. Marco Rubio defeated Texas Sen. Ted Cruz 36%-29%. Trump finished third with 21 percent. Rubio carried five districts. Cruz carried the 6th, 7th and 8th. It was the only state that Rubio carried in the nominating contest. More than 114,000 Republicans attended the caucuses, a record. In the Democratic contest, Vermont Sen. Bernie Sanders defeated Clinton 62%-38% and swept all eight congressional districts. Turnout was more than 204,000. With bipartisan support, Minnesota adopted a presidential primary for 2020.

Congressional Districts

116th Congress Lineup	5D 3R	115th Congress Lineup	5D 3R

Once-placid Minnesota likely will be the site of redistricting chaos. It was the only state that started 2019 with divided-party control of its legislature. Democrat Tim Walz, the new governor, prefers to downplay partisanship. The House delegation had five freshmen — four of whom took seats that had been held by the other party, With two seats moving in each direction, that left no net change of five Democrats and three Republicans, though there's no guarantee that any of the freshmen will be reelected in 2020. Compounding the prospective pain is the near-certainty that the 2020 census will trim one seat from Minnesota in reapportionment, its first cutback since 1962. The scenario seems custom-made for a court review — and perhaps a court drawing of the map, from the start.

No matter who holds the redistricting pen, a few governing points remain relevant. Of the eight current districts, two are urban (the Twin Cities), two are suburban and one is exurban; the remaining three are mostly rural and sprawling — to the north, west and south. In 2018, Democrats took the two suburban seats and Republicans took two of the rural seats; the third rural seat, held by Democrat Collin Peterson, had the largest vote for Donald Trump in 2016 of any Democratic-held district in the nation. Two decades ago, four of the state's eight seats were rural. The population shifts within Minnesota continue to be away from those rural areas. That seemingly will make it difficult to preserve three entire districts (of seven) that are separate from the metro area. Historically, Minneapolis and St. Paul each have dominated their own district — with some suburban appendages. Combined, the Twin Cities will have roughly the number of residents required for one district, post-2022. But civic pride — and Democratic interests — likely would react adversely to a single MSP district. The suburbs seem likely to hold even, at least. But even that is not guaranteed.

In short, expect lots of blood from all sides. This will not be Minnesota Nice.

Tim Walz (D)

Elected 2018, term expires 2023, 1st term; b. Apr 06, 1964, West Point, NE; Saint Mary's University of Minnesota; Chadron State College (NE), B.S., 1989; Minnesota State University, Mankato, M.S., 2001; Lutheran; Married (Gwen Whipple Walz); 2 children.

Military Career: U.S Army National Guard, 1981-2005.

Elected Office: US House, 2007-2018.

Professional Career: Teacher, Pine Ridge Indian Reservation, SD, 1984; Teacher, People's Republic of China, 1989-1990; Founder, Educational Travel Adventures, 1991-2006; H.S. teacher, 1989-2006.

Office: 130 State Capitol, 75 Rev. Dr. Martin Luther King Jr. Blvd.,St. Paul, 55155; 651-201-3400; Fax: 651-797-1850; Website: state.mn.us

Lt. Gov.: Peggy Flanagan (D) **Atty. Gen:** Keith Ellison (D) **Sec. of State:** Steve Simon (D)

State Legislature: Senate: 32D, 35R **House:** 75D, 59R

Election Results

Election	Name (Party)	Vote (%)
2018 General	Tim Walz (D)..	1,393,096 (54%)
	Jeff Johnson (R)...	1,097,705 (42%)
	Chris Wright (LMNP)..	68,667 (3%)
2018 Primary	Tim Walz (D)..	242,832 (42%)
	Erin Murphy (D)...	186,969 (32%)
	Lori Swanson (D)...	143,517 (25%)

Prior winning percentage: House: 2016 (50%), 2014 (54%), 2012 (58%), 2010 (49%), 2008 (63%), 2006 (50%)

Rep. Tim Walz was elected governor of Minnesota in 2018, becoming the first Minnesota Democrat to succeed a Democratic governor who had served a full eight years. On Election Day, Walz won strong support in the Twin Cities, the state's Democratic core, but he also fared better than other recent Democrats in the "Greater Minnesota" outstate regions, especially so in the state's rural southern tier, which Walz had represented in the House.

Walz grew up in Nebraska and joined the Army National Guard when he was 17. When he retired from the Guard 24 years later, in 2005, he held the rank of command sergeant major. Walz earned his teaching degree in Nebraska, taught school in China for a year through a Harvard University program, and later established an educational travel company that helped high school students study in China. He and his wife moved to Minnesota in 1996 to take teaching jobs in Mankato. There, he taught high school geography and coached the football team to two state championships.

Walz got into politics relatively late in life — he was 42 when he ran for Congress. In 2004, President George W. Bush made an appearance in the area as part of his reelection campaign. Walz took two students to the event, where Bush campaign staffers demanded to know whether he supported the president and barred the students from entering after discovering one had a sticker for Democratic candidate John Kerry. Walz suggested that it might be bad PR for the Bush campaign to bar an Army veteran, and he and the students were allowed in. Walz said the experience sparked his interest in politics, first as a volunteer for the Kerry campaign and then as a congressional candidate.

In 2006, Walz challenged six-term Republican Rep. Gil Gutknecht, an affable conservative who was not considered especially vulnerable. The district had sent Republicans to Washington for 102 of the previous 114 years. Walz was not a polished campaigner, but he struck a chord with his opposition to declining middle-class wages and tax cuts for high earners, as well as Congress' failure to hold Bush accountable on the Iraq war. He supported abortion rights and opposed a ban on same-sex marriage. Walz ran as a political outsider and painted Gutknecht as too closely tied to Bush. His military experience and football coaching gave an aura of authenticity to his campaign that made him harder to attack. Walz won, 53%-47%, and became the highest-ranking enlisted soldier ever to serve in Congress.

Walz assembled a mostly centrist voting record. He opposed the creation of the Troubled Asset Relief Program to assist the financial services industry because he said it didn't do enough to protect homeowners from foreclosure. His championing of gun owners' rights earned him the National Rifle Association's endorsement. He voted for the Keystone XL pipeline. But he backed most of President Barack Obama's chief initiatives, including the health care overhaul and the cap-and-trade bill to reduce carbon emissions.

On the Agriculture Committee, Walz secured increased access to credit and conservation opportunities for farmers in the 2008 farm bill. In the debate over the 2012 farm bill, he urged House Republicans to take up the committee-passed version instead of seeking a better bill. "Perfect is what you get in heaven," he said. "The U.S. House of Representatives is closer to hell." In 2012, the House passed a version of his bill barring the use of inside information by lawmakers to make financial trades and requiring members to disclose their investments.

Walz has been heavily involved in veterans' issues, including suicide prevention and improving the treatment of traumatic brain injuries. In 2012, he and Republican Rep. Jeff Denham of California helped enact a bill to make it easier for veterans to find jobs using skills acquired through military training. In 2016, he helped enact a bill to provide annual evaluations of mental health for all veterans and to create suicide prevention programs in the Department of Veterans Affairs. In 2015, Walz sought the top Democratic slot on the Veterans' Affairs Committee and had support from several veterans' organizations. But he lost to Corrine Brown of Florida, who benefited from seniority and the support of Democratic leaders. Instead, Democratic Leader Nancy Pelosi tapped Walz to chair her quarterly roundtables on veterans' issues. In 2017, after Brown had been indicted and then defeated in the Democratic primary, Walz finally took the senior Democratic post on the committee.

Walz faced competitive reelections in 2010 and 2014, but his biggest election scare came in 2016, in a rematch with Republican Jim Hagedorn, whose father Tom Hagedorn had represented the district in the 1970s. Walz held a fundraising advantage of more than 4-to-1, and the national parties paid little attention to this contest. But Hagedorn became a surprise threat late in the campaign by linking himself closely to the presidential campaign of Donald Trump, whose message proved to be popular in rural Minnesota. Walz won, 50.3%-49.6% -- a margin of 2,547 votes. Two years later, after Walz gave up the seat to run for governor, Hagedorn won it for the GOP.

As Democratic Gov. Mark Dayton was closing out his two terms in office, Walz faced state Rep. Erin Murphy and state Auditor Rebecca Otto in the June Democratic-Farmer-Labor convention. Murphy won the party's endorsement, likely because Walz's voting record, attuned to his rural district, clashed with the agenda preferred by the party's more progressive activists from the Twin Cities. But the party convention is non-binding, and Walz soldiered on to the August primary, where he won 42 percent, outpacing Murphy with 32 percent and, in a late entry, Attorney General Lori Swanson with 25 percent. Walz balanced his ticket by naming as his running mate state Rep. Peggy Flanagan, who had represented a district in the Twin Cities metro area and who had headed the Children's Defense Fund in the state; Flanagan was also a member of the White Earth Band of Ojibwe.

The Republicans also had a contested primary, pitting former two-term Gov. Tim Pawlenty against Jeff Johnson, a commissioner in Hennepin County, which includes Minneapolis and its suburbs. National Republicans and their business allies saw Pawlenty as a strong contender and sent substantial funding his way, but Johnson – who had failed to oust Dayton in 2014 – found success by lashing himself to Trump. Johnson won the state convention endorsement (Pawlenty had skipped the convention, irking some party regulars) and then prevailed over Pawlenty in the primary, 53%-44%. "Pawlenty was the wrong candidate in the wrong year, a misplaced establishment Republican turned Washington lobbyist who tried to shoehorn himself into the party of Trump," Dan Balz wrote in the Washington Post.

The general election was never particularly competitive. Walz had a war chest roughly double Johnson's, and it was bolstered by substantial support from the Alliance for a Better Minnesota, a pro-Democratic group that ran ads hitting Johnson over health care. Johnson called for lower taxes and less regulation, while Walz focused on education – leveraging his former profession – and health care. Johnson accused Walz of being soft on immigration enforcement, while Walz said he saw little in Johnson's record to suggest an ability to work across party lines. Stylistically, "Johnson's answers are as crisp as his well-ironed shirts, while Walz likes to meander like a geography teacher caught up in the wonders of a faraway archipelago," wrote J. Patrick Coolican in the Minneapolis Star-Tribune.

On election day, Walz won, 54%-42%. Walz ended up winning more votes than any gubernatorial candidate in the state's history, even collecting 25,000 more than Hillary Clinton had two years earlier; Johnson, by contrast, fell about 225,000 votes short of Trump's total in 2016. Walz won 21 counties, more than double the nine Clinton had won. He flipped Anoka County, a GOP-leaning Twin Cities suburb, as well as several counties in his old southern-tier district and a few in northern and western Minnesota; Walz's positions on the environment, which were to the right of Twin Cities liberals, may have helped in those regions. Calculations by the St. Paul Pioneer-Press found that Walz flipped 573 Trump precincts, compared with just 22 Clinton precincts flipped by Johnson. Equally important for Walz, Democrats took over the state House from the GOP. The state Senate, which had only one seat up in the election, remained narrowly in GOP hands. Subsequently, the GOP won a special state Senate election in a rural district, further accentuating the state's rural-urban divide and expanding the GOP majority, posing a threat to Walz's agenda. (Minnesota now has the only legislature in the nation with split-partisan control.)

After taking office, Walz's first official act was to create a diversity commission, which included not just familiar categories of racial, ethnic and gender diversity but geographic as well, a nod to more rural parts of the state. Even though he was the first governor in 20 years to come into office with a budget surplus, he supported a gasoline tax hike to fund roads, and also pushed an option to buy into the state-run MinnesotaCare health plan, both policies that had been sought by Dayton but were opposed by the GOP legislature. On a $2.6 billion project to replace Line 3 -- a pipeline supported by businesses and labor unions but opposed by environmental groups and Indian tribes -- Walz continued Dayton's legal efforts to oppose proceeding with the project, despite saying during the campaign that he was open to it.

Amy Klobuchar (D)

Elected 2006, term expires 2024, 3rd term, b. May 25, 1960; Plymouth; Yale University (CT), B.A., 1982; University of Chicago (IL), J.D., 1985; Congregationalist; Married (John Bessler); 1 child.

Elected Office: Hennepin County Attorney, 1998-2006.

Professional Career: Practicing attorney, 1985-1998.

DC Office: 425 DSOB 20510, 202-224-3244, Fax: 202-228-2186, klobuchar.senate.gov

State Offices: Minneapolis, 612-727-5220; Moorhead, 218-287-2219; Rochester, 507-288-5321; Virginia, 218-741-9690.

Committees: Senate Democratic Steering Committee Chairman. *Agriculture, Nutrition & Forestry*: Conservation, Forestry & Natural Resources; Livestock, Marketing & Agriculture Security; Nutrition, Agricultural Research & Specialty Crops; Rural Development & Energy. *Commerce, Science & Transportation*: Communications, Technology, Innovation & the Internet; Manufacturing, Trade & Consumer Protection; Subcommittee on Security; Subcommittee on Transportation & Safety. *Joint Economic. Judiciary*: Antitrust, Competition Policy & Consumer Rights (RMM); Border Security & Immigration; Crime & Terrorism; Oversight, Agency Action, Federal Rights & Federal Courts. *Rules & Administration (RMM)*.

Group Ratings

	ADA	ACLU	AFL-CIO	LCV	ITI	COC	HAFA	ACU	CFG	FRC
2018	-	64%	-	100%	-	50%	3%	5%	5%	0%
2017	100%	C	100%	100%	C	29%	C	0%	0%	0%

Key Votes of the 115th Congress

1. Obama-care revision	N	5. Gun regulations	N	9. Kavanaugh confirmation	N
2. Tax Cuts	N	6. Family planning regs	N	10. Saudi arms sales	Y
3. Dodd-Frank revision	N	7. Gorsuch confirmation	N	11. FISA rules	Y
4. Omnibus appropriations	Y	8. Immigration restrictions	N	12. Military aid in Yemen	Y

Election Results

Election	Name (Party)	Vote (%)	Cand. Spent	Ind. Exp. Support	Ind. Exp. Oppose
2018 General	Amy Klobuchar (D)...................... 1,566,174	(60%)	$9,022,199	$62,915	
	Jim Newberger (R)........................... 940,437	(36%)	$231,131	$15,697	$101
	Dennis Schuller (LMNP)..................... 66,236	(3%)			
2018 Primary	Amy Klobuchar (D)........................ 557,306	(96%)			

Prior winning percentages: 2012 (65%), 2006 (58%)

When Democrat Amy Klobuchar, Minnesota's senior senator, declared for her party's presidential nomination in February 2019, it presented a marked contrast with three female Democratic colleagues — California's Kamala Harris, Massachusetts' Elizabeth Warren and New York's Kirsten Gillibrand — who had entered the race for the White House just weeks earlier. Unlike the solidly blue coastal states of other women, who are aligned with the party's progressive wing, Klobuchar's Midwestern home state is a political battleground — and her voting record has been more centrist. Her rhetoric also has been lower key, and her emphasis has been on legislative proposals with a prospect of near-term passage, rather than serving as idealistic goalposts in the party's next platform. If Klobuchar has sometimes been dinged by critics for not taking on the difficult, controversial issues associated with her Minnesota Senate forebears — ranging from Hubert Humphrey to Eugene McCarthy to Paul Wellstone — the former prosecutor can claim one of the leading records of legislative accomplishment in today's frequently gridlocked Senate.

"I tend not to be a spear-thrower," Klobuchar told the Minneapolis Star Tribune in 2013. "To some people, that means I'm being overly careful. I am careful with how I say things. ... I don't complain about the state of things. I don't do it in my speeches, and I don't do it one-on-one. I try to look for solutions." As she prepared to seek a third Senate term in 2018 — in a state that President Donald Trump had come within 2 percentage points of carrying two years earlier — Klobuchar told MinnPost that the constant of her Senate tenure had been that she "works in the middle."

"I'm willing to stand my ground and find common ground," she said. In doing so, she has regularly sought to reach across the political aisle — Republican John Hoeven from neighboring North Dakota is a good friend, as was the late Arizona Sen. John McCain — to the point that some home-state liberals have been known to take pokes at her as "the last moderate Republican in Minnesota."

Klobuchar's cross-party appeal in a Rust Belt state — she is considered Minnesota's most popular politician — is clearly a major selling point for her backers, given Trump's narrow 2016 victories in several states in that region. But, as she launched her presidential bid in a blinding snowstorm in Minneapolis, the figurative obstacle ahead was whether a Democratic Party electorate moving leftward was looking for a consensus-oriented pragmatist. "I think Democrats are looking for someone who is the partisan bomb-thrower. She's the senator next door, not the bomb-thrower next door," Minnesota Republican consultant Mark Drake told The Washington Post, alluding to Klobuchar's 2015 memoir, "The Senator Next Door."

Klobuchar has not only been floated as a presidential candidate since her first re-election to the Senate in 2012, she was mentioned as a possible attorney general or Supreme Court nominee during President Barack Obama's second term. She was born in the Minneapolis suburb of Plymouth, the daughter of longtime Star Tribune columnist Jim Klobuchar. On her father's side, Klobuchar is the descendant of Slovenian immigrants who settled in northern Minnesota's Iron Range; her grandfather worked in the iron mines along with many others of Eastern European ancestry. Klobuchar serves potica, a traditional Slovenian holiday nut roll, at weekly Thursday meetings she holds for visiting constituents when the Senate is in session. Growing up, Klobuchar helped her father recover from alcoholism, a battle both later documented in memoirs. It was an experience to which Klobuchar publicly referred in fall 2018, when, as a member of the Senate Judiciary Committee, she earned widespread praise for her handling of a testy exchange with Supreme Court nominee Brett Kavanaugh during a nationally televised hearing.

Klobuchar graduated from Yale University, spending summers pounding stakes into the ground for the Minnesota Highway Department. Her thesis, on the machinations behind the building of Minneapolis' Hubert H. Humphrey Metrodome, was later published as a book titled "Uncovering the Dome." As an undergraduate, Klobuchar interned for Vice President Walter Mondale, and, after earning a law degree from the University of Chicago, worked with the 1984 presidential nominee at a Minneapolis law firm. Klobuchar later characterized Mondale as "an incredibly important mentor" who "encouraged me to believe that someday I could actually run for office." That goal was realized in 1998 when Klobuchar was elected county attorney in Minneapolis; she served two terms. She spearheaded a crackdown on gun crimes and was credited with securing nearly 300 homicide convictions.

There was controversy surrounding Klobuchar's management of the county attorney's office, which resurfaced just before the launch of her presidential bid. During her first Senate run in 2006, the head of the union representing many workers in her office wrote a letter opposing her, citing her "shameful treatment of her employees." At the time, Klobuchar contended the letter was backlash over salary negotiations. But recent accounts of Klobuchar's Senate tenure presented a picture different from her "Minnesota nice" public persona. LegiStorm found that, during Klobuchar's first decade on Capitol Hill, her office had the highest rate of staff turnover of any in the Senate. HuffPost reported in early 2019 that several potential hires declined to sign on with her presidential campaign owing to her reputation as a difficult boss. HuffPost quoted sources as saying then-Senate Democratic Leader Harry Reid spoke to Klobuchar in 2015 and told her to change her behavior. A spokesman said Reid didn't recall the conversation. "I love our staff," Klobuchar told Politico. "And yes, I can be tough. And yes, I can push people. ... I have, I'd say, high expectations for myself. I have high expectations for the people who work for me. But I have high expectations for this country, and that's what we need."

Klobuchar launched her 2006 Senate bid after Democratic Mark Dayton (later the state's governor) announced he would not seek re-election to the Senate. She won the endorsement of the Minnesota Democratic-Farmer-Labor Party after several prominent party members announced they would not run. In the general election, she faced Republican Rep. Mark Kennedy, who sought to distance himself from the Iraq War and President George W. Bush: It did him little good in what turned out to be a strong Democratic year. Klobuchar slammed Kennedy as a "rubber stamp" for Bush and touted her record as a prosecutor, even as Kennedy sought to highlight an increasing rate of violent crime in Minneapolis. Klobuchar consistently led in the polls and won on Election Day, 58%-38%, to become the first woman elected to represent Minnesota in the Senate.

While Klobuchar has been a mostly reliable Democratic vote in the Senate, several floor vote analyses in recent years have underscored her centrist tendencies. Recent Almanac vote rankings put her in the ideological middle of the Democratic Caucus. In a FiveThirtyEight rating of how often a senator has voted with Trump's position, Klobuchar's score is nearly twice as high as that of Harris, and more than double that of Cory Booker of New Jersey, Gillibrand, Bernie Sanders of Vermont or Warren.

Klobuchar serves on the Commerce, Science and Transportation Committee, where a major focus of her work has been consumer protection. Shortly after she was first elected, and when a 6-year-old sustained serious injuries from a swimming pool drain in a Minneapolis suburb, Klobuchar sponsored a bill, ultimately signed into law, banning swimming pool covers that fail to meet entrapment safety standards and requiring automatic drain shutoffs. The next year, after disclosures about lead in children's toys made in China, Klobuchar sponsored provisions in a child safety bill — which became law — that banned lead in children's products and required that toys contain batch numbers to make recalls easier. It prompted some Minnesota Republicans to pin a derisive nickname — "Senator of Small Things" — on her. Asked about this in an interview shortly before her presidential launch, Klobuchar bristled, telling The New York Times: "Not for a minute do I view these as small things. They're big things for the people whose kids' lives were saved."

Klobuchar's centrist tendencies have prompted griping from the left as well. LGBTQ activists complained she should have been quicker to support ending the military's "don't ask, don't tell" ban on openly gay service members, and environmentalists were angered at her efforts to remove Minnesota wolves from the federal endangered species list. In other cases, she has been comfortable with the left in the Senate. Klobuchar has a lifetime score of 95 percent from the League of Conservation Voters. She has vowed to rejoin the Paris climate accord, from which Trump withdrew the U.S., if elected. Klobuchar also joined what has been dubbed the Senate's 2020 Caucus in opposing a bill in early 2018 to roll back portions of the Dodd-Frank financial reform law.

At the same time, Klobuchar has avoided joining in calls by member of the party's left wing for free four-year college — she favors free community college — and abolishing Immigration and Customs Enforcement. And unlike most of the Senate's other White House contenders, she has not signed on to Sanders' "Medicare for All" legislation. She told The New York Times the proposal should be considered but advocated a "sensible transition," such as giving people the option of voluntarily buying into the program. On health care, Klobuchar has focused her efforts on bringing drug prices down. Working with Republican Chuck Grassley of Iowa, Klobuchar has pushed to allow importation of less expensive prescription drugs from Canada, as well as to lift the ban on the federal government negotiating for cheaper drug prices under Medicare Part D. Klobuchar's emphasis on seeking less divisive issues where bipartisan progress seems achievable has led to a record of legislative productivity that has been a selling point in her presidential bid: A 2016 assessment by Medill News Service found her to be the senator who sponsored or co-sponsored the most bills that became law.

According to Klobuchar, two dozen bills on which she was the lead Democrat — ranging from increasing funding for the nation's water infrastructure to improving telephone service in rural areas — were signed into law during the first two years of the Trump administration. Meanwhile, she recently has been active on several telecommunications and online issues. She has pushed a proposal to expand high-speed broadband to all rural households by 2022, and, in tandem with Louisiana Republican John Kennedy, introduced legislation to toughen online privacy in wake of revelations about Facebook's data mining. Klobuchar is ranking Democrat on the Rules Committee, which has jurisdiction over election law. Following reports of covert Russian interference in the 2016 election via online advertising, she introduced the "Honest Ads Act" in late 2017. It would subject online political ads to disclosure requirements similar to those imposed on radio and TV spots.

Among the bills signed by Trump at the end of 2018 was a measure dealing with sexual harassment — the product of months of negotiation between the House and Senate. The lead Senate sponsors were Klobuchar and Rules Committee Chairman Roy Blunt of Missouri. The new law holds members of Congress liable for harassment and retaliation for claims of harassment, while requiring them to reimburse the federal government for settlements in such cases. A year earlier, Klobuchar had taken over sponsorship of a sexual harassment bill drafted by her in-state colleague, Democrat Al Franken, before allegations of improper sexual advances led to his resignation. According to The Washington Post, that legislation — which proposed grants to help train law enforcement personnel in questioning of victims of sexual assault — was prompted by the rape of a University of Minnesota student.

The late 2017 episode culminating in the resignation of Franken — the onetime "Saturday Night Live" mainstay who served with Klobuchar for nearly nine years — was particularly awkward for her. Franken enjoyed a base of support among progressives in Minnesota and nationally who often have viewed Klobuchar skeptically; many of them felt Franken had been forced out of office prematurely. When the initial allegations against Franken surfaced, Klobuchar condemned his behavior and called for an Ethics Committee investigation. But several weeks later, when the latest in a series of subsequent allegations prompted more than half of the Senate Democratic Caucus to call for his resignation, Klobuchar refrained. "I felt I was in a different role as his colleague, that I'm someone that has worked with him for a long time. There's a lot of trust there, and I felt it was best to handle it in that way," she told CNN after Franken announced he would resign. During a panel discussion several months later, Klobuchar was quoted by Newsweek as calling Franken a friend who has "had two acts and he's still going to have a third." While disputing he had been forced out — Klobuchar contended Franken had made his own choice after concluding the allegations against him would have made it difficult to do his job — she emphasized the need for "due process" amid the #MeToo movement.

Another frequent interest of Klobuchar's has been combating human trafficking, most recently involving two pieces of legislation co-authored by South Dakota Republican John Thune and signed by Trump at the beginning of 2018. Three years earlier, Klobuchar was among the sponsors of a comprehensive human trafficking measure signed into law by Obama — but not before it roiled the Senate Democratic Caucus and created some uncomfortable moments for Klobuchar. In early 2015, the bipartisan, seemingly noncontroversial bill sailed through the Judiciary Committee. It was only when it was poised to be taken up on the Senate floor that several Democrats noticed a provision expanding the scope of the so-called Hyde Amendment, which bars federal dollars from being spent on abortions.

The standoff over the human trafficking bill ended up creating a six-week controversy that stalled the confirmation of Loretta Lynch as attorney general and caused strains among Senate Democrats. Klobuchar raised eyebrows by seeking to shift blame to a staff aide for failing to alert her to the anti-abortion provision. Asked later about the personal toll of the episode, Klobuchar told Politico: "Not the most pleasant."

At the outset of the Trump administration, Klobuchar was part of her party's solid opposition to the confirmation of Alabama Republican Sen. Jeff Sessions as attorney general. She cited Sessions' opposition to the 2013 reauthorization of the Violence Against Women Act, first passed in 1994.

However, Klobuchar sided with several Rust Belt Democrats on confirming Commerce Secretary Wilbur Ross — partly because of home-state concerns. During a Commerce Committee hearing, Klobuchar praised Ross for his stand against "dumping" of Chinese steel in the United States — a practice widely blamed for layoffs and plant shutdowns in Minnesota's Iron Range. In all, Klobuchar voted against 11 of 23 nominations to the Cabinet and other top administration posts that came before the Senate in the first months of Trump's administration. By comparison, several other members of the "2020 Caucus" — Booker, Gillibrand, Harris, Sanders and Warren — voted against 18 to 20 of the original Trump nominees.

Klobuchar was also part of the solid bloc of Democrats to support a filibuster of the Supreme Court nomination of Neil Gorsuch. But it was her role in the confirmation of Trump's next high court nominee, Kavanaugh, that boosted her national profile in a televised exchange that went viral. At a Judiciary Committee hearing on allegations of sexual assault against Kavanaugh by Christine Blasey Ford — charges which Kavanaugh denied — Klobuchar sought to probe whether Kavanaugh had experienced memory loss because alcohol use. Noting her father's long battle with alcoholism, she then referred to Kavanaugh's written testimony acknowledging that he occasionally had too many drinks.

"Was there ever a time when you drank so much that you couldn't remember what happened, or part of what happened the night before?" Klobuchar asked. "

You're asking about, you know, blackout. I don't know. Have you?" Kavanaugh replied.

The onetime prosecutor pressed. "Could you answer the question, judge? So ... that's not happened? Is that your answer?"

Kavanaugh came back at her. "Yeah, and I'm curious if you have," he responded.

"I have no drinking problem, judge," Klobuchar replied.

"Yeah, nor do I." Kavanaugh said.

Klobuchar ended the exchange: "OK, thank you."

After a break, Kavanaugh apologized for responding to her question with a question. "This is a tough process. I'm sorry about that," Kavanaugh told Klobuchar, who accepted the apology. Her decision to end the testy exchange without grandstanding, and by letting Kavanaugh's performance speak for itself, won her widespread praise for persistence and a quiet toughness. It also made for a contrast to the frequent histrionics of the current president. When, following her snow-saturated campaign kickoff, Klobuchar was asked by reporters if she were tough enough to take on Trump, she shot back: "I'd have loved to see him sitting out here in the snow for an hour giving this speech."

In 2012, Klobuchar crushed her opponent, state Rep. Kurt Bills, by 65%-31%, to secure a second term. It was the highest share of the vote by a Minnesota Senate candidate in nearly four decades. Klobuchar carried all but two of the state's 87 counties. Klobuchar's 2018 opponent, state Rep. Jim Newberger, tied himself closely to Trump. Her victory margin — 24 percentage points — was down from 2012, but she carried 42 counties Trump had won two years earlier. Part of this record of success has been attributed to constituent service: She visits each of Minnesota's 87 counties at least once a year. Several years ago, Franken wisecracked to a Minneapolis audience: "Amy wanted to be with us tonight, but she discovered there was one county in Minnesota where her popularity was below 70 percent. So, she's up there pumping gas and cleaning windshields."

She lined up behind Hillary Clinton's candidacy two years before Election Day 2016, was among three dozen names floated as a running mate in a leaked email from Clinton's campaign chair and was given a high-profile speaking spot at the Democratic National Convention in Philadelphia. But that didn't prevent Klobuchar from doing the kinds of things future presidential contenders often do.

During the 2014 election cycle, she traveled to a dozen states, delivering keynote speeches and raising campaign funds for Democrats. During that period, she made four trips to Iowa — Minnesota's neighbor to the south and where the first delegates to presidential nominating conventions are chosen. Her proximity to Iowa, and her campaigning with down-ballot candidates there in recent years, could give her an early advantage in the 2020 race. Klobuchar is known for a sharp wit — which she flashed during an Iowa delegation breakfast at the 2012 Democratic National Convention in North Carolina. Tweaking former Alaska Gov. Sarah Palin's much-parodied statement about her state's proximity to Russia, Klobuchar said, "I can see Iowa from my porch!"

Tina Smith (D)

Appointed 2018, term expires 2020, 1st term, b. Mar 04, 1958; Albuquerque, NM; Stanford University (CA), B.A.; Dartmouth College Tuck School of Business (NH), M.B.A.; Religion not stated; Married (Archie Smith); 2 children.

DC Office: 720 HSOB 20510, 202-224-5641, Fax: 202-224-0044, smith.senate.gov

State Offices: Duluth, 218-722-2390; Moorhead, 218-284-8721; Rochester, 507-288-2003; Saint Paul, 651-221-1016.

Committees: *Agriculture, Nutrition & Forestry*: Commodities, Risk Management & Trade; Livestock, Marketing & Agriculture Security; Rural Development & Energy (RMM). *Banking, Housing & Urban Affairs*: Economic Policy; Housing, Transportation & Community Development; Securities, Insurance & Investment. *Health, Education, Labor & Pensions*: Children & Families; Employment & Workplace Safety. *Indian Affairs*.

Group Ratings

	ADA	ACLU	AFL-CIO	LCV	ITI	COC	HAFA	ACU	CFG	FRC
2018	-	67%	-	100%	-	50%	5%	5%	5%	0%

Key Votes of the 115th Congress

1. Obama-care revision	N/A	5. Gun regulations	N/A
2. Tax Cuts	N/A	6. Family planning regs	N/A
3. Dodd-Frank revision	N	7. Gorsuch confirmation	N/A
4. Omnibus appropriations	Y	8. Immigration restrictions	N

9. Kavanaugh confirmation	N
10. Saudi arms sales	N/A
11. FISA rules	N
12. Military aid in Yemen	Y

Election Results

Election	Name (Party)	Vote (%)		Cand. Spent	Ind. Exp. Support	Ind. Exp. Oppose
2018 Special	Tina Smith (DFL)	1,370,540	(53%)			
	Katrina Housley (R)	1,095,777	(42%)			
	Sarah Wellington (LMNP)	95,614	(4%)			
2018 Primary	Tina Smith (DFL)	433,705	(76%)			
	Richard Painter (DFL)	78,193	(14%)			

After spending much of her political career as a behind-the-scenes staffer and operative, Democrat Tina Smith suddenly — and quite unexpectedly — found herself in the spotlight in late 2017. The resignation of Democrat Al Franken, amid allegations of improper sexual advances toward several women, led to the appointment of Smith as Minnesota's junior senator after three years as lieutenant governor. The latter post was Smith's first experience in elected office, and she entered the Senate not well-known to many voters — while facing a special election in less than a year. She went on to comfortably win the remaining two years of Franken's term in a state that President Donald Trump lost by less than 2 percentage points in 2016 and has planned to seek a full Senate term in 2020.

If Smith and the state's senior senator, Democrat Amy Klobuchar, are not quite the Minnesota twins, the two share far more than gender: Both women, a couple of years apart in age, have reputations as low-key politicians intent on seeking and achieving consensus. While pledging repeatedly to be a "fierce advocate" after her appointment to the Senate by Gov. Mark Dayton, Smith — during her time as chief of staff to Minneapolis Mayor R.T. Rybak and later to Dayton — was nicknamed the "velvet hammer" in political circles for her ability to prod disparate interests into agreement without creating rancor. Smith "deserves a lot of credit for things that I've gotten credit for," Rybak told the MinnPost, adding, "She's just kind of wired to find common ground."

Both Smith and Klobuchar also claim former Vice President Walter Mondale — who once occupied the Senate seat Smith now holds — as their political mentor. Born Christine Flint in Albuquerque, New Mexico, Smith grew up in Santa Fe —where she owns a second home. Her husband of more than 30 years, Archie Smith, is an investor who has specialized in medical device stocks: His professional background came into play in an attack ad aimed at his wife during the 2018 Senate race. Tina Smith earned a bachelor's degree from Stanford University and an MBA from the Tuck School of Business at Dartmouth College before moving to Minnesota to work at General Mills as a marketing executive. She left to form her own marketing and public relations firm.

Smith in 1998 managed the unsuccessful gubernatorial bid of Ted Mondale, Walter Mondale's son. Four years later, when Democratic Sen. Paul Wellstone died in a plane crash a week and a half before his reelection, Walter Mondale was nominated as a last-minute replacement. Smith ran Mondale's brief bid, which he lost to Republican Norm Coleman. Smith went on serve as vice president of public affairs for Planned Parenthood of Minnesota, North Dakota and South Dakota before becoming Rybak's chief of staff in 2005. Two years later, when the Interstate 35 bridge that crosses the Mississippi River in Minneapolis collapsed, killing 13 people, it was left to Smith to navigate the difficult relationship between the offices of Democrat Rybak and Republican Gov. Tim Pawlenty. "Tina was the one, more than anybody, who pulled those two offices together and had them acting almost as one," Rybak recalled years later.

In 2010, Smith managed Dayton's successful campaign for governor before becoming his chief of staff. As Dayton prepared to seek re-election in 2014, his ticket mate from four years earlier — Lt. Gov. Yvonne Prettner Solon — announced she would not run again, acknowledging the absence of a close working relationship with the governor. Dayton moved to replace her with a close adviser: Smith. In Minnesota, the post of lieutenant governor, with no specified duties, had traditionally been a dead-end job. After Dayton's re-election, Smith redefined it. She often served as his administration's public face, while also continuing in her accustomed behind-the-scenes role, including representing Dayton in budget negotiations with state legislative leaders. With Dayton barred from seeking a third term, there was speculation he was setting Smith up to run in his stead. But she decided in 2016 not to seek the governorship and appeared headed back to private life — until Franken became a casualty of the accelerating #MeToo movement.

At the outset of 2017, Franken — a comic mainstay of NBC's "Saturday Night Live" before entering politics — was riding high, amid buzz as a potential presidential candidate. "Perhaps the SNL writer-turned-progressive pugilist is the ideal Democratic politician for the Trump era. Like the president-elect, he excels at insult comedy," CBS political analyst Will Rahn wrote shortly before Trump was sworn in. But, in November 2017, radio anchor Leeann Tweeden alleged Franken forcibly kissed her in 2006, two years before his initial run for Senate; a posed photo emerged showing Franken reaching for her breasts while she slept on a flight.

Franken, while saying he did not remember the incident in the same manner as Tweeden, issued a public apology. As other women came forward with similar allegations, his Democratic colleagues grew increasingly uncomfortable — while initially refraining from going further than calling for an Ethics Committee investigation. But pressure increased on Democrats to demonstrate a no-tolerance policy toward sexual harassment in advance of a December 2017 special election in Alabama — where alleged sexual advances by the Republican nominee, Roy Moore, toward several teenage girls decades earlier had put the national GOP on the defensive. When, in early December, yet another allegation against Franken surfaced, it quickly triggered calls for his resignation from more than half of the Senate Democratic Caucus. A day later, Franken announced he would resign.

Smith was sworn in to the Senate on Jan. 3, 2018. Her status as Franken's successor initially required something of a political tightrope act: In Minnesota, there were many who not only missed Franken's outspoken progressive advocacy, but who also felt that he had not gotten a fair chance to defend himself. In March, during a podcast interview with Politico, she went out of her way to avoid mentioning Franken's name, opting instead to focus on the economic implications of the #MeToo movement. When the publication sent out a summary of the podcast with a headline identifying her as "Franken's replacement," she bristled — tweeting, "Hi there, @politico — the name is Tina Smith, and I'm a U.S. Senator for the great state of Minnesota." She was more conciliatory three months later during an appearance on MSNBC, during which she characterized Franken as a "great leader in Minnesota" and a "champion for a lot of issues that matter to women."

"If someone wants to enter the U.S. Senate, it's hard to imagine more complicated and challenging circumstances than [Smith] has faced," Steven Schier, a retired politics professor of politics at Carleton College, told MinnPost. "Up against an immediate re-election, she is dealing with the Franken fallout and she's having to learn a new job." Smith took a lesson from Franken's early days in the Senate, albeit for different reasons, keeping a tight focus on matters back home with the special election coming up fast. She was assigned to the Agriculture Committee. With a new five-year farm bill being debated, it allowed Smith to visibly advocate for rural Minnesota. Among her bragging points: a farm bill provision with grants to establish broadband service in remote, low-income rural areas.

Smith's floor votes during her first year resembled those of Klobuchar, putting both in the ideological middle of the Democratic Caucus. Representing a state where Trump ran strongly in 2016, Smith avoided directly attacking the president in the Senate and on the campaign trail. "I think that it is up to the voters of this country to decide whether he is fit for office," Smith told Politico. "I strongly disagree with him on almost everything. But I also believe that my state didn't send me to Washington, D.C., or any of us to Washington, D.C., to just throw bombs and fight."

Smith's leading primary challenger was University of Minnesota law professor Richard Painter, a former Republican who had been ethics counsel in the George W. Bush White House. A sharp critic of Trump — who he said should be impeached — Painter, in an apparent pitch for diehard Franken supporters, said an Ethics Committee investigation into the allegations against Franken should have been conducted before any conclusions were reached. Smith largely ignored Painter and won the primary, 76%-14%.

Pawlenty was eyed as the most potent Republican challenger to Smith but declined to run — opting instead for an unsuccessful bid to retake the governorship. State Sen. Karin Housley easily won the GOP nomination against two opponents, setting up Minnesota's first all-woman Senate race. Housley's husband was considered a major asset to her campaign. Phil Housley is a NHL Hall of Fame defenseman widely regarded as the best player ever produced by hockey-loving Minnesota. Karin Housley, meanwhile, took aim at Smith's spouse. In one of the more negative ads of the 2018 election cycle, the Housley campaign accused Smith of profiting from the opioid crisis via her husband's ownership of stock in Abbott Laboratories, which was the original marketer of OxyContin. The 30-second spot, in which actors depicting the Smiths are shown drinking champagne on a beach, was called misleading by journalistic fact checking operations. Smith's husband's ownership of between $250,000 and $500,000 in stock was originally in Minnesota-based St. Jude Medical, which Abbott Laboratories had taken over — nearly a decade and a half after Abbott had stopped marketing OxyContin. Smith, whose campaign literature asserted she was "standing up to Big Pharma" — her first Senate bill sought to increase consumer access to less expensive generic drugs — fired back. She accused Housley of siding with the pharmaceutical industry by voting against legislation — which passed the Minnesota Senate in mid-2018 — to impose millions of dollars in fees on the drug companies to address the opioid crisis.

Housley, who appeared at a rally with Trump in Rochester in early October, vowed not to be a "rubberstamp" for the president's policies as she derided Smith as a "political insider" and "career politician." When Smith did not appear for a debate at a Minneapolis TV station in mid-October — citing a scheduling conflict — Housley ran a final campaign spot showing the empty podium. "Tina Smith may have gone to Washington, but she still hasn't shown up for us," Housley said in the ad. Smith's campaign took in more than $8 million through the middle of October, outraising Housley by more than 2-1. She won 53%-42% — doing better than Franken had in 2014.Housley said in early 2019 that she had been encouraged to seek a 2020 rematch against Smith, but had not yet decided whether to do so.

Jim Hagedorn (R)

Elected 2018, 1st term, b. Aug 04, 1962; Blue Earth; George Mason University, B.A., 1992; Lutheran; Single.

Professional Career: Legislative Assistant, U.S. Rep. Arlan Strangeland, 1984-1991; U.S. Department of the Treasury, Director for Legislative and Public Affairs for the Financial Management Service, 1991 to 1998, Congressional Affairs Officer, Bureau of Engraving & Printing.

DC Office: 325 CHOB 20515, 202-225-2472, hagedorn.house.gov

State Offices: Mankato, 507-323-6090; Rochester, 507-323-6090.

Committees: *Agriculture*: Livestock & Foreign Agriculture; Subcommittee Nutrition, Oversight & Department Operations. *Small Business*: Contracting & Infrastructure; Rural Development, Agriculture, Trade & Entrepreneurship.

Election Results

Election	Name (Party)	Vote (%)	Cand. Spent	Ind. Exp. Support	Ind. Exp. Oppose
2018 General	James Hagedorn (R)............................ 146,200	(50%)	$1,563,469	$184,143	$4,741,756
	Dan Feehan (D)................................ 144,885	(50%)	$4,116,048	$3,855,465	$6,911,307

Freshman Republican Jim Hagedorn was elected in his third consecutive campaign for the district along the southern tier of Minnesota. After narrowly losing his challenge two years earlier to Democratic Rep. Tim Walz, he won an even more slender victory for the open seat, when Walz ran successfully for governor. Hagedorn spent much of his working life in the Washington area in management posts at the Treasury Department. Tom Hagedorn, his father, served four terms in the House representing a similar area, until he lost reelection in 1982 to Democrat Tim Penny and remained in Washington as a lobbyist.

Hagedorn was raised in Washington and on the family farm near Truman Minnesota, while his father served in Congress. He graduated from George Mason University and worked for Rep. Arlan Stangeland, another Minnesota Republican. At the Treasury Department, he was director for legislative and public affairs for the Financial Management Service, and congressional affairs officer for the Bureau of Engraving and Printing.

He claimed credit for the decision—which was approved in legislation—to start electronic funds transfer for hundreds of millions of annual federal payments. In his campaign bio, he said that he stopped a Bush administration plan in 2005 to merge the federal currency and coin agencies, which Hagedorn said would have cost taxpayers $500 million.

In 2010, he lost his initial bid for the seat in the Republican primary. In two challenges as the GOP nominee against Walz, who outspent him more than 4-to-1 in each campaign, Hagedorn criticized the influx of immigrants and refugees, including to the 1st District. In 2016, Hagedorn closely linked himself to the presidential campaign of Donald Trump, though he received scant support from House Republicans. He lost that contest by fewer than 2,600 votes.

Hagedorn's seeming inevitability in 2018 ran into some stumbling blocks. State Sen. Carla Nelson challenged him in the Republican primary. She cited her record in elected office, including support from the National Rifle Association, and criticized Hagedorn for having settled in the nation's capital. Hagedorn responded that Nelson was raised in Iowa and that he had the support of local Republican leaders. With the advantage of greater name recognition, he prevailed, 60%-32%.

Democratic nominee Dan Feehan, a former Army Ranger in Iraq, shared with Hagedorn an extended residency in the Washington area — where he was a deputy assistant secretary of Defense, handling readiness issues. With his youthful energy and more than twice as much campaign spending as Hagedorn, Feehan appealed for bipartisanship, including the need for health care and immigration reform.

Republicans criticized Feehan's affiliation with the Washington-based Center for a New American Security, which they described as a liberal think tank—though James Mattis, Trump's Defense Secretary, had served on its board. In this heavily agricultural district, where Trump's tariffs on farm products had become problematic, Hagedorn backed the president.

In its editorial endorsing Feehan, the Winona Daily News praised him as "the candidate who values compromise," and cited Hagedorn for "fearmongering" on immigration and "parroting the rhetoric from Trump's campaign rallies and tweets." Feehan got a boost from Walz's campaign for governor, where he ran strongly in his home district. Both parties spent millions of dollars on the contest.

This time, Hagedorn finished on the up side of a narrow outcome—with a lead of 1,315 of 291,000 that were cast. Feehan led in the two largest counties: Rochester-based Olmstead and Mankato-based Blue Earth. Hagedorn showed broader strength across the district, taking 16 of the 21 counties. In one of only three House districts that switched to Republicans in 2018 – two of them in Minnesota -- Hagedorn likely will face a competitive challenge for reelection.

MN-1: Southern Minnesota

Cook Partisan Voting Index: R+5

Population		Race and Ethnicity		Income	
Total	670,131	White	86.3%	Median Income	$59,989
Land area (sq. miles)	11,974	Black	3%	District Income Rank	179
Pop/ sq mi	56	Latino	6.2%	Poverty Rate	11.4%
Born in State	68.4%	Asian	2.6%	With health insurance	94.5%
Age Groups		Two or more races	1.5%	Cash public assistance	2.7%
Under 18	23.1%	Other	0.3%	Food stamp/SNAP	8.2%
18-34	22.9%	**Education**		**Work**	
35-64	37.6%	H.S grad or less	38.5%	White Collar	16.4%
Over 64	16.4%	Some college	33.8%	Sales and Service	37.6%
Military		College Degree, 4 yr	18.1%	Blue Collar	26%
Veteran/ Active Duty	8.2%	Post grad	9.7%	Government	10.8%

2012 Pres. Vote	Obama	170,377	(49%)	Romney	165,720	(48%)		
2016 Pres. Vote	Trump	181,647	(53%)	Clinton	130,831	(38%)	Johnson	13,881	(4%)
	McMullin	6,915	(2%)					

Rochester: The Mississippi River flows majestically southeast from Minneapolis and St. Paul, cutting through rolling hills and, where it widens, forming calm lakes. This far north, the westward tide of Yankee migrants thinned out; most settlers following the railroads on the flood plains west of the river after the Civil War were Germans and Scandinavians, bringing their families to a terrain much like the Rhineland and to the rolling uplands beyond, which resemble the northern European plain.

A little to the west is Rochester, home to the renowned Mayo Clinic, founded in 1863 when English-born physician William Mayo set up a practice to examine inductees into the Union Army. Today, 1.3 million people annually visit Mayo clinics in three states (Arizona and Florida, in addition to Minnesota) for cancer treatment and other illnesses. With more than 35,000 people employed in Rochester, that city is prosperous and has been the fastest-growing metropolitan area in Minnesota. The growth will continue, with Mayo's $6 billion plan for a high-tech medical center that will compete for what has been called the "global medical tourism industry" for health and wellness, with 22 projects planned by Mayo over two decades — plus a $250 million redevelopment of the riverfront area -- in what officials style as their "warm, hospitable" community. Mayo and community leaders have worried about the impact for employees and patients of President Donald Trump's executive orders to limit immigration and refugees; they have urged him to ease up on restrictions. (Nearly 30 percent of doctors and surgeons in the United States are immigrants.)

In Mower County, Austin is the headquarters of the Hormel meatpacking firm, which produces "miracle meat" Spam, Hormel chili and Dinty Moore stew. This was the southern locus of the 1862 Dakota Uprising, which resulted in the simultaneous hangings of 38 Dakota warriors at Mankato. Many of the bodies were dug up at night by doctors — including William Mayo — for use in medical research. To the north is Le Sueur, where Minnesota Valley Canning Co., later renamed Green Giant, was founded; a 55-foot statue of the iconic giant is a feature in Blue Earth. The farther west you go, the more frequently you find communities with a German heritage. Many small towns in southern Minnesota are now filling up with Hispanic farmworkers. The Somali communities in Rochester and Faribault — a small town to the west — each exceed 4,000, of the more than 50,000 Somalis statewide. Still, the overall minority population in the area remains small.

The 1st Congressional District of Minnesota includes most of the state's two southern tiers of counties. It stretches over 250 miles, from the South Dakota border to the Wisconsin border. This historically was a political borderland, with Civil War Republicans in the east and Farmer-Laborites more common in the west, but the traditions have been upended. Rochester had long been a Republican stronghold, but like many Northern white-collar areas, it has trended Democratic. With its tradition of staunch unionism, Austin has remained solidly Democratic-Farmer- Labor. To the west, the population-losing farm counties between Mankato and the South Dakota border now vote solidly Republican. This is one of three mostly rural districts in Minnesota that were Democratic-held and had double-digit percentage drops in the Democratic presidential vote in 2016: In the 1st, it went from 49 percent for Barack Obama in 2012 to 38 percent for Hillary Clinton.

Angie Craig (DFL)

Elected 2018, 1st term, b. Feb 14, 1972; W. Helena, AR; University of Memphis, B.A., 1994; Lutheran; Married (Cheryl Greene); 4 children.

Professional Career: Executive, St. Jude Medical; Newspaper Reporter.

DC Office: 1523 LHOB 20515, 202-225-2271, craig.house.gov

State Offices: Burnsville, 651-846-2120.

Committees: *Agriculture*: Commodity Exchanges, Energy & Credit; General Farm Commodities & Risk Management; Livestock & Foreign Agriculture. *Small Business*: Investigations, Oversight & Regulations; Rural Development, Agriculture, Trade & Entrepreneurship. *Transportation & Infrastructure*: Aviation; Highways & Transit; Railroads, Pipelines & Hazardous Materials; Water Resources & Environment.

Election Results

Election	Name (Party)	Vote (%)		Cand. Spent	Ind. Exp. Support	Ind. Exp. Oppose
2018 General	Angela D. Craig (D)...........................	177,958	(53%)	$5,074,876	$1,306,822	$3,029,754
	Jason Lewis (R)..................................	159,344	(47%)	$2,903,205	$38,236	$4,794,257
2018 Primary	Angela D. Craig (D)..		(100%)			

Freshman Democrat Angie Craig won a rematch against Republican Rep. Jason Lewis, who narrowly defeated her in 2016 when they were competing for an open seat. In this swing district, where the presidential vote has been tight in recent elections, Craig rode the national surge of political and financial support for Democratic women running in suburban areas. For Lewis, whose victory in 2016 had been something of a surprise following his controversial career as a radio talk show host, some of his earlier problems became a factor in his downfall. Craig was the only House first-termer who reversed a setback two years earlier against the same opponent.

Craig has a compelling life story. She was raised by her single mother in a trailer park in Arkansas and graduated from the University of Memphis. As a lesbian, before gay marriages were recognized, she won a major legal battle in 2000, when a judge in Tennessee gave her custody of her child, with her then-partner as the adoptive parent. Years later, Craig married her wife in Minnesota and they have four children.

She became a top executive of two medical-device companies, which are part of a major industry in the Twin Cities area. During a decade with St. Paul-based St. Jude Medical Foundation, which specialized in cardiovascular technology, Craig supervised communications and directed the company's political action committee -- whose contributions went chiefly to Republicans. She stepped down as senior vice president of global human resources.

Running in 2016 against Lewis, who had built a devoted audience for more than two decades as a nationally syndicated conservative radio talk show host based in the Twin Cities area, Democrats seized on his countless incendiary comments and said that many were racist or sexist. Lewis happily modeled himself after Trump. Craig was a superior fundraiser, with $4 million (including nearly $1 million of self-financing) to $1 million for Lewis. Each party and its allies spent about $3 million for its candidate. Defying expectations, Lewis won, 47%-45%. Craig suffered from the 8 percent that went to a liberal-leaning independent candidate.

In her 2018 campaign, Craig defeated Jeff Erdmann at the DFL district convention. Erdmann, a high school civics teacher who styled himself as a working-class candidate and criticized Craig's millions of dollars in campaign spending, withdrew before the primary.

In contrast to her 2016 contest against Lewis, Craig gave less attention to Trump and focused more on the incumbent's votes in Congress — including the large tax cuts, which she described as "trickle-down economics," and repeal of the Affordable Care Act. "I never talk about the president,"

Craig told the Minnesota Post. "We've got to tell people what we're going to fight for. We have to tell them what we care about." Lewis responded that he had sought bipartisanship, including on criminal justice reform. He also talked up the achievements of Congress and Trump. "Lots of good things come to a halt if we don't prevail," he told the Post.

National news organizations, such as CNN and BuzzFeed News, recycled some of Lewis's earlier provocative remarks from his radio talk show, including his defense of men who inappropriately touch women. Craig grew more eager to contend that such comments, plus Lewis's support for the confirmation of Brett Kavanaugh to the Supreme Court, did not represent "Minnesota values."

Like other leading House Democratic challengers, Craig had a big fundraising advantage over the incumbent. Lewis's battle became more uphill after House Republican campaign strategists acknowledged weeks before the election that the party was reducing its financial support for him. Craig's 53%-47% win confirmed that assessment. Her defeat in 2016 likely will be a reminder that suburban politics continue to shift.

MN-2: Twin Cities

Cook Partisan Voting Index: R+2

Population		Race and Ethnicity		Income	
Total	692,389	White	81.9%	Median Income	$80,403
Land area (sq. miles)	2,438	Black	4.4%	District Income Rank	50
Pop/ sq mi	284	Latino	5.9%	Poverty Rate	6.8%
Born in State	67.5%	Asian	4.6%	With health insurance	95.3%
		Two or more races	2.6%	Cash public assistance	2.4%
Age Groups		Other	0.6%	Food stamp/SNAP	5.6%
Under 18	25.3%				
18-34	21.2%	**Education**		**Work**	
35-64	41%	H.S grad or less	28.6%	White Collar	12.5%
Over 64	12.5%	Some college	33.2%	Sales and Service	39.2%
		College Degree, 4 yr	26.4%	Blue Collar	19.4%
Military		Post grad	11.8%	Government	11%
Veteran/ Active Duty	7.6%				

2012 Pres. Vote	Romney	184,576	(49%)	Obama	184,802	(49%)		
2016 Pres. Vote	Trump	176,088	(46%)	Clinton	171,396	(45%)	Johnson	16,565 (4%)

South Suburbs: Driving south from the Twin Cities, one encounters big-box stores, catering to the youngish families that live nearby in new housing developments and who work in managerial, business and technical careers. Many come from elsewhere, attracted by Minnesota's strong economy and pleasant living (provided they can tolerate its cold winters). They have turned places such as Eagan, Lakeville, Apple Valley, Mendota Heights and Burnsville in Dakota County into fast-growing suburbs. The upscale suburbs of Scott County grew by an impressive 63 percent since 2000. Dakota, which with 415,000 remains about triple the size of Scott, has grown by 18 percent during that time. In recent years, these suburban areas have begun to see an influx of lower-income residents, attracted by the good schools and low crime rates. In his book Shot All to Hell, Mark Gardner wrote about when Northfield was the site in 1876 of the final bank robbery attempt of Jesse James and his gang.

This area has been attractive to the corporate world. In Eagan, across the Mississippi River from the MSP airport, several prominent businesses filled the space after Lockheed Martin closed its plant in 2013. The Minnesota Vikings of the NFL relocated their training camp in 2018, and planned a conference center and a practice stadium. Also based in Eagan is Sun Country Airlines. Lakeville, with its 100 miles of trails and many lakes, has been ranked in Money magazine's "50 best places to live." Drive farther south on Interstate 35 and U.S. 52 — a little farther every year — and suddenly you are in farm country. Northfield is the home of Carleton College and its late professor-turned-liberal-senator, Paul Wellstone, who died with his wife in an airplane crash while campaigning for reelection in 2002.

These suburbs and hamlets make up the 2nd Congressional District of Minnesota. Like several districts in the state, this has become a battleground. Dakota County, just south of St. Paul, casts about 60 percent of the votes in the district; historically, Dakota was marginally Democratic, although today it is more of a swing county. Neighboring Scott County has the highest median income in the state, and is rapidly growing and heavily Republican, though it casts about one-third as many votes as Dakota. Donald Trump won this district by one percentage point — a bit more than 4,000 votes.

Dean Phillips (DFL)

Elected 2018, 1st term, b. Jan 20, 1969; St. Paul; Brown University (RI), B.A., 1991; University of Minnesota, M.B.A., 2000; Jewish; Divorced; 2 children.

Professional Career: President & Chief Executive Officer, Phillips Distilling Company, 1993-2012; Co-Founder, Penny's Coffee.

DC Office: 1305 LHOB 20515, 202-225-2871, Fax: 202-225-6351, phillips.house.gov

State Offices: Minnetonka, 952-563-4593.

Committees: *Ethics. Financial Services*: Oversight & Investigations; Subcommittee on Diversity & Inclusion. *Foreign Affairs*: Africa, Global Health, Global Human Rights & Internat'l Orgs; Western Hemisphere, Civilian Security, & Trade.

Election Results

Election	Name (Party)	Vote (%)		Cand. Spent	Ind. Exp. Support	Ind. Exp. Oppose
2018 General	Dean Phillips (D)	202,404	(56%)	$6,214,779	$1,576,324	$5,321,293
	Erik Paulsen (R)	160,839	(44%)	$5,861,093	$713,168	$4,294,764
2018 Primary	Dean Phillips (D)	56,677	(82%)			
	Cole Young (D)	12,784	(18%)			

Freshman Democrat Dean Phillips, a businessman and heir of a prominent Minnesota family, was elected to a seat in the Minneapolis suburbs that Republicans had held for several decades. In his first bid for elected office, he rode the Democratic surge in upscale suburbs across the nation. He defeated Rep. Erik Paulsen, an active lawmaker on the tax-writing Ways and Means Committee. The contest was costly for both sides, though House Republicans conceded their dim prospects several weeks before the election and shifted their campaign funds elsewhere. Phillips was one of three House Democratic newcomers in the Twin Cities area.

Phillips grew up in Minnesota. His father, an Army captain, was killed in Vietnam when Phillips was six months old. His mother remarried the owner of the locally based Phillips Distilling Co. He graduated from Brown University and got his master's in business administration from the University of Minnesota. After working a few years with a start-up cycling business, he joined Phillips Distilling and eventually became president. He was proudest, he later said, of the new Prairie Vodka that his team created, with a co-op of three family-owned organic corn growers in Minnesota.

Phillips left the distilling firm and helped to start a gelato business that became the largest gelato brand in the nation. During his business career, he participated in numerous community-service projects, including a global youth-empowerment initiative. The Phillips family has had many philanthropic legacies in Minnesota. "I am a fiscally responsible, socially inclusive and, yes, fortunate man … with a strong, independent voice of reason, a focus on new ideas, and a commitment to principled and courageous leadership," he wrote on his campaign website. Abigail Van Buren, also known as the advice columnist Dear Abby, was his grandmother.

In what had been a safely Republican district, Paulsen focused on tax and trade issues that boost Minnesota businesses. He fit comfortably with GOP moderates. During the 2016 presidential campaign, he objected to many actions of Donald Trump and said, "I will not be voting for him." Paulsen faced a well-funded reelection challenge that year and won, 57%-43%.

As he launched his challenge to Paulsen, Phillips said, "Congress needs a new generation of leaders willing to place principles over party." Paulsen's vote in May 2017 for the House GOP bill to repeal the Affordable Care Act "really ended my time on the bench," he told the Minnesota Post. Potential challengers for the DFL nomination largely stepped aside.

In responding to campaign charges, Paulsen sought to distance himself from Trump. He ran an ad citing his environmental credentials, as an opponent of mining near the wilderness area in northern Minnesota. Republican ads attacked Phillips for his alleged failure to provide adequate health insurance coverage to his employees and cited an $89 interest charge for his late property tax payment. Phillips sought to downplay his wealth and used little of his own money to finance the campaign.

Each candidate spent about $6 million. House Republicans added more than $1 million, before including Paulsen's campaign among the first half-dozen contests where they withdrew party support. Rep. Jason Lewis in an adjacent Twin Cities district was another GOP incumbent in that early group.

During the final week before the election, an upbeat Paulsen told reporters that he was confident about the outcome. Phillips won, 56%-44%. In Hennepin County, which cast more than 80 percent of the vote, Phillips took 57 percent. The two candidates split two other counties, with smaller margins.

With a successful start to his political career, Phillips might replicate his practice in the business world of seeking additional opportunities. But Phillips, who is Jewish, encountered unexpected early turmoil when he demanded that Democratic Rep. Ilhan Omar, another first-term member from an adjacent district, apologize for public comments that he viewed as anti-Semitic, according to news reports in March 2019.

MN-3: Twin Cities

Cook Partisan Voting Index: D+1

Population		Race and Ethnicity		Income	
Total	703,785	White	78.2%	Median Income	$85,012
Land area (sq. miles)	527	Black	7.3%	District Income Rank	38
Pop/ sq mi	1335.3	Latino	4.4%	Poverty Rate	5.9%
Born in State	62.3%	Asian	7.1%	With health insurance	95.7%
		Two or more races	2.5%	Cash public assistance	2.8%
Age Groups		Other	0.4%	Food stamp/SNAP	5.3%
Under 18	23.9%				
18-34	19.5%	**Education**		**Work**	
35-64	42.2%	H.S grad or less	22.1%	White Collar	14.4%
Over 64	14.4%	Some college	29.7%	Sales and Service	38%
		College Degree, 4 yr	31.4%	Blue Collar	14%
Military		Post grad	16.8%	Government	8.7%
Veteran/ Active Duty	6.9%				

2012 Pres. Vote	Obama	199,093	(50%)	Romney	195,802	(49%)		
2016 Pres. Vote	Clinton	201,833	(50%)	Trump	164,259	(41%)	Johnson	16,012	(4%)
	McMullin	8,348	(2%)					

West Suburbs: Over the past half century, Minnesota's two-headed metropolis has spread out from the neat streets inside the city limits of Minneapolis and St. Paul into the countryside all around. People have sorted themselves out geographically. In the lower lands along the Mississippi and Minnesota rivers, where rail lines fan out from the Twin Cities, are the blue-collar suburbs, with modest houses and warehouses and factories near the tracks. Inland, around the lakes Minnesota is so proud of, in subdivisions with curved streets hugging the hills, are more affluent neighborhoods, quiet and unflashy in the Minnesota way but comfortable whether blanketed with snow or with a nearby lake glinting in the summer sun.

At the freeway interchanges, some of the Twin Cities' innovations can be seen — Southdale shopping center in Edina, the first enclosed mall; huge indoor water parks; and the giant Mall of America in Bloomington, with its 5.4 million square feet, 500-plus stores, 85 eating options, 14 movie screens, 25 rides, and 11,000 year-round employees. The mall attracts 40 million people annually. Phase Two, with another 5.6 million square feet, has been planned to appeal to upscale patrons who travel a greater distance; construction was delayed by changes in financing. To the west is Eden Prairie, with its 17 lakes, which Money magazine has named the best medium-sized U.S. city. For years, this was a high-growth area. That trend slowed in the 2010 census when 26 suburbs in the Twin Cities area lost population. But the metro area had an 8 percent increase from 2010 to 2017, including many cities in the 3rd District. Work began in November 2018 on the 14.5 mile extension of the Green Line light-rail from Eden Prairie to Target Field, the downtown Minneapolis home of baseball's Minnesota Twins, with completion expected in 2023.

The 3rd Congressional District of Minnesota consists mostly of the Hennepin County suburbs of the Twin Cities. Less than 20 percent of the district is in parts of Anoka and Carver counties. On the north side of the district is working-class Brooklyn Park, long a Democratic-Farmer-Labor Party stronghold, where professional wrestler-turned-governor Jesse Ventura began his political career as mayor. On the south is middle-income Bloomington. To the west are Edina, Plymouth, Wayzata and other towns around Lake Minnetonka, all traditionally Republican. The 3rd is the home of Minnesota's traditional Republican establishment. Like many Northern suburban districts, it has moved toward the Democrats in recent years. For many years, the district had been close to evenly matched in presidential contests. In 2016, Hillary Clinton led by a wider margin, 50%-41%.

Betty McCollum (DFL)

Elected 2000, 10th term, b. Jul 12, 1954; Minneapolis; Saint Catherine University, B.S., 1986; Roman Catholic; Divorced; 2 children.

Elected Office: N. State Paul City Council, 1986-1992; MN House, 1992-2000.

Professional Career: Teacher; Retail Sales & Management.

DC Office: 2256 RHOB 20515, 202-225-6631, Fax: 202-225-1968, mccollum.house.gov

State Offices: St. Paul, 651-224-9191.

Committees: *Appropriations*: Agriculture, Rural Development, FDA & Related Agencies; Defense; Interior, Environment & Related Agencies (Chmn).

Group Ratings

	ADA	ACLU	AFL-CIO	LCV	ITI	COC	HAFA	ACU	CFG	FRC
2018	-	86%	-	97%	-	67%	6%	4%	2%	0%
2017	100%	C	92%	100%	C	43%	C	7%	5%	0%

Key Votes of the 115th Congress

1. Obama-care revision	N	5. Family planning regs	N	9. Guantanamo prisoners	Y
2. Tax Cuts	N	6. Body cameras/immigration	Y	10. Ground missiles, limit	Y
3. Omnibus appropriations	Y	7. Abortion ban	N	11. Defense Dept. spending	Y
4. Dodd-Frank revision	N	8. Concealed carry	N	12. FISA rules	N

Election Results

Election	Name (Party)		Vote (%)	Cand. Spent	Ind. Exp. Support	Ind. Exp. Oppose
2018 General	Betty McCollum (D)	216,865	(66%)	$883,013	$1,639	
	Greg Ryan (R)	97,747	(30%)	$19,299	$5,000	
	Susan Pendergast Sindt (LMNP)	13,776	(4%)			
2018 Primary	Betty McCollum (D)	86,842	(91%)			
	Muad Hassan (D)	5,398	(6%)			

Prior winning percentages: 2016 (58%), 2014 (61%), 2012 (62%), 2010 (59%), 2008 (68%), 2006 (70%), 2004 (58%), 2002 (62%), 2000 (48%)

Democrat Betty McCollum, first elected in 2000, has been an assertive voice as a senior member of the Appropriations Committee, where she chairs an influential subcommittee and sometimes works with Republicans. McCollum has been an ally of Speaker Nancy Pelosi, whom she calls a mentor.

McCollum grew up in North St. Paul and graduated from the College of St. Catherine. She was a substitute social studies teacher, while working as a retail sales manager at a Sears department store and raising two children. After her daughter suffered a fractured skull in a fall from a slide in a city park, McCollum worked with local officials to add sand to soften the area around the slide. She ran for the North St. Paul City Council and was elected on her second try. In 1992, she was elected to the state House after defeating incumbents in both the primary and general elections.

When the congressional seat opened, McCollum was endorsed by the Democratic-Farmer-Labor Party. She faced three opponents in the primary. With the DFL's backing, McCollum won 50 percent to 23 percent for state Sen. Steve Novak. Republicans nominated state Sen. Linda Runbeck, a vigorously anti-abortion candidate. McCollum opposed cutting taxes before Congress paid down the national debt. Runbeck, who took conservative positions on health care and education, attacked McCollum and her Democratic allies for running "hateful, vicious attack ads." Former Ramsey County prosecutor Tom Foley, a longtime DFLer, ran on Gov. Jesse Ventura's Independence Party. Once again, McCollum won unexpectedly easily, 48%-31%, with 21 percent for Foley.

McCollum has a staunchly liberal voting record. Her Almanac vote ratings have ranked her among the most liberal 10 percent of the House. As chair of the Appropriations Interior-Environment Subcommittee, she has jurisdiction over one of her longtime interests: funding for Indian tribes across the nation, especially for school construction. She has sought to limit cutbacks at the Environmental Protection Agency and the National Park Service, including spending for the National Mall. "I don't make headlines," she told the Pioneer Press. "A lot of stuff I work on is not visible to the public." McCollum has advocated major changes in Appropriations operations, including an end to the practice of adding policy-focused "riders" to spending bills and the reinstatement of "earmarks" for specific projects rather than continued control by the executive branch. Minnesota Attorney General Keith Ellison, who served 12 years in the House with McCollum, told the Star-Tribune in January 2019, "It's a small group of people [who Pelosi takes into her confidence] and Betty is one of those people."

McCollum has taken firm stands on limiting federal support for professional sports. She was successful in ending military support for NASCAR, a passion in the Republican-dominated South. "The Defense Department said it didn't have anything that could be cut. Seven million dollars to sponsor a car and we're cutting cops, we're cutting teachers, we're cutting programs for homeless vets?" she told The New York Times. The move triggered hate mail and angry blog posts, but the Army joined the Navy and Marine Corps in 2013 in abandoning the sponsorships. In December 2018, she appeared to shut down an attempt by Dan Snyder, owner of the Washington Redskins, to arrange a land swap to win approval for a new football stadium on federal parkland. In part, she objected to the team's name as offensive to Native Americans. "That's not something the federal government should be condoning, encouraging or be a part of," she told The Washington Post.

McCollum has highlighted splits among Minnesotans, including Democrats, with her proposal to restrict most copper-nickel mining in the national forest near Minnesota's Boundary Waters Canoe Area Wilderness. In January 2019, she objected to a proposal by the Trump administration to renew mineral leases at the site. McCollum told the Star-Tribune that her action illustrated her plan, as subcommittee chair, "to be putting a spotlight on stuff they're trying to roll back."

McCollum has taken an interest in overseas issues. Encouraging lawmakers to view the World Bank more positively, she founded a caucus advocating more dialogue with the global financier. In December 2018, she won enactment of her proposal for increased funds to combat global tuberculosis, malaria and AIDS, especially among children. She has filed legislation to prohibit Israel, which she said in a 2018 speech practiced "apartheid," of using U.S. funds for "the military detention, interrogation, abuse or ill treatment of Palestinian children."

McCollum has been reelected easily. In a routine rematch with Republican Greg Ryan in 2018, she increased her vote to 66 percent, from 58 percent in 2016. After having earlier run even with Ryan in Washington County, which cast one-fourth of the total vote, she got 55 percent in 2018. In Ramsey, she took 70 percent.

MN-4: Twin Cities   **Cook Partisan Voting Index: D+14**

Population		Race and Ethnicity		Income	
Total	701,130	White	67.5%	Median Income	$66,041
Land area (sq. miles)	332	Black	9.7%	District Income Rank	128
Pop/ sq mi	2108.7	Latino	6.6%	Poverty Rate	12.7%
Born in State	61.1%	Asian	12.1%	With health insurance	94.2%
		Two or more races	3.3%	Cash public assistance	4.3%
Age Groups		Other	0.7%	Food stamp/SNAP	11.1%
Under 18	23.7%				
18-34	25.2%	**Education**		**Work**	
35-64	37.7%	H.S grad or less	29.4%	White Collar	13.4%
Over 64	13.4%	Some college	27.8%	Sales and Service	39.2%
		College Degree, 4 yr	26.1%	Blue Collar	15.9%
Military		Post grad	16.8%	Government	13.1%
Veteran/ Active Duty	6.2%				

2012 Pres. Vote	Obama	231,511	(62%)	Romney	131,521	(35%)		
2016 Pres. Vote	Clinton	223,803	(61%)	Trump	111,163	(30%)	Johnson	13,513 (4%)

St. Paul: Above the Mississippi River bluffs stand St. Paul's two most distinctive landmarks: the Minnesota state capitol and Archbishop John Ireland's Cathedral of St. Paul. The city's origins are more colorful than its pious name and status as state capital might imply. Its original name was "Pig's Eye," after the tavern set up by the first European settler in the area, Pierre "Pig's Eye" Parrant. The area was settled mainly by Catholic Irish and German immigrants in the 1850s, as opposed to the Protestant Swedes and Yankees who settled Minneapolis. St. Paul became a major transportation hub, a railroad center and river port, while Minneapolis, upriver at the Falls of St. Anthony, became the nation's largest grain milling center. Both industries stoked the ire of farmers in the Dakotas who were forced to deal with them to make a living. With the large curve in the river, St. Paul borders a longer stretch of the Mississippi than any other city. Beneath the capitol and the cathedral, the skywalk-linked downtown is home to the Ordway Center for the Performing Arts, the headquarters of Minnesota Public Radio.

Beyond the cathedral is Summit Avenue, on which capitalists like the Great Northern Railway's James J. Hill built grandiose Romanesque houses. Along with Monument Avenue in Richmond and Meridian Street in Indianapolis, (two other state capitals) it remains one of America's grand 19th century residential boulevards. The parallel Grand Avenue is home to a pleasant commercial strip with a walkable, urban feel. The Minnesota state fairgrounds are in nearby Falcon Heights, where each year a new "Princess Kay of the Milky Way" is crowned; she and the other finalists sit in a walk-in cooler for six hours while their effigies are carved into 90-pound blocks of butter.

The area has become home to Hmong immigrants, some of whom were recruited by the Central Intelligence Agency during the Vietnam War and resettled here after Laos fell to the communists in 1975. From 2010 to 2017, the Asian population of Ramsey County grew by 16,000 persons and 27 percent, while the white population grew by about 6,000 and less than 1 percent. More than 30,000 in the county spoke Hmong. A spacious indoor marketplace on St. Paul's east side called Hmong Village caters to their shopping. In 2017, the first Hmong-American was elected as a county judge. Ramsey County grew 7 percent from 2010 to 2017, a notable increase from the previous decade. In October 2018, plans were unveiled to redevelop a 122-acre site in Highland Park that had been an assembly plant for Ford autos until 2011 and will include 3,800 housing units. Also underway is residential redevelopment along the riverfront in an area that had been the home of West Publishing.

Minnesota's 4th Congressional District is based in St. Paul. Even before the Democratic-Farmer-Labor Party was formed in 1944, St. Paul was a firmly Democratic part of Minnesota. The 4th includes all of Ramsey County, which hasn't voted for a Republican presidential candidate since it narrowly went for Calvin Coolidge in 1924. In 2016, it was the strongest Democratic county in the state. To the north, it takes in two-thirds of Washington County, which is more evenly balanced politically. To the east are the St. Croix River and Wisconsin. The 61 percent for Hillary Clinton in 2016 was consistent with recent Democratic performance — though not so Democratic as Minneapolis and the 5th District to the west.

Ilhan Omar (DFL)

Elected 2018, 1st term, b. Oct 04, 1982; Mogadishu, Somalia; University of Minnesota; North Dakota State University, B.A., 2011; Muslim; Married (Ahmed Hirsi); 3 children.

Elected Office: MN House, 2012-2018

Professional Career: Community Health Educator, University of Minnesota & MN Department of Education; Senior Policy Aide, Minneapolis City Council.

DC Office: 1517 LHOB 20515, 202-225-4755, omar.house.gov

State Offices: Minneapolis, 612-333-1272.

Committees: *Budget. Education & Labor*: Higher Education & Workforce Investment; Workforce Protections. *Foreign Affairs*: Africa, Global Health, Global Human Rights & Internat'l Orgs; Oversight & Investigations.

Election Results

Election	Name (Party)	Vote (%)		Cand. Spent	Ind. Exp. Support	Ind. Exp. Oppose
2018 General	Ilhan Omar (D)	267,703	(78%)	$819,609	$69,835	
	Jennifer Zielinski (R)	74,440	(22%)	$19,426	$2,500	
2018 Primary	Ilhan Omar (D)	65,237	(48%)			
	Margaret Kelliher (D)	41,156	(30%)			
	Patricia Torres Ray (D)	17,629	(13%)			

Freshman Democrat Ilhan Omar was elected with one of the most unlikely congressional profiles. After Rep. Keith Ellison unexpectedly decided to run for state attorney general on the eve of the filing deadline, the Somali-born Omar was the most adept candidate in the 10-week primary to succeed him in the heavily Democratic district. She easily defeated opponents with more political experience and became one of several Democratic women from minority groups who won House seats in 2018 as relative newcomers to politics. Like Ellison, Omar is Muslim. With Rep. Rashida Tlaib of Michigan, she was one of the first two Muslim women elected to the House.

After escaping the capital of Mogadishu during the Somalia civil war in 1991, when she was eight years old, Omar lived with her family in a Kenyan camp of 30,000 refugees for four years before emigrating to the United States; her mother had died earlier. Referring to her grandfather's position as director of Somalia's National Marine Transport, Omar was quoted in a 2016 profile of her in the Minneapolis City Pages, "You go from knowing a life of certainty and joy to one where everything is uncertain."

Settling in Minneapolis, which has attracted a large Somali community, Omar developed an interest in politics while she was in high school and became an interpreter for her grandfather at local meetings. After graduating from North Dakota State University, she used her background in nutrition and public health issues to work with community groups and political figures. In 2016, she defeated a longtime Democratic representative to win a seat in the state House.

Following Ellison's decision to leave the House, the early party frontrunner was Margaret Kelliher, a former state House Speaker who narrowly lost the Democratic-Farmer-Labor nomination for governor to Mark Dayton in 2010. In an editorial that endorsed Kelliher to succeed Ellison, the Minneapolis Star Tribune noted Omar's "compelling life story," but said that her "accomplishments are lean," with "apparent overstatement on her campaign website." Omar, who was endorsed by Minneapolis Mayor Jacob Frey and other local political leaders, described herself as "the bold, progressive voice we need" and "an organizer."

In an early sign of shifting local politics, Omar won the non-binding endorsement of the DFL convention; Kelliher did not compete. The showdown was "a tug-of-war not over ideology, but between old guard and new guard," the Minneapolis Post reported. When Ellison spoke to the convention and asked how many of the delegates participated in the 2006 convention that nominated him, "perhaps a dozen" of the roughly 200 participants raised their hand.

The primary became a contest between "a consensus-oriented dealmaker" and the activists of "the multicultural left," Steven Scheier, a political science professor at Carleton College, told the

Post. Omar and Kelliher were the biggest spenders in the six-candidate primary contest, with a bit more than $500,000 each. With a large turnout of 135,000 voters, Omar won with 48 percent of the vote to 30 percent for Kelliher. Patricia Torres Ray, a Latina who had served 12 years in the state Senate, got 13 percent.

Omar's rapid political rise was a striking success for Somali immigrants. During a campaign stop in Minnesota on the eve of the 2016 election, Donald Trump had described them as "dangerous" and said that some were "spreading their extremist views." Omar, a strong critic of Trump, called the nation's immigration system "fundamentally unjust." Their clashing approaches are symptomatic of the nation's rapidly changing politics.

Soon after taking office, Omar became the center of controversy for multiple incidents of remarks that many other House Democrats condemned as anti-Semitic or hostile to American supporters of Israel. In March, the House responded by passing a resolution, with virtually unanimous support, that condemned all forms of hate. Speaker Nancy Pelosi was slow to defend Omar when she was widely criticized for referring to the September 2001 attacks on the United States as "some people did something." Some House Republicans demanded that Democrats remove Omar from her seat on the Foreign Affairs Committee.

MN-5: Twin Cities   Cook Partisan Voting Index: D+26

Population		Race and Ethnicity		Income	
Total	702,022	White	63.1%	Median Income	$58,693
Land area (sq. miles)	136	Black	16.5%	District Income Rank	188
Pop/ sq mi	5174.9	Latino	9.2%	Poverty Rate	16.4%
Born in State	55%	Asian	6.2%	With health insurance	92.2%
		Two or more races	3.9%	Cash public assistance	5.9%
Age Groups		Other	1.1%	Food stamp/SNAP	13.1%
Under 18	20.8%				
18-34	31.4%	**Education**		**Work**	
35-64	36.3%	H.S grad or less	28.4%	White Collar	11.5%
Over 64	11.5%	Some college	26.8%	Sales and Service	38.7%
		College Degree, 4 yr	28.2%	Blue Collar	14.7%
Military		Post grad	16.5%	Government	11.5%
Veteran/ Active Duty	5.4%				

2012 Pres. Vote	Obama	274,635	(73%)	Romney	89,643	(24%)		
2016 Pres. Vote	Clinton	273,402	(73%)	Trump	68,535	(18%)	Johnson	12,558	(3%)
	Stein	7,522	(2%)					

Minneapolis: From almost nowhere in Minneapolis today can you see the geographic feature that created the city: the Falls of St. Anthony, where rapids still course beneath low downtown bridges. In olden days, every riverboat had to stop here — these are the only significant waterfalls on the upper Mississippi River — and the waterpower generated by the falls was the energy source first for the pioneers' grist mills and then for the giant grain mills that processed northern Great Plains wheat into food for the United States. By 1890, Minneapolis and St. Paul made up one of America's largest urban areas, living mainly off grain. Today, grain is still important to Minneapolis; after all, the headquarters for General Mills is located in nearby Golden Valley. But Minneapolis is also a center of high technology, banking and finance. In a 2015 story in The Atlantic, headlined "The Miracle of Minneapolis," writer Derek Thompson argued that "fiscal equalization" accounts for the success. "By spreading the wealth to its poorest neighborhoods, the metro area provides more-equal services in low-income places, and keeps quality of life high just about everywhere."

The city of Minneapolis and a few of its older suburbs make up the 5th Congressional District. In the southwest corner are the affluent neighborhoods around Lake Calhoun and Lake Harriet -- long built-up and proudly maintained. Not far away are Minneapolis' skywalk-laced downtown skyscrapers and the museum quarter on the hill above Hennepin Avenue. Straddling the Mississippi is the University of Minnesota, which has fostered the area's cutting-edge biotechnology research and medical innovations, and nearby Dinkytown, a student area where Robert Zimmerman discovered folk music and reinvented himself as Bob Dylan. The Witch's Hat Water Tower in Prospect Park is believed to be the inspiration for Dylan's classic "All Along the Watchtower." Left-leaning in its politics, the area is a product of Minneapolis's unique brand of liberalism, which is drawn from the

Yankee tradition of clean government, the Scandinavian tradition of cooperative enterprise, and the industrial-labor tradition of economic redistribution. In 2017, the city became one of the first in the nation to set a $15 minimum wage. Economic growth has accelerated in recent years. The expected population increase of about 40,000 between 2010 and 2020 would be the largest for Minneapolis since 1950, when the city peaked at 522,000. Tourism has been strong, including the Super Bowl in less than balmy February 2018. The MSP airport expects to complete a $1.6 billion renovation in 2022. The city's development plan for 2040 envisioned an increased supply of affordable housing and more population density around transit stations.

Most of the 5th District has been low on the income scale. Except for a small section of Anoka County near Coon Rapids, all of the district is in Hennepin. Many of the working-class neighborhoods of small frame houses and ample parks are now kept up by new immigrants, and 37 percent of the district is nonwhite, the highest percentage in the state. To the northeast, behind the railroad and warehouse district along the Mississippi, are many Hmong from Laos. Hennepin County is also home to increasingly influential African immigrants, including many Somalis, and Brooklyn Center has a large concentration of Liberians. The Jewish community here has increased with immigrants from the former Soviet Union. The resulting district is the most heavily Democratic in the state. Hillary Clinton won 73 percent of the vote in 2016.

Thomas Emmer (R)

Elected 2014, 3rd term, b. Mar 03, 1961; South Bend, IN; Saint Thomas Academy (MN); Boston College (MA), Att., 1980; University of Alaska, Fairbanks, B.A., 1984; William Mitchell College of Law (MN), J.D., 1988; Roman Catholic; Married (Jacqueline Samuel Emmer); 7 children.

Elected Office: Independence City Council, 1995-2002; Delano City Council, 2003-2004; MN House, 2004-2010 (Deputy Minority Leader, 2007-2008).

Professional Career: Attorney; radio talk show host.

DC Office: 315 CHOB 20515, 202-225-2331, Fax: 202-225-6475, emmer.house.gov

State Offices: Otsego, 763-241-6848.

Committees: National Republican Congressional Committee Chairman. *Financial Services*: Investor Protection, Entrepreneurship & Capital Markets; Nat'l Security, International Development & Monetary Policy.

Group Ratings

	ADA	ACLU	AFL-CIO	LCV	ITI	COC	HAFA	ACU	CFG	FRC
2018	-	18%	-	0%	-	75%	72%	76%	69%	100%
2017	0%	C	16%	0%	C	93%	C	89%	88%	100%

Almanac Ratings 2017-18

	Economy	Social	Foreign	Composite
Liberal	3%	7%	3%	4%
Conservative	97%	94%	97%	96%

Key Votes of the 115th Congress

1. Obama-care revision	Y	5. Family planning regs	Y	9. Guantanamo prisoners	N
2. Tax Cuts	Y	6. Body cameras/immigration	N	10. Ground missiles, limit	N
3. Omnibus appropriations	N	7. Abortion ban	Y	11. Defense Dept. spending	Y
4. Dodd-Frank revision	Y	8. Concealed carry	Y	12. FISA rules	N

Election Results

Election	Name (Party)	Vote (%)		Cand. Spent	Ind. Exp. Support	Ind. Exp. Oppose
2018 General	Tom Emmer (R)............................	192,931	(61%)	$1,598,756	$18,101	
	Ian Todd (D).....................................	122,332	(39%)	$75,151	$921	$2,500
2018 Primary	Tom Emmer (R).............................	34,250	(77%)			
	A.J. Kern (R).....................................	7,897	(18%)			
	Patrick Munro (R).........................	2,575	(6%)			

Prior winning percentages: 2016 (66%), 2014 (56%)

Republican Tom Emmer, elected in 2014, is a former talk-show host and an ardent conservative. He settled in comfortably and sought far less attention than his predecessor, Michele Bachmann, the tea party leader and one-time presidential contender. Emmer's occasional cooperation with party leaders was rewarded following the 2018 election with the challenging assignment to chair the National Republican Congressional Committee. He likely will be judged on whether Republicans regain House control in November 2020.

Emmer was born in South Bend Indiana, where his father was completing a degree at Notre Dame, and grew up in Edina. He got his bachelor's degree in political science at the University of Alaska, and his law degree from William Mitchell College. His great-grandfather founded a lumber business in Minneapolis that his family continued to run, under the name of Viking Forest Products. Emmer practiced law at his own firm and served on the city councils of Independence and Delano before winning election to the state Assembly. His GOP colleagues voted him deputy majority leader.

In 2010, Emmer easily won the Republican nomination for governor and challenged Democrat Mark Dayton. He staked out a very conservative platform for his blue-leaning state. Along with calls to cut spending and taxes and to promote socially conservative values, he proposed a constitutional amendment requiring a supermajority in the legislature to approve any federal law before it could take effect in the state. The national Republican wave was not quite strong enough to lift him over Dayton, who won by 8,770 votes of the 2.1 million cast. Emmer subsequently launched a radio talk show in the Twin Cities.

After Bachmann announced her retirement in 2013, Emmer was the immediate frontrunner. He coasted to his primary victory with 73 percent of the vote in a low-turnout race. In the general election, which was not seriously contested, Emmer had close to a 10-to-1 fundraising advantage. He won, 56%-38%, and took all eight counties.

Emmer quickly showed that he intended to be a player in Congress, with a willingness to cross party lines. A week after his election, he said that he was impressed with the leadership style of Speaker John Boehner. "I am being very — and I will be very — deliberate," he told USA Today. "I'm here to accomplish something." With Democratic Rep. Grace Meng of New York, he filed a bill to accelerate the visa process for physicians from overseas to work in U.S. hospitals. He helped to organize an effort by freshmen House Republicans to send a letter to President Barack Obama with their support for approval of the Trans-Pacific Partnership. In 2016, he joined the bipartisan congressional delegation that accompanied Obama to Cuba. Citing the potential market for agricultural exports from Minnesota, he called for lifting the U.S. trade embargo on Cuba.

On the Financial Services Committee, Emmer in 2016 won House passage of his bill to reduce the regulatory requirements imposed by the Financial Stability Oversight Council, which the Dodd-Frank law created in 2010. In May 2018, when broader changes were made to Dodd-Frank, that bill included Emmer's provision to adjust disclosure requirements on home mortgages, especially for smaller lending institutions. The reforms, he said, "will empower individual Americans and give them more opportunity." He was among the lawmakers who joined President Donald Trump at the White House signing ceremony.

Emmer disagreed with conservatives who opposed funding the Homeland Security Department to increase their leverage over immigration policy, and warned in 2015 that a government shutdown was a bad idea. "Two wrongs don't make a right," he said. The leader of the Minnesota Tea Party Alliance responded that he was "very disappointed" by his early votes. Emmer defended what he called his incremental approach, and seemed to make a pointed and informed jab at Bachmann, his erstwhile ally, about how to succeed in Congress. "If you want to go out there and make a lot of noise, maybe you're going to get people from all across the country to send you a lot of money, and that's great because then you can increase your own brand. But you'll never change the inside of the building," he told the St. Cloud Times.

After serving In 2017-18 as one of two deputy chairs of the NRCC, where he focused on its future operations, Emmer was unopposed for chairman following the 2018 election. He voiced optimism about GOP prospects and minimized the implications of the party's 40-seat House loss in 2018. "There's a narrative that people are trying to build out there that somehow there's been this shift, this political realignment, in the suburbs," he said in an interview with National Journal. "That's not true. It isn't there." He said that Republicans needed to do a better job with independent voters in highlighting their economic success. Emmer had an early clash with Rep. Elise Stefanik of New York and others who said that House Republicans needed to be more aggressive in seeking women candidates. He said that it would be "a mistake" for the NRCC to take sides in GOP primaries. Stefanik tweeted in response: "NEWSFLASH…I wasn't asking for permission."

Emmer's collaboration with the more establishment wing of his party could position him for another run for statewide office, perhaps an eventual bid for the Senate, though the uphill challenges for Republicans in Minnesota might be an incentive to seek additional influence in the House. Emmer has been reelected easily. In 2016, he got 69 percent of the GOP primary vote against two opponents, including an outspoken critic of immigration policy.

MN-6: Twin Cities Exurbs   Cook Partisan Voting Index: R+12

Population		Race and Ethnicity		Income	
Total	694,849	White	89.7%	Median Income	$76,698
Land area (sq. miles)	2,882	Black	3%	District Income Rank	65
Pop/ sq mi	241.1	Latino	2.7%	Poverty Rate	7.2%
Born in State	77.7%	Asian	2.3%	With health insurance	96.2%
		Two or more races	1.9%	Cash public assistance	2.4%
Age Groups		Other	0.5%	Food stamp/SNAP	6.3%
Under 18	25.8%				
18-34	22.1%	**Education**		**Work**	
35-64	40.4%	H.S grad or less	33%	White Collar	11.7%
Over 64	11.7%	Some college	37.4%	Sales and Service	39.8%
		College Degree, 4 yr	21%	Blue Collar	24%
Military		Post grad	8.5%	Government	10.8%
Veteran/ Active Duty	7.9%				

2012 Pres. Vote	Romney	205,652	(56%)	Obama	151,238	(41%)			
2016 Pres. Vote	Trump	218,546	(59%)	Clinton	123,329	(33%)	Johnson	15,314	(4%)

St. Cloud: The earliest settlers of Minneapolis and St. Paul lived within walking distance of the mills and factories and rail yards where they worked. As the first streetcars and then automobiles allowed them to live farther from their jobs, they spread out in the Twin Cities and then all around the lake-strewn countryside. The flatlands are bleak here when the winter sun struggles to pierce gray clouds, but even so, the creativity and productivity of Minnesotans have turned the countryside into some of the nation's most pleasant suburbs. Taking maximum advantage of their lakes, they refurbished old towns and farmhouses and built comfortable homes in new subdivisions.

The 6th Congressional District of Minnesota is a suburban and exurban area north and west of St. Paul and Minneapolis. It includes a mix of upscale and working-class suburbs in Anoka County, which has about one-third of the voters. More distant, up the Mississippi River, are Wright, Sherburne and Benton counties, which have nearly doubled from a combined total of 141,000 people in 1990 to 269,000 in 2017. Electrolux Co., which has been headquartered in St. Cloud since the 1940s, announced in January 2018 that it will shut down its local plant and consolidate its freezer production in Anderson South Carolina, with an expected local loss of 1,800 jobs. In February 2018, the Catholic Diocese of St. Cloud declared bankruptcy to facilitate its payment of sex-abuse claims against clergy members. Similar actions were taken earlier by the dioceses in Minneapolis, St. Paul and Duluth.

The district includes the eastern half of St. Cloud-based Stearns County, a heavily German-Catholic area and a stronghold of anti-abortion sentiment. The city is 81 percent white, but its demographics have changed. The 1990s brought an influx of Vietnamese, Chinese and Japanese immigrants. Since they first arrived in 2000, more than 10,000 Somalis have moved in and started businesses or worked at local meat-processing plants. Many of them have settled in St. Cloud from elsewhere in the United States after learning of the tight-knit local Somali community. As a group, they are disproportionately young and many have struggled economically. Federal and local investigators have reviewed charges that Somalis in the public schools of St. Cloud have suffered civil rights violations, and there have been allegations of bullying of young Somalis. Business leaders have sought to educate local citizens about the Somali culture. In September 2016, there were new tensions following a knife attack in which a Somali injured 10 at a local mall before he was shot and killed by an off-duty police officer. A year later, the city council rejected on a 6-to-1 vote a resolution to call for an end, at least temporarily, to resettlement of refugees in St. Cloud; it approved an alternative in support of the city as a "just and welcoming community."

The district is solidly Republican. Donald Trump got an overwhelming 58%-33% win, his second-largest Minnesota margin.

Collin Peterson (DFL)

Elected 1990, 15th term, b. Jun 29, 1944; Fargo, ND; Moorhead State University (MN), B.A., 1966; Lutheran; Single3 children; 4 grandchildren.

Military Career: U.S. Army National Guard 1963-1969

Elected Office: MN Senate, 1976-1986.

Professional Career: Accountant, 1966-1990.

DC Office: 2204 RHOB 20515, 202-225-2165, Fax: 202-225-1593, collinpeterson.house.gov

State Offices: Detroit Lakes, 218-847-5056; Marshall, 507-537-2299; Redwood Falls, 507-637-2270; Thief River Falls, 218-683-5405; Willmar, 320-235-1061.

Committees: *Agriculture (Chmn)*: Ex Officio membership on all subcommittees. *Veterans' Affairs*: Health; Oversight & Investigations.

Group Ratings

	ADA	ACLU	AFL-CIO	LCV	ITI	COC	HAFA	ACU	CFG	FRC
2018	-	42%	-	20%	-	82%	28%	39%	41%	75%
2017	40%	C	62%	14%	C	85%	C	26%	12%	56%

Key Votes of the 115th Congress

1. Obama-care revision	N	5. Family planning regs	Y	9. Guantanamo prisoners	Y
2. Tax Cuts	N	6. Body cameras/immigration	N	10. Ground missiles, limit	Y
3. Omnibus appropriations	N	7. Abortion ban	Y	11. Defense Dept. spending	Y
4. Dodd-Frank revision	Y	8. Concealed carry	Y	12. FISA rules	Y

Election Results

Election	Name (Party)	Vote (%)		Cand. Spent	Ind. Exp. Support	Ind. Exp. Oppose
2018 General	Collin Peterson (D)	146,672	(52%)	$1,477,349	$2,583	
	Dave Hughes (R)	134,668	(48%)	$215,468	$43,000	
2018 Primary	Collin Peterson (D)		(100%)			

Prior winning percentages: 2016 (53%), 2014 (54%), 2012 (60%), 2010 (55%), 2008 (72%), 2006 (70%), 2004 (66%), 2002 (65%), 2000 (69%), 1998 (72%), 1996 (68%), 1994 (51%), 1992 (50%), 1990 (54%)

Collin Peterson, first elected in 1990, is one of the few conservative "aggies" left in the increasingly progressive, diverse and metropolitan Democratic Caucus. He has the dubious honor of holding the Democratic seat that leans most heavily Republican and he often has stymied the hopes of GOP political operatives. With his impressive longevity, he regained his chairmanship of the Agriculture Committee, where he works well with like-minded lawmakers in both parties representing rural regions. "I am just a country boy, and I am doing the best I can," he once said.

Peterson grew up on a farm in Baker, just across the Red River from Fargo North Dakota. He graduated from Moorhead State College, then started a certified public accounting business in Detroit Lakes. In 1976, he was elected to the state Senate. In 1982, he ran for the House but lost in the Democratic-Farmer-Labor Party caucus, then set out to prove that he's nothing if not persistent. He tried three more times, losing to Republican Arlan Stangeland in 1984 and 1986 (by only 121 votes that year) and losing a DFL primary in 1988. In 1990, when the St. Cloud Times reported that Stangeland made 341 credit card calls to a woman who was not his wife, Peterson won with a robust 54 percent of the vote.

In office, Peterson has been known as a free spirit, wearing cowboy boots and playing guitar in a bipartisan rock band called the Second Amendments. He has performed with Willie Nelson at Farm Aid concerts and he has co-chaired the Rock and Roll Caucus with Democratic Rep. Marcia Fudge of Ohio. He is candid with Capitol Hill reporters, sometimes revealing more about the thinking of Republicans than do GOP lawmakers themselves. He has acted as his own campaign consultant and pilot, flying his single-engine plane to stops around the district.

Peterson regularly has had the distinction of the most conservative voting record of any House Democrat, according to the Almanac vote ratings. On environmental issues, he takes the view of his constituents, who hunt and fish as a way of life and often see environmentalists' policies as hindrances. He has supported lifting trade restrictions on Cuba, a move favored by farmers eager for another export market. He backs labor unions, a vital Democratic constituency. He has supported Speaker Nancy Pelosi on the theory, he said, that only a liberal can tell liberals what to do. Their cooperation has been mutually rewarding.

When Peterson first chaired Agriculture in 2007, he had a bumpy time. "There were people in my party who were skeptical of me taking that position. I was seen as a renegade, a maverick," he told National Journal in 2013. He had been a skeptic of the Republicans' 1996 Freedom to Farm Act and he joined the bipartisan majority that restored government controls when the farm program was renewed in 2002. In the mid-2000s, Peterson called for extending the Conservation Reserve Program to keep millions of additional acres of farmland idle to produce switchgrass and plant waste that could be used to make ethanol.

Peterson has regularly worked with Republicans to achieve many of his goals on several farm bill since then. It has not always been easy. In 2008, it took six short-term extensions of the bill and two votes to override President George W. Bush's veto. Peterson sought an income limit of $900,000 annually for subsidy payments, and the final deal set a ceiling of $750,000 for farmers receiving direct payments. It also barred payments to persons with more than $500,000 in nonfarm income. He finally got his permanent disaster fund so that farmers could get their aid more quickly following a drought or flood. Peterson, the former accountant, has proved adept at figuring the costs of commodity programs.

Many of Peterson's views are a throwback to earlier political times. A fiscal conservative and founding member of the Blue Dog Coalition, he opposed many of President Barack Obama's major initiatives. In his Republican-leaning district, Peterson voted against both the 2009 economic stimulus bill and the Affordable Care Act, and in favor of dozens of GOP attempts to repeal the latter. With Dan Lipinski of Illinois and Stephen Lynch of Massachusetts, he is among three remaining Democrats in the House who voted against the health care overhaul. He voted against the New Year's Day 2013 budget deal aimed at averting the so-called "fiscal cliff" and supports a balanced-budget constitutional amendment. He opposes abortion rights and gun control.

Peterson has been cooperative on a few big issues, but generally only after extracting legislative concessions. He said in 2009 that the Democrats' cap-and-trade bill to limit carbon emissions was "an urban-dominated bill" that catered to the environmental lobby. As part of his support for the deal, Peterson insisted that the Agriculture Department, rather than the Environmental Protection Agency, oversee the carbon emissions offset program for farmers. The bill passed the House, but it died in the Senate.

In 2010, on the major financial industry regulatory bill, Peterson struck an agreement with Financial Services Chairman Barney Frank of Massachusetts that preserved for the Commodity Futures Trading Commission some oversight of agricultural commodities trading. The deal stopped Frank's committee from grabbing jurisdiction of the commission.

Peterson had hoped a five-year farm bill could be passed in 2012, but that task became impossible because House Budget Committee Chairman Paul Ryan's GOP budget blueprint called for unacceptably steep reductions while ending direct payments to farmers. Another complication arose over Peterson's desire to come up with a new program for the dairy industry. His proposal would let the government manage the milk supply by setting production limits for farmers enrolling in a market-stabilization program. House Speaker John Boehner derided his measure as "Soviet-style" management of the farm program. In 2014, Congress cleared a bill that accommodated Peterson and most Democrats with only small trims in food-stamp programs.

On the farm bill that was enacted in 2018, Peterson once again played a balancing role between the farm interests on the Agriculture Committee and congressional Democrats who firmly opposed cutbacks in food stamps. He resisted attempts by both sides to tilt the measure their way and said that its enactment was "a miracle," though the final agreement passed overwhelmingly in both the House and Senate. He took credit for, among other things, "expanded, affordable risk management options for dairy farmers" and "permanent, mandatory funding for priorities like the Local Food & Farmers Market Promotion Program."

Taking over in 2019 as Agriculture chairman, Peterson said that his priorities were oversight of the Trump administration's implementation of the new farm bill and steps to limit Trump's trade war with China, which he said was "taking a toll on Minnesota manufacturers and farmers." He voiced hostility toward the support by many Democrats for climate-change legislation. "I think a lot of them would like us to quit farming," he told Politico in January 2019. With Reps. Bennie Thompson of Mississippi at the Homeland Security Committee and Nydia Velazquez of New York at Small Business, Peterson is one of three chairmen who previously held their post.

Republicans have been eager for Peterson to retire, which they believe would make it nearly certain that they would take his seat. He typically has won reelection easily. Despite the Republican wave in 2010, Peterson prevailed 55%-38%. Four years later, Republicans were confident they could finally beat him. The National Republican Congressional Committee recruited state Sen. Torrey Westrom; outside groups poured millions into ads depicting Peterson as out of touch for his use of a taxpayer-subsidized plane to get around his district. Peterson touted his work on the farm bill and won, 54%-46%, his closest margin in 20 years. Peterson was not intimidated. "They [Republicans] energized me last time, they got me fired up," he told the Star Tribune. In two contests since then against lightly financed David Hughes, a former Air Force officer, Peterson was held to 52 percent. In September 2018, Trump tweeted his endorsement of Hughes against "Pelosi liberal puppet Peterson." He seems unlikely to survive beyond the 2022 round of redistricting, when Minnesota likely will lose a House seat.

MN-7: Western Minnesota   Cook Partisan Voting Index: R+12

Population		Race and Ethnicity		Income	
Total	663,307	White	89%	Median Income	$54,863
Land area (sq. miles)	33,429	Black	1.3%	District Income Rank	231
Pop/ sq mi	19.8	Latino	4.5%	Poverty Rate	11.4%
Born in State	72.5%	Asian	0.8%	With health insurance	94%
		Two or more races	1.6%	Cash public assistance	3%
Age Groups		Other	2.7%	Food stamp/SNAP	8.5%
Under 18	23.5%				
18-34	20.3%	**Education**		**Work**	
35-64	37.5%	H.S grad or less	41.9%	White Collar	18.7%
Over 64	18.7%	Some college	36.2%	Sales and Service	37.8%
		College Degree, 4 yr	15.8%	Blue Collar	29.5%
Military		Post grad	6%	Government	13.6%
Veteran/ Active Duty	8.8%				

2012 Pres. Vote	Romney	180,334	(54%)	Obama	147,750	(44%)			
2016 Pres. Vote	Trump	208,215	(61%)	Clinton	104,566	(31%)	Johnson	12,523	(4%)

Moorhead: The fabled Mississippi River begins modestly in Minnesota's Itasca State Park, 2,552 miles from the Gulf of Mexico. At that point, it can be crossed by foot on stepping-stones. The country in which the river begins has made its own contributions to American literature. More than a century ago, Sinclair Lewis grew up in the town of Sauk Centre, which provided grist for his critical but affectionate portrayals of small-town America in Main Street and Babbitt. In those years, this seemingly placid country was seething with rage, as WASP nationalists banned German from schools, renamed sauerkraut "liberty cabbage," and boycotted German-American businesses. This was also once prime logging country. Although that industry is in long-term decline here, Bemidji is still home to giant statues of Paul Bunyan and Babe the Blue Ox. On the North Dakota border is Moorhead, the largest city in the district (pop. 43,000). Moorhead was the planned destination of Ritchie Valens,

Buddy Holly and J.P. "The Big Bopper" Richardson when their airplane took off from Clear Lake
Iowa in a snowstorm in 1959; the plane crashed, and singer/songwriter Don McLean committed Feb.
3 to the ages as "the day the music died." Moorhead has regained prominence as the site — with
Fargo, across the Red River -- of a planned 30-mile flood-diversion project that has been designed to
prevent a recurrence of the devastating floods of 1997 and 2009, and has been projected to cost more
than $2 billion. The two states have designed the dam so that the new channel would flow mostly
through North Dakota.

This is great farming country, the start of the wheat fields that sweep across the Dakotas and into
Montana. Even today, farmers toil against the elements to make a profitable living, although many
acres have been taken out of production by the federal Conservation Reserve Program. Farmers have
turned to corn and soybeans, which have more markets and uses. This area is the nation's leading
producer of sugar beets and a leading supplier of turkeys. On the banks of Plum Creek, near Walnut
Grove, is where Laura Ingalls Wilder's family came on the way west to South Dakota in the Little
House books. Southwest of Walnut Grove is Pipestone National Monument. Native Americans have
used rocks collected from the quarries here to make ceremonial pipes for centuries. In Pipestone
County, the largest solar project in Minnesota — covering 390 acres -- is projected for completion
in 2020.

The 7th Congressional District of Minnesota covers almost all the western part of the state. Its
southeastern corner extends to 30 miles from Minneapolis. From the Canadian border to the southern
end of the district is roughly a 400-mile drive. It takes in the wheat-farming plains adjoining North
Dakota as well as exurban German Catholic areas, with their farm villages named for saints. This has
been the fourth most productive farm district in the nation.

In a benchmark of cultural change, DFL Rep. Coya Knutson was defeated for reelection in this
district in 1958 when her husband, Andy, issued a plaintive statement urging her to come home from
Washington and make his breakfast again. She was the only incumbent Democrat to lose in that
heavily Democratic year; they divorced shortly thereafter. In 2016, the 7th had a new distinction:
Donald Trump took it, 61%-31%, the most Republican district in the state and the most Republican
district in the nation that elected a Democrat in 2016.

Pete Stauber (R)

Elected 2018, 1st term, b. May 10, 1966; Duluth; Lake Superior State
University, B.S., 1988; Catholic; Married (Jodi Stauber); 4 children.

Elected Office: Hermantown City Council, 2001-2005; City
of Hermantown, MN Council, 2011-2013; Saint Louis County
Commissioner, 2013-2018.

Professional Career: Area Commander, Duluth Police Department,
1995-2017; Player, Detroit Red Wings NHL Hockey Team.

DC Office: 126 CHOB 20515, 202-225-6211, stauber.house.gov

State Offices: Brainerd, 218-355-0862; Cambridge, 763-552-3359;
Chisholm, 218-355-0726; Hermantown, 218-481-6396.

Committees: *Small Business*: Contracting & Infrastructure (RMM); Economic Growth, Tax &
Capital Access. *Transportation & Infrastructure*: Aviation; Highways & Transit; Railroads, Pipelines
& Hazardous Materials.

Election Results

Election	Name (Party)	Vote (%)	Cand. Spent	Ind. Exp. Support	Ind. Exp. Oppose
2018 General	Pete Stauber (R)............................	159,364 (51%)	$1,726,805	$311,146	$1,009,373
	Joe Radinovich (D)........................	141,950 (45%)	$2,361,006		
	Ray Sandman (Ind.)........................	12,741 (4%)	$20,995		

Freshman Republican Pete Stauber was a notable exception in the 2018 election: He replaced a
Democratic member of the House, Rick Nolan, who exited under pressure at home following three
recent terms (plus three terms in the 1970s, prior to his initial retirement). Stauber benefited from the

shifting politics of Minnesota and the popularity of President Donald Trump in rural America. As a former elite hockey player and longtime police officer who had become active in local government, he mirrored the values of the Northland.

A native of Duluth, Stauber became well-known for his hockey exploits in high school and at Lake Superior State University, where his team was the national collegiate champion. A highlight of that experience—and the spur to his political career — came when President Ronald Reagan hosted the team at the White House. Stauber played three years of minor-league hockey in the Detroit Red Wings organization — chiefly for Adirondack in the East Coast Hockey League. He and his five brothers owned a summer hockey camp and a sporting-goods store in Duluth.

With his bachelor's degree in criminal justice, Stauber joined the Duluth Police Department, where he eventually became an area commander and served 22 years. While an officer, he was shot twice in separate incidents and was president of the local law-enforcement union. He entered politics as a city council member for eight years in suburban Hermantown (population, 9,513). In 2012, he was elected to the Duluth-based St. Louis County Commission.

When Nolan retired, after barely surviving two narrow reelections, Stauber quickly became the consensus choice of local Republicans. He embraced the district's abundant natural resources, which often have been politically controversial. "I'm the only candidate who will make the following statement: I support iron ore and precious metal mining," he told the International Falls Journal newspaper. The Obama administration had imposed a moratorium on mining in the local Boundary Waters wilderness area. Under President Donald Trump, local iron production got a boost from his increased tariffs on steel imports; he also lifted some of the Boundary Waters restrictions.

In the GOP primary, perennial candidate Harry Welty criticized Stauber as "a Trump cheerleader." That wasn't a problem for Republican voters, who gave Stauber 90 percent of the vote.

Democratic nominee Joe Radinovich, previously a state representative and Nolan's campaign manager, separated himself from Stauber on some issues. He criticized the tax cut that congressional Republicans enacted in 2017 and defended tax increases that he supported when he was in the Legislature. Citing tragedies in his family that resulted from firearms incidents, Radinovich said that he backed stronger background checks on gun sales. Responding to campaign ads that cited a criminal charge that was filed against him for marijuana use when he was a teenager, which subsequently was dropped, he said during a debate, "I've made mistakes in my life and I think that makes me more human."

In an inexpensive media market, the contest drew large expenditures from outside groups, plus comparable spending from the two candidates. The Democratic Congressional Campaign Committee cut back its support in October, following polls that showed Stauber with a comfortable lead. Stauber won 51%-45%, though Radinovich took 57 percent of the vote in Duluth-based St. Louis County, which cast one-third of the vote.

Stauber was only the second Republican elected in this district since 1946. The other one was defeated in 2012, after having served one term. That should be a lesson for him not to take the seat for granted.

MN-8: Northeastern Minnesota   Cook Partisan Voting Index: R+4

Population		Race and Ethnicity		Income	
Total	663,113	White	91.9%	Median Income	$53,950
Land area (sq. miles)	27,908	Black	1%	District Income Rank	243
Pop/ sq mi	23.8	Latino	1.7%	Poverty Rate	12.3%
Born in State	78.9%	Asian	0.8%	With health insurance	94.4%
		Two or more races	2.1%	Cash public assistance	3.6%
Age Groups		Other	2.5%	Food stamp/SNAP	9.9%
Under 18	21.3%				
18-34	19.8%	**Education**		**Work**	
35-64	39.9%	H.S grad or less	40.1%	White Collar	19%
Over 64	19%	Some college	36.9%	Sales and Service	42.1%
		College Degree, 4 yr	15.6%	Blue Collar	25.5%
Military		Post grad	7.4%	Government	14.4%
Veteran/ Active Duty	10.3%				

2012 Pres. Vote	Obama	186,761	(52%)	Romney	166,977	(46%)		
2016 Pres. Vote	Trump	194,779	(54%)	Clinton	138,665	(38%)	Johnson	12,618 (4%)

Duluth, Northern Twin Cities: In the 1860s, prospectors in Minnesota's Arrowhead region, northwest of Lake Superior in the low hills of the Mesabi Range, happened upon one of the nation's largest veins of iron ore. They moved on, looking for gold. But in the 1880s, Duluth banker George Stone and Philadelphia financier Charlemagne Tower started mining the Iron Range. Rail lines were built southward to the port of Duluth to carry the ore, plus abundant grains, to freighters for shipment across the Great Lakes. With its signature aerial lift bridge traversing its shipping channel, Duluth is nestled on dramatic bluffs over the often frozen waters of Lake Superior — one of the most beautiful settings for a city in North America, though also one of the most isolated. Its city plan was drawn up by architect Daniel Burnham, who also planned Chicago, and its splendid turn-of-the-century buildings still celebrate the triumph of technology and civilization over wilderness and the elements.

For most of the 20th century, about 100,000 people lived on the Iron Range and another 100,000 in Duluth, most of them descendants of America's 1880-1924 wave of immigration: Italians, Poles, Serbs, Croats, Swedes, Finns and Eastern European Jews. In this punishing environment, they built solid houses with reliable central heating. The work was hard, the hours long and the pay low. The churches were the main community institutions. Even after living conditions improved vastly in the booming growth following World War II, periods of economic distress persisted. More efficient iron mines and steel mills needed fewer workers. The Trump administration in September 2018 gave what the Minneapolis Star-Tribune described as "a major victory" to the local mining industry when it reinstated two long-expired mineral leases near the Boundary Waters Canoe Area Wilderness. Environmental groups and some local businesses filed lawsuits. Many in the industry also welcomed the tariffs that President Donald Trump imposed on steel imports. At a political rally in Duluth in June 2018, Trump said that winning Minnesota in the 2020 presidential election would be "really, really easy."

The port still ships large quantities of grain. Rising commodity prices brought new mining companies to the area to explore extraction of copper, nickel and other nonferrous metals. The new airport terminal in Duluth was dedicated in 2015 in honor of former local Democratic Rep. Jim Oberstar, who chaired the Transportation and Infrastructure Committee, from which he steered much of the financing for the project. The terminal has spurred economic development, including resorts for adventure tourists. The new sports competition included the winter ultra-marathon, a 135-mile endurance contest of walking, running, cycling and skiing from International Falls to Tower.

The 8th Congressional District of Minnesota includes Duluth and the Iron Range, plus much of the state's north woods and lake country to the west and south. Duluth-based St. Louis County is the largest in the district, with about 30 percent of the voters. The population in the county and Duluth has remained flat for three decades. The district extends south to the boundaries of the Twin Cities metro area, to Isanti and Chisago counties, where young families are building new homes in pleasant old lakeside towns. Those fast-growing exurban and largely Republican counties have become an increasingly dominant part of the district, even as the Duluth area remains Democratic. From 1946 through 2008, the district elected only two congressmen, both Democrats. Oberstar had worked for the first, John Blatnik, who chaired the same committee. Issues like gun control and environmental regulation have sometimes moved those areas toward the Republicans. As with the two other rural districts in Minnesota that surround the Twin Cities metro area on three sides, the 2016 election brought a huge shift. In a district that President Barack Obama in 2012 took, 52%-46%, Donald Trump won 54%-38%.

MISSISSIPPI

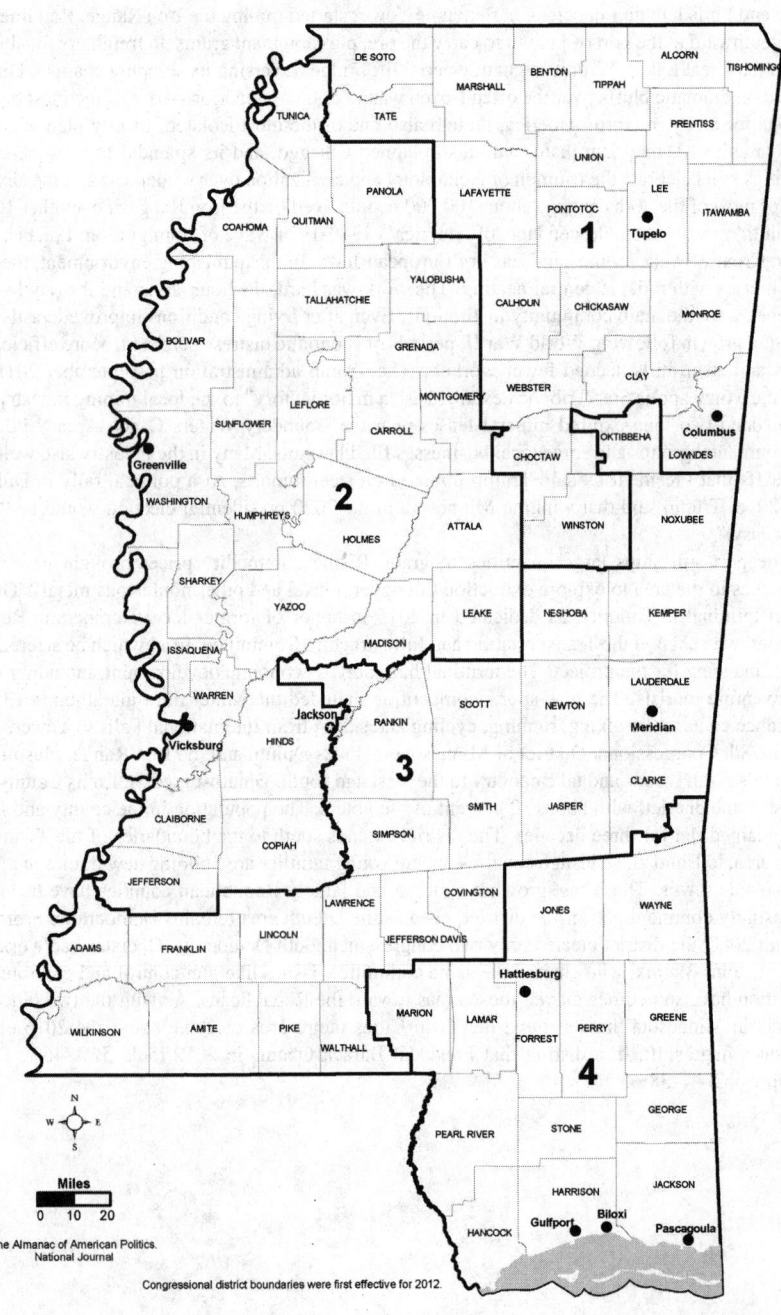

The Almanac of American Politics.
National Journal

Congressional district boundaries were first effective for 2012.

In 2018, Mississippi demonstrated that it was not immune from the nation's political trends – but also that it felt them much more weakly than other parts of the country. In a special Senate election, African-American Democrat Mike Espy improved his party's performance across the state, and particularly in its urban and suburban areas. But the heavily rural state still handed Republican Cindy Hyde-Smith an eight-point special election victory.

This green land was settled in a rush in Jacksonian America, mostly by small farmers heading west from Georgia and south from Tennessee, and also by a few big planters who made, and sometimes lost, vast fortunes, built grand mansions, brought thousands of slaves in ship holds and coffles, and sent their sons to fight in the Civil War. For a century afterward, as planters and engineers drained the Delta lands, Mississippi -- with its racial segregation, subsistence farmers, sharecroppers and low wages -- lived apart from most of America. William Faulkner's Mississippi never knew giant factories, the rushes of immigration, or the burgeoning of the suburbs that characterized much of 20th-century America. Mississippi never developed great cities: Its two commercial hubs, Memphis and New Orleans, lie just outside its borders.

But if Mississippi did not thrive in commerce, it did produce great art. Mississippi gave us the blues (from the impoverished Mississippi Delta south of Memphis) and Elvis Presley (who was born in Tupelo). It produced writers like Faulkner, Eudora Welty, Walker Percy and Shelby Foote. The state with a low literacy rate has produced an inordinate number of Pulitzer Prize winners for literature. These authors' works were informed by a sense of the tragic that is less evident in other parts of America, where life is a triumphant sales pitch or a labor-saving invention. For years, no other state had such a painful contrast between image and reality, between an ideal sincerely strived for and the tawdry facts of everyday life. Gracious trees on the lawns of antebellum mansions and golden-haired women in white dresses on the veranda, alongside black servants and retainers: This was once the ideal, at least for some. Behind the ideal stood loose-jointed frame houses and unpainted back-country stores, shotgun shacks without plumbing, and poor white crossroads. As author David Sansing wrote, "We at one time have the scent of magnolias and the smell of burning crosses."

Mississippi still ranks low on many quality-of-life scales. It had the nation's worst-performing health care system as rated by the Commonwealth Fund and 49th by the United Health Foundation, and its schools were rated 47th in the nation by Education Week. Still, the gulf between Mississippi and the rest of the country has narrowed. In recent years, the state has done particularly well in vaccinating its children, and it has cut teenage births significantly. Per capita income in Mississippi was 36 percent of the national average in 1940. But it had risen to 67 percent in 1990 and to about 70 percent today -- still well below average but, given its lower cost of living, a level recognizably American. Nearly every classroom in the state is air-conditioned and is wired for the internet.

In 1940, Mississippi had an economy based on low-wage, subsistence, or sharecropper agriculture and a system of racial segregation often enforced by violence. The economy once depended on cotton, but no longer: In the mid-20th century, mechanization spawned a mass migration of African Americans from Mississippi to northern industrial cities like Chicago, profoundly changing both. Manufacturing jobs have declined here as elsewhere in recent years, but northeast Mississippi around Tupelo remains the center of the nation's upholstered furniture industry, and the state ranks in the top 10 for automotive manufacturing jobs, including a Nissan plant in Canton, just north of Jackson, a Toyota plant in Tupelo, a Yokohama Tire facility in West Point, and a $1.5 billion Continental Tire plant near Jackson. DeSoto County, in the Memphis suburbs, saw its population grow by 10 percent between 2010 and 2017, while two suburban counties near Jackson – Rankin and Madison – grew by 7 percent and 10 percent, respectively. Statewide, however, the population has increased by less than 1 percent in that period. Sociologist Mimmo Parisi of Mississippi State University pegs the low growth rate to the decline in teenage births and the fact that Mississippi is not a magnet for Hispanics. At 3 percent, Mississippi has the smallest percentage of Hispanics in the South.

The Gulf Coast has big military installations, with Air Force intelligence units and the Navy's Seabees, as well as the Stennis Space Center. The huge Ingalls shipyard is in Pascagoula, and many of the military's and CIA's unmanned aerial vehicles are built on the Gulf Coast or in Columbus. In the mid-1960s, the United States even conducted a pair of nuclear tests in salt domes 28 miles southwest of Hattiesburg, the only such blasts east of the Rockies. Then there is gambling. Mississippi approved it in 1990, and big companies have built casinos in economically struggling Tunica County south of

Memphis, on riverboats on the Mississippi River, and on the Gulf Coast. Gambling brings in more than $2 billion a year in direct revenues, but Mississippi casinos are threatened by the expansion of gambling in neighboring states. The state has fallen from third to seventh nationally in casino gaming revenue since 2007, and gaming revenues fell 2 percent from 2016 to 2017.

Mississippi's economy has faced other travails over the last decade. The main force of Hurricane Katrina made landfall in Hancock County, where in 2005 it wiped out the towns of Waveland and Bay St. Louis. In a few hours, waves up to 55 feet high destroyed one-quarter of the structures in Biloxi and Gulfport; floodwaters swept 10 miles inland, and the storm ultimately killed 238 people in Mississippi. More quickly than New Orleans, Mississippi set about rebuilding its coast, though in 2016 the federal government suspended reimbursement of almost $30 million of recovery funds due to insufficient state oversight. Further disaster struck with major floods in 2011 and a massive tornado outbreak in 2014 that killed 14 and destroyed hundreds of structures.

An older generation would be astonished by relations between whites and blacks, who make up 38 percent of the population – the highest of any state. Forty years ago, blacks held no public offices in Mississippi. Voters in recent years have elected many black officials, most of them in local or school board posts, including black mayors in Vicksburg, Jackson, Hattiesburg, Greenville and Natchez. In recent years, more than a quarter of the legislature was African-American – a national high – and perhaps spurred by memories of the franchise denied, black turnout rates in Mississippi have exceeded white turnout in some recent elections. After four decades, prosecutors hunted down and tried Ku Klux Klan members who had killed civil rights activists in the 1960s. Former Republican Gov. Haley Barbour signed bills authorizing a civil rights curriculum in public schools and a civil rights museum in Jackson, which opened in 2017. The Jackson airport is named for the assassinated civil rights leader Medgar Evers. In 2013, Mississippi belatedly ratified the 13th amendment to the U.S. Constitution, which abolished slavery in 1865.

But race has hardly disappeared as an issue; it still hovers over everyday interactions in Mississippi to a degree it doesn't in most other places, and it remains uncomfortably present in some Mississippi elections. In 2000, voters approved a ballot measure to remove the ban on interracial marriage from the state constitution — but a full 41 percent voted to keep the no-longer-enforced language on the books. A year later, 65 percent of voters chose to retain the Confederate battle cross — a symbol offensive to many — in the state flag. Such skirmishes have continued, with mixed results. In 2016, Republican Gov. Phil Bryant issued a proclamation designating April as Confederate Heritage Month -- without mentioning slavery.

Once almost unanimously Democratic but ready to support breakaway segregationist presidential candidates like Strom Thurmond in 1948 and George Wallace in 1968, Mississippi is now reliably Republican. It was Richard Nixon's No. 1 state in 1972, Ronald Reagan gave a high-profile speech at the Neshoba County Fair in 1980, and it has been solidly Republican in presidential elections since then. Republicans have held both Senate seats since John Stennis retired in 1988. On the federal level, Democrats now control only the black-majority district the party has held since 1986 and which Rep. Bennie Thompson has represented since 1993; it includes the Delta and much of metro Jackson.

A turning point in the state's shift from Democratic to Republican leadership came in 2003, when Haley Barbour, emphasizing his Yazoo City roots over his decades as a Washington powerbroker, unseated Democratic Gov. Ronnie Musgrove. Barbour was re-elected in 2007 and by 2011 both chambers of the legislature had switched from Democratic to Republican control. That same year, Lt. Gov. Phil Bryant beat Hattiesburg Mayor Johnny DuPree, the first black Democratic gubernatorial nominee, 61%-39%. Bryant easily won reelection in 2015. Today, Attorney General Jim Hood is the only statewide elected Democrat. Voting in Mississippi runs along racial lines, with whites heavily Republican in most contests and blacks heavily Democratic. In 2014, black support arguably carried aging and comparatively moderate Sen. Thad Cochran to victory in a hard-fought Senate primary runoff against tea party-aligned Chris McDaniel.

Mississippi has often sought to enact a cutting-edge conservative agenda. In 2016, Bryant signed legislation to allow guns to be carried in belt and shoulder holsters without a permit, and to let churches allow certain parishioners to carry concealed weapons on their premises. That same year, Bryant signed a law to allow government officials and businesses cite religious objections to refuse some services to same-sex couples, and in 2018, he signed a ban on abortion after 15 weeks of gestation. The courts, however, haven't always gone along, ruling the LGBT law and the abortion law unconstitutional. In 2019, the legislature and Bryant tried again, enacting a "fetal heartbeat" bill that would be even stricter than the previous measure.

In 2018, the special election runoff to succeed Cochran, who had resigned due to poor health, attracted an unusual degree of national interest. The race pitted appointed Republican Sen. Cindy Hyde-Smith, a white cattle farmer and former state agriculture commissioner, against Democrat Mike Espy, an African-American former congressman and agriculture secretary. Hyde-Smith took heat for supporting laws that "make it just a little more difficult" for some voters to cast a ballot and for posing with Confederate symbols. Espy tended not to play up these episodes on the campaign trail. With the press doing much of that work for him, he mostly stuck to policy differences. Hyde-Smith ended up winning, 54%-46%, but her share of the vote fell by six percentage points compared with Cochran's 2014 victory and by four points from Donald Trump's win in 2016. Espy garnered 71 percent more votes than the Democratic Senate nominee had in 2014, and he increased his winning margin in Hinds County (Jackson) by 19 percentage points while cutting into the GOP's winning margins in four other populous counties – Rankin (suburban Jackson), Harrison and Jackson (the Gulf Coast), and DeSoto (suburban Memphis) – by between five and eight percentage points. But this improvement was incremental, not game-changing, for the Democrats. "While other states, with smaller African-American populations, have elected statewide leaders, the glass ceiling in Mississippi has remained not only impervious but unreachable," wrote Jimmie Gates in the Jackson Clarion-Ledger.

Population		Race and Ethnicity		Income	
Total	2,986,220	White	57.0%	Median Income	$42,009
Land area (sq. miles)	46,923	Black	37.5%	State Income Rank	50
Pop/ sq mi	63.6	Latino	3.0%	Poverty Rate	21.5%
Born in state	71.5%	Asian	1.0%	With health insurance	86.4%
		Two or more races	1.1%	Cash public assistance	2.5%
Age Groups		Other	0.5%	Food stamp/SNAP	17.3%
Under 18	24.3%				
18-34	23.2%	Education		Work	
35-64	37.9%	H.S grad or less	47.0%	White Collar	31.5%
Over 64	14.6%	Some college	31.7%	Sales and Service	41.1%
		College Degree, 4 yr	13.3%	Blue Collar	27.3%
Military		Post grad	8.0%	Government	18.1%
Veteran/ Active Duty	8.1%				

Presidential Politics

2016 Primary (D)	Clinton (D)	187,334 (82%)	Sanders (D)	37,748 (17%)			
2016 Primary (R)	Trump (R)	196,659 (47%)	Cruz (R)	150,364 (36%)	Kasich (R)	36,795	(9%)
	Rubio (R)	21,885 (5%)					
2016 Pres. Vote	Trump (R)	700,714 (58%)	Clinton (D)	485,131 (40%)			
2012 Pres. Vote	Romney (R)	710,746 (55%)	Obama (D)	562,949 (44%)			

Mississippi voted for Jimmy Carter in 1976 and came within 12,000 votes of doing so again in 1980. But starting in 1984, Democratic presidential nominees have won between only 37 and 44 percent here. The state's Delta region with its heavy African-American population hugs the Mississippi River and votes Democratic. The rest of the state, stretching from Tupelo in the north, to the suburban Jackson counties of Madison and Ranking, to Biloxi on the Gulf Coast, votes Republican. Mississippi followed its historical norm in 2016: Donald Trump defeated Hillary Clinton 58%-40%.

Mississippi has held a presidential primary in the second week of March since 1988. The 2016 GOP contest saw a record turnout of 416,270 votes, with Trump defeating Texas Sen. Ted Cruz, 47%-36%. Ohio Gov. John Kasich finished a distant third. Trump won 75 of the state's 82 counties; Cruz won the other seven. On the Democratic side, African Americans accounted for more than 70 percent of the primary electorate, and their overwhelming support gave Clinton an 83%-17% victory. In the 2nd and 3rd districts, Bernie Sanders didn't break the 15 percent threshold needed to qualify for convention delegates. Democratic turnout was 227,164, barely half of the 434,000-plus record Democratic turnout in 2008.

Congressional Districts

116th Congress Lineup	1D 3R	115th Congress Lineup	1D 3R

Redistricting in Mississippi has become relatively straightforward. Of its four districts, three typically have at least a 60 percent Republican vote in presidential elections and the 2nd District — with its African-American majority — has at least a 60 percent Democratic vote. With GOP control of the governor and legislature expected to continue, Republicans have reason to remain satisfied. And the African-American community likely will be wary of options to attempt to spread its strength over two districts in this racially polarized state with a 38 percent black population. Adding to that challenge, the population of the 2nd has lagged behind the other three districts since 2010.

The dynamics following the 2010 census had an unusual procedural twist. Some Republicans were fearful that the Obama Justice Department would deny approval to any map that didn't create a second African-American seat. So they filed suit asking federal judges to step in, because any map drawn by a federal court did not need to win Justice Department sign-off. The end-around worked. When the legislature failed to meet its deadline, the court put its own proposal into place. The map made only minor changes. Mississippi has not had a competitive election for a House district during this decade. That pattern likely will continue.

Phil Bryant (R)

Elected 2011, term expires 2020, 2nd term; b. Dec. 9, 1954, Moorhead; U. of Southern MS, B.S. 1977, MS Col., M.S. 1988; Methodist; Married (Deborah); 2 children.

Elected Office: MS House, 1991-1996; State Auditor, 1999-2008; MS Lt. Governor, 2008-2011.

Professional Career: Deputy Sheriff, Hinds County Sheriff's Office, 1976-1981; Insurance investigator, 1981-91; State auditor appointee, 1996-1999.

Office: 550 High St, Jackson, 39205; 601-359-3150; Fax: 601-359-3741; Website: governorbryant.ms.gov.

Lt. Gov.: Tate Reeves (R) **Atty. Gen:** Jim Hood (D) **Sec. of State:** Del Hosemann (R)

State Legislature: Senate: 19D, 33R House: 45D, 74R, 2I, 1V

Election Results

Election	Name (Party)	Vote (%)
2015 General	Phil Bryant (R)...	476,697 (66%)
	Robert Gray (D)...	231,643 (32%)
2015 Primary	Phil Bryant (R)...	254,779 (92%)
	Mitch Young (R)...	22,628 (8%)

Prior winning percentage: 2011 (61%)

Mississippi Gov. Phil Bryant, elected in 2011 and reelected four years later, is a Republican who succeeded term-limited Haley Barbour. Bryant had served as lieutenant governor under Barbour, and he has pleased conservatives with his willingness to go even further to the right than his patrician predecessor, especially on social issues.

Bryant was born in Moorhead in the Mississippi Delta. His father was a diesel mechanic and his mother a homemaker. His family eventually relocated to South Jackson, where Bryant finished high school. He worked in a tire store to earn extra money and decided that he needed more schooling. "Changing tires five-and-a-half days a week made me decide I would check out community college," Bryant told the Biloxi-based Sun Herald. He later earned a bachelor's degree in criminal justice from the University of Southern Mississippi. Bryant worked as a deputy sheriff and later spent time in the private sector as an insurance investigator.

Bryant first ran for office in 1991, winning a state House seat in Rankin County. In 1996, he was appointed state auditor by Republican Gov. Kirk Fordice. Bryant was elected to two full terms as auditor in 1999 and 2003 before being elected on the Barbour ticket as lieutenant governor in 2007. He became a favorite of tea party groups for his tough stance on illegal immigration. Bryant presided over the state Senate, which put him in the middle of some heated legislative battles, including redistricting in 2011. With Barbour term-limited, Bryant sought to succeed him. Despite his ties to the popular incumbent, Bryant had to fight off four other candidates in the Republican primary. He won with 59 percent, exuding more of a common touch than Barbour but less national influence. In the general election, Bryant faced Democrat Johnny DuPree, mayor of Hattiesburg and the state's first African-American gubernatorial nominee. The campaign was relatively low-key and congenial. Bryant won easily, 61%-39%.

Bryant's state budget proposal called for cutting his own office expenses, and he later sold the state jet, which Barbour had used extensively, for $2 million (though he kept a prop plane). On social issues, he signed into law a bill requiring all physicians at abortion clinics to be board-certified gynecologists and to have admitting privileges at a local hospital. Amid unemployment rates persistently above the national average, Bryant was a tireless promoter of economic development, and he used conservative talk radio to promote his agenda.

On health care, Bryant squabbled for months with state Insurance Commissioner Mike Chaney over whether to establish an insurance exchange under the Affordable Care Act. Bryant's position — that the state not set up an exchange — won out. Then, after the Supreme Court allowed states to opt out of the law's Medicaid expansion provision, Bryant pushed passionately against expanding Medicaid in Mississippi, though his opposition was not shared by residents. A January 2019 Millsaps College/Chism Strategies survey found that 60 percent of Mississippi voters backed Medicaid expansion, with 29 percent opposed.

In 2014, Bryant signed three bills curbing organized labor, which was already weak in the state. "Just to be blunt about it: We just don't want unions involved in our businesses or our public sector," Bryant said upon signing the bills. He also signed a bill to allow residents to carry concealed guns without a permit. On criminal justice, he signed a bill requiring convicts to serve at least 50 percent of their sentence, and at least 25 percent for those convicted of a nonviolent offense — a less stringent requirement than previously, and with added flexibility for judges to impose sentences that don't include incarceration. One aim was to reduce the cost of a corrections budget that had been growing rapidly.

In 2015, Bryant burnished his conservative credentials, criticizing the federal government for its "troubling" decision to send roughly 200 of the 30,000 unaccompanied children who crossed the U.S.-Mexico border to family members or guardians in Mississippi, and vetoing a bill critical of Common Core educational standards because it wasn't tough enough. Bryant was already coasting to a reelection victory in 2015 when the Democratic primary produced a stunner – Robert Gray, a truck driver and political novice who had barely campaigned, managed to beat the establishment-backed candidate, trial lawyer Vicki Slater, by 20 points. In November, Bryant won, 67%-32%, in a race mostly overshadowed by the battle over a ballot measure that would have stiffened enforcement of a law that required certain levels of K-12 education funding. The measure failed.

After winning reelection, he signed a tax cut totaling $415 million over 12 years, including a phase-out of the state's corporate franchise tax, an increase in the threshold for paying income taxes, and cuts to self-employment taxes. He also pursued a solidly conservative social agenda, including a law allowing businesses and government officials to deny some services to LGBT couples that had drawn objections from some business leaders; in October 2016, a federal court found the law unconstitutional. Meanwhile, Bryant said he would "do everything humanly possible to stop any plans from the Obama administration to put Syrian refugees in Mississippi." Bryant was one of a handful of sitting governors to campaign for Donald Trump, and he raised money for the GOP nominee in Mississippi.

Bryant began 2017 by instituting his fourth round of budget cuts or withdrawals from the state's "rainy day" fund in two years. Bryant also had to grapple with rising costs for Medicaid – part of the reason he had opposed expansion, and also part of the reason why Bryant decided to push for a state lottery, an idea that had bounced around for decades but had historically faced opposition from religious groups and the casino industry. After a hiccup in the state House, Bryant and his allies were able to get a bill passed during a special session in August 2018. The measure directed up to $80 million a year for 10 years for roads and bridges, with any excess going to public education. Opponents were able to kill a proposal to permit video gambling. The special session approved earmarking 35 percent of the state's online sales tax for bridge replacement and authorizing $300 million in borrowing and proceeds from sports betting to support infrastructure improvements. The session also approved a plan for allocating the state's $750 million settlement from the BP oil spill, with three-quarters going to coastal counties and one-quarter going to interior counties.

He signed a ban on abortion after 15 weeks of gestation – one of the nation's most restrictive laws – though it was eventually blocked in the courts. Bryant also signed a law that banned sanctuary cities, saying that state and municipal entities and colleges could not bar employees from asking about someone's immigration status. Its effect was largely symbolic, however, since only one city, Jackson, had established such a policy, and the state has one of the smallest foreign-born populations in the country. Bryant also signed legislation to end the use of prisons to incarcerate people who were unable to pay their fines or other court fees. But Bryant vetoed a bill that would have ended the practice of stripping driver's licenses from drug offenders; prison officials had expressed concern about a separate provision that would have eased the supervision fees paid by inmates who were released from prison.

Bryant continued strengthening his ties with Trump – he was one of several governors who collectively nominated Trump for the Nobel Peace Prize in 2018. But he worried the White House with his appointment that year of the relatively unknown Cindy Hyde-Smith to the Senate seat vacated by Thad Cochran. Bryant made some enemies among the right flank of the GOP by freezing out Chris McDaniel, who narrowly lost a challenge to Cochran in 2014 and had been seeking a way into the Senate. McDaniel initially sought to challenge GOP Sen. Roger Wicker, who faced reelection in 2018, but when Cochran announced his departure, McDaniel switched to that race. When Bryant tapped Hyde-Smith, McDaniel refused to step aside. McDaniel's "opportunistic behavior," Bryant said, "is a sad commentary for a young man who once had great potential." McDaniel failed to make the runoff in the all-party special election. Bryant didn't seem to be hurt by the spat; his approval rating remained robust, and Hyde-Smith won the Senate runoff in November, though not without turbulence. Bryant also appointed some younger policy wonks who are expected to carry on his legacy – Shad White as state auditor and Andy Gipson as secretary of agriculture and commerce.

In 2019, Bryant signed a strict "fetal heartbeat" bill, despite the prospect of a long court battle to enforce it. "we will all answer to the good lord one day," he tweeted. "I will say in this instance, 'I fought for the lives of innocent babies, even under the threat of legal action.'" Meanwhile, Bryant is term-limited. His lieutenant governor, Tate Reeves, has been the heavy favorite for the Republican nomination. While the Democratic bench in Mississippi is thin, Attorney General Jim Hood – a rare Democratic statewide officeholder in the Deep South – is expected to make a credible run.

Roger Wicker (R)

Elected 2007, term expires 2024, 2nd full term, b. Jul 05, 1951; Pontotoc; University of Mississippi, B.A., 1973; University of Mississippi, J.D., 1975; Baptist; Married (Gayle Long Wicker); 3 children; 5 grandchildren.

Military Career: U.S. Air Force 1976-198; U.S. Air Force Reserve 1980-2004

Elected Office: Tupelo city judge pro temp., 1986-1987; MS Senate, 1988-1994; U.S. House, 1995-2007.

Professional Career: Staff, U.S House Rules Committee, 1980-1982; Practicing attorney, 1982-1994; Lee County public defender, 1984-1987; Board Of Visitors, U.S Naval Academy, 2005.

DC Office: 555 DSOB 20510, 202-224-6253, Fax: 202-228-0378, wicker.senate.gov

State Offices: Gulfport, 228-871-7017; Hernando, 662-429-1002; Jackson, 601-965-4644; Tupelo, 662-844-5010.

Committees: *Armed Services*: Airland; Cybersecurity; Seapower. *Commerce, Science & Transportation (Chmn)*: Ex Officio membership on all subcommittees. *Environment & Public Works*: Clean Air & Nuclear Safety; Fisheries, Water, and Wildlife; Transportation & Infrastructure. *Rules & Administration*.

Group Ratings

	ADA	ACLU	AFL-CIO	LCV	ITI	COC	HAFA	ACU	CFG	FRC
2018	-	10%	-	7%	-	90%	68%	86%	59%	100%
2017	0%	C	0%	0%	C	86%	C	80%	81%	100%

Almanac Ratings 2017-18

	Economy	Social	Foreign	Composite
Liberal	6%	6%	0%	4%
Conservative	94%	94%	100%	96%

Key Votes of the 115th Congress

1. Obama-care revision	Y	5. Gun regulations	Y	9. Kavanaugh confirmation	Y
2. Tax Cuts	Y	6. Family planning regs	Y	10. Saudi arms sales	N
3. Dodd-Frank revision	Y	7. Gorsuch confirmation	Y	11. FISA rules	Y
4. Omnibus appropriations	Y	8. Immigration restrictions	Y	12. Military aid in Yemen	N

Election Results

Election	Name (Party)	Vote (%)		Cand. Spent	Ind. Exp. Support	Ind. Exp. Oppose
2018 General	Roger Wicker (R)	547,619	(59%)	$6,015,451	$278,125	$76,000
	David Baria (D)	369,567	(40%)	$871,176	$1,501	
2018 Primary	Roger Wicker (R)	130,118	(83%)			
	Richard Boyanton (R)	27,052	(17%)			

Prior winning percentages: 2012 (57%), 2008 (55%), House: 2006 (66%), 2004 (79%), 2002 (71%), 2000 (70%), 1998 (67%), 1996 (68%), 1994 (63%)

History will remember election night 2016 for one of the most monumental upsets at the top of the ballot. Senate Republicans will also recall the time they defended 24 seats, nine in states that Barack Obama carried in either 2008 or 2012, and kept their majority intact. While President Donald Trump's coattails helped, Mississippi's Roger Wicker was praised by his colleagues for his stint as chairman of the National Republican Senatorial Committee, which included raising $120 million over two years. For his efforts, Wicker got a seat at the leadership table of Majority Leader Mitch McConnell. Appointed in 2007 to fill the vacancy created by the resignation of Trent Lott, a powerful Mississippian who had served as both majority and minority leader, Wicker has comfortably been elected twice in a state that has not elected a Democrat to the Senate since 1982.

Even with his leadership role, Wicker has distanced himself from Trump at times, most notably in March 2019, when Wicker was one of 12 GOP senators who voted to overturn the president's declaration of a national emergency on the southern border to get more money for a border wall. Wicker worried that Trump's use of the national emergency law to bypass Congress could set a dangerous precedent. Elsewhere, Wicker has criticized Trump on trade and foreign policy, including when Trump wanted to withdraw U.S. troops from Syria.

Wicker grew up in the North Mississippi town of Pontotoc. His father was a conservative Democrat, a state senator and a circuit judge. He attended public schools and as a teenager became interested in Republican politics. From then on, his career was intertwined with two Mississippians on Capitol Hill: Lott and Thad Cochran. He was a page in the House and campaigned door-to-door for Cochran in his first race for Congress. At the University of Mississippi, Wicker served in student government and earned bachelor's and law degrees. He spent four years in the Air Force Judge Advocate General's Corps.

Wicker worked for Lott on the House Rules Committee. After he returned to Mississippi, he served as the public defender in his wife's hometown of Tupelo. In 1987, he was elected to the state Senate, the first Republican from North Mississippi since Reconstruction. He helped draft the state's strict abortion law and was a leading advocate of government-sponsored vouchers for private school tuition.

In 1994, Democratic Rep. Jamie Whitten retired after having been the longest-serving member of the House and chairman of the powerful Appropriations Committee, leaving big shoes to fill. Pent-up demand produced crowded primaries, attracting six Republicans and three Democrats. On the strength of support from Tupelo, Wicker finished first in the GOP primary and later won the runoff against Grant Fox, a young former aide to Cochran, 53%-47%. He easily defeated Democratic state Rep. Bill Wheeler, 63%-37%, in the general election.

Wicker compiled a solidly conservative voting record in the House. He got a seat on Appropriations, an unusual prize for a freshman. In those days, appropriators retained an atmosphere of bipartisanship. Wicker worked quietly in subcommittees to secure funding for his low-income district, including Yalobusha River flood control and an interstate highway through DeSoto County. He delivered research dollars to Mississippi universities, and he worked with Lott to attract defense technology firms to the state. Citizens Against Government Waste gave him the dubious distinction of No. 1 earmarker in the House for securing $176 million in projects, most of it for his district. "I am a fiscal conservative, and I believe in keeping spending low," Wicker said later. "But once the national budget is set, I think it is only fair to fight for our fair share for Mississippi." He reluctantly supported the GOP's earmark ban in 2011.

In November 2007, Lott announced his resignation from the Senate. Wicker wanted the seat, but so did GOP Rep. Chip Pickering and Netscape founder James Barksdale. Gov. Haley Barbour appointed Wicker. Mississippi Democrats had not seriously contested a Senate race in 20 years, but with renewed hope, they nominated former Gov. Ronnie Musgrove, whom Barbour had ousted in 2003. It was a battle between old friends: Wicker and Musgrove had both been elected to the state Senate for the first time in 1987 and they roomed together in Jackson.

Musgrove criticized Wicker for his support of earmarks and called him a "poster child" for a moratorium on pork-barrel spending. Musgrove hinted at ethical misconduct, criticizing Wicker for securing a $6 million earmark, not sought by the Pentagon, for Aurora Flight Sciences to build drones in North Mississippi. Company executives has contributed $17,000 to his campaign and hired his former chief of staff to lobby for the project. Wicker said the effort was all about bringing high-paying jobs to Mississippi. Wicker outspent Musgrove, $6.2 million to $5.3 million, though the Democratic Senatorial Campaign Committee pumped in more than enough money to compensate. Wicker won 55%-45%; 82 percent of white voters backed Wicker and 92 percent of black voters supported Musgrove.

In the Senate, Wicker has continued his conservative record, especially on social issues. In 2015, he drew attention when he cast the lone "no" vote against Democratic Sen. Sheldon Whitehouse's amendment to get Republicans to acknowledge on record that climate change is occurring. Wicker called it a "gag" and said he agreed "with the more than 31,000 American scientists who do not believe the science on this matter is settled." After Congress voted in 2010 to repeal the "don't ask, don't tell" ban on openly gay service members, Wicker co-sponsored a bill forbidding same-sex marriages on military bases.

Wicker often has had a home-state focus. As chairman of the Armed Services Seapower Subcommittee, he secured funding in the 2016 defense spending bill for a new naval destroyer and a big-deck amphibious ship. Two years later, Trump signed into law Wicker's SHIPS Act, which declared the Navy's official policy to achieve a 355-ship fleet, many of which would be built in Mississippi. On the full committee, he is next in line after Chairman Sen. Jim Inhofe of Oklahoma. On the Commerce Committee, Wicker has sought more broadband access for rural areas and complained that the Federal Communications Commission was setting internet speed artificially high. He was the lead sponsor of a bill to extend a Safe Drinking Water Act program to assist public water systems in small and rural communities, which was enacted in 2015.

Wicker's seat on Commerce would give him a voice in the congressional debate if the Trump administration puts forward a comprehensive infrastructure plan. Wicker called Mississippi's decision to raise its gas tax in 1987 to pay for a state infrastructure bill a "grown-up approach." He has said that he would support increasing the federal gas tax, if Trump supported it too.

In 2012, Wicker defeated Albert Gore — a retired United Methodist minister and distant relative of the former vice president — who ran a bare-bones campaign, 57%-41%. In 2014, he helped Cochran survive an aggressive primary challenge from tea party-backed Chris McDaniel. In the runoff, Cochran narrowly edged McDaniel with outreach to African-American voters.

His assistance for Cochran aided his bid for the NRSC chairmanship. When seeking the post, one of his first calls was to Lott, who told him, "Golly, Roger, why would you want that job?

It's the toughest job in the Senate leadership," Congressional Quarterly reported. As chairman, he faced a formidable task: Republicans were defending 24 seats; Democrats were defending 10. GOP incumbents lost only two seats: in Illinois and New Hampshire, both of which Trump lost.

In 2018, Wicker prepared for McDaniel to try again to oust an incumbent. Unlike Cochran, who was slow to realize the serious challenge, Wicker built a $3.1 million war chest. He stashed away the endorsements of some leaders who backed McDaniel in 2014. The possible sequel was short-lived as Trump endorsed Wicker. A few days later, Cochran announced his resignation and McDaniel ran for the vacant seat. Wicker faced a long-shot challenge from Democratic state House Minority Leader David Baria, who tagged Wicker as "Roger the dodger" for refusing to debate him. The snub made little difference: Wicker won 58%-39%.

Cindy Hyde-Smith (R)

Appointed 2018, term expires 2020, 1st term, Brookhaven, MA; Lawrence County Academy (MS); Copiah-Lincoln Community College (MS), A.A., 1979; University of Southern Mississippi, 1981; Baptist; Married (Michael Smith); 1 child.

DC Office: 702 HSOB 20510, 202-224-5054, Fax: 202-224-5321, hydesmith.senate.gov

State Offices: Gulfport, 228-867-9710; Jackson, 601-965-4459; Oxford, 662-236-1018.

Committees: *Agriculture, Nutrition & Forestry*: Commodities, Risk Management & Trade; Conservation, Forestry & Natural Resources; Livestock, Marketing & Agriculture Security (Chmn). *Appropriations*: Agriculture, Rural Development, FDA & Related Agencies; Department of Homeland Security; Department of the Interior, Environment & Related Agencies; DOL, HHS & Education & Related Agencies; Energy & Water Development; Legislative Branch (Chmn). *Energy & Natural Resources*: Energy; National Parks; Public Lands, Forests & Mining. *Rules & Administration*.

Group Ratings

	ADA	ACLU	AFL-CIO	LCV	ITI	COC	HAFA	ACU	CFG	FRC
2018	-	0%	-	8%	-	86%	N/A	82%	62%	100%

Key Votes of the 115th Congress

1. Obama-care revision	N/A	5. Gun regulations	N/A	9. Kavanaugh confirmation	Y
2. Tax Cuts	N/A	6. Family planning regs	N/A	10. Saudi arms sales	N/A
3. Dodd-Frank revision	N/A	7. Gorsuch confirmation	N/A	11. FISA rules	N/A
4. Omnibus appropriations	N/A	8. Immigration restrictions	N/A	12. Military aid in Yemen	N

Election Results

Election	Name (Party)	Vote (%)		Cand. Spent	Ind. Exp. Support	Ind. Exp. Oppose
2018 General	Cindy Hyde-Smith (R)	486,769	(54%)	$5,109,442	$3,132,460	$1,111,312
Runoff	Mike Espy (D)	420,819	(46%)	$6,975,054	$2,440,281	$3,527,421
2018 General	Cindy Hyde-Smith (R)	389,995	(41%)			
	Mike Espy (D)	386,742	(41%)			
	Chris McDaniel (R)	154,878	(16%)		$731,387	$973,737

In a state that has elected few women, Mississippi Republican Cindy Hyde-Smith has found a way to make her mark. Before joining the Senate, she was the state's first female commissioner of agriculture and commerce. And when Gov. Phil Bryant appointed her to succeed Republican Sen. Thad Cochran, who resigned in March 2018 after serving nearly 40 years, she made history again, this time as the first woman Mississippi sent to Congress. Though the White House, Republican operatives and Senate Majority Leader Mitch McConnell urged Bryant to consider other people, he chose her. And she later won a special election to serve the remainder of Cochran's term — making Mississippi the 49th state to elect a woman to Congress; only Vermont has failed to achieve that distinction.

While Republicans were worried that Hyde-Smith would be slammed for switching parties, it was instead an offhand comment about "attending a public hanging" that presaged a series of stories that turned her campaign against former Agriculture Secretary Mike Espy, a Democrat, into a debate on race in a state that has seen some of the worst racial violence in the nation's history. Espy would have been the first black senator from Mississippi since Reconstruction.

In the Senate, Hyde-Smith has been a reliable Republican vote and rarely critical of President Donald Trump. She literally wrapped his support around her campaign RV as she sought to discourage potential GOP spoilers who could have made a Democratic upset more likely.

Hyde-Smith was born in Brookhaven, Mississippi but grew up east of there in Monticello. Her father, a truck driver, taught her how to drive a tractor when she was seven. Hyde-Smith recalls being a "major tomboy," riding horses and dirt bikes. According to The Washington Post, she met her future husband, Michael Smith, when a customer in her mother's beauty shop set them up on a blind date. She later attended Copiah-Lincoln Community College and graduated from the University of Southern Mississippi with degrees in criminal justice and political science. The couple live in Brookhaven, where Smith's family has raised beef cattle for four generations.

She began her career working for the American Cancer Society in Mississippi. Later, she was a lobbyist in Washington for the National Coalition on Health Care and the Southern Coalition for Safer Highways. She was elected in 1999 to the state Senate, where she built a reputation for working on agricultural issues. As chairwoman of the Agriculture Committee for eight years, she successfully championed legislation to protect farmers from eminent domain after a 2005 Supreme Court decision. In 2010, she switched parties to become a Republican, joining more than a dozen officials who had left the Democratic Party in a two-year span after Barack Obama's election as president. Building on her background as a farmer, Hyde-Smith ran and won her first statewide race to become commissioner of agriculture and commerce in 2011, taking 57 percent of the vote. She won re-election in 2015 with 61 percent.

Cochran, who was first elected to the House in 1972 and the Senate six years later, in recent years had had been the subject of rumors about his fading health. They became public in October 2017 when Politico reported that the 79-year-old appeared frail and confused during a brief interview. As chairman of the Appropriations Committee, he hadn't spoken on the Senate floor all year and had only introduced two minor bills. In late March, he announced his resignation. He died in May 2019.

Hyde-Smith was not among Republicans' top choices for a successor. Bryant and state Secretary of State Delbert Hosemann topped the list. Trump reportedly said he would not endorse Hyde-Smith because of her Democratic past. The other name that loomed was state senator and tea party conservative Chris McDaniel. McDaniel and his supporters were still incensed over what they felt was a stolen Senate seat after his 2014 primary challenge to Cochran fell just short. This time, McDaniel had the backing of former White House chief strategist Steve Bannon, who wanted him to take out Mississippi Sen. Roger Wicker. But Trump endorsed Wicker shortly before McDaniel was expected to announce his primary challenge, leading McDaniel to decide that competing against Hyde-Smith was a better move.

Because it was a special election, there was no primary. So, it would be Hyde-Smith, Espy, McDaniel and little-known Democrat Tobey Bartee on the ballot. Hyde-Smith, the incumbent, carried the support of the National Republican Senatorial Committee and other outside groups aligned with the GOP leadership. The U.S. Chamber of Commerce committed to $750,000 in ads on her behalf. Hyde-Smith slammed McDaniel as a "liar" and refused to debate him saying "my guys are saying that's like handing him a $200,000 campaign donation." McDaniel pushed back, but he lacked the fire he brought in 2014. Hyde-Smith led him 41%-16%. Espy had a surprisingly strong second-place finish, virtually even with Hyde-Smith.

Hyde-Smith appeared to have everything she needed to close out a victory. But on Nov. 11, a video caught her telling a supporter, "If he invited me to a public hanging, I'd be on the front row." The clip was posted on Twitter and went viral. Soon Espy, the NAACP and Democrats demanded an apology for a remark that for many dredged up the worst in the state's history. Several large businesses organizations, including Walmart, Major League Baseball and Pfizer, asked for Hyde-Smith to return their PAC donations.

In response, Hyde-Smith released a statement calling her words an "exaggerated expression of regard." But her entire record was under the microscope and reporters kept finding more threads to pull. In the following days, several revelations came to light: as a state senator, she proposed renaming a stretch of highway after Jefferson Davis; in 2014 photo captioned "Mississippi history at its best!" she could be seen wearing a Confederate hat at visiting Davis' homestead; and she attended a private high school that appeared to open its doors just as a court order enforcing integration of public high schools in the state went into effect.

Those incidents gave Espy hope that he could pull off an upset. But the former Clinton Cabinet official was in a tough spot. Politically, he could not be too critical of Trump or express strongly liberal positions. He had to find a way to excite black voters, but not alienate white moderates. Espy was also dogged by fact that he resigned as Agriculture secretary when he was indicted for receiving improper gifts. He was eventually acquitted. But many voters remembered his messy exit. The Republican National Committee sent 100 staffers to Mississippi just before the runoff, and Trump campaigned with Hyde-Smith at two stops. She won 54%-46%.

In the Senate, Hyde-Smith has kept Cochran's seat on Appropriations. Mississippi has long depended on its delegation to bring home federal dollars. She also chaired the Agriculture Subcommittee on Livestock, Marketing and Agriculture Security. Addressing a growing concern back home, Hyde-Smith introduced legislation to respond to chronic wasting disease, a contagious and fatal neurological disease that affects white-tailed deer, which are common in the state. She partnered with Wicker on a successful bill to make the home of civil rights icons Medgar and Myrlie Evers a national monument.

Hyde-Smith got attention when she and Sen. Shelley Moore Capito of West Virginia sat behind Sen. Susan Collins of Maine when Collins announced in a 45-minute Senate speech that she would vote to confirm Supreme Court nominee Brett Kavanaugh. Hyde-Smith said that she and Capito, whose desks were not behind Collins, wanted to make their colleague, who had received death threats during the confirmation fight, feel a little more at ease.

Trent Kelly (R)

Elected 2015, 2nd full term, b. Mar 01, 1966; Union; East Central Community College (MS), A.A., 1986; University of Mississippi Business School, B.A., 1989; University of Mississippi Law School, J.D., 1994; Army War College, M.A., 2010; Methodist; Married (Sheila Kelly Hampton); 3 children.

Military Career: U.S. Army National Guard 1985-pres. (Iraq)

Elected Office: Tupelo City Prosecutor, 1999-2011; 1st Circuit Judicial District Attorney, 2012-2015.

Professional Career: Practicing attorney, 1995-1999.

DC Office: 1005 LHOB 20515, 202-225-4306, Fax: 202-225-3549, trentkelly.house.gov

State Offices: Columbus, 662-327-0748; Corinth, 662-687-1525; Eupora, 662-258-7240; Hernando, 662-449-3090; Tupelo, 662-841-8808.

Committees: *Agriculture*: Conservation & Forestry; Livestock & Foreign Agriculture. *Armed Services*: Military Personnel (RMM); Seapower & Projection Forces. *Small Business*: Investigations, Oversight & Regulations; Rural Development, Agriculture, Trade & Entrepreneurship.

Group Ratings

	ADA	ACLU	AFL-CIO	LCV	ITI	COC	HAFA	ACU	CFG	FRC
2018	-	14%	-	0%	-	75%	81%	80%	72%	100%
2017	0%	C	8%	0%	C	93%	C	89%	90%	100%

Almanac Ratings 2017-18

	Economy	Social	Foreign	Composite
Liberal	0%	7%	0%	2%
Conservative	100%	93%	100%	98%

Key Votes of the 115th Congress

1. Obama-care revision	Y	5. Family planning regs	Y	9. Guantanamo prisoners	N
2. Tax Cuts	Y	6. Body cameras/immigration	N	10. Ground missiles, limit	N
3. Omnibus appropriations	N	7. Abortion ban	Y	11. Defense Dept. spending	Y
4. Dodd-Frank revision	Y	8. Concealed carry	Y	12. FISA rules	Y

Election Results

Election	Name (Party)	Vote (%)	Cand. Spent	Ind. Exp. Support	Ind. Exp. Oppose
2018 General	Trent Kelly (R)............................... 158,245	(67%)	$628,696	$1,921	
	Randy Wadkins (D)............................ 76,601	(32%)	$140,513		
2018 Primary	Trent Kelly (R)..	(100%)			

Prior winning percentages: 2016 (69%), 2015 special (70%)

Republican Trent Kelly in 2015 won a competitive primary in a special election. Appointed to the Armed Services Committee to take advantage of his lengthy military experience, Kelly has quietly settled into his seat.

Kelly graduated from the business school and law school at the University of Mississippi, then earned a master's degree in strategic studies from the U.S. Army War College. Kelly has been in the National Guard since the mid-1980s as an engineer, and achieved the rank of colonel. He served in Iraq during the Gulf War, then had two tours of duty during the Iraq War, where he commanded 670 troops. He received two Bronze Stars and numerous other military honors. He became Tupelo's city prosecutor in 1999, and held that position for 12 years before he was elected district attorney for seven rural counties in the northeast corner of the state.

After Rep. Alan Nunnelee died, 13 candidates filed for the special election. Of the 12 Republicans, not one was from DeSoto County, which is the population center of the district. That led to a wide-open contest, with none of the candidates posting big fundraising hauls. Mike Tagert, the northern Mississippi transportation commissioner, had the support of former Republican Gov. Haley Barbour. But Kelly received contributions from Nunnelee's campaign fund, assistance from the late congressman's former consultant and an aide, and an important endorsement from his widow, Tori. In the "jungle primary," Walter Zinn, the only Democrat, led with 17.4 percent, Kelly got 16.3 percent, and Tagert finished third with 12.7 percent. Given the Republican tilt of the district, it was no surprise that Kelly won the runoff with 70 percent of the vote.

In Kelly's first year, the House passed his bill to make it easier for Small Business Administration representatives to review contract requests from small businesses. The measure later was included in the House version of the annual defense spending bill. In 2018, he co-sponsored with Florida Democratic Rep. Al Lawson a bill to allow large prime contractors to take credit for subcontracting to smaller businesses, which passed the House. He developed a working relationship with neighboring Democratic Rep. Bennie Thompson, including their joint opposition to a Senate resolution to switch the regulation of catfish from the Agriculture Department to the Food and Drug Administration. Catfish farming is big business in Mississippi.

In 2017, Kelly achieved his goal of a seat on the Armed Services Committee. He also chaired the Oversight and Investigations Subcommittee at Small Business, where he examined how the SBA and other federal agencies could operate programs that affect small businesses in a more cost-effective manner. In an interview with the Jackson Clarion-Ledger, he said that what bothered him most about the House is, "There are so many opportunities where we as members like each other — we just disagree on policy." Kelly has remained a reliable GOP vote, though he told the Northeast Mississippi Daily Journal in 2018 that he'll "never be a guy who votes party lines on anything. I vote on the values I have." Kelly said he was "apprehensive" about some of President Donald Trump's trade policies, particularly how they would affect agriculture in the district, but added, "I trust our president."

During the 2016 campaign, he said that neither party's presidential candidate was "perfect." But, he added, Trump would be "much better than" Hillary Clinton at leading the nation. Kelly has won comfortable re-elections. In 2018 he faced his most active Democratic challenger, Ole Miss biochemistry professor Randy Wadkins; Kelly won easily, 67%-32%.

MS-1: Northeast Mississippi

Cook Partisan Voting Index: R+16

Population		Race and Ethnicity		Income	
Total	757,425	White	67.3%	Median Income	$44,819
Land area (sq. miles)	10,573	Black	27.3%	District Income Rank	375
Pop/ sq mi	71.6	Latino	3.2%	Poverty Rate	18.1%
Born in State	63.7%	Asian	0.8%	With health insurance	87.5%
		Two or more races	1.3%	Cash public assistance	2.5%
Age Groups		Other	0.2%	Food stamp/SNAP	14.5%
Under 18	24.2%				
18-34	22.6%	**Education**		**Work**	
35-64	38.3%	H.S grad or less	48.4%	White Collar	14.9%
Over 64	14.9%	Some college	31.6%	Sales and Service	39.5%
		College Degree, 4 yr	12.8%	Blue Collar	31.1%
Military		Post grad	7.1%	Government	14.5%
Veteran/ Active Duty	7.4%				

2012 Pres. Vote	Romney	197,980	(62%)	Obama	118,435	(37%)
2016 Pres. Vote	Trump	203,135	(65%)	Clinton	100,780	(32%)

Memphis area, Tupelo: The university town of Oxford — the "Jefferson" of William Faulkner's fictional Yoknapatawpha County — sits on a divide between the hill country of Mississippi and the flat farmlands of the Mississippi Delta. Named for Oxford England, it is home to the University of Mississippi, where violence broke out in 1962 when James Meredith became the school's first black student. Ole Miss, as it is known, now houses Meredith's papers in its library. Under student pressure, the university in 2015 removed the state flag because it featured the Confederate battle flag within its design. As debate over Confederate memorials grew across the country, Ole Miss again came under scrutiny. The university decided to repair a statue depicting a nameless Confederate soldier instead of getting rid of it after it was damaged in 2017, though it did add a plaque trying to put its presence in context: "It must also remind us that the defeat of the Confederacy actually meant freedom for millions of people."

To the west is the Delta, with a large African-American majority, and DeSoto County, just south of Memphis and Mississippi's fastest-growing county, including a nearly 11 percent increase from 2010 to 2017. The relatively affluent DeSoto has become a magnet for Memphis commuters looking for affordable housing, better schools and lower taxes across the state line. DeSoto has become very aggressive in economic development and has taken business from Memphis. East of Oxford is the hill country, which stretches to where the Tennessee River nicks the northeast corner of Tishomingo County. This was traditional farming country, but it is now more engaged in small manufacturing.

The Golden Triangle in the Starkville area has become a center for aerospace research, including work on unmanned air vehicle designs for surveillance and communications. The biggest town in the northeast corner is Tupelo, home to an upholstered furniture industry that has survived more prosperously than furniture centers elsewhere. Tupelo was the birthplace of Elvis Presley in 1935, and the family's two-room house today is open to visitors. The town produces many Christian conservatives, the kind of townsfolk who were shocked by Presley's music and hip-swirling dance moves in the early days of rock 'n' roll. The American Family Association, a fundamentalist Christian organization, is based there. In 2013, Tupelo elected as mayor Democrat Jason Shelton , who later ordered the state flag not to be flown over the city's police department. The Tupelo region got a big economic boost when Toyota in 2011 opened an assembly plant in nearby Blue Springs. In 2018 the company announced a $170 million expansion that will add 400 jobs. Several suppliers have sprung up nearby. Clay County has become a tire-manufacturing center.

The 1st Congressional District of Mississippi includes Southaven (the district's biggest city), Oxford, Tupelo and most of the hill country. This once-conservative Democratic territory has become solidly Republican in national politics. Even with rural Clay and Marshall counties voting for Hillary Clinton, Donald Trump got 65 percent of the district vote.

Bennie Thompson (D)

Elected 1993, 13th full term, b. Jan 28, 1948; Bolton; Tougaloo College, B.A., 1968; Jackson State University (MS), M.S., 1972; Methodist; Married (London Johnson Thompson); 1 child ; 2 grandchildren.

Elected Office: Bolton Board of Aldermen, 1968-1972; Bolton Mayor, 1973-1980; Hinds County supervisor, 1980-1993.

Professional Career: County Supervisor, Hinds Co., MS; Mayor (Bolton, MS)

DC Office: 2466 RHOB 20515, 202-225-5876, Fax: 202-225-5898, benniethompson.house.gov

State Offices: Bolton, 601-866-9003; Greenville, 662-335-9003; Greenwood, 662-455-9003; Jackson, 601-946-9003; Marks, 662-326-9003; Mound Bayou, 662-741-9003.

Committees: *Homeland Security (Chmn)*: Ex Officio membership on all subcommittees.

Group Ratings

	ADA	ACLU	AFL-CIO	LCV	ITI	COC	HAFA	ACU	CFG	FRC
2018	-	81%	-	86%	-	64%	2%	0%	5%	0%
2017	95%	C	97%	94%	C	38%	C	4%	5%	0%

Almanac Ratings 2017-18

	Economy	Social	Foreign	Composite
Liberal	95%	96%	95%	95%
Conservative	6%	4%	5%	5%

Key Votes of the 115th Congress

1. Obama-care revision	N	5. Family planning regs	N	9. Guantanamo prisoners	Y
2. Tax Cuts	N	6. Body cameras/immigration	Y	10. Ground missiles, limit	Y
3. Omnibus appropriations	Y	7. Abortion ban	N	11. Defense Dept. spending	Y
4. Dodd-Frank revision	N	8. Concealed carry	N	12. FISA rules	N

Election Results

Election	Name (Party)	Vote (%)	Cand. Spent	Ind. Exp. Support	Ind. Exp. Oppose
2018 General	Bennie Thompson (D)	158,921 (72%)	$988,531		
	Troy Ray (I)	48,104 (22%)			
2018 Primary	Bennie Thompson (D)	(100%)			

Prior winning percentages: 2016 (67%), 2014 (68%), 2012 (67%), 2010 (62%), 2008 (69%), 2006 (64%), 2004 (58%), 2002 (55%), 2000 (65%), 1998 (71%), 1996 (60%), 1994 (54%), 1993 special (55%)

Bennie Thompson, first elected in 1993 and now the longest-serving African-American elected official in Mississippi, has been a liberal Democratic fixture in an otherwise deeply conservative Republican state. His national profile increased again when he returned in 2019 to chair the House Homeland Security Committee, where he has clashed with President Donald Trump and his stringent immigration policies.

Thompson grew up in Bolton, in Hinds County outside Jackson, and graduated from Tougaloo College and got a master's degree from Jackson State University. He was elected alderman in Bolton in 1969, at age 21, and elected mayor four years later. A longtime volunteer firefighter, he got the first fire engine for Bolton and also a street named after the Rev. Martin Luther King Jr. In 1980, he became a Hinds County supervisor. A lifelong grassroots activist and labor organizer, he led voter-registration drives and successfully encouraged other African Americans to run for office. He organized associations of Mississippi black mayors and supervisors.

After Democratic Rep. Mike Espy exited Congress to become President Bill Clinton's Agriculture secretary, Thompson ran for the seat in an all-party primary. He came out ahead of Henry

Espy, the congressman's brother and mayor of Clarksdale, 28%-20%. Hayes Dent, an aide to Gov. Kirk Fordice, led Republicans with 34 percent. Voting in the runoff was largely along racial lines, and Thompson won 55%-45%, with his margin coming mostly from Hinds County. Mike Espy returned in 2018 for an unsuccessful Senate campaign.

Thompson has a staunchly liberal voting record. He initially made little attempt to win white votes in his district, making roughly as few concessions across the racial divide as white lawmakers had earlier made. In time, he moderated his votes and reached out to whites, including some of the district's large farmers. He backs expansion of Medicaid, and accused Republican Gov. Phil Bryant of refusing to go along with the health care plan of President Barack Obama "just because a black man created it," Buzzfeed reported. In 2018, Thompson slammed Bryant for signing onto a lawsuit that opponents said would have gutted pre-existing condition protections from the Affordable Care Act. In 2014, Thompson drew widespread attention for comments in an interview with a New Nation of Islam radio show in which he called Supreme Court Justice Clarence Thomas an "Uncle Tom" and accused Senate Republican Leader Mitch McConnell of being racist toward Obama.

The locus of his legislative activity has been the Homeland Security Committee, where Thompson has focused on the needs of first responders. He has been vocal about the threat of computer-based attacks and successfully pushed back in 2012 against Republican calls to scale back the Homeland Security Department's role in favor of defense and intelligence agencies. For years, Thompson had a sometimes-productive relationship with New York Rep. Peter King, then the top Republican on the committee. The two worked together to restructure the Federal Emergency Management Agency after its failures in the aftermath of Hurricane Katrina in 2005. House Republicans wanted it to become an independent agency. The two called for keeping it within the Homeland Security Department, but with the kind of autonomy the Coast Guard has. They came to an agreement, but when Thompson demanded an additional $3 billion to improve state and local communications capability, the deal foundered.

As chairman in 2007, Thompson shepherded through the House the unfinished recommendations of the 9/11 commission. He enacted a requirement to screen all passenger jet and ship cargo. He worked with King to pass annual Homeland Security authorization bills, only to have the Senate ignore them. Back in the minority after Republicans regained control of the House, Thompson was named a vice chair of a House Democratic task force on gun violence formed after the December 2012 school massacre in Newtown Connecticut. He regularly gets "F" ratings from the National Rifle Association. Thompson, an avid hunter, says the ratings don't reflect sportsmen's views.

Thompson became a vocal critic of Trump and his policies. "The President's desperate attempts to militarize our southern border and tease out unconstitutional immigration policy are nothing more than political stunts and must be called out as such," Thompson said. After two children who had been held in detention facilities at the border died while in custody, Thompson promised "robust" oversight in an interview with NPR.

Thompson clashed with Homeland Security Secretary Kirstjen Nielsen, as the government partially shut down when Congress and Trump disagreed about funding a border wall. "Your border security presentation submitted to Congress today is yet another example of the misinformation and outright lies the Trump administration has used to make the case for the president's boondoggle border wall," Thompson wrote to Nielsen; she resigned in April 2019. After an inspector general report surfaced in January 2019 saying that child separations at the border had been even higher than first reported, Thompson and other Democratic chairmen said the document was "proof that the Trump administration secretly hatched a plan to separate thousands of vulnerable children from their parents and place them in federal custody in order to deter those seeking refuge in the United States." Thompson said he was a "believer in technology" along the Mexican border and that "if we do it right, then we can get -- I'm convinced -- the kind of border security that we need."

Thompson has encountered occasional campaign opposition. In 2002, he was reelected by a less than impressive 55%-43% against Republican challenger Clinton LeSueur, a consultant to the Yazoo Community Action Agency. State Rep. Chuck Espy, nephew of the former representative, challenged him in the 2006 primary, but Thompson prevailed 64%-35%. He has faced no serious challengers since. He did not attend the presidential inaugural in January 2017, stating that criticism by Trump of Democratic Rep. John Lewis was "far beneath the dignity of the office of the president." When Trump attended the opening of the Mississippi Civil Rights Museum, both Lewis and Thompson boycotted, calling Trump's attendance an "insult."

MS-2: Mississippi Delta   **Cook Partisan Voting Index: D+14**

Population		Race and Ethnicity		Income	
Total	716,972	White	30.7%	Median Income	$34,074
Land area (sq. miles)	15,552	Black	65.7%	District Income Rank	432
Pop/ sq mi	46.1	Latino	2.1%	Poverty Rate	29%
Born in State	83.8%	Asian	0.5%	With health insurance	85%
		Two or more races	0.6%	Cash public assistance	3.5%
Age Groups		Other	0.4%	Food stamp/SNAP	24.1%
Under 18	25.2%				
18-34	23.8%	**Education**		**Work**	
35-64	37%	H.S grad or less	50.8%	White Collar	14%
Over 64	14%	Some college	30.4%	Sales and Service	43.8%
		College Degree, 4 yr	11.6%	Blue Collar	27.3%
Military		Post grad	7.2%	Government	21.5%
Veteran/ Active Duty	5.9%				

2012 Pres. Vote	Obama	219,273	(66%)	Romney	109,180	(33%)
2016 Pres. Vote	Clinton	185,501	(64%)	Trump	102,159	(35%)

Jackson: "The Mississippi Delta," wrote native David Cohn, "begins in the lobby of the Peabody Hotel in Memphis and ends on Catfish Row in Vicksburg." For centuries, the flooding Mississippi and Yazoo rivers left their sediments here, producing a fertile, dark soil. Ironically, what may well be America's richest agricultural land has been home for more than a century to many of its poorest people. Crisscrossed by rivers and famously disease-ridden, the Delta wasn't much settled until after the Civil War. Then, Reconstruction-era profit-seeking operators used late 19th century technology to drain the land, line the river with levees and build railroads on tracks above the rise of the river. Black sharecroppers and field hands worked here in conditions little better than bondage. From this episode of industrial farming came both great misery and great art: Clarksdale in Coahoma County, where Martin Luther King in 1958 held the first meeting of the Southern Christian Leadership Conference, was the real birthplace of blues music, the home of W.C. Handy and Muddy Waters, John Lee Hooker, Ike Turner and Sam Cooke. Greenville on the Mississippi has produced writers of the caliber of Walker Percy and Shelby Foote. Yazoo City produced author Willie Morris and bluesman Skip James. Today, Vicksburg's antebellum mansions and battlefield monuments are popular tourist attractions. In 2017, the new Mississippi Civil Rights Museum opened in Jackson.

Twentieth century technology changed life in the Delta. The mechanical cotton-picking machine, invented in 1944, came along just as Northern factories were seeking low-wage workers. The great exodus to Chicago and other Northern cities accelerated, and the Delta's population has been declining ever since. In the decade ending in 2010, each of the 16 counties in the Delta suffered a double-digit population loss. Income levels remain very low, the teen pregnancy rate high and infant mortality at Third World levels. Yet there are signs of hope. Soybeans have become a big-dollar crop here and poultry farms have become a major enterprise. The Delta produces most of the nation's catfish, though the annual catch has decreased from about 600 million pounds of catfish production to 350 million pounds in 2018. To counter the foreign production, catfish farmers have turned to promoting the health of their catfish, as opposed to those raised in polluted areas of Vietnam.

Not far from Memphis, Tunica County is one of the nation's poorest, its struggling economy dependent on the area's seven casinos, which help to generate 10 million visitors and 15,000 tour buses annually. The Tunica casinos saw a 5.7 percent drop in revenue in 2017 and the shuttering of one casino. GreenTech Automotive, a clean energy startup once chaired by former Virginia Gov. Terry McAuliffe, opened nearby in 2014 a 300,000-square-foot plant, which produced its two-seat battery-powered MyCar electric vehicle for use chiefly at stadiums and on large campuses. But the company filed for bankruptcy in 2018, and never fully delivered on 350 jobs it promised the region. Just north of the affluent suburbs of Jackson, Nissan operates a 6,400-employee factory in Canton. The company expanded its production line for Altima sedans. The United Auto Workers has made several costly bids to unionize the plant. All have failed, most recently in 2017, when more than 60 percent of the roughly 3,600 employees opposed the union.

The 2nd Congressional District of Mississippi includes the entire Delta, with the Mississippi riverfront from Tunica almost to Natchez. It includes most of heavily African-American Jackson and surrounding Hinds County, except for the affluent Belhaven neighborhood. Nearly one-third of the population is in Hinds, which is 71 percent African American. This black-majority district includes a few counties in the east that are majority white and vote Republican. But the political tone of the district is set by the African-American neighborhoods in Jackson and the Delta counties. In 2016, the 2nd was the only Mississippi district to vote for Hillary Clinton. She got 64 percent of the vote.

Michael Guest (R)

Elected 2018, 1st term, b. Feb 04, 1970; Woodbury, NJ; Mississippi State University, B.A., 1992; University of Mississippi, J.D., 1995; Baptist; Married (Haley Guest); 2 children.

Professional Career: Madison and Rankin Counties, Assistant District Attorney, 1994-2008, District Attorney, 2008-2018.

DC Office: 230 CHOB 20515, 202-225-5031, Fax: 202-225-5797, guest.house.gov

State Offices: Brandon, 769-241-6120; Meridian, 601-693-6681; Starkville, 662-324-0007.

Committees: *Ethics.* *Foreign Affairs*: Europe, Eurasia, Energy & the Environment; Western Hemisphere, Civilian Security, & Trade. *Homeland Security*: Border Security, Facilitation & Operations; Emergency Preparedness, Response & Recovery.

Election Results

Election	Name (Party)	Vote (%)		Cand. Spent	Ind. Exp. Support	Ind. Exp. Oppose
2018 General	Michael P. Guest (R)	160,284	(62%)	$932,765		
	Michael Evans (D)	94,461	(37%)			
	Matthew Holland (Ref)	2,526	(1%)			
2018 Primary	Michael P. Guest (R)	31,572	(65%)			
	Whit Hughes (R)	16,950	(35%)			

Freshman Republican Michael Guest was elected following more than a decade as prosecutor of the two largest counties in his district. Although he was forced into a runoff to get the nomination in the comfortably Republican district, he led by nearly two-to-one margins in each round of the intra-party battle. Guest was widely supported by Mississippi's Republican establishment, including Gov. Phil Bryant. He replaced retiring Republican Rep. Gregg Harper, who chaired the House Administration Committee.

Guest graduated from Mississippi State University and got his law degree from the University of Mississippi. Following 12 years as assistant district attorney, he was elected in 2007 as the district attorney for Madison and Rankin counties, which include nearly half the voters in the district. He was a leader of local civic groups, including the Foundation for Rankin County Public Schools and Mississippi Crime Stoppers.

In the campaign, Guest said his top priority was improved enforcement along the Mexican border, including the construction of a wall to reduce illegal immigration and drugs. Handling complex cases as prosecutor "has taught me to always be prepared, the importance of standing on my principles, and how to work with others to accomplish what is right," he told the Jackson Free Press.

Whit Hughes, a health care development officer and the other contender in the GOP runoff, was a former basketball star at Mississippi State University. He was closely connected to former Gov. Haley Barbour--as finance chairman in his successful 2003 campaign and then as deputy director of the Mississippi Development Authority. "Guest and Hughes did little to differentiate from each other on policy issues during the campaign," Mississippi Today reported.

The two leading candidates were also closely matched in fundraising, with a bit more than $500,000 each in their competition for the nomination. Guest benefited from his greater prominence in the two counties that are the core of the district. In the first round of voting on June 5, Guest got

45 percent to 22 percent for Hughes. Running third with 16 percent was Perry Parker, a businessman from the more rural part of the district and former international financier.

The runoff three weeks later had a similar pattern. In Rankin County, his home county, which cast 30 percent of the vote in the runoff, Guest took more than 80 percent of the total votes and led Hughes by nearly 10,000. In smaller Madison, Guest led by almost 2,000 votes. Overall, he won by nearly 15,000 votes—with a 65%-35% margin.

In November, Guest easily defeated the Democratic nominee, state Rep. Michael "Big Country" Evans. At age 48 when he entered the House, he might eventually have the opportunity for a statewide bid.

MS-3: South Central Mississippi   Cook Partisan Voting Index: R+13

Population		Race and Ethnicity		Income	
Total	748,858	White	59.6%	Median Income	$44,530
Land area (sq. miles)	12,754	Black	35.1%	District Income Rank	381
Pop/ sq mi	58.7	Latino	2.4%	Poverty Rate	19.9%
Born in State	76.8%	Asian	1%	With health insurance	87.9%
		Two or more races	0.8%	Cash public assistance	1.9%
Age Groups		Other	1%	Food stamp/SNAP	14.2%
Under 18	23.9%				
18-34	23.3%	**Education**		**Work**	
35-64	37.8%	H.S grad or less	44%	White Collar	15%
Over 64	15%	Some college	30.5%	Sales and Service	38.9%
		College Degree, 4 yr	15.6%	Blue Collar	24.8%
Military		Post grad	10%	Government	19.2%
Veteran/ Active Duty	7%				

2012 Pres. Vote	Romney	204,232	(60%)	Obama	133,114	(39%)
2016 Pres. Vote	Trump	198,768	(61%)	Clinton	118,805	(37%)

Jackson Suburbs: The Neshoba County fair has been held every August since 1889 in the town of Philadelphia. What started as a farmer's picnic has become the traditional place where Mississippi politicians announce their candidacies, with the crowds watching to take their measure. Devotees call it "Mississippi's Giant House Party," and many stay for the entire week. The crowds are also there to watch the races on the state's only legal horse track. But nationally, Philadelphia and Neshoba County are known for something less harmonious. There is no memorial, except engraved stones at two African-American churches, to mark the events of the summer of 1964, when three civil rights workers, two white and one black, were murdered for the crime of urging black American citizens to register to vote. It wasn't until June 2005 that a jury of nine whites and three blacks convicted Edgar Ray Killen, by then an 80-year-old preacher and sawmill operator, of manslaughter and sentenced him to three life sentences. In November 2014, President Barack Obama commemorated the 50th anniversary when he awarded a posthumous presidential Medal of Freedom to James Chaney, Andrew Goodman and Michael Schwerner.

The 3rd Congressional District of Mississippi has its population centers in the Jackson suburbs in Rankin County and south Madison County, plus the affluent neighborhoods of northeast Jackson in Hinds County. East and north of Jackson, subdivisions, shopping centers and office complexes have sprouted in the countryside. In June 2018, the Jackson Clarion-Ledger reported that construction and new businesses were "hopeful signs of a coming rebirth" in downtown Jackson and was reaching "a tipping point" that could benefit the entire area. A different kind of wealth has opened in the southwest corner of the district, as oil gushers burst forth from fracked wells. In late 2018, an Australian company was drilling the first of at least six planned wells near Gillsburg.

From the Jackson suburbs, the 3rd stretches north to Starkville, home of Mississippi State University, and south almost to Laurel. In the southwest, which extends to the Louisiana border, it includes Natchez, where 668 antebellum mansions and other properties with live oaks sit atop bluffs overlooking the Mississippi River. Natchez -- settled in 1716, two years before New Orleans — was ranked second by Lonely Planet in 2016 as the most exciting destination to visit in the United States. In the middle of the district are Neshoba County and Meridian. The district's political tradition remained Democratic for decades, but its preference has become strongly Republican, even with its 35 percent black population. In 2016, Donald Trump won the district, 61%-37%.

Steven Palazzo (R)

Elected 2010, 5th term, b. Feb 21, 1970; Gulfport; University of Southern Mississippi, B.B.A., 1994; University of Southern Mississippi, M.S., 1996; Roman Catholic; Married (Lisa Palazzo); 3 children.

Military Career: U.S. Marine Corps Reserves 1988-1996; MS Army National Guard 2007-pres. (Gulf War)

Elected Office: MS House, 2007-2010.

Professional Career: FO, Biloxi Housing Authority; Owner, Palazzo & Co. PLLC.

DC Office: 2349 RHOB 20515, 202-225-5772, Fax: 202-225-7074, palazzo.house.gov

State Offices: Gulfport, 228-864-7670; Hattiesburg, 601-582-3246; Pascagoula, 228-202-8104.

Committees: *Appropriations*: Commerce, Justice, Science & Related Agencies; Homeland Security.

Group Ratings

	ADA	ACLU	AFL-CIO	LCV	ITI	COC	HAFA	ACU	CFG	FRC
2018	-	4%	-	0%	-	82%	63%	70%	52%	100%
2017	0%	C	16%	0%	C	93%	C	78%	66%	100%

Almanac Ratings 2017-18

	Economy	Social	Foreign	Composite
Liberal	5%	6%	3%	5%
Conservative	95%	94%	98%	95%

Key Votes of the 115th Congress

1. Obama-care revision	Y	5. Family planning regs	Y	9. Guantanamo prisoners	N
2. Tax Cuts	Y	6. Body cameras/immigration	N	10. Ground missiles, limit	N
3. Omnibus appropriations	Y	7. Abortion ban	Y	11. Defense Dept. spending	Y
4. Dodd-Frank revision	Y	8. Concealed carry	Y	12. FISA rules	Y

Election Results

Election	Name (Party)	Vote (%)		Cand. Spent	Ind. Exp. Support	Ind. Exp. Oppose
2018 General	Steven Palazzo (R).............................	152,633	(68%)	$635,520	$2,153	
	Jeramey Anderson (D)........................	68,787	(31%)	$133,052		
	Lajena Sheets (Ref)............................	2,312	(1%)			
2018 Primary	Steven Palazzo (R).............................	30,370	(70%)			
	E. Brian Rose (R)...............................	12,664	(30%)			

Prior winning percentages: 2016 (65%), 2014 (70%), 2012 (64%), 2010 (52%)

Republican Steven Palazzo, who unexpectedly won his seat in 2010, is a fervent fiscal and social conservative representing an area where Hurricane Katrina caused severe damage and imposed huge costs. He drew considerable attention for voting against paying Hurricane Sandy claims on the East Coast without offsetting cuts. As a member of the Appropriations Committee, he has become more amenable to spending, though he has still struggled to balance that with his tea party inclinations along with lingering conservative unrest in his district.

Palazzo was born and raised in Gulfport, where five generations of his family have called south Mississippi home. After graduating from high school and enrolling for a semester at his local community college, Palazzo enlisted in the Marine Corps. From 1988 to 1996, Palazzo was assigned to the 3rd Force Reconnaissance Company, gathering intelligence and taking tours of duty in Kuwait and Saudi Arabia during the Persian Gulf War. He remained active in the military following his full-time service, joining the Mississippi Army National Guard and supporting base operations at Camp Shelby for Operation Iraqi Freedom. In Congress he would go on to serve as co-chairman of the National Guard Caucus. After returning from his tours of duty Palazzo earned his bachelor's and master's degrees in accounting from the University of Southern Mississippi. He worked in accounting positions at various firms, primarily in the construction industry. In 2001, he and his then-wife started the accounting practice Palazzo & Co., which grew into an international firm specializing in individual income tax returns for expatriates.

In 2007, Palazzo was elected to the state House. Two years later, he decided to challenge popular veteran Blue Dog Democrat Gene Taylor. Taylor lost his home to Katrina, was in good stead with the National Rifle Association, had one of the most conservative voting records among House Democrats, and had spoken out against many of his party's major initiatives, including health care reform.

But even Taylor couldn't survive the pro-Republican environment of 2010. Palazzo portrayed him as an enabler of the Democratic agenda for his vote for Nancy Pelosi as House Speaker, which he said showed Taylor's support for a "liberal socialist agenda." Taylor touted his conservative positions and even boasted to his local newspaper that he voted for Republican John McCain for president in 2008. It wasn't enough, and Palazzo won 52%-47%.

In the House, Palazzo joined the Tea Party Caucus and the Republican Study Committee, calling for sharp reductions in spending. He opposed the New Year's Day 2013 budget deal aimed at averting the so-called fiscal cliff, saying it failed to cut enough. That year, he added an amendment to the Pentagon spending bill to ban same-sex marriage ceremonies on military bases; it was dropped in the Senate. Palazzo found ways to protect defense spending. He added money to a defense spending bill to buy land to expand a National Guard facility in his district, as well as for ship design and feasibility studies at Ingalls Shipbuilding in nearby Pascagoula. Recalling his attacks on Taylor for pork-barrel spending, Democrats and watchdog groups accused Palazzo of hypocrisy. He continued to pursue the military interests of his district, including $1 billion in the 2015 defense spending bill for the Navy's LPD-28 amphibious assault ship, which would be built at Ingalls; he also got a provision to discourage downsizing at Keesler Air Force Base

Following the 2012 election, Palazzo drew the most attention of the 67 House Republicans who voted against the bill to provide $9.7 billion in government borrowing to pay claims from Superstorm Sandy, which did considerable damage in the Northeast. He contended the measure should have made offsetting spending cuts. Most other GOP lawmakers from coastal areas backed the bill, prompting the Biloxi Sun Herald to say of Palazzo, "Seldom has a single vote in Congress appeared as cold-blooded and hard-headed." Aware of the political damage, Palazzo toured Sandy-stricken areas and then co-signed a letter calling on colleagues to support a larger aid bill.

In 2014, Palazzo survived an unusual re-election contest when Taylor changed parties and challenged him in the Republican primary. Having determined that it was "impossible" for a Democrat to win, Taylor offered himself as the candidate best-equipped to deliver for the 4th District. Palazzo barely avoided a run-off, winning 51%-43%.

But internal tensions remained. After more than one hour of a "man to man" conversation with John Boehner the evening before the vote, Palazzo decided that he was "willing to give the Speaker and his team a last chance to put us back on a conservative path for America." Two months later, Palazzo got a coveted seat on the Appropriations Committee and styled himself as an insider. "Serving as an appropriator is a privilege and a tremendous responsibility that I don't take lightly," he said.

Palazzo has continued to pursue his conservative agenda. In January 2016, he filed a resolution to censure President Barack Obama for his executive order to restrict private gun sales. He voiced support when the Mississippi legislature went on record in opposition to the U.S. Supreme Court's recognition of same-sex marriages.

In 2018, Palazzo faced conservative radio host Brian Rose in the GOP primary. Rose, an Air Force veteran, raised questions about Palazzo's military record, alleging he had sought special favors in getting assigned to Camp Shelby instead of going to Iraq, along with "fraudulently" seeking a hardship discharge from the National Guard. Palazzo brushed aside the accusations and defeated Rose, 70%-30. The Biloxi Sun Herald alleged in early 2017 that Palazzo was dodging constituents and not publicizing his district events. Still, he has cruised to reelection.

MS-4: Southeast Mississippi

Cook Partisan Voting Index: R+21

Population		Race and Ethnicity		Income	
Total	762,965	White	68.9%	Median Income	$44,782
Land area (sq. miles)	8,044	Black	23.4%	District Income Rank	376
Pop/ sq mi	94.8	Latino	4.1%	Poverty Rate	19.4%
Born in State	62.6%	Asian	1.5%	With health insurance	84.9%
		Two or more races	1.7%	Cash public assistance	2.1%
Age Groups		Other	0.4%	Food stamp/SNAP	16.9%
Under 18	24%				
18-34	23.3%	**Education**		**Work**	
35-64	38.1%	H.S grad or less	45.1%	White Collar	14.6%
Over 64	14.6%	Some college	34%	Sales and Service	42.8%
		College Degree, 4 yr	13.1%	Blue Collar	26.2%
Military		Post grad	7.8%	Government	17.8%
Veteran/ Active Duty	12%				

2012 Pres. Vote	Romney	199,354	(68%)	Obama	92,127	(31%)
2016 Pres. Vote	Trump	196,652	(69%)	Clinton	80,045	(28%)

Gulfport/Biloxi, Hattiesburg: Coastal Mississippi has gone through several transformations in its history. French explorers founded Biloxi in 1699, before New Orleans or St. Louis, and made it the capital of an empire extending across the Rocky Mountains. Two hundred years later, rich people from New Orleans came to this section of the Gulf Coast in the summer to get away from yellow fever and to rest on Victorian verandas. Six American presidents have vacationed here. There is also a military flavor to the Gulf Coast. Biloxi's Keesler Air Force Base, one of the elite bases in the world, trains 28,000 aviators annually. Pascagoula, the largest military shipbuilder in the nation and the largest private employer in the state, is home to about 12,000 workers over 800 acres at the Huntington Ingalls Shipyard, whose gray, hangar-like buildings and skeletons of ships under construction loom over the landscape. In December 2018, the Coast Guard awarded a contract of more than $930 million to build two new national security cutters.

The region's economic growth was put on hold for several years after these coastal communities took a direct hit from Hurricane Katrina in August 2005. From Waveland to Pascagoula, about 80 miles were obliterated: Beachfront cottages, fishing villages, hotel casinos, oil-drilling platforms and refineries all were either cruelly swamped or swept away. The homes of Confederate President Jefferson Davis in Biloxi and former Senate Majority Leader Trent Lott in Pascagoula were destroyed. The eye of the monster storm passed over the region, and in an instant, countless livelihoods were gone and property losses reached tens of billions of dollars.

If there was a saving grace, many of the communities had a clean slate to start over, with more control over the building of high rises and strip malls that had started to overwhelm more distinctive properties, especially in Biloxi. In 2018, SeaOne Holdings signed a 40 year lease to build its Fuels Supply Project to transport natural gas and gas liquids, adding up to 1,800 construction jobs, about half of them permanent. Following the setback that the gulf areas suffered with the massive BP oil spill in 2010, the huge fines from the recovery helped the state to set more rigorous standards to restore the coast and its facilities. Hurricane Nate hit the Gulf in October 2017, which caused about $2.5 billion in losses for oil production. The industry bounced back, and in March 2018 the Interior Department leased millions of offshore acres off the Mississippi coast and nearby for new oil and gas development.

The heart of the 4th Congressional District are the three Gulf Coast counties, which include more than 40 percent of the population. The rest of the district's people live inland, in farm counties or around Hattiesburg and Laurel. It has long been Republican territory. In 2017, Biloxi Republican Mayor Andrew "FoFo" Gilich announced that, in an effort to make all tourists feel welcome, city buildings would no longer fly the state flag, which still featured a portion of the Confederate battle emblem. Gilich faced a primary challenge a few months after he announced his stance, but easily won. In 2016, the district gave 69 percent of the vote to Donald Trump. The district, which has the smallest African-America population in Mississippi, has become the most Republican in the state.

MISSOURI

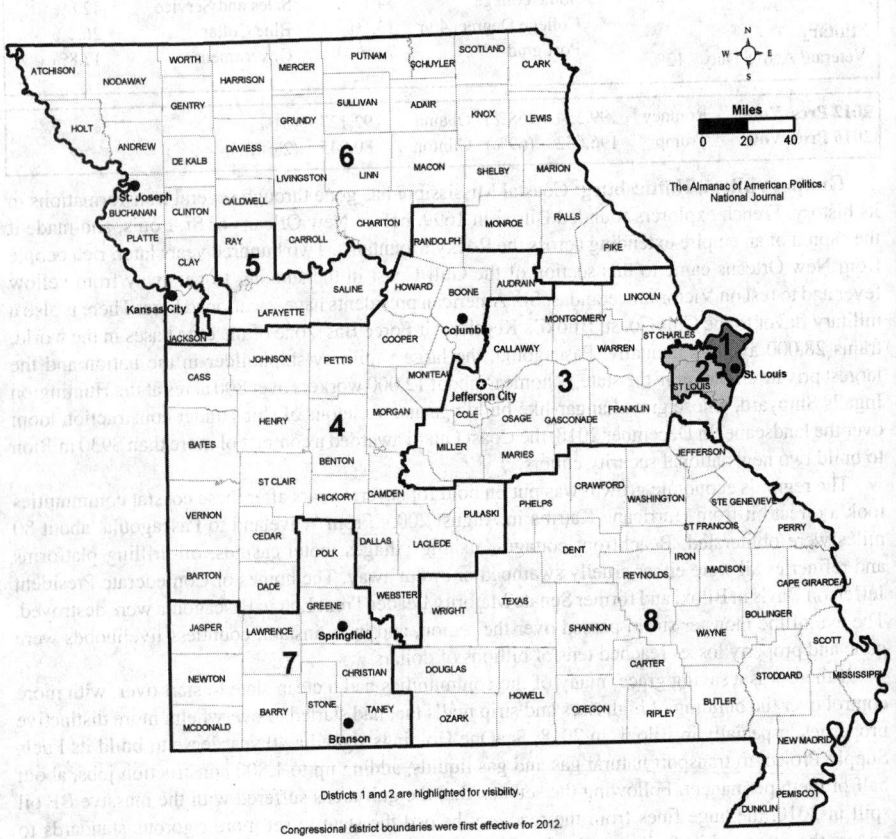

Districts 1 and 2 are highlighted for visibility.

Congressional district boundaries were first effective for 2012.

The Almanac of American Politics.
National Journal

For a century, Missouri was one of America's political bellwether states. It voted for every presidential winner but one from 1904 to 2004; the exception came in 1956, when it narrowly backed Adlai Stevenson. As recently as 2008, John McCain defeated Barack Obama by fewer than 4,000 votes in the state. But those days are gone. In 2012, Mitt Romney defeated Obama by 10 percentage points. Four years later, Donald Trump won by almost 19 points, inspiring a wave that swept Republicans into every statewide office on the ballot that year, four of them previously held by Democrats. Then, in the 2018 midterms, Republican Josh Hawley defeated two-term Sen. Claire McCaskill, one of the last elected Missouri Democrats. "Missouri has just become quite a Republican, conservative state," said Saint Louis University political scientist Ken Warren.

The Gateway Arch, rising gracefully over the Mississippi River, is a worthy tribute to St. Louis and Missouri as the gateway to the American West, but it is no longer a gleaming symbol of vigor and prosperity. This land was part of France's thinly settled North American empire; St. Louis, just below the swirling confluence of the Missouri River and the Mississippi, was founded by Pierre Laclède and Auguste Chouteau in 1764, while further south in Missouri, the French began mining in the Old Lead Belt as early as 1720. All this and much more was acquired by the United States as part of the Louisiana Purchase of 1803. On May 14, 1804, at Thomas Jefferson's direction, Meriwether Lewis, William Clark and the Corps of Discovery set out from St. Louis on their expedition to the Pacific. St. Louis was then the one well-established city in America's interior, with an aristocracy of French merchants, a brawling bourgeoisie of Yankee and Southern frontiersmen and fur traders, and a proletariat of black slaves. Statehood came in 1821, and for years thereafter the frontier democracy was a passage for westward expansion, captured in the paintings of George Caleb Bingham. West of St. Louis, new areas were settled: St. Joseph was the eastern terminus of the Pony Express; Westport, now part of Kansas City, was a starting point of the Oregon and California Trails; Independence, identified by Joseph Smith as the site of the Second Coming, was settled by Mormons who left after Gov. Lilburn Boggs ordered them "exterminated"; and Hannibal, on the Mississippi River, was where a boy named Sam Clemens engaged in pranks and watched the early steamboats that he would later chronicle as Mark Twain.

Missouri was also a focus of the furious battle over slavery. It was the northernmost slave state in the 1850s, when Missouri ruffians rode across the border and killed antislavery settlers in the Kansas Territory. The state had its own bloody civil war in the hill counties along the Missouri River and in the southwest. After the war, in 1874, the Eads Bridge opened, one of the few spans on the Mississippi; St. Louis' Cupples Station was then the largest rail hub in the world. At the turn of the 20th century, Missouri was the fifth-largest state, and St. Louis was the fourth-largest city, site of the 1904 World's Fair, and one of the few cities with two Major League Baseball teams, the Cardinals and the Browns. Missouri was also the national center of the mule trade (Harry Truman's father's line of work), an important business at a time when half of Americans lived on farms and motorized tractors had not yet been invented.

After the 1900 census, Missouri had 16 congressional districts, twice the number it has now. In the 20th century, Americans increasingly headed toward the coasts, and eventually to Florida and Texas. (Major-league teams left too: baseball's Browns, who moved to Baltimore in 1954, and Kansas City's Athletics, who decamped to Oakland in 1968; football's Cardinals, who moved to Phoenix in 1988; and their NFL successor the Rams, who moved back to Los Angeles in 2016.) Missouri was the geographic center of the nation's population in the 2010 census: An imaginary, flat map of the United States population, if everyone weighed the same, would balance in Texas County. However, Missouri has seen below-average population growth since 1900, and today it is the 18th-largest state. Since the 2010 census, the state has grown by barely 2 percent. Inside its narrow 19th century boundaries, the city of St. Louis had 856,796 in 1950 and 622,000 people in 1970 but only 308,626 in 2017. St. Louis County, which does not include the city's population, has been pretty stable: 952,000 people in 1970 and 996,726 in 2017. The three counties around St. Louis County have grown – Franklin and Jefferson counties by about 2 percent since 2010 and the Republican bastion of St. Charles County by 9 percent. But the state's fastest-growing area is the Lake of the Ozarks region in central and southwest Missouri, around the country music center of Branson. Taney County, which includes Branson, has grown by 6.7 percent since 2010, fed by an influx of modest-income retirees looking for traditional lifestyles and inexpensive recreation. (The quest for relaxed recreation turned tragic in 2018, when an amphibious "duck" boat on an excursion on nearby Table Rock Lake sank in a storm, killing 17.)

Transportation manufacturing remains important in Missouri, employing tens of thousands of workers at plants owned by Boeing, Ford, General Motors and the auto supply firms Yanfeng USA and TG Missouri, among others. St. Louis is home to Express Scripts, the largest pharmacy benefit manager in the country, as well as the investment firm Edward Jones and Enterprise Rent-A-Car. Other major companies native to the state — McDonnell Douglas, TWA, Ralston Purina, May Department Stores, Monsanto, Anheuser-Busch — have been acquired by outside competitors and multinationals or disappeared entirely. In recent years, GDP and job growth has been modest, and farmers have had to deal with severe flooding on the Missouri River in 2011, drought conditions in 2012, and then flooding again in 2016.

Overall, the state is 82 percent white, 12 percent African American, 4 percent Hispanic and 2 percent Asian. Missouri has some tough immigration laws, even as it has attracted relatively few immigrants; not quite 4 percent of residents are foreign-born. The existence of such a small minority population has profoundly shaped the state's political direction. Unlike more diverse states such as Colorado and Nevada, Missouri has not been pushed toward the Democrats by a growing minority population. Rural, conservative and largely white areas – with farms and small towns thick with churches and modest shopping centers and laced with man-made lakes and boat launches – have flexed their political muscle. Only one city outside the two big metro areas, Springfield, has a population in excess of 150,000, and in the state's rural heartland, life — and politics — seem not to have changed much over the past half-century. Missouri has permissive gun laws, including the right to carry a concealed weapon without a permit, and it has only one remaining abortion provider.

Once-obscure Ferguson, a city of 21,000 in St. Louis County where two-thirds of the population is African American, attracted intense national attention when it was rocked by riots in 2014 following the shooting of an unarmed black teenager, Michael Brown, by a white police officer who was later cleared of criminality by a Justice Department investigation. A St. Louis County grand jury had previously declined to indict the officer. Brown's death became an inspiration for the Black Lives Matter movement, which led protests and marches in cities across the country. A Justice Department probe found that the Ferguson police department engaged in abusive policing. The Missouri legislature responded in 2015 by enacting a law to curb the use of traffic fines as a revenue stream to fill municipal coffers, a practice that disproportionately affects the poor and that had inflamed tensions. Those tensions continued into late 2015 at the University of Missouri, where months of protests, including a threatened walkout by the football team, led to the resignation of the university system president, the voluntary demotion of the chancellor of the main campus, and difficulties recruiting minority athletes.

Historically, Missouri's political landscape was not just a mixture of urban and rural – its Civil War political divisions still held, too. Democrats dominated in Little Dixie in the northeast, an area first settled by Virginians, and in the northwest, which had been settled by southerners. Republicans, meanwhile, held sway in the Ozarks in the southwest, which was pro-Union, while the southeast was split, like next-door downstate Illinois. (This is the only state whose name is pronounced two ways, depending on where you're from. In metro St. Louis, they say "Mizuree." In the rest of the state it's "Mizuruh.") By 2000, however, these political patterns were fading. The large metro areas became even more Democratic, while the culturally conservative remainder of the state turned sharply Republican.

For a while, the parties were in a state of balance: In the state's 10 contests for president, senator and governor between 2000 and 2008, only two were decided by wide margins. In the eight other contests, Republicans got between 47 percent and 53 percent of the vote, Democrats between 46 percent and 50 percent. Since then, the balance has shifted to a strong GOP tilt, led by a relatively large contingent of evangelical voters and culminating in Trump's sweeping victory. Trump won 112,000 more votes in the state than Mitt Romney had four years earlier, as Hillary Clinton was winning 153,000 fewer votes than Obama had in 2012. In both elections, the county-by-county map was a sea of red, with both Obama and Clinton winning only St. Louis city, St. Louis County, Jackson County (Kansas City), and Boone County (Columbia, home of the University of Missouri's largest campus). Even a suburban county like Jefferson, near St. Louis, saw its Republican margin expand from 12 percentage points in 2012 to 35 points in 2016, with GOP candidates winning every contested race in the county. Even more worrisome for Democrats, a number of its statewide candidates in 2016 had seemed strong until the Election Night wipeout, notably Jason Kander, who lost a bid against GOP Sen. Roy Blunt despite an impressive television ad showing him assembling a firearm blindfolded.

The 2018 midterm elections only reinforced the conclusion that the Democratic brand in the state was in the doldrums. Indeed, the party was unable to take advantage of the sexual misconduct scandal that enveloped GOP Gov. Eric Greitens and led to his resignation barely a year after he won office in 2016. McCaskill – a scrappy competitor who had won two terms in the Senate after serving as state auditor – lost to Hawley, the Republican attorney general. Despite her incumbency, McCaskill didn't even match Kander's share of the vote two years earlier, and unlike Democrats elsewhere in the country, she was unable to make headway in suburban counties as she lost whatever support she'd had in more rural areas. The turning point in the race was likely the contentious confirmation battle over Supreme Court nominee Brett Kavanaugh, which united Republicans, particularly after McCaskill came out against the confirmation.

The one silver lining for Democrats was an uncanny streak of policy victories by progressives in ballot measures. In August 2018, voters by a 2-to-1 margin rejected a right-to-work law signed by Greitens. Then, in November, voters decided to legalize medical marijuana, raise the minimum wage to $12 by 2023, and approve an ethics and transparency measure that also overhauled the state's legislative redistricting process in a way that could ameliorate the GOP's embedded advantages. But those results have been the exceptions. The old model for Democratic success in Missouri – a centrist approach that played well enough outside the big cities to put the party over the top when combined with a strong urban vote – has become a thing of the past.

Population		Race and Ethnicity		Income	
Total	6,075,300	White	79.8%	Median Income	$51,542
Land area (sq. miles)	68,742	Black	11.5%	State Income Rank	36
Pop/ sq mi	88.4	Latino	4.0%	Poverty Rate	14.6%
Born in state	66.1%	Asian	1.8%	With health insurance	89.6%
		Two or more races	2.2%	Cash public assistance	2.1%
Age Groups		Other	0.6%	Food stamp/SNAP	12.2%
Under 18	22.9%				
18-34	22.9%	Education		Work	
35-64	38.5%	H.S grad or less	41.7%	White Collar	35.9%
Over 64	15.7%	Some college	30.1%	Sales and Service	41.8%
Military		College Degree, 4 yr	17.5%	Blue Collar	22.3%
Veteran/ Active Duty	9.5%	Post grad	10.7%	Government	12.2%

Presidential Politics

2016 Primary (D)	Clinton (D)	312,285 (50%)	Sanders (D)	310,711 (49%)			
2016 Primary (R)	Trump (R)	383,631 (41%)	Cruz (R)	381,666 (41%)	Kasich (R)	94,857 (10%)	
	Rubio (R)	57,244 (6%)					
2016 Pres. Vote	Trump (R)	1,594,511 (57%)	Clinton (D)	1,071,068 (38%)	Johnson (L)	97,359 (3%)	
2012 Pres. Vote	Romney (R)	1,482,440 (54%)	Obama (D)	1,223,796 (44%)			

Before 1904, Democratic strength in Missouri outside of St. Louis and Kansas City made the state more Democratic in presidential races than the nation. Since 2000, Republican strength in the numerous rural counties outside the two big metros has made it more Republican than the nation. In 2016, voters in the Show Me State favored Donald Trump over Hillary Clinton, 57%-38%. Clinton carried only St. Louis and three of the state's 114 counties: Boone, home to the University of Missouri at Columbia; Jackson, Kansas City; and St. Louis County, the largest vote producer in the state and also home to Ferguson, the site of 2014 racial unrest. Some political observers say that Trump's law-and-order rhetoric played well in the aftermath. "Across the state of Missouri, I think the predominant opinion is that the governor did not crack down enough on protests, and I think that's unfortunately an attitude that has taken hold," St. Louis African-American Alderman Antonio French told Huffingtonpost.com a month before the election.

Missouri provided two of the closest presidential primaries of the 2016 campaign. In the March 15 Republican primary, Trump edged Texas Sen. Ted Cruz by 1,965 votes out of more than 920,000 cast — essentially a 41%-41% tie. Trump carried the St. Louis metropolitan area and most of the rural counties in the state, while Cruz won the Kansas City metro, the Columbia metro, Springfield, Joplin and several surrounding Ozark Mountain counties where many evangelical voters reside. On the Democratic side, Clinton squeaked out a 50%-49% victory over Vermont Sen. Bernie Sanders in which the margin was 1,574 votes out of some 630,000 cast. She won St. Louis County and the city, as well as Jackson, while Sanders won Boone and Greene (Missouri State University) counties and suburban-exurban counties around Kansas City and St. Louis. They split rural counties, with Clinton winning along the Mississippi River and Sanders taking more counties in the western part of the state. Clinton's 18,000-vote margin in St. Louis County contributed most to her victory.

Congressional Districts

116th Congress Lineup	2D 6R	115th Congress Lineup	2D 6R

At first blush, prospects for redistricting in Missouri appear relatively straightforward. Following the 2012 redistricting, there has been no partisan change in the House delegation of six Republicans and two Democrats, with the Democrats based in the urban centers of St. Louis and Kansas City. Only the 2nd District of Rep. Ann Wagner in the St. Louis suburbs has been remotely competitive since then. No change is likely in the size of the delegation. Republicans control the governorship and the legislature, though the June 2018 ascension of Gov. Mike Parson to replace the scandal-ridden Eric Greitens has created uncertainty on the GOP side. Assuming no partisan switches in the 2020 election, Republicans likely will seek to extend Wagner's district farther into the exurbs and exchange some parts of her district with the 3rd District of Rep. Blaine Leutkemeyer. Their two districts already share parts of Jefferson and St. Charles counties outside of St. Louis.

But other options exist under different political or legal scenarios. Wagner's district, instead, could exchange voters with the heavily Democratic 1st District of Rep. Lacy Clay in St. Louis city and county. Although Clay in the past has resisted moves to add Republican voters to his district, he easily could sacrifice enough Democrats to threaten Wagner without endangering his own prospects. Assuming that Democrats take the Missouri map to court, they likely would need to agree in advance with Clay about the implications for his district. Following the 2010 census, when the state lost one seat from what had been a 6-3 delegation, Republicans in the legislature passed a map to protect Clay and eviscerated Democratic Rep. Russ Carnahan's district in the St. Louis suburbs. In what became an ugly clash between black and white Democrats, the legislature eventually passed the Republican-drawn map, which protected Clay in his showdown with Carnahan in the Democratic primary in 2012.

Although Missouri's once-influential centrist Democrats in the House had become a relic of the past, the weakening of Republicans in suburbs across the nation — including St. Louis — will place a premium on both parties to identify neighborhoods that have changed their partisan instincts in the past decade and others that might change in the next few years. As for the Kansas City-based 5th District of Democratic Rep. Emanuel Cleaver, a GOP-drawn map theoretically could place him at risk. But such a map would jeopardize Republicans in the neighboring 4th or 6th District. Plus, keeping the 5th safely Democratic might be a Democratic demand in a possible bargain over changes in the St. Louis area.

Mike Parson (R)

Assumed office in 2018, term expires 2021, 1st term; b. Sept. 17, 1955, Wheatland; University of Maryland, Att.; University of Hawaii, Att.; Christian; Married (Teresa); 2 children.

Military Career: U.S Army, 1975-1981.

Elected Office: Polk County Sheriff, 1993-2005; MO House, 2005-2011; MO Senate, 2011-2017; MO Lt. Gov., 2017-2018.

Office: 201 W Capitol Ave #216, Jefferson City, 65101-9500; 573-751-3222; Fax: 573-526-3291; Website: mo.gov

Lt. Gov.: Mike Kehoe (R) **Atty. Gen:** Eric Schmitt (R) **Sec. of State:** Jay Ashcroft (R)

State Legislature: Senate: 10D, 24R **House:** 46D, 114R, 3V

Mike Parson was elevated to the governorship of Missouri after the shocking -- and shockingly fast -- fall from grace of onetime rising star Eric Greitens, who resigned the governorship after less than 18 months, under threat of impeachment due to a scandal in which he allegedly blackmailed a mistress using compromising photographs. Parson moved up and is considered the polar opposite of Greitens – a longtime, low-profile fixture in the legislature who succeeded a governor who styled himself as a brash outsider opposed to politics-as-usual. Parson is expected to seek a full term in 2020, though he could face a challenge within his own party from the right.

Parson was raised on a farm in Wheatland Missouri and served for six years in the military police corps, including stints in Germany and Hawaii. He never earned a bachelor's degree, but he took night courses at the University of Maryland and the University of Hawaii during his Army service. Parson worked as a deputy in the Hickory County sheriff's office and then as a criminal investigator in the Polk County sheriff's office; he also bought a gas station, a farm and other real estate holdings. Parson served as the elected sheriff of Polk County from 1992 to 2004, when he won a seat in the state House. He was elected to the state Senate in 2010, where he rose to majority whip. Parson's legislative achievements included an expansion of the state's castle doctrine, which self-protection from intruders, and legislation that enshrined farming and ranching rights in the state constitution. Former state Rep. Chris Kelly, a Democrat, told the Columbia Missourian that Parson is "not flashy or spectacular, but he's smart and knows how to make good decisions."

Parson initially sought the state's open gubernatorial seat in 2016, but facing a large field of GOP contenders, including Greitens, he switched to the lieutenant governor's race. In a strong Republican year, Parson won the general election, 55%-40%, against a Democratic candidate with a long Missouri pedigree – Russ Carnahan, a former congressman whose late father Mel served as governor, whose mother Jean served in the Senate, and whose sister Robin served as Missouri's secretary of state. Parson won 112 of the state's 114 counties. In office, Greitens and Parson tended to be ideologically similar, although the two clashed over the federal low-income housing tax credit. (Greitens worked aggressively to end the state's participation in the program, while Parson defended it.) Stylistically, though, the two were near polar opposites.

Greitens, a decorated Navy SEAL with stints in Afghanistan and Iraq, seemed to have been "conjured from a consultant's wildest dreams," as the Washington Post's David Von Drehle wrote. Greitens prevailed in a bitter four-way GOP primary in 2016, then defeated Democrat Chris Koster in the general election by a five-point margin, succeeding two-term Democratic Gov. Jay Nixon. Greitens' positioning as an outsider – bolstered by his non-political resume -- resonated. "We have a political class of corrupt consultants, well-paid lobbyists and career politicians who have been in Jefferson City for decades," Greitens said when announcing his run, adding that "they have produced nothing for us but embarrassment and failure."

Greitens entered office as the first Missouri Republican governor to serve with GOP supermajorities in both legislative chambers, but it wasn't long before the scandal made Greitens radioactive. It revolved around an affair he'd had with his hairdresser prior to announcing his gubernatorial bid; Greitens was accused of taking a semi-nude picture of the woman while she was blindfolded and lashed to exercise equipment, then telling her that he would release the picture if she didn't keep quiet. Greitens denied wrongdoing, but the allegations produced an indictment (the charges were eventually dropped) as well as a legislative investigation and the threat of impeachment. Greitens' aggressively anti-establishment style had already rubbed many of his fellow Republicans the wrong way, so GOP legislators were not reluctant to call for his resignation. In June 2018, just a year and a half after taking office, Greitens resigned. Parson was reportedly herding cattle on his farm when he heard the news; upon taking office, he vowed a "fresh start" for the state.

As governor, Parson signed legislation to ban marriages for 15-year-olds, a practice that had drawn the state negative attention nationally; under the new law, 16- and 17-year-olds could still marry, but only with the approval of at least one parent. The law also eliminated the statute of limitations for child abuse and for sexual offenses against minors. Parson said he would pursue funding to maintain and upgrade the state's roads and bridges; an expansion of state efforts to support early childhood education; and a statewide database to monitor physicians' prescriptions as a way to curb the spread of opioids. He also opened the door to adding sexual orientation and gender identity to the list of classes protected from discrimination, the Kansas City Star reported. Missouri conservatives grumbled that parson was implementing too moderate a record, though it was unclear whether he would face a serious primary challenge in 2020. He did receive applause from the right in May 2019 when he signed a bill banning abortions after eight weeks, with no exception for rape or incest.

Roy Blunt (R)

Elected 2010, term expires 2022, 2nd term, b. Jan 10, 1950; Niangua; Southwest Baptist University (MO), B.A., 1970; Southwest Missouri State University, M.A., 1972; Baptist; Married (Abigail Blunt); 4 children; 6 grandchildren.

Elected Office: MO Secretary of State, 1984-1993; U.S. House, 1997-2011.

Professional Career: H.S. teacher, 1970-1973; Greene County clerk, 1973-1985; Adjunct instructor, Drury College, 1976-1982; President, SW Baptist University, 1993-1996.

DC Office: 260 RSOB 20510, 202-224-5721, Fax: 202-224-8149, blunt.senate.gov

State Offices: Cape Girardeau, 573-334-7044; Columbia, 573-442-8151; Kansas City, 816-471-7141; Springfield, 417-877-7814; St. Louis, 314-725-4484.

Committees: Senate Republican Policy Committee Chairman. *Appropriations*: Agriculture, Rural Development, FDA & Related Agencies; Department of Defense; Department of the Interior, Environment & Related Agencies; DOL, HHS & Education & Related Agencies (Chmn); State, Foreign Operations & Related Programs; Transportation, HUD & Related Agencies. *Commerce Science & Transportation*: Communications, Technology, Innovation & the Internet; Aviation & Space; Security; Transportation & Safety. *Intelligence.   Rules & Administration (Chmn).*

Group Ratings

	ADA	ACLU	AFL-CIO	LCV	ITI	COC	HAFA	ACU	CFG	FRC
2018	-	5%	-	7%	-	90%	62%	82%	59%	100%
2017	0%	C	0%	0%	C	86%	C	83%	78%	100%

Almanac Ratings 2017-18

	Economy	Social	Foreign	Composite
Liberal	0%	0%	0%	0%
Conservative	100%	100%	100%	100%

Key Votes of the 115th Congress

1. Obama-care revision	Y	5. Gun regulations	Y	9. Kavanaugh confirmation	Y
2. Tax Cuts	Y	6. Family planning regs	Y	10. Saudi arms sales	N
3. Dodd-Frank revision	Y	7. Gorsuch confirmation	Y	11. FISA rules	Y
4. Omnibus appropriations	Y	8. Immigration restrictions	Y	12. Military aid in Yemen	N

Election Results

Election	Name (Party)	Vote (%)		Cand. Spent	Ind. Exp. Support	Ind. Exp. Oppose
2016 General	Roy Blunt (R)................................. 1,378,458	(49%)		$13,690,121	$1,619,549	$15,738,323
	Jason Kander (D)............................ 1,300,200	(46%)		$12,867,419	$6,305,759	$21,999,506
	Jonathan Dine (L)............................... 67,738	(2%)				
2016 Primary	Roy Blunt (R).................................... 481,444	(73%)				
	Kristi Nichols (R)............................. 134,025	(20%)				

Prior winning percentages: 2010 (54%), House: 2008 (69%), 2006 (67%), 2004 (70%), 2002 (75%), 2000 (74%), 1998 (73%), 1996 (65%)

Republican Roy Blunt, Missouri's senior senator, is one of the few lawmakers who's risen to the leadership ranks in both chambers of Congress: In 2019, he was chosen to lead the Republican Policy Committee, making him the fourth-ranking GOP senator. Blunt barely survived a tough race in 2016, riding President Donald Trump's coattails and his state's strong shift toward the GOP to overcome questions about his family's lobbying work and his K Street ties. In the latest chapter of Blunt's five-decade political career, the consummate political insider and backroom deal-maker has served as a top lieutenant of Senate Majority Leader Mitch McConnell and chairman of the Senate Rules Committee. He has also been a key player on the powerful Appropriations Committee and a loyal foot soldier for Trump, though he's split with the president on some foreign policy and trade issues.

Blunt grew up on a farm in Niangua, near Springfield in southwest Missouri. His father, Leroy Blunt, was a dairy farmer who was elected a state representative in 1978 by defeating the mother of former Democratic Sen. Claire McCaskill. By then, the younger Blunt's political career was well underway. He graduated from Southwest Baptist University in 1970 and earned a master's degree there in 1972. He got his start in politics the same year, volunteering in the unsuccessful congressional campaign of Republican John Ashcroft — later governor, senator, and U.S. attorney general. In 1973, then-GOP Gov. Kit Bond named the 23-year-old Blunt as Greene County clerk. He lost a race for lieutenant governor in 1980. Four years later, he was elected Missouri secretary of state, becoming the first Republican to win that office in half a century. He served two terms and then ran for governor in 1992, narrowly losing the GOP primary. He spent four years as president of Southwest Baptist University before running for an open House seat based in Springfield in 1996. He won with two-thirds of the vote and held the solidly Republican district for six more terms.

In the House, Blunt had a conservative voting record containing occasional centrist votes on social issues. In 2006, he won passage of his Combat Meth Epidemic Act, the first comprehensive approach to fighting the supply of methamphetamine. He sponsored a measure creating an internet database of federal spending, along with then-Sen. Barack Obama. Blunt's greater impact in the House was in his leadership roles, which gave him a say in shaping major legislation produced by the Republican majority.

Blunt was one of 10 original members of then-Texas Gov. George W. Bush's presidential exploratory committee in 1999. That same year, House Majority Whip Tom DeLay, a Texas Republican, made him chief deputy whip, an important leadership stepping stone. Blunt had a reputation as a good listener with a light touch — Bush had described him as "a leader who knows how to raise his sights and lower his voice." Blunt's job was to make certain that bills the leadership hoped to pass were palatable to conservatives. Blunt frequently met with lobbyists and organizing groups around issues like trade, taxes and energy, while raising substantial sums for GOP candidates. When DeLay replaced Majority Leader Dick Armey of Texas in 2002, Blunt took the whip post.

As whip, he met his toughest challenge in passing the 2003 bill to create a prescription drug benefit as part of Medicare. In a controversial vote in which the roll call was held open for three hours, he was able to persuade two Republicans to switch their votes. But there were rocky moments. In 2003, the House leadership was embarrassed by disclosures in The Washington Post that Blunt had quietly sought to insert into a homeland security bill a provision benefiting tobacco giant Philip

Morris the previous year. At the time, Blunt was dating his future wife, then a Philip Morris lobbyist. Blunt's son Andrew, also a lobbyist, was working for Philip Morris in Missouri. Blunt defended the provision, dropped after other House leaders objected to it, as "good policy" aimed at curbing bootlegged cigarette sales. The flap came on the heels of another episode for which Blunt took heat: According to The Wall Street Journal, he was behind a last-minute effort to block a German-owned competitor of UPS — another client of his son's — from expanding in the United States.

In 2005, Blunt held two leadership posts: as acting majority leader and whip after DeLay was forced to step down when he was indicted on charges of violating election laws. It was a heavy burden for Blunt, and during the next three months, House Republicans struggled to pass bills. Blunt ran to keep his new job as majority leader when DeLay announced he'd step down in early 2006; Blunt said he had the votes to prevail, but he faced a fierce challenge from John Boehner of Ohio. DeLay's controversies involving well-heeled lobbyists indirectly hurt Blunt, himself viewed as being cozy with K Street. Blunt led on the first ballot in the Republican Conference, coming within a half-dozen votes of the needed majority. On the second ballot, Boehner prevailed, 122-109. Blunt suffered the double indignity of losing his bid and looking like a whip who couldn't count votes.

Blunt remained majority whip and developed a smooth working relationship with Boehner. In September 2008, Boehner gave him the thankless task of negotiating the $700 billion financial bailout bill, which proved to be wildly unpopular with fellow Republicans. Blunt stepped down as whip to make way for his chief deputy, Rep. Eric Cantor of Virginia, after the 2008 elections. "Ten years of asking people to do things they don't want to do is a long time," Blunt told reporters.

His path to the speakership blocked, Blunt saw an opportunity across the Capitol. In February 2009, Bond — who had helped launch Blunt's political career almost four decades earlier — announced he would not seek re-election, and Blunt geared up for a race to replace his mentor. He scared off potentially competitive GOP challengers and won the primary over an underfunded tea party opponent, taking 71 percent of the vote. The state's rightward shift and a great midterm year for Republicans put Blunt in the driver's seat against state Secretary of State Robin Carnahan, heir to a Missouri Democratic dynasty whose surname brought her instant name recognition. Blunt ran hard against the Affordable Care Act, a law that was toxic in that year for Democrats, and tied Carnahan to President Obama and Democratic policies unpopular with conservative voters.

Carnahan tried to paint Blunt as the insider in the race. But her family ties made it a stretch for voters to see her as an outsider: Her father was a popular governor, her mother had served two years as an appointed senator and both her grandfather and brother served in the House. Carnahan sought to link Blunt to corruption, with one ad featuring a Fox News clip in which anchor Chris Wallace mentioned Blunt inserting the provision favorable to Philip Morris into the homeland security legislation. It mattered little to Missouri voters. Blunt won 54%-41%.

Months after taking office, when a tornado devastated the town of Joplin and killed 159 people, Blunt pushed for a strong federal relief effort to help the battered community from his former House district. When Cantor, by then majority leader with Republicans in House control, suggested that the disaster relief aid should be offset with budget cuts, Blunt told Politico, "We need to prioritize spending, and this needs to be a priority."

Blunt didn't wait long to seek a Senate leadership position. In late 2011, he ran for vice chairman of the Republican Conference against Wisconsin Sen. Ron Johnson, another freshman, with the race portrayed as a battle between the establishment and tea party wings of the GOP. Despite Johnson's efforts to pitch himself as a fresh conservative face, Blunt prevailed in a secret ballot that reportedly went 25-22. His victory came shortly after Republican presidential aspirant Mitt Romney selected him as his primary liaison to win support from House and Senate lawmakers. Blunt's wife became one of the Romney campaign's "bundlers" to gather checks from other supporters.

An issue later that year was personal for Blunt: When Russian President Vladimir Putin announced in 2012 that he would ban U.S. adoptions of Russian children in retaliation for a law enabling the Obama administration to target Russian human rights violators, Blunt led an effort to persuade Putin to allow adoptions that had been completed. He told the story of how he and his wife had adopted a son born in a Russian orphanage in 2004.

When Republicans regained the majority after the 2014 elections, Blunt became chairman of the Appropriations subcommittee with jurisdiction over the Labor, Health and Human Services, and Education departments — giving him an influential voice in the allocation of a large portion of the federal government's domestic discretionary budget. Blunt led an unsuccessful effort to end Obama's program that gave legal protections to undocumented immigrants brought to the U.S. as children and was among just five senators who opposed the nomination of Ash Carter as Defense secretary, accusing Obama of micromanaging the Pentagon without laying out a clear national security strategy to combat ISIS.

As he prepared for re-election in 2016, Blunt followed other Republican senators who veered to the right to pre-empt a tea party primary challenge. Blunt remained the subject of grumbling among some conservative groups, although his Almanac vote ratings in 2015 pegged him as the fifth-most conservative Senate Republican. In the GOP primary, he got 73 percent of the vote against three challengers.

But the real threat to his re-election wasn't his conservative credentials — it was his coziness with lobbyists in a year in which voters in both parties were fed up with Washington insiders.

Blunt's wife, Abigail, was the global head of governmental affairs for the Kraft Heinz Co., and had been a lobbyist for the Altria Group, the parent company of Philip Morris. Three of his adult sons were registered lobbyists, too. His oldest son, Matt, who was Missouri's governor from 2004 to 2008, was president of the American Automotive Policy Council, which represents the Big Three automakers. His son Andrew ran a Missouri-based lobbying firm, whose clients have included AT&T, American Airlines, MillerCoors and Motorola. He has managed each of his father's Senate campaigns.

In the general election, Blunt faced Missouri Secretary of State Jason Kander, a politically talented 35-year-old former Army intelligence officer who emphasized his youth and service in Afghanistan while attacking Blunt's close ties with Washington and lobbyists.

Blunt's ads described Kander as "too liberal for Missouri," and he said that the challenger shared the views of Hillary Clinton. Kander ran a widely viewed ad that showed him assembling a rifle while he was blindfolded and discussing his support for gun rights. The race remained close throughout the fall, with Kander gaining steadily in the polls. Blunt won 49%-46%, underperforming Trump by 16 percentage points. While Blunt may have been the epitome of the "swamp" that Trump spent his campaign attacking, Trump unquestionably helped him prevail.

As Senate Rules Committee chairman, Blunt officiated Trump's inauguration ceremony. That position also made him the top negotiator on overhauling Congress' notoriously weak sexual harassment payment policy. He negotiated a compromise that passed in late 2018 that required members to pay out of pocket for some settlements and court judgments instead of using taxpayer dollars. Some criticized the compromise for capping how much lawmakers would have to pay, but the deal was an improvement over past policy.

Blunt has occasionally criticized the president but hasn't done much to stand in Trump's way. Blunt was one of many Republicans who criticized the Trump administration for separating migrant families at the U.S.-Mexico border, saying "separating families does not meet the standard of who we are as a country." He wasn't happy when Trump slapped trade sanctions on China but opposed other colleagues' efforts to push a bill undoing those sanctions. A member of the Senate Intelligence Committee, Blunt has blasted Trump's foreign policy, warning that Russia and North Korea are bad actors that can't be trusted, and publicly disagreed with Trump when the president claimed that Russia didn't meddle in the 2016 elections. But he canceled a hearing on a bipartisan bill to improve election cybersecurity that he claimed to support in late 2018 after the Trump administration made clear that it opposed the bill. While other Republicans broke with Trump for refuting his own intelligence agents' assessment that Saudi Arabia's crown prince was behind the murder of journalist Jamal Khashoggi, a U.S. resident, Blunt defended Trump's assessment.

"The president's pretty different," Blunt said in early 2018, according to Roll Call. "And not necessarily in a bad way. He's getting a lot of things done."

Josh Hawley (R)

Elected 2018, term expires 2024, 1st term, b. Dec 31, 1979; Springdale, AR, AZ; Stanford University (CA), A.B., 2002; Yale Law School (CT), J.D., 2006; Evangelical; Married (Erin Morrow); 2 children.

Elected Office: MO Attorney General 2016-2018.

Professional Career: Supreme Court Law Clerk, Chief Justice John Roberts; Attorney, Hogan Lovells US, LLP

DC Office: 212 RSOB 20510, 202-224-6154, hawley.senate.gov

Committees: *Aging. Armed Services*: Emerging Threats & Capabilities; Seapower; Strategic Forces. *Homeland Security & Government Affairs*: Federal Spending Oversight & Emergency Management; Investigations. *Judiciary*: Antitrust, Competition Policy & Consumer Rights; Border Security & Immigration; Crime & Terrorism (Chmn). *Small Business & Entrepreneurship*.

Election Results

Election	Name (Party)	Vote (%)	Cand. Spent	Ind. Exp. Support	Ind. Exp. Oppose
2018 General	Josh Hawley (R)............................. 1,254,927	(51%)	$11,392,122	$1,666,100	$30,427,230
	Claire McCaskill (D)...................... 1,112,935	(46%)	$36,808,683	$5,346,006	$40,544,816
2018 Primary	Josh Hawley (R)................................. 389,006	(59%)			
	Tony Monetti (R)........................... 64,718	(10%)			
	Austin Petersen (R)....................... 54,810	(8%)			
	Kristi Nichols (R)................................ 49,554	(8%)			
	Christina Smith (R)........................ 34,948	(5%)			

At 39, Josh Hawley became the Senate's youngest member. A fast-rising star in the Republican Party, a constitutional lawyer and a staunch social conservative, Hawley capitalized on Missouri's strong rightward shift to defeat battle-hardened incumbent Democratic Sen. Claire McCaskill in 2018 and become his state's junior senator.

Hawley was born in Springdale, Ark. His family moved to Missouri when he was a child, and he grew up in Lexington, a small town east of Kansas City. His father was a banker and GOP activist who hosted George W. Bush while Bush was working on his father's 1988 presidential campaign. Hawley's mother was a schoolteacher. Despite being Presbyterian, his parents sent him to an all-boys Catholic school in Kansas City. Hawley went on to Stanford University, where he studied constitutional law and wrote for conservative campus publications. He interned in Washington at the conservative Heritage Foundation and connected with columnist George Will, who would become a champion of Hawley's political career.

Hawley briefly taught high school in London after graduation before heading to Yale Law School, where he became president of the conservative Federalist Society. He clerked with a conservative appeals court judge in Colorado before landing a clerkship with Supreme Court Chief Justice John Roberts. There he met his wife, Erin, another Roberts clerk. During that time, he published a biography of President Theodore Roosevelt.

After a brief stint at a D.C. law firm, Hawley left to work for the Becket Fund for Religious Liberty, a nonprofit firm that works on First Amendment cases affecting faiths. There, he participated in Burwell v. Hobby Lobby, in which the Supreme Court ruled that some private companies did not need to follow Affordable Care Act requirements that their insurance plans cover birth control.

Hawley returned home in 2011 to teach at the University of Missouri's law school while keeping his job at Becket. He passed on a run for attorney general in 2012 but ran in 2016. He won by a huge margin and was the only statewide candidate to outpace President Donald Trump's 18-percentage-point margin of victory in the state and became the state's first Republican attorney general in more than two decades.

Hawley promised during that campaign that he would stick around to do his job — he even ran an ad attacking "career politicians just climbing the ladder, using one office to get another." But state and national GOP leaders looking for a consensus candidate who could defeat McCaskill had other plans for him.

Republicans were desperate to avoid a replay of the 2012 campaign, in which a crowded field — and some primary meddling by McCaskill — led to controversial Rep. Todd Akin, who self-immolated with his "legitimate rape" remarks, winning the nomination. Republican Rep. Ann Wagner had long been gearing up for a run, but her 2016 criticism of Trump made her a ripe target for a right-wing challenge, and she opted not to run. State and national Republicans turned their eyes to Hawley. Establishment-aligned Republicans, including Sen. Roy Blunt, former Sens. John Danforth and Kit Bond, former Ambassador to Belgium Sam Fox, and Senate Majority Leader Mitch McConnell, urged him to run. Even Vice President Mike Pence joined the effort, and Hawley launched his campaign just 10 months after being sworn in as attorney general.

Hawley at first kept Trump at arm's length, skipping an August visit from the president, and his closeness to the anti-Trump Danforth had some right-wing Republicans threatening a primary. In response, Hawley met people in Trump's orbit, including former campaign advisers David Bossie and Steve Bannon. He showed up the next time Trump was in town — and was rewarded with a presidential endorsement. Hawley stuck to Trump for the rest of the race, and the president returned to Missouri six times to campaign for him.

McCaskill had been in politics for 36 years — Hawley was 2 years old when she first ran for the state Legislature in 1982. He was lauded as an all-star recruit by Republicans who at the time appeared to be struggling to land strong candidates. As the race wore on, he went from hero to goat as McCaskill far outpaced him in fundraising — she ended up spending $37 million to Hawley's $11 million, forcing Republican outside groups to make up the difference. Republican operatives grumbled about Hawley's work ethic as stories surfaced of him skipping GOP events, ignoring reporters — including right-wing radio hosts — and hitting the gym in the middle of work days. Some also grew nervous he could repeat Akin's gaffe-fueled implosion when audio of him and pastors blaming human trafficking on the sexual revolution surfaced.

Whatever Hawley's missteps, they paled in comparison to then-Missouri Republican Gov. Eric Greitens, whose extramarital affair and alleged attempts to blackmail his mistress into keeping quiet threw the party into chaos for the first half of 2018. Hawley initially said he didn't have the power to investigate Greitens, allowing Democrats to hammer him for protecting the scandal-plagued governor. Hawley later launched an investigation into Greitens' charity, infuriating the governor's remaining allies. The drama played out until Greitens resigned in June 2018.

McCaskill also hammered Hawley on health care. As attorney general, he'd joined a multistate lawsuit to overturn the Affordable Care Act's requirement that insurance companies cover pre-existing conditions, and McCaskill flayed him for that. Hawley responded with an ad saying his son had a pre-existing condition and claiming that McCaskill was lying about his position, without saying how she was wrong.

McCaskill had proved herself to be a tough adversary over the years, but her approval ratings were underwater for most of the year. The polls rarely topped 45 percent — a bad position for an incumbent.

Hawley bear-hugged Trump more than almost any other 2018 candidate. He defended the Trump administration's policy of separating immigrant and refugee families at the U.S.-Mexico border even as many other Republicans called on Trump to end the policy.

McCaskill had voted to confirm fewer Trump nominees than other red-state Democrats, including high-profile votes against Supreme Court nominees Brett Kavanaugh and Neil Gorsuch. Hawley and his allies hammered her in ads for those votes, painting her as an anti-Trump obstructionist. That argument got a huge boost in early October, when McCaskill voted against confirming Kavanaugh to the Supreme Court after an intense, polarizing battle. McCaskill never led again in the polls, as the fight breathed life into the GOP base.

McCaskill was caught between her base and wooing the conservative-leaning independents she needed to win the race. She faced blowback from liberals for an ad she ran in which a man said McCaskill wasn't "one of those crazy Democrats," and throughout the campaign she was dogged by questions about whether she'd been supportive enough of the black community in a state in which racial tensions have roiled politics since a white police officer in Ferguson shot to death an unarmed black teenager, Michael Brown, in 2014. She was caught on camera saying she "can give up a few votes in the Bootheel" in the state's rural southeast if she did well enough around St. Louis — a comment Hawley used in ads to argue McCaskill didn't care about rural Missouri.

Hawley faced one more crisis before Election Day. Reports surfaced that his political team had directed his government staff on what work to do and that government staff used personal email accounts in an apparent attempt to circumvent state sunshine laws. That wasn't enough to hurt him in the election but set off an investigation from Missouri's secretary of state shortly after the election that continued in early 2019.

Hawley defeated McCaskill 51% to 46 %, carrying 110 of the state's 114 counties. McCaskill was undone by rural Missouri's embrace of the GOP and black voters' low turnout. In 2016, African-Americans made up 14 percent of the vote. In 2018, according to exit polls, they made up 8 percent.

While Hawley was a staunch champion of Trump on the campaign trail, he showed a bit of independence after being sworn in. Hawley was one of 11 GOP senators who bucked Trump and voted for a bill that would have overturned the Trump administration's decision to lift sanctions on a top Russian plutocrat close to Vladimir Putin.

Hawley got a spot on the Senate Judiciary Committee, an assignment the legal expert had eagerly sought. He also secured spots on the Armed Services and Homeland Security committees, two more high-profile spots for a freshman senator.

Lacy Clay (D)

Elected 2000, 10th term, b. Jul 27, 1956; St. Louis; John F. Kennedy School of Government; Harvard University; University of Maryland - College Park, B.S., 1983; Roman Catholic; Divorced; 2 children.

Elected Office: MO House, 1983-1990; MO Senate, 1991-2001.

Professional Career: Assistant doorkeeper, U.S. House, 1976-1983; Paralegal, 1988-1998; Real estate agent, 1986-2000.

DC Office: 2428 RHOB 20515, 202-225-2406, Fax: 202-226-3717, lacyclay.house.gov

State Offices: Florissant, 314-383-5240; St. Louis, 314-367-1970; St. Louis, 314-669-9393.

Committees: *Financial Services*: Consumer Protection & Financial Institutions; Housing, Community Development & Insurance (Chmn); Subcommittee on Diversity & Inclusion. *Natural Resources. Oversight & Reform*: Subcommittee on Civil Rights & Civil Liberties.

Group Ratings

	ADA	ACLU	AFL-CIO	LCV	ITI	COC	HAFA	ACU	CFG	FRC
2018	-	89%	-	86%	-	58%	8%	5%	11%	0%
2017	100%	C	95%	94%	C	43%	C	8%	5%	0%

Almanac Ratings 2017-18

	Economy	Social	Foreign	Composite
Liberal	95%	96%	95%	95%
Conservative	6%	4%	5%	5%

Key Votes of the 115th Congress

1. Obama-care revision	N	5. Family planning regs	N	9. Guantanamo prisoners	Y
2. Tax Cuts	N	6. Body cameras/immigration	Y	10. Ground missiles, limit	Y
3. Omnibus appropriations	Y	7. Abortion ban	N	11. Defense Dept. spending	Y
4. Dodd-Frank revision	N	8. Concealed carry	N	12. FISA rules	N

Election Results

Election	Name (Party)	Vote (%)		Cand. Spent	Ind. Exp. Support	Ind. Exp. Oppose
2018 General	Lacy Clay (D)	219,781	(80%)	$649,290		
	Robert Vroman (R)	45,867	(17%)			
	Robb Cunningham (Lib)	8,727	(3%)			
2018 Primary	Lacy Clay (D)	81,812	(57%)			
	Cori Bush (D)	53,250	(37%)			

Prior winning percentages: 2016 (76%), 2014 (73%), 2012 (79%), 2010 (74%), 2008 (88%), 2006 (73%), 2004 (73%), 2002 (70%), 2000 (75%)

Democrat William Lacy Clay was first elected in 2000 to the seat that his father, Bill Clay, held for 32 years. In recent years, he has survived serious conflicts in his St. Louis district and in his political life. With seniority, he has taken on a prime legislative niche for the nation's housing policy. The half-century lock that the Clays have held on the district is second only to the nine-decade control by the Dingell family in its suburban Detroit district.

Born in St. Louis, Clay, who goes by "Lacy," moved to the Washington area at age 12 after his father's election to the House. He attended public schools in suburban Silver Spring Maryland and then the University of Maryland, studying by night for seven years while he worked as a House staffer by day. He had started law classes at Howard University when he returned to St. Louis for a special election to the state House in 1983. Party leaders appointed him the Democratic nominee. Eight years later, party leaders again chose him to run in a special election for a safely Democratic state Senate seat.

In 1999, his father announced that he would retire from Congress, after helping to enact many labor and education laws. Clay wanted to take his father's place, but he had a serious primary contest. St. Louis Councilman Charlie Dooley, an African American with a base of support in the mostly white suburbs of St. Louis County, raised nearly $400,000. Dooley said the office should not be "inherited," and he attacked what he called Clay's old-style tactics of political threats and bossism. The St. Louis Labor Council and Missouri AFL-CIO, long allied with Bill Clay, declined to endorse his son, but more than 30 locals did. The candidate played up his father's name and revved up the still reliable machine. He won the primary 61%-28% over Dooley, winning St. Louis City 76%-12% and the county, where twice as many votes were cast, 49%-39%. In the general election, Clay won 75%-22%.

In the House, Clay has had a mostly liberal voting record in the Almanac vote ratings. He is active in the Congressional Black Caucus, where his father was a founding member. Clay is usually low-key and can be diplomatic in resolving differences among other lawmakers. "He's a peacemaker," fellow Missouri Democratic Rep. Emanuel Cleaver told the St. Louis Post-Dispatch. "He has just the right personality to take the temperature up, or bring it down." Clay also can be a dealmaker. He agreed to support Nancy Pelosi over Steny Hoyer for Democratic whip in 2001 only after securing a promise of $5 million to clean up contaminants at an Army plant in his district.

Clay has worked to protect voting rights for blacks and is the main proponent of creating a national Civil Rights Trail, with markers linking important sites in the civil rights movement, including those in St. Louis. On the Financial Services Committee, he became chairman in 2019 of the Housing, Community Development Insurance Subcommittee. He was a leading advocate for continuing the authority of the Export-Import Bank, which supported $339 million in exports from his district, Clay said. He did not play a prominent role during the 2018 rollback of the Dodd-Frank banking regulatory law.

The riots that followed the police shooting in August 2014 of an unarmed black man in Ferguson, a city in his district, raised Clay's profile. He criticized police for a "heavy-handed" approach to peaceful demonstrations and said that law enforcement organizations needed more diversity in their ranks. He called on the federal government to take over the investigation into the shooting, which he called a "murder," saying in a radio interview: "I have absolutely no confidence in the Ferguson police, the county prosecutor. I know we won't get a fair shake there." In 2015, he filed legislation that called for more "sensitivity training" for local police, and threatened the loss of federal law-enforcement funds to cities that don't require independent investigations when police use deadly force.

After Missouri lost a seat in the 2010 reapportionment, Republicans eliminated the neighboring district of Democratic Rep. Russ Carnahan, who decided to challenge Clay. The newly drawn 1st District included 70 percent of Clay's old district and just 30 percent of Carnahan's. Clay ran a radio ad featuring representatives of two prominent black churches urging listeners to stand behind "leaders like Lacy Clay and President Obama." The Post-Dispatch endorsed Carnahan, saying that Clay "has coasted on the organization that his father and predecessor built but without being as deeply and continuously involved in local issues as Bill Clay was." Clay won the primary, 63%-34%. Reflecting the demographic shifts in the area, Clay ran more strongly in St. Louis County, where he got 66 percent of the vote, than in the city, where he had 60 percent.

Clay has survived competitive primary challenges since then from well-known community leaders. In 2016, state Sen. Maria Chappelle-Nadal, a supporter of Sen. Bernie Sanders in the presidential primary and a leader of the protests in Ferguson in 2014, told the audience, "You must ask yourself a question: Is 48 years too long for one family?" After President Barack Obama endorsed him, she responded that Clay was "quite accustomed to riding on someone else's coattails to win elections." Clay had a huge fundraising advantage over Chappelle-Nadal, who raised only $78,000. He won the primary, 63%-27%, with similar advantages in both the city and county. Two years later, Cori Bush, a nurse and community activist who also was a leader of the Ferguson protests, spent $100,000 and narrowed the gap to 57%-37%. Perhaps significantly, Clay led in St. Louis city by only 51%-43%; he took 60 percent of the county vote.

MO-1: St. Louis   Cook Partisan Voting Index: D+29

Population		Race and Ethnicity		Income	
Total	736,659	White	40.9%	Median Income	$43,445
Land area (sq. miles)	225	Black	49.4%	District Income Rank	393
Pop/ sq mi	3268.8	Latino	3.4%	Poverty Rate	19.8%
Born in State	69.1%	Asian	3%	With health insurance	88.1%
		Two or more races	2.7%	Cash public assistance	2.4%
Age Groups		Other	0.5%	Food stamp/SNAP	19.1%
Under 18	22.1%				
18-34	27%	**Education**		**Work**	
35-64	38%	H.S grad or less	37.3%	White Collar	12.9%
Over 64	12.9%	Some college	31.6%	Sales and Service	46%
		College Degree, 4 yr	17.7%	Blue Collar	17%
Military		Post grad	13.5%	Government	10.8%
Veteran/ Active Duty	7.4%				

2012 Pres. Vote	Obama	280,194	(80%)	Romney	66,286	(19%)		
2016 Pres. Vote	Clinton	246,107	(77%)	Trump	60,136	(19%)	Johnson	7,948	(3%)

St. Louis City, County: For a century or more, St. Louis seemed the center of America: the starting point for the Lewis and Clark expedition in 1804, the locus half a century later of the Dred Scott slavery case, and the site of the 1904 World's Fair, which introduced the hotdog and the ice cream cone and got 19 million people to Meet Me in St. Louis. Its 630-foot-high Gateway Arch is just below the point where the waters of the Missouri surge into the Mississippi, about halfway between Lake Superior and New Orleans, between the Atlantic and the Pacific. This was the first major American city west of the Mississippi River and, for many years, Chicago's rival as the transportation hub of America. It was a heavily German city, with a Teutonic solidity and orderliness that distinguished it from the surrounding Southern-accented rural terrain. From Mitteleuropa came the founders of St. Louis's great businesses — the Anheuser-Busch brewery, May Company department stores, Joseph Pulitzer's St. Louis Post-Dispatch — and its first great politician, Carl Schurz, the senator and Interior secretary. There is almost a European aura to Forest Park, the site of the 1904 fair, and the mansion-lined private streets nearby.

St. Louis no longer occupies as central a place in the national consciousness and the central city itself has largely emptied out. It has dropped below Baltimore as the 20th largest metro area in the nation. The German order that made so many people comfortable living in close quarters and commuting by streetcar has yielded to an American desire for suburban spaces and the less restrictive automobile. St. Louis' population peaked at 856,000 in 1950; now it is at its lowest level since the late 19th century — 308,626 in 2017, an 11 percent decrease from 2000. In recent years, downtown St. Louis has been spruced up: A new Busch Stadium opened in 2006 with a panoramic view of the Arch and downtown. The national park surrounding Gateway Arch was refurbished in 2018, as a section of Interstate 44 was covered over and the accompanying museum was expanded to provide a more complete portrait of St. Louis' significance. Still, the life of the city continued to struggle. In 2008, local icon Anheuser-Busch was taken over by Belgium-based Inbred. The Anheuser-Busch Inbred corporate offices and factory operations have remained along the Mississippi just south of the Arch, though the worldwide headquarters are in Belgium and a U.S. commercial strategy office has shifted to New York City. The city suffered a civic blow, though it may have avoided a ruinous financial deal, when the St. Louis Rams of the National Football League returned to Los Angeles in 2016 and settled lawsuits after the city refused to satisfy the team owner's demand for a new stadium. In 2018, USA Today ranked St. Louis the third-worst city in which to live, behind Detroit and Flint Michigan.

About 10 miles up Interstate 70 from the Arch is the suburb of Ferguson, which became a center of riots and heated discussion of police practices following the shooting death in August 2014 of Michael Brown, an unarmed 18-year-old, by police officer Darren Wilson. A short time earlier, Brown and a friend had been videotaped in a local convenience store, apparently stealing cigars. The next day, the county police chief said that Brown had assaulted Wilson. Like other parts of St. Louis County, Ferguson (pop. 21,059) has a majority-black population, 67 percent in this case. But the minority white population had managed to keep control of the local government and the police department. As the details of Brown's death spread, there were growing protests and then riots in the streets of Ferguson, with police using tear gas and arresting dozens of persons. A fragile calm eventually was restored until November, when the county prosecutor announced that a grand jury had decided not to indict Wilson, which resulted in additional protests.

News accounts described how several municipalities in St. Louis County, including Ferguson, had profited from poverty and from police and court actions that resulted from often petty offenses, which added to the economic and social dislocation. In a March 2015 report, a panel of outside experts working with the Justice Department found persistent racial bias by Ferguson authorities, who had used arrest warrants to raise large sums for the operation of the city. The city agreed to major changes in local laws and police practices, including improved use of social media to share information — a problem at the heart of the 2014 breakdown.

The 1st District takes in all of St. Louis, plus about two-fifths of the people in suburban St. Louis County. It includes all of the predominantly African-American suburbs north of the city, including Ferguson, plus Bellefontaine Neighbors, Spanish Lake and Black Jack. It includes working-class St. Ann, part of Bridgeton and, west of the city, the affluent suburb of University City. African Americans, a 49 percent plurality in the district, account for far more than half the votes in Democratic primaries. Given that the population of St. Louis city is 47 percent black, the portion of the district that is in St. Louis County has a slight majority of blacks. Overall, the county is 27 percent black; St. Louis and Clay (Kansas City) counties are the two reliably Democratic counties in Missouri. The 1st is heavily Democratic, although the party organization has been weakened by the loss of patronage and by state approval of term limits. Hillary Clinton got a comfortable 77 percent.

Ann Wagner (R)

Elected 2012, 4th term, b. Sep 13, 1962; St. Louis; Cor Jesu Academy (MO), 1980; University of Missouri, B.S., 1984; Roman Catholic; Married (Raymond T. Wagner Jr.); 3 children.

Professional Career: Manager, Hallmark Cards; Manager Ralston Purina; MO Director, George H. W. Bush reelection campaign, 1992; Chair, MO Republican Party, 1999-2005; Co-chair, Republican National Committee, 2001-2005; U.S. ambassador to Luxembourg, 2005-2009; Chairwoman, Roy Blunt for Senate campaign, 2009-2010.

DC Office: 2350 RHOB 20515, 202-225-1621, Fax: 202-225-2563, wagner.house.gov

State Offices: Ballwin, 636-779-5449.

Committees: *Financial Services*: Investor Protection, Entrepreneurship & Capital Markets; Subcommittee on Diversity & Inclusion (RMM). *Foreign Affairs*: Asia, the Pacific & Nonproliferation; Europe, Eurasia, Energy & the Environment.

Group Ratings

	ADA	ACLU	AFL-CIO	LCV	ITI	COC	HAFA	ACU	CFG	FRC
2018	-	4%	-	0%	-	92%	83%	91%	62%	100%
2017	0%	C	3%	0%	C	93%	C	93%	81%	100%

Almanac Ratings 2017-18

	Economy	Social	Foreign	Composite
Liberal	4%	8%	0%	4%
Conservative	96%	92%	100%	96%

Key Votes of the 115th Congress

1. Obama-care revision	Y	5. Family planning regs	Y	9. Guantanamo prisoners	N
2. Tax Cuts	Y	6. Body cameras/immigration	NV	10. Ground missiles, limit	N
3. Omnibus appropriations	Y	7. Abortion ban	Y	11. Defense Dept. spending	Y
4. Dodd-Frank revision	Y	8. Concealed carry	Y	12. FISA rules	Y

Election Results

Election	Name (Party)	Vote (%)	Cand. Spent	Ind. Exp. Support	Ind. Exp. Oppose
2018 General	Ann Wagner (R)............................... 192,477	(51%)	$4,008,797	$86,452	$20,076
	Cort Van Ostran (D)........................... 177,611	(47%)	$2,254,252	$56,887	$1,342
2018 Primary	Ann Wagner (R)................................. 72,173	(90%)			
	Noga Sachs (R)............................. 8,115	(10%)			

Prior winning percentages: 2016 (59%), 2014 (64%), 2012 (60%)

A former Republican National Committee co-chair and fundraiser, Ann Wagner was elected in 2012 by overpowering her opponents financially and with her political expertise. She spent her first several years in Congress as one of the GOP conference's biggest stars, but she faced questions about her next moves as her fourth term started.

Wagner grew up in the St. Louis suburbs, where her father ran a carpet store and her grandfather owned a paint business. At an all-girls Catholic school, she acted in musicals, playing the female roles at all-boys' schools. Her father wanted to see his daughter get a business degree. She graduated with one from the University of Missouri, then went to work for Hallmark Cards and Ralston Purina. Her involvement in politics began in 1989 when her husband, Raymond, took a job with John Ashcroft, then governor of Missouri. She oversaw Missouri's redistricting after the 1990 census, and ran the Missouri campaign for President George H.W. Bush in 1992, which he lost both nationally and in the state. In 1999, Wagner became chair of the Missouri GOP. Both chambers of the General Assembly went Republican in 2002, for the first time in 54 years. President George W. Bush named her ambassador to Luxembourg, and for four years she rotated her family between Missouri and the tiny European nation.

It wasn't until 2012 — with two of her children out of the house, the third a high school senior, and a Democratic administration that she said was mortgaging her children's future — that she decided to run for office. After GOP Rep. Todd Akin announced his ill-fated bid for the Senate, she announced for his seat, quickly raising money, with substantial contributions from employees of St. Louis-based Enterprise Rent-A-Car, where her husband was an executive. Some Republicans accused Enterprise of essentially buying her the seat, but her campaign said the donations merely reflected the employees' trust in her. Initially, Wagner seemed likely to have a fight on her hands. But Republican Ed Martin, who had unsuccessfully challenged Democratic Rep. Russ Carnahan in 2010, dropped out of the race. And Carnahan, whose district had been dismantled in redistricting, decided to challenge fellow Democrat William Lacy Clay rather than run against Wagner. That left Democrat Glenn Koenen, a former food pantry executive director, who faced insurmountable odds. Wagner won, 60-37 percent.

Wagner has had a conservative voting record on economic and foreign policy issues and has ranked a bit more centrist on social issues, according to Almanac ratings. As one of four House members from Missouri to serve on the Financial Services Committee, she has tended to their home state's large financial community. Outside of her committee work, Wagner has worked closely with Democratic Rep. Carolyn Maloney of New York on the issue of human trafficking.

Wagner has found roles within the House GOP. She was chosen leader of the freshman class, and played a prime role in the recruitment of candidates by the National Republican Congressional Committee. When Rep. Steve Scalise of Louisiana became whip in June 2014, he selected Wagner as one of five senior deputy whips. She had become politically close to Scalise since her 2012 campaign, when he subbed at a campaign appearance for her on the day after her father died. Wagner spent much of the 2014 cycle dedicated to recruiting female Republican candidates, with mixed success. After she decided not to run in 2016 for chairwoman of the NRCC, she became vice-chair for fundraising. She again considered running for the top position after the 2018 midterms, only to back down after it became clear that Minority Leader Kevin McCarthy did not support her, according to The New York Times.

She has been reelected easily, though her victory in 2016 fell to 59%-38% against lightly financed Democrat Bill Otto. Following the release of the controversial "Access Hollywood" video in October

2016, she withdrew her endorsement of Donald Trump and said that Mike Pence should replace him at the top of the ticket. A few days before the election, she said that she would vote for Trump. Following the election, she said that she looked forward to working with him. After much speculation, Wagner decided against challenging Sen. Claire McCaskill in 2018.

She finished that cycle with a narrow 51%-47% win over Democrat Cort VanOstran. Wagner outspent the challenger, $4 million to $2.3 million, and the contest received little attention from the national parties. As a result, the DCCC listed her district as a top pick-up target. For 2020, Wagner will need to stay in touch at home.

MO-2: St. Louis   Cook Partisan Voting Index: R+8

Population		Race and Ethnicity		Income	
Total	762,444	White	87.2%	Median Income	$79,339
Land area (sq. miles)	466	Black	3.7%	District Income Rank	56
Pop/ sq mi	1637	Latino	2.7%	Poverty Rate	5.4%
Born in State	65.8%	Asian	4.4%	With health insurance	95.1%
		Two or more races	1.7%	Cash public assistance	0.9%
Age Groups		Other	0.3%	Food stamp/SNAP	4%
Under 18	21.9%				
18-34	19.3%	**Education**		**Work**	
35-64	40.8%	H.S grad or less	24.1%	White Collar	18%
Over 64	18%	Some college	27.2%	Sales and Service	37.8%
		College Degree, 4 yr	28.9%	Blue Collar	12.5%
Military		Post grad	19.9%	Government	8.1%
Veteran/ Active Duty	8%				

2012 Pres. Vote	Romney	235,374	(57%)	Obama	170,786	(42%)		
2016 Pres. Vote	Trump	220,727	(52%)	Clinton	177,731	(42%)	Johnson	16,078 (4%)

St. Louis County, suburbs: Just as the geographic center of U.S. population has moved west from St. Louis to rural Texas County, so has the center of metropolitan St. Louis moved farther west from the Gateway Arch on the Mississippi River. Now the midpoint is suburban St. Louis County, established in 1876 when the city, tired of paying for dusty back roads, separated itself from the sticks. That year, there were 350,000 people in the city and 31,000 in the county. In 2017, there were about 309,000 in the city and 1 million in St. Louis County. The area's office center is fast moving out along the Daniel Boone Expressway (U.S. 40) to Chesterfield. Near the city-county border is Grant's Farm, where Ulysses S. Grant lived in the 1850s and where Anheuser-Busch bred the Budweiser Clydesdales.

The 2nd Congressional District of Missouri consists of central and western St. Louis County, part of St. Charles County across the Missouri River, and a small sliver of Jefferson County to the south. Along the expressway, in the center of St. Louis County, are long-settled suburbs: Kirkwood, LaDue, and high-income Town and Country, where one-acre lots for sale remain common. In Chesterfield, Pfizer broke ground for a new research campus. But Bayer announced in late 2018 it would eliminate 4,200 jobs -- a result of its acquisition of the Creve Coeur-based Monsanto biotech company. Chesterfield has the most expensive housing in the area, and upscale shopping. Ballwin is a growing center for immigrants with biotech and health care jobs. For the district, more than four-fifths of the population is in St. Louis County, which has had a big increase in racial minorities. But they are mostly in the 1st District. The 2nd is 87 percent white. St. Louis County has a new district attorney: Wesley Bell, a former councilman from nearby Ferguson, defeated the county's longtime prosecutor Robert McCulloch in an August 2018 primary. McCulloch became a focal point of criticism for his handling in 2014 of a police shooting that led to riots in Ferguson.

These have been historically Republican areas, more so in the newer family-oriented subdivisions than in the leafy precincts of the older enclaves. Fast-growing St. Charles County, where the supply of available land and affordable housing has tightened, has more people and casts more votes than the city of St. Louis, though its Republican vote has become smaller than in the more outlying counties of the St. Louis exurbs. From 2000 to 2010, it gained nearly 27,000 jobs, even as the number of jobs in St. Louis city dropped 14 percent. This district voted for Donald Trump in 2016, 52%-42%, a five-point decline from Mitt Romney's performance in 2012. Of the six Republican-held districts in Missouri, this is the most suburban, wealthiest and best-educated, and the only one where the Trump vote was below 63 percent and the GOP share fell from 2012. Suburban St. Louis, like demographically similar places elsewhere, became a growing problem for the GOP in the midterms.

Blaine Luetkemeyer (R)

Elected 2008, 6th term, b. May 07, 1952; Jefferson City; Lincoln University (MO), B.A., 1974; Catholic; Married (Jackie Luetkemeyer); 3 children; 4 grandchildren.

Elected Office: MO House, 1999-2005.

Professional Career: Bank examiner, State of MO, 1974-1976; Loan officer, Bank of St. Elizabeth, 1978-2008; President, Luetkemeyer Ins. Agency, 1978-2008; Director, MO div. of tourism, 2007-2008.

DC Office: 2230 RHOB 20515, 202-225-2956, Fax: 202-225-5712, luetkemeyer.house.gov

State Offices: Jefferson City, 573-635-7232; Washington, 636-239-2276; Wentzville, 636-327-7055.

Committees: *Financial Services*: Consumer Protection & Financial Institutions (RMM); Housing, Community Development & Insurance.

Group Ratings

	ADA	ACLU	AFL-CIO	LCV	ITI	COC	HAFA	ACU	CFG	FRC
2018	-	4%	-	0%	-	92%	62%	80%	56%	100%
2017	0%	C	8%	0%	C	93%	C	78%	71%	100%

Almanac Ratings 2017-18

	Economy	Social	Foreign	Composite
Liberal	4%	4%	3%	3%
Conservative	96%	97%	97%	97%

Key Votes of the 115th Congress

1. Obama-care revision	Y	5. Family planning regs	Y	9. Guantanamo prisoners	N
2. Tax Cuts	Y	6. Body cameras/immigration	N	10. Ground missiles, limit	N
3. Omnibus appropriations	Y	7. Abortion ban	Y	11. Defense Dept. spending	Y
4. Dodd-Frank revision	Y	8. Concealed carry	Y	12. FISA rules	Y

Election Results

Election	Name (Party)	Vote (%)		Cand. Spent	Ind. Exp. Support	Ind. Exp. Oppose
2018 General	Blaine Luetkemeyer (R)	211,243	(65%)		$2,007	
	Katy Geppert (D)	106,589	(33%)	$27,284		
	Donald Stolle (Lib)	6,776	(2%)			
2018 Primary	Blaine Luetkemeyer (R)	95,385	(80%)			
	Chadwick Bicknell (R)	24,000	(20%)			

Prior winning percentages: 2016 (68%), 2014 (68%), 2012 (64%), 2010 (77%), 2008 (50%)

Republican Blaine Luetkemeyer, first elected in 2008, has a firm political grip on a large swath of suburban and rural Missouri. He once worked in the banking business and has been a conservative advocate of the industry on the Financial Services Committee, where he was a leading player in the GOP rollback of banking regulations in 2017-18. He has moved up the seniority ladder and could be positioned before long to take over the top GOP post on the panel..

Luetkemeyer has Missouri roots that stretch back five generations. He grew up in St. Elizabeth, where his father worked as an insurance agent and then owned a bank. Luetkemeyer was a star high school baseball player, but his Major League tryouts were unsuccessful. He graduated from Lincoln University, a historically black college in Jefferson City, with a degree in political science. He and his wife settled on his great-grandfather's farm in St. Elizabeth. In addition to farming, he joined his family's banking operations and founded the Luetkemeyer Insurance Agency. He was elected in 1999 to the state House, where he was an active legislator. He campaigned for Missouri treasurer in 2004 but lost in the Republican primary. In 2007, Luetkemeyer was appointed director of the Missouri Division of Tourism.

The House seat opened when Republican Rep. Kenny Hulshof ran unsuccessfully for governor. Luetkemeyer was the Republican favorite in a five-way GOP primary. The conservative anti-tax group Club for Growth endorsed GOP state Rep. Bob Onder, but Luetkemeyer gained a critical endorsement from Missouri Right to Life. He led the field with 40 percent to 29 percent for Onder. In the general election, he faced state Rep. Judy Baker, a health care consultant from Columbia. Luetkemeyer emphasized his farming background. He raised $2.8 million, two-thirds of it his own money; Baker raised $1.7 million. Baker carried populous Boone County (Columbia), but Luetkemeyer took the rural counties and those west of St. Louis. In a Democratic year, he won 50%-47.5%.

Luetkemeyer joined the Tea Party Caucus and established himself as a devout fiscal and social conservative. He dismissed President Barack Obama's economic stimulus as a "large-scale failure." He successfully amended a House-passed bill in 2011 to bar the United States from contributing to the United Nation's Intergovernmental Panel on Climate Change, which he said engaged in "dubious science." Luetkemeyer introduced a bill in 2012 barring the Health and Human Services Department from forcing organizations to provide contraceptive and sterilization coverage in violation of their religious beliefs.

On the Financial Services Committee, Leutkemeyer scorned the Democrats' Dodd-Frank Wall Street reform law as detrimental to small banks. The regulations, he said, had led to "unintended" restrictions of some small and mid-sized banks. In a speech to bankers, he called Massachusetts Democratic Sen. Elizabeth Warren the "Darth Vader of the financial services world." (She replied that she saw herself "more as a Princess Leia type.") He and Democratic Rep. David Scott of Georgia enacted a bill in 2012 eliminating the physical fee-warning notices on automatic-teller machines in favor of having them displayed on-screen. He organized conservative support for the reauthorization of the Export-Import Bank, which many on the right opposed as corporate welfare.

As Housing Subcommittee chairman in 2015-16, Leutkemeyer worked closely with Democratic Rep. Emanuel Cleaver of Missouri to enact in 2016 what he called "comprehensive legislation which represents real reforms to our nation's housing programs." He was especially unhappy with what he saw as inadequate funding of the mutual mortgage insurance fund, which he said might require another bailout. In 2016, the House passed his bill to end the Obama administration's Operation Choke Point, which was designed to investigate consumer fraud but allegedly had terminated legitimate banking accounts that had supported industries such as guns and tobacco that it disliked.

In 2017, Luetkemeyer became chairman of the Financial Institutions and Consumer Credit Subcommittee, where he said his goal was to "to ensure all Americans have access to the tools they need to reach financial independence." Working with the Trump administration, he used that position to reduce — but not eliminate — Dodd-Frank regulations. Because of resistance in the Senate, plus that chamber's 60-vote requirement to force most legislative action, "you can only do rifle shots that are very narrow in focus," he told Politico. He failed to achieve his goal of reining in the Consumer Finance Protection Bureau with management by a multi-member commission rather than by a single administrator.

He remained mostly positive about President Donald Trump, including his use of tariffs. "The Chinese have been the bullies of trade and dumping poor products here for years," Leutkemeyer told a local newspaper in May 2018. "We are trying to push back." Two weeks prior to the mid-term election, he told the St. Louis Post-Dispatch that congressional Republicans needed to defer to Trump. "His popularity as a whole is a lot better than what Congress's is. ... So therefore [he] sets the agenda."

With his business and legislative backgrounds, Luetkemeyer voiced interest in filling the vacancy for the top Republican at the Financial Services Committee, following the 2018 election. But he deferred to Rep. Patrick McHenry of North Carolina, who had more seniority plus leadership experience. With the prospect that McHenry could return to the leadership track, Leutkemeyer might have other opportunities to lead the panel. He has breezed to reelection every two years. Despite encouragement from some Republicans, he decided not to run for governor in 2016.

MO-3: East-central Missouri

Cook Partisan Voting Index: R+18

Population		Race and Ethnicity		Income	
Total	775,379	White	91%	Median Income	$60,476
Land area (sq. miles)	6,852	Black	3.3%	District Income Rank	174
Pop/ sq mi	113.2	Latino	2.5%	Poverty Rate	10.4%
Born in State	75.2%	Asian	1%	With health insurance	91.8%
		Two or more races	1.8%	Cash public assistance	1.8%
Age Groups		Other	0.4%	Food stamp/SNAP	9%
Under 18	23.7%				
18-34	21.4%	**Education**		**Work**	
35-64	40%	H.S grad or less	42.8%	White Collar	14.9%
Over 64	14.9%	Some college	31.8%	Sales and Service	41.3%
		College Degree, 4 yr	16.8%	Blue Collar	24.9%
Military		Post grad	8.4%	Government	12.1%
Veteran/ Active Duty	9.5%				

2012 Pres. Vote	Romney	218,926	(62%)	Obama	127,104	(36%)		
2016 Pres. Vote	Trump	254,321	(67%)	Clinton	106,245	(28%)	Johnson	13,524	(4%)

St. Louis area: Missouri was the first state settled west of the Mississippi, and the folks who settled it were a picture of pioneer diversity. Virginians and other Southerners made their way to counties north of the Missouri River, while Germans settled around the small capital, Jefferson City. A taste of that diversity can be found in the capitol, with its mural by Thomas Hart Benton, great-grandnephew of one of Missouri's first senators, who championed hard money and westward expansion for 30 years and lost his seat for opposing the expansion of slavery. The painting depicts dance hall girls, black coal miners and a mother diapering an infant. Fulton is the home of Westminster College, where former Prime Minister Winston Churchill, accompanied by President Harry Truman, told the world in 1946: "From Stettin in the Baltic to Trieste in the Adriatic, an iron curtain has descended across the continent." In the small town of Washington, Meerschaum Co. remains the largest and oldest manufacturer of corn cob pipes in the world. It has been continually operating in its brick factory since 1869 and a few decades ago, it shipped up to 25 million pipes each year. In recent years, its annual production has been less than a million pipes

The 3rd Congressional District covers east-central Missouri, stretching from Jefferson City to the western St. Louis exurbs of St. Charles and Jefferson counties, and extends like a claw to the Mississippi Rivers both north and south of St. Louis County and city. Its population base is in the western parts of fast-growing St. Charles County, which has about one-third of the voters. Because it manufactures trucks and vans, the General Motors plant in Wentzville, which has more than 4,000 workers, was not directly affected by the more than 14,000 layoffs that GM announced in its November 2018 restructuring. The local GM facility has been a boon to parts suppliers, which had been hurt by the closing of Ford and Chrysler plants in the area. In Jefferson City, business leaders have continued to explore options to build a Missouri River port. They contend that cargo vessels would be more efficient than barges in carrying shipping containers the 100 miles from Columbia to the Mississippi River.

The district is solidly Republican, with every county voting for Donald Trump in his 67%-28% win.

Vicky Hartzler (R)

Elected 2010, 5th term, b. Oct 13, 1960; Harrisonville; University of Missouri, B.S., 1983; Central Missouri State University, M.S., 1992; Evangelical; Married (Lowell Hartzler); 3 children.

Elected Office: MO House, 1995-2001.

Professional Career: Teacher, 1983-1994; Spokeswoman, Coalition to Protect Marriage, 2004; Appointee, MO Women's Cncl., 2005-2010; Owner, Hartzler Equipment Co.

DC Office: 2235 RHOB 20515, 202-225-2876, hartzler.house.gov

State Offices: Columbia, 573-442-9311; Harrisonville, 816-884-3411; Lebanon, 417-532-5582.

Committees: *Agriculture*: Biotechnology, Horticulture & Research; Livestock & Foreign Agriculture. *Armed Services*: Seapower & Projection Forces; Tactical Air & Land Forces (RMM).

Group Ratings

	ADA	ACLU	AFL-CIO	LCV	ITI	COC	HAFA	ACU	CFG	FRC
2018	-	4%	-	0%	-	91%	62%	76%	58%	100%
2017	0%	C	8%	3%	C	93%	C	78%	71%	100%

Almanac Ratings 2017-18

	Economy	Social	Foreign	Composite
Liberal	4%	4%	6%	4%
Conservative	96%	97%	94%	96%

Key Votes of the 115th Congress

1. Obama-care revision	Y	5. Family planning regs	Y	9. Guantanamo prisoners	N
2. Tax Cuts	Y	6. Body cameras/immigration	N	10. Ground missiles, limit	N
3. Omnibus appropriations	Y	7. Abortion ban	Y	11. Defense Dept. spending	Y
4. Dodd-Frank revision	Y	8. Concealed carry	Y	12. FISA rules	Y

Election Results

Election	Name (Party)		Vote (%)	Cand. Spent	Ind. Exp. Support	Ind. Exp. Oppose
2018 General	Vicky Hartzler (R)	190,138	(65%)	$1,142,179	$9,254	
	Renee Hoagenson (D)	95,968	(33%)	$433,956		
	Mark Bliss (Lib)	7,210	(2%)			
2018 Primary	Vicky Hartzler (R)	74,226	(74%)			
	John Webb (R)	26,787	(27%)			

Prior winning percentages: 2016 (68%), 2014 (68%), 2012 (60%), 2010 (50%)

Republican Vicky Hartzler, who was elected in 2010 when she defeated the Democratic chairman of the House Armed Services Committee, has created her own niche at the panel. A former activist who led the movement to ban same-sex marriage in Missouri, she retained her focus on social conservative issues, some of which are military-related. Hartzler has advocated the interests of the large military bases in her district. She gave serious thought to running for the Senate in 2018.

Hartzler has spent her entire life in rural Cass County, where she grew up on the family farm. After getting her bachelor's degree in education at the University of Missouri, she worked as a high school home economics teacher for 11 years. Later, she got her master's in education at the University of Central Missouri. She and her husband, Lowell, resided on a 1,600-acre farm outside Harrisonville, where they raised corn, soybeans and cattle and ran the Hartzler Equipment Co., which sold farming equipment. Her career changed in 1994 when she got a phone call from a friend while she was grading papers, urging her to run for state representative. "He asked me to think about it and pray about it, and I did," Hartzler said. "After 30 days, I knew I was supposed to run." She served three terms in Missouri's House, where she overhauled the state's adoption law. With the adoption of her daughter, she had a special interest in the topic.

In 2004, Hartzler headed the Coalition to Protect Marriage in Missouri, a campaign to add an amendment to the state's constitution banning same-sex marriage. Despite being outspent 17-to-1 by pro-gay-marriage groups, the amendment passed with 71 percent of the vote. She wrote the book *Running God's Way: Step by Step to a Successful Political Campaign*, a detailed guide for Christian candidates.

Her bid to unseat Ike Skelton, the powerful chairman of the Armed Services Committee, drew the interest of tea party groups. In the conservative district, Skelton had relied on crossover GOP voters during his 17 terms in the House. Hartzler assailed his votes with "the liberal leadership" for the $787 billion economic stimulus bill and an energy bill imposing caps on carbon emissions. Hartzler tried to turn Skelton's image as a wise legislative elder into a negative; "So many people in Washington [are] removed from rural America. Ike's lost touch," she said. Skelton raised $3 million and outspent Hartzler 3-to-1. She won, 50%-45%.

Republican leaders made good on their promise to give Hartzler a seat on Armed Services. Using that platform to pursue social issues, she added a provision to the defense bill in 2011 defining marriage as a union between a man and a woman for the purpose of military benefits and policy. The provision was dropped in conference with the Senate. She filed a bill preventing military veterans convicted of sexual abuse of children from being buried in Arlington National Cemetery. She added an amendment to the defense bill that would have banned gender reassignment surgery for members of the military. In July 2017, the House voted down her provision, 214-209, with 24 Republicans opposing her. Later that month, President Donald Trump said that transgenders would not be permitted to serve in the military, due chiefly to the medical costs.

As chairwoman of the Oversight and Investigations Subcommittee, the interests of her district remained paramount. The House in 2015 approved her provision for construction at Whiteman Air Force Base of a Consolidated Stealth Operations and Nuclear Alert Facility. She took credit for approval of 12 additional F/A-18F Super Hornet aircraft, large parts of which have been built at the Boeing plant in St. Louis.

After supporting House Republican spending cuts, defense-hawk Hartzler found that the tight-budget demands of fiscal hawks can be objectionable. She opposed the New Year's Day 2013 bipartisan deal aimed at averting the so-called "fiscal cliff." In 2015, she urged Congress to end budget "sequestration" and warned that automatic cuts in Defense Department spending threatened "impending devastation to our military." In 2019, as part of the House minority for the first time, she became the ranking Republican on the Tactical Air and Land Forces Subcommittee, whose jurisdiction over Army and Air Force acquisitions meshes with the interests of her district.

Continuing her work on social issues beyond the Pentagon, Hartzler in 2015 joined the special House committee charged with investigating abortion providers, including Planned Parenthood, following the release of undercover videos about the group. Also that year, she filed a resolution to veto a law passed by the District of Columbia that would ban discrimination against LGBT students attending religious schools, which she said "infringed on the fundamental right of religious freedom."

In 2016, Hartzler said that some comments by Donald Trump were "undefendable," but that she supported him because of the policies he advocated. After his first year as president, she praised Trump for having "really fulfilled his campaign promises," especially on abortion-related issues, including the selection of judges. When Trump suggested cash subsidies for farmers who had lost overseas markets because of his tariffs, Hartzler told reporters in July 2018, "farmers want trade, not aid." But she declined to criticize. "He has an unconventional approach" and the outcome of the trade talks "will be the final determinant," she added.

At home, Hartzler has not been seriously challenged for reelection. Following the 2016 election, she explored a challenge to Democratic Sen. Claire McCaskill. Facing daunting fundraising demands, she said, "this race is for another solid conservative to pursue and win."

MO-4: West-central Missouri

Cook Partisan Voting Index: R+17

Population		Race and Ethnicity		Income	
Total	762,923	White	86.8%	Median Income	$48,015
Land area (sq. miles)	14,401	Black	4.6%	District Income Rank	341
Pop/ sq mi	53	Latino	3.8%	Poverty Rate	16.6%
Born in State	62.6%	Asian	1.5%	With health insurance	88.9%
		Two or more races	2.7%	Cash public assistance	2.3%
Age Groups		Other	0.6%	Food stamp/SNAP	12.3%
Under 18	22.5%				
18-34	25.5%	Education		Work	
35-64	36.3%	H.S grad or less	45.5%	White Collar	15.7%
Over 64	15.7%	Some college	29.7%	Sales and Service	40.9%
		College Degree, 4 yr	15.1%	Blue Collar	24.7%
Military		Post grad	9.6%	Government	16.9%
Veteran/ Active Duty	13.6%				

2012 Pres. Vote	Romney	201,702	(61%)	Obama	119,932	(36%)			
2016 Pres. Vote	Trump	222,141	(65%)	Clinton	99,858	(29%)	Johnson	13,316	(4%)

Columbia: Roughly equidistant from St. Louis and Kansas City, Columbia in central Missouri has emerged as an economic hub in its own right. Nicknamed the Athens of Missouri, Columbia surpassed Independence in 2015 to become the fourth-largest city in the state, with a population that increased 12 percent from 2010 to 2017. The University of Missouri is the biggest employer in the city. A number of graduates have remained in the city to work in the health care and insurance industries. In 2015, allegations of racism plus multiple budget cuts led to widespread campus protests, including by its football team, and resulted in the resignation of the university president. That resulted in a decline of applications to the school, especially by African Americans, and a reduction in enrollment from nearly 35,000 in 2015 to 31,000 in 2017. In 2018, following campus reforms, the number of freshmen increased, though not enough to prevent a further overall decline to 29,400. Improvements at Columbia Regional Airport more than doubled the passenger load from 2014 to 2018. The widening of the main runway and plans for a new terminal — in place of the current hangar for passengers -- led to expanded service by American and United Airlines.

The 4th Congressional District occupies Columbia and rural west central Missouri. Columbia's Boone County includes about one-fourth of the district's voters. It was one of just three counties in the state to support Hillary Clinton in 2016, 49%-43%. South of Kansas City, the district includes fast-growing Belton and Raymore in ancestrally Democratic Cass County, where Donald Trump got 65 percent in 2016. There are two big military bases here: Fort Leonard Wood in Pulaski County, where Marines, sailors and airmen train in joint exercises with Army troops; and Whiteman Air Force Base, near Knob Noster in Johnson County, from which B-2 stealth bombers have flown to drop precision-targeted bombs in Afghanistan. The Air Force has plans to upgrade its B-2 fleet, of which 20 are based at Whiteman. That total fleet is scheduled to be replaced in the late 2020s by the new B-21 Raider bombers.

The district overall has become safely Republican, despite its Democratic heritage. Like other non-urban parts of Missouri, Trump scored a big increase in Republican support in the 4th, to 65%-29%.

Emanuel Cleaver (D)

Elected 2004, 8th term, b. Oct 26, 1944; Waxahachie, TX; Murray State College (OK), Att., 1964; Prairie View Agricultural and Mechanical University (TX), B.S., 1972; St. Paul School of Theology, Kansas City (MO), M.Div., 1974; Methodist; Married (Dianne Cleaver); 4 children (twins); 3 grandchildren.

Elected Office: Kansas City Council, 1979-1991; Mayor, Kansas City, 1991-1999.

Professional Career: Pastor, 1970-present; Radio talk-show host, 2002-2004.

DC Office: 2335 RHOB 20515, 202-225-4535, Fax: 202-225-4403, cleaver.house.gov

State Offices: Higginsville, 660-584-7373; Independence, 816-833-4545; Kansas City, 816-842-4545.

Committees: *Financial Services*: Housing, Community Development & Insurance; Nat'l Security, International Development & Monetary Policy (Chmn). *Homeland Security*: Transportation & Maritime Security. *Select Committee on the Modernization of Congress.*

Group Ratings

	ADA	ACLU	AFL-CIO	LCV	ITI	COC	HAFA	ACU	CFG	FRC
2018	-	87%	-	97%	-	58%	9%	4%	23%	0%
2017	100%	C	97%	89%	C	36%	C	4%	5%	0%

Almanac Ratings 2017-18

	Economy	Social	Foreign	Composite
Liberal	89%	90%	65%	81%
Conservative	11%	10%	35%	19%

Key Votes of the 115th Congress

1. Obama-care revision	N	5. Family planning regs	N	9. Guantanamo prisoners	NV
2. Tax Cuts	N	6. Body cameras/immigration	Y	10. Ground missiles, limit	NV
3. Omnibus appropriations	Y	7. Abortion ban	N	11. Defense Dept. spending	NV
4. Dodd-Frank revision	N	8. Concealed carry	N	12. FISA rules	N

Election Results

Election	Name (Party)	Vote (%)		Cand. Spent	Ind. Exp. Support	Ind. Exp. Oppose
2018 General	Emanuel Cleaver (D)	175,019	(62%)	$1,149,793		
	Jacob Turk (R)	101,069	(36%)	$65,944	$2,351	
2018 Primary	Emanuel Cleaver (D)		(100%)			

Prior winning percentages: 2016 (59%), 2014 (52%), 2012 (61%), 2010 (53%), 2008 (64%), 2006 (64%), 2004 (55%)

Democrat Emanuel Cleaver, first elected in 2004, is an ordained minister who is known for his leadership of the Congressional Black Caucus and his work on housing issues, as well as his efforts to improve civility in Congress. In the Missouri way, he displayed an independence in his public actions. In 2019, he was disappointed that he failed to become chairman of the Housing Subcommittee.

Cleaver grew up in Waxahachie Texas, in a three-room shack with no plumbing or electricity. He graduated from Prairie View A&M University, moved to Kansas City and earned a divinity degree, then became pastor of St. James United Methodist Church. He was elected to the city council in 1979 and as mayor in 1991. In city hall, Cleaver voiced support for the Clinton administration's changes in welfare policy, which he described as "corrective surgery." He backed expansion of downtown's Bartle Hall Convention Center and supported renovation of the deteriorating Liberty Memorial, the country's largest World War I memorial. After leaving office, he hosted a radio talk show.

When the seat became open, Cleaver faced former National Security Council aide Jamie Metzl in the Democratic primary. Metzl hammered him on ethics issues, questioning the propriety of a loan that Cleaver took out to purchase a car wash and his failure to pay $36,000 in back taxes on the business. Cleaver won the primary 60%-40%. In the general election, Cleaver faced Republican businesswoman Jeanne Patterson, who spent $3 million of her own money. Like Metzl, she made an issue of Cleaver's ethics, though there was no evidence that he was involved in any crimes. He said that Patterson was politically inexperienced and was trying to buy the seat. Cleaver won 55%-42%.

In the House, Cleaver's voting record in the Almanac vote ratings placed him near the center of the Democrats. In his first term, he was one of 22 members, all Democrats, who opposed a Republican House-passed resolution expressing support for Christmas that he dismissed as a sop to social conservatives. He opposed the 2011 deal to raise the federal debt limit, describing it to an audience back home as a "sugar-coated Satan sandwich" that would cost jobs and hurt the poor. He has sponsored bills to promote financial literacy and to make it easier for students to vote. During her initial reign as Speaker, Nancy Pelosi designated Cleaver to act as a liaison with mayors and faith communities.

Cleaver chaired the Black Caucus in 2011-12 at a time when members often expressed dissatisfaction with President Barack Obama for failing to do more to help low-income minorities. Cleaver tried to walk a fine line between joining in the criticism and working to ensure the reelection of the nation's first black president. "With 14 percent [black] unemployment, if we had a white president, we'd be marching around the White House. ... The president knows we are going to act in deference to him in a way we wouldn't to someone white," he told The Root in September 2012.

Cleaver periodically has taken the spotlight on issues involving race. After the August 2014 fatal police shooting of an unarmed black teenager in Ferguson Missouri touched off riots there, he defended Obama's decision not to visit the city, even as he told MSNBC that it "resembles Fallujah" because of the militarized law-enforcement presence, which he called "un-American." Cleaver filed a bill in 2015 to make it a civil rights violation for police to set criminal or traffic violations for the purpose of raising local revenue.

As ranking member of the Housing and Insurance Subcommittee from 2015 to 2018, Cleaver made affordable housing his priority. With Republican Rep. Blaine Luetkemeyer of Missouri, who chaired the subcommittee, he enacted in 2016 what they described as the most significant changes in federal housing programs in a quarter-century. The measure included a streamlining of the inspection and income review process for families living in Section 8 housing, improved condo ownership opportunities and increased access to rural housing loans. In June 2018, he spearheaded a bipartisan call to update the regulations for loan approval by the Federal Housing Administration for condos and multi-unit housing.

When Democrats took the majority in 2019, Cleaver hoped to become chairman of the Housing subcommittee. Instead, Rep. Lacy Clay — also from Missouri -- asserted his seniority. "If you accept the concept of seniority, you have to sometimes accept some things that you don't like," he said. Clay also had been more of a Democratic leadership loyalist. Instead, Cleaver became chairman of the National Security, International Development and Monetary Policy Subcommittee at Financial Services.

With West Virginia Republican Rep. (and now Senator) Shelley Moore Capito in 2011, Cleaver resurrected their idea for a "Civility Caucus," and Cleaver issued regular pronouncements to colleagues stressing the importance of collegiality. "Bees cannot sting and make honey at the same time; they have to make a choice," he said.

Cleaver stirred some unhappiness among Democrats in 2018 when he emphasized his close working relationship with Republican Rep. Kevin Yoder, who represented the district across the state line in Kansas. In his tight reelection contest, Yoder featured an image of Cleaver in a campaign ad and cited him during a debate. Cleaver objected, but Yoder continued the ad. "A lot of Democrats ... did begin to call me and say, 'Hey, what's going on," Cleaver told The Kansas City Star. "They were upset." Yoder lost to challenger Sharice Davids.

In 2018, Cleaver faced Republican Jacob Turk for the seventh time. After having run their closest campaign in 2014, a 52%-46% win for Cleaver, the incumbent regained his more customary victory margin in 2018, 62%-36%. Especially during their years in the minority, Cleaver was outspoken among Democrats who believed that they needed to change their leadership team, including Pelosi.

MO-5: Kansas City Metro　　　　　　　　**Cook Partisan Voting Index: D+7**

Population		Race and Ethnicity		Income	
Total	761,929	White	64.1%	Median Income	$48,178
Land area (sq. miles)	2,425	Black	21.7%	District Income Rank	336
Pop/ sq mi	314.2	Latino	8.9%	Poverty Rate	16.7%
Born in State	60.6%	Asian	1.8%	With health insurance	87%
		Two or more races	2.6%	Cash public assistance	2.9%
Age Groups		Other	1%	Food stamp/SNAP	13.4%
Under 18	23.2%				
18-34	24.2%	**Education**		**Work**	
35-64	38%	H.S grad or less	42%	White Collar	14.6%
Over 64	14.6%	Some college	30.8%	Sales and Service	43.5%
		College Degree, 4 yr	17.4%	Blue Collar	22.2%
Military		Post grad	9.9%	Government	11.3%
Veteran/ Active Duty	8.3%				

2012 Pres. Vote	Obama	198,356	(59%)	Romney	132,632	(39%)			
2016 Pres. Vote	Clinton	179,354	(55%)	Trump	130,051	(40%)	Johnson	12,098	(4%)

Jackson County: Kansas City, named after a state it isn't in and a river it doesn't touch, is the center of one of America's largest metro areas, the biggest on the central Great Plains. The first settlers here started little towns on the bluffs the Missouri River — Independence, Kansas City, Westport — that coalesced a few decades later. Here, traders on the Santa Fe Trail passed through on their way to cross the Sand Hills of Kansas to reach Mexican territory, and pioneers headed for Oregon and California. Kansas City was a rail center and, in the 1920s, had one of the largest stockyards in the country, a major commercial center with lean skyscrapers, and the Country Club Plaza, the first drive-to shopping center in America. Harry Truman grew up on a farm now in the suburb of Grandview and lived in his wife's family's house in Independence, the old county seat just to the east. The city is famous for its National Negro Leagues Baseball Museum, its historic jazz district that has been home to musicians like Scott Joplin, Charlie Parker and Count Basie, and for its much-praised barbecue. The redevelopment downtown includes the Kauffman Center for the Performing Arts. More than 20,000 people live downtown, most of them millennials. That increase has been accompanied by a small reduction in the black population in the city from 31 percent in 2000 to 29 percent in 2017. (Kansas City, Kansas is about one-third the size of its counterpart.)

A 2.2 mile downtown streetcar, which started service in May 2016, had modest ridership. In June 2018, a small turnout of voters in a mail-in election approved a 3.7 mile extension to the University of Missouri's Kansas City campus, with financing from increases in local sales and property taxes. That service was projected to start in 2023.

The 5th Congressional District of Missouri includes most of Kansas City, the largest city in Missouri, plus Grandview and the bulk of Independence. On Election Night 1948, when just about everyone thought he would lose, Truman was not far away in the resort town of Excelsior Springs. Most of the Kansas City area's landmarks, including the Truman home, are here, but much of the metropolitan area's growth has been across the state line in Kansas. About 40 percent of the voters live in Kansas City, which is overwhelmingly Democratic. Another 40 percent live in surrounding Jackson County, which leans a bit Republican. The remainder reside in suburban Clay County and three small counties toward the rural center of Missouri. 22 percent of the district's residents are African-American, the second highest percentage among Missouri districts. Hillary Clinton got 55 percent of the vote.

Sam Graves (R)

Elected 2000, 10th term, b. Nov 07, 1963; Tarkio; University of Missouri, B.S., 1986; Baptist; Married (Lesley Graves); 3 children.

Elected Office: MO House, 1992-1994; MO Senate, 1994-2000.

Professional Career: Farmer.

DC Office: 1135 LHOB 20515, 202-225-7041, Fax: 202-225-8221, graves.house.gov

State Offices: Hannibal, 573-221-3400; Kansas City, 816-792-3976; St. Joseph, 816-749-0800.

Committees: *Armed Services*: Intelligence, Emerging Threats & Capabilities. *Transportation & Infrastructure (RMM)*: Ex Officio membership on all subcommittees.

Group Ratings

	ADA	ACLU	AFL-CIO	LCV	ITI	COC	HAFA	ACU	CFG	FRC
2018	-	4%	-	0%	-	82%	64%	72%	46%	100%
2017	0%	C	18%	0%	C	93%	C	85%	76%	100%

Almanac Ratings 2017-18

	Economy	Social	Foreign	Composite
Liberal	8%	12%	3%	7%
Conservative	92%	88%	98%	93%

Key Votes of the 115th Congress

1. Obama-care revision	Y	5. Family planning regs	Y
2. Tax Cuts	Y	6. Body cameras/immigration	N
3. Omnibus appropriations	Y	7. Abortion ban	Y
4. Dodd-Frank revision	Y	8. Concealed carry	Y

9. Guantanamo prisoners	N
10. Ground missiles, limit	N
11. Defense Dept. spending	Y
12. FISA rules	Y

Election Results

Election	Name (Party)	Vote (%)		Cand. Spent	Ind. Exp. Support	Ind. Exp. Oppose
2018 General	Sam Graves (R)	199,796	(65%)	$1,348,641	$1,779	
	Henry Martin (D)	97,660	(32%)	$26,451		
	Dan Hogan (Lib)	7,953	(3%)			
2018 Primary	Sam Graves (R)		(100%)			

Prior winning percentages: 2016 (68%), 2014 (67%), 2012 (65%), 2010 (69%), 2008 (59%), 2006 (62%), 2004 (64%), 2002 (63%), 2000 (51%)

Republican Sam Graves, first elected in 2000, took over in 2019 as ranking member of the Transportation and Infrastructure Committee, where he hoped to address the widespread desire for far-reaching infrastructure legislation. As chairman of the Highways and Transit Subcommittee, he was instrumental in the enactment in 2015 of the first long-term highway bill in more than a decade. He earlier headed the Small Business Committee, where he battled Democrats over federal regulations on business.

Graves is a lifelong resident of Tarkio in the northwest corner of the state. An Eagle Scout, he regularly played "Taps" on his bugle at local cemeteries, a practice he has continued in his district each Memorial Day. He graduated from the University of Missouri with a degree in agronomy, farmed with his father and brother, and joined the Farm Bureau. He ran for the state House in 1992 and beat a longtime Democratic incumbent. Two years later, he was elected to the state Senate. He attracted attention with a five-hour filibuster against a school desegregation bill that he said put rural areas at a disadvantage, but the bill eventually passed.

Graves ran for the House when Democratic Rep. Pat Danner dropped her bid for reelection just minutes before the filing deadline. Not by accident, the immediate favorite to succeed her was her son, state Sen. Steve Danner, also a Democrat. Graves entered the race within the short window provided by state law and drew support from national Republicans. Against an opponent who attacked him as the darling of extremist party leaders, Graves won the primary, 68%-17%. In the general, Danner billed himself as a conservative Democrat and switched from pro-abortion rights to opposition. In an editorial endorsing Graves, The Kansas City Star said that Danner's switch showed that he "engaged in raw opportunism at the slightest opportunity." Graves won 51%-47%.

Graves has mostly been a rock-solid conservative, though he sometimes has deviated. He opposed barring the use of funds to administer the Davis-Bacon Act, which requires prevailing union wages on federal projects. He has remained a hardliner on immigration. He amended a fiscal 2013 spending bill to stop the Obama administration's family unity waiver system, which allowed illegal immigrants who are married to U.S. citizens to remain with their spouses while their green-card status is reviewed.

As chairman of the Small Business Committee, Graves was a regular critic of the Obama administration. He held hearings on the Environmental Protection Agency's failure to comply with a law requiring agencies to analyze the effects of regulations on small entities and to consider less burdensome alternatives. He opposed an effort to make more businesses eligible for a tax credit under the 2010 health care law; the credit was designed to help businesses afford health insurance for their workers. Graves worked with Democrats to pass a series of bills in 2012 aimed at fixing small business contracting problems. More changes were needed in federal contracting to encourage small businesses, he said. In December 2014, he told the Associated Press that he had made the committee "relevant" and forced the administration to analyze the burdens that regulations placed on small business.

With his new focus on transportation programs, Graves said that a long-term solution was needed for funding shortfalls in the highway trust funds. On a bipartisan basis, he and Transportation and Infrastructure Committee chairman Bill Shuster of Pennsylvania secured enactment in 2015 of the five-year Fixing America's Surface Transportation (FAST) Act, which permitted the development of user-funded tools as an alternative to gasoline taxes to finance the highway trust fund; the new law required that each state spend at least 15 percent of its funds to maintain and repair rural bridges. That left the door open for a more sweeping bill, which President Donald Trump has advocated, though he was slow to offer details.

Pointing out the need for more funds and the reduced consumption of gasoline, Graves has encouraged public-private partnerships for new highways, though he objects to toll roads. He has opposed increases in the gasoline tax as economically regressive and has backed a fee on the miles that a vehicle has traveled. The federal gas tax, which is 18.4 cents per gallon, was last raised in 1993, though every state but two impose a gas tax at least that high. The Trump administration "should be credited for taking bold, concrete steps to expedite the completion of critical projects," Graves wrote for The Kansas City Star in May 2018.

An experienced private pilot, Graves co-chairs the House's General Aviation Caucus and contends that government needs to better understand the impact of its aircraft regulations. At home, Graves has sought to compel the Army Corps of Engineers to emphasize flood control on the Missouri River, telling the St. Joseph News-Press that the agency's focus on environmental recovery over levee operations and maintenance was "out of whack." His work on highway and aviation issues, plus his district's borders on both the Missouri and Mississippi rivers, positioned Graves to jump over more senior Republicans and replace the term-limited Shuster as the senior Republican on the full committee.

Graves was the subject of an ethics investigation for his role in arranging testimony before his committee by a family friend. The matter touched off a public squabble in 2009 between the new Office of Congressional Ethics and the House Ethics Committee. OCE recommended that the case be investigated further, but the Ethics Committee found deficiencies in the recommendation and voted unanimously to clear Graves. He and other Republicans in January 2017 reportedly cited that experience to seek a House rules change to restrict the powers of the OCE, which Speaker Paul Ryan short-circuited.

In 2008, national Democrats were excited when former Kansas City Mayor and St. Joseph native Kay Barnes announced she would challenge Graves. But Graves attacked Barnes for "San Francisco values" and supporting "a homosexual agenda" because her picture had appeared in a gay magazine; he won, 59%-37%. His recent victory margins have exceeded 2-to-1.

MO-6: Northern Missouri   **Cook Partisan Voting Index: R+16**

Population		Race and Ethnicity		Income	
Total	763,913	White	88%	Median Income	$57,614
Land area (sq. miles)	18,199	Black	4.1%	District Income Rank	198
Pop/ sq mi	42	Latino	4%	Poverty Rate	12.1%
Born in State	64.9%	Asian	1.3%	With health insurance	91%
		Two or more races	2.2%	Cash public assistance	1.8%
Age Groups		Other	0.5%	Food stamp/SNAP	8.9%
Under 18	23.9%				
18-34	21.6%	**Education**		**Work**	
35-64	38.9%	H.S grad or less	43.4%	White Collar	15.6%
Over 64	15.6%	Some college	29.2%	Sales and Service	40.3%
		College Degree, 4 yr	17.9%	Blue Collar	24.4%
Military		Post grad	9.5%	Government	13.9%
Veteran/ Active Duty	9.4%				

2012 Pres. Vote	Obama	199,298	(60%)	Romney	133,185	(39%)			
2016 Pres. Vote	Trump	226,783	(64%)	Clinton	110,474	(31%)	Johnson	14,252	(4%)

Kansas City suburbs: The rolling fields along the Missouri River in northwest Missouri were settled in a rush in the late 19th century. These lands lost people for most of the 20th century as fewer hands were needed on farms. But increased efficiencies lately have led to resurgent production. In recent years, the meatpacking business has expanded in St. Joseph and has drawn many Hispanics. Barge traffic on the Missouri has successfully reopened, following an increase in water levels and record corn and soybean crops. Record-high shipments were reported along the river in 2018. Although barges move more slowly, many farmers have praised their greater reliability and lower costs than other modes of transportation.

In 2008, Rock Port in the northwest corner was the first town in the country to get all of its energy from wind power. Despite numerous applications for wind energy, the Missouri Public Service Commission in August 2017 balked at granting approval and passed the buck to the counties to certify transmission lines. That delayed the 95-mile project of the Grain Belt Express Clean Line in northeast Missouri. Some area farmers have objected that transmission lines for wind power interfere with their crops or reduce property values. The overall economy of northern Missouri remained sluggish. Twenty local counties lost population from 2000 to 2010.

In the northeast corner is Little Dixie, the swath of Missouri along the Mississippi River. This area was settled by southerners from Kentucky and Virginia. Its most famous native son is Mark Twain, born Samuel Langhorne Clemens in Hannibal, then as now a little town on bluffs overlooking the river. Hannibal was the thinly disguised St. Petersburg of Twain's classics, The Adventures of Tom Sawyer and The Adventures of Huckleberry Finn.

Hannibal is on the eastern edge of the 6th Congressional District, which takes in all or parts of 36 counties in northern Missouri, stretching more than 200 miles from Kansas and Nebraska to Illinois and the outskirts of St. Louis. On the western edge is the river town of St. Joseph, the biggest city north of Kansas City, which was the starting point for the Pony Express and its roughly 10-day transport of mail to Sacramento. The 6th also takes in the Kansas City suburbs of Clay and Platte and a sliver of eastern Jackson County. That area casts about half of the district's vote. The historic political tradition here was mostly Democratic. But the rural vote, as across the nation, has been tempered by dislike for national Democrats and has moved solidly Republican. The Kansas City suburb of Clay County traditionally was a reliable national bellwether, but it has swung the GOP's way too: Democrat Al Gore won in 2000 by one vote. Republican Donald Trump carried Clay by 12 percentage points in 2016, and the overall district, 64%-31%.

Billy Long (R)

Elected 2010, 5th term, b. Aug 11, 1955; Springfield; Missouri Auction School; University of Missouri, Att., 1976; Missouri Auction School, 1979; Presbyterian; Married (Barbara Long); 2 children.

Professional Career: Talk show host, 1999-2006; Realtor, 1978-2010; Owner, Billy Long Auctions.

DC Office: 2454 RHOB 20515, 202-225-6536, Fax: 202-225-5604, long.house.gov

State Offices: Joplin, 417-781-1041; Springfield, 417-889-1800.

Committees: *Energy & Commerce*: Communications & Technology; Environment & Climate Change; Health.

Group Ratings

	ADA	ACLU	AFL-CIO	LCV	ITI	COC	HAFA	ACU	CFG	FRC
2018	-	8%	-	3%	-	73%	80%	68%	63%	100%
2017	20%	C	11%	0%	C	92%	C	84%	82%	100%

Almanac Ratings 2017-18

	Economy	Social	Foreign	Composite
Liberal	5%	15%	0%	7%
Conservative	95%	85%	100%	93%

Key Votes of the 115th Congress

1. Obama-care revision	Y	5. Family planning regs	Y	9. Guantanamo prisoners	N
2. Tax Cuts	Y	6. Body cameras/immigration	N	10. Ground missiles, limit	N
3. Omnibus appropriations	N	7. Abortion ban	NV	11. Defense Dept. spending	Y
4. Dodd-Frank revision	Y	8. Concealed carry	Y	12. FISA rules	Y

Election Results

Election	Name (Party)	Vote (%)		Cand. Spent	Ind. Exp. Support	Ind. Exp. Oppose
2018 General	Billy Long (R)	196,343	(66%)	$1,213,716	$1,638	
	Jamie Schoolcraft (D)	89,190	(30%)	$54,881		
	Benjamin Brixey (Lib)	10,920	(4%)			
2018 Primary	Billy Long (R)	68,438	(65%)			
	Jim Evans (R)	18,383	(18%)			
	Lance Norris (R)	10,884	(10%)			
	Benjamin Holcomb (R)	7,416	(7%)			

Prior winning percentages: 2016 (68%), 2014 (64%), 2012 (64%), 2010 (63%)

Republican Billy Long, elected in 2010, brought a looser style to the House. His orientation has been tea party and rural, and his campaign motto was an anti-Beltway "Fed Up!" He has forged occasional alliances with Democrats. To break the tension, he sometimes resorts to his expertise as an auctioneer.

Long grew up in Springfield, where he developed an interest in Republican politics at an early age. When he was 9 years old, he told the Springfield News-Leader, he would ride his bike to pass out bumper stickers for a Greene County sheriff's candidate. After briefly attending the University of Missouri to study business, he became interested in real estate and attended auction school, eventually starting a company that would conduct as many as 200 auctions a year. He has been inducted into both the national and Missouri auctioneers' halls of fame. He spent six years as a morning-drive talk show host for an AM station covering southwest Missouri.

When Roy Blunt successfully sought a Senate seat, Long ran as a plain-talking conservative who would clamp down on federal spending and set Congress straight. He billed his lack of government service as a plus. "We have enough political experience in Washington D.C. to choke a horse," he told the Associated Press. "That's exactly the problem." In the GOP primary, he defeated seven other candidates, including two veteran state senators, with more than 37 percent of the vote. In the fall, Long advocated a constitutional amendment to limit the federal government's taxation powers and for repeal of the Democrats' health care law. He wore a cowboy hat and inveighed against "elitist politicians." In this Republican bastion, Long won 63%-30%.

Long has made good on his promise to try to change Washington's ways, though he eventually went along. He voted for a conservative budget alternative with deeper cuts than the version by Budget Committee Chairman Paul Ryan. He adamantly opposed President Barack Obama's 2013 proposals intended to reduce gun violence, including limiting the sale of ammunition clips to those holding 10 rounds or fewer. "If you're lying in bed at 4 in the morning and four people kick your door in, would you like to be restricted to five shots or six shots?" he asked the News-Leader. On the water resources bill that was enacted in December 2016, he got a provision to end a freeze on construction permits for docks on Table Rock Lake, which is near Branson. Long won bipartisan praise for his role in the disaster response to the deadly Joplin tornado in 2011, working closely with the Obama administration to provide funding to the ravaged area. "It was a lot heaped onto a freshman," Missouri Democratic Rep. Lacy Clay told the News-Leader. "But you could see him right before our eyes grow into the job and grow into his responsibility."

On the Energy and Commerce Committee, Long won bipartisan support in 2016 for his amendment to the 21st Century Cures bill to improve information to consumers about new pharmaceuticals. In 2017, when the Republican-controlled House narrowly voted to repeal the Affordable Care Act, Long briefly became the center of attention when he tweeted that he would vote against the GOP bill. When he objected that the alternative would not provide sufficient coverage for persons with pre-existing conditions, Republican leaders agreed to add $8 billion to cover such contingencies. That deal was sealed when Long was summoned to the White House — with Republican Rep. Fred Upton, who had similar concerns -- to meet with President Donald Trump. After further discussion, the mavericks agreed to support the bill. Long described his role to the News-Leader: "I'm a member of the Show-Me caucus, just one guy."

Some of Long's votes — such as supporting a raise in the federal debt limit and reauthorizing the Export-Import Bank — annoyed conservatives back home, and he has drawn primary challengers in his four reelection bids. Long has been held to between 60 and 65 percent of the vote in each case, enough to get his attention but not to force big changes. He retained some of his down-home style: At a committee hearing in September 2018, when a protestor sought to interrupt testimony by the chief executive of Twitter, Long launched an imaginary call of an auction and eventually drowned out the protestor, who was removed by the police.

In October 2016, Long "deplored" 11-year-old comments by Donald Trump about groping women. But he criticized Republicans such as Speaker Ryan who distanced themselves from Trump. "If everyone backs away from our nominee for president, that's going to spell disaster down-ticket," Long said. "No one's seen anything like this election before. It's a movement." He became a usually reliable supporter of Trump as president. When Sen. Mitt Romney wrote a harsh op-ed about Trump, Long tweeted that Romney should "get over himself."

MO-7: Western Ozarks

Cook Partisan Voting Index: R+23

Population		Race and Ethnicity		Income	
Total	768,753	White	88.5%	Median Income	$44,601
Land area (sq. miles)	6,273	Black	1.9%	District Income Rank	380
Pop/ sq mi	122.5	Latino	4.9%	Poverty Rate	16.5%
Born in State	57.8%	Asian	1.2%	With health insurance	87.1%
		Two or more races	2.4%	Cash public assistance	1.9%
Age Groups		Other	1.2%	Food stamp/SNAP	12.4%
Under 18	22.9%				
18-34	23.6%	**Education**		**Work**	
35-64	36.9%	H.S grad or less	44.2%	White Collar	16.6%
Over 64	16.6%	Some college	31.8%	Sales and Service	43.9%
		College Degree, 4 yr	15.8%	Blue Collar	23.9%
Military		Post grad	8.3%	Government	10.8%
Veteran/ Active Duty	9.7%				

2012 Pres. Vote	Romney	220,146	(66%)	Obama	98,889	(30%)		
2016 Pres. Vote	Trump	240,700	(70%)	Clinton	84,415	(25%)	Johnson	12,163	(4%)

Springfield, Joplin: One of the biggest tourist destinations in America today is Branson Missouri, something almost no one would have predicted 40 years ago. Branson has only 11,000 year-round residents, but it thrives thanks to the surging popularity of country and western music. It has more than 50 theaters and 57,000 seats — more than Broadway and equaling Las Vegas — and has become a hub for nonstop, low-cost entertainment, attracting 9 million visitors a year. As The Kansas City Star put it, each attraction is "more church-loving, more family-friendly, more country than the next." The 150-feet high Ferris wheel that had operated at Chicago's Navy Pier opened in 2016. Nearby are fishing, boating and plenty of shopping. These diversions have made southwest Missouri the fastest-growing part of the state, generating new businesses and attracting retirees as well as vacationers. Branson even has its own privately financed small airport, a new concept in the United States but more familiar elsewhere. The Spirit of 76 master plan to upgrade much of the commercial center was placed on hold in 2017, until financing was resolved. In March 2018, a $446 million indoor/outdoor water park and resort was proposed.

Springfield is the biggest city in southwest Missouri and the self-styled "buckle of the Bible Belt." It is home to more than 200 churches, including the headquarters of the Assemblies of God, one of the nation's largest Protestant denominations. In 2015, 51 percent of voters agreed in a referendum to repeal the city's prohibitions on LGBT discrimination. Advocates of the anti-discrimination provisions fought back and restored the earlier prohibitions in a 2016 referendum, which also got 51 percent. Southwest Missouri is dairy country and home to a growing poultry industry; the state ranks fourth in the nation for turkey production. Latinos have been moving into McDonald County to work in chicken-processing plants; roughly 1,000 of the 1,600 employees at the Tyson Foods chicken plant in Noel were minorities, including about 500 from Somalia.

In Jasper County, the city of Joplin (pop. 52,288) has been mostly rebuilt following a devastating May 2011 tornado that killed 158 people and heavily damaged or destroyed 2,000 buildings, including a hospital and schools. With winds exceeding 200 miles per hour, it was the deadliest tornado in the United States since 1950.

The 7th Congressional District of Missouri includes Springfield and Joplin. This area has been Republican territory since 1861, when it opposed secession. Pro-union Springfield changed hands several times as Missouri staged its own civil war, and now it is the most Republican part of Missouri. In 2016, Donald Trump won all the counties here, many by 2-to-1 margins. He took the district, 70%-25%.

Jason Smith (R)

Elected 2013, 3rd full term, b. Jun 16, 1980; St. Louis; Trinity College, Cambridge (England); Missouri State University, B.S., 2001; Oklahoma City University Law School (OK), J.D., 2004; Assembly of God; Marital status unknown.

Elected Office: MO House, 2005-2013.

Professional Career: Farmer, practicing Attorney, 2004-2013.

DC Office: 2418 RHOB 20515, 202-225-4404, Fax: 202-226-0326, jasonsmith.house.gov

State Offices: Cape Girardeau, 573-335-0101; Farmington, 573-756-9755; Poplar Bluff, 573-609-2996; Rolla, 573-364-2455; West Plains, 417-255-1515.

Committees: House Republican Conference Secretary. *Budget. Ways & Means*: Trade.

Group Ratings

	ADA	ACLU	AFL-CIO	LCV	ITI	COC	HAFA	ACU	CFG	FRC
2018	-	11%	-	3%	-	70%	85%	88%	80%	100%
2017	0%	C	8%	0%	C	92%	C	93%	92%	100%

Almanac Ratings 2017-18

	Economy	Social	Foreign	Composite
Liberal	2%	11%	3%	5%
Conservative	98%	89%	98%	95%

Key Votes of the 115th Congress

1. Obama-care revision	Y	5. Family planning regs	Y	9. Guantanamo prisoners	N
2. Tax Cuts	Y	6. Body cameras/immigration	N	10. Ground missiles, limit	N
3. Omnibus appropriations	N	7. Abortion ban	Y	11. Defense Dept. spending	Y
4. Dodd-Frank revision	NV	8. Concealed carry	Y	12. FISA rules	Y

Election Results

Election	Name (Party)	Vote (%)		Cand. Spent	Ind. Exp. Support	Ind. Exp. Oppose
2018 General	Jason Smith (R)...............................	194,042	(73%)	$1,215,811	$1,809	
	Kathy Ellis (D)....................................	66,151	(25%)	$181,044		
2018 Primary	Jason Smith (R)...		(100%)			

Prior winning percentages: 2016 (74%), 2014 (67%), 2013 special (67%)

Republican Jason Smith, who won a special election in 2013, has quietly become a House GOP leader, especially on tax policy. A fervent advocate of limited government, Smith serves on the Ways and Means Committee and on the GOP leadership team. Age 32 when he entered the House, Smith will have plenty of opportunity to move up the leadership ladder. He had an unusual rhetorical clash with a Democrat on the House floor in early 2019.

Smith grew up as the son of a church pastor in Salem Missouri, and he still runs the family farm that his great-grandfather started. At the University of Missouri, he received degrees in agricultural economics and business administration. He earned his law degree from Oklahoma City University. After returning to run the family farm and practice law, he became alarmed by "the harm that the overbearing government was inflicting on Missourians and our economy," according to his campaign website. He won a seat in the state House in 2005 and rose to majority whip and speaker pro tempore. He sought to amend the state constitution to protect farmers' rights, which he said was necessary to protect Missouri farmers from out-of-state animal rights groups and "environmental extremists." He joined social conservatives on gun rights and abortion-related legislation.

He ran for the House seat when Republican Rep. Jo Ann Emerson, a veteran of the Appropriations Committee, resigned to become president of the National Rural Electric Cooperative Association. Smith campaigned on his opposition to President Barack Obama's health care law and other issues of strong interest to the GOP base. "Voters do not want Obamacare, they are tired of burdensome and costly regulations and they know our $16 trillion national debt is a ticking time bomb," he said.

Democratic nominee Steve Hodges, a state representative with pro-gun rights and anti-abortion views, made an issue of Smith's missed state legislative votes during the special election campaign and criticized his support for an unpopular state sales tax hike. Hodges got little help from national Democrats, and Smith touted himself in positive ads as a "commonsense conservative." Smith raised just over $500,000. The result wasn't close. Smith won 67%-27%, and took all 30 counties except for two in the bootheel. He has been reelected with ease.

On the Natural Resources Committees, Smith sought to defend the interests of rural America: opposed to excessive regulations, in search of new markets for farmers and ranchers, and protecting his constituents' way of life. He strongly objected to tentative plans by the Obama administration to restrict recreational use of the Ozarks National Scenic Riverways, and vowed to fight "tooth and nail" to resist any change.

With his seat on Ways and Means, he runs the risk of confusion with a more senior Smith (Adrian) on the committee who is a young policy nerd from neighboring Nebraska. Jason Smith criticized the lack of clarity in the tax code. When Congress approved tax cuts in December 2017, he said that he was "honored to be part of the team" that cut taxes for working families and repealed the "individual mandate" in the Affordable Care Act. The bill "delivers" what President Donald Trump requested, Smith said. In April 2018, the House unanimously passed a bill that he cosponsored with Democratic Rep. Teri Sewell of Alabama that streamlined Internal Revenue Service audit procedures and sought to restore collaboration in disputes with taxpayers.

In January 2017, Smith praised the numerous executive orders that Trump issued during his opening days in office for having "done more to help working-class Americans" than President Barack Obama did in eight years. In February 2018, he was 1 of 67 House Republicans – and the only GOP elected leader -- who voted against the budget deal that included spending agreements for the remainder of the fiscal year. "I hate that I couldn't support it," Smith said. "You don't want to be on an island by yourself. But we also have to get serious about cutting spending."

In contrast to some other Republicans at Ways and Means, Smith praised Trump's tariffs. He acknowledged that Missouri farmers faced a "bumpy, roller-coaster ride" because of international trade disputes, the Southeast Missourian reported in July 2018. But he added, "I am very supportive of our president. I have trust that he knows what he is doing." Following the election, Smith was reelected without opposition as GOP Conference Secretary. He reportedly would have been interested in running for Republican Whip if the position had been vacant.

In a partisan exchange in the House during the partial government shutdown in January 2019, Smith shouted across the aisle "Go back to Puerto Rico" in the direction of Democratic Rep. Tony Cardenas of California, who has Mexican ancestry, The Washington Post reported. After nobody responded when Cardenas asked who had said that, Smith apologized to him in a phone call later that day and said that he was referring to a group of House Democrats who had recently visited Puerto Rico.

MO-8: Southeast Missouri   **Cook Partisan Voting Index: R+24**

Population		Race and Ethnicity		Income	
Total	743,300	White	90.6%	Median Income	$40,529
Land area (sq. miles)	19,901	Black	4.6%	District Income Rank	410
Pop/ sq mi	37.4	Latino	2%	Poverty Rate	20%
Born in State	73.2%	Asian	0.6%	With health insurance	87.5%
		Two or more races	1.6%	Cash public assistance	2.6%
Age Groups		Other	0.4%	Food stamp/SNAP	18.5%
Under 18	22.7%				
18-34	20.7%	**Education**		**Work**	
35-64	38.9%	H.S grad or less	55.6%	White Collar	17.7%
Over 64	17.7%	Some college	28.6%	Sales and Service	41.6%
		College Degree, 4 yr	9.8%	Blue Collar	30.3%
Military		Post grad	5.9%	Government	14.7%
Veteran/ Active Duty	10.2%				

2012 Pres. Vote	Romney	201,522	(66%)	Obama	97,982	(32%)		
2016 Pres. Vote	Trump	239,652	(75%)	Clinton	66,884	(21%)	Johnson	7,980 (3%)

Cape Girardeau: The southeast quadrant of Missouri is part river valley, part industrial mining and part agriculture. For years, there has been a population outflow from the Missouri Bootheel, as machines replaced low-wage farm workers and crops shifted from cotton to rice, corn and soybeans. Dairy cattle, pigs, apples and berries, plus some timber, are among the area's other products. The area is also home to Missouri's Lead Belt, a mining region rich in ore minerals such as lead, zinc, copper, silver and cadmium. Reynolds and Iron counties produced about 70 percent of the nation's lead, but many of the local mines recently have closed because of environmental contamination. Ste. Genevieve County has the nation's largest cement plant, which sparked a mini-economic boom after it opened at a huge limestone quarry in 2009 and produced four million metric tons per year. The area has suffered industrial shutdowns. Doe Run Resources Corp., the largest lead producer in the country, closed its smelter in 2013 after 120 years, following an agreement with Missouri and the Environmental Protection Agency. The company destroyed its contaminated buildings and agreed to clean up 4,000 nearby properties, but continued to produce metal from recycled lead. The Noranda Aluminum smelting plant in New Madrid, which had 850 local jobs, declared bankruptcy in February 2016 and closed its operations following lower aluminum prices. In March 2018, the smelter resumed operations, following President Donald Trump's decision to impose tariffs on imported aluminum.

Carrying many of these industrial goods to market is the Mississippi River, which Mark Twain might not recognize today. The river is hidden behind levees, which ordinarily screen small towns and river roads from rows of barges tethered together, full of coal and corn and soybeans. The Mississippi today is an industrial waterway. But it was never really all that romantic. Twain's steamboats, as he was at pains to point out, were dangerous, noisy contraptions, forever blowing up or getting embedded in roots and branches in the river currents. This is one of the oldest settled parts of the United States. French pioneers founded such Missouri towns as Cape Girardeau in the late 1700s. New Madrid has had some of the most powerful earthquakes in the nation; the most famous was in 1811-12. Recent seismic activity has raised a 90 percent likelihood of at least a 6.0 earthquake along the fault sometime in the next 50 years, according to the U.S. Geological Survey.

The 8th District, the largest in Missouri, covers its southeast corner, including rural Ste. Genevieve County, the site of Missouri's oldest permanent settlement, and takes in southern Jefferson County in the suburbs of St. Louis. It includes Plato, the tiny Missouri village named the population midpoint of the country based on 2010 census data. The Bootheel was once solidly Democratic, though the mining counties have mostly lost their traces of Democratic sentiment and Republicans have held it since 1980. In 2016, it surpassed the 7th District with the largest Republican vote in Missouri. Donald Trump won here, 75%-21%.

MONTANA

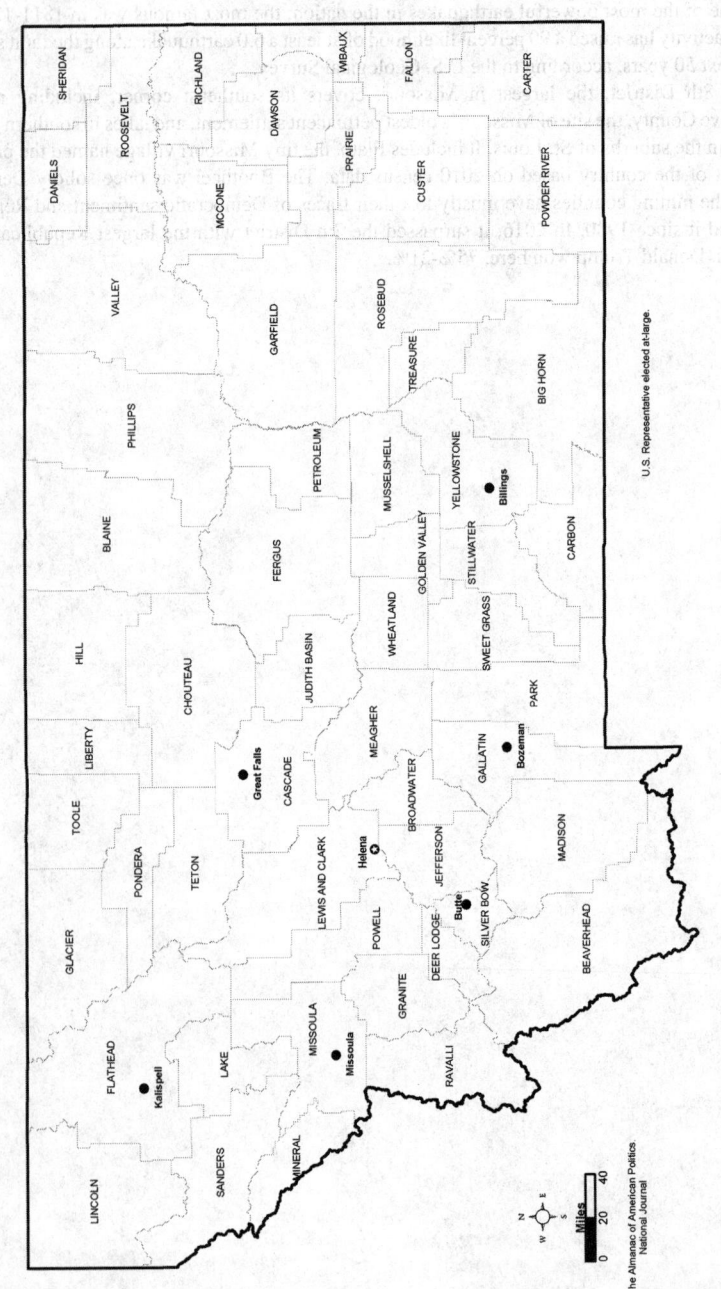

U.S. Representative elected at-large.

Montana prides itself as "The Last Best Place," and in waves, Americans have agreed. The state's natural beauty and open spaces have drawn a steady stream of newcomers, boosted in some cases by advances in telecommuting. Its population grew by 13 percent in the 1990s and another 10 percent between 2000 and 2010. Since 2010, it has increased by another 6 percent. Among all "micropolitan" areas in the United States, those between 10,000 and 50,000 in population, two Montana cities ranked first and third in population gains between 2016 and 2017 – Bozeman, a university town, and Kalispell, near Glacier National Park. Other areas have grown as well, including Missoula, the state's other major university town; Helena, the state capital; and Billings, the only Montana city ever to exceed 100,000 residents. Yet because Montana is the fourth-largest state in area, it ranks third from the bottom in population density, meaning that the state isn't close to filling up. Montana remains a land of great empty vistas, with mountains in the west and vast plateaus and plains in the east.

In April 1805, Meriwether Lewis, William Clark and their pirogues wended up the Missouri River just past the Yellowstone River into what is now Montana. To celebrate July 4, 1976, the historian Stephen E. Ambrose (who would retire to Helena and write the Lewis and Clark history Undaunted Courage) took his family to Lemhi Pass, where Lewis was the first U.S. citizen to cross the Continental Divide. Ambrose noted that the terrain was little changed from when the Corps of Discovery passed through. Even earlier, dinosaurs roamed, their remains scattered more densely and uncovered more frequently than in any other state. Almost nowhere is the wilderness out of sight. It has the Lower 48's largest population of grizzly bears and bison. Montana sits atop the spine of the continental United States, spanning the Rockies so that on Interstate 15 one can cross the Continental Divide three times.

The first settlers here were itinerant trappers seeking fur and miners seeking gold, silver and copper. They built ramshackle towns and, in a few cases, gained sudden wealth, which made them kings not of their barren homestead but of the metropolises back East. Then came the workers who built and serviced the Northern Pacific and Great Northern railroads, followed by wheat farmers and ranchers. Statehood arrived in 1889, less than a century after Lewis and Clark. On the verge of statehood, dozens of millionaires lived in Helena; in today's dollars, roughly $3.6 billion in gold was taken from the city's fabled Last Chance Gulch.

Montana's mining economy gave the state a radical, class-warfare political tradition. On one side was the Anaconda Mining Co., which until 1959 owned five of Montana's six daily newspapers, the Montana Power Co., and, in effect, many of the state's politicians. The company had strong allies in the Stockgrowers Association and the Farm Bureau. On the other side were progressives like Sen. Thomas Walsh, who exposed the Teapot Dome scandal, and Sen. Burton Wheeler, a New Dealer who broke with President Franklin Roosevelt over court-packing and isolationism. Allied with them were the labor unions (Montana has no right-to-work law and has been the most pro-union Rocky Mountain state) and pork-barrel beneficiaries (for a while in the 1930s, Montana received more federal money per capita than almost any other state). In 1912, Montana voters passed the Corrupt Practices Act to curb corporate influence in elections, striking a major blow against the Copper Kings. The act stood for a century until plaintiffs cited the Citizens United decision in a successful U.S. Supreme Court challenge. But the impetus remained; in 2015, Democratic Gov. Steve Bullock signed a measure that requires certain nonprofit groups to disclose their spending in state races, and in May 2018 a federal appeals court upheld it.

For years, the focus of the skirmishing was Butte, with its gold and copper mines; its gamblers, bootleggers and millionaires; and its company goons, union thugs and IWW organizers. Butte and surrounding Silver Bow County had 60,000 people in 1920 — the fourth highest in the Rocky Mountain states, behind only the counties containing Denver, Salt Lake City and Phoenix — but only 34,000 in 2017. The mines are mostly closed, their ore depleted; the stone temples of commerce are grim. Most spectacular is Butte's Berkeley Pit — a disused open copper mine more than a mile in diameter that's now filled with a toxic brew of contaminated groundwater.

As mines gradually closed after Butte's population peak in 1920, agriculture — especially wheat growing and cattle grazing — became the mainstay of Montana's economy. Class warfare died down, but the state's muscular personality has been resilient, stemming from its mountain men, miners and cowboys. Hunting and fishing opportunities abound; development in the small cities and resort areas has not been enough to drive the game away. Montana's libertarian streak persists: For a stretch in the 1990s, the state had no speed limit, and after one was re-imposed by the courts, lawmakers raised it to 80 miles per hour in 2015, becoming only the fifth state with a limit that high.

Over the past quarter-century, Big Sky country attracted at first a trickle and then a flood of affluent Americans who purchased second homes here — high-visibility movie stars and billionaires such as CNN founder Ted Turner, but also ordinary people buying small spreads near Big Sky, McLeod or Bozeman, or around Flathead Lake, Big Timber and Whitefish. Some newcomers, from California and other urban states, are putting down roots amid the coffee houses and gambling parlors one finds along many of Montana's highways. These new Montanans have added a spark of energy and inventiveness to a population that had consisted of people left behind when others moved elsewhere. (They have also pushed up housing prices in many high-demand areas beyond the reach of many potential homeowners.) There has been little immigration – the state is less than 1 percent black, and the biggest minority group is Native Americans, at 6.5 percent. The Hispanic population has climbed fairly quickly, but starting at a small base, from 2.9 percent in 2010 to 3.6 percent in 2017.

In addition to such mainstays as construction and agriculture, Montana now generates an estimated $1.7 billion in revenue annually from its rapidly growing high-tech industry. Even bigger is the state's tourism industry, driven by pilgrimages to Yellowstone and Glacier national parks; tourism brought a record 12.5 million visitors in 2017. The state's biggest economic challenge over the long term is likely to be aging: The state expects nearly one-fifth of today's labor force to retire over the next decade, and in rural areas, up to 10,000 jobs could disappear over the next five years as small-business owners retire without anyone willing to take over. Indeed, the state's consistently tight labor market has been a hindrance to companies looking to expand.

The boom in the Bakken shale oil field near the North Dakota border helped the state's economy for a while. Montana Democrats as well as Republicans have been big boosters of building the Keystone XL pipeline that will run south from Alberta through Montana to Oklahoma; it was approved under President Donald Trump following long delays under his predecessor, Barack Obama. But the boom was followed by a bust, with the number of active drilling rigs falling almost to zero in the eastern part of the state. Montana's sizable coal reserves also face increasing difficulty due to national shifts in how electricity is generated and environmental regulations. The fossil-fuel economy has had other drawbacks for the state: To the west, occasional accidents have spilled tens of thousands of gallons of crude oil into the Yellowstone River. In recent years, the state has tentatively begun to harness its abundant renewable energy resources, particularly the wind on the sparsely populated plains. A proposed $1 billion facility is being planned near remote Martinsdale to store power generated by the sun and wind; it would use this power to pump water uphill, generating electricity when needed by letting the water fall downhill through turbines. Under Obama, the Interior Department settled with Devon Energy to cancel oil and gas leases on federal lands sacred to the Blackfeet Tribe, but the lease was reinstated by the courts and remains subject to litigation.

In 2014, Obama signed a measure to increase wilderness area by 250,000 acres, the first such additions in the state in more than three decades. The American Prairie Reserve, funded by Manhattan and Silicon Valley millionaires, is buying up land in the northern plains to create a 500,000-acre preserve where 5,000 buffalo (and tourists) would be able to roam, though it's facing opposition from ranchers. There are lively political arguments over grizzly bears, whose numbers fell from as many as 100,000 in the Lewis and Clark era to 136 in 1975, and over the gray wolves that were reintroduced to Montana in the 1990s. Wolf hunting is now allowed, and some wildlife experts say that the grizzlies have gotten used to human beings and vice versa, which might be bad for both. After a modest recovery for the species, a limited grizzly hunt was scheduled for 2018; it would have been the first since the 1970s, but a federal judge blocked it.

Montana's senators have often had an impact in Washington far greater than the state's share of the national population, going back to the days of Walsh and Wheeler. Mike Mansfield, who was a professor of Far Eastern history, was elected to the Senate in 1952. He served as majority leader from 1961 to 1976, after which he was appointed ambassador to Japan by President Jimmy Carter. Max Baucus was scion of the family that owns the Sieben Ranch. He was elected to the House in 1974 at age 32 and to the Senate in 1978; in 2001, he became ranking Democrat on the Senate Finance Committee and held that position or the chairmanship until his retirement in 2014, when he became Ambassador to China. Montana lost its second House seat in the reapportionment following the 1990 census. Census Bureau projections now suggest that Montana will regain its second seat following reapportionment in 2020.

Montana has often elected Democratic governors, most recently the feisty populist rancher Brian Schweitzer in 2004 and 2008 and state Attorney General Steve Bullock in 2012 and 2016. Increasingly, though, Montana has favored conservatives' fierce opposition to higher taxes and federal government dictates. Montana has not elected a Democrat to the House since 1996, and other than Bill Clinton's victory 1992, it has been reliably Republican in presidential races. Since 1993, Democrats have won the outright majority in the state House or Senate only once.

In 2016, Trump won the state by 21 points, exceeding the statewide margins of Mitt Romney in 2012 (13 points) and John McCain in 2008 (3 points). Bullock narrowly won reelection that year, but Republicans successfully flipped three other statewide offices that had been held by Democrats – secretary of state, auditor and superintendent of public instruction. In the special election to succeed Rep. Ryan Zinke, who Trump tapped as his Interior secretary, Republican Greg Gianforte won despite a late incident in which he body-slammed a reporter; Gianforte eventually pled guilty to misdemeanor assault. Zinke, meanwhile, had a turbulent tenure in Trump's cabinet, eventually resigning under pressure amid investigations, including a probe of real estate deals in his home of Whitefish. Despite aggressive support by Trump, the GOP was unable to oust Democratic Sen. Jon Tester in 2018. Facing Matt Rosendale, the Republican state auditor, Tester pulled out a narrow victory, 50%-47%. Tester lost three counties he'd previously won, notably Yellowstone (Billings), but he milked enough extra votes out of Missoula County, Lewis & Clark County (Helena), and Gallatin County (Bozeman) to win. Tester's victory suggested that while Democrats face an uphill climb in Big Sky state, the party's outlook is not as hopeless as in some other states in the Mountain West.

Cook Partisan Voting Index: R+11

Population		Race and Ethnicity		Income	
Total	1,029,862	White	86.6%	Median Income	$50,801
Land area (sq. miles)	145,546	Black	0.4%	State Income Rank	39
Pop/ sq mi	7.1	Latino	3.6%	Poverty Rate	14.4%
Born in state	54.5%	Asian	0.7%	With health insurance	88.3%
		Two or more races	2.4%	Cash public assistance	2.1%
Age Groups		Other	6.3%	Food stamp/SNAP	10.2%
Under 18	22.0%				
18-34	22.2%	**Education**		**Work**	
35-64	38.7%	H.S grad or less	36.4%	White Collar	36.5%
Over 64	17.1%	Some college	33.0%	Sales and Service	41.3%
		College Degree, 4 yr	20.6%	Blue Collar	22.2%
Military		Post grad	10.1%	Government	17.5%
Veteran/ Active Duty	11.0%				

Presidential Politics

2016 Primary (D)	Sanders (D)	65,156 (52%)	Clinton (D)	55,805 (44%)			
2016 Primary (R)	Trump (R)	115,594 (74%)	Cruz (R)	14,682 (9%)	Kasich (R)	10,777	(7%)
2016 Pres. Vote	Trump (R)	279,240 (56%)	Clinton (D)	177,709 (36%)	Johnson (L)	28,037	(6%)
2012 Pres. Vote	Romney (R)	267,928 (55%)	Obama (D)	201,839 (42%)	Johnson (L)	14,165	(3%)

With its three electoral votes and remote location, Montana doesn't see much of presidential candidates. But it was a close state in 1992, when Democrat Bill Clinton carried it by three percentage points, and in 1996, when he lost by the same margin. The state voted 59%-39% for President George W. Bush in 2004, but went only 50%-47% for John McCain. In 2016, the state swung further in the GOP direction and Donald Trump defeated Hillary Clinton 57%-38%. Trump won 50 of the state's 56 counties. Clinton carried only Glacier, home to a huge Blackfeet Indian reservation; Missoula, with the University of Montana; Silver Bow, where Butte was once known as "the Gibraltar of unionism;" Deer Lodge, home to what was once the largest copper smelter in the world; Big Horn, home to a substantial Crow Indian Reservation; and Gallatin, home to Montana State University in Bozeman.

Trump carried Flathead County, with its affluent new migrants, and Lewis and Clark County, with its government employees who work in the state capital of Helena, and everything else.

Montana holds its presidential primaries in June when nominations have usually long since been decided. In 2016, the Republican primary was a non-event — Trump had already captured the GOP nomination and won 74 percent of the vote. The Democratic contest was more spirited. Vermont Sen. Bernie Sanders defeated Clinton 52%-42%. The Vermonter, who campaigned in the state while Clinton did not, carried the two major university counties, Missoula and Gallatin, and his advantage there more than accounted for his statewide margin of victory.

Congressional Districts

116th Congress Lineup	1R	115th Congress Lineup	1R

Steve Bullock (D)

Elected 2012, term expires 2021, 2nd term; b. Apr. 11, 1966, Missoula; Claremont McKenna Col., B.A. 1988; Columbia U., J.D. 1994; Catholic; Married (Lisa); 3 children.

Elected Office: MT Attorney General, 2008-2012.

Professional Career: Chief legal counsel, MT Secretary of State, 1996-1997; Executive Assistant Attorney General, MT Department of Justice, 1997-2001; Practicing attorney, 2001-2004, 2005-2008; Adjunct professor, George Washington University School of Law, 2001-2004; Acting chief deputy, MT Department of Justice, 2001.

Office: 1301 E 6th Ave, Helena, 59620-0801; 406-444-3111; Fax: 406-444-5529; Website: governor.mt.gov.

Lt. Gov.: Mike Cooney (D) **Atty. Gen:** Tim Fox (R) **Sec. of State:** Corey Stapleton (R)

State Legislature: Senate: 20D, 30R **House:** 42D, 58R

Election Results

Election	Name (Party)	Vote (%)
2016 General	Steve Bullock (D)	255,933 (50%)
	Greg Gianforte (R)	236,115 (46%)
	Ted Dunlap (L)	17,312 (3%)

Prior winning percentage: 2012 (49%)

Democrat Steve Bullock was elected governor of Montana in 2012. A popular state attorney general, he was reelected four years later despite the headwinds of Donald Trump's rout in the state. Bullock's experience as a Democrat governing a largely Republican state led to his campaign as a possible dark horse candidate for president in 2020.

Bullock was born in Missoula and raised in Helena, where his newspaper delivery route included the governor's mansion. He received his undergraduate degree from Claremont McKenna College and his law degree from Columbia University. After a brief stint at a law firm following his graduation from law school, Bullock returned to his home state in 1996 to be chief legal counsel to Democratic Secretary of State Mike Cooney (whom he would tap two decades later as a replacement lieutenant governor). Bullock rose through the ranks in the state Justice Department and ran for attorney general in 2000. He lost in the Democratic primary and then moved to Washington D.C. to join the law firm of Steptoe & Johnson and to teach as an adjunct professor at George Washington University Law School. He returned to Montana in 2004 to work in private practice in Helena.

Bullock did better in his second try for attorney general in 2008, winning a three-way Democratic primary with 42 percent and taking 53 percent in the general election. He created a state prescription drug registry and a 24/7 sobriety program, which held repeat DUI offenders accountable by requiring them to submit to, and pay for, regular blood alcohol tests. He also developed a Children's Justice Center to improve law enforcement's ability to track down and prosecute child predators. He supported Montana's century-old ban on corporate campaign contributions, fighting for it until it was struck down by the U.S. Supreme Court. And he became known for teaming with Gov. Brian Schweitzer's administration on public-lands access laws.

While Bullock had a more buttoned-down style, he portrayed his candidacy as a continuation of Schweitzer's work. After the primary, he told the Missoulian that the race is about "what sort of progressive Montana we want this to be." After eight years of Democratic control of the governorship, Montana Republicans felt they were in a solid position to pick up the governor's office, but they had an acrimonious seven-way primary. Rep. Rick Hill won the GOP nomination but had to work to unite the party behind his candidacy and to replenish his campaign coffers; that gave Bullock a head start on the general election. Hill was also hobbled by campaign-finance revelations and the presence of a Libertarian candidate on the general election ballot, a common occurrence in Montana. Libertarian candidate Ron Vandevender won 3.8 percent of the vote on Election Day, and his 18,160 votes may have cost Hill the election. Bullock came out on top by 7,571 votes, 48.9%-47.3%.   In his initial State of the State speech in January 2013, Bullock appealed to lawmakers for cooperation, saying, "We need each other if we are going to make progress." This olive branch stood in contrast to Schweitzer's antagonistic relationship with the GOP-led legislature, sometimes punctuated by his use of red-hot "veto" branding irons in front of the capitol. But Bullock ended up using the veto against the GOP almost as much as his predecessor, including on taxes and firearm bills. Meanwhile, the GOP legislature worked to stymie many of Bullock's initiatives, including an expansion of Medicaid under the Affordable Care Act and a $37 million proposal for state-funded preschools. Bullock was unafraid to take a few other liberal positions, including support for overturning the state's ban on same-sex marriage and for efforts to oppose a possible transfer of federal land to the state.

One setback for Bullock was his selection of Lt. Gov. John Walsh as the temporary successor for Democratic Sen. Max Baucus, who resigned in 2014. Revelations about plagiarism in a paper he had written at the Army War College pushed Walsh out of the race for seat. Then, Bullock's handpicked successor as lieutenant governor, Angela McLean, left her post amid reports of acrimony between her and Bullock.

But Bullock had better luck on health care and campaign finance, overcoming Republican opposition. As was the case in 2013, the legislature in 2015 tabled his Medicaid expansion proposal. But Bullock worked with moderate Republicans to draft a compromise expansion plan that won approval in the legislature and eventually enabled tens of thousands of Montanans to sign up for the program. Meanwhile, after the Supreme Court put the kibosh on the state's campaign finance law, Bullock worked with Republican and Democratic lawmakers to craft a bill that required disclosure by certain nonprofit groups spending on state races. He signed it into law in 2015, and it was upheld in the courts the following year. Bullock also negotiated a water-rights compact with the Confederated Salish and Kootenai Tribes.

Bullock began his 2016 re-election bid as chairman of the Democratic Governors Association. But winning the governorship in a red state was no easy task. Greg Gianforte, a Bozeman tech entrepreneur, won the GOP primary and sought to paint Bullock as a captive of the national Democratic Party. Gianforte spent more than $6 million from his own pocket and ran more television ads than were aired in any 2016 gubernatorial race, according to the Center for Public Integrity. But with the DGA's help, Bullock raised enough money to remain competitive. Ultimately, Bullock defeated Gianforte by just under 19,000 votes. The incumbent won 12 counties, twice the number Hillary Clinton did on the same ballot, and generally by much larger margins. (Bullock and his campaign organization paid a $3,000 fine to avoid a lawsuit stemming from his use of the state plane for campaign purposes, which they had delayed reporting in the required disclosures. Gianforte, meanwhile, won the special election for Montana's open House seat the following year. And in June 2019, he announced that he will run again for governor in 2020.)

Bullock brought out his veto pen again in 2017. He rejected a bill to ban the use of sharia and other foreign laws in Montana courts, saying "there is absolutely no need for this bill" and warning that it could be an "endorsement for anti-Muslim sentiments and activity." He also vetoed a pair of gun-rights bills, one to allow guns in post offices and another to allow gun owners to carry a concealed weapon without government permission. But Bullock signed a bipartisan legislative package that updated the state's sexual assault laws, including an extension of the statute of limitations. He flexed his executive powers in ways that sidestepped the legislature. He signed an order in 2018 to protect "net neutrality" on the internet by requiring that service providers with state contracts not promote or discriminate against certain types of digital traffic. That made Bullock the first governor anywhere to sign such an order, although it risked legal and regulatory turbulence. Separately, Bullock signed an order requiring state contractors to disclose donations they make to nonprofit advocacy groups; opponents called it starter dough for an enemies list.

The highest-profile fight of 2018, however, concerned the renewal of Medicaid expansion. Facing a looming sunset of the program in 2019, supporters put an initiative on the ballot to leverage new tobacco tax revenues to fund the state's future program costs. But on Election Day, even as voters were approving Medicaid expansion ballot measures in Idaho, Nevada and Utah, the Montana measure fell short. To prevent Montana from becoming the first state to drop Medicaid expansion after approving it, Bullock responded to the initiative's loss by proposing a budget that would continue the program; his budget would raise $50 million annually from tax increases on purchasers of tobacco and liquor, hotel guests, investment advisers, and people who rent cars. Similar tax hikes had previously failed amid Republican opposition.

Meanwhile, Bullock turned his sights to possibility of a presidential bid. In 2017, he established the Big Sky Values PAC, which funded trips to key states, including one to the Iowa State Fair. (Underlining the challenges of reconciling national and state priorities, Bullock caused a stir at home when he said in a CNN interview that he could support a ban on some semi-automatic weapons.) In a nonpartisan vein, Bullock took the reins of the National Governors Association in mid-2018. "Bullock's political calling card these days is that he is a Democrat who won reelection by four points on the day that Trump was winning his state by 20 points," wrote the Washington Post's Dan Balz. "That won't get you elected president, but it's enough to start a conversation."

In May 2019, he entered the contest, with a centrist appeal and a good-government message to "take our democracy back."

Jon Tester (D)

Elected 2006, term expires 2024, 3rd term, b. Aug 21, 1956; Havre; University of Great Falls (MT), B.S., 1978; Christian Church; Married (Sharla Tester); 2 children; 2 grandchildren.

Elected Office: Big Sandy School Board, 1983-1992, Chairman, 1986-1991; MT Senate, 1998-2006, Minority Leader, 2003-2005, pres., 2005-2006.

Professional Career: Operations Management, Procter & Gamble, 1984- 97; Vice President., Clair Daines Construction, 1997-2000; Gen. Manager/Vice President., Right-Now Technologies, 2000-2012.

DC Office: 311 HSOB 20510, 202-224-2644, Fax: 202-224-8594, tester.senate.gov

State Offices: Billings, 406-252-0550; Bozeman, 406-586-4450; Butte, 406-723-3277; Great Falls, 406-452-9585; Helena, 406-449-5401; Kalispell, 406-257-3360; Missoula, 406-728-3003.

Committees: *Appropriations*: Agriculture, Rural Development, FDA & Related Agencies; Department of Defense; Department of Homeland Security (RMM); Department of the Interior, Environment & Related Agencies; Energy & Water Development; Military Construction & Veteran Affairs & Related Agencies. *Banking, Housing & Urban Affairs*: Financial Institutions & Consumer Protection; Securities, Insurance & Investment. *Commerce, Science & Transportation*: Communications, Technology, Innovation & the Internet; Subcommittee on Aviation & Space. *Indian Affairs. Veterans' Affairs (RMM)*.

Group Ratings

	ADA	ACLU	AFL-CIO	LCV	ITI	COC	HAFA	ACU	CFG	FRC
2018	-	81%	-	93%	-	70%	5%	14%	5%	0%
2017	70%	C	100%	84%	C	29%	C	4%	4%	0%

Almanac Ratings 2017-18

	Economy	Social	Foreign	Composite
Liberal	79%	79%	89%	83%
Conservative	21%	21%	11%	17%

Key Votes of the 115th Congress

1. Obama-care revision	N	5. Gun regulations	Y	9. Kavanaugh confirmation	N
2. Tax Cuts	N	6. Family planning regs	N	10. Saudi arms sales	Y
3. Dodd-Frank revision	Y	7. Gorsuch confirmation	N	11. FISA rules	N
4. Omnibus appropriations	Y	8. Immigration restrictions	N	12. Military aid in Yemen	Y

Election Results

Election	Name (Party)	Vote (%)		Cand. Spent	Ind. Exp. Support	Ind. Exp. Oppose
2018 General	Jon Tester (D)	253,876	(50%)	$22,410,746	$3,892,048	$18,519,787
	Matt Rosendale (R)	235,963	(47%)	$5,522,453	$5,182,081	$15,651,214
	Rick Breckenridge (Lib)	14,545	(3%)			
2018 Primary	Jon Tester (D)	114,948	(100%)			

Prior winning percentages: 2012 (49%), 2006 (49%)

Democrat Jon Tester won his third close Senate contest in 2018, taking more than 50 percent of the vote for the first time. With his signature flattop haircut and his plain-spoken western manner inveighing against "D.C. politicians," he doesn't come across like a typical Democrat, but he has compiled a more liberal voting record than other red-state Democratic colleagues.

Tester grew up in a farming family, on the same prairie land his grandparents homesteaded almost a century ago near the tiny town of Big Sandy. His family ran a butcher shop behind their barn; at 9, Tester lost three fingers from his left hand in a meat grinder. The accident, he has said, changed him from a saxophone player to a trumpeter. He earned a music degree from the University of Great Falls and taught music at an elementary school before devoting himself to farming. He has raised wheat, hay, alfalfa, barley, buckwheat, lentils, millet, and peas and served on the local Soil Conservation Service Committee. He then switched to organic farming. "In the '80s, we realized we had to do something to add value to our product. … That's when we made the conversion to organic," He told Esquire magazine. "It's been a blessing for us. Before we converted, when we sprayed weeds, I just planned on being sick for about a week."

Tester's political career began on the Big Sandy School Board, on which he served a decade. In 1998, when his neighbor, a Republican state senator, decided not to seek re-election, Tester ran for and won the seat. In 2002, he became minority leader, then Senate president in 2005 after Democrats won a majority. In that role, he helped pass a budget that cut taxes for small businesses and middle-class families while increasing funding for public education. When the 2005 legislative session adjourned, Tester challenged three-term Republican Sen. Conrad Burns.

In the primary, Tester faced two-term state Auditor John Morrison, a former president of the Montana Trial Lawyers Association and the son of a state Supreme Court justice. Running as an unabashed populist, Tester gained support from Daily Kos and other progressive internet groups, and in Montana he assembled a formidable grassroots operation with hundreds of volunteers. He beat Morrison 61%-35%.

Tester was taking on the only Republican senator Montana voters had ever re-elected. But by 2006, the 71-year-old conservative incumbent had two serious problems. The first was his connection to disgraced lobbyist Jack Abramoff. Burns was the largest congressional recipient of campaign donations from Abramoff's clients, and he faced campaign accusations that he "sold his vote" and betrayed Montana's American Indian population by earmarking funds for Abramoff's Indian clients in other states. Burns' second handicap was a gaffe-prone style, which was ill-suited for the YouTube era. In 2006, while discussing the war on terrorism, he spoke of enemies who "drive taxicabs in the daytime and kill at night."

It was a bare-knuckled campaign. Burns spent $9 million, $3.5 million more than Tester, and argued that Tester was too liberal for Montana because of his opposition to the Patriot Act and links to "radical environmentalists" and left-wing bloggers. But Montana voters have a strong libertarian streak, putting Tester's privacy and foreign policy views in the state's mainstream, and Tester was not so easily caricatured as a liberal. His haircut, highlighted in a television ad filmed at the Riverview Barber Shop in Great Falls, and stocky farmer's build, combined with his 3,000 acre farm and down-to-earth style tempered the criticism. The race was decided by 3,562 votes.

Arriving in Washington, Tester stressed the importance of transparency and accountability in government, distancing himself from the questionable practices that hurt his predecessor. He co-sponsored a Republican bill to ban former members of Congress from ever lobbying and joined a group of senators seeking to ban secret holds on legislation and nominations, a longtime Senate practice. Tester drew notice for posting his daily schedules on the internet, a Senate first. In 2015, his bill to streamline the federal hiring process for its civil servants was signed into law by President Barack Obama. He was distinctive in other ways, too. He has brought to Washington beef he'd butchered himself.

Tester has supported abortion rights and same-sex marriage and taken a nuanced view of gun rights. He co-sponsored with Republican Sen. John McCain of Arizona an amendment to repeal Washington D.C.'s gun control laws. And early in Obama's presidency, Tester and fellow Montana Democratic Sen. Max Baucus made it clear they would oppose any attempt to reinstate the ban on military-style weapons. But after the 2012 elementary school massacre in Newtown Conn., Tester was one of the few red-state Democrats to back the bipartisan legislation from Democratic Sen. Joe Manchin of West Virginia and Republican Sen. Pat Toomey of Pennsylvania to tighten background checks for gun purchases. He voted against a 2016 proposal to close the "gun show loophole" in background checks because it didn't have an exemption for sales and gifts between family members.

Tester has a libertarian view on surveillance issues. He was one of eight senators led by GOP Sen. Rand Paul of Kentucky to filibuster the Patriot Act's reauthorization in 2015, though he backed the eventual compromise legislation. More recently, he voted against President Donald Trump's first nominee for CIA director, former GOP Rep. Mike Pompeo of Kansas, saying he was concerned about Pompeo's views on surveillance and "enhanced interrogation."

Baucus's departure to become ambassador to China in early 2014 gave Tester the chairmanship of the Indian Affairs Committee. In his first few months, he impressed tribal observers with his energy, getting more than a dozen bills through the panel dealing with housing, education, water rights. He also passed a legislative remedy for a 2009 Supreme Court decision that limited the Interior Department's ability to take lands into trusts for tribes. Indian Country Today praised Tester's "shoe leather diplomacy," including visits to Native American communities to gauge education, health and environmental programs. He called protecting the Badger-Two Medicine area near Glacier National Park in Montana, a place sacred to the Blackfeet Tribe but long a bone of contention with oil and gas companies. Tester and Montana's junior senator, Republican Steve Daines, have repeatedly won committee-level approval of federal recognition for the Little Shell Tribe of Chippewa Indians. A companion bill passed the House in 2018 but failed in the Senate.

Tester has tested the boundaries of party loyalty. He was one of only two Democrats in October 2011 to join Republicans in a filibuster of Obama's jobs bill; he said it contained "tax gimmicks" that did not address deficit reduction. He aroused the ire of left-wing bloggers in December 2010 when he voted against the DREAM Act, which would have provided a path to citizenship for undocumented immigrants who were brought to the U.S. as children. Tester has since reversed his position on the issue and was critical of Trump when the president moved to end the Deferred Action for Childhood Arrivals program that gives those same immigrants legal protections.

Tester has cut a moderate profile on the Banking, Housing, and Urban Affairs Committee, helping community banks and often siding with Republicans to push deregulation. That's made him a top recipient of banking industry donations. He worked in 2009 on the law that banned certain credit card fees and deadlines and provided an extra week for paying bills. A year later, he sponsored a successful amendment requiring large banks to pay higher Federal Deposit Insurance Corp. fees. He sought to block limits on the "swipe fees" that banks and credit card companies charge stores for debit card transactions, arguing that the fee limits would hurt small rural banks, but the effort fell short.

In early 2018, Tester was a key player in helping Republicans roll back the sweeping Dodd-Frank financial reforms that were enacted after the 2008 financial crisis. The bill, pushed hard by regional banks and credit unions, exempted about two dozen financial companies with assets between $50 billion and $250 billion from the same level of Federal Reserve scrutiny reserved for the largest banks. "The Main Street banks, community banks and credit unions didn't create the crisis in 2008, and they were getting heavily regulated," Tester told The New York Times, claiming that "there's not one thing in this bill that gives Wall Street a break." Liberals, including Massachusetts Sen. Elizabeth Warren, disagreed. But the bill passed with moderate Democrats' support.

None of Tester's statewide races has been easy. In 2012, he faced a tough race in a presidential election year when Obama was deeply unpopular in his home state. His opponent was Republican Denny Rehberg, who was well-known statewide as Montana's sole House member. In October 2011, the nonpartisan Center for Responsive Politics found that Tester, despite running as an outsider, had accepted more campaign contributions from lobbyists than any other member of Congress. Republicans also pointed to Tester's financial support from large banks as evidence of his hypocrisy.

Rehberg relied on the standard Republican strategy of attacking his opponent as a liberal Obama ally, citing Tester's vote in favor of the president's health care law, though that strategy took a hit when it was revealed that the National Republican Senatorial Committee had photoshopped Tester's face on to a man's body who embracing Obama in one of its ads. The man was obviously not Tester: He had had all his fingers. Tester defended his Obamacare vote as being "about being able to get health care without breaking the bank." He took a page from the national Democratic playbook in sowing doubt about Rehberg's support for Social Security and Medicare and blasted Rehberg for having sued his local fire department over what Rehberg said was an ineffective job fighting a wildfire on his property. Tester won 49%-45%; Obama lost the state by 14 points.

Tester's campaign-trail acumen helped him to take over as chairman of the Democratic Senate Campaign Committee; he had to defend just 10 seats, while the GOP had 24 up for re-election. Despite Tester's misgivings about the job's intense fundraising demands, he helped the committee out-raise the NRSC by more than $40 million for the cycle. But Democrats failed to recapture Senate control, picking up just two seats in a disappointing election cycle and losing races in which they once appeared to have the edge in Wisconsin and Pennsylvania.

Tester headed into 2018 with a target on his back: Trump had won his state by 20 points, a big swing from Obama's two-point loss there in 2008. Republicans were hopeful they could find a top-tier candidate to challenge Tester, but Trump removed the potential challenger who many believed to be Tester's biggest re-election threat when he chose Republican Rep. Ryan Zinke to become Interior secretary. Tester gleefully introduced Zinke at his committee confirmation hearing and voted for his confirmation.

Republicans failed in their efforts to recruit popular Montana Attorney General Tim Fox to run. They were left with second-tier candidates, and state Auditor Matt Rosendale emerged from the primary to face Tester in June. Rosendale, like Tester, sported a flattop haircut. But he also had a thick Maryland accent — he didn't move to Montana until the early 2000s, after making his millions in real estate. Rosendale branded himself a rancher, but documents showed that he'd never worked his family ranch and instead had kept working as a developer. Out-of-state developers are despised by many native Montanans who are dismayed by development and the steady influx of outsiders in the state.

Despite Rosendale's flaws as a candidate, he still had one huge asset: Trump. Tester became the ranking Democrat on the Senate Veterans' Affairs Committee in 2017, and infuriated Trump when he blocked the president's second nominee to head the Department of Veterans Affairs, Ronny Jackson. Tester regularly voted against Trump's nominees in 2017, and in early 2018 he was the only red-state Democrat to stand with his party against reopening the government after Democrats engineered a short-term shutdown over Trump's refusal to help Dreamers after moving to end the DACA program protecting them. Tester's rationale wasn't about immigration; he didn't like that the short-term funding bill didn't fund Montana hospitals. Trump spent at least as much time and energy trying to take out Tester as any other Democrat in the country after swearing Tester would have a "big price to pay" for blocking Jackson. Donald Trump Jr. joined Rosendale on the campaign trail several times.

Tester touted his Montana roots and work on the Veterans Affairs' Committee. And like many Democrats, he touted his defense of the Affordable Care Act. That included an ad in which he talked about how he'd lost his fingers and how his parents had to pay for the hospital visit themselves because of "junk insurance" plans he said Rosendale wanted to allow back in.

Tester led the entire race, but like other red-state Democrats, saw polls head in the wrong direction in the final month as the polarizing hearings over Supreme Court nominee Brett Kavanaugh returned Republicans to their party. Tester prevailed with 50.3 percent of the vote; Rosendale got 46.8 percent. That was the first time that Tester took a majority of the vote.

Steve Daines (R)

Elected 2014, term expires 2020, 1st term, b. Aug 20, 1962; Van Nuys, CA; Montana State University, Bozeman, B.S., 1984; Presbyterian; Married (Cindy Daines); 4 children.

Elected Office: U.S. House, 2013-2015.

Professional Career: Music teacher, F.E. Miley Elementary, 1978-1980; Custom butcher, T-Bone Farms, 1978-1998; Farmer, T-Bone Farms, 1978-present.

DC Office: 320 HSOB 20510, 202-224-2651, Fax: 202-228-1236, daines.senate.gov

State Offices: Billings, 406-245-6822; Bozeman, 406-587-3446; Great Falls, 406-453-0148; Helena, 406-443-3189; Kalispell, 406-257-3765; Missoula, 406-549-8198; Sidney, 406-482-9010.

Committees: *Appropriations*: Department of the Interior, Environment & Related Agencies; Financial Services & General Government; Military Construction & Veteran Affairs & Related Agencies; State, Foreign Operations & Related Programs; Transportation, HUD & Related Agencies. *Energy & Natural Resources*: Energy; National Parks (Chmn); Public Lands, Forests & Mining. *Finance*: Energy, Natural Resources & Infrastructure; Health Care; International Trade, Customs & Global Competitiveness. *Indian Affairs*.

Group Ratings

	ADA	ACLU	AFL-CIO	LCV	ITI	COC	HAFA	ACU	CFG	FRC
2018	-	33%	-	14%	-	78%	78%	82%	73%	100%
2017	0%	C	0%	0%	C	86%	C	92%	94%	100%

Almanac Ratings 2017-18

	Economy	Social	Foreign	Composite
Liberal	6%	6%	17%	9%
Conservative	94%	94%	83%	91%

Key Votes of the 115th Congress

1. Obama-care revision	Y	5. Gun regulations	Y	9. Kavanaugh confirmation	NV
2. Tax Cuts	Y	6. Family planning regs	Y	10. Saudi arms sales	N
3. Dodd-Frank revision	Y	7. Gorsuch confirmation	Y	11. FISA rules	N
4. Omnibus appropriations	N	8. Immigration restrictions	N	12. Military aid in Yemen	Y

Election Results

Election	Name (Party)	Vote (%)		Cand. Spent	Ind. Exp. Support	Ind. Exp. Oppose
2014 General	Steve Daines (R)	213,709	(58%)	$6,668,759	$377,362	$303,790
	Amanda Curtis (D)	148,184	(40%)	$968,388	$39,751	$43,265
	Roger Roots (L)	7,933	(2%)			
2014 Primary	Steve Daines (R)	110,565	(83%)			
	Susan Cundiff (R)	11,909	(9%)			
	Champ Edmunds (R)	10,151	(8%)			

Prior winning percentages: House: 2012 (53%)

Republican Steve Daines was elected Montana's junior senator in 2014. Shifting into politics after a successful business career, he became the second Republican from Montana since Joseph M. Dixon joined the chamber in 1913, when senators were still appointed by state legislatures. Soft-spoken with a sunny disposition, Daines pays particular attention to energy and land use issues important to Montana and has emerged as a reliable ally of President Donald Trump.

Daines grew up in Bozeman, where his father started a home-construction business. He studied chemical engineering at Montana State University. During his senior year, he became one of the youngest delegates at the 1984 Republican National Convention. Daines spent 13 years with consumer goods giant Procter & Gamble, managing operations in the United States before moving his young family for a six-year stint with the company in Hong Kong and China. In 1997, Daines left P&G to join the family construction business in Bozeman. Three years later, he got a call from entrepreneur Greg Gianforte, founder of RightNow Technologies, asking him to come on board as vice president of customer service. Daines has since returned the favor, supporting Gianforte in his failed 2016 gubernatorial run and backing his controversial but successful run for Congress a few months later.

Daines dipped into local politics in 2007 when he and his wife, Cindy, founded GiveitBack.com, a nonprofit that pushed for the return of the state's $1 billion budget surplus to taxpayers. Not long after that, former Arkansas Gov. Mike Huckabee asked Daines to serve as Montana state chairman for his presidential campaign. Daines also chaired Montana's delegation to the 2008 Republican National Convention. That same year, he ran for lieutenant governor on a ticket with former state Sen. Roy Brown, but they failed to oust Democratic Gov. Brian Schweitzer.

Two years later, Daines announced his intention to challenge Democrat Jon Tester for his Senate seat. But when Rep. Denny Rehberg said in February 2011 that he would run against Tester, Daines dropped out of the Senate race to vie for Rehberg's vacated House seat. He won with 53 percent of the vote.

Daines compiled a conservative voting record in the House, supporting a budget crafted by Rep. Paul Ryan and voting for a measure to ban abortions after 20 weeks of pregnancy. The House in 2013 passed his bill to expand hydropower production in Montana, and he amended several other bills to include provisions specific to his state's energy production.

Daines's rise to the Senate included some good fortune. Rehberg left politics after losing the 2012 race to Tester. The state's other Democratic senator, Max Baucus, resigned his seat when President Barack Obama named him ambassador to China in 2014. Daines jumped into the race, just 14 months after his election to the House. When Schweitzer declined to run, Democrats turned to Lt. Gov. John Walsh, a retired Army general who had been tapped by Democratic Gov. Steve Bullock to succeed Baucus. But in June, The New York Times published a bombshell story, reporting that Walsh had plagiarized large portions of his master's thesis at the Army War College. Walsh's muddled response made matters worse. In August, shortly before the ballot deadline, he exited the race. The party chose state Rep. Amanda Curtis to take his place, but a race that had already favored the well-funded Daines in a strong year for Republicans turned into a rout. Daines defeated Curtis 58%-40%.

Daines took seats on two panels of special interest to Montana — Energy and Natural Resources and Indian Affairs — as well as Appropriations. The first Senate bill he introduced was the Balanced Budget Accountability Act, which would have forced lawmakers to balance the budget or give up their salaries. He urged approval of the Keystone XL pipeline and decried federal regulations that curbed timber harvests.

Daines has chaired the Western Caucus, a coalition of western Republicans focused on land use and energy issues. In 2017, he introduced a bill that would open a half-million acres of Montana land for development by removing them from a federal Wilderness Study Areas list. He and other western GOP senators proposed a wildfire management bill in 2017.

He has worked across the aisle on several measures, including legislation to reauthorize the Federal Land and Water Conservation Fund, which protects and conserves public lands. The 50-year-old program's funding lapsed in late 2018, but Congress restored the coverage in February 2019. Daines sponsored a bill to bar energy development on the North and Middle forks of the Flathead River, and worked with Tester to push for federal recognition of the Little Shell Tribe of Chippewa Indians. The former tech executive led successful efforts to expand broadband and cell phone coverage, with the FCC approving expanded wireless broadband access for 1 million people in Montana and Wyoming in response to his efforts.

In 2019, Daines secured a spot on the Senate Finance Committee. He and Republican Sen. James Lankford of Oklahoma are the first senators in 75 years to serve simultaneously on Finance and Appropriations. He chaired the Energy panel's National Parks subcommittee.

Daines has been a steady ally of Trump, even as he has split with the president on some foreign policy and trade issues. Daines, a free-trader, helped engineer a $300 million deal that allowed Montana ranchers to sell beef to China, but he defended Trump's decision to start a trade war with that country. He said he believed U.S. intelligence officials' assessment that Russia meddled in the 2016 presidential election and he pressed Russian officials not to interfere in future elections during a visit to the country, though he steadily defended Trump when the president rejected the intelligence agencies' assessment. In late 2018, he visited Afghanistan and said it would be a mistake to withdraw troops, disagreeing with Trump's view.

Daines threatened to vote against the Republicans' sweeping tax cuts in late 2017 because he was concerned that the package helped big companies more than small businesses. He got what he wanted — a bigger tax cut for pass-through businesses. The change cut his own taxes significantly, according to an analysis from the Billings Gazette.

He opposed his state continuing its Medicaid expansion program unless it defunded Planned Parenthood. He also tried to put Democrats on the spot in 2017 by introducing a single-payer health bill, a move that Democrats voted against. In late 2018, he called on Senate leaders to eliminate the filibuster and authorize funding for Trump's long-demanded border wall along the U.S.-Mexico border.

Daines played a bit role in the drama of Brett Kavanaugh's Supreme Court nomination. Republicans needed every vote, but he had a conflict he couldn't skip: his daughter's wedding. Republican Sen. Lisa Murkowski of Alaska, who opposed Kavanaugh, agreed to vote "present" so Daines wouldn't have to miss the festivities.

Daines faced re-election in 2020. If Democratic Gov. Steve Bullock were to drop his presidential bid and run for the seat, Daines could have a tough fight. But it was unclear whether Democrats would find a top-tier challenger.

Greg Gianforte (R)

Elected 2017, 1st full term, b. Apr 17, 1961; San Diego, CA; Stevens Institute of Technology, B.E., 1983; Stevens Institute of Technology, M.S., 1983; Christian - Non-Denominational; Married (Susan Gianforte); 4 children.

DC Office: 1222 LHOB 20515, 202-225-3211, Fax: 202-225-5687, gianforte.house.gov

State Offices: Billings, 406-969-1736; Great Falls, 406-952-1280; Helena, 406-502-1435.

Committees: *Energy & Commerce*: Communications & Technology; Consumer Protection & Commerce; Health.

Group Ratings

	ADA	ACLU	AFL-CIO	LCV	ITI	COC	HAFA	ACU	CFG	FRC
2018	-	11%	-	3%	-	83%	47%	68%	74%	100%
2017	0%	C	-	9%	C	100%	C	61%	40%	100%

Almanac Ratings 2017-18

	Economy	Social	Foreign	Composite
Liberal	25%	22%	4%	17%
Conservative	76%	78%	96%	83%

Key Votes of the 115th Congress

1. Obama-care revision	N/A	5. Family planning regs	N/A
2. Tax Cuts	Y	6. Body cameras/immigration	N
3. Omnibus appropriations	N	7. Abortion ban	Y
4. Dodd-Frank revision	Y	8. Concealed carry	Y

9. Guantanamo prisoners	N
10. Ground missiles, limit	N
11. Defense Dept. spending	Y
12. FISA rules	Y

Election Results

Election	Name (Party)	Vote (%)		Cand. Spent	Ind. Exp. Support	Ind. Exp. Oppose
2018 General	Greg Gianforte (R)	256,661	(51%)	$9,547,639	$761,621	$691,038
	Kathleen Williams (D)	233,284	(46%)	$3,761,806	$259,614	
	Elinor Swanson (Lib)	14,476	(3%)	$3,979		
2018 Primary	Greg Gianforte (R)	(100%)				

Prior winning percentages: 2017 special (50%)

Republican Greg Gianforte won a special election in May 2017 for the seat vacated by Republican Rep. Ryan Zinke, who was President Donald Trump's first secretary of Interior. The contest, which received a disproportionate amount of national attention and dollars in the intense political environment that followed Trump's election, was capped by an unusual election-eve incident at Gianforte's headquarters in Bozeman, when he slammed to the floor a reporter for a British newspaper who asked his views about changes in the Affordable Care Act. Gianforte, whose career in the House received less notoriety, considered running again for governor in 2020. He narrowly lost his bid in 2016.

Gianforte, a New Jersey transplant, moved to Montana and started the technology firm RightNow Technologies, which he sold to Oracle for $1.8 billion. As the GOP nominee against Gov. Steve Bullock in 2016, he got a majority of the GOP convention votes on the first ballot against five other candidates. Bullock won in November, 50%-46%.

The special election for the House seat was triggered when the Senate, on a 68-31 vote, confirmed Zinke on March 1, 2017. The major parties selected their nominees in conventions four and five days later at the same hotel in Helena. Democrats nominated Rob Quist, a musician with a local wood band, whose public service included 11 years on the Montana Arts Council and as an ambassador for Montana to its sister state in Japan. Quist, who rarely was seen without a cowboy hat, highlighted his support during the 2016 presidential campaign for Sen. Bernie Sanders of Vermont, who made campaign appearances on his behalf.

With Quist as the nominee, the Democratic Congressional Campaign Committee concluded that his prospects were dim and gave him little financial support. That dismayed many party activists who saw an opportunity to take a Republican-held seat, especially in the contentious political climate.

Gianforte ran into problems during the campaign in clarifying his view on how Congress should respond on health care reform. When asked whether he would support the recent House-passed Republican plan, he initially said that he would not respond until the Congressional Budget Office had issued its analysis. The CBO issued its report on the day before the Montana election. That led Ben Jacobs, a Washington-based reporter for the Guardian newspaper, to cite the CBO in seeking Gianforte's reaction. The candidate later acknowledged that he reacted poorly to the questioning. After Gianforte threw him to the floor, Jacobs showed that his glasses had been broken and he went to a local hospital for X-rays.

In the subsequent 24 hours, prominent state newspapers withdrew their endorsements of Gianforte and he was charged with a misdemeanor by the local sheriff. The impact on voters appeared to be negligible and Gianforte apologized to the reporter as he delivered his victory speech. National Republicans initially seemed dumbfounded by the incident. "There's no call for this, no matter what — under any circumstance," said Speaker Paul Ryan, though there was no House review or sanctions following the incident. Gianforte won the special election, 50%-44%. Days later, Gianforte pleaded guilty to a misdemeanor assault and got a six-month deferred sentence; he was ordered to provide community service and to take anger-management classes. He apologized in court and said he took "full responsibility." For his part, Trump embraced Gianforte's action. "Any guy that can do a body slam, he's my kind of — he's my guy," the president told a campaign rally in Montana in October 2018.

Quist spent more than $6 million for his campaign — a huge amount for a two-month contest in a state with low advertising costs. Gianforte also spent millions of dollars, including $1 million in self-financing. The two candidates benefited from more than $7 million in outside spending, chiefly by national party groups and their allies; a majority of those funds were spent on behalf of Gianforte, largely for negative ads on Quist.

He faced another competitive and expensive campaign in 2018, this time against Kathleen Williams, who had worked as a resource economist with the Forest Service and nonprofit conservation groups. In its editorial endorsing Williams, the Missoulian wrote, Gianforte had failed to seek consensus and was "the kind of leader who prefers to give orders, rather than follow them." His victory margin, 51%-46%, was similar to the special election.

In 2019, Gianforte gained a seat on the Energy and Commerce Committee, where he said that he would "promote responsible development of our energy resources and make health care more affordable and accessible." With Bullock term-limited in 2020, Gianforte announced in June 2019 his entry into what was shaping up as a wide-open contest to succeed him. If he survived a likely competitive GOP primary, Democrats in Montana made clear that he faced a rough contest. State legislators promoted a bill to increase the penalty for assaulting a journalist, with stiffer prison terms.

NEBRASKA

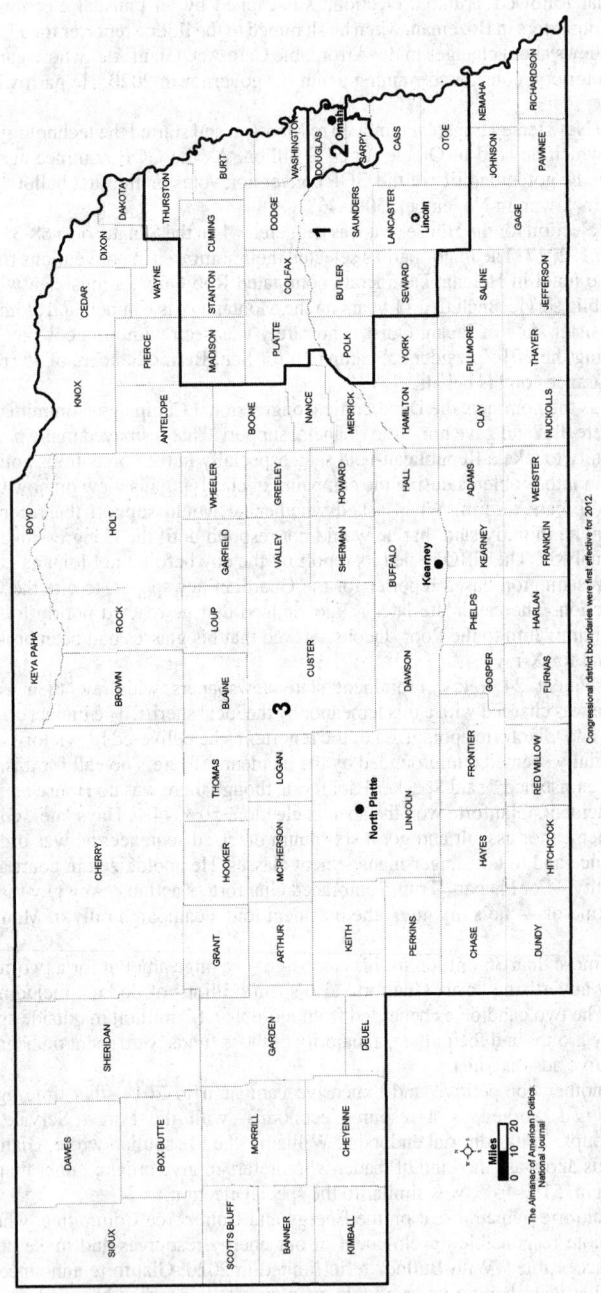

Congressional district boundaries were first effective for 2012

The Almanac of American Politics,
National Journal

Miles
0 10 20

Nebraska – America's top beef producer and home to the most feed cows of any state – has long been, and remains, one of the most Republican states in the nation. But Nebraska's largest and fastest-growing metropolitan area, Omaha, is politically marginal and, thanks to the state's eccentric Electoral College rules, it gave one of its five electoral votes to Barack Obama in 2008 and came within two percentage points of doing so again for Hillary Clinton in 2016, even as Donald Trump was winning the state with 60 percent of the vote.

The first travelers on the Oregon Trail in the 1840s called what they saw when they crossed the Missouri River and moved west along the Platte River "the sea of Nebraska." The state's ruggedly beautiful sandhills, a blanket of grass tucked roughly over submerged sand dunes, bloom atop the Ogalalla Aquifer and cover about a quarter of the state. In Nebraska, you can see nothing but rolling fields for miles on end, sectioned off here and there by barbed wire fences and perhaps, in the distance, a grain elevator towering over a tiny town and its railroad depot. The Platte is not actually a single river, but a braid of streams that weaves a silver chain around sandbars and islands, flooding the level floor of the Nebraska plain — a mile wide, the saying goes, and six inches deep. (The state's name means "flat water" in the Omaha and Oto languages.) Settlers in Nebraska sliced the top level of earth to prepare for planting, using the layers of sod to construct rustic but practical homes.

Nebraska became a territory with the 1854 Kansas-Nebraska Act. At the time, Nebraska "stretched west from the Missouri River to the Continental Divide in the Rocky Mountains and north to Canada," covering more than 351,000 square miles of the Great Plains and the Rockies, David Hendee wrote in the Omaha World-Herald on the sesquicentennial of statehood in 2017. Within a decade, the Nebraska Territory was chopped up – to help create the Colorado Territory in 1861, the Dakota Territory the same year, and the Idaho Territory two years later. The Homestead Act of 1862 promoted white settlement; 45 percent of all land in Nebraska was taken up by homesteaders, a higher percentage than any other state. "People came to Nebraska because they saw opportunities to get rich," Nebraska Wesleyan University historian Ronald Naugle told Hendee. Statehood was tied up in post-Civil War conflict between President Andrew Johnson and radical Republicans over civil rights. Initially the state intended to restrict voting to free white males, but the radical Republicans insisted on removing the restriction. Twice, Johnson vetoed the measure before the state agreed to remove the restriction, and statehood arrived in 1867.

The state was largely settled in a single rush in the 1880s, when its population increased from 452,000 to 1 million. Omaha became a major railroad center and farming and food products reigned as the main businesses. Czechs, Germans and Danes came to work the factories in Omaha and farms on the Plains — Willa Cather tells the story beautifully in her novels. Nebraska was a major destination for Volga Germans, ethnic Germans who had settled in Russia; they bequeathed runza, a meat-in-bread delicacy kept alive in the state by a popular chain of casual restaurants of that name. For about a century, Nebraska remained pretty much the same. From 1890 to 2010, its population rose from 1 million to just 1.8 million. This is not what its founders envisioned. They hoped that Nebraska would develop a diversified farming, industrial and commercial economy like the ones that emerged in Illinois, Missouri and Ohio. But climate is hard to predict. Rains were plentiful in the 1880s, but the 1890s were years of drought, and Nebraska abruptly stopped growing. Many rural counties, and even Omaha, lost population. Nebraska exported people for 100 years: 48 percent of Nebraskans in 1890 were children, but in 2017 only 28 percent were.

For a long time, the creative energies in the American economy seemed to have skipped over the Great Plains and moved west. In the popular imagination, Nebraska has made even less of an imprint than the neighboring farm states of Iowa and Kansas, which helps explain why the state tourism office in 2018 settled on a tongue-in-cheek advertising tagline: "Honestly, it's not for everyone." State tourism director John Ricks explained to the World-Herald that Nebraska has typically ranked as the least likely state that tourists plan to visit, so to make them listen, "we had to shake people up."

Since 1990, Nebraska has been growing relatively robustly for the first time in decades. Its population grew 16 percent between 1990 and 2010 — more than the increase in the previous 60 years combined — and since 2010, it has risen by another 5 percent. Growth has been concentrated around Omaha: Douglas County, which includes Omaha, has seen population increase 8.2 percent since 2010; its suburban neighbor, Sarpy County, rose 13.6 percent in the same period. Lancaster County, which includes the state capital of Lincoln, increased 9.8 percent. These three counties accounted for the entirety of the state's population increase during that period, and then some, with the rest of the state losing population. Emblematic of rural Nebraska's difficulties was the demise of onetime outdoor-retail giant Cabela's, headquartered in Sidney, a small town in western Nebraska. Amid pressure from an activist investor, Cabela's allowed itself to be bought out by Bass Pro Shops, a major rival, in 2017. At its peak, Cabela's had supported 2,000 jobs in Sidney, equal to about a quarter of the town's population; most of the employees who remained and weren't kept on in residual operations were offered generous buyouts.

The Hispanic share of Nebraska's population has risen from 2 percent in 1990 to 10.5 percent today, a higher share of the population than in such diverse states as Virginia, Georgia, Pennsylvania and Michigan. Many Hispanics came from Texas and Mexico to work in meatpacking factories in such places as Colfax County (Schuyler), which is 45 percent Hispanic, and Dawson County (Lexington), which is 33 percent Hispanic. Meanwhile, the state's Asian population is growing quickly -- though starting from a small base -- due to an influx of South Asians from such places as Bhutan, Myanmar (Burma), Nepal and Thailand. Partly as a result, Nebraska's population is no longer quite so elderly. In 2017, Nebraska was tied for fifth among states for children as a percentage of its population, and the state ranked in a tie for 34th for its share of those 65 and older.

Without a housing bubble and with an economy based on agriculture, Nebraska escaped the worst of the Great Recession. The unemployment rate hasn't even touched 4 percent since May 2012. In late 2018, unemployment had settled in at 2.8 percent, ranking among the eight best states nationally. The state's median income is slightly higher than the national average, and those dollars can go further with the state's low cost of living. Measured by cash receipts, Nebraska ranks first in the country for cattle, third in corn and feed crops, and seventh in pork. Nebraskans cheered when Japan opened its market to U.S. beef in January 2013 and when China said it would do so in September 2016. In 2019, Nebraska sought to become the second state after Missouri to pass a law preventing plant-based food products from being labeled as "meat."

Despite Trump's continued support from the state's voters, his administration's actions posed threats to the economic order. The retaliation prompted by Trump's tariffs risked significant harm to Nebraska farmers; two Nebraska counties, Colfax and Dixon, were judged by the Brookings Institution to be among the 15 counties in the United States facing the biggest risks from tariff blowback. GOP Sen. Ben Sasse retorted to Trump by saying that "kooky 18th century protectionism will jack up prices on American families" and that such trade policies are "going to make it 1929 again." Meanwhile, a crackdown on employers who hire illegal immigrants caught the meatpacking economy, a linchpin of rural Nebraska, in a bind of its own making. In August 2018, nearly 400 law enforcement officers executed raids in six Nebraska communities that included 17 criminal arrest warrants for employers and individuals.

Omaha, for its part, has been thriving economically, and not just because America's second-richest man, Warren Buffett, lives there. Omaha is home to four Fortune 500 companies: Buffett's Berkshire Hathaway, Union Pacific, the construction, engineering and mining giant Kiewit, and Mutual of Omaha. The area also harbors such large employers as Green Plains Renewable Energy, TD Ameritrade and Valmont Industries, which manufactures linear irrigation equipment and windmill support structures. Lincoln, with its skyscraper state capitol and University of Nebraska, has a solid economic base as well. On Saturdays during the fall, when the 'Huskers (Nebraskans don't say Cornhuskers) play in Lincoln, nearly all the 92,000 seats at Memorial Stadium are filled, which equates to roughly one out of every 20 people in the state. Trump's decision to green-light the Keystone XL pipeline from Canada to Nebraska gave the state's energy industry reason for optimism. But even after Trump's approval, the project remained bogged down over what path it should take through the state; in addition, a judicial ruling ordered additional reviews of its financial viability, safety protections and other concerns.

The sudden boom of the 1880s and the bust of the 1890s produced the most colorful — and atypical — politics of Nebraska's history: the populist movement and William Jennings Bryan, the "silver-tongued orator of the Platte." Bryan was only 36 when he delivered his "Cross of Gold" speech at the 1896 Democratic National Convention and was swept to the nomination. "From the first sentence, the audience was with me," recalled Bryan in his memoirs. But the country wasn't. Bryan was so radical that Democratic President Grover Cleveland wouldn't support him, although he still won 47 percent of the popular vote in the first of his three unsuccessful attempts at the presidency. Since Bryan's time, Nebraska's most notable politician has been George Norris. In 1934, Norris spurred adoption of the state's unicameral, nonpartisan legislature, in which every bill gets a public hearing where anyone can speak. In Washington, Norris sponsored the Norris-LaGuardia Anti-Injunction Act, the first federal pro-union legislation, and the Tennessee Valley Authority Act. But most Nebraskans were repelled by the New Deal, which they believed threatened their way of life.

Although it has sometimes elected Democratic governors and senators – James Exon, Bob Kerrey and Ben Nelson each served in both offices -- Nebraska over the past half-century has grown increasingly Republican. The state hasn't elected a Democrat to statewide office in more than a decade. Unusually for a strongly Republican state, the Nebraska legislature voted to abolish the death penalty in 2015. Republican Gov. Pete Ricketts vetoed the bill, but the legislature overrode him. Then, with Ricketts' support, a measure to reject the legislature's move qualified for the ballot, and in 2016, the measure passed with 57 percent of the vote. In August 2018, Nebraska executed its first convict since 1997, becoming the first state to use the synthetic opioid fentanyl as part of the lethal drug cocktail.

In the 2016 presidential race, Trump widened Mitt Romney's margin in the state by four points. All told, 62 percent of Clinton's votes in the state came from Douglas County (Omaha) and Lancaster County (Lincoln). Two years later, Ricketts won a second term by a slightly larger margin than he'd achieved in 2014, and Republicans easily swept Nebraska's other statewide offices. Democrats nursed hopes that they could flip the Omaha-based 2nd Congressional District, but the party nominated Kara Eastman, a candidate widely considered to be too far to the left; she ended up losing to incumbent Republican Don Bacon, 51%-49%, despite the strong Democratic election year. The one silver lining for Democrats was the statewide passage of a ballot measure to expand Medicaid through the Affordable Care Act, a policy change that had been consistently blocked by Ricketts and his fellow Republicans. The measure passed with 54 percent of the vote, putting pressure on Ricketts to implement the voters' will – and to figure out whose taxes to raise or programs to cut to pay for it.

Population		Race and Ethnicity		Income	
Total	1,893,921	White	79.8%	Median Income	$56,675
Land area (sq. miles)	76,824	Black	4.6%	State Income Rank	24
Pop/ sq mi	24.7	Latino	10.5%	Poverty Rate	12.0%
Born in state	64.9%	Asian	2.2%	With health insurance	91.0%
		Two or more races	2.0%	Cash public assistance	1.9%
Age Groups		Other	0.9%	Food stamp/SNAP	8.8%
Under 18	24.8%				
18-34	23.4%	**Education**		**Work**	
35-64	37.1%	H.S grad or less	35.8%	White Collar	36.8%
Over 64	14.7%	Some college	33.6%	Sales and Service	39.8%
		College Degree, 4 yr	20.4%	Blue Collar	23.4%
Military		Post grad	10.2%	Government	13.8%
Veteran/ Active Duty	8.9%				

Presidential Politics

2016 Primary (D)	Clinton (D)	42,692 (53%)	Sanders (D)	37,744 (47%)			
2016 Primary (R)	Trump (R)	122,327 (61%)	Cruz (R)	36,703 (18%)	Kasich (R)	22,709 (11%)	
	Carson (R)	10,016 (5%)					
2016 Pres. Vote	Trump (R)	495,961 (59%)	Clinton (D)	284,494 (34%)	Johnson (L)	38,946 (5%)	
2012 Pres. Vote	Romney (R)	475,064 (60%)	Obama (D)	302,081 (38%)			

Over the past 50 years, Nebraska has voted an average of 60 percent Republican in presidential elections, more than any other state except Utah, Idaho and Wyoming. In 2016, Donald Trump came close to hitting that mark, defeating Hillary Clinton 59%-34%. Nebraska is one of two states (Maine is the other) that allocate two of its Electoral College votes to the statewide winner and the others to the winners in each of the congressional districts. In 2008, Barack Obama managed to carry the 2nd District, Omaha and its suburbs, 50%-49%, by just 3,370 votes out of 277,809 cast. John McCain carried the state overall, 57%-42%. Thus, one Nebraska Electoral Vote went to Obama, the first time a Democrat picked up any of the state's Electoral College votes since 1964. The Clinton campaign aired television ads in the Omaha media market in hopes of repeating Obama's 2008 coup. She also campaigned with Omaha investment billionaire Warren Buffett. The 2nd was close, but Trump led, 49%-45%. Trump won 91 of the state's 93 counties, all but Douglas (Omaha) and Lancaster (Lincoln).

The May 10 GOP primary came shortly after Trump became the de facto Republican nominee, but Texas Sen. Ted Cruz, who had withdrawn from the race after he lost the May 3 Indiana primary, mischievously said he might get back into the GOP contest if Nebraska Republicans rejected Trump. No such thing happened and Trump captured 62 percent of the vote to 18 percent for Cruz. Republican Gov. Pete Ricketts endorsed Trump after he became the presumptive nominee. Ricketts' father, who co-founded TD Ameritrade based in Omaha and bought the Chicago Cubs, donated millions of dollars to Our Principals PAC, which had earlier run anti-Trump ads in the primaries. In the March 5 Democratic caucuses, Vermont Sen. Bernie Sanders defeated Clinton, 57%-43%. Clinton defeated Sanders in the non-binding Democratic primary two months later, 53%-47%.

Congressional Districts

116th Congress Lineup	3R	115th Congress Lineup	3R

Nebraska has had three congressional districts since the 1960 census. Boundaries can generate strong feelings in Nebraska if only because it has been one of just two states where Electoral College votes are apportioned by congressional district. The unicameral legislature is technically nonpartisan, but in reality Republicans have long controlled the process. With the tight presidential vote in the 2nd District in 2016, plus its competitive congressional battleground, Republicans have added incentive to eliminate the Electoral College anomaly.

As the sparse western two-thirds of the state has shed residents, the western 3rd District has needed to expand, and the Lincoln-based 1st District and Omaha-based 2nd District have needed to shrink. In 2011, Republicans' top priority was to shore up the 2nd. So, the legislature passed a map trading politically mixed Bellevue and Offutt Air Force Base south of Omaha to the 1st District in exchange for the deeply Republican western half of Sarpy County, making the 2nd about a percentage point safer overall. To give neighboring Republican Jeff Fortenberry extra insurance, legislators shifted very conservative Platte County from the 3rd to the 1st. To offset the move, the "Big Third" now stretches 460 miles from Wyoming to Missouri and Iowa and includes all or part of 75 counties, more than any other district in the country. That helped Republicans in 2012. But the 2nd then resumed its highly competitive status, with House incumbents ousted the next two cycles. There is no guarantee that the return to GOP normalcy will continue. Unless Republican redistricters want to divide Omaha, which seems unlikely, their options are limited.

Pete Ricketts (R)

Elected 2014, term expires 2023, 2nd term; b. Aug. 19, 1964, Nebraska City; U. of Chicago, B.A., M.A.; Catholic; Married (Susanne); 3 children.

Professional Career: Customer Services, Senior VP Strategy & Business Devel., Senior Vice President of Product Development, Senior Vice President of Marketing, COO at Ameritrade, 1993-2005; Founder, Drakon, LLC.

Office: 1445 K St, Lincoln, 68509-4848; 402-471-2244; Fax: 402-471-6031; Website: governor.nebraska.gov.

Lt. Gov.: Mike Foley (R) **Atty. Gen:** Doug Peterson (R) **Sec. of State:** John Gale (R)

State Legislature: Unicameral, bipartisan

Election Results

Election	Name (Party)	Vote (%)
2018 General	Pete Ricketts (R)...	411,812 (59%)
	Bob Krist (D)..	286,169 (41%)
2018 Primary	Pete Ricketts (R)...	138,292 (81%)
	Krystal Gabel (R)..	31,568 (19%)

Republican Pete Ricketts' last name was well known in Nebraska before he ever tried for public office. His father, Joe, had founded the company that became TD Ameritrade, based outside of Omaha, and the family owns Major League Baseball's storied franchise, the Chicago Cubs. He won the governorship in 2014 and was reelected with ease in 2018.

Ricketts is one of four children, and the eldest son. On the campaign trail, he told voters that growing up in Omaha, he and his siblings were latchkey kids in a middle-class home where both parents worked and his father built a financial empire. He graduated from Westside High School in Omaha and attended the University of Chicago, earning a bachelor's degree in biology and an MBA. After college, Ricketts joined the family business, rising to president and chief operating officer.

He left TD Ameritrade in 2005 to run against incumbent Democratic Sen. Ben Nelson in 2006. Republicans were not looking for a wealthy scion to be their standard-bearer against Nelson, who was a former two-term governor born in the small plains town of McCook, which had also produced Nebraska icon George Norris. But a number of other notable Republicans, including Gov. Dave Heineman, former Gov. Mike Johanns, and Reps. Lee Terry and Tom Osborne all passed on the race, so Republicans rallied around Ricketts, who could self-fund his campaign. Running on a platform of tax cuts and smaller government, Ricketts won the primary, but in the general election he backed a guest-worker program for immigrants, enabling Nelson to run to his right and call for securing the border. Ricketts, with his investment background, also came out in favor of private Social Security accounts, something Nelson opposed. Ricketts plowed almost $12 million of his own money into the race and outspent Nelson almost 2-to-1. But on Election Day, he lost by a nearly 2-to-1 margin.

For the next five years, Ricketts served on the Republican National Committee, building his connections to the party establishment, grassroots activists in Nebraska and GOP political players around the country. He also invested in startups, served on various boards, and developed philanthropic interests. He founded Drakon LLC, based in Omaha, a management firm that supports local entrepreneurs and new growth companies, and the Platte Institute for Economic Research, a conservative think tank based in Omaha.

When he ran for governor in 2014, Ricketts got endorsements from Wisconsin Gov. Scott Walker, Indiana Gov. Mike Pence, House Budget Committee Chairman Paul Ryan of Wisconsin and Sen. Ted Cruz of Texas, among others – potential White House hopefuls who may have been looking to woo Ricketts' father and his super PAC, as well as his brothers Todd and Tom. (Pete Ricketts' sister Laura was the exception; she was one of 27 high-profile gay and lesbian "bundlers" for President Barack Obama in 2012. Ricketts frequently had to explain how he disagreed with Laura over same-sex marriage, though he always added, "I love her.") Ricketts' main rival for the GOP nod was Attorney General Jon Bruning, who had lost a 2012 Senate primary to longshot Deb Fischer, thanks in part to a last-minute TV ad blitz for Fischer that was funded by Joe Ricketts. Bruning repeatedly accused the Ricketts family of using its wealth to buy another victory, but in a field of six candidates, Ricketts was able to edge Bruning, 27%-26%. Ricketts' Democratic opponent, Center for Rural Affairs Executive Director Chuck Hassebrook, took a few stabs at making Ricketts' family fortune an issue, but it went nowhere; Ricketts overwhelmed Hassebrook, 57%-39%, as he carried 89 of the state's 93 counties. Ricketts' campaign spent roughly $7 million, including almost $1 million from his personal checkbook and more than $1 million from his family members — more than twice what Hassebrook spent.

Entering office, Ricketts enjoyed a state budget surplus and a favorable economy, but that did not help him prevail in a number of tests with the legislature in 2015. First, Nebraska lawmakers overrode Ricketts's veto of a gas-tax hike. Ricketts said the increase would hurt "hardworking Nebraskans," but the legislature wanted the estimated $75 million generated annually by the tax increase for state road repair and maintenance, and didn't want to have to cut any other spending to get it. The legislature voted to override Ricketts' veto of a bill that would allow immigrants who were brought into the country illegally as children to get a driver's license; the governor called the measure "an inappropriate benefit to non-citizens." Most spectacularly, the legislature overrode his veto of a bill to end the state's death penalty, becoming the first conservative state in more than four decades to do so. On this issue, the governor was ultimately successful – with his support, voters qualified a ballot measure to reinstate the death penalty, and in 2016, it passed easily.

The veto overrides continued in April 2016 with a bill that would allow children who were brought to the country illegally by their parents to acquire occupational licenses. The bill had been supported by business leaders – another indication that Ricketts and the business community were not always on the same page. (Opposing a business-supported effort to protect LGBT workers was another example.) A happier outcome came from a $450 million transportation bill that Ricketts signed; the bill was designed to complete the state's 600-mile expressway system by 2033. Ricketts also courted business in Japan, China, Hong Kong and Macau -- potential consumers of Nebraska beef.

In January 2016, Ricketts initially declined to meet President Barack Obama during his first presidential visit to the state, then reversed course after an outcry and greeted him at the airport. In that fall's campaign, Ricketts took the unusual step of financially supporting several challengers to members of the legislature who had voted to override one or more of his vetoes. Even though the unicameral legislature is officially nonpartisan, the targeted lawmakers were unofficially Republicans, and Ricketts' offensive did not play well in some GOP circles. Of the 17 members who eventually joined the freshman class, Ricketts had supported eight financially; three of them had ousted Republican antagonists. Strategically, the gambit worked well for the governor. In 2017, he avoided being overridden on vetoes of a felon voting rights bill and on $56.5 million in spending cuts. Meanwhile, the 2018 budget process turned out to be much smoother, attracting no veto fights. One of the budget bills also included a provision to eliminate Title X federal funding for Planned Parenthood, a priority for the state's anti-abortion caucus.

Ricketts, meanwhile, solidified his ties to Trump, joining a White House energy roundtable and a post-World Series visit for the Cubs in 2017 and building relationships with Environmental Protection Agency Administrator Scott Pruitt, Health and Human Services Secretary Tom Price, Agriculture Secretary Sonny Perdue and Commerce Secretary Wilbur Ross. Despite Trump's protectionist agenda, which put Nebraska farmers at risk, Ricketts didn't put much distance between himself and the president, at least in his public comments. He downplayed China's retaliatory tariffs on pork products as "part of the overall trade negotiations the Trump administration has," and touted the U.S.-Mexico-Canada Agreement that the administration negotiated to replace the North American Free Trade Agreement." In December 2018, Trump tapped Ricketts to serve on a trade policy advisory committee.

Ricketts had no trouble winning a second term, defeating state Sen. Bob Krist, the Democratic nominee, 59%-41% -- a slightly larger margin than he'd assembled in 2014, even though Ricketts lost Douglas County (Omaha), which he had won four years earlier. The bigger surprise was that a ballot initiative to expand Medicaid under the Affordable Care Act also passed, 54%-46%. Ricketts had consistently fought Medicaid expansion; after the election, the governor said implementation would be complex, but it appeared that the state would eventually expand the program to include able-bodied adults with no children. In March 2019, the state experienced massive flooding, causing 64 of the state's 93 counties to declare an emergency; Ricketts called it "the most widespread disaster we've had in our state's history". As for his future plans, Ricketts told the Omaha World-Herald before the election that if he won, "I'm staying. All four years." He ruled out a 2020 Senate run, though he didn't rule out a Senate bid after he'd finished his tenure as governor.

Deb Fischer (R)

Elected 2012, term expires 2024, 2nd term, b. Mar 01, 1951; Lincoln; University of Nebraska, Lincoln, B.S., 1988; Presbyterian; Married (Bruce G. Fischer); 3 children; 3 grandchildren.

Elected Office: NE Legislature, 2005-2012; Valentine Rural High School Board of Education, 1990-2004.

Professional Career: Rancher, 1972-2012.

DC Office: 454 RSOB 20510, 202-224-6551, Fax: 202-228-1325, fischer.senate.gov

State Offices: Kearney, 308-234-2361; Lincoln, 402-441-4600; Norfolk, 402-200-8816; Omaha, 402-391-3411; Scottsbluff, 308-630-2329.

Committees: *Agriculture, Nutrition & Forestry*: Livestock, Marketing & Agriculture Security; Nutrition, Agricultural Research & Specialty Crops (Chmn); Rural Development & Energy. *Armed Services*: Emerging Threats & Capabilities; Readiness & Management Support; Strategic Forces (Chmn). *Commerce, Science & Transportation*: Communications, Technology, Innovation & the Internet; Manufacturing, Trade & Consumer Protection; Subcommittee on Security; Subcommittee on Transportation & Safety (Chmn). *Rules & Administration*.

Group Ratings

	ADA	ACLU	AFL-CIO	LCV	ITI	COC	HAFA	ACU	CFG	FRC
2018	-	14%	-	7%	-	80%	69%	81%	63%	100%
2017	0%	C	0%	0%	C	86%	C	76%	77%	100%

Almanac Ratings 2017-18

	Economy	Social	Foreign	Composite
Liberal	0%	0%	0%	0%
Conservative	100%	100%	100%	100%

Key Votes of the 115th Congress

1. Obama-care revision	Y	5. Gun regulations	Y	9. Kavanaugh confirmation	Y
2. Tax Cuts	Y	6. Family planning regs	Y	10. Saudi arms sales	N
3. Dodd-Frank revision	Y	7. Gorsuch confirmation	Y	11. FISA rules	Y
4. Omnibus appropriations	N	8. Immigration restrictions	Y	12. Military aid in Yemen	N

Election Results

Election	Name (Party)	Vote (%)		Cand. Spent	Ind. Exp. Support	Ind. Exp. Oppose
2018 General	Deb Fischer (R)	403,151	(58%)	$4,983,235		
	Jane Raybould (D)	269,917	(39%)	$2,078,587	$36,068	
	Jim Schultz (Lib)	25,349	(4%)			
2018 Primary	Deb Fischer (R)	128,157	(76%)			
	Todd Watson (R)	19,661	(12%)			
	Jack Heidel (R)	9,413	(6%)			

Prior winning percentages: 2012 (58%)

Nebraska's senior senator, Deb Fischer, was the only Republican in the country to flip a Senate seat in 2012, when President Barack Obama cruised to reelection. Since then she has become a reliable Republican vote while eschewing the spotlight — in stark contrast to the state's junior senator, Ben Sasse. Fischer garnered a reputation for quietly and methodically building the votes for her priorities — unsurprisingly, this has made her a loyal Republican vote and a member of Senate Majority Leader Mitch McConnell's leadership team, as the Kentuckian is also known for holding his cards close. Even on an issue like trade, where Fischer follows the traditional party line of favoring free trade and not President Donald Trump's tariff heavy approach, Fischer avoided public confrontations with the president. She has said she has gained more ground by staying out of the news. In another sign of her close work with the administration, Fischer teamed with the president's daughter Ivanka Trump to include a pilot family leave program in the Republican-led tax rewrite of 2017.

Fischer has sought to reach out to Democrats on some issues while maintaining a low profile as a nuts-and-bolts legislator. She declined an invitation to speak at the 2016 Republican National Convention — not because of concerns about the nominee-in-waiting, Trump, but rather because convention organizers were looking for a "more political speech" than she wanted to give. "I do realize it's a political convention — but I'm kind of known as a policy person, so I wanted to focus on that," Fischer told The Omaha World-Herald. But it was politics that gave her a rare moment in the national spotlight a couple of months later: After a decade-old recording of Trump making lewd comments about women surfaced, Fischer called on Trump to drop off the ticket, only to reverse herself days later.

Fischer grew up in Lincoln, the state capital, where her mother, Florence Strobel, was an elementary school teacher and her father, Jerry Strobel, spent many years as an engineer in the Nebraska Department of Roads, ending his career heading the department in the late 1980s. Transportation funding would later be a legislative focus for Fischer at the state and federal levels. She attended the University of Nebraska, where she met her husband, Bruce Fischer. She left school to marry him, and the couple settled on the Fischer family ranch in Valentine, in northern Nebraska. Despite growing up in what she described as the "big small town" of Lincoln, Fischer said she had little trouble adjusting to ranching life. She honed one talent often associated with farm wives: "She's infamous for her pie-making," her husband told the World-Herald shortly after Fischer was nominated for the Senate. "She doesn't do it very often, but it's a darn-sure treat when she does." As her three sons grew, Fischer returned to the University of Nebraska in Lincoln and earned a degree in education in 1988.

Her first run for elected office came two years later, when she won a seat on the Valentine Rural High School Board of Education. She went on to become president of the Nebraska Association of School Boards and serve on the Nebraska Coordinating Commission for Postsecondary Education, the state's oversight agency for higher education institutions. In 2004, Fischer won a seat in Nebraska's unicameral Legislature, representing a district that sprawled across a dozen counties — an area the size of New Jersey. She was unopposed for a second term in 2008. During her first term, an upheaval in the Legislature gave Fischer the chairmanship of the Transportation and Telecommunications Committee. Among her biggest achievements was passing legislation to shift about $70 million of the state's sales tax revenues to road construction on an annual basis.

Barred by law from seeking a third term in the state Legislature in 2012, Fischer entered the race to succeed retiring Democratic Sen. Ben Nelson. Nelson, like Fischer's opponent Bob Kerrey, had served as governor before winning a Senate seat. While Nelson had accumulated one of the most conservative voting records among members of his party, he took intense political heat for his crucial 2009 vote in favor of Obamacare.

Fischer began her Senate bid as the underdog in a primary against state Attorney General Jon Bruning and state Treasurer Don Stenberg. Bruning enjoyed the support of the GOP establishment, while tea party leaders rallied behind Stenberg. Fischer, however, steadily gained traction as Stenberg and Bruning turned their fire on each other. She also benefitted from the endorsement of one tea party favorite, 2008 vice presidential nominee Sarah Palin, along with a last-minute television ad blitz funded by wealthy businessman Joe Ricketts, founder of Omaha-based TD Ameritrade stock brokerage firm. Fischer won the primary with 41 percent of the vote; Bruning got 36 percent and Stenberg took 19 percent.

In the general election, Kerrey — having held office as governor and senator throughout the 1980s and 1990s — was considered the Democrats' best hope in a state where nearly half of all voters identify as Republicans and only about one-third as Democrats. Although Kerrey was a household name, many voters were turned off by the fact that he had been living out of state since leaving the Senate in 2000; he served as president of the New York's New School University from 2001 to 2010.

Fischer vowed not to serve more than two terms in the Senate and backed a constitutional amendment for congressional term limits. She stressed her family's ranching background and her work in the state Legislature on issues important to rural Nebraska. Kerrey made an issue of her family's use of grazing rights on 11,000 acres of federal land, calling her a "welfare rancher." He dubbed her a "bad neighbor" for suing an elderly couple in the 1990s in a dispute over ownership of more than 100 acres along the Snake River and suggested Fischer had used her influence in the Legislature to bar the couple from later selling the land in question to the state. Fischer's campaign called such attacks a "transparent act of desperation." In the end, Fischer won all but a handful of counties throughout the state and won 58%-42%. Kerrey's loss ended almost four decades of Nebraska splitting its Senate delegation.

One of Fischer's first votes in the Senate, in early 2013, was against Obama's nomination of another former Nebraska senator, Republican Chuck Hagel, as secretary of Defense. She cited what she termed Hagel's "confusing and contradictory" testimony before the Armed Services Committee, of which she was then a newly appointed member. In opposing Hagel, Fischer parted company with Republican Mike Johanns, then Nebraska's senior senator, whom Fischer had called a role model. Few were particularly surprised by her vote since Hagel, who was viewed as a moderate and had been critical of President George W. Bush's strategy in the Iraq War, had backed Kerrey in the fall election.

Fischer's philosophy has put her in the Republican mainstream on issues ranging from taxes to abortion rights. She has used her seat on the Environment and Public Works Committee to excoriate the Environmental Protection Agency for what she has called "extreme overreach" in its regulatory regimen. But she has shown a pragmatic streak, declining to go as far as other conservatives who have called for abolishing the EPA and the Education Department.

Fischer joined Republican leadership in 2015 — as counsel to the majority leader — and has been called upon to promote GOP alternatives on issues such as pay equity and family leave. In 2017, Fischer reintroduced a proposal to provide tax incentives to businesses that offer employees two weeks of paid family leave each year. But advocacy groups for paid leave criticized Fischer's legislation because it was optional — and not as generous as the leading Democratic bill, which proposed guaranteeing workers two-thirds of their pay for up to 12 weeks. Working alongside Ivanka Trump, Fischer got a two-year trial program. Despite the criticism of its limited scope, this was the first-ever national family leave policy. She has worked with independent Sen. Angus King of Maine to extend the leave program. At the end of 2018, Fischer and Iowa Sen. Joni Ernst battled each other for conference vice chairwomanship. Despite being more senior and less critical of Trump, Fischer lost.

On the Commerce Committee, Fischer joined a bipartisan group seeking to promote the economic potential of the internet of things, an expanding market of consumer products in which information can be transmitted without a computer. She stuck to her philosophy of limited government regulation, claiming that legislation she proposed had prompted the Food and Drug Administration to back off from regulating Fitbit and other wearable devices. She also partnered with Minnesota Democrat Amy Klobuchar to expand rural broadband access.

The Nebraska Republican later chaired the Armed Service subcommittee on strategic forces and Agriculture panel on research and specialty crops. She helped secure funding for new Veterans Affairs facilities in Omaha and Lincoln and money for a new runway at Offutt Air Force Base in Bellevue, home to U.S. Strategic Command, which oversees the nation's nuclear and missile arsenals. The late Sen. John McCain, who chaired the Armed Services Committee, sometimes called her "the hammer."

For the most part, Fischer has had a good working relationship with the more outspoken Sasse, who succeeded Johanns in early 2015. But Sasse's adamant opposition to Trump as the party's nominee — he went so far as to advocate a third-party conservative alternative — created some awkward moments. At the Nebraska Republican State Convention in May 2016, delegates overwhelmingly approved a resolution — aimed at Sasse — that condemned a possible third-party candidacy. The force behind the resolution was Sam Fischer, a state political operative who is Deb Fischer's nephew. Sam Fischer and an aide to the senator denied she had any involvement in the resolution. But Politico reported that the view in state political circles was that the nephew would not have acted without his aunt's tacit approval. The senators have continued to differ over Trump, with Fischer giving him a " B" halfway through his term, adding that only trade kept him from an "A," while Sasse issued scorching statements and muses about leaving the Republican Party. She later told the Scottsbluff Star Herald that Sasse had "other avenues he's going down."

Fischer joined at least a dozen of her GOP Senate colleagues in urging Trump to step down from the national ticket following the October 2016 release of the "Access Hollywood" tape. She took some criticism when she became the first of that group to reverse herself and say she would support him after all.

In her 2018 reelection, Fischer faced off against Lincoln City Councilwoman Jane Raybould. Raybould had sought to make Fischer's closeness to Trump an issue but struggled to raise money and was swamped by Fischer in rural Nebraska. The senator rarely addressed Raybould even after Raybould called Fischer "corrupt" during their only debate. Fischer won 58%-39%.

Ben Sasse (R)

Elected 2014, term expires 2020, 1st term, b. Feb 22, 1972; Plainview; Yale University (CT), M.A.; Yale University (CT), M.Phil; Oxford University (UK), 1992; Harvard University, A.B., 1994; Saint John's College (MD), M.A., 1998; Yale University (CT), Ph.D., 2004; Lutheran; Married (Melissa Sasse); 3 children.

Professional Career: Chief of Staff, U.S Department of Justice Office of Legal Policy, 2004-2005; Chief of Staff, U.S Rep. Jeff Fortenberry, 2005; Assistant Professor, University of TX-Austin 2005-2006; Counselor to secretary, Health & Human Services; Assist. Assist. Sec. Health & Human Services, 2007-2009; President, Professor University of TX-Austin, 2009; Midland University 2010-2014.

DC Office: 107 RSOB 20510, 202-224-4224, sasse.senate.gov
State Offices: Kearney, 308-233-3677; Lincoln, 402-476-1400; Omaha, 402-550-8040; Scottsbluff, 308-632-6032.

Committees: *Banking, Housing & Urban Affairs*: Economic Policy; Financial Institutions & Consumer Protection; National Security & International Trade & Finance (Chmn). *Intelligence. Joint Economic. Judiciary*: Constitution; Oversight, Agency Action, Federal Rights & Federal Courts (Chmn); Subcommittee on Intellectual Property.

Group Ratings

	ADA	ACLU	AFL-CIO	LCV	ITI	COC	HAFA	ACU	CFG	FRC
2018	-	18%	-	14%	-	80%	83%	86%	93%	100%
2017	0%	C	0%	0%	C	86%	C	96%	95%	100%

Almanac Ratings 2017-18

	Economy	Social	Foreign	Composite
Liberal	6%	6%	4%	5%
Conservative	94%	94%	97%	95%

Key Votes of the 115th Congress

1. Obama-care revision	Y	5. Gun regulations	Y	9. Kavanaugh confirmation	Y
2. Tax Cuts	Y	6. Family planning regs	Y	10. Saudi arms sales	N
3. Dodd-Frank revision	Y	7. Gorsuch confirmation	Y	11. FISA rules	Y
4. Omnibus appropriations	N	8. Immigration restrictions	N	12. Military aid in Yemen	N

Election Results

Election	Name (Party)	Vote (%)		Cand. Spent	Ind. Exp. Support	Ind. Exp. Oppose
2014 General	Ben Sasse (R)	347,636	(64%)	$5,864,653	$1,681,914	$297,050
	Dave Domina (D)	170,127	(32%)	$1,227,205		$18,597
	Jim Jenkins (I)	15,868	(3%)	$354,598		
2014 Primary	Ben Sasse (R)	110,802	(49%)			
	Sid Dinsdale (R)	50,494	(23%)			
	Shane Osborn (R)	47,338	(21%)			
	Bart McLeay (R)	12,840	(6%)			

Ben Sasse was the last of the "bear den" to make his maiden speech on the Senate floor in late 2015, nearly a year after the Nebraska junior senator and his Republican classmates became the party's majority makers. But in a class with a former Fortune 500 CEO (Georgia's David Perdue), a noted foreign policy hawk (Arkansas' Tom Cotton) and a member already considered for the vice presidency (Iowa's Joni Ernst), Sasse found a way to stand out by speaking up. After the retirements of Sens. Bob Corker of Tennessee and Jeff Flake of Arizona, he has become one of President Donald Trump's few remaining vocal GOP critics in the Senate. And while other senators carefully chose their public fights with Trump, Sasse has waylaid the president on everything from trade, foreign policy and migrant family separation to the content of Trump's tweets. Even on topics on which his colleagues are critical of Trump, the former college president with four degrees stands out for his short, stinging statements. Such criticism of the commander in chief has not gone unnoticed.

For his part, Sasse has said politics cannot be a panacea for America's problems and that he thinks "every morning" about leaving the Republican Party, viewing himself as an "independent conservative who caucuses with the Republicans." In 2020, the prospect of him facing a primary challenger and sharing a ballot with Trump will be worth watching. In 2016, when Trump was the party's front-runner, the Nebraska Republican went even further, utilizing a steady stream of tweets and a couple of lengthy Facebook manifestos to blister Trump and question both his conservativism and behavior. "You brag abt many affairs w/ married women. Have you repented?" Sasse tweeted at Trump in late January 2016, before the Iowa caucuses. Sasse's vow not to support Trump as the party's nominee made him a leading member of the "Never Trump" movement within the Republican Party — and earned him a rebuke from the Nebraska GOP. At the state convention in late spring, delegates condemned Sasse's call for a third-party conservative alternative to Trump. Sasse was undeterred. The movement to swipe back at the junior senator was backed by fellow Nebraska Sen. Deb Fischer's nephew. Politico reported it was unlikely such a move would have occurred without his aunt's blessing.

Sasse is a fifth-generation Nebraskan who spent his childhood summers working in soybean and corn fields; he bears a scar on his forehead from a boyhood fall from a hayloft. He was born in the tiny town of Plainview in northeastern Nebraska and went to high school in nearby Fremont. Sasse departed his home state for nearly two decades before returning in 2009 to head a struggling university. He was recruited by Harvard University, thanks to his prowess as a high school wrestler. ("@BenSasse looks more like a gym rat than a U.S. Senator. How the hell did he ever get elected?" Trump later tweeted in response to Sasse's criticisms.) Sasse earned his undergraduate degree while spending a junior year abroad at the University of Oxford and then worked for a year at the Boston Consulting Group — the financial firm where Mitt Romney had gotten his start — before returning to school. He collected a master's degree from St. John's College in Annapolis, Md., while tutoring House pages on Capitol Hill and then earned two more master's degrees from Yale University before getting a doctorate in American history from Yale. That led to a teaching post at the University of Texas' Lyndon B. Johnson School of Public Affairs. Examples of his erudition: The book worm devoted a chapter of his book "The Vanishing American Adult" to building a "5-foot bookshelf" for his "family canon" of books, and with his wife, he homeschools their three children.

But Sasse spent most of the five years after earning his doctorate working in Washington, first for the Justice Department and then briefly as chief of staff to Nebraska Republican Rep. Jeff Fortenberry and then consulting for the Homeland Security Department. He was at the Health and Human Services Department the last two years of George W. Bush's presidency, first as a counselor to the secretary and later, following Senate confirmation, as HHS assistant secretary for planning and evaluation. At the end of the Bush administration, Sasse returned to Fremont to become president of Midland University, a 130-year-old Lutheran school that had financial difficulties. At 37, he was among the youngest college presidents in the country; during the 2014 campaign, he boasted of executing a "turnaround job" that has made Midland University what he termed "one of the fastest growing [schools] in the Midwest." He ended lifetime tenure for professors, persuaded some to take buyouts and brought about a takeover of a rival school.

In early 2013, Republican Mike Johanns, a former Nebraska governor and secretary of Agriculture, announced he would retire from the Senate after just one term. Sasse said he would run for the seat about a month after former state Treasurer Shane Osborn had announced he would run. As a Navy pilot, Osborn briefly had been detained by the Chinese in 2001 after a midair collision with a Chinese fighter jet forced him to make an emergency landing.

In the primary, Osborn sought to cast Sasse not only as too close to Washington but also insufficiently conservative: Sasse had penned a column in 2009 for U.S. News and World Report calling Medicare Part D, the prescription-drug benefit passed by a GOP-controlled Congress during the Bush administration, "enormously successful" and a "viable model for reform." But conservative groups rallied around Sasse as he headed to the top of the polls, and the Club for Growth and the Senate Conservatives Fund spent heavily on his behalf. Campaign visits by Sen. Ted Cruz of Texas and former Alaska Gov. Sarah Palin cemented Sasse as the conservative choice in the primary. In January 2014, Sasse was featured on the cover of National Review as a "rising conservative star." Sasse prevailed in a three-way primary, winning with 49 percent of the vote; Osborn got 21 percent. National Democrats made no serious attempt to contest the seat in November and Sasse easily won the general election.

A month before his maiden Senate speech in November 2015, Sasse — while watching a football game at home — tweeted: "New to politics & in deference to tradition I've spent first 9mos in Senate keeping head down, interviewing older members/listening/learning." His first couple of years in the chamber were punctuated by his frequent use of social media, especially Twitter, where he spoke of his love for Husker football, efforts to instill the value of hard work in his then-14-year-old daughter and responded to the news of the day. He later imposed upon himself a six-month "sabbath" from social media and now posts far less frequently.

In his first floor speech — attended by about three dozen of his colleagues — Sasse bemoaned "a real institutional decline in the Senate in recent decades;" he blamed both parties. Underlying this process-oriented critique was an apparent conviction that the long-term priorities the Senate ought to debate involve the basic role of the federal government — which Sasse feels need to be sharply curtailed. His votes against proposals that he feels exceed the scope of the federal government — including those broadly embraced by both parties — have exasperated even some fellow Republicans. In March 2016, Sasse was on the losing end of a 94-1 vote on a bill aimed at combating opioid abuse that later became law. When asked for comment by The New York Times on Sasse's vote, then-New Hampshire GOP Sen. Kelly Ayotte, a sponsor of the measure, rolled her eyes: "Whatever, dude."

At the end of February 2016, Sasse posted a lengthy "Open Letter to Trump Supporters" likening Trump and President Barack Obama in their views of executive power. "Much like President Obama, [Trump] displays essentially no understanding of the fact that, in the American system, we have a constitutional system of checks and balances, with three separate but co-equal branches of government." Sasse wrote. "The law is king, and the people are boss. But have you noticed how Mr. Trump uses the word "Reign" — like he thinks he's running for King? It's creepy, actually." Sasse's push for a third-party conservative alternative to Trump prompted speculation about the senator as a possible candidate, but he disavowed interest — citing his family and Senate duties. When those efforts failed, he announced he would write in Trump's running mate, Mike Pence, for president in November.

Several months after taking office, Sasse introduced the Winding Down Obama Care Act, which was seen as a potential Republican fallback position if the Supreme Court failed to uphold a key provision of the Affordable Care Act — subsidies to the federal health insurance exchange — in June 2015. Sasse's bill proposed to do away with the ACA subsidies, replacing them with general tax credits that would disappear within 18 months. He argued this would give the Republican-controlled Congress time to come up with an alternative to Obamacare. But, as the debate over repeal of the law was joined in earnest in early 2017, Sasse — once hailed as "Obamacare's Nebraska Nemesis" by the National Review — was playing a secondary role. "I'm trying to figure out how to add value, wherever I can, in that fight," Sasse told The Omaha World-Herald.

Sasse's committee assignments changed significantly in 2017: He moved to the Armed Services Committee, where Fischer was already serving, and the Judiciary Committee. He gave up his seat on the Agriculture Committee — marking the first time in nearly a half-century that no Nebraskan served on that panel. That caused consternation among some state farm groups. "I will engage in no less activity in listening to Nebraska farmers and producers about their priorities and concerns," Sasse told the Lincoln Journal Star. Fischer joined the Ag panel in 2018. In 2019, he gave up his seat on Armed Services to join the Intelligence Committee and also became the Republican Senate appointee on the Cyberspace Solarium Commission. The 13-member commission was Sasse's creation and was enacted in the 2018 National Defense Authorization Act. The panel was mandated to deliver a report on cybersecurity policy by September 2019.

Outside of the Senate, Sasse has authored two books since his election "The Vanishing American Adult" and "Them: Why We Hate Each Other — and How to Heal." Both have been New York Times bestsellers, but they are very different than the usual political tomes.

His frequent criticisms of Trump would offer an obvious avenue to a potential primary opponent for his reelection in 2020, though running to the right of Sasse on policy issues would be difficult. The 2017 American Conservative Union rankings pegged him as one of the six most conservative members in the chamber. There was speculation once again that he could challenge Trump, this time in 2020. Before the midterms, he said, "noxious weed control board of Dodge County, Nebraska, is the far more probable scenario for me." Sasse also said he was seriously considering not running again and spending more time with his family.

Jeff Fortenberry (R)

Elected 2004, 8th term, b. Dec 27, 1960; Baton Rouge, LA; Franciscan University (OH), M.Th.; Louisiana State University, B.A., 1982; Georgetown University (DC), M.P.P., 1986; Franciscan University (OH), M.A., 1996; Roman Catholic; Married (Celeste Gregory Fortenberry); 5 children.

Elected Office: Lincoln City Council, 1997-2001.

Professional Career: Staffer, U.S. House Comm. on Ag., 1986; Research Association, Gulf South Research Inst., 1987-1989; Assistant Director, Baton Rouge Downtown Dev. District, 1989-1992; Sales rep., Sandhills Publishing, 1995-2004.

DC Office: 1514 LHOB 20515, 202-225-4806, Fax: 202-225-5686, fortenberry.house.gov

State Offices: Fremont, 402-727-0888; Lincoln, 402-438-1598; Norfolk, 402-379-2064.

Committees: *Appropriations*: Agriculture, Rural Development, FDA & Related Agencies (RMM); State, Foreign Operations & Related Programs.

Group Ratings

	ADA	ACLU	AFL-CIO	LCV	ITI	COC	HAFA	ACU	CFG	FRC
2018	-	7%	-	20%	-	82%	44%	56%	41%	100%
2017	0%	C	19%	17%	C	93%	C	65%	48%	100%

Almanac Ratings 2017-18

	Economy	Social	Foreign	Composite
Liberal	4%	4%	13%	7%
Conservative	96%	97%	87%	93%

Key Votes of the 115th Congress

1. Obama-care revision	Y	5. Family planning regs	Y	9. Guantanamo prisoners	N
2. Tax Cuts	Y	6. Body cameras/immigration	N	10. Ground missiles, limit	N
3. Omnibus appropriations	Y	7. Abortion ban	Y	11. Defense Dept. spending	Y
4. Dodd-Frank revision	Y	8. Concealed carry	Y	12. FISA rules	Y

Election Results

Election	Name (Party)	Vote (%)		Cand. Spent	Ind. Exp. Support	Ind. Exp. Oppose
2018 General	Jeff Fortenberry (R)	141,712	(60%)	$635,772		
	Jessica McClure (D)	93,069	(40%)	$69,787		
2018 Primary	Jeff Fortenberry (R)		(100%)			

Prior winning percentages: 2016 (70%), 2014 (69%), 2012 (68%), 2010 (71%), 2008 (70%), 2006 (58%), 2004 (54%)

Republican Jeff Fortenberry, elected in 2004, has taken a prime slot on agriculture issues at the Appropriations Committee. He has a reputation as a brainy policy expert and something of a centrist. At the same time, he has occasionally defended President Donald Trump. In the tradition of many Nebraskans (including former Sens. Chuck Hagel and Bob Kerrey), Fortenberry takes a strong interest in foreign policy.

Fortenberry grew up in Baton Rouge Louisiana, where his father was a life insurance salesman and his mother worked as a 4-H Club extension agent. When Fortenberry was 12, his father was killed in a car accident. "It taught me a hard lesson that you wouldn't want to wish on any other child — you have to figure out a lot of things on your own," he told Esquire magazine. Fortenberry got the political bug early as a page to a Democratic state senator, but switched to the Republican Party after he graduated from Louisiana State University. He earned a master's degree in theology from Franciscan University of Steubenville Ohio, and another in public policy from Georgetown University. For a time, he studied for the priesthood. He moved to Nebraska to take a public relations position with Sandhills Publishing, a publisher of trade magazines for the trucking, aircraft and computer industries, and later got into the sales end of the business. In 1997, he won a seat on the Lincoln City Council. He served for four years, focusing on neighborhood concerns and growing the police force.

When the House seat opened in 2004, three candidates mounted competitive campaigns for the Republican nomination: Fortenberry; Curt Bromm, the speaker of the state's unicameral legislature; and Greg Ruehle, a former executive vice president of the Nebraska Cattlemen Association. The moderate Bromm lost momentum after a barrage of negative television ads financed by the Club for Growth, a national anti-tax group that supported Ruehle. Fortenberry, a social conservative, drew criticism from his opponents as a single-issue candidate, but his superior grassroots operation and fundraising carried him to victory. Fortenberry won with 39 percent of the vote, to 33 percent for Bromm and 21 percent for Ruehle. In Lincoln's Lancaster County, he got 52 percent. In November, Fortenberry faced state Sen. Matt Connealy, a farmer from Decatur who sought to exploit GOP divisions. Fortenberry promised to improve trade policies for farmers and to support ethanol development. He focused on socially conservative themes: opposition to abortion rights, support of capital punishment and a ban on same-sex marriage. He won 54%-43%, losing only two American Indian reservation counties.

In the House, Fortenberry has moved over time to the ideological center. His Almanac vote ratings have ranked him among moderate Republicans on foreign policy issues. He backed the 2011 compromise to raise the federal debt limit as well as the New Year's Day 2013 budget deal aimed at averting the so-called fiscal cliff. He was one of a handful of Republicans who signed a Democratic discharge petition seeking to force a floor vote on a stalled farm bill. Earlier, he supported President George W. Bush on the Iraq war, won House approval of an increase in visas for Iraqi translators, and enacted a bill barring U.S. assistance to governments using children as soldiers.

His legislative work has been chiefly on the Appropriations Committee. After Democrats took control of the House in 2018, Fortenberry was named ranking member of the agriculture subcommittee. He supported extension of the Export-Import Bank of the United States on the basis that "we don't have a perfect world." He has co-chaired the Caucus on Religious Minorities in the Middle East, the Congressional Study Group on Europe and the Nuclear Security Working Group. In 2016, the House unanimously passed a resolution that he authored with Democratic Rep. Anna Eshoo of California that labeled Islamic State atrocities against Christian groups in Syria and Iraq as "genocide." Later, he called for the creation of a nation for Christians in the Middle East. In the summer of 2018, the White House selected Fortenberry to help lead a delegation to northern Iraq to investigate the difficulties minority Christians targeted by ISIS were facing. As a result, he proposed an American-sponsored but Iraqi-led training mission to integrate Christians, Yazidis, Shia Muslims and others into a security force to help stabilize and secure the region.

Fortenberry started off skeptical of Trump during the 2016 campaign. After initially urging him to withdraw as the presidential nominee following the early October 2016 release of the Access Hollywood video with his lewd comments on women, Fortenberry said a few days later that he would vote for Trump. When his 17-year-old daughter in tears told Fortenberry, "Daddy, you've got to do something — Trump hates women," he relayed the story to vice presidential nominee Mike Pence during a meeting with other House Republicans and urged the Trump campaign to reach out to women. After the meeting, Pence privately thanked him for his comment, said Fortenberry, who has five daughters. Fortenberry has come around on Trump, to some degree. "Many people love him; many do not. But I think it's best to look at outcomes," Fortenberry told the Lincoln Star Journal, citing low unemployment and advancement opportunities for minorities. "And I've never had better interaction with an administration. I find them willing to help." Fortenberry called Trump's efforts to engage with North Korean dictator Kim Jong Un toward denuclearization "historic" and "bold." On trade, he supported Trump's efforts to renegotiate the North American Free Trade Agreement and has been pro-tariffs, while arguing that the GOP's tax reform bill would also spur investment in manufacturing.

In 2006, Fortenberry's first reelection campaign was against former Democratic Lt. Gov. Maxine Moul, who made the Iraq war an issue. Even with ample fundraising, Moul's campaign did not catch fire. Fortenberry won 58%-42%. Until 2018, Fortenberry hadn't been held below 68 percent of the vote. Running against Democrat Jessica McClure, who challenged the incumbent's "complacency" with the Trump administration and his vote to repeal the Affordable Care Act, Fortenberry won 60%-40%.

NE-1: Eastern Nebraska

Cook Partisan Voting Index: R+11

Population		Race and Ethnicity		Income	
Total	636,147	White	82.4%	Median Income	$57,047
Land area (sq. miles)	8,879	Black	2.9%	District Income Rank	203
Pop/ sq mi	71.7	Latino	8.9%	Poverty Rate	12%
Born in State	66.5%	Asian	2.6%	With health insurance	91.6%
		Two or more races	2.1%	Cash public assistance	2.4%
Age Groups		Other	1.2%	Food stamp/SNAP	8.5%
Under 18	24.2%				
18-34	25.3%	Education		Work	
35-64	36.2%	H.S grad or less	34.7%	White Collar	14.3%
Over 64	14.3%	Some college	34.5%	Sales and Service	40%
		College Degree, 4 yr	20.4%	Blue Collar	23.7%
Military		Post grad	10.4%	Government	16.2%
Veteran/ Active Duty	9.6%				

2012 Pres. Vote	Romney	152,021	(57%)	Obama	108,082	(41%)			
2016 Pres. Vote	Trump	158,576	(56%)	Clinton	100,106	(36%)	Johnson	14,025	(5%)

Lincoln: The eastern half of Nebraska, between the Missouri River and the 98th parallel, was laid out in relentless Midwestern mile-square grids and became some of America's prime farmland during the 1880s. Here the Plains have completed most of their gentle decline from the Rockies to sea level, and the land has contours just regular enough, and weather just favorable enough, to make farming economically viable. The area was settled by Yankee-descended farmers from the Midwest and immigrants from Germany and other countries. Traces of the immigrant heritage can still be found. Many people from Luxembourg, for example, settled along the Platte River in Butler County, where St. Mary's Presentation Parish still has a statue of Our Lady of Luxembourg. Not far away are villages with names that recall other immigrant groups — Prague (Czechs), Malmo (Swedes), Aloys (Germans).

Today, a new wave of immigrants is coming to eastern Nebraska, including Latinos from Mexico and the southwest United States, to work in the region's meatpacking factories, and Vietnamese refugees coming to Lincoln. Fremont, a town of 26,000 northwest of Omaha that is about 15 percent Hispanic, made national news in 2010 when voters overwhelmingly approved an ordinance mandating immigration background checks for anyone seeking to rent an apartment or house; the ordinance faced legal challenges until 2014, when the Supreme Court declined to rule on its legality, leaving a lower court ruling in place upholding the policy. Voters in nearby Scribner overwhelmingly approved a similar ordinance in 2018. In January 2017, hundreds of protesters gathered outside the state capital to rally against President Donald Trump's executive order limiting immigration from some Muslim-majority countries. In June 2018 a vandal threw a brick through the window of the Nebraska Republican Party headquarters in Lincoln, and spray-painted "ABOLISH ICE" on the sidewalk outside.

The 1st Congressional District of Nebraska includes 16 counties and parts of two others in the eastern slice of the state. It surrounds but does not take in Omaha-based Douglas County, which is in the 2nd District. Taking up almost half the district is Lancaster, home to Lincoln and the main campus of the University of Nebraska, which has many scientific units that receive large research grants. Growing and affluent, Lincoln's median income exceeds the national average and its unemployment rate — 2.3 percent in December 2018 — has been among the lowest in the nation. The city is home to more than 100 companies and government agencies with 250 or more workers, including a strong manufacturing sector. In the smaller towns, there are many farm equipment and meatpacking factories. Costco is building a chicken processing plant in Fremont, though some residents in Lancaster County aren't happy about it, citing traffic and environmental concerns. A few miles from Omaha, the district includes the eastern part of fast-growing Sarpy County and the city of Bellevue, home of Offutt Air Force Base, headquarters of the Strategic Air Command. In June 2016 the Pentagon said it will repair Offutt's runway, though the project likely won't be completed until 2020.

Politically, Lincoln is fond of moderate Democrats but is still, on balance, Republican in national contests. In 2016, Lancaster was one of two counties — along with Douglas — that voted for Hillary Clinton, but by a scant 310 votes. The remaining counties were secure for Donald Trump, who took 56 percent of the district vote, compared with 57 percent for Mitt Romney in 2012. The district has not elected a Democrat to Congress since 1964.

Don Bacon (R)

Elected 2016, 2nd term, b. Aug 16, 1963; Momence, IL; Northern Illinois University, B.A., 1984; Officer Intelligence School (CO), 1986; Squadron Officer School (AL), 1989; Navigator/Electronic Warfare School (CA), 1992; University of Phoenix, Mast. Deg., 1995; Air Command and Staff College (AL), 1998; National War College (DC), Mast. Deg., 2004; Massachusetts Institute of Technology, 2006; Eckerd College Leadership Development Institute (FL), 2009; University of Virginia Darden School of Business, Mast. Deg., 2009; Christian - Non-Denominational; Married (Angie Bacon); 4 children.

Military Career: U.S. Air Force 1985-2014

Professional Career: Military Advisor, Rep. Jeff Fortenberry, 2014-2015; Assistant Professor, University of Bellvue , 2014-2017.

DC Office: 1024 LHOB 20515, 202-225-4155, bacon.house.gov
State Offices: Omaha, 402-938-0300.

Committees: *Agriculture*: Livestock & Foreign Agriculture; Subcommittee Nutrition, Oversight & Department Operations. *Armed Services*: Intelligence, Emerging Threats & Capabilities; Tactical Air & Land Forces.

Group Ratings

	ADA	ACLU	AFL-CIO	LCV	ITI	COC	HAFA	ACU	CFG	FRC
2018	-	7%	-	6%	-	92%	48%	72%	50%	100%
2017	0%	C	8%	6%	C	93%	C	78%	73%	100%

Almanac Ratings 2017-18

	Economy	Social	Foreign	Composite
Liberal	4%	4%	5%	4%
Conservative	96%	97%	95%	96%

Key Votes of the 115th Congress

1. Obama-care revision	Y	5. Family planning regs	Y	9. Guantanamo prisoners	N
2. Tax Cuts	Y	6. Body cameras/immigration	N	10. Ground missiles, limit	N
3. Omnibus appropriations	Y	7. Abortion ban	Y	11. Defense Dept. spending	Y
4. Dodd-Frank revision	Y	8. Concealed carry	Y	12. FISA rules	Y

Election Results

Election	Name (Party)	Vote (%)		Cand. Spent	Ind. Exp. Support	Ind. Exp. Oppose
2018 General	Don Bacon (R).............................	126,715	(51%)	$2,472,117	$678,355	$77,083
	Kara Eastman (D).............................	121,770	(49%)	$2,457,122	$324,027	$1,340,637
2018 Primary	Don Bacon (R).............................		(100%)			

Prior winning percentages: 2016 (49%)

Republican Don Bacon, elected in 2016 in this usually reliable Republican district in Nebraska, was the only GOP candidate nationwide that year who defeated a Democratic incumbent; two years later, as the Democratic establishment's preferred candidate lost the primary, Bacon narrowly survived amid a 40 seat loss for the GOP. His high-level military career was apt for this district, and prepared him for his seat on the Armed Services Committee.

Bacon grew up on a farm in Illinois, earning his bachelor's degree in political science at Northern Illinois University in 1984. The following year, he joined the Air Force, where he served for nearly 30 years and retired as a brigadier general. He specialized in electronic warfare, intelligence, reconnaissance and public affairs. He deployed four times to the Middle East, and commanded an electronic warfare squadron during the invasion of Iraq. In 2009, he was selected as Europe's top Air Force wing commander and later commanded Offutt Air Force Base outside of Omaha. After leaving the Air Force, Bacon worked for Republican Rep. Jeff Fortenberry of Nebraska as his military adviser and focused on Offutt. He received two master's degrees, from the University of Phoenix and the National War College in Washington D.C. As an assistant professor at Bellevue University, he taught courses on leadership and American values.

In 2016, he challenged Rep. Brad Ashford, who was one of two Democrats in 2014 to oust a House Republican incumbent. With this district's slight Republican lean, Ashford immediately became a top GOP target for 2016. Bacon, with his superior fundraising, became the frontrunner for the Republican nomination against Chip Maxwell, a more outspoken conservative who had been an editorial writer for the Omaha World-Herald. The primary was unusually robust. Maxwell accused the National Republican Congressional Committee of siding with Bacon. During the primary, the Democratic Congressional Campaign Committee spent more than $400,000 in ads that extolled Maxwell's conservative credentials, which revealed their concern about Bacon. That may have backfired. Running as a political outsider, Bacon won the primary, 66%-34%.

In the general, Ashford and Bacon discussed foreign policy at length and criticized each other's ads, including references to the Islamic State and claims of improper uses of U.S. military photos. In a debate, Ashford separated himself from President Barack Obama's nuclear deal with Iran and efforts to close the U.S. prison in Guantanamo Bay. Bacon parted company with the criticism of NATO by Republican presidential nominee Donald Trump. "I'm not a blank check for party or president," Bacon said. Ashford led by nearly 9,000 votes in Douglas County, but Bacon won on the basis of his 60 percent of the vote in Sarpy, even though that county cast less than 20 percent of the total vote. He won overall, 48.9%-47.7%, a margin of 3,464 votes.

Bacon got special attention from Republican leaders, including seats on the Armed Services and Agriculture committees. He passed a bill to help Gold Star families have better access to benefits at military bases. He passed another bill, named in honor of a fallen Omaha police officer, to allow immediate relatives of immigrant first responders killed in the line of duty to process their immigration applications more quickly. Bacon carved out a moderate profile on immigration, supporting money for a border wall in certain places and pushing for a pathway to citizenship for young immigrants brought to the country illegally by their parents. He was critical of Trump's decision to withdraw from the Paris climate accord. But Bacon was a stalwart behind other GOP policies, including the tax overhaul

Ashford ran again in 2018. In a race that largely flew under the radar, the moderate Ashford faced an unexpected challenge from progressive nonprofit CEO Kara Eastman. She criticized Ashford for his GOP past, supported "Medicaid for All" and had the backing of the Progressive Change Campaign Committee. "I'm tired of hearing Democrats don't have a backbone," she said in one direct-to-camera ad. "That we don't stand for anything. That changes now." EMILY's List, which supports pro-abortion rights women candidates, stayed neutral in the primary, while the Democratic Congressional Campaign Committee was already helping Ashford. In a surprise to many national Democrats who had viewed Ashford as one of their best candidates, Eastman narrowly prevailed, 51.4%-48.6%.

Republicans were enthusiastic about what they saw as an easier race. Eastman's strategy wasn't to win over Republican moderates as the Blue Dog Ashford had done, but to excite the progressive base. She backed a $15 minimum wage, "free" college tuition and no restrictions on abortion – issues that play better in coastal cities than in Omaha. Her positions helped rake in plenty of cash from activists, though the national party was slow to embrace her. National GOP groups carpet-bombed the district with ads painting Eastman as out of touch and pointing to her wilder days in college contrasted with Bacon's military bona fides. Bacon ultimately withstood the blue tide, prevailing 51%-49%. Bacon again lost Douglas County, this time by 6,500 votes; but he led by more than 11,000 votes in Sarpy.

Eastman said she will run again, as has another Ashford – not Brad, but his wife, Ann Ashford. So another moderate vs. progressive fight could divide Democrats in 2020, with Bacon the potential beneficiary.

NE-2: Greater Omaha   Cook Partisan Voting Index: R+4

Population		Race and Ethnicity		Income	
Total	652,312	White	73.1%	Median Income	$62,572
Land area (sq. miles)	510	Black	9.5%	District Income Rank	152
Pop/ sq mi	1279.7	Latino	11.1%	Poverty Rate	11.9%
Born in State	60.2%	Asian	3.2%	With health insurance	90.8%
		Two or more races	2.5%	Cash public assistance	1.6%
Age Groups		Other	0.5%	Food stamp/SNAP	9.5%
Under 18	26.4%				
18-34	24.4%	**Education**		**Work**	
35-64	37.6%	H.S grad or less	30.4%	White Collar	11.6%
Over 64	11.6%	Some college	30.7%	Sales and Service	41%
		College Degree, 4 yr	25.3%	Blue Collar	17.6%
Military		Post grad	13.6%	Government	10.6%
Veteran/ Active Duty	8.3%				

2012 Pres. Vote	Romney	140,976	(53%)	Obama	121,889	(46%)		
2016 Pres. Vote	Trump	137,564	(47%)	Clinton	131,030	(45%)	Johnson	13,245	(5%)

Omaha: Omaha is the commercial heart of Nebraska and the largest city on the Great Plains north of Kansas City and west of Minneapolis. It got its start from the government, when President Abraham Lincoln picked it as the eastern terminus of the Union Pacific railroad, from which emerged the stockyards and livestock exchange that made it a thriving town. Over the years, Omaha filled up with cattle hands and European immigrants, especially Germans and Czechs. It developed fine civic institutions, from the Joslyn Art Museum to Boys Town, an orphanage founded by the Rev. Edward Flanagan in 1917 and the subject of a 1938 movie. Today, the facility is a gender-neutral home for troubled youth.

Though a major city by the 1880s, Omaha has remained small enough to be intimate. One doesn't feel distant, physically or psychologically, from the other side of town. The older, less affluent part of Omaha is on the Missouri River across from Council Bluffs Iowa. Downtown and the riverfront have experienced substantial growth and development, and a $290 million effort to revitalize the Omaha waterfront is also planned. The 45-story First National Bank Tower is the tallest structure between Minneapolis and Denver. To the west, the city has flourished with the rise of upscale neighborhoods and shopping malls. Omaha has entered the Wall Street vernacular as the place where investor Warren Buffett — ranked by Forbes in 2016 as the world's second-richest person — lives and works. Buffett was a high-profile supporter of President Barack Obama and his so-called "Buffett Rule" — that wealthy people should pay a greater share of taxes — became a frequent Democratic talking point. His annual Berkshire Hathaway shareholder meeting of around 40,000 investors is Omaha's biggest gathering each year, serving as a major showcase for the city and a boost for its hotels, shops and restaurants.

Omaha has recently experienced a construction boomlet, with a $370 million cancer center with more than 4,600 employees at the University of Nebraska Medical Center, a $2 billion sewer separation project, and expansions into new buildings of the headquarters of Omaha-based TD Ameritrade and Tenaska, an energy company. While Omaha's economy remains dependent on overseas sales of food, it has also become the headquarters of more than 30 insurance companies and the nation's telecommunications hub, employing more than 20,000 people at more than two dozen telemarketing centers. The Omaha Chamber of Commerce has promoted its "Prosper Omaha" initiative, which is aiming to boost the city's population, infrastructure investments and business opportunities by 2040. Millennials have been 38 percent of this expanding workforce. Its 6 percent increase in millennials between 2005 and 2015 was the fifth-highest percentage increase among major U.S. cities. However, the elderly population has grown over the past decade too, with a 37 percent spike in residents over 65 as baby boomers age. The city has become more ethnically diverse: As of 2017, it was about 12 percent African American and 14 percent Hispanic.

The 2nd Congressional District includes Omaha and all of Douglas County. Omaha has long had competitive politics, with Democrats strong on the south side around the stockyards and the northeast and Republicans strong on the west side. As Omaha and Nebraska have boomed, they have become more Republican, and increasingly the Republican primary decides elections. The district includes nearly two-thirds of more-conservative Sarpy County, but not Offutt Air Force Base, which is in the 1st District. In 2016, Hillary Clinton won Douglas County, 48%-46%. But, with his big lead in Sarpy, Donald Trump prevailed in the district, 47%-45%. This has been the least conservative district in Nebraska and Democrats can prevail in local and national elections under the right circumstances.

Adrian Smith (R)

Elected 2006, 7th term, b. Dec 19, 1970; Scottsbluff; Liberty University (VA), Att., 1990; University of Nebraska, Lincoln, B.S., 1993; Evangelical; Married (Andrea Smith); 1 child.

Elected Office: Gering City Council, 1994-1998; NE Legislature, 1998- 2006.

Professional Career: Realtor, Buyer Realty, 1997-2006; Owner, My Other Garage, 2003-2006.

DC Office: 502 CHOB 20515, 202-225-6435, Fax: 202-225-0207, adriansmith.house.gov

State Offices: Grand Island, 308-384-3900; Scottsbluff, 308-633-6333.

Committees: *Ways & Means*: Health; Select Revenue Measures (RMM).

Group Ratings

	ADA	ACLU	AFL-CIO	LCV	ITI	COC	HAFA	ACU	CFG	FRC
2018	-	4%	-	3%	-	83%	59%	80%	76%	100%
2017	0%	C	8%	0%	C	92%	C	81%	85%	100%

Almanac Ratings 2017-18

	Economy	Social	Foreign	Composite
Liberal	3%	7%	0%	3%
Conservative	97%	94%	100%	97%

Key Votes of the 115th Congress

1. Obama-care revision	Y	5. Family planning regs	Y	9. Guantanamo prisoners	N
2. Tax Cuts	Y	6. Body cameras/immigration	N	10. Ground missiles, limit	N
3. Omnibus appropriations	Y	7. Abortion ban	Y	11. Defense Dept. spending	Y
4. Dodd-Frank revision	Y	8. Concealed carry	Y	12. FISA rules	Y

Election Results

Election	Name (Party)	Vote (%)		Cand. Spent	Ind. Exp. Support	Ind. Exp. Oppose
2018 General	Adrian Smith (R)	163,650	(77%)	$1,081,141	$5,000	
	Paul Theobald (D)	49,654	(23%)	$71,120		
2018 Primary	Adrian Smith (R)	50,878	(66%)			
	Kirk Penner (R)	20,116	(26%)			
	Arron Kowalski (R)	4,461	(6%)			

Prior winning percentages: 2016 (100%), 2014 (75%), 2012 (74%), 2010 (70%), 2008 (77%), 2006 (55%)

Republican Adrian Smith, elected in 2006, is an unwavering conservative who uses his seat on the Ways and Means Committee and his low-key style to focus intently on the rural issues important in his district. In 2017, he became chairman of its Human Resources Subcommittee. After Republicans lost their majority in 2019, he became the ranking member on the Select Revenue Measures Subcommittee, which handles tax legislation

Smith hails from a politically active family; his father is a former county Republican chairman, and his mother has been the state GOP secretary. But the most significant political influence in Smith's life was President Ronald Reagan. When he was in fourth grade, Smith recalls, adults around him were weighing Reagan's attributes against those of Democrat Jimmy Carter, and it sunk into the boy's head that Reagan favored a strong defense. "It just made sense to me that we needed a strong military," said Smith, whose congressional office is filled with portraits of the former president.

At 23, shortly after graduating from the University of Nebraska, he won election to the City Council in his hometown of Gering. Four years later, he knocked off a Democratic incumbent to win the first of two terms in the state legislature. There, Smith devoted his efforts to opposing abortion rights, protecting Nebraskans' right to bear arms, fighting tax increases and blocking efforts to expand casino gambling. He also worked as a real estate agent and owned a storage business.

In 2005, Smith joined the race for the open seat of retiring Rep. Tom Osborne. Leading the crowded Republican primary field were Grand Island Mayor Jay Vavricek and John Hanson, who had been Osborne's district director. Smith championed tax incentives to attract new residents and encourage local investment. Smith's opponents charged that he betrayed rural Nebraska by accepting more than $300,000 in contributions from members of the Club for Growth, a national anti-tax group that opposes farm subsidies. Smith, who supported caps on subsidies, parried by touting his support from the Nebraska Farm Bureau. Smith won the nomination with 39 percent of the vote.

In the general election, Democrats fielded an unusually strong nominee: Yale-educated cattle rancher Scott Kleeb, who called for changes in farm policy to emphasize niche markets, and accused Smith of "distorting the truth" about the Club for Growth's opposition to farm subsidies. Smith portrayed Kleeb as a political carpetbagger who grew up overseas on military bases and attended schools in Colorado and Connecticut before settling in Nebraska on a family-owned ranch. Kleeb was competitive financially. Still, Smith won 55%-45%. He has easily won reelection since.

In Washington, Smith is a member of the Tea Party Caucus, and he once answered a survey from the conservative Heritage Foundation about what makes him happy by responding, "Having the freedom to pursue opportunities relating to my faith while upholding the ideals of our Founding Fathers." Smith has pushed for strict fiscal discipline, and in February 2018 voted against a bipartisan budget agreement, saying the deal "does not take the necessary steps to rein in our national debt." As founder and co-chairman in 2015 of the Modern Agriculture Caucus, Smith promoted scientifically based policies to move agriculture forward and to educate other lawmakers about the issues that farmers face. On the annual defense spending bill in 2016, Smith won approval of his amendment to prevent the exclusion of meat from the Defense Department's food service program manual.

On Ways and Means, Smith has focused on agriculture and trade issues. He sought to ensure that agriculture was part of the talks held by a U.S.-European Union working group that met to consider a trade agreement. He has been a leading voice in calling for repeal of the estate tax. He has advocated lower corporate tax rates to keep the United States more competitive in the world economy, and he contends that free-trade agreements are good for the nation's overall economy, especially agriculture. When President Donald Trump formally abandoned U.S. participation in the Trans-Pacific Partnership three days after he was inaugurated, Smith responded, "Our country should be a leader in writing the rules of the global economy, rather than allowing other world powers to take our place." When the tariffs prompted retaliatory ones that worried many in the agriculture community, Smith nevertheless argued that farmers in his district still backed the president. He supported the United States-Mexico-Canada Agreement that Trump championed to replace NAFTA.

With his safe seat and his relative youth, his seniority at Ways and Means has positioned Smith to take the top Republican slot on the tax-writing committee within a decade.

NE-3: Central and Western Nebraska

Cook Partisan Voting Index: R+27

Population		Race and Ethnicity		Income	
Total	605,462	White	84.5%	Median Income	$51,735
Land area (sq. miles)	67,435	Black	1.2%	District Income Rank	274
Pop/ sq mi	9	Latino	11.5%	Poverty Rate	12%
Born in State	68.4%	Asian	0.7%	With health insurance	90.5%
		Two or more races	1.3%	Cash public assistance	1.7%
Age Groups		Other	0.9%	Food stamp/SNAP	8.4%
Under 18	23.8%				
18-34	20.4%	**Education**		**Work**	
35-64	37.3%	H.S grad or less	42.4%	White Collar	18.5%
Over 64	18.5%	Some college	35.8%	Sales and Service	38.4%
		College Degree, 4 yr	15.2%	Blue Collar	29.5%
Military		Post grad	6.6%	Government	14.6%
Veteran/ Active Duty	8.8%				

2012 Pres. Vote	Romney	182,067	(70%)	Obama	72,110	(28%)			
2016 Pres. Vote	Trump	199,821	(74%)	Clinton	53,358	(20%)	Johnson	11,676	(4%)

North Platte: West of Grand Island, Nebraska is wheat and livestock country. For miles on end there are rolling brown fields, only occasionally interrupted by barbed wire fences. The wind, rain and tornadoes that come suddenly remind you that the original settlers likened this part of the country to an ocean and thought themselves in their wooden wagons almost as helpless as passengers at sea in a rowboat. Settlers passed through here on the Oregon, California and Mormon trails in the 1840s, then set down roots in the 1880s. But the rain they hoped for fell too unreliably, and wheat lands gave way to pasture and open range. It is a beautiful but hard land, exacting much from its people, as the novels of western Nebraska's Willa Cather make poignantly clear. Chimney Rock — a clay and sandstone spire that marked a good camping spot and offered reliable spring water for travelers and their animals — was the landmark that travelers on the way west most frequently mentioned in their journals. This symbol of westward expansion now graces the Nebraska issue of the U.S. quarter.

Dozens of small counties in the region today have fewer people than they did in 1900. Severe droughts in recent years have seemed a kind of endpoint for some, as reservoirs and aquifers began to run dry and ranchers sold off their thinning herds. Still, many farmers have found ways to adapt. The $17.7 billion value of farm production sold in this large area was higher than any other congressional district in the nation, according to the Census of Agriculture in 2012. That total included $7.7 billion for cattle. Economic life also sets records in other industries. In North Platte, according to Union Pacific, Bailey Yard is the world's largest railroad classification yard, covering 2,850 acres and handling 14,000 rail cars every 24 hours. The 103-mile Union Pacific line from North Platte east to Gibbon is the busiest freight rail corridor in the world, with 139 trains a day passing through. The railroads employ about 8,000 people in Nebraska. The booming economy in North Platte has recently led to a shortage of housing.

In 2016, Missouri-based Bass Pro Shops took control of Cabela's in a $5.5 billion merger. Despite initial reassurances by Bass Pro, the move raised fears about the future of Sidney, the small town near the Colorado line where 2,000 were employed by Cabela's. In March 2018, about 700 workers took buyout packages from Bass Pro. When the Keystone XL oil pipeline was proposed to go through the environmentally sensitive Sandhills area in north central Nebraska, many Cornhusker politicians pushed to have it rerouted. President Barack Obama rejected the company's application in 2012 in part, he said, because of concerns about this region. That set off a new round of review. Four days after he took office, President Donald Trump approved completion of the final segment for Keystone. The pipeline was given a revised route, though legal hurdles remained.

The 3rd Congressional District is geographically massive, reaching roughly 460 miles from the Wyoming border to the Iowa border and larger than the state of New York. The district takes in all or part of 75 counties, more than any other district in the nation. In 2016, it became even more solidly Republican. Donald Trump won the district, 74%-20%.

NEVADA

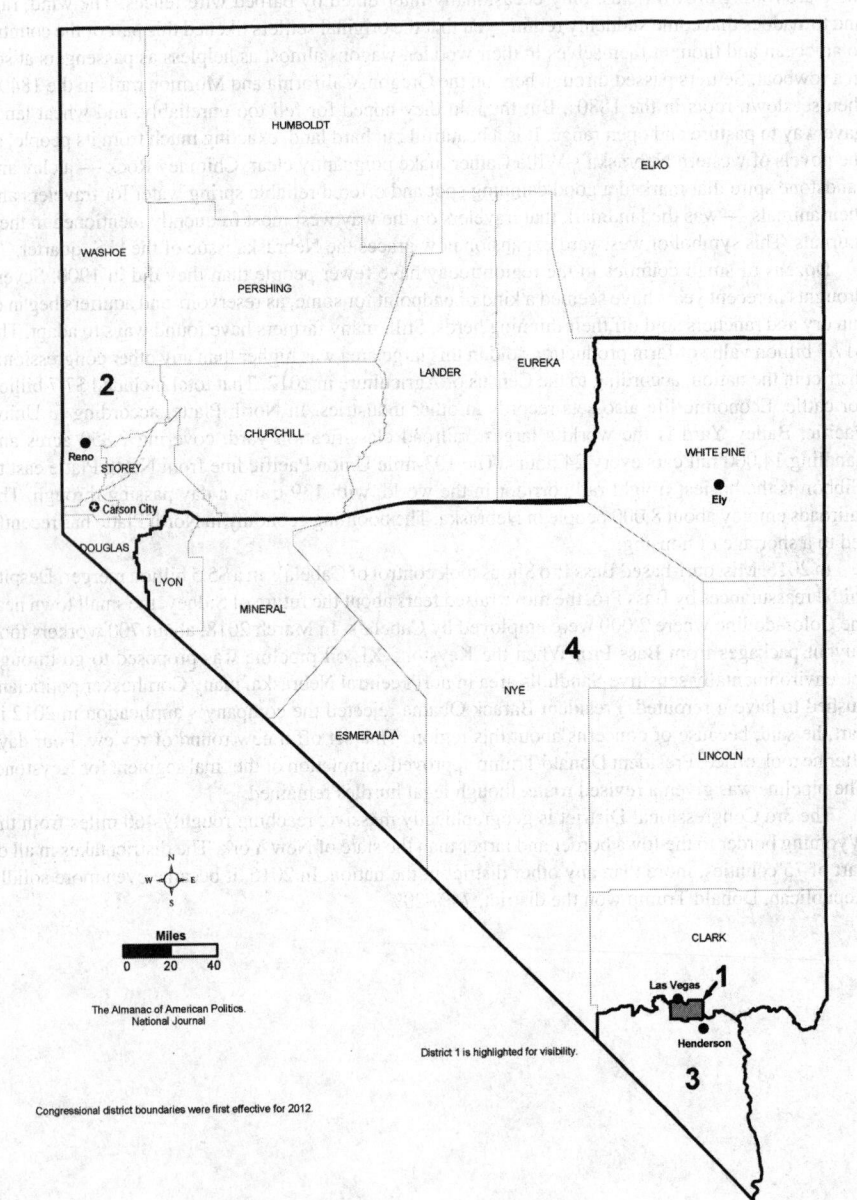

HUMBOLDT

ELKO

WASHOE

PERSHING

EUREKA

2

LANDER

CHURCHILL

WHITE PINE

Reno

STOREY

Ely

Carson City

DOUGLAS

LYON

MINERAL

4

NYE

ESMERALDA

LINCOLN

CLARK

Miles

0   20   40

Las Vegas   1

Henderson

3

District 1 is highlighted for visibility.

Congressional district boundaries were first effective for 2012.

Nevada fuses two important, and divergent, demographic groups in today's political scene – minorities and blue-collar whites. The state is 28 percent Hispanic (the fifth highest of any state), 8 percent black and 8 percent Asian (the sixth highest) – all prime voting groups for Democratic candidates. Nevada's white population, meanwhile, accounts for only about 50 percent of the population -- the sixth smallest of any state -- but it includes many with prickly views about the federal government, which owns more than 85 percent of the state's land. These voters are receptive to Republicans, especially those aligned with Donald Trump. Mix in economic upheaval during the Great Recession and you have the recipe for a politically volatile state. After a Republican sweep in 2014, Nevada Democrats showed notable strength in two subsequent election cycles, suggesting that demographics may have given them a modest edge for the near future.

Nevada has been a land of boom and bust from its very beginnings as a territory. The evidence of the latest boom is apparent as your plane descends at Las Vegas' McCarran International Airport. You see a pyramid rising from the desert; just across the street from a Sphinx-like lion are New York City-style skyscrapers. Nearby are a fair-sized Eiffel Tower, the gondolas of Venice, and a flaming pirate ship. But there have been signs of bust — giant hotels and condominiums with no lights on at night, retail space up for rent, subdivisions where many houses are unoccupied, and a seamy side of town expertly mined by CSI, the flagship of the long-running TV crime procedural. All this is set in one of North America's most forbidding landscapes, a bowl-shaped desert valley rimmed by barren peaks.

The natural parts would have looked familiar to the prospectors who first came to mine silver and gold in Virginia City, on a mountain 6,700 feet above sea level, or to Mark Twain and Bret Harte, who documented the heyday of the Comstock Lode, which beginning in 1859 produced $500 million worth of silver within two decades. President Abraham Lincoln's Republicans made Nevada a state in 1864, even though it did not meet the population requirement, in order to win three more electoral votes. But the silver boom went bust, and by 1900, Nevada had only 42,000 residents, down 68 percent from its 1880 peak. For a time, it seemed questionable whether Nevada was viable as a state. In the early 1930s, when there were still only 91,000 Nevadans, the government was about to go bankrupt. So Nevada decided to roll the dice. It reduced its residency requirement for divorce to six weeks and legalized gambling. The state catered to what most Americans considered sin — casinos, pawnshops, divorce mills, quick-wedding chapels, and legal brothels. (Nevadans remain below-average in church attendance.) It turned out to be good business. The 6.75 percent gambling receipts tax generated enough revenue to make it unnecessary for Nevada to impose income, corporate or inheritance taxes.

From mining boom to gambling boom, Nevada has been a second-chance state, a place for outcasts to succeed and misfits to rebound. Only a quarter of the state's residents were born in Nevada, a rate well below even Florida's, and that percentage has been steady for a half-century. Nevada has been an avenue of success for ethnic groups who faced roadblocks elsewhere. The four owners of the Comstock Lode — MacKay, Fair, Flood and O'Brien — were Irishmen. The first big hotel on the Las Vegas strip, the Flamingo, was built in 1946 by the Jewish gangster Bugsy Siegel, who was later gunned down in his Beverly Hills home. Most of the big casinos were owned by mobsters until industrialist Howard Hughes — a different kind of outcast — bought them up in the late 1960s. The job market has consistently attracted minorities. But Nevada's median income is 7 percent below the national average, and it was one of the lowest-ranked states for supporting advanced industry in 2015, according to a Brookings Institution study. A big reason: The state is not highly educated. Only 18 percent of residents had a college degree in 2016, ranking Nevada fifth to last in the nation. As for K-12 schools, only New Mexico ranked worse for education in the Annie E. Casey Foundation's 2018 Kids Count report, the third straight year Nevada was ranked 49th.

Gaming (the state's preferred term for gambling) has generated enormous growth: The 91,000 people in the state who decided to legalize gambling has grown into a population of just under 3 million today. Las Vegas was a dot on the map when gambling became legal, a one-traffic-light crossroads in Clark County with 8,532 people countywide. Now, Clark County has 2.2 million. Las Vegas' 23,000 hotel rooms in 1973 mushroomed into roughly 150,000 today. Reno, known as "the biggest little city in the world," now has about 465,000 people in its metro area. Nevada was America's fastest-growing state in the 1960s, 1970s, 1980s, and 1990s and from 2000 to 2007. For a long historical moment, gaming was a good economic bet. But in 2007, gaming revenues declined even before the national economy fell into recession. Nevada suddenly went bust, with the decline in gaming revenues cascading into a housing and construction crash. Nevada's unemployment rate peaked at 13.7 percent in late 2010 and was in double digits for more than four years straight. Nevada recorded the nation's steepest fall in homeownership rates between 2004 and 2012. Foreclosure rates peaked at nearly 10 percent of households, and more people left the state than moved there from other states from 2008 to 2011 — in all, a sharp reversal of fortune.

As the nation began to recover, so did Nevada. Clark County has grown by 13 percent in population since 2010, operating with a revised business model. With some form of gambling available in all of the lower 48 states and with neighboring California dotted with Indian casinos, Las Vegas promoted itself as a family destination, not just a gambling den. While gaming accounted for 58 percent of Nevada casino revenues in 1996, it was only 42 percent by 2017, and on the Strip specifically, the share fell to 34 percent. The Strip has become a luxury shopping center with world-class restaurants. (In 2018, the Supreme Court took away Nevada's monopoly on sports betting, which could further accelerate the shift.) The casinos continue to cater to high rollers, even sending private planes to fly them in, but they face increasing competition for rich Chinese and Japanese players; Macau's gaming revenues are bigger than Las Vegas'. Las Vegas has become a major player for convention business, and it attracted its first major-league sports team, the National Hockey League's Golden Knights, for the 2017-2018 season. (They proceeded to reach the Stanley Cup finals, falling to the Washington Capitals.) And the city's second pro sports team is on its way. In 2016 the legislature approved a financing plan for a $1.9 billion domed stadium to house the NFL's Oakland Raiders; they are slated to arrive in 2020.

Nevada continued to rank high nationally in foreclosures, with upticks in activity as late as 2018. Still, Las Vegas housing has gained ground, as the median price of previously owned single-family homes hit $280,000 in 2018 – more than twice as high as its low point, if still lower than the 2006 level of $315,000, according to the Greater Las Vegas Association of Realtors. This has made Las Vegas a buyer's market for people tiring of the Pacific Coast's high cost of housing. The Los Angeles Times' Steve Lopez wrote about the surge of Californians moving to Las Vegas: "Moving to get a better job or move up the workplace chain is nothing new. But what's going on here seems different — people leaving not for better jobs or pay, but because housing elsewhere is so much cheaper they can live the middle-class life that eludes them in California." In an effort to diversify its economic base, Las Vegas is counting on such businesses as Amazon, shoe retailer Zappos, and data firm Switch Inc., as well as a developing medical sector that's piggybacking on the University of Nevada's medical school. Solar energy firms, including Tesla, Sunrun and Vivint Solar, were strengthened after Gov. Brian Sandoval signed a law effectively reversing a 2015 Public Utilities Commission vote to end "net metering," which allows solar panel-owning homeowners to be paid for the power they send back to the grid. Meanwhile, Nevada legalized cannabis in 2017, and in its first year the industry produced $530 million in taxable sales and supported an estimated 8,300 jobs, according to the Nevada Dispensary Association.

Reno, for its part, has sunk in the gaming rankings without Las Vegas' luxury attractions. But Washoe County, which includes Reno, has a low cost of living and a pleasant combination of sun and ski slopes; population has increased 9 percent in the county since 2010, and economic diversification is proceeding with a big push from the state. Apple received $89 million in tax breaks to build a data center in Reno; then, with $1.3 billion in state incentives, electric automaker Tesla and Panasonic teamed up to build the biggest battery factory in the world nearby, directly employing a projected 7,000 workers. The factory expanded to produce parts for Tesla's Model 3 sports car, though vehicle production has experienced some delays.

For all its distinctiveness, Nevada has been similar to the nation politically. A silver-producing state, it voted three times for the free-silver populism of William Jennings Bryan, but since his final candidacy in 1908, Nevada has voted only twice for the loser of a presidential election — Gerald Ford in 1976 and Hillary Clinton in 2016. Nevada twice provided Bill Clinton and George W. Bush narrow victories and, with its increasingly Hispanic electorate, twice provided somewhat bigger margins for Barack Obama. Between 2000 and 2018, it elected one Democratic and one Republican senator and produced divided House delegations.

For years, Nevada sent politically shrewd Democrats to Washington and kept them there to protect the interests of a state heavily dependent on the federal government. The most enduring figure in recent Nevada politics was Harry Reid. In 1982, he won election to the House and in 1986 ran for the Senate and won. He became majority leader in 2007. Keeping him in this position was of immense importance to the gaming industry and the Culinary Union, which represents some 57,000 casino employees and has a crackerjack political organization. When the federal government planned to build a national nuclear waste repository at Yucca Mountain, 90 miles from Las Vegas, Reid fought it mightily — and successfully. In 2014, Reid lost his Senate majority, suffered a serious accidental injury and decided to retire. A different kind of power rests with Sheldon Adelson, a casino magnate, who has been a Republican mega-donor and since 2015 the owner of the Las Vegas Review-Journal.

In 2014, the GOP flipped control of the state legislature (the first time they managed to win both chambers since 1985) and won every statewide office. In 2016, Democrats won back both chambers as Hillary Clinton took the state's electoral votes. Support from nonwhites proved crucial to Clinton's victory. Trump ran strongly among white voters – well enough to cut Obama's six-point margin in 2012 down to less than three points against Clinton.

The state would soon be touched by some of the era's most divisive cultural issues. In 2017, gunman Stephen Paddock perched in a Las Vegas hotel high-rise and trained his bump-stock-fitted semi-automatic rifle on attendees of a country music concert, killing 58 and injuring more than 800 -- the deadliest mass shooting in U.S. history. Early the following year, a federal judge threw out criminal charges against Cliven Bundy, a Nevada rancher who had led an armed standoff against federal officials, challenging their rights to regulate federally owned land. And in May 2018, opponents of sanctuary cities received a judicial go-ahead to present voters with a ballot measure, though not before 2020.

The 2018 election cycle was a busy one for Nevada, and Democrats all but ran the table. Democrats Jackie Rosen and Steve Sisolak won a Senate seat and the governorship, respectively, performing a point or two better than Clinton had in 2016. Democrats also defended two open House seats and flipped the offices of lieutenant governor, attorney general, treasurer and controller. The GOP was able to hold only the secretary of state's office, eking out a 6,000-vote victory. In the legislature, Democrats extended their control and became the first state to have a female-majority legislature. Voters approved a measure to make voter registration automatic, by a 60%-40% margin. Meanwhile, in an only-in-Nevada electoral development, Dennis Hof – the larger-than-life owner of the Love Ranch brothel, the focus of an HBO reality series – died as Election Day approached, on the heels of a 72nd birthday party attended by celebrities and the porn elite. It was too late to remove his name from the ballot and, running in a safe GOP legislative district, the Trump-style Republican won the election posthumously.

Population		Race and Ethnicity		Income	
Total	2,887,725	White	50.5%	Median Income	$55,434
Land area (sq. miles)	109,781	Black	8.4%	State Income Rank	28
Pop/ sq mi	26.3	Latino	28.2%	Poverty Rate	14.2%
Born in state	25.9%	Asian	7.9%	With health insurance	86.0%
		Two or more races	3.4%	Cash public assistance	3.1%
Age Groups		Other	1.6%	Food stamp/SNAP	12.3%
Under 18	23.2%				
18-34	23.1%	**Education**		**Work**	
35-64	39.1%	H.S grad or less	42.5%	White Collar	28.4%
Over 64	14.6%	Some college	33.9%	Sales and Service	52.6%
		College Degree, 4 yr	15.6%	Blue Collar	18.9%
Military		Post grad	8.1%	Government	11.9%
Veteran/ Active Duty	9.8%				

Presidential Politics

2016 Caucus (D)	Clinton (D)	6,440 (53%)	Sanders (D)	5,785 (47%)			
2016 Caucus (R)	Trump (R)	34,531 (46%)	Rubio (R)	17,940 (24%)	Cruz (R)	16,079 (21%)	
2016 Pres. Vote	Clinton (D)	539,260 (48%)	Trump (R)	512,058 (46%)	Carson (R)		(5%)
	Johnson (L)	37,384 (3%)					
2012 Pres. Vote	Obama (D)	531,373 (52%)	Romney (R)	463,567 (46%)			

After going heavily Republican in the 1980s, Nevada voted narrowly, by a margin of three-tenths-of-one percent, for Bill Clinton in 1992. Since then, it has been a battleground in every presidential election and has voted for the winner in each race — until 2016, when Hillary Clinton defeated Donald Trump 48%-46%. Clinton's victory came by winning Clark County (Las Vegas), which regularly accounts for about two-thirds of the state's total vote. Her 82,170-vote margin in Clark was more than triple her 27,202 statewide winning margin. Clinton also carried Washoe County (Reno), but by less than 3,000 votes. Trump won the state's other 15 counties, once referred to as the "cow counties" for their cattle-grazing, which vote heavily Republican. The growing number of Hispanic voters in Nevada — many of whom live in Clark — is another asset for Democratic presidential candidates. Both campaigns spent heavily to contest the state, and overall turnout jumped by more than 100,000 votes from 2012. The Las Vegas Review-Journal, owned by casino magnate GOP donor Sheldon Adelson, was one of a handful of newspapers that endorsed Trump in the general election. Adelson, along with his wife Miriam, gave more than $20 million to various entities to help elect Trump.

A significant change in Nevada politics took place in 2008: For the first time, it became an important part of the presidential nominating process. The Democratic National Committee, under heavy pressure from then-Senate Majority Leader Harry Reid, chose Reid's home state as one of four allowed to hold early contests, along with Iowa, New Hampshire and South Carolina. Republicans went along with the idea to give regional balance to the opening salvo of the nominating race. Both parties agreed to conduct caucuses. In 2016, Trump scored a huge victory in the GOP caucuses, defeating Florida Sen. Marco Rubio 46%-24%. Texas Sen. Ted Cruz finished third with 21 percent. Cruz won two of the cow counties, Elko and Lincoln, and Trump won the other 15. Turnout soared above the 75,000-mark, more than double the nearly 33,000 who attended the 2012 GOP caucuses. On the Democratic side, Clinton held off Vermont Sen. Bernie Sanders, winning 53 percent of the county delegates to 47 percent for Sanders. Democratic turnout was estimated to be 84,000, down from more than 117,000 who attended in 2008 when Clinton beat Obama, 51%-45%. Clinton handily won Clark and five other counties. The Democratic contest ended in an unruly May state party convention where Sanders delegates tossed chairs protesting what they viewed as unfair procedures benefiting Clinton. Members of both parties entertained the notion of switching Nevada to a presidential primary in 2020, but that idea failed to gain traction.

Congressional Districts

116th Congress Lineup	3D 1R	115th Congress Lineup	3D 1R

Nevada's population surged 66 percent in the 1990s and 35 percent in the 2000s, leading the nation each time. The boom may finally be subsiding, but the state has rocketed from one district in 1980 to four in 2012. In 2011, partisan control was split and tension ran high. Democrats in charge of the legislature, including several eyeing a promotion to Congress, passed maps creating one safely Republican seat in northern Nevada and three Democratic-leaning seats in Clark County. Republican Gov. Brian Sandoval vetoed the maps on the grounds that Latinos had accounted for 46 percent of the state's growth between 2000 and 2010 and deserved a majority Latino seat based in the northeast quadrant of metro Las Vegas. Democrats decried Sandoval's position as a veiled attempt to pack Democratic voters and create three Republican-leaning seats in the process. The debate fractured Latino advocacy groups, and the legislature adjourned in a stalemate.

Carson City District Judge James Todd Russell appointed three independent special masters — a county elections administrator, a former state legislative research director and a lawyer — to draw a map. The trio submitted a diplomatic plan that created a safely Democratic, 43 percent Latino 1st District and preserved a Republican-leaning 2nd District in the north. They created a slightly more Republican 3rd District including Henderson to the south, and a new Democratic-leaning 4th District linking substantially Latino North Las Vegas with several rural counties to the north. The result in 2012 was an even 2-2 split.

Since then, multiple developments have shaped the contours for the next round of redistricting. In 2016, Democrats gained two seats to take 3-1 control of the delegation. They also regained control of the legislature. In 2018, they secured their redistricting lock when they won the election for governor.

Still, as they seek to reinforce their swing seats, Democrats will face renewed pressure from Latinos eager to win a House seat.

Steve Sisolak (D)

Elected 2018, term expires 2023, 1st term; b. Dec. 26, 1953, Milwaukee, WI; University of Wisconsin, Milwaukee, B.S., 1974; University of Nevada, Las Vegas, M.B.A, 1978; Married (Kathy Ong); 2 children (2 from previous marriage)

Elected Office: Member, NV Board of Regents, 1999-2008; Member, Clark County Commission, 2009-2019, Vice chair, 2011-2013, Chair, 2013-2019.

Office: 101 N. Carson St., Carson City, 89701; 775-684-5670; Fax: 775-684-5683; Website: nv.gov

Lt. Gov.: Kate Marshall (D) **Atty. Gen:** Aaron Ford (D) **Sec. of State:** Barbara Cegavske (R)

State Legislature: Senate: 13D, 8R **House:** 28D, 13R, 1V

Election Results

Election	Name (Party)	Vote (%)
2018 General	Steve Sisolak (D)	480,007 (49%)
	Adam Laxalt (R)	440,320 (45%)
2018 Primary	Steve Sisolak (D)	72,749 (52%)
	Chris Giunchigliani (D)	56,511 (40%)

Steve Sisolak – a longtime commissioner in Clark County, which includes Las Vegas – became the first Democrat to win the Nevada governorship in two decades, defeating Republican Adam Laxalt by four percentage points in 2018. "He's been called a bully and a bulldozer, but also a dealmaker and a moderate," the Reno Gazette-Journal has written. "For critics, he's at once too conservative and too liberal — a union-busting budget hawk and a union-loving tax-and-spender. It speaks to Steve Sisolak's political staying power that he's been so many things to so many people for so long." Sisolak entered office in a strong position, with expanded Democratic majorities in the legislature.

Sisolak grew up in Wauwatosa Wisconsin, near Milwaukee. His father worked as a General Motors design engineer; his mother worked in a convenience store. When Sisolak was 10, his father found himself laid off for three years. Sisolak worked his way through college at the University of Wisconsin-Milwaukee. He came to Las Vegas in 1976 to pursue an MBA at the University of Nevada-Las Vegas. After earning his degree, Sisolak built a direct-marketing business and raised two daughters as a single father. In 1979, during a snowstorm, the power went out as Sisolak's appendix was being operated on, and he nearly died. That brought him back to Catholicism; he's said that he attends mass daily.

From 1999 to 2008, Sisolak served on the Nevada Board of Regents, then served on the Clark County Commission from 2009 to 2019, the final six years as its chairman. On the commission, "he comes across like a gadfly in politician's clothes, demanding accountability for every dollar spent and questioning policies he thinks make no sense," the Las Vegas Review-Journal wrote in 2010. At times he was accused of being too close to unions, but he also "alienated the firefighters' union so much that he received email telling him not to expect red trucks if his house goes up in flames," the newspaper reported. Critics accused him of playing close to the ethical edge. In 2005, he won a $16 million settlement in an eminent domain case, in which he argued that county height limits near McCarran International Airport hurt the value of land he owned nearby. Then, after he was on the county commission, it awarded a six-figure contract to the attorney who had won him the settlement. "From towing and cab companies to real estate developers and trash haulers, Sisolak has been no stranger to well-publicized controversies about his votes on matters that affected a campaign donor," the Reno Gazette-Journal wrote. But Sisolak championed the Vegas Golden Knights expansion NHL team and a stadium deal that enabled the Oakland Raiders to move to Las Vegas in 2020.

Sisolak considered running for governor in 2014 against popular Republican incumbent Brian Sandoval, but decided against it. Sandoval had been elected Nevada's first Latino governor in 2010 and was reelected with token opposition in 2014. Handsome and telegenic, Sandoval was initially heralded as a trailblazer in Republican circles, but his un-Republican stances on abortion, immigration and tort reform – exacerbated by his support for a tax hike to boost spending on education in 2015 – led Sandoval to become increasingly isolated within the GOP. Notably, Sandoval broke with Republican Attorney General Adam Laxalt on several occasions, including Laxalt's desire to join a multistate lawsuit against President Barack Obama's executive actions on immigration.

Laxalt easily won the 2018 gubernatorial primary over state Treasurer Dan Schwartz. On the Democratic side, the main contenders were both Clark County commissioners – Sisolak and Chris Giunchigliani. Giunchigliani, bolstered by a late robocall from Hillary Clinton, ran to Sisolak's left, spotlighting a questionnaire he had filled out during a 1996 candidacy in which he opposed medical marijuana, same-sex marriage and expanded gun control measures. Sisolak brushed off the criticism, saying that his views had shifted leftward enough to fit comfortably into the 2018 Democratic mainstream. "Like many people, you learn and grow as times change," he told the Reno Gazette Journal. As a top city official, Sisolak played a high-profile role in the 2017 mass shooting in Las Vegas that left 58 dead; he later called bump stocks, which enabled that massacre, "killing machines" that should be banned immediately. While Giunchigliani won the backing of the Nevada State Education Association and the Sierra Club, Sisolak had the crucial support of former Senate Majority Leader Harry Reid, who, even in declining health, controlled a legendary Democratic political machine. Sisolak ended up winning, 52%-40%.

Sisolak's general election opponent had a golden name in the state: Paul Laxalt, the candidate's grandfather, had served as a Republican governor and senator from Nevada. To win his 2014 race for attorney general, Laxalt pulled off the unprecedented achievement of losing the state's two big urban counties (Washoe, which includes Reno, and Clark) yet winning the more rural counties by large enough margins to cancel out the urban losses. In late 2017, longtime Nevada political observer Jon Ralston of the Nevada Independent called Laxalt the early "favorite" to become the state's next governor, although Ralston raised several concerns that would indeed come to hamper the Republican's candidacy, including a lack of experience, a thin history of living in the state (Laxalt had grown up in Washington D.C.), and a contentious four years as attorney general. Embarrassingly for the candidate, a dozen Laxalt family members penned an op-ed opposing their relative in the Reno Gazette-Journal, saying they wanted to "protect" the family name "from being leveraged and exploited." They highlighted Laxalt's policies on illegal immigration, which they say disrespected the family's history in the United States, which began with a legal Basque immigrant in 1900. Laxalt's aunt even appeared in a Sisolak campaign ad.

Sandoval pointedly did not endorse his fellow Republican Laxalt, and while the outgoing governor never officially endorsed Sisolak, the Democrat aligned himself with some of Sandoval's most popular policies, especially his efforts to boost spending on schools. The national political environment gave Sisolak some wind at his back. The 2018 election had a strongly Democratic lean, and a closely watched Senate race involving vulnerable incumbent Republican Dean Heller gave Nevada added attention. "The Democratic Party nationally needs to emulate what Nevada has been doing since the beginning of 2015, which is organizing early, organizing everywhere," Democratic National Committee chair Tom Perez told NPR. President Donald Trump's endorsement of Laxalt probably did not help him. Sisolak won, 49%-45%, and he swept into office with a bigger Democratic majority in the legislature and Democratic takeovers of the offices of lieutenant governor, attorney general, treasurer and controller.

Once in office, Sisolak signed an executive order establishing a sexual harassment task force, and in his first State of the State address, he backed funding increases for health care and education as well as a minimum-wage boost. He reiterated his support for banning bump stocks and said he backed increasing the state's energy standard to 50 percent renewable by 2030. He proposed renaming McCarran International Airport in honor of Reid – Pat McCarran's controversial tenure in the Senate had increasingly drawn scrutiny – while rechristening Reno's airport in honor of Paul Laxalt, his opponent's grandfather.

Catherine Cortez Masto (D)

Elected 2016, term expires 2022, 1st term, b. Mar 29, 1964; Las Vegas; University of Nevada, Reno, B.S., 1986; Gonzaga University School of Law, J.D., 1990; Catholic; Married (Paul Masto).

Elected Office: NV Attorney General, 2007-2015.

Professional Career: Federal Prosecutor, U.S Attorney's Office DC; Chief of Staff, NV Governor Bob Miller.

DC Office: 516 HSOB 20510, 202-224-3542

State Offices: Las Vegas, 702-388-5020; Reno, 775-686-5750.

Committees: Democratic Senatorial Campaign Committee Chairman. *Banking, Housing & Urban Affairs*: Economic Policy (RMM); Financial Institutions & Consumer Protection; Housing, Transportation & Community Development. *Energy & Natural Resources*: Energy; Public Lands, Forests & Mining; Water & Power (RMM). *Finance*: Health Care; International Trade, Customs & Global Competitiveness; Social Security, Pensions & Family Policy. *Indian Affairs*. *Rules & Administration*.

Group Ratings

	ADA	ACLU	AFL-CIO	LCV	ITI	COC	HAFA	ACU	CFG	FRC
2018	-	62%	-	100%	-	50%	3%	9%	5%	0%
2017	70%	C	100%	89%	C	29%	C	0%	4%	0%

Almanac Ratings 2017-18

	Economy	Social	Foreign	Composite
Liberal	90%	90%	60%	80%
Conservative	10%	10%	40%	20%

Key Votes of the 115th Congress

1. Obama-care revision	N	5. Gun regulations	N	9. Kavanaugh confirmation	N
2. Tax Cuts	N	6. Family planning regs	N	10. Saudi arms sales	Y
3. Dodd-Frank revision	N	7. Gorsuch confirmation	N	11. FISA rules	Y
4. Omnibus appropriations	Y	8. Immigration restrictions	N	12. Military aid in Yemen	Y

Election Results

Election	Name (Party)	Vote (%)		Cand. Spent	Ind. Exp. Support	Ind. Exp. Oppose
2016 General	Catherine Cortez Masto (D)	521,994	(47%)	$17,148,576	$6,552,180	$42,462,146
	Joe Heck (R)	495,079	(45%)	$11,707,759	$12,978,487	$38,915,182
2016 Primary	Catherine Cortez Masto (D)	81,971	(81%)			
	Allen Rheinhart (D)	5,650	(6%)			

Democrat Catherine Cortez Masto is the first Hispanic-American woman to serve in the Senate, narrowly winning a 2016 election in a battleground state. She also became the first female senator to represent Nevada when she succeeded Harry Reid, the longtime godfather of the state's Democratic Party — who anointed Cortez Masto as his successor on Capitol Hill. Reid was the Senate Democratic leader for more than a decade. And, just two years after replacing him, Cortez Masto followed Reid's path into the leadership ranks to lead the Democratic Senatorial Campaign Committee.

Cortez Masto is a lifelong Nevadan whose paternal grandfather immigrated to the state from Mexico; the other side of her family is Italian. Her father, Manny Cortez, an attorney and ally of Reid, was a major player in Nevada politics for three decades — as a member of the Clark County Commission and later as president of the powerful Las Vegas Convention and Visitors Authority. Cortez oversaw a major expansion of the city's airport and the inception of the iconic "what happens here, stays here" marketing campaign: Both moves were credited with reviving the popularity of the nation's longtime gambling mecca.

Cortez Masto earned a degree from the University of Nevada, Reno before getting her law degree from Gonzaga University. After practicing law in Las Vegas, she served as Democratic Gov. Bob Miller's chief of staff. She spent a couple of years in Washington, D.C., as a prosecutor in the U.S. attorney's office before returning to Nevada as an assistant county manager in Clark County on issues relating to juvenile detention alternatives and child services. In 2006, she was elected state attorney general. She went after methamphetamine labs and focused on prosecuting sex trafficking and domestic abuse cases. During her second term, Cortez Masto befriended the attorney general in California, Kamala Harris, who would also be elected to the Senate in 2016. The women went after several large banks for their foreclosure and lending practices after the 2008 financial crisis. The settlement of a suit against the Bank of America yielded nearly $2 billion for Nevada homeowners — a point widely advertised during Cortez Masto's Senate bid.

But Cortez Masto faced controversy in 2008 when she charged Republican Lt. Gov. Brian Krolicki with mismanaging a state-run college savings program in his previous role as state treasurer. At the time, Krolicki was considering a 2010 run against Reid. Krolicki and his defenders decried the felony prosecution as political — and suggested Reid was behind it. Reid denied any involvement. Just days before Krolicki was scheduled to stand trial, the Las Vegas Review-Journal reported that Cortez Masto's husband, retired Secret Service agent Paul Masto, was hosting a fundraiser for a Democrat seeking Krolicki's lieutenant gubernatorial post; Cortez Masto said she had been unaware of the event until contacted by the newspaper. Shortly after that, the indictment against Krolicki was dismissed. Cortez Masto was easily reelected the next year, but her rising star status had acquired some dents.

Term-limited as attorney general, Cortez Masto declined to take on popular Republican Gov. Brian Sandoval. She was named second in command of the Nevada System of Higher Education — a post she resigned from after just three months when Reid, in March 2015, opted not to seek a sixth Senate term after injuring himself while exercising. He threw his support behind Cortez Masto within hours of announcing his decision, telling Nevada Public Radio: "She has a background that really is significantly powerful. I hope she runs, and if she does I will help her." Reid had an interest in seeing his seat filled by the Senate's first Latina: It would cement his decades long effort to bring Hispanics and immigrants into the Nevada Democratic Party. Cortez Masto announced a week and a half later, and Reid told the Review-Journal, "We got our wish." His strong support helped Cortez Masto clear the primary field.

Sandoval, also Hispanic-American, was the strongest potential Republican candidate but declined to leave the governorship in the middle of his second term. Cortez Masto faced three-term GOP Rep. Joe Heck, an Iraq War veteran from a highly competitive district encompassing much of suburban Las Vegas. Heck easily won the Republican primary against Sharron Angle, Reid's 2010 tea party-aligned challenger. Cortez Masto's ads highlighted her family's immigrant roots and featured endorsements from President Barack Obama, who had twice carried the state. Heck touted his experience as a military physician and ran as a law-and-order candidate, attacking Cortez Masto for the state's rising violent crime rate. Cortez Masto outspent him $18.6 million to $11.7 million. That was dwarfed by $90 million in independent expenditures that poured into state. About $50 million of that was intended to benefit Heck in a race that national Republicans saw as their best chance to pick up a Senate seat in 2016.

Of the independent expenditures, at least $9 million came from the conservative billionaire Koch brothers. While Cortez Masto remained circumspect in her rhetoric, Reid played attack dog: In an allusion to the Koch brothers, he termed Heck "an absolute stooge for these right-wing nut cases" in comments to The New York Times. But it was Republican presidential candidate Donald Trump's harsh rhetoric about immigration and other matters that proved the major headache for Heck in a rapidly diversifying state. Heck held a narrow lead in the polls for much of the election cycle and tried to keep Trump at arm's length; he endorsed Trump only after the latter had secured the presidential nomination. After the "Access Hollywood" video of Trump bragging about sexually assaulting women surfaced in the fall of 2016, Heck retracted his endorsement. "I cannot in good conscience continue to support Donald Trump," Heck told a rally; some Republicans in the crowd booed him. But as Trump recovered politically in the campaign's closing weeks, Heck backed off, calling Trump "qualified" to be president and refusing to say how he would vote. Meanwhile, Cortez Masto ran ads tying Heck to Trump and showing his earlier endorsement of the GOP presidential candidate.. Trump lost Nevada — and likely pulled Heck down with him. Hillary Clinton carried the state 47.9% - 45.5%, while Cortez Masto edged Heck 47.1% - 44.7%. Heck carried every county in the state but one: Cortez Masto's base of Clark County, where more than 70 percent of the state's residents live. Cortez Masto won Clark by 82,000 votes — three times her statewide margin of 27,000.

Cortez Masto has placed in the centrist wing of Senate Democrats, according to the Almanac vote ratings. So did her record of voting against 10 of Trump's first 23 nominations to Cabinet and other high-ranking administration posts. Several of the party's most outspoken liberals voted against nearly twice as many of those nominees. Cortez Masto rebuked the nomination of Treasury Secretary Steven Mnuchin, who had headed a bank that foreclosed on thousands of Nevadans during the housing crisis.

Consistent with her status as a vocal critic of Trump's immigration moves — as well as the first Latina senator whose home state population was approaching 30 percent Hispanic — she introduced as her first bill a measure that would have undone a Trump executive order that made almost all undocumented immigrants priorities for deportation and sought to block funding for "sanctuary cities" that didn't fully cooperate with immigration authorities. "When he's talking about 'bad hombres,' he's talking about my family," Cortez Masto told MSNBC during a fight between Trump and Mexico's president shortly after she took office. "Really, the only bad hombre in this scenario is the one who's sitting in the White House." In late 2018, when Trump vowed to end birthright citizenship via executive order, Cortez Masto said, "Our president continues to promote hate in America, undermine our country's values and attack our Constitution."

Cortez Masto has carefully dealt with several initiatives from the Democrats' progressive wing. In mid-2018, amid controversy over Trump's later-reversed policy of separating migrant families at the southern border, Cortez Masto said the United States needs to "be doing everything it can" to reunify families — including repatriating more than 460 adults deported without their children. But she sidestepped questions about calls from the party's left to abolish the Immigration and Customs Enforcement. While accusing the Trump administration of empowering "rogue agents" and creating an "inhumane deportation force," Cortez Masto was quoted by The Nevada Independent as saying: "Do I think we should abolish Homeland Security Investigations as part of ICE? Absolutely not. They're going after international criminals, they're going after human trafficking and child pornography."

Cortez Masto confronted another hot-button issue in October 2017 after a gunman killed 58 and wounded more than 800 during a concert along the Las Vegas Strip — the worst mass shooting in modern U.S. history. She signed on to a bill, authored by California Democrat Dianne Feinstein, to ban "bump stocks," which modify semi-automatic weapons to fire as quickly as automatic weapon. While Trump promised to ban bump stocks via executive order — which he did at the end of 2018 — Cortez Masto earlier that year joined Arizona Republican Jeff Flake, a frequent Trump critic, to argue that legislation was needed as a more permanent solution. During the 2016 campaign, the National Rifle Association and affiliates spent more than $2.5 million against Cortez Masto.

Cortez Masto aggressively carried on Reid's efforts to block a nuclear waste repository at Yucca Mountain, 90 miles northwest of Las Vegas. Congress voted in 1987 to designate that location for a repository, but Reid bottled up funding until the Obama administration halted the site licensing process in 2010. After taking office, Trump proposed funding to restart that process. The House voted for a bill to do so in mid-2018, but Cortez Masto and Republican Sen. Dean Heller of Nevada blocked action in the Senate. "Presidential hopefuls shouldn't bother coming to Nevada if they support Yucca Mountain," Cortez Masto told the Review-Journal. "Congress already wasted more than $15 billion on a hole in the ground that over 55 percent of Nevadans oppose." During the 2018 elections, with Heller battling to save his seat, Trump told a Reno-based TV station that he would be "very inclined" to oppose the project if it did not have local support. Cortez Masto asked for an official administration position on the matter, saying, "Continuing to request funds to build Yucca Mountain in your forthcoming budget request to Congress will only make President Trump's remarks meaningless."

Cortez Masto's appointment to chair the DSCC came after she raised a reported $10 million for Democratic candidates and organizations during the 2018 cycle while campaigning for Senate candidates in eight states — including Democrat Jacky Rosen, who ousted Heller. She became only the second woman to hold the DSCC top post. The first, Patty Murray of Washington, leveraged it to rise to the No. 3 spot in the Senate Democratic leadership. And Cortez Masto's ambitions are likely to draw speculation. After her first year in the Senate, Cortez Masto was asked by the Las Vegas Sun whether she could fill Reid's shoes. "When I was on the campaign trail, people would ask me that all the time," she replied, "and I would say, 'Yeah, not only am I going to fill those shoes, I'm going to do it in heels.'"

Jacky Rosen (D)

Elected 2018, term expires 2024, 1st term, b. Aug 02, 1957; Chicago, IL; University of Minnesota, B.A., 1979; Jewish; Married (Larry Rosen); 1 child.

Elected Office: US House, 2017-2019

Professional Career: Business Owner; Computer programmer/software developer.

DC Office: 144 RSOB 20510, 202-224-6244, rosen.senate.gov

State Offices: Las Vegas, 702-388-0205; Reno, 775-337-0110.

Committees: *Aging. Commerce, Science & Transportation*: Communications, Technology, Innovation & the Internet; Manufacturing, Trade & Consumer Protection; Subcommittee on Aviation & Space; Subcommittee on Security. *Health, Education, Labor & Pensions*: Employment & Workplace Safety; Primary Health & Retirement Security. *Homeland Security & Government Affairs*: Investigations; Regulatory Affairs & Federal Management. *Small Business & Entrepreneurship*.

Group Ratings (House)

	ADA	ACLU	AFL-CIO	LCV	ITI	COC	HAFA	ACU	CFG	FRC
2018	-	67%	-	94%	-	67%	8%	9%	24%	0%
2017	60%	C	84%	97%	C	71%	C	4%	0%	13%

Key Votes of the 115th Congress (House)

1. Obama-care revision	N	5. Family planning regs	N
2. Tax Cuts	N	6. Body cameras/immigration	Y
3. Omnibus appropriations	N	7. Abortion ban	NV
4. Dodd-Frank revision	Y	8. Concealed carry	N

9. Guantanamo prisoners	N
10. Ground missiles, limit	N
11. Defense Dept. spending	Y
12. FISA rules	Y

Election Results

Election	Name (Party)	Vote (%)	Cand. Spent	Ind. Exp. Support	Ind. Exp. Oppose
2018 General	Jacky Rosen (D)............................	490,071 (50%)	$26,196,746	$5,613,546	$20,883,471
	Dean Heller (R)................................	441,202 (45%)	$13,764,061	$4,149,738	$36,310,801
2018 Primary	Jacky Rosen (D)............................	110,567 (83%)			

Prior winning percentages: House: 2016 (47%)

Few sent to Congress, past or present, can match the rapid — and unlikely — ascent of Democrat Jacky Rosen, Nevada's junior senator. Three years before her election to the Senate, Rosen was president of a synagogue in suburban Las Vegas — and unknown to most Nevadans. But after narrowly winning a seat in the House in 2016, she launched a Senate bid a mere eight months later in a state that, while trending blue, remains among the nation's most politically competitive. Rosen ousted Republican Dean Heller, who had never lost an election in three decades in public office. She became the first woman to move from the House to the other side of the Capitol after just one term. According to the website Smart Politics, only 19 male House freshmen have accomplished this feat since direct election of senators was initiated in 1913.

Rosen launched her political career at the end of 2015, when she was recruited to run for an open House seat by Senate Minority Leader Harry Reid. Rosen agreed to run after more than a dozen better-known prospects reportedly turned down Reid. Born Jacklyn Spektor, her father was an auto dealer whose parents were Jewish emigrants from Russia and Austria. Raised in the Chicago suburbs, she graduated from the University of Minnesota in 1979 with a degree in psychology while honing an interest in computer science. Rosen's parents moved to Las Vegas while she was in college. She worked as a cocktail waitress at Caesars Palace on the Las Vegas Strip one summer and then moved to the city after graduation — when she was hired as a computer programmer at Summa Corp., the holding company for the business interests of reclusive billionaire Howard Hughes.

Rosen worked in computer programming and management positions for two other large corporations, Citibank and Southwest Gas, before starting an independent consulting business. The scope and nature of that business later would become an issue in her race against Heller. Among her clients was the radiology practice where her husband, Larry Rosen, whom she married in the early 1990s, was a partner. But for much of the quarter of a century before she entered politics, Jacky Rosen found herself in a situation that many other female baby boomers did: preoccupied with raising a child and caring for her husband's aging parents. She got involved in Congregation NerTamid, a synagogue in Henderson — 16 miles south of Las Vegas — which boasts the largest membership of any Jewish temple in the state. Putting her computer skills to use, Rosen worked to ensure the synagogue's computers were ready for the year 2000 and became the temple's president in 2013.

When three-term Republican Rep. Joe Heck decided to run for the Senate in 2016, Reid sought to recruit a candidate who could win Heck's politically marginal district, which, since its creation 14 years earlier, had only once been captured by a Democrat. After Reid struck out with numerous potential candidates possessing extensive political and business backgrounds, Rosen was recommended to him by state Judge Elissa Cadish, a member of NerTamid. During her Senate bid, Rosen was asked by the Nevada Independent if she would have considered running for Congress if she had not been approached by Reid. She laughed: "That's a good question. I got approached, so here I am. I guess I never had a chance to think about that."

With Reid's support, Rosen had little trouble winning the Democratic primary. In the general election, she faced businessman Danny Tarkanian, son of legendary University of Nevada, Las Vegas basketball coach Jerry Tarkanian. It was one of the closest and most expensive House campaigns of 2016. Tarkanian, an outspoken conservative, had previously lost four election campaigns; he won the Republican nomination with just 32 percent of the vote in a seven-way primary. Rosen and Tarkanian each raised $2 million, but Democratic groups and their allies spent more than $6 million to boost Rosen's profile — while also running extensive advertising that described Tarkanian's business practices as shady. Tarkanian largely failed to respond to the charges, but Republican groups spent more than $9 million on his behalf. Unlike other Republican candidates in Nevada, Tarkanian remained loyal to presidential nominee Donald Trump, who won the district by a single percentage point. Rosen proved successful with what the Las Vegas Sun described as her "under the radar" strategy, winning 47.2%-46.0% and fewer than 4,000 votes.

Rosen's Almanac vote rating placed her among moderate House Democrats representing swing districts. She joined the House Problem Solvers Caucus, a group equally split between Democrats and Republicans. But she was soon off and running again: Rosen launched her Senate bid in July 2017. Rosen won the Democratic primary with 83 percent of the vote.

Heller had been appointed to the Senate seat in 2011 after scandal-plagued Republican John Ensign resigned. Heller served three terms as Nevada secretary of state before being elected to the House in 2006. Carving out a reputation as a centrist, Heller showed a willingness to buck his party early in his Senate tenure. He was elected to a full term by a one-point margin in 2012, a year President Barack Obama carried Nevada. Heller entered the 2018 cycle as the most vulnerable Senate Republican and the only one seeking reelection in a state that Hillary Clinton had won in 2016. Heller soon found himself squeezed between a Republican governor and a Republican president on the hot-button issue of repealing of the Affordable Care Act — to say nothing of trying to straddle a conservative Republican base and a rapidly diversifying and increasingly Democratic electorate.

Heller was critical of Trump throughout the 2016 campaign, later refusing to say whether he had voted for the president. Early in the Trump administration, Heller was among several GOP senators who criticized early Republican legislation to repeal Obamacare. Initially, Heller lined up with Nevada Republican Gov. Brian Sandoval, who had appointed him to the Senate: Sandoval was critical of the repeal efforts because of their effect on federal Medicaid funds coming into the state to insure low-income residents. In July 2017, Heller voted against two Republican-sponsored proposals to repeal the ACA — but split from Sandoval to back a third option that, while not touching Medicaid, was estimated to leave millions of Americans without insurance. After that measure narrowly failed, Heller co-sponsored another proposal that would have led to cuts in Medicaid, although that plan was never brought to a vote. Heller's shift was an effort to mend fences with Trump, who had used a White House event just before the Obamacare repeal debate to all but threaten the Nevadan. "This was the one we were worried about," Trump said, gesturing toward Heller, while adding, "Look, he wants to remain a senator, doesn't he?"

The Heller-Trump relationship warmed in the months after, as Trump nudged Tarkanian out of a primary challenge to Heller in favor of another run for the House, while Heller in public and private appearances increasingly praised the president and his policies. But Heller's shift on Obamacare repeal left him the object of suspicion among many Republicans, while providing no shortage of fodder for Democrats. "He's not hard-enough red meat for the Republicans, not moderate enough to satisfy the nonpartisan folks," David Damore, a UNLV political scientist, told The New York Times. Rosen ran ads featuring footage of Heller's awkward White House appearance with Trump; one ad featured an inflatable tube man blowing back and forth, while a narrator derided Heller as "Sen. Spineless." Trump — appearing before the Nevada GOP State Convention in mid-2018 — called Rosen "Wacky Jacky." Trump said: "Now, that name didn't come from me. That's a name that people have known because people that know her, that's what they call her." In fact, it was not a name that had gained currency even among critics of the restrained, often scripted Rosen. But Trump's comments highlighted Republican efforts to define a candidate who remained largely unknown statewide.

Rosen's limited political background was a two-edged sword: It gave critics little at which to take aim, but also opened her to attacks for lack of accomplishment. "She is literally the generic Democrat," Damore said, referring to her nonspecific candidate profile. The Heller campaign launched ads taking issue with Rosen's claims that she had "built a business" — noting there was no evidence that she ever held a business license with the state or the city of Henderson. But state officials told the Reno Gazette-Journal that, before 2003, Rosen would not have been required to obtain a license if she didn't hire anyone; her campaign said she operated a one-woman unnamed consultancy between 1993 and 2002. Rosen suggested the attacks were sexist. "They wouldn't say the same thing to a man: No one ever asks a man if he feels qualified," she told the Nevada Independent. Heller attacked Rosen's legislative record, with one ad saying: "Zero. That's the number of bills Jacky Rosen passed in Congress before announcing she was running for the Senate." The Rosen campaign responded by pointing to eight bills she had co-sponsored that passed the House before she had lunched her Senate bid.

Rosen advocated for a mainstream Democratic agenda but treaded cautiously in a swing state. She criticized Trump's tax cut plan but stopped short of calling for its repeal. She supported adding a public insurance option to Obamacare but did not favor the "Medicare for All" proposal pushed by party progressives. Nor did she endorse progressives' calls for abolishing the Immigration and Customs Enforcement agency as she pushed for immigration reform. Obama appeared at a rally on her behalf, while Trump flew into the state twice to bolster Heller. In Las Vegas in September, the president called Heller to the stage, where the senator praised Trump for the state of the economy. "Mr. President, it's a pleasure to work with you and putting Nevada back to work," Heller said. Trump responded: "We started off slow — but I've had no better friend in Congress than Dean Heller."

Heller's strategy of tying himself to Trump was risky in a state where the president's approval rating was hovering below 40 percent: Rosen repeatedly mentioned figures showing Heller voting with Trump's position 96 percent of the time. But the race remained close. Rosen had a clear money advantage. She raised and spent $26 million; Heller had less than $14 million. Of the $66 million in independent expenditures that poured into the state, $40 million was spent on Rosen's behalf. Heller's strategy rested on energizing the Republican rural base in northern Nevada, while hoping the statewide vote would follow traditional patterns — in a state where Democratic turnout has tended to ebb significantly in off-years. Rosen defeated Heller 50%-45%, a difference of nearly 59,000 votes — more than twice the statewide margin by which Rosen's Senate colleague, Catherine Cortez Masto, won in 2016. While Heller carried 15 of the state's 17 counties, Rosen won the two biggest: Clark County, home to Las Vegas, and Washoe County, which contains Reno.

For her new colleagues wondering how Rosen would fare as a political neophyte, there was this observation from Democratic Rep. Lois Frankel of Florida, who helped recruit Rosen for the 2016 House run. "The minute I found out she was a synagogue president, I knew she could do anything," Frankel told Politico. "There's nothing like the politics of a synagogue."

Dina Titus (D)

Elected 2012, 5th term, b. May 23, 1950; Thomasville, GA; College of William and Mary (VA), A.B., 1970; University of Georgia, M.A., 1973; Florida State University, Ph.D., 1976; Greek Orthodox; Married (Thomas Clayton Wright).

Elected Office: U.S. House, 2008-2010; NV Senate, 1988-2008.

Professional Career: Professor, University of NV, Las Vegas, 1977-2011; Professor, N. TX St. University, 1975-1976.

DC Office: 2464 RHOB 20515, 202-225-5965, Fax: 202-225-3119, titus.house.gov

State Offices: Las Vegas, 702-220-9823.

Committees: *Foreign Affairs*: Asia, the Pacific & Nonproliferation; Europe, Eurasia, Energy & the Environment. *Homeland Security*: Oversight, Management & Accountability; Transportation & Maritime Security. *Transportation & Infrastructure*: Aviation; Economic Dev't, Public Buildings & Emergency Management (Chmn); Highways & Transit.

Group Ratings

	ADA	ACLU	AFL-CIO	LCV	ITI	COC	HAFA	ACU	CFG	FRC
2018	-	89%	-	89%	-	40%	10%	8%	17%	0%
2017	85%	C	95%	100%	C	46%	C	8%	5%	0%

Almanac Ratings 2017-18

	Economy	Social	Foreign	Composite
Liberal	94%	95%	92%	94%
Conservative	6%	5%	8%	6%

Key Votes of the 115th Congress

1. Obama-care revision	N	5. Family planning regs	N	9. Guantanamo prisoners	Y
2. Tax Cuts	N	6. Body cameras/immigration	Y	10. Ground missiles, limit	Y
3. Omnibus appropriations	N	7. Abortion ban	NV	11. Defense Dept. spending	Y
4. Dodd-Frank revision	N	8. Concealed carry	N	12. FISA rules	N

Election Results

Election	Name (Party)	Vote (%)		Cand. Spent	Ind. Exp. Support	Ind. Exp. Oppose
2018 General	Dina Titus (D)	100,707	(66%)	$543,647		
	Joyce Bentley (R)	46,978	(31%)			
2018 Primary	Dina Titus (D)	20,898	(79%)			
	Reuben D'Silva (D)	5,659	(21%)			

Prior winning percentages: 2016 (62%), 2014 (57%), 2012 (64%), 2008 (47%)

Democrat Dina Titus was elected to Nevada's 1st District House seat in 2012 after losing reelection two years earlier in a more competitive district. An open seat gave the former political science professor an opportunity to move to a liberal, Las Vegas-based district that was safe for a Democrat.

Raised in Tifton Georgia, Titus retained her thick Southern drawl. "I get teased a lot because I haven't lost the accent, but that's kind of become part of how people know me," she told National Journal. Her upbringing gave her a strong interest in politics. She recalls listening to local politicians talk shop at her grandfather's Greek restaurant across from the courthouse. Her father ran for city council, and her Republican "black sheep" uncle, as she puts it, served in the Georgia legislature.

Titus attended the College of William and Mary, where she majored in political science; she later obtained a master's degree from the University of Georgia and a doctorate from Florida State University. After teaching at the University of North Texas, she joined the faculty at the University of Nevada, Las Vegas. She taught there for 34 years, until she retired in 2011. Titus has authored two works on Nevada history, Bombs in the Backyard: Atomic Testing and American Politics, and Battle Born: Federal-State Relations in Nevada During the Twentieth Century. Her husband, Tom Wright, is a Latin American history professor at UNLV. In 1988, Titus put her political knowledge to use and was elected to the Nevada Senate, where she was minority leader for 16 years. She became an advocate for people with disabilities. In 2006, she lost a run for governor to Republican Jim Gibbons.

In 2008, Titus ran for the House, defeating Republican incumbent Jon Porter. That tenure was short-lived. She was swept out of office by the Republican wave in 2010, losing a bruising battle to Joe Heck by 1,748 votes out of more than 314,000 cast. She ran in 2012 in the 1st District, with its 2-1 Democratic edge in voter registration. In November, she largely avoided engaging Republican Chris Edwards, a Navy officer making his first foray into politics. She won, 64%-32% and has been easily reelected since.

Following her return to the House, Titus was the ranking Democrat on the Veterans' Affairs Subcommittee on Disability Assistance and Memorial Affairs. She filed bills that would overturn the VA's prohibition on doctors signing off on marijuana for patients and to permit same-sex couples to be eligible for veterans' benefits. On the Transportation and Infrastructure Committee Titus has been an enthusiastic advocate of reopening rail service from Las Vegas to Los Angeles. Amtrak shut down the line in 1997, but efforts to revive it with high speed rail have moved ahead.

Titus has strongly opposed creating a nuclear waste dump at Yucca Mountain, and slammed the Trump administration after it sent a half metric ton of plutonium to the Nevada National Security Site at Yucca Mountain, complaining that officials "treat Nevada as the dumping ground for the nation's nuclear waste." She has been a staunch ally of the gaming industry, and slammed the Department of Justice for efforts to block online gambling expansion. She has championed liberal causes as well, introducing the Greater Leadership Overseas for the Benefit of Equality (GLOBE) Act to promote LGBTQ equality worldwide. Following the Las Vegas massacre in 2017, she pushed to revive a federal ban on some types of semi-automatic weapons. In the majority in 2019, Titus chaired the subcommittee on Economic Development, Public Buildings, and Emergency Management, which positioned her for oversight of President Donald Trump's real estate holdings – including the government lease for the Trump Hotel in Washington D.C., which prompted constitutional litigation, and his alleged efforts to influence the FBI headquarters across from his hotel.

Titus voiced interest in a 2016 run to succeed retiring Senate Majority Leader Harry Reid. But Reid, with whom Titus had a distant relationship, was firmly behind former state Attorney General Catherine Cortez Masto. Titus decided "I just love representing Nevada's 1st District." Having lost two elections in the past decade, she was circumspect about giving up her safe seat. She pondered a challenge to Republican Sen. Dean Heller in 2018, even releasing an early poll showing her competitive. But Titus again ran up against Reid, who made clear he thought that more moderate freshman Rep. Jacky Rosen would be the best challenger. As Rosen quickly locked up the support of state and national Democrats, Titus again decided that she preferred to remain in the House.

NV-1: Las Vegas   **Cook Partisan Voting Index: D+15**

Population		Race and Ethnicity		Income	
Total	692,075	White	31.3%	Median Income	$40,225
Land area (sq. miles)	105	Black	10.8%	District Income Rank	413
Pop/ sq mi	6622.7	Latino	45.5%	Poverty Rate	21.2%
Born in State	23.5%	Asian	8.2%	With health insurance	78.6%
		Two or more races	2.8%	Cash public assistance	3.9%
Age Groups		Other	1.4%	Food stamp/SNAP	20.5%
Under 18	22.8%				
18-34	25.4%	**Education**		**Work**	
35-64	39%	H.S grad or less	55.8%	White Collar	12.8%
Over 64	12.8%	Some college	28.9%	Sales and Service	61.3%
		College Degree, 4 yr	10.6%	Blue Collar	20.9%
Military		Post grad	4.6%	Government	6.8%
Veteran/ Active Duty	7.4%				

2012 Pres. Vote	Obama	123,205	(65%)	Romney	60,812	(32%)		
2016 Pres. Vote	Clinton	121,321	(62%)	Trump	64,233	(33%)	Johnson	5,406	(3%)

Las Vegas: Las Vegas, that garish and improbable city, had a fittingly colorful beginning. It began as a Paiute Indian settlement that in the late 1700s served as a watering stop for Spanish priests making the 1,200-mile trek between New Mexico and California. By the 1800s, the Old Spanish Trail, as it came to be known, was used by horse and mule smugglers, by explorers like John C. Fremont, and by Mormon emigrants heading west. Las Vegas was still a small crossroads when Nevada, its mining industry a shambles, legalized gambling in the 1930s. The WPA Guide to Nevada, published in 1940 when the city had 10,000 people, describes a prim Las Vegas: "Relatively little emphasis is placed on the gambling clubs and divorce facilities — though they are attractions to many visitors — and much effort is being made to build up cultural attractions."

All that changed after World War II, when gangster Bugsy Siegel built the Flamingo hotel and casino on what became the Strip, south of the city limits. Pseudo-romantic architectural themes became the order of the day (flamingos are found in the waters of Florida, not in the deserts of Nevada), and one casino followed another. Organized crime provided much of the money and muscle for Las Vegas, and investment capital came from Teamsters pension funds. In the late 1960s, eccentric billionaire Howard Hughes moved into the Desert Inn, bought most of the casinos, and hired Mormons to run them. After Hughes abruptly left town, most of his hotels eventually were torn down, and other operators built huge casinos. Lately, the city has claimed eight of the 10 largest hotels in the world.

By the 1990s, diversification became the buzzword. Las Vegas began to produce more family-oriented entertainment, shopping, and even high art, with the Bellagio's museum-quality collection on view. Las Vegas built the largest convention center in the nation. But the city has not neglected its core clientele: people who fly in from elsewhere to be entertained, and to be, for a weekend, maybe even a little naughty. "What happens in Vegas stays in Vegas," remained the unofficial motto. The flashy Oscar Goodman, a former mob lawyer, was elected mayor and actively promoted the city. Barred from seeking a fourth term in 2011, his wife, Carolyn, succeeded him. She continued his habit of taking scantily clad showgirls to events promoting the city, and planned a third term in 2019.

Because of the city's dependence on leisure-time spending, the recession hit hard here and persisted long after other areas recovered, though there has been something of a rebound. The more affordable cost of living has attracted many middle-class Californians to Las Vegas, where they find lower taxes and cheaper rents or can buy good-sized homes for less than $300,000. In October 2018, casinos posted their best month in five years with more than $1 billion in revenue. The new visitors were more interested in shopping, concerts and nightlife. Major entertainers such as Britney Spears and Celine Dion finished residencies, while Lady Gaga launched hers and rapper Cardi B was scheduled to follow. The newest big business in Vegas has become professional sports. The Oakland Raiders planned to move their NFL franchise to the desert in 2020. After extended debate, the legislature approved increased hotel taxes to support bonds for Clark County to build a huge new stadium to house the team. The Las Vegas Golden Knights, the city's NHL expansion franchise, made it to the Stanley Cup finals in its first season, before losing to the Washington Capitals in June 2018.

In October 2017, Las Vegas was the site of the deadliest mass shooting in U.S. history after a 64 year-old gunman opened fire on a concert by country singer Jason Aldean at the Route 91 Harvest Music Festival, which attracted more than 30,000 people. The shooter executed the attack from his 32nd floor Mandalay Bay hotel room, killing 58 people and leaving more than 800 injured from the shooting and the panic that ensued. The gunman committed suicide. Mandalay Bay was sued by many of the victims and their families. MGM, which owned the hotel, made an unusual move of also suing the victims, not seeking money but trying to shield itself from liability.

The 1st Congressional District of Nevada consists of the inner core of Las Vegas that visitors are most likely to see. They cross into it as soon as they drive their rental cars out of the lot at McCarran International Airport. On the three-mile Strip are the nation's 11 largest hotels, each with thousands of rooms that extend far back on their properties. The District is 46 percent Hispanic, the highest proportion in the state, and is the only solidly Democratic district in Nevada. The 62 percent vote for Hillary Clinton in 2016 fell from 65 percent for President Barack Obama in 2012.

Mark Amodei (R)

Elected 2011, 4th full term, b. Jun 12, 1958; Carson City; University of Nevada, Reno, B.A., 1980; University of the Pacific McGeorge School of Law (CA), J.D., 1983; Presbyterian; Divorced; 2 children.

Military Career: U.S. Army, Judge Advocate General's Corps 1984-1987

Professional Career: NV Assembly, 1997-1998; NV Senate, 1999-2010.

DC Office: 104 CHOB 20515, 202-225-6155, Fax: 202-225-5679, amodei.house.gov

State Offices: Elko, 775-777-7705; Reno, 775-686-5760.

Committees: *Appropriations*: Financial Services & General Government; Interior, Environment & Related Agencies.

Group Ratings

	ADA	ACLU	AFL-CIO	LCV	ITI	COC	HAFA	ACU	CFG	FRC
2018	-	4%	-	14%	-	92%	42%	63%	47%	100%
2017	0%	C	21%	6%	C	92%	C	80%	56%	100%

Almanac Ratings 2017-18

	Economy	Social	Foreign	Composite
Liberal	6%	3%	5%	5%
Conservative	94%	97%	95%	96%

Key Votes of the 115th Congress

1. Obama-care revision	Y	5. Family planning regs	NV	9. Guantanamo prisoners	N
2. Tax Cuts	Y	6. Body cameras/immigration	N	10. Ground missiles, limit	N
3. Omnibus appropriations	Y	7. Abortion ban	Y	11. Defense Dept. spending	Y
4. Dodd-Frank revision	Y	8. Concealed carry	Y	12. FISA rules	Y

Election Results

Election	Name (Party)	Vote (%)		Cand. Spent	Ind. Exp. Support	Ind. Exp. Oppose
2018 General	Mark Amodei (R)	167,435	(58%)	$1,000,583	$77,070	
	Clint Koble (D)	120,102	(42%)	$145,418	$10,329	
2018 Primary	Mark Amodei (R)	42,351	(72%)			
	Sharron Angle (R)	10,837	(18%)			
	Joel Beck (R)	5,006	(9%)			

Prior winning percentages: 2016 (58%), 2014 (66%), 2012 (58%), 2011 special (62%)

Republican Mark Amodei won a 2011 special election to fill the seat of GOP Sen. Dean Heller. A former state Senate president pro tempore and state party chairman, Amodei is a small-government conservative whose governing experience has allied him with the party establishment in pushing for legislation on multiple fronts, though he remained a voice for compromise on immigration reform. With Heller's loss in 2018 and Democrats' success in other districts, Amodei became the lone Republican in the Nevada delegation.

Amodei grew up in Carson City, Nevada's capital, the son of an Italian immigrant father who worked for the state Forestry Division and a mother who was a physician. He attended the University of Nevada, Reno, where he joined ROTC, and earned a law degree from the University of the Pacific's McGeorge School of Law. He joined the Army and became a prosecutor for the Judge Advocate General Corps, handling criminal matters. After opening a law practice in his hometown, Amodei was elected to the state Assembly and then to the state Senate, where he chaired the Judiciary Committee and took his leadership post. In 2007, Amodei became president of the Nevada Mining Association. He said that he saw no conflict of interest, but a year and a half later he stepped down from the organization because, he said, he didn't want to have a "distracting" dual role during the legislative session.

In 2009, Amodei announced a challenge to Senate Majority Leader Harry Reid, portraying himself as a commonsense conservative who could appeal to independent voters. He dropped out of the contest six months later, explaining that he was able to raise only about $80,000, a pittance compared to Reid's multimillion-dollar war chest. When Heller was appointed to the Senate in May 2011 to replace Republican John Ensign, who resigned amid a sex scandal with the wife of one of his former aides, Amodei won the nomination with ease. In the special-election matchup, Democratic state Treasurer Kate Marshall boasted of support from the National Rifle Association and said that she would have voted against increasing the federal debt ceiling, which Amodei also opposed. Amodei played up his more conservative credentials, calling for tax cuts, a balanced budget amendment to the Constitution and opening more public lands to oil and gas production. He used an ad with his mother to deflect Medicare attacks. The National Republican Congressional Committee pumped in more than $600,000 to pummel Marshall, and the Democratic Congressional Campaign Committee never came to her rescue. Amodei won, 58%-36%.

Amodei has been an often pragmatic conservative in the House who emphasizes spending discipline. He has brought a homespun approach to his job and says lawmakers need to talk more with each other. Democratic Rep. John Garamendi of California told the Reno Gazette-Journal that Amodei "knows the legislative process." They worked together in 2016 to enact the Lake Tahoe Restoration Act to "keep Tahoe blue."

On the Appropriations Committee, he won approval of his provision to protect the water rights of private landholders. As vice chairman of the Western Caucus, Amodei has concentrated on natural resource issues. In contrast to the hardline opposition of many in Nevada, he said that the Yucca Mountain proposed burial site for high-level nuclear waste storage should be examined instead as a potential home for nuclear reprocessing and research. Nevada could become "the worldwide leader in reprocessing the fuel so it becomes a commodity instead of trash," he told the Nevada Appeal in 2016.

He clashed with President Donald Trump's first Interior Secretary Ryan Zinke, getting caught on tape addressing a GOP dinner in a profanity-laden tirade after Zinke hadn't alerted him to a shakeup at the Nevada branch of the Bureau of Land Management, according to the Reno Gazette Journal. Citing concerns about Medicaid cuts and changes, Amodei initially wavered in 2017 on whether he would support the American Health Care Act, the GOP's effort to repeal Obamacare. After receiving assurances, Amodei eventually offered his support; the bill died in the Senate. In a 2015 interview with the Sparks Tribune, Amodei said that the problems of immigration are "eminently solvable," except that "everybody's got a political angle." In his view, "I'd rather be criticized for trying to do something because I'm tired of defending nothing." After Trump tried to halt the Deferred Action for Childhood Arrivals (DACA) program, Amodei joined a group of Republicans critical of GOP leaders for stalling on a solution. Amodei's district is nearly one-fourth Hispanic.

Amodei has flirted with higher office but hasn't pulled the trigger, and he has easily won reelection in his congressional district. During the final weeks of the 2016 contest, while he was the Nevada campaign chairman for Trump, he said that some of the criticism and outrage over Trump's comments about women were "appropriate and deserved." But he stood by Trump. "I am genuinely concerned about the future of our country, and who will set the tone," Amodei said. "The present political wars have accomplished nothing. I want to try a new direction." In 2018 Amodei faced a primary challenge from tea party activist Sharron Angle, who had unsuccessfully challenged Reid in 2010. Angle slammed Amodei's openness to immigration reform as "amnesty," but she had paltry fundraising and her bid never gained traction. Amodei won 72%-18%.

NV-2: Northern Nevada   **Cook Partisan Voting Index: R+7**

Population		Race and Ethnicity		Income	
Total	702,115	White	67%	Median Income	$58,607
Land area (sq. miles)	55,830	Black	1.8%	District Income Rank	189
Pop/ sq mi	12.6	Latino	22.1%	Poverty Rate	13%
Born in State	30.6%	Asian	3.8%	With health insurance	88.3%
		Two or more races	2.8%	Cash public assistance	3.1%
Age Groups		Other	2.5%	Food stamp/SNAP	10.1%
Under 18	22.3%				
18-34	22.4%	**Education**		**Work**	
35-64	39.3%	H.S grad or less	38.3%	White Collar	16%
Over 64	16%	Some college	35.6%	Sales and Service	45.3%
		College Degree, 4 yr	16.4%	Blue Collar	22.6%
Military		Post grad	9.6%	Government	15.3%
Veteran/ Active Duty	10.6%				

2012 Pres. Vote	Romney	155,186	(53%)	Obama	131,540	(45%)			
2016 Pres. Vote	Trump	169,631	(52%)	Clinton	129,317	(40%)	Johnson	13,966	(4%)

Reno: Outside of metro Las Vegas, huge, empty and mountainous Nevada has only one sizable population center, a cluster of small cities and towns near the border with California: the casino cities of Reno and Sparks, the small capital of Carson City, the restored Comstock Lode boomtown of Virginia City, and the resort areas that surround (and endanger) the deep, impossibly blue waters of Lake Tahoe. Reno is so remote from Las Vegas that the only quick way to get there is by air; it takes more than nine hours to drive, although the spectacularly stark scenery makes it time well spent. Ghost towns that once bustled with miners dot the parched, sand-swept deserts, and in some places the land remains distinctly rutted from the wagon trains that crossed here more than 100 years ago. Today, Nevada's small towns survive on mining, ranching and, in some cases, servicing the human sins of greed and lust: Nevada's legal brothels are generally found in the small, desert counties. Another distinction is the Basque influence. Immigrant Basque shepherds once tended their flocks in remote portions of northern Nevada; Basque festivals, social clubs and restaurants can still be found in Winnemucca and Elko.

The military has holdings in the Nevada interior, including Fallon Naval Air Station, home to the Navy Fighter Weapons "Top Gun" School. Many places in Nevada depend on other federal government programs: The Newlands Irrigation Project near Fallon was among the first of its kind. Nevada's gold-mining operations, booming since 2000, do not have to pay royalties to the government, thanks to the Mining Act of 1872. The spread of legalized gambling throughout the country has hurt Reno. In 2016, it had only 7 percent of the casino revenues in Nevada.

The area has become a tech hub, with solar and wind-energy enterprises and high-precision technologies. Reno has sold itself as close to Silicon Valley but with a lower cost of living, though it has struggled to meet demands for new housing and infrastructure. Northern Nevada expected to add about 50,000 jobs — many of them tech-related -- between 2014 and 2019, a business group reported. Electric-car manufacturer Tesla Motors built a huge factory near Sparks, with lower-cost cell production for its batteries, and planned to increase its workforce to 20,000 eventually. The facility, which it called the Gigafactory, produced more lithium ion batteries annually than were produced worldwide in 2013. Apple opened a massive solar plant in the Reno area to power its huge data centers; it runs on 100 percent green energy and powered 200,000 servers. Cryptocurrency millionaire Jeffrey Berns bought an enormous plot of land for $170 million, planning a new center for his Blockchains LLC company.

The 2nd Congressional District of Nevada takes in Reno and Carson City in territory that covers nearly the northern half of Nevada. It includes Churchill, Pershing, Humboldt and Elko counties. Washoe County, which includes Reno and Sparks, has nearly two-thirds of the district's population. Washoe was an important swing county in the 2016 presidential election; Hillary Clinton won it, 46%-45%. Donald Trump won each of the outlying counties with more than 60 percent of the vote and took the 2nd comfortably, 52%-40%. This was the only Nevada district where he won a majority of the vote.

Susie Lee (D)

Elected 2018, 1st term, b. Nov 07, 1966; Canton, OH; Carnegie Mellon University, B.S., 1989; Carnegie Mellon University, M.P.A., 1990; Catholic; Married (Dan Lee); 2 children.

Professional Career: Non-Profit Executive; Board President, Communities in School.

DC Office: 522 CHOB 20515, 202-225-3252, susielee.house.gov

State Offices: Las Vegas, 702-963-9336.

Committees: *Education & Labor*: Civil Rights & Human Services; Higher Education & Workforce Investment. *Veterans' Affairs*: Economic Opportunity; Technology Modernization (Chmn).

Election Results

Election	Name (Party)	Vote (%)		Cand. Spent	Ind. Exp. Support	Ind. Exp. Oppose
2018 General	Susie Lee (D)	148,501	(52%)	$4,974,997		
	Danny Tarkanian (R)	122,566	(43%)	$2,284,907	$24,633	$5,854,133
2018 Primary	Susie Lee (D)	25,475	(67%)			
	Michael Weiss (D)	3,115	(8%)			
	Eric Stoltz (D)	2,759	(7%)			
	Jack Love (D)	2,208	(6%)			

Freshman Democrat Susie Lee comfortably won her swing seat, with endorsements from leading state and national Democrats plus huge financial support. Lee, who described herself as a "philanthropist," founded and directed organizations that support the homeless and other needy individuals. Her initial political success followed a more controversial campaign two years earlier for a neighboring House seat in which Lee was attacked for her self-financing and faced charges of seeking to buy the seat; she ran third in that Democratic primary. Her husband, Dan Lee, has been a prominent casino executive. Lee succeeded Democratic Rep. Jacky Rosen, who was elected to the Senate.

Lee, a native of Canton Ohio, grew up in a working-class family. "We didn't have much, but we had enough," she told the Las Vegas Review-Journal, which profiled her "humble beginnings." Lee got her bachelor's degree and a master's in public administration from Carnegie Mellon University. She settled in Las Vegas, where her activities included the founding of a homeless shelter, creation of an after-school program and a stint as board president of the Communities in School program.

When Lee ran in the 4th District in 2016, news reports focused on her husband's hefty earnings from casino businesses, which financed nearly one-half of the $1.6 million she spent. PolitiFact confirmed that the Lees owned 17 homes — 14 of which they rented — and a private plane. She got 21 percent in the Democratic primary, which was won by Ruben Kihuen, the son of Mexican-born immigrants. He stepped down after one term, following charges of sexual misconduct.

In contrast to other recent Democratic primaries for open seats in Nevada, which were highly competitive, Lee quickly emerged as the party favorite in 2018. Some unhappy Democratic activists, plus her opponents, cited her in criticizing the Democratic Congressional Campaign Committee for favoring high-income candidates. "The Washington D.C. and Nevada Democratic establishment anointed Susie Lee for her ease of access to large amounts of money," complained Jack Love, one of her opponents. "Political candidates should be chosen based on a contest of ideas, not the size of their bank accounts." Lee raised more than $1.4 million for the primary against six other candidates, none of whom raised more than $22,000. She got 67 percent of the vote.

Danny Tarkanian, Lee's Republican opponent, was well-known in Nevada as the son of a former prominent college basketball coach — and a perennial candidate who had lost at least six campaigns in Nevada, including a 47%-46% defeat against Rosen for the House seat in 2016. Tarkanian initially challenged Sen. Dean Heller in the 2018 GOP primary. Prominent Republicans, backed by President Donald Trump, convinced him that he had greater likelihood of success if he switched to another bid for the House. Running against eight other candidates, Tarkanian won the primary with 44 percent.

In the general election, Tarkanian attacked Lee as "part of the wealthy elite" and "out of touch" with voters. Tarkanian had his own problems in business, including the ownership of a failed bank in California, which resulted in his filing for bankruptcy. Lee criticized his opposition to the Affordable Care Act and the barriers that Trump had imposed to immigration. "I'm running for Congress because D.C. has quit working for working families," she told Nevada Public Radio.

In a district that Trump won in 2016 by fewer than 3,300 votes and Tarkanian lost by a similar total, the contest started as a toss-up. Lee emerged with several advantages, including the surge in Democratic fundraising that led her to more than double Tarkanian's spending, and the overall political climate. She had an easy 52%-43% win. The recent history of this district, where two Democrats and two Republicans split the six elections from 2006 to 2016, suggests that she cannot take it for granted.

NV-3: Southern Las Vegas area

Cook Partisan Voting Index: R+2

Population		Race and Ethnicity		Income	
Total	762,236	White	57.2%	Median Income	$67,191
Land area (sq. miles)	2,849	Black	6.7%	District Income Rank	117
Pop/ sq mi	267.6	Latino	17%	Poverty Rate	9.2%
Born in State	22.3%	Asian	13.7%	With health insurance	90.3%
		Two or more races	4.2%	Cash public assistance	2%
Age Groups		Other	1.3%	Food stamp/SNAP	6.2%
Under 18	22.1%				
18-34	22.2%	**Education**		**Work**	
35-64	40.4%	H.S grad or less	32.5%	White Collar	15.3%
Over 64	15.3%	Some college	35.7%	Sales and Service	52%
		College Degree, 4 yr	20.9%	Blue Collar	13%
Military		Post grad	10.9%	Government	11%
Veteran/ Active Duty	9.4%				

2012 Pres. Vote	Romney	138,238	(49%)	Obama	140,501	(49%)	
2016 Pres. Vote	Trump	154,814	(48%)	Clinton	151,552	(47%) Johnson	9,971 (3%)

Henderson: Las Vegas, "The Meadows" in Spanish, began as a stop along the Old Spanish Trail trading route between Santa Fe and California in the 1830s. Water from artesian wells had created vast grasslands in the area and let traders replenish their supplies. In the early 20th century, Las Vegas was a terminus of the Las Vegas & Tonopah Railroad, a link to Nevada's silver mines. Even at the end of the 1930s, soon after gambling was legalized in Nevada, it was still a town of less than 10,000. Then came decades of amazing growth, as Las Vegas became America's destination for gambling and entertainment. From 2000 to 2008, the Las Vegas metropolitan area grew by 36 percent, to 1.9 million, making it one of the five fastest-growing metropolitan areas in America. It spread across the desert in every direction from the few blocks around Fremont Street that it occupied in the 1930s, and today it is an exuberant, undisciplined and chaotic city. Following the fast pace of building, Las Vegas was particularly hard hit by the crisis in the credit markets, and the red-hot real estate market tanked. The metro area had the highest foreclosure rate in the nation in 2010, according to RealtyTrac. By May 2018, foreclosures in the area had dropped to fourth-worst.

The 3rd Congressional District covers the southern part of Clark County and several Las Vegas suburbs. It includes retiree communities, small blue-collar towns such as Blue Diamond, and a variety of planned, and often gated, areas like Summerlin South, where young families have sought job opportunities and retired baby boomers have purchased vacation homes. Gypsum Resources has planned to build thousands of homes near Blue Diamond, but local groups for several years have stalled the project with the County Commission because of their concern about damage to the ecosystem. Southeast of Las Vegas, the district takes in the population hub of Henderson and Boulder City, originally built for federal workers at Hoover Dam. (Under an old agreement with the federal government, Boulder City is the only place in Nevada where gambling and prostitution are prohibited.) After the dam was completed, many of the workers unexpectedly decided to stay in the desert. The sale of liquor was legalized in 1969. In August 2018, the first 15-mile section of Interstate 11 opened with a bypass around Boulder City, through the Eldorado Mountains overlooking Lake Mead. In the desert outside of Boulder City, a solar plant opened in 2017, with 288,000 panels that can yield 100 megawatts of power. Henderson resumed its rapid growth following the recession and has a population of 285,000. To accompany their move to Las Vegas in 2020, the Oakland Raiders said they will locate their corporate headquarters and practice facility in Henderson. Fun fact: Henderson provides tours of its "Artisan Booze" district.

The 3rd includes the Nevada half of Lake Mohave on the Arizona border, plus the state's southernmost tip, including Searchlight, the hometown of former Senate Majority Leader Harry Reid. The 3rd, with a 17 percent and growing Latino population, is politically competitive. Donald Trump in 2016 took it, 48%-47%.

Steven Horsford (D)

Elected 2018, 2nd term, b. Apr 29, 1973; Las Vegas; University of Nevada, Reno, B.A., 2014; Baptist; Married (Dr. Sonya Horsford); 3 children.

Elected Office: NV Senate, 2004-2012, Majority Floor Leader 2009-2012; U.S. House, 2013-2015.

Professional Career: NV Legislature Education Committee, Legislative Aide 1995; R&R Advertising, Account Representative 1996; Culinary Training Academy, Chief Executive Officer 2001-2012; R&R Partners, Inc., Senior Vice President, Strategic Integration and Partnerships; Managing Director, Washington, DC Office 2015-2018; Nevada Partners (Employment Training), President of the Board, Chief Executive Officer.

DC Office: 1330 LHOB 20515, 202-225-9894, horsford.house.gov

State Offices: North Las Vegas, 702-963-9360.

Committees: *Budget. Natural Resources*: National Parks, Forests & Public Lands. *Ways & Means*: Health.

Election Results

Election	Name (Party)	Vote (%)		Cand. Spent	Ind. Exp. Support	Ind. Exp. Oppose
2018 General	Steven Horsford (D)	121,962	(52%)	$2,231,105	$5,083,977	$2,893,618
	Cresent Hardy (R)	102,748	(44%)	$868,220	$1,952	$3,773,320
2018 Primary	Steven Horsford (D)	22,730	(62%)			
	Patricia Spearman (D)	5,613	(15%)			
	Amy Vilela (D)	3,388	(9%)			
	Allison Stephens (D)	2,216	(6%)			
	John Anzalone (D)	2,134	(6%)			

Prior winning percentages: 2012 (50%)

Democrat Steven Horsford won a return trip to the House, where he served one term before he unexpectedly lost reelection in 2014. His Democratic-leaning seat has experienced surprising turmoil since it was created in 2012, when Nevada gained a fourth district. Since then, no incumbent has won reelection, though Horsford is the first member to win a second term. He replaced Democrat Ruben Kihuen, who decided against seeking reelection under pressure from national and state Democrats following allegations of improper sexual behavior with a female staffer.

Horsford grew up in a rough-and-tumble neighborhood in West Las Vegas. The oldest of four, he had responsibility forced on him early in life. His mother struggled with drug and alcohol problems. He attended the University of Nevada, Reno, but had to drop out to support his family when his father was shot and killed during a robbery at a store where he worked. Well-connected to the state's hospitality industry, Horsford was CEO of the Culinary Training Academy of Las Vegas, which trained workers for jobs on the Strip. He served eight years in the state Senate, including a stint as majority leader.

When he ran for the new congressional district in 2012, Horsford dodged primary opposition. In the general, he defeated Danny Tarkanian, who has become a perennial Republican contender, 50%-42%. During his one term in the House, he was viewed as a rising star.

He was the victim of several factors in his reelection bid, including his excessive confidence against Republican Cresent Hardy, a state legislator who was significantly outspent. Hardy benefited from the popularity of Brian Sandoval, who was overwhelmingly reelected that year, a small Democratic turnout, and $1.1 million in late spending by a Republican Super PAC. Hardy won, 49%-46%.

In 2016, the district's Democrat lean reasserted itself as the presidential election and an open Senate seat nearly doubled voter turnout. Hardy was challenged by Democrat Ruben Kihuen, who was born in Mexico and moved to the United States as a child with his working-class parents. Kihuen served 10 years in the legislature, including two years as Senate majority whip. He defeated Hardy, 49%-45%.

Kihuen's House career imploded after BuzzFeed News reported in early December 2017 that he had made repeated advances toward a staffer during the 2016 campaign. House Minority Leader Nancy Pelosi and other Democrats demanded that he resign. Kihuen rejected those calls, but he announced two weeks after the revelations that he would not seek reelection.

Horsford, who had settled in Washington and opened a public relations firm, announced his candidacy in January 2018. "There are some things that I learned [in 2014] and that I will do differently about this campaign," he told the Nevada Independent. "First is, I will run a very grassroots, community-oriented campaign, listening to voters."

Horsford faced credible opposition in the primary, including the expected criticism that he had lost touch with his former constituents. "I am the best person in this race because when I moved here in 2005, I never left," said state Sen. Pat Spearman. Horsford had numerous advantages, including the endorsement of the Democratic Congressional Campaign Committee and a large fundraising lead. In the six-candidate contest, Horsford got 62 percent of the vote to 15 percent for Spearman and 9 percent for progressive activist Amy Vilela. Hardy, who also faced a six-candidate field to win the Republican nomination, was well-financed for his rematch with Horsford. "The people of Nevada fired him four years ago," he told the voters. But state and national politics had changed since 2014. This time, Horsford proved that his frontrunner status was warranted. Hardy led in the six rural counties, which cast barely 10 percent of the vote, but Horsford won, 52%-44%. On his return to the House, he got a seat on the Ways and Means Committee.

NV-4: Central Nevada   Cook Partisan Voting Index: D+3

Population		Race and Ethnicity		Income	
Total	731,299	White	45.7%	Median Income	$56,603
Land area (sq. miles)	50,998	Black	14.3%	District Income Rank	207
Pop/ sq mi	14.3	Latino	29.4%	Poverty Rate	14.2%
Born in State	27.5%	Asian	5.5%	With health insurance	86.5%
		Two or more races	3.6%	Cash public assistance	3.4%
Age Groups		Other	1.5%	Food stamp/SNAP	13.4%
Under 18	25.6%				
18-34	22.6%	Education		Work	
35-64	37.8%	H.S grad or less	44.9%	White Collar	14%
Over 64	14%	Some college	34.8%	Sales and Service	52.4%
		College Degree, 4 yr	13.6%	Blue Collar	20.2%
Military		Post grad	6.7%	Government	14.7%
Veteran/ Active Duty	12%				

2012 Pres. Vote	Obama	136,124	(54%)	Romney	109,329	(44%)			
2016 Pres. Vote	Clinton	137,070	(50%)	Trump	123,380	(45%)	Johnson	8,041	(3%)

Northern Las Vegas area: A vast majority of the land in Nevada is owned by the federal government — a constant source of tension with local officials, ranchers, loggers and miners. Their pursuits, frequently solitary and often ornery, shaped Nevada's culture from its earliest days. On the desolate frontier, speculation runs wild: Art Bell used to broadcast his popular radio show about the paranormal, aliens and other unexplained phenomena from tiny Pahrump. The federal government's top-secret aviation experiments at places like Area 51 on the Nellis Air Force Gunnery Range have stoked UFO lore to the point that adjoining Route 375 was rededicated as the Extraterrestrial Highway in 1996.

Anti-establishment views also flourish here in more mainstream ways. Nevada residents and most of its politicians have long opposed a nuclear waste repository 1,000 feet beneath Yucca Mountain, 90 miles northwest of Las Vegas. Congress finally approved the project in 2002. President Barack Obama shelved it and a commission recommended alternative storage options. With the arrival of President Donald Trump, Republicans — including some in Nevada — considered new options, though most Nevadans remained steadfast opponents. Another controversy was the December 2015 agreement by the legislature to provide more than $300 million in tax incentives to the Faraday Future company to build an electric-car plant in north Las Vegas, as a competitor to Tesla. In 2017, Faraday returned the cash to the state and abandoned its plan days after a court in China froze the assets of the company's founder.

The vast interior away from Las Vegas includes the 3-million-acre Nellis Air Force range. Also found here is the Energy Department's Nevada National Security Site, which was created by President Harry Truman. More than 800 underground tests of nuclear weapons were conducted here, as well as 100 above-ground tests, before they ended in 1962. The explosions left the Rhode Island-sized facility pockmarked with unstable "subsidence craters" as far as the eye can see. In a potentially significant twist, Nye County officials in 2015 approved the shipment of uranium waste from Oak Ridge National Laboratory in Tennessee to a landfill at the nuclear site. In December 2018, the Nevada attorney general sued the Trump administration after discovering that it had secretly shipped plutonium to the site from South Carolina. Yucca Mountain also is located in Nye County.

The 4th District is a rural and suburban mix that sprawls across most of southern Nevada. It contains much of North Las Vegas and stretches north into the state's interior. The northern part of Clark County, as well as Esmeralda, Mineral, White Pine (and the city of Ely), Nye and Lincoln counties are in the district. Clark County, which dropped from 61 percent non-Hispanic white in 2000 to 45 percent in 2015, has become one of the largest majority-minority counties in the nation, with 31 percent Hispanic, 12 percent black and 10 percent Asian. Nearly 90 percent of the district vote is cast in Clark. Democrats had a voter registration edge of 46%-33% and Hillary Clinton took the 4th in 2016 by four percentage points. The district, which is 29 percent Hispanic and 14 percent black, has become competitive.

NEW HAMPSHIRE

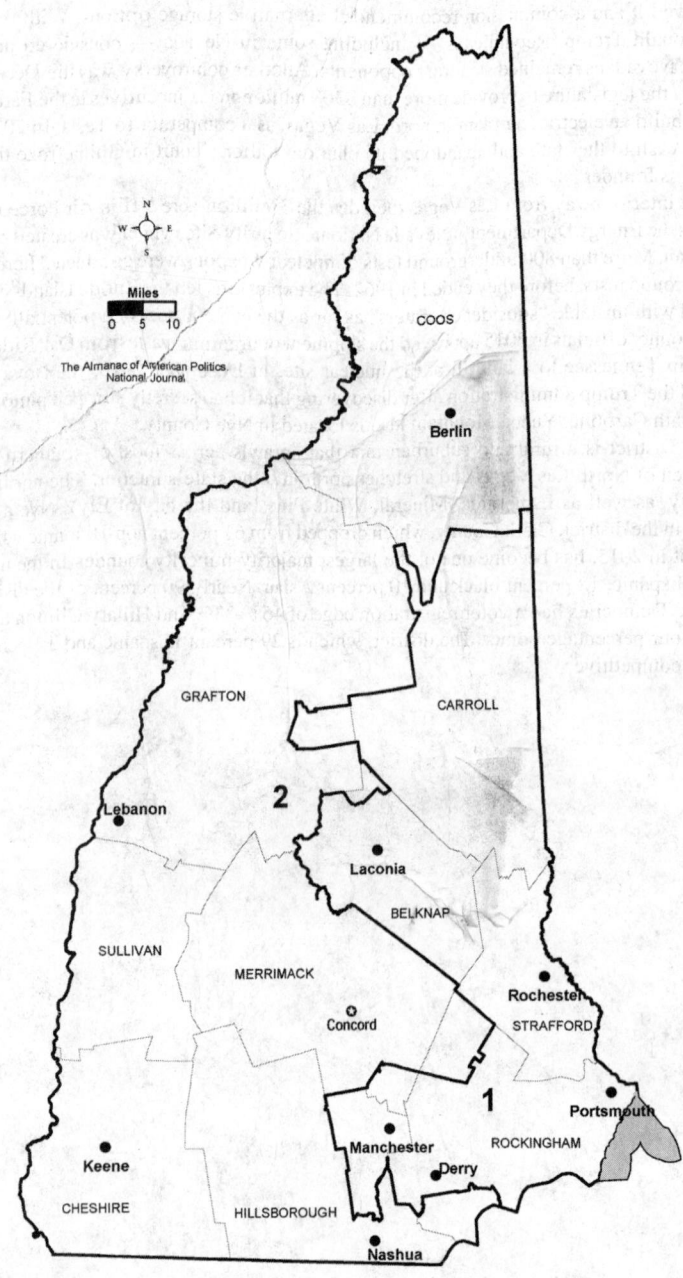

Congressional district boundaries were first effective for 2012.

Though it is home to just .41 percent of the nation's population, New Hampshire becomes the center of the political universe every four years, especially in the winter -- the place where the contest for the American presidency starts and is temporarily focused, where every vote is avidly sought and endlessly analyzed, handshake by handshake. The state, once solidly Republican, has also become a competitive hotbed for Democrats and Republicans in recent years.

In June 1788, New Hampshire voted to ratify the Constitution and, as the ninth state to do so, put the document into effect. New Hampshire has been quirky from its beginnings. In a country that prides itself on its feistiness and freedom from outside direction, the state has always been even feistier and more lightly fettered by authority. Before the Revolutionary War, New Hampshire was almost an outlaw colony, its great fortunes made by poachers in the king's forests and smugglers avoiding taxes. Boxed-in by bossy Puritan Massachusetts on two sides (Maine was part of that colony and state until 1820), New Hampshire embodied the spirit of Revolutionary War General John Stark's words, "Live free or die." New Hampshire was the first colony with an independent government and was fighting the British even before the Minutemen stood at Lexington and Concord.

In the early republic, New England merchants turned inland and built textile mills along fast-flowing rivers. The Amoskeag Mills in Manchester, lining the Merrimack River for a mile, were once the largest cotton mills in the world, employing 17,000 people and producing enough cloth every two months to extend around the world. Around the mills grew a city of red-brick dormitories and three-family frame houses filled with immigrants from Quebec, Ireland, Poland and Greece, set down amid villages of dirt roads and flinty Yankee farmers and mechanics. New Hampshire held to its traditions of local government and little external control, and for years refused to join most other states in enacting an income or sales tax, or to provide statewide guidance of schools and social services.

Instead, low taxes proved to be New Hampshire's fortune. From 1960 to 1990, the state's population grew by 83 percent, more than double the national rate of 39 percent. During that time and through the 1990s, it had the fastest growth in the Northeast, attracting businesses from Massachusetts and other high-tax states. It became a location of choice for entrepreneurs and technology innovators. The bedraggled New Hampshire of 60 years ago, of poor Yankee farmers and French Canadian mill hands, has been overtaken by one of the nation's most prosperous economic communities. The low taxes that spurred New Hampshire's growth would probably have been raised in the late 1960s or early 1970s, as they were in so many states at the time, but for the leadership of Manchester's Union Leader newspaper and its proprietor, William Loeb. The paper (now the New Hampshire Union Leader) insisted that governors and legislators "take the pledge" to vote for no sales or income tax and, from 1970 to 1998, almost all did — and the two who didn't were defeated.

The result was that education and social welfare remained local responsibilities. At the same time, New Hampshire boasted the highest average SAT scores in the country and had the brainpower to participate fully in New England's technology boom. The old Amoskeag Mills were converted to offices, and once-grimy Manchester is now a high-tech center. Fidelity Investments, BAE Systems, Liberty Mutual and Timberland are big employers, and New Hampshire has had one of the highest growth rates in information technology jobs and the highest percentage of citizens with internet access.

Since 1990, New Hampshire's growth has slowed. One reason is the cost of housing. Another is that New Hampshire's comparative advantage over Massachusetts in tax rates has diminished. New Hampshire also has high property taxes. In a series of decisions, the state Supreme Court tried to push the legislature into passing a broad-based (i.e., sales or income) tax by forcing more state spending to overcome inequality of resources in different cities and towns, but that has been resisted by all Republicans and many Democrats. A 2018 U.S. Supreme Court decision requiring the collection of taxes on out-of-state online sales terrified political leaders into calling a special legislative session to blunt the requirement, but they were unable to enact a law in their first attempt.

New Hampshire remains an affluent state. Its median income is among the highest in the nation; the unemployment rate peaked at only 6.6 percent in mid-2009, and by December 2018, it had fallen to 2.5 percent, tied for second best in the nation. This was not problem-free: Such a tight labor market poses problems for employers. In addition, New Hampshire faces a "silver tsunami" – it had the third-oldest population measured by median age in 2016, trailing only neighboring Vermont and Maine. The state is 93 percent white (ranking fourth nationally), 1 percent black (one of only eight states with such a small percentage), 3 percent Hispanic and 3 percent Asian. In combination with its tight labor market and aging population, the state's low diversity has become so worrisome that business, government, and nonprofit officials recently launched an effort to push diversification.

The biggest concern recently has been a sharp rise in opioid use. In 2017, New Hampshire ranked third nationally in per capita overdose deaths, behind only West Virginia and Ohio. New Hampshire is significantly more affluent than these two states, but a combination of factors -- high prescription rates, historically low spending for addiction treatment, the libertarian attitude embodied in the state's motto – has contributed to the problem. New Hampshire's political architecture is quirky. The state House has 400 members — one representative for every 3,391 residents, with each lawmaker paid just $100 a year. (California, by comparison, has one Assembly member for every 494,463 residents, and they are paid $110,459 annually.) Meanwhile, there's a five-member, elected "executive council" that is essentially a fourth branch of government — one that's able to stymie the governor, who as a result is structurally one of the nation's weakest. There's little impetus among voters to change the way the government works. "We've never had a major scandal, there's no widespread corruption and it's pretty transparent," Tom Rath, a former state attorney general and former Republican National Committee member, told Governing.

The lever with which this small state has sometimes moved the political world is its first-in-the-nation presidential primary. Residents are well-schooled in politics, are willing to show up in the snow for town halls, and take the process seriously. The state fiercely defends its first-in-the-nation prerogative, led for decades by Secretary of State Bill Gardner. New Hampshire gave a huge boost to Dwight Eisenhower's candidacy in 1952 and prompted the retirement of Lyndon Johnson in 1968. It helped launch Jimmy Carter in 1976, Ronald Reagan in 1980, George H.W. Bush in 1988, and Bill Clinton in 1992, who had his "Comeback Kid" moment in the Granite State.

New Hampshire has some Democratic roots: It voted for Andrew Jackson over Massachusetts neighbor John Quincy Adams, and its only president, Franklin Pierce, was a Democrat (and a coddler of slaveholders). But from 1856 to World War II and beyond, New Hampshire voted mostly Republican, with Yankee Protestant farmers outvoting Irish and French-Canadian Catholic mill workers. Manchester and Nashua, formerly Democratic, trended toward Republicans. In the presidential elections from 1972 to 1988, the state voted on average 8 percent more Republican than the nation.

Over the past three decades, though, New Hampshire has become much more Democratic and has become important in presidential elections not just as a primary state but as a target in the general election, albeit one with a small number of electoral votes. The shift began when local housing prices crashed in the early 1990s. Much of New Hampshire is part of the Boston metro area, and like most non-Southern metro areas, it has trended Democratic in response to the Republicans' conservative stands on cultural issues. And if New Hampshire voters don't like broad-based taxes, many don't much like politicized religion either. In the 2016 general-election exit poll, just 15 percent of New Hampshire respondents identified as born-again or evangelical Christians, below the national percentage of 26 percent. Below the presidential level, the state has been one of the nation's swingiest, with governor's offices, Senate seats, House seats and legislative chambers switching parties on a semi-regular basis.

In 2016, Donald Trump bounced back from a loss in the Iowa caucuses with a big win in the New Hampshire primary. Trump didn't prevail in November, but he came extraordinarily close, losing to Hillary Clinton by less than half a percentage point – the second-closest state in the nation percentage-wise. Other races were similarly close: Democrat Maggie Hassan defeated Kelly Ayotte for a Senate seat by about 1,000 votes, and Republican Chris Sununu won the gubernatorial race by 12,000 votes. Sununu's win enabled the Republicans to take full control of state government for the first time since 2002.

In 2018, Sununu was reelected, but the Democrats seized both chambers of the legislature, led by a wave of younger legislative candidates. The most compelling race, however, came after Election Day – the race to win legislators' support for secretary of state. Despite his storied tenure, Gardner rubbed many Democrats the wrong way when he joined the Presidential Advisory Commission on Election Integrity convened by Trump. Colin Van Ostern, who had lost to Sununu in 2016, challenged Gardner and broke tradition by raising a quarter-million dollars. Gardner retained enough support from establishment figures in both parties to prevail – on the second ballot, and by just one vote over the minimum required.

Population			Race and Ethnicity			Income		
Total	1,331,848		White	90.9%		Median Income	$71,305	
Land area (sq. miles)	8,953		Black	1.2%		State Income Rank	7	
Pop/ sq mi	148.8		Latino	3.4%		Poverty Rate	8.1%	
Born in state	41.9%		Asian	2.5%		With health insurance	92.5%	
			Two or more races	1.7%		Cash public assistance	2.6%	
Age Groups			Other	0.2%		Food stamp/SNAP	7.6%	
Under 18	19.8%							
18-34	21.3%		Education			Work		
35-64	42.4%		H.S grad or less	35.1%		White Collar	40.3%	
Over 64	16.5%		Some college	28.8%		Sales and Service	39.8%	
			College Degree, 4 yr	22.3%		Blue Collar	19.9%	
Military			Post grad	13.8%		Government	13.2%	
Veteran/ Active Duty	9.6%							

Presidential Politics

2016 Primary (D)	Sanders (D)	152,193 (60%)	Clinton (D)	95,355 (38%)				
2016 Primary (R)	Trump (R)	100,735 (35%)	Kasich (R)	44,932 (16%)	Cruz (R)	33,244 (12%)		
	Rubio (R)	30,071 (11%)	Bush (R)	31,341 (11%)	Christie (R)	21,089 (7%)		
2016 Pres. Vote	Clinton (D)	348,526 (47%)	Trump (R)	345,790 (46%)	Johnson (L)	30,777 (4%)		
2012 Pres. Vote	Obama (D)	369,561 (52%)	Romney (R)	329,918 (46%)				

Before Donald Trump won the 2016 election, New Hampshire had lost a bit of its kingmaker status: the three previous presidents all captured the White House without first winning the state's revered primary. New Hampshire began conducting the first-in-the-nation primary in 1920. Since 1952, when candidates' names were first put on the ballot, it has exerted inordinate influence on the presidential selection process. The arguments for having early contests in small states is that they provide a venue in which candidates meet voters in person, listen to them, share their vision for the country, and allow citizens to gauge their character. Like Iowa, New Hampshire's retail politics offers little-known candidates the ability to propel themselves into the national spotlight. In the 1970s, the national Democratic Party tried to confine primaries to a "window" in which New Hampshire would have competition. But New Hampshire, with its don't-tread-on-me tradition, insisted it would hold its primary before the window if necessary, confident that candidates and reporters would still pay it heed even if its small delegation was not seated at the national convention as punishment. New Hampshire Secretary of State William Gardner has been in his job since 1976 and has the unilateral authority to select a primary date, a power he has wielded effectively to thwart any state that might attempt to crowd New Hampshire on the primary starting line. (Gardner, the longest serving secretary of state in the nation, won his 22nd two-year term in 2018 when the state legislature re-elected him 209-205.)

New Hampshire has long had more registered Republicans than Democrats, but "undeclared" registrants are the largest bloc of voters in the state, eclipsing the 400,000 mark in the last presidential election. They can vote in either party's presidential primary and on occasion they have provided the margin of victory for both Democratic and Republican winners. Once upon a time, the state's registered Democrats were mill workers in Manchester and other factory towns, ethnics who rejected the state's Yankee Republican establishment. Those days are long gone. The two largest cities, Manchester and Nashua, lean Democratic but can vote Republican. Democratic strength is more pronounced in the state capital of Concord and in clusters of towns around universities, including the areas around Durham (University of New Hampshire), Keene (Keene State College) and Hanover (Dartmouth College). The New Hampshire counties across the Connecticut River from Vermont are Democratic — a sort of East Vermont. Republican support can be found in the small towns and suburbs around Nashua and Manchester to which many commuters to Boston-area jobs moved in search of lower real estate and tax bills.

In 2008, despite the Republican registration advantage, there was higher turnout on the Democratic side — a harbinger of the November results. Hillary Clinton trailed Barack Obama after his win in the Iowa caucuses, but shortly before the primary, at a coffeehouse in Portsmouth, Clinton was asked how she was withstanding the rigors of campaigning, and in response she seemed to tear up as she talked about her hopes for the country. Her vulnerability generated sympathy and Clinton edged Obama 39%-36%. On the Republican side, John McCain edged Mitt Romney, 37%-32%, on his strength among independent voters. The victory revived McCain's candidacy. In 2012, New Hampshire was the site of intensive GOP campaigning. For Romney this was a must-win state: Voters knew him from his 2008 run, and he owned a summer home in Wolfeboro. Romney won the primary 39%-23% over Texas Rep. Ron Paul, whose flinty libertarianism helped him run strongest in the North Country. Former Utah Gov. Jon Huntsman came in third with 17 percent, running strongest around Concord and the Connecticut River Valley counties.

The 2016 primary was memorable for the state's voters, who turned to firebrands in both parties. Ohio Gov. John Kasich skipped the Iowa caucuses and lavished his attention on New Hampshire, holding more than 100 town hall meetings in the state. Former Florida Gov. Jeb Bush brought his mother, former First Lady Barbara Bush, to his town halls to help draw crowds. Trump campaigned vigorously in the state after his defeat in the Iowa caucuses. His raucous rallies that attracted thousands seemed to mock the state's tradition of meet-and-greets with earnest voters in living rooms. Moreover, Trump engaged in a public fight with The Union-Leader, the venerable voice of conservatism in New Hampshire, calling its publisher a "low-life." The paper ran front-page editorials attacking Trump and the animosity persisted into the general election when the paper broke a century-long streak of endorsing GOP nominees and backed Libertarian Gary Johnson. But the celebrity billionaire's brashness appealed to Republican primary-goers and Trump defeated Kasich 35%-16%. In the top 25 wealthiest towns in New Hampshire based on their median household income, Trump's average vote was 31 percent. In the bottom 25 downscale towns, Trump's average vote was 40 percent. On the Democratic side, Clinton started out with a substantial lead, but Sanders' popularity among young voters and his attacks on Wall St. fueled his 60%-38% victory. Sanders scored heavily in university towns, but he also won working-class communities like Berlin and Somersworth where Clinton had swamped Obama.

Until the 1992 election, political reporters left New Hampshire the day after the primary and never returned in the fall, since it was assumed that the state would go Republican. But in six of the seven elections since 1992, New Hampshire has voted Democratic. It has often been close: Bill Clinton in 1992, George W. Bush in 2000, and John Kerry in 2004 won the state by just one point. Hillary Clinton defeated Trump by less than 3,000 votes, or three-tenths of 1 percent. The falloff in Democratic votes was notable in working-class and old mill towns -- more than 10 points in Berlin, Claremont, Franklin and Rochester. Obama captured all four in 2012. In 2016, Trump won the latter three and Clinton narrowly carried Berlin, but the Democratic vote there fell by almost 20 percentage points. Research by University of New Hampshire professor Dante J. Scala found that several such "Trump towns" swung toward Democratic candidates in the 2018 midterms, "more sharply" than municipalities with more college-educated voters.

Congressional Districts

116th Congress Lineup	2D	115th Congress Lineup	2D

New Hampshire's two congressional districts have had roughly the same boundaries since 1881, neatly separating the Merrimack River mill towns of Manchester and Nashua, the state's largest cities, along a mostly north-south line. That was originally done to split the Catholic Democratic vote, and for years the arrangement helped Republicans hold both districts. But lately, New Hampshire's movement away from its Yankee Republican roots and its high share of independent voters have led to wild gyrations: Both seats swung to Democrats in the wave of 2006, then to Republicans in 2010, and back to Democrats in 2012 and again in 2016. The flinty 2nd District along Vermont's border has crept more Democratic than the eastern 1st District, with its tax-averse Massachusetts exiles, but it remains competitive.

In the 1st District, four consecutive contests between Republican Frank Guinta and Democrat Carol Shea-Porter that resulted in four consecutive defeats of the incumbent were followed in 2018 by the victory of Democrat Chris Pappas, whose statewide ambitions might result in a relatively short tenure. With the added volatility of divided party control of state government, with a two-year term for governor, probably the only predictability in the next redistricting is that it will be unpredictable.

Chris Sununu (R)

Elected 2016, term expires 2021, 2nd term; b. Nov. 5, 1974, Salem; Massachusetts Institute of Technology, BS 1998; Catholic; Married (Valerie); 3 children.

Elected Office: NH Executive Councilor, 2011-2017.

Professional Career: Engineer 1998-2006; Owner and Director, Sununu Enterprises 2006-2010

Office: 107 N. Main St., Concord, 03301; 603-271-2121; Fax: 603-271-7640; Website: governor.nh.gov.

State Legislature: Senate: 14D, 10R **House:** 233D, 167R

Election Results

Election	Name (Party)	Vote (%)
2018 General	Chris Sununu (R)...	302,764 (53%)
	Molly Kelly (D)..	262,359 (46%)
2018 Primary	Chris Sununu (R)..	91,025 (100%)

Chris Sununu, a member of one of New Hampshire's most durable political families, won a Democratic-held open seat in 2016 and then won reelection by a larger margin in 2018, despite a national Democratic wave and the GOP's simultaneous loss of both legislative chambers. Sununu's victory marked the first time a Republican managed to win reelection as governor in 24 years, and it mirrored the reelection wins of moderate Republican governors in the blue states of Massachusetts, Vermont and Maryland.

Sununu, who entered office as the nation's youngest governor, is a son of John H. Sununu, the former three-term governor of New Hampshire and chief of staff to President George H.W. Bush, and Nancy Sununu, a former chairwoman of the New Hampshire Republican Party. He is the brother of former Sen. and Rep. John E. Sununu. His father was legendary for his prickly nature. "Unlike the reserved Yankee reputation of many New England pols, the Sununu family brings a different brand to elected politics: combat," James Pindell wrote in the Boston Globe. Though Chris Sununu was a native of Salem New Hampshire, he graduated from a suburban Virginia high school because his father was working in Washington at the time. As a youngster, Sununu attended National Governors Association meetings and hung out with Chelsea Clinton, whose father, future president Bill Clinton, was then the governor of Arkansas. At the Massachusetts Institute of Technology, Sununu earned a degree in civil and environmental engineering, and for a decade he worked as an environmental engineer. He also served as CEO of Waterville Valley Ski Resort. His father didn't think that Chris, among his eight children, would end up going into politics, the Concord Monitor reported. But in 2010, Sununu won a seat on the state's executive council, an unusual "fourth branch of government" whose five members must approve most state contracts and confirm gubernatorial appointees. Sununu was reelected in 2012.

He set his sights higher when Maggie Hassan, the state's two-term Democratic governor, decided to challenge Republican Sen. Kelly Ayotte. Sununu joined a GOP primary field that included state Rep. Frank Edelblut, state Sen. Jeanie Forrester, and Manchester Mayor Ted Gatsas. The September primary ended up as mainly a race between Sununu and Edelblut, who ran an insurgent campaign to Sununu's right. Sununu edged Edelblut by fewer than 1,000 votes – 31 percent for Sununu, 30 percent for Edelblut, 21 percent for Gatsas, and 18 percent for Forrester. Meanwhile, on the Democratic side, the easy winner was Colin Van Ostern, who like Sununu was an incumbent member of the executive council. Van Ostern had worked for Stonyfield Yogurt, Southern New Hampshire University and Dartmouth College.

The two nominees shared an opposition to a state sales or income tax – a third-rail of New Hampshire politics – but Sununu proposed shrinking the size of government and instituting a right-to-work law, while Van Ostern supported making the state's Medicaid expansion permanent. Sununu irritated people on both sides of the abortion divide by voting as an executive councilor against renewing a state contract with Planned Parenthood in 2015 and then later voting to restore the funding. During the short sprint to Election Day, polls showed the race to be competitive.

Sununu won by two percentage points, or a little over 12,000 votes. That would ordinarily be considered a close race – but in the context of the other statewide contests that year, it was a veritable landslide. In the presidential contest, Hillary Clinton won by fewer than 3,000 votes, while in the Senate race, Hassan won by about 1,000 votes. Sununu showed electoral strength, particularly compared with Hassan's reelection two years earlier. Whereas Hassan won by a 13-point margin in 2014 and took all 10 of the state's counties that year, Van Ostern won just four.

In office, Sununu worked with a Republican-controlled legislature to sign a bill that got rid of licensing requirements for carrying a concealed pistol or revolver. Sununu achieved a significant victory when he signed a bill to partially fund all-day kindergarten, which conservative Republicans had opposed but which the public favored. Sununu also signed a bill to decriminalize marijuana. But he saw right-to-work legislation hit a roadblock in the state House, thanks to more than two dozen Republicans siding with Democrats and labor unions.

Sununu had another busy legislative year in 2018, with an ideologically mixed set of initiatives. He signed bills to bolster mental health services and child protection; to set water- and air-quality standards; to overhaul permitting for wetlands affected by development; to ban discrimination over gender identity; and to prohibit "gay conversion" therapy. Sununu pleased Democrats by signing a Medicaid expansion bill, which he had previously opposed. "This is probably the biggest single piece of landmark legislation I have been involved with as governor," Sununu bragged. Democratic celebrations were undercut by Sununu's insistence on including work requirements for beneficiaries, a plan the Trump administration later approved. Meanwhile, several legislative initiatives failed: a bill of rights for crime victims; state support for private school tuition and home schooling; and paid family and medical leave. Sununu also vetoed a bill to repeal the state's death penalty.

But the biggest controversy came when Sununu signed a GOP-backed bill to tighten voting requirements starting in 2019. The measure mandated that voters register their vehicles in the state and either have a valid New Hampshire driver's license or pledge to secure one within 60 days of casting a ballot. Sununu had originally opposed a similar bill, but relented when the state Supreme Court, in a 3-2 decision, cleared it as constitutional.

It's unusual for New Hampshire governors to be ousted after just one term, and Sununu was no exception. The Democratic primary pitted former state Sen. Molly Kelly against former Portsmouth mayor and 2016 gubernatorial candidate Steve Marchand. Marchand ran to Kelly's left, and Kelly snagged a few more establishment endorsements than Marchand did, but there were no dramatic differences between the two candidates, and Kelly won the primary, 66%-34%. Kelly, who had worked her way through college as a single mother, advocated a higher minimum wage, efforts to improve college affordability, and paid family leave; Sununu touted his low-tax agenda and the strong state economy on his watch, which included one of the nation's lowest unemployment rates. One of the strongest contrasts came in a debate, when the candidates each were asked for an occasion when they bucked their party. Sununu cited the bills on kindergarten and Medicaid, but Kelly seemed stumped. Ultimately, Sununu won, 53%-46%, including a victory in Merrimack County (Concord), which he had lost in 2016. It was a somewhat narrower margin than might have been expected, given Sununu's approval rating in the 60s and Kelly's lack of funding and national support. Still, it was a clear win – and a rarity for the New Hampshire GOP in 2018, as the party lost control of both legislative chambers in the same election. The legislative lineup posed a new challenge for the incumbent governor, but also an opportunity to double down on a more moderate agenda. In early 2019, Sununu's political intentions gained national attention when he said that he was considering a bid for the Senate in 2020. But he later said he would not run against Sen. Jeanne Shaheen.

Jeanne Shaheen (D)

Elected 2008, term expires 2020, 2nd term, b. Jan 28, 1947; St. Charles, MO; Shippensburg University (PA), B.A., 1969; University of Mississippi, M.S., 1973; Protestant - Unspecified Christian; Married (William Shaheen); 3 children; 7 grandchildren.

Elected Office: NH Senate, 1990-1996; NH Governor, 1997-2003.

Professional Career: Teacher, 1969-1971; A.A., University of NH, 1973-1974; Parents' Association Program Coordinator, 1982-1986; Manager, seasonal retail business, 1973-1976; Campaign Manager, Carter/Mondale NH presidential campaign, 1979- 80; Hart, NH pres. campaign, 1983-1984; McEachern, NH Governor campaign, 1986-1988.

DC Office: 506 HSOB 20510, 202-224-2841, Fax: 202-228-3194, shaheen.senate.gov
State Offices: Berlin, 603-752-6300; Claremont, 603-542-4872; Dover, 603-750-3004; Keene, 603-358-6604; Manchester, 603-647-7500; Nashua, 603-883-0196.

Committees: *Appropriations*: Commerce, Justice, Science & Related Agencies (RMM); Department of Homeland Security; DOL, HHS & Education & Related Agencies; Energy & Water Development; State, Foreign Operations & Related Programs. *Armed Services*: Emerging Threats & Capabilities; Readiness & Management Support; Seapower. *Ethics. Foreign Relations*: Europe & Regional Security Cooperation (RMM); Near East, South Asia, Central Asia & Counterterrorism; West Hem Crime Civ Sec Dem Rights & Women's Issues. *Small Business & Entrepreneurship.*

Group Ratings

	ADA	ACLU	AFL-CIO	LCV	ITI	COC	HAFA	ACU	CFG	FRC
2018	-	62%	-	93%	-	60%	5%	10%	6%	0%
2017	95%	C	100%	100%	C	29%	C	0%	4%	0%

Almanac Ratings 2017-18

	Economy	Social	Foreign	Composite
Liberal	97%	97%	49%	81%
Conservative	3%	3%	51%	19%

Key Votes of the 115th Congress

1. Obama-care revision	N	5. Gun regulations	N	9. Kavanaugh confirmation	N
2. Tax Cuts	N	6. Family planning regs	N	10. Saudi arms sales	Y
3. Dodd-Frank revision	Y	7. Gorsuch confirmation	N	11. FISA rules	Y
4. Omnibus appropriations	Y	8. Immigration restrictions	N	12. Military aid in Yemen	Y

Election Results

Election	Name (Party)	Vote (%)		Cand. Spent	Ind. Exp. Support	Ind. Exp. Oppose
2014 General	Jeanne Shaheen (D)	251,184	(52%)	$16,436,371	$1,402,045	$10,104,403
	Scott Brown (R)	235,347	(48%)	$9,163,652	$3,913,621	$13,027,425
2014 Primary	Jeanne Shaheen (D)	Unopposed				

Prior winning percentages: 2008 (52%); Governor: 2000 (49%), 1998 (66%), 1996 (57%)

Democrat Jeanne Shaheen, New Hampshire's senior senator, is the first woman in U.S. history to be elected both governor and senator, as well as the first in New Hampshire history elected to either of those offices. She has been a political fixture in the Granite State for four decades, first coming to notice not as a candidate but as a behind-the-scenes political operative, engineering victories for Jimmy Carter and Gary Hart in the state's first-in-the-nation presidential primary. Since being elected to the Senate in 2008, Shaheen has been a reliable Democratic vote, adept at balancing partisan loyalties with the reality that she represents a state that has become a hypersensitive political bellwether. She once taught a university course on how elected officials can overcome partisanship, and she has sought to put her lessons into practice by frequently reaching across the aisle in her legislative efforts.

On Capitol Hill, Shaheen has acquired a reputation as a disciplined politician who stays on message and refrains from headline-grabbing sound bites. Her low-key style has obscured her increasing influence on foreign policy matters. In fall 2016, Shaheen was the first senator to call for hearings into allegations of Russian interference in that year's presidential race, and she was a strong supporter of legislation the following year to tighten sanctions against Russia. The Russians retaliated. They placed Shaheen on a "blacklist" and refused to grant her a visa to travel to their country in early 2018 as part of a congressional delegation.

Shaheen has served notice that she plans to seek a third term in 2020, after narrowly winning re-election in 2014 against a political transplant, former Massachusetts Sen. Scott Brown. Born Cynthia Jeanne Bowers, she grew up in the suburbs of St. Louis Missouri, where her father was in the shoe manufacturing business and her mother was a church secretary. Shaheen can trace her Native American lineage to Pocahontas. "I actually have the family tree to show that," she told CNN in 2017. Shaheen graduated from Shippensburg College in Pennsylvania with a degree in education; after teaching for a couple of years, she earned a master's degree in political science from the University of Mississippi. She was raised in a Republican family and cast her first presidential vote for Richard Nixon in 1968. But she registered as a Democrat while at Shippensburg, where her activities reflected the campus activism of the era: She successfully challenged a curfew that applied to women but not men.

While in Mississippi, Shaheen came to admire Carter, then Georgia's governor, for his efforts to foster racial integration. In 1973, she moved to New Hampshire, where she worked as a teacher and ran a seasonal silver and leather business with her husband, attorney Bill Shaheen, a New Hampshire native who has been a behind-the-scenes political power in the state. The Shaheens were among Carter's earliest New Hampshire supporters when, in 1975, the former Georgia governor began laying the groundwork for his long-shot bid for the presidency. Carter won the 1976 New Hampshire primary, and, after winning the White House, appointed Bill Shaheen as U.S. attorney for New Hampshire. In 1980, Jeanne Shaheen was Carter's state campaign director and guided him to a 10 percentage point win in the primary over the insurgent candidacy of Massachusetts Sen. Ted Kennedy. Four years later, another long shot, Colorado Sen. Hart, recruited Shaheen to manage his New Hampshire presidential primary effort. Hart defeated the Democratic front-runner, Walter Mondale, by 9 points.

At the time, Democrats had limited success in winning statewide office in then-solidly Republican New Hampshire. Shaheen oversaw two unsuccessful efforts to elect Democrat Paul McEachern as governor in the mid- and late 1980s. In 1990, "I decided all the men I'd been working for hadn't gotten it done, so I needed to run myself," she told CNN years later. She won election to the state Senate, where she supported expanded health care coverage and term limits on federal and state legislators. In 1996, Shaheen ran for governor and faced State Board of Education Chairman Ovide Lamontagne, a strong conservative, in the general election. Shaheen took what is referred to in New Hampshire as "the pledge" — a promise to oppose an income or sales tax. Such a vow had long been politically sacrosanct in a state that has prided itself as the only one in the nation not to impose a broad-based tax. Shaheen won 57%-39%, becoming just the fifth Democrat in more than 100 years to serve as governor.

Shaheen won more funding from the Legislature for kindergarten programs and signed a bill creating a needle-exchange pilot program. She vetoed bills that would have abolished the estate tax and the death penalty. In 1997, a state Supreme Court ruling outlawed New Hampshire's system of local school financing. Shaheen proposed increasing revenues through slot machine gambling and a hike in the tobacco tax, but the court invalidated her plan in 1998. That year, when her two-year term was up, Shaheen was re-elected with 66 percent of the vote. She abandoned her pledge to oppose an income or sales tax but was still re-elected in 2000 — but only on a 5 point margin. The controversy over school funding continued, and the GOP-controlled Legislature refused to pass either an income or sales tax.

Shaheen ran for the Senate in 2002, as Republicans faced a divisive primary in which Rep. John Sununu, son and namesake of a former governor and White House chief of staff, defeated the incumbent, Robert Smith, 53%-45%. Smith had angered GOP leaders when, after a failed bid for the 2000 Republican presidential nomination, he temporarily left the party. Shaheen backed President George W. Bush's tax cuts and the invasion of Iraq. But her abandoning of the tax pledge came back to haunt her, and Sununu won 51%-46%. In the 2004 election season, Shaheen served as national chairman of Democrat John Kerry's presidential campaign and was credited with reviving his campaign in the early primaries — including helping orchestrate a victory in New Hampshire.

After Kerry's general election loss, Shaheen became director of the Kennedy School of Government's Institute of Politics at Harvard University.

Shaheen insisted she had no interest in running for office again. But after the 2006 elections, New Hampshire Democrats pressed her to seek a rematch with Sununu. In September 2007, Shaheen quit her job at Harvard and announced she was running again. While the 2008 Senate campaign had the same candidates as six years earlier, it took place in a very different political environment. In 2002, Shaheen had emphasized areas in which she agreed with Bush and congressional Republicans; in 2008, she emphasized her disagreements with them. Shaheen led in polls throughout the campaign, but Sununu rebounded after gas prices reached $4 a gallon and he criticized Shaheen's opposition to offshore oil drilling. But he lost ground in October 2008, when he voted for a $700 billion bailout of the financial industry, which Shaheen, like many nonincumbent candidates in both parties, opposed. This time, Shaheen won — 52%-45% — for the first Democratic Senate victory in New Hampshire since 1974.

Although Shaheen has stuck with her party's leadership on most major votes, her Almanac rankings placed her in the less liberal half of the Senate Democratic Caucus. While her party loyalty was rewarded with an Appropriations Committee seat in 2013, her commitment to reaching across the aisle was underscored by the four-year legislative journey of an energy efficiency bill she co-authored with Ohio Republican Rob Portman. The original legislation, introduced in 2011, sought to increase energy efficiency in buildings by offering mortgage incentives and getting the federal government more involved in working with manufacturers. Finally, in spring 2015, a stripped-down version of the bill was passed and signed into law by President Barack Obama after it was twice stalled by unrelated controversies.

As the Affordable Care Act was debated during Shaheen's first year on Capitol Hill, she got several provisions into the final bill, including one to close a loophole that had allowed drug companies to avoid competition from generic drugs. On another health issue, Shaheen's interest has been personal: Her granddaughter has Type 1 diabetes and participated in a medical trial for an artificial pancreas. The senator has been involved in numerous efforts to highlight the problems associated with juvenile diabetes and worked to persuade the Food and Drug Administration to issue "clear and reasonable guidance" on artificial pancreas devices. In recent years, she has refrained from embracing the "Medicare for All" plan pushed by her Vermont neighbor, Sen. Bernie Sanders, and other leading progressives. But she backed an unsuccessful effort to add a "public option" when the Affordable Care Act was passed, and, in early 2019, introduced legislation to give those between 50 and 64 the option of buying into Medicare.

Throughout her second term, Shaheen has focused on a problem that had become an epidemic in her home state: opioid addiction. New Hampshire ranked third nationally in per capita deaths from drug overdoses, according to the Centers for Disease Control and Prevention. At the end of 2015, Shaheen called for a $600 million appropriation to address a "national public health emergency." While the Comprehensive Addiction and Recovery Act sponsored by Shaheen was signed into law in July 2016, it contained no immediate funding. However, most of that bill's initiatives were funded six months later when Obama, as one of his last major acts in office, signed the 21st Century Cures Act with $1 billion to combat opioid addiction over a two-year period. In early 2018, Shaheen and other members of her state's congressional delegation successfully pushed to boost funding to $6 billion nationally as part of a bipartisan budget deal.

Despite representing a state where Republicans still hold a registration edge over Democrats, Shaheen has not shied away from the culture wars. As a member of the Armed Services Committee, she got provisions into the fiscal year 2013 defense authorization bill to repeal a policy denying military women abortion coverage in cases of rape or incest. She got wording into the fiscal 2016 defense authorization bill to increase access to birth control for women covered by military health programs. "Almost 15 percent of our military are now women, but the military has not developed a comprehensive program to make sure they have access to family planning, contraception and counseling," Shaheen said. Another measure signed into law in late 2016 — authored by Shaheen and two other New England Democrats, Richard Blumenthal of Connecticut and Patrick Leahy of Vermont — required that rape kits be preserved for the entire relevant statute of limitations and that victims be notified in writing 60 days before the kits are destroyed. While the requirement applied only to federal cases, the legislation included incentives for states to give survivors more information at the time they report sexual crimes.

In late 2017, Trump signed a Shaheen-authored bill titled the "Women, Peace and Security Act," requiring the president to submit a strategy to Congress "to improve the participation of women in peace and security processes, conflict prevention, peace building, and decision-making institutions."

It reflected concerns by Shaheen— the only woman on the 21-member Foreign Relations panel — about men's dominance in executive branch positions dealing with foreign policy. "There have been some people who have appeared before the Foreign Relations Committee … who have been a little condescending," Shaheen told Politico, while declining to name names. But in one episode related by the publication, Secretary of State Mike Pompeo — during a hearing in summer 2018 — repeatedly interrupted and snapped at Shaheen as she questioned him after Trump's Helsinki summit with Russian President Vladimir Putin. At the end of the hearing, Foreign Relations Committee ranking member Bob Menendez accused Pompeo of "demeaning" the New Hampshire senator.

When Gina Haspel was nominated by Trump to succeed Pompeo as head of the CIA, Shaheen in May 2018 was among just six Senate Democrats to vote to confirm her — allowing Haspel to squeak through on a 54-45 vote to become the CIA's first female director. Most Democrats refused to support Haspel because of her involvement in torturing terrorism suspects after 9/11. While calling torture inconsistent with the nation's values, Shaheen said she had "been impressed by the strong support for [Haspel's] nomination within the agency and the respect she has earned from her many years of service." Meanwhile, Shaheen's concerns about cybersecurity led her to sponsor legislation, which became law in December 2017, to bar federal government use of software from Russia's Kaspersky Lab — an enterprise she described as having "extensive ties to Russian intelligence." Barely two weeks after the bill was signed, Russia denied Shaheen a visa to travel there in early 2018. The congressional delegation was cancelled after two Republicans on the Foreign Relations panel also scheduled to go called it off in solidarity with Shaheen.

On the domestic front, Shaheen has pressed to end men's monopoly on money — at least on the images on U.S. currency. In April 2015, she boosted the campaign to put a woman on the face of the $20 bill in 2020, the centennial of the women's suffrage. Her legislation directed the Treasury Department to establish a panel to decide the matter. A month later, the "Woman on the 20s" campaign announced that Harriet Tubman had won its online poll to replace Andrew Jackson on the $20 bill, and the Obama administration committed to the change in spring 2016. But, as she pressed on the matter in mid-2018, Shaheen was told by Treasury Department officials that neither new designs for the $20 bill nor plans to put Tubman's image on it had been finalized. Shaheen told The New York Times that she was "severely disappointed by the Trump administration's failure to prioritize the redesign of the $20 bill."

With a WMUR/University of New Hampshire poll in February 2013 giving her a 59 percent approval rating, Shaheen was an early favorite to win a second term the next year. But the dynamics of the race changed when Brown announced for the Republican nomination. Four years earlier, he had capitalized on public unease over passage of the Affordable Care Act to win a special election to fill the Senate seat left vacant by Kennedy's death in solidly blue Massachusetts. In 2012, he was defeated 54%-46% by Elizabeth Warren, as Massachusetts Democratic voters came out in force to re-elect Obama.

Brown and his wife sold their Massachusetts home and moved to New Hampshire, where they long had owned a vacation home. His Granite State Senate bid gained traction by relentlessly seeking to tie Shaheen, a co-chair of the 2012 Obama campaign and a leading Obama surrogate that year, to the president. Brown repeatedly charged she had voted with Obama's position 99 percent of the time. Obama, despite having twice won the state, had seen his popularity there nosedive. A WMUR poll in August 2014 shocked political observers when it showed Shaheen with a 46%-44% lead. She hung on to win with 52 percent of the vote — blocking Brown's bid to become the first person in 135 years to represent two different states in the Senate.

While there was early speculation that Shaheen, who turns 73 in 2020, might forgo a bid for a third term, she told TV station WMUR in January 2019, "I do intend to run again in 2020." Gov. Chris Sununu and former Sen. Kelly Ayotte — narrowly ousted by Shaheen's colleague, Sen. Maggie Hassan, in 2016 — were the leading potential challengers. But Ayotte, defeated with Trump at the top of the ticket, was said to be reluctant to run again in a presidential year. In March 2019, Sununu said, "I don't rule anything out" and called Shaheen "very vulnerable." Polls showed Shaheen and Sununu, both popular figures in the state, neck-and-neck in a hypothetical matchup. Two months later, Sununu announced he would seek re-election as governor while attacking Shaheen, declaring, "We all know that I would defeat Jeanne Shaheen, but others can too." But his move left state Republicans without a top-tier challenger to Shaheen's re-election.

Maggie Hassan (D)

Elected 2016, term expires 2022, 1st term, b. Feb 27, 1958; Boston, MA; Brown University (RI), A.B., 1980; Northeastern University Law School (MA), J.D., 1985; United Church of Christ; Married (Thomas Hassan); 2 children.

Elected Office: NH Governor, 2013-2016; NH Senate, 2004-2010, Majority Leader, 2008-2010.

Professional Career: Practicing attorney, 1996-2009; Association General counsel, Brigham & Women's Hosp., 1993-1996; Practicing attorney, 1985-1992; Information officer, MA Department of Social Services, 1980-1982.

DC Office: 324 HSOB 20510, 202-224-3324, Fax: 202-228-0581, hassan.senate.gov

State Offices: Berlin, 603-752-6190; Concord, 603-622-2204; Manchester, 603-622-2204; Nashua, 603-880-3314; Portsmouth, 603-433-4445.

Committees: *Finance*: Energy, Natural Resources & Infrastructure; Fiscal Responsibility & Economic Growth (RMM); Health Care. *Health, Education, Labor & Pensions*: Children & Families; Primary Health & Retirement Security. *Homeland Security & Government Affairs*: Federal Spending Oversight & Emergency Management (RMM); Investigations. *Joint Economic*.

Group Ratings

	ADA	ACLU	AFL-CIO	LCV	ITI	COC	HAFA	ACU	CFG	FRC
2018	-	62%	-	100%	-	60%	5%	14%	5%	0%
2017	95%	C	100%	100%	C	29%	C	0%	4%	0%

Almanac Ratings 2017-18

	Economy	Social	Foreign	Composite
Liberal	97%	97%	67%	87%
Conservative	3%	3%	34%	13%

Key Votes of the 115th Congress

1. Obama-care revision	N	5. Gun regulations	N	9. Kavanaugh confirmation	N
2. Tax Cuts	N	6. Family planning regs	N	10. Saudi arms sales	Y
3. Dodd-Frank revision	Y	7. Gorsuch confirmation	N	11. FISA rules	Y
4. Omnibus appropriations	Y	8. Immigration restrictions	N	12. Military aid in Yemen	Y

Election Results

Election	Name (Party)	Vote (%)		Cand. Spent	Ind. Exp. Support	Ind. Exp. Oppose
2016 General	Maggie Hassan (D)	354,649	(48%)	$18,399,896		
	Kelly Ayotte (R)	353,632	(48%)	$17,281,997	$5,671,191	$52,308,296
	Aaron Day (I)	17,742	(2%)			
2016 Primary	Maggie Hassan (D)	Unopposed				

Prior winning percentages: Governor: 2014 (53%), 2012 (55%)

When, after months of effort, national Democrats persuaded Gov. Maggie Hassan to forgo a bid for a third term in favor of a run against Republican Sen. Kelly Ayotte, it marked one of their biggest recruiting coups of the 2016 election cycle. Ayotte and Hassan were regarded as perhaps New Hampshire's most popular politicians, and persuading Hassan to run was key to the Democratic strategy of putting enough seats in play to retake the Senate majority. While the party fell short of the latter goal, the recruitment of Hassan paid off, as she was one of just two Democrats nationwide to win a Senate race against an incumbent Republican that year. The other was Tammy Duckworth of Illinois.

Hassan's election made her only the second woman in U.S. history to have served both as a governor and a senator. The first was Hassan's colleague, Democratic Sen. Jeanne Shaheen, whom Hassan considers a mentor. In a chamber where relationships between senators from the same state are often tenuous and sometimes strained owing to past rivalries and future ambitions, the two women representing the Granite State are notable for their closeness. Shaheen helped launch Hassan's political career two decades ago by naming her to a state advisory board. In the Senate, they have been remarkably similar in voting records and operating styles: Both are regarded as highly disciplined politicians who choose their words carefully to remain on message. In fact, during her 2016 race against Ayotte, Hassan at times was so disciplined that she was dinged for repeating talking points and coming off as stiff in media interviews, according to the Concord Monitor.

Born Margaret Wood, Hassan grew up steeped in politics. Raised in the upscale Boston suburb of Lincoln, she was the daughter of Robert C. Wood, a MIT political science professor who was an adviser to John F. Kennedy during the 1960 presidential campaign. Wood later played a leading role in creating the Department of Housing and Urban Development under President Lyndon B. Johnson before serving as president of the University of Massachusetts and superintendent of the Boston school system. A stream of influential guests coursed through the Wood household, and dinner conversations often focused on current events. "My father used to actually go around the table person by person and ask them what they thought, so everybody from family members to our guests were expected to either think out loud or have an opinion, and we did," Hassan told the New Hampshire Union Leader. Hassan earned her undergraduate degree at Brown University and her law degree at Northeastern University and practiced law in Boston — including a stint as a corporate attorney for Brigham and Women's Hospital.

She and her husband, Tom Hassan, met as undergraduates at Brown. The Hassans' connection to New Hampshire dates back to the late 1980s when Tom Hassan was appointed to the faculty of the Phillips Exeter Academy, an elite prep school that he later headed. The couple has two children, one of whom, an adult son, has cerebral palsy. Maggie Hassan credits him with inspiring her career in public service, which began in 1999 when then-Gov. Shaheen appointed Hassan as a citizen adviser to the state's Adequacy in Education and Finance Commission. Hassan had become involved in disability rights activism while working to ensure the elementary school attended by her son, Ben, could accommodate his needs. She often has recalled her feelings while watching her son, then 3, get picked up by the bus for his first day of pre-school. "That really got me focused on the work that other families and advocates and elected leaders had done so that, on that day, my son wasn't in an institution," she told Roll Call. "He was going to school and he was having a chance to learn and make friends." Ben Hassan was featured in the first TV ad of his mother's 2016 Senate campaign.

In 2002, Hassan lost a state Senate contest to incumbent Republican Russell Prescott but came back two years later and beat him — serving six years until he reclaimed the seat in 2010. During her three terms, Hassan held several leadership positions, culminating with majority leader. One of her initial accomplishments was helping to pass a bill offering universal kindergarten: At the time, New Hampshire was the only state in the nation without such a law. As majority leader, she proposed a bill in 2010 to set up a commission to regulate health care costs. As the Affordable Care Act was being debated in Washington, state Republicans jabbed at the idea as "Maggie Care." The bill that passed established the commission, but without authority to limit rates. A year earlier, Hassan was more successful on the issue of same-sex marriage. Several of her Democratic colleagues were reluctant to tackle the subject, but Hassan persuaded them to move ahead — and she played an integral role in New Hampshire becoming one of the first states to legalize same-sex marriage, six years before the Supreme Court ruling that recognized such unions nationwide.

After Democratic Gov. John Lynch announced in September 2011 that he would not seek a fifth two-year term, Hassan got into the gubernatorial race. She promised to restore $50 million in funding for the University System of New Hampshire that the Legislature had cut in exchange for a two-year tuition freeze. She also backed a proposed casino on the Massachusetts border to raise revenue in a state that stands alone in its lack of a broad-based tax. Hassan easily won a three-way Democratic primary; her Republican opponent in November was attorney Ovide Lamontagne, a hard-line conservative who had run unsuccessfully for governor in 1996 against Shaheen and then lost to Ayotte in the 2010 Senate primary. Polls in the campaign's final weeks showed a close race, but President Barack Obama's strong showing helped Hassan to a 55%-43% victory. A historic milestone accompanied Hassan's victory: For the next two years, New Hampshire was the first state ever to have a female governor and an all-female congressional delegation.

Taking office with a House that had been returned to Democratic control but a Senate that remained in Republican hands, Hassan stressed the need for bipartisanship: It paid off when the two-year budget that she signed her first year passed the Senate unanimously and cleared the 400-member House with fewer than 20 dissenting votes. She made good on one campaign vow when her first budget restored the cuts made to the university system during the Republicans' 2011-2012 control of the Legislature. But she fell short in delivering on her promise to legalize casino gambling at a time when neighboring states were moving to do so. In her second year in office, Hassan secured bipartisan support to expand Medicaid under the Affordable Care Act. The expansion allowed 50,000 low-income New Hampshire residents to receive subsidized health care and covered substance abuse treatment in a state besieged by heroin and opioid addiction.

In 2014, Hassan faced Republican Walt Havenstein, the former CEO of defense contractor BAE Systems — an international firm with a significant presence in New Hampshire. He pumped $2 million of his own money into his bid. But Hassan prevailed 53%-47% during an election cycle inhospitable to Democrats nationally. Hassan had a bumpy second term, as she faced an all-Republican Legislature. She vetoed bills that would have curbed the Common Core education standards and allowed the concealed carrying of firearms without a license. She also had to deal with a protracted budget impasse with the Legislature in her second year after vetoing a Republican-authored budget over objections to business tax cuts it contained. On the issue that had brought her into politics, she signed the nation's first law banning sub-minimum wages for people with disabilities. In spring 2015, a string of favorable poll results in a hypothetical Senate matchup fueled continuing speculation that she would challenge Ayotte. Republicans seemed to have little doubt about Hassan's intentions; by the end of summer, GOP-allied outside groups had spent more than $2 million in ads seeking to weaken her political standing. In September, a Democratic-aligned PAC was up with a second ad to counter the Republican media effort against Hassan, and, a month later, she announced her Senate bid.

First elected in the Republican wave year of 2010, Ayotte was facing the voters again in a purple state that had trended Democratic in presidential years over the previous quarter-century. During Ayotte's first term, her voting record took a turn to the political center, and she sought to play up her differences with her party's leadership on issues ranging from immigration to air pollution. In a July 2016 interview with Boston magazine, Ayotte characterized herself as "independent" four separate times and boasted repeatedly of working "across the aisle" in a clear effort to draw a distinction with Hassan. "I'm not hesitant to take on my party or the other side. I don't see that same level of independence from her," Ayotte said. Hassan, in turn, pointed to her dealing with legislatures partly or totally under Republican control. "I have a real record of working with members of the opposite party, having disagreements with them, to be sure, but then getting results," Hassan told USA Today.

As polls gave Democratic presidential nominee Hillary Clinton a significant lead in New Hampshire over Donald Trump, Hassan relentlessly sought to tie Ayotte to Trump. Ayotte, meanwhile, was bedeviled by trying to thread the needle between assuaging Trump's base of GOP supporters and appealing to the independents who make up 40 percent of the state's electorate. When it became apparent Trump would be his party's nominee, the Ayotte campaign initially said she would "support" Trump but not "endorse" him — a semantical exercise greeted in political circles with at best puzzlement and at worst ridicule. For months, she stuck by her support of the nominee, even as Trump took public swipes at Ayotte for her efforts to distance herself from him. In early October, the "Access Hollywood" tape with Trump making lewd comments about women emerged, prompting Ayotte to disavow him and say she would write in the name of GOP vice presidential nominee Mike Pence for president. An outside group aligned with Clinton ran ads accusing Ayotte of "running away [from Trump] to save her political career."

On Election Day, Hassan came out on top by just over 1,000 votes out of more than 708,000 cast. By the time it was over, spending had exceeded $131 million. Spending by the candidates themselves totaled $38 million, with Ayotte expending about $1 million more than Hassan. But Hassan enjoyed a $10 million advantage in the more than $93 million pumped in by outside groups. It was the second most expensive Senate race in the country in 2016, according to the Center for Responsive Politics.

During Hassan's first year in the Senate, Almanac vote ratings scored her as slightly more liberal than Shaheen, although both senators placed well within the more centrist segment of the Democratic Caucus. In voting on 22 nominees for Cabinet and other top-ranking executive branch positions in early 2017, the two New Hampshire senators had identical records: They opposed confirmation of half of Trump's nominees. But in a rare split a year later, Hassan and Shaheen came down on opposite sides when Gina Haspel was nominated to be the CIA's first female director. Hassan joined most Democrats in voting against Haspel, saying, "I agree with my colleague Sen. John McCain that her record and her perspective on torture are disqualifying."

Hassan gained notice during the confirmation hearing of Betsy DeVos, Trump's choice for Education secretary. As a new member of the Health, Education, Labor and Pensions Committee, Hassan pressed DeVos on the issue that had gotten her into politics 20 years earlier: disability rights. When DeVos said that enforcement of the rights of students with disabilities was best left to the states, Hassan pounced. She asked DeVos if she were aware that such matters were governed by federal law, the Individuals with Disabilities Education Act. "I may have confused it," DeVos said. Hassan Responded: "I have to say, I'm concerned that you seem so unfamiliar with it." She also charged that DeVos' support for private school vouchers would turn public schools "into warehouses for the most challenging kids with disabilities or other kinds of particular issues."

In April 2017, after a video showing a passenger being dragged off an overbooked United Airlines flight went viral, Hassan — then a member of the Commerce, Science and Transportation Committee — introduced legislation to strengthen passenger rights in such situations. It became law as part of a Federal Aviation Administration authorization bill signed by Trump in late 2018. Hassan also succeeded in adding provisions to the FAA measure to ensure air travel accommodations consider the needs of all people with disabilities. Hassan got a coveted slot on the Finance Committee in 2019, and she took on political responsibilities as chairwoman of the Women's Senate Network — an arm of the Democratic Senatorial Committee charged with working to elect women.

Closer to home, Hassan found herself dealing with the issue that had emerged as a crisis during her tenure as governor: opioid abuse. With New Hampshire ranking third nationally in per capita deaths from drug overdoses, she sought to turn up the heat on the White House. In a February 2018 Time magazine op-ed three months after release of a report by a Trump-appointed commission on the issue, Hassan wrote, "We have seen almost no action from the administration on the commission's recommendations, and the Trump administration has not been willing to lead in pushing for additional federal resources." Shortly afterward, as part of a two-year bipartisan spending deal on Capitol Hill, Hassan and Shaheen boosted funds to combat the opioid epidemic to $6 billion, up from $1 billion the previous two years. Hassan and other New Hampshire members succeeded in changing the formula for allocating funds to translate into a more than seven-fold increase in money directed to New Hampshire to fight opioid addiction.

Chris Pappas (D)

Elected 2018, 1st term, b. Jun 04, 1980; Manchester; Harvard College (MA), B.A., 2002; Greek Orthodox; Single.

Elected Office: NH House, 2002-2006; Hillsborough County Treasurer, 2007-2011; NH Executive Council, 2013-18.

Professional Career: Co-Owner & Operator, Puritan Restaurant.

DC Office: 323 CHOB 20515, 202-225-5456, pappas.house.gov

State Offices: Dover, 603-285-4300.

Committees: *Transportation & Infrastructure*: Coast Guard & Maritime Transportation; Highways & Transit; Water Resources & Environment. *Veterans' Affairs*: Economic Opportunity; Oversight & Investigations (Chmn).

Election Results

Election	Name (Party)	Vote (%)		Cand. Spent	Ind. Exp. Support	Ind. Exp. Oppose
2018 General	Christopher C. Pappas (D)	155,884	(54%)	$2,090,554	$620,304	
	Eddie Edwards (R)	130,996	(45%)	$1,202,298	$58,249	$604,142
	Dan Belforti (Lib)	4,048	(1%)			
2018 Primary	Christopher C. Pappas (D)	26,875	(42%)			
	Maura Sullivan (D)	19,313	(30%)			
	Mindi Messmer (D)	6,142	(10%)			
	Naomi Andrews (D)	4,508	(7%)			

Freshman Democrat Chris Pappas built on his strong local roots and political experience to defeat vigorous opponents in both the primary and general elections. At age 38, he had served in elected office since 2002 — most recently, on the influential state Executive Council. Pappas was well-known locally as the hands-on co-owner of Puritan Backroom, a popular Manchester restaurant that his family has operated for more than a century. He replaced Democratic Rep. Carol Shea-Porter, who retired after having served four terms—during which she lost two reelection campaigns.

Pappas, whose paternal great-grandfather emigrated from Greece as a young man, got his bachelor's degree from Harvard University in 2002 and was elected later that year to the state House. After four years in that position, he served four years as treasurer of Hillsborough County. In the Republican year of 2010, he lost reelection by 17 votes — the only setback of his career. He returned in 2012 to win a seat on the five-member Executive Council, defeating the Republican to whom he had lost two years earlier. Pappas had been widely expected for some time to run for Congress or a statewide office.

With Shea-Porter's retirement, Pappas was the early frontrunner to succeed her. He was supported by many of his state's Democratic leaders, including its two senators. His road to the Democratic nomination grew more complicated when Maura Sullivan, who had two degrees from Harvard and was an Iraq war veteran, entered the contest. Sullivan held senior jobs at the Veterans Affairs and Defense departments in the Obama administration and was well-financed, though largely from out-of-state.

The chief controversy surrounding her campaign was that she was a native of the Chicago area and had explored a campaign in 2018 for a House seat in Illinois until deciding to settle in New Hampshire. Sullivan responded that she had enjoyed vacations with her family in New Hampshire and that she campaigned for Shea-Porter when she was at Harvard. Pappas largely avoided direct attacks on Sullivan's residency, though he urged all candidates to sign a "Homegrown Candidate Pledge" that they would raise at least half of their campaign funds from the district.

In the 11-candidate field, Pappas and Sullivan raised far more money than the others. Sullivan reported $2 million in spending, while Pappas spent nearly $1 million prior to the primary. Some of his opponents criticized Pappas for not supporting more specific policies, especially on health care. Sullivan sought to link herself to the demand for more women to serve in Congress, though that argument was more difficult in New Hampshire — where all four members of the congressional delegation were Democratic women. Pappas won the nomination with 42 percent of the vote to 30 percent for Sullivan. Among the other candidates was Levi Sanders, son of the Vermont senator, who finished seventh with 2 percent of the vote.

The Republican nominee, Eddie Edwards, ran a small business and had been a local police chief. He embraced President Donald Trump and conservative views and was well-financed, though less than Pappas. A notable feature of the November contest in grassroots New Hampshire was their bios: Edwards is African American and Pappas is openly gay. Those personal details did not appear to be major factors for most voters.

With his victory, Pappas was well-positioned to await an opening for a Senate bid. As far back as 2015, in a profile in the New Hampshire Union-Leader, leading state Democrats agreed that he was a prime prospect for such an option.

NH-1: Eastern New Hampshire   Cook Partisan Voting Index: R+2

Population		Race and Ethnicity		Income	
Total	670,467	White	91.2%	Median Income	$72,003
Land area (sq. miles)	2,464	Black	1.3%	District Income Rank	81
Pop/ sq mi	272.1	Latino	3.3%	Poverty Rate	8%
Born in State	41.7%	Asian	2.4%	With health insurance	92.4%
		Two or more races	1.7%	Cash public assistance	2.7%
Age Groups		Other	0.2%	Food stamp/SNAP	7.5%
Under 18	19.8%				
18-34	21.9%	**Education**		**Work**	
35-64	42.3%	H.S grad or less	33.9%	White Collar	16%
Over 64	16%	Some college	29.1%	Sales and Service	40.5%
		College Degree, 4 yr	23.4%	Blue Collar	19%
Military		Post grad	13.6%	Government	12.8%
Veteran/ Active Duty	9.8%				

2012 Pres. Vote	Obama	179,148	(50%)	Romney	173,419	(48%)		
2016 Pres. Vote	Trump	179,259	(48%)	Clinton	173,344	(46%)	Johnson	15,994	(4%)

Manchester: The greatest growth in New Hampshire over the past two decades has been in the southeast and south-central parts of the state — the Seacoast and the Manchester area. Manchester was once famous for the Amoskeag Mills, the world's largest textile mill complex. In the first half of the 20th century, it was the quintessential mill town, with a few mansions for mill owners and managers and closely packed neighborhoods of frame houses for mill workers, many of them immigrants — from Quebec, Ireland and Greece. A quarter of New Hampshire residents claim French or French-Canadian ties, and racial minorities are sparse here. By the beginning of the 21st century, Manchester was something quite different: a high-tech city, with big shopping malls at freeway interchanges, a spiffy new airport and downtown arena, a more prominent university presence, spruced-up neighborhoods, and growth extending to the wooded suburbs all around. The "Queen City is becoming hip," New Hampshire magazine wrote in August 2018. "Manufacturing, in a way, still exists here – but rather than textiles, it's in the form of engineered human tissues at the Advanced Regenerative Manufacturing Institute.

The Seacoast, within easy commuting distance of Massachusetts, is a collection of towns of ancient pedigree and high-tech growth along the 18-mile coastline. The biggest city on the coast is Portsmouth, the colonial capital of New Hampshire, with its busy naval shipyard and old seaport with well-preserved homes and a solid local economy that includes many art galleries and bars. In 2017, the shipyard had 2,600 civilian employees who lived in New Hampshire and 3,800 in Maine. In March 2018, a $158 million bridge opened from Portsmouth to Kittery Maine, replacing a 76-year-old span. Pease International Tradeport, which had been the site of an Air Force Base until 1991, now houses more than 250 businesses and nearly 10,000 jobs on the Seacoast.

The 1st Congressional District of New Hampshire includes the Manchester area and the Seacoast from Manchester and next-door Bedford, its affluent suburb, east to Portsmouth. It extends north to include Laconia and gentrifying Lake Winnipesaukee, studded with summer resorts and new mansions, including the $10 million vacation home in Wolfeboro of freshman Republican Sen. Mitt Romney of Utah. Politically, this is the slightly more Republican of New Hampshire's two congressional districts. It has been the destination of many people fleeing high taxes in Massachusetts.

Portsmouth, with its trendy coffee shops, is Democratic, as are Durham, home of the University of New Hampshire, and nearby Dover, once a mill town and now the second fastest-growing city in the state. Most of the smaller towns on the Seacoast and to the north have been solidly Republican, though that is changing. Donald Trump won this swing district in 2016, 47%-46%.

Ann Kuster (D)

Elected 2012, 4th term, b. Sep 05, 1956; Concord; Dartmouth College, A.B., 1978; Georgetown University Law Center (DC), J.D., 1984; Christian Church; Married (Brad Kuster); 2 children.

Professional Career: Owner, Newfound Strategies, 2011-2013; Practicing lawyer, 1984-2010; Legislative aide, U.S. Rep. Pete McCloskey, 1978-1981.

DC Office: 320 CHOB 20515, 202-225-5206, Fax: 202-225-2946, kuster.house.gov

State Offices: Concord, 603-226-1002; Littleton, 603-444-7700; Nashua, 603-595-2006.

Committees: *Energy & Commerce*: Energy; Health; Oversight & Investigations.

Group Ratings

	ADA	ACLU	AFL-CIO	LCV	ITI	COC	HAFA	ACU	CFG	FRC
2018	-	74%	-	89%	-	70%	6%	14%	13%	0%
2017	90%	C	95%	94%	C	57%	C	0%	0%	11%

Almanac Ratings 2017-18

	Economy	Social	Foreign	Composite
Liberal	81%	91%	76%	83%
Conservative	19%	9%	24%	17%

Key Votes of the 115th Congress

1. Obama-care revision	N	5. Family planning regs	N	9. Guantanamo prisoners	Y
2. Tax Cuts	N	6. Body cameras/immigration	Y	10. Ground missiles, limit	Y
3. Omnibus appropriations	Y	7. Abortion ban	N	11. Defense Dept. spending	Y
4. Dodd-Frank revision	Y	8. Concealed carry	N	12. FISA rules	Y

Election Results

Election	Name (Party)	Vote (%)		Cand. Spent	Ind. Exp. Support	Ind. Exp. Oppose
2018 General	Ann Kuster (D).................................	155,358	(56%)	$2,607,597	$4,423	
	Steve Negron (R)...............................	117,990	(42%)	$415,392	$1,709	
	Justin O'Donnell (Lib)........................	6,206	(2%)			
2018 Primary	Ann Kuster (D)...		(100%)			

Prior winning percentages: 2016 (50%), 2014 (61%), 2012 (50%)

Democrat Ann McLane Kuster, elected in 2012, has emphasized bipartisanship in both her legislative work and her campaigns. She has achieved some success in Congress dealing with opioid addiction and veterans' health issues. With her new seat on the Energy and Commerce Committee, she gained additional opportunities to shape the debate.

Kuster was born in Concord and is part of a prominent political family in the Granite State. Her great-grandfather John McLane served as governor from 1905 to 1907, while her father, Malcolm McLane, was mayor of Concord and an unsuccessful gubernatorial candidate in 1972. Her mother, Susan McLane, was a Republican state legislator for 25 years. "Politics was sort of a way of life in our family," Kuster said.

Kuster worked on the 1972 presidential campaign of Republican Rep. Pete McCloskey of California, an anti-Vietnam War candidate who launched a quixotic challenge against President Richard Nixon. Kuster later graduated from Dartmouth College and worked in McCloskey's Washington office for three years. Kuster earned her law degree from Georgetown University and returned to Manchester to practice law. She spent many years in Concord as a lobbyist and adoption lawyer. "I represented women with unplanned pregnancies from age 14 to 40, and they ranged from living in their car to living in the nicest neighborhoods in town," she said. "Unplanned pregnancy is an equal-opportunity affliction." Kuster also became immersed in politics, and toured New Hampshire with Barack Obama during his 2008 presidential campaign.

In 2010, Kuster faced off against veteran Republican Rep. Charlie Bass, and was the underdog in a strong year for Republicans. She criticized his role in securing tax rebates for wood-pellet stove buyers before investing in a wood-pellet stove company himself. Bass denied any wrongdoing, but the issue gave her momentum. The incumbent Bass was outspent 2-to-1, but he eked out the victory 48%-47%. Their rematch two years later came in a political climate more favorable to Kuster. She supported the Democrats' 2010 health care overhaul, and Bass called the law a "bureaucratic boondoggle." Kuster again outspent Bass by more than a million dollars and had a comparable advantage in outside money. This time she won, 50%-45%.

In the House, Kuster has had several accomplishments on veterans' issues. During her first term, the House passed her bill to improve health care options for veterans. In 2016, she won support for her bill to create opportunities for veterans to become physicians after their military service. Her interest in opioid addiction extended to the broader community. New Hampshire has been among the states with the highest rates of opioid overdoses. That year, she enacted two proposals that sought additional treatment for addiction that related to mental health or substance abuse. She enacted another bill that assured federal jurisdiction over offenses committed by U.S. personnel stationed in Canada for border-security initiatives.

In 2018, Kuster organized a bipartisan heroin and opioid task force to seek a comprehensive response, both at home and in Washington. That led to passage of multiple bills dealing with treatment, recovery, prevention and law enforcement — including the creation of opioid recovery centers in states that were hardest hit by the epidemic, and loan repayment programs for students who become professionals in treatment of substance abuse. "At a time of heightened partisanship, it's rare in Washington to have such a large group of members put their differences aside," she said.

In the New Hampshire swing-seat tradition, Kuster has continued to have competitive campaigns. In 2014, she faced a challenge from state Rep. Marilinda Garcia, a young conservative Latina activist. Kuster called her opponent "naïve," and won 55%-45%. Against underfunded Republican challenger

Jim Lawrence in 2016, Kuster was held to a 50%-45% win. In 2018, she faced state Rep. Steve Negron, a businessman who emphasized his support for President Donald Trump. Kuster criticized Republican tax cuts but cast herself in bipartisan terms, including her work on opioids. Speaking in a campaign ad, she said, "the truth is, both parties, need to stop playing games and work together on the problems we face," which she called "the New Hampshire way." Kuster outspent Negron, $2.6 million to $415,000 and won, 56%-42%.

Kuster received unusual attention in October 2016 following the revelations by Trump of his groping of women. In interviews with New Hampshire reporters, she described publicly for the first time how she had been assaulted as a young woman, including an incident four decades earlier when she was working for McCloskey. While seated during a lunch on Capitol Hill next to famed South African heart-transplant surgeon Christiaan Barnard, who died in 2001, she said she realized that his hand was underneath her skirt. "I was just shocked. I didn't feel anything. I didn't know what to do. I was in the middle of a meeting. I didn't have the presence of mind to leave," Kuster told the New Hampshire Union Leader.

Kuster gained positive notice when she led Democratic women in "raise the roof" dance moves after Trump unexpectedly noted the increased number of women in the House — mostly Democrats and mostly wearing white for that evening -- during his State of the Union message in February 2019. "Raise the roof" means "raising expectations, and fulfilling our goals and our dreams," she told a reporter, after she was positively depicted in a sketch on Saturday Night Live that week.

NH-2: Western New Hampshire

Cook Partisan Voting Index: D+2

Population			Race and Ethnicity		Income	
Total	661,381		White	90.7%	Median Income	$70,531
Land area (sq. miles)	6,489		Black	1.1%	District Income Rank	90
Pop/ sq mi	101.9		Latino	3.5%	Poverty Rate	8.2%
Born in State	42.2%		Asian	2.6%	With health insurance	92.7%
			Two or more races	1.7%	Cash public assistance	2.5%
Age Groups			Other	0.3%	Food stamp/SNAP	7.6%
Under 18	19.8%					
18-34	20.9%		**Education**		**Work**	
35-64	42.4%		H.S grad or less	36.4%	White Collar	16.9%
Over 64	16.9%		Some college	28.5%	Sales and Service	39%
			College Degree, 4 yr	21.1%	Blue Collar	20.7%
Military			Post grad	14%	Government	13.6%
Veteran/ Active Duty	9.5%					

2012 Pres. Vote	Obama	190,413	(54%)	Romney	156,499	(44%)			
2016 Pres. Vote	Clinton	175,182	(48%)	Trump	166,531	(45%)	Johnson	14,783	(4%)

Nashua, Concord: Political reporters covering New Hampshire's first-in-the-nation primary usually stay in Manchester, the state's largest city and within an hour's drive of the rest of the state except for the North Country. Yet there are other noteworthy cities and towns in New Hampshire. Concord, north of Manchester, is the state capital. On one side of Main Street is the handsome, small, granite capitol, and on the other you can usually find the headquarters of the two political parties and many candidates: an entire state's politics within 100 yards. Nashua, south of Manchester and on the Massachusetts line, is twice the size of Concord and the state's second-largest city, a technology and financial services center that has been mostly booming for three decades. Local officials have been exploring the start of rail service from Nashua to Boston. To the east is prosperous and growing Salem, first chartered in 1750 and the largest of the border suburbs.

To the west near the Vermont border, past the pleasant country around Mount Monadnock, is Keene (pop., 22,949), the hub of southwest New Hampshire, and the largest city in the state north or west of Concord. The town has built a "creative economy" that attracts artists and cultural events. To the north are towns along the Connecticut River; some are mill towns, and some are vacation enclaves. Hanover, home of Dartmouth College, is a tiny, picturesque town set in the mountains. Farther north is Littleton, where the local tax base more than tripled between 1995 and 2018. Every political reporter's itinerary has to include a trip, usually by plane, to the little lumber mill city of Berlin in the middle of the North Country, where the last paper mill has closed; biomass and other forms of renewable energy have been growing, with subsidies from the state. At Dixville Notch in the White Mountains, the town's handful of voters cast their ballots at a minute past midnight and provide the first reported returns in every presidential election.

The 2nd Congressional District of New Hampshire includes Concord, Nashua, Salem, Keene, the Connecticut River counties, Hanover, Berlin and Dixville Notch. It includes Mount Washington, with its spectacularly violent weather and winds that have been measured up to 231 miles per hour; entrepreneurs have considered wind power plants, but the manager of its state park said the location was too windy and icy to be practical. The district takes in the Bretton Woods resort, where the world monetary system was established at a conference in 1944.

Politically, this region is mixed, though it has become the more Democratic of New Hampshire's two congressional districts. The area between Mount Monadnock and Keene and the territory running north along the Connecticut River to Hanover and Dartmouth had become very Democratic, much like Vermont across the river. In 2016 Hillary Clinton led Donald Trump by only 48%-45%, a significant tightening of the double-digit leads that Barack Obama had in his two campaigns. A state map shows that many of the interior towns had moved from blue to red.

NEW JERSEY

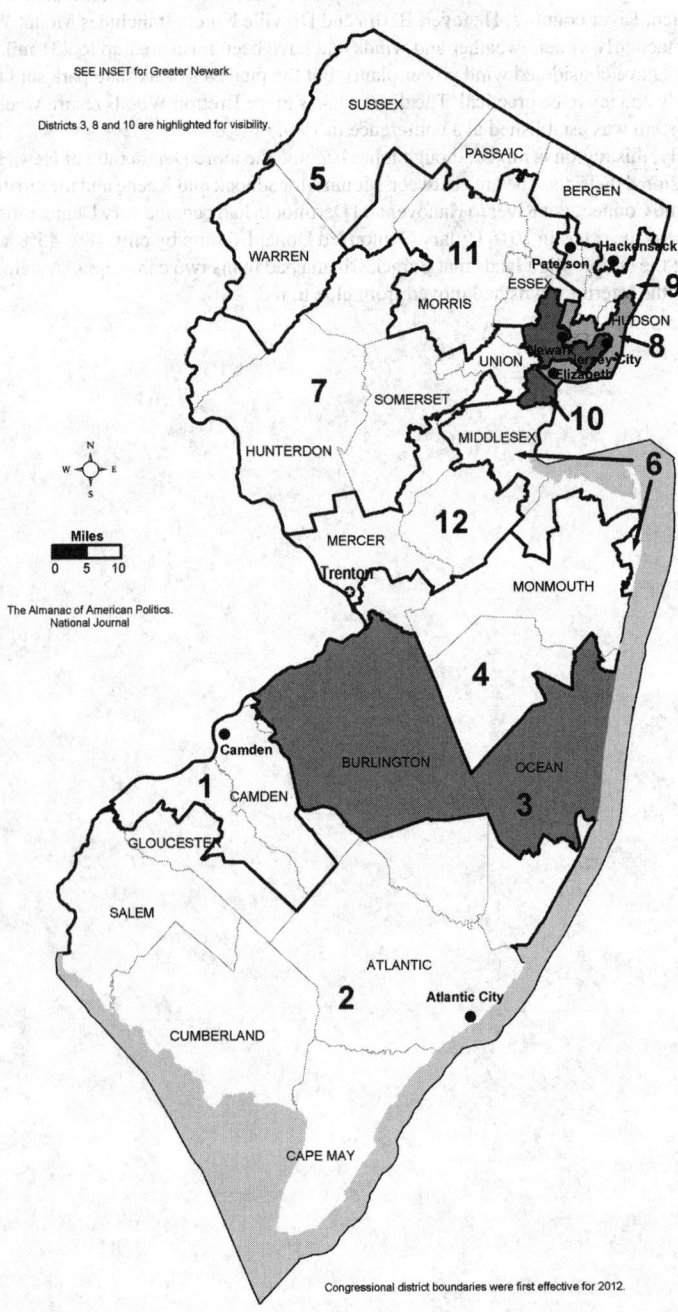

SEE INSET for Greater Newark.

Districts 3, 8 and 10 are highlighted for visibility.

SUSSEX

PASSAIC

BERGEN

5

11

WARREN

Hackensack

Paterson

MORRIS

ESSEX

9

HUDSON

8

Newark Jersey City

Elizabeth

UNION

7

SOMERSET

10

HUNTERDON

MIDDLESEX

6

12

MERCER

Trenton

The Almanac of American Politics.
National Journal

MONMOUTH

4

Camden

BURLINGTON

OCEAN

1

CAMDEN

3

GLOUCESTER

SALEM

ATLANTIC

2

Atlantic City

CUMBERLAND

CAPE MAY

Congressional district boundaries were first effective for 2012.

New Jersey leaned Republican from the 1940s through the 1980s, but over the past two decades it has become a Democratic bastion due to a growing immigrant population and the presence of many affluent suburbanites who reject the GOP's conservative stands on cultural issues. The state hasn't been a presidential battleground for a generation, and no Republican has won a Senate election since 1972.

From its notoriety as the setting for the mobster series The Sopranos to the grating stereotypes of its citizens on Jersey Shore, New Jersey gets a bad rap, and it has for a long time. During his two years as governor, Woodrow Wilson said, just a tad defensively, New Jersey is "a sort of laboratory in which the best blood is prepared for other communities to thrive on." Its early settlers included Dutch in towns behind the Palisades on the Hudson and Quakers on Delaware River bottomlands opposite Philadelphia. From the start, New Jersey was plagued by rival claims from its neighbors and, still defensive in the 1980s, went to the Supreme Court to argue that it and not New York owns the Statue of Liberty and Ellis Island. New Jersey eventually got most of the acreage, but New York got the immigrant museum and the Great Hall, which are built on fill land. For a century after the American Revolution, New Jersey was a modest, slow-growing, even backward state. It became known as the Garden State because of its vegetable farms, which supplied the tomatoes for Campbell's Soup, based in Camden. (In 1954, Gov. Robert Meyner vetoed a bill to add the nickname to license plates, saying, "I do not believe that the average citizen of New Jersey regards his state as more peculiarly identifiable with gardening for farming than any of its other industries or occupations." But the legislature overrode the veto, and the phrase remains.)

While Jersey City, Newark and Camden grew to be significant cities in their own right, New Jersey's proximity to New York and Philadelphia attracted immigrants and inventors. Thomas Edison churned out inventions in his laboratory at Menlo Park and gave birth to General Electric and Bell Labs. On open fields near large labor pools, U.S. automakers built assembly plants in the years after World War II, and the container port on the New Jersey side of New York Harbor overshadowed the crumbling docks of Manhattan and Brooklyn. Much of the pharmaceutical industry came to be concentrated in New Jersey, including the headquarters of Merck, Johnson & Johnson, Bristol-Myers Squibb, Novartis and Schering-Plough. Connected to Wall Street by Hudson River tunnels and ferries, New Jersey became the home of finance professionals and lawyers. This economy gave the state a high median income, a well-educated workforce and a prosperous middle class, with a high concentration of scientists and engineers. But while New Jersey has long had one of the highest median household incomes of any state — currently second in the nation at more than $80,000 – it also has, by some measures, some of the starkest income inequality in the nation. While about 12 percent of households have incomes above $200,000, the state's poverty rate remains higher than it was in 2008, before the Great Recession.

Physically, New Jersey has been transformed in recent decades. The oil tank farms, concrete ribbons of turnpike and Meadowlands swamps — places where young people would "meet 'neath that giant Exxon sign / that brings this fair city light," in the words of native son Bruce Springsteen — are still there, but they have been joined by sports palaces and office complexes. The Singer factory in Elizabeth, the Western Electric factory in Kearny and the Ford Motor plant in Mahwah are all gone, replaced by shopping centers and hotels. The intersection of Interstates 78 and 287 has become a major shopping and office edge city. U.S. 1 north from ivy-draped Princeton University to New Brunswick, home of the state university, Rutgers, has become one of the nation's high-tech centers. The state is overrun by municipalities -- 565 of them, with 590 school districts. This, combined with the home-rule tradition by which they handle their affairs, has shaped the state's politics, including its high property taxes.

Within New Jersey's close boundaries is great diversity — geographically, from beaches to mountains; demographically, from old Quaker stock to new Hispanic arrivals; and economically, from inner-city slums to hunt-country mansions. Although New York writers are inclined to look on New Jersey as a land of 1940s diners and 1970s shopping malls, the state much more closely resembles the rest of America than does Manhattan, although drivers will find some peculiarities, such as jug-handle intersections (to make a left turn, you exit to the right and then cross over after the light has changed), and the nation's only remaining state-imposed ban on self-service gas stations. The row houses one used to encounter upon emerging from the Holland Tunnel are now joined by office and apartment towers and, a few miles further out, by the skyscrapers of Newark and its performing arts center. Further out still are comfortably packed middle-income suburbs and the horse country around Far Hills, old industrial cities such as Paterson and Trenton (also the state capital), and dozens of suburban towns and small factory cities. In South Jersey is the desolate (and ecologically unique) expanse known as the Pine Barrens, where Christopher Moltisanti and Paulie ("Walnuts") Gualtieri of The Sopranos spent an uncomfortable winter's night trying to dispose of a Russian mobster.

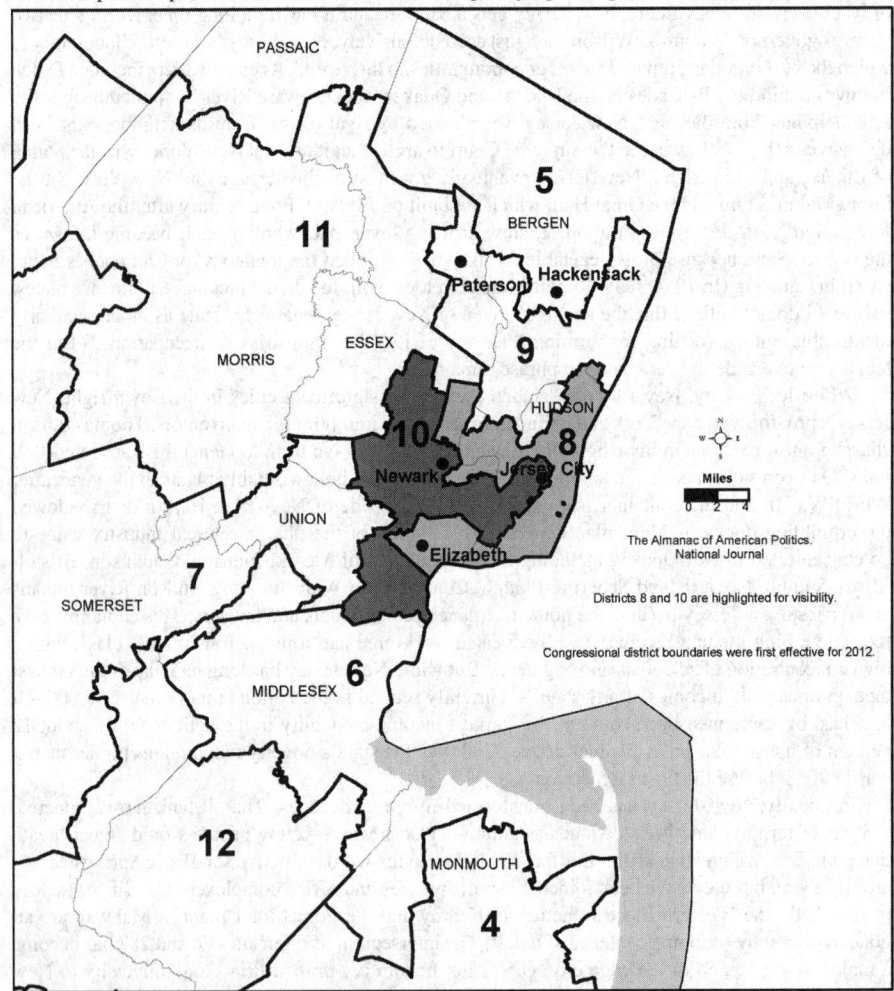

New Jersey has long been a magnet for immigrants, though more so in the vicinity of New York City than adjacent to Philadelphia. In its post-World War II years of rapid growth, the state was a quilt pattern of WASPs, Irish, Italians, Jews and Hungarians (the nation's largest concentration of the latter was in Middlesex County). Small-town-like suburbs that had been centered on Dutch Reform or Episcopal churches became heavily Catholic or Jewish. Today, New Jersey's population is 14 percent black, 20 percent Hispanic (ranking eighth nationally), 9 percent Asian (third behind Hawaii and California), and 56 percent white (ranking among the bottom 10 states). Hudson County, which includes Jersey City opposite Manhattan, was the home of hundreds of thousands of Irish, Italian, Polish and Jewish immigrants in the early 20th century; it is now 12 percent black, 15 percent Asian, and 43 percent Hispanic. Immigrants are also plentiful in the small, middle-American towns of Bergen County: Filipinos in Bergenfield, Guatemalans in Fairview, Koreans in Leonia, Indians in

Lodi, and Chinese in Palisades Park. The old industrial cities of Elizabeth and Paterson are majority Hispanic, and Newark is majority black.

Overall, the state's population has grown by barely more than 1 percent since the 2010 census. The state's fastest growth came in Hudson (Jersey City), Middlesex (New Brunswick and Edison) and Bergen (Hackensack) counties, which all have grown by between 4.6 percent and 9.2 percent since the last census. One weak spot has been millennials, who aren't fond of the state's car-dependent suburbs and who, in any case, are often unable to afford the high cost of housing. New Jersey has the nation's highest rate of 18-to-34-year-olds living with their parents, CityLab reported. United Van Lines calculations put New Jersey atop its list of outbound-moving states in 2018. "Born to Run" indeed.

Economically, New Jersey was hit hard by the recession and then was hobbled again by superstorm Sandy, which struck in October 2012. A storm surge hit the Jersey Shore from Cape May to Sandy Hook and peaked at eight-and-a-half feet. Damage was substantial on barrier-island communities and in low-lying land next to New York Harbor and the Passaic and Hackensack rivers. For a time in 2016, New Jersey ranked first in the nation in foreclosures. Meanwhile, gaming revenue – the lifeblood of Atlantic City – has sunk thanks partly to the spread of casinos to nearby Pennsylvania. Casino revenue in A.C. was 44 percent lower in 2018 than in 2006, and even the casino Donald Trump touted as "the eighth wonder of the world" in 1990 -- the Trump Taj Mahal -- shut its doors as its founder was running for president. But two new casinos have opened in the city, including the Hard Rock – the rebranded Taj Mahal. Combined with newly legal sports betting, A.C. has seen a modest bump in gaming revenues. Meanwhile, the state's biomedical industry sustained serious hits, a combination of expiring drug patents, a spate of mergers and the gravitation of research to university-based labs in places like Massachusetts and California.

State government has helped build New Jersey's identity, but it also has placed heavy burdens on its private sector. In the 1970s, Democratic Gov. Brendan Byrne pushed through an income tax in a state that, until that point, had far lower taxes than New York. A revolt crested against Democratic Gov. Jim Florio's tax increase in 1990, leading to his defeat in 1993 by Republican Christine Todd Whitman. In the 1990s, crime and welfare rolls dropped, but auto insurance and property taxes remained the highest in the nation. Health insurance premiums skyrocketed, thanks to state mandates requiring all policies to cover all manner of treatments. Meanwhile, property taxes kept rising.

On a map showing statewide election results, Democrats have generally carried the spine of the state, on either side of the Amtrak corridor and through the South Jersey suburbs of Philadelphia. Republicans have carried the outlying areas, most of the Jersey Shore on the east, and the affluent suburban and exurban areas on the northwest. Other factors beyond demographics have helped Democrats. New Jersey's high-earning, relatively well-educated voters tend not to vote in often crucial primaries — 41 percent are not registered with either of the major parties — and those who do vote tend to defer to the choices of county and city political machines, which possess varying degrees of competence and cronyism. For candidates in both parties, it is a great advantage to have the designation of the local county party on the primary ballot. Meanwhile, because New Jersey's primary TV news outlets come from out-of-state, residents don't always know what's going on in Trenton. It also makes it expensive to run a statewide campaign, because New York and Philadelphia are among the nation's priciest media markets.

Republican Chris Christie won the governorship in 2009 and was easily reelected in 2013, but shortly after his victory, he faced investigations into the closing of a lane on the George Washington Bridge, which was believed to be a way to punish a Democratic mayor who spurned Christie's reelection effort. Other stumbles piled up – Christie's presidential bid cratered, voters back home got restless about the time he spent away from the state, and eyebrows were raised when he became the first establishment Republican to back Trump (only to be purged from the transition team after Trump won). He earlier took grief from some conservatives for buddying up to President Barack Obama in the wake of Sandy. After these developments – and after Hillary Clinton's 14-point victory in the 2016 presidential race – New Jersey turned even bluer. In 2017, Democrat Phil Murphy won the race to succeed Christie as governor, 56%-42%; working with a lopsidedly Democratic legislature, he set about enacting such progressive priorities as paid sick leave and gun control. In the 2018 midterms, Sen. Bob Menendez, who had faced corruption charges that ended in a mistrial, still managed to defeat a credible and deep-pocketed Republican opponent by double digits. Even more strikingly, Democrats ousted two House incumbents and flipped two GOP-held open seats, leaving the delegation with a whopping 11 Democrats and just one Republican. Even as Trump enjoys his golf club in Bedminster, New Jersey doesn't look like it will be promising territory for Republican candidates anytime soon.

Population		Race and Ethnicity		Income	
Total	8,960,161	White	56.1%	Median Income	$76,475
Land area (sq. miles)	7,354	Black	12.7%	State Income Rank	2
Pop/ sq mi	1,218.4	Latino	19.7%	Poverty Rate	10.7%
Born in state	52.4%	Asian	9.4%	With health insurance	90.3%
		Two or more races	1.7%	Cash public assistance	2.4%
Age Groups		Other	0.5%	Food stamp/SNAP	9.2%
Under 18	22.3%				
18-34	21.8%	Education		Work	
35-64	40.8%	H.S grad or less	38.7%	White Collar	41.7%
Over 64	15.1%	Some college	23.1%	Sales and Service	40.7%
		College Degree, 4 yr	23.4%	Blue Collar	17.6%
Military		Post grad	14.7%	Government	13.4%
Veteran/ Active Duty	5.2%				

Presidential Politics

2016 Primary (D)	Clinton (D)	566,247 (63%)	Sanders (D)	328,058 (37%)			
2016 Primary (R)	Trump (R)	360,212 (80%)	Kasich (R)	59,866 (13%)	Cruz (R)	27,874	(6%)
2016 Pres. Vote	Clinton (D)	2,148,278 (55%)	Trump (R)	1,601,933 (41%)			
2012 Pres. Vote	Obama (D)	2,125,101 (58%)	Romney (R)	1,477,568 (41%)			

New Jersey used to be a close state in close presidential races. In the 1980s, the vast suburban expanses leaned toward Republicans. But Democrats have won the past seven elections. Lately, GOP nominees have barely cleared the 40 percent mark. The suburbs, with many secular voters, reject GOP positions on cultural issues, and rising immigrant communities have generally voted Democratic. As a result, New Jersey, which had voted 56%-43% for George H.W. Bush in 1988, voted 56%-40% for Al Gore over George W. Bush in 2000. In 2012, it was one of five states where President Barack Obama increased his percentage over his 2008 numbers. In 2016, Hillary Clinton dispatched Donald Trump, 55%-41%. Trump won the northwestern section of New Jersey that includes the state's two fastest growing counties, Hunterdon and Somerset, home to Trump National Golf Club in Bedminster. Those counties and Morris are among the wealthiest in the country. Trump ran close to Clinton in South Jersey, with its working-class suburbs of Philadelphia, farms around Vineland and Millville, and beach communities in Atlantic, Cape May and Ocean counties. Clinton rolled up her biggest margins in Jersey City, Newark and Union City. She also ran well in Passaic and Paterson, old industrial centers that attracted immigrants from Italy and Eastern Europe in the early 1900s, but now have large Hispanic populations.

For years, New Jersey held its presidential primary in early June, but it was usually overshadowed by the California primary on the same day. In 2008, the primary was in February on Super Tuesday. Democratic turnout was 1.1 million, nearly double the previous record, and Clinton beat Obama 54%-44%. She carried Jewish and Latino voters, while Obama carried blacks and did well in high-income suburbs. Turnout on the Republican side was 566,000, more than ever before. John McCain defeated Mitt Romney by a surprisingly large 55%-28% margin. New Jersey moved back to a June primary to save money. In 2016, Trump was the de facto GOP nominee and rolled up 80 percent of the vote in the June 7 primary. The night before the primary, the Associated Press and CNN reported that Clinton had acquired enough delegates to claim the Democratic nomination. The next day she defeated Vermont Sen. Bernie Sanders, 63%-37%.

Congressional Districts

116th Congress Lineup	11D 1R	115th Congress Lineup	7D 5R

For the past three redistricting cycles, New Jersey employed a bipartisan redistricting commission, made up of 12 members — six Democrats and six Republicans — appointed by party leaders in the legislature. The members picked a dispassionate tie-breaking arbiter. In 1991 and 2011, the outcome was the Republicans' plan. In 2001, the 13 congressional incumbents agreed on a bipartisan, if contorted, map and submitted it to the commission. The arbiter liked the incumbent-protection plan. The consistent result was a House delegation that remained closely balanced: a 7-5 split for the Democrats, prior to the 2018 election.

But politics and election outcomes in New Jersey have changed. The state's quaint traditions of bipartisan redistricting and a divided delegation have become relics, and it's unlikely that they will be revived for the foreseeable future. Democrats picked up four suburban seats in 2018 — defeating two Republican incumbents, pushing a third into early retirement and taking the fourth seat when a safe Republican retired and the GOP could not find a credible candidate. With the seat they gained in 2016, the 6-6 delegation of 2012 had turned 11-1 Democratic Even the surviving Republican-held 4th District is no longer iron-clad, especially if 20-term incumbent Rep. Christopher Smith decides to retire. In addition, Democrats have taken secure control of the governor's office and hold large majorities in the legislature. In December 2018, Trenton Democratic leaders unexpectedly revealed their intentions to reinforce their control of the delegation with a nakedly partisan constitutional amendment to overhaul redistricting procedures, which raised alarms among reformers—as well as the surviving Republicans. "They are seeking to make Republicans a permanent minority by essentially writing gerrymandering into the state constitution," The New York Times reported. Ultimately, that plan was so egregious that it caused some blushing Democratic loyalists to rebel and shelve the proposal, at least for the short term.

But unless Republicans find a way to become more competitive in New Jersey campaigns, starting with their attempts to take back in 2020 some of the five House seats they have lost since 2012, the next round of redistricting seems likely to reinforce Democratic supremacy. With their control, Democrats likely will find ways to turn most of their recently won seats into reliable sinecures.

Phil Murphy (D)

Elected 2018, term expires 2022, 1st term; b. Aug. 16, 1957, Needham, MA; Harvard University, B.A.; University of Pennsylvania, M.B.A.; Unknown; Married (Tammy); 4 children.

Elected Office: US Ambassador to Germany, United States Department of State, 2009-2013.

Office: 125 W. State St, Trenton, 08608; 609-292-6000; Fax: 609-292-3454; Website: nj.gov/governor

Lt. Gov.: Sheila Oliver (D)

State Legislature: Senate: 26D, 14R **House:** 54D, 26R

Election Results

Election	Name (Party)	Vote (%)
2017 General	Phil Murphy (D)..	1,203,110 (56%)
	Kim Guadagno (R)..	899,583 (42%)
2017 Primary	Phil Murphy (D)..	243,643 (56%)
	Jim Johnson (D)...	110,250 (22%)
	John S. Wisniewski (D)...	108,532 (22%)

Phil Murphy, a former Goldman Sachs executive and U.S. Ambassador to Germany, won New Jersey's governorship in 2017 in his first run for public office. Murphy, who succeeded two-term Republican Gov. Chris Christie, pursued one of the most liberal policy agendas in the nation, although splits within the state Democratic Party stymied some of his signature campaign promises during his first year in office.

Murphy grew up in Newton Massachusetts in what he has described as a working-class home (or "middle class on a good day," as he often put it). Murphy worked his way through Harvard University and later earned a degree from the University of Pennsylvania's Wharton School of Business. He spent more than two decades with Goldman Sachs, eventually spending four years posted in Germany and three in Hong Kong. Shortly before leaving Goldman Sachs, Murphy was tapped by acting New Jersey Gov. Richard Codey to chair a panel studying the state's pension system. He stepped further into politics in 2006, when he was named national finance chair of the Democratic National Committee under chairman Howard Dean, the former Vermont governor and 2004 presidential candidate. After Barack Obama won the presidency, he tapped Murphy as ambassador to Germany, a post he held from 2009 to 2013.

In the run-up to the 2017 gubernatorial contest, Democrats were salivating at the chance to succeed Christie, whose approval rating was in the dumps due to the "Bridge-gate" scandal and his support for Donald Trump. Several Democrats were interested in the race, including state Senate President Steve Sweeney, but Murphy moved aggressively and he easily won the nomination. On the Republican side, the outgoing lieutenant governor, Kim Guadagno, won her primary with similar ease. In the general election, Guadagno attacked Murphy as someone whose wealth made it hard to identify with ordinary New Jersey residents, and whose years with Goldman Sachs echoed the resume of Jon Corzine, the Democrat who lost reelection to Christie in 2009. Murphy, for his part, worked to lash Guadagno to Christie's administration, as well as to Trump. The candidates also differed sharply on policy. Guadagno warned voters that Murphy would raise their taxes; Murphy staked out more aggressive stances on gun control and marijuana than his Republican opponent. Notably, Murphy energized progressives with his support for such policies as sanctuary status for undocumented immigrants and a $15 minimum wage. National handicappers never considered the race to be especially competitive; Murphy prevailed, 56%-42%. Exit polls found that eight of every 10 voters disapproved of Christie, making his tenure a bigger driver of the vote than Trump's. Murphy won the support of a broad coalition, including women, minorities, younger voters and independents. Guadagno won senior citizens and white voters, but even among those groups, she won by smaller margins than Christie had four years earlier.

With solid Democratic majorities in the legislature, Murphy was able to chalk up some legislative victories. He signed laws on equal pay, paid family leave, gun control, a ban on drilling for oil and gas in state waters, renewable energy, automatic voter registration, and a restoration of funding for Planned Parenthood. The budget he signed in June 2018 included a surtax on incomes higher than $5 million and a tax hike on some corporations, and it directed money toward schools and the NJ Transit commuter rail system. A Murphy appointee, Attorney General Gurbir Grewal, acted to limit local police forces' ability to ask about immigration status and made it harder to hand over undocumented immigrants for deportation. But differences with Sweeney, the powerful Senate leader, prevented progress on other priorities, including a $15 minimum wage and marijuana legalization. Despite many shared policy priorities, the relationship between Murphy and Sweeney was widely seen as distant, stemming partly from lingering tensions from the 2017 primary season and partly from differences over the New Jersey Education Association, which Murphy had embraced and Sweeney had fought. "Sweeney is more centrist," Carl Golden, a former Republican operative told Vox.com. "And Sweeney also has a much more capable political feel than the governor does." And in 2019, open warfare emerged between Murphy and George Norcross, the Democratic boss of southern New Jersey, further complicating Murphy's attempts to govern.

Murphy experienced a few areas of turbulence unrelated to the skirmishes with Sweeney and Norcross. Katie Brennan, who served in Murphy's administration, accused former Murphy campaign aide Albert J. Alvarez of sexual assault, and she criticized Murphy for hiring him even though transition officials were aware of her allegation. Alvarez was not charged with a crime, but he resigned from his senior post; Murphy ordered an investigation and Brennan eventually sued the state, Murphy's campaign, and Alvarez. Meanwhile, Murphy fended off questions about the big-dollar support of a group that did not release information about its donors. Overall, though, Murphy's efforts won him solid, if not spectacular, approval ratings among voters, and he began to take on a higher national profile when he was named vice chairman of the Democratic Governors Association for 2019. That left Murphy poised to become chairman of the group in the presidential election year of 2020 – and possibly a candidate for a cabinet job if a Democrat were to win.

Bob Menendez (D)

Appointed 2006, term expires 2024, 3rd term, b. Jan 01, 1954; New York, NY; St. Peter's College (NJ), B.A., 1976; Rutgers University Law School (NJ), J.D., 1979; Roman Catholic; Divorced; 2 children.

Elected Office: Union City Board of Education, 1974-1982, CFO, 1978-1982; Union City Mayor, 1986-1992; NJ Assembly, 1987-1991; NJ Senate, 1991-1992; U.S. House, 1993-2006.

Professional Career: Practicing attorney, 1980-1992.

DC Office: 528 HSOB 20510, 202-224-4744, Fax: 202-228-2197, menendez.senate.gov

State Offices: Barrington, 856-757-5353; Newark, 973-645-3030.

Committees: *Banking, Housing & Urban Affairs*: Economic Policy; Housing, Transportation & Community Development (RMM); Securities, Insurance & Investment. *Finance*: Health Care; International Trade, Customs & Global Competitiveness; Taxation & IRS Oversight. *Foreign Relations (RMM)*.

Group Ratings

	ADA	ACLU	AFL-CIO	LCV	ITI	COC	HAFA	ACU	CFG	FRC
2018	-	76%	-	100%	-	50%	3%	14%	5%	0%
2017	85%	C	100%	89%	C	17%	C	0%	4%	0%

Key Votes of the 115th Congress

1. Obama-care revision	N	5. Gun regulations	N	9. Kavanaugh confirmation	N
2. Tax Cuts	N	6. Family planning regs	N	10. Saudi arms sales	Y
3. Dodd-Frank revision	N	7. Gorsuch confirmation	N	11. FISA rules	N
4. Omnibus appropriations	Y	8. Immigration restrictions	N	12. Military aid in Yemen	Y

Election Results

Election	Name (Party)	Vote (%)		Cand. Spent	Ind. Exp. Support	Ind. Exp. Oppose
2018 General	Bob Menendez (D)	1,711,654	(54%)	$10,858,720	$1,000,136	$8,852,569
	Bob Hugin (R)	1,357,355	(43%)	$42,683,739	$431,307	$15,649,323
2018 Primary	Bob Menendez (D)	262,477	(62%)			
	Lisa McCormick (D)	158,998	(38%)			

Prior winning percentages: 2012 (59%), 2006 (57%), House: 2004 (76%), 2002 (78%), 2000 (79%), 1998 (80%), 1996 (79%), 1994 (71%), 1992 (64%)

Early in the early 1980s, Democrat Bob Menendez — now New Jersey's senior senator — testified in a corruption case against Union City Mayor William Musto, a onetime mentor for whom Menendez had been an aide. Then in his late 20s, Menendez wore a bulletproof vest during the trial because of death threats. That chapter of his life was widely retold, with some measure of irony, more than three decades later when Menendez himself was hit with corruption charges — becoming only the 12th sitting senator to be indicted. It overshadowed his legislative work, which has focused on foreign policy, and forced him to spend the latter half of his second Senate term seeking to exonerate himself. An 11-week federal trial of Menendez and his co-defendant — Salomon Melgen, a wealthy Florida eye surgeon, whom the senator characterized as a longtime friend and supporter — ended in a hung jury in November 2017. The Justice Department decided against retrying the case. The Senate Ethics Committee admonished Menendez for bringing "discredit" upon that chamber, and his seat was in political jeopardy before he hung on to win in 2018 in a solidly blue state.

Allegations surrounding his relationship with Melgen had dogged Menendez since early 2013, beginning with a series of published reports as Menendez was assuming the Foreign Relations Committee chairmanship. When criminal charges were brought in April 2015, a Justice Department spokesman described it as "a bribery scheme in which Menendez allegedly accepted gifts from Melgen in exchange for using the power of his Senate office to benefit Melgen's financial and personal interests." The gifts that Menendez allegedly received included luxury vacations, pricy golf outings and more than $750,000 in campaign contributions. In turn, Menendez was accused of intervening with federal officials after a finding that Melgen had overbilled Medicare by nearly $9 million, working to protect Melgen's $500 million port security contract with the Dominican Republic, and obtaining U.S. visas for several of Melgen's foreign girlfriends. But Menendez's legal team argued the gifts from Melgen were simply generosity from one close friend to another and not tied to any quid pro quo.

When Menendez was indicted, he relinquished his role as ranking Democrat on the Foreign Relations Committee — a post to which he was reinstated nearly three years later after the charges were dropped. He spent almost two years as the panel's chairman before Senate Democrats lost their majority in 2014. Menendez's seniority has provided him with a prominent perch to lambaste overseas policy regardless of the party in power: He has sharply criticized both the Obama and Trump administrations.

When appointed in January 2006 to fill a vacant seat, Menendez became only the second Cuban-American to serve in the Senate. He grew up in Union City, the son of a carpenter and a seamstress — both Cuban immigrants who arrived in the United States before he was born. By the time Menendez graduated from nearby St. Peter's College — now St. Peter's University — he was a member of the Union City School Board — elected when he was just 20. He earned a law degree at Rutgers University. Shortly after his testimony helped convict Musto, Menendez lost a bid to oust his former boss at the polls. But in 1986, with Musto imprisoned, a 32-year-old Menendez was elected mayor of Union City, an area that is home to the largest concentration of Cuban-Americans in the United States outside Miami. Menendez was elected to the New Jersey General Assembly in 1987 and to the state Senate in 1991; he served simultaneously as mayor and state legislator, then a common practice in New Jersey.

In 1992, Menendez was easily elected to an open House seat. Ambitious and hard-driving, Menendez has been admired — if not always warmly regarded — for his prodigious fundraising and strategic savvy. In 2002, as the Democrats eyed recapturing the House majority, Menendez raised $4 million for the party and its candidates. The Democrats fell short of the majority, but Menendez accumulated chits. After California's Nancy Pelosi defeated Maryland's Steny Hoyer for party whip, the job of caucus chairman — then No. 3 in the party hierarchy — opened. Menendez, with Hoyer's support, defeated Pelosi-backed Rosa DeLauro of Connecticut, 104-103.

When Democratic Sen. Frank Lautenberg announced his retirement in 1999, Menendez was expected to run for the seat. But New Jersey Sen. Robert Torricelli, then the Democratic Senatorial Campaign Committee chairman, preferred Jon Corzine, a wealthy former investment banker who could self-finance his campaign. Corzine was elected; three years later, when Torricelli was forced to abandon his own run for reelection amid controversy over acceptance of gifts from a businessman who had pleaded guilty to violating federal election laws, Lautenberg returned to the Senate.

When Corzine was elected governor in 2005, Menendez made it known that he would run for the Senate. Menendez had amassed more than $4 million, enough to scare away primary challenges. Corzine appointed Menendez to fill out the remaining year of his Senate term. In 2006, Menendez faced state Sen. Tom Kean Jr., son and namesake of a popular former governor. The race featured the bare-knuckled politics for which New Jersey is known. Kean sought to call attention to Menendez's activities and influence in Hudson County — a Democratic bastion with a history of machine politics and corruption. Two months before the election, U.S. Attorney Chris Christie subpoenaed records from a lease arrangement between Menendez and an anti-poverty group for which Menendez had sought federal funding and that had paid him $300,000 in rent on a building he owned in Union City. It was then revealed the Kean campaign's opposition researchers had contacted a former Hudson County executive in federal prison on corruption charges. Menendez struck back with a TV spot: "Federal prisoner 25038-050. He's Tom Kean Jr.'s newest adviser." Menendez won 53%-44%.

On foreign policy, Menendez has been among the most hawkish Democrats. This led to conflicts while President Barack Obama was in office — differences accentuated when Menendez became Foreign Relations chairman. Some Cuban-American supporters suggested that the indictment was payback by the Obama administration for Menendez's hard-line stances — although he publicly disavowed such suggestions.

Menendez's stance on Cuba reflected widespread animosity toward the Castro regime among many of his Cuban-American constituents. When Obama moved in late 2014 to restore diplomatic relations with Cuba, Menendez told reporters, "I think it stinks." In 2017, when President Donald Trump ordered a rollback of several aspects of Obama's Cuba initiative, Menendez praised it as "step in the right direction," contending, "Allowing the Castro regime, as the previous administration did, to steadily and unilaterally reintegrate into the global economy without firm commitments to improve conditions for the Cuban people only emboldened an oppressive dictatorship to tighten its stranglehold over its citizens." Menendez also irritated the Obama White House with his outspoken opposition to the Iran nuclear agreement; he was one of only four Senate Democrats to vote against the treaty in late 2015. But, when Trump announced in May 2018 he was withdrawing from the agreement, Menendez was sharply critical: "Trump is risking U.S. national security, recklessly upending foundational partnerships with key U.S. allies in Europe and gambling with Israel's security."

Tensions between Menendez and the Trump administration escalated on other foreign policy fronts. In October 2018, Secretary of State Mike Pompeo accused Menendez of "putting our nation at risk" by holding up Senate votes on 60 State Department nominees. Menendez responded on the Senate floor in March 2019: "When the White House, either through negligence or incompetence, sends us unvetted, unqualified nominees incapable and often times offensive, my staff and I must exercise due diligence on behalf of the American people." A month earlier, Menendez introduced a bill to step up pressure on Russia as he assailed "Trump's willful paralysis in the face of Kremlin aggression." In a floor speech, Menendez went so far as to raise "the entirely legitimate question of whether Donald Trump could be compromised by the Russian government." Citing a series of revelations, Menendez said, "The American people deserve to know … if Trump is an agent of the Russian Federation."

Menendez has been a major player on immigration. Comprehensive legislation he introduced in 2010 failed to become law, but one of its components — the DREAM Act, offering those brought to the country illegally as children a path to citizenship — was put into policy two years later by an Obama executive order establishing the Deferred Action for Childhood Arrivals program. In 2013, Menendez was among a bipartisan group of eight senators that crafted a reform proposal; it passed the Senate by a wide margin but was never taken up by the House. In early 2018, Menendez was again part of a bipartisan group that came up with a compromise to retain protections for those covered by DACA — which Trump had earlier moved to withdraw — while providing funds to satisfy Trump's insistence on a U.S.-Mexico border wall. The deal fell apart when Trump declined to endorse it. In early 2019, when Trump's demand for funding for a southern border wall led to a protracted government shutdown, Menendez rejected an invitation to appear at a White House signing ceremony for a human trafficking bill he had sponsored. "I did not want to be a potted plant for the president's despicable policies as it relates to immigrants and the whole question of the southern border," Menendez told NJ Advance Media.

Menendez was DSCC chairman in the 2010 election cycle. The economic downturn and initial public discontent with the newly passed Affordable Care Act worked against him. But, under Menendez's leadership, the DSCC outraised its GOP counterpart. Even though Democrats lost six seats, it marked the first time in 100 years that the party in power held on to the Senate while losing control of the House.

As Menendez took over the DSCC, he got a coveted slot on the Finance Committee. In that role, he backed unsuccessful attempts to add a "public option" to the Affordable Care Act. That incensed New Jersey tea party activists, who launched a recall effort in early 2010. Menendez called it an unconstitutional "political stunt" and the state Supreme Court sided with him, halting the effort. In 2012, Republicans struggled to find a top-tier challenger. The task fell to state Sen. Joe Kyrillos, a friend of Christie. Kyrillos took in $4.6 million, but Menendez again demonstrated his fundraising prowess, raising more than $17 million. He won 59%-39%.

Within months of that victory, trouble was brewing for Menendez, as news outlets reported he had possibly violated Senate rules by accepting and not reporting two round-trip flights to the Dominican Republic in 2010 from Melgen, whose medical offices had been raided by the FBI. Menendez paid the estimated $58,500 cost of the flights and related expenses, while saying the matter "unfortunately fell through the cracks." Menendez ultimately repaid Melgen more than $112,400 to comply with the Ethics Committee's decision in his case, according to disclosure reports filed in early 2019. Four months before his joint trial with Menendez began, Melgen was convicted in a separate case in Florida on 67 counts of Medicare fraud, which the judge said involved theft of at least $73 million. He was sentenced to 17 years in prison.

Menendez denied any wrongdoing when indicted on charges that included bribery, conspiracy and making false statements; he later blamed the allegations on a smear campaign by the Castro regime. He ignored calls to resign as the trial was delayed multiple times as he fought to dismiss the case. In March 2017, the Supreme Court denied his request to dismiss many of the counts, setting up a September trial in Newark. In November, after four days of jury deliberations, District Judge William Walls declared a mistrial. One juror told reporters that, by a 10-2 margin, the jury had supported finding Menendez not guilty — in the belief that the exchange of gifts and favors between Menendez and Melgen was consistent with what good friends did for each other.

In January 2018, the Justice Department announced it would retry the case. But, less than a week later, Walls threw out seven of the 18 counts, including those involving Menendez's efforts on Melgen's behalf in the Medicare billing dispute and the port security contract. In his ruling, Walls wrote that the prosecution wanted the court "to fashion speculative inferences under the conclusory generalizations of context, chronology, escalation, concealment, and a pattern of corrupt activity — each of which is empty of relevant evidential fact." Quoting Gertrude Stein, the judge concluded, "There is no there there." Looming over Walls' ruling — and indirectly referenced by him during the trial — was a 2016 Supreme Court ruling involving former Virginia Gov. Bob McDonnell, which had narrowed the legal bounds of political corruption cases. Citing the "impact" of Walls' decision, the Justice Department reversed itself and said it would not retry Menendez and Melgen.

Menendez moved to line up endorsements for reelection from virtually every major state Democratic official. But the court case had taken its toll politically; a Quinnipiac University poll taken as the trial got underway showed 50 percent of likely voters felt he did not deserve to be reelected. After the mistrial, Senate Majority Leader Mitch McConnell called on the Ethics Committee "to immediately investigate Sen. Menendez's actions, which led to his indictment." In an April 2018 letter of admonishment approved unanimously, the six-member panel found Menendez had "knowingly and repeatedly" violated Senate rules. "You demonstrated disregard for these standards by placing your Senate office in Dr. Melgen's service at the same time you repeatedly accepted gifts of significant value from him," the panel wrote. "Your assistance to Dr. Melgen under these circumstances demonstrated poor judgment, and it risked undermining the public's confidence in the Senate." Two months later, Menendez's political vulnerability was apparent as Lisa McCormick, a newspaper publisher virtually devoid of campaign funds and unknown statewide, received nearly 40 percent of the vote in the Democratic primary.

By that time, Republican Bob Hugin had spent $2 million on attack ads aimed at Menendez. Ironically, Hugin, like Menendez, had grown up in Union City in modest circumstances. He went on to make a fortune in the biopharmaceutical industry and ended up spending $36 million from his own pocket in seeking to become the first New Jersey Republican elected to the Senate since 1972. Hugin spent heavily on TV ads reminding voters of the charges on which Menendez had been tried. Menendez responded with spots targeting Celgene — the biotech firm Hugin headed before resigning to run for Senate — for sharply increasing the price of a key cancer drug and paying $280 million to settle a Justice Department lawsuit over the marketing of two cancer drugs for unapproved treatments. Two Hugin ads sought to revive unsubstantiated allegations — carried by conservative news sites when Menendez's relationship with Melgen first came under scrutiny — that Menendez had hired underage prostitutes in the Dominican Republic. Dominican police later said an attorney there had paid three woman to make up the stories. Menendez called Hugin the "slimiest of slimeballs" for airing the charges.

National Democratic strategists became alarmed when, in mid-October, private tracking polls had Menendez ahead by only 2 points, according to The New York Times. As Democrats scrambled to protect seats in 10 states won by Trump, a super PAC with ties to Senate Minority Leader Chuck Schumer was compelled to spend $7.6 million to prop up Menendez in a state where Hillary Clinton beat Trump by 14 points in 2016. Menendez's personal campaign account spent about $11 million, barely one-fourth of the $43 million spent by Hugin. It drew primarily on Hugin's own assets. But of the $26 million in independent expenditures, about two-thirds was spent on Menendez's behalf.

Menendez could largely thank Trump for winning: The president's approval ratings in New Jersey were stuck in the mid-30s. "Your vote is all that stands between us and a Trump Republican Senate," Menendez said in one ad in the closing days of the campaign. Hugin, who had donated $200,000 to Trump's campaign, distanced himself from the president on issues ranging from immigration to abortion, while vowing to "stand up to Trump" in a closing TV spot. A Quinnipiac University polling analyst told Roll Call that, while squeamish about pulling the lever for a candidate recently tried for bribery, many voters "may hold their nose to cast a ballot" for Menendez because they wanted "to keep [the] seat in the 'D' column in a blue state where …Trump consistently remains unpopular." Menendez was reelected, 54%-43%. Menendez's Hudson County base and the neighboring Democratic stronghold of Essex County (Newark) provided two-thirds of his 350,000-vote statewide margin.

In his election night speech, Menendez — defiant throughout his legal ordeal — appeared to acknowledge he faced work to repair the damage to his 45-year political career. "I pledge to spend every day fighting for you and your families and to earn back your respect."

Cory Booker (D)

Elected 2013, term expires 2020, 1st full term, b. Apr 27, 1969; Washington, DC; Stanford University (CA), B.A., 1991; Stanford University (CA), M.A., 1992; The Queens College, University of Oxford (UK), 1994; Yale Law School (CT), J.D., 1997; Baptist; Single.

Elected Office: Newark City Council, 1998-2002; Newark Mayor 2006-2013.

Professional Career: Practicing attorney.

DC Office: 717 HSOB 20510, 202-224-3224, Fax: 202-224-8378, booker.senate.gov

State Offices: Camden, 856-338-8922; Newark, 973-639-8700.

Committees: *Environment & Public Works*: Clean Air & Nuclear Safety; Superfund, Waste Management, & Regulatory Oversight (RMM); Transportation & Infrastructure. *Foreign Relations*: Africa & Global Health Policy; Internat'l Dev Instit & Internat'l Econ, Energy & Environ Policy; State Dept & USAID Mngmnt, Internat'l Ops & Internat'l Dev (RMM). *Judiciary*: Antitrust, Competition Policy & Consumer Rights; Border Security & Immigration; Crime & Terrorism. *Small Business & Entrepreneurship*.

Group Ratings

	ADA	ACLU	AFL-CIO	LCV	ITI	COC	HAFA	ACU	CFG	FRC
2018	-	86%	-	100%	-	40%	5%	14%	20%	0%
2017	95%	C	100%	100%	C	29%	C	0%	4%	0%

Almanac Ratings 2017-18

	Economy	Social	Foreign	Composite
Liberal	100%	100%	97%	99%
Conservative	0%	0%	4%	1%

Key Votes of the 115th Congress

1. Obama-care revision	N	5. Gun regulations	N	9. Kavanaugh confirmation	N
2. Tax Cuts	N	6. Family planning regs	N	10. Saudi arms sales	Y
3. Dodd-Frank revision	N	7. Gorsuch confirmation	N	11. FISA rules	N
4. Omnibus appropriations	N	8. Immigration restrictions	N	12. Military aid in Yemen	Y

Election Results

Election	Name (Party)	Vote (%)	Cand. Spent	Ind. Exp. Support	Ind. Exp. Oppose
2014 General	Cory Booker (D)............................... 1,043,866	(56%)	$16,871,163	$1,452,027	$534,109
	Jeff Bell (R)... 791,297	(42%)	$599,118	$86,711	
2014 Primary	Cory Booker (D)........................... Unopposed				

Prior winning percentages: 2013 special (55%)

Ever since Democrat Cory Booker, New Jersey's junior senator, arrived on Capitol Hill, the question has been when, not if, the telegenic former Rhodes scholar would run for president. So, there was little surprise when, after visiting two dozen states during the 2018 election cycle, Booker launched a White House bid in February 2019. Booker was a force in national Democratic politics even before winning an October 2013 special election to the Senate: For seven years before that, he attracted bountiful media coverage as mayor of Newark — New Jersey's largest municipality, which had long been a poster child for the problems and challenges confronting urban America. Booker is a charismatic campaigner whose speeches — frequently focused on civil rights — can both mesmerize listeners and bring a crowd to its feet. And he was perhaps the most social media savvy contender in the crowded Democratic presidential field. That could boost the 50-year-old's appeal to millennials as he also competes with his Senate colleague, California's Kamala Harris, for the sizable African-American vote in several key primary states.

Like Harris, Booker is often compared to Barack Obama: Both men started as community organizers and were involved in local politics before reaching the Senate in their mid-40s. As he campaigned for his party's 2020 nomination, Booker was aiming to reassemble the coalition that made Obama president by relying on an upbeat message. But Booker possesses a resume notable for seeming contradictions, which has attracted skepticism from both sides of the political aisle. Much of what has been written about Booker in recent years has raised the question of his "authenticity." It is an issue that he has acknowledged, even as it has irritated him. "My closest friends say to me, 'When I have conversations with people, they ask that question: Is he for real?'" Booker told New York magazine in late 2018. "It's frustrating to me that people don't think you can be earnest and sincere in this game anymore. "Booker's considerable oratorical skills have on occasion left him with self-inflicted rhetorical wounds. As mayor of Newark, he frequently spoke of a drug dealer who appears to have been made up. Years later, he faced mockery from some quarters after what he termed his "'I am Spartacus' moment" during high-profile hearings over hearings of Brett Kavanaugh's Supreme Court nomination.

The bigger question about Booker's presidential aspirations is whether he can win over enough of a Democratic base that is increasingly populist, uncompromising on economic issues and skeptical of anyone with Wall Street ties. Booker is a sponsor of such recent progressive initiatives as "Medicare for All" and the "Green New Deal." But his outspoken defense of the private equity industry during 2013 continues to be cited by progressives to question whether he is really one of them. And, in early 2017, he earned scorn from the left when he was one of just 13 Democrats to vote against a largely symbolic amendment to import prescription drugs from Canada. (New Jersey is home to several major pharmaceutical companies.) The financial and pharmaceutical industries have been major donors to Booker, who in 2017 sought to defuse the issue by placing a "pause" on accepting contributions from drug companies "because it arouses so much criticism." He announced a year later he would no longer accept donations from any corporate PAC.

Booker is one of only six black members elected to the Senate since Reconstruction, a group that also includes Obama and Harris. Booker was born in Washington, D.C. — his parents were IBM business executives — but was raised in the affluent, predominantly white New York suburb of Harrington Park, New Jersey. Barely five years after the passage of the Civil Rights Act of 1964, the family had a hard time buying a home there because of racial bias. "My parents tried to move us into a neighborhood with great public schools, but Realtors wouldn't sell us a home because of the color of our skin," Booker said in a video announcing his presidential bid. "A group of white lawyers, who had watched the courage of civil rights activists, were inspired to help black families in their own community, including mine. And they changed the course of my entire life." Booker was named to the All-USA high school football team and played tight end at Stanford University — where he earned a bachelor's degree and a master's in sociology. As a Rhodes scholar, he studied at Oxford University before graduating from Yale Law School.

In 1998, Booker ran successfully for the Newark City Council, 25 miles south of where he had grown up. In his last year of law school, he had begun working in Newark as a tenants' rights advocate, soon moving into Brick Towers — one of the city's poorest and most violent housing projects. He lived in that project until the city housing authority razed it in 2006, the year he was elected mayor. Booker then bought a home nearby in Newark's predominantly African-American Central Ward, where he still lives. In 2002, he challenged longtime Mayor Sharpe James, a fellow Democrat and African-American who was twice his age. The bitter race prompted the federal government to send in observers on Election Day. The campaign became the subject of a documentary film called "Street Fight" that was nominated for an Oscar and helped make Booker a rising political star. Booker lost 53%-47%. Afterward, he practiced law and worked for civic organizations as he geared up for a rematch in 2006. But, after five terms, James declined to run again — and was indicted and convicted on corruption charges soon after leaving office. Booker won 72 percent of the vote against a former James deputy, and a slate of his political allies rode his coattails to the City Council.

As mayor, Booker built an impressive network of celebrity friends and acquaintances in the technology, finance and entertainment sectors: His contacts brought in $400 million in philanthropic efforts for the city. But his star power was a double-edged sword: He faced criticism for traveling the country to tend to his influential network and build his national profile at the expense of dealing with the day-to-day problems of his constituents. Former Washington Post reporter Dale Russakoff— whose book, The Prize, was a behind-the-scenes account of Booker's highly touted effort to revamp the city's school system — told NPR that while Booker had an "incredible talent" at "framing issues and getting the nation to pay attention to them," he struggled with the "patient, tedious, kind of unglamorous work of taking those promises and hammering them out into a different reality." Even some longtime political allies groused about the time he spent on the road.

Booker was elected promising a renaissance of one of the nation's most troubled cities. On the upside, the city achieved a balanced budget for the first time in a decade, opened new parks and spent more on mass transit. But he was unable to make a lasting dent in the notorious crime rate. A Star-Ledger story noted the city had 83 homicides and 2,850 other violent crimes in 2003 under James — compared with 95 homicides and 3,220 violent crimes in 2012, the last full year of Booker's mayoralty. His push to improve the schools received mixed grades. A member of Booker's celebrity network, Facebook co-founder Mark Zuckerberg, contributed $100 million, matched by a similar amount of public and private funds; Booker and New Jersey Republican Gov. Chris Christie joined Zuckerberg to announce the donation to great fanfare on "The Oprah Winfrey Show." The initiative doubled the number of students attending public charter schools, which significantly outperform public schools in Newark. But the overall changes didn't show the widespread success many had hoped for. Zuckerberg largely abandoned his plan to use Newark as a national model for education reform amid criticism of Booker and Christie's top-down approach.

Still, Booker was easily reelected in 2010. His persona as the city's savior gained near-mythical dimensions after he shoveled an elderly resident's walk when a city plow failed to show up and after he rescued a neighbor from a burning house in 2012. Booker formed a friendship with Obama and was a featured speaker at the 2012 Democratic National Convention. But Booker created a particularly uncomfortable moment for Obama when, on NBC's "Meet the Press," he criticized Democratic attacks on Republican presidential nominee Mitt Romney's work at Bain Capital — a leading private equity firm — as "crap" and "nauseating." He also contended painting Wall Street "with broad brushes" was unfair to "the good people who work there." Booker was less defending Romney than sticking up for the private equity industry, which is important to New Jersey. But the comments continue to haunt him among members of his party's left wing.

In January 2013, Booker announced plans to seek the Senate seat held by Democrat Frank Lautenberg when it opened in 2014. The 89-year-old Lautenberg had health problems and was all but certain to retire. But he publicly bristled at what he regarded as a lack of deference by Booker — whose eagerness created some political fallout when Lautenberg's death from viral pneumonia in June 2013 triggered a special election that October. Members of the Lautenberg family endorsed Rep. Frank Pallone, saying "gimmicks and celebrity status won't get you very far in the real battles that Democrats face in the future." Pallone attracted labor backing, including from the state's teachers, who opposed Booker's support of charter school expansion and changes in teacher tenure laws. Booker won a four-way Democratic primary with 59 percent of the vote; runner-up Pallone got 20 percent. But Booker also collected some political dents along the way. The New York Times reported that, while full-time mayor of a struggling city, he had founded an internet startup on the side designed to make it easier to collect and share videos; financial backing had come from friends such as Winfrey and Google executive Eric Schmidt. To put the controversy behind him, Booker stepped down from the company's board and donated his ownership interest to charity.

Booker's general election opponent was Steve Lonegan, former mayor of the New York suburb Bogota and state director of the tea party-affiliated Americans for Prosperity. His right-wing profile made him a decided underdog in a state that had not elected a Republican senator since 1972. Booker overwhelmed Lonegan in fundraising, taking in more than $11 million; Ivanka Trump was among his donors. But Lonegan managed to make the race closer than many had expected, partly because of a national political climate that was turning difficult for Democrats. Booker created some problems with ill-conceived tweets to a dancer at a strip club. There was also renewed scrutiny about claims to a relationship with the drug dealer he called T-Bone — another episode that has haunted him politically. In early days as mayor, Booker often spoke of how T-Bone had once threatened him but later came to him to recount a difficult childhood and seek help staying out of prison. The Star-Ledger had been unable to find evidence that T-Bone existed, and — during the 2013 race — a Rutgers University historian who was a Booker supporter told National Review that Booker had admitted to him T-Bone was a composite character. Booker dodged the issue in a Washington Post interview shortly after that. Several years before the Senate race, Booker had said T-Bone "is an archetype of so many people that are out there. He is 1,000 percent a real person."

While such controversies enabled Lonegan to cut into Booker's lead, Booker still pulled off a solid victory: 55%-44%. He won a full term in 2014 by a similar margin — 56%-42% — defeating conservative activist and public affairs consultant Jeff Bell — who had run for the same seat in 1978 and lost to Democrat Bill Bradley. Booker's term is up in 2020. In November 2018, the state Legislature passed what was dubbed "Cory's Law," allowing people to appear on the ballot for Congress and the presidency at the same time.

Like other high-wattage figures elected to the Senate, Booker initially sought to keep a low profile and focus on state-specific issues. Just 44 when sworn in, he told reporters that he "absolutely… unequivocally" was not interested in running for president or vice president in 2016. Nonetheless, he was reported by New York magazine to have been among Democratic presidential nominee Hillary Clinton's top three choices for a running mate. Immediately after the 2016 elections, Booker took a seat on Foreign Relations, shoring up his foreign policy credentials. In 2018, he and Harris joined the Judiciary Committee.

Striving to show bipartisanship soon after his election, Booker sought to make friends with conservative Texas Sen. Ted Cruz, meeting for a three-hour dinner that Booker later described to a local Fox News station as "one of the best constitutional law discussions since I got out of law school." He joined with another tea party standard-bearer, Kentucky Sen. Rand Paul, on a bill in early 2015 to remove the threat of federal prosecution against medical marijuana patients in states where it is legal. In 2017, Booker went a step further by introducing legislation to legalize recreational marijuana; it was a shift from two years earlier, when he had declined to support legalization in an interview with Vox. Booker reintroduced the marijuana legislation in early 2019, while also seeking to burnish his progressive credentials on another front: He appeared with a rival presidential contender, Vermont Sen. Bernie Sanders, to promote legislation aimed at lowering what Booker termed "the outrageous and unjustifiably high cost of prescription drugs." According to The Hill, Booker defended himself when asked about his vote two years earlier against importation of drugs from Canada, saying it had come on a "late night messaging amendment" and that he had gone to work soon afterward to draft an importation bill with adequate safety standards.

Booker's most notable effort in working across the aisle bore fruit in late 2018, when a major criminal justice reform bill was signed into law — including increased discretion for federal judges when sentencing those convicted of drug-related offenses. Initially, Booker worked closely with South Carolina Republican Tim Scott — the Senate's only other African-American at the time — to craft a reform package. A separate Booker-Scott "opportunity zones" proposal providing tax benefits to businesses that invest in depressed areas made its way into the 2017 Republican-sponsored tax reform bill. He later collaborated with another GOP conservative, Utah's Mike Lee — as well as Judiciary chairman Chuck Grassley, a Republican, and Democratic Whip Dick Durbin — on a bill that won bipartisan backing. But, amid opposition from several hard-line conservatives, the bill died in 2016 when Majority Leader Mitch McConnell declined to bring it to the floor. Booker vowed to redouble his efforts to pass the legislation, and later did — with an unlikely assist from President Donald Trump, whose adviser and son-in-law Jared Kushner negotiated with McConnell. "One of the top reasons I wanted to run for the United States Senate was to get legislation like this done," Booker told NJ Advance Media. "Our criminal justice system is a cancer on the soul of this country."

With 2020 looming, Trump appeared to notice Booker as a potential opponent: At an October 2018 news conference, the president derided Booker's tenure in Newark, calling him a "horrible mayor." According to Politico, Booker responded by saying: "I will never let him pull me so low as to hate him. I'm going to continue to be a voice in this country for the love, for bringing the nation together, not driving the nation apart." However, as he has shifted left, Booker has emerged as one of Trump's harshest critics, taking a hard partisan edge rarely seen earlier in his career. At the 2016 Democratic National Convention, he delivered a soaring speech that slammed Trump while touting a more hopeful America: It earned comparisons to the stirring speech Obama delivered at the 2004 convention, both for the passion of its delivery and the sweep of the narrative. As with Obama 12 years earlier, it intensified speculation about Booker's national ambitions.

Early in the Trump administration, Booker led the charge against Trump's nomination of then-Alabama Sen. Jeff Sessions as attorney general because of what he described as Sessions' long record of "hostility" toward minorities — apparently becoming the first senator to testify against a fellow senator's Cabinet confirmation. He tied with Harris in voting "no" on 18 of Trump's initial 22 nominations to the Cabinet and other high-ranking administration positions: Among Senate Democrats, only three fellow 2020 presidential contenders — New York's Kirsten Gillibrand, Massachusetts' Elizabeth Warren and Sanders — opposed more nominees. His votes against confirmation included Betsy DeVos for Education secretary, notwithstanding her role in pushing the Newark school reform experiment he oversaw a decade earlier. And, during a Judiciary Committee hearing in January 2018, Booker yelled at Homeland Security Secretary Kirstjen Nielsen while questioning her about a White House meeting at which Trump reportedly had referred to several African nations as "shithole countries." When Nielsen said she couldn't recall if Trump had used that language, Booker responded, "Your silence and amnesia is complicity."

Eight months later at a Judiciary Committee hearing on Kavanaugh's nomination, Booker — charging that committee Republicans were hiding behind arguments of privacy and national security in refusing to publicly release relevant documents — announced that, as an act of "civil disobedience," he would release 12 pages of emails relating to an internal discussion of racial profiling during Kavanaugh's time as a White House counsel. When a Republican committee member, Majority Whip John Cornyn, suggested that a senator could be ousted for releasing such material and read aloud the relevant rules, Booker dared Cornyn to try to do so, as Booker's Democratic colleagues came to his defense.

"This is about the closest I'll probably ever have in my life to an 'I am Spartacus' moment," Booker said, alluding to the 1960 film about a slave uprising against the Roman Empire. A problem: the documents at issue had been cleared for public release the morning of the hearing, making Booker's statements appear more theatrics than bravery. Booker later told CNN he did not know at the time the emails had been cleared for release. Booker sought to walk back his comments a bit, telling The Hill he did not intend to compare himself to Spartacus. But Booker said he had no regrets, adding, "Itdoesn't take away from the larger point. ... We have documents that have been hidden from the public that shouldn't have been hidden from the public." It was not the only time during the Kavanaugh hearings that Booker's choice of words caused blowback: He retreated from an assertion that those who supported putting Kavanaugh on the Supreme Court were "complicit in evil" after those comments sparked criticism, including from Kavanaugh. "I've been exuberant in my beliefs and I've learned a lot through this process," Booker told the Judiciary Committee. "Some of my comments have been referenced numerous times, and I know that I have not been as precise and allowed my comments to be mischaracterized."

If he becomes president, Booker would be the first White House occupant who could claim ancestors who were slaves. And he would be the second bachelor president since James Buchanan was elected in 1856. In an interview with the Philadelphia Inquirer in late 2018, Booker said he doesn't consider that to be an issue because "the norms of family relationships have changed dramatically." And, after years of avoiding direct answers to questions about his sexual orientation, he told the Inquirer that, if he were gay, he would live openly. "I'm heterosexual," he said. "Every candidate should run on their authentic self, tell their truth, and more importantly ... talk about their vision for the country."

Donald Norcross (D)

Elected 2014, 3rd full term, b. Dec 13, 1958; Camden; Camden County College (NJ), A.S., 1979; Lutheran; Married (Andrea Doran); 3 children; 2 grandchildren.

Elected Office: NJ Assembly, 2010; NJ Senate, 2010-2014.

Professional Career: Electrician; Assistant business Manager, Local 351, Int'l Brotherhood of Electrical Workers; President, Southern NJ AFL-CIO.

DC Office: 2437 RHOB 20515, 202-225-6501, Fax: 202-225-6583, norcross.house.gov

State Offices: Cherry Hill, 856-427-7000.

Committees: *Armed Services*: Seapower & Projection Forces; Tactical Air & Land Forces (Chmn). *Education & Labor*: Health, Employment, Labor & Pensions; Higher Education & Workforce Investment.

Group Ratings

	ADA	ACLU	AFL-CIO	LCV	ITI	COC	HAFA	ACU	CFG	FRC
2018	-	79%	-	86%	-	58%	6%	4%	17%	0%
2017	80%	C	97%	91%	C	57%	C	4%	5%	11%

Almanac Ratings 2017-18

	Economy	Social	Foreign	Composite
Liberal	95%	98%	79%	91%
Conservative	5%	2%	21%	9%

Key Votes of the 115th Congress

1. Obama-care revision	N	5. Family planning regs	N	9. Guantanamo prisoners	Y
2. Tax Cuts	N	6. Body cameras/immigration	Y	10. Ground missiles, limit	Y
3. Omnibus appropriations	N	7. Abortion ban	N	11. Defense Dept. spending	Y
4. Dodd-Frank revision	N	8. Concealed carry	N	12. FISA rules	Y

Election Results

Election	Name (Party)	Vote (%)		Cand. Spent	Ind. Exp. Support	Ind. Exp. Oppose
2018 General	Donald Norcross (D)	169,628	(64%)	$1,295,169	$28,158	
	Paul Dilks (R)	87,617	(33%)	$12,575		
2018 Primary	Donald Norcross (D)	39,788	(84%)			
	Robert Carlson (D)	4,570	(10%)			
	Scot John Tomaszewski (D)	2,953	(6%)			

Prior winning percentages: 2016 (60%), 2014 (57%), 2014 special (57%)

Democrat Donald Norcross, who was first elected in 2014, is a usually reliable ally of Democratic leaders and organized labor. He has gained influence on the Armed Services Committee, where he keeps a close eye on New Jersey interests.

Norcross graduated from Camden County College. He started his career as an electrician, installing power lines in refineries and on the top of bridges. Later, he became a business manager for the International Brotherhood of Electrical Workers, and president of the Southern New Jersey AFL-CIO. Norcross jumped into politics in 2009, when he won election to the state Assembly. A year later, he was appointed to fill a state Senate seat. He was a leading backer of the state's constitutional amendment to raise the minimum wage as well as a bill providing tax incentives to businesses that operate in hard-hit areas. On some social issues — notably charter schools — Norcross has staked out more centrist positions.

Norcross got his opening when longtime Democratic Rep. Robert Andrews resigned to take a job at a Philadelphia law firm. With Andrews' backing, he lined up endorsements from key Democrats across South Jersey. Not only was he the favored Democrat in a blue district, but his brother, George Norcross III, has been a longtime power broker in the state and owned a majority stake in The

Philadelphia Inquirer. (George Norcross divested his interest in the newspaper soon after his brother's campaign began.) Norcross's two primary opponents, Frank Minor and Frank Broomell, tried to play up his entrenched political ties as a liability. But he handily defeated them with 72 percent of the primary vote.

Republican Garry Cobb, a local talk-radio personality and former Philadelphia Eagles linebacker, emphasized that he was an outsider who was not part of the "Norcross machine" and that he wanted to clean up politics in South Jersey. But he was outspent $2.1 million to $108,000 and Norcross won by a comfortable, though less than overwhelming, 57%-39%.

In addition to his seat on Armed Services, Norcross sits on the Education and Labor panel. His Almanac vote ratings have been toward the center of the House, especially on foreign policy. He occasionally has gone his own way on key votes. He supported approval of the Keystone XL pipeline, which has been strongly backed by many labor unions but opposed by most Democrats. And he opposed President Barack Obama's nuclear deal with Iran, saying that "a better deal can be achieved," though he said that the October 2017 decision by President Donald Trump to decertify the agreement was "reckless" and "could harm our alliances." In January 2018, he was one of 65 House Democrats who voted for the FISA bill to expand government surveillance authority. He serves on the leadership-controlled House Democratic Steering and Policy Committee, where he has the largely honorary title of parliamentarian.

As a Democratic leader on issues dealing with organized labor, Norcross has worked with others to counter the setback to unions in the Supreme Court's 2018 ruling in the Janus case, which dealt with compulsory membership. "Our goal is to make sure the next generation of workers has a fair playing field to earn enough to take care of a family and retire with dignity," he said. Norcross filed the Toxics by Rail Accountability and Community Knowledge (TRACK) Act, which would improve safety measures for rail shipments of hazardous materials and was based on recommendations that followed a 2012 train derailment in Paulsboro. "I was an electrician for many, many years, and understanding some of the complex issues in trying to get the economy growing is something I deal with every day," he said.

In 2019, Norcross became chairman of the Armed Services Subcommittee on Tactical Air and Land Forces, which handles funding for aviation and helicopter platforms. He has consistently pledged support for the military installations based in New Jersey, especially nearby Joint Base McGuire-Dix-Lakehurst. With others, he took credit for the provision in the 2017 defense spending bill to locate at McGuire the upgraded fleet of KC-46 refueling tankers, which he said "make our base an indispensable starting point for national security missions on the East Coast." He vowed to protect the base in the event of creation of a base-closure review.

In 2016, he faced a primary challenge from Alex Law, a 25-year-old political newcomer and supporter of Sen. Bernie Sanders in the presidential campaign, who had been a consultant for IBM. Law ran against the "Norcross machine," which he said had been "marked by corruption and political cronyism." Norcross outspent him more than 20-to-1 and got 70 percent of the vote. He has breezed to reelection against Republicans.

NJ-1: Philadelphia suburbs   Cook Partisan Voting Index: D+13

Population		Race and Ethnicity		Income	
Total	730,635	White	63%	Median Income	$67,666
Land area (sq. miles)	350	Black	16.2%	District Income Rank	110
Pop/ sq mi	2087.4	Latino	13.3%	Poverty Rate	11.8%
Born in State	55%	Asian	5.1%	With health insurance	92.2%
		Two or more races	2%	Cash public assistance	3.4%
Age Groups		Other	0.4%	Food stamp/SNAP	11.3%
Under 18	22.6%				
18-34	22.5%	**Education**		**Work**	
35-64	40.1%	H.S grad or less	42.5%	White Collar	14.8%
Over 64	14.8%	Some college	27%	Sales and Service	42.7%
		College Degree, 4 yr	19.8%	Blue Collar	17.9%
Military		Post grad	10.7%	Government	13.9%
Veteran/ Active Duty	6.5%				

2012 Pres. Vote	Obama	212,236	(66%)	Romney	110,377	(34%)		
2016 Pres. Vote	Clinton	199,386	(60%)	Trump	118,880	(36%)	Johnson	6,512	(2%)

Camden: The closely built streets of Camden, across the Delaware River from Philadelphia, have seen a fair amount of history. This was where the poet Walt Whitman lived when he wrote some of the versions of his Leaves of Grass. It was an immigrant-jammed industrial city then, with tinkerers and inventors. In 1894, a Camden machinist named Eldridge Johnson produced the Victor Talking Machine, the birth of the recorded music industry and a company that became RCA Victor in 1929. A few years later, the new Campbell Soup Co. began producing condensed soups. Camden remained for years a major industrial locus on the New Jersey side of the Delaware River, not the broadest and certainly not the most picturesque of Atlantic estuaries, but probably the East Coast's premier industrial waterway, with a concentration of steel mills, chemical plants, and oil tank farms equal to any in the country. The flatlands all around, mostly ignored in the 19th century, had easy access to cheap water transportation and plenty of skilled labor from the Philadelphia area. For a quarter-century starting in the 1940s, this was one of the country's fastest-growing industrial areas.

In the 1980s and 1990s, Camden emptied out. Many of its factories had closed. Its neighborhoods were beset by crime, its mostly minority residents were heavily dependent on public assistance and its mayor was convicted of doing favors for Philadelphia's organized crime leaders. From 2002 to 2010, the state controlled its finances and government. Camden continues to struggle. Census figures released in 2012 showed Camden with a poverty rate of 42 percent, the highest in the nation. Since then, an influx of jobs modestly lowered the rate to 37 percent, though the population had dropped by 3 percent. In 2017, its median household income of $26,200 remained the lowest in the state, where the average was $76,500. After having the highest crime rate in the nation for several years, violent crime in 2017 was the lowest in 30 years.

Camden has had some bright spots: a redeveloped riverfront park, the New Jersey aquarium and a state-of-the-art amphitheater. Rowan University in 2012 opened a $139 million medical school in the city, the first new medical college in New Jersey in 35 years. As part of the "eds and meds" strategy, it was joined by a health sciences center in 2017. The port of Camden rebounded, spurred by Del Monte's large fruit-processing plant and increased steel imports. In April 2018, Subaru opened its new corporate headquarters — one of 30 companies that received state tax breaks to move into Camden. Many of the new offices are in a waterfront project. Critics pointed out shortcomings, including that Subaru and others moved from nearby sites chiefly because of huge tax incentives, there was no guarantee of new jobs for residents of Camden, and the leases might be as short as 15 years. Still, almost any progress in Camden has been radical change. "We have a safer city now, we have better schools, we're working on cleaning up our city, we're working on providing adequate housing," mayor Frank Moran told the Camden Courier Post, when he took office in January 2018.

The 1st Congressional District is greater Camden, the Delaware riverfront from Palmyra south to a point across the river from the Delaware state line. The district includes two-thirds of adjacent Gloucester County, an area that is nearly one-third of the district, plus a small slice of Burlington County. The 1st is traversed by Black Horse Pike and White Horse Pike, which connect Philadelphia to its South Jersey suburbs. Many of the nearby boroughs and townships developed over the past half-century as a result of flight from Camden. Haddonfield, an old-fashioned community filled with galleries and shops, was once described by The Philadelphia Inquirer as "a Norman Rockwell picture come to life." The district is 16 percent black and 13 percent Hispanic; those two groups comprise nearly equal shares of virtually all of Camden's population. Politically, the district remains safe for Democrats. Hillary Clinton led Donald Trump, 60%-36%.

Jeff Van Drew (D)

Elected 2018, 1st term, b. Feb 23, 1953; New York, NY; Rutgers University (NJ), B.S., 1975; Fairleigh Dickinson University, D.D.S., 1979; Veterans Administration New Jersey Healthcare; Lyons and East Orange Veterans Hospitals, D.D.S., 1979; Catholic; Married (Ricarda Drew); 2 children.

Elected Office: Dennis Township Fire Commissioner, 1983-1986; Cape May County Board of Chosen Freeholders, 1994-1997; Dennis Township Mayor, 1997-2003; NJ General Assembly, 2002-2007; NJ Senate,2009-2018.

Professional Career: Dentist; Volunteer Fire Fighter

DC Office: 331 CHOB 20515, 202-225-6572, vandrew.house.gov

State Offices: Mays Landing, 609-625-5008.

Committees: *Agriculture*: Biotechnology, Horticulture & Research; Commodity Exchanges, Energy & Credit; General Farm Commodities & Risk Management; Subcommittee Nutrition, Oversight & Department Operations. *Natural Resources*: Water, Oceans & Wildlife.

Election Results

Election	Name (Party)	Vote (%)		Cand. Spent	Ind. Exp. Support	Ind. Exp. Oppose
2018 General	Jeff Van Drew (D)............................. 136,685	(53%)		$1,733,289	$1,232,467	
	Seth Grossman (R)......................... 116,866	(45%)		$296,298		$39,917
2018 Primary	Jeff Van Drew (D)............................... 16,901	(57%)				
	Tanzie Youngblood (D)........................... 5,495	(19%)				
	Will Cunningham (D)............................. 4,795	(16%)				
	Nathan Kleinman (D)............................. 2,467	(8%)				

Jeff Van Drew was an exception in the large freshman class of House Democrats, especially from the Northeast: He won his primary as the moderate, experienced, older and male candidate. He had an easy ride in both the primary and general elections for a seat that Republican Frank LoBiondo had held for 12 terms, while receiving at least 58 percent of the vote, until he decided to retire. National Democrats had recruited Van Drew for this seat for several years, despite his conservative views on issues such as gay rights and gun control, because they viewed him as the Democrat most likely to flip the seat.

Van Drew graduated from Rutgers University and got a doctorate in dental science from Fairleigh Dickinson University. As a family dentist for more than 35 years, he was president of the New Jersey Dental Society. After serving in several local offices in Cape May County and for six years in the state General Assembly, he was elected in 2007 to the state Senate, where he chaired the Community and Urban Affairs Committee. Following LoBiondo's retirement announcement, he became the frontrunner for the seat.

In the primary, his opponents and liberal interest groups criticized Van Drew's relatively moderate viewpoints and bipartisan approach, especially on social issues, though he voiced conventional Democratic views on many economic issues. When he initially denied that he received a $1,000 campaign contribution from the National Rifle Association, a high school student responded, "Senator, you lied!"

"We're just too divided," Van Drew told voters in response. "Our country most needs consensus builders." Soon after he announced his candidacy, Democratic leaders in all eight counties across the district endorsed Van Drew, whom they largely viewed as the strongest candidate. He also won early backing from the House's Blue Dog Coalition of centrist Democrats. Van Drew benefited from superior fundraising: The $1 million that he raised prior to the June primary more than tripled the total of the three other candidates, all of whom were newcomers to Democratic campaigns.

Van Drew won the primary with 57 percent of the vote against three more liberal opponents who split the remaining vote, though he likely would have prevailed against a single opponent. Trailing behind him were Tanzie Youngblood, a retired African-American teacher, who had 19 percent, and Will Cunningham, an openly gay African-American attorney and former Obama administration official, with 16 percent. His primary win was "disappointing [to] progressive activists wary of his voting record" in Trenton, the Huffington Post wrote.

In the general election, Van Drew's Republican opponent self-destructed and the national GOP conceded the contest at an early point. Prior to the primary, National Republican Congressional Committee Chairman Rep. Steve Stivers candidly called the district a "recruitment hole" for the GOP. Their nominee, Seth Grossman, a former talk-show host, reportedly had connections to white supremacist groups.

After Grossman described diversity as "a bunch of crap and un-American" and shared a website post that referred to African Americans as a "threat to all who crossed their paths," Stivers withdrew the NRCC's endorsement and the party turned its attention to stiff challenges elsewhere in New Jersey. Still, Van Drew's victory was a surprisingly narrow 53%-45%, which could open the door to future competitive contests. He was one of 15 House Democrats who did not vote for Nancy Pelosi in the January 2019 selection of a new Speaker.

NJ-2: South Jersey   Cook Partisan Voting Index: R+1

Population			Race and Ethnicity			Income		
Total	726,894		White	65.7%		Median Income	$62,007	
Land area (sq. miles)	2,092		Black	11.7%		District Income Rank	158	
Pop/ sq mi	347.4		Latino	15.9%		Poverty Rate	13.5%	
Born in State	59.9%		Asian	4%		With health insurance	90.5%	
			Two or more races	2.3%		Cash public assistance	3.3%	
Age Groups			Other	0.3%		Food stamp/SNAP	12.5%	
Under 18	21.8%							
18-34	20.5%		**Education**			**Work**		
35-64	40.4%		H.S grad or less	47.8%		White Collar	17.3%	
Over 64	17.3%		Some college	26.5%		Sales and Service	45.8%	
			College Degree, 4 yr	17%		Blue Collar	21%	
Military			Post grad	8.6%		Government	17.2%	
Veteran/ Active Duty	7.4%							

2012 Pres. Vote	Obama	166,908	(54%)	Romney	141,480	(46%)			
2016 Pres. Vote	Trump	162,486	(50%)	Clinton	147,656	(46%)	Johnson	6,596	(2%)

Atlantic City, Philadelphia exurbs: The builders of the Camden & Atlantic Railroad in 1852 may not have known it, but when they extended their line to the little inlet town of Absecon, they were launching one of America's first beach resorts, Atlantic City. Like all resorts, it was a product of developments elsewhere — of industrialization and spreading affluence. In the years after the Civil War, Atlantic City and the Jersey Shore, from Brigantine to Cape May, became a seaside resort, and Atlantic City developed its characteristic features: the boardwalk in 1870, the amusement pier in 1882, the rolling chair in 1884, salt water taffy in the 1890s, and the Miss America pageant in 1921. In the book Boardwalk Empire, author Nelson Johnson argues that to attract tourists, a powerful alliance of local politicians and racketeers allowed gambling, prostitution and Sunday liquor laws to be flouted. "Nothing could interfere with the visitors' fun or they might stop coming," he writes. But a long period of decline came after World War II, and by the early 1970s Atlantic City was grim, featuring a bedraggled convention hall (site of the 1964 Democratic National Convention), empty hotels and bleak streets.

Then in 1977, New Jersey voters legalized casino gambling in Atlantic City, and gleaming new hotels sprang up, big-name entertainers came in, and the resort became more stylish than it had been in 90 years. But it hasn't been that way for everyone: Casino and hotel jobs tend to be low-wage, and decrepit neighborhoods begin just feet from the casinos' massive parking lots. For years, its dozen casinos had net annual revenues nearly as high as Las Vegas' casinos. Then, the recession hit the entertainment sector hard. From 2005 until 2016, casino revenues dropped more than 50 percent, to a bit more than $2 billion. As The Washington Post wrote in October 2016, Donald Trump helped to orchestrate this "casino-industry bubble," during which he had three corporate bankruptcies, the final one in 2010. His hundreds of millions of dollars in losses helped him to offset income elsewhere. Republican Gov. Chris Christie in 2011 signed legislation easing regulatory oversight of the casinos, which angered watchdog groups that said it was unfair to single out gambling for special treatment. After five of the casinos closed and others sought tax relief as gambling revenues continued to drop, a turnaround arrived in 2018, with the state's legalization of sports gambling. Two new casinos opened and total gambling revenue increased 20 percent by the end of the year. Still, Atlantic City remained under state control, which began in November 2016. In 2017, Atlantic County retained the highest foreclosure rate of any metropolitan area in the nation.

Other beach resorts lie south of Atlantic City. There is Wildwood, with its refurbished 1950s motels, and also Cape May, with its lovingly preserved Victorian houses. West of the Jersey Shore are swamps and flatlands, the Pine Barrens and abundant vegetable fields that gave New Jersey its "Garden State" nickname. The number of farms decreased 10 percent between 1997 and 2012, though agriculture remained the third largest sector of the state's economy. Restrictions on immigration were "a big challenge" facing local farmers, The Press of Atlantic City wrote in July 2018.

The 2nd Congressional District covers the southern end of New Jersey. Atlantic is the largest county, with more than 35 percent of the population. Politically, it has Democratic leanings in the chemical industry towns along the Delaware River and in Vineland and a Republican presence in Cape May County. In 2016, Trump won this hometown district, 50%-46%. The 2nd was one of three New Jersey districts where he got a majority, all of them south of the New York City suburbs.

Andrew Kim (D)

Elected 2018, 1st term, b. Jul 12, 1982; Boston, MA; Deep Springs College (CA); University of Chicago (IL), B.A., 2004; University of Oxford (UK), B.A., 2004; Oxford University (England), M.Phil, 2007; Presbyterian; Married (Kammy Kim); 2 children.

Professional Career: Foreign Affairs Officer, U.S. Department of State, 2009-2013; Director for Iraq, National Security Council, 2013-2015.

DC Office: 1516 LHOB 20515, 202-225-4765, Fax: 202-225-0778, kim.house.gov

State Offices: Marlton, 856-703-2700; Toms River, 732-504-0490.

Committees: *Armed Services*: Intelligence, Emerging Threats & Capabilities; Readiness. *Small Business*: Economic Growth, Tax & Capital Access (Chmn); Innovation & Workforce Development.

Election Results

Election	Name (Party)	Vote (%)		Cand. Spent	Ind. Exp. Support	Ind. Exp. Oppose
2018 General	Andrew Kim (D)............................ 153,473	(50%)	$6,266,142	$303,919	$4,855,075
	Tom MacArthur (R)........................ 149,500	(49%)	$4,580,132	$250,063	$7,381,182
2018 Primary	Andrew Kim (D)............................	(100%)			

Freshman Democrat Andy Kim, a former national security official during administrations of both parties, narrowly won a hard-fought contest against a tenacious incumbent. He was the first Korean-American elected to Congress as a Democrat. Kim defeated Republican Rep. Tom MacArthur, who made a point of voting for Republican legislation, which he occasionally helped to shape. Of the four New Jersey Democrats in 2018 who won House seats that had been held by Republicans, Kim ran in the district where President Donald Trump had his best showing in the 2016 election.

Kim, who went to high school in Cherry Hill, graduated from the University of Chicago with a degree in political science. As a Rhodes scholar, he studied U.S. policy in Iraq while he was at Oxford University in England. Kim worked at the State Department and was a civilian adviser to Gen. David Petraeus in Afghanistan. He was Iraq director of the National Security Council under President Barack Obama, where he helped to set policy for dealing with the ISIS terrorist network. He returned to New Jersey from his residence in Washington D.C. shortly before he announced his first election campaign.

Running against MacArthur, who had been a wealthy insurance executive, Kim sought to depict the incumbent as an out-of-touch millionaire. MacArthur had played a leading role in early 2017 in cutting a deal for the final version of the House Republican-passed bill to repeal the Affordable Care Act. Later that year, he was the only one of the five House Republicans from New Jersey who voted for passage of tax-cut legislation. That measure stirred heated objections in his home state because of its cap on deductions for state and local taxes. Without his effort to secure a $10,000 allowance, MacArthur said, there would have been no deduction.

Kim won the Democratic nomination without opposition. With parents who had moved from impoverished childhood to become successful professionals, Kim said, "There is nothing I'd rather do than serve my country," while putting the interests of the nation above partisan politics.

During their final debate a week before the election, MacArthur accused Kim of voicing generalities in calling for new policies on health-care and other issues. He would not have made such charges, he said, if Kim "didn't speak in gauzy generalities all the time and actually gave specific proposals for solving things." Kim replied that MacArthur often took his words and would "twist them out of context." He added that MacArthur voted for a tax bill that was "a bad deal for New Jersey." MacArthur defended the legislation, including his decision to go a separate direction from all others in the state's congressional delegation. "I don't relish being alone. But I didn't go to Congress for other people to tell me how to vote."

Kim outspent MacArthur, $6.3 million to $4.8 million. MacArthur self-financed $1.4 million of his campaign fund. In addition, the combined national parties and their allies spent more than $12 million. Kim won 50%-49%. The candidates split the two large counties in the district. Kim led by about 33,000 votes in Burlington, which was nearly 60 percent of the district. MacArthur took the smaller Ocean County by 30,000 votes.

Kim was the first Democrat elected in this district in more than 100 years. He faced the prospect of the most competitive reelection contest of New Jersey's four House freshmen.

NJ-3: South Central New Jersey

Cook Partisan Voting Index: R+2

Population		Race and Ethnicity		Income	
Total	737,263	White	75.6%	Median Income	$77,540
Land area (sq. miles)	900	Black	10.2%	District Income Rank	62
Pop/ sq mi	819.5	Latino	7.8%	Poverty Rate	6.7%
Born in State	61.1%	Asian	3.7%	With health insurance	94.3%
		Two or more races	2.4%	Cash public assistance	1.7%
Age Groups		Other	0.4%	Food stamp/SNAP	5.7%
Under 18	20.7%				
18-34	19.4%	**Education**		**Work**	
35-64	41%	H.S grad or less	38.7%	White Collar	18.9%
Over 64	18.9%	Some college	28.1%	Sales and Service	43.1%
		College Degree, 4 yr	21.7%	Blue Collar	16.8%
Military		Post grad	11.5%	Government	17.4%
Veteran/ Active Duty	9.7%				

2012 Pres. Vote	Obama	179,028	(52%)	Romney	163,204	(48%)			
2016 Pres. Vote	Trump	187,703	(51%)	Clinton	165,090	(45%)	Johnson	7,639	(2%)

Burlington and Ocean Counties: The Pine Barrens of New Jersey are one of the last vacant spots on the eastern seaboard — not quite terra incognita, but still not thickly populated. Encroached on by the Philadelphia suburbs of South Jersey and the Delaware River on the west and burgeoning retirement developments of the Jersey Shore on the east, the 1 million acres of heavy forest and white sand, with their unusual plant life, are crossed mostly by narrow two-lane roads. For years, the Pine Barrens were seen as a barrier to development. Only recently have environment-minded Jerseyites come to see the relatively unspoiled area as a natural treasure. There are a few small towns here, plus Joint Base McGuire-Dix-Lakehurst, the giant amalgamation of an Air Force base, Army military reservation and training site, and Navy air station, which is the second-largest employer in New Jersey, behind the state government. In a major long-term victory for the facility, the Joint Base has become the home of Boeing's KC-46A air-refueling tankers. The new planes are replacing the base's older-model KC-10 refueling planes.. The base completed in 2017 the largest military solar energy installation in the Northeast, with more than 50,000 solar panels.

East of the Pine Barrens is Ocean County, including the barrier islands from Mantoloking south to Stafford, with older communities on the beachfront and larger clusters of new subdivisions and condominiums inland. Here you can find the house in Seaside Heights where several seasons of MTV's Jersey Shore were set. After a six-year hiatus, the series resumed in 2018, though Mike "The Situation" Sorrentino, in real life, faced prison time for tax evasion. Ocean County has been the fastest-growing part of New Jersey, a kind of Frost Belt Florida, with many retirees from New York and North Jersey eager to leave urban crime and high taxes. But it hasn't been all paradise lately; Hurricane Sandy in 2012 damaged more than 40,000 buildings in the county, its 20-foot waves smashing boardwalks and flooding dunes. Years later, thousands of homeowners and renters were still struggling with claims for recovery assistance from the state. In Lacey Township, the Oyster Creed Generating Station — the oldest nuclear-power plant in the nation — shut down service in September 2018; about 300 of the 400 employees were retained for the decommissioning, which was expected to take eight years and cost $980 million.

The 3rd Congressional District of New Jersey spans the Pine Barrens and thousands of acres of farmland, plus the Joint Base. It includes large parts of Burlington and Ocean counties, including several suburban Philadelphia townships. Nearly 60 percent of the population resides in Burlington; Ocean County is more Republican-leaning. The 3rd is comfortable, but not affluent, suburban territory. Donald Trump in 2016 won the district, 51%-45%. This is likely to remain a swing district.

Chris Smith (R)

Elected 1980, 20th term, b. Mar 04, 1953; Rahway; Worcester College (England), 1974; Trenton State College (NJ), B.A., 1975; Roman Catholic; Married (Marie Hahn Smith); 4 children.

Professional Career: Sales Executive, family-owned sporting goods business, 1975-1980; Executive Director, NJ Right to Life, 1976-1978.

DC Office: 2373 RHOB 20515, 202-225-3765, Fax: 202-225-7768, chrissmith.house.gov

State Offices: Freehold, 732-780-3035; Hamilton, 609-585-7878; Plumsted, 609-585-7878.

Committees: *Foreign Affairs*: Africa, Global Health, Global Human Rights & Internat'l Orgs (RMM); Western Hemisphere, Civilian Security, & Trade.

Group Ratings

	ADA	ACLU	AFL-CIO	LCV	ITI	COC	HAFA	ACU	CFG	FRC
2018	-	19%	-	60%	-	83%	30%	40%	28%	100%
2017	35%	C	57%	49%	C	86%	C	38%	24%	78%

Almanac Ratings 2017-18

	Economy	Social	Foreign	Composite
Liberal	39%	18%	10%	22%
Conservative	61%	82%	90%	78%

Key Votes of the 115th Congress

1. Obama-care revision	N	5. Family planning regs	Y	9. Guantanamo prisoners	N
2. Tax Cuts	N	6. Body cameras/immigration	Y	10. Ground missiles, limit	N
3. Omnibus appropriations	Y	7. Abortion ban	Y	11. Defense Dept. spending	Y
4. Dodd-Frank revision	Y	8. Concealed carry	N	12. FISA rules	Y

Election Results

Election	Name (Party)	Vote (%)		Cand. Spent	Ind. Exp. Support	Ind. Exp. Oppose
2018 General	Chris Smith (R)	163,065	(55%)	$1,528,237	$42,038	
	Josh Welle (D)	126,766	(43%)	$1,823,992		$12,000
2018 Primary	Chris Smith (R)		(100%)			

Prior winning percentages: 2016 (64%), 2014 (68%), 2012 (64%), 2010 (69%), 2008 (66%), 2006 (66%), 2004 (67%), 2002 (66%), 2000 (63%), 1998 (62%), 1996 (64%), 1994 (68%), 1992 (62%), 1990 (63%), 1988 (66%), 1986 (61%), 1984 (61%), 1982 (53%), 1980 (57%)

Republican Chris Smith, first elected in 1980, combines outspoken opposition to abortion with an equally passionate commitment to human rights, whoever the perpetrator may be. Such independence does not always sit well with Republican leaders, though Smith's tenacity has made him one of the most successful legislators at guiding bills into law. Even though he is tied for the third-senior Republican in the House, his independence has led to setbacks in his quest for a committee chairmanship. But that independence yielded endorsements from some liberal groups and helped him to survive reelection in 2018, when the House GOP lost its four other seats in New Jersey.

Smith grew up in the Trenton area, worked in his family's sporting goods business, and, after graduating from the College of New Jersey with a degree in business administration, he became executive director of the New Jersey Right to Life Committee in 1976. Four years later, he ran for the House in the Trenton-centered district and defeated 26-year Rep. Frank Thompson, a Democrat convicted in the Abscam bribery scandal.

He has won enactment of more than 50 bills since he took office, according to congressional websites. Smith "has a gift for embracing issues that touch nerves and generate publicity," Bob Braun, a columnist for The Star-Ledger of Newark, once wrote. In 2018, he enacted legislation to extend AIDS relief overseas, assist victims of genocide by terrorist groups and fund programs that combat sex trafficking around the world.

A devout Roman Catholic, Smith is best known for his unwavering fight against legalized abortion. He has worked to stop abortions in military hospitals, and he persuaded the George W. Bush administration to reinstate Reagan-era restrictions denying federal funds to family-planning organizations that promote abortions abroad. (Three days after President Donald Trump took office, he rescinded President Barack Obama's executive order that had removed the earlier restrictions.) Smith was a prime mover of legislation to ban "partial birth" abortions. After Republicans regained control of the House in 2011, Smith passed a bill taking away tax benefits from employee-sponsored health insurance plans that offer abortion coverage. Critics said his bill was a step toward outlawing abortions.

Smith has long crusaded for his Unborn Child Pain Awareness Act, which would require doctors to inform pregnant women that some experts say that a fetus can feel pain after 20 weeks of gestation. The House passed the bill in 2015, after agreeing to limits to accommodate several House GOP women. He has a bill to revoke the Food and Drug Administration's approval of the abortifacient RU-486, which Smith calls "baby pesticide." He has opposed federal funding for embryonic stem cell research, which uses excess embryos from in vitro fertilization, but he has been a champion of other stem cell research. In 2005, Congress enacted his Stem Cell Therapeutic and Research Act, which funds research and therapy using umbilical cord stem cells plus cells from bone marrow transplants. In the 2016 campaign, Smith was a co-chair of the Pro-Life Coalition for Trump.

Smith has brought his strong moral views to his work against human rights abuses abroad. He has sharply criticized China for its forced sterilizations and abortions, and its persecution of Christians and other religious minorities. As a result, he opposed normalizing trade relations with the country. Smith has condemned Russia for barring entry of foreign Catholic priests, and he criticized the Saudis for treating foreign servants as slaves.

Overall, Smith has been one of the most moderate members of the House GOP. In 2009, he was one of eight Republicans to support the House-passed energy bill imposing a cap-and-trade system to limit greenhouse gas emissions. He cosponsored the so-called "card check" bill aimed at making it easier for unions to organize work sites by eliminating secret-ballot elections.

Earlier, he dramatized his willingness to buck his party for the sake of his beliefs and to accept the consequences when, as chairman of the Veterans' Affairs Committee, Smith angered budget conservatives by pushing expanded benefits for veterans. In a major breach of party protocol, he voted for the Democratic spending plan because it contained more money for the Veterans Affairs Department. In 2005, the Republican Steering Committee booted Smith from his chairmanship. Since then, Smith's bids to chair the Foreign Affairs Committee have been thwarted when GOP leaders chose more reliable conservatives. Instead, Smith has been the senior Republican on the tailor-made Subcommittee on Africa, Global Health, Global Human Rights and International Organizations.

Smith's devotion to principle and his reputation for tending to constituent problems have made him popular in the 4th District, which has become safely Republican. In 2018, Democratic challenger Joshua Welle, a Navy veteran and founder of a software company that worked with the Pentagon on cybersecurity, said voters wanted "someone with the courage to hold [Trump] accountable." He outspent Smith, $1.8 million to $1.5 million. — the first campaign in which Smith or his opponent exceeded $1 million. Smith was among the few Republicans endorsed by the AFL-CIO and former

Rep. Gabby Giffords's gun-control group. He won, 55%-43% -- the first time since 1984 that he received less than 61 percent of the vote.

Following the election, Smith said he was aided during the campaign by his votes against the Republican-passed tax cuts and repeal of the Affordable Care Act. "I vote my conscience and I vote my district," he said. He added that he would be working with Democrats on local transportation and tax issues.

NJ-4: Central New Jersey

Cook Partisan Voting Index: R+8

Population		Race and Ethnicity		Income	
Total	741,766	White	77.6%	Median Income	$80,949
Land area (sq. miles)	692	Black	6.2%	District Income Rank	49
Pop/ sq mi	1072.1	Latino	10.4%	Poverty Rate	9.5%
Born in State	59.5%	Asian	4.2%	With health insurance	92.7%
		Two or more races	1.4%	Cash public assistance	1.6%
Age Groups		Other	0.2%	Food stamp/SNAP	6.6%
Under 18	24.4%				
18-34	19%	**Education**		**Work**	
35-64	38.8%	H.S grad or less	34.9%	White Collar	17.8%
Over 64	17.8%	Some college	25.6%	Sales and Service	41.9%
		College Degree, 4 yr	24.4%	Blue Collar	15.5%
Military		Post grad	15%	Government	14.9%
Veteran/ Active Duty	6.7%				

2012 Pres. Vote	Romney	180,437	(55%)	Obama	148,621	(45%)			
2016 Pres. Vote	Trump	198,859	(55%)	Clinton	146,191	(41%)	Johnson	7,184	(2%)

Monmouth and Ocean Counties: An invisible and not-well-defined line divides North Jersey and South Jersey. North of the line, people watch New York television stations, eat hero sandwiches and root for the Yankees. South of the line, they watch Philadelphia television, eat hoagies and root for the Phillies. The state capital of Trenton lies south of the line, which passes east somewhere around Six Flags Great Adventure in the Pine Barrens and heads southeast past Lakewood and Brick to the Jersey Shore. On both sides of the line, a stronger New Jersey identity has developed. The big cities — New York and Philadelphia — are not all that close, particularly when traffic is heavy, which is often. The economy of central New Jersey has its own character, with big pharmaceutical companies and the consolidated Joint Base McGuire-Dix-Lakehurst. (The German zeppelin Hindenburg exploded while docking in 1937 at what was then called Lakehurst Naval Air Station.)

No less a true New Jersey persona than Bruce Springsteen was raised in Freehold Borough, the subject of his bleak portrayal in "My Hometown." Freehold Township, which grew 15 percent from 2000 to 2010, is now a city of 35,000. Local news stories report that millennials are choosing these suburban areas; they resist exorbitant housing costs in New York City and they prefer open space. The Asbury Park Press reported in July 2018, "a growing number moving from cities back to the suburbs." Lakewood, the area's biggest town, has become the fastest-growing area in New Jersey and home to the nation's largest population of Orthodox Jews outside of Brooklyn -- they live in crowded housing and account for more than 60 percent of Lakewood's population of 103,000, an increase from 45,000 in 1990. Local school enrollments have declined because most of the children attend private religious schools. There have been claims of welfare abuses and tensions with local minority groups. Other locals resisted when some of its members sought to become homebuyers in nearby Tom's River. After reducing its project to 66 acres and settling a lawsuit by environmentalists, Six Flags won approval for "the world's first solar-powered theme park..

The Fourth Congressional District of New Jersey is based in Monmouth County, which has about 60 percent of its population, with parts of Mercer County and the fast-growing exurban Ocean County making up the rest. The district has become relatively safe for Republicans. Donald Trump got 55 percent of the vote here in 2016, the same as Mitt Romney got in 2012. In each case, the 4th was the best GOP district in New Jersey.

Josh Gottheimer (D)

Elected 2016, 2nd term, b. Mar 08, 1975; Livingston; University of Pennsylvania, B.A., 1997; Harvard Law School (MA), J.D., 2004; Jewish; Married (Marla Brooke Tusk Gottheimer); 2 children.

Professional Career: Special Assistant and Speechwriter, President Bill Clinton, 1998-2001; Senior Counselor, Federal Communications Commission, 2010-2012.

DC Office: 213 CHOB 20515, 202-225-4465, Fax: 202-225-9048, gottheimer.house.gov

State Offices: Glen Rock, 201-389-1100; Hackensack, 973-814-4076; Newton, 973-940-1117; Ringwood, 973-814-4076; Vernon Township, 973-814-4076; Washington, 973-814-4076.

Committees: *Financial Services*: Investor Protection, Entrepreneurship & Capital Markets; Nat'l Security, International Development & Monetary Policy; Subcommittee on Diversity & Inclusion.

Group Ratings

	ADA	ACLU	AFL-CIO	LCV	ITI	COC	HAFA	ACU	CFG	FRC
2018	-	64%	-	80%	-	75%	8%	16%	18%	20%
2017	60%	C	79%	83%	C	71%	C	7%	8%	11%

Almanac Ratings 2017-18

	Economy	Social	Foreign	Composite
Liberal	66%	76%	27%	56%
Conservative	34%	24%	73%	44%

Key Votes of the 115th Congress

1. Obama-care revision	N	5. Family planning regs	N	9. Guantanamo prisoners	N
2. Tax Cuts	N	6. Body cameras/immigration	Y	10. Ground missiles, limit	N
3. Omnibus appropriations	Y	7. Abortion ban	N	11. Defense Dept. spending	Y
4. Dodd-Frank revision	Y	8. Concealed carry	N	12. FISA rules	Y

Election Results

Election	Name (Party)	Vote (%)		Cand. Spent	Ind. Exp. Support	Ind. Exp. Oppose
2018 General	Josh Gottheimer (D)	169,546	(56%)	$2,845,418	$571,521	
	John McCann (R)	128,255	(43%)	$933,058	$13,104	$557,889
2018 Primary	Josh Gottheimer (D)		(100%)			

Prior winning percentages: 2016 (51%)

Democrat Josh Gottheimer, elected in 2016 by defeating a veteran Republican incumbent, has pressed for bipartisanship, to the occasional discomfort of each party. As a self-styled problem solver, he has sought to revive the fading brand of political centrism. Gottheimer's approach has played well politically for him at home. He could become a model for some of the four Democrats from New Jersey who took Republican-held seats in 2018.

Born and raised in New Jersey, Gottheimer was introduced to politics as a high school student, when he served as a page for Democratic Sen. Frank Lautenberg. He got his bachelor's at the University of Pennsylvania, then became a Thouron Fellow at Oxford University in England. After working on the rapid response team for Bill Clinton during his 1996 reelection campaign, he joined the Clinton administration as a speechwriter from 1998 until 2001. Gottheimer attended law school at Harvard University, while working for the 2004 presidential campaigns of Wesley Clark and then John Kerry. Following that election, Gottheimer worked for Ford Motor Co. and later became executive vice president for Burson-Marsteller and an official for Microsoft. On the staff of the Federal Communications Commission, he was its first director of public-private initiatives.

His race against Rep. Scott Garrett was heavily funded on both sides as Democrats fought to unseat the seven-term Republican who was the most conservative member of New Jersey's congressional delegation. His uncompromising views on reining in federal spending and banking regulation made him a player on the House Budget and Financial Services committees and as a founder of the conservative Freedom Caucus. But they set him apart from his Garden State colleagues and he appeared to have lost touch with key parts of his upscale district. He attracted largely negative attention when he said he would not support the National Republican Congressional Committee because it was financing candidates who are homosexual. He had never secured his Bergen County-based voters, who had been moving to the left in any case.

Gottheimer talked about governing from the center with a broad coalition of support in his Republican-leaning district. He supported tax cuts and fewer regulations and opposed President Barack Obama's nuclear deal with Iran. Gottheimer benefited from record fundraising for a House candidate from New Jersey -- $4.8 million that he raised, plus another $6 million in support from Democratic groups and allies. Garrett raised $2.4 million and had less than $1 million in outside support. Gottheimer won 51%-47%, with a 56%-42% lead in Bergen. In Garrett's base of Sussex and Warren counties, the turnout and Garrett's lead were too small to make a difference. In an unusual but not unprecedented scenario, Garrett refused to cooperate in the post-election transition.

In some ways, Gottheimer followed Garrett's model once in office: He took a seat on the Financial Services Committee and was one of nine House Democrats in January 2017 to vote for a bill that eased restrictions on the Securities and Exchange Commission Later, he joined additional Democrats who worked with Republicans to reduce the Dodd-Frank financial regulations on banks. More steps should be taken, he added, to increase consumer access to credit.

Gottheimer showed the contrast to Garrett when he became co-chair of the bipartisan Problem Solvers Caucus, which has equal numbers of Democrats and Republicans and can act only with three-fourths in agreement. "I've got to do whatever I can to be at the table," he told The Wall Street Journal in July 2017. The group has made proposals — such as higher taxes to pay for more defense spending, or reduction in the authority of party leaders — that each party might oppose for separate reasons. At a meeting with President Donald Trump in September 2017, caucus members urged him to find common ground on immigration and taxes, for example; they failed to attain that objective on either issue. Following the election, the caucus — including some of its Republicans — persuaded Nancy Pelosi to agree to rules changes designed to "break the gridlock" in the House by encouraging action on legislation with bipartisan support. In the Almanac vote ratings, Gottheimer was among the half-dozen most conservative House Democrats. He ranked high among Democrats voting with Trump.

At home, Gottheimer faced Republican challenger John McCann, a former legal counsel to the Bergen County sheriff, who said that Gottheimer lacked familiarity with local issues and that he was "a vote for Nancy Pelosi." Gottheimer was endorsed by the U.S. Chamber of Commerce. He won more easily than two years earlier, 56%-42%, though McCann took each of the three smaller counties in the district. Later, some liberal groups complained about his objections to Pelosi and said that he was influenced by his large campaign funding from Wall Street groups. An ad that ran in Politico complained that Gottheimer "votes with Trump more than he votes with you."

NJ-5: Northern New Jersey   Cook Partisan Voting Index: R+3

Population		Race and Ethnicity		Income	
Total	745,615	White	69.6%	Median Income	$98,863
Land area (sq. miles)	991	Black	4.7%	District Income Rank	15
Pop/ sq mi	752.2	Latino	13.5%	Poverty Rate	5.6%
Born in State	52.2%	Asian	10.6%	With health insurance	93.6%
Age Groups		Two or more races	1.3%	Cash public assistance	1.4%
Under 18	22.3%	Other	0.3%	Food stamp/SNAP	4.2%
18-34	18.4%	**Education**		**Work**	
35-64	42.8%	H.S grad or less	31%	White Collar	16.5%
Over 64	16.5%	Some college	22.3%	Sales and Service	38.2%
Military		College Degree, 4 yr	29%	Blue Collar	14.3%
Veteran/ Active Duty	5.3%	Post grad	17.6%	Government	12.6%

2012 Pres. Vote	Romney	172,451	(52%)	Obama	162,318	(49%)			
2016 Pres. Vote	Trump	178,058	(48%)	Clinton	173,969	(47%)	Johnson	8,014	(2%)

Bergen County: The northern edge of New Jersey was settled three centuries ago by the Dutch, for whom this plateau of land behind the Hudson River Palisades seemed a natural part of Nieuw Amsterdam. The Dutch influence is seen in old, steep-roofed farmhouses and in many of the place names — Bergen County, Cresskill, Closter. But overall, northernmost New Jersey has the well-settled look of so many northeastern suburbs, with touches of both affluence and small-town hominess, crisscrossed at its edges with limited-access highways and shopping centers. Since the late 1950s, Paramus has been transformed from celery farms to the site of three shopping malls and numerous shopping centers that do more than $5 billion a year in retail sales. After more than 15 years of promises and delay, the American Dream mega-mall was scheduled to open in the summer of 2019, with the largest indoor theme park in the Western Hemisphere. Along the New Jersey Turnpike and five miles from Times Square, the $5 billion "Xanadu" was a high-stakes test of the future of retailing — in a suburban area that has been on the cutting edge of fancy malls.

Not far away are Saddle River and Franklin Lakes, with multimillion-dollar houses on multi-acre lots, and Park Ridge, with office buildings and condominiums. Bergenfield has many people of Filipino descent, and it's known locally as "Little Manila." In Bergen County overall, the population has grown to 20 percent Hispanic and 17 percent Asian. Bergen is the last urban county in the nation that widely complies with "Blue Law" limitations on Sunday retailing — and the only county in New Jersey that has decided not to "opt out" of the law. An advocacy group, Modernize Bergen County, has taken steps on a referendum to challenge the practice. But its supporters have been unable to obtain sufficient signatures for a referendum, and many small business owners prefer not having to worry about the malls on one day during the week. A few decades ago, two similar referenda were defeated. In the northeast corner of the district, tiny Alpine (population: 1,890) has had the distinction of the wealthiest ZIP code in the nation and a median home value exceeding $2.6 million. Taxes are relatively low, because many of the services are privatized.

The 5th Congressional District of New Jersey comprises most of northern Bergen County, plus a swath of North Jersey stretching west to the upper reaches of the Delaware River. This is the only district in New Jersey that stretches from the Delaware to the Hudson. Nearly three-fourths of its population is in Bergen County. Farther west are exurban and comfortably Republican Sussex and Warren counties, both of which have seen an aging tax base and population losses since 2010. In 2016, Donald Trump took the district, 48%-47%.

Frank Pallone (D)

Elected 1988, 16th term, b. Oct 30, 1951; Long Branch; Middlebury College (VT), B.A., 1973; Tufts University Fletcher School of Law and Diplomacy (MA), M.A., 1974; Rutgers University Law School (NJ), J.D., 1978; Roman Catholic; Married (Sarah Hospodor Pallone); 3 children.

Elected Office: Long Branch City Council, 1982-1988; NJ Senate, 1983-1988.

Professional Career: Assistant Professional, Rutgers University, 1979-1980; Practicing attorney, 1981-1983; Instructor, Monmouth College, 1984-1986.

DC Office: 2107 RHOB 20515, 202-225-4671, Fax: 202-225-9665, pallone.house.gov

State Offices: Long Branch, 732-571-1140; New Brunswick, 732-249-8892.

Committees: *Energy & Commerce (Chmn)*: Ex Officio membership on all subcommittees.

Group Ratings

	ADA	ACLU	AFL-CIO	LCV	ITI	COC	HAFA	ACU	CFG	FRC
2018	-	93%	-	91%	-	50%	9%	8%	23%	0%
2017	95%	C	100%	100%	C	36%	C	4%	5%	0%

Almanac Ratings 2017-18

	Economy	Social	Foreign	Composite
Liberal	100%	100%	97%	99%
Conservative	0%	0%	3%	1%

Key Votes of the 115th Congress

1. Obama-care revision	N	5. Family planning regs	N	9. Guantanamo prisoners	Y
2. Tax Cuts	N	6. Body cameras/immigration	Y	10. Ground missiles, limit	Y
3. Omnibus appropriations	N	7. Abortion ban	N	11. Defense Dept. spending	N
4. Dodd-Frank revision	N	8. Concealed carry	N	12. FISA rules	N

Election Results

Election	Name (Party)	Vote (%)	Cand. Spent	Ind. Exp. Support	Ind. Exp. Oppose
2018 General	Frank Pallone (D)............................. 140,752	(64%)	$1,233,551	$5,795	
	Rich Pezzullo (R)............................ 80,443	(36%)	$37,146		
2018 Primary	Frank Pallone (D)............................. 23,621	(86%)			
	Javahn Walker (D)........................ 3,770	(14%)			

Prior winning percentages: 2016 (64%), 2014 (60%), 2012 (63%), 2010 (55%), 2008 (67%), 2006 (69%), 2004 (67%), 2002 (66%), 2000 (68%), 1998 (57%), 1996 (61%), 1994 (60%), 1992 (52%), 1990 (49%), 1988 (52%), 1988 special (52%)

Democrat Frank Pallone, elected in 1988, has made his mark in a steady rise to the powerful position of chairman of the Energy and Commerce Committee. Promising an activist agenda, he faced pressure from party progressives to deliver, especially on environmental issues — which initially launched his political career. During four years as the committee's ranking Democrat while Republicans were in control, Pallone had several bipartisan achievements. Over the years, he has shown dexterity as one of his party's chief messengers and in adapting to internal changes — though he has fallen short in bids for a home-state Senate seat.

Pallone is the son of a disabled Long Branch policeman. He became an environmentalist in 1969, when as a Middlebury College freshman in Vermont he worked for that state's first-in-the-nation bottle deposit law. After getting a master's degree in international relations from Tufts University and a law degree from Rutgers, he was elected to the Long Branch City Council at age 31, and to the New Jersey Senate a year later.

Pallone ran in a special election for a House seat that a Democrat had long held. The district leaned Republican, but residents were angry about untreated sludge, plastic containers and medical waste washing up on the beach. Pallone's bumper sticker, which didn't mention party affiliation, said, "Stop Ocean Dumping." That, combined with his conservative views on taxes and crime, helped him win 52 percent of the vote.

He has had a continuing interest in protecting the New Jersey shoreline. In 2006, he won passage of a bill to reduce and prevent debris in the marine environment. Two years later, he was the lead sponsor of a bipartisan bill to rebuild American fisheries, in part by requiring a review of factors that lead to over-fishing. Pallone was chief sponsor of a 2015 law that placed restrictions on the sale or distribution of personal care products that contain synthetic plastic microbeads, which can pollute waterways. New Jersey earlier passed its own law to ban the products.

As chairman of Energy and Commerce's Subcommittee on Health, Pallone helped steer to passage in 2009 the Democrats' expansion of the Children's Health Insurance Program, which he called "a down payment to ensuring that all Americans have access to affordable health care." On the Democrats' economic stimulus bill, he backed an increase in the federal matching rate for Medicaid as a step to reduce the program's financial burden on states. During the health care overhaul debate that year, he shuttled among various factions of Blue Dogs and progressives to urge flexibility. After the bill was enacted in 2010 and Republicans tried to repeal it, Pallone was among its most outspoken defenders.

Pallone clashed with President Barack Obama on coastal issues. After the BP oil spill in the Gulf of Mexico in 2010, he and other Democrats implored Obama to oppose oil and gas drilling off the East Coast. After criticizing as "unthinkable" an initial plan by Obama for partial approval of drilling, Pallone welcomed the administration's later reversal, including a five-year moratorium, though he continued to urge a permanent ban on offshore drilling anywhere in the Atlantic.

He criticized the administration's response to Superstorm Sandy, which devastated many of his district's coastal communities in 2012. He repeatedly demanded that the Federal Emergency Management Agency provide mobile homes for thousands of stranded residents, then criticized its delivery of a mere 50 trailers. To improve local communications during emergencies, Pallone crafted the Securing Access to Networks in Disasters (SANDY) Act, which the House passed in 2017. He stepped up his criticism when President Donald Trump OK'd seismic tests as a possible prelude to oil drilling in the Atlantic. "We will continue to fight the administration's dangerous environmental policies in New Jersey, the courts and in Congress," he said in December 2018.

He has channeled the interests of his district's large Asian population. In a bow to the many persons of Armenian descent, Pallone helped push congressional approval of normalizing trade relations with Armenia. He sponsored the resolution that labeled the 1915 killing of Armenians by Ottoman Turks as genocide, which Turkey vehemently opposed. He has been active on issues involving India and has introduced a resolution condemning violence against the Hindus known as Kashmiri Pandits.

When Rep. Henry Waxman retired in 2014 as ranking Democrat on Energy and Commerce, Rep. Anna Eshoo was actively supported by her longtime friend, then-Minority Leader Nancy Pelosi, as his successor. The Pelosi-controlled Democratic Steering and Policy Committee had endorsed Eshoo, 30-19. But Eshoo was edged out by Pallone, 100-90, in secret balloting by the Democratic Caucus. Pallone highlighted that he had four years more seniority than Eshoo, which appealed to many in the Congressional Black Caucus, which includes many longtime members who benefit from seniority. He acknowledged the big boost from Minority Whip Steny Hoyer, who has had numerous battles with Pelosi.

After moving into his new position, Pallone sought to reduce the fractiousness on the panel. In 2016, the committee was instrumental in enacting the bipartisan Twenty First Century Cures Act, which advanced a series of medical-research innovations. Also that year, the committee completed the long-delayed update of chemical safety laws. The new law resolved numerous manufacturing and public-health issues related to New Jersey and gave new authority to the Environmental Protection Agency to evaluate existing and new chemicals.

With the Democratic takeover of the House — abetted by the gain of four seats in his home state — Pallone stepped in as chairman with multiple interests. "We will push an aggressive agenda to rebuild America, combat climate change, make health care and prescription drugs more affordable, and protect peoples' privacy," especially with social media, he said, when he was officially approved as chairman. He promised robust oversight of the Trump administration. Pallone has responded cautiously to the "Medicare for all" proposal. "The votes aren't there," he told reporters, while pressing instead for steps to reinforce Obamacare.

He immediately faced an internal clash when advocates — especially Democratic newcomers — demanded creation of a separate committee to handle climate-related issues, including their call for a "green new deal." Pallone insisted that Energy and Commerce was fully equipped and prepared to address those issues. Activists held a demonstration at his congressional office to protest his opposition. Pallone met with the group and sought to assure them of his solidarity with their goals. He proved largely successful internally, when Pelosi withheld legislative authority from the select committee and named Democratic Rep. Kathy Castor of Florida to chair the panel; she has been a Pallone ally at Energy and Commerce. Other House committee chairmen supported Pallone.

Since 1994, Pallone has been reelected with at least 60 percent of the vote, with two exceptions. In 1998, he faced a tough challenge from 28-year-old Republican Mike Ferguson, an ally of former GOP Gov. Thomas Kean. An insurance group unhappy with Pallone's support of President Bill Clinton's plan to regulate health maintenance organizations spent nearly $2 million on Ferguson's campaign. Pallone won 57%-40%. In 2010, he drew another formidable opponent in Republican Anna Little, the mayor of Highlands. With strong tea party backing, Little blasted Pallone's efforts to pass the health care bill. Pallone was bolstered by newspaper endorsements and kept his seat, 55%-44%.

He has had a continuing interest in the Senate, without risking his House seat. When Democratic Sen. Jon Corzine ran for governor in 2005, Pallone endorsed him. Corzine was elected, but he disappointed Pallone by appointing Rep. Robert Menendez to his Senate seat. After Democratic Sen. Frank Lautenberg died in 2013, Pallone ran in the special election and appealed to party regulars. Newark Mayor Cory Booker easily won the Democratic primary with 59 percent to 20 percent for Pallone, the runner-up. Now that he has the Energy and Commerce gavel — and with Senate Democrats in the minority — perhaps his patience in the House has served him well.

NJ-6: East-Central New Jersey **Cook Partisan Voting Index: D+9**

Population		Race and Ethnicity		Income	
Total	745,204	White	47.7%	Median Income	$80,087
Land area (sq. miles)	216	Black	9.5%	District Income Rank	53
Pop/ sq mi	3457.2	Latino	21.8%	Poverty Rate	10.2%
Born in State	49.8%	Asian	18.9%	With health insurance	90.1%
		Two or more races	1.6%	Cash public assistance	2%
Age Groups		Other	0.4%	Food stamp/SNAP	7.8%
Under 18	21.8%				
18-34	24.7%	**Education**		**Work**	
35-64	40.6%	H.S grad or less	38.7%	White Collar	12.9%
Over 64	12.9%	Some college	22.2%	Sales and Service	38.9%
		College Degree, 4 yr	23.3%	Blue Collar	19.4%
Military		Post grad	15.8%	Government	12.5%
Veteran/ Active Duty	4%				

2012 Pres. Vote	Obama	163,428	(62%)	Romney	99,564	(38%)
2016 Pres. Vote	Clinton	162,858	(56%)	Trump	117,679	(40%)

Middlesex and Northern Monmouth Counties: For generations, great transportation arteries have brought people out of the huge central cities of New York and Philadelphia and into the flatlands and hills of New Jersey — to vacation, to raise families, to work toward affluence and to build communities. The railroads of the late 19th century created the towns of the Jersey shore. After 1874, when the first train from New York City reached Long Branch, the shore became the summer home of seven presidents from Grant to Wilson (James Garfield, convalescing after he was shot, died there in 1881), and of New York racehorse owners and socialites. Over time, the ambiance degraded, and the fishing pier and much of the boardwalk went up in flames in 1987. A shopping and dining complex took its place. Plans for commuter ferries from these Jersey communities to Manhattan, which were common decades ago, have not moved much beyond the discussion stage. One potential applicant is the Pier Village resort in Long Beach, which is owned by the family of Jared Kushner, son-in-law of President Donald Trump.

The freight rail lines in the New York-Philadelphia corridor sparked electrical and chemical industries here — many of them building on the inventions of Thomas Edison, produced in his Menlo Park laboratory just off the rail lines. Today, a 131-foot tower stands as a memorial to the inventor. The same corridor was the site of America's first cloverleaf intersection, at the junction of U.S. 1 and U.S. 9. The New Jersey Turnpike roars past oil tank farms and petrochemical plants, major rail lines and the oily waters of Raritan Bay. Superstorm Sandy devastated much of this area in 2012. In 2018, the state's environmental protection department was reviewing options for flood-control plans to protect the coast and inland waterways. In Sayerville, a developer planned to start construction in 2019 of a $2.5 billion project — Riverton — with a marina, office space, parks and 2,000 residential units.

The 6th Congressional District inelegantly ties together these great transportation nodes, and the upward mobility that has taken place around them. The district is shaped like a backward capital F, with a string of towns running from Piscataway down the Atlantic coast to Long Branch and Asbury Park. Middlesex County accounts for two-thirds of the district's population, with the remainder in Monmouth County. The two largest localities are Woodbridge and Edison Township — an industrial area that has housed some of America's great research and development facilities. Asbury Park, which began as a Christian resort and was immortalized in the music of Bruce Springsteen, has claimed some progress in its plans for economic revival, especially for summer homes. The district has become majority-minority: 22 percent Latino, 19 percent Asian and 10 percent black. It has the third-largest share of Asians of any district on the East Coast, behind two in New York City. The largest and fastest-growing group is Indians, whose "Little India" community in once-abandoned areas of Woodbridge and Edison attracts Asian business interests from elsewhere in the Northeast. Emirates airline serves this community with a daily flight from Newark to Dubai and beyond; the Indian community provides about one-third of its U.S. passengers.

This is a safe Democratic district. The presidential contest tightened in 2016, when Hillary Clinton led Donald Trump, 56%-40%.

Tom Malinowski (D)

Elected 2018, 1st term, b. Sep 15, 1965; Slupsk, Poland; Oxford University (UK); Oxford University (UK); Divorced; 1 child.

Professional Career: Special Assistant, U.S. Sen. Danial Patrick Moynihan, 1988; Research Assistant, Institute for Human Sciences, 1992; Research Assistant, Ford Foundation, 1993; Policy Planning Staff and Speechwriter, U.S. Department of State, 1994-1998; Senior Director, National Security Council, 1998-2001; Washington Director, Human Rights Watch, 2001-2013; Assistant Secretary of State for Democracy, Human Rights, and Labor, U.S. Department of State, 2014-2017.

DC Office: 426 CHOB 20515, 202-225-5361, malinowski.house.gov

State Offices: Somerville, 908-547-3307.

Committees: *Foreign Affairs*: Middle East, North Africa & International Terrorism; Oversight & Investigations. *Transportation & Infrastructure*: Highways & Transit; Railroads, Pipelines & Hazardous Materials; Water Resources & Environment.

Election Results

Election	Name (Party)	Vote (%)		Cand. Spent	Ind. Exp. Support	Ind. Exp. Oppose
2018 General	Tom Malinowski (D)	166,985	(52%)	$6,188,595	$1,000,307	$3,569,286
	Leonard Lance (R)	150,785	(47%)	$2,626,112	$2,591,028	$3,982,883
2018 Primary	Tom Malinowski (D)	26,172	(67%)			
	Peter Jacob (D)	7,503	(19%)			
	Goutam Jois (D)	5,507	(14%)			

Democrat Tom Malinowski won his traditionally Republican district in his first bid for elected office. With his national security experience in the Clinton and Obama administrations, most prominently on human rights issues, he was among the most seasoned Washington players in the freshman class. He defeated Rep. Leonard Lance, a wonky five-term Republican who had survived close primary challenges from more conservative opponents but had become secure in general elections. Like many incoming Democrats, Malinowski significantly outspent the incumbent.

Born in Poland, Malinowski settled with his mother in Princeton when he was age six. He graduated from the University of California, Berkeley, and, as a Rhodes scholar, earned his master's degree in political science at Oxford University. Following brief stints with Democratic Sen. Daniel Patrick Moynihan and the Ford Foundation, he spent four years on the policy planning staff at the State Department. In 1998, he joined the Clinton White House as a speechwriter at the National Security Council.

During the presidency of George W. Bush, Malinowski was Washington Director for Human Rights Watch, where he was an outspoken critic of military and intelligence tactics during the U.S. "war on terror." He continued in that position during the first term of the Obama presidency. Republican Sen. John McCain said that he was "forever grateful" to Malinowski for his role in the fight in Congress to end the use of "enhanced interrogation techniques" that McCain and others likened to torture. With Secretary of State John Kerry, Malinowski returned to government as assistant secretary for democracy, human rights and labor. In that position, his portfolio included protection of religious minorities targeted by ISIS and sanctions against North Korea.

Malinowski launched his campaign with criticism of Lance for supporting Republican legislation that was "harmful to our district," and attacks on President Donald Trump for having challenged "everything that I've worked for on behalf of our country." During the Democratic primary, he said, "The big question is who can win and who can be effective if he wins." Runner-up Peter Jacob, a social worker who supported the "Medicare for all" proposal and was backed by groups associated with Sen. Bernie Sanders, had lost to Lance in 2016, 54%-43%. With the crucial endorsement of county Democratic committees in the district, which were impressed by his superior fundraising, Malinowski won the primary with 67 percent of the vote.

Lance struggled to balance party loyalty with growing antagonism by his constituents toward Trump, including frequent protests at Lance's district office. During a campaign debate, Lance — who voted against House Republican health care and tax bills in 2017 — said that he maintained his support for moderate Republican positions and called Malinowski a "carpetbagger" who had spent most of his career in Washington.

"I got more legislation passed as a non-member of the United States Congress than Leonard Lance has ever gotten passed as a member," Malinowski responded. He criticized Lance for failing to be more outspoken in opposing Trump and he promised checks on one-party government. In its editorial endorsement of Malinowski, The Newark Star-Ledger dismissed Lance's influence and said, voters "can no longer afford effete lawmakers who feed Trump's dogmatic arrogance."

As with other leading Democratic challengers in 2018, Malinowski's surge of fundraising prior to the election resulted in spending for his campaign that more than doubled Lance's expenditures. In his 52%-47% victory, he easily took Union and Somerset counties, which cast more than half the total vote. Lance won the outlying counties. With the prospect that Malinowski will face a competitive reelection challenge in 2020, Republicans likely will test whether he has returned to his familiar ground as a "Washington insider." In April 2019, Tom Kean Jr., the minority leader in the state Senate and son of the former governor, announced his challenge to Malinowski. Kean ran for the House in 2000, but lost in the Republican primary to Mike Ferguson, who won the seat. Weeks after Kean's announcement, Malinowski was among the first Democratic freshmen who won a formerly Republican seat to call for an impeachment investigation of Trump.

NJ-7: North-Central New Jersey — Cook Partisan Voting Index: R+3

Population		Race and Ethnicity		Income	
Total	745,147	White	71.7%	Median Income	$109,061
Land area (sq. miles)	970	Black	4.6%	District Income Rank	4
Pop/ sq mi	768	Latino	12.1%	Poverty Rate	4.9%
Born in State	56.5%	Asian	9.8%	With health insurance	94.6%
		Two or more races	1.4%	Cash public assistance	1.3%
Age Groups		Other	0.5%	Food stamp/SNAP	3.5%
Under 18	23.2%				
18-34	17.4%	**Education**		**Work**	
35-64	44.2%	H.S grad or less	27.2%	White Collar	15.2%
Over 64	15.2%	Some college	20.6%	Sales and Service	36.1%
		College Degree, 4 yr	29.5%	Blue Collar	12.6%
Military		Post grad	22.7%	Government	12.1%
Veteran/ Active Duty	4.8%				

2012 Pres. Vote	Romney	178,318	(53%)	Obama	157,285	(47%)		
2016 Pres. Vote	Clinton	180,525	(48%)	Trump	176,386	(47%)	Johnson	9,794 (3%)

Somerset, Union and Hunterdon Counties: The transportation arteries beneath First Watchung Mountain played a large role in New Jersey's development. The rail lines of the late 19th century opened up commuter suburbs. In the 1940s, the four lanes of U.S. 22 made those communities readily accessible by car. Next, Interstate 78, completed in the mid-1980s, put Newark only an hour's distance from the Pennsylvania line. An enormous shopping mall and office development, which included the headquarters of AT&T, rose up in the horse country around Far Hills and Bernardsville, where the likes of Malcolm Forbes and Charles Engelhard owned huge estates. (New Jersey claims more horses per square mile than any other state.) Nearby is the town of Bedminster, more than 40 miles from Manhattan and the site of Trump National Golf Club, which President Donald Trump turned into an informal "summer White House." Some of the employees at the club reportedly have been undocumented immigrants. These towns are in Somerset County, with a median household income in 2017 of $106,000, the 12th highest among U.S. counties. Somerset has become an active tourist destination, including for beer and wine enthusiasts.

Nearby, fast-growing Hunterdon County has the nation's seventh highest median household income, at $111,000. Hunterdon lost about 2 percent of its population between 2010 and 2017, chiefly because some of its kids have grown up and moved away. To the east, Diamond Nation in Flemington is a 35-acre baseball and softball complex and the site of many tournaments. Flemington was also the setting of the "trial of the century," in the kidnapping and murder of the 20-month-old son of aviator Charles Lindbergh.

The 7th Congressional District of New Jersey covers several generations of suburban development. It crosses the breadth of the state, from the edge of Pennsylvania's Lehigh Valley in the west to parts of Union County in the east. It is an agglomeration of places, and includes parts of five counties and all of Hunterdon. The largest slice of population is the 32 percent in Somerset County, with 25 percent in Union County and about 18 percent in Hunterdon County. The district usually favors Republicans, but not overwhelmingly. Trump in 2016 had less appeal in these upscale precincts. He trailed Hillary Clinton, 48%-47%. This was the only one of the five districts in New Jersey that Republicans held at the time, where Clinton led, albeit narrowly.

Albio Sires (D)

Elected 2006, 8th term, b. Jan 26, 1951; Bejucal, Cuba; Middlebury College (VT), M.A., 1985; Saint Peter's College (NJ), M.A., 1985; Roman Catholic; Married (Adrienne Sires); 1 stepchild.

Elected Office: West New York Mayor, 1995-2006; NJ Assembly, 2000-2006, speaker, 2002-2006.

Professional Career: H.S. Spanish & ESL teacher, 1975-1985; Special Assistant, NJ Department of Comm. Affairs, 1985; Part-owner, A.M. Title Agency, 1986-2006.

DC Office: 2268 RHOB 20515, 202-225-7919, Fax: 202-226-0792, sires.house.gov

State Offices: Elizabeth, 908-820-0692; Jersey City, 201-309-0301; West New York, 201-558-0800.

Committees: *Budget. Foreign Affairs*: Europe, Eurasia, Energy & the Environment; Western Hemisphere, Civilian Security, & Trade (Chmn). *Transportation & Infrastructure*: Highways & Transit; Railroads, Pipelines & Hazardous Materials.

Group Ratings

	ADA	ACLU	AFL-CIO	LCV	ITI	COC	HAFA	ACU	CFG	FRC
2018	-	74%	-	89%	-	60%	6%	4%	16%	0%
2017	90%	C	97%	97%	C	46%	C	8%	5%	11%

Almanac Ratings 2017-18

	Economy	Social	Foreign	Composite
Liberal	100%	94%	75%	90%
Conservative	0%	6%	25%	10%

Key Votes of the 115th Congress

1. Obama-care revision	N	5. Family planning regs	N	9. Guantanamo prisoners	N
2. Tax Cuts	N	6. Body cameras/immigration	Y	10. Ground missiles, limit	Y
3. Omnibus appropriations	Y	7. Abortion ban	N	11. Defense Dept. spending	Y
4. Dodd-Frank revision	N	8. Concealed carry	N	12. FISA rules	Y

Election Results

Election	Name (Party)	Vote (%)		Cand. Spent	Ind. Exp. Support	Ind. Exp. Oppose
2018 General	Albio Sires (D)	119,881	(78%)	$428,947		
	John Muniz (R)	28,725	(19%)	$5,006		
2018 Primary	Albio Sires (D)		(100%)			

Prior winning percentages: 2016 (77%), 2014 (77%), 2012 (78%), 2010 (74%), 2008 (75%), 2006 (78%)

Democrat Albio Sires, who won a special election in 2006, is the only Cuban-American Democrat in the House. He is an old-style political boss who remains influential in Hudson County. Sires concentrates on local issues, and on foreign policies that affect his district, including his continued tough stance against leftist regimes south of the border. Despite his willingness to go his separate way from other Democrats, he took the strategic chairmanship of the Western Hemisphere Subcommittee.

Sires, who was born in Cuba, remembers the book-burning following the Communist revolution there. His family fled Fidel Castro's regime in 1962 when he was 10. He attended St. Peter's College on a four-year basketball scholarship — he is 6-feet-4-inches tall — then earned a master's degree from Middlebury College. He became a high school Spanish teacher.

On his fourth try, he was elected mayor of West New York as a Republican in 1995 and held that post until 2006. He focused on creation of more affordable housing in the small but densely populated town and won praise for merging the fire department with three neighboring departments. He switched parties in 1999 and, with the support of his new party's leaders, defeated a veteran Democratic incumbent to win a state House seat. With strong support from Democratic Gov. Jim McGreevey in 2002, he became speaker of the Assembly.

After Democratic Gov. Jon Corzine appointed Rep. Robert Menendez as his replacement in the Senate, Sires became the frontrunner for the House seat. In the primary, he faced a fierce challenge from Joe Vas of Perth Amboy, who likewise was a state House member and a mayor. Vas assailed Sires as a puppet of the Hudson County Democratic machine. Sires responded by depicting Vas as soft on crime and won the support of most leading Democrats, except for his longtime rival Menendez, who remained neutral. Sires crushed Vas 80%-20% in Hudson County, which cast 74 percent of the total vote. Overall, he won 72%-28%. Sires won the general, 78%-19%, and has been reelected easily since. With his lieutenants, he has gained growing control of the Democratic organization in the county.

In the House, Sires established a voting record that has placed him toward the middle of the House, especially on foreign policy, according to the Almanac vote ratings. He allied himself with South Florida members who have wanted to keep U.S. sanctions on Cuba in place, including travel and economic aid. As ranking Democrat on the Foreign Affairs Committee's Western Hemisphere panel, he opposed President Barack Obama's opening to Cuba in 2014 as "naïve and disrespectful," and said that the effort to "encourage a form of Cuban glasnost is a dangerous miscalculation." He remained a harsh critic of the steps to establish diplomatic relations with Cuba, and advocated retention of the embargo. In 2015, Sires opposed Obama's agreement with Iran on nuclear fuel. He said that the timeframe for the agreement was too short and he objected that Iran would be "allowed to enhance its nuclear and weapons capabilities." Taking the gavel of the Western Hemisphere Subcommittee in 2019, he threatened stiffer sanctions against anti-American regimes.

On the Transportation and Infrastructure Committee, he was successful in convincing the Army Corps of Engineers to raise the Bayonne Bridge's height to accommodate larger ships. He introduced legislation to revitalize urban parks, and to help commuters find alternative ways to get to work. In 2015, he was one of 28 House Democrats who opposed Obama and sided with some unions in support of the Keystone XL pipeline. In 2018, he criticized President Donald Trump for failing to support the Gateway tunnel project under the Hudson River.

In the 2010 election, Sires was a vice chair of the Democratic Congressional Campaign Committee, in charge of member participation and outreach. After Democrats lost their majority, he called for Speaker Nancy Pelosi to step down. His comments didn't endear him to Democratic leaders, nor did the fact that he raised significantly less money than other DCCC leaders. Following the 2018 election, he was among the cadre of Democrats who sought an alternative to Pelosi as Speaker, though he eventually supported her.

NJ-8: Jersey City/Newark Area   Cook Partisan Voting Index: D+27

Population		Race and Ethnicity		Income	
Total	774,492	White	25.3%	Median Income	$57,012
Land area (sq. miles)	55	Black	8.5%	District Income Rank	205
Pop/ sq mi	14161.5	Latino	54.6%	Poverty Rate	17.6%
Born in State	37%	Asian	8.8%	With health insurance	80.7%
		Two or more races	1.4%	Cash public assistance	4%
Age Groups		Other	1.3%	Food stamp/SNAP	16.6%
Under 18	21.7%				
18-34	28.9%	**Education**		**Work**	
35-64	39%	H.S grad or less	49.7%	White Collar	10.4%
Over 64	10.4%	Some college	18.8%	Sales and Service	41.4%
		College Degree, 4 yr	19.9%	Blue Collar	25.1%
Military		Post grad	11.7%	Government	9.5%
Veteran/ Active Duty	2.1%				

2012 Pres. Vote	Obama	161,443	(79%)	Romney	42,896	(21%)
2016 Pres. Vote	Clinton	173,834	(75%)	Trump	49,336	(21%)

Hudson County: Standing in New York Harbor since 1886, the Statue of Liberty has been the symbol of America's receptiveness to immigrants. The statue is on the New Jersey side of the harbor, and so is, as the U.S. Supreme Court ruled in 1998, most of Ellis Island, where immigrants once were processed, though the museum is on the New York side of the island. So it's natural that the towns atop the granite and gneiss ridge of Hudson County, overlooking the harbor, became immigrant territory. Many children and grandchildren of Irish and Italian immigrants stayed in Hudson County, living in the same neighborhoods, working on the same docks or in the factories, and voting the dictates of the same political machine. Hudson County was the setting of one of America's classic political machines, undisciplined by any metropolitan elite. From 1917 to 1949, the boss of Hudson County was Frank ("I am the law") Hague. His machine chose governors and U.S. senators, prosecutors and judges, and had influence in the White House of Franklin D. Roosevelt. Hague collected high taxes from industries clustered here, which then passed them on to consumers. In return, he gave them an orderly city, free of most crime and vice, and a workforce insulated against racketeers and militant unions.

Hudson County has changed. New immigrants arrived — refugees from Fidel Castro's Cuba, and other Latinos and Asians. Union City has gained a mix of Colombian, Ecuadoran, Peruvian, Dominican and Filipino immigrants. Starting in the 1980s, huge new condominium and office developments went up in Jersey City, housing big banks, securities firms and, later, internet businesses. By 2018, the waterfront in Jersey City had been fully built-out, with a high and growing skyline, and many parts had gentrified with young families settling in. Upscale young singles moved into Hoboken's five-story Victorians; they were a quick commute through the PATH tubes to Wall Street or Greenwich Village. In Hoboken, the home of Frank Sinatra and the Oreo cookie, shopping and apartment complexes have taken up the waterfront sites where factories were common (and where the classic movie On the Waterfront was filmed). Hoboken attracts urban professionals plus a growing number of families seeking affordable housing; the city, which grew by 42 percent from 2000 to 2017, has been called the "Millennial Capital" of New Jersey. In 2017, Hoboken elected as mayor a Sikh who was unfairly accused in campaign flyers of being a "terrorist." Since 2010, the 9 percent population increase in Hudson made it the fastest-growing county in the state. Bayonne has become a cruise ship port. Its 5,780-foot-long bridge, built in 1931, has been raised from 151 feet to 215 feet high so it is tall enough for super-sized container ships. The project was completed in June 2017 — six months ahead of schedule, at a cost of $1.6 billion for the bridge and $2.1 billion for the dredging of the harbor. A former military terminal at Bayonne was sold in 2018 and converted to industrial warehouse space, with 2,700 jobs.

The 8th Congressional District includes much of Hudson County, plus most of the immigrant entry ports along the water and the bustling docks along the Hudson River and New York Bay. It takes in Hoboken and Elizabeth, now 64 percent Hispanic; nearly half of Newark; West New York and Weehawken; parts of Jersey City and Bayonne; working-class Harrison, an aging factory town where

European immigrants have been replaced by Hispanic immigrants; and part of industrial Kearny. The district is 55 percent Hispanic, by far the largest percentage in the state; 44 percent of the population is foreign-born. In Jersey City, many are from India. About 70 percent of the district is in Hudson, plus sections of Essex and Union and a thin slice of Bergen County. The district lines in Hudson and Essex counties were drawn like pieces of a jig-saw puzzle to assure that the 8th District is heavily Hispanic and the 10th District is heavily black. In 2016, Hillary Clinton got 75 percent of the vote.

Bill Pascrell (D)

Elected 1996, 12th term, b. Jan 25, 1937; Paterson; Fordham University (NY), B.S., 1959; Fordham University (NY), M.A., 1961; Roman Catholic; Married (Elsie Marie Botto Pascrell); 3 children; 3 grandchildren.

Military Career: U.S. Army 1961-1962; U.S. Army Reserve 1962-1967

Elected Office: President, Paterson Board of Education, 1979-1982; NJ Assembly, 1988-1997, Minority Leader pro temp; Paterson Mayor, 1990-1996.

Professional Career: H.S. teacher, 1960-1974; Director, Paterson Department of Public Works, 1974-1977; Director, Paterson Department of Policy, 1977-1987.

DC Office: 2409 RHOB 20515, 202-225-5751, Fax: 202-225-5782, pascrell.house.gov
State Offices: Englewood, 201-935-2248; Lyndhurst, 201-935-2248; Passaic, 973-472-4510; Paterson, 973-523-5152.

Committees: *Ways & Means*: Social Security; Trade.

Group Ratings

	ADA	ACLU	AFL-CIO	LCV	ITI	COC	HAFA	ACU	CFG	FRC
2018	-	78%	-	91%	-	58%	6%	8%	4%	0%
2017	85%	C	97%	97%	C	43%	C	4%	5%	11%

Almanac Ratings 2017-18

	Economy	Social	Foreign	Composite
Liberal	98%	96%	87%	94%
Conservative	2%	4%	13%	6%

Key Votes of the 115th Congress

1. Obama-care revision	N	5. Family planning regs	N	9. Guantanamo prisoners	Y
2. Tax Cuts	N	6. Body cameras/immigration	Y	10. Ground missiles, limit	Y
3. Omnibus appropriations	Y	7. Abortion ban	N	11. Defense Dept. spending	Y
4. Dodd-Frank revision	N	8. Concealed carry	N	12. FISA rules	N

Election Results

Election	Name (Party)	Vote (%)		Cand. Spent	Ind. Exp. Support	Ind. Exp. Oppose
2018 General	Bill Pascrell (D).................................	140,832	(70%)	$1,010,637		
	Eric Fisher (R).......................................	57,854	(29%)			
2018 Primary	Bill Pascrell (D).................................	23,365	(86%)			
	William Henry (D).................................	3,911	(14%)			

Prior winning percentages: 2016 (70%), 2014 (69%), 2012 (74%), 2010 (63%), 2008 (71%), 2006 (71%), 2004 (70%), 2002 (67%), 2000 (67%), 1998 (62%), 1996 (51%)

Bill Pascrell, elected in 1996, has thrived as an old-style, favor-trading pol with a feisty Jersey-guy demeanor On the House Ways and Means Committee, he suffered a setback in January 2019 when his fellow Democrats replaced him as the top Democrat on the Trade Subcommittee, with a more internationalist Democrat. In a delegation filled with new Democratic members virtually half his age and with his own recent health problems, Pascrell's long-expected plan to deliver his seat to his son had become a more timely scenario.

He grew up in Paterson, the grandson of Italian immigrants. His father worked for the railroad, and Pascrell was the first one in his family to graduate from college. He worked his way through Fordham University, served in the Army, then taught high school for 14 years. From there Pascrell went into politics, first as director of Paterson's public works department, and then as school board president. In 1987, he was elected to the New Jersey Assembly. In 1990, Pascrell was elected mayor of Paterson but continued to serve in the Assembly — a common practice in New Jersey until the legislature voted in 2007 to stop the practice.

In 1996, Pascrell challenged first-term Republican Rep. Bill Martini, whom Pascrell portrayed as the tool of an "extremist" House leadership; his ads showed Martini's face on a puppet being manipulated by House Speaker Newt Gingrich. Despite Martini's support from the Sierra Club and labor unions, Pascrell won 51%-48%.

Pascrell has compiled a conventional liberal voting record, especially on economic issues. He has voted for some restrictions on abortion, including a parental notification requirement. In 2002, he voted to authorize the use of force in Iraq and, on the Homeland Security Committee, he was a voice for improved communications among first responders. "How is it we can talk to people on the moon, but we can't talk one block away?" Pascrell asked. He authored the Firefighter Investment and Response Enhancement (FIRE) Act in 2001 and has fought regularly to increase grants to local fire and police departments.

As a member of Ways and Means, Pascrell has worked with labor and consumer groups to promote "fair trade," and to expand the Trade Adjustment Assistance program for workers who have lost their jobs. He has become an increasingly harsh critic of international trade agreements. During his early days in the House, he had a bumper sticker hanging in his office that said "NAFTA is Shafta," a caustic reference to the North American Free Trade Agreement. Despite pleas from Obama administration officials, Pascrell strongly opposed giving authority to the president to negotiate the Trans-Pacific Partnership and he later praised President Donald Trump for withdrawing the proposal. In January 2017, he became the ranking Democrat on the Trade Subcommittee.

Two years later, he appeared to have been surprised when Ways and Means Democrats, back in the majority, chose Rep. Earl Blumenauer of trade-friendly Oregon to chair the subcommittee. Under party rules, the more-senior Blumenauer was approved in an up-or-down vote, without Pascrell getting his own vote. There were things about the selection process "that I absolutely did not like," he told reporters. At that point, Pascrell had few options. Other Democrats offered little public explanation for their action, which may have resulted from a combination of factors — including internal rivalries and Pascrell's failure to protect his interests with committee chairman Richard Neal of Massachusetts. He didn't help himself when he earlier joined Democrats who urged a delay in election of party leaders as they sought an alternative to Nancy Pelosi as Speaker.

Pascrell has been successful with some pet projects. A bill to designate Paterson's Great Falls as a 120-acre national historical park was enacted in 2009. The following year, the House passed his bill calling for development of a new set of concussion-management guidelines for student athletes. That bill was part of his focus on research for traumatic brain injuries. Showing that "all politics is local," he objected to a proposal to place a woman on the $10 bill in place of local icon Alexander Hamilton. Instead, he suggested that a woman go on the $20 bill in place of Andrew Jackson.

As his party's political fortunes declined, Pascrell was among the Democrats who were open in venting frustrations. When President Barack Obama's spokesman Robert Gibbs speculated that the Democrats' House majority was in doubt in the 2010 election, Pascrell told The Washington Post, "What the hell do they think we've been doing the last 12 months? We're the ones who have been taking the tough votes."

Pascrell showed survivor skills when the 2011 redistricting placed his seat in jeopardy. The new 9th District included his home base of Paterson, but it contained a large share of Democratic colleague Steve Rothman's former Bergen County-based district. Rothman set up a primary showdown. Pascrell hammered Rothman for running against him rather than facing Republican Rep. Scott Garrett in the new 5th District. (Garrett was defeated in 2016.) In a battle of turnout, Pascrell's Passaic County machine outmatched Rothman's Bergen County team and he won 61%-39%.

Since then, Pascrell's campaigns have been uneventful. He got unwanted attention when he was overcome by heat at a local event and was briefly hospitalized in July 2018. William Pascrell III, the legal counsel to Passaic County and an ally of Paterson Mayor Andre Sayegh, reportedly has been groomed for when his father, who turned 82 in January 2019, decides to step down.

NJ-9: Northeast New Jersey   **Cook Partisan Voting Index: D+16**

Population		Race and Ethnicity		Income	
Total	758,209	White	38.8%	Median Income	$64,936
Land area (sq. miles)	95	Black	9.3%	District Income Rank	133
Pop/ sq mi	7952.7	Latino	36.9%	Poverty Rate	15.3%
Born in State	43.9%	Asian	13.3%	With health insurance	85.2%
		Two or more races	1.3%	Cash public assistance	2.5%
Age Groups		Other	0.4%	Food stamp/SNAP	15.3%
Under 18	22.6%				
18-34	23.2%	**Education**		**Work**	
35-64	40.1%	H.S grad or less	46.2%	White Collar	14.1%
Over 64	14.1%	Some college	20.7%	Sales and Service	40.3%
		College Degree, 4 yr	21.5%	Blue Collar	23.4%
Military		Post grad	11.6%	Government	10.4%
Veteran/ Active Duty	3.2%				

2012 Pres. Vote	Obama	173,070	(69%)	Romney	77,988	(31%)
2016 Pres. Vote	Clinton	177,953	(64%)	Trump	91,696	(33%)

Southern Bergen County, Paterson: Paterson is one of the few American cities that has turned out pretty much as planned. It was the brainchild of Alexander Hamilton, who in the 1790s journeyed 20 miles from Manhattan to the Great Falls of the Passaic River in New Jersey. Watching the water surge down 72 feet — the highest falls along the East Coast — he predicted an industrial city would rise on the site. Hamilton formed the Society for Establishing Useful Manufactures, which opened a calico factory in 1794, and got Pierre L'Enfant, the designer of Washington D.C., to design Paterson (named after then-Gov. William Paterson). In 1836, Samuel Colt began manufacturing revolvers there. One of the first American locomotives, the Sandusky, was built in Paterson in 1837. Paterson ultimately became America's "Silk City," employing 25,000 silk mill workers before the great strike of 1913 led by the radical Industrial Workers of the World. Throughout, Paterson attracted immigrants from England, Ireland and, after 1890, Italy and Poland.

The city continues to attract immigrants today, even if its economy produces more service jobs than manufacturing jobs. It has a lively artists' community in its postindustrial setting, and downtown's "Little Palestine" reflects the city's sizable Arab community — Palestinians, Lebanese, Jordanians; Syrian refugees have settled here since their civil war in 2011. Striving to match the more robust Newark and Jersey City — and the cultural legacy of its founder, Hamilton -- Paterson has suffered from deep-seated poverty and corruption of its politicians and police. In 2018, newly elected mayor Andre Sayegh — his parents were Syrian and Lebanese — sought to encourage optimism with a "One Paterson" campaign.

The 9th Congressional District is based chiefly in the urban parts of Bergen and Passaic counties. It also takes in the leafy suburbs of Englewood, Palisades Park and fast-growing Edgewater, where dwellers in luxury apartment houses brag about their views of New York City but a federal lawsuit in January 2018 charged corruption by town officials with a local developer. The high-rise towers of Fort Lee became famous in 2013 when top aides to Gov. Chris Christie decided to slow traffic to the George Washington Bridge, an incident that led to felony convictions and an erosion of Christie's cachet. The district also takes in East Rutherford and the Meadowlands Sports Complex, which is along Interstate 95. Once 8,400 acres of wetlands and home to thousands of species of animals and plants, the Meadowlands was developed in the 1970s. A generation later, the state built the $1.6 billion MetLife Stadium at that site for the National Football League's Giants and Jets. In October 2018, the EPA announced a $330 million clean-up of mercury waste in a nearby creek.

A bit more than half the voters reside in Bergen County, with about 40 percent in Passaic and the remainder in a small slice of Hudson. This was a growth area in the 1950s and 1960s, as New Yorkers moved out of the city. It lost population in the next two decades, as young people moved farther out. Now, the population is rising with the influx of new immigrants, many of them low-income. From 2000 to 2017, the number of Hispanics in Bergen County doubled to 190,000 (now, 20 percent of 948,000), and in Passaic County, the Latino population grew to 42 percent of the 513,000 residents. With 37 percent Hispanic and 13 percent Asian, the 9th has become a minority enclave, though Democrats' share of the presidential vote has remained roughly 65 percent.

Donald Payne (D)

Elected 2012, 4th full term, b. Dec 17, 1958; Newark; Kean College (NJ), Att., 1978; Baptist; Married (Bea Payne); 3 children (triplets).

Elected Office: Freeholder-at-large, Essex County, 2005-2012; At-large rep., Newark City Council, 2006-2012, President 2010-2012..

Professional Career: NJ highway authority, 1990-1996; District leader, Newark's South Ward, 1992-2013.

DC Office: 103 CHOB 20515, 202-225-3436, Fax: 202-225-4160, payne.house.gov

State Offices: Hillside, 862-229-2994; Jersey City, 201-369-0392; Newark, 973-645-3213.

Committees: *Homeland Security:* Border Security, Facilitation & Operations; Emergency Preparedness, Response & Recovery (Chmn). *Transportation & Infrastructure:* Aviation; Highways & Transit; Railroads, Pipelines & Hazardous Materials.

Group Ratings

	ADA	ACLU	AFL-CIO	LCV	ITI	COC	HAFA	ACU	CFG	FRC
2018	-	93%	-	91%	-	55%	8%	4%	19%	0%
2017	95%	C	97%	97%	C	36%	C	4%	5%	0%

Almanac Ratings 2017-18

	Economy	Social	Foreign	Composite
Liberal	94%	97%	100%	97%
Conservative	7%	3%	0%	3%

Key Votes of the 115th Congress

1. Obama-care revision	N	5. Family planning regs	N	9. Guantanamo prisoners	Y
2. Tax Cuts	N	6. Body cameras/immigration	Y	10. Ground missiles, limit	Y
3. Omnibus appropriations	Y	7. Abortion ban	N	11. Defense Dept. spending	N
4. Dodd-Frank revision	N	8. Concealed carry	N	12. FISA rules	N

Election Results

Election	Name (Party)	Vote (%)		Cand. Spent	Ind. Exp. Support	Ind. Exp. Oppose
2018 General	Donald Payne (D)	175,253	(88%)	$563,246		
	Agha Khan (R)	20,191	(10%)			
2018 Primary	Donald Payne (D)	38,206	(92%)			
	Aaron Fraser (D)	3,442	(8%)			

Prior winning percentages: 2016 (86%), 2014 (85%), 2012 (88%), 2012 special (97%)

Donald Payne Jr., elected in 2012 to succeeded his father, has been a reliable Democratic vote and has made few waves. He has focused on homeland security and infrastructure issues, which are vital to his metropolitan region.

A Newark native, Payne became involved in politics as a teenager when he founded and became president of the Newark South Ward Junior Democrats. He attended Kean College (now Kean University) and studied graphic arts, but did not graduate. At 21, he began working in the tolls division of the New Jersey Highway Authority; a back injury prompted him to give up the job a few years later. In 1996, at the age of 27, he became a school bus monitor with the Essex County Educational Services Commission, and went on to become director of student transportation for the county. In 1992, Payne was elected by local Democrats to the party position of South Ward leader in Newark. In 2006, Payne was elected to the Newark Municipal Council and was its president from 2010 to

2012. He co-founded Embracing Arms, a nonprofit youth-advancement organization that sponsors public service projects for young people.

Following the death of his father, Rep. Donald Payne Sr., who served 23 years and died of cancer, Payne entered the Democratic primary. His family pedigree made him a heavy favorite. Not only was his father the first African-American member of Congress to represent New Jersey, but his uncle, William Payne, served in the New Jersey General Assembly for 10 years. Payne Jr. had the backing of the powerful Democratic Party machines in Essex, Hudson and Union counties.

Political opponents and journalists raised questions about his readiness for Congress. In an editorial board meeting with The Star-Ledger before the election, Payne named creating jobs as his chief priority, but declined to provide specific details. He was vague about how he would deal with several other issues. The newspaper editorialized, "The dispiriting truth is that his claim to the seat is based entirely on his last name. He has only the vaguest grip on key federal issues. He is simply not ready for the job, and hasn't done his homework." Payne won the primary election with 60 percent of the vote, beating out fellow Newark Councilman Ron Rice and state Sen. Nia Gill. He got 88 percent in the general election in the solidly Democratic district and appears to have become entrenched.

On the Homeland Security Committee, after having served as the ranking Democrat, he became chairman in 2019 of the Emergency Preparedness, Response and Communications Subcommittee. He has noted that the area surrounding Exit 13A of the New Jersey Turnpike, which provides access to Elizabeth and the Newark Airport, has been described by homeland security officials as the "most dangerous two miles in America" because of its cluster of industrial and transportation infrastructure.

Payne won House passage of the bipartisan SMART Grid Study Act of 2014, which seeks to examine ways to upgrade and strengthen the nation's electric grid to protect critical infrastructure from natural disasters and cyberattacks. The annual defense spending bill that was enacted in 2016 included Payne's provision that required decision-makers in disaster-response planning to gain a complete understanding of a community's vulnerabilities so that homeland security grants can have appropriate priority.

Payne has a seat on the Transportation and Infrastructure Committee — an apt assignment, given the extensive air, rail, port and highway services in his district. In 2018, the House passed his bill to create a public area security working group to work with airports and other transportation facilities. The provision was enacted as part of a broader aviation bill. He called for an increase in the gasoline tax to pay for infrastructure repairs.

With Republican Rep. Markwayne Mullin of Oklahoma, Payne created and co-chairs the Congressional Men's Health Caucus. He has called attention to his father's death from colo-rectal cancer and the need for cancer screenings.

NJ-10: Newark/Jersey City area — Cook Partisan Voting Index: D+36

Population		Race and Ethnicity		Income	
Total	754,301	White	19.5%	Median Income	$50,413
Land area (sq. miles)	76	Black	50.7%	District Income Rank	301
Pop/ sq mi	9935.5	Latino	20%	Poverty Rate	19%
Born in State	50.3%	Asian	7.2%	With health insurance	85.5%
		Two or more races	1.5%	Cash public assistance	4.6%
Age Groups		Other	1.1%	Food stamp/SNAP	17.5%
Under 18	23.3%				
18-34	25.5%	**Education**		**Work**	
35-64	39.3%	H.S grad or less	45.9%	White Collar	11.9%
Over 64	11.9%	Some college	25.7%	Sales and Service	46.6%
		College Degree, 4 yr	18.5%	Blue Collar	19.6%
Military		Post grad	10%	Government	15.3%
Veteran/ Active Duty	3.4%				

2012 Pres. Vote	Obama	240,052	(88%)	Romney	31,352	(12%)	
2016 Pres. Vote	Clinton	233,822	(85%)	Trump	35,111	(13%)	

Essex County: Newark was once the heart of New Jersey. All of the main transportation arteries led there, and its corporate headquarters buildings were the tallest in the state. In 1930, 442,000 people lived in Newark, one of every nine in New Jersey. The city fell on hard times in the latter half of the 20th century. Whole sections of the city were dominated by criminals and deserted by most law-abiding residents. By the year 2000, there were just 273,000 people left in Newark, representing one in every 30.

In recent years, Newark has been attempting a turnaround. Population was up to 285,000 in 2017. New office buildings have joined the Prudential and Public Service Enterprise Group headquarters; and the New Jersey Performing Arts Center has been popular with city-dwellers seeking a less expensive experience than Manhattan. There are new restaurants and trendy bars, plus a new downtown arena. Facebook founder Mark Zuckerberg in 2010 gave $100 million to Newark public schools — conditioned on matching grants. But his program ran into bureaucratic problems, including with state officials, and it fell short of expectations. Crime remained intolerably high and downtown office buildings had plenty of empty spaces. Still, there have been positive developments. After reaching out to gang members to try to reduce crime, Mayor Ras Baraka worked with business groups on expansive plans for a new commercial center and public park in downtown. In February 2018, Newark finally regained control of its public schools — after 22 years of state control.

All of this activity led some to describe Newark as "the new Brooklyn." Intending that as a compliment, they view Newark as "the place to be," with real estate still inexpensive, busy arts and education scenes, plenty of transportation options, plus an enthusiasm. Developers "are aiming to build the critical mass needed for Newark to improve its image and fill new towers with residents who prize affordability and easy access to mass transit," Bloomberg News wrote in 2017. The fear, in some quarters, is the kind of gentrification that has overtaken Jersey City and Hoboken. "No gentrification" was the sign on the podium where Baraka spoke in December 2018, as he drew together leaders from other sectors to discuss topics such as land use, housing and building. "We do not want to wait for the market to dictate to us how to develop and move in our city," he said, with a reference to the "saturation" that has hit those other locales.

The nearby infrastructure continued to expand. At Newark Liberty International Airport, a glass and aluminum facility that has been greatly expanded for international carriers, the $2.3 billion overhaul of Terminal A was completed in October 2018. Port Newark-Elizabeth Marine Terminal is part of the larger Port of New York and New Jersey, the busiest container port on the East Coast.

The 10th Congressional District of New Jersey is centered in Essex County, with about 60 percent of its total population, including the majority of Newark. Other parts of Essex extend to Republican suburbs. Smaller parts of the 10th take in Hudson and Union counties. The district includes the predominantly African-American city of East Orange, plus parts of Bloomfield, West Orange, Jersey City and Bayonne. Drawn to maximize the African-American vote, it is a 51 percent black-majority district and one of the most heavily Democratic in the nation. Hillary Clinton took 85 percent of the vote in 2016.

Mikie Sherrill (D)

Elected 2018, 1st term, b. Jan 19, 1972; Alexandria, VA; U.S. Naval Academy (MD), B.S., 1994; London School of Economics and Political Science, Mast. Deg., 2003; Georgetown University (DC), J.D., 2007; Catholic; Married (Jason Hedberg); 4 children.

Military Career: U.S. Navy 1994-2003

Professional Career: Federal Prosecutor.

DC Office: 1208 LHOB 20515, 202-225-5034, sherrill.house.gov

State Offices: Parsippany, 973-526-5668.

Committees: *Armed Services*: Seapower & Projection Forces; Tactical Air & Land Forces. *Science, Space & Technology*: Investigations & Oversight (Chmn); Research & Technology.

Election Results

Election	Name (Party)	Vote (%)		Cand. Spent	Ind. Exp. Support	Ind. Exp. Oppose
2018 General	Mikie Sherrill (D)............................. 183,684	(57%)		$7,790,530	$3,123,608	
	Jay Webber (R)............................ 136,322	(42%)		$1,640,973	$343,315	$1,869,336
2018 Primary	Mikie Sherrill (D)................................ 35,338	(77%)				
	Tamara Harris (D)............................ 6,615	(15%)				

Freshman Democrat Mikie Sherrill switched party control of one of the most wealthy and old-line Republican districts in the nation. A first-time candidate, she brought to her campaign an impressive profile of military and civilian service, plus experience as a lawyer. She replaced veteran Republican Rep. Rodney Frelinghuysen, who was serving as chairman of the House Appropriations Committee when he decided to retire in the face of shifting politics within both his district and Congress. Once Frelinghuysen stepped aside, Sherrill's overwhelming fundraising advantage facilitated her notably easy victories in both the primary and general elections.

Sherrill was born in Alexandria Virginia and graduated from high school in nearby Reston. Following graduation from the U.S. Naval Academy, she was part of the first class of women who were eligible for combat following flight training. As a helicopter pilot, she was deployed to Italy, where her squadron supported the Sixth Fleet during the invasion of Iraq. While in the Navy, she served as a Russian policy officer.

Sherrill retired as a lieutenant commander, and got a master's from the London School of Economics and her law degree from Georgetown University. She practiced with a large law firm in New York City and spent a year in the office of the U.S. Attorney in New Jersey.

She declared her candidacy in May 2017, eight months before Frelinghuysen announced his retirement after 24 years; his father earlier had served 22 years in the House. Constituent groups had criticized his limited responses to local queries, while he also voted against the tax and health care policies of President Donald Trump and the Republican-controlled Congress. "This whole atmosphere has worn him down," a long-time friend of Frelinghuysen told the New Jersey Daily Record. Other local sources said that he saw "the handwriting on the wall," with a tough reelection campaign.

As the early frontrunner in the Democratic primary, Sherrill gained support from House Democratic leaders and other party allies. She spent about as much as the other four Democrats in that contest and won with 77 percent of the vote. Tamara Harris, a local social worker with backing from the Congressional Black Caucus, was the runner-up with 14 percent in the primary; she had criticized Sherrill's support from "corporate special interests."

Republican nominee Jay Webber initially appeared to pose a challenge to Sherrill. A state Assemblyman for a decade and former chairman of the New Jersey Republican Party, he had long been viewed as a potential successor to Frelinghuysen, though Webber's views were more conservative. The candidates clashed on an array of policy issues, including immigration, guns and Israel. Sherrill attacked Webber's support for Republican-enacted tax cuts, which had been criticized locally because they eliminated tax breaks for high-income earners.

The Newark Star-Ledger endorsed Sherrill in an editorial that described her as a "centrist" with a "sterling background," while criticizing Webber for his "bear hug of President Trump" and calling him "a strict ideologue in the state legislature." In a sign of how local and national politics had shifted from Frelinghuysen's dominance of the district, where he never faced a serious reelection challenge, Sherrill raised more than five times as much in campaign funds as did Webber. She got a further boost from national party support.

In Sherrill's 57%-42% win, she took three of the four counties, losing only more-rural Sussex. Her success and the defeat of GOP Rep. Leonard Lance in the adjacent district gave Democrats control of New Jersey's eight House districts in the metropolitan New York area. Her convincing victory left questions of how Republicans can again become competitive locally.

NJ-11: North-Central New Jersey

Cook Partisan Voting Index: R+3

Population		Race and Ethnicity		Income	
Total	743,033	White	73.8%	Median Income	$107,027
Land area (sq. miles)	505	Black	3.4%	District Income Rank	7
Pop/ sq mi	1471.4	Latino	10.9%	Poverty Rate	4.3%
Born in State	58.5%	Asian	9.9%	With health insurance	94.8%
		Two or more races	1.7%	Cash public assistance	1.1%
Age Groups		Other	0.2%	Food stamp/SNAP	2.8%
Under 18	21.4%				
18-34	18.6%	**Education**		**Work**	
35-64	42.8%	H.S grad or less	27.6%	White Collar	17.2%
Over 64	17.2%	Some college	19.6%	Sales and Service	37%
		College Degree, 4 yr	31.2%	Blue Collar	11.1%
Military		Post grad	21.6%	Government	13.1%
Veteran/ Active Duty	4.8%				

2012 Pres. Vote	Romney	183,427	(53%)	Obama	163,183	(47%)			
2016 Pres. Vote	Trump	185,696	(48%)	Clinton	182,334	(47%)	Johnson	7,911	(2%)

Morris and Essex Counties: Morris County, west of the Watchung Mountains, was one of the first inland parts of the United States to be settled. It has long been a place of comparative wealth, the home of skilled craftsmen working in the water mills and iron forges in the 19th century. But only in the late 20th century did it come into its own, as one of the most affluent parts of the United States. With its $107,000 median household income, Morris County was among the 10 wealthiest counties in the nation in 2017.

The very rich have lived here for many decades, connected to Manhattan by commuter rail. But starting in the 1970s, new residents rushed out through the newly completed interstates. Prompted by court-required zoning changes, old farms and woods were cleared to make way for new subdivisions. This is not just a bedroom community. New Jersey's economic energy, entrepreneurial creativity and research expertise are found in office complexes and corporate headquarters. Large forested areas of state parkland remain, and preservation of the state's Highlands region, a 1,000-square-mile forest-and lake-filled oasis, has been a priority. The Highlands Council, tasked with protecting the area from development, fueled controversy as the state legislature overturned a development plan by a pro-business ally of lame-duck Republican Gov. Chris Christie. Local environmentalists had battled constantly with Christie. Subsequently, the conservation-minded appointee of Democratic Gov. Phil Murphy pledged to appreciate "how unique and special the Highlands region is." In September 2018, Morris County asked the U.S. Supreme Court to review a state Supreme Court decision that it could not spend preservation funds on religious properties.

The 11th Congressional District of New Jersey takes in about three-fourths of Morris County, including the county seat of Morristown, Randolph and Rockaway. Half of the district is in Morris, one-fourth is in western Essex, and there are small parts of Passaic and Sussex. This area is family territory, with relatively few singles. It is predominantly white, though the minority population has grown to 11 percent Hispanic and 10 percent Asian. The 11th still leans Republican, with a moneyed caste. In 2016, Donald Trump won 48%-47%, a drop from the 52 percent that the GOP presidential candidates took in the two previous elections.

Bonnie Watson Coleman (D)

Elected 2014, 3rd term, b. Feb 06, 1945; Camden; Rutgers University (NJ), Att.; Thomas Edison State College (NJ), B.A., 1985; Baptist; Married (William E. Coleman Jr.); 1 child; 2 stepchildren; 3 grandchildren.

Elected Office: NJ Assembly, 1998-2014, Majority Leader, 2006-2009.

DC Office: 2442 RHOB 20515, 202-225-5801, Fax: 202-225-6025, watsoncoleman.house.gov

State Offices: Ewing, 609-883-0026.

Committees: *Appropriations*: Interior, Environment & Related Agencies; Labor, Health & Human Services, Education & Related Agencies; Transportation, HUD & Related Agencies. *Homeland Security*: Oversight, Management & Accountability; Transportation & Maritime Security.

Group Ratings

	ADA	ACLU	AFL-CIO	LCV	ITI	COC	HAFA	ACU	CFG	FRC
2018	-	96%	-	94%	-	50%	6%	4%	15%	0%
2017	95%	C	97%	89%	C	43%	C	7%	5%	11%

Almanac Ratings 2017-18

	Economy	Social	Foreign	Composite
Liberal	98%	100%	94%	98%
Conservative	2%	0%	6%	2%

Key Votes of the 115th Congress

1. Obama-care revision	N	5. Family planning regs	N	9. Guantanamo prisoners	N
2. Tax Cuts	N	6. Body cameras/immigration	Y	10. Ground missiles, limit	Y
3. Omnibus appropriations	N	7. Abortion ban	N	11. Defense Dept. spending	N
4. Dodd-Frank revision	N	8. Concealed carry	N	12. FISA rules	N

Election Results

Election	Name (Party)	Vote (%)		Cand. Spent	Ind. Exp. Support	Ind. Exp. Oppose
2018 General	Bonnie Watson Coleman (D)............ 173,334	(69%)		$610,872		
	Daryl Kipnis (R).................................. 79,041	(31%)		$21,687		
2018 Primary	Bonnie Watson Coleman (D).......	(100%)				

Prior winning percentages: 2016 (63%), 2014 (61%)

Democrat Bonnie Watson Coleman, easily elected in 2014 to an open seat, was a well-regarded state legislator and has been an activist for liberal causes, She gained recognition for her legislative skills at the Homeland Security Committee and won a seat on the Appropriations Committee when Democrats took House control.

Watson Coleman grew up in a political family, with her father, a state assemblyman, often guiding debates at the dinner table. She graduated from Thomas Edison State College. Her public service began in 1966, when she went to work for the state public safety department's civil rights division. She later headed the civil rights office of the state's Department of Transportation before taking on senior roles at the Department of Community Affairs. In 1997, she was elected to the General Assembly, where she rose through the ranks to become majority leader. She was the first African-American woman to chair the State Democratic Committee. Watson Coleman promoted staunchly liberal positions on issues such as gun control, the minimum wage and women's health care funding, and worked to reduce recidivism among state prisoners. She took an active role in legislation on identity-theft protection and expansion of urban enterprise zones.

When Democratic Rep. Rush Holt, a leading progressive in Congress, said that he would step down, Watson Coleman announced her bid. She got a boost from the Progressive Change Campaign Committee, major unions and liberal women's groups such as EMILY's List. In the June primary, only state Sen. Linda Greenstein posed any real competition. Watson Coleman topped the field with 43 percent to 28 percent for Greenstein, who ran relatively close only in her Middlesex County base. Watson Coleman breezed in November with 61 percent against Republican Alieta Eck, who sought to become the first woman physician among House members but was outspent 6-to-1.

Watson Coleman initially focused her committee work on Homeland Security. In 2015, the House-passed Cybersecurity Protection Advancement Act included her amendment to encourage public awareness and education on personal cybersecurity issues. The House passed her Homeland Security Drone Assessment and Analysis Act, the goal of which was "clarifying the framework for drone manufacturers and enthusiasts alike," she said. As the senior Democrat on the Oversight Subcommittee, Watson Coleman criticized the Transportation Security Administration for its Quiet Skies programs that tracked domestic air travelers and asked for the legal justification for collecting intelligence on U.S. citizens. In combative Republican-led hearings on the FBI's investigation during the 2016 election, she took her shots at GOP inquisitors and said that they were "out of control."

With Democratic Reps. Robin Kelly of Illinois and Yvette Clark of New York, Watson Coleman founded the Congressional Caucus on Black Women and Girls. Its objective was to create public policy that "eliminates significant barriers and disparities experienced by black women." Following the election of Donald Trump as president, she became outspoken in leading protest marches and political mobilization. In her tough attacks, she sought to censure him following his reaction to the violence in Charlottesville, tweeted that he was a "racist" while he was delivering his State of the Union message in 2018, and accused him of "treason" following his meeting in Helsinki with Russian President Vladimir Putin.

In 2019, Watson Coleman got a seat on the House Appropriations Committee, similar to the niche that she held while serving in Trenton. The spending decisions made at that committee, she said, "are a direct representation of our national values." As the only congressional appropriator from New Jersey, she replaced Republican Rep. Rodney Frelinghuysen, who was committee chairman before he retired in 2018. She noted her interest in funding regional infrastructure, including the long-discussed Gateway Project with New York City.

Watson Coleman had a cancerous tumor removed from her lung and said in October 2018 that she was cancer-free following chemotherapy treatment. That episode, she told a Democratic meeting in New Jersey, "fortified my resolve to make sure that all Americans have access to world-class health care."

NJ-12: Central New Jersey

Cook Partisan Voting Index: D+16

Population		Race and Ethnicity		Income	
Total	757,602	White	47.3%	Median Income	$83,770
Land area (sq. miles)	412	Black	16.7%	District Income Rank	42
Pop/ sq mi	1837.8	Latino	17%	Poverty Rate	9.2%
Born in State	46.9%	Asian	16.6%	With health insurance	90.5%
		Two or more races	1.5%	Cash public assistance	2%
Age Groups		Other	0.8%	Food stamp/SNAP	7%
Under 18	22.2%				
18-34	21.8%	**Education**		**Work**	
35-64	41.1%	H.S grad or less	35%	White Collar	14.9%
Over 64	14.9%	Some college	21%	Sales and Service	37.5%
		College Degree, 4 yr	24.2%	Blue Collar	15.5%
Military		Post grad	19.8%	Government	13.4%
Veteran/ Active Duty	4.2%				

2012 Pres. Vote	Obama	198,155	(67%)	Romney	96,520	(33%)
2016 Pres. Vote	Clinton	204,660	(65%)	Trump	100,043	(32%)

Middlesex County, Trenton: New Jersey politics is centered in Trenton. The city has been a manufacturing mecca since the 19th century, when it was the setting for the Lenox and Boehm china factories and the old Roebling ironworks, which produced parts for many of the great American bridges. It is a city "that can often feel like two urban areas rolled into one," The New York Times wrote in June 2018. One is the State House and its accompanying buildings for lobbyists and state employees. The other is the "bleak landscape" that they leave behind each day of dilapidated warehouses and a famous but no longer apt sign, "Trenton Makes, the World Takes." The lifeline for Trenton is U.S. 1, on any day crowded with cars taking high-salaried workers and clerical help to one of the East Coast's thickest concentrations of office buildings. The highway also is now a locus of telecommunications and pharmaceutical research, and a vital artery to the brain centers of Princeton and Rutgers.

The 12th Congressional District includes Trenton, which is 51 percent African American and 36 percent Hispanic. It stretches east to East Brunswick, with a significant Asian population, and South River, a city that has attracted Polish, Russian and Portuguese immigrants. In February 2018, East Brunswick announced a plan to create a "city-like vibe" and to redevelop its downtown area, which was filled with vacant buildings and empty parking lots. Princeton University, which provides $1.6 billion in economic output for New Jersey and supports more than 13,000 jobs, said it would spend $1 billion on campus facilities from 2017 to 2022. In Trenton, the weak economy has forced continuing cutbacks in operations. Its poverty rate of 27 percent is close to that of Newark. In September 2018, Gov. Phil Murphy signed an executive order intended to revitalize Trenton, in which the state committed to identifying funds and resources to implement local initiatives.

In the north, the district takes in Plainfield, Scotch Plains and modest-income suburbs such as Franklin. Much of the district's population is in Middlesex County and the more heavily Democratic and Princeton-based Mercer County. Somerset and Union counties have small slices of the district. As recently as two decades ago, with different boundaries, this was a highly competitive district that House Republicans frequently won. Back then, it had a small minority population, in contrast to the growing 17 percent each for African Americans, Hispanics and Asians. The district has become safe for Democrats. Hillary Clinton got 65 percent of the vote in 2016.

NEW MEXICO

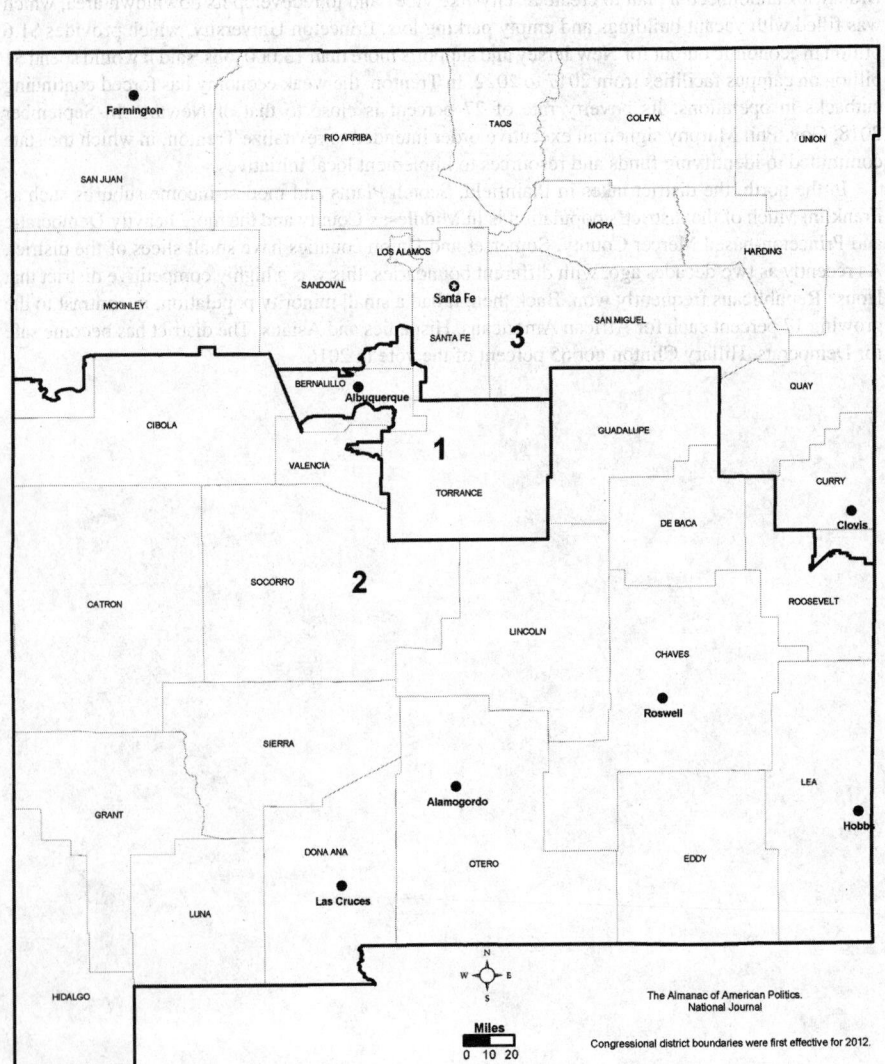

The Almanac of American Politics.
National Journal

Congressional district boundaries were first effective for 2012.

New Mexico has a higher percentage of Latino residents than any other state, and that has shaped its political transition in recent decades. Republican presidential candidates won the state in every election from 1968 to 1988, but Democrats have won it every four years since, except for 2004. While the state was decided by 366 votes in 2000 and fewer than 6,000 votes in 2004, it has barely been a battleground in ensuing elections. In 2018, non-white candidates, all Democrats, won all three of the state's House seats, the first time that happened in any state with at least a three-member delegation.

New Mexico is the northernmost salient of the great Indian-Spanish civilizations of the Cordillera, the mountain chain that extends south to Mexico and through Central and South America to the southern end of Chile. It has some of the oldest settlements in America and some of its newest technologies, often in surrealistic proximity to one another. The oldest permanently inhabited city in the United States is not Plymouth Massachusetts or Jamestown Virginia or St. Augustine Florida; it is probably Acoma, which thrived in what is now New Mexico long before the Spanish conquistadors arrived in 1540, and which has been continuously inhabited for more than 470 years since. While the settlers of Jamestown and Plymouth were building flimsy wood houses, the Indians in New Mexico were living in extensive dwellings hundreds of years old, made with the adobe that is still the characteristic building material here. They used small pebbles as mulch to retain scarce moisture on the rocky desert land.

Nearly five centuries later, much of what makes New Mexico distinctive derives from centuries of indigenous architecture and artistic traditions. The Spanish settled in Santa Fe in 1609, and while their imprint remains, their hold on the town was often tenuous. There are almost two dozen federally recognized Indian tribes in New Mexico, including reservations of the Navajo, the Jicarilla Apache, the Mescalero Apache, the Fort Sill Apache, and the Zuni. A substantial minority of today's New Mexicans are descendants of those Indians, or the Spanish, or both. New Mexico's population is 48 percent Hispanic and almost 10 percent Native American. It's 38 percent white, tied with California for the second lowest in the nation (after Hawaii), and 2 percent black, the lowest of any state in the southern half of the United States. Relatively few Hispanics are immigrants -- only about 10 percent of the state population is foreign born – and relations with Mexico are arguably less fraught than they are in other border states, owing to the relatively short length of the border and the sparse population nearby.

Modern New Mexico got a boost from science and technology. It was to a remote mesa called Los Alamos that Gen. Leslie Groves brought his Manhattan Project scientists during World War II to build a secret town and develop a secret weapon that would, in two explosions, end the war and change the course of history. Los Alamos is still a government laboratory crucial to producing U.S. nuclear weapons, and in 2016 the federal government took steps toward restarting production of plutonium "pits" for the nuclear arsenal. New Mexico has other high-tech sites as well: White Sands Missile Range near Alamogordo, where the first atomic bomb was detonated in July 1945; Sandia National Laboratories near Albuquerque, a non-nuclear weapons research facility with one of the fastest computers in the world, used to simulate nuclear explosions; and the Very Large Array National Radio Astronomy Observatory on the Plains of San Agustin, 50 miles west of Socorro. Facebook is building a data facility south of Albuquerque that will be powered exclusively by solar power, while regulators in New Mexico have approved Xcel Energy's plan for huge wind farms along the border with Texas.

But science has limits. At the federal Waste Isolation Pilot Plant (WIPP) carved into a salt bed near Carlsbad, the U.S. deposits transuranic radioactive waste. In 2014, a 55-gallon drum of nuclear waste buried in a salt mine cavern burst apart, shutting down the disposal site. It took until 2017 for the facility to be determined safe enough to receive new shipments. Meanwhile, at the western edge of White Sands in Sierra County is Spaceport America, an 18,000-acre facility in the New Mexico desert built with more than $215 million in state and local tax dollars to support space tourism. The bipartisan list of boosters included former Democratic Gov. Bill Richardson and Republican Gov. Susana Martinez. Billionaire Richard Branson predicted that his Virgin Galactic would be ferrying passengers on space tours by 2014 for up to $250,000 a ticket. Those hopes were dashed in October 2014, when Virgin Galactic's SpaceShipTwo rocket plane broke up on a test flight and crashed. Virgin Galactic remains the spaceport's primary tenant and continues working toward a civilian launch.

New and old New Mexico intermingle in varying proportions in this land of majestic vistas. Historic Acoma shares its nickname, "Sky City," with a nearby casino. The Hispanic and Indian cultures predominate north and west of Albuquerque, with picturesque old towns and active pueblos, low-income Indian reservations, and lavish gambling resorts. A prized variety of chili peppers is cultivated in the Hatch Valley just as it was centuries ago. In the middle of the state is Albuquerque, which, with federal spending, grew from a small desert community of 35,000 in 1940 into a Sun Belt metropolitan area of almost 911,000 today. The city's economy is based on technology and there, as everywhere in New Mexico, government is a prime employer. This high-tech New Mexico, however, coexists with hardship, a dichotomy expertly mined by the acclaimed TV series Breaking Bad, set in the office parks, strip malls and neighborhoods of Albuquerque.

Unlike the rest of the country, unemployment remained stuck around 6.5 percent in 2015 and 2016, and by late 2018 it still had the fifth-highest rate in the country at 4.7 percent. New Mexico's median income ranks fifth from the bottom, 23 percent lower than the national average, and its 19.7 percent poverty rate ranked the third highest of any state, behind only Mississippi and Louisiana. The state ranked second-highest in child poverty and highest in food insecurity among children, at 26 percent. Homelessness has been a stubborn problem in Albuquerque. One bright spot is tourism, which has grown for seven straight years, and another is the arts, especially in Santa Fe and Taos. Over the years, the state's stunning scenery and unique culture have attracted writers such as D.H. Lawrence and painters such as Georgia O'Keeffe. More recently, Netflix has produced extensive television content in the state.

In recent years, though, the biggest economic plus in New Mexico has been the petroleum industry. Oil production hit a new record in 2017, thanks to increased drilling in the Permian Basin in southeastern New Mexico. And there's more where that came from: Two subterranean structures, the Wolfcamp Shale and the Bone Spring Formation, contain the biggest oil and gas reserves the U.S. Geological Survey has ever confirmed. The oil boom has, in turn, provided a gusher for state finances – $1.1 billion in extra revenue in 2019. But automation in the industry has meant that fewer workers are needed than in the past, meaning population and employment in the oil patch have stagnated even as production has surged. Meanwhile, the natural gas industry in the San Juan Basin in the northwestern part of the state has sagged, largely due to falling prices.

New Mexico's population is up by 1.5 percent since 2010, but there has been a divergence between major metro areas and rural regions. The four biggest counties -- Bernalillo (Albuquerque), Dona Ana (Las Cruces), Santa Fe (Santa Fe), and Sandoval (the northern suburbs of Albuquerque, including Rio Rancho) – collectively grew by 3.2 percent between 2010 and 2017, but the rest of the state was down by almost 1 percent over the same period. The residents who are moving away pose a challenge for economic growth. "We are losing young people, and we are losing people who are educated," Jeff Mitchell, an economist with the Bureau of Business and Economic Research, told the Las Cruces Sun News. Another worry is water: Snowpacks are down, leaving 99 percent of the state in drought in 2018, with the northern one-third of the state in extreme drought. Elephant Butte reservoir, the state's largest, hit its lowest level since the early 1970s. Further complicating the issue is the oil and gas industry's heavy reliance on water for fracking, and the potential risk of contamination.

For many years, New Mexico politics was a somnolent business. Local bosses — first Republican, later Democratic — controlled the large Hispanic vote. Elections in many counties featured irregularities that would have made a Chicago ward committeeman blush. Politics was a family business in New Mexico that could rival the House of Windsor, most strikingly the extended Luján family, which includes the newly elected governor. Michelle Luján Grisham, a Democrat, succeeded Martinez, a two-term Republican, and she came into office with solid majorities in both chambers of the legislature. In 2018, Democrats also flipped the state's sole Republican-held House seat. Such electoral successes suggest that Democrats will have a largely free hand in running the state for the near future, although Republican counties are pushing back against one-party rule in the capital by pushing initiatives such as local right-to-work ordinances.

Population		Race and Ethnicity		Income	
Total	2,084,828	White	38.2%	Median Income	$46,718
Land area (sq. miles)	121,298	Black	1.8%	State Income Rank	44
Pop/ sq mi	17.2	Latino	48.2%	Poverty Rate	20.6%
Born in state	53.3%	Asian	1.3%	With health insurance	87.5%
		Two or more races	1.6%	Cash public assistance	2.8%
Age Groups		Other	8.9%	Food stamp/SNAP	17.0%
Under 18	23.9%				
18-34	23.2%	**Education**		**Work**	
35-64	37.1%	H.S grad or less	41.4%	White Collar	35.7%
Over 64	15.8%	Some college	31.7%	Sales and Service	44.1%
		College Degree, 4 yr	15.1%	Blue Collar	20.1%
Military		Post grad	11.8%	Government	22.1%
Veteran/ Active Duty	10.1%				

Presidential Politics

2016 Primary (D)	Clinton (D)	111,334 (52%)	Sanders (D)	104,741 (48%)				
2016 Primary (R)	Trump (R)	73,908 (71%)	Cruz (R)	13,925 (13%)	Kasich (R)	7,925	(8%)
2016 Pres. Vote	Clinton (D)	385,234 (48%)	Trump (R)	319,667 (40%)	Johnson (L)	74,541	(9%)
2012 Pres. Vote	Obama (D)	415,335 (53%)	Romney (R)	335,788 (43%)	Johnson (L)	27,788	(4%)

New Mexico was a battleground state in the first two presidential elections in this century but subsequently fell off the list. In 2000, after some ragged vote counting, the state gave a 366-vote margin to Al Gore. In 2004, it reported a 5,988-vote margin for George W. Bush. The 2008 contest was another story, with Barack Obama deploying a superior campaign organization in the state and beating John McCain 57%-42%. In 2012, former Republican Gov. Gary Johnson was running on the Libertarian ticket and won 4 percent in his home state, while Obama posted a 53%-43% victory over Mitt Romney. Johnson more than doubled his Libertarian vote to 9 percent when he ran again in 2016, and Hillary Clinton defeated Donald Trump, 48%-40%. Clinton handily won the three largest vote-producing counties in the state: Bernalillo (Albuquerque), Santa Fe, and Dona Ana (Las Cruces, home to New Mexico State University), and narrowly carried the fourth largest, Sandoval (suburban and exurban Albuquerque), which contains several Native American reservations. Trump carried the eastern part of the state, which includes "Little Texas," where cattle ranching, cotton farming and oil drilling exert a conservative influence that makes this the most Republican region in the state.

New Mexico traditionally held its presidential primary in June. For 2008, the race between Barack Obama and Hillary Clinton was close, and it took nine days to count all the votes, including 17,000 provisional ballots. Clinton won 49%-48%. In 2016, the Democratic contest was again spirited. Vermont Sen. Bernie Sanders narrowly carried the four-county Albuquerque region, but Clinton won the rest of the state and the primary, 52%-48%. The recent Republican primaries have come after the nomination has been resolved and they have been largely ignored.

Congressional Districts

116th Congress Lineup	3D	**115th Congress Lineup**	2D 1R

New Mexico's three congressional districts have remained substantially the same since the state gained a third seat in 1982: the heavily Hispanic and Democratic 3rd district in Santa Fe and the north, the more rural and Republican 2nd district in the south, and the competitive Albuquerque 1st in the middle. Both parties have held all three seats at various points. As the 1st District moved away from Republicans, the prevailing balance shifted from a 2-to-1 Republican edge to a 2-to-1 Democratic advantage. But those dynamics might be changing again.

For the next redistricting, Democrats have a strong hand. After winning two open House seats in 2018, including the 2nd for the first time in a decade, they control the entire delegation. Plus, they added the governor's office to their majorities in the legislature. They likely will seek to increase the Democratic vote share in the 2nd, though they likely would raise objections from Albuquerque leaders if they force extensive changes in the relatively compact 1st in the current map. Republicans hope to win back the 2nd in 2020, which could give them a bit more leverage in redistricting.

Michelle Lujan Grisham (D)

Elected 2018, term expires 2023, 1st term; b. Oct 24, 1959, Los Alamos; University of New Mexico; b.E., 1981; University of New Mexico, J.D., 1987; Roman Catholic; Widow; 2 children.

Elected Office: Secretary, NM Department of Health, 2004-2007; Commissioner, Bernalillo County, 2010-2012; US House, 2013-2018.

Professional Career: Director, NM State Agency on Aging, 1991-2002; Secretary, NM Aging & Long-Term Services Department, 2002-2004; Co-owner, Delta Consulting Group, 2008-present.

Office: 490 Old Sante Fe Trail, Room 400, Santa Fe, 87501; 505-476-2200; Fax: 505-476-2226; Website: governor.state.nm.us

Lt. Gov.: Howie Morales (D) **Atty. Gen:** Hector Balderas (D) **Sec. of State:** Maggie Toulouse Oliver (D)

State Legislature: Senate: 25D, 16R, 1V **House:** 46D, 24R

Election Results

Election	Name (Party)	Vote (%)
2018 General	Michelle Lujan Grisham (D)..	398,368 (57%)
	Steve Pearce (R)...	298,091 (43%)
2018 Primary	Michelle Lujan Grisham (D)..	116,754 (66%)
	Jeff Apodaca (D)..	38,975 (22%)
	Joseph Cervantes (D)..	20,169 (12%)

Michelle Lujan Grisham, a member of a family dynasty in her state, took back New Mexico's governorship for the Democrats in 2018, after serving three terms in the House. Her grandfather, Eugene Lujan, was the state supreme court's first Latino chief justice; her uncle, Manuel Lujan Jr., was a GOP congressman and Interior secretary; her apparently distant cousin, Rep. Ben Ray Luján, represents the 3rd District. Lujan Grisham succeeded another Latina governor – Republican Susana Martinez – in the heavily Hispanic state.

The daughter of a dentist, Lujan Grisham was born in Los Alamos and attended high school in Santa Fe. Her sister Kimberly was diagnosed with a brain tumor at 2 and died at 21; affordable health care would become a major policy focus for Lujan Grisham in both state and local government. After earning bachelor's and law degrees from the University of New Mexico, she was named director of the State Bar of New Mexico's Lawyer Referral for the Elderly Program, which provides basic legal services to seniors. In 1991, then-Gov. Bruce King appointed Lujan Grisham director of the New Mexico State Agency on Aging. In 1997, she went undercover as a stroke victim in an Albuquerque nursing home; she said her two-day stay was the "longest weekend in her life," the Journal reported. Lujan Grisham remained in the aging post for 13 years, serving under a Republican governor as well as two Democrats — a point she later emphasized as evidence of her bipartisan efforts. Ex-Gov. Gary Johnson, one of her former Republican bosses, told the Journal that Lujan Grisham was "a great communicator" who "really cared. I thought she was the genuine article."

In 2004, Lujan Grisham's college sweetheart and husband of 22 years, Gregory Alan Grisham, collapsed while jogging and died the next day from a ruptured cerebral aneurysm. Three years later, Lujan Grisham filed a wrongful death lawsuit, seeking damages from an Albuquerque physician who had misdiagnosed him with migraines, but the suit was dismissed. After her husband's death, Lujan Grisham was named secretary of the New Mexico Department of Health, which had 3,800 employees and a $440 million budget. In 2007, the Justice Department filed a lawsuit against New Mexico in response to substandard conditions and practices at the state-run Fort Bayard Medical Center. A settlement was reached in four days. Lujan Grisham resigned a month later, telling the Albuquerque Journal that overseeing the Department of Health was the "hardest job on the planet."

In 2008, Lujan Grisham made an unsuccessful run for New Mexico's 1st District seat, placing third in the Democratic primary. Two years later, she won a race for commissioner of Bernalillo County (Albuquerque). When Rep. Martin Heinrich ran for the Senate in 2012, Lujan Grisham started as a long-shot candidate to succeed him in the House. She said her real-life hardships gave her insight into voters' problems. "As a widow and a caregiver and a single mother, I'm living the experience that New Mexicans are," she told the Journal. Her primary opponents, state Sen. Eric Griego and former Albuquerque Mayor Marty Chavez, attacked each other and did not take her seriously until it was too late. Lujan Grisham won the primary with 40 percent, defeating Griego with 35 percent and Chavez with 25 percent. In the general election, she easily defeated former state Rep. Janice Arnold-Jones, 59%-41%, and later won reelection easily.

Lujan Grisham served as the ranking Democrat on the Agriculture Subcommittee on Conservation and Forestry, an important post for New Mexico, which has more than 9 million acres of Forest Service land. Following the 2016 election, Lujan Grisham took on new partisan dimensions. In the House, she chaired the Congressional Hispanic Caucus, which has been open only to Democrats and which took a leading role opposing Trump policies. In December 2016, Lujan Grisham announced her candidacy to succeed Martinez, who had become the first Hispanic woman governor of any state when she was elected in 2010. While Martinez was a rising GOP star who easily won reelection in 2014, her pragmatic instincts left her out of step in a GOP with Trumpian impulses.

Lujan Grisham faced a competitive, and messy, Democratic primary against state Sen. Joseph Cervantes and Jeff Apodaca, a media executive and the son of former Gov. Jerry Apodaca. Her opponents raised questions about Lujan Grisham's past connections to a health care firm that had a state contract to run a high-risk insurance pool. But with the help of a large war chest, she won two-thirds of the votes in the state party convention and then prevailed in the primary with a similar percentage, easily outpacing Apodaca with 22 percent and Cervantes with 12 percent. On the Republican side, Rep. Steve Pearce ran for the nomination unopposed, enabling him to start the general election campaign with a big edge in campaign funding. Pearce, a former Air Force and commercial pilot and businessman, had initially been elected to the House in 2002, ran unsuccessfully for Senate in 2008, then won back his old seat in 2010. As a House member, Pearce moved further rightward, often joining with the GOP's anti-leadership activists.

Policy-wise, the race between Lujan Grisham and Pearce offered a fairly conventional liberal-vs.-conservative faceoff. The Democrat advocated a minimum-wage increase, universal pre-kindergarten and legalization of recreational marijuana; the Republican backed right-to-work legislation, pro-resource-extraction policies and work requirements for Medicaid recipients. Pearce attacked his opponent's business ties that had come up in the primary, saying that a Lujan Grisham victory would bring New Mexico back to the "cronyism" days of former Democratic Gov. Bill Richardson. Pearce, though, faced questions of his own about his business interests, including how his firms involved in leasing oilfield equipment could shape his views on energy policy. Former Gov. Jerry Apodaca broke with his party and endorsed Pearce, calling him "the only candidate willing to collaborate across party lines."

But it didn't matter in the end: Lujan Grisham won, 57%-43%, almost exactly reversing the parties' showings four years earlier, when Martinez defeated Democrat Gary King. Pearce won more votes in 2018 than Martinez had in 2014, BUT the number of Democratic votes shot up by 82 percent over what King won in 2014 and even exceeded the number that Hillary Clinton won in 2016. Lujan Grisham was victorious in about three times as many counties as King, flipping the state's two most populous, Bernalillo and Dona Ana (Las Cruces), and shifting the winning margin toward Democrats in those counties by 33 and 30 percentage points, respectively.

In office, Lujan Grisham leveraged the state's flush coffers from an oil and gas boom into an enacted budget increase of about 12 percent, including a boost in pay for teachers and state workers. She staked out differences with Trump, whom she had used successfully as a cudgel against Pearce during the campaign. In January 2019, as a debate over building a border wall raged, Lujan Grisham visited her state's border with Mexico and told reporters, "While I've been to this area of the border many times, I haven't seen anything to indicate that we have an emerging crisis here at the border."

Tom Udall (D)

Elected 2008, term expires 2020, 2nd term, b. May 18, 1948; Tucson, AZ; Prescott College (AZ), B.A., 1970; Cambridge University (England), LL.B., 1975; University of New Mexico Law School, J.D., 1977; Mormon; Married (Jill Cooper Udall); 1 child.

Elected Office: NM Attorney General, 1990-1998; U.S. House, 1998-2008.

Professional Career: Clerk, 10th Circuit Court of Appeals, 1977; Assistant U.S Attorney, Dist. of NM, 1978-1981; Practicing attorney, 1981-1983, 1985-1990; Chief counsel, NM Health & Environment Department, 1983-1984.

DC Office: 531 HSOB 20510, 202-224-6621, Fax: 202-228-3261, tomudall.senate.gov

State Offices: Albuquerque, 505-346-6791; Carlsbad, 575-234-0366; Las Cruces, 575-526-5475; Portales, 575-356-6811; Santa Fe, 505-988-6511.

Committees: *Appropriations*: Agriculture, Rural Development, FDA & Related Agencies; Department of Defense; Department of the Interior, Environment & Related Agencies (RMM); Energy & Water Development; Military Construction & Veteran Affairs & Related Agencies. *Commerce, Science & Transportation*: Communications, Technology, Innovation & the Internet; Manufacturing, Trade & Consumer Protection; Aviation & Space; Transportation & Safety; Security. *Foreign Relations*: East Asia, the Pacific & International Cybersecurity Policy; Internat'l Dev Instit & Internat'l Econ, Energy & Environ Policy; State Dept & USAID Mngmnt, Internat'l Ops & Internat'l Dev; West Hem Crime Civ Sec Dem Rights & Women's Issues. *Indian Affairs. Rules & Administration.*

Group Ratings

	ADA	ACLU	AFL-CIO	LCV	ITI	COC	HAFA	ACU	CFG	FRC
2018	-	76%	-	100%	-	50%	5%	9%	5%	0%
2017	90%	C	100%	89%	C	29%	C	0%	4%	0%

Almanac Ratings 2017-18

	Economy	Social	Foreign	Composite
Liberal	94%	94%	92%	93%
Conservative	6%	6%	8%	7%

Key Votes of the 115th Congress

1. Obama-care revision	N	5. Gun regulations	N	9. Kavanaugh confirmation	N
2. Tax Cuts	N	6. Family planning regs	N	10. Saudi arms sales	Y
3. Dodd-Frank revision	N	7. Gorsuch confirmation	N	11. FISA rules	N
4. Omnibus appropriations	Y	8. Immigration restrictions	N	12. Military aid in Yemen	Y

Election Results

Election	Name (Party)	Vote (%)		Cand. Spent	Ind. Exp. Support	Ind. Exp. Oppose
2014 General	Tom Udall (D).....................................	286,409	(56%)	$8,736,822	$154,367	$173,814
	Allen Weh (R).................................	229,097	(44%)	$3,630,413	$70,867	
2014 Primary	Tom Udall (D).............................. Unopposed					

Prior winning percentages: 2008 (61%) House: 2006 (75%), 2004 (69%), 2002 (100%), 2000 (67%), 1998 (53%)

Democrat Tom Udall, New Mexico's senior senator, belongs to a political clan once referred to as the "Kennedys of the West." His father, Stewart Udall, was a member of the House from Arizona from 1955 to 1961, when he resigned to become Interior secretary in the Kennedy and Johnson administrations. His uncle, Mo Udall, took over the House seat and held it for 30 years, while mounting a competitive bid for the Democratic presidential nomination in 1976. For 16 years, Tom Udall served on Capitol Hill with his first cousin Mark Udall (Morris Udall's son) when the latter represented Colorado in the House and Senate. But, unlike the Kennedy dynasty, this one has a bipartisan component: Republican Gordon Smith, whose mother was a Udall, represented Oregon in the Senate from 1997 to 2009. Smith, now president of the National Association of Broadcasters, is a second cousin. So is Utah Republican Sen. Mike Lee, an outspoken conservative.

In March 2019, Tom Udall announced that he will retire in 2020 — likely marking the first time in 66 years that no Udall will serve in Congress. He will be 71 when he steps down but promised "more chapters in my public service." As the campaign for his seat likely will reinforce, one of his legacies has been the shift of New Mexico to an increasingly Democratic state.

For the most part, Udall has been a reliable liberal. Unsurprisingly — given both his family heritage and career choices before Congress — Udall has frequently focused on environmental issues on Capitol Hill. And if he has exhibited a sharp tongue — in mid-2018, he on multiple occasions likened the Trump administration's plan to house families of undocumented immigrants on military bases to the internment of Japanese-Americans during World War II — his amiable demeanor has enabled him to work with senators across the ideological spectrum. His skepticism about military commitments abroad has brought him into alliances with libertarian-minded Republicans like Kentucky Sen. Rand Paul and Lee.

Udall grew up in Tucson Arizona and McLean Virginia, a Washington suburb. He attended Prescott College in Arizona and then earned two law degrees — one at University of Cambridge in England and another the University of New Mexico. After working as a prosecutor in a U.S. attorney's office, he was chief counsel to the New Mexico Department of Health and Environment before going into private practice.

Since Udall had grown up in politics — he was 6 when his father was elected to Congress — it seemed a question of when, not if, he ran for public office. In 1982, when New Mexico's 3rd District was created, the then-34-year-old Udall sought the Democratic nomination and finished last among four candidates. The winner was Democrat Bill Richardson, later New Mexico's governor. In 1988, Udall ran in the 1st District to succeed longtime GOP Rep. Manuel Lujan. Udall won the Democratic nomination but lost the general election. Two years later, Udall won a race for attorney general, winning a four-way primary and coming out on top in November by a 2-1 margin. He focused on the environment and consumer protection; he successfully sued the federal government to delay the planned opening of the Waste Isolation Pilot Plant, the nation's first deep underground nuclear waste burial site, in far southeastern New Mexico. He was re-elected easily in 1994.

In 1997, when Richardson resigned to become the Clinton administration's United Nations ambassador, Republican Bill Redmond, a Christian minister, won in an upset, thanks largely to a Green Party nominee who siphoned 17 percent of the vote in the special election. In 1998, Udall decided he had a shot at the seat, given the House district's Democratic tilt. As for the third-party threat, he said, "I intend to make peace with the Greens." He succeeded, taking 53 percent of the vote. Udall easily won re-election four times. In the House, he was assigned to the Natural Resources Committee, on which his father had served and which his uncle had chaired.

When the Democrats took control of the House in 2007, Udall sponsored an amendment to an energy bill that year requiring 15 percent of electricity to be generated from renewable sources, not including nuclear power, by 2020. The House Democratic leadership supported this amendment, and the bill passed 220-190. But the Senate refused to accept Udall's proposal, and it was dropped from the final legislation. After 9/11, Udall opposed several Bush administration initiatives: He voted against the 2002 resolution authorizing the Iraqi War and the Patriot Act, which greatly expanded law enforcement's powers to investigate terrorists. He proposed revisions to limit police authority to obtain search warrants and restore civil liberty protections for libraries and bookstores. As a House member, he endorsed single-payer health insurance proposals similar to the "Medicare for All" plan later floated by Vermont Sen. Bernie Sanders, which Udall cosponsored in 2017.

After Republican Sen. Pete Domenici announced he would not seek re-election in 2008, Udall's entry into the race quickly cleared the Democratic field. The other two members of the state's House delegation, Reps. Heather Wilson and Steve Pearce, faced off for the Republican nomination. Domenici endorsed Wilson a few days before the June primary — but Pearce narrowly won, 51%-49%. The primary depleted Pearce's war chest, and Udall outspent him by more than $3 million. Pearce painted Udall as captive to the Democratic Party's liberal wing and its "hippie" traditions. A former oil executive, Pearce hammered Udall for his opposition to energy exploration in environmentally sensitive areas. Udall responded he was for a "do-it-all" approach to energy. He won 61%-39%, running 4 percentage points ahead of Democratic presidential nominee Barack Obama.

Since 2017, Udall has served as ranking Democrat on the Indian Affairs Committee, a politically significant slot for a senator from a state in which more than 10 percent of residents are of American

Indian ancestry. New Mexico ranks second nationally, behind Alaska, in the percentage of Native Americans in its population. Udall has served on the Appropriations Committee, a key position for a state as dependent on federal largesse as his; 27.5 million acres, more than a third of New Mexico's land area, are federally owned. "New Mexico depends significantly more on federal funding than it does on state revenue," Udall told the Albuquerque Journal, explaining why he had decided not to run for the state's open gubernatorial seat in 2018. Soon after the 2016 elections, Udall acknowledged he was considering a bid for governor, saying he had "heard from many New Mexicans urging me to run." But, a month later, he said he would remain on Capitol Hill, citing his seniority and the Democrats' upcoming battles with the Trump administration. "This is not the time to weaken our position in Washington," Udall said.

Immigration has been in the forefront of these battles: When the Senate Democratic leadership got behind an immigration reform compromise in early 2018, Udall was one of just three Democrats to oppose it — joining his New Mexico junior colleague, Martin Heinrich, and California's Kamala Harris. It would have protected the children of undocumented immigrants who entered the U.S. as minors — Dreamers — while providing $25 billion for border security as a concession to President Donald Trump's demand for a border wall. In a statement, Udall and Heinrich — whose state includes about 180 miles of the 1,900-mile U.S.-Mexico border — decried "a $25 billion boondoggle" while accusing Trump of "unabashedly ransoming the lives of Dreamers as bargaining chips to achieve one of his most bigoted and divisive ideas." With only limited support from the majority Republicans, the legislation failed. A year later, Udall and Maine Republican Susan Collins were lead sponsors of the resolution passed by the Senate disapproving of Trump's plan to declare a national emergency at the southern border to obtain funding for the wall. Udall argued the issue was less about the border wall than "standing up for the Constitution."

Udall and Paul teamed up to advocate for a faster troop withdrawal from Afghanistan in 2011. In 2019, they introduced legislation giving the Defense Department 45 days to formulate a plan for withdrawing U.S. troops within a year. Alluding to 18 years of involvement, Udall said: "Soon, U.S. service members will begin deploying to Afghanistan to fight in a war that began before they were born. As we face this watershed moment, it's past time to change our approach to the longest war in our country's history." During the Obama administration, Udall and Lee joined with two other senators on a 2015 letter urging an end to the program to train and equip Syrian opposition fighters. In a statement, they said the effort had "endangered Americans and further escalated conflict in the region."

On the domestic front, perhaps Udall's most notable bipartisan effort was as lead Democratic negotiator in talks to update the nation's chemical-safety laws — picking up the mantle from the late New Jersey Democrat Frank Lautenberg. With the backing of industry groups and some environmental organizations, the measure won Environment and Public Works Committee approval in 2015. Still, other environmental groups criticized it as doing little to improve the status quo, and Udall's role stoked the ire of some Democrats, notably California Sen. Barbara Boxer, who wanted a tougher stance toward the industry. Boxer later was assuaged after winning changes to the final legislation. The bill cleared the Senate by voice vote and was signed by Obama.

Environmentalists backing the legislation praised it for strengthening the Environmental Protection Agency's oversight of hazardous chemicals. Industry officials, who had complained of having to comply with a hodgepodge of state laws, were pleased they would be dealing with a single federal regimen. But in 2018, the Trump administration — under heavy lobbying by the industry — scaled back protocols for determining risks for chemicals on the market. According to The New York Times, the EPA would exclude from its calculations potential exposure from the substances' presence in the air, ground or water, and limit its focus to possible harm caused by direct contact in the workplace or elsewhere. Udall complained the law's requirement of a comprehensive risk analysis was being ignored. "Pruitt's EPA is failing to put the new law to use as intended," Udall said, alluding to Trump's first EPA administrator, Scott Pruitt.

In recent years, Udall has pressed for action on an issue he inherited from his father: expansion of the Radiation Exposure Compensation Act. The law compensates those whose health was affected by living down wind of Cold War nuclear tests — "downwinders" — or working in uranium mining and milling. Stewart Udall represented downwinders in court for many years, and his efforts helped spur passage of RECA in 1990. Tom Udall has pressed since 2010 to expand coverage to downwinders and uranium workers in New Mexico and several other Western states not included in the original act. When the Senate Judiciary Committee held a 2018 hearing on the issue, Udall noted it was eight years after he had first requested a hearing on a similar proposal. "As we are witnessing injustice at the border and remembering the shame of Japanese internment, I am also reminded of the grave injustice done to the Cold War victims of radiation," he said. "They came to me and my father in 1977, and we never gave up on their cause." The legislation failed to move, but Udall got language into the annual Defense Department authorization bill expressing that all victims of radiation exposure be compensated.

While a supporter of Hillary Clinton in the 2016 Democratic presidential primaries, Udall teamed with Sanders to introduce a long-shot constitutional amendment allowing Congress and the states to "set reasonable limits on the raising and spending of money by candidates and others to influence elections," including distinguishing between "natural persons and corporations." It was aimed at curbing the 2010 Supreme Court decision that opened the way for unlimited spending by corporations and labor unions in federal elections. When Democrats controlled the Senate, his similar proposal attracted 54 votes, but short of the 60 needed to advance amid a Republican filibuster. In 2019, Udall introduced the Senate companion to a reform package that had cleared the Democratic-controlled House, covering ethics laws, voter access and campaign finance. While Senate Majority Leader Mitch McConnell, a longtime foe of campaign finance reform, said the bill would not be taken up, Udall vowed to force debate using procedural maneuvers — while acknowledging passage would be a long-term proposition. "Reform is not for the short-winded," he said.

Udall easily won re-election in 2014 over businessman Allen Weh, a retired Marine who largely self-funded his campaign, beating him 56%-44%. His victory was bittersweet: It came as the Democrats lost the Senate majority amid a Republican wave in which his cousin Mark Udall was among the political casualties. Whether he would have sought a third term in 2020 if Democrats held Senate control or the Colorado seat was hypothetical. Just as Udall would have been an overwhelming favorite following a 2018 election with a strong performance by Democrats in New Mexico, his party seemed likely to hold the seat. Democratic Rep. Ben Ray Lujan was the early frontrunner for the nomination—and successor to Udall. But Lujan drew a major primary opponent: New Mexico Secretary of State Maggie Toulouse Oliver. In her April 2019 announcement, she said: "...Now it's time to change the face of the Senate by electing the first woman senator from New Mexico."

Martin Heinrich (D)

Elected 2012, term expires 2024, 2nd term, b. Oct 17, 1971; Fallon, NV; University of Missouri, B.S., 1995; University of New Mexico, Att., 2002; Lutheran; Married (Julie Heinrich); 2 children.

Elected Office: Albuquerque City Council, 2003-2007, President 2005-2006; U.S. House, 2009-2013.

Professional Career: Contractor, Phillips Laboratories; Executive Director, Cottonwood Gulch Foundation, 1997-2002; NM natural resources trustee, 2006-2008.

DC Office: 303 HSOB 20510, 202-224-5521, Fax: 202-228-2841, heinrich.senate.gov

State Offices: Albuquerque, 505-346-6601; Farmington, 505-325-5030; Las Cruces, 575-523-6561; Roswell, 575-622-7113; Santa Fe, 505-988-6647.

Committees: *Armed Services*: Cybersecurity; Emerging Threats & Capabilities; Strategic Forces (RMM). *Energy & Natural Resources*: Energy (RMM); National Parks; Public Lands, Forests & Mining. *Intelligence*.

Group Ratings

	ADA	ACLU	AFL-CIO	LCV	ITI	COC	HAFA	ACU	CFG	FRC
2018	-	76%	-	93%	-	56%	5%	14%	5%	0%
2017	90%	C	100%	95%	C	29%	C	0%	4%	0%

Almanac Ratings 2017-18

	Economy	Social	Foreign	Composite
Liberal	94%	94%	82%	90%
Conservative	6%	6%	18%	10%

Key Votes of the 115th Congress

1. Obama-care revision	N	5. Gun regulations	N	9. Kavanaugh confirmation	N
2. Tax Cuts	N	6. Family planning regs	N	10. Saudi arms sales	Y
3. Dodd-Frank revision	NV	7. Gorsuch confirmation	N	11. FISA rules	N
4. Omnibus appropriations	Y	8. Immigration restrictions	N	12. Military aid in Yemen	Y

Election Results

Election	Name (Party)	Vote (%)		Cand. Spent	Ind. Exp. Support	Ind. Exp. Oppose
2018 General	Martin Heinrich (D).......................	376,998	(54%)	$6,304,882	$7,431	
	Mick Rich (R)................................	212,813	(31%)	$995,732		
	Gary Johnson (Lib)........................	107,201	(15%)	$388,636		$1,012,259
2018 Primary	Martin Heinrich (D).......................	152,145	(100%)			

Prior winning percentages: 2012 (51%); House: 2010 (52%), 2008 (56%)

Democrat Martin Heinrich was elected New Mexico's junior senator in 2012 after a campaign in which he portrayed himself as a younger version of the man he succeeded: Democratic Sen. Jeff Bingaman, who spent three decades as a centrist Democrat representing a battleground state that had trended from red to blue during his tenure. Like Bingaman, Heinrich has established a voting record that puts him in the middle of the Senate Democratic Caucus. Heinrich is among the few engineers in Congress. He has frequently focused on issues relating to energy and technology — areas of interest to New Mexico, home to several large federal government laboratories. Heinrich has heightened his national profile as a member of the Senate Intelligence Committee, amid that panel's probing of Russian interference in the 2016 presidential election.

An avid hunter, Heinrich was once a member of the National Rifle Association but has spoken out in favor of several gun control measures as a senator. He was born in Fallon, Nev., son of a utility company lineman and a factory worker. He grew up not far from Columbia, Mo., where he attended the University of Missouri and earned a degree in mechanical engineering — while building and racing solar-powered cars. Heinrich took a job doing mechanical drawings at an Albuquerque laboratory. However, he soon went to work for AmeriCorps, President Bill Clinton's public service initiative for recent college graduates. He was later executive director of the Cottonwood Gulch Foundation, which runs adventure programs in the Southwest, and started a political consulting business. Heinrich enjoyed a swift political ascent, beginning with election to the Albuquerque City Council in 2003, when he was 32. His signature issue was increasing New Mexico's minimum wage. In 2006, as council president, he worked with city business leaders and community activists to produce a gradual increase.

Encouraged by then-Democratic Gov. Bill Richardson, Heinrich announced he would challenge six-term GOP Rep. Heather Wilson for the 1st District seat in 2008. National Democrats backed Heinrich's candidacy, and he won 44 percent of the primary vote to defeat three other hopefuls — including Michelle Lujan Grisham, who would later succeed him in the House and is now New Mexico's governor. After Wilson decided to run for the Senate — she lost in the primary — Republicans fielded a strong replacement in Bernalillo County Sheriff Darren White. Heinrich tied White to the unpopular incumbent president by reminding voters that White had served as George W. Bush's county re-election chairman in 2004. White questioned Heinrich's business practices, charging that although nonprofits had paid him for advocacy work, he hadn't registered as a lobbyist. Heinrich said the law had not required him to register when he was a consultant from 2002 to 2005 in the successful effort to gain federal protection for a wilderness area 35 miles from Albuquerque. Thanks in part to that year's national Democratic wave, Heinrich easily won, 56%-44%. In 2010, he withstood a Republican wave to win re-election by 4 percentage points.

While supporting many of President Barack Obama's major initiatives, including the 2010 Affordable Care Act, Heinrich sought to avoid being a down-the-line Democrat during his House tenure. He endorsed spending cuts in some appropriations bills and, like many Western lawmakers, backed gun owners' rights. The NRA endorsed Heinrich for re-election in 2010 — citing his vote for an amendment to allow guns in national parks. During the Affordable Care Act debate, Heinrich pushed successfully to include long-sought legislation to improve Native Americans' health care and later counted this among his major achievements in the House. "That was something that had been out there for 12-14 years in Congress," he told the Albuquerque Journal. "The negotiations to get that passed … was a real coup for New Mexico." More than 10 percent of New Mexico's population is American Indian.

As a member of the Natural Resources Committee, Heinrich introduced a bill in 2009 aimed at creating clean energy jobs by providing a dedicated funding stream for the Bureau of Land Management to process a backlog of clean energy project applications. A decade later, while refraining from signing on to the "Green New Deal" — a nonbinding resolution pushed by the party's progressive wing that called for achieving "net zero greenhouse gas emissions" — Heinrich advocated working toward total reliance on renewable energy. "We can have a future reliable, cheap, resilient grid that is 100 percent powered by clean energy," he told Greentech Media. "I think in my lifetime that is completely doable."

New Mexico's Democratic establishment was eager for Heinrichto run for the Senate as soon as Bingaman announced his retirement. Heinrich drew a competitive Democratic primary opponent in state Auditor Hector Balderas — but the party rallied around the more politically experienced Heinrich, and he won with 59 percent of the vote. That set up a general election matchup against Wilson. A former Air Force officer, Wilson was the political protégé of popular former GOP Sen. Pete Domenici. In taking on Wilson, Wilson stressed her independence from her party, running a biographical ad that played up her military record without mentioning she was a Republican. She got outside financial help from conservative groups. Heinrich benefited from the Obama re-election campaign's heavy presence in the state. Heinrich defeated Wilson 51%-45% and won their mutual home base — Bernalillo County, which encompasses Albuquerque, 54%-43%. Wilson went on to serve as Air Force secretary under President Donald Trump.

On the Senate Intelligence Committee, Heinrich emerged as a sharp critic of what he considered overly broad federal surveillance of private individuals. After the National Security Agency's bulk collection of phone records was revealed in 2013, he charged that it was "a major invasion of Americans' privacy and has done little if anything to further the fight against terrorism." The program was curtailed in the 2015 Patriot Act reauthorization. Later, when the committee investigated possible assistance by Russia to Trump's 2016 presidential campaign, Heinrich gained attention for his pointed questioning of a tight-lipped then-Attorney General Jeff Sessions. As Sessions repeatedly said it would be "inappropriate" to answer questions about conversations with the president, Heinrich later told CNN: "He seemed to invent a brand new legal standard of 'appropriateness.' This is not a backyard barbecue. You either answer the question under oath or you invoke executive privilege." Via Twitter, a Princeton University professor dubbed the performance "the Heinrich maneuver."

Recent vote ratings put Heinrich in the ideological middle of Senate Democrats. His views have evolved in at least one area: gun control. After receiving the backing of the NRA six years earlier, Heinrich appeared on the Senate floor in June 2016 to support Connecticut Democrat Chris Murphy on a proposal denying the sale of firearms to those on the government's terrorist-watch list. Heinrich joined most Democrats in voting for the plan, which failed on a largely party-line vote. He also supported a bipartisan proposal to block gun sales to those on the no-fly list, which is less expansive than the terrorist-watch list. The latter measure also failed to advance, but Heinrich reintroduced it in 2018 — while co-sponsoring legislation to ban "bump stocks" that allow semi-automatic firearms to fire like automatic weapons. The onetime NRA member told Roll Call in March 2018: "My frustration with them as a group is they just aren't part of any solutions. They're ideologically pure, and they're not interested in doing anything. … I just don't think that's in any way responsible."

A hunting and camping enthusiast, Heinrich has zeroed in on land issues on the Energy and Natural Resources Committee. He has worked to ensure hunting and fishing access to lands owned by the federal government, while criticizing calls to transfer federal land to state-government control. He and his senior colleague, Democrat Tom Udall, pushed for years to create wilderness areas in much of the Organ Mountains-Desert Peaks region of southern New Mexico — which had been declared a national monument by Obama in 2014. Legislation by Heinrich and Udall to designate more than 240,000 acres of the national monument as wilderness — which bars construction of roads and use of mechanized vehicles, while allowing hiking and horseback riding — became law as part of a major public lands and conservation bill signed in March 2019.

All told, the bill designated nearly 275,000 acres of new wilderness areas throughout New Mexico. Heinrich represents a state in which 47 percent of the population — the highest percentage in the nation — is Hispanic. In January 2019, he led 19 other Senate Democrats in introducing a bill to protect Dreamers — children of undocumented immigrants who arrived in the U.S. as minors — from possible deportation. The bill would have barred the Homeland Security Department — which oversees the Deferred Action for Childhood Arrivals program created during the Obama administration — from sharing information collected on DACA participants with immigration and law enforcement agencies. When the Senate Democratic leadership got behind a legislative compromise in early 2018 that included preserving DACA, Heinrich was one of just three Senate Democrats to vote against it. He and Udall objected to another provision of the compromise that would have provided $25 billion for border security to underwrite Trump's proposed southern border wall. "New Mexicans support smart border security measures, but President Trump's border wall is a symbol of everything that's wrong with this administration," they said in a joint statement.

One of the bigger splashes of Heinrich's first term came when he was cast with his Arizona Republican colleague Jeff Flake in a Discovery Channel reality show: "Rival Survival." It featured the bipartisan duo — who periodically collaborated on legislation before Flake's retirement in 2019 — spending six days with minimal supplies on the isolated island of Eru, in the Marshall Islands. "We wanted to show that Republicans and Democrats can get along and survive together," Flake told The Washington Post. Heinrich and Flake later tried to advance the bipartisan approach by holding a Senate lunch for members of both parties; typically, the parties hold their luncheons separately.

As Heinrich prepared to seek re-election, term-limited Republican Gov. Susana Martinez ruled out a challenge to him. Rep. Steve Pearce was mentioned as a possible candidate but instead ran unsuccessfully for governor. Mick Rich, an Albuquerque contractor and state Labor and Industrial Commission member making his first run for office, was unopposed for the GOP nomination. Libertarians slated former Gov. Gary Johnson — the Libertarian nominee for president in 2016.

Johnson's presence enlivened debates during the fall campaign, as he and Heinrich argued over whether Johnson's call to sharply downsize federal spending would adversely affect the economically important presence of military bases in New Mexico. Johnson's longtime support for legalization of marijuana was largely eliminated as an issue: Heinrich, after declining to go beyond backing medical marijuana in his first campaign, said in the spring of 2018, "It's time to legalize marijuana." Rich, while emphasizing his support for Trump, criticized Heinrich for moving his family to D.C.'s Maryland suburbs. "He has become a Washington politician," Rich said. "He has abandoned New Mexico." It had little effect: Heinrich defeated Rich 54%-31%, as Johnson trailed with 15 percent.

Debra Haaland (D)

Elected 2018, 1st term, b. Dec 02, 1960; Winslow, AZ; University of New Mexico, B.A., 1994; University of California, Los Angeles, 2000; University of New Mexico Law School, J.D., 2006; Catholic; Single1 child.

Professional Career: Manager, Native American Vote Program; tribal Administrator, Pueblo of San Felipe, Tribal Administrator.

DC Office: 1237 LHOB 20515, 202-225-6316, haaland.house.gov

State Offices: Albuquerque, 505-346-6781.

Committees: *Armed Services*: Military Personnel; Readiness. *Natural Resources*: Indigenous Peoples of the United States; National Parks, Forests & Public Lands (Chmn).

Election Results

Election	Name (Party)	Vote (%)		Cand. Spent	Ind. Exp. Support	Ind. Exp. Oppose
2018 General	Debra A. Haaland (D)	147,336	(59%)	$1,837,810	$325,998	$19,461
	Janice Arnold-Jones (R)	90,507	(36%)	$316,183		
	Lloyd Princeton (Lib)	11,319	(5%)	$74,755		
2018 Primary	Debra A. Haaland (D)	25,444	(41%)			
	Damon Martinez (D)	16,182	(26%)			
	Antoinette Sedillo Lopez (D)	12,919	(21%)			
	Paul Moya (D)	3,691	(6%)			

First-term Democrat Debra Haaland won a safely Democratic seat, following a competitive primary. She became one of the first two Native American women elected to Congress. Haaland ran on a liberal agenda and was a strong critic of President Donald Trump, especially on immigration issues. "Congress has never heard a voice like mine," she told The Albuquerque Journal, citing her experience as a single mother who struggled through poverty to get her education. Haaland succeeded Rep. Michelle Lujan Grisham, who was elected governor of New Mexico.

With her father serving in the Marine Corps for 30 years and her mother in the Navy, Haaland spent her early years living on military bases. She got her bachelor's and law degrees from the University of New Mexico, while raising her daughter as a single mother. A former Pueblo tribal administrator, she directed business operations of tribal gambling activities in the state.

Haaland worked on statewide Democratic campaigns to rally support among Native Americans. In 2014, she ran for lieutenant governor with Gary King, candidate for governor; their ticket lost, 57%-43%. As state Democratic chairman, she helped the party regain control of the state legislature two years later.

She protested locally in 2017 when Trump referred to Sen. Elizabeth Warren as "Pocahontas." As Haaland later told The Huffington Post, "He doesn't get to decide who is Indian and who is not Indian." In that interview, she cited her own participation in protests with the Standing Rock Indian Reservation in North Dakota over the proposed Dakota Access pipeline. "Is there anyone in Congress who went to Standing Rock to stand up for Native folks? No," she said. "If I'm in Congress, I would go."

In her campaign for the House, Haaland was endorsed by labor unions, progressive women's groups and the Congressional Black Caucus. With her attacks on Trump's immigration policies, she cited her own family's unhappy experience with government-forced family separation programs. Her advocacy of Native Americans included an economic component. Haaland listed her top priorities as expansion of renewable energy and opposition to oil-company drilling on tribal lands, especially in New Mexico.

Her chief opponents in the six-candidate Democratic primary were Damon Martinez, a top aide to former Democratic Sen. Jeff Bingaman and the local U.S. attorney for two years during the Obama administration, and law professor Antoinette Sedillo Lopez. Each benefited from several hundred thousand dollars of spending by outside groups: a bipartisan veterans' group for Martinez, and Latino activists for Sedillo Lopez. In candidate fundraising, Haaland and Sedillo Lopez each raised a bit more than $1 million; Martinez received about $750,000.

Haaland won the primary with 41 percent of the vote to 26 percent for Martinez and 21 percent for Sedillo Lopez. More than 90 percent of the vote was cast in Albuquerque-based Bernalillo County. She also led in the small share of votes cast in four outlying counties. In November, she defeated Republican Janice Arnold-Jones, a business owner and former state legislator.

With another first-term Democrat, Sharice Davids of Kansas, Haaland joined two other Native Americans already in Congress: Reps. Tom Cole and Markwayne Mullin, both Republicans from Oklahoma.

When. Sen. Tom Udall announced in March 2019 that he would not seek a third term in New Mexico, Haaland told supporters that she was thinking about running for his seat. But she decided a few days later to seek reelection to the House—an apparent acknowledgment that she would have been hard-pressed to defeat Rep. Ben Ray Lujan, the early Democratic frontrunner for the seat.

NM-1: Central New Mexico

Cook Partisan Voting Index: D+7

Population		Race and Ethnicity		Income	
Total	691,746	White	40.2%	Median Income	$49,277
Land area (sq. miles)	4,600	Black	2.4%	District Income Rank	322
Pop/ sq mi	150.4	Latino	49.4%	Poverty Rate	18.5%
Born in State	53%	Asian	2.2%	With health insurance	89.1%
		Two or more races	1.8%	Cash public assistance	2.5%
Age Groups		Other	4%	Food stamp/SNAP	15.7%
Under 18	22.2%				
18-34	24%	**Education**		**Work**	
35-64	38.6%	H.S grad or less	35.9%	White Collar	15.2%
Over 64	15.2%	Some college	31.6%	Sales and Service	43.7%
		College Degree, 4 yr	17.9%	Blue Collar	16.7%
Military		Post grad	14.7%	Government	19.7%
Veteran/ Active Duty	9.8%				

2012 Pres. Vote	Obama	155,915	(55%)	Romney	111,749	(40%)		
2016 Pres. Vote	Clinton	147,250	(52%)	Trump	100,132	(35%)	Johnson	30,767 (11%)

Albuquerque: New Mexico's past and future come together in its single metropolis, Albuquerque. The city's Spanish and Indian past is memorialized in its name (for a 17th-century Spanish nobleman), its age (founded in 1706) and its quaint Old Town. But Albuquerque's future is decidedly high-tech. For decades, Sandia National Laboratories, Kirtland Air Force Base and the University of New Mexico have attracted scientists and engineers to Albuquerque and promoted private-sector technology growth. The city's minor-league baseball team is the Isotopes, named in part to honor the area's association with the Atomic Age. When rocket scientist Robert Goddard moved here in 1930 and nuclear scientist J. Robert Oppenheimer reconnoitered the site in 1940, Albuquerque was still a town of 35,000 at the junction of the Rio Grande River and old U.S. 66, which paralleled the Santa Fe Railroad. "A dirty, red sod-hut tortilla desert highway city," novelist Tom Wolfe wrote.

Now, metro Albuquerque, spreading out from Bernalillo County into Sandoval and Valencia counties, has more people — 913,000 in 2017 — than all of New Mexico did when the scientists first arrived. The University of New Mexico has become a magnet for biotechnology, with more than a dozen local startups working to commercialize UNM's biomedical discoveries. Intel's facility in Rio Rancho, which had suffered several years of job losses — from 3,300 in 2013 to 1,100 -- due to the decline of its advanced chip-making, started to bounce back in 2018 with the introduction of silicon photonics, a new microprocessing technology that permits faster data transfer over longer distances. The city's prosperous neighborhoods have climbed the gently rising heights to the east; poorer residents have spread north and south along the Rio Grande. Hemmed in by the Sandia Mountains and by federal installations, growth is moving west and north. In November 2018, the county approved the first phase of Santolina, a planned 22-square-mile development west of Albuquerque that within a few decades might house 90,000 residents and create 75,000 jobs; some skeptical community groups were concerned about sprawl and scant water resources.

In the Old Town centered on the plaza, some of the adobe buildings date to the 18th century. Every October, Albuquerque hosts the International Balloon Fiesta, which features more than 500 hot-air balloons and many resident balloonists. The annual Gathering of Nations typically attracts more than 700 tribes, along with 100,000 participants and spectators. Producers began work in early 2019 on Breaking Bad, a movie version of the popular television series about a high school chemistry teacher turned meth kingpin, which was set and filmed here for five years. At the same time, Netflix planned to take over a large production studio, which will create up to 1,000 jobs. Tim Keller, who was elected mayor in 2017, highlighted his experience with heavy-metal music.

The 1st Congressional District includes almost all of Albuquerque and some of its suburbs. It is 49 percent Hispanic and takes in most of Bernalillo County, all of sparsely populated Torrance County in the desert, and small corners of Sandoval, Santa Fe and Valencia counties. More than 90 percent of the vote is in Bernalillo. The past two Democratic presidential candidates had double-digit wins in the county. Until 2008, the district elected only Republicans to Congress. With additional Latino voters, it has grown more Democratic. Hillary Clinton won the district, 52%-35%.

Xochitl Torres Small (D)

Elected 2018, 1st term, b. Nov 15, 1984; Portland, OR; Georgetown University (DC), Bach. Deg., 2007; University of New Mexico Law School, J.D., 2015; Lutheran; Married (Nathan Small).

Professional Career: Field Representative, U.S. Sen. Tom Udall, 2009-2012; Judicial Law Clerk, Hon. Robert C. Brack, 2015-2016; Attorney, Kemp Smith.

DC Office: 430 CHOB 20515, 202-225-2365, Fax: 202-225-9599, torressmall.house.gov

State Offices: Las Cruces, 575-323-6384.

Committees: *Armed Services*: Readiness; Tactical Air & Land Forces. *Homeland Security*: Border Security, Facilitation & Operations; Oversight, Management & Accountability (Chmn).

Election Results

Election	Name (Party)	Vote (%)		Cand. Spent	Ind. Exp. Support	Ind. Exp. Oppose
2018 General	Xochitl Liana I. Torres-Small (D). 101,489	(51%)		$4,537,008	$656,363	$3,049,138
	Yvette Herrell (R)............................ 97,767	(49%)		$1,301,318		
2018 Primary	Xochitl Torres-Small (D)............... 25,395	(73%)				
	Madeleine Hildebrandt (D)...................... 9,577	(27%)				

Xochitl Torres Small, who narrowly won a Republican-held seat, was one of the few incoming Democrats in 2018 who took a largely rural district. Her experience as a Senate aide helped to educate her about the issues in the area where she was raised. Torres Small benefited from divisions among local Republicans in her campaign to succeed Republican Rep. Steve Pearce, who ran unsuccessfully for governor. Her victory gave Democrats complete control of the New Mexico delegation.

Torres Small grew up in Las Cruces and graduated from Georgetown University. She returned home to get her law degree from the University of New Mexico. She joined the staff of Sen. Tom Udall, where she was his field representative in rural New Mexico. After clerking for a federal judge in her home state, Torres Small joined Kemp Smith, a Texas-based law firm, where she focused on water-rights issues. Her husband, Nathan Small, had served in the New Mexico House since 2016.

In the Democratic primary, Torres Small had the quiet support of the Democratic Congressional Campaign Committee, whose chairman was Rep. Ben Ray Lujan of New Mexico. Her opponent Madeleine Hildebrandt, a Coast Guard veteran, was backed by some progressive groups. She accused Torres Small of representing clients of her law firm that want to sell water rights, rather than local farmers and ranchers. With her better-organized campaign, Torres Small won, 73%-27%.

Republican nominee Yvette Harrell, who served eight years in the state House, had a tough contest in the GOP primary, which had four candidates. Pledging to join the conservative House Freedom Caucus, she clashed with Monty Newman, a former chairman of the state Republican Party. Newman was backed by moderate Gov. Susana Martinez, who told the Albuquerque Journal that Herrell's support of oil and gas interests raised questions about her ability to represent New Mexico "in a fair and reasonable way." Herrell led Newman, 49%-32%.

Against Torres Small, Herrell avoided debates and appeared confident of victory. Vice President Mike Pence spoke at a rally for Herrell in the final days of the campaign. The Albuquerque Journal endorsed Herrell, citing her legislative experience and support for limited government.

Torres Small had a big advantage in campaign funds. She spent about $4.5 million, compared with $1.3 for Herrell. Ads for Torres Smith downplayed her party label, sought to cast her as a centrist with local roots and showed her shooting a firearm in an open field. Herrell responded with an ad that mocked the gun use by Torres Small; a Republican ad called her "another out-of-touch liberal."

Torres Small won, 51%-49%. In Dona Ana, her home county and the largest in the district, she got 65 percent of the vote and led Herrell by 18,000 votes, which was far more than her overall lead. In a successful election year for Democrats in New Mexico, she may have benefited from the party's statewide candidates who pulled a larger share of the vote.

The last Democrat to win this district was Harry Teague, a conservative oil-company owner. He served one term and lost reelection in 2010 to Pearce, 55%-45%. Torres Small, with a different persona than Teague, hoped for a longer tenure.

NM-2: Southern New Mexico

Cook Partisan Voting Index: R+6

Population		Race and Ethnicity		Income	
Total	696,944	White	37.1%	Median Income	$42,508
Land area (sq. miles)	71,739	Black	1.7%	District Income Rank	398
Pop/ sq mi	9.7	Latino	54.4%	Poverty Rate	22.9%
Born in State	49.9%	Asian	0.7%	With health insurance	87.3%
		Two or more races	1.3%	Cash public assistance	3.5%
Age Groups		Other	4.8%	Food stamp/SNAP	20.3%
Under 18	25.1%				
18-34	23.7%	Education		Work	
35-64	35.1%	H.S grad or less	48.1%	White Collar	16.1%
Over 64	16.1%	Some college	31.3%	Sales and Service	45.6%
		College Degree, 4 yr	12.5%	Blue Collar	25.1%
Military		Post grad	8.1%	Government	22.9%
Veteran/ Active Duty	10.7%				

2012 Pres. Vote	Romney	119,168	(52%)	Obama	103,438	(45%)			
2016 Pres. Vote	Trump	117,212	(50%)	Clinton	93,362	(40%)	Johnson	18,903	(8%)

Las Cruces: Southeastern New Mexico is a disparate landscape: endless sagebrush-strewn acreage and then, suddenly, 9,000-foot mountain peaks rising along the Continental Divide. (The Robledo Mountains, says the Smithsonian Institution, are the world's greatest repository of pre-dinosaur-era fossil tracks.) The eastern part of this region — places like Lovington and Hobbs — speaks with a Texas twang rather than a northern New Mexico lilt. In Little Texas, as southeastern New Mexico is known, oil has been the economic mainstay. Cattle ranching is common, and cotton is grown on irrigated land. Roswell, the site of a supposed flying saucer landing in 1947, is now home of the International UFO Museum and Research Center. Farther west is White Sands National Monument, with its immaculate gypsum dunes and specially evolved animals with white coloration that allows them to elude predators in the harsh environment.

Virgin Galactic, a company started by billionaire Richard Branson, leased land near White Sands to build the nation's first commercial spaceport (called Spaceport America). Despite initial setbacks, including the crash in 2014 of Virgin Galactic's SpaceShipTwo Enterprise, the $218 million facility has grown more active, with several dozen rocket launches. NASA has tested several new technologies, as have the Italian Space Agency and several American aerospace companies. Close by is Alamogordo, not far from where the first atomic bomb was exploded in the empty land at 5:29:45 a.m. Mountain War Time on July 16, 1945.

Las Cruces, New Mexico's second-largest city, has grown at rates well above the statewide average, thanks to migrants from Mexico coming up the Rio Grande. For decades, Anglo and Mexican ranchers across the border spoke "the common language of cattle," and communities frequently shared public services with their cross-border neighbors, not hindered by a wall or other major barrier. This largely empty 150-mile section of the U.S.-Mexico border remains sleepier than elsewhere. In Eunice, along the Texas line, a $4 billion commercial uranium enrichment plant has been built, the first such facility licensed by the Nuclear Regulatory Commission. It takes fuel from nuclear power plants around the world. Surrounding Lea County, where the population grew 6 percent from 2010 to 2017, accounts for more than half the oil production of New Mexico, the third-largest state producer in the nation.

The 2nd Congressional District of New Mexico covers the southern part of the state, reaching to Albuquerque's southern suburbs. Demographically and politically it is diverse. It includes most of Little Texas — majority Anglo and solidly conservative — but also politically marginal Las Cruces and the Indian country around the pueblos, which is strongly Democratic. The district is 54 percent Hispanic and 5 percent Indian. Las Cruces-based Dona Ana County, the population center, has about one-third of the voters. Many Latinos here are migrant workers and not part of an organized, Democratic voting bloc. The district in 2016 voted for Donald Trump, 50%-40%, a wider margin than the GOP wins in the two previous presidential elections.

Ben Ray Luján (D)

Elected 2008, 6th term, b. Jun 07, 1972; Santa Fe; University of New Mexico, Att., 1995; New Mexico Highlands University, B.A., 2007; Roman Catholic; Single.

Elected Office: NM public reg. comm., 2004-2008, Chairman, 2005-2007.

Professional Career: NM deputy state treas., 2002-2003; Director admin. services, CFO, NM Cultural Affairs Department, 2003-2004.

DC Office: 2323 RHOB 20515, 202-225-6190, Fax: 202-226-1528, lujan.house.gov

State Offices: Farmington, 505-324-1005; Gallup, 505-863-0582; Las Vegas, 505-454-3038; Rio Rancho, 505-994-0499; Santa Fe, 505-984-8950; Tucumcari, 575-461-3029.

Committees: House Assistant Speaker. *Energy & Commerce*: Communications & Technology; Consumer Protection & Commerce; Health. *Select Committee on the Climate Crisis.*

Group Ratings

	ADA	ACLU	AFL-CIO	LCV	ITI	COC	HAFA	ACU	CFG	FRC
2018	-	89%	-	97%	-	58%	8%	4%	21%	0%
2017	100%	C	97%	100%	C	50%	C	4%	5%	0%

Almanac Ratings 2017-18

	Economy	Social	Foreign	Composite
Liberal	100%	98%	69%	89%
Conservative	0%	2%	31%	11%

Key Votes of the 115th Congress

1. Obama-care revision	N	5. Family planning regs	N	9. Guantanamo prisoners	N
2. Tax Cuts	N	6. Body cameras/immigration	Y	10. Ground missiles, limit	Y
3. Omnibus appropriations	N	7. Abortion ban	N	11. Defense Dept. spending	Y
4. Dodd-Frank revision	N	8. Concealed carry	N	12. FISA rules	N

Election Results

Election	Name (Party)	Vote (%)		Cand. Spent	Ind. Exp. Support	Ind. Exp. Oppose
2018 General	Ben Lujan (D)	155,201	(63%)	$1,453,078	$279	
	Jerald Steve McFall (R)	76,427	(31%)			
	Christopher Manning (Lib)	13,265	(5%)	$5,136		
2018 Primary	Ben Lujan (D)		(100%)			

Prior winning percentages: 2016 (62%), 2014 (62%), 2012 (63%), 2010 (57%), 2008 (57%)

Democrat Ben Ray Luján, who was elected in 2008, chaired the Democratic Congressional Campaign Committee for four years, including the party's successful performance in 2018. He reaped his reward when Speaker Nancy Pelosi designated him as assistant speaker, which placed him in the mix of contenders for a top party leadership post. Those prospects were upended when Sen. Tom Udall announced on March 25, 2019, that he will not seek reelection and Lujan a few days later announced his candidacy to succeed him. That placed Lujan in a growing list of Democrats who moved on from House leadership because of the uncertainty of Pelosi's departure plans.

A seventh-generation New Mexican, Luján is the son of Ben Luján, a former state House speaker and legendary figure in state politics. The younger Luján has sought to establish his own niche by focusing on complex topics important to the state, especially energy and technology. He was born in Santa Fe and grew up on his family's farm, where he and his three siblings helped raise cattle, sheep and chickens. Luján worked as a card dealer in a casino while attending classes at New Mexico Highlands University. After graduating, he had several state jobs, including chief financial officer and director of administrative services at the Department of Cultural Affairs.

Luján launched into electoral politics in 2004, when he was elected to the New Mexico Public Regulation Commission. As chairman, his most pressing issue was the failure of Qwest Communications to invest a promised $788 million in its New Mexico communications network. Under Luján's leadership, the PRC ordered Qwest to invest in infrastructure or refund the money to customers. When Qwest refused, Luján and the PRC took the company to the New Mexico Supreme Court. In 2006, the court sided with the commission, and Qwest finally agreed to spend $270 million in the state. He worked with commissioners from other states in the West to create regional solutions to climate change.

When Udall ran successfully for the Senate, Luján got 40 percent of the vote at the Democratic convention to 30 percent for Donald Wiviott, a developer; both were included on the primary ballot, along with Benny Shendo, former head of the New Mexico Indian Affairs Department. Wiviott ran ads claiming Luján's father had helped him secure his job as deputy state treasurer. Luján claimed that Wiviott's Texas trailer parts company had been charged by the Federal Trade Commission with price-fixing. Shendo caused the race's biggest controversy when he implied at a candidate forum that Luján was gay, which drew criticism from local gay rights groups. Luján picked up endorsements from Gov. Bill Richardson, local labor unions and the Sierra Club. Wiviott spent almost $1.6 million of his own money. Lujan, who spent half that amount, won with 42 percent to Wiviott's 26 percent and Shendo's 16 percent. The general election was a foregone conclusion. Luján has not faced serious competition since.

Luján has had some moderate strokes in his voting record. He sided with northern New Mexico ranchers in 2011 in their fight against the U.S. Forest Service over reducing cattle-grazing allotments within the Santa Fe and Carson National Forests, a position that dismayed state environmental groups. He has filed legislation to authorize additional money for victims of diseases caused by uranium mining and nuclear tests, many of whom are citizens of the Navajo nation. He supports the natural gas industry, which has a strong presence in the northwest corner.

On the Energy and Commerce Committee, he has worked on two of his pet causes: alternative energy and Los Alamos National Laboratory's non-nuclear weapons scientific research. In a 2015 speech to the New Mexico legislature, Luján urged creation of a public-private consortium for the state's two national labs to bid on federal contracts. Earlier, he organized the bipartisan Technology Transfer Caucus to funnel research from the labs to the private sector. His committee work has included legislation to treat and prevent opioid abuse, which has become a crisis in New Mexico.

Luján expressed interest in running for the open Senate seat in 2012. When Rep. Martin Heinrich was the preferred choice of national Democrats, Luján stepped aside. He was rewarded following the 2014 election when, in a surprise move, Pelosi chose him to head the DCCC over higher-profile House Democrats. Pelosi described Luján as "a dynamic and forward-looking leader with fresh energy and ideas."

But the 2016 campaign revealed little change in DCCC strategy and resulted in widespread disappointment. Democrats grumbled that Pelosi and her close team of operatives remained in control, that they failed to put enough House seats in play in a competitive cycle and that they ran cookie-cutter campaigns that failed to connect with voters, especially in swing states. Like the presidential campaign of Hillary Clinton, House Democrats fell short in reaching out to unhappy voters to whom Donald Trump appealed. Starting the cycle with their smallest number of seats since 1928, they regained only six seats.

Luján acknowledged those shortcomings and other second-guessing in a December 2016 letter to House Democrats, in which he promised "a more inclusive messaging strategy, the need for more member-driven recruitment, and an interest in setting up a regional structure to better tap the expertise of our members." He gained another term at DCCC without opposition.

Abetted by the grassroots anger toward Trump, Lujan had several factors in his favor in 2018: The organized "resistance" of Democratic women, especially in the suburbs; more systematic recruitment of candidates; huge fundraising; and more than three dozen open Republican seats, in part a symptom of GOP disillusionment with Trump. Following disappointing setbacks in special elections for four GOP-held seats in early 2017, Lujan took a disciplined approach to the calendar and use of resources, including a willingness to take sides in primaries. "We need to do a better job in understanding that we're talking about real people," he told the Los Angeles Times in July 2017. He rejected the use of litmus tests, including on abortion rights, for candidates.

The resulting 40-seat gain was beyond what most Democrats — and other observers — had forecast. After other aspirants stepped aside, Lujan was unopposed for the new position of assistant speaker, with upgraded responsibilities defined by Pelosi. As he described his position, Luján said, "I will welcome ideas from all corners of our caucus to build our agenda, protect our majority, hold the

Trump administration and congressional Republicans accountable, and make a positive difference in peoples' lives."

But Lujan's focus quickly shifted when Udall announced his retirement. Seeking to become his successor for the second time, Lujan announced a week later that he will run for Udall's seat. He said that he was "humbled by all of the outreach encouraging me to run." In a sign of Lujan's early strength, no other credible Democrat—or Republican—immediately stepped forward to enter the contest. The Democratic Senatorial Campaign Committee endorsed Lujan on April 18 and said that it would do "all we can to support [him] in this campaign." But that did not stop Secretary of State Maggie Toulouse Oliver from stepping in to challenge Lujan, in what seemed likely to be a competitive primary.

NM-3: Northern New Mexico   Cook Partisan Voting Index: D+8

Population		Race and Ethnicity		Income	
Total	696,138	White	37.2%	Median Income	$48,925
Land area (sq. miles)	44,959	Black	1.3%	District Income Rank	327
Pop/ sq mi	15.5	Latino	40.7%	Poverty Rate	20.3%
Born in State	56.9%	Asian	1.2%	With health insurance	86.1%
		Two or more races	1.7%	Cash public assistance	2.3%
Age Groups		Other	17.9%	Food stamp/SNAP	15.1%
Under 18	24.4%				
18-34	21.9%	**Education**		**Work**	
35-64	37.7%	H.S grad or less	40.7%	White Collar	16%
Over 64	16%	Some college	32.2%	Sales and Service	43.3%
		College Degree, 4 yr	14.8%	Blue Collar	19.2%
Military		Post grad	12.3%	Government	24.1%
Veteran/ Active Duty	9.8%				

2012 Pres. Vote	Obama	155,983	(58%)	Romney	104,871	(39%)			
2016 Pres. Vote	Clinton	144,622	(52%)	Trump	102,323	(37%)	Johnson	24,871	(9%)

Santa Fe: "The dancing ground of the sun" is what the Pueblo Indians called the land of northern New Mexico, where the long vistas, dotted with low-lying scrub, are painted in pastel hues in the cold light and clear air. For 100 years, artists have been coming here, attracted by the scenery and by a unique civilization that is part Indian, part Anglo, part Spanish, and a little Mexican. (Northern New Mexico was under Mexican control from 1821 to 1846.) The Indians were here first and built adobe pueblos, including some of the world's earliest apartment buildings. The Spanish conquistadors and priests brought the Catholic religion, the baroque architectural accents, and the Spanish language. The Palace of the Governors, built in Santa Fe in 1610, is now a museum on Santa Fe's Plaza and is the nation's oldest extant public building. Zoning laws vigorously enforce the height and adobe-like appearance of buildings in the historic district.

Along the back roads in Rio Arriba and Taos counties, one can find a religion that mixes Catholicism with adaptations of Indian festivals, buildings not that much different from the old pueblos, and a standard of living reminiscent of the Indian past, sometimes punctuated by high rates of drug abuse and alcoholism. It's quite a contrast with the ski lodges in the Taos Valley, the high-security research facilities of Los Alamos — which has the second-highest median income of any city in the nation (behind Washington D.C.) and has among the most Ph.D.s per capita, thanks to National Laboratory — and the affluent lifestyles of modern-day Santa Fe.

The 3rd Congressional District of New Mexico contains most of the state's historic Spanish-speaking and Indian regions. This district, similar in size to Pennsylvania, runs from the High Plains along the Texas border, past the haunting Sangre de Cristo Mountains, through the vast ridges and isolated buttes in the center, to the windy and dusty desert-like plains. With 96,000 residents, a 10 percent increase from 2010 to 2017, Rio Rancho began as a retirement community in the 1960s and has become the district's most populous city. In Farmington-based San Juan County, a lower-income area that suffered a 2 percent population decline from 2010 to 2017, the utility company's plan to close its coal-fired power plant by 2022 caused protests over increased costs. But the artsy state capital of Santa Fe, which has the most museums of any city in the nation except New York, remains its lively and dominant center. The economy in Santa Fe has remained strong, with a "gray" growth as the number of residents 65 and older has come close to surpassing those 18 and younger. In 2018, an annual Hispanic fiesta agreed to requests by Native American tribes to drop positive references to the Spanish conquest. The district's Hispanic population is 41 percent, the lowest of the state's three districts. Another 19 percent of the population is Indian, the highest in the state. Concentrated in and around the Navajo reservation in the west (and outside of Santa Fe), many of the district's Indians live in abject poverty.

The politics of northern New Mexico have been unique. For years, votes were bartered in Spanish by Republicans and Democrats, often cynically, sometimes corruptly. Loyalties ran to families and communities more than to principles or parties. Those traditions evolved. Hispanics and Indians are solidly Democratic. In Santa Fe and Taos, the upscale and many elderly migrants have produced a strong liberal tilt. In 2016, Hillary Clinton took the district, 52%-37%.

NEW YORK

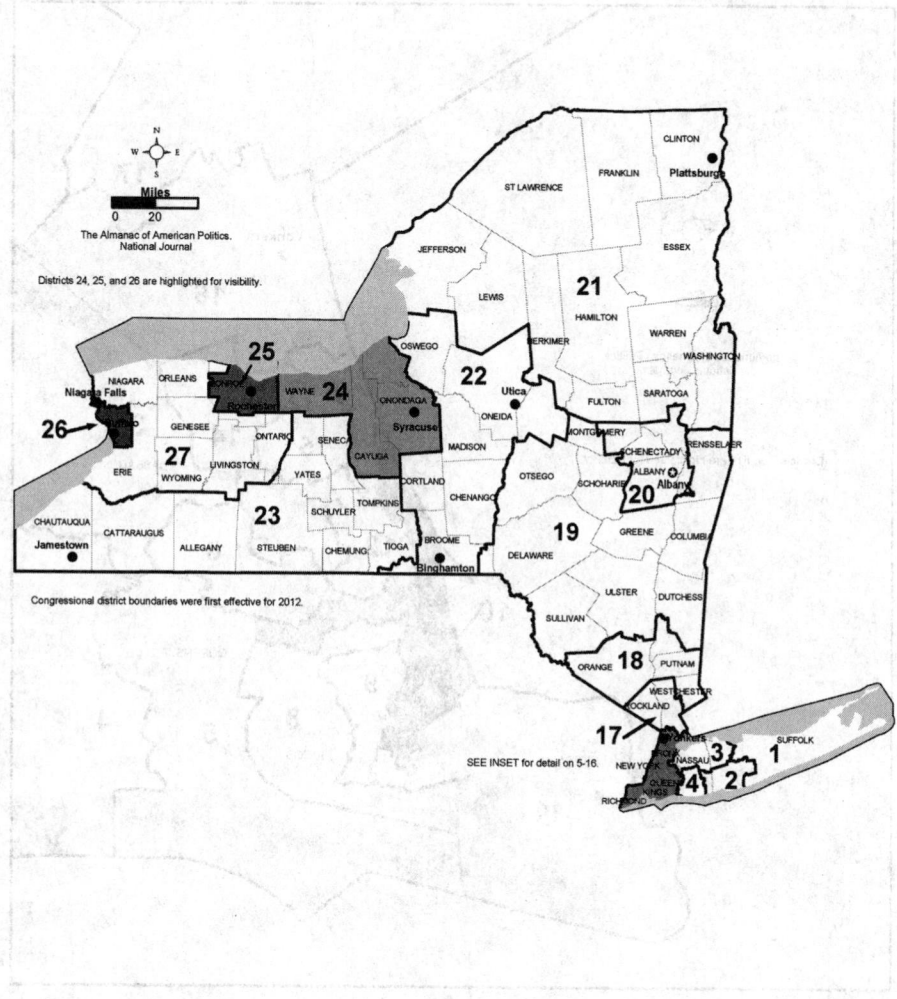

New York may no longer be the giant among states it once was, but it still packs plenty of heft. Based on gross domestic product, New York City alone would rank among the 20 largest economies in the world. In politics, the state's governor, Andrew Cuomo, has long been considered presidential timber; its senior senator, Charles Schumer, is his party's minority leader; and its junior senator, Kirsten Gillibrand, was an early candidate for president in 2020. Hakeem Jeffries is the fourth-ranking House Democratic leader. Until Justice Antonin Scalia's death, four Supreme Court justices hailed from New York City. The President of the United States, Donald Trump, lived in a luxury skyscraper he built in midtown Manhattan. And the chairmen of at least two House committees that have been investigating Trump – Jerrold Nadler of Judiciary and Eliot Engel of Foreign Affairs – hail from Manhattan and the Bronx, respectively.

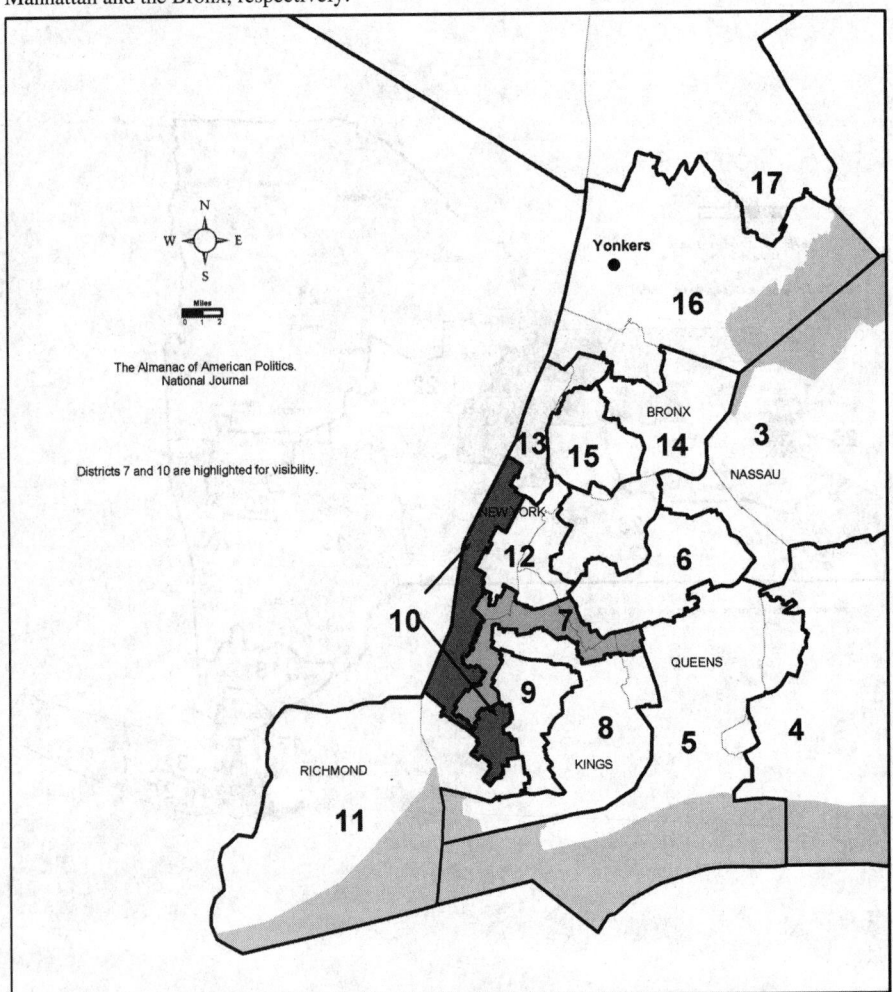

Congressional district boundaries were first effective for 2012.

"Even old New York was once Nieuw Amsterdam," the old song goes. Today's New York — America's largest city, financial capital, artistic and media center, and largest immigrant destination — seems far removed from once tiny, rough-hewn Nieuw Amsterdam. But this is a city with a certain enduring character that goes back to its birth. Fewer than 2 percent of today's New Yorkers are descended from the Dutch of Nieuw Amsterdam, but the character of the place, including its tolerance, endures in daily life and in its great institutions and helps explain its miraculous growth. Combine Amsterdam and America, Dutch character with British-born political freedoms and American military strength, and you have the opportunity to build a city-state that can lead the world — and become the natural target of terrorists who hate that civilization. In some fields – culture, finance, media -- New York City remains, in the words of "Hamilton," the greatest city in the world.

New York was not always the nation's leader. In 1776, it was only the seventh most populous colony. Only in the 19th century did the descendants of Dutch patroons, Huguenot refugees, British West Indies traders, and Yankee farmers become the nation's most successful merchants and capitalists, forging the first routes to the great American interior, including the Erie Canal that cut through the valleys of the Hudson and Mohawk rivers, and building grand brownstone mansions on broad midtown Manhattan avenues. That early diversity provides one clue to New York's success. If New York has been cynical, ready to cooperate with Loyalists and Revolutionaries, it has also been tolerant, ready to accept anyone smart or rich enough to be counted a success. It has been propelled upward at each stage, forging ahead of London as a financial and manufacturing center by World War I and staying ahead of surging Chicago and Los Angeles by incorporating every immigrant wave and consistently rewarding intelligence and hard work, with little concern about preserving hierarchies.

New York state's success has been a product not only of market economics, but also of government and politics. The English saw New York as a pivotal point in North America, the connecter of its northern and southern colonies and an avenue to the interior. That is why the 30-year-old James, Duke of York, as Lord High Admiral, ordered the fleet to take Nieuw Amsterdam in 1664; the city and state are named for the man who was later King James II. The Iroquois, the most deeply rooted and militarily strong Native Americans, were kept in place for 100 years by an alliance with British troops and then were driven out of their homelands in Upstate New York after the Revolution.

New York led the nation in political innovation. Martin Van Buren's Albany Regency was the first state political machine, an ally of New York City's Tammany Hall. Van Buren invented or institutionalized the Democratic Party, the national convention and the inaugural parade. His adversaries, Thurlow Weed and William Seward, formed the Whig Party and ultimately became Republicans. Noting that Van Buren's Democrats were winning large margins from Irish Catholics and other immigrants, the Whigs and Republicans also made bids for the newcomers' votes. Both parties – the Republicans upstate and the Democrats downstate -- served the function of mediating between the divergent interests of the urban masses and the farmers and burghers. This conflict is still evident in New York -- city and country, immigrant and native, the Big Apple and the apple-knockers.

Both parties also worked to protect New Yorkers against the untrammeled workings of free economic and political markets. Tammany Democrats embarked on an unprecedented, labor-intensive campaign to build infrastructure — the bridges and tunnels that made Greater New York possible. The tradition carried on from the time of Mayor Abram Hewitt, elected in 1886 over the single-taxer Henry George and the 27-year-old Theodore Roosevelt, up through the time of Gov. Al Smith in the 1920s and his protégé Robert Moses, who built bridges, tunnels, highways, beaches and the World's Fairs of 1939 and 1964, laying the groundwork for modern-day New York City, though also embedding infrastructure with a more mixed legacy for urban planning and the environment. New York City took its current form in 1898 when Manhattan (the nation's largest city) and Brooklyn (the fourth-largest) banded together with the Bronx, Queens and Staten Island to form a megalopolis. Progressive Republicans worked to create civil service laws and bureaucratized purchasing and spending to protect taxpayers from corrupt party machines. The Democratic Tammany machine led by Charles F. Murphy and the talented young men he advanced, Smith and Robert Wagner, responded to the 1911 Triangle Shirtwaist fire — in which hundreds of women jumped 11 floors to their death because fire escapes were blocked — by passing labor and safety laws. In the 1920s, the New York metro area produced the nation's first regional plan. New York pioneered public housing and fair housing laws, industry-wide unions (in the garment trades), rent control and dairy price controls to help both New York City tenants and Upstate farmers.

Statewide elections were exceedingly close, with Democrats carrying the New York City Catholic vote and Republicans winning Upstate Protestants. Swing votes were cast by more than 1 million Jewish immigrants, who supported a generous welfare state but mistrusted the Tammany machine and valued civil rights. (For most of its history, New York has used a "fusion voting" system under which candidates can run on multiple ballot lines.) The politician who combined these appeals most cannily was Fiorello LaGuardia, a nominal Republican but almost a socialist, an Episcopalian who was half Jewish as well as Italian, and the man who, as mayor of New York City from 1933 to 1945, built much of the public housing and many of the civic monuments that still stand. Incensed that New York had no airport, he built what is now LaGuardia within a year. Both parties produced politicians whose positions appealed to these swing voters. At a time when the national media was much more heavily concentrated in Manhattan than in Washington, many became nationally prominent and often presidential candidates: Democrats Smith, Wagner, Franklin Roosevelt and Averell Harriman; Republicans Thomas Dewey, Wendell Willkie and Nelson Rockefeller. Dwight Eisenhower, then president of Columbia University, was a New Yorker when he won the presidency in 1952.

At a time when the economy was roaring, the country was becoming accustomed to working in big units — being employed by big corporations, represented by big unions, regulated by big government — and in this, New York was a natural leader. The financial dominance of Wall Street and the big banks was protected by federal regulation. The high-technology thrust of America in the mid-20th century was directed by big companies headquartered in New York's suburbs or Upstate: Corning, General Electric and IBM, Eastman Kodak and Xerox.

But in the last quarter of the 20th century, New York's public strengths became weaknesses. The state that was clearly the national leader of a big-unit America — "Mad Men" America — lost the leadership role once growth had shifted to small economic units and where flexibility and adaptability had become more important than centralized planning. Competition emerged overseas and elsewhere in the United States, and New York's institutions, practices and infrastructure became ossified. Welfare state benefits became too expensive; measures meant to protect against corruption stifled innovation. Rent control kept housing scarce, school bureaucracies and teacher unions stifled inspired teaching, and public hospitals rationed care. The government that intended to aid growth was cutting it off — not completely, but enough to explain why New York state, which grew 45 percent in population from 1930 to 1970, grew only 6 percent from 1970 to 2010, while California grew 87 percent and Texas 125 percent.

People and businesses started voting with their feet, especially during the terms of Mayor John Lindsay, a liberal Republican turned Democrat who caved to municipal unions' demands and borrowed against next year's revenues to pay this year's bills. Two years after he left office, that approach brought the city to the brink of bankruptcy in 1975. In the 1970s, the population of New York, city and state, dropped by nearly 700,000, an unprecedented hemorrhage of talent and productivity. Retrenchment followed, and private financiers and the state government took control of city government, cut spending, and negotiated cutbacks in jobs and salaries with public employees' unions. In the 1980s, Wall Street boomed, and Manhattan once again brimmed with confidence. Taxes were cut further under Democratic Mayor Edward Koch (1978-89) and Democratic Gov. Mario Cuomo (1982-94) and public employees' unions were for a time reined in. But institutional problems remained. New York's legislature remained tightly controlled by the two chambers' leaders — the Democratic Assembly speaker from New York City and the Republican state Senate president from Upstate or the suburbs, solidified after the mid-1970s through self-reinforcing gerrymanders. They engaged in classic political logrolling, lavishing taxpayers' dollars on each other's pet projects. Public employees' unions reestablished their stranglehold. The mild recession of the early 1990s struck New York with force. Big Upstate companies — Xerox, Kodak, IBM — suffered serious reverses, which only worsened with the advent of new technologies. A private sector that had grown little if at all beyond Wall Street could no longer finance the growing demands of the state.

By the end of the 1990s, New York seemed to have gotten back on track. Republican Mayor Rudolph Giuliani, first elected in 1993, cut crime and welfare rolls in half and cut hard deals with the unions. Republican Gov. George Pataki, first elected in 1994, delivered huge tax and spending cuts. Wall Street and the financial services industry boomed in the late 1990s, to the point that the jobs lost in the early-1990s recession were replaced. Then came Sept. 11, 2001.

It was a beautiful late-summer morning, the sunshine lighting a blue sky above the skyscrapers of Manhattan, commuters hurrying through the streets and subways to work. At 8:46 a.m., the first plane hit the North Tower of the World Trade Center. When the second plane hit the South Tower 17 minutes later, it was clear that America was under attack, even as office workers fled the burning buildings and New York firefighters streamed in. The terrorists had chosen to attack the seat of government in Washington — the Pentagon and a second target saved by the heroes of United Flight 93 — and the seat of commerce in New York to inflict the maximum possible damage. The people of New York, like those at the Pentagon and on United 93, responded with courage and determination. Firefighters, police officers, and rescue workers risked death to help others. Strangers helped strangers. People who had no experience with disaster figured out how to cope and help others. In less than a week, the New York Stock Exchange reopened.

Giuliani and Pataki performed well in the national spotlight. But New York faced an economic downturn and a turn in the course of government. Despite heroic efforts at recovery, Manhattan and New York lost 200,000 jobs in 2001 and 2002. Downtown real estate values tumbled as financial services firms decentralized and sought office space elsewhere. Giuliani was term-limited. Media billionaire Michael Bloomberg, previously a Democrat, became a Republican and spent $70 million of his own money on his way to victory. The financial industry boomed as never before, generating revenues far beyond expectations — until the underlying driver of the boom, mortgage-backed securities, imploded in September 2008, with repercussions internationally, nationally and locally.

New York City's economy grew largely because of the boom in financial services, while its population growth was fueled almost entirely by immigration. The city's population grew 2 percent from 2000 to 2010, to nearly 8.2 million, and the four close-in suburban counties grew by 3 percent. But this small change masked much greater movements. The elderly moved out, heading to Florida and other warmer climes, and middle-income workers and young blue-collar workers headed to lower-cost and lower-tax states like the Carolinas, Georgia and Florida. Moving in, meanwhile, were immigrants who streamed into outer-borough neighborhoods and created new businesses, churches and neighborhood institutions — Afro-Caribbeans in Flatbush; Chinese in Flushing, Borough Park, and on Staten Island; Colombians and Mexicans in Corona; Pakistanis and Bangladeshis in Jackson Heights; Greeks in Astoria; Russians in Brighton Beach; and Dominicans in Washington Heights and much of the Bronx. At the same time, the city's black population declined; Hispanics now outnumber blacks in every borough except Brooklyn. More than one-quarter of the residents of Queens are Asians; nationally, New York state ranks fourth for its percentage of Asian residents.

Today's immigrants are arriving in a different sort of city. New York has long since lost most of its manufacturing jobs, and many corporate headquarters have moved elsewhere. The tech sector employs an estimated 320,000 people. The financial-services industry pays enormous salaries and bonuses to those at the very top and generates service jobs for those who tend to the needs of the rich. But finance was sent reeling by the meltdown of 2008, and although salaries rebounded to their highest post-recession level in 2018, volatility in the markets and a bleeding of finance-sector jobs to other states, including Texas and Pennsylvania, have brought worries.

The outer boroughs, particularly Brooklyn, started to experience a revival during the Bloomberg years, as artisanal-minded, latte-swilling hipsters helped gentrify older neighborhoods; these areas became iconic through HBO's "Girls" and other depictions in the media. Hillary Clinton ran her 2016 presidential campaign from Brooklyn. The liberal drift was made clear by the 2013 mayoral victory of Bill de Blasio to succeed Bloomberg as mayor. It came amid slackening support for Bloomberg's anti-crime stop-and-frisk policy, particularly among minorities most at risk from the strategy. But growing pains have created quality-of-life concerns. Despite de Blasio's efforts, homelessness is well above its level even 10 years prior, due largely to skyrocketing housing costs. New York City's subway system, meanwhile, grappled with broad public frustration, caused by a combination of high ridership, aging infrastructure and inefficient investment.

In the suburbs, meanwhile, the problems stemmed from having much higher property taxes than in the city. The high property taxes are in effect tuition to good suburban school districts -- New York spends more per pupil than any other state, 90 percent above the national average -- but the burden becomes heavy when the kids go off to college. Places like Levittown, buzzing with young families moving from Brooklyn in the 1950s, aged and lost population. Immigrant communities coalesced in low-income suburbs whose first residents had departed. But New York's suburbs have not necessarily been attractive to new businesses — the hedge-fund sector blossomed across the state line in Greenwich Connecticut. The right-of-center Tax Foundation ranked New York 48th in the nation for its business climate in 2019, ahead of only California and New Jersey.

Upstate New York has even deeper problems. Medicaid mandates have forced Upstate counties to drastically raise property taxes, which now rank as the nation's highest relative to values. New York is the leading producer of yogurt and third for milk, but the dairy sector has been hammered by low prices, with the number of dairy farms falling by one-quarter over the past decade. Large, formerly paternalistic companies have been shedding jobs. Buffalo, once one of the nation's great steel producers, has turned into a center for the debt-collection industry. Since the 2010 census, New York state has seen population growth below 1 percent, and it was bifurcated -- up by about 6 percent in New York City, and down by more than 2 percent elsewhere. In fact, New York registered the fastest population decline of any state from 2017 to 2018, enough to potentially cost the state not one but possibly two House seats after the 2020 census. Since 2010, 42 out of 50 Upstate counties have lost population.

In races for statewide office, New York has been voting heavily Democratic. Albany's long-festering problems with ethics and corruption have come to a head in recent years. Eliot Spitzer, elected governor in 2006, visited high-end prostitutes, got caught and resigned; his successor, David Paterson, had such low job approval ratings that he decided not to seek a full term. Longtime power players in the legislature — Assembly Speaker Sheldon Silver, a Democrat, and Senate Majority Leader Dean Skelos, a Republican — were indicted on separate federal corruption charges and convicted.

In the 2016 presidential election, Clinton (of Westchester) won New York state easily, though with a margin a few percentage points smaller than Obama's four years earlier. The results illustrated the growing split between metro and rural areas: The cumulative share of Democratic votes from New York City, Long Island and Westchester increased from 59 percent in 2012 to 67 percent in 2016, but Trump (of Queens) won almost 484,000 more votes than Mitt Romney had in 2012 and won 19 counties that had voted for Obama, sometimes in massive shifts.

In 2018, Cuomo won a third term despite lingering concerns over ethics in Albany. The same year, the Republican Party, almost hopeless in statewide races, lost its remaining toehold in New York – the state Senate – and both legislative chambers were headed by African-Americans. The Democrats flipped three Republican congressional seats, two Upstate and one based in Staten Island, leaving the Democrats with a 21-6 advantage in the delegation. Another sign of changing times was the upset victory by a young Latina socialist, Rep. Alexandria Ocasio-Cortez, in a diverse Queens-Bronx district; she rocketed to social media-driven political stardom nationally but regularly ruffled feathers, particularly when she helped torpedo a plan by Amazon.com to establish a second headquarters in Long Island City. Meanwhile, as Congress and federal prosecutors delved deep into Trump's business practices and holdings-- and as the legislature passed a bill that would make public some of Trump's tax returns -- New York City was poised to remain in a familiar place: the national spotlight.

Population		Race and Ethnicity		Income	
Total	19,798,228	White	55.9%	Median Income	$62,765
Land area (sq. miles)	47,126	Black	14.4%	State Income Rank	15
Pop/ sq mi	420.1	Latino	18.8%	Poverty Rate	15.1%
Born in state	63.1%	Asian	8.3%	With health insurance	92.4%
		Two or more races	1.8%	Cash public assistance	3.4%
Age Groups		Other	0.7%	Food stamp/SNAP	15.2%
Under 18	21.2%				
18-34	24.3%	Education		Work	
35-64	39.3%	H.S grad or less	40.2%	White Collar	40.2%
Over 64	15.2%	Some college	24.6%	Sales and Service	43.3%
		College Degree, 4 yr	19.9%	Blue Collar	16.5%
Military		Post grad	15.4%	Government	15.3%
Veteran/ Active Duty	5.0%				

Presidential Politics

2016 Primary (D)	Clinton (D) 1,133,980 (58%)	Sanders (D) 820,256 (42%)	
2016 Primary (R)	Trump (R) 554,522 (60%)	Kasich (R) 231,166 (25%)	Cruz (R) 136,083 (15%)
2016 Pres. Vote	Clinton (D) 4,556,142 (59%)	Trump (R) 2,819,557 (37%)	Johnson (L) 176,600 (2%)
2012 Pres. Vote	Obama (D) 4,485,741 (63%)	Romney (R)2,490,431 (35%)	

When Hillary Clinton faced Donald Trump in 2016 — the first time that two New Yorkers were the major party nominees since 1944 when Franklin Roosevelt faced Thomas Dewey — the turnout in the Empire State rose some 10 percent. But the state was an afterthought in the general election. In the first half of the 20th century, New York was the dominant state in presidential politics. It had the most electoral votes (peaking at 47 from 1932 to 1948) and it was usually the most evenly divided between the two parties. Dewey, then the GOP governor, came within five percentage points of FDR in 1944. In 1948, he beat Harry Truman there. But in the 21st century, New York has seen its Electoral College clout drop from 33 in 2000 to 29 in 2016 — tied with Florida (and likely to lose one or two more after the 2020 reapportionment) — while becoming heavily Democratic. In 1988, Republican George H.W. Bush was beaten only 52%-48%.

How did this Democratic dominance come to pass? One reason is that Jewish voters, who did not identify strongly with either major party in the first half of the 20th century, became strong Democrats in the second. Increases in the percentages of black, Hispanic and Asian voters also raised the Democratic percentage. White Catholic voters took conservative positions on cultural issues like crime and abortion in the 1970s and 1980s, but today, these voters and their descendants are more likely to take liberal stands on cultural issues like gun control and gay rights. Republican allegiance in the New York City suburbs — on Long Island and in the upscale commuter towns of Rockland and Westchester counties — faded away starting in 1992. In 2012, the only county in the New York City metropolitan area that was still casting its ballots for GOP presidential hopefuls was tiny Putnam. And urban millennials of all races align Democratic.

Clinton defeated Trump, 59%-37%, but he captured Suffolk County, the first time a Republican carried that suburban enclave since President Bush in 1992. In the Hudson River Valley, Trump won back exurban Orange County, as well as Rensselaer and Saratoga. Upstate, he won blue-collar Oswego, Niagara -- which includes suburbs of Buffalo -- and several other rural central New York counties. In New York City, Trump won only the Borough of Staten Island.

Typically, the New York Republican presidential primary draws little attention. In 2016, Texas Sen. Ted Cruz wooed Orthodox Jewish voters in Brooklyn, but Trump reminded his home state that the Texan had once disparaged "New York values." Ohio Gov. John Kasich repeatedly indulged in deli cuisine in the Big Apple. But Trump easily won the April 19 GOP primary, swamping Kasich 60%-25%, winning 61 of the state's 62 counties. Kasich won Manhattan where Trump resides, but only by about 1,000 votes. From this convincing victory, Trump's march to the GOP nomination was virtually unimpeded.

The Democratic race was an equally important moment for Clinton. In the runup to New York, she had lost one primary (Wisconsin) and four caucuses to Vermont Sen. Bernie Sanders. Clinton had easily captured the 2008 Democratic presidential primary over Barack Obama, 57%-40%, carrying 26 of the 29 congressional districts. Still, Sanders was a native of Brooklyn, many of the state's Democratic primary voters are die-hard liberals, and the rough-and-tumble tabloid media culture of New York City can throw even experienced candidates off stride. But it was Sanders who ran into a political buzz saw. A New York Daily News editorial board interview went poorly and Sanders offered few details on how he planned to break up the big banks on Wall Street, one of his signature issues. Then Sanders blasted Clinton on whether she was qualified to serve as president, a charge that seemed implausible to many New Yorkers who had elected her to the Senate twice. With the support of the entire New York Democratic establishment, Clinton handily defeated Sanders 58%-42%, even though the Vermonter outspent her on television advertising. Turnout was just shy of 2 million, eclipsing the previous record of 1.9 million in 2008. Clinton won 21 of the state's 27 congressional districts, losing six relatively rural ones upstate. Whether the state moves its primary to March, it will remain a major Democratic battleground.

Congressional Districts

| 116th Congress Lineup | 21D 6R | 115th Congress Lineup | 18D 9R |

The next round of redistricting is shaping up as a nightmare for New York, especially its Republicans. Based on the Census Bureau's estimates for 2020, with the state barely increasing its population during the current decade, projections by redistricting experts list New York as the only state likely to lose two seats. Under that scenario, experience and logic suggest that one would be eliminated from 10 districts Upstate (north of Westchester County) and the other seat would be eliminated from the 17 districts between Westchester and the eastern end of Long Island. Because New York City has had a notable increase in population in the past few years, while most suburban counties have been stagnant or losing, the total of 12 seats that are based in the city stand a good chance of being preserved — though some of those districts could be realigned significantly due to factors such as personal ambitions or minority-group demands.

Based on the election results in 2018, Democrats likely will control the legislature and the governor's office in redistricting for the first time in many cycles. With the House Democrats having gained three seats (by defeating three Republican incumbents), two Upstate and one based in Staten Island, Democrats can only speculate whether they will use redistricting to reinforce those gains or to reverse potential switches in the 2020 election. The fact that their two Upstate pickups — the 19th and the 22nd— border each other and are sprawling areas without a significant urban center raises the prospect that those two districts could face major change. Another relevant factor is that the elimination of two districts almost certainly would target at least one Republican. Currently, the six GOP seats include two that are based largely in Suffolk County, three in western New York (from Syracuse to Buffalo) and the other in the North Country. Depending on the fate of the current freshman Democrats, those two GOP clusters could become targets.

The rigors of musical chairs have become familiar in this state. When John F. Kennedy was elected president in 1960, New York elected 43 members, California 30 and Florida eight. In 2012, New York and Florida each elected 27 members and California 53. Reapportionment has been carnage time for New York: the state lost five districts in the 1980 census, three in 1990, and two each in 2000 and 2010. In recent cycles, those decisions have been made largely by three power brokers: the state Senate president (who until 2018 was Republican), Assembly speaker (a Democrat), and a veto-wielding governor. Next time, the partisan dynamics in Albany will shift.

In 2012, a deadlock in the legislature kicked the conflict to a federal three-judge panel, which appointed a special master in case the legislature fail. As it turned out, the court map was met with reluctant acceptance. The plan even-handedly eliminated retiring Democrat Maurice Hinchey's Upstate seat and the Queens seat of Republican special-election winner Bob Turner, who hadn't expected to win reelection anyway. That election downsized the delegation from 22 Democrats and 7 Republicans to 21-6. Subsequently, Republicans gained three seats (two of them Upstate) after 2012. But the Democrats returned to 21 seats in 2018. It's a good bet that many in the delegation have begun to calculate how they can avoid getting a short straw in 2022.

Andrew Cuomo (D)

Elected 2010, term expires 2023, 3rd term; b. Dec. 6, 1957, Queens; Fordham U., B.A. 1979; Albany Law Schl., J.D. 1982; Catholic; Divorced; 3 children.

Elected Office: NY Attorney General, 2006-2010.

Professional Career: Assistant District Attorney, Manhattan, 1984-1985; Practicing attorney, Blutrich Falcone & Miller, 1985-1988; Founder, Housing Enterprise for the Less Privileged, 1988-1993; Assistant Secretary, Department of Housing & Urban Development, 1993-1997; U.S Secretary, Department of Housing & Urban Development 1997-2001.

Office: NYS State Capitol Building, Albany, 12224; 518-474-8390; Fax: 518-474-1513; Website: governor.ny.gov.

Lt. Gov.: Kathy Hochul (D) **Atty. Gen:** Letitia James (D) **Sec. of State:** Rossana Rosado (D)

State Legislature: Senate: 40D, 22R, 1V **House:** 106D, 43R, 1I

Election Results

Election	Name (Party)	Vote (%)
2018 General	Andrew Cuomo (D)	3,635,340 (60%)
	Marcus Molinaro (R)	2,207,602 (36%)
2018 Primary	Andrew Cuomo (D)	1,021,169 (65%)
	Cynthia Nixon (D)	537,192 (35%)

Democrat Andrew Cuomo won his third term as governor of New York in 2018, matching the victory tally of his father, Mario Cuomo. After piling up accomplishments in office – but also enduring corruption convictions of officials within his circle – Cuomo in 2018 survived a primary challenge from his left from actress Cynthia Nixon, then defeated the nominee of the state's diminished Republican Party by a 24-point margin in November. Heading into his third term, Cuomo said he had no plans to run for president, but as governor he faced both new opportunities and new challenges from the newly installed Democratic majority in the state Senate. "Cuomo can be irritating, confounding, and egotistical. He can also be engaging, intense, and charismatic," Edward-Isaac Dovere wrote in The Atlantic in March 2019. "He deliberately stands apart from the leftward tilt of his party, but his record of bills signed into law on many core progressive issues is unmatched by any other Democrat, in D.C. or the states, with the possible exception of Jerry Brown. He wins in landslides, but most politicians in New York and beyond can't stand him."

Cuomo was born in Queens and grew up in the middle-class neighborhood of Hollis, the second of five siblings. He showed an early aptitude for repairing and building automobiles. He graduated from Fordham University in 1979, one year after his father was elected lieutenant governor, and from Albany Law School in 1982.

He began working for his father's campaign for governor that year and received credit for masterminding his come-from-behind primary victory against New York City Mayor Ed Koch. However, some critics said the younger Cuomo was too willing to engage in dirty politics, "the muscle that helped win Mario three terms as governor of New York," as New York magazine put it. He spent several years as an aide to his father as the governor's national profile skyrocketed in the wake of his keynote speech at the 1984 Democratic National Convention.

After a short stint in the Manhattan district attorney's office, Cuomo in 1986 founded the Housing Enterprise for the Less Privileged (HELP USA), a nonprofit organization dedicated to helping the homeless. He left his private law practice in 1989 to run the group, which became a national model for its formula of offering shelter but also job training, education, drug treatment and other assistance. Two years later, he married Kerry Kennedy, the daughter of Robert F. Kennedy, in a widely publicized union that was described as a merger of two Democratic political dynasties.

Cuomo's work at HELP caught the attention of Arkansas Gov. Bill Clinton, who asked Cuomo to serve on his presidential transition team in 1992 and then as assistant secretary of community planning and development at HUD. After Clinton's reelection in 1996, Cuomo took over as secretary of the department. He won praise for his energetic efforts to make housing more affordable, but he also adopted policies to broaden home ownership for low-income Americans that contributed to the housing crisis a decade later. One of those policies was a dramatic rise in the number of loans that government-sponsored mortgage giants, Fannie Mae and Freddie Mac, were required to buy. HUD also produced rules that explicitly forbade imposing new reporting requirements on the two enterprises.

Cuomo returned to New York in 2001 with the intention of running for governor the following year. But he did himself in with some brash and ill-advised remarks. He said that Republican Gov. George Pataki had done little after 9/11 other than hold New York Mayor Rudy Giuliani's coat. He also angered African Americans who had been looking to State Comptroller Carl McCall as their party's "next in line" candidate. Cuomo dropped out of the race before the primary, and McCall lost to Pataki. Around the same time, Cuomo became engaged in a bitter public divorce and child custody battle with his wife. Cuomo largely disappeared from the public eye for several years. In 2006, he came back to run for state attorney general when the incumbent, Eliot Spitzer, ran for governor. He patched up his differences with Democrats and won the primary with ease, then easily beat the Republican nominee, former Westchester District Attorney Jeanine Pirro, 58%-40%. Signaling his ambition for higher office, Cuomo conducted investigations on a wide range of topics, including alleged misdeeds within the financial industry – an issue that had propelled Spitzer to the governorship. He also ended up investigating Spitzer for using the state police to gather information about then-state Senate Majority Leader Joseph Bruno.

When Spitzer resigned in disgrace in 2008 over revelations that he had been the client of a prostitution ring, Lt. Gov. David Paterson took over. Paterson, the state's first African-American governor, took some bold budget stands and inspired many with his ability to overcome blindness, but his job ratings were the lowest in state history. He eventually acceded to the demands of the Obama White House and decided not to run for a full term. In May 2010, Cuomo announced his candidacy, declaring the state had slipped from being a "national model" under his father to a "national disgrace." In the general election, Cuomo faced Carl Paladino, a real estate executive who self-funded his campaign. The New York tabloids dubbed Paladino "Crazy Carl" for his sometimes outrageous statements (he also became close to Donald Trump). Cuomo had little trouble rolling to a landslide 63%-33% victory.

In office, Cuomo was fiscally cautious – in his first year, he struck a budget deal that reduced year-to-year spending by about 2 percent without raising taxes – but he was liberal on social issues. He carefully organized a broad coalition to support legalizing same-sex marriage, which the state Senate had defeated two years earlier. In the end, six senators who had voted against a legalization bill in 2009 voted for one in June 2011, including three Republicans, and New York became the largest state yet to permit such unions. Political commentators of all stripes said the governor's maneuvering was masterful, and national gay activists as well as prominent liberals began opening their wallets to him. Cuomo also worked more smoothly with the legislature than any of his recent predecessors. He entered 2012 with his highest job-approval rating as governor — 62 percent in the Siena poll. His name began popping up on the early lists of 2016 presidential prospects; even his father stoked speculation at his 80th birthday party.

In 2013, Cuomo called for action on gun control in the wake of the Newtown Connecticut school massacre. He proposed tightening the definition of so-called assault weapons and lowering the maximum magazine capacity. He quickly got the legislation into law, which caused his job-approval rating to dip below 60 percent; while downstate Democrats remained in his corner, his support among Republicans, and voters Upstate generally, suffered. His standing eroded further in 2014 after his administration reportedly sought to thwart the progress of an independent panel he had established to investigate corruption, after it had begun delving into issues that involved him and his political supporters. Cuomo's explanation was that a recently passed ethics law had strengthened anti-bribery laws and achieved roughly nine of its 10 goals. But the one unmet goal, a system of publicly financed campaigns that cut off unlimited donations, was seen by the governor's critics as the most important.

This episode helped Cuomo draw a Democratic primary challenger in Zephyr Teachout, a Fordham University law professor. Observers saw a duality in Cuomo's first term: Substantive tactical achievements, undercut by political mistakes. "The state has gone from a $10 billion deficit in 2010 to a projected $6 billion surplus," New York magazine wrote. "He's restored functionality, if not total rationality, to a state government that had become a national embarrassment," including the passing of four on-time budgets and the state's highest credit rating in more than four decades. Yet Cuomo "underestimated the anger of the state's left wing" and, on the ethics issue, acted in ways that "fueled the perception that he views himself as above the democratic process." The New York Times refused to endorse either candidate in the primary. Cuomo prevailed, 63%-34%, but Teachout's showing was stronger than expected. In the general election against Westchester County Executive Rob Astorino, Cuomo used his 9-to-1 fundraising advantage to pull out a victory, but with just 54 percent, well below the 65 percent figure with which his father had won a second term.

In 2015, the legislative landscape experienced an earthquake, as Assembly Speaker Sheldon Silver, a Democrat, and Senate Majority Leader Dean Skelos, a Republican, were both arrested on federal corruption charges; ultimately, both were convicted. (After their initial convictions were thrown out, both were re-tried and convicted again in 2018.) Feeling pressure from his party's progressive wing, Cuomo went around the legislature to set in motion a minimum wage boost for fast-food workers, and he traveled to Havana to promote engagement and trade with Cuba. The year also brought a string of personal and professional challenges. Mario Cuomo died at 82, and the governor's girlfriend, Food Network cooking show host Sandra Lee, was diagnosed with breast cancer. (She was later declared cancer free.) Meanwhile, Cuomo was mired in a loud feud with New York City Mayor Bill de Blasio, who went so far as to call reporters into his office to tell them about their strained relationship. A string of polls in 2015 showed Cuomo's approval ratings falling into the low-to-mid 40s.

Cuomo put significant political capital into building efforts, including a new Tappan Zee bridge and a rebuild of LaGuardia Airport. But ethics reemerged as an issue in November 2016 when Joe Percoco, a close aide to Cuomo, and Alain Kaloyeros, the former president of SUNY Polytechnic Institute, were indicted in an alleged bribery scheme. In time, concern about Cuomo's inability to clean up Albany helped create room for a new primary challenger in 2018 – actress Cynthia Nixon, best known for playing lawyer Miranda Hobbes on Sex and the City. Nixon criticized the incumbent for being insufficiently liberal, as well as for the ethical problems in his circle, a line of attack that became especially timely when Percoco was convicted in March 2018 and Kaloyeros was found guilty four months later. "For any other governor in America, this would be earth-shattering," Nixon said after the Kaloyeros conviction. "But in Andrew Cuomo's Albany, it was just a Thursday." Nixon attracted significant public attention – in addition to her celebrity status, she had called Immigration and Customs Enforcement a "terrorist organization" and handed out bongs to promote marijuana legalization. But on primary day, Cuomo won, 65%-35%. Establishment candidates for lieutenant governor and attorney general also won their primaries.

Further down the ballot, however, a tectonic shift was occurring in the legislature. For seven years, renegade Democrats had joined forces with Republicans to control the Senate – a longstanding irritant to progressive Democrats, and arguably a relief to Cuomo, who was able to use the GOP's control to burnish his bipartisan bona fides and excuse his moderate stances to the restive left of his party. But in April 2018, Cuomo negotiated a deal for members of the maverick Independent Democratic Conference to rejoin their fellow Democrats. That still left Democrats one seat short of the number necessary to flip control, but it showed the way the winds were blowing. On primary day, liberal challengers defeated six of the eight breakaway Democrats; Democrats picked up control of the chamber in November. Nixon's candidacy, meanwhile, had pushed Cuomo to the left on certain issues, such as marijuana legalization. Cuomo's general election race against Dutchess County executive Marcus J. Molinaro was never close, despite Molinaro's argument that Cuomo led "the most corrupted state government in America." Cuomo won, 60%-36%.

The start of Cuomo's third term brought some legislative successes but also some controversy. He quickly signed a long-blocked package of bills on electoral reform, including provisions for early voting, new campaign-finance restrictions, an end to the split primary dates for federal and state offices, automatic voter registration transfers, and advance registration for those who are 16 or 17 years old. He signed another long-delayed bill to protect abortion rights in the event the Supreme Court overturned Roe v. Wade. The bill allowed practitioners other than licensed physicians to perform the procedure and permitted abortions until the moment of birth. Archbishop Timothy Cardinal Dolan of New York called passage of the law a "tragic moment in the history of our state." Meanwhile, Cuomo – along with his new ally de Blasio – promoted New York in the high-stakes quest to become Amazon.com's second headquarters. Initially, Cuomo and de Blasio cheered as the giant online retailer chose Queens' Long Island City as one of two sites, along with Arlington Virginia. But some local politicians, including freshman Rep. Alexandria Ocasio-Cortez, raised concerns about the billions of dollars of tax breaks the two had promised Amazon and criticized the company's working conditions. Irked by the less-than-unified political support, the retailer pulled its offer. The battle of Long Island City was unlikely to be the last difficult balancing act Cuomo would face during his third term.

Chuck Schumer (D)

Elected 1998, term expires 2022, 4th term, b. Nov 23, 1950; Brooklyn; Harvard University, B.A., 1971; Harvard University, J.D., 1974; Jewish; Married (Iris Weinshall); 2 children; 1 grandchild.

Elected Office: NY Assembly, 1975-1980; U.S. House, 1981-1999.

Professional Career: U.S. Representative; Attorney

DC Office: 322 HSOB 20510, 202-224-6542, Fax: 202-228-3027, schumer.senate.gov

State Offices: Albany, 518-431-4070; Binghamton, 607-772-6792; Buffalo, 716-846-4111; Melville, 631-753-0978; New York, 212-486-4430; Peekskill, 914-734-1532; Rochester, 585-263-5866; Syracuse, 315-423-5471.

Committees: Senate Minority Leader. *Rules & Administration.*

Group Ratings

	ADA	ACLU	AFL-CIO	LCV	ITI	COC	HAFA	ACU	CFG	FRC
2018	-	67%	100%	100%	-	50%	3%	9%	5%	0%
2017	100%	C	100%	100%	C	29%	C	0%	4%	0%

Almanac Ratings 2017-18

	Economy	Social	Foreign	Composite
Liberal	97%	97%	75%	90%
Conservative	3%	3%	25%	10%

Key Votes of the 115th Congress

1. Obama-care revision	N	5. Gun regulations	N	9. Kavanaugh confirmation	N
2. Tax Cuts	N	6. Family planning regs	N	10. Saudi arms sales	Y
3. Dodd-Frank revision	N	7. Gorsuch confirmation	N	11. FISA rules	N
4. Omnibus appropriations	Y	8. Immigration restrictions	N	12. Military aid in Yemen	Y

Election Results

Election	Name (Party)	Vote (%)		Cand. Spent	Ind. Exp. Support	Ind. Exp. Oppose
2016 General	Chuck Schumer (D)	5,182,006	(71%)	$13,854,876	$100,000	$39,600
	Wendy Long (R)	1,988,261	(27%)	$685,926	$3,003	
2016 Primary	Chuck Schumer (D)	Unopposed				

Prior winning percentages: 2010 (66%), 2004 (71%), 1998 (55%); House: 1996 (75%), 1994 (73%), 1992 (89%), 1990 (80%), 1988 (78%), 1986 (93%), 1984 (72%), 1982 (79%), 1980 (77%)

Just out of Harvard Law School, Democrat Chuck Schumer, New York's senior senator, ran for a New York Assembly seat — over the objections of his mother. "Don't run, you'll never win," she is said to have advised her son. She wanted him to instead accept a job from a leading New York law firm. Not only did Schumer win, he has not lost an election in the intervening 4½ decades. Just months before her 89th birthday in early 2017, Selma Schumer saw her son become the first New Yorker to assume party leadership in the Senate since the roles of majority and minority leader were created a century ago. But it fell short of the role to which Chuck Schumer aspired: majority leader. In 2016, Senate Democrats came up three seats short of realizing the widespread expectation that they would regain the majority surrendered just two years earlier.

And so Schumer found himself in a delicate balancing act between disparate factions of his party as he searched for a workable strategy to confront another tough-talking New Yorker: President Donald Trump. Schumer has since won high marks from both ideological wings of his fractious caucus, notwithstanding some periodic strains with its energized progressive faction. He established a working — if sometimes tense — relationship with his Republican counterpart, Majority Leader Mitch McConnell of Kentucky: Under McConnell's predecessor as majority leader and Schumer's as the top Senate Democrat, Harry Reid of Nevada, relations between Senate party leaders hit a low point. Meanwhile, the Schumer-Trump relationship can best be described as love-hate, with occasional interludes of bipartisan bonding punctuated by name-calling.

After the 2016 elections, the Democratic Party's left wing and its Senate allies were in no mood to offer anything but massive resistance to the conservative agenda of a president they regarded as little more than an Electoral College fluke. Grassroots activists organized rallies outside the apartment of the avowedly liberal — albeit pragmatic — Schumer, waving signs reading, "Grow a spine, Chuck" and chanting, "Filibuster everything!" Squeezing Schumer from the other side were Democratic centrists up for re-election in states Trump had won in 2016 by landslides — and whose preservation was key to the party regaining Senate control in the foreseeable future. Democrats faced a challenging electoral map in 2018 — they had to defend 26 Senate seats, compared with the GOP's nine — and they lost a net two seats, and Schumer again fell short of his goal of heading the majority. His role was further diminished as House Democrats recaptured a majority, elevating California's Nancy Pelosi to the speakership. But Schumer and Pelosi — former House colleagues and once members of the same dinner group — forged a close working relationship that, in early 2019, forced Trump to retreat from a standoff that had shut down the government for more than a month.

First elected to the Senate in 1998 after nearly two decades in the House, Schumer began his rise in Senate leadership as chairman of the Democratic Senatorial Campaign Committee in the 2006 election cycle — helping his party to become the majority in the Senate, which his party controlled for eight years. He then ascended to vice chairman of the Democratic Caucus, the No. 3 party post, and later assumed responsibility for Senate Democrats' policy and political messaging. When Reid, the Senate Democratic leader, announced his retirement in early 2015, he anointed Schumer over another would-be successor, Whip Dick Durbin of Illinois. Reid's move put an end to a long, behind-the-scenes rivalry between Schumer and Durbin, who for a dozen years were midweek roommates in a Capitol Hill townhouse — an arrangement that inspired the sitcom "Alpha House."

The image that accompanied Schumer throughout the early part of his career — part brash partisan, part publicity hound — persists in some quarters. Former Senate Majority Leader Bob Dole once wisecracked that the most dangerous place to be in Washington was between Schumer and a TV camera. Fellow New York lawmakers often upstaged by Schumer came up with a word to describe the experience: "Schumed." But those who know him well say he has mellowed — to a degree. "Most people don't evolve. He is someone who has, in ways that enable him to be more successful than he would have been," Howard Wolfson, a top New York political operative who worked on Schumer's first Senate race, told The New York Times in late 2016. "If you think about him circa 1998, he was very focused on press, somewhat parochial in his view of the world and very partisan. He has evolved into someone who is very focused on results rather than flash, and very much able and interested in working with the other party to get things done." The current-day Schumer often appears to have his cellphone attached to the side of his head as he traverses the Capitol corridors, reaching out to colleagues to counsel and cajole. If there is a rap on the onetime political enfant terrible, it is that he wants to be loved rather than feared: One Democratic senator told Politico that Schumer is "not as iron-fisted, not as old-school, not as personally intimidating" as Reid was.

Schumer grew up in and around Brooklyn's Flatbush neighborhood, where his father had a small exterminating business. He graduated first in his class at James Madison High School, also the alma mater of Supreme Court Justice Ruth Bader Ginsburg and Vermont Sen. Bernie Sanders. Schumer graduated from Harvard College and Harvard Law School but never practiced law. With his law degree fresh in hand in 1974, he won election as the youngest member of the New York Assembly since Theodore Roosevelt in the early 1880s.

In 1980, weeks before his 30th birthday, Schumer was elected to an open House seat. His career was threatened almost as soon as it started. Because of the 1980 reapportionment, New York stood to lose five House seats and, under the Voting Rights Act, the state was under pressure to create a second majority-minority district in Brooklyn. Consequently, Schumer's district was widely regarded as being on the chopping block. But, exhibiting the fundraising prowess that would later help him climb the leadership ladder, Schumer quickly accumulated a large campaign treasury. It saved him: The neighboring district of a House member with more seniority but a smaller campaign bank account was eliminated instead. Schumer obtained a seat on the House Banking Committee, recognizing its importance to Wall Street, just across the East River from his home borough. He served on the Judiciary Committee and chaired its Crime Subcommittee, sponsoring the 1994 crime bill that banned assault weapons and created "three strikes" mandatory life terms for repeat violent offenders. He was House sponsor of the Brady Bill, which created waiting periods for handgun purchases; it passed over the strong opposition of the National Rifle Association.

In early 1997, Schumer considered seeking the governorship. But Republican Gov. George Pataki's strong job approval ratings instead persuaded him to run against GOP Sen. Alfonse D'Amato. D'Amato's initial win in 1980 had been considered something of a fluke, but he had won reelection twice despite the state's Democratic tilt — thanks in large measure to assiduous constituent service. As Banking Committee chairman in the GOP-controlled Senate, he excelled at raising money. Schumer faced serious primary opposition from a field that included Geraldine Ferraro, the 1984 vice presidential nominee. Having little difference with his rivals on social issues, Schumer focused on pocketbook concerns. He was much better financed. In September, he won the four-way primary with 51 percent of the vote; Ferraro got 26 percent. Schumer immediately launched an attack on D'Amato, saying the incumbent had told "too many lies for too long," which echoed D'Amato's earlier criticisms of his opponents as "too liberal for too long." Late in the campaign, D'Amato suffered self-inflicted damage after it leaked out that, in a closed meeting before a Jewish group, he had called Schumer a "putzhead," Yiddish slang for "jerk." Although outspent, Schumer won 55%-44%.

When outgoing first lady Hillary Clinton was elected two years later to succeed retiring New York Democrat Daniel Patrick Moynihan, many wondered how the ambitious Schumer would take to being overshadowed by a junior colleague regarded as a potential presidential candidate. At times, Schumer did appear irked by the wattage of Clinton's celebrity. "It took a while for us; we're both Type-A personalities," Schumer recalled in a Washington Post interview during Clinton's 2016 White House campaign. "We had to learn ... that working together was a lot better than working separately." Schumer endorsed Clinton's unsuccessful 2008 bid for the party's presidential nomination. Her subsequent appointment as Barack Obama's secretary of State made Schumer indisputably New York's lead senator. When Democratic Gov. David Paterson dithered over appointing a successor to Clinton in 2009, Schumer weighed in on behalf of little-known Rep. Kirsten Gillibrand. Schumer took his new colleague under his wing, helping lay the political foundation for Gillibrand to acquire national visibility.

Conscious of New York's traditional upstate/downstate political divide, Schumer vowed when first elected to visit every one of the state's 62 counties each year. In his first re-election, in 2004, he raised more than $27 million and won 71%-24%, a record margin for a New York Senate race — until Gillibrand received 72 percent of the vote in 2012. With the Senate under Democratic control for only an 18-month period during his first term, Schumer again eyed a run for governor in 2006 — when Pataki's retirement opened that job. But the issue was settled when Reid named Schumer as DSCC chairman, with a seat on the influential Finance Committee as an enticement to remain on Capitol Hill.

The task facing Schumer in 2006 was formidable: The lineup of Senate seats up for grabs left Republicans with more targets than Democrats. But he persuaded four Democratic senators from states that President George W. Bush carried in 2004 not to retire. He then demonstrated his pragmatic side as he worked on getting strong challengers to Republican incumbents. In Pennsylvania, Schumer — a strong supporter of abortion rights — recruited state Treasurer Bob Casey Jr., son of the late governor known for his vocal opposition to abortion; the younger Casey ousted Republican Sen. Rick Santorum. In Virginia, Schumer backed Jim Webb, a decorated Vietnam veteran who served as the Reagan administration's Navy secretary, over liberal lobbyist Harris Miller; Webb won a narrow victory in the primary and went on to defeat heavily favored GOP Sen. George Allen. Schumer's success in helping win a Democratic majority prompted Reid to ask him to stay on as head of the DSCC for the 2008 election season. On top of the six seats picked up in 2006, the Democrats saw a net gain of eight in 2008: A 45-seat minority had become a 59-seat majority in the span of just over two years. Seldom had one senator made such a difference in the partisan composition of the body.

Reid created the position of vice chairman of the Democratic Caucus for him. Schumer effectively became the confidential adviser to the new majority leader, putting Schumer —known for private flashes of temper over the years — in the position of counseling the hot-tempered, often difficult Reid. After the 2010 elections, which saw the Democratic majority diminished by a half-dozen seats, Reid named Schumer to chair the Democratic Policy and Communications Center, with the role of sharpening the party's appeal to the middle class. The pragmatism he has displayed in his leadership roles has won him strong support among party moderates. After the Democrats' loss of the Senate majority in 2014, several moderates urged Schumer to challenge Reid, according to Politico. But Schumer rebuffed the moderates' pleas. "Reid made me [who I am]," Schumer is reported to have said. Four months later, Reid announced his retirement and anointed Schumer as his successor,

If Schumer was a key congressional ally for Obama's policy agenda, they had some highly visible differences. In late 2016, as Obama was leaving office, Schumer led the effort to override his veto of a bill that allowed families of 9/11 victims to sue Saudi Arabia for possible involvement in the World Trade Center attacks: It was the only time that Congress overrode an Obama veto. A year earlier, when Obama sought "fast track" negotiating authority to expedite a 12-nation Pacific trade deal, Schumer opposed the president. "I don't believe in these agreements anymore," he told The Wall Street Journal. "I've changed." Trump abandoned pursuit of the trade agreement after taking office; in 2018, in a rare policy accord with Trump, Schumer told a New York radio station, "I'm closer to him on trade than I was to either Obama, a Democrat, or Bush, a Republican, because we've got to get tougher on China." It prompted a private note from Trump, thanking Schumer and suggesting they work together on the issue.

But, just weeks later, Trump was calling him names on Twitter after Schumer criticized the president for withdrawing from the Iran nuclear agreement negotiated by the Obama administration. "Senator Cryin' Chuck Schumer fought hard against the Bad Iran Deal, even going at it with President Obama, & then Voted AGAINST it! Now he says I should not have terminated the deal," Trump wrote. The "Cryin' Chuck Schumer" epithet cropped up in the first weeks of the Trump administration after Schumer teared up at a news conference while criticizing the president's effort to ban citizens from some Muslim-majority nations from entering the U.S. Trump sneered: "I'm going to ask him who is his acting coach." In 2015, Schumer opposed the Iran deal, on the grounds that decreased sanctions would eventually enable Iran to have a nuclear weapon. He did not actively lobby against approval, and his opposition was viewed as a bow to the politics of New York, whose Jewish population is the nation's largest. In criticizing Trump's decision to withdraw from the pact, Schumer argued that "pulling out precipitously without our allies involved does not achieve any of the goals we need to achieve and hurts Americans in different ways."

Such episodes highlight Schumer's roller coaster relationship with Trump. Indeed, efforts to define their relationship often begin by noting they both grew up in New York's outer boroughs, albeit Trump was raised in a Queens neighborhood considerably tonier than Schumer's Brooklyn turf. The two men fit the stereotype of New Yorkers widely held west of the Hudson River: Both crave the spotlight and won't shy away from a political street brawl. How close they were before their current incarnations appears to be — like much else between them — a matter of dispute. Before taking office in January 2017, Trump told MSNBC: "I think I'll be able to get along well with Chuck Schumer. I was always very good with Schumer. I was close to Schumer in many ways." But Schumer earlier disputed the two were ever close. "He was not my friend. We never went golfing together, even had a meal together," Schumer told Politico. During his days as a frequent Democratic campaign donor, Trump contributed to Schumer's campaigns and held a fundraiser at his Florida estate when Schumer chaired the DSCC in 2008; the event raised $230,000.

Schumer offered early olive branches. "If he is going to agree on issues like trade and transportation infrastructure in a very real way with us, we have an obligation to pursue it," Schumer told The New York Times shortly after Trump's election. But, following blowback from his left wing, Schumer took a harder line. "The only way we're going to work with [Trump] is if he moves completely in our direction and abandons his Republican colleagues," Schumer told CNN in January 2017. Trump responded via Twitter by calling Schumer the "head clown" of Democrats. But just eight months later, Trump — to the visible discomfiture of Republican congressional leaders — sided with Schumer by backing a three-month extension of the federal debt ceiling. For the White House, it facilitated a $15 billion aid package for hurricane victims. For Schumer, it pushed further action on the debt ceiling to the end of 2017 — when it would converge with a government funding deadline and give Schumer and Pelosi increased negotiating leverage on several key Democratic concerns, like extending the Obama administration's Deferred Action for Childhood Arrivals program — which protected "Dreamers" — that Trump had moved to end.

Schumer was picked up on a hot mic in the Senate saying, Trump "likes us. ... He likes me anyway." This era of good feeling did not last. When Schumer and Pelosi emerged from a dinner with Trump saying there was a deal to protect Dreamers — immigrants who had arrived in the U.S. illegally as children — from deportation, White House officials put out the word that the two Democrats had gone beyond what Trump had accepted. Several weeks later, Trump sniped via Twitter: "'Chuck and Nancy' ... want illegal immigrants flooding into our Country unchecked, are weak on Crime and want to substantially RAISE Taxes. I don't see a deal!" That prompted Schumer and Pelosi to pull out of a scheduled White House meeting, as Schumer complained about inconsistency between Trump's public and private statements. In January 2018, Schumer led Senate Democrats into a government shutdown after a spending bill failed to include protections for 1.8 million Dreamers. The shutdown ended after just three days amid fears of voter backlash from Democratic moderates seeking re-election in red states. Schumer's handling of the matter spurred grumbling among his caucus' progressive wing, as activists again demonstrated in front of his Brooklyn apartment.

But nearly a year later, Schumer and Pelosi — newly restored as House speaker — were the political winners in a record 35-day government shutdown, triggered by Trump's refusal to sign a bill without funding for his proposed southern-border wall. Schumer and Pelosi's united front was credited with keeping Democratic moderates from bolting; Trump relented after polls showed the White House taking the brunt of voters' blame for the protracted shutdown. In February 2019, he signed a bill to keep the government operating for the rest of the fiscal year, while receiving only a fraction of the $5.7 billion he had demanded for a wall. While Democrats had blocked much of the wall funding, the bill offered no final resolution on long-term protections for Dreamers.

Schumer's interest in immigration policy goes back to his time on the House Judiciary Committee, when he contributed key provisions to immigration laws passed in 1986 and 1990. In 2013, Schumer was a member of the bipartisan "Gang of Eight" that crafted a comprehensive immigration compromise. It passed the Senate in July 2013, with 14 Republicans joining the entire Democratic Caucus in backing it, but the Republican-controlled House refused to take it up. In January 2018, Schumer — as part of the deal to end the three-day government shutdown — won a commitment from McConnell to hold a floor debate on immigration. Schumer succeeded in holding his caucus together: 46 of 49 Senate Democrats voted for a compromise that contained a path to citizenship for the Dreamers and gave the Trump administration $25 billion for border security. But just eight Republicans backed it, and the legislation fell a half-dozen votes short of the 60 vote needed to advance.

Schumer's relationship with McConnell had a rocky beginning. "If they were looking for 10 different ways to get off to a bad start, this would be 11," Tennessee GOP Sen. Lamar Alexander, a friend of both Schumer and McConnell, told The Washington Post in early 2017. It started with the Democrats slow-walking the confirmation of Trump's Cabinet nominees: Schumer angered McConnell when he was one of only six Democrats to vote against confirming Transportation Secretary Elaine Chao — McConnell's wife. "She would not commit to spending money on transportation," Schumer later told The New York Times.

Schumer faced his first major test when Trump, days after taking office, nominated federal Judge Neil Gorsuch to the Supreme Court. Schumer sought to restrain the more hard-line members of his caucus, as he constructed a strategy to ramp up opposition to Gorsuch while seeking to avoid charges of obstructionism. With many Senate Democrats still fuming over McConnell's refusal to hold hearings or a vote on Obama's high court nominee for the seat — Judge Merrick Garland — Oregon Sen. Jeff Merkley — before Gorsuch's nomination was unveiled — announced plans to filibuster any Trump nominee to succeed the late Justice Antonin Scalia. Schumer buttonholed Merkley to chide him against making the fight about retribution for Garland, Politico reported. While warning publicly that the Democrats would fight any nominee who wasn't "mainstream," Schumer privately urged his caucus members to hold off on full-scale opposition until the nominee's record had been vetted via hearings. Once that process was completed, Schumer called for a filibuster.

The outcome was not a happy one for Schumer and his caucus: McConnell invoked the "nuclear option," changing Senate rules so that all presidential nominations would no longer be subject to filibuster. It allowed Gorsuch to be confirmed, while diminishing the leverage of the Democratic minority over future Supreme Court openings under Trump — as occurred little more than a year later when federal Judge Brett Kavanaugh was nominated to succeed retiring Supreme Court Justice Anthony Kennedy. Defenders of McConnell's move pointed a finger at Reid, who, in 2013, had executed a similar rules change in response to GOP resistance to Obama administration nominees. In that instance, the rules were changed to end the filibuster for presidential appointments except for the Supreme Court. Weeks before McConnell invoked his version of the nuclear option in 2017, Schumer expressed regret that Reid had opened the door to it four years earlier. "I will say it was a mistake," he told the New Yorker. He also expressed "the hope that the Republican leader and I can find a way to build a firewall around the legislative filibuster. ... Let's find a way to further protect the 60-vote rule for legislation." McConnell insisted there was no appetite within the GOP caucus to end the legislative filibuster. Subsequently, Schumer dropped hints that he might join other Senate Democrats who have openly said they would limit the filibuster on legislation if they won Senate control.

There have been some signs of rapport between McConnell and Schumer. In February 2018, they negotiated a deal to raise the debt ceiling while providing an additional $300 billion over two years for defense and domestic programs. The same month, Schumer appeared at a lecture series at the McConnell Center at the University of Louisville, bearing a bottle of Brooklyn-distilled bourbon for the Kentuckian — whom Schumer praised for agreeing to the open floor debate on immigration.

Schumer diplomatically overlooked McConnell's 2017 moves icing out Democrats in health care and tax reform debates. "We really do get along despite what you read in the press," Schumer said. McConnell added: "Robust debate is not unusual. But at every critical moment in this country, we've come together to do what is needed to be done to move the ball down the field."

Such comity aside, the McConnell-Schumer relationship faced major strains during the battle over Kavanaugh's nomination. With the minority having limited leverage after the exercise of the nuclear option in the Gorsuch nomination, Schumer wasted no time in declaring his intentions. "I will oppose Judge Kavanaugh's nomination with everything I have. The stakes are simply too high for anything less," he tweeted after the nomination was unveiled. Schumer, a former Judiciary Committee member, plotted procedural guerilla tactics with the panel's Democrats to obtain more Kavanaugh-related records. By the White House's count, Democrats interrupted Judiciary Chairman Chuck Grassley 44 times during the first hour of confirmation hearings. Later, amid negotiations with attorneys for Christine Blasey Ford — who had come forward with allegations of decades-old sexual against Kavanaugh — Grassley complained on Twitter: "I feel like I'm playing 2nd trombone in the judiciary orchestra and Schumer is the conductor." When the highly charged debate reached the Senate floor in October 2018, McConnell and Schumer all but called each other liars. Referring to McConnell, Schumer spoke of "the blatant falsehoods he tells day after day after on this floor," shouting, "Give me a break."

McConnell accused Schumer of "a mudslide of wild, uncorroborated accusations ... each more outlandish than the last." It didn't stop there: In spring 2019, McConnell's avowed aim of expediting the installation of a new generation of conservative judges collided with Schumer's use of the same type of delaying tactics that McConnell had employed on judicial nominations during the Obama administration. McConnell corralled enough Republican votes to retrigger his nuclear option of two years earlier — reducing the time allowed for debate on sub-Cabinet officials and district court judges from 30 hours to just two hours once cloture was invoked. With Democrats complaining that the Trump administration had broken a long tradition of consulting senators from the other party on judicial appointments, Schumer accused McConnell of seeking to turn the Senate into a "conveyor belt" for judicial nominees and chided Senate Republicans for allowing McConnell's "debasement of the Senate." In turn, McConnell charged Schumer had set the precedent for filibustering judges when, in 2001, he persuaded fellow Democrats to block a Bush appeals court nominee. "He started this whole thing," McConnell, said, glaring at Schumer.

Before becoming minority leader, Schumer served on the Banking Committee. While he shifted to support more oversight and regulation of the banking and investment industries after the 2008 financial crisis, he is still eyed suspiciously by some party progressives because of his longtime status as a steadfast ally of Wall Street — a major home-state state constituency. In early 2018, an effort to roll back sections of the 2010 Dodd-Frank financial regulatory overhaul created significant friction within the Democratic Caucus — as well as a leadership challenge for Schumer. While Schumer, who had voted for the Dodd-Frank bill, opposed the Republican-sponsored rollback measure, he did not try to sway the nearly one-third of Senate Democrats who voted for it; this group included vulnerable moderates up for re-election and under pressure from community banks in their states. Massachusetts Sen. Elizabeth Warren, a leading progressive, sent out a fundraising email criticizing Democrats who had voted for what she called the "Bank Lobbyist Act," leading to a nasty encounter between moderates and progressives during a caucus meeting. Schumer met with Warren and reportedly urged her — to little avail — to aim her criticism at the bill and not individual senators.

The Sept. 11, 2001 attacks hit home for Schumer: Growing up in Brooklyn in the 1960s, he watched the World Trade Center towers being constructed in the distance. Six weeks before his election to the House in 1980, he was married at the Windows on the World restaurant, on the 107th floor of the north tower. When the hijacked planes struck the World Trade Center, his oldest daughter, Jessica, was attending high school nearby, and it was several hours before Schumer and his wife could determine that she was all right. Schumer immediately requested $20 billion in aid for New York, which Bush approved. In turn, the Bush administration got Schumer's help in rallying support for its centerpiece anti-domestic terrorism law, the Patriot Act.

Schumer easily won a third term in 2010, defeating Republican Jay Townsend, owner of a market research firm, 66%-32%. Running for a fourth term in 2016, Schumer overwhelmed Wendy Long, a Manhattan attorney active in conservative circles, 71-27%. Schumer spent nearly $13 million on the campaign — more than 18 times what Long spent — and transferred another $6 million to the DSCC to assist candidates in competitive races. After his re-election, Schumer headed off an intraparty battle in the Senate as he prepared to take over as leader. Reid's decision in late February 2015 to anoint Schumer as his successor prompted Durbin to cede the leader's position. But for months afterward, Schumer declined to endorse Durbin for re-election as Democratic whip — straining relations between the former roommates. Not eager for a family squabble after the disappointing results of the 2016 elections, Schumer split the proverbial baby: Durbin stayed on as whip, while Washington Sen. Patty Murray, who had been eyeing a run for whip, was elevated to the new post of assistant Democratic leader, No. 3 in the hierarchy. Asked about Schumer in mid-2018, Durbin told Politico, "We've had good, honest conversations about our relationship, and it's never been better."

Several months into his leadership, Schumer won praise for holding his caucus together during the debate over repealing the Affordable Care Act: Combined with splits in the Republican ranks, the party's unity stymied efforts by Trump and McConnell to kill Obamacare. Less than three years earlier, after the Democrats' drubbing at the polls in 2014, Schumer had created widespread controversy when he gave a speech chastising his party for pushing the Affordable Care Act at the beginning of the Obama administration — rather than focusing on jobs and income growth. "Unfortunately, Democrats blew the opportunity the American people gave them," Schumer said, while making clear he still backed Obama's signature legislative achievement. "We took their mandate and put all of our focus on the wrong problem: health care reform."

He has been a proponent of focusing Democratic efforts on the middle class; he often has said his political reference point is an imaginary Long Island couple convinced that politicians devote too much attention to the very rich and very poor. In the aftermath of 2016, Schumer voiced a view prevalent among leading Democrats that the party had failed to appeal to voters struggling economically — and he set out to reverse that before the 2018 midterm election. "We did not have a sharp, strong, populist enough economic message," he told The New Yorker. "If you ask average voters, 'What did we stand for?' they say we weren't Trump. It wasn't good enough." In mid-2017, he rolled out an economic platform that included a $15 an hour minimum wage, a comprehensive child care proposal and a $1 trillion infrastructure package. As the 2020 elections loomed, Schumer told The Atlantic: "To me, the three biggest issues that we face as a country are climate change, disparity of income and the erosion of the middle class, and voting." The latter was a reference to Schumer's plans to emphasize strengthening the Voting Rights Act and promoting universal registration, issues of key concern to disenfranchised minorities. In an appeal to both millennials and progressives, he said Democrats planned to "go on offense on climate change" while also advocating liberalization of marijuana laws.

If Schumer's effort to regain the majority was thwarted by a difficult political map in 2018, it could be stymied in 2020, in part, by recruitment challenges — as some of the same candidates he eyed for Senate runs were looking to contend in the crowded race for the Democratic presidential nomination. He already appeared to be looking further into the future, if necessary, to land the prize he thought would be his in 2016. "It's better than last time," Schumer told Politico in assessing his prospects of becoming majority leader in 2020. But, in allusion to 2022, he added, "It's not as good as two years from now."

Kirsten Gillibrand (D)

Elected 2009, term expires 2024, 2nd full term, b. Dec 09, 1966; Albany; Dartmouth College, B.A., 1988; University of California, Los Angeles, J.D., 1991; Roman Catholic; Married (Jonathan Gillibrand); 2 children.

Elected Office: U.S. House, 2007-2009.

Professional Career: Practicing attorney, 1991-2006; Special counsel, HUD, 2000.

DC Office: 478 RSOB 20510, 202-224-4451, Fax: 202-228-0282, gillibrand.senate.gov

State Offices: Albany, 518-431-0120; Buffalo, 716-854-9725; Lowville, 315-376-6118; Melville, 631-249-2825; New York, 212-688-6262; Rochester, 585-263-6250; Syracuse, 315-448-0470; Yonkers, 845-875-4585.

Committees: *Aging. Agriculture, Nutrition & Forestry*: Commodities, Risk Management & Trade; Livestock, Marketing & Agriculture Security (RMM); Nutrition, Agricultural Research & Specialty Crops. *Armed Services*: Cybersecurity; Personnel (RMM). *Environment & Public Works*: Clean

Air & Nuclear Safety; Superfund, Waste Management, & Regulatory Oversight; Transportation & Infrastructure.

Group Ratings

	ADA	ACLU	AFL-CIO	LCV	ITI	COC	HAFA	ACU	CFG	FRC
2018	-	86%	-	100%	-	40%	5%	9%	19%	0%
2017	100%	C	100%	100%	C	14%	C	0%	4%	0%

Almanac Ratings 2017-18

	Economy	Social	Foreign	Composite
Liberal	100%	100%	100%	100%
Conservative	0%	0%	0%	0%

Key Votes of the 115th Congress

1. Obama-care revision	N	5. Gun regulations	N	9. Kavanaugh confirmation	N
2. Tax Cuts	N	6. Family planning regs	N	10. Saudi arms sales	Y
3. Dodd-Frank revision	N	7. Gorsuch confirmation	N	11. FISA rules	N
4. Omnibus appropriations	N	8. Immigration restrictions	N	12. Military aid in Yemen	Y

Election Results

Election	Name (Party)	Vote (%)		Cand. Spent	Ind. Exp. Support	Ind. Exp. Oppose
2018 General	Kirsten Gillibrand (D)	4,056,931	(67%)	$10,492,703	$47,032	$609,250
	Chele Farley (R)	1,998,220	(33%)	$1,370,237	$15,000	
2018 Primary	Kirsten Gillibrand (D)		(100%)			

Prior winning percentages: 2012 (72%), 2010 special (63%); House: 2008 (62%), 2006 (53%)

Democrat Kirsten Gillibrand, New York's junior senator, was appointed in 2009 to fill the seat vacated by Hillary Clinton when she was named secretary of State — and, in the years that followed, Gillibrand signaled she wants to follow Clinton in pursuit of national office as well. So it came as little surprise when, in January 2019, Gillibrand announced she was joining the crowded contest for the 2020 Democratic presidential nomination. Just two months earlier, Gillibrand easily had won a second full Senate term, and, during the only debate of that campaign, she responded to a question about her future intentions by asserting that, if re-elected, "I will serve my six year term." When asked about her shift in plans after the joining the race, Gillibrand told reporters: "I continue to fight for New Yorkers as I've always done. But I believe the urgency of this moment now is we have to take on President Trump and what he is doing."

In a Senate Democratic Caucus with no shortage of outspoken Trump critics, there has been no one who has built a more anti-Trump voting record than Gillibrand. In the early months of the Trump administration, Gillibrand voted against confirming 20 of 22 Trump nominees for the Cabinet and other high-ranking positions. Two rival presidential contenders, Vermont Sen. Bernie Sanders and Massachusetts Sen. Elizabeth Warren, placed second with 19 no votes. FiveThirtyEight said Gillibrand broke with Trump's position more than any other senator. And, in the 2017 Almanac vote ratings, she was one of only two senators to score a 100 percent liberal voting score. It is emblematic of the surprising evolution of a canny politician who, serving in the House a decade ago, was known for her anti-immigration and pro-gun rights stances. To criticism that her transformation has been fueled by opportunism, Gillibrand has responded with a combination of candor and contrition. In a February 2018 appearance on CBS' "60 Minutes," she said she was "ashamed" of some of her past positions, adding: "As I've gotten older, I've learned more about life. And sometimes you're wrong, and you've got to fix it. And if you're wrong, just admit it and move on."

The "60 Minutes" profile dubbed Gillibrand "the political face of the #MeToo movement." While her emphasis on legislation to combat sexual assault dates to 2013, the emergence of the #MeToo movement four years later made her a focus of attention — not all of it positive. In December 2017, she became the first senator to call on colleague Al Franken of Minnesota to step down amid allegations of inappropriate sexual behavior; Gillibrand later took heat when some Democrats questioned whether Franken had been treated fairly. A month earlier, she told The New York Times that President Bill Clinton should have resigned the presidency over the Monica Lewinsky scandal. While some felt Gillibrand had exhibited candor given the potential downside to any future ambitions, others saw expediency — after years of her readily relying on support and assistance from Bill and Hillary Clinton. Neither of the Clintons responded publicly, but Philippe Reines, a longtime adviser to Hillary Clinton, lit into Gillibrand via Twitter: "Over 20 yrs you took the Clintons' endorsements, money, and seat. Hypocrite. Interesting strategy for 2020 primaries. Best of luck."

Born Kirsten Rutnik in the New York capital of Albany, she comes from a politically wired family with bipartisan connections. Her father, Douglas Rutnik, is an attorney and lobbyist who has had close ties to several leading New York Republicans, including former Sen. Al D'Amato— for whom Gillibrand interned in college. Her grandmother Polly Noonan was a prominent Democratic activist and longtime companion of Albany Mayor Erastus Corning, who held that office for more than 40 years in the political machine run by Daniel O'Connell. Gillibrand attended the exclusive all-girls Emma Willard School in Troy, just across the Hudson River from Albany. She graduated from Dartmouth College, where she majored in Asian studies and attained fluency in Mandarin; she was among the first Dartmouth students to visit China after the country was opened to students from the United States.

Gillibrand earned her law degree at the University of California, Los Angeles and spent most of the 1990s working for Davis, Polk & Wardwell, a prominent New York-based firm. Her clients included tobacco giant Philip Morris, then the subject of numerous criminal probes and civil lawsuits: Gillibrand helped defend the company against allegations that it lied about the existence of internal research on the health effects of smoking. Toward the end of the Clinton administration, she was a special counsel to Housing and Urban Development Secretary Andrew Cuomo, who later became governor of New York, and then joined another major New York law firm, Boies, Schiller & Flexner. She raised money for Clinton's first Senate campaign in 2000, and five years later, launched what appeared to be a quixotic campaign against four-term Rep. John Sweeney in the upstate region where she had grown up.

In 2006, Sweeney was considered a rising Republican star and had a seat on the Appropriations Committee. He had never faced a serious re-election challenge in a district that, for the previous century, had elected Democrats on only the rarest occasions. As late as August, polls showed him with a solid lead. However, Gillibrand, aided by a national wave that enabled the Democrats to regain control of the House and Senate, triumphed in what turned into one of that year's nastier races. Sweeney attacked Gillibrand as a carpetbagger who actually lived in a New York City high-rise and contrasted his working-class background with her prep school pedigree. Gillibrand demanded that Sweeney release police reports from arrests in 1977 and 1978 and an automobile accident in 2001. A week before the election, the Albany Times Union reported Sweeney's wife had called the police in December 2005 to complain the legislator was "knocking her around." Sweeney at first insisted the report was "false and concocted by our opposition" but eventually conceded the police had been called to his home. Gillibrand won 53%-47%.

Reflecting her district, she joined the Blue Dog Coalition, a group of conservative Democrats, and her voting record received a 100 percent score from the National Rifle Association. Gillibrand boasted she kept two rifles under her bed and that, growing up in a family of hunters, she "always believed in protecting hunters' rights." She co-sponsored legislation denying amnesty and benefits to undocumented immigrants; in a 2007 interview, Gillibrand said "you have to close the borders" as a first step to "right size" immigration, according to CNN. Gillibrand's fundraising prowess, combined with her moderate-to-conservative stance on issues, paid off in 2008 as she defended her seat against state Republican Chairman Sandy Treadwell — who spent nearly $6 million of his own money in the nation's most expensive House race that year. She won 62%-38%.

After the elections, when Sen. Clinton became President-elect Barack Obama's choice for secretary of State, Gov. David Paterson seriously thought about appointing Caroline Kennedy, daughter of President John F. Kennedy, to succeed her. But after Kennedy performed poorly in a New York Times interview and during an upstate "listening tour," she withdrew. Two days later, in January 2009, Paterson announced he was appointing Gillibrand — who, at 42, became the Senate's youngest member at the time.

The reaction to the appointment by El Diario, New York City's dominant Spanish-language newspaper, was an unflattering photo of Gillibrand with the headline: "Anti-immigrante." Gillibrand quickly moved to modify some of her positions that were out of step with the statewide Democratic electorate. The day after her appointment, at a rally in Harlem, she won applause by vowing flexibility on gun control. "I was somebody who was not as focused on this as I should have been, as a House member," she told Politico years later, tearfully describing encounters with families wounded by gun violence. "Meeting these families devastated me, broke my heart." Gillibrand subsequently opposed legislation that would have allowed licensed gun owners to carry concealed firearms across state lines and repealed the Washington, D.C.'s tough gun laws; in the House, she had supported a bill lifting gun restrictions in the nation's capital. Within two years, her NRA score grade went from "A" to "F."

At least three Democratic members of the New York House delegation — concerned over Gillibrand's past stances and piqued at being passed over for the appointment in favor of a colleague with less seniority — seriously mulled challenging her in the 2010 primary. But, one by one, the potential opponents dropped out. Gillibrand benefited from the assistance of two powerful patrons: Obama and New York Sen. Chuck Schumer, by then a member of the Senate Democratic leadership. The White House, fearing an expensive primary could cost the Democrats a seat in 2010, mounted a full-court press, with both the president and Schumer lobbying would-be challengers to stay out. And Schumer — known for being less than thrilled during the years he had to share the spotlight with Clinton — seemed to delight in taking his new colleague under his wing. He pressed Senate leaders to give her the committee assignments she desired and introduced her to deep-pocketed donors.

Gillibrand's poll numbers remained lackluster throughout 2009. But former New York Mayor Rudy Giuliani and former Gov. George Pataki both took a pass on a Senate run, leaving the Republicans without a top-tier candidate. The GOP nominated former Rep. Joseph DioGuardi, who had not held public office in two decades. Despite a rough year for Democrats nationally, Gillibrand easily won 63%-35% to fill the final two years of Clinton's term. In 2012, she was up for a full six-year term. Wendy Long, a lawyer active in conservative circles, got the Republican nod. Gillibrand outspent Long by nearly 20-1 and won by 72%-26%: It stands as a record margin in a New York Senate race, slightly ahead of Schumer's 71 percent margins in 2004 and 2016. In 2018, Gillibrand largely ignored her opponent, private equity executive Chele Farley, on her way to a 67%-33% victory. She spent just $1.4 million from July to September, leaving $10.3 million in her treasury with which to start a presidential bid.

Gillibrand began burnishing her national image early in her Senate tenure. In 2012, she founded a political action committee, Off the Sidelines, to mobilize female candidates. Gillibrand cemented her reputation as a fundraising powerhouse: In each of the past three election cycles, Off the Sidelines has distributed more to candidates than any Senate leadership PAC, according to the nonpartisan Center for Responsive Politics. During this period, the PAC funneled more than $1.7 million to federal candidates, including $538,000 in 2018 — when Off the Sidelines backed more than 90 female candidates nationwide.

The first issue to bring Gillibrand widespread attention as a senator was her call for repeal of the "don't ask, don't tell" policy barring openly gay military service members. It was another about-face from her House tenure, during which the Human Rights Campaign gave her the lowest rating of New York's Democratic representatives for not backing policies allowing for same-sex marriage as well as for gays to serve openly in the military. She introduced legislation in July 2009, at a time when interest in the issue was lagging: Its leading champion, Massachusetts Sen. Ted Kennedy, was dying of cancer. Gillibrand lobbied former House colleagues and fellow senators, pushed for hearings, and set up a website featuring videos of LBGTQ veterans telling their stories. "If you care about national security, if you care about our military readiness, then you will repeal this corrosive policy," she said in an emotional floor speech. It became law at the end of 2010, earning her widespread praise from progressive and gay rights groups.

In 2012, Gillibrand introduced the Family and Medical Leave Act to guarantee workers at least two-thirds pay for up to 12 weeks annually for health-related leave. The bill made little progress —it was reintroduced in 2015 and 2017 — but served to tout the national Democratic Party's stance on the issue. As the party's progressive wing emerged as a force, Gillibrand not only co-sponsored its legislative touchstones, such as "Medicare for All" and the "Green New Deal," she also advocated doing away with Immigration and Customs Enforcement, which she told CNN had become a "deportation force." A decade earlier, she voted in the House to increase funding for ICE to work with local law enforcement to increase deportations. Described by Politico early in her Senate career as the "go-to advocate for the financial services industry," Gillibrand by 2018 was describing herself as a "populist," as she co-sponsored Sanders' legislation for a tax on financial transactions in the stock market. While she joined several other potential presidential contenders that year in renouncing corporate PAC contributions, Gillibrand continued courting Wall Street donors to back her presidential bid, CNBC reported; the securities and investment industry has been the second leading source of contributions to her congressional campaigns, according to the Center for Responsive Politics.

Gillibrand's involvement with the issue with which she is most identified began in 2013, when she introduced a bill to remove the military chain of command from handling sexual assault cases. It pitted Gillibrand against Missouri Democrat Claire McCaskill. As members of the Armed

Services Committee, both aggressively lobbied colleagues on behalf of rival approaches. Gillibrand's proposal fell five votes short of overcoming a Republican filibuster in March 2014; McCaskill's more incremental alternative, to reform the process for handling assault allegations while keeping responsibility within the chain of command, passed the Senate unanimously with Defense Department support. Gillibrand refused to concede on the matter, even though her approach fell 10 votes short when it came up again in 2015. In January 2017, she was the only dissenter in the 98-1 vote to confirm former Marine Gen. James Mattis as Trump's first Defense secretary. Gillibrand said her opposition arose out of concern for civilian control of the military: Mattis had been retired from the military for only four years and required a waiver to head the Defense Department. But a conservative publication, Independent Journal Review, suggested Gillibrand was carrying a "vendetta" because Mattis had been among the generals who resisted removing sexual assault cases from the military chain of command.

Despite their disagreements, Gillibrand and McCaskill forged an alliance on legislation to deal with the problem of sexual assaults on college campuses: A bill initially introduced in 2014 that would have required schools to establish a standardized process to respond to sexual assaults. Also, they headed off legislation that would have prevented universities from investigating cases of sexual assault, mandating instead that such allegations be reported to law enforcement. When Gillibrand and McCaskill, both members of sororities as undergraduates, learned that national organizations representing fraternities and sororities were lobbying for the bill, they summoned representatives of these groups and persuaded them to withdraw their support.

In December 2017, after seven women had come forward with allegations of sexual misconduct against Franken, Gillibrand told a women's conference in Washington that she was angry and that his behavior "can't be tolerated anywhere." But she stopped short of calling for his resignation. That changed a day later, when yet another allegation surfaced. "Enough is enough," Gillibrand wrote on Facebook, becoming the first of Franken's Democratic colleagues to call for his resignation. It set off a political stampede; by the end of the day, a majority of the Senate Democratic Caucus had joined her. Notwithstanding what some saw as more serious allegations lodged at the time against Republican Roy Moore — a candidate in an Alabama special Senate election accused of making advances on underage women — Gillibrand told a news conference: "I think when we start having to talk about the differences between sexual assault and sexual harassment and unwanted groping you are having the wrong conversation. You need to draw a line in the sand and say none of it is … acceptable." A day later, Franken announced he would resign.

In the weeks before Franken's departure from the Senate, a backlash set in — with much of it targeted at Gillibrand. Several senators reportedly voiced private remorse at having joined what they considered a rush to judgment; the most senior Senate Democrat, Patrick Leahy of Vermont, expressed regret on Vermont Public Radio for having called on Franken to resign instead of allowing the Ethics Committee to complete its investigation of the matter. In interviews with Politico, more than a dozen leading Democratic fundraisers — many of them women — vowed never again to donate or fundraise for Gillibrand or said they would do so only if she ended up as the party's nominee. One of them, Susie Tompkins Buell — a co-founder of the Esprit and North Face clothing brands — said the episode had "stained [Gillibrand's] reputation as a fair player," adding, "I heard her referred to as 'She would eat her own,' and she seems to have demonstrated that." Gillibrand, in a New York magazine interview announcing her presidential campaign, fired back: "You know, if a few very wealthy donors across the country are angry that I stood up for women who were demeaned and devalued by a sitting U.S. senator, that's on them."

In 2014, playing off the name of her leadership PAC, Gillibrand published a memoir: "Off the Sidelines: Speak up, Be Fearless, and Change Your World," about her efforts to get women into politics. Hillary Clinton wrote the foreword. The book deviated from the usual tomes on the subject by offering self-help and diet advice and drew attention when Gillibrand wrote about unnamed male colleagues commenting on her weight. One expressed concern she might become "porky," while another assured her she was attractive even when she was heavier because "I like my girls chubby." In the book, she also confronted the lurking doubts about her intellectual heft that accompanied her arrival in the Senate, acknowledging she was seen by some as a "parakeet" without original thoughts. She said she sought to learn from such critics rather than exact revenge. "I was new at my job, and I needed to address my inexperience and weaknesses head-on," she wrote.

Gillibrand started off her presidential bid as a long shot: She barely registered in the polls in early primary states, and, as of early spring 2019, just one of the 21 Democrats in the New York House delegation had endorsed her candidacy — a contrast to the home-state support being accorded her Senate colleagues in the contest. She suffered an early embarrassment when it was disclosed that a female staffer had resigned from her Senate office several months earlier in protest over the office's handling of a sexual harassment complaint against Gillibrand's military aide and longtime driver. Gillibrand defended her office's response, saying the complaints were "fully investigated." But when Politico, which first reported the story, presented her with additional allegations of workplace misconduct by the accused aide, her office opened a new investigation and ended up dismissing him.

Seeking to underscore her claim of being the most anti-Trump candidate in the field — and perhaps hoping to get a rise out of the mercurial commander in chief — Gillibrand formally announced her presidential run in late March 2019 in front of the Trump Tower in Manhattan. Before entering politics, Trump had contributed $4,800 to Gillibrand's 2010 Senate campaign, according to Federal Election Commission disclosure reports. Gillibrand got Trump's attention in December 2017, when three women who a year earlier had accused the president of sexual assault before he entered politics renewed their charges. Gillibrand called on Trump to resign, citing his "numerous" and "credible" accusers. Via Twitter, Trump resorted to suggestive language, characterizing Gillibrand as a "lightweight" who "would come to my office 'begging' for campaign contributions not so long ago (and would do anything for them)." Gillibrand, who learned of the early morning tweet while attending a Senate Bible study session, quickly fired back: "It was a sexist smear attempting to silence my voice, and I will not be silenced on this issue." She said she would donate Trump's campaign contributions — a total of $6,000 — to an anti-sexual violence organization.

Lee Zeldin (R)

Elected 2014, 3rd term, b. Jan 30, 1980; East Meadow; State University of New York - Albany, B.A., 2001; Albany Law School, J.D., 2003; Jewish; Married (Diana Zeldin); 2 children (twins).

Military Career: U.S. Army 23-27; U.S. Army Reserves 2007-pres. (Iraq)

Elected Office: NY Senate, 2011-2014.

Professional Career: Practicing attorney.

DC Office: 2441 RHOB 20515, 202-225-3826, zeldin.house.gov

State Offices: Patchogue, 631-289-1097.

Committees: *Financial Services*: Housing, Community Development & Insurance; Oversight & Investigations. *Foreign Affairs*: Middle East, North Africa & International Terrorism; Oversight & Investigations (RMM).

Group Ratings

	ADA	ACLU	AFL-CIO	LCV	ITI	COC	HAFA	ACU	CFG	FRC
2018	-	14%	-	9%	-	75%	62%	80%	57%	100%
2017	5%	C	29%	9%	C	86%	C	73%	54%	89%

Almanac Ratings 2017-18

	Economy	Social	Foreign	Composite
Liberal	18%	12%	10%	13%
Conservative	82%	88%	90%	87%

Key Votes of the 115th Congress

1. Obama-care revision	Y	5. Family planning regs	Y	9. Guantanamo prisoners	N
2. Tax Cuts	N	6. Body cameras/immigration	N	10. Ground missiles, limit	N
3. Omnibus appropriations	N	7. Abortion ban	Y	11. Defense Dept. spending	Y
4. Dodd-Frank revision	Y	8. Concealed carry	Y	12. FISA rules	Y

Election Results

Election	Name (Party)	Vote (%)		Cand. Spent	Ind. Exp. Support	Ind. Exp. Oppose
2018 General	Lee Zeldin (R)...................................	139,027	(52%)	$4,688,810	$328,468	$533,336
	Perry Gershon (D)............................	127,991	(47%)	$5,034,036	$454,979	$175,000
2018 Primary	Lee Zeldin (R)...................................		(100%)			

Prior winning percentages: 2016 (58%), 2014 (53%)

Republican Lee Zeldin, elected in 2014 against a Democratic incumbent, brought a burst of energy and occasional independence to the House. In a district that remained competitive and facing a well-financed challenger in 2018, he was responsive to local sentiments, including his opposition to Republican tax cuts that capped the deduction for state and local taxes employed by his affluent and highly taxed constituents.

Zeldin was raised in Shirley New York and received his bachelor's degree from the State University at Albany before earning his law degree at Albany Law School. He received an Army commission as a second lieutenant, spent four years on active duty, and deployed to Iraq in 2006 with an infantry battalion of paratroopers from the 82nd Airborne Division; he remained in the Army Reserve as a major. Zeldin opened a law practice, and in 2010 won election to the state Senate, where he led an effort to fund a pilot program for soldiers suffering from post-traumatic stress disorder. He also led a bid to scale back a transportation-authority payroll tax and sought to end fees for saltwater fishing.

Democratic Rep. Tim Bishop, who had served since 2003, defeated Zeldin in 2008, 58%-42%, but the party gap subsequently narrowed. In his second challenge to Bishop, Zeldin said that he would no longer be dragged down by voter fatigue with George W. Bush's presidency and the Iraq War. The American Action Network and the National Republican Congressional Committee spent nearly $4 million accusing Bishop of being a corrupt Washington insider. Bishop aired two ads to tell voters he was not under FBI investigation for helping a donor secure a fireworks permit for a bar mitzvah. Bishop attacked Zeldin for accepting contributions from industries that he said were polluting New York. Zeldin scored a key endorsement from Newsday, which said that Bishop "does not have a significant voice in Congress" and that "Long Island needs this seat at the Republican table." Zeldin got 53 percent of the vote and won with surprising ease.

Zeldin kept a busy pace. In 2015, the House gave voice-vote approval to his amendment to permit states to refuse to comply with Common Core education standards; it subsequently became law. He worked with Democratic Rep. Sean Patrick Mahoney of New York to gain approval of their Safe Bridges Act as part of the highway bill in 2015. Their proposal restored funding to the highway trust fund specifically for bridges and overpasses. On the Financial Services Committee in 2018, Zeldin won unanimous House passage of his bill to clarify rules for banks to create "living wills" for large financial institutions that might be facing jeopardy.

As co-chairman of the House Republican Israel Caucus — with David Kustoff of Tennessee, he is one of two Jewish Republicans in the House -- Zeldin said that President Barack Obama's conflicts with Israeli Prime Minister Benjamin Netanyahu were an opportunity for House Republicans to increase their Jewish ranks. "President Obama is operating as if he doesn't grasp who truly are America's friends and enemies in that region of the world," he told Bloomberg News. Zeldin defended as "completely true" the comments by President Donald Trump in August 2017 that blamed "both sides" for the violent protests in Charlottesville Virginia. In 2019, as ranking Republican on the Foreign Affairs Subcommittee on Oversight and Investigation, Zeldin said that his goal was to "treat our adversaries as our adversaries, and our friends as our friends."

National Democrats have designated Zeldin as a top target. In 2016, the strategy of their challenger, Anna Throne-Holst, was to link Zeldin to Trump. That might not have been wise, given Trump's double-digit victory in the district. Both candidates were lavishly funded, with more than $5 million available for each side. Zeldin won, 59%-41%.

In 2018, Zeldin faced Perry Gershon, a real-estate financier and political newcomer, who attacked Zeldin for his vote to repeal the Affordable Care Act and fought for what he called traditional "values." Zeldin continued his embrace of Trump and the president's allies, including a fundraising event that featured Steve Bannon, a former top Trump aide. After Zeldin in November 2017 voted against the Republican tax cuts, claiming they would have an adverse impact on New York, Speaker Paul Ryan canceled his appearance at a fundraising event.

Gershon spent $5 million—including nearly $2 million of self-funding—to $4.7 million for the incumbent. Zeldin had his closest win, 51%-47%.

NY-1: Eastern Long Island   Cook Partisan Voting Index: R+5

Population		Race and Ethnicity		Income	
Total	721,210	White	75.2%	Median Income	$90,378
Land area (sq. miles)	650	Black	4.8%	District Income Rank	28
Pop/ sq mi	1109.5	Latino	14.3%	Poverty Rate	7.1%
Born in State	77.9%	Asian	4.1%	With health insurance	94%
		Two or more races	1.2%	Cash public assistance	1.9%
Age Groups		Other	0.5%	Food stamp/SNAP	6.2%
Under 18	21.3%				
18-34	20.4%	Education		Work	
35-64	41.5%	H.S grad or less	36.8%	White Collar	16.8%
Over 64	16.8%	Some college	27.9%	Sales and Service	41.9%
		College Degree, 4 yr	18.9%	Blue Collar	18.4%
Military		Post grad	16.5%	Government	19.6%
Veteran/ Active Duty	6.3%				

2012 Pres. Vote	Obama	146,708	(50%)	Romney	145,115	(49%)			
2016 Pres. Vote	Trump	183,233	(54%)	Clinton	141,900	(42%)	Johnson	7,217	(2%)

Brookhaven: Long Island — "the Island" to most New Yorkers — is the largest and most populous island in the mainland United States. It stretches 118 miles, from the two-century-old Montauk Point lighthouse on a crumbling bluff to Fort Hamilton at the foot of the Verrazano-Narrows Bridge. Ranging from 12 to 20 miles wide, Long Island is ringed by gentle hills and cliffs above Long Island Sound and sand-spit beaches that front the Atlantic Ocean. Including the populations of Brooklyn and Queens, some 7.7 million people live there, more than in all but 12 states. Brooklyn, at the island's western end, is urban and thickly settled, while the Hamptons in the east are manicured countryside, preserved as a playground for the New York elite. For trend-watchers: In 2018, real-estate experts said that sales were declining in the Hamptons, and the elite increasingly were drawn to the Hudson River valley for luxury vacation spots.

More important economically — and politically — are the areas immediately west of the Hamptons: the suburbs created in the post-World War II migration out of the city. Developers looking for cheaper land for aircraft factories, shopping centers, subdivisions and office parks found them first in Nassau County, just east of Queens, and then farther out in Suffolk County. Suffolk attracted young families of Irish and Italian descent looking for more space and less crime. More recently the county has been attracting Latinos, who have grown to 20 percent of the population, compared with 9 percent black in Suffolk. The island's economy soured as defense plants were decimated by the end of the Cold War, and young people fled older suburbs for jobs elsewhere. In 2017, the Long Island Power Authority approved a plan to build a 15-turbine wind farm at sea and run cables from Rhode Island to Montauk, with a 2022 target date for completion. The project, a key part of Gov. Andrew Cuomo's clean-energy program, drew opposition from commercial fisherman worried about the loss of large beds of scallops.

The 1st Congressional District of New York consists of the eastern end of Long Island and Suffolk, with about half of the county's population. It runs as far west as Smithtown on the North Shore and Patchogue on the South Shore. It includes Shelter Island, located between the north and south forks of Long Island's "fishtail," and Plum Island. It takes in Brookhaven National Laboratory, a physics research lab. Also in the 1st are the Hamptons and most of Fire Island National Seashore, the only federal wilderness area in New York state and a magnet for gay vacationers for decades. Suffolk County was long one of the most conservative parts of New York — Richard Nixon won 70 percent of the vote here in 1972 — but it has not been very conservative by today's national standards. The district voted solidly for Democrat Al Gore in 2000 and went for Republican George W. Bush in 2004 by less than 1 percent — a September 11 effect. Donald Trump was popular here, with a 54%-42% win. Other than Staten Island, Suffolk was the only county that Trump won in New York

City or its suburbs (including Connecticut and New Jersey). His tough talk on crime and immigration had local appeal.

Pete King (R)

Elected 1992, 14th term, b. Apr 05, 1944; New York; St. Francis College (NY), B.A., 1965; University of Notre Dame Law School (IN), J.D., 1968; Roman Catholic; Married (Rosemary Wiedel King); 2 children; 2 grandchildren.

Military Career: U.S. Army 1968-1973; NY National Guard 1968-1974

Elected Office: Hempstead Town Council, 1977-1981; Nassau County comptroller, 1981-1992.

Professional Career: Practicing attorney, 1968-1972, 1978-1981; Deputy Attorney, Nassau County, 1972-1974; Executive Assistant, Nassau County Executive, 1974-1976; General counsel, comptroller, 1977.

DC Office: 302 CHOB 20515, 202-225-7896, Fax: 202-226-2279, peteking.house.gov

State Offices: Massapequa Park, 516-541-4225.

Committees: *Financial Services*: Investor Protection, Entrepreneurship & Capital Markets; Nat'l Security, International Development & Monetary Policy. *Homeland Security*: Emergency Preparedness, Response & Recovery (RMM); Intelligence & Counterterrorism.

Group Ratings

	ADA	ACLU	AFL-CIO	LCV	ITI	COC	HAFA	ACU	CFG	FRC
2018	-	3%	-	29%	-	92%	37%	52%	38%	100%
2017	15%	C	49%	11%	C	86%	C	52%	25%	89%

Almanac Ratings 2017-18

	Economy	Social	Foreign	Composite
Liberal	22%	24%	5%	17%
Conservative	78%	76%	95%	83%

Key Votes of the 115th Congress

1. Obama-care revision	Y	5. Family planning regs	Y	9. Guantanamo prisoners	N
2. Tax Cuts	N	6. Body cameras/immigration	N	10. Ground missiles, limit	N
3. Omnibus appropriations	Y	7. Abortion ban	Y	11. Defense Dept. spending	Y
4. Dodd-Frank revision	Y	8. Concealed carry	N	12. FISA rules	Y

Election Results

Election	Name (Party)	Vote (%)	Cand. Spent	Ind. Exp. Support	Ind. Exp. Oppose
2018 General	Peter King (R)................................	128,078 (53%)	$2,924,047		
	Liuba Grechen Shirley (D)...............	113,074 (47%)	$1,739,027	$9,905	
2018 Primary	Peter King (R)..	(100%)			

Prior winning percentages: 2016 (62%), 2014 (65%), 2012 (52%), 2010 (71%), 2008 (54%), 2006 (53%), 2004 (54%), 2002 (65%), 2000 (51%), 1998 (58%), 1996 (47%), 1994 (49%), 1992 (43%)

Republican Pete King, first elected in 1992, has grown from a loquacious maverick to a serious player on domestic security matters. His penchant for quotable quips has made him a constant presence on cable television, though his New York accent and intensity have grown out of place in the increasingly conservative Republican Conference. He has had occasional cooperation with the like-minded Donald Trump. But King has voiced his disdain for some of those around the president.

King grew up in Sunnyside Queens. His parents were Irish immigrants and Democrats, his father a New York City police detective. He went to St. Francis College and law school at the University of Notre Dame, and he clerked one summer at former Republican President Richard Nixon's law firm with a Long Islander named Rudolph Giuliani. After law school, he followed the trek to the suburbs and became part of the Nassau County Republican machine. He worked as a lawyer and staffer in county government. He was elected to the Hempstead town council in 1977 and as county comptroller in 1981. When the seat opened in 1992, King ran and won the GOP primary. In the general election, King ran as a fiscal conservative and abortion rights opponent. He won 50%-46%, and has gone largely unchallenged since.

King's voting record ranks him near the ideological center of the House, as the Almanac vote ratings confirmed. He has been more conservative on foreign policy, but with distinctive interests. He is far to the left of most Republicans on gun control, lamenting "a love affair with guns, almost a religious fervor" following shootings in February 2018 at the high school in Parkland Florida and filing a bill with Democratic Rep. Bennie Thompson of Mississippi to expand background checks for firearm purchases at gun shows. On immigration issues, King is an outspoken conservative. He opposes racial quotas and preferences, as well as bilingual education. He supports English-only laws and opposes aid to illegal immigrants. He moved back to the center in 2012 when he challenged anti-tax activist Grover Norquist's never-raise-taxes pledge. Norquist angrily accused him of trying to "weasel out" of an agreement; King called Norquist "a lowlife."

King was long an ardent supporter of the Irish Republican Army. He had a role in 1998 peace negotiations, carrying messages between the IRA and the Irish government. But in 2005, after the suspected involvement of Sinn Féin, the IRA's political arm, in a bank robbery and a highly publicized murder, King called for the IRA to disband. He has written three novels about politics and diplomacy in Northern Ireland. In one of them, Deliver Us From Evil, a thinly disguised Long Island congressman is the protagonist.

After the September 11 attacks, in which 160 of his constituents died, King became more of a Republican regular and focused on legislation to prevent a repeat. In 2005, GOP leaders tapped King to be chairman of the Homeland Security Committee. The following year, he was the first House Republican to attack the Bush administration's plan to give control of six major U.S. ports to a company in Dubai in the United Arab Emirates, and he subsequently helped to enact tighter controls on port security.

King sharpened his rhetoric on terrorist threats following the election of President Barack Obama. When the Homeland Security Department issued a report in 2009 about domestic right-wing extremism, King complained that the agency "has never put out a report talking about 'look out for mosques.'" The Council on American-Islamic Relations called his remarks "bigoted." King stood his ground. After Republicans regained House control in 2010, he held hearings on "the radicalization of the American Muslim community and homegrown terrorism." Islamic leaders said they feared a witch hunt, and King acknowledged that his stance carried risks. The hearings resulted in massive publicity and round-the-clock security for King following reports of threats against him. Some Muslim groups, citing his past support for Irish terrorists, accused him of a double standard. King responded, "The fact is, the IRA never attacked the United States. And my loyalty is to the United States."

In 2014, King blasted Obama for withdrawing troops from Iraq and accused him of helping foster the rise of the Islamic State of Iraq and the Levant (ISIL). He said that the terrorist group was more powerful than al-Qaida was on September 11 and described the president's handling of Iraq as "shameful." King won House approval in 2016 and again in 2017 of his bill to tighten defenses against insider threats at the Homeland Security Department.

Over the years, King has been a provocative and frequent presence on radio and television. When Republican leaders abruptly pulled from the House floor a $60 billion relief bill for Superstorm Sandy in January 2013, two months after the storm ravaged the East Coast, King declared on CNN, "There's some dysfunction in the Republican leadership." After the legislation passed easily, King told Newsday that he has felt like a "second-class citizen in the Republican caucus" as it became more Southern-oriented. In November 2017, he voted against the Republican tax cuts, claiming a "devastating" local impact from limiting the deduction for state and local taxes.

King picked fights with Texas GOP Sen. Ted Cruz, even before he became a presidential candidate. When Cruz attempted to defund the Affordable Care Act, prompting a partial government shutdown in October 2013, King told MSNBC: "We have to start going after him by name. ... It's really time to speak out against him." If Cruz had won the Republican nomination, King said, "I think that I'll take cyanide."

Despite his friendship with Trump ally Giuliani, King did not endorse Trump until he wrapped up the nomination. During the presidential transition, King met with him at Trump Tower and urged him to consider a Muslim domestic surveillance program. When Trump issued an executive order a few days after he took office that imposed a temporary immigration ban on several Muslim-majority countries with records of supporting terrorism, King said that it was "overdue."

Citing Trump's actions on immigration and calling him "an outer borough guy," King told City and State New York later in 2017, "we're getting along very well." Still, he said in another interview that former top Trump aide Steve Bannon was "like some disheveled drunk that wandered onto the political stage." During the January 2019 government shutdown, he said that Trump "should stand up to the Freedom Caucus on the right."

In 2018, King faced an unusually stiff reelection challenge from Liuba Grechen Shirley, who worked on human-rights issues at the United Nations and for nonprofit groups. She ran a grassroots campaign dismissing King's self-styled centrism and spent $1.7 million to the incumbent's $2.9 million. Newsday wrote in its endorsement of King, "In these extraordinary times, experience and bipartisanship are needed." Grechen Shirley had a 5,000-vote lead in Suffolk — a red flag for Democratic-controlled redistricting. King led by 20,000 in his Nassau base, which cast half as many votes, and he won overall, 53%-47%.

NY-2: South-Central Long Island   Cook Partisan Voting Index: R+3

Population		Race and Ethnicity		Income	
Total	721,061	White	62.3%	Median Income	$94,336
Land area (sq. miles)	182	Black	9.4%	District Income Rank	22
Pop/ sq mi	3961.7	Latino	23.3%	Poverty Rate	6.8%
Born in State	75.4%	Asian	3.1%	With health insurance	93.3%
		Two or more races	1.3%	Cash public assistance	2.2%
Age Groups		Other	0.5%	Food stamp/SNAP	7.2%
Under 18	22.3%				
18-34	22.1%	Education		Work	
35-64	41.6%	H.S grad or less	42.7%	White Collar	14%
Over 64	14%	Some college	27.4%	Sales and Service	45.3%
		College Degree, 4 yr	17.7%	Blue Collar	20.2%
Military		Post grad	12.2%	Government	16.7%
Veteran/ Active Duty	5.4%				

2012 Pres. Vote	Obama	140,817	(52%)	Romney	128,791	(47%)
2016 Pres. Vote	Trump	165,908	(53%)	Clinton	137,680	(44%)

Islip: At the end of World War II, Suffolk County was largely given over to potato fields. It was also directly in the path of one of the major suburban migrations of our day. On the highways that Robert Moses built to connect his parks to the middle-class parts of New York City came tens of thousands of young veterans and their families, forsaking the row-house neighborhoods where they had grown up for comparatively spacious lots and single-family houses. The first wave of postwar migration moved into Nassau County, starting in 1947, when 300 families moved into 750-square-foot houses that sold for $6,990, with no money down for veterans. The location was Levittown — America's first mass-produced suburb, where delivery trucks dropped off piles of prefabricated materials 60 feet apart, to be picked up by roving teams of specialized workers with power tools. By the time the final house was sold for $9,500 in 1951, Levittown, a former potato field, had become synonymous with instant suburbanization. This wave represented a cross-section of all but the poorest New Yorkers: almost half Catholic, about one-quarter Jewish, and one-quarter Protestant. As Long Island developed its own employment base, the next wave of migration was more Catholic and less Jewish, more blue-collar (aircraft manufacturers were big Suffolk employers) and less white-collar, more Democratic in ancestral politics.

The 2nd Congressional District of New York takes in Massapequa and Levittown, where the median sale price of a home increased in 2018 to $449,000. These areas in the eastern part of Nassau County are generally Republican, but only about one-third of the district's population resides in Nassau. Most of its residents live in more Democratic areas in the southwest corner of Suffolk County, where the district stretches from Amityville and Babylon east through Bay Shore and Islip to Sayville and Bayport — one community after another strung out along Sunrise Highway. The district takes in Brentwood, which is two-thirds Hispanic and has a per capita income barely half the average in Suffolk. Several news stories described the many murders in the local Latino community linked to the MS-13 gang, which left what Pro Publica described in 2018 as "killing fields" of immigrant teenagers, especially in Brentwood; the community has suffered further from "a larger breakdown between the police department and Latino immigrants." Near Islip, officials abandoned plans to expand MacArthur Airport, after concluding that the financial cost of an international terminal was too high. In April 2018, Suffolk County officials announced plans for a $1 billion development near the airport, which would include a large sports arena, plus a hotel and retail shops.

As with other Suffolk-based districts, Donald Trump strengthened Republican support, with a 53%-44% win in 2016.

Thomas Suozzi (D)

Elected 2016, 2nd term, b. Aug 31, 1962; Glen Cove; Boston College (MA), B.S., 1984; Fordham University School of Law (NY), J.D., 1989; Roman Catholic; Married (Helene Suozzi); 3 children.

Elected Office: Glen Cove Mayor, 1994-2001; Nassau County Executive, 2002-2009.

Professional Career: CPA; Practicing Attorney.

DC Office: 214 CHOB 20515, 202-225-3335, Fax: 202-225-4669, suozzi.house.gov

State Offices: Huntington, 631-923-4100; Little Neck, 718-631-0400.

Committees: *Ways & Means*: Oversight; Select Revenue Measures.

Group Ratings

	ADA	ACLU	AFL-CIO	LCV	ITI	COC	HAFA	ACU	CFG	FRC
2018	-	77%	-	97%	-	67%	10%	12%	33%	0%
2017	70%	C	92%	97%	C	64%	C	8%	0%	11%

Almanac Ratings 2017-18

	Economy	Social	Foreign	Composite
Liberal	70%	92%	56%	73%
Conservative	30%	8%	44%	27%

Key Votes of the 115th Congress

1. Obama-care revision	N	5. Family planning regs	N	9. Guantanamo prisoners	N
2. Tax Cuts	N	6. Body cameras/immigration	Y	10. Ground missiles, limit	Y
3. Omnibus appropriations	N	7. Abortion ban	N	11. Defense Dept. spending	Y
4. Dodd-Frank revision	Y	8. Concealed carry	N	12. FISA rules	Y

Election Results

Election	Name (Party)	Vote (%)		Cand. Spent	Ind. Exp. Support	Ind. Exp. Oppose
2018 General	Tom Suozzi (D)	157,456	(59%)	$1,319,423	$47,030	
	Dan DeBono (R)	109,514	(41%)	$440,022		
2018 Primary	Tom Suozzi (D)		(100%)			

Prior winning percentages: 2016 (53%)

Tom Suozzi, elected to the House in 2016 in a political comeback for a one-time boy wonder on Long Island, showed interest in consensus-building in the House. He was successful in his bid for a prominent niche: a seat on the Ways and Means Committee.

A native of Glen Cove, Suozzi graduated from Boston College and got his law degree from Fordham University. He was the mayor of Glen Cove, a position that his father — and two other Suozzis -- have held, then served eight years in the more powerful office of Nassau County executive, the first Democrat to hold that position in three decades. In 2004, he spearheaded FixAlbany.com, an initiative that targeted corruption in New York state politics and sought to enact a limit on local Medicaid expenses. Not surprisingly, the initiative ruffled some Democratic chieftains, as well as

Republicans, in Albany. From 2006 until 2013, he lost three campaigns: an uphill Democratic primary for governor against Eliot Spitzer, followed by two unexpected defeats for county executive. In private life, he led a state commission that proposed the first statewide cap on property taxes, which subsequently was enacted. He worked as a senior adviser at the investment bank Lazard Freres and as a litigator at the Shearman & Sterling law firm.

When Rep. Steve Israel, a House Democratic leader, announced his decision to step down, Suozzi quickly voiced interest. The contenders included three other officeholders: North Hempstead councilwoman Anna Kaplan, who had the support of EMILY's List, which supports Democratic women who back abortion rights; Steve Stern, a Suffolk County legislator; and former North Hempstead Supervisor Joe Kaiman. The late June primary had a low turnout of about 20,000 voters. Suozzi won with 35 percent to 22 percent for Stern (who got more than half the vote in Suffolk), 22 percent for Kaiman and 16 percent for Kaplan.

In the peculiar general election, Suozzi faced Jack Martins, a construction businessman who served six years in the state Senate and earlier was the mayor of Mineola. When a federal judge ruled in August that another Republican candidate had been improperly excluded from the primary ballot and scheduled a new GOP primary for Oct. 6, Martins sought to delay the general election until Dec. 6. There was speculation that Martins believed that it would be an advantage for him not to appear on the ballot with Donald Trump and Hillary Clinton. Shortly before Labor Day, the judge denied Martins' motion. Then, on Sept. 14, a federal appeals court canceled the rescheduled primary. The result, wrote David Wasserman of the Cook Political Report, was that the National Republican Congressional Committee "cooled" its enthusiasm and shifted its attention elsewhere. Suozzi doubled the fundraising of Martins and won, 53%-47%. Martins got 51 percent of the vote in Suffolk, but he lost narrowly in Nassau and by nearly 2-to-1 in Queens.

During his first term, Suozzi got seats on the Armed Services and Foreign Affairs committees. He was a lead sponsor of a bill to hold China responsible for its mistreatment of Uighur Muslims. But he voiced frustration with the limits of the minority party. "I want to get things done. So, I need to build new relationships," he told Newsday. As co-chair of the bipartisan Problem Solvers Caucus, he helped to prepare House rules changes to encourage more open debate; that became one of many deals to which Nancy Pelosi agreed to gain support for her return as Speaker.

With an opening for a New York Democrat on Ways and Means, Suozzi called for a revival of the federal deduction for state and local taxes, a popular notion in his high-tax state. Also competing for the position was first-termer Alexandria Ocasio-Cortez, who was backed by progressive groups. Suozzi called himself a "fiscal conservative," but said that he had progressive views on issues such as poverty and immigration. He benefited from his background as a certified public accountant, plus the tradition that freshmen rarely are assigned to Ways and Means.

In 2018, Republican Dan DeBono, an investment adviser and a former Navy SEAL, complained about business influence on both parties and supported the trade war of President Donald Trump. Suozzi outspent him, $1.5 million to $461,000 and won, 59%-41% in the comfortably Democratic cycle.

NY-3: Northern Long Island, Eastern Queens   Cook Partisan Voting Index: D+1

Population		Race and Ethnicity		Income	
Total	731,138	White	68.7%	Median Income	$108,136
Land area (sq. miles)	255	Black	3.1%	District Income Rank	5
Pop/ sq mi	2868.1	Latino	10.7%	Poverty Rate	5.6%
Born in State	69.9%	Asian	15.4%	With health insurance	95.3%
		Two or more races	1.5%	Cash public assistance	1.1%
Age Groups		Other	0.6%	Food stamp/SNAP	3.8%
Under 18	21.6%				
18-34	17.4%	**Education**		**Work**	
35-64	41.8%	H.S grad or less	27.4%	White Collar	19.2%
Over 64	19.2%	Some college	20.6%	Sales and Service	38%
		College Degree, 4 yr	27.6%	Blue Collar	11.4%
Military		Post grad	24.5%	Government	14.7%
Veteran/ Active Duty	4.7%				

2012 Pres. Vote	Obama	155,451	(51%)	Romney	147,617	(48%)	
2016 Pres. Vote	Clinton	178,288	(51%)	Trump	156,942	(45%)	

Huntington: The North Shore of Long Island is "Gatsby country," where peninsulas jutting out into the Sound are covered with vast green lawns leading to the mansions of America's great capitalists. Nineteenth-century millionaires commuted by steam yacht from Manhattan to their estates in what is now Queens or Nassau County. In the early 20th century, the richest people in business and show business spent their leisure time here, playing croquet while their servants unloaded bootleggers' boats at their private docks. Inland, behind the expansive lawns, Long Island was still farm country, with little villages clustered at railroad stations, occasional colonial-era houses, and acres of billboard-strewn wasteland on the highways to New York City. But as the city grew outward, affluent neighborhoods developed in Douglaston on the water, just beyond the middle-class Flushing area of Queens inland, and the Great Neck peninsula became a very affluent, mostly Jewish suburb. Farther out, on Sands Point and Oyster Bay, old estates alternated with more modest homes originally built for servants and newer subdivisions. The Sagamore Hill home of President Theodore Roosevelt at Oyster Bay has been restored at a cost of $10 million. Historical alert: Local researchers contend that F. Scott Fitzgerald, in writing The Great Gatsby, may have imagined a site in Connecticut, not Long Island, the New York Times reported in May 2018.

In Glen Cove, work has begun on the Gravies Point development — a Superfund clean-up site -- with $1 billion in building along the waterfront, with parks, marinas and an amphitheater, plus 1,100 residences. Growth in Glen Cove, just west of Oyster Bay, has encouraged a commuter ferry to Manhattan, though a temporary terminal sat empty in 2018 while proposals for high-cost service were reviewed. For the longer term, local environmentalists voiced concern that a potential plan for new sea gates to limit flooding in New York City could adversely affect areas along Long Island Sound. "We love New York City but we don't want to be sacrificed to protect it," a local activist told Newsday in October 2018.

The 3rd Congressional District of New York ties together a disparate collection of New York City neighborhoods and suburbs. About one-third of its votes are cast in Suffolk County, where the political leanings are more conservative than elsewhere in the district. Close to 15 percent live at the western end of the district, in upscale neighborhoods of Queens near the Throgs Neck and Bronx-Whitestone bridges to the Bronx and points north: Douglaston, Bellaire and Beechurst. This area, more affluent than other portions of Queens, is heavily Democratic. In the middle — politically, as well as geographically — is northern Nassau County. Roughly half of the district's population lives here, many in the posh neighborhoods abutting or near Long Island Sound. This affluence largely continues inland; the median household incomes in Jericho, where nearly one-third of the population is Asian, exceeded $156,000 per year. The district has been politically competitive. Even with Donald Trump's improved performance in the Suffolk part of the district, Hillary Clinton raised Democratic performance elsewhere and led, 51%-45%.

Kathleen Rice (D)

Elected 2014, 3rd term, b. Feb 15, 1965; New York City; Catholic University of America (DC), B.A., 1987; Touro Law Center, J.D., 1991; Roman Catholic; Single.

Elected Office: Nassau County District Attorney, 2006-2015.

Professional Career: Assistant District Attorney, Brooklyn; Assistant U.S. Attorney, 1999-2005.

DC Office: 2435 RHOB 20515, 202-225-5516, Fax: 202-225-5758, kathleenrice.house.gov

State Offices: Garden City, 516-739-3008.

Committees: *Homeland Security*: Border Security, Facilitation & Operations (Chmn); Cybersecurity, Infrastructure Protection & Innovation. *Veterans' Affairs*: Economic Opportunity; Oversight & Investigations.

Group Ratings

	ADA	ACLU	AFL-CIO	LCV	ITI	COC	HAFA	ACU	CFG	FRC
2018	-	75%	-	91%	-	83%	9%	12%	19%	0%
2017	85%	C	97%	100%	C	50%	C	7%	5%	0%

Almanac Ratings 2017-18

	Economy	Social	Foreign	Composite
Liberal	83%	98%	89%	90%
Conservative	18%	2%	11%	10%

Key Votes of the 115th Congress

1. Obama-care revision	N	5. Family planning regs	N	9. Guantanamo prisoners	Y
2. Tax Cuts	N	6. Body cameras/immigration	Y	10. Ground missiles, limit	Y
3. Omnibus appropriations	Y	7. Abortion ban	N	11. Defense Dept. spending	Y
4. Dodd-Frank revision	Y	8. Concealed carry	N	12. FISA rules	Y

Election Results

Election	Name (Party)	Vote (%)	Cand. Spent	Ind. Exp. Support	Ind. Exp. Oppose
2018 General	Kathleen Rice (D)............................	159,535 (61%)	$1,404,907		
	Ameer Benno (R).............................	100,571 (39%)	$49,689		
2018 Primary	Kathleen Rice (D).......................................	(100%)			

Prior winning percentages: 2016 (60%), 2014 (53%)

Democrat Kathleen Rice, a veteran Nassau County prosecutor who built a reputation for being tough on drunken drivers, won an open seat in 2014. For a junior lawmaker, she has shown an unusual willingness to challenge authority — namely, that of now-Speaker Nancy Pelosi. Increasingly, it became apparent that her assignments to second-tier committees have been no coincidence.

Born in Manhattan and raised in Garden City, Rice was one of 10 children borne by an only-child mother. She graduated from Catholic University in Washington, and got her law degree from Touro Law Center in Central Islip Long Island. Rice registered as a Republican in 1984 and did not vote until 2002, Newsday reported in 2010. She responded that her lack of voting was a "mistake."

She began her legal career as an assistant district attorney in Kings County, prosecuting burglaries, robberies and sexual assaults. For six years, she was an assistant U.S. attorney in Philadelphia, where she handled white-collar crimes, corporate fraud, gun and drug cases, and public corruption. Rice was elected Nassau County's district attorney in 2005, defeating a Republican who held the job for three decades, and quickly developed a reputation for prosecution of drunken drivers. She worked to pass legislation imposing harsher penalties on those who had children in the car or who injured other motorists. Rice went after cheating on college admission tests, working to improve test security. She was co-chair of the Moreland Commission to Investigate Public Corruption in New York State, and was president of the state's District Attorneys Association.

As her political ambition increased, Rice ran in the five-candidate Democratic primary for state attorney general in 2010. She trailed eventual winner Eric Schneiderman, 34%-32%, though she led in counties outside of New York City. In Nassau, she was the only countywide Democrat to win reelection in 2013.

In her campaign for Congress, Republican nominee Bruce Blakeman ran negative ads against Rice, accusing her of being anti-woman for her workplace policies as district attorney and her refusal to fire a staffer who made sexist and racially offensive comments on Twitter. As a new D.A., Rice had told part-timers (many of them women caring for children) that they had to become full-timers or leave the office. She told Newsday at the time that the county "deserves victims' advocates that are full time." With the support of numerous women's groups, she won, 53%-47%. Rice steadily increased her margin in her next two elections.

Rice serves on the Homeland Security Committee, where she chairs the Border Security, Facilitation and Operations Subcommittee. She also serves on the Veterans Affairs Committee. Rice is not, however, on the House Judiciary Committee, thanks to her rebellious nature. Rice has spent much of her time as one of the foremost critics of Pelosi. Rice blamed Pelosi when Democrats underperformed House pickup expectations in 2016, and she kept up the criticism throughout 2017 and 2018. According to Politico, Rice said Pelosi "set women back -- and quite frankly, our party back decades" after Pelosi did not more forcefully try to push Rep. John Conyers of Michigan out of Congress amid sexual harassment allegations; Conyers resigned in December 2017.

After the 2018 election, Rice publicly opposed Pelosi's return as Speaker. Pelosi won the gavel anyway, and Rice would soon pay a price. In January 2019, her Democratic colleagues from New York made a push for her to serve on the Judiciary Committee, only to see the re-empowered Pelosi block that effort. Rice likely will be stymied in the House for as long as Pelosi leads Democrats.

Rice briefly considered running for state attorney general amid turmoil surrounding the resignation of Schneiderman in 2018. Rice cited the timing of his resignation and a state law that prohibited candidates from seeking two offices simultaneously as her reasons for passing on the race —though those factors didn't stop Rep. Sean Patrick Maloney from his unsuccessful primary bid for the office. Despite her tangles with Pelosi, Rice remains a rising star within New York politics. It's widely speculated that she might make another statewide run in the not-too-distant future.

NY-4: Southern Nassau County
Cook Partisan Voting Index: D+4

Population		Race and Ethnicity		Income	
Total	724,387	White	57.1%	Median Income	$100,387
Land area (sq. miles)	111	Black	13.9%	District Income Rank	14
Pop/ sq mi	6534.8	Latino	20.5%	Poverty Rate	6.8%
Born in State	70.2%	Asian	6.6%	With health insurance	93.1%
		Two or more races	1.5%	Cash public assistance	1.5%
Age Groups		Other	0.5%	Food stamp/SNAP	5.7%
Under 18	22%				
18-34	21.7%	**Education**		**Work**	
35-64	40.3%	H.S grad or less	34.7%	White Collar	16%
Over 64	16%	Some college	23.9%	Sales and Service	42.5%
		College Degree, 4 yr	22.8%	Blue Collar	14.9%
Military		Post grad	18.6%	Government	16.7%
Veteran/ Active Duty	4.4%				

2012 Pres. Vote	Obama	165,876	(56%)	Romney	129,049	(43%)
2016 Pres. Vote	Clinton	179,845	(53%)	Trump	147,469	(44%)

Hempstead: Nassau County has long been on the cutting edge of American suburban life. It is the home of one of the earliest suburbs: Garden City, founded in 1869 with wide avenues and single-family homes. After World War II, it pioneered large-scale suburban development, as freeways replaced highways, and shopping centers sprang up at intersections. Many of the middle- and upper-income residents continue to depend on the Long Island Railroad to speed them to jobs in New York City. Prominent sites include the county seat of Mineola; Hofstra University in Hempstead, which has held a presidential debate during the past three general elections; and Roosevelt Field, where Charles Lindbergh took off for Paris in 1927. The fate of this historic airstrip perhaps typifies the extent of suburbanization in Nassau County: It's now the site of an upscale shopping mall, with a longstanding conflict over the exact spot of Lindbergh's departure, either at an escalator in the shopping center or just behind a parking garage near a Best Buy.

The 4th Congressional District of New York comprises Garden City and the towns around it. It is one of six districts in the state that is wholly included within a single county. The 4th takes in several suburbs along the Jericho Turnpike — New Hyde Park, Mineola, Westbury — as well as a large swath of southern Nassau County. This territory includes Hempstead, Uniondale, Rockville Centre and part of ethnically diverse Valley Stream, as well as most of the predominantly Jewish "Five Towns" — the railway suburbs of Lawrence, Cedarhurst, Hewlett and Woodmere; Inwood is in the neighboring 5th District. Jones Beach, a state park with more than six miles of an expansive ocean beachfront and 2,400 acres for maritime entertainment, hosts about 6 million annual visitors. In 2015, the New York Islanders professional hockey team abandoned the 43-year-old Nassau Coliseum and had a reverse migration to the full-service Barclays Center in rejuvenated Brooklyn. Their move into the city didn't work out. In 2019, the Islanders returned part-time to the Coliseum, while a new arena was under construction.

Nassau County was traditionally Republican, and Garden City remains that way. But the county has become more diverse and more Democratic. Hempstead typifies these emerging changes. Once swing territory that served as the political base of Republican Sen. Alfonse D'Amato, non-Hispanic whites in the village make up just 6.6 percent of the population. Nearby Roosevelt is only 2 percent non-Hispanic white. The district includes the old resort areas around Lido Beach and Long Beach and suburban Merrick, Bellmore and Wantagh; these areas are more marginal. Hillary Clinton won the district, 53%-43%. Overall, she got 52 percent of the vote in Nassau.

Gregory Meeks (D)

Elected 1998, 11th term, b. Sep 25, 1953; Harlem; Adelphi University (NY), B.A., 1975; Howard University Law School (DC), J.D., 1978; African Methodist Episcopal; Married (Simone-Marie Meeks); 3 children.

Elected Office: NY Assembly, 1992-1998.

Professional Career: Assistant District Attorney, Queens County, 1978-1983; NY St. Commission of Investigations, 1984-1985; Judge, NY St. Workers' Compensation Board, 1985-1992.

DC Office: 2310 RHOB 20515, 202-225-3461, Fax: 202-226-4169, meeks.house.gov

State Offices: Arverne, 347-230-4032; Jamaica, 718-725-6000.

Committees: *Financial Services*: Consumer Protection & Financial Institutions (Chmn); Investor Protection, Entrepreneurship & Capital Markets. *Foreign Affairs*: Europe, Eurasia, Energy & the Environment; Western Hemisphere, Civilian Security, & Trade.

Group Ratings

	ADA	ACLU	AFL-CIO	LCV	ITI	COC	HAFA	ACU	CFG	FRC
2018	-	81%	-	100%	-	67%	10%	8%	25%	0%
2017	90%	C	95%	89%	C	54%	C	4%	5%	11%

Almanac Ratings 2017-18

	Economy	Social	Foreign	Composite
Liberal	89%	97%	87%	91%
Conservative	11%	3%	13%	9%

Key Votes of the 115th Congress

1. Obama-care revision	N	5. Family planning regs	N	9. Guantanamo prisoners	Y
2. Tax Cuts	N	6. Body cameras/immigration	Y	10. Ground missiles, limit	Y
3. Omnibus appropriations	Y	7. Abortion ban	N	11. Defense Dept. spending	NV
4. Dodd-Frank revision	N	8. Concealed carry	N	12. FISA rules	Y

Election Results

Election	Name (Party)	Vote (%)		Cand. Spent	Ind. Exp. Support	Ind. Exp. Oppose
2018 General	Gregory Meeks (D)............................	160,500	(99%)	$913,555		
2018 Primary	Gregory Meeks (D)............................	11,060	(82%)			
	Carl Achille (D).......................................	1,288	(10%)			
	Mizan Choudhury (D)............................	1,200	(9%)			

Prior winning percentages: 2016 (85%), 2014 (80%), 2012 (75%), 2010 (76%), 2008 (67%), 2006 (70%), 2004 (70%), 2002 (65%), 2000 (69%)

Democrat Gregory Meeks, first elected in 1998, is a liberal who is more sympathetic to business than are other New York City Democrats — sometimes to the unhappiness of organized labor. In part, that reflects the commercial interests of his international district. As the senior African American in the delegation, Meeks wields growing influence with his committee assignments.

Meeks grew up in public housing projects in Harlem. He was inspired by his mother, who went back to school when her four children were older and who encouraged volunteerism. After graduating from Adelphi College and Howard University law school, Meeks moved to Far Rockaway. He became an assistant district attorney and a workers' compensation judge. He was elected to the state Assembly in 1992 and became an ally of Democratic Rep. Floyd Flake, a minister whose Allen African Methodist Episcopal Church congregation grew from 1,400 members in 1976 to more than 20,000 members.

When Flake resigned, Meeks won a majority of Democratic committee members at an endorsement meeting and thus became the party's nominee in a special election. Democratic state Sen. Alton Waldon and Assemblywoman Barbara Clark ran as independents. With the support of Flake and civil rights leaders, Meeks won 57 percent of the vote, to Waldon's 21 percent and Clark's 13 percent. Since then, he has not faced a serious challenge.

Meeks has a voting record toward the center of House Democrats. He has been active in the business-oriented New Democrat Coalition. On the Financial Services Committee, he has been an occasional ally of Wall Street interests. When the House in May 2018 took final action on the rollback of the Dodd-Frank financial-regulatory law, he said that he could not "in good conscience" vote for it, chiefly because it exempted many banks from some mortgage disclosure requirements. But he praised provisions in the bill that he sponsored, including benefits for minority-owned banks and credit unions, and encouragement of the use of alternative data in underwriting mortgages.

In 2019, as chairman of the Financial Services Subcommittee on Consumer Protections and Financial Institutions, he said that he hoped to encourage the notion that "the relationship between Wall Street and Main Street should not be as antagonistic." He called for more racial and ethnic diversity among board members of publicly traded companies. Meeks was among a group of moderate Democrats on the committee who were expected to push back against the more progressive views of committee chairwoman Rep. Maxine Waters of California and others — including the first-term Democrat from Queens, Rep. Alexandria Ocasio-Cortez, whom he recommended for the panel.

Meeks has backed numerous free-trade agreements. In 2015, he was one of the few outspoken Democratic supporters of President Barack Obama's Trans-Pacific Partnership. These agreements promised new opportunities for JFK airport and its many auxiliary businesses. He has joined African-American members in seeking to ensure that legislation addresses minorities' issues. He previously was ranking Democrat on the Foreign Affairs Subcommittee on Europe, Eurasia and Emerging Threats, where he has talked about the need for "working with allies" and contrasted the approach of President Donald Trump who, Meeks said, "has us stepping back from the world stage."

His financial ethics have become fodder for New York's major dailies in recent years. The Federal Election Commission in 2006 reprimanded Meeks for using more than $6,000 in 2004 campaign funds for a personal trainer and other expenses. In 2010, The New York Times wrote that despite acknowledging that he has no more than a few thousand dollars in his savings account, he "lives a life worthy of a jet-setter," staying in luxury hotels, driving a taxpayer-leased $1,000-a-month Lexus and buying a $1 million house built by a developer who was a campaign contributor. He told the newspaper that he observed all campaign finance laws. Meeks blamed the negative attention on conservative groups out to undermine Democrats.

A Queens immigration lawyer, Albert Baldeo, who was arrested for campaign finance fraud in a 2010 special-election bid to serve on the city council, told The New York Post he gave Meeks a break on rent for office space in a building he owned because he wanted the congressman to have a presence in his area. House rules prohibit members from receiving below-market rent. Meeks told the newspaper, "My office complied with the law and continues to do so." In 2015, Baldeo was sentenced to 18 months in prison for witness tampering.

The support by Meeks for the Trans-Pacific trade deal led some national unions to threaten a primary challenge in 2016. Democratic state Sen. James Sanders, an ally of organized labor, filed to challenge him but dropped out of the primary shortly before the deadline. He changed his mind, he said, so he could work with other Democrats to secure a majority in the state Senate. In both 2016 and 2018, Meeks won the Democratic primary with 82 percent of the vote in low-turnout contests. He ran unopposed in November 2018.

Meeks was selected without opposition in March 2019 to chair the Queens Democratic Party, replacing former Rep. Joe Crowley. The post gives Meeks an influential role in selecting local candidates, including judges.

NY-5: Southeast Queens, Western Nassau

Cook Partisan Voting Index: D+37

Population		Race and Ethnicity		Income	
Total	784,341	White	10.9%	Median Income	$66,094
Land area (sq. miles)	52	Black	47.2%	District Income Rank	126
Pop/ sq mi	15118.4	Latino	19.6%	Poverty Rate	12.4%
Born in State	49.7%	Asian	13.8%	With health insurance	90.3%
		Two or more races	3%	Cash public assistance	4.4%
Age Groups		Other	5.3%	Food stamp/SNAP	17.8%
Under 18	22.4%				
18-34	24.5%	**Education**		**Work**	
35-64	39.9%	H.S grad or less	48.1%	White Collar	13.2%
Over 64	13.2%	Some college	27.1%	Sales and Service	51%
		College Degree, 4 yr	16.3%	Blue Collar	19.9%
Military		Post grad	8.5%	Government	18.5%
Veteran/ Active Duty	3%				

2012 Pres. Vote	Obama	200,004	(90%)	Romney	22,026	(10%)
2016 Pres. Vote	Clinton	211,667	(85%)	Trump	31,322	(13%)

JFK Airport: A half-century ago, there was a small black community in southern Queens, near Jamaica Bay. Since then, many African-American families have bought houses and raised their families in neighborhoods that fan east from there. They fought to maintain the relatively spacious streets, relishing the plenitude of natural light, safe schools and good neighborhood stores. There is block upon block of low-rise, frame and brick houses, built mostly from the 1920s to the 1950s, in the neighborhoods of Springfield Gardens and Laurelton, St. Albans and Rosedale, Cambria Heights and Queens Village. This part of Queens today is home to New York City's largest concentration of middle-class black homeowners, with a median income higher than white households in Queens. Showing the community's economic strength, multiple developers have launched plans for new residential towers and retail space. Some of them are near the Jamaica rail terminal, which is about a 15-minute ride from JFK Airport. Also planned is an upgrade of the rail station, a busy hub for most trains on the Long Island Railroad. On Wareham Place, in the small upper middle class neighborhood of Jamaica Estates, is the Tudor home built by Fred Trump where Donald Trump lived from his birth until he was four years old.

The 5th Congressional District of New York contains all these southeast Queens neighborhoods, plus other less affluent sections of southern Queens. It is bounded on the north, more or less, by Grand Central Parkway. To the east, the Nassau County line has melted away as the unofficial boundary between black and white Long Island. The district now takes in some precincts in southwestern Nassau, with about 15 percent of the district voters: Inwood, Valley Stream and Elmont, which is the home of the Belmont Stakes, the third jewel in horse racing's annual Triple Crown. Belmont Park is the site of a planned new arena to house the New York Islanders hockey team. To the south, it includes Rockaway Peninsula, with never-completed vast swaths of government-financed housing that were planned by Robert Moses in the 1950s and 1960s. The beach and its boardwalk have reopened following $140 million in repairs and restoration that were required following the devastation in 2012 of Superstorm Sandy; the changes radically altered the landscape in what has been termed a "managed retreat" from the coast. With the start of ferry service to Manhattan, the area has become a more attractive commute. In the middle of all this is John F. Kennedy International Airport, the largest international gateway for air travelers entering the United States. The airport has generated 230,000 jobs in the area. Airlines have invested billions of dollars in upgrading terminals, some of which had sunk to third-world levels. In October 2018, New York Gov. Andrew Cuomo announced a $13 billion plan for the airport to further improve its transportation systems and create two large international terminals, including more gates, but no additional runway as some had hoped; airlines will provide much of the funding.

The 5th Congressional District is 47 percent African American, 20 percent Hispanic and 14 percent Asian. Richmond Hill and Ozone Park, just northwest of JFK, were previously white ethnic neighborhoods, but now have sizable numbers of Latinos and Asians. It has the highest median income of the Queens-based districts. Politically, it has been in the top 2 percent of the country's most-Democratic districts. The vote in 2016 for Hillary Clinton dropped to 85 percent. Perhaps some of Trump's former neighbors remained loyal to him.

Grace Meng (D)

Elected 2012, 4th term, b. Oct 01, 1975; Queens; University of Michigan, B.A., 1997; Yeshiva University Benjamin N. Cardozo School of Law (NY), J.D., 2002; Christian Church; Married (Wayne Kye); 2 children.

Elected Office: NY Assembly, 2009-2012.

Professional Career: Practicing attorney, 2003-2013.

DC Office: 2209 RHOB 20515, 202-225-2601, Fax: 202-225-1589, meng.house.gov

State Offices: Flushing, 718-358-6364; Forest Hills, 718-358-6364.

Committees: *Appropriations*: Commerce, Justice, Science & Related Agencies; Homeland Security; State, Foreign Operations & Related Programs. *Ethics*.

Group Ratings

	ADA	ACLU	AFL-CIO	LCV	ITI	COC	HAFA	ACU	CFG	FRC
2018	-	81%	-	100%	-	58%	6%	4%	17%	0%
2017	80%	C	97%	100%	C	42%	C	4%	5%	11%

Almanac Ratings 2017-18

	Economy	Social	Foreign	Composite
Liberal	98%	100%	95%	98%
Conservative	2%	0%	5%	3%

Key Votes of the 115th Congress

1. Obama-care revision	N	5. Family planning regs	N
2. Tax Cuts	N	6. Body cameras/immigration	Y
3. Omnibus appropriations	Y	7. Abortion ban	N
4. Dodd-Frank revision	N	8. Concealed carry	N

9. Guantanamo prisoners	Y
10. Ground missiles, limit	Y
11. Defense Dept. spending	N
12. FISA rules	N

Election Results

Election	Name (Party)	Vote (%)		Cand. Spent	Ind. Exp. Support	Ind. Exp. Oppose
2018 General	Grace Meng (D)................................	111,646	(90%)	$924,268		
	To Hillgardner (G)........................	11,209	(9%)			
2018 Primary	Grace Meng (D)................................		(100%)			

Prior winning percentages: 2016 (72%), 2014 (72%), 2012 (60%)

Democrat Grace Meng, elected to the House in 2012 as the first Asian American from New York, has made her mark in the Democratic Party and as a member of the House Appropriations Committee, where she has pursued an eclectic mix of interests.

Meng was born and raised in Queens. Her parents had left Taiwan in the early 1970s. After studying history at the University of Michigan, she got her law degree from Yeshiva University's Cardozo School of Law. She did pro bono work for Sanctuary for Families, and joined a law firm. She worked as a volunteer on several New York political campaigns, including Hillary Clinton's reelection to the Senate in 2006.

Her father, Jimmy Meng, served one term in the state Assembly and did not seek reelection following reports of legal problems in his campaign. After residency issues disqualified her in 2006, she then defeated his successor. During four years in Albany, Meng enacted a measure to eliminate the word "Oriental" from state documents referring to people of Asian descent. When she ran for the open seat, Meng received the backing of the Queens Democratic Party, several Asian-American advocacy groups and the powerful New York Hotel and Motel Trades Council. She won the Democratic primary against three other contenders, with 53 percent of the vote to 25 percent for runner-up Assemblyman Rory Lancman.

She had little trouble in the general election against Republican Daniel J. Halloran, a member of the New York City Council. The contest became raucous after Halloran accused Meng of running a campaign of "ethnocentrism" based on her roots, referred to her as a "Chinese national" and falsely accused her of having dual citizenship. She won, 68%-31%, and has not been seriously challenged since. Meng persevered through an embarrassing episode, when her father was arrested in 2014 and accused of soliciting $80,000 from a friend facing criminal charges, claiming he could bribe prosecutors. Jimmy Meng pleaded guilty to wire fraud and was sentenced to one month in prison.

Much of her work has reflected the international interests of her district. She filed a bill with Republican Rep. Tom Emmer of Minnesota to direct the State Department to speed up visa approvals for international physicians who are slated to work at U.S. hospitals. In 2015, Meng was the first House Democrat to oppose the Obama administration's nuclear agreement with Iran, which she described as "simply too dangerous for the American people." In 2016, she enacted a law modeled on her New York statute to remove from U.S. law "Oriental," a word that she called "insulting and outdated," and replace it with "Asian American."

On domestic issues, the House twice passed her bill to prohibit a practice known as "spoofing," which has been described as deliberately changing one's cell phone ID when texting another person — a practice used to steal money and personal information. She was a founder and co-chair of the Kids' Safety Caucus. She filed a bill to expand access to free or reduced-price feminine hygiene products, as part of health care legislation. Speaker Paul Ryan denied her request to use House office allowances to provide such products on Capitol Hill. "There have been so many times where I'm sitting around the table and I realize that I might be the only Asian-American, I might be the only woman of color at that table," she told City and State New York in May 2017.

She pursued those interests with her seat on Appropriations. She gained prominence during a hearing when she questioned Commerce Secretary Wilbur Ross about the use of citizenship questions in the 2020 census. Following his denial of such a plan, subsequent disclosures led Meng to accuse him of not responding truthfully. 'Hate being lied to!" she tweeted in October 2018. She followed up by demanding a Justice Department review of Ross' response, and filing a bill to prevent use of such questions.

After a temporary appointment in 2016 as a vice-chair of the Democratic National Committee, Meng won a full term in that position in 2017. She defended DNC Chairman Tom Perez when he made personnel changes, which she said were designed to improve "the culture and the ecosystem of the party nationally." Meng voiced interest in early 2019 in the vacancy to chair the Queens Democratic Party. The position went, instead, to Rep. Gregory Meeks.

NY-6: Central Queens   Cook Partisan Voting Index: D+16

Population		Race and Ethnicity		Income	
Total	742,207	White	34.7%	Median Income	$61,648
Land area (sq. miles)	30	Black	3.5%	District Income Rank	159
Pop/ sq mi	24923	Latino	19.4%	Poverty Rate	13.5%
Born in State	43%	Asian	39.7%	With health insurance	88.2%
		Two or more races	2%	Cash public assistance	2.5%
Age Groups		Other	0.7%	Food stamp/SNAP	10.1%
Under 18	18.8%				
18-34	22.5%	**Education**		**Work**	
35-64	42.1%	H.S grad or less	42%	White Collar	16.6%
Over 64	16.6%	Some college	22.1%	Sales and Service	46%
		College Degree, 4 yr	21.5%	Blue Collar	15.9%
Military		Post grad	14.2%	Government	13%
Veteran/ Active Duty	2.4%				

2012 Pres. Vote	Obama	125,495	(68%)	Romney	57,455	(31%)
2016 Pres. Vote	Clinton	134,970	(65%)	Trump	66,487	(32%)

Forest Hills, Flushing: More than a half-century ago, most of the neighborhoods in New York's outer boroughs were virtually all-white. Most of these areas had filled with descendants of the great mass of immigrants who came from eastern and southern Europe between 1890 and 1924 and from northern Europe earlier — Irish and Italians, Jews and Hungarians, Poles and Czechs and Greeks. A few parts of Queens were WASPy and high-income. Forest Hills in Queens, with its famous tennis stadium and large Tudor houses, was a notable example.

But the only thing permanent in New York is change. The 1960s saw pitched battles in city politics between John Lindsay, a liberal Manhattan Republican, and his mostly outer-borough opponents. During Lindsay's reign as mayor, middle-class New Yorkers fled the city's high taxes and crime-addled neighborhoods, while Forest Hills was the site of sometimes violent protests when Lindsay attempted to place low-income housing projects in the neighborhood. The result was a population decline; Queens had four congressional districts and large portions of two others at the end of the 1960s, while today it is barely entitled to three. Some of this neighborhood change would have happened anyway. Neighborhoods settled by immigrants in the 1920s were full of old people, and increasing numbers of African Americans were eager to move in.

In recent years, the overall picture in Queens has brightened. It has become the borough with the most residential growth in New York City. With the surge of new jobs across the city, Queens was set to pass Brooklyn in 2020 in the number of new housing projects, the Wall Street Journal reported in October 2018. The number of new residential units in Queens rose 243 percent in the first half of 2018, compared with a year earlier. Even with the increased supply, the growing demand has forced up rents and the cost of new housing. The 8 percent one-year increase for Queens rentals in July 2018 was the highest in the nation. Much of the growth was in areas with large numbers of recent immigrants

The 6th Congressional District is the only district that is entirely in Queens. It begins near the border of Nassau County, at Fresh Meadows, and runs west through Pomonok and the old rail suburbs of Kew Gardens and Forest Hills. It continues west to Rego Park, which has many 1950s high-rise apartments; Middle Village; Glendale; and part of Maspeth. Across Flushing Bay from LaGuardia Airport (which is in the 14th District), it takes in Flushing, long a modest-income white ethnic neighborhood and now about 70 percent Asian, with several Chinese dialects. The New World Mall in downtown Flushing is the largest indoor Asian mall on the East Coast. West of 138th Street, Queens is dominated by Taiwanese and ethnic Chinese from Malaysia, Vietnam and Thailand. Shops have an urban "Chinatown" feel and feature a wide variety of delicacies. (New York City has three Chinatowns — one each in Manhattan and Brooklyn, with the largest in Queens.) The area east of 138th Street is predominantly Korean. With more than 130 languages spoken in Queens, some call it the "Borough of Diversity."

The district has grown to 40 percent Asian American (the largest share for any district not in a Pacific Coast state), with 19 percent Latino and 4 percent black. While there are pockets of Republican voting, especially around Middle Village and Kew Gardens Hills, it is solidly Democratic. Hillary Clinton led Donald Trump, 65%-32%. That was her lowest vote in the 10 Democratic-held districts in New York City.

Nydia Velázquez (D)

Elected 1992, 14th term, b. Mar 28, 1953; Yabucoa, PR; University of Puerto Rico (Rio Piedras), B.A., 1974; New York University, M.A., 1976; Roman Catholic; Married (Paul Bader).

Elected Office: NY City Council, 1984-1986.

Professional Career: Faculty, University of PR, 1976-1981; Adjunct Professional, Hunter College, 1981-1983; Special Assistant, U.S. Rep. Edolphus Towns, 1983; Migration Director, PR Department of Labor & Human Resources, 1986-1989; Director, PR Department of Community Affairs in the U.S., 1989-1992.

DC Office: 2302 RHOB 20515, 202-225-2361, Fax: 202-226-0327, velazquez.house.gov

State Offices: Brooklyn, 718-599-3658; Brooklyn, 718-222-5819; New York, 212-619-2606.

Committees: *Financial Services*: Consumer Protection & Financial Institutions; Housing, Community Development & Insurance; Oversight & Investigations. *Natural Resources*: Water, Oceans & Wildlife.

Group Ratings

	ADA	ACLU	AFL-CIO	LCV	ITI	COC	HAFA	ACU	CFG	FRC
2018	-	96%	-	100%	-	50%	6%	4%	15%	0%
2017	100%	C	100%	100%	C	36%	C	4%	5%	0%

Almanac Ratings 2017-18

	Economy	Social	Foreign	Composite
Liberal	100%	97%	97%	98%
Conservative	0%	3%	3%	2%

Key Votes of the 115th Congress

1. Obama-care revision	N	5. Family planning regs	N	9. Guantanamo prisoners	Y
2. Tax Cuts	N	6. Body cameras/immigration	Y	10. Ground missiles, limit	Y
3. Omnibus appropriations	N	7. Abortion ban	N	11. Defense Dept. spending	N
4. Dodd-Frank revision	N	8. Concealed carry	N	12. FISA rules	N

Election Results

Election	Name (Party)	Vote (%)		Cand. Spent	Ind. Exp. Support	Ind. Exp. Oppose
2018 General	Nydia Velazquez (D)............................ 146,687	(93%)		$624,100		
2018 Primary	Nydia Velazquez (D)...	(100%)				

Prior winning percentages: 2016 (91%), 2014 (83%), 2012 (79%), 2010 (79%), 2008 (67%), 2006 (73%), 2004 (10%), 2002 (55%), 2000 (63%), 1998 (64%), 1996 (83%), 1994 (58%), 1992 (55%)

Nydia Velázquez, first elected in 1992 and the only Puerto Rican woman elected as a member of Congress, reclaimed the top post of the Small Business Committee -- one of three returning committee chairs when Democrats regained House control in 2019. Sometimes called La Luchadora — "The Fighter" -- she also is a senior member of the Financial Services Committee, which oversees companies with many employees who are her constituents. With the changes in her district, her constituents increasingly include entrepreneurs and managers, in addition to blue-collar workers.

She grew up in Puerto Rico as one of nine children of sugar-cane field workers. Although her father never finished elementary school, he was a political leader in her hometown of Yabucoa and inspired her to pursue politics as a career. She studied political science at the University of Puerto Rico and taught there in the 1970s. After graduate school in New York City, she went to work for local Democratic Rep. Edolphus Towns. In 1983, she became the first Hispanic woman elected to the New York City Council.

When the new district was created in 1992, Velázquez was a major contender in the Democratic primary. She had to overcome nine-term Rep. Stephen Solarz. Velázquez was endorsed by Mayor David Dinkins and civil rights leader Jesse Jackson. In a light turnout, she beat Solarz 34%-28%. She easily won in November.

Velázquez has a solidly liberal voting record, with occasional pro-business votes on economic issues. Velázquez has been a leading voice on issues related to Puerto Rico and the ongoing debate over changing the commonwealth's status. She favors a process that would allow the people of Puerto Rico to determine the status of the island, and has filed legislation authorizing a constitutional convention that would produce a recommendation that would then be subject to a referendum. The results would be submitted to Congress for approval. During the House debate in 2016 on debt relief for Puerto Rico, she was unhappy about the anti-union measures in the bill. "The reality is that Republicans are in control and we have no choice but to compromise," she said in a statement. Following the devastation left by Hurricane Maria after it tore through Puerto Rico in September 2017, Velazquez took the lead in demanding enhanced disaster assistance, including additional Medicaid funds — beyond what the Republican-controlled Congress would approve. When President Donald Trump low-balled the death-toll on the island, she sought an independent commission to determine the facts. Earlier, she said that his tweets that federal aid would be limited were "unpresidential" and "shameful."

As chairwoman of the Hispanic Caucus in 2009, Velázquez repeatedly pressed President Barack Obama to move comprehensive immigration reform higher on his agenda. When vehement GOP opposition made clear that such a battle was unwinnable, she worked to separate the DREAM Act, a bill providing a path to legal status for the children of illegal immigrants who attend college or serve in the military. The House approved that bill in late 2010, but Senate supporters could not reach the 60-vote threshold to overcome a filibuster. Later, the Senate passed comparable measures but they went nowhere in the Republican-controlled House.

Much of her legislative work has focused on the Small Business Committee. During the Bush administration, Velázquez joined with Republicans to reinstate an SBA loan program that had guaranteed lenders a 75 percent payback if a borrower defaulted on loans of up to $750,000. Velázquez initiated an annual scorecard to show whether the federal government had met its goal of granting 23 percent of contracts to small businesses. She charged that the SBA repeatedly fell short of its goal of granting more loans to women.

As the panel's chairwoman in 2009, Velázquez praised the Obama administration for requiring the nation's largest banks to report monthly on how much they lend to small businesses. She criticized an administration proposal to give $30 billion of the Troubled Asset Relief Program to community banks for small business, but without any conditions that the money actually be used for small business loans. "Taking $30 billion and simply handing it to banks — in the hopes that they will make loans — is not sound policy," she said. The administration dropped the idea of using TARP money. While in the House minority, she enacted a bill to improve the disaster-assistance programs of the SBA. In 2018, she worked with Republican Rep. Steve Chabot of Ohio to enact changes in small-business loans to raise lending caps and strengthen credit-risk management.

Back in control in 2019, Velázquez's priorities included expansion of SBA lending and contract-assistance programs plus oversight of President Donald Trump's immigration, trade and tax policies that she said "are harming small firms." She sought assurances that improvements in housing and schools would be part of legislation to expand public infrastructure.

A longtime combatant in New York City's political wars, Velázquez has rarely faced serious major-party opposition. In the 2016 primary, she faced a credible challenger: Yungman Lee, a banker in Chinatown, who raised $417,000, which was about half of Velázquez's total. Lee got half of the vote in Manhattan, though that borough cast only one-fourth of the total vote. Velázquez got 69 percent in vote-heavy Brooklyn and defeated Lee overall, 62%-27%. Following the 2018 election, she became an early mentor to Rep. Alexandria Ocasio-Cortez, the first-termer from Bronx who created anxiety in the New York delegation with talk of supporting challenges to other incumbents. The two had a "long, long conversation" about congressional dynamics, Velázquez told Politico in January 2019.

NY-7: Northern Brooklyn, Lower East Side of Manhattan

Cook Partisan Voting Index: D+38

Population		Race and Ethnicity		Income	
Total	750,580	White	30.1%	Median Income	$52,724
Land area (sq. miles)	16	Black	7.8%	District Income Rank	262
Pop/ sq mi	46446.8	Latino	41%	Poverty Rate	24.9%
Born in State	46.2%	Asian	18.7%	With health insurance	87.8%
		Two or more races	1.7%	Cash public assistance	4.7%
Age Groups		Other	0.7%	Food stamp/SNAP	26.4%
Under 18	22.9%				
18-34	29.9%	**Education**		**Work**	
35-64	36.5%	H.S grad or less	51.8%	White Collar	10.7%
Over 64	10.7%	Some college	16%	Sales and Service	45.1%
		College Degree, 4 yr	20%	Blue Collar	16.3%
Military		Post grad	12.2%	Government	9.2%
Veteran/ Active Duty	1.5%				

2012 Pres. Vote	Obama	156,860	(89%)	Romney	18,378	(10%)	
2016 Pres. Vote	Clinton	177,664	(86%)	Trump	21,198	(10%)	

Downtown Brooklyn: In 1957, amid a vast wave of Puerto Rican migration to New York, Leonard Bernstein wrote the music for West Side Story, which featured Romeo as an Italian American and Juliet as a Manhattan Puerto Rican. Before World War II, there were 60,000 Puerto Ricans in New York City. Three decades later, with cheap airfares and no need to go through passport control, there were 800,000. But as the city's industrial base grew stagnant, the number declined, and young

New Yorkers of Puerto Rican descent increasingly returned there or moved to Florida. By the late 1990s, New York City was experiencing a large influx of Latinos from places not under the U.S. flag. Even though New York still has the largest Puerto Rican population outside of that island, most arriving Hispanics in the city today come from the Dominican Republic, Colombia, Mexico, Panama and Peru.

The 7th Congressional District of New York was designed to stitch together many of these diverse people. About 75 percent of the district's population is in Brooklyn, with the remainder split between Queens and Manhattan. Each borough runs along the East River. Overall, the district is 41 percent Hispanic and 19 percent Asian (mostly Chinese). Of the Hispanics, one-third are Puerto Rican. Chinese, predominantly in Brooklyn, have joined Dominicans as the largest foreign-born groups in the city. But this is New York, so it takes in many other ethnicities as well.

In Brooklyn, the district hugs the upscale Brooklyn Heights waterfront, with its stunning views of Lower Manhattan, and nearby Carroll Gardens, with young professionals intermingled with Italian immigrants. Inland is Downtown Brooklyn, which has attracted a critical mass of business and residential development to become a "city that never sleeps" in its own right. To the south is Sunset Park, once the home of Irish, Polish and Norwegian immigrants, and now filled with Chinese, Puerto Ricans, Colombians and Ecuadorans; also here are comfortable neighborhoods with brownstones plus new workplaces for the formerly Manhattan-based garment industry. Industry City in Sunset Park (a 16-building site for tech start-ups) and the Domino Sugar project in Williamsburg (office buildings, parks and 2,800 apartments) were listed by the Business Insider website in July 2017 among the 11 mega-projects that were expected to transform the city in the next two decades.

North of Brooklyn Heights is DUMBO (Down Under the Manhattan Bridge Overpass), with artists in old industrial lofts that have become the most expensive real estate in Brooklyn. The old Brooklyn Navy Yard, which built ships more than two centuries ago and employed 70,000 during World War II but shut down in 1966, now houses a vibrant and rapidly growing industrial park, including new centers for tech companies and the largest movie and television production complex outside Hollywood. Williamsburg has recent Latino arrivals as well as the young and hip; many of its Orthodox Jews have been priced out of the area and moved to the exurbs of New York and New Jersey. Inland, the district takes in Bushwick, a former slum that became a beachhead in Brooklyn's urban renewal, and multi-ethnic Cypress Hills. In the Red Hook area in the southwest corner of Brooklyn, rapid gentrification has supplanted public housing. Planners have envisioned a 246-acre waterfront development with relocation of a longstanding container terminal and perhaps 45,000 residential units, which would be twice the size of Battery Park City in lower Manhattan.

In Manhattan, the 7th District includes parts of the Lower East Side, East Village and Chinatown. The neighborhood known as Little Italy has become a few blocks of restaurants surrounded by the expanded Chinatown and gentrified neighborhoods. The small salient in Queens includes Woodhaven. The 86 percent of the vote for Hillary Clinton in 2016 ranked it as the most Democratic in Brooklyn and Queens and in the top 2 percent of the most Democratic districts in the nation.

Hakeem Jeffries (D)

Elected 2012, 4th term, b. Aug 04, 1970; Brooklyn; State University of New York, Binghamton, B.A., 1992; Georgetown University (DC), M.P.P., 1994; New York University Law School, J.D., 1997; Baptist; Married (Kennisandra Jeffries); 2 children.

Elected Office: NY Assembly, 2007-2012.

Professional Career: Clerk, Judge Harold Baer, 1997-1998; Practicing attorney, 1999-2003; Counsel, Viacom, 2004-2005; Assistant General counsel, CBS Broadcasting, 2006.

DC Office: 2433 RHOB 20515, 202-225-5936, Fax: 202-225-1018, jeffries.house.gov

State Offices: Brooklyn, 718-373-0033; Brooklyn, 718-237-2211.

Committees: House Democratic Caucus Chairman. *Budget*. *Judiciary*: Courts, Intellectual Property & Internet; Crime, Terrorism & Homeland Security.

Group Ratings

	ADA	ACLU	AFL-CIO	LCV	ITI	COC	HAFA	ACU	CFG	FRC
2018	-	83%	-	91%	-	55%	8%	4%	18%	0%
2017	100%	C	100%	97%	C	46%	C	4%	5%	0%

Almanac Ratings 2017-18

	Economy	Social	Foreign	Composite
Liberal	96%	98%	97%	97%
Conservative	4%	2%	3%	3%

Key Votes of the 115th Congress

1. Obama-care revision	N	5. Family planning regs	N	9. Guantanamo prisoners	Y
2. Tax Cuts	N	6. Body cameras/immigration	Y	10. Ground missiles, limit	Y
3. Omnibus appropriations	Y	7. Abortion ban	N	11. Defense Dept. spending	N
4. Dodd-Frank revision	N	8. Concealed carry	N	12. FISA rules	N

Election Results

Election	Name (Party)	Vote (%)		Cand. Spent	Ind. Exp. Support	Ind. Exp. Oppose
2018 General	Hakeem Jeffries (D).........................	180,376	(94%)	$704,154		
	Ernest Johnson (C)............................	9,997	(5%)			
2018 Primary	Hakeem Jeffries (D)................................		(100%)			

Prior winning percentages: 2016 (93%), 2014 (81%), 2012 (78%)

Democrat Hakeem Jeffries, elected in 2012, has brought energy and a spirit of consensus-building to his office. In November 2018, he was elected chairman of the House Democratic Caucus, a major move up the leadership ladder, which positioned him for increased influence. Jeffries has been successful with bipartisan legislation at the Judiciary Committee. That has spurred rumblings of a possible primary challenge from more progressive Democrats.

Jeffries was born and raised in the Crown Heights neighborhood of Brooklyn and graduated from the State University at Binghamton. He pledged Kappa Alpha Psi, the predominantly African-American fraternity, where he received the nickname "Kool Ha," for his measured speech. He went to Georgetown University for a master's degree in public policy and later earned a law degree from New York University. He clerked for a federal judge, and worked for large corporate clients at Paul, Weiss, Rifkind, Wharton & Garrison, a law firm known for launching the careers of prominent New York Democrats.

After two unsuccessful campaigns against an entrenched incumbent in the state Assembly, Jeffries won an open seat in 2006. He worked on affordable housing issues and got a bill signed into law forcing the elimination of the New York City Police Department's "stop-and-frisk" database. He took on political reforms, including a proposal for an independent congressional redistricting process. When the House seat opened, Jeffries faced City Councilman Charles Barron in the Democratic primary. A former Black Panther, Barron had a history of making inflammatory statements critical of Israel and of Jews; local Democrats called him "a hate-monger" and "a bigot." Jeffries raised $1.4 million and won the primary in a rout, defeating Barron 72%-28%. That was tantamount to victory in the heavily Democratic district.

On the Judiciary Committee, Jeffries has focused much of his time on law-enforcement issues. In 2015, he helped to enact the Slain Officer Family Support Act, which he introduced with Republican Rep. Peter King of New York. The bill extended the tax deadline for charitable contributions to the families of two Brooklyn police officers who were killed in Bedford-Stuyvesant. Following protests against alleged police excesses in several cities, including Brooklyn, he filed a bill to bar the use of chokeholds, which he called a deprivation of civil rights. "It's not sufficient simply to ban a policy through departmental practice. We've got to elevate it, embed it in law, if we really and truly want to end it," he told CNN.

In 2017, Jeffries and Republican Rep. Doug Collins of Georgia took the lead in the House in enactment of the First Step Act, a bipartisan measure advocated by President Donald Trump that overhauled criminal justice procedures, including sentencing guidelines. The duo, who had collaborated on earlier issues, worked closely together at the Judiciary Committee and in public forums. "Our friendship is based on a respect that is deeper than legislation," Collins, who became the senior Republican on Judiciary in 2019, told Politico.

Jeffries appears to have staked his future as a House leader. In December 2016, he was selected as one of three co-chairs of the House Democratic Policy and Communications Committee. "Jeffries has quickly become a national voice for our party and our caucus," Democratic Leader Nancy Pelosi wrote. In February 2017, he said that he was not running for mayor. "The stakes are so high in Washington D.C. right now, and I want to be part of the effort to turn the situation around. It would be a dereliction of duty to abandon ship at the moment when times are tough," he said. At a Martin Luther King Day celebration in January 2019, Jeffries referred to Trump as "a hater in the White House ... the grand wizard," though he qualified that the president is not racist.

His selection as Democratic Caucus chairman resulted from a generational and demographic showdown with Rep. Barbara Lee of California, a more senior member of the Congressional Black Caucus and an ally of Pelosi. At age 48, Jeffries benefited as a younger voice joining a leadership team in which the top three Democrats were in their late-70s, though plenty of other rising Democratic stars have tired of waiting for the current team to step down. He offered a three-part appeal: a commitment that Democrats are "strongest when everyone is on the playing field," a plan to act aggressively on a bold legislative agenda that includes adequate communication to avoid "the type of mischaracterizations that took place when Barack Obama was president," and "the best defense is a good offense" against what he termed "the right-wing onslaught in this country." His 123-113 victory left some intra-party bruises, with Lee — who was supported by several former CBC leaders — claiming that she was the victim of ageism. A spokesman for first-term Rep. Alexandria Ocasio-Cortez of New York said that she was "disappointed" with the outcome; her allies reportedly considered a primary challenge to Jeffries.

Jeffries has been reelected three times without major party opposition.

NY-8: Brooklyn　　　　　　　　　　　　　　　Cook Partisan Voting Index: D+36

Population		Race and Ethnicity		Income	
Total	772,709	White	23.4%	Median Income	$49,556
Land area (sq. miles)	30	Black	51%	District Income Rank	318
Pop/ sq mi	26052.2	Latino	17.8%	Poverty Rate	22.5%
Born in State	52.6%	Asian	5.5%	With health insurance	91.8%
		Two or more races	1.6%	Cash public assistance	5.7%
Age Groups		Other	0.8%	Food stamp/SNAP	25.6%
Under 18	21.8%				
18-34	26.3%	**Education**		**Work**	
35-64	38%	H.S grad or less	45.7%	White Collar	13.9%
Over 64	13.9%	Some college	23.3%	Sales and Service	47%
		College Degree, 4 yr	19.3%	Blue Collar	15.2%
Military		Post grad	11.8%	Government	18%
Veteran/ Active Duty	2.6%				

2012 Pres. Vote	Obama	209,422	(89%)	Romney	23,861	(10%)
2016 Pres. Vote	Clinton	215,689	(84%)	Trump	34,356	(13%)

Bedford-Stuyvesant: African Americans began settling in Brooklyn's Bedford-Stuyvesant neighborhood in the 1930s, with the opening of the subway line that was celebrated in Duke Ellington and Billy Strayhorn's "Take the 'A' Train." After World War II, the pace accelerated, as crime and crowding in Harlem — as well as a large influx of African Americans from the South — drove black New Yorkers to the aging but solid brownstones of "Bed-Stuy." When job growth slowed, Bed-Stuy faced more than its share of poverty and crime. After a 1966 visit by New York's two senators, Democrat Robert F. Kennedy and Republican Jacob Javits, Bed-Stuy won a Model Cities designation, which brought the establishment of the Bedford-Stuyvesant Restoration Corporation, the first such community development organization in the United States.

Even as the black community expanded across Brooklyn, Bed-Stuy became almost as powerful a symbol of black New York as Harlem, thanks in part to the films of Spike Lee, a Brooklyn native, who hosts an annual block party. His Do the Right Thing, shot on Stuyvesant Avenue between Lexington Avenue and Quincy Street, succinctly captured the racial tensions then brewing in the old neighborhood. The neighborhood gave birth to rappers Jay-Z and Notorious B.I.G. With smart planning, the Bed-Stuy neighborhood's stately, Hopperesque architecture largely avoided the wrecking ball, and community vigilance kept the streets maintained. The revitalized residential area developed a Caribbean flavor that, combined with handsome brownstones and new shops and galleries, led to a wave of gentrification, with a population exceeding 150,000 and more than 1,900 businesses -- including the arrival in April 2018 of its first Starbucks. In 2018, a townhouse sold for $6 million in Bed-Stuy, which has had the largest increase in the sale of million-dollar homes of any neighborhood in the city. Owners of the nearby Barclays Center in 2018 began a $50 million renovation to convert the large Paramount Theater, a surviving Jazz Age movie house on Flatbush Avenue, into an entertainment and educational center. New York University launched its move into a $500 million science and engineering center in downtown Brooklyn. In December 2018, Gov. Andrew Cuomo updated the state's $1.4 billion "Vital Brooklyn" plan, including social improvements.

The 8th Congressional District of New York takes the shape of a sideways "U" as it rambles across Brooklyn. It begins in Fort Greene, a rising arts area, and from there runs east and south through Clinton Hill, Bed-Stuy and East New York. Less than 5 percent of the district is in Queens, taking in Lindenwood and Howard Beach, an Italian neighborhood that was the home of Mob boss John Gotti. The district runs along the Belt Parkway and the edge of Jamaica Bay through Spring Creek and Canarsie, which have become substantially black neighborhoods mainly due to Caribbean immigrants who prized the backyards and single-family homes.

The district continues through parts of heavily African-American Flatlands and the equally heavily white neighborhoods of Bergen Beach, Marine Park and Mill Basin. It includes the Coney Island peninsula, which was an island before the city filled in Coney Island Creek. Today, it is a diverse collection of neighborhoods and home to the famous theme park, site of the annual hot-dog eating contest and including an amphitheater for year-round entertainment. Brighton Beach, part of Coney Island, has more Russian Jewish immigrants than any other district in the nation. As part of its comeback from the devastation of Superstorm Sandy in 2012, developers have been building thousands of new apartments on Coney Island; their project includes steps to respond to the rising sea level. These factors have slightly reduced the minorities to 51 percent black and 18 percent Hispanic. Hillary Clinton, with 85 percent of the vote in 2016, showed that this remains one of the most Democratic districts in the nation.

Yvette Clarke (D)

Elected 2006, 7th term, b. Nov 21, 1964; Brooklyn; State University of New York - Medgar Evers College; Oberlin College (OH), 1986; African Methodist Episcopal; Single.

Elected Office: NY City Council, 2002-2007.

Professional Career: Childcare specialist, Erasmus Neighborhood Fed., 1987-1989; Legislative aide, Sen. Velmanette Montgomery, 1989-1991; Executive Assistant, NY Workers' Compensation Board, 1992-1993; Youth program Director, Hospital League/Local S.E.I. University 1199 Training & Upgrading Fund, 1993-1997; Business Development Director, Bronx Overall Development Corporation, 1997-2001.

DC Office: 2058 RHOB 20515, 202-225-6231, Fax: 202-226-0112, clarke.house.gov
State Offices: Brooklyn, 718-287-1142.

Committees: *Energy & Commerce*: Communications & Technology; Environment & Climate Change; Oversight & Investigations. *Homeland Security*: Border Security, Facilitation & Operations; Emergency Preparedness, Response & Recovery.

Group Ratings

	ADA	ACLU	AFL-CIO	LCV	ITI	COC	HAFA	ACU	CFG	FRC
2018	-	93%	-	100%	-	50%	6%	4%	15%	0%
2017	95%	C	100%	97%	C	50%	C	4%	5%	11%

Almanac Ratings 2017-18

	Economy	Social	Foreign	Composite
Liberal	96%	100%	97%	98%
Conservative	4%	0%	3%	2%

Key Votes of the 115th Congress

1. Obama-care revision	N	5. Family planning regs	N	9. Guantanamo prisoners	Y
2. Tax Cuts	N	6. Body cameras/immigration	Y	10. Ground missiles, limit	Y
3. Omnibus appropriations	N	7. Abortion ban	N	11. Defense Dept. spending	N
4. Dodd-Frank revision	N	8. Concealed carry	N	12. FISA rules	N

Election Results

Election	Name (Party)	Vote (%)		Cand. Spent	Ind. Exp. Support	Ind. Exp. Oppose
2018 General	Yvette Clarke (D)	181,455	(89%)	$862,607		
	Lutchi Gayot (R)	20,901	(10%)	$3,500		
2018 Primary	Yvette Clarke (D)	16,202	(53%)			
	Adem Bunkeddeko (D)	14,350	(47%)			

Prior winning percentages: 2016 (92%), 2014 (81%), 2012 (78%), 2010 (85%), 2008 (69%), 2006 (75%)

Democrat Yvette Clarke, elected in 2006, is a liberal who concentrates on immigration and other issues important to her diverse constituency. As vice chair of the influential Energy and Commerce Committee, she was positioned for activity on a wide range of issues. Clarke, who has been a leader of the Congressional Black Caucus, survived a close contest in the 2018 Democratic primary.

She was born in the Flatbush section of Brooklyn to immigrant parents from Jamaica. As a young girl, she tagged along to political meetings and events with her mother, Una Clarke, who in 1991 became the first Jamaican elected to the New York City Council. Yvette Clarke attended Oberlin College in Ohio but fell short of graduating by six credit hours. She returned to New York, helped train child care workers, worked as a state legislative aide and served as business development director for the Bronx Overall Economic Development Corporation. In 2001, when term limits forced her mother off the City Council, Clarke defeated four other candidates to succeed her in the predominantly Caribbean area of Flatbush and East Flatbush.

From its creation in 1968 until 2006, the congressional district had been represented by just two people, both Democrats — trailblazer Shirley Chisholm, the first black woman elected to Congress and a 1972 presidential candidate, and Major Owens, who succeeded her in 1982. Clarke's mother had run unsuccessfully against Owens, an African American, in the 2000 Democratic primary, a bitter contest that exposed divisions between the local Caribbean-American community and the African-American community.

In the 2006 primary for the open seat, after Owens retired, Clarke navigated a competitive primary field. New York City Councilman David Yassky, who is white, was called a "colonizer" for running in a majority-black district by Chris Owens, a health industry administrator and son of the retiring lawmaker. By the end of August, Yassky had raised more than $1.3 million, exceeding the other three candidates' combined fundraising. Clarke's status as the only woman in the contest and her support among Caribbean Americans were helpful. With the endorsement of the Service Employees International Union's powerful Local 1199, which turned out votes, Clarke defeated Yassky 31%-27%; Owens got 19 percent.

Clarke has had a staunchly liberal voting record. She joined some Black Caucus members who expressed frustration with what they considered President Barack Obama's lack of focus on helping minorities. "What we are asking for is that the president use his bully pulpit to look at a more far-reaching, deeper-penetrating jobs initiative. ... The level of unemployment in our communities is unacceptable," she told National Public Radio in 2010. In 2014, she was more aggressive than other Black Caucus members in calling for an investigation of reports that House Majority Whip Steve Scalise of Louisiana spoke to a white supremacist group. Notably, Scalise was defended by fellow Louisianan Cedric Richmond, who two years later defeated Clarke for the CBC chair. With Reps. Bonnie Coleman Watson of New Jersey and Robin Kelly of Illinois, Clarke in 2016 organized a Caucus on Black Women and Girls to bring "a balance in the dialogue about black Americans." She reportedly sought the CBC chairmanship again in 2018, when Karen Bass of California won.

One of Clarke's priorities has been immigration, specifically the DREAM Act providing in-state college tuition breaks and other benefits to children of illegal immigrants. In 2008, the House passed her bill to create an appeals process for individuals alleging denial of rights in homeland security investigations. In February 2017, she filed a bill to block President Donald Trump's executive actions that targeted sanctuary cities. "Without sanctuary in New York City, undocumented immigrants are forced to live with the fear that any contact with the government — even a call to the local police precinct to report a crime — could result in deportation," she said. With Rep. Hakeem Jeffries, also of Brooklyn, she sponsored legislation in 2018 to posthumously award a Congressional Gold Medal to Chisholm.

On Energy and Commerce, Clarke worked on legislation to urge the Federal Communications Commission to encourage small businesses to participate in spectrum auctions. In 2016, she complained about that the FCC didn't do enough to promote diversity in minority-focused programming. With her position as vice chair of the committee after Democrats regained House control, Clarke said, the 2018 election showed the public desire for "progress and advances in achieving a quality of life that surpasses that of prior generations."

For her first decade in the House, Clarke did not face a serious reelection challenge. That changed in the 2018 primary, when Adam Bunkeddeko — a 30-year-old native of Uganda and a Harvard Business School graduate with experience in community organizing — said that the district had reached "a new inflection point" and that Clarke had failed to enact a bill during her 11 years in Congress. Clarke responded that Bunkeddeko "recently moved to the community and has nothing to show for it." The challenger gained support in the white, gentrified parts of the district, according to news reports. A New York Times editorial endorsed Bunkeddeko for his "refreshing" big thinking and wrote that Clarke's major accomplishments were "regrettably far between." Clarke outspent the challenger, $1.1 million to $309,000, and won, 53%-47% -- a clear signal of future vulnerability.

NY-9: Brooklyn · Cook Partisan Voting Index: D+34

Population		Race and Ethnicity		Income	
Total	746,279	White	31.7%	Median Income	$53,047
Land area (sq. miles)	16	Black	47%	District Income Rank	251
Pop/ sq mi	48023.1	Latino	11.6%	Poverty Rate	18.6%
Born in State	47%	Asian	7.2%	With health insurance	90.6%
		Two or more races	2%	Cash public assistance	4.5%
Age Groups		Other	0.5%	Food stamp/SNAP	21.8%
Under 18	22.5%				
18-34	25.9%	**Education**		**Work**	
35-64	38%	H.S grad or less	41.2%	White Collar	13.6%
Over 64	13.6%	Some college	22%	Sales and Service	45.4%
		College Degree, 4 yr	21.2%	Blue Collar	13.1%
Military		Post grad	15.6%	Government	16.1%
Veteran/ Active Duty	1.9%				

2012 Pres. Vote	Obama	202,361	(85%)	Romney	33,045	(14%)
2016 Pres. Vote	Clinton	211,812	(83%)	Trump	36,600	(14%)

Flatbush, Crown Heights: Brooklyn. Just saying the word in a comedian's monologue used to elicit laughter. It evoked an accent of twisted English, a raucous, in-your-face style, a sense of humor with an edge, and the chip-on-the-shoulder assertiveness of those sure they will always be in second place. As its name testifies, Brooklyn was a separate community from the 17th century on, and in the 19th century, it was one of the largest cities in the country, with its own celebrities — Henry Ward Beecher, Walt Whitman, John Roebling. By 1898, when the five boroughs were welded into Greater New York, 1 million people lived in Brooklyn. In 1913, a transit agreement was struck to link the city's then-independent lines and triple the track to 619 miles. The agreement helped Brooklyn expand well beyond its established neighborhoods near the Brooklyn Bridge.

Suddenly, Manhattan factory workers no longer had to live in the crowded Lower East Side tenements that social reformer Jacob Riis had exposed in the 1890s. They moved in droves into neighborhoods of three- to five-story apartments and four-family houses. Brooklyn grew from 1.1 million in 1900 to 2.6 million in 1930. The old Brooklynites were mostly Protestant — Dutch, Yankee and German, plus some Catholic Irish. The new Brooklynites were heavily Italian and Jewish, and they populated the sports and entertainment businesses for a long generation, making their hometown nationally famous.

Around the time Jackie Robinson suited up for the Brooklyn Dodgers in 1947 as the first black player in Major League Baseball, Brooklyn was experiencing an influx of African Americans into Brownsville and Crown Heights near Ebbets Field. Just as rapid was the flight of ethnic whites, driven away by "blockbusting," in which unscrupulous real estate brokers stoked white fears, then bought homes cheaply and resold them for higher prices. In a different sort of white flight, "Dem Bums" left for Los Angeles in 1958 and Ebbets Field was knocked down and replaced by an apartment complex.

Today, Kings County, which is coterminous with Brooklyn, is New York's largest county, the nation's eighth largest -- ranked between Miami-Dade and Dallas. With a growing population that was back to 2.6 million in 2017, there has been great vitality among upwardly mobile Hispanic, Asian, Caribbean and Russian immigrants, among middle-class blacks, and among new generations of Italians and Jews. In many areas, the demands for jobs and businesses have exceeded local supply. In 2016, Brooklyn had the least affordable housing of any county in the nation. Lower-income groups found themselves priced out. A year later, its population declined by 2,100, less than one-tenth of 1 percent, the only one of the 10 largest counties with a decline.

The 9th District of New York, the only district that is entirely in Kings County, begins southeast of downtown Brooklyn. At the far northwestern tip is the Barclays Center, a large arena that is home to basketball's Brooklyn Nets; the New York Islanders hockey franchise, after moving in 2015 from Nassau County to Barclays, made plans for a new arena at Belmont Park. Deeper into the district are some of Brooklyn's jewels: the Grand Army Plaza, the Parisian-style Eastern Parkway (the world's first six-lane parkway), the Brooklyn Public Library, the Brooklyn Museum and the Brooklyn Botanic Garden, with its Japanese landscaping and placid duck ponds.

Park Slope, on Prospect Park's west side, has become affluent, filling up with young professionals who welcome the easy commute to Manhattan. On the east side of Prospect Park is Crown Heights, with its mix of modest apartment buildings and nicely restored row houses. Prospect Park South is an upscale neighborhood whose stately late Victorian-era mansions contrast sharply with the vibrant street life nearby in Flatbush's Little Haiti. At the southern end of the district are Midwood, Homecrest and Sheepshead Bay, mostly white communities with substantial Jewish populations. Most of these neighborhoods have great diversity. The district's gentrifying population has dipped to 47 percent black, with12 percent Hispanic. Politically, the 9th is overwhelmingly Democratic, though it ranked barely behind three other Brooklyn and Queens-based districts — the 5th, 7th and 8th— in support for Hillary Clinton in 2016.

Jerrold Nadler (D)

Elected 1992, 14th term, b. Jun 13, 1947; Brooklyn; Columbia University (NY), Bach. Deg., 1969; Fordham University School of Law (NY), J.D., 1978; Jewish; Married (Joyce L. Miller); 1 child.

Elected Office: NY Assembly, 1977-1992.

Professional Career: Legislative Assistant, NY Assembly, 1972; Law clerk, 1976.

DC Office: 2132 RHOB 20515, 202-225-5635, Fax: 202-225-6923, nadler.house.gov

State Offices: Brooklyn, 718-373-3198; New York, 212-367-7350.

Committees: *Judiciary (Chmn).*

Group Ratings

	ADA	ACLU	AFL-CIO	LCV	ITI	COC	HAFA	ACU	CFG	FRC
2018	-	86%	-	100%	-	58%	8%	4%	12%	0%
2017	100%	C	97%	100%	C	29%	C	7%	5%	0%

Key Votes of the 115th Congress

1. Obama-care revision	N	5. Family planning regs	N	9. Guantanamo prisoners	Y
2. Tax Cuts	N	6. Body cameras/immigration	Y	10. Ground missiles, limit	Y
3. Omnibus appropriations	Y	7. Abortion ban	N	11. Defense Dept. spending	N
4. Dodd-Frank revision	N	8. Concealed carry	N	12. FISA rules	N

Election Results

Election	Name (Party)	Vote (%)		Cand. Spent	Ind. Exp. Support	Ind. Exp. Oppose
2018 General	Jerrold Nadler (D)...............................	173,095	(82%)	$1,341,340		
	Naomi Levin (R)...............................	37,619	(18%)	$71,365		
2018 Primary	Jerrold Nadler (D)...............................	(100%)				

Prior winning percentages: 2016 (78%), 2014 (79%), 2012 (70%), 2010 (76%), 2008 (63%), 2006 (74%), 2004 (64%), 2002 (55%), 2000 (64%), 1998 (71%), 1996 (66%), 1994 (67%), 1992 (60%)

Democrat Jerrold Nadler, first elected in 1992, is chairman of the House Judiciary Committee, a crucial position during the presidency of Donald Trump. An adversary since the 1980s in conflicts over real estate development on the West Side of Manhattan and a strong civil libertarian, Nadler initially took a deliberate approach to review of legal issues surrounding the president and a possible congressional response. He faced a difficult challenge in managing the tensions among House Democrats on policy options as well as the politics of responding to Trump. He grew familiar with the public spotlight in representing the district that was the chief target of terrorists in September 2001 and in helping to manage the daunting cleanup that resulted.

Nadler was born in Brooklyn and moved around with his family as a child. His parents bought a chicken farm in New Jersey, but the business failed, and they moved back to the city. His father ran a gas station on Long Island and owned an auto parts store. Interested in politics from a young age, Nadler campaigned for Democrat Eugene McCarthy for president in 1968 while at Columbia University, where he roomed with Dick Morris, who would later become a top adviser to President Bill Clinton.

After getting his law degree from Fordham University, Nadler ran for the New York Assembly in 1976, at age 29. In the primary, he beat Ruth Messinger, the Democratic nominee for mayor in 1997, by 73 votes. In 1992, he suddenly had the opportunity to run for Congress. Representative Ted Weiss, long an Upper West Side icon, died the day before the September primary, which he won posthumously. The nomination was decided by a convention of almost 1,000 county Democratic committee members. Nadler won 62 percent of the votes to secure the nomination and thus the election.

Nadler's leftward leanings are evident in his fondness for the New Deal. He told a New York audience in 2012 that President Franklin Roosevelt's economic program "put into practice regulations on corporations and banks to prevent economic catastrophes — regulations that worked until they were dismantled, starting in the 1980s." He said Republicans have been misguided in cutting social programs and in letting large corporations pay little or no taxes. After Superstorm Sandy ravaged New York and other states in October 2012, he said the Federal Emergency Management Agency under President Barack Obama was ill-equipped to handle large urban disasters and that New York City needed higher seawalls and waterproofed electric power facilities.

With Ground Zero from the 9/11 attacks as part of his district, Nadler has had a continuing focus on the consequences and the cleanup. In late 2010, he helped steer into law a long-delayed post-September 11 measure providing more than $4 billion in compensation to first responders suffering health problems — a development he called "without a doubt the proudest moment of my 34-year career in government." In 2015, he was the original sponsor of the bill that Congress enacted to assure lifetime health benefits for 9/11 survivors. "I am proud of my country today for fulfilling our commitment to never leaving the wounded on the battlefield," he said. That legislation was named for James Zadroga, a city police officer who died in 2006 from toxins at the site.

As the longtime liberal pillar on the Judiciary Committee, Nadler has been a counterweight to lawmakers of both parties seeking expanded police powers to crack down on terrorism. Nadler insists that he is not unsympathetic to their cause. But he has worked to protect detainees' habeas corpus rights. When the House voted in 2012 to extend a warrantless wiretapping program, he bemoaned how much power it gave to presidents. A vigorous opponent of the USA Patriot Act, the Bush administration's centerpiece anti-terrorism law, he was a leader of the bipartisan coalition that crossed ideological lines to narrow the law's scope and limit the collection of bulk data by the National Security Administration. The renamed USA Freedom Act, which the House enacted in 2015, was "the first significant reform of government surveillance carried out by the federal government since 1978," he said.

On domestic issues, he led the fight in the House against proposals to ban same-sex marriage and has blasted the National Rifle Association's resistance to gun control legislation. He called suggestions for putting armed guards in schools "ludicrous and insulting." Another issue on which he has worked with Republicans has been the protection of creative performers — many of whom are his constituents — with a proposal to require that radio stations pay royalties to the record companies that own copyrights to records that are played over the airwaves.

Nadler took over the top Democratic post on Judiciary in December 2017 when Rep. John Conyers of Michigan — first elected in 1964, and the panel's top Democrat for more than two decades — resigned under pressure following reports of sexual harassment of congressional aides. Nadler, who was next senior on the committee, was challenged by Zoe Lofgren of California, a longtime ally of Nancy Pelosi, who cited her work at the committee on the impeachments of Richard Nixon (when she was a staffer) and Bill Clinton, plus her expertise on immigration and the need for more women to lead House committees. Nadler contended that his expertise in constitutional law made him "the best person to sit in that chair." He won, 118-72.

While in the minority at Judiciary, Nadler said that a Democratic-run committee would review charges that were raised against Supreme Court Justice Brett Kavanaugh during his Senate confirmation hearings in September 2018. "It is not something we are eager to do," he told The New York Times. "But the Senate having failed to do its proper constitutionally mandated job of advise and consent, we are going to have to do something to provide a check and balance." He said that he wanted to investigate the increased reports of hate crimes directed against minority groups.

As he prepared to chair the Judiciary Committee, Nadler made clear that the panel would vigorously pursue various allegations. "There is plenty for the Judiciary Committee to look into right now," he told CNN in January 2019. (Early in 2017, he had filed a "resolution of inquiry," which would have required the Justice Department to provide to the House documents related to Trump's finances; the committee rejected his resolution in a series of party-line votes.) He said the panel would end its investigation of the FBI that Republicans had initiated. He pledged communication — and occasional cooperation -- with GOP committee members. "There need not be surprises here," he said.

Nadler has been an activist on district-related issues at the Transportation and Infrastructure Committee. He has fought to add rail service east of the Hudson and to subsidize Amtrak. His biggest idea has been a rail-freight tunnel under the Hudson. Lack of such a line has meant that New York gets only a tiny share of its freight by rail; a new tunnel could mean cheaper freight and therefore lower prices. Nadler has been a strong proponent of high-speed passenger rail and the Moynihan rail terminal at Penn Station. In the 1990s, he successfully fought developer Donald Trump's attempts to alter the West Side Highway to accommodate his proposed luxury housing project in rail yards. Trump in turn called Nadler a "hack." Since then, their mutual hostility—including tweets—has deepened.

On foreign policy, Nadler opposed the Iraq war resolution in 2002. Regarding Afghanistan, he said in 2010, "An intelligent policy is not to try to remake a country that nobody since Genghis Khan has managed to conquer." In 2015, he supported Obama's nuclear agreement with Iran, a difficult vote for many of his Jewish constituents. "My conclusion is that this deal — of the available alternatives to us, not what might or should have been — is the best," he told the Times.

Nadler faced unusual competition for reelection in 2016, which he easily survived. In the primary, Oliver Rosenberg, a 30-year-old former investment banker, called his vote for the Iran nuclear deal "disastrous." Rosenberg, who self-financed $367,000, said that Nadler was out of touch with younger voters. The outcome suggested otherwise. Nadler won the primary with 89 percent. The general election was a reprise of sorts. Republican Philip Rosenthal said that Nadler's Iran vote was "an existential threat" to both Israel and to New York City. A lawyer with a business in data analytics, Rosenthal raised only $74,000. Nadler, who raised $1.6 million for the campaign, won 78%-22%, including 57 percent in Brooklyn. In 2018, Nadler got 82 percent against Republican Naomi Levin, a pro-Trump political newcomer, who spent $79,000.

The question that hovered over Nadler was whether he would become the third chairman of the Judiciary Committee in the past half-century to conduct an impeachment inquiry of a president. On that, Nadler showed abundant caution—telling reporters and others that the question dealt not only with the specifics of Trump's offenses but with the political context of whether a large cross-section of the public would support that option and its consequences. "Just because it's an impeachable offense does not mean he should be impeached. It's a different judgment," he told The New Yorker in February 2018. "To initiate impeachment, we would have to be convinced…that those impeachable offenses are so serious that the constitutional order is threatened if he's not impeached and removed from office." In May, after the Justice Department rejected the demand by Judiciary Committee Democrats for access to the to the complete report of special counsel Robert Mueller's investigation of Russian interference in the 2016 election, Nadler led the committee's party-line vote to hold in contempt Attorney General William Barr. In June, the House voted to authorize the committee to seek court action to enforce its subpoena of the documents.

NY-10: Lower Manhattan, Southern Brooklyn   Cook Partisan Voting Index: D+26

Population		Race and Ethnicity		Income	
Total	740,752	White	62.7%	Median Income	$87,826
Land area (sq. miles)	14	Black	3.6%	District Income Rank	32
Pop/ sq mi	51982.6	Latino	12.6%	Poverty Rate	16.7%
Born in State	44.2%	Asian	18.6%	With health insurance	93.8%
		Two or more races	2%	Cash public assistance	2.2%
Age Groups		Other	0.5%	Food stamp/SNAP	12%
Under 18	19.6%				
18-34	28.3%	**Education**		**Work**	
35-64	37.6%	H.S grad or less	26.9%	White Collar	14.5%
Over 64	14.5%	Some college	12.7%	Sales and Service	32.4%
		College Degree, 4 yr	30.5%	Blue Collar	8%
Military		Post grad	29.9%	Government	7.4%
Veteran/ Active Duty	2.2%				

2012 Pres. Vote	Obama	173,487	(74%)	Romney	58,970	(25%)
2016 Pres. Vote	Clinton	205,114	(78%)	Trump	49,179	(19%)

West Side, Borough Park: Over the course of the 20th century, New York City spread so far beyond its original boundaries in Lower Manhattan that, for a while, it became easy to forget how pivotal the southern end of the island had been in making the city what it is today. That changed in an instant on the morning of Sept. 11, 2001, when al-Qaida terrorists flew two hijacked jets into the twin towers of the World Trade Center, killing nearly 3,000 people and laying waste to 13 city blocks. The terrorists struck the tallest buildings in the nation's biggest city, toppling a complex whose name embodied American capitalism. The city, nation and world were forever altered.

Lower Manhattan has long been home to Wall Street and the Financial District. Over the years, it has represented America's striving spirit in other ways as well. The Brooklyn Bridge, begun in 1869 just a few blocks east of the Twin Towers site and completed in 1883, was half again as long as any bridge then standing and seven times higher than any building in the adjoining boroughs. The Holland Tunnel, built in 1927, was the first underwater vehicular tunnel built anywhere in the world. Just offshore are Ellis Island, now split between New York and New Jersey, where members of the great immigration wave first set foot on American soil, and the Statue of Liberty, the symbol of freedom they saw as they sailed in.

Infrastructure remains a local preoccupation. Repairs of the Brooklyn Bridge began in 2010, with costs that have escalated at least 60 percent to more than $800 million, with additional repairs required as the result of damage caused by Superstorm Sandy in 2012 plus the need to reinforce its foundations. The Port Authority Bus Terminal on the West Side, originally opened in 1950 and generously described as decrepit, has generated plans for billions of dollars of renovation and expansion to accommodate greatly increased demand. The Hudson Yards, a web of rail tracks on 34th Street near the Hudson River, has become the platform for a massive real-estate development that a growing new neighborhood of skyscrapers, on a scale that has been compared to the building of Rockefeller Center in the 1930s. At the World Trade Center site, a new skyscraper that opened in 2018 was the third since the September 11 attacks; one more tower is expected, plus a new performing arts center. Other major tenants have moved in. In the West Village, Google in 2018 purchased two prime sites for a total of $3.4 billion, which will give the tech giant a local workforce of more than 14,000.

From the Battery, at the southern tip of Manhattan, the 10th Congressional District of New York runs north up the island's west side, covering the Financial District and many neighborhoods. Battery Park City has attractive, modern apartments and parks — with what reportedly are the most expensive rents in the nation. Sophisticated TriBeCa has artists' lofts and an annual film festival that has spurred economic and cultural revitalization. Art galleries have thrived in Chelsea, and SoHo has become an international shoppers' paradise. Greenwich Village, home of New York University, has long had a taste for the radical, though some of its ideas have become mainstream: Led by Jane Jacobs, its successful fight against the proposed Lower Manhattan Expressway popularized historic preservation and urbanism. A leading antagonist at the time was the local builder, Donald Trump. Clinton is the economically diverse incarnation of the old slum known as Hell's Kitchen. In Midtown, the district boundary is mostly along Eighth Avenue. At 57th Street, it cuts east to Fifth Avenue and includes most of Central Park, then continues north along Amsterdam Avenue as it excludes Harlem. The Upper West Side is home to Lincoln Center, while the northern end of the district at 122nd Street takes in Morningside Heights, site of Columbia University. This strip of Manhattan has gained renown among transportation planners for the Gateway Project with New Jersey -- proposed rail tunnels under the Hudson River that are needed to expedite commerce in the Northeast and to replace antiquated portals, at a cost exceeding $10 billion.

The venerable apartment buildings along Central Park West, West End Avenue and Riverside Drive, and the brownstones on the cross streets, house some of the country's most dedicated liberals. These professional people were satirized on Seinfeld, the long-running sitcom that resonated far beyond Manhattan. In the 1950s, West Siders took up the reform banner and finally killed off the ancient and ailing Tammany Hall Democratic machine.

The slice of the 10th District in Brooklyn, which includes fewer than 20 percent of the voters, includes a very different set of neighborhoods. Borough Park has one of the nation's largest Orthodox Jewish communities, with Yiddish-language ATMs and Russian bathhouses. Jews have a long history in the city. After World War I, as many as 400,000 disembarked each year at Ellis Island until a 1924 law virtually shut down immigration. Today, New York has the largest Jewish population of any city other than Tel Aviv. The Russians, many of whom live close to poverty, are anti-socialist. The Hasidic Jews of Borough Park are conservative and hostile to racial preferences, and they favor tough police treatment of crime; Trump got two-thirds of their votes Even with these conservative enclaves, the district remains at the cultural and financial heart of national liberalism. Hillary Clinton got 77 percent of its vote in 2016.

Max Rose (D)

Elected 2018, 1st term, b. Nov 28, 1986; Brooklyn; Wesleyan University (CT), B.A., 2008; London School of Economics (England), M.S., 2009; Jewish; Married (Leigh Byrne).

Military Career: U.S. Army 2012-2014; U.S. Army National Guard 2013-pres. (Afghanistan, WIA)

Professional Career: Special Assistant to Ken Thompson and Director of Public Engagement, Brooklyn District Attorney's Office; Chief of Staff, Brightpoint Health.

DC Office: 1529 LHOB 20515, 202-225-3371, maxrose.house.gov

State Offices: Staten Island, 718-667-3313.

Committees: *Homeland Security*: Emergency Preparedness, Response & Recovery; Intelligence & Counterterrorism (Chmn). *Veterans' Affairs*: Health; Oversight & Investigations.

Election Results

Election	Name (Party)	Vote (%)	Cand. Spent	Ind. Exp. Support	Ind. Exp. Oppose
2018 General	Max Rose (D)... 101,823	(53%)	$4,153,751	$299,432	
	Daniel Donovan (R).......................... 89,441	(47%)	$2,666,932		
2018 Primary	Max Rose (D)..................................... 11,539	(63%)			
	Michael DeVito Jr. (D)........................... 3,642	(20%)			
	Omar Vaid (D)............................. 1,589	(9%)			

Freshman Democrat Max Rose was the surprise winner of what had been the only Republican-held district in New York City. In his first political campaign, he ran on his experience as an Afghanistan war veteran and in social-service positions at home. He defeated GOP Rep. Daniel Donovan, whose chief concern at the start of 2018 was a primary challenge from former Rep. Michael Grimm, who had given up the seat after pleading guilty to tax fraud. After defeating Grimm's attempted return, Donovan seemed in good shape in a district that President Donald Trump won in 2016 and where he had many personal connections. Instead, Rose struck a chord in running against political insiders.

A native of Brooklyn, Rose graduated from Wesleyan University and got a master's degree in philosophy and public policy from the London School of Economics. After enlisting in the Army, he was an infantry officer in Afghanistan, where an improvised explosive device struck his vehicle and caused extensive injuries.

After leaving active military service, Rose became director of public engagement for the district attorney in Brooklyn, working with ex-offenders. He later served as chief of staff for Brightpoint Health, which operated medical clinics in New York.

With his proudly independent constituency, Rose cautiously balanced his neutrality on Trump with opposition to local and national Democratic leaders. "I've seen how broken our government and politics have become," he said, in launching his campaign. "The real division is between the American people and the political class," including Donovan, he later told Politico. Rose easily won the primary with 63 percent of the vote against five other candidates.

The Republican primary between Donovan and Grimm was far more contentious. The contest pitted the incumbent -- the former district attorney on Staten Island, who secured Trump's endorsement — against his predecessor, who had been charged with lying to federal investigators about hiring undocumented immigrants at his restaurant. After Grimm pleaded guilty in 2015 and served prison time, Donovan easily won a special election to succeed him, plus a full term in 2016.

Grimm embraced Trump — despite the president's endorsement of Donovan — and sought to rally conservatives behind his attempted comeback with his contention that law enforcement officials had unfairly prosecuted him. Donovan contrasted his own lengthy record to Grimm's problematic history. Spending more than twice as much in campaign funds, Donovan defeated Grimm, 63%-37%.

In the general election, Donovan continued to run on his record and initially ignored Rose. The challenger caught the attention of the political community when he revealed in early October that his campaign had raised $1.5 million during the past three months and had far more cash on hand than did Donovan. Rose styled himself as "an independent-minded veteran ... with a focus on local, non-ideological issues," City & State New York reported. Asserting that he would get the job done, Rose criticized office-holders in both parties and complained about traffic and subway delays.

Donovan reminded voters of his independence in voting against House Republican-passed tax cuts and repeal of the Affordable Care Act. He dismissed Rose as "a carpetbagger" and a Brooklyn-based candidate.

Voters were impressed with the political outsider. In his 53%-47% victory, Rose not surprisingly took 60% of the vote in Brooklyn, which cast one-fourth of the total vote. Unexpectedly, he also led — though narrowly — in the Staten Island vote. Since 1980, Michael McMahon in 2008 had been the only Democrat to win the Staten Island district; after one term, he lost reelection to Grimm. With his post-election interest in a 2020 challenge, Grimm fed speculation that he had encouraged the defeat of Donovan. Other Republicans expressed interest, too. In the House, Rose charted a centrist course as an activist freshman.

NY-11: New York City   Cook Partisan Voting Index: R+3

Population		Race and Ethnicity		Income	
Total	733,750	White	60.7%	Median Income	$69,192
Land area (sq. miles)	66	Black	6.9%	District Income Rank	98
Pop/ sq mi	11146.1	Latino	16.8%	Poverty Rate	14%
Born in State	62.7%	Asian	13.6%	With health insurance	93.2%
		Two or more races	1.7%	Cash public assistance	3.7%
Age Groups		Other	0.4%	Food stamp/SNAP	14.3%
Under 18	22%				
18-34	22.4%	**Education**		**Work**	
35-64	40.1%	H.S grad or less	42.8%	White Collar	15.5%
Over 64	15.5%	Some college	23.1%	Sales and Service	42.5%
		College Degree, 4 yr	20.5%	Blue Collar	16.8%
Military		Post grad	13.7%	Government	18.5%
Veteran/ Active Duty	4.1%				

2012 Pres. Vote	Obama	110,088	(52%)	Romney	100,811	(47%)
2016 Pres. Vote	Trump	133,232	(53%)	Clinton	108,807	(44%)

Staten Island, South Brooklyn: Staten Island is part of New York City, yet is a land apart, closer geographically and culturally to New Jersey than to the city's other boroughs. Its inclusion in Greater New York as part of the great 1898 consolidation was something of an afterthought. It was connected to the rest of the city only by ferry or through Bayonne New Jersey, until the Verrazano-Narrows Bridge — one of Robert Moses' last and most impressive infrastructure achievements — opened to traffic in 1964. Hilly Staten Island (or Richmond County) is the state's southernmost county, one-tenth as densely populated as Manhattan. That's after it grew 27 percent between 1990 and 2017, one of the largest increases in New York state. Its rate of home ownership, 70 percent, is double that of New York City as a whole.

Ethnically, Staten Island has the highest percentage of residents of Italian ancestry in the nation. The signs on coffee shops read Caffe and on delicatessens, Salumeria. The Staten Island Ferry docks at St. George. The north and south shores that spread out from there are notable for their pleasant Victorian homes, while the island's west shore is industrial marshland, where the 2,200-acre Freshkills park — three times as large as Central Park and on top of the former landfill that collected more than 50 years of the city's trash — has begun to take shape, with varieties of plant and animal life, though the formal opening is projected for 2036. Staten Island's interior consists of scrubland that has become blocks of suburbia for New Yorkers who like a small-town ambience. In St. George, Empire Outlets, a $350 million shopping and entertainment complex with extensive waterfront and the first outlet mall in New York City, was scheduled to open in the spring of 2019. Population growth, plus limited public transit, has brought significant traffic congestion to the island, which depends on cars more than the other boroughs. Construction of a $613 million seawall and 20-foot levy on the eastern shore of the island that were designed to limit or delay a repeat of the devastating floods in 2012 from Superstorm Sandy has been redesigned and delayed until 2022.

Culturally, Staten Islanders are more conservative than people from the other boroughs, particularly those from Manhattan, which is an 18-minute ferry ride away. Fed up with the city's high income taxes and social programs, Staten Island residents voted in 1993 for secession, but the legislature never carried out their wish. In that same election, Staten Islanders provided the margin of victory for Republican Mayor Rudy Giuliani. The Giuliani years contributed a new ferry terminal, additional shops, and hundreds of new houses near cleaned-up beaches. Recent years have featured some demographic shifts. The northern shore of Staten Island has gained African-American and Asian population centers on the corners of the island, with a large Hispanic community in between and the traditional Italian neighborhoods on the southern side.

The 11th Congressional District of New York is made up of Staten Island plus neighborhoods in the southwest corner of Brooklyn. These include heavily Catholic and Italian Bay Ridge, Dyker Heights and part of Bensonhurst, middle-class enclaves with large single-family brownstones that are nowhere near a subway stop and largely impervious to the gentrification spreading across Brooklyn. John Travolta danced to fame in the film Saturday Night Fever on the streets of Bensonhurst and

Bay Ridge. Staten Island overall remains New York's whitest borough, with the fewest immigrants. It was 19 percent Hispanic, 12 percent black and 10 percent Asian in 2017. As a whole, the district is 17 percent Hispanic, 14 percent Asian and 7 percent black. Not surprisingly, Donald Trump won this district, 53%-44%. In the county itself, Trump won 56 percent of the 177,000 votes. Staten Island was twice the size of the next largest county in the state that Trump won: Niagara, in the northwest corner.

Carolyn Maloney (D)

Elected 1992, 14th term, b. Feb 19, 1946; Greensboro, NC; University Dijon, Paris (France); New School for Social Research (NY); Greensboro College (NC), Bach. Deg., 1968; Presbyterian; Widow (Clifton Maloney); 2 children.

Elected Office: NY City Council, 1982-1992.

Professional Career: Community affairs Coordinator, Board of Ed. Welfare ed. program, 1972-1975; Staff, Board of Ed. cntr. for career & occupational ed., 1975-1976; Sr. program analyst, NY Assembly committee, 1977-1979; Legislative aide, NY Assembly & NY Senate, 1979-1982.

DC Office: 2308 RHOB 20515, 202-225-7944, Fax: 202-225-4709, maloney.house.gov

State Offices: Astoria, 718-932-1804; Brooklyn, 718-349-5972; New York, 212-860-0606.

Committees: *Financial Services*: Housing, Community Development & Insurance; Investor Protection, Entrepreneurship & Capital Markets (Chmn). *Oversight & Reform*: Subcommittee on Civil Rights & Civil Liberties. *Joint Economic (VChmn)*.

Group Ratings

	ADA	ACLU	AFL-CIO	LCV	ITI	COC	HAFA	ACU	CFG	FRC
2018	-	89%	-	97%	-	50%	8%	4%	15%	0%
2017	95%	C	95%	97%	C	33%	C	8%	5%	0%

Almanac Ratings 2017-18

	Economy	Social	Foreign	Composite
Liberal	98%	95%	87%	93%
Conservative	2%	5%	14%	7%

Key Votes of the 115th Congress

1. Obama-care revision	N	5. Family planning regs	N	9. Guantanamo prisoners	Y
2. Tax Cuts	N	6. Body cameras/immigration	Y	10. Ground missiles, limit	Y
3. Omnibus appropriations	N	7. Abortion ban	N	11. Defense Dept. spending	Y
4. Dodd-Frank revision	N	8. Concealed carry	N	12. FISA rules	N

Election Results

Election	Name (Party)	Vote (%)		Cand. Spent	Ind. Exp. Support	Ind. Exp. Oppose
2018 General	Carolyn Maloney (D)...........................	217,430	(86%)	$2,302,285		
	Eliot Rabin (R)...................................	30,446	(12%)	$31,067		
2018 Primary	Carolyn Maloney (D)...........................	26,742	(60%)			
	Suraj Patel (D)...................................	18,098	(40%)			

Prior winning percentages: 2016 (83%), 2014 (77%), 2012 (72%), 2010 (71%), 2008 (66%), 2006 (76%), 2004 (81%), 2002 (61%), 2000 (60%), 1998 (66%), 1996 (61%), 1994 (59%), 1992 (42%)

Democrat Carolyn Maloney, first elected in 1992, is known for her forceful efforts on behalf of women and consumers and has been a prolific legislator on Capitol Hill. Her seniority has positioned her for influence on two prime House committees, including Financial Services, where she chairs a key subcommittee and is more willing than many other Democratic lawmakers to listen to bankers — many of whom are her constituents -- but not necessarily to support their interests.

Born and educated in North Carolina, she visited New York at the age of 22, loved it, and "just stayed." She taught adult-education classes in East Harlem and, from 1977 to 1982, was an influential legislative staffer in Albany. She was elected to the New York City Council in 1982. Redistricting in 1992 made the Silk Stocking district more Democratic, and Maloney ran against incumbent Bill Green, an independent Republican who shared Manhattan's cultural liberalism. But he was poorly positioned to appeal to voters in the working-class outer-borough neighborhoods that had been added to the district. Maloney lost the Manhattan part of the district 50%-44% but carried Queens heavily, winning 50%-48% overall.

Maloney has a mostly liberal voting record. On the Financial Services Committee, she had a hand in crafting the Dodd-Frank Wall Street overhaul in 2010, working with Democratic Sen. Richard Durbin of Illinois to achieve a compromise on interchange fees charged on consumers' debit cards. The fees had been an area of contention between merchants worried about their high rates and the financial industry's worries that lower fees would not cover their costs. In 2009, she enacted her bill to promote more transparent practices by credit card companies and to restrict lending practices. Even though she has many constituents in banking, Maloney had tough rhetoric for bankers who took millions of dollars in bonuses after their firms received federal bailout money in 2008. But she opposed in early 2010 a proposed .25 percent tax on stock transactions above $100,000.

She opposed Republican-led efforts to weaken the law and she criticized as lax the Trump administration's enforcement of Dodd-Frank. "We have essentially taken the cop off the beat," she said during an April 2018 hearing. In 2019, Maloney was selected to chair the restructured Investor Protection, Entrepreneurship and Capital Markets Subcommittee at Financial Services, where she is the next-senior Democrat behind Chairwoman Maxine Waters of California.

A leader of the Women's Caucus, Maloney drew national attention in 2012 for walking out of an Oversight and Government Reform Committee hearing on contraception and religious liberty after pointing out its all-male witness list. "What I want to know is, where are the women?" she asked. She also blasted GOP efforts to bar funding for Planned Parenthood. When conservatives that year removed expanded protections for lesbians and Native Americans in a reauthorization of the Violence Against Women Act, Maloney called it "as chilling and callous as anything I have seen come before this Congress in modern times." The House passed her 2008 bill to give eight weeks of paid leave to federal employees for the birth or adoption of a child. In 2017, she reached out to first daughter Ivanka Trump to seek common ground on paid-leave legislation.

With part of her district in Lower Manhattan and close to Ground Zero, Maloney has been heavily involved in the government response to the September 11 attacks. She was outspoken in urging President George W. Bush to quickly send New York the $20 billion that Congress approved for cleanup and recovery. In 2010, she and several other New York members steered into law a long-delayed measure to compensate September 11 first responders with health problems. In 2015, she took the lead in extending those benefits to cover the entire life of survivors.

Maloney made a bid for the top Democratic slot on Oversight and Government Reform after Democrats lost the House majority in 2010. She lost to the less senior Elijah Cummings of Maryland, 119-61, in the Democratic Caucus. Cummings reportedly had the pivotal backing of Minority Leader Nancy Pelosi. In 2019, she became vice chair of the Joint Economic Committee, where the gavel rotates every two years between the House and the Senate.

Maloney was bitterly disappointed when Democratic Gov. David Paterson appointed the less-seasoned Rep. Kirsten Gillibrand to the Senate seat vacated by Hillary Clinton in 2009. Maloney publicly questioned Gillibrand's stances on issues such as gun control and curbing illegal immigration, and she began raising money for a primary challenge in 2010. Gillibrand quickly moved left in the Senate, and in August 2009 Maloney reluctantly heeded the calls of President Barack Obama and senior New York Democrats to give her a clear path to the nomination.

In 2018, Maloney faced an unusually competitive primary challenge from Suraj Patel, a hotel executive and former Obama campaign aide who appealed to Millennials seeking change and said that Maloney had been ineffective. With sizable fundraising from contributors of Indian descent, Patel spent more than $1 million. Maloney won, 60%-40%, chiefly by taking nearly two-thirds of the vote in the Manhattan portion of the district; the candidates were nearly even in Queens and Patel led in Brooklyn, which had the smallest turnout. The vote in the primary was more than double the total from 2016.

NY-12: New York City   **Cook Partisan Voting Index: D+31**

Population		Race and Ethnicity		Income	
Total	732,140	White	64.7%	Median Income	$100,828
Land area (sq. miles)	15	Black	4.4%	District Income Rank	12
Pop/ sq mi	49502.4	Latino	14%	Poverty Rate	11%
Born in State	41.9%	Asian	13.8%	With health insurance	94.1%
		Two or more races	2.4%	Cash public assistance	1.6%
Age Groups		Other	0.6%	Food stamp/SNAP	6.1%
Under 18	11.7%				
18-34	36.1%	**Education**		**Work**	
35-64	37%	H.S grad or less	15.9%	White Collar	15.2%
Over 64	15.2%	Some college	12.2%	Sales and Service	28.7%
		College Degree, 4 yr	39.2%	Blue Collar	4.5%
Military		Post grad	32.8%	Government	7.1%
Veteran/ Active Duty	2.4%				

2012 Pres. Vote	Obama	205,662	(77%)	Romney	57,489	(22%)
2016 Pres. Vote	Clinton	255,601	(82%)	Trump	41,384	(13%)

Manhattan's East Side, Queens Astoria: The Upper East Side of Manhattan is home to people with more accumulated wealth than anywhere else in the world. Its western border was established at Fifth Avenue in 1857, when work began on Central Park; originally a swampy, rocky slum, it was completed in 1873. During the 1880s, the avenues — Fifth, Madison, Park, Lexington, Third, Second, First — were paved, and rich New Yorkers as well as many who had made their money elsewhere, built mansions on Fifth Avenue. With its elevated train line, Third Avenue was lined with walk-ups for working-class commuters. The side streets off Fifth Avenue were filled with massive brownstones shielded from the industrial haze along the East River.

The Upper East Side began taking on its present character in 1913, when Grand Central Terminal opened and the New York Central rail line was buried under Park Avenue. What had been a filthy railroad cut became a broad boulevard lined with grand apartment buildings. The federal income tax, passed the same year, had the unintended consequence of encouraging New York's rich to dispense with grand mansions and live, quietly and out of sight, in apartment buildings where doormen protected their privacy. Although New York has been transformed by gleaming postmodern skyscrapers, its most enduring landmarks are products of the first half of the 20th century: the Flatiron Building, built in 1902; Grand Central, in 1913; the Chrysler Building, in the 1920s; and the Empire State Building and Rockefeller Center, in the 1930s. The United Nations headquarters, the world's first glass-fronted skyscraper, went up after World War II. The Upper East Side remains a world apart from ordinary folks. The neighborhood is overwhelmingly white and expensive.

The 12th Congressional District of New York includes the Upper East Side. It begins at East 96th Street, the historic dividing line between Manhattan's wealthiest and poorest neighborhoods, and runs south through Murray Hill and Gramercy Park all the way to Houston Street, with a few salients protruding further south. It takes in Alphabet City, with its unique lettered avenue names, almost all of the East Village, with its pricey lofts and busy nightlife, and much of the Lower East Side. The district's cultural landmarks are among the world's finest: the Museum of Modern Art, the Guggenheim, the Whitney Museum of American Art, and the Frick Collection. Midtown Manhattan's skyscrapers are also here, along with Times Square and the Theatre District. Roosevelt Island, once dubbed Welfare Island and home to massive hospital and prison complexes, was renamed and transformed in the 1970s into an ethnically diverse residential neighborhood. Cornell University has opened on that island a 12-acre "tech campus," in affiliation with the Technion-Israel Institute of Technology and with a $100 million gift from former Mayor Michael Bloomberg's philanthropies. Nearly 80 percent of the district resides in Manhattan.

Across the East River in Queens, the 12th encompasses Long Island City and vibrant, historically Greek Astoria, now with many Asians, Latinos and Arabs. Some politicians and neighbors in and close to Long Island City caused a furor when they objected to the November 2018 announcement by Amazon to establish one of its two new office centers in their locale, despite the approval of Gov. Andrew Cuomo and Mayor Bill deBlasio. (The other site was set for Arlington Virginia.) Their continuing objections to the government incentives to Amazon and the impact on local lifestyle, plus grassroots threats to slow the requisite approval by various agencies led Amazon to reverse its decision, which had been expected to directly create 25,000 jobs. Even without Amazon, nearby areas have been booming — with new housing (both luxury and low-income) plus gentrification. Still in the early planning stage is a project to turn the 180-acre Sunnyside Yard — a huge rail hub — into a residential and office complex, which would dwarf the massive Hudson Yards project on the Lower West Side of Manhattan. In the northwest corner of Brooklyn, another 10 percent of the district takes in parts of trendy Williamsburg, gritty East Williamsburg, and working-class yet gentrifying Greenpoint — the site of a large new community.

The district historically has been dominated by its affluent and highly educated voters, leaders in securities, publishing, advertising, entertainment, broadcasting and communications. Historically, they mistrusted the city's usually Democratic immigrant masses. But as the Republican Party increasingly took on cultural conservatism and its Southern accents, the attitude of the Manhattan elite shifted from "silk stocking" liberal Republican to leftish Democratic.

In recent years, a new local address has consumed the business and political worlds: Trump Tower, on Fifth Avenue, two blocks south of Central Park. Trump purchased the property in 1979 and created what his publicists describe as the first super-luxury high-rise property in New York to include high-end retail shops, office space and residential condominiums. Once he gained political prominence, its location in the heart of one of the world's busiest and most expensive shopping areas created a costly and disruptive security nightmare. Government security officials took offices in the building, and paid high rent to the landlord -- their new boss -- though his local visits became rare. This district, one of the wealthiest in the nation, gave 82 percent of its vote in 2016 to Hillary Clinton. Trump likely did not expect a thumbs-up from these neighbors.

Adriano Espaillat (D)

Elected 2016, 2nd term, b. Sep 27, 1954; Santiago, Dominican Republic; New York University and Rutgers University Leadership for Urban Executives Institute; University of New York Queens College (NY), B.S., 1978; Roman Catholic; Married (Marthera Madera Espaillat); 2 children.

Elected Office: NY Assembly, 1996-2010; NY Senate, 2010-2016.

Professional Career: Coordinator, New York City Criminal Justice Agency, 1980-1988; Director, Washington Heights Victim Services Community Office, 1992-1994; Director, Project Right Start, 1994-1996.

DC Office: 1630 LHOB 20515, 202-225-4365, Fax: 202-226-9731, espaillat.house.gov

State Offices: Bronx, 718-450-8241; New York, 212-663-3900.

Committees: *Foreign Affairs*: Oversight & Investigations; Western Hemisphere, Civilian Security, & Trade. *Small Business*: Economic Growth, Tax & Capital Access. *Transportation & Infrastructure*: Highways & Transit; Water Resources & Environment.

Group Ratings

	ADA	ACLU	AFL-CIO	LCV	ITI	COC	HAFA	ACU	CFG	FRC
2018	-	89%	-	100%	-	50%	9%	4%	18%	0%
2017	95%	C	100%	97%	C	36%	C	4%	5%	0%

Almanac Ratings 2017-18

	Economy	Social	Foreign	Composite
Liberal	99%	100%	97%	99%
Conservative	1%	0%	3%	1%

Key Votes of the 115th Congress

1. Obama-care revision	N	5. Family planning regs	N	9. Guantanamo prisoners	Y
2. Tax Cuts	N	6. Body cameras/immigration	Y	10. Ground missiles, limit	Y
3. Omnibus appropriations	N	7. Abortion ban	N	11. Defense Dept. spending	N
4. Dodd-Frank revision	N	8. Concealed carry	N	12. FISA rules	N

Election Results

Election	Name (Party)	Vote (%)	Cand. Spent	Ind. Exp. Support	Ind. Exp. Oppose
2018 General	Adriano Espaillat (D)...................... 180,035	(95%)	$315,059		
	Jineea Butler (R)........................... 10,268	(5%)	$5,581		
2018 Primary	Adriano Espaillat (D)............................	(100%)			

Prior winning percentages: 2016 (89%)

Adriano Espaillat, after narrowly losing two primary challenges to the incumbent, took the open seat in 2016. Espaillat's Dominican background marked the gentrification of Harlem and the shift of what had been a legendary African-American district to a Hispanic majority. He became an outspoken critic of President Donald Trump, sometimes taking dramatic steps to call attention to his policies.

Espaillat was born in Santiago in the Dominican Republic. He arrived in the United States with his mother and sister at the age of nine and overstayed his visa. He described himself as the first undocumented immigrant elected to Congress, though he had become a citizen in his late 20s. He graduated from Bishop Dubois High School, a Roman Catholic school in Harlem, and got his bachelor's from Queens College. He took graduate courses in public administration at New York University and Rutgers University. He got involved in legal services, as a courts coordinator for the New York City Criminal Justice Agency and later as a certified resolution mediator for the Washington Heights Inwood Conflict Resolutions and Medication Center. In Washington Heights, he was the director of Project Right Start, a national initiative designed to combat substance abuse by educating parents.

In 1996, Espaillat successfully challenged a 16-year Assemblyman in the Democratic primary and became the first Dominican American elected to a state legislature. He chaired the New York State Black, Puerto Rican, Hispanic and Asian Legislative Caucus. After 14 years, he was elected to an open seat in the state Senate. In 2012, and again in 2014, he challenged Democratic Rep. Charlie Rangel in bitter affairs, reflecting the changes in the minority community and the ethical problems that Rangel had experienced in his later years, which resulted in his censure by the House and forced him to step aside in 2010 as chairman of the tax-writing Ways and Means Committee. Espaillat argued that Rangel had overstayed his welcome in Congress after more than 40 years, but Rangel's surrogates maintained that his seniority and experience were valuable to the district.

In 2012, Rangel outspent Espaillat by 5-to-1 and won by 1,086 votes, 44.5%-42%. In 2014, Espaillat had become more familiar to voters and was more competitive financially, spending $716,000 for the campaign to $1.5 million for Rangel. But the outcome was little changed. In the four-candidate primary, Rangel 48%-43%. When Rangel retired in 2016, he endorsed influential state Assemblyman Keith Wright, his longtime protégé. The large number of serious African-American contenders in the June primary benefited Espaillat. With nine Democratic candidates, Espaillat won 36 percent of the vote to 34 percent for Wright. Wright led by 159 votes in Manhattan, but Espaillat got nearly half the vote in the Bronx. His victory in November was a formality. In 2018, he was reelected without a Democratic primary.

Espaillat became an assertive advocate on immigration and a harsh critic of President Donald Trump. In September 2017, he was arrested outside of Trump Tower in New York with two other House Democrats urging action on behalf of undocumented immigrants. In June 2018, Espaillat joined another small group of members who shouted at Trump as he walked past them while he was at the Capitol for a meeting. House Democratic Whip Steny Hoyer said that their action was "not appropriate." In November 2017, he was among six House Democrats who filed impeachment resolutions against Trump, accusing him of obstruction of justice.

In 2019, Espaillat got a seat on the Transportation and Infrastructure Committee and said that he will work with others on legislation "that will tackle the numerous transportation challenges our communities face on a daily basis." He is the whip for the Hispanic Caucus and chairs its task force for transportation, infrastructure and housing.

NY-13: Manhattan's Upper West Side　　　Cook Partisan Voting Index: D+43

Population		Race and Ethnicity		Income	
Total	782,402	White	13.8%	Median Income	$39,490
Land area (sq. miles)	10	Black	24.6%	District Income Rank	418
Pop/ sq mi	76331.9	Latino	54.7%	Poverty Rate	28.3%
Born in State	46.3%	Asian	4.5%	With health insurance	89%
		Two or more races	1.7%	Cash public assistance	5.5%
Age Groups		Other	0.5%	Food stamp/SNAP	31.8%
Under 18	20.6%				
18-34	30.3%	Education		Work	
35-64	37.1%	H.S grad or less	48.9%	White Collar	12%
Over 64	12%	Some college	20.6%	Sales and Service	51.5%
		College Degree, 4 yr	18.1%	Blue Collar	13.9%
Military		Post grad	12.3%	Government	12.3%
Veteran/ Active Duty	2.1%				

2012 Pres. Vote	Obama	219,319	(95%)	Romney	10,558	(5%)
2016 Pres. Vote	Clinton	232,925	(92%)	Trump	13,727	(5%)

Harlem, Washington Heights: Harlem, for many years America's most famous black ghetto, has turned from grim times to major social evolution. In the late 19th century, Harlem was a commuter neighborhood, first for Germans and then for Jews and Italians. After the turn of the century, real estate speculators began constructing blocks of impressive brownstones, hoping to capitalize on the impending arrival of the subway. Overbuilding led to high vacancy rates. Some landlords agreed to rent to African Americans, as long as they were willing to pay a premium. After generations of being shunted from one neighborhood to the next as the city developed, black residents were willing, and the neighborhood soon turned into the locus of New York City's African-American community. Many great Americans — W.E.B. DuBois, Thurgood Marshall, Ralph Ellison, Joe Louis — lived in Harlem's Sugar Hill.

The rosters of the Apollo Theater on 125th Street in the 1920s and 1930s were filled with the names of great artists. Then, the WPA Guide described Harlem as "the spiritual capital of Black America." Starting with a riot in the summer of 1964, Harlem endured deterioration. Hundreds of brownstones were abandoned or pulled down. As successful black families moved out, Harlem's population shifted increasingly toward welfare dependency and criminal gangs. Its population declined by a third between 1970 and 1990. In the 1990s, Harlem began to recover. The federal government provided $300 million in investment capital, and the huge drop in crime under Mayor Rudy Giuliani made Harlem real estate valuable again. Brownstones were renovated, vacant city buildings sold off, neighborhood schools upgraded and arts spaces opened. Harlem became an enterprise zone, with favorable federal and state tax treatment. Younger African Americans returned. The façade of the Apollo Theater was restored, a new Harlem pier constructed, supermarkets and chain stores opened. In 2001, former President Bill Clinton opened his post-presidential office at 55 West 125th Street in Harlem.

Politically, Harlem has been heavily Democratic since the 1930s, when blacks switched from the Republican Party of Abraham Lincoln to the Democratic Party of Franklin Roosevelt. Harlem got its own congressional district in 1944 and elected Adam Clayton Powell Jr., minister at the Abyssinian Baptist Church and a brilliant orator. He was instrumental as chairman of the Education and Labor Committee when it crafted many of the Great Society programs, but lost his power when the House refused to seat him because of ethical issues.

Today, the 13th Congressional District of New York includes not just Harlem but all of Upper Manhattan, south to 122nd Street on the far west side and lower into Manhattan along both sides of the northern part of Central Park. On the west side, the district includes portions of the liberal Upper West Side. On the east side, it's East Harlem, once known as Spanish Harlem. This area had been Italian and was Fiorello LaGuardia's political base, before it became Puerto Rican. Today, it is dominated by Mexicans and Dominicans and gentrifying whites, some of whom like the close-in location but have had conflicts with local preservationists and residents who want to keep their low rents and worry about "whitewashing." Some investors have received tax breaks as an incentive to develop these areas. At the northern tip of Manhattan, the district takes in Washington Heights and Inwood, both heavily Latino, with lower incomes and more affordable housing; nearly half their population of about 220,000 are immigrants, with two-thirds Dominican. In 2018, a report by the Citizens Committee for the Children found that economic conditions had improved in these areas, but continued to trail African-American neighborhoods elsewhere in the city. Increased housing costs have forced some Dominicans out of the neighborhood. Across the Harlem River in the Bronx, the district includes Marble Hill and heavily Hispanic Kingsbridge. Those neighborhoods in the Bronx are about 20 percent of the district.

Overall, the district is 55 percent Hispanic and 25 percent African American, figures that testify to ongoing decades of black flight from Harlem and the continuing inflow of immigrants from the Western Hemisphere. These changes have altered the identity of Harlem and the 13th. For now, this remains overwhelmingly Democratic territory. Hillary Clinton had her second-best showing in the nation in the district in 2016 when she got 92 percent of the vote. It trailed only the adjacent 15th District in New York.

Alexandria Ocasio-Cortez (D)

Elected 2018, 1st term, b. Oct 13, 1989; Bronx; Boston University (MA), B.A., 2011; Catholic; Single.

Professional Career: Educational Director, National Hispanic Institute; Founder, Brook Avenue Press.

DC Office: 229 CHOB 20515, 202-225-3965, ocasio-cortez.house.gov

State Offices: Jackson Heights, 718-662-5970.

Committees: *Financial Services*: Consumer Protection & Financial Institutions; Investor Protection, Entrepreneurship & Capital Markets. *Oversight & Reform*: Subcommittee on Civil Rights & Civil Liberties; Subcommittee on Environment.

Election Results

Election	Name (Party)	Vote (%)		Cand. Spent	Ind. Exp. Support	Ind. Exp. Oppose
2018 General	Alexandria Ocasio-Cortez (D)..............	110,318	(78%)	$1,707,910		$633,303
	Anthony Pappas (R).........................	19,202	(14%)			
2018 Primary	Alexandria Ocasio-Cortez (D)..............	16,898	(57%)			
	Joseph Crowley (D).............................	12,880	(43%)			

Freshman Alexandria Ocasio-Cortez became a sensation for national Democrats after she unexpectedly defeated 10-term Rep. Joseph Crowley in the primary. The virtually unknown 28-year-old challenger first drew attention as the giant-killer who defeated the longtime party boss in New York City and ambitious chairman of the House Democratic Caucus, who had been widely viewed as a leader of the upcoming generation of House Democrats.

Her media spotlight, which can glow brightly in New York, intensified as she described her humble background and her bold ambitions for the Democrats' future. Although that agenda had its limitations in parts of Middle America, Ocasio-Cortez enhanced her cachet by forming alliances with other relatively young Democratic women — especially racial minorities — who emerged during the 2018 campaign.

Born in the Bronx — her mother was born in Puerto Rico and her father was a Bronx native — Ocasio-Cortez grew up in in Westchester County. While attending Boston University, where she got a bachelor's degree, she pursued her interest in income inequality and worked on immigration issues for Sen. Edward Kennedy. Returning to the Bronx, she worked in Manhattan as a bartender and as a waitress in a taco stand. She created a small publishing firm, with books for children about urban life, and she taught Hispanic students. In 2016, she was a local organizer for the presidential campaign of Sen. Bernie Sanders.

Running against Crowley, who had not faced a Democratic challenge since 2004, Ocasio-Cortez gained attention with a two-minute video that began, "Women like me aren't supposed to run for office." A member of the Democratic Socialists of America, she gained support from Sanders alumni and national progressive groups. In her diverse district, she launched her campaign "with the mission of bringing together a broad coalition of groups and communities to listen to their needs and give everyone an open and transparent seat at the table."

Crowley, longtime chairman of the Queens Democratic Party, initially relied on his party organization and did not take the challenger seriously until days before the primary. He sent a surrogate to their only scheduled debate. His campaign routinely gained the endorsement of prominent state and local Democratic officials, and spent $3.6 million (much of it for direct mail) to a bit more than $500,000 for Ocasio-Cortez. Even with his belated moves, The New York Times headlined after the outcome, "Crowley never saw defeat coming." (Nor did the Times.)

In a district that Ocasio-Cortez said had been marred by "generations of backroom dealing" — Crowley gained his seat after his predecessor quit following the filing deadline and party bosses selected him as the successor — voter turnout typically had been low, to the benefit of the insiders. In this primary, the challenger had the momentum in the scant turnout of just short of 30,000. In Crowley's base of Queens, which cast more than two-third of the vote, Ocasio-Cortez took 59 percent. With her 53 percent of the vote in the Bronx, her overall victory was, 57%-43%. Post-election vote analysis showed that she ran well in gentrifying neighborhoods. Crowley became a Washington-based lobbyist.

National and local news media—which had largely ignored the primary prior to the vote—showed a surge of interest in Ocasio-Cortez's success. At events in New York and in several House primary contests across the nation, where she had limited success, she described her platform as "a nation of dignified health care, tuition-free higher education, quality employment, and justice for all." Her policies included "Medicare for all," abolition of the Immigration and Customs Enforcement agency and the shutdown of private prisons.

As the youngest woman ever elected to Congress, Ocasio-Cortez embraced the national attention, including social media. She generated support for her far-reaching "Green New Deal," which was more aspirational than a legislative proposal. Her maverick style and occasional struggle with details created tensions with other Democrats—including Speaker Nancy Pelosi, who downplayed the impact of the newcomer. Ocasio-Cortez remained aware that Crowley's failure to tend to his grassroots led to his downfall.

NY-14: New York City   Cook Partisan Voting Index: D+29

Population		Race and Ethnicity		Income	
Total	721,690	White	22.8%	Median Income	$54,753
Land area (sq. miles)	28	Black	9.4%	District Income Rank	232
Pop/ sq mi	25510.4	Latino	49%	Poverty Rate	16.2%
Born in State	44%	Asian	16.9%	With health insurance	84.8%
		Two or more races	1.3%	Cash public assistance	4.1%
Age Groups		Other	0.5%	Food stamp/SNAP	17.2%
Under 18	20.2%				
18-34	26.6%	**Education**		**Work**	
35-64	40%	H.S grad or less	53.6%	White Collar	13.2%
Over 64	13.2%	Some college	20.5%	Sales and Service	49.4%
		College Degree, 4 yr	16.8%	Blue Collar	21.5%
Military		Post grad	9.1%	Government	11.7%
Veteran/ Active Duty	2.1%				

2012 Pres. Vote	Obama	136,783	(81%)	Romney	30,978	(18%)	
2016 Pres. Vote	Clinton	151,407	(77%)	Trump	38,560	(20%)	

Eastern Bronx, Northern Queens: Along the East River, LaGuardia Airport has struggled with short runways and poor commuter access. On more than one occasion, Gov. Andrew Cuomo has promised to upgrade it into a "21st century airport." with plans for two new terminals. He heralded a significant step in that direction with a ribbon-cutting ceremony in November 2018 that marked the opening of 11 new gates. Previewing further improvements by 2022, he added, "It's going to be a magnificent facility and it's going to be what New York deserves." Also underway with a 2022 completion date was construction of an above-ground AirTrain link at LaGuardia to subway and

Long Island Railroad lines at Willets Point, near Citi Field. This first-ever rail link to the airport will provide access to both the city and island.

Nearby in Queens is College Point, a middle-class neighborhood. Further south and west are Jackson Heights, home to Little India and a sizable Latino community; East Elmhurst; and Woodside, a long-settled enclave with recent immigrants. Corona was once predominantly Italian and African American (Louis Armstrong, Duke Ellington, and Malcolm X lived here), but it then became home to Dominican and Ecuadoran immigrants and many Asians. More recently, Corona has become the most popular housing site in Queens for millennials. Also in northern Queens are Ditmars, increasingly popular with professionals, as well as Steinway, where the plant that makes pianos for North and South American distribution is still located. Close enough to LaGuardia that it could be the site of an additional runway is Rikers Island, which opened in 1932 and has become over-crowded. Mayor Bill de Blasio in 2017 announced plans for smaller detention centers in all the boroughs except Staten Island, with his hope to close Rikers in a decade.

Across the bridge, the Bronx derives its name from its original European settlements. Jonas Bronck, a Swede who emigrated to the New World, started a farm, and once wrote that his new homeland was "a veritable paradise and needs but the industrious hand of man to make it the finest and most beautiful region in the world." His name was given to a nearby river, then to a borough, and it became a county in 1914. Real growth began in 1910, when the subways started connecting these neighborhoods with job sites in Manhattan. The Bronx was rapidly transformed by hundreds of thousands of immigrants flooding to the open spaces northeast of the Harlem River. Today, these neighborhoods are filling with Latinos, with more Mexicans than Puerto Ricans, and many from the Dominican Republic and elsewhere in the Caribbean and Latin America. In Parkchester, the immigrants arrived from Ecuador and Bangladesh. Out past Eastchester Bay is City Island, a Cape Cod-like resort area with boat makers and plenty of seafood restaurants that still looks like it did half a century ago.

These Bronx and Queens neighborhoods make up the 14th Congressional District of New York.

Other prominent locales include the Bronx Zoo and New York Botanical Garden in the Bronx, and the New York Mets home at Citi Field in Queens. The district is a polyglot; it is 49 percent Hispanic, 17 percent Asian and 9 percent black. More than two-thirds of the voters reside in Queens. Not long ago, Republicans were competitive here. Redistricting and demographic changes reversed GOP expansion. Hillary Clinton won the district with more than three-fourths of the vote.

Jose Serrano (D)

Elected 1990, 15th full term, b. Oct 24, 1943; Mayaguez, PR; Lehman City College (NY), Att., 1961; Roman Catholic; Divorced; 5 children.

Military Career: U.S. Army 1964-1966

Elected Office: District 7 School Board, 1969-1974; NY Assembly, 1975-1990.

Professional Career: Banker, 1961-1969.

DC Office: 2354 RHOB 20515, 202-225-4361, Fax: 202-225-6001, serrano.house.gov

State Offices: Bronx, 718-620-0084.

Committees: *Appropriations*: Commerce, Justice, Science & Related Agencies (Chmn); Financial Services & General Government; Interior, Environment & Related Agencies.

Group Ratings

	ADA	ACLU	AFL-CIO	LCV	ITI	COC	HAFA	ACU	CFG	FRC
2018	-	89%	-	100%	-	50%	6%	4%	15%	0%
2017	100%	C	100%	97%	C	36%	C	4%	5%	0%

Almanac Ratings 2017-18

	Economy	Social	Foreign	Composite
Liberal	100%	100%	100%	100%
Conservative	0%	0%	0%	0%

Key Votes of the 115th Congress

1. Obama-care revision	N	5. Family planning regs	N	9. Guantanamo prisoners	Y
2. Tax Cuts	N	6. Body cameras/immigration	Y	10. Ground missiles, limit	Y
3. Omnibus appropriations	N	7. Abortion ban	N	11. Defense Dept. spending	N
4. Dodd-Frank revision	N	8. Concealed carry	N	12. FISA rules	N

Election Results

Election	Name (Party)	Vote (%)	Cand. Spent	Ind. Exp. Support	Ind. Exp. Oppose
2018 General	Jose Serrano (D)	124,469 (96%)	$178,827		
	Jason Gonzalez (R)	5,205 (4%)			
2018 Primary	Jose Serrano (D)	(100%)			

Prior winning percentages: 2016 (95%), 2014 (90%), 2012 (86%), 2010 (86%), 2008 (75%), 2006 (76%), 2004 (75%), 2002 (65%), 2000 (73%), 1998 (74%), 1996 (71%), 1994 (68%), 1992 (64%), 1990 (66%)

Democrat José Serrano, who won his seat in a 1990 special election, is chairman of an Appropriations subcommittee that funds federal agencies in which Serrano has a strong interest. They include spending for federal agencies that handle law enforcement, immigration and the census. In March 2019, he cited health problems in announcing that he will not seek reelection in 2020.

Born in Mayagüez Puerto Rico, he grew up in the Mill Brook project in Mott Haven. After serving in the Army, he worked at a bank and as a school administrator. Serrano moved up while other Bronx politicians fell by the wayside because of corruption. He was elected to the New York Assembly in 1974 and chaired its Education Committee. In 1985, he ran for Bronx borough president, bucking the Democratic organization, and nearly won. Then in 1990, Rep. Robert García was convicted of accepting money from the minority contractor Wedtech. His conviction was later reversed, but his resignation paved the way for Serrano's election to the House.

Serrano once described himself as being "to the left of the left." The Almanac vote ratings have ranked him among the top 2 percent of the most liberal members of the House. He rarely casts a vote that sides with conservatives. Serrano was the only House member from New York City who voted in 2008 against the federal bailout for banks and other financial services companies. He said he couldn't justify giving money to the wealthy people he believed created the problem. A big local priority for Serrano has been restoration of the Bronx River, and he delivered more than $30 million for the effort.

On Appropriations, where he had spent a decade as the top Democrat on the Financial Services Subcommittee, he took over in 2017 as senior Democrat on the Commerce, Justice, Science Subcommittee, where he has focused on spending and enforcement issues for his economically struggling district. "I will do everything in my power to ensure adequate funding for these agencies, which guarantee that our fundamental constitutional rights are respected and protected," he said. As chairman in 2019, his priorities included insistence that the Commerce Department not include a question about citizenship on the 2020 census form. With Democratic Rep. Nita Lowey, who represents a nearby district in New York and chairs Appropriations, Serrano had become an important local resource.

Another of his issues has been statehood for Puerto Rico, which he has called an American "colony." A proponent of a long-stalled referendum to determine the island's status, he got a bill through the House in 2010 calling for a two-step process. In 2016, with the island's finances in disarray, he supported the Puerto Rico Oversight, Management, and Economic Stability Act, which was designed to approve debt reorganization and encourage financial stability. Noting that he had found it "disheartening and difficult" as Congress ignored earlier pleas for action, he added, "In a Republican-led Congress, this compromise legislation is the only one with a possibility of getting to the president's desk. There is no realistic alternative." Serrano said that the financial crisis had demonstrated that as a commonwealth, Puerto Rico had been "treated unfairly and unequally," and that debate was needed on the two best alternatives -- statehood or independence.

Serrano gave renewed attention to the island following the devastation caused by Hurricane Maria in September 2017. Noting that he felt "very much a part" of where he was born, he said that the extensive recovery efforts were "my first priority." Later, he said that the Trump administration handled those needs as "an afterthought," and repeated his claim that "Puerto Rico is in a colonial relationship with the United States," though its residents ought to have the same rights as "I have living in New York." He renewed his call for statehood.

Serrano's attempts to join the Democratic leadership have been stymied. In 1998, he ran for Democratic Caucus vice chairman as "the candidate who refuses to raise money to buy your vote for leadership." He lost out to the less-senior Robert Menendez of New Jersey, who later became a senator. Serrano briefly toyed with running against newly appointed Sen. Kirsten Gillibrand in the 2010 primary because of concerns over her centrist voting record. He passed, and Gillibrand moved left once she was in the Senate.

Serrano had become "alienated from the Bronx political establishment" and Democratic officials had sought another candidate for his seat, the New York Observer reported in 2015. Before she decided on her successful challenge to Rep. Joe Crowley in the 14th District, Alexandria Ocasio-Cortez initially filed to run against Serrano in the 2018 primary. (With nine write-in votes, she led the field for the Reform Party nomination to oppose Serrano, but she declined to accept the ballot listing.) But there was no sign of a recent political challenge to Serrano, nor any attempt to demonstrate his unpopularity. In his March 2019 retirement announcement, Serrano said that he had learned in recent months that his Parkinson's Disease "will eventually take a toll." Democrats are certain to retain his seat. His son, state Sen. Jose Serrano, cited family factors in stating that he would not seek to succeed him. He praised his father's impact. "When I was a child growing up in the 1970s, the Bronx was burning. Now, it's thriving."

NY-15: Bronx — Cook Partisan Voting Index: D+44

Population		Race and Ethnicity		Income	
Total	758,424	White	2.4%	Median Income	$27,351
Land area (sq. miles)	15	Black	28.2%	District Income Rank	435
Pop/ sq mi	52161.2	Latino	66%	Poverty Rate	38.2%
Born in State	51.2%	Asian	1.8%	With health insurance	87.6%
Age Groups		Two or more races	0.8%	Cash public assistance	9.6%
Under 18	28.1%	Other	0.8%	Food stamp/SNAP	47.6%
18-34	28%	**Education**		**Work**	
35-64	34.5%	H.S grad or less	62.9%	White Collar	9.4%
Over 64	9.4%	Some college	23.9%	Sales and Service	61.8%
Military		College Degree, 4 yr	9.6%	Blue Collar	20%
Veteran/ Active Duty	2%	Post grad	3.6%	Government	12.2%

2012 Pres. Vote	Obama	171,364	(97%)			
2016 Pres. Vote	Clinton	179,454	(94%)	Trump	9,371	(5%)

South Bronx: It may not quite be "the beautiful Bronx," as borough historian Lloyd Ultan calls it, but the Bronx has rebounded from rock bottom. The borough began its modern development in 1906 with the arrival of the first subway, which allowed the children of immigrants to move from grim Lower East Side tenements to spacious walk-up apartments flooded with light. The population grew from 200,000 in 1900 to 1.2 million in 1930. Its population hit nearly 1.5 million in 1950. Four years later, Supreme Court Justice Sonia Sotomayor was born in a South Bronx tenement before her family moved into the nearby Bronxdale Houses public housing project. The years prior to mid-century were the peak days for the Bronx, when Babe Ruth, Lou Gehrig and Joe DiMaggio knocked home runs out of Yankee Stadium, art deco apartment buildings were built along the Grand Concourse, and shoppers thronged Tremont Avenue stores.

In the mid-1960s, several factors led to the destruction of Bronx neighborhoods. Rent control guaranteed that many owners of low-rent property wouldn't maintain it. Once empty, buildings were torched for the insurance money, sometimes as many as four blocks a week. A decline in low-skill jobs in Manhattan and the Bronx led to a rise in welfare dependency and crime, and empty building shells became the perfect venue for drug dealing. A vicious cycle emerged: Crime drove away jobs, producing more crime. The 13-year, $250 million effort to build the Cross-Bronx Expressway — a brainchild of Robert Moses that crossed 113 streets and avenues, hundreds of utility mains and 10 mass-transit lines — made things worse.

The borough's eventual saviors were churches and creative community groups that built single-family bungalows and small-scale apartment projects for the elderly, single-parent families and the homeless. As immigrants from the Dominican Republic, Jamaica, Ecuador and Central America settled in, the population began to rise. Today, nearly 1.5 million people live in the Bronx, as new immigrants revive neighborhoods that had been given up for dead. Businesses — warehouses, distribution centers and small industrial parks — have begun to move back in. In 2016, the Bronx led the other boroughs in new homes and apartments authorized for construction. A promising development has been the city's plans to improve 30 blocks of the waterfront in Mott Haven along the Bronx side of the Harlem River, including the city's first soccer stadium. In 2018, South Bronx residents — intent on improving their neighborhood — objected to city plans to locate a new detention center there. Yet, incomes remain low in the South Bronx, drug overdose rates have been among the highest in the nation and the borough has the highest poverty rate in the state.

The 15th Congressional District of New York, which is the only district entirely in the Bronx, includes most of the South Bronx. It is bounded by the Harlem River on the west; the East River on the south; Westchester Creek, the Cross Bronx Expressway, and Bronx Park (home of the Bronx Zoo) on the east; and it goes just past Fordham Road on the north. It includes the gentrifying Belmont to the north, the industrial flatlands of Bruckner Boulevard, and Hunts Point, where meat and produce markets supply the city's tony restaurants, with some new housing. The district is 28 percent black, and it has the highest share of Hispanics — 66 percent — of any New York district; in 2017, it increased to 2 percent white. It has long had New York's largest concentration of Puerto Ricans, but about 69 percent of Hispanics are now from other parts of Latin America. Poverty here remains endemic. The 15th District has the lowest median income in the nation. As longstanding Democratic territory, it is extreme in other ways. The 15th was the most Democratic district in the nation in 2016, giving Hillary Clinton 94 percent of the vote.

Eliot Engel (D)

Elected 1988, 16th term, b. Feb 18, 1947; Bronx; Hunter-Lehman College (NY), B.A., 1969; City University of New York - Herbert H. Lehman College, M.S., 1973; New York University Law School, J.D., 1987; Jewish; Married (Patricia Ennis Engel); 3 children.

Elected Office: NY Assembly, 1977-1988.

Professional Career: Teacher, guidance counselor, NYC Public Schools, 1969-1977; Bronx Democratic District ldr., 1974-1977.

DC Office: 2426 RHOB 20515, 202-225-2464, Fax: 202-225-5513, engel.house.gov

State Offices: Bronx, 718-796-9700; Bronx, 718-320-2314; Mount Vernon, 914-699-4100.

Committees: *Energy & Commerce*: Health. *Foreign Affairs (Chmn)*.

Group Ratings

	ADA	ACLU	AFL-CIO	LCV	ITI	COC	HAFA	ACU	CFG	FRC
2018	-	93%	-	100%	-	50%	6%	4%	15%	0%
2017	85%	C	100%	97%	C	50%	C	4%	6%	11%

Almanac Ratings 2017-18

	Economy	Social	Foreign	Composite
Liberal	97%	98%	75%	90%
Conservative	3%	2%	25%	10%

Key Votes of the 115th Congress

1. Obama-care revision	N	5. Family planning regs	N	9. Guantanamo prisoners	Y
2. Tax Cuts	N	6. Body cameras/immigration	Y	10. Ground missiles, limit	N
3. Omnibus appropriations	N	7. Abortion ban	N	11. Defense Dept. spending	Y
4. Dodd-Frank revision	N	8. Concealed carry	N	12. FISA rules	N

Election Results

Election	Name (Party)	Vote (%)	Cand. Spent	Ind. Exp. Support	Ind. Exp. Oppose
2018 General	Eliot Engel (D)................................ 182,044	(100%)	$1,697,798		
2018 Primary	Eliot Engel (D).................................... 22,160	(74%)			
	Jonathan Lewis (D)........................ 4,866	(16%)			
	Joyce Briscoe (D)................................ 1,772	(6%)			

Prior winning percentages: 2016 (94%), 2014 (72%), 2012 (66%), 2010 (69%), 2008 (66%), 2006 (68%), 2004 (60%), 2002 (55%), 2000 (70%), 1998 (72%), 1996 (67%), 1994 (61%), 1992 (60%), 1990 (52%), 1988 (55%)

Democrat Eliot Engel, elected in 1988, has worked on international issues of interest to his district's varied foreign-born and low-income residents. As chairman of the Foreign Affairs Committee, he is one of four New York Democrats to hold a top committee post. He has backed many downtrodden ethnic groups and has been a stalwart defender of Israel, which resulted in an unusual conflict with a first-term committee member soon after he became chairman.

Engel is the son of a welder and grew up in the Bronx. He graduated from Hunter-Lehman College, got a master's in guidance and counseling from the City University of New York, then taught and was a guidance counselor in the New York City public schools. After 14 years, he returned to school for a law degree from New York Law School. In 1977, at age 30, he was elected to the New York Assembly in a special election to replace a convicted incumbent. He won election to the House in 1988, replacing Democratic Rep. Mario Biaggi, who also had been convicted of bribery.

Engel's once strongly liberal voting record has become more moderate, especially on foreign policy, if only because his party has shifted to the left. In the Almanac vote ratings, his score on international issues has placed him toward the center of the House. On Foreign Affairs, which has a lower profile than its Senate counterpart, he has forged a good working relationship with senior Republicans. He and Ed Royce of California, the committee's chairman when Republicans had House control, issued many joint news releases, notably on Israel and the Middle East. With Royce's Foreign Affairs predecessor, Ileana Ros-Lehtinen of Florida, Engel worked on legislation to rein in Syria's weapons program and promote human rights there. She called him "a principled man ... an incredible freedom fighter."

Engel occasionally sought to deflect Republican criticism of the Obama administration. At a 2013 hearing at which committee members sharply questioned outgoing Secretary of State Hillary Clinton about security flaws that led to the attack on the U.S. consulate in Benghazi Libya, Engel noted that House Republicans had cut diplomatic security funding. Engel has written laws relating to Albania and Kosovo, Cyprus and Irish affairs, and co-authored a law that addressed child slave labor in the cocoa fields of Africa. He was successful in encouraging some collaboration between Obama and Republicans, including enactment in 2016 of laws that encouraged engagement with nations in the Caribbean and sought to preserve international cultural antiquities.

On some issues, Engel is a foreign-policy hawk. He supported the Gulf War resolution in 1990, the bombing of Serbia to get a settlement in Bosnia, and the use of force in Iraq in 2002, though he criticized President George W. Bush's handling of that conflict. He was one of three lawmakers to participate in a 2011 documentary, Iranium, which sounded alarms about Iran's pursuit of nuclear weapons. After the agreement was reached in 2015, he was an outspoken opponent and said that the deal might "strengthen Iran's position as a destabilizing and destructive influence across the Middle East." Such views have sparked some complaints by progressive groups about Engel and his influence among House Democrats.

Engel had a personal tradition of staking out an aisle seat many hours before the start of the annual State of the Union address so he can shake the president's hand or occasionally give him a hug. In February 2009, CNN anchor Anderson Cooper called Engel "pathetic" for waiting more than 12 hours for President Barack Obama's address to Congress. Engel replied that Cooper was "pathetic" for failing to share his enthusiasm. He later told The Journal-News that constituents loved him for it:

"It'll be September, October and people will say they saw me on TV." But he abandoned that practice when President Donald Trump made his first address to Congress in February 2017.

Engel opposed many of Trump's foreign policy actions. Despite his opposition to Obama's deal with Iran, he opposed Trump's decision to withdraw from the agreement. Even with its flaws, he wrote in USA Today in October 2017, "our ongoing commitment to the agreement could help prevent further destabilization in the Middle East." As Trump prepared to meet NATO leaders in July 2018, Engel co-authored an opinion article for CNN that argued "NATO is not, as Trump has stated, taking advantage of the United States." In January 2019, contrary to Trump, he said that U.S. armed intervention in Venezuela was "not an option." An exception was his support for Trump's decision to move the U.S. embassy in Israel from Tel Aviv to Jerusalem, a step that Engel said "helps correct a decades-long indignity."

Taking over as Foreign Affairs chairman in 2019, Engel said that diplomacy and economic development were "critical to our national security" and that he planned a renewed emphasis on U.S. overseas alliances, especially NATO. Reinforcing the need for Congress to serve as "a co-equal branch of government," he said, he created a new Oversight and Investigations Subcommittee to probe Trump's management of foreign policy, including whether the president's business dealings have affected those actions.

During his first two months as chairman, Engel twice issued harsh criticism in response to comments by Democratic Rep. Ilhan Omar of Minnesota, a new member of the committee, that some American Jews had an "allegiance" to Israel. "It's unacceptable and deeply offensive to call into question the loyalty of fellow American citizens because of their political views, including support for the U.S.-Israel relationship," Engel said in a March 1 statement. "Rep. Omar's comments were outrageous and deeply hurtful." Weeks earlier, Omar had apologized in response to similar criticism.

On the Energy and Commerce Committee, where he has retained a seat, Engel has worked on a wide range of subjects, from climate change to cell phone theft. He joined a bipartisan group of lawmakers who sponsored a 2009 measure requiring half of all new cars sold in the U.S. to be flex-fuel vehicles capable of burning any combination of ethanol, methanol and gasoline. The automobile industry fought the measure, and it was not added to the House-passed energy bill that year. In 2010, he enacted a bill that made it illegal to use false caller IDs to trick people into revealing personal information.

Engel has had a handful of spirited election opponents. In the 2000 primary, Assemblyman Larry Seabrook attacked Engel for living in suburban Maryland. Engel won 50%-41%. After redistricting made his district more suburban in 2002, Engel had vigorous competition from Rockland County Executive Scott Vanderhoef, a Republican who criticized Engel for voting against tax cuts and defense spending. Engel won 63%-34%. In the 2018 Democratic primary, Engel faced three opponents — including Jonathan Lewis, who self-funded most of his $900,000 in spending. Lewis, a financial executive, said Engel was too dependent on campaign contributions from special-interest groups and that he needed to be more "visible" on local issues. Engel led Lewis 74%-16%.

NY-16: Southern Westchester County, North Bronx

Cook Partisan Voting Index: D+24

Population		Race and Ethnicity		Income	
Total	745,855	White	36.8%	Median Income	$68,246
Land area (sq. miles)	78	Black	30.7%	District Income Rank	105
Pop/ sq mi	9517.1	Latino	24.9%	Poverty Rate	12.9%
Born in State	56.2%	Asian	5.1%	With health insurance	92%
		Two or more races	1.6%	Cash public assistance	3.5%
Age Groups		Other	0.9%	Food stamp/SNAP	14.2%
Under 18	22.2%				
18-34	21.8%	**Education**		**Work**	
35-64	39.6%	H.S grad or less	37.9%	White Collar	16.4%
Over 64	16.4%	Some college	22.8%	Sales and Service	44.1%
		College Degree, 4 yr	20.4%	Blue Collar	13.7%
Military		Post grad	18.9%	Government	15.6%
Veteran/ Active Duty	3.6%				

2012 Pres. Vote	Obama	197,364	(74%)	Romney	68,373	(26%)
2016 Pres. Vote	Clinton	212,644	(75%)	Trump	63,590	(22%)

Yonkers, New Rochelle: The northeastern Bronx wasn't settled until the early 20th century, when it became a collection of middle-class neighborhoods clustered around subway stops, places where the children of immigrants left behind Manhattan's gloomy tenements and walk-ups and basked in the sunlight, wide avenues and hilly vistas. Different ethnic groups collected here: Irish in Kingsbridge; well-to-do WASPs and Jews in Riverdale; and middle-class blacks in Williamsbridge. When neighboring areas in the South Bronx began to deteriorate, many residents fled to Westchester County.

The 16th Congressional District of New York includes the bulk of these Bronx neighborhoods, and a broad swath of Westchester County. It is divided into three parts of similar size. South of the Westchester County line and west of the Bronx River Parkway, the area is about 70 percent white and heavily Democratic. This portion has the century-old Van Cortlandt Park, at 1,146 acres, New York City's fourth-largest park. On opposite sides of the park are Riverdale and leafy Woodlawn, still a magnet for Irish immigrants. The second section of the district is the southern edge of Westchester. It extends from Yonkers, which is the most populous city in the county and 36 percent Hispanic, across the Bronx River Parkway into Mount Vernon, which is 67 percent African American. The sprawling Co-op City is here, consisting of 35 buildings that house more than 35,000 residents in 15,000 apartments that were built by a consortium of labor unions in the late 1960s — the largest affordable-housing development in the nation. Nearby, Metro-North plans to open a transit stop in 2022. Yonkers suffered from high debt during the recession and received additional state aid. After an environmental clean-up along the Hudson River waterfront, more than $2.5 billion of new housing was underway in 2018; the city has promoted itself to millennials and others as relatively inexpensive, with a 30-minute rail commute to Grand Central Station.

The district's third section, to the north in Westchester, stretches from Hastings-on-Hudson eastward to Mamaroneck on Long Island Sound. This section pushes well into Westchester County suburbs, all the way to a touch short of the Connecticut border. It includes a number of affluent suburbs, many within easy reach of Grand Central via the Metro North rail lines — Bronxville, Tuckahoe, Eastchester, New Rochelle, Scarsdale, Larchmont, Mamaroneck and Rye. New Rochelle, which has begun work on a planned $4 billion in downtown redevelopment, received $10 million from the state in 2018 for revitalization.

Historically, Westchester was a Republican county, with a successful GOP machine and an electorate of white-collar professionals who naturally preferred the political party that opposed the big city political bosses and labor union leaders. Today, party registration in Westchester is majority-Democratic, after an influx of racial and ethnic minorities and of Jews who broke down many barriers to residence after World War II. Overall, the parts of the richly diverse 16th have had a major transformation. It is 31 percent African American and 25 percent Hispanic — and solidly Democratic, with an increase to 75 percent for Hillary Clinton in 2016.

Nita Lowey (D)

Elected 1988, 16th term, b. Jul 05, 1937; Bronx; Mount Holyoke College (MA), B.S., 1959; Jewish; Married (Stephen Lowey); 3 children; 8 grandchildren.

Professional Career: Assistant for Econ. Devel. & Neighborhood Preservation, NY Secretary of st.; Deputy Director, Div. of Econ. Opportunity, 1975-1985; NY Assistant Secretary of st., 1985-1987.

DC Office: 2365 RHOB 20515, 202-225-6506, Fax: 202-225-0546, lowey.house.gov

State Offices: New City, 845-639-3485; White Plains, 914-428-1707.

Committees: *Appropriations (Chmn):* Ex Officio membership on all subcommittees.

Group Ratings

	ADA	ACLU	AFL-CIO	LCV	ITI	COC	HAFA	ACU	CFG	FRC
2018	-	79%	-	91%	-	58%	8%	4%	12%	0%
2017	90%	C	95%	100%	C	36%	C	7%	5%	0%

Almanac Ratings 2017-18

	Economy	Social	Foreign	Composite
Liberal	97%	100%	89%	95%
Conservative	3%	0%	11%	5%

Key Votes of the 115th Congress

1. Obama-care revision	N	5. Family planning regs	N	9. Guantanamo prisoners	Y
2. Tax Cuts	N	6. Body cameras/immigration	Y	10. Ground missiles, limit	Y
3. Omnibus appropriations	Y	7. Abortion ban	N	11. Defense Dept. spending	Y
4. Dodd-Frank revision	N	8. Concealed carry	N	12. FISA rules	Y

Election Results

Election	Name (Party)	Vote (%)	Cand. Spent	Ind. Exp. Support	Ind. Exp. Oppose
2018 General	Nita Lowey (D).............................	170,168 (88%)	$763,394		
2018 Primary	Nita Lowey (D)...........................	(100%)			

Prior winning percentages: 2016 (99%), 2014 (54%), 2012 (58%), 2010 (65%), 2008 (58%), 2006 (63%), 2004 (57%), 2002 (51%), 2000 (57%), 1998 (55%), 1996 (57%), 1994 (53%), 1992 (52%), 1990 (59%), 1988 (53%)

Democrat Nita Lowey, first elected in 1988 and a formidable insider among House Democrats, took the reins of the Appropriations Committee in 2019. She became the first woman to hold that slot and the most powerful female head of any congressional committee. She was largely successful in her first showdown when she joined others who stood against President Donald Trump's attempt to use the leverage of a partial government shutdown in a bid to get money for a wall on the border with Mexico. In the lore surrounding the hard-bargaining Lowey, the late Republican Rep. Henry Hyde of Illinois referred to her as the "perfumed ice pick." Lowey framed that quote and an ice pick in her office.

Lowey was born in the Bronx. After graduating from Mount Holyoke College with a degree in marketing, she moved to Queens, where she became a homemaker raising three children. She got involved in politics when her neighbor, Mario Cuomo, got Lowey to assist his 1974 campaign for lieutenant governor. He lost that race but was appointed New York secretary of state and hired Lowey as his assistant in 1975. She remained a top official in his administration until she ran for Congress.

In the Democratic primary for an open seat, Lowey faced Hamilton Fish III, who was politically well connected but, as a former publisher of The Nation, was considerably to the left of Lowey. She won 44%-36%. In the general election, two-term Republican Rep. Joseph DioGuardi was dogged by charges of illicit contributions. Lowey won 50%-47%, while spending $657,000 of her own money.

Lowey styles herself mostly as liberal, although she has been more moderate on foreign policy. She has been a strong advocate of aid to Israel and voted for the 2002 Iraq war resolution. Her ties to Nancy Pelosi were evident in 2012 when she defeated Marcy Kaptur of Ohio for the ranking Democratic slot on Appropriations, even though Kaptur had more seniority. As ranking Democrat on the State and Foreign Operations Subcommittee, Lowey worked closely with Texas Republican Kay Granger, who was that panel's chairwoman until 2017. They warned the Palestinian Authority that any unilateral moves toward statehood jeopardized U.S. funding. Lowey opposed GOP proposals to cut U.S. contributions to international financial organizations, arguing that American companies' access to foreign markets would be impaired.

On an overseas topic separate from her work at Appropriations, Lowey has won passage of two of her bills designed to promote education around the world: the Education for All Act that is designed to help the 263 million children, adolescents and young adults who are not enrolled in school, which the House approved in 2016; and the Reinforcing Education Accountability in Development (READ) Act, which was passed in 2017. "We cannot build the world we want for ourselves, and for future generations, without making education the center of our efforts," Lowey said.

Lowey has been a big supporter of biomedical research and helped increase spending on cancer research at the National Institutes of Health. She worked to combat drunken driving, advocating the increased use of ignition interlock devices to impede repeat offenses. Pursuing her interest in feminist issues, she has backed funds for international family planning, including abortion. She has actively supported the National Endowment for the Arts.

Lowey reportedly played a key behind-the-scenes role in loosening restrictions on derivatives in the 2010 Dodd-Frank financial industry overhaul law that would have negatively affected New York's banking industry. That provision became a controversial part of the 2014 year-end omnibus spending bill when Lowey — working with Sen. Barbara Mikulski of Maryland — cut a deal with Republican appropriators to permit an exemption for big banks from derivatives regulation. In exchange, Lowey got an additional $185 million in spending for banking regulators. That agreement raised major objections from Pelosi and other liberal Democrats, but the appropriators held firm. President Barack Obama went along with the agreement.

Presiding over Appropriations in January 2019, Lowey said, "Democrats will make government work for the people," and she drew the contrast to Republicans who "have governed from crisis to crisis of their own making." Lowey's allies weren't shy about the opportunities with her powerful post. Asked by a reporter what her chairmanship would mean for New York, Gov. Andrew Cuomo responded with one word: "Money!" Lowey immediately made clear her opposition to funding a border wall with Mexico — which Republicans had not pushed during the previous two years when they controlled the House. "We will invest in other programs that will make us safer," she told a local reporter following the election.

Inheriting the government shutdown that began in the closing days of the previous Congress, she filed alternatives to open other parts of the government while Congress tried to resolve the conflict over border security. Aided by Pelosi, who spent more than a decade on Appropriations before she became party leader, Lowey said, "It is critical that we reopen the federal government ... while allowing time for negotiation on border security." Ultimately, the 34-day shutdown ended in late January when Trump threw in the towel, amid reports of growing adverse consequences, including reduced manpower to monitor airplanes in the air traffic control system. That deal gave Congress three more weeks to resolve details on border security. The bipartisan negotiators — including Lowey's friend Granger, who had become the top Republican on the committee -- agreed to give Trump barely one-fourth of the $5.7 billion that he requested, for fencing, not a wall. The president reluctantly signed the bill and decided to take the controversial step of invoking his "emergency power" to secure funds for the wall.

Since Lowey's first election, the boundaries of her district have been radically altered three times by redistricting, but she has been reelected by wide margins. She thought about a Senate bid in 2000, but deferred to first lady Hillary Clinton, and she was an enthusiastic supporter of Clinton's two presidential campaigns. Her party loyalty and avid fundraising led Minority Leader Dick Gephardt to appoint her to chair the Democratic Congressional Campaign Committee for the 2002 election. That year, the GOP's six-seat gain was an acute disappointment to Lowey. In 2008, she was mentioned as a possible Senate successor after Clinton became secretary of State, but the plum fell to Democratic Rep. Kirsten Gillibrand.

When redistricting in 2012 gave Lowey a district in which just over half of the constituents were new to her, she drew a stronger GOP candidate in Rye Town Supervisor Joe Carvin. But she won 64 percent of the vote. In the more Republican-leaning 2014 cycle, Lowey got 56 percent against Republican Chris Day, a retired Army captain who served in Iraq and Afghanistan, whom she outspent by more than 10-to-1. In 2016 and 2018, she was reelected without major-party opposition.

If Lowey steps down from the seat, Republicans could run a competitive campaign. Such a contest would be all the more interesting, given widespread speculation that Chelsea Clinton and her family have had their eye on the seat. "I'll retire when I'm ready to retire," Lowey — age 81 and reinvigorated -- said about that scenario.

NY-17: Northern Westchester, Rockland Counties

Cook Partisan Voting Index: D+7

Population		Race and Ethnicity		Income	
Total	742,801	White	60%	Median Income	$95,454
Land area (sq. miles)	383	Black	9.9%	District Income Rank	19
Pop/ sq mi	1941.3	Latino	22.1%	Poverty Rate	10.6%
Born in State	62.4%	Asian	5.9%	With health insurance	92.2%
		Two or more races	1.6%	Cash public assistance	1.4%
Age Groups		Other	0.4%	Food stamp/SNAP	7.9%
Under 18	24.7%				
18-34	20.7%	Education		Work	
35-64	39.3%	H.S grad or less	32.5%	White Collar	15.3%
Over 64	15.3%	Some college	21.8%	Sales and Service	40.6%
		College Degree, 4 yr	23.7%	Blue Collar	13%
Military		Post grad	22%	Government	14.6%
Veteran/ Active Duty	4.1%				

2012 Pres. Vote	Obama	167,884	(57%)	Romney	123,125	(42%)
2016 Pres. Vote	Clinton	186,437	(58%)	Trump	122,339	(38%)

White Plains: Blessed with some of America's loveliest scenery and easily accessible from Manhattan by train, Westchester County has some of America's earliest suburbs, where grand estates were built by millionaires — Jay Gould's Gothic revival Lyndhurst and John D. Rockefeller's spectacular Kykuit. Today, Westchester still looks suburban, but with the patina of age. It has little commuter railroad stations across from faux Tudor drugstores, soda fountains and cobblestone post offices. But it also has shopping malls and plenty of corporate headquarters, from IBM to Pepsi. In recent years, Westchester also has been drawing biotech companies. In January 2019, officials unveiled a new bio-tech campus, planned for Valhalla, that is expected to feature 8,000 jobs, chiefly in life sciences. Development slows north of White Plains, where Westchester is crossed by the first of several mountain ridges — the closest the Appalachians come to the ocean. In Ossining, on the Hudson River, looms the famed Sing Sing maximum security prison.

The 17th Congressional District of New York contains the largest share of Westchester County, including its northern and western sections: Port Chester, White Plains, Tarrytown, Armonk and Chappaqua, where former President Bill Clinton and Hillary Clinton have a home. Facebook Chairman and CEO Mark Zuckerberg was born in White Plains and grew up in Dobbs Ferry, now the southernmost town in the district on the east bank of the Hudson River. Also here are Yorktown Heights and Peekskill, where George Pataki was mayor before becoming governor. Westchester magazine in 2014 described White Plains as the heart of the county that "combines a suburban environment with urban sophistication for a great living and working experience." The twin Indian Point nuclear reactors are scheduled to shut down in 2020, largely because of fears about the safety risk to New York City. In the era of Donald Trump, Republicans in Westchester have lost some of their approval — and control of county management.

Across the Tappan Zee — a stretch in the Hudson River so wide that Henry Hudson believed he had finally discovered the Northwest Passage to the Pacific Ocean upon entering it — the district takes in all of Rockland County, which comprises about 40 percent of the residents of the 17th and is the second fastest-growing county in the state. First settled by Dutchmen, Rockland was studded by little towns that grew up as if they were 1,000 miles from Gotham, but which eventually thrived on their proximity to the city once the Palisades Interstate Parkway and Tappan Zee Bridge were built in the 1950s. Today, Rockland is a triangular stretch of suburbia. Its demographics have changed; Haverstraw, on the banks of the Hudson, has a large share of Dominicans; Kaser, a village in the inland town of Rampao, has a large community of Romanians. Orangetown is the site of several large high-tech data centers. The second span of the eight-lane, 3.1 mile Mario Cuomo Bridge to replace the deteriorating Tappan Zee opened in September 2018; the old bridge was destroyed in five seconds by dynamite charges in January 2019. The $4 billion cost will be paid from future toll revenue of the New York Thruway. Westchester and Rockland counties had the highest property-tax revenues in the nation in 2016.

The 17th District is 22 percent Hispanic and 10 percent black. In her home district, Hillary Clinton won, 58%-38%.

Sean Maloney (D)

Elected 2012, 4th term, b. Jul 30, 1966; Sherbrooke, Canada; Georgetown University (DC), Att., 1986; University of Virginia, B.A., 1988; University of Virginia School of Law, J.D., 1992; Roman Catholic; Married (Randy Florke); 3 children.

Professional Career: Practicing attorney, 1993-1997, 2004-2006, 2009-present; Staff Secretary, President Bill Clinton, 1997-2000; Founder & COO, Kiodex, 2000-2003; First deputy Secretary, Gov. Eliot Spitzer, 2007-2008.

DC Office: 2331 RHOB 20515, 202-225-5441, Fax: 202-225-3289, seanmaloney.house.gov

State Offices: Newburgh, 845-561-1259.

Committees: *Agriculture*: Biotechnology, Horticulture & Research; Commodity Exchanges, Energy & Credit. *Permanent Select on Intelligence*: Counterterrorism, Counterintelligence & Counterproliferation; Defense Intelligence & Warfighter Support. *Transportation & Infrastructure*: Aviation; Coast Guard & Maritime Transportation (Chmn); Highways & Transit.

Group Ratings

	ADA	ACLU	AFL-CIO	LCV	ITI	COC	HAFA	ACU	CFG	FRC
2018	-	75%	-	89%	-	67%	8%	12%	19%	0%
2017	80%	C	97%	94%	C	64%	C	7%	5%	11%

Almanac Ratings 2017-18

	Economy	Social	Foreign	Composite
Liberal	77%	96%	45%	72%
Conservative	23%	4%	55%	28%

Key Votes of the 115th Congress

1. Obama-care revision	N	5. Family planning regs	N	9. Guantanamo prisoners	N
2. Tax Cuts	N	6. Body cameras/immigration	Y	10. Ground missiles, limit	N
3. Omnibus appropriations	N	7. Abortion ban	N	11. Defense Dept. spending	Y
4. Dodd-Frank revision	Y	8. Concealed carry	N	12. FISA rules	Y

Election Results

Election	Name (Party)	Vote (%)	Cand. Spent	Ind. Exp. Support	Ind. Exp. Oppose
2018 General	Sean Maloney (D)	139,564 (55%)	$1,887,334		
	James O'Donnell (R)	112,035 (45%)	$269,236		
2018 Primary	Sean Maloney (D)	(100%)			

Prior winning percentages: 2016 (56%), 2014 (48%), 2012 (49%)

Elected in 2012, Sean Patrick Maloney of New York was a staffer on Bill Clinton's presidential campaigns and a West Wing aide. He has brought the former president's brand of centrism and a notable ambition. Maloney fell short in 2018 in his bids for statewide office and a House leadership post. He has been a productive legislator, even when House Democrats were in the minority.

Maloney was born in Quebec Canada, where his father worked in the lumber industry. He grew up in Hanover New Hampshire, attended Georgetown University for two years and then transferred to the University of Virginia, where he got a bachelor's in international relations and stayed on to earn a law degree. Maloney worked on Clinton's 1992 campaign as a deputy to Susan Thomases, then the chief scheduler. In the 1996 reelection campaign, he was director of surrogate travel. After that, he snagged a job in the White House as the No. 3 official under Chief of Staff John Podesta. Maloney later became staff secretary, responsible for coordinating the flow of information to the president.

After Clinton left office, Maloney worked as the chief operating officer at Kiodex, a firm that developed risk management tools. He made his first bid for office in 2006, when he lost badly to Andrew Cuomo in the Democratic primary for attorney general. Maloney became first deputy secretary to Gov. Eliot Spitzer and, after Spitzer resigned, to Gov. David Paterson. Maloney came under a cloud for possible obstruction of justice following a scheme to release damaging information about then-Senate Majority Leader Joseph Bruno's travel. Bruno was convicted on federal corruption charges, but he was later acquitted in a retrial.

When Maloney ran for the House seat in 2012, his role in Albany became an issue in the five-way Democratic primary. The New York Times editorial board said that during law-enforcement review of the charges, Maloney "appeared to be most interested in holding back the staff's personal emails from investigators." Still, he won the primary handily. He led his closest competitor, Cortlandt Town Council Member Richard Becker, 48%-32%. Against first-term Rep. Nan Hayworth, Maloney painted Hayworth as a tea party extremist, citing her votes for Rep. Paul Ryan's budget and for cutting funding for Planned Parenthood. Hayworth outraised him $3.3 million to $2.3 million and had a comparable edge in outside assistance. Maloney eked out a win, 52%-48%.

Maloney, who is gay, married in 2014 his longtime partner, Randy Florke, a prominent real estate agent and interior designer. He has co-chaired the Congressional LGBT Equality Caucus. He has been an active legislator, though with occasional embellishment. In summarizing his work during his first term, Maloney claimed credit for introducing 10 bills that were signed into law. In most of those cases, he appeared to have been a cosponsor of legislation, which often was changed prior to enactment.

Maloney sparked a furor in the House in May 2016 when he offered an amendment to prevent federal contractors from engaging in job discrimination on the basis of sexual orientation. The proposal lost, 213-212, after Republican leaders used strong-arm tactics to urge some of their members to switch their votes. Maloney again offered his amendment the following week and it easily passed, though his provision died in the Senate. He was successful on two other initiatives in 2016. The Federal Aviation Administration reauthorization included his amendment to hire more air traffic controllers, with priority to military veterans. The House passed his bill to require an advisory committee of the Food and Drug Administration to recommend procedures for use of certain new opioids.

In 2019, as chairman of the Coast Guard and Maritime Transportation Subcommittee, Maloney said his top priority was protecting the Hudson River, which he called "a national treasure" and a key to local commerce. He cited his past opposition to Coast Guard proposals for new anchorage sites along the river, which had drawn strong local protests and eventually were suspended. He also gained a coveted assignment to the Intelligence Committee.

In 2014, Maloney won a rematch with Hayworth. This time, Maloney outraised his opponent, $4.3 million to $3.5 million, and assistance from super PACs gave him another $2 million. In a Republican year, he won 49.7%-47.9%, and led in three of the four counties, losing only Putnam. In 2016, his opponent Phil Oliva, an aide to the Westchester County executive, accused Maloney of exaggerating or lying about his legislative successes. Oliva raised $224,000 to Maloney's $3.6 million and was limited in getting his message out. Maloney won, 56%-44%.

Following the election, Maloney raised questions about the operations of the DCCC during the 2016 campaign, including its strategy and financing of candidates. In February 2017, Maloney told The Washington Post, "We can win [in districts] where we used to struggle, and we're struggling a bit where we used to win." The DCCC got much-improved results in 2018 with its 40-seat gain, including three in New York.

Maloney had an unusual campaign season in 2018. He ran again for attorney general in a wide-open Democratic primary, citing his experience in the private sector and opposing the Trump administration in Washington. With approval of a state judge, he ran for both the statewide post and for reelection to his House seat; under New York's unusual election law, those primaries were held in separate months. If he had won the September primary for attorney general, he said that he would have given up his House seat, for which he had won the June primary. Instead, though spending more than the combined total of his opponents, he finished third with 25 percent of the vote in the four-candidate primary, which was won by Letitia James. In his House campaign, Republican challenger James O'Donnell criticized Maloney for placing his attention elsewhere. Maloney won, 55%-45%.

Following the election, he ran for DCCC chairman. When he was hospitalized for a bacterial infection, he dropped out of the contest, which Rep. Cheri Bustos of Illinois won. It was not clear that Maloney had strong support against the three other candidates.

NY-18: Lower Hudson Valley   **Cook Partisan Voting Index: R+1**

Population		Race and Ethnicity		Income	
Total	723,244	White	69%	Median Income	$82,543
Land area (sq. miles)	1,353	Black	8.8%	District Income Rank	45
Pop/ sq mi	534.4	Latino	16.5%	Poverty Rate	9.8%
Born in State	70.7%	Asian	3.1%	With health insurance	94.4%
		Two or more races	2%	Cash public assistance	2%
Age Groups		Other	0.6%	Food stamp/SNAP	8.7%
Under 18	23.5%				
18-34	21.2%	**Education**		**Work**	
35-64	40.8%	H.S grad or less	36%	White Collar	14.5%
Over 64	14.5%	Some college	28.5%	Sales and Service	43%
Military		College Degree, 4 yr	19.9%	Blue Collar	17.2%
Veteran/ Active Duty	7.3%	Post grad	15.6%	Government	17.7%

2012 Pres. Vote	Obama	149,610	(51%)	Romney	137,144	(47%)			
2016 Pres. Vote	Trump	152,142	(49%)	Clinton	146,188	(47%)	Johnson	7,930	(3%)

Newburgh, Poughkeepsie: The great interior of America can be said to begin where the Hudson River squeezes through a series of Appalachian ridges at the Hudson Highlands. This chokepoint became a barrier to British military power during the Revolutionary War, when American forces put a chain across the river to keep the British from sailing north. Benedict Arnold betrayed his country over control of this part of the Hudson, and the new nation built its military academy high on the cliffs at West Point. The Hudson was the impetus for the builders of the Erie Canal and the water-level New York Central Railroad, two great projects that made New York City the port of the American interior.

The 18th Congressional District of New York covers much of the southern Hudson Valley, sprawling across four counties. West of the Hudson, the district includes all of Orange County, which takes in about half the voters in the district; it has trailed only Rockland as the state's fastest-growing county outside New York City, with an 11 percent increase between 2000 and 2015, though it has barely changed since then. There, old farming villages like Warwick adjoin mountains, farms and new middle-income subdivisions on the nation's biggest deposit of muck soil outside the Everglades. Orange County includes Kiryas Joel, a Hasidic Jewish settlement with more than 20,000 residents, many of whom moved from Brooklyn to find room for their large families. In January 2019, Kiryas Joel separated from Monroe and renamed itself Palm Tree — the first new town in New York in 35 years. With county approval, the $500 million Legoland theme park was set to open in 2020 — the largest such theme park in the world and the third in the United States, in addition to California and Florida. Also in Orange, the heirs to railroad baron E.H. Harriman successfully resisted plans by Caesars Entertainment to locate a large casino and resort complex next to their parkland; instead, the site was approved for residential development. Stewart International Airport expanded its terminal and nearly doubled its passenger load, including service to Europe with low-cost carrier Norwegian Air. The airport renamed itself "New York International," though it is 60 miles north of New York City.

East of the river, the 18th takes in all of Putnam County and more than half of Dutchess County, including Poughkeepsie, home of Vassar College, and Wappingers Falls. In Poughkeepsie, which has suffered many years of economic hard times, robust development attracted young professionals after officials approved a booming waterfront plan along the Hudson. IBM planned to open in 2019 a center for quantum computing. The district takes in the lightly populated northeastern reaches of Westchester County, around Somers, North Salem and Lewisboro.

The region has proved attractive to white-collar workers seeking reasonably priced housing in low-crime areas. This has led to population growth at a time when many other areas of the state have been losing residents. Politically, Putnam County is reliably Republican; the rest of the district is swing territory or leans slightly Democratic, resulting in a district that tends to end up near the national average. Donald Trump won the district, 49%-47%.

Antonio Delgado (D)

Elected 2018, 1st term, b. Jan 28, 1977; Schenectady; Colgate University, B.A., 1999; Oxford University (England), M.A., 2001; Harvard University Law School (MA), J.D., 2005; Married (Lacey Delgado); 2 children.

Professional Career: Attorney, Akin, Gump, Strauss, Hauer & Feld; Music Label Owner.

DC Office: 1007 LHOB 20515, 202-225-5614, delgado.house.gov

State Offices: Kingston, 845-443-2930.

Committees: *Agriculture*: Biotechnology, Horticulture & Research; Commodity Exchanges, Energy & Credit. *Small Business*: Economic Growth, Tax & Capital Access. *Transportation & Infrastructure*: Highways & Transit; Water Resources & Environment.

Election Results

Election	Name (Party)	Vote (%)	Cand. Spent	Ind. Exp. Support	Ind. Exp. Oppose
2018 General	Antonio Delgado (D)............................	147,873 (51%)	$8,987,722	$639,667	$6,367,113
	John Faso (R)................................	132,873 (46%)	$3,826,176	$1,691,166	$6,227,559
2018 Primary	Antonio Delgado (D)..............................	8,576 (22%)			
	Pat Ryan (D)..	6,941 (18%)			
	Gareth Rhodes (D).................................	6,890 (18%)			
	Brian Flynn (D)....................................	5,245 (14%)			
	Jeff Beals (D).....................................	4,991 (13%)			
	David Clegg (D).....................................	4,257 (11%)			

Democrat Antonio Delgado, elected in 2018, won a contentious campaign that gained national attention, as Republicans sought to demonize aspects of his diverse career. One of the most robust fundraisers in House campaigns, he also was among the African-American newcomers who won districts that leaned Republican and had small minority populations. Delgado defeated Republican Rep. John Faso, a freshman with extensive experience as a state lawmaker and lobbyist who asserted his independence from President Donald Trump.

A native of Schenectady, which is in the adjacent 20th District, Delgado graduated from Colgate University, where he was a leading player on the school's championship basketball team. He studied at Oxford University as a Rhodes Scholar, and got his law degree from Harvard University. In Los Angeles, he was a music-company executive and produced his own rap album, which he said was designed to empower young people with its focus on social justice. He returned to New York, where he represented large businesses and was a litigator with the large Washington-based law firm of Akin, Gump, Strauss, Hauer & Feld.

"I've lived a narrative that's hard to come by," Delgado told the Albany Times-Union. He described his life story as "one of upward mobility," but lamented that the American dream had become out of reach for many Americans, especially in upstate New York.

Days after Trump was inaugurated, Delgado decided to run for Congress — his first bid for political office — and called Trump's election "a moment of awakening." With Faso seen as a vulnerable reelection target, he faced six other candidates in the Democratic primary. They included businessmen Brian Flynn and Pat Ryan, who each spent more than $1 million, and Gareth Rhodes, a former aide to New York Gov. Andrew Cuomo.

Delgado raised the most money for the primary, and he highlighted his local roots; his parents had both worked at a large General Electric plant, which closed. He won the primary with 22 percent of the vote, to 18 percent for Ryan and Rhodes and 14 percent for Flynn. Delgado was the frontrunner in Ulster County, which cast the largest share of the vote, and he led in four of the other 10 counties.

Faso, who voted for repeal of the Affordable Care Act but opposed the tax cuts passed by House Republicans, sought to depict himself as a bipartisan problem-solver and opposed to wasteful spending. His campaign highlighted Trump-style themes that critics said were laced with racial messages and stoked fear of crime. He ran an ad that attacked Delgado as an outsider who moved to the district for the campaign, and as a "big-city rapper," with lyrics that were profane and politically radical.

Delgado responded that he was addressing issues such as income inequality and climate change. His campaign messages included the need for improved health care services and his pledge to be a "true independent actor" in Congress. Delgado's spending of $9 million more than doubled Faso's account, though the incumbent received more than $3 million in national-party support.

Delgado, with his 51%-46% victory, won the three largest counties, which are the closest to New York City: Ulster, where he had his biggest edge, Dutchess and Columbia. Faso took seven of the remaining eight counties in the more rural parts of the district. In a district represented by three Republicans during 20 of the previous 24 years, Delgado should expect a competitive reelection challenge. In April 2019, the Washington Post profiled Delgado's visits to his district, where he focused on local economic concerns but raised—or received—scant references to Trump.

NY-19: Central Hudson Valley, the Catskills   **Cook Partisan Voting Index: R+2**

Population		Race and Ethnicity		Income	
Total	705,473	White	84.9%	Median Income	$60,494
Land area (sq. miles)	7,937	Black	4%	District Income Rank	173
Pop/ sq mi	88.9	Latino	7.2%	Poverty Rate	12.5%
Born in State	75.2%	Asian	1.7%	With health insurance	93.7%
		Two or more races	1.9%	Cash public assistance	2.4%
Age Groups		Other	0.3%	Food stamp/SNAP	10.6%
Under 18	18.9%				
18-34	21%	**Education**		**Work**	
35-64	41.4%	H.S grad or less	42.1%	White Collar	18.7%
Over 64	18.7%	Some college	29.6%	Sales and Service	41.7%
		College Degree, 4 yr	15.5%	Blue Collar	21.1%
Military		Post grad	12.8%	Government	19.2%
Veteran/ Active Duty	7.8%				

2012 Pres. Vote	Obama	157,279	(52%)	Romney	138,384	(46%)			
2016 Pres. Vote	Trump	162,266	(50%)	Clinton	140,517	(44%)	Johnson	10,235	(3%)
	Stein	6,434	(2%)						

Dutchess and Ulster Counties: The Hudson River, an avenue of commerce in colonial days and an inspiration to artists in the early republic, is still one of America's great sights, although it is no longer central to the nation's consciousness and politics. The classic mansions overlooking the river, like Clermont, built by Robert Livingston, who financed the first steamboat, are reminders of the daring nature of the 18th century spirit. The Hudson gave birth to America's passionate party politics. On a visit to this area in the 1790s, James Madison and Aaron Burr welded the Virginia-New York alliance that changed the course of American political history. Nearby is Kinderhook, the home of Martin Van Buren, the innkeeper's son who, in concert with Andrew Jackson, invented the torchlight parade, the national party convention, and, many argue, the Democratic Party. Later in the 19th century, the Hudson was lined with the palaces of the nation's first great millionaires and the comfortable country homes of New York's gentry. One of the latter, Springwood in Hyde Park, was the birthplace and home of Franklin Roosevelt, who, even as president, was most comfortable looking out over his sloping lawn to the river, where he liked to go iceboating in the winter.

On the other side of the Hudson loom the Catskills, where Rip Van Winkle was said to have fallen asleep for 20 years after drinking with nine pipe-playing dwarfs. Eventually, the area became part of a great pathway west, along the Erie Lackawanna and Delaware & Hudson railroad lines, with engines steaming over giant viaducts and along narrow river valleys through the mountains. Later in the 19th century, huge kosher hotels were built in Sullivan County in the Catskills, the resort area popularly known as the Borscht Belt. These thrived when Jews were excluded from other resorts but fell on hard times in the late 20th century. Today, there is little passenger train service, and the Catskills are bypassed by major airlines. A new generation of inns and boutique hotels has sought to create a niche in recent years.

The sprawling 19th Congressional District of New York connects these two regions into a single district. It extends from north of Albany to the exurbs of New York City. Like most of the Upstate districts, its boundaries are relatively straight, in contrast to past gerrymanders. It includes seven full counties and parts of four others. It is a collection of small towns and villages. The largest locale is Kingston (pop. 23,169) and only one other place, Hyde Park, has more than 20,000 residents. Like most of Upstate, all but one of these counties (Rensselaer) lost population between and 2010 and 2017. The 19th bends around the Albany metropolitan area in the north, taking in a bit of the Mohawk Valley, and the Baseball Hall of Fame in Cooperstown. In Ulster is Bethel, where the 1969 Woodstock music festival took place. A huge Resorts World casino, with more than 2,000 jobs, opened in Sullivan County in 2018. Its initial financial reports were not positive. Roosevelt lore has contributed to more robust tourism in Dutchess County.

Ulster, the largest county, is solidly Democratic at the national level. Like most of Upstate, Republicans fare better at the local level and even control the county legislature. The district was once solidly Republican, part of a tradition that dated to the Civil War (Franklin Roosevelt never carried his home territory except when he ran for the state Senate in 1910.) Today, it is swing territory: Donald Trump won here, 50%-44%. Barack Obama carried the district twice.

Paul Tonko (D)

Elected 2008, 6th term, b. Jun 18, 1949; Amsterdam; Clarkson University (NY), B.S., 1971; Roman Catholic; Single.

Elected Office: Montgomery County Board of Supervisors, 1976-1983, Chairman, 1981; NY Assembly, 1983-2007.

Professional Career: NY Department of Transportation, 1972-1974; NY Department of Public Service, 1974-1983; President & CEO, NY St. Energy Research & Development Authority, 2007-2008.

DC Office: 2369 RHOB 20515, 202-225-5076, Fax: 202-225-5077, tonko.house.gov

State Offices: Albany, 518-465-0700; Amsterdam, 518-843-3400; Schenectady, 518-374-4547.

Committees: *Energy & Commerce*: Energy; Environment & Climate Change (Chmn); Oversight & Investigations. *Natural Resources*: National Parks, Forests & Public Lands. *Science, Space & Technology*: Environment; Research & Technology.

Group Ratings

	ADA	ACLU	AFL-CIO	LCV	ITI	COC	HAFA	ACU	CFG	FRC
2018	-	89%	-	94%	-	67%	4%	4%	5%	0%
2017	100%	C	97%	100%	C	36%	C	4%	5%	0%

Almanac Ratings 2017-18

	Economy	Social	Foreign	Composite
Liberal	100%	97%	100%	99%
Conservative	0%	3%	0%	1%

Key Votes of the 115th Congress

1. Obama-care revision	N	5. Family planning regs	N	9. Guantanamo prisoners	Y
2. Tax Cuts	N	6. Body cameras/immigration	Y	10. Ground missiles, limit	Y
3. Omnibus appropriations	Y	7. Abortion ban	N	11. Defense Dept. spending	N
4. Dodd-Frank revision	N	8. Concealed carry	N	12. FISA rules	N

Election Results

Election	Name (Party)	Vote (%)		Cand. Spent	Ind. Exp. Support	Ind. Exp. Oppose
2018 General	Paul Tonko (D)	176,811	(67%)	$807,825		
	Joe Vitollo (R)	89,058	(33%)			
2018 Primary	Paul Tonko (D)		(100%)			

Prior winning percentages: 2016 (68%), 2014 (59%), 2012 (64%), 2010 (57%), 2008 (55%)

Democrat Paul Tonko, elected in 2008, came to Congress with an extensive background in energy issues and parlayed his expertise into a seat on the powerful Energy and Commerce Committee, where he has dealt with similar types of industrial problems that are common to his district. In 2019, as a subcommittee chairman, his domain expanded to include climate change. He has had some bipartisan accomplishments.

The grandson of Polish immigrants, Tonko was born in the old mill town of Amsterdam New York, where he still lives. He graduated from Clarkson University with a degree in engineering. Attracted from a young age to public service, he built his career in state government, first at the New York Department of Transportation and then as an engineer at the Department of Public Service, the state's utilities regulator. His says his working-class background gave him an appreciation for the "underdog" that remains the underpinning of his political beliefs.

In 1974, at age 26, he became the youngest person elected to the Montgomery County Board of Supervisors, and later became board chairman. Tonko won a seat in the state Assembly in 1983 and served for nearly a quarter century. He won passage of a law requiring health insurers to cover most mental illnesses and another requiring social workers to report all cases of suspected child abuse to the state. He exercised his greatest influence over state energy policy, serving as chairman of the Assembly's energy committee for 15 years, until he resigned to head the state's Energy Research and Development Authority.

When the House seat opened, most of the local Democratic establishment lined up behind Tonko. He won important union endorsements, plus the backing of the Working Families Party. With few differences between the candidates on major issues, the local support likely made the difference. Outraised and outspent by both opponents, Tonko sailed to victory with 40 percent of the vote to 30 percent for Tracey Brooks, a former staffer for Democratic Sen. Hillary Clinton. In the general, Tonko faced Republican Jim Buhrmaster, a Schenectady County legislator; he won. 62%-35%.

Tonko has focused on the issue he knows best, energy policy. Even as a freshman, while Democrats controlled the House, Tonko was quick to exploit his policy expertise. He got a bill through the House in 2009 creating an $800 million research program in wind energy technologies, which would benefit GE in his district. Another of his bills, which passed the same year, created a research program to improve the efficiency of gas turbines used in power generation systems that convert heat into energy.

While Democrats were in the minority, much of Tonko's work was defensive. On Energy and Commerce, he was at the vanguard of defending the Environmental Protection Agency against GOP attacks. He co-chaired the Sustainable Energy and Environment Coalition. On spending bills, he sought to protect EPA's authority to regulate carbon emissions. He worked to undo Republican cutbacks to the Weatherization Assistance Program, which improves home energy efficiency through insulation and superior equipment. On the Science, Space and Technology Committee, he worked in 2015 to protect federal research funds that had been directed at Upstate manufacturing facilities.

Tonko pushed ahead with his own proposals. In 2016, the House passed his bill to encourage citizen activities in the federal government to accelerate scientific research. It was enacted as part of a broader package of innovation measures. In 2018, Tonko won enactment of his bill to require increased testing of local drinking water systems.

In the majority, Tonko became chairman of the renamed Environment and Climate Change Subcommittee, which has jurisdiction over the Clean Air Act. "We don't have the time or resources to let this president and his allies in Congress sit on their hands for another two years," he declared. He held an early hearing on warming global temperatures. Climate-change activists have complained that Tonko was not moving fast enough. Protestors rallied on the steps of his office in Albany and demanded that he support the "Green New Deal" proposal backed by many progressive Democrats and their environmental allies. But Tonko was skeptical about the vague guidelines of that proposal, which did not define specific policy action. He also clashed with activists by voicing reservations about the need for a select committee on climate change and responding that House committees "should be allowed to do their work." Speaker Nancy Pelosi created a select committee but did not give it legislative authority.

On other issues, Tonko worked to expand low-income children's access to healthy meals. He has sought to promote mental-health parity, as he did in Albany. The Almanac vote ratings have consistently ranked Tonko among the most liberal members.

Tonko has had little trouble winning reelection. Albany Times Union columnist Marv Cermak described him in 2011 as "a super-duper campaigner who shows up all over the place," and said "If there is a chink in his armor, colleagues and media types agree it's his penchant for long-winded speeches." On the other hand, he resists hyper-partisanship. "He is frustrated that partisan politics are overshadowing science, math and reason," the Albany Business Review reported in February 2018. In the politically divided Congress, Tonko has the opportunity to address that problem.

NY-20: Capital Region   Cook Partisan Voting Index: D+7

Population		Race and Ethnicity		Income	
Total	727,071	White	76.7%	Median Income	$64,154
Land area (sq. miles)	1,231	Black	8.6%	District Income Rank	142
Pop/ sq mi	590.5	Latino	6.2%	Poverty Rate	12%
Born in State	75.5%	Asian	5%	With health insurance	95.3%
		Two or more races	2.8%	Cash public assistance	2.7%
Age Groups		Other	0.7%	Food stamp/SNAP	11.7%
Under 18	20%				
18-34	25.2%	**Education**		**Work**	
35-64	38.8%	H.S grad or less	33.6%	White Collar	16%
Over 64	16%	Some college	29%	Sales and Service	41.8%
		College Degree, 4 yr	20.4%	Blue Collar	14.8%
Military		Post grad	17%	Government	21.7%
Veteran/ Active Duty	7.2%				

2012 Pres. Vote	Obama	186,460	(59%)	Romney	122,230	(39%)			
2016 Pres. Vote	Clinton	175,384	(53%)	Trump	131,557	(40%)	Johnson	12,538	(4%)

Albany, Schenectady: As readers of novelist laureate William Kennedy know, Albany is an antique city. Its solid row houses recall its 19th century prosperity. Its once-teeming lumberyards, railroad car shops, restaurants and hotels have the patina of age and the accumulated grime of decades of coal smoke burned during six-month-long winters. Its history dates to 1609, when Dutch traders from Henry Hudson's ship Half Moon set up a fur trading post. Hudson, his son, and seven crew members were set adrift amidst a mutiny in James Bay, Canada, two years later and never seen again, but the trading post endured. The Dutch built Fort Orange on the banks of the Hudson in 1624 so seagoing ships could dock at the edge of the great, gloomy forests near the confluence of the Hudson and the Mohawk. Albany became one of America's biggest lumber towns.

A few miles upriver, Troy was a steel town rivaling Pittsburgh in the 1840s, greatly advantaged by its proximity to the mouth of the Erie Canal. That is where meatpacker Samuel Wilson supplied beef rations to soldiers during the War of 1812; we know Wilson today as "Uncle Sam." Lately, a gentrified Troy has been bustling with antique shops, though many former industrial properties remain vacant. Schenectady, a few miles up the Mohawk, was the site of Charles Steinmetz's fabled General Electric laboratories and long remained a GE town.

In addition to state government, Albany had one of the nation's most famed Democratic political machines, dating to 1921, when Daniel O'Connell, his brothers, and local aristocrat Edwin Corning took control of City Hall. The machine was sustained by legions of city and county employees, by a certain creativity when it came to counting votes, and by the raffish atmosphere of the speakeasies during Prohibition. Curiously, the machine made possible the transformation of Albany into the shinier metropolis it is today. Mayor Corning and Republican Gov. Nelson Rockefeller collaborated on a smorgasbord of civic improvement projects: Empire State Plaza with 11,000 employees in 10 government buildings on 98 acres; the distinctive, ovoid performing arts center known as the Egg; and a renovated Union Station.

The economy in the Capital Region has been stronger than elsewhere in Upstate, with a population gain of 17,000 between 2010 and 2017. The area has remained vibrant with renewable energy jobs and high-tech manufacturing. GE has new plants producing digital X-ray equipment and advanced batteries, though its 5,000-plus area employees are a shadow of the 40,000 in heavy manufacturing at Schenectady Works during World War II. The port of Albany has spent $50 million on an expansion to move additional cargo — partly as an inducement for GE to remain in the area; with the continued downsizing of the company, that might be a risky bet.

The 20th Congressional District of New York includes most of the Albany metropolitan area: all of Albany and Schenectady counties, which take in nearly two-thirds of the district population; most of Montgomery County, including Amsterdam; parts of Rensselaer County, including Troy;

and much of Saratoga County. The horse-race track at Saratoga Springs, operating since 1863 and reportedly the oldest sports venue in the nation, in 2018 completed a major upgrade, including the grandstand. Politically, Democratic voters in Albany and Troy outweigh the Republican tilt of the outer counties and make this a comfortably Democratic district. As in other Upstate districts, the Democratic presidential vote fell in 2016. Hillary Clinton got 53 percent of the vote.

Elise Stefanik (R)

Elected 2014, 3rd term, b. Jul 02, 1984; Albany; Harvard University, Bach. Deg.; Roman Catholic; Engaged (Matthew Manda).

Professional Career: Staff, President George W. Bush, 2006-2009; Staff, Vice President. candidate Paul Ryan, 2012; Director Communications, Foreign Policy Initiative; Sales, marketing & mgmt operations, Premium Plywood Products.

DC Office: 318 CHOB 20515, 202-225-4611, Fax: 202-226-0621, stefanik.house.gov

State Offices: Glens Falls, 518-743-0964; Plattsburgh, 518-561-2324; Watertown, 315-782-3150.

Committees: *Armed Services*: Intelligence, Emerging Threats & Capabilities (RMM); Readiness. *Education & Labor*: Civil Rights & Human Services; Higher Education & Workforce Investment. *Permanent Select on Intelligence*: Intelligence Modernization & Readiness; Strategic Technologies & Advanced Research.

Group Ratings

	ADA	ACLU	AFL-CIO	LCV	ITI	COC	HAFA	ACU	CFG	FRC
2018	-	14%	-	51%	-	100%	24%	32%	29%	100%
2017	10%	C	39%	43%	C	86%	C	41%	24%	67%

Almanac Ratings 2017-18

	Economy	Social	Foreign	Composite
Liberal	32%	20%	10%	21%
Conservative	68%	80%	90%	79%

Key Votes of the 115th Congress

1. Obama-care revision	Y	5. Family planning regs	Y	9. Guantanamo prisoners	N
2. Tax Cuts	N	6. Body cameras/immigration	N	10. Ground missiles, limit	N
3. Omnibus appropriations	Y	7. Abortion ban	Y	11. Defense Dept. spending	Y
4. Dodd-Frank revision	Y	8. Concealed carry	Y	12. FISA rules	Y

Election Results

Election	Name (Party)	Vote (%)		Cand. Spent	Ind. Exp. Support	Ind. Exp. Oppose
2018 General	Elise Stefanik (R)	131,981	(56%)	$2,980,681	$86,955	
	Tedra Cobb (D)	99,791	(42%)	$1,495,823	$3,176	
2018 Primary	Elise Stefanik (R)		(100%)			

Prior winning percentages: 2016 (65%), 2014 (53%)

Republican Elise Stefanik, elected to an open seat in 2014 that had been Democratic-held, has taken advantage of her opportunities. When she took office, she was the youngest woman ever elected to Congress. The politically adept Stefanik is a rising and prominent Republican star. With good connections to House leaders, she has worked to entrench herself politically, with apparent success.

Born and raised in Albany, Stefanik grew up among entrepreneurs, with both parents running a wholesale plywood business. She became politically engaged during her college years at Harvard, and upon graduation she landed a job with the Bush administration's Domestic Policy Council. She worked in the White House chief of staff's office, and later joined Tim Pawlenty's presidential campaign as policy director. After Pawlenty withdrew, she worked for Rep. Paul Ryan of Wisconsin when he became the running mate for Mitt Romney, advising him on vice presidential debate preparation.

After Blue Dog Democratic Rep. Bill Owens announced his retirement, Stefanik unveiled her House bid and earned the backing of the National Republican Congressional Committee's "Young Guns" program, which supports new talent. With nearly $800,000 in help from Karl Rove's American Crossroads — making a rare intervention in a GOP primary — Stefanik dispatched Republican Matt Doheny in the June primary, 61%-39%. A Wall Street investment banker, Doheny had run twice against Owens, and lost each time by two percentage points.

Democrats faced problems in recruiting, and their nominee, Aaron Wolff, was a filmmaker who was a resident of Brooklyn. His only claim to the North Country was that his family owned some land. In the general, Stefanik moderated from the customary GOP line on some issues. She signaled willingness to compromise on raising the minimum wage, and proposed expanding Medicare as part of an alternative to the Affordable Care Act. She refused to sign Grover Norquist's anti-tax pledge, arguing that she was beholden to voters, not lobbyists. Her campaign came under criticism for lacking a district address and for property-tax delinquency in Washington. Stefanik benefited from nearly $2 million in party-related assistance, far more than Democrats spent for Wolff, who also suffered from an active campaign by Green Party candidate Matt Funicello. Stefanik pulled away to a surprisingly comfortable win, with 55 percent of the vote to 34 percent for Wolff and 11 percent for Funicello. She won nine of the 12 counties, losing three in the northeast corner of the state.

Stefanik has drawn considerable publicity, nearly all of it favorable. CBS News featured her with an online story headlined, "Is Elise Stefanik the future of the GOP?"

Stefanik's committee assignments put her at the forefront of national security policy. On the Armed Services Committee, she is the ranking member of the Emerging Threats and Capabilities Subcommittee, which oversees counterterrorism programs and the proliferation of weapons of mass destruction. She also serves on the often-contentious Intelligence Committee. As a member of the Education and Labor Committee, she worked with Democratic Rep. Cheri Bustos of Illinois to provide more flexible access to Pell Grants.

Stefanik has had multiple party assignments. She is a member of the House GOP steering committee, a group that holds enormous sway over committee assignments. At the National Republican Congressional Committee, she spent the 2018 cycle as the vice chair for recruitment, the first woman to hold that position. She recruited more than 100 Republican women to run for office. Only one, West Virginia's Carole Miller, was elected to the House. The party's female ranks dwindled to 13 House members. Stefanik announced in December 2018 that she would step back from NRCC duties and instead focus on taking a more active role in supporting women candidates in primaries. NRCC Chairman Tom Emmer called the move "a mistake." Stefanik tweeted that she wasn't asking permission.

Democrats have backed away from competing for her district. In both 2016 and 2018, her challengers received virtually no party assistance. In 2018, she coasted to victory, 56%-42%, over Tedra Cobb. Stefanik kept her distance from Donald Trump during the 2016 campaign, when she voiced occasional criticism and said that she would be "an independent voice for the district." After he became president, she criticized Trump for his handling of the immigration and refugee bans, which she said was "rushed and overly broad."

In a gracious moment after the 2018 midterms, Stefanik took to Twitter to congratulate Democratic Rep. Alexandria Ocasio-Cortez, who surpassed her as the youngest woman ever elected to Congress. "I proudly hand off that mantle to you," Stefanik wrote. "Work hard to encourage the next generation of women who follow!"

NY-21: Northern New York

Cook Partisan Voting Index: R+4

Population		Race and Ethnicity		Income	
Total	712,223	White	90.2%	Median Income	$53,402
Land area (sq. miles)	15,115	Black	3%	District Income Rank	247
Pop/ sq mi	47.1	Latino	3.4%	Poverty Rate	14%
Born in State	77.3%	Asian	1%	With health insurance	93.7%
		Two or more races	1.5%	Cash public assistance	3.2%
Age Groups		Other	1%	Food stamp/SNAP	14.6%
Under 18	20.7%				
18-34	23.1%	**Education**		**Work**	
35-64	39.8%	H.S grad or less	46.2%	White Collar	16.4%
Over 64	16.4%	Some college	30.5%	Sales and Service	43.6%
		College Degree, 4 yr	12.8%	Blue Collar	23.2%
Military		Post grad	10.4%	Government	21%
Veteran/ Active Duty	11.8%				

2012 Pres. Vote	Obama	138,889	(52%)	Romney	122,471	(46%)			
2016 Pres. Vote	Trump	150,481	(53%)	Clinton	111,760	(39%)	Johnson	11,620	(4%)
	Stein	5,577	(2%)						

Glens Falls, Watertown: Some early 19th century visionaries believed that the North Country of Upstate New York — a battleground in both the Revolutionary War and the War of 1812 — was the land of the future. Politician Gouverneur Morris, French slave trader James LeRay, and Dutch silver speculator David Parish bought up thousands of acres between the Adirondacks and the St. Lawrence River and tried to unload them on farmers unaware of the shortness of the growing season and the unnavigability of the river. These developers left behind grand mansions, but their hopes for huge profits were frustrated when the Erie Canal turned the stream of settlement westward, and Canadians built their new capital of Ottawa far north of the river. But northern New York was not without its business successes: It was in Watertown in 1878 that 26-year-old Frank Woolworth put a sign over a table of odds and ends that read "Any Article 5 Cents," starting America's first retail chain and inventing the concept of discount stores.

More recently, the North Country has looked to government for help. The St. Lawrence Seaway proved too small for most oceangoing freighters and remains frozen three months of the year. Plan 2014, a binational agreement with Canada to return the St. Lawrence River to more natural flowing patterns, took effect in 2016. Fort Drum, despite the Army's preference for warm-weather training sites, has been the home since 1985 of the 10th Mountain Division, a 10,000-person light infantry division near Watertown. The unit performed valiantly in difficult environs in Afghanistan and Iraq. In 2017, the economic impact of Drum slightly improved for the region. Another economic bright spot: In Massena and Plattsburg -- places with abandoned aluminum plants -- companies use the cheap electricity derived from St. Lawrence River dams to fuel computer servers that produce Bitcoins, a digital currency. Private developers have built big malls in Watertown and Massena, with the cheap dollar attracting Canadian tourism and shopping, as even New York taxes are lower than Ontario's. In March 2019, The Atlantic found in a national survey that Watertown and the surrounding area were among the most "politically tolerant" places in the United States, based on the openness of local people to other points of view.

The 21st Congressional District of New York covers most of the North Country, starting at Lake Champlain, running westward along the St. Lawrence Seaway and over the Adirondacks Forest Preserve to Lake Ontario. Lake Placid is here, site of the 1980 Olympic Games and the famous "Miracle on Ice," when a heavily favored Soviet hockey team was upset by an upstart American squad. It stretches to the edges of Saratoga Springs to the southeast, and near Oswego and Syracuse to the southwest. Malone, located near the Canadian border, was the boyhood home of Almanzo Wilder, the protagonist of wife Laura Ingalls Wilder's children's book "Farmer Boy." The district has only a few population centers, including Plattsburgh on Lake Champlain, Watertown near Lake Ontario, and Gloversville and Glens Falls in the south. Each is home to fewer than 30,000 residents, with population declining from 2010 to 2017. Warren County is known as "catheter valley" because of its many medical-device companies that make such products.

Geographically it is the largest district in New York and one of the largest in the East. It is ancestrally Republican but more inclined toward moderates than conservatives and increasingly divided in its partisan loyalties. Clinton, Franklin and St. Lawrence counties in the northeast corner along the Vermont border have been solidly Democratic since the 1990s. The southwestern counties are more heavily Republican. Overall, the district is competitive. Donald Trump ran well ahead of his national performance, with a 53%-39% win.

Anthony Brindisi (D)

Elected 2018, 1st term, b. Nov 22, 1978; Utica; Siena College (NY), B.S., 2000; Albany Law School, J.D., 2004; Catholic; Married (Erica McGovern); 2 children.

Elected Office: Utica School Board,2009-2011; NY Assembly, 2011-2018.

Professional Career: Small Business Owner; Attorney, Brindisi, Murad, Brindisi & Pearlman, LLP.

DC Office: 329 CHOB 20515, 202-225-3665, brindisi.house.gov

State Offices: Binghamton, 607-242-0200; Utica, 315-732-0713.

Committees: *Agriculture*: Biotechnology, Horticulture & Research; Livestock & Foreign Agriculture. *Veterans' Affairs*: Economic Opportunity; Health.

Election Results

Election	Name (Party)	Vote (%)		Cand. Spent	Ind. Exp. Support	Ind. Exp. Oppose
2018 General	Anthony J. Brindisi (D)....................... 127,715	(51%)		$4,587,361	$584,804	$6,702,952
	Claudia Tenney (R).......................... 123,242	(49%)		$3,042,204	$520,744	$8,201,219
2018 Primary	Anthony J. Brindisi (D).....................................	(100%)				

Freshman Democrat Anthony Brindisi won a swing district in upstate New York that has elected diverse members in recent years. He styled himself as an advocate of "principled bipartisanship" and claimed success with that approach during four terms in the state's Democratic-dominated Assembly. He narrowly defeated first-term Rep. Claudia Tenney, a conservative Republican who clashed with her moderate Republican predecessor. One of three Democrats who defeated GOP incumbents in New York in 2018, Brindisi's margin was the tightest.

A native of Utica in his district, Brindisi graduated from Siena College and got his law degree from Albany Law School. As a member of the school board in Utica, where he practiced law, he led a project to renovate outdated school buildings. In 2011, he was elected to the Assembly, where he focused on job training and education, including passage of his plan to encourage diplomas for high school students. An example of his occasional collaboration across party lines in Albany was the support that he received from the National Rifle Association, which gave him a perfect rating; the NRA did not extend its support to his congressional bid.

Tenney, who served four years in the Assembly, waged a bitter GOP primary challenge to Rep. Richard Hanna in 2014, which she narrowly lost, leaving bad blood within the party. When she decided to run again in 2016, Hanna retired after three terms and he opposed her in the primary, which Tenney won with 42 percent of the vote against two opponents. Hanna's continued opposition led him to support an independent candidate in the general election. That split the vote in the three-way contest, which Tenney won with 47 percent of the vote. She was boosted by Donald Trump's double-digit win in the district.

In 2018, both candidates won their nomination without opposition. With Trump supporting Tenney, including his participation at a fundraising event in Utica three months before the election, she appeared to have unified GOP voters following her two contentious primaries. "I'm here for Claudia," Trump told the local crowd, in what reportedly was the first presidential visit to the area in 70 years. "She has helped us so much." Tenney cited the alleged mob ties of Brindisi's father, a lawyer who had represented organized-crime figures and pleaded guilty to cocaine possession in 1991. In response, the campaign manager for Brindisi accused Tenney of "blatant and false attacks on Italians." Some local Republicans joined criticism of her "ethnic smear."

Brindisi attacked Tenney for "marching in lockstep with the hard right on critical issues" in Congress. He kept his distance from House Democratic leaders and was more circumspect about taking on Trump. "People see Claudia Tenney as part of the same rigged system that President Trump campaigned against," he told a campaign rally in Binghamton. He told a local reporter that he and Tenney "really didn't work together too much on issues" when they served together in Albany.

Brindisi's $4.6 million in spending gave him an advantage over Tenney. In addition, the two parties spent a total of about $16 million on the campaign. In his 51%-49% victory, Brindisi won the two largest counties in the district — Broome, which was the core of his victory margin, and Oneida. Tenney took five smaller, rural counties. In this district, neither party can take the outcome for granted.

NY-22: Central New York

Cook Partisan Voting Index: R+6

Population		Race and Ethnicity		Income	
Total	704,369	White	87.7%	Median Income	$51,482
Land area (sq. miles)	5,077	Black	3.8%	District Income Rank	277
Pop/ sq mi	138.7	Latino	3.6%	Poverty Rate	15.5%
Born in State	80.7%	Asian	2.7%	With health insurance	94.9%
		Two or more races	1.8%	Cash public assistance	4%
Age Groups		Other	0.3%	Food stamp/SNAP	16.1%
Under 18	20.7%				
18-34	23%	**Education**		**Work**	
35-64	38.8%	H.S grad or less	44.8%	White Collar	17.5%
Over 64	17.5%	Some college	30.8%	Sales and Service	43%
		College Degree, 4 yr	14%	Blue Collar	21.8%
Military		Post grad	10.3%	Government	18.9%
Veteran/ Active Duty	8.7%				

2012 Pres. Vote	Romney	136,500	(49%)	Obama	135,172	(49%)			
2016 Pres. Vote	Trump	158,913	(54%)	Clinton	114,016	(39%)	Johnson	12,349	(4%)

Utica, Binghamton: One of the first American frontiers was the Mohawk River Valley of Upstate New York. But from the establishment of Fort Orange in 1624 in what is now Albany until the Revolutionary War, white settlers did not dare move west along the Mohawk. The British used their Iroquois allies as a buffer against the French and in turn kept New England Yankees from moving westward. Only after the French were driven from North America in 1759 did the pressures for westward settlement prevail. Once the Revolutionary War started, Iroquois dominion ended. The later digging of the Erie Canal was an engineering feat that hastened the westward push. In 1811, it cost more to ship goods 30 miles inland from New York City than to send them to England. But after eight years of work by 9,000 men, the canal opened in 1825, ahead of schedule and on budget, effectively tying together the nation and guaranteeing the preeminence of New York City in America's economy.

When the New York Central built its water-line rail route to the west, the Mohawk Valley became one of the nation's early industrial centers. The little Oneida County hamlets of Utica and Rome, where the canal builders had to dig through the route's highest ground, became sizable factory towns. First settled by New England Yankees, these towns attracted a new wave of immigration from the Atlantic coast in the early 20th century, including many Italian and Polish Americans.

The 22nd Congressional District of New York drops from Lake Ontario to the Pennsylvania border in a strip east of Syracuse, as it sprawls through all or parts of eight counties in central New York, most of them lightly populated. The biggest cities are Utica and Rome in Oneida County and Binghamton in Broome County. Each county takes in about 30 percent of the district. This part of Upstate New York has been bypassed by economic growth for decades. Oneida County's population has dropped 15 percent since it peaked in the 1970 census. A similar pattern applied in Broome, which has lost about 13 percent during that time -- and 15,000 jobs from 2007 to 2017. Since 2010, Oneida and Broome, respectively, lost another 4 percent and 2 percent of their population. With these losses, it's no surprise that Oneida has become a popular spot for refugees and immigrants from across the world. More than 16,000 refugees have settled in Utica in the past 40 years, while the overall population dropped by more than 20,000 during that period. In a once economically dynamic area, the largest employer in central New York has become Oneida Nation's Turning Stone Resort Casino, which operates a huge retail outlet and entertainment complex with 4,700 employees; in January 2019, the resort announced plans to partner with Caesars Entertainment to offer sports betting. State government has completed dredging for Utica Harbor, which is the successor to the Erie Canal in Utica. In 2018, developers were negotiating for purchase of nearby land.

Politically this area had been Republican since the party came into existence in the 1850s, and the GOP maintains a registration advantage in every county except Broome. After Barack Obama got 49 percent in each of his elections, Donald Trump won the district, 54%-39%, and took all eight counties.

Tom Reed (R)

Elected 2010, 5th full term, b. Nov 18, 1971; Joliet, IL; Alfred University (NY), Bach. Deg., 1993; Ohio Northern University College of Law, J.D., 1996; Roman Catholic; Married (Jean Reed); 2 children.

Elected Office: Corning Mayor, 2008-2010.

Professional Career: Clerk, private firm, 1995; Association Attorney, private firm, 1996-1999; Owner, Law Office of Thomas W. Reed II.

DC Office: 2263 RHOB 20515, 202-225-3161, Fax: 202-226-6599, reed.house.gov

State Offices: Corning, 607-654-7566; Geneva, 315-759-5229; Jamestown, 716-708-6369; Olean, 716-379-8434.

Committees: *Ways & Means*: Health; Social Security (RMM); Worker & Family Support.

Group Ratings

	ADA	ACLU	AFL-CIO	LCV	ITI	COC	HAFA	ACU	CFG	FRC
2018	-	15%	-	17%	-	92%	34%	54%	51%	100%
2017	5%	C	32%	11%	C	93%	C	58%	47%	78%

Almanac Ratings 2017-18

	Economy	Social	Foreign	Composite
Liberal	11%	17%	10%	13%
Conservative	89%	83%	90%	87%

Key Votes of the 115th Congress

1. Obama-care revision	Y	5. Family planning regs	Y	9. Guantanamo prisoners	N
2. Tax Cuts	Y	6. Body cameras/immigration	Y	10. Ground missiles, limit	N
3. Omnibus appropriations	N	7. Abortion ban	Y	11. Defense Dept. spending	Y
4. Dodd-Frank revision	Y	8. Concealed carry	Y	12. FISA rules	Y

Election Results

Election	Name (Party)	Vote (%)		Cand. Spent	Ind. Exp. Support	Ind. Exp. Oppose
2018 General	Tom Reed (R).....................................	130,323	(54%)	$3,519,183	$324,264	$12,600
	Tracy Mitrano (D)...........................	109,932	(46%)	$1,734,248	$40,221	
2018 Primary	Tom Reed (R).................................	(100%)				

Prior winning percentages: 2016 (58%), 2014 (58%), 2012 (52%), 2010 (57%)

Republican Tom Reed, who took office in 2010, is a pragmatic and low-key centrist who has styled himself as a "problem solver" willing to cross the party line. On the Ways and Means Committee, he has worked on tax and trade issues and has become the top Republican on the Social Security Subcommittee. He failed in a party leadership bid, but showed influence in working with Democrats in 2018 on House rules reforms — some of which Nancy Pelosi accepted to assure that she would become Speaker.

Reed was born in Joliet Illinois, the youngest of 12 children. His father was an Army veteran and Silver Star recipient who fought in World War II and Korea, but he accidentally died of carbon monoxide poisoning while working on his car when Reed was two years old. Reed's surviving family soon moved to Corning New York, where his mother had grown up. She stayed home to take care of the children, relying on her late husband's military death benefits and Social Security checks for financial support. Reed got his bachelor's at Alfred University in western New York. He went to law school at Ohio Northern University College, then worked at a law firm in Rochester before he returned to Corning to start his own firm. He was elected mayor in 2007.

He first ran for a vacant seat after the Democratic incumbent resigned following inappropriate behavior with staff aides. Reed was unchallenged for the Republican nomination. Democratic nominee Matthew Zeller, an Afghanistan combat veteran, argued that he would protect Social Security and create jobs more effectively than would Reed, who focused his message on reducing the deficit and shrinking government. Zeller raised $457,000, compared with Reed's $1 million. Capitalizing on the Republican wave, Reed won, 57%-43%.

Reed has mostly stuck with his party on major legislation, though his Almanac vote ratings have ranked him near the center of the House. He impressed leadership by getting the support of colleagues for free trade agreements with Colombia, Panama and South Korea. In 2011, he got a prized seat on Ways and Means, rare for a freshman. In 2015, he backed a change that Republicans made in House rules to prevent a transfer of funds from the Social Security retirement system as "a short-term Band Aid" to fix the serious financial shortfall in the federal disability program. Later that year, he enacted his Trade Facilitation and Trade Enforcement Act, which was largely a law-enforcement measure that overhauled the Customs and Border Protection agency.

After the 2014 election, Reed ran against two other candidates for chairman of the House Republican Policy Committee, which has been viewed as a stepping-stone to higher leadership positions. On the showdown second ballot, he lost to Luke Messer of Indiana, 137-90.

In 2017, Reed took over as Republican co-chair of the bipartisan Problem Solvers Caucus, whose objective was "fighting for commonsense principles that impact all Americans – Democrat, Republican, independent – everyone," he said. With the partisan line-drawing that year on the major health care and tax policies, which Reed helped to shape at Ways and Means, the caucus initially had little influence. But he joined members of both parties in the group who worked prior to the 2018 election to propose in the new Congress rules changes that were designed to open the House floor to debate of additional legislation, including amendments. After extended negotiations with Pelosi resulted in their agreement in late November, Reed praised her for having "opened up the door to giving power back to members." Despite unspecified threats from Republican leadership of "consequences," Reed was one of three Republicans who took the unusual step of voting for the new majority party's rules package — including those changes — when Democrats took control of the House in January.

In a significant opportunity, Reed in January 2019 became ranking Republican on the Social Security Subcommittee at a time when leading House Democrats were eager to address long-term financing demands facing the retirement and disability trust funds. "We will work together with Democrats for the American people to protect this program and ensure Social Security is around for future generations," said Reed, who had personal familiarity with its benefits. The appointment indicated that he did not face immediate consequences for his independence on the House rules changes.

On local issues, Reed added an amendment to the House-passed fiscal 2013 energy and water spending bill to increase money for cleanups at sites such as his district's West Valley Demonstration Project, a former nuclear fuel reprocessing facility in Ashford. In 2018, the House passed his bill to authorize long-term funding for West Valley. Although the Senate did not act, Congress continued to approve annual spending for the project in appropriations bills.

Reed has faced competitive Democratic challengers from the Ithaca-based eastern edge of his district. In 2012, Nate Shinagawa, the 28-year-old vice chairman of the Tompkins County Legislature, attacked Reed for his support of hydraulic fracturing for natural gas. Reed said he supported an exemption for drilling in the Finger Lakes. He eked out a win, 52%-48%. In 2014, Martha Robinson, chairwoman of the Tompkins Legislature, strongly opposed fossil-fuel production in New York and changes in the Social Security cost-of-living adjustment. She raised more money than Shinagawa, but was outpaced, $3.4 million to $2.3 million. Reed won, 62%-38%, an indication that he had become entrenched in his seat. In 2018, he faced Tracy Mitrano, a cybersecurity expert who had overseen digital information policy at Cornell University. Reed called her "an extreme Ithaca liberal." She spent $1.7 million to $3.5 million for Reed. Reed won, 54%-46%, though he continued to win every county except for Tompkins, where Mitrano got 76 percent.

As with other Upstate House members, redistricting in 2022 could pose problems for Reed. He likely will have an advantage with his secure political base on the Southern Tier.

NY-23: Southern Tier   Cook Partisan Voting Index: R+6

Population		Race and Ethnicity		Income	
Total	706,305	White	88.5%	Median Income	$49,433
Land area (sq. miles)	7,372	Black	2.7%	District Income Rank	320
Pop/ sq mi	95.8	Latino	3.8%	Poverty Rate	16.3%
Born in State	74.4%	Asian	2.4%	With health insurance	92.9%
		Two or more races	1.9%	Cash public assistance	3.2%
Age Groups		Other	0.6%	Food stamp/SNAP	14.8%
Under 18	20.4%				
18-34	24.1%	Education		Work	
35-64	38.3%	H.S grad or less	44.6%	White Collar	17.2%
Over 64	17.2%	Some college	29.5%	Sales and Service	40.8%
		College Degree, 4 yr	13.5%	Blue Collar	23.7%
Military		Post grad	12.4%	Government	16.1%
Veteran/ Active Duty	9%				

2012 Pres. Vote	Romney	137,307	(50%)	Obama	133,940	(48%)			
2016 Pres. Vote	Trump	158,158	(54%)	Clinton	115,014	(39%)	Johnson	11,749	(4%)

Jamestown, Ithaca: The Southern Tier of New York is one of the nation's forgotten stretches of territory, yet it has an interesting and distinctive history. Elmira was the hometown of Mark Twain's beloved wife, Olivia, and it is where Twain is buried. On Lake Chautauqua, not far from Lake Erie, a training camp for Methodist Sunday school teachers was founded in 1874. In summers, on wide green lawns and in Victorian-style gazebos, some 25,000 people heard educational talks and inspirational lectures from the likes of William Jennings Bryan. The area has an Indian presence, with small reservations as wells as the Seneca-Iroquois National Museum in Salamanca, plus miles and miles of dairy farms. Sheltered by hills, the lands at the edge of Upstate New York's deep lakes constitute the nation's largest grape-growing area outside California.

Corning is the headquarters of Corning Glass Works, a company successful over the years not only in manufacturing but also in its artistic distinction, which is showcased at a well-visited glass museum. Its long-term prospects have improved dramatically, with heavy demand for its fiber optics and other high-tech components. The Fortune 500 company makes key components of the liquid crystal display (LCD) glass used in flat-screen televisions and computers. But the company produces and sells much of that display glass overseas, including in Beijing. At its Big Flats plant in Corning, the company announced in 2017 its plan to manufacture Valor glass, which is used by the pharmaceutical industry to reduce breakage. In Jamestown, where it employs 1,700 workers, the Cummins Co. manufactures more efficient engines for industry and heavy-duty trucks. Gov. Andrew Cuomo's ban on fracking in New York has caused complaints by landowners along the Southern Tier, who contend that towns across the state line in Pennsylvania have benefitted from drilling the oil shale.

The 23rd Congressional District of New York is centered on the state's Southern Tier, extending from Chautauqua near Erie across the Pennsylvania line almost to Binghamton, more than halfway to the Massachusetts line. To the north, it includes the central Finger Lakes: giant gorges torn into the Earth's crust by expanding glaciers, and then naturally dammed up by the debris deposited when the glaciers retreated. Nearby Seneca Falls was the birthplace of the women's rights movement in 1848, when Boston transplants Elizabeth Cady Stanton and Lucretia Mott produced a Declaration of Sentiments that initiated the push for suffrage. The town is believed to be the inspiration for Bedford Falls in the classic film, It's a Wonderful Life. In the small town of Celoron, a statue honors Lucille Ball, the hometown native who became a renowned comedian. In nearby Jamestown, the $50 million National Comedy Center opened in August 2018, with more than 50 interactive exhibits. USA Today ranked it as the best new museum of the year. Ithaca has become the economic bright spot of the district. Its 3 percent growth in 2017 was the best in the state and the airport is expected to open its expanded terminal in late 2019.

The addition of the heavily Democratic university town of Ithaca made the district more competitive at the federal level; Republicans still perform well locally. President Barack Obama lost this district by two percentage points in 2012, after winning it by one point in 2008. In 2016, Donald

Trump won the district by 15 points and took every county by a double-digit margin except for Ithaca-based Tompkins, where he lost nearly 3-to-1.

John Katko (R)

Elected 2014, 3rd term, b. Nov 09, 1962; Syracuse; Niagara University, B.A., 1984; Syracuse University - College of Law (NY), J.D., 1988; Roman Catholic; Married (Robin Katko); 3 children.

Professional Career: Sr. trial Attorney, U.S. Securities & Exchange Comm., 1991-1995; Prosecutor, NY Northern District U.S. Attorney office; Assistant U.S. Attorney, U.S. Justice Department, 1995-2013.

DC Office: 2457 RHOB 20515, 202-225-3701, Fax: 202-225-4042, katko.house.gov

State Offices: Auburn, 315-253-4068; Lyons, 315-253-4068; Oswego, 315-423-5657; Syracuse, 315-423-5657.

Committees: *Homeland Security*: Cybersecurity, Infrastructure Protection & Innovation (RMM); Transportation & Maritime Security. *Transportation & Infrastructure*: Aviation; Highways & Transit.

Group Ratings

	ADA	ACLU	AFL-CIO	LCV	ITI	COC	HAFA	ACU	CFG	FRC
2018	-	22%	-	43%	-	83%	26%	36%	34%	100%
2017	5%	C	45%	26%	C	93%	C	48%	38%	67%

Almanac Ratings 2017-18

	Economy	Social	Foreign	Composite
Liberal	29%	22%	16%	22%
Conservative	71%	78%	84%	78%

Key Votes of the 115th Congress

1. Obama-care revision	N	5. Family planning regs	Y	9. Guantanamo prisoners	N
2. Tax Cuts	Y	6. Body cameras/immigration	Y	10. Ground missiles, limit	N
3. Omnibus appropriations	Y	7. Abortion ban	Y	11. Defense Dept. spending	Y
4. Dodd-Frank revision	Y	8. Concealed carry	Y	12. FISA rules	Y

Election Results

Election	Name (Party)	Vote (%)		Cand. Spent	Ind. Exp. Support	Ind. Exp. Oppose
2018 General	John Katko (R)...............................	136,920	(53%)	$2,984,541	$569,270	$2,509,193
	Dana Balter (D)...............................	123,226	(47%)	$2,372,187	$133,497	$1,037,205
2018 Primary	John Katko (R)...............................	(100%)				

Prior winning percentages: 2016 (61%), 2014 (60%)

Republican John Katko, first elected in 2014, has become relatively secure in what had been a political swing district He has focused his legislative attention on homeland security and the transportation needs of Upstate. He had a setback in seeking the top GOP slot on the Homeland Security Committee.

Katko grew up in Onondaga County, then attended Niagara University and Syracuse University's law school. He worked for a D.C. law firm before taking a position at the Securities and Exchange Commission. In two decades at the Justice Department, he was a federal prosecutor in Virginia's Eastern District and worked for the narcotics and dangerous drugs section of the criminal division. During that time, he joined multiple organized crime and drug enforcement-related prosecutions with the U.S. Attorney's Office in Syracuse. He contends that his successful prosecution of a major gang case led to a significant drop in the violent crime rate in Syracuse.

Katko retired from the Justice Department to challenge Democratic Rep. Dan Maffei, who was elected in 2012 with just 49 percent of the vote, as President Barack Obama won 57 percent in the district. Maffei had an unusual streak of participating in five consecutive elections with alternating party control of the seat. Katko tried to depict Maffei as an out-of-touch Beltway insider. He pointed to his purchase of a $700,000 house in the Washington area. Maffei emphasized his moderate stripes and nonideological pragmatism and tried to poke holes in Katko's record as a prosecutor. Katko complained that such campaign attacks "destroyed my character." Katko won with surprising ease, 60%-40%, and he took all four counties. Onondaga was the tightest, with 53 percent for Katko.

In the House, Katko chaired the Transportation Subcommittee on the Homeland Security Committee. He passed several bills, which later were enacted as part of the reauthorization of the Federal Aviation Administration. Those measures called for a review of the Transportation Security Administration's security and staffing procedures, enhanced the security of overseas flights and revised TSA's expedited security program. He also took the leadership of a bipartisan Task Force on Combating Terrorist and Foreign Fighter Travel. In 2017-18, his productive legislative work included enactment of bills to encourage recruitment and retention at the Secret Service, stiffen requirements for biometric transportation security cards and promote more innovative transportation security.

He showed occasional independence from the House GOP leadership, as when he voted in 2015 to oppose both the final version of the annual budget plan and a plan to overturn a District of Columbia law that banned workplace discrimination over employees' reproductive decisions but provided no faith-based exemptions. Katko's Almanac vote ratings have placed him in the center of the House and among the most centrist Republicans, though he was a bit more conservative on foreign policy issues. A survey by the Lugar Center and a Georgetown University institute ranked him 7th in bipartisanship among 435 House members in 2017. He voted against the repeal of the Affordable Care Act, though he voted for the GOP tax cuts.

In November 2018, Katko sought the ranking Republican position at the Homeland Security Committee. In the backroom vote of a GOP leadership panel, he lost to Rep. Mike Rogers of Alabama, who had more seniority. He became the senior Republican on the Cybersecurity, Infrastructure Protection and Innovation Subcommittee.

Not surprisingly, Katko has been a prime Democratic reelection target. After Syracuse Mayor Stephanie Miner decided not to challenge him in 2016, Democrats rallied around Colleen Deacon, who had been the Syracuse district director for Sen. Kirsten Gillibrand. During a debate, she suggested that Katko had misled voters into believing that he was more independent than was the case. "When the chips are down, he stands with his do-nothing Republican colleagues on the issues that matter," Deacon said. Katko responded that she was a tool of Democratic leaders. "She is 100 percent in the tank with not only her party, but Hillary Clinton," he said. Both candidates were well-financed in their cheap-media market. Katko outraised Deacon, $2.7 million to $1.5 million. In an outcome that was similar to 2014, Katko won 61%-39%, with a narrow lead in Onondaga.

In 2018, Democrats suffered from internal divisions. All four Democratic county organizations endorsed Dana Balter, a professor of public administration at Syracuse University. The Democratic Congressional Campaign Committee favored Juanita Perez Williams, who ran unsuccessfully for mayor of Syracuse in 2017 and was a former city official. Balter won the primary, 62%-38%. In the general election, Democrats targeted Katko's vote for the tax bill, which they said favored the wealthy. Katko spent $3 million to $2.4 million for Balter. The two national parties and their allies spent more than $4 million on the contest. Katko was one of the few House Republicans from a metro area to survive the Democratic onslaught. He won, 53%-47%. Balter got 51 percent of the vote in Onondaga County, but Katko took at least 60 percent in each of the three outlying counties.

NY-24: North-Central New York   **Cook Partisan Voting Index: D+3**

Population		Race and Ethnicity		Income	
Total	712,307	White	81.9%	Median Income	$55,603
Land area (sq. miles)	2,389	Black	8%	District Income Rank	222
Pop/ sq mi	298.2	Latino	4.3%	Poverty Rate	14.7%
Born in State	79.6%	Asian	2.8%	With health insurance	94.5%
		Two or more races	2.5%	Cash public assistance	3.6%
Age Groups		Other	0.6%	Food stamp/SNAP	14.2%
Under 18	21.5%				
18-34	23.1%	**Education**		**Work**	
35-64	39.5%	H.S grad or less	38.8%	White Collar	15.9%
Over 64	15.9%	Some college	30.7%	Sales and Service	42.4%
Military		College Degree, 4 yr	17.3%	Blue Collar	19.4%
Veteran/ Active Duty	7.9%	Post grad	13.2%	Government	16.7%

2012 Pres. Vote	Obama	171,502	(57%)	Romney	123,534	(41%)			
2016 Pres. Vote	Clinton	151,021	(49%)	Trump	139,763	(45%)	Johnson	13,090	(4%)

Syracuse Metro: Syracuse is a Middle American city in the middle of Upstate New York, halfway between Albany and Buffalo on the Erie Canal and the old New York Central Railroad, which were for years the nation's major east-west transportation routes. Built on a swamp that was a salt spring, Syracuse is the home of many practical-minded inventions — the dental chair, Stickley mission furniture, the drive-in bank teller, and the serrated knife. It is the site of the New York State Fair, which attracts more than 1 million visitors annually; of Syracuse University, which plays basketball and football inside the Carrier Dome, the largest domed stadium on a college campus; and of the Museum of Automobile History, home to the largest private collection of automobiles and automobile-related objects in the world.

Nearby, the agricultural hinterland is rich with specialty crops like wine grapes, and its industrial jobs are mostly high-skill. Still, there were 20,000 fewer manufacturing jobs here in 2018 than there were in 2000. An example is Carrier, which once manufactured air-conditioning equipment in Syracuse and employed 7,000 workers; now, it is owned by Connecticut-based United Technologies and has 1,300 workers in Syracuse. Poverty in Syracuse remains deep-seated, with 50 percent of children living below the poverty line and the ninth-worst poverty rate in the nation in 2017. The good news is that housing in Syracuse is among the most affordable in the nation, with a median home value of $91,000. The growing communities of immigrants and refugees have been driving the limited economic growth. In November 2018, the airport opened a new terminal.

The 24th Congressional District of New York centers on Syracuse and surrounding Onondaga County, which takes in two-thirds of the voters in the 24th. From 1990 to 2017, the city lost 12 percent of its population, while the county remained nearly even. West of Syracuse is territory that dips south from Lake Ontario, with all of Cayuga County, home of abolitionist Harriet Tubman. Near Rochester, in Wayne County, is the village of Palmyra, where Joseph Smith had his vision of the angel Moroni and received the golden tablets that led him to found the Church of Jesus Christ of Latter-day Saints. To the north, the district includes the city of Oswego, whose port facilities on Lake Ontario have made it an attractive tourist destination.

Historically, Syracuse was Republican, partly out of antipathy to New York City. Like much of Upstate, this has become a politically competitive area. Following President Barack Obama's double-digit victory margins in his two elections, the 2016 election narrowed to a 49%-45% win for Hillary Clinton.

Joseph Morelle (D)

Elected 2018, 1st full term, b. Apr 29, 1957; Utica; State University of New York at Geneseo, B.A., 1986; Roman Catholic; Married (Mary Beth Morelle); 3 children (1 deceased).

DC Office: 1317 LHOB 20515, 202-225-3615, Fax: 202-225-7822, morelle.house.gov

State Offices: Rochester, 585-232-4850.

Committees: *Budget. Education & Labor:* Early Childhood, Elementary & Secondary Education; Health, Employment, Labor & Pensions. *Rules:* Legislative & Budget Process; Rules & Organization of the House.

Election Results

Election	Name (Party)	Vote (%)		Cand. Spent	Ind. Exp. Support	Ind. Exp. Oppose
2018 General	Joseph D. Morelle (D)	159,244	(59%)	$1,819,215		
	James Maxwell (R)	110,736	(41%)	$981,590		
2018 Primary	Joseph D. Morelle (D)	16,245	(46%)			
	Rachel Barnhart (D)	7,003	(20%)			
	Robin Witt (D)	6,158	(17%)			
	Adam McFadden (D)	6,103	(17%)			

Joe Morelle stood out in the House Democrats' freshman class. He was an older white male with an extensive political background in a year when that profile had become the exception for newly elected lawmakers. With his strong base of local support, he easily surmounted the potential stigma of a long career in the tarnished New York state Assembly, where he served six years as majority leader. He replaced another political veteran: 16-term Rep. Louise Slaughter, who died in March 2018 and was an influential ally of Speaker Nancy Pelosi as chairwoman of the Rules Committee when Democrats controlled the House.

Morelle, a native of the Rochester area, graduated from the State University of New York at Geneseo. He served two terms in the Monroe County Legislature before he was elected to the Assembly in 1990. His assignments included the chairmanship of both the Insurance and Tourism committees. As majority leader, he was instrumental in enacting gun-control legislation in 2013. When powerful Assembly Speaker Sheldon Silver was indicted on federal corruption charges in January 2015 and was forced to step down, Morelle spent a week as interim Speaker; he had little chance to win the top post, given the dominance of New York City Democrats in the Assembly.

While serving in Albany, Morelle was the founder and chief executive of MMI Technologies, a small software firm that worked with local health care and manufacturing firms. That business background, the Rochester Business Journal reported, made him "a point man for business in the Democratic-controlled and mostly liberal Assembly." Morelle also served nearly a decade as Democratic chairman in Monroe County.

Although the aging Slaughter had slowed down physically and her reelection margins had narrowed, her death shortly before the campaign-filing deadline created local interest in what was expected to be an uneventful contest. In the Democratic primary, Morelle faced three opponents, who split support from progressive groups. With his support from the Monroe County Democratic Committee in the abbreviated campaign, Morelle was criticized by his opponents as a political insider. "We need different experiences," Rachel Barnhart, a citizen activist who had been a local television reporter, said during a candidate debate. Also running were Rochester City Council member Adam McFadden and Brighton Town Board member Robin Wilt.

In its endorsement of Morelle for the Democratic nomination, the Rochester City Newspaper cited "his long experience in local and state politics and his political connections and influence," which would make him "an effective member of Congress." Morelle also benefited from raising more than $800,000 for the primary, which was eight times more than the combined total reported by his three opponents. In the June primary, Morelle got 45 percent of the vote to 20 percent for Barnhart; the other two Democrats had limited appeal beyond their local political bases.

Republican nominee Jim Maxwell, a longtime neurosurgeon and political newcomer, gained some attention by self-funding half of his $1 million campaign. Maxwell attacked Morelle as "a career politician steeped in the ways of corruption and gridlock," and he focused heavily on health care issues, including proposals to reduce costs. But House Republicans directed their attention and resources to endangered GOP incumbents elsewhere in upstate New York, and Maxwell gained little traction in the House Democratic tide during the 2018 election. Morelle won, 59%-41%. In the House, he was one of three freshmen assigned to the Rules Committee.

NY-25: Monroe County   Cook Partisan Voting Index: D+8

Population		Race and Ethnicity		Income	
Total	721,651	White	70.2%	Median Income	$54,715
Land area (sq. miles)	510	Black	14.9%	District Income Rank	233
Pop/ sq mi	1414.5	Latino	8.5%	Poverty Rate	15.1%
Born in State	73.9%	Asian	3.7%	With health insurance	95.4%
		Two or more races	2.2%	Cash public assistance	4.4%
Age Groups		Other	0.4%	Food stamp/SNAP	15.4%
Under 18	21.3%				
18-34	24.6%	**Education**		**Work**	
35-64	38.2%	H.S grad or less	34.2%	White Collar	15.9%
Over 64	15.9%	Some college	29%	Sales and Service	41.4%
		College Degree, 4 yr	20.6%	Blue Collar	15.7%
Military		Post grad	16.4%	Government	12.2%
Veteran/ Active Duty	6.2%				

2012 Pres. Vote	Obama	187,753	(59%)	Romney	125,897	(39%)			
2016 Pres. Vote	Clinton	182,896	(55%)	Trump	128,955	(39%)	Johnson	12,514	(4%)

Rochester Metro: Rochester, with a metropolitan area of just over 1 million, is a major city of Upstate New York and was one of America's first boomtowns. Here, the Genesee River descends in a 100-foot drop known as High Falls, which powered the city's early industries. Rochester became known as Flour City for the mills that served western New York farmers. Rochester was also the home base of women's suffrage leader Susan B. Anthony and abolitionist Frederick Douglass, and a popular center of 19th century tent revivals.

It became one of the early high-tech cities, after a bank clerk named George Eastman marketed the first still camera and film for Thomas Edison's motion picture camera. Later, Bausch & Lomb developed its lens business in Rochester. The optics and imaging industry continues to be a significant regional employer. The industries it has produced — Bausch & Lomb, Eastman Kodak and Xerox, which started here as Haloid before moving its headquarters to Connecticut in 1969 — thrived on technical innovation, precision workmanship, high reliability and customer service. They gave Rochester an affluent and well-educated population as well as fine civic institutions, including the George Eastman House, one of the world's leading repositories of photographic and motion picture history.

In recent decades, Rochester's big employers have fallen on tough times, and young professionals have been leaving the area. Kodak was hard hit by competition from digital cameras, and although it locally employed 1,500 people (of 6,000 worldwide) in 2018, the workforce was down from 60,000 people in 1981. In 2012, it filed for bankruptcy and reemerged a year later as what it called "a technology company focused on imaging for business." Xerox has continued to decline in size but maintained a significant presence in the area, with a payroll of about 3,100. In July 2018, it closed its office in downtown Rochester and moved those remaining employees to suburban Webster. The city's population — 332,000 in 1950 — has dropped in each census since then, to 208,000 in 2017; the overall metropolitan area has grown by less than 10 percent in the past 40 years. The University of Rochester is the largest employer, with 30,000 on its payroll. In October 2018, the Rochester airport completed an $80 million renovation, including new security technology in the terminal.

The 25th Congressional District of New York is a compact district that is entirely within Rochester's Monroe County. All but a small northwest corner of the county is in the 25th. Heavily

Democratic areas in Rochester mix with more marginal suburbs in a district that is comfortably but not overwhelmingly Democratic. Hillary Clinton performed better here than in other Upstate districts, with a 55%-39% win over Donald Trump.

Brian Higgins (D)

Elected 2004, 8th term, b. Oct 06, 1959; Buffalo; Buffalo State College (NY), B.S., 1984; Buffalo State College (NY), M.A., 1985; Harvard University John F. Kennedy School of Government (MA), M.A., 1996; Catholic; Married (Mary Jane Hannon); 2 children.

Elected Office: Buffalo City Council, 1988-1994; NY Assembly, 1999-2004.

Professional Career: Chief of Staff, Erie County Leg., 1994-1998; Lecturer, Buffalo St. College, 2000-2003.

DC Office: 2459 RHOB 20515, 202-225-3306, Fax: 202-226-0347, higgins.house.gov

State Offices: Buffalo, 716-852-3501; Niagara Falls, 716-282-1274.

Committees: *Budget. Ways & Means*: Health; Social Security; Trade.

Group Ratings

	ADA	ACLU	AFL-CIO	LCV	ITI	COC	HAFA	ACU	CFG	FRC
2018	-	67%	-	91%	-	58%	4%	4%	5%	0%
2017	90%	C	95%	100%	C	62%	C	4%	5%	11%

Almanac Ratings 2017-18

	Economy	Social	Foreign	Composite
Liberal	100%	90%	77%	89%
Conservative	0%	10%	23%	11%

Key Votes of the 115th Congress

1. Obama-care revision	N	5. Family planning regs	N	9. Guantanamo prisoners	Y
2. Tax Cuts	N	6. Body cameras/immigration	Y	10. Ground missiles, limit	N
3. Omnibus appropriations	Y	7. Abortion ban	N	11. Defense Dept. spending	Y
4. Dodd-Frank revision	N	8. Concealed carry	N	12. FISA rules	Y

Election Results

Election	Name (Party)	Vote (%)		Cand. Spent	Ind. Exp. Support	Ind. Exp. Oppose
2018 General	Brian Higgins (D)	169,166	(73%)	$554,635		
	Renee Zeno (R)	61,488	(27%)			
2018 Primary	Brian Higgins (D)		(100%)			

Prior winning percentages: 2016 (75%), 2014 (68%), 2012 (75%), 2010 (61%), 2008 (74%), 2006 (79%), 2004 (51%)

Democrat Brian Higgins, who was elected in 2004 and devotes his energies to reviving the Buffalo area's economy, is well-placed on the House Ways and Means Committee, with its work on tax and trade issues. He has advocated a trillion-dollar plan to upgrade the nation's infrastructure. After keeping his distance from Nancy Pelosi, he was one of the first renegades to reach an agreement to support her for Speaker following the 2018 election.

Higgins grew up in Buffalo, the son of a skilled tradesman who was prominent in local politics. His mother was a schoolteacher. Higgins graduated from Buffalo State College, where he later became an instructor, and got a master's degree in public administration from Harvard. A political junkie, he launched his career with staff jobs in the Erie County sheriff's office, the state Assembly, and the county legislature. In 1993, after six years on the Buffalo City Council, he ran for county comptroller and lost. In 1998, he was elected to the Assembly and served three terms. In a district crowded with unionized workers, Higgins reminded voters that his father and uncle were bricklayers and he stressed his Irish heritage.

When the House seat opened after Republican Rep. Jack Quinn retired, five Democrats sought the nomination. Higgins was the favorite of party leaders, organized labor and The Buffalo News, which called him "an unusually productive member of a largely dysfunctional legislative body" in Albany. He won the primary with 44 percent of the vote. In the contentious general election, Higgins reminded voters that Republican nominee Nancy Naples, a former Merrill Lynch executive in Manhattan, supported many of President George W. Bush's policies, which he claimed shifted the tax burden from the rich to the middle class. He ran on a platform of making health care more widely available. Naples criticized Higgins for supporting tax increases in Albany. Higgins won 51%-49%, about a 3,800-vote victory, in what was then a far more competitive district.

On Ways and Means, he initially opposed the 2010 deal to extend the expiring Bush-era tax cuts because it would not extend the Renewal Communities program, which had brought $150 million in development to the district. But he eventually went along with the deal, saying "the cost of inaction would be far worse for western New York families and seniors." After the Republican takeover of the House in 2011 removed junior Democrats from seats on Ways and Means, Higgins served on the Homeland Security and Foreign Affairs panels.

With increased seniority, he regained his Ways and Means seat in 2017. His priorities included the New Markets Tax Credit program, the solar investment tax credit and tax simplification for middle-class families. He cosponsored the Social Security 2100 proposal to expand benefits and pay for them with increased taxes on higher-income earners. He has been the chief proponent of legislation to expand Medicare to permit early buy-in by those who are age 50.

Hoping to kick off a debate about the importance of infrastructure, he has repeatedly filed a bill calling for $1.25 trillion to be spent over five years to rebuild roads, bridges, railroads, ports and airports. "The time is now for nation-building here at home," he said, while noting that 81 bridges in Erie County have been deemed structurally deficient. He helped create, and co-chaired, a Revitalizing Older Cities Task Force and has sought tax credits to transform older neighborhoods.

In the debate over gun control, Higgins once sided with gun owners, voting in favor of a 2011 amendment to block federal efforts to demand reports from gun dealers on sales of multiple semi-automatic rifles. After the Newtown Connecticut school massacre in 2012, he called for "meaningful reforms" to gun laws.

As Democrats prepared to take House control following the 2018 election, Higgins had signed a letter with 15 other House Democrats stating their opposition to Pelosi as Speaker and the need for more assertive leadership. After several discussions, the two of them made a deal in which Higgins supported Pelosi for Speaker in exchange for her agreement to schedule action in 2019 on both his Medicare and infrastructure bills and that he would be given a leading role in those debates. "I have renewed confidence that more voices will be heard, that members will each have greater opportunities to advance policies," he said in a statement, adding that his earlier "principled stand" required a "pragmatic outlook" to succeed.

Since developing skin cancer, Higgins has become a leader of the Cancer Caucus and worked on cancer research, introducing bills to establish a national cancer trust fund and pushing for money for Buffalo's Roswell Park Cancer Institute. He helped to broker an agreement with the New York Power Authority for local financial aid, including waterfront improvements, in exchange for its long-term right to operate the Niagara Power Project.

Higgins has been reelected easily in what has become a safe district. The declining population of Buffalo could prove perilous during the 2022 redistricting.

NY-26: Western New York

Cook Partisan Voting Index: D+11

Population		Race and Ethnicity		Income	
Total	715,764	White	69.2%	Median Income	$47,127
Land area (sq. miles)	219	Black	17.8%	District Income Rank	351
Pop/ sq mi	3266.4	Latino	6.2%	Poverty Rate	19%
Born in State	79.2%	Asian	4%	With health insurance	95.4%
		Two or more races	2.2%	Cash public assistance	3.8%
Age Groups		Other	0.6%	Food stamp/SNAP	20.3%
Under 18	20.6%				
18-34	25.8%	**Education**		**Work**	
35-64	37.2%	H.S grad or less	38.9%	White Collar	16.4%
Over 64	16.4%	Some college	30.3%	Sales and Service	46%
		College Degree, 4 yr	17.1%	Blue Collar	17.2%
Military		Post grad	13.6%	Government	15.6%
Veteran/ Active Duty	7.5%				

2012 Pres. Vote	Obama	193,362	(64%)	Romney	103,743	(34%)		
2016 Pres. Vote	Clinton	175,336	(58%)	Trump	115,558	(38%)	Johnson	8,632 (3%)

Buffalo Metro: With its massive 1920s City Hall overlooking the Niagara River and Lake Erie, Buffalo declares itself to be a city of substance. The butt of jokes about the snow from Lake Erie that supposedly keeps it immobilized half the year, Buffalo also can claim credit for building a heavy industrial base in the late 19th and early 20th centuries, as America's No. 1 grain milling center and as a major steel producer. By 1910, it had installed the first electric street light, produced the world's largest office building (Ellicott Square), and erected one of the earliest skyscrapers. It also played a part in producing two presidents: Grover Cleveland was mayor of Buffalo, and Millard Fillmore worked in nearby East Aurora. Today, the area still benefits from cheap hydroelectric power, but the Lackawanna steel mills are shuttered and grain milling waned after the St. Lawrence Seaway opened in the 1950s. Buffalo was eclipsed by the larger Great Lakes industrial cities of Chicago, Detroit and Cleveland.

Buffalo was the nation's 15th-largest city in 1950, when it had a population of 580,000. By 2018, it was 75th-largest, with a population reduced by more than half to about 259,000. As a further insult, right across Buffalo's Peace Bridge is the richest part of Canada, the "Golden Horseshoe," from Niagara Falls through Hamilton to Toronto. Still, Buffalo retains considerable assets: a high-skill labor force, inexpensive real estate, including a gentrified and handsome waterfront on a now-cleaner Lake Erie, and some impressive cultural institutions. The area has had some encouraging economic developments. General Motors spent $296 million on equipment for engine production at its Tonawanda plant. Both the Tonawanda and Lockport plants, which have nearly 3,000 employees, survived GM's extensive job cutbacks that were announced in November 2018. Panasonic teamed with the electric-car company Tesla to make solar cells and modules at Tesla's SolarCity factory in south Buffalo. As of January 2019, the workforce of 800 was short of the companies' pledge to create 1,400 jobs by 2020, in exchange for the state building the SolarCity factory as part of Gov. Andrew Cuomo's Buffalo Billion plan, an economic development initiative during his first term.

The 26th Congressional District of New York includes all of Buffalo and the cities and townships abutting it, and nearly two-thirds of Erie County. To the north, it takes in a small slice of Niagara County with Niagara Falls and North Tonawanda. About 90 percent of the district is in Erie County. The large number of Eastern European settlers, many of whom hailed from Poland, gave Buffalo a Democratic tilt early on. Unlike much of Upstate, it began electing Democrats with some regularity in the 1860s, and almost exclusively after the 1930s. Today, the district is solidly Democratic. Hillary Clinton got 57 percent of the vote. Local voters can be quirky: independent presidential candidate Ross Perot won 28 percent of the vote in Buffalo in 1992 — his best showing in any urban center.

Chris Collins (R)

Elected 2012, 4th term, b. May 20, 1950; Schenectady; North Carolina State University, B.S., 1972; University of Alabama, Birmingham, M.B.A., 1975; Roman Catholic; Married (Mary Sue Collins); 3 children; 4 grandchildren.

Elected Office: Erie County Executive, 2007-2011.

Professional Career: Westinghouse Electric, 1972-1983; Founder & CEO, Nuttall Gear Corporation, 1983-1997; Entrepreneur, 1998-2007.

DC Office: 2243 RHOB 20515, 202-225-5265, Fax: 202-225-5910, chriscollins.house.gov

State Offices: Clarence, 716-634-2324; Geneseo, 585-519-4002.

Group Ratings

	ADA	ACLU	AFL-CIO	LCV	ITI	COC	HAFA	ACU	CFG	FRC
2018	-	7%	-	9%	-	92%	42%	72%	45%	100%
2017	0%	C	14%	3%	C	93%	C	81%	52%	100%

Almanac Ratings 2017-18

	Economy	Social	Foreign	Composite
Liberal	5%	6%	7%	6%
Conservative	95%	94%	93%	94%

Key Votes of the 115th Congress

1. Obama-care revision	Y	5. Family planning regs	Y	9. Guantanamo prisoners	N
2. Tax Cuts	Y	6. Body cameras/immigration	N	10. Ground missiles, limit	N
3. Omnibus appropriations	Y	7. Abortion ban	Y	11. Defense Dept. spending	Y
4. Dodd-Frank revision	Y	8. Concealed carry	Y	12. FISA rules	Y

Election Results

Election	Name (Party)	Vote (%)		Cand. Spent	Ind. Exp. Support	Ind. Exp. Oppose
2018 General	Chris Collins (R)............................	140,146	(49%)	$1,791,747	$5,000	
	Nate McMurray (D).......................	139,059	(49%)	$1,229,323		$146,173
2018 Primary	Chris Collins (R)............................		(100%)			

Prior winning percentages: 2016 (67%), 2014 (67%), 2012 (49%)

Republican Chris Collins, a self-made multimillionaire, was elected in 2012 by narrowly defeating first-term Democratic Rep. Kathy Hochul, who had won a special election. Following a quiet three years, he became the first member of Congress to endorse Donald Trump for president. The result, as the Buffalo News wrote, turned Collins "from back-bencher to power broker."

As a child, Collins' family moved around the country with his father's job transfers at General Electric. After high school in Hendersonville, North Carolina, he earned a bachelor's degree in mechanical engineering from North Carolina State and a master's in business administration from the University of Alabama at Birmingham. He went to work for Westinghouse in Buffalo and planned to spend his career climbing the corporate ladder there, as his father did at GE. Westinghouse promoted him to take over its plant, where he already was the general manager of the industrial gear division. He ran the Nuttall Gear Corp., which eventually reverted to private ownership after he sold it.

Former local Rep. Bill Paxon, a House Republican leader in the 1990s, persuaded Collins to get into politics. He challenged veteran Democratic Rep. John LaFalce in 1998, hoping to benefit from dissatisfaction with the local economy, but Collins lost, 57%-41%. He returned to business as an entrepreneur, spending the next 10 years working on almost two dozen financially distressed and bankrupt companies in the Buffalo area.

In 2007, New York Republicans again tapped Collins, this time to run for Erie County executive. "Erie County was effectively bankrupt, and I was now known as a fix-it guy," Collins told National Journal. He ran as an independent on a platform of business know-how and won with 64 percent of the vote. He lost reelection in 2011 in this Democratic county. The defeat became a positive break for his career. Collins said his experience at the county level inspired him to head to Washington, where he hoped to apply his budget experience. "If there's ever anything that's broken, it is Congress," Collins said.

In 2012, he thought that redistricting gave him a chance. Democrats accused Collins of neglecting the county's infrastructure, but he stayed focused on his business background. "Unlike my opponent and President Obama, who think we can tax our way to prosperity, I'm saying we need to grow our way to prosperity, by having a balanced budget and having some certainty for business on the financial side," Collins said. He benefitted from heavy campaign spending from outside GOP groups and beat Hochul, 51%-49%. He has been reelected with token opposition.

With a seat on the Energy and Commerce Committee, Collins has styled himself as a pragmatic problem-solver. As part of the bipartisan 21st Century Cures Act, he won committee support for his plan to simplify the approval of new medical treatments for the market, with adaptive clinical trials that monitor patients. Calling the measure "common sense," he said that his proposal "makes sure these drugs come through the [Food and Drug Administration] process faster." Collins promoted hydraulic fracturing for natural gas in New York.

Collins showed occasional independence. In 2015, the Buffalo News praised him as one of 75 House Republicans who supported the plan to keep open the Homeland Security Department rather than engage in "a suicide charge" against President Barack Obama's proposed easing of immigration enforcement. "I didn't come here to lurch from crisis to crisis," Collins said. In June, he joined most House Democrats, and abandoned Obama and most House Republicans, when he voted against a plan to expedite congressional action on the president's proposed Trans Pacific Partnership. He objected that the trade deal failed to stop overseas currency manipulation.

When Collins decided to endorse Trump in February 2016, he instructed his staff to ask the campaign whether he should seek media attention. "A few hours later he was surprised to receive a voicemail from Trump thanking him for his support and encouraging him to go big," Politico reported. Collins saved the message on his phone. He organized a small number of House members into the "Trump Caucus." They were a "pretty lonely group," he recounted. He became Trump's chief salesman to other lawmakers. Following the election, Collins became a go-to person on behalf of the new president and his team. Trump responded with appreciation. Among his initial steps as he prepared to deal with Congress, Trump requested Speaker Paul Ryan to designate Collins as his liaison to lawmakers. Ryan called Collins that night to say that it was a done deal. "Mr. Trump, I have come to find out, very much values loyalty," Collins told Politico.

Collins turned down the opportunity to join the new administration. Instead, in the heady days of the transition, he became a "clearinghouse for everything coming out of Congress" about the new president and his team, Collins said to the News. He was especially interested in appointments of federal officials in western New York.

Not surprisingly, Collins agreed with Trump on virtually every issue. When many colleagues in Congress criticized Trump's executive orders limiting access to the United States by refugees and immigrants, Collins responded, "These are people who just need to get some backbone." One exception was his strong opposition to Trump's call for biometric tests at border crossings, which Collins said would "significantly delay" access from Canada, including in the Buffalo area.

His high visibility on behalf of Trump increased local attention. When critics threatened protests, Collins said that he never held town-hall meetings and never would. "Because what you get are demonstrators who come and shout you down and heckle you," Collins told a local TV station.

His August 2018 indictment created another campaign headache for Republicans by putting a safe seat into play when they were struggling to retain their majority. Collins insisted that he was innocent. He announced a few days after the indictment that it was in "the best interests" of his constituents, the Republican Party and Trump for him to "suspend" his reelection campaign. "I will fill out the remaining few months of my term," he said on Aug. 11.

On Sept. 17, he reversed that decision for several legal and political reasons, including the obstacles posed by state law for withdrawing so close to the election. "Because of the protracted and uncertain nature of any legal effort to replace Congressman Collins, we do not see a path allowing Congressman Collins to be replaced on the ballot," his lawyer said. During the next seven weeks, he had little contact with voters or with the news media. He ran campaign ads and spent $1.8 million, leaving a balance in his campaign account of only $200,000.

Democratic challenger Nate McMurray, a lawyer and the town supervisor of Grand Island, spent $1.2 million, including a campaign ad in which he said — without naming Collins -- "We are tired of name-calling and corruption." He received late campaign support from national Democrats, who had no interest in the contest prior to the August indictment.

Following a recount and challenges that lasted more than a month, Collins won by 1,087 votes out of 279,205 that were cast. Collins narrowly won Niagara and four other counties. McMurray took Erie by 6,300 votes and two other counties.

With the continuing uncertainty over the political future of Collins, whose trial was set for February 2020, other local Republicans explored campaigns for the seat.

NY-27: Northwestern New York

Cook Partisan Voting Index: R+11

Population		Race and Ethnicity		Income	
Total	718,095	White	91.8%	Median Income	$63,010
Land area (sq. miles)	3,973	Black	2.4%	District Income Rank	148
Pop/ sq mi	180.7	Latino	2.6%	Poverty Rate	9%
Born in State	85%	Asian	1.1%	With health insurance	95.6%
		Two or more races	1.3%	Cash public assistance	2.1%
Age Groups		Other	0.8%	Food stamp/SNAP	8.8%
Under 18	20.4%				
18-34	19.8%	**Education**		**Work**	
35-64	42.2%	H.S grad or less	39.1%	White Collar	17.6%
Over 64	17.6%	Some college	31.5%	Sales and Service	40.3%
		College Degree, 4 yr	16.7%	Blue Collar	22.3%
Military		Post grad	12.7%	Government	16%
Veteran/ Active Duty	8.5%				

2012 Pres. Vote	Romney	180,681	(55%)	Obama	140,136	(43%)			
2016 Pres. Vote	Trump	206,867	(59%)	Clinton	122,106	(35%)	Johnson	13,162	(4%)

Buffalo and Rochester Suburbs: The destination of the Erie Canal, the great engineering project that made New York the Empire State, is Lake Erie. The final 100 miles of the canal passed through the rolling countryside of western New York when it was scarcely occupied, except by American Indians. The appropriately named Lockport was founded as a site for locks on the canal. Later, the land was settled mostly by New England Yankees, with cultural folkways quite different from those of New York City. By the end of the 19th century, much of the farmland found here had become dominated by heavy industry, especially in Buffalo, where the Yankees were joined by Irish, Italian and Polish immigrants who came to work in the factories. For most of its history, western New York had an economy more prosperous than that of the rest of the country, as is visible in the solid houses and schools, stores and factories built to weather the Upstate winters. But in recent decades, economic growth has lagged behind the rest of the nation. Many of Buffalo's factories have closed. The slow growth and population decline have frequently spilled over to the suburbs that sprang up around the city in outer Erie County. In some ways, the region has a Midwest flavor, culturally as well as economically. People speak not in the pungent accents of New York City, but in flat Midwestern tones.

The 27th Congressional District of New York covers much of western New York. It extends from the suburbs that surround Buffalo to suburbs southeast of Rochester, plus the northwest corner of Monroe County. In between are rural areas and small towns, including Attica, scene of a terrible prison uprising in 1970. The district has elected influential national Republicans such as Jack Kemp and Bill Paxon. With population changes, the size of the district has expanded. Erie and Niagara counties have been reduced to 60 percent of the district, though Erie remains its heart. Politically, these suburbs are ancestrally Republican country, based on Upstaters' general distrust of New York City. It is the most Republican district in the state by most measures. Donald Trump's 59%-35% win in 2016 was his best performance in his home state.

NORTH CAROLINA

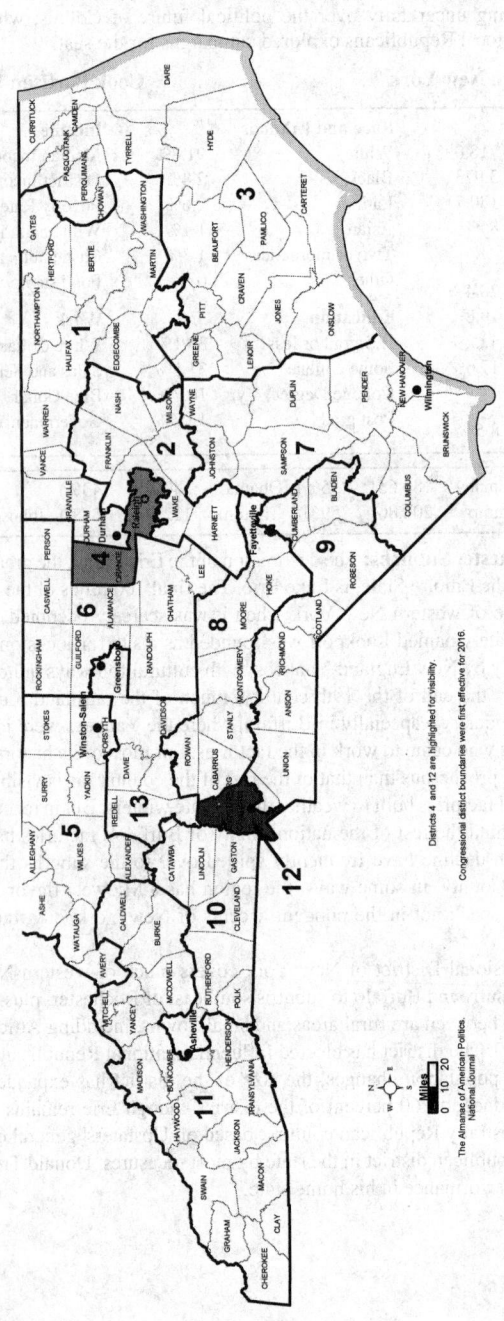

Districts 4 and 12 are highlighted for visibility.

Congressional district boundaries were first effective for 2016.

The Almanac of American Politics,
National Journal

In few states today is the political climate more polarized between Democrats and Republicans – and between rural, urban and suburban areas – than in North Carolina. Bolstered by rapid population growth from other states, North Carolina, and particularly its suburban areas, has become a hard-fought battleground, especially over the direction of state government. Beginning in 2010, North Carolina Republicans enjoyed large legislative majorities and increasing success in winning races at all levels. But in 2018, after seemingly endless battles over control of the state's levers of power, voters dialed back their support for Republicans, electing enough Democrats to break the GOP's legislative supermajorities, and in turn bolstering Democratic Gov. Roy Cooper's leverage in policy debates.

In the early republic, when Virginia and South Carolina produced statesmen and had grand plantation cultures, North Carolina was often called a valley of humility between two mountains of conceit. It joined the Confederacy only after those two neighbors did. After the Civil War, North Carolina developed its tobacco industry and enticed textile mills south from New England, while its hardwood forests produced raw material for furniture factories. Textile mills were prevalent in the Piedmont region as owners saw in the South an opportunity for cheap land, cheap labor and state governments eager to foster pro-business, anti-union climates. In the following decades, the industry continued to expand and drastically improved the economy of the South. The mill industry became the main source of industrial paid labor for white southerners. While it was one of the lowest paying manufacturing industries, the jobs were valued because there were few other options other than agricultural or service work.

The tobacco-textile-furniture trio enabled North Carolina to grow faster than the national average in the 1920s and 1930s, but the state began to lag in the 1950s. Then, two developments transformed the state. In 1959, Gov. Luther Hodges established Research Triangle Park between Raleigh and Durham. With synergy from nearby universities — Duke, North Carolina, and North Carolina State — the region became one of the leading research centers in the United States. The second development was Charlotte's emergence as the No. 2 city in financial assets behind New York, a status that owes much to the state's expansive banking laws.

These twin developments explain how North Carolina has become one of the fastest-growing and largest states. Its population more than doubled between 1970 and 2018, from 5.1 million to 10.4 million. In the same period, the city of Charlotte grew from 241,000 to 826,000 and Raleigh grew from 123,000 to 449,000. Since the 2010 census, the state as a whole has grown by a healthy 8.5 percent, probably enough to add another seat in Congress, but several populous counties have expanded by rates even higher than that: Wake County (Raleigh) grew by 20.3 percent, Mecklenburg County (Charlotte) by 17.2 percent, Durham County (Durham) by 16.4 percent, and Guilford County (Greensboro) by 8.7 percent, with Buncombe County (Asheville) not far behind at 8.2 percent. As the state has shifted from old-line manufacturing in textiles and furniture to fast-growing industries, including pharmaceuticals and aerospace, so have its exports. Fitting for a state that was home to the first flight at Kitty Hawk, the state's top export is now civilian aircraft engines and parts. Just behind are various categories of medical exports; the Triangle, as the Raleigh-Durham area is commonly known, is one of the world's leading pharmaceutical and medical device centers. Highly skilled people from the Northeast have flocked to the state: The jurisdiction of Cary in the Triangle, jokingly referred to as "Containment Area for Relocated Yankees," has grown 25 percent since 2010. High-tech firms are also sprouting farther west in the Piedmont Triad of Greensboro, Winston-Salem and High Point. In 2017, Site Selection magazine ranked North Carolina No. 1 in the country for its business climate, and in 2018, Forbes followed suit. North Carolina has the nation's second-least unionized labor force, trailing only neighboring South Carolina, leaving its labor costs among the lowest in the nation. Immigrants seeking jobs in construction and in meat and chicken factories have pushed the Hispanic population up to 9 percent.

Urban, affluent, high-tech North Carolina, however, is not the only North Carolina: The state ranks second to Texas in its number of rural residents with 3.2 million. The state's predominantly rural counties saw taxable wages decline by 3 percent in the past decade, compared with a 6 percent increase in suburban counties and a 15 percent increase in urban counties, the NC Rural Center calculated. Most rural jurisdictions lost population, which, combined with lower education levels, has made attracting business difficult. "Many rural counties in the eastern part of the state are 40 miles from a natural gas line, a non-starter for some corporations," the Wall Street Journal noted. The 2018 federal approval for the $5 billion, 600-mile Atlantic Coast Pipeline, running from West Virginia to Pembroke, North Carolina, offered some hope for economic progress.

North Carolina's agriculture sector is significant -- the state is the nation's third-ranking producer of broilers, the biggest producer of sweet potatoes, the second-biggest for Christmas trees. Notably, it ranks second in hog production, with big feedlots in the southeastern portion of the state. Hurricane Florence – which dropped a record 30-odd inches of rain in 2018 and ranked among the top 10 most expensive storms in U.S. history – spotlighted the problems of hog-waste lagoons, dozens of which overflowed amid the flooding. Concerns over the lagoons have become so contentious that neighbors have sued for damages to their quality of life –so the legislature, looking to protect the industry, enacted limits on such lawsuits. The psychic draw of rural North Carolina runs deep: If Charlotte is proud of its downtown bank towers and modern art museum, it is also proud of its Billy Graham Museum and the NASCAR Hall of Fame. But all is not well in North Carolina. The textile industry largely moved offshore, although efforts are under way to promote a "dirt-to-shirt" movement akin to "farm-to-table" for artisanal food. Meanwhile, the federal government's 2004 buyout of tobacco quotas greatly diminished that sector, with further concern generated by retaliatory tariffs by China, which buys more tobacco from the state than any other country. High Point still hosts annual furniture industry shows, but much of the production has gone elsewhere, including China. Median income remained in the bottom quarter of states.

Big-government liberalism provided an impetus toward spending on education, but by 2018 the publication Education Week ranked North Carolina's public schools only 40th best in the nation, and teachers marched to the state capitol seeking higher pay and still more spending on the poorly performing public school system. The state has historically invested in highways and amenities, including the nation's first state-funded symphony and state high schools for science, mathematics and the arts. A different philosophical strand, religious conservatism, has provided a communitarian spirit and charitable impulses, as well as a moral undertone that anchors those who might go astray. The state's racial conflicts were never as intense as they were in Alabama or Mississippi, though the Greensboro sit-ins in 1960 were a pivotal, and effective, moment in the civil rights movement. Yet in a state with an African-American population of 22 percent -- the seventh-highest of any state -- the legacy of segregation persists. Racial tensions divided Durham in 2006, when its prosecutor wrongly accused three white Duke lacrosse players of raping an African-American dancer. Race has been an issue in the state's moves to tighten its voting procedures and draw congressional and legislative district lines, and the police shooting of Keith Lamont Scott in Charlotte heightened tensions in 2016. After the white nationalist rally in Charlottesville Virginia, in 2017, vandals toppled a Confederate statue at a courthouse in Durham. The "Silent Sam" confederate statue on the University of North Carolina campus was also toppled by protesters. It was moved to storage, the subject of negotiations between a largely Republican-appointed governing board and campus officials.

During the latter part of the 20th century, Republicans tended to win federal elections in North Carolina, and Democrats tended to do well in state elections. The exemplars of these traditions were Republican Sen. Jesse Helms and Democratic Gov. Jim Hunt, each of whom was elected to statewide office five times. But in the first two decades of the new millennium, a polarized, increasingly party-line politics evolved, waged partly on economic issues but even more on cultural attitudes. Barack Obama narrowly won the state in 2008, bolstered by high turnout by minorities and affluent whites. But conservatives fought back. Aided by Democratic sales- and income-tax increases in 2009, the Great Recession and fatigue from 20 years of Democratic state government, the Republicans achieved big legislative majorities in the 2010 election, the first period of GOP control since Reconstruction. Two years later, Republican Pat McCrory was elected governor. He ran as a centrist, pro-business mayor of Charlotte, but the legislature produced a virtual assembly line of conservative legislation and dared McCrory to use his veto. Despite some tensions and a few vetoes, McCrory mostly acceded to their wishes.

Over the course of several years, the GOP enacted a partisan redistricting map, a constitutional amendment to ban same-sex marriage, cuts to unemployment benefits, a tax overhaul that eliminated elements of progressivity in the code, a law requiring voters to show ID along with a shorter early-voting period, an increase in the waiting period for abortions, and a repeal of a state law to commute the death penalty if racial bias in sentencing could be shown. It didn't take long for a liberal backlash to coalesce – a running series of protests known as "Moral Mondays," led by Rev. William Barber III of the state NAACP. In the meantime, federal court decisions invalidated all or part of some of the laws passed by the GOP, including the redistricting and voting measures.

The backlash mushroomed in March 2016, when Republicans passed a bill known as H.B. 2. The measure had been spurred by Charlotte's enactment of a non-discrimination ordinance on sexual orientation. The state bill preempted local ordinances and required people to use bathrooms that coincided with one's birth gender. This time, allies of the LGBT community peeled off sizable portions of the business community, who feared, with reason, that national groups would boycott the state. Indeed, PayPal and Deutsche Bank were among those to pull out of projects in the state, and the NCAA and NBA canceled major events; the Associated Press projected the full economic hit to be $3.76 billion over 12 years. Democrats – including McCrory's Democratic challenger, Cooper – hammered away at Republicans for inviting economic hardship. In time, the law became an albatross for McCrory, and after the election, the two sides agreed to repeal the law in March 2017. On the upside, the compromise brought back the NBA All-Star game and generally kept the issue from hindering economic development.

The drama over state government at times overshadowed the 2016 presidential election in North Carolina, but it too was hard-fought and close. Both Donald Trump and Hillary Clinton returned again and again to the state, and key surrogates such as Barack and Michelle Obama stumped there as well. Trump ended up winning, doubling Mitt Romney's two-point winning margin in 2012 to four points, thanks to a strong showing in rural areas. But in addition to Cooper's victory, the Democrats held the attorney general seat he had vacated and seized a majority on the nominally nonpartisan Supreme Court. In the 2018 midterms, Democrats finally won enough legislative seats to break the GOP's supermajority, and voters rejected the two most controversial Republican-backed constitutional amendments, which would have weakened the governor's hand in filling judicial vacancies and the state election board. (Voters did support a Republican-backed amendment to require a photo ID to vote.) A Democrat won a state supreme court seat and the court's Republican chief judge resigned. Cooper filled the vacancy with a Democratic appeals court judge, giving the Democrats a 6-1 majority. Despite Cooper's increased leverage, the rest of his first term promised continued partisan battles among the legislature, the governor and the courts.

Population		Race and Ethnicity		Income	
Total	10,052,564	White	63.6%	Median Income	$50,320
Land area (sq. miles)	48,618	Black	21.2%	State Income Rank	40
Pop/ sq mi	206.8	Latino	9.1%	Poverty Rate	16.1%
Born in state	57.0%	Asian	2.7%	With health insurance	87.9%
Age Groups		Two or more races	2.1%	Cash public assistance	1.8%
Under 18	22.8%	Other	1.4%	Food stamp/SNAP	13.7%
18-34	22.7%	**Education**		**Work**	
35-64	39.4%	H.S grad or less	39.2%	White Collar	36.9%
Over 64	15.1%	Some college	31.0%	Sales and Service	40.5%
Military		College Degree, 4 yr	19.2%	Blue Collar	22.6%
Veteran/ Active Duty	9.9%	Post grad	10.6%	Government	14.4%

Presidential Politics

2016 Primary (D)	Clinton (D)	622,915 (55%)	Sanders (D)	467,018 (41%)			
2016 Primary (R)	Trump (R)	462,413 (40%)	Cruz (R)	422,621 (37%)	Kasich (R)	145,659 (13%)	
	Rubio (R)	88,907 (8%)					
2016 Pres. Vote	Trump (R)	2,362,631 (50%)	Clinton (D)	2,189,316 (46%)	Johnson (L)	130,126 (3%)	
2012 Pres. Vote	Romney (R)	2,270,395 (50%)	Obama (D)	2,178,391 (48%)			

Republicans have carried North Carolina in 10 of the last 12 presidential elections. The only Democratic victories came in 1976, when southerner Jimmy Carter won the state and 2008, when

Barack Obama's campaign built an organization that was able to take advantage of a 2007 state law permitting same-day voter registration and the growing appeal of early voting to mobilize large numbers of college students and African Americans.

The recent arrivals of many Hispanics and affluent professionals in the state's Research Triangle provided opportunities for Democrats to compete in the GOP-leaning state. In his 2012 reelection bid, Obama was unable to repeat his success. After Republican lawmakers passed and the governor signed into law in early 2016 legislation to restrict the use of public bathrooms to people's biological gender, a backlash further roiled the state's politics. On Nov. 8, Donald Trump defeated Hillary Clinton, 50%-46%. North Carolina was vigorously contested on both sides and saw more television ads than any state other than Florida and Ohio. Trump's 173,000-vote victory was helped by higher GOP margins in rural counties in both the eastern and western parts of the state. Turnout of black voters was off from its 2008 and 2012 levels. Clinton captured 24 of the state's 100 counties. She performed well in the Research Triangle -- Durham, Orange and Wake counties. She boosted the Democratic vote in Charlotte as well. And she carried Winston-Salem and Greensboro. But GOP numbers leapt in places like Burke, Caldwell, Haywood, McDowell, Rutherford, Surry and Wilkes counties in the Blue Ridge and Smokey Mountain region of the western part of the state. Those rural and largely white counties were Republican to begin with, but in some cases Trump's vote reached 76 percent. Much has been made of the Democrats' ability to turn out their supporters before Election Day, and indeed, Clinton won the early vote in North Carolina (in-person plus absentee-by-mail) by almost 78,000 votes. But Trump beat Clinton by more than 251,000 votes cast on Election Day (including provisional ballots). A three-judge panel on the U.S. Court of Appeals for the 4th Circuit had suspended North Carolina's stricter voter ID and voter-access law three months before the election, but some Democrats still complained that the measure had a chilling effect on minority voting.

North Carolina's primary has occasionally played a role in presidential politics. In 1976, after five straight losses, Ronald Reagan won his first major victory over Gerald Ford in the Republican primary, reenergizing his campaign that went all the way to the convention in Kansas City. After Obama trounced Clinton in the 2008 primary, he was the de-facto Democratic nominee. In 2016, the state moved its primary up to March 15. In the GOP primary, Trump narrowly defeated Texas Sen. Ted Cruz, 40%-37%. Trump carried dozens of rural and small-town counties in the west and east. Cruz won the Research Triangle as well as Winston-Salem and Greensboro metros. Clinton beat Sanders 55%-41%, and carried 83 of 100 counties.

Congressional Districts

116th Congress Lineup	3D 8R 2V	115th Congress Lineup	3D 10R

North Carolina is projected to gain the 14th House seat that it fell barely short of taking after the 2010 census. As of early 2019, numerous variables made it difficult to envision the outcome, short of a virtual guarantee that the state faced another partisan and legal brawl.

Among the immediate uncertainties:

*The Supreme Court was expected to rule by June 2019 on an appeals-court decision in August 2018 that held the state's redistricting plan an unconstitutional partisan gerrymander.

*With Democrats holding the governor's office and Republicans retaining control of the legislature, though no longer with super-majorities, the outcome of elections in 2020 for those offices was highly unpredictable.

*Meanwhile, the two parties were competing to resolve a disputed November 2018 contest for a Charlotte-area district that the state board of elections had thrown out following allegations of improper handling of absentee ballots. A Democratic victory would mark the first party switch since 2014 in the delegation, which Republicans have controlled 10-3.

Since the 1990s, North Carolina has been the epicenter of race-based redistricting litigation. The initial focus was a long, skinny new black-majority 12th District that went to the U.S. Supreme Court four times. Throughout these battles, Democrats managed to retain partisan control of the delegation. That ended in 2011, when North Carolina was the site of Democrats' worst redistricting devastation, the seeds of which were sown 15 years prior. In 1996, Democrats in charge of the General Assembly exempted redistricting matters from new gubernatorial veto powers, reasoning they would always hold the legislature but voters might occasionally elect a Republican governor. In the ultimate tale of unintended consequences, Republicans shocked even themselves by taking over the legislature by large margins in 2010, rendering Democratic Gov. Bev Perdue helpless to foil their map makeover. Republicans quickly released and passed a new plan that unraveled and reversed the Democrats' 2002 map, and then some. They packed Democratic voters into three of the state's 13 seats: an African-American majority 1st District covering parts of rural northeastern counties and heavily black neighborhoods in Durham; an almost comically gerrymandered and liberal 4th District connecting the academic haven of Chapel Hill, black neighborhoods in Raleigh and faraway Fayetteville; and an even more tightly packed African-American majority 12th District knifing along the I-85 corridor in a strip from Charlotte to Winston-Salem and Greensboro. Republicans drew the other 10 seats at least 10 percentage points more Republican than the national average. By 2014, their handiwork eviscerated four of the state's seven Democrats.

The redistricting battles have continued. In 2015, the litigation resulted in yet another new map. The GOP-controlled legislature was given the opportunity to redraw the districts. With their lengthy experience in litigation and demographics, the map-drawers believed they had found a way to ensure what they thought were 10 secure Republican districts. The gross geographic gerrymanders were largely eliminated and the new districts took similar partisan leanings. Only the uncertain outcome of the tossed-out election in the 9th District threatened the GOP's continued success. In the meantime, the appeals court ruling that the legislature had crafted a partisan gerrymander presented new issues for the Supreme Court, which historically has been cautious in its rulings on redistricting and where two newly confirmed justices in the previous two years raised additional uncertainties.

In drawing the new 14th district after the 2020 census, even the Republicans would be hard-pressed to draw themselves a secure 11th seat. With the prospect that the courts will continue to intervene, Democrats likely will have an opportunity to gain at least one seat. Given population trends, options include "fair-fight" districts in one or both of the state's chief population centers: Mecklenburg and Wake counties.

Roy Cooper (D)

Elected 2016, term expires 2021, 1st term; b. Jun. 13, 1957, Nashville; Univ. of North Carolina Chapel Hill, BA 1979; Univ. of North Carolina, JD 1982; Presbyterian; Married (Kristin); 3 children.

Elected Office: NC House 1987-1991; NC Senate 1991-2000; NC Attorney General 2001-2017

Office: 116 W Jones St, Raleigh, 27699-0301; 919-814-2000; Fax: 919-733-2120; Website: governor.nc.gov.

Lt. Gov.: Dan Forest (R) **Atty. Gen:** Josh Stein (D) **Sec. of State:**   Elaine Marshall (D)
State Legislature: **Senate:** 21D, 29R **House:** 55D, 65R

Election Results

Election	Name (Party)	Vote (%)
2016 General	Roy Cooper (D)	2,309,190 (49%)
	Pat McCrory (R)	2,298,927 (49%)
	Lon Cecil (L)	102,986 (2%)
2016 Primary	Roy Cooper (D)	710,658 (69%)
	Ken Spaulding (D)	323,774 (31%)

Roy Cooper, a Democrat who had served four terms as North Carolina's attorney general, narrowly ousted Republican Gov. Pat McCrory in 2016 amid public dissatisfaction with H.B. 2, a bill that preempted local non-discrimination ordinances on sexual orientation, requiring, among other things, that people use bathrooms corresponding with their birth gender. In his first two years in office, Cooper fought seemingly endless battles with the GOP-controlled legislature, including against repeated efforts to strip his powers as governor. But Cooper achieved an important victory in the 2018 elections, as Democrats broke the Republican supermajorities in the House and Senate, making it easier for Cooper to make his vetoes stick, starting in 2019.

Cooper was born and raised in a rural portion of east-central North Carolina. He earned a bachelor's degree in psychology and political science and a law degree at the University of North Carolina. While Cooper was still in law school, then-Gov. Jim Hunt, a Democrat, named him to a state goals and policy board. Upon graduation, Cooper joined the family law firm, handling civil suits and personal injury and insurance cases; he also served as a Sunday school teacher and deacon at his Presbyterian church. Cooper served in the state House from 1987 to 1991, and in the state Senate from 1991 to 2001 -- part of that time as majority leader. In 2000, Cooper ran for attorney general against Republican Dan Boyce. It was a hard-fought race, with Cooper airing ads accusing Boyce of overbilling in a class-action lawsuit against the state. (The overbilling allegation prompted a 14-year legal battle that ended with Cooper apologizing.) After outspending Boyce four-to-one, Cooper won the race by five points. He later won reelection three times, serving 16 years. As attorney general, Cooper oversaw the increased use of DNA testing and sought tougher sentences for child predators and pornographers. He took over the bogus Duke lacrosse rape case after Durham District Attorney Mike Nifong recused himself; Cooper re-investigated the allegations and cleared the players of all charges.

In 2013, Cooper actively opposed a voter-ID and election overhaul law driven by the Republican legislature. This and other stances made it increasingly clear that Cooper was aiming for a gubernatorial run against McCrory in 2016. McCrory, a seven-term mayor of Charlotte, had run for governor in 2012 touting a pragmatic, "middle way" philosophy based on pro-business policies and little emphasis on social issues – an approach that had worked for him as a Republican serving on the city level, and that embodied the kind of centrism that had historically carried both Republicans and Democrats to the governor's mansion. (Indeed, Cooper's rise to prominence came as a mirror image to McCrory's – he was a moderate Democrat able to win rural and small-town votes.) Once in office, however, McCrory had to work with a Republican-dominated legislature that had little interest in pragmatic centrism and a strong desire to control the agenda, which often included socially conservative issues. McCrory sometimes clashed with GOP legislators and vetoed their bills, but more often he signed them, including the election overhaul bill (later overturned in the courts), a tax overhaul that flattened brackets, and an abortion waiting period.

The biggest threat to McCrory's hopes for reelection came from H.B. 2. The types of business interests who had historically aligned with McCrory were unhappy, fearing boycotts and economic pullouts that indeed materialized within weeks. In the campaign, Cooper made opposition to H.B. 2 – and particularly its effect on the state's economy – a cornerstone of his message. He also advocated increased funding for K-12 education. Cooper's approach resonated – at least, enough to defeat McCrory by a little over 10,000 votes. Donald Trump carried the state, but McCrory underperformed the top of the ticket in some of the industrial areas of the Piedmont and western North Carolina. The McCrory camp raised the specter of election fraud, but election boards headed by Republicans disagreed. In December, the incumbent conceded.

Even then, it wasn't over. In an echo of the then-Democratic legislature's actions to remove the governor from the redistricting process in the 1990s, Republican legislators passed laws to strip some of Cooper's powers. In December 2016, the two parties failed to come to agreement on how to repeal

H.B. 2. Finally, in March 2017 – after Cooper had become governor and after the Associated Press had estimated that the state would suffer $3.76 billion over 12 years in lost business – the two sides agreed to a repeal. However, the repeal measure contained a provision sought by Republicans that continued for three years a restriction on the types of local ordinances that had precipitated H.B. 2 in the first place. The three-year moratorium was a bitter pill for LGBT advocates, and Cooper signed it unhappily, saying it wasn't his "preferred solution."

Rhetorically, Cooper came out in favor of removing Confederate monuments after the white nationalist march in Charlottesville, writing, "Some people cling to the belief that the Civil War was fought over states' rights. But history is not on their side. We cannot continue to glorify a war against the United States of America fought in the defense of slavery. These monuments should come down." A year later, Cooper pulled back North Carolina National Guard members from serving at the U.S.-Mexico border in protest of the Trump administration policy of family separations; he also spoke out against Trump's trade policy, saying that retaliatory tariffs would put millions of dollars of North Carolina agricultural exports at risk.

On a few limited issues, Cooper was able to act without being blocked by the legislature. He pledged to oppose a Trump administration proposal to drill for oil and gas offshore, reversing the position previously articulated by McCrory. He also signed an executive order setting a state goal of cutting greenhouse gas emissions by 40 percent by 2025, effectively keeping North Carolina within the terms of the Paris climate accord, which Trump had pulled the U.S. out of. In September 2018, Cooper led the recovery from Hurricane Florence, which left some three dozen North Carolinians dead and caused widespread damage. Meanwhile, Cooper saw two of his vetoes sustained – one of a bill that would have let nonprofits hold gambling fundraisers, and another of a bill that critics said would have permitted the spraying of "garbage juice" at landfills.

More often – much more often – Cooper's efforts were stymied. His campaign pledge to expand Medicaid under the Affordable Care Act stalled, and his vetoes of budget bills were overridden in both 2017 and 2018. The 2017 bill, he said, "prioritizes tax breaks for the wealthy and corporations and comes up short for education and the economy." (The spending plan cut his office budget by $1 million.) Cooper criticized the 2018 budget on similar grounds. Both measures were enacted with strong Republican support. By January 2019, Cooper had vetoed 28 bills, including several that sought to limit the governor's powers. Many of the bills about gubernatorial authority went through various stages of vetoes, overrides, lower court decisions and judicial appeals. One that became law after an override was a bill to make judicial elections partisan. Another reduced the number of Court of Appeals judges from 15 to 12 through attrition, although by early 2019, Republicans were considering scrapping it.

The voters spoke on Election Day 2018, when they rejected – by solid, 3-to-2 margins – a pair of legislature-backed ballot measures to weaken the governor's powers. One would have given legislators the power to appoint election board members, while the other would have enabled legislators to fill judicial vacancies. All five living former governors, including McCrory, joined with Cooper in opposition. In an even more important Election Day development, Democrats won enough seats in the state House and Senate to break the GOP's veto-proof supermajority, giving Cooper crucial leverage despite continued GOP majorities. As the 2020 election cycle began, a Public Policy Polling survey found Cooper leading in head-to-head matchups against five possible GOP challengers, with McCrory the closest at 45%-41%. With North Carolina likely to be a presidential battleground state, the 2020 gubernatorial election is expected to be closely watched nationally. Republicans plan their national convention in Charlotte in August 2020.

Richard Burr (R)

Elected 2004, term expires 2022, 3rd term, b. Nov 30, 1955; Charlottesville, VA; Wake Forest University (NC), B.A., 1978; Methodist; Married (Brooke Fauth Burr); 2 children.

Elected Office: U.S. House, 1995-2005.

Professional Career: National sales Manager, Carswell Distributing, 1978-1994.

DC Office: 217 RSOB 20510, 202-224-3154, Fax: 202-228-2981, burr.senate.gov

State Offices: Asheville, 828-350-2437; Rocky Mount, 252-977-9522; Wilmington, 910-251-1058; Winston-Salem, 336-631-5125.

Committees: *Aging. Finance*: Energy, Natural Resources & Infrastructure; Health Care; Taxation & IRS Oversight. *Health, Education, Labor & Pensions*: Children & Families; Employment & Workplace Safety; Primary Health & Retirement Security. *Intelligence (Chmn)*.

Group Ratings

	ADA	ACLU	AFL-CIO	LCV	ITI	COC	HAFA	ACU	CFG	FRC
2018	-	6%	-	14%	-	89%	62%	77%	59%	100%
2017	0%	C	0%	0%	C	86%	C	80%	76%	100%

Almanac Ratings 2017-18

	Economy	Social	Foreign	Composite
Liberal	0%	0%	0%	0%
Conservative	100%	100%	100%	100%

Key Votes of the 115th Congress

1. Obama-care revision	Y	5. Gun regulations	Y	9. Kavanaugh confirmation	Y
2. Tax Cuts	Y	6. Family planning regs	Y	10. Saudi arms sales	N
3. Dodd-Frank revision	Y	7. Gorsuch confirmation	Y	11. FISA rules	Y
4. Omnibus appropriations	NV	8. Immigration restrictions	Y	12. Military aid in Yemen	N

Election Results

Election	Name (Party)	Vote (%)	Cand. Spent	Ind. Exp. Support	Ind. Exp. Oppose
2016 General	Richard Burr (R)	2,395,376 (51%)	$12,398,612	$2,293,659	$26,170,688
	Deborah Ross (D)	2,128,165 (45%)	$20,299,019	$3,001,651	$28,311,467
	Sean Haugh (L)	167,592 (4%)	$4,298		
2016 Primary	Richard Burr (R)	627,354 (61%)			
	Greg Brannon (R)	257,331 (25%)			
	Paul Wright (R)	86,940 (9%)			

Prior winning percentages: 2010 (55%), 2004 (52%); House: 2002 (70%), 2000 (93%), 1998 (68%), 1996 (62%), 1994 (57%)

Senate Intelligence Chairman Richard Burr took on the dicey responsibility of pursuing a bipartisan probe into Russian interference in the 2016 presidential election. That placed the North Carolina Republican, who has been regarded as a hard-working and consistent conservative, in an unfamiliar setting: the spotlight. In collaboration for the most part with Sen. Mark Warner of Virginia, the committee's ranking Democrat, Burr took the panel in a very different direction than its House counterpart, which was full of partisan fireworks. In his third term that he has said will be his last, he showed a political independence that can be atypical in the Senate.

A distant relative of Aaron Burr, the nation's third vice president, Richard Burr grew up a minister's son in Winston-Salem and was a high school and Wake Forest University football star. He then spent nearly two decades in sales for Winston-Salem-based Carswell Distributing, a wholesaler of lawn and garden equipment and home heating appliances. His first run for office was in 1992, against nine-term Democratic Rep. Steve Neal. Although outspent 3-1, he lost by a relatively narrow

53%-46%. Neal retired in 1994 and Burr ran again, this time winning 57 percent of the vote in a Republican wave year. Burr did not have a serious challenge in four re-election bids.

On the House Energy and Commerce Committee, Burr worked to streamline the Food and Drug Administration's drug and medical device approval process, which he argued would speed lifesaving products to the market. With broad bipartisan support, his FDA Modernization Act became law in 1997. He also helped set up the National Institute for Biomedical Imaging and Bioengineering at the National Institutes of Health.

In his last year in the House, 2004, Burr fought to end the tobacco quota system that had been in place since 1938. The entire North Carolina delegation favored it; tobacco quotas had been cut back in recent years and seemed likely to be again. At issue was whether the buyout should be coupled with FDA regulation of tobacco. Burr favored the buyout without FDA regulation, arguing that the toxicity of cigarettes should be regulated by the Centers for Disease Control and Prevention. In the conference committee, he held out for the buyout without FDA regulation; Senate conferees yielded, and the bill was enacted to reflect his preferences.

Burr had promised to serve only five terms in the House, and he made clear his interest in running for the Senate. In 2002, when GOP Sen. Jesse Helms announced he would retire, Burr deferred to Elizabeth Dole, who had the backing of the Bush White House. Two years later, Democratic Sen. John Edwards opted to run for president over seeking re-election, and Burr had the shot he was waiting for. He had serious opposition from Erskine Bowles, President Bill Clinton's onetime chief of staff, who had lost the 2002 Senate race 54%-45% to Dole. Bowles had deep roots in North Carolina: His father, Skipper Bowles, had been the Democratic nominee for governor in 1972. As Clinton's top aide, Bowles negotiated the 1997 legislation that produced a balanced federal budget for the first time in decades.

Each candidate spent about $13 million. Bowles started running ads in May, while Burr held back until September and, having conserved resources, had a money advantage in the final two months. Bowles touted his ability to work with both parties while depicting Burr as a captive of special interests, especially pharmaceutical and tobacco companies. Burr linked Bowles to Clinton's policies on tax increases, welfare for immigrants and trade with China. Bush carried North Carolina 56%-44% in his re-election bid, and Burr beat Bowles 52%-47%. Later, when Bowles co-chaired President Barack Obama's fiscal commission, he had kind words for Burr: "I think by the grace of God we both ended up in the exact right jobs for North Carolina. ... I can tell you from firsthand experience nobody works harder or is smarter than this guy in Washington."

In the Senate, Burr has shown little interest in calling attention to himself. He told The Charlotte Observer in 2009: "I tend to be more of a policy guy than I am a guy who shows up on the 24-hour talk shows or a guy who goes to the floor and speaks." He has leaned conservative on cultural issues and initially toward the center on foreign policy, although he moved further to the right after Obama became president. His voting record places him in the middle of the Republican conference.

One of his most significant legislative achievements came in his first year in the Senate, when he won enactment of a law to create the Biomedical Advanced Research and Development Authority to develop vaccines and other countermeasures to bioterrorism and pandemics. It was a continuation of Burr's efforts in the House after 9/11. It was among several notable instances of Burr reaching across the political aisle.

In 2010, Burr surprised his conservative supporters when he voted to end the "don't ask, don't tell" law banning openly gay service members. In 2015, he voted to give married same-sex spouses Social Security and veterans benefits they have earned. Burr occasionally has shown a willingness to take on more-conservative colleagues; he said in 2013 that talk of shutting down the federal government over opposition to the Affordable Care Act was "the dumbest idea I've ever heard." A year later, he worked on a comprehensive alternative to the ACA that retained many of the law's most popular elements but guaranteed coverage to those with pre-existing medical conditions only if they maintained "continuous coverage."

One area where Burr has taken a strong conservative line is immigration. In 2006, he voted against an immigration overhaul because he said it would lead to "blanket amnesty" for undocumented immigrants. During negotiations on a compromise bill the following year, Burr supported the "touchback" amendment that would have forced undocumented immigrants to return to their home countries before applying for visas. When the amendment was voted down, he voted against the compromise measure. He vowed to keep an open mind as a bipartisan group of his colleagues drafted a comprehensive immigration reform proposal in 2013, but he voted against the bill, saying it didn't do enough to secure the border.

As ranking Republican on the Veterans' Affairs Committee in 2014, after a scandal erupted at the Veterans Affairs Department over mismanagement and overly long waits for patients, Burr — who represents a state with more than 800,000 veterans — found himself at the center of an acrimonious spat. He wrote an open letter charging that the staffs at various veterans groups have "ignored the constant VA problems expressed by their members and is more interested in their own livelihoods and Washington connections than they are to the needs of their own members." His comments produced outrage; an official at Disabled American Veterans said the senator "shows no interest in pursuing serious policy solutions, preferring instead to launch cheap political attacks on the integrity of leaders of veterans organizations that do not agree with him."

Having taken over as Intelligence Committee chairman in 2015, Burr had an at times bumpy relationship with the panel's ranking member, Dianne Feinstein of California — who had chaired the panel for six years. Feinstein had commissioned a staff investigation of the CIA's use of torture after 9/11. It produced a critical report longer than 6,700 pages, although only a 500-page summary was declassified and released publicly. Burr lambasted the report's conclusions that the CIA's torture program had proved ineffective, calling the report "fiction," and fought declassification of the report. After becoming chairman, he wrote to Obama asking that copies of the full classified report sent to the White House and other parts of the executive branch be returned — apparently fearing the report could become available under the Freedom of Information Act. Feinstein opposed Burr's request, later telling the New Yorker, "I was surprised and somewhat suspicious about who put him up to it." The White House declined to return or destroy copies of the report.

Burr resisted reining in the power of intelligence agencies in the face of domestic snooping revelations and fought to turn back attempts at greater openness when sections of the Patriot Act came up for reauthorization. "If I had my way, with the exception of nominees, there would never be a public intelligence hearing," he told reporters in 2014. A year later, Burr helped lead the charge to reauthorize the law, fighting against bipartisan efforts to curtail the program's bulk collection of Americans' phone records. He and Senate Majority Leader Mitch McConnell did all they could to renew the act unaltered, even after the House passed a bill with changes by overwhelming bipartisan margins. After an attempt to force a short-term extension of the law failed and the Patriot Act expired, McConnell relented and allowed a vote on the House-passed measure. Burr was among 32 senators to vote against the changes. "I am disappointed in the final bill and, quite frankly, am very concerned about the new system's ability to keep up with the threats we face," he said.

In 2016, Burr got behind Trump when it was clear that he would be the party's nominee. At one point, the usually low-key senator compared himself to the bombastic billionaire. "He's a very nontraditional candidate, and he's run a very nontraditional campaign," Burr told reporters at the Republican National Convention. "Most in Washington would probably say that describes me to a 'T,' and so I can associate with Donald Trump very well." He later signed on as a national security adviser to the Trump campaign, while downplaying the possibility of Russian interference in the election to benefit Trump. "I have yet to see anything that would lead me to believe that's the case," Burr told Foreign Policy magazine in early October. He called his congressional colleagues' warnings "probably incorrect," adding, "They give the impression there's one cyber-problem in the world: Russia and the elections, and that's a huge understatement."

Burr vowed impartiality as his panel's investigation of Russian interference — and possible collusion between Moscow and the Trump campaign — got underway in early 2017. "I'll admit that I voted for [Trump]. ... But I've got a job in the United States Senate, and I take that job extremely seriously," Butt said. "It overrides any personal beliefs that I have or loyalties that I might have." He quickly developed a cordial relationship with Warner, who had replaced Feinstein as the committee's senior Democrat and had a history of working well with Republican Senators. With Burr emphasizing the need to determine what had happened during the election, they worked together on much of the investigation and often held joint news conferences. "Contrary to maybe popular belief," Burr told reporters in March 2017, he and Warner were partners.

The committee leaders had little to say in 2017 about their closed-door inquiry, with Burr stressing the extended commitment of his personal time and obligation to protect classified information. By March 2018, he told reporters, "It is clear the Russian government was looking for vulnerabilities in our election system" during 2016. But he said that the Russian interference was not responsible for Trump's victory and he rejected suggestions that Trump had "colluded" with Russia. As the committee inquiry continued, Burr made a point of avoiding meetings at the White House and didn't heed Trump's pleas to stop investigating, as Republicans had done in the House. Instead, Burr said after the 2018 elections that he expected that the review would continue well into 2019, including the committee's final report.

Burr criticized Rep. Devin Nunes of California, then then chairman of the House Intelligence Committee, for his handling of that panel's investigation. In February 2018, when Nunes released a memo that alleged wrongdoing by the Justice Department in its surveillance of a Trump adviser, Burr said, "I don't think there was any need for a memo to be released."

Displaying his increased independence in other areas, Burr said that Trump was "misguided" when he cast "blame on both sides" after the protests by white supremacist groups in Charlottesville in August 2017. He was the decisive vote in June 2018 when the Senate rejected $15 billion in cuts of previously approved spending. He opposed, in particular, the elimination of $16 million for the Land and Water Conservation Fund, which has been one of his favorite programs.

Burr has sought to move up the Senate leadership ladder. In 2007, he lost a bid for Republican Conference chairman to Lamar Alexander of Tennessee. In 2009, he was named chief deputy whip. In 2011, Burr said he intended to run for Republican whip, the No. 2 leadership slot, after Jon Kyl of Arizona announced his retirement. Burr changed his mind in March 2012 and said he would rather focus on legislation, clearing the way for John Cornyn of Texas to take the job.

When he faced re-election in 2010, there was speculation Burr could encounter serious opposition, considering Obama's victory in North Carolina in 2008 and Dole's defeat for re-election that year. Moreover, polls showed Burr had a low profile in the state. But the strongest possible Democratic challenger, state Attorney General Roy Cooper, declined to run. (Cooper is now the state's governor.) Secretary of State Elaine Marshall emerged from the Democratic primary with little money. Burr raised $11 million, nearly four times as much as his opponent. He won 55%-43%.

Democrats also had recruiting difficulties in 2016, when Burr again came up for re-election. Former Sen. Kay Hagan, narrowly ousted by Republican Thom Tillis in 2014, declined to take on Burr — as did Obama Secretary of Transportation Anthony Foxx, a former Charlotte mayor. Former state Rep. Deborah Ross, a Raleigh attorney, eventually was embraced by the state Democratic establishment. Initially, the faceoff was not high on the list of competitive Senate races. But Burr was weighed down by a couple of other factors beyond his control: the unpopularity of GOP Gov. Pat McCrory, who ended up losing to Cooper, and the "bathroom bill" passed by the North Carolina General Assembly — which required transgender people to use bathrooms in government buildings consistent with the gender on their birth certificates. Burr sought to distance himself from the law, telling HuffPost: "The Legislature botched what they were trying to do. It was far too expansive."

Burr created some problems for himself. To the frustration of GOP officials, he did not campaign in earnest until late September. Ross sought to paint Burr as a Washington insider and accused him of voting to privatize Medicare and cut Social Security benefits — charges that Burr disputed. Meanwhile, Burr and his GOP allies sought to tie Ross to several unpopular stances taken by the state chapter of the American Civil Liberties Union, of which Ross was a former director. Burr pulled out a 51%-45% win — mirroring Trump's 50%-46% victory in the state. Although short of the $111 million spent in the Hagan-Tillis contest, spending in the Burr-Ross race approached $84 million. The candidates themselves spent about $32 million, with Ross outspending the incumbent by $8 million. That was dwarfed by nearly $60 million from outside spending groups.

Months before the votes were counted, Burr said that, if he won, it would be his last term.

"It's real simple: I'm beginning to get old," Burr, who will be 67 in 2022, told reporters at the Republican National Convention. "I still look forward to getting back into the private sector before retirement even comes into the picture. I never envisioned retiring out of the Congress."

Burr will have an opportunity to take on new responsibilities during what he has said will be his final two years as a senator. With the retirement in 2020 of Alexander, Burr will be next in line to chair the Senate Health, Education, Labor & Pensions Committee, assuming Republicans retain Senate control. Switching from oversight of federal intelligence agencies to the handling of domestic social policy might be a welcome change for Burr.

Thom Tillis (R)

Elected 2014, term expires 2020, 1st term, b. Aug 30, 1960; Jacksonville, FL; University of Maryland University College, B.S., 1996; Catholic; Married (Susan Tillis); 2 children.

Elected Office: Board of Commissioners, Cornelius, NC, 2003-2005; NC House, 2007-2014.

Professional Career: Life insurance company consultant, 1981-1982; Executive and Manager, PricewaterhouseCoopers, IBM, 1983-2009.

DC Office: 113 DSOB 20510, 202-224-6342, Fax: 202-228-2563, tillis.senate.gov

State Offices: Charlotte, 704-509-9087; Greenville, 252-329-0371; Hendersonville, 828-693-8750; High Point, 336-885-0685; Raleigh, 919-856-4630.

Committees: *Armed Services*: Airland; Personnel (Chmn); Seapower. *Banking, Housing & Urban Affairs*: Economic Policy; Financial Institutions & Consumer Protection; Securities, Insurance & Investment. *Judiciary*: Border Security & Immigration; Crime & Terrorism; Oversight, Agency Action, Federal Rights & Federal Courts; Subcommittee on Intellectual Property (Chmn). *Veterans' Affairs*.

Group Ratings

	ADA	ACLU	AFL-CIO	LCV	ITI	COC	HAFA	ACU	CFG	FRC
2018	-	14%	-	7%	-	75%	59%	80%	52%	100%
2017	0%	C	0%	0%	C	86%	C	83%	82%	100%

Almanac Ratings 2017-18

	Economy	Social	Foreign	Composite
Liberal	6%	6%	5%	5%
Conservative	94%	94%	95%	95%

Key Votes of the 115th Congress

1. Obama-care revision	Y	5. Gun regulations	Y	9. Kavanaugh confirmation	Y
2. Tax Cuts	Y	6. Family planning regs	Y	10. Saudi arms sales	N
3. Dodd-Frank revision	Y	7. Gorsuch confirmation	Y	11. FISA rules	Y
4. Omnibus appropriations	N	8. Immigration restrictions	Y	12. Military aid in Yemen	NV

Election Results

Election	Name (Party)	Vote (%)		Cand. Spent	Ind. Exp. Support	Ind. Exp. Oppose
2014 General	Thom Tillis (R)	1,423,259	(49%)	$10,513,963	$13,033,391	$37,000,532
	Kay Hagan (D)	1,377,651	(47%)	$24,851,013	$7,789,136	$20,462,687
	Sean Haugh (L)	109,100	(4%)			
2014 Primary	Thom Tillis (R)	223,174	(46%)			
	Greg Brannon (R)	132,630	(27%)			
	Mark Harris (R)	85,727	(18%)			

Republican Thom Tillis, North Carolina's junior senator, benefited from the Republican wave in the 2014 election to pull off a narrow win over Democratic Sen. Kay Hagan in what was, up to that point, the most expensive Senate campaign in history. Since then, he has struggled to find a balance between supporting Senate Republican initiatives and President Donald Trump and demonstrating his independence and centrist tone as a senator, especially as he looked ahead to the prospect of another close campaign in 2020. Democrats have continued to remind voters that Tillis often took sharp partisan positions when he was speaker of the North Carolina House before he became a senator.

Tillis was born in Jacksonville Florida, one of five siblings. By the time he was 17, his family had moved 20 times as his parents sought work, at one point living in a trailer park. While he graduated near the top of his high school class, he and his siblings "weren't wired to go to college," he told an interviewer shortly after becoming House speaker. He took a job as a warehouse records clerk — later earning a bachelor's degree in technology management, at 36, through University of Maryland-University College, a largely online institution. By that time, he was a partner at the international accounting and consulting firm PriceWaterhouseCoopers. He previously worked for now-defunct Wang Laboratories. He remained at PriceWaterhouseCoopers after it was taken over by IBM and advised banks and other corporations. It was his work for Charlotte-based NationsBank — which later became Bank of America after a merger — that brought him to North Carolina in 1998.

After he settled in Cornelius, a Charlotte suburb, his political rise was little short of meteoric. After getting his start as the president of the PTA at his daughter's high school, he served as a town commissioner before winning election to the state House in 2006. Four years later, Republicans flipped the state House and Tillis was chosen as the fifth GOP speaker in state history. He touted his business background in winning election to the House and later managing it. "A democratic institution is by definition not a business. But there is the business of running the Legislature, which I think we're doing pretty well," he told Business North Carolina magazine in 2012. Critics on the left, however, suggested a contradiction between Tillis' initial political image and his later persona. "He goes to the General Assembly as a business conservative and then votes for or enables some of the most far-right legislation in our state's history," Chris Fitzsimon, executive director of the liberal N.C. Policy Watch, told The Charlotte Observer during Tillis' campaign for Senate.

A business-oriented conservative, Tillis helped enact laws that included restructuring North Carolina's tax code to reduce personal and business income taxes, eliminating the estate tax, and capping the gasoline tax. On his watch, state House Republicans also took on social issues. They passed bills to allow guns in bars and on college campuses and to require women to watch a narrated ultrasound before abortions. The abortion measure was later struck down by a federal judge. In 2013, the Tillis-led House created outrage among civil rights groups when it repealed a law allowing citizens to register to vote and cast a ballot on the same day while adopting a requirement that voters had to present one of six state-approved ID cards at the polls. Democrats attacked Tillis for those moves and for cutting funds from the University of North Carolina system and dragging his feet on teacher pay increases — charges that became a prominent feature in Hagan's Senate campaign ads. Nonetheless, some conservatives griped that Tillis wasn't going far enough in pushing changes through the General Assembly.

Indeed, Tillis faced resistance from his right while taking on Hagan in 2014. While a programmatic social and fiscal conservative, he was not a fire-breather — and had no trouble picking up the support of the state's GOP establishment. That helped him prevail in an eight-way primary with 46 percent of the vote, more than the 40 percent needed to avoid a runoff. But for two months after the May primary, pressure from conservatives in the Statehouse kept Tillis focused on his day job more than was helpful for a candidate in a nationally targeted race.

Hagan's seat was high on national Republican lists of pickup opportunities: The incumbent had ousted Republican Sen. Elizabeth Dole in 2008, a good year for Democrats when Barack Obama became only the second Democratic presidential nominee in more than four decades to carry North Carolina. Hagan had backed Obama on his chief legislative priorities. Tillis' main campaign objective was to tie Hagan to Obama, highlighting her support for the Affordable Care Act. He accused his rival of skipping an Armed Services Committee hearing on the threat of the Islamic State to raise campaign money, a particularly potent attack in a state with two large military bases and 800,000 veterans. If tea party activists in the state remained lukewarm at best toward his candidacy, Tillis had the support of major outside groups like Americans for Prosperity, American Crossroads and the U.S. Chamber of Commerce. These organizations spent months and millions of dollars attacking Hagan via television ads.

Hagan responded by campaigning against what she characterized as Tillis' extreme agenda on issues ranging from abortion to education to taxes. "At every opportunity he has fought for policies that are taking our state backwards," Hagan said during an October debate. "Speaker Tillis feels that those who have the most should get the most help." Hagan also emphasized her opposition to a statewide ban on same-sex marriage, which Tillis said he would continue to defend. The North Carolina Constitution's ban on same-sex marriage was overturned in 2014 by a federal judge, prompting Tillis to say during the October debate, "We're in a dangerous time in this country where the president has appointed liberal activist judges — and Sen. Hagan has endorsed them or confirmed them — that are literally trying the legislate from the bench."

As Hagan turned her attention toward turning out her base — focusing on equal pay for women, Tillis' opposition to a minimum wage increase and North Carolina Republicans' push to constrain ballot access — Tillis tightened his message: He hammered Hagan on national security issues like

ISIS and the Ebola outbreak as well as problems at the Department of Veterans Affairs. Tillis edged Hagan 48.8%-47.2%, the Republicans' closest win of the election cycle; the margin was 45,000 votes out of more than 2.9 million cast. Polls showed neither candidate was well-liked on Election Day — but Obama's low popularity in the state likely was the crucial blow for Hagan. The contest stood as the most expensive Senate race in history — until 2016, when it was supplanted by that year's Pennsylvania Senate battle. Total spending in the Hagan-Tillis faceoff came to $111 million, with more than two-thirds of that, $77 million, from outside groups. Hagan outspent Tillis by more than 2-1.

In some of his early actions in the Senate, Tillis appeared much the same lawmaker who had steered the North Carolina House sharply to the right. He backed a state push to add anti-abortion "choose life" license plates and called the Department of Justice's investigation into the restrictive voting laws and gerrymandered congressional map he had helped pass in the state House a "waste of resources." He voted against Obama's nomination of Loretta Lynch, a North Carolina native, to be attorney general. But he did vote for a bill to give married same-sex spouses Social Security and veterans' benefits they had earned, despite his opposition to same-sex marriage. His scores in the Almanac vote ratings have put him in the middle of the Republican Conference.

He actively reached out to Democrats, seeking to hit the reset button and shed the image he had brought to Capitol Hill. Just weeks after taking office, he became the only Republican to join 13 Democratic senators on a bill to create a mechanism for monitoring conflicts worldwide and detecting early warning signs that might enable the United States to prevent genocides. He also co-authored legislation with Democratic Sen. Tom Carper of Delaware to ensure payments made to eugenics victims did not affect their eligibility for federal benefits like Medicaid and food stamps. The measure, signed by Obama in late 2016, was aimed at protecting the victims of compulsory sterilization programs that operated in 33 states as recently as the 1970s.

Tillis initially endorsed Florida Sen. Marco Rubio for the 2016 Republican presidential nomination but was a steadfast supporter of Trump from late spring — when Trump had clearly secured the nomination — through the election. "Anybody who doesn't support the Republican nominee ... is a RINO," Tillis said, referring to the acronym "Republican in name only." He added: "We have to recognize that more than anything else, we have to unite. At the end of the day, we're all Republicans."

Tillis was circumspect after Trump's and congressional Republicans' victories in 2016. "Since the election, I've heard some of my fellow Republicans claim that the party received a decisive mandate from voters," Tillis noted in an op-ed page column published in The Charlotte Observer. "Let's be clear: the American people didn't give the GOP a stamp of approval or a mandate to ram through an ideologically-driven, far-right agenda. If the election was a mandate for anything, it was for elected officials in both parties to break through the gridlock to finally start producing results.

"I, for one, have no intention of sitting down and watching another re-run of the same divisive partisanship we see year after year. ... I'll be reaching across the aisle to find opportunities to work with Democrats on the issues that desperately need to be addressed," he wrote.

When, early in his presidency, Trump issued an executive order imposing a temporary ban on immigration from seven predominantly Muslim countries, Tillis and Missouri Democrat Claire McCaskill and New Hampshire Democrat Jeanne Shaheen sent a letter to the Defense Department protesting the treatment of two Iraqis who had aided U.S. forces but were detained at New York's John F. Kennedy International Airport. Tillis said he supported tighter screening of refugees but that "there is a lot of confusion surrounding the order" and that it needed to be "refined."

Tillis suggested he might not seek re-election unless a bipartisan criminal justice reform measure — within the jurisdiction of the Judiciary Committee, of which Tillis is a member — became law. The bill, intended to reduce mandatory minimum sentences for those with drug convictions and increase rehabilitation programs for prisoners, had cleared the Judiciary panel by a wide margin but was stalled in late 2016 by a handful of hard-line conservatives. It returned to the committee's agenda in 2017. Tillis made the issue one of his top priorities. "I don't run again until 2020, and if we're not able to get things like this done, I don't have any intention of coming back," he said to applause at a juvenile justice forum. "It is time to tell the far-left and the far-right to get productive or get out of the way because we need to solve this problem." With support from Trump's son-in-law, Jared Kushner, the First Step Act was enacted in the lame-duck session after the 2018 elections.

Amid his overtures across the political aisle, Tillis has not abandoned his partisan instincts. For much of 2016, he pursued a leadership role at the National Republican Senatorial Committee, the Senate GOP's campaign arm. For a time, Tillis and Cory Gardner of Colorado — also elected in 2014 from a purple state — floated the idea of co-chairing the NRSC. But Tillis threw his support behind Gardner to chair the panel and became his deputy in for the 2018 election cycle.

Tillis took other steps to play down his partisanship. In April 2018, he filed a bill limiting Trump's ability to interfere with the investigation of special counsel Robert Mueller by permitting Mueller to appeal a possible removal — arguing for such protections regardless of which party controls the White House. Democrats praised the proposal, while many conservatives criticized Tillis and warned that Trump voters would react adversely. Separately, in response to threats from Russia, he created a bipartisan Senate group with Shaheen to demonstrate the chamber's commitment to NATO. He opposed Trump's nominee, Michael Dourson, for chemical safety regulation by the Environmental Protection Agency because of concerns about water contamination at Camp Lejeune in North Carolina; Dourson withdrew his name in December 2017.

Tillis sided with Trump on other issues. He reportedly told a closed-door meeting of GOP activists that Brett Kavanaugh "will be one of the greatest Supreme Court justices." In November 2018, he said that the president was right to send troops to the border with Mexico to stop illegal immigration. In what seemed a dramatic break, he wrote an op-ed published in The Washington Post in February 2019 in which he opposed Trump's plan to declare a national emergency at the southern border to use funds from other programs to finance a border wall. He cited his responsibility as a member of Congress to "preserve the separation of powers and to curb the kind of executive over-reach that Congress has allowed to fester for the better part of the past century." But when the Senate voted in March on a resolution to reject the emergency plan, Tillis sided with Trump and party regulars.

In January 2019, The Charlotte Observer editorial board wrote that it agreed with many of Tillis' moderate positions. But, it added, "when faced with an opportunity to put action behind his words, Tillis is instead getting in line with Republican senators" when "the big moments arrive." It characterized his political strategy as: "Keep those Trump backers happy, but talk a good centrist game in hopes of grabbing enough moderates to win" re-election in 2020. His political fate likely will not rest with editorial writers. But Tillis can expect Democrats to challenge his attempts to strike a balance.

G.K. Butterfield (D)

Elected 2004, 8th full term, b. Apr 27, 1947; Wilson; North Carolina Central University, B.A., 1971; North Carolina Central University School of Law, J.D., 1974; Baptist; Divorced; 3 children; 3 grandchildren.

Military Career: U.S. Army 1968-1997

Elected Office: NC Superior Court, 1988-2001, 2002-2004; NC Supreme Court, 2001-2002.

Professional Career: Practicing attorney, 1974-1988.

DC Office: 2080 RHOB 20515, 202-225-3101, Fax: 202-225-3354, butterfield.house.gov

State Offices: Durham, 919-908-0164; Wilson, 252-237-9816.

Committees: *Energy & Commerce*: Communications & Technology; Energy; Health. *House Administration. Joint Library.*

Group Ratings

	ADA	ACLU	AFL-CIO	LCV	ITI	COC	HAFA	ACU	CFG	FRC
2018	-	85%	-	91%	-	50%	2%	4%	2%	0%
2017	95%	C	95%	91%	C	57%	C	0%	0%	13%

Almanac Ratings 2017-18

	Economy	Social	Foreign	Composite
Liberal	95%	95%	98%	96%
Conservative	6%	5%	2%	4%

Key Votes of the 115th Congress

1. Obama-care revision	N	5. Family planning regs	NV	9. Guantanamo prisoners	Y	
2. Tax Cuts	N	6. Body cameras/immigration	Y	10. Ground missiles, limit	Y	
3. Omnibus appropriations	Y	7. Abortion ban	N	11. Defense Dept. spending	N	
4. Dodd-Frank revision	N	8. Concealed carry	N	12. FISA rules	N	

Election Results

Election	Name (Party)	Vote (%)	Cand. Spent	Ind. Exp. Support	Ind. Exp. Oppose
2018 General	G.K. Butterfield (D)......................	190,457 (70%)	$485,158		
	Roger Allison (R)...............................	82,218 (30%)	$28,799		
2018 Primary	G.K. Butterfield (D)................	(100%)			

Prior winning percentages: 2016 (69%), 2014 (73%), 2012 (75%), 2010 (59%), 2008 (70%), 2004 (64%)

Democrat G.K. (George Kenneth) Butterfield, who won a special election in 2004, rarely makes headlines but has been a key behind-the-scenes strategist for Democratic leaders and the Congressional Black Caucus. He has been a close ally of Rep. James Clyburn of South Carolina, who regained his position of majority whip, and has been a consistent voice for economic revival among low-income African Americans, especially in rural areas.

Butterfield grew up in Wilson County, where his father was a dentist and the first black elected official in Wilson in the 20th century; he lost his seat in 1957 when the white majority switched voting procedures to at-large elections. His mother was a schoolteacher for 48 years. In 1963, at age 16, Butterfield joined his father in Washington when Martin Luther King Jr. delivered his "I have a dream" speech. He got his bachelor's and law degrees from North Carolina Central University and participated in many registration drives after enactment of the Voting Rights Act. As a civil rights lawyer, Butterfield took on voting rights cases. He joined hospital employees at Duke University in their drive to organize a union. As a Superior Court judge for 12 years, he handled thousands of civil and criminal cases in 46 counties until 2001, when Democratic Gov. Michael Easley appointed him to the state Supreme Court. After Butterfield lost election in 2002 to a full term, Easley appointed him as a special Superior Court judge.

In the special election that resulted when the first-term incumbent resigned, Butterfield said that his priorities would be strengthening the rural economy and halting U.S. job losses. He won 71%-27% and has not been seriously challenged since.

Butterfield has a solidly liberal voting record. He has focused on an array of racial-discrimination issues. He helped to settle claims of up to 74,000 African-American farmers who were discriminated against when applying for Agriculture Department loans and programs between 1983 and 2010. He lobbied to include an exhibit in the Capitol Visitor Center on the slave labor that was employed in building the Capitol and on the careers of the 22 African Americans who served in Congress during and after Reconstruction. He pressed Obama administration officials for the appointment of an African American to fill a vacancy for federal judge in North Carolina's Eastern District.

A longtime friend of Clyburn, Butterfield managed his successful campaign for majority whip in 2006. Butterfield became a chief deputy whip under Clyburn and retained the position with Democrats in the House minority. A longtime leader of the Black Caucus, he was less confrontational toward President Barack Obama than were other CBC members. Along with Clyburn, he was among the few who supported funding of the wars in Iraq and Afghanistan.

As CBC chairman, Butterfield led a delegation to Ferguson Missouri in 2015 to call for "transformative changes" nationwide in police practices. During a meeting of CBC members with Obama, he told the president that "black America continues to be in a state of emergency." He has met frequently with leaders of Silicon Valley to demand more diversity in the tech industry. At those meetings, and in an April 2018 hearing with Facebook CEO Mark Zuckerberg, he criticized the limited progress. An increase from 2 to 3 percent in the share of the workforce that is black "does not meet the definition of building a racially diverse community," Butterfield said, who urged a strategy to increase diversity in the tech industry.

With his connections to Democratic leaders, Butterfield has a seat on the influential Energy and Commerce Committee, where he has worked to prohibit states from passing on their Medicaid costs to counties. In his low-income district, many counties spend more of their property-tax revenues on Medicaid than on public schools. He worked with Republican Rep. Michael McCaul of Texas to enact in 2012 a bill allowing pharmaceutical companies to receive faster Food and Drug Administration reviews of profitable drugs in return for developing treatments for rare pediatric diseases.

Following the 2018 election, when Democrats had back-room discussions about changes in their leadership, Butterfield made the case for Clyburn to move up a notch or two. When Nancy Pelosi and Steny Hoyer clinched their bids to retain their top-two positions, Butterfield said that Democrats needed to retain an African-American among their top leaders. "I understand that there is a pretty strong argument that we need fresh blood in the leadership and I respect that view. But now is not the time to make any significant changes in the top three among our leaders," he told the News & Observer. "To change the lineup would disrupt the caucus at a time when we need to be united." The status quo survived.

NC-1: Northeastern North Carolina   Cook Partisan Voting Index: D+17

Population		Race and Ethnicity		Income	
Total	750,304	White	42.1%	Median Income	$41,998
Land area (sq. miles)	5,878	Black	44.2%	District Income Rank	401
Pop/ sq mi	127.7	Latino	8.7%	Poverty Rate	21.7%
Born in State	65.9%	Asian	2%	With health insurance	86.9%
		Two or more races	2.1%	Cash public assistance	1.7%
Age Groups		Other	0.9%	Food stamp/SNAP	19.3%
Under 18	21.6%				
18-34	25.2%	**Education**		**Work**	
35-64	38.1%	H.S grad or less	45.4%	White Collar	15.1%
Over 64	15.1%	Some college	27.8%	Sales and Service	40.6%
		College Degree, 4 yr	15.8%	Blue Collar	23.5%
Military		Post grad	11%	Government	16.9%
Veteran/ Active Duty	7.2%				

2012 Pres. Vote	Obama	244,107	(68%)	Romney	113,493	(31%)			
2016 Pres. Vote	Clinton	240,217	(67%)	Trump	108,565	(30%)	Johnson	7,041	(2%)

Durham, Greenville: In colonial days, the eastern portion of North Carolina was a smaller version of the Chesapeake Bay colonies of Virginia and Maryland. A fertile land laced by rivers and inlets, it had tobacco plantations and farms with docks on waterways accessible to the ocean and so to London. In 1890, James B. Duke founded the American Tobacco Co. in Durham, and began mass production of cigarettes. Today, East Carolina survives with remnants of Tobacco Road and is still largely inhabited by descendants of the original white settlers and black slaves of 250 years ago. They live in small towns and cities. Tobacco was a labor-intensive crop that for many years produced yields of $4,000 an acre; a family lucky enough to have a tobacco quota could make a living off 40 acres. In 2004, Congress enacted a $10 billion buyout of quota holders.

North Carolina's tobacco production, which peaked at 1 billion pounds in 1951, dropped to 360 million pounds in 2017 and the industry's political influence has diminished, though its yield had stabilized and remained larger than that of the next six states combined. More of the local business in this area has turned to hog farming, where its $2 billion in sales make North Carolina the third-largest state for production, behind Iowa and Minnesota. Food-processing plants have replaced textile mills. Reser's Fine Foods began operations locally in 1950 with a potato-salad recipe, and now has 3,000 employees who produce deli foods and salads in the United States and Mexico, with its headquarters in the tiny town of Halifax. CSX rail company has been building a $214 million "intermodal" terminal in Edgecombe County near Rocky Mount; completion was expected in 2020.

The 1st Congressional District of North Carolina covers much of the old tobacco country of East Carolina. The 2016 redistricting significantly straightened out its boundaries, which had been ranked among the most gerrymandered districts in the nation. The chief population center is Durham, where the district takes in Duke University. Duke is an anchor for the Research Triangle area, whose facilities attract scholars from across the globe in a wide variety of fields and were ranked fourth in the nation in 2015 for tech jobs. The population of the county grew by 40 percent between 2000 and 2017, when it reached 312,000. Durham is overwhelmingly Democratic. Hillary Clinton took 79 percent of the presidential vote in 2016. The only other urban area in the district is Greenville-based Pitt County, nearly half of which is in the 1st with the remainder in the 3rd District.

The rest of the district is a swath of mostly rural, heavily African-American counties in the northeastern portion of the state. These are Democratic precincts in a variety of cities and small towns along North Carolina's coastal plain, including Roanoke Rapids, Tarboro, Wilson and parts of Albemarle Sound, but none of the Outer Banks. Even with robust Durham, the mostly rural district is among the lowest in the nation in its median income. In rural Warren County, the Raleigh News & Observer reported in December 2018, a relic of Tobacco Road that was prosperous in the mid-20th century faces many of the problems common in rural America: "the loss of manufacturing, a decline in small farming and youth leaving for better opportunities."

The district is 44 percent African American overall. This is one of three solidly Democratic North Carolina districts where Hillary Clinton got an identical 67 percent of the presidential vote in 2016.

George Holding (R)

Elected 2012, 4th term, b. Apr 17, 1968; Raleigh; Wake Forest University (NC), B.A., 1991; University of Saint Andrews (Scotland), Att., 1992; Wake Forest University (NC), J.D., 1996; Baptist; Married (Lucy E. Herriott); 4 children.

Professional Career: Practicing lawyer, 1996-1999; Legislative aide, Sen. Jesse Helms, 1999-2001; Practicing lawyer, 2001-2002; Assistant U.S. Attorney, E. District of NC, 2002-2006; U.S. Attorney, E. District of NC, 2006-2011.

DC Office: 1110 LHOB 20515, 202-225-3032, Fax: 202-225-0181, holding.house.gov

State Offices: Raleigh, 919-782-4400.

Committees: *Budget. Ethics. Ways & Means*: Health; Trade.

Group Ratings

	ADA	ACLU	AFL-CIO	LCV	ITI	COC	HAFA	ACU	CFG	FRC
2018	-	7%	-	3%	-	75%	92%	84%	86%	100%
2017	0%	C	8%	0%	C	93%	C	96%	92%	100%

Almanac Ratings 2017-18

	Economy	Social	Foreign	Composite
Liberal	0%	7%	0%	2%
Conservative	100%	94%	100%	98%

Key Votes of the 115th Congress

1. Obama-care revision	Y	5. Family planning regs	Y	9. Guantanamo prisoners	N
2. Tax Cuts	Y	6. Body cameras/immigration	N	10. Ground missiles, limit	N
3. Omnibus appropriations	N	7. Abortion ban	Y	11. Defense Dept. spending	Y
4. Dodd-Frank revision	Y	8. Concealed carry	Y	12. FISA rules	Y

Election Results

Election	Name (Party)	Vote (%)		Cand. Spent	Ind. Exp. Support	Ind. Exp. Oppose
2018 General	George Holding (R)............................	170,072	(51%)	$2,756,907	$45,633	$1,357,790
	Linda Coleman (D).......................	151,977	(46%)	$1,588,445	$562,127	$1,939,368
	Jeff Matemu (Lib).............................	9,655	(3%)	$22,750		
2018 Primary	George Holding (R)...............................	17,979	(76%)			
	Allen Chesser II (R)........................	5,612	(24%)			

Prior winning percentages: 2016 (57%), 2014 (57%), 2012 (57%)

Former federal prosecutor George Holding, elected in 2012, has been blessed with many good breaks in his political career. Redistricting that year all but guaranteed Republican success. Following another redistricting in 2016, Holding survived the kind of contest that many House members most fear: a matchup with a member from the same party. The biggest plus for Holding was that the new district contained far more of his former district than of Rep. Renee Ellmers' former district. He won in a rout. On the Ways and Means Committee, he was "thrilled" to have contributed to the crafting of the 2017 tax cuts. A year later, he survived a competitive reelection challenge.

Holding grew up in Raleigh in a wealthy family. He gave his first public speech at age 11 to dedicate a statue of his recently deceased father, the chairman of a prominent local bank. He entered Massachusetts' prestigious Groton School and graduated from Wake Forest University. During those years, Holding developed an interest in conservative ideas and worked as a summer intern for his state's conservative Republican Sen. Jesse Helms. After Holding graduated from Wake Forest law school, he clerked for a federal judge and worked at a law firm. He rejoined Helms as a legislative counsel, where he concentrated on business, tax and tobacco issues.

In 2006, President George W. Bush nominated him as a U.S. attorney. He prosecuted numerous local politicians, including former Gov. Mike Easley for campaign finance irregularities. His most prominent case was that of former Democratic Sen. John Edwards, and the nearly $1 million his supporters paid to Edwards' mistress, Rielle Hunter, during his 2008 presidential campaign. Holding resigned to run for Congress before the case was argued in court. In June 2012, a jury deadlocked on five of the six felony counts, prompting the Justice Department to drop the charges.

His campaign for the open House seat turned acrimonious. Holding's chief opponent in the primary was Wake County Commission Chairman Paul Coble, a nephew of Helms. Coble accused Holding of politicizing Edwards' indictment and said that he took "dirty money" from trial lawyers. Holding's fundraising advantage of more than 6-to-1, including $319,000 in self-financing, helped his victory, 44%-34%. In the general election, Democrat Charles Malone accused Holding of being "surrounded by wealth" and therefore out of touch. Malone raised only $18,000, compared with his opponent's $1.7 million. Holding won, 57%-43%.

Holding fit comfortably in the Republican establishment. His Almanac vote ratings have ranked him among the most conservative members of the House. He won a seat on Ways and Means and set tax reform as a top priority, "including closing loopholes and stopping fraud." In 2015, the House approved his IRS Bureaucracy Reduction and Judicial Review Act, which he said would streamline Internal Revenue Service reviews by "allowing groups to declare their tax-exempt status rather than wait for endless amounts of time to gain approval." He called the IRS "an agency in turmoil."

At home, the Republican-controlled legislature in late February 2016 approved the new redistricting plan for North Carolina, in response to a court order. Holding's string of good fortune continued. Ellmers, who had defeated a Democratic incumbent in 2010 and quickly became a GOP leadership ally, confronted a nightmarish set of circumstances following the redistricting: no obvious district in which to run, a brief interval for the campaign, her occasional splits with Republican dogma, and Holding's $1.4 million fundraising advantage, plus more than $1 million in support from GOP and conservative groups. In addition, she was the target of a notably public whisper campaign about an alleged affair with then-House Majority Leader Kevin McCarthy, which each of them denied.

Harding won an unexpectedly easy victory, with 53 percent to 24 percent for Ellmers and 23 percent for Greg Brannon, a physician and tea party favorite who had lost primaries to each of the state's GOP senators. In November, he defeated his little-known Democratic opponent, Marine Corps veteran John McNeil, 57%-43%.

With the election of President Donald Trump, tax reform became a top priority and the truncated deliberations began at Ways and Means. The big reduction in the estate tax was like a dream come true four decades later, Holding said, as the House prepared to approve the bill in November 2017. His father, chairman of First Citizens Bank, died when Holding was 10 years old. "A great deal of the wealth that he accumulated went to the federal government," Holding told the Raleigh News & Observer. "So, I feel like I'm a day late and a dollar short achieving that."

Asked about the Democratic attacks that the bill benefits the wealthy, Holding said, "Hey, it benefits everybody." (His family continued to own the controlling share of the Raleigh-based bank.) The legislation, he added, showed how Ways and Means "changes the entire world." Passage of that legislation would be "the key to American greatness." The House passed the bill, 227-205, with all Democrats opposed.

In 2018, Holding received his first robust Democratic challenge from Linda Coleman, an African-American former state legislator whose motto was "health care, education, jobs." Coleman, who had little to say about Trump, simply said that Holding was "conservative." As NBC News wrote about the contest, "Neither of the candidates is a charismatic viral sensation or a fiery ideologue." Polls showed that it was a close contest, with a private Harding poll reportedly showing him losing. He spent $2.8 million to Coleman's $1.6 million; the contest attracted close to $4 million in money from the national parties and outside groups.

Harding won 51%-46%, a margin of 18,000 votes. Coleman led in Wake by 2,400 votes, while Harding took the five suburban and exurban counties. He won, Harding told an Election Night party, because "the economy is doing great because [of] a lot of the policies we've been able to enact in Washington the last two years, and I'm really happy that that message got through."

NC-2: East-Central North Carolina   Cook Partisan Voting Index: R+7

Population		Race and Ethnicity		Income	
Total	806,396	White	66.5%	Median Income	$64,502
Land area (sq. miles)	2,698	Black	19.3%	District Income Rank	140
Pop/ sq mi	298.8	Latino	9.5%	Poverty Rate	11.4%
Born in State	53.4%	Asian	1.7%	With health insurance	90.3%
		Two or more races	2.2%	Cash public assistance	1.4%
Age Groups		Other	0.7%	Food stamp/SNAP	10.5%
Under 18	26.4%				
18-34	19.3%	**Education**		**Work**	
35-64	41.6%	H.S grad or less	34.4%	White Collar	12.7%
Over 64	12.7%	Some college	30.8%	Sales and Service	38.5%
		College Degree, 4 yr	23.1%	Blue Collar	18.8%
Military		Post grad	11.6%	Government	16.6%
Veteran/ Active Duty	10.5%				

2012 Pres. Vote	Romney	199,397	(55%)	Obama	159,397	(44%)		
2016 Pres. Vote	Trump	210,842	(53%)	Clinton	172,612	(43%)	Johnson	12,564	(3%)

Raleigh Metro, Rocky Mount: A generation ago, Raleigh was a sleepy state capital, moderately prosperous but not very big or showy, while the small cities to the east, such as Rocky Mount, had economies built around tobacco and textile factories, the railroad and later Interstate 95. Just a few miles from the center of town, farm fields started, dotted by country towns with barbecue restaurants and churches. Today, the booming metropolitan areas of North Carolina have spread far beyond the old city and county lines into the adjacent counties. Wake County, which includes Raleigh, grew 71 percent between 2000 and 2017, to a population of nearly 1.1 million; Raleigh is about 45 percent of the total and also is fast-growing. Once-rural roads are clogged in the morning with commuters headed for jobs in new office parks, and income levels have risen far above what they once were. Raleigh is 29 percent African American, compared with 21 percent for the county.

Much of this territory makes up the 2nd Congressional District of North Carolina. Nearly half its residents live in Wake County. Rolesville is a fast-growing boom town in northern Wake County, where farmlands have been converted into subdivisions and commercial development. Its population has increased from less than 1,000 in 2000 to nearly 8,000 in 2017, with median household income about 30 percent higher than in the county as a whole. The town has built lots of affordable housing for workers in Raleigh and Research Triangle. But, as the News & Observer wrote in February 2018, "elected leaders hope to eventually see a restaurant and shopping district." Raleigh has long had an active Lebanese community, which celebrates an annual cultural festival. Zebulon is a growing business area, including the pharmaceutical firm GlaxoSmithKline, which employs about 1,000 and produces respiratory drugs and inhalers. The 2nd draws in the affluent Republican suburbs and exurbs that surround Raleigh, such as Wake Forest and Holly Springs.

The 2nd extends to a collection of crossroads towns — including, from north to south on the interstate, Rocky Mount in Nash County, Smithfield in Johnston and Dunn in Harnett. Overall, the district's voters lean comfortably Republican, as was the case with each of the state's 10 redrawn GOP-held districts in the 2016 redistricting. Donald Trump won 52 percent.

NC-3: Vacant (V)

DC Office: 2333 RHOB 20515, 202-225-3415, Fax: 202-225-3286, jones.house.gov

State Offices: Greenville, 800-351-1697; Havelock, 252-565-6846; Jacksonville, 252-565-6846.

The Feb. 10, 2019, death of Republican Rep. Walter Jones triggered a special election for the vacancy, which Republicans were widely favored to retain. They contended with a July primary runoff and the special election scheduled for September before they could fill the opening. Fresh faces, with national party support, emerged among Republicans in the special election.

Jones, who was first elected in 1994, survived as one of his party's leading iconoclasts against campaigns by party regulars to take him out. A devout social conservative, he was the GOP's most fervently antiwar House member. Although party leaders often treated him as an outcast and he faced numerous primary challenges, Jones showed little regret. He grew up in eastern North Carolina. His father, Walter Jones Sr., was a Democratic representative who served for a quarter-century and chaired the Merchant Marine and Fisheries Committee.

The younger Jones, then a Democrat, was elected in 1982 to the state House, where he often broke with party leaders. In 1992, he ran in the new black-majority 1st District after his father retired. He led the primary with 38 percent; he lost the runoff to Democrat Eva Clayton, an African American who got 55 percent. In 1993, the resourceful Jones switched to the Republican Party to run in the 3rd District. This pitted him against four-term Rep. Martin Lancaster, a Democrat who had worked earnestly on local projects. Lancaster voted for President Bill Clinton's budget and tax bills and his crime legislation, while failing to persuade Clinton to drop the cigarette tax from health care legislation. Jones ran an ad showing Lancaster jogging with Clinton, with the voiceover message: "How'd Martin Lancaster get so out of touch? Well, look who he's running around with in Washington." Jones won 53%-47%.

Jones' voting record began consistently conservative and hawkish, but over the years he moderated on foreign policy. He underwent a remarkable reversal on the war in Iraq. Jones voted in 2002 to authorize the use of force in Iraq, as did all but six House Republicans. Not long afterward, he was profoundly affected by a local Marine's funeral, setting the stage for an unlikely conversion to passionate war critic. Jones began writing letters to the families of every soldier killed in Iraq and Afghanistan, calling them his "mea culpa to my Lord" for voting for the war. His independence from his party cost Jones top Republican posts on the Armed Services Committee. Democrats approached him about switching parties, but he declined, saying his opposition to abortion rights would make him ill at ease in the party.

His outspoken criticism of the Iraq war brought Jones serious primary challengers. In 2008, Onslow County Commissioner Joe McLaughlin, a former Army Ranger, called Jones "a poster boy for the Left." Jones seemed to benefit from Iraq fatigue among voters, even among military families; he won, 59%-41%. In the 2014 primary, he faced Taylor Griffin, a native of eastern North Carolina who worked more than a decade in Washington, both in government and as a lobbyist. The margin narrowed to 51%-45%. Two years later, Phil Law, a supervisor for Hewlett-Packard who earlier served four years in the Marine Corps, joined Griffin in challenging Jones. Both ran active campaigns and raised a total of nearly $500,000; Jones raised $673,000. Jones won an unexpectedly large 65 percent of the vote.

In what became his final campaign, the victory margin for Jones tightened again in the 2018 primary. He was challenged by Law a second time and by Scott Dacey, a member of the Craven County Commission and registered lobbyist who embraced the policies of President Donald Trump. Dacey nearly matched the $570,000 that Jones spent in the campaign. Law spent about $90,000. Jones won the primary with 43 percent to 29 percent for Law and 28 percent for Dacey. He took 15 of the 17 counties, with Dacey winning two small counties. With his extended illness, Jones was absent from the House throughout late 2018.

Following Jones's death, 17 Republicans competed for the nomination in the special election. With the North Carolina requirement that the winner receive at least 30 percent of the vote, the initial focus was on which 2 of the 17 contenders would lead the April 30 vote. Law ran again, but he raised scant campaign funds. The leading spenders in the Republican contest turned out to be the two candidates who were the front-runners on the first ballot. Each was a doctor with key national party support: State Rep. Greg Murphy, a urologist, was supported by Rep. Mark Meadows, also of North Carolina, who chaired the Freedom Caucus; Joan Perry, a pediatrician, was backed by the Winning for Women political action and Rep. Elise Stefanik of New York, who was encouraging women candidates. Murphy got 23 percent to 15 percent for Perry.

Allen Thomas, the former mayor of Greenville, got 50 percent of the vote to win the six-candidate Democratic primary. He faced an uphill challenge in the September 10 contest against the winner of the Republican run-off.

NC-3: Coastal North Carolina

Cook Partisan Voting Index: R+12

Population		Race and Ethnicity		Income	
Total	754,005	White	67.6%	Median Income	$48,484
Land area (sq. miles)	7,213	Black	20%	District Income Rank	334
Pop/ sq mi	104.5	Latino	7.7%	Poverty Rate	15.8%
Born in State	52.7%	Asian	1.5%	With health insurance	87.9%
		Two or more races	2.7%	Cash public assistance	2.3%
Age Groups		Other	0.5%	Food stamp/SNAP	14.6%
Under 18	22.1%				
18-34	26.1%	**Education**		**Work**	
35-64	35.9%	H.S grad or less	40.5%	White Collar	15.9%
Over 64	15.9%	Some college	37%	Sales and Service	43.4%
		College Degree, 4 yr	14.6%	Blue Collar	23.9%
Military		Post grad	7.9%	Government	21.4%
Veteran/ Active Duty	21.7%				

2012 Pres. Vote	Romney	185,743	(58%)	Obama	130,472	(41%)			
2016 Pres. Vote	Trump	198,972	(60%)	Clinton	120,964	(37%)	Johnson	8,490	(3%)

Jacksonville, Outer Banks: Nearly 500 years ago, Giovanni da Verrazano, a Florentine explorer under the flag of France, sailed past the Gulf Stream and landed on a sandspit island he thought was the outer edge of China. It was the Outer Banks of North Carolina. These are probably America's most unstable barrier islands, constantly changing shape and cut by new inlets as they are battered by ocean currents and storm winds. The islands were settled early by Europeans. Sir Walter Raleigh's Roanoke colony was founded here in 1587, near present-day Manteo, then vanished shortly thereafter when supply ships diverted themselves to loot Spanish galleons rather than deliver their badly needed cargo. Edward Teach, better known as Blackbeard, and other pirates lurked in Pamlico and Albemarle sounds behind the islets.

History is very much alive on the Outer Banks. An antique form of English is spoken by some on Ocracoke Island, reachable only by ferry and largely insulated from the commercialization of the upper islands. A pack of about 100 feral horses — believed to be the last remaining descendants of late-16th century Spanish mustangs — roams free in a 12,000-acre sanctuary in Corolla; fears of their extinction have led the Fish and Wildlife Service to approve the introduction of other horses. The 208-foot lighthouse on Cape Hatteras, America's tallest, looks out on some of the most treacherous currents in the Atlantic. The sands along Kitty Hawk, with their winds, brought the Wright brothers to the Outer Banks to undertake mankind's first heavier-than-air flight in December 1903. The Outer Banks are prime vacation and retirement country, with affluent beachfront communities on both the coastal and sound side. Kill Devil Hills has the most millionaires per capita in the state. Those visitors benefit from a new 2.8 mile bridge from the mainland that opened in February 2019, replacing an outdated bridge. In February 2017, the largest wind farm in the Southeast began operations on land near Elizabeth City, with 104 turbines. Rising sea levels on the Outer Banks have raised concerns by residents and activists worried about climate change, though few seem worried enough to leave. The islands mostly escaped the impact of Hurricane Florence, which caused punishing damage to the mainland in September 2018.

Inland, vestiges of the area's 18th-century past can be seen in New Bern with its reconstructed Tryon Palace, the governor's house when this was the capital, and in the tiny, well-preserved town of Edenton on Albemarle Sound, where 51 women in 1774 protested the taxing of tea and cloth. It is considered the first women's political protest on American shores. Further south, amid swamps outside of Jacksonville, is the Marine Corps' Camp Lejeune. With its 14 miles of beachfront and 80 live-fire ranges, it is home base for about 40,000 enlisted Marines and officers, and the Corps' largest base; including families, veterans and civilian employees, the wider community is about 170,000 persons. On the other side of the Croatan National Forest is Cherry Point, the world's largest Marine Corps air station.

The 3rd Congressional District of North Carolina covers the Outer Banks and the coastal plain of North Carolina from the Virginia border nearly to Wilmington. Redistricting in 2016 added Elizabeth City and Washington and removed the minority communities in Wilmington. The three largest counties are inland: Onslow, Craven and Pitt (which is shared with the 1st District). With the new district lines, Donald Trump won with 60 percent.

David Price (D)

Elected 1986, 16th term, b. Aug 17, 1940; Erwin, TN; Mars Hill College (NC), Att., 1959; The University of North Carolina System, B.A., 1961; Yale University (CT), B.D., 1964; Yale University (CT), Ph.D., 1969; Baptist; Married (Lisa Kanwit Price); 2 children; 2 grandchildren.

Elected Office: U.S. House, 1986-1994.

Professional Career: Legislative aide, U.S. Sen. Bartlett, 1963-1967; Professor, Yale University, 1969-1973, Duke University, 1973-1986, 1995-1996; Executive Director, NC Dem. Party, 1979-1980, Chairman, 1983-1984; Staff Director, DNC Comm. on President Nominations, 1981-1982.

DC Office: 2108 RHOB 20515, 202-225-1784, Fax: 202-225-2014, price.house.gov

State Offices: Chapel Hill, 919-967-7924; Raleigh, 919-859-5999.

Committees: *Appropriations*: Homeland Security; State, Foreign Operations & Related Programs; Transportation, HUD & Related Agencies (Chmn). *Budget*.

Group Ratings

	ADA	ACLU	AFL-CIO	LCV	ITI	COC	HAFA	ACU	CFG	FRC
2018	-	86%	94%	94%	-	58%	6%	4%	12%	0%
2017	100%	C	92%	100%	C	43%	C	4%	0%	0%

Almanac Ratings 2017-18

	Economy	Social	Foreign	Composite
Liberal	100%	100%	100%	100%
Conservative	0%	0%	0%	0%

Key Votes of the 115th Congress

1. Obama-care revision	N	5. Family planning regs	N	9. Guantanamo prisoners	Y
2. Tax Cuts	N	6. Body cameras/immigration	Y	10. Ground missiles, limit	Y
3. Omnibus appropriations	Y	7. Abortion ban	N	11. Defense Dept. spending	N
4. Dodd-Frank revision	N	8. Concealed carry	N	12. FISA rules	N

Election Results

Election	Name (Party)	Vote (%)		Cand. Spent	Ind. Exp. Support	Ind. Exp. Oppose
2018 General	David Price (D)	247,067	(72%)	$651,535		
	Steve Von Loor (R)	82,052	(24%)			
	Barbara Howe (Lib)	12,284	(4%)	$2,712		
2018 Primary	David Price (D)	52,203	(77%)			
	Michelle Laws (D)	11,120	(16%)			
	Richard Watkins (D)	4,391	(7%)			

Prior winning percentages: 2016 (68%), 2014 (75%), 2012 (75%), 2010 (57%), 2008 (63%), 2006 (65%), 2004 (64%), 2002 (61%), 2000 (62%), 1998 (57%), 1996 (54%%),1992 (65%), 1990 (58%), 1988 (58%), 1986 (56%)

Democrat David Price was first elected in 1986, lost the seat in 1994, and regained it in 1996. Since his return, he has distinguished himself as an influential Appropriations subcommittee "cardinal" and a thoughtful voice on education, security and urban issues. A longtime political science professor, Price has remained a working scholar who has shared his insights on Congress. He is among the dozen longest-serving House Democrats.

Price grew up in East Tennessee, the son of a school principal and an English teacher. He is an interesting blend of political scientist, practical politician and lay Baptist preacher. He attended the

University of North Carolina at Chapel Hill, worked as a young aide on Capitol Hill, earned a degree in divinity and a doctorate in political science at Yale University, and taught there for four years. In 1973, he became a political science professor at Duke. He was executive director of the North Carolina Democratic Party in the 1980 election season and chairman in 1983-84. With Democratic Gov. Jim Hunt, Price helped develop North Carolina's robust straight-ticket politics.

In 1986, he ran for the House and beat Republican freshman Rep. Bill Cobey. In 1994, Price lost the seat, 50.4%-49.6%, to Fred Heineman, a former New York City police officer and Raleigh police chief in the 1970s. Two years later, Price outspent Heineman in a rematch, winning 54%-44%.

Price has written four books about Congress, including The Congressional Experience, which focuses on his life as a lawmaker. The polarization of the two chambers has made him pessimistic about finding agreement to solve the nation's fiscal problems. "Our capacity to take them on in the bipartisan fashion that history teaches us is almost always necessary is far weaker" than it was in the 1990s, he said in 2010. Circumstances subsequently proved him correct, and they have worsened.

His Education Affordability Act, which he considers his proudest achievement, was folded into the 1997 Balanced Budget Act. It made interest on student loans tax-deductible and allowed penalty-free withdrawals from individual retirement accounts for education expenses. Price founded and now chairs the House Democracy Partnership, a bipartisan, 20-member commission that seeks to strengthen democracy by mentoring more than a dozen legislatures across the world.

From 2007 through 2010, Price chaired the Homeland Security Appropriations Subcommittee. He sought higher levels of spending for homeland security measures, like support for first responders, than were requested by the Bush administration. In 2007, the House passed Price's bill establishing a code of conduct for private security contractors in Iraq and Afghanistan. A target of the bill was North Carolina-based Blackwater, whose controversial activities in Iraq included the shooting of 17 people in a Baghdad square. After President Barack Obama took office, Price crafted spending bills that rejected the administration's proposal to hold criminal trials for terror suspects in New York City and restored budget cuts that the administration had made to the Coast Guard. In 2010, he called increased drug trafficking and violence on the U.S. border "an emergency" that merited as much attention as the wars in Afghanistan and Iraq.

In 2015, Price switched to ranking Democrat on the Transportation, HUD Appropriations Subcommittee. He joined a bipartisan group of senior appropriators who strongly opposed a proposal from the Transportation and Infrastructure Committee to create a separate air traffic organization outside the Federal Aviation Administration and removed from the annual appropriations process. The oversight and funding role of Congress, they wrote, was critical "in the operation of our nation's air traffic system." As subcommittee chairman in 2019, his plans included oversight of the Housing and Urban Development Department to enforce "adequate property standards" and to hold the Trump administration accountable. Another priority was to "rebuild our broken infrastructure system."

Price has been active on campaign finance law. He sponsored the "stand by your ad" requirement for candidates to appear in the full frame of television ads reading their disclaimers on the air, so they would more likely be held responsible for negative ads. His proposal was enacted in the 2002 campaign reform law. He has sought a similar requirement for internet ads and said the Supreme Court's Citizens United decision allowing unlimited spending by corporations, labor unions and wealthy individuals contributed to the flow of misleading ads. "The least we can do is inform viewers who has bought the ads they are seeing," he said. In 2019, the Democrats' House-passed "good government" legislation included Price's longstanding proposal to give a tax break for small campaign contributions. He criticized plans by Democratic National Committee Chairman Tom Perez to reduce the number and authority of elected officials serving as "super delegates" at the party convention. He suggested renaming them as "delegates" and reducing their independent influence.

Price has nurtured local projects for appropriations support, including $272 million for a new Environmental Protection Agency complex in Research Triangle Park, plus defense- and technology-related programs for universities in his district. He helped to get the Obama administration's support for $545 million to finance the Raleigh-to-Charlotte high-speed rail corridor. In 2016, he took the lead in seeking to relax restrictions on the Centers for Disease Control and Prevention to conduct research on gun violence.

Since his return to the House in 1996, Price has been reelected by wide margins. After Democratic Rep. Brad Miller decided to retire rather than face Price in a primary following the 2012 redistricting, he had a secure seat, at least until redistricting in 2022, when Price will be 82.

NC-4: Research Triangle   **Cook Partisan Voting Index: D+17**

Population		Race and Ethnicity		Income	
Total	825,295	White	56.4%	Median Income	$66,982
Land area (sq. miles)	733	Black	21.9%	District Income Rank	119
Pop/ sq mi	1126.5	Latino	10.3%	Poverty Rate	12.5%
Born in State	43.2%	Asian	8.4%	With health insurance	89.5%
		Two or more races	2.3%	Cash public assistance	1.3%
Age Groups		Other	0.6%	Food stamp/SNAP	7.4%
Under 18	22.3%				
18-34	28.6%	**Education**		**Work**	
35-64	38.7%	H.S grad or less	22.9%	White Collar	10.4%
Over 64	10.4%	Some college	23.9%	Sales and Service	36.9%
		College Degree, 4 yr	30.9%	Blue Collar	12.5%
Military		Post grad	22.2%	Government	16.1%
Veteran/ Active Duty	5.8%				

2012 Pres. Vote	Obama	248,572	(64%)	Romney	134,409	(35%)		
2016 Pres. Vote	Clinton	281,535	(67%)	Trump	116,368	(28%)	Johnson	14,632	(4%)

Raleigh, Chapel Hill: Back in the 1950s, few people would have predicted that the countryside around Raleigh and Durham would become one of America's high-tech boom areas. But Democratic Gov. Luther Hodges did, and he started the 6,900-acre Research Triangle Park as a research and development industrial park between the musty state capital of Raleigh and the Lucky Strike-manufacturing city of Durham. With the drawing power of three universities — North Carolina State in Raleigh, Duke in Durham, and the University of North Carolina in Chapel Hill — Research Triangle Park slowly began attracting top R&D organizations, which in turn spawned a dynamic entrepreneurial sector. Today, this is among the top tech centers in the nation, with big-name employers that include IBM, Cisco Systems, GlaxoSmithKline and RTI International. Fidelity and Credit Suisse have brought the financial sector to the RTP. Slightly more than half of the 275 employers are in biotech and life sciences or information technology.

A sleepy metro area that once trailed the nation in income is now a vibrant, affluent metropolis and the prime engine of North Carolina's growth. From 2010 to 2017, Wake and Mecklenburg (Charlotte) counties accounted for nearly half the state's growth. The Triangle has one of the highest concentrations of Ph.D.s in the nation. Local officials shifted their transit plans from light-rail to diesel, and added bus service in dedicated lanes. They envision four "bus rapid transit" lines from downtown Raleigh by 2027.

Still, the region prides itself on its homier touches. Barbecue is a serious business here. College basketball is the other major preoccupation, and UNC, N.C. State, and Duke (in the neighboring 1st District) have fielded more March Madness contenders than any similarly sized area. UNC attracted different attention in August 2018 when student protestors took down the "Silent Sam" statue, a tribute to the Confederacy.

The combination of upscale and down-home has proved to be a popular draw. From 1990 to 2014, the Raleigh-Durham-Cary "combined statistical area" (in Census Bureau jargon) more than doubled in population, from 855,000 to 2.1 million. Many of the new arrivals are from the North; locals joke that the fast-growing town of Cary is an acronym for "Containment Area for Retired Yankees." The new arrivals are changing the politics of the region as well. Just as Northern immigrants helped bring Republicanism to the South in the 1950s and 1960s, today they have made this the most heavily Democratic region in the state.

The 4th Congressional District of North Carolina is the core of the Research Triangle, with three-fifths of Raleigh-based Wake County, a small tuck in the southern part of Durham County and all of Orange County, which includes Chapel Hill. About four-fifths of the residents are in Wake, which grew 19 percent from 2010 to 2017. The 4th -- 22 percent black and 10 percent Hispanic -- is the most heavily Democratic district with a non-Hispanic white majority population in the South. Like the minority-majority 1st and 12th districts, the latest version of this district has continued to accentuate its Democratic vote, though the 2016 redistricting left it far less gerrymandered. Hillary Clinton increased the Democratic vote to 67 percent.

Virginia Foxx (R)

Elected 2004, 8th term, b. Jun 29, 1943; Bronx, NY; Lees McRae College (NC), 1961; Appalachian State Teachers College (NC), Att., 1963; University of North Carolina Chapel Hill (UNC), Bach. Deg., 1968; University of North Carolina Chapel Hill (UNC), M.A., 1972; University of North Carolina, Greensboro, Ed.D., 1985; Roman Catholic; Married (Thomas A. Foxx); 1 child; 2 grandchildren.

Elected Office: Watauga Board of Education, 1976-1988; NC Senate, 1994-2004.

Professional Career: Owner, Grandfather Mountain Nursery, 1976-2004; Professor, Assistant Dean of General College, Appalachian St. University, 1976-1985; President, May-land CC, 1987-1994.

DC Office: 2462 RHOB 20515, 202-225-2071, Fax: 202-225-2995, foxx.house.gov
State Offices: Boone, 828-265-0240; Clemmons, 336-778-0211.

Committees: *Education & Labor (RMM). Oversight & Reform:* National Security.

Group Ratings

	ADA	ACLU	AFL-CIO	LCV	ITI	COC	HAFA	ACU	CFG	FRC
2018	-	4%	-	3%	-	83%	74%	92%	83%	100%
2017	0%	C	8%	0%	C	93%	C	93%	82%	100%

Almanac Ratings 2017-18

	Economy	Social	Foreign	Composite
Liberal	2%	3%	0%	2%
Conservative	98%	97%	100%	98%

Key Votes of the 115th Congress

1. Obama-care revision	Y	5. Family planning regs	Y	9. Guantanamo prisoners	N
2. Tax Cuts	Y	6. Body cameras/immigration	N	10. Ground missiles, limit	N
3. Omnibus appropriations	Y	7. Abortion ban	Y	11. Defense Dept. spending	Y
4. Dodd-Frank revision	Y	8. Concealed carry	Y	12. FISA rules	Y

Election Results

Election	Name (Party)	Vote (%)		Cand. Spent	Ind. Exp. Support	Ind. Exp. Oppose
2018 General	Virginia Foxx (R)	159,917	(57%)	$2,136,509	$5,000	
	Denise Adams (D)	120,468	(43%)	$336,825	$26,336	$2,500
2018 Primary	Virginia Foxx (R)	32,654	(81%)			
	Dillon Gentry (R)	5,703	(14%)			
	Cortland Meader (R)	2,063	(5%)			

Prior winning percentages: 2016 (58%), 2014 (61%), 2012 (58%), 2010 (66%), 2008 (58%), 2006 (57%), 2004 (59%)

Republican Virginia Foxx, first elected in 2004, is a vocal conservative who has been savvy in gaining influence. She held a Republican leadership position for four years, and then chaired the House Education and the Workforce Committee for two years. A former teacher and university administrator, she pledged to cut back on federal rules and return education policy to a more traditional state-federal relationship. Her sweeping proposal to overhaul federal higher-education programs stalled in 2018, apparently due to insufficient support to win House passage. Although liberal critics dismiss her as a loose cannon, she has raised herself by the bootstraps and moved into a position to influence major social policy changes.

Foxx grew up in the hardscrabble hollows of western North Carolina; she lived in a home that didn't have running water or electricity until she was 14. She got her bachelor's in English from the University of North Carolina in Chapel Hill and her doctorate in education from UNC-Greensboro, and had a diverse background before she was elected to Congress. She owned with her husband a nursery and landscape company, and she taught sociology and was assistant dean of the General College at Appalachian State University. Later, she was president of Mayland Community College.

She served 12 years on the Board of Education of Watauga County. In 1994, Foxx was elected to the state Senate, where she sponsored a constitutional amendment to ban same-sex marriage and a bill to deny Social Security benefits to undocumented immigrants. She actively supported gun rights and home schooling, and she opposed abortion rights.

In 2004, Foxx was one of five candidates in a hotly contested Republican primary for an open seat. Winston-Salem Councilman Vernon Robinson, a retired Air Force officer who campaigned as "the black Jesse Helms," finished first with 24 percent of the vote. Foxx was second, with 22 percent, just 511 votes ahead of Ed Broyhill, the son of former Republican Sen. James Broyhill. In a hard-fought, four-week runoff campaign, Robinson aired several controversial ads highlighting his tough position on illegal immigrants. Foxx warned voters that Robinson's aggressive style would make him a weak general election candidate who would lose the district for the GOP. She won 55%-45%. In the general election, Foxx won relatively easily, 59%-41%.

Foxx has been close to House GOP leaders and has had a nearly perfect conservative record in the Almanac vote ratings. She was elected Republican Conference secretary in 2012 when she defeated Rep. Jeff Denham of California to become one of three women to take leadership roles that year.

Foxx has not been afraid to speak her mind in her home-spun style. She was one of only 11 House members who voted against a $52 billion relief bill following Hurricane Katrina in 2005 because, she said, there was too little accountability in how the money would be spent. During the health care debate in 2009, she remarked that the public had more to fear from the legislation than from terrorists. During debate on a hate crimes bill named for Matthew Shepard, a Wyoming man tortured and murdered allegedly because of his sexual orientation, she said naming the bill for Shepard was "a hoax" because, she argued, he wasn't gay. She later apologized. Republican leaders saw her as a useful attack dog.

On the Education Committee, Foxx has said the Education Department imposes burdensome regulations on colleges. She is an advocate of for-profit colleges and community colleges. On talk radio in 2012, she expressed her disdain for people taking out student loans. "I have very little tolerance for people who tell me that they graduate with $200,000 of debt or even $80,000 of debt, because there's no reason for that." President Barack Obama later repeated her remarks at a campaign stop at the University of North Carolina. "Can you imagine saying something like that?" he asked. Still, Foxx found common ground with Obama in 2013 during renewal of the student-loan program. They tied the rate to the 10-year Treasury bond in what Foxx termed a "market-based approach."

When the chairmanship of the committee opened in 2016, Foxx was eager to take the post. She had curried favor with GOP leaders and Republicans were about to lose their only woman chair. Foxx won the position without opposition. At the committee, her targets have included overtime rules at the Department of Labor, plus restrictions imposed by the National Labor Relations Board. In March 2017, Foxx was one of three House chairs who brought the leadership-drafted American Health Care Act to the House floor, where it was pulled because Republicans were divided on how to replace Obamacare. After additional tinkering, the bill passed in early May but subsequently died in the Senate. Also in March 2017, her committee approved a bill to permit employers to seek genetic information as part of employee wellness programs. Critics said that employees who declined to participate would be adversely treated for health insurance. "We do not ask for people's genetic information," Foxx said. The House took no action on the bill.

Her chief initiative was her PROSPER (Promoting Real Opportunity, Success and Prosperity through Education Reform) Act to add performance standards for most universities and roll back many regulations on academia, especially on the for-profit and online education sectors. "A hard truth that students, families and institutions must face is that the promise of a post-secondary education is broken," Foxx said, in releasing the proposal in December 2017. The proposal was opposed by committee Democrats and received scant support from most of the traditional education groups in Washington, who had grown comfortable with status quo. Education Secretary Betsy DeVos supported the measure. By June 2018, the Inside Higher Education publication reported "vocal opposition" to the legislation and doubts among many Republicans; Sen. Lamar Alexander of Tennessee, who chaired the counterpart Senate committee, had decided to defer the issue for the year.

In her safely Republican district, Foxx has been reelected by modest margins against low-profile opponents. In 2012, The Winston-Salem Journal, the largest newspaper in her district, endorsed her Democratic challenger, Elisabeth Motsinger. The newspaper said Foxx "has accomplished little" for the district and "represents the calcification of the political process and is therefore an impediment to reasoned political compromise." Regardless, she has remained popular with her political base. In 2016, she was challenged in the Republican primary by Pattie Curran, who said that Foxx had moderated her views. "She's establishment and I'm not," Curran told a local reporter. Foxx won 68 percent of the vote and easily took every county.

In 2018, Foxx faced Democratic challenger Denise Adams, a member of the Winston Salem City Council who claimed "my fingerprints all over" the reinvention of that city. When Adams questioned whether she had voted against hurricane-relief funding, Foxx said she had voted for a broader funding bill. Foxx outspent Adams, $2.1 million to $$337,000 and won 57%-43%.. Perhaps significantly for the longer term, Adams got 56 percent in each of the two largest counties, Forsyth and Watauga, which cast more than half the total vote.

NC-5: Northwest North Carolina   Cook Partisan Voting Index: R+10

Population		Race and Ethnicity		Income	
Total	749,093	White	72.9%	Median Income	$44,052
Land area (sq. miles)	3,969	Black	14.4%	District Income Rank	387
Pop/ sq mi	188.7	Latino	9.5%	Poverty Rate	18.7%
Born in State	64.9%	Asian	1.4%	With health insurance	88.1%
		Two or more races	1.4%	Cash public assistance	1.6%
Age Groups		Other	0.6%	Food stamp/SNAP	13.2%
Under 18	21.5%				
18-34	22%	Education		Work	
35-64	39.5%	H.S grad or less	43.8%	White Collar	17%
Over 64	17%	Some college	30%	Sales and Service	40.6%
		College Degree, 4 yr	16.7%	Blue Collar	24.6%
Military		Post grad	9.5%	Government	12.7%
Veteran/ Active Duty	8%				

2012 Pres. Vote	Romney	195,291	(56%)	Obama	146,243	(42%)		
2016 Pres. Vote	Trump	205,332	(57%)	Clinton	142,369	(39%)	Johnson	10,302	(3%)

Winston-Salem: From the Atlantic Ocean, the terrain of North Carolina rises slowly through the Piedmont, a transitional land of modest hills that lies between the coastal plain and the Blue Ridge Mountains. The Blue Ridge, named for the mysterious blue haze that blankets it, provides the headwaters of the New River — ironically named given that it is the oldest river in North America — which cuts majestic crevasses as it flows north to West Virginia. The lower Piedmont lands of North Carolina were first settled by independent-minded Scots-Irish farmers and by followers of British and German sects like the Moravians. This was hardscrabble farm country before the Civil War, with few slaves. By the late 19th century, it was becoming industrialized, with textile mills alongside streams, furniture factories not far from hardwood forests, and R.J. Reynolds' cigarette factories in the growing city of Winston-Salem.

Today, the Winston-Salem area's pharmaceutical companies, banking institutions and high-skill Piedmont factories have largely supplanted the tobacco and textile industries. At a former R.J. Reynolds Tobacco plant, the booming Wake Forest Innovation Quarter focuses on medical education and biotech research. A smaller and more urban version of the Research Triangle less than 100 miles to the east, it is a broad partnership among the city, state, university and the private developer, with 3,700 workers in more than 170 companies, five colleges with 1,800 degree-seeking students and 8,000 workforce trainees. Its mission is to drive economic growth with "diverse people, a unique mixed-use environment and a welcoming culture." The biennial National Black Theater Festival, which drew more than 60,000 attendees in 2017, has become a prominent weeklong event.

Aside from Winston-Salem, the region has remained rural. Places of interest include chicken-raising Wilkes County, the remnants of the socks-manufacturing plant of Hanes-Brand in Mount Airy, and Appalachian State University in Boone (named for Daniel), which has become a center for resurgent pride in the culture of Appalachia, a region often the target of either pity or condescension. In 2018, NBC News profiled economically struggling Wilkes County, where half the residents are evangelical Christians, as an example of the changing Republican Party. Residents referred to President Donald Trump, who got 76 percent of the vote in 2016, as "the last hope for an America in decline."

All these places are in the 5th Congressional District. It includes all of Forsyth County and Winston-Salem. Nearly half of the district's residents reside in Forsyth, which is 27 percent black.

Hillary Clinton in 2016 won the county, 54%-43%. To the west, the remainder of the district takes in nine counties and a small part of Catawba, with small cities and towns in the heavily Republican Piedmont and mountain areas. The only other area of Democratic strength is in Watauga County, with the university. These rural areas have sparse minority population. The district as a whole is 14 percent black. Donald Trump won 57 percent.

Mark Walker (R)

Elected 2014, 3rd term, b. May 20, 1969; Dothan, AL; Trinity Baptist College (FL), Att., 1988; Houston Community College System, Att., 1990; Piedmont International University (NC), B.A., 1999; Baptist; Married (Kelly Walker); 3 children.

Professional Career: Sales & business Manager, automotive company, 1991-1996; Church minister & official, 1998-2014.

DC Office: 1725 LHOB 20515, 202-225-3065, Fax: 202-225-8611, walker.house.gov

State Offices: Asheboro, 336-626-3060; Graham, 336-229-0159; Greensboro, 336-333-5005.

Committees: House Republican Conference Vice Chairman. *Education & Labor*: Higher Education & Workforce Investment; Workforce Protections. *Homeland Security*: Cybersecurity, Infrastructure Protection & Innovation; Intelligence & Counterterrorism (RMM). *House Administration*.

Group Ratings

	ADA	ACLU	AFL-CIO	LCV	ITI	COC	HAFA	ACU	CFG	FRC
2018	-	4%	-	0%	-	75%	96%	96%	86%	100%
2017	0%	C	5%	0%	C	92%	C	96%	90%	100%

Almanac Ratings 2017-18

	Economy	Social	Foreign	Composite
Liberal	5%	9%	0%	5%
Conservative	95%	91%	100%	95%

Key Votes of the 115th Congress

1. Obama-care revision	Y	5. Family planning regs	Y	9. Guantanamo prisoners	N
2. Tax Cuts	Y	6. Body cameras/immigration	N	10. Ground missiles, limit	N
3. Omnibus appropriations	N	7. Abortion ban	Y	11. Defense Dept. spending	Y
4. Dodd-Frank revision	Y	8. Concealed carry	Y	12. FISA rules	Y

Election Results

Election	Name (Party)	Vote (%)		Cand. Spent	Ind. Exp. Support	Ind. Exp. Oppose
2018 General	Mark Walker (R)	160,709	(57%)	$714,912		
	Ryan Watts (D)	123,651	(43%)	$296,123		
2018 Primary	Mark Walker (R)		(100%)			

Prior winning percentages: 2016 (59%), 2014 (59%)

Republican Mark Walker, elected to an open seat in 2014, was an ordained minister who framed his campaign in religious terms and ran as a Washington outsider. He showed his insider skills as chairman of the Republican Study Committee and later as a leader of the House Republican Conference. He has clashed occasionally with conservative leader Rep. Mark Meadows, another North Carolina Republican.

Walker was born in Dothan Alabama, and grew up in Pensacola Florida, where his father was a minister. He got his bachelor's degree in religious studies at Piedmont Baptist College. Most of his professional career was spent serving churches in the Greensboro region. He devoted time to helping local and state Republicans in campaigns and engaging in civic affairs.

The firmly GOP open seat attracted a scrum of nine Republican candidates. The initial frontrunner was Phil Berger Jr., the district attorney for Rockingham County. Boosted by name recognition and endorsements from the GOP establishment, Berger topped the primary field at 34 percent of the vote, with Walker at 25 percent. In the runoff, Walker built up his campaign base in Guilford County while underscoring his outsider credentials. He rejected signing on to activist Grover Norquist's anti-tax pledge because he said he did not want to be beholden to "a guy in Washington." With turnout low and much of the vote from the defeated candidates in the primary turning toward the insurgent, Walker won 60%-40%. He took 65 percent in Guilford County, which cast a bit more than half the vote in the runoff.

The general election was a breeze for Walker in the Republican stronghold. Democratic challenger Laura Fjeld spent nearly $900,000, which was slightly more than the total Walker spent in his three contests. Walker won, 59%-41%.

Walker was the first freshman Republican to pass a bill in 2015, when the House passed his Human Traffic Detection Act. It was designed to improve the training of workers at the Homeland Security Department to intercept human traffickers and their victims.

Walker became an active member of the Republican Study Committee (RSC), the mainstream group of House conservatives that has worked more closely with GOP leaders than has the Freedom Caucus. Following the 2016 election, he was successful in an insurgent campaign to chair the group, even though board members initially sided with more experienced Rep. Andy Harris of Maryland. Walker described his ambitious plans: "Looking at the election results, it is clear the American people want to reclaim constitutional principles and reinvigorate our economy. It is unacceptable for us not to deliver on the faith the voters have invested in us."

He emphasized the need for Republicans to repeal — and replace — the Affordable Care Act.

Walker got on board after President Donald Trump and House GOP leaders agreed to his suggested changes — some of them on behalf of the RSC — including work requirements for able-bodied beneficiaries of Medicaid and abortion restrictions. Walker described the RSC role as "effective conservatism ... standing up for conservative values but doing so in the right tone, the right spirit." When Senate Republicans countered with a scaled-back alternative to the House-passed reform of the health care law, which was dubbed the "skinny repeal," Walker dismissed it as "ugly to the bone." Later in 2017, as congressional Republicans had failed to deliver on many of their promises, Walker warned that the scant productivity could be "catastrophic" politically.

Walker occasionally was depicted as more cooperative than Meadows, the head of the Freedom Caucus. Many viewed "the two Marks," with their shared home state, as rivals for influence.

"Mark Walker is the right-wing and Mark Meadows is the righter-wing" Claremont McKenna College government professor John Pitney — who has written extensively about House Republicans — told USA Today. Walker objected when senior House Republicans failed to support the party program. After Appropriations Committee Chairman Rodney Frelinghuysen of New Jersey in November 2017 voted against the Republican tax-cut legislation, Walker told House Speaker Paul Ryan than Frelinghuysen should be stripped of his chairmanship. Ryan did not take action, though Frelinghuysen a few weeks later announced his retirement. Following the 2018 election, Walker was elected without opposition as vice chairman of the GOP Conference.

On other issues, Walker has been an outspoken proponent of aid for historically black colleges and universities, which are prominent in North Carolina. In February 2017, he sponsored a conference in Washington on steps to increase federal support. Later, he filed a bill to require more planning by federal agencies with the HBCUs. In 2019, Walker became the ranking Republican on the Homeland Security Subcommittee on Intelligence and Counterterrorism. National security threats increased the need for "partnerships and coalitions that deliver results," he said.

In his redrawn district, Walker has not faced a serious primary challenge. He has been reelected with 59 percent and then 57 percent of the vote. In each contest, Walker trailed in Guilford and Chatham counties. In November 2018, the Greensboro News & Record endorsed his reelection. "Walker is a mixed bag on policies. But he is reasonable," the editorial contended. "And by and large, he hasn't engaged in the scorched-earth warfare that characterizes much of Congress today." When Republican Sen. Thom Tillis voiced concerns about Trump's border policies, Walker opened the door to challenging Tillis in the 2020 GOP primary. In June 2019, Walker said that he would run for reelection to the House.

NC-6: North-Central North Carolina   **Cook Partisan Voting Index: R+9**

Population		Race and Ethnicity		Income	
Total	757,229	White	66.1%	Median Income	$47,256
Land area (sq. miles)	3,911	Black	20%	District Income Rank	348
Pop/ sq mi	193.6	Latino	9.9%	Poverty Rate	16.5%
Born in State	65.1%	Asian	1.6%	With health insurance	87.9%
		Two or more races	1.8%	Cash public assistance	2.2%
Age Groups		Other	0.6%	Food stamp/SNAP	14.9%
Under 18	22.9%				
18-34	19.8%	**Education**		**Work**	
35-64	40.7%	H.S grad or less	45.1%	White Collar	16.6%
Over 64	16.6%	Some college	31.3%	Sales and Service	40%
		College Degree, 4 yr	15.4%	Blue Collar	27.7%
Military		Post grad	8.3%	Government	13.9%
Veteran/ Active Duty	8.2%				

2012 Pres. Vote	Romney	193,609	(56%)	Obama	149,414	(43%)			
2016 Pres. Vote	Trump	201,385	(56%)	Clinton	148,693	(41%)	Johnson	8,741	(2%)

Greensboro, The Piedmont: The rolling hills of the Piedmont, which are really the foothills of the long ridges of the Appalachian Mountains, are a geographic feature that helped define North Carolina politically. The Piedmont was settled not by the aristocratic planters who typified the Southern lowlands, but by the more hardscrabble Scots-Irish who colonized the Appalachian regions. These settlers clustered in small towns, usually around a mill or a factory. Even today, there isn't a large population center between High Point and the ancient sand dunes in the Sandhills region toward Fayetteville. Instead, the landscape is a collection of small towns, places like Asheboro and Siler City, burial place of Francis Bavier, best known as Aunt Bee on The Andy Griffith Show. Some of these areas have faced hard times. Medical device manufacturer Teleflex had more than 600 employees in Asheboro, but it shut down in 2017. In Rockingham County, the MillerCoors brewery — a 1,365-acre site -- and the affiliated Ball Cannery closed and were purchased by a demolition company in 2018. The closure followed a lengthy dispute between Miller and Pabst Brewing, which had an agreement to handle most of the beer production. Chatham County has ambitious plans for a planned community near Pittsboro. Chatham Park, which had been home to 4,000, was projected to grow to 60,000. Following completion in 2018 of a brewery, hotel and senior housing, new development was planned for a hotel and shops; the site had been a trailer park.

In Burlington-based Almanace County, a voting-rights controversy gained national attention in 2018 when the local prosecutor filed felony charges against 12 individuals who had voted in violation of a state law that prohibits voting by convicted felons — including while they remain on probation or post-release supervision. Many of the "Almanace 12," nine of whom were African-Americans, said they were not aware of the restrictions and their names had not previously been removed from the voting rolls. The local district attorney said that he was committed to strict prosecution of the law. At least nine of the group pleaded guilty to subsequent misdemeanor charges, without additional prison time, and the judge waived court costs, the Burlington Times-News reported in August 2018.

The 6th Congressional District of North Carolina takes in these Piedmont towns plus the eastern parts of greater Greensboro, which collectively contain more than half of its residents. Much of Greensboro's downtown has shifted to the 13th District. Greensboro-based Guilford County is the chief part of the 6th that is politically competitive. Almanace is the second-largest county. This was once a swing area of the state, but now the Piedmont, where about one-third of the district's population lives, is solidly Republican, especially Asheboro-based Randolph County. In 2016, Donald Trump got 56 percent.

David Rouzer (R)

Elected 2014, 3rd term, b. Feb 16, 1972; Landstuhl, Germany; Fund for American Studies; North Carolina State University, B.A., 1994; North Carolina State University, B.S., 1994; Southern Baptist; Single.

Elected Office: NC Senate 2009-2012.

Professional Career: PAC coordinator, 1996; Congressional aide, 1996-2000, 2001-2005; University official, 2000-2001; Administrator, U.S. Department of Agriculture, 2005-2006; Owner, consulting company, 2006-present; Owner, cleaning products business, 2009-present.

DC Office: 2439 RHOB 20515, 202-225-2731, Fax: 202-225-5773, rouzer.house.gov

State Offices: Bolivia, 910-253-6111; Four Oaks, 919-938-3040; Wilmington, 910-395-0202.

Committees: *Agriculture*: Commodity Exchanges, Energy & Credit; Livestock & Foreign Agriculture (RMM). *Transportation & Infrastructure*: Aviation; Highways & Transit; Water Resources & Environment.

Group Ratings

	ADA	ACLU	AFL-CIO	LCV	ITI	COC	HAFA	ACU	CFG	FRC
2018	-	7%	-	3%	-	75%	82%	76%	72%	100%
2017	0%	C	5%	3%	C	93%	C	93%	88%	100%

Almanac Ratings 2017-18

	Economy	Social	Foreign	Composite
Liberal	2%	7%	0%	3%
Conservative	98%	94%	100%	97%

Key Votes of the 115th Congress

1. Obama-care revision	Y	5. Family planning regs	Y	9. Guantanamo prisoners	N
2. Tax Cuts	Y	6. Body cameras/immigration	N	10. Ground missiles, limit	N
3. Omnibus appropriations	N	7. Abortion ban	Y	11. Defense Dept. spending	Y
4. Dodd-Frank revision	Y	8. Concealed carry	Y	12. FISA rules	Y

Election Results

Election	Name (Party)	Vote (%)		Cand. Spent	Ind. Exp. Support	Ind. Exp. Oppose
2018 General	David Rouzer (R)	156,809	(56%)	$1,204,104		
	Kyle Horton (D)	120,838	(43%)	$858,043		
2018 Primary	David Rouzer (R)		(100%)			

Prior winning percentages: 2016 (61%), 2014 (59%)

Republican David Rouzer was elected in 2014 as the first Republican to represent southeastern North Carolina since the late 19th century. He settled in at the Agriculture Committee and was influential in the enactment of the farm bill in 2018. Rouzer has styled himself as an expert in public relations and legislative strategy, though he kept a low profile in the district.

Rouzer was born in Landstuhl Germany and was raised in Durham North Carolina. He attended North Carolina State University's College of Agriculture, where he received his bachelor's degree in three majors: agricultural business management, agricultural economics and chemistry. He spent much of his career in Washington as an aide to two home-state Republican senators, Jesse Helms and Elizabeth Dole; as a Bush administration appointee in the Agriculture Department; and as a lobbyist for tobacco companies.

During four years in the state Senate, Rouzer co-chaired the Agriculture and Environment Committee. He became known for his vocal support of a North Carolina law banning the state's use of scientific predictions of how much the sea level will rise in developing coastal policy. The law, passed in 2012, drew criticism from environmental groups, which said it amounted to denial of scientific evidence of climate change.

In 2012, Rouzer challenged centrist Democratic Rep. Mike McIntyre, an independent and once-untouchable incumbent. Rouzer had more than $4 million in support from party groups; McIntyre had $1.9 million in party assistance and spent $2.3 million of his campaign funds. McIntyre squeaked out a 50.1%-49.9% win, a lead of 654 votes. When McIntyre announced his retirement after nine terms, the seat became an easy pickup for Republicans in 2014.

The real contest was in the primary, where Rouzer's chief opponent was attorney Woody White. Not surprisingly given the stakes, the campaign got nasty: White accused Rouzer of being a Beltway lobbyist, and Rouzer derided White's work as a trial lawyer. With more money, more establishment support and more name recognition, Rouzer won, 53%-40%. In the general, Rouzer campaigned as an unabashed conservative. Democratic nominee Jonathan Barfield, a commissioner in New Hanover County and a local real estate agent, said he did not want to see U.S. boots on the ground in Syria. National Democrats and their allies had no presence in their longtime bastion. Rouzer spent nearly $1.5 million for the entire campaign, compared with $60,000 for Barfield, and won 59%-37%.

Rouzer got a rare chairmanship for a freshman at the Agriculture Subcommittee on Livestock and Foreign Agriculture, which was well-suited to his background. He talked up export promotion and "the overarching benefits that market development funding brings the U.S. agricultural industry as a whole." He noted growing concerns about devastating animal diseases, especially for livestock, and "the linkages between agriculture and national security."

As a member of the House-Senate conference committee that crafted the final version of the 2018 farm bill, Rouzer took credit for two related provisions: $300 million in mandatory funding for research and coordination for animal disease preparedness, and $150 million for deployment of a U.S. vaccine bank for Foot and Mouth Disease.

On other issues, Rouzer talked up familiar proposals from the conservative arsenal: shutting down the Education Department and requiring drug tests for welfare recipients. In 2018, he was a rare House Member from a coastal district who supported off-shore drilling in the Atlantic Ocean.

Rouzer breezed to a routine reelection in 2016 against Wesley Canteen, a CPA and attorney in Wilmington who was uncontested for the Democratic nomination. Casteen had run in the 7th as an independent in 2014 and got 4 percent of the vote. This time, he rallied the Democratic base vote, but little more. Rouzer outraised him nearly 100-to-1 and won, 61%-39%.

His 2018 contest was a more competitive challenge from Kyle Horton, an internal-medicine physician who was a native of the district but a political newcomer. Horton, who opposed off-shore seismic testing and drilling for oil and gas, took issue with Rouzer on the topic and said their district was "definitely at the epicenter of so many climate challenges." Rouzer, who refused to debate with her, outspent Horton, $1.4 million to about $900,000. He won more narrowly, 56%-43%; Horton took Wilmington-based New Hanover by nearly 5,000 votes.

NC-7: Southeast North Carolina   Cook Partisan Voting Index: R+9

Population		Race and Ethnicity		Income	
Total	777,138	White	67.7%	Median Income	$45,716
Land area (sq. miles)	5,940	Black	19.2%	District Income Rank	368
Pop/ sq mi	130.8	Latino	9.4%	Poverty Rate	19.3%
Born in State	60.3%	Asian	0.8%	With health insurance	86.3%
		Two or more races	2%	Cash public assistance	1.7%
Age Groups		Other	0.8%	Food stamp/SNAP	15.8%
Under 18	21.4%				
18-34	21.3%	**Education**		**Work**	
35-64	39.3%	H.S grad or less	42.8%	White Collar	18%
Over 64	18%	Some college	32.4%	Sales and Service	42.3%
		College Degree, 4 yr	16.7%	Blue Collar	25.7%
Military		Post grad	8.1%	Government	14.7%
Veteran/ Active Duty	10.6%				

2012 Pres. Vote	Romney	194,178	(56%)	Obama	148,026	(43%)			
2016 Pres. Vote	Trump	206,192	(57%)	Clinton	142,782	(40%)	Johnson	8,950	(3%)

Wilmington, Goldsboro: At the end of the 19th century, North Carolina's lengthy attachment to the Democratic Party and white supremacy seemed to be weakening. A fusion ticket of Populists and Republicans had taken over the state legislature in 1894, and the state elected a rotund, racially egalitarian Republican named Daniel Russell as governor two years later. At the epicenter of this not-so-quiet revolution was Wilmington, a bustling majority-black city then. It was truly revolutionary, but the changes fell short. The run-up to the 1898 elections was marked by increasing violence and assertion of racial supremacy by many whites. In the ensuing vote, Democrats recaptured the statehouse, though a biracial governing coalition was elected in Wilmington. That, too, was short-lived. A white mob instigated a violent protest, and hundreds of African Americans fled to the nearby woods and swamps. The biracial government was forced to resign at gunpoint in the only violent coup d'état in American history. Wilmington became a majority-white city, which it remains to this day.

The coastal counties of southern North Carolina recently have grown smartly. The military has kept things afloat, as have tourism and growing retirement communities. From 1990 to 2017, the population of Wilmington-based New Hanover County increased by about 89 percent, and Brunswick County to the south more than doubled. This metropolitan area was the second fastest-growing in the nation from 2015 to 2016. The region has some of the busiest movie and television production facilities outside Los Angeles, with more than a dozen credits. South of Wilmington, the Army runs the 16,000-acre Military Ocean Terminal at Sunny Point, the Army's main deep-water port on the East Coast. It is the largest military ammunition port in the world, and often is referred to as "the FedEx of the sea" because it is almost always open.

Inland, hogs outnumber humans by more than 30-1 in Duplin County. Smithfield Foods in Tar Heel runs the largest pork production plant in the world. The smell of hog manure, some of it stored in open-air pits, is a big problem. Farther north in Wayne County is Goldsboro, a former railroad crossing in the exurbs of Raleigh that has been losing jobs and population. Goldsboro had a 22 percent drop in median income between 2000 and 2017, among the worst in the nation.

The 7th Congressional District of North Carolina covers much of this territory. It is ancestrally Democratic, and it was the final white-majority district in the state that hadn't elected a Republican since Reconstruction. That anomaly was resolved in 2014, after redistricting in 2012 made the 7th the second-most Republican district in the state. The 2016 redistricting restored the minority communities of the Wilmington area to the new 7th and added Goldsboro. New Hanover and Brunswick include half the voters in the 7th. The area has remained comfortably Republican. Donald Trump won it in 2016, 57%-40%.

Richard Hudson (R)

Elected 2012, 4th term, b. Nov 04, 1971; Franklin, VA; University of North Carolina, Charlotte, B.A., 1996; Methodist; Married (Ms. Renee Hudson); 1 child.

Professional Career: Deputy chief of Staff, Rep. Robin Hayes, 2000- 05; Chief of Staff, Rep. Virginia Foxx, 2005-2006; Chief of Staff, Rep. John Carter, 2006-2008; Chief of Staff, Rep. Mike Conaway, 2008-2011; President, Cabarrus Marketing Group, 2011-present.

DC Office: 2112 RHOB 20515, 202-225-3715, Fax: 202-225-4036, hudson.house.gov

State Offices: Concord, 704-786-1612; Fayetteville, 910-997-2070; Pinehurst, 910-246-5374.

Committees: *Energy & Commerce*: Consumer Protection & Commerce; Energy; Health.

Group Ratings

	ADA	ACLU	AFL-CIO	LCV	ITI	COC	HAFA	ACU	CFG	FRC
2018	-	4%	-	0%	-	83%	89%	83%	72%	100%
2017	0%	C	3%	0%	C	92%	C	96%	96%	100%

Almanac Ratings 2017-18

	Economy	Social	Foreign	Composite
Liberal	5%	3%	2%	4%
Conservative	95%	97%	98%	96%

Key Votes of the 115th Congress

1. Obama-care revision	Y	5. Family planning regs	Y	9. Guantanamo prisoners	N
2. Tax Cuts	Y	6. Body cameras/immigration	N	10. Ground missiles, limit	N
3. Omnibus appropriations	Y	7. Abortion ban	Y	11. Defense Dept. spending	Y
4. Dodd-Frank revision	Y	8. Concealed carry	Y	12. FISA rules	Y

Election Results

Election	Name (Party)	Vote (%)	Cand. Spent	Ind. Exp. Support	Ind. Exp. Oppose
2018 General	Richard Hudson (R)....................... 141,402	(55%)	$2,023,384	$15,000	
	Frank McNeill (D)............................ 114,119	(45%)	$642,297		
2018 Primary	Richard Hudson (R)....................	(100%)			

Prior winning percentages: 2016 (59%), 2014 (65%), 2012 (53%)

Republican Richard Hudson, elected in 2012, used a boost from redistricting to take control of a formerly Democratic-held seat, but had to adjust to changes from a subsequent redrawing of his district lines. A former senior congressional staffer and usually a party regular, he has worked on health and energy issues from his seat on the Energy and Commerce Committee.

Hudson grew up in the Charlotte area, and has a good political bloodline. He helped his grandfather run for the Roanoke Rapids City Council, where he served for 30 years. He put up yard signs for Republican Sen. Jesse Helms. Hudson was student-body president at the University of North Carolina at Charlotte, where he got a bachelor's degree. After college, he worked in Washington, as chief of staff to GOP Reps. Mike Conaway and John Carter of Texas and Virginia Foxx of North Carolina. He was deputy chief of staff for local Rep. Robin Hayes, who lost this seat to Democrat Larry Kissell in 2008. In November 2011, two months after moving back to the district, Hudson said he had a sense that God had a higher purpose for his life and was calling him to run for Congress.

Republicans made Kissell's seat a top 2012 takeover target. Hudson led the first round in the five-candidate primary with 32 percent, setting up a runoff with former Iredell County Commissioner Scott Keadle. When Keadle tried to portray Hudson as a Washington insider out of touch with the district, Hudson maintained that his experience on Capitol Hill created connections that would allow him to be more effective than most freshmen. He cruised to a runoff win, 64%-36%.

In the general, Hudson turned the tables by painting Kissell as the Beltway insider. He blamed the incumbent for moving the country toward "skyrocketing debt" and for "out-of-control spending." He accused Kissell of flip-flopping to try to save his seat. "I don't know where my opponent stands on many issues, it depends which day of the week it is," he told The Fayetteville Observer. Kissell stressed his vote against the Affordable Care Act. But styling himself as a conservative Blue Dog who was distant from Obama alienated black voters. Hudson took the seat, 53%-45%.

On Energy and Commerce, he has sought to unleash the energy resources of North Carolina and to replace the Affordable Care Act with "a health care system that puts patients first." He helped to form the Atlantic Offshore Energy Caucus, which was designed to promote policies that explore and expand energy production on the Outer Continental Shelf. In 2017, the House unanimously passed his bill to allow emergency medical technicians to dispense medications, subject to general approval of local medical directors. He chaired the agriculture policy group of the House Republican Policy Committee.

Showing his GOP establishment brand during debate in 2017 on repeal of the Affordable Care Act, Hudson criticized Freedom Caucus members who objected to leadership proposals to deliver on the party's promise. "It defies me to understand where they're coming from," he told Politico.

He breezed to reelection in 2014 with 65 percent of the vote against Democratic challenger Antonio Blue, the mayor of tiny Dobbins Height (pop. 855). In 2016, redistricting created more robust challenges for Hudson, with opponents who had credible financial support. In the Republican primary, he faced Tim D'Annunzio, a former Army paratrooper who went into the military-equipment business. D'Annunzio, who had run for Congress during the previous three cycles, self-financed most of his $239,000 campaign. He won narrowly in Cumberland, Hoke and Moore counties. Hudson had big margins in the western counties, including 82 percent of the vote in Cabarrus, and won 65%-35%.

In the general, Hudson faced Tom Mills, a veteran Democratic consultant in the area who founded the website, politicsnc.com. The candidates shared doubts about new international trade agreements and agreed on the need to protect U.S. citizens from the Islamic State. They disagreed on other issues, including gun control and immigration. Hudson raised $2 million overall to $400,000 for Mills. The national parties and their allies spent little money here. In the two biggest counties, Hudson got 62 percent in Cabarrus and Mills got 60 percent in Cumberland. Hudson took four other counties with margins of up to 78 percent and won overall, 59%-41%. After the election, Mills wrote a scathing piece for Politico in which he ripped the Democratic Congressional Campaign Committee for its failure to give attention to him or his campaign.

In 2018, Frank McNeill, the former mayor of Aberdeen and a fuel dealer, contrasted his local roots to Hudson, who "has lived in Washington his whole life." In a low-decibel contest, Hudson won, 55%-45%. His share of the vote in exurban Cabarrus dropped to 56 percent.

NC-8: South-Central North Carolina   Cook Partisan Voting Index: R+8

Population		Race and Ethnicity		Income	
Total	772,777	White	61.3%	Median Income	$50,110
Land area (sq. miles)	2,955	Black	22.3%	District Income Rank	311
Pop/ sq mi	261.5	Latino	10%	Poverty Rate	15.4%
Born in State	53.8%	Asian	2.2%	With health insurance	88.9%
		Two or more races	2.9%	Cash public assistance	1.3%
Age Groups		Other	1.3%	Food stamp/SNAP	13.1%
Under 18	24.3%				
18-34	24.4%	**Education**		**Work**	
35-64	37.2%	H.S grad or less	38.6%	White Collar	14.1%
Over 64	14.1%	Some college	35.8%	Sales and Service	42.7%
		College Degree, 4 yr	17.1%	Blue Collar	23.3%
Military		Post grad	8.5%	Government	18.3%
Veteran/ Active Duty	18.5%				

2012 Pres. Vote	Romney	174,278	(55%)	Obama	141,249	(44%)		
2016 Pres. Vote	Trump	185,920	(56%)	Clinton	136,191	(41%)	Johnson	9,128 (3%)

Eastern Charlotte Suburbs, Fayetteville: In the Carolina Piedmont, from Atlanta to Durham along Interstate 85, lie the remnants of America's once-mighty textile industry. These sites included Concord and Kannapolis, the latter named for its founding company, Cannon Mills. While eastern Carolina was settled by Englishmen, the Piedmont was settled mainly by Scots and diverse groups like Quakers and Moravian sects, coming down the Blue Ridge from Pennsylvania through Virginia. These migratory patterns were reflected in Civil War divisions and continue to some degree in current voting habits. The textile mill towns along the interstate were anti-secession and have long been Republican.

To the east is military-focused Fayetteville, which is centered on Fort Bragg — operating since 1918 and accounting for half of the area's economic activity. Racial integration on the post took place long before it did in the city. The Army base styles itself as the largest military base in the world, which has had more than 54,000 active-duty military personnel. This is the home of the famed 82nd Airborne Division, which specializes in forcible-entry operations. In 2014, the 82nd lost its "airborne" status because of the high cost of maintenance, plus injuries to the paratroopers and others. The area is home to 100,000 Army retirees and family members.

These separate areas are the end points of the 8th Congressional District, which stretches across the southern part of the state with five mostly rural and heavily Republican counties between them. They recently have moved in very different directions. Cabarrus County, which includes the southern end of the textile corridor around Kannapolis and Concord, has been fed by migration from Charlotte and has moved beyond its small-town roots to become a booming exurban county. The county grew by 58 percent from 2000 to 2017. Concord, with an influx of technology jobs, was the 14th-fastest growing small city in the nation from 2011 to 2017. In January 2018, proposals were unveiled for $300 million of downtown economic revitalization. Cabarrus casts one-fourth of the district's votes. Fayetteville-based Cumberland County is less robust economically, with growth of 10 percent since 2000. It leans Democratic.

The 2016 redistricting of the 8th District added Cumberland from the Raleigh-based 4th and lost to the 9th District a string of counties from Union to Robeson along the South Carolina border. What had been a political swing area has become a much more Republican district. Donald Trump in 2016 led, 56%-41%.

NC-9: Vacant (V)

DC Office: 224 CHOB 20515, 202-225-1976, Fax: 202-225-3389, pittenger.house.gov
State Offices: Charlotte, 704-362-1060.

The North Carolina Board of Elections scheduled a new contest after it decided not to accept the results of the November 2018 election. Republican Mark Harris had narrowly led that contest. But the outcome was challenged following allegations of absentee-voter fraud by an operative working on his behalf. Following a lengthy investigation and a February 2019 hearing by the board, Harris supported the call for a new election. The election was scheduled for September, unless a primary runoff caused a delay until November. Citing medical problems, Harris did not run again.

In the May 14 primary, state Sen. Dan Bishop won the Republican nomination against nine other candidates. Democratic entrepreneur Dan McCready, who was the runner-up in the earlier disputed election, remained his party's nominee as he sought to become the first Democrat to win this seat since 1952.

In addition to the nullification of the November result, the 2018 election was unusual for other reasons. Harris, an evangelical minister seeking his first elected office, won the GOP primary over Republican Rep. Robert Pittenger, a former real estate investor who served three terms. That marked a turnaround of a 2016 contest, when Harris lost by 134 votes to Pittenger. Harris won the bitter rematch by 828 votes. Pittenger refused to endorse Harris and said he should apologize for his false charges. Harris was the only House GOP candidate in 2018 who defeated an incumbent in either party — though he ultimately failed to win the seat.

The bitter GOP residue gave an added boost to McCready — an Marine Corps veteran of the Iraq war and a successful businessman with a solar-energy company. He pledged bipartisanship and fiscal discipline, and said that Harris' social views were too conservative for the district.

McCready's spending of more than $6 million tripled Harris' total for the campaign. Harris got a boost from $1 million in spending by the House Republican Super PAC. The conservative Club for Growth ran an ad that accused McCready of shady business practices in seeking favors for his solar company from "pay-to-play politicians."

Harris led by 905 votes. In the two largest counties, which cast nearly two-thirds of the total vote, Harris took Union by 17,500 votes and McCready led in Mecklenburg by more than 9,000 votes. McCready led in five of the six outlying counties. But when Harris had an unexpectedly big lead in that sixth county — Bladen — election officials noticed unusual patterns to the results and discovered suspicious practices with the handling of absentee ballots that had been collected for the Harris campaign by a local operative, Leslie Dowless. Harris denied any wrongdoing. But the fraud allegations were sufficient that the board of election delayed routine certification. That left the 9th District as the only one without a representative when Congress convened on Jan. 3, 2019. In the House, the new Democratic majority was prepared to investigate the apparent irregularities, depending on the local outcome.

In February, the state board held a weeklong hearing in February to review the charges. Harris' son John, as the dramatic concluding witness, said that he had earlier suspicions that Dowless was a "shady character" and that he had warned his father, despite the confidence of the senior Harris in Dowless's actions. John Harris emotionally concluded, "I love my father" and that he had no family animosity but that his father had made mistakes. The following morning, Mark Harris said that public confidence "had been undermined" by the hearing and that the testimony warranted a new election. The bipartisan board unanimously agreed. Dowless did not testify at the hearing.

Prior to the hearing, the Republican-controlled legislature had passed a bill requiring new primaries if the November election was not certified. McCready and other Democrats initially objected — preferring Harris as the GOP nominee — but they decided not to challenge the new procedure. To the relief of many Republicans, Harris was not a candidate.

Bishop took an unexpectedly strong 48 percent of the vote in the GOP primary. Bishop earlier gained prominence as the chief legislative sponsor of North Carolina's controversial "bathroom" bill restricting use by transgenders, which was subsequently repealed. He outspent the other candidates in the GOP primary, though the National Association of Realtors spent more than $1 million on behalf of Leigh Brown; she finished fourth. With Republican campaign assistance, Bishop moved quickly to seek to tie McCready to national Democrats.

NC-9: Southern North Carolina   Cook Partisan Voting Index: R+8

Population		Race and Ethnicity		Income	
Total	772,073	White	60.5%	Median Income	$56,003
Land area (sq. miles)	3,874	Black	18.9%	District Income Rank	217
Pop/ sq mi	199.3	Latino	7.9%	Poverty Rate	15.6%
Born in State	57.2%	Asian	2.5%	With health insurance	89.3%
		Two or more races	2.1%	Cash public assistance	1.6%
Age Groups		Other	8%	Food stamp/SNAP	15.2%
Under 18	25.4%				
18-34	19.9%	**Education**		**Work**	
35-64	40.7%	H.S grad or less	38%	White Collar	14%
Over 64	14%	Some college	28.9%	Sales and Service	39%
		College Degree, 4 yr	21.9%	Blue Collar	21.5%
Military		Post grad	11.2%	Government	12.6%
Veteran/ Active Duty	8.4%				

2012 Pres. Vote	Romney	183,971	(55%)	Obama	145,174	(44%)			
2016 Pres. Vote	Trump	186,926	(54%)	Clinton	147,162	(42%)	Johnson	9,841	(3%)

Southern Charlotte Suburbs: "An agreeable village but in a damn rebellious country," recorded British Revolutionary War Gen. Charles Cornwallis when, before the unpleasantness at Yorktown, he visited Charlotte. Settled by Scots-Irish and German colonists who came down from Pennsylvania along the Blue Ridge Mountains, Charlotte has been a rapidly growing metropolitan area and the largest in North Carolina. Before the California gold rush, Charlotte was the gold-mining capital of the country; in 1837, the U.S. Mint established a branch here. And the city continues its preoccupation with the financial sector today. It is headquarters to one of the nation's biggest banks, Bank of America. In booming Union County, more than two dozen aerospace manufacturers — with more than 4,000 employees — produce high-precision metal and plastic parts for airplanes around the world. Local high schools and community colleges train these workers. Union has occasionally struggled with its neighbors. In February 2018, its economic development board decided to withhold its $67,000 dues to the Charlotte Regional Partnership. Board members contended that they needed to promote Union County's interests.

The 9th Congressional District has been a microcosm of the changes that have taken place in the South in the past century. In 1928, it elected Republican Charles A. Jonas to Congress. The result was considered a fluke — he lost two years later — but in truth it was a precursor of trends in urban areas across the region. In 1952, the congressman's son, Charles R. Jonas, won the Charlotte district, and this time held it for another nine elections; Republicans subsequently retained control.

Although redistricting in 2016 radically changed the 9th, the Republican portions of Charlotte remained the constant factor. What had been a relatively compact district that stretched north and south of the city evolved with a population base in the southern parts of Charlotte in Mecklenburg County, plus rapidly growing Union County. Union increased from 124,000 in 2000 to 231,000 in 2017. Matthews, whose population doubled to 32,000 from 1990 to 2017, has been among the hot real-estate markets south of Charlotte. These areas include about 60 percent of the voters in the district. The remainder of the 9th sprawls east to include four mostly rural counties that extend east along the South Carolina border and then hooks north to Bladen and a small share of Fayetteville-based Cumberland County. Robeson County, which is the home of the Lumbee Tribe, leans Democratic. For decades, the Lumbees have sought to gain full congressional recognition. In the closing days of the Obama administration, the Interior Department reversed its previous opposition. The black population in the 9th increased from 13 percent to 20 percent, though its political leaning showed little change. Donald Trump in 2016 got 54 percent of the vote.

Patrick McHenry (R)

Elected 2004, 8th term, b. Oct 22, 1975; Charlotte; North Carolina State University, Att., 1997; Belmont Abbey College (NC), B.A., 2000; Roman Catholic; Married (Giulia Cangiano McHenry); 2 children.

Elected Office: NC House, 2002-2004.

Professional Career: Real estate broker, 2000-2002; Special Assistant to the U.S. Secretary of Labor, 2001.

DC Office: 2004 RHOB 20515, 202-225-2576, Fax: 202-225-0316, mchenry.house.gov

State Offices: Black Mountain, 828-669-0600; Gastonia, 704-833-0096; Hickory, 828-327-6100.

Committees: *Financial Services (RMM).*

Group Ratings

	ADA	ACLU	AFL-CIO	LCV	ITI	COC	HAFA	ACU	CFG	FRC
2018	-	4%	-	9%	-	91%	63%	84%	52%	100%
2017	0%	C	8%	0%	C	93%	C	93%	82%	100%

Almanac Ratings 2017-18

	Economy	Social	Foreign	Composite
Liberal	3%	0%	2%	2%
Conservative	97%	100%	98%	98%

Key Votes of the 115th Congress

1. Obama-care revision	Y	5. Family planning regs	Y	9. Guantanamo prisoners	N
2. Tax Cuts	Y	6. Body cameras/immigration	N	10. Ground missiles, limit	N
3. Omnibus appropriations	Y	7. Abortion ban	Y	11. Defense Dept. spending	Y
4. Dodd-Frank revision	Y	8. Concealed carry	Y	12. FISA rules	NV

Election Results

Election	Name (Party)	Vote (%)		Cand. Spent	Ind. Exp. Support	Ind. Exp. Oppose
2018 General	Patrick McHenry (R)	164,969	(59%)	$1,942,461		
	David Wilson Brown (D)	113,259	(41%)	$121,746		
2018 Primary	Patrick McHenry (R)	34,173	(71%)			
	Gina Collins (R)	6,664	(14%)			
	Jeff Gregory (R)	3,724	(8%)			

Prior winning percentages: 2016 (63%), 2014 (61%), 2012 (57%), 2010 (71%), 2008 (58%), 2006 (62%), 2004 (64%)

Patrick McHenry, a Republican first elected in 2004, has evolved from a highly partisan GOP guerilla fighter in his early years in the House into a talented insider with both leadership and committee experience seeking to move the party's agenda. His new position as ranking Republican on the Financial Services Committee offers mutual opportunities with the large financial sector in Charlotte. As the former chief deputy to GOP Whip Steve Scalise, McHenry is prominent in the next generation of Republicans seeking future influence. Despite being the youngest member in the North Carolina delegation, he is tied with Virginia Foxx as the most senior of its 10 Republicans.

McHenry grew up in Cherryville as the youngest of five children and graduated from Belmont Abbey College, where he was president of the state College Republicans. After school he worked as a real estate broker. As a young conservative, he cut his political teeth on his strenuous opposition to the Clintons. He once dressed up in an Abraham Lincoln costume at a North Carolina appearance by Bill Clinton after Clinton was accused by Republicans of rewarding big contributors with overnight stays in the Lincoln Bedroom in the White House. McHenry worked on several Republican campaigns in North Carolina and was appointed to a job in the Labor Department. In 2002, he was elected to the state House.

When McHenry ran for an open seat, his chief competition in the Republican primary was Catawba County Sheriff David Huffman. Both made conservative Christian values their main issue. After Huffman finished first with 35 percent and McHenry second with 26 percent, the four-week runoff campaign took a negative turn. Huffman questioned McHenry for hosting noisy late-night parties at his house, which also served as a residence for his campaign staff, a claim rebutted by McHenry's neighbors. McHenry accused Huffman of campaign finance irregularities. He ran an energetic, door-to-door grassroots campaign, billing himself as a "pro-life, pro-gun, anti-gay-marriage" Christian conservative. He won the runoff by just 85 votes after a recount, rolling up huge majorities in the counties close to his Gaston County home. He easily won the general election and has not faced a serious challenge since.

At age 29, McHenry arrived as the youngest member of the House. Instead of quietly learning the ropes, he made repeat appearances on talk shows to serve up red meat and sound bites. On the House floor, he took on Democrats no matter how powerful or senior. In 2007, he accused Speaker Nancy Pelosi of California of abusing her office by using military jets to fly home to San Francisco during congressional recesses. In 2009, he sidled up to the "birther" movement by saying at a town hall forum that "I haven't seen evidence one way or the other" of President Barack Obama's U.S. citizenship. He backed away from the comment the next day.

When Republicans took control of the House in 2011, he became more substantive as chairman of a subcommittee specializing in government bailouts, such as the Troubled Asset Relief Program for the financial industry. He told The Charlotte Observer that TARP was "a very uneven response from the federal government," with some banks bailed out and others, notably Charlotte-based Wachovia, forced to merge. He got into a hostile exchange at a 2011 hearing with Elizabeth Warren, then a Harvard professor who helped create the Consumer Financial Protection Bureau as part of the Dodd-Frank financial services overhaul. Supporters of Warren, who soon gained greater prominence among Democrats, posted thousands of angry comments on McHenry's Facebook page.

McHenry won enactment in 2011 of his bill allowing financial institutions involved in multiple transactions to combine them into one contract, something helpful to the banking industry in Charlotte. With his district on the outskirts of the city, his constituents include many banking executives. McHenry passed a provision in the jobs bill enacted in 2012 that allowed companies to more easily raise equity through social media and online platforms. In 2016, he filed a bill to expedite regulatory approval of new products for financial technology companies.

Behind the scenes, he helped his friend Scalise win election as chairman of the Republican Study Committee, the caucus of the House's mainstream conservative members. When Scalise became majority whip in the fallout from Eric Cantor's surprise primary defeat in 2014, he repaid the favor, appointing McHenry as his chief deputy. Like Scalise, McHenry spent much of his time courting his longtime conservative allies, not always successfully. For his new job, McHenry abandoned his earlier presence on the media circuit and went underground. "Some [lawmakers] know on day one how to be effective in this institution; others, it takes time — and I was in that camp," McHenry told The Wall Street Journal in 2015.

Given the economic plight of the textile industry, McHenry often voted against trade deals, as he did in 2005 on a pact proposed with Central America and in 2010 on a Haiti trade relief bill. His leadership post created a new twist in 2015 as he engaged in countless discussions to rally support from GOP members for the trade promotion authority request from Obama.

The nearly fatal shooting of Scalise at a congressional baseball practice in June 2017 placed him in charge of the whip team for several months. McHenry largely succeeded in continuing with business-as-usual during often stressful circumstances. "You've got to put in the understanding with people, not simply drive them on some issue, but very much get a sense of where they are and why they are where they are and that gives you a sense of where they can be," he said in described his responsibilities in a September 2017 interview with the Raleigh News & Observer.

The North Carolina delegation has included troublemakers for GOP leaders, including Rep. Mark Meadows, who represents the adjacent district and has chaired the rebellious Freedom Caucus. McHenry's responsibilities to help win enactment of the agenda of Trump and congressional Republicans created additional challenges as he tried to manage the conservative renegades. He praised the president's ability to "adapt and change in his interactions with members of the House."

When Republicans lost House control in the 2018 election, McHenry took advantage of the opening for the ranking minority member on the Financial Services Committee, with Rep. Maxine Waters as committee chairwoman. He pledged to "fight back against any efforts by Democrats to use this committee to roll back our successes from the past two years or use the committee as the launch pad for endless, partisan investigations."

In an initial showing of cooperation, Waters and McHenry cosponsored a bill to direct the Securities and Exchange Commission to review corporate executive investment plans. On other committee issues, McHenry called for a review of how technology was reshaping banking. In taking on his new responsibilities, he also said that he would increase his campaign fundraising and party support. In all likelihood, he eventually will have opportunities to return to GOP leadership.

McHenry has had little trouble at election time. He faced several GOP primary challengers who accused him of being insufficiently conservative, but won each contest easily.

NC-10: West-Central North Carolina — Cook Partisan Voting Index: R+12

Population		Race and Ethnicity		Income	
Total	749,120	White	77.9%	Median Income	$45,783
Land area (sq. miles)	2,589	Black	11.8%	District Income Rank	366
Pop/ sq mi	289.4	Latino	6.3%	Poverty Rate	15.8%
Born in State	65%	Asian	1.6%	With health insurance	88%
		Two or more races	1.7%	Cash public assistance	2.5%
Age Groups		Other	0.5%	Food stamp/SNAP	15.1%
Under 18	21.5%				
18-34	20.3%	**Education**		**Work**	
35-64	40.9%	H.S grad or less	44.6%	White Collar	17.3%
Over 64	17.3%	Some college	31.7%	Sales and Service	40.6%
		College Degree, 4 yr	15.7%	Blue Collar	27.3%
Military		Post grad	8%	Government	11.6%
Veteran/ Active Duty	8.5%				

2012 Pres. Vote	Romney	199,027	(58%)	Obama	137,474	(40%)		
2016 Pres. Vote	Trump	216,943	(60%)	Clinton	129,104	(36%)	Johnson	9,088	(3%)

Gastonia, Asheville: In 1790, one of the most important decisions in North Carolina's history was made — in Pennsylvania. That was when 19-year-old Michael Schenck decided to leave his family farm in Lancaster and settle in western North Carolina. In 1813, on a small creek west of Lincolnton, Schenck built the first cotton mill south of the Potomac River. In 1816, he brought in investors and erected the Lincoln Cotton Mills on the South Fork of the Catawba River, which operated until the Civil War. The North Carolina textile industry was born and soon dominated in an area that had specialized in corn, cotton and whiskey production. After the Civil War, the surfeit of cheap labor and fast-flowing streams on the Piedmont made it a perfect locus for manufacturing. By the end of the 19th century, North Carolina had more textile plants than Connecticut, Maine or Vermont. These companies relied on the "Rhode Island model" of development, where towns were put up around the mills and whole families were placed in small, company-owned homes.

Ground zero for the industry was Gaston County and nearby towns. By the 1930s, there were 570 mills within a 100-mile radius of Gastonia. The relationship between workers and management was often uneasy. Gastonia was the site of a massive strike at Loray Mills in the late 1920s, led by the communist-dominated United Textile Workers, which erupted in violence and resulted in the deaths of the local police chief and Ella May Wiggins, the unofficial balladeer of the union who penned tunes such as "A Mill Mother's Song" and "The Big Fat Boss and the Workers." Today, the textile industry is in decline and Gastonia has slower growth than most of the area surrounding Charlotte. Still, the western Piedmont continues to excel in making things. Developers have found new uses for abandoned mills. Asheville has had a spurt of technology-related manufacturing plus craft breweries. Gaston County has explored options to extend light-rail service from Charlotte, which could also serve the Charlotte airport.

The 10th Congressional District of North Carolina is centered on Gastonia, where a quarter of the district's votes are cast. To the north, it takes in Lincoln County and most of Hickory's Catawba County. To the west are Cleveland and Rutherford counties. The 10th has gained most of heavily Democratic Asheville, a popular artistic and retirement mecca with its well-preserved and gentrified historic structures in styles ranging from Gothic Revival to Art Deco. Asheville-based Buncombe, with one-fifth of the population, is a blue island in a deep red sea and an economic oasis amid extensive poverty. Those new lines reduced the Republican advantage in the 10th, but the district retained a strong GOP tilt. The other seven counties remain solidly Republican. Donald Trump took 60 percent here in 2016, his second-best performance in the state.

Mark Meadows (R)

Elected 2012, 4th term, b. Jul 28, 1959; Verdun, French Republic; Florida State University, Tallahassee, Att.; University of South Florida, B.A., 1981; Christian Church; Married (Debbie Meadows); 2 children; 1 grandchild.

Professional Career: Director, customer relations & public safety, Tampa Electric, 1983-1986; Owner, sandwich shop, 1986-1990; Real-estate developer, 1990-2012.

DC Office: 2160 RHOB 20515, 202-225-6401, Fax: 202-226-6422, meadows.house.gov

State Offices: Hendersonville, 828-693-5660; Lenoir, 828-426-8701; Spruce Pine, 828-765-0573; Waynesville, 828-452-6022.

Committees: *Oversight & Reform*: Government Operations (RMM); National Security; Subcommittee on Civil Rights & Civil Liberties. *Transportation & Infrastructure*: Economic Dev't, Public Buildings & Emergency Management (RMM); Highways & Transit.

Group Ratings

	ADA	ACLU	AFL-CIO	LCV	ITI	COC	HAFA	ACU	CFG	FRC
2018	-	19%	-	0%	-	75%	98%	91%	94%	100%
2017	5%	C	3%	0%	C	93%	C	100%	98%	100%

Almanac Ratings 2017-18

	Economy	Social	Foreign	Composite
Liberal	0%	13%	3%	6%
Conservative	100%	87%	97%	95%

Key Votes of the 115th Congress

1. Obama-care revision	Y	5. Family planning regs	Y	9. Guantanamo prisoners	N
2. Tax Cuts	Y	6. Body cameras/immigration	NV	10. Ground missiles, limit	N
3. Omnibus appropriations	N	7. Abortion ban	Y	11. Defense Dept. spending	Y
4. Dodd-Frank revision	Y	8. Concealed carry	Y	12. FISA rules	N

Election Results

Election	Name (Party)	Vote (%)		Cand. Spent	Ind. Exp. Support	Ind. Exp. Oppose
2018 General	Mark Meadows (R)	178,012	(59%)	$1,145,557		
	Phillip Price (D)	116,508	(39%)	$225,456		
	Clifton Ingram (Lib)	6,146	(2%)			
2018 Primary	Mark Meadows (R)	35,665	(86%)			
	Chuck Archerd (R)	5,639	(14%)			

Prior winning percentages: 2016 (64%), 2014 (63%), 2012 (57%)

With his leadership role in the House Freedom Caucus, Republican activist Mark Meadows, elected in 2012, has become the chief conservative renegade in the House. With his trusted pal, Rep. Jim Jordan of Ohio, he has made frequent maverick moves that alienated party leaders. Meadows played a key role in Speaker John Boehner decision to resign in 2015. The election of Donald Trump gave him additional influence as an adviser and outspoken defender of the president, even though Meadows occasionally has gone his own way on legislation.

Meadows was born in the 42nd Army Field Hospital in Verdun France, while his father was stationed abroad. His father was a draftsman; his mother, a surgical nurse. He attended high school in the Tampa area and got a degree in business management from the University of South Florida. After college, he worked for Tampa Electric, but he and his wife, Debbie, whom he met in Tampa, dreamed of living in North Carolina. Instead of waiting to retire, they moved there in 1986. They started a small sandwich shop in the resort town of Highlands, and ran it for a few years before they sold it and turned to real estate investments.

A self-described history buff, Meadows was drawn to conservative politics. He was the only person who showed up for a precinct meeting of his local Republican Party in rural North Carolina, thus becoming precinct chairman and eventually county chairman. He worked on behalf of GOP candidates for 25 years and was a delegate to party conventions.

In the 2012 Republican-controlled redistricting, Rep. Heath Shuler was one of four Democrats who were targeted. When his district became significantly more conservative, Shuler decided to retire. Meadows faced six Republicans in the May primary. He led with 38 percent of the vote. He trounced tea party activist Vance Patterson, 76%-24%, in the runoff campaign. In November, Meadows faced Shuler's former chief of staff, Hayden Rogers, who received significant financial backing from local business and labor interests. Rogers ran ads espousing his "mountain values" and sought to depict his opponent as wealthy and out of touch. He spent $726,000 but received little national party assistance. Meadows focused heavily on opposition to President Barack Obama. He took 12 of the 17 counties and won his first elected office, 57%-43%.

In the House, Meadows joined other conservative activists. In 2015, he was among nine founding members of the Freedom Caucus, which pressed House Republicans to pursue a more conservative agenda. That year, he was one of 25 Republicans who did not vote for Boehner for Speaker; he explained that he was reflecting the widespread view of his constituents that they wanted a new direction. Meadows took an interest in investigative work, and he became chairman of the Subcommittee on Government Operations, whose jurisdiction includes federal employees. He created a "tipline" for them to report problems. The committee approved his bill to prohibit government workers from using their computers to surf pornographic websites.

Meadows took several steps that offended House Republican leaders. His June 2015 vote against a rule for debating trade legislation — on top of his vote against Boehner plus his failure to pay dues to the National Republican Congressional Committee — led Oversight and Government Reform Chairman Jason Chaffetz of Utah to strip his subcommittee chairmanship. After angry conservatives threatened retaliatory moves to weaken his control of the committee, Chaffetz quickly reversed himself and Meadows regained his gavel. On the eve of the August recess, he filed a resolution designed to oust Boehner. Meadows said that he hoped for a "family discussion." At the end of September, Boehner announced that he would step down as Speaker.

The election of Trump initially raised doubts about the influence of the Freedom Caucus, as Republicans prepared for what they expected would be a busy legislative agenda. As it turned out, Meadows became an outspoken critic of the initial House Republican plan to revise the Affordable Care Act, and he pressed for changes that further reduced the scope of President Barack Obama's landmark law. Trump targeted Meadows for the initial setback, with a caustic tweet that the Freedom Caucus had "saved Planned Parenthood & Ocare." And he not so jokingly threatened Meadows at a White House meeting with conservatives, "I'm coming after you," if the House failed to pass a bill. Reinforced by grassroots conservative encouragement to hold firm, Meadows resumed negotiations for his approach. He was instrumental in crafting what became the trigger for the House-passed agreement.

Later, Meadows opposed Trump's international trade war and reportedly urged him not to impose steep tariffs. Meadows told reporters that he pursued the private discussions because Congress was not equipped to reverse the president. He also was unhappy about the business-as-usual approach on federal spending by most Republicans — in both Congress and the White House. "Meadows may be the most frustrated man in Washington," Politico headlined a story in February 2018.

Even though he made little headway with Trump, Meadows gained influence via his frequent conversations with the president — by phone and in person. He scored points by publicly criticizing the Justice Department and FBI for their handling — both past and present — of investigations of Trump; in July 2018, Meadows filed an impeachment resolution against Rod Rosenstein, the deputy attorney general because of his objections to requests to provide documents to Congress. In late 2018, their comfort level had reached the point that Trump reportedly considered tapping Meadows as White House chief of staff.

With the Republican loss of House control in the 2018 election, the legislative leverage of the Freedom Caucus was further reduced. Meadows moved to lead opposition to Democratic investigations of Trump, especially at the Oversight committee. With his ally Jordan in place as the senior Republican at that panel, the two of them sought to undermine the opposition attacks.

Meadows faced a three-year investigation by the House Ethics Committee into sexual harassment charges that had been filed against his former chief of staff, Kenny West. In November 2018, the committee ruled that Meadows broke House rules by "by failing to take appropriate steps" in managing his office; he was fined more than $40,000 to cover his aide's salary for a time when the committee determined that West should have been removed from Meadows' staff. Meadows responded that he took "good faith steps" after he learned of the problem.

At home, Meadows has won easy reelection. In September 2015, a few days before Boehner announced his resignation, The Hill reported that local Republicans were discussing the possibility of a primary challenge, with national party encouragement. GOP Rep. Patrick McHenry, who represents the district adjacent to Meadows, acknowledged the rumors but denied that he had anything to do with them. In 2018, Meadows faced a token primary challenge from Chuck Archerd, who said he supported Meadows and ran only because of speculation that the incumbent might resign to join the Trump administration. Meadows won, 86%-14%.

NC-11: Western North Carolina   Cook Partisan Voting Index: R+14

Population		Race and Ethnicity		Income	
Total	746,213	White	86.4%	Median Income	$43,833
Land area (sq. miles)	6,606	Black	3.1%	District Income Rank	388
Pop/ sq mi	113	Latino	6%	Poverty Rate	16.3%
Born in State	59.8%	Asian	1.2%	With health insurance	86.7%
		Two or more races	1.6%	Cash public assistance	2%
Age Groups		Other	1.8%	Food stamp/SNAP	13.6%
Under 18	19.5%				
18-34	19%	Education		Work	
35-64	40%	H.S grad or less	43.3%	White Collar	21.5%
Over 64	21.5%	Some college	32%	Sales and Service	41.8%
		College Degree, 4 yr	15.5%	Blue Collar	26.7%
Military		Post grad	9.1%	Government	14.8%
Veteran/ Active Duty	9.6%				

2012 Pres. Vote	Romney	201,258	(59%)	Obama	132,079	(39%)			
2016 Pres. Vote	Trump	230,018	(62%)	Clinton	123,790	(34%)	Johnson	10,246	(3%)

Asheville: Steeped in the hues that gave them the name Blue Ridge, the heavily wooded mountains of North Carolina seem placid and ancient. Geologically, they are some of the oldest ranges in the world; they began forming 400 million years ago, when plant life was just beginning to spread across the continents. In the early 20th century, this hardscrabble country, around the county seats of Lenoir and Morganton, became a manufacturing area. Textile mill owners moved their operations from New England to western North Carolina for its low-wage workforce. After the collapse of the residential furniture industry in Grand Rapids Michigan during the Great Depression, furniture manufacturing took hold in the region because of the abundance of hardwood forests.

Economic interests have continued to evolve. Textiles are a low-wage industry that typically represent the first stage in industrial development, migrating to cheaper venues when wages rise. And furniture has faced competition from Asia. So the region has increasingly turned to technology. In 2015, Google announced that it was the first customer of a Duke Energy program to bring renewable power from a nearby solar farm. Tourism has become a major local business. The Blue Ridge Parkway is the main route that feeds into the Great Smoky Mountains, which cross into Tennessee. In 2017, the Smokies hosted 11.3 million visitors and were rated the most popular park in the National Park Service. The scenery along the parkway attracted 16 million visitors — the largest total of any park unit. In 2018, for the first time since the Parkway was built in the 1930s, arborists cut some trees to improve the views. With $2 billion from tourism, the Asheville area's unemployment rate was below 3 percent in 2018 -- the lowest in the state.

The 11th District of North Carolina includes the Catawba Valley and consists of small, mountainous counties in far western North Carolina. The local politics once were volatile. From 1978 through 2012, the western North Carolina district switched between the parties seven times and threw out six incumbents. About a third of the district's residents live in the stretch of counties along the Tennessee border. These include some of the most reliably Republican locales in the nation. Another third of the district comes from the Asheville and Hendersonville areas. Republican redistricters removed the most heavily Democratic precincts in Asheville to the 10th District, though the remaining parts of Buncombe County can be competitive. Retiree-friendly Henderson County is heavily Republican. In 2016, Donald Trump got 62 percent in the 11th, which remained the strongest GOP-performing district in North Carolina.

Alma Adams (D)

Elected 2014, 3rd term, b. May 27, 1946; High Point; North Carolina Agricultural and Technical State University, 1968; North Carolina Agricultural and Technical State University, M.S., 1972; Ohio State University, Ph.D., 1981; Baptist; Divorced; 2 children; 4 grandchildren.

Elected Office: Guilford Cty., School Board, 1984-1986; Greensboro City Council, 1987-1994; NC House, 1994-2014.

Professional Career: Professor, Bennett College, 1972-2012.

DC Office: 2436 RHOB 20515, 202-225-1510, Fax: 202-225-1512, adams.house.gov

State Offices: Charlotte, 704-344-9950.

Committees: *Agriculture*: Subcommittee Nutrition, Oversight & Department Operations. *Education & Labor*: Higher Education & Workforce Investment; Workforce Protections (Chmn). *Financial Services*: Subcommittee on Diversity & Inclusion.

Group Ratings

	ADA	ACLU	AFL-CIO	LCV	ITI	COC	HAFA	ACU	CFG	FRC
2018	-	85%	-	94%	-	64%	4%	4%	12%	0%
2017	100%	C	95%	100%	C	43%	C	0%	0%	0%

Almanac Ratings 2017-18

	Economy	Social	Foreign	Composite
Liberal	96%	98%	93%	96%
Conservative	4%	2%	7%	4%

Key Votes of the 115th Congress

1. Obama-care revision	N	5. Family planning regs	N	9. Guantanamo prisoners	Y
2. Tax Cuts	N	6. Body cameras/immigration	Y	10. Ground missiles, limit	Y
3. Omnibus appropriations	Y	7. Abortion ban	N	11. Defense Dept. spending	N
4. Dodd-Frank revision	N	8. Concealed carry	N	12. FISA rules	NV

Election Results

Election	Name (Party)	Vote (%)		Cand. Spent	Ind. Exp. Support	Ind. Exp. Oppose
2018 General	Alma Adams (D)	203,974	(73%)	$311,802		
	Paul Wright (R)	75,164	(27%)			
2018 Primary	Alma Adams (D)	38,849	(86%)			
	Keith Young (D)	2,549	(6%)			

Prior winning percentages: 2016 (67%), 2014 (75%), 2014 special (75%)

Democrat Alma Adams, elected in 2014, has pursued occasional bipartisanship on causes of personal interest. When redistricting in 2016 removed her longtime base, she showed political dexterity in moving 90 miles to her new home, despite some local objections. In the majority, she was selected to chair the Workforce Protections Subcommittee.

Adams arrived in Washington as a rarity: a lawmaker with a fine-arts background. She grew up in New Jersey, with her single mother who did domestic work. She got her bachelor's degree from North Carolina A&T State University, a master's and her doctorate in art education and multicultural education from Ohio State University. Until 2012, she taught art history at Bennett College, a historically black women's college. She got her first taste of politics in the 1980s, with election to the Guilford County School Board and the Greensboro City Council; she was the first African-American woman elected to the school board. A single mother from a working-class African-

American community, she focused on educational and housing disparities. She helped organize Greensboro for the 1988 presidential campaign of Jesse Jackson.

In 1994, Adams was appointed to the state Assembly, where she chaired the Legislative Black Caucus and became known as "the minimum-wage lady" because of her advocacy. Adams is known for her hats. "It's a part of my wardrobe," she told National Public Radio in 2015. "I started wearing hats because I was sick a lot. And I remember my grandmother telling me, 'Cover your noggin; you'll stay healthy.'" Serving in Congress has expanded her collection from 903 when she started to 1,108, as of September 2017.

The departure of Rep. Melvin Watt, who held the seat from 1993 until President Barack Obama nominated him to head the Federal Housing Finance Agency, set off a scramble. Seven Democrats jumped into the race. Adams was backed by progressive and abortion-rights organizations that funneled at least $186,000 to super PACs that took aim at her top Democratic rival, Malcolm Graham, a former Charlotte city council member and state senator. Organized labor was another major ally.

In a heavily Democratic district, the candidates largely agreed on the core issues: supporting the Affordable Care Act, opposing the decision of Republican Gov. Pat McCrory to block Medicaid expansion, and taking aim at Republican efforts to curtail early voting. Adams emphasized her participation in the Democratic pushback in a state where partisan politics had become fractious. She easily topped the field in the primary with 44 percent to 24 percent for Graham. She got 75 percent in her general election victory, which was a foregone conclusion.

Adams displayed her activism on numerous issues. With Republican Rep. Bradley Byrne of Alabama, she founded the Historically Black Colleges and Universities Caucus. In 2016, the House passed their bill with improvements in capital financing of HBCUs. Adams introduced with Democratic Rep. Rosa DeLauro the Paycheck Fairness Act for gender equality on wages, and she filed a measure to raise the federal minimum wage to $12 hourly by 2020. She said that voting must be made easier for all Americans, and claimed that mandatory voter ID laws did the opposite.

In 2016, Adams filed the Small and Disadvantaged Businesses Act, which called for a review of government purchasing procedures. That measure was enacted as part of that year's defense spending bill. Earlier, the House approved her amendment calling on the Pentagon to assure that service members have enough resources and treatment for post-traumatic stress disorder.

In 2019, Adams was tapped to chair the Education and Labor Subcommittee on Workforce Protections. She listed her top priorities as an increase in the minimum wage and a requirement of equal pay for equal work. She filed a paycheck fairness bill to update the 2009 Lily Ledbetter Fair Paycheck Act, which was designed to make it easier to sue for gender discrimination. Adams also gained a seat on the Financial Services Committee, a useful assignment for her district.

When redistricting reduced her district to only Mecklenburg County, Adams claimed that she picked up roots from her home in Greensboro to run in the Democratic primary. The Charlotte Observer, saying that it preferred "someone with a better grounding in Charlotte's history, culture and neighborhoods," endorsed Graham, who ran again, and cited his "deep varied local experience." Graham ran an ad with the slogan, "A house is not a home." State Rep. Tricia Cotham, another candidate, said that Adams was "intentionally deceiving" voters by claiming that she had changed her residence. Adams had a big fundraising advantage. Memos that had been hacked from the computers of the Democratic Congressional Campaign Committee revealed its assistance for Adams, who raised more than $900,000, to about $100,000 for each of her chief challengers. Adams got 43 percent to 29 percent for Graham and 21 percent for Cotham.

By 2018, Adams appeared to have entrenched herself. In the Democratic primary, she got 86 percent against three challengers. The runner-up with 6 percent was Keith Young, a city council member in Asheville, who evidently was less skillful in establishing a local connection.

NC-12: Mecklenburg County   **Cook Partisan Voting Index: D+18**

Population		Race and Ethnicity		Income	
Total	830,510	White	40.1%	Median Income	$56,061
Land area (sq. miles)	420	Black	36.6%	District Income Rank	215
Pop/ sq mi	1975.8	Latino	14.6%	Poverty Rate	15.4%
Born in State	41.9%	Asian	5.5%	With health insurance	85.2%
		Two or more races	2.6%	Cash public assistance	1.7%
Age Groups		Other	0.6%	Food stamp/SNAP	12.7%
Under 18	24.5%				
18-34	27.8%	**Education**		**Work**	
35-64	38.6%	H.S grad or less	31.4%	White Collar	9.1%
Over 64	9.1%	Some college	29.2%	Sales and Service	41.4%
		College Degree, 4 yr	26.5%	Blue Collar	18.1%
Military		Post grad	12.9%	Government	8.8%
Veteran/ Active Duty	6.1%				

2012 Pres. Vote	Obama	232,581	(68%)	Romney	107,627	(31%)			
2016 Pres. Vote	Clinton	243,693	(67%)	Trump	101,178	(28%)	Johnson	11,425	(3%)

Charlotte: "This is perhaps the Negro's temporary farewell to Congress," began the peroration of the last speech given by George White, an African-American lawyer from Tarboro North Carolina, and a Republican, in his last days in the House in 1901. Segregation was being imposed by law, and blacks were informally but effectively driven from the voting rolls in the rural South. The conclusion of White's speech proved prophetic: "Phoenix-like, he will rise up some day and come again. These parting words are in behalf of an outraged, heart-broken, bruised, and bleeding, but God-fearing people, faithful, industrious, loyal people — rising people, full of potential force." When White said his farewell, most North Carolina blacks lived on farms or in tiny towns. Through the 20th century, few moved to the textile towns, where most mills hired only whites, but some moved to its larger cities. After the Voting Rights Act of 1965, their "potential force" began to be felt in the state legislature. Some blacks won in white-majority constituencies, notably Charlotte Mayor Harvey Gantt. The next African Americans elected to Congress from North Carolina after White resulted when the Democratic legislature after the 1990 census drew two irregularly shaped black-majority districts. The winners in 1992 were Eva Clayton in the mostly rural and small-town 1st District and Melvin Watt in the mostly urban 12th District.

Charlotte-based Mecklenburg County and Raleigh-based Wake are the two largest counties and they include about one-fifth of the population in North Carolina, but they accounted for half of the population gain from 2010 to 2017. Charlotte, which is about 80 percent of Mecklenburg has a boosterish pride in its capacity for accommodation. The downside of its rapid growth is that the city has had the worst sprawl of 15 fast-growing metro areas. Construction by a private contractor of two toll lanes in each direction for 26 miles on Interstate 77 was expected to be completed by mid-2019. Charlotte has promoted cultural development and entertainment. It boasts the NASCAR Hall of Fame and a $50 million performing arts center across from the 60-story Bank of America tower. The city has long been the financial center for North Carolina and much of the South. In 2017, Allstate Insurance announced that it was expanding its local workforce with 2,250 additional workers. Republicans will hold their national convention in Charlotte in the summer of 2020, even though city and county have scant GOP office-holders. Democrats had a successful convention in Charlotte in 2012, when they renominated President Barack Obama.

The 12th Congressional District of North Carolina has been the most litigated district in the country since the 1990s and has been the focus of no fewer than four cases that went to the Supreme Court. It originally comprised a series of black precincts connected in some places by nothing wider than the lanes of Interstate 85, and it stretched 160 miles from Gastonia to Durham. Over the years, it grew a bit shorter. The district, among the most gerrymandered in the nation, concentrated Democratic strength of any color, helping to make nearby districts more Republican. Finally, in the 2016 redistricting, the 12th took on regular lines and was entirely in Mecklenburg. The immediate outcome was the same: The district remained a Democratic island that bordered four Republican-held districts, with three others nearby in western North Carolina.

The district is 37 percent black and 15 percent Hispanic — compared with 54 percent and 15 percent in the old 12th. The Hispanic share is the largest of any district in the state. The changes reduced the vote in 2012 for President Barack Obama from 79 percent, among the highest in the nation in 2008, to 68 percent. In 2016, Hillary Clinton won 67 percent here.

Ted Budd (R)

Elected 2016, 2nd term, b. Oct 21, 1971; Winston-Salem; Appalachian State University (NC), B.S., 1994; Dallas Theological Seminary (TX), M.Th., 1998; Wake Forest University (NC), M.B.A., 2007; Christian - Non-Denominational; Married (Amy Kate); 3 children.

Professional Career: Investment analyst; Business owner.

DC Office: 118 CHOB 20515, 202-225-4531, budd.house.gov

State Offices: Advance, 336-998-1313; High Point, 336-858-5013.

Committees: *Financial Services*: Consumer Protection & Financial Institutions; Subcommittee on Diversity & Inclusion.

Group Ratings

	ADA	ACLU	AFL-CIO	LCV	ITI	COC	HAFA	ACU	CFG	FRC
2018	-	14%	-	3%	-	75%	98%	100%	97%	100%
2017	0%	C	3%	0%	C	93%	C	100%	95%	100%

Almanac Ratings 2017-18

	Economy	Social	Foreign	Composite
Liberal	0%	7%	3%	3%
Conservative	100%	94%	97%	97%

Key Votes of the 115th Congress

1. Obama-care revision	Y	5. Family planning regs	Y	9. Guantanamo prisoners	N
2. Tax Cuts	Y	6. Body cameras/immigration	N	10. Ground missiles, limit	N
3. Omnibus appropriations	N	7. Abortion ban	Y	11. Defense Dept. spending	Y
4. Dodd-Frank revision	Y	8. Concealed carry	Y	12. FISA rules	N

Election Results

Election	Name (Party)	Vote (%)		Cand. Spent	Ind. Exp. Support	Ind. Exp. Oppose
2018 General	Ted Budd (R)	147,570	(52%)	$1,957,431	$828,409	$1,253,080
	Kathy Manning (D)	130,402	(46%)	$4,119,665	$571,294	$2,007,742
2018 Primary	Ted Budd (R)		(100%)			

Prior winning percentages: 2016 (56%)

Ted Budd, elected in 2016 as a political newcomer, became an active member of the Financial Services Committee, where he worked with banking groups to roll back the Dodd-Frank financial regulatory law. He survived a more competitive campaign in his first reelection campaign than in his initial contest.

Budd grew up on a 300-acre cattle and commercial chicken farm and he continues to reside there in the town of Advance, which had a population of 1,171 in 2018. His father built a janitorial supply house into a facility-services company that employed 3,400 people in 10 states, The Charlotte Observer reported. He graduated from Appalachian State University, where he worked on phone banks for Republican Sen. Jesse Helms. He got graduate degrees in theology from Dallas Theological Seminary and in business administration from Wake Forest University. Budd met his wife, Amy Kate, while they were on a mission trip to the former Soviet Union. He worked for his father's company and owned his own gun store and shooting range, which he called ProShots. He opposes gun control, and he views terrorism and mental health problems as the chief causes of gun-related violence.

The Republican primary included 17 candidates, none of whom spent sizable amounts of money. Budd raised about $150,000 for the primary, which was more than any of the next three candidates in the contest. He got a big boost from the Club for Growth, which viewed him as a true outsider and spent $500,000 on his behalf, with ads that highlighted his conservative values and firm resolve. In a remarkably low-turnout contest for a new seat, Budd got 6,340 votes and won the primary with 20 percent. Three other candidates were next in line with 10 percent each: John Blust, Hank Henning and Julia Howard. Budd won Davie and Davidson counties, finished second in Iredell, third in Guilford, which cast about one-third of the vote, and fourth in Rowan, which had the lowest vote.

In the general election, Budd faced Democrat Bruce Davis, a Marine Corps veteran who owned a child development center in High Point and served 12 years as a Guilford County commissioner. The two candidates had similar views on several issues, including support of gun ownership, opposition to the Trans-Pacific Partnership, and the need to address Islamic extremism. Davis disagreed with Budd's support for a wall on the southern border to keep out illegal immigrants. Davis raised only $91,000 and had scant opportunity to get his message out compared with Budd, who raised nearly $600,000 overall. Budd won, 56%-44%. Davis won 60 percent in Guilford, which cast slightly more than half the vote. Budd won Davie, Davidson and Iredell by margins of more than two-to-one.

In the House, he got a seat on the Financial Services Committee, where he said he would be "using my real world experience to roll back the restrictive regulations that strangle job creation in this country." With a Republican-controlled Congress and White House, his timing was right. He took a special interest in repealing the Durbin amendment to the Dodd-Frank banking law. Sponsored by Democratic Sen. Richard Durbin of Illinois, that provision placed limits on the rates that credit-card companies could charge retailers for their "swipe fees." In a statement, Budd said, "Command and control government policies benefit powerful interests as much as they do the disadvantaged." With strong support for the Durbin proviso from small business groups, Budd's initiative proved a step too far. Still, the American Bankers Association supported Budd and Democratic Sen. Jon Tester of Montana in its first broadcast ads of the midterms. "Rep. Budd understands the important role North Carolina banks play in the economy," said the president of the North Carolina Bankers Association.

That support proved useful to Budd in the 2018 campaign, when he faced a more organized and better financed challenge for reelection. Democrat Kathy Manning, a Greensboro attorney and civic activist, said her top issue was the need for more affordable and accessible health care. She criticized Budd for the failure of Republican-passed legislation to protect patients with pre-existing conditions. In an election-eve appearance, House Speaker Paul Ryan praised Budd as an "impact player" and warned of a "green wave of [campaign] money coming at us." Manning spent an impressive $4.1 million to $2 million for Budd; outside groups spent more than $4 million on the contest. Budd won, 52%-46%. Manning led in Guilford, 62%-37%, a margin of 34,000 votes. Budd survived with more than 70 percent of the vote in Davidson and Davie counties.

NC-13: North-Central North Carolina   Cook Partisan Voting Index: R+6

Population		Race and Ethnicity		Income	
Total	762,411	White	64.8%	Median Income	$48,679
Land area (sq. miles)	1,832	Black	21.9%	District Income Rank	331
Pop/ sq mi	416.2	Latino	7.7%	Poverty Rate	16.3%
Born in State	60.7%	Asian	3.4%	With health insurance	88.3%
		Two or more races	1.7%	Cash public assistance	1.9%
Age Groups		Other	0.5%	Food stamp/SNAP	13.9%
Under 18	22.3%				
18-34	22.4%	**Education**		**Work**	
35-64	39.7%	H.S grad or less	40.3%	White Collar	15.6%
Over 64	15.6%	Some college	31.6%	Sales and Service	40.6%
		College Degree, 4 yr	18.8%	Blue Collar	24.9%
Military		Post grad	9.3%	Government	11.2%
Veteran/ Active Duty	7.6%				

2012 Pres. Vote	Romney	188,114	(53%)	Obama	163,603	(46%)		
2016 Pres. Vote	Trump	193,990	(53%)	Clinton	160,204	(44%)	Johnson	9,678	(3%)

Greensboro, High Point: For more than half a century, furniture store managers and owners from all over the country twice a year have converged on the huge Furniture Mart in High Point, the center of the U.S. furniture business. The giant trade show put on by manufacturers has attracted about 75,000 visitors and 2,000 exhibitors from 100 nations. The furniture business grew here early in the 20th century because of the hardwoods in the mountains not far to the west and the abundance of low-wage labor in the flatlands not far to the east. For many years, the furniture business has proven more resilient than textiles and tobacco. Recently, it has faced serious competition from China, though it continues to call itself the "Furniture Capital of the World." The North Carolina Commerce Department estimated that more than 35,000 workers were employed statewide in furniture manufacturing.

The Triad area — Greensboro, High Point and Winston-Salem — has scrambled for new sources of economic growth to keep pace with booming Raleigh-Durham and Charlotte. In 2018, Site Selection magazine ranked the area second in the nation for its appeal to new and expanded businesses. FedEx has a hub at Piedmont Triad International Airport, between Winston-Salem and Greensboro, plus a "super hub" ground sorting facility that has 750 workers. That has led other firms to plan distribution centers to utilize the "aerotropolis," otherwise known as a city built around an airport. In 2018, FedEx announced that it was doubling its airport work force to more than 800.

Created in the 2016 redistricting, the 13th Congressional District has no overlap with the previous 13th, which was east of Raleigh. It was formed with pieces of five districts under the old map, from west of Raleigh and north of Charlotte. Along with two-thirds of Guilford, the district includes all of Davie and Davidson, most of Iredell and one-third of Rowan. Iredell has had rapid growth as the Charlotte metro area has expanded deeper into the suburbs; that has jeopardized the county's status as the leading dairy-producer in the state. Lexington-based Davidson County, in the heart of the Piedmont, styles itself as the Barbecue Capital of the World and features many renowned golf courses.

Politically, the 13th is divided into two distinct parts. Guilford, which has nearly half the population, leans Democratic. Hillary Clinton got 59 percent in the county, which is 41 percent black. The four counties to the west are comfortably Republican with large white majorities. It has had the lowest Republican presidential support of the 10 GOP-leaning districts in North Carolina. In 2016, Donald Trump led, 53%-44%.

NORTH DAKOTA

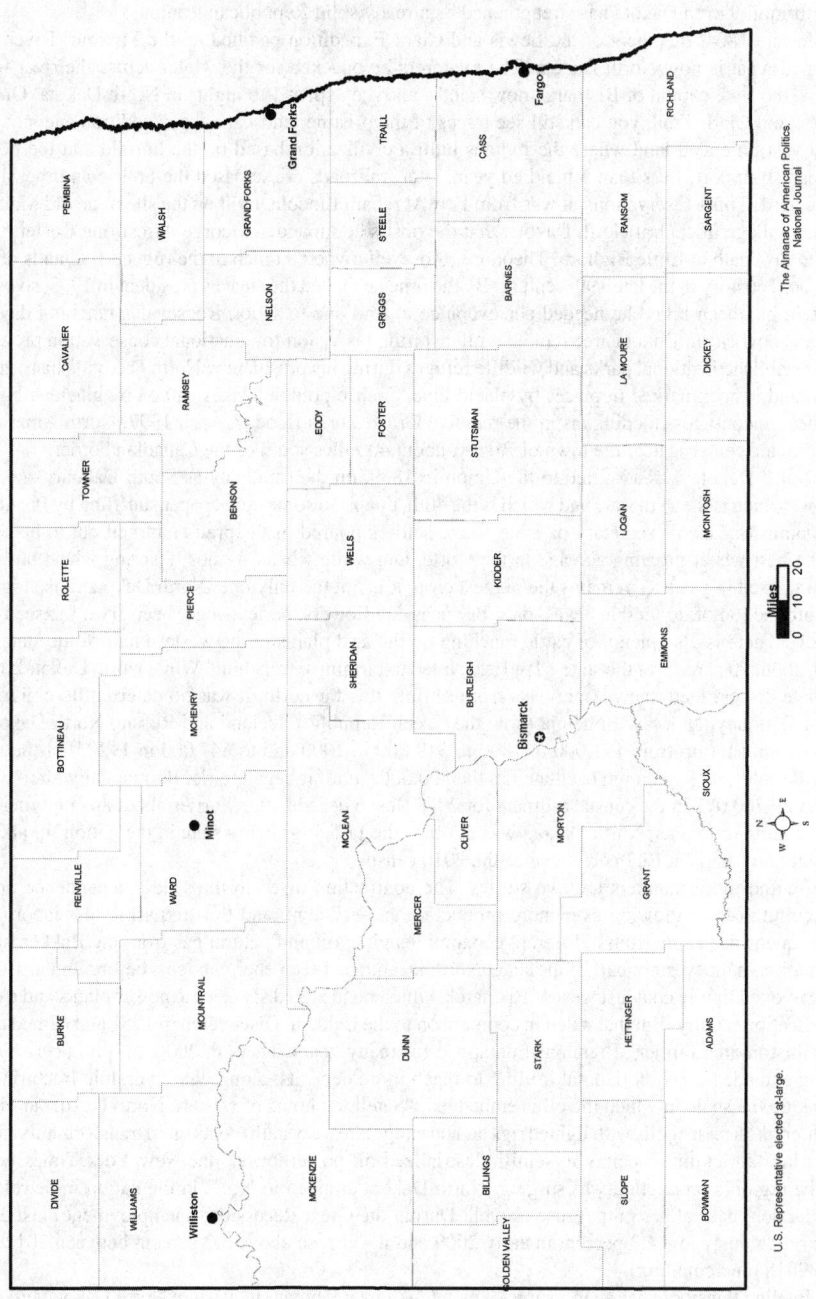

U.S. Representative elected at-large.

For a state that is one of the most remote in the Lower 48, North Dakota has been much in the news in recent years – first for a shale-oil boom that transformed the western part of the state, then for protests by Native Americans and others against the Dakota Access Pipeline. Amid the ferment and turmoil, North Dakota has strengthened its already solid Republican leanings.

In late 1804, members of the Lewis and Clark Expedition paddled up the Missouri River and reached what is now North Dakota. The explorers bivouacked for the winter across the river from where the state capital of Bismarck now stands, and they spent 146 nights in North Dakota. On the Lewis and Clark Trail, you can still see traces of the pristine landscape the expedition encountered — a vast unfenced land where the Indians built a civilization based on the buffalo and the horse, a Spanish import. Less than a hundred years later, railroads crisscrossed the prairie and the Sioux were herded onto reservations; it was from Fort Abraham Lincoln, built on the site of an old Mandan Indian village in central North Dakota, that the post's commander, George Armstrong Custer, rode out to his death at Little Bighorn. Theodore Roosevelt owned a ranch in the rugged Badlands of the Dakota Territory in the late 19th century. By the time he visited the state as president in 1903, so many buffalo had been killed he needed perseverance to find one to shoot. Roosevelt's ranching days in what is now North Dakota are credited with inspiring his vision for a national conservation program that established national parks and wildlife refuges during his presidency. North Dakota's lush, green farmland is pockmarked in places by placid blue "prairie pothole" lakes carved by glaciers; but its flatness encourages flooding, as in the massive Grand Forks flood in April 1997. North America's geographic center is near the town of Rugby, about 40 miles south of the Canadian border.

North Dakota was admitted to the Union in 1889, on the same day as South Dakota -- no one knows which is the 39th state and which is the 40th, thanks to some quick paper shuffling by President Benjamin Harrison's secretary of State -- and settlers poured in. Its prairies turned out to be some of the best wheat-growing acreage in the world, and while wheat — mostly spring wheat but also durum, used in pasta — remains the biggest crop, it is not the only one. North Dakota ranks high in the production of dry edible beans, oats, dry peas, sunflowers, barley, sugar beets, rye, flaxseed and canola. There is also plenty of cattle ranching on the arid plains in the western half of the state; all told, about 90 percent of the state's land is devoted to farming or ranching. While North Dakota's cold climate discouraged many Americans from settling this far north, it was no deterrent to emigrants from Germany, Norway, Bohemia (now the Czech Republic), Iceland and Russia. North Dakota's population shot up from 191,000 in 1890 to 319,000 in 1900 and to 647,000 in 1920. For the next nine decades, its population oscillated in the 600,000s, until it began to rise dramatically after 2007, reaching 760,077 in the census estimate for 2018. Just a decade after worries about an emptying-out of the northern plains, North Dakota was at times the fastest-growing state in the nation. In all, the population has risen 12.7 percent since the 2010 census.

Behind those numbers are two stories. The contraction owed to the state's dependence on an agriculture sector growing ever more productive and efficient, and thus requiring less labor. The subsequent rise came from a different economic engine: oil and natural gas from the Bakken shale formation in the western part of the state. North Dakota had seen energy booms before. In the 1970s, it developed lignite coal just west of Bismarck, which bequeathed six electric power plants and a coal gasification facility. But that paled in comparison to the Bakken. Discovered in 1951 and named after a Williston-area farmer, it remained untapped for many years. Then, in 2006, oil producers began using extended-reach horizontal drilling to reach more deposits, along with hydraulic fracturing to break up the shale in which the oil is embedded. "Satellite photos of western North Dakota at night, aglitter like a metropolis with lighted rigs and burning flares, crystallized its rapid transformation from tight-knit agricultural society to semi-industrialized oil powerhouse," the New York Times wrote as the region's production was surging. North Dakota climbed to No. 2 in the nation in petroleum production; natural gas output rose as well. During the Great Recession, unemployment maxed out at a ridiculously low 4.3 percent in early 2009 and never rose above 3.2 percent between 2012 and late 2018 (and counting).

Fueling this boom has been a surge of men (and fewer women) to western North Dakota, lured by annual earnings of $100,000 and more. Initially, many lived in RVs or modular living pods lined up on farm fields, because Williston, improbably, had become the nation's highest average rent for an entry-level apartment. Ten counties in the region registered double-digit population increases in the first half-decade after the 2010 census, led by Williams County (58 percent) and McKenzie County (102 percent). In what is the seventh-whitest state in the country, the share of African Americans and Hispanics more than doubled, from a small base, thanks to the new work available for qualified out-of-staters. The state also saw the nation's biggest percentage increase in foreign-born residents between 2010 and 2017, including refugees settled from Congo, Iraq and Somalia. Trucks carrying water in for fracking and oil out for refining jammed the two-lane roads and buckled the pavement; there were long lines at stores and fast-food takeout lanes, and schools were strained. In Williston, "the first thing you see leaving the Amtrak station is two strip clubs that cater to the wave of men coming into town from the oil fields, their pockets stuffed with cash," NPR reported. This milieu spawned human and drug trafficking, organized crime and homicides — a situation worrisome enough that the FBI opened an office there.

But the energy sector is volatile, and beginning in 2015, with lower prices on the global market, production declined. This didn't necessarily show up in the unemployment figures – workers would often leave the state when work dried up – but the number of operating rigs fell by three quarters. Worker deaths spiked, and the lack of government regulation attracted questions. The New York Times calculated that North Dakota regulators collected just one-thirtieth the fines on industry that Texas collected over the same period.

Native Americans, already afflicted with greater poverty, risked becoming another potential casualty of the oil boom. For 10 months starting in 2016, the Standing Rock Sioux, joined by the Cheyenne River Sioux and a small group of celebrities and other supporters, camped out to oppose the $3.7 billion Dakota Access Pipeline, which would run for 1,170 miles from North Dakota to Illinois. Living in teepees and rallying behind the cry "Mni wiconi!" – "water is life" – they said the pipeline would threaten drinking water supplies and harm ancestral lands. Work was temporarily halted by the Obama administration. But President Donald Trump reversed that decision as one of his first actions. The remaining demonstrators were cleared in February 2017 after burning some of their teepees as a final act of protest (and leaving tons of trash behind); tensions between the protest camp and nearby ranchers had become so heated that one state lawmaker proposed a bill to legalize running over protesters in the road as long as it was done accidentally. (The bill was defeated in the state House.) For Native Americans – the state's largest minority group – choosing between economic growth and cultural and environmental protection was often wrenching. "We would like to see more drilling," Indian official Gene McCowan told Reuters. "But we are caught in a bind because people are concerned about fracking and how that will affect the earth and water."

In time, increased technological efficiency helped North Dakota's petroleum sector recover, allowing it to be profitable even in periods of lower prices. "Today North Dakota's oil companies are producing record amounts of oil with half as many drilling rigs," NPR reported in late 2018. Another factor was the Dakota Access Pipeline, which significantly cut transportation costs. Having reached a flow of 500,000 barrels a day, the industry began mulling how to construct additional pipeline capacity. As the industry matured, the rough boomtowns slowly transitioned into stability as families replaced itinerants and as sturdier roads and new schools, retail stores and recreation centers were built.

Politics until recently was shaped by agriculture, not oil. When farm prices are high, it is often because of low production; when they are low, farmers seek protection. The boosterish optimism of the first settlers was soon followed by cries, reverberating with varying intensity, for government protection against market forces. Since commodity prices tend to fall during periods of economic growth, there was often a countercyclical force at work in North Dakota politics — a tendency to vote against the national trends, and a radical strain going back to the 1910s. That strain also owes much to the Scandinavian and German origins of many of the state's early settlers, who produced orderly small towns and grain cooperatives and supported the Nonpartisan League, which operated as a faction within the Republican Party from its founding in 1915 until its alliance with the Democratic Party in 1956.

The NPL appealed to marginal farmers, cut off in many cases from the wider American culture by language and geographical barriers and seemingly at the mercy of the grain millers in Minneapolis, the railroads in St. Paul, the banks in New York City and the commodity traders in Chicago. The NPL's program was socialist — government ownership of railroads and grain elevators — and its members, like most North Dakota ethnics, opposed going to war with Germany in 1917 and in 1940-41. The NPL often determined the outcome of the usually decisive Republican primary, but sometimes swung its support to the otherwise heavily outnumbered Democrats, instituting reforms and creating the state-owned Bank of North Dakota and a state grain elevator.

One reason local Democrats thrived for years while the state steadily voted Republican for president was that politics was personal in a place where most everyone knows everyone else. But in a sign of the times, the GOP-led state government tightened its voter ID law in 2013. After a long-running legal battle, it was finally given the go-ahead just weeks before the 2018 election, drawing national criticism for requiring everyone, including Native Americans, to have a street address to vote. Many residents on reservations had traditionally used post office box numbers for mail and identification.

North Dakota's combination of light taxation and regulation on the one hand and the state-owned Bank of North Dakota on the other has encouraged business startups. But communal closeness has produced an innate cultural conservatism. Bills to ban discrimination based on sexual orientation have been rejected on multiple occasions; the state joined a lawsuit to challenge the Obama administration's transgender schools policy; and Republican Gov. Jack Dalrymple in 2013 signed what was widely regarded at the time as the nation's strictest anti-abortion law. (The law was overturned by the courts, and North Dakota voters separately rejected a ballot measure in 2014 that would have defined life as beginning at conception.) In 2018, North Dakota voters turned down a marijuana legalization ballot measure by a 3-to-2 margin.

With rare exceptions, such as Democrat Heidi Heitkamp's narrow Senate victory in 2012, North Dakota has become a solidly Republican state. Heitkamp fared significantly better than Hillary Clinton two years earlier when she ran for another term in 2018, but it still wasn't nearly close enough to win, as she lost to GOP Rep. Kevin Cramer, 55%-44%. Heitkamp saw her share of the statewide vote fall by six percentage points compared with her 2012 race, and she won only 12 counties rather than 24. Her losing margins in such populous counties as Burleigh (Bismarck) and Ward (Minot) ballooned by double digits – another sign of the Democrats' deep challenges in North Dakota. For the first time since 1960, the state's federal delegation is all Republican. The GOP holds all 12 statewide elected offices and large majorities in both legislative chambers.

Cook Partisan Voting Index: R+16

Population		Race and Ethnicity		Income	
Total	745,475	White	85.7%	Median Income	$61,285
Land area (sq. miles)	69,001	Black	2.3%	State Income Rank	16
Pop/ sq mi	10.8	Latino	3.3%	Poverty Rate	11.0%
Born in state	63.6%	Asian	1.3%	With health insurance	92.0%
		Two or more races	2.0%	Cash public assistance	2.0%
Age Groups		Other	5.3%	Food stamp/SNAP	7.2%
Under 18	22.9%				
18-34	27.0%	**Education**		**Work**	
35-64	35.7%	H.S grad or less	34.8%	White Collar	36.1%
Over 64	14.4%	Some college	36.2%	Sales and Service	38.9%
		College Degree, 4 yr	21.1%	Blue Collar	25.0%
Military		Post grad	7.8%	Government	15.7%
Veteran/ Active Duty	9.4%				

Presidential Politics

2016 Caucus (D)	Sanders (D)	253 (64%)	Clinton (D)	101 (26%)			
2016 Pres. Vote	Trump (R)	216,794 (63%)	Clinton (D)	93,758 (27%)	Johnson (L)	21,434 (6%)	
2012 Pres. Vote	Romney (R)	188,163 (58%)	Obama (D)	124,827 (39%)			

In the past 20 presidential elections North Dakota has voted only once for a Democratic nominee: Lyndon Johnson in 1964. So it came as no surprise that Donald Trump defeated Hillary Clinton here, 63%-27%. Clinton carried just two of the state's 53 counties, Rolette and Sioux, where the Native American population exceeds 75 percent. North Dakota was the state that turned most Republican in the 2016 election: Trump's margin over Clinton was 36 percentage points, a whopping 16-point increase from Mitt Romney's margin over Barack Obama in 2012. No other state saw such a large jump. Democrats can be competitive in North Dakota if they win Cass (Fargo) and Grand Forks (home to the University of North Dakota) counties, which have a relatively high share of white-collar workers. Republican strength is in the central and western part of the state where oil and natural gas production from the Bakken shale formation has had a significant impact on the state's economy.

North Dakota Democrats and Republicans use caucuses to help select their national convention delegates. In 2016 the state GOP declined to include a presidential preference poll at the first stage of its caucuses, opting to elect individuals to its state party convention, who would then select a delegation to the national Republican confab in Cleveland that was technically unbound to any candidate. When the state convention was held April 3, Texas Sen. Ted Cruz's campaign, as it had in other states with similar formats, got many of his supporters elected as national convention delegates. After Cruz suspended his campaign, many of the Cruz delegates switched their allegiance to Trump. The Democratic caucuses were held June 7. Vermont Sen. Bernie Sanders campaigned in Bismarck and won 64 percent of the county delegates selected to the state convention to Clinton's 26 percent, with 10 percent uncommitted.

Congressional Districts

116th Congress Lineup	1R	115th Congress Lineup	1R

Doug Burgum (R)

Elected 2016, term expires 2020, 1st term; b. Aug. 1, 1956, Arthur; North Dakota State University, BA 1978; Stanford University, MBA 1980; Married (Kathryn); 3 children.

Professional Career: CEO, Great Plains Software 1983-2001; Senior Vice President, Microsoft Business Solutions Group,2001-2007; Founder, Arthur Ventures.

Office: 600 E. Boulevard Ave., Bismarck, 58505-0001; 701-328-2200; Fax: 701-328-2205; Website: governor.nd.gov.

Lt. Gov.: Brent Sanford (R) **Atty. Gen:** Wayne Stenehjem (R) **Sec. of State:** Al Jaeger (R)
State Legislature: Senate: 10D, 37R **House:** 15D, 79R

Election Results

Election	Name (Party)	Vote (%)
2016 General	Doug Burgum (R)...	259,863 (77%)
	Marvin Nelson (D)...	65,855 (19%)
	Marty Riske (L)...	13,230 (4%)
2016 Primary	Doug Burgum (R)...	68,042 (59%)
	Wayne Stenehjem (R)...	44,158 (39%)

Doug Burgum, a successful software entrepreneur, was elected governor of North Dakota in 2016 after winning the Republican primary as an underdog and then prevailing easily in the general election. North Dakota voters, who have not voted Democratic for governor since 1988, made Burgum the third out of the state's four most recent governors to ascend to the office without having held a lower elective office. Burgum took the reins of a state that has grown substantially from oil and gas production, but which experienced ups and downs that affected the state's fiscal picture.

Burgum grew up near tiny Arthur, northwest of Fargo, and attended North Dakota State University, where he was a cheerleader. He earned an MBA at Stanford before returning to North Dakota. In 1983, he mortgaged the family farm to get into the computer business. He became CEO of Fargo-based Great Plains Software, expanded the company, took it public in 1997, then sold it to Microsoft for $1.1 billion in 2001, when it had 1,200 local employees. Burgum then led Microsoft Business Solutions for six years before founding a group to revitalize downtown Fargo and establishing a venture-capital firm.

After Gov. Jack Dalrymple said he would not seek another term, Burgum announced his intention to run for the seat. With a deep Republican bench in the state, others were ahead of him in the establishment queue, notably long-serving state Attorney General Wayne Stenehjem. Burgum seized the outsider's mantle, touting his business experience ("when I think about the governor's job, I like it because it's a CEO position," Burgum told Fortune) and announcing that he would forgo his gubernatorial salary if elected. At the state Republican convention in April, he finished a distant third behind Stenehjem and state Rep. Rick Becker. In the June primary, Stenehjem had the endorsements of Dalrymple, Sen. John Hoeven and most Republican state lawmakers. But amid a $1.6 billion state budget shortfall and the Republican surge for Donald Trump, Burgum's outsider approach proved to be more effective with rank-and-file primary voters. Burgum endorsed Trump in May and spoke more favorably about him than Stenehjem did. Burgum defeated Stenehjem, 59%-39%, carrying 49 of North Dakota's 53 counties.

The general election was anticlimactic, as the Democrats put up under-funded state Rep. Marvin Nelson. Burgum won, 77%-19%. That 58-point margin was double Dalrymple's already substantial 29-point victory in 2012. Nelson won only two counties, down from the six won by the Democratic nominee in 2012. Strikingly, Burgum increased the GOP's winning margins from 2012 by roughly double digits in each of the state's four most populous counties – Cass (Fargo), Burleigh (Bismarck), Ward (Minot) and Grand Forks.

Upon taking office, Burgum kept most of Dalrymple's cabinet and sought more extensive spending cuts to balance the state budget with declining tax revenues from oil and gas. Drawing from his own background, Burgum touted the role of technology in economic growth and the diversification of the state's economy. In his first state of the state address, he choked up while telling the story of a young man he had met in Fargo who was homeless, suffering from addiction to methamphetamine, and facing a parole violation. "Jail time without rehab is not a cure for addiction," Burgum said. "We need to start treating addiction like the chronic disease it is, and by moving these services upstream we will save lives and we will save taxpayer money." His wife, Kathryn Helgaas Burgum, overcame alcohol addiction and now spearheads a statewide "Recovery Reinvented" initiative. (In 2019, Burgum signed a bill eliminating mandatory minimums for some drug crimes. And another bill effectively decriminalizing small amounts of marijuana.)

Burgum supported the Dakota Access Pipeline, which had drawn intense protests on environmental and cultural grounds from the Standing Rock Sioux tribe and a band of celebrity allies. Burgum said he offered a "fresh start" to critics of the pipeline, which was eventually green-lighted by Trump. Weeks after taking office, Burgum signed a bill to allow the carrying of concealed firearms without a permit. The state's fiscal picture had a roller-coaster couple of years, due in part to fluctuating conditions in the oil and gas industry. Burgum signed a budget in 2017 that cut general fund spending by 28 percent. Two years later, with the industry in a better position, he proposed a larger budget, including increases for K-12 education, roads, behavioral health and employee pay. Burgum urged spending a portion of the state's Legacy Fund – a voter-created account funded by oil and gas revenue – on such projects as a proposed Theodore Roosevelt Presidential Library and infrastructure for developing and deploying drones. The focus on unmanned aircraft "will ensure that North Dakota remains America's proving ground" for drones, "which is good for our economy and taxpayers," he said.

Burgum and the legislature skirmished over the limits of the governor's line-item veto powers. The state Supreme Court ruled in 2018 that several of Burgum's vetoes had been too surgical. But the court also found that the legislature had invested too much power in a small committee to make budget decisions during the long stretches when the legislature was out of session. The latter part of the court's decision raised the question of whether the legislature needed to meet annually instead of for 80 days every two years. Meanwhile, Burgum established a task force to reconsider how the state's 11 public colleges and universities were governed. "We've got these powerful economic forces that are being driven by rapid changes in technology," Burgum told Inside Higher Ed, arguing that it's "time to take a look and say, 'Does a governance model that was built in 1939 give all the tools to our higher education system that it needs to allow them to be nimble and responsive in a time of rapid change?'" After 10 months of deliberations, the panel recommended establishing one board for community and regional institutions and one each for the state's two research institutions. "With increased bandwidth, these boards would work more directly with institutions and enhance accountability of their leadership. And they would be better able to focus more deeply on the institutions' individual missions, challenges and opportunities," Burgum wrote in applauding the panel's recommendation. The proposal would need approval from voters.

John Hoeven (R)

Elected 2010, term expires 2022, 2nd term, b. Mar 13, 1957; Bismarck; Dartmouth College, Hanover (NH), B.A., 1979; Northwestern University Kellogg School Management (IL), M.B.A., 1981; Roman Catholic; Married (Mikey Hoeven); 2 children; 3 grandchildren.

Elected Office: ND Governor, 2000-2010.

Professional Career: Executive Vice President., First Western Bank, 1986-1993; President & CEO, Bank of ND, 1993-2000.

DC Office: 338 RSOB 20510, 202-224-2551, Fax: 202-224-7999, hoeven.senate.gov

State Offices: Bismarck, 701-250-4618; Fargo, 701-239-5389; Grand Forks, 701-746-8972; Minot, 701-838-1361.

Committees: *Agriculture, Nutrition & Forestry*: Commodities, Risk Management & Trade; Nutrition, Agricultural Research & Specialty Crops; Rural Development & Energy. *Appropriations*: Agriculture, Rural Development, FDA & Related Agencies (Chmn); Department of Defense; Department of Homeland Security; Energy & Water Development; Military Construction & Veteran Affairs & Related Agencies; Transportation, HUD & Related Agencies. *Energy & Natural Resources*: Energy; National Parks; Public Lands, Forests & Mining. *Indian Affairs (Chmn)*.

Group Ratings

	ADA	ACLU	AFL-CIO	LCV	ITI	COC	HAFA	ACU	CFG	FRC
2018	-	5%	-	7%	-	90%	62%	73%	47%	100%
2017	0%	C	0%	0%	C	86%	C	80%	77%	100%

Almanac Ratings 2017-18

	Economy	Social	Foreign	Composite
Liberal	0%	0%	0%	0%
Conservative	100%	100%	100%	100%

Key Votes of the 115th Congress

1. Obama-care revision	Y	5. Gun regulations	Y	9. Kavanaugh confirmation	Y
2. Tax Cuts	Y	6. Family planning regs	Y	10. Saudi arms sales	N
3. Dodd-Frank revision	Y	7. Gorsuch confirmation	Y	11. FISA rules	Y
4. Omnibus appropriations	Y	8. Immigration restrictions	Y	12. Military aid in Yemen	N

Election Results

Election	Name (Party)	Vote (%)		Cand. Spent	Ind. Exp. Support	Ind. Exp. Oppose
2016 General	John Hoeven (R)	268,788	(79%)	$2,055,899		
	Eliot Glassheim (D)	58,116	(17%)	$32,799		
	Robert Marquette (L)	10,556	(3%)			
2016 Primary	John Hoeven (R)	Unopposed				

Prior winning percentages: 2010 (76%), Governor: 2008 (74%), 2004 (71%), 2000 (55%)

North Dakota's senior senator, John Hoeven, became the first Republican Senator from that state in 24 years. He presided over the state's new prosperity — from an oil and gas boom — for a decade as governor and was elected to the Senate in a breeze. He has been a reliable member of the GOP team, though he occasionally has taken issue with President Donald Trump — especially on home state issues. His re-election in 2016 with 78 percent of the vote reaffirmed his popularity.

Hoeven was born in Bismarck and grew up in Minot. His father was a banker who in 1969 took over the First Western Bank & Trust of Minot, which became a family business. Hoeven started working there as a bookkeeper at 15. He graduated from Dartmouth College and went on to earn his master's degree in business administration from Northwestern University. He later returned home to become First Western Bank's executive vice president. In 1993, he was chosen to head the Bank of North Dakota, the only state-owned bank in the country, by a board that included his predecessor as governor, Republican Ed Schafer, and then-Attorney General Heidi Heitkamp, a Democrat. Under Hoeven's stewardship, the bank's worth rose from $990 million to $1.6 billion, and its loan portfolio increased from $200 million to $1 billion. Hoeven's banking career and successful investments have placed him among the 25 wealthiest members of Congress, according to Roll Call's survey of congressional assets. Financial disclosure forms show him with a net worth of at least $17 million and possibly as much as $73 million.

Though he's credited with putting North Dakota in the red column, Hoeven had declared himself a Democrat as recently as four years before his 2000 election as governor. In a 1996 letter to a local newspaper, Hoeven wrote: "I have always been moderate in my political views, but now that I am considering elective office, I realize I must join a political party and stick to it. I have decided to join the Democratic-NPL Party because I believe that is the best fit for my views." The Bank of North Dakota was created in 1919 at the initiative of the Nonpartisan League, a coalition of reformers and radicals that was a major force in North Dakota for decades before it merged with the state Democratic Party in 1960. When the letter surfaced during Hoeven's 2010 Senate bid, his campaign manager, Don Larson, told Talking Points Memo that, shortly after writing the letter, Hoeven "realized his views were more in line with the Republicans than the Democrats. So, he got involved with the Republican Party, became a Republican district chairman, helped Republican candidates around North Dakota and then ran for and won the governorship. Before that, he had not been involved in politics at all, either as a Republican or a Democrat." Throughout his tenure as governor and a senator, Hoeven has been in the conservative Republican mainstream on most social issues, ranging from abortion to gun control. Unlike those in the party's tea party wing, Hoeven has been open to committing increased funds for education and infrastructure; while he was governor, the state budget increased dramatically, especially for those categories.

In 2000, after Schafer retired, Hoeven ran for governor against Heitkamp. He cited his work attracting and retaining local jobs and organizing the effort to keep Minot Air Force Base off the government's base closure list. He called for economic development in the state with an emphasis on the technology industry and on improving education, and he pledged more money for teacher training and salaries. He won 55%-45%, as Heitkamp was compelled to all but end her campaign after she was diagnosed with breast cancer.

As governor, Hoeven used North Dakota's burgeoning state revenues to fund programs to stimulate economic development. In 2002, he announced an ambitious research and development program, borrowing $50 million for university projects to commercialize new technology. From 2005 to 2007, more than $40 million in state funds and double that amount in private funds were invested in several research centers. Much of this was aimed at exploiting North Dakota's abundant energy resources, including oil, coal, ethanol, wind, and hydrogen. In 2002, he announced his EmPower North Dakota energy plan, aimed at building three biodiesel plants by 2015 and having wind supply 10 percent of the state's electricity by 2015. By 2014, wind energy supplied 17.5 percent of electricity generated in North Dakota.

During his second term, Hoeven submitted budgets with reductions in local property taxes and big increases in education spending, especially for raising teachers' salaries. Despite the pleas of national Republicans, he opted not to challenge Democratic Sen. Kent Conrad in 2006. In 2008, he won a third term against state Sen. Tim Mathern, capturing nearly 75 percent of the vote. By all indications, Democratic Sen. Byron Dorgan was planning to run for a fourth term — he had been raising money for the campaign — until he stunned Senate colleagues in January 2010 by saying he would retire. Shortly thereafter, Hoeven announced he was running for the open Senate seat, criticizing President Barack Obama's economic agenda and what he called the overly bureaucratic overhaul of the health care system. He didn't have to campaign very hard. Democratic nominee state Sen. Tracy Potter struggled for attention and momentum. Hoeven spent $4 million; Potter spent $28,000. Hoeven won 76%-22%.

Hoeven got seats on the Appropriations and Agriculture committees; he worked on the 2014 farm bill that renewed federal agriculture and nutrition programs. Hoeven supported an earlier version of the bill that cleared the Senate in 2012, which ended direct payments to farmers but included a new form of crop insurance favored by farm-state senators outside the South. Both features were included in the final 2014 legislation. Hoeven also worked to ensure that the legislation contained an extension of the sugar program — important to North Dakota, one of the nation's leading producers of sugar beets, but controversial among critics who complain it has raised the cost of sugar for consumers.

On the next farm bill, in 2018, Hoeven called crop insurance "the primary risk management tool for many producers" and cited a countercyclical safety net that he added to the coverage that was designed to reduce disparity in protection between counties. He worked on another provision in the final agreement to ensure producers have access to enough capital. "This increased credit is especially helpful to young producers," he said.

On the Energy and Natural Resources Committee, Hoeven advocated a national energy plan similar to EmPower North Dakota — an approach that encompassed renewable and traditional energy resources. He was an outspoken critic of Obama's decision to block construction of the Keystone XL pipeline, which was designed to carry 100,000 barrels of oil a day from Canada to the Gulf Coast, partly through North Dakota. In 2012, Hoeven offered a bill to reinstate the project; even with the support of 11 Democrats, it failed to attain the 60 votes needed to stymie a filibuster. With the Senate in Republican control in 2014, Hoeven led the effort to allow the pipeline to move ahead; it cleared the House and Senate. Pipeline advocates fell five votes short of the two-thirds majority needed to override Obama's veto. Hoeven helped get the pipeline OK'd in early 2017 by Trump.

Hoeven played a leading role in another pipeline controversy. In 2016, members of the Standing Rock Sioux Tribe protested the Dakota Access pipeline — built to transport 470,000 barrels of oil daily from North Dakota to Illinois — that grazes its reservation. Tribal opponents of the project said it violated a 170-year-old treaty with the U.S. government and that a leak in the pipeline — routed to run under a reservoir adjacent to the reservation — could have disastrous consequences for drinking-water supplies. As the Sioux were joined by thousands of Native American allies, the protests attracted international attention as a symbol of the continuing fight for Native American rights. Hoeven rebuked the protests as often violent and disruptive of the economic livelihood of farmers and ranchers in the area.

In a Senate speech in November, Hoeven dismissed the arguments against the pipeline as specious, noting, the pipeline had been "twice challenged and twice upheld — including by the Obama administration's own appointees" and saying "the federal courts found that the Army Corps had followed the appropriate process, the Standing Rock Sioux Tribe was properly consulted and the project could lawfully proceed." However, while Obama was still in office, the Army Corps of Engineers denied an easement to allow pipeline builders to burrow under the reservoir. As it had with the Keystone pipeline, the Trump administration quickly reversed that decision and granted the easement, although tribal leaders vowed to continue to fight.

Given this history, Hoeven's ascension in early 2017 to the normally low-profile chairmanship of the Senate Indian Affairs Committee stirred controversy among progressive activists. In December 2018, he won enactment of his bill to give Native American tribes greater flexibility to manage their energy resources by streamlining their agreement with the Interior Department. The measure was supported by tribes in North Dakota, where about one-fifth of state's oil production is on the Fort Berthold Indian Reservation.

While he has targeted federal regulations that he thinks have stifled innovation and are onerous for state and local governments, Hoeven is not a hard-line conservative. He was one of 15 Republicans to vote to reauthorize the Violence Against Women Act in 2012. In early 2013, he supported the bipartisan immigration overhaul pushed by Republican Sens. Marco Rubio of Florida and John McCain of Arizona and was one of 12 Republicans to vote to raise the limit on how much debt the government could amass. Later that year, he was one of only nine Senate Republicans to back a bipartisan budget deal crafted by the chairmen of the Senate and House budget committees that conservative groups criticized as spending too much.

Continuing his gubernatorial efforts to spur economic development through commercialization of technology, Hoeven joined Democratic Sen. Cory Booker of New Jersey in 2015 on legislation to set guidelines for drones — an effort to promote increased commercial use of unmanned aircraft. At the end of 2016, he helped gain approval from the Federal Aviation Administration for a drone test site in Grand Forks. That site became the first in the nation to have beyond-line-of-sight operability.

In the 2016 campaign, Hoeven spent more than $2 million while running against state Rep. Eliot Glassheim. Glassheim, owner of a Grand Forks used-book store called Dr. Eliot's Twice Sold Tales, spent a mere $33,000. Hoeven won in a 78%-17% blowout, running 15 points ahead of Trump in the state. He took 52 of 53 counties: Glassheim won only Sioux, the only county entirely within the boundaries of the Standing Rock Sioux reservation.

Hoeven was rated as the GOP Senator who most consistently supported his party in 2017 and 2018, according to Pro Publica. In the Almanac vote ratings for that period, his scores were solidly conservative. Still, he voiced concern that while Trump's tariffs might benefit steel and other industries, "we want to be very careful to make sure that it doesn't hurt our [farmers'] ability to export in other areas." And he said early drafts of the Senate bill to repeal and replace the Affordable Care Act would have adversely affected health care providers in North Dakota; he voted for the final version, which failed to win Senate approval.

After a trip to Moscow in July 2018 with seven other Republican senators, Hoeven faced criticism about their secret dealings with Russian officials. "In a long political career in which he has avoided being nicked, being called a 'Red Square Republican' must sting a little," the West Fargo Pioneer editorial board wrote. Still, the challenges faced by Republicans seemed unlikely to affect Hoeven's support at home.

Kevin Cramer (R)

Elected 2018, term expires 2024, 1st term, b. Jan 21, 1961; Rolette; Concordia College (MN), B.A., 1983; University of Mary (ND), M.A., 2003; Evangelical; Married (Kris Neumann); 5 children (1 deceased); 5 grandchildren.

Elected Office: ND Public Service Commission, 2003-2012; U.S. House 2013-2019.

Professional Career: Director, Harold Schafer Leadership Foundation, 2001-2003; Director, ND tourism, 1993-1997; Chairman, ND Republican Party, 1991-1993.

DC Office: 400 RSOB 20510, 202-224-2043, cramer.senate.gov

State Offices: Fargo, 701-232-5094; Minot, 701-837-6141.

Committees: *Armed Services*: Airland; Emerging Threats & Capabilities; Strategic Forces. *Banking, Housing & Urban Affairs*: Economic Policy; Financial Institutions & Consumer Protection; Housing, Transportation & Community Development. *Budget. Environment & Public Works*: Clean Air & Nuclear Safety; Fisheries, Water, and Wildlife (Chmn); Transportation & Infrastructure. *Veterans' Affairs*.

Group Ratings (House)

	ADA	ACLU	AFL-CIO	LCV	ITI	COC	HAFA	ACU	CFG	FRC
2018	-	4%	-	3%	-	91%	42%	78%	51%	100%
2017	0%	C	16%	0%	C	93%	C	81%	58%	100%

Key Votes of the 115th Congress (House)

1. Obama-care revision	Y	5. Family planning regs	NV	9. Guantanamo prisoners	N
2. Tax Cuts	Y	6. Body cameras/immigration	N	10. Ground missiles, limit	N
3. Omnibus appropriations	Y	7. Abortion ban	N	11. Defense Dept. spending	Y
4. Dodd-Frank revision	NV	8. Concealed carry	Y	12. FISA rules	Y

Election Results

Election	Name (Party)	Vote (%)		Cand. Spent	Ind. Exp. Support	Ind. Exp. Oppose
2018 General	Kevin Cramer (R)	179,720	(55%)	$6,121,645	$807,062	$7,244,464
	Heidi Heitkamp (D)	144,376	(44%)	$18,948,236	$1,896,604	$8,518,167
2018 Primary	Kevin Cramer (R)	61,529	(88%)			
	Thomas O'Neill (R)	8,509	(12%)			

Prior winning percentages: House: 2016 (69%), 2014 (56%), 2012 (55%)

Republican Kevin Cramer was elected to the Senate in 2018 — the culmination of a long career in North Dakota politics that has had its ups and downs. He defeated Democratic Sen. Heidi Heitkamp 55%-44% — by far, the widest margin of the four GOP challengers who ousted Democratic senators in 2018. Although he hit some bumps on the campaign trail, Cramer benefited from what has become an overwhelming tilt to Republicans in his home state plus the eventual support of President Donald Trump. Heitkamp showed the resilience that had been the mark of her political career. But the odds were stacked against her and polls had shown for weeks before the election that her defeat was likely. Cramer, who served three terms in the House before his Senate election, had been a state GOP chairman and public utility commissioner. He has tended to his home state's oil and gas business.

Cramer grew up in Kindred, southwest of Fargo. Throughout high school, he worked for the same electric cooperative as his father. He got his bachelor's degree from the Lutheran Church-affiliated Concordia College in Minnesota, where he was a pre-seminary student majoring in social work. Cramer was inspired to get involved in politics by Ronald Reagan, whom he described as a "joyful conservative." He was a campaign aide to Sen. Mark Andrews in his failed 1986 re-election bid and worked for the state Republican Party, where he rose to executive director. At 30, he was the youngest-ever state party chairman. A self-described leader of a GOP "youth movement," he was courted by national party bigwigs. Looking back, Cramer said, he was "naïve enough" to be "quite bold — you might say reckless, even."

After serving as state tourism director, he ran for the House in 1996. Cramer lost to Democratic Rep. Earl Pomeroy 55%-43%. After the loss, Cramer became the state's economic development director. He ran for the House seat a second time but again lost to Pomeroy. He later called that run a political mistake that cost him the state party's endorsement when he ran for the seat in 2010. That year, in his third try, he dropped out before the GOP primary. From 2003 to 2012, he served on North Dakota's public service commission, helping oversee an energy-driven boom in the state economy. He worked for a foundation offering faith-based training for students at the University of Mary in Bismarck, where he earned a master's in management.

When Republican Rep. Rick Berg ran for the Senate in 2012, Cramer tried again, spurning the state party's endorsement and taking his campaign directly to the primary. He beat party-backed Brian Kalk, a fellow public service commissioner, 55%-45%. Against Democrat Pam Gulleson, a former state representative, Cramer ran as a strong social conservative, saying on his campaign website, "I hope you know that my public service is an extension of my service to Christ." He called himself "a strong advocate for the free market system." Gulleson was competitive financially, but the state's Republican tilt gave the win to Cramer by 13 percentage points.

In the House, Cramer advocated for a host of North Dakota interests. He often told President Barack Obama "you're welcome" for the huge economic boost to the nation from oil and gas drilling in North Dakota and urged Obama to open more federal lands to production. He was one of the few congressional Republicans to support Obama's move to normalize relations with Cuba. In addition to the opportunity for agriculture sales, he said that the move was "an opportunity to influence an oppressed country." In 2016, he won enactment of a measure to set procedures for criminal background checks of adults working in foster care or tribal social service agencies. His Almanac vote ratings put him toward the center of the House Republican Conference.

On Energy and Commerce, Cramer took an interest in proposals designed to protect electricity consumers from higher costs imposed by Environmental Protection Agency regulation of power plants. He was an enthusiastic advocate for the completion of the Dakota Access pipeline, and he criticized the "political expediency" of the Obama administration for its delay in the face of court challenges. "I can't wait for the adults to be in charge on Jan. 20," Cramer said after the 2016 elections.

In 2014, Cramer faced a competitive contest with Democratic state Sen. George Sinner, the son of former Gov. George Sinner. The challenger complained that Cramer's campaign ads were dishonest and proposed "truth in politics" legislation. Cramer responded that his ads were true and that Sinner's proposal would violate the free speech guarantee of the First Amendment. Cramer won 56%-39%. His next re-election campaign was routine.

As one of seven House members who served single-district states, Cramer was well-positioned to run for Senate when the opportunity knocked. He was the front-runner among possible challengers to Heitkamp. Before their faceoff became official, both took steps to show their ambition and their reluctance to face each other in the election.

Soon after Heitkamp met with Trump in New York after the 2016 elections and showed interest in joining his Cabinet, reports surfaced that she was under consideration for Agriculture secretary. Cramer, in turn, had a well-publicized meeting with Senate Majority Leader Mitch McConnell to discuss the possibility that he would run in the special election for a vacant seat. At about the same time, he had his own meeting with Trump in New York to discuss the possibility of becoming secretary of Energy. During the presidential campaign, he had written a white paper for Trump about energy policy and his skepticism about climate change. Neither Heitkamp nor Cramer was selected for the Cabinet, though their political dances with Trump had begun.

While not having announced for a second term, Heitkamp was actively raising campaign funds in early 2017. "I'm taking the steps to prepare to run but am still in the process of making a decision," she said. While GOP leaders thought Cramer was the strongest challenger to Heitkamp, some Republicans were concerned about his penchant for making controversial comments. They were worried about a repeat of the 2012 campaign, in which Heitkamp narrowly defeated Berg, who was hurt by what was widely viewed as a poorly run campaign.

Despite facing an uphill fight to be re-elected, which was laid bare by Trump's 63%-27% win in North Dakota in 2016, Heitkamp maximized her opportunities. On the Senate Banking, Housing and Urban Affairs Committee, her strong support for the rollback of the Dodd-Frank financial reforms was instrumental in the bipartisan approval of the Senate-passed bill. She was the only Democrat to attend the White House bill-signing ceremony, where she stood in front of other supporters — including Cramer — and directly at Trump's side. Her efforts were applauded in endorsements by the American Bankers Association and other industry groups; Americans for Prosperity, the political network of the conservative Koch brothers, took the unusual step of backing a Democratic incumbent in a priority contest, including digital ads.

In June 2018, The Washington Post headlined a story about Cramer: "GOP candidate seethes as Trump embraces Democratic senator." Trump's positive remarks about and meetings with Heitkamp made other large conservative campaign donors reluctant to offend the president. The Club for Growth, for example, stayed neutral in the contest. As a result, Heitkamp outspent Cramer, $19 million to $6 million.; party committees from both sides spent more than $15 million on the contest — huge sums for a sparsely populated state. Reflecting the views of his home state's businesses, Cramer voiced disagreement with Trump's tight restrictions on immigrants. Trump's tariffs' adverse effects on North Dakota farmers — who included the three largest soybean producers in the nation — became another concern for Cramer.

These factors helped explain Cramer's caution and some public doubts about launching his candidacy. As he tended to his campaign, his victory gained a sense of inevitability. Cramer was bolstered by Trump's appearances at three rallies before the election. By mid-September, he had a double-digit lead in public polls. Probably the final strike against Heitkamp's election prospects was her opposition to Supreme Court nominee Brett Kavanaugh. Heitkamp, who was one of three Democratic senators who voted to confirm Neil Gorsuch to the court in 2017, concluded that Kavanaugh was "tearing our country apart;" she tried to shift the discussion to other issues, which proved difficult during the dramatic Senate hearings. Her decision on Kavanaugh "may just have been the final blow," Jennifer Duffy wrote in the Cook Political Report.

Cramer's victory marked the first time since 1960 that Republicans controlled both Senate seats from North Dakota.

Kelly Armstrong (R)

Elected 2018, 1st term, b. Oct 08, 1976; Dickinson; University of North Dakota, B.A., 2000; University of North Dakota, B.A., 2000; University of North Dakota School of Law, J.D., 2003; Lutheran; Married (Kjersti Armstrong); 2 children.

Elected Office: ND Senate, 2012-2018.

Professional Career: Attorney; Vice President, Armstrong Corp.

DC Office: 1004 LHOB 20515, 202-225-2611, armstrong.house.gov

State Offices: Bismarck, 701-354-6700; Fargo, 701-353-6665.

Committees: *Judiciary*: Antitrust, Commercial & Administrative Law; Constitution, Civil Rights & Civil Liberties; Immigration & Citizenship. *Oversight & Reform*: Subcommittee on Environment. *Select Committee on the Climate Crisis*.

Election Results

Election	Name (Party)	Vote (%)		Cand. Spent	Ind. Exp. Support	Ind. Exp. Oppose
2018 General	Kelly M. Armstrong (R)...................... 193,568	(60%)		$1,651,300	$44,384	
	Mac Schneider (D)........................... 114,377	(36%)		$732,556	$271,004	
	Charles Tuttle (I)................................ 13,066	(4%)				
2018 Primary	Kelly M. Armstrong (R)........................ 37,364	(56%)				
	Tom Campbell (R)......................... 17,861	(27%)				
	Tiffany Abentroth (R).................... 5,921	(9%)				
	Paul Schaffner (R)............................... 5,243	(8%)				

Republican Kelly Armstrong brought a diverse background as a House freshman. At home, he was a lawyer and a leader of his family business in energy and farming. His political experience included service in the state Senate, chairman of the state Republican Party and an ally of North Dakota's governor, Doug Burgum. When the House seat opened after GOP Rep. Kevin Cramer decided to challenge Sen. Heidi Heitkamp, his chief party rival withdrew after Armstrong was endorsed by the state Republican convention. During the campaign, he showed independence from President Donald Trump by criticizing the trade war with China as harmful to his home state's soybean exports.

Armstrong got his bachelor's and law degrees from the University of North Dakota. He served as vice president of Armstrong Corp., his family's oil and gas business, which has been active in farming and other commercial activities in the booming energy-production region in the western part of the state. Harold Hamm of Oklahoma, a billionaire oil investor and a pioneer of North Dakota drilling, has been a partner of the Armstrong projects. Hamm also has been a prominent financier of Republican politics, both nationally and in North Dakota.

Elected to the state senate in 2012, Armstrong chaired the Judiciary Committee. He helped to enact measures on issues ranging from criminal sentences to disputes over private mineral ownership.

Cramer announced his ultimately successful campaign for the Senate in February 2018, leaving Republicans a brief period to select a House candidate to succeed him. Armstrong, who called himself "a conservative guy with a conservative record," stepped down as chairman of the state party. That experience proved helpful as he won the endorsement of the Republican convention in April. State Sen. Tom Campbell, a potato farmer who had been seeking the GOP nomination to oppose Heitkamp before Cramer entered that contest, was the distant runner-up at the convention. Campbell subsequently reversed his decision to run in the House primary, though he was too late to remove his name from the ballot.

Armstrong, who described himself as a "Trump Republican," showed some independence from the president. In an interview with the Grand Forks Herald following the GOP convention, he warned that Chinese retaliation to the president's tariffs would harm North Dakota's soybean exports and other parts of the state's agriculture industry. "This cannot happen," he said.

In November, Armstrong defeated Democrat Mac Schneider, a former state Senate minority leader, 60%-36%.

OHIO

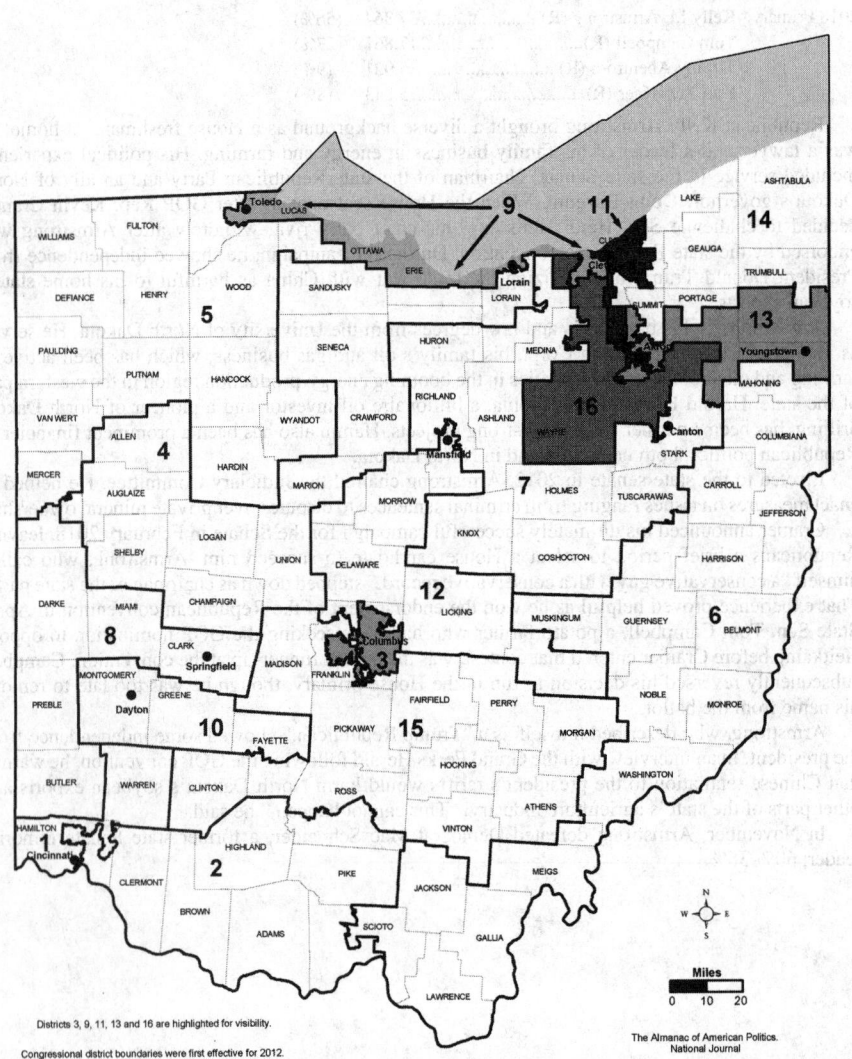

Districts 3, 9, 11, 13 and 16 are highlighted for visibility.

Congressional district boundaries were first effective for 2012.

The Almanac of American Politics.
National Journal

Ohio, a crossroads of the Midwest, was for a long time a bellwether state politically – it has not voted for a presidential loser since 1960. True to form, Ohio backed Barack Obama by three points in 2012 and Donald Trump by eight points in 2016. But Ohio's demographics – notably its disproportionately aging, white, working-class population – is putting the state's role as a bellwether in jeopardy, underlined by Ohio Republicans' strong showing in the otherwise Democratic-friendly midterm elections of 2018.

Ohio was the first entirely American state. The original 13 started as British colonies, and the next three — Vermont, Kentucky and Tennessee — were spun off from them. But Ohio sprang, Athena-like, from the head of Congress, as the first state formed from the Northwest Territory. The Northwest Ordinance of 1787 established 6-mile-square townships, which imposed geometric order on diverse new American landscapes to the west. It set aside one square mile per township for public schools, and the land was soon peppered with schoolhouses and small colleges, the foundation stones of a literate republic. The ordinance prohibited slavery at a time when most northern states still had it, opening the way for free labor to clear fields, raise crops, and build mills and factories. In less than half a century, the former wilderness wrested from British-aided Indian control only in 1796 was one of the most productive parts of the young republic. In the years after the Civil War, Ohio became one of the great industrial states, the original headquarters of John D. Rockefeller's Standard Oil, the site of major steel mills along the narrow Cuyahoga and Mahoning rivers, and the location of the biggest soap companies, machine tool makers and tire manufacturers. Dayton was the home of the Wright brothers, who developed the airplane; Akron was the home of Harvey Firestone, B. F. Goodrich and F. A. Seiberling of Goodyear — the great tire manufacturers. Cincinnati was and is the headquarters of Procter & Gamble.

Ohio was settled by New Englanders in the northeast (in the Western Reserve) and by Virginians in the southwest, creating a split between the Southern-accented counties south of the National Road and U.S. 40 and the Yankee-accented cities and towns to the north. In the middle were the Amish, who moved west from Pennsylvania. (By 2013, Ohio was home to almost 74,000 Amish in 61 settlements, just slightly behind Pennsylvania; in places like Holmes County, their horse-drawn buggies are a common sight.) This split heritage was an early reason why Ohio became a closely divided state politically — and a nationally pivotal one. Ohio produced the winning candidate for president in 1896 and 1900, William McKinley, who inaugurated a 34-year period of mostly Republican national majorities. McKinley's Republicans were for high tariffs and hard money and had a friendly regard for workers and even some unions, but they had no patience with large unions. They preached a nationalist Americanism tempered by wariness about making major commitments abroad. Republicans were the majority in this increasingly industrial Ohio, losing rural Butternut counties but carrying the big industrial cities of the north.

Then came the Great Depression of the 1930s, and Ohio became the scene of class warfare, with sit-down strikes and victories for industrial unions in autos, steel and tires. CIO cities — Cleveland, Akron, Youngstown and Toledo — moved sharply toward the Democrats, while places with fewer union members, such as Cincinnati and Columbus, stayed Republican. The political fighting was fierce and the stakes were high. CIO leaders hoped to organize the entire workforce, but Republican leaders like Ohio Sen. Robert Taft feared that union control of business would imperil freedoms and throttle the economy. In the 1930s and 1940s, unions made great gains, but Taft prevailed in hotly contested campaigns in 1944 and 1950, allowing him to curb union power with such legislation as the Taft-Hartley Act of 1947. Ohio thrived in the industrial economy after World War II, with new auto and auto-parts plants going up and its population rising. In those years it was often said that Ohio was a great test market – close to the national average in income levels, urban-rural balance, ethnic mix and partisan proclivities. The typical American voter, wrote Richard Scammon and Ben Wattenberg in 1970, was a Dayton housewife whose brother-in-law was a machinist and who was hoping one of her children might go to college.

But Ohio is not so typical today: It remains industrial in an increasingly post-industrial country. In Ohio, manufacturing accounted for 16.6 percent of state GDP in 2017, compared with 12 percent for the nation as a whole. The ArcelorMittal steel mill in Cleveland – once again operating after being closed in 2002 – makes specialized, advanced-technology steel that allows it to compete against cheaper foreign competitors. But like other industrial operations in an era of automation, the mill employs far fewer employees than it once did. Ohio's manufacturing economy has been shrinking relative to other sectors of the economy. Manufacturing accounted for 18.2 percent of Ohio's jobs in 2000 but just 12.5 percent in 2017; the number of manufacturing workers in the state declined by 324,000 during that span. Median income has remained mired in the bottom third of states.

Still, Ohio was slowly adapting to new economic realities. The recovery of the auto industry after the Great Recession boosted Ohio. Site Selection magazine ranked greater Cincinnati fifth among large metro areas for economic development; Columbus ranked eighth. Akron, once hailed as the tire and rubber capital of the world, has attracted new jobs in polymers, information technology and biomedical engineering, and its jobless rate has fallen below the state average. The development of the Marcellus and Utica shale formations that lie under much of eastern Ohio, has been driven by horizontal drilling and hydraulic fracturing — fracking — enabled drillers to tap into huge reservoirs of oil and natural gas. The growth in health services is underscored by the economic impact of the world-renowned Cleveland Clinic, which has helped midwife hundreds of biomedical firms, including Invacare, Philips Healthcare and Steris. Agriculture remained a significant industry; Ohio ranks second nationally in egg production, third in tomatoes and pumpkins, fifth in bell peppers, and sixth in sweet corn and cucumbers. But the state suffered a blow in November 2018, when General Motors announced plans to shutter its Lordstown plant near Youngstown that had produced the Chevy Cruze. While the steel industry showed signs of expansion amid tariffs imposed by Trump, the gains were scattered; the Trump trade policy worried the state's carmakers, who used steel as an input, and Ohio's soybean farmers, who feared retaliatory tariffs on the one-third of their $2.5 billion crop that's exported to China. Meanwhile, Ohio's opioid overdose death rate ranked second only to neighboring West Virginia.

The state's population has stagnated in recent decades. Between 1970 and 2010, Ohio's population grew by only 8 percent, a lower rate than any other state except New York, West Virginia, Pennsylvania and Iowa. Since the 2010 census, Ohio's population has grown by just 1.3 percent, putting the state in danger of losing one of its 16 House seats after the 2020 census. During that period, only two of the state's 10 most populous counties grew by more than 2 percent, led by Franklin County (Columbus), which expanded by a healthy 9.8 percent. "Columbus, home of the state capital and Ohio State University, is riding a knowledge economy into prosperity. Buildings are going up and being renovated as new businesses arrive chasing a growing population," wrote NBC News' Dante Chinni and Deepa Shivaram. By contrast, they wrote, Montgomery County (Dayton) has seen its population decline slightly since 2010, and both the city and the county have seen their median household incomes fall by more than $9,000 during that time. The jobs that remain pay less.

African Americans make up 12 percent of the population, a reflection of the great northward migration of 1940-65. But part of the reason for Ohio's slow population growth has been a relative lack of Hispanics: The state ranks in the bottom 10 for the percentage of residents who are Hispanic. The percentage of foreign-born residents in Ohio is about 4 percent, far below the national average of 13 percent.

Cleveland has moved past its days as the "mistake by the lake" in the 1960s and '70s. The city still faces some challenges, including a 2015 consent decree to impose new standards and monitoring on the use of force by the city's police department, the progress on which was deemed lagging in 2018. However, downtown Cleveland has blossomed – a clear lesson that visitors and media took away from the 2016 Republican National Convention. Indeed, 2016 was a banner year for the city. The city opened the renovated Public Square, transforming the asphalt-heavy, traffic-snarled plaza into a lush urban park designed by landscape architect James Corner, who had designed Manhattan's celebrated High Line. In the spring, the NBA's Cleveland Cavaliers, led by local hero LeBron James, won the championship and prompted a massive victory parade. Then in the fall, the Cleveland Indians made it to the World Series, losing in extra innings in the seventh game to the Chicago Cubs.

Post-New Deal, Ohio has had two politically distinct regions. Traditionally, Northeast Ohio — centered on Cleveland and extending west to Toledo and south and east to the factory towns of Akron and Canton, Youngstown and Warren — has been the state's Democratic heartland, with the highest percentages of union members and African Americans. The other part of Ohio — south and west of the industrial belt and including Columbus, Cincinnati and Dayton — was never as heavily unionized and in national elections tended to vote Republican, like most of neighboring Indiana, although not always by wide margins. These patterns began shifting in recent years. Metro Columbus has trended Democratic and provided key votes for Barack Obama in 2008 and 2012. At the same time, the hill country along the Ohio River — coal country and now shale oil country — has trended sharply Republican.

These shifts intensified in the 2016 presidential election. It became clear during the campaign that, given its demographics, Ohio was ripe for Trump to flip to the GOP column. On Election Day, it was a romp: A three-point winning margin for Obama in 2012 became an eight-point margin for Trump in 2016. Clinton's raw vote total fell by a stunning 433,000 compared with Obama in 2012, as Trump outperformed Mitt Romney by 180,000. Clinton won eight counties, half as many as Obama. Even in some of the counties that remained blue, the Democratic margins narrowed significantly, shrinking by 25 points in Mahoning County (Youngstown), by 14 points in Lorain County (west of Cleveland), by 12 points in Lucas County (Toledo), and by seven points in Summit County (Akron).

Democrats across the country generally fared well in the 2018 midterms, but that wasn't the case in Ohio. While populist, labor-friendly Democratic senator Sherrod Brown was reelected, a credible Democratic gubernatorial candidate, Richard Cordray, lost to Republican Mike DeWine, and the GOP won the other four statewide executive offices on the ballot. When the Cook Political Report issued its initial handicapping for the 2020 presidential race, Ohio, the onetime bellwether, was rated Likely Republican. Still, Democrats could find a measure of hope in two developments. First, despite being badly outnumbered in the legislature, Democrats teamed up with some Republicans to elect Larry Householder, the more moderate of two Republican candidates for House speaker. Second, the state moved forward on a new plan for redistricting that promised to produce a more competitive map than the strongly Republican one enacted after the 2010 census. The procedural changes passed the legislature with bipartisan support and won the voters' endorsement by a 3-to-1 margin.

Population		Race and Ethnicity		Income	
Total	11,609,756	White	79.6%	Median Income	$52,407
Land area (sq. miles)	40,861	Black	12.1%	State Income Rank	34
Pop/ sq mi	284.1	Latino	3.6%	Poverty Rate	14.9%
Born in state	75.1%	Asian	2.0%	With health insurance	92.6%
		Two or more races	2.3%	Cash public assistance	3.1%
Age Groups		Other	0.2%	Food stamp/SNAP	14.2%
Under 18	22.6%				
18-34	22.2%	**Education**		**Work**	
35-64	39.3%	H.S grad or less	43.8%	White Collar	36.0%
Over 64	15.9%	Some college	29.0%	Sales and Service	40.6%
		College Degree, 4 yr	17.0%	Blue Collar	23.4%
Military		Post grad	10.2%	Government	12.0%
Veteran/ Active Duty	8.5%				

Presidential Politics

2016 Primary (D)	Clinton (D)	696,681 (56%)	Sanders (D)	535,395 (43%)	
2016 Primary (R)	Kasich (R) 933,886 (47%)	Trump (R) 713,404 (36%)	Cruz (R) 264,640 (13%)		
2016 Pres. Vote	Trump (R) 2,841,006 (51%)	Clinton (D) 2,394,169 (43%)	Johnson (L) 174,498 (3%)		
2012 Pres. Vote	Obama (D) 2,827,709 (51%)	Romney (R)2,661,437 (48%)			

In the last 31 presidential elections, Ohio has sided with the winner in all but two: 1944, when it cast its votes for Thomas Dewey over Franklin D. Roosevelt; and 1960, when it favored Richard Nixon over John F. Kennedy. No Republican has ever captured the White House without carrying Ohio. No Democrat, given recent electoral vote arithmetic, can ignore it.

The critical role that Ohio plays was reflected in the intensity of campaigning there in 2016. Second only to Florida, Ohio saw the biggest barrage of television ads. Hillary Clinton pulled out all the stops in her quest to corral the state's 18 electoral votes. In the closing days of the campaign, Beyonce and Jay Z headlined a concert in Cleveland. At a separate event, basketball superstar LeBron James introduced Clinton. Trump campaigned vigorously too, but without the support of one of his chief rivals for the GOP nomination, Ohio Gov. John Kasich, who never endorsed him. And after

Trump's taped comments about groping women were released in early October, a number of Ohio Republicans, including Sen. Rob Portman and State Auditor Dave Yost, repudiated their support. Yet amid all that strife, Trump handily defeated Clinton, 52%-44%. Clinton won just eight of the state's 88 counties: Athens (Ohio University), Cuyahoga (Cleveland), Franklin (Columbus), Hamilton (Cincinnati), Lorain (working-class Cleveland suburbs), Lucas (Toledo), Mahoning (Youngstown), and Summit (Akron). It was a remarkable turnaround from the 2008 and 2012 presidential elections, when Barack Obama won. In dozens of counties, the falloff in the percentage of voters who cast ballots for Clinton compared with the percentage who voted for Obama was dramatic. Agricultural counties like Marion and Tuscarawas where Obama was competitive with Romney in 2012 became more than 30-point Trump blowouts. Blue-collar counties like Ashtabula, Ottawa, Sandusky and Trumbull, all carried by Obama in 2012, flipped to Trump in 2016. Trump's criticism of trade deals like NAFTA — a striking policy departure from recent GOP presidential nominees — and his vow to restore manufacturing jobs played well in these depressed Rust Belt counties. Ashtabula went from a 12-point Obama victory to a 19-point Trump win. Obama won Trumbull by 22 points; Trump beat Clinton there by six.

In 1996, Ohio switched its presidential primary from May to March. In 2008, the Republican contest was effectively over when Ohio voted. Mike Huckabee remained an active candidate, but John McCain beat him 60%-31%, carrying all 88 counties. There was a spirited contest on the Democratic side, with Clinton besting Obama 53%-45%. She ran well in the Mahoning Valley steel and the Democratic-leaning smaller industrial counties along the Ohio River. In 2012, the March 7 GOP primary was a pivotal contest between Mitt Romney and Rick Santorum. Romney won narrowly, 38%-37%, and secured his path to the GOP nomination.

In 2016, the March 15 GOP presidential primary featured a spirited Trump-Kasich faceoff. Trump accused Kasich of being an "absentee governor," and blasted him for voting for NAFTA when he was in the House. Kasich, who was fond of saying he ran an "unwavering, positive" campaign, nonetheless noted the "toxic atmosphere" at Trump rallies and told a town hall before the primary, "Ohio is going to send a message that we don't accept those kinds of tactics." Buckeye voters gave their governor a 47%-36% victory. But the GOP results pointed toward Trump's strength in the state in the fall: he won 32 of the state's counties, most of which were in an arc from the Mahoning Valley in the northeast corner through the Appalachian region and along the Ohio River to the outskirts of Cincinnati. In the Democratic primary, Clinton rallied party regulars and cruised to a 56%-43% victory. She enjoyed the backing of the state's senior Democrat, Sen. Sherrod Brown. Clinton handily carried five counties she lost in the 2008 Democratic primary: Cuyahoga, Delaware, Franklin, Hamilton and Montgomery. She won 72 counties in all. Ohio does not have partisan registration, so voters are free to choose which party primary they participate in.

Congressional Districts

116th Congress Lineup	4D 12R	115th Congress Lineup	4D 12R

Ohio is projected to lose one seat in the next reapportionment. As was the case following the most recent redistricting, Republicans may find that they again are victims of their own success.

Following the 2010 census, the state lost two House seats in the reapportionment. That reduced the delegation to 16 members, the fewest since Ohio was frontier country in the 1820s. During the previous decade, the map had been somewhat competitive: Democrats won a 10-8 majority in 2008 and Republicans a 13-5 majority in 2010. Even with their complete control of redistricting, GOP strategists conceded that they had too many Democrats to allocate if they wanted to keep all 13 of their seats. To resolve the dilemma, they forced one pair of Democrats to run against each other in the Cleveland-Toledo area, and they weakened another Democrat by creating a heavily Democratic seat in the Akron-Youngstown corridor that favored Rep. Tim Ryan. Furthermore, for decades, Republicans had cracked Columbus into multiple districts to shortchange Democrats. But the state capital was growing and attracting progressive-minded voters at such a rate that neither the Republican-held 12th nor 15th might hold until 2020. So, under the watchful guidance of House Speaker John Boehner of Ohio, Republican legislative aides hatched an innovative scheme.

Republicans would pack Democrats into a new Columbus 3rd District. The creation of a Columbus Democratic vote sink would produce a beneficial ripple effect, allowing Republicans to shore up their freshmen and keep a 12-4 advantage.

The legislature and Gov. John Kasich easily approved the plan. To attract enough support to achieve the two-thirds support required to avoid a veto referendum in the next election, Republicans plotted minor changes designed to appease enough Democrats. Chiefly, those were allies of Toledo-based Marcy Kaptur, who got the better draw of the new district with Cleveland-based (and former presidential candidate) Dennis Kucinich. Republican Steve Austria, a low-key sophomore, retired, given the option of running in a district that favored Dayton-based Republican Mike Turner. Republicans got the 12-4 delegation they envisioned in a state that Barack Obama twice won.

Reforms of Ohio's redistricting procedures gained support after the 2014 election. Spurred by Republican Secretary of State Jon Husted, a bipartisan coalition voted for a compromise plan that transferred redistricting authority from a handful of statewide elected officials to a broader group that would require support from both parties. The plan, which was approved by 71 percent of voters in a November 2015 referendum, has limitations. At Boehner's urging, the new procedures did not apply to the state's congressional map, at least initially. In May 2018, voters approved a new referendum for congressional districts. The new rules require support for a redistricting plan by at least half of the members of each party in the legislature and limit the splitting of counties. If the legislature deadlocked, then a commission of elected officials would draw the map; without sufficient bipartisan support, the map would be subject to revision after four years. In May 2019, a three-judge federal court created a new wrinkle when it ruled that the Ohio congressional map was an unconstitutional partisan gerrymander that deprived many voters of their rights. In a unanimous ruling, the court ordered the state to draw new maps for the 2020 election, but the Supreme Court delayed that order, at least temporarily. Ohio Republicans have defended their map as an incumbent-protection plan.

Even if Republicans retain control of congressional redistricting, their House delegation again may have maxed out. Until 2018, none of the 12 GOP members had been seriously challenged for reelection. After Republican Rep. Pat Tiberi resigned early that year in one of those Columbus-area districts, Republican Troy Balderson struggled in the special election. Still, he held on. If that pattern continues through 2020, Republicans may discover that they face a situation comparable to a decade earlier when they had to sacrifice one of their own members. If they are unable to squeeze enough Democratic voters into three districts, one option is that the 12th Republican who has drawn the short straw could be matched in a "fair fight" with one of the three Democrats in northeast Ohio — though the African-American majority 11th District likely would be protected. In that scenario, the Republicans facing the greatest jeopardy would be those in the 6th, 7th, 14th and 16th districts. Many of the remaining Republicans in the Ohio delegation would find their districts moved a bit to the east.

Mike DeWine (R)

Elected 2018, term expires 2023, 1st term; b. Jan. 05, 1947, Springfield; Miami University of Ohio, B.S., 1969; Ohio Northern University, J.D., 1972; Roman Catholic; Married (Frances); 8 children.

Elected Office: Greene County Prosecutor, 1977-1981; OH Senate, 1981-1982; US House, 1983-1991; OH Lt. Gov., 1995-1997; US Senate, 1995-2007; OH Attorney General, 2011-2018.

Professional Career: Attorney.

Office: Riffe Center, 77 S. High St., 30th Floor,Columbus, 43215; 614-466-3555; Fax: 614-466-9354; Website: governor.ohio.gov

Lt. Gov.: Jon Husted (R) **Atty. Gen:** Dave Yost (R) **Sec. of State:** Frank LaRose (R)

State Legislature: Senate: 9D, 24R **House:** 38D, 61R

Election Results

Election	Name (Party)	Vote (%)
2018 General	Mike DeWine (R)..	2,231,917 (50%)
	Richard Cordray (D)...	2,067,847 (47%)
2018 Primary	Mike DeWine (R)..	499,639 (60%)
	Mary Taylor (R)..	335,328 (40%)

Mike DeWine, a fixture in Ohio politics for four decades, was elected governor in 2018, bucking a national Democratic edge in that year's midterms. DeWine, who became Ohio's oldest-ever governor at 72, defeated Democrat Richard Cordray, whom he had previously ousted as state attorney general in 2010. DeWine notched a three-point victory over Cordray in his bid to succeed term-limited Republican Gov. John Kasich, who had grown more popular among Ohio Democrats than Republicans after Kasich's criticism of President Donald Trump and departures from conservative orthodoxy.

DeWine grew up in Yellow Springs, the home of liberal Antioch College, where his family owned a successful seed business. DeWine's great-great-great-grandfather came from Ireland during the potato famine and settled in Yellow Springs. His mother, Jean, wrote a conservative column for the local Yellow Springs News in the 1960s. DeWine met his future wife, Frances Struewing, when they were first graders. They began dating during high school and married while both were attending Miami University. DeWine earned a law degree from Northern Ohio University and settled in Cedarsville, where he and his wife for years hosted an annual ice cream social. There, DeWine was elected Greene County prosecutor in 1976 at age 29. He resisted plea bargaining; once, in order to nail a drug dealer, he put up the collateral to get $50,000 in cash to stage a buy.

In 1980, at 33, he was elected to the state Senate. In 1982, when incumbent Clarence Brown ran for governor, DeWine won a six-way Republican primary for a seat in Congress with 69 percent of the vote. In 1990, he was elected lieutenant governor. Two years later, DeWine sought to unseat legendary astronaut and Democratic Sen. John Glenn. It was a hard-hitting campaign, as DeWine attacked Glenn for his part in the Keating Five political corruption case. Democrats brought up DeWine's 31 overdrafts on the House bank and the occasion in which he fell asleep during the Iran-Contra hearings. Glenn won, 51%-42%, but it was his closest general election margin ever. In 1994, DeWine ran for Senate again, this time to fill the seat of retiring Democrat Howard Metzenbaum. Metzenbaum was backing his son-in-law – Joel Hyatt, the founder of a legal chain – to succeed him. Hyatt narrowly won the Democratic primary, while DeWine defeated former National Institutes of Health Director Bernadine Healy in the GOP primary by a more comfortable margin. DeWine won in November, 53%-39%. In 2000, Democrats initially thought DeWine might be vulnerable, but no top-tier candidate surfaced; after vastly outspending his challenger – Ted Celeste, brother of former Democratic Gov. Dick Celeste – DeWine prevailed, 60%-36%, winning 83 of 88 counties.

A common motif of DeWine's time in Congress was a concern for children and families, shaped by the loss of his 22-year-old daughter Becky in a car accident in 1993. As chairman of the Appropriations Subcommittee on the District of Columbia – regarded on Capitol Hill as a thankless post -- DeWine worked to reform the city's child welfare system. He was also chief sponsor of a bill to make it a crime to injure or kill a fetus in the course of a federal crime; it passed, 61-38. A bipartisan bill he sponsored to provide $82 million for teen suicide prevention became law in 2004. On other issues, he worked with Democrats to back legislation on federal regulation of tobacco and antitrust enforcement. He bucked his party on drilling in the Arctic National Wildlife Refuge in 2002 and 2003, and joined the Gang of 14, a group of bipartisan moderates who opposed getting rid of the Senate filibuster. DeWine took a special interest in Latin America, traveling often to Haiti, Colombia and other countries. DeWine lost his Senate seat in 2006 to Democrat Sherrod Brown. DeWine defeated Cordray, the incumbent, to become attorney general in 2010. DeWine served two terms as attorney general.

DeWine announced he was running for governor at his family ice cream social. He was running to succeed Kasich, whose career in Ohio politics was almost as long as his own, including 18 years in the House and two terms as governor. In 2016, Kasich ran for president and outlasted 15 rivals before conceding the nomination to Trump. After the nomination was settled, the Trump and Kasich camps – both nationally and in Ohio – found themselves at odds. Kasich declined an offer to address the Republican National Convention in his home state, instead making the rounds of satellite events where he usually touted Republican themes without promoting the party's candidate. When he cast his early vote for president, Kasich said he wrote in Sen. John McCain's name rather than casting a ballot for Trump.

With GOP opinion of Kasich in the dumps, the initial Republican primary included DeWine, Lt. Gov. Mary Taylor, Secretary of State Jon Husted, and Rep. Jim Renacci. But early on, DeWine tapped Husted as his running mate, while Renacci chose to challenge Brown in the Senate contest instead. That left DeWine facing Taylor in a bare-knuckled fight for the nomination. Taylor had been an ally of Kasich, but as the campaign went on, she became more and more critical of the shape-shifting governor, seeking to align herself with the Republican base. The party establishment, however, strongly favored DeWine. The State Republican Party Central Committee gave DeWine its endorsement by a 59-2 vote. When the voters weighed in, DeWine defeated Taylor, 60%-40%.

The Democratic primary included Cordray, onetime Cleveland mayor and former Rep. Dennis Kucinich, former state Senate Minority Leader Joe Schiavoni, and former Ohio Supreme Court Justice Bill O'Neill. O'Neill drew attention – not exactly positive – for his preemptive revelation, amid a "national feeding frenzy about sexual indiscretions," that in the past 50 years, "I was sexually intimate with approximately 50 very attractive females." The primary eventually narrowed to a two-man contest – the progressive Cordray vs. the even more progressive Kucinich.

Cordray had served as Ohio solicitor general and was elected twice as treasurer in Franklin County (Columbus). He was elected state treasurer in 2006, then won a special election to fill a scandal-related vacancy as attorney general in 2008. After losing to DeWine in 2010, Cordray was tapped as the first director of the federal Consumer Financial Protection Bureau, where he boasted of recouping $12 billion for 30 million Americans. Kucinich, meanwhile, had a far more eclectic, even eccentric, record. The onetime "boy mayor" later served in Congress and ran quixotic campaigns for president in 2004 and 2008. For a time, it seemed like the left-leaning Democratic electorate might flock to him in the gubernatorial race. "Populist causes that he has championed forever despite derision and dismissal — universal health care, free college tuition, rethinking trade agreements, reining in the surveillance state, bringing troops home, making huge investments in infrastructure — are now mainstream positions within his own party," wrote David Montgomery in the Washington Post. "Kucinich has long been tuned to a political frequency that few heard until it became a roar." But Cordray also boasted progressive support, including from President Barack Obama, Sen. Elizabeth Warren and the state AFL-CIO, and his sober style seemed the safer choice for voters concerned about electability in November. Kucinich attacked Cordray for being soft on guns, while Cordray took issue with Kucinich's ties to the Assad regime in Syria. Backed by a superior war chest, Cordray won 62 percent, with Kucinich at 23 percent, Schiavoni at 9 percent and O'Neill at 3 percent.

The general election between DeWine and Cordray was dubbed a contest of nerds. Cordray was a multiple winner of Jeopardy! who "tweets Ohio trivia and strange observations regularly," the Cleveland Plain Dealer noted. DeWine, for his part, had an old-school approach, "handing out thousands of his wife's cookbooks a year" and arguably outwalking anyone in a small-town parade, the paper wrote. Cordray focused on health care, particularly on protecting Kasich's expansion of Medicaid under the Affordable Care Act; DeWine walked a tightrope on that issue, favoring scrapping the expansion during the primary but backing continuation, with some modifications, in the general election. The two also divided over social issues, including abortion, transgender rights and marijuana legalization. DeWine opposed Issue 1, a ballot measure that would reform the criminal justice approach to low-level drug crimes, while Cordray strongly favored it. For months, Kasich stayed out of the campaign, but despite efforts by Cordray to woo the outgoing governor and his supporters, he eventually campaigned for his fellow Republican.

DeWine prevailed, 50%-47%, even as other midwestern GOP gubernatorial candidates were losing. The Ohio contest reflected the statewide – and national – trend of Democrats cleaning up in more urbanized areas and Republicans doing the same in rural regions. Among the state's 10 most populous counties, Cordray won seven – Cuyahoga (Cleveland), Franklin (Columbus), Hamilton (Cincinnati), Summit (Akron), Lucas (Toledo), Lorain (Cleveland vicinity), and Mahoning (Youngstown). The only top-10 counties DeWine won were Montgomery (Dayton, by less than 1,000 votes), Butler (north of Cincinnati) and Stark (Canton). However, the cumulative returns from less populated areas added up to a DeWine victory. In May 2019, DeWine signed a "heartbeat bill" that would ban abortions after a fetal heartbeat is detected; it had been vetoed by Kasich. He also signed a 10.5 cent gas tax to fund road repairs.

Sherrod Brown (D)

Elected 2006, term expires 2024, 3rd term, b. Nov 09, 1952; Mansfield; Yale University (CT), B.A., 1974; Ohio State University, M.A., 1979; Ohio State University, M.P.A., 1981; Lutheran; Married (Connie Schultz); 2 children; 2 stepchildren; 6 grandchildren.

Elected Office: OH House, 1974-1982; OH Secretary of State, 1982-1990; U.S. House, 1993-2007.

Professional Career: Professor, OH St. University Mansfield, 1979, 1981, 1991.

DC Office: 503 HSOB 20510, 202-224-2315, Fax: 202-228-6321, brown.senate.gov

State Offices: Cincinnati, 513-684-1021; Cleveland, 216-522-7272; Columbus, 614-469-2083; Lorain, 440-242-4100.

Committees: *Agriculture, Nutrition & Forestry*: Commodities, Risk Management & Trade (RMM); Nutrition, Agricultural Research & Specialty Crops; Rural Development & Energy. *Banking, Housing & Urban Affairs (RMM)*: Ex Officio membership on all subcommittees. *Finance*: Health Care; International Trade, Customs & Global Competitiveness; Social Security, Pensions & Family Policy (RMM). *Veterans' Affairs*.

Group Ratings

	ADA	ACLU	AFL-CIO	LCV	ITI	COC	HAFA	ACU	CFG	FRC
2018	-	76%	-	100%	-	50%	3%	9%	5%	0%
2017	95%	C	100%	95%	C	29%	C	0%	4%	0%

Almanac Ratings 2017-18

	Economy	Social	Foreign	Composite
Liberal	97%	97%	88%	94%
Conservative	3%	3%	12%	6%

Key Votes of the 115th Congress

1. Obama-care revision	N	5. Gun regulations	N	9. Kavanaugh confirmation	N
2. Tax Cuts	N	6. Family planning regs	N	10. Saudi arms sales	Y
3. Dodd-Frank revision	N	7. Gorsuch confirmation	N	11. FISA rules	N
4. Omnibus appropriations	Y	8. Immigration restrictions	N	12. Military aid in Yemen	Y

Election Results

Election	Name (Party)	Vote (%)		Cand. Spent	Ind. Exp. Support	Ind. Exp. Oppose
2018 General	Sherrod Brown (D)	2,355,923	(53%)	$23,969,911	$4,855,471	$674,215
	Jim Renacci (R)	2,053,963	(47%)	$5,036,235	$491,708	$57,006

Prior winning percentages: 2012 (51%), 2006 (56%); House: 2004 (67%), 2002 (69%), 2000 (65%), 1998 (62%), 1996 (60%), 1994 (49%), 1992 (53%)

Now in his mid-60s, Democrat Sherrod Brown, Ohio's senior senator, has held elected office virtually his entire adult life. But, despite being on presidential nominee Hillary Clinton's shortlist for a running mate in 2016, Brown for years insisted he had little interest in a White House bid of his own. To run for president, "you have to really want the job. I don't really want the job," Brown told the Cleveland Plain Dealer's editorial board in October 2018. His view changed just weeks later, however, after comfortably winning a third term in a state that voted for President Donald Trump by an 8 percentage point margin two years earlier. "I mean — every politician who can put a complete sentence together, from a big state, somebody has said to them at some point, 'You oughta think about running'," Brown told New York magazine. "But it never occurred to me to actually do it until ... the response to election night." Brown said he had been overwhelmed by the number of people urging he consider a presidential run after a victory speech in which he characterized his campaign as a "blueprint for America in 2020" — particularly in Ohio and other Midwestern states that had swung to Trump in 2016 after going for President Barack Obama four years earlier.

In the weeks that followed, he touted his electoral success as proof that Democrats could pursue a progressive agenda — Brown boasted he would be the only candidate in a Democratic presidential debate to have voted against the Iraq War in 2002 and to have endorsed same-sex marriage two decades earlier — while also appealing to Trump's white, working-class base. Brown advocated an emphasis on what he coined "the dignity of work," with a platform that included not only raising the federal minimum hourly wage but also bolstering collective-bargaining rights and using the tax system to prod major corporations to share more of their profits with the workforce. "For too long, Democrats have not focused on these issues," he said before embarking on a tour of early presidential primary states. "We seem so happy about our success in the suburbs. But at the same time, we've been losing the working-class areas by bigger and bigger margins." But, in March, Brown said his tour had reassured him his party was focusing on organized labor and workers more than it had in 2016 and announced he had decided to remain in the Senate — where, as ranking Democrat on the Banking, Housing and Urban Affairs Committee, he has taken repeated aim at Wall Street. "The pull on me was always do my work here," he said just outside the Senate chamber.

The Senate seat Brown has occupied since his initial 2006 election had been held for nearly two decades by the late Howard Metzenbaum, with whom Brown is sometimes compared. Metzenbaum, a self-made multimillionaire, was dubbed "the last angry liberal." But he positioned himself as a populist whose frequent attacks on big business and other powerful interests gave him an appeal that transcended ideological lines in a perennial battleground state. In addition to being a friend of labor unions and a foe of the nation's big banks, Brown has been an outspoken critic of trade agreements; his views on trade are far closer to Trump's than they were to Obama's. Brown worked with the White House in 2018 as Trump revised the North American Free Trade Agreement, which Brown had voted against during his first term in the House. "I will get a number of Trump voters because I fought for the things that Trump campaigned on long before he did," Brown told Bloomberg News during his re-election race, adding that, except for trade, "I'm not a supporter of his." In an applause line he often used on the stump in 2018, Brown said: "The White House looks like a retreat for Wall Street executives, except for the days when it looks like a retreat for pharmaceutical executives. Right now, the special interests are prioritized over hardworking families."

Brown's rhetoric can be acidic. "When I see some fascist dictator called a populist, or I see Donald Trump called a populist, it just rankles me," he told Yahoo News in early 2019. "I mean, why do anyone even describe Trump as a populist? Because he says he's 'for people' and he has big rallies? So did Mussolini." Behind this sharp tongue is a personal style that is often cheerful and informal. Besides his fondness for wearing sneakers — always American-made — and off-the-rack suits sold not far from his Cleveland home, Brown is known for a voice that sounds perpetually hoarse and a mop of tousled hair that frequently appears in need of a comb. He is so often described as "rumpled" that it appears to be part of his given name. Brown loves to talk about baseball; "Damn Yankees" is the beginning of his personal email address. "I really didn't grow up with this dream of running for president," he told The Washington Post while exploring a White House candidacy. "My dream was to play center field for the Cleveland Indians."

Brown grew up in Mansfield in northeast Ohio. The son of a physician, he graduated from Yale University in 1974 and went directly to the campaign trail, winning a seat in the Ohio House that November as he was turning 22. He earned master's degrees in education and public administration from Ohio State University while serving in the Legislature. In 1982, he was elected secretary of state and worked to increase voter registration and turnout. After two terms, he lost in 1990 to Republican Bob Taft, a scion of Ohio's most famous political family and later the state's governor. It didn't take long for Brown to make a political comeback. In 1992, he won an open House seat that stretched from the western suburbs of Cleveland south to Akron. With solid labor support, Brown campaigned hard against NAFTA, which Congress eventually approved in 1993, while championing universal health care. He won 53%-35%. He had a close call in the Republican wave year of 1994, but, after that, was regularly re-elected with more than 60 percent of the vote.

Brown was among the most voluble "fair-trade" House members from the manufacturing-reliant Great Lakes region, attacking a string of trade agreements and free-trade policies that followed NAFTA. In 2005, he helped lead the effort to defeat the U.S.-Central American free trade agreement, which cleared the House by just two votes. One of two books he published during his House years was titled "Myths of Free Trade: Why American Trade Policy Has Failed."

Brown had eyed a return to statewide office, but, in 2005, initially said he would not challenge two-term Republican Sen. Mike DeWine. That left Iraq veteran Paul Hackett as the Democratic front-runner. But there were questions among party insiders about Hackett's viability as a candidate; Brown reconsidered and entered the race. Hackett withdrew, and Brown breezed to the Democratic nomination. DeWine, meanwhile, suffered from association with the Bush administration and from various scandals associated with the Republican-controlled state government. Brown charged that DeWine — elected governor in 2018 — was a "rubberstamp" for Bush. Brown won 56%-44%, carrying the major population centers and the area east of Interstate 77, where his opposition to free trade resonated in coal- and steel-dependent counties.

In the Senate, Brown's voting record has been as reliably liberal as it was in the House, even though he represents a state that has long been politically marginal and, in recent years, trended red. In 2015, Almanac vote rankings put him in a three-way tie for the Senate's most liberal voting record. However, he has refrained from co-sponsoring recent high-profile initiatives touted by fellow progressives — "Medicare For All" and the "Green New Deal." He has authored legislation to expand Medicare to allow a buy-in at 55. "I want to get something done: I see too many 58-year-olds and 62-year-olds whose plants have closed going without insurance," he said in early 2019. "Then, we move towards Medicare for All. But I just don't know how it happens in this political climate." Representing a coal-producing state, Brown has tread carefully on environmental issues. In 2010, the last time the Senate seriously endeavored to pass a climate change bill, he was point man for a bloc of Democrats that dubbed itself the "Brown Dogs;" its members refused to support the bill without more protections for U.S. firms on carbon emissions. More recently, he has worked to make Ohio a leader in wind energy production.

"In a place like Mansfield Ohio, where I grew up, which used to have six or eight major manufacturers and five dozen small manufacturers, most of them are gone," Brown told HuffPost in 2015. "The rest of them, by and large, will be gone, if we don't take care of worker enforcement on trade law and if we don't help those workers that lose their jobs." At the beginning of Obama's first term, as Congress passed a $787 billion economic stimulus measure, he fought to include requirements that the money be used on U.S.-made goods. The provision was included in versions of the bill that passed the House and Senate, but the final legislation allowed goods to be purchased from some of America's largest trading partners. He led a 2012 effort to persuade Obama to file a series of trade cases against China, which he accused of unfairly subsidizing auto-parts makers. With Trump in office, Brown split from many Democratic colleagues fearful of a trade war when he praised Trump's April 2018 imposition of tariffs on steel and aluminum from China and several U.S. allies. The "action finally sends a clear message to our trading partners that we aren't going to allow them to cheat Americans out of their jobs and infect global markets," he said.

Shortly after the 2016 elections, Brown wrote Trump urging renegotiation of NAFTA and received a note back from the president reading: "Great letter. I will never let our workers down. Best wishes!" Brown worked with administration officials — notably Trade Representative Robert Lighthizer, a native of Ashtabula Ohio — as deals were reached to replace NAFTA. But, after initially offering tentative praise for the new U.S.-Canada-Mexico trade agreement, he objected to what he considered insufficient protections for workers. "The work is not done yet," Brown told CNN, adding, "We can go back to the table with the Mexicans and the Canadians and do stronger labor standards." Brown also urged Trump to withdraw from the Trans-Pacific Partnership, a 12-nation trade pact negotiated by Obama; Trump did that, within a week of taking office.

In 2015, Brown became ranking member on the Banking Committee. Before the 2014 elections, with Senate control in the balance, one bank executive anonymously told The Washington Post that the prospect of Brown becoming committee chairman was "frightening." The next two years were not productive for the Banking panel, amid a bumpy relationship between Brown and the chairman, Alabama Republican Richard Shelby. The two produced competing bills to revise the 2010 Dodd-Frank law on financial reforms; Shelby's bill cleared the panel but went no further, amid the prospect of a Democratic filibuster. Brown was happy to see Idaho Republican Mike Crapo replace Shelby as chairman at the end of 2016, because of GOP term limit rules. "We have a working relationship. He's way more conservative than I am, but he's straightforward and honorable," Brown said of Crapo, according to The Hill.

In early 2017, it appeared Crapo and Brown were poised to pursue a bipartisan approach to change Dodd-Frank. But, at the end of October, Brown announced he and Crapo had been unable to reach a compromise. Crapo then began negotiations with several Democratic moderates, some of whom were up for re-election in states that had voted overwhelmingly for Trump in 2016. The upshot was a bill signed by Trump after passing the Senate 67-31 in spring 2018 — with 17 Democrats backing it. It opened an acrimonious rift within the Senate Democratic Caucus: While supporters of the measure pointed to relief for community banks and local credit unions, liberal populists such as Brown and Massachusetts' Elizabeth Warren blasted a provision that loosened regulations on banks with assets greater than $50 billion but less than $250 billion. Bemoaning what he called "collective amnesia" about the banking crisis a decade earlier, Brown warned on the Senate floor: "This legislation threatens to undo important rules protecting us from risk. [It] again puts taxpayers on the hook for bailouts."

For many years, Brown has worn a lapel pin with a canary in a cage to commemorate underground miners who worked before the protections later added by labor unions and government safety inspections. In late 2016, Brown and West Virginia Democrat Joe Manchin led a group of coal-state senators who threatened to block a funding bill needed to keep the government in operation unless a program providing health care benefits to miners was extended. Such a provision was included in a government funding bill that passed in early 2017 — but it left open the issue of shoring up miners' pension plans. Brown successfully pushed to include in a February 2018 budget deal a provision creating a special committee to deal with financially troubled multiemployer pension plans, including one covering nearly 70,000 Ohio Teamsters. But the panel, co-chaired by Brown and Utah Republican Orrin Hatch, failed to reach agreement. Brown advocated a plan to create a low-interest, 30-year loan program for troubled pension plans.

In 2012, as Brown sought a second term, 35-year-old Ohio Treasurer Josh Mandel, raised $19 million and was aided by $23.5 million in spending by outside conservative groups. The two candidates regularly accused each of lying, while Mandel labeled Brown's support for the auto industry bailout "un-American." Brown spent more than $24.5 million, and liberal outside groups funneled in another $15 million. Boosted by Obama's substantial political investment in Ohio, Brown turned what was a neck-and-neck race in August into a 51%-45% win. Obama carried the state, 50%-48%, over Republican Mitt Romney.

Rep. James Renacci abandoned a bid for governor in 2018 and ran for the Senate. With the endorsement of Trump and the state GOP establishment, Renacci won a five-way May primary with 47 percent of the vote. Renacci was a multimillionaire businessman before entering Congress, and the White House recruited him in part because of his ability to self-finance. Despite loaning his campaign $8 million, he used less than $300,000 and repaid himself the rest.

Brown raised $28.7 million and outspent Renacci by nearly 5-1: $24 million to $5 million. There was only $6 million in outside spending, more than 80 percent of it on Brown's behalf. With Brown leading by double digits in most polls, Renacci was largely written off by national Republicans: After an initial ad buy in June, his campaign did not go back on the air until October's second week. Still, the contest developed into one of the nastiest of the 2018 cycle. On issues, it was a faceoff between an anti-Trump Democrat and a pro-Trump Republican — except for trade: Brown reiterated his endorsement of Trump's tariffs, while Renacci was ambivalent about the president's actions in this area. Taking little for granted in a state increasingly Republican, Brown ran ads attacking Renacci for his wealth and lengthy fight to avoid paying nearly $360,000 on his 2000 taxes. When Renacci's campaign finally went on TV in the closing weeks, it focused on an issue generally avoided by Republicans in previous campaigns: Brown's contentious 1986 divorce from his first wife.

The ads aired after Brown's vote against confirming Brett Kavanaugh, the subject of sexual assault allegations, to the Supreme Court. Brown told the Plain Dealer he had decided to oppose Kavanaugh's nomination before the allegations surfaced in September 2018; he added that he had found Kavanaugh's accuser, Christine Blasey Ford, more credible than the nominee. Citing filings from Brown's divorce proceeding, Renacci's ads highlighted that the incumbent's former wife, Larke Recchie, had gotten a restraining order against him after alleging Brown had been rough with her. Brown repeated past statements denying any violence toward Recchie, who is remarried — and now a political supporter of her ex-husband. She recorded a campaign ad decrying Renacci's effort to bring the matter into the political arena, while contending the divorce proceedings had led "only to angry words." Renacci continued to hammer Brown during three debates over what he called "substantiated claims of abuse;" Brown called Renacci and his allegations "despicable." In a mid-October session with the Cincinnati Enquirer's editorial board, Renacci said he had heard abuse allegations against Brown from "multiple women" but that they had not been substantiated. An attorney for Brown sent a cease-and-desist letter to Renacci, calling the charges "false and libelous."

Brown won 53.4%-46.6%, as Republicans swept Ohio's statewide executive offices. Brown took only 16 of the 88 counties, but again captured the population centers and most of traditionally Democratic northeast Ohio. While it was unclear whether Renacci's attacks had an effect, there was later speculation about the role they might have played in Brown's decision to forgo a national campaign. He told the Plain Dealer shortly after his re-election that, if he decided to run for president, he expected Trump, "who has made a career of attacking people personally," would recycle the allegations that Renacci had used again him.

Brown married Pulitzer Prize-winning columnist Connie Schultz in 2004. His 2012 re-election bid created professional complications: She resigned after 18 years with the Plain Dealer, telling colleagues "it has become painfully clear that my independence, professionally and personally, is possible only if I'm no longer writing for the newspaper that covers my husband's Senate race on a daily basis." Schultz, who teaches journalism at Kent State University, wrote a 2007 book titled "... And His Lovely Wife: A Memoir From the Woman Beside the Man."

Rob Portman (R)

Elected 2010, term expires 2022, 2nd term, b. Dec 19, 1955; Cincinnati; Cincinnati Country Day School, 1974; Dartmouth College, B.A., 1979; University of Michigan Law School, J.D., 1984; Methodist; Married (Jane Portman); 3 children.

Elected Office: U.S. House, 1993-2005.

Professional Career: White House Legislative Affairs Director, 1989-1991; U.S trade rep., 2005-2006; Director, Office of Management & Budget, 2006-2007; Practicing attorney, 1984-1988, 2007-2010.

DC Office: 448 RSOB 20510, 202-224-3353, Fax: 202-224-9075, portman.senate.gov

State Offices: Cincinnati, 513-684-3265; Cleveland, 216-522-7095; Columbus, 614-469-6774; Toledo, 419-259-3895.

Committees: *Finance*: International Trade, Customs & Global Competitiveness; Social Security, Pensions & Family Policy (Chmn); Taxation & IRS Oversight. *Foreign Relations*: Africa & Global Health Policy; Europe & Regional Security Cooperation; State Dept & USAID Mngmnt, Internat'l Ops & Internat'l Dev; West Hem Crime Civ Sec Dem Rights & Women's Issues. *Homeland Security & Government Affairs*: Investigations (Chmn); Regulatory Affairs & Federal Management. *Joint Economic*.

Group Ratings

	ADA	ACLU	AFL-CIO	LCV	ITI	COC	HAFA	ACU	CFG	FRC
2018	-	10%	-	7%	-	80%	62%	76%	50%	100%
2017	0%	C	0%	0%	C	100%	C	68%	72%	92%

Almanac Ratings 2017-18

	Economy	Social	Foreign	Composite
Liberal	0%	0%	3%	1%
Conservative	100%	100%	97%	99%

Key Votes of the 115th Congress

1. Obama-care revision	Y	5. Gun regulations	Y	9. Kavanaugh confirmation	Y
2. Tax Cuts	Y	6. Family planning regs	Y	10. Saudi arms sales	N
3. Dodd-Frank revision	Y	7. Gorsuch confirmation	Y	11. FISA rules	Y
4. Omnibus appropriations	Y	8. Immigration restrictions	Y	12. Military aid in Yemen	N

Election Results

Election	Name (Party)	Vote (%)		Cand. Spent	Ind. Exp. Support	Ind. Exp. Oppose
2016 General	Rob Portman (R)	3,118,567	(58%)	$33,851,658	$3,264,568	$15,540,944
	Ted Strickland (D)	1,996,908	(37%)	$10,231,752	$4,827,629	$34,525,870
2016 Primary	Rob Portman (R)	1,336,686	(82%)			
	Don Elijah Eckhart (R)	290,268	(18%)			

Prior winning percentages: 2010 (57%), 2004 (72%), 2002 (74%), 2000 (74), 1998 (76%), 1996 (72%), 1994 (77%), 1993 special (70%)

For Republican Rob Portman, Ohio's junior senator, election to the Senate in 2010 was just another stop for a consummate insider whose career has alternated between Capitol Hill and the White House. After serving in the administration of President George H.W. Bush — to whom Portman occasionally has been compared, both in his center-right views and even-keeled modesty — Portman won a Cincinnati-based House seat in a 1993 special election, only to head back up Pennsylvania Avenue a dozen years later when he was appointed U.S. trade representative and later director of the Office of Management and Budget by President George W. Bush. After his arrival in the Senate, it appeared that another White House stint might be in his future. Portman was on 2012 GOP presidential nominee Mitt Romney's short list of possible running mates, and, early in the 2016 election cycle, he made the requisite visits to Iowa and New Hampshire as he mulled a presidential bid himself. But in December 2014, Portman cited the new GOP majority in the Senate as a key factor in not seeking the presidency.

His decision turned out to be good news for Republicans looking to hang on to a Senate seat in the perennial battleground of Ohio. Portman's re-election appeared at risk early in the 2016 cycle, as some polls showed him trailing the likely Democratic nominee, former Gov. Ted Strickland, by nearly double digits. Portman ended up handily winning a second term after running a well-executed campaign, during which he kept his distance from his party's presidential nominee: Donald Trump. Portman endorsed Trump only in the most perfunctory terms after the latter emerged as the party's all-but-certain nominee, and ended up not voting for him — announcing he would instead write in the party's vice presidential nominee, Indiana Gov. Mike Pence, after the October 2016 disclosure of the "Access Hollywood" tapes in which Trump was heard making lewd comments about grabbing women. However, with Trump in the White House, Portman has been a reliable vote for most of the president's policies, notwithstanding occasional differences in areas such as immigration and international trade. In January 2019, Portman endorsed Trump for a second term, telling Independent Journal Review: "I work with him every day. I disagree with him publicly and privately when appropriate, but I also get a lot done, and I get that done with him."

Portman grew up in Cincinnati, where his father in 1960 started a small forklift distribution company. The five-employee firm grew into a 350-person operation before being sold to a Dutch conglomerate in 2004. Portman's grandfather in 1926 purchased the Golden Lamb Inn in the Cincinnati suburb of Lebanon, which had opened in 1803 and says it's Ohio's oldest continuously operated business. A dozen presidents have stayed at the hotel, now owned by Portman and his siblings. As an undergraduate at Dartmouth College, he hung out with a crowd nicknamed the "Granola Gang," known for its love of the outdoors; many of its members later volunteered for the Peace Corps or went to work in the renewable energy field. Portman took a semester off to work for Republican Rep. Bill Gradison, whom he would later succeed, and, after graduation, worked on the advance team for George H.W. Bush's 1980 presidential campaign. It was the beginning of a long association with the Bush family.

After earning a law degree at the University of Michigan, Portman was hired by a leading Washington lawyer/lobbying firm, Patton, Boggs and Blow. He returned to Cincinnati to practice law before coming back to Washington in 1989 as an associate White House counsel and then head of the Office of Legislative Affairs. Portman was back practicing law in Cincinnati when, in January 1993, Gradison resigned his House seat to head a Washington-based trade association. Portman ran in a special election to fill the vacancy, with former first lady Barbara Bush recording a radio ad for him. He won a seven-candidate primary and then the general election in a blowout. He was easily re-elected six times to the GOP-dominated district.

Portman got on the House Ways and Means and Budget committees and became known for his fiscal conservatism and ability to work across the aisle. He co-chaired the National Commission on Restructuring the Internal Revenue Service and won broad support for repeal of the 3 percent excise tax on telephone service. Portman worked with his then-House and current-Senate colleague Maryland Democrat Ben Cardin on issues ranging from land conservation to welfare reform to pensions. He helped revise 401(k) rules to make it easier for small businesses to offer pension plans.

In 2005, President George W. Bush appointed Portman as U.S. trade representative. A year later, Bush appointed him OMB director; the president nicknamed him "The Mule" in tribute to Portman's persistence in trying to push the federal budget toward balance. "I wanted to offer a balanced budget over five years, and a lot of people didn't," he later told The Hill. During the Bush administration, Portman befriended Brett Kavanaugh, who was associate White House counsel and later staff secretary. In September 2018, Portman introduced Kavanaugh before the Senate Judiciary Committee after the latter had been nominated by Trump to the Supreme Court. During the highly charged floor debate on Kavanaugh's confirmation, Portman defended him against sexual assault allegations: "If the new normal is 11th hour accusations, toxic rhetoric like calling a candidate 'evil' and those of us who support him 'complicit in evil,' and guilt without any corroborating evidence, who would choose to go through that?" Portman asked. "How many good public servants have we possibly already turned away by this display?"

Portman left OMB in 2007 and returned to Cincinnati, where he joined a law firm and taught a class at Ohio State University's John Glenn School of Public Affairs. When Republican Sen. George Voinovich announced that he would not run for a third term, Portman entered the contest to replace him. Despite his long record, Portman had virtually no name recognition beyond the Cincinnati area. Unfazed, Portman campaigned around the state in blue jeans and a windbreaker while raising serious money: $16.5 million. In the fall campaign, Lt. Gov. Lee Fisher — who had emerged from a fractious Democratic primary — derided Portman's association with the Bush family: "Rob Portman had his hands on the steering wheel as George W. Bush drove us off the cliff and into the deepest economic ditch in most of our lives." But Fisher was strapped for cash — much of the $6.4 million he had raised was spent in the primary — and Portman asserted Ohio had lost 400,000 jobs while Fisher was Strickland's "jobs czar" from 2007 to 2008. Portman fended off criticism of his work as trade representative by saying he would make enforcement of trade laws a high priority. Portman won 57%-39%, carrying 82 of 88 counties.

In the Senate, Portman's government experience and personable demeanor quickly earned him respect and friendship from members of both parties. In an institution in which some adults have a reputation for exhibiting juvenile behavior, Portman is regularly described as a "grown-up." It's a description he has self-deprecatingly waved off, quipping, "When your hair starts to turn more gray, as mine has been, people are going to call you a grown-up." His voting record has been conservative, but not extremely so.

Portman attracted widespread attention in 2013 when he reversed his opposition to same-sex marriage after he disclosed that his 21-year-old son, Will, had come out as gay. It made him the first Republican senator to openly support same-sex marriage. Some conservatives vowed to oppose him for renomination in 2016, but a serious primary challenger did not emerge. In a 2014 interview with The Associated Press — a year before the Supreme Court ruling that legalized same-sex marriage nationwide — Portman said, "I feel very comfortable in taking a position of respecting people for who they are, which is what I think ultimately same-sex marriage is about." Also present for that interview was his wife, Jane Portman, who grew up in a Democratic family and, in the 1980s, was a staffer to future Senate Democratic Leader Tom Daschle of South Dakota. She has laughingly referred to the "consolidation agreement" when she and Rob Portman married: She agreed to become a Republican and he agreed to become a Methodist.

Just months after Portman was sworn into the Senate, a standoff between the Obama White House and Republican congressional leaders over raising the federal debt limit resulted in a deal that created the Joint Select Committee on Deficit Reduction. Portman was one of three Senate Republicans appointed to the panel, which was charged with finding an additional $1.5 trillion in budget savings over a 10-year period. As the late November 2011 deadline approached, efforts to come up with an agreement faltered. Portman and Massachusetts Democratic Sen. John Kerry were devoted cyclists, and took numerous bike rides together as they informally discussed ways to move forward. But the deadline passed with the panel in a partisan deadlock.

Portman later teamed with Montana Democrat Jon Tester on a 2012 bill to prevent federal government shutdowns. He has introduced similar legislation in every Congress since and was still trying amid a standoff between the White House and congressional Democrats that shut down the government for a record 35 days beginning in December 2018. Portman expressed hope the latter episode would build support for his proposal, which calls for an automatic "continuing resolution" at current spending levels if Congress fails to enact annual appropriations bills. While his latest legislation attracted more than half of Senate Republicans — but no Democrats — as co-sponsors in early 2019, Portman told reporters, "Finally, there is a sense that we are tired of this. ... I am hearing this from Republicans and Democrats alike, even those who are not on my bill, that we need to do something."

Portman was among the first senators to call attention to the opioid epidemic. With statistics for Ohio showing a death every three hours from an opioid overdose, Portman joined four other Republicans to back a March 2016 effort led by New Hampshire Democrat Jeanne Shaheen to add $600 million for treatment and prevention programs to a bill funding continued government operations. The move failed because of opposition from Senate GOP leaders. But President Barack Obama later that year signed the 21st Century Cures Act, which included $1 billion to combat opioid abuse over a two years. When an $8.4 billion bipartisan bill aimed at the problem was signed by Trump in October 2018, it included several Portman-authored provisions — most notably one requiring the U.S. Postal Service to screen packages shipped from overseas for fentanyl. A month later, a report by the Homeland Security Subcommittee on Investigations, chaired by Portman, called out a Virginia pharmaceutical company for raising the price of its version of naloxone — an opioid overdose antidote — by more than 600 percent. After the subcommittee's finding was disclosed on CBS' "60 Minutes," the firm, Kaleo, announced it would make a generic version of naloxone available at a far lower price.

The effort to get rid of Obamacare would also have translated into a significant loss of Medicaid funds to Ohio, which prompted Portman to hide his plans until shortly before the legislation was brought to the floor in July 2017. Portman joined a half-dozen other Republicans in opposing the "partial repeal" bill favored by hard-line conservatives, but he voted for the option that came the closest to passing — the "skinny repeal," a bare-bones measure that was an attempt to attract enough votes to move to conference committee with the House, where a comprehensive bill could be written. It failed narrowly, as three Republicans joined all Democrats in opposition.

Portman has navigated between his high-profile past as a negotiator of trade agreements and the widespread skepticism toward such deals in his home state — where "free trade" has been widely blamed for reduced employment and a shrinking manufacturing base. In 2015, he was at odds with members of his own party as he pushed an amendment to Obama's request for "fast track" negotiating authority to expedite a 12-nation trade deal known as the Trans-Pacific Partnership. Teaming with Michigan Democrat Debbie Stabenow, Portman unsuccessfully sought an amendment to require the White House to establish "enforceable rules" to combat currency manipulation. The effort was backed by the nation's automakers, who charged they were being undercut by Japan's undervaluing of the yen. But the Wall Street Journal's conservative editorial board called it a "killer amendment," while suggesting Portman was "abandoning his policy chops in favor of reelection politics." Portman early the next year came out against the draft TPP agreement. The Ohio Teamsters cited his opposition to the TPP in endorsing his 2016 re-election campaign.

The TPP never came before Congress for a vote before the end of the Obama administration, and Trump withdrew the United States from the agreement days after entering the White House. Nearly two years into the Trump administration, Portman — in a speech to the conservative Heritage Foundation — praised the president's hard line on trade relations with China. "China has been violating and circumventing our trade laws for decades," Portman said. "I think the Trump administration now has China's attention, and I applaud the president for taking a tough stand." But he also disagreed with Trump's use of a 1962 law — known as Section 232 — to impose tariffs based on national security. Alluding to an investigation launched by the Commerce Department into whether imports of autos and auto parts were damaging U.S. national security, Portman was quoted by the Columbus Dispatch: "Autos help run our economy. They don't run a national security risk." Portman, co-sponsor of a bill to make it harder for presidents to cite national security in imposing tariffs on goods with little relation to the military, noted Trump had previously used Section 232 to impose tariffs on steel and aluminum. "Broadly imposing tariffs on our allies risks them retaliating by putting tariffs on our products," Portman warned — pointing to Canada responding to the Trump administration's moves with $12 billion worth of tariffs on U.S. goods, "including agricultural products from Ohio."

Portman split with Trump in early 2019 when he was among 12 Senate Republicans to support a resolution disapproving the president's declaration of a national emergency at the southern border — a move by the White House to bypass Congress and siphon military money for a border wall. While he backed the border wall, Portman expressed concern about the usurpation of congressional powers. He said it "opens the door for future presidents to implement just about any policy they want and to take funding from other areas Congress has already decided upon without Congress' approval." The previous year, Portman took issue with Trump's immigration policies, as he joined in widespread criticism of the administration's policy of separating immigrant children from their families at the U.S.-Mexico border. Portman complained the policy, later reversed under pressure, was further aggravating a problem uncovered by his subcommittee: the failure of the Department of Health and Human Services to adequately track unaccompanied immigrant children placed with sponsors in the U.S. Portman chaired a hearing on the issue after it was revealed human traffickers had forced teenagers from Guatemala to work on farms in central Ohio.

In 2012, Portman put his Ohio organization behind Romney before the state's crucial primary, which the former Massachusetts governor won by just over 10,000 votes. He and Romney got along well, and Portman later assumed the role of Obama in Romney's debate preparation sessions. But

Portman's close association with the unpopular George W. Bush was probably a mark against him in the vice presidential sweepstakes, along with the perception that his personality was —well, bland. Those who know him say such characterizations are off the mark; in fact, he has a reputation as a prankster, and his outdoor exploits include smuggling a kayak into China in the 1980s to paddle the Yangtze River. In 2016, after earlier suggesting he would not make an endorsement in that year's race for the GOP presidential nomination, Portman threw his support behind his home-state governor, John Kasich. It was something of a surprise, given Portman's ties to the Bush family and the presence of former Florida Gov. Jeb Bush in the contest. But it presumably helped solidify Portman's home-state party base, as polls showed his re-election in jeopardy.

National Democrats initially thought they had scored a coup in recruiting Strickland to take on Portman in 2016, but the former governor ran a problem-plagued campaign. Portman again demonstrated his fundraising prowess: By July 2016, he had raised more than $15 million, more than twice as much as Strickland had. It allowed Portman to go on air during the summer with negative ads, to which the Strickland campaign was slow to respond. Some of Portman's ads accused Strickland of poor management of state finances. When the Strickland campaign finally went on air, it was with an ad that sought to rebut Portman's attacks by attributing the state's difficult situation to the Great Recession. "They say I lost jobs and drained the rainy-day fund," Strickland said in opening the ad, thereby giving Portman's charge additional exposure — and causing some Democratic operatives to wince.

While Portman has been viewed with suspicion by the GOP's tea party wing, he got a big assist from the billionaire Koch brothers, the tea party's financial angels — who were determined to see the Senate remain in Republican control. Groups aligned with the Kochs poured nearly $12 million for advertising into the race, with most of it coming before Labor Day. By that time, the advertising blitz had sliced Strickland's favorability ratings in half. National Democratic strategists withdrew large ad buys scheduled for the first part of September. Portman captured 84 of 88 counties and scored a 58%-37% victory — running well ahead of Trump's 51%-43% win in the Buckeye State.

Steve Chabot (R)

Elected 2010, 12th term, b. Jan 22, 1953; Cincinnati; College of William and Mary (VA), B.A.; Northern Kentucky University Salmon P. Chase College of Law (KY), J.D.; Roman Catholic; Married (Donna Chabot); 2 children; 1 grandchild.

Elected Office: Cincinnati City Council, 1985-1990; Hamilton County Commission, 1990-1994; U.S. House, 1995-2009.

Professional Career: Teacher, St. Joseph School, 1975-1976; Practicing attorney, 1978-1994.

DC Office: 2408 RHOB 20515, 202-225-2216, Fax: 202-225-3012, chabot.house.gov

State Offices: Cincinnati, 513-684-2723; Lebanon, 513-421-8704.

Committees: *Foreign Affairs*: Middle East, North Africa & International Terrorism. *Judiciary*: Courts, Intellectual Property & Internet; Crime, Terrorism & Homeland Security. *Small Business (RMM)*.

Group Ratings

	ADA	ACLU	AFL-CIO	LCV	ITI	COC	HAFA	ACU	CFG	FRC
2018	-	3%	-	3%	-	92%	88%	96%	92%	100%
2017	0%	C	3%	0%	C	93%	C	100%	92%	100%

Almanac Ratings 2017-18

	Economy	Social	Foreign	Composite
Liberal	2%	0%	0%	1%
Conservative	99%	100%	100%	100%

Key Votes of the 115th Congress

1. Obama-care revision	Y	5. Family planning regs	Y	9. Guantanamo prisoners	N
2. Tax Cuts	Y	6. Body cameras/immigration	N	10. Ground missiles, limit	N
3. Omnibus appropriations	Y	7. Abortion ban	Y	11. Defense Dept. spending	Y
4. Dodd-Frank revision	Y	8. Concealed carry	Y	12. FISA rules	Y

Election Results

Election	Name (Party)	Vote (%)		Cand. Spent	Ind. Exp. Support	Ind. Exp. Oppose
2018 General	Steve Chabot (R)	154,409	(51%)	$3,008,495	$1,471,935	$2,321,730
	Aftab Pureval (D)	141,118	(47%)	$3,842,297	$334,029	$3,533,122
2018 Primary	Steve Chabot (R)	41,298	(83%)			
	Samuel Ronan (R)	8,324	(17%)			

Prior winning percentages: 2016 (59%), 2014 (63%), 2012 (58%), 2010 (52%), 2006 (52%), 2004 (60%), 2002 (65%), 2000 (53%), 1998 (53%), 1996 (54%), 1994 (56%)

Republican Steve Chabot first came to the House in the historic GOP Class of 1994. After losing reelection in 2008, he returned two years later as the most senior member of another huge freshman class. He reclaimed his status as one of the chamber's most conservative members. As Small Business Committee chairman, he claimed credit for removing obstacles to American entrepreneurism. He had another close reelection in 2018 but benefited from a more favorable redistricting.

Chabot grew up in the Cincinnati area and graduated from La Salle High School. He earned a degree in history and physical education from the College of William & Mary. He took night classes at Northern Kentucky University to get his law degree while teaching at an elementary school during the day. Chabot won a seat on the Cincinnati City Council, where he served for four years. He followed that with a four-year stint on the Hamilton County Commission. During that time, Chabot tried to find innovative ways to reduce the cost of government, such as using jail inmates for some public services.

In 1994, Chabot was among the successful conservative Republicans who ended 40 years of Democratic control of the House. For 14 years, he sometimes took politically risky stands opposing federal spending on projects in his district and was a leader on social issues, particularly opposition to abortion rights. In 2003, on the Judiciary Committee, he helped enact a ban on "partial-birth" abortions, and he pushed a bill to prevent minors from crossing state lines to get abortions. Chabot was a House manager during the 1998 impeachment of President Bill Clinton.

Chabot lost his seat in 2008 when Democrat Steve Driehaus defeated him by five percentage points. In a rematch, Chabot in 2010 criticized the incumbent for voting for the Affordable Care Act and the $787 billion economic-stimulus package. Driehaus defended the actions of Democrats, including the health care overhaul, which he called "the right thing" to do. Each candidate raised about $2 million. Chabot won, 52%-46%.

When he returned to the House, Chabot used his seniority to become chairman of the Foreign Affairs Subcommittee on the Middle East and South Asia. He criticized the Obama administration's policies in the region and called its explanation of events before and after the deadly 2012 attack at the U.S. consulate in Benghazi Libya, "ham-handed at best and a cover-up at worst." During the next two years, he chaired the Asia and the Pacific Subcommittee. He filed the Burma Human Rights and Democracy Act, which restricted military aid to that country and signaled the Obama administration to move more cautiously to normalize relations. In December 2018, he won House passage of a resolution that condemned the military in the renamed Myanmar for its genocide of Rohingya Muslims. As co-chair of the Taiwan Caucus, Chabot angered the Chinese government with his resolution that facilitated more meetings between Taiwan and the United States.

On domestic issues, he filed a bill to revamp the Section 8 housing initiative for low-income residents, calling it "a broken program that rewards dependency on government with our tax dollars." He crusaded against federal funding of Cincinnati's streetcar project on economic grounds. In 2014, Chabot enacted a bipartisan bill to strengthen the law school clinic certification program of the Patent and Trademark Office, which he said would encourage innovation. His Almanac voting record has been nearly perfect conservative.

For four years, he chaired the Small Business Committee. "If there's one thing government can do for small business, it's to get the heck off their backs," Chabot told the Associated Press. In June 2018, he enacted his bill that reorganized the Small Business Administration's loan program and increased its lending authority. "It's cumbersome, it takes too long, there's far too much paperwork. It just intimidates a lot of people," he said.

Following the 2018 election, Chabot made a bid for the vacancy as the ranking Republican on the Judiciary Committee, citing his lengthy experience. But he lost to Doug Collins of Georgia, who had closer ties to GOP leaders. Chabot's bid may have been handicapped by the bid of Jim Jordan, another Ohioan, for the top post. Chabot resumed his position as the ranking Republican on Small Business.

After redistricting made the 1st District substantially more Republican by adding solidly GOP Warren County, Chabot won reelection easily. "Unless Steve Chabot commits a felony, he will be there for as long as he wants to be," Hamilton County Democratic Party Chairman Tim Burke lamented to The Cincinnati Enquirer.

Not all Democrats accepted that caution. In 2018, Chabot was challenged by Aftab Pureval, the clerk of courts for Hamilton County, who styled himself as a moderate and claimed that the incumbent had lost touch with his district. The campaign got nasty with national Republicans running ads accusing Pureval — who was a first-generation American of Indian descent — of working on behalf of the Libyan government. Pureval responded that the law firm for which he worked had represented Libya long before he was hired. Pureval was criticized when a supporter secretly did work for the Chabot campaign. Chabot won 51%-47%. Pureval had a 20,000 vote lead in Hamilton County. Chabot prevailed with two-thirds of the vote in Warren, where he led by 33,000. This was a case where artful redistricting likely was a savior for the GOP.

OH-1: Southwest Ohio   Cook Partisan Voting Index: R+5

Population		Race and Ethnicity		Income	
Total	733,390	White	69.1%	Median Income	$55,897
Land area (sq. miles)	687	Black	21.9%	District Income Rank	219
Pop/ sq mi	1067.6	Latino	3%	Poverty Rate	15.9%
Born in State	72.4%	Asian	3.4%	With health insurance	93%
		Two or more races	2.3%	Cash public assistance	3.8%
Age Groups		Other	0.4%	Food stamp/SNAP	13.7%
Under 18	24.4%				
18-34	23%	**Education**		**Work**	
35-64	38.8%	H.S grad or less	38.4%	White Collar	13.8%
Over 64	13.8%	Some college	27.7%	Sales and Service	40.8%
		College Degree, 4 yr	21.3%	Blue Collar	18.5%
Military		Post grad	12.6%	Government	10.4%
Veteran/ Active Duty	7.3%				

2012 Pres. Vote	Romney	190,501	(52%)	Obama	168,195	(46%)			
2016 Pres. Vote	Trump	185,025	(51%)	Clinton	160,988	(44%)	Johnson	11,250	(3%)

Western/Northern Cincinnati Metro: Cincinnati, with its long-settled good looks, was Ohio's first major metropolis, a heavily German beehive of riverboats and sausage factories, nicknamed in the 1850s "Porkopolis." In the 19th century, it was the nation's fourth-largest city, and at the outbreak of the Civil War, it was a chief destination for slaves on the Underground Railroad. The National Underground Railroad Freedom Center is now located downtown. In the middle of the city is Mill Creek, named by the advocacy group American Rivers the most endangered urban river in North America in 1997. Two decades later, fish and wildlife had returned to the Mill Creek, with a reduction of sewage, the cleanup of nearby contaminated sites and improved local planning.

The Cincinnati area was the site of great innovations: the first municipal fire department; the first professional baseball team, the Red Stockings, who began playing in 1869; and the nation's first concrete skyscraper, the 15-story Ingalls building built in 1902. Cincinnati spawned not flashy but solid industries, including America's biggest concentration of machine tool makers and the Procter & Gamble soap business. General Electric has its Global Operations Center downtown, with more than 1,300 employees. In suburban Evendale, the company maintains a huge jet-engine manufacturing facility. With more than 9,000 employees in southwest Ohio, GE is the largest manufacturer statewide. P&G opened in 2017 its new Beauty Innovation Center, a $300 million expansion of its campus in Mason.

Downtown, Fountain Square shows off well-maintained skyscrapers plus a revival of museums, arts institutions and retail shops. Old ethnic neighborhoods on the west side, crowded with brick row houses on steep hills, maintain their thick local accents and special foods, from German sauerbraten to Cincinnati chili. With fewer recent immigrants than comparable northern cities, Cincinnati's population declined in every decade from 1940 until 2010. From 2010 until 2017, the population was growing and has become younger -- an increase of 4,400 residents in the city and 11,400 in Hamilton County. In the metro area, which remained the largest in the state, there was 6 percent growth during that period.

The 1st Congressional District of Ohio includes almost all of Cincinnati, except for parts of its affluent eastern side. It contains most of Cincinnati's distinctive neighborhoods, like Over-the-Rhine, named for its heavily German-American early population. This was a premier entertainment district until the late 1910s, when Prohibition shut down the breweries. With increased African-American population, it was the epicenter of race riots in 2001, though it has been gentrifying since then. The district takes in Avondale, once the center of Cincinnati's Jewish population, but now more than 90 percent African American; Hebrew Union College, the oldest extant Jewish seminary in the Americas, is just to the west of the neighborhood. Hillary Clinton won Hamilton County, 53%-43%, one of only eight she took statewide. The district takes in overwhelmingly Republican Warren County, which in 2016 had the second-highest median household income in the state, behind Delaware County.

Historically, Cincinnati was an island of Republicanism in a sea of Democratic sentiment. Today, the reverse is true. It has an overwhelmingly Democratic urban core, but beyond that, the rest of the district is largely Republican. The 1st includes most of the heavily Republican middle-class suburbs and exurbs to the west of the city and some Democratic-leaning inner suburbs to the north. The district is divided into three roughly equal parts: the city, the Hamilton suburbs and Warren County. Donald Trump got 51 percent, while Mitt Romney got 52 percent in 2012. This was one of only two Republican-held districts in Ohio where the GOP presidential vote declined.

Brad Wenstrup (R)

Elected 2012, 4th term, b. Jun 17, 1958; Cincinnati; University of Cincinnati, B.A., 1980; Rosalind Franklin University (IL), B.S., 1985; William M. Scholl College of Podiatric Medicine, Rosalind Franklin University (IL), 1985; Roman Catholic; Married (Monica Klein); 1 child.

Military Career: U.S. Army Reserve Medical Service Corps 1998-pres. (Iraq)

Professional Career: Physician, Wellington Orthopedic & Sports Medicine, 1999-2013; Private practice, 1986-1999.

DC Office: 2419 RHOB 20515, 202-225-3164, Fax: 202-225-1992, wenstrup.house.gov

State Offices: Cincinnati, 513-474-7777; Peebles, 513-605-1380.

Committees: *Permanent Select on Intelligence*: Counterterrorism, Counterintelligence & Counterproliferation; Defense Intelligence & Warfighter Support (RMM). *Ways & Means*: Oversight; Worker & Family Support.

Group Ratings

	ADA	ACLU	AFL-CIO	LCV	ITI	COC	HAFA	ACU	CFG	FRC
2018	-	3%	-	0%	-	92%	70%	92%	61%	100%
2017	0%	C	3%	0%	C	93%	C	96%	86%	100%

Almanac Ratings 2017-18

	Economy	Social	Foreign	Composite
Liberal	0%	4%	0%	1%
Conservative	100%	97%	100%	99%

Key Votes of the 115th Congress

1. Obama-care revision	Y	5. Family planning regs	Y	9. Guantanamo prisoners	N
2. Tax Cuts	Y	6. Body cameras/immigration	N	10. Ground missiles, limit	N
3. Omnibus appropriations	Y	7. Abortion ban	Y	11. Defense Dept. spending	Y
4. Dodd-Frank revision	Y	8. Concealed carry	Y	12. FISA rules	Y

Election Results

Election	Name (Party)	Vote (%)		Cand. Spent	Ind. Exp. Support	Ind. Exp. Oppose
2018 General	Brad Wenstrup (R)...............................	166,714	(58%)	$1,450,355		
	Jill Schiller (D)...................................	119,333	(41%)	$581,349		
2018 Primary	Brad Wenstrup (R)...	(100%)				

Prior winning percentages: 2016 (65%), 2014 (66%), 2012 (59%)

Republican Brad Wenstrup, elected in 2012 when he defeated the Republican incumbent in the primary, is a foot surgeon and Iraq War veteran. He used those experiences to become an influential player on national security issues. In 2018, he won a seat on the Ways and Means Committee. He earned the gratitude of many in the House when his medical skills — and quick response — probably helped to save the life of Rep. Steve Scalise following the shooting at a baseball practice in 2017.

Wenstrup was born and raised in Cincinnati. His father was an optician, and his mother worked at a Stein Mart department store. As a kid, Wenstrup thought about a career in medicine as well as serving in the military. He got his bachelor's degree from the University of Cincinnati and a medical degree from the Scholl College of Podiatric Medicine in Chicago. His medical practice was incorporated into Wellington Orthopedic & Sports Medicine. He joined the Army Reserve in 1998 and served as a combat surgeon in Iraq in 2005 and 2006. "I tell people, it's the worst thing I ever had to do, but the best thing I ever got to do," he said. Not long after the prisoner-abuse scandal at the Abu Ghraib prison erupted, he was stationed at a combat support hospital within the prison walls. He treated U.S. troops, civilians and some enemy combatants.

Politics grew more intriguing to Wenstrup when he returned from Iraq. "I started to see people in Washington making military decisions that have never served, making health care plans that have never seen a patient or dealt with insurance companies or Medicaid and Medicare," he said. Running for mayor of Cincinnati in 2009 against incumbent Democrat Mark Mallory, Wenstrup lost but took a respectable 46 percent of the vote in the Democratic-leaning city.

In 2011, he launched a primary challenge to Rep. Jean Schmidt, who had sometimes offended colleagues in Washington and Ohio and was dubbed "Mean Jean" in the blogosphere. Wenstrup was endorsed by the Ohio Liberty Council, a coalition of tea party groups. Wenstrup ran an ad attacking Schmidt's votes to raise the debt limit and to support the Wall Street bailout, while mentioning that she planted a kiss on President Barack Obama at the State of the Union address. He won the nomination, 49%-43%. He has not faced a serious primary challenge since then.

When Congress completed action on the defense spending bill in 2018, Wenstrup cited his work on the Armed Services Committee to increase military readiness of troops with gear designed to reduce the risk of injury and to require an intelligence report on the interference by Russia and China in U.S. elections. In 2016, he served on a House task force that investigated accusations from intelligence analysts that senior Obama administration officials responsible for operations in the Middle East had watered down their assessments. The report concluded that the military had taken a rosy view. "We still do not fully understand the reasons and motivations behind this practice, and how often the excluded analyses were proven ultimately to be correct," Wenstrup said.

Veterans issues have drawn Wenstrup's attention. In 2015, he praised the Veterans Affairs Department for integrating its record-keeping with Ohio's automatic prescription reporting system. He passed bills in the House that improved the electronic processing by the Veterans Benefits Administration of claims for educational assistance, and established the Veterans Economic Opportunity and Transition Administration to assist veterans with health, education assistance and vocational rehabilitation. Those measures became part of a broader veterans bill that was enacted in 2016. In 2017, as chairman of the Health Subcommittee at Veterans Affairs, Wenstrup won committee approval of his bill to ban smoking inside VA facilities — striking a 25-year mandate to require smoking areas. The House did not act on the bill.

With his interest in national security issues, he has served on the Intelligence Committee. He rejected attacks by President Donald Trump and his allies against senior Justice Department officials for their handling of surveillance activities related to opposition research during the 2016 presidential campaign. In 2019, he became ranking Republicans on the panel's Subcommittee on Defense Intelligence and Warfighter Support. He cited his familiarity during military service with "the importance of reliable intelligence on the battlefield."

Wenstrup's medical experience in stressful circumstances proved invaluable when he happened to be with a group of House Republicans at an early-morning baseball practice in June 2017. When a gunman shot and seriously wounded then-Majority Whip Steve Scalise of Louisiana, Wenstrup applied a tourniquet to care for Scalise until a rescue squad arrived. Nearly four months later, when Scalise made a dramatic return to the House, he said that Wenstrup "saved my life." Wenstrup, who remained a colonel in the Army Reserve, received a Pentagon award for valor.

Filling a vacancy on Ways and Means in early 2018, Wenstrup said he wanted to focus on actions to reduce opioid abuse, including steps to reduce what he considered the excessive writing of prescriptions by physicians. He became the only committee member who was a doctor.

At home, Wenstrup in 2018 had his closest election. Democrat Jill Schiller, who was a White House aide during the Obama administration, said that her top issue was expanded health-insurance coverage. Schiller—who spent $581,000 compared with $1.2 million for Wenstrup—took 55 percent in Hamilton County, which cast nearly half the total vote. Wenstrup rolled up huge majorities in the remaining seven counties and won, 58-41%.

OH-2: Southern Ohio   Cook Partisan Voting Index: R+9

Population		Race and Ethnicity		Income	
Total	726,067	White	85.7%	Median Income	$54,888
Land area (sq. miles)	3,222	Black	8.4%	District Income Rank	230
Pop/ sq mi	225.4	Latino	2%	Poverty Rate	14.1%
Born in State	74.6%	Asian	1.4%	With health insurance	93%
		Two or more races	2.1%	Cash public assistance	2.5%
Age Groups		Other	0.4%	Food stamp/SNAP	13.6%
Under 18	22.9%				
18-34	21.3%	**Education**		**Work**	
35-64	40.2%	H.S grad or less	42.1%	White Collar	15.6%
Over 64	15.6%	Some college	26.8%	Sales and Service	39.5%
		College Degree, 4 yr	19%	Blue Collar	20.9%
Military		Post grad	12.1%	Government	11%
Veteran/ Active Duty	8%				

2012 Pres. Vote	Romney	194,385	(55%)	Obama	155,036	(44%)		
2016 Pres. Vote	Trump	197,856	(55%)	Clinton	140,786	(39%)	Johnson	12,111	(3%)

Eastern Cincinnati Metro: Back in the 1850s, Cincinnati, with its large German population, was heavily Republican and anti-slavery. The city's ethnic character and political preference, like its physical appearance, remained pretty well fixed for a long time. Cincinnati attracted fewer European immigrants than did Great Lakes industrial cities such as Cleveland, Detroit and Chicago, so the New Deal had less impact on the local political dynamic. Appalachian immigrants who settled here in the 1940s to work in the factories were typically Republicans. Economically, it was never a strong union town, and culturally it is conservative.

The city of Ripley was a hub for the Underground Railroad, a natural point of egress from the South because the Ohio River narrows near the city. In 1838, escaped slave Eliza Harris leapt from one ice floe to the next, while carrying her 2-year-old son, to cross the river and make it to the city. A young abolitionist and Underground Railroad participant named Harriet Beecher Stowe lived in Cincinnati at the time and likely borrowed from Harris' experiences to create one of the most riveting scenes in Uncle Tom's Cabin.

The area to the east on the Ohio River includes distinctly different places — "the richest to the poorest, and everything in between," as one area mayor put it. Chillicothe, on the Scioto River and the first capital of Ohio, had a 2 percent population drop from 2010 to 2017. That area has suffered from the opioid epidemic, with a rising death rate. Heroin overdoses have become an almost daily occurrence, a local police captain wrote in Vox in 2017. "People are silent about their addiction or an addiction in their family — until it's too late." In Portsmouth, work on the Energy Department's uranium cleanup project to decontaminate and decommission the Portsmouth Gaseous Diffusion

Plant reached a major milestone in 2018, with the turnover of the first 80 acres of formerly toxic property for possible development by a community group; the original site was 3,700 acres.

Ohio's 2nd Congressional District includes the eastern edge of Cincinnati, taking in Hyde Park Square, with its farmer's market and many shops and boutiques; most of the largely affluent suburbs of eastern Hamilton County; and the fast-growing suburbs of Clermont County. In once-rural Clermont, Miami Township has become a bedroom community and a center of commercial development along the Interstate 275 loop. The metropolitan parts of the district, with more than 70 percent of the people, are mostly affluent and Republican. The counties farther east are less well off, with most of the old factories gone and with pockets of high unemployment and poverty. The district still leans substantially Republican, and Democrats have rarely competed here. In 2016, Donald Trump took the district, 55%-39%. In rural Pike County, which has a lengthy Democratic tradition, Trump got 67 percent of the vote.

Joyce Beatty (D)

Elected 2012, 4th term, b. Mar 12, 1950; Dayton; Central State University (OH), B.A., 1972; Wright State University (OH), M.S., 1974; University of Cincinnati, Att., 1979; Baptist; Married (Justice Otto Beatty Jr.); 2 stepchildren; 2 grandchildren.

Elected Office: OH House, 1999-2008.

Professional Career: Sr.Vice President., OH St. University, 2008-2013; President, Joyce Beatty & Associates, 1992-2013; Director, Montgomery County Department of Comm. Human Services, 1983-1992; Director, Adult & Elderly services, Montgomery County Mental Health Board, 1983; Professor, Capital University, 1979-1992; Professor, Sinclair Community College, 1975-1983; Caseworker, City of Dayton, 1971-1975.

DC Office: 2303 RHOB 20515, 202-225-4324, Fax: 202-225-1984, beatty.house.gov
State Offices: Columbus, 614-220-0003.

Committees: *Financial Services*: Housing, Community Development & Insurance; Oversight & Investigations; Subcommittee on Diversity & Inclusion (Chmn). *Joint Economic*.

Group Ratings

	ADA	ACLU	AFL-CIO	LCV	ITI	COC	HAFA	ACU	CFG	FRC
2018	-	86%	-	83%	-	55%	4%	5%	2%	0%
2017	95%	C	95%	100%	C	57%	C	4%	5%	11%

Almanac Ratings 2017-18

	Economy	Social	Foreign	Composite
Liberal	94%	98%	92%	95%
Conservative	6%	2%	8%	5%

Key Votes of the 115th Congress

1. Obama-care revision	N	5. Family planning regs	N	9. Guantanamo prisoners	Y
2. Tax Cuts	N	6. Body cameras/immigration	Y	10. Ground missiles, limit	Y
3. Omnibus appropriations	Y	7. Abortion ban	N	11. Defense Dept. spending	Y
4. Dodd-Frank revision	N	8. Concealed carry	N	12. FISA rules	N

Election Results

Election	Name (Party)	Vote (%)		Cand. Spent	Ind. Exp. Support	Ind. Exp. Oppose
2018 General	Joyce Beatty (D)................................	181,575	(74%)	$739,684		
	Jim Burgess (R)....................................	65,040	(26%)			
2018 Primary	Joyce Beatty (D)...		(100%)			

Prior winning percentages: 2016 (69%), 2014 (64%), 2012 (68%)

Democrat Joyce Beatty's election to the House in 2012 gave Ohio its first African-American member outside of Cleveland. Consistent with the spirit of Columbus, Beatty often takes a consensus-building approach and has worked with Republicans. She looks after the large academic and financial interests of her constituents. Chairing a new subcommittee in 2019, she pressed for increased diversity, including racial, in the nation's banks.

Beatty is the daughter of a brick mason and stay-at-home mom. Her parents moved from the inner city to a predominantly white neighborhood in Dayton with better schools when Beatty was young. She did her undergraduate work in speech and psychology at Central State University and later earned a master's degree in counseling from Wright State University, both in Ohio. Beatty's interest in politics was fueled by hearing Jesse Jackson speak at the 1984 Democratic National Convention. She owned her own management consulting business and had several jobs in local government and academia, eventually becoming senior vice president for engagement and outreach at Ohio State University. She served in the Ohio House for nearly a decade, including a stint as minority leader. She was instrumental in passing measures that helped women without health insurance get cancer screenings, reined in home foreclosures and encouraged financial literacy education. Her husband, Otto Beatty Jr., is an attorney and was a member of the state House for nearly two decades until he resigned and was succeeded by his wife.

When she entered the race in the new Columbus-based district, Beatty cited her knowledge of how to "make a payroll" and her ability to work with businesses and labor unions to bring jobs to central Ohio. She drew on her background to make education a central focus of her campaign, calling for making college more affordable and encouraging public-private partnerships to work on job-training initiatives with community colleges and training centers. With the endorsement of Columbus Mayor Michael Coleman and strong financial support from labor unions, her toughest opponent in the primary was former Rep. Mary Jo Kilroy, who had served one term in the 15th District and was defeated in 2010. Beatty took the primary, 38%-35%. She easily won in November. During the campaign, Minority Leader Nancy Pelosi joined her at a district forum on health care policy, and Beatty spoke at the Democratic convention on the role of women in the economy.

On the Financial Services Committee, Beatty has a useful platform for the robust financial sector in Columbus. In 2015, she filed the Housing Financial Literacy Act to improve first-time homebuyers' financial knowledge. She has been a leading advocate for placing a woman on the $20 bill, and praised the Obama administration plan in 2016 for Civil War-era abolitionist Harriett Tubman to replace President Andrew Jackson on the currency. She urged that the Treasury Department act more speedily than its original timetable, which could extend until 2030. As of early 2019, the Trump administration had delayed a final decision.

As chairwoman of the new Diversity and Inclusion Subcommittee in 2019, which she urged committee Chairwoman Maxine Waters of California to create, she filed a bill with her "Beatty" rule. That required an interview of at least one racial minority when there was an opening for the head of one of the regional Federal Reserve banks. "It's hard to believe that in 2018, in the Federal Reserve's 105-year history, only one African American has ever served as a Reserve Bank president," she said. With that partly symbolic step, Beatty added, she planned to encourage the entire financial-services industry to look more like America. "It's about changing the culture, the quality of service and the benefits to constituents or customers."

Beatty has carried forward her professional experience with intercollegiate athletics. She called for more research on neurological disorders and brain injuries. "Talk is not enough," she said, referring to the actions of the NCAA governing board. During her first term, Beatty praised the Big Ten universities when they adopted a plan similar to what she had advocated to guarantee that students who receive athletic scholarships may keep the award until they graduate.

With Republican Rep. Ann Wagner of Missouri, Beatty won House passage of legislation to combat sex trafficking in the United States by making it easier for people to report incidents. The bill was enacted in 2015 as part of broader legislation on the issue. Subsequently, Beatty joined other lawmakers in criticizing the Justice Department for slow implementation of the law. In April 2018, she and Wagner enacted a bill to penalize website operators that facilitate online sex trafficking.

Beatty took her pursuit of bipartisanship an additional step by creating the Civility Caucus with Republican Rep. Steve Stivers, who serves a neighboring district. "There may be times as the underdog that I will want to talk about people who are unhinged and undisciplined and making appalling statements that are counter to civility and what I stand for," she told the Columbus Dispatch.

Following the 2018 election, Beatty became vice chair of the Congressional Black Caucus. She was an early supporter of Nancy Pelosi for Speaker and kept that commitment even when there was talk of Rep. Marcia Fudge, another African-American Democrat from Ohio, as a potential challenger.

OH-3: Franklin County   Cook Partisan Voting Index: D+19

Population		Race and Ethnicity		Income	
Total	770,797	White	52.4%	Median Income	$45,253
Land area (sq. miles)	228	Black	32.8%	District Income Rank	370
Pop/ sq mi	3380.7	Latino	6.4%	Poverty Rate	22.5%
Born in State	66.6%	Asian	3.9%	With health insurance	88.8%
		Two or more races	4.1%	Cash public assistance	3.5%
Age Groups		Other	0.3%	Food stamp/SNAP	19.8%
Under 18	24.6%				
18-34	29.7%	**Education**		**Work**	
35-64	35.7%	H.S grad or less	42.7%	White Collar	10%
Over 64	10%	Some college	29.5%	Sales and Service	45.1%
		College Degree, 4 yr	18.4%	Blue Collar	20.5%
Military		Post grad	9.4%	Government	13%
Veteran/ Active Duty	7%				

2012 Pres. Vote	Obama	217,969	(70%)	Romney	90,434	(29%)		
2016 Pres. Vote	Clinton	210,489	(66%)	Trump	89,634	(28%)	Johnson	9,210 (3%)

Columbus Metro: In 1972, the first Almanac of American Politics noted that Columbus had just surpassed Cincinnati to become Ohio's second-largest city. Today, Columbus is by far the largest city in the state, with a gain of 90,000 from 2010 to 2017. Franklin County grew by 9 percent during the 2000s and another brisk 11 percent in the seven subsequent years. In 2017, the population of the metro area was nearly 2.1 million, now surpassing the Cleveland metro area and expecting to replace metro Cincinnati by 2024, and it is booming while much of the state has stagnated or declined. The reasons are simple: location, location, location ... and government. Not only the geographical center of Ohio, the city lies just a one-day truck drive from more than half of the nation's population, making it the perfect location for a Midwestern hub. It is also the capital of the nation's seventh-most-populous state and home to the Ohio State University system's flagship campus. Columbus, NBC News reported in September 2018, "is riding a knowledge economy into prosperity." Its median age is seven years younger than the rest of Ohio and its share of residents with a college degree is eight percentage points higher.

In a region known for its blue-collar accents, Columbus has retained a distinctly white-collar flavor and attracted the type of upscale, enterprising people who have produced much of America's growth in recent years. It is home to four Fortune 500 companies. The area is the home of the Battelle Memorial Institute, the think tank that helped invent photocopying, compact discs and the Universal Product Code. Columbus has been rated as one of the best cities for a start-up business. Its leaders point to an inviting civic culture.

The city's rapidly growing foreign-born population — Latinos, Koreans, Ethiopians, Chinese, Russian Jews and Somalis — exceeds 11 percent. In January 2017, Mayor Andrew Ginther signed an executive order supporting the settlement of refugees in Columbus, though the travel ban and other restrictions of the Trump administration resulted in a big cut in new refugees. This population growth brought political change. Columbus had been Democratic during the Civil War years but became reliably Republican in the late 1800s. As the metropolitan area grew, more people headed for the suburbs and one of the largest Republican cities in the country slowly became Democratic again.

The 3rd Congressional District represents a bow by Republicans to political and demographic realities. Columbus had traditionally been split between the 12th and 15th districts, enabling suburban areas to trump Democratic-leaning portions of the city even in landslide Democratic years. Republicans chose to protect the 12th and 15th and create a Democratic "vote sink" in Franklin County, the only district in the state entirely contained in a single county. The 3rd takes in the skyscrapers of downtown Columbus; heavily Jewish Bexley, the site of the governor's mansion; the capitol, with the statue of President William McKinley out front; most of the university (except for the Ag Lab) plus its neighborhoods; the capital further south at the curve of the Scioto River; city slums;

and the Democratic portions of upscale New Albany and Westerville. The district includes working-class, mixed-race communities west of the city, like Greater Hilltop and Franklinton, which has begun to revitalize. These sometimes-disparate areas have Democratic voting patterns in common. The 3rd is the second-most Democratic district in Ohio. Hillary Clinton won here, 66%-28%.

Jim Jordan (R)

Elected 2006, 7th term, b. Feb 17, 1964; Urbana; University of Wisconsin, B.S., 1986; Ohio State University, M.A., 1991; Capital University (OH), J.D., 2001; Evangelical; Married (Polly Jordan); 4 children; 2 grandchildren.

Elected Office: OH House, 1994-2000; OH Senate, 2000-2006.

Professional Career: Assistant wrestling coach, OH St. University, 1987-1995; Wrestling camp coach, clinician, 1987-2006.

DC Office: 2056 RHOB 20515, 202-225-2676, Fax: 202-226-0577, jordan.house.gov

State Offices: Bucyrus, 419-663-1426; Lima, 419-999-6455; Norwalk, 419-663-1426.

Committees: *Judiciary*: Constitution, Civil Rights & Civil Liberties; Courts, Intellectual Property & Internet. *Oversight & Reform (RMM)*.

Group Ratings

	ADA	ACLU	AFL-CIO	LCV	ITI	COC	HAFA	ACU	CFG	FRC
2018	-	21%	-	3%	-	75%	98%	100%	98%	100%
2017	5%	C	3%	0%	C	93%	C	100%	98%	100%

Almanac Ratings 2017-18

	Economy	Social	Foreign	Composite
Liberal	2%	10%	8%	7%
Conservative	98%	90%	92%	93%

Key Votes of the 115th Congress

1. Obama-care revision	Y	5. Family planning regs	Y	9. Guantanamo prisoners	N
2. Tax Cuts	Y	6. Body cameras/immigration	N	10. Ground missiles, limit	N
3. Omnibus appropriations	N	7. Abortion ban	Y	11. Defense Dept. spending	Y
4. Dodd-Frank revision	Y	8. Concealed carry	Y	12. FISA rules	N

Election Results

Election	Name (Party)	Vote (%)		Cand. Spent	Ind. Exp. Support	Ind. Exp. Oppose
2018 General	Jim Jordan (R)	167,993	(65%)	$1,567,860	$1,074	
	Janet Garrett (D)	89,412	(35%)	$689,313		
2018 Primary	Jim Jordan (R)	56,191	(85%)			
	Joseph Miller (R)	9,646	(15%)			

Prior winning percentages: 2016 (68%), 2014 (68%), 2012 (58%), 2010 (72%), 2008 (65%), 2006 (60%)

Republican Jim Jordan, elected in 2006, has endeared himself to conservatives while annoying his party's leaders with his confrontational approach. He took over in 2019 as the top Republican on the Oversight and Reform Committee, where he served as a relentless ally of President Donald Trump. Jordan's first platform was as chairman of the Republican Study Committee. Later, he was a founder and the first chairman of the House Freedom Caucus, which conservative members on economic and social policy organized as a forum for their resistance to President Barack Obama's agenda. Jordan has been an assertive force among House Republicans, as he has chiefly sought to stifle the plans of others rather than to press his own legislation. But he has fallen short in leadership bids.

Jordan grew up in Champaign County and graduated from Graham High School, where he was a champion wrestler. At the University of Wisconsin, he won two NCAA wrestling championships in the 134-pound weight class and was inducted into the Badger Hall of Fame. With his bachelor's in economics, Jordan worked as an assistant wrestling coach at Ohio State University, where he earned a master's degree in education before getting a law degree at Capital University. (Years later, in 2018, charges were raised, and quickly dismissed, that he was aware of sexual-harassment allegations in the wrestling program.) Soon, he began thinking about elected office. "You get married and have kids, and you get sick of having the government take your money and tell you what to do," he told columnist George Will in 2011. He won a state House seat in 1994 and served six years before he won a tough primary for the state Senate. His solidly conservative record included legislation creating Ohio's "Choose Life" license plates, a ban on same-sex marriage and government vouchers for private-school tuition.

Jordan ran for the House when Republican Rep. Michael Oxley retired as chairman of the Financial Services Committee. In the six-way Republican primary, he had the most name recognition plus support from Ohio Right to Life, the National Rifle Association and the national anti-tax group Club for Growth. With the benefits of geography and connections, Jordan won 51 percent, carrying eight of 11 counties. Findlay real estate developer Frank Guglielmi self-financed $1.6 million and carried his home county and one other to get 30 percent. In the solidly Republican district, Democrats barely mounted a competitive campaign.

In the House, Jordan established an unfailingly conservative voting record, with consistent perfect scores and a 100 percent lifetime rating from the American Conservative Union. "With the exception of the military, the federal government doesn't do anything very well," he told the Mansfield News Journal. He said he weighs all issues based on whether they benefit families. He is a father of four whose desk calendar is crowded with his children's athletic schedules.

With his right-wing bona fides well established, Jordan became head of the 170-member Republican Study Committee in 2011, when the GOP reclaimed control of the House. Jordan vowed to be independent of the leadership, saying his group would lobby lawmakers just as vigorously as did the Republicans' formal whip team.

Under Jordan's guidance, the RSC unveiled a congressional budget plan that called for cuts of $2.5 trillion in planned spending over 10 years. When the House approved a measure in March to keep the government running temporarily as Speaker John Boehner and Obama tried to hammer out an agreement on spending cuts, Jordan was openly scornful. "We must do more than cut spending in bite-sized pieces," he said. That summer, Jordan dug in his heels during the showdown over whether to raise the federal debt limit. He denied speculation that he and allies were eager to shut down the government and said he was not out to undercut Boehner, who held the neighboring district. When Republicans and Obama failed to reach a budget deal in early 2013 and triggered across-the-board spending cuts under the sequester, Jordan shrugged that it "won't be the end of the world" and marked an important step toward savings.

As the founding chairman in January 2015 of the House Freedom Caucus, whose chief purpose was to move the Republican agenda to the right, he created a new base for friction with Boehner. Those divisions became apparent in the next few months, notably opposition by Jordan and others in the Freedom Caucus to giving trade promotion authority to Obama, and their demand that new limits on national security data collection go even further. Despite his high regard among the rebels and his continued poor-mouthing of GOP leaders, Jordan pointedly was not among the conservatives who voted for alternatives when Boehner was reelected as House Speaker in 2013 and 2015, nor was he directly involved with the internal pressure campaign that ultimately led Boehner to step down as Speaker in September 2015.

With Republicans in control of the White House and Congress after the 2016 election, some Republicans speculated that Jordan would lose his leverage as Trump and Speaker Paul Ryan took command. Jordan disagreed. "I actually think our influence is as strong as ever," he told The New York Times a week after the election.

Initially at least, Jordan proved to be correct. In March 2017, he and his Freedom Caucus allies stood firm against party leaders, whom they criticized for failing to keep their promise to repeal the Affordable Care Act. Singling out Jordan and two others, an unhappy Trump tweeted in response, "The Freedom Caucus will hurt the entire Republican agenda if they don't get on the team, & fast. We must fight them, & Dems, in 2018!" A few weeks later, Jordan and others in the Freedom Caucus cut a deal with Republican Rep. Tom MacArthur of New Jersey, which would make it easier for states to get waivers from some requirements of the health care law. That was a critical step to the House's passage of the repeal measure and helped to spare Jordan potential blame for House inaction.

In May 2018, a similar scenario of Republican infighting played out when Jordan and other Freedom Caucus members voted against House passage of a bill to extend farm programs.

Conservatives objected that the bill did not impose stricter work requirements on recipients of food stamps. The following month, following extended backroom negotiations, Jordan led a group of eight conservatives who switched their previous opposition to the farm bill when Republican leaders agreed to oppose separate immigration legislation.

Jordan became a vocal defender of Trump and persistent critic of special counsel Robert Mueller and his investigation of the 2016 presidential campaign. The president viewed Jordan and Rep. Mark Meadows of North Carolina, his successor as Freedom Caucus chairman, as his "tough-talking, unapologetic allies," Politico reported in July 2018, despite their separate tactics "that made [House] leadership look feckless or worse." On Air Force One, Trump told reporters, "Jim Jordan is one of the most outstanding people I've met since I've been in Washington."

The limits of the support for Jordan among House Republicans became apparent when he challenged Rep. Kevin McCarthy for minority leader a week after the party's setbacks in the 2018 election. On Fox News, Jordan complained that House GOP leaders failed to demonstrate the "same intensity" toward party goals and presidential support that conservatives had shown on behalf of Trump. The outcome was not close. McCarthy won, 159-43.

In December, Jordan had another setback in his bid to become the senior Republican on the Judiciary Committee, where he again pledged to be an aggressive advocate for Trump. Instead, the McCarthy-controlled panel gave the position to Rep. Doug Collins of Georgia, who had held a House GOP leadership position. In what seemed a consolation prize, Jordan agreed not to press for a vote on the Judiciary panel and he got the vacant top GOP slot on the Oversight committee — defending Trump in Democratic investigations.

Jordan has survived intraparty conflicts at home. During preparation for the 2012 redistricting in Ohio, The Columbus Dispatch reported that Boehner's allies were considering retaliation through a plan that would make Jordan's seat substantially more competitive. Boehner denied any such effort, and Jordan's new district became securely Republican, though it moved well beyond his thinly populated base in western Ohio. The changes have posed scant reelection problems for Jordan. The next round of redistricting could pose a new set of internal challenges.

OH-4: Central Ohio   Cook Partisan Voting Index: R+14

Population		Race and Ethnicity		Income	
Total	711,332	White	88%	Median Income	$51,697
Land area (sq. miles)	4,665	Black	5%	District Income Rank	275
Pop/ sq mi	152.5	Latino	3.6%	Poverty Rate	13.5%
Born in State	82.1%	Asian	0.8%	With health insurance	93.4%
		Two or more races	2.3%	Cash public assistance	3%
Age Groups		Other	0.3%	Food stamp/SNAP	13%
Under 18	22.7%				
18-34	20.7%	**Education**		**Work**	
35-64	40.2%	H.S grad or less	51.5%	White Collar	16.4%
Over 64	16.4%	Some college	31%	Sales and Service	37.7%
		College Degree, 4 yr	11.2%	Blue Collar	33.7%
Military		Post grad	6.4%	Government	10.8%
Veteran/ Active Duty	9%				

2012 Pres. Vote	Romney	185,521	(56%)	Obama	139,189	(42%)			
2016 Pres. Vote	Trump	208,736	(64%)	Clinton	99,626	(30%)	Johnson	11,741	(4%)

Lima, Sandusky: Central and western Ohio look mostly like farmland to the traveler. Yet this is manufacturing country, indeed one of America's premier manufacturing areas, where the economy is based on factories in small towns and on rural highways. These places seem far from anywhere "important," yet the region has been quietly prosperous most of the years since World War II. While there have been some manufacturing job losses, most of this area emerged from the recession in better shape than other parts of the state.

Each population center has its own pet industry: In Lima, which had big gains in jobs and median income in 2017, the Joint Systems Manufacturing Center has been building versions of the Abrams tank since 1980. In January 2019, it got a $700 million contract to upgrade 174 of the battle tanks, with a workforce of about 1,000. A month earlier, the JSMC got a contract to build a new tank prototype — good news for a facility that came close to shutting down a few years earlier during a time of smaller Pentagon budgets. Also in Lima, Ford spent $500 million to develop "EcoBoost" technology for its F-150 pick-up truck. Dannon in Minster in 2017 announced an expansion of what once was the world's largest yogurt plant, with adaptations for the transition to Greek yogurt; the Chobani plant in Idaho surpassed it as the largest. In Jackson Center, Airstream was scheduled to complete in 2019 the expanded production of its iconic trailers, with a workforce of about 1,200. Honda has invested more than $6 billion in Marysville and East Liberty since it opened its first plant in Union County, for motorcycles, in 1979. Today, it employs about 15,000 Ohioans and is the largest automobile employer in the state. Production of the hybrid Honda Accord returned to Marysville from Japan in 2018. That plant can assemble about 440,000 vehicles each year. Many other local companies provide parts and supplies.

These small towns have historical significance. Marion was the home of President Warren G. Harding and socialist Norman Thomas; the latter, as a young boy, delivered the newspaper edited by the former. Fremont, settled by abstemious Yankees, was the home of President Rutherford B. Hayes, whose wife, Lucy, served only lemonade in the White House. Today it is home to an aromatic Heinz ketchup plant; it produces daily the equivalent of 4.1 million 14-ounce bottles, the most in the world. Tiny Milan is the birthplace of the inventor and capitalist Thomas Edison, while Tiffin still has St. Paul's United Methodist Church, the first public building in the United States to be wired for electricity. Wapakoneta, a typically Ohioan-Indian name, is the hometown of Neil Armstrong, the first man to walk on the moon, and the site of the Neil Armstrong Air and Space Museum.

This terrain in central Ohio makes up the 4th Congressional District. The district extends north and east into Seneca, Sandusky, Erie and Lorain counties, and the outer Cleveland suburbs. But it has been carefully wedged into the countryside to avoid metro areas, including Dayton and Toledo. The GOP lean of the small towns mitigates the impact of places like Oberlin College, one of the most liberal colleges in the country and the first to admit African Americans (1835) and women (1841). Donald Trump in 2016 got 64 percent of the vote.

Bob Latta (R)

Elected 2007, 6th full term, b. Apr 18, 1956; Bluffton; Ohio Northern University, Att., 1975; Bowling Green State University (OH), B.A., 1978; University of Toledo College of Law (OH), J.D., 1981; Roman Catholic; Married (Marcia Sloan Latta); 2 children.

Elected Office: Wood County commissioner, 1991-1996; OH Senate, 1997- 2001; OH General Assembly, 2001-2007.

Professional Career: Attorney, 1981-1991.

DC Office: 2467 RHOB 20515, 202-225-6405, Fax: 202-225-1985, latta.house.gov

State Offices: Bowling Green, 419-354-8700; Defiance, 419-782-1996; Findlay, 419-422-7791.

Committees: *Commission Congressional Mailing Standards.* *Energy & Commerce*: Communications & Technology (RMM); Consumer Protection & Commerce; Energy.

Group Ratings

	ADA	ACLU	AFL-CIO	LCV	ITI	COC	HAFA	ACU	CFG	FRC
2018	-	7%	-	0%	-	75%	66%	92%	64%	100%
2017	0%	C	5%	0%	C	93%	C	89%	85%	100%

Almanac Ratings 2017-18

	Economy	Social	Foreign	Composite
Liberal	2%	7%	0%	3%
Conservative	98%	94%	100%	97%

Key Votes of the 115th Congress

1. Obama-care revision	Y	5. Family planning regs	Y	9. Guantanamo prisoners	N
2. Tax Cuts	Y	6. Body cameras/immigration	N	10. Ground missiles, limit	N
3. Omnibus appropriations	N	7. Abortion ban	Y	11. Defense Dept. spending	Y
4. Dodd-Frank revision	Y	8. Concealed carry	Y	12. FISA rules	Y

Election Results

Election	Name (Party)	Vote (%)	Cand. Spent	Ind. Exp. Support	Ind. Exp. Oppose
2018 General	Bob Latta (R).. 176,569	(62%)	$1,474,445	$1,039	
	John Michael Galbraith (D)................... 99,655	(35%)	$205,248		
	Don Kissick (Lib).................................... 7,393	(3%)			
2018 Primary	Bob Latta (R)....................................... 45,732	(74%)			
	Todd Wolfrum (R)................................ 10,385	(17%)			
	Bob Kreienkamp (R)............................. 5,897	(10%)			

Prior winning percentages: 2016 (71%), 2014 (67%), 2012 (57%), 2010 (68%), 2008 (64%), 2007 special (57%)

Republican Bob Latta, who was elected in 2007 to the seat that his father, Delbert Latta, earlier held for 30 years, has a conservative voting record like his father. He has been a practical legislator on the Energy and Commerce Committee, where he has become a GOP leader on communications policy — mostly from a free-market perspective.

Bob Latta was born in Ohio but split his early years between his native Bluffton and Washington D.C. Helping his father's campaigns, Latta says he learned the business of catering to constituents. Young Latta frequently interrupted his homework to answer their phone calls and remembers his father following up with federal agencies to get results from the bureaucracy. While attending Bowling Green State University, he volunteered in his father's office, where he met his wife, Marcia, who worked for his father. When he graduated from law school at the University of Toledo, his father had one bit of career advice for him: Don't get into politics.

He followed that guidance and practiced law for several years. When his father retired in 1988, the 31-year-old couldn't pass on the opportunity to follow in his footsteps. Paul Gillmor, a Republican state senator, had been waiting for a congressional seat to open up during Del Latta's long tenure. After a spirited race, Gillmor beat Latta by just 27 votes out of 57,361 cast. Latta retreated to local politics, on the Wood County Commission and then to the Ohio legislature. One of his major efforts was to repeal the estate tax for most Ohioans. An avid hunter, Latta championed longer hunting seasons and expanded wildlife reserves.

After Gillmor in September 2007 died at his Washington home, Latta ran for the open seat. His chief primary opponent was state Sen. Steve Buehrer, who was backed by the Club for Growth, which ran several ads attacking Latta as an advocate of higher taxes. Latta attacked Buehrer for accepting donations from Tom Noe, a former Ohio fundraiser for President George W. Bush and a convicted money launderer. It came to light that Latta had also taken money from Noe. Latta defeated Buehrer by 2,542 votes out of 74,191 cast. Democrat Robin Weirauch had backing from labor unions and the abortion-rights group EMILY's List. She attacked Latta on economic issues and his support for the Iraq war. Latta won 57%-43%.

Latta's Almanac voting record has been nearly perfect conservative. On the Energy and Commerce Committee, he initially made energy independence his central issue. He successfully amended a House-passed air-quality bill in 2011 to require the Environmental Protection Agency to take costs into account in setting standards under the Clean Air Act. As vice chairman of the Congressional Sportsmen's Caucus, Latta castigated an Obama administration proposal to reclassify pocketknives that can be sprung open with one hand as switchblades. Congress enacted a bill that overturned the rule. Latta's Protect Our Great Lakes Act, which was designed to reduce algal blooms by prohibiting discharge of dredged material into the lakes, evolved and was enacted in 2015 as his Drinking Water Protection Act.

Latta has taken an interest in technology. In 2010, he was the first House member to release an iPhone app. He filed in 2011 a resolution declaring that to continue aggressive growth in telecommunications and technology industries, the federal government "should get out of the way and stay out of the way." He co-chaired the Republican New Media Caucus and the Rural Broadband Caucus. With Democratic Rep. Jerry McNerney of California, another member of Energy and

Commerce, Latta started the Wi-Fi Caucus. They addressed aspects of the digital divide between communities with and without internet access.

As chairman of the Digital Commerce and Consumer Protection Subcommittee, Latta in September 2017 got voice-vote passage in the House of his bill to set a policy framework for autonomous, self-driving vehicles. "U.S. companies are investing major resources in the research and development of this tech and should not be held up by regulatory barriers," he said. The Senate did not act on the bill. His subcommittee gave bipartisan approval in June 2018 to a bill that provided a framework for policy on the broadly defined "internet of things." His proposal, he said, was designed to encourage discussion of best practices and "who is doing what."

In the minority in 2019, Latta was ranking Republican on the Communications and Technology Subcommittee. His goals, he said, included "increasing access to high-speed broadband" and assuring that the United States remained "a leader of this cutting-edge technology." In January 2019, he told an industry audience that government should not stand in the way of innovators.

Latta has won reelection by wide margins. His closest race was in 2012. The Toledo Blade endorsed his Democratic opponent, Angela Zimmann, a college professor, and said Latta "has not been pragmatic or constructive." Latta outspent her nearly 3-to-1 and won convincingly, 57%-39%.

OH-5: Northwest Ohio   Cook Partisan Voting Index: R+11

Population		Race and Ethnicity		Income	
Total	722,212	White	89.3%	Median Income	$56,458
Land area (sq. miles)	5,626	Black	2.7%	District Income Rank	209
Pop/ sq mi	128.4	Latino	5%	Poverty Rate	11.2%
Born in State	79.1%	Asian	1.3%	With health insurance	94.5%
		Two or more races	1.5%	Cash public assistance	1.8%
Age Groups		Other	0.2%	Food stamp/SNAP	9.8%
Under 18	22.6%				
18-34	22.1%	Education		Work	
35-64	38.9%	H.S grad or less	43.2%	White Collar	16.4%
Over 64	16.4%	Some college	30.8%	Sales and Service	37.5%
		College Degree, 4 yr	15.8%	Blue Collar	29.2%
Military		Post grad	10.1%	Government	11.8%
Veteran/ Active Duty	8.3%				

2012 Pres. Vote	Romney	195,060	(54%)	Obama	159,659	(44%)			
2016 Pres. Vote	Trump	214,661	(59%)	Clinton	124,407	(34%)	Johnson	15,370	(4%)

Toledo Area, Bowling Green: Undergirded by limestone, as flat and fertile as any place in America, northwest Ohio was economically productive from the time it was settled. That settlement came relatively late. Conflicts with Native Americans played a large role in the delay. In 1791, near Fort Recovery in Mercer County, the U.S Army was routed by a confederation of Indian tribes: Only 48 of the 1,000 soldiers led into battle escaped unharmed, and a quarter of them died. Three years later, the Battle of Fallen Timbers near present-day Maumee put a temporary end to outright conflict between Indians and Americans, and the ensuing Treaty of Greenville set aside northwestern Ohio for Native American use; the area wasn't made formally available for white settlement until the end of Tecumseh's War some 20 years later. What we know today as fecund farmland was part of a giant swamp in the early 1800s. The Great Black Swamp, left behind by a retreating glacier thousands of years earlier, ran from present-day Sandusky to the outskirts of Fort Wayne Indiana. It wasn't drained until the mid-1800s.

Today, this is prime industrial country. Its limestone, rail connections, and location between Lake Michigan and Lake Erie have spurred a factory economy that financially is far more important than agriculture. After the first settlements, northwest Ohio grew steadily for many decades, with Germany supplying many of the immigrants. Its small factories supplied the big auto plants in Detroit and northeast Ohio. Growth lagged in the 1980s when the domestic industry collapsed, but rebounded somewhat as small firms sold not only to the Big Three but to foreign customers. Honda has dozens of suppliers in the area. The plan by General Motors to shut down in 2019 its Lordstown plant in northeast Ohio raised concerns about the impact on parts suppliers. In February 2018, leaders of the

Regional Growth Partnership — a private planning group -- listed $4 billion in new investments, with 4,000 jobs, during the previous year, with the potential of $12 billion in additional projects.

The 5th Congressional District sweeps across northwest Ohio, including the suburbs of Toledo, the university town of Bowling Green, the Marathon Petroleum home in Findlay, and the towns of Napoleon and Defiance en route to Ohio's borders with Michigan and Indiana. Its factories are numerous and widespread. Bowling Green is the site of the state's first wind turbines. By 2017, the Columbus Dispatch reported, the wind industry was generating $1 billion statewide, with proposals that would more than triple the 255 active turbines. Napoleon has the world's largest Campbell soup plant. Upper Sandusky (more than 60 miles inland from Sandusky on Lake Erie) is home to about 30 industrial firms; it promotes its "small town living with big business appeal." In November 2017, voters in Bowling Green rejected a proposal that would have banned gas pipelines in their city.

This had been a solidly Republican district. Nearly one-third of the district is in suburban Lucas County, though its Toledo neighborhoods are mostly in the solidly Democratic 9th District. With adjacent Wood County, the area surrounding Toledo accounts for about one-half of the district. From 2010 to 2017, Lucas lost 3 percent of its population and Wood gained 4 percent. The outlying areas are strongly Republican. As with several other mostly rural Ohio districts, Donald Trump in 2016 boosted the Republican presidential performance here to 59 percent.

Bill Johnson (R)

Elected 2010, 5th term, b. Nov 10, 1954; Roseboro, NC; Air Command and Staff College (AL); Troy University (AL), B.S., 1979; Georgia Institute of Technology, M.S., 1984; Protestant - Unspecified Christian; Married (LeeAnn Johnson); 4 children; 6 grandchildren.

Military Career: U.S. Air Force 1973-1999

Professional Career: President, Johnson-Schley Mgmt. Group, 1999-2003; Owner, J2 Business Solutions, 2003-2006; Director, Lockheed Martin, 2005; CIO, Stoneridge Inc., 2006-2010.

DC Office: 2336 RHOB 20515, 202-225-5705, Fax: 202-225-5907, billjohnson.house.gov

State Offices: Cambridge, 740-432-2366; Ironton, 740-534-9431; Marietta, 740-376-0868; Salem, 330-337-6951.

Committees: *Budget. Energy & Commerce*: Communications & Technology; Energy; Environment & Climate Change.

Group Ratings

	ADA	ACLU	AFL-CIO	LCV	ITI	COC	HAFA	ACU	CFG	FRC
2018	-	4%	-	0%	-	92%	47%	72%	54%	100%
2017	0%	C	26%	0%	C	93%	C	74%	57%	100%

Almanac Ratings 2017-18

	Economy	Social	Foreign	Composite
Liberal	8%	4%	0%	4%
Conservative	92%	97%	100%	96%

Key Votes of the 115th Congress

1. Obama-care revision	Y	5. Family planning regs	Y	9. Guantanamo prisoners	N
2. Tax Cuts	Y	6. Body cameras/immigration	N	10. Ground missiles, limit	N
3. Omnibus appropriations	Y	7. Abortion ban	Y	11. Defense Dept. spending	Y
4. Dodd-Frank revision	Y	8. Concealed carry	Y	12. FISA rules	Y

Election Results

Election	Name (Party)	Vote (%)		Cand. Spent	Ind. Exp. Support	Ind. Exp. Oppose
2018 General	Bill Johnson (R)............................ 172,774	(69%)	$1,422,398	$1,095
	Shawna Roberts (D)........................ 76,716	(31%)	$26,624	
2018 Primary	Bill Johnson (R)............................ 50,271	(84%)		
	Robert Blazek (R)........................ 9,501	(16%)		

Prior winning percentages: 2016 (71%), 2014 (58%), 2012 (53%), 2010 (50%)

Republican Bill Johnson, elected in 2010 in what was a Democratic bastion not long ago, had been a business consultant and founded an anti-tax group. After learning the ropes, he has become an active member of the Energy and Commerce Committee, where he has been a zealous opponent of environmental regulation and an advocate of more business-friendly government. Wisely in this district, he has been an enthusiastic — though mostly low-profile -- ally of President Donald Trump.

Johnson was born in Roseboro North Carolina and raised on his family's cotton and tobacco farm. He joined the Air Force when he was 17. While serving, he graduated with a degree in computer science from Alabama's Troy University. Later, he earned his master's degree in computer science from Georgia Tech. In the military, he was stationed at many bases. As a director at U.S. Special Operations Command, he briefed congressional and intelligence officials. He retired from the military in 1999 as a lieutenant colonel, having managed communications and computer systems. He worked for multiple tech companies and became an information-technology consultant, especially for the military. He moved to Ohio in 2006, when he began working for Stoneridge, which makes electronic components for automobiles. Upset that shoppers were pouring across the border into Pennsylvania to buy certain goods free of sales taxes, Johnson in 2009 founded an organization called the Ohio Sales Tax Reform Incentive with the goal of creating tax holidays for shoppers.

He challenged two-term Democratic Rep. Charlie Wilson. In the GOP primary, he defeated Donald Allen, a veterinarian, 43%-37%. Wilson cast fiscally conservative votes and backed gun rights, but he voted for the Democrats' $787 billion economic stimulus bill and the Affordable Care Act. Johnson characterized Wilson as a puppet of liberal House Speaker Nancy Pelosi and out of touch with his constituents. Wilson accused Johnson's company of exporting jobs. Johnson replied that the company created jobs in Ohio and called Wilson's attacks "the desperate act of a career politician who cannot defend his record for his tax-and-spend policies." Johnson benefited from ads by the U.S. Chamber of Commerce that attacked Wilson as "Party-Line Charlie." Johnson won, 50%-45%, while Wilson was outspending him almost 2-to-1, though each benefited from national party spending.

Johnson's voting record moved closer to the center as he adopted more liberal positions on foreign policy. His Almanac vote ratings ranked him near the middle of Republicans in the House. He was an adamant critic of the Obama administration. He won House passage in 2012 of his "Stop the War on Coal Act," which barred the Environmental Protection Agency from restricting greenhouse gas emissions, quashed stricter fuel efficiency standards for cars and gave states control over disposal of coal byproducts.

On the Energy and Commerce Committee, Johnson advocated the interests of coal and promoted energy independence. In 2015, the House passed his bill to expedite exports of liquefied natural gas by setting a deadline for federal approval. After a trip to four European nations, he said that they were "begging" for U.S. energy exports so they could reduce their dependence on Russia. At a July 2016 committee hearing, he called the EPA "un-American" and said that the agency was "draining the lifeblood out of our businesses." Democrats criticized him as "extreme." In April 2018, he won committee approval of a bill to streamline approval of small-scale LNG facilities. On the House Budget Committee, Johnson ran unsuccessfully in January 2018 to fill the vacancy for chairman. Rep. Steve Womack of Arkansas was the easy winner of that contest.

In February 2017, Trump used one of his first bill-signings to enact a Johnson measure to overturn a regulation on mining waste that President Barack Obama had approved shortly before he left office. Johnson said that the sole purpose of the rule was "to put a death knell into the coffin of the coal industry." He has become a reliable advocate for Trump. "You don't have to like what he says," Johnson told a Lincoln Day dinner in Athens in April 2018. "But you can't argue with the idea of returning America to that age of innovation and ingenuity."

Wilson sought a comeback in 2012 and loaned his campaign more than $400,000 to keep pace with Johnson, who tried to preserve his outsider status with ads referring to his rival as "Congressman

Charlie Wilson." Wilson got about $2 million in help from the DCCC, but the anti-tax lobbying group Americans for Tax Reform spent more than $3 million on Johnson's behalf. Johnson won again, 53%-47%. In 2014, Johnson faced Democrat Jennifer Garrison, a lawyer who served six years in the state Assembly and described herself as "pro-life, pro-gun and pro-coal." She called Johnson "the face of Washington dysfunction." Johnson outspent her $1.9 million to $900,000. He won 58%-39% and took 17 of the 18 counties. In 2016, Johnson outraised his opponent by more than 100-to-1 and won, 71%-29%, evidence that Democrats had turned their attention elsewhere.

OH-6: Ohio River Valley   **Cook Partisan Voting Index: R+16**

Population		Race and Ethnicity		Income	
Total	703,764	White	94.5%	Median Income	$46,048
Land area (sq. miles)	7,215	Black	2.2%	District Income Rank	362
Pop/ sq mi	97.5	Latino	1.1%	Poverty Rate	16.5%
Born in State	69.8%	Asian	0.4%	With health insurance	91.9%
		Two or more races	1.5%	Cash public assistance	2.7%
Age Groups		Other	0.3%	Food stamp/SNAP	16.6%
Under 18	21.2%				
18-34	19.1%	**Education**		**Work**	
35-64	40.8%	H.S grad or less	55.5%	White Collar	18.9%
Over 64	18.9%	Some college	28.6%	Sales and Service	41.2%
		College Degree, 4 yr	9.9%	Blue Collar	30.4%
Military		Post grad	5.9%	Government	12.4%
Veteran/ Active Duty	9.7%				

2012 Pres. Vote	Romney	176,602	(55%)	Obama	136,518	(43%)		
2016 Pres. Vote	Trump	221,872	(69%)	Clinton	85,501	(27%)	Johnson	8,833	(3%)

Steubenville: In the years after the American Revolution, shipping goods downriver by raft was cheaper than sending them over the Appalachian Mountains, and so the Ohio River became a great highway of commerce. From Pittsburgh, where the Allegheny and Monongahela Rivers meet to form the Ohio, the river led south and west toward the Mississippi and the great port of New Orleans. For hundreds of miles, it twisted this way and that through mountains and rolling hills, land that marked the boundary between post-Revolutionary Virginia and the Northwest Territory, between slaveholding territory and free soil as determined by the Confederation Congress of 1787. Across this boundary, settlers made their way in those years to Ohio — Yankees and, in larger numbers, Virginians.

By the late 19th century, the Ohio was an industrial river. Coal was nearby, barge transportation was available, and railroads were built in the narrow valleys between the hills. Steel mills went up on the riverfront. This produced prosperity for a while, but it also produced pollution — Steubenville on the Ohio River once had the nation's dirtiest air — and after the old-line steel industry fell on hard times, the Ohio River was lined with some of the most impoverished parts of America. So many people left what became known as Appalachia to find jobs in Detroit and the big industrial cities that the road to the north was called the Hillbilly Highway. Even with mandates from the Clean Air Act, the pollution in much of the area from coal-fired power plants remains. Locally, many landowners reaped a windfall after rising prices made feasible the extraction of vast reserves of oil and natural gas from the Marcellus and Utica shale beds miles under their land. In December 2018, President Donald Trump's trade war, which was designed to benefit areas like this, was credited with reopening a steel mill in Mingo Junction that had been closed for 10 years. In January 2019, the local economic progress ranked Steubenville and Jefferson County first in the nation for its percentage gain in construction jobs.

The 6th Congressional District of Ohio is a string of counties running 325 miles along the Ohio River, plus part of the Mahoning Valley. It includes Canfield and a few small suburbs of Youngstown in Mahoning County. Nearby are Steubenville, once known as "Sin City" and home to Rat Pack crooner Dean Martin, and Hanoverton, the home for nearly two centuries of the Spread Eagle Tavern — a Republican hangout. The district curves along the lightly populated stretch of the river south from Marietta, past the old industrial town of Ironton, and extends to Wheelersburg, which is not quite in the Cincinnati metro area. For most of its length, the district extends one or two counties from the river.

This mix of communities has become a Republican enclave with a cultural conservatism much like that of West Virginia and eastern Kentucky across the river. The population is 95 percent white, the third highest in the nation, but with the lowest median income of any Republican-held district in Ohio. In 2016, Trump won this district, 69%-27%. That margin, the largest in Ohio, was all the more extraordinary given that Mitt Romney in 2012 won, 55%-43%. In Columbiana, the Republican chairman called the area, "the very epicentre of the Trump groundswell." The only local patch of blue in the district is a small piece — less than 10 percent — of university-based Athens County.

Bob Gibbs (R)

Elected 2010, 5th term, b. Jun 14, 1954; Peru, IN; Ohio State University Agricultural Technical Institute, A.A.S., 1974; Methodist; Married (Jody Gibbs); 3 children.

Elected Office: OH House, 2003-2008; OH Senate, 2008-2010.

Professional Career: Technician, OH Ag. Research & Devel. Center, 1974-1978; Owner, Hidden Hollow Farms, 1978-2004; Owner, Gibbs Enterprises.

DC Office: 2446 RHOB 20515, 202-225-6265, Fax: 202-225-3394, gibbs.house.gov

State Offices: Ashland, 419-207-0650; Canton, 330-737-1631.

Committees: *Oversight & Reform*: Subcommittee on Environment. *Transportation & Infrastructure*: Coast Guard & Maritime Transportation (RMM); Highways & Transit.

Group Ratings

	ADA	ACLU	AFL-CIO	LCV	ITI	COC	HAFA	ACU	CFG	FRC
2018	-	4%	-	0%	-	92%	71%	80%	57%	100%
2017	0%	C	8%	0%	C	93%	C	85%	80%	100%

Almanac Ratings 2017-18

	Economy	Social	Foreign	Composite
Liberal	2%	4%	0%	2%
Conservative	99%	97%	100%	98%

Key Votes of the 115th Congress

1. Obama-care revision	Y	5. Family planning regs	Y	9. Guantanamo prisoners	N
2. Tax Cuts	Y	6. Body cameras/immigration	N	10. Ground missiles, limit	N
3. Omnibus appropriations	Y	7. Abortion ban	Y	11. Defense Dept. spending	Y
4. Dodd-Frank revision	Y	8. Concealed carry	Y	12. FISA rules	Y

Election Results

Election	Name (Party)	Vote (%)		Cand. Spent	Ind. Exp. Support	Ind. Exp. Oppose
2018 General	Bob Gibbs (R)	153,117	(59%)	$1,722,903	$1,099	$216,138
	Ken Harbaugh (D)	107,536	(41%)	$2,953,875	$40,938	$92,828
2018 Primary	Bob Gibbs (R)	42,274	(78%)			
	Patrick Quinn (R)	6,211	(11%)			
	Terry Robertson (R)	5,765	(11%)			

Prior winning percentages: 2016 (64%), 2014 (100%), 2012 (56%), 2010 (54%)

Republican Bob Gibbs, elected in 2010, is a hog farmer and ex-state farm bureau president who takes seriously agriculture and public works projects. As chairman of the Water Resources and Environment Subcommittee, he was a prime dispenser of congressional pork — or, as his website described his domain, "cost effective water infrastructure improvements that provide jobs." He has avidly sought to cut back excessive regulations. In 2019, he took on a new water-based assignment as ranking Republican on the Coast Guard and Maritime Transportation Subcommittee.

Gibbs grew up on the west side of Cleveland, "as far away from agriculture as you can get," he said. After working in the garden center of his high school, he enrolled in Ohio State University's Agricultural Institute. Gibbs went into business in Holmes County with his Hidden Hollow Farms, where he mostly raised market hogs. His two terms as president of the Ohio Farm Bureau Federation sparked his interest in politics. In 2002, Gibbs won a seat in the Ohio House. He was elected six years later to the Senate, where he chaired the Ways and Means Committee. He focused on agriculture, small business and private property issues. He co-authored a 21 percent cut in Ohio's personal income tax rates.

Gibbs challenged two-term Democratic Rep. Zack Space, a self-described moderate and a prolific fundraiser. They attacked each other on climate change, health care reform and the "don't ask, don't tell" policy prohibiting gay men and women from serving openly in the military. Republicans blasted Space for his vote for the 2009 House-passed bill to create a cap-and-trade system to reduce greenhouse-gas emissions. Space ran ads with footage of Gibbs telling an audience, "I'm a free-trader," and tying him to trade deals that, Space said, sent Ohio jobs overseas. Space outspent Gibbs, $2.9 million to $1.1 million; each had more than $1 million in national party help. In the 2010 Republican tidal wave, Gibbs won easily, 54%-40%.

With a boost from Speaker John Boehner, Gibbs got the Water Resources subcommittee chairmanship -- a prime plum for a freshman. He enacted in 2014 the Water Resources Reform and Development Act, the first such reauthorization since 2007. The law reformed the review process of the Army Corps of Engineers for the nation's ports and flood control projects, "deauthorized" $18 billion in inactive projects and included no specific earmarks. But Gibbs worked to provide clear guidance to the Army Corps for new projects. "Typically, it would take 10 to 15 years to complete the studies necessary prior to beginning construction. WRRDA will reduce that time to three years so that projects are able to begin as they are needed and create jobs," he summarized. He noted, in particular, the need to protect the health of Great Lakes ports. Subsequently, Gibbs said he was "disappointed" with the slow pace and the priorities of the Army Corps in its implementation of the new law.

Gibbs used his position to blast the Environmental Protection Agency. The House in 2011 passed his Reducing Regulatory Burdens Act, which prevented the implementation of a court order requiring pesticide applications in and around U.S. waters to be covered by Clean Water Act permits. In 2015, the House passed his bill to nullify the EPA's proposed Waters of the United States (WOTUS) rules, which Gibbs described as "a vast expansion of federal jurisdiction." His measure deadlocked in the Senate.

The election of President Donald Trump became a policy breakthrough for Gibbs. In February 2017, he joined a White House ceremony where Trump signed an executive order that overturned Obama's WOTUS rules. Trump called those rules one of the worst examples of government "run amok." Gibbs praised Trump for keeping his campaign promise. Subsequently, a federal judge in South Carolina blocked the Trump administration's move to suspend the water rules. On the farm bill that was enacted in 2018, Gibbs took the lead in the House on a provision that encouraged farmers to make more use of clean-water sources. In 2019, as the senior Republican on the Coast Guard Subcommittee, he pursued his interest in water navigation, especially on the Great Lakes.

Redistricting gave Gibbs a district in which six of the 10 counties were completely new to him, but the new district leaned more Republican. In 2012, Democrats nominated Joyce Healy-Abrams, who ran a corporate record-keeping business and whose brother, William Healy, was mayor of Canton. She spent $905,000 to $1.3 million for Gibbs. Healy-Abrams won 55 percent of the vote in Stark, but Gibbs rolled up big majorities in the other counties and won 56%-44%.

In 2018, Democratic challenger Ken Harbaugh, a Navy veteran with support from veterans groups, spent $3 million to $1.7 million for Gibbs. His campaign theme was "country over party" and he styled himself as a political centrist. The Cleveland Plain Dealer endorsed Harbaugh, though it said that his campaign views were "noticeably thin;" it criticized Gibbs for his "blind partisanship" in support of Trump. Gibbs won, 59%-41%; he took all 10 counties, with 51 percent in Stark.

OH-7: North-Central Ohio   **Cook Partisan Voting Index: R+12**

Population		Race and Ethnicity		Income	
Total	724,257	White	91%	Median Income	$52,532
Land area (sq. miles)	3,865	Black	3.9%	District Income Rank	263
Pop/ sq mi	187.4	Latino	2.1%	Poverty Rate	12.7%
Born in State	83%	Asian	0.6%	With health insurance	90.1%
		Two or more races	2.1%	Cash public assistance	4.1%
Age Groups		Other	0.2%	Food stamp/SNAP	12.4%
Under 18	23.5%				
18-34	19.8%	**Education**		**Work**	
35-64	39.3%	H.S grad or less	52.1%	White Collar	17.4%
Over 64	17.4%	Some college	27.9%	Sales and Service	40%
		College Degree, 4 yr	13.1%	Blue Collar	30.1%
Military		Post grad	6.8%	Government	10.3%
Veteran/ Active Duty	9.1%				

2012 Pres. Vote	Romney	179,375	(54%)	Obama	147,567	(44%)		
2016 Pres. Vote	Trump	205,572	(62%)	Clinton	107,942	(33%)	Johnson	10,856 (3%)

Canton, Cleveland Suburbs: A little more than a century ago, Canton was at the center of American politics. It was already an industrial city, though without the huge steel mills of Youngstown or Cleveland. Its high-skill workers were fashioning new kinds of plows and reapers, making watches and, beginning in 1899, roller bearings. It did not attract masses of immigrants, its factories did not run on harsh stopwatch discipline, and the class-warfare politics of other northern Ohio industrial cities did not take root here. Canton's most famous citizen was Republican President William McKinley, who rose to the rank of major at age 22 in the Civil War and was later elected to Congress. In 1896, he campaigned for president from his front porch in Canton, meeting with delegations brought in by train from around the country. This spectacle, displaying both technological virtuosity and personal modesty, sounded a reverberating note in American politics, as did the McKinley platform — the "full dinner pail," the gold standard and the enforcement of law and order in labor relations — a platform that mostly severed the Democrats' ties to northern blue-collar whites until the 1930s.

Today, Canton remains based on manufacturing and has had some recovery from job losses With a boost from President Donald Trump's tariffs, the Republic Steel plant in July 2018 added a new shift of workers. In 2017, community leaders issued a report warning that surrounding Stark County was growing "smaller, older and poorer," unless there was major economic development. Canton has become best known as the home of the Professional Football Hall of Fame, with a roof shaped like a football. The Canton Bulldogs were one of the first teams in the Ohio League, the predecessor to the modern National Football League. The NFL has pursued lavish plans for a $700 million, 200-acre Hall of Fame village in Canton, which has been described as sports and entertainment "Disney for football fans" and is scheduled to open in 2020, the centennial of the league. Planned facilities include a university for coaches, an Institute for the Integrity of Officials, eight turf fields, a four-star hotel and conference center, a 5,500-seat performance center, a retirement complex and retail space. The area includes Holmes County, which has moved toward becoming the first Amish-majority county in the nation. Ashland is a rural county where Johnny Appleseed lived on what is now Ashland University. The campus includes the Ashbrook Center, which has become a hub for conservative academicians and politicians.

The 7th Congressional District of Ohio is a hodgepodge of counties forming a crescent across northeastern Ohio and avoiding Democratic areas of Cleveland, Akron and Lorain. It includes all of Canton, the old Ohio and Erie Canal town of Massillon, and most of Stark County, which has about a third of the district's population. Much of the area west and southwest of Canton is part of the Appalachian Plateau. The remaining swath of lightly populated counties arches west to Knox County on the outskirts of Columbus and north to North Ridgeville and Avon nearly to Lake Erie in Lorain County. The district extends through Medina County in the outer reaches of the Cleveland metropolitan area. The Stark County portions of the district are Democratic, but the rest is mostly

Republican and the net result is that the 7th District leans Republican. In 2016 Donald Trump had a 62%-33% lead over Hillary Clinton.

Warren Davidson (R)

Elected 2016, 2nd full term, b. Mar 01, 1970; Troy; University of Notre Dame (IN), M.B.A.; U.S. Military Academy - West Point (NY), B.A., 1995; Married (Lisa Davidson); 2 children.

Military Career: U.S. Army 1995-2000

DC Office: 1107 LHOB 20515, 202-225-6205, Fax: 202-225-0704, davidson.house.gov

State Offices: Springfield, 937-322-1120; Troy, 937-339-1524; West Chester, 513-779-5400.

Committees: *Financial Services*: Investor Protection, Entrepreneurship & Capital Markets; Oversight & Investigations.

Group Ratings

	ADA	ACLU	AFL-CIO	LCV	ITI	COC	HAFA	ACU	CFG	FRC
2018	-	26%	-	3%	-	75%	95%	100%	98%	100%
2017	0%	C	3%	0%	C	93%	C	96%	98%	100%

Almanac Ratings 2017-18

	Economy	Social	Foreign	Composite
Liberal	0%	16%	8%	8%
Conservative	100%	84%	92%	92%

Key Votes of the 115th Congress

1. Obama-care revision	Y	5. Family planning regs	Y	9. Guantanamo prisoners	N
2. Tax Cuts	Y	6. Body cameras/immigration	N	10. Ground missiles, limit	N
3. Omnibus appropriations	N	7. Abortion ban	Y	11. Defense Dept. spending	Y
4. Dodd-Frank revision	Y	8. Concealed carry	Y	12. FISA rules	N

Election Results

Election	Name (Party)	Vote (%)	Cand. Spent	Ind. Exp. Support	Ind. Exp. Oppose
2018 General	Warren Davidson (R)..................... 173,852	(67%)	$406,807		
	Vanessa Enoch (D)............................... 87,281	(33%)	$40,977		
2018 Primary	Warren Davidson (R)............................	(100%)			

Prior winning percentages: 2016 (69%), 2016 special (77%)

Warren Davidson won a special election in June 2016 to replace Speaker John Boehner, who had resigned from the House. With his business background, he has centered his work at the Financial Services Committee. He has been an active member of the Freedom Caucus, though —unlike some of the group's members — he does not automatically support the views of President Donald Trump.

Davidson grew up in Sydney, which is between Dayton and Lima. In high school, he was not a motivated student. As Davidson recounted to The Cincinnati Enquirer, he told a guidance counselor during his senior year that he wanted to attend West Point. She told him, "Baby, that's not going to happen." Instead, he enlisted in the Army. He gained a series of promotions and became an elite Army Ranger. He witnessed the fall of the Berlin Wall while he was serving in Germany. With this background, he eventually won an appointment to West Point, where he graduated with a degree in American history.

When he left the military, he returned home and planned to join his father's tool-making manufacturing business. But, The Enquirer reported, the business was "floundering" and his father was "leery of change." Davidson started his own tool-making business. He was successful and bought out his father. The company grew from 20 employees to more than 200. During that time, he got an MBA from Notre Dame University and settled in Concord Township, where he served two years as a trustee. He was appointed to the position after having lost an election for the seat.

After Boehner resigned, Davidson voiced interest in running. Republican Rep. Jim Jordan of the neighboring district arranged an appointment for him with the Washington-based Club for Growth. Davidson won the endorsement. "It was a pretty easy call for us," said Andrew Roth, the group's vice president of government affairs told The Enquirer. "He doesn't mince words. It was clear that what he was telling us was based on principle." That support proved vital when the Club spent $1.1 million on behalf of Davidson during the primary. His two chief opponents, Bill Beagle and Tim Derickson, raised $500,000 and $300,000, respectively. Each was a member of the state legislature. For the entire campaign, Davidson raised nearly $1 million.

The 15-candidate March primary for the special election attracted a turnout of about 130,000. Davidson won with 32 percent of the vote to 24 percent for Derickson and 20 percent for Beagle. Derickson led in Butler and Beagle led in Miami, the two counties with the largest turnouts. Davidson ran second in those counties and led elsewhere. Davidson defeated Democrat Corey Foister, 77%-12%, with a thin turnout. Foister was described as a 25-year-old whose biggest political achievement was serving in student government at Northern Kentucky University.

Davidson joined the invitation-only Freedom Caucus, the group that spurred Boehner's downfall and where Rep. Jordan has been a leader. By 2018, he expressed interest in becoming the group's leader once Rep. Mark Meadows of North Carolina stepped down. He talked up Jordan in his unsuccessful bid to take over as GOP leader following the 2018 election. At the end of the year, Davidson was among the House members who took a hard line during the government shutdown in demanding that Congress approve funds for a border wall with Mexico. He also proposed alternative funding for the wall, including crowdfunding appeals and the use of digital currency such as bitcoin.

Davidson got a seat on the Financial Services Committee. In 2017, he filed with freshman Rep. Ted Budd of North Carolina the "Drain the Swamp" bill, which required that each federal agency relocate its employees across the nation and retain no more than 10 percent of its staff in the Washington area. He filed with Democratic Rep. Darren Soto of Florida a bill to permit the regulation of so-called crypto-currencies separately from securities law. One purpose was to prevent the flight of those funds to uncontrolled off-shore jurisdictions. Their goal, Davidson said, was to promote "American leadership in this innovative space." Bitcoin has had few consumer protections, as its value has gyrated widely.

Davidson voiced occasional disagreements with Trump. At a local farm forum in March 2018, he opposed the president's trade war with China and said that he was "very concerned" about the adverse impact on farm commodities. Later, he said that he was frustrated by "the amount of spending" that Trump approved, including farm legislation and hurricane relief. "The oath of office says to support and defend the Constitution, not support the president," Davidson told The Cincinnati Enquirer in October 2018.

OH-8: West-Central Ohio

Cook Partisan Voting Index: R+17

Population		Race and Ethnicity		Income	
Total	725,385	White	86.3%	Median Income	$55,913
Land area (sq. miles)	2,450	Black	5.9%	District Income Rank	218
Pop/ sq mi	296	Latino	3.3%	Poverty Rate	12.8%
Born in State	74.4%	Asian	1.8%	With health insurance	93.3%
		Two or more races	2.3%	Cash public assistance	3.2%
Age Groups		Other	0.3%	Food stamp/SNAP	12.1%
Under 18	23.8%				
18-34	21.7%	**Education**		**Work**	
35-64	38.9%	H.S grad or less	47.2%	White Collar	15.6%
Over 64	15.6%	Some college	29%	Sales and Service	39.8%
Military		College Degree, 4 yr	15.1%	Blue Collar	26%
Veteran/ Active Duty	9%	Post grad	8.8%	Government	10.8%

2012 Pres. Vote	Romney	211,446	(62%)	Obama	124,407	(36%)			
2016 Pres. Vote	Trump	223,215	(65%)	Clinton	104,929	(30%)	Johnson	10,948	(3%)

Cincinnati and Dayton Suburbs, Springfield: Since the early 20th century, the far west edge of Ohio — where U.S. 40, the old National Road, heads into Indiana — was some of the nation's prime industrial country. The Great and Little Miami rivers drain south into the Ohio, and the Miami and Erie Canal system continues its northward march to Toledo. The small cities and towns around and between Dayton and Cincinnati were rising industrial country a century ago. In the years since, they have weathered economic downturns and sought to adapt to changing markets and circumstances. Butler County, in between the two cities, was dominated by the large factory towns of Hamilton and Middletown, which suffered downturns during the recession but now style themselves as "reinvention cities." Butler is reliably Republican and has had an economic boom since the recession, with a big increase in retail vendor licenses.

Butler's population has grown with the outflow of people from Cincinnati and Dayton, an increase of 14 percent from 2000 to 2017. The county has five universities, including Miami in Oxford. The center of growth has been West Chester Township, situated on Interstate 75 south of Wright-Patterson Air Force Base and rated by Money magazine as one of the best places to live in the nation. It has attracted an Amylin Pharmaceuticals facility, which produces diabetes medication and is owned by AstraZeneca. CFM manufactures jet engines in a partnership between GE and French-owned Safran. The town remains the home of former House Speaker John Boehner.

The 8th Congressional District of Ohio includes all of Butler County. It extends north along the Indiana border to take in Preble County and Darke County, the birthplace of Phoebe Ann Moses, later known as sharpshooter Annie Oakley. The district includes Clark County, with economically depressed Springfield, where manufacturing has collapsed, the poverty rate is 26 percent and residents are disproportionately aging. Its declining population is at a 90-year low, with a 10 percent drop from 2000 to 2017. In 2016, the Pew Research Center listed Springfield as tied with Goldsboro North Carolina as the cities with the largest decline in economic status since 2000. Springfield votes Democratic, but its presence does not alter the partisan balance of the district, which has been comfortably Republican. About half the voters are in Butler County and 20 percent are in Clark. Donald Trump got 64 percent of the vote in 2016. He surpassed that in Ohio only with his 69 percent in the 6th District.

Marcy Kaptur (D)

Elected 1982, 19th term, b. Jun 17, 1946; Toledo; St. Ursula Academy (OH), Att.; University of Wisconsin, B.A., 1968; University of Manchester (England), Att., 1974; University of Michigan, M.A., 1974; Massachusetts Institute of Technology, Att., 1981; Catholic; Single.

Professional Career: Urban planner, Lucas County Planning Comm., 1969-1975; Urban planning consultant, 1975-1977; White House Assistant Director for Urban Affairs, 1977-1980; Deputy Secretary, National Consumer Coop. Bank, 1980-1981.

DC Office: 2186 RHOB 20515, 202-225-4146, Fax: 202-225-7711, kaptur.house.gov

State Offices: Cleveland, 216-767-5933; Lorain, 440-288-1500; Toledo, 419-259-7500.

Committees: *Appropriations*: Commerce, Justice, Science & Related Agencies; Defense; Energy & Water Development & Related Agencies (Chmn).

Group Ratings

	ADA	ACLU	AFL-CIO	LCV	ITI	COC	HAFA	ACU	CFG	FRC
2018	-	79%	-	94%	-	58%	4%	4%	2%	0%
2017	100%	C	97%	97%	C	36%	C	4%	5%	0%

Almanac Ratings 2017-18

	Economy	Social	Foreign	Composite
Liberal	100%	92%	93%	95%
Conservative	0%	8%	7%	5%

Key Votes of the 115th Congress

1. Obama-care revision	N	5. Family planning regs	N	9. Guantanamo prisoners	Y
2. Tax Cuts	N	6. Body cameras/immigration	Y	10. Ground missiles, limit	Y
3. Omnibus appropriations	Y	7. Abortion ban	N	11. Defense Dept. spending	Y
4. Dodd-Frank revision	N	8. Concealed carry	N	12. FISA rules	N

Election Results

Election	Name (Party)	Vote (%)		Cand. Spent	Ind. Exp. Support	Ind. Exp. Oppose
2018 General	Marcy Kaptur (D)	157,219	(68%)	$377,677		
	Steven Kraus (R)	74,670	(32%)			
2018 Primary	Marcy Kaptur (D)	41,502	(86%)			
	Joshua Garcia (D)	7,029	(15%)			

Prior winning percentages: 2016 (69%), 2014 (68%), 2012 (73%), 2010 (59%), 2008 (74%), 2006 (74%), 2004 (68%), 2002 (74%), 2000(75%), 1998 (81%), 1996 (77%), 1994 (75%), 1992 (74%), 1990 (78%), 1988 (81%), 1986 (78%), 1984 (56%), 1982 (58%)

Democrat Marcy Kaptur, first elected in 1982, has set the record for the longest-serving woman in the House. Kaptur is a plainspoken Democrat and a dedicated opponent of free trade who does not always toe the party line, but whose old-fashioned ways have proven popular at home. In 2019, she highlighted the importance of Ohio as "a leader in the energy industry" as she chaired the Appropriations Subcommittee on Energy and Water Development.

Kaptur grew up in a blue-collar neighborhood in Toledo, the daughter of Polish-American parents who worked at local auto plants. The family also operated a small grocery store, but her father sold it to get a job with health benefits. "It broke his heart," she said. She has spent almost her entire career in public service. She graduated from the University of Wisconsin, the first in her family to attend college, got a master's degree from the University of Michigan, then spent eight years as an urban planner in Toledo. She worked on urban revitalization in the Jimmy Carter White House. She interrupted her studies for a doctorate at M.I.T. to return home and run for office. In 1982, she challenged first-term Republican Rep. Ed Weber and won 58%-39%, despite being outspent 3-to-1.

Kaptur has long been convinced that Toledo and places like it have lost jobs and industry because of unfair trade practices and low-wage competition from countries like Mexico and China. She was featured prominently in left-wing filmmaker Michael Moore's 2009 movie Capitalism: A Love Story. "I have always said there's a great injustice being done here, because the power rests with a handful of megabanks and millions of Americans are being affected," she told The Toledo Blade when the film opened.

She criticized President Bill Clinton for ignoring Democrats opposed to the 1993 North American Free Trade Agreement. In 1995, she made a rousing speech on trade before Texas businessman Ross Perot's United We Stand Party. Perot, running as a third-party candidate for president in 1996, offered her the vice presidential nomination, but she turned it down. She was a vocal opponent of normal trade relations with China and the Central American Free Trade Agreement.

Reflecting on those early trade wars years later, Kaptur criticized Nancy Pelosi's support of NAFTA. "That's where the real knife was put in the flesh," she said. When Pelosi announced in 2007 an agreement with Treasury Secretary Hank Paulson on principles for international trade policy, an uninvited Kaptur glared from the back of the room. She strongly opposed trade agreements with Colombia, Panama and South Korea that passed the House in 2011. When the House narrowly voted in 2015 to give trade promotion authority to President Barack Obama, Kaptur slammed proponents who she said sold out "working families and American industries that have been the backbone of the U.S. economy for decades."

Kaptur has departed from party orthodoxy on abortion. She opposes federal funding for the procedure, though she has also voted against proposals to deny federal money to Planned Parenthood. She contended that federal funds were not used for abortions, and that Planned Parenthood provided valuable medical care for women.

On the Appropriations Committee, Kaptur in 2012 hoped to fill the vacancy as the ranking Democrat. But the post instead went to Nita Lowey of New York, who had six fewer years of seniority but was a more predictable liberal and a favorite of Pelosi, who earlier served on the committee. Kaptur became ranking Democrat on the Energy and Water Development Subcommittee. She is a strong advocate of Ohio-produced alternative energy such as ethanol and biofuels. Kaptur has also promoted solar energy, a growing industry in Toledo.

In 2019, as subcommittee chairwoman, she invoked Ohio's long history in energy innovation and suggested that she could help to promote those interests. "Many, many of the firms in Ohio, or the inventors who are patenting, don't necessarily see the institutions here in Washington as being a helpful partner to them," Kaptur told an interviewer with Spectrum News. "And I think we need a little more shoulder-to-the-wheel in that arena." She also has emphasized her continued protection of the Great Lakes, which she describes as "the largest collection of fresh water on the planet."

Prior to the House ban on earmarks, Kaptur in 2010 ranked 24th for her district among the top earmark recipients, according to the group Taxpayers for Common Sense. She once challenged Republicans on Appropriations to limit farm payments, but when they threatened her favorite spending projects, she backed off. "I may be blockheaded sometimes, but I'm not stupid," Kaptur said.

Kaptur keeps close tabs on her district. A constituent gave her the idea to sponsor the legislation that created the World War II Memorial on the National Mall. She is exceedingly popular in the Toledo area and rarely has faced a credible challenge. In 2012, Ohio lost two congressional seats. Republicans drawing the new map put her in a district with Cleveland-based Democratic Rep. Dennis Kucinich. Though Kucinich's bids for president had made him a national hero to hard-core progressives, he had a reputation at home for hobnobbing with celebrities and not accomplishing much for the district. Kaptur defeated Kucinich in the Democratic primary, 56%-40%, putting an end to his 16-year House career. In Lucas County, she led 94%-4%. Since then, she has had no primary opposition and has breezed to reelection. She appears secure, at least until the next redistricting.

Kaptur's dealings with Pelosi and other Democratic leaders have continued to evolve. In 2002, she ran a quixotic, one-day campaign for minority leader against Pelosi but, predictably, got nowhere. In 2008, she challenged Xavier Becerra of California for Democratic Caucus vice chair and lost badly, 175-67. She backed Pelosi for minority leader in 2011 when her hold on power within the caucus had grown tenuous. The two appeared to have reached an entente following the 2018 election when Kaptur gave early and enthusiastic support to her return as Speaker, even as other Ohio Democrats explored possible leadership challenges. In a statement, Kaptur said, "No possible candidate can match Nancy Pelosi's indefatigable, consistent determination to restore a Democratic majority against tremendous odds."

In 2018, Kaptur exceeded the 35 years of House service of Republican Rep. Edith Nourse Rogers of Massachusetts, who had held the longest tenure for a woman. (Barbara Mikulski of Maryland retained the record of 40 years of combined House and Senate service.) She is the second most-senior House Democrat, behind only Steny Hoyer of Maryland. In an interview with National Public Radio, Kaptur reflected on the changes in the nation. "I was rejected when I applied to the U.S. Air Force Academy, to Notre Dame University when I was first seeking to go to college, and to the FBI because I was a woman," she said. Now, women have a major presence at each of those institutions.

As for the House, Kaptur cited her belief in what she called the Marshmallow Maxim. "You get here and it's like you run into this big marshmallow, this mammoth marshmallow," she added. "And it kind of absorbs you, and it's so hard to work your way through in order to get passage to do something different for the country."

OH-9: Lakefront   Cook Partisan Voting Index: D+14

Population		Race and Ethnicity		Income	
Total	710,563	White	68.4%	Median Income	$42,346
Land area (sq. miles)	465	Black	15.7%	District Income Rank	400
Pop/ sq mi	1529.2	Latino	11.1%	Poverty Rate	20.6%
Born in State	75.9%	Asian	1.4%	With health insurance	91.8%
		Two or more races	3.1%	Cash public assistance	3.9%
Age Groups		Other	0.3%	Food stamp/SNAP	21%
Under 18	22.4%				
18-34	23.4%	**Education**		**Work**	
35-64	39%	H.S grad or less	46.5%	White Collar	15.2%
Over 64	15.2%	Some college	31.8%	Sales and Service	44.1%
		College Degree, 4 yr	14%	Blue Collar	25%
Military		Post grad	7.8%	Government	11.5%
Veteran/ Active Duty	7.9%				

2012 Pres. Vote	Obama	217,169	(68%)	Romney	99,213	(31%)			
2016 Pres. Vote	Clinton	177,147	(58%)	Trump	110,178	(36%)	Johnson	9,495	(3%)

Toledo, Cleveland Suburbs: Lake Erie, the southernmost and shallowest of the Great Lakes, played a critical role in the history of America's interior. For decades, its shoreline was the locus of a four-way battle among French, Indian, British and American claimants. Additional conflicts over various claims to the area made by the various American colonies bubbled underneath. Once the federal government finally assumed full control of the Lake Erie shoreline in 1800, development proceeded quickly. Cleveland, at the mouth of the Cuyahoga River, had a population of 1,000 in 1830. Toledo and Cleveland became the biggest cities once the Ohio & Erie and Miami & Erie canals were completed. All the towns benefited from the trade that flowed from the Atlantic seaboard, up the Erie Canal to Buffalo, across the lake and into the burgeoning American interior. The canal traffic declined in the late 1800s, but Lake Erie retained an important role in the economy. Erie contains only 2 percent of the water of the Great Lakes, but 50 percent of its fish. It houses one of the largest commercial freshwater fisheries in the world, including a large yellow perch yield. Port Clinton bills itself as the "Walleye Capital of the World" and drops a plastic walleye in place of a glittering ball on New Year's Eve.

Fiat Chrysler in 2017 shut down its Toledo assembly line for Jeep Cherokees and moved their production to Belvidere Illinois. In its place, the company upgraded its plant to produce Jeep Wranglers and then pick-up trucks. Its local workforce remained at about 5,000. Gritty Lorain has survived decades of job losses and shutdowns as a steel town. That changed, modestly and perhaps temporarily, as the result of President Donald Trump's trade war, which placed domestic steel production as a high priority. Republic Steel set the delayed reopening by mid-2019 of its plant that had closed in March 2016. But the U.S. Steel plant, idled in 2015, remained shut down. The high-tech economy has made some local inroads, including innovative ways to clean up the environmental degradation left behind by earlier industries. Pollution poses a continued threat to the native fisheries. The canals brought in invasive species — most recently Asian carp — while runoff from farms still promotes algae blooms. In March 2018, the state's environmental agency designated the western part of Lake Erie as an "impaired" waterway.

The 9th Congressional District sprawls across the Lake Erie shoreline, rarely venturing more than 10 miles inland and sometimes less than a mile or two. From Toledo-based Lucas County, with about 30 percent of its voters, it goes east through Port Clinton and Sandusky, home to the giant Cedar Point amusement park, with some of the country's fastest roller coasters, and on to Lorain and Avon Lake. About 40 percent are in Cuyahoga County, where the district takes in western Cleveland, including Hopkins International Airport. This portion includes some inner suburbs, such as revived Lakewood, with its many Victorian-era houses. (Three other districts include parts of Cuyahoga.) Toledo and Cleveland rank fifth and twelfth among the nation's cities in their population loss from 2010 to 2017. The two ends of the district, which are 120 miles apart, have shared other features: generally blue-collar economies and Democratic voting patterns. That changed a bit in 2016. With a minority population of about 30 percent and a large white blue-collar cadre, the 58 percent for Hillary Clinton dropped from the 68 percent that Barack Obama got in 2012.

Michael Turner (R)

Elected 2002, 9th term, b. Jan 11, 1960; Dayton; Ohio Northern University, B.A., 1982; Case Western Reserve University School of Law (OH), J.D., 1985; University of Dayton (OH), M.B.A., 1992; Presbyterian; Divorced; 2 children.

Elected Office: Dayton Mayor, 1993-2001.

Professional Career: Practicing attorney.

DC Office: 2082 RHOB 20515, 202-225-6465, Fax: 202-225-6754, turner.house.gov

State Offices: Dayton, 937-225-2843.

Committees: *Armed Services*: Strategic Forces (RMM); Tactical Air & Land Forces. *Permanent Select on Intelligence*: Defense Intelligence & Warfighter Support; Strategic Technologies & Advanced Research.

Group Ratings

	ADA	ACLU	AFL-CIO	LCV	ITI	COC	HAFA	ACU	CFG	FRC
2018	-	14%	-	14%	-	100%	40%	52%	41%	100%
2017	5%	C	32%	6%	C	93%	C	63%	46%	89%

Key Votes of the 115th Congress

1. Obama-care revision	N	5. Family planning regs	Y	9. Guantanamo prisoners	N
2. Tax Cuts	Y	6. Body cameras/immigration	N	10. Ground missiles, limit	N
3. Omnibus appropriations	Y	7. Abortion ban	Y	11. Defense Dept. spending	Y
4. Dodd-Frank revision	Y	8. Concealed carry	Y	12. FISA rules	Y

Election Results

Election	Name (Party)	Vote (%)		Cand. Spent	Ind. Exp. Support	Ind. Exp. Oppose
2018 General	Michael Turner (R)	157,554	(56%)	$1,442,017		$4,258
	Theresa Gasper (D)	118,785	(42%)	$1,171,543	$24,596	
2018 Primary	Michael Turner (R)	43,047	(80%)			
	John Anderson (R)	6,192	(12%)			
	John Mitchell (R)	4,693	(9%)			

Prior winning percentages: 2016 (64%), 2014 (65%), 2012 (60%), 2010 (68%), 2008 (63%), 2006 (59%), 2004 (62%), 2002 (59%)

Republican Mike Turner, first elected in 2002, is a former Dayton mayor who has retained his strong interest in urban issues. He has gained significant influence and a growing voice on national security policy, which he has used on behalf of his district's military presence.

Turner grew up in Dayton, where his father spent his career with General Motors. He graduated from Ohio Northern University, Case Western law school and the University of Dayton business school, and became a corporate lawyer. At age 33, he narrowly defeated a scandal-tainted Democratic incumbent to win the first of two terms as Dayton mayor. He created Rehabarama, an acclaimed private-public partnership to rehabilitate neglected housing in Dayton's historic neighborhoods. He narrowly lost reelection in 2001.

Republican leaders recruited him to challenge Democratic Rep. Tony Hall, who had served 12 terms but was vulnerable following redistricting changes. A week after Turner announced he was running for Congress, President George W. Bush nominated Hall as ambassador to the U.N. Food and Agriculture Organization in Rome. In the Republican primary, Turner faced fierce opposition from newspaper publisher Roy Brown, grandson and son of former Reps. Clarence Brown and Clarence Brown Jr. Brown spent $1.3 million of his own money, largely on ads attacking Turner's record on taxes and lambasting him for being insufficiently conservative. Turner defeated Brown 80%-14%. The Democratic nominee was Rick Carne, Hall's chief of staff. With little support from his national party, he raised nearly $600,000, and benefited from a local appearance by actor -- and Dayton native -- Martin Sheen. Turner won 59%-41%.

Turner has supported his party on most major issues, though he has shown occasional independence. The Almanac vote ratings have ranked him toward the center of the House, especially on economic issues. He has voted against conservative efforts to cut science funding and to eliminate such agencies as the Legal Services Corporation and the National Endowment for the Arts. He has helped to save the Community Development Block Grant program. In May 2019, he was one of 20 House Republicans who voted against the GOP plan to repeal and replace the Affordable Care Act, which he said "will leave our most vulnerable citizens with inadequate health coverage."

Turner has remained focused on urban issues and formed a caucus of former mayors serving in Congress. He worked on House-passed legislation to accelerate the cleanup of polluted brownfields by making it easier for communities to apply for federal grants. He has promoted the kind of public-private partnerships that he used for economic development in Dayton.

On the Armed Services Committee, especially while he was chairman of its Tactical Air and Land Forces Subcommittee, Turner has offered protection from Defense Department cuts for

Wright-Patterson Air Force Base, which is the largest single-site employer in Ohio. He said that the base added 10,000 jobs since he was first elected. He has worked to make Dayton into a center for unmanned aerial vehicle research and testing, and he was strongly critical of the Obama administration's funding cuts for missile defense. Turner was a leader of the House Republicans' strategy to ignore requirements to "sequester" spending until the deficit was reduced. In 2016, he opposed President Barack Obama's proposed budget cuts for the military, which Turner said "could break the Army." With his seat on the Intelligence Committee, Turner has worked to retain the National Air and Space Intelligence Center headquarters at Wright-Patt.

Turner and Democratic Rep. Niki Tsongas of Massachusetts led the bipartisan Military Sexual Assault Prevention Caucus. In August 2018, they criticized the Veterans' Affairs Department for improper handling of assault claims. Turner has tried for years to get Congress to pass a law aimed at protecting service members from losing custody of their children because of military deployments; the measure passed the House and stalled in the Senate.

As ranking Republican on the Strategic Forces Subcommittee in 2019, Turner raised extensive questions about creation of the proposed Space Force, including its impact on the Wright-Patterson base. He said it was important that the new unit remain under the control of the Air Force. In 2014, when there was an opening for chairman of the Armed Services Committee, Turner deferred to Rep. Mac Thornberry of Texas, but made clear his interest in the next such vacancy. Thornberry is term-limited in 2020 as the senior Republican.

In July 2015, Turner endorsed Ohio Gov. John Kasich at the start of his campaign for the Republican presidential nomination. During a December interview with CNN, he said that Donald Trump was "not qualified to … hold any elective office." In May 2016, Turner endorsed Trump, without citing his name, "because Hillary Clinton would be an awful president, as she has shown a blatant disregard for our laws." He harshly criticized some of Trump's actions as president. He said that the president's comments following his July 2018 meeting with Russian president Vladimir Putin were "deeply damaging" for U.S. relations in Europe. In a December 2018 letter to Trump, Turner wrote that suggested cuts in Pentagon spending would be "disastrous." In February 2019, he was one of 13 House Republicans who backed the Democrat-sponsored resolution opposing Trump's declaration of a national emergency to finance a wall at the border with Mexico; Turner called the president's plan "a dangerous precedent."

In 2018, Turner faced his first serious reelection challenge. Democrat Theresa Gasper, a political newcomer and former Republican, said the election of Trump prompted her to run. She attacked the president's immigration policies, including family separation at the Mexican border. She added that Turner has supported Trump's policies and that he had not sufficiently addressed the problems of Dayton. Turner defended his record and outspent Gasper, $1.4 million to $1.3 million. He was reelected, 56%-42%, the lowest vote share in his nine terms. He took 53 percent in Dayton-based Montgomery County. Following the election, Gasper said she will run again in 2020.

OH-10: Montgomery County   Cook Partisan Voting Index: R+4

Population		Race and Ethnicity		Income	
Total	720,851	White	75%	Median Income	$50,316
Land area (sq. miles)	1,130	Black	16.7%	District Income Rank	306
Pop/ sq mi	638.1	Latino	2.7%	Poverty Rate	16.6%
Born in State	69.1%	Asian	2.2%	With health insurance	92.5%
		Two or more races	2.9%	Cash public assistance	3.1%
Age Groups		Other	0.4%	Food stamp/SNAP	14.4%
Under 18	22.1%				
18-34	23.2%	**Education**		**Work**	
35-64	38%	H.S grad or less	37.5%	White Collar	16.7%
Over 64	16.7%	Some college	33.3%	Sales and Service	41.3%
		College Degree, 4 yr	16.8%	Blue Collar	20.1%
Military		Post grad	12.3%	Government	15%
Veteran/ Active Duty	11.4%				

2012 Pres. Vote	Romney	179,772	(50%)	Obama	172,981	(48%)		
2016 Pres. Vote	Trump	178,674	(51%)	Clinton	153,346	(44%)	Johnson	11,898 (3%)

Dayton Area: For decades, the underestimated Dayton has held its own against bigger cities for fostering creative American genius in commerce. It has strong traditions of tinkering and innovation, practical organization and mechanical dreaming, as well as small-town neighborliness. Just south of the old National Road that spans the Midwest was the home of James Ritty, who in 1879 invented the cash register, that indispensable instrument of retail trade that led to the establishment in 1884 of the National Cash Register Co. Tom Watson Sr., an employee of NCR, feuded with owner John Henry Patterson and went off in a huff to found International Business Machines, better known by its initials, IBM. In 1887, George Huffman moved the Davis Sewing Machine Co. to Dayton, and in 1892 began producing Huffy bicycles. Around the same time, Wilbur and Orville Wright experimented with kites and gliders and constructed the first wind tunnel in the world and the first heavier-than-air flying machine, which they took to windy Kitty Hawk North Carolina for a test flight in 1903. A few years later, Dayton's Charles Kettering invented the automatic starter for cars and became one of the leaders of the budding automobile industry. Not long ago, Montgomery County was home to the most patents per capita of any county in the United States. Boston took away that title.

Dayton's economy in recent years suffered serious setbacks , though there have been signs that it has been bouncing back. During the latest recession, DHL closed an air cargo hub at the Wilmington Air Park in Clinton County, costing the region 10,000 jobs. In a major psychological and economic blow for the city, NCR departed to suburban Atlanta in 2009, taking away Dayton's last Fortune 500 company and the 1,300 jobs it provided. An encouraging feature has been General Electric, which has a huge presence in southwest Ohio and employs 1,200 in the Dayton area. It builds jet engines here, and has a center that develops advanced electric power systems for aircraft, ships and hybrid automobiles, including a partnership with Boeing. A former General Motors assembly plant has been converted to a highly automated automotive glass factory, which is a Chinese subsidiary; the pay scales for employees have been cut roughly in half. Dayton remains "a manufacturing town," with those plants covering 13 percent of its workforce, NBC News reported in September 2018.

Dayton-area universities and Wright-Patterson Air Force Base have made the area a magnet for technology companies. That includes the world's most advanced centrifuge, which is used for aerospace medical research. Wright-Patt has more than 27,000 military and civilian employees. Plans for development of the military's new Space Force at other facilities have raised questions about the implications for Wright-Patt. In 2018, Site Selection magazine ranked Dayton as eighth in the nation for business expansion projects in cities with fewer than 1 million people. In 2016, Bloomberg News listed Dayton among the post-industrial cities with bargain real estate and pockets of economic promise. About half its homebuyers are younger than 35.

The 10th Congressional District of Ohio includes all of Dayton and surrounding Montgomery County, which is about three-fourths of the district. To the east, it includes Greene County, with upscale Beaver Creek and middle-class Fairborn, and most of rural Fayette County, which is about midway from Dayton to Columbus. This has been a Republican-leaning district, although not overwhelmingly so. Donald Trump increased the GOP vote to 51 percent, a smaller increase than in other districts in Ohio.

Marcia Fudge (D)

Elected 2008, 6th full term, b. Oct 29, 1952; Cleveland; Ohio State University, B.S., 1975; Cleveland State University Marshall College of Law (OH), J.D., 1983; Baptist; Single.

Elected Office: Warrensville Heights Mayor, 2000-2008.

Professional Career: Practicing attorney; Aide, U.S. Rep. Stephanie Tubbs Jones, 1991-2000.

DC Office: 2344 RHOB 20515, 202-225-7032, Fax: 202-225-1339, fudge.house.gov

State Offices: Akron, 330-835-4758; Warrensville Heights, 216-522-4900.

Committees: *Agriculture*: Conservation & Forestry; Subcommittee Nutrition, Oversight & Department Operations (Chmn). *Education & Labor*: Civil Rights & Human Services; Health, Employment, Labor & Pensions. *House Administration*.

Group Ratings

	ADA	ACLU	AFL-CIO	LCV	ITI	COC	HAFA	ACU	CFG	FRC
2018	-	85%	-	89%	-	58%	4%	4%	2%	0%
2017	100%	C	97%	100%	C	36%	C	4%	5%	0%

Almanac Ratings 2017-18

	Economy	Social	Foreign	Composite
Liberal	95%	98%	95%	96%
Conservative	6%	2%	5%	4%

Key Votes of the 115th Congress

1. Obama-care revision	N	5. Family planning regs	N	9. Guantanamo prisoners	Y
2. Tax Cuts	N	6. Body cameras/immigration	Y	10. Ground missiles, limit	Y
3. Omnibus appropriations	Y	7. Abortion ban	N	11. Defense Dept. spending	N
4. Dodd-Frank revision	N	8. Concealed carry	N	12. FISA rules	N

Election Results

Election	Name (Party)	Vote (%)	Cand. Spent	Ind. Exp. Support	Ind. Exp. Oppose
2018 General	Marcia Fudge (D)..............................	206,138 (82%)	$596,700		
	Beverly Goldstein (R)...................	44,486 (18%)	$18,468		
2018 Primary	Marcia Fudge (D)...	(100%)			

Prior winning percentages: 2016 (80%), 2014 (80%), 2012 (100%), 2010 (83%), 2008 (85%)

Democrat Marcia Fudge, elected in 2008, has parlayed her organizational and networking skills into leadership of the Congressional Black Caucus and an active role in the Democratic Caucus. She has been an outspoken advocate of change among House Democrats. With her allies, she opened the door for new leadership hopefuls — including herself. In a conciliatory move, Speaker Nancy Pelosi arranged a subcommittee for Fudge to chair that gave her a platform to investigate alleged election abuses

Like many African Americans of her generation, Fudge was greatly influenced by the civil rights movement and got active politically when she was young. During high school, Fudge volunteered with get-out-the-vote efforts for "Young Folks for Stokes," young people helping to elect Carl Stokes mayor of Cleveland. After getting her bachelor's in business administration from Ohio State University, she received her law degree from Cleveland State University. She practiced mainly criminal defense law in the Cleveland area until she went to work for her mentor and friend, Rep. Stephanie Tubbs Jones.

Fudge and Tubbs Jones had met as members of the national Delta Sigma Theta Sorority alumnae association. Fudge later served as national president of the group of predominantly African-American women. When Tubbs Jones became the Cuyahoga County prosecutor, Fudge was her administrative assistant. When Tubbs Jones was elected to Congress in 1998, Fudge followed her to Washington as chief of staff. After a few years, Fudge pursued her own elected office. After the Warrensville Heights mayor resigned, she was the first African-American woman to be elected mayor of the city. She focused on economic development and claimed credit for creating 3,000 jobs and bringing in $500 million.

Tubbs Jones died unexpectedly from a cerebral aneurysm after having won the Democratic primary for another term. Fudge called each member of the district's Democratic Executive Committee, which selected a replacement on the ballot. She explained why she would be the best choice to carry on Tubbs Jones' legacy. The committee nominated Fudge with 175 votes. She won the general election with 85 percent of the vote.

Fudge has been a staunch and passionate liberal. As chair of the CBC in 2013-14, she assailed the automatic across-the-board spending cuts that were imposed after the two parties failed to reach a budget agreement. "If we allow this sequester to happen, we're saying that our political agendas are more important than the ability to take care of our families," she said. When lawmakers unveiled a statue of civil rights icon Rosa Parks at the Capitol, she noted the irony of the event occurring on the same day that several conservative Supreme Court justices raised sharp questions about the Voting Rights Act. Fudge earlier drew attention for her proposal to rein in the powers of the independent

Office of Congressional Ethics, after it found that Fudge's chief of staff "improperly influenced" information given to the House Ethics Committee about an annual Caribbean trip for Black Caucus members. But neither party has been willing to take responsibility for shutting down that office.

Representing an urban area, Fudge has been outspoken on the Agriculture Committee in defending food stamps. In 2017, she became the senior Democrat on the panel's Conservation and Forestry Subcommittee. Although her district had few farms or forests, Fudge used the committee niche during debate on the 2018 farm bill to oppose House Republicans' proposals for work requirements. With bipartisan Senate support in the House-Senate conference committee, she largely prevailed. In 2019, Fudge gained direct influence over the program as chairwoman of the Nutrition, Oversight and Department Operations Subcommittee. Earlier, as ranking Democrat on the Education and the Workforce Subcommittee on Early Childhood, Elementary and Secondary Education, Fudge helped to enact bipartisan changes in the No Child Left Behind Act.

Fudge has been active in the national party. At the Democratic convention in Philadelphia in 2016, she presided for many hours after Rep. Debbie Wasserman Schultz unexpectedly stepped down as DNC chairwoman. After that election, she said that Democrats "have to build our party from the ground up and I think that we've not been doing that." She was a vocal supporter of her neighboring Rep. Tim Ryan in his challenge to Nancy Pelosi as minority leader. Following the leadership vote, Fudge bluntly claimed "a great first step" for change. "I think anytime you've been in office as long as Nancy and you lose a full third of your caucus, it's significant," she told Politico.

After the House Democrats' election success in 2018, Fudge continued to press for internal changes. With Pelosi foes struggling to find a prospective challenger, Fudge said that an African-American woman should be part of the leadership team and that Pelosi had not wrapped up the requisite 218 votes. For a short time, she said that she was considering a bid for Speaker. But her interest ran into numerous obstacles, including the support of many Black Caucus members for Majority Whip James Clyburn and the support of many women for Pelosi — including two other House Democrats from Ohio.

Seeing the opportunity to neutralize a prospective opponent, Pelosi reached out to Fudge. Within a few days, Fudge agreed to take the gavel of the House Administration Elections Subcommittee, where she planned to make the case and prepare legislation to reinstate and overhaul a provision of the Voting Rights Act that the Supreme Court had ruled against in 2013. In exchange, Fudge undermined the rebels by agreeing to support Pelosi. With her Nutrition Subcommittee post, that gave Fudge the unusual cachet of two chairmanships. And she remained in play for future opportunities.

At home, Fudge focused on the continuing tensions in Cleveland. In 2015, she embraced as "a turning point" for police-community relations the consent decree between the city and the Justice Department that promised systemic changes. In her overwhelmingly Democratic district, Fudge has faced token opposition in primary and general elections.

OH-11: Cuyahoga County   **Cook Partisan Voting Index: D+32**

Population		Race and Ethnicity		Income	
Total	697,927	White	37.3%	Median Income	$35,930
Land area (sq. miles)	244	Black	52.9%	District Income Rank	429
Pop/ sq mi	2855	Latino	4.2%	Poverty Rate	26.8%
Born in State	73.2%	Asian	2.5%	With health insurance	92%
		Two or more races	2.6%	Cash public assistance	5.5%
Age Groups		Other	0.5%	Food stamp/SNAP	26.7%
Under 18	22.3%				
18-34	24.2%	**Education**		**Work**	
35-64	37.7%	H.S grad or less	43.1%	White Collar	15.8%
Over 64	15.8%	Some college	30.2%	Sales and Service	44.9%
		College Degree, 4 yr	14.7%	Blue Collar	18.4%
Military		Post grad	12%	Government	12.7%
Veteran/ Active Duty	6.9%				

2012 Pres. Vote	Obama	299,107	(83%)	Romney	57,787	(16%)
2016 Pres. Vote	Clinton	260,311	(80%)	Trump	55,013	(17%)

Cleveland, Downtown Akron: Like most great American cities, Cleveland grew in great bursts of migration, during periods when the economy expanded and attracted low-wage workers from around the country and the world. After the Ohio and Erie Canal connected Lake Erie with the Ohio

River in the 1830s, Cleveland became a critical destination for goods traveling from the north to the interior and vice versa. Its greatest surge of growth started in the 1890s and lasted through the 1920s, when the city was transformed from a bustling city of 250,000 to a burgeoning metropolis of over 900,000. Tens of thousands of immigrants from central and southern Europe arrived, looking for jobs in the steel and automobile factories. Bohemians came to the tightly packed neighborhoods along Broadway, Hungarians settled in the northeast, Jews lived north of University Circle along East 105th Street, and Italians ran produce markets along Mayfield Road. As heavy industries geared up for World War II and enjoyed years of prosperous growth afterward, another surge of immigrants came, this time from the South.

These bursts of migration led to political changes. A string of ethnic mayors — Frank Lausche, Anthony Celebrezze, Ralph Locher — was followed by the election in 1967 of Carl Stokes, the nation's first black big-city mayor. Cleveland had racially polarized politics for much of the 1970s. Even so, the west side stayed mostly white, and Cleveland did not have a black majority until the 2000 census; its 2017 population declined to 385,000 and was only 42 percent of what it was in 1950. In a hopeful sign, the loss of 81,000 people from 2000 to 2010 was reduced by only 11,000 in the next seven years. Nearly all Clevelanders exalted in the NBA title that their Cavaliers, led by Akron-native LeBron James, won in 2016. This was the first professional championship for the city since 1964, when the football Browns won the NFL. Two years later, he escaped to Los Angeles, where he had other professional interests. And there was new hope for the woebegone Browns. More significantly for Cleveland, the economy grew in 2017, including a hopeful turnaround in manufacturing. And the downtown improvements, which James helped to create, appear to have spurred new development.

For decades, Akron was the rubber capital of the world. The four largest tire companies had their headquarters and factories here, with close to 60,000 workers in the rubber industry in the 1930s. By the 1980s, those plants had largely shut down, except for the production of a few specialty tires. Goodrich, Firestone and General left town to manufacture tires with cheaper labor in the South, and then outside the country. Goodyear remained, with an impressive new office building plus its innovation center. One positive result was that the air was cleaner, and the smell of rubber was gone. The population dropped from 290,000 in 1960 to 198,000 in 2017. Like Cleveland, where the influx of new residents from around the world has enriched the city, Akron has benefited from immigration. Many refugees have moved into North Hill — from Myanmar and Bhutan, and more recently from Iraq and Syria. In his hometown, James and his foundation left behind a partnership with the local schools to aid low-income kids.

The 11th Congressional District of Ohio includes most of the east side of Cleveland, plus the suburbs just to the east. Some of these areas — East Cleveland, Warrensville Heights — are mostly black. Others, like Shaker Heights, are mostly white. Still others, like the old Slavic enclave of Garfield Heights, are populated by the heirs of the ethnic whites who settled Cleveland in the early 20th century. The district includes exurbs of Cleveland, minority segments of downtown, plus Fairlawn and a few other suburbs of Akron. Nearly one-third of Summit County is in the district, which accounts for about 15 percent of its population. The 11th exists for two reasons: To provide a minority-majority district in compliance with the Voting Rights Act, and to satisfy the desire of Republicans in control of redistricting to place as many Democrats as possible in a single district and protect Republicans in nearby districts. The 11th is 53 percent black, and is among the most heavily Democratic districts in the nation. Hillary Clinton took 80 percent in 2016.

Troy Balderson (R)

Elected 2018, 1st full term, b. Jan 16, 1962; Zanesville; Muskingum College (OH); Ohio State University; Christian Church; Married (Angie Albright); 1 child.

DC Office: 1221 LHOB 20515, 202-225-5355, Fax: 202-226-4523, balderson.house.gov

State Offices: Worthington, 614-523-2555.

Committees: *Science, Space & Technology*: Research & Technology. *Small Business*: Contracting & Infrastructure; Innovation & Workforce Development (RMM). *Transportation & Infrastructure*: Aviation; Highways & Transit; Railroads, Pipelines & Hazardous Materials.

Group Ratings

	ADA	ACLU	AFL-CIO	LCV	ITI	COC	HAFA	ACU	CFG	FRC
2018	-	-	-	0%	-	-	-	-	-	100%

Election Results

Election	Name (Party)	Vote (%)		Cand. Spent	Ind. Exp. Support	Ind. Exp. Oppose
2018 General	Troy Balderson (R)	175,677	(51%)	$2,505,825	$2,717,023	$982,182
	Danny O'Connor (D)	161,251	(47%)	$8,139,412	$487,638	$4,754,929
2018 Primary	Troy Balderson (R)	19,552	(29%)			
	Melanie Leneghan (R)	18,777	(28%)			
	Tim Kane (R)	11,491	(17%)			
	Kevin Bacon (R)	9,711	(14%)			
	Carol O'Brien (R)	4,415	(7%)			

Prior winning percentages: 2018 special (50%)

Republican Troy Balderson in 2018 won two elections in three months to secure a vacant seat that the GOP had long controlled. Each outcome was close and produced high anxiety among Republicans, with Democrats outspending Balderson and his allies and placing him on the political defensive in a prelude to the Democrats' big gains in November in suburban districts similar to this one — though they failed to make a breakthrough in Ohio. Balderson, a veteran state legislator from the rural part of the district, replaced Republican Rep. Pat Tiberi, an influential member of the Ways and Means Committee, who resigned in January 2018 to become president of the Ohio Business Roundtable.

A native of Zanesville, Balderson took business administration classes at Muskingum College and Ohio State University but did not graduate. He owned and operated a family farm and was general manager of the family's auto dealership in Zanesville. He won election to the state House in 2008 and was appointed in 2011 to a seat in the state Senate, where he chaired the Energy and Natural Resources Committee. He calls himself a "principled conservative" who opposes abortion, supports gun rights and believes that government should create an environment for economic growth.

In the special election following Tiberi's resignation, Balderson was endorsed by Tiberi. He had close ties to retiring GOP Gov. John Kasich, who held this House seat for 18 years prior to Tiberi and was an early supporter of Kasich's presidential campaign in 2016. He narrowly won the competitive Republican primary in May 2018 against nine other candidates. Of the 68,000 votes cast, Balderson led by 775 votes -- 29 percent to 28 percent — against runner-up Melanie Leneghan, the trustee for Liberty Township, who ran as a supporter of President Donald Trump and was backed by conservative Republican Rep. Jim Jordan, also of Ohio. Democratic nominee Danny O'Connor, who handily defeated six other candidates in his primary, had been elected as recorder of Franklin County.

In their initial faceoff, Balderson's campaign ads attacked national Democratic leaders — including then-Minority Leader Nancy Pelosi -- and their liberal agenda. O'Connor attacked the pending Republican tax bill as "a corporate tax giveaway." Balderson emphasized his background and seemed more comfortable in the rural part of the district, which had a smaller share of the vote. O'Connor's Franklin County base was the most populous part of the district. In the high turnout for an August special election, Balderson won 50.1%-49.3%, a margin of 1,680 votes of the 208,000 that were cast. In Franklin County, O'Connor got 65 percent and led by more than 22,000 votes. Balderson led in the other six counties, including a 2-to-1 lead in Muskingum, his home county.

With barely a chance to catch their breath, Balderson and O'Connor plunged into the general election. O'Connor maintained his large financial advantage. In the two campaigns combined, he outspent Balderson $8.1 million to $2.5 million. National Republican groups spent more than $6 million on behalf of O'Connor. Another difference in the November election was the growing political expectation that Democrats would win the House majority. The national Democratic momentum failed to give a boost to O'Connor. Balderson won 51%-47%, a margin of more than 14,000 votes — a sign of the district returning to its roots. He narrowed O'Connor's lead in Franklin to 62 percent. Balderson took 55 percent in Delaware County and got at least 60 percent of the vote in each of the other five counties.

Balderson got a seat on the Transportation and Infrastructure Committee. As a junior member of the Republican-heavy delegation, he could be at risk in the 2022 redistricting, when Ohio is expected to lose a House seat.

OH-12: Central Ohio   Cook Partisan Voting Index: R+7

Population		Race and Ethnicity		Income	
Total	761,758	White	86%	Median Income	$69,159
Land area (sq. miles)	2,272	Black	4.5%	District Income Rank	99
Pop/ sq mi	335.3	Latino	2.5%	Poverty Rate	9.8%
Born in State	73%	Asian	4%	With health insurance	93.9%
		Two or more races	2.8%	Cash public assistance	2.1%
Age Groups		Other	0.3%	Food stamp/SNAP	9.4%
Under 18	23.8%				
18-34	21.4%	**Education**		**Work**	
35-64	40.5%	H.S grad or less	33.5%	White Collar	14.3%
Over 64	14.3%	Some college	26.3%	Sales and Service	38%
		College Degree, 4 yr	25.4%	Blue Collar	16.4%
Military		Post grad	14.8%	Government	13.7%
Veteran/ Active Duty 8%					

2012 Pres. Vote	Romney	207,339	(54%)	Obama	167,507	(44%)			
2016 Pres. Vote	Trump	205,978	(52%)	Clinton	162,218	(41%)	Johnson	14,308	(4%)

Northern Columbus Metro: Columbus was overshadowed by its much larger cousins for most of its existence — Cincinnati to the south and Cleveland to the north. It remained a surprisingly small town for the capital of such an important state. Today, Columbus is a major metropolis and, with 880,000 people in 2017, has breezed past the total of Cleveland and Cincinnati. Columbus' Franklin County has grown close to 1.3 million, surpassing Cleveland's Cuyahoga in 2016. With this explosive growth has come sprawl in all directions. Most American cities grew up around a coastline or river, which tended to direct their growth. The plains to the north and west of Columbus have done little to inhibit growth, while the rolling hills that mark the end of the Appalachian Plateau to the south and east provide no meaningful barrier to expansion.

The 12th Congressional District contains a northern slice of the city and Franklin County, with portions of the University District filled with pre-World War II Craftsman-style bungalows, as well as the more spacious homes of Clintonville, one of the original "streetcar" communities. It takes in suburbs to the north and east: Worthington, increasingly indistinguishable from the encroaching city; newly fashionable Dublin, with its lush Muirfield Village Golf Club; Gahanna; and upscale New Albany.

To the north is fast-growing Delaware County, home to the highly-rated Columbus Zoo and traditionally Republican. It last voted for a Democratic presidential candidate in 1916. Its upscale suburbs help give Delaware the highest median income of any county in Ohio. Growth here has spread to the northern townships. In May 2018, the Columbus Dispatch reported that Evans Farm is a "new urbanist" project of business, with more than 2,000 homes in Orange Township mostly within walking distance. Outside of Columbus' orbit, Licking County is home to picturesque Granville and Denison, its small liberal arts college. Industrial parks across the county have attracted new manufacturing companies. Newark, an old manufacturing town that was in decay, has started to revive its downtown area — including a historic district. Corn fields have turned into business parks. Rural Zanesville, with its famous "Y"-shaped bridge, provides the only real center of Democratic voting strength outside Franklin County.

Franklin is the population center in the 12th District, with about one-third of the vote, but Delaware and Licking are not far behind. Filling the new 3rd district with Democratic precincts in the center of Columbus following the 2012 redistricting produced a significant shift in the 12th. A district that Barack Obama won in 2008 with 54 percent was transformed into one that John McCain would have won with 54 percent. In 2016, Donald Trump took 52 percent.

Tim Ryan (D)

Elected 2002, 9th term, b. Jul 16, 1973; Niles; Dickinson School of Law's International Law Program (Italy), Att.; Youngstown State University (OH), Att., 1992; Bowling Green State University (OH), B.A., 1995; Franklin Pierce College Law Center (NH), J.D., 2000; Catholic; Married (Andrea Zetts); 1 child; 2 stepchildren.

Elected Office: OH Senate, 2000-2002.

Professional Career: Aide, U.S. Rep. Jim Traficant, 1995-1997.

DC Office: 1126 LHOB 20515, 202-225-5261, Fax: 202-225-3719, timryan.house.gov

State Offices: Akron, 330-630-7311; Warren, 800-856-4152; Youngstown, 330-740-0193.

Committees: *Appropriations*: Defense; Legislative Branch (Chmn); Military Construction, Veterans Affairs & Related Agencies. *Joint Library*.

Group Ratings

	ADA	ACLU	AFL-CIO	LCV	ITI	COC	HAFA	ACU	CFG	FRC
2018	-	86%	-	94%	-	55%	4%	4%	2%	0%
2017	100%	C	94%	94%	C	30%	C	4%	5%	0%

Almanac Ratings 2017-18

	Economy	Social	Foreign	Composite
Liberal	98%	97%	82%	92%
Conservative	2%	4%	19%	8%

Key Votes of the 115th Congress

1. Obama-care revision	N	5. Family planning regs	N	9. Guantanamo prisoners	Y
2. Tax Cuts	N	6. Body cameras/immigration	Y	10. Ground missiles, limit	Y
3. Omnibus appropriations	Y	7. Abortion ban	N	11. Defense Dept. spending	Y
4. Dodd-Frank revision	N	8. Concealed carry	N	12. FISA rules	N

Election Results

Election	Name (Party)	Vote (%)		Cand. Spent	Ind. Exp. Support	Ind. Exp. Oppose
2018 General	Tim Ryan (D)	153,323	(61%)	$1,495,292		
	Christopher DePizzo (R)	98,047	(39%)	$90,686		$25,000
2018 Primary	Tim Ryan (D)	54,967	(87%)			
	John Luchansky (D)	4,908	(8%)			
	Robert Crow (D)	3,195	(5%)			

Prior winning percentages: 2016 (68%), 2014 (69%), 2012 (73%), 2010 (54%), 2008 (78%), 2006 (80%), 2004 (77%), 2002 (51%)

Tim Ryan, a Democrat elected in 2002 at age 29, has been a pro-union centrist who is usually a party regular and tries to encourage occasional hope for his economically battered constituency. His views on guns and abortion have moved to the left. Following the 2016 election, he criticized Minority Leader Nancy Pelosi's handling of that year's campaign and challenged her bid for another term. He lost the Democratic Caucus vote, 134-63, which many viewed as an indication that Ryan might be part of the post-Pelosi leadership. When Democrats regained House control in 2018 and Pelosi was the beneficiary, Ryan quietly stepped aside. He kept busy with his growing seniority at the Appropriations Committee. Several times, he has considered a bid for statewide office in Ohio. Recently, his ambitions have gone national.

Ryan grew up in Niles, was a star quarterback before a knee injury ended his career, and graduated from Bowling Green State University. His first job was with Rep. James Traficant, a blue-collar and often maverick Democrat. In 2000, after graduating from Franklin Pierce Law Center, Ryan was elected to the state Senate. His opening to run for Congress came when the increasingly flaky Traficant was forced to resign in disgrace after his conviction in 2002 for racketeering and bribery.

Akron-based Rep. Tom Sawyer, a Democrat who had been thrown into the district by redistricting, was the early favorite to succeed Traficant. He outspent Ryan nearly 6-to-1 and had the perks of incumbency. But Sawyer had voted for the 1993 North American Free Trade Agreement, and he was one of the few Rust Belt Democrats to vote for normalizing trade relations with China. Ryan hammered on these votes in the Mahoning Valley. He was endorsed by the National Rifle Association in a district with many hunters. With greater voter intensity in Youngstown than in Akron, Ryan defeated Sawyer 41%-27%. In the general, Ryan slammed state Rep. Ann Womer Benjamin and the GOP legislature for votes that he said led to higher tuition at state universities. Republicans fired back with ads highlighting several disorderly conduct charges lodged against Ryan while he was in college. The district's Democratic leanings and Ryan's labor support proved decisive. He won 51 percent of the vote to 34 percent for Womer Benjamin and 15 percent for Traficant, who ran from jail as an independent.

Ryan has leaned to the left on economic policy. His splits with Democrats on abortion rights and gun control initially placed him closer to the center on social issues, but he has shifted and worked with others to seek common ground. After the deadly school massacre in Newtown Connecticut, he held meetings with gun enthusiasts and law enforcement officials to try to "thread the needle" on a solution to gun violence. With Democratic abortion-rights advocate Rosa DeLauro of Connecticut, he sponsored the Reducing the Need for Abortion and Supporting Parents Act, with federal dollars to fight teen pregnancy and increased aid for women who become pregnant. In 2015, he said that his position had "evolved" further. "I have come to believe that we must trust women and families — not politicians — to make the best decisions for their lives," he wrote in the Akron Beacon-Journal.

In 2006, Ryan endeared himself to Pelosi when he was a vocal backer of her close ally John Murtha of Pennsylvania in his unsuccessful bid for majority leader against Steny Hoyer of Maryland. That earned Ryan a seat on the Appropriations Committee. He used that niche to secure earmarked projects for his hard-pressed district. Those practices ended when Speaker John Boehner ended earmarks after Republicans regained control in 2011.

Reflecting his district, Ryan has remained a harsh critic of international trade deals. For several years, he sponsored the Chinese Currency Act, a proposal to counter China's alleged manipulation and undervaluation of its currency. He has co-chaired the Congressional Manufacturing Caucus, which seeks to revive the nation's industrial base and to revise its trade policy. Ryan has not been impressed by the efforts of President Donald Trump to address those problems. When General Motors in November 2018 announced the shutdown of its Lordstown plant in his district, Ryan criticized his failure to contribute to the revival of manufacturing in the Mahoning Valley. "What we've gotten instead are broken promises and petty tweets."

Ryan has drawn attention for his meditation. He attended a five-day retreat after the 2008 election, turning off his two BlackBerrys and gradually reducing how often he talked until he maintained a 36-hour period of silence. "My mind and body were in the same place at the same time, synchronized in a way I had rarely experienced," he told the Beacon Journal. He wrote a book in 2012, A Mindful Nation: How a Simple Practice Can Help Us Reduce Stress, Improve Performance, and Recapture the American Spirit, and he has spent 45 minutes a day practicing "mindfulness" — something he says stressed-out Washingtonians and corporate executives should try. In 2015, he expanded his spiritual revival to include healthier eating, with a book, The Real Food Revolution: Healthy Eating, Green Groceries, and the Return of the American Family Farm. He became a devotee of hot yoga.

When House Democrats convened after their traumatic 2016 election, Ryan joined those calling for political introspection. Some Democrats, mostly junior, were looking for an alternative to Pelosi, who had been Democratic leader for 14 years, all but four of them in the minority. They urged Ryan to run. In a letter to House Democrats, he agreed. "Keeping our leadership team completely unchanged will simply lead to more disappointment in future elections," he wrote.

Although his voting record was more centrist and consensus-driven than that of Pelosi, his two-week campaign was more generational and geographic, especially in the wake of their party's election setbacks in Ohio and elsewhere in the nation's heartland. His 63 votes, though dismissed by Pelosi, were potentially a springboard when House Democrats have their inevitable leadership changes.

Ryan has not faced serious reelection problems. His political dilemma at home has been a repeated refusal to step up the ladder for other offices. Pelosi and her allies mocked his contest against her as a way to get more publicity for a statewide bid. He had considered a run for the Senate in 2006 but decided against challenging more senior Democrat Sherrod Brown. Democratic Gov. Ted Strickland discussed a shared ticket with Ryan in 2010, but Ryan decided to remain in the House, largely because of his new influence at Appropriations; all but one of the 10 Democrats senior to him in 2019 were more than 20 years older than Ryan. He took another serious look at running for governor in 2014 after Strickland said he wouldn't run, but announced that it still wasn't worth the risk to give up his committee seat. He turned down the opportunity to run for the Senate in 2016, with the explanation that he wanted to be close to his "new and growing family." In 2017, he said he would not run for governor in 2018 because "I believe the best way to serve my community, my state and my country is to remain in the United States Congress."

The balancing act continued in early 2019, as he occasionally talked like a presidential candidate and showed up in battleground Democratic primary states. In April 2019, Ryan announced that he was running for president, with an appeal to "working-class" voters and other economically struggling areas. Meanwhile, he had become an Appropriations "cardinal," as chairman of the Legislative Branch Subcommittee — a niche that gave him an opportunity to address the working needs of many House members and left Pelosi and other senior Democrats to rely on him for their spending requests. In his mid-40s and with many Democrats demanding change, ideological and generational, Ryan likely will have other opportunities — inside the Capitol and beyond.

OH-13: Northeast Ohio

Cook Partisan Voting Index: D+7

Population		Race and Ethnicity		Income	
Total	710,834	White	80.8%	Median Income	$43,753
Land area (sq. miles)	894	Black	11.4%	District Income Rank	389
Pop/ sq mi	794.9	Latino	3.2%	Poverty Rate	17.8%
Born in State	77%	Asian	1.7%	With health insurance	92.2%
		Two or more races	2.6%	Cash public assistance	4.3%
Age Groups		Other	0.3%	Food stamp/SNAP	17%
Under 18	20.1%				
18-34	23.6%	Education		Work	
35-64	38.8%	H.S grad or less	49.5%	White Collar	17.5%
Over 64	17.5%	Some college	28.2%	Sales and Service	44.6%
		College Degree, 4 yr	14.8%	Blue Collar	25.4%
Military		Post grad	7.6%	Government	11.3%
Veteran/ Active Duty	8.8%				

2012 Pres. Vote	Obama	212,082	(63%)	Romney	120,913	(36%)			
2016 Pres. Vote	Clinton	163,600	(51%)	Trump	142,738	(44%)	Johnson	8,810	(3%)

Youngstown, Akron Area: For nearly a century, the Mahoning Valley — between the Lake Erie docks that unload iron ore from Great Lakes freighters and the coalfields of western Pennsylvania and West Virginia — was a steel capital of the United States. The first blast furnace opened in 1803, and the first coal mine opened in 1826. Canals followed, and in 1892 the first steel mill was built. The valley soon filled up with mills, converters and furnaces. But in the 1950s and 1960s, worldwide overcapacity in steel grew as almost every developing country decided it needed its own steel mills. After a 119-day strike in 1959, an agreement between the United Steelworkers and management boosted wages and fringe benefits to levels that helped price domestic steel out of the market. When the oil shock of the 1970s produced sharply higher energy prices and a collapse in the U.S. auto and steel markets, every plant in the Mahoning Valley closed, with a loss of 40,000 jobs.

Steel has since revived, although not at its previous peak and not in Youngstown. The high-wage living standard of the area vanished. Organized crime infiltrated local government, and a federal investigation in the late 1990s led to more than 70 convictions; among those sentenced were a prosecutor, a sheriff and a congressman. In 2017, Youngstown's population was 64,600, little more than a third its size in the 1950s, when the area stopped growing. Since 2000, two-thirds of the manufacturing jobs in the area have disappeared. The city has struggled to rebound, though it managed to attract a few high-tech firms, including the Turning Technologies software company, whose goal was to make technology more affordable and user-friendly. The region has also become a locus for shale drilling. Still, there is some benefit to the weak economy. In 2018, the Youngstown area had the second-lowest home prices in the nation, higher than only Cumberland Maryland. The median price for a single-family home was $90,200.

The 13th Congressional District of Ohio encompasses most of the Mahoning Valley industrial area: Youngstown, Warren and most of Trumbull County. It includes nearly all of Portage County and the less-minority parts of Summit County and Akron. Mahoning, Trumbull and Summit, with similar shares of the population, comprise most of the district. It contains two loci of 1970s protest — Kent State University, where four students were killed by National Guardsmen, and Lordstown, site of the General Motors plant where workers purposely built shoddy cars to protest the tedium of the assembly line. After a pick-up in production following the recession, Lordstown's auto-based facility grew obsolescent as market demand shifted to SUVs and trucks — plus, increasingly, hybrid and autonomous vehicles. In November 2018, GM announced that it was closing Lordstown in the spring of 2019, with its previously downsized workforce of about 1,250. Amid the pain, some local workers hoped that another auto manufacturer might find the facility a worthwhile investment.

Of the four Democratic-held district in Ohio, this Rustbelt patchwork is the least Democratic and least urban. Support for Hillary Clinton fell to 51 percent in 2016. The Democratic lead in Mahoning County dropped from 63%-35% in 2012 to 50%-47%. Whether Donald Trump could retain support in this area, where economic distress remained acute, was viewed as a key test of his presidency.

Dave Joyce (R)

Elected 2012, 4th term, b. Mar 17, 1957; Cleveland; University of Dayton (OH), B.S., 1979; University of Dayton (OH), J.D., 1982; Roman Catholic; Married (Kelly Joyce); 3 children.

Elected Office: Prosecutor, Geauga County, 1988-2013.

Professional Career: Public defender, Geauga County, 1985-1988; Public defender, Cuyahoga County, 1983-1984.

DC Office: 1124 LHOB 20515, 202-225-5731, Fax: 202-225-3307, joyce.house.gov

State Offices: Mentor, 440-352-3939; Twinsburg, 330-357-4139.

Committees: *Appropriations*: Financial Services & General Government; Interior, Environment & Related Agencies (RMM).

Group Ratings

	ADA	ACLU	AFL-CIO	LCV	ITI	COC	HAFA	ACU	CFG	FRC
2018	-	14%	-	14%	-	83%	40%	60%	46%	100%
2017	10%	C	34%	11%	C	93%	C	59%	51%	89%

Almanac Ratings 2017-18

	Economy	Social	Foreign	Composite
Liberal	9%	4%	10%	8%
Conservative	91%	97%	90%	92%

Key Votes of the 115th Congress

1. Obama-care revision	N	5. Family planning regs	Y	9. Guantanamo prisoners	N
2. Tax Cuts	Y	6. Body cameras/immigration	N	10. Ground missiles, limit	N
3. Omnibus appropriations	Y	7. Abortion ban	Y	11. Defense Dept. spending	Y
4. Dodd-Frank revision	Y	8. Concealed carry	Y	12. FISA rules	Y

Election Results

Election	Name (Party)	Vote (%)	Cand. Spent	Ind. Exp. Support	Ind. Exp. Oppose
2018 General	Dave Joyce (R)................................... 169,809	(55%)	$2,601,945	$276,249	
	Betsy Rader (D)................................. 137,549	(45%)	$2,185,943	$64,386	$90,950
2018 Primary	Dave Joyce (R)...	(100%)			

Prior winning percentages: 2016 (63%), 2014 (63%), 2012 (54%)

Republican David Joyce, a former prosecutor who was elected in 2012 against a weak opponent after the GOP incumbent unexpectedly retired following the primary, quickly showed his political skills when he got a seat on the Appropriations Committee. In 2019, he became the ranking Republican on its subcommittee that deals with environmental issues, which dovetailed with his interest in protecting the water quality of the Great Lakes. Although he occasionally goes his own way, Joyce usually is a reliable member of the GOP establishment and politically secure at home.

Joyce, born in Cleveland, is the son of a coal salesman. He went to the University of Dayton, where he got his bachelor's in accounting and earned a law degree. He said that he expected to get a job at a national accounting firm, but he was told during interviews that he would have little opportunity for trial work. Instead, he took a job as a public defender in Cuyahoga County, eventually moving to nearby Geauga County. Rising through the ranks quickly, Joyce was elected as the youngest prosecutor in Geauga County's history. He worked in political campaigns, starting on phone banks for then-Cleveland Mayor George Voinovich. In 1999, he organized "Prosecutors for Bush," with George W. Bush's presidential campaign.

In July 2012, nine-term GOP Rep. Steven LaTourette made a stunning announcement that he would not seek reelection, despite having won the GOP primary. Without giving specifics, he said that the political climate "has increased the toll that it takes on a person." He soon suffered serious health problems and died of cancer in 2016. Needing a new candidate. a group of 14 Republican leaders selected Joyce, a friend of LaTourette with a credible background and no political record to attack. Democratic nominee Dale Blanchard, an obscure accountant and a 10-time candidate for Congress, continued to run despite pressure to step aside for a stronger challenger. Joyce ran a mostly positive campaign and generally did not engage Blanchard. He won, 54%-39%.

Although Joyce has been more of a party regular than his predecessor, his Almanac vote ratings have ranked him near the center of the House and as the most moderate member of the Ohio delegation. He got a seat on the Appropriations Committee, where he said his priority was to reduce the size and scope of government. In May 2017, Joyce was one of 20 Republicans who voted against House passage of a bill to repeal and replace the Affordable Care Act. He said that it was "unacceptable" that premiums for people with pre-existing conditions "could potentially skyrocket." He showed independence in filing a bill to permit each state to go its own way in deciding whether to legalize marijuana. Joyce co-chaired the Congressional Cannabis Caucus, a bipartisan group in the House.

On Appropriations, Joyce has identified spending that he favors. He has pursued bipartisan efforts to restore the environmental health of the Great Lakes, with $300 million in annual funding. In 2016, Joyce claimed a victory when enactment of water resources legislation included a provision for the Great Lakes states to create an action plan to determine future funding projects. That bill continued regular dredging of the Cuyahoga River, with removal of dangerous sediments. In both 2017 and 2018, Joyce worked with the Ohio delegation and got the full $300 million; President Donald Trump had proposed eliminating the funds. With Joyce taking over in 2019 as ranking Republican on the Appropriations Subcommittee on Interior and the Environment, long-term funding appeared secure for restoration of the Great Lakes, which Joyce termed "the greatest natural resources and economic powerhouses we have in the United States."

After handing Joyce his seat on a silver platter, Democrats promised a more serious effort in 2014. They failed again. In the Republican primary, Joyce won 55%-45% over pro-life state Rep. Matt Lynch, who was helped by tea party groups. Joyce had more than $600,000 in help from the

U.S. Chamber of Commerce, American Hospital Association and a Super PAC run by LaTourette, whose daughter won Lynch's seat in the state House. Michael Wager, a Democratic fundraiser and former chairman of the Cleveland-Cuyahoga County Port Authority, ran ads that called his opponent "greedy" and criticized him for flying first-class. Wager was a disappointing challenger in a poor year for Democrats in Ohio. Joyce won, 63%-33%. In 2016, Joyce breezed past two rematches. In the GOP primary, Lynch voiced similar tea party themes. Joyce increased his margin to 64%-36%. Wager tried again in 2016, with rhetorical boosts from national Democrats but not much else. He spent $240,000 to $2 million for Joyce and lost 63%-37%.

In 2018, Joyce faced a well-funded and credible challenger. Democrat Betsy Rader, an attorney who handled employment discrimination cases, said she was "horrified" by Trump's proposed budget cuts. She told The Cleveland Plain Dealer that "she has nothing against Joyce personally," but that he had "gone missing" in failing to attend a town-hall meeting organized by supporters of Obamacare. Joyce, who outspent Rader $2.6 million to $2.5 million, gained attention with an unusual campaign ad in which he cited his willingness to challenge Trump on behalf of the Great Lakes. "I'll do what's right for northeast Ohio, even if it means standing up to my own party," he said in the ad. He won, 55%-45%. Rader led narrowly in Cuyahoga and Summit counties.

OH-14: Northeast Ohio   Cook Partisan Voting Index: R+5

Population		Race and Ethnicity		Income	
Total	718,257	White	89.1%	Median Income	$64,870
Land area (sq. miles)	1,953	Black	4.4%	District Income Rank	134
Pop/ sq mi	367.7	Latino	2.7%	Poverty Rate	8.6%
Born in State	76.5%	Asian	2.1%	With health insurance	93.6%
		Two or more races	1.5%	Cash public assistance	1.8%
Age Groups		Other	0.2%	Food stamp/SNAP	8.1%
Under 18	21.9%				
18-34	18.1%	**Education**		**Work**	
35-64	41.4%	H.S grad or less	38.2%	White Collar	18.6%
Over 64	18.6%	Some college	27.5%	Sales and Service	38.9%
		College Degree, 4 yr	21.1%	Blue Collar	20.3%
Military		Post grad	13.2%	Government	10.6%
Veteran/ Active Duty	8.4%				

2012 Pres. Vote	Romney	192,895	(51%)	Obama	180,026	(48%)		
2016 Pres. Vote	Trump	197,943	(53%)	Clinton	155,561	(42%)	Johnson 11,325	(3%)

Cleveland and Akron Suburbs, Ashtabula: The imprint of the westward track of New England Yankee migration is still apparent today on the shores of Lake Erie in northern Ohio. The British crown had granted the Colony of Connecticut all the land due west of its borders in 1662. Connecticut ceded most of this land in 1786 in exchange for the newly created federal government taking over its Revolutionary War debts, but it retained a 3 million-acre claim in Ohio for its excess population, which became known as the Western Reserve. As European claims to North America subsided and Native Americans were placed on reservations or relocated, these Yankees, cooped up in New England for 200 years, moved west, through Upstate New York, across Ohio and Michigan to Chicago, and on to Kansas, Oregon and California.

During the Civil War, the Western Reserve, ceded by Connecticut to the federal government in 1800, produced some of the nation's strongest opposition to slavery and hardiest support of the Union armies and the Republican Party; Lake Erie ports were prime transit points for the Underground Railroad to Canada. Its thrifty, hardworking, well-educated citizens built communities with fine schools and, with their accumulated savings, invested in what became some of the nation's leading industries. Now, like Connecticut and Massachusetts, northeastern Ohio has moved toward a post-industrial economy. Small, adaptive business units with highly skilled workers are the growth sectors. In February 2018, a private economic development report found that northeast Ohio remained globally competitive in manufacturing and that the number-one challenge for businesses was finding skilled workers to meet the expected demand and to replace retiring workers. Another report found that the economy in the area was diversifying beyond manufacturing. In March 2018, FirstEnergy filed a notice that it would shut down by 2021 its nuclear power plant in Lake County, plus others near Toledo and Pittsburgh. The company later filed for bankruptcy; it was losing money because of the low price of natural gas and other fuels. In February 2019, the local Star Beacon newspaper reported that Ashtabula, which was hit hard by the decline of the steel industry, was close to a deal with a company in South Africa to become the site of a pig-iron production facility; it would be the first such plant in the United States.

The 14th Congressional District of Ohio takes in parts or all of seven counties of northeast Ohio and the old Western Reserve. It includes the suburbs of eastern and southern Cleveland-based Cuyahoga County; northern Summit; some of Portage to the east; and Geauga. The largest are Lake County, which has nearly one-third of the population, and Summit. The more diverse areas are rural Ashtabula, home to a historic port district, 18 covered bridges and several wineries, and the northern part of Trumbull County, which is industrial and close to Youngstown. Historically, the area was Republican. Since the 1930s, it has remained politically competitive, as Cleveland and the industrial centers on Lake Erie became more Democratic. The 14th District has enough Republican territory to give a GOP lean. Donald Trump got 53 percent of the vote in 2016. In Ashtabula, he got 56 percent and was the first Republican to win the county since Ronald Reagan.

Steve Stivers (R)

Elected 2010, 5th term, b. Mar 24, 1965; Cincinnati; Ohio State University, B.A., 1989; Ohio State University, M.B.A., 1996; U.S. Army War College (PA), M.A., 2012; Methodist; Married (Karen Stivers); 2 children.

Military Career: OH Army National Guard 1988-pres. (Iraq)

Elected Office: OH Senate, 2003-2008.

Professional Career: Legislative aide; Lobbyist.

DC Office: 2234 RHOB 20515, 202-225-2015, Fax: 202-225-3529, stivers.house.gov

State Offices: Hilliard, 614-771-4968; Lancaster, 740-654-2654; Wilmington, 937-283-7049.

Committees: *Financial Services*: Investor Protection, Entrepreneurship & Capital Markets; Nat'l Security, International Development & Monetary Policy (RMM).

Group Ratings

	ADA	ACLU	AFL-CIO	LCV	ITI	COC	HAFA	ACU	CFG	FRC
2018	-	8%	-	11%	-	90%	46%	63%	43%	100%
2017	0%	C	31%	3%	C	93%	C	69%	43%	100%

Almanac Ratings 2017-18

	Economy	Social	Foreign	Composite
Liberal	10%	9%	5%	8%
Conservative	90%	91%	95%	92%

Key Votes of the 115th Congress

1. Obama-care revision	Y	5. Family planning regs	Y	9. Guantanamo prisoners	N
2. Tax Cuts	Y	6. Body cameras/immigration	N	10. Ground missiles, limit	N
3. Omnibus appropriations	Y	7. Abortion ban	Y	11. Defense Dept. spending	Y
4. Dodd-Frank revision	NV	8. Concealed carry	Y	12. FISA rules	Y

Election Results

Election	Name (Party)	Vote (%)		Cand. Spent	Ind. Exp. Support	Ind. Exp. Oppose
2018 General	Steve Stivers (R)............................	170,593	(58%)	$3,367,990		
	Rick Neal (D).................................	116,112	(40%)	$1,309,302	$130,429	
2018 Primary	Steve Stivers (R)........................		(100%)			

Prior winning percentages: 2016 (66%), 2014 (66%), 2012 (62%), 2010 (54%)

Republican Steve Stivers, elected in 2010, had the challenging assignment in 2017-18 of chairing the National Republican Congressional Committee. After the House GOP lost 40 seats, he suffered the inevitable second-guessing and offered some hindsight judgments about other Republicans. He resumed his work on the Financial Services Committee, dealing with issues where he had extensive personal background. As an economic conservative and a social centrist, he may have additional opportunities to be part of the next generation of Republican leaders in the House.

Stivers grew up in the Cincinnati suburbs, moved to Columbus to attend Ohio State University, and never left, except for deployments with the Ohio Army National Guard. For most of his career, he was associated with the Ohio legislature. He was a staffer in the state Senate, and in 1995 began working as a lobbyist for BankOne, which was based in Columbus (and later absorbed into Bank of America). He was appointed by the Senate in 2003 to fill the seat of a retiring state senator. Soon afterward, he served tours in Kuwait and Iraq, for which he received a Bronze Star. In the 2006 election, he ran his campaign from Iraq and won. Stivers was vice chairman of the Finance Committee, supporting state budgets that cut property taxes and froze tuition at state universities. He remained active in the Ohio Army National Guard, where he was promoted in 2017 to brigadier general.

When Republican Rep. Deborah Pryce retired in 2008, Democrats nominated Franklin County Commissioner Mary Jo Kilroy. After initially declining amid speculation that he wanted to be Ohio Senate president, Stivers entered the contest. He campaigned as a moderate, with a blend of support for abortion rights and fiscal discipline plus his military experience. Kilroy emphasized her background as a former Columbus school board president and slammed Stivers for his stint as a bank lobbyist. Stivers portrayed Kilroy as "way outside the mainstream," too liberal for the district, and a captive of big labor. In a strongly Democratic year, Kilroy won 46%-45%, a margin of 2,312 votes.

In her one term, Kilroy was a faithful supporter of the majority Democrats' programs, including the cap-and-trade bill to reduce carbon emissions and the Affordable Care Act. Stivers called the health law's mandate to buy insurance "very dangerous" and said the legislation would be a heavy burden on small business. Kilroy portrayed him as a flip-flopper, arguing that he had supported an individual mandate and a carbon emissions bill in the past. They raised roughly $2.7 million each, but the Democratic Congressional Campaign Committee abandoned the race in October as unwinnable. Stivers prevailed 54%-41%. Kilroy made an unsuccessful comeback bid in 2012, when she narrowly lost in the Democratic primary to Joyce Beatty in the new heavily Democratic 3rd District.

In the House, Stivers was a loyalist to Speaker John Boehner and "the type of sensible moderate that most Ohioans want to see," The Columbus Dispatch wrote in endorsing him for reelection. He joined the centrist Main Street Partnership as well as the conservative Republican Study Committee. On the Financial Services Committee, Stivers has worked with other Republicans to rein in the excesses of the Dodd-Frank banking law. In his attempt to boost the housing market, the House in 2015 passed his bipartisan Capital Access for Small Community Financial Institutions bill.

At Boehner's behest, Stivers served on a party task force on cybersecurity and worked with other allies of the Speaker to find ways to boost infrastructure spending. He served two years on the House Rules Committee, the "arm of the leadership," but gave up that assignment after Boehner stepped down.

Stivers has been deeply involved in party activities. He initially worked with Rep. Steve Scalise of Louisiana to recruit GOP candidates for the NRCC. When Scalise was elected in 2014 as GOP whip, Stivers was selected as one of his top deputies. Following the 2016 election, he became NRCC chairman, after easily defeating Rep. Roger Williams of Texas. In that position, Stivers faced the usual mid-term challenges for the party controlling the White House, plus the unconventional political style of President Donald Trump. His initial tests were four special-election contests in the spring of 2017 to replace House Republicans who joined the Trump administration. The GOP retained each of those seats, but their victories were narrow and closer than in the past, especially the record-setting costly contest for a district in the Atlanta suburbs — a signal of the problems that would confront Stivers.

Stivers contended with internal problems and other intra-party divisions. In the battleground suburban districts, House Republican members — and their voters — were distancing themselves from Trump. Stivers said that Trump could be helpful even in those districts, at least with groups of voters on a selective basis. When Rep. Ryan Costello of Pennsylvania decided to retire after court-ordered redistricting made his district an uphill climb, Stivers said that Costello suffered from "a lack of intestinal fortitude" for the challenge, though he later backed off the criticism. He did not back down late in the campaign when he "strongly condemned" Rep. Steve King of Iowa for his failure to "stand up against white supremacy and hate in all forms;" the NRCC withdrew its financial support and King barely survived reelection.

Stivers was second-guessed for spending millions of dollars on behalf of individual GOP incumbents, such as Barbara Comstock of Virginia and Mike Coffman of Colorado, whose prospects were viewed as hopeless by many Republicans. They held the type of suburban seats that Stivers represented and that had been the core of the House GOP majority in the past. Stivers was dealt a bad hand with numerous political factors that were largely out of his control, including the large number of GOP retirements in vulnerable seats, plus the Democrats' enthusiastic supporters and fundraising advantage.

Although the contest received little attention, Stivers had his most serious challenger since he was elected to the House. Rick Neal, a former Peace Corps volunteer and international aid worker and a political newcomer, campaigned for "affordable health care" and criticized Stivers for leaving behind his own district "when he took a new job raising money for his fellow Republicans in Congress." Neal waged what The Columbus Dispatch described as "a scrappy battle," in which he took issue with what Stivers described as his objective of "civility" in Congress, given the NRCC's support for "divisive, nasty attacks ads all over the country." Stivers, who responded that all the ads were accurate and fair, spent $3.4 million in the cycle to $1.3 million for Neal. He won, 58%-40%. Neal took Athens County and the outcome in Columbus-based Franklin was a virtual toss-up.

As Republicans struggled to come to terms with their loss of 40 House seats (pending the delayed outcome of a new election in the 9th District of North Carolina after the first results were thrown out), Stivers resumed his focus at the Financial Services Committee. As ranking Republican on its National Security, International Development and Monetary Policy Subcommittee, he said his objective was "a safer and more prosperous America."

OH-15: Central Ohio   Cook Partisan Voting Index: R+7

Population		Race and Ethnicity		Income	
Total	749,429	White	89.3%	Median Income	$61,004
Land area (sq. miles)	4,739	Black	3.9%	District Income Rank	167
Pop/ sq mi	158.1	Latino	2%	Poverty Rate	12.3%
Born in State	77.1%	Asian	2.3%	With health insurance	93.5%
		Two or more races	2.1%	Cash public assistance	2.4%
Age Groups		Other	0.3%	Food stamp/SNAP	12.4%
Under 18	22%				
18-34	23.8%	**Education**		**Work**	
35-64	39.9%	H.S grad or less	42%	White Collar	14.3%
Over 64	14.3%	Some college	27%	Sales and Service	38.8%
		College Degree, 4 yr	19.3%	Blue Collar	20.9%
Military		Post grad	11.7%	Government	16.4%
Veteran/ Active Duty	8.5%				

2012 Pres. Vote	Romney	180,487	(52%)	Obama	161,187	(46%)		
2016 Pres. Vote	Trump	196,762	(55%)	Clinton	141,648	(39%)	Johnson	12,381	(3%)

Southern Columbus Metro, Athens: Not long ago, when Columbus was a smaller and more provincial city, a Republican could compete there. But as that city and its metro area have become the largest -- and continually growing — part of Ohio, the new arrivals have been younger and they leaned Democratic. In state government, on the Ohio State campus and in the growing financial-services sector, a Republican struggled to survive. Coincidentally for Republicans, that growth in the heart of the state left the area with nearly enough people to fill three congressional districts, rather than the two of the past. This happened at the same time that its population statewide resulted in a loss of two House seats. For Republican redistricters in 2011, the solution became obvious: Create a heavily Democratic district based in the city, and carefully draw the two outlying districts to make them safely Republican.

That partisan shift resulted in radical changes in the 15th Congressional District. Only about 39 percent of the old 15th was preserved. A slim majority of the district's residents live in Columbus and its suburbs, mostly in the southern parts of the metro area. In a vast swath of mostly Republican counties stretching from the exurbs of Cincinnati nearly to West Virginia — disparate areas were stitched together to help prevent a non-Columbus Republican from amassing a power base in a primary election. About 40 percent of the population is in Franklin County, with 20 percent in adjacent Fairfield.

The parts of Columbus were mostly south of the capital and the campus: half of the Short North neighborhood just north of downtown, an up-and-coming area with a large gay population and many of the fashionable new clubs and restaurants of Columbus, though high real estate costs have forced some businesses to move elsewhere; a few other downtown communities; the old money suburb of Upper Arlington; and the up-and-coming suburbs of Hilliard and Grove City, which grew 27 percent and 15 percent, respectively, from 2010 to 2017. In Fairfield, downtown Lancaster has combined its historic roots and downtown revitalization to create an attractive community.

The only Democratic county is Athens, the poorest county in the state and home of Ohio University, the oldest college west of the Appalachians. Athens has been one of 31 counties in the Appalachian region that has been listed as "distressed," and it was one of only eight counties in Ohio to vote for Clinton in 2016. Nearby is Hocking Hills, the most visited state park in Ohio, with features that include a cave, a gorge, nature preserves, log cabins and access to the 1,444-mile Buckeye Trail that circles most of the state. The district has a distinct Republican lean. Donald Trump took 55 percent of the vote.

Anthony Gonzalez (R)

Elected 2018, 1st term, b. Sep 18, 1984; Avon Lake; Ohio State University, B.A., 2007; Stanford University (CA), M.B.A., 2014; Catholic; Married (Elizabeth Gonzalez); 1 child.

Professional Career: Indianapolis Colts, Wide Receiver 2007-2011; New England Patriots, Wide Receiver 2012-2012; Manager, InformedK12.

DC Office: 1023 LHOB 20515, 202-225-3876, anthonygonzalez.house.gov

State Offices: Canton, 330-599-7037; Strongsville, 440-783-3696.

Committees: *Financial Services*: Housing, Community Development & Insurance; Nat'l Security, International Development & Monetary Policy; Subcommittee on Diversity & Inclusion. *Science, Space & Technology*: Environment; Research & Technology.

Election Results

Election	Name (Party)	Vote (%)		Cand. Spent	Ind. Exp. Support	Ind. Exp. Oppose
2018 General	Anthony E. Gonzalez (R)............ 170,029	(57%)		$1,833,825	$451,000	
	Susan Moran Palmer (D).................... 129,681	(43%)		$364,821		
2018 Primary	Anthony E. Gonzalez (R)............ 34,327	(53%)				
	Christina Hagan (R)........................ 26,380	(41%)				
	Michael Grusenmeyer (R)........ 3,977	(6%)				

Freshman Republican Anthony Gonzalez was elected in his first campaign. Before entering politics, he had extensive experience in the public spotlight as a star football player at Ohio State University and then for five years as a wide receiver with the Indianapolis Colts in the National Football League. Gonzalez brought to the campaign a compelling life story as the grandson of refugees from Cuba, the son of a successful businessman and the manager of his own enterprises. As the frontrunner against both his GOP and Democratic opponents, he succeeded Rep. Jim Renacci, who was the unsuccessful Republican challenger to Sen. Sherrod Brown.

Gonzalez proudly embraced his grandfather, who was a successful lawyer in Cuba before he fled with his family to Miami in 1960, when their lives were in jeopardy following the takeover by Fidel Castro. They settled in Ohio, where his father started up a steel plant on the west side of Cleveland. At Ohio State, where Gonzalez got an athletic scholarship, the team won two Big Ten championships during his career.

Following his career with the NFL's Colts, where he was a first-round draft choice, Gonzalez got a master's in business administration from Stanford University. That led to his work as chief operating officer for Chalk Schools, a San Francisco-based tech company that sought to reduce excessive paperwork in public schools.

Returning to Ohio to run for Congress, Gonzalez won the GOP primary against state Rep. Christina Hagan, who had served eight years in the state House. Hagan more closely identified with President Donald Trump. Her ardent pro-gun and anti-abortion views drew support from conservative leaders. She criticized Gonzalez for his lack of political experience. "Legislating isn't quite as easy as catching a football," she said in an interview with Fox News. At age 29, Hagan would have been the youngest Republican woman elected to Congress.

Gonzalez, while mostly avoiding discussion of Trump, emphasized his own policy and campaign themes. He more than doubled Hagan's campaign financing and benefited from $300,000 in expenditures by the U.S. Chamber of Commerce. House Republican Leader Kevin McCarthy of California contributed to his campaign during the primary.

Gonzalez won the primary, 53%-41%. In Cuyahoga County, which had the largest turnout with a bit more than one-third of the vote, Gonzalez took 59 percent. Hagan led narrowly in her base of Stark County, plus nearby Portage, and Gonzalez took the other three counties.

In November, Gonzalez handily defeated Democrat Susan Palmer, a health product sales executive and another political newcomer. She had limited campaign funds and received scant national-party assistance in this GOP-friendly district. In his 57%-43% victory, he narrowly won Cuyahoga County, which was nearly 40 percent of the total vote, and had a big lead in the five other counties. Gonzalez gained the distinction as the first Hispanic Republican in the House from outside the Sunbelt.

OH-16: Northern Ohio   Cook Partisan Voting Index: R+8

Population		Race and Ethnicity		Income	
Total	722,933	White	91.8%	Median Income	$64,625
Land area (sq. miles)	1,205	Black	2.1%	District Income Rank	137
Pop/ sq mi	599.8	Latino	2.2%	Poverty Rate	7.4%
Born in State	78%	Asian	2.2%	With health insurance	93.9%
		Two or more races	1.6%	Cash public assistance	1.9%
Age Groups		Other	0.2%	Food stamp/SNAP	6.7%
Under 18	21.5%				
18-34	19.3%	**Education**		**Work**	
35-64	40.7%	H.S grad or less	38%	White Collar	18.5%
Over 64	18.5%	Some college	29%	Sales and Service	38.9%
		College Degree, 4 yr	21.1%	Blue Collar	20.9%
Military		Post grad	11.9%	Government	10.9%
Veteran/ Active Duty	8.3%				

2012 Pres. Vote	Romney	199,697	(54%)	Obama	169,106	(45%)		
2016 Pres. Vote	Trump	207,149	(56%)	Clinton	145,670	(39%)	Johnson	11,451	(3%)

Cleveland/Akron/Canton Suburbs: The rapidly growing Cleveland of the early-1900s — it went from 93,000 residents in 1870 to more than 900,000 in 1930 — was crammed into a compact area. The eclectic mix of newcomers that populated the city sorted itself into Cleveland's so-called "cosmo wards:" Italians in Big Italy to the southeast of Public Square; Croats, Serbs and Slovenians in the St. Clair area on the northeast side of town; Irish in Whiskey Island to the west of downtown; Russians, Germans, Poles and Slovaks in the Ohio City and Tremont areas near present-day Newburgh Heights; and Czechs and Poles in Praha and Slavic Village to the north of present-day Garfield Heights. The cosmo wards began to empty out in the 1950s as the original immigrants died off and their children fled to the suburbs. For a half-century, Cleveland's population has been in decline. Only 14 percent of the population of Greater Cleveland now lives in the city itself, the lowest share since before the Civil War.

The now-graying great-grandchildren of those immigrants live in places like those found in the 16th Congressional District of Ohio, a political creation whose precincts are bound more by Republican voting habits than by any coherent geographic locale. About 40 percent of the district's votes are cast in Cuyahoga County, mostly in Cleveland's western outer suburbs: comfortable places like Westlake, a stone's throw from Lake Erie, plus Strongsville and North Royalton. Many residents here tend to be descended from the Hungarians and Bohemians who settled southwest of Public Square, near present-day Brooklyn.

The district also takes in exurban Medina County, Portage and Stark (but not including Canton) counties, and Wayne County, home to the College of Wooster. In 2018, Wayne was ranked among the five strongest "micropolitan" areas in the nation, a reference to economically growing communities with a population between 10,000 and 50,000. The county is the headquarters of Smuckers, whose familiar consumer brands have included Smucker jellies and Folgers coffee; in recent years, it has added Big Heart pet foods and Ainsworth Pet Nutrition. The southern part of Wayne County is Amish country, where people drive horse-drawn tractors, eschew automobiles and electricity (except from their own generators), and quit school after the eighth grade. Tourism has been a growth industry in the Amish region, with a profusion of restaurants, bed-and-breakfasts, and gift shops. The 16th leans Republican just enough to avoid serious Democratic challenges. Donald Trump won 55 percent in 2016.

OKLAHOMA

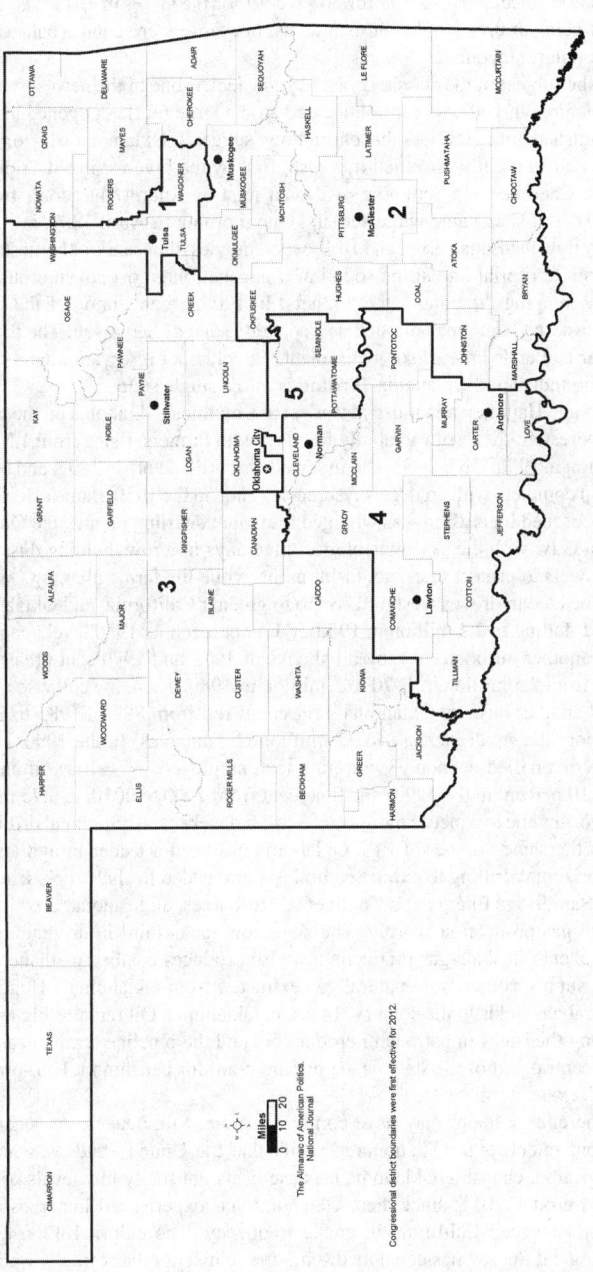

Congressional district boundaries were first effective for 2012.

Miles
0 10 20

It wasn't that long ago that Democrats held some sway in Oklahoma. They controlled the state House until 2004, the state Senate until 2008, and the governorship until 2010. Since then, though, the GOP has had a virtual lock on the state. Not a single county in Oklahoma has voted Democratic in a presidential election since 2000 – a 308 for 308 record for the GOP. In 2018, Oklahoma Democrats notched modest gains in urban and suburban areas, but those were counterbalanced by the party's continued erosion in rural counties.

Oklahoma, the subject of the classic Broadway musical, is one of the newest states, the 46th to be admitted to the Union, in 1907. Its capitol, located atop a large oil field, opened in 1917, though the dome was not finished until 2002. As that chronology suggests, Oklahoma's history has been a story of sudden stops and starts. It was settled in a rush, first by the Five Civilized Tribes — Chickasaw, Choctaw, Creek, Cherokee and Seminole — driven west by Andrew Jackson's troops on the Trail of Tears in the 1830s. Then came white settlers. One morning in April 1889, in the great land rush memorialized by novelist Edna Ferber and Hollywood movies, thousands of homesteaders drove their wagons across the territorial line at the sound of a gunshot, the most adventurous or unscrupulous of them literally jumping the gun — the Sooners. In 1905, a convention of the Civilized Nations sought to have eastern Oklahoma admitted as a separate state of Sequoyah. The federal government turned a deaf ear and ended the tribal government, parceled out reservation land to tribe members, and combined the Indian and Oklahoma Territories into a single state.

The Rodgers and Hammerstein musical was set in a mythical Oklahoma on the brink of statehood in 1906. Soon thereafter, the territory rapidly filled up with farmers, rising from 1.5 million people in 1907 to 2.4 million in 1930. Oil helped. The first well was drilled here in 1897, and by 1920 Tulsa was an oil boom town complete with art deco skyscrapers. Then in the 1930s came a decade of bust — and dust — as soil loosened by erosion was whipped into giant swirling clouds: the Dust Bowl. "People sat in Oklahoma City, with the sky invisible for three days in a row, holding dust masks over their faces and wet towels to protect their mouths at night, while the farms blew by," wrote author John Gunther. Okies headed in droves west on U.S. 66 to greener California, and Oklahoma's population steadily declined, falling to 2.2 million in 1950. It did not reach its 1930 level again until 1970.

Then came another oil boom. As the oil shocks of 1973 and 1979 sent prices up, Oklahoma's population rose from 2.5 million in 1970 to 3 million in 1980. Then, the collapse of oil prices in the 1980s produced another bust, as Oklahoma's rig count fell from 882 in 1982 to 232 in 1983. The 1990 census reported a small increase to 3.1 million Oklahomans. In the 1990s, Oklahoma began building a more diversified economy, with high-tech employers as well as oil and gas firms. The population rose 10 percent in the 1990s and 9 percent from 2000 to 2010, to 3.75 million. Higher oil prices made it worthwhile to squeeze more from marginal wells, and horizontal drilling allowed more production with the same number of rigs. Oklahoma has been a leader in hydraulic fracturing, or fracking, and horizontal drilling to extract natural gas embedded in shale rock. Chesapeake Energy, Devon Energy, SandRidge Energy and Continental Resources, all headquartered in Oklahoma City, increased natural gas production sharply. The state now ranks third in dry natural gas production nationally and seventh in shale-gas production; it also produces coalbed methane, and much of the nation's helium supply comes from natural gas extracted from Oklahoma's Hugoton field. Of the 100 largest natural gas fields in the country, 14 are in Oklahoma. Oil remains big as well. Oklahoma ranks sixth among the states in petroleum production, and the pipeline terminus and storage hub of Cushing, in the central part of the state, is the pricing point for benchmark U.S.-produced crude oil, known as West Texas Intermediate.

However, the energy boom may have come at a price: earthquakes. As recently as 1990, the Soviet Union sent scientists to Oklahoma to verify that the United States was not testing nuclear weapons underground, choosing Oklahoma because of its unusually low levels of seismic activity. That all changed around 2011; since then, Oklahoma has experienced hundreds of quakes a year and occasionally exceeded California in quake frequency. The culprit isn't fracking per se, the Oklahoma Geological Survey has concluded – it's the reinjection back into "disposal wells" of the water produced in drilling. Tighter regulation instituted by the Oklahoma Corporation Commission in 2015 has coincided with a reduction in quakes – 903 in 2015, 623 in 2016 and 304 in 2017 – but the level remains far higher than it was a decade earlier, and concerns continue because building codes in the state were never intended to handle quakes. Meanwhile, Oklahoma has joined Texas in signing legislation to prevent Oklahoma cities and counties from banning fracking on their own.

The growth of the energy business has juiced the state's capital. The area around its stockyards, the nation's largest, has become a tourist attraction, and civic leaders have channeled the North Canadian River (and renamed a portion of it the Oklahoma River) to create North America's premier rowing center, even if the arid landscape does not match verdant Henley-on-Thames. At the same time, Oklahoma has been investing in renewable energy. Oklahoma now ranks second to Texas in electricity generation from wind. In Oklahoma, wind can also be a serious problem. Between 1890 and 2013, metropolitan Oklahoma City saw at least 156 tornadoes — about one each year, including the 2013 EF5 that killed 24 in and around Moore. The state also has 10 hydropower plants; Oklahoma has more man-made lakes than any other state.

Despite its oil riches, Oklahoma has its share of problems. It has the second-highest percentage of divorced residents in the nation, the health system ranks 50th in the nation according to the Commonwealth Fund, and median income ranks in the bottom 10 states. Oklahoma has the third-highest rate of teenage pregnancy, ranks 11th in violent crime, and is eighth from the bottom in bachelor's degrees. Two studies found that Oklahoma police in 2015 killed people more often than those in any other state. A decline in oil revenues, exacerbated by repeated tax cuts, came home to roost under Republican Gov. Mary Fallin. In April 2018, teachers staged a walkout in search of higher pay that left one-fifth of schools operating only four days a week. The teachers sought a $3.3 billion boost – a $10,000 teacher raise over three years, a $7,000 raise for support staff and a cost-of-living increase for teacher pensions. Ultimately, teachers ended their walkout with a smaller sum signed into law. (As she signed the smaller increase, Fallin dismissed the teachers' complaints as akin to a "teenage kid that wants a better car.")

On the upside, unemployment in the state has been mild, peaking at 7.1 percent in late 2009; by early 2019, it was 3.2 percent. In addition to energy jobs, the healthy workforce statistics stemmed from a more stable housing market and some good years for agriculture. Oklahoma ranks fourth in the nation in number of farms, in the top five states for cattle, and in the top three states for rye, canola, hay and winter wheat. Statewide, the population has increased by a healthy 4.9 percent since 2010, concentrated in Canadian County (the western suburbs of Oklahoma City, with 21 percent growth), Oklahoma County (Oklahoma City, 10 percent), Cleveland County (the southern Oklahoma City suburbs and Norman, 11 percent) and Tulsa County (8 percent). The numbers in rural Oklahoma declined, however: Between mid-2016 and mid-2017, no fewer than 49 of Oklahoma's 77 counties lost residents.

Amid all this change, Oklahoma's Indian identity has persisted. With only one small reservation, Oklahomans of Indian ancestry — 9 percent of the population — have made their way forward in the larger society while still cherishing their heritage. There has been much intermarriage over the years, and many Oklahomans — and not a few of its politicians — proudly claim Indian blood. Such murky ancestral ties caused problems for Massachusetts Sen. Elizabeth Warren, an Oklahoma native whose claims of Native American family history came under scrutiny; her attempts to use DNA testing to prove her lineage outraged the Cherokee leadership, and Warren eventually apologized. There is an ongoing struggle to keep the Cherokee, Choctaw, Chickasaw and Seminole languages from dying out — you can see street signs in the Cherokee alphabet in Tahlequah, the Cherokee Nation's capital. The state has other minorities as well – in fact, white students are now a minority in the state's public schools. Hispanics, who account for 10 percent of the state's population, are concentrated in the two big cities and in meatpacking counties in the west. Just 7 percent are black, mostly residents of Oklahoma City and Tulsa. The latter was the site of the Tulsa race riot of 1921, "a firestorm of hatred and violence that is perhaps unequaled in the peacetime history of the United States," as historian John Hope Franklin called it. The violence by white mobs destroyed nearly 40 square blocks of African-American homes and businesses and likely killed between 75 and 100 people, yet the carnage was largely forgotten for decades. More than seven decades later, on April 19, 1995, the state's other major city, Oklahoma City, was the site of mass slaughter when a truck bomb placed by anti-government domestic terrorists blew apart the Alfred P. Murrah Federal Building, killing 168.

Historically, Oklahoma saw big Democratic margins in eastern counties and in Little Dixie in the southeast, while northwestern Oklahoma, settled by Kansans, has always been Republican. Starting in the 1950s, Tulsa and Oklahoma City leaned Republican too. Then, in the last decade or two, parts of the state outside the metro regions moved sharply away from their Democratic heritage. This evolution has made Oklahoma one of America's most Republican states. It has not voted Democratic for president since 1964, and since 1966, it has elected only one Democratic senator, David Boren. In 2010, more than 70 percent of voters approved a state constitutional amendment to prevent courts from considering sharia law in judicial decisions. The state GOP is fractured between tea partiers, Chamber of Commerce types, movement conservatives, evangelicals and others, but Democrats are usually too weak to take advantage. In 2016, Donald Trump won the state by a 36-point margin. He tapped Oklahoma's strongly pro-energy attorney general, Scott Pruitt, to head the Environmental Protection Agency; he resigned in June 2018 amid a flood of investigations into his office spending, housing arrangements and allegedly evasive record-keeping about meetings with lobbyists.

The partisan tide turned – slightly – during the Trump era. In 2017, Democrats won a flurry of legislative special elections, and in June 2018 Oklahoma voters approved medical marijuana by a double-digit margin despite opposition from Fallin, GOP Sen. James Lankford, the Oklahoma State Medical Association, the Oklahoma Sheriffs' Association and the Oklahoma District Attorneys Association. In November, Democrat Kendra Horn surprised even some in her own party by defeating Rep. Steve Russell in an Oklahoma City-based district that hadn't voted for a Democrat in more than four decades. The trends that catapulted Horn were echoed in urban and suburban areas. Even as Democrat Drew Edmondson was losing the gubernatorial race statewide to Republican Kevin Stitt by 12 points – a margin similar to the one in the 2014 gubernatorial race – he posted marked improvement in and around Oklahoma City. While the 2014 Democratic nominee lost Oklahoma County by five points, Edmondson won it by 14 points, and while the Democrat lost Cleveland County in 2014 by six points, Edmondson won it by five. In Oklahoma County, the number of votes cast for the Democratic gubernatorial nominee spiked by 77 percent between 2014 and 2018, and it jumped by 71 percent in Cleveland County. In the meantime, two Democratic women won previously Republican legislative districts in the Oklahoma City area. Still, Republicans gained legislative seats overall by flipping Democratic-held seats in rural areas, and Republican candidates for lieutenant governor, attorney general and state treasurer won their races by larger margins than Stitt did – another sign that Republican dominance in Oklahoma isn't reversing any time soon.

Population		Race and Ethnicity		Income	
Total	3,896,251	White	66.5%	Median Income	$49,767
Land area (sq. miles)	68,595	Black	7.2%	State Income Rank	41
Pop/ sq mi	56.8	Latino	10.1%	Poverty Rate	16.2%
Born in state	60.9%	Asian	2.0%	With health insurance	85.1%
		Two or more races	6.9%	Cash public assistance	2.9%
Age Groups		Other	7.3%	Food stamp/SNAP	13.4%
Under 18	24.5%				
18-34	23.9%	Education		Work	
35-64	36.9%	H.S grad or less	44.0%	White Collar	34.1%
Over 64	14.7%	Some college	31.2%	Sales and Service	41.2%
		College Degree, 4 yr	16.6%	Blue Collar	24.6%
Military		Post grad	8.3%	Government	16.7%
Veteran/ Active Duty	10.1%				

Presidential Politics

2016 Primary (D)	Sanders (D)	174,228 (52%)	Clinton (D)	139,443 (42%)			
2016 Primary (R)	Cruz (R)	158,078 (34%)	Trump (R)	130,267 (28%)	Rubio (R)	119,633 (26%)	
	Carson (R)	28,601 (6%)					
2016 Pres. Vote	Trump (R)	949,136 (65%)	Clinton (D)	420,375 (29%)	Johnson (L)	83,481 (6%)	
2012 Pres. Vote	Romney (R)	891,325 (67%)	Obama (D)	443,547 (33%)			

Since the FDR era, Oklahoma has voted only twice for a Democratic presidential candidate: Harry Truman in 1948 and Lyndon Johnson in 1964. The last Democratic nominee to carry a county in Oklahoma was Al Gore in 2000 (he won nine out of 77). Traditionally, Tulsa and Oklahoma City were

Republican strongholds, but starting in 2004 the counties outside the two big metro areas have been voting more Republican than the state average in presidential elections. In 1996, Bob Dole defeated Bill Clinton 48%-40%, but Clinton won nearly half the counties. Most of those were in the region's old Indian Territory, where in-migration from Texas, Arkansas and especially Mississippi brought with it Democratic traditions -- the region became known as "Little Dixie." But in 2016, Donald Trump crushed Hillary Clinton, 65%-29%. In 66 counties he won 70 percent or more of the vote. Clinton's best county was Oklahoma (Oklahoma City) where she won 41 percent of the vote. In the 2008 Democratic primary, Clinton handily beat Obama 55%-31%. Obama carried Oklahoma County (Oklahoma City), and Clinton carried all the others, with big margins in eastern counties near her longtime home in Arkansas. In 2016, Vermont Sen. Bernie Sanders defeated Clinton 52%-42%. This time Clinton won only two counties -- Oklahoma and Osage -- which comprise the Osage Nation Reservation. Oklahoma was one of five states Clinton won in the 2008 primaries that she lost in 2016. The others were Indiana, New Hampshire, Rhode Island and West Virginia.

Republican presidential primaries have been closer. John McCain beat Mike Huckabee 37%-33% in 2008 and Rick Santorum beat Mitt Romney 34%-28% in 2012. In 2016, Texas Sen. Ted Cruz spent more than $800,000 on television ads, more than the rest of the GOP candidates combined, and defeated Trump 34%-28%. Marco Rubio won 26 percent. The competitive race drew a GOP record 459,992 primary voters.

Congressional Districts

116th Congress Lineup	1D 4R	115th Congress Lineup	5R

Oklahoma redistricting following the 2010 census was a breeze. Republicans controlled the process for the first time and they had little incentive to rock the boat. Dan Boren, whose family name is revered in state politics, was the sole Democrat in the delegation, but he voted with Republicans more often than any other Democrat in the House. All five incumbents, including Boren, agreed to minimal changes in their districts, and legislators passed them with a yawn. Then, Boren surprised observers and made the GOP job even easier by announcing his retirement at age 37, from what had long been known as the Little Dixie district — a former Democratic stronghold in the southeast. Fiercely conservative Republican Markwayne Mullin easily picked up the seat the following November. From 2012 through 2016, Republicans won each of the five districts with at least 57 percent of the vote.

Then, the unexpected happened. Democrat Kendra Horn took the 5th District from Republican Rep. Steve Russell — with some help from GOP over-confidence and shifting demographics in Oklahoma City. Even if Horn manages to win reelection, Democratic prospects of retaining the seat in the 2022 redistricting seemed dim — given solid GOP control of the legislature and the governor's office, plus the certain Republican desire to reclaim the entire delegation. One Republican option would be to shift some Democratic-leaning precincts in Oklahoma County to the 4th District, which already has 10 percent of that county, and add nearby Republican strongholds to the 5th.

Kevin Stitt (R)

Elected 2018, term expires 2023, 1st term; b. Dec. 28, 1972, Milton, FL; Oklahoma State University, B.S., 1996; Unknown; Married (Sarah); 6 children;

Professional Career: CEO, Gateway Mortgage Group, 2000-2018; Loan Officer, First City Financial, 1998-2000.

Office: 2300 N. Lincoln Blvd., Room 212,Oklahoma City, 73105; 405-521-2342; Fax: 405-521-3353; Website: ok.gov

Lt. Gov.: Matt Pinnell (R) **Atty. Gen:** Mike Hunter (R)

State Legislature: Senate: 9D, 39R **House:** 24D, 77R

Election Results

Election	Name (Party)	Vote (%)
2018 General	Kevin Stitt (R)	644,579 (54%)
	Drew Edmondson (D)	500,973 (42%)
	Chris Powell (Lib)	40,833 (3%)
2018 Primary runoff	Kevin Stitt (R)	164,892 (55%)
	Mick Cornett (R)	137,316 (45%)
2018 Primary	Mick Cornett (R)	132,806 (29%)
	Kevin Stitt (R)	110,479 (24%)
	Todd Lamb (R)	107,985 (24%)
	Dan Fisher (R)	35,818 (8%)
	Gary Jones (R)	25,243 (6%)

Republican Kevin Stitt was elected governor of Oklahoma in 2018, sealing GOP dominance in the state despite weak approval ratings for the outgoing Republican governor, Mary Fallin. Stitt, founder of a mortgage company and a first-time candidate, defeated the outgoing lieutenant governor and the longtime mayor of Oklahoma City in the primary runoff, then defeated a Democratic former attorney general in November, always portraying himself as an outsider who could shake up the capital.

Stitt, a fourth-generation Oklahoman, grew up in Norman, where his father was a pastor, and spent summers in Skiatook, where his grandfather owned a dairy farm. He is a member of the Cherokee Nation, making him the first Native American to be elected governor in the United States. Stitt earned his bachelor's degree at Oklahoma State University, working his way through college as a door-to-door book salesman. In his late twenties – with just $1,000 and a computer, he has often said – Stitt founded Gateway Mortgage, turning it into a company with $16 billion in loans, 1,200 employees and 164 field offices in 41 states by 2018. He stepped down as CEO shortly before securing the GOP nomination. The company's record drew questions from opponents, who cited a Business Insider article after the 2008 financial crisis that called Gateway one of the "15 shadiest mortgage lenders." The label was based on reporting by Center for Public Integrity that found the company with a relatively high default rate of 11.9 percent. Stephen Curry, Stitt's successor as CEO, acknowledged to the Associated Press that the firm's default rate was high, but that it stemmed from the challenging times in the lending industry. "Gateway's performance may have been worse than average, but nowhere extreme enough to be considered shady," Curry told the AP, adding that the company's record improved substantially in later years.

Stitt was one of the contenders to succeed Fallin, who had been elected in 2010 as the state's first female chief executive and was easily reelected in 2014. Her record of cutting taxes, curbing abortion rights and relaxing handgun restrictions pleased conservatives, but an oil and gas downturn hit the state – and the state budget – hard, lowering Fallin's approval ratings during her second term. Her final year in office was dominated by a teacher walkout, driven by spending cuts that had left one-fifth of schools operating only four days a week and that left teacher salaries second-to-last in the nation. Fallin ultimately signed legislation raising teacher salaries by $6,100 for teachers and $1,250 for support staff – less than what the teachers had been seeking, but enough to end the walkout.

With Fallin leaving office after eight years, the race for the 2018 Republican nomination was heavily contested. The primary featured 10 candidates, though only three of them were considered to be in the top tier: Mick Cornett, the outgoing four-term Oklahoma City mayor; two-term Lt. Gov. Todd Lamb; and Stitt. Lamb had long since distanced himself from Fallin, but his establishment ties and career-politician label posed problems with the electorate. The little-known Stitt spent more than $2 million from his own pocket prior to primary day to raise his profile. Cornett finished first with 29 percent; Stitt pulled slightly ahead for the second runoff spot. In the runoff, Stitt continued spending his own money, positioning himself as a political outsider and emphasizing his loyalty to President Donald Trump and his immigration policies (although Trump didn't publicly endorse Stitt until after he won the nomination). In ads, Cornett rejected the notion that he was disloyal to Trump, calling the charge "Bull Stitt." Stitt won, 55%-45%, with Cornett running strong in the central part of the state and Stitt performing well everywhere else, including in his home base of Tulsa County. Meanwhile, in the Democratic primary, former 16-year attorney general Drew Edmondson easily defeated state Sen. Connie Johnson, 61%-39%.

Stitt framed Edmondson as part of the Oklahoma political establishment, but Edmondson questioned whether a political outsider like Stitt could be successful as governor. (When the Tulsa World looked at voting records, it found that Stitt had not even voted in a gubernatorial race since at least 1999.) Edmondson backed expanding Medicaid under the Affordable Care Act – a course Oklahoma had consistently rejected – while Stitt opposed such a move. Edmondson said he'd support higher taxes, while Stitt ruled out tax increases, even saying he disagreed with the tax hikes previously approved by the legislature to fund the teacher pay raises. In a state where Trump's approval rating remained above water, Stitt made use of Trump's endorsement as well as a visit from Vice President Mike Pence during a rally at Oral Roberts University. The National Rifle Association also took out ads against Edmondson. Bolstered by nearly $5 million in his own funds, Stitt won all but four of the state's counties, though he notably lost Oklahoma County (Oklahoma City) and Cleveland County (Oklahoma City suburbs and Norman), both of which had voted for Fallin in 2014. Edmondson won his home base of Muskogee County – by one vote.

By the time Stitt took office, the state was looking at an improved budget picture – a $600 million surplus – and he floated the idea of an additional $1,200 pay raise for teachers. He proposed raising the state's rainy-day fund from $874 million to $1 billion as a hedge against the boom-and-bust pattern of the energy sector. On an issue with bipartisan support, Stitt backed efforts to ease sentencing for non-violent offenders. He signed a series of executive orders that restructured the cabinet, increased transparency requirements on the use of contract lobbyists by state agencies, and gave agency managers more flexibility in hiring. He signed a bill allowing Oklahomans to carry firearms without a permit or training – a measure that Fallin had vetoed over safety concerns. And he signed legislation that strengthened the governor's authority over hiring and firing the heads of the state's five largest agencies.

Jim Inhofe (R)

Elected 1994, term expires 2020, 4th full term, b. Nov 17, 1934; Des Moines, IA; University of Tulsa (LK), B.A., 1973; Presbyterian; Married (Kay Kirkpatrick Inhofe); 4 children (1 deceased); 16 grandchildren.

Military Career: U.S. Army 1957-1958

Elected Office: OK House, 1967-1969; OK Senate, 1969-1977, Republican leader, 1975-1977; Tulsa Mayor, 1978-1984; U.S. House, 1987-1995.

Professional Career: Businessman, land developer, 1962-1986.

DC Office: 205 RSOB 20510, 202-224-4721, Fax: 202-228-0380, inhofe.senate.gov

State Offices: Enid, 580-234-5105; McAlester, 918-426-0933; Oklahoma City, 405-208-8841; Tulsa, 918-748-5111.

Committees: *Armed Services (Chmn). Environment & Public Works*: Clean Air & Nuclear Safety; Superfund, Waste Management, & Regulatory Oversight; Transportation & Infrastructure. *Small Business & Entrepreneurship.*

Group Ratings

	ADA	ACLU	AFL-CIO	LCV	ITI	COC	HAFA	ACU	CFG	FRC
2018	-	10%	-	14%	-	80%	76%	91%	61%	100%
2017	0%	C	0%	0%	C	86%	C	80%	88%	100%

Almanac Ratings 2017-18

	Economy	Social	Foreign	Composite
Liberal	6%	6%	0%	4%
Conservative	94%	94%	100%	96%

Key Votes of the 115th Congress

1. Obama-care revision	Y	5. Gun regulations	Y	9. Kavanaugh confirmation	Y
2. Tax Cuts	Y	6. Family planning regs	Y	10. Saudi arms sales	N
3. Dodd-Frank revision	Y	7. Gorsuch confirmation	Y	11. FISA rules	Y
4. Omnibus appropriations	Y	8. Immigration restrictions	N	12. Military aid in Yemen	N

Election Results

Election	Name (Party)	Vote (%)		Cand. Spent	Ind. Exp. Support	Ind. Exp. Oppose
2014 General	Jim Inhofe (R)	558,166	(68%)	$5,152,276	$7,250	
	Matt Silverstein (D)	234,307	(29%)	$471,194		
2014 Primary	Jim Inhofe (R)	231,131	(88%)			

Prior winning percentages: 2008 (57%), 2002 (57%), 1996 (57%), 1994 special (55%), House: 1992 (53%), 1990 (56%), 1988 (53%), 1986 (55%)

Republican Jim Inhofe, Oklahoma's senior senator, moved into the top ranks of influential senators when he became Armed Services Committee chairman in September 2018, following the death of Sen. John McCain. In the previous months, Inhofe had served as acting chairman while McCain was at home in Arizona fighting brain cancer. During that time, Inhofe managed the Senate-House agreement on a defense spending bill in which the Republican-controlled Congress gave President Donald Trump much of the GOP's wish list for military spending. Earlier in the year, Inhofe was forced by Senate GOP rules to give up the chairmanship of the Environment and Public Works Committee after three terms. But his policy influence on energy and environment issues remained strong as several of his former aides and Oklahoma allies took top positions in the Trump administration — though some of them had a rocky road. Facing re-election in 2020, Inhofe's chief potential obstacle appeared to be his age: He'll be 85 on Election Day 2020. Rarely reluctant to express his views, Inhofe seemed comfortable with Trump, though he sometimes objected to his tweets.

Inhofe's political career dates back more than a half-century. He grew up in Tulsa, served in the Army, and worked in real estate and insurance. He was elected to the state House in 1966 and to the state Senate in 1969. During his time in the state Senate, he earned a bachelor's degree from the University of Tulsa. As a state legislator, he promoted a balanced budget constitutional amendment. His career then hit a couple of bumps at a time when now-solidly Republican Oklahoma still tilted Democratic. In 1974, Inhofe ran for governor and lost to Democrat David Boren — whom he later succeeded in the Senate — 64%-36%. Two years later, he ran for the House against Democratic Rep. Jim Jones and lost. Inhofe made a political comeback by winning election as mayor of Tulsa in 1978, an office he held until 1984.

When Jones left to run unsuccessfully for Senate in 1986, Inhofe was elected to his House seat. He was re-elected three times, albeit with uninspiring margins: He was held to 53 percent of the vote on two occasions. Negative publicity from a family business lawsuit and charges of campaign finance irregularities impaired his support in what was even then a strongly Republican district. Inhofe's most notable accomplishment while in the House was reforming the arcane rules for discharge petitions, used chiefly by the minority party to force a floor vote on legislation bottled up in committee. For years, House rules kept secret the names of signers of discharge petitions until they reached 218, when suddenly they were made public; anonymity allowed lawmakers to claim they had worked to bring legislation to the floor, when they in fact had done the opposite. That was changed in 1993, and one of the first bills to benefit from the new rules was an aviation liability reform bill co-sponsored by Inhofe, an avid flyer of small airplanes. The legislation limited the liability of small-airplane manufacturers in lawsuits resulting from crashes.

In 1994, when conservative Democrat Boren resigned from the Senate to become president of the University of Oklahoma, Rep. Dave McCurdy, a moderate Democrat, was the initial front-runner in the special election to fill the last two years of Boren's term. But the Clinton administration's unpopularity among conservatives was too much for McCurdy, who had voted for 1993 budget increases and tax hikes and for the 1994 crime bill with its ban on assault weapons. Inhofe won 55%-40%. In the Senate, Inhofe was elected president of the large GOP freshman class of 11, as Republicans regained the Senate majority.

In the Almanac's vote ratings, Inhofe consistently has been among the most conservative senators. For many years, he has been an outspoken leader of the GOP faction that disputes the mainstream scientific view of global warming — which holds that carbon dioxide emissions will cause catastrophic climate change absent action by the United States and other major nations. In 2003, Inhofe termed the contention that man-made emissions have caused global warming "the greatest hoax ever perpetrated on the American people." Nearly a decade later, in 2012, he published a book: "The Greatest Hoax: How the Global Warming Conspiracy Threatens Your Future." He came armed with a snowball as a prop during a Senate floor speech in 2015. Inhofe suggested climate change was due to forces beyond the control of modern civilization. "Climate is changing, and climate has always changed. There's archeological evidence of that. There's biblical evidence of that. There's historic evidence of that," he said.

Representing a major petroleum-producing state, Inhofe has been an avid proponent of oil drilling in the Arctic National Wildlife Refuge, as well as more oil and gas exploration throughout the nation at large. After the April 2010 BP oil spill in the Gulf of Mexico, he opposed a Democratic initiative to remove the $75 million cap on damages for offshore drilling accidents. Environmental activist Robert F. Kennedy Jr. in 2012 called Inhofe "Big Oil's top call girl."

Inhofe's first stint as chairman of the Environment and Public Works Committee was from 2003 to 2007, when Democrats regained the majority. He devoted much of his attention to a major nonenvironmental responsibility of the panel — reauthorization of the federal surface transportation bill funding highways and transit systems. By early 2004, Inhofe had hammered out an agreement in the Senate for a six-year, $318 billion transportation bill. The House-passed bill was $275 billion. The two versions had significant political differences. Inhofe's goal was to guarantee that every state got 95 percent of its gas tax money back. With the conflict deadlocked, the issue was deferred to 2005. By that time, GOP leaders were eager to cut a final deal with President George W. Bush, and Inhofe agreed to a scaled-down bill of $286 billion.

It took another decade for Congress to agree on the next long-term surface transportation measure, after a period of short-term extensions of two years or less. In 2015, President Barack Obama signed a five-year, $305 billion extension of the highway bill into law. By that time, the Republicans had regained Senate control and Inhofe was back for his third and final term as Environment and Public Works chairman. Left unresolved was a long-term solution to funding the nation's transportation infrastructure: Gas tax revenues continued to decline because of more fuel-efficient vehicles, and lawmakers resisted increasing the per gallon amount of the tax. Trump had promised to address that challenge. Initial prospects for cooperation between Inhofe and Barbara Boxer of California, the senior Democrat on the committee for many years, had appeared dim. He spoke out strongly against her bill to impose a mandatory cap on carbon dioxide emissions, which died in the Senate in 2008. But Inhofe insisted their working relations were nonetheless good. Indeed, after they worked together in 2012 to pass a two-year surface transportation bill extension, Boxer told reporters that Inhofe "has been just the best partner for me as chairman ... in the best traditions of how the highway bill has been done until now."

Besides the surface transportation measure, perhaps the most notable accomplishment of Inhofe's final term as Environment and Public Works chairman was a revision to the federal Toxic Substances Control Act in 2016. Before his death in 2013, New Jersey Democratic Sen. Frank Lautenberg had worked for years to improve the much-criticized law, which had remained largely unchanged since its enactment in 1976. The changes cleared Inhofe's panel in 2015 on a bipartisan vote, with backing from some environmental groups — which felt it gave Environmental Protection Agency significantly increased powers — and industry, which liked the fact that, going forward, it provided a single federal regulatory regimen rather than a patchwork of state laws. Inhofe negotiated with New

Mexico Democratic Sen. Tom Udall, as Boxer — and several other environmental groups — initially resisted the bill as not going far enough to regulate industry. She was assuaged after winning some changes, and the final bill cleared the Senate floor on a voice vote.

Inhofe initially served as the top Republican on the Armed Services Committee from 2013 to 2014 after term limits forced McCain to step aside as that panel's ranking minority member. In 2015, with the Republicans back in the majority, McCain was able to claim the Armed Services chairmanship under the GOP term limit rules, and Inhofe returned to Environment and Public Works' top slot. Inhofe began his tenure atop Armed Services by crusading against his former Senate colleague Nebraska Republican Chuck Hagel's bid to become Obama's secretary of Defense. While other senators said that Hagel's inadequate support for Israel was a cause for concern, Inhofe went even further: He suggested that Hagel was "cozy" with countries promoting terrorism because Iran had expressed support for his nomination. Although the switch from McCain to Inhofe as committee chairman in 2018 was relatively smooth, not least because the Oklahoman had earlier served as the panel's top Republican, the two brought different styles. With his quick temper and experience as a Naval Academy graduate and pilot who was a prisoner of war for six years during the Vietnam War, McCain wasn't shy about voicing his views and demanding accountability from the Pentagon brass. Inhofe, by contrast, usually refrained from public criticism of military officials and was less familiar with the operational side.

Inhofe had a more conservative record than the famously independent McCain and he had a more positive relationship with Trump. He acknowledged that tension when Trump initially refused to lower the flag over the White House after McCain's death. "John McCain is partially to blame for that because he is very outspoken," Inhofe told reporters during the flag controversy. "He disagreed with the president in certain areas and wasn't too courteous about it."

The annual defense spending bill that Congress approved in 2018 became law in August, two weeks before McCain died, and it was named in his honor. The legislation, which had much of Inhofe's imprint, increased military spending by $160 billion over two years. That reflected, in part, the transition from Obama to Trump. Congressional Republicans, including Inhofe, welcomed the increase. The new chairman also took credit for added funding of military facilities in his home state, including for the new KC-46 tanker, stationed at Altus Air Force Base, and upgrades of the B-52 bomber, some of which have been stationed at Tinker Air Force Base.

Even with the gush of military spending that Congress had recently approved, Inhofe began his first full year as chairman with warnings about the threats that the nation continued to face, especially because the Pentagon budget had been downsized in earlier years. "China and Russia have increased all during the years that we have decreased," he told the Senate in January 2019. "It would take over 40 years to modernize a fleet that's already too old and too small."

Inhofe has for years regularly flown airplanes and is one of the few certified commercial pilots in Congress. He flew around the world following the historic route of Wiley Post, the first pilot to fly solo around the globe. But he has had several close calls, most recently a July 2016 forced landing in northeastern Oklahoma amid severe weather; he was 81. A decade earlier, in 2006, Inhofe encountered problems when the experimental plane he was flying spun out of control and suffered significant damage on landing in Tulsa, though he and an aide escaped injury. In 2010, his apparent flouting of air safety rules became a serious issue. Inhofe set his six-seat Cessna down on a clearly closed runway at a South Texas airport and just narrowly missed hitting a group of construction workers during an aborted landing attempt. The Federal Aviation Administration ordered him to take remedial flying lessons but did not take away his pilot's license.

An unrepentant Inhofe contended he had been cleared to land, and he responded with what he called a pilot's bill of rights that gave pilots accused of wrongdoing more authority to review the evidence against them. It was signed into law in 2012. Inhofe didn't stop there: In 2015, he introduced "Pilots Bill of Rights 2," which became law in mid-2016 as part of a FAA authorization bill. In November 2013, Inhofe's son Perry Inhofe died when the small single-engine plane he was flying crashed in Oklahoma. Discussing how the loss affected him, Jim Inhofe told NBC News: "You don't change in terms of your positions, in terms of what you believe in, but you change in terms of your understanding of individuals."

Inhofe was re-elected by almost identical margins in 2002 and 2008, both somewhat smaller than recent Republican presidential margins in Oklahoma. In 2002, he defeated former Gov. David Walters, who had years earlier pleaded guilty to a misdemeanor count of violating campaign finance laws, 57%-36%. In 2008, he beat state Sen. Andrew Rice 57%-39%. In 2014, he won a fourth full term with a more convincing 68 percent of the vote against little-known Democratic challenger Matt Silverstein. The previous year, Inhofe had quadruple bypass surgery to repair extreme blockages in his arteries. When asked by reporters about his plans when his current term ends in 2020, he has responded that he has no plans to retire.

In 2016, Inhofe's first choice for the Republican presidential nomination was Florida Sen. Marco Rubio. But, when it became clear that Trump would be the nominee, Inhofe reportedly forged ties through his Alabama Sen. Jeff Sessions — later, Trump's first attorney general — and was named an adviser to the Trump campaign on national security and regulatory issues. Environmental groups weren't laughing in early 2017. "Inhofe was like the original climate denier in chief. He was one of the first people spouting this gibberish — fact-free but dangerous gibberish," Gene Karpinski, president of the League of Conservation Voters, told The Washington Post. "Now he and his cronies have far more reach and are far more dangerous than they've ever been."

Trump's selection of Scott Pruitt to run the EPA initially was a big boost for Inhofe and his home state. Pruitt had twice been elected as Oklahoma attorney general and he made his mark fighting environmental and energy regulations of the Obama administration. He pursued that approach even more vigorously as one of Trump's top officials. But Pruitt got into trouble with some questionable ethical and financial decisions in how he ran EPA and lived in the nation's capital. He became the target of numerous investigations in Congress and even within the Trump administration for his handling of official funds, including for travel and security costs.

When Pruitt resigned in July 2018, that was hardly the end of Inhofe's influence in the enforcement of environmental policy. Andrew Wheeler, who succeeded Pruitt at EPA, had been staff director at the Environment and Public Works Committee when Inhofe was chairman. Other former Inhofe aides became part of Wheeler's inner circle. "With these Inhofe staff, you get all of the Pruitt policy and none of the Pruitt baggage," an energy lobbyist told E&E News.

Inhofe remained a strong ally of Trump on most policy issues, especially environmental and military policy. But he was less enamored of Trump's style. "I have to admit — confession's good for the soul — every time I hear that a tweet is coming out, I cringe a little," he told an audience of Defense officials in December 2018, according to The Hill. "But how else can he circumvent a media that hates him?"

If Inhofe decided to call it quits in 2020, there has been speculation that Pruitt would be eager to return to Oklahoma politics and succeed him. That has raised questions about both Inhofe's intentions and public sentiment about Pruitt in their home state. If Inhofe seeks another term, he's unlikely to encounter any problems.

James Lankford (R)

Elected 2014, term expires 2022, 1st full term, b. Mar 04, 1968; Dallas, TX; University of Texas, B.S., 1990; Southwestern Theological Baptist Seminary (TX), M.Div., 1994; Baptist; Married (Cindy Lankford); 2 children.

Elected Office: U.S. House 2011-2014.

Professional Career: Youth camp Director, Baptist Gen. Convention of OK, 1995-2009.

DC Office: 316 HSOB 20510, 202-224-5754, lankford.senate.gov

State Offices: Oklahoma City, 405-231-4941; Tulsa, 918-581-7651.

Committees: *Appropriations*: Department of Homeland Security; DOL, HHS & Education & Related Agencies; Financial Services & General Government; Legislative Branch; State, Foreign Operations & Related Programs. *Finance*: Fiscal Responsibility & Economic Growth; Health Care; Social Security, Pensions & Family Policy. *Homeland Security & Government Affairs*: Investigations; Regulatory Affairs & Federal Management (Chmn). *Indian Affairs*.

Group Ratings

	ADA	ACLU	AFL-CIO	LCV	ITI	COC	HAFA	ACU	CFG	FRC
2018	-	10%	-	7%	-	80%	80%	91%	86%	100%
2017	0%	C	0%	0%	C	86%	C	88%	100%	100%

Key Votes of the 115th Congress

1. Obama-care revision	Y	5. Gun regulations	Y	9. Kavanaugh confirmation	Y
2. Tax Cuts	Y	6. Family planning regs	Y	10. Saudi arms sales	N
3. Dodd-Frank revision	Y	7. Gorsuch confirmation	Y	11. FISA rules	Y
4. Omnibus appropriations	N	8. Immigration restrictions	Y	12. Military aid in Yemen	N

Election Results

Election	Name (Party)	Vote (%)		Cand. Spent	Ind. Exp. Support	Ind. Exp. Oppose
2016 General	James Lankford (R)............................ 980,892	(68%)	$3,079,878	$2,000		
	Mike Workman (D)............................ 355,911	(25%)				
	Robert Murphy (L)............................... 43,421	(3%)				
	Sean Braddy (I)..................................... 40,405	(3%)		$4,518		
2016 Primary	James Lankford (R)........................ Unopposed					

Prior winning percentages: 2014 special (68%), House: 2012 (59%), 2010 (63%)

A decade ago, Republican James Lankford was a little-known church camp director without political experience. Today, he is Oklahoma's junior senator, first elected in 2014 after four years in the House in which he rose rapidly to occupy a position in the GOP leadership. Since coming to the Senate, Lankford has chaired the subcommittee overseeing the federal government workforce, and he has reached across the political aisle on proposals ranging from personnel policy to governmental effectiveness and transparency. With his low-key style, he managed an unusual feat in 2019 by gaining seats on the Senate's two most powerful committees: Appropriations and Finance. If he keeps his hands clean and stays in touch with his solidly Republican state, the wonders of seniority could make him a very influential senator within a couple of decades.

Lankford grew up impoverished in Dallas. His parents divorced when he was 4, and, with his mother and older brother, he moved into the garage behind his grandparents' house. Lankford has said he became a Christian when he was 8 and that his religion has helped him endure tough times. He graduated from the University of Texas with a degree in secondary education and then earned a master's degree in divinity from the Southwestern Baptist Theological Seminary. In 1995, Lankford began working for the Baptist General Convention of Oklahoma. A year later, he was made director of the Falls Creek Christian youth summer camp, which touts itself as the largest religious camp in the world. He was in charge of organizing activities for more than 50,000 campers each summer.

In 2009, Lankford resigned to run for the Oklahoma City-based House seat of GOP Rep. Mary Fallin after she decided to run for governor. With grassroots support among conservative Christians — Southern Baptists constitute a significant portion of Oklahoma's population — Lankford led in the initial round of voting and then won 65 percent of the vote in the primary runoff against state Rep. Kevin Calvey, who had the backing of national Republicans. Lankford also benefited from tea party support. In the general election, Lankford easily defeated Democratic attorney Billy Coyle, taking 63 percent of the vote even though he was running in the least conservative of Oklahoma's five districts.

In the House, Lankford got a seat on the Oversight and Government Reform panel and won committee passage of several bills, including a measure setting standards to promote transparency in the awarding of federal grants. On the Budget Committee, he became a firm supporter of Republican Chairman Paul Ryan's push to cut spending. Politico named him and California Democrat Karen Bass as the freshmen "most likely to succeed."

When there was an opening for chairman of the Republican Policy Committee after the 2012 elections, Lankford quietly lined up support. Making the case that he provided fresh blood from the large GOP Class of 2010, he was elected without opposition to the party's No. 5 post, a sign of respect from ambitious colleagues. In his leadership post, he tried to define agenda items beyond the typical week-ahead congressional perspective, and he described his role as serving as the "eyes and ears" of then-Speaker John Boehner in the Republican Conference. As it turned out, he had little time to make an impact: He left the House sooner than Boehner.

GOP Sen. Tom Coburn, a physician first elected to the Senate in 2004, was battling prostate cancer and announced in January 2014 that he would resign at the end of that year rather than serve out the final two years of his term. Lankford jumped into the Senate race. Despite his earlier backing from tea party interests, he rankled some in the movement by joining the GOP leadership and with some of his votes. "We won't support Congressman Lankford's bid for the Senate because of his past votes to increase the debt limit, raise taxes and fund Obamacare," an official of the tea party-aligned Senate Conservatives Fund said at the time.

Several of the tea party's most visible figures — including former vice presidential nominee Sarah Palin, Texas Sen. Ted Cruz and Utah Sen. Mike Lee — coalesced around T.W. Shannon, the former speaker of the Oklahoma House, in the Republican Senate primary. An African-American who also is a member of the Chickasaw Nation, Shannon's candidacy was seen by some of his high-profile supporters as an opportunity to rebut criticisms of the Republican Party as lacking in racial diversity. "The Democrats accuse us of not embracing diversity? Oh, my goodness. He is it," Palin said at an April event also attended by Cruz and Lee.

Meanwhile, Coburn, who had emerged as one of the Senate's most outspoken conservatives, said he would remain out of the contest. But, two weeks before the primary, he released a statement calling Lankford "a man of absolute integrity." It was intended as a criticism of outside groups that had been hammering Lankford and not an endorsement but was widely perceived as the latter. Lankford ran an ad featuring Coburn's words and drew on his long-standing support from the Southern Baptist community, including former Arkansas Gov. Mike Huckabee.

Lankford defeated Shannon 57%-34%; the remaining 9 percent was spread among five other candidates. The outcome was a surprise — particularly for conservative groups that were planning a big push for Shannon in an August runoff that would have resulted if no candidate got more than 50 percent of the vote. In the solidly conservative Sooner State, the GOP nomination assured Lankford's election in November to fill the remainder of Coburn's term. He received 68 percent of the vote against Democratic state Rep. Connie Johnson, the first woman and the first African-American to be nominated for the Senate from Oklahoma. In his bid for a full term in 2016, Lankford faced no primary challenger and received a similar percentage of the vote against Democratic political operative Mike Workman.

In the Senate, Lankford got a plum assignment to the Appropriations Committee, on which he became chairman of the Legislative Branch Subcommittee in 2017. That post can be useful for exchanging favors with well-connected officials on Capitol Hill, though approving more than $4 billion in spending for Congress is not a priority for which most fiscal conservatives — like Lankford — seek public acclaim. He used a seat on the Intelligence Committee to gain increased visibility in early 2017, making the rounds of cable news shows while the panel investigated allegations of Russian interference in the 2016 president election.

Lankford has taken a particular interest in freedom of religion. When the Senate granted President Barack Obama expedited authority to negotiate the proposed Trans-Pacific Partnership in 2015, Lankford won inclusion of an amendment into the measure that U.S. trading partners should encourage religious freedom. He noted that a U.S. commission monitoring international religious freedom had urged the State Department to designate Vietnam as a country of particular concern. Nearly two years later, after President Donald Trump had taken office, Lankford sponsored a resolution with Florida Republican Marco Rubio and Delaware Democrat Chris Coons "reaffirming the commitment of the United States to promoting religious freedom" and pointing to a recent Pew Center finding that nearly 80 percent of the world's population lives in countries where freedom of religion is highly restricted.

Some of Lankford's efforts in the name of religious freedom have been controversial. In 2015, he introduced resolutions of disapproval aimed at overturning two measures passed by the District of Columbia City Council designed to protect the right to an abortion and the rights of gay student groups. Lankford voiced concern that those policies could restrict the rights of others, including religious groups. In 2017, he filed a bill to overturn a 1954 provision in the tax code — included at the behest of influential Sen. Lyndon B. Johnson — that prohibited ministers and leaders of nonprofits from advocating for or against political candidates if they wanted to keep their organizations' tax-exempt statuses. "The federal government and the IRS should never have the ability to inhibit free speech," Lankford said. Three months after Lankford introduced his legislation, Trump issued an executive order "promoting free speech and religious liberty" that also took aim at the Johnson amendment. But Lankford and other social conservatives failed to make legislative progress, and the law remained intact after Congress completed its sweeping revision of the tax code in 2017. He reintroduced his proposal in 2019, emphasizing First Amendment rights.

Lankford has worked with other libertarian-minded Republicans to reduce mandatory questionnaires from the Census Bureau that they viewed as overly intrusive of personal privacy. As chairman of the Homeland Security and Governmental Affairs Subcommittee on Regulatory Affairs and Federal Management, Lankford has worked across the aisle on several bills. Citing an increase in embezzlement of government benefits by dishonest representatives of retirees, he got legislation through the Senate in 2015 to give U.S. attorneys the power to prosecute retiree representatives who misuse funds. Lankford collaborated with Democratic colleagues Cory Booker of New Jersey and Mark Warner of Virginia on one of the last measures that Obama signed before leaving office. The law made permanent what is known as the Presidential Innovation Fellows program, which since 2012 has paired outside technology experts and entrepreneurs with high-ranking civil servants to solve challenges facing the public sector. He was a leader among Republicans seeking to reduce the time available for discussion in the Senate after a majority has voted to close debate on a presidential nomination — from 30 hours to two hours. His proposal would permit the Senate to "function appropriately again," he said.

Inside the Senate, Lankford pulled off a coup in January 2019 when he and Republican Steve Daines of Montana gained seats on the Finance Committee while remaining as members of Appropriations; they reportedly were the first senators to have such dual assignments in several decades. The caveat for Lankford was that he lost, at least temporarily, his seniority and subcommittee chairmanship at Appropriations.

Because Lankford largely hews to the party line in public pronouncements, it created a bit of a stir when, shortly before Trump took office, a transcript of a private conference call in which he expressed nervousness about the incoming president leaked. Alluding to Trump's criticism of trade agreements throughout the campaign, Lankford told a group of Oklahoma business executives, Trump "has reassured me that he is a trade person and does want deals — he just wants a good deal, but I have never heard what a good deal is."

Lankford continued to distance himself from Trump's leadership. When the president spoke positively about his meeting with Russian President Vladimir Putin in Helsinki in July 2018, Lankford tweeted, "I trust the assessments of Dan Coats, Gina Haspel & their [intelligence] teams more than I trust a former KGB agent." Two months earlier, he said in an interview on MSNBC, "I don't consider the president a role model for my kids. ... I don't speak that way. I don't tweet that way. I don't interact with people that way. I don't treat my staff the way that he treats his staff."

Kevin Hern (R)

Elected 2018, 1st full term, b. Dec 04, 1961; Belton, MO; University of Arkansas-Little Rock, B.S., 1986; University of Arkansas-Little Rock, M.B.A., 1999; Evangelical; Married (Tammy Hern); 3 children.

DC Office: 1019 LHOB 20515, 202-225-2211, Fax: 202-225-9187, hern.house.gov

State Offices: Tulsa, 918-935-3222.

Committees: *Budget. Natural Resources*: Energy & Mineral Resources; Indigenous Peoples of the United States. *Small Business*: Economic Growth, Tax & Capital Access (RMM); Innovation & Workforce Development.

Election Results

Election	Name (Party)	Vote (%)		Cand. Spent	Ind. Exp. Support	Ind. Exp. Oppose
2018 General	Kevin R. Hern (R)..............................	150,129	(59%)	$2,729,529		$345,508
	Tim Gilpin (D)............................	103,042	(41%)	$382,071		
2018 Primary	Kevin R. Hern (R)............................	40,401	(55%)			
Runoff	Tim Harris (R)...................................	33,155	(45%)			
2018 Primary	Tim Harris (R)...................................	28,431	(28%)			
	Kevin R. Hern (R)..............................	23,466	(23%)			
	Andy Coleman (R)...........................	22,608	(22%)			
	Nathan Dahm (R)............................	20,868	(20%)			
	Danny Stocksill (R)...............................	8,100	(8%)			

Freshman Republican Kevin Hern of Oklahoma won his first bid for elected office. A successful businessman, Hern earlier had participated in local government and political activities. Hern positioned himself as a relative centrist in the competitive primary, and some Republicans criticized him as not sufficiently conservative. He replaced Rep. Jim Bridenstine, who resigned in April 2018 to become administrator of the National Aeronautics and Space Administration.

Hern described his life as a child living in poverty and on government assistance, including food stamps. He got his bachelor's degree from Arkansas Tech University, where he majored in engineering, and an MBA from the University of Arkansas. Early in his professional career, he worked for several companies — including the Rockwell aerospace firm, where he wrote computer programs. His turning point in business came in 1999, when he bought two McDonald's franchises in Muskogee Oklahoma. At the time, he later said, he came home "to a house with no furniture and a sleeping bag as a bed."

Eventually, Hern owned 10 McDonald's restaurants and he took a national leadership position with the company, chairing the systems economic team for more than 3,000 franchisees. With his profits, he expanded into other businesses. He took on additional projects, including chairman for four years of the finance committee of the Oklahoma Turnpike Authority and finance committee chairman of the Oklahoma Republican Party.

The crucial contest in the campaign to succeed Bridenstine was the wide-open GOP primary, which featured five candidates. Hern was endorsed by the business-friendly Republican Main Street Partnership. His chief opponents were Tim Harris, who served 16 years as district attorney for Tulsa County and taught constitutional law, and Andy Coleman, a retired military intelligence officer who was backed by the Club for Growth and other national conservative groups. Harris led the first round of voting with 27 percent of the vote, to 23 percent for Hern and 22 percent for Coleman. Hern qualified for the runoff, with his 858-vote lead over Coleman.

In the two-month runoff campaign, Harris emphasized law-enforcement issues and his experience in government. Hern embraced President Donald Trump, attacked Harris as a "career politician" and called for term limits. Harris voiced reservations about Trump's policies on international trade and said the President "has to temper some of his verbiage," the Tulsa World reported. The Club for Growth ran ads that attacked Hern's political contributions to Democratic candidates in past campaigns.

Hern spent more than $2 million in the primary, including $1.5 million in personal and bank loans to his campaign; Harris spent about $480,000. Hern won the runoff, 55%-45%. In Tulsa County, which cast nearly 80 percent of the vote and where Harris was well-known, Hern took 53 percent. Hern increased his vote total by about 17,000 over the primary; Harris's total grew by less than 5,000 votes.

Democratic nominee Tim Gilpin, a Tulsa attorney and former state education official, described himself as the "serious candidate." He criticized Trump and Republican handling of issues such as tax cuts and changes to the Affordable Care Act. With scant national-party assistance, Gilpin's campaign struggled financially.

In this district, which last elected a Democrat to Congress in 1984 (when the House delegation for Oklahoma had five Democrats and one Republican), Hern was on safe ground in seeking to emulate Trump as "somebody who brings a different perspective"—in his campaign, and as he learned the ropes in Congress.

OK-1: Tulsa Area   Cook Partisan Voting Index: R+17

Population		Race and Ethnicity		Income	
Total	789,968	White	65%	Median Income	$52,927
Land area (sq. miles)	1,632	Black	8.5%	District Income Rank	256
Pop/ sq mi	484.1	Latino	10.9%	Poverty Rate	14.8%
Born in State	58.4%	Asian	2.7%	With health insurance	85.7%
		Two or more races	7.4%	Cash public assistance	2.5%
Age Groups		Other	5.6%	Food stamp/SNAP	12.3%
Under 18	25.3%				
18-34	23.2%	**Education**		**Work**	
35-64	37.6%	H.S grad or less	38%	White Collar	13.9%
Over 64	13.9%	Some college	32.4%	Sales and Service	41.6%
		College Degree, 4 yr	20.3%	Blue Collar	21.6%
Military		Post grad	9.4%	Government	10.2%
Veteran/ Active Duty	8.5%				

2012 Pres. Vote	Romney	188,961	(66%)	Obama	98,321	(34%)	
2016 Pres. Vote	Trump	191,343	(61%)	Clinton	101,757	(33%) Johnson	18,406 (6%)

Tulsa: The gushers of the 1905 Glenn Pool discovery made Tulsa one of America's oil boomtowns, settled not just by people from the immediate hinterland but also by Midwesterners and New Englanders of Yankee stock. In the 1920s, as its art deco skyscrapers rose on the heights above the Arkansas River, it was still a raw town, but one bent on becoming more cultured. It was optimistic and ready to seek economic change, yet culturally and politically conservative, with a Yankee elite and an American Indian heritage recalled today in one of the nation's best collections of Western art at the Gilcrease Museum — left by oil millionaire Thomas Gilcrease, who was one-eighth Creek Indian. Tulsa, also the home of Oral Roberts University, has remained cosmopolitan and conservative. In 2019, an exhibition opened at eight sites to commemorate Black Wall Street, the 1921 massacre in which a white mob burned black neighborhoods and killed more than 300 people in Tulsa.

In recent decades, Tulsa has boomed and occasionally busted. The "Vision 2025" tax of six-tenths of a cent has helped pay for everything from Arkansas River protection work to new university buildings to upgrades at city parks and golf courses. In 2018, Gathering Place — a 66-acre, $465 million park — opened in the downtown area. The American Airlines maintenance center in Tulsa is the largest such facility in the world, with 5,200 employees at the maintenance base; in 2018, the airline added engine service to the workload. That presence spurred other aerospace-related development in Tulsa, which has become the base of the Oklahoma Aerospace Alliance. More than 500 aerospace firms in the state have an annual output of about $14 billion, including more than 20,000 workers in Tulsa. The next two largest companies are aerospace-components manufacturer NORDAM, which filed for bankruptcy in 2018 and was acquired by Gulfstream, and Spirit AeroSystems, a Boeing supplier that assembles fuselages.

The 1st Congressional District of Oklahoma includes Tulsa, Wagoner and Washington counties, and small slices of Rogers and Creek counties —with about 80 percent in Tulsa. The political tradition here is heavily Republican, strengthened in recent decades by opposition to national Democrats' cultural liberalism. Donald Trump got 61 percent of the vote here in 2016, but the 1st ranked only fourth among the five Oklahoma districts in its vote for Trump. It's not likely that Republican presidential candidates will need to worry about Oklahoma any time soon.

Markwayne Mullin (R)

Elected 2012, 4th term, b. Jul 26, 1977; Tulsa; Missouri Valley College, Att., 1996; Oklahoma State University Institute of Technology, Assc. Deg., 2010; Pentecostal; Married (Christie Mullin); 5 children (twins).

Professional Career: Owner, Mullin Plumbing, 1996-present.

DC Office: 2421 RHOB 20515, 202-225-2701, Fax: 202-225-3038, mullin.house.gov

State Offices: Claremore, 918-283-6262; McAlester, 918-423-5951; Muskogee, 918-687-2533.

Committees: *Energy & Commerce*: Environment & Climate Change; Health; Oversight & Investigations.

Group Ratings

	ADA	ACLU	AFL-CIO	LCV	ITI	COC	HAFA	ACU	CFG	FRC
2018	-	7%	-	3%	-	75%	66%	80%	70%	100%
2017	0%	C	11%	0%	C	93%	C	85%	87%	100%

Almanac Ratings 2017-18

	Economy	Social	Foreign	Composite
Liberal	0%	7%	0%	2%
Conservative	100%	94%	100%	98%

Key Votes of the 115th Congress

1. Obama-care revision	Y	5. Family planning regs	Y	9. Guantanamo prisoners	N
2. Tax Cuts	Y	6. Body cameras/immigration	N	10. Ground missiles, limit	N
3. Omnibus appropriations	N	7. Abortion ban	Y	11. Defense Dept. spending	Y
4. Dodd-Frank revision	Y	8. Concealed carry	Y	12. FISA rules	Y

Election Results

Election	Name (Party)	Vote (%)		Cand. Spent	Ind. Exp. Support	Ind. Exp. Oppose
2018 General	Markwayne Mullin (R)	140,451	(65%)	$1,665,609	$147,465	
	Jason Nichols (D)	65,021	(30%)	$121,977		
	John Foreman (I)	6,390	(3%)			
2018 Primary	Markwayne Mullin (R)	32,654	(54%)			
	Jarrin Jackson (R)	15,204	(25%)			
	Brian Jackson (R)	6,907	(12%)			
	John McCarthy (R)	5,549	(9%)			

Prior winning percentages: 2016 (71%), 2014 (70%), 2012 (57%)

Republican plumber Markwayne Mullin, elected in 2012, has been an outspoken conservative, but a more reliable vote for the GOP leadership than some other junior Republicans. As a member of the Energy and Commerce Committee, he has taken an interest in rural issues. A fitness buff, he has led early morning workout sessions for a devoted bipartisan following of House members.

Mullin was born in Tulsa and grew up in Westville, a small town on the Arkansas line, as the youngest of seven children. His father ran a small plumbing business, which Mullin took over at age 19 after briefly attending Missouri Valley College. He expanded the company from six employees to more than 100. He hosted a local talk show advising callers on home repair. Mullin, a Cherokee, operates the Oklahoma Fight Club in Broken Arrow, a training center for jujitsu and mixed martial arts. He earned an associate's degree in business from the Oklahoma State University Institute of Technology in Okmulgee.

Mullin was one of six Republican candidates for the open seat of retiring Democratic Rep. Dan Boren, who was one of the House's last conservative Southern Democrats. Arguing that it was "time to fire Barack Obama," he became the frontrunner. His fundraising outpaced that of his GOP rivals, although a good portion was self-financed. In the primary, he coasted to a first-place finish with 42 percent of the vote. In the runoff, state Rep. George Faught accused Mullin of carpetbagging when property records showed that he had claimed homestead tax exemptions in Wagoner County, outside the district. Mullin labeled Faught a career politician and won the runoff handily, 57%-43%.

In September, news broke that Mullin Plumbing had received about $370,000 in federal economic stimulus money for housing projects with the Cherokee and Muscogee nations. Mullin had campaigned heavily against Obama's stimulus program, and Democratic nominee Rob Wallace accused him of acting like an "out-of-touch, typical Washington politician." Mullin claimed not to know that the projects got stimulus money, but documents from the Cherokee Nation contradicted that assertion. Other business practices of Mullin came under fire. Those attacks mostly fell flat. Mullin outspent Wallace, $1.7 million to $1.2 million, and won, 57%-38%.

On Energy and Commerce, Mullin has provided an "Oklahoma business owner perspective" on its broad agenda of regulatory and health care issues. He took on an unusual adversary, when he filed a bill in 2016 to require the rapidly growing Ultimate Fighting Championship to disclose more information about its finances, including how it handles its martial-arts competitors. He also sponsored a bill to extend safety protections to those fighters. In 2018, Mullin enacted a bill to extend health coverage in sparsely served rural areas. Other bills that he has enacted include procedures for low-volume auto manufacturers to meet federal regulations and several bills related to Indian tribes. In July 2017, the House passed his bill to transfer authority over pipelines and power transmission lines that cross international borders from the State Department to the Federal Energy Regulatory Commission; the Senate did not act on the measure.

Mullin has taken a personal approach to his work. He used his fitness expertise to bond with members from both parties, including interval training exercises at the House gym and the formation with Democratic Rep. Donald Payne of New Jersey of the Men's Health Caucus.

In 2016, Mullin had a competitive primary against Jarrin Jackson, a West Point graduate who served two tours of duty in Afghanistan. Jackson criticized Mullin for having "only voted to grow government" and for perhaps backing away from his earlier campaign pledge to serve only three terms in the House. Three months before the primary, Mullin had issued a brief statement to The Oklahoman that he and his wife "will continue to seek the Lord's guidance and do what is best for our family and the 2nd District of Oklahoma" on his term-limits pledge. Citing Mullin's uncertainty, former Oklahoma Sen. Tom Coburn endorsed Jackson. Current Sens. Jim Inhofe and James Lankford endorsed Mullin. He won the primary, 63%-37%.

In 2018, Mullin said that he had found that his term-limits pledge was a "mistake" and "I'm going to learn from" it. With the support of President Donald Trump, Mullin added, he can "make a difference" in Washington. Jackson ran again in the primary; not surprisingly, he attacked Mullin for abandoning his pledge. Mullin spent $1.7 million — nearly 10 times as much as Jackson — and won·54%-25% over Jackson; two other candidates split the remaining vote. In the general election, Democrat Jason Nichols, the mayor of Tahlequah, ran an active campaign and spent $126,000; he did not raise the term-limits issue. Mullin won easily. 65%-30%.

In August 2018, the House Ethics Committee ruled that Mullin improperly took $40,000 from his plumbing business, which he had turned over to his wife after his initial election, and required that he return the funds to the business. The committee said that an accounting error led Mullin to "inadvertently fail" to comply with its earlier guidance. An unhappy Mullin responded that the ruling "proves that you can no longer be a citizen legislator" in Congress.

OK-2: East Oklahoma   Cook Partisan Voting Index: R+24

Population			Race and Ethnicity			Income		
Total	748,004		White	64.4%		Median Income	$41,089	
Land area (sq. miles)	20,995		Black	3.4%		District Income Rank	406	
Pop/ sq mi	35.6		Latino	5%		Poverty Rate	19.8%	
Born in State	61.5%		Asian	0.6%		With health insurance	81.4%	
			Two or more races	9.9%		Cash public assistance	3.8%	
Age Groups			Other	16.6%		Food stamp/SNAP	17.4%	
Under 18	23.6%							
18-34	21%		**Education**			**Work**		
35-64	37.5%		H.S grad or less	52.7%		White Collar	17.9%	
Over 64	17.9%		Some college	30.6%		Sales and Service	41.3%	
			College Degree, 4 yr	11.4%		Blue Collar	29.8%	
Military			Post grad	5.4%		Government	20%	
Veteran/ Active Duty	10%							

2012 Pres. Vote	Romney	170,983	(68%)	Obama	81,179	(32%)			
2016 Pres. Vote	Trump	198,155	(73%)	Clinton	62,022	(23%)	Johnson	11,667	(4%)

Tulsa Suburbs, Muskogee: The land that is now northeast Oklahoma used to be Indian territory, the place where in the 1830s the Five Civilized Tribes were driven from Georgia and Alabama over the Trail of Tears. A sizable minority here report their race as American Indian. The Native American identity is highest in the hilly counties west of the Ozarks of Arkansas, where county names — Cherokee, Osage, Sequoyah — recall the Civilized Tribes. The street signs in scenic Tahlequah, the Cherokee capital since 1839, are written in both English and Cherokee. The Creek Nation chose its tribal site in Okmulgee in the belief that tornadoes would not strike the area; history has proven the choice correct so far — tornadoes have done minimal damage here. Bicyclists from the Cherokee Nation have an annual three-week trip for 950 miles across seven states to retrace the Trail of Tears. South of Indian country is Oklahoma's Little Dixie, settled between 1889 and 1907 by white Southerners, most of them poor.

This pleasant land of gentle hills and man-made lakes recently has grown at a healthy pace with population spread from Tulsa. Interstate highways and turnpikes connect people to jobs in more-vibrant metropolitan areas, while the lakes have spurred resort and retirement communities. The largest city here is Muskogee, an old railroad community with a manufacturing economy that had slowed in recent years; despite efforts at local revival, the population of both Muskogee city and county dipped 3 percent from 2010 to 2017. The largest local employer is a Georgia-Pacific paper mill, with 800 workers. Natural-gas production has been increasing in this area, which is part of the Anadarko Basin. In 2017, a local field was the third most active in the nation, behind two in Texas. Of the several dozen rigs, many have been operating with modern horizontal wells.

The 2nd Congressional District includes eastern Oklahoma, except for the Tulsa area. It borders on four states and takes in Muskogee; Claremore, Will Rogers' hometown; and McAlester, hometown of former House Speaker Carl Albert. The median income here is the lowest of the five districts in Oklahoma and in the bottom 10 percent nationwide. McAlester is the site of a massive Army ammunition plant that manufactures non-nuclear bombs and is the largest local employer. In 2017, the plant began work to upgrade and extend the life of 1,400 Stinger missiles, which can be shoulder-launched or mounted on a vehicle or helicopter. The area was ancestrally Democratic. Since the retirement in 1976 of Albert, a New Deal Democrat who presided over the House during the Watergate scandal, the area has become as solidly Republican as most of Oklahoma. The 2016 election confirmed that the vestiges of Yellow Dog Democrats had mostly disappeared from Little Dixie: Donald Trump won the presidential vote, 73%-23%.

Frank Lucas (R)

Elected 1994, 13th term, b. Jan 06, 1960; Cheyenne; Oklahoma State University, B.S., 1982; Baptist; Married (Lynda Bradshaw Lucas); 3 children; 2 grandchildren.

Elected Office: OK House, 1988-1994.

Professional Career: Farmer & rancher.

DC Office: 2405 RHOB 20515, 202-225-5565, Fax: 202-225-8696, lucas.house.gov

State Offices: Yukon, 405-373-1958.

Committees: *Financial Services*: Consumer Protection & Financial Institutions; Nat'l Security, International Development & Monetary Policy; Subcommittee on Diversity & Inclusion. *Science, Space & Technology (RMM)*.

Group Ratings

	ADA	ACLU	AFL-CIO	LCV	ITI	COC	HAFA	ACU	CFG	FRC
2018	-	4%	-	6%	-	92%	44%	71%	52%	100%
2017	0%	C	18%	6%	C	93%	C	74%	55%	100%

Almanac Ratings 2017-18

	Economy	Social	Foreign	Composite
Liberal	5%	4%	0%	3%
Conservative	95%	97%	100%	97%

Key Votes of the 115th Congress

1. Obama-care revision	Y	5. Family planning regs	Y	9. Guantanamo prisoners	N
2. Tax Cuts	Y	6. Body cameras/immigration	N	10. Ground missiles, limit	N
3. Omnibus appropriations	Y	7. Abortion ban	Y	11. Defense Dept. spending	Y
4. Dodd-Frank revision	Y	8. Concealed carry	Y	12. FISA rules	Y

Election Results

Election	Name (Party)	Vote (%)		Cand. Spent	Ind. Exp. Support	Ind. Exp. Oppose
2018 General	Frank Lucas (R)................................. 172,913	(74%)		$621,986		
	Frankie Robbins (D)............................ 61,152	(26%)				
2018 Primary	Frank Lucas (R)..	(100%)				

Prior winning percentages: 2016 (78%), 2014 (79%), 2012 (75%), 2010 (78%), 2008 (70%), 2006 (68%), 2004 (82%), 2002 (76%), 2000 (59%), 1998 (65%), 1996 (64%), 1994 (70%)

Republican Frank Lucas, who won a 1994 special election, is a soft-spoken, unflashy farmer and rancher who has become a senior and savvy lawmaker. As chairman of the Agriculture Committee until 2015, he eventually found a way to bridge deal-oriented lawmakers from farm states and budget-conscious conservatives. After being term-limited as chairman, he moved to new niches at other committees. In 2019, in the minority, he became the senior Republican on the Science, Space and Technology Committee, where he made early bipartisan moves..

Lucas' family roots in western Oklahoma extend more than 100 years; he owns a 480-acre farm and cattle ranch in Roger Mills County. He studied agricultural economics at Oklahoma State University, where he was active in the College Republicans and student government. He was elected to the Oklahoma House at age 28 after losing two races. He shared an office there with Jim Reese, who became the state's secretary and commissioner of agriculture. "He's not a showboat," Reese told The New York Times in 2012. "He just goes about doing his work and tries to work with everybody and is not about getting credit for himself."

He ran for Congress when veteran conservative Democratic Rep. Glenn English resigned to head the National Rural Electric Cooperative Association. In the primary, he trailed state Sen. Brooks Douglass, who campaigned from his Oklahoma City base, 36%-34%. In the runoff, Lucas ridiculed "some Johnny-come-lately dressed up like a drugstore cowboy" and carried the rural areas to win 56%-44%. In the general, he faced Dan Webber, the 27-year-old press secretary for Democratic Sen. David Boren. Lucas ran an ad depicting the Capitol and saying, "This is where Dan Webber has worked his entire adult life." The ad displayed a picture of Oklahoma farmland and said, "This is where Frank Lucas has worked his entire adult life." Lucas won 54%-46%. At age 34, he settled in for a lengthy tenure.

Lucas' voting record is mostly conservative. As shown by his Almanac vote ratings, he has occasionally broken from conservative orthodoxy on economic matters. He has voted against GOP amendments to abolish or cut funding for federal programs such as rural airport subsidies and the Economic Development Administration.

For many years, his chief base was the Agriculture Committee. On the 2002 farm bill, Lucas helped to unravel the 1996 Freedom to Farm Act and its rollback of government subsidies, although he had once embraced the law and its conservative philosophical underpinnings. Lucas helped write provisions to control erosion, aid farmers hit by drought, and protect air and water quality. He successfully fought a plan to reduce the number of Farm Service Agency field offices. In the minority during work on the 2008 farm bill, Lucas strongly opposed an overhaul of farm programs as "a threat to the nutrition of the whole, entire world," and he mostly succeeded in preserving subsidies for his district, which ranked 14th in subsidies between 1995 and 2009. With an eye on his district, Lucas helped to write the final provisions in the 2005 energy bill governing rural grants and biodiesel tax credits. He has been a proponent of government support for alternative fuels, particularly switchgrass.

As chairman in 2011, he found himself leading a committee full of freshmen and new members who did not share his bipartisan leanings. He worked closely with Agriculture's ranking Democrat Collin Peterson of Minnesota to report a five-year farm bill from the committee in 2012. But the measure never came to a vote that year in the full House. Some conservatives wanted deeper cuts to the food stamp program, which Democrats fiercely resisted. In a closed-door GOP meeting, House Speaker John Boehner reportedly criticized the committee bill's dairy provisions — which contained a new market stabilization plan that major milk processors strongly opposed — as "communism." The delays frustrated Lucas, who labored for months to strike a deal acceptable to House GOP leaders, whom he referred to as "the management."

In 2013, the legislation he managed to get to the floor looked to be a conservatives' dream: It cut spending $40 billion over 10 years, including $20 billion from the food stamp program, and it had bipartisan support from Peterson and many other farm-state Democrats. Discontented conservatives passed an amendment to give states the option of imposing work requirements on food stamp recipients, a move that shattered the delicate political coalition behind the bill. Despite a desperate last-minute plea by Lucas on the House floor, the farm bill failed on final passage, 195-234. Sixty-two Republicans voted against it while only 24 Democrats voted for it. At one point, he lamented, "it shouldn't be this hard to pass a farm bill."

When he finally passed the bill in 2014, which Lucas called his "single biggest accomplishment" as chairman, he said that its "fundamental guise" was that it became an insurance measure in place of the direct payment program for farm commodities. The House passed the bill, 251-166, with bipartisan support in 2014. After term limits forced him to step down as Agriculture chairman in 2015, he remained active on the committee. When a final deal was reached in 2018, he praised it for "protecting the safety net for producers" and "maintaining critical conservation programs."

Lucas found himself, like other term-limited House GOP chairmen, looking for opportunities to remain relevant. When Jeb Hensarling of Texas, the hard-edged chairman at Financial Services, refused to give him a subcommittee chairmanship or other influence, Lucas pursued another Texas chairman — Lamar Smith at Science, Space and Technology — and became vice chairman of that committee. Lucas shaped a bipartisan bill to improve weather forecasting and research capabilities (useful tools for farmers), which was enacted in 2017. With his Democratic ally Peterson, Lucas in 2015 passed a bill to create a science advisory board to promote fairness and independence at the Environmental Protection Agency.

Moving into his leadership role on the Science Committee in 2019, he said that he wanted more data collected from satellites to chart short-term and long-term weather. That information would be useful to energy entrepreneurs as well as farmers. Tulsa is the home of many aerospace contractors. With what he called "a solid relationship" with Democratic Rep. Eddie Bernice Johnson of Texas, who chaired the committee, Lucas filed two bills on the opening day of the new Congress: to combat sexual harassment in science and engineering, and to improve water conservation and resources for clean water.

Lucas has been reelected by wide margins — at least 67 percent since 2000. Despite the unhappiness of national conservative groups, he has not faced serious competition in GOP primaries. The Club for Growth threatened, but failed, to recruit a primary opponent in 2014 after he scored in the bottom third among Republicans in the anti-tax group's legislative ratings. He said that the criticism didn't bother him. "Any time I have to choose between the influences of D.C. political groups and my fellow Oklahomans, I will always side with my fellow Oklahomans," he told the Tulsa World.

OK-3: Western and Central Oklahoma   Cook Partisan Voting Index: R+27

Population		Race and Ethnicity		Income	
Total	773,867	White	74.3%	Median Income	$50,439
Land area (sq. miles)	34,117	Black	3.6%	District Income Rank	300
Pop/ sq mi	22.7	Latino	9.7%	Poverty Rate	15.2%
Born in State	64.4%	Asian	1.4%	With health insurance	86.8%
		Two or more races	5%	Cash public assistance	2.5%
Age Groups		Other	6.1%	Food stamp/SNAP	11.3%
Under 18	24.4%				
18-34	23.9%	**Education**		**Work**	
35-64	36.6%	H.S grad or less	46.9%	White Collar	15.1%
Over 64	15.1%	Some college	30.6%	Sales and Service	39.4%
		College Degree, 4 yr	15.3%	Blue Collar	28.5%
Military		Post grad	7.2%	Government	18.3%
Veteran/ Active Duty	9.4%				

2012 Pres. Vote	Romney	199,390	(74%)	Obama	70,346	(26%)			
2016 Pres. Vote	Trump	216,078	(74%)	Clinton	61,179	(21%)	Johnson	16,160	(6%)

Suburbs of Oklahoma City and Tulsa: Settled at the turn of the 20th century, western Oklahoma is a fertile land forever at the mercy of the elements. The western plains are scorching hot under the summer sun and blown frozen by bitter winter winds. Visitors to the Tallgrass Prairie Preserve, maintained by the Nature Conservancy near Pawhuska, can experience what settlers found when they arrived here: a swaying ocean of 10-foot-high grasses filled with insects emitting a dull, incessant roar. Many rural counties here are not much more populated than they were 100 years ago. Today, local entrepreneurs see the possibility of economic revival in another abundant natural resource: the wind. Kansas company TradeWind has purchased multiple wind farm properties in western Oklahoma. As of 2018, 11 of those projects had begun operations. Two of those wind farms have long-term contracts with large corporations: Anheuser-Busch, T-Mobile and Google. Developers proposed a transmission line that could transform the prairie into a national wind energy hub. After the original developer shut down, a new company — Chicago-based Invenergy — took control of the Osage County transmission project in November 2018 and entered an agreement with an electric cooperative to start producing power in late 2020.

Solar power has increased in the Panhandle, with a subsidiary of Arkansas Electric Cooperatives owning a 1-megawatt solar project in Hooker. The region is home to the world's largest plot of switchgrass, and there are hopes that it too can become a profitable source of alternative energy. In 2010, the state government set a goal of making Oklahoma 15 percent dependent on renewable energy by 2015. In 2018, nearly one-third of the state's electricity came from renewables — a higher share than all but two states.

The 3rd Congressional District includes Oklahoma's western plains and nearly half of the state's land. It includes the university town of Stillwater, and Osage County, site of the state's lone Indian reservation. A few of the southern counties, settled by farmers crossing the Red River from Texas, are ancestrally Democratic. Farmers coming south from Kansas settled most of these plains, and they were heavily Republican. In February 2019, Altus Air Force Base became the home of a squadron of KC-46 refueling tankers. To the west in the Panhandle is Beaver County, which claims to be the cow-chip-throwing capital of the world. Hispanic population has grown to 24 percent, with many moving here to work on hog farms and in meatpacking plants. One of the largest operations is Seaboard Corp.'s plant in Guymon, which has more than 3,000 employees. Texas County, a wheat-growing area in the Panhandle, is 46 percent Hispanic, the highest percentage in the state. This has been the most Republican district in the state, and among the top 10 for the GOP nationwide. Donald Trump got 74 percent of the vote in 2016.

Tom Cole (R)

Elected 2002, 9th term, b. Apr 28, 1949; Shreveport, LA; Grinnell College (IA), B.A., 1971; Institute for Historical Research - London (England), B.A., 1972; Yale University (CT), M.A., 1974; University of London - Queens College (England), 1978; University of Oklahoma (OK), Ph.D., 1984; Methodist; Married (Ellen Elizabeth Decker Cole); 1 child.

Elected Office: OK Senate, 1988-1991.

Professional Career: Staff, U.S. Rep. Mickey Edwards, 1982-1984; OK GOP Chairman, 1985-1989; Executive Director, NRCC, 1991-1995; OK Secretary of st., 1995-1999; Chief of Staff, RNC, 1999-2000; Political consultant, 2000-2002.

DC Office: 2207 RHOB 20515, 202-225-6165, Fax: 202-225-3512, cole.house.gov
State Offices: Ada, 580-436-5375; Lawton, 580-357-2131; Norman, 405-329-6500.

Committees: *Appropriations*: Defense; Labor, Health & Human Services, Education & Related Agencies (RMM). *Rules (RMM)*.

Group Ratings

	ADA	ACLU	AFL-CIO	LCV	ITI	COC	HAFA	ACU	CFG	FRC
2018	-	4%	-	9%	-	92%	47%	21%	43%	100%
2017	5%	C	18%	9%	C	93%	C	74%	56%	100%

Almanac Ratings 2017-18

	Economy	Social	Foreign	Composite
Liberal	4%	2%	0%	2%
Conservative	96%	98%	100%	98%

Key Votes of the 115th Congress

1. Obama-care revision	Y	5. Family planning regs	Y	9. Guantanamo prisoners	N
2. Tax Cuts	Y	6. Body cameras/immigration	N	10. Ground missiles, limit	N
3. Omnibus appropriations	Y	7. Abortion ban	Y	11. Defense Dept. spending	Y
4. Dodd-Frank revision	Y	8. Concealed carry	Y	12. FISA rules	Y

Election Results

Election	Name (Party)	Vote (%)		Cand. Spent	Ind. Exp. Support	Ind. Exp. Oppose
2018 General	Tom Cole (R)	149,227	(63%)	$1,824,880		
	Mary Brannon (D)	78,088	(33%)	$5,267		
	Ruby Peters (I)	9,323	(4%)			
2018 Primary	Tom Cole (R)	55,929	(65%)			
	James Taylor (R)	30,461	(35%)			

Prior winning percentages: 2016 (70%), 2014 (71%), 2012 (68%), 2010 (unopposed), 2008 (66%), 2006 (65%), 2004 (78%), 2002 (54%)

Tom Cole, first elected in 2002, is a politically savvy and experienced Republican who has become a key ally of House GOP leaders. As chairman of the Appropriations subcommittee that handles discretionary spending for health and education programs, he has been an active policy leader for the GOP. Following the 2018 election, he failed in his bid to become the senior Republican on Appropriations, but got an impressive consolation prize: the top GOP slot on the traffic-cop Rules Committee, while retaining his spending post. Cole has remained a frequent source for reporters seeking to understand the GOP's inner workings.

Cole grew up in Moore, south of Oklahoma City. He is a fifth-generation Oklahoman, and his mother was a state representative and senator. He is a member of the Chickasaw Nation tribe; more than half of the nation's Chickasaw Indians live in his district. Until 2019, Oklahoma GOP colleague Markwayne Mullin and Cole were the only Native Americans in Congress; they were joined by first-term Democrats from Kansas and New Mexico. Cole's father served in the Air Force and later worked at Tinker Air Force Base. Cole graduated from Grinnell College, got a master's degree at Yale University, and a Ph.D. in British history at the University of Oklahoma, studying for a year at the University of London. From 1985 to 1989, he was the Oklahoma Republican Party chairman. In 1988, he was elected to the state Senate.

He moved to Washington in 1991 to become executive director of the National Republican Congressional Committee, and over the next decade held jobs as the appointed Oklahoma secretary of state, president of a polling and political consulting firm in Oklahoma City, and chief of staff for the Republican National Committee during the 2000 election. When Republican Rep. J.C. Watts announced that he would not seek reelection, Cole was the early frontrunner. Despite his party connections and an endorsement from Watts, he faced formidable opposition from attorney Marc Nuttle. The two shared positions on most issues and extensive party connections. Nuttle had been Cole's predecessor at the NRCC and worked on Pat Robertson's 1988 presidential campaign. In the showdown between the strategists, Cole won 60%-33%.

In the general election, he had tough competition from former state Senate Majority Leader Darryl Roberts, who appealed to the "yellow dog" Democratic tradition that had remained strong in the Red River counties. Cole countered by linking Roberts to past Democratic presidential nominees he had supported, and described him as "pro-tax, pro-abortion, and pro-lawsuit." Cole won 54%-46% and has been reelected with ease.

Cole has a voting record that usually fits with mainstream conservatives. From his plum seat on the Appropriations Committee, he tends to the needs of his district's military installations and supports federal programs that help his constituents. In the wake of the influence-peddling scandal involving Republican lobbyist Jack Abramoff, who represented several tribes, Cole strongly opposed the proposed limits on the right of tribes to contribute to political campaigns. In 2018, he continued his efforts to protect Native American rights by enacting a bill that expanded the definition of eligibility for tribal membership.

In late 2013, Cole took an expanded role in critical budget talks with Senate Democrats, as one of four House Republicans appointed by Speaker John Boehner to a conference committee seeking to end the partisan brinkmanship that had led to a 16-day government shutdown in October. Working with then-Budget Committee Chairman Paul Ryan, Cole was a skillful conciliator trusted by mainstream Republicans and conservative enough to maintain credibility with the restive tea party faction. Earlier, during the late 2012 negotiations over tax and spending to avoid the so-called "fiscal cliff," he urged his party to accept a tax-cut extension for all but the highest-earning Americans. A profile on the Politico website that October likened him to "the friendly uncle sent out to smoke a cigar and explain to the neighbors what all the noise is about in the basement."

The appropriator has warned about the need to control entitlement spending. He filed a bipartisan proposal that called for a bipartisan commission to recommend steps to guarantee the solvency of Social Security for decades to come. "Without immediate changes that modernize the current system, Social Security will not be able to pay the benefits that American workers have earned and have come to rely upon," Cole warned in 2015.

For four years, Cole was an Appropriations "cardinal" as chairman of the Subcommittee on Labor, Health and Human Services, Education and Related Agencies. In recent years, that spending bill typically made little progress toward agreement with the Senate and instead became part of a status quo "continuing resolution" in the new fiscal year. With Republican Sen. Roy Blunt of Missouri, a Cole ally when he served in the House, serving as chairman of the counterpart Senate panel, they were successful in reaching House-Senate consensus on those major spending categories. Their agreement in 2018 was the first time since 1996 that their bill was enacted — with bipartisan support -- before the start of the fiscal year. Cole called it "a monumental moment," though Republicans lost House control five weeks later.

In a sign of his increasing value to Ryan and GOP leaders, he was named in 2017 as vice chairman of the leadership-driven Rules Committee. Along with his seat on the Budget Committee, he became the eyes and ears — and occasionally a gentle enforcer — for Republican strategists. Following the 2018 election, Kevin McCarthy, House GOP leader, selected Cole to fill the vacancy as top Rules Committee Republican, though in the minority. Cole said that he would "ensure Republicans remain heard and influential." Earlier, he was unsuccessful in his bid to take the top post at Appropriations. He lost to Kay Granger of Texas, who had more seniority, plus the support of the influential Texas delegation. Granger named Cole as the vice ranking member of the committee and he remained as the senior Republican on the Labor-HHS panel.

Campaign politics have been a longstanding part of Cole's portfolio in the House. Following the dismal 2006 election for Republicans, he became chairman of the NRCC, where he had cut his teeth as a political strategist years earlier. He expanded the playing field of competitive seats, but his tenure was a difficult time for the GOP. The party suffered a rough transition to the minority with many retirements, and the committee was $19 million in debt. The biggest obstacle was largely out of Cole's control: President George W. Bush's low public approval ratings, which made reelection an uphill climb for Republicans in competitive seats. The party lost 24 seats during the cycle.

Cole found his way back into Boehner's good graces through aggressive fundraising, plus his savvy combination of legislative skills and political instincts. He called Republicans who voted against Boehner for Speaker in 2015 "pretty unprofessional and very disappointing." Later, both Ryan and McCarthy tapped him as a skillful legislative tactician.

OK-4: South-Central Oklahoma   Cook Partisan Voting Index: R+20

Population		Race and Ethnicity		Income	
Total	780,488	White	71.2%	Median Income	$54,310
Land area (sq. miles)	9,777	Black	6.6%	District Income Rank	237
Pop/ sq mi	79.8	Latino	8.4%	Poverty Rate	13.7%
Born in State	60.9%	Asian	2.3%	With health insurance	87.6%
		Two or more races	6.7%	Cash public assistance	2.4%
Age Groups		Other	4.9%	Food stamp/SNAP	11.6%
Under 18	23.7%				
18-34	25.8%	**Education**		**Work**	
35-64	36.6%	H.S grad or less	42.8%	White Collar	13.9%
Over 64	13.9%	Some college	32.4%	Sales and Service	41.7%
		College Degree, 4 yr	16.3%	Blue Collar	22.9%
Military		Post grad	8.6%	Government	21.3%
Veteran/ Active Duty	13.3%				

2012 Pres. Vote	Romney	175,956	(67%)	Obama	86,357	(33%)		
2016 Pres. Vote	Trump	194,160	(66%)	Clinton	83,648	(28%)	Johnson	17,617	(6%)

Parts of Oklahoma City, Norman: In the years after 1900, the brown hills west of Oklahoma City and north of the Red River suddenly filled up with farmers riding north from Texas, past the quenched green lands of the east toward the bare pasturelands of the west. The first settlers here arrived just as the buffalo were dying out, down from an estimated 60 million animals to no more than 1,000. So in 1901, Republican President William McKinley established the nation's first wildlife preserve in the Wichita Mountains, 25 miles northwest of Lawton. Fifteen bison were donated by the New York Zoological Society and arrived at the preserve via rail in 1907 — a major factor in the survival of the species. Today, this habitat supports grazing for Rocky Mountain elk, white-tailed deer and Texas longhorn cattle.

Government has played a role in the survival of the people, too. Population in southwest Norman, which housed the world's first school of petroleum geology and is now home to the National Weather Center; Tinker Air Force Base in southern Oklahoma City; and the Army Field Artillery School at Fort Sill in Lawton. Tinker will provide maintenance for the new fleet of B-21 Raider stealth bombers (replacing the B-1 and B-2), when they become operational in the mid-2020s. In January 2019, the base had 26,000 employers — the largest employer in the state. With 120,000 people, Norman is the third-largest city in Oklahoma, with booming commercial and residential development underway. In 2015, 72 percent of voters approved the Norman Forward initiative, with $148 million of capital improvements financed by bonds and a half-cent increase in the sales tax for 15 years. Early projects included a new library, aquatic centers and public art projects. In November 2018, the initiative's oversight board found that lower revenues and unexpected costs had led to possible delays. In 2018, the Norman city council agreed on a transition to 100 percent renewable energy by 2035.

The 4th Congressional District of Oklahoma begins smack dab in the middle of the state not far from the capitol in Oklahoma City, and spreads south and west to cover half of Oklahoma's Red River Valley. Demographically, this district is becoming more suburban, but the cultural tone remains countrified. Norman-based Cleveland County is about 40 percent of the population; Oklahoma County is less than 10 percent. The area is at the heart of Tornado Alley. Moore, outside Oklahoma City, has been the site of several deadly strikes, including one in 1999 that remains the strongest ever recorded. In 2013, an EF-5 tornado struck Moore, killing 24 people, damaging at least 12,000 buildings, and leveling entire neighborhoods, including two elementary schools; its estimated $2 billion in damage placed it among the most costly tornados in the nation's history. Ancestrally, this is Democratic country. But Norman, Lawton and the Oklahoma City outskirts have voted solidly Republican since the 1990s.

Kendra Horn (D)

Elected 2018, 1st term, b. Jun 09, 1976; Chickasha; University of Tulsa (LK), B.A., 1998; Southern Methodist University Law School (TX), J.D., 2001; Methodist; Divorced.

Professional Career: Braumiller and Rodriguez, LLC, 2000-2002; Self Employed Attorney 2002-2003; Press Secretary, U.S. Rep. Brad Carson, 2004-2005; Director, Communications and Manager of Government Affairs, Space Foundation, 2005-2008; Director of Marketing and Congressional Relations, WP Aerospace, 2008-2009.

DC Office: 415 CHOB 20515, 202-225-2132, horn.house.gov

State Offices: Oklahoma City, 405-602-3074.

Committees: *Armed Services*: Readiness; Strategic Forces. *Science, Space & Technology*: Energy; Space & Aeronautics (Chmn).

Election Results

Election	Name (Party)	Vote (%)		Cand. Spent	Ind. Exp. Support	Ind. Exp. Oppose
2018 General	Kendra Horn (D)	121,149	(51%)	$1,177,209	$429,664	
	Steve Russell (R)	117,811	(49%)	$881,069	$112,521	
2018 Primary Runoff	Kendra Horn (D)	22,067	(76%)			
	Tom Guild (D)	7,043	(24%)			
2018 Primary	Kendra Horn (D)	34,892	(44%)			
	Tom Guild (D)	14,251	(18%)			
	Elysabeth Britt (D)	10,752	(14%)			
	Eddie Porter (D)	7,844	(10%)			
	Leona Kelley-Leonard (D)	6,697	(9%)			
	Tyson Meade (D)	4,530	(6%)			

Democrat Kendra Horn was among the least expected members of the 2018 freshman class. Her challenge to Republican Rep. Steve Russell was largely ignored by national Democratic groups and political pundits. Horn ran an energetic campaign that voiced national party themes, with an emphasis on voter unhappiness with state Republicans. As the first Democrat elected to Congress from Oklahoma since 2010, her victory shocked local and national political observers in both parties. The district has been a Republican bastion, though its GOP presidential vote has been the lowest in the state.

A native of Chickasaw Oklahoma, Horn graduated from the University of Tulsa and got her law degree from Southern Methodist University. After a few years of practicing law, she served as press secretary for Democratic Rep. Brad Carson, who served one term and ran unsuccessfully for the Senate in 2004. Horn joined the Washington office of the Space Foundation, an advocacy group for space exploration. She managed political campaigns for Democrats in Oklahoma and was a founder of Women Lead Oklahoma, which promoted civic engagement by women.

When Horn announced her candidacy in July 2017, she noted the recent success of other Democrats in Oklahoma City and Tulsa. That was due, in part, to the unpopularity of Republican Gov. Mary Fallin — who made controversial budget decisions, including tax increases, because of falling state revenue from the oil industry.

"People here have so much more in common than our differences," Horn told a reporter for CapitolBeatOK. "We need to get down to brass tacks and work together in making the state better." In the Democratic primary, she got 44 percent of the vote against five other candidates. In the runoff against Tom Guild, who was endorsed by national progressive groups but ran a shoe-string campaign, Horn won 76%-24%.

Russell, a longtime Army officer who served in Iraq, had been easily elected to two terms in the House, where he served on the Armed Services Committee. He said that his objective was to fight waste in government, including in the military.

Horn discussed problems with health care and education, and "the need to change how things are done in Washington." In their sole debate, Russell said that Horn had run ads that were "nasty" and "deceitful," referring to her criticism of his contributions from the oil and gas industry. He dismissed her references to problems in Oklahoma, suggesting that she run for the state legislature.

Horn and Russell each raised about $1 million for the campaign, though Russell left a large amount in the bank on Election Day. National parties sent scant funds to the contest. In late October, the Cook Political Report reviewed the contest and wrote that "it would take a tsunami" for Horn to win. That wave hit Oklahoma City, though barely.

In "a political upset for the history books," The Oklahoman reported, Horn defied "expectations, polls, experts, opponents and history itself." She won, 51%-49%, with 52 percent in Oklahoma County, which cast nearly 90 percent of the vote. Russell took the two outlying counties. His campaign was "slow from the start," according to the newspaper's analysis.

Horn was the first Democrat to win the district since the 1970s. She may have been helped by Democrat Drew Edmondson, who got 54 percent in Oklahoma County, though he lost statewide in his bid for governor. She faced challenges in finding a niche among House Democrats and would be hard-pressed to avoid becoming a one-term wonder. Horn got a boost with the assignment to chair the Science, Space and Technology Subcommittee on Space and Aeronautics — an unusual opportunity for a freshman.

OK-5: Oklahoma City Area   **Cook Partisan Voting Index: R+10**

Population		Race and Ethnicity		Income	
Total	803,924	White	57.7%	Median Income	$49,560
Land area (sq. miles)	2,074	Black	13.4%	District Income Rank	317
Pop/ sq mi	387.6	Latino	16.2%	Poverty Rate	17.6%
Born in State	59.6%	Asian	3.1%	With health insurance	84.2%
		Two or more races	5.5%	Cash public assistance	3.5%
Age Groups		Other	4.1%	Food stamp/SNAP	14.6%
Under 18	25.6%				
18-34	24.8%	**Education**		**Work**	
35-64	36.5%	H.S grad or less	39.8%	White Collar	13.1%
Over 64	13.1%	Some college	30%	Sales and Service	42.3%
		College Degree, 4 yr	19.4%	Blue Collar	21.8%
Military		Post grad	10.7%	Government	14.9%
Veteran/ Active Duty	9%				

2012 Pres. Vote	Romney	156,035	(59%)	Obama	107,344	(41%)			
2016 Pres. Vote	Trump	149,400	(53%)	Clinton	111,769	(40%)	Johnson	19,631	(7%)

Oklahoma City: Oklahoma City, like many state capitals, was not the spontaneous creation of commerce but the deliberate creation of government, sited in the geographic center of the state on what turned out to be oil land. Rigs were pumping crude on the grounds of the capitol until 1989. The land here is browner and more eroded by creeks than the rolling Oklahoma farmland to the east. Oklahoma City's population grew briskly from 506,000 in 2000 to 644,000 in 2017, a 27 percent increase. A survey of housing affordability in 2019 ranked Oklahoma City as the third most affordable city in the United States; the top two were Pittsburgh and Rochester.

Oklahoma City was scarred by a profound tragedy: the day in April 1995 when a bomb destroyed the Alfred P. Murrah Federal Building, killing 168 people and injuring more than 680. Five years later, the Oklahoma City National Memorial opened on the site of the blast. Local pride spiked in 2008 when the Seattle SuperSonics of the National Basketball Association relocated to the city and became the Oklahoma City Thunder, the state's first major sports franchise. The team's run to the NBA finals in 2012 energized the city's fan base. But, alas, the team's star players escaped for more cosmopolitan venues and its title prospects waned. A local builder planned to complete by 2020 redevelopment of the historic First National Center — with its Art Deco exterior -- into a hotel, with retail stores and apartments. Also underway downtown was a new convention center. In 2018, streetcar service started along five miles of track. All of this activity was bolstered by the growing number of young professionals moving into the city, plus an increase in the minority population (19 percent Hispanic and 15 percent black).

The 5th Congressional District is centered in Oklahoma City and includes most of Oklahoma County. It takes in Pottawatomie and Seminole counties to the east. Oklahoma County, which is the least-red in the state, casts nearly 90 percent of the vote. In 2016, Donald Trump took the district, 53%-40% -- a drop from the 59 percent the Republican presidential nominees took in 2008 and 2012 and a notable contrast to the more than 70 percent for Trump in the adjacent 2nd and 3rd districts. The local influx of new voters has been trending Democratic. In 2018, four state legislative seats in Oklahoma County flipped from Republican to Democratic. "Minorities and millennials turn Oklahoma City blue," The Oklahoman newspaper headlined following the election.

OREGON

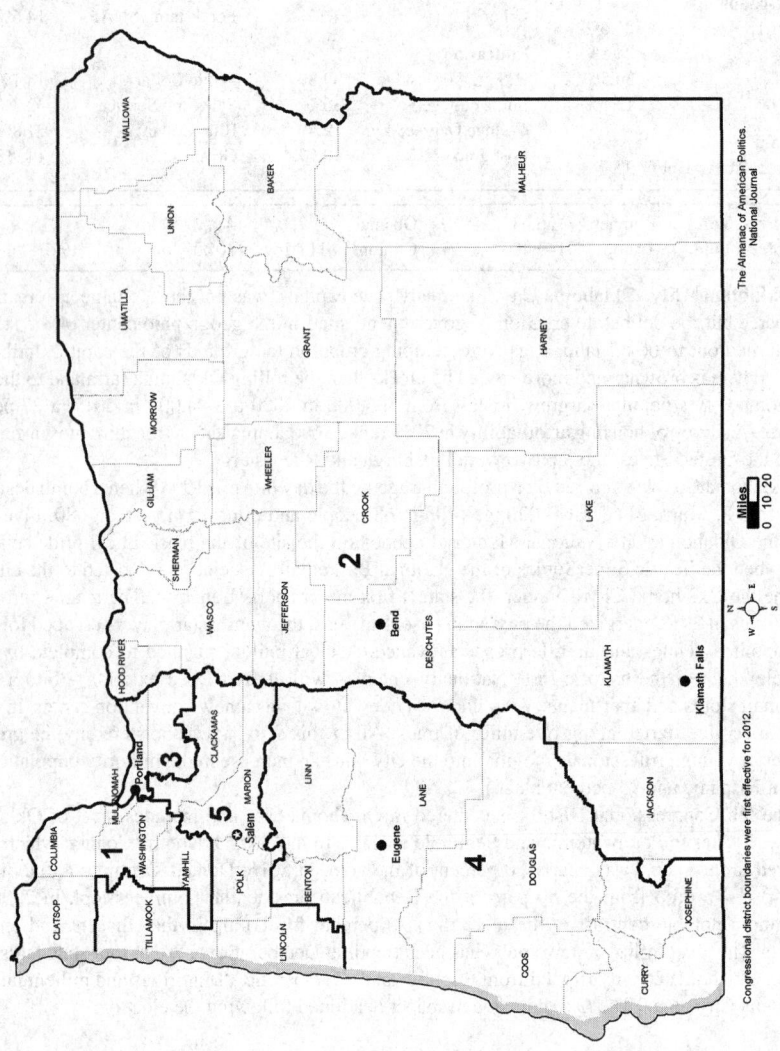

Congressional district boundaries were first effective for 2012.

Almost half of Oregon's population lives in the counties in and around Portland, the city whose hippie-liberal sensitivities were lovingly satirized by Fred Armisen and Carrie Brownstein in the television comedy series Portlandia. Residents of the Portland area have had mixed feelings about this portrayal, but its underlying truth helps explain how Oregon became a blue state, even as much of the rest of Oregon is as rural and Republican as other portions of the American West.

Oregon is an experimental commonwealth, a laboratory of reform, a maker of national trends — with varying results. Bike trails now exist throughout the country. You can find light-rail trams in many central cities, but not so many solar energy-powered, plug-in stations for electric cars. Oregon produces (or has manufactured in China) Nike sneakers and Pendleton shirts, but its handcrafted ales don't travel far from the Oregon Brewers Festival. For all its modern advances, however, you can still see much of the same Oregon that Lewis and Clark saw in 1805, when they came down the Columbia River gorge, past the Willamette River to the Pacific Ocean. A few years later, in 1811, John Jacob Astor set up his fur trading post at Astoria. But few Americans came overland until the 1840s, when New England Yankees and Missouri farmers drove wagons along the Oregon Trail and floated down the Columbia to the well-watered Willamette Valley.

In this remote spot, nearly 2,000 miles from the Mississippi River frontier and 700 miles from the small Mexican settlements in California, they built an orderly, productive society — a kind of western New England. It grew steadily, with a few booms: in the early 1900s as timber harvesting surged; during World War II, when Kaiser shipyards in Portland and Vancouver churned out "Liberty" and "Victory" ships; and then again in the 1970s, when homebuilding skyrocketed and Oregon's natural environment began to be widely appreciated. The settlers brought town-meeting attitudes to Oregon. This was the second state after South Dakota to give people direct decision-making via the initiative and referendum, an innovation widely copied elsewhere. Oregon pioneered the election of senators by popular vote and, with Michigan in 1908, the recall of elected officials. It was the first state to institute Labor Day. It was first to sanction assisted suicide and to adopt mail-in ballot elections.

Oregon has a darker strain of history, too. When the state's constitution was written, it included a provision that barred the relocation of any African American in the state, and another that precluded black ownership of real estate. "Oregon is the only state in the United States that actually began as literally whites-only," Winston Grady-Willis, director of Portland State University's School of Gender, Race and Nations, told the Washington Post. The Klan had a significant presence in the state in the early 20th century and communities of skinheads flourished in the 1980s. It took until 1959 for Oregon to ratify the post-Civil War 15th Amendment, which guaranteed the right to vote. While the "Portlandia" image of "kombucha-swilling, artisan knot-loving, bicycle-riding haven" (as the Oregonian newspaper summarized it) is based in reality, the state's racist heritage has become increasingly visible in recent years. In Portland, violent far-right groups have engaged in clashes with violent far-left antifa. In 2017, a man screamed anti-Muslim insults on a commuter train and proceeded to stab two men to death and injure a third. Meanwhile, in the winter of 2016, a breakaway group of armed protesters occupied the headquarters of the Malheur National Wildlife Refuge in the state's rural, southwestern corner, decrying federal encroachment on private lands and prompting a 41-day standoff that led to one death and more than a dozen guilty pleas for conspiracy and trespassing. In 2018, a sympathetic President Donald Trump pardoned the ranchers whose five-year sentences for arson had sparked the occupation; within months, his administration had restored their grazing permit.

Oregon grew much faster than the national average in the 1940s, when war industries brought thousands of people to the West Coast, and again in the 1970s, when the pleasant environment attracted so many young people that the state's population shot up by 26 percent. Containing growth became the hot local issue. "Come and visit us again and again," Republican Gov. Tom McCall told outsiders. "But for heaven's sake don't come here to live." At his prodding, the legislature in 1973 passed a law that limited development, and in the 1990s, the Portland metropolitan area sharply restricted growth and sprawl. These measures were also popular in the university towns of Eugene and Corvallis and to a lesser extent in the suburbs. The lumber industry, which for decades accounted for most of Oregon's exports, was already sliding when it took another major blow in the 1990s from federal land-use restrictions imposed to protect the threatened spotted owl. While Oregon has remained a leader in producing Christmas trees, federal and state regulation, productivity gains from technology advances, and greater automation have all contributed to slack employment in the timber sector.

But as rural areas seethed over land-use policies, those same regulations attracted environment-minded migrants to Portland and the university towns. And some of those newcomers helped build the state's new economy. The growth of high-tech companies around Portland was such that the area became known as Silicon Forest, where Intel, the largest tech employer in the state, shares the stage with homegrown firms like Mentor Graphics, FEI Co. and Rentrack Corp. The tech industry accounted for a disproportionate number of the state's job gains in the most recent economic rebound, and those jobs were high-paying. Oregon is also a top exporter; the Portland region ranks as the seventh most trade-dependent metro area, according to the Brookings Institution. By far, the biggest export consists of semiconductors and electronic components at $7.7 billion, thanks largely to Intel. The port of Portland also ships more than a billion dollars of motor vehicles and agricultural crops every year. Befitting Oregon's location on the Pacific Rim, the state's top trading partners save Canada are in Asia, including China, Malaysia and Vietnam. One new line of business – legalized recreational marijuana, approved by voters in 2014 – is growing. Unlike most products for sale in the state, marijuana is taxed at 17 percent.

Healthy post-recession growth caused state revenues to soar and trigger the state's "kicker" rebate to Oregon taxpayers. In 1980, voters agreed to a proposal that Oregon's legislators devised to ward off the tax revolt that had swept neighboring California in the late 1970s: when personal income tax receipts grew by more than 2 percent above the state's projections, the excess would be rebated to taxpayers. A comparable kicker was established for corporate income tax revenue, but in 2012, voters approved a ballot measure requiring that any corporate kicker revenue be deposited in the state school fund. Then, in 2018, discussion increased about ending the kicker and instead using the added revenue to fill school reserve coffers. According to the Oregon Business Council, more than 60 percent of poll respondents favored the switch.

While Oregon's population growth rate has fallen from its earlier peaks, the state is still expanding at a healthy clip, up 9.2 percent since 2010. Its three biggest counties – Multnomah, Washington and Clackamas, each in the Portland metro area – have each grown by between 8 and 11 percent since 2010. Oregon's population is 2 percent black, 13 percent Hispanic and 4 percent Asian, and metro Portland, with its hugely progressive core neighborhoods, is America's whitest big city -- 77 percent white and 6 percent African American. Washington County in suburban Portland, is increasingly diverse ethnically – 10 percent Asian and 16 percent Hispanic. The state capital of Salem and farming counties east of the Cascades have relatively high Hispanic percentages.

Though it was founded by New England churchmen, Oregon has America's highest percentage of self-described agnostics (8 percent) according to the Pew Research Center's 2014 U.S. Religious Landscape Study. The religiously unaffiliated form the core constituency for some of the state's policy innovations over the last two generations, when Oregon legalized most abortions prior to the Supreme Court's Roe v. Wade decision, decriminalized medical marijuana, and legalized assisted suicide in referendums in 1994 and 1997, to the point that doctors can prescribe but not administer lethal drugs. In 2007, the Democratic-controlled legislature imposed limits on smoking, banned discrimination on the basis of sexual orientation and mandated recycling of discarded electronics. Oregon eagerly expanded Medicaid under the Affordable Care Act, adding 438,000 mostly able-bodied adults to the rolls. When costs skyrocketed, voters in 2018 approved tax increases on health care providers to pay for it. Meanwhile, the state has some of the oldest sanctuary policies for undocumented immigrants, and in 2018, voters rejected a ballot measure that would have overturned the sanctuary law. Oregon was also among the most active states in filing lawsuits opposing the Trump administration's immigration policies. Sometimes, though, Oregon's liberals moved faster than the state's voters. Oregonians narrowly rejected a 2014 ballot measure requiring labels on genetically engineered foods by 837 votes. And same-sex marriage came relatively late to Oregon, thanks to a 2004 amendment to the state constitution that barred it.

Voting in Oregon has featured huge margins for progressive candidates and positions in Portland, Eugene and Corvallis and huge conservative margins in counties east of the Cascades and in much of southwestern Oregon, where discontent over the policies that decimated the logging industry has lingered. There are no polls open on Election Day – there really is no Election Day -- and voters have until that night to get their ballots to an election clerk.

In 2016, presidential voting patterns in Oregon didn't change as markedly as they did in some other states, as Hillary Clinton defeated Donald Trump by a 50%-39% margin -- essentially the same gap as in 2012. (In 2016, Libertarian Gary Johnson won 5 percent and Green Party nominee Jill Stein got 2.6 percent.) In the midterm elections two years later, no House seats switched hands, but, mirroring national patterns, Democrats made gains in suburban areas while Republicans made progress in white working-class areas. Democratic Gov. Kate Brown was reelected in 2018, with strong majorities in both chambers, and liberal ballot measures prevailed. In early 2019, the only Republican to win statewide in years, Secretary of State Dennis Richardson, died of brain cancer. Oregon has more women in senior legislative leadership roles than any other state, according to Rutgers University's Center for American Women and Politics. Ironically, those female leaders in 2018 had to grapple with their imperfect handling of explosive sexual harassment allegations in the legislature.

Population		Race and Ethnicity		Income	
Total	4,025,127	White	76.5%	Median Income	$56,119
Land area (sq. miles)	95,988	Black	1.8%	State Income Rank	26
Pop/ sq mi	41.9	Latino	12.7%	Poverty Rate	14.9%
Born in state	46.1%	Asian	4.1%	With health insurance	91.2%
		Two or more races	3.6%	Cash public assistance	3.9%
Age Groups		Other	1.4%	Food stamp/SNAP	17.8%
Under 18	21.5%				
18-34	22.8%	Education		Work	
35-64	39.4%	H.S grad or less	33.2%	White Collar	38.1%
Over 64	16.3%	Some college	34.5%	Sales and Service	41.1%
		College Degree, 4 yr	20.1%	Blue Collar	20.7%
Military		Post grad	12.2%	Government	13.6%
Veteran/ Active Duty	9.3%				

Presidential Politics

2016 Primary (D)	Sanders (D)	360,829 (56%)	Clinton (D)	269,846 (42%)			
2016 Primary (R)	Trump (R)	252,748 (64%)	Cruz (R)	65,513 (17%)	Kasich (R)	62,248 (16%)	
2016 Pres. Vote	Clinton (D)	1,002,106 (50%)	Trump (R)	782,403 (39%)	Johnson (L)	94,231 (5%)	
	Stein (G)	50,002 (3%)					
2012 Pres. Vote	Obama (D)	970,488 (54%)	Romney (R)	754,175 (42%)			

Oregon has the distinction of being the site of the first presidential broadcast debate. During the 1948 GOP primary, Portland radio station KEX hosted Thomas Dewey and Harold Stassen, who debated whether the Communist Party should be outlawed. The debate was carried on national radio networks and some 40 million Americans tuned in to listen for an hour without commercial interruption. Dewey opposed the proposition, won the debate and the primary, and carried the state in the general election. Oregon regularly tilted Republican in close presidential contests, voting for other losing GOP nominees in 1960 and 1976. Still, it has now voted for the Democratic presidential candidate in eight consecutive elections, voting more Democratic than the nation in the past four. In 2016, Hillary Clinton defeated Donald Trump 50%-39%. Clinton won Multnomah County (Portland), the state's largest vote producer, by a whopping 73%-17%. She also won Portland suburban counties, Clackamas and Washington, Lane County (Eugene), and four others. Trump won the remaining 28 counties.

Oregon holds its presidential primary in late May. In 2008, when the race between Clinton and Barack Obama was still raging, Obama carried Oregon 59%-41%, with especially large margins in Multnomah and the university towns. Eight years later, Vermont Sen. Bernie Sanders beat Clinton, 56%-42%, winning all but one small rural county. Oregon Democratic Sen. Jeff Merkley was the only one of Sanders' Senate colleagues to endorse him. The GOP primary was held after all of Trump's Republican rivals had withdrawn from the race and he won 64 percent of the vote.

Congressional Districts

116th Congress Lineup	4D 1R	115th Congress Lineup	4D 1R

Oregon is projected to gain the sixth seat that it narrowly missed following the 2010 census. The good news for Democrats is that they now control the governorship and the legislature. That is likely to continue through the next redistricting cycle. The challenge that Democrats face is whether they can create a safe seat for their party in a delegation that has four Democrats and one Republican. The 4th and 5th districts have been competitive in presidential elections, and each seat might be at risk if the current incumbent retires. The Portland-based 1st and 3rd Districts have plenty of Democrats to sacrifice, though the map-drawers probably would need to divide the city to create a new Democratic-leaning district; that likely would meet resistance. Alternatively, Democrats could draw the new district to give their candidate a reasonable opportunity in a competitive district. The Republican-controlled 2nd District east of the Cascade Mountains could sacrifice its growing number of Democratic voters in Bend-based Deschutes County.

In 2011, the legislature accomplished something that it hadn't been able to do in more than 100 years: It passed its own congressional redistricting plan. The prospects had seemed unlikely because the parties were tied at 30 seats apiece in the state House. But there was a compromise to be had: Democrats wanted to shift Corvallis, home of Oregon State University, to the Eugene-based 4th District. In the deal, Democrats let the 3rd pick up some of Democrat Kurt Schrader's already tiny share of Portland, keeping his 5th District competitive. That kind of deal might be more difficult to pull off with the complexities created by an additional seat. Traditionally progressive Oregon is the last West Coast state without an independent redistricting commission of some kind.

Kate Brown (D)

Assumed office in 2015, term expires 2023, 1st full term; b. Jun. 21, 1960, Torrejón de Ardoz, Spain; U. of CO Boulder, B.A. 1981; Northwestern Schl. of Law, J.D. 1985; Married (Dan); 2 children.

Elected Office: OR House, 1991-1996; OR Senate, 1997-2008, Majority Leader, 2004; OR Secretary of State, 2008-2015.

Professional Career: Practicing attorney; Instructor, Portland State University.

Office: 900 Court St. NE, Rm. 160, Salem, 97301-4047; 503-378-4582; Fax: 503-378-8970; Website: oregon.gov.

Atty. Gen: Ellen Rosenblum (D) **Sec. of State:** Leslie Cummings (R)

State Legislature: Senate: 18D, 11R, 1V **House:** 38D, 22R

Election Results

Election	Name (Party)	Vote (%)
2018 General	Kate Brown (D)	934,498 (50%)
	Knute Buehler (R)	814,988 (44%)
	Patrick Starnes (I)	53,392 (3%)
2018 Primary	Kate Brown (D)	324,451 (84%)
	Ed Jones (D)	33,464 (9%)
	Candace Meville (D)	29,110 (8%)

Prior winning percentage: 2016 (51%)

Kate Brown won her second election as governor of Oregon in 2018, almost four years after succeeding scandal-plagued Gov. John Kitzhaber, a fellow Democrat. Brown, the nation's first openly bisexual governor, faced a competitive reelection contest in 2018 against Republican Knute Buehler, but she ended up winning almost the same share of the vote – 50 percent -- as she'd won in the 2016 special election and as Kitzhaber had won in 2014.

Brown was born in Spain, where her father served in the Air Force, but she grew up in Minnesota. She received a bachelor's degree in environmental conservation, with a certificate in women's studies, from the University of Colorado at Boulder, then obtained her law degree from Lewis & Clark College in Portland. She practiced family law in Portland and worked for a nonprofit legal services group. Brown got her start in politics in 1991 when, while working as an advocate for the Women's Rights Coalition, she was appointed by the Multnomah County Board of Commissioners to fill a vacancy in the Oregon House. A year later, the state representative who Brown replaced, Judy Bauman, wanted her seat back and challenged Brown in the Democratic primary. Bauman had stronger political connections, but Brown went door-to-door and waged a vigorous grassroots campaign, winning the primary by seven votes. In 1996, Brown won a seat in the Oregon Senate and quickly was named its Democratic caucus leader. Brown married in 1997, and publicly acknowledged her bisexuality after The Oregonian reported on it when she was a state lawmaker. She rose to majority leader in 2004, becoming the first woman to occupy that post.

Brown ran for secretary of state in 2008 and won, 51%-46%. In that post, Brown attracted attention for helping Oregon implement an online voter-registration system and for using iPad technology to make voting more accessible to people with disabilities. But in 2012, she came under fire when her office notified two candidates for labor commissioner that their elections would be held in November instead of the following May, a move that critics said appeared to be aimed at helping the Democratic candidate. In her reelection bid, the Oregonian endorsed Buehler – her future gubernatorial opponent – saying her decision had "eroded public confidence in Brown, if not the office itself." But Brown won reelection anyway.

Prior to his resignation, Kitzhaber was a giant figure in Oregon politics. During the summer before his reelection, he became engaged to Cylvia Hayes, who ran an environmental consulting business. But investigative reporting by Willamette Week in 2014 raised questions about whether Hayes had benefited financially from her relationship with the governor and whether she had properly disclosed the consulting fees she had been paid. Although Kitzhaber won his race, the controversy didn't die down. It reached a crescendo in February 2015, and Kitzhaber stepped down. Brown, the next in line as secretary of state, became governor.

On the whole, lawmakers seemed to welcome Brown and her more collegial approach; Kitzhaber was seen by some as aloof and arrogant. Brown emphasized the need to restore trust in government and within months she signed an ethics package. Separately, she signed a bill that would automatically register voters who obtained or renewed their driver's license, becoming the first state to make voter registration automatic. Brown also signed other progressive measures approved by the state legislature, including mandatory paid sick leave for most Oregon workers; more permissive rules for acquiring a medical-marijuana card; a bill making it illegal for employers to ask about an applicant's criminal background on job applications; a new system for collecting data about racial profiling by law enforcement officers; an employee-funded workplace-based retirement savings program; a bill to end "conversion therapy" for homosexuality; and protections for transgender students. The most controversial measure, however, was a bill Brown signed in 2015 to require a background check for most private sales of guns. Reaction to the measure highlighted the divide between the Portland region and the state's rural areas.

Brown's second year in office began with a crisis, as an armed group protesting federal land policies occupied the headquarters of the Malheur National Wildlife Refuge, in rural southeast Oregon. Brown vented frustration with federal officials' take-it-slow approach – local residents, she said during the standoff, "have been overlooked and underserved by federal officials' response." The incident ended after 41 days, with one protester dead; more than a dozen people eventually pled guilty to conspiracy and trespassing charges. (In 2018, President Donald Trump pardoned the cattle ranchers whose legal case had initially inspired the armed occupation.) The Malheur refuge takeover, combined with lingering anger at Brown's gun control policies, raised concerns about the governor's safety. In July 2016, The Oregonian reported that Brown's security procedures had been tightened and coordination with the FBI had increased. Two months later, Brown was burned in effigy on the front steps of the state capitol by gun-rights demonstrators.

Despite such tensions, Brown had legislative successes in 2016. She signed a phased-in minimum wage increase scaled to three different territories – Portland, rural areas, and everywhere else. She signed new protections for tenants, and she allowed jurisdictions to require builders to include housing priced below market rates. Lawmakers also approved new renewable energy mandates; a lodging-tax increase; a boost for the backlogged testing of rape kits; the lifting of the statute of limitations on rape; and permission for banks to take on marijuana businesses as clients. One problem, however, remained unsolved -- how to tackle the state's $22 billion in unfunded pension liabilities.

Brown ran in a 2016 special election for the final two years of Kitzhaber's term. She faced William "Bud" Pierce, a moderate former president of the Oregon Medical Association. During a debate, Pierce said well-educated and accomplished women are less susceptible to sexual harassment; after an outcry, he apologized. Republicans hadn't won an Oregon gubernatorial race since 1982 and Brown courted opposition from pro-gun Republicans by accepting a $250,000 campaign donation from former New York City mayor and gun control advocate Michael Bloomberg. In the end, she won by less than the polls had indicated -- seven points.

As Brown prepared for another election in just two years, she had a productive time with the legislature. In 2017, she signed a measure to keep private any changes transgender people make on their birth certificates; Oregon was the second state with such a measure, following California. She also signed one of the most pro-abortion-rights laws in the nation, requiring abortion coverage and birth control without any co-pay, and allotting state funds to pay for abortions for non-citizens who aren't permitted to sign up for Medicaid. The following year, Brown signed a bill to require internet providers who do business with the state to maintain so-called net neutrality, while signing another measure to close the "boyfriend loophole" that had permitted gun access for those convicted of domestic violence against non-married intimate partners. Brown signed an executive order to ban offshore drilling. She also persuaded her fellow Democrats to support a narrowly tailored tax cut for an estimated 6,000 sole proprietors. Meanwhile, Brown and Attorney General Ellen Rosenblum went to court to protect the state's longstanding sanctuary-state law, a stance that would receive the voters' support in November when a ballot measure for its repeal failed by nearly a 2-to-1 margin.

In the 2018 GOP primary, Buehler, an orthopedic surgeon and state legislator, prevailed against a split conservative field, winning 46 percent against Trump-aligned businessman Sam Carpenter, with 29 percent, and former Navy pilot Greg Wooldridge, with 20 percent. Buehler ran a center-right campaign, backing abortion rights and saying climate change needed to be tackled; he was bolstered by millions of dollars donated by Nike co-founder Phil Knight. Buehler criticized Brown's record on educational achievement, mental health, foster care and the state's pension challenges. Buehler sought to distance himself from Trump, who was unpopular in the state. but Brown got a boost in October when independent candidate Patrick Starnes dropped out and endorsed the incumbent, saying that she would be best positioned to enact campaign finance reform, Starnes' highest-profile issue. Brown won, 50%-44%. Compared with Kitzhaber's 2014 win, Brown performed about four percentage points better in populous Multnomah and Washington counties.

After her reelection, Brown sought support for a plan to curb carbon emissions that had stalled in previous legislative sessions and called for the partial repeal of the tax cut she had pushed just six months earlier. She sought $700 million in new taxes and fees, saying she would spend it on K-12 education. The legislature quickly passed new taxes she proposed on hospitals and health insurance carriers.

Ron Wyden (D)

Elected 1996, term expires 2022, 4th full term, b. May 03, 1949; Wichita, KS; University of California, B.A., 1969; Stanford University (CA), B.A., 1971; University of Oregon Law School, J.D., 1974; Jewish; Married (Nancy Bass Wyden); 5 children (2 from previous marriage).

Elected Office: U.S. House, 1981-1996.

Professional Career: Co-Director & co-founder, OR Gray Panthers, 1974-1980; Director, OR Legal Svcs. for the Elderly, 1977-1979; Instructor, University of OR, 1976, Portland St. University, 1979, University of Portland, 1980.

DC Office: 221 DSOB 20510, 202-224-5244, Fax: 202-228-2717, wyden.senate.gov

State Offices: Bend, 541-330-9142; Eugene, 541-431-0229; La Grande, 541-962-7691; Medford, 541-858-5122; Portland, 503-326-7525; Salem, 503-589-4555.

Committees: *Budget. Energy & Natural Resources:* Energy; Public Lands, Forests & Mining (RMM); Water & Power. *Finance (RMM):* Ex Officio membership on all subcommittees. *Intelligence. Joint Taxation.*

Group Ratings

	ADA	ACLU	AFL-CIO	LCV	ITI	COC	HAFA	ACU	CFG	FRC
2018	-	86%	-	100%	-	50%	3%	5%	15%	0%
2017	95%	C	100%	95%	C	14%	C	0%	4%	0%

Almanac Ratings 2017-18

	Economy	Social	Foreign	Composite
Liberal	100%	100%	92%	97%
Conservative	0%	0%	8%	3%

Key Votes of the 115th Congress

1. Obama-care revision	N	5. Gun regulations	N	9. Kavanaugh confirmation	N
2. Tax Cuts	N	6. Family planning regs	N	10. Saudi arms sales	Y
3. Dodd-Frank revision	N	7. Gorsuch confirmation	N	11. FISA rules	N
4. Omnibus appropriations	Y	8. Immigration restrictions	N	12. Military aid in Yemen	Y

Election Results

Election	Name (Party)	Vote (%)		Cand. Spent	Ind. Exp. Support	Ind. Exp. Oppose
2016 General	Ron Wyden (D)...............................	1,105,119	(57%)	$6,565,807		
	Mark Callahan (R)...............................	651,106	(33%)		$37,221	
	Eric Navickas (G)..................................	48,823	(3%)			
2016 Primary	Ron Wyden (D).................................	501,903	(84%)			
	Kevin Stine (D).............................	78,287	(13%)			

Prior winning percentages: 2010 (57%), 2004 (63%), 1998 (61%), 1996 special (48%), House: 1994 (73%), 1992 (77%), 1990 (81%), 1988 (99%), 1986 (86%), 1984 (59%), 1982 (78%), 1980 (72%)

Democrat Ron Wyden, Oregon's senior senator, is tied with Sen. Chuck Schumer of New York as the second long-serving Democrat on Capitol Hill, behind only Sen. Patrick Leahy of Vermont. He arrived in the Senate via a special election in January 1996, after a decade and a half in the House. He is the senior Democrat on the tax-writing Finance Committee, though partisanship in recent years has reduced his influence as a member of the minority party. He has pursued an array of eclectic interests. As a member of the Intelligence Committee, Wyden has emerged as perhaps the Senate's most implacable critic of government efforts to expand electronic surveillance of citizens for the sake of national security.

Wyden has relentlessly worked to bridge the partisan divide on such high-wattage issues as health care — to the consternation of his Democratic colleagues. In 2013, he became chairman of the Senate Energy and Natural Resources Committee. Just over a year later, when Montana Sen. Max Baucus resigned to become ambassador to China, Wyden briefly took the Finance Committee gavel — bringing along his reputation for trying to craft bipartisan deals on highly polarizing issues. "Sometimes folks tease him, [saying] 'If Ron Wyden hasn't used the word bipartisan in a sentence today, it's not our Ron,'" Alaska Sen. Lisa Murkowski, the ranking Republican on the Energy and Natural Resources panel when Wyden was chairman, told The Oregonian in 2013. "But then he's genuine about it, and it's important to him." During the Trump administration, such opportunities have been scant.

Wyden was born in Wichita, Kansas, while his father, Peter, a journalist, was working for the Wichita Eagle. Peter shortened the family surname from Weidenreich three years before his son was born; both Wyden's father and his mother, Edith, were Jews who had fled Nazi Germany. Presaging Wyden's involvement in overseeing U.S. intelligence policy years later, Peter Wyden was trained as a U.S. spy during World War II and returned to Europe to help run an Allied propaganda campaign aimed at Nazi-held territory. Ron Wyden grew up in California, graduated from Stanford University and moved to Oregon to attend the University of Oregon Law School. After graduating in 1974, he founded the Oregon chapter of the Gray Panthers, an advocacy group for the elderly. Under Wyden, the group ventured into electoral politics by sponsoring a successful referendum reducing the price of dentures.

As a 19-year-old undergraduate, Wyden worked as a campaign driver for Sen. Wayne Morse, who became a mentor — and whose Senate seat Wyden now occupies. In 1968, the famously independent-minded Morse, an early opponent of the Vietnam War, got a challenge in the Democratic primary from former Rep. Robert Duncan, a supporter of the war. Morse won the primary, but lost the general election to a young Republican state legislator, Bob Packwood. Twelve years later, at 31, Wyden launched a primary challenge to Duncan. In the sometimes small world of Oregon politics, Duncan had returned to the House representing the Portland-based 3rd District. Wyden won the primary 60%-40% and easily captured the heavily Democratic seat in 1980. As a member of the Energy and Commerce Committee, his interests included health care, energy and telecommunications.

Wyden's path to the Senate was opened by the Senate Ethics Committee's decision in September 1995 to expel Packwood for sexually harassing aides and lobbyists. Wyden, who had long eyed the seat, ran in the special election to replace Packwood, who resigned before the scheduled expulsion vote. With his base in Portland, Wyden had greater name recognition than his rivals. But he had spirited opposition in the primary, but won 50%-44% win. The Republican nomination went to state Senate President Gordon Smith, a moderate. Smith, a frozen-vegetable tycoon from Eastern Oregon, spent $2 million of his own money. Most polls suggested a dead heat, and negative ads flooded the airwaves. Wyden won, 48%-47%. Ten months later, Smith won the state's other Senate seat after Republican Mark Hatfield retired.

Wyden and Smith became friends and collaborators, holding dozens of joint town meetings across Oregon and having lunch every Thursday with their chiefs of staff. Facing a tough re-election campaign in 2008 against Democrat Jeff Merkley, Smith boasted of bipartisanship in ads that included images of Wyden. Merkley narrowly won.

Wyden has sought other opportunities to pursue counterintuitive political alliances and creative ideas. In early 2009, he and Maine Republican Sen. Olympia Snowe predicted that high-dollar bonuses and "golden parachutes" for executives of financial companies being bailed out by U.S. taxpayers would be unpopular with the public, and they won passage of a provision in that year's economic stimulus bill to prevent such payments. But the stipulation was dropped from the final bill at the insistence of aides to President Barack Obama, who argued that employees might sue to keep their bonuses. Public anger boiled over in March 2009 after lucrative bonuses were paid to employees of troubled insurance giant AIG.

One of the more memorable moments of Wyden's career came during a 2013 Intelligence Committee meeting. He asked then-Director of National Intelligence James Clapper, "Does the [National Security Agency] collect any type of data at all on millions or hundreds of millions of Americans?"

Clapper replied, "No, sir."

"It does not?" Wyden pressed.

"Not wittingly," Clapper answered.

Three months later, whistleblower Edward Snowden created a national firestorm by leaking thousands of NSA documents that proved Clapper had not been straight with Wyden. Snowden, in a column in 2014, said that Clapper's answer to Wyden had been a "major motivating factor" in his decision to leak information illustrating the extent to which intelligence agencies were electronically collecting information on U.S. citizens. Clapper later acknowledged he had answered Wyden in the "least most untruthful manner."

After Snowden's revelations, Wyden achieved success in 2015, when the revised USA Freedom Act reined in the government's ability to collect phone data. It put Wyden in yet another bipartisan alliance, this time with libertarian-minded Sen. Rand Paul of Kentucky. Two years earlier, Wyden was the only Democrat to stand on the floor while Paul filibustered John Brennan's nomination to be director of the CIA — a protest of the Obama administration's use of drone strikes overseas. Wyden voted to confirm Brennan, but he called on the administration to produce more documents about its drone policy.

In January 2017, Wyden battled President Donald Trump's first nominee for CIA director, then-Rep. Mike Pompeo, forcing a six-hour debate on the Senate floor before Pompeo was confirmed. Wyden took aim at an op-ed piece that Pompeo had written a year earlier that called for re-establishing programs collecting Americans' metadata, which Congress had restricted in 2015. Pompeo said such metadata should be combined with publicly available financial and lifestyle information into a "comprehensive searchable database." Wyden said on the Senate floor: "I have never heard an idea so extreme, so overarching and so intrusive of Americans' privacy. We are headed into dangerous times." Many of those restrictions enacted in 2015 were due to expire in 2019, after Pompeo left the CIA to become secretary of State.

Wyden's interest in the internet goes back to the mid-1990s. He was an early champion of internet freedom, often siding with the tech sector against Hollywood and other content producers who sought strict anti-piracy laws. He and then-California Republican Rep. Christopher Cox sponsored a three-year ban on taxation of access to the internet that passed in 1998. The ban on such taxes was extended several times until Congress made the prohibition permanent in 2016.

Wyden's efforts to cross the aisle on health care date to the George W. Bush's presidency. He was one of 11 Senate Democrats to vote for the Republican-authored Medicare prescription drug law in 2003. "It wasn't a bill I would have written. But I thought it was the right thing to do to get started," he said. Later, with Snowe, he sponsored a bill to allow the federal government to negotiate drug prices with pharmaceutical companies.

As Obama's health care overhaul was debated in 2009, Wyden joined Republican Bob Bennett of Utah on a bill to replace the tax exclusion for employer-provided health insurance with a tax deduction for individuals to buy insurance from private insurers. The Obama administration and key Senate committee chairmen disagreed that changes in tax incentives alone would achieve the goal of insuring millions of Americans without health insurance. "Ron Wyden's brand is as a guy who wants to get things done," Bennett, who lost re-election in 2010, later said. "Anything he does with a Republican who is reasonable builds that brand, even if it doesn't come to fruition. ... He's built this brand and he loves it."

Wyden did not get a lot of love from his own party when, in December 2011, he joined forces with Rep. Paul Ryan of Wisconsin — then chairman of the House Budget Committee and later House speaker — to offer a plan to partially privatize and radically transform Medicare. The Democratic Party had already campaigned against — and condemned — Ryan's budget blueprint to change Medicare, and Wyden's move undermined the party's message. The Obama White House said the plan would "end Medicare as we know it." The Wyden-Ryan plan would have allowed insurers to compete with traditional Medicare and give patients subsidies they could use for either fee-for-service Medicare or private insurance.

The next summer, Ryan was chosen as Republican Mitt Romney's running mate in the presidential race. In arguing that Ryan's Medicare plan had bipartisan support, the Romney campaign cited Wyden. By then, Wyden had disavowed the plan. He denounced Romney's claims and sought to downplay his involvement with the plan by noting he had not drafted actual legislation with Ryan. But critics on the left complained that Wyden "gave cover" to Ryan while the Republicans were on the political defensive.

Wyden has long promoted a broad restructuring of the tax code, including reductions in tax rates and an expansion of the tax base by eliminating tax preferences and deductions. In 2010, he and Republican Judd Gregg of New Hampshire sponsored a measure with three income tax brackets — 15 percent, 25 percent and 35 percent — a lower corporate tax rate and immediate expensing of inventory and equipment for businesses with receipts under $1 million. Wyden has reintroduced the bill, undaunted by the challenge that Congress has become too polarized to find common ground on a bipartisan tax reform.

During his short-lived Finance chairmanship, which ended with the Republican takeover of the Senate in 2015, Wyden ran the committee with a lighter touch than his predecessors had — he even granted subcommittee chiefs more freedom to hold their own hearings. He didn't achieve much of what he wanted, in part because the leaders of his own party were leery of his independent ways. As The Washington Post put it, Wyden was "shoved aside by his majority leader, snubbed by his House counterpart and handcuffed by his president." The newspaper published a quote from a former aide to then-Senate Democratic Leader Harry Reid, Jim Manley, that was dismissive of Wyden's leadership style. "He's prone to quixotic causes and never really got into the nitty-gritty of the legislative process," Manley said.

The debate over the Trans-Pacific Partnership trade deal in 2015 allied Wyden with the Obama White House — albeit on the opposite side from most Democratic senators. Representing a Pacific Rim state heavily dependent on exports, Wyden was one of his party's most notable free-trade voices. Oregon is "the face of the opportunity to grow more good-paying jobs" from trade, he told the Post. Wyden and 11 other Democrats joined most Republicans in voting to give Obama expedited negotiating authority for the 12-nation trade deal. His critics expressed their dismay: Activists back home chased him with a blimp and an RV and AFL-CIO President Richard Trumka visited Portland just to scold Wyden and other free-trade backers in the state's delegation. Trump withdrew from the deal after taking office.

Wyden's attention to state issues, and his visibility at home — he holds forums in all 36 counties every year — have arguably made him the state's most popular and enduring politician. Wyden has been a staunch defender of Oregon's landmark assisted-suicide law. He irritated allies in the environmental movement by backing a proposed liquefied natural gas terminal at Coos Bay in southern Oregon; he touted its potential for jobs, but opponents said it would lead to significant greenhouse-gas emissions. When a company in 2016 withdrew its application for a liquefied natural gas site at the mouth of the Columbia River in northwest Oregon amid strong local opposition, Wyden said he was relieved, adding, "I shared the concerns that the … project would have had negative environmental and economic impacts."

With Merkley, Wyden opposed the 2018 nomination of Ryan Bounds, a federal prosecutor in Oregon, to a judgeship on the 9th U.S. Circuit Court of Appeals. On the Senate floor, they read extensive excerpts from earlier writings by Bounds that Wyden described as "appalling stuff" in its "disdain for multicultural values." In an unusual concession by Senate Republicans, Bounds' nomination was withdrawn in July 2018 after it became clear that he lacked support for confirmation. Wyden voiced relief, perhaps prematurely, hoping the move meant "the Senate [was] coming to its senses on judges."

In 2016, Wyden won a fourth full term 57%-33%, defeating Republican Mark Callahan, a perennial candidate who surprised even himself by winning a four-way primary for the GOP nomination.

After the election of Trump, Wyden voiced worry about other nations, especially Russia, hacking U.S. government computers — including in Congress. In September 2018, he wrote to Senate leaders, saying their security office had claimed it lacked the authority to defend senators and their aides. "This must change," he wrote. "Russia continues its attack on our democracy, and the Senate simply does not have the luxury of further delays." In March 2019, he and Republican Sen. Tom Cotton of Arkansas — another member of the Intelligence Committee — requested that Senate authorities immediately inform senators if their computer networks get hacked.

In early 2019, Wyden backed House Ways and Means Committee Chairman Richard Neal's attempts to obtain Trump's tax returns. He filed a bill that affirmed the authority of Congress to require the delivery of such records. "For four decades dating back to the Watergate era, presidents and candidates releasing their taxes has been the lowest ethical bar to clear," he told The Oregonian. His call for congressional activism was a reminder of the potential ramifications if Democrats regain Senate control and Wyden takes back the Finance Committee gavel.

Jeff Merkley (D)

Elected 2008, term expires 2020, 2nd term, b. Oct 24, 1956; Myrtle Creek; Stanford University (CA), B.A., 1979; Princeton University Woodrow Wilson School of Public and International Affairs (NJ), M.P.P., 1982; Lutheran; Married (Mary Sorteberg); 2 children.

Elected Office: OR House, 1999-2008, Speaker, 2007-2008.

Professional Career: President fellow, Office of the Secretary of Defense, 1982-1985; National security analyst, CBO, 1985-1989; Executive Director, Portland Habitat for Humanity, 1991-1994; Director of housing development, Human Solutions, 1995-1996; President, World Affairs Council of OR, 1996-2003.

DC Office: 313 HSOB 20510, 202-224-3753, Fax: 202-228-3997, merkley.senate.gov

State Offices: Bend, 541-318-1298; Eugene, 541-465-6750; Medford, 541-608-9102; Pendleton, 541-278-1129; Portland, 503-326-3386; Salem, 503-362-8102.

Committees: *Appropriations*: Agriculture, Rural Development, FDA & Related Agencies (RMM); Department of the Interior, Environment & Related Agencies; DOL, HHS & Education & Related Agencies; Energy & Water Development; State, Foreign Operations & Related Programs. *Budget*. *Environment & Public Works*: Clean Air & Nuclear Safety; Fisheries, Water, and Wildlife; Transportation & Infrastructure. *Foreign Relations*: East Asia, the Pacific & International

Cybersecurity Policy; Internat'l Dev Instit & Internat'l Econ, Energy & Environ Policy (RMM); State Dept & USAID Mngmnt, Internat'l Ops & Internat'l Dev.

Group Ratings

	ADA	ACLU	AFL-CIO	LCV	ITI	COC	HAFA	ACU	CFG	FRC
2018	-	86%	-	100%	-	40%	5%	9%	19%	0%
2017	100%	C	100%	100%	C	14%	C	0%	4%	0%

Almanac Ratings 2017-18

	Economy	Social	Foreign	Composite
Liberal	100%	100%	92%	97%
Conservative	0%	0%	8%	3%

Key Votes of the 115th Congress

1. Obama-care revision	N	5. Gun regulations	N	9. Kavanaugh confirmation	N
2. Tax Cuts	N	6. Family planning regs	N	10. Saudi arms sales	Y
3. Dodd-Frank revision	N	7. Gorsuch confirmation	N	11. FISA rules	N
4. Omnibus appropriations	N	8. Immigration restrictions	N	12. Military aid in Yemen	Y

Election Results

Election	Name (Party)	Vote (%)	Cand. Spent	Ind. Exp. Support	Ind. Exp. Oppose
2014 General	Jeff Merkley (D)	814,537 (56%)	$11,147,553	$198,099	$1,320,547
	Monica Wehby (R)	538,847 (37%)	$3,896,848	$747,941	$322,424
2014 Primary	Jeff Merkley (D)	256,365 (93%)			

Prior winning percentages: 2008 (49%)

Democrat Jeff Merkley, Oregon's junior senator, has attracted a following among activists beyond Oregon for a willingness to aggressively pursue his agenda. "I'm absolutely a risk-taker," Merkley said, "and it kind of catches people off guard." In spring 2016, Merkley became the only senator to endorse his colleague, Bernie Sanders of Vermont, for the Democratic presidential nomination. His hard-charging tactics have caused him to run afoul of the Democratic leader, Chuck Schumer of New York, at times.

In June 2018, Merkley received extensive news coverage when he traveled to a site along the southern border in McAllen, Texas, where hundreds of migrant children were housed after having been separated from their families. He sought entry into the facility as a senator, but the police denied him access. He said that the Trump administration had acted to "deliberately inflict trauma on [asylum-seekers'] children." Merkley explored a run for president in 2020. Among the hurdles: Oregon lawmakers were unwilling to change a state law that would have prohibited him from running for president while also seeking re-election to the Senate. He decided instead to put "all my efforts in through the Senate," he told Oregon Public Broadcasting in January 2019.

Merkley was born in Myrtle Creek in Oregon's Douglas County, where his parents worked at a sawmill. The sawmill closed when Merkley was 2, and his father went to work as a logger and a homebuilder in the neighboring town of Roseburg. When those jobs disappeared, the family moved to Portland, where his father took a job as a mechanic. He still resides in the East Portland neighborhood in which he grew up, and his kids went to the same schools that he attended. "My parents lived with an ethic of making sure they saved and spent very little money on frills," he recalled.

In high school, Merkley spent a summer in Ghana as part of the American Field Service Exchange Program. At Stanford University, he earned a bachelor's degree in international affairs. As an intern with the Carnegie Endowment for International Peace in 1980, he and a fellow intern traveled through Central America by bus. He earned a master's degree in public policy from Princeton University, landed a presidential fellowship at the Pentagon in 1982 and worked as an analyst in the Congressional Budget Office.

Merkley returned to Portland in the early 1990s and accepted a job as director of the city's Habitat for Humanity chapter, where he concentrated on affordable housing and skills training for at-risk youth and low-income families. He worked for the World Affairs Council in Oregon. Merkley was elected to the state House in 1998, having campaigned on a platform to improve the state's school system. In 2003, state House Democrats cited his consensus-building ability as they chose him for minority leader. Merkley exhibited his no-holds-barred side as he campaigned on behalf of Democratic candidates in 2006, including running a television ad that accused the Republican House speaker of covering up suspected sexual misconduct by her brother-in-law. State Republicans condemned the ad as over the line. Democrats won control of the Oregon House for the first time in 16 years, and Merkley was elected speaker.

He had a busy two years as speaker. The Legislature passed an expanded indoor smoking ban and extended more rights to same-sex couples. Merkley pushed through an ethics bill aimed at curbing gifts from lobbyists to lawmakers. He took on Oregon's payday loan industry with a bill that imposed an interest rate cap of 36 percent annually on consumer loans of less than $50,000, and he negotiated establishment of a rainy-day fund to protect schools and other state services from recessions; an increase in the state's corporate minimum tax paid for the fund. The Oregonian called the session "one of the most successful ... of recent years."

In 2008, after two House Democrats passed on the opportunity to challenge GOP Sen. Gordon Smith, Schumer — then chairman of the Democratic Senatorial Campaign Committee — recruited Merkley. "The fact that I ended up in that campaign was a real shock to me," Merkley reminisced years later. National Democrats thought he would appeal to the same voters who had elected the moderate and pragmatic Smith to two terms. Despite the endorsements and financial backing of his national party, Merkley faced stiff primary competition from liberal activist and political consultant Steve Novick, who had opposed Merkley's elevation to House minority leader five years earlier. Merkley initially ignored Novick and focused his campaign on Smith. But Novick labeled Merkley as pro-war for a vote cast in favor of a 2003 resolution that praised both President George W. Bush and U.S. troops for courage in the war against Iraq. Merkley won the primary 45%-42%.

The general election was among the most expensive and closely watched contests of 2008. Smith had broken with his party by voting for higher automobile mileage standards and against oil drilling in the Arctic National Wildlife Refuge. Merkley allied himself with Democratic presidential nominee Barack Obama and his campaign theme of change. The message resonated in a state where Bush's approval ratings were particularly weak. Smith touted his reputation for bipartisanship, particularly his good relationship with fellow Oregon Sen. Ron Wyden, a Democrat. He attempted to distance himself from Bush, running ads that featured shots of Wyden, Sen. Ted Kennedy of Massachusetts and even Obama. Merkley won 49%-46%. Smith had outraised Merkley $13 million to $7 million, but the DSCC and other outside groups poured in $11 million to help Merkley. The election gave Oregon two Democrats in the Senate for the first time in 40 years.

"When he was running, people didn't expect him to be quite as progressive as he turned out to be," Tim Carpenter of the Progressive Democrats of America said. Arriving on Capitol Hill just months after the financial crisis of 2008 began, Merkley hammered Wall Street. During debate over the 2010 Dodd-Frank law on financial regulation, he joined Democrat Carl Levin of Michigan to craft a tough version of the "Volcker Rule" banning banks from engaging in risky investment practices that may have contributed to the crisis. Their provision remained in the final bill, albeit in a weakened version.

Merkley was one of 11 Democrats to oppose Obama's nomination of Ben Bernanke in 2010 for a second term as Federal Reserve chairman. He contended Bernanke was partly at fault for the recession and was the wrong person to trust with an economic recovery. Four years later, Merkley was among the progressives whose opposition stymied Obama's plan to nominate former Treasury Secretary Larry Summers to succeed Bernanke; the party's left wing saw Summers as too accommodating to Wall Street. Merkley also joined progressive Democrats in the debate over the Affordable Care Act, as they unsuccessfully pushed for a Senate vote on a government-run "public option" to compete with private insurers.

Merkley has courted progressive activists outside the Beltway. "He gets the value of an inside-outside partnership — of really using pressure from around the country to get Washington, D.C., to pay attention," said Adam Green, co-founder of the Progressive Change Campaign Committee. In turn, some progressive activists floated his name as a running mate for Clinton before the Democratic National Convention in July 2016. Notwithstanding his limited name recognition outside his home state and a reputation as a less-than-fiery stump speaker, they argued Merkley would bring progressive enthusiasm to the ticket. Three months earlier, Merkley had stood alone among his Senate colleagues in endorsing Sanders. "It doesn't feel lonely, it just feels right," Merkley told The Atlantic, adding, "I think we need to fundamentally change the system that has been so deeply moving towards consolidation of power by the very few."

Earlier, when Senate Democrats were in the majority, Merkley lobbied outside groups to support efforts to restrict the GOP's ability to block progressive-backed legislation via a filibuster. "The clear and undeniable fact is that the Senate is broken," he said. "Thoughtful deliberation does not occur and far too much gets lost in a tangle of obstruction and delay." Merkley joined Democratic Sen. Tom Udall of New Mexico on a proposal to ban filibustering of motions to proceed to legislation. Initially, Senate leaders resisted their efforts. But in 2013, Majority Leader Harry Reid pushed through a no-filibuster rule for most judicial and executive-branch appointments — expanded in 2017 by the GOP and Majority Leader Mitch McConnell, in the face of a filibuster of President Donald Trump's Supreme Court nominee.

By that time, with the Democrats in the minority, Merkley's perspective on filibustering had shifted. In January 2017, even before Trump nominated Neil Gorsuch to the high court, Merkley vowed to filibuster the nominee — utilizing Senate procedures to exact revenge for McConnell's refusal to allow hearings or a vote on Obama's nominee for the same seat, Merrick Garland, a year earlier. According to Politico, an irritated Schumer warned Merkley about making the battle about retribution for Garland instead of the nominee's merits. Shortly before McConnell's move to change the filibuster rules on nominations, Merkley delivered the eighth-longest floor speech in Senate history; it was nearly 15 hours and 30 minutes long. He charged the Republicans had "stolen" a Supreme Court seat and detailed Democratic concerns about Gorsuch. McConnell already had set the vote on the Senate rules change, and Merkley's move did not delay Senate business.

Merkley was aligned with Sanders, Warren and other leading progressives — and against most Oregon legislators, as well as Obama — in opposing the Trans-Pacific Partnership trade deal in 2015. While free trade receives notable support in export-friendly Oregon, Merkley opposed the pact. "Here we are repeating the same basic structure of the other agreements with no changes for America and therefore no improvement for the workers," he said in a floor speech.

As a follow-on to his advocacy for extending rights to same-sex couples while speaker of the Oregon House, Merkley played a leading role in drafting and moving the Employment Non-Discrimination Act, which would protect members of the LGBTQ community from job discrimination. The legislation passed 64-32 in November 2013 with bipartisan backing. The bill didn't make it out of the House. Prominent on Merkley's office wall is a letter from Kennedy — for years the Senate's leading liberal voice — turning over leadership on the issue to Merkley.

Representing a state where the sale of both medical and recreational marijuana is legal, Merkley has filed legislation since 2015 to allow Veterans Affairs physicians to discuss marijuana as a treatment option for pain and symptoms related to post-traumatic stress disorder. With Republican Sen. Steve Daines of Montana — another state where medical marijuana is legal — Merkley sponsored a bill to make medicinal cannabis easier to access for veterans. In both 2015 and 2016, the Senate and House approved amendments to appropriations bills for which Merkley had advocated. But the marijuana language was quietly stripped in House-Senate conference committees. Merkley blasted the removal as "outrageous" but failed to get the provision reinserted.

In 2018, he made progress on steps to legalize hemp and make it readily available. This time, he had the vital assistance of McConnell, who has become an advocate for hemp, a productive home-state crop; hemp is derived from a cannabis plant but does not provide a high like marijuana and is typically used as a fiber. With Wyden and Rand Paul, the other two senators from their states, Merkley and McConnell won approval of the Hemp Farming Act as part of the sweeping farm bill that was enacted in December 2018. That legislation defined hemp as an agricultural commodity and removed it from the list of controlled substances. Merkley welcomed the result. "This is a cash crop that hasn't been allowed to meet its full economic potential because of outdated restrictions," he said. Meanwhile, Merkley teamed with Democratic Sen. Cory Booker of New Jersey on a bill that would legalize marijuana nationwide.

Merkley returned to the southern border in December 2018, this time with several other congressional Democrats, and visited an encampment where 2,700 migrant children were being held near El Paso. "This is a child prison strategy that inflicts trauma on children," he said. "It's part of the broader strategy of the Trump administration. ... It's completely unacceptable." He was again denied access to the facility. Republicans accused him of grandstanding.

Republicans hoped to unseat Merkley in 2014 by seeking to portray him as out of touch with most Oregon voters. Monica Wehby, a pediatric neurosurgeon with moderate positions, took 50 percent of the vote in a five-way GOP primary. Subsequent media reports alleged that Wehby had "stalked" her ex-husband and a former boyfriend. No charges were ever filed, and Wehby blamed Democrats for trying to "shred" her family. But she never recovered politically from the allegations. Freedom Partners, a group connected to the conservative billionaire Koch brothers, poured money into the race in a year when Democrats suffered a net loss of nine Senate seats. Merkley won 56%-37%. By spring 2019, no Republican had stepped forward to challenge him for re-election to the Senate.

Suzanne Bonamici (D)

Elected 2012, 4th term, b. Oct 14, 1954; Detroit, MI; Lane Community College (OR), A.A.; University of Oregon Law School, J.D.; University of Oregon (OR), B.A., 1980; Episcopalian; Married (Michael H. Simon); 2 children.

Elected Office: OR House, 2007-2008; OR Senate, 2008-2011.

Professional Career: Attorney, Federal Trade Commission, 1983-1986; Practicing attorney, 1986-1989; Legislative aide, 2001-2006.

DC Office: 2231 RHOB 20515, 202-225-0855, Fax: 202-225-9497, bonamici.house.gov

State Offices: Beaverton, 503-469-6010.

Committees: *Education & Labor*: Civil Rights & Human Services (Chmn); Higher Education & Workforce Investment. *Science, Space & Technology*: Environment; Investigations & Oversight. *Select Committee on the Climate Crisis.*

Group Ratings

	ADA	ACLU	AFL-CIO	LCV	ITI	COC	HAFA	ACU	CFG	FRC
2018	-	86%	-	97%	-	58%	8%	4%	17%	0%
2017	95%	C	95%	100%	C	43%	C	7%	5%	0%

Almanac Ratings 2017-18

	Economy	Social	Foreign	Composite
Liberal	97%	98%	97%	98%
Conservative	3%	2%	3%	2%

Key Votes of the 115th Congress

1. Obama-care revision	N	5. Family planning regs	N	9. Guantanamo prisoners	Y
2. Tax Cuts	N	6. Body cameras/immigration	Y	10. Ground missiles, limit	Y
3. Omnibus appropriations	Y	7. Abortion ban	N	11. Defense Dept. spending	N
4. Dodd-Frank revision	N	8. Concealed carry	N	12. FISA rules	N

Election Results

Election	Name (Party)	Vote (%)		Cand. Spent	Ind. Exp. Support	Ind. Exp. Oppose
2018 General	Suzanne Bonamici (D)	231,198	(64%)	$526,249		
	John Verbeek (R)	116,446	(32%)			
	Drew Layda (Lib)	15,121	(4%)		$0	
2018 Primary	Suzanne Bonamici (D)	69,774	(92%)			

Prior winning percentages: 2016 (60%), 2014 (57%), 2012 (60%), 2012 special (54%)

Democrat Suzanne Bonamici, who won a special election in 2012, usually has been a reliable liberal. The chief exception has been that she is responsive to the needs and overseas interests of local businesses, often to the dismay of unions on international trade issues. Her coastal district has increased her advocacy on climate change.

Bonamici was born in Detroit and grew up in the small town of Northville Michigan. Her father worked at a local bank, and her mother was a piano teacher. After high school, Bonamici traveled with friends in a van to Oregon, fell in love with the state and moved to Eugene. "It was a very '70s thing to do," Bonamici told The Oregonian. She attended Lane Community College and worked at a legal-aid center in Eugene. Bonamici got her bachelor's and law degrees from the University of Oregon. She moved to Washington D.C. to take a job as a consumer protection lawyer at the Federal Trade Commission. There, she met her husband and they relocated to Oregon, where Bonamici was a lawyer in private practice. After working as a legislative assistant in the Oregon House of Representatives, she won her own state House seat and focused on consumer protection. She was appointed to fill a vacancy in the state Senate and then was elected.

When Democratic Rep. David Wu resigned amid charges of improper sexual advances, Bonamici jumped into the Democratic primary in the special election. She faced off against state Labor Commissioner Brad Avakian and state Rep. Brad Witt; both opposed U.S. trade pacts with Colombia, Panama and South Korea that were being debated in Congress. Bonamici initially declined to take a position and drew criticism for indecisiveness. She then came out in favor of the South Korea pact. She raised the most money of the three candidates and won with 66 percent of the vote.

In the general, Bonamici faced Rob Cornilles, a sports business consultant. Cornilles played up his business experience and kept his distance from the national GOP. Bonamici ran an ad attacking Cornilles for an old federal tax lien against his business over failure to pay payroll taxes. The Democratic Congressional Campaign Committee moved early to paint Cornilles as a tea party extremist. The DCCC, EMILY's List and other liberal interest groups poured millions into the race, while national Republican groups mostly stayed away. Bonamici won, 54%-40%.

On the Education and the Workforce Committee, she focused on making college more affordable and reforming the No Child Left Behind Act. On the renewal of student-loan legislation in 2014, she worked with others to add increased financial counseling for recipients. She was a founder of the bipartisan Congressional STEAM Caucus, which encourages innovation in science, technology, engineering, art and design, and math education. In 2019, Bonamici became chairwoman of the revamped Subcommittee on Civil Rights and Human Services, where she promised "meaningful oversight" of the Trump administration and steps to "expand opportunities for people of all backgrounds."

As the ranking Democrat on the Science, Space and Technology Subcommittee on Environment in 2015, she focused on global climate change, including ocean policy. In 2017, she enacted her bill to improve warnings and education in coastal communities about the threat of tsunamis. With Republican Rep. Don Young of Alaska, she wrote an op-ed in 2018 about the economic stakes in protecting the health of the oceans, including marine life. In 2019, she co-chaired the Oceans Caucus and was a member of the Select Committee on the Climate Crisis, where she pledged to fight for comprehensive policies to "protect our planet."

In 2015, Bonamici was one of 28 House Democrats who voted to give trade promotion authority to President Barack Obama, whose prospective Trans-Pacific Partnership was touted as an economic boon for West Coast companies and ports. "Our economy is increasingly global, and trade done right creates jobs, helps businesses grow and puts our country on stronger economic footing," she said. She cited the benefits for local wheat and potato farmers. She accompanied Obama on a visit to Nike headquarters, where he said that the deal would benefit Oregon companies. A few days later, AFL-CIO President Richard Trumka spoke in Portland and warned that he was "blowing the whistle, quite frankly" on Bonamici and other Portland-area Democrats in Congress for being on "the wrong side" of TPP, which he said most Oregonians opposed.

Bonamici has been reelected easily. Despite the threat of a challenge backed by organized labor or a loss of enthusiasm among her base, she suffered neither. In the Democratic primary in 2016, her opponent was Shabba Woodley, a 25-year-old videographer who had no money or political experience and read poetry to a reporter. Bonamici won the primary with 90 percent of the vote. Likewise, her Republican opponent, Brian Heinrich, was a sales representative who was running his first campaign. He did not file a campaign-finance report. Bonamici won, 60%-37%, and retained support from a broad array of interest groups. She was reelected in 2018 with no Democratic primary and with comparable ease.

OR-1: Northwest Oregon

Cook Partisan Voting Index: D+9

Population		Race and Ethnicity		Income	
Total	817,756	White	71.7%	Median Income	$70,350
Land area (sq. miles)	3,007	Black	1.6%	District Income Rank	93
Pop/ sq mi	271.9	Latino	14.5%	Poverty Rate	10.8%
Born in State	44.1%	Asian	7.5%	With health insurance	92.2%
		Two or more races	3.9%	Cash public assistance	2.8%
Age Groups		Other	0.8%	Food stamp/SNAP	12.8%
Under 18	23%				
18-34	22.9%	**Education**		**Work**	
35-64	40.5%	H.S grad or less	28%	White Collar	13.6%
Over 64	13.6%	Some college	31.7%	Sales and Service	38.4%
		College Degree, 4 yr	24.9%	Blue Collar	17.8%
Military		Post grad	15.3%	Government	10.3%
Veteran/ Active Duty	8.2%				

2012 Pres. Vote	Obama	200,993	(57%)	Romney	140,462	(40%)			
2016 Pres. Vote	Clinton	219,369	(55%)	Trump	132,195	(33%)	Johnson	22,061	(6%)
	Stein	9,036	(2%)						

Western Portland Area: Just over the hills from downtown Portland are the valleys and interstices between green mountains of suburban Washington County. This was once farm country, with 39,000 people in 1940; now it has almost 575,000 and is an integral part of metro Portland. Its population zoomed up 70 percent between 1990 and 2010, with an increase of another 59,000 in the next seven years. Its towns enjoy a high-tech, healthy-lifestyle affluence, cushioned by protected forests and anchored by major employers that include Tektronix, Intel, IBM and Columbia Sportswear. Like Silicon Valley, the Silicon Forest has an environment that appeals to a highly skilled workforce. Nestled at the foot of mountains, it is woodsy and even rustic, but is outfitted with all the comforts of modern life. The Asian population of the county is 11 percent.

Near Beaverton is the world headquarters of Nike, housed in 22 buildings spread over 200 acres, with 12,000 local employees. Intel is the largest private employer in the state with 20,000, many of them at a 530-acre campus in Hillsboro, with plans in early 2019 for a huge expansion of the campus to house the next generation of computer chips. The company controls about 96 percent of the chip market; the tech industry's move away from standard chips has led Intel to new markets, such as data and memory. Biotech firm Genentech has a presence in Hillsboro.

The 1st Congressional District of Oregon includes the western slice of Portland and all of suburban Washington County, which includes two-thirds of the voters. It extends nearly 100 miles northwest from Portland along the Columbia River to the rain-swept port of Astoria on the Pacific Coast, where Lewis and Clark spent the winter of 1805-06. (The event is memorialized at the Lewis and Clark National Historical Park.) Yamhill County and Beaverton are known for wineries. Astoria, which retains many century-old buildings, has been a popular site to shoot movies. Like Oregon overall, the 1st was historically New England Republican, electing only Republicans to Congress from 1892 to 1972. It trended left on cultural issues, and since 1974 it has elected only Democrats. Hillary Clinton won 55 percent of the presidential vote in 2016.

Greg Walden (R)

Elected 1998, 11th term, b. Jan 10, 1957; The Dalles; University of Alaska, Att., 1975; University of Oregon, B.S., 1981; Episcopalian; Married (Mylene Ann Simons Walden); 1 child.

Elected Office: OR House, 1989-1995, Majority Leader, 1991-1993; OR Senate, 1995-1997.

Professional Career: Press Secretary, U.S. Rep. Denny Smith, 1981-1984, chief of Staff, 1984-1986; Owner, Columbia Gorge Broadcasters Inc., 1986-2008.

DC Office: 2185 RHOB 20515, 202-225-6730, Fax: 202-225-5774, walden.house.gov

State Offices: Bend, 541-389-4408; La Grande, 541-624-2400; Medford, 541-776-4646.

Committees: *Energy & Commerce (RMM)*: Ex Officio membership on all subcommittees.

Group Ratings

	ADA	ACLU	AFL-CIO	LCV	ITI	COC	HAFA	ACU	CFG	FRC
2018	-	7%	-	6%	-	92%	41%	64%	45%	100%
2017	0%	C	29%	9%	C	92%	C	74%	43%	100%

Almanac Ratings 2017-18

	Economy	Social	Foreign	Composite
Liberal	8%	4%	10%	7%
Conservative	92%	97%	90%	93%

Key Votes of the 115th Congress

1. Obama-care revision	Y	5. Family planning regs	Y	9. Guantanamo prisoners	N
2. Tax Cuts	Y	6. Body cameras/immigration	N	10. Ground missiles, limit	N
3. Omnibus appropriations	Y	7. Abortion ban	Y	11. Defense Dept. spending	Y
4. Dodd-Frank revision	Y	8. Concealed carry	Y	12. FISA rules	Y

Election Results

Election	Name (Party)	Vote (%)		Cand. Spent	Ind. Exp. Support	Ind. Exp. Oppose
2018 General	Greg Walden (R)	207,597	(56%)	$4,551,369		
	Jamie McLeod-Skinner (D)	145,298	(39%)	$1,302,289		
	Mark Roberts (I)	15,536	(4%)			
2018 Primary	Greg Walden (R)	71,543	(78%)			
	Paul Romero (R)	15,181	(17%)			
	Randy Pollock (R)	5,514	(6%)			

Prior winning percentages: 2016 (72%), 2014 (70%), 2012 (69%), 2010 (74%), 2008 (70%), 2006 (67%), 2004 (72%), 2002 (72%), 2000 (74%), 1998 (62%)

Greg Walden, elected in 1998, has emerged as one of the Republican Party's most highly regarded inside strategists. After two successful terms as chairman of the National Republican Congressional Committee, he became chairman of the influential Energy and Commerce Committee in 2017. That made for a rocky start as Walden and other senior committee members worked behind the scenes with GOP leaders in a frantic effort to deliver on their promise to repeal and replace the Affordable Care Act. After that eventual failure, he took action on other health care issues before Republicans lost their House majority. Unexpectedly, Walden encountered political problems at home.

Walden grew up on an 80-acre cherry orchard near The Dalles in the Columbia River Gorge. His father ran radio stations that had been in the family since the 1930s and also served in the state House. Walden followed both pursuits. As a young man, he was a disc jockey and talk show host. Then, he got involved in politics as press secretary and chief of staff for local Republican Rep. Denny Smith from 1981 to 1987. Walden returned to Hood River to run the family's five-station broadcast business,

Columbia Gorge Broadcasters. In 1988, he was elected to the state House, eventually becoming majority leader.

When the 2nd District seat opened in 1998, Walden ran and faced substantial primary opposition from Perry Atkinson, a Christian broadcaster who was backed financially by Gary Bauer's Campaign for Working Americans. Walden stayed competitive by raising $500,000 and prevailed over Atkinson with 55 percent of the vote. In the anticlimactic general election against a conservative Democrat, Walden won 61%-35%. He went 20 years before he faced a competitive reelection challenge in his comfortably Republican district.

In the House, Walden has been a mainstream Republican who leans to the center on cultural issues. He caught the eye of Republican leaders with his political knowledge, knack for forming friendships and devotion to the party agenda. In early 2010, Minority Leader John Boehner picked Walden to chair the Republican leadership. When Republicans reclaimed the majority that fall, Walden helped steer the GOP's transition to power, handling issues ranging from rules changes governing debate to steps to economize on House operations.

After the 2012 election, Walden was unanimously elected chairman of the NRCC. Although the midterm environment was considered highly favorable for his party, Walden's confidence in a wave election startled even fellow Republicans. Walden touted a "Drive for 245," which would require a double-digit increase in Republican seats. Some Republicans dismissed it as an unrealistic fundraising ploy, and lamented the Democrats' ability to outraise them. Two junior Republicans floated the idea of challenging Walden for another term. Some anonymous Republicans wondered in print whether he was too nice. That talk disappeared after Republicans reaped 247 seats, their largest House majority since 1928. Walden was unopposed for another term as NRCC chairman.

Walden has kept busy on the policy side. In 2011, he took over as chairman of the Energy and Commerce Telecommunications Subcommittee, a prime niche for an ex-broadcaster. As a critic of the Federal Communications Commission and its Obama-era policies, he waged a fierce battle against the regulators. Walden filed legislation that would require the FCC to justify any rule change by identifying market implications or potential harm to consumers. His bill passed the House in 2012, but the Democratic-controlled Senate did not take it up.

Walden clashed with the FCC and vowed to upend its proposed internet rules, known as "net neutrality," which prohibit tiered pricing by phone and cable companies; many Republicans viewed them as excessive interference in the market. His bill passed the House in 2011 but also died in the Senate. Walden co-authored a letter to Obama asking him to halt net neutrality rules expected to take effect. The administration ignored his letter. In 2015, the FCC under Chairman Tom Wheeler issued its final net neutrality rules. Although Walden pursued legislative alternatives, the Obama administration's embrace of Wheeler left his critics with few options. That quickly changed after the 2016 election when President Donald Trump named new leaders at the FCC. One of their first actions was repeal of the net neutrality rules.

Walden has had a hand in national issues that affect his rural district. He played a central role in 2003 in assembling bipartisan support for the Healthy Forests Restoration Act, which was a legislative response to wildfires raging across the West worsened by unlogged dry timber. Walden has worked to curb regulations under the Endangered Species Act by encouraging a greater role for outside scientists to review government proposals. In an effort to restore timber payments to rural counties, he joined forces with home-state Democrats. In 2015, Walden added to a time-urgent Medicare bill his plan, cosponsored by Oregon Democratic Rep. Peter DeFazio, to give hundreds of millions of dollars of aid to rural counties that suffered from reduced timber sales.

Going into the 2016 campaign cycle, Walden and the NRCC were widely expected to be on the defensive. Although the GOP majority seemed secure, a double-digit loss of seats was considered likely. His task became all the more challenging when Trump had a limited, or chilly, relationship with many House Republicans, who worried that he had become a drag on their own election prospects. In the end, some benefited from Trump's relative strength in exurban and rural districts; Democrats failed to take advantage of opportunities in suburban districts where Trump ran relatively poorly. With the NRCC's strategic advice and spending in battleground districts, the GOP's loss of only six House seats was viewed as an impressive accomplishment for Walden.

During that campaign, his eyes were on a bigger prize: With Fred Upton of Michigan term-limited as Energy and Commerce chairman after 2016, Walden quietly made known his interest in taking the reins. His chief opponent was John Shimkus of Illinois, who had impressive accomplishments on energy and environmental issues. Walden had the big advantage of having protected the Republican majority for four years. He won with the support of many Republicans who owed their seat — or their chairmanship — to him. Speaker Paul Ryan reportedly backed Walden, despite the seniority advantage for Shimkus.

As committee chairman, Walden turned his attention to Republican efforts to revise the Affordable Care Act. Prior to the 217-213 passage of the bill in May 2017, Walden and others on his committee worked with Ways and Means Republicans plus GOP leaders in the painstaking deliberations to build majority support. Their objective, he said, was "how to best achieve the goals of protecting America's sickest patients and maintaining market stability … without Obamacare's unpopular individual mandate." Two months later, the bill died in the Senate.

Walden was more successful with other proposals. In December 2017, he enacted a bill to authorize the Food and Drug Administration to approve emergency uses for medical products that reduce deaths and injuries in a military emergency. He enacted a separate bill to speed up FDA's approval process for many generic drugs and to encourage the development of inexpensive hearing aids. In October 2018, he coordinated final action on sweeping legislation designed to treat and reduce incidents of opioid addiction.

Given his experience at the NRCC, Walden was hopeful that these legislative results would improve reelection prospects for House Republicans. In that sense, he fell short. At home, Walden encountered his most competitive reelection challenge. Democrat Jamie McLeod-Skinner, a former civic administrator, said that it was time for the nation to "get back to basics," especially on health care. She avoided negative attacks. McLeod-Skinner had the support of several liberal groups and spent $1.3 million. Walden spent $4.6 million. He won, 56%-39%, his first reelection with less than 67 percent of the vote. McLeod-Skinner took the population center of Bend-based Deschutes County by 1,000 votes.

Following the election, Walden showed increased independence from Trump. In February 2019, he was one of 13 House Republicans who voted with Democrats to oppose the president's declaration of a national emergency to finance a wall at the border with Mexico. "I strongly object to any president acting outside of those explicit authorities to spend money that Congress has not appropriated for specific initiatives," he said.

OR-2: Eastern Oregon   Cook Partisan Voting Index: R+11

Population		Race and Ethnicity		Income	
Total	794,957	White	80.3%	Median Income	$48,797
Land area (sq. miles)	69,443	Black	0.6%	District Income Rank	329
Pop/ sq mi	11.4	Latino	13.5%	Poverty Rate	16.1%
Born in State	44.4%	Asian	1%	With health insurance	89.8%
		Two or more races	2.7%	Cash public assistance	3.6%
Age Groups		Other	1.9%	Food stamp/SNAP	20.2%
Under 18	22%				
18-34	20%	**Education**		**Work**	
35-64	38.6%	H.S grad or less	39.5%	White Collar	19.4%
Over 64	19.4%	Some college	36.3%	Sales and Service	43.5%
		College Degree, 4 yr	15.4%	Blue Collar	24.5%
Military		Post grad	8.8%	Government	14.6%
Veteran/ Active Duty	11.1%				

2012 Pres. Vote	Romney	196,568	(56%)	Obama	139,940	(40%)			
2016 Pres. Vote	Trump	215,711	(55%)	Clinton	139,059	(35%)	Johnson	18,600	(5%)
	Stein	8,191	(2%)						

Medford, Bend: The Cascade Mountains that wall off eastern Oregon from the rest of the state are a magnificent chain of once active volcanic mountains that drain almost every drop of moisture out of the air blowing in from the Pacific Ocean. They separate green, wet western Oregon from brown, parched eastern Oregon. The eastern part has 70 percent of the state's land, but only around half a million of its 4 million people, many of whom still make their living off the land: beef and dairy cattle, timber and lumber, fish from the Columbia River, and wheat and sugar beets from the irrigated plains. The effect of the Cascades can be felt in the one place they are breached —the Columbia River Gorge. Here, funneled winds pound in steadily from the west, making the confluence of the Columbia and Hood rivers the best windsurfing site in the United States. One of the world's largest wind farms, Shepherds Flat, became operational here in 2012.

The 2nd Congressional District of Oregon covers nearly three-fourths of the state: everything east of the Cascades and the southernmost valley between the Cascades and the Coast Range. Much of this land is forested and unpopulated. In Bend and the surrounding area, sawmills have closed, but the wilderness and high desert plateau have attracted software developers, outdoor activity, upscale tourists and telecommuters. With its 23 percent growth between 2010 and 2017, Bend has been one of the fastest-growing cities in the nation. CNBC reported in March 2018 that the city is so appealing — and relatively cheap — that some workers commute to their Silicon Valley jobs, in California. The influx of techies has shifted politics toward the center in surrounding Deschutes County, the largest in the district.

In the town of The Dalles, Google operates a data center on 30 acres of land on the Columbia River. The facility was a pioneer when it opened in 2006. Since then, Google has expanded its campus with a total investment of close to $2 billion. Oregon is an appealing site for these power-intensive facilities because it has no sales tax. To the south, other tech giants — including Apple and Facebook -- have taken advantage of property tax breaks and opened huge data centers in once-tiny Prineville. With expanded solar energy, the area has quickly boosted its electrical power. "Maybe Prineville will be visible from outer space," the Oregonian speculated in February 2018.

The 2nd District has been heavily Republican. This is part of the leave-us-alone Rocky Mountain Basin, not the hipster West Coast. Court decisions protecting the spotted owl hurt the logging industry here. In 2009, rural Jackson County saw its last remaining large sawmill dismantled; it had 91 in its heyday. In 2014, according to The Oregonian, "the pendulum had swung so far that Oregon's high-tech industry accounted for the same number of workers and share of wages as the forest sector did in the 1970s." This has become the only district in Oregon where Republican presidential candidates are competitive. Donald Trump got 55 percent of the vote.

Earl Blumenauer (D)

Elected 1996, 12th full term, b. Aug 16, 1948; Portland; Lewis & Clark College (OR), B.A., 1970; Northwestern Law School, Lewis and Clark College (OR), J.D., 1976; Married (Margaret Kirkpatrick Blumenauer); 2 children.

Elected Office: OR House, 1973-1978; Multnomah County Commissioner, 1978- 86; Portland City Council, 1986-1996.

Professional Career: Assistant to President, Portland St. University, 1970-1977; Portland Community College Board of Director, 1975-1981.

DC Office: 1111 LHOB 20515, 202-225-4811, Fax: 202-225-8941, blumenauer.house.gov

State Offices: Portland, 503-231-2300.

Committees: *Ways & Means*: Health; Trade (Chmn).

Group Ratings

	ADA	ACLU	AFL-CIO	LCV	ITI	COC	HAFA	ACU	CFG	FRC
2018	-	93%	-	97%	-	45%	13%	13%	38%	0%
2017	100%	C	92%	100%	C	36%	C	8%	5%	0%

Almanac Ratings 2017-18

	Economy	Social	Foreign	Composite
Liberal	98%	95%	97%	97%
Conservative	2%	5%	3%	3%

Key Votes of the 115th Congress

1. Obama-care revision	N	5. Family planning regs	N	9. Guantanamo prisoners	Y
2. Tax Cuts	N	6. Body cameras/immigration	Y	10. Ground missiles, limit	Y
3. Omnibus appropriations	N	7. Abortion ban	N	11. Defense Dept. spending	N
4. Dodd-Frank revision	N	8. Concealed carry	N	12. FISA rules	N

Election Results

Election	Name (Party)	Vote (%)		Cand. Spent	Ind. Exp. Support	Ind. Exp. Oppose
2018 General	Earl Blumenauer (D)......................	279,019	(73%)	$1,035,347		
	Tom Harrison (R)...............................	76,187	(20%)			
	Marc Koller (I)................................	21,352	(6%)			
2018 Primary	Earl Blumenauer (D).........................	91,226	(91%)			
	Ben Lavine (D)......................................	6,008	(6%)			

Prior winning percentages: 2016 (72%), 2014 (72%), 2012 (75%), 2010 (70%), 2008 (75%), 2006 (74%), 2004 (71%), 2002 (67%), 2000 (67%), 1998 (84%), 1996 (67%)

Democrat Earl Blumenauer, who won a special election in 1996, has pursued an idiosyncratic approach that is socially liberal with a "smart growth" economic approach that has sought to combat urban sprawl. On the Ways and Means Committee, he unexpectedly was selected chairman of the International Trade subcommittee despite support of some — but not all -- trade deals that in recent years has placed him among a minority of Democrats. He is known for his distinctive bow ties and bike rides.

Blumenauer grew up in Portland and graduated from Lewis and Clark College and its Northwestern Law School. In his teens, he was inspired by the civil rights and anti-war movements of the 1960s. In college, he headed a statewide campaign to lower Oregon's voting age. He has held public office for almost all his adult life. In 1972, at age 23, he was elected to the Oregon House. He subsequently was elected as a Multnomah County commissioner and as a Portland city councilor; in the latter job, he also served as commissioner of public works.

He championed many of the policies that have made Portland distinctive — regional light-rail transit, curbside recycling and aggressive land-use planning. He encouraged bicycle riding and "regional rail summits," which bring neighborhood residents into the planning for higher densities at transit nodes. Blumenauer has had some setbacks, notably when he lost the 1992 mayoral race. He was the obvious successor when Ron Wyden was elected to the Senate, and he won the special election 68%-25%. His campaign slogan was "Vote Earl, Vote Often." In his Democratic bastion, he has never drawn less than 67 percent of the vote since and has not faced a serious primary challenge.

Blumenauer has had a consistently liberal voting record, as shown by his Almanac vote ratings. He has been a lead sponsor of a bill allowing states to legalize medical marijuana and to regulate it in a manner similar to alcohol. "We're still arresting two-thirds of a million people for use of a substance that a majority feel should be legal," Blumenauer told The Associated Press. In 2015, the House narrowly defeated a proposal that he cosponsored to give states the authority to legalize marijuana. In April 2016, Rolling Stone profiled him as the "top legal pot advocate," and quoted him saying there has been a "sea change" in support within Congress.

Blumenauer, who has ridden his bicycle everywhere he travels around Washington, formed a Congressional Bike Caucus. Blumenauer was astonished to find that the House subsidized parking for employees, but not mass transit; now employees can get subsidized transit fares. He is interested in what seem like quixotic projects now, but may seem less so in time: an interstate highway system for bicycle paths and reduced dependence on driving as a tool to improve public health. "The rise of bicycles is a metaphor for change in this country," Blumenauer says. To rescue the depleted highway trust fund, he has called for a 15-cent hike per gallon in the federal gas tax over a three-year period, plus eventual movement toward a mileage-based tax. GOP leaders did not permit a vote on his plan during debate of a highway bill in 2015. When Democrats took House control in 2019, he sought to make increased transportation funding a top priority.

On economic issues, he has actively promoted trade across the Pacific, a key element of Portland's economy. He was an outspoken supporter of approving Trade Promotion Authority for President Barack Obama, noting in 2015 that "Oregon will not only be able to export more of its products, but also its values," including human rights, worker rights and environmental protections. He was caustic in criticizing other House Democrats, including party leaders, for their votes against extending trade adjustment assistance for workers adversely affected by overseas trade deals. "Political gamesmanship within our party won out over substance," he said. He complained that tariffs imposed on U.S.-designed footwear imported from Asia discriminate against companies like Oregon's Nike.

With what critics have called his "business-friendly" background, he won a majority of the 25 Ways and Means Democrats to become Trade Subcommittee chairman when they organized the committee in January 2019. In the seniority-based selection, which started with an up-or-down vote on the most senior member seeking a post, Blumenauer was selected over Rep. Bill Pascrell of New Jersey. The outcome was significant because the House faced a busy trade agenda, including review of President Donald Trump's revision of the U.S. trade deal with Canada and Mexico. Blumenauer insisted that he was not a single-minded free-trader. In an interview with Huffington Post, he said that he had voted against trade agreements with Central America and Colombia and that he had been "all over the Obama people because they weren't aggressive enough" in enforcing trade rules. In August 2018, he criticized Trump's "senseless" tariffs for "inflicting unnecessary damage to Oregon's agriculture."

In April 2017, Blumenauer filed a bill to create a panel of former presidents and vice presidents to issue a statement if they determine a president is "unable to discharge the powers and duties of office" and should be removed from office, consistent with the 25th Amendment to the Constitution. He told reporters in Portland that his proposal was directed at Trump and that he had spoken with professionals who believed that "clinical" problems were driving the president's behavior," The Oregonian reported. Five other House Democrats cosponsored his proposal.

OR-3: Multnomah County · Cook Partisan Voting Index: D+24

Population		Race and Ethnicity		Income	
Total	820,929	White	71.4%	Median Income	$60,395
Land area (sq. miles)	1,074	Black	5.1%	District Income Rank	175
Pop/ sq mi	764	Latino	11.2%	Poverty Rate	16.1%
Born in State	43.7%	Asian	6.7%	With health insurance	90.9%
		Two or more races	4.2%	Cash public assistance	4.4%
Age Groups		Other	1.5%	Food stamp/SNAP	18.7%
Under 18	20.1%				
18-34	26.1%	**Education**		**Work**	
35-64	41.3%	H.S grad or less	28.8%	White Collar	12.5%
Over 64	12.5%	Some college	31.5%	Sales and Service	39.7%
		College Degree, 4 yr	24.6%	Blue Collar	17.5%
Military		Post grad	15.2%	Government	12.1%
Veteran/ Active Duty	6.7%				

2012 Pres. Vote	Obama	268,004	(72%)	Romney	91,733	(25%)			
2016 Pres. Vote	Clinton	282,402	(68%)	Trump	89,631	(22%)	Johnson	14,294	(4%)
	Stein	12,886	(3%)						

Greater Portland: Postmodern skyscrapers rising above the riverfront and below a range of hills: This is downtown Portland. The city — which would have been named Boston if a coin toss had gone the other way — started here, along the Willamette River just before it flows into the Columbia. Downtown Portland was once a dowdy place, proper in a New England kind of way, with a few formal buildings above the warehouses and factories. But the past four decades here have witnessed an explosion of affluence and creativity, symbolized by handsome high-rises, restored Victorian storefronts, a downtown transit trolley, and a light-rail line known as MAX (for Metropolitan Area Express). The population of the city increased 11 percent from 2010 to 2017.

On the Pacific Rim, Portland makes much of its living on trade with Asia. It has become a home to high-tech industries, particularly in the Silicon Forest suburbs. Local government also has produced change. Metro, the regional agency established just as growth was accelerating, is a counterweight against the endless population sprawl outward. The city encouraged development of high-density commercial space and housing around transit stops, and bicycle paths wind throughout the metropolitan area. In a 2016 survey based on Bike Score ratings, Portland ranked fifth as the nation's most bicycle-friendly large city, though it remained first in the share of commuters who bicycle to work. Local leaders have sought to make Portland the nation's leader for biodiesel and other renewable fuels. In 2018, the local transit authority started using electric buses, with a goal to eliminate diesel buses by 2034. In becoming a city focused on renewable energy, Portland has attracted political and cultural liberals. In 2017, Portland ranked fifth in the nation in the Clean Tech Leadership Index.

The city's hipster sensibility was satirized on the IFC television show Portlandia, which featured Carrie Brownstein and Fred Armisen and had its final episode in March 2018. In its farewell to the program, The Oregonian wrote that the city had "a complicated love/hate relationship" with the show, including "some fist-waving locals who blame Portlandia for ruining Portland." In 2018, a survey ranked the Portland metro area second behind San Francisco in the share of its population that is gay, lesbian, bisexual or transgender. In other ways, the city is notably less diverse: its population is 5 percent African American and 11 percent Hispanic. In 2016, The Atlantic headlined a story about the city, "The Racist History of Portland, the Whitest City in America." In 2018, protests in the downtown area sometimes grew violent, with small numbers of conservatives who, at least in part, were challenging the liberal caricature of the city.

The 3rd Congressional District of Oregon includes most of Portland, including downtown. It also takes in Multnomah County east of the city and a small part of suburban Clackamas County to the south, which includes a bit more than 10 percent of its voters. Politically, the 3rd remains dominated by progressives. In 2016, Hillary Clinton got 76 percent of the vote in Multnomah County and 68 percent in the district.

Peter DeFazio (D)

Elected 1986, 17th term, b. May 27, 1947; Needham, MA; Tufts University (MA), B.A., 1969; University of Oregon, Att., 1971; University of Oregon, M.S., 1977; Roman Catholic; Married (Myrnie Daut).

Military Career: U.S. Air Force 1967-1971

Elected Office: Lane County Board of Commissioners, 1983-1986, chmn, 1985-1986.

Professional Career: District Director, U.S. Rep. James Weaver, 1977-1982.

DC Office: 2134 RHOB 20515, 202-225-6416, Fax: 202-226-3493, defazio.house.gov

State Offices: Coos Bay, 541-269-2609; Eugene, 541-465-6732; Roseburg, 541-440-3523.

Committees: *Transportation & Infrastructure (Chmn)*: Ex Officio membership on all subcommittees.

Group Ratings

	ADA	ACLU	AFL-CIO	LCV	ITI	COC	HAFA	ACU	CFG	FRC
2018	-	79%	-	97%	-	55%	6%	4%	17%	0%
2017	85%	C	89%	100%	C	57%	C	4%	0%	11%

Almanac Ratings 2017-18

	Economy	Social	Foreign	Composite
Liberal	95%	89%	95%	93%
Conservative	5%	11%	5%	7%

Key Votes of the 115th Congress

1. Obama-care revision	N	5. Family planning regs	N	9. Guantanamo prisoners	Y
2. Tax Cuts	N	6. Body cameras/immigration	Y	10. Ground missiles, limit	Y
3. Omnibus appropriations	Y	7. Abortion ban	N	11. Defense Dept. spending	N
4. Dodd-Frank revision	N	8. Concealed carry	N	12. FISA rules	N

Election Results

Election	Name (Party)	Vote (%)		Cand. Spent	Ind. Exp. Support	Ind. Exp. Oppose
2018 General	Peter DeFazio (D)	208,710	(56%)	$1,027,346		
	Art Robinson (R)	152,414	(41%)	$163,010		
2018 Primary	Peter DeFazio (D)	78,575	(92%)			
	Daniel Arcangel (D)	6,672	(8%)			

Prior winning percentages: 2016 (56%), 2014 (59%), 2012 (59%), 2010 (55%), 2008 (82%), 2006 (62%), 2004 (61%), 2002 (64%), 2000 (68%), 1998 (70%), 1996 (66%), 1994 (67%), 1992 (71%), 1990 (86%), 1988 (72%), 1986 (54%)

Peter DeFazio, a Democrat first elected in 1986, is a persistent — and sometimes outspoken — populist who doesn't mind showing his independence from his party or loudly criticizing the conservative ideas he disdains. With his lengthy tenure, he planned to use his influential post as chairman of the Transportation and Infrastructure Committee to press for sweeping legislation to expand the nation's infrastructure.

DeFazio grew up in Massachusetts, moved to Oregon for graduate school, was a bike mechanic and went to work for Democratic Rep. Jim Weaver. In 1982, DeFazio moved to Springfield and won a seat on the county commission. When Weaver retired in 1986, DeFazio won his House seat in close contests. He beat Bill Bradbury 34%-33% in the primary and took the general election 54%-46%.

DeFazio has compiled a record that seems to satisfy both liberal Eugene and the more conservative parts of the district: The Almanac vote ratings have shown that he's liberal on most issues, and moderate on social issues. An original founder of the loose-knit Progressive Caucus, he channeled the anger that millions of working Americans suffered during the boom years before the economic collapse in 2008 and the recession.

DeFazio often takes idiosyncratic or maverick views. He introduced a bill in 2011 allowing people to opt out of the health care law's individual mandate reviled by Republicans — but only if they waived the right to any government-backed medical help for at least three years. He voted against climate legislation in 2009 putting caps on carbon emissions, he said, because there were better ways to reduce greenhouse gas emissions, such as a carbon tax. Sometimes, his views are enacted: He took the lead in 2007 in the House effort to permit airline pilots to carry guns in the cockpit. Although the Bush administration initially opposed it, DeFazio won by an astonishing 250-175. The Senate followed suit.

In 2013, DeFazio was ranking Democrat on the Natural Resources Committee. He promised to "push for a 21st century energy policy that promotes conservation and the development of renewable resources on federal lands and waters." But the next two years were an unusually quiet legislative period. In 2014, the committee passed his bipartisan bill to save West Coast fishermen millions of dollars by refinancing high-interest federal loans for fishing vessels in a program that had been created in 2003 to address over-capacity; the House didn't act on the measure. DeFazio strongly opposed Republican efforts to revise the Endangered Species Act.

DeFazio was the only member of Congress to oppose the final economic stimulus bill in 2009 after backing the original House version, saying it did not sufficiently boost transportation spending. In 2012, he made sure that a surface transportation bill contained a temporary extension of federal payments for Oregon counties. DeFazio has called for replacing the federal gasoline tax with a per-barrel tax on oil. "What if we got rid of the tax that people don't like and move it upstream to something that most people don't like — the oil industry?" he asked The Oregonian.

When he took the top Democratic post on Transportation and Infrastructure after the 2014 election, DeFazio urged Congress to get serious about fixing what he called the nation's decaying transportation facilities and stop "relying on short-term patches for longstanding problems." He called for financing the highway trust fund with a one-time 14 percent transition tax on foreign earnings by U.S. companies, followed by a 19 percent minimum tax on their global profits. He pledged bipartisan cooperation and said that his goals were "job creation, increased efficiency and strategic growth." In 2015, the Republican-controlled Congress approved a highway bill, but not with DeFazio's taxes.

Long before it became the consensus position for congressional Democrats, he had been a critic of international trade deals. He opposed the Clinton-era North American Free Trade Agreement and was a leader in the fight against normal trade relations with China. In 2015, he was an outspoken foe of granting authority to President Barack Obama to expedite his prospective Trans-Pacific Partnership. The agreement, he said, was "informed and manipulated by corporate interests" and would have "relegated Congress to be used as a doormat… [for an agreement that] has been negotiated in secret and will export jobs, drive down U.S. wages, and undermine U.S. sovereignty." The House approved the presidential authority the following week, with support from the other three Democrats from Oregon.

After Republican Sen. Bob Packwood resigned in 1995, DeFazio ran in the special election. His opposition to gun control and NAFTA provided clear contrasts with Portland liberal Democratic Rep. Ron Wyden. The better-funded Wyden won the primary 50%-44% and prevailed in the general. Until 2010, DeFazio routinely won reelection by more than 60 percent in his marginal district. That year,

Republican Art Robinson held him to 55 percent of the vote after getting a boost from outside groups' ads tying DeFazio to House Speaker Nancy Pelosi. Robinson, a biochemist who owns a sheep ranch, received hundreds of thousands of dollars of support from Robert Mercer, a hedge-fund manager who became a prominent supporter of Donald Trump in the 2016 campaign. DeFazio faced Robinson in the next four elections. He got between 56 percent and 59 percent in those contests. Robinson continued to receive sizable Super PAC support, though he was largely ignored by Republican groups.

After Trump was elected and called for extensive new building of infrastructure, DeFazio said that he would be willing to work with him. But he added, "I will not hesitate to fight short-sighted proposals that seek to privatize our transportation systems, jeopardize American jobs and manufacturing, or gut critical regulations that protect our workers and communities." He filed a new financing plan, with an annual increase of one cent in the gasoline tax, plus authorization for the Treasury Department to issue 30-year bonds to finance highway construction. The president delayed in sending a financing proposal and congressional Republicans hesitated to take the lead. DeFazio applauded Trump's decision to withdraw from the Trans-Pacific Partnership.

Taking over as committee chairman in January 2019, DeFazio said that he would push for a bipartisan deal that would require Trump to be "fully on-board" with any increase in the gas tax or other new funding. "I will fight for commonsense, comprehensive solutions to address the major issues facing our aging, 20th century infrastructure and champion a smarter, greener infrastructure that helps to reduce carbon pollution," he said. He also supported a tax on securities transactions.

At his committee, which has jurisdiction over the General Services Administration, DeFazio has demanded information about GSA's lease agreement with the Trump International Hotel on Pennsylvania Avenue. In January 2019, he warned that he might subpoena GSA for the details, including Trump's possibly unconstitutional conflicts of interest.

OR-4: Southwest Oregon   Cook Partisan Voting Index: EVEN

Population		Race and Ethnicity		Income	
Total	785,159	White	84.2%	Median Income	$46,558
Land area (sq. miles)	17,274	Black	0.8%	District Income Rank	358
Pop/ sq mi	45.5	Latino	7.7%	Poverty Rate	18.4%
Born in State	46.8%	Asian	2.3%	With health insurance	91.4%
		Two or more races	3.8%	Cash public assistance	3.9%
Age Groups		Other	1.3%	Food stamp/SNAP	20.3%
Under 18	19.1%				
18-34	23.7%	Education		Work	
35-64	37.6%	H.S grad or less	35.3%	White Collar	19.6%
Over 64	19.6%	Some college	38.1%	Sales and Service	42.8%
		College Degree, 4 yr	16%	Blue Collar	22.4%
Military		Post grad	10.6%	Government	17.1%
Veteran/ Active Duty	11.2%				

2012 Pres. Vote	Obama	188,563	(51%)	Romney	163,931	(45%)			
2016 Pres. Vote	Clinton	180,872	(45%)	Trump	180,318	(44%)	Johnson	19,141	(5%)
	Stein	11,675	(3%)						

Eugene, Albany: Eugene is nestled in the southernmost bit of lowland in Oregon's Willamette Valley, and is surrounded by mountains on three sides. It is a farming center, a lumber provider and, most notably, a university town. In 1876, the University of Oregon was established, a symbol of the state's strong Yankee cultural ethic. Eugene and next-door Springfield, which has become a center for the manufacture of computer chips, have grown into comfortable midsized towns. Eugene has bicycle paths along the riverbanks and its main streets. It likes to bill itself as the "Running Capital of the Universe" — Phil Knight and his former University of Oregon track coach, Bill Bowerman, started Nike here, the first soles formed on a waffle iron. Now the third-largest city in Oregon, Eugene has small-town ambience and urban sensibilities, and its progressive voters have been vital to Democrats statewide. A longtime contributor, Knight in 2016 donated $500 million to the University of Oregon for its new science campus. Critics — including journalist Joshua Hunt, who in 2018 wrote a book, University of Nike -- have contended that the university has provided commercial benefits to Nike.

Beyond Eugene and Springfield are southwest Oregon's green-clad mountains. For years, the region cut more timber than anywhere else in the country. But Timber Country, including forest-product businesses, has struggled. Recent economic development has been diverse, with gains in health care, tourism and retiree migration from California. Springfield is the putative home of the popular television show "The Simpsons," according to its creator, Oregon native Matt Groening. The largest employer in the real Springfield is Peace Health, a Catholic health care and hospital system, whose prominence has spurred residential development in the area. Local groups have protested the proposed Jordan Cove liquefied natural gas terminal and a 229-mile pipeline in coastal Coos County. Despite earlier setbacks to the project, the Trump administration in early 2019 continued its efforts to revive the site for overseas exports.

The 4th Congressional District of Oregon includes Eugene, Springfield and surrounding Lane County. It includes the state's other main college town, Corvallis, home to Oregon State University. Also in the 4th is Douglas County and the southern half of Oregon's stunning Pacific coastline, a roughly 200-mile drive to the California border. About half the voters are in Eugene-based Lane County. Eugene is heavily Democratic, while Douglas County votes Republican; the travails of the logging industry hurt the Democrats here. The 4th has leaned Democratic but is far more blue-collar and less liberal than the Portland area's districts. Hillary Clinton led Donald Trump by a few hundred votes in this district in 2016.

Kurt Schrader (D)

Elected 2008, 6th term, b. Oct 19, 1951; Bridgeport, CT; Cornell University (NY), B.A., 1973; University of Illinois, B.A., 1975; University of Illinois College of Veterinary Medicine (IL), D.V.M., 1977; Episcopalian; Married (Susan Mora); 5 children.

Elected Office: OR House, 1997-2003; OR Senate, 2003-2008.

Professional Career: Former aide, AK gov.; Veterinarian, 1978-2008.

DC Office: 2431 RHOB 20515, 202-225-5711, Fax: 202-225-5699, schrader.house.gov

State Offices: Oregon City, 503-557-1324; Salem, 503-588-9100.

Committees: *Energy & Commerce*: Communications & Technology; Energy; Health.

Group Ratings

	ADA	ACLU	AFL-CIO	LCV	ITI	COC	HAFA	ACU	CFG	FRC
2018	-	75%	-	63%	-	83%	13%	25%	35%	0%
2017	70%	C	77%	73%	C	71%	C	11%	6%	0%

Almanac Ratings 2017-18

	Economy	Social	Foreign	Composite
Liberal	68%	69%	94%	77%
Conservative	32%	31%	7%	23%

Key Votes of the 115th Congress

1. Obama-care revision	N	5. Family planning regs	N	9. Guantanamo prisoners	Y
2. Tax Cuts	N	6. Body cameras/immigration	Y	10. Ground missiles, limit	Y
3. Omnibus appropriations	Y	7. Abortion ban	N	11. Defense Dept. spending	N
4. Dodd-Frank revision	Y	8. Concealed carry	Y	12. FISA rules	N

Election Results

Election	Name (Party)	Vote (%)		Cand. Spent	Ind. Exp. Support	Ind. Exp. Oppose
2018 General	Kurt Schrader (D)	197,187	(55%)	$569,359	$46,763	
	Mark Callahan (R)	149,887	(42%)	$28,425		
2018 Primary	Kurt Schrader (D)	59,196	(87%)			
	Peter Wright (D)	9,002	(13%)			

Prior winning percentages: 2016 (54%), 2014 (54%), 2012 (54%), 2010 (51%), 2008 (54%)

Kurt Schrader, elected in 2008, has been a business-oriented Democrat in a district that is divided between urban and rural. A veterinarian and organic farmer, he has dealt with health care and energy issues on the Energy and Commerce Committee. Schrader has urged change in the Democratic leadership and has been an outspoken critic of Nancy Pelosi; he was one of 15 House Democrats who did not support her in the January 2019 vote for Speaker. He has remained a leader of the centrist Blue Dog Democrats.

Schrader was born in Bridgeport Connecticut, where his father was a chemical engineer. He studied government and got a degree at Cornell University, then received his doctorate in veterinary medicine at the University of Illinois. He settled in Oregon and ran two veterinary clinics in Canby. From his farm, he sold organic fruits and vegetables. Schrader entered politics on the Canby planning commission, assisting in development of the city's land-use plan. He was elected to the state House, where he served six years, followed by another six in the state Senate. He was co-chairman of the Joint Ways and Means Committee, where he pushed legislation to tax new construction to pay for schools. He developed a reputation as a conservative Democrat and opposed his party on increasing the minimum wage.

When the House seat opened, Schrader lent his campaign $130,000 during the primary and won more than 54 percent of the vote against three opponents. In the general, he faced Republican shipping entrepreneur Mike Erickson, who was the GOP nominee two years earlier. The general election was initially considered wide open. This was George W. Bush territory in 2000 and 2004, but a surge in new voters gave Democrats their first voter-registration advantage in 12 years. Erickson was unable to shake allegations about an earlier relationship with a woman for whose abortion he had paid. Schrader received endorsements from the Oregon Farm Bureau and several newspapers, and got financial help from the Democratic Congressional Campaign Committee. Erickson outspent Schrader by more than $1 million, but Schrader prevailed 54%-38%. He has retained roughly that share of the vote since.

Schrader has been willing to go his own way from his party. He has been co-chair of the fiscally conservative Blue Dog Coalition and was one of 22 House Democrats in 2012 to support fellow Blue Dog Jim Cooper's unsuccessful budget proposal based on the bipartisan Simpson-Bowles commission's recommendations. He has voted for Republican alternatives to weaken the 2010 health care law by allowing consumers to purchase insurance plans that don't meet the terms of that law. He originally cosponsored the DREAM Act for children of illegal immigrants but later voted against it, saying he wanted a more comprehensive immigration reform. In 2015, he voted for the Keystone XL pipeline from Canada, the only Democrat from Oregon to support the project. Also that year, he was among only 28 House Democrats voting for trade promotion authority, though three of them were from Oregon. In 2019, he continued to serve as chairman of the Blue Dog political action committee.

Schrader has been an outspoken critic of the Supreme Court's Citizens United decision in 2010 that eased campaign finance restrictions, and has proposed a constitutional amendment to allow congressional regulation of campaign contributions and spending. He joined the nonpartisan No Labels group, which has urged a bipartisan congressional agenda. And he has participated in the bipartisan Problems Solvers Caucus. On social issues, Schrader has frequently crossed the party line. In December 2017, he was one of six Democrats who voted for a Republican-sponsored bill to permit gun-owners licensed for concealed carry to use their weapons in all 50 states. Schrader said that the bill, which was supported by the National Rifle Association, would have strengthened background checks. In April 2018, he cosponsored a bill to override a federal court decision that instructed operators of dams to spill more water to assist endangered salmon; all but eight House Democrats voted against it. The issue has remained controversial in the West, where salmon stocks have been depleted along the Columbia and Snake rivers, with their multiple dams.

On Energy and Commerce, Schrader advocated more spending on renewable energy and access to health coverage without increased government regulations. With Republicans holding House control, he praised the panel's bipartisan handling of several bills, and claimed some credit.

National Republicans went after Schrader in 2010 and recruited state Rep. Scott Bruun, who accused him of not being the fiscal hawk he claimed and of going "on a world-class spending spree with your money." Schrader parried that Bruun wanted to privatize Social Security. Schrader won 51%-46%. After redistricting changes made the district slightly more favorable for Republicans, they nominated in 2014 Clackamas Commissioner Tootie Smith, a conservative who once raffled off a Glock pistol to raise campaign funds. Schrader won 54%-39% and led in all seven counties. Two years later, he again got 54 percent, this time against Colm Willis, the top lobbyist for Oregon Right to Life. In the 2016 primary, Schrader was challenged by a former state representative who decided to run after Schrader said that he supported the Trans-Pacific trade deal. Schrader won with 72 percent of the vote. In 2018, he had no primary opposition and he got 55 percent against a light-spending Republican in November.

Following the 2018 election, Schrader was among 16 Democrats who signed a letter vowing to oppose Pelosi for Speaker. Even after many dissidents decided to support Pelosi, he said that her selection could jeopardize the Democrats' majority in 2020. Some Democratic activists in Oregon threatened a primary challenge to Schrader.

OR-5: West-Central Oregon   Cook Partisan Voting Index: EVEN

Population		Race and Ethnicity		Income	
Total	806,326	White	75.4%	Median Income	$59,704
Land area (sq. miles)	5,190	Black	1%	District Income Rank	183
Pop/ sq mi	155.4	Latino	16.4%	Poverty Rate	13.2%
Born in State	51.7%	Asian	2.7%	With health insurance	91.5%
		Two or more races	3.2%	Cash public assistance	4.6%
Age Groups		Other	1.4%	Food stamp/SNAP	16.7%
Under 18	23.2%				
18-34	21.4%	**Education**		**Work**	
35-64	38.8%	H.S grad or less	34.9%	White Collar	16.6%
Over 64	16.6%	Some college	35%	Sales and Service	42.3%
		College Degree, 4 yr	19.1%	Blue Collar	22.6%
Military		Post grad	10.9%	Government	15%
Veteran/ Active Duty	9.5%				

2012 Pres. Vote	Obama	172,986	(50%)	Romney	161,482	(47%)			
2016 Pres. Vote	Clinton	180,404	(46%)	Trump	164,548	(42%)	Johnson	20,135	(5%)
	Stein	8,214	(2%)						

Salem, Clackamas County: The Willamette River Valley was the great Promised Land at the end of the Oregon Trail, shielded from the cold storms of the Pacific by mountains but squeezing most of the moisture out of the clouds in the form of rain, fog and persistent mist. New England Yankees planted small towns they called Salem and Oregon City, founded schools and colleges, built tall-spired churches and eventually Salem's distinctive Art Deco state capitol, a few blocks east of the river. This was one of the few valleys in the West that settlers found readily suitable for agriculture. The soil is fertile, and the plain created by the waters of the Willamette sweeping down from the mountains is broad. Ironically in this environmentally friendly state, agricultural and polluted stormwater runoff have continued to make the river among the dirtiest in the nation. The Willamette Valley is home to a burgeoning wine industry with more than 750 wineries, as of 2018, many of which are known for their pinot noir. By some measures, Oregon is the third-largest wine producing state, behind California and Washington.

Salem and Eugene have battled for the distinction of Oregon's second-largest city, after Portland. Salem, the state capital, has pulled slightly ahead; its 22 percent Hispanic population is more than twice the share in Eugene. In Wilsonville, German-based Siemens owns Mentor Graphics, a sophisticated electronic-design company with 1,000 employees at its 53-acre headquarters campus. In 2015, Microsoft began to manufacture giant touch screens in Wilsonville, with a retail price up to $22,000, depending on size. But the company shut the facility two years later and switched the product to its larger operations in China.

The 5th Congressional District of Oregon includes much of the northern Willamette Valley. The district has about 40 percent of its voters in Clackamas County on the outskirts of Portland; more than three-fourths of Clackamas is in the 5th. It spreads south to Salem-based Marion County, which has one-third of the voters and is home of Willamette University, the oldest university in the West. It crosses the Coast Range to take in Lincoln and Tillamook counties, which are fishing, logging and cheese-making communities. In the thinly populated coastal areas, Newport has a busy port and a state beach. The Coast Guard announced in 2014 that it was removing its local helicopter because of budget pressures, but Congress responded to local pressure and agreed to retain the Newport base, at least temporarily, in Coast Guard legislation that was enacted in 2018. Historically, the valley was Republican, but it has trended Democratic. Overall, the 5th has remained competitive. In 2016, Hillary Clinton took the district, 46%-42%.

PENNSYLVANIA

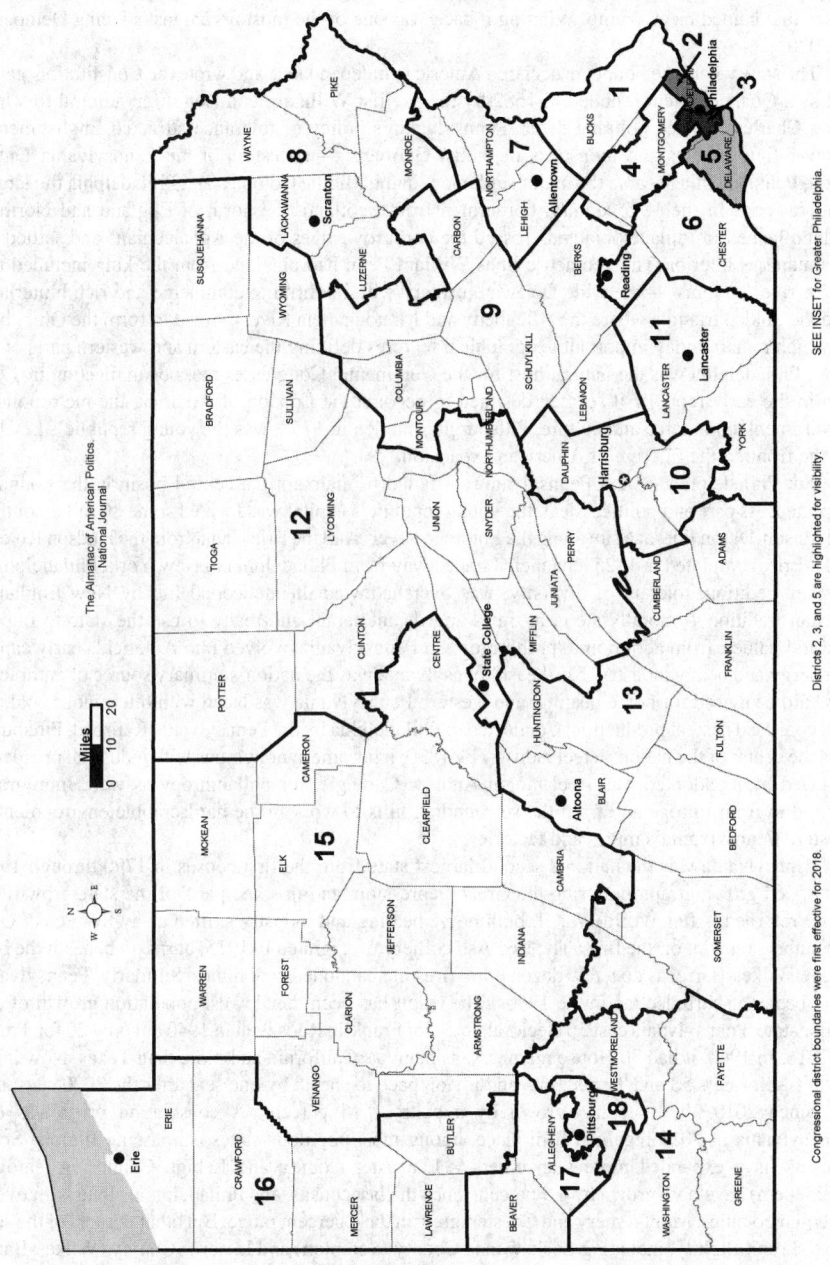

The Almanac of American Politics.
National Journal

Districts 2, 3, and 5 are highlighted for visibility.   SEE INSET for Greater Philadelphia.

Congressional district boundaries were first effective for 2018.

Pennsylvania has long been a state targeted by Democrats and Republicans alike, with competitive contests at almost every level of government. But the Keystone State hadn't voted Republican for president since 1988 – until 2016, when it stunned the nation by backing Donald Trump over Hillary Clinton by about 44,000 votes, joining Michigan and Wisconsin as the Rust Belt states that helped elect Trump. Winning it back was one of the most urgent tasks facing Democrats in 2020.

The state where the Founders declared American independence and wrote the Constitution started out as a Quaker haven, founded in 1682 by the pacifist William Penn, son of an admiral to whom King Charles II owed political debts. Pennsylvania's policy of tolerance attracted Englishmen of many religious sects and thousands of pietist Germans — ancestors of the Pennsylvania Dutch. Soon, Pennsylvania became the major settlement in the Middle Colonies and Philadelphia the largest colonial port. In the 18th century, bordermen from Scotland, the north of England and Northern Ireland landed in Philadelphia and crossed the corduroy ridges of the Appalachians and settled the mountainous interior. The geometric lines William Penn had obtained from the king included two major river systems — the wide Delaware estuary with its thriving commerce and rich hinterland, and the golden triangle where the Allegheny and Monongahela Rivers joined to form the Ohio, both of which remain today important geographical features defining the eastern and western parts of the state. Philadelphia was the natural host for the Continental Congresses that began meeting in 1774, and in the early republic it seemed destined to become the London of America, the metropolis of government, commerce and culture. Pittsburgh, founded in 1758, was the young republic's key hub on the frontier, the fulcrum of American expansion.

But Philadelphia — and Pennsylvania — failed to maintain the central position the Founders expected. As part of a political deal, the young republic's capital was located some 80 miles south of the Mason-Dixon line, at a site along the Potomac River. And the Erie Canal from the Hudson River to Lake Erie, completed in 1825, channeled trade away from Philadelphia to New York. Philadelphia's Quaker tradition, tolerant of diversity, was overshadowed in intellectual life by New England's Puritan tradition -- morally stern, at times angrily intolerant and ready to use the state to impose cultural values, from abolition to prohibition. So Pennsylvania evolved into America's early capital of energy and heavy industry. Northeast Pennsylvania was the nation's primary source of anthracite, the hard coal used for home heating, and western Pennsylvania was laced with bituminous coal, the soft coal used in steel production. Connected to Philadelphia by the Pennsylvania Railroad, Pittsburgh was the center of the nation's steel industry by 1890; it became synonymous with industrial prosperity and, led by its adopted son, steel mogul Andrew Carnegie, for philanthropy as well. Immigrants poured in from Europe and from the surrounding hills to work in the hardscrabble environment of western Pennsylvania's mines and factories.

Pennsylvania was the nation's second-largest state from the first census in 1790 through 1940. It stopped growing rapidly during the Great Depression, and in some parts of the state growth has never returned. After World War II, both home heating and industry shifted away from coal. Only the embers remain, or, the fires: The Red Ash colliery fire, ignited in 1915, burns on beneath the hills above Wilkes-Barre, as do a few dozen other fires in abandoned coal mines. Similarly, Pennsylvania steel began a sharp decline in the 1960s. The result has been the slowest population growth of any major state. Pennsylvania cast 36 electoral votes for Franklin Roosevelt in 1940 but only 20 for Trump in 2016. In 1960, it had 30 House members, as many as California and more than Texas. Now it has 18 to California's 53 and Texas' 36 – and it's on pace to shrink by one seat after the 2020 census.

Since 2010, the state has grown by a paltry 0.75 percent. A consolation prize was that Pennsylvania in 2017 regained fifth place among most populous states, surpassing Illinois. Some pockets have expanded more than others – Lancaster County and Lehigh County (Allentown-Bethlehem) have both grown by 4.9 percent since the last census, and Philadelphia, along with two of its collar counties, Montgomery and Chester, grew in the 4 percent range. But other corners of the state have shrunk slightly, including Lackawanna County (Scranton) and Luzerne County (Wilkes-Barre) in the northeast, and Erie County in the northwest. Some smaller counties have contracted more than that. Relatively few outsiders moved in. This has made the state increasingly old -- only four others (Florida, West Virginia, Maine and Vermont) have a higher percentage of residents age 65 and over. Pennsylvania remains one of the whitest big states — 11 percent black, 7 percent Hispanic, and 3 percent Asian. Pockets of the state, however, have seen rapid Hispanic increases, notably Hazleton in Luzerne County, a shift that has prompted bitter battles over illegal immigration.

Inset for Greater Philadelphia

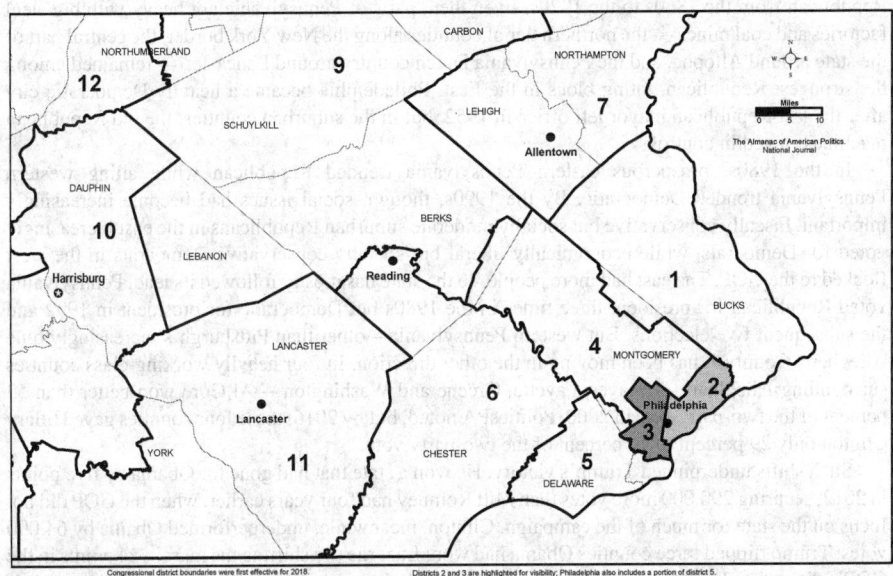

Economically, Pennsylvania has begun to perk up a bit over the past two decades. Big hospitals have replaced big steel mills as employers in metro Pittsburgh, and metro Philadelphia and the surrounding countryside have experienced diversified economic growth, though manufacturing remains important outside the big cities. Manufacturing employment in Pennsylvania has declined by 35 percent since 2000, a significantly faster rate than the national decline of 25 percent. Some municipalities have become insolvent. Pennsylvania has held state taxes down more than many of its Northeastern neighbors, which has been a factor in luring New Yorkers to retire near the Delaware Water Gap and the Poconos. Hispanics from New York and North Jersey are also moving out Interstate 78 to work in Reading, Allentown and Bethlehem. As for the City of Brotherly Love, it has become a hip destination with impressive cultural and nightlife amenities. Agriculture remains a significant industry in Pennsylvania – it ranks among the top seven states for production of eggs, milk, pumpkins, apples, grapes, and peaches, and ranks first nationally in mushroom production, centered on Kennett Square in Chester County, "The Mushroom Capital of the World." (The recent emergence of the invasive spotted lanternfly has put some of Pennsylvania's fruit crops at risk.) The state's median income ranks slightly below the national average.

James Carville once famously described the state as Pittsburgh and Philadelphia with Alabama in between. It's those parts in the "T" of rural Pennsylvania, once the site of the world's first oil well and first commercial nuclear power plant, that are getting a renewed taste of being a major economic engine. The Marcellus Shale beneath 60 percent of Pennsylvania and much of upstate New York contains the nation's largest reserves of natural gas embedded in hard rock. It can be brought to the surface by hydraulic fracturing, or fracking. With the development of horizontal drilling, fracking became commercially feasible in 2004, and there are now wells through much of the western and northern parts of the state, making Pennsylvania the second biggest producer of natural gas after Texas. Environmental groups have charged that fracking can pollute drinking water sources, but development has transformed portions of the state economically.

For generations after the Civil War — whose turning point is often pegged to quiet Gettysburg — Pennsylvania was the most Republican of the large states, due in part to the legacy of Abraham Lincoln and the Union, and due in part to the steel industry and high tariffs. Its Republican machines built parties that were representative not of one ethnic segment, but had a place for just about everyone. In 1932, Pennsylvania was the only big state that stuck with Republican Herbert Hoover

over Democrat Franklin Roosevelt. But then the political landscape changed. The New Deal, John L. Lewis' United Mine Workers and the CIO industrial union movement, and a series of bloody strikes made industrial Pennsylvania almost as Democratic in the late 1930s and 1940s as it had been Republican from the 1860s to the 1920s. Even then, parts of Pennsylvania not heavy with big steel factories and coal mines — the northern tier of counties along the New York border, the central part of the state around Altoona, and the Pennsylvania Dutch country around Lancaster — remained among the strongest Republican voting blocs in the East. Philadelphia became a heavily Democratic city after the last Republican mayor left office in 1952, but in the suburban counties, the old Republican machines stayed in control.

In the 1980s, prosperous eastern Pennsylvania trended Republican while ailing western Pennsylvania trended Democratic. By the 1990s, though, social issues had become increasingly important. Fiscally conservative but socially moderate suburban Republicans in the east increasingly voted for Democrats, while economically liberal but socially conservative Democrats in the west flocked to the GOP. The east had more people, so the state has mostly followed its lead. Pennsylvania voted Republican for president three times in the 1980s but Democratic for president in 1992 and the subsequent five elections. But western Pennsylvania – other than Pittsburgh's increasingly blue Allegheny County – has been moving in the other direction. In four heavily working-class counties surrounding Allegheny -- Beaver, Fayette, Greene and Washington -- Al Gore won better than 53 percent of the two-party vote in 2000, PoliticsPA noted, but by 2016, those four counties gave Hillary Clinton only 29 percent to 40 percent of the two-party vote.

Such shifts underpinned Trump's victory. He won a state that had gone for Obama by five points in 2012, securing 290,000 more votes than Mitt Romney had four years earlier, when the GOP did not focus on the state for much of the campaign. Clinton, meanwhile, underperformed Obama by 64,000 votes. Trump flipped three counties Obama had won: Luzerne (by shifting the margin 24 points in the GOP's direction), Erie (by shifting it 19 points), and Northampton (Easton, by shifting it nine points). Trump also moved the needle in several blue-collar counties, but not quite enough to win; notably, these included Clinton's (and Joe Biden's) ancestral county of Lackawanna, where the margin shifted from a 27-point Democratic win in 2012 to a three-point victory in 2016. The silver lining for Clinton was her ability to improve on Obama's performance in more affluent and educated cities and suburbs. She flipped Philadelphia-area Chester County from red to blue, as well as Centre County, the home of Penn State University. But Trump managed to wring more votes from less-populated areas, and they added up. The cumulative Republican improvement over 2012 in just five western Pennsylvania counties – Beaver, Fayette, Greene, Washington and Westmoreland – was almost enough by itself to supply Trump's statewide winning margin. The same could be said for Trump's improvement in Luzerne and Lackawanna. In these regions, a combination of social conservatism, support for gun rights and energy development, and a frayed union legacy delivered votes to Trump.

If 2016 was a disappointment for Pennsylvania Democrats, 2018 was undeniably a comeback. The run of good fortune began, unobtrusively enough, in 2015, when the Democrats seized three open seats on the Pennsylvania Supreme Court, giving the party a 5-2 edge. In 2018, the court threw out the congressional district lines that, despite the state's overall competitive nature, had given the GOP a consistent 13-5 House delegation lead. The court-drawn replacement map strengthened what had already been looking like a good cycle for Democratic House candidates. On Election Day, Democrats pulled into a 9-9 tie in the delegation, aided by four Republican incumbents being nudged into retirements; these gains proved to be an early signal of the Democrats' march to the House majority. The Democrats also came within three points of winning two other districts and within five points in a third. Meanwhile, Gov. Tom Wolf and Sen. Bob Casey, both Democrats, were reelected by double digits. Such victories gave the party hope that Trump's victory in 2016 would be reversed in 2020.

Population		Race and Ethnicity		Income	
Total	12,790,505	White	77.3%	Median Income	$56,951
Land area (sq. miles)	44,743	Black	10.6%	State Income Rank	22
Pop/ sq mi	285.9	Latino	6.8%	Poverty Rate	13.1%
Born in state	72.8%	Asian	3.2%	With health insurance	92.9%
		Two or more races	1.8%	Cash public assistance	3.2%
Age Groups		Other	0.3%	Food stamp/SNAP	13.0%
Under 18	21.0%				
18-34	22.5%	Education		Work	
35-64	39.4%	H.S grad or less	45.7%	White Collar	37.7%
Over 64	17.1%	Some college	24.3%	Sales and Service	40.7%
		College Degree, 4 yr	18.3%	Blue Collar	21.6%
Military		Post grad	11.8%	Government	10.4%
Veteran/ Active Duty	8.0%				

Presidential Politics

2016 Primary (D)	Clinton (D)	935,107 (56%)	Sanders (D)	731,881 (44%)			
2016 Primary (R)	Trump (R)	902,593 (57%)	Cruz (R)	345,506 (22%)	Kasich (R)	310,003 (19%)	
2016 Pres. Vote	Trump (R)	2,970,733 (48%)	Clinton (D)	2,926,441 (47%)	Johnson (L)	146,715 (2%)	
2012 Pres. Vote	Obama (D)	2,990,274 (52%)	Romney (R)	2,680,434 (47%)			

Was Pennsylvania the ultimate battleground in the 2016 election? Unlike its Rustbelt neighbors Michigan and Wisconsin, both Donald Trump and Hillary Clinton campaigned vigorously there, saturating the state with television ads. And Democrats held their national convention in Philadelphia. It doesn't have the demographic diversity of other presidential battlegrounds like Florida and Virginia, but it is a state where the shifting politics of wealthier suburbs and blue-collar communities have been apparent for several elections.

Pennsylvania has been seriously contested in just about every presidential election since 1976, but only once in that time, in 2008, has any candidate received more than 52 percent of the vote. For Democrats today, their winning coalition in Pennsylvania relies less on working class and union voters in Western Pennsylvania and the Lehigh Valley and more on suburbanites in the four vote-rich counties — Bucks, Chester, Delaware and Montgomery — surrounding Philadelphia. Many of those blue-collar voters are Catholics and white ethnics who were drawn to the GOP because of its conservative stance on abortion and other social issues. The reverse was happening in the Philadelphia suburbs where college-educated voters were alienated by the Republicans' courtship of evangelicals and rightward drift on social issues. These suburbanites were happy to vote for Democratic candidates so long as they didn't lurch too far to the left on economic issues. In 2008, Barack Obama defeated John McCain 54%-44%. He carried the Philadelphia suburbs 57%-42%. With Joe Biden as his running mate, Obama carried the Northeast, a 15-county region, 54%-45%, which includes Lackawanna County. Obama's margins throughout the state dipped in 2012, but he still managed to win the Philadelphia suburbs 54%-45% and carry the state 52%-47%.

In 2016, Hillary Clinton won the Philadelphia suburban counties by a greater margin, 55%-42%. In the largely rural and solidly Republican central part of the state, Clinton's vote dropped about five percentage points from Obama's totals, but it collapsed in the northwest: In 2012, Obama won the area, 51%-48%; in 2016, Trump prevailed there 55%-42%, a 16-point swing to the GOP. Pittsburgh (Allegheny County) has transformed itself from a steel town to a technology hub and contributes 2-out-of-5 votes cast in the west and votes Democratic. But it was the only county in the 20-county region that backed Clinton in 2016. Even Erie County, a former Democratic blue-collar bastion, backed Trump, 49%-47%. Trump carried western Pennsylvania 54%-42%. With all these shifts, Trump eked out a 49%-48% victory and became the first Republican since George H.W. Bush in 1988 to carry the state.

Since 1924, Pennsylvania has held its presidential primary in April. It was a battleground in the 2008 Democratic primary, when it gave Clinton a 55%-45% victory over Obama, who had his "basket of deplorables" moment when he spoke at a fundraiser about Pennsylvanians in small towns who were "bitter" about their economic straits and who "cling to guns or religion." In 2016, Pennsylvania

Democrats were good to Clinton again: she defeated Vermont Sen. Bernie Sanders by a similar 56%-44%. Clinton carried Philadelphia and its suburban counties by relatively large margins and won the Lehigh Valley, Pittsburgh and most of western Pennsylvania. Sanders tended to run better in rural counties. On the Republican side, Donald Trump defeated Texas Sen. Ted Cruz 57%-22%, capturing all 18 of the state's congressional districts. Ohio Gov. John Kasich, a Pittsburgh-area native, was once seen as a potential contender, but won only 19 percent of the vote.

Congressional Districts

116th Congress Lineup	9D 9R	115th Congress Lineup	5D 13R

In February 2018, Pennsylvania Democrats convinced the state Supreme Court to issue a mid-decade redistricting. The 4-3 ruling eviscerated the previous Republican-drawn map and replaced it with a new map largely along the lines that Democrats had proposed. The resulting upheaval left a 9-9 delegation that the GOP had previously controlled, 12-6. Republicans, who have succeeded with their share of partisan redistricting gambits in other states, were outraged — not surprisingly. The results were a reminder of the power of redistricting, whatever the timing or whoever the map-drawer. The district revisions in swing areas — chiefly, in the suburbs outside Philadelphia — were so dramatic that three GOP incumbents (Pat Meehan, Charlie Dent and Ryan Costello) threw in the towel and their party made little, if any, effort to contest the new seats; for other personal and political reasons, Meehan and Dent might have stepped down, even without the changes. The redistricting resulted in the defeat of a fourth House Republican (Keith Rothfus) in the Pittsburgh suburbs, though the GOP managed to retain its 4-2 control of districts in western Pennsylvania; that, in turn, reflected a pick-up by Democrat Scott Lamb in a special election in March 2018, which was waged with the earlier district lines.

Among the notable results of the election changes in 2018, a total of six incumbents (including one Democrat) decided not to seek reelection; two other incumbents (Rothfus and Lamb) ran against each other. All four newly elected Democrats in the Philadelphia area were women. The other three freshmen were Republican men from central and western parts of the state. Four of those seven had not previously held elected office. With Pennsylvania expected to lose another seat following the 2020 census and with political power likely to remain divided in Harrisburg between a Democratic governor and Republican-controlled legislature, the likely prospect is that another court-drawn map will cause new upheaval and unpredictable partisan consequences in 2022. In the meantime, a few competitive House elections were likely in 2020.

History offers useful insights into the complexities of Pennsylvania redistricting. Republicans held the governorship and legislative majorities in both 2001 and 2011, and were in firm control of redistricting. In 2001, under heavy pressure from White House strategist Karl Rove, they overreached. Republicans could have eliminated two of the Democrats' 10 seats and called it a day; instead they attempted to claim 13 of 19 seats by pairing three sets of Democratic incumbents. With Republicans having overplayed their hand and two of their incumbents damaged by scandals, Democrats in Pennsylvania gained by 2008 six seats that the GOP had intended as its own. Then, in their party's national wave of 2010, Republicans' regained five of those seats and reversed Democrats' 12-7 edge.

By 2011, Republicans had learned their lesson. Needing to cut a seat while protecting 12 of their own, including five in districts that President Barack Obama had carried in 2008, Republicans retained all their seats and picked up one more when they carefully merged two junior House Democrats in the west in such a way that neither could plausibly run elsewhere but either would still be vulnerable in a general election; both ran, and lost, in the same district in 2012. The new Republican plan ruthlessly sewed the state, particular the Philadelphia suburbs, into a crazy quilt. Montgomery County, about the population of one district, was split five ways to boost three suburban Republicans. In the three elections from 2012 to 2016, Republicans emerged with what appeared to be a lock-tight 13-5 delegation in what has been an essentially 50-50 state.

Democrats finally turned the tables, in a June 2017 lawsuit filed by the League of Women Voters of Pennsylvania that challenged the congressional map as an unconstitutional partisan gerrymander. The case moved expeditiously through the state courts. Democratic Gov. Tom Wolf played an instrumental role, in working with state Democrats to offer legal arguments and an alternative. The Republican-controlled legislature objected to the proceedings and defended the existing boundaries. On Jan. 22, 2018, the Democratic-dominated state Supreme Court ruled that the map violated the state constitution and ordered the legislature to submit a new plan. When Republican lawmakers refused, Stanford University law professor Nathaniel Persily prepared the new map, following guidance by the court — and with alternatives submitted by Democrats and others.

Moving quickly, Persily presented his alternative, which the court — on a 4-3 vote -- imposed on Feb. 19. Republican objections in state and federal courts were dismissed. As the New York Times reported, its analysis showed that the new map was a more favorable partisan alternative for Democrats than all 500 simulations that were prepared by a redistricting expert. It had the advantage, according to the Times, of "achieving partisan symmetry in an evenly divided state." It also met the redistricting dictates of relatively straight boundaries and a minimum number of divided counties. With slam-dunk victories for Democrats in several of the open seats, each party took nine seats in November, though Republicans narrowly survived in three of those contests.

The result was the first case in which any congressional redistricting plan has been overturned as a partisan gerrymander, though the violation was based on the Pennsylvania constitution. The Republican response was aptly summarized by GOP Rep. Costello, whose gerrymandered district in the Philadelphia suburbs was a target of the redistricting critics. He decided not to seek reelection. "I was surprised and am still absolutely shocked that the Supreme Court got away with what it did," he told a local reporter. "Their objective was to take me out politically, and that's what they did." Costello was not the first politician across the country to voice such outrage. And he likely won't be the last.

Tom Wolf (D)

Elected 2014, term expires 2023, 2nd term; b. Nov. 17, 1948, York; Dartmouth Col., B.A. 1972; U. of London, M.A. 1978; MA Inst. of Technology, PhD 1981; Episcopalian; Married (Frances); 2 children.

Professional Career: Peace Corps, India; CEO & President, Wolf Organization, 1986-2006, Chairman & CEO, 2009-present; Secretary of Revenue, Governor Ed Rendell, 2007-2009.

Office: Main Capitol Building, Rm. 225, Harrisburg, 17120; 717-787-2500; Fax: 717-772-8284; Website: governor.pa.gov.

Lt. Gov.: John Fetterman (D) **Atty. Gen:** Josh Shapiro (D)

State Legislature: Senate: 22D, 26R, 2V **House:** 93D, 108R, 2V

Election Results

Election	Name (Party)	Vote (%)
2018 General	Thomas Wolf (D)...	2,895,652 (58%)
	Scott Wagner (R)..	2,039,882 (41%)
2018 Primary	Thomas Wolf (D)...	749,812 (100%)

Pennsylvanians elected Democrat Tom Wolf, a wealthy latecomer to politics, as their governor in 2014, shattering Pennsylvania's rigid, post-World War II pattern of the two parties trading off the governorship every eight years. Despite tortured budget battles in his first three years, Wolf won by an even larger margin in 2018.

Born in York and raised in Mount Wolf — named for his great-great-grandfather — Wolf earned degrees from Dartmouth College, the University of London and the Massachusetts Institute of Technology. During that time, he interrupted his studies to join the Peace Corps, serving two years in a village in India. After graduation, Wolf went to work for the family business, initially employed as a forklift operator at the Wolf Organization, a cabinet and building-materials company. In 1985, Wolf and two cousins bought the company and more than doubled its size. After selling the company to a private-equity firm in 2006, Wolf was tapped by Democratic Gov. Ed Rendell to be state revenue secretary in 2007 and 2008. Wolf intended to mount a campaign for governor to succeed Rendell, who was term-limited, but when the family business was on the brink of bankruptcy and collapse, Wolf abandoned the campaign, repurchased the company and restored it to solvency. He stepped down as CEO in 2013 to focus on his 2014 bid for governor, targeting first-term Republican Gov. Tom Corbett, who was saddled with low approval ratings.

Democratic Rep. Allyson Schwartz was anointed the early frontrunner in the primary, and state Treasurer Rob McCord and former state Environmental Protection Secretary Kathleen McGinty ran as well. But Wolf poured $10 million of his own money into the race, allowing him to blanket the airwaves from January 2014 until the May primary, which Wolf won easily with 58 percent of the vote. (Wolf later tapped McGinty as his chief of staff.) In the general, Wolf had the air and campaign strategy of an incumbent, bolstered by double-digit leads in the polls. Corbett touted his tax cuts and his efforts to reduce the size of government, rein in spending and bring businesses back to Pennsylvania. But Wolf hammered away at weak job growth under Corbett and accused him of slashing school funding. Wolf said that, unlike Corbett, he would raise taxes on the fast-growing natural gas industry. Scrutiny of Corbett's role as attorney general in the investigation of former Penn State assistant football coach Jerry Sandusky on accusations of child molestation became another albatross for the incumbent. Wolf won the high-spending race with 55 percent of the vote.

Wolf came into office stressing transparency. He introduced a website to track expenses by cabinet secretaries and signed a gift ban, and he refused the gubernatorial salary and residence and paid out of pocket for office space for the state police officers assigned to protect him. Meanwhile, he moved to broaden the state's Medicaid expansion under the Affordable Care Act, and he ordered a moratorium on the death penalty. But budget issues proved the most intractable. Wolf came into office facing a $2 billion budget gap – and two Republican-controlled legislative chambers. In June 2015, Wolf vetoed the first GOP budget. That instigated a battle that lasted until March 2016 and that included skirmishes not only over revenues and spending but also vetoes of GOP-backed changes to the state pension system and to tightly regulated liquor sales. The standoff also led to a credit downgrade for the state and fears of layoffs and closed public schools. Ultimately, Wolf allowed a budget to become law without signing it.

The relationship between Wolf and lawmakers grew lower-key and generally more productive. In 2016, he signed a medical-marijuana law, and issued an executive order protecting persons from discrimination based on sexual orientation and gender identity. Wolf signed bipartisan legislation to overhaul the state liquor system, including permission for grocery stores to sell wine and for wine to be shipped directly to customers, as well as an extension of hours at state liquor stores. He signed new regulations governing horizontal oil and gas drilling. And he signed several measures aimed at curbing opioid addiction, including restrictions on prescriptions for minors and requirements that medical professionals check a database before issuing prescriptions. The 2016 election was a downer for Pennsylvania Democrats, as presidential nominee Hillary Clinton lost the state and Republicans expanded their majorities by three seats in the state Senate and two seats in the state House. That gave Senate Republicans their widest edge in the Senate in seven decades. It was enough to override vetoes if Republicans stuck together.

In 2017, Wolf and the legislature faced the biggest budgetary shortfall since the recession; the independent legislative fiscal office projected a deficit of about $3 billion for the two-year fiscal period ending in June 2018. Wolf once again allowed the budget to be enacted without his signature, and it took another three months before the two sides could come up with enough funding to close the budget gap. "This is not the way government is supposed to work," he told reporters. It took until June 2018 for the two sides to finally notch a harmonious budget session, as Wolf signed a $32.7 billion spending package, bolstered by projections of strong revenue gains. Wolf signed an executive order to raise state employees' and contractors' minimum wages to $12 initially and to $15 an hour in 2024. Wolf signed a bipartisan criminal-justice reform bill that sealed nonviolent criminal records after an individual had been free of convictions for 10 years. Wolf also wielded his veto pen: He vetoed one bill that would have banned abortions at 20 weeks, and a business-backed, union-opposed measure that would have limited the prescriptions permitted for injured workers. For the fourth consecutive year, Republicans blocked Wolf's proposal to institute a severance tax on natural gas drilling. Wolf also played a key role in the state's redistricting battle: After the state Supreme Court struck down the congressional district map as a Republican gerrymander, Wolf rejected the alternative proposed by legislative Republicans, which effectively left the courts to draw the new maps, which proved to be significantly more favorable to the Democrats.

Wolf faced no opposition in the Democratic primary, although primary voters did knock out the lieutenant governor, Mike Stack, in favor of John Fetterman, with Wolf's tacit support. Stack had a controversial term in office that included scrutiny of his family's treatment of state employees. Fetterman, the burly, 6-foot-8 mayor of Braddock in Allegheny County, had attracted attention for his black T-shirt and jeans, as well as his grassroots brand of progressivism. He had performed respectably in a longshot 2016 Senate bid. (He also grew up near Wolf's ancestral hometown.)

The GOP, meanwhile, held a raucous primary between state Sen. Scott Wagner, businessman and former McKinsey consultant Paul Mango, and attorney Laura Ellsworth. As Lancasteronline.com put it, Wagner sold himself "as a farm-raised businessman who owns a trash-hauling company and isn't afraid to get on the back of a garbage truck or clean the company toilets," while Mango played up his status "as a West Point graduate handed his degree from Grand Old Party icon Ronald Reagan, going on to Harvard, then learning how to reinvigorate businesses." Wagner and Mango railed against each other in TV ads, many self-funded; Mango hit his opponent as "slumlord Wagner," "sleazy bail bondsman Wagner," and "deadbeat dad Wagner," while Wagner responded by calling Mango a "phony" and a "real liberal." Wagner adopted an outspoken, Trumpian style, while Mango attacked him for being insufficiently conservative on social issues. Ellsworth, who had chaired the Greater Pittsburgh Chamber of Commerce, adopted a more pragmatic image, but she failed to catch fire with the GOP base. Wagner won with 44 percent, followed by Mango with 37 percent and Ellsworth with 19 percent.

In the general election, Wolf outspent the Republican and was aided by the Democratic lean of the 2018 cycle. Wagner attracted national criticism for remarks he made in a video posted on his campaign's Facebook page in which he told Wolf, "Between now and Nov. 6, you better put a catcher's mask on your face, because I'm going to stomp all over your face with golf spikes." The only debate between Wolf and Wagner garnered attention mostly for being moderated by Alex Trebek, the longtime host of "Jeopardy!" By October, Wagner announced that he was "tapped out" of personal resources to fund his campaign.

Wolf won, 58%-41%; he collected nearly 1 million more votes than in his 2014 victory. Wolf lost ground in more rural areas, failing to repeat his 2014 victories in Lawrence, Greene, Fayette, Cambria, Clinton, Northumberland, Cumberland, Schuylkill and Carbon counties, and losing ground in Lackawanna (Scranton) and Luzerne (Wilkes-Barre). But those shortcomings were more than evened out by gains in the Philadelphia area; he improved his winning margins by 13 points in Delaware County, by 15 points in Bucks and Montgomery counties, by 20 points in Chester County, and by 150,000 votes in Philadelphia. He also fared well in Allegheny County (Pittsburgh), increasing his winning margin by 20 points. And even in southwestern counties Wolf lost, such as Fayette, Greene, Washington and Westmoreland, Wolf improved upon Hillary Clinton's 2016 performance.

Democrats made gains in both legislative chambers but not enough to flip partisan control. Early in his second term, Wolf proposed a $34.1 billion budget with increases for public schools. He pursued a pared-back tax agenda, including a retooled severance tax that would be devoted to infrastructure rather than the general fund. He called for the minimum wage to be raised in stages to $15. He signed an executive order setting a target for carbon emissions that was 26 percent below 2005 levels in 2025, and 80 percent below in 2050. He floated the idea of legalizing recreational marijuana. A Franklin & Marshall College poll in late March 2019 found a majority – 51% -- saying Wolf's job performance was "excellent" or "good."

Bob Casey (D)

Elected 2006, term expires 2024, 3rd term, b. Apr 13, 1960; Scranton; College of The Holy Cross (MA), B.A., 1982; Catholic University of America (DC), J.D., 1988; Roman Catholic; Married (Terese Foppiano Casey); 4 children.

Elected Office: PA auditor General, 1997-2005; PA State Treasurer, 2005-2007.

Professional Career: Practicing attorney, 1988-1996.

DC Office: 393 RSOB 20510, 202-224-6324, Fax: 202-228-0604, casey.senate.gov

State Offices: Allentown, 610-782-9470; Bellefonte, 814-357-0314; Erie, 814-874-5080; Harrisburg, 717-231-7540; Philadelphia, 215-405-9660; Pittsburgh, 412-803-7370; Scranton, 570-941-0930.

Committees: *Aging (RMM)*. *Agriculture, Nutrition & Forestry*: Conservation, Forestry & Natural Resources; Livestock, Marketing & Agriculture Security; Nutrition, Agricultural Research & Specialty Crops (RMM). *Finance*: Health Care; International Trade, Customs & Global Competitiveness (RMM); Social Security, Pensions & Family Policy. *Health, Education, Labor & Pensions*: Children & Families (RMM); Employment & Workplace Safety.

Group Ratings

	ADA	ACLU	AFL-CIO	LCV	ITI	COC	HAFA	ACU	CFG	FRC
2018	-	57%	-	93%	-	50%	5%	9%	5%	13%
2017	90%	C	100%	100%	C	29%	C	0%	4%	0%

Key Votes of the 115th Congress

1. Obama-care revision	N	5. Gun regulations	N	9. Kavanaugh confirmation	N
2. Tax Cuts	N	6. Family planning regs	N	10. Saudi arms sales	Y
3. Dodd-Frank revision	N	7. Gorsuch confirmation	N	11. FISA rules	Y
4. Omnibus appropriations	Y	8. Immigration restrictions	N	12. Military aid in Yemen	Y

Election Results

Election	Name (Party)	Vote (%)		Cand. Spent	Ind. Exp. Support	Ind. Exp. Oppose
2018 General	Bob Casey (D)..................................... 2,792,437	(56%)	$19,869,640	$769,690	$36,085
	Lou Barletta (R)............................ 2,134,848	(43%)	$7,423,020	$89,756	$2,321,087
2018 Primary	Bob Casey (D)..	(100%)			

Prior winning percentages: 2012 (54%), 2006 (59%)

Bob Casey, Pennsylvania's senior senator, navigated a tricky political balance in 2018 as he sought a third term. In one of the three blue states that narrowly swung the 2016 presidential election to Donald Trump and that has a history of electing Republicans statewide, he needed to motivate swing voters to vote against Trump — and for himself. That required him to reassure progressive Democrats that they did not need to worry about his long-standing apostasy on abortion-related issues. Casey's brand of economic populism had some overlap with Trump's —and with some blue-collar Democrats, but not with the party's suburban voters. He supported the president's international trade war, including tariff increases. On those economic issues, he was closer to Trump than was Pennsylvania's Republican senator, Pat Toomey, who was an outspoken opponent of the president on trade. As it turned out, Casey was re-elected in a cakewalk, as his Republican challenger failed to reignite the Trump coalition. His victory was the latest example of the appeal Casey, like his father before him, has had with his state's voters.

Born in the former coal town of Scranton in northeast Pennsylvania, the oldest son in a large Irish-Catholic family, Casey grew up in the Green Ridge neighborhood — also the boyhood home of former Vice President Joe Biden. His father, Bob Casey Sr., served as a state senator and Pennsylvania's auditor general; he lost three Democratic primaries for governor before winning that office in 1986 and serving two terms. He was a feisty, tradition-minded practitioner of New Deal-style politics but was best known nationally for his steadfast opposition to abortion and his frequent clashes with national party leaders over that issue. In 1992, he was prevented from speaking at the Democratic National Convention, a decision related to his abortion stance but also brought on by his skepticism of Bill Clinton.

Casey Jr. graduated from the College of the Holy Cross in Massachusetts. He taught in an inner-city Philadelphia school for the Jesuit Volunteer Corps and earned his law degree from The Catholic University of America in Washington, D.C. He practiced law in Scranton and then began his political career by winning election in 1996 as state auditor general. He was re-elected in 2000, and, two years later, he ran as a cultural conservative with strong labor support in a nasty and expensive primary for governor against former Philadelphia Mayor Ed Rendell. Casey voiced similar views on abortion as his late father had as he sought unsuccessfully to follow his footsteps into the governor's mansion. Casey's negative ads tarnished his image, but he showed resilience by returning in 2004 to win the state Treasurer's Office.

A year later, national Democrats were looking for a strong challenger to two-term Republican Sen. Rick Santorum, a high-profile social conservative with a red-state following and blue-state constituency. First in the House and then in the Senate, Santorum showed a knack for winning elections against tough odds — but the state's political landscape had shifted considerably since his first election to the Senate in 1994. Casey was waiting to make another run for governor in 2005 when New York Sen. Chuck Schumer — then head of the Democratic Senatorial Campaign Committee — wanted him to run for the Senate and quickly cleared the field to avoid a cash-draining primary. While Casey's opposition to abortion rights made him anathema to many cultural liberals in the Philadelphia area, Schumer believed Casey could make inroads into Santorum's culturally conservative base — particularly in the western part of the state, where Santorum lived. Meanwhile, as the Democratic alternative to Santorum, Casey would be acceptable to anti-abortion voters in suburban Philadelphia, Schumer reasoned. The national party's heavy-handed involvement in recruiting Casey rankled many Democrats in the state. But resistance to Casey's candidacy faded in the run-up to the election, as he maintained a sizable lead over Santorum in the polls.

Though Santorum was being mentioned as a potential presidential candidate, his standing at home was tenuous. In the summer of 2005, he released a book titled, "It Takes a Family: Conservatism and the Common Good." Published a year before Santorum stood for re-election, the book didn't have the best timing for a frank discourse on some of the most divisive cultural issues of the day. Santorum's support of the unpopular Bush administration in 2006 didn't help him either. Casey's socially conservative positions — at the time, he opposed gun control and same-sex marriage — helped cut into Santorum's advantage outside the state's metropolitan areas. The two candidates raised a combined $43 million. Santorum outspent Casey by more than $8 million, but it wasn't enough. Casey won 59%-41%, becoming the first Pennsylvania Democrat elected to a full Senate term since 1962.

In the Senate, Casey has been a reliable supporter of his party's agenda and has moved leftward on several social issues. He angered some anti-abortion groups in 2011 when he voted against denying federal funds to Planned Parenthood, saying the group provides many family planning services beyond abortion. He used a similar line of argument in 2014 when he supported a bill to overturn the Supreme Court's Hobby Lobby decision, another move that irked some abortion foes. The legislation was an effort to put congressional Democrats on record in favor of forcing most businesses to offer employees a full range of contraceptive coverage, even if the businesses' owners raised religious objections. "The health care service that's at issue here is contraception, which means prior to conception," Casey told the Philadelphia Inquirer that year, even as he said, "I'm a pro-life Democrat, always have been, always will be." Christopher Borick, a political scientist at Muhlenberg College, told the newspaper, "He has remained a pro-life Democrat, but one who has stretched the bounds of that definition."

Casey held to his traditional anti-abortion stand in spring 2015, voting with three other Democrats and most Republicans to advance a bill related to human trafficking. Most Democrats supported a filibuster of the measure over a provision they believed would expand the scope of the so-called Hyde amendment, which bars federal dollars from being spent on abortions. He signed on to the anti-abortion view in 2015 and again in 2018 when he joined two Democratic senators — Joe Donnelly of Indiana and Joe Manchin of West Virginia — to vote to start debate on a bill to prohibit abortions after 20 weeks of pregnancy. A Pennsylvania official of Planned Parenthood, who seemed reconciled to Casey's views, offered a nuanced view when she told the Pittsburgh Post-Gazette in early 2017 that he had "become more comfortable in distinguishing the women's health work we do" from abortion. In a July 2018 interview with Politico, Casey said that he remained a "pro-life Democrat," which meant, "I try to support policies that help women and children both before and after birth."

Casey reversed himself on two other social issues of perennial controversy: gun control and same-sex marriage. In 2013, he supported a measure — co-authored by his colleague Toomey — to expand background checks for gun owners. The bill, which came after the 2012 school shooting in Newtown, Connecticut in which more than two dozen were killed, failed to overcome a filibuster. Two years before the Supreme Court legalized same-sex marriage nationwide, Casey dropped his opposition to same-sex marriage. In 2016, after the massacre at a gay club in Orlando, he reinforced his shift on guns with a proposal to restrict sales to or ownership for those convicted hate crimes.

On the Senate Finance Committee, Casey has been a party regular on economic issues. He has shared the skepticism of other Democrats from Rust Belt states toward international trade deals. "Our workers are losing over and over again when you have these trade agreements," Casey told the Allentown-based Morning Call. He voted against South Korea, Panama and Colombia trade agreements that became law in 2011, and, in 2015, was among the large majority of Democrats to oppose giving President Barack Obama "fast track" negotiating authority to expedite a 12-nation Pacific trade agreement.

Casey serves on the Health, Education, Labor and Pensions Committee, where he has taken an interest in issues affecting children and families. He has consistently promoted legislation to award grants to states that provide full-day prekindergarten programs, while complaining that Congress has ignored the business community's support for investment in early childhood education. "It's been terribly frustrating," he told the Easton Express-Times. He has been an avid booster of funding for the Children's Health Insurance Program, which is similar to a program his father instituted in Pennsylvania.

Like other coal-state senators, Casey had his differences with the Obama administration on environmental and energy policies. Responding in late 2014 to the administration's proposed climate change rules, Casey, emphasizing his commitment to environmental protection, said that a plan by the Environmental Protection Agency was necessary. But he asked for revisions, saying the plan set the carbon emissions target for Pennsylvania too high. In 2015, he was one of only eight Democrats to support an unsuccessful effort to override Obama's veto of the Keystone XL pipeline, a project opposed by environmentalists.

Republicans hoped to unseat Casey in 2012, but they had a hard time recruiting a top-tier candidate to take on the well-funded incumbent. Former coal executive Tom Smith, who spent almost $5 million of his own money, won the nomination with almost 40 percent of the vote. Initially, Smith was given little chance to beat Casey. But Smith went on the attack, calling Casey "Sen. Zero" and claiming he had accomplished little in the Senate. As a precaution, Casey kept his distance from Obama. His supporters worried he was underestimating Smith. "They've run a noncampaign up until now," Rendell told the Scranton Times-Tribune just weeks before the general election. Around that time, Smith invested another $10 million into his campaign, flooding the airwaves with attack ads. Casey won endorsements from most of the state's major newspapers. Smith outspent him, $21 million to $14 million, but Casey hung on to win, 54%-45%; the margin was half of big as it was in his victory over better-known Santorum. He ran slightly ahead of Obama, who took the state with 52 percent of the vote.

Heading into the 2018 campaign, Casey saw that the political tide again was shifting. In early 2017, he spoke out against several of Trump's Cabinet nominees and went to the Philadelphia airport to join a protest of Trump's executive order banning entry of citizens of seven majority-Muslim nations. Although he had incentive to reach out to the Democratic base, the reality was that he had been moving in recent years to the left on social issues. Still, the cautious Casey was mindful of the 2016 results in Pennsylvania: Democrats had narrowly lost high-stakes presidential and Senate contests. That spring, Republican Rep. Lou Barletta said he was thinking about challenging Casey and that he had received encouragement from Trump. Barletta, an early and outspoken supporter of Trump, shared Casey's home ground in northeastern Pennsylvania.

In his customary way, Casey played to both sides as he responded to Trump's actions as president. He supported Trump's increased tariffs, especially on steel and aluminum. "I commend the president for announcing his intent to take action to protect our steelworkers from countries like China that cheat on trade," he said in March 2018. Strikingly, Toomey took issue with that action, which he called "a big mistake." Both Pennsylvania senators serve on the Finance Committee, where they sometimes cancel each other's vote — not always in line with the views of their respective parties. In July, Casey said Trump "shamed the office of the presidency" during his "dangerous and reckless" news conference with Russian President Vladimir Putin after their meeting in Helsinki. In February 2019, he opposed Trump's attempts to declare an emergency at the southern border and build a wall there with funds taken from other federal accounts, including nearly $200 million that had been approved for military construction in the Keystone State "I will fight like hell to keep this funding and these projects up and running in Pennsylvania," Casey said.

Barletta followed Trump's 2016 small-town strategy instead of Toomey's more-suburban emphasis in his close re-election that year. Local pundits said that the contest would be "a referendum on Trump." But Barletta was no Trump. And politics in Pennsylvania shifted between 2016 and 2018. Midterm turnout dropped by about 1 million voters, with anti-Trump voters in the suburbs more motivated than many of Trump's core voters. Barletta had problems building his name recognition and selling his message, and Casey outspent him, $20 million to $7.4 million. Casey won 56%-43%. Casey won 15 counties, including big majorities in most of the heavily populated areas.

At 58 when he began his third term, Casey retained options. His seniority had lifted him close to a top committee post in the Senate. Or, he could still seek to satisfy his ambition to follow his father as governor in Harrisburg. He quickly ruled out a 2020 run for president, though public demand for his candidacy had not seemed loud. "After two months of considering it, I have concluded that the best way for me to fight for the America that so many of us believe in is to stay in the U.S. Senate," he said in a January 2019 statement to CNN.

Pat Toomey (R)

Elected 2010, term expires 2022, 2nd term, b. Nov 17, 1961; Providence, RI; La Salle Academy (RI); Harvard University, B.A., 1984; Roman Catholic; Married (Kris Toomey); 3 children.

Elected Office: Allentown Government Study Commissioner, 1994-1996; U.S. House, 1999-2005.

Professional Career: Investment banker, Chemical Bank, 1984-1986; Investment banker, Morgan Grenfell, 1986-1990; Financial consultant, Springfield Ltd., 1990-1991; Restaurateur, 1990-2001; President, Club for Growth, 2005-2009.

DC Office: 248 RSOB 20510, 202-224-4254, Fax: 202-228-0284, toomey.senate.gov

State Offices: Allentown, 610-434-1444; Erie, 814-453-3010; Harrisburg, 717-782-3951; Johnstown, 814-266-5970; Philadelphia, 215-241-1090; Pittsburgh, 412-803-3501; Wilkes-Barre, 570-820-4088.

Committees: *Banking, Housing & Urban Affairs*: Financial Institutions & Consumer Protection; National Security & International Trade & Finance; Securities, Insurance & Investment (Chmn). *Budget. Finance*: Health Care (Chmn); International Trade, Customs & Global Competitiveness; Taxation & IRS Oversight.

Group Ratings

	ADA	ACLU	AFL-CIO	LCV	ITI	COC	HAFA	ACU	CFG	FRC
2018	-	6%	-	0%	-	89%	85%	100%	100%	100%
2017	0%	C	0%	0%	C	86%	C	84%	100%	100%

Almanac Ratings 2017-18

	Economy	Social	Foreign	Composite
Liberal	0%	0%	0%	0%
Conservative	100%	100%	100%	100%

Key Votes of the 115th Congress

1. Obama-care revision	Y	5. Gun regulations	Y	9. Kavanaugh confirmation	Y
2. Tax Cuts	Y	6. Family planning regs	Y	10. Saudi arms sales	N
3. Dodd-Frank revision	Y	7. Gorsuch confirmation	Y	11. FISA rules	Y
4. Omnibus appropriations	NV	8. Immigration restrictions	Y	12. Military aid in Yemen	N

Election Results

Election	Name (Party)	Vote (%)	Cand. Spent	Ind. Exp. Support	Ind. Exp. Oppose
2016 General	Pat Toomey (R)............................ 2,951,702	(49%)	$27,373,876	$15,146,525	$59,455,201
	Kathleen McGinty (D)................. ... 2,865,012	(47%)	$14,968,292	$14,558,232	$47,543,382
	Edward Clifford (L)...................... 235,142	(4%)			
2016 Primary	Pat Toomey (R)............................ Unopposed				

Prior winning percentages: 2010 (51%), House: 2002 (57%), 2000 (53%), 1998 (55%)

In his improbable re-election in 2016, Republican Pat Toomey, Pennsylvania's junior senator, showed his political evolution in his state's complex politics. He had taken a different path to victory than did Donald Trump, who won even more narrowly in the Pennsylvania presidential contest that day. With an emphasis on the suburban battlegrounds outside Philadelphia, Toomey succeeded with more of a coalition-building appeal. Toomey is one of only two surviving Republican senators from the New England and Mid-Atlantic regions — areas that were the heart of the Republican establishment a few decades ago. Despite this status, Toomey mostly retained his Main Street Republican views and his role as a busy Senate insider, including a willingness to challenge Trump.

His latest success was all the more notable because of the contrast with the political approach he took before 2010, when he won a similarly narrow election to the Senate. In those earlier days, Toomey spent several years as the president of the Club for Growth, a national organization that has spent generously to support conservative candidates who share its views. As head of the group, he frequently backed candidates opposed by the local party establishment in Republican primary contests, sometimes taking on incumbent Republicans in the process. During his first term in the Senate, Toomey remained steadfast in his devotion to the Club for Growth's core principles of lower taxes and less spending. But, facing re-election in a state that had become reliably blue in presidential elections, he moved perceptibly to the center on some social issues. The most noteworthy example came in 2013, when Toomey — a gun-rights supporter with an "A" rating from the National Rifle Association — broke with his party to sponsor expanded background checks on would-be gun purchasers.

A New Englander by birth, Toomey grew up in Providence, Rhode Island, the third of six children of a union worker and a part-time church secretary. He graduated from Harvard University, paid for by scholarships and earnings from part-time jobs. After college, he worked in investment banking — founding a successful international financial services consulting firm and amassing considerable wealth. After six years on Wall Street, Toomey moved to Allentown, where he joined his brothers to start Rookies Restaurant and Sports Bar, which grew into a statewide chain. In 1994, he was elected to the Allentown Government Study Commission, where he pushed to lower taxes and require the City Council to have a supermajority to raise taxes.

As one of six candidates in the 1998 Republican primary for an open House seat, Toomey advocated individual Social Security investment accounts, a flat tax to replace the income tax system and term limits for members of Congress; he promised to serve only six years. He won the close primary with 27 percent of the vote. In the general election, he won 55%-45%. He was twice re-elected with a similar margin in a district that had consistently voted for Democrats in presidential elections since 1992.

In the House, Toomey focused primarily on economic issues, pushing to limit spending and force Congress to set aside money for debt reduction. Toomey ran in 2004 for the Senate seat held by then-Republican Arlen Specter. Specter was supported by President George W. Bush and conservative Pennsylvania colleague, Sen. Rick Santorum. Specter raised far more money than Toomey, while spotlighting the projects he had obtained for the state over his 24 years in the Senate, Toomey criticized Specter's voting record as too liberal and emphasized the latter's support from trial lawyers. Specter won 51%-49%, by a margin of 17,000 votes out of more than 1 million cast. Specter carried metro Philadelphia, his home, with 57 percent of the vote, but Toomey carried metro Pittsburgh with 58 percent.

In 2005, Toomey signed on as the head of the Club for Growth, a post he held until 2009 and which enabled him to make contacts around the country with conservative activists and major fundraisers. He defended the group's strategy in 2008 after Oklahoma Rep. Tom Cole, then chairman of the National Republican Congressional Committee, excoriated the Club for Growth's involvement in a contentious Ohio congressional primary. "The problem I have with the club is, I think they're stupid,"

Cole told The New York Times. "They spend more money beating Republicans than Democrats." In a Wall Street Journal op-ed piece titled "In Defense of RINO Hunting," — which used a derogatory term meaning "Republican in Name Only" —Toomey shot back: "This is the argument of politicians who care more about maintaining power than using that power to implement conservative policies." In recent years, the Club for Growth has stopped targeting Republican Senate incumbents.

Toomey challenged Specter again in 2010 after the incumbent cast one of three Republican votes for the Democrats' $787 billion economic stimulus bill. In April 2009, Specter announced he was switching parties to become a Democrat, saying he did not want to put his service at the mercy of Republican primary voters. Specter had a rocky path to the Democratic nomination, despite his backing from party heavyweights. Two-term Democratic Rep. Joe Sestak, a retired Navy admiral, entered the race. Sestak won the primary 54%-46%, carrying all but three counties: Philadelphia and those containing Harrisburg and Scranton. Sestak's independence left intraparty scars that affected his candidacy in 2016, when he sought a rematch against Toomey.

The general election presented a clear contrast on issues: Sestak had voted not only for the stimulus bill, but for the Democrats' health care overhaul and their cap-and-trade bill to limit carbon emissions. Toomey called for extending the Bush-era tax cuts for everyone, including the wealthiest bracket, and for lower corporate and capital gains tax rates. He spent $17 million, while Sestak spent $12 million, much of it in the primary. In a year in which Republicans rode a political wave, Toomey beat Sestak 51%-49%.

In the Senate, Toomey has shown a preference for serious policy over sound bites. He has won praise for articulating conservative ideals in a manner that has not offended those who disagree. He introduced legislation making permanent an earmark ban on pet projects in spending bills; it did not pass, but continuing opposition to earmarks has resulted in a prohibition of the practice.

Toomey gained attention while floating a couple of far-reaching plans to reduce the deficit. When a standoff developed in 2011 between President Barack Obama and Republican congressional leaders over raising the federal debt ceiling, Toomey disputed warnings from the Treasury Department and business leaders that a failure to raise the debt ceiling risked a financial default; he argued the United States could prioritize its payments to avoid a true default. Although he voted against the bill that ended the crisis by raising the federal debt ceiling, he was one of three Republican senators appointed to the Joint Committee on Deficit Reduction — the "Supercommittee" — that was created by the legislation. The committee, evenly divided between Democrats and Republicans and House and Senate, was charged with coming up with at least $1.2 trillion in budget savings over a 10-year period.

The committee's efforts ended in partisan stalemate. Toomey, with the support of several other Republicans, floated a proposal to raise $400 billion in revenue — the majority coming from a reduction in tax breaks — coupled with $800 million in spending cuts. But the Democrats reportedly rejected Toomey's plan because it did not phase out the Bush era tax cuts for the wealthiest Americans. Toomey's proposal aimed to balance the budget in nine years with defense cuts already proposed by then-Defense Secretary Robert Gates, along with an overhaul of Medicaid into a block grant program. His plan did not touch two popular entitlement programs: Medicare and Social Security.

In 2013, with a coveted seat on the Finance Committee, Toomey supported the compromise on taxes and spending to avoid the "fiscal cliff." But he blunted criticism from conservatives who didn't like the deal by saying Republicans needed to be ready to shut down the government in future debates over raising the deficit. "We absolutely have to have this fight over the debt limit," he said. In October of that year, Toomey was one of just 18 senators to vote against the spending deal to end a 16-day federal government shutdown, saying he opposed the new borrowing it allowed.

Toomey's first-term record on social issues was variable. In late 2010, he favored repealing the military's ban on openly gay service members. Although he reiterated shortly before the Supreme Court's 2015 ruling on same-sex marriage that he believes marriage should be between a man and a woman, he voted for several measures that acknowledged gay rights. They included domestic violence protections for LGBTQ people, a ban on workplace discrimination and a requirement that groups receiving federal money do not discriminate based on sexual orientation.

In his decision to team with West Virginia Democratic Sen. Joe Manchin in April 2013 on a compromise on gun control, Toomey caused a ripple across Capitol Hill. Their proposal called for expanding background checks to gun shows and online sales while maintaining record-keeping provisions that law enforcement officials said were essential in tracking criminal gun use. Toomey said that, while the volatile issue was "not something I sought," he considered it important to take action. The measure came after the December 2012 school shooting in Newtown Connecticut, in which 26 people, most of them children, were killed. The Manchin-Toomey proposal fell five votes short of the 60-vote supermajority needed to overcome a filibuster because only three Republicans joined Toomey in supporting the measure, which was strongly opposed by the NRA. At a subsequent event at which he was honored by the families of Newtown victims, Toomey said that, despite the fallout from his conservative base, he would "do it again in a heartbeat," The Washington Post reported. Later, Toomey said he regretted his bill hadn't passed and "that it took me so long before I raised my voice on this very important issue."

In 2015, national Democratic leaders spent months searching for an alternative candidate to Sestak to take on Toomey. Finally, in August, Katie McGinty entered the contest, hoping to rally the support of feminists, organized labor and environmentalists. Republicans pointed out that the former Al Gore aide ran a distant fourth in the 2014 primary for governor. In a view that became more prevalent in post-election second guessing, some Democrats argued that Sestak, given his outsider appeal and narrow loss to Toomey in a year unkind to Democrats, would have been a formidable challenger in a rematch, notwithstanding his scratchy relations with Democratic leaders. McGinty won the primary 43%-33%.

Toomey presented himself as more well-rounded than a politician who cared only about cutting taxes and regulations, his campaign strategist Jon Lerner told Roll Call after the election. Emphasizing that Toomey had not backed away from his conservatism, Lerner said, "It was an attempt to put something else on top of it, it was a tonal aspect. It was a guy who's thoughtful, a guy who's serious." He sought to demonstrate this approach on several issues, including opposition to the Iranian nuclear agreement and the response to sanctuary cities, in addition to his actions on the federal debt and gay rights.

The approach was designed to appeal, in particular, to voters in the Philadelphia suburbs. The results there showed his success. He narrowly won in Bucks and Chester counties, and lost narrowly in Montgomery and Delaware counties. In the four counties combined, Toomey got about 48 percent of the vote; Trump only got 43 percent. Trump outperformed Toomey in blue-collar strongholds outside Pittsburgh, which responded to more socially conservative appeals. Toomey won every other county west of the Philadelphia suburbs, including Centre and Dauphin, which Trump narrowly lost. During the campaign, Toomey would not endorse Trump, though he said on Election Day that he voted for Trump. The Senate contest was one of the most expensive in congressional history. In addition to nearly $50 million in spending by the candidates, outside groups spent more than $130 million, which was split about evenly between the two parties.

After the election, Toomey worked on significant Republican policies. On the Finance Committee, where several of the senior Republicans were focused elsewhere as chairmen of other committees, he worked with party leaders to seek common ground on major health care and tax bills in 2017. He had played a similar role earlier in the decade during the unsuccessful debt-reduction negotiations.

As Senate Republicans failed to repeal the Affordable Care Act in July 2017, Toomey said that he could not reach common ground on alternatives that might draw support from Democrats. "I'm not interested in perpetuating a failed system and just throwing more dollars at it," he told the Pittsburgh Post-Gazette. "I've expended an awful lot of political time and energy and political capital. It's really important to me and it'll be extremely disappointing if we don't get this done."

After the GOP meltdown on health care legislation, Toomey had a more rewarding experience with the party's measure to cut taxes. In reviewing Toomey's "intimate role" on the tax bill, the Allentown Morning Call gave him credit for crafting the key deal that set the amount of the cuts, for serving as a public "cheerleader" for the bill and for making a closing pitch to the final undecided Republican senators. "Let's face it, he was central," Sen. Bob Corker of Tennessee, who was part of the deal-making, told The Washington Post in December 2017. For that story, Toomey described his experience as "gratifying and fulfilling."

As chairman of the Banking, Housing and Urban Affairs Subcommittee on Financial Institutions and Consumer Protection, he helped prepare the Senate bill to alter the 2010 Dodd-Frank banking regulation law. Trump signed the measure in May 2018.

Toomey faced his limits as a team player on steps that Trump took overseas. In March 2018, he called the president's tariff hikes "very, very counter-productive." He told a telephone town hall in July that Trump's meeting with Russian President Vladimir Putin was "very troubling" and showed "inexplicable blindness." In March 2019, he was one of 12 senators who voted to reject Trump's declaration of an emergency at the southern border to secure funds for a border wall.

At home, Democratic Lt. Gov. John Fetterman said before his 2018 election that he planned to use that position as a bully pulpit to challenge Toomey's re-election in 2022. "It's hard to ignore Pat Toomey and what he's talking about," Fetterman told City & State Pennsylvania.

Brian Fitzpatrick (R)

Elected 2016, 2nd term, b. Dec 17, 1973; Levittown; LaSalle University, Bach. Deg., 1996; Pennsylvania State University, M.B.A., 2001; Pennsylvania State University School of Law, J.D., 2001; Roman Catholic; Single.

Professional Career: Judicial Clerk, Eastern District of PA, 2001-2002; Special Agent, FBI.

DC Office: 1722 LHOB 20515, 202-225-4276, Fax: 202-225-9511, brianfitzpatrick.house.gov

Committees: *Foreign Affairs*: Europe, Eurasia, Energy & the Environment; Middle East, North Africa & International Terrorism. *Transportation & Infrastructure*: Aviation; Highways & Transit; Railroads, Pipelines & Hazardous Materials.

Group Ratings

	ADA	ACLU	AFL-CIO	LCV	ITI	COC	HAFA	ACU	CFG	FRC
2018	-	29%	-	83%	-	83%	27%	24%	28%	80%
2017	20%	C	47%	71%	C	93%	C	44%	38%	67%

Almanac Ratings 2017-18

	Economy	Social	Foreign	Composite
Liberal	39%	26%	16%	27%
Conservative	61%	74%	84%	73%

Key Votes of the 115th Congress

1. Obama-care revision	N	5. Family planning regs	Y	9. Guantanamo prisoners	N
2. Tax Cuts	Y	6. Body cameras/immigration	Y	10. Ground missiles, limit	N
3. Omnibus appropriations	Y	7. Abortion ban	Y	11. Defense Dept. spending	Y
4. Dodd-Frank revision	Y	8. Concealed carry	N	12. FISA rules	Y

Election Results

Election	Name (Party)	Vote (%)	Cand. Spent	Ind. Exp. Support	Ind. Exp. Oppose
2018 General	Brian Fitzpatrick (R)....................... 169,053	(51%)	$3,328,411	$2,096,102	$2,553,799
	Scott Wallace (D)............................. 160,745	(49%)	$13,526,504	$359,201	$8,921,540
2018 Primary	Brian Fitzpatrick (R)....................... 31,394	(67%)			
	Dean Malik (R)............................. 15,461	(33%)			

Prior winning percentages: 2016 (54%)

Republican Brian Fitzpatrick, elected in 2016, succeeded his brother, GOP Rep. Mike Fitzpatrick, who retired to keep his term-limits pledge. The latest Fitzpatrick has deep experience with law enforcement, where he pursued political corruption and global terrorism. His expertise in campaign-finance and election laws is unusual for a member of Congress. He has often shown independence from GOP leaders on high-stakes votes. That likely served Fitzpatrick well in 2018, as he withstood a costly reelection challenge and survived as the only remaining House Republican in the Philadelphia suburbs; three others retired and Democrats took their seats.

Brian Fitzpatrick, who is 10 years younger than his brother Mike, was raised in Bucks County. He got his bachelor's degree from LaSalle University and his MBA and law degrees from Penn State University. He has been a licensed certified public accountant and an attorney. Fitzpatrick served as a special assistant U.S. attorney focused on drug crimes. He graduated first in his class at Quantico, the FBI academy, and served for 15 years as an FBI supervisory special agent. During the war in Iraq, Fitzpatrick was embedded with U.S. Special Forces. In his portfolio with the FBI, he was the national director for its Campaign Finance and Election Crimes Enforcement Program and was a national supervisor for its political corruption unit. In 2015, he was an inaugural recipient of the FBI Director's Leadership Award.

Mike Fitzpatrick retired after having served eight years between 2005 and 2017 (he lost reelection in 2006 and regained his seat four years later.) Although Brian Fitzpatrick was a newcomer as a political candidate and had not resided in the 8th District for many years, his last name and bio were obvious assets. When he entered the contest, early frontrunner state Rep. Scott Petri dropped out. The Republican primary became a low-key contest in which the candidates had few major differences and Fitzpatrick's two opponents raised less than $50,000 between them; he raised $2.2 million for the cycle. He won that contest with 78 percent of the vote.

His Democratic challenger, state Rep. Steven Santarsiero, took his far more competitive primary, 54%-46%, against Shaughnessy Naughton, who was backed by EMILY's List, which supports Democratic women who favor abortion rights. Santarsiero said that Fitzpatrick had spent little time in the district for many years prior to their campaign, and that "it's clear that if his last name were not Fitzpatrick, he wouldn't be running." Local reporters said that Fitzpatrick was rarely available for interviews. His ads described him as "Levittown's own," and he emphasized his professional credentials and national security expertise. He did not endorse Donald Trump during the campaign and said that he could not vote for him. Santarsiero raised $2.8 million for the cycle. Each candidate benefited from more than $7 million in national party support. In a district where the presidential election was virtually even, Fitzpatrick had a comfortable 54%-46% win.

In the House, Fitzpatrick quickly showed his independence. In January 2017, he was one of nine Republicans who voted against the plan to permit expedited House votes on health care reform. He said that Trump's initial executive order to limit entry by refugees to the United States "entirely misses the mark." That early pattern continued. He opposed the House GOP plan to replace the Affordable Care Act. Following Trump's meeting in Helsinki with Russian President Vladimir Putin in July 2018, Fitzpatrick said that Trump was "manipulated" and that he was "frankly sickened by the exchange" between the two presidents in describing their meeting.

In January 2019, Fitzpatrick was one of seven House Republicans who voted to end the partial government shutdown and was among 13 Republicans in February who opposed Trump's declaration of a national emergency to justify funding construction of a wall along the border with Mexico. Also that month, he was the only Republican who joined 50 Democrats in sponsoring a bill that affirmed support for the Paris climate agreement that Trump had rejected.

Fitzpatrick faced a daunting reelection challenge from Scott Wallace, who self-financed about 90 percent of the $13.5 million that his campaign spent. Wallace, whose grandfather Henry Wallace was vice president under Franklin Roosevelt, was estimated to have a net worth exceeding $100 million — largely from the sale of a family business. He ran a foundation that contributed to many strongly liberal causes; some of those recipients, including the Black Panthers and anti-Israel groups, became the focus of Republican campaign attacks. Wallace sought to link Fitzpatrick to Trump and to Republican attempts to cut back government health spending. Fitzpatrick continued to distance himself from the president and highlighted his attempts to rebuild the political center. He was endorsed by the AFL-CIO and by the Philadelphia Inquirer, which wrote that "Fitzpatrick's emphasis on bipartisanship is a breath of fresh air."

Fitzpatrick spent $3.3 million and was aided by $11 million in national GOP assistance. He won, 51.3%-48.7%, a margin of 8,300 votes. Wallace led by about 2,500 votes in the small part of the district that is in Montgomery County. Following the election, Republicans gave him a seat on the Transportation and Infrastructure Committee.

PA-1: Northern Philadelphia Suburbs   **Cook Partisan Voting Index: R+2**

Demographics data for new House districts were not prepared by the Census Bureau prior to our editorial deadline.

2012 Pres. Vote	Obama	180,413	(50%)	Romney	174,516	(49%)		
2016 Pres. Vote	Clinton	189,327	(49%)	Trump	181,716	(47%)	Johnson	9,729	(3%)

Bucks County: Bucks County was one of Pennsylvania founding father William Penn's three original settlements and the launching point for George Washington's crossing of the frigid Delaware River to surprise English and Hessian forces on Christmas Day 1776. But it has had a split personality from the start. Upper Bucks County was at once a bucolic paradise of rolling hills and creeks. In the 1920s, Bucks County's well-settled farmland, old fieldstone houses and covered bridges captured the imagination of writers and artists, attracting the New York theatrical crowd — Oscar Hammerstein,

Moss Hart, Dorothy Parker and S.J. Perelman. Doylestown, the county seat, has beautiful old homes and several impressive museums. New Hope remains a popular weekend spot, with its hip boutiques and restaurants.

After World War II, its location between Philadelphia and Trenton New Jersey brought industrial Lower Bucks County to the forefront. The ocean-navigable Delaware River and several rail lines resulted in huge new developments: U.S. Steel's Fairless Works, one of the few big postwar steel plants, and the Levitt organization's second Levittown in what had been a swamp between U.S. 13 and U.S. 1. The steel mill closed in 1991. A wind turbine plant moved onto part of the site. In September 2018, highway crews opened a four-mile section of I-95 in Bucks, thus filling the final gap in the 1,917-mile interstate highway from Houlton Maine to Miami Florida; while county officials and residents argued for decades about the location of the link, the area was served by the Pennsylvania Turnpike and another expressway. Development in Bucks came later than in other suburban Philadelphia counties, where most blue-collar immigration settled decades earlier. Fairless Works and Levittown, with their tightly packed homes filled with blue-collar workers, became Democratic. Upper Bucks was a Republican bastion for many decades. As the area began to attract trendy New Yorkers, it has increasingly favored Democratic policies such as green space programs to keep developers away. Tourism and conventions are big business in Bucks. Overall, Bucks County has remained politically marginal.

The 1st Congressional District of Pennsylvania includes all of Bucks County. Its small part of northeast Montgomery County is slightly more than 10 percent of the district. The redistricting in 2018 had less impact here than in any other district in the state. The modest change from the old 8th District, which already had relatively compact boundaries, moved its Montgomery County townships to the south along the Northeast Extension of the Pennsylvania Turnpike -- from the area surrounding Upper Hanover to Franconia and Hatfield townships, including the borough of Lansdale. Bucks has a notably small minority population of 5 percent for both Hispanics and Asians, plus 4 percent for blacks, and the third-highest median household income of any county in the state (behind Chester and Montgomery). The district has hosted some of the most hotly contested House races in the country, and it remained competitive. In both the 2012 and 2016 presidential elections, the outcome was virtually even. The latest redistricting changes increased the Democratic vote by about 1 percent.

Brendan Boyle (D)

Elected 2014, 3rd term, b. Feb 06, 1977; Philadelphia; University of Notre Dame (IN), B.A., 1999; Harvard University John F. Kennedy School of Government (MA), M.P.P., 2005; Roman Catholic; Married (Jennifer Morgan); 1 child.

Elected Office: PA House, 2009-2014.

Professional Career: Radio broadcaster; Management Consultant; Adjunct Professional, Drexel University.

DC Office: 1133 LHOB 20515, 202-225-6111, Fax: 202-226-0611, boyle.house.gov

State Offices: Philadelphia, 215-426-4616.

Committees: *Budget. Ways & Means*: Oversight; Select Revenue Measures; Social Security.

Group Ratings

	ADA	ACLU	AFL-CIO	LCV	ITI	COC	HAFA	ACU	CFG	FRC
2018	-	82%	-	91%	-	58%	6%	5%	18%	0%
2017	85%	C	95%	94%	C	62%	C	4%	5%	11%

Almanac Ratings 2017-18

	Economy	Social	Foreign	Composite
Liberal	94%	94%	83%	91%
Conservative	6%	6%	17%	9%

Key Votes of the 115th Congress

1. Obama-care revision	N	5. Family planning regs	N	9. Guantanamo prisoners	Y
2. Tax Cuts	N	6. Body cameras/immigration	Y	10. Ground missiles, limit	N
3. Omnibus appropriations	N	7. Abortion ban	N	11. Defense Dept. spending	Y
4. Dodd-Frank revision	N	8. Concealed carry	N	12. FISA rules	Y

Election Results

Election	Name (Party)	Vote (%)		Cand. Spent	Ind. Exp. Support	Ind. Exp. Oppose
2018 General	Brendan Boyle (D)............................	159,600	(79%)	$775,381	$6,819	
	David Torres (R).............................	42,382	(21%)			
2018 Primary	Brendan Boyle (D)............................	23,641	(65%)			
	Michele Lawrence (D)....................	12,974	(35%)			

Prior winning percentages: 2016 (100%), 2014 (67%)

Democrat Brendan Boyle in 2014 took an unconventional route to victory by sweeping the north Philadelphia wards in his demographically mixed district, while his higher-spending rivals in the Democratic primary focused on upscale Montgomery County. The court-ordered redistricting in 2018 provided a boost for Boyle by removing Montgomery County from his district and locating it entirely in Philadelphia. Another positive step was his selection in 2019 to the tax-writing House Ways and Means Committee. He and his brother, state Rep. Kevin Boyle, are politically ambitious and have sought to expand their reach.

Raised by working-class parents in northeast Philadelphia, Boyle was the first in his family to go to college. After his bachelor's in government at Notre Dame, he got a master's degree in public policy at Harvard's John F. Kennedy School of Government. In 2008, he was elected to the state House. Kevin was elected two years later, making them the first pair of siblings to serve together in the state House.

When Democratic Rep. Allyson Schwartz ran unsuccessfully in the Democratic primary for governor, Boyle was one of four Democrats seeking to replace her. They included former Rep. Marjorie Margolies, who is Chelsea Clinton's mother-in-law. Boyle was financially outgunned by the three other Democratic contenders. Each spent at least $1.5 million in the primary, while Boyle spent only $900,000 for his entire campaign. Boyle hit the pavement with old-school populism and held 225 voter events that played up his grassroots candidacy, noting that his father was a public-transit maintenance worker and his mother a school crossing guard. He got a boost from union support, with a labor-backed PAC spending $350,000 on Boyle's behalf, plus a crucial endorsement by then-Rep. Robert Brady, boss of the Philadelphia Democratic organization. NARAL, a leading abortion-rights group, accused him of "tap dancing around votes he took that would throw roadblocks in front of women seeking reproductive health care."

Boyle's targeted route to victory went decidedly through Philadelphia, where he got 70 percent of the vote, with Brady's help. He called himself "a Northeast guy." He finished a distant fourth with only 16 percent in Montgomery, which cast 54 percent of the primary vote. But that was enough to give him the victory with 41 percent, to 27 percent for runner-up Margolies, whose Clinton ties were not enough to overcome a disorganized campaign. In the general election, the contest was never in doubt. Boyle won 67%-33%, and took 75 percent of the vote in Philadelphia.

At the St. Patrick's Day reception at the White House in March 2015, President Barack Obama gave a shout-out to Boyle, plus his brother and father. He told the immigrant story of their father, who was born in Donegal. His Almanac vote ratings have ranked Boyle toward the center of the House, especially on foreign policy.

In 2017, Boyle got a seat on the Budget Committee, where he joined other Democrats in attacking Republican plans to repeal and replace the Affordable Care Act. He said that the GOP alternative broke the promises made by Donald Trump during his presidential campaign. With Democratic Rep. Marc Veasey of Texas, he organized the Blue Collar Caucus for Democrats to reach out to Trump voters. In 2019, he gained additional influence with his seat on Ways and Means. That made him, he said, "one of the youngest members of Congress' oldest committee" at what he termed a "relatively early" point in his career.

In February 2017, Philadelphia magazine ran a lengthy profile of the Boyle brothers that described their skill in reaching out to working-class voters, a constituency with which national Democrats had been falling short, they said. "Now that I've been inside the room of the Democratic Congressional

Campaign Committee, one of the first questions that's asked when we're looking to recruit a Democratic candidate for Congress is: Can that person self-fund?" Brendan Boyle said critically. He added that Democrats need to "widen the tent" to include voters with different views on abortion and guns, for example.

In 2016, Boyle was reelected without opposition from either party. Two years later, he faced token challenges. In March 2018, the Philadelphia Inquirer reported, former City Councilman Bill Green — whose father and grandfather were influential members of the House — filed papers for his candidacy. But he changed his mind just before the filing deadline because of legal uncertainty whether he could retain his membership on a local school board. Green told the Inquirer that he might have had enough support to win the party endorsement. A Boyle spokesman responded, "It would have been awfully difficult to beat" the incumbent.

PA-2: North Philadelphia   **Cook Partisan Voting Index: D+15**

Demographics data for new House districts were not prepared by the Census Bureau prior to our editorial deadline.					

2012 Pres. Vote	Obama	210,112	(77%)	Romney	59,321	(22%)
2016 Pres. Vote	Clinton	207,154	(73%)	Trump	70,663	(25%)

Delaware River areas: Everywhere in Philadelphia, American history is close at hand. Independence Hall is where Americans in the 1780s drew up the Constitution, and not far away are the restored townhouses of Society Hill. Nearby sits the Liberty Bell and its signature crack. City founder William Penn was a Quaker, a member of one of the 17th-century sects that prized reason, and he imposed order on his new environment: no cow-path street patterns here, but a grid of numbered and named streets. Penn's "City of Brotherly Love" grew to be a commercial and industrial metropolis that spread out over the countryside until it was the young nation's largest city. Since 2005, the metro area has dropped from the fourth-largest in the nation to seventh.

Expansion of container cargo facilities plus additional dredging at the port, which are part of a $300 million capital improvement plan to accommodate ultra-large container vessels and to double overall capacity, have resulted in the fastest-growing port on the Atlantic coast. Plans were underway to build an 11-acre park over Interstate 95 that would redesign Penn's Landing and integrate the city with the riverfront.

Northeast Philadelphia is relatively new urban territory, with more than half its houses built after 1950. Many of Philadelphia's Hispanics, who are mostly from Puerto Rico, live in the industrial wards along the Delaware River. Other wards in the Northeast have remained mostly white and blue-collar. Tripadvisor recommends Fishtown, which is centered on Frankford Avenue, for "some of the coolest hipster neighborhood bars in the city." Nearby is Northern Liberties, another gentrifying neighborhood that has received national recognition and is not far from Center City. Kensington, a more troubled area to the north, has suffered from a wave of opioid-related deaths.

The 2nd Congressional District of Pennsylvania contains North Philadelphia and eastern sections of Philadelphia along the Delaware River. It extends south to Franklin Square. The new 2nd District, now entirely in Philadelphia, takes about 40 percent of the old 1st District and half of the 13th. It does not include areas that were based in Center City and South Philadelphia or Delaware and Montgomery counties. To keep the neighboring 3rd District an African-American majority, the 2018 redistricting decreased the black population of the 2nd. But this is a two-thirds majority-minority and solidly Democratic district.

Dwight Evans (D)

Elected 2016, 2nd full term, b. May 16, 1954; Philadelphia; Community College of Philadelphia, A.A., 1973; La Salle College (PA), B.A., 1975; Baptist; Single.

Elected Office: PA House, 1980-2016.

Professional Career: Teacher, Philadelphia Public Schools.

DC Office: 1105 LHOB 20515, 202-225-4001, Fax: 202-225-5392, evans.house.gov

Committees: *Small Business*: Investigations, Oversight & Regulations. *Ways & Means*: Health; Worker & Family Support.

Group Ratings

	ADA	ACLU	AFL-CIO	LCV	ITI	COC	HAFA	ACU	CFG	FRC
2018	-	86%	-	94%	-	58%	4%	4%	2%	0%
2017	100%	C	100%	94%	C	43%	C	4%	5%	0%

Almanac Ratings 2017-18

	Economy	Social	Foreign	Composite
Liberal	96%	100%	94%	97%
Conservative	4%	0%	7%	4%

Key Votes of the 115th Congress

1. Obama-care revision	N	5. Family planning regs	N	9. Guantanamo prisoners	Y
2. Tax Cuts	N	6. Body cameras/immigration	Y	10. Ground missiles, limit	Y
3. Omnibus appropriations	Y	7. Abortion ban	N	11. Defense Dept. spending	Y
4. Dodd-Frank revision	N	8. Concealed carry	N	12. FISA rules	N

Election Results

Election	Name (Party)	Vote (%)		Cand. Spent	Ind. Exp. Support	Ind. Exp. Oppose
2018 General	Dwight Evans (D)	287,610	(93%)	$1,094,250	$794	
	Bryan Leib (R)	20,387	(7%)	$8,770		
2018 Primary	Dwight Evans (D)	73,800	(81%)			
	Kevin Johnson (D)	17,548	(19%)			

Prior winning percentages: 2016 (90%)

Democrat Dwight Evans won the Democratic primary in 2016 against 11-term Rep. Chaka Fattah, who was convicted on corruption charges two months later. Evans, who had been influential and well-known locally during his 36 years in the state House, had the support of Democratic state and city leaders. In the House, he became a leadership loyalist and got a seat on the Ways and Means Committee, where he said that he would address the consequences of income inequality.

Evans was born in Philadelphia and got his bachelor's degree from La Salle University. He went to work as a teacher in Philly and for the Urban League as a community activist. In 1980, he was elected as a state representative, where he began a busy legislative career. He led the effort to win approval in 1986 of a new downtown convention center in his home town. He helped to create the Public Transportation Assistance Fund, which was a dedicated funding source for mass transit. He was an author of the state's charter school program, which increased the school choices for parents and their children.

For 20 years, Evans was the chairman or senior Democrat on the House Appropriations Committee, where he directed funds to communities across the state. In 2010, he was stripped of the position following an internal squabble among Democrats. As chairman of the Budget Committee of the Southeast Pennsylvania Transportation Authority, Evans participated actively in labor negotiations, including the weeklong transit strike in 2016 that was settled on the eve of Election

Day. Evans had several unsuccessful runs for higher office, including governor and lieutenant governor and two bids for mayor.

Evans got his big opening when Fattah was indicted in July 2015 on federal corruption charges — including bribery, money laundering and mail fraud — for his mixing of personal and campaign finances when he ran for mayor in 2007. Fattah remained in the House, but he was required to step down as senior Democrat on the Commerce, Justice, Science Appropriations Subcommittee. Evans was endorsed by, among others, Pennsylvania Gov. Tom Wolf and Philadelphia Mayor Jim Kenney, each of whom Evans had endorsed when they sought their current office. Many of the ward leaders in the Democratic organization stayed with Fattah. Despite his decades serving in Harrisburg, Evans styled himself as a reformer.

Fattah, who was beleaguered by legal bills, raised only $220,000 to $1.5 million for Evans. In the four-candidate April primary, Evans won 42%-35%. Fattah resigned from the House three days after his conviction. In January 2017, he began to serve his sentence of 10 years in prison, one of the longest-ever criminal sentences for a current or former member of Congress. In the general election, Evans got 90 percent of the vote against Republican James Jones. He won a simultaneous special election for the remainder of Fattah's term, and took office a week after the election. In August 2018, a federal appeals court threw out Fattah's convictions for bribery — citing improper instructions to the jury — but upheld the other criminal counts.

Evans joined the Agriculture Committee, where he worked on hunger and nutrition programs during debate on the farm bill in 2018. He had spent time on related issues during his years in Harrisburg. A week after President Donald Trump took office, Evans joined local Democrats in criticizing the new administration's decision to deny admission to Syrian refugees who reportedly were seeking to enter the nation legally at the Philadelphia airport. He called the prohibition "cruel and unusual ... [and] a very sad day in the city of Brotherly Love." In 2018, Evans called for the removal of cannabis and hemp from federal drug-sentencing schedules, which he said have targeted African-American males. He won enactment of his bill to reduce costs for small business owners who apply for a loan with the Small Business Administration.

In 2019, with his seat on Ways and Means, Evans planned to pursue action on his bill to allow public school buildings to qualify for a rehabilitation tax credit. An unusual aspect was that Democratic Rep. Brendan Boyle also was assigned to Ways and Means on that same day. They hold adjacent districts in Philadelphia, which gives the city additional clout on tax and social-welfare legislation. Evans also serves as vice chairman of the Small Business Committee.

PA-3: West Philadelphia, Center City   Cook Partisan Voting Index: D+40

Demographics data for new House districts were not prepared by the Census Bureau prior to our editorial deadline.					

2012 Pres. Vote	Obama	340,116	(92%)	Romney	28,074	(8%)
2016 Pres. Vote	Clinton	339,564	(91%)	Trump	26,216	(7%)

City Hall: Looking out over the Schuylkill River north of Center City Philadelphia, you can still see the landscape painted 100 years ago by Philadelphia artist Thomas Eakins: the tightly packed but formidable rowhouses, the old fieldstone houses of Germantown and the boat houses below the small Greek temples of the Water Works. West Philadelphia's long-established black neighborhoods run across the Schuylkill on either side of Market Street. Pennsylvania was the first state to abolish slavery, thanks to William Penn and his Quaker legacy, and Philadelphia has been home to a large African-American community since before the Civil War.

Northwest Philadelphia includes distinguished old neighborhoods such as Chestnut Hill, with its cobblestone streets and classic architecture. East Falls was the childhood home of Grace Kelly, who grew up to be a Hollywood starlet and princess of Monaco. Some neighborhoods here continue to suffer from poverty and blight. But in recent years, city officials have made a concerted effort to bring young, affluent people back to the city.

For all its historical grandeur, Philadelphia seldom has had a city government to be proud of. Its employees' retirement fund's obligations of $11 billion were only 45 percent funded in 2018. It has had crime-ravaged neighborhoods, with the highest rates of the nation's 10 largest cities. The more than 300 homicides in 2017 were the most since 2012. Also that year, the adult poverty rate of 26 percent was the highest in the nation for big cities. (In 2017, Phoenix replaced Philadelphia as the nation's fifth-largest city.) There are signs of renewal. Center City remains attractive to young professionals — a growing number with families. In October 2018, Bloomberg reported, the city ranked third with the greatest income inequality, behind Atlanta and New Orleans.

The 3rd Congressional District takes in the African-American neighborhoods in West Philadelphia, and north Philadelphia west of 15th Street. It includes City Hall, an ornate building where a statue of city founder William Penn stands 37 feet high, well-heeled Rittenhouse Square, the Philadelphia Zoo (America's first), and the University of Pennsylvania and Drexel University across the Schuylkill. It also includes most of Fairmount Park, the largest landscaped urban park in the world, which climaxes at the Philadelphia Museum of Art, where a Rocky-like run up the steps has become de rigueur for tourists. For many, including visitors, the 30th Street train station is the heart of the district. A $10 billion master plan envisioned a new concourse, connections to local rail and bus lines, and long-term development of the area over the tracks — which occupies 88 acres of prime urban real estate.

Also here is much of 18th century Philadelphia: Independence Hall; the U.S. Mint; and historic Christ Church, where George Washington and Benjamin Franklin worshipped. The district takes in Chinatown, Society Hill, the Northern Liberties village, Penn's Landing, two miles of prime real estate along the Delaware River, and Old City, with its flourishing night life. The National Constitution Center is on Independence Mall. The massive Gallery Mall shopping area, part of wider-scale development between City Hall and Independence Mall, was transformed into the Fashion District across three city blocks and was scheduled to open in late 2019. A less expensive, but also controversial, move has been the replacement of the station's iconic flipboard with a new digital listing of its train schedule; that was the last such board maintained by Amtrak.

The court-ordered redistricting in 2018 had little impact on the politics of the district, which has been among the five most Democratic districts in the nation. The chief geographic shifts were the addition of Center City and the historic areas of the city in exchange for the removal of about 10 percent of the old 2nd District that had been located in a few wealthy suburbs on the Main Line of Montgomery County. As a result, the new 3rd — like the new 2nd — is entirely in Philadelphia. Together, they cover nearly 95 percent of the city; the remainder is in the Delaware County-based 5th District.

Madeleine Dean (D)

Elected 2018, 1st term, b. Jun 06, 1959; Glenside; La Salle University (PA); Montgomery County Community College; University of Pennsylvania, Att.; Widener University School of Law - Delaware, J.D., 1984; Christian Church; Married (Patrick J. Cunnane); 3 children; 1 grandchild.

Elected Office: PA House, 2012-2018.

Professional Career: Counsel, Cunnane Bicycle Company, Inc.; General Law Practice Attorney; Philadelphia Daily News, Contributor

DC Office: 129 CHOB 20515, 202-225-4731, dean.house.gov

State Offices: Glenside, 215-884-4300; Norristown, 610-382-1250.

Committees: *Financial Services*: Oversight & Investigations; Subcommittee on Diversity & Inclusion. *Judiciary*: Constitution, Civil Rights & Civil Liberties; Crime, Terrorism & Homeland Security.

Election Results

Election	Name (Party)	Vote (%)		Cand. Spent	Ind. Exp. Support	Ind. Exp. Oppose
2018 General	Madeleine Dean (D)	211,524	(64%)	$1,181,848	$326,271	$100,000
	Dan David (R)	121,467	(36%)	$502,378	$25,000	
2018 Primary	Madeleine Dean (D)	42,749	(73%)			
	Shira Goodman (D)	9,714	(17%)			
	Joe Hoeffel (D)	6,456	(11%)			

Democrat first-termer Madeleine Dean had the easiest path to the House of the four Philadelphia-area Democratic newcomers to the Pennsylvania delegation. She also had the most political experience of that group. Probably her biggest challenge was navigating the complex redistricting changes in her Montgomery County-based seat. Rep. Brendan Boyle had represented a large chunk of that county, but he switched to a district that is entirely in Philadelphia. In the once-competitive battleground, which has become solidly Democratic, Dean's victory in the primary virtually assured her election in November.

Dean offered a diverse background. A graduate of LaSalle University and Widener University Law School, she had been a lawyer, writer and teacher. She practiced law with the Philadelphia Trial Lawyers, where she became executive director, and she later opened a three-woman firm that practiced general law. As a writer, she contributed to local newspapers and taught writing as an English professor at LaSalle.

Dean launched her political career in 2012, when she was elected to the first of three terms in the state House. In Harrisburg, she was vice-chair of the Finance Committee and co-chaired the PA Safe Caucus, a coalition that sought to curb gun violence through action and awareness; she filed legislation to ban the use of bump stocks with firearms. As a member of the Governor's Commission for Women, she advised on policies that promoted equality issues ranging from sexual assault to business initiatives. That advocacy led to her focus on the need for more women in politics.

In 2017, Dean announced her campaign for lieutenant governor. But she switched her plan when the state Supreme Court in February 2018 approved a new congressional redistricting map. State Sen. Daylin Leach, who finished fourth in the 2014 Democratic primary when Boyle won an open seat, dropped his bid to run in the revised Montgomery County district because of sexual-harassment claims.

After no strong contender showed interest during the brief filing period, Dean launched what she called a "once in a lifetime opportunity to serve." Her campaign was endorsed by labor unions and EMILY's List, the Democratic abortion-rights group. She emphasized the lack of women in the Pennsylvania delegation, though two women had been elected to earlier versions of this district during the previous quarter-century: Marjorie Margolies and Allyson Schwartz, each of whom turned down the opportunity to return to Congress. In addition to her support from other prominent local Democrats, The Philadelphia Inquirer endorsed Dean as "the person who seems better prepared to not only represent Pennsylvanians but counter" President Donald Trump.

In what became a surprisingly easy contest, her chief opponent appeared to be former Rep. Joe Hoeffel, who served three terms in the Montgomery County-based district (prior to Schwartz) before he ran unsuccessfully against Republican Sen. Arlen Specter in 2004. Hoeffel was under-financed in his bid to return to Congress and had lost support from party regulars. Also competing in the primary was Shira Goodman, a gun-control advocate who was new to electoral politics. Dean won 73 percent of the vote, with runner-up Goodman getting 17 percent.

In November, Dean got 64 percent of the vote against Republican Dan David, a political newcomer who started up an equities research firm. In the House, Dean got prime committee assignments on Financial Services and Judiciary.

PA-4: Northwestern Philadelphia Suburbs   Cook Partisan Voting Index: R+11

Demographics data for new House districts were not prepared by the Census Bureau prior to our editorial deadline.

2012 Pres. Vote	Obama	203,585	(56%)	Romney	155,372	(43%)		
2016 Pres. Vote	Clinton	221,308	(57%)	Trump	147,219	(38%)	Johnson	9,663	(3%)

Montgomery County: Montgomery County is the proximate hinterland of Philadelphia: rolling hills cut on one side by the Schuylkill River and at intervals by the Pennsylvania and Reading Railroad lines radiating outward from Center City. Older suburbs, both rich and modest, grew up around rail stations, with comfortable houses within walking distance for commuters. Farther out are 18th and 19th century villages, once surrounded by farm fields, now encroached upon by subdivisions where people depend on cars, not rail lines, to get to work. Historically, the moderate Republican style of politics in Montgomery was set by Ivy League graduates. In the 1990s, the county swung toward Democrats in national politics, with abortion rights and other cultural issues usually trumping economic concerns. Now, as in much of the nation's suburbia, Republican influence has become scarcer. Montgomery County had the fastest growth in the region from 2013 to 2016 and it has been the second most affluent county, behind Chester, in the state. It is a distant third as the most populous county, behind Philadelphia and Allegheny.

In Horsham, downsizing of the Willow Grove Naval Air Station resulted in plans for a large housing development following an environmental clean-up of the area. Instead, local officials approved the land for open-space preservation. Parts of Willow Grove have been revived as a home to pilots of unmanned military drone aircraft flying missions over conflict zones across the world. Just to the east of Valley Forge, where Gen. George Washington and his men spent the terrible winter and spring of 1777-78, is the King of Prussia mall. With three expansions in recent years and more than 450 stores, it has gained the distinction of the largest amount of leased space of any mall in the nation. The Mall of America in Minnesota retained the record for the most stores. In January 2018, plans were approved to extend SEPTA high-speed rail service to the mall.

The 4th Congressional District of Pennsylvania is 97 percent in Montgomery County and largely unified the county in one district for the first time since 2002; the remaining three percent is in Berks County. Two small salients, which border Bucks and Delaware counties in the 1st and 5th Districts, include an additional 15 percent of the county. Prior to the latest changes, only 55 percent of the voters were in Montgomery; in that earlier district, the remainder were chiefly in Northeast Philadelphia. The new 4th is one of four solidly Democratic districts in the Philadelphia metro area — two of them in the city and two others based in Montgomery and Delaware counties. The loss of Northeast Philadelphia from the old 13th District reduced the Democratic base vote here by a few percent. The return to Republican control of this area, which predominated as recently as 1998, seems a distant prospect.

Mary Gay Scanlon (D)

Elected 2018, 1st full term, b. Aug 30, 1959; Syracuse, NY; Colgate University, B.A., 1980; University of Pennsylvania Law School, J.D., 1984; Catholic; Married (Mark Scanlon); 3 children.

DC Office: 1535 LHOB 20515, 202-225-2011, Fax: 202-226-0280, scanlon.house.gov

State Offices: East Lansdowne, 610-626-1913.

Committees: *Judiciary*: Antitrust, Commercial & Administrative Law; Constitution, Civil Rights & Civil Liberties; Immigration & Citizenship. *Rules*: Legislative & Budget Process; Rules & Organization of the House. *Select Committee on the Modernization of Congress.*

Election Results

Election	Name (Party)	Vote (%)		Cand. Spent	Ind. Exp. Support	Ind. Exp. Oppose
2018 General	Mary Gay Scanlon (D)	198,639	(65%)	$1,624,753	$158,223	
	Pearl Kim (R)	106,075	(35%)	$466,781		
2018 Primary	Mary Gay Scanlon (D)	17,220	(28%)			
	Ashley Lunkenheimer (D)	9,291	(15%)			
	Richard Lazer (D)	9,095	(15%)			
	Molly Sheehan (D)	6,216	(10%)			
	Gregory Vitali (D)	5,726	(9%)			
	Lindy Li (D)	4,236	(7%)			
	Theresa Wright (D)	3,149	(5%)			

Freshman Democrat Mary Gay Scanlon scored her victory with a big boost from redistricting in the revamped Delaware County-based district. A longtime legal activist, Scanlon had scant experience in elected office beyond her tenure on the Wallingford-Swarthmore School Board. She campaigned on her extensive resume on education issues and her background in the area's legal community. Republican Rep. Pat Meehan, who had been elected to four terms, resigned from the seat in April 2018, following disclosure of his settlement of a sexual-harassment claim with a female staffer. The court-ordered redrawing of district lines made it virtually impossible for Meehan — or any other Republican — to win the seat.

Scanlon was born in upstate New York, where her father and grandfather were local judges. A graduate of Colgate University and the University of Pennsylvania Law School, Scanlon served 14 years as the national pro bono counsel at Ballard Spahr, a large Philadelphia-based law firm where she supervised the public-oriented legal services. (Her husband, Mark Stewart, was chairman of the firm, where he has been a prominent litigator.)

Working with the Education Law Center of Pennsylvania, Scanlon's expertise included federal laws on special education; at home, she worked with statewide councils implementing those laws. She co-chaired the Philadelphia Bar Association's Commission on Children at Risk and served as president of her school board, where she was a member for eight years. "With the rise of the corporate social responsibility movement, pro bono work has become an important indicator [of] a law firm's values," she wrote for a legal journal in 2009.

In her extensive portfolio, Scanlon helped to win two class-action lawsuits on behalf of children with disabilities. She worked on voting-rights issues, including allegations of voter suppression and gerrymandering. Her efforts on behalf of women included successful pursuit of fair pay and equitable treatment of the U.S. national women's hockey and soccer teams. When President Donald Trump sought a travel ban targeting several majority-Muslim nations shortly after he took office, Scanlon led a team of lawyers defending international passengers arriving at U.S. airports. "I am running to continue doing that work, just in a new forum," she told The Philadelphia Inquirer in an interview prior to the primary.

The Democratic primary was a wide-open contest, with 10 candidates — including six women. None had been widely known in the population center of Delaware County. Scanlon benefited from the endorsement of the Inquirer, which praised her "deep understanding of pressing national, state, and local issues." Former Philadelphia Mayor and Gov. Ed Rendell appeared prominently in her advertising, which described Scanlon as a "progressive Democrat... [who] will fight for us."

Richard Lazer, a former deputy mayor for labor of Philadelphia who was endorsed by organized labor and Sen. Bernie Sanders, drew early attention. But he failed to grow beyond his local electoral base. The other leading contender was Ashley Lunkenheimer, a former federal prosecutor who then worked with a group to expand Medicare and Medicaid services. Scanlon and Lunkenheimer, the leading fundraisers among the Democrats, each loaned at least $300,000 to their campaigns.

Scanlon won the primary with 28 percent of the vote; Lunkenheimer got 15.3 percent and Lazer had 15 percent. In Delaware County, which cast 70 percent of the vote, Scanlon got 33 percent — double the vote for Lunkenheimer. She took a similar share in the Montgomery County sliver of the district, which cast nearly 10 percent of the vote. Lazer got 41 percent in the Philadelphia portion, where Scanlon got 8 percent; but Lazer ran poorly in the suburban counties. In November, Scanlon defeated Pearl Kim, the daughter of immigrants who became a prosecutor and law-enforcement official.

In the House, Scanlon got leadership assignments as vice-chair of the Judiciary Committee and a member of the Rules Committee.

PA-5: Southern and Western Philadelphia Suburbs

Cook Partisan Voting Index: R+13

Demographics data for new House districts were not prepared by the Census Bureau prior to our editorial deadline.

2012 Pres. Vote	Obama	223,545	(63%)	Romney	125,724	(36%)		
2016 Pres. Vote	Clinton	230,060	(62%)	Trump	126,361	(34%)	Johnson	6,828	(2%)

Delaware County: A century ago, Delaware County, southwest of Philadelphia, was already filling up, with industrial towns strung out along the rail lines paralleling the Delaware River and residential suburbs along the inland commuter lines. Politics in Delaware County in those days was run by a Republican machine headed by state Sen. John McClure. Such was his power that, in 1960, presidential candidate Richard Nixon stopped by the ailing McClure's home to pay homage. McClure exercised his influence through the War Board, a 15-member panel that decided on all nominations for public office. The board technically went out of business in 1975, but one of its products, Tom Judge, remained county Republican chairman until 2010. In 2017, Democrats for the first time won countywide offices, and won seats on the county council for the first time since 1980.

The area is filled with colonial history. At the Brandywine Battlefield, Gens. George Washington and Henry Knox unsuccessfully tried to prevent British forces from taking Philadelphia during the Revolutionary War. Villanova University, the oldest Catholic university in Pennsylvania and the home of the NCAA basketball champions in 2016 and 2018, is in Radnor. A driving economic force here is Boeing's plant in Ridley Park, with 4,600 employees, where the V-22 Osprey and H-47 helicopters have been assembled for decades. In September 2018, the Air Force announced a new $2.4 billion deal with Boeing to build MH-139 helicopters, to replace the aging "Huey" copters that have protected the nation's intercontinental ballistic missile bases. To the south, past artsy Swarthmore College and along the Delaware River, is impoverished Chester, where the school system went bankrupt in 2012. Following the order of a federal judge, the state bailed out the city. In recent decades, blacks have moved out of Philadelphia into adjacent Delaware County in large numbers, and cultural liberalism has led many affluent suburbs to vote Democratic. In the 1988 presidential race, Delaware County voted 60%-39% for Republican George H.W. Bush. Hillary Clinton got 60 percent in the county in 2016.

The 5th Congressional District of Pennsylvania covers all of Delaware County. The remaining 20 percent of the district is chiefly in once heavily Italian South Philadelphia, where the Delaware River turns its southerly direction to the west as it heads toward Delaware Bay. That area takes in the city's stadium and arena complex, the CSX rail yards, as well as Pat's and Geno's, well-established haunts for late-night cheesesteaks. At the Wells Fargo Arena, Democrats nominated Hillary Clinton for president at their 2016 convention. A small section extends northwest from the city line into the upscale Ardmore and Bryn Mawr sections of Montgomery County. The new 5th replaced the unconventional shape of the old 7th, which had been one of the most discredited gerrymanders in post-2010 redistricting, as it meandered to parts of Chester and Berks counties and a few conservative precincts in Lancaster County. The Washington Post described it as "Goofy Kicking Donald Duck." The Philadelphia Daily News complained that it was "a new poster child for why we must find a better way to do redistricting." Making the lines more regular and adding parts of the city switched the district from marginal territory to more than 60 percent Democratic.

Chrissy Houlahan (D)

Elected 2018, 1st term, b. Jun 05, 1967; Patuxent River, MD; Stanford University (CA), B.S., 1989; Massachusetts Institute of Technology, M.S., 1994; Married (Bart Houlahan); 2 children.

Military Career: U.S. Air Force 1989-1992; U.S. Air Force Reserves 1992-2006

Professional Career: Chief Operating Officer, AND1 Basketball; Founding Chief Operating Officer, B-Lab, ; Chemistry Teacher, Teach for America Corps; President, Chief Operating Officer and Chief Financial Officer, Springboard Collaborative.

DC Office: 1218 LHOB 20515, 202-225-4315, houlahan.house.gov

State Offices: Reading, 610-295-0815; West Chester, 610-883-5050.

Committees: *Armed Services*: Intelligence, Emerging Threats & Capabilities; Readiness. *Foreign Affairs*: Africa, Global Health, Global Human Rights & Internat'l Orgs; Asia, the Pacific & Nonproliferation. *Small Business*: Innovation & Workforce Development.

Election Results

Election	Name (Party)	Vote (%)		Cand. Spent	Ind. Exp. Support	Ind. Exp. Oppose
2018 General	Chrissy Houlahan (D)........................	177,704	(59%)	$2,950,594	$290,814	
	Greg McCauley (R)............................	124,124	(41%)	$214,651		
2018 Primary	Chrissy Houlahan (D)....................................		(100%)			

Democrat Chrissy Houlahan, a political newcomer, had an unusually easy ride to Congress. With her military background, business experience and recent political activism, she was one of the prime recruits for House Democrats in the 2018 cycle. Houlahan won the Democratic nomination without opposition after entering the contest early. Following the last-minute decision by two-term Republican Rep. Ryan Costello not to seek reelection in the face of an adverse political climate and redistricting changes, she easily defeated in November a token opponent who was largely written off by the GOP.

Houlahan got her bachelor's degree in engineering from Stanford and a master's in technology and policy from the Massachusetts Institute of Technology. As a captain in the Air Force Reserve, she worked on missile-defense systems. Following her military service, she helped to start up and became chief operating officer of And1 Basketball, a successful t-shirt company. Later, she became president of a Philadelphia-based non-profit that sought to improve literacy in inner-city schools.

Her political activism was launched in January 2017 when she organized a busload of women traveling to the Washington Women's March to protest the inauguration of President Donald Trump. Following that experience, Houlahan decided to run for Congress. By summer, she won the support of the Democratic Congressional Campaign Committee and EMILY's List, which supports Democratic women who favor abortion rights.

That positioned her for an uphill challenge to Costello, who won his two campaigns with 56 and 57 percent of the vote in a district that Hillary Clinton won by 2,299 votes in 2016. Costello had been prepared for the contest, but he was knocked off-balance by the state Supreme Court redrawing of district lines in February 2018, which measurably jeopardized his reelection. "I was ... absolutely shocked that the Supreme Court got away with what it did," he told a local reporter. "Their objective was to take me out politically, and that's what they did."

In his announcement on the eve of the filing deadline for candidates, he also cited the political tumult created by Trump. "It's very difficult to move forward in a constructive way today," said Costello, who was an emerging leader of House Republican centrists. "Plus, I think there is a lot of hate out there, from the left especially, and it's a very angry environment. It is a sad commentary on the state of our culture and political environment."

Costello's late decision angered GOP leaders and made it nearly impossible for other candidates from either party to enter the campaign. Houlahan added to the steep challenge facing potential opponents with her prolific financing: $2.8 million raised and $2.2 million cash on hand by mid-year. Her Republican opponent, Greg McCauley, a tax lawyer with little political experience, had less than 10 percent of those totals.

Perhaps the biggest stumbling block that Houlahan faced during the campaign were reports of sweatshop labor at the Chinese firms that manufactured her company's sportswear, plus allegations of large pay raises at the nonprofit she led, which were uncovered by Republican researchers. Her campaign dismissed the charges as "grossly misleading," and McCauley had little success in stirring the pot.

Her 59%-41% November victory included 59 percent of the vote in the once-Republican leaning Chester County core of the district. In the House, she got a seat on the Armed Services Committee and was named freshman leader of the New Democrat Coalition of party moderates.

PA-6: Southeast Pennsylvania   Cook Partisan Voting Index: R+2

Demographics data for new House districts were not prepared by the Census Bureau prior to our editorial deadline.

2012 Pres. Vote	Obama	169,037	(51%)	Romney	158,475	(48%)		
2016 Pres. Vote	Clinton	185,866	(52%)	Trump	153,034	(43%)	Johnson 10,169	(3%)

Chester County, Reading: The gentle hills of southeastern Pennsylvania, settled in the 18th century by Quaker townsmen, Welsh farmers, German peasants and members of pietistic sects who became known as the Pennsylvania Dutch, were America's first polyglot interior. Before and after independence, a diverse lot looking for tolerance in the area above Philadelphia and the Delaware River found a land that yielded riches, first in crops, then in ironworking. In Revolutionary times, the area was countryside, a long day's ride from the markets and docks of Philadelphia. Then, rail lines were built from Philadelphia: The Main Line of the Pennsylvania Railroad headed west to industrial Pittsburgh and the Midwest, and the Reading Railroad headed northwest through Berks County and the anthracite coalfields beyond. Factories were built in some of the towns, and many farms continued to thrive, but by the late 19th century, some of the land had become commuter territory. The area along the Main Line was affluent suburbia for the masses, or a large part of them. Parts of Chester County, such as the refined farm country of Chadds Ford, have been home to generations of Wyeth artists. In 2017, Democrats won the four countywide offices that were on the ballot — the first-ever victory by the party; all four were women.

Much of this area has a kinship with Philadelphia, which is about 50 miles to the east, but it also offers idyllic, rustic living. Chester has a disproportionate share of well-educated voters. Its $92,000 median household income in 2017 was the highest in Pennsylvania, though it has dipped in the national rankings. Its 4 percent population growth from 2010 to 2017 was the highest in the Philadelphia area. With the rich soil, fruits and vegetables are a pillar of the local economy. Kennett Square is the Mushroom Capital of the World. It grows two-thirds of domestic consumption. The industry employs about 8,600 workers; most of them are permanent residents because many of the mushroom farmers have six crops each year, most of them indoors. In September, the annual mushroom festival — a mile-long street fair -- attracts about 100,000 attendees.

The 6th Congressional District of Pennsylvania was the only district in the state that retained its number, but the 2018 redistricting made significant political revisions. It was redrawn to include all of Chester County plus about half of Berks County, including heavily urban — and Democratic — Reading. An old industrial town that inspired John Updike's Rabbit novels and many of his short stories, Reading has become 65 percent Hispanic and ranked recently among the poorest cities in the nation; its median household income of $29,000 in 2017 was half that of overall Berks County and less than one-third of the average in Chester County. The old 6th was an oddly shaped configuration that snaked through nearly two-thirds of Chester County, clipped the northwest corner of Montgomery County and the southeast corner of heavily Republican Lebanon County and stretched through the center of Berks County but did not include Reading. Prior to the latest redistricting, other parts of Chester County were in the old Republican-held 7th and 16th Districts.

Those changes turned an artfully drawn Republican-held seat into a district where Republicans in 2018 threw in their cards. Chester is the population center, with three-fourths of the population. The northern, and more Republican, portion of Berks was shifted to the 9th District. Chester was a battleground in 2016. Hillary Clinton won the county, 53%-43%, a margin of more than 25,000 votes. Clinton would have won the new 6th by nearly 10 percentage points after having won the earlier version by less than one point in 2016.

Susan Wild (D)

Elected 2018, 1st full term, b. Jun 07, 1957; Wiesbaden, Germany; American University (DC), B.A., 1978; George Washington University (DC), J.D., 1982; Jewish; Divorced; 2 children.

DC Office: 1607 LHOB 20515, 202-225-6411, wild.house.gov

State Offices: Allentown, 484-781-6000; Easton, 610-333-1170.

Committees: *Education & Labor*: Health, Employment, Labor & Pensions; Workforce Protections. *Ethics. Foreign Affairs*: Africa, Global Health, Global Human Rights & Internat'l Orgs; Europe, Eurasia, Energy & the Environment.

Election Results

Election	Name (Party)	Vote (%)		Cand. Spent	Ind. Exp. Support	Ind. Exp. Oppose
2018 General	Susan Ellis Wild (D)....................... 140,813		(54%)	$3,245,530	$562,917	$221,067
	Marty Nothstein (R)....................... 114,437		(43%)	$812,039	$130,944	$1,741,843
	Tim Silfies (Lib)...................................... 8,011		(3%)	$15,638		
2018 Primary	Susan Ellis Wild (D)....................... 15,262		(34%)			
	John Morganelli (D)............................ 13,754		(30%)			
	Greg Edwards (D)........................... 11,602		(25%)			
	Roger Ruggles (D)............................ 2,467		(5%)			

Freshman Democrat Susan Wild, in her first bid for political office, won hard-fought primary and general-election contests. One of four newly elected House Democratic women from southeast Pennsylvania, she was the only one who ran in a swing district following the court-drawn redistricting in February 2018. She succeeded Republican Charlie Dent, a leader of House GOP moderates, who decided not to seek reelection and resigned in May. Wild, an experienced trial lawyer, had been the part-time solicitor of Allentown for more than two years while the mayor was tried and convicted for corruption.

Wild lived for more than a decade in the Washington D.C. area, where she got her bachelor's degree at American University and law degree from George Washington University, and worked for a local law firm for five years. In 1988, she settled in the Allentown area and practiced law for three decades. As a partner and the head of the litigation group in the prominent Allentown-based Gross McGinley firm, Wild handled hundreds of cases and described herself as an expert in the use of legal technologies for a courtroom practice. Her clients included health care practitioners, insurance companies and local governments.

In 2015, following her selection by Allentown Mayor Ed Pawlowski, Wild was approved by the city council to serve as the city's part-time solicitor. Her tenure was a chaotic time, as Pawlowski was charged in a federal indictment for pay-to-play crimes that occurred before Wild became a city official. She resigned to run for Congress shortly before Pawlowski was convicted in March 2018. "No evidence was presented during the trial signaling Wild participated in Pawlowski's criminal scheme," The Allentown Morning Call reported. Prosecutors said that Wild cooperated with the investigation, though her role was an issue during the campaign.

In running for the House, Wild embraced local concerns. "It's working-class families that deserve a break in this economy — not big city billionaires and wealthy corporations," she said. Wild was well-positioned among the three chief Democrats in the primary. She was the only woman running against two men, and she was a relatively mainstream Democrat. The alternatives were Greg Edwards, an African-American pastor who was supported by Sen. Bernie Sanders and progressive groups, and John Morganelli, the more-conservative Northampton County district attorney for 25 years, who occasionally spoke positively about President Donald Trump. Both criticized House Democratic campaign strategists for their lack of support.

Wild "built a network of volunteers and experienced campaigners and attracted interest among outside groups that invested more than $360,000 in the race," The Morning Call reported, while noting that she had been largely unknown to voters when the campaign began. EMILY's List, which supports Democratic women candidates who back abortion rights, was a leading ally.

Wild ran well in the suburbs, while Edwards was strong with urban voters and Morganelli relied on his local base. She won the primary with 34 percent of the vote, to 30 percent for Morganelli and 25 percent for Edwards. In the two counties that dominated the redrawn district, Wild led by nearly 4,000 votes in Lehigh and Morganelli led by nearly 3,000 in Northampton; Wild won overall by 1,508 votes.

Republicans initially were hopeful about their nominee, Marty Nothstein, a Lehigh County commissioner. He was well-known among many voters after having won an Olympic gold medal for cycling in 2000. But "GOP operatives and insiders have been sharply critical of his campaign, marked by sluggish fund-raising," the Philadelphia Inquirer reported in September.

Wild won, 53%-43%, and led in each of the three counties. She benefited from the opposition to Trump in many suburbs. The district is sufficiently competitive that she cannot take reelection for granted.

PA-7: Lehigh Valley   **Cook Partisan Voting Index: R+1**

> Demographics data for new House districts were not prepared by the Census Bureau prior to our editorial deadline.

2012 Pres. Vote	Obama	158,645	(53%)	Romney	137,641	(46%)		
2016 Pres. Vote	Clinton	160,346	(48%)	Trump	156,771	(47%)	Johnson	8,272	(2%)

Allentown, Bethlehem: Billy Joel's song "Allentown" was a source of both controversy and praise upon its release in 1982. Its grim picture of closed factories, joblessness and human despair resonated with some area residents, while others found the song derisive and inaccurate. Joel was actually singing about the neighboring town of Bethlehem and the struggles of Bethlehem Steel, which was dissolved in 2003. Fences were mended when a petition drive helped bring Joel to play a concert at Lehigh University's Stabler Arena. The empathy Joel showed toward the region's economic plight has generated mostly pleasant memories.

Today's Lehigh Valley has a much more diverse economy, with a mix of regional health care networks, telephone call centers for insurance companies and banks, and long-surviving manufacturing industries. The valley's population increased almost 12 percent from 2000 to 2010. Growth slowed to 3 percent in the next seven years, though that was still better than most of Pennsylvania. Commuters seeking to avoid big-city housing costs are connected by Interstate 78 to New York City and by the Northeast Extension to Philadelphia. The region has a cluster of colleges — Lehigh, Muhlenberg and Moravian — and a strong newspaper in The Morning Call. Still, the area has been shedding manufacturing jobs, and even its health care sector was struggling. In Allentown, the 2014 opening of a new $200 million hockey arena was described as "the biggest happening in 30 years." After the merger of the Kraft and Heinz companies led to the shutdown of its large plant in Upper Macungie Township, the company sold the old factory in 2017 to an Atlanta-based developer who replaced it with two large warehouses. Planned development in Allentown of a $425 million, 12-building commercial and residential complex along the Lehigh River was delayed after it broke ground in 2015. In Easton, old industrial buildings have become a magnet for artists seeking inexpensive loft and warehouse space.

The 7th Congressional District of Pennsylvania includes the Lehigh Valley, covering all of Allentown-based Lehigh County and Bethlehem-based Northampton County. Half the population is in Lehigh, about 42 percent is in Northampton and the remainder is in a southern slice of Monroe County, which is more rural. These lines are far more compact than the old 15th District, which extended west almost to Harrisburg. The loss of those exurban areas marginally shifted the district from its previous Republican lean to a slight Democratic lean — though Lehigh and Northampton have been politically competitive and the 7th is more competitive than suburban districts closer to Philadelphia.

Matthew Cartwright (D)

Elected 2012, 4th term, b. May 01, 1961; Erie; Hamilton College (NY), A.B., 1983; Temple University School of Law (PA), Att., 1984; University of Pennsylvania, J.D., 1986; Roman Catholic; Married (Marion Munley); 2 children.

Professional Career: Practicing attorney, Munley, Munley & Cartwright, 1986-2012.

DC Office: 1034 LHOB 20515, 202-225-5546, Fax: 202-226-0996, cartwright.house.gov

State Offices: Hawley, 570-576-8005; Hazleton, 570-751-0050; Tannersville, 570-355-1818.

Committees: *Appropriations*: Commerce, Justice, Science & Related Agencies; Financial Services & General Government; Military Construction, Veterans Affairs & Related Agencies. *Natural Resources*: Energy & Mineral Resources; Indigenous Peoples of the United States.

Group Ratings

	ADA	ACLU	AFL-CIO	LCV	ITI	COC	HAFA	ACU	CFG	FRC
2018	-	61%	-	91%	-	58%	6%	8%	2%	20%
2017	85%	C	89%	97%	C	36%	C	7%	5%	0%

Almanac Ratings 2017-18

	Economy	Social	Foreign	Composite
Liberal	100%	81%	84%	88%
Conservative	0%	19%	16%	12%

Key Votes of the 115th Congress

1. Obama-care revision	N	5. Family planning regs	N	9. Guantanamo prisoners	Y
2. Tax Cuts	N	6. Body cameras/immigration	Y	10. Ground missiles, limit	Y
3. Omnibus appropriations	Y	7. Abortion ban	N	11. Defense Dept. spending	Y
4. Dodd-Frank revision	N	8. Concealed carry	N	12. FISA rules	Y

Election Results

Election	Name (Party)	Vote (%)		Cand. Spent	Ind. Exp. Support	Ind. Exp. Oppose
2018 General	Matt Cartwright (D)	135,603	(55%)	$2,511,007	$92,691	$556,367
	John Chrin (R)	112,563	(45%)	$2,183,537	$1,239	
2018 Primary	Matt Cartwright (D)		(100%)			

Prior winning percentages: 2016 (54%), 2014 (57%), 2012 (60%)

Scranton lawyer and political newcomer Matt Cartwright was elected in 2012 after he toppled 10-term Rep. Tim Holden in the 2012 Democratic primary by running to the left in a redrawn district. With a seat on the Appropriations Committee, he took on the Pennsylvania tradition of servicing local constituents. Declining blue-collar support for Democrats and a big-spending challenger in 2018 forced Cartwright to scramble for reelection.

Cartwright was born in Erie. His mother earned a law degree but didn't practice law. After his father served in the Army during World War II, that wartime experience with radar technology led to a job with General Electric and relocation to Toronto, where Cartwright got his bachelor's degree from Hamilton College. He studied at the London School of Economics and Political Science. He earned his law degree from the University of Pennsylvania and practiced law in Philadelphia for several years. He and his wife moved to Scranton to join the law firm of his father-in-law, Robert Munley. Cartwright represented consumers tangling with large corporations on a variety of civil claims. He served on the board of governors of the American Association for Justice, a trial lawyers' group.

Cartwright decided to take on Holden, who had been severely damaged by the Republican-orchestrated redistricting. "I had always thought about running for high political office, and I was kind of waiting for the stars to line up," Cartwright said. "And, you know, they don't hold the door open for you. You kind of have to muscle your way in." For the Democratic primary, Cartwright raised around $600,000, much of it from fellow trial lawyers. Cartwright ran as a progressive, pushing for environmental protections and criticizing corporate tax breaks. The two candidates differed on health care. Cartwright supported the 2010 Affordable Care Act. Holden had voted against it while serving his more conservative district. The new Democratic district was better suited to Cartwright's liberal views than to Holden's centrism. The challenger won the primary, 57%-43%, with more than 70 percent of the vote in both Lackawanna and Luzerne. In the general election, Cartwright defeated Scranton Tea Party founder Laureen Cummings, 60%-40%.

With Rep. Joaquin Castro of Texas, Cartwright was elected one of two presidents of the Democratic freshman class. During his first two years, he took credit for having developed and introduced 60-plus bills, more than any other House Democrat. He filed a proposed constitutional amendment to reverse the Supreme Court's ruling in the Citizens United case that overturned some restrictions on federal campaign financing. True to his campaign promise, Cartwright mostly voted the party line.

In the Almanac vote ratings, he has been more liberal on economic issues and conservative on foreign policy. He was part of a bipartisan group that enacted in 2016 the Megabyte Act, which reduced government costs for software licenses. Cartwright made a big personal move that year when he filled the vacancy on the Appropriations Committee, which resulted when Democrat Chaka Fattah of Pennsylvania resigned after his criminal conviction. Explaining his selection to the Wilkes-Barre Times Leader, Cartwright said, "As soon as I got to Washington, I set about the business of making friends. And the best way to make friends is to be a friend."

Following the 2018 election, he won election in the Democratic Caucus as one of three co-chairs of the Democratic Policy and Communications Committee, working to develop the party's agenda and message. In March 2019, the House passed his bill to provide incentives for energy efficiency in public schools.

In the 2016 election, Cartwright showed that he needed to work to secure his seat. Little-known Republican challenger Matt Connolly, a real estate investor who campaigned against excessive federal regulations and unfunded mandates on local governments, said that Cartwright's views were "not aligned with this district." Connolly raised a mere $31,000 to nearly $1 million for Cartwright. The outcome was unexpectedly close, 54%-46%. In 2018, in the redrawn district, he faced a well-funded challenger. John Chirin, an investment banker who had been a managing director at JP Morgan Chase and then joined his wife's investment advisory firm, offered his "practical business experience;" prior to the campaign, Chirin, a native of the Lehigh Valley, had been living in Short Hills New Jersey. He ran ads attacking Cartwright for voting for sanctuary cities. In a meeting with the Times Leader editorial board, Cartwright cited his increased seniority on Appropriations. Former vice president — and Scranton native — Joe Biden made an election-even campaign stop. Cartwright, who outspent Chirin $2.5 million to $2.2 million, won 55%-45% -- with 64 percent in Lackawanna and 53 percent in Luzerne.

PA-8: Northeast Pennsylvania   **Cook Partisan Voting Index: R+1**

Demographics data for new House districts were not prepared by the Census Bureau prior to our editorial deadline.

2012 Pres. Vote	Obama	158,884	(55%)	Romney	124,449	(43%)	
2016 Pres. Vote	Trump	165,168	(53%)	Clinton	135,590	(43%) Johnson	5,742	(2%)

Scranton, Wilkes-Barre: "Coal is the theme song of this city in the hills," the WPA Guide said of Scranton in 1940, but even as those words were written, the anthracite kingdom around Scranton and Wilkes-Barre was crumbling. In the 19th century, anthracite had become America's main home heating fuel, and the valley along the East Branch of the Susquehanna River was the No. 1 source. Thousands of immigrants flocked to the valley, settling in a chain of little cities north and south of Wilkes-Barre and Scranton. They took jobs with long hours, modest pay, poor working conditions and high death rates — facts of life that made the violently pro-union Molly Maguires popular here and that spawned periodic clashes between workers and the Pinkerton security forces hired by the industrial moguls.

While the supply of coal was endless, demand proved fleeting. Anthracite production peaked in 1917, with long strikes in 1922 and 1925 quickening the conversion to oil and gas. Demand for anthracite began to fall in the 1920s and plummeted in the 1940s. The counties containing Wilkes-Barre and Scranton, Luzerne and Lackawanna, had 755,000 people in 1930 and 528,000 in 2017. Scranton is the birthplace of former Vice President Joe Biden, and Hillary Clinton's paternal grandparents were natives. Scranton's $16 million budget shortfall in 2012 threatened to push the city into bankruptcy. Crisis was averted and the city was expected to end its "distressed" status by 2020. As of November 2018, three industrial parks were under construction in the Nanticoke area.

Hazleton is a small city that gained national notoriety for its crackdowns on illegal immigrants, which were repeatedly contested in the courts and not implemented. Those problems have subsided with a combination of new warehouse jobs, "white flight" to nearby towns and a population that has become more than 50 percent Hispanic. By contrast, Pike County on the Delaware River has had significant growth and was the state's second-fastest growing county from 2000 to 2010, with many of its new residents fleeing higher taxes in New Jersey and New York; growth has been flat since 2010. The Pocono Mountains are a destination for weekend skiers and, for a few days each

November, for bear hunters. In April 2018, developers unveiled plans for Pocono Springs, a $350 million entertainment center, with completion of the first phase scheduled for 2021. It would be located adjacent to Kalahari Waterpark, the largest such facility in North America.

The 8th Congressional District takes in the Democratic strongholds Scranton and Wilkes-Barre, and nearly all of surrounding Lackawanna and Luzerne Counties. The remaining 30 percent of the population is in the more rural Pike and Wayne counties and most of Monroe; the eastern boundaries of these counties drop from New York to New Jersey. The relatively straight lines of the new 8th replaced the irregularly shaped 17th district, which had been drawn by Republican redistricters to include Democratic bastions and protect nearby GOP districts. Democratic performance in these blue-collar areas took a sharp and unexpected downward turn in the 2016 election. The old district shifted from a double-digit victory in 2012 for President Barack Obama — with Biden – to a double-digit loss in 2016 for Hillary Clinton against Donald Trump. The court-drawn redistricting changes in 2018 had scant partisan impact.

Daniel Meuser (R)

Elected 2018, 1st term, b. Feb 10, 1954; Babylon, NY; Cornell University (NY), B.A., 1986; Cornell University (NY), B.A., 1986; Catholic; Married (Shelley Van Acker); 3 children.

Elected Office: Secretary, PA Department of Revenue, 2011-2015

Professional Career: Executive, Pride Mobility Products, 1988-2008.

DC Office: 326 CHOB 20515, 202-225-6511, meuser.house.gov

State Offices: Pottsville, 570-871-6370.

Committees: *Budget*. *Education & Labor*: Health, Employment, Labor & Pensions; Higher Education & Workforce Investment. *Veterans' Affairs*: Economic Opportunity; Health.

Election Results

Election	Name (Party)	Vote (%)		Cand. Spent	Ind. Exp. Support	Ind. Exp. Oppose
2018 General	Daniel P. Meuser (R)	148,723	(60%)	$2,138,643	$156,344	
	Denny Wolff (D)	100,204	(40%)	$1,532,869		
2018 Primary	Daniel P. Meuser (R)	26,866	(53%)			
	George Halcovage (R)	12,162	(24%)			
	Scott Uehlinger (R)	11,721	(23%)			

Republican freshman Dan Meuser easily won the redrawn seat that was the successor to the district represented by Lou Barletta, who ran unsuccessfully against Democratic Sen. Bob Casey. Meuser, who embraced Barletta and President Donald Trump, had been a fixture in the local business community and earlier held a prominent position in state government. Shortly after Barletta announced his Senate campaign in 2017, Meuser was the leading Republican to announce for the seat. He stuck with his plans, even with the significant local disruptions from the redistricting plan the state Supreme Court approved in February 2018. After getting 53 percent of the vote against two other candidates in the GOP primary, he breezed to victory in November.

Meuser spent most of his professional life in business. After graduating from Cornell University, he settled in Luzerne County and joined Pride Mobility Products, which he built with his father and brother and managed for more than two decades. He became president of the company — an industry leader in the manufacturing of power wheel-chairs, scooters and other personal mobility products.

Meuser made an earlier bid for Congress. In 2008, he lost a contentious primary for the Republican nomination in the district in the northeast corner of Pennsylvania, which was held at the time by Democratic Rep. Christopher Carney; two years later, Republican Tom Marino won that seat. From 2011 to 2015, he held the powerful state office of Secretary of Revenue under Gov. Tom Corbett, a Republican for whom Meuser had been a major contributor in the 2010 campaign. During his four years in government, Meuser said, the Council on State Taxation raised the rating of his department from D to A-minus.

Making another run in 2018, Meuser had a huge fundraising advantage in the GOP primary for the open seat. He raised nearly $1 million against his two opponents: Schuylkill County Commissioner George Halcovage and former CIA station chief and Fox News analyst Scott Uehlinger. With his endorsement by the Trump-supporting Making America Great PAC, he described himself as "a problem-solving conservative" with "a record of success in business and the public sector" and a commitment to helping Trump implement his agenda.

In the primary, Meuser took 53 percent of the vote to 24 percent for Halcovage and 23 percent for Uehlinger. He ran strongly in the five northern counties in the district, where he got between 61 and 85 percent of the vote. Uehlinger took his base in Berks County and Halcovage narrowly won Schuylkill; in those two counties, Meuser was second.

Democrats nominated Denny Wolff — a dairy farmer who shared Meuser's executive experience in Harrisburg, as secretary of agriculture under former Democratic Gov. Ed Rendell. Wolff ran a credible campaign in the general election. But in the face of the strong Republican tilt of the district and national Democrats' focus on several nearby districts, he was out-matched by the fundraising dominance of Meuser; he won 60%-40%. Perhaps the most significant political challenge Meuser will face is the uncertain impact of redistricting in 2022 on a district that sprawls across a wide area of eastern Pennsylvania, with no central urban core.

PA-9: East-Central Pennsylvania   **Cook Partisan Voting Index: R+19**

Demographics data for new House districts were not prepared by the Census Bureau prior to our editorial deadline.

2012 Pres. Vote	Romney	164,938	(57%)	Obama	118,959	(41%)		
2016 Pres. Vote	Trump	205,191	(65%)	Clinton	97,810	(31%)	Johnson	8,369 (3%)

Exurbs of Lancaster and Wilkes-Barre: In the late 19th and early 20th centuries, towns existed in Berks and Schuylkill counties solely to mine rich veins of anthracite coal, which long served as the nation's chief energy supply. These mountain towns were less orderly, filled with tough-talking miners and factory workers — the Pennsylvania that novelist John O'Hara knew growing up and wrote about in the 1930s and 1940s. Although the big companies abandoned the mines long ago, some local entrepreneurs still go deep underground to blast their way into the anthracite. With incentives from the Trump administration's trade policies, several abandoned coal mines in Schuylkill have reopened, though the surrounding towns have been hollowed out by economic distress.

Pottsville is the home of Yuengling lager (known locally as "Vitamin Y") and produced the Maroons, the team that may have won the 1925 National Football League championship. The league disputed the claim, to the eternal chagrin of Pottsville. The city's ties to coal country are emblematic of the hardscrabble roots of the NFL in the old Rust Belt.

The 9th Congressional District is centered in the small cities of east-central Pennsylvania, west of Philadelphia. Two-thirds of the population is in the three largest and adjacent, counties: Berks, Schuylkill and Lebanon. The portion of Berks does not include economically distressed Reading, which is in the 6th District. The remainder of the new 9th is in the more rural area to the north, including the small part of Luzerne County that is not in the 8th District.

Redistricting in 2018 shifted to the south the old 11th District, where Luzerne was the largest county. For decades, that area leaned Democratic. When Republican redistricting in 2011 removed Wilkes Barre, Scranton and other Democratic urban centers, the district became solidly Republican. It increased from 52 percent for John McCain in the 2008 presidential election to 60 percent for Donald Trump in 2016. The latest round of redistricting further entrenched GOP control in the 9th, which is the party's strongest district in the outskirts of Philadelphia. The fact that Democrats have abandoned these blue-collar areas but have become entrenched not far away in upscale Montgomery County illustrates how the politics of the state — and nation — have turned upside-down in the past half-century.

Scott Perry (R)

Elected 2012, 4th term, b. May 27, 1962; San Diego, CA; U.S. Army War College (PA), M.S.; Pennsylvania State University, B.S., 1991; Church of the United Brethren in Christ; Married (Christy Perry); 2 children.

Military Career: PA Army National Guard 1980-pres. (Iraq)

Elected Office: PA House, 2007-2012.

Professional Career: Dock worker, Dauphin Distribution, 1981-1982; Insurance sales agent, 1984-1985; Co-owner, Hydrotech Mechanical Services, 1993-present.

DC Office: 1207 LHOB 20515, 202-225-5836, Fax: 202-226-1000, perry.house.gov

State Offices: Harrisburg, 717-603-4980.

Committees: *Foreign Affairs*: Asia, the Pacific & Nonproliferation; Oversight & Investigations. *Transportation & Infrastructure*: Aviation; Railroads, Pipelines & Hazardous Materials.

Group Ratings

	ADA	ACLU	AFL-CIO	LCV	ITI	COC	HAFA	ACU	CFG	FRC
2018	-	21%	-	3%	-	75%	96%	92%	95%	100%
2017	5%	C	3%	0%	C	93%	C	96%	99%	100%

Almanac Ratings 2017-18

	Economy	Social	Foreign	Composite
Liberal	3%	7%	3%	5%
Conservative	97%	93%	97%	95%

Key Votes of the 115th Congress

1. Obama-care revision	Y	5. Family planning regs	Y	9. Guantanamo prisoners	N
2. Tax Cuts	Y	6. Body cameras/immigration	N	10. Ground missiles, limit	N
3. Omnibus appropriations	N	7. Abortion ban	Y	11. Defense Dept. spending	Y
4. Dodd-Frank revision	Y	8. Concealed carry	Y	12. FISA rules	N

Election Results

Election	Name (Party)	Vote (%)	Cand. Spent	Ind. Exp. Support	Ind. Exp. Oppose
2018 General	Scott Perry (R).............................	149,365 (51%)	$1,410,268	$453,178	$774,963
	George Scott (D)............................	141,668 (49%)	$2,135,617	$591,063	$1,400,079
2018 Primary	Scott Perry (R)...	(100%)			

Prior winning percentages: 2016 (66%), 2014 (75%), 2012 (60%)

Republican Scott Perry was elected in 2012 after easily prevailing in a crowded primary in which he started as an underdog. With an agenda that emphasized a leaner federal government, gun rights, traditional marriage and his lengthy military career, Perry became an active member of the House Freedom Caucus and voiced interest in becoming a leader. In 2018, redistricting made his district more competitive and was a factor in his close reelection. Democrats contended that his views had grown out of sync with his district.

Perry was born in San Diego but moved at age 7 to central Pennsylvania, where he lived in a home without electricity or plumbing. He grew up in what he described to National Journal as a "little dysfunctional and a little disjointed family." After graduating from high school, Perry worked as an auto mechanic before enlisting in the Pennsylvania Army National Guard. He became an instructor pilot and distinguished himself as a helicopter pilot -- rising to the rank of brigadier general. While a state representative, he served for a year in Iraq, flying 44 missions. He has commanded the Fort Indiantown Gap National Training Site and remained active as an assistant adjutant general at headquarters.

With his bachelor's in business administration from Penn State University, Perry and a partner built a contracting firm specializing in meter calibration and line work for municipalities. In 2002, the

Pennsylvania attorney general's office accused Perry of falsifying reports to the state Environmental Protection Department. The matter ended with a $5,000 fine and his record being expunged. Perry maintained his innocence.

As a past president of the Pennsylvania Young Republicans, Perry was elected to the state House in 2006. He expanded the law allowing residents to use deadly force in self-defense. He bucked Republican Gov. Tom Corbett by proposing legislation that would have declined federal money to fund insurance exchanges under the Affordable Care Act.

When he ran for the House, Perry's past legal troubles were raised in the seven-person Republican primary, but they never got traction. He got endorsements from Corbett and GOP Sen. Pat Toomey. Retiring Rep. Todd Platts offered kind words about him in a mailer to voters, but not an endorsement. He benefited from his military background. Perry was outspent 2-to-1, but won 54 percent of the primary vote. In November, he had no trouble in what was a heavily Republican district.

In the House, Perry was a co-founder of the post-9/11 veterans' caucus. As a member of the Foreign Affairs Committee, he has taken a hard line on overseas issues. In 2014, when the Iraqi military lost control of major parts of their country, he voiced bitterness as he recalled his own service. "Right now, I wonder what that was all about. What was the point of all of that?" In 2015, he criticized President Barack Obama's "lack of leadership" in dealing with terror threats overseas and worried publicly about the potential threat to the homeland from domestic jihadists. But he backed away from an earlier charge that Obama was "working collaboratively with what I would say is the enemy of freedom."

After President Donald Trump met with Russian President Vladimir Putin in Helsinki in July 2018, Perry told a town-hall meeting that news coverage of the two standing next to each other "makes you feel uncomfortable." He added that he didn't object to the meeting "as long as it gets us where we need to go," Roll Call reported. On Foreign Affairs in 2019, Perry deferred to less-senior Republicans who took ranking positions on subcommittees.

In July 2017, the House, on a 185-234 vote, defeated Perry's move to strip from the annual defense spending bill a provision that would have blocked a Pentagon study of the impact of climate change on national security. The proposed review "detracts from the central mission of securing our nation against enemies," he told the House. On the Homeland Security Committee, the House passed his bill in 2017 to improve management of the vehicle fleet at the Department of Homeland Security. Following the 2018 election, Perry left that panel, where he had become a senior Republican.

As an active member of the Freedom Caucus, Perry supported the partial government shutdown that Trump hoped would result in funding of a wall along the border with Mexico. He was one of three members seeking to succeed Rep. Mark Meadows of North Carolina as the group's chairman, with a vote expected later in 2019. Some conservatives suggested that Perry was being "groomed for the job" by caucus leaders, The Hill reported in November 2018.

At home, Perry faced Harrisburg Democratic Mayor Linda Thompson in the 2014 election. She campaigned against the "dysfunction" in Congress but raised less than $9,000 and was not well known outside of her Democratic base. Perry won 75%-25%. In 2016, Perry got 66 percent of the vote against Joshua Burkholder, who got the Democratic nomination as a write-in candidate.

In 2018, Perry faced his first well-financed challenger — George Scott, a retired Army lieutenant colonel and Lutheran pastor who ran "common sense" ads to contrast himself to Perry. He cited, for example, the need for gun safety and more "compassionate" treatment of immigrants at the border. In endorsing Scott, the York Daily Record criticized Perry's participation in the Freedom Caucus, with its "their way or the highway" approach. Scott outspent Perry, $2.1 million to $1.4 million, with outside groups on both sides spending more than $3 million. In the district that had become less Republican following the court-drawn redistricting, Perry won, 51%-49%, a margin of 7,700 votes. Scott got 54 percent of the vote in Dauphin. Perry took 56 percent in York and 53 percent in Cumberland. The Democratic Congressional Campaign Committee placed him on its early target list for 2020.

PA-10: South-Central Pennsylvania   **Cook Partisan Voting Index: R+11**

Demographics data for new House districts were not prepared by the Census Bureau prior to our editorial deadline.

2012 Pres. Vote	Romney	169,699	(52%)	Obama	148,327	(46%)			
2016 Pres. Vote	Trump	180,979	(52%)	Clinton	150,076	(43%)	Johnson	10,542	(3%)

Harrisburg, York: Harrisburg, the capital of Pennsylvania, features a string of mansions-turned-lobbying headquarters lining the banks of the Susquehanna and boasts Pennsylvania's marvelously restored capitol. Beyond that building, the city has suffered financially. In 2012, its $1.5 billion debt was the largest per capita in the nation. The legislature in 2016 tightened municipal debt procedures in an attempt to prevent a repeat of apparent abuses. During a campaign visit that summer, Donald Trump said that Harrisburg "looked like a war zone" because of its closed factories. Local business leaders and journalists disagreed. In 2018, the city was exploring options to end its participation in the state's financial distress program.

Nearby in Dauphin County are centers of American heritage. Hershey was erected by chocolate magnate Milton S. Hershey as a planned utopian village for his factory workers and their families. The surrounding area is fed by a steady flow of tourists to the Hersheypark amusement site. With automation and the smell of chocolate still in the air, the facility produced more than 70 million Kisses each day. Middletown has leafy, gridded streets and handsome homes that give no hint that it is the location of the Three Mile Island nuclear plant, which in 1979 was the site of the worst nuclear accident in U.S. history. After Exelon in May 2017 announced its plan to shut down TMI because it was no longer profitable, state legislators reviewed possible rescue options.

West of the Susquehanna River, the small town of Carlisle has a unique history as one of the unsung stories of rural Pennsylvania. In 1912, the most dominant college football team in the nation belonged to the Carlisle Indian Industrial School. The team of Native Americans starred Olympian Jim Thorpe and was coached by Glenn Scobey "Pop" Warner. "They didn't just change football. They changed prevailing ideas about Indians," wrote author Sally Jenkins in her book, The Real All Americans. The epic 1912 game between the Carlisle Indians and the U.S. Military Academy — which featured Dwight Eisenhower at linebacker — became an extension of fighting between white expansionists and Native Americans. This time, the Carlisle underdogs won, 27-6. Today, Carlisle is home to Dickinson College, the U.S. Army War College and a huge Amazon warehouse.

The area was home to the westernmost capital of the United States during the Revolutionary War: the city of York, where the Continental Congress passed the Articles of Confederation and received word from Benjamin Franklin in Paris that the French would help the colonies with money and ships. More than two centuries later, a different kind of European intervention proved more troublesome. A large Harley-Davidson manufacturing plant has been based in York, though automation and fewer sales downsized its payroll from 2,000 workers in 2009 to about 900 in early 2018. With plans to close a Harley plant in Kansas City Missouri, the York facility expected to gain 300 workers. But Harley's decision to shift some of its motorcycle operations across the Atlantic to avoid much higher tariffs prompted harsh criticism from President Donald Trump and added new uncertainty.

The 10th Congressional District of Pennsylvania is in the south-central part of the state and includes all of Dauphin County, which is the largest share of the district, plus large portions of York and Cumberland counties. Like York, Cumberland — whose 6 percent population increase from 2010 to 2017 was the fastest in the state — has remained conventionally Republican. With portions of Democratic-leaning Dauphin added to the old 4th District, plus its loss of some rural areas, redistricting in 2018 made the 10th more politically competitive.

Lloyd Smucker (R)

Elected 2016, 2nd term, b. Jan 23, 1964; Lancaster; Lebanon Valley College (PA), Att.; Franklin & Marshall College, Att., 1991; Lutheran; Married (Cynthia Smucker); 3 children.

Elected Office: Western Lampeter Board of Supervisors, 2001-2005.

Professional Career: Business Owner; West Lampeter Planning Commission.

DC Office: 127 CHOB 20515, 202-225-2411, Fax: 202-225-2013, smucker.house.gov

State Offices: Hanover, 717-969-6132; Red Lion, 717-969-6133.

Committees: *Education & Labor*: Higher Education & Workforce Investment (RMM). *Transportation & Infrastructure*: Aviation; Highways & Transit; Railroads, Pipelines & Hazardous Materials.

Group Ratings

	ADA	ACLU	AFL-CIO	LCV	ITI	COC	HAFA	ACU	CFG	FRC
2018	-	7%	-	3%	-	75%	67%	92%	80%	100%
2017	0%	C	13%	3%	C	93%	C	78%	66%	100%

Almanac Ratings 2017-18

	Economy	Social	Foreign	Composite
Liberal	3%	7%	0%	3%
Conservative	97%	94%	100%	97%

Key Votes of the 115th Congress

1. Obama-care revision	Y	5. Family planning regs	Y	9. Guantanamo prisoners	N
2. Tax Cuts	Y	6. Body cameras/immigration	N	10. Ground missiles, limit	N
3. Omnibus appropriations	N	7. Abortion ban	Y	11. Defense Dept. spending	Y
4. Dodd-Frank revision	Y	8. Concealed carry	Y	12. FISA rules	Y

Election Results

Election	Name (Party)		Vote (%)		Cand. Spent	Ind. Exp. Support	Ind. Exp. Oppose
2018 General	Lloyd Smucker (R).............................	163,708	(59%)		$1,521,027	$37,049	$20,431
	Jessica King (D)...............................	113,876	(41%)		$1,859,730	$244,963	
2018 Primary	Lloyd Smucker (R).............................	34,232	(59%)				
	Chester Beiler (R)........................	24,241	(42%)				

Prior winning percentages: 2016 (54%)

Lloyd Smucker, elected to an open seat in 2016, seemed to fit comfortably with the mostly establishment Republicans in his state delegation. He won competitive contests in both the primary and general election and styled himself as a problem-solver. Two years later, following court-ordered redistricting, Smucker was the survivor in a district that had become more safely Republican, as three other GOP members from southeast Pennsylvania walked away and were replaced by Democrats. He became the senior Republican on a subcommittee handling higher education issues.

Smucker grew up locally and attended but did not graduate from local colleges. He founded Smucker Co., a commercial construction firm that specialized in dry wall, and ran the business for a quarter-century. He served on the West Lampeter Township Planning Commission for four years and was elected to the state Senate for eight years. In Harrisburg, Smucker chaired the Senate Education Committee and mostly advocated local control over educational standards. He supported steps to encourage legalization of immigrants but was unable to enact such a measure.

When Republican Rep. Joseph Pitts retired after serving 20 years, just as his predecessor Rep. Robert Walker had done, Smucker became the frontrunner. In the primary, he faced businessman Chet Beiler, whose family-owned Amish Country Gazebos was the nation's leading retailer of custom-built gazebos. The two candidates were second cousins who graduated in the same class at Lancaster Mennonite High School. In the primary, each spent more than $600,000, with a large share self-financed. Smucker was endorsed by the Chamber of Commerce and the National Rifle Association. He won, 54%-46%, with 56 percent in Lancaster County, which cast more than 80 percent of the total vote.

The general election was competitive against Democrat Christina Hartman, a local native who was a consultant to nonprofit groups after having spent 15 years in international development. She described herself as "moderate to progressive" and said that the district was moving to the left. Her campaign ran negative ads that sought to link Smucker to GOP presidential nominee Donald Trump. In the closing weeks of the campaign, Smucker grew more enthusiastic about Trump and spoke at his rally in Lancaster. David Wasserman of the Cook Political Report wrote that Hartman ran a "surprisingly energetic campaign," and was competitive financially, even though national Democrats did not become active until late in the campaign. Smucker outraised Hartman, $1.5 million to $1.2

million, and received more than $800,000 in additional support. He won, 54%-43%. Lancaster cast about three-fourths of the total vote, of which Smucker took 59 percent.

In the House, Smucker was usually a party loyalist and made few waves. His Almanac vote ratings showed a consistently conservative pattern. He advocated steps to reduce health care costs and said that he was "very disappointed" by the initial failure of House Republicans to reform the Affordable Care Act. Smucker showed some independence and his legislative expertise when he joined the bipartisan Problem Solvers Caucus, where he said that he would "focus on navigating — not obstructing — our path forward," while maintaining his "conservative principles." After the 2018 election, he was part of the group that persuaded Nancy Pelosi to agree to its plan for more open House debates, especially on bills with bipartisan support.

Taking over in 2019 as ranking Republican on the Education and Labor Subcommittee on Higher Education and Workforce Investment, Smucker said his objectives were "improving college affordability, expanding apprenticeships and strengthening career and technical education." He added that he would draw on his experience as chairman of the Senate Education Committee in Harrisburg. In March 2019, a broad public lands bill was enacted that included Smucker's legislation to create the Susquehanna National Heritage Area, which would prepare a plan for historic preservation, natural-resource conservation and local tourism.

In his redrawn district, Smucker had another competitive primary with Beiler. In what seemed a strained relationship between the cousins, Beiler accused Smucker of being insufficiently conservative and of sending campaign mailers that had "no basis in reality." Smucker won the primary 59%-41%. That became the same result in Smucker's general-election contest with Jessica King, a Mennonite with a career of anti-poverty work. She was supported by Bernie Sanders, which helped her to raise and spend $1.9 million—more than the $1.5 million for Smucker. But that endorsement carried less weight with voters in this district.

PA-11: Philadelphia exurbs   Cook Partisan Voting Index: R+5

Demographics data for new House districts were not prepared by the Census Bureau prior to our editorial deadline.

2012 Pres. Vote	Romney	184,739	(60%)	Obama	116,048	(38%)			
2016 Pres. Vote	Trump	201,586	(60%)	Clinton	115,388	(34%)	Johnson	11,343	(3%)

Lancaster, part of York County: The Pennsylvania Dutch Country, settled by Germans in the 18th century when it was Pennsylvania's frontier, remains a distinctive part of America. These Germans were Amish and Mennonite, pietistic sects seeking religious liberty and determined to farm rich lands in the same intensive way they had in Germany. Today, many of their descendants — the Eisenhower family is the most famous example — have blended into mainstream America. But in the Dutch area around Lancaster, many "Plain People" still live in the old way, though today they are willing to use some modern devices, such as battery-powered electricity. Tourists can still see families of Plain People clad in black, clattering over the back roads in horse-drawn carriages, with scrupulously tended farms set amid rolling hills and barns decorated with hex signs. Beneath the surface, Amish communities have faced the strains of modernity and economic dislocation. In 2006, five Amish girls were killed and five others seriously wounded by a gunman at their one-room schoolhouse in Nickel Mines. In December 2017, the York Daily Record reported that some Amish were leaving Lancaster to start settlements in more rural areas. According to a book author who has written about the Amish, one factor might be that Lancaster had become too "crowded, fast paced."

With an easy drive from Philadelphia, Baltimore and Washington, the area is home to many outlet malls; the first Woolworth's store opened in Lancaster in 1879. Pennsylvania Dutch Country draws more than 8 million tourists annually. Lancaster has gained national attention for its livability. In October 2018, U.S. News & World Report rated it as the best place to retire in the United States. New York Times columnist Tom Friedman in July 2018 praised Lancaster as a model for local development. Citing "the societal innovation the town's leader's had employed to rebuild their once-struggling city," Friedman described its "adaptive coalition in which business leaders, educators, philanthropists, social innovators and the local government would work together to unleash entrepreneurship."

The Mason-Dixon Line, the historic boundary between Maryland and Pennsylvania, runs through pleasant rolling farmlands from the Susquehanna River through the Appalachian Mountains. Hanover, in York County, is a snack headquarters, home to Snyder's of Hanover and potato chip giant Utz. The city has a growing Hispanic population, many of whom work the abundant orchards near Gettysburg, which is to the west in Adams County.

The 11th Congressional District of Pennsylvania includes all of Lancaster County, plus nearly half of York County, which is along the Maryland border. Until the 1980s, Lancaster County was one of the most Republican counties in the state. Suburbanization and demographic change have reduced that share. But it remains firmly Republican, with 57 percent for Donald Trump in 2016, and is the second-fastest growing county in the state. The county includes nearly 75 percent of the population in the new 11th. (Amish rarely vote, but their social views seem consistent with the overall local attitudes.) The northern portion of York County, now in the 10th District, is less firmly Republican. Overall, the 2018 redistricting boosted the GOP base in the new 11th — the second-largest increase in the state, next to that of the adjacent 9th District. That would have given about 60 percent of the vote to Donald Trump in 2016, compared with his 50 percent in the old 16th district.

Fred Keller (R)

Elected 2019, term expires 2020, 1st term, b. Oct 23, 1965; Page, AZ; Shikellamy High School, 1984; Don Paul Shearer Real Estate School, 1995;Christian; Married (Kay); 2 children.

Elected Office: PA House, 2010-2018.

Professional Career: Operations Manager, Conestoga Wood Specialties Corporation.

DC Office: 2242 RHOB 20515, 202-225-3731, Fax: 202-225-9594

Republican Fred Keller was elected in May 2019, as the first winner of a special election since Democrats took control of the House in January. Keller replaced Republican Tom Marino, who had served four terms before resigning for health reasons three weeks after the new Congress convened. In this solidly Republican district with no major population centers, the contest was perfunctory and the outcome was expected. Keller, who was nominated at a party convention in March, styled himself as a conservative Republican with mainstream credentials. He won with 68 percent of the vote.

Marino, a former federal prosecutor who was elected in 2010 when he defeated Democratic Rep. Chris Carney, had not faced serious reelection challenges. In the House, he served on the Judiciary Committee, where he sought to reduce the adverse economic impact of federal regulations. His signature legislation was his Responsibly and Professionally Invigorating Development (RAPID) Act, which requires federal agencies to act promptly on proposals for infrastructure or energy construction. In September 2015, the House passed the bill, 233-170.

In February 2016, Marino became the fourth House Republican to endorse the presidential campaign of Donald Trump. He became an informal campaign adviser to Trump and his top aides and served as a surrogate at the Republican convention and elsewhere. In April 2017, there were multiple press reports that Trump had decided to nominate Marino as head of the White House Office of National Drug Control Policy. A month later, several news organizations reported that Marino was no longer being considered. There was very little explanation, pro or con.

Marino's resignation announcement on Jan. 16 was surprising and gave little explanation. He said little more than that he was planning to take a private-sector job. Two weeks later, he told a local newspaper — the Sunbury Daily Item -- that his resignation resulted from medical issues. "I am not well," the 66-year-old Marino said. "But I'm getting better. I had surgery and they found my lining in my kidney was deteriorating and tissue was blocking everything, so they went in and cleaned everything out." Marino said that he had battled cancer for 20 years and that he had lost his first kidney in 2009; cancer resulted in the removal of 60 percent of his other kidney in 2012.

Gov. Tom Wolf set the special election for May 21, which was a previously scheduled date for primaries in the state. Each party selected its nominee at a party convention. On Feb. 12, Democrats nominated Marc Friedenberg, a Penn State University professor who taught cyber law and the global economy. He ran against Marino in 2018 and lost, 66%-34%.

The Republican selection process was more contentious, given that the winner would likely get Marino's seat. At the Republican convention in Williamsport on March 2, the 202 delegates selected among 14 candidates. Keller won a majority on the fourth ballot. The Associated Press described him as "largely a back-bencher and one of the most conservative state House members."

Keller graduated from Shikellamy High School in Northumberland County and attended the Don Paul Shrear Real Estate School, which is a state-certified appraiser. He spent 25 years with the Conestoga Wood Specialties Corp. in Lancaster County, which manufactures cabinet doors and wood products for kitchens and bathrooms; he eventually became plant manager. He served as the auditor for Middlecreek Township in Somerset County. Keller resided in Kreamer, a township with 835 persons in a 2018 census report and an area of 1.2 square mile. In 2010, he was elected to the state House from a district serving parts of Snyder and Union counties; he served on the Appropriations and Finance committees.

The special election attracted little attention, locally or nationally. Keller raised $400,000 to $154,000 for Friedenberg, according to their pre-election reports—notably small amounts for an open-seat contest. In the rural district, Keller said that he would be "a champion for the agriculture industry" and he backed "pragmatic, conservative principles." Trump appeared at an election-eve rally at the Williamsport airport, during which he briefly introduced Keller and focused chiefly on prospects for the 2020 presidential contest. Keller won at least 63 percent of the vote in every county, except for Friedenberg's home of Penn State-based Centre County, where he took 66 percent.

PA-12: North-central Pennsylvania   Cook Partisan Voting Index: R+11

Demographics data for new House districts were not prepared by the Census Bureau prior to our editorial deadline.						
2012 Pres. Vote	Romney	172,294	(61%)	Obama	103,168	(37%)		
2016 Pres. Vote	Trump	202,538	(65%)	Clinton	91,175	(29%) Johnson 8,843 (3%)

Williamsport: The sprawling northern tier of Pennsylvania is a land of crevassed valleys and rugged mountains, crisscrossed by giant viaducts built for the railroads linking the East Coast with the Great Lakes and the mines that produced the region's anthracite coal. This area still has a throwback look to it. The region has numerous long-established small towns, with solidly built courthouses and banks and elderly citizens. It's a part of the Northeast that seems worlds away from the region's huge central cities and growing suburbs. Notable towns include Williamsport, home of the Little League World Series, and Lewisburg, home of Bucknell University. The area's most consequential member of Congress was probably David Wilmot of Bradford County, a founding member of the Republican Party. In the 1840s, he introduced the Wilmot Proviso barring slavery from the New Mexico and California territories acquired in the Mexican War, raising the issue that led proximately to the Civil War. Most people in this part of Pennsylvania have been Republicans ever since.

The rural area recently has benefited from major building and energy development. Work has begun on the Central Susquehanna Valley Thruway project, including a $156 million bridge across the Susquehanna River between rural Snyder and Northumberland counties. The project was scheduled for completion in 2024, though sections of the new 12-mile highway might open before that date. Two new Marcellus Shale-gas power plants in Lycoming and Bradford counties will convert the natural gas from nearby wells to generate enough electricity to power up to 2 million homes. Dozens of permits have been issued for drilling of natural-gas wells in Lycoming, Sullivan and Tioga counties.

The 12th Congressional District includes the less-populated areas of north-central Pennsylvania. (Democratic-leaning Scranton and Wilkes Barre are in the neighboring 8th District.) Williamsport-based Lycoming County is the population center of the 15 counties. None of them have a substantial Democratic presence. The district dips deep into central Pennsylvania west of Harrisburg in the conservative rural counties of Juniata and Mifflin. In 2018, redistricting shifted the old 10th District a bit to the west, replacing Wayne and Pike counties in the northeast corner with Potter and Clinton in the mountainous center of the state. In its southwest corner, the new 12th includes about half of Centre County, where the cutting-edge facilities of Penn State University have spawned a high-skills job market. The university has struggled to recover from the abuse scandal that rocked its powerful football team in 2011. That led to the firing and death two months later of Joe Paterno, the iconic coach, and the eventual criminal conviction of Gordon Spanier, the former university president, on one count of child endangerment. The 12th and 15th Districts are the largest in the state; combined, they extend from nearly Ohio to the Catskills in New York. Along with the adjacent 13th to the south, they also are the most Republican.

John Joyce (R)

Elected 2018, 1st term, b. Feb 08, 1957; Altoona; Pennsylvania State University, Att., 1977; Pennsylvania State University, Bach. Deg., 1979; Temple University (PA), M.D., 1983; Catholic; Married (Alice Joyce); 3 children.

Military Career: U.S. Navy, Portsmouth Naval Hospital

Professional Career: Dermatologist.

DC Office: 1337 LHOB 20515, 202-225-2431, johnjoyce.house.gov

State Offices: Altoona, 814-656-6081; Chambersburg, 717-753-6344.

Committees: *Homeland Security*: Border Security, Facilitation & Operations; Emergency Preparedness, Response & Recovery. *Small Business*: Rural Development, Agriculture, Trade & Entrepreneurship (RMM).

Election Results

Election	Name (Party)	Vote (%)		Cand. Spent	Ind. Exp. Support	Ind. Exp. Oppose
2018 General	John Joyce (R).....................................	178,533	(70%)	$1,413,784	$36,718	$349,118
	Brent Ottaway (D)...............................	74,733	(30%)	$30,484		
2018 Primary	John Joyce (R).....................................	14,828	(22%)			
	John Eichelberger (R)...........................	13,311	(20%)			
	Stephen Bloom (R)...............................	12,231	(18%)			
	Doug Mastriano (R).......................	10,509	(16%)			
	Art Halvorson (R)..........................	10,323	(15%)			

Republican first-termer John Joyce is the first representative of this west-central Pennsylvania district since 1972 who has not been named Shuster. But Joyce, a physician who styled himself as a political outsider, attracted a late endorsement and other encouragement from retiring Rep. Bill Shuster. In the decisive GOP primary, he defeated other candidates who had challenged or criticized Shuster in recent campaigns.

Bill Shuster in 2001 had succeeded his father, Bud Shuster, who served 28 years. The two Shusters had the unusual cachet that each chaired the powerful House Transportation and Infrastructure Committee, which controls the largesse for many public works programs. Each also faced ethical challenges and criticisms that they were too close to lobbyists.

An Altoona native, Joyce graduated from Pennsylvania State University, got his medical degree from Temple University and was a resident in dermatology at Johns Hopkins. Following a tour of duty with the Navy during the 1991 war in Iraq, he established his practice as a dermatologist in Altoona. He was active in community activities and became a quiet supporter of the Shusters.

Facing a six-year term limit as committee chairman, Bill Shuster's retirement had been widely expected. Joyce launched his campaign by styling himself as a political outsider and a problem-solver. He received early support from the centrist Republican Main Street Partnership, which includes Shuster among its members. With more than $900,000 in contributions, nearly half of which was from personal loans, Joyce spent more money in the primary than the other seven GOP candidates combined. With themes that he was a caring physician and "a pro-life, commonsense conservative," his ads sought to reach across the party.

The conservative Club for Growth ran ads that opposed Joyce as an occasional supporter of Democrats. In the closing days of the campaign, Shuster announced support for Joyce — who was a longtime financial supporter of the incumbent, despite Joyce's campaign criticism of "career politicians." Joyce's son Sean, a Washington lobbyist, had served as Shuster's campaign chairman, the Chambersburg Public Opinion reported.

Joyce, with 22 percent of the vote in the primary, benefited from the other candidates splitting what remained of the anti-Shuster sentiment from their geographic bases across the district. Like the Shusters, Joyce's core support was in Blair County, which cast the most votes in the primary. His chief opponents — who each received between 15 and 20 percent of the total vote -- were state Sen. John Eichelberger, who took Huntingdon County; state Rep. Stephen Bloom, who ran strongest in Cumberland County; Douglas Mastriano from Franklin County; and Art Halvorson, whose base was Bedford County. Halvorson, who had held Shuster to a 51%-49% win in the 2016 GOP primary, said following the latest outcome, "The swamp won."

In November, Democrat Brent Ottaway, a communications professor at St. Francis University, had no chance in this Republican bastion. Joyce won, 70%-30%. Older than both Shusters when they took office, he likely will require many years to attain comparable influence.

PA-13: Southwest Pennsylvania   **Cook Partisan Voting Index: D+15**

Demographics data for new House districts were not prepared by the Census Bureau prior to our editorial deadline.							

2012 Pres. Vote	Romney	195,375	(66%)	Obama	94,046	(32%)	
2016 Pres. Vote	Trump	227,448	(71%)	Clinton	81,407	(25%) Johnson	7,228 (2%)

Pittsburgh Exurbs, Altoona: The old towns of the southern tier of Pennsylvania look much as they did a century ago: farmhouses and red barns set amid rolling hills in the shadow of mountain ridges, seemingly isolated from the pulsing rhythms of modern America. During the 18th century, the Appalachian Mountains provided Quaker Pennsylvania with a rampart against Indian attacks, and allowed the commonwealth to become the richest and most populous of the colonies. In July 1863, Robert E. Lee's Confederate troops crossed the invisible Mason-Dixon line and were repelled at the Battle of Gettysburg. Not much today suggests that these hills were a frontier or the object of bloody struggle. President Dwight Eisenhower, of Pennsylvania Dutch stock, quietly spent his retirement years in Gettysburg.

The mountains became a barrier to commerce for later pioneers, and it took the aggressive capitalists who built the Pennsylvania Railroad to get trains over the ridges. Though Pennsylvania's rail links remained important, a war-bound nation in 1940 opened the road of the future here: the Pennsylvania Turnpike, the first highway in America that was able to move vehicles dependably at high speeds over long distances. The exit at Breezewood, in Bedford County, has been a traffic nightmare for generations of drivers passing through the mountains. "Breezewood pulls you into its realm because you have no choice — like a responsibility without a reason," columnist Salena Zito wrote in the Washington Examiner in January 2018. "It is not perfect and it sure isn't pretty. But there is something to be admired in its determination to not just survive, but thrive."

The region recorded a tragic mark in transportation history: On Sept. 11, 2001, United Airlines Flight 93 crashed into an empty former coalfield near Shanksville in Somerset County, killing all 40 passengers and crew on board. To Americans, the crash site became a symbol of both sadness and pride at the passengers' effort to wrest back control of the plane and possibly thwart a greater disaster, initiated by the now-famous cry of "Let's roll!" The National Park Service opened a memorial to Flight 93.

The 13th Congressional District takes in a wide swath of southern Pennsylvania, extending from east of Gettysburg almost to the northern panhandle of West Virginia and the eastern fringes of the Pittsburg metro region, with seven full counties and parts of three others. Most of the 9th is not coal country and was thus spared the boom-bust cycles of northeastern Pennsylvania. But this is still a slow-growth, low-income area today. Blair County includes the city of Altoona, which continues to wither, from 82,000 people in 1930 to 44,100 in 2017. In September 2017, Altoona ended its status as a "distressed city" receiving state aid. In Cambria County is Johnstown, the site of the cataclysmic flood in 1889 and more recently the preserve of the powerful Democratic Rep. John Murtha, an Appropriations baron who directed a disproportionate share of Defense Department contracts to his hometown prior to his death in 2010. Johnstown, whose population fell from 67,000 in 1920 to below 20,000 in 2017, has been ranked as the poorest city in Pennsylvania, with 38 percent living in poverty. The largest and fastest-growing full county in the 13th is Franklin, where several international manufacturers have built local plants; its population jumped 19 percent from 2000 to 2017.

The court-ordered redistricting moved the boundary of the district east to include all of Adams County and dropped Fayette County, which has been the western boundary. Politically, this part of Pennsylvania has been solidly Republican since 1860 and remains the strongest GOP district in the state, with little partisan shift from redistricting. In the old 9th, Donald Trump in 2016 increased the Republican presidential vote to an impressive 70 percent.

Guy Reschenthaler (R)

Elected 2018, 1st term, b. Apr 07, 1983; Pittsburgh; Pennsylvania State University, B.A., 2004; Duquesne University, J.D., 2007; Christian Church; Single.

Military Career: U.S. Navy 2007-2012 (Iraq)

Elected Office: PA Magisterial District Judge, 2013-2015; PA Senate, 2015-2018.

Professional Career: Attorney.

DC Office: 531 CHOB 20515, 202-225-2065, reschenthaler.house.gov

State Offices: Greensburg, 724-219-4200; Washington, 724-206-4800.

Committees: *Foreign Affairs*: Middle East, North Africa & International Terrorism; Oversight & Investigations. *Judiciary*: Constitution, Civil Rights & Civil Liberties; Courts, Intellectual Property & Internet; Crime, Terrorism & Homeland Security.

Election Results

Election	Name (Party)	Vote (%)		Cand. Spent	Ind. Exp. Support	Ind. Exp. Oppose
2018 General	Guy L. Reschenthaler (R)	151,386	(58%)	$1,037,767	$385,114	
	Bibiana Boerio (D)	110,051	(42%)	$574,046		
2018 Primary	Guy L. Reschenthaler (R)	23,737	(55%)			
	Rick Saccone (R)	19,274	(45%)			

Republican freshman Guy Reschenthaler restored order to a firmly Republican seat that moved into the national spotlight earlier in 2018. He might benefit as the youngest Republican to join the House delegation from Pennsylvania after retirements, redistricting and election losses devastated the once-influential group.

The political chaos in what had become a reliably partisan district ensued after veteran GOP Rep. Tim Murphy resigned in October 2017, amid reports that the married lawmaker asked his mistress to get an abortion after she believed that she was pregnant. Five months later, Democrat Conor Lamb, a political newcomer, unexpectedly won a special election to replace him. When the court-ordered redistricting made this district even more Republican, Lamb in November ran — and won — in a more favorable adjacent district against GOP Rep. Keith Rothfus.

Reschenthaler and Lamb shared in common that each defeated veteran state legislator Rick Saccone, whose moment on the national political stage as the centerpiece of campaign appearances by President Donald Trump and his retinue instead led to his two defeats in two months. Republicans might have avoided the tumult if they had initially nominated Reschenthaler, who narrowly lost to Saccone at a party convention for the special election that attracted about 200 Republican insiders. By contrast, in the redrawn district, 43,000 voters participated in the May 2018 primary in which Reschenthaler easily defeated Saccone.

A graduate of Pennsylvania State University and Duquesne Law School, Reschenthaler joined the U.S. Navy Judge Advocate General Corps. He served in Iraq, where he prosecuted terrorists from al-Qaida. Back home, he was nominated by both parties and elected as a district judge in Allegheny County. In 2015, as a Republican, he won a special election to the state Senate for what had been a Democratic-held seat. In the Senate, he claimed credit for passing a bill to outlaw sanctuary cities in Pennsylvania.

At the October 2017 closed-door GOP contest to nominate a candidate for the special election to replace Murphy, Reschenthaler led by one vote following the first ballot. But the third candidate in that contest, state Sen. Kim Ward, threw her support to Saccone, who she called "a very fiery guy." She dismissed Reschenthaler, her Senate colleague, as a "very nice young man," the Pittsburgh Post-Gazette reported. Saccone proved a poor candidate with a weak organization that failed to take advantage of Trump's personal support. In March 2018, Lamb rallied working-class voters as an alternative to Trump and defeated Saccone by 755 votes out of more than 217,000 cast.

In the May primary for a full term in the new district, Reschenthaler conveyed a youthful and patriotic appeal as "a new voice" who was "born to lead and called to serve." He welcomed the contrast to 60-year-old Saccone, who he called "an embarrassment" and "a career politician," and criticized Saccone's failure in the special election, the Post-Gazette reported. "The president said that Rick was a weak candidate. The national Republicans said his campaign was a joke." With scant public attention compared to the special election, Saccone appealed to the "grassroots." This time, Ward backed Reschenthaler.

Reschenthaler won the primary, 55%-45%. He took 58 percent in Westmoreland County and 56 percent in Washington County, the population centers of the district. Saccone took rural Fayette and Greene Counties, but they cast less than 20 percent of the total vote. Reschenthaler spent nearly twice as much money as his opponent and benefited from more than $100,000 spent by a group organized by former Rep. Murphy. With national Democratic attention having moved elsewhere, in November he easily defeated Democrat Bibiano Boerio, a businesswoman and former congressional aide.

Taking office at age 35 and with demonstrable political skills, Reschenthaler could have a lengthy tenure in the House.

PA-14: Southwest Pennsylvania   **Cook Partisan Voting Index: D+17**

Demographics data for new House districts were not prepared by the Census Bureau prior to our editorial deadline.

2012 Pres. Vote	Romney	180,082	(58%)	Obama	125,401	(41%)		
2016 Pres. Vote	Trump	209,536	(62%)	Clinton	112,882	(34%)	Johnson	7,665	(2%)

Southern and eastern Pittsburgh Suburbs: The mountains and valleys within a 100-mile radius of Pittsburgh comprise one of America's most beautiful — and economically troubled — regions. This has been tough, hardworking country ever since Scots-Irish farmers settled here in the 1790s. Their first big product was whiskey — this was the site of the Whiskey Rebellion of 1794 — but historically the most important product was bituminous coal. Discovered in the 19th century, it was the basic energy source for the production of iron and steel.

The cities and towns of Greater Pittsburgh are discontinuous, separated from each other not just by miles but by altitude. So, the region's high-income suburbs and its gritty factory towns are not concentrated in one area, but are scattered all around. This is long-settled country, with many more old towns than sparkling new suburbs. Unlike the economically diverse Pittsburgh-based Allegheny County, Westmoreland and Washington counties here are more dependent on manufacturing and more susceptible to industry-wide cuts. That, in turn, has led young people to leave to find work elsewhere. In Westmoreland, "a slipping population and evaporating jobs coincide with the county's update of its comprehensive plan, dubbed Reimagining Westmoreland County," the Pittsburgh Post-Gazette reported in July 2017. "We have no industrial base or anything to encourage people to live here," said Richard Jacobelli, the outgoing mayor of Jeannette. That city has lost 30 percent of its population since 1980, when several glass factories shut down, due largely to cheaper foreign imports. The dim signs of hope for Westmoreland have included a new "small business incubator" by Penn State University and a program by the local community college to introduce teenagers to high-tech manufacturing during their summer break from school.

Fayette County is a blue-collar area, where the loss of jobs accompanied a 4 percent drop in population from 2010 to 2017; since 1940, the population has declined 35 percent. There has been a spiraling effect as prospective employers have "struggled with hiring" because the workforce has dried up, the Post-Gazette reported in July 2018. "The truth is not a lot of people want to live in

Fayette County," said an executive with a new company in the area. The jobs problems have been "aggravated by rising substance abuse," according to the Post-Gazette. Youth poverty in Fayette has made teens vulnerable to human trafficking. One positive factor: Washington County has benefited from the growth in energy production. In 2016, it led the state in new permits for natural-gas drilling from the Marcellus Shale.

The 14th Congressional District of Pennsylvania covers the southern part of the Pittsburgh metropolitan area and the southwest corner of Pennsylvania. It includes nearly 90 percent of Westmoreland County, which is nearly half of the district population; the eastern edge of Westmoreland is part of the rural 13th District. The three other counties along both sides of the West Virginia border — Washington, Fayette and Greene — are entirely in the new 14th; Washington is the largest. All four of these counties are comfortably Republican. The court-ordered redistricting in 2018 added Fayette and part of Greene County from the old 9th District, and moved to the 17th District parts of Allegheny County that were in the old 18th District. These latest changes turned an area that already had been a struggle for Democratic candidates into a safe Republican bastion.

Glenn Thompson (R)

Elected 2008, 6th term, b. Jul 27, 1959; Bellefonte; Pennsylvania State University, B.S., 1981; Temple University (PA), M.Ed., 1998; Marywood College (PA), 2006; Protestant - Unspecified Christian; Married (Penny Thompson); 3 children.

Elected Office: Bald Eagle Area School Board, 1990-1995.

Professional Career: Therapist, Williamsport Hosp., 1982-1995; Adjunct faculty, Cambria County Comm. College, 1997-1999; Manager, Susquehanna Health Rehabilitation Services, 1995-2008; Centre County GOP Chairman, 2002-2008; Firefighter & EMT.

DC Office: 400 CHOB 20515, 202-225-5121, Fax: 202-225-5796, thompson.house.gov

State Offices: Ebensburg, 814-419-8583.

Committees: *Agriculture*: Biotechnology, Horticulture & Research; General Farm Commodities & Risk Management (RMM); Livestock & Foreign Agriculture. *Education & Labor*: Civil Rights & Human Services; Early Childhood, Elementary & Secondary Education.

Group Ratings

	ADA	ACLU	AFL-CIO	LCV	ITI	COC	HAFA	ACU	CFG	FRC
2018	-	7%	-	3%	-	83%	51%	64%	47%	100%
2017	0%	C	18%	6%	C	93%	C	74%	53%	100%

Key Votes of the 115th Congress

1. Obama-care revision	Y	5. Family planning regs	Y
2. Tax Cuts	Y	6. Body cameras/immigration	N
3. Omnibus appropriations	Y	7. Abortion ban	Y
4. Dodd-Frank revision	Y	8. Concealed carry	Y

9. Guantanamo prisoners	N
10. Ground missiles, limit	N
11. Defense Dept. spending	Y
12. FISA rules	Y

Election Results

Election	Name (Party)	Vote (%)		Cand. Spent	Ind. Exp. Support	Ind. Exp. Oppose
2018 General	Glenn Thompson (R)	165,245	(68%)	$1,357,297	$1,747	
	Susan Boser (D)	78,327	(32%)	$141,781		
2018 Primary	Glenn Thompson (R)		(100%)			

Prior winning percentages: 2016 (67%), 2014 (64%), 2012 (63%), 2010 (69%), 2008 (57%)

Republican Glenn Thompson, who won the seat in 2008, is an amiable centrist and the only Pennsylvanian to serve on the House Agriculture Committee, where he is an influential member. He played a prominent role in helping to enact the 2018 farm bill, though the final deal dropped most of the new restrictions on food stamp recipients that Thompson had moved through the House. He is a senior member of the Education and Labor Committee, where he has worked on a bipartisan basis. He could become the top Republican on one of those committees in the next few years.

A lifelong resident of Centre County, Thompson graduated from nearby Penn State. He launched his career in health care at Williamsport Hospital, where he worked as a rehabilitation services manager. He later worked as a licensed nursing home administrator. As his congressional website states about his career, "GT has touched the lives of thousands of individuals facing life altering conditions. As a result, he has become a strong advocate for increased access, affordability, quality of care, and patient choice." Thompson served as a member of the board of the Bald Eagle Area School District. He ran twice for state representative, both times unsuccessfully, but was elected to three terms as chairman of the Centre County Republican Party.

When the House seat opened, Thompson jumped into the nine-candidate primary. His hopes appeared dim against big-spending rivals. Thompson instead hit the pavement, crisscrossing the district in a low-key and low-cost campaign that emphasized his Republican positions and focused on rural issues. He called for expanding rural Medicare initiatives and spoke of the Iraq war in personal terms; his son, Logan, was injured by a landmine in 2007 while serving.

Two developments helped him break out of the pack. Less than two weeks before the primary, retiring GOP Rep. John Peterson endorsed Thompson as the candidate who would follow in his footsteps and who best understood rural issues. A week later, the Clearfield County district attorney filed charges against Derek Walker, one of his leading rivals, for allegedly breaking into his ex-girlfriend's apartment. Vastly outspent, Thompson won 19 percent of the vote to beat Walker by 835 votes. In the general election, Thompson won 57%-41%. He has not been seriously challenged for reelection.

Thompson has shown some independence. His Almanac vote ratings have ranked him toward the center of the House. He dissed tea party advocates by voting to raise the federal debt limit in 2011, to preserve rural air subsidies in 2012, and to support the tax and spending legislation that averted the so-called "fiscal cliff" in 2013. He called the latter "not perfect, but a pretty good deal." In 2014, he included in the yearend spending bill $155 million for the Essential Air Service program, which promotes rural airports and is opposed by many conservatives. In each year from 2015 to 2018, C-SPAN has reported that Thompson spoke on the House floor more often than any other member.

Rural causes have been a priority for Thompson. On the Agriculture panel, he chaired the Subcommittee on Conservation and Forestry for six years. He worked to strengthen voluntary conservation programs as part of the farm bill enacted in 2014. With many dairy farmers in his district, he filed a bill in January 2019 with Democratic Chairman Collin Peterson of Minnesota to allow participants in the school-lunch program to serve whole milk as an option. Thompson is the number-two Republican on the committee behind Rep. Mike Conaway of Texas, who is term-limited in 2020 as the senior Republican.

In 2017-18, Thompson chaired the Nutrition Subcommittee, where Republicans have placed a high priority on adding work requirements for most beneficiaries of food stamps. When the House passed its version of the farm bill in May 2018, its restrictions included 20 hours of weekly work or participation in a state-run training program for most recipients. His goal, Thompson said, was helping "hungry families be able to achieve the ultimate food security, which is a family-sustaining job." Democrats have traditionally opposed such requirements, often with the support of Senate Republicans. So, when the farm bill was included on the "to do" list for the lame-duck session after Democrats had won House control, Thompson and his allies had lost much of their leverage. "If we could get this one done with some bad modifications, it will be so much better than what will be negotiated under the Democrat majority" in 2019, Thompson said at the start of the final negotiations. Most House Republicans accepted those changes that Thompson had forecast.

Thompson has retained his interest in education issues as a member of the Education and Labor Committee. A leader of the Career and Technical Education Caucus, he partnered with Democratic Rep. Raja Krishnamoorthi of Illinois in 2018 to enact a bill that gave states more flexibility in running such programs. With Democratic Rep. Jim Langevin of Rhode Island, Thompson filed a bill that year to promote career education programs in cybersecurity.

Although Thompson does not frequently criticize President Donald Trump, he said in 2018 that the administration's program of family separation of migrants at the border with Mexico was "a practice of Third World countries," which he hoped would end soon.

PA-15: West-central Pennsylvania   **Cook Partisan Voting Index: R+13**

Demographics data for new House districts were not prepared by the Census Bureau prior to our editorial deadline.

2012 Pres. Vote	Romney	180,372	(62%)	Obama	102,921	(36%)		
2016 Pres. Vote	Trump	215,591	(69%)	Clinton	81,962	(26%)	Johnson	7,771	(2%)

Cambria and Indiana Counties: West-central Pennsylvania, isolated from the rest of the country by mountains and off the main east-west rail and highway lines until the 1970s, is one of those empty spaces that make even the Northeastern states seem lightly populated compared to the densely packed terrain of Western Europe or East Asia. This is a prime area for hunting, fishing and snowmobiling. The Allegheny National Forest sprawls across four counties and is a popular recreational area. Neatly preserved Ridgway holds the largest chainsaw carving event in the world.

For several years recently, production of natural gas deep underground in the Marcellus Shale formation generated extensive local spending and considerable optimism. In 2016, the worldwide decline in oil and gas prices led to a substantial drop in local production. That changed in 2017, with 802 new wells developed — nearly 300 more than a year earlier; the area has become the second-largest producer of natural gas in the nation, closely behind Texas. In Centre County, there has been "a quiet renaissance of manufacturing," led by small businesses, the Centre Daily Times reported in February 2018. Punxsutawney in Jefferson County is home of the legendary groundhog Phil, who predicts the arrival of spring every February 2 by looking for his shadow on Gobbler's Knob.

The 15th Congressional District of Pennsylvania, rural and sprawling, reaches more than 150 miles across the western half of the state — from the New York state border south nearly to the Mason-Dixon line and from Butler east to Bellefonte. Court-ordered redistricting removed its portion of Erie County and cut back parts of Centre County, including Pennsylvania State University, which now is in the 12th District. Those had been the two most populous and the least Republican areas of the old 5th District. In their place, the new map extended toward the exurbs of Pittsburgh. Indiana County and two-thirds of Cambria County, new to the district, have become its two largest counties, though Johnstown is in the 13th. Those shifts increased the already ample Republican vote in the district, which rivals the adjacent 13th as the most Republican in the state.

Mike Kelly (R)

Elected 2010, 5th term, b. May 10, 1948; Pittsburgh; University of Notre Dame (IN), B.A., 1970; Roman Catholic; Married (Victoria Kelly); 4 children; 10 grandchildren.

Elected Office: Butler City Council, 2006-2009.

Professional Career: Butler Area School Board, 1992-1996; Owner, Manager, Kelly Chevrolet-Cadillac Inc.

DC Office: 1707 LHOB 20515, 202-225-5406, Fax: 202-225-3103, kelly.house.gov

Committees: *Ways & Means*: Health; Oversight (RMM).

Group Ratings

	ADA	ACLU	AFL-CIO	LCV	ITI	COC	HAFA	ACU	CFG	FRC
2018	-	7%	-	6%	-	83%	68%	68%	48%	100%
2017	0%	C	27%	0%	C	93%	C	70%	65%	100%

Almanac Ratings 2017-18

	Economy	Social	Foreign	Composite
Liberal	6%	6%	0%	4%
Conservative	94%	94%	100%	96%

Key Votes of the 115th Congress

1. Obama-care revision	Y	5. Family planning regs	Y	9. Guantanamo prisoners	N	
2. Tax Cuts	Y	6. Body cameras/immigration	N	10. Ground missiles, limit	N	
3. Omnibus appropriations	N	7. Abortion ban	Y	11. Defense Dept. spending	Y	
4. Dodd-Frank revision	Y	8. Concealed carry	Y	12. FISA rules	Y	

Election Results

Election	Name (Party)	Vote (%)	Cand. Spent	Ind. Exp. Support	Ind. Exp. Oppose
2018 General	Mike Kelly (R)................................... 135,348	(52%)		$37,110	$2,000
	Ronald DiNicola (D)......................... 124,109	(47%)	$1,693,488	$869,726	
2018 Primary	Mike Kelly (R)..	(100%)			

Prior winning percentages: 2016 (100%), 2014 (61%), 2012 (55%), 2010 (56%)

Republican Mike Kelly, who defeated a Democratic incumbent in 2010, is an ex-college football player and auto dealer who has been known for his fiery pep talks to colleagues behind closed doors. He has been mostly loyal to his party and its leaders. On the Ways and Means Committee, he has advocated core issues for House Republicans. In 2019, as part of the minority for the first time, he defended President Donald Trump against what Kelly viewed as excessive investigations by the panel's Democrats.

Kelly was born in Pittsburgh and four years later his family moved to Butler, where his father started a small automobile business, working seven days a week. "He took the cars off the trains himself, and he serviced them himself. And he built a business, based around a strong work ethic, which was similar to his parents. It's pretty much the story of western Pennsylvania," Kelly said. In high school, Kelly was an all-state football player and was recruited to play for the University of Notre Dame. But he tore up a knee during his freshman year and dislocated it again in his sophomore season, ending his football career. After college, he worked as a salesman in the family business, Kelly Chevrolet-Cadillac, eventually becoming general manager. He bought the dealership from his father, and expanded it to include Hyundai and Kia autos. In 2005, Kelly was elected to the Butler City Council.

Running for Congress in 2010, Kelly's toughest opponent in the primary was business executive Paul Huber. He eked out a victory by 954 votes out of 54,000 cast. His general election foe was Rep. Kathy Dahlkemper, a Democrat who in 2008 had narrowly defeated the Republican incumbent. Dahlkemper opposed abortion rights, but she took heat from conservatives for voting for the Affordable Care Act. She outspent Kelly by about 3-to-2. He stressed his football background, which was an asset in the football mecca of western Pennsylvania, and he promised to cut government spending and curtail interference with small business. With the strong Republican wave at his back, Kelly won 56%-44%.

During the 2011 fight over raising the debt limit, he gave what Rep. Peter King of New York called a well-delivered "Knute Rockne-type speech" to rally conservatives. "Mike Kelly's the one that steps up to the microphone and says, 'Hey, we're all in this together. ... Nobody in this room is going to get everything they want. Let's go do this,'" Republican Rep. Austin Scott of Georgia told the Pittsburgh Tribune-Review.

On Ways and Means, Kelly won approval in 2015 of his bill to remove protections for Internal Revenue Service employees who improperly review or reveal taxpayer information. The committee approved his bill to improve the transparency of Medicare Advantage programs for individuals who have enrolled. He co-founded the bipartisan Retirement Security Caucus to encourage more savings. Kelly has been a vocal advocate of expanded international trade, which he said is a boost for workers and assures that the nation "is leading, shaping, and dominating the global economy." He strongly backed trade promotion authority for President Barack Obama, a step that he said would be "a crucial victory to the principles of American dominance, domestic prosperity, and government accountability that we hold so dear." In 2017, he was an avid proponent of the Republican-passed tax cuts, which he later said had "successfully revived our economy."

During the 2016 presidential campaign, Kelly was an enthusiastic supporter of Donald Trump. "Only a Trump presidency can undo the current damage caused by explosive government growth and chart a new direction," he wrote for CNN in October 2016. That loyalty would become helpful for Trump when Kelly took over in 2019 as ranking Republican on the Oversight Subcommittee at Ways and Means, where he said he would serve "as a guardian of America's precious taxpayer dollars." Democratic efforts to get the president's tax returns would be "an abuse of power [and] open a Pandora's box" and "set a very dangerous precedent," he said at a committee meeting in February.

At home, Kelly easily won reelection in 2012 and 2014 against active Democratic challengers. In 2016, he had no major-party opposition. Encouraged by the redistricting changes, Democrats in 2018 gave Kelly his first serious contest. Democratic challenger Ron DiNicola, a criminal defense lawyer who narrowly lost a bid for the seat in 1996, attacked Kelly for his vote to repeal the Affordable Care Act and said that Congress was "corrupt." Democrats accused Kelly of profiting from a section in the recent tax-law changes that aided auto dealers. During an October campaign rally in Erie, Trump said "Mike is strong on crime … and he is really great on jobs." Kelly outspent DiNicola, $3 million to $1.7 million, and won, 52%-47%. DiNicola took 59 percent of the vote in Erie County, where he led by 20,000 votes, but Kelly swept the four outlying counties. EMILY's List, the Democratic group that supports women favoring abortion rights, listed Kelly as an early target for 2020.

PA-16: Northwest Pennsylvania   **Cook Partisan Voting Index: R+11**

Demographics data for new House districts were not prepared by the Census Bureau prior to our editorial deadline.	

2012 Pres. Vote	Romney	159,083	(52%)	Obama	144,205	(47%)		
2016 Pres. Vote	Trump	187,203	(57%)	Clinton	122,582	(38%)	Johnson	9,392	(3%)

Erie, Pittsburgh Exurbs: The best natural harbor on Lake Erie is in Erie Pennsylvania, protected by the Presque Isle ("almost an island") peninsula — a cowlick-shaped, seven-mile-long sand spit blanketed by mature forest, with a lighthouse dating to 1872. Erie is in Pennsylvania's far northwest corner, closer to Cleveland (about 100 miles) than to Pittsburgh (125 miles). There are farmlands here, and even some woods, but the land between the Great Lakes and the basin of the Ohio River has been prime heavy industry territory for more than a century. The jeep, which Gen. George Marshall called America's greatest contribution to World War II, was invented in Butler County. In the 1990s, under Republican Gov. Tom Ridge, who grew up in Erie, the state spent $100 million on the city's waterfront to develop a cruise ship terminal, hotel and convention center, a ballpark for the double-A Erie SeaWolves baseball team, and a renovated Warner Theatre.

The effort spruced up a dying downtown, but it didn't buffer Erie from a new downturn during which International Paper, American Meter, Gunite/EMI and American Sterilizer laid off employees and closed plants. General Electric Transportation, which had remained the area's largest industrial employer, in July 2017 announced the end of locomotive production in Erie, citing the decline in freight rail traffic. That resulted in a loss of 575 jobs. In May 2018, what remained of the GE division was sold to Wabtec, a Pittsburgh-based rail-equipment company known as the Westinghouse Air Brake Company. At that time, 2,000 workers remained of the more than 15,000 who once worked locally for GE, which had been a force in Erie for more than a century. "The GE of the past has been gone for a long time," said Erie County Executive Kathy Dahlkemper. Erie officials have created a downtown innovation district that they envision as a hub for cybersecurity and data science.

The 16th Congressional District of Pennsylvania occupies the northwest corner of the state. It takes in all of Erie County and two-thirds of Butler County outside Pittsburgh. The court-ordered redistricting in 2018 resulted chiefly in population switches with the new 15th District to the east: The 16th added the portion of Erie County that had been in the old 5th District in exchange for Armstrong. The 16th continues to cover Meadville, where the company Talon invented the zipper, and Grove City and Grove City College, a Christian liberal arts school. It includes New Castle and the old glass industry borough, Ford City. About two-fifths of the population is in Erie, and one-fifth in Butler. The population of the city of Erie declined 30 percent from 1960 to its 2018 total of 97,400. The growing number of refugees coming to the city -- about 18 percent of the population — was slowed by restrictions imposed by the Trump administration. The redistricting changes increased the Democratic vote in the district by a few percentage points, though it remained comfortably Republican.

Conor Lamb (D)

Elected 2018, 1st full term, b. Jun 27, 1984; Washington, DC; University of Pennsylvania, B.A., 2006; University of Pennsylvania Law School, J.D., 2009; Catholic; Married.

DC Office: 1224 LHOB 20515, 202-225-2301, Fax: 202-225-1844, lamb.house.gov

State Offices: Monaca, 724-206-4860.

Committees: *Science, Space & Technology*: Energy (Chmn); Environment. *Veterans' Affairs*: Health; Technology Modernization.

Key Votes of the 115th Congress

1. Obama-care revision	N/A	5. Family planning regs	N/A	9. Guantanamo prisoners	N/A
2. Tax Cuts	N/A	6. Body cameras/immigration	N/A	10. Ground missiles, limit	N/A
3. Omnibus appropriations	N/A	7. Abortion ban	N/A	11. Defense Dept. spending	N/A
4. Dodd-Frank revision	N	8. Concealed carry	N/A	12. FISA rules	N/A

Election Results

Election	Name (Party)	Vote (%)		Cand. Spent	Ind. Exp. Support	Ind. Exp. Oppose
2018 General	Conor Lamb (D)................................	183,162	(56%)	$8,727,393	$991,208	$7,733,408
	Keith Rothfus (R)..............................	142,417	(44%)	$3,565,782	$168,300	$679,580
2018 Primary	Conor Lamb (D)...	(100%)				

Prior winning percentages: 2018 special (50%)

Democrat Conor Lamb achieved the unusual distinction of winning two House elections in less than eight months in 2018 in two notably different House districts in the Pittsburgh metro area. One was a special election, in which he defeated a relatively weak Republican opponent by fewer than 800 votes. In the second, in a new district that changed significantly in the court-ordered redistricting, Lamb defeated a veteran GOP incumbent by more than 40,000 votes. Lamb, a political newcomer, kept his distance from Democratic Leader Nancy Pelosi. His dual successes were a harbinger of the national election changes and offered useful tips to other centrist Democrats running in suburban districts. In each contest, Lamb had a big lead in the Allegheny County part of his district but trailed in all the outlying counties.

Lamb, a native of Mount Lebanon, went to Central Catholic High School in Pittsburgh. He got his bachelor's and law degrees from the University of Pennsylvania. He served four years on active duty in the Marine Corps and remained in the Marine Corps Reserve, with the rank of captain. That was followed by work as a prosecutor in the U.S. attorney's office in Pittsburgh, where he handled narcotics cases and worked to build partnerships between law enforcement and hard-hit communities.

Lamb's political opportunity opened when veteran Republican Rep. Tim Murphy — a physician who became a leader in Congress on mental health issues -- resigned in October 2017. His decision followed news reports in Pittsburgh that Murphy had urged his mistress to have an abortion, despite his own pro-life views; it turned out that she was not pregnant. The reports also described his allegedly abusive treatment of his congressional aides. Under pressure at home and from House GOP leaders, Murphy quit what he had turned into a safely Republican seat.

Lamb brought a profile that was old-style, blue-collar Democrat, in some ways. He embraced organized labor and was an advocate of gun ownership. As a devout Catholic, he said, he opposed abortion but he did not favor new anti-abortion laws. In the Republican-leaning district during the special election, he styled himself as a bipartisan problem-solver. He was widely viewed as the underdog in a district that President Donald Trump had won by 20 points.

But Lamb got a boost when Republicans at their closed-door party convention narrowly selected state Rep. Rick Saccone as their nominee. He proved to a be a weak fundraiser and communicator who struggled with the national attention that the special-election received from party leaders and the news media. Saccone sought to turn the contest into a referendum on Trump, who made a campaign appearance on his behalf; other officials of the Trump administration also embraced Saccone. Lamb sought to remain neutral on the president, whose increased tariffs were popular in parts of the steel-producing region.

Lamb won by 755 votes in the March 2018 special election, which had a turnout of nearly 230,000 votes. He led, 57%-42%, in Allegheny County, which cast more than 40 percent of the vote. Saccone won handily in the more exurban and rural parts of the district, but he fell short of the 15,000-vote lead that Lamb had built in Allegheny. Following four close special elections in 2017 in which Republicans narrowly retained each of their seats, the outcome was the first House district that changed parties since the 2016 election.

Meanwhile, the legal victory by Democrats in their court challenge to the Republican-drawn redistricting plan in 2012, caused major changes of district lines across Pennsylvania. Among other things, the old 18th District that Lamb had won became even more Republican. Lamb decided that he had a better chance in a neighboring district that had a large share of Allegheny County, including some precincts in the district that Lamb had won. That placed Lamb in a contest in the new 17th District with three-term Republican Rep. Keith Rothfus. (In the heavily Republican new 14th District, Saccone ran again. But he lost the GOP primary to Guy Reschenthaler, who easily won the district in November.)

The fiscally conservative Rothfus was a mainstream Republican. When he was first elected in 2012, after having narrowly lost his first congressional campaign in 2010, he was the beneficiary of redistricting that drew a Republican-leaning seat, plus a bitter primary between two Democratic incumbents who were forced into the new district.

The Rothfus-Lamb contest initially seemed a toss-up between two incumbents in the new district where Trump had led by about two points in 2016. But Lamb benefited from extensive favorable publicity that resulted from his special-election victory and the national surge in Democratic support in 2018, especially in suburban areas. Lamb continued his campaign strategy of not discussing Trump and of running an upbeat strategy of political change. Citing the need for new leadership, he said that he would not support Pelosi in a vote for House Speaker.

With polls showing that Lamb had a double-digit lead, the National Republican Congressional Committee — which was hard-pressed to salvage dozens of vulnerable seats — in mid-September canceled its planned ads on behalf of Rothfus, a sure sign of its pessimistic view of his prospects. Lamb won, 56%-44%. This time, he had a nearly 43,000-vote lead in Allegheny.

Lamb kept his promise and was one of 15 House Democrats who did not vote for Pelosi for Speaker. Still, he got two plums in the new Congress: vice chairman of the Veterans' Affairs Committee and chairman of the Science, Space and Technology Subcommittee on Energy.

PA-17: Allegheny County   **Cook Partisan Voting Index: R+1**

Demographics data for new House districts were not prepared by the Census Bureau prior to our editorial deadline.

2012 Pres. Vote	Romney	187,021	(52%)	Obama	170,774	(47%)	
2016 Pres. Vote	Trump	188,250	(49%)	Clinton	178,625	(46%)	Johnson 10,569 (3%)

Northern and western Pittsburgh suburbs: Pittsburgh was built on the unlikeliest terrain of any major U.S. city. Just about the only level places in the city or its suburbs are the bottomlands along the rivers. Everything else is built on hills that approach the magnitude of mountains. Only a propitious location, where the Allegheny and Monongahela rivers join to form the Ohio, and the confluence of economically valuable natural resources — coal from the mountains and iron ore from the Great Lakes — can explain why a large metropolitan area sprang up there.

This is long-settled country, with many more old towns than new suburbs. The population in the area has been declining, but with some increase in high-wage jobs to counter an ongoing loss of blue-collar jobs. With government aid, companies in the area have developed improved batteries and energy storage. The massive $6 billion ethane cracker plant along the Ohio River in Beaver County — powered by natural-gas reserves from the Marcellus Shale -- has created as many as 6,000 construction jobs. When the petrochemical facility is completed, as soon as 2021, it expects a permanent payroll of 600 workers. The project is the most significant economic development in the region in 40 years, local officials report. Perhaps optimistically, they view the facility — and others that might follow — as successors to the steel industry. Southwestern Pennsylvania is also football country: Joe Namath was a grandchild of a Hungarian immigrant steelworker from Beaver Falls, and Joe Montana and Dan Marino -- other Hall of Fame quarterbacks -- hailed from the region.

The Allegheny County suburbs north of Pittsburgh include old-money Fox Chapel and Sewickley, which have attracted the region's high-tech wealth. In the North Hills are affluent McCandless and more middle-class Ross. In contrast to adjacent Beaver and Butler counties, which have gained many young families and are comfortably Republican, the Allegheny suburbs — which include many senior citizens — have remained politically marginal. Several small towns in Allegheny County have had above-average growth since 2010, especially those that are close to the Pittsburgh airport.

The 17th Congressional District stretches from the Ohio border to the suburbs surrounding Pittsburgh on all but its eastern side. It varies economically from the shrinking rust belt cities of Aliquippa and Beaver Falls to comfortable Pittsburgh suburbs. Nearly three-fourths of the population is in Allegheny County. The remainder is all of Beaver County and the southwest corner of Butler in Cranberry Township. In the court-ordered redistricting in 2018 Republican-leaning areas in northern Westmoreland County plus Johnstown-based Cambria that were in the old 12th District were removed. The 17th added large parts of the western and southern Allegheny suburbs. Those changes made the new district virtually a political toss-up, based on 2016 presidential results.

The changes reversed recent gains by Republicans in the old 12th District and elsewhere in southwest Pennsylvania, which were abetted by the GOP-controlled redistricting in 2012 that had been a disaster for Democrats. That year, both Democratic incumbents in the Pittsburgh suburbs lost their seats and — with a boost from creative GOP map-drawers — were replaced by one Republican. More painfully for Democrats, the four seats that they held in the southwest corner in 2002 were reduced to one a decade later. The 2018 redistricting changes were part of a long-running evolution in the region that likely faces a few more twists.

Mike Doyle (D)

Elected 1994, 13th term, b. Aug 05, 1953; Swissvale; Pennsylvania State University, B.S., 1975; Roman Catholic; Married (Susan Erlandson Doyle); 4 children.

Elected Office: Swissvale Borough Council, 1977-1981.

Professional Career: Ins. agent, 1975-1977; Executive Director, Turtle Creek Valley Citizens Union, 1977-1979; Chief of Staff, PA Sen. Frank Pecora, 1979-1994; Co-founder/owner, Eastgate Ins. Agency, 1983-present.

DC Office: 306 CHOB 20515, 202-225-2135, Fax: 202-225-3084, doyle.house.gov

Committees: *Energy & Commerce*: Communications & Technology (Chmn); Energy.

Group Ratings

	ADA	ACLU	AFL-CIO	LCV	ITI	COC	HAFA	ACU	CFG	FRC
2018	-	86%	-	91%	-	58%	4%	4%	2%	0%
2017	100%	C	95%	97%	C	50%	C	4%	5%	0%

Almanac Ratings 2017-18

	Economy	Social	Foreign	Composite
Liberal	96%	100%	100%	99%
Conservative	4%	0%	0%	1%

Key Votes of the 115th Congress

1. Obama-care revision	N	5. Family planning regs	N	9. Guantanamo prisoners	Y
2. Tax Cuts	N	6. Body cameras/immigration	Y	10. Ground missiles, limit	Y
3. Omnibus appropriations	Y	7. Abortion ban	N	11. Defense Dept. spending	N
4. Dodd-Frank revision	N	8. Concealed carry	N	12. FISA rules	N

Election Results

Election	Name (Party)	Vote (%)	Cand. Spent	Ind. Exp. Support	Ind. Exp. Oppose
2018 General	Mike Doyle (D).. 231,472	(100%)	$504,958		
2018 Primary	Mike Doyle (D).. 52,080	(76%)			
	Janis Brooks (D)..................................... 16,549	(24%)			

Prior winning percentages: 2016 (74%), 2014 (100%), 2012 (76.9%), 2010 (69%), 2008 (91%), 2006 (90%), 2004 (100%), 2002 (100%), 2000 (69%), 1998 (68%), 1996 (56%), 1994 (55%)

Mike Doyle, an ardently pro-labor Democrat first elected in 1994, has become a senior member of the Energy and Commerce Committee, where he has shown deal-making skills. As chairman of the subcommittee handling communications and technology issues, his early initiative was a bill to restore regulations designed to impose restrictions on use of the spectrum, which Republicans had repealed. He also showed interest in forcing accountability by giant social-media firms.

Of Irish and Italian descent, Doyle grew up in the Monongahela Valley town of Swissvale and worked in steel mills during summers off from Penn State. He became an insurance agent and was elected to the Swissvale Borough Council at age 24. In 1978, he became chief of staff to state Sen. Frank Pecora, a Republican. In 1994, Doyle, who followed his boss in switching to the Democratic Party, ran for the House seat vacated by Republican Rep. Rick Santorum, who was elected to the Senate. With endorsements from labor unions and community leaders, he won the seven-candidate primary. In November, he faced John McCarty, an aide to the late Republican Sen. John Heinz. McCarty was pro-abortion rights and Doyle opposed abortion rights. Doyle also campaigned for sweeping health care changes. In a Republican year, he won 55%-45%.

Doyle initially had a mixed voting record, often on the right on cultural issues. Over the years, he became more of a progressive populist. His Almanac vote ratings have been almost perfectly liberal. As a pro-life Catholic, he helped broker the deal on abortion during the final days of the 2010 health care debate that brought on board other anti-abortion members of his party. When Republicans regained control, he complained that GOP budgets would "eviscerate" social services. In a private meeting, he reportedly compared Republicans' negotiating tactics to those of terrorists. Conservative bloggers and commentators heaped criticism on him, and he said, "I wasn't out to defame anybody."

On Energy and Commerce, his focus has been on high-tech initiatives, including increased availability of broadband services in underserved areas. On the Communications and Technology Subcommittee, he has supported policies such as modernized 911 services, greater competition for devices and services, and protection of the open internet. In 2017, Doyle joined other senior Democrats on the committee calling for the Federal Communications Commission to investigate Russian media interference in the 2016 election. In 2018, he called for a federal agency to assure that social-media companies make proper use of data. Recent abuses, he said, have shown that "self-regulation hasn't worked."

When Democrats took House control in 2019, Doyle's initial priority was to restore "net neutrality" rules that Democrats had approved at the FCC during the Obama administration but that Republicans repealed when they took control in 2017. His bill, which he called the "Save the Internet Act," would prohibit internet service providers from creating tiered services with different pricing and service options. His legislation "puts consumers first by once again putting a cop on the beat at the FCC," Doyle said. Most Republicans opposed the proposal.

During the 2009 debate over cap-and-trade legislation, which would have capped carbon emissions while allowing companies to trade emissions credits, he vigorously advocated the interests of steel and other job-creating Rust Belt industries, even as he worked out a compromise with environmentalists. The House-passed bill died in the Senate, largely because of opposition from Rust Belt Democrats. When Republicans in 2011 voted to restrict the Environmental Protection Agency's power to regulate emissions, Doyle accused the GOP of "scaring the American people" into wrongly believing that failure to curb EPA's authority would cause gas prices to rise.

Doyle has worked to reduce foreign imports. During debate over the Keystone XL pipeline, he unsuccessfully offered an amendment that would have required at least three-quarters of the iron and steel in the pipeline to be made in North America. In December 2016, Republicans defeated his effort to add a "buy America" provision to a water infrastructure bill. Doyle founded and co-chaired the House Distributed Generation Caucus, which promotes decentralized power generation technology that is fuel efficient and environmentally friendly.

Doyle has been politically untouchable at home. In 2016, he got 74 percent of the vote against Republican Lenny McAllister, who has hosted local radio and television talk shows. In 2018, he was challenged in the Democratic primary by Janis Brooks, a community activist and former pastor. Doyle got 76 percent in that contest.

Following the 2018 election, Doyle said in an interview with a public radio station in Pittsburgh that he wished that Democrats had "choices" in the selection of party leaders. "A new generation of Democrats [is] ready to assume the mantle and they've been blocked from doing that." He added that he supported Nancy Pelosi for Speaker in what would be "her final term as the Speaker."

PA-18: Allegheny County   Cook Partisan Voting Index: D+17

Demographics data for new House districts were not prepared by the Census Bureau prior to our editorial deadline.

2012 Pres. Vote	Obama	222,095	(63%)	Romney	123,265	(35%)		
2016 Pres. Vote	Clinton	225,321	(62%)	Trump	125,266	(34%)	Johnson	7,903	(2%)

Pittsburgh metro: The Golden Triangle is the inevitable focus of Pittsburgh, the tip of land where the Allegheny and Monongahela rivers come together to form the Ohio. It has been a strategic site for more than 200 years. During the French and Indian War, British Gen. Edward Braddock's army was heading to Fort Duquesne, with George Washington helping lead the way, when it was ambushed and famously defeated in 1754. A few years later, the first American city west of the Appalachian chain was carved out of the wilderness and named after the English statesman William Pitt. Pittsburgh did nicely when railroads became ascendant because rail lines tend to run along the riverside. Then Andrew Carnegie, a Scottish immigrant, foresaw that steel would replace iron for railroad bridges. He built a steel factory in Pittsburgh, one blessed with ready deposits of coal and access to iron ore via the Great Lakes. Carnegie built his capacity to the point that when he sold out in 1901, the resulting U.S. Steel Corp. held a near-monopoly.

As the steel industry and other blue-collar industries contracted over the years, so did Pittsburgh. In 1940, it was the nation's 10th largest city, with 672,000 people. In 2017, it was the 65th largest, with 302,000. The population loss has been easing, with an increase in young people. Economic diversity helped Pittsburgh survive the recession better than other Rust Belt cities. The University of Pittsburgh Medical Center is the largest employer in the region. Carnegie Mellon University has been a pioneer in machine-learning technologies, including for self-driving cars. In 2015, local icon H.J. Heinz purchased Chicago-based Kraft Foods and the company described itself as "global" and "co-headquartered" in the two cities. The city has a rich cultural heritage. Pop artist Andy Warhol grew up in Pittsburgh and the Warhol Museum is located in the downtown area. The predominantly black Hill District inspired playwright August Wilson's chronicles, and along the Monongahela River is the town of Clairton, where The Deer Hunter was filmed. The Brookings Institution in 2017 ranked Pittsburgh third among 100 metro areas in a combination of productivity, wage increases and standard of living. In February 2018, a columnist for Bloomberg described the city as a "growing mecca for millennials" who enjoy "an art scene, fashionable neighborhoods and a lively downtown." In October 2018, Pittsburgh suffered a painful incident when a gunman killed 11 Jewish worshippers at a Sabbath service inside the sanctuary of a synagogue in upscale Squirrel Hill.

The 18th Congressional District of Pennsylvania includes Pittsburgh and the mostly working-class suburbs to the east, south and west. All of it is in Allegheny County. The district remains safely Democratic, but the 2018 redistricting reduced by a few percentage points the Democratic vote in the old 14th District. The Pittsburgh neighborhoods that it lost — chiefly in areas to the west (such as Green Tree and Carnegie) and north (Penn Hills and Verona) of downtown -- shifted to the new 17th to boost Democrats and make that district more competitive. In return, the district smoothed out some missing pieces from the southeastern part of Allegheny County. The 18th has become less of a Democratic island in increasingly Republican southwest Pennsylvania.

RHODE ISLAND

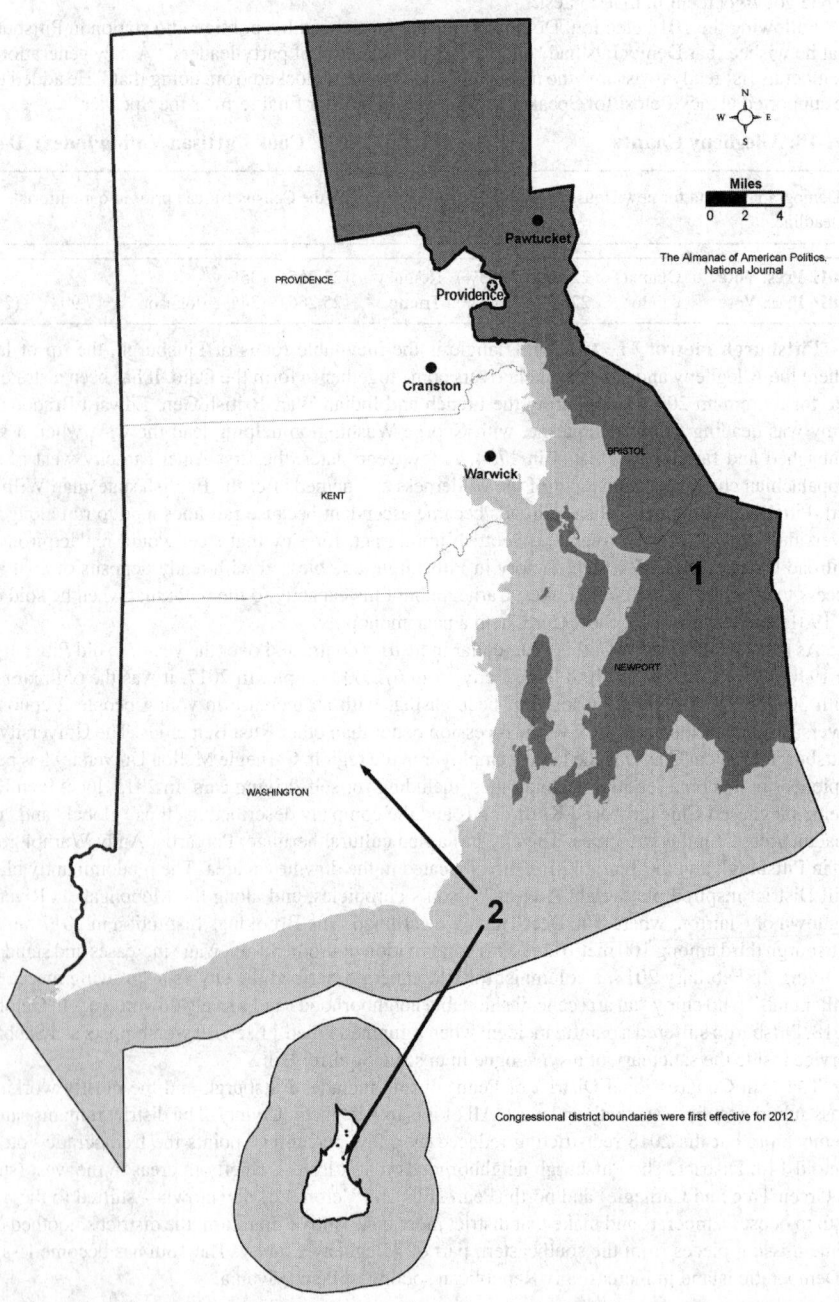

PROVIDENCE

Pawtucket

Providence

Cranston

BRISTOL

Warwick

KENT

NEWPORT

1

WASHINGTON

2

Miles
0   2   4

The Almanac of American Politics.
National Journal

Congressional district boundaries were first effective for 2012.

Rhode Island has a lopsidedly Democratic legislature and a Democratic governor, and it supported Hillary Clinton for president by double digits. But more so than in almost any other blue state, Rhode Island's Democratic party is so dominant that it has been riven by a bitter dispute between a moderate-to-conservative establishment in the legislature and a more progressive insurgency.

"Little Rhody," the nation's smallest state in size, has often been set apart, with a turbulent history. It was founded by Roger Williams as a refuge for religious dissenters -- "the sewer of New England," as the Puritan Cotton Mather put it. It has been a successful trading community since the late 17th century and a leader in manufacturing since Samuel Slater replicated from memory an English water-powered cotton textile mill in Pawtucket in 1791. Rhode Island profited from slavery (two-thirds of America's slaves arrived from Africa on ships owned by Rhode Islanders) and war (the state boomed during the Civil War), and it carried its tradition of tolerating just about anything into its politics. Rhode Island refused to pay its share for the Revolutionary War and declined to send delegates to the 1787 Constitutional Convention. It delayed joining the union until the other 12 states already had.

In the 1930s, Rhode Island had something resembling a political revolution. Thousands of immigrants from Ireland, Italy, Portugal and French Canada came to the state to work in textile mills, and the colony founded by dissident Protestants became the most heavily Catholic state in the nation – 41 percent, according to a 2017 estimate, three quarters of whom are non-Hispanic whites. Yankee Republicans tried to appeal to Catholics by running French Canadians for office. But national events — including Catholic Democrat Al Smith's presidential candidacy in 1928 and Franklin Roosevelt's New Deal — moved Catholic voters toward the Democrats. Then came a revolution. In 1935, although they had won only 20 of the 42 state Senate seats, Democrats under Gov. Theodore Green refused to seat two Republicans. With the lieutenant governor breaking the tie, they voted Democrats into the seats and proceeded in 14 minutes to declare the state Supreme Court vacant, to abolish state boards that controlled Democratic cities, to increase the power of the governor, and to reorganize state government to purge Republicans. It was a faint echo of the Dorr Rebellion of the 1840s, in which a growing urban middle class violently rose up against the small rural elite that controlled state government. The uprising of the 1930s similarly ended the political control of Rhode Island's "Five Families" — the Browns, Metcalfs, Goddards, Lippitts and Chafees — who owned or ran many of the textile mills, the Rhode Island Hospital Trust (long the largest bank), the Providence Journal-Bulletin, Brown University, the Rhode Island School of Design and the state Republican Party. Democrats have won most elections since.

Rhode Island today has a diverse ethnic and racial mix: 7 percent African American, 15 percent Hispanic and 3 percent Asian. Nearly one-fifth describe their ancestry as Irish, and another one-fifth as Italian. About one of every six are French or French Canadian, while one of every 11 are Portuguese, many from the Azores. But if the population is diverse, it has been extremely slow-growing in recent years, increasing by just three-tenths of a percentage point since 2010; Providence accounted for all of these gains and then some, with the rest of the state losing population. This slow growth likely will drop Rhode Island to one House seat after the 2020 census – the first time in more than two centuries that the state's representation will have been so small. (As it happens, Providence played host to the census' only full-scale "dress rehearsal" in 2018; observers expressed concern about its ability to achieve a full enumeration of the region's diverse and multi-lingual population.)

Rhode Island has experienced a long and often painful economic transformation -- from blue collar to white collar, and from textiles toward technology. In the early 1990s, the state suffered job losses when the naval air base at Quonset Point and the state's costume jewelry manufacturers shed jobs; neighboring Massachusetts, with a more educated population and a much bigger high-tech sector, surged ahead. A 2016 paper by the Federal Reserve Bank of Cleveland found that after 1980, Providence and its metro area saw the country's most dramatic shift from manufacturing jobs toward work that requires a college degree. Another study by the Boston Federal Reserve found that manufacturing employment in the state fell by 57 percent between 1990 and 2015.

Today, Rhode Island's median income exceeds the national average, but one of every six children live in poverty, tied with Maine for the worst in New England, according to the Annie E. Casey Foundation. Food insecurity rose by almost half between 2007 and 2017, and child abuse cases rose by a quarter between 2008 and 2017. The state has attracted investment in the biosciences, such as an Amgen manufacturing plant in the Providence suburbs, but well below the level of neighboring Massachusetts. Still, in 2018, toy giant Hasbro floated the idea of leaving its headquarters in Pawtucket, a city that was already reeling from the impending loss of the Boston Red Sox AAA farm team to Worcester Massachusetts. Meanwhile, with its low-lying areas under threat, the state in 2018 sued 21 defendants, including ExxonMobil, BP, Chevron, and Shell, for knowingly contributing to climate change. Rhode Island became home to the nation's first operational offshore windfarm, a 30-megawatt project off Block Island.

The anti-corruption group Coalition for Integrity rates Rhode Island's ethics laws among the strongest in the country, yet Rhode Island is sometimes called "Rogues Island" for its history of public corruption. The rogues gallery includes former Gov. Edward DiPrete, who served time after pleading guilty to bribery and extortion charges in 1998; Joseph Bevilacqua and Thomas Fay, two chief justices of the state Supreme Court, who resigned while they were under investigation in 1986 and 1992; longtime House Speaker John Harwood, who resigned in 2002 after reports that he had sexually harassed a researcher in the legislature; and Senate President William Irons, who resigned in 2004 after an investigation by the state Ethics Commission of lawmakers who voted on legislation while they were working for companies that benefited from those bills. The grim parade continued in 2014, when the FBI raided the home and office of then- House Speaker Gordon Fox, who quickly resigned his post and later pleaded guilty to bribery and related charges. Then, in 2016, House Finance Chairman Raymond Gallison resigned and was later charged with stealing from the estate of a deceased client. But no political figure embodied Rhode Island's spotty ethical history better than Buddy Cianci, the Providence mayor who spent time in a "federally funded gated community" for assaulting with a fire log a man whom he accused of having an affair with his wife. Later, after becoming a radio talk show host, Cianci was reelected as mayor in 1990, before resigning again amid federal racketeering charges that ultimately led to another conviction. Cianci died in 2016.

From 1940 to 1980, Democrats won every election in Rhode Island for House seats, and the state has backed the Democrat in every presidential election since Ronald Reagan's 49-state landslide in 1984. Democrats currently hold all of Rhode Island's four seats in Congress, with Sens. Jack Reed and Sheldon Whitehouse well-positioned to hold on as long as their Democratic predecessors Theodore F. Green, John Pastore and Claiborne Pell (24, 24 and 36 years, respectively). Republicans have done better with the governor's office. Starting in 1994, Republicans Lincoln Almond and Donald Carcieri were elected governor twice each; in 2010, Lincoln Chafee, former Republican Sen. John Chafee's son, was elected as an independent. It wasn't until 2014 that Democrats returned to the governor's chair as Gina Raimondo, the state's first female governor, won office. Despite early indications of a tough reelection race, she easily won a second term in 2018. In the 2016 presidential election, Clinton won Rhode Island by 16 points – a substantial victory, though a narrower one than Barack Obama's 28 point spread in 2012.

Explaining the Democrats' dominance in Rhode Island requires some important caveats. The party has become so strong in the state that its big tent has experienced some rips and tears. During the 2018 election cycle, tensions flared between a restive progressive wing and the more moderate Democratic establishment, which, with the support of the influential Catholic Church, has bottled up legislation on abortion rights and assisted suicide. Rhode Island is the rare Democratic state where many legislative Democrats are pro-life; many of them are also aligned with the National Rifle Association. The party, led by influential House Speaker Nicholas Mattiello, took heat for backing moderate candidates in the Democratic primary, including one who had supported Trump in 2016; after some federal and statewide Democrats officeholders expressed their displeasure, the party backed down from some of the endorsements. Progressive candidates ended up making incremental gains in the 2018 elections, and Mattiello – who survived a tight election and retained his speakership – declared himself after the election to be "the firewall" against "ultra left-wing groups." It was a sign that intra-party tensions should remain for the foreseeable future.

Population		Race and Ethnicity		Income	
Total	1,056,138	White	73.2%	Median Income	$61,043
Land area (sq. miles)	1,034	Black	5.5%	State Income Rank	18
Pop/ sq mi	1,021.6	Latino	14.6%	Poverty Rate	13.4%
Born in state	56.8%	Asian	3.3%	With health insurance	93.3%
		Two or more races	2.3%	Cash public assistance	3.4%
Age Groups		Other	1.2%	Food stamp/SNAP	16.1%
Under 18	19.9%				
18-34	24.4%	**Education**		**Work**	
35-64	39.6%	H.S grad or less	40.6%	White Collar	38.1%
Over 64	16.1%	Some college	26.4%	Sales and Service	43.3%
		College Degree, 4 yr	19.8%	Blue Collar	18.6%
Military		Post grad	13.1%	Government	12.2%
Veteran/ Active Duty	7.5%				

Presidential Politics

2016 Primary (D)	Sanders (D)	66,993 (55%)	Clinton (D)	52,749 (43%)			
2016 Primary (R)	Trump (R)	39,221 (64%)	Kasich (R)	14,963 (24%)	Cruz (R)	6,416 (10%)	
2016 Pres. Vote	Clinton (D)	252,525 (54%)	Trump (R)	180,543 (39%)	Johnson (L)	14,746 (3%)	
2012 Pres. Vote	Obama (D)	279,677 (63%)	Romney (R)	157,204 (35%)			

Rhode Island has been one of the most Democratic states in presidential elections. Hillary Clinton easily beat Donald Trump 54%-39%, but that was a significant drop from Barack Obama's 63%-35% victories in both 2008 and 2012. Registered Democrats outnumber Republicans in Rhode Island by more than three-to-one, but unaffiliated voters make up a plurality of the electorate. Rhode Island is also the most Catholic state in the country, but many Catholics vote with their party rather than with their bishop. White ethnic voters dominate the political culture of the state and places like Johnston, North Providence, West Warwick and Woonsocket can tilt more Republican for a candidate who is conservative on social issues and crime, but is not hostile to bigger government. All of these locales saw their vote for Clinton fall by 13 to 17 percentage points from Obama's levels in 2012.

Clinton underperformed Obama's 2012 showing by 27,000 votes, while Trump over-performed Mitt Romney by 23,000. Of the state's five counties, one switched from blue to red -- Kent (Warwick), which went from an 18-point Obama victory to a narrow win by Trump. The other four counties remained Democratic, although Providence County saw its margin shift by 14 points toward the GOP, Washington County (Narragansett) saw its margin shift by seven points, and Bristol County saw its shift by two points. Only Newport County gravitated in Clinton's direction, by just one point. The Providence Journal found that Clinton "drew her support from the wealthiest and poorest places, while Trump drew his from the middle." The newspaper further noted that "all of the communities that touch saltwater voted for Clinton, and all but four of the state's inland communities went for Trump."

Rhode Island used to hold a presidential primary in early-to-mid March, but in 2011 the state legislature moved the date back in hopes of increasing its relevance in a regional Eastern states primary. The state succeeded somewhat: In the final days before the April 26 primary, all four of the top contenders in 2016 campaigned in Rhode Island. Donald Trump defeated Ohio Gov. John Kasich 64%-24%. Trump captured all 39 of the state's cities and towns except for comfortably suburban Barrington. Vermont Sen. Bernie Sanders defeated Clinton 55%-43%, winning all but Barrington, East Greenwich and Pawtucket.

Congressional Districts

116th Congress Lineup	2D	115th Congress Lineup	2D

Rhode Island held onto its two districts in the 2010 census, though not by much, and now houses the least populous districts in the country. Census Bureau projections are that the state won't be so lucky next time.

Redistricting hasn't been much of a problem since the state lost its third seat in 1932: Providence is split and both districts are overwhelmingly Democratic —though a Republican occasionally has been elected against a flawed Democrat.

In 2011, the legislature approved a new 18-member Special Commission on Reapportionment, an advisory panel comprising eight legislators and six citizens appointed by the majority leaders (Democrats), and four legislators appointed by the minority. The commission needed to shift only about 7,000 residents from the 1st District to the 2nd, and could have easily done so by tweaking a few lines in Providence. But freshman Democrat David Cicilline was polling abysmally in the 1st. At his request, the commission drafted a map shifting three northern towns Cicilline had lost in 2010 — Smithfield, North Smithfield and Burrillville — into Democrat Jim Langevin's 2nd District in exchange for more of liberal Providence, moving nearly 100,000 residents. Langevin, though popular, would have none of it. The commission proposed exchanging only Burrillville for a smaller share of Providence, giving Cicilline one extra percentage point of insurance. The legislature and governor approved. Since then, Cicilline and Langevin have won easily.

The state is preparing for a political nightmare when the 2020 census likely will strip its second House seat, and the two Democrats — or their successors — will be forced to run against each other, unless one steps aside. Langevin has made moves in that direction with suggestions that he was thinking of running for governor in 2022. Cicilline likely would find that an appealing option. But there's no guarantee that the two Democrats — each of whom has gained influence in the House — will avoid a showdown.

Gina Raimondo (D)

Elected 2014, term expires 2023, 2nd term; b. May. 17, 1971, Smithfield; Harvard U., B.A. 1993; Rhodes Scholar, Oxford U., PhD; Yale Law Schl., J.D. 1998; Catholic; Married (Andy Moffitt); 2 children.

Elected Office: RI Treasurer, 2010-2014.

Professional Career: Clerk, Judge Kimba Wood; Founder & Senior Vice President, Village Ventures; Co-founder, Point Judith Capital.

Office: 82 Smith St., Providence, 02903; 401-222-2371; Fax: 401-222-2012; Website: governor.ri.gov.

Lt. Gov.: Dan McKee (D) **Atty. Gen:** Peter Neronha (D) **Sec. of State:** Nellie Gorbea (D)

State Legislature: Senate: 33D, 5R **House:** 66D, 9R

Election Results

Election	Name (Party)	Vote (%)
2018 General	Gina Raimondo (D)	198,122 (53%)
	Allan Fung (R)	139,932 (37%)
	Joseph Trillo (I)	16,532 (4%)
	Bill Gilbert (Mod)	10,155 (3%)
2018 Primary	Gina Raimondo (D)	67,370 (57%)
	Matt Brown (D)	39,518 (34%)
	Spencer Dickinson (D)	10,987 (9%)

Democrat Gina Raimondo — a Harvard graduate, Rhodes scholar, Yale-trained lawyer and venture capitalist — was elected Rhode Island's first woman governor in 2014, as the state was struggling to recover from the Great Recession. In 2018, following improvements in the economy and enactment of taxpayer-funded community college tuition, Raimondo won reelection, first defeating a primary challenge from her left and then winning a general-election rematch against Republican Allan Fung by an impressive 16-point margin.

Raimondo's personal history reads like the script for a made-in-Rhode Island public service ad. Her grandfather arrived from Italy at age 14, and learned English by studying at the Providence Public Library. Her father is a World War II Navy veteran from a family of butchers who used the GI Bill to become the first in his family to attend college. Raimondo grew up in a tight-knit family in Smithfield and graduated with honors from Harvard, where she was named top economics student in her class. Though she's under 5-foot-3, she played rugby in college, which may have helped her prepare for her state's rough-and-tumble politics. She received a doctorate from Oxford University on a Rhodes scholarship and earned a law degree from Yale Law School. She clerked for a federal judge, then entered the venture-capital business. She says she decided to enter politics after she saw libraries in the state shutting down, a painful development considering her grandfather's experience.

While Raimondo is a Democrat in one of the nation's bluest states, she has typically positioned herself as a pro-business, reformist politician rather than a creature of the party establishment and its key interest groups, such as organized labor. She was elected Rhode Island treasurer in 2010 and set about overhauling the public-employee pension system. Central Falls, a city of about 19,000 people, filed for bankruptcy in 2011 under the weight of underfunded and overly generous pensions — its retiree health benefit liability was five times the city's annual revenues. Meanwhile, Providence was grappling with the 1991 decision by then-mayor Buddy Cianci to award 6 percent annual increases in pension benefits to hundreds of city employees. Raimondo warned that Rhode Island had the largest unfunded pension debt per capita of any state, spending 10 cents of every dollar of tax revenue on the pensions of 21,000 former public employees, with that amount poised to double within five years. So in 2011, Raimondo crafted a pension law that froze automatic cost-of-living increases and raised retirement ages. Additional legislation required some state workers and teachers to move a portion of their retirement savings into 401(k)-style accounts. It passed with bipartisan support and was signed into law in 2012, but public-employee unions were livid.

The governorship came open in 2014 after independent Lincoln Chafee's decision not to seek another term. At first, it appeared the Democratic primary was headed toward a battle between Raimondo and Providence Mayor Angel Taveras, running as a progressive who would win support from labor unions. But then former U.S. Education Department official Clay Pell, grandson of the late Democratic Sen. Claiborne Pell, got into the race, and union support was divided, with firefighters, police, supermarket clerks and city employees backing Taveras and the teachers union — unhappy with Taveras' support of charter schools — siding with Pell. Raimondo benefited from the split and won the primary with 42 percent of the vote.

Raimondo sought to mend fences with organized labor in the general election. She stumped to raise the state minimum wage to $10.10 an hour, and benefited when her Republican opponent – Fung, the Cranston mayor – came out against raising the minimum wage and in favor of right-to-work legislation that would ban union shops from requiring non-members to pay dues. Raimondo won, 41%-36%. Perennial candidate Robert Healey, running on the Moderate Party line, took 21 percent.

Raimondo got off to an inauspicious start when she attended a Washington D.C. conference and criticized the state's budget process. The Rhode Island governor has relatively weak powers, including a requirement that many appointments be approved by the state Senate and the absence of line-item veto powers enjoyed by 44 other governors. Her criticism prompted a rebuke from Democratic House Speaker Nicholas Mattiello, after which Raimondo called Mattiello to apologize and went to his office to smooth things over. After that flap, Raimondo quietly worked with lawmakers on a budget that ended up winning unanimous approval in the House and near-unanimous approval in the Senate. The budget created new economic-development programs, exempted most Social Security benefits from state taxes, removed the sales tax on energy for businesses, cut Medicaid spending, increased funding for K-12 education, raised the tax on cigarettes by 25 cents to $3.75 a pack, lowered the state's corporate minimum tax, established a state infrastructure bank and raised the state minimum wage to $9.60 an hour.

The budget also authorized the state to settle the lawsuit brought by unions challenging its pension reforms. Earlier, the state and the unions had averted a trial and agreed to soften the reforms by modifying retirement ages, increasing defined benefits for longtime public employees and permitting more chances for inflation adjustments. In 2016, Fortune magazine named Raimondo to its list of the World's 50 Greatest Leaders on the basis of her work on pensions. But she took some heat for the pension investment fund's annual loss in 2015, the first since the financial crisis in 2008. She had long advocated the use of hedge funds to maximize income, but critics were irked by their high fees and secrecy – and now by their weak performance. In September 2016, the State Investment Commission unanimously backed a move to relinquish half of the state's $1.1 billion hedge funds investments.

In February 2016, Raimondo signed a bill to fund bridge repairs through a mix of borrowing, refinancing and new tolls on trucks, and in July she signed a renewable energy package. Raimondo suffered an embarrassment over the launch of a tourism campaign in early 2016. Residents were puzzled by the slogan "Rhode Island – Cooler and Warmer," and matters only worsened when a video affiliated with the campaign was discovered to have included footage of Iceland. (Wags called it "Rhode Iceland.") Within days, the marketing director was out, and so was the slogan. And some criticized the governor for being too fond of incentives to boost business projects, partly a legacy of the disastrous tax breaks the state had previously given 38 Studios, a video-game business founded by former baseball player Curt Schilling.

In early 2017, the unemployment rate fell below the national average for the first time since 2005. "Raimondo is a pure centrist, New Way technocrat at heart," the conservative Weekly Standard noted approvingly, and the right-of-center Tax Foundation gave her an award. (One high-profile economic development effort didn't pan out: Raimondo and legislative leaders agreed to support a mini-Fenway Park project in downtown Pawtucket in a failed effort to retain the Boston Red Sox's AAA affiliate. The team took a more generous offer from Worcester Massachusetts.) Raimondo notched other accomplishments in the second two years of her first term: a budget surplus, an array of tax cuts, a further minimum wage hike to $10.50, a paid sick leave law, and taxpayer-funded tuition and fees at the Community College of Rhode Island for two years for qualifying students.

Still, Raimondo's approval ratings were only so-so, and heading into her reelection campaign she initially seemed to face a competitive race. "These are tempestuous times in the tiny teacup of Rhode Island politics, with Democrats struggling to find unity, Republicans hoping to gain relevance and independents relishing the idea of upsetting the whole darn system," Governing magazine wrote in July 2018, as the primaries approached. Raimondo's first challenge was on her left, from onetime secretary of state Matt Brown. Critics were unhappy not just with aspects of her pro-business record but also the seeming dominance of the Democratic Party's moderate wing on social issues such as abortion. While abortion rights were roughly as popular among rank-and-file Rhode Island voters as they were in other blue states, the Democratic leadership, including Mattiello, was hesitant to push the issue, given particularly aggressive opposition by the state's Catholic Church hierarchy. Raimondo's portrait was removed from her Catholic high school after she spoke to Planned Parenthood; Providence Bishop Thomas Tobin called her appearance with the group "an inexcusable lack of moral courage."

Brown attacked her policies as corporate giveaways and argued for reversing of some of her pension changes. Brown was backed by Justice Democrats and the Bernie Sanders-aligned Our Revolution, but Raimondo, with a bigger war chest, attacked Brown in television ads that targeted a complicated fundraising scheme he'd used in his unsuccessful 2006 Senate campaign. Brown also suffered from having been away from state politics for about a decade. Raimondo received support from Mattiello and others in the party establishment. She pledged to expand the taxpayer-funded tuition program to include University of Rhode Island and Rhode Island College and to seek universal pre-kindergarten for four-year-olds. She defeated Brown, 57%-34%, winning 35 of the state's 39 cities and towns. In the quieter GOP primary, Fung prevailed, winning 56 percent against House Minority Leader Patricia Morgan, who won 40 percent.

In addition to Raimondo and Fung, the general election featured several third-party candidates, including longtime Republican state Rep. Joe Trillo, who aligned with Trump, and Anne Armstrong, of the pro-marijuana Compassion Party. Fully in the spirit of Rhode Island political weirdness, Armstrong was charged with possession of 48 pounds of marijuana, while it came out during the campaign that Trillo had been charged in 1975 for assaulting Mattiello, then a 12-year-old neighborhood kid, with a caulking gun. As the campaign progressed, Raimondo pulled away. The Republican Governors Association, which had gotten involved in the race when it seemed like the GOP had a shot, pulled its advertising on behalf of Fung in October. In what became the most expensive gubernatorial campaign in state history, Raimondo defeated Fung, 53%-37%, with Trillo getting 4 percent. Raimondo won every county but Kent, which she lost by fewer than 250 votes.

After her victory, Raimondo was named chair of the Democratic Governors Association. Yet her position within the party was more complicated. New York Times columnist Frank Bruni wrote after her reelection that Raimondo "winces at talk of a top marginal tax rate of 70 percent and cringes at the growing use of 'corporatist' as a slur against Democratic politicians deemed too cozy with business interests." Raimondo told Bruni that Democrats "have become the party that is anti-business. We need to be the party of work."

Jack Reed (D)

Elected 1996, term expires 2020, 4th term, b. Nov 12, 1949; Cranston; La Salle Academy (RI), 1967; U.S. Military Academy (NY), B.S., 1971; Harvard University John F. Kennedy School of Government (MA), M.P.P., 1973; Harvard University School of Law (MA), J.D., 1982; Roman Catholic; Married (Julia Hart Reed); 1 child.

Military Career: U.S. Army 1967-1979; U.S. Army Reserve 1979-1991

Elected Office: RI Senate, 1985-1991; U.S. House, 1991-1997.

Professional Career: Association Professor, U.S Military Acad. at West Point, 1977-1979; Practicing attorney, Southerland, Asbill & Brennan, Edwards & Angell, 1982-1990.

DC Office: 728 HSOB 20510, 202-224-4642, Fax: 202-224-4680, reed.senate.gov
State Offices: Cranston, 401-943-3100; Providence, 401-528-5200.

Committees: *Appropriations*: Commerce, Justice, Science & Related Agencies; Department of Defense; Department of the Interior, Environment & Related Agencies; DOL, HHS & Education & Related Agencies; Military Construction & Veteran Affairs & Related Agencies; Transportation, HUD & Related Agencies (RMM). *Armed Services (RMM)*. *Banking, Housing & Urban Affairs*: Financial Institutions & Consumer Protection; Housing, Transportation & Community Development; Securities, Insurance & Investment.

Group Ratings

	ADA	ACLU	AFL-CIO	LCV	ITI	COC	HAFA	ACU	CFG	FRC
2018	-	62%	-	100%	-	50%	3%	9%	5%	0%
2017	95%	C	100%	100%	C	29%	C	0%	4%	0%

Almanac Ratings 2017-18

	Economy	Social	Foreign	Composite
Liberal	90%	90%	67%	82%
Conservative	10%	10%	33%	18%

Key Votes of the 115th Congress

1. Obama-care revision	N	5. Gun regulations	N	9. Kavanaugh confirmation	N
2. Tax Cuts	N	6. Family planning regs	N	10. Saudi arms sales	Y
3. Dodd-Frank revision	N	7. Gorsuch confirmation	N	11. FISA rules	Y
4. Omnibus appropriations	Y	8. Immigration restrictions	N	12. Military aid in Yemen	Y

Election Results

Election	Name (Party)	Vote (%)		Cand. Spent	Ind. Exp. Support	Ind. Exp. Oppose
2014 General	Jack Reed (D)..................................... 223,675	(71%)	$4,649,761	$5,576	$4,115
	Mark Zaccaria (R)............................ 92,684	(29%)	$54,031		
2014 Primary	Jack Reed (D)................................ Unopposed				

Prior winning percentages: 2008 (73%), 2002 (78%), 1996 (63%), House: 1994 (68%), 1992 (71%), 1990 (59%)

Since he was first elected in 1996, Democrat Jack Reed, Rhode Island's senior senator, has been numbered among the Senate's most respected policy wonks, making his influence felt on banking issues and national security matters. Reed is a graduate of the United States Military Academy and one of the few senators of his generation with military experience. Reed hoped to chair the Senate Armed Services Committee one day. His role in the Senate's long-standing bipartisanship on the Pentagon has been challenged by two recent developments: the 2016 election of President Donald Trump and the August 2018 death of Republican Sen. John McCain, who had chaired the panel.

As the top Democrat on Armed Services since 2015, Reed collaborated closely with McCain. The two had an unusually respectful relationship, based partly on their common experience as military academy graduates with lengthy service. During a February 2016 interview with WPRI in Reed's home state, McCain described their partnership: "We work together, never surprise each other. ... We also happen to be good friends, which is very helpful. That's not always the case with a Republican and Democrat." In an interview with NPR days before McCain died, Reed said, "his whole demeanor was one of encouraging bipartisan participation in the committee." That spirit was jeopardized by Reed's disagreements with Trump over the president's support for Saudi Arabia in its war in Yemen and his antagonism toward NATO allies.

Rhode Island has tended to send scions of the state's blue-blooded families to the Senate; Theodore Green, Reed's predecessor once removed, traced his ancestry to the colonists who arrived with Roger Williams, Rhode Island's founder, in 1636. Reed is an exception to this political pattern: He grew up in working-class Cranston, just outside Providence, as the second of three children of a school custodian and a housewife. Disappointed that she never got to go to college, Mary Reed prepared her children for success in school. She insisted on music and art classes for Jack beginning at 5. Her son, fascinated by history and World War II as a child, decided he wanted to attend the U.S. Military Academy in West Point, New York. At LaSalle Academy, a Catholic prep school in Providence, he played football.

After graduating from West Point in 1971, Reed served in the 82nd Airborne Division and received a master's degree from Harvard's Kennedy School of Government. After eight years of active duty, Reed enrolled in Harvard Law School. He spent another 12 years in the Army Reserve, retiring with the rank of major. Throughout his life, he has maintained connections to West Point, teaching there briefly in the late 1970s, serving on the academy's governing board and choosing its chapel as the site of his wedding in 2005.

After graduation from law school, Reed was an associate at a Washington, D.C. law firm before returning to Rhode Island in 1983 to work for Providence-based Edwards & Angell, then one of the state's oldest and most prominent law firms. A year later, at 35, Reed won public office for the first time, beating an incumbent in the primary for the state Senate, where he served six years. During his tenure, Reed headed a commission that investigated a corruption scandal involving the Rhode Island Housing and Mortgage Finance Corporation, a state agency created to make affordable loans to low-income Rhode Islanders. When Republican Claudine Schneider gave up her House seat in 1990 to run against Sen. Claiborne Pell, Reed ran for Congress. He captured 49 percent of the vote in a four-way field for the Democratic nomination. In the general election, he won 59%-41%.

In 1995, when Pell announced his retirement after six terms, Reed ran to succeed him. Reed had no serious competition for the Democratic nomination and faced state Treasurer Nancy Mayer in the general election. National Republicans spent nearly $1 million on ads attacking Reed as a liberal for opposing bills requiring welfare recipients to work and supporting labor unions — not especially harmful charges in largely liberal, heavily unionized Rhode Island. Reed spent $2.7 million to Mayer's $773,000. His biography was his message: Reed launched his campaign in a public school conference room named for his late father, he stressed his bootstraps rise from a working-class background and he called for education spending to help others achieve the same success. He won 63%-35%. He has not had serious competition for re-election since.

As a member of the Armed Services Committee, his influence on defense issues is such that former Defense Secretary Robert Gates said Reed was instrumental in persuading him to stay on the job in the early years of the Obama administration. "In terms of reaching out to me, and whether I would stay on, Obama couldn't have picked a person I was more willing to listen to or respected more than Jack," Gates told Rhode Island Monthly in 2012. Reed — on at least two occasions when Obama was president — reportedly rejected opportunities to become Defense secretary. One occurred just after the 2014 elections, when Defense Secretary Chuck Hagel was eased out. A Reed spokesman told the Providence Journal at that time that Reed "has made it very clear that he does not wish to be considered for secretary of Defense or any other Cabinet position."

When Obama was a Democratic presidential candidate, Reed accompanied him on a 2008 trip to Iraq and Afghanistan, and Obama later considered him as a potential running mate until Reed ruled himself out. During Obama's first year, as the new president was mulling strategy in Afghanistan, Reed expressed doubts about sending more troops and said the burden of proof was on commanders to justify a troop increase; Obama was sympathetic with that viewpoint, as Reed knew. Reed has traveled to Iraq and Afghanistan frequently, often straying from the safe zones — thanks to his military background and his close relationships with many military commanders.

In the final months of Obama's presidency, Reed said that his decision to maintain U.S. troops in Afghanistan and provide support to the country's armed forces "have laid the foundation for a sustainable U.S. and international security presence in Afghanistan," and he urged the incoming Trump administration to continue a "conditions-based approach" in Afghanistan. He said, "It is critical that we not cede space or territory to Iranian influence."

As of 2018, Reed had visited Afghanistan 17 times and Iraq 20 times since 2003. In a February 2019 hearing, he warned about reports that Trump was planning large cutbacks in U.S. troops to Afghanistan. "In considering the prospect of conflict termination, we must also weigh the cost of getting it wrong," he said.

Reed opposed the 2002 Iraq War resolution. When American forces entered Iraq months later, he argued that Defense Secretary Donald Rumsfeld grossly underestimated the strength of anti-American insurgents in Iraq and failed to send in adequate troops and equipment. In 2005, after a trip to Iraq, he said: "I think my criticism has been accurate, certainly in the operations in this region, in that we didn't organize ourselves for the appropriate occupation and stabilization" after the overthrow of Iraqi leader Saddam Hussein. Reed was at the forefront of Democratic efforts in 2006 to persuade Bush to redeploy forces in Iraq, calling for a "phased redeployment" in six months, with no deadline for complete withdrawal and with some U.S. forces remaining to train Iraqi security forces. That proposal lost 60-39.

Reed has long backed efforts to permanently increase the size of the Army. In 2004, he and Chuck Hagel, then a Nebraska Republican senator, called for an increase of 30,000 troops, and the Senate agreed to 20,000. In 2006, Reed worked with Republican leaders to add $3.7 billion for more soldiers and Marines, and he sponsored an amendment to add $10 billion to replace damaged or destroyed equipment. While Reed defended in 2012 Obama's plans to shrink the size of the Army and Marines, he later expressed concern about the effect on the armed forces of the 2011 Budget Control Act. That bipartisan deal created automatic spending cuts — so-called sequestration — while putting both defense and domestic spending limits in place. In 2015, Reed and McCain told leaders of the Senate Budget Committee that those limits "which require nearly $1 trillion of defense spending cuts over 10 years … have become a national security crisis of the first order."

When Trump became president, Reed voiced mixed sentiments. He welcomed the increased Pentagon spending, which has boosted local jobs in submarine building at General Dynamics Electric Boat. In March 2018, Reed was one of only 10 Democratic senators who voted against a resolution that would have ended U.S. troop support for Saudi Arabia's involvement in Yemen's civil war. He voiced concern about the consequences of withdrawal. But he reversed his position later in the year, spurred in part by the grisly killing of Saudi journalist Jamal Khashoggi at the Saudi consulate in Istanbul. "I think we should terminate the aerial refueling. I don't think it provides any control over [Saudi] behavior," Reed told reporters in October 2018. He criticized Trump for having too cozy a relationship with Saudi leaders. "This outrageous [killing of Khashoggi] can't be followed by a business-as-usual arms deal," he added.

Reed warned that Trump and other Republicans should not dismiss facts about possible Russian interference in the 2016 presidential election "because they are, for some reason, inconvenient." In July 2018, the Senate approved on a 97-2 vote Reed's motion to reaffirm support for NATO, amid concern about Trump's ambivalence. "Our allies are starting to wonder whether they can rely on the United States to come to their defense in a crisis." When Sen. Jim Inhofe of Oklahoma took over as Armed Services Committee chairman after McCain's death, it was uncertain whether the Republican successor would continue McCain's independence.

On most issues, Reed has had a solidly liberal voting record. In 2009, a National Journal examination of roll call votes dating to the 1980s found him to be the most liberal senator, slightly ahead of Barbara Boxer of California and Ted Kennedy of Massachusetts. In recent years, he has remained among the most-liberal senators in the Almanac vote ratings.

Sometimes overlooked in Reed's high-profile status as a defense expert is his grounding in financial issues. In his Banking Committee portfolio, he played a key role in the crafting of the Dodd-Frank financial regulation law in 2010. The committee chairman, Connecticut Democrat Christopher Dodd, asked Reed to work with New Hampshire Republican Judd Gregg on the derivatives issue. According to "Act of Congress," a book by Washington Post editor Robert Kaiser on the making of Dodd-Frank, Reed spent months working with Gregg to craft a regulatory framework in the complex area of derivatives — financial contracts based on the value of other assets, from interest rates to corn and soybeans. "Reed was an atypical senator," Kaiser wrote. "A small, compact man with a formidable intellect, he did mountains of homework. He mastered complicated issues."

In 2008, as his home state was buffeted by the Great Recession — Rhode Island was among the 10 states with the most subprime mortgage foreclosures — Reed played a quiet, but major role in securing an agreement on a foreclosure rescue bill. It included an affordable housing fund that he had been seeking since 2002. New York Democrat Chuck Schumer told The New York Times, "Once again, Jack does it in his quiet, steadfast way, and it is extremely effective." Reed has used his position as ranking Democrat on the Appropriations Subcommittee on Transportation, Housing and Urban Development to protect home-state interests, including his removal of a provision from the transportation funding bill in 2015 that would have eliminated more than $8.5 million from the Rhode Island Public Transportation Authority.

In 2005, Reed, whom friends long joked was married to his work, married for the first time in his mid-50s. His wife, Julia Hart, was working in the Senate's Interparliamentary Services Office when she and Reed met in 2002 — on a congressional delegation trip to Afghanistan. He is only the third senator — all Democrats — to hold his Senate seat since 1937. Green served 24 years and retired at 93; Pell served for 36, retiring at 77. Each chaired the Foreign Relations Committee. Based on those precedents — and Rhode Island's blue voting patterns — Reed is well-positioned to remain an influential force in the Senate for years to come, though he continues to await the opportunity to become chairman. He's a virtual lock for re-election in 2020.

Sheldon Whitehouse (D)

Elected 2006, term expires 2024, 3rd term, b. Oct 20, 1955; New York City, NY; Yale University (CT), B.Arch., 1978; University of Virginia Law School, J.D., 1982; Episcopalian; Married (Sandra Thornton Whitehouse); 2 children.

Elected Office: RI Attorney General, 1999-2003.

Professional Career: RI special Assistant Attorney General, 1984-1990; Legal counsel, Governor Bruce Sundlun, 1991; Policy Director, Governor Bruce Sundlun, 1992; Director, RI Department of Business Regulation, 1992-1994; U.S Attorney for RI, 1994-1998; Practicing attorney, 2003-2006.

DC Office: 530 HSOB 20510, 202-224-2921, Fax: 202-228-6362, whitehouse.senate.gov

State Offices: Providence, 401-453-5294.

Committees: *Budget. Environment & Public Works*: Clean Air & Nuclear Safety (RMM); Fisheries, Water, and Wildlife; Transportation & Infrastructure. *Finance*: Energy, Natural Resources & Infrastructure; Health Care; Taxation & IRS Oversight. *Judiciary*: Constitution; Crime & Terrorism (RMM); Oversight, Agency Action, Federal Rights & Federal Courts; Subcommittee on Intellectual Property.

Group Ratings

	ADA	ACLU	AFL-CIO	LCV	ITI	COC	HAFA	ACU	CFG	FRC
2018	-	64%	-	100%	-	50%	3%	9%	5%	0%
2017	95%	C	100%	100%	C	29%	C	0%	4%	0%

Almanac Ratings 2017-18

	Economy	Social	Foreign	Composite
Liberal	97%	97%	67%	87%
Conservative	3%	3%	33%	13%

Key Votes of the 115th Congress

1. Obama-care revision	N	5. Gun regulations	N	9. Kavanaugh confirmation	N
2. Tax Cuts	N	6. Family planning regs	N	10. Saudi arms sales	Y
3. Dodd-Frank revision	N	7. Gorsuch confirmation	N	11. FISA rules	Y
4. Omnibus appropriations	Y	8. Immigration restrictions	N	12. Military aid in Yemen	Y

Election Results

Election	Name (Party)	Vote (%)		Cand. Spent	Ind. Exp. Support	Ind. Exp. Oppose
2018 General	Sheldon Whitehouse (D)	231,477	(61%)	$4,732,417	$49,716	
	Robert Flanders Jr. (R)	144,421	(38%)	$1,191,815		$155,000
2018 Primary	Sheldon Whitehouse (D)	89,140	(77%)			
	Patricia Fontes (D)	26,947	(23%)			

Prior winning percentages: 2012 (65%), 2006 (54%)

Democrat Sheldon Whitehouse, since first being elected in 2006 from one of the country's bluest states, has emerged as one of the Senate's most vocal liberals — particularly on climate change. Much of his energy has been devoted to keeping the flame alive on a host of liberal causes unlikely to be enacted into law anytime soon. He has been outspoken in seeking to control the influence of money in elections.

He explored those themes in more detail in his 2017 book, "Captured: The Corporate Infiltration of American Democracy." In its introduction, Whitehouse offered insight into his workplace. "In the Senate, I see every day how power works in the political sphere. I see who's got it. I see who uses it. I see how they use it. I see the devices by which that power is applied," he wrote. "Never in my life have I seen such a complex web of front groups sowing deliberate deceit to create public confusion about issues that should be clear. The corporate propaganda machinery is of unprecedented size and sophistication."

Whitehouse is one of many congressional liberals in recent decades to come from a background of wealth and privilege. He is a descendant of Charles Crocker, one of California's "Big Four" men who built the Central Pacific Railroad. Whitehouse's grandfather was a diplomat, as was his father, Charles Whitehouse, a World War II Marine pilot who was U.S. ambassador to Laos and Thailand in the 1970s. He was born in New York City and grew up overseas, including in Cambodia, South Africa, the Philippines and Guinea; as a teenager, he taught English to Vietnamese children in Saigon. He graduated from St. Paul's preparatory school, Yale University and the University of Virginia Law School.

Whitehouse moved to Rhode Island in 1984 to take a job as an assistant state attorney general. He was appointed a top staffer to Democratic Gov. Bruce Sundlun in 1991, and served two years as the head of the state's Department of Business Regulation under Sundlun. In 1994, on the recommendation of Democratic Sen. Claiborne Pell, a family friend, Whitehouse was appointed U.S. attorney for Rhode Island. Whitehouse launched an undercover investigation that resulted in the conviction of Providence Mayor Buddy Cianci on corruption charges. He also focused on environmental cleanup, leading an investigation that resulted in the largest fine in state history for an oil spill in Narragansett Bay.

In 1998, Whitehouse ran for state attorney general. In the three-way Democratic primary, his opponents portrayed him as an inexperienced, fox-hunting patrician trying to buy his way into public office. Whitehouse was better-known than his two opponents and he got the nomination, capturing about half of the total vote. In the general election, the Republican nominee, state Treasurer Nancy Mayer, forced Whitehouse to concede he had tried drugs as a student and questioned whether he was tough enough for the job. Whitehouse later told the Providence Journal: "The book on me was, 'Smart kid, works hard, but, you know, has no common touch, can't relate to people, will be a disaster.' In fact, I got advice from some political types to run sort of a Rose Garden strategy. You know, 'Don't go out, don't let people see you, 'cause if they see you, they're not going to like you. Just mail your resume around, you know, and spend a lot of money on television.'"

The tide began to turn in his favor after highly negative ads by Mayer on the drug issue backfired in the absence of evidence that the incident was more than a short chapter from Whitehouse's distant past. He won 67%-33%. By 2002, he was viewed as a strong contender for governor. He lost the Democratic primary by 926 votes to former state Sen. Myrth York, who outspent him, 2-1.

Whitehouse had considered running for the Senate in 2000. Republican Sen. John Chafee had announced he would not seek a fifth term. But Chafee — who had been a roommate of Whitehouse's father while they were undergraduates at Yale — died in November 1999. Republican Gov. Lincoln Almond appointed the senator's son, Lincoln Chafee, then mayor of Warwick, to fill the vacancy; Whitehouse deferred his bid and Chafee was elected to a full term. In 2006, Chafee faced a primary challenge from Cranston Mayor Steve Laffey, a conservative and a sharp-elbowed campaigner backed by a national anti-tax group, the Club for Growth. Though Chafee won the primary 54%-46%, he had little cash remaining.

Whitehouse had an easy time in the Democratic primary to take on Chafee. The general election pitted two candidates of fairly similar views who shared an upper-crust background: Chafee was an heir of one of Rhode Island's most prominent families, whose members had held high office in the state going back to the 1870s. Both candidates backed abortion rights, gun control and federal funding of stem cell research. Whitehouse campaigned against the unpopular Bush administration, running ads with the tagline, "Finally, a Whitehouse in Washington you can trust." He won 54%-46%.

Whitehouse was one of eight new Democratic senators whose elections gave the party a majority in the Senate. He quickly gained recognition as a fierce critic of the Bush administration. Whitehouse blasted Attorney General Alberto Gonzales for firing U.S. attorneys for what Democrats alleged were political motivations. After Gonzales resigned, Whitehouse opposed the nomination of Michael Mukasey as attorney general for refusing to say whether water boarding was illegal.

With President Barack Obama in office, Whitehouse became a stalwart administration defender. In the Almanac vote ratings, he has consistently ranked among the most liberal senators. Whitehouse irked conservatives when he said on the Senate floor that opposition to Obama's health care reform measure was driven in part by "right-wing militias and Aryan support groups." Later, in 2012, he charged that House Budget Committee Chairman Paul Ryan's budget blueprint "gets rid of Medicare in 10 years and turns it into a voucher program," which the fact-checking site PolitiFact rated as false.

Whitehouse has gained attention with a series of weekly Senate floor speeches on the dangers he believes are posed by climate change. He began giving speeches on the subject in April 2012, accusing Congress of "sleepwalking through history." Speaking weekly when the Senate was in session, he claimed he never had to give the same speech twice because of the breadth of the topic. Whitehouse credits his wife Sandra, a marine scientist, with helping him recognize the importance of oceans in everyone's lives. In the process, he has become perhaps Congress' most persistent voice on the hazards of climate change.

In March 2018, as he began his 200th speech, Whitehouse told the Senate: "The most obvious fact standing plainly before me is not the measured sea level rise at Naval Station Newport. It is not the 400 parts per million carbon dioxide barrier we have broken through in the atmosphere. It is not the new flooding maps that coastal communities like Rhode Island's must face. It is not the West aflame. It is not even the uniform consensus about climate change across universities, national laboratories, scientific societies, and even across our military and intelligence services. The fact that stands out for me, here at No. 200, is the persistent failure of Congress to even take up the issue of climate change. One party will not even talk about it. One party in the executive branch is even gagging America's scientists and civil servants and striking the term 'climate change' off of government websites."

Whitehouse has pushed for more funding of ocean protection, including creation of a National Endowment for the Oceans, Coasts and Great Lakes. He has tried to make the idea of carbon fees on industries that emit carbon pollution more politically acceptable by crafting it as revenue neutral, with corporate tax cuts and rebates for taxpayers. In 2014, he formed an alliance with Democratic Sen. Joe Manchin of West Virginia. Manchin visited Rhode Island to see the effect of climate change firsthand; Whitehouse toured coal and energy resources in West Virginia.

On the Senate Judiciary Committee, Whitehouse got into a tussle with chairman Chuck Grassley over the panel's probe into Russian interference in the 2016 presidential election. In June 2017, they and other committee members tentatively agreed to staff interviews with key campaign officials. Months later, Whitehouse tweeted that the committee review, under pressure from the Trump White House, had moved toward an inquiry into Hillary Clinton's campaign. "Your insinuation is baseless," Grassley responded in a letter to Whitehouse.

In 2018, Whitehouse won a long-sought assignment to the Finance Committee and gave up his seat on the Health, Education, Labor and Pensions panel. He spoke out against "Trump tax breaks" and stepped up his own proposals for new tax breaks.

Whitehouse has been re-elected easily, though his share of the vote has averaged a few points less than that of Democratic Sen. Jack Reed, his home-state colleague. In 2012, his Republican opponent was software executive Barry Hinckley, who campaigned as a moderate on social issues, while calling for the repeal of Obamacare and supporting offshore oil drilling. Whitehouse won 65%-35%.

In April 2018, Lincoln Chafee said that he planned to challenge Whitehouse in the Democratic primary. After losing to Whitehouse in 2006, Chafee had been elected governor as an independent and then ran an eccentric campaign for the Democratic presidential nomination in 2016. He told the Providence Journal that supporters of Sen. Bernie Sanders had encouraged him to seek his former Senate seat because they were unhappy that Whitehouse had supported Hillary Clinton in the 2016 contest. Chafee criticized Whitehouse for failing to challenge warrantless wiretapping and for opposing a Senate resolution to end U.S. support for Saudi Arabia's involvement in Yemen's civil war and said "we should have a debate" on those issues. A month later, Chafee abandoned his plan. "Discretion is the better part of valor," he told a reporter. Whitehouse got 77 percent of the vote against a little-noticed Democratic primary challenger and defeated Republican Robert Flanders 61%-38%. Flanders, a former state Supreme Court justice, referred to the incumbent as "silver spoon Sheldon" and criticized his focus on climate change.

David Cicilline (D)

Elected 2010, 5th term, b. Jul 15, 1961; Providence; Brown University (RI), B.A., 1983; Georgetown University Law Center (DC), J.D., 1986; Jewish; Single.

Elected Office: RI House, 1995-2003; Providence Mayor, 2003-2011.

Professional Career: Public defender, 1986-1987; Practicing attorney; Faculty, Roger Williams Law School.

DC Office: 2233 RHOB 20515, 202-225-4911, Fax: 202-225-3290, cicilline.house.gov

State Offices: Pawtucket, 401-729-5600.

Committees: *Foreign Affairs*: Europe, Eurasia, Energy & the Environment; Middle East, North Africa & International Terrorism; Oversight & Investigations. *Judiciary*: Antitrust, Commercial & Administrative Law (Chmn); Crime, Terrorism & Homeland Security.

Group Ratings

	ADA	ACLU	AFL-CIO	LCV	ITI	COC	HAFA	ACU	CFG	FRC
2018	-	85%	-	100%	-	58%	9%	8%	14%	0%
2017	95%	C	95%	100%	C	36%	C	7%	5%	0%

Almanac Ratings 2017-18

	Economy	Social	Foreign	Composite
Liberal	100%	97%	95%	97%
Conservative	0%	4%	5%	3%

Key Votes of the 115th Congress

1. Obama-care revision	N	5. Family planning regs	N	9. Guantanamo prisoners	Y
2. Tax Cuts	N	6. Body cameras/immigration	Y	10. Ground missiles, limit	Y
3. Omnibus appropriations	Y	7. Abortion ban	N	11. Defense Dept. spending	N
4. Dodd-Frank revision	N	8. Concealed carry	N	12. FISA rules	N

Election Results

Election	Name (Party)	Vote (%)		Cand. Spent	Ind. Exp. Support	Ind. Exp. Oppose
2018 General	David Cicilline (D)	116,099	(67%)	$897,333		
	Patrick Donovan (R)	57,567	(33%)			
2018 Primary	David Cicilline (D)	47,762	(78%)			
	Christopher Young (D)	13,474	(22%)			

Prior winning percentages: 2016 (65%), 2014 (60%), 2012 (53%), 2010 (51%)

Democrat David Cicilline, elected in 2010 with a niche as a gay and often outspoken liberal lawmaker, gained two plum assignments when Democrats took House control. They give him potentially busy platforms in the party leadership and at the Judiciary Committee. The former mayor of Providence, Cicilline had a rocky start in the House when his popularity plummeted with news of his messy stewardship of the city's finances. But he has recovered politically at home.

Cicilline was born in Providence, the middle of five children. His parents eloped when his Jewish mother was 16 and his Catholic father 17. He grew up celebrating the traditions of both religions, and now identifies as Jewish. His father was a criminal-defense attorney. Cicilline attended Brown

University, where he majored in political science and founded, along with classmate John F. Kennedy Jr., a chapter of the College Democrats. He was active in student government and worked two jobs waiting tables. Cicilline came out as gay in college and says he was fortunate to have a supportive family. After getting a law degree from Georgetown University, he worked in Washington as a public defender for juveniles.

He returned to Rhode Island to campaign for the state Senate. He lost that bid, but ran for the state House two years later and won. In the legislature, he pushed to raise the legal age to buy a gun from 13 to 18, introduced a bill creating a needle exchange program for drug users, and fought attempts to restrict abortion rights. In 2002, he was elected to the first of two terms as mayor of Providence, becoming the first openly gay mayor of a state capital city. He campaigned as a reformer, promising to clean up the city after the two-decade reign of Buddy Cianci, who was convicted of corruption. As the city's revenue shriveled in the recession, he laid off nearly 500 employees and raised property taxes. Cicilline was president of the National Conference of Democratic Mayors.

When Democratic Rep. Patrick Kennedy decided not to seek reelection, Cicilline won the primary with 37 percent of the vote against three opponents. In the general election, he campaigned as a pragmatist seeking to create jobs. Republican state Rep. John Loughlin focused on the state's poor economy and said he would balance the federal budget. Cicilline spent $2 million to $800,000 for Loughlin and won 51%-45%. The unexpectedly close outcome in a heavily Democratic district highlighted national Republican strength in 2010 and residual problems for Cicilline.

Cicilline spent his first term under a cloud from his actions as mayor. The Providence Journal reported in early 2011 that the city had a $180 million deficit for the next two fiscal years and that its reserve fund was almost depleted. A nonpartisan bond rating agency, Fitch Ratings, criticized Cicilline's administration for "imprudent budgeting decisions." Cicilline said he had to use reserve money to prevent sharp cuts to city programs. He went on an apology tour to acknowledge he should have been more forthcoming about Providence's fiscal problems.

Cicilline established a solidly liberal voting record. He spoke out forcefully against proposed GOP budget cuts to programs for low-income citizens, and he tried without success to amend spending bills to take money from Afghanistan reconstruction and apply it to deficit reduction. On the Judiciary Committee, he criticized Facebook and its chairman, Mark Zuckerberg, for lying to Congress about its data-sharing practices and for turning "a blind eye to the spread of hate speech and Russian propaganda on its platform." That led to his selection in 2019 to chair the Antitrust, Commercial and Administrative Law Subcommittee, where his agenda included the goal to "hold big tech companies accountable." He gained notice when he launched hearings on the anti-competitive practices of Facebook and Google, which he described as part of an extended investigation.

While in the House minority, Cicilline filed legislative proposals that had no prospects in a Republican-controlled Congress, but they gave Democrats and progressives talking points. In 2015, following the shooting deaths of nine people in a Charleston South Carolina church, he filed legislation to prohibit gun purchases by children, people with a criminal record and those with a mental illness. "While I understand that some in Congress would prefer not to have this debate right now, it is critical that we find the political will to finally address these urgent concerns," Cicilline said. He has pushed another bill to reinstate a ban on certain classes of semi-automatic weapons. He has sponsored legislation for automatic voter registration in the 50 states, which shifts the burden for registering from the individual to the state. The proposal gives citizens a 21-day period to opt out of registration.

Following the 2018 election, Speaker Nancy Pelosi created a new leadership position that was intended for Cicilline: chairman of the Democratic Policy and Communications Committee, with responsibility to develop a policy agenda and communications strategy to unify Democrats in Congress and beyond. He was elected without opposition.

In 2012, he turned back a Democratic challenge from businessman Anthony Gemma, who was the runner-up in the 2010 primary. Gemma accused Cicilline of voter fraud. The incumbent called the allegation "absolutely absurd" and won 62%-38%. His general election rival was Republican Brendan Doherty, a former state police superintendent. Cicilline outspent Doherty, $2.4 million to $1.5 million, and each received generous party support. Cicilline again won modestly, 53%-41%, while President Barack Obama took the district with 66 percent of the vote. Since then, Cicilline has won more comfortably against lightly funded opponents.

Cicilline and his friends have talked up his interest in climbing further up the leadership ladder.

RI-1: Eastern Rhode Island   **Cook Partisan Voting Index: D+14**

Population		Race and Ethnicity		Income	
Total	532,360	White	67.8%	Median Income	$56,013
Land area (sq. miles)	268	Black	7.3%	District Income Rank	216
Pop/ sq mi	1982.8	Latino	17.1%	Poverty Rate	15.3%
Born in State	50.5%	Asian	3.5%	With health insurance	92.4%
		Two or more races	2.6%	Cash public assistance	3.4%
Age Groups		Other	1.6%	Food stamp/SNAP	18.5%
Under 18	20.5%				
18-34	25%	**Education**		**Work**	
35-64	38.7%	H.S grad or less	42.1%	White Collar	15.8%
Over 64	15.8%	Some college	25%	Sales and Service	43.2%
		College Degree, 4 yr	19.4%	Blue Collar	19.1%
Military		Post grad	13.4%	Government	10.8%
Veteran/ Active Duty	7.5%				

2012 Pres. Vote	Obama	141,306	(66%)	Romney	68,723	(32%)			
2016 Pres. Vote	Clinton	130,682	(59%)	Trump	75,510	(34%)	Johnson	6,767	(3%)

Parts of Providence, Newport: Economic woes have hit hard in some Rhode Island cities, and have not been easy to shake. Central Falls declared bankruptcy in 2011, becoming the second city in the nation to exhaust its pension fund; it significantly cut benefits for retirees under court direction. In 2012, Providence, on the brink of bankruptcy, averted fiscal disaster by cutting back pensions and education spending, and raising property taxes. Since then, each city has continued to struggle with its finances. In Pawtucket, the loss of resources has become daunting. After years of futile discussions with city and state officials, the AAA baseball franchise affiliated with the Boston Red Sox announced in August 2018 that it will relocate 40 miles away in Worcester Massachusetts, where it will have a taxpayer-financed new stadium and a growing metropolis. In December 2018, the chief executive of Hasbro, the Fortune 500 toy company that has been headquartered in Pawtucket for more than a half-century and employs 1,600 locally, announced that the company was exploring all options for its new headquarters location — in Pawtucket, elsewhere in Rhode Island or beyond — and planned a decision in the next six months. These dispiriting conditions contrast sharply with the comfortable — in some cases, aristocratic — lifestyle only a few miles away, in parts of Providence and in tony towns along Narragansett Bay. In October 2018, a study by economists at Brown University found that Providence, known for its progressive political base, "is among the most unequal cities in the country," with pockets of prosperity alongside areas of deep poverty.

The 1st Congressional District is the eastern half of Rhode Island, divided from the state's other congressional district by a boundary line that circles around the state capital on three nearby streets and extends about 40 miles from Woonsocket along the Massachusetts border to Newport and Little Compton along the Atlantic Ocean. The district takes in much of Providence, including the elite East Side and College Hill around Brown University. Lower-income South Providence is the only sizable part of the district west of the Providence River. In recent years, the once down-on-its-luck city has revived physically, with an accessible waterfront adjacent to downtown, active night life and restoration of neighborhoods around the state capitol. The district captures all of next-door Pawtucket, whose Slater Mill is known as the birthplace of the American Industrial Revolution. Pawtucket created an arts district downtown and has rehabbed many of its abandoned mills into lofts for artists and commercial space for entrepreneurs.

The onetime textile mill towns of the Blackstone Valley, Woonsocket and Central Falls (with an area of one square mile) are in the 1st, along with high-income Barrington and Bristol along the eastern coast of Narragansett Bay. To the south, on the ocean, is the old city of Newport, with its restored 18th-century houses and summer "cottages" that are more like mansions, plus the smaller island of Jamestown. Newport has been home to the America's Cup races and has hosted a popular jazz festival every summer since 1954, with productions occasionally elsewhere. It is also the site of the oldest synagogue in North America, where George Washington once told a congregation that the United States gives "to bigotry no sanction, to persecution no assistance." Ethnically, the 1st District is the more French-Canadian and the less Italian of Rhode Island's two congressional districts.

Politically, it is the more strongly Democratic, though the party's vote in each district dropped several points in the 2016 presidential election.

Jim Langevin (D)

Elected 2000, 10th term, b. Apr 22, 1964; Providence; Rhode Island College, B.A., 1990; Harvard University John F. Kennedy School of Government (MA), M.P.A., 1994; Roman Catholic; Single.

Elected Office: RI House, 1989-1995; RI Secretary of St., 1995-2001.

Professional Career: RI Secretary of State; State Representative

DC Office: 2077 RHOB 20515, 202-225-2735, Fax: 202-225-5976, langevin.house.gov

State Offices: Warwick, 401-732-9400.

Committees: *Armed Services*: Intelligence, Emerging Threats & Capabilities (Chmn); Seapower & Projection Forces; Tactical Air & Land Forces. *Homeland Security*: Cybersecurity, Infrastructure Protection & Innovation; Intelligence & Counterterrorism.

Group Ratings

	ADA	ACLU	AFL-CIO	LCV	ITI	COC	HAFA	ACU	CFG	FRC
2018	-	68%	-	94%	-	58%	9%	12%	4%	20%
2017	95%	C	92%	100%	C	36%	C	7%	5%	0%

Almanac Ratings 2017-18

	Economy	Social	Foreign	Composite
Liberal	97%	87%	83%	89%
Conservative	3%	13%	17%	11%

Key Votes of the 115th Congress

1. Obama-care revision	N	5. Family planning regs	N	9. Guantanamo prisoners	Y
2. Tax Cuts	N	6. Body cameras/immigration	Y	10. Ground missiles, limit	Y
3. Omnibus appropriations	Y	7. Abortion ban	N	11. Defense Dept. spending	Y
4. Dodd-Frank revision	N	8. Concealed carry	N	12. FISA rules	Y

Election Results

Election	Name (Party)	Vote (%)		Cand. Spent	Ind. Exp. Support	Ind. Exp. Oppose
2018 General	Jim Langevin (D)............................ 126,476	(64%)		$717,908		
	Salvatore Caiozzo (R)................... 72,271	(36%)		$3,335		
2018 Primary	Jim Langevin (D).....................................	(100%)				

Prior winning percentages: 2016 (58%), 2014 (62%), 2012 (56%), 2010 (60%), 2008 (70%), 2006 (73%), 2004 (75%), 2002 (76%), 2000 (62%)

Democrat Jim Langevin, elected in 2000, is the first quadriplegic to serve in Congress and has worked on behalf of others with similar physical challenges. He has been a leader in promoting policies on cybersecurity and other national security issues on the Armed Services and Homeland Security committees, and chairs a key subcommittee.

Langevin grew up in Warwick and as a boy hoped to become an FBI agent. in 1980, at age 16, when he was a police cadet in the Boy Scout Explorer program, he was shot by a police officer when a gun accidentally discharged. The bullet went through his upper back and throat and damaged the upper part of his spinal column, leaving him a quadriplegic. He received a $2.2 million settlement from the city of Warwick. Although he disliked the attention it brought him, he says he became determined to do something meaningful with his life. He worked as an intern at the state House and for Sen. Claiborne Pell. While a student at Rhode Island College, where he got his bachelor's, he was elected to the state House, where he styled himself as a reformer. He got a master's degree in public administration from the John F. Kennedy School of Government at Harvard. In 1994, Langevin was elected Rhode Island's secretary of state.

When the House seat opened, Langevin's strongest opponent was Kate Coyne-McCoy, executive director of the Rhode Island Association of Social Workers, who criticized his opposition to abortion rights. Langevin had support from many Democratic leaders and some unions, and won the party's convention endorsement. Coyne-McCoy waged an aggressive campaign financed by unions, health care workers and EMILY's List. Langevin called her positions "unrealistic and extreme." She said, "There's no such thing as being too liberal." He spoke often about the accident that paralyzed him. "Certainly, being disabled is part of who I am, but it doesn't define me," he said. Langevin defeated Coyne-McCoy, 47%-29%. In the general, Rodney Driver, nominee of the Conscience for Congress Party and a retired mathematics professor, spent $300,000 of his retirement savings. Langevin won easily, 62%-21%.

The House chamber in the Capitol was made wheelchair-accessible for Langevin, with two seats in the front removed to give him space to maneuver and to talk to colleagues. At his urging, Speaker Nancy Pelosi agreed to changes to make all parts of the chamber, including the speaker's rostrum, accessible. In July 2010, he became the first person in a wheelchair to preside over the House. In February 2018, he opposed a Republican-passed bill he said would weaken compliance with the Americans with Disabilities Act. "I am saddened that Congress sent a message to people with disabilities that we are not equal or worthy of the same civil rights protections as other," he said.

Langevin has been a member of the Democratic whip team. In 2005, he sided with conservatives in the case of Terri Schiavo, a severely brain-damaged Florida woman in a court battle over removing her life-sustaining feeding tube. He returned to the liberal fold on embryonic stem cell research, which anti-abortion groups opposed. Langevin took the view that the research might alleviate suffering from certain diseases and injuries, which drew heat from the Roman Catholic bishop of Providence. With Rep. Dan Lipinski of Illinois, he has been one of two Democrats in the Pro-Life Caucus.

Langevin has sponsored several gun-control bills, including increased inspections of firearms dealers' sales records and stiffened penalties for dealers who have been untruthful. In 2006, Langevin won passage of a bipartisan bill that established a respite program for caregivers of individuals with special needs. He was a staunch supporter of the Democrats' health care initiative in 2009 and 2010. His Almanac vote ratings have been liberal on economic issues and more centrist on cultural and foreign policy issues.

On the Armed Services Committee, Langevin worked successfully to thwart the Obama administration's proposed cut in production of Virginia-class submarines in Rhode Island and Connecticut. As ranking Democrat, and now chairman, of the Intelligence, Emerging Threats and Capabilities Subcommittee, he has been an expert and leading policymaker on cybersecurity programs and what he has termed "the increasingly competitive security environment," including "new forms of hybrid warfare and cyber intrusions." Langevin was the chief House sponsor of a bill to establish cybersecurity offices in the White House and Homeland Security Department and give the president emergency powers to act during a cybersecurity crisis. The House passed the bill in 2010, but it died in the Senate. During the Obama administration, he called the failure of the Office of Personnel Management to create a risk-based cyber strategy "simply unacceptable,"

After a cyber expert was removed from the National Security Council staff of President Donald Trump, Langevin filed legislation to require an advocate for cybersecurity be in the room when budget and policy decisions are made and to develop the workforce needed to address cybersecurity issues. For the private sector, he won approval of his amendment in June 2018 for the Homeland Security Department to disclose vulnerabilities in industry systems. He has filed a bill to require companies to notify victims of a cybersecurity breach. "Americans put a lot of trust in companies by giving them personal and private information, and they should have confidence that their data is secure," Langevin said.

State and national Democrats urged Langevin to challenge Republican Sen. Lincoln Chafee in 2006, but abortion rights groups objected to his candidacy. In 2017, he said in an interview that he might run for governor "at some point in the future," but not in 2018. Making such a move in 2022 would avoid a showdown when reapportionment is expected to eliminate one of Rhode Island's two House seats. Still, he might be in position by then to chair a House committee.

RI-2: Western Rhode Island   **Cook Partisan Voting Index: D+6**

Population		Race and Ethnicity		Income	
Total	523,778	White	78.8%	Median Income	$65,736
Land area (sq. miles)	765	Black	3.6%	District Income Rank	131
Pop/ sq mi	684.4	Latino	12%	Poverty Rate	11.4%
Born in State	63.3%	Asian	3.1%	With health insurance	94.2%
		Two or more races	1.9%	Cash public assistance	3.4%
Age Groups		Other	0.6%	Food stamp/SNAP	13.7%
Under 18	19.4%				
18-34	23.6%	**Education**		**Work**	
35-64	40.6%	H.S grad or less	38.9%	White Collar	16.4%
Over 64	16.4%	Some college	27.9%	Sales and Service	43.5%
		College Degree, 4 yr	20.2%	Blue Collar	18.2%
Military		Post grad	12.9%	Government	13.6%
Veteran/ Active Duty	7.5%				

2012 Pres. Vote	Obama	138,371	(60%)	Romney	88,481	(38%)		
2016 Pres. Vote	Clinton	121,843	(50%)	Trump	105,033	(43%)	Johnson	7,979 (3%)

Parts of Providence, Warwick, Cranston: For a small state, Rhode Island plays a major role in the construction of the nation's submarine fleet. The Electric Boat company, a division of General Dynamics, has sprawling plants in Quonset Point — a few miles from Warwick -- and across the Connecticut line in Groton and New London. The combined workforce exceeds 15,000 and has been growing steadily, with plans to manufacture a new class of ballistic missile submarines, which were scheduled for production starting in 2020. The Quonset Point shipyard already has been producing a class of attack submarines. The increased workload resulted in ground-breaking in June 2018 for a new $800 million facility a short distance down Narragansett Bay in North Kingston, which was expected to hire at least 1,300 workers.

The 2nd Congressional District is the western half of Rhode Island. The largest cities are working-class Cranston and more upscale Warwick, which has been the second-largest in the state. But its lead of 2,259 persons over Cranston in 2010 had narrowed to 669 by 2017, and it was only a matter of time before Cranston took the number-two slot behind Providence. One reason why Cranston has had more growth has been because it had more undeveloped land, while Warwick had little space for growth. Cranston was reportedly the inspiration for FOX's animated comedy Family Guy, with a cultural edge; the show, which has run for several seasons and has been one of the most popular on the network, was set in the fictitious town of Quahog, which happens to be a Rhode Island species of clam. The 2nd includes the fastest-growing part of the state, South County, which is not an official place but the common name for Rhode Island south of East Greenwich. This area takes in the affluent suburbs and beachfront communities along Narragansett Bay, the Kingston home of the University of Rhode Island, and the area around Westerly, where many residents work at the Electric Boat shipyards in Groton.

Another important segment of the economy is sailing and tourism. In addition to its rolling farmland (this is Rhode Island, so there is not much acreage), the district includes communities along the bay and the ocean, where many people still make their living building boats and catching fish. The Block Island Wind Farm began to produce energy in 2017 from the nation's first off-shore wind farm. The five-turbine, 30-megawatt facility, which is three miles off the coast, uses a submarine cable to connect to the mainland and is expected to power 17,000 homes. Wind farms on land are cheaper to build, but those in the ocean have stronger winds.

This has been a comfortably Democratic district. President Barack Obama twice won with 60 percent of the vote. In 2016, Hillary Clinton won by only 50%-43%. Donald Trump ran strongly in the small towns.

SOUTH CAROLINA

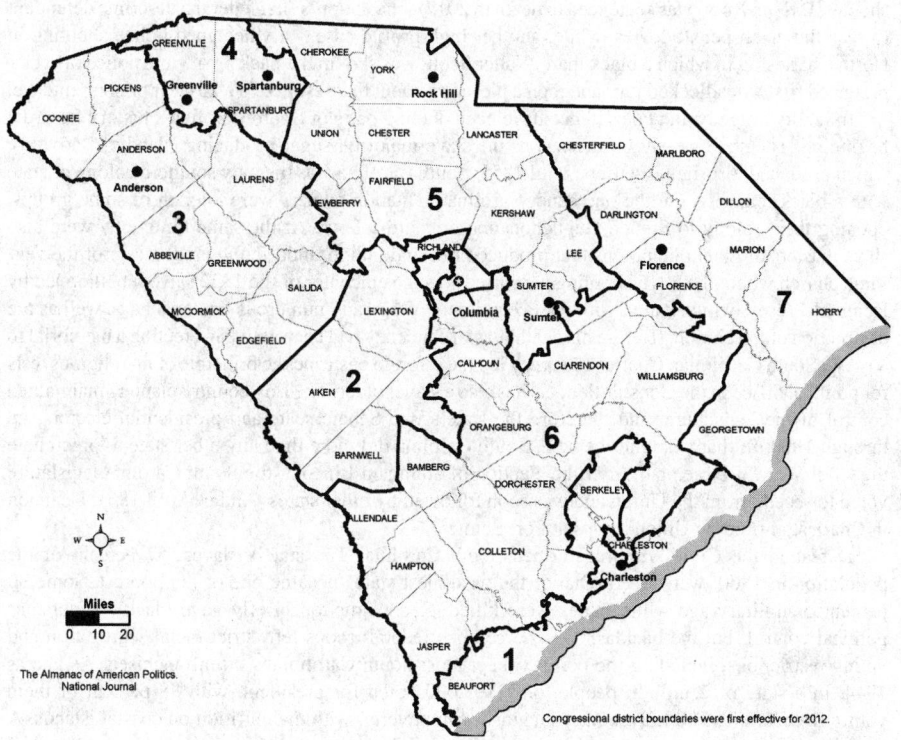

The Almanac of American Politics.
National Journal

Congressional district boundaries were first effective for 2012.

History is inescapable anywhere, but especially so in the South — as Americans have been reminded in recent years, when South Carolina has repeatedly been vaulted into the headlines for tragic incidents and efforts at reconciliation.

In 2015, a gunman with a history of white supremacist beliefs entered a historic African-American church in Charleston, sat down for Bible study, and then systematically gunned down nine black worshippers — including the pastor, state Sen. Clementa Pinckney – as he squeezed the trigger more than 75 times. Amid the mourning, a debate about an old subject — race and Confederate heritage — reemerged. Critics said the state should finally do what it had previously balked at — remove the Confederate battle flag from the state capitol grounds in Columbia, where it had flown, in one way or another, since the depths of the civil rights conflict in 1962. Republican Gov. Nikki Haley, who prior to the killings had shown little interest in following her predecessors' (failed) efforts to pull down the flag, offered her support for removal, and the tide began to turn. The legislature gave its approval, and on July 10, 2015, the flag was lowered from the statehouse grounds for good. The shooter, Dylann Roof, was sentenced to death in 2017 -- the nation's first federal hate-crime defendant to face the death penalty. Meanwhile, another high-profile case – a videotaped police shooting in North Charleston in which a black man, Walter Scott, was shot in the back by a white police officer – produced first a deadlocked jury and then a plea agreement that resulted in a 20-year prison sentence.

In reality, tragedy and coexistence have been dueling parts of South Carolina's history from the beginning. The state's early influence was the slave-majority, sugar-producing island of Barbados, which produced its original settlers; until 1855, South Carolina was the only southern colony or state with a black majority. On the one hand, Carolina plantation owners were tolerant of some groups, opening their colony to French Huguenots and Sephardic Jews. At the same time, they were also slave masters of giant plantations that produced rice and indigo. Indeed, the predecessor of the very same church where the 2015 shootings occurred was the epicenter of the 1822 slave rebellion led by Denmark Vesey, which ended with the execution of Vesey and numerous lieutenants, as well as the destruction of the church. (Before his death, Pastor Pinckney had been active in erecting a memorial to Vesey.) South Carolinian Charles Pinckney led the effort to enshrine the principle of no religious tests for political office in the Constitution; he was also a slaveholder. The Lowcountry planters maintained control of the legislature, and therefore the state's two Senate seats and presidential electors, up through 1860. In that year and the next, South Carolina did more than any other state to precipitate the Civil War. In December, after the election of Abraham Lincoln, the South Carolina legislature voted to secede from the Union and was soon followed by other states. And in April 1861, a cannon in Charleston fired on Union troops at Fort Sumter.

Defeat in the Civil War transformed South Carolina. The state's slaves, 57 percent of the population in 1860, were freed. One of the wealthiest states became one of the poorest. Some 30 percent of military-age white males were killed. Reconstruction briefly gave black Republicans political control, but the backlash was fierce once federal troops left; strict racial segregation and voting restrictions, including the poll tax, kept most South Carolinians disenfranchised. As late as 1944, in a state of 2 million people, only 103,000 voted for president, with 88 percent of them voting Democratic. The Lowcountry languished in poverty, with malnutrition on coastal islands. A silver lining was architectural — the old mansions of Charleston were not replaced by commercial buildings, and instead were saved by the nation's first local historic preservation movement (and rebuilt after Hurricane Hugo in 1989), cementing the city's culture and civic pride. Mostly white Upstate South Carolina, with a growing textile industry, took the political lead, led by such politicians as Pitchfork Ben Tillman (governor 1890-94, senator 1895-1918) and a close friend's son, Strom Thurmond (governor 1947-51, senator 1954-2003).

In the last few decades, this once underdeveloped state has taken steps forward. Most South Carolina whites opposed integration, but unlike in Alabama and Mississippi, the effort was mostly not punctuated by violence. The Civil Rights Act of 1964 and the Voting Rights Act of 1965 ended legal segregation of public accommodations and workplaces and brought blacks into the electorate. Democratic (and later Republican) Sen. Thurmond, who staged a record-setting filibuster of the 1957 Civil Rights Act, began appointing black staffers and signed off on a black federal judge. By the 21st century, the state elected Haley, a daughter of immigrants from India, and then Tim Scott, an

African-American, to the House and later to the Senate, respectively; in this strongly conservative state, their ideology was what mattered.

In many ways, the biggest change has been economic. Forty years ago, much of South Carolina's economy depended on military bases and big textile mills in the Interstate 85 corridor around Greenville and Spartanburg. Then South Carolina became the most aggressive state in the South in seeking new industry. It advertised its business climate, with one of the nation's lowest rates of unionization and taxation and a willingness to splurge on tax incentives. Crucially, Democratic Gov. (later Sen.) Ernest Hollings spearheaded the creation of the state's technical colleges, which today educate and train hundreds of thousands of residents a year. Michelin opened the first of several South Carolina plants in 1975, and the first BMW vehicles rolled off the Spartanburg assembly line in 1992. Volvo chose a South Carolina site 30 miles northwest of Charleston as the location of its first North American assembly plant, while smaller companies built factories throughout much of central and Upstate South Carolina.

Navy bases were the mainstay of Charleston's economy in the 1970s, but they were closed in the early 1990s, subsequently becoming a center of aircraft production, particularly after Boeing in 2009 chose North Charleston to build a plant to assemble its 787 Dreamliner. The aircraft giant now employs 6,800 people in the Charleston area, though the company has been enmeshed in a contentious battle over unionization; one major organizing effort was rejected in a vote, but a narrower one succeeded in 2018. Charleston has become a major port, which is especially helpful for the state's international exporters; the state has scrambled to line up the funds to carry out a $558 million, multi-year plan to dredge Charleston Harbor so container ships can traverse it regardless of tidal conditions. Charleston's downtown has not only survived but thrived, thanks in large part to the creative energy of longtime Mayor Joseph P. Riley Jr., who was first elected in 1975 and who served for 40 years. With a keen aesthetic eye, he made the city's historic center a magnet for tourists; statewide, tourism has grown consistently, reaching $21.2 billion in 2016, an amount bigger than the $16 billion statewide impact of the military. By late 2018, the unemployment rate had fallen to 3.3 percent, slightly below the national average.

Through the 1960s, few people except military personnel moved to South Carolina. That has changed in a big way. In 2018, United Van Lines reported that South Carolina was the sixth-most popular destination for interstate moves. Since 2010, the population has grown by 9.7 percent, with growth fastest on and near the coast – 20 percent in Horry County (Myrtle Beach) and Berkeley County (the northern suburbs of Charleston), 17 percent in Dorchester County (the northwestern suburbs of Charleston), 15 percent in Beaufort County (Hilton Head), and 13 percent in Charleston County (Charleston). Another growth area has been the York County suburbs of booming Charlotte, North Carolina; it grew by 17 percent. These booming areas attract tourists and affluent retirees eager to spend days with pleasant weather on the golf course and in time-shares. The newcomers are disproportionately white and conservative; South Carolina's population is 27 percent black (tied for the fifth highest in the nation, although far below African-Americans' near-majority of the 1940s) and 6 percent Hispanic. The fastest-growing portion of South Carolina's population now consists of those 85 and older, and by 2030, the state is expected to have more residents 65 and older than children in school.

Despite the economic gains, South Carolina had no locally headquartered company on the Fortune 500 list in 2018, and business leaders worried about the impact of President Donald Trump's protectionist trade policies. After tariffs began to hit, BMW shifted some of its production to China, and Daimler, which was building a plant in North Charleston, said it might need to follow suit; Volvo warned that it may hire fewer workers at its plant. The state's exports fell in 2018 for the first time in years, and television maker Element Electronics near Columbia shut down entirely due to higher costs from tariffs. But the state's Republican politicians hung with Trump for the most part, saying they hoped the approach would produce long-term gains despite short-term pain.

Not even the export-driven growth has managed to extinguish poverty in many areas of the state. In 2016, five whole counties and parts of several others reported more than 95 percent of their schoolchildren qualifying for free or reduced-cost lunches or Medicaid. Statewide median income is 16 percent below the national average, and the poverty rate is a few percentage points higher than the national average. South Carolina ranked in the bottom quarter of states for the percentage of residents with a college degree, and large percentages of new – and even experienced – teachers have left the state's schools, and even the profession entirely, according to The State newspaper.

The demographic changes have moved South Carolina politically toward Republicans. Politics cleaves the electorate along racial lines, and the hard math of the population figures — whites have an easy majority — makes it difficult for Democrats to win statewide. South Carolina has voted for Republicans for president in every election but one since 1960 – in 1976, when son of the South Jimmy Carter was running. With some bare-knuckled help from wunderkind strategist Lee Atwater, former Gov. Carroll Campbell built a Republican Party capable of electing statewide officials and legislative majorities. In 1988, Campbell and Atwater, who was by then George H.W. Bush's campaign manager, set up the early Republican presidential primary on the Saturday before Super Tuesday, which enabled Bush to clinch the nomination that year. It did the same for Bob Dole in 1996, for George W. Bush in 2000, and for John McCain in 2008. The only hiccup came in 2012, when Newt Gingrich won the state.

In 2016, Donald Trump won all but two counties in South Carolina's primary, and easily won the state in the general election. South Carolinians remained supportive of the embattled president, which led such leading GOP figures as Sen. Lindsey Graham and Gov. Henry McMaster to cement close ties with Trump. Haley, as U.N. ambassador, and former Rep. Mick Mulvaney, in several White House positions including acting chief of staff, served in high-profile administration roles. Trump helped push GOP primaries toward loyalists, including a primary challenger who ousted Rep. Mark Sanford for being insufficiently supportive. That move backfired in the general election when the Democrats flipped the seat, but that race was the exception. Not even a long-unfolding investigation of Richard Quinn, a powerbroker with deep influence in the legislature who was indicted on perjury charges in April 2019, hurt Republican prospects in the state, despite several indictments of legislators and other political figures. Today, even attractive Democratic candidates find it hard to secure more than 45percent of the vote in South Carolina.

Population		Race and Ethnicity		Income	
Total	4,893,444	White	63.8%	Median Income	$48,781
Land area (sq. miles)	30,061	Black	27.0%	State Income Rank	42
Pop/ sq mi	162.8	Latino	5.5%	Poverty Rate	16.6%
Born in state	57.2%	Asian	1.5%	With health insurance	87.9%
		Two or more races	1.8%	Cash public assistance	1.4%
Age Groups		Other	0.6%	Food stamp/SNAP	14.0%
Under 18	22.3%				
18-34	22.8%	Education		Work	
35-64	38.6%	H.S grad or less	42.9%	White Collar	33.7%
Over 64	16.3%	Some college	30.1%	Sales and Service	42.5%
		College Degree, 4 yr	17.2%	Blue Collar	23.9%
Military		Post grad	9.8%	Government	15.2%
Veteran/ Active Duty	10.6%				

Presidential Politics

2016 Primary (D)	Clinton (D)	272,379 (73%)	Sanders (D)	96,498 (26%)		
2016 Primary (R)	Trump (R)	240,882 (32%)	Cruz (R)	165,417 (22%)	Rubio (R)	166,565 (22%)
	Bush (R)	58,056 (8%)	Kasich (R)	56,410 (8%)	Carson (R)	53,551 (7%)
2016 Pres. Vote	Trump (R)	1,155,389 (55%)	Clinton (D)	855,373 (41%)	Johnson (L)	49,204 (2%)
2012 Pres. Vote	Romney (R)	1,071,645 (55%)	Obama (D)	865,941 (44%)		

In presidential general elections, South Carolina has been reliably Republican for a long time. It was the only Deep South state to vote for Richard Nixon over George Wallace in 1968. Since then, it has voted Democratic only once, for Jimmy Carter in 1976. In 2016, the state held to its GOP tendencies and Donald Trump defeated Hillary Clinton 55%-41%. Trump won 31 of the state's 46 counties. Clinton carried Charleston and Richland and did well in the counties with a higher African-American population. The state's presidential primaries are less predictable, but more important. Since 1980, when Republicans began using a primary to allocate their national convention delegates,

South Carolina played a pivotal role in determining nearly every contested GOP race. And with an early spot on the calendar, it also played a major role in the 2008 Democratic race.

The primary's significance for Republicans started when Ronald Reagan defeated John Connolly in 1980. Connolly had the backing of the state's legendary Sen. Strom Thurmond. Reagan's 55%-30% victory confirmed his widespread popularity among Southern Republicans and helped propel him to the GOP nomination. In 1987, GOP operative Lee Atwater craftily scheduled the GOP primary for the Saturday before Super Tuesday, a collection of mostly Southern primaries that many of the region's Democrats had organized, hoping to push their party toward choosing a moderate Southern standard bearer. Instead, South Carolina moved Republicans toward choosing a moderate Southern Republican, George H.W. Bush of Texas, who won a 49%-21%-19% victory over GOP Senate leader Bob Dole and evangelical champion Pat Robertson. That victory was a precursor of Bush's sweep of the Southern primaries that clinched the nomination for him three years later. In 1992, Bush beat Pat Buchanan 67%-26%, squashing Buchanan's claims to conservative Southern support. Four years later, Dole, after his disappointing showings elsewhere, won an impressive 45%-29% victory over Buchanan. In 2000, former GOP governors Carroll Campbell and David Beasley supported George W. Bush as he beat John McCain 53%-42% in a particularly bruising and bitter contest that left relations between McCain and Bush strained throughout the latter's presidency. In 2008, McCain defeated former Arkansas Gov. Mike Huckabee 33%-30%. The Arizonan's victory established him as the frontrunner for the nomination and gave him momentum that he carried into the Florida primary 10 days later and then the subsequent Super Tuesday contests. The 2012 Republican primary was held just 10 days after New Hampshire. The hot candidate turned out to be Newt Gingrich, who defeated Mitt Romney 40%-28%.

The 2016 edition of the South Carolina GOP primary was another Republican slugfest. Trump questioned Texas Sen. Ted Cruz's citizenship and threatened to sue him over a negative television ad, which featured Trump describing himself in 1999 as "very pro-choice." In a debate, Trump accused former President George W. Bush of lying about the presence of weapons of mass destruction in Iraq in the run-up to the 2003 U.S.-led invasion of that country. After that debate the former president made his only appearance at a campaign rally for his brother, Jeb. Florida Sen. Marco Rubio won endorsements from the state's popular junior senator, Tim Scott, and more importantly, Gov. Nikki Haley. Sen. Lindsey Graham, who had been a candidate for the nomination but withdrew from the race a couple months before the primary, endorsed Bush. But it was Trump's fiery rhetoric and disdain for the GOP establishment and the media that excited South Carolina Republicans and enabled him to defeat Rubio, 33%-23%. Cruz finished third with 22 percent and Bush's 8 percent prompted him to withdraw from the race.

The state's two political parties — not the state government — conduct presidential primaries in South Carolina, and they can choose to hold them on different days. In 2008, the Democratic National Committee chose South Carolina as the only state other than New Hampshire to hold an early primary. The most coveted endorsement was that of Rep. James Clyburn, the House Majority Whip and an African American who can be a force in a presidential primary in which the electorate is more than 50 percent black. Candidates and surrogates flock to his annual spring fish fry in Columbia, where the crowd consumes more than 1,000 pounds of whiting. Clyburn didn't endorse in 2008. Turnout in the Democratic primary was a record 532,000 voters, and Barack Obama won a crushing victory, defeating Hillary Clinton 55%-26%. Years later in his memoir, Clyburn, who had voted for Obama, wrote that he received a 2 a.m. phone call the day after the primary from Bill Clinton blaming him for his wife's defeat and vowing, "If you bastards want a fight, you damn well will get one." The 2016 Democratic primary was much less contentious and saw a reversal of fortune for Clinton, who had consolidated African-American support, particularly in the South. She was endorsed by Clyburn one week before the primary, while her rival, Vermont Sen. Bernie Sanders, dispatched rap singer Killer Mike to the state in hopes of rallying younger blacks to his candidacy. It didn't work. Clinton won more than 80 percent of black voters.

Despite this rich history, some South Carolina Republicans in early 2019 backed an idea to cancel their 2020 primary to indicate their support for president Trump's re-nomination. While this was somewhat controversial, it was not unprecedented: Republicans cancelled their primary in 1984 and 2004, and Democrats did likewise in 1996 and 2012 in deference to their respective incumbent presidents who were seeking a second term.

Congressional Districts

116th Congress Lineup	2D 5R	115th Congress Lineup	1D 6R

In the redistricting of 2022, as was the case a decade earlier, Republicans likely will split the seven districts of South Carolina so that they get six of the seats and Democrats get one seat that reaches into several urban and rural areas to create an African-American majority, as has been the case in the 6th District. Once again, the GOP seems certain to hold the governorship and solid majorities in both houses of the legislature. The key question will be where, and how, Democrats push for a second district that has at least a sizable African-American influence and perhaps a majority. That likely would require reduction of black voters in the 6th, and carving up the 5th or the 7th. In 2011, the Obama Justice Department tersely granted preclearance. A group of six Democratic voters sued to block the map on the grounds it failed to create a second African-American seat, but a three-judge panel upheld the map. Subsequently, Republicans controlled all six of their districts until an internal GOP split in the 2018 campaign unexpectedly gave Democrats control of the Charleston-based 1st District. If Republicans do not regain that seat in the 2020 election, they likely will set an additional priority of recapturing and reinforcing GOP control there.

The 2011 redistricting had another twist that might remain relevant. In that case, the state House passed a proposal adding its new 7th District in the Pee Dee region anchored by Myrtle Beach and surrounding Horry County, a rapidly growing Republican bastion. But something unexpected happened on the road to final passage. The state Senate, including ambitious Republicans from the Lowcountry region, surprised the House with its own scheme, placing the new 7th District in the Charleston suburbs and Beaufort to the south. The map's plotters had brought on board several Democrats who believed the Senate version would give them a better shot in the 7th District. The impasse created by Republican infighting threatened to send the entire matter to federal court. After all, African-Americans were 28 percent of the state's population in 2010 — roughly the same as now. Finally, Republicans in the two chambers reached a compromise, greased by support from Upstate legislators, to place the 7th District in the Pee Dee, which would have the most blacks of any district in the state other than the 6th. Gov. Nikki Haley signed the map. Since then, Tom Rice has easily held the new 7th District for the GOP.

Based on the previous precedent, the keys to the outcome will include the predisposition of the Justice Department and the judges who might hear the case, plus the ability of Democrats to unify around an alternative that carries legal and political support for them to gain a second seat.

Henry McMaster (R)

Assumed office in 2017, term expires 2023, 1st full term; b. May. 27, 1947, Columbia; Univ. of South Carolina, BA 1969; Univ. of South Carolina, J.D 1973; Presbyterian; Married (Peggy); 2 children.

Military Career: U.S Army JAG, 1969-1975.

Elected Office: Chairman, SC Republican Party, 1993-2002; SC Attorney General 2003-2011; SC Lt. Governor, 2015-2017.

Professional Career: Legislative Assistant to U.S Sen. Strom Thurmond, 1973-1974; SC Law Enforcement Coordinating Committee head, 1981-1985;

Office: State House, 1100 Gervais St., Columbia, 29201; 803-734-2100; Fax: 803-734-5167; Website: governor.sc.gov.

Lt. Gov.: Pamela Evette (R) **Atty. Gen:** Alan Wilson (R) **Sec. of State:** Mark Hammond (R)

State Legislature: Senate: 19D, 27R **House:** 44D, 78R, 2V

Election Results

Election	Name (Party)	Vote (%)
2018 General	Henry McMaster (R)	921,342 (54%)
	James E. Smith, Jr. (D)	784,182 (46%)
2018 Primary runoff	Henry McMaster (R)	184,286 (54%)
	John Warren (R)	159,349 (46%)
2018 Primary	Henry McMaster (R)	155,723 (42%)
	John Warren (R)	102,390 (28%)
	Catherine Templeton (R)	78,705 (21%)
	Kevin Bryant (R)	24,790 (7%)

Henry McMaster, a longtime Republican officeholder in South Carolina who had lost a gubernatorial primary to Nikki Haley in 2010, was elevated from lieutenant governor in 2017 after Haley, by then in the middle of her second term as governor, was confirmed as President Donald Trump's pick to be U.S. ambassador to the United Nations. In 2018, McMaster won a full term, but not before becoming the first modern South Carolina governor in either party to be forced into a primary runoff.

McMaster, a native of Columbia, received his bachelor's degree from the University of South Carolina in 1969 and his law degree from the same university four years later. He served a year as a legislative assistant to Sen. Strom Thurmond, after which he built a private practice in South Carolina. In 1981, President Ronald Reagan appointed McMaster to serve as U.S. attorney. During his four years in the post, his office helped convict more than 100 people for importing nearly $1 billion in illegal drugs. In 1986, McMaster ran against longtime Democrat Sen. Ernest Hollings, but lost. Four years later, he ran for lieutenant governor and lost again. In 1991, then-Gov. Carroll Campbell appointed McMaster to the state Commission on Higher Education, and for most of the 1990s he headed the state Republican Party.

McMaster finally won an elected statewide office -- attorney general -- in 2002. After securing the GOP nomination in a contested primary, McMaster defeated Democrat Steve Benjamin, 56%-44%, and he easily won a second term four years later. As attorney general, McMaster took a leading role in opposing the Affordable Care Act. He threw his hat into the ring for the open-seat gubernatorial race in 2010. The large Republican primary field also included Lt. Gov. André Bauer, Rep. Gresham Barrett, state Sen. Larry Grooms, and state Rep. Nikki Haley; Haley won the primary and then the governorship in November. In 2014, McMaster ran for lieutenant governor, taking the Republican primary and defeating Democrat Bakari Sellers in the general election, 59%-41%. During her six years as governor, Haley had attracted national attention as the first woman and the first racial minority to lead the Palmetto State. With Haley's confirmation for the U.N. post in January 2017, McMaster at last became governor, at age 69.

Coming into office, state legislators said they were hoping he'd be a dealmaker and easier to get along with than either Haley or her predecessor, Mark Sanford, both of whom were perceived to have sharp elbows. But as it turned out, McMaster's early tenure in office featured plenty of legislative drama. McMaster vetoed a bill that would have raised the state's gasoline tax for the first time since 1987, but the measure to help fix the state's crumbling roads – which received support from the party's business wing – was ultimately overridden in the legislature by large, bipartisan margins. He also drew fierce legislative opposition to a spending-bill veto that would have allotted $20.5 million to replace aging and fire-prone school buses; McMaster said it was unwise to earmark lottery funds for that purpose rather than for scholarships, the highest-profile use of lottery funds. The legislature overwhelmingly overrode this veto, too. Both vetoes were widely believed to be fodder for the GOP's anti-tax, small-government base as McMaster headed into what promised to be a tough primary season.

McMaster made other moves that pleased the GOP base. He asked the federal government to stop the resettlement in South Carolina of refugees from the countries targeted by Trump's travel ban; he signed an executive order protecting a foster care agency that limited its services to Christian families; and he vetoed almost $16 million in women's health services to end state funding for Planned Parenthood. McMaster also worked, unsuccessfully, to block a proposed tariff that could have hit Samsung washing machines being built in a newly opened plant in the state, and sought to derail a Trump administration plan to allow drilling off the Atlantic coast. (In January 2019, after he had won reelection, the state filed suit against the administration's plan to conduct offshore seismic testing for oil and gas.) McMaster, joined by the state's congressional delegation, fought the Trump administration's plan to shut down a partially built facility at the Savannah River Site that would reprocess plutonium from weapons into nuclear fuel. He also urged a sale of Santee Cooper, a state-owned electric utility saddled with $4 billion in nuclear-related debts, though some in the legislature pushed back on the idea.

In the primary, McMaster faced former state agency head Catherine Templeton, Lt. Gov. Kevin Bryant, former Lt. Gov. Yancey McGill, and businessman John Warren. McMaster received endorsements from South Carolina Citizens for Life and the National Rifle Association, and he touted a strong economy. "When you're winning, you don't fire an experienced coach and hire a rookie," McMaster said at a fundraiser. "You give him four more years and keep on winning!" But his opponents attacked him as an apostle of a tired and corrupt political establishment. Late in the campaign, Warren gained ground by leveraging his outsider profile. Warren, a 39-year-old Marine veteran from Upstate, owned a mortgage lending firm; a relatively late entrant in the race, he spent $3 million from his own pocket, including a heavy run of television ads. McMaster finished first with 42 percent, followed by Warren with 28 percent, Templeton with 21 percent, Bryant with 7 percent, and McGill with 2 percent. That was only enough for a McMaster showdown with Warren. On the eve of the runoff, Trump visited South Carolina to promote McMaster, who had been the first statewide official anywhere to back Trump before the state's 2016 primary. As was the case in other Republican primaries in 2018, Trump had the magic touch: McMaster defeated Warren in the runoff, 54%-46%, ceding only a few counties in Warren's Upstate home base. South Carolina Republicans "picked the candidate Trump liked over the Trump-like candidate," The State newspaper wrote.

In the general election – running for the first time on a ticket with a lieutenant governor candidate, following a change in state law – McMaster faced Democratic state Rep. James Smith, who Democrats considered a strong candidate. Smith was an Afghanistan combat veteran and an experienced legislative hand who had easily won a three-way primary with the support of national Democratic leaders. But McMaster benefited from a fundraising edge and strong marks for handling the economy. Compared with Democrats running elsewhere in 2018, Smith couldn't go full-blast against Trump, because he remained popular among many voters. McMaster won, 54%-46%. Below the surface, Democrats gained some ground. Smith's share of the vote was about five percentage points higher than Democrats had won in the 2014 gubernatorial contest, and the party expanded its winning margin in Charleston County (Charleston) and Richland County (Columbia) by 14 and five points, respectively. Democrats also narrowed the GOP's winning margin in Beaufort (Hilton Head) and Greenville counties by 18 and 16 points, respectively. But for Democrats, gaining those final few percentage points to score a statewide victory remained elusive, and looked to remain so for the foreseeable future.

Lindsey Graham (R)

Elected 2002, term expires 2020, 3rd term, b. Jul 09, 1955; Central; University of South Carolina, B.S., 1977; University of South Carolina, M.P.A., 1978; University of South Carolina School of Law, J.D., 1981; Baptist; Single.

Military Career: U.S. Air Force 1982-1988; SC Air National Guard 1989-1995; U.S. Air Force Reserve 1995-2015 (Afghanistan & Iraq)

Elected Office: SC House, 1992-1994; U.S. House, 1995-2003.

Professional Career: U.S Air Forces Europe Circuit Trial Counsel, 1984-1988; Assistant Oconee County Attorney, 1988-1992; Practicing attorney, 1988-1994; Judge advocate, McEntire Air National Guard Base, 1989-1994; Central, SC, city Attorney, 1990-1994.

DC Office: 290 RSOB 20510, 202-224-5972, Fax: 202-224-3808, lgraham.senate.gov

State Offices: Columbia, 803-933-0112; Florence, 843-669-1505; Greenville, 864-250-1417; Mt. Pleasant, 843-849-3887; Pendleton, 864-646-4090; Rock Hill, 803-366-2828.

Committees: *Appropriations*: Commerce, Justice, Science & Related Agencies; Department of Defense; DOL, HHS & Education & Related Agencies; Energy & Water Development; State, Foreign Operations & Related Programs (Chmn); Transportation, HUD & Related Agencies. *Budget. Foreign Relations*: Africa & Global Health Policy (Chmn); Internat'l Dev Instit & Internat'l Econ, Energy & Environ Policy; Near East, South Asia, Central Asia & Counterterrorism. *Judiciary (Chmn)*: Ex Officio membership on all subcommittees.

Group Ratings

	ADA	ACLU	AFL-CIO	LCV	ITI	COC	HAFA	ACU	CFG	FRC
2018	-	9%	-	7%	-	90%	59%	71%	42%	100%
2017	5%	C	7%	5%	C	67%	C	75%	86%	100%

Almanac Ratings 2017-18

	Economy	Social	Foreign	Composite
Liberal	9%	9%	8%	9%
Conservative	91%	91%	92%	91%

Key Votes of the 115th Congress

1. Obama-care revision	Y	5. Gun regulations	Y	9. Kavanaugh confirmation	Y
2. Tax Cuts	Y	6. Family planning regs	Y	10. Saudi arms sales	N
3. Dodd-Frank revision	Y	7. Gorsuch confirmation	Y	11. FISA rules	Y
4. Omnibus appropriations	Y	8. Immigration restrictions	Y	12. Military aid in Yemen	NV

Election Results

Election	Name (Party)	Vote (%)		Cand. Spent	Ind. Exp. Support	Ind. Exp. Oppose
2014 General	Lindsey Graham (R)	672,941	(55%)			
	Brad Hutto (D)	456,726	(38%)			
	Thomas Ravenel (I)	47,588	(4%)			
	Victor Kocher (L)	33,839	(3%)			
2014 Primary	Lindsey Graham (R)	178,093	(56%)			
	Lee Bright (R)	48,704	(15%)			
	Richard Cash (R)	26,246	(8%)			
	Det Bowers (R)	23,071	(7%)			
	Nancy Mace (R)	19,560	(6%)			
	Bill Connor (R)	16,847	(5%)			

Prior winning percentages: 2008 (58%), 2002 (54%), House: 2000 (69%), 1998 (100%), 1996 (60%), 1994 (60%)

Republican Lindsey Graham, South Carolina's senior senator, may have had the biggest — and most confounding — political transformation of any lawmaker over the past two years. First elected to the House in 1994 and to the Senate in 2002, Graham was once seen as a maverick alongside his late friend Arizona Sen. John McCain, who was unafraid to challenge his party and collaborate with Democrats. Now, Graham has morphed into one of President Donald Trump's most loyal allies, after having called him a "kook" and "unfit for office" during his own short-lived presidential campaign. But for Graham, this unorthodox pairing has been helpful as he wields even more power in the Senate, taking over in 2019 as chairman of the Senate Judiciary Committee. And while Graham still brought his hawkish defense beliefs to the forefront in the GOP caucus, his relationship from Trump may have finally endeared him to conservatives back home who had long been skeptical of his true colors.

Graham grew up in Pickens County, where his parents owned a tavern in the textile mill town of Central. Both his parents died young, while Graham was attending the University of South Carolina, and he became his younger sister's legal guardian so that she could receive his military benefits. He was first in his family to graduate from college; and he received a law degree from the University of South Carolina. He was an Air Force prosecutor who worked on assignments overseas, including one case that led to major changes in the service's drug testing program for soldiers. In 1988, he returned home and practiced law in Seneca. In 1992, he was elected to the state House. Graham was called to active duty and served stateside during the Gulf War. In 1995, he joined the Air Force Reserve and served as a senior instructor in the Judge Advocate General's school and as a reserve judge on the Air

Force Court of Criminal Appeals. He was awarded the Bronze Star in 2014 for meritorious service for his role as a senior legal adviser to the Air Force during combat operations in Afghanistan. Graham retired from the reserves in June 2015 just as he was launching his ill-fated presidential campaign.

In 1994, with the retirement of 20-year Democratic Rep. Butler Derrick, Graham ran for the House. Graham won the Republican primary with 52 percent of the vote. In the general election, he faced state Sen. Jim Bryan. Graham called for term limits, supported more defense spending and opposed gays openly serving in the military. His attitude toward the Clinton administration and Democratic leadership was unequivocal. "I'm one less vote for an agenda that makes you want to throw up," he said. Graham won 60%-40%, a smashing victory in a district that had been represented only by Democrats since Reconstruction.

In the House, Graham had a solidly conservative voting record but did not always support the Republican leadership. In the summer of 1997, he was among a small group of junior House members who plotted with some senior lawmakers to oust Speaker Newt Gingrich, who by then had lost the confidence of his Republican troops. The attempt failed. In a Republican Conference meeting, Majority Leader Dick Armey of Texas, one of the plotters, said no member of the leadership was involved; Graham said that was untrue.

As a member of the House Judiciary Committee, Graham played a major role in the 1998 impeachment of President Bill Clinton. In the Senate trial, Graham's folksy manner and clear description of Clinton's offenses — "Where I come from, a man who calls someone up at 2:30 in the morning is up to no good" — made him one of the most effective GOP impeachment managers. In 2000, Graham was one of McCain's staunchest supporters in his first bid for the presidency.

In 2002, Graham ran for the seat of Republican Sen. Strom Thurmond, who was 99 and did not seek a ninth term. There had not been an open South Carolina Senate seat since 1941. Graham had no opposition in the Republican primary. His work on impeachment and the McCain campaign made him well-known and popular statewide, and he had the endorsements of three former governors and Thurmond. Democrats portrayed him as lacking in substance and recruited Alex Sanders, president of the College of Charleston who in 1985 was appointed to the state Court of Appeals.

Sanders was a gifted raconteur, charming and well-connected around the state. He was a solid fundraiser as well, raising $4.2 million — less than Graham's $6.2 million, but a considerable achievement for a candidate consistently behind in the polls. Sanders supported the Bush tax cuts and Iraq War, but he opposed the death penalty — on religious grounds — and a constitutional amendment to allow criminalization of flag burning. Graham hammered him on the death penalty and the flag amendment, but most of all, labeled him as a liberal, saying Sanders would advance the agenda of Sens. Hillary Clinton of New York and Ted Kennedy of Massachusetts. Graham won 54%-44% and took the place of a senator first elected in the year before he was born. Graham and Clinton have had a love-hate relationship. She cited him as one of the Republicans she worked best with while in the Senate and called him after the 2015 Charleston church shooting, but he was a vocal critic of her tenure as secretary of State. During the closing weeks of the 2016 presidential race, he called for a special prosecutor to investigate the emails that she kept on a private server when she was secretary of State.

Graham has long combined a foreign policy hawkishness with sometimes surprising breaks with his party on domestic issues. After the Supreme Court legalized same-sex marriage nationwide, he said the party should accept the ruling and drop language calling for a constitutional amendment barring same-sex marriage nationwide from its platform. Graham was the only Judiciary Committee Republican to support President Barack Obama's choice of Sonia Sotomayor for the Supreme Court in 2009, saying the president deserved the prerogative to nominate a qualified person of his choice even if the GOP disagreed with her ideology. He took the same position a year later when Obama nominated Solicitor General Elena Kagan for the court. He praised her intellect and, he said, "She's funny, and that goes a long way in my book."

But his limits of understanding the other side were tested amid Trump's nomination of Brett Kavanaugh to the Supreme Court in 2018. After the initial confirmation hearing, allegations surfaced from psychology professor Christine Blasey Ford, who said Kavanaugh had sexually assaulted her while he was drunk at a high school party decades earlier. Kavanaugh denied the allegations, and a subsequent public hearing with both the nominee and accuser testifying was held. Republicans on the committee — all white men — had hired a female prosecutor to question Blasey Ford, cognizant of the optics. At first, most also ceded their time to the prosecutor when it was Kavanaugh's turn, but Graham was the first not to do so. He erupted in anger, accusing Senate Democrats of "the most unethical sham since I've been in politics. ... Boy, you guys want power. God, I hope you never get it." Seething, Graham pointed out he had been willing to cross the aisle and vote for Obama's nominees, but Democrats wouldn't consider doing so. "This is not a job interview. This is hell," the senator said. His indignation shocked many Democrats as he was attacking a woman who said she had been sexually assaulted, but Graham was undeterred. "I know I'm a single white man from South Carolina and I've been told to shut up, but I will not shut up," he said. His impassioned defense of Kavanaugh, who was eventually confirmed, won praise from the White House and Trump allies in conservative spheres who had once mocked the sometimes centrist senator.

But his aggressively confrontational stance was nothing new. He took similar tacks in several high-profile issues involving national security. He and McCain led a successful push to derail U.N. Ambassador Susan Rice's chances to become secretary of State after they sharply questioned her role in responding to the deadly September 2012 terrorist attack on the U.S. consulate in Benghazi, Libya. Graham told Fox News that Secretary of State Clinton "got away with murder" for not foreseeing the threat in Benghazi. The two senators were at the forefront of opposing the nomination of their former colleague Republican Chuck Hagel of Nebraska to become secretary of Defense because of what they considered his insufficient support for Israel and hawkishness on Iran, although Hagel was confirmed. And he warned in June 2014 that the "seeds of 9/11 are being planted all over Iraq and Syria" in calling for a more aggressive U.S. response in both nations.

Graham has taken a sharp turn to the right on fiscal and social policy. During the 2012 showdown over spending and taxes, he faulted Obama for not "manning up" and told Fox News his party needed to take a tough approach on the next vote to raise the federal debt limit. "We're not going to let Obama borrow any more money, or any American Congress borrow any more money, until we fix this country from becoming Greece," he said. Meanwhile, Graham took a hard line against new gun control measures including a ban on assault weapons. Graham stuck by his view that tighter gun control wasn't necessary even after the murders of nine black churchgoers by a white man in Charleston in June 2015, though he suggested he would support more enforcement of background check laws already on the books. Breaking with other Republican candidates, he said there's "no doubt" the murders were racially motivated but initially demurred when asked if he thought the Confederate flag should be removed from official use in the state, calling it "part of who we are." Later, he backed South Carolina Gov. Nikki Haley when she called for the removal of the Confederate flag from Statehouse grounds after the Charleston shooting.

In 2017, he and Republican Sen. Bill Cassidy of Louisiana proposed a plan to repeal and replace the Affordable Care Act, which would have turned Obamacare funding into state block grants. It was rejected by the White House. Graham later admitted he was far out of his policy comfort zone on health care.

Graham had worked in a bipartisan fashion on immigration, an issue with which he has long grappled. In 2006 and 2007, Graham supported the McCain-Kennedy and Kennedy-Kyl immigration bills, positions that got him in considerable trouble with conservatives who opposed giving undocumented immigrants a path toward citizenship. Radio talk show host Rush Limbaugh belittled him as "Lindsey Grahamnesty," and the Greenville County Republican Party voted to censure him. Graham's public comments suggesting that immigration bill opponents were "bigots" did not help his cause.

Undeterred, Graham joined a group of senators, four Democrats and four Republicans, that hammered out a plan in early 2013 to tighten border security, visa tracking and workplace verification in exchange for providing a path toward citizenship for the country's estimated 11 million undocumented workers. "I am confident, very confident, that if I help solve this problem in a way that we won't have 20 million illegal immigrants 20 years from now, not only will I get re-elected, I can look back and say I was involved in something that was important," he told McClatchy. The bill passed by a wide margin in the Senate, but House GOP leaders refused to take it up in the face of withering criticism from conservative talk radio. Graham later joined conservatives in calling for an end to birthright citizenship, a position that incensed his usual immigration allies. After the 2016 elections, he again turned more conciliatory when he said that legal protections should be given to undocumented immigrants who arrived in the United States as children. During the campaign, he criticized Trump for his hostility toward immigrants. "My party is in a hole with Hispanics. The first rule of politics when you're in a hole is stop digging. And somebody needs to take a shovel out of Donald Trump's hand."

But, as on other issues, once Graham allied with Trump, his rhetoric and policy positions on immigration began to change. He supported Trump's call to end birthright citizenship and took a much harder line on Muslim immigration and purported, but unproven, links to possible terrorism. Using words that seemed straight out of Trump's mouth, Graham said in November 2017 that the president "is right to make sure when somebody comes into the country from a place where radical

Islam [flourishes] ... we're going to ask extra hard questions." And he added that Trump was "right to slow down who comes into this country" and applauded him for recognizing "that we're in a religious war" — a stark shift from the Graham who in 2011 convened a hearing on "Protecting the Civil Rights of American Muslims" and said that "if I don't stand up for" religious freedom for Muslims, "you won't stand up for mine." Amid the 35-day government shutdown in late 2018 and early 2019 over funding for a southern border wall, the senator tried to broker a comprehensive reform push despite initially saying he was "glad [Trump] picked this fight" because capitulating would "probably [be] the end of his presidency." During negotiations, Graham said he'd "never been more depressed about moving forward than I am right now." When Trump declared a national emergency to obtain funding for the wall, Graham applauded.

Before his transformation, Graham had varied experiences in national politics. Comparing his political style to McCain's, Graham told The New York Times: "I've never been a Luke Skywalker; I'm a much more calculating guy than that. I understand that you just don't charge into these things based on some moral belief that you're right and the other guy's wrong." Without much of a threat to his own re-election bid, Graham in 2008 traveled the country with McCain, then then Republican presidential nominee. McCain, Graham, and Democratic Sen. Joe Lieberman of Connecticut formed a bipartisan triumvirate on the campaign trail, dubbed the Three Amigos. Graham's support helped McCain in the pivotal January 2008 South Carolina primary, in which McCain redeemed his 2000 loss by winning with 33 percent of the vote. "There's nobody I trust more than Lindsey Graham," McCain told the Myrtle Beach Sun News.

Graham lost one of his best friends when McCain died from brain cancer in August 2018. "The void to be filled by John's passing is more than I can fill. Don't look to me to replace this man," Graham said in a tearful speech from the Senate floor, next to McCain's desk that was draped in black. "There is a little John McCain in all of us, and the little John McCain practiced by a lot of people can make this a really great nation." But to others, McCain's death only magnified the evolution Graham had undergone, especially as remembrances of the late senator's patriotism and war career rolled in — which stood in stark contrast to Trump, who had belittled the former prisoner of war and said he wasn't a war hero. In his first TV interview after McCain's death — on Trump's favorite morning show, "Fox and Friends" — Graham defended the president and attacked the investigation into possible Russian collusion in the 2016 presidential election. "Plenty of corruption at the Department of Justice and the FBI. Should be stunning. Not one Democrat seems to care," Graham said. He told The Washington Post in October 2018 that, "I'm not living my life going forward around John McCain."

Graham had long mused about running for president. He launched his campaign in June 2015, with a heavy focus on national security. "I want to be president to protect our nation that we all love so much from all threats foreign and domestic," he said in his announcement speech. Graham began the campaign as a long-shot candidate, and he failed to rise above that status or gain much positive attention. With Trump taking an "America First" approach, Graham argued for a more aggressive national security strategy. Early in the campaign, he got under Trump's skin so much that the billionaire businessman called him a "light-weight" and urged supporters at his rallies to call Graham's cellphone. When Trump said that Graham's friend McCain was not a war hero because he had been captured and held prisoner in North Vietnam, Graham called Trump "a jackass." Graham ended his campaign in December 2015 after failing to break out of the second tier of presidential candidates.

After Trump's election victory, Graham joined Sen. Ben Cardin of Maryland, the senior Democrat on the Foreign Relations Committee, in voicing concern about Russian attempts to influence the election. They took the lead in the Senate in demanding that Trump retain economic sanctions on Russia. When Graham and McCain said that Trump's ban on citizens from seven majority-Muslim countries from entering the United States — one of his first actions as president — would "become a self-inflicted wound in the fight against terrorism," the new president tweeted that they were "sadly weak on immigration" and "always looking to start World War III."

However, his relationship with Trump began to evolve around the time that McCain was diagnosed with cancer. The two played golf together often and Trump frequently called Graham for advice. "I'm going to try to stay in a position where I can have input to the president," Graham told The New York Times in October 2017. "I can help him where I can, and he will call me up and pick my brain. Now, if you're a United States senator, that's a good place to find yourself." And, in the same interview, he admitted there was also an ulterior electoral motive: "He's very popular in my state. When I help him, it helps me back home." Earlier, in an April 2017 interview with Fox News, Graham said, "I am like the happiest dude in America right now. ... We have got a president and a national security team that I've been dreaming of for eight years." In February 2019,

Graham reminded The New York Times Magazine that McCain, too, had to reinvent himself as more conservative when he faced primary challenges in 2010. "If you don't want to get re-elected, you're in the wrong business. ... I have never been called this much by a president in my life." He lashed out at other Republicans who dared to criticize Trump, including his onetime immigration reform collaborator, Arizona Sen. Jeff Flake, who retired in 2018 rather than face a Trump-inspired primary challenge. Democrats bemoaned the disappearance of the Graham they once knew. "People have black armbands on around the Democratic Caucus because it feels like we've lost Lindsey Graham," Missouri Sen. Claire McCaskill told NPR in November 2018 after she lost her re-election bid. "He is someone who was willing to step outside that bubble from time to time and really do the hard work on issues like immigration. " Notably, in 2018, Graham campaigned against Senate Democrats for the first time, targeting those who had opposed Kavanaugh's nomination, reneging on his past practice to never campaign against colleagues.

Another notable shift was on his approach to the Russia investigation. Far from his partnership with Cardin in voicing concerns over that country's interference in the 2016 elections, Graham downplayed the need for a bill he had once co-authored to protect the man leading it, special counsel Mueller, because no one in their "right mind" would fire him. Graham had also once defended Jeff Sessions as attorney general, saying in 2017 there would be "holy hell to pay" if Trump fired him. But after Trump forced Sessions out in November 2018, Graham did an about face, defending Trump's move and saying that "every president deserves an attorney general they have confidence in and they can work with."

There have remained flashes of Graham's formerly "maverick" self, and some accounts have posited that Graham has simply sidled up to Trump to try to wield the most influence on defense issues, especially on a president with an often incoherent foreign policy and strong isolationist beliefs. In late 2018, he criticized Trump's decision to withdraw troops fighting ISIS from Syria, saying on the Senate floor that such a move would be "dishonorable" to allies in the region and "a stain on the honor of the United States." Graham also lamented Defense Secretary Jim Mattis' resignation over the announcement. He also broke with Trump after Washington Post columnist Jamal Khashoggi was murdered inside the Saudi consulate in Istanbul, arguing that Saudi Crown Prince Mohammed bin Salman must be held accountable even as Trump wanted to give him a pass because of their alliance and saying that the prince had said he didn't know about the murder. On Fox News, Graham said, "Nothing happens in Saudi Arabia without MBS knowing it."

Graham took the gavel of the Senate Judiciary Committee in 2019. He promised to "push for the appointment and Senate confirmation of highly qualified conservative judges to the federal bench and aggressive oversight of the Department of Justice and FBI." And he said he would reopen probes into Hillary Clinton, again one of Trump's top talking points. "We need a special counsel to look at all this," he told Fox News host Sean Hannity about Clinton's use of a private email server, "but I intend to look at it." Graham also planned a "deep dive" into FBI and Justice Department surveillance of Trump campaign advisers during the 2016 race. One of his earliest actions was to get William Barr confirmed as Trump's second attorney general. However, he also might use his role to push for comprehensive immigration reform, saying before he took the gavel that "on immigration, there's a deal to be had." Given Graham's recent conversion to Trump ally, Democrats who had once worked with him on the issue were skeptical.

Any threat of an intraparty battle for Graham in 2020 no longer seemed a real worry. While he had been booed frequently at county conventions, he began getting applause. Graham's move to the right has given Democrats renewed hope they might be able to mount a competitive challenge to his re-election. In February 2019, former South Carolina Democratic Party Chairman Jaime Harrison announced his campaign, with the backing of national Democrats. But South Carolina hasn't sent a Democrat to the Senate since 1998, and given that Trump won the state by 14 percentage points and plans to be on the ballot again, it's a longshot. And if he does survive that re-election, the more interesting question might be which version of Graham returns to the Senate.

Tim Scott (R)

Appointed 2013, term expires 2022, 1st full term, b. Sep 19, 1965; North Charleston; Presbyterian College (SC), Att., 1984; Charleston Southern University (SC), B.S., 1988; Evangelical; Single.

Elected Office: Charleston County Council, 1995-2008, Chairman, 2007-2008; SC House, 2009-2010; U.S. House, 2011-2013.

Professional Career: Partner, real estate firm; Owner, Tim Scott Allstate.

DC Office: 104 HSOB 20510, 202-224-6121, Fax: 202-228-5143, scott.senate.gov

State Offices: Columbia, 803-771-6112; Greenville, 864-233-5366; North Charleston, 843-727-4525.

Committees: *Aging. Banking, Housing & Urban Affairs:* Financial Institutions & Consumer Protection (Chmn); National Security & International Trade & Finance; Securities, Insurance & Investment. *Finance:* Energy, Natural Resources & Infrastructure (Chmn); Fiscal Responsibility & Economic Growth; Health Care; International Trade, Customs & Global Competitiveness. *Health, Education, Labor & Pensions:* Children & Families; Employment & Workplace Safety; Primary Health & Retirement Security. *Small Business & Entrepreneurship.*

Group Ratings

	ADA	ACLU	AFL-CIO	LCV	ITI	COC	HAFA	ACU	CFG	FRC
2018	-	5%	-	7%	-	80%	71%	86%	58%	100%
2017	0%	C	0%	0%	C	86%	C	84%	90%	100%

Almanac Ratings 2017-18

	Economy	Social	Foreign	Composite
Liberal	0%	0%	0%	0%
Conservative	100%	100%	100%	100%

Key Votes of the 115th Congress

1. Obama-care revision	Y	5. Gun regulations	Y
2. Tax Cuts	Y	6. Family planning regs	Y
3. Dodd-Frank revision	Y	7. Gorsuch confirmation	Y
4. Omnibus appropriations	Y	8. Immigration restrictions	Y

9. Kavanaugh confirmation	Y
10. Saudi arms sales	N
11. FISA rules	Y
12. Military aid in Yemen	N

Election Results

Election	Name (Party)	Vote (%)		Cand. Spent	Ind. Exp. Support	Ind. Exp. Oppose
2016 General	Tim Scott (R)	1,241,609	(61%)	$4,751,790	$161,399	
	Thomas Dixon (D)	757,022	(37%)	$35,176		
2016 Primary	Tim Scott (R)	Unopposed				

Prior winning percentages: 2014 special (61%); House: 2012 (62%), 2010 (66%)

Republican Tim Scott, South Carolina's junior senator, has had a remarkable ascent in local and state politics and has become a prominent national spokesman on topics from conservatism to police practices — and racism in the Trump era, setting himself often apart from his party. Scott was appointed to the Senate by Gov. Nikki Haley in January 2013 after GOP Sen. Jim DeMint resigned to lead the conservative Heritage Foundation think tank. Since then, as the first black GOP lawmaker to be elected statewide in the South and the Senate's first, and so far only, black Republican since 1979, Scott has easily won two elections. He previously served one term in the House. Scott has remained ambitious, seeking to influence the selection of the GOP presidential nominee in 2016.

In the cauldron of South Carolina Republican politics, Scott has shown that he should be taken seriously, and he could be a rising star within the GOP if he chooses — or if the party allows him to be, depending on its direction.

Scott and his siblings were raised by a single mother who worked 16-hour days as a nurse's assistant. Scott got his first job at 13. He was on the verge of flunking out of high school when he met the man who he has said changed his life: John Moniz, the owner of a Chick-fil-A next to the movie theater where Scott worked and where he would regularly buy French fries, the only food he could afford. Moniz, a Christian, became a father figure for Scott, teaching him the value of personal discipline and hard work. In a speech at the 2012 Republican National Convention, Scott said Moniz taught him that "having a job is a good thing, but creating jobs was even better." Scott finished high school and went on to earn a partial football scholarship to Presbyterian College in Clinton, S.C. He transferred to Charleston Southern University, where he earned a bachelor's degree in political science.

Scott went on to run an insurance company, own part of a real estate agency and win a seat on the Charleston County Council. Just after his first election, in 1995, he received a handwritten note of congratulations from Republican Sen. Strom Thurmond of South Carolina, who had run for president on a pro-segregation platform in 1948. Thurmond's past didn't stop Scott from accepting the job as statewide co-chairman of Thurmond's final senatorial campaign in 1996. Asked how an African-American could help Thurmond, Scott told The New York Times, "The Strom Thurmond I knew had nothing to do with that" and noted that Thurmond's views on race had evolved. He later served as chairman of the council and was elected to one term in the state House.

In 2010, Scott ran for an open House seat in the 1st District, which includes Charleston. In the GOP primary, he faced opposition from candidates with better name recognition, including Carroll Campbell III, son of former South Carolina Gov. Carroll Campbell Jr., and Paul Thurmond, the late senator's son. Scott got help from national Republican organizations and was the front-runner in the primary. He took 47 percent of the vote, which was just short of avoiding a runoff; Thurmond took second. There were few policy differences between the two, although Thurmond did not share Scott's willingness to abide by term limits and swear off earmarked spending. Scott claimed that in his 15 years in elected office, he never voted for a tax increase. His conservative credentials won him praise from prominent Republicans like former Alaska Gov. Sarah Palin and former House Speaker Newt Gingrich. In the runoff, Scott defeated Thurmond 68%-32%. In the general election, he easily beat Democrat Ben Frasier, a retired federal worker, 65%-29%. His race appeared to be a nonissue for the district's voters, about 70 percent of whom were white.

As a House member, Scott's voting record was marginally more moderate than those of the rest of South Carolina's deeply conservative delegation. He was less outspoken than the state's other members. He joined conservatives in refusing to support a 2011 bill to raise the federal debt limit, a 2012 tax and spending compromise to avert a "fiscal cliff" and several leadership-backed spending bills to keep the government running. Republican leaders didn't mind; they realized his value to their party and heaped praise on him. Scott served as a deputy whip and a freshman-class liaison to the leadership, and he was given a seat on the influential Rules Committee.

The decision by DeMint to quit the Senate after he suffered setbacks in the 2012 election with the defeat of some Tea Party candidates whom he had supported, which contributed to Republicans' failure to win Senate control, turned attention to whom Haley would appoint. Haley, who is Indian-American, chose Scott over four other finalists, a decision she said was based on his devotion to the state and his ability to advocate for it. "It is very important to me, as a minority female, that Congressman Scott earned this seat," she said. His selection proved extremely popular with Republicans.

At first, Scott mostly shunned the public spotlight, turning down several opportunities to raise his national profile and didn't seek to highlight his race. He concentrated on getting to know the state, holding numerous town halls and meeting constituents in creative circumstances, such as volunteering incognito at a local Goodwill store to talk about their problems without tipping them off that he was a politician. In 2014, he flew under the national radar without serious primary or general election opposition, winning 61 percent of the vote.

But when major race-related events shook South Carolina, Scott embraced his unique position. After a white policeman killed Walter Scott [no relation], an unarmed black man in Scott's hometown of North Charleston in April 2015, the senator was one of the first to support issuing body cameras to police officers and introduced a bill to provide millions of dollars for police departments to acquire them. Similar legislation became law in South Carolina in early June. Weeks later, when nine black churchgoers were murdered by a white supremacist in Charleston, Scott joined Haley and other South Carolina leaders to back a move to remove the Confederate flag from Statehouse grounds. During an emotional speech on the Senate floor, Scott choked up when repeating comments from a relative of a victim that "this evil attack would lead to reconciliation, restoration and unity in the nation." He later said on the Senate floor that he had been subject to racial discrimination at the Capitol. "I have felt the anger, frustration, sadness and humiliation that comes with feeling like you're being targeted for nothing more than being yourself," Scott said in a floor speech detailing how he'd been racially profiled throughout his life.

Once President Donald Trump was elected, Scott began separating himself from his party by opposing many of Trump's judicial and administration nominees, often raising comments about past statements or actions on race. In 2017, Senate Majority Leader Mitch McConnell was forced to withdraw Trump's nomination of Ryan Bounds to the Ninth Circuit Court of Appeals after Scott announced he would oppose Bounds — and persuaded Florida Sen. Marco Rubio to do so, too — after past racist writings surfaced. In late 2018, Scott also helped derail Thomas Farr's nomination to the District Court for the Eastern District of North Carolina after he was scrutinized for defending a controversial voter ID law and other possible suppression of black voters in North Carolina. Scott wrote in The Wall Street Journal about those votes, telling his party that "the solution isn't simply to decry 'racial attacks.' Instead, we should stop bringing candidates with questionable track records on race before the full Senate for a vote." However, Scott has not been complimentary of Democratic efforts to address race and has criticized Senate Minority Leader Chuck Schumer for opposing a South Carolina judicial nominee because he was white and would be replacing two black men that President Barack Obama had nominated. "Perhaps Senate Democrats should be more worried about the lack of diversity on their own staffs than attacking an extremely well-qualified judicial nominee from the great state of South Carolina," Scott tweeted.

Scott was deeply critical of Trump's response to violent protests by neo-Nazi groups in Charlottesville Virginia in August 2017. The president claimed there were "some very fine people on both sides" amid the clashes between white supremacists and counterprotesters. "What we want to see from our president is clarity and moral authority," Scott told VICE News. "And that moral authority is compromised when Tuesday happened. There's no question about that." Trump later reached out to Scott and the two met. Scott told CBS afterward that the president "was very clear that the perception that he received on his comments was not exactly what he intended with those comments." However, Trump repeated his earlier comments the next day.

There were areas where Scott worked with the Trump administration. As a member of the Senate Finance Committee, Scott successfully pushed in 2017 for his "Investing in Opportunity Act," which encouraged private capital investment in distressed communities via tax advantages. "I'm not talking about an imaginary or statistical single parent household. ... I'm talking about my momma and our income and her hard work and the loss of chances to do cool stuff because you don't have money to do it," Scott told USA Today. He also worked with Ivanka Trump to expand the child tax credit in the GOP's tax overhaul and praised her as someone who has "a strong, powerful backbone." And Scott successfully inserted a provision in the 2018 farm bill to allow the heirs of property owners to qualify for federal farm programs — something especially important to black farmers in the South.

Scott joined with New Jersey Democratic Sen. Cory Booker to introduce a bill for tax credits for businesses to create more apprenticeship programs. The idea received bipartisan praise. Scott, Booker and California Sen. Kamala Harris — the Senate's only three black members — introduced a bill to make lynching a federal hate crime; it passed unanimously in early 2019.

Scott was influential in passing the First Step Act in 2018, bipartisan criminal justice reform legislation that overhauled sentencing guidelines. He called Trump "the MVP" for helping get the bill across the finish line, but it was Scott and other lawmakers like Utah Sen. Mike Lee who persuaded undecided senators to support it. However, he was unsuccessful at getting his Walter Scott Act, named after the unarmed black man who was fatally shot by a white North Charleston policeman in 2015, included in the criminal justice reform overhaul. The Walter Scott Act would have forced states receiving federal law enforcement funding to keep track of certain data points for each officer-involved shooting.

In July 2016, Scott told the Senate that there was no single solution to law enforcement problems affecting racial minorities. "Believe it or not, the government is not the answer to what ails us," he said. He called for improved police training, increased personal interaction between law enforcement officers and community groups, and federal legislation to provide broader assistance — including expanded police use of body cameras. His critics pointed out that he received "F" ratings from the NAACP on its annual scorecards, supported voter ID laws many civil rights groups view as discriminatory against minorities, and refused to endorse a congressional fix to the Voting Rights Act after the Supreme Court struck down a key enforcement provision of the law. He also has been a loud advocate for school choice, a more controversial issue. Scott believes it can improve education for poor and minority children. "There is a trend that can be broken at its foundation if we focus first on education and second on work skills," he said on ABC's "This Week" in 2015.

Scott had an easy election in 2016. Perhaps the most notable aspect was that his 61 percent of the vote was 6 percentage points ahead of Trump's performance in the state on Election Day. The chief difference in their performances was that Scott took 56 percent of the vote in his home county of Charleston, where Trump ran behind to Hillary Clinton and took 43 percent.

With Rep. Trey Gowdy's encouragement, local Republicans discussed the possibility that Scott and Gowdy would together campaign for governor in 2018, when Haley was term-limited. But that possibility dimmed when Trump appointed Haley as ambassador to the United Nations and Lt. Gov. Henry McMaster became governor and later won a full term. Gowdy, Scott's best friend in Congress, retired in 2018 and said that he did not want to seek office again. But Scott appeared to have plenty of interest in remaining in his seat — and possibly seeking higher office. The two published a book together in 2017 titled "Unified: How Our Unlikely Friendship Gives Us Hope for a Divided Country" about their close bond that transcended their backgrounds and racial lines. "The truth is that after the 2015 Mother Emanuel Church shooting, I found myself turning to a white guy in the aftermath," Scott told CBS News during their book tour. "It became clear to me that there is a chance to bridge real gaps in this country. ... Are there lessons within this friendship that can help our nation that seems to be so polarized?"

Gowdy heaped praise on Scott, saying, "I would love Tim Scott to run for president, whether it's 2024 — whenever it fits his heart."

Joe Cunningham (D)

Elected 2018, 1st term, b. May 26, 1982; Kuttawa, KY; College of Charleston, Att., 2002; Florida Atlantic University, B.S., 2005; Northern Kentucky University, J.D., 2014; Christian Church; Married (Amanda Cunningham); 1 child.

Professional Career: Ocean Engineer, Turrell, Hall & Associates, 2005-2010; Law Clerk, Boone County Commonwealth Attorney's Office, 2012-2014.

DC Office: 423 CHOB 20515, 202-225-3176, cunningham.house.gov

State Offices: Beaufort, 843-521-2530; Mount Pleasant, 843-352-7572.

Committees: *Natural Resources*: Energy & Mineral Resources; Water, Oceans & Wildlife. *Veterans' Affairs*: Economic Opportunity; Technology Modernization.

Election Results

Election	Name (Party)	Vote (%)		Cand. Spent	Ind. Exp. Support	Ind. Exp. Oppose
2018 General	Joe Cunningham (D)...................... 145,455	(51%)		$2,374,593	$418,141	$242,894
	Katie Arrington (R)......................... 141,473	(49%)		$1,574,191		
2018 Primary	Joe Cunningham (D)...................... 23,493	(72%)				
	Toby Smith (D)............................... 9,366	(29%)				

Democrat Joe Cunningham was elected in 2018 in the second surprising result of the year for local Republicans. In a coastal district that had not elected a Democrat since 1980, he struck a chord with his opposition to off-shore drilling, which had become a controversial local issue. He drew a contrast with the GOP nominee, Katie Arrington, who had pulled off one of the biggest upsets of the 2018 campaign when she defeated veteran Rep. Mark Sanford in the Republican primary.

Arrington, a relative newcomer, was too conservative for many voters in the Charleston area. Cunningham benefited from the lingering animosity between Sanford and Arrington, who had received support in the primary from President Donald Trump.

Cunningham, a native of Kentucky, graduated from Florida Atlantic University with a degree in ocean engineering and worked with environmental groups. He got his law degree from the Chase College of Law at Northern Kentucky University, then returned to South Carolina, where he had started his undergraduate years. His experiences as an ocean engineer and an attorney led him to the view that "it took teams working together and listening to one another" to solve complex problems, he said when he launched his campaign. Cunningham won the Democratic nomination with nominal opposition.

The Republican primary played a vital role in the election. Arrington, an expert on cybersecurity who ran her own contracting company, was a fresh face in local politics. She benefited from voter fatigue with Sanford, the disgraced former governor who returned to the House in 2013 after his personal life had become a national punch line.

Running as a political outsider and Trump ally in her campaign against Sanford, Arrington exploited the questions that he raised during the 2016 presidential campaign about Trump's business practices, plus Sanford's criticism of Trump's policies in the White House. "We have to support our president's agenda," she told The Washington Post prior to the primary.

Sanford was slow to defend his own record and Arrington outspent him in the primary. Sanford spent about $500,000 in the contest, although he had $1.5 million remaining in his campaign account. With support from a Trump tweet that was critical of Sanford a few hours before the voting ended, Arrington won, 51%-47%.

Running against Arrington, Cunningham spotlighted his opposition to the Trump administration's plan to open parts of the Atlantic Ocean to off-shore drilling. Although she voiced questions about the drilling later in the campaign, Arrington initially supported Trump's actions during a debate with Sanford. "It was the focal point of the whole campaign," said the state leader of the Sierra Club.

Sanford, who opposed the nearby oil exploration and was neutral in the general election, told The Island Packet newspaper that Cunningham's victory was a reaction to Trump's leadership style and that the public focus on off-shore drilling was a "proxy issue" for the quality of life. Sanford added that Cunningham's friendly social-media style contrasted to Arrington's "hyper-partisan" approach. With his first election bid in this Republican-leaning district, Cunningham deftly distanced himself from leaders of both parties.

Cunningham won, 51%-49%. Arrington won four of the five counties in the district. But Cunningham took 57 percent in Charleston County, which cast nearly half the total vote. His victory shocked members of both parties. "We lost because Mark Sanford could not understand this was about the conservative movement and not him," Arrington told Election Night supporters.

The interest of Arrington and Sanford, among other Republicans, in seeking the nomination in 2020 raised the prospect of another GOP bloodbath.

SC-1: Lowcountry   Cook Partisan Voting Index: R+10

Population		Race and Ethnicity		Income	
Total	748,066	White	70.6%	Median Income	$64,118
Land area (sq. miles)	1,548	Black	18.6%	District Income Rank	144
Pop/ sq mi	483.3	Latino	6.4%	Poverty Rate	10.8%
Born in State	43.2%	Asian	1.8%	With health insurance	89.1%
		Two or more races	2.2%	Cash public assistance	1%
Age Groups		Other	0.4%	Food stamp/SNAP	7.4%
Under 18	21.9%				
18-34	23.2%	**Education**		**Work**	
35-64	38.2%	H.S grad or less	30%	White Collar	16.7%
Over 64	16.7%	Some college	31%	Sales and Service	41.9%
		College Degree, 4 yr	24.4%	Blue Collar	17.9%
Military		Post grad	14.5%	Government	16.4%
Veteran/ Active Duty	14%				

2012 Pres. Vote	Romney	174,391	(58%)	Obama	119,833	(40%)		
2016 Pres. Vote	Trump	178,181	(54%)	Clinton	134,541	(40%)	Johnson	12,450	(4%)

Charleston, Hilton Head: Looking out across the harbor to Fort Sumter are the glorious mansions of the Battery, gazing on the same view that the hot-blooded young swells of Charleston did in April 1861, when they fired the shots that began the Civil War. Today, there are few more beautiful urban scenes in America than the pastel "single houses" of Charleston, built flush with the sidewalk, turning their shoulders to the streets, with open piazzas inside their iron gateways facing south to catch the breeze. Founded in 1670, Charleston was blessed with one of the finest harbors on the Atlantic, at the point where, Charlestonians like to say, the Ashley and Cooper rivers meet to form the Atlantic Ocean. Cargoes of rice, indigo, cotton and slaves crossed its docks, enriching the white planters and merchants who dominated the state's economic and political life. After the war, Charleston became an economic backwater, enabling the old buildings to survive. The loving restorations of recent years have made the center city look better than ever and have attracted a considerable tourist trade.

Charleston's old society — descended from planters from Barbados, French Huguenots, Sephardic Jews and the second sons of English gentry — was once a leading force in American political life. The hotheads in the gallery disrupted the 1860 Democratic National Convention here so boisterously that it adjourned and reconvened in Baltimore, while Southern Democrats split off and nominated their own candidate, enabling Abraham Lincoln to win with 38 percent of the popular vote. The history of black South Carolinians, memorialized in George Gershwin's Porgy and Bess, is noteworthy, but the tale of slavery, once hidden under a blanket of politeness, was slow to emerge. Many plantations near Charleston have added programs on the history of slavery to tours once dominated by romantic tales of the old South. The decision by Gov. Nikki Haley to remove the Confederate flag from the state capitol grounds following the racially motivated 2015 shootings that killed nine worshippers at Mother Emanuel AME Church in downtown Charleston -- accelerated that rethinking. In 2018, the Charleston City Council formally apologized for its role in slavery, the slave trade and Jim Crow. The Old Slave Mart Museum, the onetime site of slave auctions, has opened, detailing the city's history along with displaying African-American arts and crafts, and the city is building a $100 million, 40,000-square-foot International African American Museum where slave ships once docked; 100,000 slaves took their first steps in America here, and historians estimate that 90 percent of African Americans can trace at least one ancestor to that spot.

Charleston remains one of the top tourist destinations in the world -- ranked for five years straight by Travel + Leisure magazine as the best city in the U.S. to visit -- but inequality persists. An analysis from the College of Charleston found that around 60 percent of downtown Charleston's restaurant and hotel workers live outside the peninsula. Tour guides take visitors around in horse-drawn carriages along the cobblestone streets. Those guides had been required to pass a test from a roughly 500-page manual about the city's history and architecture to get a license, but in 2018 a federal judge struck down that requirement, saying it violated free speech rights.

The 1st Congressional District of South Carolina stretches along the coast from Charleston down to Hilton Head. It includes the coastal parts of Beaufort County, taking in the old county seat of Beaufort and the carefully manicured developments of Hilton Head Island, plus parts of burgeoning inland suburbs in Berkeley and Dorchester counties. It includes the heavily white Battery and the area west of the Ashley River, but not the African-American areas to the north in downtown Charleston. About 40 percent of the population of the 1st is in Charleston, another 40 percent in the inland counties, and 20 percent in Beaufort. The old mansions in Beaufort provided the backdrop for novelist Pat Conroy, who also wrote of Charleston's tony "South of Broad" aristocratic world. Meanwhile, the posh condominium developments and golfing resorts around Hilton Head help drive up Beaufort County's population, which increased 13 percent between 2010 and 2016. On nearby St. Helena Island, slave owners escaping the heat and the mosquitoes ran largely absentee operations, thus allowing Gullah culture — a fusion of English and African elements — to thrive, which lingers in the Lowcountry today. The district takes in the Marine Corps' Parris Island training base and an air station at Beaufort.

This is comfortable Republican country, but the conservatism of the Lowcountry — the term for South Carolina's coastal counties, including Charleston — is more economic and less cultural than the conservatism of the Upstate region. Many voters here oppose offshore drilling, favor environmental restrictions -- the city voted to ban plastic bags, straws and foam containers by 2020 -- and efforts to curb sprawl. The area has moderated as more northern retirees also settle here. Donald Trump won the 1st, 53%-40%, his lowest performance in the state's six Republican districts.

Joe Wilson (R)

Elected 2001, 9th full term, b. Jul 31, 1947; Charleston; Washington and Lee University (VA), B.A., 1969; University of South Carolina, J.D., 1972; Presbyterian; Married (Roxanne Dusenbury McCrory Wilson); 4 children; 7 grandchildren.

Military Career: U.S. Army Reserve 1972-1975; South Carolina Army National Guard 1975-2003

Elected Office: SC Senate, 1985-2001.

Professional Career: Practicing attorney, 1972-2001.

DC Office: 1436 LHOB 20515, 202-225-2452, Fax: 202-225-2455, joewilson.house.gov

State Offices: Aiken, 803-642-6416; West Columbia, 803-939-0041.

Committees: *Armed Services*: Readiness; Strategic Forces. *Foreign Affairs*: Europe, Eurasia, Energy & the Environment; Middle East, North Africa & International Terrorism (RMM).

Group Ratings

	ADA	ACLU	AFL-CIO	LCV	ITI	COC	HAFA	ACU	CFG	FRC
2018	-	4%	-	3%	-	92%	63%	76%	50%	100%
2017	0%	C	8%	0%	C	93%	C	89%	78%	100%

Almanac Ratings 2017-18

	Economy	Social	Foreign	Composite
Liberal	3%	0%	0%	1%
Conservative	97%	100%	100%	99%

Key Votes of the 115th Congress

1. Obama-care revision	Y	5. Family planning regs	Y
2. Tax Cuts	Y	6. Body cameras/immigration	N
3. Omnibus appropriations	Y	7. Abortion ban	Y
4. Dodd-Frank revision	Y	8. Concealed carry	Y

9. Guantanamo prisoners	N
10. Ground missiles, limit	N
11. Defense Dept. spending	Y
12. FISA rules	Y

Election Results

Election	Name (Party)	Vote (%)		Cand. Spent	Ind. Exp. Support	Ind. Exp. Oppose
2018 General	Joe Wilson (R)	144,642	(56%)	$1,341,997		
	Sean Carrigan (D)	109,199	(43%)	$159,159		
2018 Primary	Joe Wilson (R)		(100%)			

Prior winning percentages: 2016 (60%), 2014 (62%), 2012 (96%), 2010 (54%), 2008 (54%), 2006 (63%), 2004 (65%), 2002 (84%), 2001 special (73%)

Republican Joe Wilson, elected in 2001, has a reputation in his committee work roles as a hard-working fiscal and defense hawk. With his seniority, he has been a mentor to many junior Republicans. Still, he remains known as the lawmaker who breached congressional decorum in 2009 by shouting, "You lie!" during President Barack Obama's health care address to Congress.

Wilson grew up in Charleston and graduated from Washington & Lee University and the University of South Carolina law school. He got his Republican stripes as an aide to Rep. Floyd Spence and then for Sen. Strom Thurmond. Wilson was deputy general counsel at the Energy Department during the Reagan administration. He practiced law in West Columbia for 25 years while working on several political campaigns. In 1984, he was elected to the state Senate, where he chaired the Transportation Committee. Throughout this period, he served as a staff judge advocate in the South Carolina Army National Guard. All four of Wilson's sons have been Eagle Scouts and served in the military, two of them in Iraq. His son, Alan, was reelected state attorney general in 2018.

In 2001, when Spence died after more than 30 years in the House, Wilson became the frontrunner to replace his longtime friend and mentor. In the special election, he won the Republican primary with 76 percent of the vote and defeated his Democratic opponent easily.

With a seat on the Armed Services Committee, he has concentrated on military issues. In the fiscal 2013 defense authorization bill, he kept alive some of the Air Force's Global Hawk unmanned surveillance planes after the Pentagon had sought to retire them. At a 2013 hearing, Wilson rebuked outgoing Secretary of State Hillary Clinton for not going on Sunday talk shows to discuss the terrorist attack in Benghazi Libya, saying one of her priorities should have been "telling correct information" to the public. Wilson criticized Obama for "holding our military hostage" with the across-the-board defense cut "sequester" that took effect that year after the president and Congress failed to reach a comprehensive spending deal.

Wilson has advocated a closer military relationship with India, and he traveled frequently to Iraq and Afghanistan to review those conflicts when U.S. forces were engaged. He urged President Donald Trump to loosen restrictions on the U.S. military fighting the Taliban rebels in Afghanistan. In 2017-18, Wilson chaired the Readiness Subcommittee, to provide the resources for the military to respond to what he described as an "unprecedented readiness crisis."

Wilson was unknown outside of his district, and barely known in Washington, before his outburst during Obama's September 2009 speech at the Capitol. As Obama was answering what he called critics' "bogus claims" about his health care legislation, Wilson called out, "You lie!" His behavior provoked stinging criticism on editorial pages and talk shows around the country. He apologized to Obama in a phone call but rebuffed Democratic demands for a more public apology from the well of the House. His South Carolina Democratic colleague, Majority Whip James Clyburn, alleged there was a taint of racism in Wilson's reaction, noting that no other president in memory had been the target of a similar breach in protocol during a joint session. The House passed a "resolution of disapproval" on a mostly party-line vote. The incident continued to follow Wilson, and during a contentious town hall in 2017 amid the ultimately unsuccessful repeal of Obamacare, a crowd taunted him with "You lie!" chants.

Wilson typically has joined most other South Carolina Republicans in opposing trade promotion authority for presidents. In 2011, he refused to support a trade deal with South Korea, which competed against his state's textile industry. Ironically, despite their antipathy for Obama, Wilson and three other House Republicans from South Carolina voted in 2015 to give him trade promotion authority for the Trans-Pacific Partnership. After a Department of Energy decision imperiled the Mixed Oxide Fuel Fabrication Facility project at the Savannah River Site, Wilson and others in the South Carolina delegation met with Trump to lobby for reversal of the decision.

On the Education and the Workforce Committee, Wilson worked with Democrats to make permanent the child adoption tax credit. He failed to get the top Republican slot on the committee when it came open in 2009. Although he had more seniority, he lost out to John Kline of Minnesota. After Kline stepped down in 2016, Wilson supported Rep. Virginia Foxx of North Carolina as the next chairman. In 2019, he vied for the ranking Republican slot on the House Foreign Affairs Committee after working vigorously to help vulnerable Republicans in the 2018 cycle to boost his chances, doling out $1.8 million to more than 100 candidates and incumbents. Even though Wilson had more seniority and had made a case that his working relationship with the new chairman, Eliot Engel of New York, would be an asset, he lost out to Rep. Michael McCaul of Texas.

Wilson has typically been reelected by wide margins. In 2018, he had his closest reelection challenge since 2010, besting Army veteran Sean Carrigan 56%-43%. Carrigan attacked him for his support for Trump and for not taking Russian interference in U.S. elections seriously enough. Wilson's victory was more comfortable than that of many Republicans across the country, but a constant reminder that Democrats will continue to use that "you lie" outburst against him. In another faux pas in 2018, Wilson was among the politicians tricked by comedian Sacha Baron Cohen for his HBO show "Who Is America?" The actor had posed as an Israeli anti-terror expert and duped Wilson into appearing to support arming kindergarteners.

SC-2: West-Central South Carolina

Cook Partisan Voting Index: R+12

Population		Race and Ethnicity		Income	
Total	697,001	White	66.7%	Median Income	$57,042
Land area (sq. miles)	3,022	Black	23.2%	District Income Rank	204
Pop/ sq mi	230.6	Latino	5.5%	Poverty Rate	13.3%
Born in State	53.1%	Asian	1.9%	With health insurance	89.6%
		Two or more races	2.2%	Cash public assistance	1.3%
Age Groups		Other	0.5%	Food stamp/SNAP	12.2%
Under 18	23.1%				
18-34	22.7%	**Education**		**Work**	
35-64	39.6%	H.S grad or less	36.9%	White Collar	14.6%
Over 64	14.6%	Some college	29.8%	Sales and Service	40.7%
		College Degree, 4 yr	20.9%	Blue Collar	20.8%
Military		Post grad	12.4%	Government	19%
Veteran/ Active Duty	12.4%				

2012 Pres. Vote	Romney	171,829	(62%)	Obama	101,354	(37%)			
2016 Pres. Vote	Trump	176,615	(57%)	Clinton	119,812	(38%)	Johnson	8,289	(3%)

Parts of Columbia Metro, Aiken: In 1786, soon after the Revolutionary War, the South Carolina legislature decided to move the state capital away from the Charleston aristocracy and into the interior, away from a city named after a king to a new city named after a discoverer of America. So began Columbia. The State House was built on high ground above the Congaree River in a town of one-and-a-half story houses with first-floor porticos, dormers and raised brick basements — "Columbia cottages." In 1865, Gen. William Tecumseh Sherman's army burned almost everything here but the State House — something remembered by a local Presbyterian minister's eight-year-old son, whose name was Thomas Woodrow Wilson. Columbia recovered but grew slowly, with the state government, the state university, the Army's Fort Jackson, and local insurance companies providing steady employment.

Columbia's politics were personified by Jimmy Byrnes, the Democrat who was elected to Congress in 1910 and returned from top posts in the administrations of Franklin D. Roosevelt and Harry Truman to serve as governor. Byrnes adamantly opposed the Brown v. Board of Education decision in 1954. Since then, upwardly mobile white South Carolinians have turned Republican. Metro Columbia is competitive: Richland County, which is 47 percent African-American, votes Democratic and gave 64 percent of the vote to Hillary Clinton in 2016. Across the river, Lexington County is 15 percent black and heavily Republican and gave 66 percent to Donald Trump.

The 2nd Congressional District of South Carolina includes parts of metro Columbia, excluding black neighborhoods in central and north Columbia that are in the black-majority 6th District. It contains the city's affluent white neighborhoods and the spread-out towns and countryside beyond. It includes all of Lexington and Aiken counties. Aiken, with its horsey trappings for polo and steeplechase, has long attracted affluent transplants. About 40 percent of the vote is in Lexington, and 30 percent is in Richland. The Midlands area overall has been rapidly growing, and in 2017 the financial website SmartAsset found that Columbia gained the second most millennials in the country, behind only Seattle. The Columbia metro area's population, including both Richland and Lexington counties, is projected to double by 2050. Fort Jackson in Columbia trains 70,000 Army soldiers each year, most of them basic trainees. Aiken County, which runs along the Georgia border, has grown in recent years thanks to employers such as Bridgestone Tires, Kimberly-Clark Corp., Shaw Industries carpet and flooring and UPS. At a plant in Lexington, Michelin manufactures radial and earthmover tires.

The district takes in Barnwell County and the Savannah River Site near Aiken, which from 1954 to 1991 was one of the nation's nuclear weapons manufacturing complexes. Since then, the 310 square miles have been undergoing a multibillion-dollar cleanup, an important economic driver regionally. The state has pursued extensive litigation with the federal government over the project. In February 2017, a federal judge dismissed part of the lawsuit seeking compensation for the delay, but continued to review the pace of the cleanup. In May 2018, the Department of Energy announced it would shutter the Mixed Oxide (MOX) Fuel Fabrication Facility at the site, threatening thousands of jobs as the nuclear material was moved to New Mexico. By October, an appeals court had backed the move and the shutdown looked likely.

The district is comfortably Republican, though the vote for Donald Trump in 2016 dropped to 57 percent.

Jeff Duncan (R)

Elected 2010, 5th term, b. Jan 07, 1966; Greenville; Clemson University (SC), B.A., 1988; Baptist; Married (Melody Duncan); 3 children.

Elected Office: SC House, 2002-2010.

Professional Career: Assistant Vice President., M.S. Bailey & Son, 1989-1993; Assistant Vice President., Palmetto Bank, 1993-1995; President, J. Duncan & Assocs., 1995-2010.

DC Office: 2229 RHOB 20515, 202-225-5301, Fax: 202-225-3216, jeffduncan.house.gov

State Offices: Anderson, 864-224-7401; Clinton, 864-681-1028.

Committees: *Energy & Commerce*: Energy; Environment & Climate Change; Oversight & Investigations.

Group Ratings

	ADA	ACLU	AFL-CIO	LCV	ITI	COC	HAFA	ACU	CFG	FRC
2018	-	19%	-	0%	-	70%	98%	100%	96%	100%
2017	0%	C	3%	0%	C	92%	C	93%	91%	100%

Almanac Ratings 2017-18

	Economy	Social	Foreign	Composite
Liberal	2%	5%	3%	4%
Conservative	98%	95%	97%	96%

Key Votes of the 115th Congress

1. Obama-care revision	Y	5. Family planning regs	Y	9. Guantanamo prisoners	N
2. Tax Cuts	Y	6. Body cameras/immigration	N	10. Ground missiles, limit	N
3. Omnibus appropriations	N	7. Abortion ban	Y	11. Defense Dept. spending	Y
4. Dodd-Frank revision	Y	8. Concealed carry	Y	12. FISA rules	N

Election Results

Election	Name (Party)	Vote (%)		Cand. Spent	Ind. Exp. Support	Ind. Exp. Oppose
2018 General	Jeff Duncan (R)	153,338	(68%)	$539,808		
	Mary Geren (D)	70,046	(31%)	$296,180		
2018 Primary	Jeff Duncan (R)		(100%)			

Prior winning percentages: 2016 (73%), 2014 (71%), 2012 (67%), 2010 (66%)

Republican Jeff Duncan, elected in 2010 to an open seat, has often gone his own way from GOP leadership. His deeply held conservative beliefs can prompt fierce rhetoric, which angers Democrats but plays well among his like-minded colleagues and at home.

Duncan was born in Greenville. His family moved frequently, mostly in the Carolinas, as they followed his father's job as a textile industry manager tasked with turning around underperforming plants. He got his bachelor's at Clemson University, where he was a wide receiver on the football team and majored in political science. After college, he worked as a community banker and then for a real estate auction company, which inspired him to start his own real estate marketing firm that specialized in auctions. In the state House, he worked on updating the funding formula for education and on lowering taxes. In 2009, Duncan sponsored a bill creating an alternative state budget that did not use federal stimulus money, as a way of protesting President Barack Obama's $787 billion measure.

In the six-candidate GOP primary for the House seat, Duncan was endorsed by the anti-tax group Club for Growth, built a 2-to-1 fundraising advantage and prevailed in a runoff with 51 percent of the vote against businessman Richard Cash. In the general, he faced token Democratic opposition in the solidly Republican district. He has widened his victory margin in each of his four reelections.

Duncan believes in the "Jeffersonian principles of limited governments, free markets and individual liberties," and says the federal government has gone beyond its constitutional authority. In 2011, he became the first member of Congress to receive a perfect score from the conservative activist group Heritage Action. A member of the Tea Party Caucus, Duncan has been part of the cadre of conservatives who have voted against GOP leadership priorities. In January 2015, he voted against giving John Boehner another term as Speaker. Soon after that, he quit as a member of the Republican whip team and was among the GOP rebels who helped to create the Freedom Caucus. Duncan is also a steadfast supporter of gun rights, and in 2017 sponsored the Hearing Protection Act to legalize silencers; the congressman suffered damage in his left ear during his youth as a result of not using proper noise suppressors when he was hunting with his dad.

Duncan was an active member of the Foreign Affairs Committee. In 2012, he enacted a bill that called for a strategy to address the Iranian threat in the Western Hemisphere. At a hearing in 2013 on the terrorist attack in Benghazi Libya, he rebuked outgoing Secretary of State Hillary Clinton for "gross negligence" in allowing the consulate there to "become a death trap." As chairman of the Subcommittee on the Western Hemisphere, Duncan was outspoken in his opposition to President Barack Obama's opening of diplomacy to Cuba. He filed a bill calling for immediate and mandatory deportation of any non-citizen or permanent resident who has been entered into the terrorist screening database.

On the Energy and Commerce Committee, which he joined in 2017, he supported the Mixed Oxide Fuel Fabrication Facility (MOX) at the Savannah River Site, which was opposed by Trump's Energy Department. Calling it "part of God's "intelligent design," Duncan supported offshore drilling, telling a group at Lander University that "God gave us the ability to discover there are resources known as fossil fuels inside the Earth that we can extract." Duncan used his committee post to grill Facebook CEO Mark Zuckerberg during his April 2018 appearance before the committee, arguing that the social media site has censored conservative and Christian content unfairly. Duncan gave Zuckerberg at pocket copy of the U.S. Constitution, asking him, "This is maybe a rhetorical question, but why not have a community standard for free speech and freedom of religion that is simply a mirror of the First Amendment with algorithms that have a viewpoint that is neutral? Why not do that?"

During the presidential campaign, Duncan criticized as "horrendous and indefensible" comments about women by Donald Trump. Then, he added, "I continue to be more concerned with Hillary Clinton's actions than I am with Donald Trump's words." He became a steadfast supporter of Trump's policies as president, though he said in a speech back in South Carolina that "I'm proud of this president. Now, I'm not proud about what he says or how he says it, and maybe not proud of what he's done in the past. But from the time he was sworn into office until now, he has kept his eye on the Americans." He backed Trump's initial plans to withdraw troops from Syria and called for the impeachment of deputy attorney general Rod Rosenstein, who Trump had frequently criticized over special counsel Robert Mueller's investigation.

Duncan had been interested in running for governor in 2018, when there was the prospect of an open seat. That option faded in January 2017 when Henry McMaster succeeded Nikki Haley after she became ambassador to the United Nations. He might look to move up if there is an open Senate seat or for the next gubernatorial vacancy.

SC-3: Northwestern South Carolina   **Cook Partisan Voting Index: R+19**

Population		Race and Ethnicity		Income	
Total	677,940	White	74.1%	Median Income	$44,345
Land area (sq. miles)	5,268	Black	18.4%	District Income Rank	384
Pop/ sq mi	128.7	Latino	4.7%	Poverty Rate	17.9%
Born in State	65.7%	Asian	0.9%	With health insurance	88.1%
		Two or more races	1.7%	Cash public assistance	1.3%
Age Groups		Other	0.3%	Food stamp/SNAP	14.5%
Under 18	21.8%				
18-34	22%	**Education**		**Work**	
35-64	38.7%	H.S grad or less	48.7%	White Collar	17.5%
Over 64	17.5%	Some college	30.3%	Sales and Service	40%
		College Degree, 4 yr	13.3%	Blue Collar	29.4%
Military		Post grad	7.8%	Government	14%
Veteran/ Active Duty	9.1%				

2012 Pres. Vote	Romney	170,084	(65%)	Obama	89,439	(34%)			
2016 Pres. Vote	Trump	190,605	(67%)	Clinton	82,618	(29%)	Johnson	5,616	(2%)

Anderson, Greenville Suburbs: The Upstate in South Carolina was once many days' travel by wagon from the Lowcountry plantations along the coast. It was first settled by Scots-Irish farmers, including the family of future Vice President John C. Calhoun, around the time of the Revolutionary War. The pioneers wanted to make big plantations of these forests, but the land was too hilly for the labor-intensive rice crops grown in the Lowcountry and sometimes too cold for cotton. So, relatively few slaves were brought here and the land became mostly small farms. Today, the racial and cultural tone of the Upstate shows traces of these roots. Clemson University was founded here by Calhoun's son-in-law and is one of the state's two land-grant institutions. (South Carolina State, a historically black university in Orangeburg, is the other.) This is a mostly white part of the South, with a hell-of-a-fella tone to daily life and a tradition-minded slice of Middle America.

Yet it is not untouched by change. The textile factories and mills have been shutting down, and a way of life in many of these rural areas has vanished with them. In 2018, one of the area's oldest textile plants, Alice Manufacturing Co., closed its doors in Easley after 50 years, resulting in 175 jobs lost. On the positive side, high-tech and automobile manufacturers have expanded, with growth throughout the Upstate. In 2018, Michelin -- which has its North American headquarters in nearby Greenville -- reopened a dormant jumbo tire plant in Anderson County. Overall, Anderson has seen the third highest job growth in the state over the past decade, with 21 new companies and 38 that planned to expand. The county is now home to manufacturing centers such as Electrolux appliances, First Quality tissue products and Glen Raven fabrics. Bosch, the second-largest plant in Anderson, announced a $45 million expansion in 2018, and there's a growing presence and influence of German companies in the Upstate. In 2016, Clemson became part of a $300 million program, including support from the Defense Department, to expand textile manufacturing and technology. The football team's national championship victories in 2017 and 2019 were feel-good moments for the university and the state, with a boost in fundraising and applications for admission.

The 3rd Congressional District of South Carolina follows the Georgia border from Augusta through the tree-harvesting country around McCormick County to Appalachian foothills along the North Carolina border. The 18 percent black population is the smallest of any district in the state. The southern part of the 3rd has a few heavily African-American areas, including Edgefield County, where Sen. Strom Thurmond first won public office in the 1930s. Anderson is the largest county in the district, with nearly 30 percent of the voters.

This part of South Carolina, ancestrally Democratic, began trending Republican in the 1950s as cultural issues became more important in this fervently religious region. Donald Trump won 67 percent of the vote here in 2016, his best showing in a South Carolina district.

William Timmons (R)

Elected 2018, 1st term, b. Apr 30, 1984; Greenville; Christ Church Episcopal School (SC); George Washington University (DC), B.A., 2006; University of South Carolina, Mast. Deg., 2009; University of South Carolina, J.D., 2010; Church of Christ; Single.

Elected Office: SC Senate, 2016-2018.

Professional Career: Staff Assistant, Sen. Bill Frist, 2006-2007; Prosecutor, SC 13th Circuit Solicitor's Office.

DC Office: 313 CHOB 20515, 202-225-6030, timmons.house.gov

State Offices: Greenville, 864-241-0175; Spartanburg, 864-583-3264.

Committees: *Budget. Education & Labor*: Early Childhood, Elementary & Secondary Education; Higher Education & Workforce Investment. *Select Committee on the Modernization of Congress.*

Election Results

Election	Name (Party)	Vote (%)		Cand. Spent	Ind. Exp. Support	Ind. Exp. Oppose
2018 General	William Timmons (R)	145,321	(60%)	$1,250,443	$174,546	$468,227
	Brandon Brown (D)	89,182	(37%)	$66,515		
	Guy Furay (A)	9,203	(4%)	$68,922		
2018 Primary	William Timmons (R)	37,096	(54%)			
Runoff	Lee Bright (R)	31,236	(46%)			
2018 Primary	Lee Bright (R)	16,742	(25%)			
	William Timmons (R)	12,885	(19%)			
	Dan Hamilton (R)	12,494	(19%)			
	Josh Kimbrell (R)	7,465	(11%)			
	James Epley (R)	5,386	(8%)			
	Stephen Brown (R)	5,078	(8%)			

First-term Republican William Timmons was elected as the more mainstream candidate in a hard-fought primary. He narrowly won the GOP runoff against Lee Bright, an outspoken conservative who generated controversy as a state legislator and in his 2014 primary challenge to Sen. Lindsey Graham. The general election became an afterthought in the solidly Republican district. Timmons replaced retiring Rep. Trey Gowdy, who chaired the House Oversight and Government Reform Committee and was an aggressive investigator for House Republicans.

Timmons, part of a prominent family in the Greenville business community, graduated from George Washington University and got his master's and law degrees from the University of South Carolina. He worked in the state prosecutor's office and later started his own small businesses in the Greenville area. In 2016, he defeated a veteran Republican incumbent to win election to the state Senate.

Bright had been a controversial figure in the Legislature for his conservative views on social issues, such as defense of flying the Confederate flag on State House grounds and a limitation on the rights of transgender people. In his 2014 challenge to Graham, Bright attacked the senator's collaboration with "gun grabbers" in attempts at gun-control legislation; he was criticized during that campaign for his plan to give away an AR-15 rifle at a raffle during a political event. He was a distant runner-up in that primary with 15 percent to Graham, who got 56 percent. In 2016, Bright narrowly lost the GOP primary to retain his state Senate seat. Then-Gov. Nikki Haley, among other leading Republicans, backed his opponent.

In their contest for the House seat, Timmons said that Bright had a "history of embarrassing stunts" and that he had run a "dirty, name-calling campaign" against him, including references to Timmons's wealthy family background. "He is going to say things that embarrass you, and it is going to cause problems for the Upstate," warned Timmons, who contrasted his own skills as a thorough prosecutor. Bright dismissed Timmons as the "establishment-backed candidate."

With his base in Spartanburg County, where he more than doubled the vote for Timmons, Bright led with 25 percent of the vote in the initial round of voting in the 13-candidate Republican field.

Bolstered by his narrow lead in Greenville County, Timmons finished second—following a recount-- by a scant 391 votes over state Rep. Dan Hamilton.

That forced a runoff two weeks later, which took on larger dimensions within the national party. Timmons was endorsed by Sen. Marco Rubio of Florida; Bright had the support of Sen. Ted Cruz of Texas. The Club for Growth spent more than $400,000 on advertising that attacked Timmons for his inadequate support of President Donald Trump. Overall, he had a big fundraising advantage, with $1.4 million — including $1.1 million in personal loans -- to $343,000 for Bright. Timmons prevailed, 54%-46%. This time, Timmons led in both counties, with similar margins. Nearly two-thirds of the vote was cast in Greenville.

In November, Timmons easily defeated Brandon Brown, a local businessman. As one of the youngest members of the freshman class, he was positioned for a lengthy career in Congress.

SC-4: Upcountry   Cook Partisan Voting Index: R+15

Population		Race and Ethnicity		Income	
Total	708,271	White	68.6%	Median Income	$51,198
Land area (sq. miles)	1,299	Black	18.7%	District Income Rank	282
Pop/ sq mi	545.1	Latino	8.2%	Poverty Rate	14.3%
Born in State	56%	Asian	2.4%	With health insurance	87.7%
		Two or more races	1.7%	Cash public assistance	1.3%
Age Groups		Other	0.4%	Food stamp/SNAP	11.7%
Under 18	23.4%				
18-34	22.8%	Education		Work	
35-64	38.8%	H.S grad or less	39.3%	White Collar	15%
Over 64	15%	Some college	30%	Sales and Service	40%
		College Degree, 4 yr	19.5%	Blue Collar	24%
Military		Post grad	11.2%	Government	10.7%
Veteran/ Active Duty	8.1%				

2012 Pres. Vote	Romney	170,623	(62%)	Obama	99,359	(36%)		
2016 Pres. Vote	Trump	181,637	(60%)	Clinton	103,848	(34%)	Johnson	8,171	(3%)

Greenville and Spartanburg: A century ago, Northern investors seeking sites for textile mills looked at the Upstate of South Carolina and found what was described then as "mild climate, abundant water power, proximity to the cotton fields, and plenty of native labor already accustomed to a low standard of living." As mills fled New England, textile factories settled along the Southern Railway and Seaboard Coast Line tracks between Charlotte and Atlanta, especially in the Piedmont of South Carolina. The textile country might look bucolic, but Greenville, Spartanburg and the dozens of mill towns thick in the surrounding countryside became as industrial as Lancashire or the Ruhr. In the days before child labor laws, factory work sometimes began at age 6, condemning workers to a life of illiteracy. Escapes to a brighter future, such as the brilliant but brief baseball career of West Greenville's "Shoeless" Joe Jackson, were rare.

Today, along Interstate 85, which parallels the Southern Railway, little remains of what was once the largest textile-producing area in the United States. In 2016, Greenville Online reported that the 18 textile mills that were operating a century earlier within three miles of downtown had been reduced to three. But the multinational corporations that have sprung up in their place have spurred Greenville to become the fourth fastest growing city in the country, with a 20 percent uptick from 2000 to 2016.

Financial sweeteners, tax incentives, the absence of unions, and solid infrastructure — airports, highways and the busy Port of Charleston — attracted an enormous BMW plant in Spartanburg that marked its 25th anniversary in 2017, announcing an expansion to boost its annual production rate to 450,000 vehicles and nearly double its current payroll of 9,000 over the coming years, bringing its total investment there to more than $9 billion. About 70 percent of the vehicles are exported to 140 countries, which exceeds the exports of GM and Ford combined. A few days before his inauguration, Donald Trump complained about BMW's plans to build a new factory in Mexico, warning those imports would be subject to a 35 percent tax. The company defended its commitment to the U.S. market. Local leaders warned Trump that they feared those jobs would leave for China and could cause other layoffs in South Carolina. The Greer plant, BMW's largest in the world and its first outside Germany, manufactures many of its X-series cars and planned to add its new X7 SUV.

Michelin is another large employer in the Greenville area, with more than 4,000 workers at several plants. In 2016, GE Power opened its first advanced manufacturing center, which employed 3,200. Greenville's revitalized downtown boasts fancy hotels and restaurants, which cater to the new corporate manager class, along with glitzy condos, apartments and other mixed-use developments. Falls Park along the Reedy River Falls boasts a unique 370-foot curved European-style suspension bridge -- supported by a single suspension cable -- that's at the heart of the still-growing downtown. Greenville has become a top place for investors and new business incubators, boasting about five young businesses per 1,000 people in 2014, nearly as many as in Boston and Chicago.

The 4th Congressional District of South Carolina includes about 90 percent of Greenville and Spartanburg counties, with nearly two-thirds living in Greenville. Along with Anderson, Greenville and Spartanburg comprise the largest population area in South Carolina, with more than 1 million residents. Culturally, the 4th ranges from conservative to very conservative, with strong influence from Greenville's many evangelical and fundamentalist churches. Bob Jones University is here as well. It dropped its ban on interracial dating in 2000 (finally regaining its tax-exempt status in 2017 three decades after losing it because of that ban), but students are still prohibited from smoking, drinking, dancing and wearing jeans or shorts to class. Here, the real political divide is between religious and economic conservatives. As the city continues to grow and diversify, that gap has shrunk. It's a top destination for young people too, many of whom stay in the area after graduating from Furman University or nearby Clemson. Large subdivisions have sprouted between Greenville and Spartanburg, and newcomers have brought religious and ethnic diversity. Greenville has growing numbers not only of Catholics and Jews, but also of Muslims, Buddhists, Hindus, Baha'is, and even has a gay-oriented church. Hispanics grew from 4 percent of Greenville County's population in 2000 to 9 percent in 2015. The 4th remains comfortably Republican. Trump got 60 percent of the vote in 2016.

Ralph Norman (R)

Elected 2017, 1st full term, b. Jun 20, 1953; York County; Presbyterian College (SC), B.S., 1975; Presbyterian; Married (Elaine Rice); 4 children; 16 grandchildren.

DC Office: 319 CHOB 20515, 202-225-5501, Fax: 202-225-0464, norman.house.gov

State Offices: Rock Hill, 803-327-1114.

Committees: *Budget. Oversight & Reform*: Government Operations. *Science, Space & Technology*: Energy; Investigations & Oversight (RMM).

Group Ratings

	ADA	ACLU	AFL-CIO	LCV	ITI	COC	HAFA	ACU	CFG	FRC
2018	-	17%	-	0%	-	67%	95%	92%	88%	100%
2017	0%	C	-	0%	C	100%	C	89%	91%	100%

Key Votes of the 115th Congress

1. Obama-care revision	N/A	5. Family planning regs	N/A	9. Guantanamo prisoners	N
2. Tax Cuts	Y	6. Body cameras/immigration	Y	10. Ground missiles, limit	N
3. Omnibus appropriations	N	7. Abortion ban	Y	11. Defense Dept. spending	Y
4. Dodd-Frank revision	Y	8. Concealed carry	Y	12. FISA rules	N

Election Results

Election	Name (Party)	Vote (%)		Cand. Spent	Ind. Exp. Support	Ind. Exp. Oppose
2018 General	Ralph W. Norman Jr. (R)................ 141,757	(57%)	$1,845,612	$77,353	$417,173
	Archie Parnell (D)........................... 103,129	(42%)	$1,988,002	$34,952	$35,000
	Michael Chandler (CNP).......................... 3,443	(1%)			
2018 Primary	Ralph W. Norman Jr. (R).............	(100%)			

Prior winning percentages: 2017 special (51%)

Republican Rep. Ralph Norman was first elected in a June 2017 special election to succeed former Rep. Mick Mulvaney, who resigned to join the Trump administration, first as director of the Office of Management and Budget and later as acting chief of staff. The special election was closer than expected -- a harbinger of things to come in suburban House districts in the midterm elections as a backlash to President Donald Trump. After damaging information about his Democratic opponent's past surfaced, Norman easily won a full term in 2018.

A Rock Hill native, Norman got a degree in business from Presbyterian College in Clinton South Carolina. He joined his family's real estate development company. The business began by building homes and planning subdivisions in and around Rock Hill, and expanded into commercial real estate throughout York and Lancaster counties. The ventures were highly successful.

In 2004, Norman won an open seat in the state house, winning the three-way primary with 52 percent of the vote. Two years later, he challenged longtime Democratic Rep. John Spratt, who was in line to chair the House Budget Committee. National Republicans had long lobbied the wealthy Norman to take on Spratt. The incumbent spent more than $2.6 million, double Norman's $1.3 million. In a poor year for the GOP that saw Democrats take back the House, Spratt won 57%-43%.

In 2009, Norman won back his old state House seat. When the congressional seat opened again in 2017, he couldn't resist another try. The Republican primary was hard-fought, with Norman and state Rep. Tommy Pope emerging as frontrunners. Norman received more than $700,000 of support from the Club for Growth, while Pope was backed by the Chamber of Commerce. Norman painted himself as the natural successor to Mulvaney, underscoring his support for Trump and opposition to Obamacare, saying at one forum, "If you liked Mick Mulvaney's votes, you'll like my votes." Pope cast himself as a more pragmatic figure. In the first round of voting, each got 30 percent of the vote in the seven-candidate primary; Pope led by 135 votes. The run-off was just as close. Norman prevailed by 221 votes out of the more than 35,000 tallied. Pope took 54 percent of the vote in York County, which cast slightly more than half the vote; Norman won nine of the other 10 counties.

Archie Parnell, the Democratic nominee, was new to local politics, but he had extensive experience in Washington as a tax attorney at the Justice Department and with the House Ways and Means Committee. Later, he was an international tax and trade adviser to large companies. The contest was overshadowed by another special election the same day about 200 miles west in a suburban Atlanta district that had been nearly as solidly Republican. Norman won by a much closer margin than did the GOP candidate in Georgia, 51%-48%.

Parnell started gunning to challenge Norman for a full term in 2018, and Democrats saw him as a top-tier candidate -- until divorce records surfaced from the 1970s showing he had physically abused his ex-wife. Parnell admitted to the abuse, saying that it occurred when he was in college and he "did something that I have regretted every single day since," but that it had led to a "monumental change in my life," pointing to his second marriage of 40 years and two grown daughters. Parnell's staff quit en masse and the national party largely abandoned him, but he refused to drop out. Norman refused to debate Parnell, saying, "I'm not going to debate a man who beats his wife."

During a Rock Hill event in April 2018, Norman put his loaded gun on a table while talking with women from the gun control group Moms Demand Action. Saying he was trying to make the point that guns aren't dangerous in the right hands, Norman told the Charleston Post & Courier, "I'm not going to be a Gabby Giffords.... I don't mind dying, but whoever shoots me better shoot well, or I'm shooting back" -- a reference to the former Arizona Democratic congresswoman who was shot and nearly killed during a constituent event in 2011. The Moms group said they felt "unsafe." During hearings over sexual assault allegations against Supreme Court nominee Brett Kavanaugh, Norman made an off-color joke about Justice Ruth Bader Ginsburg, who "came out saying she was groped by Abraham Lincoln."

None of that seemed to hurt Norman, who won, 57%-41%.

Norman joined the House Freedom Caucus, as he had promised. His bill to direct the Department of Energy to establish a "research program in artificial intelligence and high performance computing" to help the Department of Veterans Affairs identify potential health risks and challenges with veterans' data passed the House in September 2018. Drawing on his background as a developer, he joined Democratic Rep. Raja Krishnamoorthi of Illinois to found a House solar caucus.

SC-5: North-Central South Carolina   **Cook Partisan Voting Index: R+9**

Population		Race and Ethnicity		Income	
Total	695,549	White	65.4%	Median Income	$48,044
Land area (sq. miles)	5,506	Black	26.6%	District Income Rank	339
Pop/ sq mi	126.3	Latino	4.3%	Poverty Rate	16.5%
Born in State	57.6%	Asian	1.1%	With health insurance	89.2%
		Two or more races	2%	Cash public assistance	1.4%
Age Groups		Other	0.6%	Food stamp/SNAP	13.6%
Under 18	23.4%				
18-34	20.8%	**Education**		**Work**	
35-64	40%	H.S grad or less	46.9%	White Collar	15.8%
Over 64	15.8%	Some college	29.9%	Sales and Service	40.9%
		College Degree, 4 yr	15.3%	Blue Collar	27.4%
Military		Post grad	7.9%	Government	13.7%
Veteran/ Active Duty	10.3%				

2012 Pres. Vote	Romney	158,537	(55%)	Obama	124,561	(43%)			
2016 Pres. Vote	Trump	175,488	(57%)	Clinton	118,656	(39%)	Johnson	6,525	(2%)

Charlotte Suburbs, Sumter County: Some of the fiercest battles of the Revolutionary War were fought in South Carolina's Upstate, on hilly lands just being settled by Scots-Irish farmers moving up from the Lowcountry or down the Virginia Piedmont valley. This was a country of violent passions and unclear lines. Carolinians argued for years over which side of the North and South Carolina boundary Andrew Jackson was born on in 1767. Ever since, the fighting spirit and Calvinist faith of Upstate Carolinians have not wavered. This "Olde English District" remains intensely religious and pro-military, but it is no longer impoverished. The area has been moving on from the Civil War in other ways. In 2017, the Confederate flag and photos of local war generals were removed from a room in the courthouse in York.

For many years, the dominant industry here was textiles, traditionally the first factory enterprise of industrializing countries, with low pay and poor working conditions. With unemployment exceeding 20 percent in some small counties during the 2007-09 recession, the number of textile jobs declined markedly, though more sophisticated manufacturing has boomed. President Donald Trump's tariffs have complicated efforts, with TV-maker Element Electronics closing in Fairfield County in August 2018. In January 2018, South Korean company Samsung opened a $380 million plant in Newberry to manufacture home appliances, creating about 950 jobs over the next three years, but tariffs on washing machines threatened that endeavor. The growth of suburbia south of Charlotte in York and Lancaster counties has been rapid, and they saw the biggest growth in voter participation in the state in 2018. York had a 57 percent increase in population from 2000 to 2016 and the fastest job growth rate in the nation, with a 6.8 percent spike from March 2016 to March 2017.

Located 30 miles from downtown Charlotte and with an average home price of about $139,000 in 2015, Rock Hill has become an attractive destination for city workers looking for affordable housing, and some businesses are taking advantage, too. In May 2018, Roundtrip Mortgage Servicing Corp. moved its headquarters from Charlotte to Fort Mill, with 1,100 jobs. In Cherokee County, Gaffney is the heart of peach country. It is home to the famed Peachoid, a four-story water tower tank off Interstate 85 that is shaped like a peach. In 2015, when the tower -- which was made famous thanks to the Netflix show House of Cards -- was refurbished and painted, some tourists feared it was being dismantled. A fence was put around it in 2018 to stop vandals. South Carolina has shipped more peaches than neighboring Georgia since the 1950s, despite the latter's Peach State nickname.

The 5th Congressional District consists of all or part of 11 counties, mostly in the Upstate and some in the Midlands. Over half the population is in Lancaster and York counties and in Cherokee County, along I-85 and in the Charlotte exurbs. Politically, this Jacksonian homeland is ancestrally

Democratic but has become increasingly Republican. Much of the population growth in York and Lancaster comes from Charlotte suburban commuters with few ties here but with strong conservative views. In the outskirts of Columbia, the rural counties of Fairfield and Lee are majority-black. Sumter, which is 47 percent black, has grown only 3 percent since 2000. The district is 28 percent black. Overall, this has been a Republican district in presidential elections, and Trump got 57 percent of the vote in 2016. Demographics have placed a lid on the partisan balance. If York County and its surrounding areas continue to explode with college educated professionals, that balance could shift again.

James Clyburn (D)

Elected 1992, 14th term, b. Jul 21, 1940; Sumter; South Carolina Executive Institute, 1957; Mather Academy, Camden (SC), 1957; South Carolina State University, B.S., 1962; University of South Carolina School of Law, B.S., 1974; African Methodist Episcopal; Married (Emily England Clyburn); 3 children; 4 grandchildren.

Professional Career: Teacher, 1962-1966; Director, Charleston Neighborhood Youth Corps, 1966-1968; Executive Director, SC Comm. for Farm Workers, 1968-1971; Assistant, Gov. West, 1971-1974; SC Human Affairs Comm., 1974-1992.

DC Office: 200 CHOB 20515, 202-225-3315, Fax: 202-225-2313, clyburn.house.gov

State Offices: Columbia, 803-799-1100; Kingstree, 843-355-1211; Santee, 803-854-4700.

Committees: House Majority Whip.

Group Ratings

	ADA	ACLU	AFL-CIO	LCV	ITI	COC	HAFA	ACU	CFG	FRC
2018	-	79%	-	94%	-	58%	6%	4%	12%	0%
2017	90%	C	97%	83%	C	36%	C	4%	6%	0%

Key Votes of the 115th Congress

1. Obama-care revision	N	5. Family planning regs	N	9. Guantanamo prisoners	Y
2. Tax Cuts	N	6. Body cameras/immigration	Y	10. Ground missiles, limit	Y
3. Omnibus appropriations	Y	7. Abortion ban	N	11. Defense Dept. spending	Y
4. Dodd-Frank revision	N	8. Concealed carry	N	12. FISA rules	Y

Election Results

Election	Name (Party)	Vote (%)	Cand. Spent	Ind. Exp. Support	Ind. Exp. Oppose
2018 General	James Clyburn (D)........................ 144,765	(70%)	$985,074		
	Gerhard Gressmann (R)......................... 58,282	(28%)	$1,588		
2018 Primary	James Clyburn (D).....................	(100%)			

Prior winning percentages: 2016 (70%), 2014 (73%), 2012 (94%), 2010 (63%), 2008 (68%), 2006 (64%), 2004 (68%), 2002 (67%), 2000 (72%), 1998 (73%), 1996 (69%), 1994 (64%), 1992 (65%)

James Clyburn, a Democrat elected in 1992, is the highest ranking African-American in Congress and again serves as the House Majority Whip. With Democrats back in control, he's a major spokesman for the party, especially on issues of race, and will be an influential player in his state's important 2020 presidential primary.

Clyburn, the son of a minister, grew up in Sumter and was educated at a private, all-black boarding school. As a young man, he joined the Student Nonviolent Coordinating Committee, which took its cues from the Rev. Martin Luther King Jr.'s Southern Christian Leadership Conference. In 1960, he was one of seven people who organized the state's first sit-ins, at a five-and-dime store in the Orangeburg town square. He met his wife while in jail for three days. Clyburn worked as a teacher, as an employment counselor and in government antipoverty programs. In 1970, he ran for the South

Carolina House and lost narrowly. Democratic Gov. John West appointed Clyburn as state Human Affairs commissioner, and he served 18 years, under two Democratic and two Republican governors. He ran twice for secretary of state, losing narrowly.

Then, the new black-majority 6th District was created. Clyburn ran for the seat and won 56 percent of the vote in the Democratic primary against four African-American opponents. Clyburn was better known, ran first or second in every part of the district, and piled up 88 percent of the vote in his home county of Sumter. He became the first African American to represent South Carolina in Congress since George Washington Murray (a distant relative of his) left in 1897. He has not faced serious opposition for reelection.

In the House, Clyburn established a moderate-to-liberal voting record. He joined the moderate New Democrat Coalition, the only African-American House member to do so. Like other South Carolina lawmakers, he has been a proponent of expanding the use of nuclear power, which provides more than half of the state's electricity. On the Appropriations Committee, Clyburn focused on securing federal funds to develop the Interstate 95 corridor, which passes through rural counties in the district that historically were dependent on tobacco and cotton. The House enacted in 2006 his bill to create a Gullah/Geechee Cultural Heritage Corridor from south of Jacksonville Florida to north of Wilmington North Carolina.

After the 2002 election, Clyburn ran for vice chairman of the Democratic Caucus, arguing that the leadership needed to better reflect the party's diversity, and he prevailed over New York Rep. Gregory Meeks and California Rep. Zoe Lofgren. In 2006, he was elected Democratic Caucus chairman; later that year, after Democrats won control of the House, he was chosen majority whip, the No. 3 post.

Clyburn sought enhanced influence for his whip organization in crafting policy, a way of getting more points of view into the drafting of major legislation. He held a series of "listening sessions" with Democrats to explore options for an immigration bill. He led the Hurricane Katrina Task Force, which met regularly with local officials to coordinate the House's response to the devastation caused in 2005. "I truly believe that if the demographics of the affected areas had been different, the response of the federal government would have been different," he said in a 2007 speech in Baton Rouge. Clyburn also finessed a solution to a longstanding complaint by CBC members that they were prevented from advancing in the Democratic caucus because they couldn't pay their "dues" by raising large amounts of political donations in their disproportionately low-income districts. Clyburn persuaded Pelosi to adopt a modified system that rewarded Democrats for non-financial contributions, such as making appearances for candidates and doing press interviews.

In 2009, Clyburn got into a conflict with Republican Gov. Mark Sanford, who said that he would not use all of the money available to South Carolina from the $787 billion economic stimulus bill. Clyburn called the action a "slap in the face" to the predominantly black constituents who would benefit. He wrote a clause into the bill that enabled state legislatures to bypass governors who rejected the money. Clyburn took on another South Carolina conservative, Rep. Joe Wilson, after he infamously called out "You lie!" during President Barack Obama's health care address to Congress in 2009. Clyburn pressed a resolution formally reproaching Wilson for a breach of House rules, which passed on a largely party-line vote.

When Democrats lost the House majority in 2010, they lost one spot in their leadership lineup. An intense, behind-the-scenes battle shaped up for the No. 2 position between Clyburn and former Majority Leader Steny Hoyer of Maryland. To avoid a divisive outcome, Pelosi created the new job of assistant leader and made it the No. 3 post in the minority hierarchy. Clyburn took that position.

Clyburn's new job wasn't well-defined, but he became one of his party's main messengers. After the Newtown Connecticut school massacre, he compared the push for gun control to the civil rights movement. When Obama's health care law was a hot topic on the 2012 campaign trail, he told a gathering of South Carolina Democrats, "Do not be afraid to use the term 'Obamacare.' You should be proud of Obamacare." He spoke out forcefully against state voter-identification laws that he said disenfranchised minority voters.

As the most prominent black politician in the state, Clyburn has been a player in South Carolina's often pivotal Democratic presidential primary. In 2004, after his initial candidate, Rep. Dick Gephardt of Missouri, withdrew following the Iowa caucuses, Clyburn endorsed frontrunner John Kerry rather than South Carolina native John Edwards, who represented North Carolina in the Senate. Although he did not take sides in the 2008 primary, he clashed with Hillary Clinton when she seemed to suggest that President Lyndon Johnson, in signing the Civil Rights Act of 1964, had a more important role than King and other key civil rights figures at the time. He later wrote in his 2014 memoir Blessed Experiences: Genuinely Southern, Proudly Black that an angry Bill Clinton called to blame him for his wife's defeat in the primary.

In February 2016, Clyburn enthusiastically endorsed Hillary Clinton a week before the South Carolina primary. During the closing weeks of the general election, Clyburn publicly urged the Clinton campaign to step up its activity in minority neighborhoods to assist in down-ballot contests. He turned out to be correct about the lack of grassroots enthusiasm. In January 2017, after President Donald Trump voiced repeated accusations of voter fraud in 2016, Clyburn joined Democratic Rep. Elijah Cummings of Maryland in requesting details from state election officials and attorneys general. With several viable African-American candidates seeking the Democratic nomination in 2020, Clyburn's endorsement will again be a valuable prize.

Clyburn has carved out his own, often more anti-Trump, space from others in leadership. In 2017, he backed opening debate over possible impeachment against the president, over the concerns of Pelosi and Hoyer. Just ahead of Trump's first State of the Union address, Clyburn told CNN that "I can only equate one period of time with what we experience now, and that was what was going on in Germany around 1934, right after the 1932 elections when Adolf Hitler was elected chancellor." Clyburn faced criticism for being too slow to call for longtime Michigan Rep. John Conyers to step down after he was accused of sexual harassment. Initially, Clyburn cast doubt on the allegations against his fellow CBC member, telling The Times that, "You can't jump to conclusions with these type of things. For all I know, all of this could be made up." Clyburn was also caught on video seemingly suggesting that politicians should be held to a different standard than other men who had been brought down by the rising #MeToo movement, asking "Who elected them?" Amid social media backlash, Clyburn backtracked a bit.

Ahead of the 2018 elections, Clyburn said that if Democrats didn't win back the House, given their prime position amid rising dissatisfaction with Trump, their entire leadership team should be replaced. Once they were victorious, Clyburn re-assumed the position as majority whip. He was reelected unanimously after Colorado Rep. Diana DeGette dropped her bid amid pressure from the CBC. Clyburn said he would consider running for Speaker if Pelosi didn't have the necessary votes amid a revolt of some within the caucus. Pelosi eventually quelled any rising rebellion, with a promise that the trio of septuagenarian leaders -- herself, Hoyer and Clyburn -- would serve no more than four more years to make way for a new generation of Democratic leadership. In early 2019, Clyburn joined other CBC members in seeking reparations for African-Americans.

Clyburn, who will be 80 in July 2020, has shown no signs of slowing down. "My health is good. I feel fine," Clyburn told The State after former state Rep. Bakari Sellers, a CNN analyst and former Clyburn intern, said he "will be raring and ready" to run for the 6th District seat whenever Clyburn retires. The congressman's three daughters are all politically active, and at least one, Jennifer Clyburn Reed, has expressed interest in following her father in the seat. "There is one office that I know a little bit more than others," Reed told the Post and Courier. "People are like, 'You can start small,' and I'm like, 'I don't know too much about those.' That learning curve [for Congress] won't be as much for me as it would be for someone else." Clyburn replied: "I don't know whether she will run for office, but I know if she is planning to run for my seat, she's going to have to wait for a while."

SC-6: Central South Carolina   **Cook Partisan Voting Index: D+19**

Population		Race and Ethnicity		Income	
Total	667,841	White	35.4%	Median Income	$35,546
Land area (sq. miles)	8,063	Black	56.6%	District Income Rank	430
Pop/ sq mi	82.8	Latino	4.8%	Poverty Rate	25.1%
Born in State	69.7%	Asian	1.1%	With health insurance	85.6%
		Two or more races	1.6%	Cash public assistance	1.9%
Age Groups		Other	0.5%	Food stamp/SNAP	22.4%
Under 18	21.3%				
18-34	28.2%	**Education**		**Work**	
35-64	35.7%	H.S grad or less	51.4%	White Collar	14.8%
Over 64	14.8%	Some college	29.3%	Sales and Service	47%
		College Degree, 4 yr	12.1%	Blue Collar	25.8%
Military		Post grad	7.2%	Government	18.9%
Veteran/ Active Duty	10.1%				

2012 Pres. Vote	Obama	206,857	(73%)	Romney	73,588	(26%)
2016 Pres. Vote	Clinton	179,272	(67%)	Trump	79,798	(30%)

Parts of Charleston and Columbia: South Carolina's coastal lowlands and islands are laced with sluggish rivers and swamps. Its early settlers, planters from Barbados, brought thousands of slaves from Africa, and colonial South Carolina quickly became one of the richest parts of North America, with dazzling Georgian architecture in Charleston and classic plantation gardens. The planters built great irrigation systems and grew rice, cotton and the dye-plant indigo, all heavily in demand in Britain and elsewhere. All this wealth, of course, was built on the slave labor of countless African Americans. In colonial times, a majority of South Carolinians were slaves, as were a majority of lowland residents. South Carolina's black heritage has left a lasting imprint on American culture. Gullah, a mixture of English, French and African dialects, is still spoken on the Sea Islands, and Gullah customs survive — oyster roasts and sweet potato feasts at Christmas, handmade dolls and sweetgrass baskets. The poverty that was the almost universal lot of lowland blacks after the Civil War has eased only in the last generation, as development came to the coast and cultural isolation dissipated. But many African Americans decided not to wait for progress. They long ago abandoned South Carolina for opportunities in the North.

At the Emanuel African Methodist Episcopal Church in downtown Charleston -- which sits within the 1st District by just one block -- a 21-year-old white gunman in 2015 opened fire on a Bible study group, killing nine people before he escaped and was captured a few hours later driving in North Carolina. The victims included the church pastor, Clementa Pinckney, who also was a state senator. "Emanuel A.M.E. Church is the rock upon which the A.M.E. Church throughout the South is built," local Rep. James Clyburn said at a prayer vigil the next day. Dylann Roof, who had earlier produced amateur videos that featured white-supremacist objects and themes, was convicted in December 2016 of the nine murders; a month later, he became the first federal hate-crime defendant sentenced to death on murder charges.

The 6th Congressional District of South Carolina, created in 1992 as a black-majority district, takes in the black central city neighborhoods of Charleston, North Charleston and Columbia, but leaves out their affluent white areas, both urban and suburban. Columbia-based Richland has about 30 percent of the population; Charleston and Orangeburg are close to 15 percent each. The remainder of the district is mostly rural. The poorer counties that run along the I-95 corridor, from southern Florence County to Jasper County along the Georgia border, have been given the distressing moniker "Corridor of Shame" after a 2005 documentary highlighted the lack of attention paid to rural, dilapidated schools that are largely minority and low-income, leaving many students illiterate and unable to meet state standards. But with dropping population in many of these counties such as Orangeburg, they may face a decrease in state funding after the 2020 census.

The 6th includes most of Orangeburg County, home of the historically black South Carolina State University. Orangeburg was the scene of a massacre in 1968, when three black students were killed and 27 were wounded by police while protesting a segregated bowling alley. The troopers involved were tried and acquitted. In Boeing's North Charleston assembly plant, adjacent to the airport the company laid off about 200 people in June 2017, only months after President Donald Trump made the company his first post-inauguration stop to tout his trade and economic policies. In 2017, Chinese Wanli Tire Corp. announced it would build a manufacturing plant in Orangeburg County that would employ 1,200 people.

Republicans packed the 6th District with African-American Democrats, hoping to ensure that the remaining six of the state's seven congressional seats would solidly favor Republicans. Hillary Clinton in 2016 won the district, 67%-30%. This area was the site of early visits by 2020 Democratic White House hopefuls, especially by black candidates California Sen. Kamala Harris and New Jersey Sen. Cory Booker, and will be vital in determining the state's important early primary.

Tom Rice (R)

Elected 2012, 4th term, b. Aug 04, 1957; Charleston; University of South Carolina, B.S., 1979; University of South Carolina, Mast. Deg., 1982; University of South Carolina School of Law, J.D., 1982; Episcopalian; Married (Wrenzie Rice); 3 children.

Elected Office: Horry County Council, 2010-2012.

Professional Career: Staff accountant, Deloitte Haskins & Sells, 1982-1984; Practicing lawyer, 1984-present.

DC Office: 512 CHOB 20515, 202-225-9895, Fax: 202-225-9690, rice.house.gov

State Offices: Florence, 843-679-9781; Myrtle Beach, 843-445-6459.

Committees: *Ways & Means*: Select Revenue Measures; Trade.

Group Ratings

	ADA	ACLU	AFL-CIO	LCV	ITI	COC	HAFA	ACU	CFG	FRC
2018	-	7%	-	0%	-	75%	83%	83%	72%	100%
2017	0%	C	3%	3%	C	93%	C	96%	85%	100%

Almanac Ratings 2017-18

	Economy	Social	Foreign	Composite
Liberal	4%	7%	0%	4%
Conservative	96%	94%	100%	96%

Key Votes of the 115th Congress

1. Obama-care revision	Y	5. Family planning regs	Y	9. Guantanamo prisoners	N
2. Tax Cuts	Y	6. Body cameras/immigration	N	10. Ground missiles, limit	N
3. Omnibus appropriations	N	7. Abortion ban	Y	11. Defense Dept. spending	Y
4. Dodd-Frank revision	Y	8. Concealed carry	Y	12. FISA rules	Y

Election Results

Election	Name (Party)	Vote (%)		Cand. Spent	Ind. Exp. Support	Ind. Exp. Oppose
2018 General	Tom Rice (R)	142,681	(60%)	$848,375		
	Robert Williams (D)	96,564	(40%)	$25,385		
2018 Primary	Tom Rice (R)	38,346	(84%)			
	Larry Hammond (R)	7,532	(16%)			

Prior winning percentages: 2016 (61%), 2014 (60%), 2012 (56%)

Republican Tom Rice was elected in 2012 with a focus on his business background and conservative politics in the growing region. Compared to the often raucous members of the state's congressional delegation, Rice has been more low-profile and focused on his legislative work. That style proved useful when he got a seat on the Ways and Means Committee, where his accounting expertise has been helpful on tax policy.

Growing up amid the sand dunes of Myrtle Beach, Rice spent most days at the beach. His mother was a schoolteacher; his father, a repairman, died when he was young. Rice worked every summer after he turned 12, busing tables at the local tourist restaurants. At the University of South Carolina, he volunteered with Big Brothers Big Sisters. He stayed at the university to earn his master's in accounting and a law degree.

Rice moved to Charlotte to work for the accounting giant Deloitte. After gaining experience on larger cases, he returned home to practice tax law and eventually open his own practice. Rice served on the board of the Myrtle Beach Haven homeless shelter and, during 10 years as president, helped it build an expanded facility. He was elected Horry County Council chairman in 2010. In that role, he focused on rebuilding the Myrtle Beach Regional Economic Development Corporation and bringing jobs to the county. He led a protest against the motorcycle rallies that take over the Grand Strand every May.

In 2012, Rice came in second in the crowded GOP primary field to former Lt. Gov. André Bauer, who raised almost double the amount of campaign cash as Rice and labeled him a "moderate" in a wave of attack ads. In the runoff, Rice crushed Bauer, 56%-44%, thanks in part to a powerful endorsement from popular GOP Gov. Nikki Haley. In the general, Rice faced former economics professor Gloria Bromell Tinubu, who ran on a platform of union advocacy. Rice got support from the state tea party and National Right to Life Committee. He outspent Bromell Tinubu a bit more than 2-to-1 and won 56%-44%. His entire margin of victory came from his base in Horry County, where he led 65%-35%.

Rice has been outspoken in his call to raise the gasoline tax by as much as 13 cents per gallon to pay for improvements to highways and bridges. "Infrastructure is the foundation on which competitiveness is based," he said. He said that the increase should be offset by cuts in income taxes. Rice has made a big push to build the local section of Interstate 73, and appealed to President Donald Trump when he visited the coast in the aftermath of Hurricane Florence, underscoring that it was a safety issue as people tried to evacuate. "We need some infrastructure, we need it terribly, we need it 50 years ago and it's ridiculous we're trying to do it right now (with sandbags)," Rice told The Charleston Post and Courier. After Democrats won back the House in 2018, Rice was hopeful about funding I-73, reasoning that infrastructure looked ripe for bipartisan agreement.

Rice disagreed with GOP conservatives who sought to shut down the Export-Import Bank, which earned him the ire of the anti-tax Club for Growth. "In a perfect world, I wish it wasn't there. And I wish that banks would step up to fill the void. But the problem is it's not a perfect world," Rice said. When he voted in 2015 to extend the Bank, he said that during the previous five years it "has facilitated $4 billion in exports from South Carolina, and has helped over 60 companies in the state." Also in 2015, he filled a vacancy on Ways and Means.

Rice has resisted entreaties to join the Freedom Caucus and has gotten some pushback from local tea party activists as a result. But local leaders praised his efforts to connect them to transportation officials and they like the influence he wields on Ways and Means, despite his low-key style. "People don't pay me for smiling," Rice told the Post and Courier. "They pay me to get results." He has criticized Trump occasionally, with a wish that he would tweet less. He opposed the president's push for offshore drilling, saying that "tapping new reserves in the Atlantic has become less and less feasible" compared to technologies such as hydraulic fracturing. Rice added that he's cognizant that his district voted overwhelmingly for the president and that "while I don't necessarily agree with his tactics, I agree with 95 percent of his policies."

In a 2014 rematch, Bromell Tinubu spent $229,000, which was one-third her total in 2012. Rice won 60 percent of the vote. Perhaps the biggest challenge facing Rice is redistricting in 2022, but his base in booming Horry County likely will serve him well.

SC-7: Pee Dee/Waccamaw Region   **Cook Partisan Voting Index: R+9**

Population		Race and Ethnicity		Income	
Total	698,776	White	64%	Median Income	$42,536
Land area (sq. miles)	5,355	Black	28.6%	District Income Rank	397
Pop/ sq mi	130.5	Latino	4.2%	Poverty Rate	19.7%
Born in State	57%	Asian	0.9%	With health insurance	86%
		Two or more races	1.6%	Cash public assistance	1.5%
Age Groups		Other	0.8%	Food stamp/SNAP	17.6%
Under 18	21.1%				
18-34	20.2%	**Education**		**Work**	
35-64	39.5%	H.S grad or less	48.7%	White Collar	19.2%
Over 64	19.2%	Some college	30.4%	Sales and Service	47.9%
		College Degree, 4 yr	13.6%	Blue Collar	23.3%
Military		Post grad	7.3%	Government	13.6%
Veteran/ Active Duty	9.7%				

2012 Pres. Vote	Romney	152,577	(55%)	Obama	124,601	(45%)
2016 Pres. Vote	Trump	173,065	(58%)	Clinton	116,626	(39%)

Myrtle Beach, Florence, Georgetown: The Pee Dee region of South Carolina was named for the river that lazily winds its way through the northern lowlands of the Palmetto State. It was here that Francis Marion's penchant for conducting lightning fast raids on larger British forces and then vanishing into the swamps earned him the name "Swamp Fox" during the Revolutionary War. In

2016, researchers raised from the muddy Pee Dee River three cannons, which Confederate forces apparently had pushed overboard from a ship in their futile battle against the oncoming forces of Gen. William Tecumseh Sherman.

The 7th Congressional District takes in almost the entire Pee Dee region. The 7th consists of two distinct areas of roughly equal size. The inland counties remain reminiscent of the Old South. Crossroads communities and farms dot the landscape, and on Labor Day weekend the Bojangles' Southern 500 fills the air around Darlington with the roar of stock car engines. Florence -- historically the hub of the Pee Dee and the only city in this portion of the district with a population in excess of 30,000 -- has experienced economic development over the past decade. In 2017, WestRock LLC announced a $470 million upgrade to its paper mill there. The county overall had new investments that created more than 1,000 jobs, with companies like Honda, McCall Farms, Otis Elevator and GE Healthcare expanding.

The second half of the district is coastal. A century ago, this was largely uninhabited forestland. Myrtle Beach wasn't incorporated until 1938. Today, the two coastal counties of the Pee Dee — Horry and Georgetown — are home to the 60-mile Grand Strand, comprising miles of beachfront and golf courses and drawing 17 million visitors annually to the year-round vacation spot. That's all without an interstate into the growing coastal cities. There's been a push for years to build Interstate 73, which would run from Michigan to Myrtle Beach. Hurricane Florence's hit the area in 2018 gave local officials another justification, arguing an interstate was necessary for evacuation. Environmentalists have opposed the plan. The storm battered the region, causing massive flooding on the coast and far inland. Losses in the state totaled more than $930 million.

The combined vote of Horry and Georgetown counties has increased to a bit more than half of the total for the district. From 2000 to 2016, Horry County (pronounced OR-e) grew 64 percent to 322,000 people, and was the fastest-growing county in the state; it expects to add another 100,000 people over the next 20 years. The Myrtle Beach metro area was the second fastest-growing in the country from 2016 to 2017, much of it migration from out-of-state. A steel mill in Georgetown shut down in 2015, causing the loss of more than 200 jobs, but there was much celebration when it reopened in June 2018 by the British company GFG. The coastal areas of the district are overwhelmingly Republican, while the inland portions of Florence and Darlington are more competitive. Rural Marion and Marlboro counties are majority-black, and they vote Democratic.

The district is 29 percent black, similar to the 5th District and the largest in the state other than the black-majority 6th District. Despite legal challenges, the Obama administration concluded that the state was not required by the Voting Rights Act to draw an additional minority-majority district. Overall, the 7th is Republican, but not overwhelmingly so. Donald Trump won 58 percent of the vote here in 2016, no longer the lowest vote of the state's six GOP-held districts.

SOUTH DAKOTA

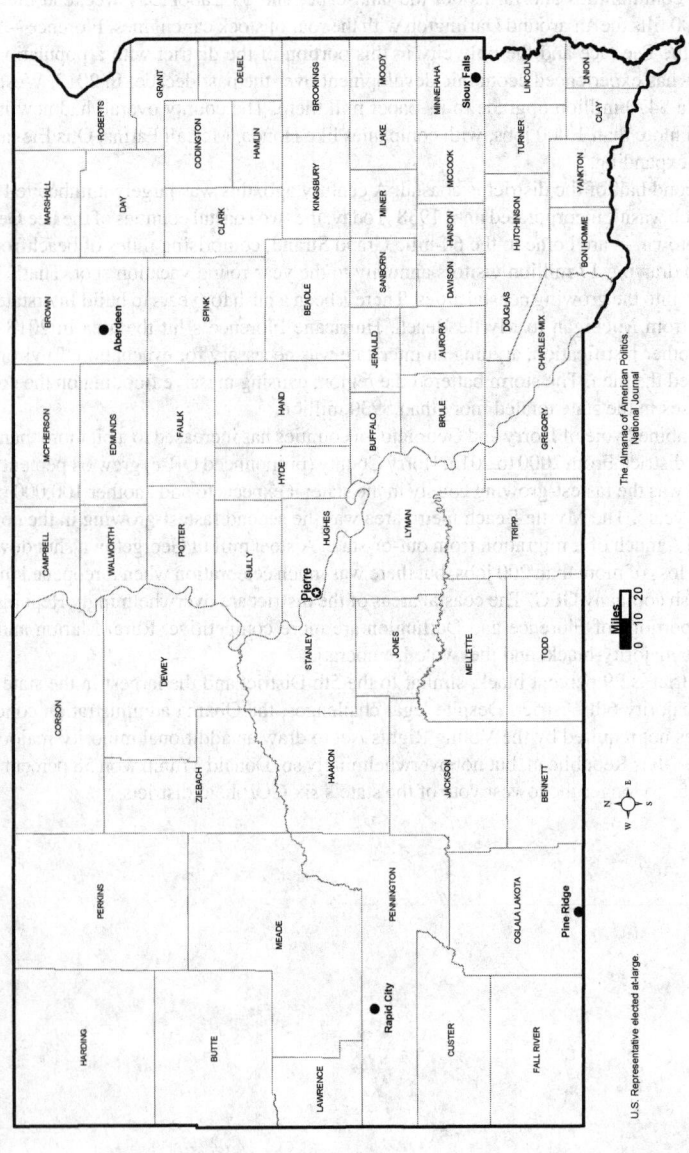

U.S. Representative elected at-large.

South Dakota is one of the most Republican states in the nation. It last supported a Democratic nominee for president in 1964, and it last elected a Democratic governor in 1974, a Democratic senator in 2006, and a Democratic House member in 2008. In the 2016 presidential election, Donald Trump won in a 30-point romp. Today, South Dakota's Republican lean is, if anything, increasing.

The Lewis and Clark expedition encountered herds of buffalo as the Corps of Discovery paddled up the Missouri River in the fall of 1804 through land where the Oglala Sioux became masters of the horses the Spaniards had imported to North America 300 years earlier. (Today, you can still see bison, bighorn sheep and elk at Custer State Park near Rapid City, a preserve on par with many of the finest national parks.) Fort Pierre was established as a fur-trading post in 1817 and Congress established the Dakota Territory in 1861, but few white men settled here until the 1880s. The Sioux remained dominant, and their warrior chief Sitting Bull, now buried on a bluff above the Missouri River, destroyed Gen. George Armstrong Custer and his 7th Cavalry at Little Big Horn in 1876 next door in Montana. Fourteen years later, many of the remaining Oglala Sioux Indians in South Dakota were massacred at Wounded Knee. After half a century of disease and a decade of setbacks against the westward advance of white settlement, the Sioux were a traumatized people.

In many ways, they still are. Indians account for 9 percent of South Dakota's population, the third-highest behind Alaska and New Mexico. (By contrast, African Americans account for less than 2 percent, ranking South Dakota in the bottom 10 states nationally, while Hispanics account for just 3.5 percent.) Most Native Americans live on reservations with proud traditions but terrible poverty. Isolated from the mainstream economic marketplace, they are beset by high rates of alcoholism, diabetes, and suicide. Five South Dakota counties – Ziebach, Todd, Buffalo, Corson, and Oglala Lakota (known as Shannon County prior to 2015) – rank among the 11 most impoverished counties in the country. In 2015, a federal judge ruled that the South Dakota Department of Social Services and other state agencies had "failed to protect Indian parents' fundamental rights" over many years when they removed hundreds of Native American children after cursory hearings and placed them in foster-care homes. In 2018, a federal appeals court sided with the state and sent the case back to a lower court.

Once the Sioux were forced to surrender their territory, white settlement of South Dakota came quickly. After gold was first discovered in the Black Hills in 1874, the mountains swarmed with settlers. Deadwood became a city of 20,000 where Calamity Jane ruled the saloons and Wild Bill Hickok was shot in the back while holding two pair — aces and eights. Because barbed wire could not fence in the buffalo, hired hunters massacred them so thoroughly that when Theodore Roosevelt visited the Dakota Territory in 1884, he had a hard time finding one to shoot. It was not long before the railroad came through, followed by permanent settlers, many of them German and Scandinavian immigrants recruited by the railroads. They built sod houses, broke the land, and set down roots. There were 98,000 South Dakotans in 1880; 401,000 in 1900; and 636,000 in 1920 — at which point settlement pretty much stopped. Farmers settled the eastern third of the state, sectioned off Midwestern-style. But moving westward, before a traveler reaches the Missouri River in the middle of the state, green turns to brown, cultivation grows sparse, and then simply stops. The West River plains are open grazing land. Beyond the 100th meridian the land is punctuated not by roads meeting every mile at precise angles, but by buttes, gullies, and grasslands sweeping to the horizon with no sign of human habitation except the occasional missile silo that once pointed toward the Soviet Union. The badlands did not get their name for nothing.

In 1979, Sioux Falls banker Thomas Reardon suggested that the state get rid of its usury law limiting interest rates; state officials agreed in 1981, and the laws they passed enticed Citibank to move its credit-card operations to Sioux Falls, where it could charge market interest rates, all in a state with no corporate or personal income taxes, and a community with a literate but lower-wage work force. It didn't take long for other companies such as Wells Fargo and Capital One to move their credit-card operations to the Sioux Falls metro area. Today, South Dakota has $3.2 trillion in bank assets, ranking second in the nation, according to the Federal Deposit Insurance Corporation. The arrival of the financial sector enabled residents of an aging agricultural state to gain exposure to and experience in the 21st century economy of finance (although Dakota farmers had been dealing with Eastern bankers for a century, sometimes unhappily). The finance sector also bequeathed Sioux Falls a secondary industry -- mail-order pharmaceuticals, which piggybacked on a logistics network that had been built to enable credit-card companies to deliver replacement cards quickly and securely to their customers. It has also become a locus for trusts for wealthy families, aided by favorable laws. In just one "modest, two-story white-brick building" at 201 South Phillips Ave. in Sioux Falls, $80 billion worth of trust assets are administered, the Financial Times reported in 2016. "America is the new Switzerland," Swiss-based lawyer David Wilson told the newspaper.

South Dakota has an unapologetically pro-business climate; the Tax Foundation ranks it third best in the country for its business-tax climate. (Some taxes, though, are readily accepted: It was a South Dakota lawsuit that led the Supreme Court, in a landmark 2018 ruling, to allow states to impose sales taxes on online merchants even if they lack a physical presence in the state.) South Dakota ranks high in credit ratings, low in foreclosures, high in repayment of college loans, and low in commute times. Still, there have been signs of modest erosion, notably in the financial-services sector. Four big banks – TCF, Capital One, Citi and Wells Fargo – had cut their in-state staffs by 2018, due in part to technology and outsourcing, the Argus Leader reported. Citi's footprint in Sioux Falls has fallen from 3,000 to 1,600. The agriculture sector, meanwhile, began a downturn around 2014, as prices for livestock, corn, soybeans and wheat fell. Farm income fell by 76 percent between 2011 and 2016 before rising again, although retaliatory tariffs from China, particularly on soybeans, spurred worry.

The generally healthy economy, particularly when bolstered by tourism, has boosted the state's population. South Dakota is coming to resemble the Rocky Mountain States, with most people concentrated around a few prosperous and growing cities and towns, while vast acreage remains vacant, punctuated by the occasional farm or ranch house. Statewide, the population has grown 8 percent since 2010, with particularly large increases in the Sioux Falls area – 10.7 percent in Minnehaha County and 28.7 percent in suburban Lincoln County. More distant locales, though, have thinned out. More than half the state's incorporated municipalities have seen flat or declining population since the 2010 census. De Smet, once home to Little House on the Prairie author Laura Ingalls Wilder, dug deep within its own pockets to move forward: The city's 1,100-odd residents donated millions of dollars to expand the local hospital and build an event center, the Sioux Falls Argus Leader reported. Philanthropy has also improved the quality of life in Sioux Falls. "The business community recognizes that we're in a low-tax state," local banker Dave Rozenboom told Bloomberg. "So in essence we're taxing ourselves. And we get to choose what to spend it on."

South Dakota's political patterns were largely set by the early 1900s. Its early settlers were mostly Midwesterners who brought their Republicanism with them, of New England Yankee and German stock primarily, and also some Norwegians. South Dakota, unlike North Dakota, never had much use for the Non-Partisan League, and unlike in Minnesota, there was never anything comparable to the Farmer-Labor Party. But the nature of the farm economy — its dependence on the great railroads and milling companies and on the vagaries of international markets — meant that South Dakota was subject to periodic farm revolts. It voted for populists and William Jennings Bryan in the 1890s, then switched to Republicans. In the summer of 1927, when Gutzon Borglum began sculpting Mount Rushmore, it welcomed President Calvin Coolidge for a vacation in Custer State Park, where he announced he would not seek another term in 1928. South Dakota briefly supported the New Deal, and it revolted against the Eisenhower administration in the late 1950s by electing to Congress a young Dakota Wesleyan University professor named George McGovern. South Dakota shared the isolationist impulse of much of the Great Plains; McGovern's opposition to the Vietnam War in the late 1960s was not a liability back home.

As in other small states, South Dakotans expect to meet and chat with their elected officials repeatedly. Pierre (pronounced "peer") is the nation's second smallest state capital city, outranking only Montpelier Vermont, and personal campaigning enabled Democrats such as Sens. Tom Daschle and Tim Johnson to be competitive in congressional elections, particularly when they articulated populist themes. In general, though, South Dakota has leaned strongly Republican. Since 2008, no Democrat has been elected to statewide office.

In the 2016 presidential election, the state became even more heavily red. Donald Trump's winning margin was 30 points, well above Mitt Romney's 18-point edge in 2012. Each of South Dakota's five most populous counties – Minnehaha, Lincoln, Pennington (Rapid City), Brown (Aberdeen), and Brookings (Brookings) -- voted Republican in both 2012 and in 2016 and shifted even more strongly toward the GOP. In 2018, the Democratic gubernatorial nominee – Billie Sutton, a legislator who was paralyzed in a rodeo accident at age 23 – ran a surprisingly strong race but ultimately lost to Republican Kristi Noem, 51%-48%. Noem began work with an overwhelmingly Republican legislature.

Cook Partisan Voting Index: R+14

Population		Race and Ethnicity		Income	
Total	855,444	White	82.7%	Median Income	$54,126
Land area (sq. miles)	75,811	Black	1.7%	State Income Rank	29
Pop/ sq mi	11.3	Latino	3.5%	Poverty Rate	13.9%
Born in state	64.7%	Asian	1.4%	With health insurance	90.3%
		Two or more races	2.4%	Cash public assistance	2.5%
Age Groups		Other	8.4%	Food stamp/SNAP	10.6%
Under 18	24.7%				
18-34	23.0%	Education		Work	
35-64	36.9%	H.S grad or less	39.1%	White Collar	35.2%
Over 64	15.4%	Some college	33.1%	Sales and Service	40.6%
		College Degree, 4 yr	19.5%	Blue Collar	24.1%
Military		Post grad	8.3%	Government	14.9%
Veteran/ Active Duty	9.8%				

Presidential Politics

2016 Primary (D)	Clinton (D)	27,047 (51%)	Sanders (D)	25,959 (49%)			
2016 Primary (R)	Trump (R)	44,867 (67%)	Cruz (R)	11,352 (17%)	Kasich (R)	10,660 (16%)	
2016 Pres. Vote	Trump (R)	227,721 (62%)	Clinton (D)	117,458 (32%)	Johnson (L)	20,850 (6%)	
2012 Pres. Vote	Romney (R)	210,610 (58%)	Obama (D)	145,039 (40%)			

South Dakota has voted Democratic for president just four times since statehood — in 1896, 1932, 1936 and 1964. But it was fairly close in five of the seven elections between 1972, when South Dakota Sen. George McGovern was the Democratic nominee, and 1996, when Democrat Bill Clinton came within 3 points of winning. Since then, its closest call for a Republican came in 2008 when John McCain carried the state 53%-45% over Barack Obama, who won the Indian reservations, several counties in the northeast and southeast, and Minnehaha County (Sioux Falls) by 587 votes out of 80,000 cast. In 2012, South Dakota gave Republican Mitt Romney a 58%-40% victory. The 2016 general election was a smashing Republican victory; Donald Trump defeated Hillary Clinton, 62%-32%, winning 61 of the state's 65 counties. He won Minnehaha, 54%-39%.

South Dakota holds a June presidential primary that seldom sees much action. In 2008 there was a robust race for the Democratic nomination, when South Dakota voted. Obama had a long list of endorsements from leading South Dakota Democrats, but Hillary Clinton, Bill Clinton and daughter Chelsea crisscrossed the state in the two weeks before the primary, and Clinton won 55%-45%. In the 2016 primary South Dakotans stuck with Clinton, giving her a narrow 51%-49% victory over Sen. Bernie Sanders.

Congressional Districts

116th Congress Lineup	1R	115th Congress Lineup	1R

Kristi Noem (R)

Elected 2018, term expires 2023, 1st term; b. Nov 30, 1971, Watertown; Mount Marty College (SD), Att.; Northern State University, Aberdeen (SD), Att., 1992; South Dakota State University, Bach. Deg., 2012; Evangelical; Married (Bryon Noem); 3 children.

Elected Office: SD House, 2007-2011; US House, 2011-2018.

Professional Career: Farmer, rancher.

Office: 500 E. Capitol Ave., Pierre, 57501-5070; 605-773-3212; Fax: 605-773-4711; Website: sd.gov/governor

Lt. Gov.: Larry Rhoden (R) **Atty. Gen:** Jason Ravnsborg (R) **Sec. of State:** Steve Barnett (R)

State Legislature: Senate: 5D, 30R **House:** 11D, 59R

Election Results

Election	Name (Party)	Vote (%)
2018 General	Kristi Noem (R)	172,912 (51%)
	Billie Sutton (D)	161,454 (48%)
2018 Primary	Kristi Noem (R)	57,598 (56%)
	Marty J. Jackley (R)	45,174 (44%)

Republican Kristi Noem was elected governor of South Dakota in 2018, becoming its first woman governor. Previously, Noem had served four terms in the House, including a stint on the influential Ways and Means Committee. Despite the state's solidly red leanings, Noem won narrowly against a charismatic Democratic lawmaker who had been paralyzed in a rodeo accident.

Noem was born in Hamlin County South Dakota. She attended college but returned home to help run the family farm after her father died in a fall into a grain bin while trying to unclog a feeder line, an accident that she discussed in her first campaign ad. She raised Angus cattle and quarter horses on a ranch with her husband, Bryon. An avid hunter of elk, pheasant and other game, Noem owned a hunting lodge and worked a variety of jobs, including a stint as a restaurant manager. She finished her bachelor's degree at South Dakota State University in 2011, when she was already serving in Congress.

After developing an interest in conservative causes, Noem ran for the South Dakota House and narrowly won in 2006, eventually becoming assistant majority leader. While serving in the legislature and Congress, she and her husband raised three children on the ranch. In 2010, Noem challenged Democratic Rep. Stephanie Herseth Sandlin. In the GOP primary, two-term secretary of state Chris Nelson had greater name recognition and experience, and state Rep. Blake Curd raised more money. But Noem, who said she didn't plan to make politics a career, struck a chord with voters, talking more about South Dakota than national issues. Noem won the primary with 42 percent, to Nelson's 35 percent and Curd's 23 percent.

With substantial campaign contributions from out-of-state Republicans, Noem outraised Herseth Sandlin; local operatives of popular Republican Sen. John Thune helped her candidacy. Outside conservative groups poured about $2 million into the race, more than three times what liberal groups spent. Herseth Sandlin, a leader of the Blue Dog Coalition of fiscally conservative House Democrats, touted her credentials as a moderate who opposed her party on several high-profile measures, including the Affordable Care Act. The state Democratic Party sought to make an issue of Noem's 20 speeding tickets and other traffic violations over two decades; she received six notices for failing to appear in court. Noem responded that she was not proud of her driving record and was working to be a better example to young drivers. In the end, Noem won 48%-46%.

In Washington, Noem was named one of two freshman class representatives to the GOP leadership. In 2011, she opposed the Environmental Protection Agency's proposal to regulate dust as part of air quality standards because of the harm the rules would do to farmers and ranchers. She joined her party in backing a budget that eliminated an Agriculture Department flood control program, but later requested federal disaster aid to cope with South Dakota's spring flooding. She worked on other issues of local interest, including House passage of a measure to transfer ownership of nine cemeteries in the Black Hills from the federal government to the communities that have managed them.

Noem became a favorite with activists on the right, and her votes generally followed the Republican leaders' wishes. On the House-Senate conference committee that hammered out the final terms of the farm bill enacted in 2014, she won approval of a retroactive livestock disaster program. Noem authored a provision that gave the Forest Service additional tools to fight the pine beetle, which had caused considerable damage in the Black Hills. In 2015, when she joined Ways and Means, that became the first time since 1978 that South Dakota did not have a member on the Agriculture Committee, a topic of some partisan grumbling at home. She said that "abysmal" customer service by the Internal Revenue Service was "inexcusable." In 2016, the House passed her bill to prevent the IRS from rehiring employees who had previously been fired for misconduct. As a co-chair of the Congressional Caucus on Women's Issues, Noem worked for bipartisan policies that affect low-income children.

In 2012, Noem faced a challenge by Democrat Matt Varilek, a former aide to Democratic Sen. Tim Johnson. Varilek impressed local observers by raising close to $1 million and hitting Noem on missing Agriculture Committee hearings. But Noem raised $2.8 million and won, 57%-43%. She won easily after that. Noem gave serious thought to running for an open Senate seat in 2014 before pulling back. (Although she criticized as "horrific" his campaign comments about groping women, Noem kept on mostly positive terms with President Donald Trump and his policies.)

Less than a week after the 2016 election, Noem announced her plan to run for governor, seeking to succeed two-term Gov. Dennis Daugaard, a Republican who had combined conservative stances on abortion and guns with more moderate ones on juvenile justice and transgender rights. In Congress, Noem played significant roles on the Republican tax bill that passed in 2017, and the farm bill in 2018. On the House-Senate conference committee on the tax bill, Noem helped to lessen the impact of the estate tax – a longtime concern dating back to the death of Noem's father. His estate left his family with an estate tax obligation, at a time when the tax's threshold was much lower. Critics said that Noem, in making the case for overhauling the tax, often oversimplified her family's situation.

Noem faced a bitter GOP primary against Attorney General Marty Jackley. Noem portrayed herself as a respite from the Pierre status quo embodied by Jackley, who had spent nearly a decade as attorney general. Noem won the primary, 56%-44%, but her treasury was drained, and some Jackley supporters were left with raw feelings. Democrat Billie Sutton didn't have to worry about a primary, enabling him to hoard campaign funds. Sutton, 34, was as strong a candidate as Democrats had put forward in South Dakota in years. He had been a champion saddle bronc rider until, at age 23, he was thrown by his horse and paralyzed from the waist down. After a stint in banking, Sutton won a state Senate seat in 2010 and became minority leader in 2015. He articulated views more in tune with the state than with the national Democratic Party – he was anti-abortion, pro-gun and anti-income-tax (although Noem sought to tie him to pro-tax views). Sutton painted the state GOP as arrogant and corrupt because of its longstanding control of Pierre, and he tried to leverage frustration with Trump's trade policies, which prompted retaliatory tariffs that hit the state's farmers hard. "The national [Democratic] party hasn't been engaged with a good message," Sutton told the New York Times. "They haven't been relating to people in the Midwest. It used to be fighting for the little guy."

Sutton found that his campaign message and his personal story were resonating; some Jackley supporters joined the bandwagon, and polls showed the race to be close. Sutton won the endorsement of the Rapid City Journal and the Sioux Falls Argus Leader. Trump visited Sioux Falls in September for a private fundraiser that netted more than $500,000; later, there were visits from Vice President Mike Pence and Sens. Lindsey Graham of South Carolina and Cory Gardner of Colorado. The Republican Governors Association invested substantially in the state, a development few would have predicted at the start of the campaign. Sutton may have been hurt down the stretch when video footage was unearthed showing him praising former Democratic presidential candidate Bernie Sanders.

Noem pulled out a victory – 51%-48%. Sutton won 22 counties, up from just four the Democrat won against Daugaard during his 2014 reelection romp. Sutton collected 47 percent more votes than Hillary Clinton had in 2016, while Noem won 29 percent fewer votes than Trump had. The Democrat flipped populous Minnehaha County (Sioux Falls), winning by seven percentage points after the Democrats had lost it by 49 points four years earlier. Sutton became the first Democratic gubernatorial nominee since 1972 to win Hughes County (Pierre) -- by five percentage points after Democrats had lost it by 66 points in 2014. Sutton also flipped Brookings County (Brookings) and Brown County

(Aberdeen). In Lincoln County (suburban Sioux Falls), the Republican margin fell from 55 points in 2014 to seven points in 2018, while in Pennington County (Rapid City) the GOP margin fell from 50 points to 12. Sutton may have carved out a promising political future should he choose to pursue it, but Noem looked forward to governing a state that has remained in line with her party.

John Thune (R)

Elected 2004, term expires 2022, 3rd term, b. Jan 07, 1961; Pierre; Biola University, B.B.A., 1983; University of South Dakota, M.B.A., 1984; Evangelical; Married (Kimberley Joe Weems Thune); 2 children; 2 grandchildren.

Elected Office: U.S. House, 1997-2003.

Professional Career: Legislative Assistant, U.S Sen. James Abdnor, 1985-1986; Special Assistant, U.S Small Business Admin., 1987-1989; Executive Director, SD Republican Party, 1989-1991; SD railroad Director, 1991-1993; Executive Director, SD Municipal League 1993-1996.

DC Office: 511 DSOB 20510, 202-224-2321, Fax: 202-228-5429, thune.senate.gov

State Offices: Aberdeen, 605-225-8823; Rapid City, 605-348-7551; Sioux Falls, 605-334-9596.

Committees: Senate Majority Whip & Assistant Majority Leader. *Agriculture, Nutrition & Forestry*: Conservation, Forestry & Natural Resources; Nutrition, Agricultural Research & Specialty Crops; Rural Development & Energy. *Commerce, Science & Transportation*: Communications, Technology, Innovation & the Internet (Chmn); Manufacturing, Trade & Consumer Protection; Subcommittee on Aviation & Space; Subcommittee on Transportation & Safety. *Finance*: Health Care; International Trade, Customs & Global Competitiveness; Taxation & IRS Oversight (Chmn).

Group Ratings

	ADA	ACLU	AFL-CIO	LCV	ITI	COC	HAFA	ACU	CFG	FRC
2018	-	10%	-	14%	-	90%	62%	82%	57%	100%
2017	5%	C	0%	0%	C	86%	C	80%	81%	100%

Almanac Ratings 2017-18

	Economy	Social	Foreign	Composite
Liberal	6%	6%	0%	4%
Conservative	94%	94%	100%	96%

Key Votes of the 115th Congress

1. Obama-care revision	Y	5. Gun regulations	Y	9. Kavanaugh confirmation	Y
2. Tax Cuts	Y	6. Family planning regs	Y	10. Saudi arms sales	N
3. Dodd-Frank revision	Y	7. Gorsuch confirmation	Y	11. FISA rules	Y
4. Omnibus appropriations	Y	8. Immigration restrictions	N	12. Military aid in Yemen	N

Election Results

Election	Name (Party)	Vote (%)		Cand. Spent	Ind. Exp. Support	Ind. Exp. Oppose
2016 General	John Thune (R)	265,516	(72%)	$2,424,179		
	Jay Williams (D)	104,140	(28%)	$59,126		
2016 Primary	John Thune (R)	Unopposed				

Prior winning percentages: 2010 (100%), 2004 (51%), House: 2000 (73%), 1998 (75%), 1996 (58%)

Republican John Thune, the senior senator from South Dakota, moved up in 2019 to Republican whip, the No. 2 position in Senate GOP leadership. He stepped down as chairman of the Commerce, Science and Transportation Committee, where he focused on transportation and communications issues — often with home-state interests. Thune is well-positioned to gain additional influence in the years ahead — perhaps more so than any other of the relatively junior GOP senators. Those prospects depend, in part, on the longevity of Republican Leader Mitch McConnell of Kentucky and the plans of Sen. John Cornyn of Texas, the previous GOP whip, who was forced to step down because of term limits. The seniority tables could leave Thune as the top Republican on the powerful Senate Finance Committee within the next decade.

He first gained national notice in 2004, when he defeated the Senate Democratic leader, Tom Daschle, in a hard-fought and costly contest. With his relative youth, extensive Capitol Hill experience and impressive fundraising, Thune has numerous opportunities inside and outside the Senate. In effect, he has become a Republican version of his predecessor.

Thune grew up in Murdo, on the dusty plains west of the Missouri River, a small town with a cluster of restaurants and motels at the interchange of Interstate 90 and U.S. Route 83. His father, the son of a Norwegian immigrant and a Navy veteran of World War II, was a teacher and the family was Democratic. Thune graduated from Biola University in La Mirada, California, and then earned an MBA from the University of South Dakota. Thune's political career dates to his freshman year of high school, when he was spotted at a grocery checkout counter by Republican Rep. Jim Abdnor, who recalled the tall boy had missed only one of six free throws in his high school basketball game the previous night. They kept in touch, and Thune joined his staff a year after finishing business school, when Abdnor was in the Senate. He worked there until Abdnor lost his 1986 bid for re-election to Daschle. Thune then worked for the Small Business Administration.

Thune returned to South Dakota in 1989 and became executive director of the state Republican Party. In 1991, he was appointed state railroad director by Gov. George Mickelson and in 1993 he became director of the South Dakota Municipal League. In 1996, Thune ran for the state's at-large House seat. The favorite in the Republican primary was Lt. Gov. Carole Hillard. But Thune attracted the support of religious conservatives and won the primary 59%-41%. In the general election, he faced Democrat Rick Weiland, a former state director for Daschle. Thune opposed all tax increases and promised to serve only three terms. He won 58%-37%. In the House, Thune was chosen as freshman class representative to the Republican leadership.

As he bumped up against his self-imposed three-term limit in the House, Thune considered running for the open governor's seat in 2002, and he was a heavy favorite to win it. But, at a White House dinner in April 2001, President George W. Bush urged Thune to challenge Democratic Sen. Tim Johnson. Thune launched his Senate bid, clearing the way for Republican Mike Rounds — now Thune's junior colleague in the Senate — to run successfully for governor. In taking on Johnson, Thune argued South Dakota would be better off with a bipartisan Senate delegation. Johnson emphasized votes he had cast for Bush administration policies in a state that had not voted for a Democratic presidential nominee since 1964. Johnson and Thune spent about $6 million each, a record amount for South Dakota; the national parties and independent groups spent much more.

The last two precincts reporting from Shannon County, which includes most of the Pine Ridge Indian Reservation and is now known as Oglala Lakota County, voted for Johnson by a margin greater than 9-1, putting him on top by 524 votes. Many Republicans urged Thune to contest the election results. In a decision that won him respect and appreciation from both parties in South Dakota, he declined and went to work as a lobbyist and consultant in Washington.

Encouraged by Republican leaders, he decided to run in 2004 against Daschle, who had beaten lightly funded opponents in 1992 and 1998. Daschle had been majority leader for 18 months in beginning in 2001, and he had been Democratic leader since 1995. In South Dakota, Thune's favorability ratings remained high; he enjoyed the full support of the Bush White House.

Thune sought to portray Daschle as the chief obstructionist to the Bush agenda in the Senate. Daschle ran ads arguing that a freshman senator could not hope to match his influence in Washington and emphasizing the federal largesse he had brought to South Dakota. He also cited his support of some Bush initiatives. But Daschle was hobbled politically by a difficult balancing act — serving as a spokesman for national Democratic policies without putting off voters in a Republican-leaning battleground state. "Sen. Daschle at the time was using his leadership position in a way that was contrary to where a majority of South Dakotans were," Thune told C-SPAN nearly a decade after that campaign. "Eventually, that caught up with him."

Thune portrayed Daschle as a political insider who lived in a $2 million house in Washington and had lost touch with folks back home. The state Republican Party sent a mailer attacking the work of Daschle's wife, an aviation industry lobbyist. It was the most expensive congressional election of the year, as both national parties and numerous third-party interest groups spent $35 million. Thune won 51%-49%; it was the first defeat for a Senate party leader since Democrat Ernest McFarland of Arizona lost to Republican Barry Goldwater in 1952. The contours of the vote were similar to

2002, although Thune significantly increased his share of the vote in the Pine Ridge and Rosebud Indian reservations.

Republicans celebrated Thune as a giant killer, and he became a talk show favorite and a fundraising star, quickly rising in the ranks. He served as vice chairman of the Senate Republican Conference before moving up to Republican Policy Committee chairman in 2009. In early 2012, Thune became chairman of the Republican Conference after Tennessee Sen. Lamar Alexander gave up that post. It made Thune the No. 3 Senate Republican, behind McConnell and Cornyn.

Thune has established a mostly conservative voting record, especially on cultural issues. His Almanac vote ratings ranked him near the center of Senate Republicans. "He is conservative, but his message usually is not bombastic, and he doesn't say things that scare off moderates and independents," the largest newspaper in Thune's home state, the Sioux Falls-based Argus Leader, said in 2013.

Taking over as Commerce Committee chairman, Thune attended to railroads, which were a specialty of his lobbying days and remain a prime interest of many farmers and businesses in South Dakota. He has been especially concerned about the availability of rail transportation for agriculture. In 2015, he won enactment of a bill to reform operations of the Surface Transportation Board, which regulates rail freight. Thune said that the changes were designed to make the board "more accountable and effective in addressing rail rate and service disputes," including severe rail backlogs and service delays that had hindered agricultural shipments. On another transportation issue that is vital to South Dakota, Thune has split with fellow conservatives who have sought to kill the Essential Air Service program, which ensures small airports get commercial flights.

Another prime issue for Thune has been net neutrality, which the Democratic majority of the Federal Communications Commission approved on a 3-2 vote in 2015. The rules were designed to ensure all internet content is treated equally by classifying internet providers as public utilities, as telephone companies have long been. Thune called the FCC action the "most radical, polarizing and partisan path possible." He told the FCC majority at a hearing of his committee: "Instead of working with me and my colleagues in the House and Senate on a bipartisan basis to find a consensus, the three of you chose an option that I believe will only increase political, regulatory and legal uncertainty, which will ultimately hurt average internet users." In February 2017, Thune filed legislation that defined net neutrality principles and codified them into law, including a measure blocking internet service providers from selectively slowing down traffic or creating special "fast lanes" for sites that pay more. After President Donald Trump selected new commissioners, the FCC rescinded the earlier rules. In May 2018, Thune said Senate Democrats for grandstanding with a bill aimed at reinstating net neutrality and said that they were unwilling to negotiate on his proposal. On an issue that is vital for rural areas, Thune pushed his bill to increase wireless broadband development by making more of the spectrum available. In October 2018, he criticized the FCC for failing to ensure "sufficient and predictable funding" of broadband to rural areas.

On the Agriculture Committee in 2017, Thune proposed a new category of land conservation, which he has called the Soil Health and Income Protection Program. The voluntary program, which compensates farmers during times of excessive crops, was approved as a pilot program in six prairie states as part of the 2018 farm bill. Thune said that his income protection program for farmers did not require a long-term commitment. Earlier, he helped author a section of the 2008 farm bill establishing a permanent disaster-relief program to provide financial aid to farmers whose crops are harmed by natural disasters. He pushed successfully to include those provisions in the 2014 farm bill and made sure they were retroactive to 2012 to cover drought losses in the Upper Midwest.

Thune has used his seat on the Finance Committee to push legislation to repeal the estate tax, which he has said disproportionately affects farmers. The Republican tax bill that was enacted in December 2017 doubled the exemption for all estates to $11.4 million. Thune also emphasized the lower rates that resulted for middle-class taxpayers. For business, he highlighted the steps toward reducing the "double taxation" on American firms operating overseas. Thune has supported proposals for a biennial budget and a presidential line-item veto as steps to encourage fiscal discipline.

After his initial close Senate races, Thune has breezed to re-election. In 2010, Democrats did not field a challenger. He became only the third Republican senator to run unopposed since direct election of senators began in 1913. Thune faced token opposition in 2016 from Jay Williams, a small businessman who spent $59,000 — 2 percent of what Thune spent during the two-year cycle. Thune won 72%-28%. With the lack of serious competition, Thune in 2016 gave $2 million to the National Republican Senatorial Committee to assist other Senate GOP candidates. In early 2019, he retained nearly $12 million in his campaign account. His investment of those funds has resulted in yearly interest and dividends of several hundred thousand dollars for his campaign fund.

After the 2018 elections, Senate Republicans tapped Thune as their whip. The fact that he ran without opposition was a tribute to his skill in garnering support from his colleagues. Some of them undoubtedly would have enjoyed serving in the position, but they realized that challenging Thune would have been a futile exercise. Given his decade of serving on the GOP leadership team, Thune's selection resulted in little immediate change, though Thune took some time to learn the nuts and bolts of his new position. On the day that Thune was selected as whip, both he and Cornyn issued statements that lavished praise on the other. As the most likely heirs to McConnell, it's fair to expect that they will cautiously eye each other as they firm up their separate teams and look for opportunities to show their strength.

Thune is young by the standards of the Senate — he turned 58 in January 2019 — and he could be an influential presence on Capitol Hill for years to come. With the election of Trump as president, options for ambitious Republicans — especially those in the Senate — have become uncertain. "That might have been the window. You never know," Thune said of his decision not to run in 2012. "Timing's everything."

Mike Rounds (R)

Elected 2014, term expires 2020, 1st term, b. Oct 24, 1954; Huron; South Dakota State University, B.S., 1977; Roman Catholic; Married (Jean Vedvei Rounds); 4 children; 6 grandchildren.

Elected Office: SD Senate, 1991-2000, Majority Leader, 1995-2000; SD governor, 2003-2010.

Professional Career: Insurance & real estate Executive.

DC Office: 502 HSOB 20510, 202-224-5842, Fax: 202-224-7482, rounds.senate.gov

State Offices: Aberdeen, 605-225-0366; Pierre, 605-224-1450; Rapid City, 605-343-5035; Sioux Falls, 605-336-0486.

Committees: *Armed Services*: Cybersecurity (Chmn); Personnel; Strategic Forces. *Banking, Housing & Urban Affairs*: Financial Institutions & Consumer Protection; Housing, Transportation & Community Development; Securities, Insurance & Investment. *Environment & Public Works*: Clean Air & Nuclear Safety; Superfund, Waste Management, & Regulatory Oversight (Chmn); Transportation & Infrastructure. *Veterans' Affairs*.

Group Ratings

	ADA	ACLU	AFL-CIO	LCV	ITI	COC	HAFA	ACU	CFG	FRC
2018	-	5%	-	7%	-	100%	60%	71%	53%	100%
2017	0%	C	0%	0%	C	86%	C	80%	76%	100%

Almanac Ratings 2017-18

	Economy	Social	Foreign	Composite
Liberal	6%	6%	0%	4%
Conservative	94%	94%	100%	96%

Key Votes of the 115th Congress

1. Obama-care revision	Y	5. Gun regulations	Y	9. Kavanaugh confirmation	Y
2. Tax Cuts	Y	6. Family planning regs	Y	10. Saudi arms sales	N
3. Dodd-Frank revision	Y	7. Gorsuch confirmation	Y	11. FISA rules	Y
4. Omnibus appropriations	Y	8. Immigration restrictions	Y	12. Military aid in Yemen	N

Election Results

Election	Name (Party)	Vote (%)		Cand. Spent	Ind. Exp. Support	Ind. Exp. Oppose
2014 General	Mike Rounds (R)................................	140,741	(50%)	$5,043,223		
	Rick Weiland (D).............................	82,456	(30%)	$20,755		
	Larry Pressler (I).............................	47,741	(17%)			
	Gordon Howie (I).................................	8,474	(3%)			
2014 Primary	Mike Rounds (R).................................	41,377	(56%)			
	Stace Nelson (R).............................	13,179	(18%)			
	Larry Rhodes (R).................................	13,593	(18%)			
	Annette Bosworth (R)...................	4,283	(6%)			

Prior winning percentages: 2006 (62%), 2002 (57%)

Like other former governors in the Senate, Republican Mike Rounds has felt the differences between the more action-oriented and less partisan responsibilities of a chief executive and the often gridlocked Senate. Arriving in the Senate in 2015, he gravitated toward a range of topics on which he could build consensus. Those interests have included cybersecurity, banking regulations and immigration enforcement. Rounds has not always been successful, given the deepening polarization in the Senate. But he has shown opportunities remain for bipartisanship.

Soon after entering the Senate, Rounds became co-chairman of the Former Governors Caucus and struck a collaborative tone with Democrat Jeanne Shaheen of New Hampshire and independent Angus King of Maine, both erstwhile governors. "Former governors are accustomed to making decisions and working across party lines to get things done," he said. "Our shared background helps us find common ground without checking our credentials at the door." He said on NBC's "Meet the Press" that other former governors in the Senate had warned him he would be frustrated.

Rounds was initially expected to walk away with the seat of retiring Democratic Sen. Tim Johnson. He won comfortably, but only after the contest took some unusual twists. His swearing-in gave South Dakota its first all-GOP congressional delegation in more than a half-century. Although the state has voted reliably Republican in presidential races, it had a history of sending Democrats to Congress, where some became highly influential — including 1972 presidential nominee George McGovern and Tom Daschle, who was Senate Democratic leader for a decade.

Rounds, named for an uncle who was killed in World War II, was born in Huron. He has lived in Pierre, the state capital, since he was 3. The eldest of 11 siblings, Rounds earned a degree in political science from South Dakota State University. In 1990, he was elected to the South Dakota Senate, where he served six years as majority leader before departing in 2000 because of term limits. In 2002, he ran for governor and won the Republican primary in one of the biggest political upsets in state history. Rounds faced former Lt. Gov. Steve Kirby and state Attorney General Mark Barnett, who waged highly negative campaigns against each other. Their attack ads were so negative they backfired, benefiting Rounds — who won with 44 percent of the vote. That fall, he won 57 percent of the vote against Democrat Jim Abbott, who had been president of the University of South Dakota.

As governor, Rounds enjoyed high approval ratings. They briefly slumped in spring 2006 after he signed a law banning all abortions except those necessary to save the mother's life. The law was challenged in court and never took effect. The statute — criticized because it did not include exceptions for rape, incest or the mother's health — was repealed by voters in a state referendum — 55%-45% — on the same day that Rounds won his second term with 62 percent of the vote. Term-limitedin 2010, Rounds was urged by some Republicans to challenge Johnson in 2008, but he declined to do so. At 2006's end, Johnson suffered a cerebral hemorrhage that required brain surgery; he had only partially recovered. At the end of 2010, Rounds returned to his insurance and real estate firm, where he had put his ownership interest in a blind trust after being elected governor.

When Johnson did not seek re-election in 2014, Rounds ran and won a five-way primary with 56 percent of the vote. After a top Democratic prospects declined to run, the national party all but threw in the towel on the seat. Rick Weiland, a former congressional aide and a two-time unsuccessful candidate for the state's at-large House seat, became the Democratic nominee.

Weiland hammered Rounds on his handling, while governor, of the so-called EB-5 visa program — which allows foreigners to obtain U.S. green cards by investing $500,000 in U.S. business projects that create jobs. The highest profile EB-5 project in the state was a beef processing plant, Northern Beef Packers that received almost $100 million from EB-5 funding but went bankrupt in 2013 — a year after it opened. The problem for Rounds was that, a month before leaving office as governor, his economic development secretary, Richard Benda, had signed a contract with a private firm, SDRC, to take over the state's EB-5 program. Benda subsequently went to work for that firm. It was later revealed that Benda failed to disclose his plans to work for SDRC while signing contracts on behalf of the state that benefitted that firm. Benda killed himself in 2013 after the South Dakota attorney general, in a draft indictment, accused him of diverting a $550,000 state grant to his own enrichment. Rounds, who acknowledged that he had been aware of Benda's conflict of interest, dropped in the polls amid voter anger over the EB-5 scandal.

Rounds campaigned on a conservative platform, favoring gun rights and opposing abortion and same-sex marriage; he advocated repeal of the Affordable Care Act and suggested during the campaign that the Department of Education should be abolished. Still, some Republicans fretted that he was not doing enough to defend himself.

Public polling revealed another problem: An independent candidate — former Republican Sen. Larry Pressler — was showing strength and was making the race a three-way contest. Pressler had served for 18 years until losing to Johnson in 1996. A Rhodes scholar and Vietnam veteran who was regarded as an oddball by colleagues on Capitol Hill, Pressler had moved back to South Dakota after living in Washington. He ran as a maverick committed to reforming the way things are done in Washington. Weiland charged that the Democratic Senatorial Campaign Committee was seeking to undercut him and boost Pressler. Rounds went along with national GOP strategists and began running ads contrasting his views on the Affordable Care Act and the Keystone XL pipeline with those of Pressler and Weiland. Rounds won comfortably, taking 50 percent of the vote; Weiland took 30 percent for and Pressler nabbed 17 percent.

Rounds arrived in the Senate as the only former governor elected in 2014. "There's no time frame there," he said of Capitol Hill in an interview soon after arriving there. "There's nobody there that seems to understand that the people outside of Washington expect results."

Rounds took his problem-solving approach to cybersecurity, especially regarding national security. That topic had attracted growing bipartisan interest after Russia hacked computers as it sought to influence the 2016 presidential election. In January 2017, Rounds became chairman of the newly created Armed Services Cybersecurity Subcommittee. He was especially interested, he said, in "the Defense Department's role in responding to an attack on our nation's civilian critical infrastructure and in deterring bad actors from conducting such an attack in the first place." It was vital, he said, to deter a potential attack on the nation's infrastructure.

With Democratic Sen. Martin Heinrich of New Mexico, Rounds spearheaded a bipartisan group of senators that sent a letter to President Donald Trump in March 2018 and urged that he issue a national strategy for deterring malicious cyber activity "as soon as possible." Emphasizing that the failure to set such a policy was bipartisan and long-standing, the senators wrote that the failure had become "an open invitation to foreign adversaries and malicious cyber actors to continue attacking the United States." They did not get an immediate response.

Rounds led another bipartisan group seeking to increase security against attacks on election systems. In September 2018, he praised Trump for issuing an executive order that imposed sanctions on foreign countries and people who interfere with U.S. elections. "Today's executive order draws a clear line in the sand and puts our adversaries on notice that we will not tolerate any meddling in our election process," Rounds said.

He fell short on a bipartisan proposal with King and other members of the Senate's self-styled Common Sense Coalition, which sought to address immigration conflicts. The unofficial group backed steps to provide a pathway to citizenship for "Dreamers" — immigrants who illegally entered the United States as children. In late January 2018, Rounds issued a statement that claimed broad bipartisan support for making permanent changes to the law for such immigrants enrolled in the Obama era Deferred Action for Childhood Arrivals program. Two weeks later, Trump tweeted that the proposal by Rounds and others was a "a total catastrophe."

As a member of the Banking, Housing and Urban Affairs Committee, Rounds looked after large banking and credit card interests in South Dakota. He helped assemble a broad Senate coalition, including 17 Democrats, that voted in May 2018 to relax the Dodd-Frank law on financial regulations. Rounds was interested in reducing regulations on small, local banks and credit unions. He cited a provision that he had sponsored and was part of the final bill, which relaxed rules on banks with less than $3 billion in assets. The result, he said, permits financial institutions to "focus on providing services to their customers."

Rounds pursued other constituent-based concerns. As chairman of the Environment and Public Works Subcommittee on Superfund, Waste Management and Regulatory Oversight, he welcomed repeal of Obama-era environmental regulations, notably rules that had given the Environmental Protection Agency new authority over water sources. In December 2018, he praised the Trump administration for issuing new regulations on water policy. They replaced Obama-era rules, which Rounds called "one of the largest federal land grabs in U.S. history."

Rounds was among several Republican senators expected to breeze to re-election in 2020.

Dusty Johnson (R)

Elected 2018, 1st term, b. Sep 30, 1976; Pierre; University of South Dakota, B.A., 1999; University of Kansas, M.P.A., 2002; Christian Church; Married (Jacquelyn Johnson); 3 children.

Elected Office: SD Public Utilities Commission, Chair 2005-2011

Professional Career: Chief of Staff, Gov. Dennis Daugaard; Management Analyst; Adjunct Professor, Dakota Wesleyan, Adjunct Professor; Senior Policy Advisor, Gov. Mike Rounds, Truman Fellow, U.S. Department of Agriculture.

DC Office: 1508 LHOB 20515, 202-225-2801, dustyjohnson.house.gov

State Offices: Aberdeen, 605-622-1060; Rapid City, 605-646-6454; Sioux Falls, 605-275-2868.

Committees: *Agriculture:* Commodity Exchanges, Energy & Credit; Subcommittee Nutrition, Oversight & Department Operations (RMM). *Education & Labor:* Civil Rights & Human Services; Health, Employment, Labor & Pensions.

Election Results

Election	Name (Party)	Vote (%)		Cand. Spent	Ind. Exp. Support	Ind. Exp. Oppose
2018 General	Dusty Johnson (R)	202,695	(60%)	$1,699,690	$72,283	$51,385
	Timothy Bjorkman (D)	121,033	(36%)	$815,793		
	Ron Wieczorek (I)	7,323	(2%)	$36,412		
2018 Primary	Dusty Johnson (R)	47,120	(47%)			
	Shantel Krebs (R)	29,551	(29%)			
	Neal Tapio (R)	24,040	(24%)			

Freshman Republican Dusty Johnson had extensive experience in government and business in South Dakota. After winning election as a state regulator and later serving as chief of staff to Gov. Dennis Daugaard, Johnson became a corporate consultant. He easily won election with a pragmatic approach in a competitive GOP primary. Compared to most other successful Republican congressional candidates in 2018, he kept his distance from President Donald Trump. In the House, he replaced Republican Kristi Noem, who was elected governor.

Johnson, a South Dakota native, graduated from the University of South Dakota and got a master's in public administration from the University of Kansas. After serving as a policy aide to Gov. Mike Rounds, he was elected in 2004 to the state's Public Utilities Commission; two years later, he became its chairman. During his tenure, Johnson took credit for "hundreds of megawatts of new electrical generation, more than 100 new cell towers, and assistance provided to thousands of consumers."

Following the 2010 election, when Johnson won another term on the commission, Daugaard tapped him as his chief of staff. In 2014, he joined the private sector as vice president of Vantage Point Solutions, a local telecommunications engineering and consulting firm.

When Noem made her long-expected move to run for governor, Johnson was an early contender to succeed her. He embraced what he called the optimistic appeal of President Ronald Reagan. "I am not going to hurl insults," Johnson told the Rapid City Journal. "I really do believe that constructive governance is about building bridges....I'm not gonna be anybody's foot soldier in Washington D.C." He criticized Trump's personal behavior and said that he was "too easily distracted" and "too thin-skinned."

During his campaign, Johnson voiced concerns about the mounting federal deficit plus the "general dysfunction" in Washington, and supported changes in how Congress handles the budget. He voiced concern that the tax cuts enacted by Republicans in 2017 will increase the federal debt. He cautioned that Trump's international trade policies could cause problems for South Dakota's farmers.

His chief primary opponent, Secretary of State Shantel Krebs, kept closer to Trump and was endorsed by several conservative groups and political leaders.

The Sioux Falls Argus-Leader endorsed Johnson as "a mature and moderate Republican voice," with "a measured voice" and "a consistency in his ideals and demeanor." He generally avoided campaign attacks on his opponents. Johnson had a slight edge over Krebs in fundraising. He benefited from more than $310,000 in independent spending by Citizens for a Strong America, a North Carolina-based super PAC that backed centrist Republicans.

Johnson won the GOP primary with 47 percent of the vote to 29 percent for Krebs and 24 percent for state Sen. Neal Tapio. Johnson led in 62 of the state's 66 counties. In November, he faced Tim Bjorkman, who served 10 years as a state court judge before stepping down in 2017 to run for the House; Johnson won, 60%-36%. In Republican-controlled South Dakota, Johnson could have additional electoral opportunities.

In the House, he took a high-profile assignment as ranking Republican on the House Agriculture Subcommittee on Nutrition, Oversight and Department Operations, which has control of the food-stamp program.

TENNESSEE

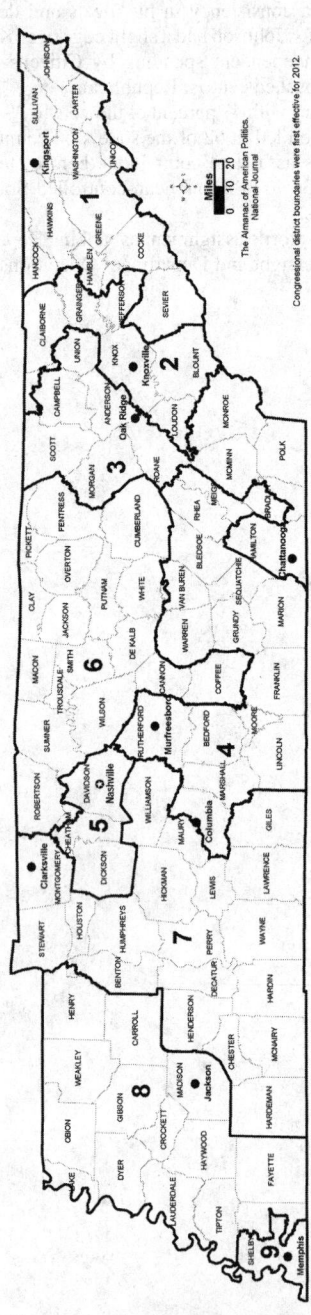

Congressional district boundaries were first effective for 2012.

The Almanac of American Politics,
National Journal

Tennessee, once a political battleground, is no longer. It has become one of the most solidly Republican states in the country, with just a few pockets of blue in its biggest cities. And while Tennessee has long been home to an influential strain of moderate Republicanism, two of the tradition's prime exemplars -- Sen. Bob Corker and Gov. Bill Haslam – are now out of politics, succeeded in 2018 by harder-edge conservative Republicans. A third, Sen. Lamar Alexander, announced that he would not run in 2020, leaving another seat likely to be filled by a more ideological warrior.

Tennessee is almost 500 miles across, closer in the east to Dover Delaware than to Memphis, and closer in the west to Dallas Texas than to Johnson City. It has had a fighting temperament since the days before the Revolutionary War, when the first settlers crossed the Appalachian ridges and headed for the rolling country in the watersheds of the Cumberland and Tennessee rivers. Tennessee became a state in 1796, the third state after the original 13. Its first congressman was a 29-year-old lawyer who was the son of Scots-Irish immigrants: Andrew Jackson. Jackson, who killed two men in duels, was a general who led Tennessee volunteers — it's still called the Volunteer State — to battle against the Creek Indians at Horseshoe Bend in 1814 and against the British at New Orleans in 1815. He was the first president from an interior state, elected in 1828 and 1832, and was a founder of the Democratic Party, now the oldest political party in the world. Jackson was a strong advocate of the union, but 16 years to the day after his death, Tennessee voted to join the Confederacy. (Today, Jackson's own party largely disowns him, while President Donald Trump made a pilgrimage to his gravesite and keeps his portrait in a prominent spot in the White House.)

Tennessee is a state with a certain civility: Both Confederate and Union generals paid respectful calls on Sarah Polk, the widow of President James K. Polk who stayed carefully neutral, in her Nashville mansion. Yet it was better known as a cultural battleground for much of the 20th century. On one side were the Fugitives, writers like John Crowe Ransom and Allen Tate, who contributed to "I'll Take My Stand," a manifesto calling for retaining the South's rural economy and heritage. (Today, the state ranks fourth in tobacco production and in the top five states for tomatoes and snap beans.) Tennessee is also known for the momentous 1925 trial in Dayton in which high school biology teacher John T. Scopes defied a state ban on teaching evolution in public schools. In 1960, John Lewis, a student at Nashville's Fisk University, organized sit-in protests at segregated lunch counters at Kress, Woolworth and McClellan stores. The protests sparked confrontations, arrests and ultimately a bombing that destroyed the home of the defense attorney for the protestors. That prompted Nashville Mayor Ben West to make a public appeal calling for an end to discrimination in the city. Within a few weeks, stores began to integrate their lunch counters and Nashville later became the first major city in the South to desegregate public facilities. The campaign became a template for student-run civil rights efforts throughout the South that Lewis, who eventually became a Georgia congressman, would heroically lead. Against this backdrop were business leaders who created the first supermarket (Piggly Wiggly), Holiday Inn and Moon Pies, and who made FedEx a global leader. The New Deal-era creation of the federal Tennessee Valley Authority also provided the state with bountiful energy, from a mix of coal, nuclear and hydropower plants.

Music is another strong Tennessee tradition. East Tennessee is one of the original homes of bluegrass music and mountain fiddling. Gospel music has long been centered in Nashville, which is also home to the Southern Baptist Convention and a center for religious publishing; justifiably, Nashville is known as the "buckle of the Bible Belt." Country music got its commercial start in Nashville, with broadcasts of the Grand Ole Opry from Ryman Auditorium in 1925, and it remains the capital of country music today. The Mississippi lowlands around Memphis, which is economically and culturally the metropolis of the Mississippi Delta, gave birth to the blues in the years from 1890 to 1920, and the blues were in turn the inspiration for Elvis Presley and countless other rock 'n' roll musicians beginning in the 1950s and 1960s. Presley's Graceland mansion is now one of the country's major tourist destinations.

While Tennessee's economy trailed the nation's through much of the 20th century, its open climate for entrepreneurism enabled it to grow mightily in the 1980s and 1990s. The absence of strong unions made Tennessee attractive, as did the relative lack of bitter racial discord, with the obvious exception being the assassination of Martin Luther King Jr. in Memphis in 1968. Alexander, governor through most of the 1980s, was a deft salesman in his efforts to bring foreign auto plants to

Middle Tennessee; Nissan opened a plant in Smyrna, south of Nashville, where the land was flat and the bedrock was strong. It has since built another and relocated its U.S. headquarters to Tennessee. Volkswagen built a $1 billion "green" plant for the Passat in Chattanooga that, after a $900 million investment, is now being used to build the Atlas, a new midsize crossover SUV. Among domestic producers, General Motors built the short-lived Saturn, a cult favorite, at Spring Hill; the plant is now producing the GMC Acadia SUV and the Cadillac XT6. All told, the state's factories now produce a new car every 20 seconds, and the broader auto industry, including suppliers, employs 134,000 people at more than 900 establishments in 88 of the state's 95 counties. Automotive exports totaled $5.8 billion in 2017, up 59 percent since 2010.

The state's population has grown 6.5 percent since 2010, with especially rapid expansion in the Nashville area. Davidson County grew by 10.7 percent, while suburban Rutherford and Williamson counties increased by 19.1 percent and 21.7 percent, respectively. In 2018, the economic-analysis firm POLICOM rated Nashville fourth among the nation's metro areas in "economic strength," up from 10th the previous two years. Meanwhile, the populations of Knox County (Knoxville) and Hamilton County (Chattanooga) grew by mid-to-high single digit percentages during the same span; among big counties, only Shelby County (Memphis) lagged with growth of 1.6 percent. Tennessee's population is 17 percent black and 5 percent Hispanic; it has almost 327,000 immigrants, about 5 percent of the state population. Tennessee ranks among the bottom 10 states in median income and in the attainment of bachelor's degrees, and the 2018 edition of America's Health Rankings placed Tennessee 42nd in overall health status, due in part to high rates of obesity and smoking. In 2018, the liberal-leaning Institute on Taxation and Economic Policy rated Tennessee's tax system the nation's sixth most regressive, thanks in large part to its heavy reliance on the sales tax, which does not exempt food and clothing. Tennesseans seem to prefer it. In 2014, voters by an almost a 2-1 margin ratified a constitutional amendment banning the adoption of any state or local personal income or payroll tax.

For more than a century, Tennessee's political divisions were rooted in Civil War loyalties. In two referenda on secession (one that failed in February 1861 and one that embraced it in June after the attack on Fort Sumter) most East Tennessee counties voted heavily for the Union and have remained heavily Republican ever since. Pro-secession counties in Middle and West Tennessee long voted heavily Democratic. Reform-minded liberal Democrats Estes Kefauver and Albert Gore Sr. became national figures, with reliable enough backing from Tennessee's yellow-dog Democratic majority to vote for civil rights bills. Gore was defeated in 1970, but he lived to see his son twice elected vice president before his death in 1998.

As the Democrats' cultural liberalism strained the ancestral loyalties of rural voters in West and Middle Tennessee, and as the surging growth in the ring of counties around Nashville created a new voting bloc that was conservative both economically and culturally, Republicans gained the upper hand. In 2004, as George W. Bush was handily carrying the state, Tennessee voters elected a Republican majority in the state Senate. By 2012, with President Barack Obama at the top of the Democratic ticket, Republicans won supermajorities in both chambers. In the space of a decade, Democrats went from controlling all three branches of state government to barely being relevant in the capital. Now, the American Conservative Union ranks the Tennessee legislature as the nation's most conservative. The rump Democratic Party has become largely urban and more progressive as old-style conservative Democrats have died or become Republicans. The only significant base of power for Democrats at the moment is in mayoral offices, which they now hold in Memphis, Nashville, Chattanooga and Knoxville. This political lineup was reinforced in the 2016 presidential election, which Trump won by 26 points

The 2018 elections may have represented a death blow to a long tradition of pragmatic, technocratic Republicanism. On the strength of Republican support in rural and exurban areas, the GOP candidates for senator and governor – Rep. Marsha Blackburn and businessman Bill Lee – won their races by 11 and 21 points, respectively. The winning party label may not have changed, but the brand of Republicanism did. Both Blackburn and Lee, along with the incoming state House speaker, Glen Casada, hail from Williamson County in Middle Tennessee, and all of them articulate a more confrontational message than was typical of politicians in the East Tennessee mold, such as former Senate Republican Leader Howard Baker, former Sen. Bill Brock, Alexander, Corker and Haslam. Places like Williamson County are "white, affluent and in the past decade have been a breeding ground for Tea Party supporters," wrote Tennessee political journalist Steve Cavendish. Just months into his speakership, Casada said he would step down in August amid controversy over lewd text messages.

The other pattern that can be seen in the 2018 electoral returns is the widening divergence between Tennessee's rural and urban areas. Even as moderate former Democratic Gov. Phil Bredesen was losing the Senate race to Blackburn by double digits, he performed strongly in the state's most populous counties. Between the 2012 and 2018 Senate races, Bredesen not only flipped Davidson County, where he had served as mayor of Nashville, but he shifted the county's margin of victory 46 percentage points in the Democrats' direction. In strongly Democratic Shelby County, Bredesen shifted the Democratic margin of victory by 25 percentage points, and while Blackburn did manage to win both Hamilton and Knox counties, the former governor whittled the GOP margins of victory in those counties by 36 and 44 percentage points, respectively. Even in Williamson County, Blackburn's home base, the GOP margin of victory fell from 59 points in the 2012 Senate race to 19 points in the 2018 race, with Bredesen jolting the Democratic vote total by 150 percent. Still, the outlook remains grim for Democrats. The performance of Karl Dean, the Democratic gubernatorial candidate, lagged Bredesen's, and even the gains notched in the Senate race by Bredesen – an unusually well-known and respected candidate – weren't enough to come within single digits of Blackburn. Prior to the election, the New York Times' Jonathan Martin framed the Senate race as "a test of whether Tennessee will remain politically distinct or become just one more reliably red bastion, like Mississippi to the south or Kentucky to the north." For now, it looks like the latter.

Population		Race and Ethnicity		Income	
Total	6,597,381	White	74.3%	Median Income	$48,708
Land area (sq. miles)	41,235	Black	16.7%	State Income Rank	43
Pop/ sq mi	160.0	Latino	5.2%	Poverty Rate	16.7%
Born in state	60.6%	Asian	1.7%	With health insurance	89.1%
		Two or more races	1.9%	Cash public assistance	2.6%
Age Groups		Other	0.4%	Food stamp/SNAP	15.7%
Under 18	22.7%				
18-34	22.6%	**Education**		**Work**	
35-64	39.3%	H.S grad or less	46.1%	White Collar	34.4%
Over 64	15.4%	Some college	27.9%	Sales and Service	41.2%
		College Degree, 4 yr	16.5%	Blue Collar	24.4%
Military		Post grad	9.6%	Government	13.6%
Veteran/ Active Duty	9.0%				

Presidential Politics

2016 Primary (D)	Clinton (D)	245,930 (66%)	Sanders (D)	120,800 (32%)			
2016 Primary (R)	Trump (R)	333,180 (39%)	Cruz (R)	211,471 (25%)	Rubio (R)	181,274 (21%)	
	Carson (R)	64,951 (8%)	Kasich (R)	45,301 (5%)			
2016 Pres. Vote	Trump (R)	1,522,925 (61%)	Clinton (D)	870,695 (35%)	Johnson (L)	70,397 (3%)	
2012 Pres. Vote	Romney (R)	1,462,330 (59%)	Obama (D)	960,709 (39%)			

Most of Tennessee is part of the Jacksonian belt of America running along the Appalachians, territory that has turned more and more Republican since 2000. In 2008, Barack Obama carried Memphis' Shelby County, which is majority African American, and Nashville's Davidson County, but he won only four of the state's other 93 counties. In 2016, Hillary Clinton won Shelby and Davidson and tiny Haywood, the only other county in the state with a majority black population. Donald Trump won the other 92 counties on his way to a 61%-35% victory.

Since 2008, Tennessee set its primary on Super Tuesday, when Clinton defeated Barack Obama 54%-40%. In 2016, Clinton defeated Vermont Sen. Bernie Sanders 66%-33%. Sanders won only three rural counties in western Tennessee. Recent GOP primaries have offered mixed results. In 2008, Mike Huckabee carried most of rural Tennessee and Shelby County and defeated John McCain 34%-32%, with the Arizonan carrying Knoxville and its suburbs. Mitt Romney carried most of metro Nashville and got 24 percent. In 2012, Rick Santorum defeated Romney 37%-28%. In 2016, Trump defeated Texas Sen. Ted Cruz 39%-25% and carried 94 of the state's 95 counties. But his five worst performing counties were the five largest GOP primary vote producers on Super Tuesday: Hamilton, Knox, Davidson, Shelby and Williamson, which Trump lost to Florida Sen. Marco Rubio. Rubio, who was endorsed by Republican Gov. Bill Haslam and former GOP Senate Majority Leader Bill Frist, finished third with 21 percent.

Congressional Districts

116th Congress Lineup	2D 7R	115th Congress Lineup	2D 7R

Republicans swept the governorship and both houses of the Tennessee legislature in 2010, earning unbridled authority to reverse the jig-sawed map Democrats had drawn in 2002. Back then, Democrats had created a fragile arrangement that gave them a 5-4 edge for eight years. Tennessee's cultural shift away from Democrats rendered the map a ticking time bomb even before the next redistricting. In 2010, Republicans defeated one incumbent and had double-digit wins in two open seats. That gave them 7-2 control of the delegation, which has not been seriously threatened since. In early 2011, there was chatter that Republicans would seek more revenge by splitting Nashville Democrat Jim Cooper's 5th District four ways. But Republicans determined the move too risky and passed a map strengthening Cooper and straightening most district lines across the state. They had enough maneuvering room to tweak two of the districts to remove potential primary foes for two of their GOP incumbents. Democrats comfortably control the Memphis-based 9th plus the 5th. Of the 36 House elections since 2012, the winner has received at least 60 percent of the vote in each, except for the first two contests in the 4th District.

With Republicans in firm control of the process, that scenario seems likely to prevail for another decade following the redistricting in 2022. Given their success during the past decade and the relatively orderly district lines, Republican redistricters seem likely to make few changes beyond the tinkering required to maintain equal populations in each district. The 8th and 9th districts in west Tennessee have grown the least, which likely will require both of them to extend a bit farther to the east.

Bill Lee (R)

Elected 2018, term expires 2023, 1st term; b. Oct. 09 1959, Franklin, TN; Auburn University, B.S.; Married (Maria); 4 children.

Professional Career: Rancher; President, Lee Company, 1992-2016, Chair, 2016-2018.

Office: Tennessee State Capitol, 1st Floor, 600 Dr. Martin L. King, Jr. Blvd., Nashville, 37243; 615-741-2001; Fax: 615-532-9711; Website: tn.gov/governor

Lt. Gov.: Rand McNally (R) **Atty. Gen:** Herbert Slatery III (R)

State Legislature: Senate: 5D, 28R **House:** 26D, 73R

Election Results

Election	Name (Party)	Vote (%)
2018 General	Bill Lee (R)..	1,336,106 (60%)
	Karl Dean (D)...	864,863 (39%)
2018 Primary	Bill Lee (R)..	289,699 (37%)
	Randy Boyd (R)......................................	191,940 (24%)
	Diane Black (R)...................................	181,719 (23%)
	Beth Harwell (R)...	120,910 (15%)

Businessman Bill Lee easily won the governorship of Tennessee in 2018, becoming the first Tennessee Republican to succeed a Republican governor since 1869. Lee's victory shattered another longstanding pattern in Tennessee: Since the 1960s, partisan control of the governor's office had changed with every new governor. This electoral habit finally came to an end as Tennessee became one of the most Republican states in the union.

Lee, a seventh-generation Tennessean from Williamson County south of Nashville, earned a mechanical engineering degree at Auburn University, then returned home to join the Lee Co., a business founded by his grandfather in 1944 that specializes in HVAC, electrical work, and plumbing. Starting in 1992, Lee served as president and CEO; by the time of his gubernatorial run, the company was employing 1,200 people and earning annual revenues of more than $220 million. The company collected $13.8 million from state contracts between 2012 and 2018, but it stopped signing new state contracts during his campaign, and Lee put his holdings into a blind trust. Separately, Lee helped operate the Triple L Ranch, a 1,000-acre farm founded by his grandparents with 300 head of Hereford cattle. Carol Ann, Lee's wife and the mother of their four children, died in a horse-riding accident in 2000. Lee eventually became close to a third-grade teacher of one of his children, and in 2008, they married. Bill and Maria Lee attended a conservative, charismatic church, and Lee served as a board member of the Men of Valor prison ministry.

Lee was one of several Republicans to enter the race to succeed two-term Gov. Bill Haslam. A major business figure in the state, Haslam had come to the governorship after serving as mayor of Knoxville. He fit with the East Tennessee tradition of pragmatic Republicanism, producing achievements in education and transportation policy. Haslam often sparred with the more conservative members of his own party in the GOP-controlled state legislature, and he declared that he would not vote for Donald Trump in 2016, even though Trump was poised to win the state by 26 points.

In addition to Lee, the Republican primary field seeking to succeed Haslam included Rep. Diane Black, state House Speaker Beth Harwell and Knoxville businessman Randy Boyd. Boyd, who spent $21 million on his candidacy, came the closest to following Haslam's more pragmatic approach, but Republican primary voters seemed to be in a mood for a more conservative choice. Black came into the race as something of a frontrunner, winning endorsements from Vice President Mike Pence and the National Rifle Association. Lee, meanwhile, framed himself as an outsider. He campaigned from an RV and a tractor, and refrained from negativity as the Boyd and Black campaigns beat up on each other. The low-key approach enabled Lee to climb in the polls. In the end, he finished first with 37 percent, followed by Boyd at 24 percent, Black at 23 percent, and Harwell at 15 percent. The Tennessean called Lee's victory "arguably the biggest Cinderella story in Tennessee Republican politics in decades."

On the Democratic side, former Nashville Mayor Karl Dean easily won the primary with 75 percent of the vote. But Dean was unsuccessful in his efforts to woo Republican moderates. Unlike the Senate contest between Republican Rep. Marsha Blackburn and former Democratic Gov. Phil Bredesen, which remained relatively close almost to the end, the gubernatorial race never became a genuinely competitive contest. Lee won, 60%-39%. Lee's 21-point margin was almost twice as large as Blackburn's 11-point victory over Bredesen. Dean exceeded 60 percent in his home county of Davidson (Nashville) as well as in the Democratic stronghold of Shelby County (Memphis), but Lee won all but one other county.

After taking office, Lee prioritized a proposal to expand school choice. Not surprisingly, this was met with opposition from the Tennessee Education Association and legislative Democrats, although another proposal, for a 2.5 percent teacher pay increase, was enacted to become effective 2021-2022. Citing what he'd seen working with the prison ministry, Lee proposed criminal justice reforms, including $10.5 million for prison-based college and high school courses, $1.7 million for specialized drug courts for nonviolent offenders, and an additional $1.5 million for GPS monitoring to avoid having to incarcerate those involved in nonviolent crimes. Lee also proposed additional funding for probation, parole and correctional officers, as well as $11 million to support behavioral health care for the uninsured mentally ill.

Lee signed executive orders to increase ethics and transparency within state government, and he said he would back a bill to outlaw abortions after a fetal heartbeat is detected. In February 2019, USA Today discovered a 1980 photograph from Lee's Auburn days in which he had posed in a Confederate uniform. That wasn't long after the discovery of a photograph of Virginia Gov. Ralph Northam's medical school yearbook page that featured one man in blackface and another in a KKK costume. Lee told the newspaper, "I never intentionally acted in an insensitive way, but with the benefit of hindsight, I can see that participating in that was insensitive and I've come to regret it." The discovery did not appear to cause a significant hit to Lee's standing in the state.

Lamar Alexander (R)

Elected 2002, term expires 2020, 3rd term, b. Jul 03, 1940; Maryville; Vanderbilt University (TN), B.A., 1962; New York University Law School, J.D., 1965; Presbyterian; Married (Leslee Buhler Buhler); 4 children; 6 grandchildren.

Elected Office: TN Governor, 1979-1987.

Professional Career: President, University of TN, 1988-1991; U.S Education Secretary, 1991-1993; Co-Director, Empower America, 1994-1995; Professor, Harvard University JFK School Of Government, 2001-2002.

DC Office: 455 DSOB 20510, 202-224-4944, Fax: 202-228-3398

State Offices: Blountville, 423-325-6240; Chattanooga, 423-752-5337; Jackson, 731-664-0289; Knoxville, 865-545-4253; Memphis, 901-544-4224; Nashville, 615-736-5129.

Committees: *Appropriations*: Commerce, Justice, Science & Related Agencies; Department of Defense; Department of the Interior, Environment & Related Agencies; DOL, HHS & Education & Related Agencies; Energy & Water Development (Chmn); Transportation, HUD & Related Agencies. *Energy & Natural Resources*: Energy; National Parks; Water & Power. *Health, Education, Labor & Pensions (Chmn)*: Ex Officio membership on all subcommittees. *Rules & Administration.*

Group Ratings

	ADA	ACLU	AFL-CIO	LCV	ITI	COC	HAFA	ACU	CFG	FRC
2018	-	5%	-	7%	-	100%	62%	81%	53%	100%
2017	0%	C	0%	5%	C	86%	C	72%	71%	92%

Almanac Ratings 2017-18

	Economy	Social	Foreign	Composite
Liberal	15%	15%	3%	11%
Conservative	85%	85%	97%	89%

Key Votes of the 115th Congress

1. Obama-care revision	Y	5. Gun regulations	Y	9. Kavanaugh confirmation	Y
2. Tax Cuts	Y	6. Family planning regs	Y	10. Saudi arms sales	N
3. Dodd-Frank revision	Y	7. Gorsuch confirmation	Y	11. FISA rules	Y
4. Omnibus appropriations	Y	8. Immigration restrictions	Y	12. Military aid in Yemen	N

Election Results

Election	Name (Party)	Vote (%)		Cand. Spent	Ind. Exp. Support	Ind. Exp. Oppose
2014 General	Lamar Alexander (R)............	850,087	(62%)	$9,378,379	$973,069	$294,406
	Gordon Ball (D).............	437,848	(32%)	$971,372		
	Joe Wilmoth (C)...................	36,088	(3%)			
2014 Primary	Lamar Alexander (R)............	330,088	(50%)			
	Joe Carr (R)............................	269,169	(41%)			
	George Flinn (R).............	34,207	(5%)			

Prior winning percentages: 2008 (65%), 2002 (54%), Governor: 1982 (60%), 1978 (56%)

Lamar Alexander, elected to the Senate in 2002, has been at the center of Tennessee and Republican politics for a half-century. With a start as an aide in the Senate and the Nixon White House, his career includes: governor of Tennessee, state university president, Education secretary and Republican presidential aspirant. His Senate years have brought added distinction, including as a GOP leader and chairman of the Health, Education, Labor and Pensions Committee. But that influence will come to an end in 2020 with Alexander's retirement. No longer worrying about re-election, Alexander has freely criticized President Donald Trump — just like his in-state colleague Bob Corker before him.

Alexander grew up Maryville, in East Tennessee between Knoxville and the Smoky Mountains, the son of a principal and a teacher. He began piano lessons at 4 and still plays. He went to Vanderbilt University, where in the early 1960s he wrote editorials for the school newspaper urging integration. He got a law degree from New York University and then clerked for Judge John Minor Wisdom of the 5th U.S. Circuit Court of Appeals. In 1966, he wrote to Republican Howard Baker, volunteering to work for Baker's Senate campaign against Democrat Frank Clement. Instead, Baker gave him a job on his Washington staff. In 1969, on Baker's recommendation, Alexander got a job with President Richard Nixon's congressional liaison, Bryce Harlow. On a trip back to Tennessee in 1970, he met Memphis dentist Winfield Dunn, who was running for governor, and Alexander agreed to manage his campaign. Dunn became the first Republican elected Tennessee governor in 50 years.

Back then, Tennessee governors were limited to one four-year term. Alexander decided that next time, he would be the candidate. In 1974, at 34, he ran for governor. In that Watergate year, he lost to Democratic Rep. Ray Blanton, 55%-44%. He ran again in 1978 — by then, Tennessee changed its law to allow two consecutive terms — and undertook a more colorful campaign strategy. Wearing a red-and-black plaid flannel shirt that would become his signature, Alexander walked 1,000 miles across Tennessee. He defeated Blanton 56%-44%.

After the election, Blanton issued many pardons of criminals, who, it turned out, were paying him bribes. The U.S. attorney urged that Alexander be sworn in three days early, and Democratic legislative leaders and the state's chief justice agreed. In a hurried ceremony, Alexander took the oath and named Fred Thompson, famous for his work as Baker's chief counsel in the Senate Watergate hearings, as special prosecutor. In office, Alexander attended a White House meeting at which President Jimmy Carter urged governors to get Japanese automakers to build cars in the United States; he flew to Japan and persuaded Nissan to build its first American plant in Rutherford County. He also persuaded General Motors to build its innovative Saturn plant in Williamson County. The plants became the spark plugs of rapid growth in the counties around Nashville. Alexander was re-elected in 1982, 60%-40%. After leaving office, he spent six months living in Australia, writing a book appropriately called "Six Months Off." In 1988, he became president of the University of Tennessee, and in 1991, President George H.W. Bush tapped him to be secretary of Education.

In 1996, Alexander sought a bigger prize: the White House. He campaigned as a plaid-shirt-wearing outsider. Of members of Congress, he said, "Cut their pay and bring them home!" He called for decentralizing government, and he had a superb fundraising organization that made Nashville a leading Republican money source in the nation. He hired top-notch political consultants and organizers in Iowa and New Hampshire. Alexander finished third in the Iowa caucuses, behind Bob Dole and Pat Buchanan and ahead of Steve Forbes. New Hampshire was his best chance for a breakthrough. Five days before the primary, Dole shrewdly ran ads attacking Alexander. Buchanan was likely to do well in New Hampshire, but probably could not be nominated. If Buchanan finished second in New Hampshire, he would likely become Dole's chief rival, smoothing Dole's path to the nomination. Dole's strategy worked: Buchanan won 27 percent of the vote, edging Dole with

26 percent. Alexander, who came in third place with 23 percent, dropped by the wayside and Dole cruised to the nomination.

Alexander briefly ran for president again in 1999, but the shirt grew old and the outsider themes failed to resonate. George W. Bush dominated the race and left little room for Alexander. His fundraising faltered and after his disappointing sixth-place finish in the August 1999 Iowa straw poll, he dropped out and endorsed Bush. He was later interviewed by Dick Cheney as a possible vice presidential nominee, but Cheney kept the job for himself. Critical of the front-loaded presidential primary calendar, Alexander in 2007 was a chief co-sponsor of legislation to implement a system of rotating regional primaries.

In March 2002, less than a month before the filing deadline, Thompson, by then a senator, announced that he would not seek re-election. He gave Alexander a heads-up on his decision, allowing him to get his campaign underway shortly after the announcement.

In the general election, his opponent was Democratic Rep. Bob Clement of Nashville. Clement, with a relatively moderate voting record that supported the Bush tax cuts and the 2002 Iraq War resolution, depicted Alexander as a political insider who became wealthy through political connections. Alexander countered that Clement, while public service commissioner in the 1970s, served on the board of one of the banks of Jake Butcher, whose banks imploded in scandal in the 1980s. Clement maintained that it was an advisory board and his work on it occurred a decade before the scandal. Alexander prevailed 54%-44%. Six years later, prominent Democrats passed on challenging Alexander's re-election and he easily defeated former state Democratic Chairman Bob Tuke 65%-32%, carrying 94 of 95 counties, including Memphis's black-majority Shelby County. It was the highest percentage ever for a Tennessee Republican senator.

In his early years in the Senate, Alexander sought to become part of his party's leadership. When Alexander's home-state colleague Bill Frist retired in 2006, GOP Whip Mitch McConnell of Kentucky was poised to replace Frist as GOP leader. Alexander courted votes to take McConnell's spot as whip. After the election, former majority leader Trent Lott of Mississippi got into the contest. Although Alexander claimed he had enough votes to win, Lott prevailed 25-24. When Lott resigned from the Senate in December 2007, Jon Kyl was elected whip and Alexander ran for Republican Conference chairman. North Carolina's Richard Burr also ran and pulled support from younger conservatives. Alexander won 31-16, although he showed deference to those on his right by striving to be inclusive.

In September 2011, he baffled much of Washington by announcing that he was resigning as conference chairman — a rare move in a town where people seldom relinquish power voluntarily. "Stepping down from the Republican leadership will liberate me to spend more time working for results on issues that I care most about," he said. He insisted that he was still a "very Republican Republican."

For the most part, Alexander has stuck to consensus party positions. He opposed Democrats' health care overhaul, telling the Tennessee Tribune that it was "arrogant in its dumping of 15 million low-income Americans into a medical ghetto called Medicaid that none of us or any of our families would ever want to be a part of for our health care." After the Newtown Connecticut school massacre in 2012 sparked debates over gun control, he told MSNBC: "I think video games are a bigger problem than guns, because video games affect people."

However, Alexander also sought bipartisan alliances and often found them — with an interest in home-state energy and environment issues. He joined Delaware Democratic Sen. Tom Carper on a bill to limit emissions of carbon dioxide and other pollutants and to create a system of emissions trading. Air pollution had been high in Knoxville and threatened the tourism industry near the Great Smoky Mountains. To counter the effects of a federal court ruling, he pushed to restrict emissions from coal-fired power plants. In 2009, he actively opposed the Democrats' cap-and-trade bill to create a system of emissions trading even though it was like the one he had supported with Carper. In 2011, he was one of six Republicans to cross party lines and vote against a move by Sen. Rand Paul of Kentucky to oppose an Environmental Protection Agency regulation that limited smog. "There's a lot I admire about our neighbors in Kentucky, including their two distinguished United States senators, but I don't want their dirty air blowing into Tennessee," Alexander told the Senate. In 2019, he and Alabama Democratic Sen. Doug Jones proposed the Automotive Jobs Act that would have delayed Trump's proposed 25 percent tariffs on imported vehicles and auto parts that would negatively affect each of their major auto-manufacturing states.

On immigration reform, Alexander joined another Delaware Democrat, Sen. Chris Coons, to introduce a measure in 2012 to create a new temporary visa for immigrants working in high-tech fields. He was one of 14 Republicans to support the "Gang of Eight" comprehensive reform bill that passed the Senate in 2013. Alexander voted for Obama Supreme Court nominee Sonia Sotomayor in 2009, although he voted against Elena Kagan a year later. He cited Kagan's action as Harvard Law School dean barring military recruiters from the school.

In 2011, Alexander helped craft bipartisan legislation to enable states to compel online retailers to collect sales taxes from consumers after previous attempts to implement internet sales taxes failed to get traction. The issue had been especially divisive in Tennessee, where Amazon began building distribution centers but dragged its feet on collecting sales taxes. He was a co-sponsor of the Stop Online Piracy Act, which was opposed by much of Silicon Valley but had the support of Nashville's country music artists and songwriters. When public opposition to the bill grew, with an internet "blackout" day sponsored by Wikipedia and Google, he conceded that it had little chance of passing.

On the HELP committee, Alexander worked on successful bills to help states ensure special education teachers meet federal standards, give parents more choice in special education services and create summer academies for teachers and students to study American history. As a former secretary of Education, Alexander opposed greater involvement by the federal government in federal student loans, comparing it with the "European-Soviet higher education model."

Since taking over as HELP committee chairman in 2015, Alexander has had remarkable legislative success, with 45 bills from his committee becoming law through early 2019. His initial top priority was a revision to the No Child Left Behind education law. He had inveighed against the 2001 law's theory that the federal government should hold states accountable for students' progress. In early 2015, Alexander joined with Sen. Patty Murray of Washington, the senior Democrat on the panel, to propose an overhaul that restored local authority while providing new protections for low-income families. A former university president and former preschool teacher, they were a formidable bipartisan duo. The Senate sent the bill to President Barack Obama on an 85-12 vote. Alexander was enthusiastic about the final bill. "It will unleash a flood of excitement and innovation and student achievement that we haven't seen in a long time," he said.

As chairman of the Appropriations Subcommittee on Energy and Water Development, Alexander gained an opportunity to promote his longtime goals of nuclear and alternative energy. He has advocated for 100 new nuclear power plants over the next 20 years and conversion of half the country's automobiles to electric power. When the Senate overwhelmingly passed his subcommittee bill in 2016, it included funds for new nuclear-energy technologies, including next-generation small modular reactors, plus research and other incentives for wind, solar and hydroelectric power.

Bipartisanship on education didn't last long. When Trump nominated Betsy DeVos as Education secretary, Alexander defended her strong advocacy of charter schools against unified Democratic opposition. Overriding objections from Democratic senators who wanted additional time for hearings during which DeVos sometimes struggled to respond, he said that he was using the same committee procedures that Democrats followed when they were in the majority and handled the nominees of a Democratic president. "I'm trying to be fair," he said in January 2017. Outside Alexander's office in Nashville, Tennessee, teacher unions and other liberal advocacy groups protested DeVos her inexperience with public schools. Alexander said that she was "on our children's side." In an unprecedented action, Vice President Mike Pence broke a 50-50 Senate tie, confirming DeVos.

The conflict over Trump's nominees paled in comparison to the challenge facing Alexander and Senate Republicans on their pledge to replace the Affordable Care Act. As chairman, he was eager to find a bipartisan solution, which initially seemed a steep challenge. After having spent six years "shooting at each other" after enactment of the law, he cautioned: "Building consensus in an environment like that is hard to do. But if we keep in mind that we're trying to help people who are hurting and trying to keep people from being hurt, then that will encourage consensus." Given that his committee had held numerous hearings, Alexander said that he accepted Senate Majority Leader McConnell's plan to draft an alternative in a Republican working group. "There's nothing new in the bill, really. We've debated it and heard it for six years," he said, as Republicans struggled to find consensus. Ultimately, his efforts with Murray to find a bipartisan way to stabilize shaky ACA markets fell short after a GOP push to repeal and replace Obamacare also failed. The HELP chairman worked on the unsuccessful Republican repeal efforts, even though GOP leaders bypassed his committee. "It wasn't ideal for them. It's not ideal for us," Alexander said at the time. "But it may be the only way you can deal with the subject at a time when people have such different opinions about the issue." Alexander and Murray continued to work on solutions, with Alexander telling the Knoxville News Sentinel in early 2019 that his top priorities during his final two years would include making the health care system more innovative and free-market driven, "helping people to know when they're buying health care what the price is." In May, they unveiled a sweeping plan to control health-care costs and eliminate so-called "surprise" medical bills.

In 2014, hoping to avoid the fate of Indiana Sen. Richard Lugar, a moderate who had lost a 2012 primary to a tea party challenger, Alexander kicked off his re-election bid early, announcing a team that included popular Republican Gov. Bill Haslam and the entire GOP Tennessee delegation except for scandal-ridden Rep. Scott DesJarlais. Some worried that a tea party-aligned rival, state Rep. Joe Carr, could catch fire in the increasingly conservative state. Alexander took no chances, spending a combined $8 million in the primary and general elections. He won the August primary 50%-41% — though notably lost his home of Blount County by 422 votes to Carr— and then defeated Knoxville Democratic attorney Gordon Ball by more than 30 percentage points in the fall.

Alexander announced in December 2018 he would not seek a fourth Senate term. "The people of Tennessee have been very generous, electing me to serve more combined years as governor and senator than anyone else from our state. I am deeply grateful, but now it is time for someone else to have that privilege," he said. His decision was met with grief by Republican and Democratic colleagues alike, with Minority Leader Chuck Schumer saying he "felt a pang of sadness" after hearing the news, as yet another veteran legislator and problem solver was heading for the exit. But his early decision allowed him to work across the aisle without fear of the primary challenge he likely would have drawn. Alexander embraced some of that newfound freedom during the 35-day government shutdown that began in December 2018. He spoke out against Trump's refusal to fund several government agencies unless there was funding for his proposed southern border wall. "Government shutdowns should be as off-limits to budget negotiations as chemical weapons are to warfare," Alexander wrote in a Washington Post op-ed. His approach stood in stark contrast to his new colleague, Sen. Marsha Blackburn, who stood firmly behind Trump's approach. When the government was reopened, Trump declared a national emergency to bypass Congress and get funds for the wall. Alexander called the move "unnecessary, unwise and inconsistent with the U.S. Constitution."

It was unlikely Democrats could compete for his seat after former Tennessee Gov. Phil Bredesen, their best centrist hope, fell short in 2018. Haslam — who declined to run after Corker retired — would be the prohibitive front-runner in the race if were to run, bringing a fundraising base and strength from his home in East Tennessee. He likely would be more in the mold of the pragmatic Alexander than the incendiary Blackburn. But if Haslam doesn't run, there would be a wide-open path for a more conservative challenger, marking a likely erasure of the type of senators the state typically has elected — not only Alexander but also Frist, Thompson and Howard Baker. Ambassador to Japan Bill Hagerty, Haslam's former economic and community development commissioner, could run if Haslam doesn't. Freshman Rep. Mark Green, who succeeded Blackburn in the House, was mulling a bid — with the encouragement of the anti-tax Club for Growth — as was Rep. David Kustoff. Another possible candidate was former Rep. Diane Black, who lost the GOP primary for governor. Vanderbilt trauma surgeon Manny Seethi was running.

Marsha Blackburn (R)

Elected 2018, term expires 2024, 1st term, b. Jun 06, 1952; Laurel, MS; Mississippi State University, B.S., 1973; Presbyterian; Married (Chuck Blackburn); 2 children; 2 grandchildren.

Elected Office: TN Senate, 1998-2002; U.S. House, 2003-2019.

Professional Career: Retail marketing consultant, 1973-1998.

DC Office: 357 DSOB 20510, 202-224-3344, Fax: 202-228-0566, blackburn.senate.gov

State Offices: Chattanooga, 423-541-2939; Jackson, 731-660-3971; Jonesborough, 423-753-4009; Knoxville, 865-540-3781; Memphis, 901-527-9199; Nashville, 629-262-8423.

Committees: *Armed Services*: Cybersecurity; Emerging Threats & Capabilities; Readiness & Management Support. *Commerce, Science & Transportation*: Communications, Technology, Innovation & the Internet; Manufacturing, Trade & Consumer Protection; Aviation & Space; Security. *Judiciary*: Antitrust, Competition Policy & Consumer Rights; Constitution; Intellectual Property. *Veterans' Affairs*.

Group Ratings (House)

	ADA	ACLU	AFL-CIO	LCV	ITI	COC	HAFA	ACU	CFG	FRC
2018	-	11%	-	3%	-	70%	85%	-	57%	100%
2017	0%	C	5%	0%	C	93%	C	96%	95%	100%

Key Votes of the 115th Congress (House)

1. Obama-care revision	Y	5. Family planning regs	Y	9. Guantanamo prisoners	N
2. Tax Cuts	Y	6. Body cameras/immigration	N	10. Ground missiles, limit	N
3. Omnibus appropriations	Y	7. Abortion ban	N	11. Defense Dept. spending	Y
4. Dodd-Frank revision	N	8. Concealed carry	Y	12. FISA rules	N

Election Results

Election	Name (Party)	Vote (%)	Cand. Spent	Ind. Exp. Support	Ind. Exp. Oppose
2018 General	Marsha Blackburn (R)...................... 1,227,483	(55%)	$16,298,206	$9,551,771	$19,797,103
	Phil Bredesen (D).............................. 985,450	(44%)	$19,285,588	$6,461,866	$22,204,717
2018 Primary	Marsha Blackburn (R)........................ 613,513	(85%)			
	Aaron Pettigrew (R)....................... 112,705	(16%)			

Prior winning percentages: House: 2016 (72%), 2014 (70%), 2012 (71%), 2010 (72%), 2008 (69%), 2006 (66%), 2004 (100%), 2002 (71%)

Republican Marsha Blackburn won a closely watched race in 2018 to become the first woman elected to the Senate from Tennessee. A conservative firebrand who was a legislative activist and influential lawmaker in the House for 16 years, she was poised to become an influential member of a GOP Conference badly in need of gender diversity. But Blackburn represented a sharp shift in senator from a pragmatic conservative— like Bob Corker, whom she replaced — to a tea party acolyte who's a fierce supporter of President Donald Trump.

Blackburn grew up in Laurel, Mississippi, where her father sold oil-field production equipment. Her interest in gardening and canning won her a 4-H college scholarship at Mississippi State University, where she majored in merchandising and clothing. She helped pay her way through college by selling books door to door for Southwestern Co., which sold educational materials that attracted many conservative students. Blackburn, however, was rejected when she first applied because she was a woman and there were concerns about a single woman going out to sell alone. The company finally hired her as one of its first saleswomen, albeit with a catch — she had to live in Mississippi with her parents, while the salesmen were allowed to go between cities. "People have been brainwashed that they think women aren't capable of this type of work," she told her college newspaper. Blackburn worked her way up and eventually became a sales manager and earned enough money to pay for her sophomore year college tuition and buy a blue Ford sedan, which she called the "Can-Do."

After graduation, she married and moved to Tennessee, settling in the tony Nashville suburb of Brentwood. Her hilltop home in Brentwood is known as "Up Yonder," named by its former owner, Grand Ole Opry star Minnie Pearl. Blackburn became director of retail fashion for the Nashville department store Castner Knott Company and later found her own marketing company. She was appointed by Republican Gov. Don Sundquist as executive director of the Tennessee Film, Entertainment and Music Commission, and her interest in politics grew. In 1992, she challenged Democrat Rep. Bart Gordon but lost 57%-41%. She then won a state Senate seat, where she built a grassroots campaign to defeat Sundquist's proposed income tax. In 2014, Tennessee voters approved a constitutional amendment that prohibited a state income tax.

When the 7th District House seat, which then stretched from the Nashville to Memphis suburbs, opened, Blackburn was the only well-known candidate from the Nashville area. Of the six other candidates, three were familiar figures in the Memphis area. She benefited from financial support of the national anti-tax Club for Growth and from attacks by the Shelby County candidates on one another. She ran as an anti-abortion, pro-gun, pro-military conservative and won the primary with 40 percent of the vote and then easily won the general election. She was the first woman elected to Congress from Tennessee without following her husband, though gender wasn't something she emphasized — even asking to be called "congressman" rather than "congresswoman."

Blackburn staked out conservative positions in the House, often seeking leadership roles. She was active on the Republican Study Committee, and in 2012 she co-chaired the Republican National Convention's platform committee. She co-sponsored the "birther" bill, requiring future presidential candidates to prove they were born in the United States, a measure that played off attacks from the right on President Barack Obama's qualifications to hold office, although the measure would not have applied to him. In 2015, she wrote a letter to the IRS challenging the tax-exempt status of the Clinton Foundation. A champion of gun owners' rights, Blackburn has boasted about her perfect marksmanship score with her Smith & Wesson .38. After the Newtown, Connecticut, elementary school massacre, she said the debate should focus on mental health because disturbed people predisposed toward violence could use "a hammer, a hatchet, a car" instead of a gun. In 2016, she chaired the House's Select Panel on Infant Lives, which was a special committee created to review allegations by anti-abortion activists of an illicit trade of fetal tissue. The panel held hearings and issued recommendations for changes in what Blackburn described as "the abortion and fetal tissue procurement industries." Democrats opposed creation of the panel and its activities.

When Republicans regained control of the House in 2011, Blackburn played a prominent role on technology policy at Energy and Commerce. A fervent advocate of the Nashville-based music industry and founder of the Congressional Songwriters Caucus, she fought to protect intellectual property rights of artists against illegal music downloads. In 2015, she co-sponsored the bipartisan Fair Play, Fair Pay bill to ensure musicians are compensated for their work. The recording industry has given her a congressional Grammy. Blackburn has often challenged the Federal Communications Commission. In 2014, the House passed on a largely party-line vote her amendment to prevent the FCC from pre-empting state laws that block the ability of cities to create local government-run broadband networks; she cited state sovereignty on behalf of her proposal, which was supported by large cable companies. In 2015, she sought to deny funding for the FCC to implement its net-neutrality rules that were designed to bar tiered pricing for internet services; she contends that such authority is solely the responsibility of Congress. In taking over in 2017 as chairwoman of the revamped Communication and Technology Subcommittee, she encouraged Ajit Pai, Trump's choice to chair the FCC, to cut back its regulations.

Blackburn was an early Trump supporter and served as a vice chairwoman of his presidential transition team, which sparked speculation that she might be named to a Cabinet position. When Corker announced in September 2017 he wouldn't run for a third term, her attention turned to the open seat. After term-limited Tennessee Gov. Bill Haslam announced he wouldn't run, Blackburn became the GOP front-runner. She made clear in her announcement video she would be a very different senator than the collegial Corker. "I'm a hard core, card-carrying Tennessee conservative. I'm politically incorrect and proud of it," Blackburn said. "I know the left calls me a wing-nut, or a knuckle-dragging conservative. And you know what? I say that's all right; bring it on."

Corker, however, soon appeared to have a change of heart. Some in the Tennessee Republican establishment had concerns about Blackburn's statewide viability — especially after popular centrist former Gov. Phil Bredesen got in on the Democratic side — and began encouraging Corker to reconsider his decision to retire. Corker's office confirmed the pressure campaign, saying he was "listening closely." Former Rep. Stephen Fincher, who was Blackburn's chief primary opponent, dropped out to encourage Corker to run. A spokeswoman for Blackburn issued an irate response: "Anyone who thinks Marsha Blackburn can't win a general election is just a plain sexist pig. ... We aren't worried about these ego-driven, tired old men." She made clear Blackburn was staying in the race, whether or not Corker jumped back in. The prospect of such a primary — which many Republicans admitted Corker likely could not win — would bleed their war chests dry, while Bredesen was left a clear path to the general election. Corker stuck with his original decision. Blackburn won the primary with 85 percent of the vote against a little-known challenger.

The rift between Blackburn and the state establishment was cause for pause, initially. And those concerns were magnified by Corker's repeated praise of Bredesen, with whom he had worked closely while mayor of Chattanooga to bring Volkswagen to the area. He gave Blackburn only a tepid endorsement, repeatedly refusing to say her name during one live TV interview. Bredesen was a strong recruit for Democrats — their last candidate to win statewide, first elected in 2002 and re-elected in 2006 with 69 percent of the vote, including carrying all of Tennessee's 95 counties. He argued the race was a test of the centrist brand he had built in the state and would show whether a Southern Democrat could still be victorious despite a national party very much disliked in Tennessee. "I'm not going up there to be lockstep in some way with what the national Democratic Party has become," Bredesen told NPR. "You have to join the party to participate in electoral politics but the party for me is an organization I belong to — it's not a religion and I don't think that I will go to hell if [Senate Minority Leader] Chuck Schumer doesn't like what I say about something or other." Instead, the low-key policy wonk tried to make issues local, holding small events with a focus on topics like agriculture and trade — emphasizing his opposition to Trump's tariffs — health care and even on hyperlocal issues like Asian Carp, an invasive species that was harming the state's fishing industry. The former businessman and health care executive also pointed out places where he agreed with Trump, such as rolling back regulations. Bredesen made the case he was the centrist, middle-of-the road choice and would bring that mentality to Washington. "Look, I very much would like my party to sort of, you know, get back to being a muscular party focusing on opportunity for middle- and working-class voters, and actually have some ideas that are practical about how to go about doing that," he told The New Yorker.

Blackburn worked to make the race as nationalized as possible — a smart strategy in a state that Trump won by 26 percentage points. The Tennessee seat was a key piece to Democrats' path to a majority — another thing Blackburn and other Republicans repeatedly emphasized. She argued that even if you may have liked Bredesen as governor, going to Washington with a "D" beside your name was a far different matter. Trump traveled to Tennessee to campaign for Blackburn several times, telling voters that she would be the best person to uphold his agenda. Her biggest break may have been the retirement of Supreme Court Justice Anthony Kennedy. Blackburn's fervent support for the president's nominee to replace him, Brett Kavanaugh, underscored just how important having a Republican vote in the Senate would be, and she stood by Kavanaugh even after he was accused of sexual assault, a charge he denied. Bredesen said he would have supported Kavanaugh's nomination. Regardless, Blackburn's poll numbers rose.

Outside money poured into the race—with $22.2 million spent hitting Bredesen compared with $19.8 million attacking Blackburn. Both had large war chests of their own—Bredesen spent $20.9 million, including $7.5 million of his own, while Blackburn spent $17.4 million. Republicans had been worried about this seat up until the end, but Blackburn won 55%-44%. Bredesen, who 12 years before had swept every county in the state, only won three counties. Blackburn's victory was a major shift in Tennessee politics — away from the genial, bipartisan lawmakers who have typically won in the state and toward vocal, conservative partisans.

Blackburn got a seat, along with Iowa Sen. Joni Ernst, on the Judiciary Committee — adding Republican women to the panel just months after their absence was especially stark during the hearings into the sexual assault allegations against Kavanaugh. Blackburn stood behind Trump during the 35-day government shutdown in December 2018 and January 2019, warning of the dangers of illegal immigration. "We know that walls work. This is about using our resources properly to protect our nation," she told the Clarksville Leaf-Chronicle. "Remember this: Until we secure that porous southern border ... every town's a border town, every state's a border state." The first bill Blackburn introduced would have taken federal funding from organizations that perform abortions — such as Planned Parenthood.

Phil Roe (R)

Elected 2008, 6th term, b. Jul 21, 1945; Clarksville; Austin Peay State University (TN), B.S., 1967; University of Tennessee, Memphis, M.D., 1973; Methodist; Married (Pam Roe); 3 children (3 from previous marriage); 2 grandchildren.

Military Career: U.S. Army 1973-1974

Elected Office: Johnson City Commission, 2003-2009, vice Mayor, 2005-2007, Mayor, 2007-2009.

Professional Career: Obstetrician/gynecologist, 1970-2008.

DC Office: 102 CHOB 20515, 202-225-6356, Fax: 202-225-5714, roe.house.gov

State Offices: Kingsport, 423-247-8161; Morristown, 423-254-1400.

Committees: *Education & Labor*: Health, Employment, Labor & Pensions. *Veterans' Affairs (RMM)*.

Group Ratings

	ADA	ACLU	AFL-CIO	LCV	ITI	COC	HAFA	ACU	CFG	FRC
2018	-	7%	-	3%	-	83%	61%	88%	59%	100%
2017	0%	C	3%	3%	C	93%	C	89%	73%	100%

Almanac Ratings 2017-18

	Economy	Social	Foreign	Composite
Liberal	4%	3%	3%	3%
Conservative	96%	97%	97%	97%

Key Votes of the 115th Congress

1. Obama-care revision	Y	5. Family planning regs	Y	9. Guantanamo prisoners	N
2. Tax Cuts	Y	6. Body cameras/immigration	N	10. Ground missiles, limit	N
3. Omnibus appropriations	Y	7. Abortion ban	Y	11. Defense Dept. spending	Y
4. Dodd-Frank revision	Y	8. Concealed carry	Y	12. FISA rules	N

Election Results

Election	Name (Party)	Vote (%)		Cand. Spent	Ind. Exp. Support	Ind. Exp. Oppose
2018 General	Phil Roe (R)..	172,835	(77%)	$533,452	$1,565	
	Martin Olsen (D).................................	47,138	(21%)	$160,524		
2018 Primary	Phil Roe (R)......................................	71,556	(74%)			
	Todd McKinley (R).............................	16,175	(17%)			
	James Brooks (R).............................	5,058	(5%)			

Prior winning percentages: 2016 (78%), 2014 (83%), 2012 (76%), 2010 (81%), 2008 (72%)

Republican Phil Roe, elected in 2008, is one of the House's physicians and he has been closely associated with his former profession. He serves on two committees dealing with health issues, regularly espouses his party's opposition to the Affordable Care Act, co-chairs the GOP Doctors Caucus and issues his news releases with "M.D." after his name. As a reliable partisan but no bomb-thrower, he was selected by House Republicans to take over in 2017 as chairman of the Veterans' Affairs Committee.

Roe grew up in Clarksville and attended a one-room schoolhouse with no running water. He graduated from Austin Peay State University and received a medical degree from the University of Tennessee. He was a captain in the Army Medical Corps, where he was stationed in South Korea near the Demilitarized Zone. He set up shop in Johnson City as an obstetrician/gynecologist and practiced for 30 years. He delivered nearly 5,000 babies, a useful way to connect with voters. In 2003, the political bug bit Roe, and he was elected to the Johnson City Commission. Roe was chosen by commission members to be vice mayor in 2005 and mayor in 2007. When the House seat opened in 2006, Roe competed in a crowded GOP primary. In a state with no runoff, he finished fourth with 17 percent of the vote, behind health care business owner David Davis, who went on to win the general election.

Davis quickly gained a reputation as a combative partisan. Without the complication of a 10-candidate field, Roe challenged him one-on-one for reelection and embarked on a grassroots campaign, talking to voters, stumping in restaurants and waving signs at busy intersections. In ads featuring an elderly grandmother trying to fill up her car with gas, Roe criticized Davis for accepting money from oil companies, attacks that resonated as gas prices spiked. Davis outspent the challenger 3-to-1, but Roe became the first challenger in more than 40 years to defeat a House member in Tennessee. His margin of victory was 482 votes. He won the district's two largest counties, Washington and Sullivan, while Davis was strong along the western edge of the district, winning Sevier and Hawkins counties. Roe defeated Democrat Robert Russell with 72 percent of the vote and has been reelected with ease since.

Roe's positions mirror the conservative bent of the district. He has an upbeat, folksy demeanor and was among the first House Republicans to join the Tea Party Caucus in 2010. With the GOP takeover of the House, he became chairman of the Education and Workforce Committee's health panel and helped to craft his party's free-market alternatives to the new law. He filed a bill in 2011 seeking to repeal an advisory board that was created to rein in Medicare spending increases. The

House passed the measure in 2012, but GOP leaders drew criticism from Democrats — including those who supported the bill — for attaching a provision setting caps on medical damage lawsuit awards, and the bill died in the Senate.

With GOP Rep. Austin Scott of Georgia and the backing of the Republican Study Committee, Roe filed in 2015 a bill to repeal the Affordable Care Act and replace it with what the authors called patient-centered reforms and free-market solutions. An attempt to revive it amid President Donald Trump's push to repeal Obamacare failed. Roe worked on the bipartisan bill that was enacted in 2015 to repeal the "doc fix," imposing new payment rules for doctors with Medicare patients. With Democratic Rep. Ami Bera of California, another doctor, Roe sought to limit drug abuse by disposing of prescription drugs that the user no longer needs. In 2019, Roe said that the Doctors Caucus would explore ways to lower the cost of prescription drugs.

After hearings by the Veterans' Affairs Committee revealed problems with Department of Veterans Affairs contracting procedures, Roe won approval in 2012 of a provision barring its employees who break the law from receiving bonuses. In 2016, he won enactment of his bill to require clinicians practicing at the VA to report directly to state licensing boards whenever they witness unacceptable behavior from other VA clinicians. After the election, Roe ran for the opening as committee chairman. He won the contest against two Colorado Republicans — moderate Mike Coffman and conservative Doug Lamborn. "There's no federal agency more in need of reform than the VA," Roe said about his plans as chairman.

The committee did just that, passing legislation to expand options for private-sector care for veterans, to modernize the disability appeal claims process and to improve the VA's technology. After Trump's first nominee for VA secretary, White House and Navy physician Ronny Jackson, withdrew amid allegations of improper behavior and fostering a hostile workplace, Roe said while he was sure Jackson had been previously vetted, he had "became a distraction, and certainly the VA doesn't need any more distractions right now."

Roe has said that he wants to delve into funding for veteran homelessness and suicide prevention. He has supported allowing the VA to do research on cannabis. In 2019, with Democratic Chairman Mark Takano of California, he took another shot at a longtime cause: providing health and disability benefits to "Blue Water" Navy veterans -- those who served on ships on the coast of Vietnam during the war and were exposed to Agent Orange, but have not been eligible for benefits other veterans received.

After the release in October 2016 of Trump's crude comments about women, Roe called them "disgusting, inappropriate and reprehensible," and said that he planned to write-in another Republican for president. With Trump as president, Roe opposed his tariffs, saying they would harm northeast Tennessee. In 2017, Roe was diagnosed with prostate cancer, but was declared cancer-free later that year after surgery. He had contemplated retiring in 2018 but ultimately decided to run for another term; he was reelected with 77 percent of the vote. He will be 75 in 2020 and, in the minority, a retirement wouldn't come as a shock. Whenever it becomes open, the district likely will attract another crowded and competitive GOP primary, but the district is all but certain to remain Republican.

TN-1: Northeast Tennessee   Cook Partisan Voting Index: R+28

Population		Race and Ethnicity		Income	
Total	712,059	White	91.6%	Median Income	$40,411
Land area (sq. miles)	4,142	Black	2.1%	District Income Rank	411
Pop/ sq mi	171.9	Latino	3.6%	Poverty Rate	18.4%
Born in State	61.4%	Asian	0.7%	With health insurance	88.3%
		Two or more races	1.7%	Cash public assistance	2.5%
Age Groups		Other	0.2%	Food stamp/SNAP	17.9%
Under 18	20.2%				
18-34	20.1%	**Education**		**Work**	
35-64	40.5%	H.S grad or less	53.7%	White Collar	19.2%
Over 64	19.2%	Some college	26.8%	Sales and Service	43.9%
		College Degree, 4 yr	12.1%	Blue Collar	26.1%
Military		Post grad	7.4%	Government	13.9%
Veteran/ Active Duty	10.1%				

2012 Pres. Vote	Romney	186,318	(73%)	Obama	65,782	(26%)		
2016 Pres. Vote	Trump	203,651	(77%)	Clinton	52,237	(20%)	Johnson	6,488	(2%)

Kingsport, Bristol, Johnson City: Between the corduroy-like ridges of the Appalachian chains, as they bend west and then south, the Great Valley of Virginia extends far into northeastern Tennessee. These ridges guide travel today (even the interstates follow the valleys here) just as they guided settlement more than 200 years ago. The land rush immediately after the Revolutionary War populated the area, mostly with Scots-Irish immigrants. These settlers and their descendants were often hot-tempered, fierce folk. In tiny Jonesborough, the early settlers attempted to establish the free state of Franklin in 1784. The original town had an ordinance requiring settlers "to within three years build a brick, stone, or well framed house, 20 feet long and 16 feet wide, and at least 10 feet in the pitche, with a brick or stone chimney" — a sort of early restrictive covenant — and many pioneer cabins, Federal-style mansions and Greek Revival churches are lovingly preserved today. In Elizabethton, European settlers established the Watauga Association in 1772, the first majority-rule system of government in America and the first permanent settlement outside of the 13 colonies. A young Andrew Jackson made his way from North Carolina to the area, set up a legal practice, and became a (typically irascible) judge before moving westward.

The building of the railroads in the 1850s determined the winners and losers for the modern era, and today some of those dormant railroad routes have been converted into biking and hiking trails. The small industrial cities that originally developed — Johnson City, Kingsport and Bristol, now collectively known as the Tri-Cities — were on the main lines of national commerce before the Civil War. The war had a different political impact here than in most of the South: Mountainous Northeast Tennessee had few slaves and, with its connection to Northern industry, was Union and Republican territory. East Tennesseans twice voted against secession. It remains heavily Republican to this day.

The area developed the sort of industrial economy that produced unions and Democrats in the North. Its skilled labor force, low electric power rates because of the Tennessee Valley Authority, and good transportation routes (rail lines and Interstates 26 and 81) spurred growth. Its small cities once boasted major paper, printing and fabric plants, although most of them are gone. With companies such as Kingsport-based Eastman Chemical Co. and Bell Helicopters taking the lead, the area has been a strong market for exports. Bristol is home to a major NASCAR track, nicknamed "The World's Fastest Half-Mile." In 2016, Bristol Motor Speedway hosted the largest crowd ever to see a college football game, with 156,990 on hand to watch Tennessee defeat Virginia Tech. Bristol, the birthplace of country music, is a split city -- half in Tennessee, half in Virginia, divided literally in the middle of State Street -- though the Tennessee side has been more economically successful. In Sevier County near Knoxville, Gatlinburg and Pigeon Forge (home of Dolly Parton's Dollywood theme park), there are more than 10,000 hotel rooms near the entrance to Great Smoky Mountains National Park, the nation's busiest. In 2018, the park had more than 11.4 million visitors, twice as many as the runner-up, Grand Canyon. Still, the Tri-Cities region has succumbed, as many poorer and rural regions have, to the opioid epidemic. In 2015, more than half the state's drug overdose deaths were in Washington County (Johnson City).

The 1st Congressional District takes in the far northeastern end of Tennessee. Sullivan and Washington counties, which make up the Tri-Cities, include 40 percent of the population. Mountain City is where fugitive murderer Tom Dula was captured before being returned to North Carolina for hanging (generations of folk musicians would eventually alter his name to the more familiar "Tom Dooley"). Greeneville was the birthplace of member of Congress and Alamo hero Davy Crockett, and the longtime home of President Andrew Johnson. Over the years, this district's politics haven't budged an inch. It hasn't elected a Democrat to the House since 1878. True to its roots, it gave Donald Trump 77 per cent of the vote: his highest in Tennessee and in the top 2 percent of GOP districts nationwide.

Tim Burchett (R)

Elected 2018, 1st term, b. Aug 25, 1964; Knoxville; University of Tennessee, B.S., 1988; Presbyterian; Married (Kelly Burchett); 1 child.

Elected Office: TN House, Member 1995-1999, TN Senate, 1998-2010; Knox County Mayor, 2010-2018.

Professional Career: Small Businessman.

DC Office: 1122 LHOB 20515, 202-225-5435, burchett.house.gov

State Offices: Knoxville, 865-523-3772; Maryville, 865-984-5464.

Committees: *Budget*. *Foreign Affairs*: Africa, Global Health, Global Human Rights & Internat'l Orgs; Europe, Eurasia, Energy & the Environment. *Small Business*: Innovation & Workforce Development; Investigations, Oversight & Regulations.

Election Results

Election	Name (Party)	Vote (%)		Cand. Spent	Ind. Exp. Support	Ind. Exp. Oppose
2018 General	Tim Burchett (R).............................	172,856	(66%)	$933,550	$2,390	
	Renee Hoyos (D).................................	86,668	(33%)	$340,927		
2018 Primary	Tim Burchett (R).............................	47,875	(48%)			
	Jimmy Matlock (R).........................	35,855	(36%)			
	Ashley Nickoles (R)........................	10,961	(11%)			

Republican Tim Burchett was elected in 2018 as the most experienced officeholder among the House GOP freshmen. His 24 years in state and local elected positions ran counter to the "outsider" persona that was popular among many House freshmen across the nation. In his heavily Republican district, Burchett survived a bruising primary contest. His victory marked the first time since 1964 that the seat was not held by one of the Duncans, a father and son team who typically were backbenchers but remained attentive to local politics in their Knoxville-based district. Retiring Rep. Jimmy Duncan showed his declining influence with his endorsement of Burchett's chief opponent and unfriendly comments about his successor.

Burchett, a Knoxville native, graduated from the University of Tennessee. In his first job, he sold mulch; government regulations put him out of business, he later complained. He served four years in the state House and 12 years in the Senate before winning election in 2010 as mayor of Knox County — a separate post from the mayor of the city of Knoxville.

During eight years as county mayor, he took credit for reducing taxes and the county's debt. He called himself a "limited libertarian," who believed that individuals should be responsible for their own actions. "I've never seen where government has come into a situation and made things better," he told Cityview magazine. In that 2017 interview, he said that both "national parties have continuously failed us." With Burchett's position term-limited in 2018, he planned to seek another office. When Duncan announced his retirement in August 2017, Burchett days later said he would seek to replace him.

His chief opponent was Jimmy Matlock, who owned a chain of local tire and auto-repair shops and served 12 years in the state House. He styled himself as the more-conservative candidate, and was endorsed by leaders of the House Republican Freedom Caucus. Duncan supported Matlock, citing his "real heart for service."

The primary was marked by frequent attacks between the two frontrunners. Matlock charged that Burchett backed tax increases when he served in the Legislature and that he supported a Democrat to lead the Senate. Burchett filed a complaint with the Federal Election Commission contending that Matlock used his auto shops to run ads to promote his candidacy. Each candidate raised a bit more than $500,000 for the primary; Matlock's total included $175,000 in personal loans.

Five other candidates entered the GOP primary, but none of them gained significant support. Sarah Nickloes, the only woman in the field, received national publicity for her experience in the Air Force as commander of an aircraft tanker. The political action committee of the Republican Main Street Partnership spent more than $100,000 for ads on her behalf.

Burchett won the primary with 48 percent of the vote to 36 percent for Matlock and 11 percent for Nickloes. His lead of more than 17,000 votes in Knox County, which cast a bit more than half the total vote, accounted for his overall advantage of about 12,000 votes. Matlock won his home county of Loudon with 71 percent and also took neighboring Blunt County. Burchett took the four smaller counties north of Knoxville.

Democrat Renee Hoyos, executive director of the Tennessee Clean Water Network, who opposed Burchett in November, styled herself as a problem-solver and said voters wanted a change from "the same old, same old." With his 66%-33% victory, Burchett upheld the district's tradition as a Republican stronghold since the 19th century.

TN-2: East Tennessee   **Cook Partisan Voting Index: R+20**

Population		Race and Ethnicity		Income	
Total	732,230	White	86.2%	Median Income	$50,711
Land area (sq. miles)	2,321	Black	6.1%	District Income Rank	295
Pop/ sq mi	315.5	Latino	3.9%	Poverty Rate	15.4%
Born in State	59.8%	Asian	1.6%	With health insurance	90.6%
		Two or more races	1.8%	Cash public assistance	2.2%
Age Groups		Other	0.3%	Food stamp/SNAP	13.7%
Under 18	21%				
18-34	23.2%	**Education**		**Work**	
35-64	39%	H.S grad or less	41.5%	White Collar	16.8%
Over 64	16.8%	Some college	28.3%	Sales and Service	42.2%
		College Degree, 4 yr	18.4%	Blue Collar	21.1%
Military		Post grad	11.7%	Government	13.8%
Veteran/ Active Duty	9.1%				

2012 Pres. Vote	Romney	186,362	(67%)	Obama	85,510	(31%)			
2016 Pres. Vote	Trump	188,973	(65%)	Clinton	86,217	(30%)	Johnson	10,457	(4%)

Knoxville: Knoxville, the largest city in East Tennessee, was the state's first capital. It is nestled between mountain ridges where the Holston and French Broad rivers join to form the Tennessee River. It was established not long after the first wave of pioneers came through the gaps and down the mountains of the Appalachian chain. During the Civil War, it was Union territory, and it has remained Republican in allegiance and progressive on civil rights ever since.

Its Republican heritage has been affected by another tradition, that of the Tennessee Valley Authority. A bold program when created in the 1930s, it is now part of the fabric of life in East Tennessee, sometimes criticized as it has reached capacity to produce hydroelectric power and begun to rely more on nuclear power. In a competitive electricity market, TVA has labored under billions of dollars in debt mostly incurred in building its nuclear plants. In 2018, the Department of Energy awarded Knoxville-based Analysis and Measurement Services Corp. a $2.8 million grant to test the age-related wear in nuclear reactors' electrical cables. Heavy ozone pollution in Knoxville led the Environmental Protection Agency to impose growth limits, so TVA spent several billion dollars to reduce pollution at its coal-fired power plants. The result has improved local air quality and the EPA has ruled that the Knoxville area met its ozone standard. Even with its more rigorous standards, the American Lung Association in 2016 gave Knoxville an "F" for air quality, though it has improved slightly since then.

Knoxville has overcome other setbacks and grown, at times robustly. The University of Tennessee's football complex, Neyland Stadium, on fall Saturdays contains one of the nation's largest crowds, over 100,000, cheering on the Volunteers. Women's basketball has historically been nearly as popular as football here. In 2009, Lady Vols' Coach Pat Summitt became the first Division I basketball coach, men's or women's, to win 1,000 career games. She retired in 2012 with a diagnosis of early-onset Alzheimer's disease, after having won 1,098 games and eight national championships, and died in 2016. In spring 2016, a new bridge for walkers and bikers opened across the Tennessee River from the campus to South Knoxville.

The 2nd Congressional District of Tennessee includes Knoxville and Knox County, plus all or part of six mountainous counties to the north and south. More than 60 percent live in Knox County, where the landmark Sunsphere tower from the 1982 World's Fair remains visible from Interstate 40.

The heavily Republican district has not elected a Democratic congressman since the early 1850s. With its 65 percent vote for Donald Trump in 2016, the 2nd was at the low end of the seven Republican-held districts in Tennessee.

Chuck Fleischmann (R)

Elected 2010, 5th term, b. Oct 11, 1962; New York, NY; University of Illinois, B.A., 1983; University of Tennessee College of Law, Knoxville, J.D., 1986; Roman Catholic; Married (Brenda Fleischmann); 3 children.

Professional Career: Practicing attorney, 1987-2010.

DC Office: 2410 RHOB 20515, 202-225-3271, Fax: 202-225-3494, fleischmann.house.gov

State Offices: Athens, 423-745-4671; Chattanooga, 423-756-2342; Oak Ridge, 865-576-1976.

Committees: *Appropriations*: Energy & Water Development & Related Agencies; Homeland Security (RMM).

Group Ratings

	ADA	ACLU	AFL-CIO	LCV	ITI	COC	HAFA	ACU	CFG	FRC
2018	-	4%	-	3%	-	83%	62%	80%	54%	100%
2017	0%	C	11%	0%	C	93%	C	85%	68%	100%

Almanac Ratings 2017-18

	Economy	Social	Foreign	Composite
Liberal	3%	7%	5%	5%
Conservative	97%	94%	95%	95%

Key Votes of the 115th Congress

1. Obama-care revision	Y	5. Family planning regs	Y	9. Guantanamo prisoners	N
2. Tax Cuts	Y	6. Body cameras/immigration	N	10. Ground missiles, limit	N
3. Omnibus appropriations	Y	7. Abortion ban	Y	11. Defense Dept. spending	Y
4. Dodd-Frank revision	Y	8. Concealed carry	Y	12. FISA rules	Y

Election Results

Election	Name (Party)	Vote (%)		Cand. Spent	Ind. Exp. Support	Ind. Exp. Oppose
2018 General	Chuck Fleischmann (R)	156,512	(64%)	$558,943	$6,435	
	Danielle Mitchell (D)	84,731	(35%)	$265,938	$1,801	
2018 Primary	Chuck Fleischmann (R)	67,830	(79%)			
	Jeremy Massengale (R)	10,219	(12%)			
	William Spurlock Jr. (R)	5,359	(6%)			

Prior winning percentages: 2016 (66%), 2014 (62%), 2012 (62%), 2010 (60%)

Republican Charles (Chuck) Fleischmann was elected in 2010 to succeed GOP Rep. Zach Wamp, who ran unsuccessfully for governor. Fleischmann is more of a team player than the independent-minded Wamp. With his seat on the Appropriations Committee, where he has become the ranking Republican on the Homeland Security Subcommittee, he pursues funding for the Oak Ridge lab. He has contended with two primary challenges from Zach's son Weston, in which Fleischmann narrowly prevailed.

When he was a boy, Fleischmann's father, Max, worked in the food services business. Fleischmann lived in Philadelphia and New Jersey before finishing high school in Chicago. He graduated from the University of Illinois in three years with a bachelor's degree in political science. He got his law degree at the University of Tennessee and started his own firm in Knoxville with his wife, Brenda.

When Zach Wamp decided to retire, Fleischmann ran, saying he was "very, very upset with the way things were going in Washington D.C." In the primary, health care consultant Robin Smith, a former Republican state party chairwoman, was a formidable opponent. Fleischmann put $544,000 of his own money into the campaign and accused Smith of mismanaging funds when she chaired the GOP. Smith attacked Fleischmann's record as a personal injury lawyer, saying that he had sued gun clubs, Walmart stores and churches, all popular institutions in the state. Fleischmann defended himself by saying, "I make a living standing up for the little guy, people who have traditionally not had a voice and who have been dealt injustices and harm." Fleischmann edged out Smith, 30%-28%. In November, he defeated radio talk-show host John Wolfe, 57%-28%.

Fleischmann has been a conservative mainstay. He is capable of serving up red-meat rhetoric. Asked at a debate for his views on climate change, he responded: "I think we ought to take Al Gore, put him on an iceberg, and put him way out there." He opposed the debt ceiling hike in 2011 and the deal to avoid the so-called fiscal cliff in 2013. In 2018, the Chattanooga Free Press editorial board endorsed Fleischmann and acknowledged he had become more pragmatic as he gained seniority, writing that "while not changing his stripes, we believe he has lost some of the stridency he had in his first few years on the job and has learned the value of working with colleagues across the aisle on issues important to the state and to this district." Given the importance of international business to the Chattanooga region, Fleischmann has voiced concern over President Donald Trump's tariffs.

His position on Appropriations, especially its Energy and Water Development Subcommittee, has given Fleischmann a critical voice on an issue of vital interest to the region. In 2018, he helped secure $4.5 billion for the Oak Ridge National Laboratory. Fleischmann has repeatedly stressed the need to replace Chickamauga's deteriorating 75-year-old river lock by overhauling the project's funding mechanism, the Inland Waterway Trust Fund, for the estimated $680 million project. When the lock shut down in July 2016 because of cracked concrete, he said that its replacement was "very high on the priority list." That process finally began in 2018, with a new, larger 110-foot-by-600-foot lock made possible by an initial $78 million in funding; the replacement was set to be completed in 2024.

In February 2019, his new GOP post on the Homeland Security Subcommittee made Fleischmann a part of the bipartisan group that negotiated a deal following the 35-day government shutdown. The agreement included only $1.375 billion for border barriers -- far short of the $5.7 billion Trump wanted – but Fleischmann considered it a victory. "I do believe we were successful," he told NPR after the bill passed. "Republicans got more border wall funding. We kept the ICE beds up....There was tremendous common ground." Fleischmann later supported Trump's decision to declare a national emergency to get the rest of the border wall funds, though he said that he had constitutional concerns.

Fleischmann has survived two grueling primary fights. In 2012, he drew spirited challenges from 25-year-old Weston Wamp and dairy magnate Scottie Mayfield. He won the primary with 39 percent, as Mayfield took 31 percent and Wamp 29 percent. His Democratic opponent, acute care physician Mary Headrick, accused him of being in the pocket of special interests and blasted his proposal to cut capital gains tax rates. He coasted to a 61 percent win.

Wamp returned for another try in 2014 in what became an even tighter one-on-one primary. He called himself an "independent-minded conservative," and he courted votes from Democrats, who were eligible to vote in the primary. Fleischmann rebuked him at one debate, saying, "If he wants to run as a Democrat, let him run as a Democrat." Wamp responded that the congressman apparently believed "that Democrats have cooties and you can't talk to them." Fleischmann retorted, "They have got a lot worse than that, Weston." Fleischmann accused Wamp of being a "show horse" and supporting "amnesty" for illegal immigrants. He eked out a win, 51%-49%. The outcome in many of the counties was exceedingly close and neither candidate had an obvious base.

In 2016, the scare for Fleischmann was a contest that did not happen. Bo Watson, the veteran speaker pro tem in the Tennessee Senate, said publicly that he was giving serious thought to a primary challenge. Instead, Watson decided to stick with his influential state post. That left Fleischmann with easy campaigns in 2016 and 2018. Given his influential positions on the Appropriations panel, Fleischmann may have finally settled into this district for as long as he wants.

TN-3: East Tennessee   **Cook Partisan Voting Index: R+18**

Population		Race and Ethnicity		Income	
Total	723,001	White	82.2%	Median Income	$45,751
Land area (sq. miles)	4,570	Black	10.6%	District Income Rank	367
Pop/ sq mi	158.2	Latino	3.8%	Poverty Rate	16.6%
Born in State	64.4%	Asian	1.3%	With health insurance	90.1%
		Two or more races	1.7%	Cash public assistance	2.9%
Age Groups		Other	0.3%	Food stamp/SNAP	16.7%
Under 18	21%				
18-34	21.1%	**Education**		**Work**	
35-64	40.1%	H.S grad or less	48.8%	White Collar	17.8%
Over 64	17.8%	Some college	28.3%	Sales and Service	40.8%
		College Degree, 4 yr	14.4%	Blue Collar	25.7%
Military		Post grad	8.5%	Government	14.1%
Veteran/ Active Duty	9.1%				

2012 Pres. Vote	Romney	172,227	(63%)	Obama	95,014	(35%)		
2016 Pres. Vote	Trump	181,189	(65%)	Clinton	83,297	(30%)	Johnson	8,665 (3%)

    Chattanooga, Oak Ridge: Etching its way through the serrated ridges of East Tennessee, with some of the most vivid scenery in the Appalachian Mountain chain, is the river that gave the state its name. From Knoxville, the Tennessee River cuts through a ridge and then plunges down a long valley to the city of Chattanooga at the Georgia line. There it switches course again, winding around the tabletop Lookout Mountain and then moving into northern Alabama before eventually swinging back north to empty into the Ohio River at Paducah Kentucky. Chattanooga was just a village when it became a Civil War battlefield. It then grew to be the industrial "Dynamo of Dixie," rising to prominence as a part of the "New South." Four decades ago, it was labeled America's most polluted city. But regional political leaders, prodded by influential and civic-minded scions of its Industrial Age aristocracy, used creative measures, such as locally built electric shuttle buses, to reduce pollution and to spruce up the city's scenic river banks. With big job cuts at the Tennessee Valley Authority, the region has pinned its hopes for economic growth more on the private sector, including tourism and a large food-service industry that includes the Moon Pie and Little Debbie confectioners.

    Chattanooga is the state's fourth-largest city and in recent years has been challenging Knoxville for third place. After declining in the 1980s and stagnating in the 1990s, the city has had a double-digit increase since 2000. As old businesses have shut down, new ones have arrived, and now more than two dozen companies from 20 countries employing more than 20,000 people have found homes in the region. By 2018, Chattanooga's Hamilton County was growing new businesses at the fastest rate in the state. However, leaders in the region worried how President Donald Trump's trade war might affect the area. In early 2019, Volkswagen announced that it was building a second plant in Chattanooga, an $800 million investment that would add 1,000 jobs, to build electric vehicles set to roll out in 2020. Amazon.com has expanded its sprawling distribution center, which is the size of 28 football fields and employs more than 4,000 people -- 1,000 of whom were added in 2017.

    The technology industry is transforming more than the local economy. The city features a state-of-the-art, publicly owned, citywide fiber network. Its 10-gigabyte service reportedly makes Chattanooga the largest city with such service. The city is a growing tourist destination, featuring the popular Tennessee Aquarium and Rock City atop Lookout Mountain, narrowly situated on the Georgia side where you can see seven states. Chattanooga has moved closer to the growing orbit of metropolitan Atlanta, which is 110 miles away, and it has been discussed as a site for the latter city's second airport.

    The 3rd Congressional District of Tennessee includes Chattanooga, stretches from Georgia to Kentucky, and stops a few miles short of both Alabama and Virginia. A bit more than half of its population is in Hamilton County. The district includes Oak Ridge National Laboratory, which was secretly constructed during World War II in virgin Appalachian forest to house the facility that made uranium isotopes for the Hiroshima bomb. For years, it did not appear on maps. The district contains the Museum of Appalachia in Clinton, which maintains dozens of frontier structures, including a cabin owned by Mark Twain's father. Historically, the area was split politically, with Chattanooga voting Democratic and the mountain counties Republican. Today, it is solidly Republican. Donald Trump won 65 percent of the vote.

Scott DesJarlais (R)

Elected 2010, 5th term, b. Feb 21, 1964; Des Moines, IA, IN; University of South Dakota, B.S., 1987; University of South Dakota School of Medicine, M.D., 1991; Episcopalian; Married (Amy DesJarlais); 4 children (1 from previous marriage).

Professional Career: Practicing physician, 1993-2010.

DC Office: 2301 RHOB 20515, 202-225-6831, Fax: 202-226-5172, desjarlais.house.gov

State Offices: Cleveland, 423-472-7500; Columbia, 931-381-9920; Murfreesboro, 615-896-1986; Winchester, 931-962-3180.

Committees: *Agriculture*: Livestock & Foreign Agriculture; Subcommittee Nutrition, Oversight & Department Operations. *Armed Services*: Intelligence, Emerging Threats & Capabilities; Strategic Forces.

Group Ratings

	ADA	ACLU	AFL-CIO	LCV	ITI	COC	HAFA	ACU	CFG	FRC
2018	-	11%	-	3%	-	75%	92%	96%	70%	100%
2017	0%	C	3%	0%	C	93%	C	100%	98%	100%

Almanac Ratings 2017-18

	Economy	Social	Foreign	Composite
Liberal	0%	3%	0%	1%
Conservative	100%	97%	100%	99%

Key Votes of the 115th Congress

1. Obama-care revision	Y	5. Family planning regs	Y	9. Guantanamo prisoners	N
2. Tax Cuts	Y	6. Body cameras/immigration	N	10. Ground missiles, limit	N
3. Omnibus appropriations	N	7. Abortion ban	Y	11. Defense Dept. spending	Y
4. Dodd-Frank revision	Y	8. Concealed carry	Y	12. FISA rules	Y

Election Results

Election	Name (Party)	Vote (%)		Cand. Spent	Ind. Exp. Support	Ind. Exp. Oppose
2018 General	Scott DesJarlais (R)	147,323	(63%)	$267,101	$1,419	
	Mariah Phillips (D)	78,065	(34%)	$555,877		
	Michael Shupe (I)	7,056	(3%)			
2018 Primary	Scott DesJarlais (R)	61,994	(70%)			
	Jack Maddux (R)	26,580	(30%)			

Prior winning percentages: 2016 (65%), 2014 (58%), 2012 (56%), 2010 (60%)

Republican Scott DesJarlais, elected in 2010, has overcome explosive accusations about his personal life and unexpectedly has survived serious primary challenges, which seem to have finally passed. To do so, he has continued to show skills as a campaigner, though he's been less active as a legislator.

DesJarlais grew up in Sturgis South Dakota. He earned a bachelor's degree in chemistry and psychology from the University of South Dakota in 1987. After receiving his medical degree from the school in 1991, DesJarlais moved to Jasper Tennessee, where he practiced medicine.

The 2010 House race was DesJarlais' first bid for elected office. He challenged Rep. Lincoln Davis, a Democrat who had earned the endorsements of the U.S. Chamber of Commerce, the National Rifle Association and National Right to Life. DesJarlais billed himself as a "doctor, not a politician."

Davis made headlines with an ad featuring accusations by DesJarlais' first wife, Susan, who claimed that he physically intimidated her during their 2000 divorce and threatened to commit suicide.

DesJarlais called the charges "completely false," and the ad exposed Davis to accusations of mudslinging. Davis pointed out his votes against the Democrats' health care overhaul and cap-and-trade bill to limit greenhouse gas emissions, both unpopular in the district. But he backed the $787 billion economic stimulus. DesJarlais won 57%-39%.

DesJarlais has been a mainstream conservative. He joined fellow Tennessee Republican Charles Fleischmann in opposing an Energy Department plan to consolidate management of Oak Ridge's Y-12 weapons plant with the Pantex facility in Texas. He defended as essential outreach his unusually high spending on constituent mailings. On the flip side, C-SPAN found that he spoke on the House floor only once in 2015-16, the fewest of any House member who served the full term. "When you speak on the floor, it's usually to an empty House, so I don't think it's the best forum to reach out," he told USA Today. In the next two years, that number increased, though he still spoke sparingly. In 2017, he joined the Armed Services Committee, where he tended to the needs of Arnold Air Force Base, an advanced testing facility in Coffee and Franklin counties.

Scandal has so overshadowed DesJarlais' legislative work that survival has seemed his most significant accomplishment. According to the transcript of a phone recording made prior to his divorce made public a few weeks before the 2012 election, DesJarlais reportedly urged his pregnant mistress — who was one of his medical patients — to get an abortion. He issued a statement accusing opponents of "the same gutter politics" as his earlier race, but he later said in a letter to supporters that he encouraged the abortion because he was trying to get her to admit she wasn't pregnant. Conservatives abandoned him in droves, and national Democrats raced to assist challenger Eric Stewart, who had been seen as a long shot. The district's conservative voters gave DesJarlais the benefit of the doubt, and he defeated Stewart 56%-44%.

After the election, the state Democratic Party released court transcripts showing that DesJarlais and his ex-wife mutually agreed that she would have two abortions, and that he admitted having sex with at least two patients, three coworkers, and a drug company representative. DesJarlais later acknowledged having used "very poor judgment" but dismissed suggestions that he resign or not run again. In 2013, the Tennessee Board of Medical Examiners fined him $500 and reprimanded him for having sex with multiple patients.

In January 2013, state Sen. Jim Tracy announced a primary challenge for 2014 and began to peel off DesJarlais' donors. Tracy told supporters, "I'm a conservative in word and deed. I'm 100 percent pro-life." Tracy outraised DesJarlais and won endorsements from many in the state's GOP establishment. He campaigned on bringing "integrity" to the office, but was slow to attack DesJarlais directly. The incumbent countered that his personal life was old news, noting that he had been married for 12 years to his second wife. He emphasized his conservative values and efforts in Washington.

DesJarlais won the high-turnout primary by 38 votes. Tracy had a big lead in the population center of Rutherford County, but Desjarlais rolled up the vote in rural areas. After 18 days of recounts, Tracy continued to fault the handling of the election but said that further challenges "would not be the right thing for the Republican Party and the conservative cause in Tennessee." In November, DesJarlais faced Democrat Lenda Sherrell, an accountant, who spent more than $1 million. Republicans rallied around DesJarlais and he won, 58%-35%.

In 2016, his chief Republican challenger was Grant Starrett, a lawyer and real estate investor who worked for Mitt Romney in the 2012 presidential campaign. Starrett moved to the district in 2015 and self-financed nearly $900,000 of the $1.6 million he raised for his campaign. DesJarlais won the four-candidate contest, 52%-43%, again winning all of the counties except for the three in the eastern mountains. In 2018, DesJarlais faced a primary challenge from Jack Maddux, an underfunded former police officer; he had his smoothest primary win yet, 70%-30%, and in November was easily reelected.

In the presidential campaign, Desjarlais was an early supporter of Donald Trump and he served as his liaison to the conservative Freedom Caucus. DesJarlais has become a loyal ally of the president, especially on defense spending. DesJarlais was one of 11 members of the Freedom Caucus who filed articles of impeachment against Deputy Attorney General Rod Rosenstein, saying he was not cooperating with Congress.

TN-4: Middle Tennessee   **Cook Partisan Voting Index: R+20**

Population		Race and Ethnicity		Income	
Total	756,359	White	80.5%	Median Income	$51,166
Land area (sq. miles)	5,985	Black	8.6%	District Income Rank	284
Pop/ sq mi	126.4	Latino	6.1%	Poverty Rate	15.1%
Born in State	60.7%	Asian	1.6%	With health insurance	89.1%
		Two or more races	2.7%	Cash public assistance	2.6%
Age Groups		Other	0.3%	Food stamp/SNAP	14.6%
Under 18	23.5%				
18-34	23.2%	**Education**		**Work**	
35-64	39.2%	H.S grad or less	48.7%	White Collar	14.1%
Over 64	14.1%	Some college	28.6%	Sales and Service	39.6%
		College Degree, 4 yr	15.2%	Blue Collar	29%
Military		Post grad	7.5%	Government	13.4%
Veteran/ Active Duty	8.5%				

2012 Pres. Vote	Romney	169,508	(65%)	Obama	86,394	(33%)			
2016 Pres. Vote	Trump	189,318	(68%)	Clinton	76,133	(27%)	Johnson	7,806	(3%)

Murfreesboro Area: The invisible line between Republican and Democratic territory during the Civil War in Tennessee ran along Walden Ridge, the westernmost swelling of the Appalachians. This invisible line also separates the Tennessee Valley, which had few slaves and whose economic ties were to the North, from the rolling farmlands of Middle Tennessee, first settled by Andrew Jackson in the 1790s and resolutely Democratic from 1829, when Jackson became the first president to call himself a Democrat. This is an America of small towns, where every hamlet seems to have its own annual festival, like the RC Moon Pie Festival in Bell Buckle. Lynchburg is where Jasper Newton Daniel, better known by the nickname "Jack," began brewing his "Old No. 7" whiskey, an operation that continues to this day. In 2016, the company completed a $140 million expansion at its plant, which has 500 workers. Oddly, Moore County, where the distillery is located, is a dry county.

There is an industrial base here as well, particularly in the automobile industry. General Motors launched its Saturn brand in Spring Hill in 1990, igniting growth in the region. When the erstwhile auto giant went bankrupt in 2009, it furloughed most of its 2,700 employees. Since then, it has had an impressive comeback. Assembly-line production resumed in 2012 on the Chevrolet Equinox, and the plant produces engines and other components for GM assembly plants elsewhere. In 2017, it added a third shift and raised total employment to 3,300 workers. In 2019, GM announced it was making a $300 million investment to start building the Cadillac XT6, as well as another $22 million to shift production toward high-tech, fuel-conserving V-8 engines. Nissan has a large engine assembly plant in Decherd in Franklin County and operates a vehicle production assembly plant in Smyrna with 8,400 employees, where it also manufactures batteries for its Leaf electric cars. In 2018, Nissan announced $159 million in upgrades to its Smyrna plant.

The 4th Congressional District of Tennessee takes in all of these places. About 40 percent of its population is in Rutherford County, which has become part of suburban Nashville. Murfreesboro is the sixth-largest city in the state; with a population of 136,000, it was one of the top 15 fastest-growing large cities in the U.S. in 2017. This is the most blue-collar of Nashville's major suburban counties and the least-heavily Republican. The rest of the district is a scattering of small towns and rural areas. Dayton is where the famous Scopes Monkey Trial was held in 1925; John T. Scopes was convicted of teaching evolution and fined $100 (although the conviction was later overturned). This was once reliably blue territory, but Democrats have become scarce in most of Tennessee outside of Nashville and Memphis. Donald Trump in 2016 won the 4th with 68 percent.

Jim Cooper (D)

Elected 1982, 15th term, b. Jun 19, 1954; Nashville; University of North Carolina, Chapel Hill, B.A., 1975; Oxford University (England), M.A., 1977; Harvard University Law School (MA), J.D., 1980; Episcopalian; Married (Martha Hays Cooper); 3 children.

Elected Office: U.S. House, 1983-1995.

Professional Career: Practicing attorney, 1980-1982; Investment banker, 1995-1999; Founder & partner, investment bank, 1999-2002.

DC Office: 1536 LHOB 20515, 202-225-4311, Fax: 202-226-1035, cooper.house.gov

State Offices: Nashville, 615-736-5295.

Committees: *Armed Services*: Intelligence, Emerging Threats & Capabilities; Seapower & Projection Forces; Strategic Forces (Chmn). *Budget. Oversight & Reform*: National Security.

Group Ratings

	ADA	ACLU	AFL-CIO	LCV	ITI	COC	HAFA	ACU	CFG	FRC
2018	-	68%	-	86%	-	67%	15%	32%	33%	0%
2017	90%	C	84%	100%	C	57%	C	11%	3%	0%

Almanac Ratings 2017-18

	Economy	Social	Foreign	Composite
Liberal	82%	81%	44%	69%
Conservative	18%	19%	56%	31%

Key Votes of the 115th Congress

1. Obama-care revision	N	5. Family planning regs	N	9. Guantanamo prisoners	Y
2. Tax Cuts	N	6. Body cameras/immigration	Y	10. Ground missiles, limit	N
3. Omnibus appropriations	Y	7. Abortion ban	N	11. Defense Dept. spending	Y
4. Dodd-Frank revision	N	8. Concealed carry	N	12. FISA rules	Y

Election Results

Election	Name (Party)	Vote (%)		Cand. Spent	Ind. Exp. Support	Ind. Exp. Oppose
2018 General	Jim Cooper (D)	177,923	(68%)	$434,527		
	Jody Ball (R)	84,317	(32%)			
2018 Primary	Jim Cooper (D)		(100%)			

Prior winning percentages: 2016 (63%), 2014 (62%), 2012 (65%), 2010 (57%), 2008 (66%), 2006 (69%), 2004 (69%), 2002 (64%), 1992 (66%), 1990 (69%), 1988 (100%), 1986 (100%), 1984 (75%), 1982 (66%)

Jim Cooper, a Democrat elected in 2002 who also served from 1982 to 1994, is a brainy moderate with a tart tongue — especially when it comes to his own party's leadership. Despite the polarized political climate, he persistently seeks bipartisanship on fiscal matters. He has shifted his legislative focus chiefly to defense issues.

His father, Prentice Cooper, was governor for six years; his brother John sits on the Nashville Metro Council and ran for mayor in 2019 with calls to reduce downtown development. Jim Cooper, educated at the University of North Carolina, Oxford and Harvard Law School, was first elected in 1982 at age 28, by defeating Republican Cissy Baker, daughter of then-Senate Majority Leader Howard Baker. During his first stint in Congress, when his district was mostly rural, he spoke out against tobacco use and opposed the National Rifle Association in a state where both were popular. He participated actively in the "Group of Nine" Democrats on the Energy and Commerce Committee that produced a compromise between Michigan Democrat John Dingell, an ally of the auto industry, and California's Henry Waxman, who was pro-environmental regulation, on the Clean Air Act of 1990. In 1994, Cooper ran against Republican Fred Thompson for the Senate seat that Democrat Al Gore had vacated when he was elected vice president; in a bad year for Democrats, Thompson won, 60%-39%.

Cooper went to work as an investment banker in Nashville and as a teacher at Vanderbilt University's business school. In 2002, when the city-based district opened, Cooper joined a flurry of Democratic candidates. His toughest opponent was Davidson County Sheriff Gayle Ray, the first female sheriff in Tennessee, who had support from the EMILY's List, which supports women candidates who back abortion rights. Ray attacked Cooper's voting record on abortion. An abortion-rights supporter, Cooper said that Ray's charges were inaccurate. The AFL-CIO and The Tennessean endorsed Ray. Cooper had support from the Sierra Club and several smaller newspapers and raised twice as much money as Ray, including $700,000 in self-financing. He won the primary, 47%-23%, in a seven-candidate field. Cooper won the general election easily and has faced no serious reelection challenges since.

Since his return to Congress, he has served on the Armed Services Committee. When Democrats won back the House in 2018, he became chairman of its Strategic Forces Subcommittee, which oversees the nation's nuclear arsenal and usually acts on a bipartisan basis.

Cooper has been a consistent voice for fiscal discipline. He called for a panel to examine entitlement spending — an idea that led to President Barack Obama's creation in 2010 of the Simpson-Bowles commission on the national debt. When the House in 2012 debated Cooper's amendment to have a budget resolution based on the commission's recommendations, it drew just 38 votes. He has introduced numerous measures with GOP support. He said that finding Republicans to support him "is really not hard" but gets overlooked. "The press is only focused on the leaders," he said. "They barely know the names of the backbenchers, and those are the people who can make things happen if they choose to."

Cooper has sought to reform Congress, which he has accused of being "too lazy to prioritize." In 2012, he became the first lawmaker to sign a pledge by the activist group Rootstrikers not to lobby after leaving office. He was an early advocate of limits on spending earmarks — before the earmark moratorium, he had refused for years to seek such special-interest funding — and enforcement of pay-as-you-go rules that require tax cuts or spending increases to be offset elsewhere in the budget. A longtime proponent of increased government oversight, his bill to strengthen the independence of federal inspectors general passed Congress and became law in 2008. He has taken the lead in calling for redistricting reform by requiring that each state establish a bipartisan commission to draw House boundaries.

Cooper has been a leader of the fiscally conservative Blue Dog Coalition -- where he has described himself as "the nerd" of the group -- and an advocate of consensus-building among Democrats. He once said of his fellow Democrats under California's Nancy Pelosi, "We're just told how to vote. We are treated like mushrooms most of the time." In the January 2017 vote for House Speaker, he voted for Democratic Rep. Tim Ryan of Ohio, who earlier had challenged Pelosi within the Democratic Caucus. In 2019, he simply voted "present," joining more than a dozen Democrats in not casting their votes for Pelosi. He has continued to say that Democrats need new leadership.

With the growing influence of the party's progressive wing, it wouldn't be surprising if Cooper faced a primary challenge . Still, he would not be an easy target.

TN-5: Davidson County   **Cook Partisan Voting Index: D+7**

Population		Race and Ethnicity		Income	
Total	758,995	White	60.1%	Median Income	$52,985
Land area (sq. miles)	1,249	Black	24.7%	District Income Rank	253
Pop/ sq mi	607.9	Latino	9.3%	Poverty Rate	16.6%
Born in State	52.7%	Asian	3.2%	With health insurance	86.8%
		Two or more races	2.1%	Cash public assistance	3.8%
Age Groups		Other	0.6%	Food stamp/SNAP	13.4%
Under 18	21.6%				
18-34	28.9%	**Education**		**Work**	
35-64	37.8%	H.S grad or less	37.3%	White Collar	11.7%
Over 64	11.7%	Some college	26%	Sales and Service	40.9%
		College Degree, 4 yr	23.1%	Blue Collar	19.4%
Military		Post grad	13.5%	Government	10.8%
Veteran/ Active Duty	6.5%				

2012 Pres. Vote	Obama	152,960	(56%)	Romney	116,289	(43%)			
2016 Pres. Vote	Clinton	156,730	(56%)	Trump	105,720	(38%)	Johnson	10,431	(4%)

Nashville Metro: Country music, an art form that emerged from the settlers of the hardscrabble, mountainous counties of East Tennessee, is now a more than $2 billion-a-year business. The heart of country music is located in the city that is increasingly the cultural, political and economic heart of Tennessee: Nashville. Run out of a series of deceptively modest homes-turned-offices on Music Row, the industry congregated in Nashville because local radio station WSM had a clear channel in the 1920s from which to beam its weekly "barn dances" throughout the South. The broadcasts later became known as the Grand Ole Opry, the nation's longest continuously running radio show. Music Row has become a corporate juggernaut that views itself as more influential than the entertainment meccas on the East or West Coast. The city has about 200 recording studios, and Nashville music has more than $1 billion in sales each year. The music industry is increasingly intertwined with the television industry here. The eponymous ABC and then CMT show "Nashville" filmed here for six seasons, closing in 2018; it highlighted some of the smaller performance spaces, such as the legendary Bluebird Cafe. Honky tonks line Lower Broadway, where live music from aspiring singer/songwriters is played at all hours of the day -- a big reason why Nashville has become the country's top destination for bachelorette parties.

For years, the city's elite and its religious leaders resented the growing local influence of country music. But all three made their peace in the 1970s, and since then Nashville has become one of the South's boom cities — one of the fastest-growing metropolitan areas behind the much larger Atlanta and Dallas-Fort Worth Metroplex, though with that growth has also come wealth disparities. An agreeable quality of life, plenty of highly skilled labor, a central location and absence of urban strife have all enhanced Nashville as the largest metropolitan area in the state, with suburban growth in all directions. An estimated 100 people move into Nashville every day, which has sent real estate prices skyrocketing. The music industry has supported 57,000 jobs here -- more per capita than either New York City or Los Angeles -- and adds $10 billion to the city's economy annually. It is also a center of the for-profit health industry, the area's largest and fastest-growing employer. Amazon selected Nashville as the site of its new eastern hub of operations, bringing 5,000 corporate jobs to the area with a $230 million investment.

The dominant cultural tone in the metropolitan area is conservative — Nashville has more than 700 churches and is the headquarters for the publishing arms of the Southern Baptist Convention, United Methodist Church, and National Baptist Convention. But Nashville and Davidson County remain Democratic islands in an ocean of Republicanism. Bolstered by the defeat in 2009 of an English-only referendum in Nashville, the metro area has a large immigrant population and one of the fastest-growing foreign-born populations in the country, at nearly 12 percent. Davidson County is 60 percent white (down from 80 percent in the 1960s and 70s), more than a quarter African American, and 11 percent Hispanic, up from just 1 percent Hispanic in the 1990s.

The 5th Congressional District of Tennessee includes all of consolidated Nashville-Davidson County. Neighboring Cheatham and Dickson counties include about 10 percent of the district's population. The 5th is reliably Democratic, one of only two districts in Tennessee where a Democrat has a chance, but it is more centrist than the Memphis-based 9th District. Hillary Clinton got 56 percent of the vote.

John Rose (R)

Elected 2018, 1st term, b. Feb 23, 1965; Cookeville; Tennessee Tech University, B.S., 1988; Purdue University (IN), M.S., 1990; Vanderbilt University (TN), J.D., 1993; Christian Church; Married (Chelsea Rose); 1 child.

Elected Office: TN Commissioner of Agriculture, 2002-2003

Professional Career: Owner & President, Boson Software.

DC Office: 1232 LHOB 20515, 202-225-4231, Fax: 202-225-6887, johnrose.house.gov

State Offices: Cookeville, 931-854-9430; Gallatin, 615-206-8204.

Committees: *Financial Services*: Housing, Community Development & Insurance; Nat'l Security, International Development & Monetary Policy; Oversight & Investigations.

Election Results

Election	Name (Party)	Vote (%)		Cand. Spent	Ind. Exp. Support	Ind. Exp. Oppose
2018 General	John Rose (R)	172,810	(70%)	$2,965,513	$4,803	
	Dawn Barlow (D)	70,370	(28%)	$41,837		
2018 Primary	John Rose (R)	43,797	(41%)			
	Robert Corlew (R)	33,091	(31%)			
	Judd Mattheny (R)	16,758	(16%)			
	LaVern Vivio (R)	9,462	(9%)			

Republican John Rose was the only one of the three GOP freshmen elected in 2018 from Tennessee who held no previous elected office. A family farmer and a lawyer, Rose became wealthy after starting a technology-training business. His chief experience in government was a few months as Tennessee's commissioner of agriculture. In the contest to succeed Rep. Diane Black, who unsuccessfully sought the Republican nomination for governor, the chief battleground was the GOP primary. Rose had a larger financial war chest and a broader base of support across the district.

Rose, a native of rural Putnam County, graduated from Tennessee Tech University, got a master's degree in agricultural economics from Purdue and a law degree from Vanderbilt. After practicing law for a few years with a Chattanooga firm, he co-founded the Transcender Corp., a fast-growing provider of information technology certification training. In 2000, he and his partners sold that company for $60 million, the Tennessean reported the following year. In 2002, as he was about to leave office, Gov. Don Sundquist appointed Rose to the state's top agricultural position. He later held several public-service posts, including with the Tennessee Tech Foundation, a state conservation trust fund and the Tennessee State Fair Association.

After Black announced her bid for governor, the chief contenders to replace her were Rose and Bob Corlew, who served 30 years as a Rutherford County judge before retiring in 2014. Each was largely a self-funder, though Rose's $3 million campaign fund roughly doubled Corlew's account. Several weeks before the primary, the Volunteer State Report wrote that Corlew "has come out of the gate flat" and that Rose's "connections with both the political class and the agricultural community" made him the frontrunner. Corlew was disadvantaged because Rutherford County shifted from the 6th District to the 4th District in the 2012 redistricting.

In their campaign ads, Rose and Corlew both emphasized their support of President Donald Trump and the need for tougher enforcement of immigration laws. Rose described himself as a "businessman, farmer and outsider." In a closing ad, Corlew's unusual message that he was not Sen. Bob Corker, who was retiring, revealed that he had problems in building his name-identification. Also running was state Rep. Judd Matheny, who was backed by members of the House Republicans' Freedom Caucus. But he had far less funding than the top two candidates and failed to push beyond his base in Coffee County.

Rose won the primary with 41 percent of the vote to 31 percent for Corlew and 16 percent for Matheny, with two other candidates in the single digits. He took 15 of the 19 counties, with his largest margins in Sumner and Putnam. Corlew led Rose by 111 votes in Wilson County, which had the largest turnout, plus two smaller counties. Matheny got 64 percent in Coffee County but finished no higher than third in the other counties.

On a 69%-28% vote, Rose defeated Democratic nominee Dawn Barlow, a medical doctor who campaigned mostly on health care reform. Barlow had scant financing and gained little notice in this once-firmly Democratic district, where Vice President Al Gore got his political start in 1976 — a long time ago as a political milestone.

TN-6: Middle Tennessee   **Cook Partisan Voting Index: R+24**

Population		Race and Ethnicity		Income	
Total	746,798	White	88.7%	Median Income	$49,934
Land area (sq. miles)	6,474	Black	4.3%	District Income Rank	314
Pop/ sq mi	115.3	Latino	4.2%	Poverty Rate	14.1%
Born in State	62%	Asian	0.9%	With health insurance	90.2%
		Two or more races	1.5%	Cash public assistance	2.5%
Age Groups		Other	0.5%	Food stamp/SNAP	13.7%
Under 18	22.9%				
18-34	20.2%	**Education**		**Work**	
35-64	39.8%	H.S grad or less	50.8%	White Collar	17.1%
Over 64	17.1%	Some college	27.9%	Sales and Service	40.8%
		College Degree, 4 yr	14.2%	Blue Collar	27%
Military		Post grad	7.1%	Government	13.5%
Veteran/ Active Duty	9%				

2012 Pres. Vote	Romney	192,602	(69%)	Obama	82,276	(30%)		
2016 Pres. Vote	Trump	216,516	(72%)	Clinton	70,428	(24%)	Johnson	7,578	(3%)

Eastern Nashville Suburbs: Middle Tennessee is hilly and fertile, cut by deep, curvy rivers. The terrain was never much suited for plantation crops, and there were few big landholdings. This has long been a land of small farmers and small county-seat towns, nestled amid some of the loveliest scenery in the country. As one of the heartlands of the Democratic Party, it was the political base of President Andrew Jackson and supported him nearly unanimously in his 1832 reelection. For 140 years after Jackson, it voted solidly Democratic and elected as its representatives in Congress some of the luminaries of the national party: Cordell Hull (1907-21, 1923-31), later senator and secretary of State; Albert Gore Sr. (1939-53), later senator; and Albert Gore Jr. (1977-85), later senator and vice president.

The 6th Congressional District includes 17 Middle Tennessee counties, plus small parts of two others. These counties largely retain a rural heritage. Dan Evans, founder of the Cracker Barrel Old Country Store chain, grew up in Smithville. The populated areas evoke the small-town charm for which those stores are famous. Just over half of the district's population lives in the three counties that adjoin Nashville. These are generally upscale places with median incomes that are among the highest in the state. Sumner and Wilson, the two largest counties in the district, grew 14 and 20 percent respectively from 2010 to 2017. Sumner, which includes Nashville bedroom communities like Hendersonville, Gallatin, White House and Portland, has seen a major spike in new homes as working professionals have moved to the suburbs, along with an influx of retirees. Putnam County and Cookeville are an industry and manufacturing hub in the district. In 2018, Brazilian ceramic tile manufacturer Portobello America Inc. chose Baxter as the location of its U.S. headquarters and first U.S. production facility, investing $150 million in the county and adding 220 jobs.

Because this part of Tennessee had few African Americans, the racial politics of the 1960s largely bypassed the region, and Democratic loyalties outlasted those in other parts of the South. With Gore, Bill Clinton swept the area in 1992. As the Democratic Party became an increasingly urban coalition in the 2000s, the party's local fortunes plummeted. Its 72 percent for Donald Trump in 2016 placed it among his top 5 percent of districts nationwide. It likely will be a long time before Democrats return to competitiveness in Al Gore's former district.

Mark Green (R)

Elected 2018, 1st term, b. Nov 08, 1964; Jacksonville, FL; U.S. Military Academy - West Point (NY), B.S., 1986; University of Southern California, Mast. Deg., 1987; Wright State University (OH), M.D., 1999; Christian Church; Married (Camilla Joy Guenther); 2 children.

Military Career: U.S. Army 1987-2006 (Afghanistan & Iraq)

Elected Office: TN Senate, 2012-2018.

Professional Career: President and Chief Executive Officer, Align MD, 2006-2015.

DC Office: 533 CHOB 20515, 202-225-2811, markgreen.house.gov

Committees: *Homeland Security*: Intelligence & Counterterrorism; Transportation & Maritime Security. *Oversight & Reform*: National Security.

Election Results

Election	Name (Party)	Vote (%)	Cand. Spent	Ind. Exp. Support	Ind. Exp. Oppose
2018 General	Mark E. Green (R)........................ 170,071	(67%)	$1,763,693	$44,764	
	Justin Kanew (D)................................. 81,661	(32%)	$412,591		
2018 Primary	Mark E. Green (R).......................	(100%)			

First-term Republican Mark Green brought a diverse background to Congress: West Point graduate, flight surgeon, war veteran, founder of his own medical-services business, state senator, and a failed nomination in 2017 for Secretary of the Army. He also had the notable political mark of winning the nomination without a primary in his heavily Republican district, which opened when Rep. Marsha Blackburn ran successfully for the Senate. Green's general-election victory wasn't much more difficult. His Democratic opponent had extensive experience in Hollywood, but he was new to Tennessee and to politics.

Green, a native of Mississippi, graduated from the U.S. Military Academy with a degree in business management. During 20 years in the Army, with a final rank of lieutenant colonel, he began as an infantry officer and then served as an airborne battalion supply officer with the renowned 82nd Airborne Division. While in the Army, he attended medical school, where he was a resident in emergency care and became a flight surgeon. That background prepared Green to be in the elite crew that captured Saddam Hussein in 2003; Green wrote a book, A Night with Saddam, about his six hours of interrogation of the former Iraqi president.

Following his military service, Green founded and became chief executive of Align MD, a business that provided hospital and emergency room services. In 2015, he sold that company to a competitor for $24 million. He remained as its president for the following year, then became chief executive of the firm. The Nashville Business Journal cited Green as a Health Care Hero.

Green began his political career in 2012, when he defeated a Democratic incumbent to win a seat in the Tennessee Senate. He sponsored legislation to provide a health savings account for Medicaid beneficiaries, and he played a leading role in the phased repeal of taxes on income from savings and investment.

In April 2017, President Donald Trump nominated Green as Secretary of the Army. Critics cited Green's controversial remarks on various topics, including the status of transgender persons and the rights of Muslims in the United States. Senate Armed Services Committee Chairman John McCain said that some of Green's comments were "very concerning." When Green requested the withdrawal of his nomination, Secretary of Defense Jim Mattis had no public comment, The Washington Post reported. Green called the attacks "false and misleading," and subsequently blamed that failure on "obstruction from Senate Democrats and attacks on his Christian faith."

In January 2017, Green filed papers to run for governor in 2018. He switched that plan in October when Blackburn announced her campaign for the Senate, and he said he would seek her House seat. Initially, the Nashville Post reported, Green was "almost certain" to face opposition from other Republicans. Lee Thomas Miller, a country music songwriter, filed as a GOP candidate in November. But he withdrew a few weeks later. Despite continued speculation about a more moderate alternative, none stepped forward. Green won the primary without opposition—an unusual result for an open seat in which one party has firm control.

Democrats nominated Justin Kanew, a film producer and writer who was perhaps best-known as a former contestant on the reality TV show, The Amazing Race. Kanew moved from Los Angeles to the district in 2017. He called Green an "extremist" and urged a "return to civility." With his ample fundraising and the district's pedigree, Green won easily. He has gained notice as a potential candidate to run for the Senate to replace Lamar Alexander, who is retiring.

TN-7: Middle Tennessee   **Cook Partisan Voting Index: R+20**

Population		Race and Ethnicity		Income	
Total	752,931	White	80.7%	Median Income	$54,233
Land area (sq. miles)	9,160	Black	9.8%	District Income Rank	238
Pop/ sq mi	82.2	Latino	5%	Poverty Rate	13.9%
Born in State	53.1%	Asian	1.9%	With health insurance	90.6%
		Two or more races	2.1%	Cash public assistance	2.5%
Age Groups		Other	0.5%	Food stamp/SNAP	13.4%
Under 18	25%				
18-34	21.6%	**Education**		**Work**	
35-64	39.3%	H.S grad or less	44.2%	White Collar	14.1%
Over 64	14.1%	Some college	27.2%	Sales and Service	38.4%
		College Degree, 4 yr	18.5%	Blue Collar	24.1%
Military		Post grad	10.1%	Government	16.1%
Veteran/ Active Duty	12.9%				

2012 Pres. Vote	Romney	183,840	(66%)	Obama	91,987	(33%)		
2016 Pres. Vote	Trump	196,893	(67%)	Clinton	82,236	(28%)	Johnson	9,071	(3%)

Western Nashville Suburbs, Clarksville: Rural Tennessee north of Mississippi is mostly a sparsely settled area. Along each side of the Tennessee River, as it flows north and widens out into Kentucky Lake, are small rural communities. Many date to pre-Civil War days and have not grown much since. One of these is Waynesboro, where Davy Crockett delivered campaign speeches from the base of a huge natural stone double bridge overlooking the Buffalo River. Farther west is McNairy County, where Sheriff Buford Pusser of Walking Tall fame carried his big stick and fought organized crime until his death in a 1974 car crash. Even some of the roads have changed little; the Natchez Trace Parkway follows the same basic path as the trail carved out by prehistoric bison from Mississippi grazing lands to the salt licks of central Tennessee.

This land is complemented by two urban areas: Greater Nashville to the east and Clarksville to the north. South of Nashville is Williamson County, where the bedroom communities of Franklin and Brentwood are affluent, highly educated, and fast-growing. The county grew by more than 17 percent from 2010 to 2017 and boasts among the highest housing costs in the state. Still, those communities' attractive suburban lifestyle, low crime rates and good schools were a major factor in Amazon deciding in 2018 to locate its eastern hub there. Nissan North America took advantage of the low cost of doing business in Tennessee by moving its headquarters from California to the Cool Springs area of Franklin.

Along the Cumberland River is Clarksville, the fifth-largest city in the state, with many restored 19th-century homes and a large industrial park. In 2018, Google broke ground on a $500 million data center nearby. Straddling the Kentucky border north of Clarksville is the Army's sprawling Fort Campbell, home of the 101st Airborne Division, which has become a rapid deployment unit and is the Army's only air assault division; Campbell is the Army's fifth largest base and a military boomtown. The 2018 defense bill included more than $130 million for Fort Campbell, including a helicopter training facility, a special ops live fire range and money for on-base schools. The military community and jobs in Clarksville have helped make it the youngest city in the state; it also has one of the lowest voter turnout rates in the nation.

The 7th Congressional District covers this territory, which is the largest district in Tennessee. Close to 40 percent live in Tennessee's Central Basin, in Williamson County. Another fifth of its population lives in Clarksville-based Montgomery County, which has seen nearly 14 percent population growth since 2010. This is the wealthiest county in the state, measured by median income.

The remainder live in the lightly populated, rural counties traversing the state from northern border to southern. The area around Clarksville retains some of its historic attachment to the Democratic Party dating to the Civil War. In 2016, Donald Trump got 65 percent in Williamson and 56 percent in Montgomery. He took the district with 67 percent.

David Kustoff (R)

Elected 2016, 2nd term, b. Oct 08, 1966; Memphis; University of Memphis, B.B.A., 1989; University of Memphis School of Law, J.D., 1992; Jewish; Married (Roberta Kustoff); 2 children.

Professional Career: Practicing attorney; Chairman, Shelby County GOP, 1995-1999; U.S. Attorney, Western District of Tennessee, 2006-2008.

DC Office: 523 CHOB 20515, 202-225-4714, Fax: 202-225-1765

State Offices: Dyersburg, 731-412-1037; Jackson, 731-423-4848; Memphis, 901-682-4422.

Committees: *Financial Services*: Consumer Protection & Financial Institutions; Housing, Community Development & Insurance; Subcommittee on Diversity & Inclusion.

Group Ratings

	ADA	ACLU	AFL-CIO	LCV	ITI	COC	HAFA	ACU	CFG	FRC
2018	-	4%	-	0%	-	82%	85%	87%	59%	100%
2017	0%	C	8%	0%	C	86%	C	89%	82%	100%

Almanac Ratings 2017-18

	Economy	Social	Foreign	Composite
Liberal	0%	9%	0%	3%
Conservative	100%	91%	100%	97%

Key Votes of the 115th Congress

1. Obama-care revision	Y	5. Family planning regs	Y	9. Guantanamo prisoners	N
2. Tax Cuts	Y	6. Body cameras/immigration	N	10. Ground missiles, limit	N
3. Omnibus appropriations	Y	7. Abortion ban	Y	11. Defense Dept. spending	Y
4. Dodd-Frank revision	Y	8. Concealed carry	Y	12. FISA rules	Y

Election Results

Election	Name (Party)	Vote (%)		Cand. Spent	Ind. Exp. Support	Ind. Exp. Oppose
2018 General	David Kustoff (R)	168,030	(68%)	$1,734,806	$26,616	
	Erika Stotts Pearson (D)	74,755	(30%)	$6,838		
	James Hart (I)	5,560	(2%)	$117		
2018 Primary	David Kustoff (R)	57,741	(56%)			
	George Flint Jr. (R)	40,903	(40%)			

Prior winning percentages: 2016 (69%)

Republican David Kustoff was elected to an open seat in 2016 after winning a hard-fought primary. With his experience as a U.S. attorney in West Tennessee and his political connections to leading Republicans in the state, Kustoff was the establishment favorite in the contest.

Born and raised in Shelby County, Kustoff got his bachelor's and law degrees from the University of Memphis. He opened a law firm with Jim Strickland, a Democrat who was elected mayor of Memphis in 2016. Kustoff served in various positions for the Republican Party, including Shelby County chairman, and state chairman of the George W. Bush presidential campaigns in 2000 and 2004. He ran for Congress in the 7th District in 2002, but finished second with 20 percent, to 40 percent for Marsha Blackburn in the Republican primary, when he split the vote from Shelby County with two other local Republicans. Kustoff was nominated as U.S. attorney in 2006 and served until 2009. He gained attention for winning the conviction of state Sen. John Ford and others in the "Tennessee Waltz" political corruption trial. Later, Kustoff served on the board of the Bank of Tennessee, a community bank, and was appointed by Gov. Bill Haslam as vice chairman of the Tennessee Higher Education Commission, where he oversaw implementation of state assistance programs. Kustoff is a regimented person, waking up every day at 3:15 a.m. without fail and eating one meal a day.

When three-term GOP Rep. Stephen Fincher retired, there was a wide-open field of 13 Republican candidates, two Democrats and five independents. Kustoff emphasized his law-enforcement background by criticizing President Barack Obama for having "unfairly and severely impugned the reputation of law enforcement" officers in high-profile cases of alleged police misconduct. Other leading Republican candidates were former Shelby County Commissioner George Flinn, a radiologist and TV station owner who had two previous unsuccessful runs for Congress, Shelby County Mayor Mark Luttrell and state Sen. Brian Kelsey.

Flinn raised by far the most money with $3 million, of which $2.7 million was self-financed. Kustoff raised about $700,000 for the primary, including $100,000 from a personal loan. Kustoff won the primary with 28 percent of the vote to 23 percent for Flinn, 18 percent for Luttrell and 13 percent for Kelsey. Kustoff took nearly half the vote in Shelby County, which was a larger margin than in the overall district. Democratic nominee Rickey Hobson did not file a financial report with the Federal Election Commission, and Kustoff won the general, 69%-25%.

Flinn challenged Kustoff again in the 2018 Republican primary, and again put more than $3 million of his own money into the race. Flinn argued Kustoff wasn't conservative enough and touted his "Christian conservative" background -- which many saw as a not-so-veiled swipe at Kustoff, who is one of the few Jewish Republicans in Congress. It was Kustoff, however, who got the coveted endorsement from President Donald Trump, who tweeted that "Congressman David Kustoff has been a champion for the Trump Agenda." Despite being outspent more than three-to-one, he again defeated Flinn, 56%-40%.

Kustoff got a seat on the Financial Services Committee, where he sought to reduce the restrictions imposed by the 2010 Dodd-Frank banking law, arguing that it has hampered small business growth, especially in rural communities. In a 2017 op-ed for CNBC, he wrote that "Dodd-Frank created two Americas, but I see a unified U.S. economy that serves all Americans." Kustoff has forged a close working relationship with neighboring Memphis Democratic Rep. Steve Cohen; the two attend the same temple and are both alumni of the University of Memphis. Cohen helped to whip votes for Kustoff's first bill in the House, which would protect religious institutions; it passed 402-2. And Kustoff used his leverage with the Trump administration to successfully lobby for Clayborn Temple in Memphis to be named a National Treasure by the National Trust for Historic Preservation; striking sanitation workers in 1968 used that site as their staging ground during the civil rights movement.

TN-8: West Tennessee   **Cook Partisan Voting Index: R+19**

Population		Race and Ethnicity		Income	
Total	709,012	White	72.9%	Median Income	$55,777
Land area (sq. miles)	6,851	Black	19.9%	District Income Rank	220
Pop/ sq mi	103.5	Latino	3.2%	Poverty Rate	14.1%
Born in State	66.4%	Asian	2%	With health insurance	91.8%
		Two or more races	1.6%	Cash public assistance	2.1%
Age Groups		Other	0.3%	Food stamp/SNAP	14.7%
Under 18	23.5%				
18-34	19.7%	**Education**		**Work**	
35-64	40.3%	H.S grad or less	43.9%	White Collar	16.5%
Over 64	16.5%	Some college	27.2%	Sales and Service	39.8%
		College Degree, 4 yr	17.8%	Blue Collar	22.6%
Military		Post grad	11.1%	Government	14.4%
Veteran/ Active Duty	9.3%				

2012 Pres. Vote	Romney	202,041	(66%)	Obama	99,608	(33%)		
2016 Pres. Vote	Trump	197,432	(66%)	Clinton	90,006	(30%)	Johnson	6,370	(2%)

Memphis Suburbs, Jackson: West of Nashville and north of Memphis, the rivers roll lazily through flat or gently rolling land that has similarities to the northern end of Mississippi. Cotton and soybeans are the main crops — the annual Tennessee Soybean Festival is held in Martin, near the Kentucky border — and they often are abundant. African Americans remain in rural areas here, a reminder of the old plantation economy. Henning is the hometown of Alex Haley, who used to sit on his porch and listen to his aunts tell him stories about slave ships and the Civil War; these became his best-selling book Roots. The plantation economy also bequeathed a fierce loyalty to the Democratic Party; before 2011, much of this district hadn't been represented by a Republican since Reconstruction.

The small towns in this area are sustained by manufacturers such as the NSK automotive plant and light industry such as Dot Foods, the nation's largest food redistributor, both in Dyersburg. In 2018, Tyson Foods broke ground for a new plant in Humboldt, a $313 million investment that aimed to hire 1,600 when it opens in two years, producing fresh tray-packed chicken for retail sales. Excel Boat Co. announced a new plant in Lake County that will hire 300. The Memphis Regional Megasite, which includes 4,100 acres in Haywood and Fayette counties, was working to attract a major employer after receiving a $106 million grant from the state. Those re-developments have helped to soften the blow after other companies once prominent in the area closed – including Brown Shoe Co. and Plastech Corp. in Gibson County, where Tyson will now open, and a Goodyear Tire & Rubber Co. plant in Obion County that closed in 2011.

Crockett County, with a county seat named Alamo, is named after Davy Crockett, who represented the area for three terms in the House before he moved to Texas. The area carries the highest earthquake risk in the United States outside of the West Coast. In the early 1800s, four earthquakes rocked the region, permanently altering the topography. Perhaps the most extreme example is Reelfoot Lake, the only large natural lake in Tennessee, which was a dry area before the quakes occurred; the land dropped almost 20 feet in places before the Mississippi River filled in the newly formed depression. Kentucky Lake draws big crowds for its annual BASSfest in Henry County.

The 8th Congressional District of Tennessee includes much of this West Tennessee farmland. Its largest city is Jackson, founded shortly after the area was opened for white settlement in 1818, and the site of one of Crockett's final speeches before heading west to his doom – and immortality -- at the Alamo. Jackson has become 49 percent black. Nearby Haywood is a black-majority county. Overall, the population is 20 percent black. Suburban Shelby County east of Memphis includes 40 percent of the district population. Donald Trump got 66 percent of the vote in 2016.

Steve Cohen (D)

Elected 2006, 7th term, b. May 24, 1949; Memphis; Vanderbilt University (TN), B.A., 1971; Memphis State University - Cecil C. Humphreys School of Law (TN), J.D., 1973; Jewish; Single1 child.

Elected Office: Shelby County Commissioner, 1977-1978; TN Senate, 1982-2006.

Professional Career: Practicing attorney, 1974-2006.

DC Office: 2104 RHOB 20515, 202-225-3265, Fax: 202-225-5663, cohen.house.gov

State Offices: Memphis, 901-544-4131.

Committees: *Judiciary*: Constitution, Civil Rights & Civil Liberties (Chmn); Courts, Intellectual Property & Internet; Crime, Terrorism & Homeland Security. *Science, Space & Technology*: Investigations & Oversight; Research & Technology. *Transportation & Infrastructure*: Aviation; Highways & Transit; Railroads, Pipelines & Hazardous Materials.

Group Ratings

	ADA	ACLU	AFL-CIO	LCV	ITI	COC	HAFA	ACU	CFG	FRC
2018	-	88%	-	94%	-	50%	4%	8%	5%	0%
2017	100%	C	100%	100%	C	36%	C	7%	5%	0%

Almanac Ratings 2017-18

	Economy	Social	Foreign	Composite
Liberal	91%	97%	89%	92%
Conservative	9%	4%	11%	8%

Key Votes of the 115th Congress

1. Obama-care revision	N	5. Family planning regs	N	9. Guantanamo prisoners	N
2. Tax Cuts	N	6. Body cameras/immigration	Y	10. Ground missiles, limit	Y
3. Omnibus appropriations	N	7. Abortion ban	N	11. Defense Dept. spending	N
4. Dodd-Frank revision	N	8. Concealed carry	N	12. FISA rules	N

Election Results

Election	Name (Party)	Vote (%)		Cand. Spent	Ind. Exp. Support	Ind. Exp. Oppose
2018 General	Steve Cohen (D)	145,139	(80%)	$307,996		
	Charlotte Bergmann (R)	34,901	(19%)	$69,100		
2018 Primary	Steve Cohen (D)	67,433	(91%)			
	Kasandra Smith (D)	4,734	(6%)			

Prior winning percentages: 2016 (79%), 2014 (75%), 2012 (75%), 2010 (74%), 2008 (88%), 2006 (60%)

Democrat Steve Cohen, elected in 2006, is a rare white member of Congress representing a majority-minority district. He has easily fended off primary challenges from the district's African-American majority by maintaining one of the House's most liberal voting records, becoming an outspoken opponent of President Donald Trump and concentrating on issues of strong interest to his constituents.

Cohen is a fourth-generation Memphian and the son of a psychiatrist. At age 5, he was diagnosed with polio. Cohen got his bachelor's at Vanderbilt University and his law degree from the University of Memphis. He worked as a legal adviser for the Memphis Police Department and then started a law practice. He was elected to the Shelby County Commission and, in 1982, to the state Senate, where he served for 24 years. He became known as the father of the Tennessee State Lottery for his efforts in 2002 to pass a referendum creating a lottery, with revenue to fund college scholarships.

Cohen wanted to run for Congress in 1996 when 22-year African-American Rep. Harold Ford Sr. announced his retirement, but he found his path blocked by the incumbent's 26-year-old son, who secured the seat. He got his chance in 2006 when Harold Ford Jr. ran unsuccessfully for the Senate. As the only serious white contender among the 15 candidates who filed to run, Cohen faced criticism from local black leaders, who said that an African American should represent the district. Cohen's supporters charged that another primary foe paid for a push poll that asked, "Are you more likely to vote for a born-again Christian or a Jew?" Cohen quipped that his staunchly liberal record would make people mistake him for a black woman.

The district's black leaders did not sufficiently narrow the field, and the primary results splintered. Cohen won with 31 percent. Nikki Tinker, the former campaign manager for Ford Jr. finished second with 25 percent. The incumbent's cousin, Joe Ford Jr., finished third with 12 percent. Cohen faced a challenge in November from yet another Ford — Jake Ford, the incumbent's younger brother, who ran as an independent. Jake Ford was a high school dropout who had a few scrapes with the law, but he had support from his father and other African-American leaders who opposed Cohen. Cohen won the general election with 60 percent of the vote, ending the Ford family's 32-year hold on the district. Cohen wanted to join the Congressional Black Caucus, but CBC leaders made it clear that they objected.

Cohen worked to secure his hold on the seat. Among his first moves was a resolution apologizing for slavery. While it seemed like a relatively harmless motion that easily passed the House on a voice vote, Cohen's office was slammed with constituent calls charging the measure was a political ploy. It was approved just days before the August 2008 primary. Cohen also got a Memphis federal building and post offices named after prominent African Americans.

In that primary, African-American leaders in the district coalesced around Tinker, who staged a rematch. "He's not black, and he can't represent me," one minister told the Memphis Commercial Appeal. Tinker got financial help from the CBC and EMILY's List, the abortion-rights fundraising group that supports women candidates. But prominent black leaders from outside the district made radio ads for Cohen and donated to his campaign. He outraised Tinker by more than 2-to-1 and crushed her, 79%-19%.

On the Judiciary Committee, Cohen worked on bills to force radio broadcasters to pay money to performers and to study racial disparities in the criminal justice system. He enacted a measure in 2010 protecting authors and journalists from having foreign libel judgments honored in U.S. courts and another to help members of the National Guard and Reserve obtain bankruptcy relief. As ranking Democrat on the Constitution and Civil Justice Subcommittee, Cohen championed a bipartisan bill to make marijuana legal for some medical purposes.

After Democrats won back the House in 2018, Cohen became chairman of the renamed Constitution, Civil Rights and Civil Liberties Subcommittee. In November 2017, he and several other liberal Democrats had introduced five articles of impeachment against President Trump. "The time has come to make clear to the American people and to this president that his train of injuries to our Constitution must be brought to an end through impeachment," Cohen said. Although Democratic leaders had little appetite to proceed, he continued to call for impeachment. He vowed to use his chairmanship for aggressive oversight, with hearings on whether Trump violated the Constitution's emoluments clause by profiting from his business ventures and to examine his criticisms of the judiciary, the FBI and the press. He filed constitutional amendments to eliminate the Electoral College and prohibit presidents from pardoning themselves.

At home, he came under fire in 2018 for comments he made during the Tennessee Senate race targeting eventual winner Republican Marsha Blackburn, hitting her close ties to Trump. "Cause Marsha Blackburn, if he says, 'jump off the Harahan Bridge,' she'll jump off the Harahan Bridge. ... I wish he'd say that. She will do anything he says."

In the face of repeated primary challenges, Cohen has become entrenched. In 2010, his opponent was Willie Herenton, Memphis' first elected black mayor. Cohen was ready, with an endorsement from President Barack Obama, a popular figure in the district, as well as support from a dozen CBC members. He trounced Herenton, 79%-21%, in the primary and sailed to reelection. Two years later, his challenger was Memphis Urban League CEO and school board member Tomeka Hart. The Cook Political Report observed that her campaign "seems to be focusing more on promoting her brand than giving voters a reason to replace Cohen," and he won, 89%-11%.

Against the less well-known Ricky Wilkins in 2014, Cohen had his closest primary since he was first elected. Wilkins campaigned publicly on how Cohen's race and ethnicity differed from that of most of his constituents. Cohen won, 66%-33%. In 2018, he easily dispatched two primary challengers, winning 91 percent of the vote. Cohen signaled he plans to run again in both 2020 and 2022. The threat of a serious primary challenge now seems virtually nil.

TN-9: Shelby County   **Cook Partisan Voting Index: D+28**

Population		Race and Ethnicity		Income	
Total	705,996	White	24%	Median Income	$39,067
Land area (sq. miles)	483	Black	65.6%	District Income Rank	421
Pop/ sq mi	1460.5	Latino	7%	Poverty Rate	26.2%
Born in State	65.4%	Asian	1.7%	With health insurance	84.6%
		Two or more races	1.4%	Cash public assistance	2.5%
Age Groups		Other	0.3%	Food stamp/SNAP	23.5%
Under 18	25.4%				
18-34	26.7%	**Education**		**Work**	
35-64	36.8%	H.S grad or less	45.8%	White Collar	11.1%
Over 64	11.1%	Some college	30.5%	Sales and Service	44.8%
		College Degree, 4 yr	14.6%	Blue Collar	25.8%
Military		Post grad	9.1%	Government	13.5%
Veteran/ Active Duty	7.1%				

2012 Pres. Vote	Obama	201,171	(79%)	Romney	53,147	(21%)	
2016 Pres. Vote	Clinton	173,411	(78%)	Trump	43,233	(19%)	

Memphis Metro: Memphis had long been the largest city in Tennessee, until it lost that title in 2015 to fast-growing Nashville, which also has a much larger metropolitan area. In the state's southwestern corner, 20 miles from Mississippi's cotton fields and riverboat casinos, Memphis' share of African Americans is among the largest in the country, evidence of the city's economic heritage as a capital of the Cotton Kingdom. Big Mississippi planters used to come north to sell their crops in the courtyard of the Peabody Hotel, then make financial arrangements for the next growing season. According to tradition, ducks still famously march daily to the hotel's fountain for a dip.

The city's most celebrated tradition is blues music. Unlike Nashville's country music, which emerged from mountainous East Tennessee, the Memphis sound originated from the self-taught musical stylings of poor, rural blacks in the Mississippi Delta. Throughout the first half of the 20th century, talented black musicians migrated north to Memphis and congregated downtown on Beale Street. The blues sound was adapted by Elvis Presley, a poor white boy from rural Mississippi, in July 1954 at Sam Phillips' Sun Studio in Memphis — the birth of rock 'n' roll. In the early 1960s, Memphis again became the crucible of a new sound, soul music, which emerged as a counterpoint to rock, its increasingly white-dominated cousin. Otis Redding, Isaac Hayes, the Staple Singers, and Sam & Dave made their records at the Stax studio. The Museum of American Soul Music, at the downtown site of the Stax studio, is the world's only soul music museum and attracts about 500,000 visitors annually. Graceland, Presley's garishly decorated mansion, attracts hordes of musical pilgrims from all over the world.

Memphis is the home of the first supermarket chain: Piggly Wiggly, founded in 1916 (its symbol, Mr. Pig, has slimmed down since then). St. Jude's Children's Research Hospital is also in Memphis, opened in 1962 by actor Danny Thomas to provide free treatment for children with cancer and to advance cancer research. The biggest private employer by far is FedEx, where nearly 10,000 employees scan, sort, weigh and route 1.4 million packages on 42 miles of conveyor belts to and from 150 aircraft that arrive and depart within a six-hour period almost every night at the world's busiest cargo airport. In 2018, FedEx announced a $1 billion investment to enlarge and modernize the Memphis superhub. However, there have been economic struggles in the city too. Electrolux, a home appliance manufacturer, will close its Memphis plant by 2020, putting 530 people out of work. And studies have shown that the city lags behind other nearby cities economically, citing high tax rates and rising crime and poverty as deterrents. It's the only southern city in the Economic Innovation Group's 2017 Distressed Communities Index, ranking sixth among 100 major urban areas.

Racial discord has scarred the political life of Memphis, which has been a major site in the civil rights movement. Rev. Martin Luther King Jr., was assassinated there in 1968, and the site, the Lorraine Motel, has been converted into the National Civil Rights Museum. After the Memphis City Council sold off two public parks to dispose of Confederate statues, the GOP-controlled state legislature retaliated by refusing to allocate any money for the city's bicentennial celebration. Resurgent Beale Street is one of the few racially integrated spaces in the city, a division that holds equally true in voting. Blacks vote almost unanimously Democratic, and whites vote Republican by margins almost as great. The city has been ranked as the fourth most-segregated city in the nation; a Chalkbeat analysis in 2018 found that Memphis schools are more segregated than 50 years ago; more than half its schools are more than 90 percent black. In 2017, Memphis was sixth in the country for population loss.

The 9th Congressional District of Tennessee remains the strongest Democratic district in the state and is essential to any chance of success for Democrats running statewide. African Americans are 65 percent of the population. In 2016, Hillary Clinton won 78 percent in the district.

TEXAS

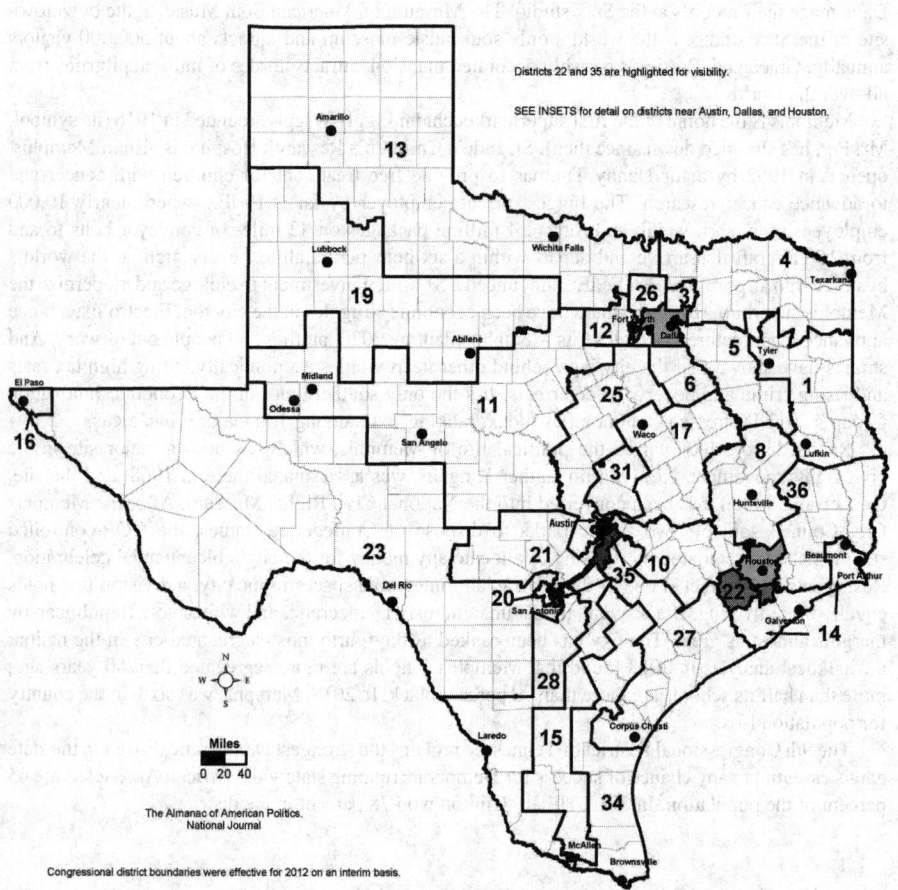

Districts 22 and 35 are highlighted for visibility.

SEE INSETS for detail on districts near Austin, Dallas, and Houston.

Amarillo

13

Lubbock

19

Wichita Falls

4

Texarkana

26 3

12   Fort Worth   Dallas

5   Tyler

1

Abilene

25   6

El Paso

Midland   11   San Angelo   Waco   17   8   Lufkin

Odessa   31   Huntsville   36

16

23   Austin   21   10

Del Rio   35

20   San Antonio   Houston   Beaumont   Port Arthur

22   14

Galveston

27

28

Laredo   15   Corpus Christi

34

McAllen   Brownsville

Miles
0 20 40

The Almanac of American Politics.
National Journal

Congressional district boundaries were effective for 2012 on an interim basis.

Texas hasn't elected a Democrat to statewide office in more than a quarter century, and it hasn't voted for a Democratic presidential candidate since Jimmy Carter. But after years of watching the state's demographics slowly shift in their direction, the Democrats have finally been on an upswing. In 2016, Texas displayed one of the nation's sharpest shifts against Donald Trump. Then, in the 2018 midterms, Senate candidate Beto O'Rourke fell just short but energized Democratic voters, turning Texas' big cities blue and many of its suburbs pink or purple. It will take a few more election cycles to determine if this was truly the Democrats' long-awaited demographic shift beginning to bear fruit, or simply a temporary reaction to Trumpism.

Inset for Austin and San Antonio

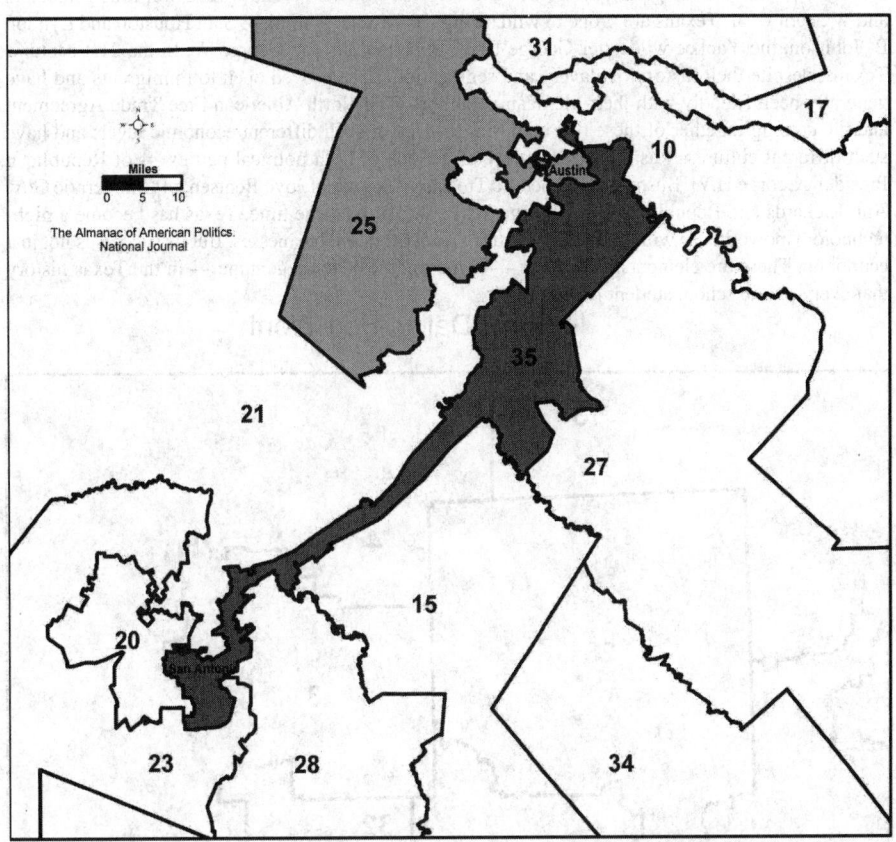

Congressional district boundaries were effective for 2012 on an interim basis.   Districts 25 and 35 are highlighted for visibility.

David Oshinsky, a former University of Texas historian, has written of Texas that "no state can match its swagger or eccentricities; no state generates more loyalty within its borders, or more controversy beyond." At its origin, Texas was an independent republic, freed from Mexico before it agreed to annexation by the United States in 1845. Today it is a nation-state, almost 29 million strong, larger in area than any of the 28 nations of the European Union and more populous than all but six. Texas has been the second-largest state in area since Alaska was admitted to the Union in 1959, and it became the second largest in population in 1994, when it surpassed New York. Texas was founded by Southerners, particularly Tennesseans, who were invited to establish their own enclave within the borders of Mexico, then dreamed of a republic with Anglo-Saxon freedoms and African-American slavery. They defended their dream to the death at the Alamo and to a bloody victory at San Jacinto. They entered the Union willingly in 1845 and left it enthusiastically in 1861.

The Texas that emerged from the Civil War was still young and poor. It began as a marshland on the border of the Third World, with an economy based on commodities, mainly cotton, when cotton prices were in long-term decline. Its farmers felt as if they were part of a colonial economy controlled by bankers and Wall Street financiers. But in 1901, oil was discovered in Beaumont, near the Gulf Coast, at a well that would be named Spindletop. "It was the greatest oil discovery in history," Texas journalist Lawrence Wright has written. "For the next nine days, until the well was capped, the gusher spurted into the air a hundred thousand barrels of oil a day — an output that exceeded the production of all the other wells in America combined." To develop Spindletop, two future oil giants were established, Gulf Oil and Texaco.

Without the underpinnings and burdens of tradition, 20th century Texas produced fabulous wealth, generously rewarding success while being unforgiving of failure. It has respect for learning and style — think of its great universities and Neiman Marcus — and it revels in rough manners and Western wear. Texans are prone to wild swings in fortune — think of Sam Houston and Lyndon B. Johnson, the Yankee wildcatter George H.W. Bush and his son George W. In the 21st century. Texans, despite their history of slavery and segregation, have proved open to immigrants and have generally been friendly with their Mexican neighbors. The North American Free Trade Agreement and the coming together of these two countries that are at such different economic levels and have such different cultures, was a project mainly of Texans of both political parties — of Republican President George H.W. Bush and Democratic Treasury Secretary Lloyd Bentsen, of Democratic Gov. Ann Richards and Republican Gov. George W. Bush. At the same time, Texas has become a high-technology powerhouse with some of the nation's most creative businesses. But its success is not just economic. There are elements of heroism — some mythical, some genuine — in the Texas history that every public school student learns.

Inset for Dallas-Fort Worth

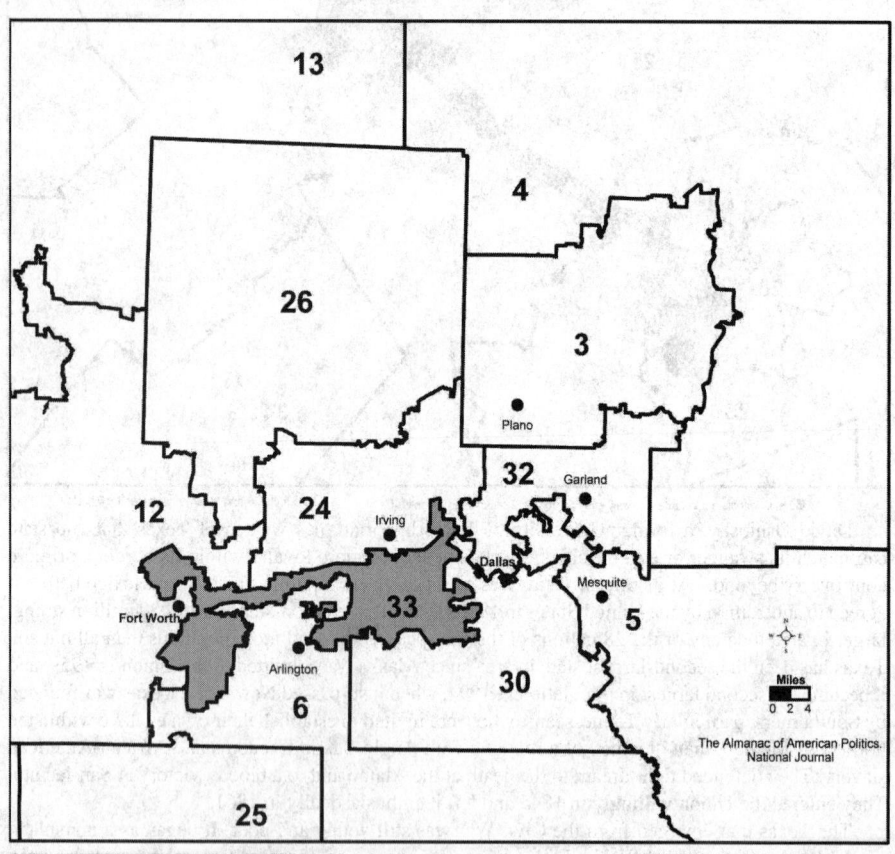

Texas became the nation's— and for a time the world's— leading producer of oil. But oil prices were subject to declines, and producers were propped up by politicians. These politicians also secured subsidies for cotton growers and contracts for defense plants and space facilities during World War II and through the Cold War. Most Texas voters stayed Democratic up to 1970 because of Confederate memories, New Deal affections, and the clout and competence of Texas Democratic officeholders. By the 1970s, Texas was no longer dependent on raw commodities. The "awl bidness" here became less a matter of extracting oil than it was playing host to the world's greatest concentration of highly skilled specialists in extracting other soil and natural gas. Also beginning in the 1960s, Texas became a center for technology with the critical mass of knowledge and finances needed to produce firms like Texas Instruments and Dell Computer and a university infrastructure in the University of Texas and Texas A&M. By 2018, there were 52 Fortune 500 companies with Texas headquarters, tying New York and barely trailing California; Texas A&M educated four of the Fortune 100 CEOs, tied with Cornell and the University of Michigan for the most of any university.

Today, oil extraction remains important in the state – revered, and still protected by politicians. Texas accounts for 37 percent of the nation's crude oil production, and recent discoveries in the Permian Basin of West Texas – the Alpine High and the Wolfcamp shale – have boosted the state's recoverable oil and gas reserves. The state has played host to key developments in horizontal drilling and hydraulic fracturing, or "fracking," and those developments have further boosted the state's footprint in resource extraction. At the same time, the fracking boom has taken a toll on roads (every well requires some 1,200 truck deliveries) and possibly on air quality; while it has produced jobs, mechanization has, over time, reduced the number. Still, the industry isn't going anywhere: A 2015 law keeps localities from banning fracking. In the meantime, Texas leads the nation in wind-powered electricity capacity. Texas ranks sixth per capita among the states in energy consumption, due in part to the needs of oil and gas drillers, combined with heavy air-conditioning loads. In typically Texas fashion, it is the only state that has a stand-alone electric grid entirely within its borders.

The oil slump of the mid 2010s did not hurt Texas' economy as severely as the 1980s oil bust, which helped tank the real estate and banking sectors. A big reason is diversification: According to the Federal Reserve Bank of Dallas, oil and mineral revenue now accounts for 5 percent of state tax revenue, half its share in the 1980s. During the post-recession recovery, foreclosure rates were well below the national average. In 2018, CNBC rated Texas the top state in the nation for business, becoming the first four-time winner.

The Dallas-Fort Worth Metroplex is rich with defense contractors and small firms that grew large through exports to Mexico; the suburb of Plano is now home to a 2 million-square-foot U.S. headquarters for Toyota, which relocated from California. Houston is home to one of the nation's busiest ports as well as firms like Schlumberger, the global oil services company. It also has many high-tech spinoffs from the enormous Texas Medical Center and from the space program. (Elon Musk's SpaceX announced in 2019 that it planned to build initial versions of its Mars space vehicle in south Texas.) Data collected by Rice University's Stephen Klineberg shows that oil and gas represented 80 percent of Houston's economy four decades ago; it's now half that. San Antonio, with the Air Force's prime hospital, has significant medical technology and biotech industries, as well as a growing cybersecurity sector. Austin became a technology center competing with California's Silicon Valley, as well as a mecca for the arts and culture. The Dallas-Fort Worth and Houston metro areas now rank as the fourth and fifth largest in the country.

By some indicators, the state is underperforming. As its public colleges prosper, the rest of the public school system complains of being cash-starved. Texas has the nation's second-lowest percentage of residents who graduated from high school. It's tied for the seventh-worst state in the nation for children in poverty, and the state's violent crime rate in 2017 was 11 percent higher than the national rate. Texas also faces health care challenges. Its 17 percent uninsured rate is easily the highest in the nation, and lawmakers have been resistant to expanding Medicaid under the Affordable Care Act. But Texas has developed a civic culture of adaptability and resilience, as it demonstrated by taking in thousands of Hurricane Katrina evacuees in 2005. In 2017, after slow-moving Hurricane Harvey dumped as much as 52 inches of rain on the Houston area, the region and its industries recovered from massive damage more quickly than expected.

Newcomers — think of the Bushes — have done much to put the stamp of Texas on the whole of the United States. The state's population grew from 21 million in 2000 to 25 million in 2010, a 21 percent increase, and by an additional 14 percent since 2010. Texas was home to four of the eight U.S. counties that gained the most residents between 2010 and 2018: Harris (Houston), Tarrant (Fort Worth), Bexar (San Antonio), and Dallas. It also had six of the 13 counties that gained the most residents between 2017 and 2018 – Harris, Tarrant and Bexar, plus Collin and Denton near Dallas and Fort Bend near Houston. Since 2010, Fort Bend County has grown by 33 percent, while Denton and Collin have grown by 29 percent and 27 percent, respectively. Even the big counties with below-average growth rates expanded at a pace that other states would envy – 11 percent in Hidalgo County (McAllen) and Dallas County, and about 5 percent in El Paso County.

Today, Texas is 43 percent non-Hispanic white, lower than any state save California, New Mexico and Hawaii. Hispanics account for 39 percent, African-Americans 12 percent and Asian-Americans 5 percent. Hispanic growth has accounted for a majority of the state's population increase since 2010. Texas has thrived in part because it has nurtured and profited from its relationship with its southern neighbor. The border is some 1,200 miles and porous. Nearly half of merchandise exports to Mexico are from Texas; the busiest truck crossing between the countries is the World Trade Bridge near Laredo and Nuevo Laredo.

Inset for Greater Houston

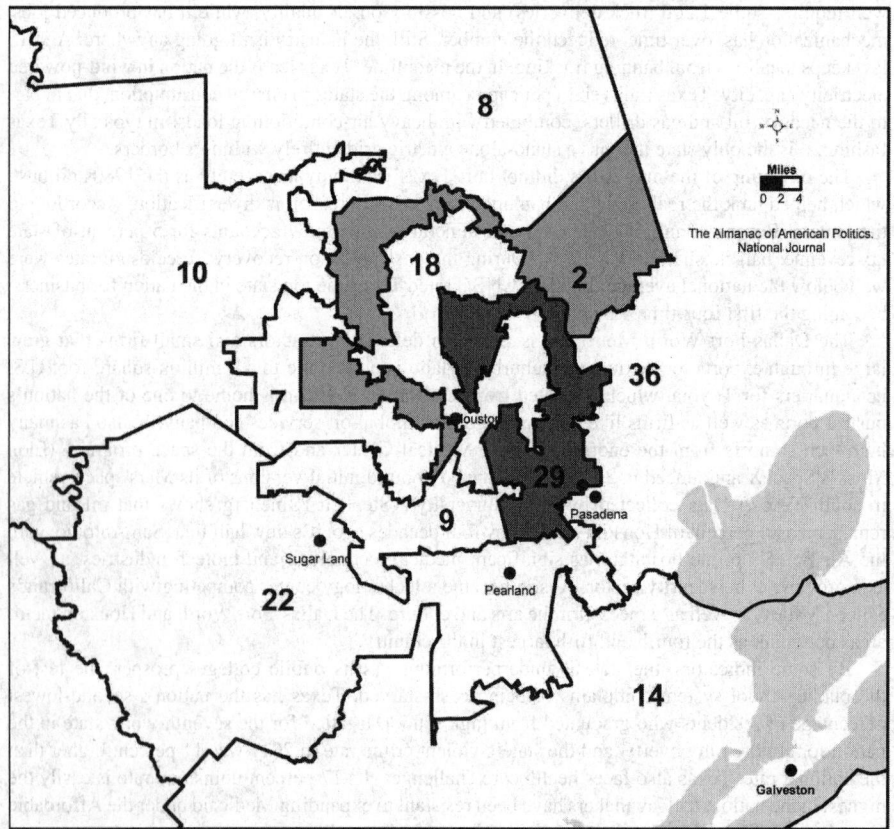

Congressional district boundaries were effective for 2012 on an interim basis.   Districts 2 and 29 are highlighted for visibility.

Politically, Republicans hold both Senate seats, almost two-thirds of the congressional seats, all nine statewide elective offices in the executive branch, all nine elected seats on the state Supreme Court, and all nine statewide elected judges on the Court of Criminal Appeals. Republicans control both houses of the state legislature, although under former Speaker Joe Straus, who retired in

2018, moderate Republicans in the House often teamed with Democrats to stifle conservative initiatives, such as school choice. Democrats have been waiting for demographic factors to undermine Republican dominance, but for years, rural, small-town GOP strongholds in Texas have punched above their weight politically. (Democratic strength in rural areas is limited to a heavily Hispanic stretch of border counties that runs from El Paso to Brownsville in the Rio Grande Valley.)

In the past two election cycles, two factors have provided Democrats with more hope than they've had in a long time. One is rapid population growth in heavily blue urban Texas. The second is the election of Trump, whose populist rhetoric was unwelcome in historically Republican suburban areas . Mitt Romney won Texas by 16 points in 2012; Trump won it by nine. Hillary Clinton increased the Democratic vote tally by about 570,000 votes, far more than Trump's increase of 115,000. In Collin, Denton and Tarrant counties, Trump's margins of victory were between 8 and 15 points smaller than Romney's, and in Travis, Harris, Dallas, El Paso and Bexar counties, the Democratic winning margin grew by between 9 and 15 points.

These trends intensified in 2018. O'Rourke fell about two and a half points short of knocking off GOP Sen. Ted Cruz, but the surge of support he inspired paid dividends elsewhere . Democratic challengers knocked off GOP Reps. John Culberson and Pete Sessions, and incumbent Republicans Dan Patrick, the lieutenant governor, and Ken Paxton, the attorney general, saw their winning margins shrink by 14 and 17 percentage points, respectively. O'Rourke flipped several counties Cruz had won in 2012 – Harris, Fort Bend, Tarrant, and the suburban Austin counties of Hays and Williamson – and he reduced the GOP margins of victory in Denton and Collin counties. Meanwhile, the O'Rourke-driven turnout enabled Democrats to capture 30 of 42 judicial seats in play on the state's courts of appeals, helping shift the balance of power on the influential mid-level courts. While the strong results for Democrats "aren't the end of the status quo, they just might be the beginning of the end," wrote Texas-based journalist Christopher Hooks in The Atlantic. According to the Cook Political Report's David Wasserman, Republicans have come close to maxing out their edge with rural whites, while Democrats still have room to grow in the state's college-educated suburbs and with Hispanic voters.

Population		Race and Ethnicity		Income	
Total	27,419,612	White	42.9%	Median Income	$57,051
Land area (sq. miles)	261,232	Black	11.7%	State Income Rank	21
Pop/ sq mi	105.0	Latino	38.9%	Poverty Rate	16.0%
Born in state	59.8%	Asian	4.5%	With health insurance	81.8%
		Two or more races	1.6%	Cash public assistance	1.5%
Age Groups		Other	0.4%	Food stamp/SNAP	12.7%
Under 18	26.3%				
18-34	24.7%	**Education**		**Work**	
35-64	37.3%	H.S grad or less	42.3%	White Collar	35.9%
Over 64	11.7%	Some college	29.0%	Sales and Service	41.4%
		College Degree, 4 yr	18.8%	Blue Collar	22.7%
Military		Post grad	9.9%	Government	13.2%
Veteran/ Active Duty	7.8%				

Presidential Politics

2016 Primary (D) Clinton (D)	936,004 (65%)	Sanders (D)	476,547 (33%)		
2016 Primary (R) Cruz (R)	1,241,118 (44%)	Trump (R)	758,762 (27%)	Rubio (R)	503,055 (18%)
2016 Pres. Vote Trump (R)	4,685,047 (52%)	Clinton (D) 3,877,868 (43%)		Johnson (L)	283,492 (3%)
2012 Pres. Vote Romney (R)	4,569,843 (57%)	Obama (D) 3,308,124 (41%)			

Jimmy Carter was the last Democrat to win Texas's then-26 electoral votes. Since the Georgian's narrow victory, the closest a Democratic nominee has come to carrying Texas was in 1996, when Texan Ross Perot split the opposition to Bill Clinton, and Bob Dole carried the state 49%-44%. In 2012, Mitt Romney carried the state 57%-41%. He lost 58%-41% in the heavily Hispanic South Texas that includes the Rio Grande Valley, San Antonio and Corpus Christi. Barack Obama also won 52%-45% in metro Austin. But Romney won a solid 54 percent in the Dallas-Fort Worth Metroplex (Collin, Dallas, Denton and Tarrant Counties) and 52 percent in metro Houston (Brazoria, Chambers,

Fort Bend, Galveston and Harris Counties). He won rural East and West Texas by 73 percent and 78 percent, respectively.

In 2016, Hillary Clinton held Donald Trump to 52%-43%, a margin of victory comparable to his victory in the battleground state of Ohio. Clinton won South Texas by roughly 59%-37%. Clinton's breakthrough of sorts came when she won the Dallas-Fort Worth area by less than a percentage point, and captured metro Houston by roughly 51%-45%. Trump won East and West Texas with roughly 73 percent and 77 percent of the vote, respectively. The comparisons to 2012 are not exact because of the greater vote for third-party candidates in 2016. Almost one-quarter of the 2016 Texas electorate was Hispanic and according to the television network exit poll they voted for Clinton by 61%-34%, a far cry from 2004, when Bush lost that group by only one percentage point. Democrats still need to improve their appeal among white voters, who Trump won by a whopping 69%-26%. Almost 1 million more Texans voted in 2016 than in 2012, up 12.2 percent.

For the first time in 20 years, Texas was an important state in the presidential nomination process in 2008. After Obama had won a string of primaries and caucuses in February, Clinton won 51%-47%. But Obama won more delegates overall because one-third of them were selected in caucuses held on primary night and more Obama voters showed up. In the 2016 Democratic presidential primary, Clinton swamped Vermont Sen. Bernie Sanders, 65%-33%. Sanders narrowly carried Travis County (Austin and University of Texas), next-door Hays, Brazos (Texas A&M University) as well as a handful of rural counties. Clinton won 239 of the state's 254 counties (two were tied).

On the Republican side in 2016, the primary was conducted as the GOP nominating contest was entering a critical phase. Texas Sen. Ted Cruz campaigned hard in the state, knowing that if he lost it, he was out. A CNN debate in Houston days before the March primary was a raucous affair with candidates hurling insults at each other. Cruz defeated Trump 44%-27% and claimed 248 of the state's counties; Trump won six.

Congressional Districts

116th Congress Lineup	13D 23R	115th Congress Lineup	11D 25R

Texas redistricting, once the plain prerogative of Anglo Democrats, now involves a complex sets of partisan, racial and legal dynamics. In the 2000 census, Texas gained two seats, and in 2010, another four. The projection is for a two or three-seat gain in 2020. In 2001, after a split legislature failed to agree on a map, a federal court drew a plan protecting 17 Democratic incumbents and adding two new Republican seats, for a 17-15 breakdown. Since then, as the Republicans' strengthening grip on state politics has coincided with a Hispanic population boom, Texas has endured what seems like a never-ending legislative and legal rollercoaster ride. The 2018 election results introduced important new dynamics: Democrats took two Republican-held seats in the Dallas and Houston suburbs, plus Latina Democrats replaced Anglo Democrats in Houston and El Paso, giving Republicans 23-13 control of the delegation. Strong Democratic performances left them with several other opportunities. Six GOP incumbents won with less than a five percent margin; three of them were partly in the suburbs or exurbs of Austin, with one each in the Dallas, Houston and San Antonio areas.

Republicans took over the legislature in 2002, and House Majority Leader Tom DeLay pressured his party to replace the court plan with a design to maximize Republican seats. Months later, 51 Texas House Democrats, who became known as the "Killer D's," fled to Oklahoma to thwart a two-thirds quorum. But Republicans eventually rammed through their map, converting a 15-17 deficit that wildly underrepresented GOP strength into a 21-11 edge in 2004 by defeating five "WD-40s" — white Democrats over age 40 — whom DeLay had targeted for extinction. In 2010, Republicans captured 23 of 32 seats, and it was Democrats rather than Republicans who were underrepresented.

In early 2011, Republicans faced a dilemma. The most rapid growth in the state had taken place in exurban counties, almost all of them Republican. But Hispanics had accounted for 65 percent of all growth between 2000 and 2010, and the state's plans were subject to review by the Obama administration's Justice Department. The prevailing interpretation of the Voting Rights Act seemed to require maximizing black- and Hispanic-majority seats. So, mindful of federal scrutiny, a group of pragmatic House Republicans lobbied legislators in Austin to simply shore up incumbents and split the four new seats evenly: two new Democratic-leaning, Hispanic-majority seats, and two new Republican seats in fast-growing exurban areas, for a 25-11 delegation.

Republican legislators, and Perry, were horror-struck by the idea of "giving" Democrats any seats. In June, they passed their own plan to split the Dallas-Fort Worth Metroplex's Hispanic population six ways, stuff Austin Democrat Lloyd Doggett into a heavily Hispanic seat stretching to San Antonio, and create three new safely Republican enclaves: one in Fort Worth's western suburbs, another in Houston's eastern suburbs, and a third running along the I-35 corridor from the fringes of the Metroplex to the outskirts of Austin. The plan created one new Democratic seat in the Rio Grande Valley.

Doggett and the Democrats immediately blasted the "Perry-mander" as a gross overreach. Hispanic advocacy groups denounced it as discriminatory and sued in a San Antonio federal court. The Justice Department declared the map had been drawn with discriminatory intent and assumed the opposition. Attorney General Greg Abbott, in an end-around attempt, sought preclearance from a three-judge panel at the U.S. Court of Appeals in Washington. Back in San Antonio, the state's own expert witness, Rice University professor John Alford, admitted on the stand the Republican map didn't create an effective new Hispanic seat. The San Antonio panel halted the map's implementation and announced its intent to draw its own interim plan if the state map did not obtain federal preclearance before the December 2011 opening of the candidate filing period.

Sure enough, the D.C. court denied Abbott's request for quick summary judgment, setting up a protracted preclearance trial. So the San Antonio judges delighted Democrats with their own plan: Not only did it preserve Doggett's existing Austin-based 25th District, it essentially drew three of four new seats for Democrats — one minority "coalition" seat in Fort Worth, and one Hispanic majority seat each in the Rio Grande Valley and San Antonio areas.

In January 2012, the Supreme Court ruled that the San Antonio court had "exceeded its mission" to fix only the districts that had violated the Voting Rights Act and faulted the court for failing to use an elected legislature's original plan as a baseline for its own. So in February, the San Antonio court issued a second interim map. This time, it resembled the Republicans' plan, except it created a new 66 percent Hispanic seat linking Dallas and Fort Worth and restored Hispanic voting strength in the San Antonio-based 23rd District. The end result was nearly identical to what Republican incumbents had lobbied for in the first place: a 2-2 division of new seats. Democrats picked up the 23rd in November, for 12 of 36 seats overall; Republicans regained that seat two years later.

Following further legal maneuvering, the San Antonio panel ruled in August 2017 that Doggett's 35th District, plus the Republican-held 27th district in Corpus Christi were discriminatory violations of the Constitution and the Voting Rights Act. But the judges failed to offer an alternative. In September 2017, the Supreme Court blocked immediate changes. In June 2018, in a 5-4 ruling that was a legal victory for Republicans, the high court found that alleged discrimination by the state was not intentional. As it turned out, Democrats turned the map to their favor in the November 2018 election, as the broader demographic and political shifts in the suburbs gave them a two-seat gain — their first pick-up of House seats in Texas since 2012.

Preparation for the political and legal thicket that is certain to accompany the 2021 redistricting will be affected by the 2020 election. Republicans will seek to recapture the two seats they lost in 2018, while Democrats likely will make competitive challenges for some of the several seats where they fell narrowly short. Regardless, Republicans will use their initial control of the next cycle in Texas to reinforce control of their newly vulnerable seats and they likely will use the state's additional seats following reapportionment to cede some — or all — of that new ground to the Democrats in 2022. With their previous best-case map that gave them 25-11 control of the delegation after the 2016 election, Republicans will be hard-pressed to avoid Democratic gains of at least one seat each in the rapidly-growing Dallas, Houston and Austin-San Antonio areas.

For Democrats, the total of their prospective gains will be accompanied by the demographic implications. Of their four freshmen following the 2018 election, they included two Latinas (in Democratic seats that previously were held by Anglo men), a white woman and an African-American man. Of the six Republican newcomers to the delegation, all were white men; overall, 21 of the 23 Republicans are white men. Hispanics (all Democrats) hold six of the 36 seats in a state where they are 39 percent of the overall population; four are in districts along the border with Mexico, and one each in Houston and San Antonio. Blacks, with 12 percent of the population, also hold six House seats — three Democrats in the Metroplex, two Democrats in Houston and one Republican in the San Antonio area. Another consequence of the 2018 election is that the return to Democratic control of the House left Texans chairing only one committee. Under Republican control of the House in 2018, the Texas delegation included seven committee chairman and three Appropriations subcommittee chairmen. Of those 10 Republicans, two retired and two lost their reelection bids. The prospect of additional turnover among Republicans — some of whom are term-limited in their committee slots — and the longer-term increase of Hispanic influence, especially among Democrats, promise new turmoil in the Texas delegation.

Greg Abbott (R)

Elected 2014, term expires 2023, 2nd term; b. Nov. 13, 1957, Wichita Falls; U. of TX, B.B.A. 1981; Vanderbilt U., J.D. 1984; Catholic; Married (Cecilia); 1 child.

Elected Office: TX State Trial Judge 129th District Court, 1992-1995; TX Supreme Court, 1995-2001; TX Attorney General, 2002-2014.

Professional Career: Practicing attorney, Butler & Binion, 1984-1992.

Office: 1100 San Jacinto Blvd., Austin, 78711-2428; 512-463-2000; Fax: 512-463-5571; Website: gov.texas.gov.

Lt. Gov.: Dan Patrick (R) **Atty. Gen:** Ken Paxton (R)

State Legislature: Senate: 12D, 19R **House:** 67D, 83R

Election Results

Election	Name (Party)	Vote (%)
2018 General	Greg Abbott (R)	4,656,196 (56%)
	Lupe Valdez (D)	3,546,615 (43%)
2018 Primary	Greg Abbott (R)	1,389,562 (90%)
	Barbara Krueger (R)	127,134 (8%)

Republican Greg Abbott once described his job as the state's attorney general this way: "I go into the office in the morning, I sue Barack Obama, and then I go home." It was that reputation that helped Abbott win the governorship in 2014, entrenching Republican domination in a state that has not elected a Democrat to statewide office since 1994. Abbott won a second term in 2018.

Abbott was born in Wichita Falls and raised in Duncanville in Dallas County. He earned a bachelor's degree in finance from the University of Texas at Austin and got his law degree from Vanderbilt University in Nashville Tennessee. The year he finished law school, in 1984, a falling tree injured Abbott while he was out for a run. The incident left him a paraplegic, and he has used a wheelchair ever since. After a stint in private practice, Abbott became an associate justice on the Texas Supreme Court in 1995, appointed to fill a vacancy by then-Gov. George W. Bush. Abbott won election twice more to the state's highest civil court, and in 2001 he resigned to run for attorney general in 2002. Abbott won reelection twice and became the longest-serving state attorney general in Texas history. As the state's highest law enforcement officer, Abbott was a pure Texas conservative. He sued the federal government more than two dozen times, on issues ranging from the Affordable Care Act to abortion, voter ID and environmental regulations. In 2005, Abbott argued before the U.S. Supreme Court on the constitutionality of the Ten Commandments monument on the Texas State Capitol grounds. The high court ruled 5-4 in his favor.

Less than a week after Gov. Rick Perry announced he would not seek another term, Abbott declared his candidacy for the job. He faced only token opposition in the GOP primary; in the general, he squared off against state Sen. Wendy Davis, whom supporters hoped would benefit from the national attention she got from her unsuccessful filibuster of a bill to ban most abortions after the 20th week of pregnancy. Democrats saw Texas, with its growing Hispanic population, as a state gradually swinging in their direction, and Davis tapped Hispanic state Sen. Leticia Van de Putte as her running mate. Abbott was joined at the top of the GOP ticket by state Sen. Dan Patrick, the nominee for lieutenant governor, and state Sen. Ken Paxton, the nominee for attorney general; both were tea party favorites who had prevailed over establishment favorites in contentious primaries and runoffs. Davis sought to portray Abbott as an Austin "insider" siding with the interests of his rich and powerful friends at the expense of "hard-working Texans." Abbott saturated the airwaves with spots that reminded voters how, despite using a wheelchair, he had persevered and succeeded in life. His ads portrayed Davis as closely aligned with Obama, who was not popular in the Lone Star State, and he featured his Hispanic mother-in-law in TV ads and on billboards to appeal to Hispanic voters. In October, the Davis campaign released the "wheelchair ad." The spot opened with a picture of a wheelchair, noted Abbott's crippling accident and said, "He sued and got millions. Since then he spent his career working against other victims." The ad then cited cases as evidence that Abbott had thwarted or ruled against other victims trying to get compensation. The ad got a lot of attention, including criticism that it was in bad taste. But there was probably nothing that was going to save Davis' campaign; Abbott ended up trouncing her, 59%-39%. Exit polls showed he won roughly 44 percent of the Hispanic vote. Abbott carried 235 of the state's 254 counties, limiting Davis to the Democratic strongholds of Dallas, El Paso and Travis County (Austin) and 16 others in the heavily Hispanic Rio Grande Valley.

Abbott made progress on some of his key agenda items in 2015. He signed legislation in May to provide $130 million in funding to school districts whose pre-kindergarten programs met certain standards, including having certified teachers and using a state-approved curriculum. The measure won bipartisan approval in the legislature. In June, Abbott steamrolled critics who said border-crossing from Mexico was at a years-long low, signing legislation that expedited hiring of law-enforcement officers on the border, increased penalties for human trafficking, and established a center to analyze border-crime data. Abbott got a further boost when a federal judge in Brownsville blocked Obama's executive order on immigration, which he had personally fought in court as attorney general.

In the 2016 presidential race, Abbott initially supported home-state Sen. Ted Cruz. Abbott, like the GOP presidential candidates, continued to articulate a tough stance on immigration. He threatened to cut funding to any public university that considered itself a "sanctuary" campus, and he kept a promise to cut state grants to Travis County Sheriff Sally Hernandez, who had moved to limit cooperation with federal immigration officials over arrestees accused of non-violent crimes. After Trump took office, Abbott praised the new president's efforts to build a border wall and to expand federal spending on border security.

In 2017, Abbott signed a measure to cut state funding for sanctuary cities. The legislature took up a "bathroom bill" that would require transgender individuals to use the bathroom of their birth sex; a similar law in North Carolina had become a target of boycotts before being repealed in 2017. As the bill worked its way through the legislature, Abbott ranged from neutral to supportive of a more moderate version; in the end, the bill failed to pass in a special session. Lawmakers did back other items from Abbott's agenda, including a measure requiring women who wanted abortion coverage to buy it in a separate insurance policy. The following year, Abbott tried again to cap property taxes, but no bill passed, and the skirmishing continued into 2019. The legislature also considered a "red flag law" that would let judges temporarily take firearms from a person deemed to be an imminent threat; Abbott indicated that he was open to the idea, but amid opposition from gun-rights advocates, the measure floundered.

Abbott remained on good terms with Trump; in April 2018, Neil Cavuto of the Fox Business Network called him Trump's favorite governor. But on occasion, Abbott broke with the president. In June 2018, Abbott wrote a letter to Trump asking him to lift the tariffs he imposed on foreign steel and aluminum, arguing that the state's oil and gas industry was hurt by higher prices. He also urged care in renegotiating the North American Free Trade Agreement, a significant driver of Texas' economy. That same month, amid a national outcry over child separations at the U.S.-Mexico border, Abbott urged lawmakers from both parties to work together on a solution. "This disgraceful condition must end; and it can only end with action by Congress to reform the broken immigration system," he wrote to the Texas delegation.

Abbott was always considered a strong favorite to win a second term. Two Democratic candidates advanced to the runoff: Dallas County Sheriff Lupe Valdez, a child of migrant workers who had previously served as a captain in the Army and as a U.S. Customs and Border Protection agent, and businessman Andrew White, son of the late Democratic Gov. Mark White. Valdez faced criticism from liberal activists for being too willing to work with federal immigration enforcement, and she was questioned about her record overseeing the Dallas County jail, which was sued by the federal government for substandard health care and facilities; the complaint was lifted after changes made on her watch. White, meanwhile, entered politics after running a fire and water damage restoration firm and then starting – and eventually selling – a home warranty business. White said he was personally pro-life, though he pledged to veto any legislation that sought to limit abortion rights. Valdez won the runoff, 53%-47%.

In the general election, Abbott far outraised Valdez, and used his money to tout his conservative stances on immigration policy and his efforts to fund pre-kindergarten. Valdez attacked Abbott for not calling a special session to generate recovery funds for Hurricane Harvey. "He calls a special session for bathrooms but does not call a special session when people are dying," she charged. The two candidates split over allowing teachers to be armed (Abbott supported it, Valdez opposed it) and over expanding Medicaid under the Affordable Care Act (with the reverse). On Election Day, Abbott won, 56%-43% -- about three points below his percentage in 2014, though still not enough to produce a genuinely competitive race. Indeed, Abbott fared about five points better than Cruz in his Senate race against Democrat Beto O'Rourke. Thanks to the O'Rourke surge and dissatisfaction with Trump, Valdez was able to flip several urban and suburban counties – Hays (Austin suburbs), Bexar (San Antonio), Harris (Houston) – shifting the margin by seven to 10 percentage points in each. O'Rourke, unlike Valdez, won Fort Bend County (Houston suburbs), as well as Tarrant (Fort Worth) and Williamson (Austin suburbs).

Abbott kicked off his second term by urging unity within the often-fractious GOP leadership and saying he would seek targeted funding for schools, including teacher pay hikes, as well as more stringent property tax caps for school districts, counties and cities.

John Cornyn (R)

Elected 2002, term expires 2020, 3rd term, b. Feb 02, 1952; Houston; Trinity University (TX), B.A., 1973; St. Mary's School of Law (TX), J.D., 1977; University of Virginia, LL.M., 1995; Church of Christ; Married (Sandra Hansen Cornyn); 2 children.

Elected Office: Bexar County District court judge, 1985-1991; TX Supreme Court, 1991-1997; TX Attorney General, 1999-2002.

Professional Career: Practicing attorney, 1977-1984.

DC Office: 517 HSOB 20510, 202-224-2934, Fax: 202-228-2856, cornyn.senate.gov

State Offices: Austin, 512-469-6034; Dallas, 972-239-1310; Harlingen, 956-423-0162; Houston, 713-572-3337; Lubbock, 806-472-7533; San Antonio, 210-224-7485; Tyler, 903-593-0902.

Committees: *Finance*: Energy, Natural Resources & Infrastructure; International Trade, Customs & Global Competitiveness (Chmn); Taxation & IRS Oversight. *Intelligence*. *Judiciary*: Border Security & Immigration (Chmn); Constitution; Crime & Terrorism; Subcommittee on Intellectual Property.

Group Ratings

	ADA	ACLU	AFL-CIO	LCV	ITI	COC	HAFA	ACU	CFG	FRC
2018	-	5%	-	7%	-	90%	65%	77%	58%	100%
2017	0%	C	0%	0%	C	86%	C	80%	81%	100%

Almanac Ratings 2017-18

	Economy	Social	Foreign	Composite
Liberal	0%	0%	0%	0%
Conservative	100%	100%	100%	100%

Key Votes of the 115th Congress

1. Obama-care revision	Y	5. Gun regulations	Y	9. Kavanaugh confirmation	Y
2. Tax Cuts	Y	6. Family planning regs	Y	10. Saudi arms sales	N
3. Dodd-Frank revision	Y	7. Gorsuch confirmation	Y	11. FISA rules	Y
4. Omnibus appropriations	Y	8. Immigration restrictions	Y	12. Military aid in Yemen	N

Election Results

Election	Name (Party)	Vote (%)		Cand. Spent	Ind. Exp. Support	Ind. Exp. Oppose
2014 General	John Cornyn (R)............................. 2,861,531	(62%)	$14,672,004	$635,391	$27,244
	David Alameel (D)......................... 1,597,387	(34%)	$5,715,984		
	Rebecca Paddock (L)...................... 133,751	(3%)			
2014 Primary	John Cornyn (R)................................ 781,259	(59%)			
	Steve Stockman (R)............................ 251,577	(19%)			
	Dwayne Stovall (R)........................... 140,794	(11%)			

Prior winning percentages: 2008 (55%), 2002 (55%)

Republican John Cornyn has been the highest ranking Texan to serve in the Senate since Lyndon Johnson. But thanks to term limits for leadership posts, he was in a bit of limbo within the GOP hierarchy as he prepared for re-election in 2020.

Cornyn has risen quickly through his party's leadership ranks since his initial election in 2002. After two terms as chairman of the National Republican Senatorial Committee, he was chosen minority whip in 2013. Two years later, after the Republicans retook control of the Senate, Cornyn became majority whip. In that role, Cornyn was well-regarded among colleagues. He was known for using the carrot over the stick and had close relationships with members of his conference. But he had to cede that post in 2019 to Sen. John Thune of South Dakota, thanks to the term limits for his party's leaders.

Cornyn, who turned 67 in 2019, has made little secret of his desire to succeed Majority Leader Mitch McConnell, telling Politico that it is "something I would be interested in doing." But McConnell, 77, holds the one GOP leadership post not subject to term limits and he has shown no interest in stepping down. "And so, I think a lot depends on what his decision is going to be," Cornyn said; each faced re-election in 2020. Even so, Senate Republicans carved out a counselor role for Cornyn, allowing him to attend leadership meetings and offer guidance.

The workload has been bumpy for Cornyn at times. Since 2013, he has shared representation of the Lone Star State with erstwhile presidential contender Ted Cruz: Cornyn and Cruz have perhaps the chilliest relationship of any two same-state senators. Cornyn is frequently overshadowed by his junior colleague. At the same time, Cornyn is the more effective legislator. In early 2018, a shaken Cornyn responded to a massacre at a Sulphur Springs church by pushing enhanced background checks for some firearm sales; later that year, he quarterbacked a sweeping criminal justice reform bill that had widespread bipartisan support.

Cornyn was born in Houston and spent much of his childhood in San Antonio. His father was an oral pathologist in the Air Force and stationed in Japan, where Cornyn went to high school. After his father retired from the service, the family settled in San Antonio. Cornyn graduated from Trinity University and St. Mary's University School of Law, both in San Antonio. He practiced law for five years with a firm that defended physicians and insurance companies in medical malpractice cases. In 1984, he ran for District Court judge in Bexar County and, at 32, upset a strong favorite in the race. In 1990, Cornyn was elected to the state Supreme Court. Five years later, he wrote the 5-4 decision upholding the state's "Robin Hood" school finance system, in which property-wealthy school districts had to send money to property-poor districts.

In 1997, Cornyn resigned from the court to run for attorney general. Facing two better-known opponents, he placed second in the initial round of the primary but won the runoff. In the general election, he faced a grizzled political veteran — former Attorney General Jim Mattox, a populist Democrat. Cornyn won 54%-44%, becoming the first Republican attorney general in Texas since Reconstruction. He argued two cases before the U.S. Supreme Court, including the Santa Fe Independent School District's defense of reading the Lord's Prayer at football games. The high court nixed it.

When GOP Sen. Phil Gramm announced he would not seek re-election in 2002, Cornyn ran and had no serious opposition in the primary. Democrats nominated two-term Dallas Mayor Ron Kirk, who was vying to become Texas' first African-American senator. Cornyn ran as a strong supporter of President George W. Bush, a former Texas governor; he called for making Bush's 2001 tax cuts permanent. He supported government vouchers for private school tuition, individual investment accounts as part of Social Security and "colorblind" standards for college and university admissions. Kirk took opposite stands on most issues, but portrayed himself as a moderate Democrat who would support Bush in many instances. Republicans ran ads linking Kirk to then-New York Sen. Hillary Clinton and liberal out-of-state contributors.

Kirk — who later served as U.S. trade representative under President Barack Obama — campaigned with a sense of humor, making fun of his bald pate, but he made some mistakes. Cornyn came out in favor of a bill in the Texas Legislature requiring district attorneys to seek the death penalty for killers of law enforcement officials after the Austin-based district attorney had not done so for the killer of a Travis County sheriff's deputy. Kirk said Cornyn was acting like he was running for district attorney and then apologized to a convention of law enforcement officials a few days later — as Cornyn met with the deputy's widow. Democrats operated on the assumption that Kirk had to win 85 percent of African Americans, 65 percent of Hispanics and 35 percent of whites to win. He achieved the first and probably achieved the second of those goals but failed to achieve the third. Cornyn won 55%-43%.

Cornyn often is described as "genial" and generally favors reasoned language over angry rhetoric. "He's quiet by nature and isn't excitable," his friend Jim Lunz, a retired San Antonio businessman, told The New Republic. "So when he does speak, you are more inclined to listen to what he has to say." Because of Cornyn's reputation, South Carolina Sen. Lindsey Graham told NPR in 2014 that Cornyn was "the best guy in the [GOP] Conference to bring us together" as Republicans prepared to assume the majority. "Nobody doubts his conservatism, but he's a very practical, let's-move-the-ball-forward kind of guy."

In contrast, Cruz has a reputation for slash-and-burn legislative tactics that have alienated senators on both sides of the aisle, including Cornyn. In the 2012 primary, in which Cruz defeated Lt. Gov. David Dewhurst, Cruz was criticized for refusing to back Cornyn's bid for GOP Senate whip. Cruz declined to endorse Cornyn when the latter faced a challenge from the right in the 2014 primary. Cornyn, in turn, stayed out of the 2016 race for the GOP presidential nomination in which Cruz emerged as the leading challenger to Trump.

"Obviously, I would have loved for Ted and I to be exactly two peas in a pod on everything," Cornyn told the Austin American-Statesman editorial board in February 2014. Days earlier, in what he described as "an uncomfortable moment," Cornyn had moved to shut down a Cruz filibuster of an increase in the federal debt ceiling. Upon Cruz's arrival on Capitol Hill, Cornyn sought to work with him — initially signing on to Cruz's effort in late 2013 to shut down the government in an effort to defund the Affordable Care Act. Cornyn subsequently withdrew his support and criticized the highly controversial tactic, which resulted in a 16-day shutdown. The Dallas Morning News' editorial page in January 2015 suggested Cornyn was often guilty of "straying from his signature sound judgment and allowing the party's extremists, including Cruz, to set an agenda that feeds gridlock." Six months later, Cornyn called out his colleague when Cruz, in a startling departure from Senate norms, accused McConnell of a "flat-out lie" on an Export-Import Bank bill. Cornyn, in a remark considered blunt by the chamber's genteel standards, responded: "I have listened to the comments of my colleague, the junior senator from Texas, both last week and this week, and I would have to say that he is mistaken."

Political necessity, however, has brought the two men closer together. Sensing a Democratic threat to Cruz from Rep. Beto O'Rourke, Cornyn endorsed Cruz in his 2018 Senate race. Cruz swiftly returned the favor in early 2019 for Cornyn, signaling that a rising Democratic tide in the state would leave no room for GOP primary fights in 2020.

With the Republicans back in the majority in 2015, Cornyn took over as chairman of Judiciary's Constitution Subcommittee. In October of that year, Cornyn led a diverse group of eight senators — including two members of the Senate Democratic leadership as well as the Republican chairman of the Judiciary panel — in introducing a major criminal justice reform measure. "This is the way the system is supposed to work —people with different views come together, find common ground. You won't get everything you want, and if your attitude is 'I get everything I want or nothing,' you'll always get nothing," Cornyn said in what some saw as a dig at Cruz. The bill proposed to reduce sentences for some nonviolent drug offenses and give judges more leeway with lower-level drug crimes while increasing rehabilitation and job-training programs for inmates to cut down on recidivism. Cornyn said it drew on reforms that had worked in Texas.

The bill cleared the Judiciary Committee on a bipartisan vote. But it then ran into objections from Cruz and several other conservative hard-liners, and, despite revisions designed to assuage the dissenters, McConnell opted not to bring it to the floor. McConnell "understandably did not want to tee up an issue that split our caucus right before the 2016 election," Cornyn told The New York Times, while expressing consternation about the demise of the legislation. "It is one of the things that makes this a frustrating place to work," he said. With support from President Donald Trump, a revised version was enacted in 2018.

Cornyn worked on immigration reform legislation in 2007 before abandoning his efforts. Arizona Republican John McCain accused Cornyn at the time of raising arcane legal issues to scuttle the bill. Cornyn said of the talks, "I didn't so much walk away as got chased away." His amendment to bar undocumented immigrants convicted of identity theft from a legalization processes was defeated 51-46. From then on, he opposed the larger immigration bill. As reform heated up in 2013 with the bipartisan "Gang of Eight" negotiations, Cornyn remained a skeptic about a comprehensive approach. He said giving undocumented immigrants a path to citizenship remained premature and insisted on focusing on border enforcement. Frank Sharry, founder of the pro-immigration group America's Voice, complained in the HuffPost that Cornyn "is famous for posing as a reformer even as he works to derail reform."

When a crisis involving Central American refugees along the border became a major controversy in 2014, Cornyn joined with Texas Democratic Rep. Henry Cuellar on a bill expediting the deportation of undocumented children from countries other than Mexico and Canada. Immigration advocates criticized the bill, saying an easier deportation process would return the children to potentially dangerous situations. Cornyn was among several border-state Republicans who took issue with Trump's call for a wall along the 1,900-mile U.S.-Mexico border, advocating instead for 700 miles of border fence.

In 2009, Cornyn became chairman of the NRSC, the campaign arm of the Senate GOP. The assignment came at a tumultuous moment in Republican politics. The emergence of anti-establishment tea party activism and candidates would dog his two terms at the helm of the committee. Democrats had gained 14 Senate seats between the 2006 and 2008 campaign cycles, when their Senate campaign committee was headed by New York Sen. Chuck Schumer; Cornyn wanted to reverse those results. Cornyn adopted Schumer's strategy of recruiting candidates who could win in states not naturally inclined to his party. It didn't always work out. Cornyn urged Gov. Charlie Crist to run in Florida and Rep. Mike Castle to run in Delaware. In Florida, former state House Speaker Marco Rubio gained steam against Crist, eventually forcing him from the party and then crushing his independent bid. Castle lost in a stunning primary upset to a tea party challenger, Christine O'Donnell, with the Democrats retaining the seat in the fall.

Despite these setbacks, Cornyn succeeded in the chairman's major duty: raising large sums. He brought in $115 million for the cycle and came close to matching the $130 million raised by rival Democrats. The Republicans gained six seats, many more than seemed likely in January 2009 but fewer than seemed possible over the summer and fall.

Cornyn got another term as NRSC chairman for the 2012 election cycle. Irritated by then-South Carolina Republican Sen. Jim DeMint's endorsements of candidates whose chances Cornyn had thought to be dim in 2010, he urged colleagues to bring concerns they had about candidates to him. Cornyn, in turn, made it plain that he would be more wary of taking sides in primaries. The upshot was that a pair of far-right Republicans became nominees: Richard Mourdock in Indiana and Todd Akin in Missouri. Both blew what were seen as nearly sure-thing opportunities after they made politically disastrous comments about rape and abortion; in 2018, Republicans captured each seat. When Republican Whip Jon Kyl of Arizona retired at the end of 2012, Cornyn ran for the position. Lamar Alexander of Tennessee said he would run for whip but later dropped out. Richard Burr of North Carolina also considered running but decided against it, giving Cornyn a clear path to the post.

At home, Democrats' attempts in 2008 to attract a well-known challenger failed. Their nominee was Houston state Rep. Rick Noriega, an Afghanistan veteran. Cornyn outraised Noriega by more than 4-1 and won 55%-43%, the same margin by which he won in 2002. He captured 36 percent of the Hispanic vote, an improvement over 2002.

After Cruz's surprise primary win over Dewhurst, an establishment Republican like Cornyn, Cornyn's biggest re-election threat in 2014 appeared to be from the right. But Cornyn assiduously courted conservatives in the state, careful not to split with Cruz's hard-line postures on most high-profile votes. His efforts, and huge early fundraising, helped scare off serious primary challengers. Even though Cruz declined to endorse him, Cornyn drew no serious tea party primary opposition—just an impulsive last-minute challenge from quirky far-right Rep. Steve Stockman. Cornyn finished way ahead of Stockman, 59%-19%. Cornyn's race against Democratic businessman David Alameel was little more than a formality; he won 62%-34%.

In the Senate, Cornyn was close to Alabama Republican Jeff Sessions, who — as Trump's attorney general — asked Cornyn to consider the FBI job after Trump fired James Comey in May 2017. Cornyn was quickly interviewed, but a week after Comey's ouster, he took himself out of the running. "Now, more than ever, the country needs a well-credentialed, independent FBI director," Cornyn said. His statement hinted at what even many of his Republican colleagues were suggesting: Given allegations that Trump had fired Comey to slow down an investigation of possible collusion by the Trump campaign with Russia in the 2016 presidential election, appointment of a partisan as FBI director — even a well-liked one such as Cornyn — would have yielded a bruising confirmation battle.

Cornyn faced re-election in 2020. He made clear that he would take the race seriously, along with his role as the party leader on the ballot whose coattails could affect down-ballot Republicans . When Rep. Joaquin Castro decided not to run, the initial Democratic frontrunner was M.J. Hegar, a military veteran who ran a well-financed and unexpectedly close—though unsuccessful--challenge to Rep. John Carter in 2018. The central question in Texas politics heading into that race was whether Cornyn's lower profile — one that elicits less passion on both sides — puts him in better shape than Cruz in 2018.

Ted Cruz (R)

Elected 2012, term expires 2024, 2nd term, b. Dec 22, 1970; Calgary, Alberta, Canada, AB; Princeton University (NJ), A.B., 1992; Harvard Law School (MA), J.D., 1995; Southern Baptist; Married (Heidi Nelson); 2 children.

Professional Career: Clerk, U.S Appeals Court, 1995; Clerk, Supreme Court Justice William Rehnquist, 1996; Attorney, Cooper, Carvin & Rosenthal, 1997-1999; Domestic policy adviser, Bush-Cheney campaign, 1999- 2000; Association deputy U.S Attorney General, 2001; Policy-planning office Director, Fed. Trade Commission, 2001-2002; Texas solicitor General, 2003-2008; Adjunct Professor, University of TX, 2004-2009; Attorney, Morgan, Lewis & Bockius, 2008-2012.

DC Office: 404 RSOB 20510, 202-224-5922, Fax: 202-228-0755, cruz.senate.gov

State Offices: Austin, 512-916-5834; Dallas, 214-599-8749; Houston, 713-718-3057; McAllen, 956-686-7339; San Antonio, 210-340-2885; Tyler, 903-593-5130.

Committees: *Commerce, Science & Transportation*: Communications, Technology, Innovation & the Internet; Subcommittee on Aviation & Space (Chmn); Subcommittee on Science, Oceans, Fisheries & Weather; Subcommittee on Security. *Foreign Relations*: Africa & Global Health Policy; Near East, South Asia, Central Asia & Counterterrorism; West Hem Crime Civ Sec Dem Rights & Women's Issues. *Joint Economic. Judiciary*: Border Security & Immigration; Constitution (Chmn); Crime & Terrorism. *Rules & Administration*.

Group Ratings

	ADA	ACLU	AFL-CIO	LCV	ITI	COC	HAFA	ACU	CFG	FRC
2018	-	23%	-	14%	-	78%	78%	95%	72%	100%
2017	5%	C	0%	0%	C	86%	C	96%	86%	100%

Almanac Ratings 2017-18

	Economy	Social	Foreign	Composite
Liberal	6%	6%	8%	6%
Conservative	94%	94%	92%	94%

Key Votes of the 115th Congress

1. Obama-care revision	Y	5. Gun regulations	Y	9. Kavanaugh confirmation	Y
2. Tax Cuts	Y	6. Family planning regs	Y	10. Saudi arms sales	N
3. Dodd-Frank revision	Y	7. Gorsuch confirmation	Y	11. FISA rules	N
4. Omnibus appropriations	N	8. Immigration restrictions	N	12. Military aid in Yemen	N

Election Results

Election	Name (Party)	Vote (%)	Cand. Spent	Ind. Exp. Support	Ind. Exp. Oppose
2018 General	Ted Cruz (R)................................ 4,260,553	(51%)	$40,647,923	$1,205,710	$3,186,483
	Beto O'Rourke (D)........................ 4,045,632	(48%)	$74,424,994	$1,770,046	$9,138,593
2018 Primary	Ted Cruz (R)................................ 1,315,146	(85%)			
	Mary Miller (R)................................. 94,274	(6%)			

Prior winning percentages: 2012 (56%)

In the modern political era, there rarely has been a senator as controversial — or who has attracted as much animosity in the clubby chamber — as Ted Cruz. Nor has the Senate seen a member whose fortunes have reversed so quickly. Once a dominant force in conservative politics, Cruz has been rebuilding his career after losing the 2016 GOP presidential nomination to Donald Trump and nearly losing his Senate seat to former Rep. Beto O'Rourke, who became a Democratic presidential candidate.

In March 2015, a little more than two years after joining the Senate, Cruz announced his presidential bid, which he ran with a hard-right ideology and an outsider's appeal. He won nearly a dozen state primaries and caucuses and raised a record amount of money in finishing as the runner-up to another outsider: Trump. Cruz was slow to rebound from the bitterness of that campaign: He was virtually booed off the stage at the Republican National Convention in July 2016 when he delivered a speech in which he refused to endorse Trump. The backlash from that episode spurred some intraparty fence-mending on his part. And Trump's unexpected victory in November prompted Cruz — whose path to the White House was blocked for at least eight years — to blunt his hard political edges.

Cruz was born in Calgary, Alberta, where his parents worked in the oil business. Thanks to an American-born mother, he is considered a natural-born citizen under the Constitution, notwithstanding Trump's suggestion during the 2016 race that Cruz's place of birth made him ineligible for the White House. His father's life story figures prominently into Cruz's political narrative. Rafael Cruz fought to overthrow Fulgencio Batista's regime in Cuba in the 1950s before fleeing to Texas at 18 with nothing more than $100 sewn into his underwear. He worked as a dishwasher for 50 cents an hour to put himself through the University of Texas, and he later started a business in Houston. There, he met Cruz's mother, an Irish-American who studied math at Rice University.

As a high school student, Ted Cruz earned a scholarship by entering speech contests organized by the Free Enterprise Institute, in which participants studied the "Ten Pillars of Economic Wisdom," a libertarian manifesto, and delivered 20-minute speeches about it. As part of the program, Cruz memorized the Constitution and traveled around Texas discussing conservative ideas. He was educated at elite East Coast universities not usually associated with political outsiders: After earning his undergraduate degree from Princeton University, where he was a champion debater, Cruz graduated from Harvard Law School and clerked for Supreme Court Chief Justice William Rehnquist.

After a few years with a Washington law firm, Cruz joined George W. Bush's presidential campaign in 2000 as a domestic policy adviser. It was there that he met his wife, Heidi Nelson Cruz, another member of the Bush team. Both were dispatched to Florida in the chaos of the recount between Bush and Democratic nominee Al Gore, which led to jobs in the Bush administration. In his autobiography, Cruz admits he was "far too cocky for my own good" in those years and "burned a fair number of bridges" that hurt his chances at landing a higher-level administration job. He served as associate deputy attorney general at the Justice Department and then as director of the Federal Trade Commission's Office of Policy Planning.

Cruz returned to Texas in 2003 when he was appointed state solicitor general, making him the first Hispanic-American to hold the position. During his five-year tenure, Cruz argued before the Supreme Court nine times and participated in a number of high-profile cases, including one in which Texas fought to execute a Mexican citizen who raped and murdered two teenage girls and another in which he defended the display of the Ten Commandments on the state Capitol grounds. Cruz in July 2012 told The Texas Tribune: "We ended up, year after year, arguing some of the biggest cases in the country. There was a degree of serendipity in that, but there was also a concerted effort to seek out and lead conservative fights." His successor, James Ho, told The New Yorker: "He was and is the best appellate litigator in the state of Texas."

Cruz was in private practice when he decided to run to replace retiring Republican Sen. Kay Bailey Hutchison in 2012. He began the race as an underdog against Lt. Gov. David Dewhurst, an influential figure in the Texas GOP establishment who had the backing of almost every prominent Republican officeholder, including Gov. Rick Perry. Dewhurst was much better-known than Cruz and had millions of dollars to throw into the race. But Cruz got the backing of national conservative heavyweights and outside groups such as the Club for Growth and FreedomWorks. Cruz sank $1 million of his own money into the primary in an effort to keep Dewhurst under 50 percent and force a runoff. In the nine-candidate first round, Dewhurst finished with 45 percent of the vote, followed by Cruz with 34 percent.

Dewhurst sought to cast Cruz as a creature of Washington, given his government experience, and suggested Cruz did not have the state's best interests in mind. Cruz portrayed Dewhurst as just another moderate Republican, though one in a position that required a large amount of deal-cutting and horse trading. Cruz trounced Dewhurst 57%-43%, capturing every major county. In the general election, he had little trouble beating former state Rep. Paul Sadler.

Within a year of his election, Cruz revealed his headstrong, take-no-prisoners legislative tactics that helped shut down the federal government for 16 days — thrilling tea party activists but infuriating Democrats and many of his Republican colleagues. "If you killed Ted Cruz on the floor of the Senate, and the trial was in the Senate, nobody would convict you," South Carolina Republican Lindsey Graham said at the Washington Press Club Foundation's congressional dinner in early 2016.

Cruz established himself as a strong voice for the right. Summarizing what he would do to enact a conservative agenda, Cruz told National Review: "What it takes is backbone, the willingness to stand and fight for those principles in the face of opposition and derision. Of those who have firm principles, even fewer have the backbones to stand for those principles when the heat is on." Underpinning such convictions was a political calculation: At least before Trump's surprise 2016 victory, the Republican Party was divided over whether success lay in seeking to energize the political right or following a more centrist approach in an effort to broaden the party's base. Cruz was firmly in the former camp.

He won ecstatic reviews from conservative activists for his aggressiveness on issues, but his hyperconfident style won him few friends of either party among his Senate colleagues. When he expounded on the origins of the Bill of Rights to California Democrat Dianne Feinstein at a Judiciary Committee hearing two months after being sworn in, she snapped: "It's fine you want to lecture me on the Constitution. I appreciate it. Just know that I've been here a long time." When Cruz aided the libertarian-leaning Sen. Rand Paul of Kentucky during the latter's 2013 filibuster of the Obama administration's nomination of John Brennan to head the CIA over the government's drone policy, Arizona Republican John McCain called Cruz and Paul "wacko birds." Cruz didn't seem to care. At a conservative awards dinner, he joked, "It is wonderful to be among friends or, as some might say, fellow wacko birds."

As 2013 progressed, Cruz eclipsed another junior Republican senator, Marco Rubio of Florida, who also came to power on the tea party wave. Cruz opposed Rubio's efforts to enact a comprehensive immigration reform bill being pushed by a bipartisan group of senators. But Cruz had an even bigger goal in mind. He sought to block a vote on a measure to fund the federal government past the Sept. 30 budget deadline unless Congress barred any funding to implement the Affordable Care Act. "I believe we can win this fight," he told reporters and conservative activists.

But other Republicans weren't buying it; North Carolina Sen. Richard Burr called it "the dumbest idea I've ever heard." In September, Cruz staged a 21-hour talk marathon on the Senate floor in which he read portions of Dr. Seuss' "Green Eggs and Ham" as a bedtime story to his two young daughters supposedly watching via C-SPAN. The resulting 16-day shutdown damaged the GOP brand, and Cruz took a significant share of the blame. "It wasn't about the shutdown. It wasn't about the Affordable Care Act. It was about launching Ted Cruz," Oklahoma GOP Sen. Tom Coburn told The Washington Post.

Indeed, the episode caused Cruz's star to shine even brighter in right-wing circles. He won several straw polls at conservative events during and after the shutdown. He traveled across the country giving speeches, accompanied by his father, who introduced him saying, "He will not compromise!" His dad also was in the spotlight later during the presidential campaign after Trump, citing a National Enquirer story, made the unfounded claim that the elder Cruz had been with Lee Harvey Oswald before the assassination of President John F. Kennedy. Ted Cruz's numbers as a potential 2016 presidential contender reached double digits in mid-2014 surveys.

By February 2014, Cruz was so emboldened he objected to a deal crafted by Republican Leader Mitch McConnell of Kentucky that would have required 51 votes instead of 60 to raise the debt ceiling. The lower threshold would have given senators like McConnell the political cover to vote against the increase while ensuring it would pass and that the government could continue to function. Cruz later acknowledged that his effort to scuttle the deal enraged his colleagues but was unrepentant. "It's part of the reason why I've said many times that I think the biggest divide we've got in this country is not between Republicans and Democrats," he told The New Yorker. "It's between entrenched politicians in Washington in both parties and the American people." Cruz's tactics created a continuing series of headaches for his in-state colleague Sen. John Cornyn, leading to a frosty relationship between the two Texans.

Cruz became the first major Republican in the presidential race when he launched his long-expected bid in March 2015 at Liberty University, a hotbed of social conservatism founded by the late Jerry Falwell. But his star had faded somewhat with the base since his first years in office — he began the race in the low single digits in national polling, stuck in the second tier of a crowded GOP field. Undeterred, Cruz kept up his bomb-throwing rhetorical approach on the campaign trail, seeking to put together a coalition of religious and economic ultraconservatives. His calls to abolish the IRS and Common Core national education standards earned regular cheers on the campaign trail. Cruz leaned hard into religious liberty arguments as well, introducing legislation for a constitutional amendment that would reinstate states' rights to bar same-sex marriage just days before the Supreme Court legalized such unions nationwide.

At first, Cruz went out of his way to maintain a "bromance" with Trump — to the point of defending the New York businessman after Trump described Mexicans coming to the U.S. as "rapists" and criminals while launching his candidacy. In contrast with the insult-laden blasts aimed at other rivals, Trump was kinder to Cruz, calling him a "nice guy." The sentiment did not last. Before the race was over, Trump had posted an unflattering picture of Heidi Cruz — on whom he threatened to "spill the beans" — while Ted Cruz had blasted Trump as a "serial philanderer" and "utterly amoral."

Cruz pulled off a surprise win in the first delegate selection contest: the Iowa caucuses — in which Trump was thought to be in the lead heading into the contest. The Cruz campaign raised $93.2 million on its own, a record for a Republican presidential primary candidate. According to a compilation by The Washington Post, this does not include another $89.6 million raised by super PACs and other independent groups supporting Cruz. In addition to Iowa and his home state of Texas, Cruz won primaries and caucuses in nine other states and outlasted two other freshman senators seeking the nomination: Paul, who dropped out after Iowa, and Rubio, who called it quits after losing his home state of Florida to Trump. But for most of the campaign after the Iowa win, Cruz had a bumpy ride. Trump recovered to win the first-in-the-nation New Hampshire primary and followed with a victory in South Carolina. On Super Tuesday in March, Trump captured seven states; Cruz took three.

Cruz scored a significant, 15-point victory over Trump in the Wisconsin primary, but, by that time, there was no mathematical possibility of Cruz winning the nomination outright. In an informal alliance with the other remaining contender besides Trump, Cruz and Ohio Gov. John Kasich pursued a strategy of seeking to deny Trump a first-ballot victory — and thereby force a contested convention. Cruz picked a former contender for the GOP nomination, businesswoman Carly Fiorina, as his running mate, as he sought to present himself as the true conservative in the race.

In the end, the animosity toward Cruz precluded him from emerging as the standard-bearer of the "Never Trump" movement. Former House Speaker John Boehner of Ohio called Cruz "Lucifer in the flesh" and a "miserable son of a bitch." Josh Holmes, McConnell's chief of staff when Cruz arrived in the Senate, told Politico, "The idea that there's ever been a spokesperson less equipped to make an argument for party unity — I don't think there is anybody." In early May, Cruz lost the Indiana primary to Trump 53%-36% and withdrew from the race, shortly before Trump's last remaining rival, Kasich, quit the contest.

Cruz announced he would seek re-election in Texas in 2018, but the blowback from his prime-time convention speech in Cleveland — including criticism of his refusal to endorse Trump — prompted speculation that his Senate seat could be at risk. "You don't come to the convention after you have lost the nomination and not support the nominee," Cornyn told Fox News Radio. "I think it was a mistake and I don't know what it means in terms of his future, but I think he miscalculated."

Cruz took steps to repair the damage: He and Cornyn co-sponsored October events in Texas to raise money for endangered Senate Republicans. A month earlier, Cruz endorsed Trump in a

Facebook post, declaring: "After many months of careful consideration, of prayer and searching my own conscience, I have decided that on Election Day, I will vote for the Republican nominee, Donald Trump. ... If you don't want to see a Hillary Clinton presidency, I encourage you to vote for him."

At that time, Trump was the clear underdog, and Cruz appeared to be contemplating a bid for the 2020 GOP nomination to run against a President Hillary Clinton. After the election, he pivoted again. According to Politico, Cruz visited Trump Tower in in mid-November and told the Trump transition team that the incoming president would need a "champion" — and volunteered for the task. "I think everyone recognizes we are in a markedly different environment today," Cruz told the newspaper in January 2017. "And that environment is going to change how everyone approaches getting our job done."

Two months later, less than a year after Trump and Cruz had slung insults at each other over their wives and respective moral standards, the two dined at the White House at Trump's invitation — accompanied by their spouses. On Capitol Hill, a kinder, gentler Cruz invited colleagues to weekly basketball games.

While some were skeptical about the authenticity of Cruz's changed modus operandi, McConnell — at a weekly luncheon of Republican senators — labeled his erstwhile tormentor "the new Ted Cruz" and Graham apologized for his much-quoted wisecrack of a year earlier. "Love is everywhere," Graham said as he and Cruz made a joint appearance on MSNBC.

In 2018, Cruz needed all the friends he could find. O'Rourke, a little-known El Paso Democrat, challenged him for the Senate. O'Rourke spent the early stages of the campaign visiting all 254 Texas counties. It was a mixture of internet savvy — most of O'Rourke's events and even car rides were livestreamed — and old-style retail politics. The result was astonishing: Cruz won by less than 3 percentage points. It was even more shocking on the financial side. O'Rourke had spent $74 million to Cruz's $41 million. That left O'Rourke running for president, built on the political capital gained from nearly defeating the conservative firebrand in one of the most conservative states.

Louie Gohmert (R)

Elected 2004, 8th term, b. Aug 18, 1953; Pittsburg; Texas Agricultural and Mechanical University, B.A., 1975; Baylor University School of Law (TX), J.D., 1977; Baptist; Married (Kathy Gohmert); 3 children.

Military Career: U.S. Army 1978-1982

Elected Office: Smith County District Court judge, 1993-2002.

Professional Career: Practicing attorney, 1982-1992; Chief justice, TX 12th Court of Appeals, 2002-2003.

DC Office: 2267 RHOB 20515, 202-225-3035, Fax: 202-226-1230, gohmert.house.gov

State Offices: Longview, 903-236-8597; Lufkin, 936-632-3180; Marshall, 903-938-8386; Nacogdoches, 936-715-9514; Tyler, 903-561-6349.

Committees: *Judiciary*: Constitution, Civil Rights & Civil Liberties; Crime, Terrorism & Homeland Security. *Natural Resources*: National Parks, Forests & Public Lands; Oversight & Investigations (RMM).

Group Ratings

	ADA	ACLU	AFL-CIO	LCV	ITI	COC	HAFA	ACU	CFG	FRC
2018	-	16%	-	3%	-	75%	94%	86%	98%	100%
2017	5%	C	11%	3%	C	93%	C	85%	83%	100%

Almanac Ratings 2017-18

	Economy	Social	Foreign	Composite
Liberal	10%	9%	14%	11%
Conservative	90%	91%	86%	89%

Key Votes of the 115th Congress

1. Obama-care revision	Y	5. Family planning regs	Y	9. Guantanamo prisoners	N
2. Tax Cuts	Y	6. Body cameras/immigration	N	10. Ground missiles, limit	N
3. Omnibus appropriations	N	7. Abortion ban	Y	11. Defense Dept. spending	N
4. Dodd-Frank revision	Y	8. Concealed carry	N	12. FISA rules	N

Election Results

Election	Name (Party)	Vote (%)		Cand. Spent	Ind. Exp. Support	Ind. Exp. Oppose
2018 General	Louie Gohmert (R)...............................	168,165	(72%)	$741,493	$16,244	$6,780
	Shirley McKellar (D)...................	61,263	(26%)	$43,907		
2018 Primary	Louie Gohmert (R)...............................	64,004	(88%)			
	Anthony Culler (R).......................	6,504	(9%)			

Prior winning percentages: 2016 (74%), 2014 (78%), 2012 (71%), 2010 (90%), 2008 (88%), 2006 (68%), 2004 (62%)

Louie Gohmert, a Republican first elected in 2004, is a devout tea party conservative with a knack for provoking Democrats and even some fellow Republicans. As an unabashed supporter of Donald Trump, Gohmert has taken on the president's critics. When Democrats regained House control in 2019, they imposed what he proudly referred to as the "Louis Gohmert rule," which limited how often a member could speak in the House on non-legislative topics.

Gohmert grew up in Mount Pleasant and graduated on an Army scholarship at Texas A&M University, where he was class president. He got a law degree from Baylor University, then served as a captain in the Army. He practiced law in Tyler and spent a decade as a district court judge. Republican Gov. Rick Perry named him chief justice of the Texas Appellate Court in 2002. He earned a reputation as a tough law-and-order judge with a knack for attracting attention. In 1996, he ordered an HIV-positive convicted car thief, as a condition of probation, to notify future sexual partners of his HIV status and to obtain written consent from them before engaging in sexual activity.

After the 2003 redistricting in Texas, Gohmert was one of six Republicans to challenge four-term Democratic Rep. Max Sandlin, who was a close ally of Minority Leader Nancy Pelosi. Gohmert led in the primary with 42 percent of the vote to 30 percent for lawyer John Graves. In the runoff campaign, few differences separated the two conservatives; Gohmert prevailed 57%-43%. Gohmert won 77 percent of the vote in his home base of Smith County, where half the votes were cast. In the general election, Gohmert linked Sandlin to the national Democratic Party and its 2004 presidential nominee, John Kerry. The result wasn't close. Gohmert beat Sandlin, 61%-38%, winning 79 percent in Smith County.

Gohmert has had some notable moments. When the bailout for the financial industry came to the House floor in 2008, he made a motion to adjourn the chamber "so we don't do this terrible thing to our nation." It was defeated 394-8. He had little regard for President Barack Obama or Hillary Clinton. During a 2016 speech to the Values Voters Summit of social conservatives, Gohmert said that Clinton was "mentally impaired." "We need to be praying for Hillary Clinton," he added. "There's special needs there." Also that year, he said on the House floor that gay people should not be sent into space.

Gohmert was among the House Republicans who vociferously complained about special counsel Robert Mueller's investigation into charges that Russia sought to influence the 2016 presidential campaign. He questioned the fairness of current officials of the Justice Department and the FBI. At a well-publicized hearing in July 2018 of the Judiciary Committee with FBI agent Peter Strzok, whose law-enforcement inquiries were challenged by Trump and his allies, Gohmert said the witness was a "disgrace" and asked "how many times did you look so innocent into your wife's eye and lie about" his reported affair with a former FBI attorney.

Gohmert often has tangled with House Republican leaders. After the 2014 election, he launched his own candidacy as conservative unhappiness with Speaker John Boehner deepened. He received three votes, including his own. Allies referred to Gohmert as "a stalking horse" who encouraged others to enter the contest. After Boehner resigned in October 2015, he was one of nine who voted against Paul Ryan for Speaker. "I simply cannot vote for a candidate who demands more power before he agrees to be Speaker," Gohmert said. In 2019, he became the top Republican on the Oversight and Investigations Subcommittee of the Natural Resources panel. With the announced retirement in 2020 of Rep. Rob Bishop of Utah as the full committee's senior Republican, Gohmert is the most senior Republican in line to take that position. That could pose awkward dynamics for GOP leaders.

Gohmert has never been reelected with less than 68 percent of the vote. In 2018, retired Army officer Shirley McKellar was his Democratic challenger for the fourth consecutive cycle. In its editorial endorsement of Gohmert in 2018, the Longview News Journal said that he was "usually far outside the mainstream of his own party," but that "Democrats must find stronger candidates" if they hope to defeat him. Gohmert won, 72%-26%.

When Democrats in January 2019 changed House rules to limit each member to one "special order" speech to the House each week, Gohmert told the Houston Chronicle that the "Louis Gohmert rule" was a compliment. "If Speaker Pelosi thought I was hurting the Republican Party, she surely would want me speaking every night," he said.

TX-1: East Texas   Cook Partisan Voting Index: R+25

Population		Race and Ethnicity		Income	
Total	713,841	White	62.5%	Median Income	$47,282
Land area (sq. miles)	7,859	Black	17.5%	District Income Rank	347
Pop/ sq mi	90.8	Latino	17.1%	Poverty Rate	18%
Born in State	71.5%	Asian	1.2%	With health insurance	81.3%
		Two or more races	1.3%	Cash public assistance	1.7%
Age Groups		Other	0.5%	Food stamp/SNAP	14.1%
Under 18	24.7%				
18-34	22.9%	**Education**		**Work**	
35-64	36.5%	H.S grad or less	46%	White Collar	15.9%
Over 64	15.9%	Some college	33.4%	Sales and Service	41.6%
		College Degree, 4 yr	14.1%	Blue Collar	28.2%
Military		Post grad	6.5%	Government	13.2%
Veteran/ Active Duty	8.4%				

2012 Pres. Vote	Romney	181,835	(72%)	Obama	69,858	(28%)		
2016 Pres. Vote	Trump	189,604	(72%)	Clinton	66,389	(25%)	Johnson	5,501	(2%)

Tyler, Longview: The gently rolling land of East Texas was settled by Tennessee farmers in the years before the Civil War. It sits at the western edge of Scots-Irish America, a swath of territory that starts in the Appalachian ridge and is inhabited by a combative, honor-bound and highly religious populace. A hundred years ago, this was one of the poorest parts of America, where farmers scratched a living off the land and hoped for good weather and decent prices in the marketplace. When a peach blight in the early 20th century wiped out much of the local fruit industry, many farmers turned to growing roses, which proved ideally suited to the climate and soil of East Texas. By the 1940s, more than half the nation's rose bushes were grown within 10 miles of Tyler, which has become known for its annual Texas Rose Festival, which draws 120,000 visitors every October. About 75 percent of the garden roses in the country have found their way through Tyler and are distributed throughout the country. The area continues to grow rapidly. In 2017, Texas demographers reported that Tyler was one of two areas in the state where the average age was decreasing; much of the population increase has resulted from domestic migration.

Longview, which in the 1870s was the western terminus of the Southern Pacific Railroad, became a trading center for wagon trains and local cotton growers and timber cutters. In 1943, the Big Inch pipeline began sending millions of barrels of crude oil from the "Black Giant" oil field near Longview — at the time, the largest ever in the state — to the East for refining. Since then, the area has become an industrial center for earth-moving equipment and chemicals. Eastman Chemical Co., which once produced chemicals for film company Eastman Kodak, has had a booming business because of lower natural gas prices; its Longview site has employed about 1,500. Geologists have identified the shale formations in east Texas as the largest reserves of natural gas in the nation. In April 2017, the U.S. Geological Survey quintupled its estimate to more than 300 trillion cubic feet. The Keystone XL pipeline runs through the district in eastern Wood and Smith counties and western Nacogdoches County. Unlike the pipeline's northern end, mired in regulatory holdups, oil began flowing through the Gulf Coast portion in 2014.

The 1st Congressional District of Texas, covering the heart of East Texas, is made up of 12 counties, the most populous being Tyler's Smith County and Longview's Gregg County, which total nearly half the population. East Texas is ancestrally Democratic, a region that responded to the populist rhetoric of presidential candidate William Jennings Bryan in the 1890s and President Franklin D. Roosevelt in the 1930s and 1940s. Republicans began making inroads in Tyler and Longview in the 1950s. By the time George W. Bush ran for reelection as Texas governor in 1998, the area was solidly Republican. Democrats held onto the district until the 2003 redistricting. GOP-friendly Smith and Gregg counties were added to the district. In the Cook Political Report's PVI listings, this is the 18th most Republican district in the nation. But it is only the 7th most Republican district in Texas.

Daniel Crenshaw (R)

Elected 2018, 1st term, b. Mar 14, 1984; Aberdeen, Scotland; Tufts University (MA), B.A., 2006; Taubman Center for State & Local Government – Harvard Kennedy School, M.P.A., 2017; Methodist; Married (Tara Crenshaw).

Military Career: U.S. Navy SEAL 2006-2016 (Afghanistan, WIA)

DC Office: 413 CHOB 20515, 202-225-6565, crenshaw.house.gov

State Offices: Kingwood, 713-860-1330.

Committees: *Budget. Homeland Security*: Emergency Preparedness, Response & Recovery; Oversight, Management & Accountability (RMM).

Election Results

Election	Name (Party)	Vote (%)		Cand. Spent	Ind. Exp. Support	Ind. Exp. Oppose
2018 General	Daniel Crenshaw (R)	139,188	(53%)	$1,737,570	$1,503,425	$719,958
	Todd Litton (D)	119,992	(46%)	$1,375,117		
2018 Primary	Daniel Crenshaw (R)	19,430	(70%)			
Runoff	Kevin Roberts (R)	8,523	(30%)			
2018 Primary	Kevin Roberts (R)	15,273	(33%)			
	Daniel Crenshaw (R)	12,679	(27%)			
	Kathaleen Wall (R)	12,524	(27%)			
	Rick Walker (R)	3,320	(7%)			

Political newcomer Dan Crenshaw brought new blood and enthusiasm as the unexpected Republican nominee in a Texas open seat in 2018. In the GOP primary, he barely survived into the runoff against a big-spending party contributor. Then he easily defeated a state legislator who was backed by business groups. Crenshaw, a retired Navy lieutenant commander who served as a SEAL for 10 years, wore a distinctive eye patch. He lost his right eye to an explosive blast that nearly killed him while he was deployed in Afghanistan in 2012.

More distinctively, the youthful Crenshaw generated excitement among suburban Houston voters. He ran as an outsider who emphasized the importance of "service before self," and appealed to young voters with his call for long-term steps to preserve Social Security. Following his easier than expected victory in the Republican runoff, the Houston Chronicle wrote that Crenshaw "became a potential star on the national stage because of his war-hero story and a charisma that is drawing younger voters."

A native of Houston, where his father worked in the oil business and traveled around the world, Crenshaw graduated from Tufts University, where he joined the Reserve Officers' Training Corps. Following his military retirement as a lieutenant commander and his recuperation from the war injuries that also badly damaged his other eye, he received a master's in public administration from Harvard's Kennedy School of Government. He returned to Houston just in time to assist as a volunteer in the recovery from the devastation of Hurricane Harvey in September 2017. That experience spurred his decision to run for Congress.

In the first round of voting in the Republican primary, he finished second by a scant 155 votes ahead of Republican donor Kathaleen Wall, who spent $6.2 million of her own funds but lacked basic skills as a campaigner. Crenshaw, by contrast, raised about $200,000 in the initial round of the contest, as he sought to introduce himself as a fresh spirit against the party insider. "You keep electing old, rich, white people to the seat — you can expect the Republican Party to be gone in 50 years," he told The Weekly Standard during the primary. "We can't keep doing that. We have to make conservatism cool and exciting again." State Rep. Kevin Roberts led the opening round with 33 percent of the vote, to 27 percent each for Crenshaw and Wall.

Roberts, the chief operating officer of a Houston law firm, began the runoff with support from much of the state's Republican establishment and he outspent Crenshaw nearly 2-to-1. He campaigned on his legislative experience plus support from conservative groups, including the National Rifle Association. Crenshaw, by contrast, styled himself as a policy expert and wrote his campaign's position papers.

His appeal was enhanced by several national appearances on Fox News. He received a late campaign boost from former Texas Lt. Gov. David Dewhurst, who criticized a negative campaign mailing from the Roberts camp for "lying about his opponent." Crenshaw was endorsed by Rep. Scott Taylor of Virginia, also a former Navy SEAL, plus Rep. Pete Sessions of Texas, for whom Crenshaw worked as an adviser on military issues. (Each of those supporters subsequently lost reelection in November.)

Crenshaw won the runoff with an impressive 70 percent of the vote. He won, 53%-46%, in November against Democrat Todd Litton, a lawyer and political activist. Although national Democrats had voiced hopes of being competitive in this contest, they instead focused elsewhere in Texas. Crenshaw embellished his cultural appeal when he responded magnanimously to a sarcastic reference to his eye patch by an entertainer on Saturday Night Live prior to the election. The following week, he appeared on the show and, after smoothing over the earlier conflict, appealed for support of veterans.

TX-2: Harris County   Cook Partisan Voting Index: R+11

Population		Race and Ethnicity		Income	
Total	767,312	White	48%	Median Income	$75,989
Land area (sq. miles)	309	Black	10.5%	District Income Rank	68
Pop/ sq mi	2485.2	Latino	31.4%	Poverty Rate	10.6%
Born in State	50.2%	Asian	7.7%	With health insurance	84.9%
		Two or more races	1.7%	Cash public assistance	1.2%
Age Groups		Other	0.6%	Food stamp/SNAP	6.4%
Under 18	24.2%				
18-34	25.4%	**Education**		**Work**	
35-64	39.8%	H.S grad or less	31%	White Collar	10.6%
Over 64	10.6%	Some college	28.1%	Sales and Service	36.8%
		College Degree, 4 yr	26.1%	Blue Collar	18.2%
Military		Post grad	14.7%	Government	9.6%
Veteran/ Active Duty	5.8%				

2012 Pres. Vote	Romney	157,094	(63%)	Obama	88,751	(36%)			
2016 Pres. Vote	Trump	145,530	(52%)	Clinton	119,659	(43%)	Johnson	10,323	(4%)

West Houston and Northern Suburbs: Houston, which remains one of the fastest growing metropolitan areas in the country, has become an internationally renowned energy hub that provides the largest share of the nation's jobs in oil and gas extraction. The city's Energy Corridor, a sprawling 4,000-acre business district on both sides of the Katy Freeway west of the city, is a state-established district whose vision is to become the world's premier location for energy-related businesses. It houses more than 300 companies and 94,000 employees, including U.S. headquarters for BP, ConocoPhillips and Shell. Northeast of downtown near Lake Houston along the Sam Houston Tollway is Generation Park, a 4,000-acre master-planned enterprise park for corporate and residential development, with office, shopping and industrial sites that could eventually host 150,000 employees. In early 2018, its 52-acre "mixed-use corporate lifestyle" Redemption Square district opened its initial retailers.

Growth in the Houston area has been phenomenal. The oil and gas rush in South Texas' Eagle Ford Shale region alone supported 155,000 jobs, according to a 2013 University of Texas-San Antonio study. Many of those field operation and management jobs have been centered in Harris

County. Harris' growth to 4.7 million to 2017 was a 37 percent increase from 2000; the metropolitan area's 16 percent growth from 2010 to 2017 was the fifth-fastest in the nation. New office space and condominiums have been concentrated on the west side of Houston.

When Hurricane Harvey devastated the Houston area in August 2017, it didn't spare these upscale sections. After long-term sedimentation had reduced the depth of Lake Houston, the flooding from the San Jacinto River was severe in nearby Kingswood and Atascocita, plus Humble, which is near the entrance to George Bush International Airport. Six months later, the Houston Chronicle reported, those communities were "still struggling to recover from Harvey" and "distinctly vulnerable to more flooding." To the west of the city, the Army Corps of Engineers made a deliberate decision to flood parts of the Energy Corridor to prevent a possible failure of massive reservoirs at the Addicks and Barker dams, which form the Buffalo Bayou through downtown. Residents in these wealthy neighborhoods filed huge lawsuits against the Army Corps.

The 2nd Congressional District of Texas is a swirl-shaped district located entirely within Harris County. It comes close to the downtown, covering Rice University, the museum district and Memorial Park, which at 1,466 acres is larger than New York City's Central Park. It also takes in the heavily Democratic neighborhood of Montrose, southwest of downtown, which has been the center of Houston's gay and lesbian community and claims President Lyndon Johnson (who lived there after he graduated from Southwest Texas State) and Howard Hughes as former residents. In 2017, Texas Monthly wrote that Montrose had been changed by gentrification but that "enough of its spirit remains intact for it to remain Houston's, and Texas's, coolest neighborhood." It is home to the only LGBT pride crosswalk in Texas. The district, which includes some of the most Republican precincts in Harris County, was the only one of the five that are mostly in Houston that voted for Donald Trump in 2016. His 52 percent of the vote in the 2nd was a big drop from the 63 percent for Mitt Romney in 2012.

Van Taylor (R)

Elected 2018, 1st term, b. Aug 01, 1972; Dallas; Harvard College (MA), A.B., 1995; Harvard Business School (MA), M.B.A., 2001; Episcopalian; Married (Anne Taylor); 3 children.

Military Career: U.S. Marine Corps 1995-1999; U.S. Marine Corps Reserve 1999-2005 (Iraq)

Elected Office: TX House, 2011-2018.

Professional Career: Director, Churchill Capital Company.

DC Office: 1404 LHOB 20515, 202-225-4201, vantaylor.house.gov

State Offices: Plano, 972-202-4150.

Committees: *Education & Labor*: Early Childhood, Elementary & Secondary Education; Health, Employment, Labor & Pensions. *Homeland Security*: Cybersecurity, Infrastructure Protection & Innovation; Oversight, Management & Accountability.

Key Votes of the 115th Congress

1. Obama-care revision	Y	5. Family planning regs	Y	9. Guantanamo prisoners	N
2. Tax Cuts	Y	6. Body cameras/immigration	N	10. Ground missiles, limit	N
3. Omnibus appropriations	Y	7. Abortion ban	Y	11. Defense Dept. spending	Y
4. Dodd-Frank revision	Y	8. Concealed carry	Y	12. FISA rules	Y

Election Results

Election	Name (Party)	Vote (%)		Cand. Spent	Ind. Exp. Support	Ind. Exp. Oppose
2018 General	Van Taylor (R)	169,520	(54%)	$3,412,936	$23,500	
	Lorie Burch (D)	138,234	(44%)	$308,803		
2018 Primary	Van Taylor (R)	45,475	(85%)			
	David Niederkorn (R)	5,052	(9%)			
	Alex Donkervoet (R)	3,185	(6%)			

Republican first-termer Van Taylor had little competition to win the seat of retiring Rep. Sam Johnson. Taylor was the only one of six House GOP freshmen from Texas who won his seat in 2018 without a primary runoff. Perhaps his biggest obstacle was to await the long-anticipated retirement of Johnson, a 28-year House veteran who was held as a prisoner of war for more than six years during the Vietnam War. Taylor largely cleared the field after Johnson announced his retirement, with support from both economic and social conservatives in the GOP. For the future, his biggest political challenge might be to keep watch on shifting demographics in his rapidly growing district.

Taylor is a Dallas native with deep Texas roots. He was a descendant of Robert Lee Blaffer, who helped to start Humble Oil Co., and he resided in Plano on land near where another great-grandfather farmed during the Depression. He got his undergraduate and business degrees from Harvard University. As a captain in the Marine Corps and a paratrooper, Taylor won awards for his service as a platoon commander and intelligence officer in Iraq, including a successful mission to rescue wounded Marines during a battle in An Nasiriyah.

In business, Taylor was a director of the Dallas-based Churchill Capital Co., a real estate investment firm that has financed many large projects across the South. He also has experience in cellular infrastructure financing and home building, and has been a board member of Texas Gulf Bank. His wife, Anne, has been an executive at another Dallas-based real estate firm.

He had an unsuccessful start in politics in 2006, when he lost to veteran Rep. Chet Edwards, 58%-40%, which was the largest victory margin in that decade for the embattled Democrat in his Waco-based district. Edwards attacked Taylor for having recently moved into the district. That setback became largely overlooked as Taylor rebuilt his political career in Collin County, more than 100 miles to the north. After serving four years in the state House, he had tea party support when he was elected to the Texas Senate in 2014. He received awards from conservative groups for his efforts to restrict government spending and taxes, and he was a consistent conservative on social issues.

Taylor won Senate adoption of a Truth in Taxation rule, which required that legislation state clearly in its first line if there is an attempt to raise taxes or fees. Americans for Tax Reform has cited the rule as a blueprint for other states. For his work in the Republican-controlled chamber, The Dallas Morning News in its endorsement described Taylor as "a solid conservative who can point to a series of bills he got passed as a state legislator with bipartisan support."

Although many local Republicans for years had their eyes on the seat held by Johnson, who retired at age 88 as the oldest member of Congress, Taylor had a virtual free ride. He received early endorsements, including the free market-oriented Club for Growth. For the GOP primary, he raised $1.8 million — including a $1 million personal loan that he mostly paid back -- compared with $54,000 for runner-up David Niederkorn, who had experience as a professor and in the Baptist ministry. Taylor swamped him in the vote, 85%-9%.

In November, he defeated Democrat Lorie Burch, an attorney, in a contest that received little attention from national Democrats or interest groups. With his surprisingly narrow 54%-44% win, Taylor will need to monitor the impact of population increases and partisan shifts north of Dallas on redistricting changes in 2022.

TX-3: Northern Dallas Suburbs   **Cook Partisan Voting Index: R+13**

Population		Race and Ethnicity		Income	
Total	816,143	White	58.4%	Median Income	$90,604
Land area (sq. miles)	481	Black	9.2%	District Income Rank	26
Pop/ sq mi	1697.2	Latino	14.7%	Poverty Rate	6.8%
Born in State	43.1%	Asian	14.6%	With health insurance	89.1%
		Two or more races	2.5%	Cash public assistance	0.8%
Age Groups		Other	0.6%	Food stamp/SNAP	3.2%
Under 18	26.6%				
18-34	20.9%	**Education**		**Work**	
35-64	42.4%	H.S grad or less	19.8%	White Collar	10.1%
Over 64	10.1%	Some college	27%	Sales and Service	36.3%
		College Degree, 4 yr	33.8%	Blue Collar	10%
Military		Post grad	19.4%	Government	9.3%
Veteran/ Active Duty	6.1%				

2012 Pres. Vote	Romney	175,383	(64%)	Obama	93,290	(34%)			
2016 Pres. Vote	Trump	174,561	(54%)	Clinton	129,384	(40%)	Johnson	12,304	(4%)

Plano, McKinney: The Dallas and Fort Worth metropolitan area, once a railroad junction and cotton-shipping center, now has 7.1 million people, the fourth largest in the nation and more than all of Texas had during World War II. More than two-thirds of them live beyond the city limits of Dallas and Fort Worth. In Dallas, the city's old elite occupies the mansions of Highland Park north of downtown, but its business and professional classes have moved farther up into Collin County's scrub-covered hills. Collin's population exploded from 67,000 in 1970 to 970,000 in 2017, with an impressive 24 percent growth since 2010. The county has the sixth-largest population and third-highest median income in Texas.

Its biggest city is Plano, with 286,000 people. The former farming community is the corporate headquarters of Dr. Pepper, J.C. Penney and HP Enterprise Services. In July 2017, Toyota opened its seven-building headquarters at a state-of-the-art campus on 100 acres near the Dallas North Tollway in Plano. Relocation costs exceeded $1 billion. Toyota executives said that the result, with about 4,200 employees, was "a more nimble, mobility-focused company, rather than just an automaker," The Dallas Morning News reported. Officials reviewed more than 100 other potential sites before they decided to shift from Torrance California. JPMorgan Chase moved 6,000 employees to its new campus in Plano in 2017. Nearby, Boeing located the headquarters of its global services division. Collin may have more rentable property than uptown and downtown Dallas combined, D Magazine reported in June 2017.

Plano and nearby Richardson have growing Asian-American populations that were 19 percent and 16 percent, respectively, in 2017. Sixty Chinese cultural organizations are based in North Texas, mostly in Collin County, serving more than 30,000 Chinese-American residents. More than 20,000 Indian-American residents moved into Collin County from 2000 to 2010, with many working at high-tech firms and medical centers in the region. Restaurants, grocery stores and boutiques cater to the Indian community. North of Plano is Frisco, which was the fastest-growing city in the nation in 2017. Nearby McKinney ranked ninth. WalletHub in 2018 listed them as the top real-estate markets nationwide. The Professional Golfers Association announced in December 2018 its plans to move its headquarters from Palm Beach Gardens Florida to a hotel and convention-center complex in Frisco.

The 3rd Congressional District of Texas, based entirely within Collin County, includes all but two small corners of the county and centers on Plano. Collin has been heavily Republican. As in other upscale suburban GOP districts in Texas, its 54 percent vote for Donald Trump in 2016 was a big drop from the 64 percent for Mitt Romney in 2012.

John Ratcliffe (R)

Elected 2014, 3rd term, b. Oct 20, 1965; Chicago, IL; University of Notre Dame (IN), B.A., 1987; Southern Methodist University Law School (TX), J.D., 1989; Roman Catholic; Married (Michele Ratcliffe); 2 children.

Elected Office: Heath City Council, 2001-2004; Heath Mayor, 2004-2012.

Professional Career: Practicing attorney; Heath Board of Adjustment, 1997-1998; Heath Planning & Zoning Commission, 1998-2001; E. TX District Chief, Anti-Terrorism & National Security, 2004-2007; U.S. Attorney, TX East District, 2007-2008.

DC Office: 223 CHOB 20515, 202-225-6673, Fax: 202-225-3332, ratcliffe.house.gov

State Offices: Rockwall, 972-771-0100; Sherman, 903-813-5270; Texarkana, 903-823-3173.

Committees: *Ethics. Homeland Security:* Cybersecurity, Infrastructure Protection & Innovation; Transportation & Maritime Security. *Judiciary:* Courts, Intellectual Property & Internet; Crime, Terrorism & Homeland Security (RMM). *Permanent Select on Intelligence:* Intelligence Modernization & Readiness; Strategic Technologies & Advanced Research.

Group Ratings

	ADA	ACLU	AFL-CIO	LCV	ITI	COC	HAFA	ACU	CFG	FRC
2018	-	6%	-	0%	-	75%	94%	91%	91%	100%
2017	0%	C	5%	0%	C	93%	C	93%	87%	100%

Almanac Ratings 2017-18

	Economy	Social	Foreign	Composite
Liberal	5%	3%	0%	3%
Conservative	95%	97%	100%	97%

Key Votes of the 115th Congress

1. Obama-care revision	Y	5. Family planning regs	Y	9. Guantanamo prisoners	N
2. Tax Cuts	Y	6. Body cameras/immigration	N	10. Ground missiles, limit	N
3. Omnibus appropriations	N	7. Abortion ban	Y	11. Defense Dept. spending	Y
4. Dodd-Frank revision	Y	8. Concealed carry	Y	12. FISA rules	Y

Election Results

Election	Name (Party)	Vote (%)		Cand. Spent	Ind. Exp. Support	Ind. Exp. Oppose
2018 General	John Ratcliffe (R)	188,667	(76%)	$511,049	$5,000	
	Catherine Krantz (D)	57,400	(23%)	$18,074		
2018 Primary	John Ratcliffe (R)	61,902	(85%)			
	John Cooper (R)	10,560	(15%)			

Prior winning percentages: 2016 (88%), 2014 (100%)

Republican John Ratcliffe, elected in 2014, won the GOP primary runoff against 91-year-old Rep. Ralph Hall, the oldest member of Congress, who was seeking his 18th term. Under those circumstances, he could have come to Congress with a well of ill will. Instead, Ratcliffe has earned the support and confidence of many within party leadership and in the Texas delegation. With his background as a federal prosecutor, Ratcliffe has worked on law-enforcement and national security issues and has gained expertise and influence on cybersecurity law.

Ratcliffe, the youngest of six children, got a scholarship to Notre Dame, where he graduated in three years, and earned his law degree from Southern Methodist University. He served eight years as mayor in the town of Heath. He took credit for the town being the only municipality in Rockwall County not to have a tax increase during those years.

He served President George W. Bush as U.S. attorney for northern and eastern Texas, where his caseload included terrorism, illegal immigration, drug trafficking, public corruption and internet child predators. During that time, he led a national operation, which resulted in the single-day arrest of more than 300 illegal immigrants and the subsequent successful prosecution of hundreds who committed identity theft and Social Security fraud, plus a $4.5 million criminal penalty for the company that hired them. Later, he became a partner in a law firm run by former Attorney General John Ashcroft.

In the primary, Ratcliffe sought to refer to the issue of Hall's age without offending seniors, who make up more than 15 percent of the district's electorate. He told voters he admired Hall as a man and as a politician, while portraying the congressman's Washington experience as a liability. After so much time in the nation's capital, "the problems are getting worse, not better," Ratcliffe said in one ad.

In terms of substance, little distinguished the two. Hall, a former Democrat who switched parties following the redistricting in 2003, had one of the most conservative voting records in the House. Ratcliffe was endorsed by the Club for Growth and the Senate Conservatives Fund. A big campaign difference was tactical: Ratcliffe pursued a data-driven approach, while Hall favored old-style stumping. The challenger cited his background in law enforcement — particularly, immigration and homeland security — as a chief reason to seek higher office.

In the six-candidate primary, Hall led 45%-29%. That triggered a runoff. With turnout one-third lower this time, committed conservatives flocked to Ratcliffe. He edged out Hall, 52.8%-47.2%, a margin of 2,372 votes, and was unopposed in November.

Ratcliffe focused on law-enforcement and national security issues with service on the Judiciary and Homeland Security committees. In 2019, he earned a slot on the House Intelligence Committee, a popular post as the panel investigated Russian interference in the 2016 elections. Some House observers viewed Ratcliffe as a successor to retired Rep. Trey Gowdy of South Carolina as a combative interrogator on pivotal committees. Republican Leader Kevin McCarthy publicly (and unsuccessfully) lobbied President Donald Trump to nominate Ratcliffe as attorney general. Ratcliffe also served on the Ethics Committee, another mark of leadership confidence in him.

Ratcliffe took a big-tent approach among Republicans. "I certainly don't see myself as an establishment guy or a leadership guy, but I also don't see myself as a bomb-thrower who's anti-establishment or [an] anti-leadership guy," he said in an interview with The Texas Tribune a month after he took office. Ratcliffe stayed busy with his work and kept his distance from junior House Republicans — including some from Texas — who have stirred the pot and demanded quick change.

In his first reelection campaign, Ratcliffe had a primary challenge from Lou Gigliotti, who finished third with 16 percent in the first round of his 2014 challenge to Hall. Gigliotti was a businessman who claimed tea party support. Ratcliffe won their rematch, 68%-21%, and again had no Democratic opposition.

When his old rival died in early 2019, Ratcliffe led the Texas delegation in a moment of silence on the House floor. "He left this Earth, went right past the moon, and our loss became heaven's gain. Godspeed Ralph Hall," he said.

TX-4: Northeast Texas　　　　　　　　　　**Cook Partisan Voting Index: R+28**

Population		Race and Ethnicity		Income	
Total	728,435	White	72.3%	Median Income	$51,945
Land area (sq. miles)	10,123	Black	10.3%	District Income Rank	271
Pop/ sq mi	72	Latino	13.5%	Poverty Rate	14.9%
Born in State	67.2%	Asian	1.1%	With health insurance	84%
		Two or more races	2.2%	Cash public assistance	1.7%
Age Groups		Other	0.8%	Food stamp/SNAP	13.2%
Under 18	24.5%				
18-34	20.4%	**Education**		**Work**	
35-64	38.7%	H.S grad or less	46.5%	White Collar	16.4%
Over 64	16.4%	Some college	32.3%	Sales and Service	40.8%
		College Degree, 4 yr	14.3%	Blue Collar	26.6%
Military		Post grad	6.9%	Government	14.4%
Veteran/ Active Duty	9.9%				

2012 Pres. Vote	Romney	189,554	(74%)	Obama	63,559	(25%)			
2016 Pres. Vote	Trump	210,587	(75%)	Clinton	60,841	(22%)	Johnson	6,530	(2%)

Eastern Dallas Area, Denison: The Red River Valley is hardscrabble farm country along an unnavigable river. First settled in the 1830s, in the days of the Texas Republic, many counties here reached their population peak around 1900, when a large extended farm family worked every 160 acres. It includes towns like Denison, due north of Dallas, best-known as the birthplace of Dwight Eisenhower, and Sherman, which was the site of a major race riot in 1930 when a black farm worker accused of rape was attacked by a white mob. To the east is Texarkana, noteworthy because its neat grid streets cross the Texas-Arkansas state line, which is straddled by the city's downtown post office. The contrast between the laws of the two states has created competition for which side of the border is more attractive. This small city and its hinterland have produced three recent presidential candidates: Ross Perot grew up in Texarkana, while Bill Clinton and Mike Huckabee hail from Hope Arkansas, just 30 miles east.

Northeast Texas in 1912 sent Democrat Sam Rayburn to Congress, where he became the powerful House Speaker from 1940 until his death in 1961 (except for two terms when Republicans had the majority). The region was once a Democratic bastion, with a sentimental regard for Confederate veterans and a seething hatred of Wall Street bankers. That was Rayburn's politics, and he arguably was the most skillful lawmaker of the 20th century. Today, Rayburn's style of politics has almost completely vanished from the area.

The 4th Congressional District of Texas is the lineal descendant of the seat that Rayburn held, and still includes his hometown of Bonham in Fannin County, which houses a Rayburn museum. But it is quite a different district today. In Rayburn's time, it was farm country, separate and distinct from citified Dallas. Today, it retains its farm counties, but they are only a short hop on the interstate from the Dallas-Fort Worth Metroplex, and about one-third of the district's residents live in the DFW metropolitan area. Rockwall County's population increased 118 percent between 2000 and 2016, while Hays County was the fastest growing county in the state between 2010 and 2017. In 2017, its median household income of $93,300 made it the second-wealthiest county in Texas. In addition to Rockwall, other population centers are Denton-based Grayson County and Texarkana-based Bowie. Less than 10 percent of the district is in suburban Collin County. Bonham is the site of the state's first new reservoir since 1999, which will pump water into northeast Dallas.

In 1940, the year Rayburn became Speaker, his district voted 90 percent for Franklin D. Roosevelt. In 2016, the 4th District voted 75% for Donald Trump, which placed it among his top 2 percent of districts in the nation.

Lance Gooden (R)

Elected 2018, 1st term, b. Dec 01, 1982; Terrell; Trinity Valley Community College (TX); University of Texas, B.A., 2004; Church of Christ; Married (Alexa Calligas).

Elected Office: TX House, 2011-2018.

Professional Career: Legislative Aide, Rep. Betty Brown; Insurance Broker.

DC Office: 425 CHOB 20515, 202-225-3484, gooden.house.gov

State Offices: Mesquite, 214-765-6789.

Committees: *Financial Services*: Diversity & Inclusion; Housing, Community Development & Insurance.

Election Results

Election	Name (Party)	Vote (%)		Cand. Spent	Ind. Exp. Support	Ind. Exp. Oppose
2018 General	Lance Gooden (R)...........................	130,617	(62%)	$882,798	$300,218	$517,300
	Dan Wood (D)...................................	78,666	(38%)	$98,699		
2018 Primary	Lance Gooden (R)...........................	23,294	(53%)			
Runoff	Bunni Pounds (R)...............................	20,542	(47%)			
2018 Primary	Lance Gooden (R)...........................	17,551	(30%)			
	Bunni Pounds (R)...............................	12,851	(22%)			
	Sam Deen (R)...................................	10,051	(17%)			
	Kenneth Sheets (R)...........................	7,024	(12%)			
	Jason Wright (R)...............................	6,690	(11%)			

Republican first-termer Lance Gooden was the superior campaigner, as he defied expectations to take the seat of retiring Rep. Jeb Hensarling, who was term-limited as chairman of the House Financial Services Committee. Gooden, whose chief opponent in the GOP primary wielded more cash and endorsements and was closely connected to Hensarling, also faced the disadvantage of running from the rural parts of a district in which the clout has been chiefly in the Dallas suburbs. Gooden's success was evidence that "all politics is local" remains an apt adage among some Republicans.

A resident of Terrell in rural Kaufman County, Gooden got bachelor's degrees in government and business administration from the University of Texas. He worked as an insurance broker and consultant for energy companies. In 2010, he was elected to the first of three terms in the state House. After losing reelection in 2014, he regained his seat two years later. His accomplishments included passage of a bill that stopped municipalities from annexing rural land into their city limits without the approval of local voters; the legislation resulted from a property conflict between Dallas and Kaufman counties. In the Legislature, he was an ally of Speaker Joe Straus, whose desire for bipartisan coalition-building sparked internal Republican conflicts.

After Hensarling announced his retirement, the frontrunner was Bunni Pounds, a Republican political consultant who earlier had been Hensarling's campaign manager. With support from the Club for Growth and other national conservative groups, she had the initial fundraising lead. Gooden, with his base in the rural part of the district, was endorsed by many local officials from those areas. He emphasized his support for "traditional values" of those rural communities, in contrast to the "establishment" support for his opponent from insiders with "no connection to our district;" they included Vice President Mike Pence, a Hensarling ally. Gooden styled himself as "a new congressman of rural Texas, by rural Texas and for rural Texas."

Gooden led the first round of voting in the March primary, with 30 percent to 22 percent for Pounds; six other candidates divided the remainder. In Dallas County, which cast about one-fifth of the vote, Gooden won only 9 percent to 24 percent for Pounds and 38 percent for Kenneth Sheets, a former state representative. Gooden won an outright majority of the vote in Kaufman and Henderson counties, which were the core of his state House district; each county cast nearly as many votes as the Dallas County portion of the district.

Gooden was endorsed as the "hands-down choice" in the runoff by The Dallas Morning News, which cited his free-market views on economic issues, plus his "strong legislative experience," in contrast to the lack of legislative background by the "doctrinaire" Pounds. The final days of the contest featured a theological conflict between the Texas Catholic Conference of Bishops, which backed Gooden, and the Pounds-supporting Texas Right to Life Political Action Committee.

In the runoff, Pounds led in Dallas and three of the outlying rural counties. Gooden again ran strongly in Kaufman and Henderson, which were the two largest county votes in the runoff, and he won, 54%-46%. Pounds outspent him by more than $200,000. Gooden benefited from significant spending by a super PAC, Our Conservative Texas Future, which was largely financed by Monty Bennett, an influential Dallas businessman, The Texas Tribune reported. In November, Gooden faced Dan Wood, a lawyer and former member of the Terrell City Council. Wood got 59 percent of the vote in Dallas County, which cast 40 percent of the vote. Gooden took at least 70 percent in each of the six outlying counties and won, 62%-38%. Redistricting in 2022 could become a factor in Gooden's future, especially with the prospect of shifts within Dallas-area districts.

TX-5: Dallas County   Cook Partisan Voting Index: R+16

Population		Race and Ethnicity		Income	
Total	740,618	White	52.9%	Median Income	$50,049
Land area (sq. miles)	5,044	Black	14.8%	District Income Rank	313
Pop/ sq mi	146.8	Latino	28.3%	Poverty Rate	16.4%
Born in State	65%	Asian	2%	With health insurance	79.2%
		Two or more races	1.4%	Cash public assistance	1.4%
Age Groups		Other	0.6%	Food stamp/SNAP	14.1%
Under 18	26.4%				
18-34	22.4%	**Education**		**Work**	
35-64	38%	H.S grad or less	49.9%	White Collar	13.2%
Over 64	13.2%	Some college	29.9%	Sales and Service	43.2%
		College Degree, 4 yr	13.4%	Blue Collar	27.4%
Military		Post grad	6.8%	Government	12.7%
Veteran/ Active Duty	7.4%				

2012 Pres. Vote	Romney	137,239	(65%)	Obama	73,085	(34%)		
2016 Pres. Vote	Trump	145,841	(62%)	Clinton	79,759	(34%)	Johnson	5,776	(3%)

Eastern Dallas Suburbs, Mesquite: Not all of Dallas is glitz and postmodern marble. East of downtown is an older Dallas with neighborhoods of old mansions, modest bungalows and shotgun houses. Some of these areas have been renovated and rebuilt, with chic cafes and trendy stores. Other once middle-class neighborhoods are filling up with immigrants from Mexico and are again noisy with children, as they were in the 1950s when people moved here not from Mexico or Central America, but from the almost all-Anglo counties of North and Central Texas.

The 5th Congressional District includes much of east and southeast Dallas County, including neighborhoods in east Dallas and suburban Mesquite, which has become a destination for immigrants moving up the economic ladder. The population of Mesquite is 39 percent Hispanic and 25 percent black. In April 2015, the Breitbart.com website ran a story headlined, "Mesquite Texas — The Gun Show Capital of America," which described its several hundred shows annually as a mix of "trade shows, swap meets and raw capitalism," with crowds that are usually male, white and over 40. Since then, Mesquite has grown and become more suburban, with a new health care center and a furniture distribution facility. In 2018, the city had a 47 percent increase in building permits from a year earlier. The district also covers a more upscale slice of Dallas inside the LBJ freeway, including parts of Lakewood and White Rock Lake.

The minority population in the district has been steadily increasing, to 28 percent Hispanic and 15 percent black in 2017. About 40 percent of the district's voters are in Dallas County. The 5th takes in six other counties in East Texas, the largest of which are Henderson and Kaufman. Anderson County was the site in 1910 of the little-noted Slocum Massacre in which a white mob attacked and killed as many as 25 black residents and forced the remainder to flee, according to a report in 2015 on Texas Public Radio. Each of the outlying counties is heavily Republican. As rural areas have swung away from Democrats, the district switched from being a battleground in the early 1990s to safely Republican. In 2016, Donald Trump won 62 percent of the vote. Aided by rural voters, that gave him a larger share than in other Dallas-area districts.

Ronald Wright (R)

Elected 2018, 1st term, b. Apr 08, 1953; Jacksonville; University of Texas, 1972; Roman Catholic; Married (Susan Mazanti); 3 children; 9 grandchildren.

Elected Office: Arlington Housing Authority Board of Commissioners, 1998-2000; Arlington City Council, Member, At-Large 2000-2004; Arlington City Council, 2004-2008.

Professional Career: Sales Representative, PVI Industries 1981-1985; Senior Project Manager, Ceramic Cooling Tower Co., 1985-2000; Weekly Columnist, Star-Telegram Newspaper, 1995-2000; District Director, U.S. Rep. Joe Barton, 2000-2008, Chief of Staff, 2009-2011.

DC Office: 428 CHOB 20515, 202-225-2002, wright.house.gov

State Offices: Arlington, 817-775-0370.

Committees: *Education & Labor*: Health, Employment, Labor & Pensions; Workforce Protections. *Foreign Affairs*: Africa, Global Health, Global Human Rights & Internat'l Orgs; Europe, Eurasia, Energy & the Environment.

Election Results

Election	Name (Party)	Vote (%)		Cand. Spent	Ind. Exp. Support	Ind. Exp. Oppose
2018 General	Ronald J. Wright (R)........................	135,961	(53%)	$697,599	$124,306	
	Jana Lynne Sanchez (D).....................	116,350	(45%)	$674,368	$2,250	
2018 Primary	Ronald J. Wright (R)........................	12,747	(52%)			
Runoff	Jake Ellzey (R).................................	11,686	(48%)			
2018 Primary	Ronald J. Wright (R)........................	20,750	(45%)			
	Jake Ellzey (R).................................	9,999	(22%)			
	Ken Cope (R)...................................	3,540	(8%)			
	Shannon Dubberly (R).................	2,884	(6%)			

Republican first-termer Ron Wright took the seat of 17-term Rep. Joe Barton, for whom Wright served as a longtime aide and had become his heir apparent. Even with his own extensive experience in city and county politics in the district, plus his conservative credentials, Wright struggled in the GOP primary against an opponent with a limited political profile. Barton, who had been prominent as chairman of the House Energy and Commerce Committee, decided not to seek reelection after a nude photo of him appeared on social media in November 2017, though he rejected demands for his resignation. Local unhappiness with Barton, who did not endorse in the GOP primary, had some negative impact for Wright's campaign.

A native of Tarrant County, Wright graduated from the University of Texas in Arlington. Following a lengthy career in the private sector, he spent more than a decade as district director and then chief of staff to Barton. During much of that time, he pursued his own career as a member of the Arlington City Council and served as mayor pro tempore. He was appointed as Tarrant County tax assessor-collector and later was elected to two terms in that position.

Although Wright did not disavow Barton following his former boss' embarrassing social-media revelations, he said that he knew nothing about those actions and criticized Barton for "some terrible mistakes and choices." He emphasized his own experience in local office and distanced himself from Barton on some issues, notably by voicing hardline opposition to rights for illegal immigrants, even with his district's population that is more than 40 percent African-American and Hispanic. Wright cited support from the business-oriented Club for Growth and pledged to join the conservative House Freedom Caucus.

His chief opponent for the GOP nomination was Jake Ellzey, a former Navy officer and fighter pilot who flew combat missions in Afghanistan and Iraq, later became an aide to President George W. Bush and worked as a commercial airplane pilot; he lost a 2014 bid for the Texas House. In the March primary, Wright led Ellzey, 45%-22%; nine other candidates split the remaining vote. Wright took 61 percent of the vote in Tarrant County, which cast nearly three-fifths of the total. Ellzey was the frontrunner in outlying Ellis and Navarro counties.

In the runoff, The Dallas Morning News recommended Ellzey for his "understanding of the issues that confront Congress," including the military and veterans, and criticized Wright's plan to join the Freedom Caucus, which it called "one of the farthest right groups on Capitol Hill." Ellzey was endorsed by former Texas Gov. Rick Perry, who had become secretary of Energy in the Trump administration. The two Republicans had comparable campaign spending.

Despite his commanding lead in the primary, Wright barely survived in the runoff, with only 52 percent of the vote. In Tarrant, he took 68 percent, but turnout in that county dipped to less than half of the total vote. Ellzey got 63 percent in Ellis and 57 percent in Navarro in the runoff. His performance was a warning of Wright's potential vulnerability in future Republican primaries.

In November, Wright faced Jana Sanchez, who won the Democratic nomination over Ruby Fay Woodridge, who had lost to Barton in 2016, 58%-39%. Sanchez, a public relations consultant with experience as a campaign manager, had some national Democratic connections. She attacked the Trump administration, especially for its immigration policies. But Democratic strategists devoted more attention to other congressional campaigns in Texas. Wright prevailed, with 53 percent of the vote, with leads of more than 2-to-1 in Ellis and Navarro. Sanchez led 52%-47% in Tarrant — another warning of Wright's future vulnerability.

TX-6: Southwest Metroplex   Cook Partisan Voting Index: R+9

Population		Race and Ethnicity		Income	
Total	759,949	White	50%	Median Income	$64,748
Land area (sq. miles)	2,148	Black	20%	District Income Rank	135
Pop/ sq mi	353.7	Latino	22.6%	Poverty Rate	11.8%
Born in State	58.8%	Asian	4.7%	With health insurance	84.8%
		Two or more races	2.2%	Cash public assistance	1.4%
Age Groups		Other	0.7%	Food stamp/SNAP	9.7%
Under 18	26.3%				
18-34	23.4%	**Education**		**Work**	
35-64	39.2%	H.S grad or less	36.5%	White Collar	11.1%
Over 64	11.1%	Some college	33.8%	Sales and Service	40.7%
		College Degree, 4 yr	20.2%	Blue Collar	22%
Military		Post grad	9.4%	Government	13.5%
Veteran/ Active Duty	7.8%				

2012 Pres. Vote	Romney	146,985	(58%)	Obama	103,444	(41%)		
2016 Pres. Vote	Trump	148,945	(54%)	Clinton	115,272	(42%)	Johnson	8,552	(3%)

Arlington, Fort Worth Area: The Dallas-Fort Worth Metroplex — a name even the locals use — has spread outward from its historic nodes in downtown Dallas and downtown Fort Worth. Although Dallas is the larger population center, much of the development has moved west, across the plains and the barely perceptible Balcones Escarpment, the geologist's boundary between green and grassy East Texas and brown, barren and hilly West Texas. The plains have been filled in with subdivisions and shopping centers under the enormous Texas sky. Among the larger suburbs is Arlington, right between Dallas and Fort Worth and an easy highway commute to both cities. Named in 1877 after Robert E. Lee's hometown in Virginia (another suburb, but not quite so booming as the Texas locale), its location has been ideal as a site for regional attractions like Six Flags over Texas and Globe Life

Park in Arlington, commissioned by the former part-owner of the Texas Rangers, George W. Bush. In 2009, the Dallas Cowboys opened the $1.1 billion domed AT&T Stadium in Arlington, which hosted the 2011 Super Bowl and the 2014 NCAA "Final Four" basketball tournament. In August 2018, developers opened in Arlington the $250 million Texas Live entertainment center, including hotel and dining facilities; in November, a new feature was the largest e-sports stadium in the United States. The Rangers have scheduled completion of their nearby new baseball stadium in 2020. (Redistricting in 2011 placed those complexes in a small area just outside the 6th District, in the 33rd District.)

The city's population of 388,000 in 2017 was 29 percent Hispanic, 22 percent African American, and 7 percent Asian. Enrollment at the University of Texas campus in Arlington reached a new high of 41,700 students in 2017, making it the second-largest in the UT system behind Austin. GM's Arlington assembly plant produces the company's popular and highly profitable SUVs and employs about 4,800 workers. In 2018, GM switched the factory entirely to wind power as part of an expansion of the plant. As Arlington has filled up, the big growth has been to the south in Mansfield, where the population increased from 28,000 to 69,000 from 2000 to 2017.

The 6th Congressional District of Texas includes most of Arlington and the southern and northeastern fringes of Fort Worth to the west. Nearly three-fourths of the people live in Arlington and Tarrant County, which is the 15th largest in the nation. To the south is Ellis County, which grew 55 percent between 2000 and 2017. Beyond Ellis is small-town Navarro County, home to the Collin Street Bakery, which ships its famed fruitcakes around the world during Christmas season each year. Ellis and Navarro lean heavily Republican and provide the partisan ballast for the 6th. This territory was ancestrally Democratic for many years, then became solidly Republican. With non-Hispanic whites declining to 50 percent of the district, the GOP margin at the presidential level has tightened.

Lizzie Fletcher (D)

Elected 2018, 1st term, b. Feb 13, 1975; Houston; William & Mary Law School (VA); Kenyon College (OH), B.A., 1997; Methodist; Married (Scott Fletcher PE); 2 stepchildren.

Professional Career: Attorney, Vinson & Elkins, Ahmad, Zavitsanos, Anaipakos, Alavi & Mensing.

DC Office: 1429 LHOB 20515, 202-225-2571, Fax: 202-226-3805, fletcher.house.gov

State Offices: Houston, 713-353-8680.

Committees: *Science, Space & Technology*: Energy; Environment (Chmn). *Transportation & Infrastructure*: Economic Dev't, Public Buildings & Emergency Management; Railroads, Pipelines & Hazardous Materials; Water Resources & Environment.

Election Results

Election	Name (Party)	Vote (%)		Cand. Spent	Ind. Exp. Support	Ind. Exp. Oppose
2018 General	Lizzie Fletcher (D)	127,959	(53%)	$6,089,442	$1,875,077	$5,164,602
	John Culberson (R)	115,642	(47%)	$3,489,959	$935,229	$7,129,678
2018 Primary	Lizzie Fletcher (D)	9,888	(68%)			
Runoff	Laura Moser (D)	4,666	(32%)			
2018 Primary	Lizzie Fletcher (D)	9,768	(29%)			
	Laura Moser (D)	8,099	(24%)			
	Jason Westin (D)	6,375	(19%)			
	Alex Triantaphyllis (D)	5,234	(16%)			
	Ivan Sanchez (D)	1,895	(6%)			

Democrat Lizzie Pannill Fletcher, elected in 2018, scored a significant victory in the battle to shift control of suburban seats from Republicans' decades-long dominance. She defeated nine-term Rep. John Culberson, who was an influential "cardinal" on the House Appropriations Committee.

Culberson was one of three Republicans — starting with George H.W. Bush — to hold the suburban Houston seat since it was created in 1966. Fletcher initially won a hard-fought primary that spurred national controversy when House Democrats intervened on her behalf against her more progressive opponent.

Fletcher, a Houston native, graduated from Kenyon College and got her law degree from William and Mary. She was a lawyer for two prominent Houston-based law firms. As a partner in a firm that specialized in business litigation, she represented a cross-section of Houstonians facing difficult legal issues. She was a co-founder of Planned Parenthood Young Leaders and worked with local charitable groups.

Culberson -- who had never faced a credible Democratic challenger even as the district grew more diverse -- became an early target of House Democrats after Hillary Clinton in 2016 took it, 48%-47%. "Changing demographics, the #MeToo movement, and [Hurricane] Harvey may give the Democrats their best chance in decades to capture the West Houston seat," headlined Houston Public Media.

The Democratic primary attracted seven contenders. None of the leading candidates had ever won an election. The frontrunners who advanced to the runoff were Fletcher and Laura Moser, a former journalist who had lived much of her adult life in the Washington D.C. area. They received 29 percent and 24 percent of the vote, respectively.

Moser cited her history of grassroots activism as she appealed to the party's progressive base. Her candidacy was damaged when House Democratic researchers uncovered a magazine story that they cited to call her a "Washington insider," out of fear that she could not defeat Culberson. For an article in Washingtonian in 2014, Moser had written, "I'd rather have my teeth pulled out without anesthesia than live in Texas," referring to a rural area where she had spent time.

Moser and her progressive allies gained more attention as she blasted the Democratic campaign committee for taking sides. Fletcher, meanwhile, reaffirmed her Texas roots and appealed to mainstream Democrats and other voters unhappy with President Donald Trump and congressional Republicans. She won the runoff, 67%-33%.

Culberson was slow to respond politically, claiming that he was busy arranging relief for victims of devastating local hurricane damage in 2017 and with his national responsibilities in the House. In their only debate, Culberson praised the House Republican alternative to the Affordable Care Act and defended his low profile. "I don't go looking for the headlines," he said. Fletcher alleged long-term failure on Culberson's part to address hurricane threats to the Houston area and questioned the honesty of his campaign claims.

In endorsing Fletcher, the Houston Chronicle said that she was "so well prepared, so knowledgeable about the job, so right for the district" and praised her for having "reclaimed the center." Although the editorial credited Culberson's handling of recent hurricane relief, it added, "his career has been spent promoting his own pet projects rather than serving the local needs of his home district."

Fletcher spent more than $6 million on the campaign, which nearly doubled Culberson's total. Each party and its allies spent more than $5 million for its candidate. Fletcher won, 53%-47%. She vowed to seek bipartisanship in Congress, but conceded that she likely will be a prime Republican target in 2020.

TX-7: Harris County   Cook Partisan Voting Index: R+7

Population		Race and Ethnicity		Income	
Total	770,276	White	43.4%	Median Income	$73,591
Land area (sq. miles)	162	Black	13%	District Income Rank	75
Pop/ sq mi	4756.6	Latino	30.5%	Poverty Rate	12.2%
Born in State	45%	Asian	10.7%	With health insurance	84.1%
		Two or more races	1.9%	Cash public assistance	1%
Age Groups		Other	0.5%	Food stamp/SNAP	6.7%
Under 18	25.8%				
18-34	24.5%	**Education**		**Work**	
35-64	39.2%	H.S grad or less	26.9%	White Collar	10.5%
Over 64	10.5%	Some college	23.8%	Sales and Service	36.6%
		College Degree, 4 yr	29.3%	Blue Collar	14.9%
Military		Post grad	20%	Government	8.4%
Veteran/ Active Duty	4.7%				

2012 Pres. Vote	Romney	143,631	(60%)	Obama	92,499	(39%)		
2016 Pres. Vote	Clinton	124,722	(48%)	Trump	121,204	(47%)	Johnson	9,126	(4%)

West Houston and Suburbs: When George H.W. Bush moved from Midland in West Texas to Houston in 1960, he bought a house in Briarwood in what were then the western outskirts of the fast-growing city. He returned to Houston in 1993 after losing his reelection bid for the presidency and built a new house one mile from his old one, near lush Memorial Park. The lavish Galleria, one of the largest malls in the United States with an ice rink and tennis club, draws more than 30 million visitors a year under its impressive glass atriums. Downtown Houston is sprouting apartment buildings. Oil companies have prospered, and many businesses moved here from the New Orleans area following the devastation of Hurricane Katrina in 2005.

The 7th Congressional District of Texas is the lineal descendant of the district that in 1966 elected Bush as the first Republican to represent Houston in the House. It occupied far more territory then, half of Harris County. It now includes only 17 percent of the county. In successive redistricting rounds, its boundaries have been pared back, as the population of the west side of Houston has skyrocketed. Today, more than 2 million people reside in an area where 350,000 lived when Bush was first elected. The district, based entirely in Harris County, includes most of the territory between the Katy Freeway (Interstate 10) and Westheimer Road from downtown. In Texas style, Katy's 26 lanes when it crosses Beltway 8 may be the widest highway in the world. The district takes in the affluent neighborhoods southwest of downtown Houston and a swath of Houston west of the 610 loop; Bellaire is the wealthiest town in Texas. Most of Houston's business and professional elite live within the district's boundaries: the partners of the big law firms, cutting-edge medical researchers and society mavens. During the torrential rains of Hurricane Harvey in August 2017, the Barker reservoir overflowed and caused extensive damage in the western end of the district. Months later, the Houston City Council imposed restrictions on building in the flood plain. In August 2018, voters in Harris County approved $250 million in bonds for flood-control projects.

Outside the loop is Gulfton, a rural area in the 1950s that became a haven for young oil workers in the 1970s and is now a predominantly Hispanic town that the Houston Chronicle called an "ersatz Ellis Island for economic refugees from Mexico and Central America." Continued surges of immigration from Mexico have strained the public schools in Gulfton, whose sprawling apartment complexes have become the most densely populated neighborhood in Houston. The district is also home to Rev. Joel Osteen's Lakewood evangelical megachurch, which describes itself as the largest congregation in the nation and draws more than 45,000 worshipers a week, with many more viewing the service on an internationally televised Sunday program.

The 7th has been a solidly Republican district, but its demographics are changing. After redistricting in 2011, this became a majority-minority district: Whites are about 43 percent of the population, Hispanics 31 percent, blacks 13 percent and Asian Americans 11 percent. Among the voting-age population, Hispanics had skewed younger and turned out to vote at a lower rate. But that pattern has changed dramatically. In a district that Mitt Romney won with 60 percent in 2012, down from George W. Bush's 66 percent in 2004, Donald Trump lost to Hillary Clinton, 48%-47%.

Kevin Brady (R)

Elected 1996, 12th term, b. Apr 11, 1955; Vermillion, SD; University of South Dakota, B.S., 1990; Roman Catholic; Married (Cathy Brady); 2 children.

Elected Office: TX House, 1991-1996.

Professional Career: Executive, The Woodlands Chamber of Commerce, 1978-1996.

DC Office: 1011 LHOB 20515, 202-225-4901, Fax: 202-225-5524, kevinbrady.house.gov

State Offices: Conroe, 936-441-5700; Huntsville, 936-439-9532.

Committees: *Joint Taxation. Ways & Means (RMM).*

Group Ratings

	ADA	ACLU	AFL-CIO	LCV	ITI	COC	HAFA	ACU	CFG	FRC
2018	-	4%	-	3%	-	91%	55%	82%	56%	100%
2017	0%	C	8%	3%	C	92%	C	89%	77%	100%

Almanac Ratings 2017-18

	Economy	Social	Foreign	Composite
Liberal	3%	0%	0%	1%
Conservative	97%	100%	100%	99%

Key Votes of the 115th Congress

1. Obama-care revision	Y	5. Family planning regs	Y	9. Guantanamo prisoners	N
2. Tax Cuts	Y	6. Body cameras/immigration	N	10. Ground missiles, limit	N
3. Omnibus appropriations	Y	7. Abortion ban	Y	11. Defense Dept. spending	Y
4. Dodd-Frank revision	Y	8. Concealed carry	Y	12. FISA rules	Y

Election Results

Election	Name (Party)	Vote (%)		Cand. Spent	Ind. Exp. Support	Ind. Exp. Oppose
2018 General	Kevin Brady (R)............................... 200,619	(73%)		$3,539,580		
	Steven David (D)................................. 67,930	(25%)		$28,962		
2018 Primary	Kevin Brady (R)..	(100%)				

Prior winning percentages: 2016 (100%), 2014 (89%), 2012 (77%), 2010 (80%), 2008 (73%), 2006 (67%), 2004 (69%), 2002 (93%), 2000 (92%), 1998 (93%), 1996 (59%)

Republican Kevin Brady, first elected in 1996, served three years as chairman of the House Ways and Means Committee. As one of the most powerful players in Congress, he sat at the starting point for much of President Donald Trump's legislative program — notably, the tax cuts that were enacted in December 2017. After Republicans lost House control in the 2018 election, Brady defended Trump's objections to efforts by House Democrats to get copies of the president's tax returns. He voiced major differences with Trump on his use of tariff increases in international trade.

Brady comes easily to his pro-business viewpoint. He grew up and went to college in South Dakota, moved in 1978 to what was then rural Texas in Montgomery County and headed The Woodlands Chamber of Commerce for 18 years. In 1990, he was elected to the Texas House. When Brady ran for the open seat in Congress, his chief opponent in the decisive Republican primary was Eugene Fontenot, a physician who said he wanted "to restore America to its Christian heritage." Brady was the choice of party regulars; Fontenot was backed by religious conservatives.

Fontenot attacked Brady for being one of two Republicans to vote against the state's concealed weapons law. Brady had opposed most gun control bills but not the concealed weapons bill. When he was 12 years old, his father, an attorney, was shot and killed while trying a case in a South Dakota courtroom. "I couldn't look Mom in the eye and vote for this," he told the Houston Chronicle after the vote. (In 2013, he said he regretted the vote. "I've been remarkably impressed with how well concealed-carry has worked in Texas," he told National Journal.) The campaign was grueling and convoluted. After Fontenot led Brady in the March primary, Brady won the April runoff 53%-47%. After the Supreme Court in June ordered a redrawing of 13 districts, Brady led Fontenot 41%-39% in an all-party primary in November. Finally, in the December runoff, turnout was sharply down and Brady won their third face-off, 59%-41%.

Brady has compiled a conservative voting record, though he has often been more of a pragmatist than other Texas conservatives. He is known for being easygoing and soft-spoken, but that doesn't mean he never gets mad. His November 2009 showdown with Treasury Secretary Timothy Geithner made national news when Brady savaged Geithner's handling of the Wall Street crisis, saying, "The public has lost all confidence in your ability to do the job." A year earlier, Brady was the only Houston-area member of the House in either party to vote for the financial industry rescue. "As much as I detest this bill, doing nothing is worse," he said.

At Ways and Means, Brady has focused on economic issues. As chairman of the Health Subcommittee in 2013, his agenda included repealing unpopular parts of the Affordable Care Act, such as a tax on medical devices. He got those bills through the House, but they stalled in the

Democratic-controlled Senate. On international trade issues, Brady persistently fought for more free-trade agreements, which he contends are essential to U.S. economic strength. For many weeks in early 2015, he worked closely with Ways and Means and House GOP leaders to win the House's narrow approval of trade promotion authority for President Barack Obama to submit his Trans-Pacific Partnership.

Much of his work has been on the tax code. Brady in 2014 got a bipartisan bill through the House to make permanent and expand the research and development tax credit. The Obama administration, however, opposed the measure because it would expand the credit without offsetting the cost. On an important local matter, Brady was a central figure in the successful effort in 2004 to make state and local sales taxes deductible in the seven states, including Texas, that have no personal income tax.

When the Ways and Means chairmanship became open after the 2014 election, Brady made his case for the job. He challenged Rep. Paul Ryan, the 2012 vice presidential nominee, who had chaired the House Budget Committee. "I'm qualified and prepared to lead this committee," Brady told Bloomberg TV. "This is all about the ideas and how we can move tax reform, trade, entitlement reform forward, so it's good to have a healthy competition."

Ryan had less seniority than Brady, but he had the support of Speaker John Boehner and made at least an implicit disavowal of plans for another national campaign. Ryan prevailed, though Brady retained his Health Subcommittee post. He seemed to benefit from running a respectful campaign.

Brady continued as the senior House Republican of the Joint Economic Committee, which studies fiscal policy but has no power to consider legislation. Brady used that post to preach the gospel of getting Washington out of the way to let the private sector create jobs. He called for reforming the Federal Reserve Board and appointing a bipartisan commission to study its operations, though the Fed's leaders took a dim view of his efforts.

His next opportunity at Ways and Means came sooner than expected amid the internal House Republican chaos. When Boehner in late September 2015 announced his resignation as Speaker under pressure, House Republicans struggled to find a successor. After other contenders fell short, Ryan became the consensus choice of virtually all Republicans and he became Speaker a month later. That created uncertainty and awkwardness at Ways and Means, especially for Brady. Although Brady seemed to be the heir apparent, Rep. Pat Tiberi of Ohio — a Boehner ally — said that he would seek the chairmanship.

Five days after Ryan became Speaker, one of his first official duties was to chair the leadership committee meeting as it selected his Ways and Means successor. Shortly before the secret-ballot vote, Ryan said he was supporting Brady. This time, Brady won. As the new chairman, he said he supported "a pro-growth agenda," with the objectives of "real steps toward fixing this broken tax code, reforming welfare, saving Social Security and Medicare for the long term and enlarging America's economic freedom to trade." (Tiberi resigned from the House in January 2018 to become head of a business group in Ohio.)

With 2016 consumed by the presidential election, Brady's start as chairman was relatively quiet. That respite ended with Republicans in control of Congress and, unexpectedly, Donald Trump as president. It took time for Brady and GOP leaders to establish a working relationship with Trump on the handling of major legislation. That resulted in missed deadlines on budget actions and an extended scramble before the House passed in May 2017 its first major legislation during the Trump presidency: the bill to repeal and revise the Affordable Care Act. On that legislation, the final deals were brokered chiefly by Ryan and other GOP leaders.

Later in the year, Brady had primary responsibility for handling the Republican tax cuts. He faced an early setback when Republicans abandoned his plan to impose a "border adjustment" tax on imports, as a tool to assist U.S. manufacturers. That proposal was actively opposed by retail groups, who ran an extended lobbying campaign. Within the House, Brady faced resistance from Republicans from high-tax states who were unhappy with his plan to limit taxpayer deductions for state and local taxes. On that issue, Brady prevailed.

Democrats complained that the Republican legislation favored the wealthy and that Ways and Means Republicans were acting mostly behind closed doors — with coordination by Ryan, the previous chairman. For Brady and his allies, failure was not an option and their party usually responds favorably to tax cuts. In November 2017, the House passed the bill, 227-205, with no Democratic support and opposition from 12 Republicans — chiefly from the high-tax states of California, New Jersey and New York. After Senate Republicans made limited tweaks, the House sent the final version to Trump a month later. "This is an incredibly exciting day for the American people, who have waited years — even decades — for a simpler, fairer tax code that will grow our economy and allow them to keep more of their hard-earned money," Brady exulted.

That was not the final move on taxes by the House Republican majority. In July 2018, Brady unveiled a "tax cut 2.0" plan, with lower rates, incentives for savings and steps to make permanent the 2017 cuts. The House planned "to look at the tax code every year — not just once a generation — to consider how we do things better," Brady said, in an indication that Republicans had not completely won the tax debate. The House passed the Brady-crafted tax-relief plan in one of its final votes before adjourning for the election. The Senate during its lame-duck session had no time to consider the bill, which had no hope after Democrats took House control.

Brady clashed with Trump on his use of tariff hikes. Resorting to his customary free-trade view, Brady told CNBC in July 2018 that "tariffs are taxes [that] impede economic growth. ... We do worry about that." Also that month, he urged Trump to resolve the "escalating trade dispute" with China.

In the minority, Brady clashed with Democratic Rep. Lloyd Doggett of Texas, who was outspoken in the new majority's attempt to gain access to Trump's tax returns. "Weaponizing the tax code for political purposes sets a dangerous precedent," Brady told reporters in February 2019.

Amid his new prominence in Washington, Brady ran into a major problem at home in 2016: his first significant Republican primary contest. He faced three challengers, who spent a total of less than $200,000, compared with the $4 million that Brady spent during the campaign cycle. Steven Toth, an ordained minister and a former state representative, was his chief challenger. In a pre-primary story, The Texas Tribune reported, "Brady is in enough trouble that outside groups -- including the leadership-aligned Congressional Leadership Fund super PAC -- are spending big to protect him." Brady barely avoided the peril of a runoff, with 53 percent of the vote to 37 percent for Toth. Brady had no opposition in November. In 2018, he had no Republican primary and was reelected routinely.

TX-8: Northern Houston Suburbs   Cook Partisan Voting Index: R+28

Population		Race and Ethnicity		Income	
Total	807,525	White	64.9%	Median Income	$66,893
Land area (sq. miles)	6,054	Black	8.2%	District Income Rank	120
Pop/ sq mi	133.4	Latino	22%	Poverty Rate	12%
Born in State	59.1%	Asian	2.8%	With health insurance	85.5%
		Two or more races	1.6%	Cash public assistance	1.2%
Age Groups		Other	0.5%	Food stamp/SNAP	7.7%
Under 18	25.5%				
18-34	22%	**Education**		**Work**	
35-64	39.7%	H.S grad or less	40.8%	White Collar	12.8%
Over 64	12.8%	Some college	29.3%	Sales and Service	40.4%
		College Degree, 4 yr	20.1%	Blue Collar	21.7%
Military		Post grad	9.8%	Government	12.9%
Veteran/ Active Duty	8.3%				

2012 Pres. Vote	Romney	195,742	(77%)	Obama	55,273	(22%)		
2016 Pres. Vote	Trump	214,605	(72%)	Clinton	70,532	(24%)	Johnson	8,418	(3%)

Montgomery County: Montgomery County, to the north of Houston, was once fenceless cattle country, dotted with roadside stands and barbecues. In 1931, wildcatter George Strake struck oil near Conroe. Thousands of other wildcatters and roughnecks quickly joined in the boom, and this became one of the richest oil-producing areas in the nation. Active production continues today.

The oil boom centered on Conroe was followed by a population and economic boom. In 1974, a planned community called The Woodlands opened 30 miles north of Houston and 15 miles south of Conroe. Development of this new city has barreled along since then, with corporate parks, glistening condo towers, pristine golf courses and a man-made waterway. Its real estate, which is among the most expensive in the Houston area, was home to more than 117,000 residents and 2,200 businesses with 68,000 employees, as of January 2019. Anadarko Petroleum, with two office towers, has been the chief corporate presence, with 3,400 employees. In early 2019, Chevron and Occidental were in a bidding war for Anadarko. The Cynthia Woods Mitchell Pavilion in The Woodlands, which opened in 1990, was listed as the third-busiest outdoor concert venue in the nation in 2018. The Woodlands is the home to five large hospitals and has styled itself as a prominent medical center. Entergy began construction in September 2018 of a $1 billion natural gas-fired power plant north of Conroe.

The 8th Congressional District includes all of Montgomery County, which was the seventh fastest-growing county in Texas, with a 30 percent increase from 2010 to 2017, and contains about two-thirds of the district's people. About 10 percent of the district is a small slice of Harris County, a few miles from George Bush International Airport. The district extends north through parts of the thinly populated Brazos Valley and covers Sam Houston National Forest and Davy Crockett National Forest. It encompasses all of seven counties and parts of two. The district takes in Huntsville, with one of Texas' oldest prisons, and "Big Sam," a 67-foot-tall statue of Sam Houston outside the town along Interstate 45. This is one of the most Republican districts in the country, and Donald Trump got 72 percent of the vote in 2016.

Al Green (D)

Elected 2004, 8th term, b. Sep 01, 1947; New Orleans. LA, LA; Tuskegee University (AL), Bach. Deg.; University of Florida, Att., 1971; Texas Southern University, Thurgood Marshall School of Law, J.D., 1973; Baptist; Marital status unknown.

Elected Office: Harris County justice of the peace, 1977-2004.

Professional Career: Practicing attorney, 1973-1977; President, Houston NAACP, 1986-1995.

DC Office: 2347 RHOB 20515, 202-225-7508, Fax: 202-225-2947, algreen.house.gov

State Offices: Houston, 713-383-9234.

Committees: *Financial Services*: Housing, Community Development & Insurance; Oversight & Investigations (Chmn); Subcommittee on Diversity & Inclusion. *Homeland Security*: Border Security, Facilitation & Operations; Emergency Preparedness, Response & Recovery.

Group Ratings

	ADA	ACLU	AFL-CIO	LCV	ITI	COC	HAFA	ACU	CFG	FRC
2018	-	86%	-	97%	-	58%	2%	4%	2%	0%
2017	100%	C	100%	100%	C	43%	C	0%	0%	0%

Almanac Ratings 2017-18

	Economy	Social	Foreign	Composite
Liberal	97%	98%	95%	97%
Conservative	3%	2%	5%	3%

Key Votes of the 115th Congress

1. Obama-care revision	N	5. Family planning regs	N	9. Guantanamo prisoners	Y
2. Tax Cuts	N	6. Body cameras/immigration	Y	10. Ground missiles, limit	Y
3. Omnibus appropriations	Y	7. Abortion ban	N	11. Defense Dept. spending	Y
4. Dodd-Frank revision	N	8. Concealed carry	N	12. FISA rules	N

Election Results

Election	Name (Party)	Vote (%)		Cand. Spent	Ind. Exp. Support	Ind. Exp. Oppose
2018 General	Al Green (D)....................................	136,256	(89%)	$405,755		
	Phil Kurtz (Lib).......................................	5,940	(4%)			
	Benjamin Hernandez (I)...............	5,774	(4%)	$16,514		
	Kesha Rogers (I)............................	5,031	(3%)	$53,359		
2018 Primary	Al Green (D)..............................		(100%)			

Prior winning percentages: 2016 (81%), 2014 (91%), 2012 (78%), 2010 (76%), 2008 (94%), 2006 (100%), 2004 (72%)

Democrat Al Green, first elected in 2004 and a champion of the homeless and poor, became the earliest and most outspoken advocate of the impeachment of President Donald Trump — even after Democrats took House control in 2019 and party leaders decided to downplay that option for fear of stoking conservative counter-action. His legislative work has focused on the Financial Services Committee, where he represents the interests of low-income groups. With his engaging demeanor, he has had some success in building bipartisanship. Like his namesake soul-singer-turned-preacher, Green is deeply religious, usually sporting a "God Is Good" lapel pin.

Green grew up in New Orleans. He attended college at Florida A&M University and graduated from Texas Southern University's law school, where he later taught. He was elected justice of the peace for Harris County in 1977 and served 26 years. For a decade, he also was president of the Houston chapter of the NAACP.

After the congressional redistricting in 2003 that largely benefited Republicans, Green saw an opening to run for Congress. The representative from the old district that covered much of this area was Chris Bell, a white Democrat elected in 2002, when he defeated a more conservative black candidate. Green said that he wanted to fight discrimination in law enforcement and he used subtle racial references on the campaign trail, including his promise to bring "a mountain of soul" to the new district. He amassed endorsements from prominent local and national black leaders. Bell responded by asking voters "not to focus on the color of my skin, but on the size of my heart." He was endorsed by the AFL-CIO, teachers unions, abortion rights groups and Democratic Minority Leader Nancy Pelosi. But he struggled as a white candidate running in a heavily minority district. Green won the primary in a landslide, 66%-31%, and faced no real opposition in the general election.

Green began with a relatively moderate voting record but has become a more liberal Democrat. The Almanac ratings have ranked him among the most liberal House member from Texas . On the Financial Services Committee, where he took over in January 2019 as chairman of the Oversight and Investigations Subcommittee, he has worked to eliminate housing practices that discriminate against minorities, at times successfully enlisting Republicans in his efforts. In 2015, the House passed his "Homes for Heroes" bill to increase housing assistance to low-income and homeless veterans, and give the topic a higher priority at the Department of Housing and Urban Development. An estimated 50,000 veterans are homeless.

Like most Texas lawmakers, Green is protective of the oil and gas industry, joining a group of Democrats in 2009 warning that President Barack Obama's proposal to raise taxes and impose new fees on the industry would hamper domestic production. Green broke with House Democrats by voting in 2012 for a bill to double the number of offshore oil and gas drilling leases, probably the smart vote in a Houston-based district that relies on oil profits. In 2015, he was one of 28 House Democrats who voted for the Keystone XL oil pipeline.

Green has focused on a diverse set of social issues. After Democrats were criticized before their 2012 convention for initially leaving the word "God" out of the party platform, Green was added as a speaker to reinforce the party's commitment to religion. At a controversial Homeland Security Committee hearing on Muslim extremism in 2011, he passionately told panel members that other groups using religion as the basis for their views, such as the Ku Klux Klan, also should be examined. As part of the congressional delegation that accompanied Obama to Cuba in 2016, Green voiced concern about the racism that he said is experienced by Afro-Cubans, who are more than one-fourth of the population on the island.

Green did not take long to advocate the impeachment of Trump. "I will not be moved. The president must be impeached," he told the House in May 2017. His position initially was based on Green's view that Trump had damaged the social fabric of the nation. The damage to American society could be "irreparable," Green said in September 2018. He filed the initial articles of impeachment, which were tabled in December 2017 on a 364-58 vote. After Democrats won the House and Speaker Pelosi said that impeachment could not go forward without bipartisan support, Green in February 2019 filed new impeachment charges, which were based on what he called "400 years of bigotry culminating in the Trump presidency."

Since 2014, Green has been reelected without major-party opposition in his safe district.

TX-9: Harris County, Eastern Fort Bend County

Cook Partisan Voting Index: D+29

Population		Race and Ethnicity		Income	
Total	780,017	White	10.9%	Median Income	$46,321
Land area (sq. miles)	166	Black	37.2%	District Income Rank	361
Pop/ sq mi	4709.1	Latino	38.8%	Poverty Rate	20.7%
Born in State	49.1%	Asian	11.6%	With health insurance	74.8%
		Two or more races	1.2%	Cash public assistance	1.9%
Age Groups		Other	0.3%	Food stamp/SNAP	18.6%
Under 18	26.6%				
18-34	27.9%	**Education**		**Work**	
35-64	36.3%	H.S grad or less	47.8%	White Collar	9.2%
Over 64	9.2%	Some college	26.8%	Sales and Service	46.4%
		College Degree, 4 yr	16.6%	Blue Collar	24.7%
Military		Post grad	8.8%	Government	11.1%
Veteran/ Active Duty	4.4%				

2012 Pres. Vote	Obama	145,332	(78%)	Romney	39,392	(21%)
2016 Pres. Vote	Clinton	151,559	(79%)	Trump	34,447	(18%)

South Houston: A half-century ago, the steaming flatlands south of Houston running down to the Gulf of Mexico did not seem a likely site for one of the world's most advanced civilizations. But spreading out in all directions from its historic center at Allen's Landing on Buffalo Bayou, Houston has become one of the great metropolises of North America. Most of the scientific work in NASA's early years was done in Houston, and the first word spoken when man landed on the moon was "Houston." It is the undisputed center of expertise in the oil business and has been at the center of innovations in fracking, leading to a resurgence in drilling throughout South Texas. The famed Astrodome, which was once the "Eighth Wonder of the World," has been closed since 2009 and came close to demolition. After voters in 2013 rejected a referendum to turn it into a giant convention center, the Harris County Commission in 2016 decided to create a parking lot on its lower two levels. Work was scheduled to start in the spring of 2019 on a renovation, which will raise its floor by 30 feet to ground level and encourage more open space for festivals and events. The projected $105 million cost will be paid by revenues and fees, with support from a non-profit conservancy.

Houston has become a medical mecca, with the giant Texas Medical Center and its 14 hospitals leaving their mark on the health care statewide. The Memorial Hermann Health System is scheduled to complete in 2020 a $650 million expansion of its 13 hospitals across Houston, including renovation of the Texas Medical Center, its original facility. The MD Anderson Cancer Center had financial problems and cut 1,000 employees in 2017, though it retained a payroll of nearly 20,000.

Twenty-one Fortune 500 companies are headquartered in Houston; all but three of them are chiefly in the energy business. This success is in part a triumph of air conditioning, which made Houston's five-month summer tolerable. Today, it is the fourth-largest city in the nation, with a population that grew 17 percent from 2000 to 2017. It is now the most ethnically diverse major metropolitan area, according to a Rice University report, citing its status as an "immigration gateway."

The 9th Congressional District of Texas slices across the southern part of metropolitan Houston in Harris County. It takes in two wedges of Fort Bend County, which form a crescent around the 22nd District and include about 30 percent of the district's voters. The 9th includes many African-American neighborhoods, low-income and middle-income, in both counties. Its population is 39 percent Hispanic and 37 percent black, although many of the former are not citizens or do not vote. Another 12 percent are Asians, many clustered along Bellaire Boulevard in the Chinese-American community. Entrepreneurial Vietnamese boat people settled in Alieve and have created quality schools, an Asian-oriented shopping mall and businesses that serve one of the largest Vietnamese communities in the nation. Overall, this is a heavily Democratic district, which gave Hillary Clinton 79 percent of the vote in 2016, her second best in Texas and barely behind the Dallas-based 30th District.

Michael McCaul (R)

Elected 2004, 8th term, b. Jan 14, 1962; Dallas; Trinity University (TX), B.A., 1984; Harvard University John F. Kennedy School of Government (MA), Att., 2002; St. Mary's University School of Law (TX), Att., 2002; Catholic; Married (Linda McCaul); 5 children (triplets).

Professional Career: Federal prosecutor, 1990-1999; Deputy Attorney General, 1999-2003; Chief, Western Div. of TX. U.S. Attorney's Office, 2003-2004.

DC Office: 2001 RHOB 20515, 202-225-2401, Fax: 202-225-5955, mccaul.house.gov

State Offices: Austin, 512-473-2357; Brenham, 979-830-8497; Katy, 281-398-1247; Tomball, 281-255-8372.

Committees: *Foreign Affairs (RMM). Homeland Security.*

Group Ratings

	ADA	ACLU	AFL-CIO	LCV	ITI	COC	HAFA	ACU	CFG	FRC
2018	-	4%	-	3%	-	92%	57%	76%	56%	100%
2017	0%	C	8%	0%	C	93%	C	89%	76%	100%

Almanac Ratings 2017-18

	Economy	Social	Foreign	Composite
Liberal	3%	0%	3%	2%
Conservative	97%	100%	98%	98%

Key Votes of the 115th Congress

1. Obama-care revision	Y	5. Family planning regs	Y	9. Guantanamo prisoners	N
2. Tax Cuts	Y	6. Body cameras/immigration	N	10. Ground missiles, limit	N
3. Omnibus appropriations	Y	7. Abortion ban	Y	11. Defense Dept. spending	Y
4. Dodd-Frank revision	Y	8. Concealed carry	Y	12. FISA rules	Y

Election Results

Election	Name (Party)	Vote (%)		Cand. Spent	Ind. Exp. Support	Ind. Exp. Oppose
2018 General	Michael McCaul (R)	157,166	(51%)	$1,639,416		
	Mike Siegel (D)	144,034	(47%)	$459,027	$34,510	
	Mike Ryan (Lib)	6,627	(2%)			
2018 Primary	Michael McCaul (R)	41,881	(80%)			
	John Cook (R)	10,413	(20%)			

Prior winning percentages: 2016 (57%), 2014 (62%), 2012 (61%), 2010 (65%), 2008 (54%), 2006 (55%), 2004 (79%)

Michael McCaul, a Republican first elected in 2004 as a protégé of Texas GOP Sen. John Cornyn, has been an activist legislator. As chairman of the Homeland Security Committee for six years, he pursued an agenda of timely issues, often on a bipartisan basis, and warned of threats facing the nation. Following the 2018 election, he switched to the top Republican post on the Foreign Affairs Committee. McCaul remained interested in a Senate seat, if available, and he has discussed with President Donald Trump a possible Cabinet appointment.

McCaul grew up in Dallas, studied business and history at Trinity University, and got his law degree at St. Mary's University, both in San Antonio. He worked as a federal prosecutor and then moved to Austin in 1999 to be a deputy to state Attorney General Cornyn. In 2002, he joined the U.S. attorney's office and was chief of the Terrorism and National Security Section for West Texas.

McCaul was one of eight candidates in the 2004 Republican primary for the newly created congressional district. The other top Republican contenders were mortgage company owner Ben Streusand and former Judge John Devine. McCaul focused on his anti-terrorism work, calling himself the only candidate who "won't have a learning curve." Streusand, based in Harris County, called for less government regulation. Devine had the support of Christian conservatives and called for a crackdown on illegal immigration. In the primary, Streusand carried seven of the eight counties to finish with 28 percent of the vote, to 24 percent for McCaul, who ran strongly in his Travis County base, and 21 percent for Devine.

In the runoff campaign, McCaul criticized Streusand's past donations to Democratic candidates, while Streusand questioned McCaul's service in the Clinton administration Justice Department. McCaul used his connections — his father-in-law is Clear Channel Communications founder and Chairman Lowry Mays — to collect major Republican endorsements. McCaul won 63%-37%, carrying both Travis and Harris counties. Roll Call in 2018 listed him as the second wealthiest member of Congress, with a net worth of at least $113 million.

In the House, McCaul has a mostly conservative voting record. Early in his career, he cast moderate votes that included requiring insurers to treat mental illness the same as other health conditions, and allowing the Food and Drug Administration to regulate tobacco products. He worked with Democratic Rep. G.K. Butterfield of North Carolina in 2012 to enact a bill encouraging companies to develop drugs for rare childhood cancers and other diseases. After Republicans took control of the House in 2011, his voting record grew more conservative, particularly on fiscal matters. McCaul earned the gratitude of House GOP leaders for leading the party's efforts in protracted 2010 ethics investigation of Democratic Rep. Charles Rangel of New York that culminated in Rangel's censure by the full House.

In 2011, as chairman of Homeland Security's Oversight, Investigations and Management Subcommittee, McCaul filed legislation to have six Mexican drug cartels designated as foreign terrorist organizations, a move that could have led to much stiffer penalties for drug traffickers. Later, he pressed Obama administration officials at a hearing over their failure to define "spill-over violence" from the drug wars in Mexico. McCaul co-sponsored a cybersecurity bill with Democratic Rep. Daniel Lipinski of Illinois that would develop standards for dealing with cyberthreats; it passed the House in 2012 but fell victim to partisan squabbling in the Senate.

McCaul has moved legislation on several fronts. In 2014, he worked with a bipartisan group to enact the National Cybersecurity Protection Act, which provided private and government digital networks additional protection against attacks. He joined the bipartisan coalition that enacted in 2015 the USA Freedom Act to reduce the bulk collection of phone data and other records by the National Security Agency. Later that year, he cited parts of a classified U.S. intelligence document to allege that terrorists were seeking to enter the nation as refugees. In November 2018, McCaul enacted a bill that strengthened the role of the Homeland Security Department in overseeing cybersecurity issues that are separate from the military.

McCaul spoke out during the final week of the 2016 presidential campaign to cite Hillary Clinton's use of her private email server while she was secretary of State as possible grounds for the House to impeach her if she was elected president. In another interview, he termed her conduct "treason." After the election, he was on Trump's initial short list to lead the Homeland Security Department and publicly voiced interest in the job. Although McCaul had advised the Trump campaign and transition team on immigration enforcement, he said in January 2017 that the new president's executive order on immigration "went too far" in restricting lawful entry.

Later that year, when Homeland Security Secretary John Kelly gave up that job to become White House chief of staff, McCaul again was considered for the job. But it had become clear that he didn't see eye-to-eye with Trump on some issues, including immigration policy and his management style. He had differences — at least in tone — with Trump's proposal for a wall on the border with Mexico. "I don't think we need a 2,000 mile wall down there," McCaul said in an interview with PBS in 2017. A year later, he criticized Trump's handling of his meeting in Helsinki with Russian President Vladimir Putin as "demoralizing" to U.S. intelligence agencies and said that he was "astounded at the inability" of Trump to criticize Russian meddling in the 2016 presidential election.

Term-limited as chairman of the Homeland Security Committee, McCaul in 2018 voiced interest in the opening at the Foreign Affairs Committee. His previous experience was an advantage in winning the position — now in the minority — over Republican Reps. Joe Wilson of South Carolina and Ted Yoho of Florida. At Foreign Affairs, he had early cooperation with Democratic Chairman Eliot Engel of New York. In February 2019, McCaul said that he was "deeply troubled" by the Trump administration's weak response to Saudi Arabia's murder of dissident Jamal Khashoggi. In May, he said that Trump's plan to circumvent Congress with arms sales to Saudi Arabia was "unfortunate and will damage certain future congressional interactions."

At home, McCaul voiced interest in the seat of Sen. Ted Cruz during the latter's presidential campaign in 2016 and later, at the national convention when many of the party faithful were unhappy with Cruz's failure to endorse Trump. Cruz eventually rebuilt his bridges with the Texas GOP.

Likewise, McCaul was mentioned as a possible successor when Cornyn was briefly considered in 2017 for the opening of FBI director. With his deep pockets and law-enforcement persona, McCaul could be a credible statewide contender.

His reelection bid in 2018 proved to be unexpectedly competitive. Democrat Mike Siegel, a civil rights lawyer in Austin, endorsed much of the progressive agenda and said that McCaul "refused to act as a check on Trump." McCaul declined to participate in campaign debates and missed a meeting with editors at the Houston Chronicle. Siegel had little national party support and was outspent by McCaul, $1.6 million to $459,000. McCaul won, 51%-47%, his narrowest outcome in eight elections. Siegel took Travis County by 50,000 votes and McCaul led in Harris by nearly 31,000. The incumbent's huge margins in the rural counties pushed him over the top.

TX-10: Western Harris County, Northern Travis County

Cook Partisan Voting Index: R+9

Population			Race and Ethnicity			Income		
Total	813,505		White	53.4%		Median Income	$72,361	
Land area (sq. miles)	5,071		Black	10.6%		District Income Rank	79	
Pop/ sq mi	160.4		Latino	28.2%		Poverty Rate	10.3%	
Born in State	57.3%		Asian	5.5%		With health insurance	86.5%	
			Two or more races	1.9%		Cash public assistance	1.1%	
Age Groups			Other	0.5%		Food stamp/SNAP	7.8%	
Under 18	25.8%							
18-34	23.4%		**Education**			**Work**		
35-64	39.5%		H.S grad or less	33.8%		White Collar	11.3%	
Over 64	11.3%		Some college	27.6%		Sales and Service	38.1%	
			College Degree, 4 yr	25.5%		Blue Collar	18.3%	
Military			Post grad	13.1%		Government	13.9%	
Veteran/ Active Duty	6.7%							

2012 Pres. Vote	Romney	159,714	(59%)	Obama	104,839	(39%)			
2016 Pres. Vote	Trump	164,912	(52%)	Clinton	135,984	(43%)	Johnson	11,251	(4%)

Austin/Houston Corridor: Two of Texas' major cities are named for leaders of the old Texas Republic, Sam Houston and Stephen F. Austin. They were not entirely attractive characters: Houston had episodes of alcoholic depression, and Austin was a slaveholder who argued that Mexico infringed on Texas' liberty when it freed its slaves. But they were also men of courage and determination who built a distinctively American culture in what was then the northeast of Mexico. Today, the two metropolises named for them are quite different in character. Houston is about commerce, the capital of the oil business, an entrepreneurial hub spread out over the swampy, humid plains north of the Gulf of Mexico. Austin is the creature of the state government headquartered in the grand capitol building and of the University of Texas, with a huge endowment of land in West Texas that turned out to be full of oil. Still, Austin has as much oil in its DNA as does Houston.

Politically, these two urban centers have moved in very different directions. The historic Austin is a liberal enclave in the heart of a conservative state. North of the capitol and the university, an entrepreneurial Austin has taken shape, one that embraces technology and the free market, and is a major center for technology start-ups and the manufacturing of computer and electronic products. It is host to the annual South by Southwest (SXSW) conference, which had more than 300,000 participants in 2018. Started in 1986 by journalists chiefly as a music festival, it has become a 10-day phenomenon of policy, culture, food, entertainment and networking. The area around north Austin and its suburbs has taken on some of Houston's character in recent years. Apple has built a campus in northwest Austin, which handles hardware technologies, customer service and human resources; its payroll of 6,200 at the end of 2018 was scheduled to grow by at least another 5,000 on a new 133-acre campus less than a mile away.

Curiously, there is no superhighway connecting the 160 miles between Austin and Houston, though there has been improved motor-coach service and discussion of a rail line. To get from one to the other, the drive goes through thinly populated counties dotted with plaques recalling the days of the Texas Republic. This area includes seven lightly populated rural counties, including Austin County and its small town of Sealy, where the same-named mattress company was founded. The town of Brenham is home to renowned ice cream manufacturer Blue Bell Creamery. The company suffered a setback with Listeria contamination that caused three deaths and closed the facility for most of 2015; three years later, it had rebounded. With its trendy shops, red-brick inns and fancy restaurants, Brenham is a popular rest stop for travelers between the two cities.

The 10th Congressional District of Texas is like a bar-bell (politically, if not visually) that connects the western suburbs of Houston with the northern precincts of Austin through a corridor of rural counties. It is split into three parts. About 38 percent live on the western edge of Houston's Harris County, a fast-growing and overwhelmingly Republican area, with lots of young families, new subdivisions and mega-churches. Another 36 percent of the voters are in Austin and Travis County, where the Democratic arm of the district includes the northern third of Austin, with one tentacle reaching northwest beyond the city limits and another dropping south to Austin State Hospital. In 2018, the congressional vote in the 10th was 63 percent Republican in Harris and 70 percent Democratic in Travis. The small towns between the two ends are heavily Republican, making the district comfortably Republican. With minority growth on each end, the Hispanic population is 28 percent and blacks account for 11 percent. In 2016, Donald Trump took 52 percent of the district vote.

Mike Conaway (R)

Elected 2004, 8th term, b. Jun 11, 1948; Borger; Abilene Christian University (TX); Texas A & M University, Commerce, B.B.A., 1970; Baptist; Married (Suzanne Conaway); 4 children; 7 grandchildren.

Military Career: U.S. Army 1970-1972

Elected Office: Midland School Board, 1985-1988.

Professional Career: Tax Manager, Price Waterhouse & Co., 1972-1980; CFO, Keith G. Graham, 1980-1981; CFO, Lantern Petroleum Co., 1981; CFO, Arbusto Energy Inc./Bush Exploration Co., 1982-1984; CFO, Spectrum 7 Energy Corporation, 1984-1986; CFO, United Bank, 1987-1990; Sr. Vice President., TX Community Bank, 1990-1992; Owner, K. Michael Conaway, CPA, 1993- 2004; TX St. Board of Public Accountancy, 1995-2002.

DC Office: 2469 RHOB 20515, 202-225-3605, Fax: 202-225-1783, conaway.house.gov
State Offices: Brownwood, 325-646-1950; Granbury, 682-936-2577; Llano, 325-247-2826; Midland, 432-687-2390; Odessa, 432-331-9667; San Angelo, 325-659-4010.

Committees: *Agriculture (RMM)*: Ex Officio membership on all subcommittees. *Armed Services*: Intelligence, Emerging Threats & Capabilities; Seapower & Projection Forces. *Permanent Select on Intelligence*: Counterterrorism, Counterintelligence & Counterproliferation; Defense Intelligence & Warfighter Support; Intelligence Modernization & Readiness.

Group Ratings

	ADA	ACLU	AFL-CIO	LCV	ITI	COC	HAFA	ACU	CFG	FRC
2018	-	3%	-	3%	-	92%	59%	84%	56%	100%
2017	0%	C	5%	0%	C	93%	C	93%	85%	100%

Almanac Ratings 2017-18

	Economy	Social	Foreign	Composite
Liberal	3%	0%	0%	1%
Conservative	97%	100%	100%	99%

Key Votes of the 115th Congress

1. Obama-care revision	Y	5. Family planning regs	Y	9. Guantanamo prisoners	N
2. Tax Cuts	Y	6. Body cameras/immigration	N	10. Ground missiles, limit	N
3. Omnibus appropriations	Y	7. Abortion ban	Y	11. Defense Dept. spending	Y
4. Dodd-Frank revision	Y	8. Concealed carry	Y	12. FISA rules	Y

Election Results

Election	Name (Party)	Vote (%)	Cand. Spent	Ind. Exp. Support	Ind. Exp. Oppose
2018 General	Mike Conaway (R).............................. 176,603	(80%)	$2,081,917		
	Jennie Lou Leeder (D)................. 40,631	(18%)	$80,542		
2018 Primary	Mike Conaway (R)............................. 62,593	(83%)			
	Paul Myers (R)................................... 12,960	(17%)			

Prior winning percentages: 2016 (90%), 2014 (90%), 2012 (79%), 2010 (81%), 2008 (88%), 2006 (100%), 2004 (77%)

Mike Conaway, a Republican first elected in 2004, is a low-profile, well-regarded conservative. He has become an all-purpose handyman who has taken on numerous assignments for his party, including generously fundraising for GOP colleagues, serving as chairman of the House Ethics and Agriculture committees, and taking over the Intelligence Committee investigation of Russian influence in the 2016 election.

Conaway grew up in Odessa, playing offensive and defensive line on the Odessa Permian High School team that won the 1965 state championship, the same school that became the inspiration for the TV show Friday Night Lights. He graduated from East Texas State University, before it became known as Texas A&M-Commerce. He worked as a certified public accountant with Price Waterhouse for, among others, George W. Bush, and was chief financial officer in Arbusto/Bush Exploration during the 1980s. After Bush became governor, he named Conaway to the state Board of Public Accountancy. Conaway later chaired the National Association of State Boards of Accountancy. In May 2003, he finished second in the all-party primary for a special election in the 19th District. In June, he lost by fewer than 600 votes in a hard-fought runoff with Republican Randy Neugebauer of Lubbock, who later won the seat.

After state Republicans pushed through a new redistricting plan that October, Conaway was the obvious front-runner in the redrawn 11th District, which is immediately south of the 19th. Veteran Democratic Rep. Charles Stenholm, who represented much of the area, decided to run against Neugebauer. Conaway's GOP primary opponent was Bill Lester, a little-known political science professor who campaigned against Bush's proposed guest worker program. Conaway supported increased documentation of people crossing the border. He won 75%- 25%. In the general election, he won 77%-22% and has been reelected with ease ever since.

Through 2016, Conaway had a lifetime rating of nearly 93 percent from the American Conservative Union. His Almanac vote ratings have ranked him among the most conservative House members. He is known for requiring his staff to read and understand the Constitution. "It's only 4,500 words — it's not like reading War and Peace," he told the Houston Chronicle. He favors state-based regulatory actions over federal ones, arguing that they are far more nimble and responsive. He was critical of Obama administration efforts to promote renewable energy and sponsored legislation to limit the purchase of biofuels, which compete against his state's oil and natural gas. He voted against the original $700 billion bailout of the financial services industry in 2008, but voted for the final version after his long-time friend President Bush called to urge his support.

As an accountant, Conaway served on the executive committee of the National Republican Congressional Committee. In 2007, he uncovered an internal fraud scheme by the committee's longtime treasurer, who had embezzled almost $1 million. Speaker John Boehner personally asked Conaway to become chairman in 2013 of the Ethics Committee, an undesirable posting but one that often brings later leadership rewards with other opportunities. Conaway said he sought to enhance Congress' low public standing by conducting investigations thoroughly and fairly. "I have a long history of accepting the responsibilities I have been offered and doing the best I can," he told the San Angelo Standard-Times. In that post, he shared a collegial relationship with the committee's top Democrat, California's Linda Sanchez.

When Oklahoma's Frank Lucas was term-limited as Agriculture chairman, Conaway solidified his hold on that job by raising more than $800,000 for other Republicans during 2014. As the new chairman, he noted that there are "fewer and fewer voices" in Congress that represent rural America, and he was honored to be one of them.

In preparing to meet his priority of a timely renewal of the farm bill in 2018, Conaway led a comprehensive committee review of the Supplemental Nutrition Assistance Program, also known as food stamps, a target for numerous fiscal conservatives' ire. He explored options for when recipients should start — and stop — receiving benefits. An overriding question on that program, he said, is the impact on the price of food. "There is sincere, bipartisan interest in ensuring that SNAP is meeting the needs of those it is intended to serve," he said in a 2016 committee report. Conaway has been willing to challenge fellow conservatives who have criticized subsidies for mohair, a fabric yielded from Angora goats. Numerous Angora farmers live in his district. Another interest of constituents was gaining better coverage for cotton in the commodity program. Conaway staked his congressional career on passing the farm bill, an accomplishment he achieved in late 2018.

Conaway has kept busy on other issues as a member of the Armed Services and Intelligence committees. When Intelligence Committee Chairman Devin Nunes of California in April 2017 stepped aside under pressure from control of that panel's investigation of Russian interference in the election following questions about his release of classified information, committee and party leaders designated Conaway to lead the high-pressure inquiry. Earlier, he did not deny that Russian computer hacks were intended to influence the election results.

Democrats who served on the House Intelligence Committee initially had high hopes for Conaway's leadership of the investigation. But the goodwill waned, as Democrats laced into Republican handling of the probe. Even so, the criticism toward Conaway was far more indirect than the vitriol expressed against Nunes. Conaway expressed interest in serving as the top Republican on that committee when an opening occurs. He has considered a run at leading the House GOP conference, though he has not stepped up when he had the opportunity.

During the 2016 campaign, Conaway was a consistent supporter of Trump. "It is what it is, awful, but by the same token, no candidate is perfect," he said, following the release in October 2016 of a controversial video with lewd comments by Trump. "I refuse to do anything that would help Hillary [Clinton] become president."

TX-11: West-Central Texas   Cook Partisan Voting Index: R+32

Population		Race and Ethnicity		Income	
Total	753,479	White	56.1%	Median Income	$54,570
Land area (sq. miles)	27,832	Black	3.6%	District Income Rank	234
Pop/ sq mi	27.1	Latino	37.7%	Poverty Rate	13.1%
Born in State	70.8%	Asian	1%	With health insurance	80.9%
		Two or more races	1.2%	Cash public assistance	1.7%
Age Groups		Other	0.4%	Food stamp/SNAP	10.5%
Under 18	25.3%				
18-34	24.3%	**Education**		**Work**	
35-64	35.2%	H.S grad or less	48.7%	White Collar	15.2%
Over 64	15.2%	Some college	30.7%	Sales and Service	40.1%
		College Degree, 4 yr	14.6%	Blue Collar	30.2%
Military		Post grad	6.1%	Government	12.7%
Veteran/ Active Duty	9%				

2012 Pres. Vote	Romney	182,438	(79%)	Obama	45,083	(20%)			
2016 Pres. Vote	Trump	193,620	(78%)	Clinton	47,468	(19%)	Johnson	6,659	(3%)

Midland, Odessa: In the 1540s, the conquistador Francisco Coronado and his men rode their horses over the plains of the land they called the Llano Estacado, or "palisaded plains," which is now West Texas. They found a vast emptiness, gradually and imperceptibly rising in elevation to the west, with only scrub vegetation and small bands of Comanche Indians. What they did not see, lying far beneath the surface, was oil, discovered in the 1940s in large amounts in the Permian Basin. When oil was found, two tiny county seats 25 miles apart suddenly became small cities — Odessa, home of the roughneck oil well workers, and Midland, the more upscale town where oil entrepreneurs lived and started their own Petroleum Club. The Permian Basin boomed in the years just after World War II. In 1940, Ector and Midland counties had a population of 26,000. By 1960, they had grown to 159,000. Midland in the 1950s was an affluent town by West Texas standards, but hardly luxurious. Air conditioning had not yet become standard in homes or schools, and there were no mansions at the edge of town, just barren desert and oil derricks. George and Barbara Bush moved to the Permian Basin in 1948 in search of success in the oil industry and room for a growing family. They rented houses in Odessa before upgrading to a series of larger, but by no means grand, ranch houses in Midland. President George W. Bush's wife, Laura, also is from Midland. Odessa is perhaps best known as the high school football-crazed town depicted in the 1990 book Friday Night Lights, later turned into a movie and hit TV series.

In an area that still yields much of the state's oil, production and land sales have increasingly been driven by new hydraulic fracturing techniques. As recently as early 2014, 536 of the 1,540 on-shore oil rigs operating in the United States were in the Permian Basin. As a result, there are few American cities that feel the swing of a boom-and-bust market quite like Midland. Tales of the 1980s oil bust are legion. In recent years, it has been all boom. In 2018, Midland had the hottest housing market in the country. Midland's population grew by 18 percent from 2000 to 2010 and an even more impressive 20 percent in the next five years. Optimistic city leaders have projected that, if the boom holds, population could double over the next three decades.

The 11th Congressional District of Texas covers much of West Texas. It sweeps through 29 counties and across 300 miles of often barren land from the New Mexico border to the outskirts of both Fort Worth and Austin. More than half the population is in Midland, Ector and Tom Green (San Angelo) counties. The district's Hispanic population has steadily increased to 38 percent. West Texas in the 1940s was, like nearly every other part of Texas, almost totally Democratic. That began to change in the 1950s. Newcomers like the Bushes were an important part of this trend. The 11th today is overwhelmingly Republican, giving Donald Trump 78 percent of the vote in 2016. Slightly behind the adjacent 13th District, it is the second-most Republican district in the nation, the same top-two results as in 2012.

Kay Granger (R)

Elected 1996, 12th term, b. Jan 18, 1943; Greenville; Texas Wesleyan University, B.S., 1965; University of Texas - Arlington, 1976; Methodist; Divorced; 3 children; 5 grandchildren.

Elected Office: Ft. Worth City Council, 1989-1991; Ft. Worth Mayor, 1991-1996.

Professional Career: Teacher, 1965-1978; Life ins. agent, 1978-1985; Chairman, Ft. Worth Zoning Comm., 1981-1989; Founder & President, Kay Granger Ins. Co. Inc.

DC Office: 1026 LHOB 20515, 202-225-5071, Fax: 202-225-5683, kaygranger.house.gov

State Offices: Fort Worth, 817-338-0909.

Committees: *Appropriations (RMM).*

Group Ratings

	ADA	ACLU	AFL-CIO	LCV	ITI	COC	HAFA	ACU	CFG	FRC
2018	-	4%	-	6%	-	83%	59%	72%	50%	100%
2017	15%	C	11%	0%	C	93%	C	85%	71%	100%

Almanac Ratings 2017-18

	Economy	Social	Foreign	Composite
Liberal	8%	3%	0%	4%
Conservative	92%	97%	100%	96%

Key Votes of the 115th Congress

1. Obama-care revision	Y	5. Family planning regs	Y	9. Guantanamo prisoners	N
2. Tax Cuts	Y	6. Body cameras/immigration	N	10. Ground missiles, limit	N
3. Omnibus appropriations	Y	7. Abortion ban	Y	11. Defense Dept. spending	Y
4. Dodd-Frank revision	Y	8. Concealed carry	Y	12. FISA rules	Y

Election Results

Election	Name (Party)	Vote (%)	Cand. Spent	Ind. Exp. Support	Ind. Exp. Oppose
2018 General	Kay Granger (R)................................ 172,557	(64%)	$1,293,233		
	Vanessa Adia (D)............................ 90,994	(34%)	$186,616		
2018 Primary	Kay Granger (R)...	(100%)			

Prior winning percentages: 2016 (69%), 2014 (71%), 2012 (71%), 2010 (72%), 2008 (68%), 2006 (67%), 2004 (72%), 2002 (92%), 2000 (63%), 1998 (62%), 1996 (58%)

Kay Granger, first elected in 1996 and the only Republican woman in its delegation, is one of the most powerful Texans in Congress. Less conservative than most other Texans, she became the top Republican on the Appropriations Committee in 2019. Granger quietly wields her power on behalf of her district, including a massive public works project and production of F-35 fighter planes in Fort Worth.

Granger grew up in Fort Worth, graduated from Texas Wesleyan College and worked as a high school journalism and English teacher in North Richland Hills. She raised three children and started her own insurance agency, which she operated for more than 20 years. In 1989, she was elected to the Fort Worth Council, and two years later was elected as the nonpartisan mayor. When the House seat became open, leaders of both parties recruited Granger.

She decided to run in the Republican primary. In a three-candidate race, she was attacked as a liberal, partly for her support of abortion rights. She won with 69 percent of the vote. Her Democratic opponent was Hugh Parmer, a former Fort Worth mayor and the challenger to GOP Sen. Phil Gramm in 1990. Parmer attacked Republican cuts in Medicare and the stewardship of House Speaker Newt Gingrich. Granger called for a balanced budget and tax cuts for business and ran on her record as mayor. She won 58%-41%, a stunning Republican victory in the district held for 18 terms by Democratic Speaker Jim Wright until 1989.

Granger's voting record has been in the center of House Republicans, as shown by the Almanac vote ratings. In 2007-08, she was vice chair of the Republican Conference, but her leadership ambitions were limited. One of Granger's legislative achievements was enactment of tax-free savings accounts for higher education expenses. In 2014, Speaker John Boehner named her to chair a working group on the border crisis, chiefly in the Rio Grande Valley. Her proposal was far less costly than the plan submitted by President Barack Obama. She takes her work seriously and she rarely seeks media attention. "Kay Granger chooses work over recognition," the Fort Worth Star-Telegram headlined a March 2015 news story.

After six years chairing the subcommittee that controls spending for the State Department and foreign aid, she took over in 2017 as chairwoman of the Defense Subcommittee. Her expertise on national security issues and local funding have been instrumental for the major defense plants in her district. Coincidentally, House Armed Services Committee Chairman Mac Thornberry represents the adjacent 13th District.

Over the years, she has kept a close eye on local Pentagon spending and worked to maintain production in her district of Lockheed Martin planes, especially the F-35 fighter jet. Her selection was all the more timely because Donald Trump following his election had tweeted, "F-35 program and cost is out of control." After the October 2016 release of Trump's crude comments about women, Granger said that he "should remove himself from consideration as commander in chief." Following the election, she said that Trump had a "mandate for change" and "I will work with whoever is the president."

The key constituent project of Granger's career has been a water control project, "Panther Island." She has directed hundreds of millions of dollars to the north side of downtown Fort Worth to reroute the Trinity River. The project's plans also have aimed to create a new entertainment district in the city. With her son, J.D. Granger, as the executive director of the Trinity River Vision Authority that has been responsible for the plan and its ballooning costs, Granger faced extended negative publicity in late 2018.

As ranking member of the Appropriations Committee, Granger prevailed over other senior Republicans on the committee. She was one of the few women with significant stature in the GOP Conference. As she rose through the committee ranks, Granger formed a close and productive working relationship with Democratic Rep. Nita Lowey of New York, who chairs Appropriations.

Granger has been reelected by wide margins. Her moderate tendencies inspired challenges in the 2010 and 2012 Republican primaries by underfunded challengers from her right, whom she dispatched with ease. She wrote a book, What's Right About America: Celebrating Our Nation's Values, published in 2006.

TX-12: Tarrant County   Cook Partisan Voting Index: R+18

Population		Race and Ethnicity		Income	
Total	773,234	White	62.8%	Median Income	$64,541
Land area (sq. miles)	1,441	Black	8.3%	District Income Rank	139
Pop/ sq mi	536.5	Latino	22.8%	Poverty Rate	11.3%
Born in State	60.5%	Asian	3.4%	With health insurance	85.2%
		Two or more races	2.1%	Cash public assistance	1.5%
Age Groups		Other	0.6%	Food stamp/SNAP	9.5%
Under 18	25.1%				
18-34	24.6%	**Education**		**Work**	
35-64	38%	H.S grad or less	37.2%	White Collar	12.3%
Over 64	12.3%	Some college	31.7%	Sales and Service	40.9%
		College Degree, 4 yr	20.9%	Blue Collar	21.3%
Military		Post grad	10.2%	Government	12.4%
Veteran/ Active Duty	9.3%				

2012 Pres. Vote	Romney	166,992	(67%)	Obama	79,147	(32%)			
2016 Pres. Vote	Trump	177,939	(62%)	Clinton	92,549	(33%)	Johnson	10,173	(4%)

Fort Worth and Western Suburbs: Fort Worth has a fair claim to being the quintessential mid-American city. It sits halfway across the continent, just west of the Balcones Escarpment that divides the dry, treeless grazing lands of West Texas from the humid green croplands of East Texas -- "where the West begins," as its 19th century boosters proclaimed, coining the slogan that's still used by the city. This was the last stop for cattle drives before they returned to Kansas. It is Southern in heritage and Northern in its advanced post-industrial economy. It has the nation's longest row of Western wear shops and one of the nation's richest families, the Basses, whose steel skyscrapers dominate the skyline. The family developed Sundance Square, a 35-block entertainment, office and retail district that has helped revive the downtown district. The area was named for the running mate of famed outlaw Butch Cassidy, who regularly frequented Fort Worth for its saloons and gambling establishments at the turn of the 20th century.

"Cowtown," "Panther City" or "Funky Town," as the city is sometimes called, surpassed Indianapolis in 2018 to become the 15th most populous city in the nation. It has a high-tech economy and has been an aviation center since the 1940s, though one that was hard hit by defense cuts. The huge Lockheed Martin plant, which employs about 14,000 people, produces numerous bombers and fighter planes, including the F-35 fighter jet. Next door is the Naval Air Station Fort Worth Joint Reserve Base, formerly Carswell Air Force Base, the home of B-52 bombers for years. The New York Times has called the city "an irresistible combination of cowboys and culture," in part because it has some of the nation's premier small museums, including the Amon Carter Museum, the Kimbell Art Museum, the Modern Art Museum of Fort Worth, and the Sid Richardson Museum. Scheduled to open in the Cultural District in November 2019 was the $540 million Dickies arena, where the sporting events will include rodeos.

City leaders have sought to tamp down the city's historic little-brother rivalry with nearby Dallas. While many in Fort Worth commute to Dallas, many of the city's residents resent the Dallas shadow. Newspaper publisher Amon Carter was known to pack a sack lunch for trips to Dallas, to avoid supporting the city's economy.

The 12th Congressional District includes about half of Fort Worth and western suburban Tarrant County, as well as all of Parker County to the west and part of Wise County to the north. About 76 percent of the population is in Tarrant, which has grown an impressive 41 percent since 2000. It has narrowed its population gap with Dallas County to less than 600,000 residents. Parts of Tarrant are in six districts, of which the 12th has the largest share. The district includes northern and western Fort Worth neighborhoods and the affluent southwest quarter beyond Texas Christian University, downtown and the stockyards. Parker County was once windswept open land around the courthouse town of Weatherford, where former House Speaker Jim Wright, a Democrat, grew up and was first elected to the House in 1954. He served two-plus years as Speaker, before he quit in 1989 in the face of ethics sanctions. Today, Parker is sprouting subdivisions; it grew 50 percent from 2000 to 2017, to a population of 133,000.

Fort Worth and Tarrant County stayed Democratic in the 1950s when Dallas went Republican. With Dallas recently swinging back to Democrats, Fort Worth and Tarrant County continued to swing Republican. The 12th District gave Donald Trump 62 percent of the vote in 2016. That changed with the 2018 midterm wave. Tarrant, the last urban Republican county in the state, fell to the Democrats when Rep. Beto O'Rourke carried the county by 4,400 votes (less than a one percentage point margin) in his challenge to Sen. Ted Cruz.

Mac Thornberry (R)

Elected 1994, 13th term, b. Jul 15, 1958; Clarendon; Texas Tech University, B.A., 1980; University of Texas Law School, J.D., 1983; Presbyterian; Married (Sally Adams Thornberry); 2 children.

Professional Career: Legislative counsel, Rep. Tom Loeffler, 1983-1985; Chief of Staff, Rep. Larry Combest, 1985-1988; Deputy Assistant Secretary of st. for Legislative affairs, 1988-1989; Practicing attorney, 1989-1994; Rancher, 1989-1994.

DC Office: 2208 RHOB 20515, 202-225-3706, Fax: 202-225-3486, thornberry.house.gov

State Offices: Amarillo, 806-371-8844; Wichita Falls, 940-692-1700.

Committees: *Armed Services (RMM).*

Group Ratings

	ADA	ACLU	AFL-CIO	LCV	ITI	COC	HAFA	ACU	CFG	FRC
2018	-	4%	-	3%	-	92%	54%	72%	50%	100%
2017	0%	C	8%	0%	C	93%	C	85%	69%	100%

Almanac Ratings 2017-18

	Economy	Social	Foreign	Composite
Liberal	4%	0%	0%	1%
Conservative	96%	100%	100%	99%

Key Votes of the 115th Congress

1. Obama-care revision	Y	5. Family planning regs	Y	9. Guantanamo prisoners	N
2. Tax Cuts	Y	6. Body cameras/immigration	N	10. Ground missiles, limit	N
3. Omnibus appropriations	Y	7. Abortion ban	Y	11. Defense Dept. spending	Y
4. Dodd-Frank revision	Y	8. Concealed carry	Y	12. FISA rules	Y

Election Results

Election	Name (Party)	Vote (%)		Cand. Spent	Ind. Exp. Support	Ind. Exp. Oppose
2018 General	Mac Thornberry (R)	169,027	(82%)	$791,887		
	Greg Sagan (D)	35,083	(17%)	$28,701		
2018 Primary	Mac Thornberry (R)		(100%)			

Prior winning percentages: 2016 (90%), 2014 (84%), 2012 (91%), 2010 (87%), 2008 (78%), 2006 (74%), 2004 (92%), 2002 (79%), 2000 (68%), 1998 (68%), 1996 (67%), 1994 (55%)

Republican Mac Thornberry, first elected in 1994, has been one of Congress' brainiest and most thoughtful members on national and domestic security issues. As chairman from 2015 to 2018 of the House Armed Services Committee, the first Texan of either party to hold that post, he was outspoken about the need for more defense spending and he challenged anybody who delayed that objective.

His great-great-grandfather, Amos Thornberry, a Union Army veteran and staunch Republican, moved to Clay County, just east of Wichita Falls, in the 1880s. A year after Amos died in 1925, his son bought the cattle ranch in sparsely populated Donley County, closer to Amarillo, which Mac Thornberry and his family now run. After college at Texas Tech and law school at the University of Texas, Thornberry worked for influential West Texas GOP Reps. Tom Loeffler and Larry Combest. He returned to practice law in West Texas, and in 1994 challenged Democratic Rep. Bill Sarpalius, whom he attacked for voting for President Bill Clinton's budget and tax legislation. He profited from news stories that Sarpalius failed to pay a company that moved him to Washington, then accepted a fee for speaking at the company's convention in Las Vegas. Thornberry won 55%-45% and has rolled up large reelection margins since. With the death of North Carolina Rep. Walter Jones in February 2019, Thornberry became the only continuously serving member of the historic GOP class of 1994.

Thornberry has a solidly conservative voting record, though he is hardly the most ideological Republican in the Texas delegation. In keeping with his scholarly nature, his official website includes a section on "Mac's reading list." The Dallas Morning News, in a January 2015 profile with a headline saying he brought "expertise, not notoriety" to his work, wrote that his office bookshelves are "filled with tomes on spy craft, military history and strategy."

On domestic issues, Thornberry has pressed for repeal of the estate tax and adoption of a national sales tax. In 2010, he enacted a bill expanding access to state veterans' homes for parents whose children died while serving in the military. He filed a bill in 2011 to help states set up special health care courts staffed by judges with health policy expertise. The judges would serve as an alternative to juries that Republicans say are inclined to award unnecessarily large damage amounts in malpractice cases. He has supported a two-year budget cycle, an idea that reform groups have said would make the budget process run far more smoothly. On a vital local issue, Thornberry won House passage in 2017 of his bill to require that the Bureau of Land Management survey the lands along the Texas side of the Red River as a step toward resolving longtime disagreements between landowners and the federal government.

Thornberry has long been at the forefront of national security issues. He was at the Pentagon for an early breakfast with Defense Secretary Donald Rumsfeld on Sept. 11, 2001. "I remember him very well receiving a note, so we decided to get out of there, he's got things to do," he told C-SPAN in 2012. In 2002, after the Sept. 11 terrorist attacks, he played a key role in creation of the Homeland Security Department. In the subsequent years, he was a force within the Armed Services Committee on terrorism and cybersecurity strategy for the country. In 2013, Thornberry led a long-term effort to reform the Pentagon's acquisition programs. Thornberry told Federal Computer Week that he wanted to change the underlying principles of acquisition instead of merely trying to eliminate wasteful programs. "I think the key is looking … to the incentives that exist in the system, both on the side of government and on the side of industry," he said.

Taking over as committee chairman, Thornberry sought to be a firm check on the Obama administration. "Congress is sometimes criticized for exercising its proper role in defense," he said in a forceful January 2015 speech that made clear he would be an activist. He cited Capitol Hill's move to block the Pentagon's decision to shut down the country's lone tank-production line and its insistence on using Predator drones as a weapon against terrorists. At the same time, though, he acknowledged that Congress can be "parochial" and get things wrong. He said that he was open to "any solution" that would stave off the steep spending cuts under automatic sequestration procedures.

Thornberry won House approval in May 2015 of the military authorization bill, which reflected the view of his committee's defense hawks that the Pentagon needed an infusion of funds for new and expanded programs. After a House-Senate agreement on the defense spending bill was vetoed by Obama in October 2015, the two sides came together when congressional leaders reached a budget agreement to raise spending caps.

Thornberry continued his interest in improving the efficiency of the Pentagon. In 2016, he set acquisition reform as a key feature of the annual defense spending bill, including steps such as more experimentation with technology, encouragement of competition and clarification of intellectual property rights of Pentagon contractors. Several of these changes gained bipartisan support and were included in the final version of what otherwise was mostly a stand-pat measure.

Although the election of President Donald Trump gave him opportunities to set Pentagon policy with a more sympathetic administration, Thornberry had early problems with Trump's freewheeling style during the 2016 campaign. "I'm troubled by some of the things Mr. Trump has said and done," he said when the GOP nominee had an extended rhetorical showdown with a Muslim family whose son had died in Iraq while serving in the Army.

Thornberry was a crucial ally of nearby Fort Worth during the Trump transition when the president-elect threatened to pull the plug on Lockheed's production of the F-35. The fighter plane is in part manufactured in Fort Worth. Thornberry and Rep. Kay Granger, a senior Republican appropriator, presented a united front to protect the plane.

When Trump in March 2017 submitted initial budget plans for the entire government, Thornberry responded that they fell short of what he had expected for rebuilding the military. "Do people at the White House understand how much damage has been done over the past several years? I don't know," Thornberry told reporters. When Congress in November completed action on the annual defense bill, he said, "We will not rebuild and fix our problems in one year or one bill. But we can head in the right direction....That's what this conference report does." The legislation increased funds beyond Trump's request for the F-35 and for overall troop levels. In July 2018, he said that the president was "right to insist" that other NATO members increase spending for their defense.

Thornberry has become a frequent Trump critic. He released a statement when Trump withdrew the United States from the Iran nuclear deal, expressing his hope that European allies were given more time to strengthen the deal. In December 2018, he said that he was "deeply disturbed" by Trump's reduction of U.S. forces from Afghanistan, which made America "less safe." Thornberry expressed reservations about Trump's emergency order to build a wall along the border with Mexico, with his fear that military money might be diverted from the Pentagon.

Thornberry lost his gavel at Armed Services when Democrats took control of the House in 2019. He was reaching the end of his tenure as the Republican leader of the committee in 2021, thanks to party term limits.

TX-13: North Texas/Panhandle | Cook Partisan Voting Index: R+33

Population		Race and Ethnicity		Income	
Total	708,616	White	63.8%	Median Income	$50,854
Land area (sq. miles)	38,349	Black	5.2%	District Income Rank	290
Pop/ sq mi	18.5	Latino	26.5%	Poverty Rate	15.7%
Born in State	66.4%	Asian	2%	With health insurance	83.4%
		Two or more races	1.9%	Cash public assistance	1.5%
Age Groups		Other	0.7%	Food stamp/SNAP	12.2%
Under 18	25.1%				
18-34	23.7%	**Education**		**Work**	
35-64	36.5%	H.S grad or less	46.9%	White Collar	14.7%
Over 64	14.7%	Some college	32.8%	Sales and Service	41.8%
		College Degree, 4 yr	14.1%	Blue Collar	28.1%
Military		Post grad	6.1%	Government	15.8%
Veteran/ Active Duty	10%				

2012 Pres. Vote	Romney	184,104	(80%)	Obama	42,521	(19%)		
2016 Pres. Vote	Trump	190,838	(80%)	Clinton	40,253	(17%)	Johnson	6,709	(3%)

Amarillo, Wichita Falls: The farther west one travels in Texas, the browner the land gets and the smaller the towns get, until you arrive at counties containing only a few hundred people each — plus quite a few more head of cattle. At that point, the land rises nearly 1,000 feet in elevation, up steep hillsides from the gullies along the rivers that for most of the year are just trickles, to the tilted tableland that makes up the High Plains of West Texas. The winds here sweep down from the Rockies, the land is barren except where irrigated, often with the now dangerously depleted waters of the Ogallala Aquifer. The land alternates between grazing areas and cotton fields. But here and there in this demanding environment — sticky hot in the summer, swept by north winds from Canada in winter, always threatened by tornadoes — comfortable cities have been built to house the people and businesses that bring forth some of the nation's most abundant oil, natural gas, helium and other elements from the earth. The area produces cotton and milo, a variety of sorghum, and is home to one of the nation's oldest cattle auctions. Researchers have discovered dangerous levels of uranium at some sites in the Ogallala Aquifer. Support has grown for greater use of renewable energy in the Panhandle, especially wind.

Around Wichita Falls is the agricultural land of the Red River Valley. Cadillac Ranch, located just off I-40 west of Amarillo, is a famous roadside sculpture featuring "10 tail-finned, brightly painted Cadillacs planted nose down in a pasture," as Texas Monthly describes it. Built in 1974, the attraction inspired the 1980 Bruce Springsteen song Cadillac Ranch. Archer City, home of novelist Larry McMurtry, was chronicled in The Last Picture Show and Texasville. Female entrepreneur Enid

Justin founded Nocona Boots in its namesake Montague County town in 1925. The boot company eventually relocated, but Nokona baseball mitts are still produced in the town. On the other side of the county, once-dry Saint Jo has become a wine-drinking destination.

The 13th Congressional District of Texas spans 39 counties and parts of two others, from the New Mexico border to just north of Denton in the Dallas exurbs. That is a Texas-sized drive of more than 450 miles. The area was long dominated by Texas Anglos, but Latinos lately have been moving here in large numbers to work in the fields or in crop processing. Still, the population in the region has been either in decline or stagnant for three decades. Today, the district is 27 percent Hispanic. Amarillo is the largest city in the heart of cowboy country. It is famously windy — windier than Chicago, in fact. Just outside town is the Pantex plant that secretly assembled and then dismantled thousands of nuclear warheads and was the epicenter of American defense in the Cold War. Much of the facility has decayed, including leaky roofs. A Pentagon study in 2016 showed $3.7 billion in deferred maintenance for nuclear-weapons facilities. Pantex has become the site of a renewable energy project that removes carbon dioxide emissions from the air. To the east, close to the Red River Valley, the district reaches but does not include Denton County at the northwest corner of the Metroplex.

Settled by Confederate veterans, the valley was heavily Democratic through the 1970s. The High Plains were for years more Republican. Both are now solidly Republican, and so is the 13th District. In 2016, Donald Trump got 80 percent of the vote here, which was his strongest performance in the nation.

Randy Weber (R)

Elected 2012, 4th term, b. Jul 02, 1953; Pearland; Alvin Community College (TX); University of Houston, Clear Lake (TX), B.S., 1977; Baptist; Married (Brenda Weber); 3 children; 7 grandchildren.

Elected Office: Pearland City Council, 1990-1996; TX House, 2008-2013.

Professional Career: Owner, Weber's Air & Heat, 1981-present.

DC Office: 107 CHOB 20515, 202-225-2831, Fax: 202-225-0271, weber.house.gov

State Offices: Beaumont, 409-835-0108; Lake Jackson, 979-285-0231; League City, 281-316-0231.

Committees: *Science, Space & Technology*: Energy (RMM). *Transportation & Infrastructure*: Coast Guard & Maritime Transportation; Railroads, Pipelines & Hazardous Materials; Water Resources & Environment.

Group Ratings

	ADA	ACLU	AFL-CIO	LCV	ITI	COC	HAFA	ACU	CFG	FRC
2018	-	14%	-	6%	-	75%	77%	76%	59%	100%
2017	0%	C	5%	0%	C	92%	C	93%	86%	100%

Almanac Ratings 2017-18

	Economy	Social	Foreign	Composite
Liberal	3%	3%	3%	3%
Conservative	97%	97%	97%	97%

Key Votes of the 115th Congress

1. Obama-care revision	Y	5. Family planning regs	Y	9. Guantanamo prisoners	N
2. Tax Cuts	Y	6. Body cameras/immigration	N	10. Ground missiles, limit	N
3. Omnibus appropriations	N	7. Abortion ban	Y	11. Defense Dept. spending	Y
4. Dodd-Frank revision	Y	8. Concealed carry	Y	12. FISA rules	N

Election Results

Election	Name (Party)	Vote (%)		Cand. Spent	Ind. Exp. Support	Ind. Exp. Oppose
2018 General	Randy Weber (R)............................ 138,942	(59%)		$570,811		
	Adrienne Bell (D).................................. 92,212	(39%)		$190,533		
2018 Primary	Randy Weber (R)........................... 33,509	(75%)				
	Bill Sargent (R)................................ 8,742	(20%)				
	Keith Casey (R)...................................... 2,291	(5%)				

Prior winning percentages: 2016 (62%), 2014 (62%), 2012 (54%)

Republican Randy Weber, who took the seat of retiring libertarian icon Rep. Ron Paul in 2012, has used his business background to craft energy legislation — a prime interest to many of his constituents. Weber joined the Freedom Caucus and posed challenges to House GOP leaders. In 2019, he made an unsuccessful bid for the top GOP slot on the Science, Space and Technology Committee.

Before he was elected to Congress, Weber had always resided within a five-mile radius of his hometown of Pearland. His father owned a gas station and later ran an RV business. After getting his bachelor's from the University of Houston, he started Weber's Air and Heat, making all the service calls as an air conditioning contractor and putting flyers on every doorstep in town to drum up business. "Did we struggle? Man, did we," Weber said, recalling the number of times the electric company threatened to turn off his power. "Nobody came to bail out Randy Weber. My company, I made it the old-fashioned way." In the 1980s, President Ronald Reagan's message of limited government inspired Weber to get politically involved. From 1990 to 1996, he served on the Pearland City Council. Twelve years later, he was elected to the Texas House, where he worked on issues ranging from veterans affairs to domestic human trafficking — usually with a strongly conservative view.

Running for the House, Weber emerged from a field of nine GOP contenders. He was endorsed by Paul and Texas Gov. Rick Perry. Weber styled himself as a devoted family man and Christian and he ran "to everyone else's right," wrote David Wasserman of the Cook Political Report. After leading the first round with 28 percent to 19 percent for Felicia Harris, an attorney and councilwoman from Pearland, he easily won the runoff with 63 percent of the vote.

Weber faced off in the general election against former Democratic Rep. Nick Lampson, who distanced himself from the national party and retained some of his local popularity from two earlier stints in the House when he served five terms and represented Jefferson County. The unique makeup of the district — thick with working-class voters —forced Republicans to work harder than expected, especially when Weber ran short of cash in the final weeks of the campaign. Each candidate spent a bit more than a million dollars. Lampson took 58 percent of the vote in Jefferson. Weber ran stronger in his base, with 68 percent in Brazoria. In the swing county of Galveston, which cast 45 percent of the total vote, Weber got 57 percent. Overall, he won, 54%-45%. He has been easily reelected against opponents whom he vastly outspent.

In the House, Weber unabashedly said that nobody would "out-conservative" him — unlike Paul, whose libertarian views on some social and foreign policy issues sometimes fit more comfortably with Democrats. In 2014, he filed a resolution condemning President Barack Obama for having routinely refused to enforce the law and said the president was provoking a constitutional crisis. "In my view, the president has not faithfully executed the law," Weber said.

He got an opportunity to deal with local issues as chairman of the Science, Space and Technology Subcommittee on Energy. When the House passed in 2017 an authorization bill for the Energy Department, it included Weber's provisions to encourage spending on advance nuclear reactor technologies. In 2018, he took the lead in the House in the enactment of the Nuclear Energy Innovation Capabilities Act, which updated programs for civilian use of nuclear energy, including advanced reactors. The legislation opened the door, he said, to "the next generation reactor designs, materials and nuclear fuels."

Weber clashed frequently with Republican leaders. In January 2015, he voted for Rep. Louie Gohmert of Texas — and against John Boehner — for House Speaker, and explained, "I voted according to my constituents' wishes." He said that he hoped his vote sent a signal to GOP leaders that "we need to be more forceful in fighting this president and his liberal agenda." After Weber voted for Rep. Daniel Webster of Florida in the October 2015 selection of a successor to Boehner, he expressed hope that Paul Ryan "will take this opportunity to forward our conservative cause, restore order in the House, and have the strength to make tough decisions."

Following the 2018 election, Weber ran for the opening of top Republican on the Science committee. He cited his familiarity with the panel and the connection of his district to its agenda. The slot went to Frank Lucas of Oklahoma — who also had oil and gas interests at home, plus the experience of chairing the Agriculture Committee and usually operating as a leadership ally.

TX-14: Gulf Coast   Cook Partisan Voting Index: R+12

Population		Race and Ethnicity		Income	
Total	737,708	White	51.1%	Median Income	$57,851
Land area (sq. miles)	2,441	Black	19.5%	District Income Rank	195
Pop/ sq mi	302.2	Latino	24.5%	Poverty Rate	15.6%
Born in State	66%	Asian	3%	With health insurance	82.6%
		Two or more races	1.5%	Cash public assistance	1.1%
Age Groups		Other	0.4%	Food stamp/SNAP	13%
Under 18	24.5%				
18-34	23%	**Education**		**Work**	
35-64	39.4%	H.S grad or less	43.8%	White Collar	13.1%
Over 64	13.1%	Some college	32.9%	Sales and Service	40.1%
		College Degree, 4 yr	15.7%	Blue Collar	24.9%
Military		Post grad	7.6%	Government	14.7%
Veteran/ Active Duty	8.3%				

2012 Pres. Vote	Romney	147,213	(59%)	Obama	97,958	(40%)		
2016 Pres. Vote	Trump	153,191	(58%)	Clinton	101,228	(38%)	Johnson	7,352 (3%)

Galveston, Beaumont-Port Arthur: The spongy land of the Texas Gulf Coast remained mostly unsettled until well into the 19th century. When oil was found at the Spindletop field near Beaumont in 1901, the area all around it boomed, first with oil exploration, then petroleum refining, then petrochemical production. The rig workers and mechanical engineers they attracted have given a kind of permanent roughneck air to the region, and it's one of the few places in Texas where unions have any strength. The Humble oil field was once the largest in Texas, and the local Humble Oil and Refining Company is now known as ExxonMobil. Galveston, on a barrier island in the Gulf, was an immigrant port until a 1900 hurricane killed thousands. It is now guarded by a 17-foot seawall and connected to the mainland by a hurricane-resistant bridge. Its cruise port in 2016 ranked fifth in total passengers and serves several of the largest cruise lines; a third cruise terminal was scheduled to open in 2021. The nearby refinery town of Texas City was home to one of the state's worst disasters: In April 1947, more than 500 people died after two freighters containing ammonium nitrate fertilizer exploded, demolishing the port. More recently, Hurricanes Gustav and Ike in 2008 shut down oil pipelines for months and toppled some platforms. To limit a possible recurrence of the "storm surge" in Galveston Bay, the Army Corps of Engineers in 2018 proposed a 70-mile coastal barrier ("Ike Dike"), which could cost about $30 billion.

The 14th Congressional District of Texas stretches along the southeast Gulf Coast, from Port Arthur and Beaumont to Freeport at its southernmost point. Nearly half the district is in the solidly Republican confines of Galveston. One-third of the population lives in Jefferson County, around the highly polluted "Golden Triangle" oil refining area of Beaumont and Port Arthur. While refineries are Port Arthur's economic lifeline, the city's downtown has been virtually abandoned, and over a quarter of residents live below the poverty level. The BP oil spill disaster and subsequent offshore drilling moratorium hurt that industry and the local shrimping economy, as well. The local economy received a boost from the 2014 opening of the southern leg of the Keystone XL pipeline from Cushing Oklahoma to the Port Arthur refineries. This industrial area is the planned site of two new huge petrochemical steam cracker plants. In January 2019, ExxonMobil began work on expansion of its refinery complex in Beaumont, which is among the largest in the nation with 2,100 employees. The construction, scheduled for completion in 2022, was expected to hire 1,800 additional workers. The company planned to spend $20 billion on new manufacturing along the Gulf Coast.

The population in Jefferson County is 34 percent African American and 21 percent Hispanic; the county leans Democratic and is about one-third of the 14th. The remaining 20 percent of the district is inland Brazoria County, home to the first capital of the Republic of Texas; about half of Brazoria is in the 14th. The district, working-class and ancestrally Democratic, since the 1980s has become safely Republican, with help from redistricting changes. Overall, the 25 percent Latino and 20 percent black population have not affected the comfortably Republican tilt. In this area, where local Rep. Ron Paul was once the favorite son in presidential campaigns, Donald Trump took 58 percent of the vote.

Vicente Gonzalez (D)

Elected 2016, 2nd term, b. Sep 04, 1967; Corpus Christi; Harvard University School of Law (MA); Embry-Riddle Aeronautical University, B.A., 1992; Texas A & M University School of Law (formerly Texas Wesleyan School of Law), J.D., 1996; Catholic; Married (Lorena Saenz).

Professional Career: Attorney and Owner, V. Gonzalez & Associates.

DC Office: 113 CHOB 20515, 202-225-2531, Fax: 202-225-5688, gonzalez.house.gov

State Offices: Benavides, 888-217-0261; Falfurrias, 361-209-3027; McAllen, 956-682-5545; San Diego, 888-217-0261; Seguin, 830-358-0497.

Committees: *Financial Services*: Housing, Community Development & Insurance; Investor Protection, Entrepreneurship & Capital Markets; Subcommittee on Diversity & Inclusion. *Foreign Affairs*: Europe, Eurasia, Energy & the Environment; Western Hemisphere, Civilian Security, & Trade.

Group Ratings

	ADA	ACLU	AFL-CIO	LCV	ITI	COC	HAFA	ACU	CFG	FRC
2018	-	82%	-	74%	-	67%	10%	32%	27%	0%
2017	70%	C	97%	71%	C	64%	C	7%	0%	11%

Almanac Ratings 2017-18

	Economy	Social	Foreign	Composite
Liberal	75%	85%	70%	77%
Conservative	25%	15%	30%	23%

Key Votes of the 115th Congress

1. Obama-care revision	N	5. Family planning regs	N	9. Guantanamo prisoners	N
2. Tax Cuts	N	6. Body cameras/immigration	Y	10. Ground missiles, limit	N
3. Omnibus appropriations	N	7. Abortion ban	N	11. Defense Dept. spending	Y
4. Dodd-Frank revision	Y	8. Concealed carry	Y	12. FISA rules	N

Election Results

Election	Name (Party)	Vote (%)	Cand. Spent	Ind. Exp. Support	Ind. Exp. Oppose
2018 General	Vicente Gonzalez (D)	98,333 (60%)	$401,960	$46,282	
	Tim Westley (R)	63,862 (39%)	$5,440		
2018 Primary	Vicente Gonzalez (D)	(100%)			

Prior winning percentages: 2016 (57%)

Democrat Vicente Gonzalez of Texas was elected in 2016 to an open seat along the border with Mexico. His years growing up had a boot-strap quality in an area that faced demanding imperatives. His professional success as a trial lawyer allowed him to mostly self-finance his campaign. In the House, he continued to show independence.

Gonzalez was born to a military family in Corpus Christi. His mother stressed the importance of education, which motivated Gonzalez to go back to high school and get his GED certificate. He attended community college classes at Del Mar College and earned his bachelor's in business aviation at Embry Riddle Aeronautical University at Corpus Christi Naval Air Station. Continuing to heed his mother's advice, he got a law degree at Texas A&M. While in law school, he interned for Democratic Rep. Solomon Ortiz of Texas to learn more about government. He founded his own law firm, which focused on business litigation, catastrophic accidents and property damage. In that work, he successfully handled several major lawsuits against South Texas school districts, which recovered millions of dollars from contractors who misspent bond money.

When Rep. Rubén Hinojosa announced his retirement, Gonzalez faced five other candidates in the Democratic primary. Gonzalez said that he self-financed his campaign so he would not have to accept corporate contributions. The $2.3 million that he spent more than doubled the total for all of his opponents combined in both parties. With the benefit of some Washington connections, Gonzalez won the endorsement of the Congressional Progressive Caucus and campaign contributions from several House Democrats, including now-Majority Leader Steny Hoyer of Maryland. In the first round of voting, Gonzalez got 42 percent; the runner-up with 19 percent was Juan "Sonny" Palacios Jr., an attorney who was a member of the Edinburg school board. Gonzalez won the runoff with 66 percent of the vote.

In the general election, Republican nominee Tim Westley was an Army veteran whose campaign slogan was "Putting God Back into Politics." He spent $16,000, which was less than 1 percent of the total for his opponent. Gonzalez won, 57%-38%. That might seem close, but it was roughly the share of the vote that Hinojosa typically received during his 10 terms as Gonzalez's predecessor. Two years later, Gonzalez had no Democratic opposition and got 60 percent against Westley.

Gonzalez showed insider skills by gaining a seat on the Financial Services Committee, where he joined the bipartisan coalition that enacted cutbacks in the Dodd-Frank banking regulatory law that had been enacted following the Wall Street meltdown. He joined the bipartisan Problem Solvers Caucus. "For too long we have fallen victim to partisan bickering and witnessed congressional inaction," he said. "Legislators must find practical, commonsense solutions to the nation's most pressing issues." A week after President Donald Trump took office, Gonzalez invited him to the Rio Grande Valley to discuss international trade policy. "I would appreciate having the opportunity to visit with you in a bipartisan way to discuss how commerce between the two nations affects border communities and the overall economy," he wrote to Trump. Instead, Trump visited other parts of the border to make other rhetorical points.

Following a meeting with Trump at the White House in January 2019, Gonzalez questioned the president's grasp of the border and called his comments "crazy" and "irrational," he said to the Houston Chronicle. "Just crazy stuff." He told the Rio Grande Guardian, an independent news service, that the root cause of the immigrant crisis was the failure of three governments in Central America — El Salvador, Guatemala and Honduras — which need economic and security aid. "Until we deal with that, we will continue to have problems," he said.

Following the 2018 election, he joined the Problem Solvers Caucus meetings with Nancy Pelosi, who needed their support to become Speaker. She agreed to the group's changes in House rules that were designed to produce more open debate. With the others, Gonzalez voted for Pelosi for Speaker.

TX-15: South Texas   **Cook Partisan Voting Index: D+7**

Population		Race and Ethnicity		Income	
Total	764,749	White	15.2%	Median Income	$42,713
Land area (sq. miles)	7,804	Black	1.7%	District Income Rank	396
Pop/ sq mi	98	Latino	81.5%	Poverty Rate	27.7%
Born in State	64.7%	Asian	1%	With health insurance	72.6%
		Two or more races	0.4%	Cash public assistance	1.9%
Age Groups		Other	0.1%	Food stamp/SNAP	25.9%
Under 18	31.5%				
18-34	24.3%	**Education**		**Work**	
35-64	33.4%	H.S grad or less	55.7%	White Collar	10.8%
Over 64	10.8%	Some college	25%	Sales and Service	47.5%
		College Degree, 4 yr	13.7%	Blue Collar	24.2%
Military		Post grad	5.6%	Government	18%
Veteran/ Active Duty	5.6%				

2012 Pres. Vote	Obama	86,941	(57%)	Romney	62,885	(42%)		
2016 Pres. Vote	Clinton	104,454	(57%)	Trump	73,689	(40%)	Johnson	4,501	(2%)

McAllen/San Antonio Corridor: A century ago, there was little but desert wilderness in the Lower Rio Grande Valley in South Texas. Only a handful of people lived anywhere near the shallow, sluggish Rio Grande. There was no U.S. Border Patrol because very few people wanted to venture across desert. Then came pioneers like Lloyd Bentsen Sr., father of the former senator and Treasury secretary, who arrived after World War I with $5 in his pocket and became one of the valley's biggest landowners; his son became a senator and Treasury secretary. Bentsen and others cleared the land and dug canals, hired Mexican and Mexican-American workers, and with irrigated water from the Rio Grande planted citrus groves, cornfields and palm windbreaks, ran cattle and drilled for oil and gas. Along U.S. 83, north of the Rio Grande, these pioneers built a string of towns with Anglo names and storefronts. But most of the people were Latino in culture and language.

The 15th Congressional District of Texas is one of three adjacent districts in the Lower Rio Grande Valley that run from the heavily populated areas along the border to just north of San Antonio; the 15th has a much smaller slice of the border than do the districts to the east and west. The days are past when ranchers and oilmen wielded absolute political power here. There is instead a robust, mostly Hispanic politics. The Hispanic population in the district is 82 percent, the second-highest in the state. Although the district includes the rural area between Corpus Christi and San Antonio, three-quarters of its residents live just north of the river in McAllen-based Hidalgo County. Reasonably priced real estate and wages that are higher than across the border contributed to fast-paced growth in the region. Hidalgo's population tripled since 1980 and increased 50 percent from 2000 to 2017, when it reached 860,000. Hidalgo has surpassed El Paso as the largest Texas metro area along the border.

The local infrastructure has barely kept up as subdivisions have replaced citrus groves. In the McAllen area, new suburbanites work just across the border in booming Reynosa as corporate managers in the low-wage "maquiladoras," or factories. Poverty is pervasive. As of 2017, 30 percent of residents lived below the poverty line, which was twice the state average. The abortion clinic in McAllen, which became a flashpoint in federal litigation over state-imposed restrictions, reopened in 2017. The region is struggling to handle crime from the trade in illegal immigration and drugs. A Gallup survey in 2014 found that McAllen had the highest rate of fear of walking alone at night. "This town built on immigration has become ground zero for the nation's nastiest political battle," The Washington Post reported in July 2018. The chain-link fenced detention center in the huge customs facility has been called the "dog kennel." The local bus terminal is "America's new Ellis Island," The New York Times wrote in the same month, though most of its arriving immigrants are effectively jailed, for a time at least.

The district is heavily Democratic in the border areas but more conservative elsewhere. Hillary Clinton carried the district with 57 percent in 2016. The 15th shares Hidalgo with the 28th and 34th Districts, but includes about 70 percent of the county population.

Veronica Escobar (D)

Elected 2018, 1st term, b. Sep 15, 1969; El Paso; University of Texas, El Paso, B.A., 1991; New York University, M.A., 1993; Catholic; Married (Michael Pleters); 2 children.

Elected Office: El Paso County Commissioner, 2007-2010.

Professional Career: El Pasoans Judge 2011-2017; Community Scholars, Executive Director; Communications Director, El Paso Mayor Raymond Caballero.

DC Office: 1505 LHOB 20515, 202-225-4831, escobar.house.gov

State Offices: El Paso, 915-541-1400.

Committees: *Armed Services*: Military Personnel; Readiness. *Judiciary*: Constitution, Civil Rights & Civil Liberties; Immigration & Citizenship.

Election Results

Election	Name (Party)	Vote (%)		Cand. Spent	Ind. Exp. Support	Ind. Exp. Oppose
2018 General	Veronica Escobar (D)	124,437	(69%)	$1,138,551	$325,905	
	Rick Seeberger (R)	49,127	(27%)	$44,807		
	Ben Mendoza (I)	8,147	(4%)	$0		
2018 Primary	Veronica Escobar (D)	30,630	(61%)			
	Dori Fenenbock (D)	10,992	(22%)			
	Norma Chavez (D)	3,325	(7%)			
	Enrique Garcia (D)	2,661	(5%)			

Democratic first-termer Veronica Escobar brought extensive experience in El Paso County politics, plus an independence at home that is similar to that of her predecessor, Beto O'Rourke, who stepped down in 2018 for his unsuccessful challenge to Sen. Ted Cruz. She and Sylvia Green, who was elected at the same time to an open seat in the Houston area, are the first Latina women from Texas elected to Congress. Representing a gateway that is on the border with Mexico, she had a strong interest in immigration issues and has been an outspoken critic of President Donald Trump's handling of those policies.

A native of the El Paso valley area, Escobar grew up near her family's dairy farm. She graduated from the University of Texas at El Paso, got her master's degree in English literature from New York University and returned home to teach Chicano literature at UTEP. She served as communications director to the El Paso mayor and was Executive Director for Community Scholars, a local non-profit organization that hired high school students to do public policy research.

When she entered public office as a county commissioner, Escobar kept her distance from the local Democratic Party, which she viewed as resistant to change and to newcomers. "The local Democratic Party has been very fractured and not as inclusive as I think it should have been," she told the El Paso Inc. website in a 2011 interview. In 2010 she was elected El Paso County judge, the chief executive manager, and held that position for seven years until she stepped down to run for Congress.

In the primary for the open seat, her chief opponent was Dori Fenenbock, a former El Paso School Board president. With the endorsement of O'Rourke plus several national Democratic-allied and progressive organizations, Escobar was the early frontrunner. Each contender spent about $1 million and they ran a spirited contest. Escobar cited her record in cleaning up and modernizing county government, and in addressing border issues such as immigration and trade. In the spirit of Sen. Bernie Sanders, she supported single-payer health care and free college tuition for those who need it. She criticized Trump as "nothing short of dangerous" and said that "injustice is at our doorstep."

Fenenbock, a former Republican and a self-styled moderate, criticized Escobar for "hypocrisy" on immigration issues. She cited the fact that Escobar's husband, Michael Pleters, became a federal immigration judge after Trump took office. Escobar criticized the negative tactics and responded that Pleters, a former state and federal prosecutor, was initially approached for the position during the Obama administration and that his job was not a political appointment. Fenenbock's supporters created a Keep El Paso Honest PAC and she was backed by former Rep. Silvestre Reyes, who served in Congress for eight terms before O'Rourke unexpectedly defeated him in the Democratic primary in 2012.

Escobar won the March primary with 61 percent of the vote to 22 percent for Fenenbock. Four other candidates split the remainder. In an April interview with The Texas Tribune, Escobar said that Trump was not fit to be president because of his "rampant corruption and collusion," and that he should be impeached. She added that Latino voters were a "sleeping giant" — a longstanding political prediction, especially in Texas — and that the "perfect combination" of inspiration and anger had motivated her and many other Democratic women to seek office in 2018. In a district that Hillary Clinton won with 68 percent in 2016, Escobar defeated Republican Rick Seeberger with that same vote share.

TX-16: El Paso area   **Cook Partisan Voting Index: D+17**

Population		Race and Ethnicity		Income	
Total	734,516	White	13.8%	Median Income	$44,891
Land area (sq. miles)	710	Black	3.4%	District Income Rank	373
Pop/ sq mi	1034	Latino	80.2%	Poverty Rate	20.4%
Born in State	56.5%	Asian	1.2%	With health insurance	79%
		Two or more races	1%	Cash public assistance	2.5%
Age Groups		Other	0.4%	Food stamp/SNAP	20.7%
Under 18	27.6%				
18-34	26.3%	**Education**		**Work**	
35-64	34.5%	H.S grad or less	44.5%	White Collar	11.6%
Over 64	11.6%	Some college	31.5%	Sales and Service	47.9%
		College Degree, 4 yr	16.3%	Blue Collar	20%
Military		Post grad	7.7%	Government	20.4%
Veteran/ Active Duty	12.2%				

2012 Pres. Vote	Obama	100,993	(64%)	Romney	54,315	(35%)		
2016 Pres. Vote	Clinton	130,784	(68%)	Trump	52,334	(27%)	Johnson	6,900	(4%)

El Paso: El Paso Texas and Ciudad Juaréz Mexico face each other across the narrow Rio Grande, their tree-shaded streets spread out below the rough brown face of Comanche Peak. Downtown El Paso is only a few blocks from the bridge to Ciudad Juaréz. The two border cities are surrounded by hundreds of miles of some of North America's most rugged and desolate landscape. El Paso is closer to San Diego than to Houston, and it's in a different time zone from the rest of the state. Still, the region has grown significantly. In the 1950s, El Paso and Ciudad Juaréz each had a population around 130,000. In 2017, there were 840,000 people in El Paso County (including 684,000 in the city of El Paso), 83 percent of them Hispanic; the Mexican census counted 1.4 million in metro Juaréz. This is a bilingual, bicultural pair of cities, where most people have a Mexican heritage.

El Paso is one of the lowest-wage and lowest-education locales in the United States, though statistically it has been one of the safest, with the lowest crime rate of any large U.S. city. After President Donald Trump in his February 2019 State of the Union message said that El Paso "used to have extremely high rates of violent crime" before the barrier along the border was reinforced, Mayor Dee Margo said that he was "wrong." Ciudad Juaréz, though struggling with drug cartel violence and crime, is one of the highest-wage cities in Mexico. At the border, undocumented immigrants released by the Immigration and Customs Enforcement agency have overwhelmed shelters and other services. In February 2019, the Trump administration announced plans to build a huge migrant processing center in the next few months.

In the wake of the North American Free Trade Agreement, maquiladora factories enhanced the cross-border economy. Much of the local economy is built on cheap, low-skill labor. South of the border, there is a large General Motors technical center The other important factor sustaining the economy has been Fort Bliss, which had a $5 billion expansion following the 2005 base closing review; as of December 2018, Bliss had 39,000 military personnel, more than 40,000 family members and nearly 13,000 civilian employees. The base is home to the First Armored Division and covers 1,700 square miles, which is nearly four times the size of Delaware. One in three jobs in El Paso depends directly or indirectly on Fort Bliss. There has been deep concern about the potentially devastating impact of another base-closing review. Most of the local job growth has been in leisure and hospitality. Only 77 percent of El Paso County residents are high school graduates.

The 16th Congressional District of Texas is based entirely in El Paso County — the city itself, the suburban fringe, Fort Bliss to the north, and rural housing settlements known as colonias, most without electricity and running water, spreading out to the east and south. The district is solidly Democratic. The remaining 9 percent of El Paso voters are in the sprawling 23rd District. In 2016, Hillary Clinton won the 16th with 68 percent of the vote.

Bill Flores (R)

Elected 2010, 5th term, b. Feb 25, 1954; Warren Air Force Base, Cheyenne, WY; Texas A and M University, B.B.A., 1976; Houston Baptist University (TX), M.B.A., 1985; Baptist; Married (Gina Flores); 2 children; 2 grandchildren.

Professional Career: Keyes Offshore, 1980-1990; Marine Drilling, 1990-1997; Western Atlas, 1997-1998; Gryphon Exploration, 2001-2005; Accountant, financial Manager, Phoenix Exploration, 2006-2009.

DC Office: 2228 RHOB 20515, 202-225-6105, Fax: 202-225-0350, flores.house.gov

State Offices: Austin, 512-373-3378; Bryan, 979-703-4037; Waco, 254-732-0748.

Committees: *Budget. Energy & Commerce*: Communications & Technology; Energy; Environment & Climate Change.

Group Ratings

	ADA	ACLU	AFL-CIO	LCV	ITI	COC	HAFA	ACU	CFG	FRC
2018	-	4%	-	3%	-	91%	71%	88%	60%	100%
2017	0%	C	3%	0%	C	93%	C	96%	85%	100%

Almanac Ratings 2017-18

	Economy	Social	Foreign	Composite
Liberal	3%	4%	0%	2%
Conservative	97%	97%	100%	98%

Key Votes of the 115th Congress

1. Obama-care revision	Y	5. Family planning regs	Y	9. Guantanamo prisoners	N
2. Tax Cuts	Y	6. Body cameras/immigration	N	10. Ground missiles, limit	N
3. Omnibus appropriations	Y	7. Abortion ban	Y	11. Defense Dept. spending	Y
4. Dodd-Frank revision	Y	8. Concealed carry	Y	12. FISA rules	Y

Election Results

Election	Name (Party)	Vote (%)		Cand. Spent	Ind. Exp. Support	Ind. Exp. Oppose
2018 General	Bill Flores (R)	134,841	(57%)	$1,271,930		
	Rick Kennedy (D)	98,070	(41%)	$78,555		
2018 Primary	Bill Flores (R)		(100%)			

Prior winning percentages: 2016 (61%), 2014 (65%), 2012 (80%), 2010 (62%)

Republican Bill Flores, a retired oil and gas executive, won his seat in 2010 by defeating a longtime Democratic incumbent and GOP nemesis. He has zealously guarded home-state interests with a seat on the Energy and Commerce Committee. As chairman of the conservative Republican Study Committee for two years, Flores showed establishment leanings. He rejected that characterization, though dissidents then created the outspoken Freedom Caucus. He has continued to keep his distance.

Flores was born at Warren Air Force Base in Cheyenne Wyoming. After his father's military tour of duty, the family moved back to Stratford, in the northern tip of the Texas Panhandle. From age 9, he helped work cattle on the family's ranch. Flores helped pay his way through Texas A&M, where he was a member of the student body government and the honor guard. He has remained active as an alumnus, donating millions of dollars to fund scholarships. After graduation, he went to work for the KPMG accounting firm and built a career as a financial manager for several large corporations, eventually settling in the oil and gas industry in Houston. He was president and chief executive officer of Phoenix Exploration.

In 2010, he had four opponents in the Republican primary. After leading 2008 GOP nominee Rob Curnock in the first round, 33%-29%, Flores won the runoff, 65%-35%. He ran against Rep. Chet Edwards, the final remaining "yellow dog" Texas Democrat, a 20-year incumbent. Edwards' standing with conservatives was damaged when House Speaker Nancy Pelosi in 2008 mentioned him as a possible Democratic vice presidential candidate. Flores targeted Edwards' vote for the 2009 economic stimulus bill. And he emphasized his own business credentials, saying that he would bring to Congress the discipline of a successful accountant. Edwards spent $3.8 million and Flores $3.3 million (including $1.5 million of his own money). Flores won by an impressive 62%-37%, carrying all but one small county.

Flores' first bills were measures to set more stringent deadlines for government approval of offshore oil and gas drilling and to extend for 12 months all leases in the Gulf of Mexico affected by Interior Department's drilling moratoriums after the massive BP spill. He successfully amended several House-passed bills to block a provision in the 2007 energy law promoting the use of alternative fuels in federal vehicles. He took heat from constituents at home for voting in 2011 to raise the federal debt limit, but opposed the tax and spending compromise in 2013 to avoid the so-called "fiscal cliff." With his seat on Energy and Commerce, the former oil executive pursued energy issues. In 2015, he joined a bipartisan coalition that sought to reduce the mandate for ethanol use by vehicles. In 2017, he worked with others on the committee to win mostly party-line House passage of legislation to improve the coordination of pipeline permits by federal and state officials, including lessons learned from the handling of the controversial Keystone XL pipeline.

Flores became active in the Republican Study Committee, which had been the caucus of the most conservative House members. He ran for chairman after the 2014 election, after years in which the RSC often spent more time attacking other Republicans than Democrats. He sought a less adversarial relationship that would still push the party agenda to the right. His chief foe was South Carolina Rep. Mick Mulvaney, an outspoken member of the GOP class first elected in 2010. After the easy victory by Flores, which was encouraged by allies of Speaker John Boehner, Mulvaney and other mavericks created the Freedom Caucus to give them a separate forum to challenge party leaders. Later, Mulvaney joined the Trump administration as director of the Office of Management and Budget and then White House chief of staff.

As RSC chairman, Flores laid out a policy agenda for the RSC that was based on five principles: expand economic opportunity, fix Washington's fiscal mess, rebuild national security, protect American values and "restrict the federal government to its constitutionally limited role." After the 2016 election, he ran for vice chairman of the Republican Conference, but was defeated by Doug Collins of Georgia. In May 2018, Flores took on the GOP renegades for their opposition to the farm bill. "The Freedom Caucus was against welfare reform," he told The Hill. "They're against farmers, too." He showed his own independence from Republican dogma following the October 2017 mass shooting during a concert in Las Vegas. With Texas Sen. John Cornyn, Flores called for a federal ban on bump stocks that can enhance the firing power of semiautomatic firearms.

Flores has been an occasional critic of Donald Trump. In the 2016 campaign, he cited the "inappropriate attacks" by Trump on a federal judge as a reason why he withheld support after Trump had wrapped up the nomination. Later, Flores endorsed him at the GOP convention. In July 2017, he told a Texas radio station, "it would be in the president's best interests if he removed all of his children from the White House," adding that they caused "some distractions."

At home, Flores had a primary challenge in 2016 from Ralph Patterson, an ordained Baptist deacon who had chaired the McLennan County Republican Party. Patterson spent $403,000 to $1.5 million for Flores, who won, 72%-18%. In 2018, he had no primary opposition and got 57 percent in his routine reelection contest. Consistent with the reduced Republican vote across Texas, that was the lowest share in his five elections.

TX-17: Central Texas   **Cook Partisan Voting Index: R+12**

Population		Race and Ethnicity		Income	
Total	750,555	White	55.1%	Median Income	$51,151
Land area (sq. miles)	7,651	Black	12.7%	District Income Rank	285
Pop/ sq mi	98.1	Latino	25.4%	Poverty Rate	18.4%
Born in State	66.8%	Asian	4.7%	With health insurance	85.1%
		Two or more races	1.8%	Cash public assistance	1.7%
Age Groups		Other	0.3%	Food stamp/SNAP	10.8%
Under 18	23.1%				
18-34	30.6%	Education		Work	
35-64	34.4%	H.S grad or less	40%	White Collar	11.9%
Over 64	11.9%	Some college	30.2%	Sales and Service	41.2%
		College Degree, 4 yr	18.9%	Blue Collar	21.3%
Military		Post grad	10.8%	Government	18.2%
Veteran/ Active Duty	7.5%				

2012 Pres. Vote	Romney	135,309	(60%)	Obama	84,531	(38%)			
2016 Pres. Vote	Trump	139,415	(56%)	Clinton	96,156	(38%)	Johnson	10,055	(4%)

Waco, College Station: Waco, about midway between Dallas and Austin, is deep in the heart of Texas. In the late 19th century, it was one of the largest cotton markets in the world, a rip-roaring town with legalized prostitution. In 1870, Waco opened across the Brazos River what was then the largest single-span suspension bridge in the United States. It became the main depot along the Chisholm Trail, which cattlemen used to drive their longhorns north to Kansas stockyards. In 1885, a Waco pharmacist concocted the first Dr. Pepper. The city has embarked on an "Imagine Waco" program to restore a walkable downtown; development along the riverfront also is underway. The city's growing tourism business, with many conventions and attractive vacation sites, in 2017 surpassed that of Austin. It had been the site of "Fixer Upper," the popular HGTV program about home-buying.

The 17th Congressional District of Texas includes all of eight counties and parts of four more, but centers on Waco and all of McLennan County, which has a third of the district's population. The southwestern tip of the district covers a small slice of northern Austin and most of socially diverse suburban Pflugerville, whose population jumped from 4,400 in 1990 to more than 63,000 residents in 2017. The other population center is Brazos County, whose largest city, College Station, is home to Texas A&M University, with nearly 70,000 students; Brazos is entirely in the 17th and is one-fourth of the population. The school's agricultural and military traditions have given it a much more conservative ambience than the similarly selective University of Texas at Austin. College Station, the sixth fastest-growing city in the nation in 2018, is the site of the George H.W. Bush Presidential Library, where the former president enjoyed spending time during his final years. Both he and his wife, Barbara, died in 2018. Following funeral services in Houston, each was interred at the site, along with their daughter Robin, who died of leukemia at age three.

The political tradition in Central Texas for more than a century after the Civil War was heavily Democratic. As recently as 1990, it voted Democratic for governor, supporting Waco native Ann Richards. Since then, the district has followed most of non-urban Texas to the Republican Party. The arm of the district that extends into Austin and Travis County is its heavily Democratic enclave. The 17th is one of five Republican-held districts that slice up small parts of the area surrounding Austin. Donald Trump won 56 percent of the district-wide vote in 2016.

Sheila Jackson Lee (D)

Elected 1994, 13th term, b. Jan 12, 1950; Jamaica, NY; New York University; Yale University (CT), B.A., 1972; University of Virginia Law School, J.D., 1975; Seventh-Day Adventist; Married (Elwyn C. Lee); 2 children; 2 grandchildren.

Elected Office: Houston City Council, 1990-1994.

Professional Career: Practicing attorney, 1975-1977, 1978-1987; Staff counsel, U.S. House Select Assassinations Committee, 1977-1978; Houston Association municipal judge, 1987-1990.

DC Office: 2079 RHOB 20515, 202-225-3816, Fax: 202-225-3317, jacksonlee.house.gov

State Offices: Houston, 713-691-4882; Houston, 713-861-4070; Houston, 713-655-0050; Houston, 713-227-7740.

Committees: *Budget. Homeland Security:* Cybersecurity, Infrastructure Protection & Innovation; Intelligence & Counterterrorism. *Judiciary:* Constitution, Civil Rights & Civil Liberties; Crime, Terrorism & Homeland Security; Immigration & Citizenship.

Group Ratings

	ADA	ACLU	AFL-CIO	LCV	ITI	COC	HAFA	ACU	CFG	FRC
2018	-	88%	-	97%	-	50%	2%	4%	5%	0%
2017	95%	C	100%	94%	C	38%	C	0%	0%	0%

Almanac Ratings 2017-18

	Economy	Social	Foreign	Composite
Liberal	93%	98%	92%	95%
Conservative	7%	2%	8%	5%

Key Votes of the 115th Congress

1. Obama-care revision	N	5. Family planning regs	N	9. Guantanamo prisoners	Y
2. Tax Cuts	N	6. Body cameras/immigration	Y	10. Ground missiles, limit	Y
3. Omnibus appropriations	N	7. Abortion ban	N	11. Defense Dept. spending	Y
4. Dodd-Frank revision	N	8. Concealed carry	N	12. FISA rules	N

Election Results

Election	Name (Party)	Vote (%)		Cand. Spent	Ind. Exp. Support	Ind. Exp. Oppose
2018 General	Sheila Jackson Lee (D)	138,704	(75%)	$642,233	$15,000	
	Ava Pate (R)	38,368	(21%)	$9,737		
	Luke Spencer (Lib)	4,067	(2%)	$6,268		
2018 Primary	Sheila Jackson Lee (D)	34,514	(86%)			
	Richard Johnson (D)	5,604	(14%)			

Prior winning percentages: 2016 (74%), 2014 (72%), 2012 (75%), 2010 (70%), 2008 (77%), 2006 (77%), 2004 (89%), 2002 (77%), 2000 (77%), 1998 (90%), 1996 (77%), 1994 (74%)

Sheila Jackson Lee, a Democrat first elected in 1994 and long known for her high staff turnover, gave up a senior subcommittee chairmanship in January 2019 following serious allegations involving her aides. Still, she remained outspoken in her committee work. Jackson Lee remains hugely popular at home, always winning at least 70 percent of the vote in elections and rarely facing a primary challenge.

A native of Queens New York, Jackson Lee graduated from Yale University and the University of Virginia law school. She practiced law in Houston, where she was a local judge and won two terms as an at-large member of the Houston City Council. After a local term-limits law took effect in 1994, she ran against Democratic Rep. Craig Washington, a talented but iconoclastic legislator. He had voted against funding for the space station, a source of many local jobs, and against the 1993 North American Free Trade Agreement, which was a boon to Houston's port traffic. Jackson Lee supported NAFTA and raised a lot of money from business interests that favored it. She won the primary, 63%-37%, and swept the general election.

The Almanac vote ratings have shown that Jackson Lee has shifted toward the center of the House in each of the three issue areas. She has been among the most prolific members of the House in proposing bills and offering amendments on the floor. In 2017-18, she filed 65 bills. Typically, her measures call for studies on one topic or another, add small amounts to spending bills, or are noncontroversial, such as one that called on Afghanistan to prohibit the use of children as soldiers. She told the Houston Chronicle that while she can ruffle feathers, she is unflagging in her desire to serve constituents. "I just want to be called an Energizer bunny that keeps on working for the people of this great district," she said.

Jackson Lee has been active on the Homeland Security Committee, especially the Border and Maritime Security Subcommittee, an assignment that suits a port city. In 2016, one of her bills was enacted. It required the Transportation Security Administration to make a comprehensive risk analysis of security threat assessment procedures for vessels and maritime facilities. In 2015 and again in 2017, the House passed her bill to require the Homeland Security Department to prepare a report on the effectiveness and availability of first responders in the case of a terrorist threat or attack.

On the Judiciary Committee, she has faced conflicting tensions from Latino constituents, who favor more generous treatment of immigrants, and African-American constituents, who see immigrants as competition for jobs. She frequently has taken the pro-immigrant side. She favors an increase in visas and access to permanent resident status. As ranking Democrat on the Subcommittee on Crime, Terrorism, Homeland Security, and Investigations for several years, Jackson Lee introduced the "Build Trust Act," which was intended to decrease the excessive reliance by some local governments on traffic fines and court costs to generate revenue to fund operations.

In January 2019, news stories reported that a former aide to the Congressional Black Caucus Foundation, which Jackson Lee chaired, had filed a lawsuit against the foundation and Jackson Lee's office, claiming that she had been wrongly fired in March 2018. The ex-staffer alleged that her supervisor at the foundation had sexually assaulted her in 2015, when she was a 19-year-old student.

Jackson Lee denied any wrongdoing on her part, including retribution against the aide, and she said that she would be exonerated. But she stepped down from her position with the foundation. And she relinquished, at least temporarily, her chairmanship of the Crime Subcommittee; that position went to Rep. Karen Bass of California, who also chairs the Congressional Black Caucus. House Democrats reportedly were prepared to strip Jackson Lee of her assignments if she did not step aside. An advocacy group supporting the victims of domestic violence said that Jackson Lee should no longer handle legislation dealing with violence against women.

Jackson Lee has been outspoken in her opposition to Donald Trump. At the Democratic convention in 2016, she delivered a speech in which she called him "a man of fear" and "willfully ignorant to the outcry of young people who want real criminal justice reform." In January 2017, during the usually routine joint session of Congress that certifies the Electoral College count, she led several House members who protested the vote count in some states. When she failed to get the required support of at least one senator, Vice President Joe Biden overruled her objections. In February 2019, she issued a statement that she would "hold this presidential administration accountable" on the various charges against Trump and that members of the Judiciary Committee "are not joking around about oversight." She also called for reparations for African-Americans and filed a House resolution to create a commission to study the concept.

In 2010, Jackson Lee faced a primary challenge from Houston City Councilman Jarvis Johnson, who cited her reputation as difficult to work with, and local lawyer Sean Roberts. Neither came remotely close to her in fundraising. She released an endorsement from President Barack Obama calling her "a tireless champion for Houston's working families." She drew 67 percent of the vote to Johnson's 28 percent and Roberts' 5 percent. She did not face another primary challenge until 2018, when she took 85 percent against Richard Johnson, an aide to a Houston-area state representative.

TX-18: Harris County   **Cook Partisan Voting Index: D+27**

Population		Race and Ethnicity		Income	
Total	766,074	White	16.3%	Median Income	$44,527
Land area (sq. miles)	235	Black	36.8%	District Income Rank	382
Pop/ sq mi	3257.1	Latino	41.8%	Poverty Rate	22.7%
Born in State	60.1%	Asian	3.7%	With health insurance	76.4%
		Two or more races	1.1%	Cash public assistance	2.4%
Age Groups		Other	0.4%	Food stamp/SNAP	19.7%
Under 18	26.7%				
18-34	28.2%	**Education**		**Work**	
35-64	36.1%	H.S grad or less	51.4%	White Collar	9%
Over 64	9%	Some college	26.8%	Sales and Service	43.6%
		College Degree, 4 yr	13.9%	Blue Collar	27.4%
Military		Post grad	7.9%	Government	10.7%
Veteran/ Active Duty	4.6%				

2012 Pres. Vote	Obama	150,129	(76%)	Romney	44,991	(23%)			
2016 Pres. Vote	Clinton	157,117	(76%)	Trump	41,011	(20%)	Johnson	5,346	(3%)

Central and Northern Houston: Within its sprawling boundaries, Houston contains income and wealth disparities as striking as any city in America, the product of an expanding city with dynamic economic growth, a high rate of immigration and the absence of centralized planning. The contrast is most obvious at the edge of Houston's gleaming downtown. Just blocks from the Heritage Plaza, Pennzoil and Bank of America buildings, and the sports complexes for baseball's Astros and basketball's Rockets are slums where many people live in unpainted frame houses with cracks wide enough to let in Houston's humid, smoggy air.

Until the 1960s, Houston had a Third World economy. It was a low-skill producer of basic commodities, where a few got rich and many lived near subsistence level. Since then, Houston has built a high-tech economy offering myriad opportunities and a wider range of economic outcomes. It has also greatly expanded its international trade. Many of Houston's African Americans and Hispanics have moved to comfortable middle-class neighborhoods. In 2007, Hispanics for the first time outnumbered Anglos in Harris County, which grew 20 percent from 2000 to 2010 and another 14 percent from 2010 to 2017. Houston accounts for about half of the county. With its rapid growth, it was expected to surpass Chicago as the third-largest city in the nation by about 2025. By 2050, state demographers project, Houston will be 60 percent Hispanic and 15 percent black. (In 2017, the 45 percent Hispanic population doubled the 23 percent black share.)

While oil has remained king, the city has diversified economically. In 2015, Forbes ranked Houston as the fastest-growing city in the nation. In 2018, the metro area led the nation in new construction jobs. The city's long tradition of limited urban planning has drawn growing criticism, especially following the devastation in August 2017 of Hurricane Harvey — the third "500-year flood" to hit the city in three years. The contrasts between rich and poor remain. In a 2014 report, the Brookings Institution ranked Houston 11th among cities with the highest income inequality. The diversity also has applied to local elections. With the retirement of three-term Mayor Annise Parker, one of the first mayors in the nation who was openly gay, voters in 2015 selected African-American state Sen. Sylvester Turner over Republican Bill King, a longtime local businessman, 50.2%-49.8%. In 2018, Republican Ed Emmett, who had been county judge (the chief executive position) since 2007, was defeated by 27-year-old Lina Hidalgo, a Democrat and native of Colombia.

The 18th Congressional District of Texas contains Houston's downtown area and the African-American and Latino neighborhoods immediately south of it. The district has two arms running beyond Loop 610 and nearly encircling the city — one is northeast, between the Eastex Freeway and Beaumont Freeway, and the larger one is northwest, between the Northwest Freeway and Interstate 45, extending east to take in George Bush Intercontinental Airport. African Americans make up a declining 37 percent of the district's population and Hispanics a rising 42 percent. This is the third most Democratic district in Texas. Hillary Clinton got 76 percent of the vote here in 2016.

Jodey Arrington (R)

Elected 2016, 2nd term, b. Mar 09, 1972; Kansas City, MO; Texas Tech University, B.A., 1994; Texas Tech University, M.P.A., 1997; Georgetown University-McDonough School of Business, 2004; Presbyterian; Married (Anne Arrington); 3 children.

Professional Career: Special Assistant, President George W. Bush, 2001; Chief of Staff, FDIC Chairman Don Powell, 2001-2005; Deputy Federal Coordinator, COO, Office of the Federal Coordinator for Gulf Cost Rebuilding, 2005-2006; Administrator, Texas Tech University, 2007-2014.

DC Office: 1029 LHOB 20515, 202-225-4005, Fax: 202-225-9615, arrington.house.gov

State Offices: Abilene, 325-675-9779; Lubbock, 806-763-1611.

Committees: *Ways & Means*: Select Revenue Measures; Social Security.

Group Ratings

	ADA	ACLU	AFL-CIO	LCV	ITI	COC	HAFA	ACU	CFG	FRC
2018	-	4%	-	0%	-	83%	78%	92%	59%	100%
2017	5%	C	5%	0%	C	92%	C	93%	83%	100%

Almanac Ratings 2017-18

	Economy	Social	Foreign	Composite
Liberal	2%	3%	0%	2%
Conservative	99%	97%	100%	98%

Key Votes of the 115th Congress

1. Obama-care revision	Y	5. Family planning regs	Y	9. Guantanamo prisoners	N
2. Tax Cuts	Y	6. Body cameras/immigration	N	10. Ground missiles, limit	N
3. Omnibus appropriations	Y	7. Abortion ban	Y	11. Defense Dept. spending	Y
4. Dodd-Frank revision	Y	8. Concealed carry	Y	12. FISA rules	Y

Election Results

Election	Name (Party)	Vote (%)		Cand. Spent	Ind. Exp. Support	Ind. Exp. Oppose
2018 General	Jodey Arrington (R)................. 151,946	(75%)		$603,941		
	Miguel Levario (D)....................... 50,039	(25%)		$89,304		
2018 Primary	Jodey Arrington (R).....................	(100%)				

Prior winning percentages: 2016 (87%)

Republican Jodey Arrington was elected in 2016 to an open seat. His narrow win in the primary runoff was tantamount to victory in this Republican stronghold. Arrington benefited from strong political connections, which resulted from his extended experience as an aide to President George W. Bush. In his second term, he got a seat on the Ways and Means Committee.

Arrington was born in Plainview, where his father was a farm equipment salesman. He earned a bachelor's and a master's degree in public administration from Texas Tech University. A high school tennis player, he was a walk-on player for the Red Raider football team. Soon after that, he joined the staff of then-Gov. Bush as a manager of appointments in state government. After Bush was elected president, Arrington become a White House special assistant to the president and associate director of presidential personnel. He was among the White House staffers who were evacuated from the building on September 11, 2001. He specialized in appointments relating to energy, the environment and natural resources. Late that year, he became chief of staff to the chairman of the Federal Deposit Insurance Corporation, who was a native of Amarillo.

In 2002, Arrington returned to Texas to become chief of staff for the Texas Tech University System, which has more than 40,000 students and a budget of about $1.3 billion. Initially, he worked for Chancellor Kent Hance, who had defeated Bush a quarter-century earlier in a campaign for Congress. Later, he was appointed vice chancellor of research and commercialization, where he helped to spur the university's growth. In 2014, he ran for the state Senate and lost the

Republican primary, 53%-30%. In the private sector, he became president of Scott Laboratories, which commercializes health care innovations.

When Rep. Randy Neugebauer retired, nine Republican candidates ran for the open seat. The chief contenders, in addition to Arrington, were Glen Robertson, who was completing four years as mayor of Lubbock, and Michael Bob Starr, who had been commander of Dyess Air Force Base near Abilene. In the first round of the primary, Starr got 48 percent of the vote in Abilene-based Taylor County. Arrington and Robertson each got 30 percent in Lubbock County, which was the base for both. The district-wide vote in the primary gave 27 percent to Arrington, 26 percent to Robertson and 21 percent to Starr, with the top two advancing to the runoff.

Arrington touted his support from Bush and many of his advisers, plus former Gov. Rick Perry, and said that he was the candidate who best represented "conservative values." Robertson said he had more political experience as mayor and as a local businessman for 38 years. Robertson had an edge in campaign spending with $1.8 million, of which 90 percent was self-financed. Arrington spent $1.3 million during the cycle. He won, 54%-46%, and led in both Lubbock and Taylor counties. In November, no Democrat had filed and Arrington took 87 percent of the vote. In 2018, he coasted to reelection. He faced no primary challenge and won 75 percent of the vote against Democrat Miguel Levario.

In the House, Arrington was assigned to the Agriculture Committee, his first choice. He said that a priority on the farm bill was the resumption of commodity coverage for cotton. That objective was bolstered by committee Chairman Mike Conaway representing the neighboring 11th District, which also is heavily rural. "I want to carry his water, help him any way I can," Arrington said. His cotton provision, with detailed specifications, was included as a rider in a disaster-relief appropriation bill that was enacted in February 2018. It restored the price support, which had been overturned in 2014 in a ruling by the World Trade Organization. The cotton crop in Texas exceeds $2 billion in annual value.

His prized seat on Ways and Means, Arrington said, expands the influence of West Texas and "the decibel of the voice of rural America." He told the Abilene Reporter News that he would "fight for free-market policies" that encourage energy production. In March 2019, Arrington welcomed the decision by the Air Force to select Dyess Air Force Base in Abilene as the only base that will house the operational test squadron and the weapons training school for the prospective B-21 bomber. The action, he said, "secures the future of Dyess as a bomber base in the 21st century."

TX-19: West Texas   **Cook Partisan Voting Index: R+27**

Population		Race and Ethnicity		Income	
Total	721,822	White	54.3%	Median Income	$48,548
Land area (sq. miles)	25,836	Black	5.9%	District Income Rank	332
Pop/ sq mi	27.9	Latino	36.5%	Poverty Rate	17.3%
Born in State	72.7%	Asian	1.4%	With health insurance	83%
		Two or more races	1.5%	Cash public assistance	1.4%
Age Groups		Other	0.5%	Food stamp/SNAP	13%
Under 18	24.9%				
18-34	27.8%	**Education**		**Work**	
35-64	34%	H.S grad or less	48%	White Collar	13.3%
Over 64	13.3%	Some college	30.2%	Sales and Service	43.2%
		College Degree, 4 yr	14.4%	Blue Collar	25.1%
Military		Post grad	7.5%	Government	16.4%
Veteran/ Active Duty	8%				

2012 Pres. Vote	Romney	160,058	(74%)	Obama	54,448	(25%)		
2016 Pres. Vote	Trump	165,384	(72%)	Clinton	53,519	(23%)	Johnson	7,849	(3%)

Lubbock, Abilene: Until water was discovered in the giant Ogallala Aquifer that lies under Lubbock and its environs, this was Indian country, a land of Army forts and cattle ranches. When the water was tapped, well into the 20th century, what had been grazing land suddenly became cotton-growing territory, with green crops grown in circles where the sprinklers reached and parched ground beyond. Lubbock became a regional center, the home of Texas Tech University, and grew rapidly at mid-century. Lubbock County's population increased from 101,000 in 1950 to 156,000 in 1960. Since then, the regional economy has grown more slowly, though it had a 9 percent gain from 2010 to 2017, when the county's population reached 305,000. Nearby Gaines County has led the nation in cotton production. Cotton growers have struggled with international competitors and adverse trade rulings, as well as pressure to reduce agricultural subsidies. The region's economy is strong. Lubbock and nearby counties have made an outsized contribution to American popular culture with a disproportionate share of renowned musicians, including Buddy Holly, Tanya Tucker, Jimmy Dean, Waylon Jennings, Mac Davis, Roy Orbison and the Dixie Chicks' Natalie Maines.

Nearly 200 miles southeast of Lubbock, over gully-ridden territory, are Abilene and the surrounding Big Country, with ranches specializing in Angora goats and sheep and exotic animals like ostriches, emus and aoudad sheep. Sweetwater, near Abilene, features an annual "rattlesnake roundup," with a noise from thousands of snakes that apparently can be fearsome. There also are cotton fields, pecan trees, mesquite and many oil wells. Some of the nation's B-1 bombers are stationed at Dyess Air Force Base. In 2018, Texas officials advocated Dyess as the principal training base for the B-21 long-range bomber, which is scheduled for delivery in the mid-2020s. Abilene is a college town, but the culture is conservative as the three most prominent schools -- Abilene Christian University, Hardin-Simmons University and McMurry University -- are all religiously affiliated. Like other parts of Texas, Abilene has become a haven for resettlement of refugees, mostly from Africa. In 2017, about 1,200 resided in Abilene, a city of 120,000.

The 19th Congressional District of Texas takes in the Lubbock and Abilene areas. The two counties combined account for about 62 percent of the district's population. In 1978, this part of West Texas was Democratic enough that in an open-seat election, voters rejected the candidacy of a young Midland oilman named George W. Bush in favor of Lubbock Democrat Kent Hance. Today, the area is heavily Republican. Bush received 77 percent of the vote in his 2004 reelection, and Republican candidate Mitt Romney won the district with 74 percent in 2012 — among their highest scores in the nation. In 2016, the vote for Donald Trump dipped to 72 percent; that was eight percentage points less than his vote in the 13th District to the north, which can be explained partly by the larger Hispanic population in the 19th.

Joaquin Castro (D)

Elected 2012, 4th term, b. Sep 16, 1974; San Antonio; Stanford University (CA), A.B., 1996; Harvard University Law School (MA), J.D., 2000; Roman Catholic; Married (Anna Flores); 2 children.

Elected Office: TX House, 2003-2013.

Professional Career: Practicing attorney, 2000-2013.

DC Office: 2241 RHOB 20515, 202-225-3236, Fax: 202-225-1915, castro.house.gov

State Offices: San Antonio, 210-348-8216.

Committees: *Education & Labor*: Higher Education & Workforce Investment. *Foreign Affairs*: Europe, Eurasia, Energy & the Environment; Western Hemisphere, Civilian Security, & Trade. *Permanent Select on Intelligence*: Counterterrorism, Counterintelligence & Counterproliferation; Intelligence Modernization & Readiness.

Group Ratings

	ADA	ACLU	AFL-CIO	LCV	ITI	COC	HAFA	ACU	CFG	FRC
2018	-	86%	-	97%	-	50%	8%	8%	15%	0%
2017	90%	C	92%	100%	C	50%	C	4%	3%	11%

Almanac Ratings 2017-18

	Economy	Social	Foreign	Composite
Liberal	96%	100%	95%	97%
Conservative	5%	0%	5%	3%

Key Votes of the 115th Congress

1. Obama-care revision	N	5. Family planning regs	N	9. Guantanamo prisoners	Y
2. Tax Cuts	N	6. Body cameras/immigration	Y	10. Ground missiles, limit	Y
3. Omnibus appropriations	N	7. Abortion ban	N	11. Defense Dept. spending	Y
4. Dodd-Frank revision	N	8. Concealed carry	N	12. FISA rules	N

Election Results

Election	Name (Party)	Vote (%)	Cand. Spent	Ind. Exp. Support	Ind. Exp. Oppose
2018 General	Joaquin Castro (D)......................... 139,038	(81%)	$678,340		
	Jeffrey Blunt (Lib).................................. 32,925	(19%)			
2018 Primary	Joaquin Castro (D).......................	(100%)			

Prior winning percentages: 2016 (80%), 2014 (76%), 2012 (64%)

Democrat Joaquin Castro was elected to his San Antonio-based seat in 2012. As a young, telegenic Hispanic, he gained prominence along with his twin brother, Julián, who became a candidate for the 2020 Democratic presidential nomination. Joaquin Castro voiced strong interest in challenging Republican Sen. John Cornyn in 2020, raising the possibility that both brothers might be running statewide at the same time. But he announced on May 1, 2019, that he will seek reelection to the House and that a potential bid for other office likely would be "something that takes me back home to Texas." Meanwhile, he grew more active in the House with Democrats in the majority, working on national security issues and on representation of Hispanic interests.

Politics is in Castro's blood. His mother, Rosie Castro, was a noted Latina activist in the 1960s and 1970s, and she instilled a belief in civil rights and equality of opportunity in her sons. Both he and his brother earned their bachelor's in political science at Stanford University. Both continued to Harvard Law School, where they graduated and then returned to San Antonio to join the politically well-connected Akin, Gump, Strauss, Hauer & Feld law firm and launch their local political careers. Joaquin Castro successfully challenged a Democratic incumbent in the Texas House in 2002, running a change-themed campaign. In the legislature, he focused on education and eventually became the Democratic floor leader. "I've always been in deep minorities" in the legislature, Castro said. "The silver lining is that you learn, almost in a Darwinian way, how to be effective without using sheer force of numbers." That included restoring education funding amid budget-cutting after the 2010 elections.

Castro has had an unusually charmed electoral history. He initially announced he would run in 2012 for Texas' new 35th Congressional District, which runs from San Antonio's east side to Austin. That pitted him against veteran Democratic Rep. Lloyd Doggett and foretold an expensive primary battle dividing two cities and two ethnic groups of Democrats. Soon, longtime Democratic Rep. Charles Gonzalez of San Antonio called Castro and said he had decided to retire. "At that point," Castro said, "it became clear I should run for my home district." No other Democrat has run against him and he has faced perfunctory Republican opposition.

Castro has pushed on various fronts to urge legislative action on immigration, including a pathway to citizenship for those in the country illegally. In 2016, he unsuccessfully pleaded to the House Rules Committee to abandon Republican efforts to force the Library of Congress to continue using the term "alien" to refer to immigrants, which he described as "a prejudicial term that's particularly offensive to Hispanics." He added, "These folks may not be U.S. citizens, but they're not from outer space."

Working on overseas issues, Castro gained House passage in 2016 of a bill that he filed with Republican Rep. Mike McCaul of Texas to create a Global Development Lab in the U.S. Agency for International Development. Their goal, he said, was "applying science and building partnerships to solve urgent, complex development challenges." On the House Intelligence Committee, Castro spoke out on the "need to determine not only the extent of Russia's attempts to undermine our election and democracy, but also whether any Americans participated in those efforts."

Following the 2018 election, in the legislative majority for the first during his career, Castro was selected as chairman of the Congressional Hispanic Caucus. A comprehensive immigration bill was a priority, he said, as was "shedding light on [President Donald] Trump's inhumane immigration policies." Democrats named him vice-chairman of the Foreign Affairs Committee; Castro said that he would assist in "pursuing a foreign policy that checks President Trump's actions, empowers Congress, and represents who we are and who we want to be as a nation." In February 2019, he took the lead in sponsoring the House-passed resolution that sought to block Trump's declaration of a national emergency along the border with Mexico to justify the transfer of federal funds to finance a wall. Trump vetoed the measure, which the House failed to override. Castro has remained active among Democrats as a chief deputy whip.

Castro has been an in-demand figure on the political circuit. During the final days of the 2016 presidential campaign, he and his brother barnstormed battleground states, plus Texas, to get out the vote for Hillary Clinton. When Julian Castro in January 2019 announced his presidential candidacy, his brother stepped forward to chair the campaign and he told The Texas Tribune that he would assist in "whatever he asks me to do."

His support for his brother grew potentially more complicated when Joaquin Castro voiced interest in challenging Republican Sen. John Cornyn for reelection in 2020. Those plans grew more active after former Rep. Beto O'Rourke said that he would not challenge Cornyn and, instead, launched his own presidential campaign. Cornyn initially responded that Castro's record was too liberal to win statewide election in Texas.

A statewide bid remains a daunting challenge for any Texas Democrat, though O'Rourke's narrow loss to Sen. Ted Cruz in 2018 encouraged some Democrats. Journalists have written for years about Castro's frequent travels to meet with grassroots Democrats across the state. When Castro announced that he would not run for the Senate, military veteran MJ Hegar—who had run unsuccessfully against Republican Rep. John Carter in 2018—already had announced her candidacy. Cornyn's campaign responded, "Shame on Chuck Schumer and DC Democrats for forcing a high profile Hispanic leader out of the Senate race." Castro dismissed speculation about the rationale for his decision as "political gossip." He has made clear that he remains upwardly mobile.

TX-20: Bexar County   **Cook Partisan Voting Index: D+10**

Population		Race and Ethnicity		Income	
Total	776,926	White	21.3%	Median Income	$50,355
Land area (sq. miles)	200	Black	4.9%	District Income Rank	304
Pop/ sq mi	3890.9	Latino	68.9%	Poverty Rate	18.4%
Born in State	65.8%	Asian	3.1%	With health insurance	82.6%
		Two or more races	1.4%	Cash public assistance	1.7%
Age Groups		Other	0.3%	Food stamp/SNAP	15%
Under 18	25.8%				
18-34	28.4%	**Education**		**Work**	
35-64	35.3%	H.S grad or less	45.2%	White Collar	10.5%
Over 64	10.5%	Some college	30.8%	Sales and Service	47.2%
		College Degree, 4 yr	15.8%	Blue Collar	20.2%
Military		Post grad	8.3%	Government	13.9%
Veteran/ Active Duty	11.2%				

2012 Pres. Vote	Obama	110,663	(59%)	Romney	74,540	(40%)		
2016 Pres. Vote	Clinton	132,363	(61%)	Trump	74,386	(34%)	Johnson	7,373	(3%)

San Antonio: With its antique past and Hispanic heritage, San Antonio is unlike any other city in the United States. It is the home of the Alamo, preserved by the Daughters of the Republic of Texas, where Davy Crockett, Jim Bowie and 184 others were killed in 1836. Its Spanish architecture recalls San Antonio's days as the most important town in Texas, when the state was part of Mexico; it contrasts with the 30-story Tower Life Building and with the armadillo-like Alamodome. Its Paseo del Rio, the Riverwalk along the tiny San Antonio River that was redeveloped in the 1970s, recalls an earlier era.

For most of the 20th century, San Antonio's economy was built on the military. What the locals call "Military City, U.S.A." remains the home of Lackland Air Force Base, Fort Sam Houston and a giant military hospital. San Antonio has many military retirees and is the largest tourist center in Texas. The city's recent strength has resulted from a diversifying economy that has attracted good-paying jobs in its booming medical research industry. Health care and biosciences have grown to a $37 billion business, led by the military units and the University of Texas Health Science Center. More than one of every six San Antonio employees works in these fields, according to the city's Chamber of Commerce. San Antonio's manufacturing center contributes more than $22 billion to the local economy, more than triple the revenue it generated in 1991. It is home to the world headquarters of Valero Energy, Clear Channel Communications and USAA Insurance. The 30 percent increase in the gross regional product of the metro area from 2011 to 2016 was the third-highest in the nation, behind San Jose and Austin.

From 2000 to 2017, San Antonio's population increased 32 percent, and it has surpassed Dallas as Texas' second-largest city, after Houston. Of its metropolitan area population of 2.5 million, 56 percent are Hispanic and that share is growing. In 2017, San Antonio had the largest population increase (24,000) of any city in the United States. In November 2018, when Texas Attorney General Ken Paxton sued San Antonio for the first alleged violation of a state law barring the practices of a sanctuary city, he cited a decision by the city's police department not to bring charges against a trailer carrying 12 undocumented individuals from Guatemala. The police department responded that its policy is not to refer individuals to immigration agencies unless they have a federal deportation warrant.

Just over half of San Antonio's population — or one-third of Bexar County -- is located in the 20th Congressional District of Texas, which is centered in its lower-income west side; the downtown area where most of the city's attractions are located is mostly in the 35th District. To dilute the Democratic vote, parts of five districts are in Bexar; only the 20th is wholly contained in the county. With a Hispanic population share of 69 percent, it is one of the state's nine Hispanic-majority districts. Hillary Clinton took 61 percent of the district vote.

Chip Roy (R)

Elected 2018, 1st term, b. Aug 07, 1972; Bethesda, MD; University of Virginia, B.S., 1994; University of Virginia, M.S., 1995; University of Texas, J.D., 2003; Baptist; Married (Carrah Roy); 2 children.

Professional Career: Counsel, U.S. Senate Subcommittee on Constitution, Civil Rights, and Property Rights, 2005; Counsel, U.S. Sen. John Cornyn 2009; Senior Counsel, U.S. Senate Subcommittee on Immigration, Refugees and Border Security, 2009; Director, Office of Texas Governor Rick Perry, Washington DC Office, 2011; Chief of Staff, U.S. Sen. Ted Cruz, 2012-2014; TX First Assistant Attorney General; Vice President of Strategy, Texas Public Policy Foundation; Senior Advisor, Governor Rick Perry; Special Assistant U.S. Attorney in the Eastern District of Texas.

DC Office: 1319 LHOB 20515, 202-225-4236, Fax: 202-225-8628, roy.house.gov

State Offices: Austin, 512-871-5959; San Antonio, 210-821-5024.

Committees: *Budget. Oversight & Reform*: Subcommittee on Civil Rights & Civil Liberties (RMM); Subcommittee on Economic & Consumer Policy. *Veterans' Affairs*: Oversight & Investigations; Technology Modernization.

Election Results

Election	Name (Party)	Vote (%)		Cand. Spent	Ind. Exp. Support	Ind. Exp. Oppose
2018 General	Chip Roy (R)	177,654	(50%)	$1,747,592	$1,221,175	$251,356
	Joseph Kopser (D)	168,421	(48%)	$3,084,330	$110,184	$257,002
	Lee Santos (Lib)	7,542	(2%)			
2018 Primary Runoff	Chip Roy (R)	18,000	(53%)			
	Matt McCall (R)	16,181	(47%)			
2018 Primary	Chip Roy (R)	19,428	(27%)			
	Matt McCall (R)	12,152	(17%)			
	William Negley (R)	11,163	(16%)			
	Jason Isaac (R)	7,208	(10%)			
	Jennifer Sarver (R)	4,027	(6%)			

Republican first-termer Chip Roy was the most politically experienced and well-connected of the six Texas Republicans in 2018 who won contests for open House seats, which were largely determined in the party primary. But his victory, 50%-48%, was the narrowest among that group. Roy, a veteran congressional aide and partisan insider who was supported by leading local Republicans plus national conservative groups, was making his own initial bid for elected office.

Even though he significantly outspent his opponent, Roy won an unexpectedly tight victory in the GOP runoff against a local businessman who ran a low-profile campaign. In November, Roy was on the other end as his Democratic challenger outspent him nearly 2-to-1. He took the seat of Rep. Lamar Smith, who retired after chairing four House committees during his 32-year House career.

Born in Maryland to Texas natives and raised in northern Virginia, Roy got his bachelor's degree and a master's degree in management information systems from the University of Virginia, plus his law degree from the University of Texas. With his blue-chip credentials, he served as a federal prosecutor with then-U.S. Attorney John Cornyn, became a senior aide when Cornyn was elected to the Senate and later was a top official for the Texas Attorney General. He also was a top aide to, among others, Texas Sen. Ted Cruz and former Gov. Rick Perry, including their separate presidential campaigns. In the private sector, Roy was an investment banking analyst and a top officer of the conservative Texas Public Policy Foundation.

"For years, Roy has operated behind the scenes on behalf of top Texas GOP officeholders," the Austin American-Statesman wrote in a campaign profile, which emphasized that he used his experience chiefly to oppose federal actions. "Now he's trying to make a name for himself as a politician in his own right." But that became an unexpectedly challenging effort.

In the March primary, Roy received 27 percent of the vote to 17 percent for Matt McCall; an unwieldy 16 other candidates split the remainder of the vote. In Bexar County, the population center of the district that cast nearly one-third of the vote, Roy barely led with 26 percent. McCall spent less than half as much money as Roy, who also benefited from more than $1 million in spending by the conservative Club for Growth.

Roy struggled in the runoff. McCall, a tea party ally who got about one-third of the vote when he ran against Smith in the 2014 and 2016 GOP primaries, criticized Roy "as an outsider in the district who is leaning hard on his political connections to get him across the finish line," The Texas Tribune reported prior to the runoff. Roy emphasized his experience in fighting for conservative principles. He won the GOP nomination by an unimpressive 53%-47%. He led McCall in Bexar and Travis, the urban anchors of the district, and also won the three exurban counties that were closest to those areas. McCall took the other five counties in the rural western part of the district, including the Hill Country.

In November, Roy faced Democrat Joseph Kopser, a businessman who once was affiliated with the Republican Party. Despite Kopser's impressive fundraising and Roy's continued learning curve, the Republican history of the district ultimately secured Roy's victory. The vote was split in three roughly equal parts: Kopser won 76 percent in Travis County; Roy took a slim 51 percent in Bexar County and rolled up huge majorities in the exurban and rural counties. In the House, Roy was positioned to take advantage of his deep familiarity with Capitol Hill, especially among Texans.

After Kopser said that he would not run again in 2020, Democrat Wendy Davis—who ran unsuccessfully for governor in 2014—said in April 2019 that she was "looking very seriously" at challenging Roy. "I want to make sure that we have the ability to win it, and I believe we do," she said in a podcast.

TX-21: Northern Bexar County, Southern Travis County

Cook Partisan Voting Index: R+10

Population		Race and Ethnicity		Income	
Total	777,686	White	62%	Median Income	$67,354
Land area (sq. miles)	5,921	Black	3.4%	District Income Rank	114
Pop/ sq mi	131.3	Latino	29%	Poverty Rate	11.3%
Born in State	58%	Asian	3.4%	With health insurance	88%
		Two or more races	2%	Cash public assistance	0.9%
Age Groups		Other	0.2%	Food stamp/SNAP	5.6%
Under 18	20.3%				
18-34	26.2%	**Education**		**Work**	
35-64	38.1%	H.S grad or less	25.6%	White Collar	15.4%
Over 64	15.4%	Some college	29%	Sales and Service	39.7%
		College Degree, 4 yr	28.7%	Blue Collar	13.3%
Military		Post grad	16.8%	Government	14.5%
Veteran/ Active Duty	10.9%				

2012 Pres. Vote	Romney	188,241	(60%)	Obama	119,220	(38%)		
2016 Pres. Vote	Trump	188,336	(52%)	Clinton	152,528	(42%)	Johnson	14,130	(4%)

San Antonio/Austin Corridor: The Balcones Escarpment is a bulwark of cracked and weathered rock that crosses Texas diagonally from the Dallas-Fort Worth Metroplex southwest to Austin and San Antonio and all the way to the Rio Grande. It separates the flatlands of central Texas from the stony hills to the north and west. It is a boundary between cropland and grazing land, between acres rich with greenery and acres whose rolling brown hills blaze out in color when the wildflowers bloom in early spring. But the Balcones Escarpment is less familiar to Texans today than the highway that runs pretty much along the same line: Interstate 35. This is one of the most heavily traveled and congested interstates in America, thick with truck traffic in the populated stretches between the Metroplex and the Mexican border even as it passes through the lightly populated near-desert between San Antonio and Laredo. I-35 connects Austin and San Antonio, two booming Texan cities with very different beginnings and different characters now.

In the counties between these two cities and in the Hill Country to the west is the Texas German country, originally settled by Germans in the mid-1800s. It consists of economically prosperous communities that were anti-slavery and politically Republican in a state whose enthusiasm for the Democratic Party had roots in Confederate loyalties and populist rebellions. Texas Germans introduced the long-barbecued beef brisket that has become synonymous with Lone Star State cuisine; an antique German dialect is sometimes heard on the streets of New Braunfels, Boerne and Fredericksburg. Parts of this area, chiefly small cities, are among the most rapidly growing in the nation. Comal and Hays, which are between Travis and Bexar counties, ranked second and fourth among the fastest-growing counties in the nation in 2017. New Braunfels ranked second among cities nationwide in 2017. San Marcos, which is about halfway between the two anchors on I-35, was the fastest-growing city in 2014. But it suffered extensive flooding from Hurricane Harvey in 2017 and sought long-term solutions to its problems in what has been called "Flash Flood Alley."

The 21st Congressional District of Texas includes much of this territory. One-third of its people are in San Antonio and Bexar County. It includes the northeast corner of the city and county, taking in Fort Sam Houston, and the affluent northside neighborhoods of Terrell Hills, Olmos Park and Alamo Heights just outside San Antonio. In the expansive Hill Country, the district takes in Gillespie County; along the Pedernales River is the LBJ Ranch, where the 36th president was born, vacationed during his presidency and is buried. When he was a New Deal congressman, Johnson famously brought electricity and other services to this hinterland, which remains countrified today.

Nearly one-third of the district is in Travis County, with parts of downtown Austin's central business district that border the University of Texas and the state capital. Amid the booming corporate development, downtown Austin has cherished its fame of more bars per capita than any other ZIP code in the nation. While Travis County was always Democratic and the Texas German country was Republican, San Antonio was mixed. As was the case in other suburban parts of Texas, Donald Trump underperformed the GOP presidential vote here; he got 52 percent, compared with 60 percent for Mitt Romney in 2012.

Pete Olson (R)

Elected 2008, 6th term, b. Dec 09, 1962; Fort Lewis, WA; Rice University (TX), B.A., 1985; University of Texas Law School, J.D., 1988; Methodist; Married (Nancy Olson); 2 children.

Military Career: U.S. Navy 1988-1995; U.S. Naval Reserve 1997-2009

Professional Career: Naval officer, 1995; Staffer, U.S. Sen. Phil Gramm, 1998-2002; Staffer, U.S. Sen. John Cornyn, 2002-2007.

DC Office: 2133 RHOB 20515, 202-225-5951, Fax: 202-225-5241, olson.house.gov

State Offices: Pearland, 281-485-4855; Sugar Land, 281-494-2690.

Committees: *Energy & Commerce*: Communications & Technology; Energy. *Science, Space & Technology*: Space & Aeronautics.

Group Ratings

	ADA	ACLU	AFL-CIO	LCV	ITI	COC	HAFA	ACU	CFG	FRC
2018	-	4%	-	0%	-	83%	73%	80%	54%	100%
2017	0%	C	5%	0%	C	92%	C	93%	88%	100%

Almanac Ratings 2017-18

	Economy	Social	Foreign	Composite
Liberal	3%	3%	0%	2%
Conservative	97%	97%	100%	98%

Key Votes of the 115th Congress

1. Obama-care revision	Y	5. Family planning regs	Y	9. Guantanamo prisoners	N
2. Tax Cuts	Y	6. Body cameras/immigration	N	10. Ground missiles, limit	N
3. Omnibus appropriations	Y	7. Abortion ban	Y	11. Defense Dept. spending	Y
4. Dodd-Frank revision	Y	8. Concealed carry	Y	12. FISA rules	Y

Election Results

Election	Name (Party)	Vote (%)		Cand. Spent	Ind. Exp. Support	Ind. Exp. Oppose
2018 General	Pete Olson (R)	152,750	(51%)	$1,853,800		$31,596
	Sri Preston Kulkarni (D)	138,153	(47%)	$1,408,056	$76,478	
2018 Primary	Pete Olson (R)	35,782	(78%)			
	Danny Nguyen (R)	6,170	(14%)			
	James Green (R)	2,521	(6%)			

Prior winning percentages: 2016 (60%), 2014 (67%), 2012 (64%), 2010 (68%), 2008 (52%)

Pete Olson, a Republican elected in 2008, has brought a lengthy pedigree in Texas politics. But his reaction to the rapid demographic shifts in his district has been uneven. His narrow reelection in 2018 made him a top Democratic target. The best hope for Olson might be a big shift for his district in redistricting if he can survive another term. On the Energy and Commerce Committee, he advocates on behalf of oil and gas interests and Houston's diverse business community. Olson is every bit as conservative as Tom DeLay, the powerful former House Majority Leader who served the district for two decades, though few lawmakers could match DeLay's clout.

A graduate of Rice University and the University of Texas Law School, Olson entered the Navy on the same day he took the Texas bar exam. He served as a naval aviator and flew anti-submarine missions, including in the Persian Gulf following the war against Iraq in 1991. He finished his military career in Washington D.C. as a liaison to the Senate. His next job was as a staff member for Republican Sen. Phil Gramm of Texas. After Gramm retired in 2002, Olson was chief of staff for his successor, Republican Sen. John Cornyn.

In 2006, DeLay resigned his seat after his 2005 indictment in Texas required him to give up his leadership post. His conviction in 2011 for money laundering and conspiracy stemming from his role funneling corporate contributions to Texas state races was overturned by the state criminal appeals court on the basis that prosecutors failed to prove that the contributions were illegal. Former Democratic Rep. Nick Lampson took advantage of local Republican disarray and won the seat.

Two years later, Shelley Sekula-Gibbs — who held the seat for a few weeks when she won a special election after DeLay resigned — finished first in the primary but with only 30 percent of the vote. Republican strategists regarded her as a weak candidate and coalesced around Olson, who won the runoff with 69 percent. In the general election, Olson touted a conservative message, while Lampson tried to tar him with DeLay's image. In a Democratic year, the district returned to its GOP roots. Olson won 52%-45%.

Olson has been a rock-solid conservative, with nearly perfect conservative Almanac vote ratings. On Energy and Commerce, he has been a staunch defender of the Texas oil and gas industry. The House passed his bill in 2012 letting power companies off the hook if they violate environmental laws while attempting to comply with federal mandates to maintain the reliability of their electricity grids during power emergencies. Olson has sought to permit more oil and gas drilling on public lands.

With Democratic Rep. Cedric Richmond of Louisiana, he co-founded the Congressional Refinery Caucus, which was designed to educate lawmakers about the industry's interests. In 2016 and again in 2017 the House passed Olson's bill to extend the time for implementation by the Environmental Protection Agency of its ozone-reduction standards under the Clean Air Act. Each time, the bill died in the Senate.

Olson has been a champion of NASA's Johnson Space Center, where many of his constituents have been employed. He called for a return of human space flight to the moon to set the stage for an eventual manned mission to Mars. He has pursued conservative initiatives. He took the lead in filing articles of impeachment against Attorney General Eric Holder for his mismanagement of the "Fast and Furious" gun-running program in Mexico. Republican leaders did not pursue the charges and Holder stepped down in 2015. In 2017, he filed a bill to prohibit the federal government from treating gender identity as a protected class unless Congress had explicitly authorized the action — a national version of the "bathroom" legislation that had generated controversy in a few states.

Olson in 2018 faced his first serious reelection challenge. Democrat Sri Preston Kulkarni, a former foreign service officer with the State Department, ran an ad describing Olson as a "do-nothing congressman" and he ran an aggressive grass-roots campaign. CNN aired a videotape of Olson, whose grassroots skills might have waned, referring to Kulkarni as "a liberal Indo-American who's a carpetbagger;" his father was a native of India. Olson outspent Kulkarni, $1.9 million to $1.4 million, though the contest received little attention from national party groups on either side until the closing days of the campaign. Olson won, 51%-46%, with narrow leads in each of the three counties.

In January 2019, the Democratic Congressional Campaign Committee listed Olson among its top 25 targets in 2020. Kulkarni said in April that he will challenge Olson again. "People wanted change in this district, and since we've built all that infrastructure, it would be a waste to start from scratch," he told the Houston Chronicle. Kulkarni could face other Democrats in the primary.

TX-22: Southern Houston Suburbs   **Cook Partisan Voting Index: R+10**

Population		Race and Ethnicity		Income	
Total	844,913	White	41.4%	Median Income	$93,667
Land area (sq. miles)	1,033	Black	13.3%	District Income Rank	23
Pop/ sq mi	818	Latino	25.2%	Poverty Rate	7.8%
Born in State	50.6%	Asian	17.9%	With health insurance	88.5%
		Two or more races	1.9%	Cash public assistance	1.1%
Age Groups		Other	0.3%	Food stamp/SNAP	6.4%
Under 18	28%				
18-34	21.1%	**Education**		**Work**	
35-64	40.9%	H.S grad or less	27%	White Collar	10%
Over 64	10%	Some college	27.8%	Sales and Service	33.8%
		College Degree, 4 yr	28%	Blue Collar	15%
Military		Post grad	17.2%	Government	12.4%
Veteran/ Active Duty	5.8%				

2012 Pres. Vote	Romney	158,452	(62%)	Obama	93,582	(37%)		
2016 Pres. Vote	Trump	159,717	(52%)	Clinton	135,525	(44%)	Johnson	9,322	(3%)

Sugar Land: The story of the Houston area's booming growth is well captured in a drive out the Southwest Freeway to Sugar Land. Much has changed from the days before the Civil War, when sugar plantations flourished here. In 2018, archeologists at the construction site for a new local school found 95 graves that they concluded were the remains of black prison laborers who worked in indentured servitude on plantations in the late 19th century. The school board decided to move the new school elsewhere and approve a historical memorial for the "Sugar Land 95." Sugar Land is a privately planned city of more than 88,000 people, with privatized water and other services. (In 1990, its population was 45,000.) The surrounding Fort Bend County has been among the nation leaders in job growth since 2000. In November 2018, a University of Houston study projected that Fort Bend would be the third-fastest growing county in the nation between 2010 and 2050, with an increase to perhaps 2.7 million. The local baseball team is the Sugar Land Skeeters, a reference to the area's uncomfortable proliferation of the biting insects.

When former House Majority Leader Tom DeLay represented the 22nd Congressional District, whites were a majority. Although much of Fort Bend's black population resides in the adjacent 9th

District, the 22nd has become a minority-majority district. Suburban Sugar Land and Fort Bend County are among the most-diverse areas in the country. Almost a quarter of the county's population is Hispanic, 21 percent is African American, and 20 percent is Asian. In 2018, voters elected as county judge — the top county executive — KP George, a Democrat and a native of India, who was described as the Indian-American with the most prominent position in local government in the United States. From 2010 to 2018, Fort Bend grew from 585,000 to 788,000 — a 35 percent increase. With growth and diversification has come wealth: The median income in the district is nearly $94,000, the highest in Texas. In 2016, Hillary Clinton took the county, 52%-45%, a 13-point swing from 2012 and an encouraging omen for Democrats. About two-thirds of the district is in Fort Bend.

The district includes 80 percent of the voters in Fort Bend County, including Sugar Land, and a bit more than half of Brazoria County, centering on Pearland, just south of Houston. In Pearland, a suburb that was positioning itself as a health care hub for the region, the population exploded from 46,000 in 2000 to 120,000 in 2017; the local economy in 2017 was the third fastest-growing in the nation. The district, which takes in a small slice of southwestern Houston, has been solidly Republican, with Mitt Romney getting 62 percent of the vote in 2012. Four years later, Donald Trump was not so good a fit and took only 52 percent.

Will Hurd (R)

Elected 2014, 3rd term, b. Aug 19, 1977; San Antonio; Texas A&M University, College Station, B.S., 2000; Christian - Non-Denominational; Single.

Elected Office: TX House, 1990-2013.

Professional Career: Operations officer, CIA, 2000-2009; Partner, Crumpton Group, 2010-2013; Senior advisor, FusionX, 2010-present.

DC Office: 317 CHOB 20515, 202-225-4511, Fax: 202-225-2237, hurd.house.gov

State Offices: Del Rio, 830-422-2040; Eagle Pass, 210-921-3130; Fort Stockton, 210-245-1961; San Antonio, 210-921-3130; Socorro, 915-235-6421.

Committees: *Appropriations*: Military Construction, Veterans Affairs & Related Agencies; Transportation, HUD & Related Agencies. *Permanent Select on Intelligence*: Defense Intelligence & Warfighter Support; Intelligence Modernization & Readiness (RMM).

Group Ratings

	ADA	ACLU	AFL-CIO	LCV	ITI	COC	HAFA	ACU	CFG	FRC
2018	-	7%	-	20%	-	92%	40%	52%	46%	100%
2017	5%	C	16%	3%	C	92%	C	70%	55%	89%

Almanac Ratings 2017-18

	Economy	Social	Foreign	Composite
Liberal	9%	7%	0%	5%
Conservative	91%	94%	100%	95%

Key Votes of the 115th Congress

1. Obama-care revision	N	5. Family planning regs	Y	9. Guantanamo prisoners	N
2. Tax Cuts	Y	6. Body cameras/immigration	N	10. Ground missiles, limit	N
3. Omnibus appropriations	Y	7. Abortion ban	Y	11. Defense Dept. spending	Y
4. Dodd-Frank revision	Y	8. Concealed carry	Y	12. FISA rules	Y

Election Results

Election	Name (Party)	Vote (%)		Cand. Spent	Ind. Exp. Support	Ind. Exp. Oppose
2018 General	Will Hurd (R)......................................	103,285	(49%)	$5,006,462	$1,072,868	$2,578,222
	Gina Ortiz Jones (D)........................	102,359	(49%)	$6,063,053	$728,714	$4,069,389
	Ruben Corvalan (Lib)............................	4,425	(2%)			
2018 Primary	Will Hurd (R)......................................	24,569	(80%)			
	Alma Arredondo-Lynch (R).....................	5,986	(20%)			

Prior winning percentages: 2016 (48%), 2014 (50%)

In a district known for its frequent change of party control, Republican Will Hurd, a former CIA officer, has done something none of the previous incumbents could achieve over the last 12 years: He has won election three times. Through extensive constituent outreach and an active legislative record, the African-American running in a heavily Hispanic district defied the odds each cycle since 2014. In a profile, Politico described him as "a phenom," with "a rare combination of competence as a policymaker, responsiveness as a representative and ferocity as a campaigner."

Hurd, a native of San Antonio, is the youngest of three children of a mixed-race couple. He graduated from Texas A&M University with a degree in computer science. As student body president, he helped a grieving campus recover from the 1999 collapse of the traditional football bonfire, which killed 12 students and injured 27 others. On the day after the September 11 attacks, he joined a new counterterrorism unit in Afghanistan. When he left the agency after nine years and returned to Texas, he became a partner in the strategic advisory firm Crumpton Group, founded by former CIA officer and counterterrorism director Henry "Hank" Crumpton. Hurd also was a senior adviser with the cybersecurity firm FusionX. The Houston Chronicle headlined him as the spy "who came in from the shadows."

Hurd ran for the House seat in 2010, and he led the first round of primary voting with 34 percent. But he lost the GOP runoff to Francisco "Quico" Canseco, 53%-47%, a margin of 722 votes. Canseco then defeated Democratic Rep. Ciro Rodriguez. In 2012, Pete Gallego, a former prosecutor and former state representative, took the seat back for Democrats, 50%-46%. In 2014, Hurd easily defeated Canseco, 59%-41%, in the runoff. Tea party supporters backed Hurd's campaign, which emphasized his intelligence service "in this time of heartbreak and troubles throughout the world." Gallego portrayed himself as a moderate Blue Dog Democrat, but Hurd criticized him as too aligned with President Barack Obama and "radical environmentalists." The race remained tight to the end. Gallego outspent Hurd, $2.7 million to $1.4 million. Each candidate was helped by more than $2.5 million in spending by national party committees and other outside groups that made huge ad purchases. Hurd won by about 2,400 votes, 49.8%-47.7%. In Bexar, Hurd led, 57%-40%.

Hurd quickly settled in and made his mark in the House, including an impressive record of legislative accomplishments. He got a plum assignment for a freshman as chairman of the Oversight and Government Reform Subcommittee on Information Technology. In a February 2015 interview with Baseline magazine, Hurd said that the nation needs to do more to prepare against a cyberattack. "We do not have clear rules of engagement for a pure digital-on-digital attack. Knowing the rules of engagement deters some of this undesirable behavior." Seven months after taking office, he enacted his bill to cut the number of information technology systems at the Homeland Security Department to reduce duplication.

Demonstrating his familiarity with national security and intelligence issues, Hurd in July 2016 had what the Express-News described as "a star-making moment." As the Oversight Committee grilled FBI Director James Comey about the bureau's investigation of Hillary Clinton's handling of her personal email server when she was secretary of State, Hurd said that Clinton had "a server in her basement that had information that was collected from our most sensitive assets and it was not protected by anyone. ... And that's not a crime? That's outrageous."

Hurd was not shy in taking on the leadership of his own party. Following the October 2016 release of the 2005 video in which Donald Trump made lewd comments about women, Hurd called them "repulsive for women and all Americans" and said that Trump should "step aside for a true conservative to beat Hillary Clinton." After Trump was elected, Hurd said that he would be able to work with him. But he found plenty of opportunities to distance himself. Five days after Trump took office and repeated that he wanted to build a wall along the border with Mexico, Hurd — whose district includes more than 800 miles of that border — said the proposed wall was "the most expensive and least effective way to secure the border." In 2017, Hurd got a plum assignment, given his background: a seat on the Intelligence Committee. That didn't keep him from being one of 20 Republicans in May who voted against House passage of the GOP's American Health Care Act.

It has been no surprise that the Democratic Congressional Campaign Committee has made Hurd a prime target. In a 2016 rematch, Gallego relentlessly sought to link him to Trump. Hurd ran a well-organized and well-financed campaign. Hurd won, 48.3%-47%, a margin of 3,000 votes. Hurd led in Bexar County by 13,600 votes and trailed with the much smaller electorate in El Paso by 14,000 votes. The margin of difference was in the district's vast rural areas.

In 2018, Hurd was one of the few perennially vulnerable Republicans who survived the 2018 Democratic midterm wave -- and it was not by much. Air Force veteran Gina Ortiz Jones launched a spirited challenge to Hurd. Both candidates spent lavishly. Ortiz Jones outspent Hurd, $6.1 million to $5 million, but she lost by 926 votes. She made plans to challenge him again in 2020.

Hurd has been widely viewed as having a prominent future among Republicans and he has been popular among colleagues. House GOP leaders have supported his career; in January 2019, they assigned him a seat on the Appropriations Committee. A month later, he was one of 13 Republicans — and the only one from Texas — who voted for the Democratic-sponsored resolution to reject Trump's call for a "national emergency" along the border to justify his transfer of funds to build a wall. "This is not a tool that the president needs in order to solve this problem," Hurd said.

TX-23: Bexar County Exurbs, West Texas   Cook Partisan Voting Index: R+1

Population		Race and Ethnicity		Income	
Total	752,067	White	24.4%	Median Income	$52,162
Land area (sq. miles)	58,059	Black	3.1%	District Income Rank	267
Pop/ sq mi	12.9	Latino	69.6%	Poverty Rate	17.8%
Born in State	64.6%	Asian	1.3%	With health insurance	80.7%
		Two or more races	1%	Cash public assistance	1.5%
Age Groups		Other	0.5%	Food stamp/SNAP	17.7%
Under 18	28.4%				
18-34	23.9%	**Education**		**Work**	
35-64	35.3%	H.S grad or less	51.3%	White Collar	12.4%
Over 64	12.4%	Some college	27.2%	Sales and Service	43%
		College Degree, 4 yr	14%	Blue Collar	27%
Military		Post grad	7.5%	Government	16.9%
Veteran/ Active Duty	9.1%				

2012 Pres. Vote	Romney	99,666	(51%)	Obama	94,419	(48%)		
2016 Pres. Vote	Clinton	115,157	(50%)	Trump	107,273	(46%)	Johnson	7,077 (3%)

San Antonio: Fifty or so miles west of San Antonio, the hills flatten out and become the parched uplands of West Texas. This is a borderland, just north of Mexico, where people are concentrated in tiny hamlets amid the empty ranchlands. Most are Hispanic. Once, Indians were the threat on this frontier. Now the challenge is a lack of water. The aquifers of West Texas are being drained, and state law still permits landowners to pump out as much water as they want. The Rio Grande, dried out by a dam in New Mexico, gets most of its water from the Rio Conchos in the Mexican state of Chihuahua. Rising above the Rio Grande are the mountains of Big Bend National Park, where in the clean air you can see for 180 miles. Texas' frontier in many ways is thriving; its remote location makes it one of the least-visited national parks. The tiny town of Marfa first became a landmark when director George Stevens and actors Rock Hudson, Elizabeth Taylor and James Dean stayed in the glamorous Hotel El Paisano and shot the movie Giant. Marfa has become known as an eccentric art colony. Near the Mexican border is Dimmit County, where more than a dozen companies have drilled thousands of wells in an oil and gas field known as the Eagle Ford shale formation. In oil-producing Loving County, the population grew from 82 to 134 residents from 2010 to 2017, which made it the fastest-growing — as well as least populous -- county in the nation. Discovery of shale oil and improved fracking techniques have opened additional parts of the Permian Basin to production.

The 23rd Congressional District of Texas is geographically the largest in the state, stretching from the outskirts of San Antonio to the edge of El Paso, from Eagle Pass and Maverick County to the New Mexico border. It takes in 23 percent of the state's land area, spanning more than 800 miles of the Texas-Mexico border and covering 29 counties. Many local communities along the border have strong views — often hostile — about national politicians who want to build a large wall here. Local residents also understand the logistical complications, especially in Big Bend.

About half of the district's population is in Bexar County, chiefly in a C-shaped ring in the county's western suburbs that surround downtown San Antonio and is the more heavily Republican part of the district. San Antonio's Mexican-American community has produced many politicians who are liberal on economic issues and civil rights but also are pro-military and at home with traditional cultural values. Only 8 percent of the 23rd is in El Paso County, which is disproportionately Democratic, as are many of the rural counties. The district is 70 percent Hispanic, but this has remained a battleground district. This was among the few seats won by Hillary Clinton that Mitt Romney carried four years earlier — narrowly, in each case.

Kenny Marchant (R)

Elected 2004, 8th term, b. Feb 23, 1951; Bonham; Southern Nazarene University (OK), B.A., 1974; Nazarene Theological Seminary (MO), Att., 1975; Nazarene; Married (Donna Walker Marchant); 4 children; 4 grandchildren.

Elected Office: Carrollton City Council, 1980-1984; Carrolton Mayor, 1984-1986; TX House, 1987-2005.

Professional Career: Founder & owner, construction & home building business, 1975-2004.

DC Office: 2304 RHOB 20515, 202-225-6605, Fax: 202-225-0074, marchant.house.gov

State Offices: Irving, 972-556-0162.

Committees: *Ethics (RMM)*. *Joint Economic*. *Ways & Means*: Health; Trade.

Group Ratings

	ADA	ACLU	AFL-CIO	LCV	ITI	COC	HAFA	ACU	CFG	FRC
2018	-	4%	-	3%	-	83%	80%	76%	65%	100%
2017	0%	C	3%	0%	C	93%	C	93%	87%	100%

Almanac Ratings 2017-18

	Economy	Social	Foreign	Composite
Liberal	2%	3%	0%	2%
Conservative	99%	97%	100%	98%

Key Votes of the 115th Congress

1. Obama-care revision	Y	5. Family planning regs	Y	9. Guantanamo prisoners	N
2. Tax Cuts	Y	6. Body cameras/immigration	N	10. Ground missiles, limit	N
3. Omnibus appropriations	Y	7. Abortion ban	Y	11. Defense Dept. spending	Y
4. Dodd-Frank revision	Y	8. Concealed carry	Y	12. FISA rules	Y

Election Results

Election	Name (Party)	Vote (%)		Cand. Spent	Ind. Exp. Support	Ind. Exp. Oppose
2018 General	Kenny Marchant (R)	133,317	(51%)	$918,286	$1,412	
	Jan McDowell (D)	125,231	(48%)	$83,225		
2018 Primary	Kenny Marchant (R)	30,310	(74%)			
	Johnathan Davidson (R)	10,425	(26%)			

Prior winning percentages: 2016 (56%), 2014 (65%), 2012 (61%), 2010 (82%), 2008 (56%), 2006 (60%), 2004 (64%)

Republican Kenny Marchant, elected in 2004, has moved into influential positions, as a senior member of the Ways and Means Committee and the top Republican on the Ethics Committee. He typically is loyal to GOP leadership and the party agenda. Mild-mannered and deeply religious, he does not have the sharp rhetorical edge of many Texas conservatives. But like other Texas

Republicans, his reelection margin has tightened significantly, prompting Democrats to list him as a campaign target in 2020.

Marchant graduated from Southern Nazarene University and became a homebuilder and successful developer. He said that he got involved in politics when the head of the local homebuilders association told him that officials planned to change the construction codes and make it more expensive to build. Marchant served a quarter-century in local elected offices, including stints on the Carrollton City Council, as Carrollton mayor, and then in the state House. He has been active in humanitarian projects around the world; the Ken Marchant Foundation funds church loans, mission projects and scholarships. He has a ranch about an hour from Dallas, where he maintains a large herd of cows and likes to fish and hunt. His assets in 2015 fell between $16 million and $32 million, according to the Center for Responsive Politics.

In the state House, he enjoyed a reputation on both sides of the aisle as a levelheaded peacemaker. Marchant was chairman of the Banking and Investments Committee, and spent four years as floor leader of the Texas House Republican caucus. He served on the House Redistricting Committee during the bitter 2003 mapping battle. Unsurprisingly, the redistricting plan couldn't have been more favorable to him. The new 24th District was heavily Republican and inhospitable to Democratic Rep. Martin Frost, its previous incumbent. Frost opted to run in the new 32nd District and lost. Marchant has thrived in the redrawn 24th.

Marchant has a solidly conservative voting record in the Almanac vote ratings. He was among the original members of the Tea Party Caucus. "My vision for America is one where government is limited, taxes are low, success is celebrated, and the public sector flourishes," he told the Fort Worth Star-Telegram in 2012. He developed a fruitful relationship with Speaker John Boehner and was one of the few Texans to back Boehner when he ran for majority leader in 2006.

On Ways and Means in 2013, Marchant chaired the tax reform working group on debt, equity and capital. In response to the political-targeting controversy at the IRS, which he said jeopardized the security of confidential taxpayer information, he prepared a bill to prohibit IRS employees from using personal email accounts for official business. The House passed the measure on a voice vote in 2015. He was an outspoken proponent of the tax cuts that Republicans enacted in 2017. "This is an historic opportunity to reject the status quo and provide real tax relief," Marchant said.

As a member of the Trade Subcommittee, he has been an enthusiastic supporter of most proposed trade agreements, including the prospective Trans-Pacific Partnership. In a notable bipartisan step in 2018, Marchant joined Democratic Rep. Brian Higgins of New York in filing a bill to permit senior citizens to use their life insurance policies to cover some health care costs, including long-term care. In 2019, he had little to say publicly when he took over as ranking Republican on the Ethics Committee — an assignment that members often choose not to highlight.

Marchant drew a spirited GOP primary challenger in 2012 in Grant Stinchfield, a former TV news investigative reporter. He accused Marchant of failing to adequately represent conservatives and chastised him for requesting in an email to a GOP operative that his "grandbabies'" schools be included in his district as part of the recent redistricting. Stinchfield won the endorsement of the Star-Telegram, which called Marchant "a good argument for term limits" and cited his lack of legislative productivity. Stinchfield spent a relatively modest $239,000. The incumbent won 68%-32%.

In 2016, Democratic nominee Jan McDowell, a certified public accountant from Carrollton, called for Congress to take a new approach based not on the interests of campaign donors but on "what benefits the greatest number of people." She spent only $21,000. Marchant won, 56%-39%. McDowell ran again in 2018 and told the Star-Telegram that "constituents can't contact" Marchant. She gained little attention and from national Democrats and spent $125,000, still a paltry sum for an affluent area. Marchant spent $918,000 and was held to a surprisingly close 51%-48% win, a lead of about 8,000 votes. His victory margin came entirely in Tarrant, where he led by 23,000 votes. Although Marchant called the close margin a "fluke," the Democratic Congressional Campaign Committee sought a challenger for 2020 who could raise more money and gain more attention than McDowell.

TX-24: North-Central Metroplex

Cook Partisan Voting Index: R+9

Population		Race and Ethnicity		Income	
Total	774,968	White	48.2%	Median Income	$70,492
Land area (sq. miles)	263	Black	11.1%	District Income Rank	91
Pop/ sq mi	2949.3	Latino	24.2%	Poverty Rate	9.1%
Born in State	45.2%	Asian	13.2%	With health insurance	84.7%
		Two or more races	2.5%	Cash public assistance	1.3%
Age Groups		Other	0.9%	Food stamp/SNAP	5.8%
Under 18	23.8%				
18-34	25.1%	**Education**		**Work**	
35-64	41%	H.S grad or less	27.4%	White Collar	10.1%
Over 64	10.1%	Some college	27.9%	Sales and Service	39.6%
		College Degree, 4 yr	28.9%	Blue Collar	15.6%
Military		Post grad	15.9%	Government	7.9%
Veteran/ Active Duty	6.1%				

2012 Pres. Vote	Romney	150,547	(60%)	Obama	94,634	(38%)			
2016 Pres. Vote	Trump	140,128	(50%)	Clinton	122,872	(44%)	Johnson	10,753	(4%)

Fort Worth Suburbs: The gigantic (larger than Manhattan Island) Dallas-Fort Worth International Airport bisects the Metroplex and its two adjacent counties with its large terminals and the Texas-sized highway network that feeds them. Its total of flight operations makes it the third largest airport in the world, with seven runways, five terminals, 165 gates and 60,000 employees in an area of 27 square miles. DFW, as the locals call it, has been a focal point for development in both Dallas and Tarrant counties. "DFW is no longer solely an airport. DFW is our home," the Fort Worth Star-Telegram wrote. New cities, with as many people as Dallas and Fort Worth had in the 1950s — Grand Prairie and Irving — grew up around the airport during the next two decades in an area that had been an open prairie. The merger of American Airlines and US Airways made the combined company the largest airline in the nation, with its headquarters remaining in Fort Worth. It remains the dominant carrier at DFW. In November 2018, the airport authority announced plans to sell about $10 billion in bonds; one possible project was the building of a sixth terminal. "Our airfield is in pretty good shape, but we're out of gates again," an executive said.

North and west of DFW are newer and more upscale suburbs in northeast Tarrant County: Southlake, with huge shopping malls and resort centers, and Grapevine, home to the largest consumer-judged wine competition in the country. The Texas 114 corridor (also known as the Northwest Freeway) has become a booming business zone from Southlake to Roanoke. Across the International Parkway in northwest Dallas County are Coppell, Farmers Branch and Carrollton. To the north are the fast-growing suburbs and exurbs of Denton County. The Dallas-Fort Worth-Arlington Metropolitan Statistical Area has passed Philadelphia as the nation's fourth-largest MSA. In 2017, it was the fastest-growing metro area.

The 24th Congressional District of Texas is based in the suburban territory around DFW Airport. The line between its two principal counties, which goes through the eastern part of the terminal, is roughly the central axis of the district. Dallas and Tarrant each provide slightly more than 40 percent of the population, with the remainder beyond Dallas in Denton County. The area in Dallas takes in part of Irving, including ExxonMobil's corporate headquarters, part of Carrollton and all of Farmers Branch and Coppell. Irving, which business executives describe as "the headquarters of headquarters," has six Fortune 500 corporate offices — the most per capita of any city in the United States. McKesson, the giant pharmaceutical company, relocated from San Francisco in early 2019. The slice in Tarrant is the strongest Republican part of the district. This has been solidly Republican territory, though the 50 percent vote for Donald Trump in 2016 was a sharp drop from the 60 percent that Mitt Romney got four years earlier.

Roger Williams (R)

Elected 2012, 4th term, b. Sep 13, 1949; Evanston, IL; Texas Christian University, B.S., 1972; Disciples of Christ; Married (Patty Williams); 2 children.

Professional Career: Owner, Roger Williams Chrysler Dodge Jeep Ram, 1971-present; Atlanta Braves farm team, 1971-1974; Baseball coach, TX Christian University, 1974-1976; TX Secretary of st., 2005-2007.

DC Office: 1708 LHOB 20515, 202-225-9896, Fax: 202-225-9692, williams.house.gov

State Offices: Austin, 512-473-8910; Cleburne, 817-774-2575.

Committees: *Financial Services*: Consumer Protection & Financial Institutions; Nat'l Security, International Development & Monetary Policy.

Group Ratings

	ADA	ACLU	AFL-CIO	LCV	ITI	COC	HAFA	ACU	CFG	FRC
2018	-	14%	-	0%	-	75%	85%	92%	64%	100%
2017	0%	C	3%	0%	C	93%	C	96%	84%	100%

Almanac Ratings 2017-18

	Economy	Social	Foreign	Composite
Liberal	3%	7%	6%	5%
Conservative	97%	94%	94%	95%

Key Votes of the 115th Congress

1. Obama-care revision	Y	5. Family planning regs	Y	9. Guantanamo prisoners	N
2. Tax Cuts	Y	6. Body cameras/immigration	N	10. Ground missiles, limit	N
3. Omnibus appropriations	N	7. Abortion ban	Y	11. Defense Dept. spending	Y
4. Dodd-Frank revision	Y	8. Concealed carry	Y	12. FISA rules	N

Election Results

Election	Name (Party)	Vote (%)		Cand. Spent	Ind. Exp. Support	Ind. Exp. Oppose
2018 General	Roger Williams (R)	163,023	(54%)	$1,616,040		
	Julie Oliver (D)	136,385	(45%)	$620,656	$23,638	
2018 Primary	Roger Williams (R)		(100%)			

Prior winning percentages: 2016 (58%), 2014 (60%), 2012 (58%)

Republican Roger Williams, a former Texas secretary of state and prolific fundraiser, in 2012 took a district that had become reliably Republican in redistricting. He has quietly gone about his work, which includes a seat on the Financial Services Committee. He suffered setbacks on two non-legislative matters in the House. In 2016, he lost a bid to chair the National Republican Congressional Committee. Plus, he faced an ethics complaint dealing with his business ownership; eventually, he got a wrist slap.

Williams grew up in Fort Worth, where his father was a Chevrolet dealer and his mother ran a needlepoint business. He distinctly remembers that, as a 14-year-old, he was the last person to shake President John Kennedy's hand as he left the Texas Hotel in Fort Worth on the morning of Nov. 22, 1963. He attended Texas Christian University on a baseball scholarship. After graduating, he played in the Atlanta Braves minor league system for four years until he injured a shoulder while sliding into first base. He returned home to run the family car dealership and to coach baseball at TCU for three years. He continues to own the dealership, which led to the ethics inquiry.

Their shared love for baseball connected Williams and George W. Bush. A former owner of the Texas Rangers, Bush invited Williams to be a regional finance chairman for his two campaigns for governor, which was Williams' first foray into politics. In 2000, Bush appointed him to run the Republican National Committee's Eagles program. Later, Gov. Rick Perry appointed him as secretary of state. He was also Perry's chief liaison to Mexico. Having voiced interest in running for the open

Senate seat that Ted Cruz later won in 2012, Williams announced in 2011 that he would instead run for the 25th District seat. The GOP-engineered changes prompted its veteran Democratic Rep. Lloyd Doggett to move to the 35th District.

Williams overwhelmingly outspent the GOP primary field and defeated tea party activist Wes Riddle in a runoff, 58%-42%. Williams ran on what he called a "pretty simple" platform. "It's lower taxes, less government, cut the spending, defend the borders, listen to your generals, and understand the 10th Amendment," he said. He generated controversy when he called President Barack Obama a socialist at a campaign event, but said he saw no reason to apologize. "Here's a man that wants to own the banks, the car manufacturers, the student loan programs," he said. "It's basically socialism versus entrepreneurialism and capitalism. That's what we're fighting." In November, Williams defeated Democrat Elaine Henderson, 58%-37%.

In the House, Williams generated controversy in seeking to award the Medal of Honor to former Navy SEAL Chris Kyle, who inspired the movie American Sniper for having killed more than 160 people during combat in Iraq, and then was the victim of a shooting at a Texas rifle range. Critics from some veterans' groups contended that Kyle did not meet the required standard of a single extraordinary act of valor. Williams disagreed, and filed his bill in 2015. The House took no action on his proposal.

After serving as finance chairman of the National Republican Congressional Committee, he voiced interest in taking over as chairman of the full committee in 2014. When House Republicans made a double-digit gain in that election, then-chairman Greg Walden of Oregon. made clear that he was not giving up the post, Williams quietly abandoned his bid. Following the 2016 election, Williams and Rep. Steve Stivers of Ohio competed to replace Walden. Stivers, who had more experience within the NRCC, won on a 143-96 vote among House Republicans.

Questions dealing with his legislation related to car dealerships led the Office of Congressional Ethics to recommend that the House Ethics Committee conduct an investigation, given his continued ownership of a large auto dealership in the Fort Worth area. Williams denied any conflict. In August 2017, the committee ended its inquiry and said that the conduct of Williams "did not create a reasonable inference of improper conduct." Its statement added a general reminder that lawmakers who take legislative actions that could affect their personal financial interests "should contact the committee before doing so." In 2018, Roll Call listed his wealth as $27.7 million, which ranked him as the 13th wealthiest member of Congress.

In 2016, Democrat Kathi Thomas, a special events planner, challenged Williams for reelection. She talked about the need for bipartisanship and getting big money out of politics. Like other Democratic challengers in Texas, she had little money to make her case. Williams won, 58%-38%, though he trailed in Travis County, 55%-40%. In 2018, Democratic challenger Julie Oliver spent $646,000. An attorney and health care finance professional, she campaigned on behalf of "Medicare for all." The victory for Williams was reduced to 54%-45%, chiefly because Oliver increased the Democratic vote in Travis to 64 percent. With close to half of the vote cast in Travis, Williams — and other Republicans working on redistricting in 2021 — might seek to reduce the portion of that county that is in his district.

TX-25: Northern Travis County; the Hill Country **Cook Partisan Voting Index: R+11**

Population		Race and Ethnicity		Income	
Total	755,821	White	68.5%	Median Income	$67,263
Land area (sq. miles)	7,621	Black	6.7%	District Income Rank	116
Pop/ sq mi	99.2	Latino	18.5%	Poverty Rate	11.2%
Born in State	57.4%	Asian	2.9%	With health insurance	87.6%
		Two or more races	2.6%	Cash public assistance	1.4%
Age Groups		Other	0.7%	Food stamp/SNAP	8%
Under 18	24.2%				
18-34	23.5%	**Education**		**Work**	
35-64	39%	H.S grad or less	32.7%	White Collar	13.3%
Over 64	13.3%	Some college	30.3%	Sales and Service	36.6%
		College Degree, 4 yr	23.6%	Blue Collar	19.4%
Military		Post grad	13.4%	Government	16.1%
Veteran/ Active Duty	12.1%				

2012 Pres. Vote	Romney	162,279	(60%)	Obama	102,433	(38%)			
2016 Pres. Vote	Trump	172,476	(55%)	Clinton	125,949	(40%)	Johnson	11,772	(4%)

Austin: Austin, the capital of the second-largest state in the country and the site of the largest capitol building, had long been styled as laid-back and countrified. After World War II, in Sen. Lyndon Johnson's time, Austin had a metropolitan population of just over 130,000. There had never been much commerce. State government provided much of the local employment. Its skies were untainted by industrial smoke. Its biggest industry was the University of Texas, now with 52,000 students and an endowment of thousands of West Texas acres that turned out to sit on top of oil. The university has long had a distinguished faculty and some of the world's great scholarly collections, including the LBJ Presidential Library and its 45 million pages of documents. The Austin of old was also the central focus of Texas' hardy but almost always outnumbered liberals, based in the university, state government and Texas Observer magazine. They mocked the business lobbyists who they were certain called the shots when the "Leg" (pronounced lej) was in session.

Today's Austin is quite a different place. Greater Austin's population stands at 2.1 million. In 2017, it was the ninth fastest-growing metro area in the nation with at least 1 million people. The city, with a 19 percent increase from 2010 to 2017, has a population of 950,000. Some businesses cater to the old liberal bastions: The upscale organic-food chain Whole Foods Market was based in Austin, until its purchase by Amazon in 2017. The tone of the area overall has grown more corporate, especially as its private sector began to make up a larger share of the local economy. The techies who settled in the Silicon Hills tended to vote Republican. Housing prices across much of the city have soared, though they still seem cheap compared with San Francisco and Boston. Travis County in March 2017 declared itself a "sanctuary" for immigrants. But when the state passed a law prohibiting such designations, the county sheriff announced a reversal of its sanctuary status.

The 25th Congressional District of Texas, which includes the capitol and the nearby UT campus, has about 30 percent of the residents of Travis County. To dilute the liberal votes cast in Austin, they have been split among five districts, of which the 25th has the largest share and is the only district that runs across the county. That part of the district leans notably Democratic, though not as much as the lower-income neighborhoods of southeast Austin, which are in the 35th District. To the west of downtown, Mopac Boulevard operates as a dividing line for the more suburban, Republican-leaning areas of the county near Lake Travis. The remaining 55 percent of the district's population resides in a string of Republican-leaning counties that include the Hill Country. This stretch extends 180 miles north to Burleson in the Fort Worth exurbs. Rural Coryell County include much of Fort Hood, which covers more than 25 percent of the county's land area, though its official home in Killeen is in the 31st District. The 25th has been a solidly Republican district, though many of its new business class did not respond well to Donald Trump. He got 55 percent of the vote in 2016.

Michael Burgess (R)

Elected 2002, 9th term, b. Dec 23, 1950; Rochester, MN; The Selwyn School (TX), 1968; North Texas State University, Dallas, B.S., 1972; North Texas State University, M.S., 1976; University of Texas-Houston, M.D., 1977; University of Texas at Dallas, M.S., 2000; Anglican; Married (Laura Burgess); 3 children; 2 grandchildren.

Professional Career: Practicing obstetrician, 1981-2003.

DC Office: 2161 RHOB 20515, 202-225-7772, Fax: 202-225-2919, burgess.house.gov

State Offices: Lake Dallas, 940-497-5031.

Committees: *Energy & Commerce*: Consumer Protection & Commerce; Health (RMM); Oversight & Investigations. *Rules*: Legislative & Budget Process.

Group Ratings

	ADA	ACLU	AFL-CIO	LCV	ITI	COC	HAFA	ACU	CFG	FRC
2018	-	11%	-	0%	-	83%	77%	84%	56%	100%
2017	0%	C	5%	0%	C	93%	C	96%	78%	100%

Almanac Ratings 2017-18

	Economy	Social	Foreign	Composite
Liberal	3%	3%	3%	3%
Conservative	97%	97%	97%	97%

Key Votes of the 115th Congress

1. Obama-care revision	Y	5. Family planning regs	Y	9. Guantanamo prisoners	N
2. Tax Cuts	Y	6. Body cameras/immigration	N	10. Ground missiles, limit	N
3. Omnibus appropriations	Y	7. Abortion ban	Y	11. Defense Dept. spending	Y
4. Dodd-Frank revision	Y	8. Concealed carry	Y	12. FISA rules	N

Election Results

Election	Name (Party)	Vote (%)		Cand. Spent	Ind. Exp. Support	Ind. Exp. Oppose
2018 General	Michael Burgess (R)............................	185,551	(59%)	$1,601,514		
	Linsey Fagan (D)................................	121,938	(39%)	$92,789		
2018 Primary	Michael Burgess (R)............................	42,290	(77%)			
	Veronica Birkenstock (R).....................	12,684	(23%)			

Prior winning percentages: 2016 (66%), 2014 (83%), 2012 (68%), 2010 (67%), 2008 (60%), 2006 (60%), 2004 (66%), 2002 (75%)

Michael Burgess, a conservative Republican physician first elected in 2002, has become an activist House leader and GOP spokesman on health care. An outspoken member of the Energy and Commerce Committee, he served as chairman of its Health Subcommittee from 2017 to 2018. Republicans failed to achieve their paramount objective during that time, but they had success on some lower-profile issues.

Burgess grew up in Denton County, the son of a physician, and graduated from the University of North Texas and the University of Texas Medical School in Houston. He trained at Parkland Hospital in Dallas and set up an obstetrics-gynecology practice in Lewisville. After 21 years in practice, Burgess made an unlikely run for Congress, his first bid for elective office. When Majority Leader Dick Armey announced in 2001 that he would not run again, there was no doubt that a Republican would succeed him in his overwhelmingly Republican district. The widespread expectation was that the winner would be the majority leader's son, Scott Armey, a former Denton County judge. Almost no one expected that the winner would be Burgess.

In the primary, Armey outspent Burgess by more than 6-to-1. With no statewide Republican contests on the ballot, there seemed to be no suspense about the outcome. Armey took 45 percent of the vote, failing to gain the required majority. Burgess won 23 percent. In the four-week runoff campaign, Burgess benefited from a series of hard-hitting articles in The Dallas Morning News about Armey's record as a county judge, which suggested he had used his position to steer county jobs and contracts to close friends. Burgess focused on health care and taxes. He had helped to draft the Texas Patients' Bill of Rights and vowed to do the same on a national level. With a low-turnout of 19,259 voters, Burgess won the runoff 55%-45%. Armey tellingly lost 60%-40% in Denton County, where he was known best. Burgess breezed to victory in November, 75%-23%. He has been reelected comfortably since.

Burgess has a reliably conservative voting record, especially on social issues, according to the Almanac vote ratings. He joined the Tea Party Caucus when it was formed in 2010. He has pushed legislation to simplify or replace the federal income tax — either with a single flat rate or with a 23 percent sales tax on goods and services. Those proposals received little attention when Republicans approved tax cuts and major changes to the tax code in 2017.

Burgess has focused his work chiefly on health care. On Energy and Commerce, he has been an effective inquisitor on the 2010 health reform law, and was a persistent opponent of Obama administration policies. His nine-part plan for health care included many ideas that GOP candidates have espoused and that have become mainstream within the party, including allowing patients to shop for insurance across state lines and limiting damages in malpractice lawsuits.

He has made a steady rise to influence, with work on a cross-section of health care issues. In 2009, Burgess joined a bipartisan agreement to permit the Food and Drug Administration to approve generic versions of biologic drugs. He was part of a bipartisan group in 2011 that proposed legislation ensuring that seniors who show signs of Alzheimer's receive a formal diagnosis from their doctor. In 2015, he filed with then-Rep. Chris Van Hollen of Maryland the Advancing Research for Neurological Diseases Act of 2015, which would create a national data collection system at the Centers for Disease Control and Prevention for disorders such as Parkinson's disease and multiple sclerosis.

In 2015, he was the chief sponsor of a landmark law when Congress resolved the "doc fix" issue that limited reimbursements for patients with Medicare coverage. The bipartisan deal, which he called the most significant entitlement reform in years, included other changes in Medicare, such as performance incentives and new payment procedures for health care providers. Several provisions from Burgess were part of the enactment in 2016 of the Twenty First Century Cures Act, including neurological research and interoperability standards for electronic health records.

When Burgess became chairman of the Health Subcommittee in 2017, he said the position is "what I asked for" when first elected to Congress. "That's going to be my life for the next two years," he told The Texas Tribune. He described his role as "educator" of other members of Congress as well as the public. In a profile, McClatchy News headlined that Burgess was "the GOP's policy wonk behind Obamacare repeal." When House action was delayed, he blamed the Freedom Caucus. "There were people who were not interested in solving the problem," Burgess said in March 2017, according to Politico. House Republicans passed a slightly revised version of their proposal a few weeks later, but it died in the Senate that summer. He led action on other health care issues. The House passed in 2017 the bipartisan Improving Access to Maternity Care Act, of which Burgess was the lead sponsor. The proposal sought to improve the availability of maternity services, a topic with which he has deep familiarity. In 2018, President Donald Trump signed the "right to try" legislation that he had advocated, which authorized dying patients to use experimental drugs that had not been approved by the Food and Drug Administration. "Why do you not want to allow these patients to exercise their right to fight for the future?" Burgess asked opponents during House debate. He advocated research into the potential medical benefits of marijuana. At home, Burgess has kept his distance from the Texas GOP establishment. He was an early supporter of Ted Cruz, including his successful Senate primary bid against Lt. Gov. David Dewhurst in 2012. Early in the 2016 campaign, he said that it would be "inappropriate" for vaccination against measles to become an issue. His position took issue with Donald Trump, who occasionally raised questions about vaccines when he was a candidate.

TX-26: Northern Metroplex   Cook Partisan Voting Index: R+18

Population		Race and Ethnicity		Income	
Total	823,749	White	64.9%	Median Income	$85,433
Land area (sq. miles)	907	Black	7.5%	District Income Rank	36
Pop/ sq mi	908.1	Latino	18.2%	Poverty Rate	7.7%
Born in State	50.1%	Asian	6%	With health insurance	89%
		Two or more races	2.8%	Cash public assistance	1.1%
Age Groups		Other	0.6%	Food stamp/SNAP	5.6%
Under 18	27.2%				
18-34	23%	**Education**		**Work**	
35-64	40.6%	H.S grad or less	26.4%	White Collar	9.2%
Over 64	9.2%	Some college	30.9%	Sales and Service	39.3%
		College Degree, 4 yr	28.9%	Blue Collar	14.7%
Military		Post grad	13.8%	Government	12.3%
Veteran/ Active Duty	7.8%				

2012 Pres. Vote	Romney	177,941	(68%)	Obama	80,828	(31%)		
2016 Pres. Vote	Trump	194,033	(60%)	Clinton	109,536	(34%)	Johnson	12,577 (4%)

Denton County: Until the Texas Land and Immigration Company settled this portion of northeast Texas with a land grant from the Texas Congress in 1841, settlers were scarce and Indian raids were common. The area now known as Denton County takes its name from John Bunyan Denton, a Methodist pioneer preacher and lawyer killed in a skirmish with Indians. Today, this area on the northern edge of the Dallas-Fort Worth Metroplex is teeming with new arrivals and filling up with young, well-educated, middle-class families. In 1940, there were 34,000 people in Denton County, and they voted 88 percent Democratic for president. Population for the county grew from 432,000 in 2000 in 836,000 in 2017, a 94 percent increase. The University of North Texas, with more than 38,000 students, is the sixth-largest in the state, while Texas Woman's University is the largest state-supported university for women in the United States (although it does accept men).

The county's chief cities are Denton, Flower Mound and Lewisville, and there is plenty of room for more growth along Interstates 35E and 35W. Truck manufacturer Peterbilt Motors, the largest employer in Denton with 2,300 employees, completed in 2017 a large expansion to improve its efficiency. Near Justin, in the southwest corner of Denton County, a pipeline allows for the production of up to 1 billion cubic feet of natural gas daily. With sophisticated imaging and drilling technology, other natural gas wells operate within 10 miles of downtown Fort Worth. The sale of GE Transportation, which manufactures rail locomotives in Fort Worth, to the local Westinghouse Air Brakes Technology firm in 2018 restored hope that the business would fare better outside of the chaos that has surrounded GE in recent years; company officials voiced confidence about continued demand for their products. More broadly, Oxford Economics, a forecasting firm, projected that Denton County from 2017 to 2022 would have the strongest economic growth of any county in the nation. Sufficient open space remains so that Denton has more horse ranches than any other county in the United States.

The 26th Congressional District of Texas is at the heart of the northern expansion of the Metroplex. It includes more than 80 percent of Denton County, and a small fragment of urban Tarrant County, including the old railroad town of Keller, now a bustling upscale suburb. There are some Democratic areas here, especially around Denton's universities. The county voted 65 percent for Mitt Romney in 2012, though it fell to 58 percent for Donald Trump in 2016. Overall, this was the second-strongest Republican district in the Metroplex for Trump; he got 60 percent here, short of the 62 percent in the 5th District.

Michael Cloud (R)

Elected 2018, 1st full term, b. May 13, 1975; Baton Rouge, LA; Oral Roberts University, Bach. Deg.; Religion unknown; Married (Rosel Cloud); 3 children.

DC Office: 1314 LHOB 20515, 202-225-7742, Fax: 202-226-1134, cloud.house.gov

State Offices: Corpus Christi, 361-884-2222; Victoria, 361-894-6446.

Committees: *Oversight & Reform*: National Security; Subcommittee on Civil Rights & Civil Liberties; Subcommittee on Economic & Consumer Policy (RMM). *Science, Space & Technology*: Energy.

Group Ratings

	ADA	ACLU	AFL-CIO	LCV	ITI	COC	HAFA	ACU	CFG	FRC
2018	-	-	-	0%	-	-	-	-	-	100%

Election Results

Election	Name (Party)	Vote (%)		Cand. Spent	Ind. Exp. Support	Ind. Exp. Oppose
2018 General	Michael J. Cloud (R)............................ 125,118	(60%)	$675,823	$539,749		
	Eric Holguin (D)............................... 75,929	(37%)	$186,909			
	James Duerr (I)...................................... 4,274	(2%)	$65,138			
2018 Primary	Michael J. Cloud (R)............................ 15,041	(61%)				
Runoff	Bech Bruun (R)...................................... 9,565	(39%)				
2018 Primary	Bech Bruun (R)..................................... 15,919	(36%)				
	Michael J. Cloud (R)............................ 14,920	(34%)				
	Chris Mapp (R)....................................... 5,356	(12%)				
	Jerry Hall (R)... 3,649	(8%)				
	John Grunwald (R)................................. 3,027	(7%)				

Republican Michael Cloud, a newcomer to public office, navigated an unusual path to Congress, including a special election to the seat of his predecessor, Blake Farenthold. The incumbent had quit following allegations of ethics violations that resulted from sexual harassment claims by a former House employee. Cloud, a veteran party activist, was the least experienced with public policy issues of the six Texas Republicans who won open House seats in 2018. He skillfully learned the political ropes and settled into his House seat, facing significant local demands for aid in recovery from Hurricane Harvey devastation in 2017. Amid the turmoil that had surrounded Farenthold, Cloud ran a relatively harmonious campaign while emphasizing his outsider status.

Cloud, a graduate of Oral Roberts University, owned a small business in which he advised on media relations. He was the communications director of the Faith Family Church in Victoria, served seven years as chairman of the Victoria County Republican Party and was a local leader of the tea party. His core message was that "Congress is broken" and failed to serve the public's interests.

He entered the GOP primary two months prior to Farenthold's decision not to seek reelection, which ensued from additional controversy that he used $84,000 in congressional funds to settle the discrimination claim from his ex-aide. (Farenthold subsequently became a lobbyist for Port Lavaca, a tourist site north of Corpus Christi. He reneged on his pledge to reimburse the $84,000.) Once Farenthold stepped aside, the frontrunner was Bech Bruun, who has held several senior positions in Texas government, including chairman of the Water Development Board. Key Republican officials, including Gov. Greg Abbott, quickly endorsed Bruun, who had a fundraising advantage in the primary.

In the first round of voting, Bruun got 58 percent of the vote in his base of Nueces County, which had the largest turnout. Cloud got 62 percent in Victoria County, his base, which had the second-largest turnout. With six other candidates splitting the vote in the 11 other mostly rural counties, Bruun led Cloud in the first round, 36%-34%. Cloud's strength grew in the May runoff. He took 85 percent of the vote in Victoria and led in each of the other counties except for Nueces, where he reduced Bruun's vote to 53 percent. Overall, Cloud won, 61%-39%.

Cloud's victory in November over Democrat Eric Holguin, a gay activist and former congressional aide, was largely a formality. Instead, attention turned to Abbott's decision to schedule a special election on June 30 so the district would have federal representation in dealing with recovery from flood damage. The filing deadline had been set prior to the runoff for the full term, which led the chief contenders in both parties to file for the remaining months of the vacant seat. In the nonpartisan primary in which a majority of all votes was required to avoid a runoff, the initial expectation was that another contest would be required in September.

Bruun reduced the suspense by endorsing Cloud following the May runoff and urging his voters to switch their allegiance. That tactic proved successful. With only 4 percent of the special-election vote going to Bruun, Cloud won 55 percent of the total vote. Cloud led narrowly in Nueces County, and comfortably elsewhere. He took his House seat in July and won a full term with 60 percent. In November, he won all 11 counties; in Nueces, which cast nearly 45 percent of the total vote, Cloud led by only 232 votes.

TX-27: Central Gulf Coast   Cook Partisan Voting Index: R+13

Population		Race and Ethnicity		Income	
Total	732,212	White	40%	Median Income	$53,040
Land area (sq. miles)	9,128	Black	4.9%	District Income Rank	252
Pop/ sq mi	80.2	Latino	52.2%	Poverty Rate	15.9%
Born in State	75.3%	Asian	1.5%	With health insurance	82.2%
		Two or more races	1%	Cash public assistance	1.5%
Age Groups		Other	0.3%	Food stamp/SNAP	14.4%
Under 18	25.3%				
18-34	22.8%	**Education**		**Work**	
35-64	37%	H.S grad or less	49.2%	White Collar	14.9%
Over 64	14.9%	Some college	31.7%	Sales and Service	43%
		College Degree, 4 yr	12.7%	Blue Collar	28.4%
Military		Post grad	6.5%	Government	14.5%
Veteran/ Active Duty	10%				

2012 Pres. Vote	Romney	131,803	(61%)	Obama	83,152	(38%)			
2016 Pres. Vote	Trump	140,787	(60%)	Clinton	85,589	(36%)	Johnson	6,491	(3%)

Corpus Christi, Victoria: The Nueces River rises on the Edwards Plateau in Central Texas, almost a half mile above sea level. From there it cascades across the Texas Hill Country and passes through the coastal plain before emptying into the Gulf of Corpus Christi. Early attempts at establishing settlements near the river's terminus were half-hearted and unsuccessful, and the area was uninhabited until Henry Lawrence Kinney and William Aubrey established a trading post on the west shore of the bay in 1839. Growth came slowly here at first; a population of 2,100 in 1870 was barely 11,000 in 1920. Hurricanes, the occasional outbreak of yellow fever and, more importantly, the lack of a deep-water port, frustrated attempts to expand the city.

Then, in 1926, the federal government completed the dredging of a shipping channel and the modern Port of Corpus Christi was born. The city's population almost tripled in the 1920s, then doubled in the 1930s. By 2017, it topped 325,000. The port is the sixth largest in the United States in total tonnage shipped, a center for exporting cotton, sorghum and grains, and importing steel and construction equipment; the port includes numerous factories and industrial plants. Barge traffic of oil has increased greatly along the Gulf Intracoastal Waterway. In November 2018, a $15 billion liquefied natural gas facility — the first in Texas -- was opened in nearby Gregory; it was the first "greenfield" liquefaction plant built in the lower 48 states. In 2016, work began on the $900 million Harbor Bridge, which will replace a nearby bridge that is nearly 70 years old; it will give larger ships entry to the port. The Naval Air Station at Corpus Christi is another major contributor to the local economy. Starting in 2010, the Eagle Ford Shale yielded more than 1.5 million barrels of daily oil production. In December 2018, work began in San Patricio County on a $10 billion petrochemical complex owned by ExxonMobil and its Saudi partner; the project expected to hire 6,000 workers for the construction. Corpus Christi's population is 62 percent Hispanic. Only 9 percent of residents were foreign-born. According to an earlier Pew Research Center report, the city had the smallest such share of any of the 60 metro areas with sizable Hispanic populations.

The 27th Congressional District of Texas is centered on Corpus Christi, and almost half its residents live in the city and surrounding Nueces County. Corpus Christi is the county seat and 90 percent of Nueces; the city extends into three adjacent smaller counties. The district takes in most of the Gulf Coast north of Corpus Christi, up to Bay City and the outskirts of Houston's suburbs. The only other city of any size in the district is Victoria, an industrial town of 68,000. An arm of the 27th reaches to Bastrop and Caldwell counties, in the Austin area, and takes in Gonzales, where the first shots of the Texas Revolution were fired. The redrawn district, unlike its predecessor, is safe Republican territory, even with its 52 percent Hispanic population. In 2016, Donald Trump got 60 percent of the district vote.

Henry Cuellar (D)

Elected 2004, 8th term, b. Sep 19, 1955; Laredo; Laredo Community College (TX), A.A., 1976; Georgetown University (DC), B.S., 1978; University of Texas School of Law, J.D., 1981; Texas A and M International University, M.B.A., 1982; University of Texas, Ph.D., 1998; Roman Catholic; Married (Imelda Rios Cuellar); 2 children.

Elected Office: TX House,1987-2001; TX Secretary of st., 2001.

Professional Career: Practicing attorney, 1981-2004; Adjunct Professional, TX A&M University, 1984-1986.

DC Office: 2372 RHOB 20515, 202-225-1640, Fax: 202-225-1641, cuellar.house.gov

State Offices: Laredo, 956-725-0639; Mission, 956-424-3942; Rio Grande City, 956-487-5603; San Antonio, 210-271-2851.

Committees: *Appropriations*: Agriculture, Rural Development, FDA & Related Agencies; Defense; Homeland Security.

Group Ratings

	ADA	ACLU	AFL-CIO	LCV	ITI	COC	HAFA	ACU	CFG	FRC
2018	-	43%	-	49%	-	91%	19%	40%	30%	40%
2017	40%	C	55%	34%	C	92%	C	22%	13%	33%

Almanac Ratings 2017-18

	Economy	Social	Foreign	Composite
Liberal	35%	43%	67%	48%
Conservative	65%	57%	33%	52%

Key Votes of the 115th Congress

1. Obama-care revision	N	5. Family planning regs	N	9. Guantanamo prisoners	N
2. Tax Cuts	N	6. Body cameras/immigration	Y	10. Ground missiles, limit	Y
3. Omnibus appropriations	Y	7. Abortion ban	Y	11. Defense Dept. spending	Y
4. Dodd-Frank revision	Y	8. Concealed carry	Y	12. FISA rules	Y

Election Results

Election	Name (Party)	Vote (%)		Cand. Spent	Ind. Exp. Support	Ind. Exp. Oppose
2018 General	Henry Cuellar (D)........................	117,494	(84%)	$687,134		
	Arthur Thomas IV (Lib).....................	21,732	(16%)			
2018 Primary	Henry Cuellar (D).......................		(100%)			

Prior winning percentages: 2016 (66%), 2014 (82%), 2012 (68%), 2010 (56%), 2008 (69%), 2006 (68%), 2004 (59%)

Henry Cuellar, elected in 2004, is one of the most conservative Hispanic Democrats, with a voting record putting him near the center of the House as a whole. Even with his coveted seat on the Appropriations Committee, he has remained a maverick — including in Texas politics. He has delivered funds to his district for its many needs, including homeland security and agriculture.

Cuellar was the oldest of eight children of migrant workers who had only elementary school educations. He graduated from Georgetown University and the University of Texas law school, and later got a Ph.D. in government from UT. With his five degrees, he claims to be the "most degreed" member of the House. From his base in Laredo, he served in the Texas House from 1986 to 2000, where he helped to author the Texas Grant college aid program. In 2001, Republican Gov. Rick Perry appointed him secretary of state even though he is a Democrat.

Cuellar resigned in 2002 to run against veteran Republican Rep. Henry Bonilla in the sprawling 23rd District. Bonilla claimed he didn't need Laredo to win. In response, the Webb County GOP chairman endorsed Cuellar. The challenger attacked Bonilla for his votes against funding for the Children's Health Insurance Program, the Family and Medical Leave Act, and Pell grants. Cuellar carried Webb County 84%-15%. When the Bexar County votes were counted, Bonilla's confidence turned out to be warranted. He won 52%-47%.

Redistricting in 2003 gave Cuellar an opportunity to run against Democratic Rep. Ciro Rodriguez of San Antonio, who was chairman of the Hispanic Caucus. Rodriguez expressed disbelief that a friend and former legislative colleague for whom he had raised money in 2002 would run against him. The ambitious Cuellar told a local reporter, "Nobody died and made him king." Cuellar criticized Rodriguez for voting against the GOP's 2003 Medicare prescription drug bill, while Rodriguez pointed out Cuellar's cooperation with Republicans as secretary of state. Cuellar was the Democratic nominee by 58 votes out of 49,000 cast. He won in November, 59%-39%.

Cuellar's voting has placed him among the most conservative Democrats. The Almanac ratings for 2015 and 2017 gave him the second-highest conservative score for a House Democrat behind Collin Peterson of Minnesota. Cuellar has been a leader of the Blue Dog Coalition of his party's fiscal conservatives. He was one of just 22 Democrats to support a failed amendment for a fiscal 2013 budget based on the recommendations of the Simpson-Bowles deficit reduction commission. He joined most of the Texas delegation in voting against lifting the financial liability cap on oil spills. In response to criticism of his independence, Cuellar often says, "I will die as a Democrat."

His middle ground positions on immigration have irritated both parties. He was the only House Democrat who voted for a bill that would have made it easier to deport unaccompanied minors from Central America. He criticized President Barack Obama and said that Obama looked "aloof and detached" by not going to the Mexican border when he was in Texas for political fundraisers in 2014. When Donald Trump became president, Cuellar attacked his proposal for a border wall as "a 14th century solution," and said that illegal immigration ought to be addressed as a 21st century problem, with steps such as military surveillance and a "virtual border." During the January 2019 partial government shutdown when Trump was seeking additional funds for a wall, Cuellar joined a bipartisan delegation to meet with the president. Later, he told reporters that Trump was "just wrong" that a wall is the only security; he continued to advocate multiple steps, such as more personnel and improved technology.

Cuellar has had success passing legislation that has benefited his district. In 2016, he enacted his bill for alternative financing arrangements to construct and maintain facilities at ports of entry along the border. The water-resources bill that became law the same month included a provision for the Army Corps of Engineers to study a flood-control project along Chacon Creek in Laredo. In a spending bill that was approved in 2017, he claimed credit for $947 million for his 10-20-30 agriculture program: at least 10 percent of funds goes to counties where 20 percent or more of the population has lived in poverty for the past 30 years. In 2018 and again in January 2019, Cuellar won House passage of his U.S.-Mexico Economic Partnership Act, which would expand educational and professional exchange programs.

In Cuellar's first reelection bid in 2006, Rodriguez challenged him in the primary but struggled to match his fundraising. Cuellar won the primary comfortably, 53%-40%. He has won reelection easily since. He got national media attention in 2018 when he sponsored a fundraising event for Texas Republican Rep. John Carter, who was facing a difficult reelection challenge. "Judge Carter is a dear friend and trusted colleague with whom I work on Appropriations," Cuellar said in a statement. He added that he raised more money for House Democrats than has any other Democrat from Texas.

In January 2019, Justice Democrats — a political committee of progressive activists that has sought to reshape the party through primary challenges — listed Cuellar as its initial target for 2020. In response, Cuellar told reporters, "I've been polling and my district is more moderate, conservative Democrats, and I think an outside group that thinks they know south Texas politics better than I do are going to find [that] out," according to Roll Call.

With his seniority on Appropriations, Cuellar was close to becoming the top Democrat on a subcommittee — assuming he retains the support of other Democrats when there is a vacancy.

TX-28: South Texas   **Cook Partisan Voting Index: D+9**

Population		Race and Ethnicity		Income	
Total	742,188	White	16.3%	Median Income	$46,733
Land area (sq. miles)	9,379	Black	4%	District Income Rank	356
Pop/ sq mi	79.1	Latino	77.5%	Poverty Rate	25.2%
Born in State	63.9%	Asian	1%	With health insurance	74.4%
		Two or more races	1%	Cash public assistance	1.6%
Age Groups		Other	0.2%	Food stamp/SNAP	23.4%
Under 18	31.2%				
18-34	23.6%	**Education**		**Work**	
35-64	34.3%	H.S grad or less	56.4%	White Collar	10.9%
Over 64	10.9%	Some college	25.7%	Sales and Service	47.6%
		College Degree, 4 yr	12.3%	Blue Collar	24.9%
Military		Post grad	5.6%	Government	17%
Veteran/ Active Duty	7.5%				

2012 Pres. Vote	Obama	101,843	(60%)	Romney	65,372	(39%)			
2016 Pres. Vote	Clinton	110,020	(58%)	Trump	72,520	(38%)	Johnson	4,401	(2%)

Laredo/San Antonio Corridor: The border country along the Rio Grande is in some ways a region all its own, a mixture of the United States and Mexico. As former Laredo Mayor Betty Flores has said, "The river for us is more like some street that we cross. It's really not a border." This is where, in "Streets of Laredo," singer Marty Robbins summoned up images of lonely cowboys on dusty streets outside of saloons in a tiny town. But that is not the Laredo of today. It is the busiest border crossing for U.S.-Mexico trade. About 20,000 trucks and railcars cross its four bridges daily; with about $303 billion in two-way trade crossing the Rio Grande in 2017, the Laredo customs district was the second busiest in the nation behind Los Angeles. Local enthusiasts refer to the Laredo area as "NAFTA on Wheels." They were hoping that the limited revisions in NAFTA that President Donald Trump reached in 2018 with his counterparts from Mexico and Canada would win quick approval from Congress and implementation. Laredo grew at a 34 percent pace in the first decade of the 21st century and another 10 percent from 2010 to 2017. Its old downtown streets are filled with Mexicans who cross the border on foot.

Laredo's Webb County had a population of 275,000 in 2017, of which 96 percent was Hispanic. Local fast-food restaurants feature enchiladas more often than hamburgers. Nearly three-fourths of all businesses are minority owned, which is the largest share in the nation. The region has its problems, including crime from the trade in illegal immigration and drugs; its positioning at the end of Interstate 35 makes it an important point of entry for both. The county retained a 27 percent poverty rate in 2017. Production in the Eagle Ford Shale increased in 2018, with 175 new permits to drill oil and gas wells.

The 28th Congressional District of Texas is centered in Laredo and Webb County, which has the largest population in the district. South along the Rio Grande, it crosses Starr County, one of the poorest counties in Texas and home of many blatant and wealthy drug smugglers. It also takes in Mission in a narrow strip of Hidalgo County. These border counties make up about two-thirds of the district. To the north, it extends through thinly settled ranch and oil well country, plus about 160,000 residents on the eastern side of Bexar County, including a small portion of San Antonio. It includes the Joint Base San Antonio, formed from the joining of Randolph and Lackland Air Force bases and Fort Sam Houston. About 78 percent of the residents of the 28th are Hispanic. The district leans Democratic locally, but Republicans sometimes do well. President George W. Bush in 2004 and some state GOP officials have carried the district as currently configured. In 2016, Hillary Clinton got 58 percent.

Sylvia Garcia (D)

Elected 2018, 1st term, b. Sep 06, 1950; San Diego; Texas Woman's University, B.A., 1972; Texas Southern University, Thurgood Marshall School of Law, J.D., 1978; Catholic; Single.

Elected Office: Presiding Judge, Houston Municipal System; City of Houston Controller, 1998-2002; Harris County Commissioner, 2003-2008; TX Senate, 2013-2018.

Professional Career: Social Worker; Attorney.

DC Office: 1620 LHOB 20515, 202-225-1688, sylviagarcia.house.gov

State Offices: Houston, 832-325-3150.

Committees: *Financial Services*: Oversight & Investigations; Subcommittee on Diversity & Inclusion. *Judiciary*: Constitution, Civil Rights & Civil Liberties; Immigration & Citizenship.

Election Results

Election	Name (Party)	Vote (%)		Cand. Spent	Ind. Exp. Support	Ind. Exp. Oppose
2018 General	Sylvia Garcia (D)	88,188	(75%)	$985,805	$137,084	
	Phillip Aronoff (R)	28,098	(24%)	$96,656		
2018 Primary	Sylvia Garcia (D)	11,727	(63%)			
	Muhammad Tahir Javed (D)	3,831	(21%)			
	Roel Garcia (D)	1,221	(7%)			

Democratic first-termer Sylvia Garcia won the open Houston-area seat that she first sought in 1992. In that contest, she was defeated by Gene Green, an Anglo who held the heavily Latino seat for the next 26 years and faced growing pressure to defer to the minority community. In 2018, Green and most of the local political establishment backed Garcia. Despite occasional setbacks, she compiled one of the most extensive records in local and state government by any member of the large freshman class. Garcia and Veronica Escobar, who won the El Paso-based 16th District, became the first two Latinas elected to Congress from Texas. "I never really wanted to be the first. I wanted to be the best," Garcia told supporters.

A native of a small farming community in west Texas, Garcia graduated from Texas Woman's University in Denton, with a degree in social work and political science. She got her law degree from Texas Southern University in Houston, where she worked at several jobs to pay for her tuition. Early in her career, Garcia was a social worker and a legal-aid attorney.

She served five terms in the appointed position as director and presiding judge of the Houston Municipal System. In the 1992 contest for the newly created Latino-majority district, Garcia ran third in the Democratic primary, with 21 percent of the vote. Six years later, she was elected Houston City Controller, the city's chief financial officer. In a further sign of the shifting local politics, she was elected in 2002 to the Harris County Commissioner's Court, the first woman and first Latina to hold that position; eight years later, she unexpectedly lost reelection to a Republican. She won a special election for the state senate in 2013.

After Green, a senior Democrat on the House Energy and Commerce Committee, announced his retirement, Garcia was the early frontrunner to succeed him. During the campaign, she said that her top national concern was passage of legislation to grant permanent legal status to "dreamers," who entered the nation as minors and lacked citizenship. In an interview with the Houston Chronicle, she said that her chief local concern was the need to protect against a repeat of the hurricane devastation that recently had jarred the Houston area.

Garcia contended with an unexpected Democratic primary challenge from Tahir Javed, a health care entrepreneur who raised $1.8 million (including $1.3 million from himself), far more than the other candidates; he had been a prominent fundraiser for Hillary Clinton in the 2016 presidential campaign. With endorsements from Indian-American groups and national Democrats, including Senate Minority Leader Chuck Schumer of New York, Javed hoped to keep Garcia below 50 percent in the primary and force a runoff. Schumer spoke at a Houston fundraising event for him, to the dismay of some Hispanic Democrats.

Garcia, who raised $700,000 for the primary, had a robust campaign organization and was supported by organized labor and EMILY's List. In the March primary, she easily prevailed with 63 percent of the vote to 21 percent for Javed; five other candidates split the remainder. Following the primary, she was more cautious in criticizing President Donald Trump than were many other House Democratic hopefuls. Citing her background as a judge, the experienced Garcia told The Texas Tribune in April 2018, "the facts are not there yet" to warrant impeachment proceedings. She has been out front with Democratic activists in leading demonstrations against Trump's policies along the border and seeking to abolish the Immigration and Customs Enforcement agency.

After a 26-year wait to enter Congress, Garcia made a quick impression. She scored with assignments to the Financial Services and Judiciary committees, including the Immigration Subcommittee.

TX-29: Harris County

Cook Partisan Voting Index: D+19

Population		Race and Ethnicity		Income	
Total	740,295	White	9.7%	Median Income	$41,301
Land area (sq. miles)	187	Black	10.6%	District Income Rank	404
Pop/ sq mi	3957.3	Latino	77.4%	Poverty Rate	25%
Born in State	57.2%	Asian	1.6%	With health insurance	68.4%
		Two or more races	0.4%	Cash public assistance	1.3%
Age Groups		Other	0.2%	Food stamp/SNAP	20.7%
Under 18	31.2%				
18-34	26.5%	**Education**		**Work**	
35-64	34.5%	H.S grad or less	68.6%	White Collar	7.8%
Over 64	7.8%	Some college	21.8%	Sales and Service	41.4%
		College Degree, 4 yr	6.9%	Blue Collar	41.7%
Military		Post grad	2.7%	Government	8.4%
Veteran/ Active Duty	3.2%				

2012 Pres. Vote	Obama	75,720	(66%)	Romney	37,909	(33%)			
2016 Pres. Vote	Clinton	95,027	(71%)	Trump	34,011	(25%)	Johnson	3,136	(2%)

East Houston and Pasadena: Many areas of Texas have large Mexican-American communities that can be traced back to statehood. But not Houston. The swampy area in what was originally called Harrisburg County had few inhabitants of any ethnicity until the 20th century. Houston and its Mexican-American community had to be built from the ground up. The city's economy was also built from the ground up, based on a combination of cotton, oil and trade via the 52-mile Houston Ship Channel. Cotton and oil were gifts of nature, though they required much human effort and ingenuity to produce in commercial quantities. The ship channel has been almost totally man's creation and a massive public works project. Along with the unsettled conditions created by the Mexican Revolution of 1910, it provided the impetus for Mexican immigration to the city.

After the sand-spit port of Galveston was destroyed by a hurricane in 1900, Houston's elders decided to dredge out Buffalo Bayou and make their inland city a seaport. When the channel officially opened in November 1914, a sluggish, 6-foot-deep creek had become a 40-foot-deep waterway that would turn Houston into one of the nation's biggest ports. Today, the channel is 45 feet deep and 530 feet wide. In the port, which is the second-largest in the nation in tonnage, more than half the cargo is energy-related. Total exports from the port of Houston exceeded imports in 2018 by about $20 billion. Nearly half of those exports were from gasoline, oil and petroleum gases. In early 2018, for the first time ever, oil exports from the port exceeded oil imports. The port is the site of the largest petrochemical complex in the nation. On its west side, Houston seems entirely a white-collar, office-bound city. But on the east and north, around the port and through the maze of refinery towers and pipelines, it remains blue-collar and a job magnet for Mexican Americans and workers from the rural South. To the south is Hobby Airport, whose art-deco terminal served the city until what is now called the George Bush International Airport opened in 1969. Hobby serves about 25 percent of the area's airline passengers. The three devastating hurricanes that struck Houston in three years, capped by Harvey in 2017, temporarily shut down refineries, pipelines and chemical plants. They were a reminder that the clout of Mother Nature had not disappeared following the destruction of Galveston more than a century earlier, though the local infrastructure had been strengthened. In August 2018, voters in Harris County approved $2.5 billion in new bonds for more than 200 flood-control projects.

The 29th Congressional District of Texas, which is entirely in Harris County, covers much of the ship channel area and working-class Houston. Its unusual shape — some say it resembles a seated dragon — connects heavily Hispanic sections north of Houston with the Hispanic community around the ship channel and Pasadena. The district wraps around the Sam Houston Tollway, taking in blue-collar neighborhoods in northeast Houston as well. In the southeast, Pasadena, once part of the giant Allen Ranch, is now a working-class city of 154,000 centered on the oil and aerospace industries. In 2017, construction began on a $820 million high-capacity marine terminal along the ship channel in Pasadena. It will chiefly handle refined petroleum products and will be able to dock Panamax-size ships; with room for expansion, completion of the initial facility was scheduled for 2020. The district is 77 percent Hispanic and firmly Democratic. Hillary Clinton got 71 percent in 2016.

Eddie Bernice Johnson (D)

Elected 1992, 14th term, b. Dec 03, 1935; Waco; St. Mary's College at the University of Notre Dame (IN), M.P.A., 1955; Texas Christian University, B.S., 1967; Southern Methodist University (TX), M.P.A., 1976; Baptist; Divorced; 1 child; 3 grandchildren.

Elected Office: TX House, 1973-1977; TX Senate, 1987-1993.

Professional Career: Registered nurse, 1955-1972; Regional Director, U.S. Department of HEW, 1977-1981; Mgmt. consultant, Sammons Corporation, 1979-1981; Owner, Eddie Bernice Johnson & Association.

DC Office: 2306 RHOB 20515, 202-225-8885, Fax: 202-226-1477, ebjohnson.house.gov

State Offices: Dallas, 214-922-8885.

Committees: *Science, Space & Technology (Chmn). Transportation & Infrastructure*: Aviation; Highways & Transit; Water Resources & Environment.

Group Ratings

	ADA	ACLU	AFL-CIO	LCV	ITI	COC	HAFA	ACU	CFG	FRC
2018	-	89%	-	94%	-	58%	4%	4%	8%	0%
2017	85%	C	100%	94%	C	50%	C	0%	0%	0%

Almanac Ratings 2017-18

	Economy	Social	Foreign	Composite
Liberal	95%	97%	90%	94%
Conservative	5%	3%	10%	6%

Key Votes of the 115th Congress

1. Obama-care revision	N	5. Family planning regs	N	9. Guantanamo prisoners	Y
2. Tax Cuts	N	6. Body cameras/immigration	Y	10. Ground missiles, limit	Y
3. Omnibus appropriations	N	7. Abortion ban	N	11. Defense Dept. spending	Y
4. Dodd-Frank revision	N	8. Concealed carry	N	12. FISA rules	N

Election Results

Election	Name (Party)	Vote (%)		Cand. Spent	Ind. Exp. Support	Ind. Exp. Oppose
2018 General	Eddie Bernice Johnson (D)	166,784	(91%)	$260,062		
	Shawn Jones (Lib)	16,390	(9%)			
2018 Primary	Eddie Bernice Johnson (D)	32,415	(64%)			
	Barbara Caraway (D)	11,641	(23%)			
	Eric Williams (D)	6,931	(14%)			

Prior winning percentages: 2016 (78%), 2014 (88%), 2012 (79%), 2010 (76%), 2008 (82%), 2006 (80%), 2004 (93%), 2002 (74%), 2000 (92%), 1998 (72%), 1996 (55%), 1994 (73%), 1992 (72%)

Eddie Bernice Johnson, a Democrat first elected in 1992, has been a revered figure in Dallas politics, an advocate for the city for nearly a half-century. Some of her younger rivals and The Dallas Morning News' editorial page have said that it's time for her to step aside, even as she acknowledged that she was considering retirement. By remaining in the House until Democrats regained control, Johnson became chairwoman of the Science, Space and Technology Committee, where she promised a more bipartisan approach, especially in contrast to her often-fractious relationship with the previous Republican chairman, a fellow Texan. At age 83 when she took the gavel, Johnson was the second-oldest House member, trailing only Republican Rep. Don Young of Alaska. When Democrats regained House control, she was the only chairman from Texas, which has a long history of influential lawmakers in both parties.

Johnson grew up in Texas, graduated from Texas Christian University with a nursing degree, and later got a master's degree in public administration at Southern Methodist University. She worked at St. Paul Hospital and was the chief psychiatric nurse at the Veterans Administration Hospital in Dallas. She told The Morning News in 1987 that she first got interested in politics in the early 1960s, when she went to buy a new hat and was shocked to learn that blacks in the city weren't allowed to try on such headgear. She organized a boycott of the store. In 1972, she was elected to the Texas House, the first black woman elected to the legislature from Dallas. She became a regional director of the Health, Education and Welfare Department under President Jimmy Carter. She was elected to the Texas Senate in 1986. As the Senate's Redistricting Committee chair in 1991, she was instrumental in creating the new 30th District and she went on to win the Democratic primary with 92 percent of the vote. She remains the only person to have held the seat.

In the House, Johnson — known by her initials "EBJ" — has a mostly liberal voting record. A former chairwoman of the Congressional Black Caucus, she was more supportive of President Barack Obama than other CBC members critical of his limited efforts for low-income and unemployed blacks. She has been attentive to business interests in Dallas. Johnson once pledged to labor unions to oppose the North American Free Trade Agreement, but she changed her mind and voted for it in 1993. Dallas is a large exporter to Mexico and many jobs depend on that trade. Johnson also sided with business on normalizing trade relations with China and was one of 28 House Democrats who backed trade promotion authority for Obama in 2015. National unions were unhappy, though she suffered no political damage.

Johnson became ranking Democrat on the Science, Space, and Technology Committee in 2011. What had long been a bipartisan committee has become increasingly polarized. At a 2013 hearing, she accused chairman Lamar Smith, a fellow Texan, of representing the interests of "industry hacks." In 2015, they clashed over his criticism of scientists at the National Oceanic and Atmospheric Administration who had studied global warming. Smith's claims that the researchers altered historical climate data were "the most outrageous statements ever made by a chair of the Committee on Science," she said. While lambasting proposed cuts in science funding, she sought to encourage more students to enter science- and technology-related fields. As a health care professional, she takes an interest in minority health issues. She has regularly filed her bipartisan bill to create a federal National Nurse for Public Health to work alongside the surgeon general.

Taking the committee gavel in 2019, Johnson focused on the panel as "the only one that really truly examines the future in a profound way." She said that her objectives included ensuring that the United States leads the world in science and innovation and has "the right educational and workforce development programs." Her hopes for bipartisanship may have been improved by the retirement of Smith and the selection of the more collegial Frank Lucas of Oklahoma as the panel's ranking Republican. As The Texas Tribune noted in an August 2018 profile of Johnson, the committee is important to her home state, which is "home to NASA's Johnson Space Center, massive oil fields, several major research universities and more than 300 miles of coastline vulnerable to hurricanes." Following the election, she told a meeting of scientists, "climate change is perhaps the biggest challenge of our time."

As a senior member of the Transportation and Infrastructure Committee, Johnson has worked to secure funds for the Interstate 30 suspension bridge over the Trinity River, and she continues to support Trinity River projects. The Trinity River Corridor toll-road project, in the works for decades and including three new suspension bridges, has remained controversial and unresolved. A pedestrian bridge that was mostly completed in 2017 was then delayed for perhaps three more years because of problems with the support cables. She has supported the Dallas-Fort Worth area's mass transit projects to alleviate traffic congestion and other area transportation priorities. She has been well-positioned as an ally of the huge Dallas-Fort Worth International Airport.

Johnson generally has sailed to reelection, though she has faced some local impatience over when she will step down. In 2012, she faced two young Democratic challengers: attorney Taj Clayton and state Rep. Barbara Mallory Caraway, who avoided criticizing Johnson directly but made clear their view that the district needed fresh representation. The Morning News endorsed Clayton, saying Johnson "once had what it takes, but now it's time for new leadership." Johnson ripped into both of her opponents, calling Clayton a stooge for Republicans and Caraway a disgruntled former aide. She won the primary with 70 percent to Caraway's 18 percent and Clayton's 12 percent. In subsequent rematches with Caraway, whose husband Dwaine Caraway is a city council member in Dallas, Johnson has won the primary with declining — but still safe — 70 percent in 2014, 69 percent in 2016 and 64 percent in 2018.

Following the 2016 election, Johnson broadly hinted that she would not seek reelection. "I want to wind it down and move on to what's out there for me," she told a local television station. By April 2017, The Morning News reported that she had changed her tune and was planning to seek one more term. If nothing else, her uncertainty and the recent futile challenges have opened the door for Johnson's potential successors to make plans. Another possible signal that Johnson has focused on her legacy: In April 2019, she received extended tributes when the century-old train station in Dallas was dedicated in her name. "If my work highlights any one thing in particular, it is that I have made it a point to help others," she said at the event.

TX-30: Dallas County   Cook Partisan Voting Index: D+29

Population		Race and Ethnicity		Income	
Total	760,204	White	15.2%	Median Income	$44,945
Land area (sq. miles)	356	Black	42.9%	District Income Rank	372
Pop/ sq mi	2133.8	Latino	38.4%	Poverty Rate	23.2%
Born in State	64.3%	Asian	1.9%	With health insurance	77.9%
		Two or more races	1.3%	Cash public assistance	1.9%
Age Groups		Other	0.2%	Food stamp/SNAP	20.2%
Under 18	28.1%				
18-34	25.2%	Education		Work	
35-64	37%	H.S grad or less	50.8%	White Collar	9.7%
Over 64	9.7%	Some college	28.9%	Sales and Service	44.5%
		College Degree, 4 yr	13.4%	Blue Collar	26.9%
Military		Post grad	6.9%	Government	12.4%
Veteran/ Active Duty	5.5%				

2012 Pres. Vote	Obama	175,637	(80%)	Romney	43,333	(20%)		
2016 Pres. Vote	Clinton	174,528	(79%)	Trump	40,333	(18%)	Johnson	4,276	(2%)

Central and Southern Dallas Metro: In 1923, Texas adopted the "white primary," which barred blacks from participating in statewide Democratic primary elections, although blacks who could pay a poll tax were permitted to vote in general elections, municipal elections, school board elections, special elections and on ballot propositions. By 1947, Dallas County had a majority-black electorate, and yet despite this, there was no congressional district in North Texas that was considered likely to elect a black representative until the creation of the 30th Congressional District in 1991. Its creation was insisted on by the then-chairwoman of the Texas Senate's redistricting committee, and the result was a grotesquely shaped district. Since then, lawsuits and four more rounds of redistricting have smoothed out the lines and left the 30th as one of two heavily minority Democratic districts in the Dallas-Fort Worth Metroplex.

The Dallas-Fort Worth metro area in 2017 surpassed Houston as the fastest growing area in the nation; in the previous year, they grew by 146,000 and 94,000, respectively. With its population of 7.4 million, Dallas continued to claim bragging rights as the largest metro area in Texas, over Houston, with its 6.9 million. Nationally, they trailed only New York, Los Angeles and Chicago. The Dallas metro area has been responding to the growth in multiple ways. Construction was scheduled to start in late 2019 on a privately financed high-speed rail train that would take 90 minutes from Dallas to Houston on an elevated 240-mile route. In 2016, the board of Dallas Area Rapid Transit approved plans for a new downtown subway line; subsequent progress was slowed by delay in federal financial support. Love Airport, which Congress in 1979 confined to short routes so that it would not interfere with the new DFW airport, was the fastest-growing airport in the nation from 2007 to 2017, with a 90 percent increase in passengers; that progress was expedited by repeal in 2014 of the Wright amendment, which was named for Rep. Jim Wright of Texas, who was the House majority leader at the time.

Today, the 30th District consists of most of the south side of Dallas, with one tentacle running northwest, out Stemmons Freeway to Love Field. In between is the "mixmaster," where three busy highways — Interstates 30, 35E and 45 — come together within a square mile, surrounding many of the prominent sites in Dallas. Further south, it embraces African-American majority towns such as Cedar Hill, Glenn Heights and upscale DeSoto, as well as minority-majority locales like Duncanville and Hutchins. The court-drawn map placed much of the district's previous Hispanic population in the newly created 33rd District. But Hispanics have continued to surge in South Dallas. The 30th District's population is now 43 percent African American and 38 percent Hispanic; the latter are mostly young and 90 percent of them are from Mexico. The growing influence of racial minorities in the city has been a major factor in Democrats' virtual takeover of Dallas County offices. In 2018, local Democrats won 12 of the 14 House seats in the Texas legislature; with the Republican redistricting map in 2012, they had six of the 14. This district is overwhelmingly Democratic and the party's strongest in Texas.

John Carter (R)

Elected 2002, 9th term, b. Nov 06, 1941; Houston; Texas Technical University, B.A., 1964; University of Texas School of Law, J.D., 1969; Lutheran; Married (Erika Carter); 4 children; 6 grandchildren.

Elected Office: Williamson County TX District Court judge, 1981-2001.

Professional Career: Practicing attorney, 1969-1981.

DC Office: 2110 RHOB 20515, 202-225-3864, Fax: 202-225-5886, carter.house.gov

State Offices: Round Rock, 512-246-1600; Temple, 254-933-1392.

Committees: *Appropriations*: Defense; Military Construction, Veterans Affairs & Related Agencies (RMM).

Group Ratings

	ADA	ACLU	AFL-CIO	LCV	ITI	COC	HAFA	ACU	CFG	FRC
2018	-	4%	-	6%	-	82%	52%	68%	50%	100%
2017	0%	C	8%	0%	C	93%	C	85%	73%	100%

Almanac Ratings 2017-18

	Economy	Social	Foreign	Composite
Liberal	7%	3%	0%	3%
Conservative	93%	97%	100%	97%

Key Votes of the 115th Congress

1. Obama-care revision	Y	5. Family planning regs	Y	9. Guantanamo prisoners	N
2. Tax Cuts	Y	6. Body cameras/immigration	N	10. Ground missiles, limit	N
3. Omnibus appropriations	Y	7. Abortion ban	Y	11. Defense Dept. spending	Y
4. Dodd-Frank revision	Y	8. Concealed carry	Y	12. FISA rules	Y

Election Results

Election	Name (Party)	Vote (%)	Cand. Spent	Ind. Exp. Support	Ind. Exp. Oppose
2018 General	John Carter (R).................................... 144,680	(51%)	$1,782,433	$3,608	$233,611
	M.J. Hegar (D)............................... 136,362	(48%)	$4,986,814	$9,326	$3,608
2018 Primary	John Carter (R)..................................... 34,513	(65%)			
	Mike Sweeney (R)............................... 18,184	(35%)			

Prior winning percentages: 2016 (58%), 2014 (64%), 2012 (61%), 2010 (83%), 2008 (60%), 2006 (59%), 2004 (65%), 2002 (69%)

John Carter, a conservative Republican first elected in 2002, has brought an ex-judge's no-nonsense perspective to his work on homeland security and immigration, and later to military construction and veterans' issues, as the top Republican of the Appropriations subcommittees dealing with those issues. "Judge Carter" has been respected as an informal leader among House Republicans. In 2018, he sweated his first tough reelection challenge since taking office against a well-founded challenger, a woman who was a former military pilot.

Carter grew up in Houston and graduated from Texas Tech University and the University of Texas law school. He practiced law in Williamson County and served as a municipal judge in Round Rock. He was appointed a district judge in 1981 by Republican Gov. Bill Clements and in 1982 stood for election. Judicial elections are partisan in Texas, and Carter was the first GOP judge elected in Williamson County. He became known as the father of the county Republican Party.

In 2001, he ran in a new Republican district stretching from Williamson County to Houston. The real contest was for the Republican nomination. Carter's main rivals were Peter Wareing, the son-in-law of Texas oilman Jack Blanton, and Brad Barton, son of Rep. Joe Barton. In the primary, Wareing led with 37 percent to 26 percent for Carter and 16 percent for Barton.

In the runoff, Carter attacked Wareing as a liberal in disguise, pointing to his campaign contributions to Democrats. When Wareing proposed that each candidate sign a "clean campaign pledge," Carter offered what he called a "homestead pledge" — a ploy to highlight his charge that Wareing was a Houston carpetbagger who had rented an apartment in the district to run for the seat. Wareing outspent Carter more than 2-to-1, but Carter won 57%-43%. He got 78 percent of the vote in Williamson County, which cast 33 percent of the vote. Carter won the general election easily.

Carter has been a reliable conservative, but not a hardliner. As an Appropriations Committee member, he opposed some of the bolder GOP proposals to cut spending in 2012, such as an across-the-board cut in energy and water spending. He fought off a Republican attempt in 2011 to sharply cut spending for military bands, arguing that they "are an integral part of the patriotism that keeps our soldiers' hearts beating fast." In 2016, he enacted his POLICE (Protecting Our Lives through Initiating COPS Expansion) Act, which was designed to increase active-shooter training for law-enforcement officers — partly in response to the 2009 shooting at Fort Hood. In 2017, he joined Republican Rep. Jeff Duncan of South Carolina in filing a bill to relax restrictions on gun silencers, which is a priority of the National Rifle Association.

As chairman of the Homeland Security Appropriations Subcommittee, Carter fought for spending more to secure the U.S.-Mexico border, but also acknowledged the need to "show compassion" to immigrants who are already in the United States. In 2015, he cooperated on the House GOP leadership strategy to use the Homeland Security spending bill to try to force President Barack Obama to back down on his executive actions to loosen restrictions on immigrants from Mexico. Senate Democrats held firm against any compromise, and Republicans eventually approved full-year funding of Carter's bill rather than force a shutdown.

In 2017, Carter switched to chair the Military Construction and Veterans Affairs Subcommittee. His work on Appropriations brought added benefits to Fort Hood, including funding of a new hospital, $61 million to upgrade the barracks and $50 million to renovate the cavalry headquarters. He has served several terms as co-chairman of the bipartisan House Army Caucus.

On immigration legislation, Carter took part in bipartisan discussions to seek a compromise on a broader measure. He quit the group in September 2013 because, he said, Obama was using the immigration issue to "advance his political agenda." With President Donald Trump demanding a wall along the border with Mexico, Carter was supportive in general terms. In April 2018, he cautioned that the demands of private landowners along the border would complicate the building of a wall. Later that year, he enacted a bill that provided additional resources to assist local prosecutors with DNA analysis. Carter earlier served on the Judiciary Committee, where he passed his Terrorist Penalties Enhancement Act and a bill to establish penalties for identity theft.

Carter served three terms in the leadership as House Republican Conference secretary and still likes to be called "Judge." In 2009, he was the chief antagonist on ethics charges against Democratic Rep. Charles Rangel, who stepped down as chairman of the Ways and Means Committee.

In 2016, Carter had a GOP primary challenge from political newcomer Mike Sweeney, who criticized Carter for his "votes to fund the Obama agenda." Sweeney, who had a successful software business, spent a mere $10,000. Carter spent $1.2 million in the campaign cycle and got 71 percent of the vote, a signal of some conservative unrest. Facing Sweeney again in the 2018 Republican primary, Carter touted his support for Trump plus the $367 million he delivered to Fort Hood; with Sweeney spending $55,000 this time, Carter won with 65 percent of the vote.

The real challenge for Carter in 2018 came from Democrat M.J. Hegar, who gained attention with a campaign ad that described her experience serving as a decorated Air Force officer in Afghanistan, where she was shot down while operating as a "search and rescue" helicopter pilot. Later, she complained, Carter refused to provide her sufficient assistance as a constituent in Round Rock. She outspent Carter, $5 million to $1.8 million, and criticized him as a "coward" for his failure to agree to a campaign debate. Carter escaped with a 51%-48% win. Hegar led by 3,500 votes in the more populous Williamson County, but Carter prevailed with a nearly 12,000-vote edge in Bell County. In March 2019, Carter might have gotten a break when Hegar announced a challenge to Republican Sen. John Cornyn in 2020.

TX-31: Central Texas   Cook Partisan Voting Index: R+10

Population		Race and Ethnicity		Income	
Total	806,513	White	56.9%	Median Income	$68,127
Land area (sq. miles)	2,154	Black	10.8%	District Income Rank	108
Pop/ sq mi	374.3	Latino	24%	Poverty Rate	9.9%
Born in State	51.5%	Asian	4.7%	With health insurance	88.9%
		Two or more races	2.9%	Cash public assistance	1.5%
Age Groups		Other	0.7%	Food stamp/SNAP	8.5%
Under 18	26.8%				
18-34	24.3%	Education		Work	
35-64	37.8%	H.S grad or less	31%	White Collar	11.1%
Over 64	11.1%	Some college	34.4%	Sales and Service	41.3%
		College Degree, 4 yr	23.1%	Blue Collar	17%
Military		Post grad	11.6%	Government	17.2%
Veteran/ Active Duty	15.6%				

2012 Pres. Vote	Romney	144,634	(60%)	Obama	92,842	(38%)			
2016 Pres. Vote	Trump	153,823	(53%)	Clinton	117,181	(40%)	Johnson	13,735	(5%)

Williamson and Bell Counties: In 1932, Williamson County was a rural backwater that cast a little more than 7,000 votes for president; Franklin Roosevelt won all but 431 of them. Today it has become a major population and business center deep in the heart of Texas, casting 200,000 votes in 2016. Its population has virtually doubled in every recent decade. It had 40,000 people in 1970 and 548,000 in 2017. Williamson County is just north of Austin, and much of this growth has been generated by the area's high-technology boom — Austin's city limits actually now spill over into Williamson. The county long ago moved beyond a bedroom suburb. Hugely successful computer producer Dell is headquartered in Round Rock (the rock, which served as an important wagon crossing, is in the middle of Brushy Creek, with wheel ruts still visible). Dell had more than 13,000 local employees, though it suffered layoffs following its merger in 2016 with EMC Corp. In December 2018, Apple announced its plan for a second campus in northwest Austin, where it expected to hire 5,000 employees. Texas 130, a 49-mile, 10-lane toll road with a speed limit of 85 miles per hour in parts, has steered more growth. Georgetown, which has become a popular retirement destination, was the fastest-growing city in the nation in 2015; it slipped to sixth-fastest in 2017, with a population increase from 28,000 in 2000 to 71,000 in 2017. In 2017, the city claimed that it was one of the first in the country that is powered entirely on renewable energy, both wind and solar; later, it reported that it also was using natural gas

Bell County, just north of Williamson County, is home to part of Fort Hood, the largest U.S. military base in the world in terms of acreage. The base is the only U.S. post capable of supporting two full armored divisions. Its mission — maintaining combat readiness, including training Army reservists in urban combat — explains its size; it covers 218,000 acres, or, 340 square miles, an area larger than New York's five boroughs. Killeen, home of the base, has been growing rapidly. In February 2019, the Austin American-Statesman reported "deplorable" housing conditions at Hood, where the barracks housed 18,000 soldiers. To the east is Temple, a rail center and the birthplace of Miriam "Ma" Ferguson, wife of Gov. James "Pa" Ferguson, who was elected governor in 1925 after her husband was impeached and convicted.

The 31st Congressional District is an unusually compact district by modern Texas standards. It is entirely contained within Bell and Williamson counties, and takes in almost all of each. Williamson has 70 percent of the population. Historically this was solidly Democratic country, devoted to the party of the Confederacy and then the New Deal. It was populated by cotton farmers who distrusted Wall Street and railroads and who trusted politicians like Sam Rayburn and Lyndon Johnson. These people took a shine to Ronald Reagan's and George W. Bush's brand of Republicanism. With the large tech workforce, the vote dropped to 53 percent for Donald Trump in 2016.

Colin Allred (D)

Elected 2018, 1st term, b. Apr 15, 1983; Dallas; Baylor University (TX), B.A., 2005; University of California, Berkeley, J.D., 2014; Religion unknown; Married (Alexandra Allred); 1 child.

Professional Career: Linebacker, Tennessee Titans, 2006-2010; Special Assistant, U.S. Department of Housi., Attorney

DC Office: 328 CHOB 20515, 202-225-2231, allred.house.gov

State Offices: Richardson, 972-972-7949.

Committees: *Foreign Affairs*: Middle East, North Africa & International Terrorism. *Transportation & Infrastructure*: Aviation; Highways & Transit; Railroads, Pipelines & Hazardous Materials. *Veterans' Affairs*: Disability Assistance & Memorial Affairs.

Election Results

Election	Name (Party)	Vote (%)		Cand. Spent	Ind. Exp. Support	Ind. Exp. Oppose
2018 General	Colin Allred (D)......................................	144,067	(52%)	$5,786,869	$728,381	$4,725,787
	Pete Sessions (R)................................	126,101	(46%)	$5,157,552	$1,383,532	$9,545,008
2018 Primary	Colin Allred (D)...........................	15,442	(69%)			
Runoff	Lillian Salerno (D)........................	7,343	(31%)			
2018 Primary	Colin Allred (D)............................	15,498	(38%)			
	Lillian Salerno (D)........................	7,400	(18%)			
	Brett Shipp (D)...............................	6,550	(16%)			
	Ed Meier (D)...................................	5,474	(14%)			
	George Rodriguez (D)............................	3,029	(8%)			

Freshman Democrat Colin Allred won a district north of Dallas that had recently shifted toward Democrats. Although a first-time candidate, he had experience in Democratic politics and with civil-rights issues as an attorney. Allred defeated Republican Rep. Pete Sessions, who served 22 years and led the GOP campaign committee when the party regained the House majority in 2010. The head of the Rules Committee, Sessions was the only House chairman who lost reelection in 2018. Hillary Clinton's 48%-46% lead in this district in 2016 signaled an opportunity for Democrats, though they oddly failed to run a candidate against Sessions that year.

Allred was raised in North Dallas and graduated from Baylor University, where he received an athletic scholarship. He played for five years as a defensive lineman for the Tennessee Titans in the

National Football League. After getting his law degree from the University of California, Berkeley, he was a special assistant in the general counsel's office at the Housing and Urban Development Department. In 2014, he entered politics as the Dallas-Fort Worth director of the Texas Democrats' voter protection program. He worked as a voting-rights litigator with the Washington-based law firm of Perkins Coie.

Following the results of the 2016 election, Democrats weren't going to repeat their mistake of not posing a challenge to Sessions. His voting record often was among the most conservative in the House, which posed a potential clash with his district, and he could be a tough partisan — both at home and in the Capitol. As chairman of the Rules Committee, he promoted the Republican message. House Democrats enthusiastically made Sessions one of their prime targets in 2018; he had not faced a serious reelection challenge since the redistricting wars of 2004.

Of the seven candidates in the Democratic primary, none of the four leading contenders had held elected office, though each had been actively involved in party politics; three of them spent at least $700,000 in the primary.

Allred was forced into a runoff, where he won the nomination easily. He led runner-up Lillian Salerno, a senior Agriculture Department official in the Obama administration, by more than 2-to-1 in each round.

Sessions sought to wrap himself in multiple wings of the Republican Party. He embraced the mantra of President Donald Trump to "make America great again." In an interview with a Dallas radio station, he called himself "the business community member of Congress." And he posed the election as a stark partisan choice: "You get somebody that's for Nancy Pelosi or you get a market-based system, which is what I have stood for." Each of those themes seemed politically outdated, given the demographic and political shifts in his district.

In an editorial, The Dallas Morning News endorsed Sessions as more experienced and wrote that he "better represents the principles of limited government that we favor." The endorsement criticized Allred for his lack of "comprehensive solutions" and his support for the Affordable Care Act. As it turned out, the newspaper was at odds with many of its readers.

Each candidate spent more than $5 million and outside groups spent another $10 million, mostly in negative ads against the opposition candidate. Allred won, 52%-46%, with more than 90 percent of the vote cast in Dallas County, where he led by 20,000 votes. The remainder was in outlying Collin County, where Sessions got 55 percent of the vote. Like other House Democrats who won Republican-held suburban seats in 2018, Allred likely will face a competitive reelection challenge. It remained to be seen which Republican wing would prevail and had the best chance of regaining the district.

TX-32: Dallas County　　　　　　　　　　　　　　**Cook Partisan Voting Index: R+5**

Population		Race and Ethnicity		Income	
Total	752,654	White	49.5%	Median Income	$68,084
Land area (sq. miles)	186	Black	12.9%	District Income Rank	109
Pop/ sq mi	4053.9	Latino	26.3%	Poverty Rate	12.4%
Born in State	50.5%	Asian	8.3%	With health insurance	83%
		Two or more races	2.5%	Cash public assistance	1.1%
Age Groups		Other	0.4%	Food stamp/SNAP	8.3%
Under 18	23.8%				
18-34	25.4%	**Education**		**Work**	
35-64	38.9%	H.S grad or less	30.7%	White Collar	11.9%
Over 64	11.9%	Some college	26%	Sales and Service	39.4%
		College Degree, 4 yr	27.3%	Blue Collar	16.9%
Military		Post grad	15.9%	Government	9%
Veteran/ Active Duty	5.7%				

2012 Pres. Vote	Romney	146,420	(57%)	Obama	106,563	(42%)			
2016 Pres. Vote	Clinton	134,895	(48%)	Trump	129,701	(46%)	Johnson	11,358	(4%)

Northern Dallas Metro: North Dallas has long been the home of the city's elite and, indeed, a slice of the nation's elite. Early in the 20th century, the richest citizens started moving away from old neighborhoods adjacent to downtown and out past Turtle Creek to the area around the suburbs of Highland Park and University Park. Dallas grew lustily from mid-century. Beyond the Park Cities, miles of affluent neighborhoods were built, especially between the Central Expressway and the Dallas

North Tollway. Gallerias and office complexes followed. An entertainment and singles apartment corridor runs along Greenville Avenue, plus working-class neighborhoods here and there, and pockets of Latino neighborhoods near the freeways. In 2018, the Texas transportation department agreed to expand a section of Interstate 635 that is east of the Central Expressway — the LBJ East project.

The Park Cities are well-heeled and over 90 percent white in increasingly diverse Dallas. University Park is the larger of the two, which have a combined population of 34,000 and median household income exceeding $200,000. After eight years in the White House, George and Laura Bush returned to their Preston Hollow neighborhood a few miles from his presidential library at Southern Methodist University; in 2018, they decided that they will be buried at the library. The much larger and still-growing urban center is Garland, with a population of 238,000, majority-minority residents and household income of $55,000. Its largest private-sector employers are the Baylor Medical Center and Kraft Foods. Just to the east in Rowlett, developers began work in 2017 on a $1 billion mixed-use development project on 260 acres along the shores of Lake Ray Hubbard, including an eight-acre constructed lagoon. After pulling back on those plans, the developer defaulted in December 2018.

North Dallas and the 32nd Congressional District of Texas reflect the political trends driving 21st century politics: As upper-income suburbanites drifted toward the Democrats and the minority population of north Dallas County increased, the district has moved leftward. The Republican-engineered redistricting in 2011 dropped the Hispanic share of the population from 43 percent to 26 percent. The district includes a thin slice of Collin County that takes in some of fast-growing, upscale Wylie; more than 90 percent of the 32nd is in Dallas County. The 32nd has Democratic pockets around racially diverse Richardson and the downtown area. Still, few were prepared for the stunning outcome in 2016, when Hillary Clinton led Donald Trump, 48%-46%.

Marc Veasey (D)

Elected 2012, 4th term, b. Jan 03, 1971; Tarrant County; Texas Wesleyan University, B.S., 1995; Christian Church; Married (Tonya Veasey); 1 child.

Elected Office: TX House, 2005-2013.

Professional Career: Staffer, Rep. Martin Frost, 1998-2004; Commercial real-estate broker.

DC Office: 2348 RHOB 20515, 202-225-9897, Fax: 202-225-9702, veasey.house.gov

State Offices: Dallas, 214-741-1387; Fort Worth, 817-920-9086.

Committees: *Energy & Commerce*: Communications & Technology; Consumer Protection & Commerce; Energy. *Small Business*: Contracting & Infrastructure; Innovation & Workforce Development.

Group Ratings

	ADA	ACLU	AFL-CIO	LCV	ITI	COC	HAFA	ACU	CFG	FRC
2018	-	86%	-	89%	-	67%	9%	20%	25%	0%
2017	80%	C	97%	91%	C	57%	C	0%	0%	11%

Almanac Ratings 2017-18

	Economy	Social	Foreign	Composite
Liberal	88%	100%	72%	87%
Conservative	12%	0%	28%	13%

Key Votes of the 115th Congress

1. Obama-care revision	N	5. Family planning regs	N	9. Guantanamo prisoners	Y
2. Tax Cuts	N	6. Body cameras/immigration	Y	10. Ground missiles, limit	Y
3. Omnibus appropriations	N	7. Abortion ban	N	11. Defense Dept. spending	Y
4. Dodd-Frank revision	Y	8. Concealed carry	N	12. FISA rules	Y

Election Results

Election	Name (Party)	Vote (%)		Cand. Spent	Ind. Exp. Support	Ind. Exp. Oppose
2018 General	Marc Veasey (D)...............................	90,805	(76%)	$1,289,423	$70,073	
	Willie Billups (R)...............................	26,120	(22%)	$55,050		
2018 Primary	Marc Veasey (D)...............................	14,998	(71%)			
	Carlos Quintanilla (D)...........................	6,233	(29%)			

Prior winning percentages: 2016 (74%), 2014 (87%), 2012 (73%)

Democrat Marc Veasey, first elected in 2012, has faced competitive primaries as an African American in this heavily Hispanic district. His deep political experience gave him a head start in the House, where he looked after the needs of local defense contractors. In the majority in 2019, he got a seat on the Energy and Commerce Committee — the only Texas Democrat on the panel, joining three Republicans from his home state. A McClatchy News profile in August 2017 described Veasey as "the future of the Democratic Party: Moderate, African-American and focused on helping Democrats reconnect with the working-class voters who abandoned them for Donald Trump on the 2016 election."

Veasey, a commercial real estate broker, was born and still lives in Fort Worth. His uncle worked for Rep. Jim Wright, the House Speaker from 1987 to 1989. After watching a White House press briefing on television in his mid-teens, Veasey remembers asking what it would take to get such a job. His uncle advised he get a college degree. After graduating from Texas Wesleyan University, Veasey held a string of jobs. As a staffer to Democratic Rep. Martin Frost, he attracted a grocery store to a poor section of Fort Worth to create jobs and enable residents to buy fresh produce. Veasey ran successfully for the state House in 2004 against an incumbent who refused to join other Texas Democrats in leaving the state to protest GOP-led redistricting. He chaired the Democratic Caucus.

His main competition in the decisive primary for the House seat was Dallas attorney Domingo Garcia. The contest polarized black voters who supported Veasey and Hispanics who largely supported Garcia; it also developed into a regional spat between Veasey from Fort Worth and Garcia from Dallas. In the initial balloting, Veasey led Garcia, 37%-25%. In the runoff, Veasey targeted black voters on his home turf. Garcia accused him of "playing the race card." But it was a good strategy. Voters in Tarrant County turned out in higher proportions than those in Dallas County.

Garcia failed to galvanize Hispanics, who outnumbered blacks four-to-one, though more narrowly among registered voters. He labeled Veasey an "errand boy for the establishment" — and then refused to apologize for use of the racially charged "boy" because, he said, he didn't mean it as a slur. Veasey won the runoff 53%-47%. He got 68 percent in Tarrant County, which cast 59 percent of the total, and he was conciliatory in his acceptance speech. "This election was about making sure North Texans were represented fairly and honestly," he said. In November, Veasey defeated Republican Chuck Bradley, 73%-26%.

At the Armed Services Committee, he tended to the interests of the many military contractors in or near his district. On the defense spending bill in 2015, he claimed credit for additional weapons procurement plus a bipartisan agreement that required the Pentagon to review how illegal immigrants were serving in the military. He was one of five Texas Democrats who split with President Barack Obama to support the Keystone XL pipeline.

With his assignment to Energy and Commerce, Veasey said he would work on health care, energy, communications and environmental issues. He and Democratic Rep. Rick Larsen of Washington filed in January 2019 a bill to remove "discriminatory" restrictions on voting participation, such as ID cards. Their measure was incorporated into the sweeping political reform bill that House Democrats passed in February.

Veasey has organized two caucuses to promote Democratic interests. The Congressional Voting Rights Caucus was designed to update the Voting Rights Act, following the 2013 ruling by the Supreme Court that struck down a key enforcement provision. With Rep. Brendan Boyle of Pennsylvania, he launched the Blue Collar Caucus to respond to what Veasey called the "scam" of President Donald Trump's outreach to workers. "Trump's focus on America's workers started and ended with his campaign rhetoric," Veasey and Boyle wrote in an op-ed in The Philadelphia Inquirer in November 2018. By contrast, their caucus was "addressing the growing economic strain felt by working families."

Veasey has faced varied primary challenges from Latino opponents. In 2014, Tom Sanchez, a telecommunications lawyer, self-financed nearly all of his $1.5 million campaign. Although outspent, Veasey won easily, 73%-27%. The 2016 primary sent a warning to Veasey. Democratic challenger Carlos Quintanilla, a self-described "activist," did not report spending any money. But his grassroots campaign gave him 52 percent in Dallas County, which cast 43 percent of the total vote. Veasey took 75 percent in Tarrant, which gave him 63 percent overall. Quintanilla ran again in 2018. Veasey increased to 70 percent his share of the smaller midterm turnout, including 57 percent of the Dallas vote.

Local Democrats have talked up the possibility that the next round of redistricting could create separate minority seats for blacks and Hispanics in the Metroplex, in addition to the longstanding 30th District. For Veasey, those dynamics could depend, in part, on a potential successor to veteran Democratic Rep. Eddie Bernice Johnson in the 30th and whether first-term Democratic Rep. Colin Allred retains the Dallas-based 32nd District. All three are African American.

TX-33: Central Metroplex   Cook Partisan Voting Index: D+23

Population		Race and Ethnicity		Income	
Total	727,777	White	14.8%	Median Income	$39,089
Land area (sq. miles)	212	Black	15.8%	District Income Rank	420
Pop/ sq mi	3433.9	Latino	66.2%	Poverty Rate	25.7%
Born in State	55%	Asian	2.2%	With health insurance	67.3%
		Two or more races	0.9%	Cash public assistance	2.6%
Age Groups		Other	0.1%	Food stamp/SNAP	23.6%
Under 18	31.4%				
18-34	26.5%	**Education**		**Work**	
35-64	34%	H.S grad or less	70.6%	White Collar	8.1%
Over 64	8.1%	Some college	19.8%	Sales and Service	43.4%
		College Degree, 4 yr	6.8%	Blue Collar	41.3%
Military		Post grad	2.8%	Government	6.9%
Veteran/ Active Duty	3.7%				

2012 Pres. Vote	Obama	86,686	(72%)	Romney	32,641	(27%)			
2016 Pres. Vote	Clinton	94,513	(73%)	Trump	30,787	(24%)	Johnson	3,157	(2%)

Parts of Fort Worth and Dallas: In the 1950s, the Dallas-Fort Worth Turnpike was built on empty land to link the two cities' downtowns. Over the next three decades, the land filled up, with as many people as the central cities had. Irving, Grand Prairie and Arlington grew up along the highway in the once impoverished region and became central to one of America's richest and most productive metropolitan areas. Major civic landmarks followed: Rangers Ballpark in Arlington, built by one-time managing partner George W. Bush, and the domed AT&T Stadium, home of the Dallas Cowboys. Arlington and Grand Prairie are in their second generation, taking on the patina of age. The turnover brought newcomers to these fast-growing areas: Arlington is now only 40 percent non-Hispanic white; Irving is 24 percent; Grand Prairie 23 percent.

The 33rd Congressional District of Texas, which covers this suburban zone, is a judicial creation. A court created the minority-majority district, which is 66 percent Hispanic and 16 percent African American. In its southeast corner, its jagged boundaries mesh with those of the African-American-controlled 30th District in Dallas. The 33rd doesn't take in many of the industrial plants in the area, but its blue-collar workforce provides much of the manpower for Northrop Grumman, General Motors, Hughes Training, Bell Textron Helicopter and Lockheed Martin, all of which have facilities in or near the district. It has neighborhoods in western Dallas, including Oak Cliff, a collection of Victorian era mansions near the Trinity River that became heavily African American and is now heavily Hispanic. Lee Harvey Oswald, who lived in a rooming house in Oak Cliff, took a cab from near Dealey Plaza to his home after killing President John Kennedy in November 1963 and then was arrested in the nearby Texas Theater.

The district includes much of Grand Prairie and Irving, as well as tiny, almost-entirely Hispanic Cockrell Hill. The $180 million Toyota Music Factory entertainment and retail venue in Irving launched operations in 2017. Across a narrow tentacle of lightly populated precincts, the district has about a third of Fort Worth, including the old stockyards, where cattle drives are still conducted twice a day by real cattle drovers. The Tarrant County part of the district includes Forest Hill and parts of Arlington, including the sports stadiums. Several major commercial and retail projects are underway in the district, including the $175 million Stockyards real estate and retail development, and the voter-approved $1 billion baseball stadium in an entertainment complex adjacent to the site where the Rangers now play. North of the stockyards, Fort Meachem International Airport planned to offer commercial service for the first time since 1998. The extensive redevelopment of the land and buildings, which the city has owned since 1925, was scheduled for completion by 2021. Tarrant and Dallas counties each have about 50 percent of the voters of the 33rd. Overall, Hillary Clinton got 73 percent in 2016, which fell short of her 79 percent in the adjacent 30th.

Filemon Vela (D)

Elected 2012, 4th term, b. Feb 13, 1963; Harlingen; St. Joseph's Academy, Brownsville, TX; Loyola University, New Orleans (LA), Att., 1982; Georgetown University (DC), B.A., 1985; University of Texas, Ausitn, J.D., 1987; Roman Catholic; Married (Rose Vela).

Professional Career: Practicing attorney, 1988-2012.

DC Office: 307 CHOB 20515, 202-225-9901, Fax: 202-225-9770, vela.house.gov

State Offices: Alice, 361-230-9776; Brownsville, 956-544-8352; San Benito, 956-276-4497; Weslaco, 956-520-8273.

Committees: *Agriculture*: Commodity Exchanges, Energy & Credit; General Farm Commodities & Risk Management (Chmn); Livestock & Foreign Agriculture. *Armed Services*: Seapower & Projection Forces; Tactical Air & Land Forces.

Group Ratings

	ADA	ACLU	AFL-CIO	LCV	ITI	COC	HAFA	ACU	CFG	FRC
2018	-	82%	-	80%	-	73%	11%	13%	24%	0%
2017	80%	C	95%	80%	C	64%	C	15%	0%	11%

Almanac Ratings 2017-18

	Economy	Social	Foreign	Composite
Liberal	75%	87%	84%	82%
Conservative	25%	13%	17%	18%

Key Votes of the 115th Congress

1. Obama-care revision	N	5. Family planning regs	N	9. Guantanamo prisoners	N
2. Tax Cuts	N	6. Body cameras/immigration	Y	10. Ground missiles, limit	N
3. Omnibus appropriations	N	7. Abortion ban	N	11. Defense Dept. spending	N
4. Dodd-Frank revision	Y	8. Concealed carry	N	12. FISA rules	N

Election Results

Election	Name (Party)	Vote (%)		Cand. Spent	Ind. Exp. Support	Ind. Exp. Oppose
2018 General	Filemon Vela (D)	85,825	(60%)	$555,431		
	Rey Gonzalez (R)	57,243	(40%)	$79,484		
2018 Primary	Filemon Vela (D)		(100%)			

Prior winning percentages: 2016 (63%), 2014 (59.5%), 2012 (61.9%)

Democrat Filemon Vela won the 34th District House seat in part on the strength of his illustrious political family. Brownsville's federal courthouse bears the name of his late father, a federal district judge who served more than two decades, and his mother was the city's first elected woman mayor. In his first elected office, Vela has focused on local concerns: the border and agriculture. He does not seem to have paid any price for his notable independence of Speaker Nancy Pelosi.

Vela was born in Harlingen and raised in nearby Brownsville. After receiving a bachelor's degree from Georgetown University and a law degree from the University of Texas, he returned to Brownsville to practice law. Vela represented school districts seeking restitution for shoddy construction by independent contractors. In one case, he won recompense for a malfunctioning air-quality control system.

When Vela launched his campaign, some political observers were surprised by the "D" next to his name. His wife was a Republican justice on the Texas Court of Appeals. Vela acknowledged that he sometimes backed GOP office-seekers. He aligned himself with the Democratic agenda, calling for "a realistic and fair way" to deal with illegal immigration, protection of Medicare and Social Security benefits, and tax cuts for small businesses as an incentive to hire workers. Undoubtedly, he was mindful of the district's Democratic tilt.

His main rival for the Democratic nomination, Cameron County District Attorney Armando Villalobos, led the field in fundraising but was indicted on federal fraud charges two weeks before the primary. Vela had a 40%-13% lead in the opening round and got 67 percent in the runoff against Denise Saenz Blanchard, who was chief of staff to former Democratic Rep. Solomon Ortiz, who represented the area for 28 years before he was defeated in 2010. Following the runoff, she told the Associated Press, "We now have a Republican who has converted to being a Democrat, who I believe is taking a seat from the Democrats." Pelosi, the House Democratic leader, headlined a fundraiser for Vela in August. He won in November, 62%-36%.

Vela showed an informed and forceful interest in immigration issues. In 2013, he resigned from the Hispanic Caucus because he felt that it was not objecting strongly enough to a provision in the Senate-passed immigration reform bill, which he believed was spending too much money on new barriers and border officials. The caucus agreed to his return. That year, he filed with Democratic Rep. Raul Grijalva of Arizona a comprehensive immigration bill in an effort to jump-start the House debate. During the 2016 campaign, he was outspoken in his opposition to Donald Trump, especially his views on immigration. Vela sent him an open letter after Trump said that he would not get a fair trial from a judge who was Hispanic in a case dealing with Trump University. "Your ignorant anti-immigrant opinions, your border wall rhetoric, and your recent bigoted attack on an American jurist are just plain despicable," he wrote. "Mr. Trump, you're a racist and you can take your border wall and shove it up your ass."

When Trump took initial steps to build a wall during his first few days as president in January 2017, Vela called it "a ridiculous proposition." Later, he said that it was "difficult to believe any Democrat would be willing to give President Trump a nickel to fund his 'big beautiful wall.'" A large border wall, Vela wrote in February 2019, "would trample on the property rights of many Texas families." Alternatively, he advocated improved security at the nation's ports of entry.

On the Agriculture Committee, Vela has focused on assuring sufficient water from the Rio Grande for South Texas farmers and he opposed cuts in food stamps. On the bipartisan farm bill that was enacted in December 2018, he took credit for a national animal disease preparedness and response program and for protections for cotton and sugar growers. In 2019, he became chairman of the General Farm Commodities and Risk Management Subcommittee. "It is imperative that we mitigate the risks inherent to farming with robust credit and insurance programs," he said. On the Armed Services Committee, he said that he would protect an army depot — with more than 3,000 employees — and two naval air stations in and near his district.

Pelosi's willingness to accommodate Vela has been notable, given his repeated calls for new Democratic leaders. "She just doesn't help our candidates in those swing districts with independent voters and Republican voters," he told CNN in June 2017. Following the House Democrats' election success in November 2018, he remained a vocal dissident who opposed her return as Speaker. "She's been in power 16 years, and the time has just come for us to have a new leader. It's just that simple," he told the Austin American-Statesman. Weeks later, when Vela was part of the final crucial group of House Democrats who agreed to support her, he cited Pelosi's decision to name Rep. Ben Ray Lujan of New Mexico as assistant speaker.

In 2014, Vela was reelected 59%-39% over Republican Larry Smith, who spent $120,000 and had a small lead among the one-third of district voters who did not reside in Cameron or Hidalgo counties. The same pattern applied in 2016 against his opponent, Rey Gonzalez Jr., who did not file a spending report for his campaign. In 2018, Gonzalez spent nearly $100,000. Vela won, 60%-40%. He has become entrenched along the border. The growth of Hispanic political power in Texas and among national Democrats could give him opportunities for increased influence.

TX-34: Southern Gulf Coast   **Cook Partisan Voting Index: D+10**

Population		Race and Ethnicity		Income	
Total	720,989	White	13.7%	Median Income	$37,568
Land area (sq. miles)	8,190	Black	1.2%	District Income Rank	426
Pop/ sq mi	88	Latino	84.1%	Poverty Rate	29.3%
Born in State	70%	Asian	0.6%	With health insurance	72.5%
		Two or more races	0.2%	Cash public assistance	2%
Age Groups		Other	0.1%	Food stamp/SNAP	24.4%
Under 18	30%				
18-34	23.7%	**Education**		**Work**	
35-64	33.2%	H.S grad or less	60.1%	White Collar	13.1%
Over 64	13.1%	Some college	24.6%	Sales and Service	48.5%
Military		College Degree, 4 yr	10.9%	Blue Collar	24.4%
Veteran/ Active Duty	5.6%	Post grad	4.5%	Government	17.5%

2012 Pres. Vote	Obama	90,885	(61%)	Romney	57,303	(38%)		
2016 Pres. Vote	Clinton	101,796	(59%)	Trump	64,767	(38%)	Johnson 4,042	(2%)

Brownsville, McAllen: At the far southern tip of Texas, just before the waters of the Rio Grande end their 1,900-mile journey from southern Colorado by washing out into the Gulf of Mexico, stands the fast-growing city of Brownsville. Situated across the river from Matamoros Mexico, it is one of the country's major border crossings, and its history has been intertwined with U.S.-Mexican relations. Fort Texas, later renamed Fort Brown, was established in the run-up to the Mexican-American War. After the war ended, land speculators bought up property nearby, and the town of Brownsville was born. The First and Second Cortina wars took place here, as a private army under Juan Cortina did battle with Texas Rangers over perceived mistreatment of Mexican-American laborers. Later, President Theodore Roosevelt notoriously gave dishonorable discharges to an entire regiment of African-American soldiers stationed in Brownsville for a purported cover-up of a murder. More than 60 years later, an investigation concluded the soldiers were innocent. President Richard Nixon granted them pardons, all but two of which were issued posthumously.

Fort Brown was decommissioned in 1946, but Brownsville still stands at the crossroads of Mexican-American relations. The 1993 North American Free Trade Agreement has lifted the economy in parts of the area, and there has been a boom in commercial construction. In February 2019, the port of Brownsville announced that it will build its second new dock in five years to accommodate the increased shipping. Officials contend that more than 8,000 jobs result directly from the port, with $3 billion in annual economic activity for Texas. Increased trade was expected to result in completion of parts of Interstate 69 through the redesignation of former state highways; supporters intend that it will link Brownsville with Port Huron Michigan. But the I-69 project has run into obstacles from state and local officials en route, fearing a loss of small-town retail transactions. More than 90 percent of the cargo in the Brownsville port is to or from Mexico. Brownsville has gained a new niche as the "ship-breaking" capital of the nation. In 2014, it dismantled a former aircraft carrier, the Constellation. The dismantling of other Navy hulks ensued, including the USS Tripoli assault ship. In February 2019, the SpaceX company of Elon Musk confirmed its plan to build and test its super-heavy booster rocket at its launch site near Brownsville. In 2017, Brownsville, which is 94 percent Hispanic, had a 31 percent poverty rate, the highest for any city in the nation. Not far from the border is Cameron Park, where people live in trailers or makeshift structures without water or sewer service. It is one of the poorest places in the nation, with an annual per capita income of $8,500 and a 47 percent poverty rate in 2017.

National politicians have made visits to Brownsville to assess its migration patterns and security needs. In June 2018, Sen. Jeff Merkley of Oregon was among several congressional Democrats who complained that they were denied access to a converted Walmart supercenter that had become the largest shelter of migrant children in the nation, with nearly 1,500 boys aged 10 to 17. In January 2019, President Donald Trump visited nearby McAllen to make his case for a border wall. Officials in Brownsville have rejected his claim that their city was plagued by crime.

The 34th Congressional District of Texas stretches nearly 300 miles while reaching across 11 counties. More than half its population is at the far southern end in Brownsville-based Cameron County and another 15 percent is in McAllen-based Hidalgo County. The rest of the district is mostly ranching country, with a handful of small towns that lean heavily Republican. Kleberg County is home to the vast grazing and oil lands of the 825,000-acre — that's 1,289 square miles, part-nuh! — King Ranch, which is bigger than Rhode Island. South Padre Island, part of the lengthy national seashore, is a popular spring-break beach destination. With its 84 percent Hispanic population, the 34th is a Democratic district. Hillary Clinton got 59 percent of the vote.

Lloyd Doggett (D)

Elected 1994, 13th term, b. Oct 06, 1946; Austin; University of Texas, B.B.A., 1967; University of Texas Law School, J.D., 1970; Methodist; Married (Libby Belk Doggett); 2 children; 4 grandchildren.

Elected Office: TX Senate, 1973-1985; TX Supreme Court justice, 1989-1994.

Professional Career: Practicing attorney, 1970-1989; Adjunct Professional, University of TX Law School, 1989-1994.

DC Office: 2307 RHOB 20515, 202-225-4865, Fax: 202-225-3073, doggett.house.gov

State Offices: Austin, 512-916-5921; San Antonio, 210-704-1080.

Committees: *Budget. Joint Taxation. Ways & Means*: Health (Chmn); Select Revenue Measures. **Group Ratings**

	ADA	ACLU	AFL-CIO	LCV	ITI	COC	HAFA	ACU	CFG	FRC
2018	-	89%	-	100%	-	50%	13%	8%	30%	0%
2017	100%	C	95%	97%	C	36%	C	7%	5%	0%

Almanac Ratings 2017-18

	Economy	Social	Foreign	Composite
Liberal	100%	100%	95%	98%
Conservative	0%	0%	5%	2%

Key Votes of the 115th Congress

1. Obama-care revision	N	5. Family planning regs	N	9. Guantanamo prisoners	Y
2. Tax Cuts	N	6. Body cameras/immigration	Y	10. Ground missiles, limit	Y
3. Omnibus appropriations	N	7. Abortion ban	N	11. Defense Dept. spending	Y
4. Dodd-Frank revision	N	8. Concealed carry	N	12. FISA rules	N

Election Results

Election	Name (Party)	Vote (%)		Cand. Spent	Ind. Exp. Support	Ind. Exp. Oppose
2018 General	Lloyd Doggett (D)..............................	138,278	(71%)	$238,568		
	David Smalling (R)........................	50,553	(26%)	$25,892		
	Clark Patterson (Lib)............................	5,236	(3%)			
2018 Primary	Lloyd Doggett (D)..		(100%)			

Prior winning percentages: 2016 (63%), 2014 (63%), 2012 (64%), 2010 (53%), 2008 (66%), 2006 (67%), 2004 (68%), 2002 (84%), 2000 (85%), 1998 (85%), 1996 (56%), 1994 (56%)

Lloyd Doggett, first elected in 1994, is a liberal Democrat and a respected voice in his party on tax and poverty issues. He has been a vocal figure in Texas politics for nearly a half-century. He has become a senior member of the House Ways and Means Committee, where he has pressed for steps to reduce prescription drug prices and took over in 2019 as chairman of the Health Subcommittee. Doggett also has been outspoken in seeking copies of President Donald Trump's tax returns and raising questions about possible tax-code violations.

Doggett grew up in Austin, finished first in his class at the University of Texas, and was student body president. At age 26, he began his lengthy and relentless career with election to the state Senate, which had been under the control of conservative Democrats. In the 1970s, as part of a large liberal bloc, he pushed for laws against job discrimination and cop-killer bullets, and for generic drugs. He has long been a close ally of trial lawyers, a strong force supporting liberal Democrats in Texas. In the legislature, he was one of the "Killer Bees" who hid out to prevent a quorum on changing the rules in the Democratic primary.

In 1984, he ran for the Senate, narrowly edging out two House members to win the Democratic nomination. He lost the general election 59%-41% to Rep. Phil Gramm, a former Democrat who had switched parties. Doggett was elected to the Texas Supreme Court in 1988. When Democratic Rep. Jake Pickle retired after 31 years, Doggett ran for his Austin-based seat. He won the Democratic primary with token opposition and took the general 56%-40%.

Doggett's Almanac vote ratings have ranked him as the most liberal Democrat in Texas. At times highly partisan, he was a frequent critic of Republican Speaker Newt Gingrich and an ally of Democratic leaders in raising continual questions about his ethics.

When Democrats controlled the House from 2007 to 2010, Doggett was influential on Ways and Means. His priorities included eliminating tax shelters and loopholes and giving the federal government power to negotiate prescription drug prices for Medicare. He sought tax incentives for purchasers of plug-in hybrid electric cars. In 2009, when President Barack Obama announced his plan to reform international tax policy, he cited Doggett's input on proposals to crack down on overseas tax evasion.

Back in the minority in the House, Doggett found ways to be effective. As the senior Democrat on the Human Resources Subcommittee at Ways and Means, he got a bill into law in 2013 setting up a national commission to examine ways to reduce the number of children who die from abuse and neglect. Texas has had the highest rate of child abuse and neglect fatalities. He worked with committee Republicans to gain House passage of a bill in 2012 to authorize the phased removal of Social Security numbers from Medicare cards to crack down on identity theft.

Doggett has become a vigorous advocate of steps to reduce prescription costs. In 2015, he enacted his proposal to give Medicare beneficiaries notification of the details of out-patient services. In September 2018, his "right to know" provisions for drug-price information were enacted with Senate allies initiating action in that chamber. Taking over as Health Subcommittee chairman in January 2019, Doggett filed a bill to increase the leverage of federal officials who administer health care, including Medicare, in their negotiation of drug prices with pharmaceutical companies. "I hope that President Trump will follow the advice of candidate Trump to find common ground with us [and] reject the advice of the Big Pharma executives he appointed to control his agenda," Doggett said.

He has been persistent in seeking votes on his proposals to force Trump to release his tax returns for closed-door review. Once Democrats won House control and gained added leverage, Doggett supported moves by Ways and Means Chairman Richard Neal to get the tax records. Sunlight is "a weapon against corruption, bias and self-dealing," he told the Houston Chronicle in February 2019.

Republicans have sought and failed with numerous redistricting schemes to end Doggett's congressional career. In 2004, the GOP stretched his district 300 miles south to the Mexican border. But he took up the challenge. As other dislocated Texas Democrats took their fight to the courts, Doggett took his case to the voters of his new district. Doggett won the primary 64%-36%, with 88 percent of the vote in Travis County and holding Leticia Hinojosa, a former district court judge from McAllen, to a standoff in her base in Hidalgo County. He won handily in November. In 2010, he drew a tough challenge from Republican Donna Campbell, a doctor and hospital emergency department director who raised $765,000. But Doggett spent $1.2 million and won 53%-45%.

In 2011, Texas Republicans again sought to carve up Doggett's stronghold, by attaching his liberal Austin base to a predominantly San Antonio district. Doggett easily won a three-way Democratic primary with 73 percent of the vote and then crushed Republican San Marcos Mayor Susan Narvaiz in November with 64 percent. In March 2017, after federal judges ruled that his district had been unconstitutionally gerrymandered, Doggett agreed and said that the GOP map "reduces the amount of accessibility and accountability of elected officials, regardless of their party."

He has remained active in home-state politics. In 2017, he condemned the "vindictiveness" and "anti-immigrant hysteria" of Texas Gov. Greg Abbott in seeking to punish Austin with a loss of state funding because of its "sanctuary" policies to protect illegal immigrants.

TX-35: Eastern Bexar County, Eastern Travis County   **Cook Partisan Voting Index: D+15**

Population		Race and Ethnicity		Income	
Total	795,361	White	25.6%	Median Income	$45,959
Land area (sq. miles)	594	Black	8.9%	District Income Rank	364
Pop/ sq mi	1339.5	Latino	62.2%	Poverty Rate	21.8%
Born in State	64.3%	Asian	1.4%	With health insurance	78.7%
		Two or more races	1.5%	Cash public assistance	2%
Age Groups		Other	0.3%	Food stamp/SNAP	17.6%
Under 18	26.4%				
18-34	29.6%	**Education**		**Work**	
35-64	35.1%	H.S grad or less	51.5%	White Collar	8.9%
Over 64	8.9%	Some college	28.6%	Sales and Service	47.8%
		College Degree, 4 yr	13.9%	Blue Collar	25%
Military		Post grad	6.1%	Government	13.7%
Veteran/ Active Duty	7.9%				

2012 Pres. Vote	Obama	105,550	(63%)	Romney	58,007	(35%)		
2016 Pres. Vote	Clinton	128,535	(64%)	Trump	61,136	(30%)	Johnson	7,664 (4%)

San Antonio/East Austin Corridor: "There are only four unique cities in America: Boston, New Orleans, San Francisco and San Antonio." This quote may well be apocryphal — it has been attributed to both Mark Twain and Will Rogers — and today one would have to add a few other cities to the list. But San Antonio still stands as a one-of-a-kind American locale. It started out as a collection of five Spanish missions, including the Mission San Antonio de Valero, better known today as the Alamo. From there it grew into a colonial capital, a hub for cattle drives, a railroad base, and eventually the heart of South Texas' increasingly transnational economy. Southerners and Mexicans played a large role in the city's growth, but Germans also settled here in large numbers in the mid-19th century. Frederick Law Olmsted referred to antebellum San Antonio as a "jumble of races, costumes, languages, and buildings," and as late as 1877, German speakers outnumbered Anglos and Mexican Americans. Even the city's politics ran against the grain. In 1920, a district that included Bexar County elected Republican Harry Wurzbach to Congress, the only member of his party the Lone Star State sent to Congress in the first half of the 20th century.

The 35th Congressional District of Texas covers many of the downtown features that helped make San Antonio unique. The Alamo, which had been maintained by the private Daughters of the Republic of Texas for 110 years, switched to management by the state's general land office soon after George P. Bush became land commissioner in 2015. The district takes in the 2.5-mile-long River Walk, lined with restaurants, museums and hotels; the 30-story, octagonal Tower Life Building; and the Alamodome, a 65,000-seat basketball/football stadium and the Henry B. Gonzalez Convention Center. On the east side of downtown, an innovation district gained initial approval by the city council in February 2019. The plans calls for it to be a center for bioscience start-ups and research. About 40 percent of the district's voters live in Bexar County.

There has been rapid growth in the often-thin strip of neighborhoods running along Interstate 35 through the outskirts of Texas Hill Country, in the German settlement of New Braunfels, the old mill town of San Marcos, and Kyle, a booming suburb of Austin. New Braunfels, with 8 percent growth in 2017, was the second-fastest growing city in the nation, behind Frisco Texas.

The remaining 30 percent of the district's population lives in southeastern Travis County, in the mostly minority neighborhoods of east Austin. The Austin airport, a former military base, which had been about even with San Antonio in its passenger load, has had a spurt in traffic and expanded its facilities with nine new gates in February 2019. More airport growth is planned. A new highway to the airport, including toll lanes, is scheduled for completion in 2020. Along Lady Bird Lake in southeast Austin, Oracle has built a new campus to focus on cloud computing technologies. It opened in 2018, with space for 10,000 employees.

The district owes its unique shape to two goals of Republicans during the 2011 redistricting. They wanted to pack as many Democrats as possible into a single district, and they wanted to make a majority-Hispanic district that would endanger longtime Austin-based Democratic Rep.

Lloyd Doggett in a primary. They attained their objective with a district that has become 63 percent Hispanic. In March 2017, a three-judge federal court ruled that the gerrymandered shape of the district was unconstitutional, though the panel did not offer a solution. A year later, the Supreme Court, in a 5-4 ruling, largely overturned that decision, though the majority agreed that the district was a racial gerrymander. Three other districts — the 10th, 21st and 25th -- cover larger parts of Austin and Travis County than does the 35th. Each is a Republican-leaning district that has consistently elected a Republican, even though the Travis County part of each of those districts votes heavily Democratic. The logic of that math, plus the continued growth in this area, suggests that the next round of redistricting will give Austin its own Democratic district, as historically was the case prior to 2005.

Brian Babin (R)

Elected 2014, 3rd term, b. Mar 23, 1948; Port Arthur; University of Texas-Houston, Att., 1969; Lamur University (TX), B.S., 1973; University of Texas-Houston, D.D.S., 1976; Southern Baptist; Married (Roxanne Babin); 5 children; 13 grandchildren.

Military Career: TX Army National Guard 1969-1975; U.S. Air Force 1975-1979

Elected Office: Woodville City Council, 1981-1982, 1984-1989; Woodville Mayor, 1982-1984; Woodville School Board, 1992-1995.

Professional Career: Dentist, 1979-2014; TX St. Board of Dental Examiners, 1981-1987; TX Historical Comm., 1989-1995; Lower Neches Valley Authority, 1999-2014.

DC Office: 2236 RHOB 20515, 202-225-1555, Fax: 202-226-0396, babin.house.gov
State Offices: Deer Park, 832-780-0966; Orange, 409-883-8075; Woodville, 409-331-8066.

Committees: *Science, Space & Technology*: Environment; Space & Aeronautics (RMM). *Transportation & Infrastructure*: Highways & Transit; Railroads, Pipelines & Hazardous Materials; Water Resources & Environment.

Group Ratings

	ADA	ACLU	AFL-CIO	LCV	ITI	COC	HAFA	ACU	CFG	FRC
2018	-	12%	-	3%	-	75%	71%	80%	61%	100%
2017	0%	C	8%	0%	C	93%	C	93%	86%	100%

Almanac Ratings 2017-18

	Economy	Social	Foreign	Composite
Liberal	2%	7%	5%	4%
Conservative	98%	93%	96%	96%

Key Votes of the 115th Congress

1. Obama-care revision	Y	5. Family planning regs	Y	9. Guantanamo prisoners	N
2. Tax Cuts	Y	6. Body cameras/immigration	N	10. Ground missiles, limit	N
3. Omnibus appropriations	N	7. Abortion ban	Y	11. Defense Dept. spending	Y
4. Dodd-Frank revision	Y	8. Concealed carry	Y	12. FISA rules	NV

Election Results

Election	Name (Party)	Vote (%)	Cand. Spent	Ind. Exp. Support	Ind. Exp. Oppose
2018 General	Brian Babin (R)..................................	161,048 (73%)	$685,009		
	Dayna Steele (D)...............................	60,908 (27%)	$856,426		
2018 Primary	Brian Babin (R)...................................	(100%)			

Prior winning percentages: 2016 (89%), 2014 (76%)

Brian Babin, a dentist and local Republican leader who was elected in 2014, has sought to bolster NASA and make his own mark as the top Republican on the Space Subcommittee, an apt assignment for his district. After four years in the majority, he had limited success. As a staunch conservative,

Babin has been a loyal ally of President Donald Trump. But he clashed with other members of the conservative Freedom Caucus and quit the group in 2017, amid internal divisions among House Republicans over their attempts to repeal the Affordable Care Act.

Babin grew up in Beaumont, attended Lamar University and got his degree in dentistry at the University of Texas at Houston; friends refer to him as "Doc Babin." After dental school, he served overseas in the Air Force, and later was an airborne artilleryman in the Army Reserve. He settled in Woodville in rural Tyler County, where he maintained his dental practice. Babin entered local politics by serving as an alderman and mayor of Woodville. He was a regional chairman for Ronald Reagan's 1980 presidential campaign and claimed some credit for the shift to the Republican Party in these parts of east Texas that had been "yellow dog" conservative Democratic territory. When the colorful Democratic Rep. Charlie Wilson retired in 1996, Babin ran for the seat, only to lose to Democrat Jim Turner 52%-46%. He tried again two years later and lost by a wider margin.

When the more suburban 36th became open in 2014, he decided to try again after a 16-year hiatus. In a 12-candidate field in the March primary, Babin ran first with 33 percent of the vote, followed by tea-party favorite Ben Streusand at 23 percent. In the May runoff, Streusand brought up Babin's role in a long-ago Texas campaign finance scandal, noting that he received $37,000 in illegal corporate money from his friend, businessman Peter Cloeren, when he ran for the House in 1996. The FEC gave Babin a relative pass, ordering him to pay $30,000 in civil fines. His years of local political work gave him the edge. Streusand, a Houston banker who lived outside the district, led in Harris County with 65 percent of the vote, but he underperformed on turnout as Harris cast only one-third of the total vote, though it had about one-half of the voters. Babin rolled up huge majorities in the rural areas, including 85 percent in his native Tyler County. He won the runoff, 58%-42%. The general election was largely a formality.

In the House, Babin has served on two committees well-suited to his district: Transportation and Infrastructure; and Science, Space and Technology. In his first year, Babin became chairman of the Space Subcommittee. His goal, he said, was to "strengthen NASA's core exploration mission, create an environment for commercial space ventures to thrive, and build a clear vision for America's space program." More specifically, he wanted to resume manned space flight as NASA's top priority, and to end NASA's reliance on other nations to send astronauts to the International Space Station. He supported expansion of commercial space flight. When he took over as chairman, Babin criticized the agency's lack of focus. "NASA's primary missions are aeronautics and human spaceflight," he told the Houston Chronicle. "We seem to have gotten off of that in many respects."

With other Texans, Babin sought to revitalize the Johnson Space Center, whose share of the NASA budget dropped from about half to less than one-fourth during the Obama administration. The 2017 NASA authorization bill, which he helped to enact, included Babin's provision to care for former astronauts and enhance public understanding of the effects of spaceflight on the human body. In 2018, Babin pursued more ambitious legislation for NASA. In April, the Science Committee approved a bill, with bipartisan support, that boosted funds for the International Space Station. Babin called it "an important step forward for America's economic competitiveness." But the bill failed to generate enough support for Republican leaders to bring it to the House floor before Congress adjourned at the end of 2018.

On his other committee, Babin won approval of two provisions in the water resources bill, which the Transportation Committee helped to enact in 2016. They improved the navigation and maintenance of the Houston Ship Channel. In September 2018, he took the leadership in creating — and then co-chairing — the I-14 Caucus, which advocated for a proposed new east-west interstate in the South that would serve "forts and ports," including Beaumont Texas.

In March 2017, Babin voiced disappointment that the Freedom Caucus — of which he was a member — delayed House approval of the revision of the Affordable Care Act. "I worked very hard to get President Trump elected," Babin said. "So we need to support that agenda." The following month, he quit the caucus and told Fox Business Network, "we have the opportunity of a lifetime … so we must make the best use of our opportunity." In May, the House narrowly passed the bill. It died in the Senate.

Babin has enthusiastically backed Trump's initiatives. The president's decision to reach out to North Korea was "a bold new tack," he wrote for USA Today in February 2019. With Democratic Rep. Ami Bera of California, Babin wrote that Trump's call in December 2017 for a return to manned space flight was "welcome and encouraging news." In each case, follow-up steps became problematic.

TX-36: Harris County, Southeast Texas

Population		Race and Ethnicity		Income	
Total	726,915	White	62.4%	Median Income	$58,115
Land area (sq. miles)	7,126	Black	8.7%	District Income Rank	194
Pop/ sq mi	102	Latino	24.7%	Poverty Rate	13.9%
Born in State	67.9%	Asian	2%	With health insurance	82.2%
		Two or more races	1.6%	Cash public assistance	1.5%
Age Groups		Other	0.4%	Food stamp/SNAP	12.6%
Under 18	25%				
18-34	22.3%	**Education**		**Work**	
35-64	39%	H.S grad or less	48.4%	White Collar	13.7%
Over 64	13.7%	Some college	32.9%	Sales and Service	38.2%
		College Degree, 4 yr	12.8%	Blue Collar	30.8%
Military		Post grad	5.9%	Government	13.5%
Veteran/ Active Duty	8.3%				

2012 Pres. Vote	Romney	175,883	(73%)	Obama	61,786	(26%)		
2016 Pres. Vote	Trump	183,176	(72%)	Clinton	64,225	(25%)	Johnson	5,704	(2%)

Eastern Houston Suburbs : East Texas is thick with landmarks of Lone Star history. There's still an Indian reservation in Polk County, and the swampland Big Thicket National Preserve reminds you of what the area looked like before humans first settled the region some 2,500 years ago. These were some of the first parts of Texas to be settled by Anglos; Anahuac in Chambers County was a port of entry for early colonists. Later, the area became a destination for other colonists during the famed "Runaway Scrape," as they fled eastward, leaving beds unmade and breakfasts sitting on the table, in the face of Santa Anna's approaching army. Today, much of East Texas looks frozen in time — farm towns that the railroads passed by and the interstates overlooked. Of course, some things have changed. Racial segregation has been abolished — this area is home to a large portion of the state's rural black population — and the isolation of the small towns has been reduced.

Urban development, sprinting outward from Houston's loop freeways, is spreading in between the pine forests and reservoirs. The industrial age is on steroids in Baytown. Exxon began production in 2018 at its petrochemical plant, with a major expansion of chemical manufacturing and its reduction in carbon emissions. Chevron completed the $6 billion expansion of its "methane cracker," which is instrumental in the production of plastics. In October 2018, a steel company from India broke ground on an expanded steel mill in Baytown. The growth of Houston's port has been an incentive for local industrial expansion.

The southeastern corner of Harris County tends to be more upscale, populated by highly educated employees of the Lyndon B. Johnson Space Center and the space and aeronautics industry that grew around it. The location of that iconic center, which opened in 1961, was influenced by its namesake. After its discouraging recent years, during which the Houston Press in 2014 reported that the JSC "lost its identity and purpose" with the demise of NASA's manned space flights and roughly half of its buildings were torn down or consolidated, several factors have contributed to a brightening of prospects. They include Texans taking key House and Senate committee positions that handle NASA finances, plus the apparent support of President Donald Trump for space exploration. His enthusiasm has included a call to return space flight to the moon and beyond, with "commercial and international partners," he said in a December 2017 policy statement. But, as The Atlantic reported in January 2019, "it seems, the president forgot all about" that ambitious goal.

The 36th Congressional District of Texas was a compromise: Both suburban Houston Republicans and East Texas Republicans wanted a new congressional district, and the result is one evenly divided between the two groups. About half of the district's population lives in a collection of eight lightly populated counties, where lumbering, farming, ranching, and oil and gas dominate. The other half of the district's population lives in the suburbs on the eastern edge of Harris County. They include blue-collar Baytown, Deer Park, La Porte and part of Pasadena, near the Houston Ship Channel. Further south are Clear Lake, Taylor Lake Village and part of Webster. The district is among the top 5 percent of the most Republican nationwide. Donald Trump got 72 percent in 2016.

UTAH

The Almanac of American Politics.
National Journal

Congressional district boundaries were first effective for 2012.

Utah has long been one of the most Republican states in the union. Those proclivities have remained, though the 2016 presidential election – featuring a Republican candidate whose behavior repulsed many in the highly religious state – scrambled the electoral map, and two years later, a Democrat narrowly won a House seat.

Other American states were founded by leaders of religious sects — Massachusetts, Connecticut, Pennsylvania — but only in colonial times and along waters navigable by ocean ships. Utah, a triumph of man over nature, was the creation of a productive and orderly civilization in a remote expanse of desert and mountain, arrayed around a desolate salt sea. It owes its settlement to the Church of Jesus Christ of Latter-day Saints, which was founded in Upstate New York nearly 190 years ago. (For years, the shorthand "LDS" was common, but the current church leadership has sought to move away from that.) There, farmer Joseph Smith said he experienced a vision in which the angel Moroni appeared and told him where to unearth several golden tablets inscribed with hieroglyphic writings. With the aid of special spectacles, Smith translated the tablets and published them as The Book of Mormon in 1830; he declared himself to be a prophet. The Mormons he led attracted thousands of converts and created their own communities. Persecuted for their beliefs, they moved west to Ohio, Missouri, and then Nauvoo Illinois, where some 15,000 members lived under Smith's theocratic rule. It was there that Smith received a revelation sanctioning the practice of polygamy and was murdered by a mob in nearby Carthage in 1844. The new church president, Brigham Young, decided to move the faithful — "the saints" — farther west into territory that was still part of Mexico and far beyond white settlement. In 1847 Young led a well-organized march across the Great Plains and into the Rocky Mountains, stopping in what became Utah. "This is the place," Mormon tradition has Young exclaiming as he stood on the western slope of the Wasatch Range and looked out over the valley of the Great Salt Lake.

Utah was transferred from Mexico to the United States by the Treaty of Guadalupe Hidalgo of 1848, but for many years, it lived apart from the rest of the nation. Young was the first governor of the Utah Territory and most settlers in Utah continued to live by the teachings of the church. The early pioneers laid out towns foursquare to the points of the compass with huge city blocks. They built sturdy houses and planted trees generously. Young's home still stands a block away from Temple Square, where the Salt Lake LDS Temple, closed to non-Mormons, stands in gleaming granite, topped by the golden angel Moroni and situated across from the oval Mormon Tabernacle, where its renowned choir sings. For 160 years, this "Zion" has attracted thousands of converts from across the United States, England, Scandinavia and all over the world. The object of religious fear and prejudice, Utah was not granted statehood until 1896, after the church had renounced polygamy. The state has grown steadily since then and remains heavily Mormon — 62 percent, according to the church, though the percentage in populous, urban Salt Lake County is 49 percent, the lowest since the 1930s.

The LDS Church accounts for only about 2 percent of Americans, but it remains distinctive in many ways. It cares deeply about its past. The church preserves America's most complete genealogical records in its Family History Library and has made them available on site and on the Internet; in 2018, the database announced that it would include same-sex couples. The church works hard to spread the faith: The most recent statistics show that 65,000 young Mormons did missionary work in the United States and abroad. (An ancillary result is that Utah has relatively low rates of military enlistment.) The missionaries' experiences give Utah the broadest inventory of people with knowledge of foreign languages of any state in the union, a nice commercial advantage, and one that played a role in the National Security Agency's decision to build a $2 billion cloud-based facility in Bluffdale, south of Salt Lake City. By law, the state now prioritizes teaching languages in public schools as early as first grade.

Mormon teaching prohibits the consumption of tobacco, alcohol, coffee and tea. Only in July 2009, amid concerns about the impact on tourism, could you finally get a drink served at a bar without joining a private club, and even then it had to be poured out of sight, behind what became known as a "Zion curtain." After years of trying, lawmakers finally got rid of the Zion curtain in 2017. The same year, the state lowered the blood alcohol limit from .08 to .05, the nation's lowest threshold. (Possibly related: Utahns buy candy at the highest rate in the United States, about 50 percent higher than the national average.)

The church encourages hard work and large families; 30 percent of Utah residents in 2017 were under 18, compared with the national average of 23 percent. On average, Mormons are better educated, work longer hours, and earn more money than Americans at large. The LDS Church has no paid clergy, but members serve in positions for which they are chosen, conducting religious services but also keeping in touch with members and counseling them when they need help. The church also maintains its own social-service organizations. While American mainline denominations have been losing members, the LDS Church is growing. Starting with just 30 members, the church took a century to reach 1 million. There were 2.9 million Mormons in 1970, 5 million in 1982 and about 16.1 million today. The United States has 6.6 million members in 14,255 congregations, but about three-fifths of LDS members today live outside the U.S.

In some ways, Utah resembles the America of the 1950s. In recent years, it has had the highest percentage of households headed by married couples and households with children, the highest fertility rate for non-Hispanic whites, the youngest median age of first marriages, and the lowest birth rate for unmarried women. Sometimes this makes its economic statistics misleading: Utah has a per capita income 14 percent below the national average — because all those kids aren't earning salaries — yet the median household income is 13 percent above the national average and the poverty rate is more than three full percentage points below the nation's as a whole. It also has the highest rate of volunteerism, and its residents have the nation's highest rate of charitable giving, according to the Chronicle of Philanthropy. Utahns' trusting nature has even prompted state Attorney General Sean Reyes to note that Utah is "sadly known for its high level of financial vulnerability to affinity fraud" — scams that take advantage of personal relationships. Utah was the first state where women voted and it elected the first female state senator. But in recent years, the percentage of women in elected office has been below the national average.

Historically, Utah has been a bastion of social conservatism. The LDS Church's opposition to abortion rights is widely shared by its membership, and the church has always discouraged gambling. It is one of only two states (Hawaii is the other) with no form of legal gambling. The church has made notable overtures to the LGBT community in recent years. In 2015, Mormon leaders worked with lawmakers to pass a measure that banned employment and housing discrimination based on sexual orientation while carving out protections for religious institutions that oppose homosexuality. A new church policy leaked later that year sent a more negative signal, saying that Mormons in same-sex unions would be considered apostates. But in April 2019, the church, under new leadership, announced that it was reversing that policy. "While we cannot change the Lord's doctrine, we want our members and our policies to be considerate of those struggling with the challenges of mortality," the church said.

Indeed, the state isn't frozen in time. While its black population – 1 percent – is among the nation's lowest, Utah's Hispanic population is now 14 percent. While that's lower than Arizona or Nevada, it still represents a sharp contrast with Utah's past, and the Utah Hispanic population is even younger than the state's population as a whole, making it a growing demographic force. This shift has evoked a different response in Utah than in Arizona. Utah businesses have been interested in maintaining an immigrant work force, and LDS leaders, many with experience as overseas missionaries, have expressed compassion. In 2018, the church threw its weight behind protection for "dreamers" who were brought illegally to the United States as children, saying that while "immigration is a complex and sometimes divisive issue . . . we believe that our first priority is to love and care for one another as Jesus Christ taught."

Overall, Utah has been on a growth spurt. From 2000 to 2010, the state's population rose 24 percent, to nearly 2.8 million — the third-highest growth rate in the nation after Nevada and Arizona. Since 2010, the state has grown by another 14 percent, and from 2016 to 2017, St. George – closer to Las Vegas than Salt Lake City – was the fastest-growing metro area in the country. Wasatch County (Heber City), Morgan County (suburban Salt Lake City and Ogden), Washington County (St. George), and Utah County (Provo) have all grown by at least 23 percent since 2010, while Davis County (suburban Salt Lake City) and Summit County (Park City) have grown by at least 13 percent.

Before World War II, Utah saw itself as a colonial victim of East Coast bankers and financiers, and Mormons saw themselves as suffering religious discrimination and bigotry — with considerable cause. Utah's income levels were well below the national average, and its cost of living was higher. In political terms, this perspective translated into Democratic allegiance. In 1940, Utah was represented by staunch New Dealers in Congress and voted 62%-38% for Franklin Roosevelt. Since then, Utah has come to see itself as a busy generator of wealth, pushing Mormons and Utahns toward the GOP, at least in ordinary circumstances. Utah has not voted Democratic for president since 1964, it hasn't elected a Democratic governor since Scott Matheson in 1980, and it hasn't sent a Democratic senator to Washington since 1970.

Salt Lake City has been the state's primary pocket of liberalism, with the resort area of Park City a close second. The neighborhoods close to the church headquarters, with their gracious old houses and a smaller street grid, have attracted academic and professional newcomers and so have become the most heavily "gentile" (the Mormon term for non-Mormons) part of the state. In 2008, Democrats won control of the Salt Lake County government and elected most of its state legislators. But Democrats have won few legislative seats in the rest of the state. The Republican dominance has grown so great that tea party factions have flexed their muscle, worrying establishment figures in the party. Prompted by an activist-dominated convention in 2010 in which insurgent Mike Lee won enough votes to keep incumbent Sen. Robert Bennett off the primary ballot, establishment Republicans pushed successfully to allow candidates alternate paths to the primary.

The 2016 presidential race in Utah was the most topsy-turvy in memory. The eventual Republican nominee, Donald Trump, got a measly 14 percent of the GOP primary vote, and was so unpopular that even Democratic nominee Hillary Clinton made the rare move of spending general election money in the state, sending a mailer to Utah voters in late August. About two weeks before the election, the Trump campaign felt pressed to dispatch vice presidential nominee Mike Pence to Salt Lake City, a move unheard of for a Republican nominee. Mitt Romney had won the state with 73 percent in 2012; Trump won it with 46 percent four years later and garnered 225,000 fewer votes statewide than Romney had. Most of the "missing" Republican vote went to Evan McMullin, a third-party Utah resident and LDS member, who took 21.5 percent. Clinton won two counties – Salt Lake County, where the margin shifted 28 points in the Democratic direction, and Summit County, where the margin shifted by 20 points.

Both parties found aspects of the 2018 midterm election to celebrate. Romney, running for the Senate with a mildly anti-Trump tone, was easily elected with 63 percent of the vote. But GOP Rep. Mia Love, a Brooklyn native of Haitian ancestry who had converted to the LDS church, narrowly lost her seat to Democrat Ben McAdams, the Salt Lake County mayor. Several ballot initiative results also pleased center-left voters in the state: Medical marijuana passed with 53 percent, an expansion of Medicaid under the Affordable Care Act passed with 53 percent, and a redistricting commission passed with just over 50 percent. But after the election, the Republican legislature sought to flex its muscles by passing a more limited Medicaid expansion, along with a compromise medical marijuana law that both sides had agreed to. There are limits to how far liberalism can go in Utah.

Population		Race and Ethnicity		Income	
Total	2,993,941	White	79.0%	Median Income	$65,325
Land area (sq. miles)	82,170	Black	1.1%	State Income Rank	13
Pop/ sq mi	36.4	Latino	13.7%	Poverty Rate	11.0%
Born in state	62.2%	Asian	2.2%	With health insurance	89.2%
		Two or more races	2.1%	Cash public assistance	1.7%
Age Groups		Other	2.0%	Food stamp/SNAP	7.7%
Under 18	30.4%				
18-34	26.3%	Education		Work	
35-64	33.0%	H.S grad or less	31.1%	White Collar	37.7%
Over 64	10.3%	Some college	36.5%	Sales and Service	41.1%
		College Degree, 4 yr	21.5%	Blue Collar	21.2%
Military		Post grad	11.0%	Government	14.5%
Veteran/ Active Duty	6.2%				

Presidential Politics

2016 Caucus (D)	Sanders (D)	62,991 (79%)	Clinton (D)	16,162 (20%)		
2016 Caucus (R)	Cruz (R)	132,904 (69%)	Kasich (R)	31,992 (17%)	Trump (R)	26,434 (14%)
2016 Pres. Vote	Trump (R)	515,231 (45%)	Clinton (D)	310,676 (27%)	McMullin (I)	243,690 (21%)
	Johnson (L)	39,608 (3%)				
2012 Pres. Vote	Romney (R)	740,600 (73%)	Obama (D)	251,813 (25%)		

Utah has been the most Republican state in seven of the last 10 presidential elections. Barack Obama's 34.4 percent showing in 2008 was the best Democratic performance since Hubert Humphrey won 37 percent of the vote in 1968. He even carried Salt Lake County, if only by 296 votes. In 2012, when Republicans nominated Mitt Romney, a Mormon who was widely known for his work in rescuing the 2002 Salt Lake City Winter Olympics, the state saw the biggest Republican swing in the nation, as Romney won 73%-25% and carried Salt Lake County 58%-38%. The 2016 presidential race was scrambled when shortly after Republicans formally nominated Donald Trump, Utah native Evan McMullin, a Mormon and former senior GOP congressional aide and ex-CIA operative, launched an independent presidential bid. His name wound up on the ballot in 11 states, including Utah. Trump won the state over Hillary Clinton, 46%-28%, with McMullin taking 21 percent, his best showing by far. Clinton carried two counties, Salt Lake and Summit (Park City). McMullin didn't win any of the state's 29 counties, but finished ahead of Clinton in 15.

While it could get overlooked in the swarm of states holding primaries on the first Tuesday in March, Utah has decided to join the pack on that date in 2020. In their caucus in March 2016, Democrats gave Vermont Sen. Bernie Sanders a 79%-20% landslide over Clinton. In the GOP caucus, Romney cut radio ads for Sen. Ted Cruz in Utah, and the Texan captured 70 percent of the vote, to Ohio Gov. John Kasich's 17 percent and Trump's 14 percent.

Congressional Districts

116th Congress Lineup	1D 3R	115th Congress Lineup	4R

Democrats managed to hold a seat in the first election after Republicans drew Utah's districts in 2012, with a new fourth seat, when they expected to sweep the delegation. And they surprisingly found a way to regain that 4th District in 2018 when Salt Lake County Mayor Ben McAdams narrowly defeated Republican Rep. Mia Love. If McAdams beats the odds again in 2020, the likelihood is that a Republican governor and legislature will reallocate a few precincts and make it very difficult for him — or any other Democrat — to prevail in 2022 in this state that has been comfortably Republican. By that time, the ambitious McAdams may have found a better opportunity with a bid for statewide office.

The next round could be a reprise of the 2012 redistricting when many Utah Republicans argued, in their party's interest, that all the state's districts should contain both urban and rural areas, splitting Democratic-leaning Salt Lake City like a "pizza pie." After lengthy debate and some Republican internal bickering, the legislature agreed the new 4th District would be a "doughnut hole," with its core in the heavily Republican suburbs south of Salt Lake City and the northern reaches of prohibitively Republican northern Utah County. Each of the remaining three districts included parts of the metropolitan area plus vast open spaces.

In 2012, Democratic Rep. Jim Matheson ran in the 4th. Like Houdini, he cheated the Republicans' plan, prevailing by 768 votes. The feat was all the more impressive in light of his opponent, Mia Love, a black Mormon small-town mayor who gained a national following. To boot, Republican presidential nominee Mitt Romney won 68 percent in the 4th. Had Republicans carved just one more Utah County precinct into the 4th, Matheson would almost certainly have lost. Still, Matheson decided that he had struggled enough, including with Democratic leaders in the House. He retired in 2014. Love prevailed twice — though by unexpectedly narrow margins, before the popularity of McAdams and the unpopularity of President Donald Trump worked against her. Republican map-drawers likely will be more rigorous in advancing their interests the next time.

Gary Herbert (R)

Assumed office in 2009, term expires 2021, 2nd full term; b. May. 7, 1947, American Fork; Brigham Young U., attended 1968-70, Mormon; Married (Jeanette); 6 children.

Military Career: UT Army National Guard, 1970-1976.

Elected Office: UT County Commissioner, 1990-2004; UT Lt. Governor, 2005-2009.

Professional Career: Realtor, Herbert & Assocs. Realtors; Co-owner, The Kids Connection, 1985-2008.

Office: 350 North State St., Suite 200, Salt Lake City, 84114-2220; 801-538-1000; Fax: 801-538-1133; Website: utah.gov/governor.

Lt. Gov.: Spencer Cox (R) **Atty. Gen:** Sean Reyes (R)

State Legislature: Senate: 6D, 23R **House:** 16D, 59R

Election Results

Election	Name (Party)	Vote (%)
2016 General	Gary Herbert (R)..	750,828 (67%)
	Mike Weinholtz (D)..	322,462 (29%)
	Brian Kamerath (L)...	34,687 (3%)
2016 Primary	Gary Herbert (R)..	165,678 (72%)
	Jonathan Johnson (R)...	63,978 (28%)

Prior winning percentage: 2012 (68%), 2010 (64%)

Republican Gary Herbert is the longest-serving governor in the nation, having assumed office in August 2009 following the resignation of Republican Gov. Jon Huntsman Jr., who became U.S. ambassador to China. Herbert was easily elected in 2010 for the remainder of that term, then won reelection on his own in 2012. He then survived a credible primary challenge in 2016. Herbert has steered a relatively moderate course despite his state's overwhelmingly Republican leanings, and his approval ratings have been consistently high.

Herbert was born in American Fork, where his father owned a construction company. He studied engineering and accounting at Brigham Young University but left school before graduating and established Herbert and Associates Realtors. He ran for the Orem City Council in 1989, losing by 32 votes. The next year, he was elected to the Utah County Commission and served as its chairman for 13 years. During his tenure, Utah County had one of the state's lowest tax rates. He entered the 1994 race to unseat Democratic Rep. Bill Orton but dropped out after struggling to raise money.

In 2003, Herbert left the Utah County Commission to run for governor. The field for the 2004 Republican primary was crowded with better known politicians, including former Rep. Jim Hansen, former Utah House Speaker Nolan Karras, and Huntsman, the son of industrialist Jon Huntsman Sr., the wealthiest man in Utah. Herbert cast himself as a "David" in a field of "Goliaths" and stressed his rural roots and ties to local government. Unable to generate enough support for his candidacy, Herbert accepted Huntsman's invitation to join his ticket as the nominee for lieutenant governor. At the time, Huntsman was perceived as lacking credibility in state politics and rural issues, two areas where Herbert was strong. The ticket won with 58 percent of the vote.

Under Utah's constitution, the lieutenant governor's sole official duty is overseeing the state Elections Office, but Huntsman expanded Herbert's responsibilities to include managing the state's public lands policies, transportation plans and homeland security operations. He pushed for the creation of a Public Lands Policy Coordination Office to help manage the state's role in land-management issues. Succeeding the outgoing Huntsman, Herbert has been unflashy and unpretentious. "He's plainspoken," the Salt Lake Tribune said in endorsing him for reelection in 2012. "With Gary, what you see is what you get." Legislatively, Herbert made few changes to Huntsman's cabinet and continued a policy of opposing most tax increases. He agreed not to veto a bill that raised the state's cigarette tax by $1 a pack to reduce an education budget shortfall from $300 million to around $10 million. He also retained a four-day workweek — since repealed — that his predecessor had initiated as a way to cut costs.

Herbert was strongly favored for election in 2010 and won the GOP nomination at the state party's convention in May with 71 percent of the vote. He ran on his state's fiscal stability during the 2007-09 recession. His Democratic opponent was Salt Lake County Mayor Peter Corroon. The state's GOP leanings and the strong election cycle for the party enabled Herbert to easily beat Corroon, 64%-32%, carrying every county except Summit (Park City).

On immigration, Herbert signed a package of bills that authorized a guest-worker program that allowed undocumented immigrants to remain in the state if they paid fines. At the same time, it required police to check the legal status of people arrested on felony or serious misdemeanor charges; established a partnership with the Mexican state of Nuevo León to allow workers to come to Utah; and allowed Utah citizens to sponsor immigrants.

Herbert addressed another controversial issue in March 2012, when he vetoed a bill that would have allowed school districts to drop sex education and required abstinence-only instruction in those that kept it. The measure had sparked emotional protests and petition drives, and Herbert argued that it "simply goes too far by constricting parental options." His action displeased conservatives, but they were mollified when he signed another measure asking the federal government to give back more than 20 million acres of land to the state.

In 2012, Herbert drew five Republican challengers but won 58 percent on the first ballot at the state's GOP convention, then proceeded to trounce runner-up Morgan Philpot, a former state representative, in the primary, 63%-37%. Herbert's Democratic opponent, Peter Cooke, was a retired Army Reserve general; Herbert won, 68%-28%, carrying every county. He even won Summit this time, 50%-47%.

After that election, Herbert began to assert a moderate approach. He signed a bill urging treatment rather than prison for drug offenders, and signed another to permit the use of cannabis oil as a medical treatment. He created a Clean Air Action Team to craft ideas for improving air quality along the Wasatch Front. He increased property taxes to spend on education and raised the gasoline tax to boost transportation initiatives. He also worked with the Obama administration to propose a middle ground on the expansion of Medicaid under the Affordable Care Act. Most strikingly, Herbert worked with leaders of the LDS church and gay-rights groups to enact a compromise measure that simultaneously outlawed discrimination against members of the LGBT community while protecting religious freedoms. At the same time, Herbert took some stands that pleased conservatives. He supported a resolution opposing federal protections for two areas, Cedar Mesa and San Rafael Swell, and signed into a law a measure that allowed firing squads for executions if no drugs were available for lethal injections.

As Herbert prepared to run for his second full term in 2016, he continued to balance conservative and moderate positions. Conservatives were pleased to see him sign the nation's first law requiring women seeking an abortion after 20 weeks to be given anesthesia. He also signed a package of measures addressing pornography. The most far-reaching provision required computer technicians to report child pornography they find, with the failure to do so a misdemeanor. Herbert also made moves to reverse his past support for the Common Core curriculum and related education reforms. He cheered moderates by approving one bill to spend $27 million over three years on homeless services, and another to spend $15 million on an expansion of Medicaid to a projected 16,000 residents. Herbert also withdrew his support for Republican presidential nominee Donald Trump in October after the emergence of a 2005 recording showing the future Republican candidate making remarks offensive to women. "While I cannot vote for Hillary Clinton," he tweeted, "I will not vote for Trump."

Herbert first faced a primary challenge from his right by Overstock.com chairman Jonathan Johnson, who received the backing of the conservative group FreedomWorks. At the diehard-dominated state GOP convention, Johnson beat Herbert, 55%-45% -- not enough to push Herbert out of the race, but enough for the challenger to secure a spot on the primary ballot. After it came out that Herbert had referred to himself at a meeting with lobbyists as "AvailableJones" – someone open to doing business in exchange for campaign contributions – Johnson attacked his comment and Herbert apologized. But critics also raised questions about Johnson's fundraising efforts; he received some $900,000 from one donor, Overstock.com founder Patrick Byrne. In the June primary, Herbert defeated Johnson, with 72 percent of the vote. In the general election, Herbert was the heavy favorite against Democrat Mike Weinholtz, a largely self-funded candidate who was chairman of a health care company. Weinholtz sent mailers pairing Herbert with Trump and Russian President Vladimir Putin, but they weren't enough to overcome the state's strong partisan leanings. Herbert won, 67%-29%.

In 2017, Herbert signed a bill to end the state's"Zion curtains," which shielded customers from the pouring of alcoholic beverages. Some lawmakers had been trying to end the practice for years without success. He also signed a resolution calling on Trump to roll back the Bears Ears National Monument in southern Utah that had been established by President Barack Obama. Later that year, Trump came to Utah to announce that he would be shrinking that monument as well as another in Utah that had been established by President Bill Clinton, Grand Staircase-Escalante National Monument. In 2018, Herbert applauded pro-resource-extraction revisions by the Trump administration to an Obama-era agreement on preserving habitat for the endangered sage grouse.

On other issues, though, Herbert burnished his moderate credentials. He signed a student-inspired resolution that acknowledged human-driven climate change; while it was non-binding, backers called the resolution a breakthrough for a conservative state. He expressed skepticism about Trump's idea of arming schoolteachers, and said he would be open to raising the purchase age for certain firearms from 18 to 21. Herbert also approved repeal of the "no promo homo" bill that prevented any "promotion" of homosexuality in schools; it had drawn a lawsuit. Herbert said he would oppose a measure to prevent transgender people from being able to change the gender on their birth certificates, and he expressed support for a bill to enhance hate-crime penalties, even though similar legislation had failed in the past. "I think the message we want to put out there is that members of the gay community, LGBTQ, are loved and welcomed and appreciated for who they are," Herbert said.

Another group to consistently win public support from Herbert was immigrants. Herbert opposed the Trump administration's restrictions on travelers from certain predominantly Muslim nations, and signed a bill to ease the renewal of drivers' licenses for refugees living in Utah. When it comes to the president, Herbert said in October 2017, "there's a lot of things to like, but there's things to be concerned about." He was especially irked after Trump mocked Utah Rep. Mia Love after she lost in the 2018 election. Herbert also threw cold water on an effort in the legislature to rename the Utah National Parks Highway after Trump.

Meanwhile, after voters passed ballot measures in November 2018 to allow medical marijuana and expand Medicaid under the Affordable Care Act, Herbert signed bills that limited the scope of both policies. The marijuana measure had been negotiated amicably prior to passage by the key players, but the Medicaid bill was more controversial, effectively reducing the number of potential beneficiaries by the tens of thousands. Still, its enactment accomplished one of Herbert's long-sought goals, and he said upon signing it that the rewrite "balancesUtah's sense of compassion and frugality." Herbert would be allowed to run for a third full term in 2020. Herbert would have been allowed to run for a third full term in 2020, but despite telling the Deseret News "never say never" in January 2019, he decided against another run. Shortly after his announcement, Lt. Gov. Spencer Cox jumped in the race. While Cox began as the frontrunner, other Republicans could contend for the open seat.

Mike Lee (R)

Elected 2010, term expires 2022, 2nd term, b. Jun 04, 1971; Mesa, AZ; Brigham Young University (UT), B.A., 1994; Brigham Young University (UT), J.D., 1997; Mormon; Married (Sharon Lee); 3 children.

Professional Career: Law clerk, Judge Samuel Alito, U.S Court of Appeals, 3rd Circuit, 1998-1999; Practicing attorney, 1999-2002; Assistant U.S Attorney, 2002-2005; Gen. counsel, Gov. Jon Huntsman, 2005-2006; Law clerk, Supreme Court Justice Samuel Alito, 2006-2007; Practicing attorney, 2007-2010.

DC Office: 361-A RSOB 20510, 202-224-5444, Fax: 202-228-1168, lee.senate.gov

State Offices: Ogden, 801-392-9633; Salt Lake City, 801-524-5933; St. George, 435-628-5514.

Committees: *Commerce, Science & Transportation*: Communications, Technology, Innovation & the Internet; Manufacturing, Trade & Consumer Protection; Subcommittee on Aviation & Space; Subcommittee on Security. *Energy & Natural Resources*: Energy; National Parks; Public Lands, Forests & Mining (Chmn). *Judiciary*: Antitrust, Competition Policy & Consumer Rights (Chmn); Border Security & Immigration; Constitution; Subcommittee on Intellectual Property. *Joint Economic (Chmn)*

Group Ratings

	ADA	ACLU	AFL-CIO	LCV	ITI	COC	HAFA	ACU	CFG	FRC
2018	-	36%	-	7%	-	60%	100%	100%	100%	100%
2017	10%	C	0%	0%	C	71%	C	96%	94%	100%

Almanac Ratings 2017-18

	Economy	Social	Foreign	Composite
Liberal	11%	11%	28%	17%
Conservative	89%	89%	73%	83%

Key Votes of the 115th Congress

1. Obama-care revision	Y	5. Gun regulations	Y	9. Kavanaugh confirmation	Y
2. Tax Cuts	Y	6. Family planning regs	Y	10. Saudi arms sales	Y
3. Dodd-Frank revision	Y	7. Gorsuch confirmation	Y	11. FISA rules	N
4. Omnibus appropriations	N	8. Immigration restrictions	N	12. Military aid in Yemen	Y

Election Results

Election	Name (Party)	Vote (%)		Cand. Spent	Ind. Exp. Support	Ind. Exp. Oppose
2016 General	Mike Lee (R).................................	760,220	(68%)	$4,420,800	$316,173	
	Misty Snow (D)...............................	301,858	(27%)	$95,199		
	Stoney Fonua (I).............................	27,339	(3%)			
2016 Primary	Mike Lee (R)................................ Unopposed					

Prior winning percentages: 2010 (62%)

Utah's senior senator is Republican Mike Lee, who was elected in 2010 by ousting the incumbent at the Republican state convention. Though low-key and outwardly unassuming, Lee has strong convictions, especially an abiding interest in spreading his tea party views. In 2016, he was an enthusiastic supporter of Texas Sen. Ted Cruz's presidential bid and refused to endorse Donald Trump in the general election. Utah Republicans consistently have been hostile to Trump.

Lee grew up in Provo, where his father, Rex Lee, was the founding dean of Brigham Young University's law school. As a youth, Mike Lee lived part time in McLean, Virginia, when his father was an assistant attorney general from 1975 to 1976 and solicitor general from 1981 to 1985. Lee remembers watching his father argue cases before the Supreme Court. "It took me a while before I realized it wasn't entirely an ordinary experience to get to do that frequently," he recalled. Lee returned to Provo at 14 and later graduated from college and law school at Brigham Young. He clerked for two federal judges, including Samuel Alito. He practiced law in Washington, D.C. and Utah, where he served as legal counsel to Republican Gov. Jon Huntsman. In 2006, after Alito was confirmed to the Supreme Court, Lee returned to Washington to clerk for him once again.

Lee said he decided to challenge 18-year Senate veteran Bob Bennett after Congress passed the 2009 $700 billion bailout of the financial industry and the $787 billion stimulus bill that President Barack Obama sought. "The Republican Party had in so many ways deviated from what it professes," Lee said. Bennett was a solid conservative, but he had voted for the Troubled Asset Relief Program for the financial industry and had been a chief supporter of bipartisan health care legislation with Oregon Democratic Sen. Ron Wyden.

Bennett was endorsed by soon-to-be presidential nominee Mitt Romney and Utah GOP Sen. Orrin Hatch. But to get on the primary ballot, he needed either 60 percent of the delegate vote or to finish first or second at the 2010 Republican State Convention. In the meantime, Lee had caught the fancy of tea party activists, who were beginning to make inroads with their attacks on government spending.

At the May convention, involving roughly 3,500 delegates from around the state, Bennett was hammered for being a member of the Appropriations Committee when the government debt kept growing. He was swept out in the second round. Business consultant Tim Bridgewater came in first with 37 percent of the vote; Lee got 35 percent of the delegates and Bennett finished third with 27 percent. When the contest went to a primary election, Lee prevailed 51%-49%. The general election was anticlimactic in this heavily Republican state. Lee easily won 62%-33%.

At 38, Lee was the youngest senator when he took office in 2011. He got some notice when he was one of the few Republicans to vote against extending the Patriot Act after expressing concern that it did not sufficiently protect civil liberties and privacy. Also that year, he penned a book titled, "The Freedom Agenda: Why a Balanced Budget Amendment is Necessary to Restore Constitutional Government." During the standoff over raising the debt limit in summer 2011, he pushed his balanced budget amendment that would have required a two-thirds vote of both houses of Congress to raise the limit on spending. When the Democratic-controlled Senate approved a plan with more modest deficit reduction, Lee voted against it. In December, he and fellow Utahn Hatch offered a balanced budget amendment that was rejected 47-53.

Lee jumped into the fray on judicial nominations. Outraged over Obama's recess appointments, he voted, from his seat on the Judiciary Committee, against Utah lawyer Robert Shelby for a federal judgeship in April 2012. He made it clear that he supported Shelby but voted "no" to protest recess appointments. His persistence was rewarded when the Supreme Court ruled unanimously in 2014 that such recess appointments were unconstitutional if made when the Senate said it is in session.

Lee's tenacity became evident in his battle to dismantle the Affordable Care Act. During the initial legal challenge to the law, Lee was active as the lawsuit wended its way to the Supreme Court. He published three health care-related YouTube videos. But the high court upheld the law's requirement that individuals must carry health insurance or face a penalty as part of the government's tax authority in 2012.

That setback did not stop Lee from targeting the law. He emerged as a leader, along with his friend and ally Cruz, in formulating the strategy to defund Obamacare. That approach led to a government shutdown in October 2013, much to the consternation of party leaders. When the 16-day shutdown ended without having made a dent in Obamacare, Lee faced widespread unhappiness in the Senate from fellow Republicans. Lee suffered back home, where the federal government is the largest employer, too. That downturn proved to be temporary as Lee rebounded by explaining his relentless push for smaller and less meddlesome government. He had the strong backing of well-funded conservative groups that were poised to spend lavishly to help him fend off would-be GOP primary challengers. As it turned out, their help was unneeded in his 2016 re-election.

Lee does not shy from bucking his party's establishment and has pressed some controversial stances. With other conservative Republicans, he co-sponsored a measure declaring that the 14th Amendment's birthright citizenship is limited to children of citizens, legal residents and members of the military and does not extend to children of undocumented immigrants. Showing his independence, he also pushed for loosening some immigration restrictions. He crossed party lines in an unusual alliance with New York Democratic Sen. Chuck Schumer to advance a visa reform bill that included helping foreigners who have invested at least $500,000 in a house in the United States. At Schumer's behest, Lee took part in bipartisan talks on a comprehensive immigration reform bill in late 2012 and early 2013 but backed out and refused to sign the group's draft giving immigrants a path to citizenship. "Reforms to our complex and dysfunctional immigration system should not in any way favor those who came here illegally over the millions of applicants who seek to come here lawfully," he said.

On foreign policy, Lee has been less hawkish than some other conservatives. In a Senate Foreign Relations Committee vote in 2011, Lee opposed a congressional resolution authorizing U.S. military involvement in Libya. He was the first GOP senator to join Kentucky colleague Rand Paul during Paul's 13-hour filibuster in 2013 that protested the Obama administration's potential use of drones to attack U.S. citizens. Lee's Almanac vote ratings mostly have been conservative, except that his scores on foreign policy votes have leaned toward the center.

During the high-stakes fight over the Trans-Pacific Partnership trade pact in 2015, Politico reported Lee had blindsided Republican leaders by failing to show up on a critical vote. Though he had stated he backed the effort, he stayed in Utah when the vote was called, because, his office said, he had a family commitment. In 2016, he pursued a quixotic bid for a GOP leadership seat, even though there appeared to be no opening.

Lee has worked hard to elect other tea party-backed candidates. In 2012, he formed a political action committee to support like-minded conservative candidates and produced a policy blueprint for them to use on the trail. Lee has traveled across the country to campaign with such candidates who are involved in tough primaries. In 2016, he coasted to re-election, 68%-27%, against Democrat Misty Snow, one of the first openly transgender people to win a major-party nomination for a congressional seat. After his enthusiastic support for Cruz during the 2016 presidential primaries, Lee was outspokenly "Never Trump" at the Republican National Convention and during the fall campaign. He complained that Republican officials violated party rules by denying the anti-Trump forces their right to participate in convention activities.

From a state where Trump got 45 percent of the vote in 2016, Lee continued to show his independence. He filed a bill to limit Trump from raising tariffs with what Lee called "unilateral trade actions." The purpose of his legislation, Lee said, was "to restore the proper balance of power between the branches of government." In February 2018, he opposed a budget deal that congressional leaders reached with Trump as "a betrayal of everything limited government conservatism stands for." A year later, he was one of 12 Republican senators who voted for a bill to oppose Trump's use of a national emergency to shift federal funds to pay for a wall on the border with Mexico. In its tracking of Senate votes as of April 2019, FiveThirtyEight found that Lee had voted against Trump during the previous two years more often than any other Republican senator except for Paul.

Lee spoke out against some of the president's foreign policy actions. Referring in April 2018 to a possible U.S. military response to conflicts in Syria, he said, "The president of the United States should come to Congress and ask for authorization before military force is used." With liberal Sen. Bernie Sanders of Vermont, Lee filed a resolution to end U.S. military support the Saudi-led coalition intervening in Yemen's civil war. "This legislation is neither liberal nor conservative. It's constitutional," he said at a news conference in February 2019. After it was passed by the Senate and House, Trump in April vetoed the measure as "an unnecessary, dangerous attempt to weaken my constitutional authorities."

Lee was a vocal supporter of the Supreme Court nomination of Brett Kavanaugh and actively lobbied other Republican senators on Kavanaugh's behalf. They had been friends since Lee clerked at the Supreme Court. Perhaps oddly, given Lee's independence of Trump, a conservative group included him on a list of 25 potential Supreme Court nominees that it submitted to Trump during the 2016 campaign. Cruz was among those who publicly urged Trump to nominate Lee to the high court.

In 2019, Lee became chairman of the Joint Economic Committee. That position rotates every two years between the Senate and House. He said that he would use the assignment to oversee his "social capital project," which he earlier launched to examine "how family, neighborhood, workplace, and religious relationships are at the core of our nation's economic success." Lee has said that these institutions are critical to the "associational life" of a locale. Utah has ranked at the top of the project's index.

Mitt Romney (R)

Elected 2018, term expires 2024, 1st term, b. Mar 12, 1947; Detroit, MI; Brigham Young University (UT), B.A., 1971; Harvard University School of Business (MA), M.B.A., 1975; Harvard University Law School (MA), J.D., 1975; Mormon; Married (Ann Davies); 5 children; 16 grandchildren.

Elected Office: MA Governor, 2003-2007.

Professional Career: Boston Consulting Group, Management Consultant, 1975-1977; Bain & Company, Vice President, 1978-1984, Chief Executive Officer, 1991-1993; Bain Capital, Founder, Managing Partner 1984-2001; Salt Lake City Winter Olympics Organizing Committee, President and Chief Executive Officer, 1999-2002.

DC Office: 124 RSOB 20510, 202-224-5251, romney.senate.gov

State Offices: Salt Lake City, 801-524-4380.

Committees: *Foreign Relations*: Europe & Regional Security Cooperation; Internat'l Dev Instit & Internat'l Econ, Energy & Environ Policy; Near East, South Asia, Central Asia & Counterterrorism (Chmn). *Health, Education, Labor & Pensions*: Children & Families; Employment & Workplace Safety; Primary Health & Retirement Security. *Homeland Security & Government Affairs*: Investigations; Regulatory Affairs & Federal Management. *Small Business & Entrepreneurship*.

Election Results

Election	Name (Party)	Vote (%)		Cand. Spent	Ind. Exp. Support	Ind. Exp. Oppose
2018 General	Mitt Romney (R)............................... 665,215	(63%)		$5,248,693	$58,790	$7,960
	Jenny Wilson (D).......................... 328,541	(31%)		$923,979		
	Tim Aalders (CNP)....................... 28,774	(3%)		$74,518		
	Craig Bowden (Lib)...................... 27,607	(3%)		$37,321		
2018 Primary	Mitt Romney (R)............................. 240,021	(71%)				
	Mike Kennedy (R)............................... 96,771	(29%)				

Prior winning percentages: Massachusetts Governor: 2002 (50%)

When he was elected Utah's junior senator in November 2018, Republican Mitt Romney earned himself a place in history: He became only the third American to serve as governor of one state and senator for another. The last person to pull off this feat was Sam Houston, governor of Tennessee from 1827 to 1829 and later a senator from the new state Texas. Romney was governor of Massachusetts from 2003 to 2007 before twice trying to win the presidency, securing the Republican nomination in 2012. He declined to make a third presidential bid in 2016, only to emerge as a scathing critic of Donald Trump, whose nomination Romney tried to derail. After Trump won the White House, the two have had a tempestuous relationship. As Romney arrived on Capitol Hill to succeed GOP Sen. Orrin Hatch, who retired after 42 years, speculation surrounding the anything-but-typical freshman focused on the extent to which he would seek to become a counterforce to a president of his own party.

While he now represents one of the nation's reddest states, Romney's previous elected office was in one of its bluest. His political journey between the two posts was marked by significant shifts in policy and outlook. During his 2002 campaign for Massachusetts governor, he said in a TV interview, "I think people recognize that I'm not a partisan Republican, that I'm someone who is moderate, and my views are progressive." A decade later, on his way to winning the presidential nomination, Romney told a gathering of right-wing activists that he had been a "severely conservative" governor. The latter assertion was greeted with widespread skepticism, if not incredulity; throughout his 2008 and 2012 White House bids, he was criticized by rivals for what they saw as flip-flopping. Romney often responded to such attacks by denying inconsistencies. "There are some folks who obviously for various political and campaign purposes will try and find some change and draw great attention to something which looks like a change, which in fact is entirely consistent," Romney was quoted as saying by The Washington Post in early 2012. "I've been as consistent as human beings can be."

Willard Mitt Romney was born in Detroit, the youngest of four children of George and Lenore Romney. He grew up in Bloomfield Hills, Michigan, as his father, CEO of American Motors, rescued the nearly bankrupt automaker. In 1962, George Romney was elected governor of Michigan, and, after an unsuccessful bid for the 1968 Republican presidential nomination, was secretary of Housing and Urban Development during President Richard Nixon's first term. Lenore Romney, his wife, unsuccessfully ran for a Senate seat from Michigan in 1970.

Mitt Romney initially enrolled in Stanford University, but — as a member of a prominent Mormon family — left after his freshman year to spend 30 months in France as a missionary for the Church of Jesus Christ of Latter-day Saints. He graduated from Mormon-founded Brigham Young University and earned degrees from both Harvard Law School and Harvard Business School, where he overlapped with George W. Bush. Romney stayed in the Boston area and became a vice president of Bain & Co., a management consulting firm. In 1984, he founded Bain Capital, an investment company that provided crucial capital to such retailers as Staples, Domino's Pizza, and Brookstone. In 1990, he returned to Bain & Co., for a year as interim CEO to rescue it from financial difficulties. During his years with Bain, he accumulated a considerable fortune: Disclosures during his 2012 presidential campaign put it as high as $250 million. He also served from 1986 to 1994 as president of the Mormons' Boston Stake, making him the rough equivalent of a bishop in the church — although he would downplay his faith throughout much of his political career.

In 1994, as Massachusetts Democrat Ted Kennedy was seeking a sixth full Senate term, Romney made his first run for office. Kennedy's approval ratings had plummeted three years earlier when his nephew William Kennedy Smith was charged with rape after a night of drinking in Palm Beach, Florida. The senator had been present that night. Polls in mid-September showed the race even, but Kennedy recovered to win 58%-41%. The Kennedy campaign produced ads on how Bain Capital's purchase of an Indiana paper plant had led to layoffs and a bitter strike. It presaged attacks on Romney's ties to Bain during the 2012 presidential primary and general elections.

Romney relinquished day-to-day management of Bain Capital in early 1999 to head the Salt Lake City Winter Olympics Organizing Committee, which was in debt and reeling from scandal. He erased a $379 million deficit, mobilized 23,000 volunteers and ran an effective security operation at the games; 87 percent of Utahans rated his performance positively. At the time, however, Romney was eyeing a campaign 2,000 miles to the east. Massachusetts Republican Lt. Gov. Jane Swift, who became acting governor in 2001 when her predecessor resigned to accept an ambassadorship, was engulfed in controversy. Amid low poll ratings, Swift dropped a bid for election in March 2002, and, hours later, Romney announced. He was embarrassed when it was disclosed he had listed his Park City, Utah, home as his principal residence for tax purposes from 1999 to 2001. He said he had intended all along to return to Massachusetts, where he owned a home in the Boston suburb of Belmont. Democrats challenged his eligibility to run, but the state Ballot Law Commission ruled in his favor.

Romney ran as a professional manager and outsider who wasn't part of the Beacon Hill crowd. The Democratic nominee was Treasurer Shannon O'Brien. O'Brien attacked Romney in debates, arguing he was out of place in Massachusetts and trying to "mask a very conservative set of belief systems." Although she avoided making an issue of his religion, she criticized him for making contributions to Brigham Young University, whose policies bar expressions of homosexuality. She also advocated legalizing same-sex marriage; Romney sidestepped the issue by saying he opposed all extramarital sex. During his 1994 Senate bid, Romney had written a letter promising a gay Republican group he would be a stronger supporter of gay rights than Kennedy. Romney won, 50%-45%.

With his business background, he was less inclined than his predecessors to make deals with the Democratic-dominated Legislature. But his major accomplishment turned out to be a plan for universal health insurance coverage enacted by working closely not only with the legislative leadership, but his erstwhile opponent, Kennedy. "Romneycare" became a model for the Affordable Care Act. (Despite that, Romney campaigned for president in 2012 while advocating repeal of Obamacare.) In signing the legislation in 2006, Romney hailed it as "an achievement that comes around once in a generation."

Romney unveiled his plan in a Boston Globe op-ed just weeks after the 2004 elections, before which he had aggressively tried and failed to get more Republicans elected to the Legislature. At a time when the state was in danger of losing $600 million in Medicaid funding because federal officials felt the money was being used for ineligible services, Romney persuaded Washington to provide funding for the experiment. It featured an individual mandate requiring all who could afford insurance to purchase it. The final compromise that emerged from the Legislature included an annual fee for companies that didn't offer health insurance. Romney initially did not voice objections but, as conservatives grumbled that it amounted to a new tax, he exercised a line-item veto over the "employer assessment" — which, as expected, was later overridden by the Legislature. While the Massachusetts health law succeeded in covering nearly all state residents, it failed to lower health care spending.

At the end of 2005, Romney announced he would not seek re-election. He became chairman of the Republican Governors Association the next year and traveled the country building a political network. Hours before leaving the governorship in early 2007, he registered a presidential exploratory committee at the Federal Election Commission. His approval ratings at home tumbled to less than 40 percent — amid extensive out-of-state travel and frequent use of liberal Massachusetts as a rhetorical foil, as he curried favor with conservatives in early presidential primary states.

Romney's views on several hot-button social issues took a turn to the right. In 2002, he had called his support for abortion rights "unequivocal" despite personal opposition to abortion. But in May 2005, he told USA Today he was "in a different place" and vetoed a bill promoting emergency contraception that he had supported during his gubernatorial run. He began to criticize Roe v. Wade and, as a presidential candidate, said the Supreme Court decision should be overturned. After he had sidestepped the same-sex marriage issue during the governor's race, a 2004 decision by the state's highest court made Massachusetts first in the nation to legalize gay marriage; Romney worked to have a constitutional amendment reversing the ruling put on the ballot. That effort was later thwarted by his Democratic successor, Deval Patrick. After saying during the 1994 Senate race that "I don't line up with the NRA" and signing an assault weapons ban as governor, Romney touted himself as a "life-long hunter" during his 2008 presidential bid, while disclosing he had recently joined the National Rifle Association.

Romney was seeking to present himself as a conservative alternative to the presumed front-runner for the 2008 Republican presidential nomination — Arizona Sen. John McCain, a political maverick who had been runner-up to Bush in the race for the 2000 nomination. After some early stumbles by McCain, Romney finished first in the quadrennial straw poll of Iowa Republican activists in August 2007. But in the Iowa caucuses the next January, Romney came in second despite heavily outspending the winner, former Arkansas Gov. Mike Huckabee. McCain, after righting his campaign, skipped Iowa to focus on the New Hampshire primary — where he defeated Romney 37%-32%, despite Romney's longtime ownership of a vacation home in the state. Romney won the primary in Michigan, where he had grown up, but finished a distant fourth to McCain in South Carolina and lost to the Arizonan in Florida. McCain had the nomination sewn up by Super Tuesday in early February, and Romney suspended his campaign several days later.

After the 2008 general election, Romney began laying the groundwork for another run, which he announced in April 2011. While he started as the front-runner, conservatives remained leery, and several contenders emerged to challenge him from the right. Minnesota Rep. Michele Bachmann won the Iowa straw poll this time but dropped out after a poor finish in the Iowa caucuses in January 2012. For a time, Texas Gov. Rick Perry was a leading alternative, but his bid collapsed after a late 2011 debate when — in one of the most embarrassing moments in presidential campaign history — he couldn't recall one of the three federal agencies he had proposed to eliminate. (It was the Energy Department, which Perry would head during the Trump administration.) In late 2011, polls showed businessman Herman Cain in a tie with Romney after Cain won a straw vote in Florida. But Cain dropped out after allegations of sexual harassment and an extramarital affair surfaced. (In his first months in the Senate, Romney joined with several other Republicans to doom a plan by Trump to appoint Cain to the Federal Reserve Board. He advised Trump to appoint someone "less partisan and more experienced in the world of economics.")

Two other hard-line conservatives fared better: Former Pennsylvania Sen. Rick Santorum battled Romney to a draw in the Iowa caucuses, and, while Romney won the New Hampshire primary, he was badly beaten by former House Speaker Newt Gingrich in South Carolina. Romney recovered after winning a half-dozen states on Super Tuesday; Santorum dropped out in April and Gingrich in early May, guaranteeing Romney the nomination. In November, Romney faced an incumbent president who was vulnerable as the national economy struggled to recover from the 2008 recession. However, Romney's selection of Wisconsin Rep. Paul Ryan — a leading proponent of reforming entitlement programs — as his running mate kicked off a debate that overshadowed the Republicans' desire to make the election a referendum on Obama's handling of the economy. A Romney-Ryan premium support proposal called for new Medicare beneficiaries, beginning in 2023, to have the option of choosing between traditional Medicare and a private health plan. Democrats attacked it as an effort to dismantle the social safety net.

In September 2012, Romney was put on the defensive after a video of a private fundraiser he had held in Florida the previous May leaked. Romney told attendees at the event: "There are 47 percent of the people who will vote for the president [Obama] no matter what ... who believe that they are victims, who believe the government has a responsibility to care for them, who believe that they are entitled to health care, to food, to housing, to you name it. ... These are people who pay no income tax. ... And, so, my job is not to worry about those people. I'll never convince them that they should take personal responsibility and care for their lives."

Obama jumped on the remarks, saying Romney was out of touch with middle class America. On Election Day, exit polls showed Obama ahead of Romney by 4-1 on the question of which candidate "cares about people like me." In a post-election interview, Romney told Fox News: "I didn't express myself as I wished I would have. ... There's no question that hurt and did real damage to my campaign." Obama won the Electoral College 332-206, with Romney carrying two more states than McCain had in 2008. In the popular vote, Romney's biggest margin of victory was in Utah, where he defeated Obama 73%-27%. In Massachusetts, he lost 61%-38%.

Romney had sold his house in Belmont in 2009, but a year later purchased a condominium there, maintaining his Massachusetts voter registration. In 2014, he switched his voter registration to Utah when he built a home next to one of his five sons in a Salt Lake City suburb. After contemplating a third presidential bid, he announced in January 2015 he would not run. But he was back in the spotlight a year later when Trump established himself as the clear front-runner for the 2016 GOP nomination. Romney demanded Trump release his income tax returns, suggesting they might contain a "bombshell." While saying he lacked proof, Romney told Fox News: "I think there is something there. Either he is not nearly as wealthy as he says he is, or he hasn't been paying the kind of taxes you would expect him to." Trump responded via Twitter, calling Romney a "dope" who "totally blew an election that should have been won." Insiders were puzzled as to why Romney had picked this fight; he had resisted releasing his own tax returns in 2012 and had never done so in his three previous runs for office.

Romney's volley turned out to be prelude to a speech at the University of Utah a month later, during which he let Trump have it with both barrels. "Donald Trump is a phony, a fraud," Romney said. "He has neither the temperament nor the judgment to be president." It was an unprecedented rebuke in the modern political era — the party's immediate past nominee devoting an entire speech to condemning the current front-runner for the nomination in withering terms. Romney urged voters in the remaining primary states to cast ballots for the candidate most likely to beat Trump to force a floor fight at the Republican National Convention. When Trump was nominated, Romney said he would not vote for him; in mid-2018 he revealed he had written in the name of Ann Romney, to whom he has been married since 1969, for president.

Romney switched to a conciliatory tone after Trump's election, telling the Deseret News, "Now the time has come for us to recognize we have a new president and we have hopes he will be successful leading our country." After the new president was sworn in, Romney said he was "off to a very strong start." Trump and Romney met twice after the election, reportedly to discuss the possibility of Romney becoming secretary of State. It appeared Trump never seriously entertained appointing Romney — who has differed with the president on issues ranging from Russia to free trade — but was instead toying with his frequent antagonist.

A more consequential discussion of Romney's future took place in March 2017, when Romney met with Hatch, the longest serving Republican in Senate history. Hatch indicated he planned to retire and urged Romney to consider running to succeed him. He presented Romney with a memo with the case for doing so, according to The Atlantic. When Trump endorsed Republican Roy Moore in a 2017 special Senate election in Alabama, amid allegations that Moore had sexually assaulted young teenage girls while he was in his 30s, Romney said the election of Moore "would be a stain on the GOP and on the nation" and that "no vote, no majority is worth losing our honor, our integrity."

As Romney was condemning Moore, Trump, during a visit to Utah, publicly said he hoped Hatch would seek re-election. It reportedly capped a series of private efforts by Trump to block Romney's ascension by persuading Hatch to stay, despite polls showing Hatch with low approval ratings and likely to face a fight if he were to run. Hatch declined to run, and Trump offered Romney "my full support and endorsement" on Twitter. At the Utah Republican state convention, Romney was forced into a June primary after losing the vote of the delegates by 51%-49% to state Rep. Mike Kennedy. Such gatherings often are not reflective of Utah's GOP electorate, and Romney defeated Kennedy 71%-29%. In November, he defeated the Democratic nominee, Salt Lake County Councilwoman Jenny Wilson, 63%-31% — running 18 percentage points ahead of the 45 percent plurality by which Trump had won Utah in 2016.

In an op-ed in the Salt Lake Tribune two days before the June primary, Romney was conciliatory toward Trump, while also offering a warning. "I will support the president's policies when I believe they are in the best interest of Utah and the nation," he wrote, noting that "the first year of his administration has exceeded my expectations." But Romney added, "I have and will continue to speak out when the president says or does something which is divisive, racist, sexist, anti-immigrant, dishonest or destructive to democratic institutions." In a Washington Post op-ed published just before he was sworn into the Senate in January 2019, Romney issued a critique reminiscent of his biting comments during the 2016 campaign. He wrote that Trump had not "risen to the mantle of the office," adding, "With the nation so divided, resentful and angry, presidential leadership in qualities of character is indispensable. And it is in this province where the incumbent's shortfall has been most glaring."

In the Senate, Romney got a seat on the Foreign Relations Committee. "To reassume our leadership in world politics, we must repair failings in our politics at home," Romney wrote in the Post op-ed. "That project begins, of course, with the highest office once again acting to inspire and unite us." The op-ed was published shortly after the resignation of Defense Secretary Jim Mattis, who quit amid disagreements over Trump's decision to withdraw U.S. troops from Afghanistan and Syria. "The Trump presidency made a deep descent in December," Romney wrote. Trump shot back on Twitter with a familiar broadside. "I won big, and he didn't. Be a TEAM player & WIN!"

In his first months in the Senate, Romney picked his shots carefully, adhering to his vow in the Post op-ed to not "comment on every tweet or fault." His voting record was the least supportive of Trump of any Republican senator, according to FiveThirtyEight ratings. Although he supported building a wall on the U.S.-Mexico border, Romney joined 11 other Republican senators in voting to overturn Trump's effort to obtain money for such a wall by issuing an emergency declaration.

Romney said the action set a bad precedent. In April, Romney broke from many Republicans who argued special counsel Robert Mueller's probe into possible collusion between Russia and Trump's 2016 campaign had exonerated the president. While saying it was "good news" that Mueller didn't find evidence to charge Trump, Romney added, "I am sickened at the extent and pervasiveness of dishonesty and misdirection by individuals in the highest office of the land, including the president."

Just before his Senate swearing-in, Romney told CNN that, while he would not challenge Trump in 2020, he was not sure he would endorse the president. "I'm going to see what the alternatives are," he said. In another CNN appearance in May 2019, Romney suggested he might vote again for his wife if Trump secured the nomination. "We'll have to wait and see how she does," he quipped.

Rob Bishop (R)

Elected 2002, 9th term, b. Jul 13, 1951; Kaysville; University of Utah, B.A., 1974; Mormon; Married (Jeralynn Hansen Bishop); 5 children; 7 grandchildren.

Elected Office: UT House, 1978-1994, speaker 1993-1994.

Professional Career: H.S. teacher, 1974-2002; Chair, UT Republican Party, 1997-2001.

DC Office: 123 CHOB 20515, 202-225-0453, Fax: 202-225-5857, robbishop.house.gov

State Offices: Ogden, 801-625-0107; Vernal, 435-781-5302.

Committees: *Armed Services*: Readiness; Strategic Forces. *Natural Resources (RMM)*: Ex Officio membership on all subcommittees.

Group Ratings

	ADA	ACLU	AFL-CIO	LCV	ITI	COC	HAFA	ACU	CFG	FRC
2018	-	11%	-	3%	-	83%	68%	88%	57%	100%
2017	0%	C	14%	0%	C	93%	C	81%	76%	100%

Almanac Ratings 2017-18

	Economy	Social	Foreign	Composite
Liberal	3%	0%	6%	3%
Conservative	97%	100%	94%	97%

Key Votes of the 115th Congress

1. Obama-care revision	Y	5. Family planning regs	Y	9. Guantanamo prisoners	N
2. Tax Cuts	Y	6. Body cameras/immigration	N	10. Ground missiles, limit	N
3. Omnibus appropriations	N	7. Abortion ban	Y	11. Defense Dept. spending	Y
4. Dodd-Frank revision	Y	8. Concealed carry	Y	12. FISA rules	N

Election Results

Election	Name (Party)	Vote (%)		Cand. Spent	Ind. Exp. Support	Ind. Exp. Oppose
2018 General	Rob Bishop (R)	156,692	(62%)	$797,119		
	Lee Castillo (D)	63,308	(25%)	$20,708		
	Eric Eliason (I)	29,547	(12%)	$231,311		
2018 Primary	Rob Bishop (R)		(100%)			

Prior winning percentages: 2016 (66%), 2014 (64%), 2012 (72%), 2010 (69%), 2008 (65%), 2006 (63%), 2004 (68%), 2002 (61%)

Republican Rob Bishop, first elected in 2002, is a leading advocate of states' rights and a sharp critic of federal management of public lands. As chairman of the Natural Resources Committee, he sought to reshape the debate, with some success. Bishop pressed President Donald Trump to rescind many of the executive actions affecting the West that were taken by President Barack Obama, especially during his final days in office. Bishop, who is term-limited at his committee and plans to retire in 2020, left the door open to a run for governor.

Bishop grew up in Davis County and graduated from the University of Utah. He became a high school history and government teacher in Box Elder County. In 1978, he was elected to the state House and served two years as House speaker. He continued working as a teacher after leaving the legislature in 1994, and also worked as a lobbyist for state Republicans and for the National Rifle Association.

When the House seat became open, both Bishop and former House Majority Leader Kevin Garn ran. As a former state party chair for four years, Bishop won 58 percent of the vote at the Republican nominating convention. With mostly similar conservative views, their chief difference was a contentious issue in Utah: the ongoing battle between banks and credit unions. The credit union lobby endorsed Bishop who, as a lobbyist in 1999, helped defeat legislation to curtail the credit unions' tax-exempt status. Bishop won the primary 60%-40%. Democrat Dave Thomas, a wealthy advertising executive and an anti-abortion rights Mormon bishop, presented himself as a fiscal conservative and "a regular guy" not tied to special interests. Bishop won, 61%-37%.

Bishop has been an active conservative voice, often on behalf of western land interests. He started a "10th Amendment Task Force" to advocate allowing states to assume control of federal programs, and proposed a constitutional amendment to allow any federal law or regulation to be overturned if two-thirds of states opposed it.

On Natural Resources, Bishop has demonstrated skill at deal-making during his long legislative career. The Standard-Examiner of Ogden, in endorsing him for reelection in 2014, praised him as "a statesman willing to both listen and work hard for his constituents." Still, Bishop sometimes has been averse to bipartisanship. Soon after taking over as chairman in 2015, he included in a border-security bill a provision to exempt from some environmental laws immigration enforcement activities within 100 miles of U.S. borders, a move that critics condemned as a ruse to bar any regulation of those lands.

Bishop has said that he wants to think broadly about the way the United States manages federal and Indian lands. But his four years as chairman before the Democrats regained House control did not produce many major changes in policy. Probably his greatest impact was convincing Trump to undo earlier presidential actions, especially by President Barack Obama, to designate new national monuments in the West. Bishop had been especially furious when Obama in his final month in office unilaterally declared the 1.3 million-acre Bears Ears National Monument in his district. "It has to be a gotcha moment where the president unveils something unilaterally," he told NPR. Bishop urged Trump to rescind or substantially cut back the Bears Ears site. In December 2017, Trump removed more than 1.1 million acres from the monument and said that the area could be leased for energy exploration. Bishop praised the presidential step to "remedy one of the largest abuses of power foisted upon Utah."

Bishop had less success in revising what he referred to as the "damn" Antiquities Act, which Obama had invoked to create Bears Ears. His chief proposal was to limit the type of sites for which the law could be used, as well as the acreage of new monuments. In October 2017, his committee on a party-line vote approved the bill, which he said would ensure "public accountability and transparency." But the House did not take up the measure in the next 14 months, a sure sign of opposition to the proposal — including from other Republicans.

Bishop has remained an active member of the Armed Services Committee; the military has numerous facilities in Utah. He urged the Trump administration to locate its proposed "space force" at Hill Air Force Base, which is in his district. He left open whether he supported the call to create a new branch of the military to take control of the mission from the Air Force.

Bishop has been comfortably reelected every two years. Prior to the 2018 election, he said that it would be his final term. That led to speculation that he might be considered for positions ranging from House Republican leader to Trump's secretary of the Interior. Bishop dismissed such options. But he did not rule out a bid for governor in 2020. A wide-open Republican primary was likely, with the expected retirement of Gov. Gary Herbert.

UT-1: Northern Utah   **Cook Partisan Voting Index: R+26**

Population		Race and Ethnicity		Income	
Total	740,424	White	81.6%	Median Income	$65,355
Land area (sq. miles)	19,561	Black	1%	District Income Rank	132
Pop/ sq mi	37.9	Latino	12.6%	Poverty Rate	10.5%
Born in State	65.2%	Asian	1.4%	With health insurance	90.8%
		Two or more races	2%	Cash public assistance	1.9%
Age Groups		Other	1.3%	Food stamp/SNAP	8.3%
Under 18	31.3%				
18-34	25.4%	Education		Work	
35-64	33.5%	H.S grad or less	33.6%	White Collar	9.8%
Over 64	9.8%	Some college	37.1%	Sales and Service	39.1%
		College Degree, 4 yr	19.9%	Blue Collar	25.2%
Military		Post grad	9.3%	Government	18.3%
Veteran/ Active Duty	7.9%				

2012 Pres. Vote	Romney	193,672	(78%)	Obama	51,098	(20%)			
2016 Pres. Vote	Trump	139,503	(49%)	McMullin	62,547	(22%)	Clinton	62,733	(22%)
	Johnson	10,231	(4%)						

Ogden, Logan: In May 1869, a motley crowd of Irish and Chinese laborers, teamsters, engineers, train crews, officials and guests from Salt Lake City gathered at Promontory Summit to watch the opening of the transcontinental railroad. Leland Stanford's blow with a silver sledge, intended to drive the ceremonial "Last Spike" into the railroad ties, missed its mark, but telegraphs nevertheless conveyed the word "done" across the nation. It wasn't just the railroad that was complete. As long as America had been America, there had been a frontier. But as the civilized East and the mostly untamed West were finally united, that frontier began to shrink and then vanish.

Ogden Utah is in many ways a microcosm of the impact the railway could have. At the time the railroad was completed, Ogden was a small farming community of 1,500 inhabitants. Had it not won the right to become the junction of the Union Pacific and Central Pacific railroads — which meant that all the passengers and shipping crossing the nation changed trains in Ogden — it might have suffered the same fate as Corinne, the nearby and forgotten town that lost out to Ogden in the competition for the railroad. The city adopted the motto, "You can't get anywhere without coming to Ogden!" Today, with a population of 87,000, Ogden has developed as a hub for outdoor sports equipment makers. Amer Sports, founded in Finland and with operations in 34 nations, has consolidated its North American operations in Ogden. As a manufacturing center for bicycles, it has become known as "biketown." Like other cities in Utah, Ogden has become a center for technology jobs.

The 1st Congressional District of Utah takes in Ogden and areas to the north of Salt Lake City. While it sprawls from the Colorado border to Idaho, about two thirds of its residents live in the stretch north of Salt Lake City from Kaysville to Brigham City. Hill Air Force Base, which houses F-35 fighter jets, is in the district, as is Utah State University, farther north in Logan. Much of the district is farm country. Great Salt Lake, which is the largest water mass west of the Mississippi River and much of which is in this district, has been disappearing — despite record rainfall in 2017. Ecologists worry about the threat to the ecosystem of the area, including wildlife. The problem has been caused largely by over-use, including for agriculture. The National Audubon Society has advocated less use of irrigation. The sands have drawn growing interest from energy companies seeking oil production. An exception to the Mormon dominance is Park City, in the mountains east of Salt Lake City, which is a fashionable ski resort and home of actor Robert Redford's annual Sundance Film Festival, the largest independent film festival in the nation. The 11-day event in 2018 attracted 125,000 attendees, two-thirds of whom were women and from Utah.

The 1st has been among the top 10 most heavily Republican districts in the nation. Mitt Romney got 78 percent in 2012. The antipathy of Mormons for Donald Trump changed that. The 49 percent for Trump in the district was his highest in the state and the 22 percent for Hillary Clinton was her lowest.

Chris Stewart (R)

Elected 2012, 4th term, b. Jul 15, 1960; Logan; Utah State University, B.S., 1984; Mormon; Married (Evie Stewart); 6 children.

Military Career: U.S. Air Force 1984-1998

Professional Career: Owner, Shipley Group, 2000-present.

DC Office: 2242 RHOB 20515, 202-225-9730, Fax: 202-225-5629, stewart.house.gov

State Offices: Salt Lake City, 801-364-5550; St. George, 435-627-1500.

Committees: *Appropriations*: Financial Services & General Government; Interior, Environment & Related Agencies. *Budget. Permanent Select on Intelligence*: Counterterrorism, Counterintelligence & Counterproliferation; Strategic Technologies & Advanced Research (RMM).

Group Ratings

	ADA	ACLU	AFL-CIO	LCV	ITI	COC	HAFA	ACU	CFG	FRC
2018	-	7%	-	3%	-	83%	70%	80%	61%	100%
2017	0%	C	8%	0%	C	93%	C	88%	87%	100%

Almanac Ratings 2017-18

	Economy	Social	Foreign	Composite
Liberal	0%	6%	3%	3%
Conservative	100%	94%	98%	97%

Key Votes of the 115th Congress

1. Obama-care revision	Y	5. Family planning regs	NV	9. Guantanamo prisoners	N
2. Tax Cuts	Y	6. Body cameras/immigration	N	10. Ground missiles, limit	N
3. Omnibus appropriations	N	7. Abortion ban	Y	11. Defense Dept. spending	Y
4. Dodd-Frank revision	Y	8. Concealed carry	Y	12. FISA rules	Y

Election Results

Election	Name (Party)	Vote (%)		Cand. Spent	Ind. Exp. Support	Ind. Exp. Oppose
2018 General	Chris Stewart (R)................................	151,489	(56%)	$876,232		
	Shireen Ghorbani (D)........................	105,051	(39%)	$430,531		
	Jeffrey Whipple (Lib)...........................	13,504	(5%)			

Prior winning percentages: 2016 (62%), 2014 (60%), 2012 (62%)

Republican Chris Stewart, a former Air Force pilot and author, won an open seat in 2012. Following impressive careers in the military and private sector, he established his credentials as a member of the Appropriations and Intelligence committees. Stewart typically takes a hard line on national security issues, which has resulted in occasional criticism of President Donald Trump.

Stewart and his nine siblings grew up on a dairy farm in southern Idaho. His parents, both Mormon, had moved there from nearby Utah. Stewart enrolled in Utah State University, serving as a Mormon missionary in Texas before completing a degree in economics. After graduating from college, he entered the Air Force. He was first in his class in both officer training school and undergraduate pilot training. In 14 years in uniform, he attained the rank of major and in 1995 set the world record for the fastest nonstop flight around the world in a B-1 Lancer. (His crew flew nearly 23,000 miles in just over 36 hours, for an average speed of about 630 mph.) He also flew rescue helicopters. Five of Stewart's six sons have served in the military.

Stewart began writing in the military and took it up full time after his discharge to spend more time with his children. After two years, he bought the Shipley Group, an energy and environment consulting firm that did government and corporate security work. While he ran the business, Stewart's writing career flourished. He has written 18 books. One of his New York Times best sellers was a collaboration in 2013 with Utah native Elizabeth Smart on the story of her kidnapping. He says that he found more meaning in writing a six-part fiction series, The Great and Terrible, a religious epic about the struggle between good and evil.

When Democratic Rep. Jim Matheson decided to run in 2012 in the newly created 4th District, Stewart got into the open-seat contest, emerging on top in an acrimonious GOP primary. Stewart prevailed with more than 60 percent of the vote in the only contest that really mattered in the heavily Republican district.

After the October 2013 government shutdown, which cost local Utah governments and businesses millions of dollars, Stewart filed a bill that would allow states to fund the operations of national parks, monuments and other facilities related to tourism and other commercial activity in the event of a future lapse of federal spending. In 2014, the House passed on a largely party-line vote his bill to revamp the selection of members to the Environmental Protection Agency's Science Advisory Board to require more representatives of state and local governments. In March 2019, enactment of a wide-ranging public lands bill included two provisions from Stewart, which increased disclosure on the settlement of claims against the United States and permitted Utah to purchase federal land along the old Pony Express route.

His seats on the Appropriations and Intelligence committees positioned him to use his Air Force experience to oversee national security activities, notably the Obama administration's nuclear-arms talks with Iran. In March 2015, Stewart wrote in The Wall Street Journal that, as a B-1 pilot, he was a military representative in arms-reduction talks with the former Soviet Union. On that basis, he contended, "the record is bare" of Iran partnering with the United States or an ally "in a productive way." Congress must do everything in its power to stop it," he said. The House and Senate failed to secure the two-thirds to prevent that. Stewart praised the decision by President Donald Trump to withdraw the United States from the "deeply flawed" agreement.

In December 2016, Stewart voiced concern that the "Cold War-esque" relationship with Russia had become difficult and dangerous, especially its cyber-attacks against American interests, including the election that year. "What Russia is doing is aggressive. It's illegal and harmful," he told a Utah reporter. On the Intelligence Committee in 2019, he was ranking Republican on the Strategic Technologies and Advanced Research Subcommittee.

During the Republican presidential primaries, Stewart supported Sen. Marco Rubio of Florida. While speaking to University of Utah students in March 2016, he called Donald Trump "our Mussolini," referring negatively to the fascist dictator of Italy. A few days before the election, he said that he would vote for Trump as "a better choice than Hillary Clinton." He occasionally disagreed with Trump's actions as president. Many of his tweets, Stewart told CNN, were "just unpresidential" and "not helpful." When Trump said that he accepted the assurances of Russian President Vladimir Putin during their meeting in Helsinki and praised him in July 2018, Stewart said, "Trump is wrong. Russia meddled in the 2016 elections. Russia is led by a former KGB thug who only understands lies and manipulations." But Stewart later applauded Trump in his policy actions as "willing to confront Vladimir Putin."

UT-2: Southwest Utah

Cook Partisan Voting Index: R+16

Population		Race and Ethnicity		Income	
Total	739,470	White	76.8%	Median Income	$59,179
Land area (sq. miles)	39,988	Black	1.1%	District Income Rank	187
Pop/ sq mi	18.5	Latino	15.4%	Poverty Rate	13.2%
Born in State	58.9%	Asian	2.4%	With health insurance	87%
		Two or more races	2%	Cash public assistance	1.9%
Age Groups		Other	2.3%	Food stamp/SNAP	8.5%
Under 18	28%				
18-34	26%	**Education**		**Work**	
35-64	33.4%	H.S grad or less	33.3%	White Collar	12.6%
Over 64	12.6%	Some college	34.7%	Sales and Service	41.9%
		College Degree, 4 yr	20%	Blue Collar	21.9%
Military		Post grad	12%	Government	15.7%
Veteran/ Active Duty	6.9%				

2012 Pres. Vote	Romney	173,513	(68%)	Obama	74,556	(29%)			
2016 Pres. Vote	Trump	130,525	(46%)	Clinton	90,686	(32%)	McMullin	47,862	(17%)
	Johnson	8,914	(3%)						

Salt Lake City: At the center of the Mormon Church is Temple Square, illuminated by 300,000 lights during Christmas week and nestled beneath the towering mountains that flank Salt Lake City. The Mormon Tabernacle is here, home to the famous choir, as is the Salt Lake LDS Temple itself, crowned with the golden angel Moroni. The area has been the focal point of Utah since Mormon leader Brigham Young, looking down at the valley and said (according to church tradition), "This is the place." Ironically, this part of Salt Lake City has become the least Mormon and most cosmopolitan part of Utah, with the state university and businesses bringing in outsiders who, flouting Mormon strictures, keep purveyors of alcohol and caffeine in business. The state has ended its private club system at bars, though prohibitions remained on bartenders pouring drinks in plain sight. In 2015, Salt Lake City elected as mayor Jackie Biskupski, who was a Democrat (which was nothing new for the city) and lesbian (which was). She ran into conflicts with the county and other officials, including on the siting of a homeless shelter. In March 2019, she cited a "serious and complex family situation" in announcing that she would not seek reelection. Several contenders already had entered the contest.

The 2nd Congressional District of Utah consists of most of Salt Lake City and the vast and mostly empty southwestern portion of the state. In Salt Lake, which includes about one-third of the district's population, it takes in the historic downtown, its distinctive Avenues District, and the airport. The county has had one Mormon chapel every 1.3 square miles, many of which are relatively small. The Milken Institute, in its annual report on best-performing cities, ranked Salt Lake City 11th in 2016, with its "well-educated workforce and relatively lower wages and business costs." The already huge reconstruction of the terminal at the airport has been expanded to add a second concourse. The first concourse was scheduled to be completed in 2020. The population of the city, which peaked at 189,000 in 1960 and then fell 15 percent by 1990 as residents moved to the suburbs, has rebounded; in 2017, it surpassed 200,000.

The neighboring open land of stark beauty, much of it federally owned, has been used roughly by humans, as a repository for hazardous wastes at civilian and military dumps in Tooele County and as a place for military experimentations at the Dugway Proving Grounds, where scientists test defenses against chemical and biological agents. About 20 percent of the district's residents live in the stretch of the Wasatch Front, between the mountains and Great Salt Lake, just north of Salt Lake City, in suburban and fairly affluent Davis County. Another 25 percent live in the stretch of lightly populated counties in the southwest corner of the state, chiefly Washington County, which is the home of Zion National Park. The park has coped with a surge of visitors, which exceeded 4.4 million in 2017.

Politically, this is a mostly Republican area, with pockets of Democratic strength in Salt Lake City. Hillary Clinton carried Salt Lake County by nearly 38,000 votes over Donald Trump in 2016. The 68%-29% win in 2012 for Mitt Romney, now a Utah senator, dropped to a 46%-32% lead for Trump four years later.

John Curtis (R)

Elected 2017, 1st full term, b. May 10, 1960; Salt Lake City; University of Utah, Salt Lake City, Att., 1979; Brigham Young University (UT), B.S., 1985; Mormon; Married (Sue Snarr); 6 children; 5 grandchildren.

DC Office: 125 CHOB 20515, 202-225-7751, Fax: 202-225-5629, curtis.house.gov

State Offices: Provo, 801-922-5400.

Committees: *Foreign Affairs*: Asia, the Pacific & Nonproliferation; Western Hemisphere, Civilian Security, & Trade. *Natural Resources*: Indigenous Peoples of the United States; National Parks, Forests & Public Lands.

Group Ratings

	ADA	ACLU	AFL-CIO	LCV	ITI	COC	HAFA	ACU	CFG	FRC
2018	-	25%	-	0%	-	83%	79%	92%	83%	100%
2017	0%	C	0%	0%	C	100%	C	-	64%	100%

Key Votes of the 115th Congress

1. Obama-care revision	N/A	5. Family planning regs	N/A	9. Guantanamo prisoners	N/A
2. Tax Cuts	Y	6. Body cameras/immigration	N/A	10. Ground missiles, limit	N/A
3. Omnibus appropriations	N	7. Abortion ban	N/A	11. Defense Dept. spending	N/A
4. Dodd-Frank revision	Y	8. Concealed carry	Y	12. FISA rules	Y

Election Results

Election	Name (Party)	Vote (%)		Cand. Spent	Ind. Exp. Support	Ind. Exp. Oppose
2018 General	John R. Curtis (R)	174,856	(68%)	$1,358,207		$247,331
	James Singer (D)	70,686	(27%)	$28,957		
	Gregory Duerden (IAP)	6,686	(3%)			
	Tim Zeidner (UUP)	6,630	(3%)			
2018 Primary	John R. Curtis (R)	66,404	(73%)			
	Christopher Herrod (R)	24,158	(27%)			

Prior winning percentages: 2017 Special (58%)

Republican John Curtis in 2017 won a special election to fill a vacancy, following a party primary in which he highlighted his independence from President Donald Trump, though he has largely supported the GOP agenda. Curtis, who was a Democrat earlier in his career, has emphasized the need for bipartisanship. He took the House seat of Republican Jason Chaffetz, a media-savvy and sometimes hard-edged conservative, who was elected to five terms and chaired the Oversight and Government Reform Committee. Chaffetz became a contributor to Fox News and left the door open for future campaigns in Utah — possibly governor in 2020.

Curtis, a native of Salt Lake City, was class president at Skyline High School. After graduating from Brigham Young University, he was a Mormon bishop and served on a mission in Taiwan. With his wife, Sue, whose family was politically active in the area, they settled in Provo; she later became president of the school board. Curtis became a salesman for a watch company and soon won the company's award for "salesman of the year." He worked for local businesses and developed his own firm: Action Target, a shooting range.

Curtis registered as a Democrat, he told the Deseret News, so that he could counter the "one-party dominance" of Utah, though he said that he continued to "sound just like a Republican." He switched to a Republican in 2006, but lost two bids for the state House. In 2009, Curtis narrowly won a non-partisan election for mayor of Provo, where he built a reputation for economic development and tight-fisted budgets. He is "a self-professed introvert" and often seeks to avoid crowds, the News reported. His chief extrovert trait has been a penchant for colorful socks, of which he owns more than 200 pairs.

Months before Chaffetz announced his surprise resignation in June 2017, Curtis had decided not to seek a third term as mayor of Provo. He moved quickly to seek the House seat. At a party convention to secure the Republican nomination for the House seat, he was defeated on the fourth ballot by Christopher Herrod. His political experience and familiarity with voters were advantages when Curtis decided to run in the GOP primary. Tanner Ainge outspent his two opponents and ran ads that linked Curtis with "tax and spend liberals" such as Nancy Pelosi. Curtis responded by emphasizing gun rights and defending his record as mayor. He was endorsed by Mitt Romney, who was elected a year later as senator from Utah.

During the campaign, Curtis said that he had written in a "good friend's name" in the 2016 presidential election, The Salt Lake Tribune reported. But he added that he wanted Trump to be successful. With surprising ease, Curtis won the August primary with 43 percent of the vote to 33 percent for Herrod and 24 percent for Ainge. He led comfortably in both Utah and Salt Lake counties, the two population centers. In this district, he was a shoo-in against Democrat Kathie Allen. He won, 58%-26%, with four other candidates splitting the remaining votes.

In the House, one of his first votes was for the Republican-crafted tax bill. Curtis said that he read the 400-plus pages before deciding to vote for it. After Trump acted to reduce the size of Bears

Ears National Monument, Curtis filed a bill to formalize that action in a statute. In his bid for his first full term, Curtis easily prevailed, 73%-27%, in a primary rematch with Herrod. And he defeated Democrat James Singer, 68%-27%. In the sweeping public lands bill that was enacted in March 2019, Curtis sponsored provisions that resolved a long-running conflict in Emery County and set rules for fish recovery in the Colorado River Storage Project. He had seats on the Natural Resources and Foreign Affairs committees.

UT-3: Central and East Utah   Cook Partisan Voting Index: R+25

Population		Race and Ethnicity		Income	
Total	740,511	White	82.8%	Median Income	$68,918
Land area (sq. miles)	20,071	Black	0.5%	District Income Rank	101
Pop/ sq mi	36.9	Latino	10.6%	Poverty Rate	11.4%
Born in State	60.8%	Asian	1.8%	With health insurance	90.5%
		Two or more races	2.1%	Cash public assistance	1.4%
Age Groups		Other	2%	Food stamp/SNAP	6.5%
Under 18	30.8%				
18-34	28.5%	**Education**		**Work**	
35-64	31.1%	H.S grad or less	22.8%	White Collar	9.6%
Over 64	9.6%	Some college	36.8%	Sales and Service	41.8%
		College Degree, 4 yr	26.6%	Blue Collar	16.3%
Military		Post grad	13.8%	Government	12.2%
Veteran/ Active Duty	4.8%				

2012 Pres. Vote	Romney	208,121	(79%)	Obama	51,791	(20%)			
2016 Pres. Vote	Trump	136,782	(47%)	McMullin	70,933	(24%)	Clinton	67,461	(23%)
	Johnson	9,580	(3%)						

Provo Area, Salt Lake City Suburbs: Provo is in a geographically isolated valley between 11,000-foot peaks of the Wasatch Range and the shores of Utah Lake. It is the third-largest city in the state and home of Brigham Young University, the heart of Mormonism and an institution long known for old-fashioned moral standards and the conservative views of its faculty. In 2018, its student population of 34,000 was 98 percent Mormon, and about 25 percent of students were married. It is annually ranked as the most-sober university in the nation. BYU is known for its welcoming of technological innovation. The Mormon commonwealth, after all, started off with a huge shortage of both labor and water, and its inhabitants were motivated to use technology to prosper in the fearsome terrain. Provo is where the vast majority of Mormon missionaries are trained; 36,000 annually have gone through Provo's Missionary Training Center, which has had the effect of producing a disproportionately high number of foreign language speakers in the area. In 2015, the 5 percent job growth in Provo was the strongest in the nation.

Today, the city is a technology center, the home of Novell and hundreds of other computer-related firms. Provo produced Philo Farnsworth, the inventor of television, and Harvey Fletcher, inventor of the hearing aid. Nearby Lehi is home to a large office site for the software maker Adobe and to Micron's master planned community for technology leadership. In January 2019, Micron announced its plan to purchase the share that its partner Intel held in their jointly operated IM Flash plant, where 1,700 employees have been developing new computer chips for use in manufacturing, in an effort to reverse the big drop in the U.S. share of the chip market. In 2018, Provo had the fastest-growing tech economy in the nation, with a 65 percent growth in tech employees from 2010 to 2017.

The 3rd Congressional District of Utah includes all or part of seven counties in central and eastern Utah. More than 50 percent of the district's residents live in Utah County and 30 percent in Salt Lake. The 3rd takes in affluent suburbs southeast of Salt Lake City, including Holladay and Cottonwood Heights. In Utah County, which grew 17 percent from 2010 to 2017, the district takes in Provo and the string of towns between the mountains and Utah Lake. The area around Moab is a destination for outdoor-loving tourists. The land is mostly owned by one federal agency or another, and there have been bitter fights between locals dependent on mining and environmentalists who want to preserve the scenery, including recently discovered dinosaur tracks. President Donald Trump fared poorly throughout Utah. He won the 3rd with 47 percent of the vote in 2016.

Ben McAdams (D)

Elected 2018, 1st term, b. Dec 05, 1974; Salt Lake City; University of Utah, B.A., 2000; Columbia University Law School (NY), J.D., 2003; Mormon; Married (Julie Mcadams); 4 children.

Elected Office: UT Senate, 2009-2013; Salt Lake City Mayor, 2013-2018.

Professional Career: Adjunct Professor, S.J. Quinney College of Law, 2007-2018; Senior Advisor, Mayor Ralph Becker; Attorney, Dorsey & Whitney.

DC Office: 130 CHOB 20515, 202-225-3011, mcadams.house.gov

State Offices: West Jordan, 801-999-9801.

Committees: *Financial Services*: Consumer Protection & Financial Institutions; Nat'l Security, International Development & Monetary Policy. *Science, Space & Technology*: Environment; Research & Technology.

Election Results

Election	Name (Party)	Vote (%)		Cand. Spent	Ind. Exp. Support	Ind. Exp. Oppose
2018 General	Ben McAdams (D)............................	134,964	(50%)	$3,291,448	$82,795	$841,181
	Mia Love (R).....................................	134,270	(50%)	$5,679,823	$1,410,028	$1,122,231

Freshman Democrat Ben McAdams prevailed in 2018 in a late count that took two weeks to tabulate. His victory was all the more surprising because of Utah's heavily Republican vote — though two-term Rep. Mia Love, his opponent, had struggled far more in her previous campaigns than other local Republicans. McAdams had been the mayor of Salt Lake County.

McAdams, a Utah native, served as a Mormon missionary in Brazil. He graduated from the University of Utah and got his law degree from Columbia University. He practiced law briefly in New York City before returning home and joining a local firm, where he specialized in securities law. He taught at the University of Utah College of Law. He was a senior adviser to Salt Lake City Mayor Ralph Becker and served four years in the state Senate. In 2012, McAdams won the first of two terms as county mayor, where his move to expand a homeless shelter proved controversial.

McAdams breezed to the Democratic nomination at a convention with 72 percent against three other candidates. He emphasized his bipartisan approach as mayor and called himself an "independent thinker." Opponents criticized his "safe" and centrist views. McAdams turned the focus on Love, whom he called "an empty seat" in addressing Utah problems.

The only black Republican woman in Congress, Love's parents were natives of Haiti. Viewed as a rising star in the House GOP, she worked on revising the Dodd-Frank banking law. Love described McAdams as a "liberal in sheep's clothing" and a "Washington D.C. insider," based on his work as a White House aide to President Bill Clinton.

McAdams criticized Love for her support of legislation favored by President Donald Trump, who was not popular in Utah. Ironically, Trump cited Love following the election for her failure to work with him. "Mia Love gave me no love, and she lost," he told reporters. She did not endorse Trump in the 2016 presidential campaign and distanced herself from other Republicans with her support of immigration reform.

During their only campaign debate, McAdams criticized Love as ineffective. "We need to judge our Congress by their outcomes, not their desires or their words," he said. Love responded that she had passed several bills. "I've taken some hits for taking on my leadership," notably on immigration, she added.

In an editorial, The Salt Lake Tribune endorsed Love, citing her membership in the Congressional Black Caucus as "a much-needed path for members of both parties to seek some of the common ground that is all too rare these days."

Love was one of the few House Republicans defeated in 2018 who had an incumbent's traditional fundraising advantage. Her nearly $5.7 million in spending nearly doubled the total for McAdams. She was aided by nearly $1 million in party spending. House Democrats spent virtually nothing for McAdams, a sign that they too were surprised by the outcome. Love denied a report that the Federal

Election Commission had questioned her possible violation of campaign rules by raising money for a primary even though she had no opponent.

The narrow victory for McAdams resulted from his 54 percent in Salt Lake County, which cast four-fifths of the total vote. Love took more than 70 percent in the other three counties. Even if he manages to win reelection in 2020, he likely would be hard-pressed to survive the subsequent perils of redistricting, when the three other districts will have plenty of Republican voters to sacrifice. McAdams has shown interest in running statewide.

UT-4: Central Utah   Cook Partisan Voting Index: R+13

Population			Race and Ethnicity			Income		
Total	773,536		White	74.9%		Median Income	$69,115	
Land area (sq. miles)	2,550		Black	1.6%		District Income Rank	100	
Pop/ sq mi	303.3		Latino	16%		Poverty Rate	9.2%	
Born in State	63.9%		Asian	3.1%		With health insurance	88.4%	
			Two or more races	2.1%		Cash public assistance	1.7%	
Age Groups			Other	2.1%		Food stamp/SNAP	7.5%	
Under 18	31.5%							
18-34	25.2%		Education			Work		
35-64	34.3%		H.S grad or less	33.5%		White Collar	9%	
Over 64	9%		Some college	37.2%		Sales and Service	41.6%	
			College Degree, 4 yr	20%		Blue Collar	21.4%	
Military			Post grad	9.2%		Government	12.1%	
Veteran/ Active Duty	5.3%							

2012 Pres. Vote	Romney	165,294	(68%)	Obama	74,368	(30%)			
2016 Pres. Vote	Trump	108,421	(39%)	Clinton	89,796	(32%)	McMullin	62,348	(22%)
	Johnson	10,883	(4%)						

Suburbs of Salt Lake City and Provo: Driving along the Wasatch Front on the 90-mile stretch of Interstate 15 from North Ogden to Provo, one passes within about five miles of two-thirds of the state's population. In Utah, 65 percent of the people occupy about 2 percent of the land area. Salt Lake City accounts for a surprisingly small portion of this: Its population of 200,000 is only slightly larger than the 189,000 it had in 1960. Suburbs and small cities stretch out to the north, south, and west of the city, and even into the foothills of the Wasatch. Salt Lake County, consequently, quadrupled its population from 275,000 in 1950 to 1.1 million in 2017.

The 4th Congressional District of Utah, the smallest district in the state, takes in much of the suburban area to the south of Salt Lake City. About 40 percent of the district's population is in Salt Lake County south of the Interstate 215 Belt Route — West Jordan, South Jordan, Sandy and Riverton — all of which are Republican. Sandy was an old mining town and West Jordan was a farming community, but their populations shot up as suburban growth took off in the 1960s. Today, West Jordan has more than 114,000 people. South Jordan and Lehi, which is farther south, are the new growth centers. Each has been among the fastest-growing cities in the nation between 2010 and 2017: 41 percent and 31 percent, respectively. Technology-related employment has expanded strongly in this area since 2010. Bluffdale is the site of the Intelligence Community Comprehensive National Cybersecurity Initiative Data Center. These are all upscale places, with median incomes well above the national average. More than 80 percent of the 4th is in Salt Lake County, where the Mormon population in 2017 fell below 50 percent for the first time since at least the 1930s. The district also takes in western Utah County, including Eagle Mountain and Saratoga Springs, which were created in the early 1990s and have grown rapidly; in May 2018, Facebook unveiled its plan for a giant data center in Eagle Mountain. Only one area in Salt Lake County has had a population drop since 2010: Draper, the site of the state prison, which was scheduled to move to make its site available for development.

This has been a solidly Republican district, which Mitt Romney won in 2012 with 68 percent of the vote, though it is the least Republican district in deep-red Utah. The antipathy toward Donald Trump throughout Utah was especially pronounced here. He won the 4th, 39%-32%, with much of the remaining vote going to Evan McMullin.

VERMONT

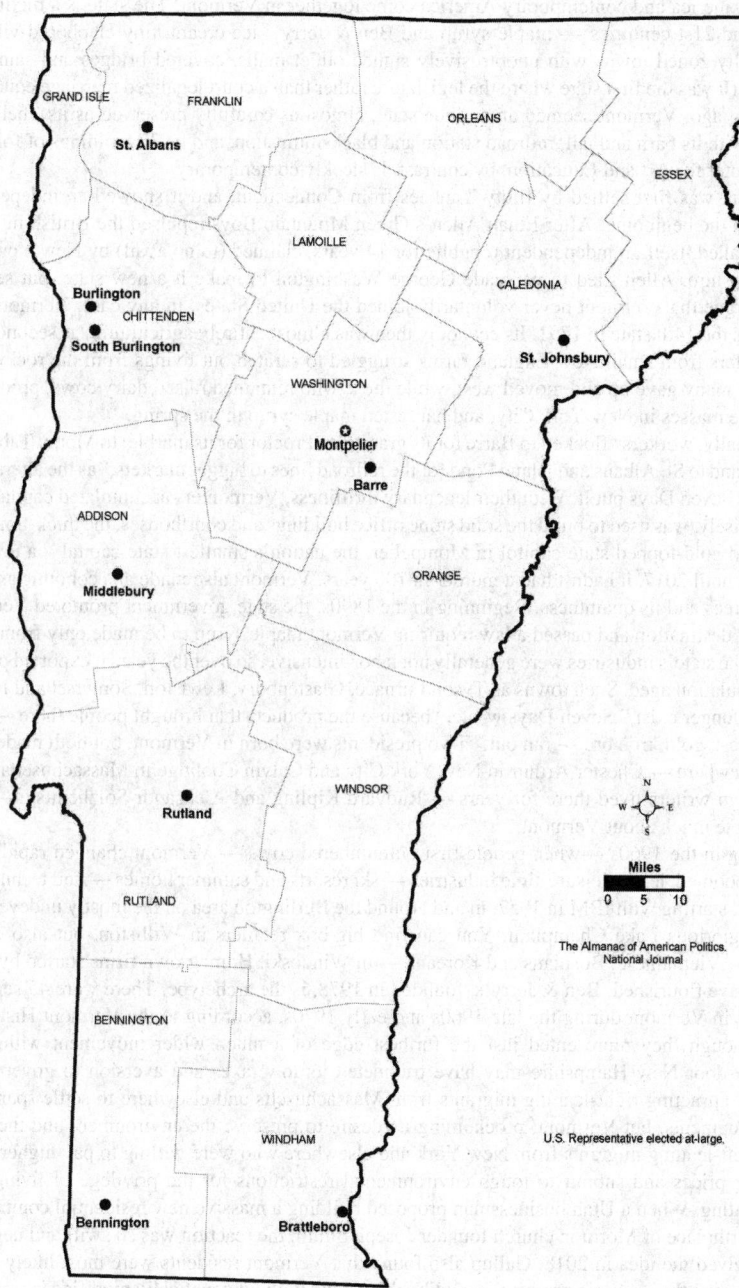

GRAND ISLE

FRANKLIN

ORLEANS

ESSEX

● St. Albans

LAMOILLE

CALEDONIA

Burlington ●
CHITTENDEN

● St. Johnsbury

South Burlington ●

WASHINGTON

ADDISON

● Montpelier

● Barre

● Middlebury

ORANGE

WINDSOR

W —— E
N
S

● Rutland

Miles

0   5   10

RUTLAND

The Almanac of American Politics.
National Journal

BENNINGTON

WINDHAM

U.S. Representative elected at-large

● Bennington

● Brattleboro

Vermont is one of the bluest states in America. But while the state has overwhelmingly elected socialist Bernie Sanders to Congress, it also elected, and reelected, Republican Phil Scott as its governor in 2016 and 2018.

Early America and contemporary America come together in Vermont. The state is a mixture of the 19th and 21st centuries — maple syrup and Ben & Jerry's ice cream, tiny clapboard villages and carefully zoned towns with unobtrusively signed outlet malls, covered bridges and same-sex marriages. (It was the first state where the legislature rather than a court legalized marriage equality.) Not so long ago, Vermont seemed an antique state, almost as carefully preserved as its Shelburne Museum, with its barn and jail, railroad station and blacksmith shop, and its 37 buildings of folk art; its new Center for Art and Education, by contrast, is sleekly contemporary.

Vermont was first settled by flinty Yankees from Connecticut, and it showed an independent streak from the beginning. After Ethan Allen's Green Mountain Boys repulsed the British in 1777, Vermont called itself an independent republic for 14 years, claimed (to no avail) by New York and New Hampshire. Allen tried to persuade George Washington to make it a new state, but several histories argue that Vermont never voluntarily joined the United States. In any case, Vermont was admitted as the 14th state in 1791. Its economy then was almost entirely agricultural, as second sons and daughters from small New England farms struggled to scratch out livings from the rocky soil. Eventually many gave up and moved west, while those who remained raised dairy cows, producing milk for the masses in New York City, and harvested maple syrup in the spring.

Eventually, workers "flocked to Barre for its granite; to Proctor for its marble; to Mount Tabor for its timber; and to St. Albans and Island Pond for the railroad lines to bigger markets," as the alternative newspaper Seven Days put it. With their legendary thriftiness, Vermonters accumulated capital that, invested wisely, was used to build the solid stone office buildings and courthouses, the thick-timbered houses, and gold-topped state capitol in Montpelier, the nation's smallest state capital – a town so sleepy that until 2017, it hadn't had a murder in 100 years. Vermont also made an economic asset of its maple trees and its quaintness. Beginning in the 1890s, the state government promoted Vermont as a tourist destination and passed a law requiring Vermont maple syrup to be made only from local trees. But the state's industries were generally not labor-intensive, so over the years it exported people and its population aged. Such towns as Tyson Furnace, Glastenbury, Lewiston, Somerset and Ricker Basin "no longer exist," Seven Days wrote, "because the products that brought people there — old-growth forest, gold, iron ore — ran out." Two presidents were born in Vermont, but both made their careers elsewhere — Chester Arthur in New York City and Calvin Coolidge in Massachusetts. Two great foreign writers lived there for years — Rudyard Kipling and Aleksandr Solzhenitsyn — but neither wrote much about Vermont.

Starting in the 1960s —when people first outnumbered cows — Vermont changed rapidly. Its economy boomed, led by leisure-time industries — ski resorts and summer homes — and technology companies, starting with IBM in 1957, in and around the Burlington area on the mostly undeveloped shores of glorious Lake Champlain. You can find big-box retailers in Williston, but also ethnic diversity — Vietnamese, Bosnians and Koreans — in Winooski. Homegrown firms started by baby boomers have flourished; Ben & Jerry's, founded in 1978, is the archetype. There were 45 separate communes in Vermont during the late 1960s and early 1970s, according to the Vermont Historical Society, though they represented just the furthest edge of a much wider movement within the state. Next-door New Hampshire may have trumpeted its low taxes and aversion to government regulation, attracting right-leaning migrants from Massachusetts and elsewhere to settle spanking-new developments, but Vermont, proclaiming its desire to preserve the environment and the past, attracted left-leaning migrants from New York and elsewhere who were willing to pay higher taxes and higher prices and submit to tough environmental restrictions for the privilege of living in a pristine setting. When a Utah businessman proposed building a massive new residential community near the birthplace of Mormon church founder Joseph Smith, the reaction was so swift and negative that he shelved the idea in 2018. Gallup also found that Vermont residents were most likely to eat produce frequently – organic produce, in all likelihood, and without genetically modified ingredients (although a landmark state law requiring the labeling of GMO foods was preempted by a federal law in 2016).

Public policy has shaped the state's arc. In 1970, Republican Gov. Deane Davis pushed through Act 250, a sweeping land-use law that helped give Vermont its environmental reputation. Housing developments and new ski resorts were required to meet 10 environmental criteria and get the approval of five different commissions, with opponents granted a right to appeal. Later, Vermont passed its own Clean Air Act, levying a tax on new cars that get less than 20 miles per gallon. It bans billboards and rooftop air conditioning units. Residents also passed Act 60, which attempted to equalize property taxes throughout the state. Vermont maintains a land trust that buys development rights to farmland to stop the disappearance of family farms. Distressed by the demise of dairy farming — the number of dairy farms has declined from 3,300 in 1983 to 699 in 2018 – the state government loans taxpayer money to help farmers buy water buffalo to produce mozzarella cheese. In 2014, two landmark events occurred in the state's energy sector: The Vermont Yankee nuclear power plant on the Connecticut River shut down after more than four decades of operation, and the city of Burlington announced that 100 percent of its electricity came from renewable sources, including renewably farmed wood chips, hydroelectric power, wind turbines and solar panels. In 2018, Vermont became the first state to legalize the importation of prescription drugs from Canada, to the chagrin of the Trump administration. Liberal policies have proven to be compatible with economic success: The unemployment rate was at 2.4 percent in February 2019, tied for the lowest in the nation.

The quintessential Vermont commercial strip is the Church Street Marketplace in downtown Burlington, a four-block pedestrian mall known for its tasteful shopping venues and street fairs — the polar opposite of the big-box stores sprouting elsewhere. Target finally opened its first Vermont location in South Burlington in 2018, making it the last state to get one. Dollar General was required to face its Chester store with clapboard wood rather than vinyl siding and keep its shopping carts off the street. For a long time, Vermont had one exception to its tight regulatory impulse – a lax policy on guns, tolerated even by leading Vermont Democrats to the consternation of others in their party who represent more urbanized areas. But that changed after the 2018 Parkland Florida high school mass shooting, as the Democratic legislature and the Republican governor worked together to enact a gun-control package.

Vermont has battled the scourge of drug addiction with better-than-average results. In 2017, Vox.com looked for a state that has "taken the opioid epidemic seriously" and found Vermont. Using a "hub-and-spoke" system that seeks to integrate intensive and follow-up care for addicts, Vermont, with bipartisan political support, has kept its overdose rate below that of its regional neighbors.

Recently, population growth in Vermont has been sluggish; between 2017 and 2018, Vermont grew (slightly) for the first time in four years. The population is also aging. Art Woolf, a University of Vermont economist, noted that the number of births in the state is at a 160-year low, and the birthrate is about 30 percent below its pace in the 1980s. When Moody's downgraded Vermont's bond rating slightly in 2018, it did so less for the state's fiscal picture than for its economic base that faces "low growth prospects from an aging population." So the state has gotten creative about attracting newcomers. It established the Remote Worker Grant Program, which provides $10,000 to anyone who moves to the state and works remotely in their existing job. Another program, Stay to Stay, brings out-of-staters on three-day-weekend vacations to such destinations as Bennington, Burlington, Brattleboro, Manchester and Rutland, hoping that that they will resettle in the state. Vermont also remains the whitest state in the nation, with blacks, Hispanics and Asian-Americans each accounting for less than 2 percent of the population. Residents were forced to do a gut check when Kiah Morris, the state's first African-American woman to be elected to the legislature, resigned from her seat in 2018 following a series of racist threats, ranging from social media attacks to vandalism at her home. The state attorney general filed no charges.

In the 19th century, Yankee Vermont was the most Republican state in the nation, voting Republican in every presidential election from 1856 to 1960. In 1936, Vermont and Maine were the only states to resist Franklin D. Roosevelt's landslide, inspiring Roosevelt's campaign manager, James Farley, to joke, "As Maine goes, so goes Vermont." For three decades thereafter, Vermont's Yankee Protestant Republicans outnumbered its French Canadian and Irish Catholic Democrats. As newcomers kept arriving, Vermont was divided politically along different lines: between liberal, highly educated newcomers and conservative, less educated, old Vermonters. A key figure was Howard Dean, who grew up on Park Avenue in New York City, was educated at Yale and moved to

Vermont, where he and his wife practiced medicine. He was elected lieutenant governor in 1986 and became governor when incumbent Republican Richard Snelling died in August 1991, learning of his elevation while treating a patient. He was elected to five terms in his own right (Vermont and New Hampshire are the last states with two-year gubernatorial terms) and set out to run for president in January 2003. His campaign took off briefly because of his full-throated opposition to the Iraq war. This was the point at which Vermont had moved way to the left on America's political spectrum.

Sanders, a self-styled socialist, has managed to hold office almost continuously in Vermont since 1981. Democrat Peter Shumlin won three terms and pursued a progressive agenda, but he also faced the limits of liberalism, even in a liberal state: He pulled back from his proposal for a single-payer health insurance system in 2014, citing the pitfalls of financing it. Republicans haven't become extinct in Vermont, but the ones who survived tended to be much more moderate than their peers within the national GOP. When Shumlin opted not to seek another term in 2016, Scott, the moderate Republican lieutenant governor, won the open seat on the same day Hillary Clinton won, although her 56 percent was well below Obama's 67 percent four years earlier.

Cook Partisan Voting Index: D+15

Population		Race and Ethnicity		Income	
Total	624,636	White	93.2%	Median Income	$57,808
Land area (sq. miles)	9,217	Black	1.2%	State Income Rank	20
Pop/ sq mi	67.8	Latino	1.8%	Poverty Rate	11.4%
Born in state	50.7%	Asian	1.5%	With health insurance	95.2%
		Two or more races	1.8%	Cash public assistance	3.8%
Age Groups		Other	0.4%	Food stamp/SNAP	12.8%
Under 18	19.2%				
18-34	22.2%	**Education**		**Work**	
35-64	41.1%	H.S grad or less	37.4%	White Collar	40.7%
Over 64	17.5%	Some college	25.9%	Sales and Service	38.7%
		College Degree, 4 yr	21.8%	Blue Collar	20.7%
Military		Post grad	15.0%	Government	14.1%
Veteran/ Active Duty	8.1%				

Presidential Politics

2016 Primary (D)	Sanders (D)	115,900 (86%)	Clinton (D)	18,338 (14%)			
2016 Primary (R)	Trump (R)	19,974 (33%)	Kasich (R)	18,534 (30%)	Rubio (R)	11,781 (19%)
	Cruz (R)	5,932 (10%)				
2016 Pres. Vote	Clinton (D)	178,573 (57%)	Trump (R)	95,369 (30%)	Johnson (L)	10,078 (3%)
	Stein (G)	6,758 (2%)				
2012 Pres. Vote	Obama (D)	199,239 (67%)	Romney (R)	92,698 (31%)		

While Vermont is the home of Sen. Bernie Sanders, the liberal champion of the 2016 election, no state has voted more often for Republican presidential candidates. From the birth of the GOP in 1856 until the 1992 election, Vermont voted once for the Democratic presidential nominee, Lyndon Johnson in 1964. Times changed. Starting in 1992, Vermonters have voted Democratic in every presidential contest. In 2008 and 2012, it was the second-most Democratic state, trailing only Barack Obama's birthplace of Hawaii (and non-state D.C.). Vermont has become solidly liberal on foreign policy and cultural issues (except gun control) and it is not very conservative on economics, either. In 2016 Hillary Clinton defeated Donald Trump, 57%-30%, dropping the state to the sixth most Democratic (seventh if you include D.C.). What dropped Democratic Party performance is that some 18,183 Vermonters wrote in Sanders' name on the general election ballot, almost 6 percent of the vote. Sanders' tally exceeded the totals garnered by Libertarian Gary Johnson and Green Party candidate Jill Stein combined. Among the state's some 250 towns and cities, Trump won a majority of the votes cast in 18 and a plurality in another 43.

The Vermont presidential primary, abolished for 1992, reappeared in 1996. In 2008, Obama and Hillary Clinton were locked in a struggle for the nomination. Obama beat Clinton 59%-39%. In 2012, Vermont voted when the Republican race was still raging. Mitt Romney led with 40 percent, to 26 percent for Ron Paul and 24 percent for Rick Santorum. In 2016, Sanders crushed Clinton, 86%-14%.

In the Republican race, Ohio Gov. John Kasich held several town-hall events, a hallmark of his New Hampshire campaign, hoping that his moderate profile would appeal to the state's voters, but Trump beat him, 33%-30%.

Congressional Districts

116th Congress Lineup	1D	115th Congress Lineup	1D

Phil Scott (R)

Elected 2016, term expires 2021, 2nd term; b. Aug. 4, 1958, Barre; Univ. of Vermont, BS 1980; Married (Diana); 2 children.

Elected Office: VT Senate 2001-2010; VT Lt. Governor 2011-2017

Professional Career: Stock Car Racer 1996-2005; Co-owner, DuBois Construction, 1986-2016.

Office: 109 State St., Montpelier, 05609-0101; 802-828-3333; Fax: 802-828-3339; Website: governor.vermont.gov.

Lt. Gov.: David Zuckerman (P) **Atty. Gen:** T. J. Donovan (D) **Sec. of State:** Jim Condos (D)
State Legislature: Senate: 22D, 6R, 2P **House:** 94D, 43R, 5I, 7P, 1V

Election Results

Election	Name (Party)	Vote (%)
2018 General	Phil Scott (R)...	151,261 (55%)
	Christine Hallquist (D)..	110,335 (40%)
2018 Primary	Phil Scott (R)...	24,142 (67%)
	Keith Stern (R)...	11,669 (33%)

Prior winning percentage: 2016 (53%)

Vermont may be one of the most liberal states in the union, but in 2016, voters elected Phil Scott -- a Republican -- as governor by an almost nine-point margin, and in 2018 they reelected him by 15 points. The 2018 election followed decades of Vermont tradition: The state has not ousted an incumbent governor since 1962.

Scott was born in Barre, earned a bachelor's degree from the University of Vermont, and co-owned a company, DuBois Construction, that he sold, as he had promised, prior to his inauguration as governor. A stock-car enthusiast, Scott also founded a program called Wheels for Warmth, which enabled Vermont residents to donate tires they no longer need, with some being resold to benefit heating-fuel assistance programs and others recycled. Scott won a race for the state Senate in 2000 and served for a decade. In 2010, he ran for lieutenant governor, which in Vermont is elected separately from the governor. In the general election, he defeated Democrat Steven Howard, 49%-42%, as Democrat Peter Shumlin was winning an open-seat gubernatorial race. As lieutenant governor, Scott started the "Vermont Everyday Jobs" initiative, in which he worked a few hours several times a month in different jobs, aiming to promote state businesses and highlight local workers. Scott was fiscally conservative but steered a moderate course overall; by the time he ran for reelection in 2012, he was endorsed by the state affiliate of the National Education Association. Scott won a second term over Democrat Cassandra Gekas, 57%-40%. Two years later, he won a third term without even facing a Democratic candidate; instead, Scott's main opponent was Dean Corren from the left-wing Progressive Party. Corren was endorsed by the senior Democrats in the state, but Scott prevailed, 62%-36%.

When Shumlin decided against running for a fourth two-year term as governor in 2016, Scott jumped into the race. First, though, Scott had to win the August GOP primary against former Wall Street executive Bruce Lisman. On the big issues – such as their stances toward business, taxation and the state's health care system – Scott and Lisman were generally on the same page. Instead, the race boiled down to a faceoff between a Montpelier insider (Scott) and a political outsider (Lisman). But with the backing of much of the party establishment, Scott won the primary, 60%-39%. In the competitive Democratic primary, state transportation secretary Sue Minter prevailed decisively over former state Sens. Matt Dunne and Peter Galbraith.

In the general election, Scott and his allies at the Republican Governors Association sought to tie Minter to Shumlin. Minter, meanwhile, declared her independence from Shumlin and touted her support from independent Sen. Bernie Sanders, the state's most popular politician, and from President Barack Obama, who cut an ad for her. The support didn't transfer, however. Scott was able to maintain his image as a moderate pragmatist in the mold of the state's two most recent Republican governors, Richard Snelling and Jim Douglas. Even as Hillary Clinton defeated Donald Trump by a 57%-30% margin, voters backed Scott over Minter, 53%-44%. (Scott had withheld his support from Trump.) Scott won all but three counties – Chittenden (Burlington), Windsor (Hartford) and Windham (Brattleboro). Scott's victory made him the only Republican to hold statewide office in Vermont.

During his first year, Scott encountered budget difficulties with legislative Democrats and their Progressive allies. Scott's effort to overhaul school-employee health care coverage – backed up by a threat to veto the budget -- irked many lawmakers and union officials. Eventually the two sides compromised, agreeing to a requirement that school districts cut their spending. Scott also vetoed a marijuana legalization bill in 2017, though by January of the following year, he reversed himself and signed a similar bill, acknowledging "mixed emotions." With the bill's enactment, Vermont became the first state to approve recreational marijuana through legislative action rather than by a popular vote. The budget battle in 2018 was also contentious; Scott vetoed initial versions of a bill, then let the measure become law without his signature. Legislative Democrats had insisted on certain tax increases, which Scott had pledged not to support. Meanwhile, Scott vetoed a range of proposed fee increases as well as a minimum wage hike to $15. Republicans in the legislature sustained Scott's vetoes.

The most consequential action addressed a topic that was once a third rail of Vermont politics: gun control. Scott and legislators enacted a package that included a ban on bump stocks and large magazines; a requirement that gun sales be handled through a licensed dealer; and permission for police to temporarily confiscate guns from individuals deemed to pose an immediate threat. In 2016, Scott had campaigned on not changing the state's gun laws, but he said he changed his mind after the mass school shooting in Parkland Florida in February 2018, as well as a case that involved a Columbine-style plan to shoot up a school in Vermont that was stopped in time. "As I processed this information, I was shocked," he told reporters. "Just 24 hours before — even in the aftermath of Parkland — I thought, as the safest state in the nation, Vermont was immune to this type of violence." Scott's change of heart made many Republicans irate: At the bill signing, he was heckled with calls of "Traitor!" and "BS!"

As the Republican base grew restive, Scott's once-charmed approval ratings sank and a primary challenger emerged. Keith Stern, a political novice and owner of Stern's Quality Produce in White River Junction, challenged Scott from the right on taxes and guns. With help from the Republican Governors Association, Scott prevailed, 67%-33%. The Democrats, meanwhile, had a four-way primary, led by Christine Hallquist, the former CEO of Vermont Electric Cooperative, and environmental advocate James Ehlers. Hallquist attracted the most notice for her bid to become the nation's first transgender gubernatorial nominee. Hallquist said the victory by Trump drove her to run; she called him a "psychotic despot" who "has decided he wants to eradicate my community." Hallquist took 48 percent of the primary vote, with 22 percent for Ehlers, 21 percent for local Democratic official Brenda Siegel, and 8 percent for 14-year-old candidate Ethan Sonneborn.

Despite national media attention, Hallquist began – and ended – the race as a heavy underdog. A big reason was Scott's ability to maintain support among moderate-to-liberal voters by openly defying Trump. Scott opposed Trump's immigration policies. He called Trump's favorable comments about the Unite the Right marchers in Charlottesville Virginia "unacceptable." He pledged to uphold the Paris climate accord after Trump pulled out. He declined to endorse Brett Kavanaugh's Supreme

Court nomination, and he opposed GOP efforts to roll back the Affordable Care Act. Hallquist struggled to gather support from national Democrats. Scott won, 55%-40%. Hallquist took only one county, Windham. The Democrats had won Chittenden by six percentage points in the 2016 gubernatorial race, but Hallquist lost it by a five-point margin. Democrats gained ground in both legislative chambers, making it harder for Republicans to sustain Scott's vetoes of progressive legislation. In 2019, as other states were passing stringent anti-abortion laws, Scott allowed a broad abortion-rights bill to become law. It's unclear what kind of future the GOP will have in Vermont. "Scott may be a natural successor to figures such as Jim Douglas, the state's Republican governor from 2003 to 2011," wrote Parker Richards in the Atlantic. "But there are fewer clear heirs to Scott."

Patrick Leahy (D)

Elected 1974, term expires 2022, 8th term, b. Mar 31, 1940; Montpelier; St. Michael's College (VT), B.A., 1961; Georgetown University Law Center (DC), J.D., 1964; Roman Catholic; Married (Marcelle Pomerleau Leahy); 3 children; 5 grandchildren.

Elected Office: VT State Attorney, Chittenden County, 1966-1974.

Professional Career: Practicing attorney, 1964-1974.

DC Office: 437 RSOB 20510, 202-224-4242, Fax: 202-224-3479, leahy.senate.gov

State Offices: Burlington, 802-863-2525; Montpelier, 802-229-0569.

Committees: *Agriculture, Nutrition & Forestry*: Conservation, Forestry & Natural Resources; Livestock, Marketing & Agriculture Security; Nutrition, Agricultural Research & Specialty Crops. *Appropriations (RMM)*: Ex Officio membership on all subcommittees. *Judiciary*: Antitrust, Competition Policy & Consumer Rights; Border Security & Immigration; Oversight, Agency Action, Federal Rights & Federal Courts; Subcommittee on Intellectual Property. *Rules & Administration*.

Group Ratings

	ADA	ACLU	AFL-CIO	LCV	ITI	COC	HAFA	ACU	CFG	FRC
2018	-	76%	-	100%	-	50%	3%	5%	5%	0%
2017	100%	C	100%	100%	C	14%	C	0%	4%	0%

Almanac Ratings 2017-18

	Economy	Social	Foreign	Composite
Liberal	100%	100%	89%	96%
Conservative	0%	0%	11%	4%

Key Votes of the 115th Congress

1. Obama-care revision	N	5. Gun regulations	N	9. Kavanaugh confirmation	N
2. Tax Cuts	N	6. Family planning regs	N	10. Saudi arms sales	Y
3. Dodd-Frank revision	N	7. Gorsuch confirmation	N	11. FISA rules	N
4. Omnibus appropriations	Y	8. Immigration restrictions	N	12. Military aid in Yemen	Y

Election Results

Election	Name (Party)	Vote (%)		Cand. Spent	Ind. Exp. Support	Ind. Exp. Oppose
2016 General	Patrick Leahy (D)	192,243	(61%)	$2,558,664		
	Scott Miline (R)	103,637	(33%)	$57,826		
	Cris Ericson (M)	9,156	(3%)			
2016 Primary	Patrick Leahy (D)	62,249	(89%)			
	Cris Ericson (D)	7,596	(11%)			

Prior winning percentages: 2010 (64%), 2004 (71%), 1998 (72%), 1992 (54%), 1986 (63%), 1980 (50%), 1974 (50%)

Democrat Patrick Leahy, Vermont's senior senator, was first elected in 1974, and, in late 2012, became the chamber's senior member. Re-elected to an eighth term in 2016, he has become the fifth longest serving senator in history. In more than four decades on Capitol Hill, Leahy has wielded influence over a wide range of issues — ranging from civil liberties to agricultural subsidies. He has chaired two Senate committees: Agriculture, from 1987 to 1995, and Judiciary, from 2001 to 2003 and again from 2007 to 2015. He could have ascended to the chairmanship of a third, Appropriations, when a vacancy occurred in 2012. But, as a former prosecuting attorney, Leahy remained at Judiciary to focus on a host of issues that have been his legislative passion.

In 2017, Leahy used the weight of his seniority to become the top Democrat on Appropriations. A year later, when Alabama Republican Richard Shelby became the Appropriations chairman, the two set out to restore "regular order" to an annual funding process plagued by partisan gridlock and brinkmanship — amid increasing reliance on stopgap continuing resolutions to keep the government running.

Leahy is a stalwart liberal known for periodic flashes of temper and can be a sharp-tongued partisan. Vice President Dick Cheney infamously told Leahy to "Go f--- yourself" after a 2004 picture-taking session at the Capitol; Cheney apparently was angered by Leahy's criticism of the activities of Halliburton, a company Cheney once headed, during the Iraq War. But Leahy arrived in the Senate in a more collegial time and has continued to reach across the aisle in an era of intensifying polarization. He has found common ground on civil liberties and criminal justice issues with some of the Senate's most outspoken conservatives, including Kentucky Sen. Rand Paul, and has enjoyed a good working relationship with his longtime Judiciary Committee colleague Iowa Republican Chuck Grassley, the second-most senior senator. But Leahy did not hesitate to lambaste Republicans' handling of Brett Kavanaugh's nomination to the Supreme Court when Grassley chaired the Judiciary panel in 2018.

Leahy grew up in Vermont when the Green Mountain State, now one of the nation's bluest, was rock-ribbed Republican. He graduated from St. Michael's College, just north of where he grew up in Burlington. He earned a law degree at Georgetown University and returned home to join the law firm of Philip Hoff, who, in 1962, had become the first Democrat since before the Civil War to win election as Vermont's governor. In 1966, Hoff appointed Leahy, then just 26, to fill a vacancy as state's attorney for Chittenden County, which includes Burlington. He was elected to full terms in 1966 and 1970.

In 1974, at 34, he ran for the Senate seat vacated by liberal Republican George Aiken, who first was elected the year Leahy was born. Leahy had made a name for himself in the pocket-sized state as a prosecutor who tried major felony cases and had a solid base in Democratic Burlington, the state's largest city, along with the thoughtful temperament Vermonters like in their public officials. In a year when Democrats benefited from the Watergate scandal, Leahy defeated Rep. Richard Mallary 50%-46% to become the first — and only — Democrat to win a Senate seat from Vermont. His colleague, Sen. Bernie Sanders, though now a force in the national Democratic Party, has run as an independent.

In 2012, a key reason that Leahy stayed at the helm of the Judiciary Committee — rather than chair Appropriations after the death of Hawaii Sen. Daniel Inouye — was that Judiciary was confronting two issues that could shape his legislative legacy. One was the first attempt at comprehensive immigration reform in six years; the other was the first major gun control legislation in nearly two decades. Leahy was an unlikely figure on the latter issue: A gun enthusiast, he was a member of his college shooting team and still enjoys the sport. In 1993, Leahy voted against passage of the so-called Brady Bill, which requires background checks for individuals purchasing firearms. Vermont continues to have one of the highest rates of gun ownership in the country — and some of the least restrictive gun laws.

After the December 2012 school massacre in Newtown Connecticut in which 27 people were killed, Leahy moved a series of bills through his committee to bar the straw purchase and trafficking of guns. His legislation included reinstatement of a ban on assault weapons, which then-Senate Majority Leader Harry Reid refused to schedule because it lacked the votes for passage. Even so, efforts to pass more modest gun control legislation fell apart when a bipartisan compromise to expand background checks to more gun buyers fell five votes short of the 60-vote threshold needed to end a filibuster.

On immigration, Leahy held hearings to try to build support for reform, while leaving much of the legislative work to a bipartisan group of eight senators. He guided the major overhaul of immigration laws, providing a path to citizenship for undocumented immigrants, through the Senate on a 68-32 vote. The GOP-controlled House never took up the measure.

Leahy's first stint as Judiciary chairman coincided with Sept. 11, 2001. He worked with the Bush administration to hammer out the sweeping law that sparked a national debate over government investigative powers at the expense of individual liberties. The original Patriot Act, enacted a month after the 9/11 attacks, was essentially the version crafted in Leahy's committee. Leahy fought attempts to expand police powers after the attacks and opposed a proposal to allow the government to detain and deport immigrants suspected of terrorism without presenting evidence in court.

In 2013, when onetime National Security Agency contractor Edward Snowden revealed the agency was collecting Americans' telephone and email data en masse, sentiment grew in Congress to restrict such authority. Leahy and Republican Mike Lee of Utah, a tea party conservative, introduced a bill to require targeted warrants to obtain Americans' data from telecommunications firms. Chairman Grassley's failure to move a bill through committee strengthened Leahy's hand. It left the Leahy-Lee measure and a proposal backed by Senate Majority Leader Mitch McConnell — to continue the law in its current form — as the major options. McConnell was forced to concede to the approach contained in the Leahy-Lee bill and a similar House-passed measure. "It's historical. It's the first major overhaul of government surveillance in decades," Leahy said after Congress stripped the NSA of authority to collect from U.S. citizens' phone and internet communications in bulk.

In January 2018, an effort by Leahy and like-minded colleagues to place restrictions in a related law — Section 702 of the Foreign Intelligence Surveillance Act — fell short. Section 702 permits the government to collect phone and email data of foreigners abroad without a warrant — even when they communicate with U.S. citizens. Leahy and Lee again teamed up on an amendment requiring the government to get a warrant to access Americans' phone and email data collected incidentally under Section 702. Their effort failed narrowly. The final measure signed into law contained a limited step toward requiring a warrant in some cases involving Americans, but Leahy said the provision was so narrow it was a "sham."

Leahy was an early supporter of Barack Obama in the 2008 presidential primaries and guided his two Supreme Court nominees, Sonia Sotomayor and Elena Kagan, through the Judiciary Committee to swift Senate confirmation. He accused Republicans of seeking to play the race card against Sotomayor, the court's first Latina justice, and of gender bias toward Kagan. As the GOP blocked numerous Obama nominees to district and appeals courts, Leahy lamented in 2013, "I have repeatedly asked Senate Republicans to abandon their destructive tactics." Soon thereafter, Reid sought to end to such tactics by invoking the "nuclear option" — changing the Senate rules to prevent filibusters for all appointees except Supreme Court justices; in 2017, Republicans under McConnell extended the move to include high court nominees.

Leahy often held up Bush's judicial nominations. He led filibusters against 10 Bush appeals court nominees, tactics about which Republicans bitterly complained. Leahy countered that the committee had approved most appellate and trial court nominees and argued he had been fairer to Bush's appointees than Republicans had been to those put forth by President Bill Clinton. When Leahy returned as chairman in 2007, he instituted "blue slip" procedures that gave all senators the ability to object to judicial nominees within their home states. "I have steadfastly protected the rights of the minority," Leahy said in 2012. "I have done so despite criticism from Democrats." Under President Donald Trump, Senate Republicans abandoned Leahy's blue slip procedures. It prompted some progressives to grumble that judgeships Obama had been unable to fill remained open to conservatives appointed by Trump.

Leahy led the criticism in 2016 when Republicans, spearheaded by McConnell, refused to hold hearings on Obama's nomination of federal Judge Merrick Garland to succeed the late Justice Antonin Scalia. "It's sleazy," Leahy told USA Today. "Have the courage to do your job and actually ask the questions." It put Leahy at odds with Grassley, whom Leahy tried to prod into breaking with McConnell to convene hearings on the nomination. It didn't work: Grassley had breakfast with Garland but went no further, and the seat remained vacant until Trump took office and nominated Judge Neil Gorsuch to fill it in early 2017.

Leahy announced he would vote against Kavanaugh before sexual assault allegations against the nominee were aired, saying he didn't believe Kavanaugh had been truthful about several policy questions. Leahy was overshadowed by junior Democratic colleagues during Kavanaugh's confirmation hearings, but his rhetoric was no less pointed. As the hearings opened in September 2018, Leahy said, "This is the most incomplete, most partisan and least transparent vetting for any Supreme Court nominee I have ever seen — and I've seen more than anyone else in the Senate. ... I'm just sorry to see the Senate Judiciary Committee descend this way." He slammed the unwillingness of Chairman Grassley and other committee Republicans to request records relating to Kavanaugh's tenure as a top aide in the George W. Bush White House. In a New York Times op-ed, Leahy contrasted his cooperation with Republicans during Kagan's 2009 confirmation to obtain records relating to her tenure as an aide in the Clinton White House.

In 2005, Leahy led the Democratic minority's questioning of Bush's Supreme Court nominees, John Roberts and Samuel Alito. Leahy surprised many when he voted to approve the conservative Roberts but voted against Alito. "This president is in the midst of a radical realignment of the powers of government and its intrusiveness into the private lives of Americans. This nomination is part of that plan," Leahy said, in opposing Alito. In 2017, he voted against Gorsuch, taking aim at not only several of Gorsuch's rulings but at what Leahy termed his "nonresponsive testimony" before the Judiciary panel. "Compared to Chief Justice Roberts, there is a yawning crevasse between the words Judge Gorsuch spoke to us and his actual record," Leahy said.

Intellectual property rights have been a major focus for Leahy, particularly as the digital age dawned, posing new challenges. He won enactment of an overhaul of the nation's patent system in 2011, ending a seven-year stalemate. But in mid-2014, Leahy was forced to throw in the towel on legislation to rein in patent trolls — firms which accumulate patents not to produce tangible goods but to use the system to extract fees and legal judgments from other companies. Leahy reportedly withdrew the measure under pressure from Reid, as the legislation faced opposition from the pharmaceutical industry and trial lawyers association. Leahy tried again in 2015, but failed to advance a patent trolling measure that he co-authored with Grassley. It was yet another collaboration between Leahy and Grassley, who have also worked together on satellite television access and cellphone unlocking technology. After the Kavanaugh hearings, they combined in early 2019 on legislation to allow the Justice Department to sue the Organization of Petroleum Exporting Countries for illegal pricing and other violations of antitrust laws.

After he became the ranking Democrat on Appropriations, Leahy forged a partnership with Shelby. Trump had recently signed "omnibus" legislation in which the 12 annual appropriations bills were merged into a hastily passed 2,200-page measure. Trump called the process "ridiculous" and vowed not to sign such legislation again. Leahy and Shelby shared longer-term concerns that the breakdown of the appropriations process — the last time all 12 annual appropriations measures were passed and individually signed was 2005 — had concentrated increasing power with congressional leaders to cut last-minute deals at the expense of rank-and-file lawmakers. "We took a couple of trips together and we talked about it, and just said, 'Unless we get this back, the Senate is really screwed,'" Leahy told The New York Times of his discussions with Shelby. "We have to get back to doing it the regular way."

Leahy and Shelby persuaded their respective party leaderships to keep "poison pill" policy riders off appropriations bills. Democrats credited Shelby for holding up his part of the bargain — often to the consternation of other Republicans seeking to advance pet causes. Shelby and Leahy by the end of 2018 had shepherded nine of the 12 annual appropriations measures to Senate passage on bipartisan votes. Those bills did not include the Department of Homeland Security measure that was a focal point in the battle over Trump's proposed southern border wall; the 35-day government shutdown obscured the progress of Shelby and Leahy in restoring the traditional appropriations process.

Leahy is ranking member of the Appropriations subcommittee with jurisdiction over the State Department and foreign aid programs and has chaired that subcommittee. He has been a major force behind the Trafficking Victims Protection Act, first passed in 2000; the law is designed to pressure foreign countries engaged in human trafficking and provide recourse to victims of the practice in the United States. Another Leahy cause is the elimination of land mines. Since 1989, he has crusaded against such devices, which are easy and cheap to implant yet difficult and expensive to remove. In 1994, he persuaded the United Nations to unanimously call for the eventual elimination of land mines. As an opponent of the U.S. embargo against Cuba, Leahy was actively involved in the successful effort to free government contractor Alan Gross from a Cuban prison in 2014 — a move that paved the way for Obama's decision to restore diplomatic relations with the island nation. Leahy was among several lawmakers who flew to Cuba to bring Gross home.

Earlier in his career, Leahy became one of the few senators to chair the Agriculture Committee who did not represent a state with crops like wheat, corn or cotton. As the panel's ranking Democrat, he worked with Indiana Republican Richard Lugar in the 1990s to phase out the subsidy system. But after their success in enacting the Freedom to Farm Act of 1996, crop prices fell. Congress took to supporting large annual subsidies of emergency relief to farmers, and in 2002, largely rolled back the 1996 act. More recently, Leahy has delivered for the roughly 1,000 dairy farms in Vermont, including steps in the 2018 farm bill to insulate dairy farmers from financial risk.

Leahy expressed second thoughts in late 2017 about his response to the controversy that led to the resignation of Minnesota Democrat Al Franken. In December, when allegations of improper sexual behavior against Franken surfaced, Leahy joined 30 other Democratic senators in calling for Franken to step down. The next day, Franken announced he would do so. Several days later, however, Leahy said the Senate Ethics Committee should have been allowed to complete its investigation before a judgment was reached on Franken's fate. "I have stood for due process throughout my years as a prosecutor," Leahy said. "I regret not doing that this time."

In Leahy's first race for Senate in 1974, 4 percent of the vote went to the candidate of the Liberty Union Party: Sanders, Vermont's junior senator since 2006. In 2016, Leahy endorsed Hillary Clinton for the Democratic presidential nomination, saying he had committed to Clinton before Sanders got into the race. When Sanders announced a second presidential run in February 2019, Leahy endorsed him. He also co-sponsored Sanders' "Medicare For All" legislation.

Leahy had a close call in his first re-election bid, surviving a 1980 challenge by a single percentage point amid a national Republican landslide. In 1986, a year more favorable for Democrats, he had little trouble defeating popular Gov. Richard Snelling and won 63%-35%. In 1992, Leahy was held to 54 percent of the vote by Republican Jim Douglas, who was later elected governor. Leahy has easily won re-election since then.

Running in 2016 at 76, Leahy faced businessman Scott Milne, who had come close to upsetting Gov. Peter Shumlin two years earlier. Milne sought to make an issue of Leahy's past advocacy of the EB-5 program, which provides foreigners with path to permanent residency in exchange for investments in U.S. projects: Milne's charges followed a Securities and Exchange Commission lawsuit alleging two Vermont developers, including one with ties to Leahy, had operated what the SEC called a "Ponzi-like scheme" to defraud foreign investors of $200 million. Leahy snapped: "If he is accusing me of doing something wrong, he should call the U.S. attorney's office." Leahy won 61%-33%. By the end of his current term in 2022, he will have reached third place on the all-time Senate seniority list—behind Robert Byrd of West Virginia and Inouye.

Around the Capitol, Leahy is known for his hobbies. He is an accomplished photographer, despite being legally blind in his left eye since birth; his work has been published in The New York Times, USA Today and several news magazines. He is a huge fan of "Batman" movies, appearing briefly in four of them, most recently "Batman v. Superman: Dawn of Justice" in 2016. He had a speaking part in "The Dark Knight" in 2008: Leahy tells the Joker, "We're not intimidated by thugs." Leahy also has been a high-profile fan of the Grateful Dead and can recite lyrics from the band's songs.

Bernie Sanders (I)

Elected 2006, term expires 2024, 3rd term, b. Sep 08, 1941; Brooklyn, NY; Brooklyn College (NY), Att., 1960; University of Chicago (IL), B.A., 1964; Jewish; Married (Jane O'Meara Driscoll); 1 child; 3 stepchildren.

Elected Office: Burlington Mayor, 1981-1989; U.S. House, 1991-2007.

Professional Career: Writer; Director, American People's Historical Soc., 1977-1981; Lecturer, Harvard University, 1989; Lecturer, Hamilton College, 1990.

DC Office: 332 DSOB 20510, 202-224-5141, Fax: 202-228-0776, sanders.senate.gov

State Offices: Burlington, 802-862-0697; St. Johnsbury, 800-339-9834.

Committees: Senate Democratic Outreach Committee Chairman. *Budget (RMM)*. *Energy & Natural Resources*: Energy; National Parks; Water & Power. *Environment & Public Works*: Clean Air & Nuclear Safety; Fisheries, Water, and Wildlife; Transportation & Infrastructure. *Health, Education, Labor & Pensions*: Children & Families; Primary Health & Retirement Security (RMM). *Veterans' Affairs*.

Group Ratings

	ADA	ACLU	AFL-CIO	LCV	ITI	COC	HAFA	ACU	CFG	FRC
2018	-	86%	-	100%	-	40%	8%	9%	26%	0%
2017	95%	C	100%	100%	C	14%	C	0%	4%	0%

Almanac Ratings 2017-18

	Economy	Social	Foreign	Composite
Liberal	100%	100%	100%	100%
Conservative	0%	0%	0%	0%

Key Votes of the 115th Congress

1. Obama-care revision	N	5. Gun regulations	N	9. Kavanaugh confirmation	N
2. Tax Cuts	N	6. Family planning regs	N	10. Saudi arms sales	Y
3. Dodd-Frank revision	N	7. Gorsuch confirmation	N	11. FISA rules	N
4. Omnibus appropriations	N	8. Immigration restrictions	N	12. Military aid in Yemen	Y

Election Results

Election	Name (Party)	Vote (%)		Cand. Spent	Ind. Exp. Support	Ind. Exp. Oppose
2018 General	Bernie Sanders (I)........................ 183,649	(67%)		$5,222,961		$2,232,449
	H. Brooke Paige (R)............................. 74,815	(27%)				
2018 Primary	Bernie Sanders (D)............................. 63,322	(94%)				
	Folasade Adeluola (D)................. 3,748	(6%)				

Prior winning percentages: 2012 (71%), 2006 (65%), House: 2004 (67%), 2002 (64%), 2000 (69%), 1998 (63%), 1996 (55%), 1994 (50%), 1992 (58%), 1990 (56%)

In late 2013, when independent Bernie Sanders, Vermont's junior senator, introduced "Medicare for All" legislation, he did so without a single co-sponsor. When Sanders again introduced the bill — which calls for private health insurance to be supplanted by a government-run single-payer plan — in late 2017, one-third of the Senate Democratic Caucus co-sponsored it. The change was emblematic of the clout the onetime backbencher had acquired after the surprising success of his 2016 campaign for the Democratic presidential nomination. Down nearly 50 percentage points in some polls when he started, Sanders battled the front-running candidate, Hillary Clinton, to the end of the primary elections. By the time he arrived at the Democratic National Convention, he had won contests in 22 states, along with 46 percent of the pledged delegates — after attracting massive crowds and energizing millennial voters, as he railed against the "billionaire class" and urged a "political revolution."

While Sanders didn't end up as the party's nominee, he could claim a major victory by having pulled the Democratic Party's center of gravity in his direction, as he campaigned on proposals ranging from free college tuition to a $15 hourly minimum wage, as well as Medicare for All. "During our 2016 campaign, when we brought forth our progressive agenda, we were told that our ideas were 'radical' and 'extreme,'" the self-described democratic socialist wrote to supporters in February 2019, launching his second presidential bid. "Three years have come and gone. And, as result of millions of Americans standing up and fighting back, all of these policies and more are now supported by a majority of Americans." Unlike four years earlier, Sanders entered the race this time as a leading contender — with national name recognition, a committed base of backers in all 50 states and a sophisticated social media operation with which to energize them, to say nothing of an ability to raise large amounts of money from a massive list of small donors.

But as Sanders faced a different political landscape than he did in 2016 — competing in a splintered Democratic field of more than 20 candidates — a key question was whether he might turn out to be a victim of his own success. He was no longer the sole alternative on the left to the party establishment choice; this time, the field also included several of his Senate colleagues as well as other aspirants espousing many of the progressive policies he had advanced. Amid a movement within the Democratic Party for greater diversity, many of these rival contenders were women and people of color — in contrast to a white male who will be 79 on Inauguration Day 2021. Sanders bristled at what he regarded as ageism — "Age is a factor! But it is one of many factors!" he told New York magazine in late 2018 — and another leading contender, former Vice President Joe Biden, is just a year younger. If elected, Sanders would be the oldest person to occupy the Oval Office.

Though he has arguably become the dominant figure of the Democratic Party's progressive wing, Sanders has made eight successful runs for the House and three for the Senate without appearing on the Democratic line on the ballot. He caucuses with Democrats in the Senate, as he did in the House, but when asked whether he identified as a Democrat on MSNBC in April 2017, Sanders replied,

"No, I'm an independent." During the same interview, he indicated his goal was nothing less than a transformation of the Democratic Party. "If the Democratic Party is going to succeed — and I want to see it succeed — it's going to have to open its door to independents. ... It's got to open its doors to working people and to young people, create a grassroots party," he said.

Such statements help explain why many in the Democratic Party establishment remain leery about Sanders and believe his behavior in 2016 contributed to Clinton's loss to now-President Donald Trump. Consequently, unlike other recent second-time presidential contenders — who have emerged as front-runners for their party's nomination — Sanders' base of support showed few signs of expansion as he embarked on his 2020 run. Many Democrats saw him as more interested in transforming the party's prevailing orthodoxy than in its near-term success — a view Clinton herself has voiced. In her post-2016 campaign memoir, "What Happened," she complained Sanders had run to "disrupt the Democratic Party" rather than to "make sure a Democrat won the White House" and that his candidacy did "lasting damage" to her campaign. Sanders responded on "The Late Show with Stephen Colbert" with a back-handed gibe: "You know, Secretary Clinton ran against the most unpopular candidate in the history of this country, and she lost. And she was upset by that. I understand that."

Behind this face of a fomenter of political upheaval, however, is a savvy strategist who has demonstrated a willingness to — yes, compromise, both during and before his congressional career. In many years as a Capitol Hill outlier, he often teamed with Republicans to chalk up legislative victories. "The thing about Bernie, which is different than most socialists, is Bernie wants to win," Garrison Nelson, a University of Vermont professor who has known Sanders for four decades, told Politico. As chairman of the Senate Veterans' Affairs Committee, Sanders steered an overhaul of the Department of Veterans Affairs into law in 2014. After closing that deal, Sanders recalled his days as mayor of Burlington in the 1980s. "When I took office, [in terms of] people who supported me on the City Council, we had two out of 13, and I had to make things happen while being in the minority," he told Roll Call. "So, I do know how to negotiate fairly. Negotiation is part of the political process. I certainly have been prepared to do that since Day One."

As his thick Brooklyn accent indicates, Sanders grew up in the Flatbush section of New York's largest borough. His father was a paint salesman who had emigrated from Poland. He graduated from James Madison High School — also the alma mater of Minority Leader Chuck Schumer, who named Sanders to a post in the Senate Democratic leadership in late 2016 — before attending Brooklyn College. He graduated from the University of Chicago, where he became involved in left-wing politics. Sanders moved to Vermont as part of the hippie migration of 1968. Sanders worked as a carpenter upon arriving in the Green Mountain State. In 1971, he ran in a special election for a vacant U.S. Senate seat as the candidate of the Liberty Union Party, winning just 2 percent of the vote. He went on to lose four statewide races. Running against Democrat Patrick Leahy, now his senior colleague, in 1974, Sanders raised his vote on the Liberty Union line to 4 percent.

Sanders' earnest persona finally won over the Burlington electorate, which in 1981 made him the city's first socialist mayor by just 10 votes. "There was anger in the air, plenty of it," the Burlington Free Press wrote years later. "Bernie Sanders, a self-proclaimed socialist of all people, had somehow stolen City Hall from" the Democrats. He served until 1989, winning re-election three times. "I am a socialist, of course I am a socialist," Sanders said during a 1983 debate, according to The Associated Press. He added, "To hold a vision that society can be fundamentally different, to believe that all people can be equal, that is not a new idea."

One-third of a century later, some Democrats feared that Sanders would revive Cold War era use of the socialist label as a pejorative against them. "Here in the United States, we are alarmed by the new calls to adopt socialism in our country," Trump said during his 2019 State of the Union address, a line soon echoed by other Republicans. Sanders afterward told NPR: "I think what we have to do ... is to do a better job maybe in explaining what we mean by socialism — democratic socialism. Obviously, my right-wing colleagues here want to paint that as authoritarianism and communism and Venezuela, and that's nonsense." Sanders sought to do that on a televised town hall hosted by Fox News in April 2019; most hands went up when the audience was asked if they would be willing to give up private health insurance for a Medicare for All-type system. "So weird to watch Crazy Bernie on @Fox News," Trump tweeted after the event, during which Sanders said: "Whether you're a conservative, a moderate, or a progressive, I don't think the American people are proud that we have a president who is a pathological liar. And it does not give me pleasure to say that."

Sanders' first congressional bid came in 1988, when Vermont's at-large House seat opened. He ran as an independent but lost by 3 percentage points to Republican Peter Smith in a three-way race. Two years later, he defeated Smith 56%-40%, becoming only the third socialist elected to the House

— and the first since the late 1920s. Sanders benefited politically from his opposition to gun control: Smith had voted to ban semi-automatic weapons, and the National Rifle Association had come out against him. Three years later, Sanders voted against the "Brady Bill," which requires background checks for those buying firearms. And in 2005, he supported an NRA-backed bill to shield gun manufacturers and dealers from most lawsuits. Sanders' early gun control stance has come to haunt him; Clinton raised it in candidate forums in 2016, and it was used in ads by a super PAC supporting her. More recently, Sanders has sided with gun control advocates — voting in 2013 to expand background checks and in 2016 to bar firearm sales to those on the government's terrorist watch list. But he has represented a state where gun ownership remains widespread, with few restrictions.

In the House, Sanders formed the Congressional Progressive Caucus with an agenda later adopted in large measure by his presidential campaign. Besides a single-payer health insurance system, it included progressive tax reform, a 50 percent cut in military spending, a national energy policy, and — a Vermont touch — support for family farms. Notwithstanding much of what he has advocated is unlikely to be enacted anytime soon — even co-sponsors of Medicare for All see it as largely aspirational in the short term — Sanders has played the long game throughout his career, hoping to influence opinion by speaking out early and often. "Everybody [now] talks about income inequality," he told The New York Times in 2015. "Well, check it out. Find out who was talking about it 20 years ago." As much as anyone, Sanders helped make the cost of prescription drugs a national issue: He was the first member of Congress to lead bus trips to Canada to buy pharmaceuticals at lower costs.

All of this played well at home, where Sanders regularly won re-election with more than 60 percent of the vote. After eight House terms, Sanders became the early front-runner for the Senate when Independent Jim Jeffords announced his retirement in 2005. Sanders quickly amassed endorsements from top Vermont Democrats; with Sanders' consent, Democrats put his name on their primary ballot and he won 94 percent of the vote. He declined the nomination and petitioned to be listed on the general election ballot as an independent. Gov. Jim Douglas, who was considered the only Republican with a real shot at defeating Sanders in 2006, declined to run. Richard Tarrant, a multimillionaire businessman, became the GOP nominee. Tarrant's ads sought to portray Sanders as an ineffective radical soft on sexual predators and drug dealers. The strategy didn't work in a small state where voters were well-acquainted with Sanders and his iconoclastic ways. Although outspent, Sanders won 65%-32%.

Sanders had no trouble winning reelection. In 2012, he dispatched underfunded Republican John MacGovern 71%-25%. In 2018, he bested Lawrence Zupan, a real estate broker and critic of the Medicare for All plan, 67%-27% — after again winning the Democratic nomination with 94 percent of the vote and declining it to run as an independent.

Sanders initially settled with surprising ease into the chamber's more structured ways. Leahy told a Vermont reporter that other senators — presumably expecting a political bomb-thrower in their midst — had confided "what a pleasant surprise [Sanders] has turned out to be" with his willingness to craft legislative deals.

His more familiar side was on display when, as the Occupy Wall Street protests energized the American left, Sanders endorsed the goals of the upstart movement. His breakout moment on the national political stage came with an eight-hour, often apoplectic, Senate speech at the end of 2010: He excoriated the extension of tax cuts for the highest-income Americans — enacted early in the Bush administration — as "Robin Hood in reverse." At one point, Sanders sarcastically asked: "How can I get by on one house? I need five houses, 10 houses! I need three jet planes to take me all over the world! Sorry, American people. We've got the money, we've got the power, we've got the lobbyists here and on Wall Street. Tough luck." The speech proved so popular it temporarily shut down the Senate video server.

In 2013, Sanders — unhappy about a guest-worker program in a bipartisan immigration bill — used his leverage to win inclusion of a $1.5 billion youth jobs plan in the legislation, which passed the Senate but was not taken up by the House. That same year, Sanders assumed the Veterans' Affairs Committee chairmanship. Revelations about the poor treatment veterans faced had forced out VA Secretary Eric Shinseki and increased support for a reform bill. Over several months, Sanders engaged in a bitter war of words with his conservative House counterpart, Florida Republican Jeff Miller, but the two struck a compromise at the end of what Sanders called "a very, very difficult process." The $17 billion package sailed through the House unanimously and drew just three dissenting votes in the Senate. It was one of the largest expansions of the federal government since Republicans had taken over the House.

Since 2015, when Republicans seized control of the Senate, Sanders has been ranking Democrat on the Budget Committee. "I have helped fight for budget and national priorities, which represent the needs of working families and not just the 1 percent," Sanders said in January 2019. When Sanders released 10 years of his income tax returns three months later, it confirmed that the onetime carpenter was now among the 1 percent: Thanks largely to proceeds from sales of his books, he and his wife, Jane Sanders, reported $1 million in annual income for both 2016 and 2017. Given his frequent targeting of the wealthiest Americans, there were suggestions that Sanders' message had been undercut by his own disclosures. "These tax returns show that our family has been fortunate," Sanders said. "I am very grateful for that, as I grew up in a family that lived paycheck to paycheck and I know the stress of economic insecurity."

In fall 2013, Sanders toured several Southern states and said he would consider running for president. He took the plunge in May 2015 after the first choice of the party's left wing, Massachusetts Sen. Elizabeth Warren, spent a year insisting she had no plans to mount a White House bid.

Like Trump, Sanders exhibited a populist appeal, albeit from the opposite end of the spectrum — and, also like Trump, was seen as a political outsider taking aim at the status quo. The latter appeared to be a key element of his allure to voters younger than 30, as he captured them by a 5-2 margin over Clinton. Sanders' fundraising efforts relied heavily on small individual donors, thereby lending credibility to his attacks on moneyed interests and their influence on the political system. Sanders' campaign collected nearly $234 million from 8 million donations, setting it apart from many of the 2016 presidential candidates fueled by super PACs and other outside groups. Sanders' fundraising success propelled his campaign through the 2016 primary season, even as the mathematical odds against his capturing the nomination mounted. In early 2019, he raised nearly $6 million in the 24 hours after announcing he would run again.

But if he had the enthusiastic support of young voters, Sanders — who represents a state that is 93 percent white — struggled to attract nonwhite voters, who cast an estimated 40 percent of the ballots during Democratic primaries and caucuses. According to exit poll data compiled by The Wall Street Journal, African-American voters favored Clinton by more than 3-1: Most of Sanders' primary season wins were in less populated states with smaller minority populations. Sanders worked in the run-up to his second presidential bid to build ties to minority communities, and his endorsements helped two African-American candidates, Andrew Gillum and Ben Jealous, win gubernatorial primaries in Florida and Maryland, respectively — albeit both lost in November. But supporters acknowledged his difficulty in expanding a message focused on class and ideology to encompass today's identity politics. "The 2020 challenge will be making sure [he] can inclusively get the class message out in a way that doesn't make it seem like he's dismissing identity issues," one Sanders adviser told New York magazine.

Also working against Sanders in 2016 were 700 superdelegates with automatic votes at the convention as elected officeholders or high-ranking party officials — a large majority of whom backed Clinton early on. That extended to Sanders' own state, where four of five superdelegates lined up behind Clinton, despite Vermont giving more than 85 percent of its primary vote to its favorite son. Among the Vermont superdelegates backing Clinton was Leahy, who said he had committed to her well before Sanders decided to run; in 2019, Leahy endorsed Sanders' second bid. Sanders' sharpest criticisms were reserved for the Democratic National Committee and what he considered its rigging of the system to bolster Clinton. The DNC's chairwoman, Rep. Debbie Wasserman Schultz, resigned just before the convention in July 2016 after a series of stolen emails confirming Sanders' suspicions were leaked.

In an olive branch to Sanders backers, the DNC in 2018 changed the party's nominating rules to reduce the influence of superdelegates. At the insistence of some members of the establishment wing, the DNC also instituted a loyalty pledge — which Sanders and other 2020 candidates signed — for its presidential candidates to "run and serve as a member of the Democratic Party." It was designed to address concerns dating to 2016 that Sanders, as an independent, might seek to run as a third-party candidate after his loss to Clinton.

In 2017, during the budget debate, Sanders called out 13 Democratic senators who voted against a largely symbolic amendment that promoted one of his longtime causes: allowing reimportation of prescription drugs from Canada. "The Democratic Party has got to make it very clear that they are prepared to stand up to powerful special interests. ... And they're not going to be doing the right thing for the American people unless they have the guts to do that," he said. A month later, one of the 13, New Jersey Sen. Cory Booker — who later joined the field seeking the party's 2020 presidential nomination — cosponsored with Sanders a bill allowing importation of pharmaceuticals from Canada. Booker, whose state is home to several large pharmaceutical firms, shifted after taking heat from progressive activists.

It was the first of several examples of Sanders' successful jawboning to effect change. In July 2018, he livestreamed a town hall with workers from several large companies, including Disney; a month later, Disney World announced it planned to raise its minimum wage to $15 per hour. In September, he introduced legislation intended to turn up the heat on Amazon. Titled the Stop Bad Employers by Zeroing Out Subsidies Act — "Stop BEZOS" — it would have required Amazon and other large employers to cover the cost of food stamps, public housing, Medicaid and other federal assistance received by its employees. Not long afterward, Amazon CEO Jeff Bezos announced the online retailer would raise its minimum wage to $15 per hour for 350,000 permanent and seasonal U.S. employees.

The launch of Sanders latest presidential bid came amid published reports of allegations by several women who said they were harassed or mistreated while working for his male-dominated campaign in 2016. Although Sanders offered multiple apologies and shook up his campaign staff heading into 2020, some detected signs of tone deafness when he was asked if he had been aware of the complaints during the campaign. "I was a little bit busy running around the country trying to make the case," he told CNN. For Sanders, it was a reminder that, as a leading candidate in 2020 as opposed to the outlier he was in 2015, his words and actions were certain to attract far greater scrutiny in the months ahead.

Peter Welch (D)

Elected 2006, 7th term, b. May 02, 1947; Springfield, MA; College of The Holy Cross (MA), B.A., 1969; University of California, Berkeley, J.D., 1973; Roman Catholic; Married (Margaret Cheney); 5 children; 3 stepchildren.

Elected Office: Elected Office: VT Senate, 1981-1989, 2002-2007, Minority Leader, 1983-1985, President pro tem, 1985-1989, 2003-2007.

Professional Career: Robert F. Kennedy fellow, 1969-1970; Practicing attorney, 1974-2006.

DC Office: 2187 RHOB 20515, 202-225-4115, Fax: 202-225-6790, welch.house.gov

State Offices: Burlington, 888-605-7270.

Committees: *Energy & Commerce*: Communications & Technology; Energy; Health. *Oversight & Reform*: National Security. *Permanent Select on Intelligence*: Counterterrorism, Counterintelligence & Counterproliferation; Defense Intelligence & Warfighter Support.

Group Ratings

	ADA	ACLU	AFL-CIO	LCV	ITI	COC	HAFA	ACU	CFG	FRC
2018	-	86%	-	94%	-	58%	8%	12%	4%	0%
2017	100%	C	95%	97%	C	36%	C	7%	5%	0%

Almanac Ratings 2017-18

	Economy	Social	Foreign	Composite
Liberal	97%	97%	98%	97%
Conservative	3%	3%	3%	3%

Key Votes of the 115th Congress

1. Obama-care revision	N	5. Family planning regs	N	9. Guantanamo prisoners	Y
2. Tax Cuts	N	6. Body cameras/immigration	Y	10. Ground missiles, limit	Y
3. Omnibus appropriations	Y	7. Abortion ban	N	11. Defense Dept. spending	N
4. Dodd-Frank revision	N	8. Concealed carry	N	12. FISA rules	N

Election Results

Election	Name (Party)	Vote (%)		Cand. Spent	Ind. Exp. Support	Ind. Exp. Oppose
2018 General	Peter Welch (D)	188,547	(69%)	$389,712		
	Anya Tynio (R)	70,705	(26%)		$8,556	
	Cris Ericson (I)	9,110	(3%)			
2018 Primary	Peter Welch (D)	54,330	(84%)			
	Daniel Freilich (D)	7,711	(12%)			

Prior winning percentages: 2016 (90%), 2014 (64%), 2012 (72%), 2010 (65%), 2008 (83%), 2006 (53%)

Vermont's only House member is Peter Welch, a Democrat first elected in 2006. He is highly regarded within his party as a strategist and spokesman. He serves as a chief deputy whip and has been active on energy and health care issues — occasionally on a bipartisan basis. One of his proposals to lower Medicare costs drew the direct interest of President Donald Trump. Welch has been viewed as the heir apparent to a Senate seat if either of Vermont's more elderly senators creates a vacancy. As he turns age 72 in 2019, he might be close to missing his chance.

Welch grew up in Springfield Massachusetts, the son of a dentist, and graduated from the College of the Holy Cross. The summer before his junior year, he worked for a Jesuit group that did community outreach in poor black neighborhoods in Chicago, where he was inspired by a speech by the Rev. Martin Luther King Jr. After graduating from law school at the University of California, Berkeley, Welch backpacked down the Pan-American Highway to Santiago Chile, then worked on a freighter that sailed to Portugal. After that, he was ready to practice law and chose White River Junction as his home. He worked as a public defender before founding his small firm.

In 1980, Welch became the first Democrat to represent Windsor County in the state Senate since the Civil War. Two years later, he became Senate minority leader. After Democrats won a majority in the Senate for the first time ever, he was elected president pro tem. He focused on environment, education and tax issues and helped establish the Housing and Land Conservation Trust, which worked to create affordable housing and to conserve farmland and forests. In 1988, Welch aimed for the House but lost the Democratic primary by 266 votes. In 1990, he ran for governor, but lost 52%-46% to Republican Richard Snelling. For some years after that, Welch was out of political life. His wife, Joan, who had been his closest adviser and campaign manager, fought cancer for nine years, and Welch at times was her full-time caregiver. She died in 2004.

In 2001, Democratic Gov. Howard Dean appointed Welch to the state Senate to fill a vacancy. In 2003, he became president pro tem once again and focused on health care issues. When Rep. Bernie Sanders, after 16 years in the House, ran for the Senate, Welch ran again for the House and won the Democratic nomination unopposed. In the general election, Welch ran as an opponent — from the start — of military action in Iraq, and he condemned the "corrupt" Republicans in Washington. He supported universal health care. Republican nominee Martha Rainville, commander of the Vermont National Guard, said she would have voted for military action in Iraq in 2002 given what was known then, but she criticized some decisions of the Bush administration. Both candidates favored abortion rights. Welch spent $1.7 million to Rainville's $1.1 million. Welch won, 53%-45%.

Welch features an understated and collegial style. On the Energy and Commerce Committee, he has helped to shape energy and climate-change legislation. He got a provision in a House-passed bill to spend billions of dollars on energy efficiency. He won committee approval of a measure to provide tax rebates to consumers for installing upgraded insulation, storm windows and other energy-efficiency aids. Practicing what he preached, he made his office the first in the House to install new lights and water fixtures to reduce energy use.

After the GOP takeover of the House, he helped liberals articulate their opposition on various issues, but Welch is not a strict partisan. He worked with Republicans on a measure in 2013 to allow states to ensure online merchants collect sales taxes in return for simplified tax procedures. He joined Republican Rep. David McKinley of West Virginia on a broad proposal that included efficiency standards for utility companies and a requirement that federally backed home mortgages must include efficiency ratings for the property. The House passed the bill in 2015 and it was enacted with Senate revisions. In November 2016, he joined a bipartisan group that enacted a bill that directed the Commerce Department to quantify the financial impact of outdoor recreation. Welch has been a member of the bipartisan citizen activist effort, No Labels.

In March 2017, Welch and Democratic Rep. Elijah Cummings of Maryland met with Trump to discuss their proposal for the federal government to negotiate lower prices for prescription-drug coverage under Medicare. Following the nearly hourlong meeting, the two Democrats said that Trump agreed to support their plan. There was no apparent follow-up. Welch strongly opposed Trump's tariffs on Canada, which has long enjoyed a lucrative trade relationship and friendly border with Vermont. "The president is abusing his authority," he said.

Back in the majority, Welch was active on multiple fronts and said it was vital to revive open debate in the House. "Too much power has landed in the Speaker's office," regardless of which party was in House control, he told Seven Days, a Vermont news site. Welch remained a chief deputy whip and he joined the Intelligence Committee, with a pledge to "protect our national security, as well as our privacy and civil liberties." He worked with Rep. Peter DeFazio of Oregon, chairman of the Transportation and Infrastructure Committee, on a wide-ranging plan to upgrade the nation's public works, including in rural areas. He endorsed the "Green New Deal" proposal of progressive Democrats.

At home, Welch has faced no serious reelection threats. In 2009, he married state Rep. Margaret Cheney, who later became a member of the Vermont Utility Commission. After a question arose about a possible conflict, he said that he would not accept campaign contributions from political action committees of companies with cases before the board. When Seven Days in 2018 raised new allegations of possible conflicts involving his wife, he responded that he does not discuss her professional work. "Her responsibilities and my responsibilities are completely separate," he said. Welch turned down an opportunity to run for governor in 2016. Even with his age, he remained a distinct possibility to seek to succeed either Sen. Patrick Leahy or Sen. Bernie Sanders if an opening occurs; they are seven and six years older than Welch.

VIRGINIA

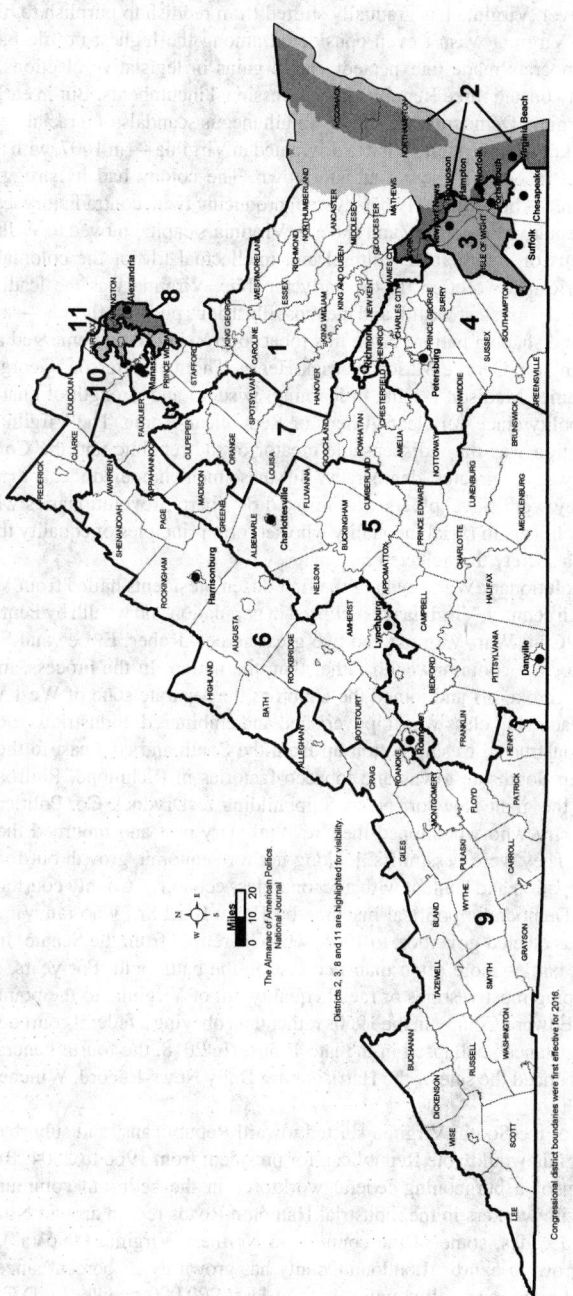

The Almanac of American Politics.
National Journal

Districts 2, 3, 8 and 11 are highlighted for visibility.

Congressional district boundaries were first effective for 2016.

N
W   E
S

Miles
0 10 20

Virginia may have been home to the capital of the Confederacy a century and a half ago, but in recent years, the commonwealth – and its political evolution – have been driven to a large degree by the increasingly diverse and government-focused suburbs of Washington D.C. Election by election, at the statewide level, Virginia has gradually shifted from reddish to purplish to bluish; by the 2016 presidential race, Virginia wasn't even considered among the highest-profile battleground states. A year later, Democrats made unexpectedly large gains in legislative elections, and in the 2018 midterms, the party ousted three Republican congressional incumbents. But in early 2019, the entire top echelon of Virginia Democrats was hit by simultaneous scandals of a racial or sexual nature.

What we now know as the United States originated in Virginia — in 1607, with the first permanent English settlement in North America at Jamestown. The colony had its struggles — with food, weather and Indians — but ultimately persevered, producing twin, contradictory legacies that shaped the nation: representative democracy and slavery. Virginia's capital moved to Williamsburg in 1699, becoming the locus of commercial, cultural and intellectual life of the colonial era, all the way through the American Revolution. In the early republic, Virginia was the leading state, with the largest population, the greatest wealth and the most illustrious political figures — a place that seemed destined to lead and shape a nation. From this tobacco-growing region emerged a group of leaders — George Washington, George Mason, Patrick Henry, Thomas Jefferson, George Wythe, Richard Henry Lee and James Madison — that in learning, wisdom and strength of character equaled any group from any polity since Periclean Athens or Republican Rome. The Virginia they led into the American Revolution was the indispensable creator of the republic and the Constitution that has held together the world's greatest democracy. But these men embodied ideals that were profoundly dichotomous. They were slaveholders who insisted on liberty, revolutionaries who insisted on the rule of law, and believers in racial inequality who set forth principles of equality that would, in time, form the basis of a society that rejected racism.

After the Revolutionary War, seven of the first dozen presidents hailed from Virginia. But in the first half of the 19th century, Virginia was eclipsed in population and wealth by Pennsylvania and New York. During the Civil War, Virginia had two great heroes, Robert E. Lee and Stonewall Jackson, but they fought for the commonwealth rather than the nation. In the process, many of Virginia's mountain counties broke off and joined the Union as the separate state of West Virginia. After the war, Virginia's leadership class was impoverished and embittered. Industrialization was haphazard. Railroads were constructed to ship cotton up from the South and coal east to the seaports. Textile mills were built in Southside towns and tobacco factories in Richmond. Railroad magnate Collis Huntington built the giant Newport News Shipbuilding & Drydock Co. Politically, Virginia was ruled by local gentry who worshipped their revolutionary past and mourned the "Lost Cause" of the Confederacy. They were pessimists, looking not for economic growth but for stability, bent on maintaining segregation and content with a second-class economy. County courthouse organizations were united in a Democratic political machine by Harry Byrd Sr., who ran Virginia politics from 1925, when he was elected governor, to 1965, when he retired from the Senate. In national politics, this machine lost battles more often than Lee lost on the battlefield. For years, the Byrd machine succeeded in keeping most vestiges of racial equality out of Virginia, to the point of closing public schools in Prince Edward County in the 1950s rather than obeying a federal court desegregation order. This "massive resistance" collapsed in the late 1950s. (In 2018, the fourth generation of politically active Byrds announced the sale of the Harrisonburg Daily News-Record, Winchester Star, and four weekly papers.)

Like the rest of the South, Virginia shifted toward Republicans, and suburban growth kept the party strong; Virginia would vote Republican for president from 1968 to 2004. But political change came in the form of a burgeoning federal workforce in the bedroom communities of Northern Virginia, along with workers in the industrial Hampton Roads region around Norfolk and Newport News. Over the decades, some of the counties in Northern Virginia ("NoVa") have become the nation's fastest-growing exurbs. Loudoun County has grown by 28 percent since the 2010 census, the fourth-highest rate among all counties with at least 200,000 people. Its D.C.-area neighbors – Prince William, Stafford and Arlington counties and the cities of Manassas, Manassas Park and Alexandria – each grew by between 13 percent and 22 percent over the same period. The city of Falls Church in the D.C. suburbs grew by 5.2 percent between 2016 and 2017 alone, more than any jurisdiction in the country with at least 10,000 residents. Further to the south, Hampton Roads grew out into swampy lands on either side of the James River and swelled due to a large military presence, while metropolitan Richmond, undeterred by the marginalization of tobacco, expanded outward, with places like New Kent County growing by 16.2 percent since 2010. Other jurisdictions also exceeded Virginia's overall growth rate of 6.7 percent, including Fredericksburg (20.3 percent), Harrisonburg (11.9 percent) and the university area of Charlottesville (10 percent). But "RoVa" (the "rest of Virginia") -- places like the Northern Neck, the two Eastern Shore counties, Southside Virginia, and the Shenandoah Valley – saw population, and in many cases the economy, stagnate. The mountains of Southwest Virginia suffered the most: Since 2010, the Appalachian counties of Bath, Buchanan, Dickenson, Tazewell and Wise have seen their populations decline by between 4.5 percent and 7.5 percent.

Virginia's population growth was accompanied by significant demographic change, especially in Northern Virginia. Statewide, the population is 19 percent black, 9 percent Hispanic and 6 percent Asian; both the black and Asian percentages ranked Virginia among the top 10 states in the nation. Virginia's immigrant population grew four times as fast as its native-born population from 2007 to 2015, the nonprofit Commonwealth Institute for Fiscal Analysis reported, with large communities of South Asians, Vietnamese, Koreans and Latinos. Virginia's northern suburbs saw the heaviest diversification. Prince William County is 22 percent Hispanic and 8 percent Asian; Fairfax County is 16 percent Hispanic and 19 percent Asian; and Loudoun County is 14 percent Hispanic and 17 percent Asian. Each of these jurisdictions was not just diverse but also affluent – Loudoun, Fairfax, Arlington, Stafford and Prince William counties and Falls Church and Fairfax cities all rank among the 20 highest-income counties in the country, thanks to the growth of the federal government and the relatively high wages and good benefits enjoyed by federal employees. Virginia ranks high in median income and educational attainment; it has the fifth-highest percentage of any state for residents with bachelor's degrees.

Growth and change produced unstable politics. In the 1970s, conservatives who left the Democratic Party and ran as independents or Republicans held Democrats at bay. In the 1980s, three moderate Democrats were elected governor — Charles Robb in 1981, Gerald Baliles in 1985 and Douglas Wilder in 1989. (Virginia is the last state that bars its governors from running for reelection, though they can run again after at least one term out of office.) The three Democratic governors did not attempt to impose a liberal agenda on an unwilling Virginia, instead arguing that government could be used effectively to improve education and build the commonwealth's economy. In the 1990s, Virginia split increasingly along ideological lines. George Allen, elected governor by a wide margin in 1993, was a Republican who believed in lower taxes and traditional cultural values. He leavened confrontational issue positions with a sunny temperament. Four years later, Republican James Gilmore made his centerpiece issue the phasing-out of the property tax on automobiles and won a 56%-43% victory. Republicans for the first time swept the top three statewide offices, and in the 1999 legislative elections Gilmore led Republicans to majorities in both chambers for the first time ever.

But the 21st century has tilted Virginia more toward the Democrats. Mark Warner won the governorship in 2001 after an intensive campaign in rural Virginia in which he paid attention to regions not blessed by 1990s growth. Warner carried Northern Virginia and the Hampton Roads area narrowly, but he also carried non-urban Virginia. Warner left office with high ratings and later became a senator.

Warner's success represented the first of several Democratic breakthroughs. While George W. Bush carried Northern Virginia in 2000, he lost it four years later, 51%-48%. The trend accelerated as Democrat Tim Kaine was elected governor in 2005 over Republican Jerry Kilgore, whose conservative stands were a tough sell in Northern Virginia as well as in suburban Richmond and Hampton Roads. Three years later, Barack Obama became the first Democratic presidential candidate to carry Virginia since 1964, and he did so by his national average of 53%-46%. A grateful Obama installed Kaine as Democratic National Committee chairman. Virginia politics zig-zagged back, at least temporarily, in 2009, amid dissatisfaction with Obama's agenda; Attorney General Bob McDonnell deemphasized cultural issues and ran instead as a job-creating candidate ready to tackle the recession. He won a smashing 59%-41% victory, the biggest margin for any Virginia governor since the last big victory of the Byrd machine in 1961. But 2009 proved to be the last year any Republican has won statewide. Virginia's relative prosperity — plus an extensive campaign organization with 60 offices, 20,000 volunteers, and 580,000 door knocks — enabled Obama to carry the commonwealth again in 2012, by the reduced margin of 51%-47%. After a money-and-influence scandal hobbled McDonnell, voters returned the governor's mansion to the Democrats, as national party fixer Terry McAuliffe defeated socially conservative attorney general Ken Cuccinelli. But voters continued to give Republicans a large margin in the state House and a narrow one in the state Senate.

In the 2016 presidential election, Clinton, with Kaine as her running mate, won Virginia by a slightly wider margin than Obama had in 2012. In Northern Virginia, such jurisdictions as Arlington, Fairfax, Loudoun and Prince William counties and the city of Alexandria pushed their winning margins by between five and 20 points in the Democrats' direction. The Richmond suburbs also moved toward the Democrats. Republicans have been "losing ethnic voters en masse" in recent elections, former Republican Rep. Tom Davis told the New York Times. "Vietnamese, Koreans used to be the backbone of my vote. They are very Republican in the way they live their lives, but I saw the immigration issue just turn it south." In August 2017, Virginia became a battleground when white nationalists and neo-Nazis converged on Charlottesville to protest the city's decision to remove a statue of Robert E. Lee. Torch-bearing marchers rallied on the University of Virginia campus at night, then, the following day, white nationalists clashed with anti-fascists downtown. Before the day was out, a 32-year-old counter-protester was dead and 19 others injured after a car driven by a white nationalist plowed into the crowd; two state troopers also died in a helicopter crash during the unrest.

In the 2017 elections, amid a backlash against President Donald Trump, Democrats fared even better than expected. The Democrats won the governorship, lieutenant governorship and the attorney general's office, and they came close to seizing control of the state House. (Control hinged on a tied race that was decided by drawing the winner's name from a bowl – a Republican, as it turned out.) The Democrats' gains were focused in suburban districts that had been turning bluer. One of the newly elected Democratic legislators, Danica Roem, ousted socially conservative, 13-term Del. Bob Marshall, becoming the first openly transgender candidate to be elected and serve as a state legislator in the country. The Democratic gains likely would have been larger had Republican legislative majorities not drawn such effective maps following the 2010 census: The Democrats won the cumulative vote for all delegate races by nine percentage points, yet they remained in the minority.

The strong Democratic showing at the ballot box paid policy dividends, as newly elected Gov. Ralph Northam persuaded enough Republicans to join him in enacting an expansion of Medicaid under the Affordable Care Act. Northam also enacted a proposal to provide dedicated funding for the D.C. area's Metro transit system – an idea that had long been a tough sell outside of Northern Virginia. Virginia Democrats had another good election season in 2018, as Kaine easily won reelection and Democratic challengers ousted three Republican incumbents in the House. But Northam didn't have long to celebrate. In early 2019, he inspired outrage on the right with comments that implied he supported infanticide for babies who survive an abortion. Soon after, it emerged that Northam's 1984 medical school yearbook page included a photograph of one man in blackface and another in a KKK outfit. Widespread outrage followed, especially after a disastrous press conference and equivocations about whether Northam was one of the people in the photos. But then two women accused Lt. Gov. Justin Fairfax of sexual assault and Attorney General Mark Herring volunteered that he had once appeared in blackface. This deflected some of the pressure from Northam, though it left Virginia and the Democratic Party with a bruised image. "Virginia is a state that for historical reasons has always imagined its political institutions and leaders as possessed of special virtue," wrote John Harris in Politico. "Now, they are known for uncommon vice."

Population		Race and Ethnicity		Income	
Total	8,365,952	White	62.6%	Median Income	$68,766
Land area (sq. miles)	39,490	Black	18.8%	State Income Rank	8
Pop/ sq mi	211.8	Latino	9.0%	Poverty Rate	11.2%
Born in state	49.3%	Asian	6.2%	With health insurance	90.1%
		Two or more races	2.9%	Cash public assistance	2.0%
Age Groups		Other	0.5%	Food stamp/SNAP	9.1%
Under 18	22.3%				
18-34	23.8%	Education		Work	
35-64	39.7%	H.S grad or less	35.3%	White Collar	43.3%
Over 64	14.2%	Some college	27.2%	Sales and Service	38.9%
		College Degree, 4 yr	21.5%	Blue Collar	17.8%
Military		Post grad	16.1%	Government	20.1%
Veteran/ Active Duty	12.5%				

Presidential Politics

2016 Primary (D)	Clinton (D)	504,791 (64%)	Sanders (D)	276,387 (35%)			
2016 Primary (R)	Trump (R)	356,896 (35%)	Rubio (R)	327,936 (32%)	Cruz (R)	171,162 (17%)	
	Kasich (R)	97,791 (10%)	Carson (R)	60,237 (6%)			
2016 Pres. Vote	Clinton (D)	1,981,473 (50%)	Trump (R)	1,769,443 (44%)	Johnson (L)	118,274 (3%)	
2012 Pres. Vote	Obama (D)	1,971,820 (51%)	Romney (R)	1,822,522 (47%)			

Long ignored in presidential politics, Virginia suddenly became a national bellwether in 2008 and 2012, when its 53%-46% and 51%-47% margins for Barack Obama were the same as those in the nation as a whole. With its diverse electorate, steady growth and urban-rural mix, Virginia is a battleground state reflective of the country. In the first half of the 20th century, it was part of the solid Democratic South. But from 1952 to 1960 it voted Republican, following the "golden silence" of Democratic Sen. Harry Byrd Sr., who declined to endorse presidential candidates, but quietly signaled his preference for the more fiscally conservative GOP standard bearers. It voted for Democrat Lyndon Johnson for president in 1964, then backed Republicans in the next 10 elections. But over time, the GOP margins narrowed. In 2008, Obama targeted Virginia from start to finish. His organizing efforts for the February primary gave him a head start when he defeated Hillary Clinton 64%-35%. Obama ran seven percentage points ahead of John Kerry in 2004 on his way to defeating John McCain. In 2012, Obama's margin over Mitt Romney was reduced, but patterns were similar. Close-in Northern Virginia D.C. suburbs voted heavily for Obama, and he narrowly carried the Northern Virginia exurbs. The vote was almost identical to 2008 in the Tidewater and metro Richmond, while Romney increased Republican margins in rural areas. Without Northern Virginia, Obama would have barely lost the state in 2012.

The growth and diversity of the Northern Virginia suburbs and exurbs will continue to make the region's voters a critical component of the Democratic coalition in the state. And while the area includes a Donald Trump golf club in Loudoun County, the Republican nominee was not a local favorite in 2016. Hillary Clinton defeated Trump 50%-44%, a margin that some believe shows the state will increasingly tilt Democratic in presidential races. That may be premature, but the Democrat tide in the suburbs is unmistakable. The immigrants, government employees, highly educated and young singles of the D.C. suburbs gave Clinton a 70%-27% advantage over Trump, better than either of Obama's margins. Clinton narrowly captured the Northern Virginia exurbs that stretch from wealthy Loudoun County to Frederick County on the border with West Virginia and south to Spotsylvania County, 49%-47%. She carried the central and eastern portions of the state that include Richmond and more rural counties with relatively high numbers of African-American voters. Sen. Tim Kaine, her running mate, was once the mayor of Richmond, and the suburban county that surrounds the city, Henrico, saw a jump in Democratic voting. Clinton won the Tidewater, 53%-43%, a bit under Obama's 57%-42% margin in 2012. The mostly rural western and central regions of the state were Trump country in 2016. He carried this area, 65%-32%. Indeed, the 15 Virginia counties that saw the greatest falloff from Obama in 2012 to Clinton were all in this region.

In the 2008 Democratic presidential primaries Obama captured the state the same day he won in neighboring Maryland and the District of Columbia, making him the clear frontrunner in the race. In the GOP competition, McCain defeated Mike Huckabee 50%-41. In 2012, the Republican primary was held on March 6. But only two candidates gathered the number of signatures required to get on the ballot; Romney beat Ron Paul 60%-40%. This was Paul's highest percentage in any 2012 primary. The 2016 primary was held on March 1, when both parties' nominations were up for grabs. The Republican contest saw Trump narrowly defeat Florida Sen. Marco Rubio, 33%-30%, in a record presidential primary turnout for either party of 1,025,617 votes. Texas Sen. Ted Cruz finished third with 17 percent. Rubio thrashed Trump in the close-in D.C. suburbs of Northern Virginia, 42%-23% and also defeated him in Loudoun and Prince William counties, the largest exurban tracts outside of Washington, foreshadowing a weakness that would become even more apparent in November. The Democratic primary was a one-sided affair in which Clinton reversed her 2008 fate and defeated Vermont Sen. Bernie Sanders, 64%-35%.

Congressional Districts

116th Congress Lineup	7D 4R	115th Congress Lineup	4D 7R

Despite above national average population growth, Virginia has failed to gain a seat in reapportionment since 1991 and the size of its delegation appeared unlikely to change in 2021. At the start of this decade, Virginia was a prime target for Democratic redistricters. Republicans had maximized their opportunities with creative map-drawing in a state that was leaning Democratic. Since then, Democrats have picked up four seats — through a combination of legal and election successes. And they might have additional opportunities.

Federal judges in 2016 ordered a mid-decade redrawing of lines following the relentless push by state Democrats, led by Gov. Terry McAuliffe, to seek court revision of the plan that had been enacted in 2011 by the Republican-controlled legislature and Gov. Bob McDonnell. That map had shored up incumbents in both parties, especially Republicans, and left the 8-3 GOP delegation — in a state whose statewide officials are all Democrats and Republican haven't won a presidential campaign since 2004. At the time, Democrats offered a competing plan converting Republican Rep. Randy Forbes' 4th District into a second minority-majority seat. The Senate Democrats' plan took on new life in October 2014, when a three-judge federal court panel ruled that the state's map was an unconstitutional violation of the 14th Amendment's civil rights protections. The court found that the legislature had improperly packed minorities into the 3rd District of Democratic Rep. Bobby Scott. After the Republican-controlled legislature was unwilling to make the sacrifice, Democrats persisted on court resolution. The judges agreed to a version of the Democrats' map, in which Petersburg and large parts of Richmond were moved to the 4th, and much of Forbes' base of Chesapeake was shifted to the 3rd District. Forbes concluded that he could not win his revised district. With little time to prepare, he ran in the revamped Virginia Beach-based 2nd District, which had none of his previous constituents. In the primary for an open seat, Forbes ran as an outsider against Del. Scott Taylor and fared poorly. In what became a missed opportunity for Democrats, Taylor won easily in November. The court's map made changes in the 1st and 7th Districts, but their Republican incumbents were unscathed. The remaining six districts in Virginia were untouched.

In 2018, the Republican collapse deepened. Three of their incumbents in suburban seats — Tidewater, the Richmond area and the Northern Virginia suburbs — succumbed to their own mistakes plus well-financed challengers who took advantage of divisions among the state's Republicans and hostility toward President Donald Trump. That left Democrats with 7-4 control of the delegation. The prospects for redistricting will be shaped significantly by whether those three Democrats survive in 2020 and whether Democrats in November 2019 finally crack the GOP's narrow majorities in each chamber of the state legislature. Another uncertainty is the role — and disposition — of federal judges, whose continued role seems inevitable. Whatever the dynamics, Democrats likely will retain control of at least three seats in Northern Virginia and one minority district in the Tidewater area; Republicans start with their two seats in the western part of the state. The shape and the outcome of the five remaining districts — from Tidewater to the center of the state -- likely will be up for grabs.

Ralph Northam (D)

Elected 2017, term expires 2022, 1st term; b. Sept. 13, 1959, Nassawadox; Virginia Military Institute, B.S., 1981; Eastern Virginia Medical School, M.D., 1984; Unknown; Married (Pam); 2 children.

Military Career: US Army, 1984-1992.

Elected Office: VA Senate, 2008-2014; VA Lt. Gov., 2014-2018.

Professional Career: Pediatric Neurologist, Children's Hospital of the King's Daughters.

Office: P.O. Box 1475, Richmond, 23218; 804-786-2211; Fax: 804-371-6351

Lt. Gov.: Justin Fairfax (D) **Atty. Gen:** Mark Herring (D)

State Legislature: Senate: 19D, 21R **House:** 49D, 51R

Election Results

Election	Name (Party)	Vote (%)
2017 General	Ralph Northam (D)	1,409,175 (54%)
	Ed Gillespie (R)	1,175,731 (45%)
2017 Primary	Ralph Northam (D)	303,846 (56%)
	Tom Periello (D)	239,505 (44%)

Ralph Northam, a low-key pediatric neurologist, rode a blue wave into the Virginia governorship in 2017. His victory was accompanied by significant Democratic gains in the state House, which enabled him to sign a Medicaid expansion bill, a policy goal that had eluded Northam's Democratic predecessor. However, his stature took a body blow when a 35-year-old medical school yearbook surfaced, showing a photograph on Northam's page that featured a pair of men in blackface and a KKK outfit.

Northam was born on Virginia's eastern shore, an isolated, tight-knit peninsula between Chesapeake Bay and the Atlantic Ocean – "a flat strip of farm fields and fishing villages, pine trees and crape myrtles and marsh grass," as The Washington Post described it. "When Northam was born in 1959, the area was connected to the rest of Virginia only by ferryboats; the 20-mile Chesapeake Bay Bridge-Tunnel linked the region to Norfolk in 1964." (The most recent governor from the eastern shore had served just before the Civil War.) Northam's father, Wescott, returned from World War II and earned a law degree, practicing locally and eventually serving as a prosecutor and a circuit court judge; his wife, Nancy, was a nurse. While still a teen, Northam worked on ferries and fishing charters. He attended Virginia Military Institute, where he served as president of the honor court, heading investigations into honor code violations that could result in expulsion. He earned his medical degree at Eastern Virginia Medical School and rose to the rank of major in the Army. His service included treating wounded soldiers from Operation Desert Storm who had been airlifted to Germany. After eight years in the Army, Northam practiced pediatric neurology and taught at his medical alma mater.

Northam was recruited to politics to challenge Nick Rerras, a Republican state senator in a district that spanned the eastern shore and portions of Hampton Roads. He won the 2007 race by eight points. In the Senate, Northam forged ties to Republicans – sometimes too much so for Democratic leaders' tastes – but also had a good relationship with Democratic Gov. Tim Kaine, who asked him to take a lead role on legislation to ban smoking in restaurants. Northam also worked against a transvaginal ultrasound mandate for women seeking abortions. In 2011, he won reelection to the state Senate.

Democratic gubernatorial candidate Terry McAuliffe recruited Northam to run for lieutenant governor in 2013, seeking geographical balance for the ticket. He easily beat Rev. E.W. Jackson, an outspoken social conservative, in November, and took office alongside McAuliffe and fellow Democrat Mark Herring, who won the race for attorney general. In office, McAuliffe moved to restore voting rights to some 200,000 convicted felons, but in a closely divided decision, the state Supreme Court overturned his action. Instead, he pursued restorations on a more piecemeal basis. Meanwhile, his repeated efforts to expand Medicaid under the Affordable Care Act were dashed by Republican majorities in the legislature.

With the Virginia governorship coming open every four years, Northam was considered the frontrunner for the Democratic nomination in 2017, but he faced a challenge from the left by former Rep. Tom Perriello. Northam, who counted most of the in-state Democratic establishment in his corner, moved to the left to compete with Perriello, who touted supportive words from Sens. Bernie Sanders and Elizabeth Warren. In addition to his reputation for bipartisanship, Northam had to explain his votes for George W. Bush in 2000 and 2004. But Northam got to Perriello's left on abortion and both candidates earned F ratings from the National Rifle Association. In an ad, Northam told primary voters that "I'm listening carefully to Donald Trump, and I think he's a narcissistic maniac." Northam, boosted by strong support from African Americans, beat Perriello 56%-44%. Meanwhile, in the GOP primary, Ed Gillespie – a Washington insider and lobbyist who made a surprisingly strong run at Democratic Sen. Mark Warner in 2014 – faced state Sen. Frank Wagner and Prince William County Board Chairman Corey Stewart. Gillespie was the clear establishment favorite against Stewart, who had loudly championed the preservation of Confederate statues, and the enactment of tough immigration policies, with a Trump-like swagger. Gillespie won – but only narrowly, 44%-43%, with Wagner taking 14 percent. Ominously for the GOP, Democrats cast 543,000 total votes in their primary, while Republicans cast 366,000.

In the general election, Northam backtracked from the "narcissistic maniac" rhetoric about Trump, but on most issues he took a progressive line. He supported a $15 minimum wage, driver's licenses for undocumented immigrants, a public option for health care (though not a single-payer system), free community college in certain fields of study and with a required year of public service, decriminalization of marijuana possession, and an assortment of gun control measures. Northam even joined in a protest at the National Rifle Association headquarters in Fairfax two weeks after the 2017 mass shooting in Las Vegas. (The gun group was airing ads for Gillespie and against Northam.)

Late in the campaign, Democrats fretted that Northam was running too quiet a campaign to break away, but in the end, he won easily, 54%-45%, much wider than McAuliffe's 2.5-percentage-point victory four years earlier. Aided by a surge in voting by white suburbanites angered by Trump, Northam managed to flip two counties that Republican Ken Cuccinelli had won four years earlier – Chesterfield, near Richmond, and Virginia Beach. Northam also extended McAuliffe's margins in the Richmond, Hampton Roads and Northern Virginia areas. In Northern Virginia's already blue Arlington, Loudoun, Prince William and Fairfax counties and the city of Alexandria, Northam increased his predecessor's margins by between eight and 15 points. Even more strikingly, Democrats nearly wiped out the GOP's 66-to-34 majority in the House, losing a shot at control only because of a tied outcome that was decided in favor of the GOP by drawing lots.

The Democratic gains in the legislature helped Northam deliver the Medicaid expansion that had eluded McAuliffe. He also vetoed a bill that would have kept cities from establishing sanctuary policies, an issue on which Northam had sent conflicting signals as a candidate, and he signed legislation to create a dedicated source of funding for the D.C. area's Metro transit system. "The blue wave is cresting in Virginia, and Northam is riding it very skillfully," longtime Virginia Commonwealth University political scientist Robert Holsworth told the Washington Post in January 2019.

But Northam would soon suffer a reversal of fortune. First, he drew the ire of anti-abortion advocates when he offered garbled remarks about a pending bill that would have eased the rules governing third-trimester abortions. Soon after, a conservative website published images of Northam's page in his 1984 medical school yearbook; it included a photograph of one man in blackface and another in a KKK costume. The reaction was immediate and viscerally negative, not least from most elected Democrats in Virginia, and was only compounded after Northam equivocated about whether he was one of the men in the picture and after he gave a peculiar press conference in which he acknowledged once wearing blackface to portray Michael Jackson in a dance contest, then seemed to consider an impromptu demonstration of a moonwalk before his wife urged him to move on. Northam's resignation seemed imminent – until the lieutenant governor, Justin Fairfax, was accused of two sexual assaults, and the attorney general, Mark Herring, acknowledged that he too had worn blackface at a college party. With the line of succession mired in controversy, Northam seemed likely to remain in office, although his stature took a big hit. He pledged to undertake efforts to better understand racial injustice throughout American history and offered to "take a harder line" on Confederate monuments. While Northam lowered his profile after the blackface scandal, he did veto a bill that would have allowed out-of-state residents to obtain a temporary concealed-carry permit if the state police did not finish reviewing an application in 90 days. He also redoubled efforts to pass other restrictions on gun rights, including universal background checks, a ban on certain types of semi-automatic weapons, and limits on the frequency of handgun purchases. It was unclear whether the Democratic officials' troubles would outweigh the party's overall gains in the commonwealth, particularly as every seat in the state House and Senate was on the line in 2019.

Mark Warner (D)

Elected 2008, term expires 2020, 2nd term, b. Dec 15, 1954; Indianapolis, IN; George Washington University (DC), B.A., 1977; Harvard University Law School (MA), J.D., 1980; Presbyterian; Married (Lisa Collis); 3 children.

Elected Office: VA Governor, 2002-2006.

Professional Career: Fundraiser, Democratic National Committee, 1980-1982; Venture capitalist, 1982-1989; Mng. Director, Columbia Capital Corporation, 1989-2001; Commonwealth Transportation Board, 1990-1994; Chairman, VA Democratic Party, 1993-1995; Chmn, Nat'l Governors Association, 2004-2005.

DC Office: 703 HSOB 20510, 202-224-2023, Fax: 202-224-6920, warner.senate.gov

State Offices: Abingdon, 276-628-8158; Norfolk, 757-441-3079; Richmond, 804-775-2314; Roanoke, 540-857-2676; Vienna, 703-442-0670.

Committees: Senate Democratic Conference Vice Chairman. *Banking, Housing & Urban Affairs*: Financial Institutions & Consumer Protection; National Security & International Trade & Finance (RMM); Securities, Insurance & Investment. *Budget. Finance*: Health Care; International Trade, Customs & Global Competitiveness; Taxation & IRS Oversight (RMM). *Intelligence (RMM). Rules & Administration.*

Group Ratings

	ADA	ACLU	AFL-CIO	LCV	ITI	COC	HAFA	ACU	CFG	FRC
2018	-	62%	-	100%	-	70%	5%	9%	5%	0%
2017	70%	C	100%	79%	C	29%	C	0%	4%	0%

Almanac Ratings 2017-18

	Economy	Social	Foreign	Composite
Liberal	90%	90%	20%	67%
Conservative	10%	10%	81%	33%

Key Votes of the 115th Congress

1. Obama-care revision	N	5. Gun regulations	N	9. Kavanaugh confirmation	N
2. Tax Cuts	N	6. Family planning regs	N	10. Saudi arms sales	N
3. Dodd-Frank revision	Y	7. Gorsuch confirmation	N	11. FISA rules	Y
4. Omnibus appropriations	Y	8. Immigration restrictions	N	12. Military aid in Yemen	Y

Election Results

Election	Name (Party)	Vote (%)		Cand. Spent	Ind. Exp. Support	Ind. Exp. Oppose
2014 General	Mark Warner (D)	1,073,667	(49%)	$18,114,108	$345,891	$321,800
	Ed Gillespie (R)	1,055,940	(48%)	$7,875,545	$486,890	$1,827,242
	Robert Sarvis (L)	53,102	(2%)	$84,949		
2014 Primary	Mark Warner (D)	Unopposed				

Prior winning percentages: 2008 (72%), Governor: 2001 (52%)

Democrat Mark Warner, Virginia's senior senator, is a former governor whose tenure in Richmond was widely seen as a template for fellow Democrats seeking ways to win and effectively govern in the states once a part of the Confederacy. Warner's success in his 2001-2005 gubernatorial tenure was such that many viewed him as a leading presidential contender in 2008, and he seriously considered running. But he instead ran for an open Senate seat that year and won by a 2-1 margin.

He has served since 2017 as the ranking Democrat on the Senate Intelligence Committee, including during its investigation of Russian efforts to influence the 2016 presidential election. Warner's close cooperation with the Republican chairman, Sen. Richard Burr of North Carolina, has been consistent with his approach to much of his Senate career — and a notable contrast to the partisan fireworks at the House Intelligence Committee.

Warner was born in Indianapolis, where his father was a safety evaluator for Aetna Life & Casualty Inc. The family moved to Connecticut when Warner was in the eighth grade. He graduated from The George Washington University, becoming the first college graduate in his family, and from Harvard Law School. Although he has emphasized his business experience in his campaigns, his first love appears to have been politics: Soon after graduating from law school in 1980, he took a job fundraising for the Democratic National Committee. In 1989, he managed Democrat Douglas Wilder's successful campaign to become the first African-American governor elected anywhere in the nation since Reconstruction.

Warner spent most of the 1980s and 1990s as a highly successful venture capitalist and gaining political contacts. While working for the DNC, Warner met then-Rep. Tom McMillen, a Maryland Democrat, who told him about the potential of cellphone markets just as the Reagan administration was about to award 1,500 free licenses for metropolitan markets. Warner cobbled together investor groups and packaged their applications in exchange for a fee and a 5 percent ownership stake if they received the licenses. The best-known of these ventures was Nextel, and Warner soon became wealthy. His average net worth in 2015 was estimated at $238 million, making him the third wealthiest member of Congress, according to an analysis of financial disclosure reports by the nonpartisan Center for Responsive Politics.

A political career remained very much on Warner's mind. From 1993 to 1995, he was Virginia Democratic Party chairman. In 1996, he ran against Republican Sen. John Warner (no relation) in what seemed a quixotic race: The incumbent Warner, elected narrowly in 1978, had won re-election in a landslide in 1984 and had no Democratic opponent in 1990. Mark Warner pitched his campaign not to his home turf in Northern Virginia, but to the Shenandoah Valley and southwest Virginia. He carried southwest Virginia but lost the part of the state outside the three big metropolitan areas by only 51%-49%, a considerable achievement for a Democrat. But John Warner's strength among moderates enabled him to carry Northern Virginia 55%-45% and to win Hampton Roads and metropolitan Richmond with smaller majorities. The result was a 52%-47% statewide win for John Warner. But it wasn't the end of upstart Mark Warner's electoral ambitions.

In the late 1990s, Mark Warner put millions of dollars into philanthropic efforts and set up regional business investment funds in Hampton Roads, Richmond, and Southside — the area south of Richmond — as well as southwest Virginia. By 1999, he had an eye on running for governor in 2001 as an entrepreneur who could bring savvy business methods to government. He picked a good year. Republican Gov. Jim Gilmore had helped elect Republican majorities in both houses of the Legislature, but then battled with them over the budget. Republicans had an intraparty fight over the gubernatorial nomination in 2001 between Lt. Gov. John Hager and Attorney General Mark Earley. After winning the nomination, Earley had little money and no clear strategy. Warner poured $5 million of his own money into his candidacy.

Warner lived in a mansion in Old Town Alexandria but avoided being typecast as an urban liberal. He characterized himself as a fiscal conservative and pledged not to raise income or sales taxes. Responding to complaints from traffic-choked Northern Virginia and Hampton Roads, he called for regional referendums on local sales tax increases for transportation. He opposed new gun control measures and wooed the National Rifle Association, which remained neutral in the contest. Warner ran ads featuring old pickups and bluegrass music, and he sponsored a local NASCAR team. He traveled to all parts of rural Virginia, much as Wilder had in 1989, to show he was in touch with everyday folks and to remind them of his investment funds and philanthropic initiatives.

Warner defeated Earley 52%-47%. He carried all major regions of the state, albeit by narrow margins. And he attracted notice from national Democrats for winning a Southern state through business-friendly, fiscally responsible policies combined with cultural conservatism — a combination Warner dubbed "radical centrism."

Once in office, Warner persuaded the Legislature to approve transportation tax referendums in Northern Virginia and Hampton Roads, but the House of Delegates rejected his education initiative in 2002. As a budget shortfall grew, Warner cut more than $850 million in spending and laid off 1,800 state employees. In November 2003, after the legislative elections and when Virginia seemed to be in danger of losing its AAA bond rating, Warner presented his new fiscal plan: a $1 billion tax increase, with increases in the income, sales, and cigarette taxes, and tax reductions for those with low incomes and in car and food taxes. In early 2004, his plan was rejected by the heavily Republican House of Delegates, which moved to increase taxes by just $520 million and provide few spending increases. But House Speaker William Howell was unable to hold his Republicans in line, and 17 of them abandoned their anti-tax positions. The Senate agreed to a $1.3 billion tax increase, more than Warner had requested, and the House went along, a major victory for the governor. By December 2004, the fiscal picture had changed: State government was facing a $1.2 billion surplus, and Warner called for more spending.

When John Warner in August 2007 announced his retirement from the Senate, Mark Warner's next move seemed obvious. He had no serious opposition for the Democratic nomination. On the Republican side, Gilmore, Warner's predecessor as governor, decided to run. At the 2008 Republican State Convention, he barely prevailed after being challenged from the right because of his support for abortion rights in some cases. It turned out not to be a seriously contested campaign. Warner argued Gilmore had left the state in poor fiscal shape and that he had turned things around as Gilmore's successor. Warner won 65%-34%, losing only two counties in the Shenandoah Valley, two exurban Richmond counties and two small independent cities. For the first time since 1970, Virginia had two Democratic senators.

In the Senate, Warner lamented the adjustment former governors face in becoming one of 100 senators. In 2013, he toyed with running again for governor, which he called "the best job I ever had," but opted against it. His driven and frenetic personality became a source of humor among his colleagues. In recounting his close working relationship with the laid-back Republican Saxby Chambliss of Georgia, Warner told reporters in 2013, "The way he starts each day is, 'Well, Mark, did you take your Ritalin today?'"

Warner's voting habits have put him in the political center. He supported President Barack Obama on the health care overhaul in 2009; during that debate, he led 11 freshman Democrats in proposing a series of amendments intended to control costs and boost accountability of the new program. He also backed the Budget Control Act of 2011 and other Obama administration efforts to raise the federal debt ceiling, but he joined Republicans in backing caps on discretionary spending.

Despite his "A" rating from the NRA, Warner said after the December 2012 Newtown, Connecticut, school massacre in which 27 were killed that "the status quo isn't acceptable" on guns. "There needs to be appropriate restrictions on these tools of mass-killing," he said. In April 2013, Warner joined most Democrats in backing a compromise measure — opposed by the NRA — to expand background checks on gun buyers. But he was among 15 Democrats to vote against an assault weapons ban and one of 10 Democrats to oppose a ban on high-capacity magazines. Warner took blowback from the party's liberal wing, as the president of MoveOn.org called Warner's votes on the latter issues "shameful." After the high school massacre in Parkland, Florida, he shifted and said he backed a ban on assault weapons. It might be impossible to reach "a perfect solution," he told The Virginian-Pilot, but "it's time for action."

As he frequently reached across the political aisle, Warner became best known for joining forces with Chambliss in leading the "Gang of Six." The group, consisting of three Republicans and three Democrats, came together in 2011 in the hopes of putting the recommendations of the bipartisan Simpson-Bowles deficit reduction commission into legislation.

By 2011, as the House and Senate faced an increase in the federal debt limit, the group had developed a $3.7 trillion deficit-reduction plan. Of that total, $2.7 trillion in cuts came from adjustments to Medicaid and Social Security. Meanwhile, federal revenues would be increased $1.1 trillion over 10 years through changes to tax deductions for home mortgage interest, charitable giving and health care insurance. But most Senate Republicans opposed any revenue increases. The Gang of Six proposal never became formal legislation, and the leadership of both parties paid the group scant attention. Warner repeatedly expressed frustration over his inability to get a deal. "In Washington there is no support group, or institutional structure, to support people doing the right thing," he told a 2012 gathering in Richmond.

Meanwhile, Warner won a seat on the Finance Committee in 2014, a plum assignment he had pursued for years. It provided him with an influential platform to pursue longtime interests in reforming the tax code and curbing entitlement spending. He worked closely with Republicans on the Senate Banking Committee to craft the bipartisan deal in 2018 that rolled back the Dodd-Frank financial regulatory law.

He retained his interest in the tech industry, occasionally raising tough questions. With Sens. Amy Klobuchar of Minnesota and John McCain of Arizona, Warner filed in 2017 legislation that would have forced social media companies to disclose who paid for online ads. "Americans deserve to know whether the ads they're seeing are generated by Americans or generated by foreign interests," he told reporters. In 2018, he circulated a white paper in which he wrote that he was "very annoyed" with Silicon Valley for its "pathetic" response to revelations of massive data breaches. "I was rubbed the wrong way by the arrogance of the technology companies and the presumption that they knew what was best for everyone," he told The Atlantic in October 2018.

After the 2010 elections, Warner was offered the chairmanship of the Democratic Senatorial Campaign Committee. His business connections made him a highly desirable candidate, but he turned down the post — which would have required him to become much more of a partisan. When Chuck Schumer of New York became Democratic leader in 2017, he named Warner and Elizabeth Warren of Massachusetts as vice chairs of the Democratic Caucus.

Warner came within 1 percentage point of losing re-election in 2014. He started the campaign as a prohibitive favorite, and polls as late as September showed him up by 20 points over his challenger, former Republican National Committee Chairman Ed Gillespie. By the end of the campaign, Warner had outspent Gillespie by 2-1, $15.7 million to $7.9 million. Warner's ad campaign attacked Gillespie, founder of a prominent Washington lobbying firm, for lobbying on behalf of Enron — the Texas-based energy firm that collapsed amid scandal in 2001. Gillespie in 2010 had helped found American Crossroads, an outside group that pumped millions into Republican campaigns around the country. But he was unable to attract the group's interest to his seemingly long-shot bid, and his own campaign couldn't afford to go on the air until October.

Two major factors conspired to almost do in Warner. First, Democratic turnout in 2014 was low nationwide — but especially low in Virginia. Warner was later criticized in Democratic circles for not getting his campaign up and running earlier in the cycle and for not doing more to turn out the vote, especially in Democratic areas such as Northern Virginia. Plus, Gillespie relentlessly tied Warner to Obama, pointing to a CQ Roll Call analysis that found Warner had voted with Obama 97 percent of the time. PolitiFact noted the 97 percent figure was based on just 419 of the 1,473 votes Warner had cast in the Senate. This line of attack proved potent. Obama's approval ratings had sunk to 40 percent after he carried the state in 2008 and 2012. Warner eked out a win by 49%-48%, a statewide margin of fewer than 18,000 votes.

Warner, who focused heavily during the campaign on the centrist, fiscally responsible persona he had developed during his time as governor, brushed aside suggestions that the election results were an indication his moderate stance no longer played well in an increasingly polarized state. "I'm going to continue to be bipartisan," he said. He attributed his close call to voters "grumpy" over congressional inaction and saying that "they want results." The voters, he added, were telling him: "'Warner, show us some more of being that change agent.' I'm taking that message to heart."

His big opportunity arrived in January 2017 when changes on the Intelligence Committee left Warner as the ranking Democrat as the panel became the Senate vehicle to investigate claims of Russian interference in the 2016 presidential election. As Warner told The New York Times, the investigation would be "probably the most important thing I've done in public life." After committee Chairman Burr — backed by Majority Leader Mitch McConnell — initially rejected demands for an inquiry, Warner organized committee Democrats to reverse his decision. With a combination of public and private pressures, Warner succeeded. As the investigation began, Warner seemed to have succeeded with his practice of bonding with a relatively pragmatic Republican senator. In this case, Warner and Burr were both mid-South white men of similar age and serious purpose. "We together, with the members of our committee, are going to get to the bottom of this," Warner told reporters in March 2017 at a news conference with Burr.

Following extensive closed-door investigation, the two committee leaders in May 2018 said that they agreed with the conclusion of the intelligence community that Russia had tried to influence the result of the election. "The Russian effort was extensive, sophisticated and ordered by President Putin himself for the purpose of helping Donald Trump," Warner said. In December, they issued a report with detailed analysis of Russia's disinformation campaign. Also in May, Warner showed some affinity with the CIA when he was one of six Democrats who voted to confirm Gina Haspel as its new director. Haspel — who had served 33 years with the CIA, mostly undercover — had been "straightforward and forthcoming" in their dealings, Warner said.

Warner seemed to have placed himself at the center of a complex international web of 21st century statecraft and competition. For the most part, he was careful to respect Burr's occasional caution with the challenges in their fact-finding. Still, he pursued some clues on his own, including his private meetings and exchanges with Russian oligarchs and others who had dealt with them. In February 2018, the conservative website Breitbart charged that Warner was responsible for "Democrat-Russian collusion."

As he prepared for his likely bid in 2020 to seek a third term in the Senate, Warner could draw confidence from the fact that Republicans had not won a statewide campaign in Virginia since 2009. But he remained mindful of his near-death experience in 2014. In the early maneuvering among Republicans, former Rep. Scott Taylor, who served one term from a Virginia Beach-based district before he was defeated in 2018, expressed some interest. Taylor's youth, background as a Navy SEAL and past campaigns in a political "swing" region could pose challenges to Warner, though Virginia's vote in the presidential election might prove at least as important to the outcome.

Tim Kaine (D)

Elected 2012, term expires 2024, 2nd term, b. Feb 26, 1958; St. Paul. MN, MN; University of Missouri, A.B., 1979; Harvard Law School (MA), J.D., 1983; Roman Catholic; Married (Anne Bright Holton); 3 children.

Elected Office: Richmond City Council, 1994-1998; Richmond Mayor, 1998-2001; VA Lt. Governor, 2002-2006; VA Governor, 2006-2010; Chairman, Democratic National Committee, 2009-2011.

Professional Career: Practicing attorney, 1983-2000; Lecturer, University of Richmond, 1987-1993, 2010-2012;

DC Office: 231 RSOB 20510, 202-224-4024, Fax: 202-228-6363, kaine.senate.gov

State Offices: Abingdon, 276-525-4790; Danville, 434-792-0976; Manassas, 703-361-3192; Richmond, 804-771-2221; Roanoke, 540-682-5693; Virginia Beach, 757-518-1674.

Committees: *Armed Services*: Readiness & Management Support (RMM); Seapower. *Budget. Foreign Relations*: Africa & Global Health Policy (RMM); Near East, South Asia, Central Asia & Counterterrorism; West Hem Crime Civ Sec Dem Rights & Women's Issues. *Health, Education, Labor & Pensions*: Children & Families; Primary Health & Retirement Security.

Group Ratings

	ADA	ACLU	AFL-CIO	LCV	ITI	COC	HAFA	ACU	CFG	FRC
2018	-	67%	-	100%	-	70%	5%	9%	5%	0%
2017	90%	C	100%	95%	C	29%	C	0%	4%	8%

Almanac Ratings 2017-18

	Economy	Social	Foreign	Composite
Liberal	97%	97%	61%	85%
Conservative	3%	3%	39%	15%

Key Votes of the 115th Congress

1. Obama-care revision	N	5. Gun regulations	N	9. Kavanaugh confirmation	N
2. Tax Cuts	N	6. Family planning regs	N	10. Saudi arms sales	Y
3. Dodd-Frank revision	Y	7. Gorsuch confirmation	N	11. FISA rules	N
4. Omnibus appropriations	Y	8. Immigration restrictions	N	12. Military aid in Yemen	Y

Election Results

Election	Name (Party)	Vote (%)		Cand. Spent	Ind. Exp. Support	Ind. Exp. Oppose
2018 General	Tim Kaine (D)	1,910,370	(57%)	$16,951,669	$108,120	$270,375
	Corey Stewart (R)	1,374,313	(41%)	$2,769,385	$39,676	$26,613
2018 Primary	Tim Kaine (D)		(100%)			

Prior winning percentages: 2012 (53%), Governor: 2005 (52%)

Democrat Tim Kaine, a former Virginia governor who was elected in 2012 as the state's junior senator, took a star turn in 2016 as his party's vice presidential nominee in a campaign that had seemed likely to cap his diverse career in local and national government and politics. Hillary Clinton's loss of that presidential campaign initially marked a retreat for Kaine, too. Kaine got his political career back on track in 2018 with an easy re-election against a Republican challenger who was out of sync with the changing politics in Virginia. The unorthodox governing style of President Donald Trump gave Kaine a more conventional foil for his continuing efforts to limit the president's authority to conduct military operations without authorization from Congress.

Born in St. Paul, Minnesota, Kaine grew up outside Kansas City. His father ran his own ironworking and welding shop, with Kaine and his younger brothers frequently helping. Kaine attended the University of Missouri, where he graduated in three years, before going to Harvard Law School. Midway through law school, Kaine left to spend nine months teaching at a Jesuit mission in Honduras. In a Washington Post interview three decades later, Kaine said of his time in Honduras: "It made a public servant out of me. ... And the Jesuits themselves kind of became my heroes." It also gave him fluency in Spanish. As the Senate debated a major immigration overhaul bill in 2013, Kaine became the first senator ever to deliver a floor speech entirely in Spanish. "I think people were probably surprised," Kaine told The New York Times afterward. "One of my people got a call by a Latino staffer in the House [who] said, 'I have waited 20 years to see this happen.'"

Kaine returned to Harvard to complete his law degree in 1983. It was there that he met his wife, Anne Holton, a daughter of Linwood Holton, Virginia's first Republican governor since Reconstruction. Anne Holton made national headlines as a child when her father, as governor from 1969-1973, ended the state's resistance to desegregation — and enrolled his children in Richmond's public schools, whose student population was largely African-American. For a time, Kaine worked for a federal judge in Macon, Georgia, while Holton was working for a federal judge in Richmond. They decided to marry and settle in Richmond. Kaine worked as a civil rights lawyer, specializing in representing those who had been denied housing because of race or disability. In 1994, he won a seat on the Richmond City Council and four years later was elected mayor. In 2001, he was elected lieutenant governor. Holton worked as a legal aid attorney before serving as a juvenile court judge; she stepped down as Virginia's secretary of education after Kaine became the Democratic vice presidential nominee.

Kaine ran for governor in 2005 against former state Attorney General Jerry Kilgore. Kaine, who held positions well to the left of Kilgore, pitched a quality-of-life agenda designed to appeal to urban and suburban voters. He emphasized tax relief for homeowners, a statewide pre-kindergarten initiative, a balanced approach to growth and new transportation solutions. Kilgore relied on hot-button issues such as the death penalty and illegal immigration, while dismissing Kaine as "too liberal for Virginia." In one Kilgore ad, a man whose son and daughter-in-law were murdered criticized Kaine for opposing the death penalty for "the worst mass murderer in modern times." Kaine said his opposition to capital punishment was based on religious convictions, and the issue gave him an opportunity to talk about his Catholic faith. Kaine emphasized that, despite his personal beliefs, he would allow executions as governor.

Kaine won 52%-46%, a victory powered by large margins in suburban Northern Virginia. In his first year, Kaine had some successes dealing with the Republican-controlled Legislature, including passage of a bill requiring rigorous teacher evaluations. Kaine did not stand in the way of four executions of death row inmates.

A year later, Kaine reached agreement with the Republican-controlled House and Senate on a $1 billion transportation bill, representing the state's biggest funding increase in two decades. Since Republicans would not agree to a significant statewide tax increase, the scheme called for borrowing up to $3 billion over 10 years and giving taxing powers to regional authorities in the two traffic-choked big metro areas, Northern Virginia and Hampton Roads. That plan was frustrated when the state Supreme Court ruled that the regional authorities couldn't raise taxes. In 2008, Kaine proposed $1.1 billion for transportation, with a penny sales tax increase in Northern Virginia and Hampton Roads. But House Republicans resisted it.

While Kaine was in Japan on a trade mission in April 2007, a Virginia Tech student opened fire on campus during classes, killing 32 people before killing himself. Kaine immediately flew home and won praise for his handling of the tragedy. Kaine in his last year in office reached agreement with House Speaker William Howell, a Republican, to ban smoking in bars and restaurants, but he failed to get the Legislature to agree to proposals for universal prekindergarten and background checks on sales at gun shows.

In February 2007, Kaine endorsed Barack Obama for the Democratic presidential nomination, the first governor to do so outside Obama's home state. He campaigned heavily for Obama in Virginia and helped him win one of his biggest primary victories there. He made Obama's list of potential vice presidential candidates. Named chairman of the Democratic National Committee in 2009, Kaine held the post until 2011.

When Democratic Sen. Jim Webb decided not to seek re-election in 2012 after serving just one term, Kaine entered the Senate race at the urging of Obama and other leading Democrats eager to find a high-profile challenger to George Allen. The son and namesake of a legendary football coach, Allen was first elected to the Senate in 2000. But he narrowly lost re-election in 2006 to Webb, after Allen sparked widespread controversy when he referred to an Indian-American aide to Webb — who had been assigned to tape Allen's public campaign appearances — with the racist term "macaca."

Kaine and Allen flooded the airwaves with ads. Kaine spent nearly $18 million; Allen spent $14.4 million. The outside group Crossroads GPS spent millions attacking Kaine, while Allen ridiculed him for accepting a position to head the DNC while still governor; Kaine criticized Allen for increased spending while in the Statehouse. Kaine hit Allen for past support of partial privatization of Social Security and then beat him 53%-47%. He said he is among roughly 20 people in U.S. history to have served as mayor, governor and senator.

Kaine was assigned to seats on the Foreign Relations and Armed Services committees. He focused on national security — and, specifically, the process for authorizing the United States to engage in military action. Kaine and Arizona Republican John McCain in 2014 introduced legislation to clarify the then-40-year-old War Powers Act — and the underlying question of the degree to which the president and Congress possess, or share, the power to initiate military action abroad. In 2016, Kaine said that it was hypocritical for the Obama administration to criticize Russia's invasion of Ukraine when it has put troops in Syria without authority. "We are carrying out escalating military operations in Syria without the permission and really even against the will of the sovereign nation," he told a Senate hearing.

In addition, Kaine has pushed repeatedly for a congressional debate and vote on a new authorization for U.S. military action against the Islamic State group. This stance put him at odds with Obama, who had asserted that an Authorization for Use of Military Force passed a week after 9/11 allowed for current U.S. military activities in and around Syria and Iraq. Kaine has contended that current military action against ISIS "goes well beyond the intent" of the 2001 AUMF. In June 2014, Kaine engaged Obama at the White House in what the senator later referred to as a "spirited discussion." Kaine is reported to have firmly told Obama that, if he intended to go to war, he would need Congress' permission, while the president — politely, but just as firmly — disagreed. Republican Jeff Flake of Arizona and Kaine advocated for an authorization for action against ISIS, but they failed.

Kaine told The New York Times in 2014 that his adamant position on this issue grew not only out of the large military presence in his home state, but also Virginia's place in the nation's founding. "They know I feel strongly about this because I'm a Virginian," Kaine said of the Obama White House. "Until we have a vote, and we live by that vote, I am going to keep pushing them hard."

Clinton's selection of Kaine as her running mate was well-received. But Kaine did not escape second-guessing. He did not excite liberal activists and his support for international trade deals did little to generate enthusiasm among blue-collar union members. Clinton based the selection, in part, on their compatibility and his preparation to do the job, She told PBS her decision showed that she was "afflicted with the responsibility gene." Kaine seemed to have little effect on the outcome of the electoral vote.

Kaine's persistent attack mode in the vice presidential debate was described by commentators as "over-caffeinated." He played the attack dog, especially against Republican presidential nominee Donald Trump. "A dark and twisted journey through the mind of Donald Trump [is] a very scary place to be," was an occasional attack line. But, like the Clinton campaign generally, he failed to convince battleground-state voters that Trump was an unacceptable choice or generate enthusiasm for the Democratic alternative. Kaine's Spanish speaking and experience in Latin America did not have a noticeable effect with Hispanic voters.

In the aftermath of the unexpected defeat, he may have become even more settled into the Senate. "I have a job to do here that in some ways may have gotten more important," Kaine told reporters when he returned to the Capitol a week after the election. "The Senate is playing more of the role of the adult in the room right now for the American government," he later told Politico.

Kaine resumed his quest to debate the use of military force, citing the new element of a president whose actions could be unpredictable or not fully explained. With Flake, he filed his resolution again. "We owe it to the American public to define the scope of the U.S. mission against terrorist organizations, including ISIS, and we owe it to our troops to show we're behind them in their mission," Kaine said in May 2017. The Republican-controlled Senate and House in 2017 and 2018 had little interest in taking on Trump. That changed after Democrats took over the House in 2019.

In a 2018 re-election campaign that turned out to be his easiest statewide contest, Kaine faced Corey Stewart, the Prince William County board chairman, whose right-wing populism and occasional demagoguery bore similarities to Trump's political style. He called himself "Trumpier than Trump." Even more than Trump, Stewart had problems unifying his party after a narrow primary win. The National Republican Senatorial Committee did not spend money on his behalf. Americans for Prosperity — the political arm of the Koch network — refused to endorse him, in part because of his hard-line opposition to immigration and international trade. Virginia Business, a statewide magazine that had not endorsed a candidate during its more than 30 years of publication, endorsed Kaine as "good for business."

In a campaign debate, Stewart criticized Kaine's record in the Senate. "He's had six years in the Senate, four of which were under a Democratic president, and he's got nothing done," Stewart said. Kaine cited his pragmatic and occasionally bipartisan approach and said that Trump had signed his bills dealing with career education and cybersecurity.

Stewart's challenge to Kaine never posed a serious threat. He spent only $2.8 million — far less than successful Democratic challengers for House seats in Virginia in 2018 — while Kaine spent $17 million. In the closing days, the incumbent focused much of his attention on aiding other Democratic candidates. Kaine won 57%-41%. In Stewart's home of Prince William County, Kaine won 65%-33%.

Kaine has said that he wants a lengthy career in the Senate, like Virginia Republican John Warner, who served for 30 years. For now, little seems to be standing in his way.

Rob Wittman (R)

Elected 2007, 6th full term, b. Feb 03, 1959; Washington, DC; Virginia Polytechnic Institute, B.S., 1981; University of North Carolina in Chapel Hill, M.PH, 1990; Virginia Commonwealth University, Ph.D., 2002; Episcopalian; Married (Kathryn Jane Sisson Wittman); 2 children; 4 grandchildren.

Elected Office: Montross Town Council, 1986-1996; Montross Mayor, 1992-1996; Westmoreland County Board of Supervisors, 1996-2005, chmn, 2004-2005; VA House, 2006-2007.

Professional Career: Environmental health specialist, VA health Department; Field Director, VA Health Department Div. of Shellfish Sanitation.

DC Office: 2055 RHOB 20515, 202-225-4261, Fax: 202-225-4382, wittman.house.gov

State Offices: Mechanicsville, 804-730-6595; Stafford, 540-659-2734; Tappahannock, 804-443-0668.

Committees: *Armed Services*: Seapower & Projection Forces (RMM); Tactical Air & Land Forces. *Natural Resources*: Water, Oceans & Wildlife.

Group Ratings

	ADA	ACLU	AFL-CIO	LCV	ITI	COC	HAFA	ACU	CFG	FRC
2018	-	11%	-	6%	-	83%	84%	92%	63%	100%
2017	0%	C	8%	3%	C	93%	C	89%	85%	100%

Almanac Ratings 2017-18

	Economy	Social	Foreign	Composite
Liberal	7%	7%	0%	5%
Conservative	93%	93%	100%	95%

Key Votes of the 115th Congress

1. Obama-care revision	Y	5. Family planning regs	Y
2. Tax Cuts	Y	6. Body cameras/immigration	N
3. Omnibus appropriations	Y	7. Abortion ban	Y
4. Dodd-Frank revision	Y	8. Concealed carry	Y

9. Guantanamo prisoners	N
10. Ground missiles, limit	N
11. Defense Dept. spending	Y
12. FISA rules	Y

Election Results

Election	Name (Party)	Vote (%)	Cand. Spent	Ind. Exp. Support	Ind. Exp. Oppose
2018 General	Rob Wittman (R)................................ 183,250	(55%)	$2,024,338	$1,104	
	Vangie Williams (D)......................... 148,464	(45%)	$307,440		$28,193
2018 Primary	Rob Wittman (R)..	(100%)			

Prior winning percentages: 2016 (60%), 2014 (63%), 2012 (56%), 2010 (64%), 2008 (57%), 2007 special (61%)

Republican Rob Wittman, who won the seat in a 2007 special election, has engaged on national security, with a focus that goes beyond the parochial concerns of his district. He combines military expertise with a professional interest in environmental protection, a pairing not often found among officials in either party. Wittman has gained growing influence in the House, especially on the Armed Services Committee, where he has worked to expand the Navy's fleet, including two new aircraft carriers. In 2018, he had his closest election ever, though it received less attention than the state's battleground districts.

Wittman was born in Washington D.C., and became a marine scientist. He has a Ph.D. in public policy and administration from Virginia Commonwealth University. Wittman served for many years as an environmental health specialist in the Northern Neck and Peninsula regions, including as field director for the state's shellfish sanitation division. His first public office was a seat on the Montross Town Council, where he served for 10 years, including four as mayor. In 1995, he began a decade on the Westmoreland County Board of Supervisors. In 2005, he was elected to the Virginia House of Delegates.

When the seat was vacant in 2007, after GOP Rep. Jo Ann Davis died of breast cancer, Republicans held a convention to choose their nominee. Wittman's chief opponent was Paul Jost, a businessman and anti-tax activist. Wittman cited his experience in public office and "the basics of good government." With help from several busloads of supporters, Jost led in early balloting, which began with 11 candidates. The key moment came after five ballots, when Davis' widower, Chuck Davis, threw his support to Wittman. Democratic nominee Philip Forgit, a school teacher and Navy reservist who won a Bronze Star in Iraq, described himself as a centrist. Wittman emphasized his conservative credentials, including his support for gun rights and opposition to abortion. Democrats paid little attention to the contest, and Wittman won 61%-37%.

Wittman got a seat on the Armed Services and Natural Resources committees. He usually sticks with Republicans on major issues but is not an automatic vote. Coming from a district with a large government presence, he is less enamored of eliminating federal programs and dramatically reducing spending than are other conservatives.

Wittman has worked with lawmakers in both parties on efforts to clean up Chesapeake Bay. In March 2019, he joined Democratic Reps. Elaine Luria and Bobby Scott to call for $455 million for pollution control in the bay and assistance to states in the watershed to manage their runoffs into its tributaries. Congress has not formally authorized the cleanup program since 2005. An advocate of an "all of the above" approach to energy resources, he has supported off-shore drilling.

Wittman has had key position on the Armed Services Committee. As chairman of the Oversight and Investigations Subcommittee in 2011, he delved into a management scandal at Arlington National Cemetery, where an Army report found mismarked graves and numerous other problems. In 2013, he became chairman of the Readiness Subcommittee. As co-chair of the Congressional Shipbuilding Caucus, he aggressively advocates expanding the fleet and he has maintained that it is more critical than ever for the military to project power around the world.

Republican Rep. Randy Forbes of Virginia lost re-election following the redistricting changes in 2016, conveniently opening for Wittman the chairmanship of the Seapower and Projection Forces Subcommittee. He grabbed that opportunity, a vital position for the extensive ship-building interests of Virginia. "As chairman, I will have the opportunity to serve both our nation and the commonwealth of Virginia, and I am committed to ensuring that our military remains the greatest fighting force the world has ever known," Wittman said.

He has made the most of the opportunity. That chairmanship was all the more attractive because of the support from President Donald Trump to expand the Navy from its roughly 285 ships to 355 ships. Wittman enthusiastically embraced that ambitious long-term objective, which could require at least 30 years to achieve, not least because Hampton Roads is home to the world's largest naval base and the headquarters for Huntington Ingalls Industries, the largest U.S. military shipbuilder.

As an immediate priority, Wittman worked in the House and with the Trump administration to win approval of two new aircraft carriers, which were part of the defense spending bill that was enacted in December 2018. When Trump's budget in March 2019 called for an early decommissioning of one of the current 12 carriers, Wittman strongly objected, calling the proposal "strategically and fiscally irresponsible."

Wittman has not been seriously threatened for reelection. In a state that has not elected a Republican statewide since 2009, he explored but then rejected possible runs for governor and the Senate in 2017 and 2018. In 2018, Wittman had his most competitive House contest. Democratic challenger Vangie Williams, who was a strategic planner with a government contractor and filed for bankruptcy years earlier because of a sick child's medical bills, proposed a "Medicare for all" system. Wittman outspent her $2 million to $307,000, but was held to a 55%-45% win — his lowest congressional vote. In a strongly Democratic year in Virginia, Williams led by nearly 10,000 votes in Prince William County — a potentially ominous implication for Wittman if Democrats control the next redistricting. Still, if he retains his hold on the district, Wittman is young enough and respected enough that he eventually could be positioned to be the top Republican on one of his two committees, especially now that his statewide plans have been curtailed.

VA-1: Eastern Virginia   **Cook Partisan Voting Index: R+8**

Population		Race and Ethnicity		Income	
Total	776,151	White	67.6%	Median Income	$83,367
Land area (sq. miles)	4,212	Black	16.1%	District Income Rank	43
Pop/ sq mi	184.3	Latino	9.3%	Poverty Rate	7.2%
Born in State	49.5%	Asian	3.1%	With health insurance	91.6%
		Two or more races	3.4%	Cash public assistance	1.3%
Age Groups		Other	0.6%	Food stamp/SNAP	6.4%
Under 18	24.1%				
18-34	20.8%	**Education**		**Work**	
35-64	41%	H.S grad or less	34.6%	White Collar	14.1%
Over 64	14.1%	Some college	29.8%	Sales and Service	39.5%
		College Degree, 4 yr	21.8%	Blue Collar	17.7%
Military		Post grad	13.9%	Government	23.4%
Veteran/ Active Duty	15.6%				

2012 Pres. Vote	Romney	206,220	(55%)	Obama	161,539	(43%)			
2016 Pres. Vote	Trump	210,618	(53%)	Clinton	161,476	(41%)	Johnson	12,298	(3%)

DC and Richmond Exurbs: When the English first sailed up the estuaries that flow into Chesapeake Bay, they were searching for gold. But they couldn't help noticing that the spot where the James River fed into the bay, now Hampton Roads, was a fine natural harbor with calm, deep water and good anchorages. So, some of them stayed and established communities farther up the river that achieved not only the high craftsmanship of Williamsburg, but endured the pitiless hardship of Jamestown and other early settlements. Tidewater Virginia brought slavery to America and tobacco to the world, and slave-raised tobacco was the center of its economy in the colonial era and in the years afterward. Today, more than 1.7 million people live in the area. Because of the heavy military presence, it's a population collected from all over the country. Like most of Northern Virginia, it has less of a southern atmosphere than other regions of the Old Dominion.

About half the population of the 1st Congressional District of Virginia lives south and east of Fredericksburg, the unofficial southern terminus of Northern Virginia. Most of the major Hampton Roads military installations are in surrounding congressional districts. But the 1st remains steeped in military culture, and the Department of Defense and NASA are significant employers. In Caroline County, Fort A.P. Hill serves as a training site for active and reserve-component units. Not far from there is the Naval Surface Warfare Center in Dahlgren, located on the Potomac River, originally established as the Navy's main proving ground for large-caliber guns.

The other half of the district's population lives in the southern reaches of exurban Washington D.C., effectively making its representative the fourth member of Congress from Northern Virginia. This part has become a political swing area, with Fredericksburg, Stafford County and portions of

Prince William and Fauquier counties. Prince William and Stafford remain the two largest counties in the district. They comprise nearly 40 percent of the population. Prince William, smaller parts of which are in two suburban Washington districts, has grown 63 percent between 2000 and 2017; it surpassed Virginia Beach in population and is the second-largest locality in Virginia, behind Fairfax County. Stafford County, which is more rural and 42 miles from Washington, also is rapidly growing, with a 57 percent increase during that time; projections are that it will more than double between 2015 and 2040. The district has a large military presence here as well, including the Quantico Marine Corps base. With drivers in this area suffering some of the worst commutes in the nation, Virginia transportation officials have prepared plans to upgrade the rail line, including additional tracks, between Richmond and Washington to reduce the time along that route by about an hour; at a cost of more than $1 billion, the changes could be completed by 2025. With its military population and growing retirement communities, the 1st has been reliably Republican in most elections and is the most Republican district in Tidewater. Donald Trump won 53 percent of the vote.

Elaine Luria (D)

Elected 2018, 1st term, b. Aug 15, 1975; Birmingham, AL; U.S. Naval Academy (MD), B.S., 1997; Old Dominion University (VA), M.E.M., 2004; Jewish; Married (Bob Blondin); 1 child ; 2 stepchildren.

Military Career: U.S. Navy 1997-2017

DC Office: 534 CHOB 20515, 202-225-4215, luria.house.gov

State Offices: Onley, 757-364-7631; Virginia Beach, 757-364-7650.

Committees: *Armed Services*: Military Personnel; Seapower & Projection Forces. *Veterans' Affairs*: Disability Assistance & Memorial Affairs (Chmn); Economic Opportunity.

Election Results

Election	Name (Party)	Vote (%)		Cand. Spent	Ind. Exp. Support	Ind. Exp. Oppose
2018 General	Elaine Luria (D)............................	139,571	(51%)	$4,227,293	$1,351,251	$1,974,994
	Scott Taylor (R).................................	133,458	(49%)	$4,011,273	$643,560	$3,431,876
2018 Primary	Elaine Luria (D)............................	17,552	(62%)			
	Karen Mallard (D)...............................	10,610	(38%)			

Freshman Elaine Luria was among several Democratic newcomers with extensive military experience. She was an officer and nuclear engineer in the U.S. Navy, which has a major presence in her district. Luria was one of three Democratic women in 2018 who ousted Republican incumbents in suburban Virginia districts. She defeated Rep. Scott Taylor, who also had a lengthy career in the Navy. He became enmeshed during the campaign in an investigation of the filing papers of an independent candidate.

A native of Birmingham Alabama, Luria graduated from the Naval Academy, where she majored in physics and history. She later received a master's degree in engineering management from Old Dominion University. Luria was trained as an officer in the surface warfare division and in Tomahawk land-attack missile launch.

During her 20-year Navy career, Luria was deployed on numerous vessels, including aircraft carriers. Much of that time was in the Middle East and western Pacific, including for support of operations in Iraq and Afghanistan. As an engineer, she operated nuclear reactors to conduct air operations. In the private sector, she started a business, Mermaid Factory, with two local shops that sold clay souvenirs of aquatic symbols. Her husband, Robert Blondin, is a retired Navy commander.

In the Democratic primary, Luria faced Karen Mallard, a school teacher who was a progressive advocate for organized labor. With early support from the Democratic Congressional Campaign Committee, which drew complaints from Mallard, Luria had a big fundraising advantage and won, 62%-38%.

Taylor, a retired Navy Seal sniper, was severely injured while on a combat mission in Iraq. He was elected in 2016, when he defeated Rep. Randy Forbes — a senior member of the Armed Services Committee — in a district that was redrawn by major redistricting changes. He easily defeated Democrat Shaun Brown, a business consultant who had lost several previous local campaigns. (Luria said that she voted in both contests for Taylor, a fellow Navy officer.) In the House, Taylor supported key Republican legislation. He occasionally showed independence from President Donald Trump, including objecting to his call to freeze federal salaries and his management of environmental issues such as off-shore drilling and clean-up of Chesapeake Bay.

In 2018, Taylor ran into problems when his campaign aides forged signatures on petitions for Shaun Brown to run as an independent against Taylor and Luria. Given her background, her candidacy likely would draw votes chiefly from Luria. Following an investigation by a special prosecutor, a local judge ordered Brown's name removed from the ballot because of what he termed "out-and-out fraud."

Taylor, who said that he fired the aides, maintained that he was aware of their assistance for Brown but that he knew nothing about their illegal actions. In a separate case days before the election, Brown was convicted of fraud in mishandling funds for a federal nutrition program for needy children.

In a campaign debate, Taylor contended that he had delivered on his campaign promises from 2016, when Luria voted for him. Luria said that his vote to repeal the Affordable Care Act ran counter to his promises. She cited the flap over Brown's candidacy to question Taylor's honesty. Each candidate spent more than $4 million and the national parties spent an additional $7 million. Citing Taylor's handling of the ballot controversy, The Virginian-Pilot endorsed Luria.

Luria won, 51%-49%. She took 51 percent of the vote in Virginia Beach, which cast about 60 percent of the vote. Taylor got 55 percent in York County, the next-largest locality in the district. Luria led in most other areas. Close results in other recent elections have shown that this is a swing district.

VA-2: Hampton Roads   Cook Partisan Voting Index: R+3

Population		Race and Ethnicity		Income	
Total	738,962	White	63.2%	Median Income	$66,487
Land area (sq. miles)	1,109	Black	19.4%	District Income Rank	122
Pop/ sq mi	666.5	Latino	7.7%	Poverty Rate	9.7%
Born in State	41.7%	Asian	5.3%	With health insurance	90.4%
		Two or more races	3.9%	Cash public assistance	1.6%
Age Groups		Other	0.5%	Food stamp/SNAP	7.7%
Under 18	21.8%				
18-34	27.3%	Education		Work	
35-64	37.3%	H.S grad or less	31%	White Collar	13.6%
Over 64	13.6%	Some college	34.9%	Sales and Service	41.8%
		College Degree, 4 yr	21.2%	Blue Collar	18.6%
Military		Post grad	12.9%	Government	22.1%
Veteran/ Active Duty	25.7%				

2012 Pres. Vote	Romney	162,384	(50%)	Obama	154,633	(48%)		
2016 Pres. Vote	Trump	158,067	(48%)	Clinton	147,217	(45%)	Johnson	12,379 (4%)

Virginia Beach, Colonial Virginia: Virginia Beach, once a sleepy beach resort, is now the state's largest city, with 450,000 people. It began attracting tourists when rail service to Norfolk began in 1883. Since then, it has become the anchor to a metropolitan area of 1.7 million people that is centered on the local Navy community -- active duty and civilian personnel, dependents, retirees and workers at the Newport News Shipyard. Virginia Beach also is home to the headquarters of the Christian Broadcasting Network, which produces The 700 Club and features evangelist Pat Robertson, the son of former Democratic Sen. A. Willis Robertson of Virginia. The city has a growing industrial base, including a large power tool plant of the German-based Stihl company. Like Norfolk, Virginia Beach is infused with military culture. The city is the base of East Coast Navy SEAL teams; these elite commandos endure punishing training, and they took on some of the military's most secretive and daring missions in Iraq and Afghanistan, including participating in the Pakistan compound raid that killed Osama bin Laden in 2011. A monument in tribute to the SEALs was dedicated in July 2017. The boardwalk helped Virginia Beach to attract a record 19 million visitors that year.

Military history of a different sort is commemorated in Yorktown, site of the decisive battle of the Revolutionary War in 1781, which is adjacent to a naval weapons station on the banks of the York River. Not far away is Williamsburg, where major parts have been restored to look as they did in colonial times; actors play the roles of colonists, which is a major tourist draw. Also in Williamsburg is the College of William & Mary, America's second-oldest college. Jamestown, with the nation's first permanent settlement, is the third leg of what has been called the "Historic Triangle." Another historic site, on a spit of land in Chesapeake Bay, is Fort Monroe, where Jefferson Davis was confined after the Civil War.

The 2nd Congressional District of Virginia includes all of Virginia Beach, plus several small cities on thin stretches of land that Virginians refer to as necks (peninsulas to outsiders). Across the Chesapeake Bay Bridge-Tunnel, the district transforms into a more placid area, including the two Virginia counties of the Delmarva Peninsula, site of the annual roundup of wild Chincoteague ponies in the national wildlife refuge. Dominion Resources operates in Accomack County what has been promoted as the largest solar power facility on the East Coast. More than 60 percent of the district's population is in Virginia Beach, and it has narrowly leaned Republican. In 2016, Donald Trump had a similar narrow lead, 48%-45%.

Bobby Scott (D)

Elected 1992, 14th term, b. Apr 30, 1947; Washington, DC; Harvard University, B.A., 1969; Boston College Law School (MA), J.D., 1973; Episcopalian; Divorced.

Military Career: U.S. Army Reserve 1970-1976; MA National Guard 1974-1976

Elected Office: VA House, 1978-1983; VA Senate, 1983-1993.

Professional Career: Practicing attorney, 1973-1991.

DC Office: 1201 LHOB 20515, 202-225-8351, Fax: 202-225-8354, bobbyscott.house.gov

State Offices: Newport News, 757-380-1000.

Committees: *Budget. Education & Labor (Chmn):* Health, Employment, Labor & Pensions.

Group Ratings

	ADA	ACLU	AFL-CIO	LCV	ITI	COC	HAFA	ACU	CFG	FRC
2018	-	93%	-	94%	-	58%	6%	4%	8%	0%
2017	95%	C	97%	100%	C	36%	C	4%	5%	0%

Almanac Ratings 2017-18

	Economy	Social	Foreign	Composite
Liberal	97%	100%	95%	97%
Conservative	3%	0%	5%	3%

Key Votes of the 115th Congress

1. Obama-care revision	N	5. Family planning regs	N	9. Guantanamo prisoners	Y
2. Tax Cuts	N	6. Body cameras/immigration	Y	10. Ground missiles, limit	Y
3. Omnibus appropriations	Y	7. Abortion ban	N	11. Defense Dept. spending	Y
4. Dodd-Frank revision	N	8. Concealed carry	N	12. FISA rules	N

Election Results

Election	Name (Party)	Vote (%)	Cand. Spent	Ind. Exp. Support	Ind. Exp. Oppose
2018 General	Bobby Scott (D)..................................	198,615 (91%)	$310,697		
2018 Primary	Bobby Scott (D)..................................	(100%)			

Prior winning percentages: 2016 (67%), 2014 (94%), 2012 (81%), 2010 (70%), 2008 (97%), 2006 (96%), 2004 (69%), 2002 (96%), 2000 (98%), 1998 (76%), 1996 (82%), 1994 (79%), 1992 (79%)

Democrat Bobby Scott, first elected in 1992, has been an influential civil libertarian, an intellectual force in the Congressional Black Caucus and an important figure in Virginia politics. In 2019, he became chairman of the House Education and Labor Committee, where he promised to uphold the party's "core values" by "advancing equity in education, expanding access to affordable health care [and] ensuring workers have a safe workplace." This new influence followed disappointment in 2016, when the prospect that Sen. Tim Kaine would be elected vice president fueled widespread speculation that Scott would gain new prominence as his Senate successor.

Scott grew up in Newport News, the son of a doctor. He got his bachelor's at Harvard University, where he was a classmate of Al Gore, and his law degree at Boston College. He served in the National Guard and Army Reserve and returned home to practice law. In 1977, he was elected to the House of Delegates, and later to the state Senate, representing a multiracial district in a community that had been shaped by the military tradition of integration.

In 1986, he ran a credible race for Congress and lost to Republican Rep. Herb Bateman, 56%-44%. In 1992, with his base in a new district that had been redrawn to have an African-American majority, Scott won the Democratic primary with 67 percent of the vote against two Richmond-based candidates. He easily won the general election to become the first African-American elected from Virginia since 1891. He has been reelected by overwhelming margins, with occasional changes in his district lines.

Scott has a solidly liberal voting record. His Almanac vote ratings have placed him among the most liberal House members, especially on social issues. As an outspoken civil libertarian on the Judiciary Committee, he raised First Amendment objections when bipartisan coalitions in 2012 passed legislation to permit states to display the Ten Commandments in schools or government buildings. After the September 11 attacks, he opposed the USA Patriot Act, the anti-terrorism law, arguing that it might promote racial profiling.

After the Newtown Connecticut elementary school massacre in 2012, Minority Leader Nancy Pelosi named Scott vice chair of the Democrats' gun-violence prevention task force. One of his legislative successes was the bipartisan Death in Custody Reporting Act, which requires states to report deaths of arrestees and prisoners. Also in 2010, he enacted the Fair Sentencing Act to narrow the discrepancies between sentences for powder and crack cocaine, an issue he had long contended led to blacks receiving disproportionately longer sentences.

Scott has been a fervent advocate of boosting funding to reduce juvenile crime. In 2016, he gained House passage of a bipartisan bill to upgrade juvenile justice programs and end what Scott called the "school-to-prison pipeline." He worked with Republicans to reduce certain mandatory drug sentences, restore judicial discretion in sentencing for some offenses, and promote alternatives to incarceration. He played a leading role in reducing national security collection of telephone metadata records, as part of a revision of the Patriot Act in 2015.

On the Education and Labor Committee, Scott has combined his longtime interest in K-12 education with a special focus on equity. In 2015, he was among the four lawmakers chiefly responsible for rewriting the No Child Left Behind education law, which Scott had contended was outdated. Despite his initial objections to Republican alternatives, he praised the final version of the Every Student Succeeds Act as "the embodiment of what we can do when we work together in Washington -- a workable compromise that does not force either side to desert its core beliefs." In a February 2017 speech at the University of Virginia, he discussed his efforts to bridge the partisan divide during what he called a "difficult" moment in Congress.

When he moved up as chairman after Democrats regained House control in 2019, Scott said his priorities included funds for school construction and renovation, steps to promote school safety, and a revival of the higher education bill that the previous Congress ad deadlocked on, including increased affordability. He planned a review of the new education law to assure that states have "a credible plan" to address achievement gaps. Scott was largely dismissive of Trump administration policies. The logic behind its proposal to merge the Education and Labor departments was "painfully thin," he said.

Scott has taken a leadership role on issues that go beyond his committee work. In 2007, he joined with then-Sens. Barack Obama of Illinois and Joe Biden of Delaware in pushing legislation to compensate black farmers who had been victims of government discrimination; the bill was enacted in 2010. Scott has been the prime sponsor of the CBC's alternative budget plan to phase out tax cuts for upper-income taxpayers and finance more spending on domestic programs. The House has routinely defeated his annual proposal. In December 2017, he strongly denied the claim by a former aide to the Congressional Black Caucus Foundation that he had touched her inappropriately four years earlier.

Scott has hosted an annual Labor Day picnic that has become a required stop for Democratic candidates for state and federal office. He used the 2011 picnic to announce that he wouldn't run for retiring Democrat Jim Webb's Senate seat, clearing the way for former Gov. Kaine to get the nomination. At the 2016 picnic, guests enthusiastically speculated that Scott would be the front-runner for Gov. Terry McAuliffe's appointment to succeed Kaine. He did not object. Privately, some Democrats worried that Scott would have been too liberal and unknown outside his district to win statewide. That became a moot point.

In the redistricting litigation over the Republican-drawn congressional map in 2016, he kept a behind-the-scenes role in encouraging a second district in the Tidewater area with a substantial minority presence. That ultimately removed from his district many African-American locales. Scott has become stronger politically, as Democrats have gained seats elsewhere in the Old Dominion and as he became one of five African-Americans chairing a House committee.

VA-3: Tidewater

Cook Partisan Voting Index: D+16

Population		Race and Ethnicity		Income	
Total	738,417	White	42%	Median Income	$52,131
Land area (sq. miles)	627	Black	45.5%	District Income Rank	268
Pop/ sq mi	1178.6	Latino	6.1%	Poverty Rate	16.7%
Born in State	55.9%	Asian	2.5%	With health insurance	88.8%
		Two or more races	3.2%	Cash public assistance	3%
Age Groups		Other	0.7%	Food stamp/SNAP	14.4%
Under 18	22.7%				
18-34	28.2%	**Education**		**Work**	
35-64	36.3%	H.S grad or less	39.2%	White Collar	12.8%
Over 64	12.8%	Some college	35.1%	Sales and Service	43.4%
		College Degree, 4 yr	15.8%	Blue Collar	22.4%
Military		Post grad	10%	Government	21.9%
Veteran/ Active Duty	19.2%				

2012 Pres. Vote	Obama	227,574	(67%)	Romney	105,946	(31%)		
2016 Pres. Vote	Clinton	205,746	(63%)	Trump	103,064	(32%)	Johnson	9,072 (3%)

Newport News, Norfolk: The U.S. Navy Atlantic fleet berthed in its home port of Norfolk is one of the most awe-inspiring sights in America, or anywhere. Norfolk has been a Navy port since 1801 and has long been recognized as having one of the best natural harbors on the East Coast, one that never freezes, has a channel 50 feet deep, and is within 750 miles of three-quarters of U.S. manufacturing capacity. The Norfolk Naval Station is the world's largest naval base, situated on 4,300 acres on Sewell's Point. Almost a quarter of the nation's uniformed military personnel are stationed in the Hampton Roads area, and the aggregation of destructive power in the line of towering gray ships is probably greater than in any other single port.

Once a small city, Norfolk is now part of a metropolitan area of 1.7 million people, anchored by Virginia Beach. The local Navy community — active duty and civilian personnel, dependents, retirees, and workers at the Newport News Shipyard — is estimated at more than 300,000, and military spending pours some $11 billion annually into the local economy. The shipyard, a division of Huntington Ingalls Industries, and Virginia's largest industrial employer, increased in 2017 to 23,000 workers, a rebound from recent job losses that were chiefly the result of military spending cutbacks in Washington. It expected to add at least 2,000 workers by 2022, given the Pentagon's budget for new ships. Work was underway with Electric Boat in Groton Connecticut on the new Columbia class nuclear submarines that will replace the Navy's Ohio-class subs. The Newport News yard is the only manufacturer of nuclear-powered aircraft carriers. In 2018, Congress approved spending for two new carriers.

The 3rd Congressional District of Virginia includes all of the majority-black city of Portsmouth, a Navy port and industrial town with a charming old section. It travels up the James River to the communities of Norfolk and Newport News, which form its population centers. In December 2018, Norfolk Southern — a Fortune 500 company — announced that it was moving its headquarters to Atlanta; two years earlier, the state had subsidized the rail company to assist in moving many of its jobs from Roanoke. The district takes in areas with high concentrations of white liberals, such as

Ghent in Norfolk. In Smithfield, where the town museum offers the "World's Oldest Ham," pork products have been iconic. That ended in 2018 when Smithfield Foods closed its final smokehouse, which had prepared the genuine Smithfield cured ham for more than 50 years. The business had been purchased by a large Chinese company.

As the result of the redistricting changes in 2016, the district no longer includes parts of Richmond. Those areas, especially the African-American neighborhoods, have shifted to the new 4th District, which gained a sizable increase in its black population. In exchange for losing Richmond, the 3rd picked up large parts of Chesapeake and Suffolk, plus Franklin, which is close to the North Carolina border. The District dropped to 46 percent black from the 56 percent black population of the old 3rd, which had been drawn to place the largest possible number of Democrats in a single district. As a result, the partisan ranking of the district dropped below the two more strongly Democratic districts in northern Virginia. In exchange, a black plurality — and Democrats -- gained control of a second district in Tidewater. In 2016, Hillary Clinton won the 3rd, 63%-32%.

A. Donald McEachin (D)

Elected 2016, 2nd term, b. Oct 10, 1961; Nuremberg, Germany; St. Christopher School (VA), 1979; American University (DC), B.S., 1982; University of Virginia Law School, J.D., 1986; Virginia Union University Samuel DeWitt Proctor School of Theology, M.Div., 2008; Baptist; Married (Colette Wallace McEachin); 3 children.

Elected Office: VA Assembly, 1996-2002, 2006-2008; VA Senate, 2008-2016.

DC Office: 314 CHOB 20515, 202-225-6365, Fax: 202-226-1170, mceachin.house.gov

State Offices: Richmond, 804-486-1840; Suffolk, 757-942-6050.

Committees: *Commission Congressional Mailing Standards. Energy & Commerce*: Communications & Technology; Energy; Environment & Climate Change. *Natural Resources*: Energy & Mineral Resources; Oversight & Investigations. *Select Committee on the Climate Crisis.*

Group Ratings

	ADA	ACLU	AFL-CIO	LCV	ITI	COC	HAFA	ACU	CFG	FRC
2018	-	77%	-	86%	-	58%	10%	4%	18%	0%
2017	95%	C	95%	89%	C	50%	C	7%	5%	0%

Almanac Ratings 2017-18

	Economy	Social	Foreign	Composite
Liberal	96%	97%	89%	94%
Conservative	4%	3%	11%	6%

Key Votes of the 115th Congress

1. Obama-care revision	N	5. Family planning regs	N	9. Guantanamo prisoners	Y
2. Tax Cuts	N	6. Body cameras/immigration	Y	10. Ground missiles, limit	Y
3. Omnibus appropriations	Y	7. Abortion ban	N	11. Defense Dept. spending	Y
4. Dodd-Frank revision	N	8. Concealed carry	N	12. FISA rules	Y

Election Results

Election	Name (Party)	Vote (%)		Cand. Spent	Ind. Exp. Support	Ind. Exp. Oppose
2018 General	Donald McEachin (D).......................	187,642	(63%)	$645,034		
	Ryan McAdams (R).......................	107,706	(36%)	$222,235		
2018 Primary	Donald McEachin (D).................		(100%)			

Prior winning percentages: 2016 (58%)

Democrat Donald McEachin was elected in 2016 to represent a district that changed significantly in a court-ordered redistricting plan, which led longtime Republican Rep. Randy Forbes to conclude that he could not win in the new district. McEachin, with extensive experience as a legislator, has taken a seat on the Energy and Commerce Committee, where he said his chief attention will be environmental protection and the promotion of renewable energy. He has focused on the need to mitigate climate change.

McEachin was born in Nuremberg Germany to an Army veteran and a public-school teacher. He grew up in Richmond, got his bachelor's from American University and law degree from the University of Virginia. He served six years in the state House of Delegates, then ran unsuccessfully in 2001 for state attorney general. "The defeat stung, and he found himself struggling to find a purpose," The Washington Post reported. McEachin enrolled in the Samuel Proctor Theological Seminary at Virginia Union University, received his master's of divinity degree and became an ordained Baptist minister. Meanwhile, he returned to the state House and later was elected to the state Senate, where he chaired the Democratic Caucus. He co-founded and practiced with his law firm in Richmond.

When a federal court reviewed redistricting in Virginia, it agreed to a version of the map proposed by Democratic Gov. Terry McAuliffe that revamped the Republican-held 4th District. It appeared to be tailor-made politically and geographically for McEachin. He ran and got 75 percent of the vote in the low-turnout Democratic primary against Ella Ward, a member of the Chesapeake City Council. After Forbes decided to run in the Virginia Beach-based 2nd District, where he lost the Republican primary, Henrico County Sheriff Mike Wade, who spent his career in law enforcement, switched from a campaign in the 7th District and won the GOP nomination for the open seat.

With McEachin running a mostly quiet campaign, the lightly funded Ward had little opportunity to engage. He referred to his opponent as "Dodging Don." Although they agreed during a campaign debate on the need for law enforcement officers to wear body cameras, Wade took offense at McEachin's claim of excessive police profiling of racial minorities. The greater problem, he said, was with individuals who have mental-health or substance-abuse problems. "When I got pulled over … I didn't have a mental health problem and I wasn't on my way to jail," McEachin responded. He won, 57%-43%, rolling up huge majorities in Richmond, Petersburg and Henrico, which cast nearly half of the vote. Ward took 64 percent of the vote in Chesapeake and won other outlying counties that had been Forbes' base in the old 4th.

During his first term, McEachin had seats on the Armed Services and Natural Resources committees, and promoted "quality of life" issues for the military and veterans. In the Tidewater tradition, he was an enthusiastic proponent of increased shipbuilding. In 2018, he was "disappointed" that the budget plan from President Donald Trump proposed only 10 new ships. He opposed plans for seismic testing for off-shore oil drilling. "Unlike the Trump administration, we have not forgotten about the Deepwater Horizon oil spill" in the Gulf of Mexico in 2010, McEachin said in December 2018. He moved to Energy and Commerce when Democrats took House control. "For me, protecting our environment is a moral obligation and an act of faith," he said, in describing his new assignment.

He found the pace in Congress slower and less stressful than serving in Richmond, he said in an interview mid-way through his first year. "The breadth of issues is like drinking water out of a fire hydrant, but we have the ability to actually dig down and figure what exactly should the right policy be, as opposed to what we did in the General Assembly," McEachin told The Virginian-Pilot.

In the 2018 campaign, Republican Ryan McAdams — a pastor and former social worker in Williamsburg, and a political newcomer -- challenged McEachin. "I'm not your normal Republican," McAdams told the Richmond Times-Dispatch, in describing his appeal to urban voters. He was outspent, $713,000 to $222,000, in a contest that received little attention from either national party. McEachin improved his victory margin to 63%-36%, with a similar pattern of taking huge majorities in Richmond and Petersburg and running behind in the outlying counties. McEachin lost more than 60 pounds in the several months prior to his reelection as the result of a medical condition caused by earlier treatment for cancer. Photos showed that he was notably slimmer.

Following revelations of medical-school yearbook photos of Democratic Gov. Ralph Northam in blackface, McEachin called on him to resign because he had "lost the authority to lead." He added that Northam's defense was "not the look that I think Virginia wants to portray to the nation." The two had served together in the state Senate.

VA-4: Southeast Virginia   **Cook Partisan Voting Index: D+10**

Population		Race and Ethnicity		Income	
Total	760,613	White	48.8%	Median Income	$54,560
Land area (sq. miles)	3,644	Black	40.9%	District Income Rank	235
Pop/ sq mi	208.7	Latino	5.2%	Poverty Rate	16.3%
Born in State	62.7%	Asian	1.8%	With health insurance	89.2%
		Two or more races	2.8%	Cash public assistance	2.7%
Age Groups		Other	0.6%	Food stamp/SNAP	13.7%
Under 18	21.3%				
18-34	25.5%	**Education**		**Work**	
35-64	39.6%	H.S grad or less	42%	White Collar	13.6%
Over 64	13.6%	Some college	29.4%	Sales and Service	43.1%
		College Degree, 4 yr	17.7%	Blue Collar	20.2%
Military		Post grad	10.9%	Government	20.1%
Veteran/ Active Duty	11.8%				

2012 Pres. Vote	Obama	217,618	(60%)	Romney	138,295	(38%)			
2016 Pres. Vote	Clinton	212,677	(58%)	Trump	134,676	(37%)	Johnson	9,595	(3%)

Richmond and its Exurbs, parts of Chesapeake: The history of American slavery literally began along the tidal expanse of the James River. Only a dozen years after the founding of Jamestown in 1607, the first slave ship sailed up the James and offloaded its human cargo, giving birth to the slave-based economy of the American South. In the 21st century, some of the big plantation houses of the Tidewater still dot the banks of the James. Charles City County — the site of William Byrd II's Westover, Benjamin Harrison III's Berkeley, and John Carter's Shirley — also was the birthplace of two successive presidents, William Henry Harrison and John Tyler. Virginia famously produced a total of eight U.S. presidents — almost 20 percent of the individuals to serve — but none for the past century.

The 4th Congressional District of Virginia travels back and forth across the James River north of Jamestown to string together black precincts and communities. Upriver on the south bank of the James, it takes in 78 percent African-American Petersburg, where much of the movie Lincoln was filmed, as well as eastern Henrico County, though three-fourths of surrounding Henrico is in the 7th District. All of Richmond is in the district, including the state's capitol, designed by Thomas Jefferson; the historic Jefferson Hotel; and the African-American neighborhoods around Church Hill, where Patrick Henry famously proclaimed "give me liberty or give me death." Monument Avenue has statues of Confederate luminaries and tennis player Arthur Ashe; initial plans in 2018 to revise the local statuary were abandoned following protests. Old tobacco warehouses on the banks of the James have been converted into loft apartments. Hollywood Cemetery is where Presidents James Monroe and John Tyler share a final resting place with 25 Confederate generals, Jefferson Davis, and Davis' son, Joseph, who died at age 5 in 1864 after falling from the Confederate White House balcony.

The district also takes in the flat lands of Southside Virginia. These were tobacco fields after the English first settled here in the 17th century. The tiny town of Wakefield is home to the Shad Planking, the iconic fish-eating event where Virginia politicians have made pilgrimages every spring for more than a half-century to meet and greet each other and voters. The gathering has been renamed as the Barbecue and Shad Homecoming (BASH), where more traditional fare has been added to the oily fish to increase the turnout. In 2017, the largest solar facility in the state was opened in Southampton County. Parts of the district are in fast-growing Chesterfield County, where the population increased 32 percent from 2000 to 2017 and surpassed Henrico. The redistricting changes in 2016 increased the African-American population in the district from 31 percent to 41 percent. Although some of the outlying areas remain Republican, the overwhelming Democratic vote in Richmond and other parts of Henrico, plus Petersburg, controls the outcome of the district. In 2016, Hillary Clinton took 58 percent of the vote.

Denver Riggleman (R)

Elected 2018, 1st term, b. Mar 17, 1970; Manassas; Burlington County College, A.A., 1996; Community College of the Air Force (AL), A.A.S., 1996; University of Virginia, Bach. Deg., 1998; Villanova University, Mast. Deg., 2007; Christian Church; Married (Christine Riggleman); 3 children.

Military Career: U.S. Air Force 1992-2003

Professional Career: Whiskey Distillery Owner.

DC Office: 1022 LHOB 20515, 202-225-4711, riggleman.house.gov

State Offices: Charlottesville, 434-973-9631; Danville, 434-791-2596.

Committees: *Financial Services*: Consumer Protection & Financial Institutions; Nat'l Security, International Development & Monetary Policy.

Election Results

Election	Name (Party)	Vote (%)		Cand. Spent	Ind. Exp. Support	Ind. Exp. Oppose
2018 General	Denver L. Riggleman III (R)..............	165,339	(53%)	$1,878,150	$666,581	$14,471
	Leslie Cockburn (D)...........................	145,040	(47%)	$3,216,736	$737,107	$1,064,989

Freshman Denver Riggleman won a campaign that had more than its share of peculiarities. Riggleman, who had no experience in elected office, spent many years in military and intelligence operations and was the successful owner of a distillery. He was the only bright light for Virginia Republicans in what was otherwise a dismal election for the party. He replaced Republican Rep. Tom Garrett, who served one term and retired after having won the nomination for reelection, amid news reports of his struggles with alcoholism.

Riggleman, a native of nearby Manassas, graduated from the University of Virginia. He served four years in the Air Force, where he was an avionics technician for C-141 military transport planes based at McGuire Air Force Base in New Jersey. He worked for the National Security Agency, where he supported science and technology development and was an intelligence officer around the world. In the private sector, he specialized in counter-terrorism as an intelligence consultant for the NSA and other federal agencies. With his wife, Christine, he built a distillery, which distributed several spirits; he had several regulatory conflicts with larger liquor companies.

When Garrett unexpectedly abandoned his reelection bid in late May, the district's 37-member Republican committee selected his successor a few days later. Riggleman reportedly won by one vote on the fourth ballot over Cynthia Dunbar, an outspoken conservative who two weeks earlier lost a Republican convention for an open seat in the neighboring 6th District. In his only other political campaign, Riggleman sought the GOP nomination for governor in 2017, but withdrew before the primary. With his advocacy of limited government, he called himself a "liberty Republican."

Democrats nominated Leslie Cockburn, who won the party convention — initially to oppose Garrett — after her chief opponent, Roger Huffstetler, withdrew shortly before the vote; a self-styled moderate, he spent $1.1 million on local caucuses that preceded the convention. Cockburn was a longtime investigative journalist who produced documentaries and other reports for national news media. She authored several books on U.S. foreign policy and other international topics.

Cockburn said that she entered politics because of her hostility to President Donald Trump. "I was really appalled by him, as a woman and as a former journalist," she said during a campaign debate. During the campaign, Republicans echoed the claims of earlier critics that her broadcasts and writings occasionally included very liberal views.

Riggleman embraced Republican policy on most economic issues. He was more independent on immigration and he condemned the white nationalist protests that led to violence in Charlottesville in August 2017. "I don't agree 100 percent with everything Trump does," he told The Washington Post. He claimed that Cockburn's principal residence was an expensive home in Washington D.C., which Cockburn denied. The campaign took an odd turn and briefly gained national attention when Cockburn accused Riggleman of being a "devotee of Bigfoot erotica," referring to a book he had written but never published. He posted a chapter on Facebook, which earlier received little attention and Riggleman described as satire.

Cockburn spent $3.2 million, nearly twice Riggleman's total. National Democrats, who had doubts about Cockburn's prospects, spent little in the contest; Republicans responded accordingly.

Riggleman won, 53%-47%. The results reinforced the district's pattern of a heavily Democratic fortress in an otherwise Republican bastion. Cockburn took 85 percent of the vote in Charlottesville and 65 percent in surrounding Albemarle County; combined, that area cast nearly one-fourth of the district vote. Riggleman won all but three of the remaining 21 counties and cities. In Virginia's rapidly shifting political landscape, he could become a target of Democratic redistricting plans following the 2020 census.

VA-5: Southside   Cook Partisan Voting Index: R+6

Population		Race and Ethnicity		Income	
Total	733,693	White	72.7%	Median Income	$52,081
Land area (sq. miles)	10,030	Black	19.6%	District Income Rank	269
Pop/ sq mi	73.2	Latino	3.6%	Poverty Rate	14.3%
Born in State	64.6%	Asian	1.7%	With health insurance	89.9%
		Two or more races	2.1%	Cash public assistance	2.1%
Age Groups		Other	0.3%	Food stamp/SNAP	11.4%
Under 18	20.2%				
18-34	21.4%	**Education**		**Work**	
35-64	39.6%	H.S grad or less	44.4%	White Collar	18.8%
Over 64	18.8%	Some college	28.2%	Sales and Service	39.9%
		College Degree, 4 yr	15.7%	Blue Collar	23%
Military		Post grad	11.7%	Government	18.6%
Veteran/ Active Duty	9.5%				

2012 Pres. Vote	Romney	188,485	(52%)	Obama	164,555	(46%)		
2016 Pres. Vote	Trump	195,190	(53%)	Clinton	154,665	(42%)	Johnson	9,230	(3%)

Charlottesville, Danville: Southside Virginia is technically defined as the parts of the commonwealth east of the Blue Ridge, west of the Fall Line and south of the James River. But it really is a cultural designation: an outcropping of Deep South culture in the Old Dominion. The eastern counties are flat and humid — frontier in the late-colonial period, plantation country by 1800, and now peanut fields and pine forests. Along U.S. 58, which snakes across southern Virginia from Virginia Beach almost to the Cumberland Gap, are the vestiges of the state's Tobacco Road, including the Tobacco Farm Life Museum of Virginia in South Hill. The largest metropolitan area in Southside is Danville, where the tobacco auction originated in 1858. Two of the most important battles for African-American equality were won northeast of Danville. The first was at Appomattox Court House, the serene little hamlet where Robert E. Lee surrendered to his onetime subordinate Ulysses S. Grant. The second was in Prince Edward County, where one of the five cases consolidated into the landmark Brown v. Board of Education case arose.

Charlottesville was the scene of a controversial "Unite the Right" protest in August 2017, which resulted in the death of a counter-protestor and the December 2018 conviction on murder charges of the automobile driver who caused her death, plus a national debate over the deepening political polarization the incident revealed. The initial protest, which had been organized to oppose removal of a statue of Confederate General Robert E. Lee, started with an evening torchlight march on the campus of the University of Virginia; it included a few hundred hooded members of the Ku Klux Klan and other white nationalists. The next day, the political Right and Left clashed in the small several block area of downtown Charlottesville. The angry exchanges turned lethal when the young driver rammed his car into a small group on the street and killed Heather Heyer, a liberal activist. President Donald Trump stoked the tensions a few days later when he refused to criticize the incendiary actions and said that there were good people — as well as blame — on "both sides." The raw feelings left by the incident also resulted in criticism of local officials; a year later, Nikuyah Walker, one of the liberal protestors, was elected mayor.

The 5th District of Virginia covers most of Southside Virginia west of metro Richmond, spreading out to the Blue Ridge Mountains. This is the heart of the district; about two-thirds of its population lives south of the James River. The district includes overwhelmingly liberal Charlottesville, with Thomas Jefferson's University of Virginia, and surrounding Albemarle County, but their 20 percent of the vote has had little impact in this district. An arm extends north to the western part of Fauquier County in the Washington D.C. exurbs. Southside Virginia was long conservative and Democratic; it was the last part of Virginia to elect a Republican to Congress. In recent decades, the district has voted predominantly Republican. Democrats running statewide have energized the Charlottesville area and the African-American precincts, especially in Danville, which is 50 percent black. Donald Trump in 2016 won 53 percent of the vote.

Benjamin Cline (R)

Elected 2018, 1st term, b. Feb 29, 1972; Stillwater, OK; Bates College (ME), B.A., 1994; University of Richmond (VA), J.D., 2007; Roman Catholic; Married (Elizabeth Rocovich); 2 children.

Elected Office: VA House, 2002-2018; Roanoke Valley Higher Education Authority Board, 2004-2018.

Professional Career: Policy Advisory & Chief of Staff, U.S. Rep. Bob Goodlatte, 1994-2002; President, New Dominion Solutions, L.L.C., 2002-2007; Assistant Commonwealth Attorney, Rockingham County and City of Harrisonburg, 2007-2013; Private Practice Attorney.

DC Office: 1009 LHOB 20515, 202-225-5431, Fax: 202-225-9681, cline.house.gov

State Offices: Harrisonburg, 540-432-2391; Lynchburg, 434-845-8306; Roanoke, 540-857-2672; Staunton, 540-885-3861.

Committees: *Education & Labor*: Higher Education & Workforce Investment; Workforce Protections. *Judiciary*: Constitution, Civil Rights & Civil Liberties; Courts, Intellectual Property & Internet; Crime, Terrorism & Homeland Security.

Election Results

Election	Name (Party)	Vote (%)		Cand. Spent	Ind. Exp. Support	Ind. Exp. Oppose
2018 General	Benjamin L. Cline (R).........................	167,957	(60%)	$880,601		$1,842
	Jennifer Lewis (D)..............................	113,133	(40%)	$411,655	$19,575	

Republican Ben Cline coasted to his first term in the House without a competitive contest among district voters. That resulted from two factors: the GOP's unusual use of a convention to select its nominee for the general election, where he squelched a limited insurrection from a conservative faction, plus the weakness of Democrats in the Shenandoah Valley region of Virginia. Cline had deep local connections. He served eight terms in the state House of Delegates, where he was a conservative leader. Cline earlier was chief of staff to his predecessor, Rep. Bob Goodlatte, who was term-limited as House Judiciary Committee chairman and retired after 13 terms.

A graduate of Bates College and the University of Richmond Law School, Cline was an assistant prosecutor in Rockingham County. He worked for Goodlatte for eight years following college. He was first elected to the state House in 2002. He chaired the Militia, Police and Public Safety Committee, where he was a strong opponent of gun control, and was vice-chair of the Finance Committee.

His successful legislation included a limitation on the use of unmanned drone aircraft by state and local law enforcement agencies. Cline was the House chairman of the Conservative Caucus. In addition to practicing law, he served as a business advisor who gave marketing assistance to internet and high-tech companies in rural areas.

For years, he had been viewed as the heir apparent in the district. Following Goodlatte's retirement, Cynthia Dunbar challenged Cline for the GOP nomination. Dunbar, a member of the Republican National Committee, who styled herself as a political outsider, criticized Cline as a "career politician" and a resident of "the swamp."

Under pressure from Dunbar, who voiced strongly conservative views on social issues and viewed the limited turnout at a convention as her best option, district GOP leaders agreed to select the nominee at a convention rather than a primary. At Dunbar's insistence, they initially included an additional stipulation that there would be only one ballot and the winner was not required to get the customary majority of convention votes.

When the convention met in May, some Republicans — including Cline -- questioned the legality of the planned procedure. Over the objections of Dunbar and her allies, they modified the rules to require a majority vote. The parliamentary conflict became a moot point. With an initial field of eight candidates and more than 2,200 voters, Cline led Dunbar on the first ballot, 52%-39%. (In an unusual effort, Dunbar two weeks later sought the GOP nomination for the open seat in the adjacent 5th District; Rep. Thomas Garrett had unexpectedly announced his retirement after having received the nomination. At a meeting of the 37-member GOP selection committee, Dunbar lost by one vote on the fourth round of secret ballots to Denver Riggleman, who won the seat in November.)

In a year marked by competitive House races across Virginia, Cline defeated Democrat Jennifer Lewis, a liberal activist, 60%-40%. Lewis won her nomination over three other candidates in the first primary that local Democrats held since 1970. During the campaign, Cline got national attention following an unusual incident in his home town of Lexington when White House press secretary Sarah Huckabee Sanders was asked to leave the local Red Hen restaurant because its employees objected to President Donald Trump. Cline called the restaurant's action "disappointing" and he tweeted an apology to Sanders. In the House, his safe district enabled him to follow in the footsteps of Goodlatte — including a seat on the Judiciary Committee.

VA-6: Shenandoah Valley   Cook Partisan Voting Index: R+13

Population		Race and Ethnicity		Income	
Total	746,117	White	79.8%	Median Income	$51,875
Land area (sq. miles)	5,930	Black	10.7%	District Income Rank	272
Pop/ sq mi	125.8	Latino	5.1%	Poverty Rate	14.5%
Born in State	63.8%	Asian	1.9%	With health insurance	89.3%
		Two or more races	2.1%	Cash public assistance	2.5%
Age Groups		Other	0.4%	Food stamp/SNAP	11%
Under 18	20.4%				
18-34	24.3%	**Education**		**Work**	
35-64	37.9%	H.S grad or less	45.4%	White Collar	17.4%
Over 64	17.4%	Some college	27.6%	Sales and Service	42.1%
		College Degree, 4 yr	16.7%	Blue Collar	23.3%
Military		Post grad	10.2%	Government	15.3%
Veteran/ Active Duty	8.7%				

2012 Pres. Vote	Romney	197,045	(59%)	Obama	132,153	(39%)		
2016 Pres. Vote	Trump	206,303	(59%)	Clinton	120,596	(35%)	Johnson	10,801	(3%)

Roanoke, Harrisonburg: The sturdy men and women who settled the Shenandoah Valley of Virginia west of the Blue Ridge were quite different from the "second sons" of the European aristocracy who cleared the marshy forests of the Tidewater and built grand plantations. Even before the Revolutionary War, Scots and Scots-Irish, German Protestants, and Mennonites and Moravians — members of religious communities and fiercely independent farmers — poured down the Great Wagon Road from Pennsylvania to the valley, planting farms and founding towns with names like Strasburg, Edinburg, Mount Jackson and Glasgow. They were looking not for the flat, mahogany colored land that Eastern tobacco growers sought, but for land that could support wheat, corn and hay — crops that could be rotated and that an individual farmer and his family could handle. A young George Washington surveyed portions of the land; what are believed to be his carved initials are still visible on Natural Bridge in Rockbridge County.

The same independent spirit nurtured the growth of higher education here. In Lexington are Washington and Lee University, which Robert E. Lee headed, and the Virginia Military Institute, where Stonewall Jackson taught philosophy and artillery tactics. Harrisonburg is the home of James Madison University. A trio of distinguished women's colleges is nearby: Mary Baldwin College in Staunton, Hollins University in Roanoke and Sweet Briar College in Sweet Briar, which was revived after nearly shutting down in 2015 because of financial woes. President Woodrow Wilson's birthplace is in Staunton. Industry flourished here more than in most of Virginia east of the Blue Ridge. In the 19th century, the Norfolk and Western Railway established its chief junction at Roanoke; as the years passed, the city became the headquarters of the railroad and many other companies. In 2015, the renamed Norfolk Southern moved its corporate headquarters to Norfolk — but soon shifted again to

Atlanta. In October 2017, Amtrak restored passenger service to Roanoke for the first time since 1979. The population of Roanoke was on the cusp of 100,000 in 2017 for the first time since 1980. The city was thriving, according to CityLab, with its attractiveness to "outdoorsy millennials," including new craft breweries and the revived downtown in a historic district. The number of available jobs increased by 2,000 in the past year, The Roanoke Times reported in September 2018. But the local poverty level remained high, at 22 percent.

The 6th Congressional District of Virginia covers the heart of the Valley of Virginia, from Front Royal to Roanoke. In recent decades, the ancestral conservatism of the region and the feisty politics of the mountain rebels have melded into a single conservative Republicanism, more populist than elitist in tone and prickly about interference from Washington and Richmond. Those roots go deep: Many of these counties have shown Republican tendencies dating back more than 100 years. In 1952, the district's voters did something extremely rare at the time: They voted out an incumbent Southern Democrat in favor of a Republican. The GOP has held the seat ever since, save for an interlude in the 1980s. Donald Trump in 2016 won 59 percent of the vote, though Hillary Clinton took Roanoke, Harrisonburg and Lexington.

Abigail Spanberger (D)

Elected 2018, 1st term, b. Aug 07, 1979; Red Bank, NJ; University of Virginia, B.A., 2001; Christian Church; Married (Adam Spanberger); 3 children.

Professional Career: Federal Law Enforcement Officer, Narcotics and Money Laundering Cases, U.S. Postal Inspection Service; Operations Officer, Central Intelligence Agency; Page, Office of U.S. Sen. Chuck Robb.

DC Office: 1239 LHOB 20515, 202-225-2815, spanberger.house.gov

State Offices: Glen Allen, 804-401-4110; Spotsylvania, 202-225-2815.

Committees: *Agriculture*: Commodity Exchanges, Energy & Credit; Conservation & Forestry (Chmn). *Foreign Affairs*: Asia, the Pacific & Nonproliferation; Europe, Eurasia, Energy & the Environment.

Election Results

Election	Name (Party)	Vote (%)		Cand. Spent	Ind. Exp. Support	Ind. Exp. Oppose
2018 General	Abigail Spanberger (D)	176,079	(50%)	$7,041,600	$676,107	$3,652,495
	David Brat (R)	169,295	(48%)	$3,185,912	$1,038,446	$3,176,005
2018 Primary	Abigail Spanberger (D)	33,210	(73%)			
	Dan Ward (D)	12,483	(27%)			

Freshman Democrat Abigail Spanberger was elected to a seat that had been a Republican stronghold. A former CIA analyst, she brought a deep national security background plus extended familiarity with the Richmond-area district. Spanberger defeated Republican Rep. Dave Brat, whose stunning victory in the 2014 primary over then-House Majority Leader Eric Cantor threw GOP leadership succession into chaos and bolstered the party's conservative faction.

Spanberger, a native of New Jersey, moved with her family to a Richmond suburb and attended high school there. She graduated from the University of Virginia, where her major was French literature, and she got a master's in business administration while living in Germany. She started her career as a law enforcement officer with the U.S. Postal Inspection Service.

At the Central Intelligence Agency, Spanberger was an operations officer who gathered intelligence on terrorism, making use of her knowledge of other languages and her experiences overseas. Agency rules barred her from discussing the details of her work. When she returned to Henrico County, she joined a consulting firm that specialized in higher education.

In declaring her candidacy, Spanberger said that she wanted to talk not only about problems, but also solutions. "Beating the drum about how terrible the president [Donald Trump] is, is just beating the drum," she told the Chesterfield Observer. "It's not actually doing something productive." In the

Democratic primary, she faced Dan Ward, a former Marine who was a pilot and worked at the State Department. Ward spent $1.1 million. Spanberger won easily, 73%-27%.

Brat, who had been an economics professor at Randolph-Macon, compiled a modest legislative record. At home, he had limited reconciliation with Cantor allies in his district and he suffered from mid-decade redistricting changes that added suburban Democrats to his constituency. In an interview with the Orange County Review prior to the election, he said that enactment of tax cuts was his proudest accomplishment in Congress, referring especially to subsequently abandoned plans for post-election tax cuts targeted to the middle class.

The Congressional Leadership Fund, a Republican Super PAC, caused a stir in the campaign when it released a confidential security-clearance application that Spanberger had filed for a job, which showed that she had taught for a short time at a Washington-area school that was financed by Saudi Arabia. Although the Postal Service said that it had mistakenly released the document, Republicans ran ads that suggested Spanberger was aiding terrorists. Her campaign responded that the ad was a smear and that she spent her career "on the front line" fighting terrorists.

In their only debate, both candidates mostly avoided talking about Trump, though Brat sought repeatedly to link his opponent to the "Nancy Pelosi liberal agenda." Brat, who noted that his defeat of Cantor had resulted in the demise of plans for House action on immigration legislation, said that Spanberger backed legislation to support undocumented immigrants. She responded that such a charge was "frankly comical," given her intelligence work to keep communities safe.

Spanberger spent $7 million, which more than doubled Brat's spending. National party groups added more than $8 million in spending for the contest.

Spanberger won, 50.3%-48.4%. She took the two largest counties, each of which cast about one-third of the total vote: Henrico, with 59 percent; and Chesterfield, which had been shifting to Democrats, with 54 percent. Brat took the other eight, mostly rural, counties. Spanberger faced the prospect of a competitive reelection, which likely would depend partly on the direction that Republicans take in selecting their nominee.

VA-7: Central Virginia   Cook Partisan Voting Index: R+6

Population		Race and Ethnicity		Income	
Total	769,141	White	67.1%	Median Income	$73,904
Land area (sq. miles)	3,119	Black	17.6%	District Income Rank	74
Pop/ sq mi	246.6	Latino	7.1%	Poverty Rate	8.2%
Born in State	55.3%	Asian	5%	With health insurance	91.4%
		Two or more races	2.7%	Cash public assistance	1.7%
Age Groups		Other	0.5%	Food stamp/SNAP	7.2%
Under 18	23.6%				
18-34	20.7%	**Education**		**Work**	
35-64	41.1%	H.S grad or less	34.1%	White Collar	14.6%
Over 64	14.6%	Some college	27.7%	Sales and Service	39.8%
		College Degree, 4 yr	23.6%	Blue Collar	17%
Military		Post grad	14.6%	Government	16.9%
Veteran/ Active Duty	9.6%				

2012 Pres. Vote	Romney	206,308	(54%)	Obama	166,748	(44%)			
2016 Pres. Vote	Trump	198,032	(50%)	Clinton	172,544	(44%)	Johnson	14,206	(4%)

Richmond Suburbs: The metro area of Richmond, now the third-largest in the commonwealth, has grown far past its city borders, covering most of suburban Henrico and Chesterfield counties and spreading into what was, until recently, countryside. As the area has grown, its tone has shifted. No longer is this the heart of the Old South. Some of these areas are closer in outlook to Washington D.C. Richmond, the centrally located capital of Virginia, still sets the tone for the commonwealth. It is home to many of the state's great institutions — Dominion Resources, Main Street banks, big law firms and the Richmond Times-Dispatch. Likewise, the city has changed, as it has become less insular and more cosmopolitan.

The 7th Congressional District of Virginia sprawls across 120 miles from southwest of Richmond to the outer reaches of the Washington exurbs, though it is centered in Henrico and Chesterfield; each county is about one-third of the population. Surrounding much of Richmond, Henrico was once a linchpin of the state Republican coalition — it gave GOP nominee Barry Goldwater 70 percent of the vote in 1964. But demographic change, especially in the eastern portion of the county, and the movement of suburbanites toward Democrats in the past two decades have changed its makeup. In 2008, Barack Obama became the first Democrat to carry Henrico since Franklin Roosevelt. In 2016, Hillary Clinton increased the Democratic vote in Henrico to 58 percent. In 2017, Henrico was 31 percent black and 6 percent Hispanic. To the south of Richmond, Chesterfield County has been exurban and largely Republican. With rapid population growth and increases to 24 percent black and 9 percent Hispanic, Chesterfield has become more competitive. Donald Trump won the county, 48%-46%, a marked tightening from Bob Dole's 60%-32% lead over Bill Clinton in 1996. Solidly Democratic Richmond is in the 4th District. Not all these areas are middle-class suburbia. "The growth of suburban poverty continues to outpace that of the city's," especially in Henrico, the Times-Dispatch reported in March 2017.

The outlying parts of the district are rural and heavily Republican. For Washingtonians willing to endure a long commute or simply wanting to get away from the metro area, Spotsylvania and Culpeper counties have become popular destinations in the Washington exurbs; each grew about 50 percent from 2000 to 2017. The redistricting in 2016 added areas west of Richmond that had been in the old 4th District, and in exchange moved New Hanover and Kent counties north and east of Richmond to the 1st District. That switch resulted in a slight increase in the Democratic vote. The demographic and redistricting shifts have made this a more competitive area. Donald Trump won, 50%-44%.

Don Beyer (D)

Elected 2014, 3rd term, b. Jun 20, 1950; Trieste, Italy; Williams College, B.A., 1972; Episcopalian; Married (Megan Carroll); 4 children; 2 grandchildren.

Elected Office: VA Lt. Governor, 1990-1998.

Professional Career: Automobile dealer; Chairman, Jobs for VA Graduates, 1999-2013; U.S. Ambassador to Switzerland and Liechtenstein, 2009-2013.

DC Office: 1119 LHOB 20515, 202-225-4376, Fax: 202-225-0017, beyer.house.gov

State Offices: Arlington, 703-658-5403.

Committees: *Joint Economic. Science, Space & Technology*: Environment; Investigations & Oversight; Space & Aeronautics. *Ways & Means*: Select Revenue Measures; Trade.

Group Ratings

	ADA	ACLU	AFL-CIO	LCV	ITI	COC	HAFA	ACU	CFG	FRC
2018	-	93%	-	86%	-	67%	8%	4%	16%	0%
2017	100%	C	100%	100%	C	50%	C	4%	5%	0%

Almanac Ratings 2017-18

	Economy	Social	Foreign	Composite
Liberal	98%	97%	90%	95%
Conservative	2%	3%	10%	5%

Key Votes of the 115th Congress

1. Obama-care revision	N	5. Family planning regs	N	9. Guantanamo prisoners	Y
2. Tax Cuts	N	6. Body cameras/immigration	Y	10. Ground missiles, limit	Y
3. Omnibus appropriations	Y	7. Abortion ban	N	11. Defense Dept. spending	Y
4. Dodd-Frank revision	N	8. Concealed carry	N	12. FISA rules	N

Election Results

Election	Name (Party)	Vote (%)		Cand. Spent	Ind. Exp. Support	Ind. Exp. Oppose
2018 General	Don Beyer (D)	247,137	(76%)			
	Thomas Oh (R)	76,899	(24%)	$61,623		
2018 Primary	Don Beyer (D)		(100%)			

Prior winning percentages: 2016 (68%), 2014 (63%)

Democrat Don Beyer easily won election in 2014 in this district, which covers the wealthy and heavily Democratic Northern Virginia suburbs. After his long record as a successful businessman and public official, he sought opportunities for bipartisanship, though he initially made few headlines. With the Democratic takeover of the House in 2019, Beyer gained new opportunities with a seat on the Ways and Means Committee, where his top priority was action on a carbon tax. He remained active as co-chair of the Safe Climate Caucus.

Beyer was born in Trieste Italy, where his father was serving as an Army officer, grew up in Washington, went to Gonzaga High School in the shadow of the Capitol, and got his bachelor's degree from Williams College. American politics is rich in examples of second and third chances, and Beyer is no exception. He built a reputation as an affable dealmaker who could work with both sides of the aisle when he served two terms as Virginia's lieutenant governor, starting in 1990. But in 1997, when he sought the prize of the governorship, he floundered in his campaign against Republican James Gilmore III, stumbling in particular over the issue of the state's contested car tax. When he lost by 10 percentage points, many Virginians thought it would mark the end of Beyer's political career.

Beyer turned toward building his family's car-dealership business, which features Volvos, but he found he couldn't stay away from politics for good. In 2004, he served as campaign treasurer for Howard Dean's presidential campaign, and in 2008 he helped raise substantial sums for the Obama campaign. He led the new administration's transition planning at the Commerce Department and was rewarded with a plum ambassadorship to Switzerland and Liechtenstein, which he held for four years.

When 12-term Democratic Rep. Jim Moran announced his retirement, Beyer promptly launched his bid and tapped his extensive network of high-level Democratic contacts. His name recognition and his connections proved to be an advantage in a crowded primary race that drew six other Democrats. Of the $2.7 million he spent, $415,000 was self-financed. He stood out in candidate forums by demonstrating a strong grasp of both foreign and domestic policy. In the June primary, he topped the field with 46 percent of the vote, followed by state Del. Patrick Hope at 18 percent. The general election is a formality in this district.

On the Science, Space and Technology Committee, Beyer worked with Republicans on cybersecurity issues, including at the Office of Personnel Management and in the banking industry. The House passed his Science Prize Competition Act, which encourages federal agencies to use prize competitions as incentives for innovative scientific research and development. A self-styled "science nerd," Beyer has said that he wants to make it easier for experts to clarify the facts on complex topics — such as climate change. Following an April 2017 hearing of the Science Committee where he said that witnesses made several "false or misleading" statements, he wrote to chairman Lamar Smith, a Texas Republican, with several "fact checks." Not surprisingly, Smith did not agree with his claims.

Beyer brought his international experience to bear as well. To the dismay of labor unions that had supported him, he was an enthusiastic backer in 2015 of President Barack Obama's request for trade promotion authority and the prospective trans-Pacific trade deal. Union threats to challenge his reelection proved empty in this upscale district. He praised Obama's nuclear-arms agreement with Iran, and took a bit of credit. As ambassador to Switzerland, he recounted, he hosted the initial discussions with Iran that launched the broader negotiations.

Beyer said he identified with the more than 70,000 federal employees in his district: Three of his four grandparents were federal employees. With the election of President Donald Trump, Beyer said his job was "to play careful defense" on behalf of federal employees.

In 2017, he unsuccessfully urged the Trump administration to comply with international climate-change agreements. In February 2019, as one of four co-chairs of a new climate-change task force of the New Democrat Coalition, Beyer said the group planned to propose "commonsense solutions" to build a green economy. With his continued leadership of the Safe Climate Caucus, Beyer said its mission was to "stand up to the White House" and "show the world that the United States has leaders who are willing to lead on climate and find bold solutions."

On the Ways and Means Committee, Beyer said he advocated a carbon tax to achieve the progressive goals of the "Green New Deal," which he supported. He endorsed "an economic mechanism that would rapidly elevate wind, solar and other clean energy and phase out carbon pollution, while minimizing the negative effects on American families."

VA-8: Northern Virginia

Cook Partisan Voting Index: D+21

Population		Race and Ethnicity		Income	
Total	787,232	White	52%	Median Income	$103,414
Land area (sq. miles)	149	Black	13.9%	District Income Rank	8
Pop/ sq mi	5274.9	Latino	19.1%	Poverty Rate	8.5%
Born in State	23.3%	Asian	11.3%	With health insurance	88.8%
		Two or more races	3.2%	Cash public assistance	1.2%
Age Groups		Other	0.4%	Food stamp/SNAP	4.5%
Under 18	20.9%				
18-34	27.6%	**Education**		**Work**	
35-64	40.8%	H.S grad or less	21.7%	White Collar	10.7%
Over 64	10.7%	Some college	16.9%	Sales and Service	31.7%
		College Degree, 4 yr	30%	Blue Collar	10.6%
Military		Post grad	31.5%	Government	23.7%
Veteran/ Active Duty	10.1%				

2012 Pres. Vote	Obama	243,746	(68%)	Romney	111,518	(31%)			
2016 Pres. Vote	Clinton	270,415	(72%)	Trump	76,854	(21%)	Johnson	10,396	(3%)
	McMullin	7,334	(2%)						

Fairfax, Arlington, Alexandria: When George Washington strolled the brick sidewalks of Alexandria on his way to market or church or Gadsby's Tavern (where he celebrated his final two birthdays), it was the largest city in Northern Virginia, and larger than Georgetown just up the Potomac River. The areas that are now Capitol Hill and downtown Washington D.C. were hills above the river's mud flats. But Washington became the national capital; as it grew, Northern Virginia seemed left behind. In 1846, the District of Columbia retroceded its land south of the Potomac — now Alexandria and Arlington — to Virginia because it seemed then that the federal government would never need it. It would be another 97 years before the first federal building was constructed on the Virginia side — the Pentagon. When that occurred, Alexandria and the rural countryside of Northern Virginia were represented in Congress by Judge Howard W. Smith, for many years the influential chairman of the House Rules Committee, a Democrat who saw as his mission the maintenance of the standards of George Washington, Thomas Jefferson and Robert E. Lee, including on racial segregation. Yet by the 1950s, the area was changing around him. New subdivision dwellers with white-collar jobs wanted schools with good academic programs, not the segregated schoolhouses Judge Smith's friends were willing to finance. Plans by Alexandria to remove a Confederate monument in the center of town have been rejected by state legislators.

Today, the onetime suburbs of Arlington and Alexandria are "edge cities," with far more liberal policies. In 2014, Arlington County led the nation with the greatest share of its people who have college degrees (72 percent) and graduate degrees (37 percent). Cranes dot its cityscape, as giant office and housing developments have sprung up from rail yards in Crystal City and from used car lots upriver in Rosslyn. Amazon announced in November 2018 the location of its second headquarters between Crystal City and Alexandria, with at least 25,000 workers and 4 million square feet of office space. The plan, renamed National Landing, was described as a "generationally transformative project." The move was accompanied by $750 million in tax incentives, with up to $295 million in transportation improvements, from the state and county — with relatively little controversy, especially compared to the quick reversal of comparable plans in New York City. For years, local commuters have found roads jammed: Washington suffers from some of the worst traffic congestion in the country, plus nagging slowdowns with its Metrorail system. In 2018, the Army completed its first expansion of Arlington National Cemetery since the 1980s; the 27 acres were removed from woodlands adjacent to nearby Fort Myer.

The 8th Congressional District of Virginia consists of Arlington County and the cities of Alexandria and Falls Church, where slightly more than half its population resides. The district covers all of Virginia that is inside the Capital Beltway except for small pockets in Annandale and McLean. The balance lives in Fairfax County, either in precincts near the perimeter of Arlington/Falls Church/ Alexandria or in areas south of the Beltway. The district takes in George Washington's Mount Vernon estate and the more rural areas around Fort Belvoir. The district is solidly Democratic. Hillary Clinton got 72 percent of the vote in 2016. This is the most Democratic district in Virginia.

Morgan Griffith (R)

Elected 2010, 5th term, b. Mar 15, 1958; Philadelphia, PA; Emory and Henry College (VA), B.A., 1980; Washington and Lee University School of Law (VA), J.D., 1983; Episcopalian; Married (Hilary Davis); 3 children.

Elected Office: VA House, 1994-2010, Majority Leader, 2000-2010.

Professional Career: Practicing attorney, 2008-2010.

DC Office: 2202 RHOB 20515, 202-225-3861, Fax: 202-225-0076, morgangriffith.house.gov

State Offices: Abingdon, 276-525-1405; Big Stone Gap, 276-525-1405; Christiansburg, 540-381-5671.

Committees: *Energy & Commerce*: Energy; Health; Oversight & Investigations. *Select Committee on the Climate Crisis.*

Group Ratings

	ADA	ACLU	AFL-CIO	LCV	ITI	COC	HAFA	ACU	CFG	FRC
2018	-	21%	-	3%	-	83%	70%	92%	68%	100%
2017	10%	C	6%	0%	C	86%	C	92%	85%	100%

Almanac Ratings 2017-18

	Economy	Social	Foreign	Composite
Liberal	7%	4%	8%	7%
Conservative	93%	96%	92%	93%

Key Votes of the 115th Congress

1. Obama-care revision	Y	5. Family planning regs	Y	9. Guantanamo prisoners	N
2. Tax Cuts	Y	6. Body cameras/immigration	N	10. Ground missiles, limit	N
3. Omnibus appropriations	N	7. Abortion ban	Y	11. Defense Dept. spending	N
4. Dodd-Frank revision	Y	8. Concealed carry	Y	12. FISA rules	N

Election Results

Election	Name (Party)	Vote (%)	Cand. Spent	Ind. Exp. Support	Ind. Exp. Oppose
2018 General	Morgan Griffith (R)............................ 160,933	(65%)	$1,116,927		
	Anthony Flaccavento (D).................. 85,833	(35%)	$1,047,897		
2018 Primary	Morgan Griffith (R)..	(100%)			

Prior winning percentages: 2016 (69%), 2014 (72%), 2012 (61%), 2010 (51%)

Republican Morgan Griffith, a former Virginia House majority leader, has used his Energy and Commerce Committee seat to protect his region's coal industry, inveigh against the Environmental Protection Agency and cut back federal regulation. Following his election in 2010, he has become entrenched in a district that his predecessor, Democrat Rick Boucher, held for 28 years. He has shown insider skills and occasional independence.

Griffith was born in Philadelphia and moved to Salem as a child. He was president of his high school student body and an avid swimmer. He attended Emory & Henry College, in part because it had just installed a new pool. He went on to get a law degree from Washington and Lee University. Griffith opened a private practice in Salem. After winning a seat in the House of Delegates in 1994, Griffith worked to repeal restrictions on gun ownership, limit abortion rights, and block a $1.4 billion tax increase. In 2000, he became the first Republican in Virginia to serve as House majority leader and earned a reputation as a skilled parliamentarian. Griffith bucked his party in 2010 when he helped draft a bill to legalize marijuana for medicinal use.

When he first ran for Congress, Griffith was at a significant financial disadvantage; Boucher outspent him, 3-to-1. Boucher, though he sought a middle ground, had been a leader at the Energy and Commerce Committee on his party's cap-and-trade bill aimed at limiting greenhouse gas emissions, which passed the House in 2009. The bill was unpopular in Appalachia's coal country. Griffith made Boucher's work on the bill a centerpiece of his campaign. He argued that the measure would have killed jobs and raised electricity costs. Boucher framed his support for the bill as a way to ensure that Congress — and not conservatives' nemesis, the EPA — had power over regulating carbon emissions. Griffith ran an ad with a video clip of President Barack Obama saying, "I love Rick Boucher." Boucher attacked Griffith as a carpetbagger who lived outside the district, running a television ad that said, "Morgan Griffith: He's not from here ... and it shows." Griffith was bolstered by nearly $2 million in spending by national party and conservative groups. As Republicans swept across the country, especially in rural areas, Griffith won 51%-46%.

In the House, Griffith has mostly been a loyal Republican, though less of an ideologue than many of his GOP classmates. He followed Boucher with a plum seat on Energy and Commerce and steered a bill through the House in 2011 that sought to limit the EPA's power to regulate boilers. He and West Virginia Republican Rep. David McKinley complained in a 2013 op-ed about "the destructive consequences of this administration's regulatory assault" on the coal industry. He contended that EPA regulations treated dairy milk spills the same as oil spills, an assertion that the fact-checking site PolitiFact labeled false. When Appalachian Power in 2015 shut down two coal-fired power plants in Virginia and three in West Virginia in response to an EPA mandate of stricter emissions standards, Griffith said the agency was threatening the stability of the electrical grid. Griffith took the lead in seeking to reverse "stream protection" regulations imposed by the Obama administration, which were designed to prevent coal debris from being dumped into nearby waters. In February 2017, he praised President Donald Trump for signing a bill to overturn the new rules and "bring relief" to coal miners.

On other issues at Energy and Commerce, Griffith focused on home-style rural and energy issues. He filed with Democratic Rep. Joyce Beatty of Ohio the Furthering Access to Stroke Telemedicine (FAST) Act, to expand Medicare coverage of health technology in rural areas. He urged the inclusion of expanded broadband services in any legislation for additional infrastructure. In 2018, Griffith won enactment of his bill to expedite permits for hydropower plants that potentially use existing infrastructure, including abandoned coal mines, and provide renewable energy. These pumped-storage facilities have been promoted by some miners. He continued to seek other opportunities for the use of coal, especially with the support of Trump.

Griffith has easily won reelection. In 2018, Democratic nominee Anthony Flaccavento launched a rematch of his challenge in 2012, which Griffith won, 61%-39%. Flaccavento ran on what he called "rural progressive" themes, including "Medicare for all," taxpayer-funded community college tuition, and protections for organized labor. A resident of the area since he arrived in the mid-1980s to run a program for the Catholic Church, Flaccavento was a consultant for local businesses. In his campaign, he avoided criticism of Trump and said that Democrats had become too liberal. He spent a bit more than $1 million, nearly as much as Griffith. Aside from taking Blacksburg-based Montgomery County, which is the largest in the district, his revival bid fell short. Griffith won, 65%-35%, reinforcing the political transformation of rural America.

VA-9: Southwest Virginia   **Cook Partisan Voting Index: R+19**

Population		Race and Ethnicity		Income	
Total	714,326	White	89.5%	Median Income	$42,438
Land area (sq. miles)	9,114	Black	5.3%	District Income Rank	399
Pop/ sq mi	78.4	Latino	2.2%	Poverty Rate	18.4%
Born in State	65%	Asian	1.3%	With health insurance	89.8%
		Two or more races	1.2%	Cash public assistance	2.9%
Age Groups		Other	0.3%	Food stamp/SNAP	14.6%
Under 18	18.7%				
18-34	22.7%	**Education**		**Work**	
35-64	39.6%	H.S grad or less	50.4%	White Collar	19%
Over 64	19%	Some college	29.3%	Sales and Service	41.6%
		College Degree, 4 yr	12.1%	Blue Collar	26%
Military		Post grad	8.1%	Government	20.1%
Veteran/ Active Duty	7.9%				

2012 Pres. Vote	Romney	196,354	(63%)	Obama	108,641	(35%)			
2016 Pres. Vote	Trump	217,837	(68%)	Clinton	86,463	(27%)	Johnson	7,481	(2%)

Blacksburg, Bristol: As early as 1765, settlements were carved out of the great Valley of Virginia, bending westward and south toward Tennessee and the Cumberland Gap. Most of these founders were of Scots-Irish lineage, and they moved to a mountainous area that developed almost apart from the rest of Virginia. The fiercely independent settlers eventually spilled into the heart of the Appalachian Mountains. Here, they followed the same political and economic development patterns as those in West Virginia, which wasn't a separate state until 1863. They were first farmers and later coal miners. Politically, this virtually all-white area opposed slavery and was skeptical, if not hostile, to the Confederacy. It is a long way from here to plantation country — the state's extreme southwest corner is closer to nine other state capitals than to Richmond. Out of the crucible of struggle between secessionists and unionists, Southwest Virginia developed a robust two-party politics after the Civil War, sooner than in the rest of the state.

In recent decades, as development moved down Interstate 81 from Roanoke to Bristol, the region has become more like the rest of Virginia. With encouragement from state officials, businesses have created jobs at high-tech companies and telephone call centers. Agriculture has thrived, especially produce and dairy, while coal mining has diminished. Coal has not entirely disappeared, either economically or socially. Big Stone Gap, a movie shot in the mining town with the same name in the southwest corner of the state that starred Ashley Judd seeking love and herself, brought attention to the area, with local festivities and a celebration of its 1970s culture.

The 9th Congressional District covers all of Southwest Virginia west of Roanoke; the city and most of Roanoke County are in the 6th District. Over the years, it became known as the "Fighting Ninth" because of its taste for raucous politics, which by and large were culturally conservative and economically populist. This is NASCAR country; Martinsville's speedway is here, and Bristol's is just across the Tennessee line. Bristol, a former rail hub, has adjacent cities on opposite sides of the state line that share many services; its Virginia locale has suffered from poor local management. Blacksburg, with a population of 45,000 plus the 33,000 students on campus at Virginia Tech University, is the largest city in the area. Buchanan County, in the far western part of the district, shows how the political winds have shifted. It gave Bill Clinton 63 percent of the vote in both 1992 and 1996, but the Democratic vote then dropped precipitously. In 2016, Donald Trump took Buchanan by a stunning 79%-19%. As Democratic support collapsed, this has become the most Republican district in the state. Even with Sen. Tim Kaine of Virginia as her running mate, Hillary Clinton fell far short. Trump won 68%-27%.

Jennifer Wexton (D)

Elected 2018, 1st term, b. May 27, 1968; Washington, DC; University of Maryland, Baltimore (UMB), B.A., 1991; College of William and Mary - Marshall-Wythe Law School (VA), J.D., 1995; Married (Andrew Wexton); 2 children.

Elected Office: VA Senate, 2014-2018.

Professional Career: Assistant Commonwealth Attorney, Loudon County 2001-2005; Attorney; Loudoun County Circuit Court Substitute Judge.

DC Office: 1217 LHOB 20515, 202-225-5136, Fax: 202-225-0437, wexton.house.gov

State Offices: Sterling, 703-234-3800.

Committees: *Financial Services*: Consumer Protection & Financial Institutions; Nat'l Security, International Development & Monetary Policy. *Science, Space & Technology*: Investigations & Oversight; Space & Aeronautics.

Election Results

Election	Name (Party)	Vote (%)		Cand. Spent	Ind. Exp. Support	Ind. Exp. Oppose
2018 General	Jennifer Wexton (D)	206,356	(56%)	$6,025,222	$776,128	$5,040,194
	Barbara Comstock (R)	160,841	(44%)	$6,360,759	$485,649	$5,570,006
2018 Primary	Jennifer Wexton (D)	22,405	(42%)			
	Alison Kiehl Friedman (D)	12,283	(23%)			
	Lindsey Davis Stover (D)	8,567	(16%)			
	Dan Helmer (D)	6,712	(13%)			

Freshman Jennifer Wexton received the largest share of the vote among the more than two dozen Democratic challengers who defeated a House Republican incumbent in the 2018 election. Her 56 percent of the vote highlighted gains that Democrats have made in the suburbs since the election of President Donald Trump, not only in Virginia but in many metro areas across the nation. Wexton defeated Republican Rep. Barbara Comstock, who received hefty financial support from national Republican groups despite her dim prospects.

Wexton, a native of Bethesda Maryland, graduated from the University of Maryland and got her law degree from the College of William & Mary School of Law. She was a prosecutor for the Commonwealth's Attorney of Loudoun County, Virginia. As a partner in the Laurel Brigade law group in Leesburg, she had an interest in mental health issues. Wexton was a member of an advisory board to the county's mental health department and handled pro bono work on behalf of abused or neglected children. For a year, she chaired the Loudoun County Bar Association.

Wexton won a special election in 2014 for the state Senate, where she pursued her interest in issues affecting children. She claimed credit for enacting 40 bills, though she had served entirely in the minority party.

In the Democratic primary, Wexton faced five other candidates. Three of them spent more than $1 million: Lindsey Davis Stover and Alison Friedman, both of whom held positions in the Obama administration, and Army veteran Dan Helmer. Opponents criticized Weston for not refusing to accept corporate campaign contributions. She won the primary with 42 percent of the vote to 23 percent for Friedman, 16 percent for Stover and 13 percent for Helmer. Wexton got 49 percent in her base of Loudoun, which cast nearly half the vote.

In the general election, both Wexton and Comstock ran extensive advertising, much of it negative. Comstock cast blame on Wexton for traffic congestion and for tolls that she had supported in the state legislature.

Wexton sought to link "Trumpstock" to President Donald Trump. The ads were replete with exaggerations and falsehoods, according to campaign observers.

In a campaign debate, Wexton described her opponent as "a masterful political chameleon." Comstock responded by defending her record of "getting results." Wexton accused Comstock of a double standard when she refused to say whether she believed allegations of sexual misconduct that had been lodged against Supreme Court nominee Brett Kavanaugh, who was a longtime friend of hers.

In an editorial endorsing Wexton, The Washington Post praised her "clear and convincing competence" and said that she would be "a breath of fresh air." The editorial added that Comstock's earlier promise to be independent of Trump had "turned to dust" and that she had been an "often unquestioning foot soldier" among GOP loyalists.

This was one of the costliest House contests in the nation. Each candidate spent more than $6 million. Total spending exceeded $25 million. Some Republicans objected during the campaign that the GOP campaign committee was wasting money here that could have been spent more effectively elsewhere. Their complaints proved to be valid.

Wexton won, 56%-44%. In suburban Loudoun and Fairfax counties, which cast nearly three-fourths of the total vote, she got 60 percent and 59 percent of the vote, respectively. Comstock won two small, outlying counties. Wexton entered the House with more legislative experience than most of her colleagues and seemed politically secure. Redistricting, plus changing local demographics, might give her even more favorable lines by 2022.

VA-10: Northern Virginia　　　　　　Cook Partisan Voting Index: D+1

Population		Race and Ethnicity		Income	
Total	813,785	White	62%	Median Income	$119,874
Land area (sq. miles)	1,372	Black	6.7%	District Income Rank	2
Pop/ sq mi	593	Latino	13.2%	Poverty Rate	4.8%
Born in State	36.4%	Asian	14%	With health insurance	92%
		Two or more races	3.5%	Cash public assistance	1.2%
Age Groups		Other	0.7%	Food stamp/SNAP	3.8%
Under 18	26.9%				
18-34	19.1%	Education		Work	
35-64	42.7%	H.S grad or less	23.8%	White Collar	11.3%
Over 64	11.3%	Some college	21.4%	Sales and Service	33.7%
		College Degree, 4 yr	30.5%	Blue Collar	12%
Military		Post grad	24.4%	Government	17.3%
Veteran/ Active Duty	9.4%				

2012 Pres. Vote	Romney	186,650	(50%)	Obama	182,432	(49%)		
2016 Pres. Vote	Clinton	210,692	(52%)	Trump	170,580	(42%)	Johnson 12,563	(3%)

Loudoun and Fairfax Counties: What we think of today as the outer suburbs and exurbs of Washington D.C. was still open country as late as World War II. Gen. George Marshall, driving from his office in the Pentagon to the old house he bought in Leesburg 40 miles away, would pass a few gas stations, crossroads villages and countless acres of farm fields. If Marshall made the trip today, his drive would take a lot longer and he would see something very different. As the federal government grew, Fairfax County's population doubled in the 1940s and very nearly tripled in the 1950s. It has continued to grow, though at a much slower rate, passing 1 million in 2002 and 1.1 million in 2011. Loudoun County, where Dulles International Airport opened in the 1960s as the outer limit to the region, lately has experienced that type of explosive growth. Its population fell just short of doubling in each of the past two decades, with an increase from 174,000 in 2000 to 398,000 in 2017. This has become the richest area of the country: Loudoun and Fairfax counties ranked first and second in the nation in median household income in 2017, with $130,000 and $118,000, respectively. Nearby Falls Church and Arlington were close behind. The Asian and Latino populations have increased rapidly in both Fairfax and Loudoun: a combined 36 percent and 33 percent, respectively.

Growth continues apace, and the Washington metro area now extends past those two counties and over the Blue Ridge into the Shenandoah Valley. No longer simply a collection of bedroom communities, Northern Virginia has become an employment center and focus of innovation in its own right. The Dulles Access Road is lined with high-tech firms and entrepreneurial startups, defense contractors and "Beltway bandit" lobbying firms. Traffic is mightily congested and Loudoun has taken steps to curb sprawl.

The 10th Congressional District covers much of Northern Virginia's western suburbs. It includes most of well-heeled McLean, home of many of Washington's political and lawyer-lobbyist elites, but it skirts the increasingly liberal — and growing -- residential enclaves in the booming Tysons commercial area. It includes the conservative Clifton area of southwest Fairfax, northern Prince William County, and the cities of Manassas and Manassas Park. Beyond the Beltway, it takes in woodsy Great Falls and the Dulles Airport corridor. It includes all of Loudoun County, which is heavily built-up in the east with some still-rural areas west of Leesburg. Middleburg, with both old and new money, is horse country with many gated mansions. Beyond the Blue Ridge, it takes in the fast-growing, Republican Winchester-based Frederick County, which not long ago was best known for its apple orchards. Winchester was the home of the Byrd family, who published the local newspaper and spawned a powerful political "machine" of conservative Democrats, led by longtime Sen. Harry Byrd, who firmly resisted racial desegregation. About 45 percent of the population is in Loudoun, and 30 percent in Fairfax.

The district was once reliably Republican. It gave George W. Bush 56 percent of the vote in 2000. With an influx of immigrants and federal workers, Northern Virginia has become notably friendlier to Democrats. Hillary Clinton in 2016 won the district, 52%-42%.

Gerald Connolly (D)

Elected 2008, 6th term, b. Mar 30, 1950; Boston, MA; Maryknoll College (IL), B.A., 1971; Harvard University, M.P.A., 1979; Roman Catholic; Married (Cathy Connolly); 1 child.

Elected Office: Fairfax County Board of Supervisors, 1995-2009, Chairman, 2004-2009.

Professional Career: Non-profit Executive; U.S. Senate aide; Defense contractor.

DC Office: 2238 RHOB 20515, 202-225-1492, Fax: 202-225-3071, connolly.house.gov

State Offices: Annandale, 703-256-3071; Woodbridge, 571-408-4407.

Committees: *Foreign Affairs*: Asia, the Pacific & Nonproliferation; Middle East, North Africa & International Terrorism. *Oversight & Reform*: Government Operations (Chmn); Subcommittee on Economic & Consumer Policy.

Group Ratings

	ADA	ACLU	AFL-CIO	LCV	ITI	COC	HAFA	ACU	CFG	FRC
2018	-	86%	-	94%	-	58%	6%	8%	8%	0%
2017	90%	C	92%	100%	C	64%	C	4%	0%	11%

Key Votes of the 115th Congress

1. Obama-care revision	N	5. Family planning regs	N	9. Guantanamo prisoners	Y
2. Tax Cuts	N	6. Body cameras/immigration	Y	10. Ground missiles, limit	Y
3. Omnibus appropriations	Y	7. Abortion ban	N	11. Defense Dept. spending	Y
4. Dodd-Frank revision	N	8. Concealed carry	N	12. FISA rules	N

Election Results

Election	Name (Party)	Vote (%)		Cand. Spent	Ind. Exp. Support	Ind. Exp. Oppose
2018 General	Gerald Connolly (D)	219,191	(71%)	$1,452,645		
	Jeff Dove (R)	83,023	(27%)	$330,822		
2018 Primary	Gerald Connolly (D)		(100%)			

Prior winning percentages: 2016 (88%), 2014 (57%), 2012 (61%), 2010 (49%), 2008 (55%)

Democrat Gerald (Gerry) Connolly, elected in 2008, is a former Capitol Hill staffer and county executive who remains an ardent champion of the federal workers and government contractors who populate his Northern Virginia district. When Democrats regained House control in 2019, his subcommittee chairmanship gave him wide-ranging jurisdiction over federal operations and many aspects of metropolitan Washington. He retains influence on international issues.

Connolly grew up in the Boston area and graduated from Maryknoll College. He considered joining the priesthood and studied for six years at a Catholic seminary. His interest in public policy led him to Washington, where he managed the American Freedom from Hunger Foundation and the U.S. Committee for Refugees. He got a master's degree from Harvard and worked for a decade on the staff of the Senate Foreign Relations Committee, where he specialized in Middle Eastern affairs and foreign aid. He left Capitol Hill to run the Washington office of Stanford Research Institute International and then became vice president of the San Diego-based defense contractor SAIC. In 1995, Connolly won a seat on the Fairfax County Board of Supervisors, and later was elected board chairman, taking responsibility for a large government at a time of rapid growth. His biggest project was the Metrorail extension to Tysons and Dulles.

In these battles, Connolly often worked with Republican Rep. Tom Davis, who continued to pay close attention to local issues. Davis, an expert on political demographics, could see that Northern Virginia was moving away from the GOP; he also was term-limited as the top Republican on the Oversight and Government Reform Committee. In 2008, he decided not to seek reelection. In the primary, Connolly faced former Rep. Leslie Byrne, whom Davis defeated in 1994. She had the backing of the national abortion rights fundraising group EMILY's List, but Connolly outpaced her finances, with support from defense contractors. In a low-turnout June primary, Connolly won by a solid 58%-33%. Republican nominee Keith Fimian, a businessman and newcomer to Northern Virginia politics, self-financed much of his campaign. Democrats attacked Fimian as too conservative on cultural issues, in contrast to Davis' moderate record; Fimian got little help from national Republicans. Connolly won 55%-43%.

Connolly has been a leader of the centrist New Democrat Coalition and he has established a moderate voting record. His Almanac vote ratings have placed him toward the center of the House, though he was more liberal on social issues. Connolly was among the Democrats who joined a majority of Republicans in backing free-trade deals with Colombia, Panama and South Korea in 2011. In 2015, he was an enthusiastic supporter among an even smaller number of House Democrats who supported trade promotion authority for President Barack Obama and his prospective Trans-Pacific Partnership deal. In turn, he was strongly criticized by labor and liberal groups that opposed the measure. Connolly's close alliance with federal employees' unions gave him some political cover.

On the Oversight and Reform Committee, Connolly has often worked well with Republicans. He was instrumental in 2014 in the enactment of the landmark Federal Information Technology Acquisition Reform Act, which was the first major overhaul of federal IT management since 1996. He enacted a bill in 2010 to encourage teleworking. When Republicans controlled the House, Connolly blasted their budget-cutting efforts that he said unfairly targeted government workers.

Taking over as chairman of the Oversight Subcommittee on Government Operations, Connolly had a busy agenda. On his House website, he listed the range of federal issues over which his panel had responsibility: "federal workforce and federal agency oversight, federal procurement and federal information policy, national drug policy, regulatory reform, the United States Postal Service, the United States Census Bureau and the District of Columbia." His immediate topics of attention included the questionnaire for the 2020 census, President Donald Trump's interest in the possible move of the FBI headquarters, management of federal information technology and a pay raise for federal employees.

Following up on his work as a Senate staffer, Connolly has been an active member of the House Foreign Affairs Committee, where he tends to voice an internationalist view. In 2017, he said that Trump's proposed budget cuts for the State Department would harm American security and diminish its leadership on the global stage. "You don't make America great again by unilaterally withdrawing from the world," he said. In 2019, he became chairman of the U.S. delegation to the NATO Parliamentary Assembly. As he described his mission, he planned to "reaffirm — with absolute clarity — the longstanding U.S. commitment to NATO and Euro-Atlantic security."

Connolly has been a harsh critic of Trump, with often cutting remarks. During the 35-day federal shutdown that began in December 2018 and was prompted by Trump's demand for funding of a wall on the border with Mexico, Connolly said in an interview on CNN: "I think the president lives in this delusional world fed by Fox News and a couple of right-wing talking heads and does not connect actions with consequences."

At home, Connolly faced a rematch with Fimian in 2010, a perilous year for Democrats. This time, Fimian did not have to rely on self-financing and raised $2.9 million to Connolly's $2.4 million. Fimian stuck to the national Republican message of "outrageous spending" and rising deficits and attacked Connolly as a "career politician." Five days after the election, Fimian conceded, having won 48.8 percent to his opponent's 49.2 percent — a margin of 981 votes out of 227,000 cast. Connolly has had it easier since then, with assistance from new district lines and the Democrats' domination of Northern Virginia.

VA-11: Northern Virginia   **Cook Partisan Voting Index: D+15**

Population		Race and Ethnicity		Income	
Total	787,515	White	46.7%	Median Income	$107,567
Land area (sq. miles)	185	Black	12.9%	District Income Rank	6
Pop/ sq mi	4254.8	Latino	18.2%	Poverty Rate	6.7%
Born in State	28.7%	Asian	18%	With health insurance	89.4%
		Two or more races	3.8%	Cash public assistance	1.2%
Age Groups		Other	0.5%	Food stamp/SNAP	4.9%
Under 18	24%				
18-34	23.5%	**Education**		**Work**	
35-64	41.4%	H.S grad or less	23.9%	White Collar	11.1%
Over 64	11.1%	Some college	21.2%	Sales and Service	35.4%
		College Degree, 4 yr	29.3%	Blue Collar	11.7%
Military		Post grad	25.7%	Government	20.9%
Veteran/ Active Duty	10.3%				

2012 Pres. Vote	Obama	212,181	(62%)	Romney	123,317	(36%)			
2016 Pres. Vote	Clinton	238,982	(66%)	Trump	98,222	(27%)	Johnson	10,253	(3%)

Fairfax and Prince William Counties: Rising on a hill west of Washington D.C., Tysons Corner was a back-country intersection 50 years ago. By the late 1980s, it was an edge city, with the largest concentration of office space to be found anywhere between Washington and Atlanta, and with a modern skyline and busy multi-lane avenues that served as arteries to the Capital Beltway. Fairfax County, which includes Tysons Corner, had been a typical postwar suburb. It had only 99,000 people in 1950, far fewer than Washington's 802,000. But in the years that followed, the trickle moving into Fairfax became a gusher. In 2018, it had 1.1 million people, nearly twice as many as Washington. Today, it is packed with mostly affluent communities, with dazzlingly high percentages of residents with college degrees and two or more cars.

In the last decade, the once-sedate "Mother Fairfax" has once again changed. Just as Tysons Corner (now referred to as simply Tysons) made it a major corporate and shopping center, developers are transforming that complex to approximate a walkable, downtown urban area. By 2050, planners envision 100,000 residents and 200,000 jobs in Tysons, which will become a 24-hour urban center. Population growth has slowed since the 1980s; the 12 percent growth rate of the 2000s was the slowest since the 1910s. The 11.7 mile extension of the Washington-area Metrorail system to Tysons and Reston, which opened in 2014, has reduced traffic congestion in that area and increased the number of shoppers who use public transit. The next Silver Line extension from Reston to Dulles Airport, which is scheduled for completion in 2020, is expected to boost the number of passengers who fly from Dulles. Meanwhile, Prince William County has been growing at a fast clip, 63 percent between 2000 and 2017, attracting the young families that Fairfax once did. Immigrants — Koreans and Vietnamese, Ethiopians and Afghans, Salvadorans and Mexicans — have put their stamp in Fairfax on what once were mostly white, heavily Protestant neighborhoods.

The 11th Congressional District of Virginia consists of much of Fairfax County and southeastern Prince William County. Stretching across northern Virginia, its southern end borders the Potomac River but its northern edge falls a bit short of the river. Republicans in control of redistricting in 2011 packed as many Democratic voters into the district as possible to shore up neighboring Republican districts. Fairfax County has had a dramatic political shift. Bill Clinton won 46 percent of the county vote in his 1996 reelection; Hillary Clinton took 64 percent in 2016. The 11th takes in sprawling Tysons, parts of Annandale that are the only area of the district inside the Capital Beltway, and also Oakton, Vienna, Fairfax City, Lorton, Burke and part of Centreville. An arm extends west to the heavily Democratic planned community of Reston, neighboring Herndon and the entrance to Dulles Airport. In Prince William County, it includes Woodbridge and Dale City, areas with large Latino immigrant populations. The district has the most federal employees of any district that does not have a military base. It is majority-minority: 18 percent Asian, 18 percent Hispanic, and 13 percent African American. It is solidly Democratic, as intended. In 2016, Hillary Clinton got 66 percent of the vote.

WASHINGTON

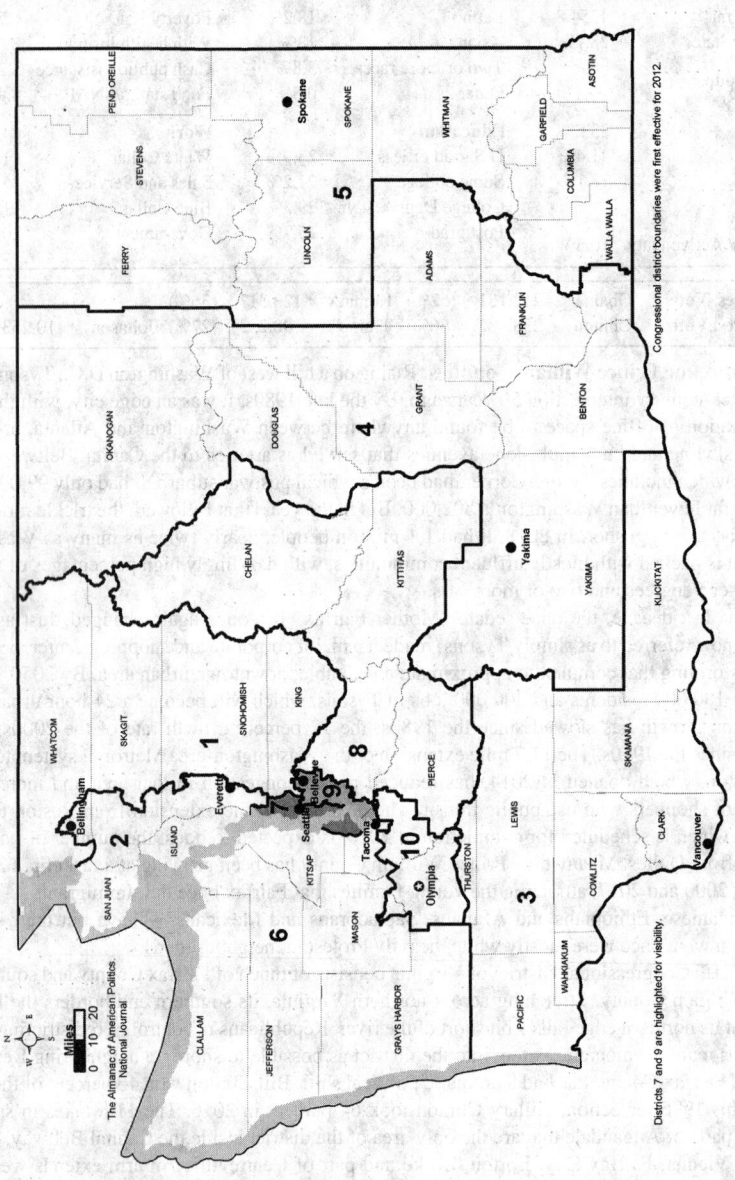

Districts 7 and 9 are highlighted for visibility.

Congressional district boundaries were first effective for 2012.

The Almanac of American Politics, National Journal

Washington is a hotbed for high-tech and export industries, disproportionately populated by affluent, well-educated, and culturally liberal residents, at least in the Seattle metropolitan area, which accounts for just over half of the state's population. As such, it embodies a key wing of the modern Democratic Party. In 2016, Washington was the rare state in which Hillary Clinton expanded on Barack Obama's 2012 margin of victory, though only modestly. At the same time, the eastern part of the state is rural and more heavily Republican.

Off in the far northwest corner of the continental United States, Washington likes to think of itself as a national trendsetter and model for the rest of the country. As the headquarters of Microsoft, Starbucks and Amazon, Washington has been on the cutting edge of innovation. An unusual environment and human creativity combined to produce these achievements. Seattle's cold, misty air and 226 overcast days a year – the cloudiest pattern of any big U.S. city -- stimulate the appetite for strong, aromatic coffee, while the torn blue jeans and flannel shirts worn year-round in this moist climate by professionals and teenagers alike created the trend made famous by Seattle-based grunge musicians. Boeing's airframe business took off during World War II because the Pacific Northwest's abundant hydroelectric power made cheap aluminum possible, and the boom in air travel in the 1980s and 1990s kept Boeing's huge assembly lines humming. Redmond-based Microsoft, founded by the tie-less and tousle-haired Bill Gates and the late Paul Allen, became one of America's great success stories as its software became embedded in the vast majority of the world's computers.

In the two decades after it became a state in 1889, Washington built a new civilization as transcontinental railroads reached the great ports of Puget Sound, the wheat-processing city of Spokane, and the region's orchard towns, fishing ports and lumber settlements. Shielded from the storms of the Pacific Ocean by the Olympic Mountains and Puget Sound, Seattle quickly became a significant American city, a lusty town full of lumbermen and railroad workers. When gold was struck in the Klondike and in Alaska, Seattle became a metropolis of miners, prospectors, and get-rich-quick operators; it is the site of the original "Skid Road," where logs were rolled downhill to the port. (Today it's in gentrified Pioneer Square.) In the years before World War I, thriving young Seattle's politics were turbulent, as class warfare pitted the radical Industrial Workers of the World (the IWW, or Wobblies) against city business and civic leaders. The businessmen, after some violence from both sides, prevailed. Adding to the area's distinctiveness was its large number of Scandinavian immigrants, with their favorable views of cooperative enterprises and government ownership.

Over time, Washington was transformed by a series of national decisions that set its course. One was government development of hydroelectric power. The Columbia River and its tributary, the Snake River, fall thousands of feet in a relatively short distance, offering far greater hydroelectric potential than any other American river system; Franklin D. Roosevelt took an interest in projects there. In 1937, Bonneville Dam was completed on the lower Columbia, followed three years later by Grand Coulee Dam, the largest man-made structure in the world at the time and still the nation's single greatest producer of electricity. When war came, Washington's hydroelectric power — the cheapest electricity in the country — made it the natural site for huge, electricity-sucking aluminum plants. The Seattle area became the home not only of shipbuilders but also of the biggest aircraft manufacturer in the country, Boeing. William Boeing founded the company in 1916 in a converted shipyard on the Duwamish River in south Seattle. The Navy had a large presence as well, with depots in Seattle, Bremerton and other locations. Further inland, the Hanford plant on the Columbia was secretly one of the government's main nuclear weapons manufacturing sites; it is currently undergoing a multi-decade, multibillion-dollar cleanup. Cheap power, aluminum, aircraft, nuclear weapons and high unionized wages — these became the starting point for the state's post-World War II economy.

Today, Washington lives less off the brawn of hydroelectric power and rail and ship tonnage, and more off the brains that made Boeing, Microsoft and Amazon global giants. Today, Washington ranks 10th in attainment of bachelor's degrees. The state hit a rough patch at the turn of the 21st century as the tech bubble burst in 2000. Microsoft also fended off a federal antitrust suit initiated in 1998, and over the next decade, the company failed to achieve the dominance in computer games and search engines that it enjoyed in PC software. In March 2001, Boeing announced it was moving its headquarters (though not its factories) to Chicago; it then saw its order book go blank after the September 11 attacks.

Washington bounced back pretty well – it now ranks in the top 10 states for median income -- but not without nagging worries. Boeing introduced its 787 Dreamliner, although the plane was grounded temporarily in 2013 while a problem with recurring battery fires was remedied. The company also got a controversial contract for the Air Force's KC-46 refueling tanker. Amid record levels of jet deliveries and revenues, the company added 4,000 jobs in 2018; that broke a six-year run of shrinking payrolls, but employment was still 20 percent below its 2012 peak. The celebrations stopped in early 2019 with back-to-back crashes of newly introduced (and once fast-selling) 737 MAX jets flown by Lion Air and Ethiopian Airlines, forcing a grounding of the fleet. Henry Harteveldt, a travel industry analyst, told Business Insider that the crashes were "a very serious problem for Boeing" and one that "I don't think will be easy to fix."

Microsoft, meanwhile, survived the antitrust case, a huge fine from the European Union, Gates' retirement, and vigorous competition from California-based Apple and Google. It now has almost 135,000 full-time employees, about 50,000 of them in metro Seattle. Starbucks cut back during the recession but has been expanding again, abroad and at home. Amazon was transformed from an internet bookseller that wreaked havoc on big bookstores to a behemoth rewriting the rules of retailing everywhere. The company expanded into streaming video and even toyed with the idea of delivery by drones; its founder, Jeff Bezos, purchased The Washington Post (in the other Washington) and proceeded to bolster its fortunes. The company had a profound impact on Seattle, creating some 45,000 jobs and counting, redeveloping large swaths of the city, and encouraging transit-oriented development, but also drawing "much of the blame for pushing up housing costs and homelessness, aggravating traffic and even diluting Seattle's identity as a quirky, laid-back city," The Post wrote in 2018. Like the tech hubs of California, Seattle became an expensive city to live in, exacerbating income inequality.

At the same time, businesses in the state fretted about President Donald Trump's protectionist agenda. An estimated 40 percent of the state's jobs are linked to international trade – from planes to cherries – and the Brookings Institution calculated that retaliatory tariffs could put 16,000 jobs at risk. In 2018, a study by a pro-trade alliance said that consumers in the state were paying as much as $100 million more for imported goods due to the trade face-off.

Buoyed by business growth, the state's population expanded 14 percent between 2000 and 2010 -- faster than Oregon or California – and it has risen another 10.1 percent since 2010. Seattle has grown 18.7 percent since 2010, the fastest pace of any of the 50 biggest U.S. cities. Washington's biggest counties have expanded by healthy rates: King County (Seattle) by 12.7 percent since 2010, and neighboring Snohomish County (Everett) and Pierce County (Tacoma) by 11.2 percent and 8 percent, respectively. Outside metro Seattle, Clark County (Vancouver, across from Portland Oregon) has grown 10.3 percent. Even Spokane County, in the slower-growing eastern half of the state, has grown 6.4 percent since 2010. Washington remains predominantly white, though the percentage has fallen in recent years; overall, the state is 12 percent Hispanic and 8 percent Asian. Some of the highest minority proportions are in agricultural areas, such as apple-growing Yakima County, a minority-majority jurisdiction that is 48 percent Hispanic and 4 percent Native American.

People continue to flock to Washington despite the growing evidence of catastrophic risk. Four of the nation's 15 most dangerous volcanoes, according to the U.S. Geological Survey, are located in the state: Mount St. Helens, which erupted spectacularly in 1980 and continues to produce periodic earthquakes; 14,000-foot Mount Rainier, situated just 60 miles from Seattle and Tacoma; Mount Baker; and Glacier Peak. Another risk is an earthquake and tsunami stemming from the obscure Cascadia subduction zone. A regional director of the Federal Emergency Management Agency told the New Yorker in 2015 that, in the worst-case scenario, "our operating assumption is that everything west of Interstate 5 will be toast," meaning 140,000 square miles and 7 million people living in and around Seattle, Tacoma and Olympia in Washington and Portland, Eugene and Salem in Oregon. Officials are working to launch ShakeAlert, a seismic detection system that will send alerts to residents using a smartphone app.

Situated in a region with abundant natural beauty, Washington has taken environmental concerns seriously, but this often has pitted green priorities against industries that created the state's original wealth. A key flashpoint has been coal – not extracted from mines in the state (the last one closed in 2006) but rather shipped by rail from places such as Wyoming, destined for terminals that would send shiploads to growing Asian economies. Activists have fought the construction of a half-dozen new cargo terminals, and their opposition has often have been successful. Port expansions for containerized cargo have generally prompted less opposition: In early 2019, the Port of Seattle was moving toward a $500 million plan to upgrade its dormant Terminal 5 to handle bigger freighters and make the port more competitive with such regional rivals as the Canadian ports of Vancouver and Prince Rupert. Indeed, the state's environmental leanings have been consistently shown to have limits. In 2016, voters rejected a ballot measure that would have taxed carbon dioxide emissions at $25 per ton, in exchange for sales tax rollbacks. The measure failed by an 18-point margin. (Some environmentalists opposed the initiative because it did not steer the anticipated revenue to their pet projects.) Two years later, voters, by a 57%-43% margin, rejected a measure to enact a carbon emissions fee with revenues funding environmental programs; it won King County by double digits but lost in rural areas and in the suburban counties of Snohomish and Pierce.

Politically, Washington was one of the most Democratic northern states in the 1930s. Roosevelt's campaign manager, James Farley, used to refer to "the 47 states and the Soviet of Washington." Its mainstream Democrats — notably Sens. Warren Magnuson and Henry "Scoop" Jackson, who represented the state in Congress for a cumulative 87 years — believed in an activist federal government that built dams, bought military aircraft and pursued an internationalist, anti-Communist foreign policy abroad. Their political strength came out of a blue-collar base, augmented by the respect big business had for their political clout. Today, the state remains one of the most unionized in the nation, but the fulcrum of the electorate has moved from blue collar to white collar, and from economic class warfare to culture wars. On balance, the Democrats have benefited. In presidential races, Washington has voted exclusively Democratic since 1988 and has elected only Democratic governors since 1984. However, a number of the state's recent gubernatorial and senatorial contests have been competitive, and the GOP holds the offices of state treasurer and secretary of state.

Politically, Washington is divided along geographic lines. The biggest share of votes comes from the three counties closest to Seattle – King, Snohomish and Pierce. Together, they accounted for 53 percent of the statewide votes cast for president in 2016. In the 1980s, King County was closely divided, with higher-income suburbs voting Republican and working-class neighborhoods in Seattle voting Democratic. But Seattle has become a relatively childless city, while Hispanics have been moving to southern King County suburbs, as a growing number of Asians relocate to suburbs like Bellevue and Redmond east of Lake Washington. All these groups tend to vote heavily Democratic. Seattle in particular has pursued a solidly progressive course, raising its minimum wage to $15 and electing Kshama Sawant, an Indian-born Trotskyist socialist, to the city council. Pierce County was long a blue-collar Democratic bastion, and that remains true in Tacoma, though it's less so elsewhere in the county. Snohomish County leans blue in many races but can be competitive.

Two other regions account for the remainder of the statewide vote. One is eastern Washington beyond the Cascade Range; this region votes consistently Republican. Cultural issues have produced results in this part of the state that are sharply at odds with the state as a whole. In 2012, when Washington endorsed same-sex marriage, it passed with 67 percent in King County but failed by 60 percent in eastern Washington. The third area that casts the remainder of the state's votes is west of the Cascades but outside King, Snohomish and Pierce. A notable portion of this region is Clark County, a fast-growing area adjoining Portland. (Washington has no income tax and Oregon no sales tax, so you can avoid lots of taxes by living in Clark County and shopping across the line.)

In the 2016 presidential race, Clinton won by 16 points, with relatively strong showings by third-party candidates – Libertarian Gary Johnson, who got 5 percent, and Green Party nominee Jill Stein, who got nearly 2 percent. In aggressively progressive King County, Clinton improved on Obama's winning margin by 10 points, whereas in Pierce County, with more white working-class voters who were receptive to Trump's message, Clinton's margin slipped to seven points from Obama's 11. Her weak performance in less-populated areas of the state meant that she had to rely more heavily on the Seattle area to win. The share of the Democratic presidential vote coming from King, Snohomish and Pierce counties rose from 55 percent in 2012 to 62 percent in 2016.

Democrats cheered other victories in 2016. Cyrus Habib, a blind Rhodes Scholar and Iranian-American lawyer-legislator with a passion for karate and jazz piano, was elected lieutenant governor.

Voters passed ballot measures to raise the statewide minimum wage and to allow courts to remove individuals' access to firearms if they are deemed to be a risk to themselves or others.

In 2018, Democrats managed to flip one of three competitive House seats, winning an open-seat contest. Meanwhile, in addition to rejecting the carbon emission fee, Washington voters said no -- by double digits -- to new soda taxes. However, voters did approve two liberal measures by wide margins: new requirements and training for police officers' use of deadly force, and a package of gun-control measures that included the imposition of background checks and waiting periods.

Population		Race and Ethnicity		Income	
Total	7,169,967	White	69.8%	Median Income	$66,174
Land area (sq. miles)	66,456	Black	3.5%	State Income Rank	10
Pop/ sq mi	107.9	Latino	12.3%	Poverty Rate	12.2%
Born in state	47.2%	Asian	8.0%	With health insurance	91.7%
		Two or more races	4.6%	Cash public assistance	3.5%
Age Groups		Other	1.8%	Food stamp/SNAP	13.3%
Under 18	22.5%				
18-34	23.8%	Education		Work	
35-64	39.3%	H.S grad or less	31.6%	White Collar	40.3%
Over 64	14.4%	Some college	33.9%	Sales and Service	38.8%
		College Degree, 4 yr	21.7%	Blue Collar	20.9%
Military		Post grad	12.7%	Government	15.9%
Veteran/ Active Duty	10.7%				

Presidential Politics

2016 Caucus (D)	Clinton (D)	420,461 (52%)	Sanders (D)	382,293 (48%)	
2016 Primary (R)	Trump (R)	455,023 (75%)	Cruz (R)	65,172 (11%)	Kasich (R) 58,954 (10%)
2016 Pres. Vote	Clinton (D) 1,742,718 (53%)	Trump (R) 1,221,747 (37%)	Johnson (L) 160,879 (5%)		
2012 Pres. Vote	Obama (D) 1,755,396 (56%)	Romney (R)1,290,670 (41%)			

For three decades, Washington was one of the most contrarian states in presidential politics, voting for Republican losers Richard Nixon in 1960 and Gerald Ford in 1976 and Democratic losers Hubert Humphrey in 1968 and Michael Dukakis in 1988. In the 1990s, it tilted Democratic, with the nation, voting for Bill Clinton twice. Since then, it has moved significantly toward the Democrats, voting 58%-40% and 56%-41% for Barack Obama in 2008 and 2012, respectively. Hillary Clinton won the state 53%-37%. The traditional partisan dividing line is the Cascades mountain range. West to the Pacific is Democratic territory. East to the Idaho border is Republican turf. Anchoring the Democratic terrain is King County, which accounts for almost one-third of the state's vote. King once had plenty of Seattle suburbs that backed moderate Republicans. But as the GOP adopted more conservative stands on social issues and Seattle became a high-tech haven that attracted younger voters, the county became a Democratic bastion. It voted for Clinton over Donald Trump, 70%-21%. Trump received 8 percent of the vote in Seattle, less than the 10 percent he garnered in the liberal temple of San Francisco. Adjoining Pierce and Snohomish counties, the next two largest vote-producers that include Seattle suburbs and exurbs, also backed Clinton. But the Obama administration's hostility toward the timber industry shifted some of the traditional allegiances in Washington. The five counties in the state that saw the biggest percentage drop-off in the Democratic vote from 2012 were in the west: Cowlitz, Gray's Harbor, Mason, Pacific and Wahkiakum. All five have lumber and logging concerns. All five backed Trump. All the counties east of the Cascades backed Trump except for Whitman, home to Washington State University.

When it came to the two parties' presidential nominating contests, there was no divide in the state. Democrats held a caucus on March 26 and Vermont Sen. Bernie Sanders walloped Clinton 73%-27% and carried every county in the state. The caucuses gave him a larger delegate boost than any other caucus or primary. For Clinton it must have felt like déjà vu all over again: In the 2008 caucuses, Obama beat Clinton 68%-31%, winning every county. Republicans held a May primary, after all of Trump's GOP rivals had withdrawn from the race and he garnered 76 percent of the vote.

For 2020, the state moved to March 10 its all mail-in presidential primary, which both parties will use to allocate their convention delegates.

Congressional Districts

116th Congress Lineup	7D 3R	115th Congress Lineup	6D 4R

In 1983, voters approved a constitutional amendment that created a bipartisan redistricting commission, made up of two Democrats and two Republicans appointed by legislative leaders. If the commission deadlocks, the issue goes to the Supreme Court; lines also can be changed by a two-thirds vote in both houses of the legislature. The Washington plan originally was lauded for encouraging cooperation and creating more districts that both parties can win. But unlike Iowa or California, where commissions are not supposed to take political considerations into account, the result in Washington has become incumbent protection.

Washington gained a House seat in the reapportionment following the 2010 census. In 2011, Democrats held a 5-4 lead in House seats, and 56 percent of the state's growth between 2000 and 2010 had taken place in the four Republican-held districts. The two Republican commissioners, including former Sen. Slade Gorton, proposed placing a new "fair fight" 10th District in the state's highly competitive northwest and North Puget Sound. The two Democrats countered with proposals putting the new 10th District in the more reliably Democratic South Puget Sound area around Olympia. Three days before their New Year's Eve deadline, the commissioners forged a compromise in a display of bipartisanship rare for the 2012 cycle. The new 10th District went to the South Sound and was a perfect fit for Democrat Denny Heck, who had lost to Republican Rep. Jaime Herrera Beutler in 2010. In exchange, Democrats strengthened two incumbent Republicans, and stretched the suburban Seattle 1st District all the way north to the Canadian border to make it marginally more competitive. Democrats have easily controlled the 1st and the 10th since then. When Republicans lost the incumbency advantage after Rep. Dave Reichert retired in 2018, Democrats took the 8th in the eastern Seattle-Tacoma suburbs.

That left Democrats with all seven districts that surround Seattle and Puget Sound. Republicans continued to hold the three seats in the hinterlands. If Democrats have the opportunity in the 2021 redistricting, their chief objective likely will be to reinforce the 8th in their favor. Their other six districts have plenty of voters to spare. Absent an improved performance in the suburbs, Republicans may be hard-pressed to take back that seat, under any circumstances. Their greater concern may be incumbent protection in their three remaining districts.

Jay Inslee (D)

Elected 2012, term expires 2021, 2nd term; b. Feb. 9, 1951, Seattle; Stanford U., 1969-70, U. of WA, B.A. 1973; Willamette U., J.D. 1976; Protestant; Married (Trudi); 3 children.

Elected Office: WA House, 1988-1992; U.S. House, 1993-1995, 1999-2012.

Professional Career: City prosecutor, Selah, WA, 1976-1984; Practicing attorney, 1976-1992, 1995-1996; Regional Director, U.S. Department of Health and Human Services, 1997-1998.

Office: 416 14th Ave SW, Olympia, 98404-0002; 360-902-4111; Fax: 360-753-4110; Website: governor.wa.gov.

Lt. Gov.: Cyrus Habib (D) **Atty. Gen:** Bob Ferguson (D) **Sec. of State:** Kim Wyman (R)
State Legislature: Senate: 28D, 20R, 1V **House:** 57D, 41R

Election Results

Election	Name (Party)	Vote (%)
2016 General	Jay Inslee (D)	1,760,520 (54%)
	Bill Bryant (R)	1,476,346 (45%)
2016 Primary	Jay Inslee (D)	687,412 (49%)
	Patrick O Rourke (R)	40,572 (3%)

Prior winning percentage: 2012 (52%); House: 2010 (58%), 2008 (68%), 2006 (68%), 2004 (62%), 2002 (60%), 2000 (55%), 1998 (50%), 1992 (51%)

Democrat Jay Inslee was narrowly elected Washington's governor in 2012, after serving 15 years in the House. He won a second term in 2016 by a nine-point margin, only about half the winning statewide margin for Hillary Clinton in the same election. In 2019, he entered the race for the 2020 Democratic presidential nomination, making the centerpiece of his candidacy the need to tackle climate change.

Inslee grew up in north Seattle, the son of a high school biology teacher and football coach. He graduated from the University of Washington and Willamette University College of Law. He moved to Selah, in Yakima County east of the Cascades, to practice law and served on the State Trial Lawyers Association board of directors. In 1988, at age 37, he was elected to the state House over a former Yakima mayor.

In 1992, when 4th District Rep. Sid Morrison ran for governor, Inslee won the general election to succeed him, 51%-49%, over Doc Hastings. In the House, Inslee voted for the Clinton budget and tax increase and for a crime bill with a ban on some types of semi-automatic weapons. In the 1994 Republican wave election, Hastings challenged Inslee and beat him, 53%-47%. After his defeat, Inslee moved to Bainbridge Island and practiced law in Seattle. In 1996, he ran for governor and finished fifth, with 10 percent of the vote, in the all-party primary. He briefly served as regional director of the U.S. Health and Human Services Department.

In 1998, Inslee decided to run for Congress again, this time in the 1st District against Republican Rep. Rick White, an economic conservative with liberal votes on some cultural issues. In the September all-party primary, White led 50%-44%. But by November, two issues changed the balance. Inslee ran ads claiming that White intended to spend 10 years in the House and then become a lobbyist, a charge his ex-wife had made in divorce papers. He also ran ads highlighting White's vote to impeach President Bill Clinton. White's vote share was also hurt by a third-party Christian conservative, Bruce Craswell. The primary numbers were reversed in November, and Inslee won 50%-44%.

In Congress, Inslee was a moderate-to-liberal Democrat. He joined in protecting the privacy of consumer financial records — an issue important to Microsoft, his largest single source of campaign funds as a congressman. When security experts reported in 2011 that Apple's iPhone could secretly track its users' movements, Inslee called for greater government oversight of data collection. On the Energy and Commerce Committee, Inslee focused on conservation and increasing renewable energy sources. As early as 2005, he introduced bills to address global warming and reduce U.S. dependence on foreign oil. When Republicans took control of the House, Inslee criticized what he called the GOP's "allergy to science," and toted a stack of more than 20 books to a March 2011 hearing, claiming they contained irrefutable evidence of the problem.

By the time two-term Democratic Gov. Christine Gregoire decided to retire in 2012, Inslee had already laid the groundwork for a bid. Nine months after launching his candidacy, he decided in March 2012 to resign his House seat to campaign full-time. Inslee's stature cleared the Democratic contenders, and he won the state's top-two primary in August with 47 percent of the vote. That set up a general-election matchup against Republican Rob McKenna, the state's attorney general, who had taken 43 percent in the primary. Republicans accused Inslee of notching no significant legislative accomplishments or attaining a leadership position.

Even though a Republican hadn't won a gubernatorial race in the state since 1980, the GOP liked McKenna's chances. As attorney general, he focused on consumer protection issues and, as president of the National Association of Attorneys General, played a key role in a $25 billion, multi-state settlement with banks over their mortgage practices. Democrats sought to tie him to the tea party movement, citing his decision to join other states in challenging the federal health care law. But McKenna campaigned as a business-friendly moderate. He played up his pro-environment beliefs and said that he did not oppose collective bargaining and would work with unions if elected. He said he personally opposed abortion, but that ultimately it was up to the woman to decide. He got help from state Republicans who played up the failure of some of the renewable-energy companies that Inslee had highlighted in a book he'd written.

Barack Obama's strong reelection showing in the state — he won with 56 percent of the vote — helped put Inslee over the top, 52%-48%. McKenna eked out a 52%-48% win in Pierce County (Tacoma) and dominated the rural eastern half of the state. Inslee decisively won King County (Seattle), 62%-38%, and took Snohomish County (Everett) 51%-49%.

In 2014, Inslee imposed a moratorium on the death penalty, covering the nine men on death row in the state. In 2015, Senate Republicans blocked his bid for a $12 statewide minimum wage. On taxes, Inslee proposed a roughly $1.5 billion package that would include a capital gains tax, a carbon tax, a hike in the cigarette tax and a tax on e-cigarettes, along with several narrower provisions. None were voted on in the Democratic-controlled state House, and six months later, following an unexpectedly strong revenue forecast, he said a tax package that extensive was no longer necessary, although individual elements might remain on the table.

For much of his term, Inslee grappled with the issue of carbon emissions cuts — a signature accomplishment if he could achieve it. In April 2014, Inslee proposed a cap-and-trade program aimed at reducing greenhouse gases in stages by 2020, 2035 and 2050, to reach target levels that had been enacted in 2008. He also urged phasing out coal-derived electricity, reducing vehicular emissions, increasing investment in alternative energy and curbing emissions by state government. But the key part of his agenda — the cap-and-trade plan — faced resistance, including from some Democrats. By June 2015, even modified versions of the proposal fell by the wayside. Meanwhile, Inslee supported the "Connecting Washington" program, which allocated billions of dollars for expanding and replacing state highways, paid for by gasoline and car taxes. He also worked with the legislature to raise salaries for school employees and cut college tuition.

Spending on K-12 education proved to be particularly thorny. A 2012 state Supreme Court ruling had upended the state's education funding system, requiring the state to pay more for teacher salaries and other basic education costs. After the ruling, lawmakers and the governor reallocated some state money to schools but never fully satisfied the court's dictates; the justices responded by levying contempt fines on the state. The issue was eventually settled in the courts, and in 2018, teachers began receiving pay bumps stemming from the lawsuit.

The 2016 election pitted Inslee against Republican Bill Bryant, a former Port of Seattle commissioner. In the August primary, Inslee took first place with 49 percent and Bryant took second with 38 percent. In the general election, Bryant attacked Inslee's oversight of the state's biggest psychiatric facility as well as the corrections system, which had released thousands of inmates too early as a result of incorrect computerized calculations. Inslee countered by touting the state's economic health and reductions in tuition at state colleges and universities; he was also a leading supporter of a ballot measure that would raise the minimum wage in steps to $13.50 an hour. Inslee beat Bryant by a nine-point margin. Democrats kept their House majority, but the GOP held their majority in the state Senate. Voters approved the minimum-wage ballot measure, but rejected one that would have imposed the nation's first carbon tax, abetted by dissatisfied environmentalists who wanted the money to be earmarked for renewable energy subsidies and other pet projects.

The $43.7 billion two-year budget Inslee signed in 2017 raised state property taxes by $1.6 billion to fund education, while also expanding online sales taxes and raising taxes on bottled water and extracted fuels. In addition to K-12 education, the budget provided raises for state workers and additional money for the state mental-health system, as well as for higher education and early childhood education. He signed a bipartisan measure to guarantee paid family leave.

Meanwhile, Inslee became a leading national Democratic voice against the immigration policies of President Donald Trump. This was not a new issue for Inslee; as early as 2015, he had taken a stand in favor of continuing to accept Syrian refugees, even as other governors, mostly Republican, sought to bar their settlement. In 2017, Washington state, led by Attorney General Bob Ferguson, became an important – and, at least initially, successful -- litigant against Trump's travel ban. Inslee received support on the issue from the state's influential tech sector, which relied on a well-functioning immigration system to hire workers from overseas. (A rewritten travel order did eventually pass muster with the Supreme Court in 2018.) Inslee signed an executive order limiting state cooperation on federal immigration enforcement, and he called the administration "morally bankrupt" and the White House "a den of deceit." When Trump made increasingly protectionist moves on trade, Inslee, the governor of an export-dependent state, spoke out. "Unfortunately, the president's erratic and unilateral moves undermine everything we've done to build up markets for our world-class products," he wrote in a CNBC op-ed in July 2018.

Closer to home, Inslee in 2018 spearheaded an effort – the nation's first – to pass a law requiring net neutrality, though it was expected to face legal challenges. He vetoed a bill that would have protected the legislature from the state's Public Records Act, signed a bill to ban "bump stocks" that make semi-automatic weapons more deadly, signed another bill to ban LGBT "conversion therapy" for those under 18, and signed a measure to guarantee that health insurers in the state cover abortions and contraception if they also cover maternity care. In October 2018, Inslee's death penalty moratorium was vindicated when the state Supreme Court abolished the practice and commuted the sentences of existing death row inmates to life in prison. In January 2019, Inslee announced that he would pardon residents who had misdemeanor convictions for marijuana. He proposed $3.7 billion in new tax revenue, including a levy on capital gains.

In March 2019, Inslee entered the presidential primary field. He made climate change the centerpiece of his campaign, and promised to forgo money from the fossil fuel industry. "There was only four minutes of climate change in the last three presidential debates" in 2016, he said in a CNN town hall. "I'm going to end that." In his state of the state address, Inslee proposed a package that included a stricter auto emissions standard, a phase-out of polluting chemicals in air conditioning, more taxpayer-funded incentives for electric vehicles, and increased energy-efficiency benchmarks for buildings. Still, Inslee began as a serious underdog in the race, and according to a Pew Research Center poll, climate change ranked among the least important issues for Democratic respondents.

Patty Murray (D)

Elected 1992, term expires 2022, 5th term, b. Oct 11, 1950; Bothell; Washington State University, B.A., 1972; Roman Catholic; Married (Robert Randall Murray); 2 children.

Elected Office: Shoreline School Board, 1985-1989, President, 1985-1986; WA Senate, 1988-1992.

Professional Career: State Senator; Teacher

DC Office: 154 RSOB 20510, 202-224-2621, Fax: 202-224-0238, murray.senate.gov

State Offices: Everett, 425-259-6515; Seattle, 206-553-5545; Spokane, 509-624-9515; Tacoma, 253-572-3636; Vancouver, 360-696-7797; Yakima, 509-453-7462.

Committees: Senate Assistant Minority Leader. *Appropriations*: Department of Defense; Department of Homeland Security; DOL, HHS & Education & Related Agencies (RMM); Energy & Water Development; Military Construction & Veteran Affairs & Related Agencies; Transportation, HUD & Related Agencies. *Budget. Health, Education, Labor & Pensions (RMM)*: Ex Officio membership on all subcommittees. *Veterans' Affairs*.

Group Ratings

	ADA	ACLU	AFL-CIO	LCV	ITI	COC	HAFA	ACU	CFG	FRC
2018	-	76%	-	100%	-	50%	3%	5%	5%	0%
2017	95%	C	100%	100%	C	29%	C	0%	4%	0%

Almanac Ratings 2017-18

	Economy	Social	Foreign	Composite
Liberal	100%	100%	82%	94%
Conservative	0%	0%	18%	6%

Key Votes of the 115th Congress

1. Obama-care revision	N	5. Gun regulations	N	9. Kavanaugh confirmation	N
2. Tax Cuts	N	6. Family planning regs	N	10. Saudi arms sales	Y
3. Dodd-Frank revision	N	7. Gorsuch confirmation	N	11. FISA rules	N
4. Omnibus appropriations	Y	8. Immigration restrictions	N	12. Military aid in Yemen	Y

Election Results

Election	Name (Party)	Vote (%)		Cand. Spent	Ind. Exp. Support	Ind. Exp. Oppose
2016 General	Patty Murray (D).............................. 1,913,979	(59%)		$5,676,043	$33,423	
	Chris Vance (R)............................... 1,329,338	(41%)		$441,718		
2016 Primary	Patty Murray (D)............................... 745,421	(54%)				
	Chris Vance (R)................................. 381,004	(28%)				

Prior winning percentages: 2010 (52%), 2004 (55%), 1998 (58%), 1992 (54%)

Patty Murray is the senior senator from Washington, first elected in 1992. She has come a long way from her entry into politics as a parent-activist. Even as Murray maintains a low-key, plainspoken style, she has become a powerful, senior backroom player, with a seat at her party's leadership table. She plays a key role in advancing Democrats' positions, especially on health care and education — a lofty status she partly ascribes to her preschool teacher training. "You don't walk into a class with 4-year-olds without a direction of where you're going to go," she told HuffPost. In 2016, she won a fifth term with her biggest election vote.

Murray grew up in the Seattle suburb of Bothell, one of seven children of a disabled World War II veteran. She graduated from Washington State University in 1972, married, and stayed home to raise her children. In 1980, she was in Olympia trying to save a parenting class she was teaching at Shoreline Community College, which was the target of budget cuts. A state legislator told her: "You're just a mom in tennis shoes. You can't make a difference." She later said, "Almost every woman I've ever met in politics got into it because she was mad about something." She won her fight over the parenting class and then ran for the Shoreline School Board. She eventually was chosen board president. In 1988, she challenged a Republican state senator, knocked on 17,000 doors and won the seat. While there, she worked on issues that resonated with voters, from school bus safety to extending a family leave bill for a parent whose child is ill or dying. In late 1991, Murray decided to run against Sen. Brock Adams, a Democrat who was under a cloud following charges of sexual molestation. He decided not to seek re-election.

Amid a crowd of better-known, conventional male politicians, Murray, with her flat, Midwestern-style accent and "mom in tennis shoes" line, attracted most of the campaign attention. In the 1992 all-party primary, her main Democratic opponent was former Rep. Don Bonker, who had narrowly lost a Senate nomination in 1988. Murray won 28 percent of the vote to Bonker's 19 percent. She sprinted to a big lead in polls against Republican Rep. Rod Chandler, who had served for a decade. She won 54% to 46% in November in what came to be called "the year of the woman."

With a largely liberal voting record, Murray is a skillful lawmaker. She is known for being attuned to the needs of Senate conservatives, being adept at ingratiating herself with veteran colleagues and recognizing and exploiting the possibility of a deal even in a partisan environment. "She's a pretty good arbiter and proxy for the caucus as a whole," Rich Tarplin, a lobbyist close to Senate Democrats, told National Journal. Murray generally leaves the spotlight for others but does not shy from asserting senatorial prerogatives. In what she calls her "angry mom" voice, she has rebuked Republican and Democratic secretaries of the Department of Veterans Affairs for proposals that would make veterans pay more for health care.

Murray became chairwoman of the Budget Committee in 2013. To counter the budget proposal offered by her House counterpart, Wisconsin Republican Paul Ryan, she unveiled a spending plan that was the first from her party since 2009. It included about $1 trillion in new revenues over 10 years, mostly from closing tax loopholes and incentives, and had about $1 trillion in spending cuts. Unlike Ryan's budget, which some House GOP moderates found draconian, her plan was geared toward getting broad Democratic support. It included $100 billion for a new "economic recovery protection plan" that would fund infrastructure projects and education programs. But in a surprise, it would have cut more than twice as much from the biggest health entitlement, Medicare, than Ryan's would have. Though Republicans vilified her proposal as unworkable, they said Murray was easy to work with. "You've allowed us to have free ability to speak out; you've been respectful," Republican Jeff Sessions of Alabama, the ranking Republican on the panel, told her at a hearing.

Murray forged a working relationship with Ryan through her combination of affability and a can-do, pragmatic style. Their partnership enabled them in December 2013 to strike a two-year budget deal that called for raising new revenue through fee increases without tax increases or changes to Social Security or Medicare. It replaced steep across-the-board spending cuts under the looming "sequester" in January with targeted spending cuts. Democrats groused about the deal, which didn't add much money for party priorities such as infrastructure spending, and it failed to close any of the tax loopholes they had targeted. But it easily passed both chambers and became law. Each chairman scored a personal achievement.

That deal with Ryan was her second—and more productive—attempt to play a leading role in chairing the Budget Committee. After the protracted standoff over raising the federal debt limit in 2011, she and Texas Republican Rep. Jeb Hensarling were named as co-chiefs of the Joint Select Committee on Deficit Reduction, the "super committee" charged with finding a bipartisan consensus on future spending in just a few months. To nearly no one's surprise, the effort was fruitless. In this case, she had less maneuverability. "The one thing the Republicans wouldn't put on the table was revenue," Murray told The Seattle Times. "I knew what a bad deal would mean for the middle class in this country. Many of us are where we are in our lives because we had a country that was there for us."

As a junior member on the Appropriations Committee, Murray made a point to get along with senior senators. After Alaska's Ted Stevens, the former GOP chairman, lost his bid for re-election in 2008, he gave Murray the desk that once belonged to Washington Democrat Warren Magnuson, who served in the Senate for nearly 40 years. When West Virginia Democrat Robert Byrd was too ill in 2007 and 2008 to manage spending bills on the floor as chairman, he gave Murray the task ahead of more senior members. Now, only Patrick Leahy of Vermont and Dianne Feinstein of California have served more years as Democrats in the Senate than Murray. Murray has delivered for her state and then some: The Washington watchdog group Taxpayers for Common Sense dubbed her the "Queen of Pork." Despite a subsequent ban on earmarking, Murray still worked to include funding for a variety of Washington projects in spending bills, including money for a Seattle light-rail system and a bridge over the Columbia River.

After the 2014 retirement of Sen. Tom Harkin, Murray became the ranking Democrat at the HELP Committee. She worked with Tennessee Republican Lamar Alexander, the chairman of the committee, on a measure to overhaul No Child Left Behind, a bipartisan legacy of President George W. Bush. She dissuaded him from writing his own bill and then seeking some moderate Democrats' support and, instead, he agreed to develop a bipartisan proposal from the start. No Child Left Behind had become unpopular because of its heavy reliance on standardized testing. "I've heard from parent after parent and teacher after teacher in Washington state who has told me that not only are students taking too many tests, oftentimes the tests are of low quality or redundant," Murray said.

Though efforts to change the law had failed for several years, Alexander and Murray crafted a proposal that cut back the heavy reliance on testing and gave states and school districts more control of academic standards and teacher and school performance. Remarkably, the HELP Committee, whose members' views span the ideological spectrum, voted unanimously for the bill in 2015. The Senate passed it 81-17.

That collaboration on the HELP Committee ended with the election of President Donald Trump. The confirmation of Betsy DeVos as Education secretary was a contentious affair. Murray complained that DeVos had not sufficiently disclosed her complex personal finances or answered questions from Democrats, who were unhappy with Alexander's rush to confirm DeVos.

Murray has positioned herself as a foe of DeVos. She has also made stopping sexual harassment a central part of her Trump agenda. The two women have clashed over a range of issues but tensions boiled over in 2018 when Murray went after DeVos on Twitter over proposed changes to the department's guidelines to universities on how to handle sexual assault and sexual misconduct. DeVos called Murray's action "unbecoming and irresponsible."

In 2018, Murray and Alexander attempted — but failed — to extend their collaboration to higher education legislation. Alexander said that Murray was no longer unwilling to negotiate. But circumstances were different this time. With Republicans in complete control of Congress and the White House, Murray had less leverage to push her objectives, like lowering tuition costs and increasing access to education for those with low incomes. Plus, Murray had little interest in House Republicans' proposal, which changed and cut back on student-aid programs. The Trump administration was content to have DeVos take some of those steps without Congress.

Alexander and Murray also ran into broader partisan problems in 2018 when they again failed to find common ground on incremental changes to the Affordable Care Act. Their discussions included ideas like giving states more flexibility in setting up their own programs in exchange for Democrats' goal of providing billions of dollars more to support the states. Despite progress between the two senators, they found themselves hamstrung by peripheral issues, especially the Republican insistence to prohibit funding of abortion in the Obamacare marketplaces. "I greatly respect the senator from

Washington and enjoy working with her, but on this issue, I think we've reached an impasse," Alexander told the Senate in March 2018.

In 2015, Murray worked with then-Senate Republican Whip John Cornyn of Texas to end a stalemate over a noncontroversial measure to combat human trafficking that became ensnared in the always-combustible abortion debate. Democrats objected to what they saw as an anti-abortion provision in the legislation that would have prevented money from the victim's fund from being used for abortions in keeping with the Hyde Amendment's prohibition on taxpayer money being used for abortion services. Murray and Cornyn led the way to a creative compromise: They clarified that money from the fines would go to non-health care concerns, which would not be subject to the Hyde prohibition, and that federal funds, which are subject to the prohibition, would cover health care.

Murray first served as the head of the Democratic Senatorial Campaign Committee in 2002. After the Sept. 11 terrorist attacks, it was a tough year for the party, which lost a net two seats. Even so, Murray impressed colleagues with her fundraising. Ten years later, Democrats faced a daunting map, and the party was on defense. Several ambitious Democrats passed on the job, but Murray stepped in to lead the committee once again. Murray and fellow Democrats picked up two seats. They got some fortunate breaks from Republicans and successful female candidates, such as Massachusetts' Elizabeth Warren, Wisconsin's Tammy Baldwin and North Dakota's Heidi Heitkamp. "Oftentimes, when you're looking at people to run, they rule the women out, saying, 'They can't win,'" Murray told The Oregonian. "I ruled them in."

In her first years on Capitol Hill, Murray was criticized as too staff-reliant. But she has grown into the role of senator. She immersed herself in Washington state issues, becoming one of the Senate's staunchest proponents of normal trade relations with China, a position strongly backed by Boeing, a major employer in Washington state. Murray also has worked to remove restrictions on abortion rights and has pushed through the Senate legislation allowing abortions in military hospitals. With then-Democratic Sen. Hillary Clinton of New York, she fought the Bush administration over allowing over-the-counter sales of the morning-after pill.

Murray's 2016 re-election was her easiest, a 59%-41% victory over Chris Vance, a former chairman of the Washington Republican Party, which failed to recruit a more formidable challenger. Vance was outspent 19-1. In earlier campaigns, Murray had won re-election three times by steadily diminishing margins. In 1998, she was challenged by Rep. Linda Smith, a Republican and a strong opponent of abortion and free trade deals. Murray raised far more money than Smith and won 58%-42%. In 2004, she faced Republican George Nethercutt, another House member, who in 1994 earned a reputation as a giant killer for defeating Democratic House Speaker Tom Foley. The mom in tennis shoes had become a hardball fundraiser. An aide put out the word to lobbyists that the senator would regard contributions to Nethercutt as hostile, even if contributors gave to her too. Murray raised $11.5 million, compared with Nethercutt's $7.7 million. Murray won 55%-43%. Republicans initially considered Murray vulnerable in 2010. They landed a top-tier recruit in former state Sen. Dino Rossi, a fiscal conservative who had twice run impressive but losing campaigns against Democratic Gov. Christine Gregoire. He criticized Murray's involvement in shaping the Democratic agenda. But Murray did not back down from her record and said Rossi would bankrupt the nation by giving tax breaks to the wealthy. She won 52%-48%.

When Senate Democratic Leader Harry Reid announced in 2015 that he would not seek re-election, Murray did not rule out a move to climb up the Democratic leadership ladder. Though she endorsed New York Sen. Chuck Schumer to succeed Reid in the top post in 2017, she declined to back Sen. Dick Durbin of Illinois to retain his position as Democratic whip. When asked by reporters whether she planned to seek the whip post, Murray sidestepped the question, saying her \focus was her own re-election. After the election and the Democratic setbacks, she decided not to challenge Durbin, who said that he had a majority of the votes. Schumer gave her more responsibilities and the title assistant Democratic leader. As the relentless Murray has shown in playing the long game, it's a good bet that she will have additional opportunities.

Maria Cantwell (D)

Elected 2000, term expires 2024, 4th term, b. Oct 13, 1958; Indianapolis, IN; Miami University of Ohio, B.A., 1980; Roman Catholic; Single.

Elected Office: WA House, 1987-1993; U.S. House, 1993-1995.

Professional Career: Owner, Cantwell & Association PR firm, 1985-1991; RealNetworks, 1995-2000.

DC Office: 511 HSOB 20510, 202-224-3441, Fax: 202-228-0514, cantwell.senate.gov

State Offices: Everett, 425-303-0114; Richland, 509-946-8106; Seattle, 206-220-6400; Spokane, 509-353-2507; Tacoma, 253-572-2281; Vancouver, 360-696-7838.

Committees: *Commerce, Science & Transportation (RMM):* Ex Officio membership on all subcommittees. *Energy & Natural Resources:* Energy; Public Lands, Forests & Mining; Water & Power. *Finance:* Energy, Natural Resources & Infrastructure; Health Care; International Trade, Customs & Global Competitiveness. *Indian Affairs. Small Business & Entrepreneurship.*

Group Ratings

	ADA	ACLU	AFL-CIO	LCV	ITI	COC	HAFA	ACU	CFG	FRC
2018	-	76%	-	100%	-	50%	5%	5%	15%	0%
2017	95%	C	100%	100%	C	29%	C	0%	4%	0%

Almanac Ratings 2017-18

	Economy	Social	Foreign	Composite
Liberal	100%	100%	77%	92%
Conservative	0%	0%	23%	8%

Key Votes of the 115th Congress

1. Obama-care revision	N	5. Gun regulations	N	9. Kavanaugh confirmation	N
2. Tax Cuts	N	6. Family planning regs	N	10. Saudi arms sales	Y
3. Dodd-Frank revision	N	7. Gorsuch confirmation	N	11. FISA rules	N
4. Omnibus appropriations	Y	8. Immigration restrictions	N	12. Military aid in Yemen	Y

Election Results

Election	Name (Party)	Vote (%)		Cand. Spent	Ind. Exp. Support	Ind. Exp. Oppose
2018 General	Maria Cantwell (D)...........................	1,803,364	(41%)	$10,393,463	$32,056	
	Susan Hutchison (R)..........................	1,282,804	(29%)			
2018 Primary	Maria Cantwell (D)...........................	929,961	(55%)			
	Susan Hutchison (R)..........................	413,317	(24%)			

Prior winning percentages: 2012 (60%), 2006 (57%), 2000 (49%), House: 1992 (55%)

Democrat Maria Cantwell, Washington's junior senator, was elected in 2000. She is active on energy, technology and tax matters, and is known for her tenacity. As the ranking member on the Energy and Natural Resources Committee, she has developed a close partnership with Republican Chairwoman Lisa Murkowski of Alaska; the two share a Northwest perspective and views on many issues. In 2017, they split when Murkowski achieved her long-sought goal of opening part of the Arctic National Wildlife Refuge to oil development.

Cantwell grew up in Indianapolis, where her father, Paul Cantwell, was a construction worker and served as county commissioner, a city councilman and a state legislator. As a child, Cantwell observed politics firsthand as her father advised union members, laborers and politicians who stopped by to talk politics. During her father's stint as an aide to Democratic Rep. Andy Jacobs of Indiana, she awoke one morning to the distinctive Boston accent of Sen. Ted Kennedy of Massachusetts downstairs.

Cantwell graduated from Miami University of Ohio, the first in her family to graduate from college. She worked in Ohio for Cincinnati mayor-turned-television personality Jerry Springer's 1982 campaign for governor. Then she worked for California Democratic Sen. Alan Cranston's presidential campaign in 1984, setting up a regional campaign office in Seattle. The Cranston campaign went nowhere, but Cantwell loved the Pacific Northwest and stayed. She moved to Mountlake Terrace, a suburban city in Snohomish County, where she organized a coalition to build a new library. In 1986, she was elected to the Washington state House.

In 1992, Cantwell ran for an open House seat and won 55%-42%, becoming the first Democrat to represent Washington's 1st District in 40 years. In the House, she showed her independence by not supporting President Bill Clinton's health care plan, but she did back a family and medical leave bill, Clinton's economic plan and NAFTA. Cantwell was a strong supporter of abortion rights and protecting the environment. She sounded early alarms about encroachments on digital privacy and persuaded the Clinton administration to drop its support of the "clipper chip," which would have enabled the government to monitor personal electronic communications. Still, she lost her 1994 bid for re-election to Republican Rick White by 4 percentage points, as Republicans rode a nationwide wave and pushed six Democrats out of the nine-person Washington delegation.

Back in the Seattle area, Cantwell joined a startup firm called Progressive Networks in 1995. Five years later, it had become RealNetworks, a leader in internet-based audio and visual software. In late 1999, her stock was worth about $40 million, and Cantwell was ready to resume her political career. She challenged Republican Sen. Slade Gorton. Gorton had an increasingly conservative record on environmental and economic issues. Insurance Commissioner Deborah Senn, who also was running, was widely considered too liberal to win. Cantwell called herself a New Democrat in the Clinton mode and backed permanent normal trade relations with China — a move that Senn opposed. But the real difference was money. Cantwell spent freely, while Senn was on television only during the two weeks right before the September all-party primary. In the first round, Gorton got the most votes: 44 percent. Cantwell got 37 percent, and Senn received 13 percent.

Cantwell said she would spend "whatever it takes" to win. At the same time, she made her support of campaign finance regulation a major issue and refused to take contributions from political action committees or large donations known as "soft money" from the Democratic Party; the party had already pumped $640,000 into the state before Cantwell won the primary. She charged that Gorton was beholden to special-interest contributors, singling out his late-night Senate amendment that paved the way for a cyanide leach gold mine in rural Okanogan County, which environmentalists were fighting. She talked about her work in tech and compared her experience with his, saying: "I've just spent the last five years in the private sector learning how to do things on the outside. Sen. Gorton's been in office for 41 years. He seems to like government a lot." Gorton described Cantwell as an old-style liberal Democrat who would have government meddling in health care, education and the environment. Overall, she spent $11.5 million — $10.3 million of it her own money — to Gorton's $6.4 million. Gorton was hurt when American Indian tribes, some flush with casino cash, weighed in against him, saying he did not respect their sovereignty when he sought to bind them to the same laws as other people.

Ballots from heavily Democratic King County put Cantwell on top by 2,229 votes out of 2.4 million cast. Cantwell carried only five counties: King (Seattle), Snohomish, Thurston (Olympia), and two small counties in the west. Gorton took 61 percent of the vote in eastern Washington.

Cantwell's voting record has been consistently liberal on social issues but moderate on economic and foreign policy matters. She was one of just nine Senate Democrats to oppose creating the Troubled Asset Relief Program for ailing financial institutions in 2008, saying the government had no business getting so deeply involved with the private sector.

To help her state's hydropower industry, which produces almost three-fourths of Washington's electricity, Cantwell has been active in efforts to remove barriers to licensing new facilities. In 2010, when the Obama administration and Democrats in Congress pushed for ultimately unsuccessful legislation aimed at curbing greenhouse gases, she jumped into the debate. Cantwell and GOP Sen. Susan Collins of Maine stepped up efforts to push their cap-and-dividend bill that skirted the idea of a carbon trading market. Instead, their bill would have capped emissions from sources such as coal mines and oil refineries, and those emitters would have been required to purchase carbon permits. The Senate failed to take action on the bill.

When Montana Sen. Max Baucus quit the Senate in early 2014 to become ambassador to China, Oregon's Ron Wyden took over the Finance Committee and Louisiana's Mary Landrieu moved into Wyden's spot as chief of Energy and Natural Resources. Cantwell nabbed the gavel on the Small Business Committee. She worked with Jim Risch of Idaho, the panel's ranking Republican, on a measure to renew the State Trade and Export Promotion program, which awards grants to states to help small businesses begin or expand exports of their products. She held separate hearings on helping veterans and women grow small businesses. After Landrieu lost re-election, Cantwell took the top Democratic seat on Energy — as a member of the minority.

Working with Chairwoman Murkowski, Cantwell put together a bill on multiple energy topics that won bipartisan approval in committee and overwhelmingly passed the Senate in 2016. "Most provisos are very modest, but that doesn't mean they're not useful," former Democratic Rep. Philip Sharp of Indiana, who has worked on energy issues for decades, told The Washington Post. "It's a positive test for the Congress being able to legislate across the bitter partisan divide, and frankly Chairman Murkowski and Sen. Cantwell deserve considerable credit." The Senate bill addressed such issues as enhancement of the electrical grid, energy efficiency in buildings and exports of natural gas. Negotiators failed to resolve differences with the House, which had passed a measure that focused more on resource production. "It is really irresponsible for our House colleagues to drop the ball," Cantwell said. She and Murkowski also collaborated on a proposal to increase the fleet of icebreakers for the Coast Guard, which has an active presence in their home states.

In 2017, President Donald Trump's nomination of former Texas Gov. Rick Perry to be Energy secretary halted bipartisanship on the Energy committee. Perry was "not the direction that the Energy Department needs to go," Cantwell said. When the Trump administration teamed with Murkowski to add Arctic oil drilling to the Republicans' sweeping 2017 tax bill, Cantwell sought to block the parliamentary maneuver but was defeated on a nearly party-line vote.

Months later, Cantwell and Murkowski resumed their collaboration, working on a sweeping public lands bill that combined more than 100 measures that previously had been introduced in the Senate. She called it "the biggest public lands package in more than a decade." It included a prohibition of new mining activities on federal land in Washington's Methow Valley and a multibillion dollar plan for more efficient water use in the Yakima basin. The package was enacted soon after the Senate passed it — on a 92-8 vote — in February 2019.

Cantwell gave up her ranking post on the Energy committee in 2019 to lead Democrats on the Commerce, Science and Transportation Committee. She replaced Sen. Bill Nelson of Florida, who lost re-election. She said that her priorities included expanding the Coast Guard's Arctic fleet and improving cybersecurity for the nation's electrical grid. On the committee, she has kept a close eye on Boeing and the rest of her state's aerospace businesses. Cantwell was the point person on the ambitious NextGen air traffic control modernization effort, which was part of the Federal Aviation Administration reauthorization bill that became law in 2012.

Cantwell also has a coveted seat on the Finance Committee. She secured passage of a 2008 measure to temporarily extend the deductibility of state sales taxes, a popular tax break in Washington because the state doesn't have a personal income tax. She objected when Republicans' eliminated that provision in their 2017 tax overhaul. The result, she said, was to "gouge middle-class taxpayers in King County and make them pay $1,000 more [to] open the Arctic Wildlife Refuge."

In 2015, Cantwell took the lead in seeking to extend the life of the U.S. Export-Import Bank — another priority for Boeing. The bank, which finances U.S. exports abroad, became the center of a fierce political debate. Tea party conservatives argued that it is a prime example of corporate cronyism and welfare to companies that don't need it. Defenders, like Cantwell, saw it as vital to U.S. competitiveness. With her home-state colleague Patty Murray, Cantwell played tough with Senate Majority Leader Mitch McConnell and won a promise for a floor vote on the bank's renewal; in return, they supported a bill to give President Barack Obama fast-track authority to negotiate new trade deals. That led to a sequence of votes in which Congress agreed to revive the bank, which has aided Boeing's jet sales. The Seattle Times editorial board said Cantwell deserved "credit for helping bring back the Ex-Im Bank."

Although a strong supporter of campaign finance regulation, Cantwell has had campaign finance problems. To fund her 2000 campaign, she had sold $5.6 million of her RealNetworks stock and had borrowed $3.8 million from a bank using the company's stock as collateral. That enabled her to run last-minute ads that were essential to her victory. The Federal Election Commission ruled in 2004 that she had violated the law by failing to disclose the terms of the loans, but it took no punitive action. With her earlier net worth of $40 million, paying off the loans should have been easy. But RealNetworks saw its stock price plummet from $80 per share in spring 2000 to $6 per share in spring 2001. Suddenly, Cantwell owed far more than the collateral was worth. Over the course of the next several years, she paid off the debt.

Cantwell's narrow victory in 2000 placed her high on Republicans' target list in 2006. National Republicans recruited Mike McGavick, chairman and chief executive officer at Safeco Insurance. McGavick, a moderate who managed Gorton's 1988 campaign and served as his chief of staff, appeared formidable. McGavick acknowledged that he had been charged with drunken driving in

1993. Cantwell faced lingering discontent from liberals in the party for her 2002 vote in favor of the Iraq War. In a Democratic year in a Democratic-leaning state, she won 57%-40%. In 2012, another good year for Democrats, Cantwell had an easy race against Republican state Sen. Michael Baumgartner. He was from eastern Washington, which hasn't produced a senator since 1934, and was unable to raise the kind of money necessary to compete with Cantwell. She won 60%-40%. In 2018, Cantwell defeated former television news anchor Susan Hutchison 58%-42%.

Suzan DelBene (D)

Elected 2012, 4th term, b. Feb 17, 1962; Selma, AL; Reed College (OR), B.A., 1983; University of Washington, M.B.A., 1990; Episcopalian; Married (Kurt Delbene); 2 children.

Professional Career: Director of Marketing, Microsoft, 1989-1998; Vice President., Drugstore.com, 1998-2000; President, CEO, Nimble Tech., 2000-2003; Vice President., Microsoft, 2004-2007; Consultant, Global Partnerships, 2008-2009; Director, WA Department of Revenue, 2010-2012.

DC Office: 2330 RHOB 20515, 202-225-6311, Fax: 202-226-1606, delbene.house.gov

State Offices: Bothell, 425-485-0085; Mount Vernon, 360-416-7879.

Committees: *Select Committee on the Modernization of Congress. Ways & Means*: Oversight; Select Revenue Measures; Trade.

Group Ratings

	ADA	ACLU	AFL-CIO	LCV	ITI	COC	HAFA	ACU	CFG	FRC
2018	-	86%	-	94%	-	75%	4%	4%	5%	0%
2017	95%	C	92%	97%	C	43%	C	4%	0%	0%

Almanac Ratings 2017-18

	Economy	Social	Foreign	Composite
Liberal	92%	98%	92%	94%
Conservative	8%	2%	8%	6%

Key Votes of the 115th Congress

1. Obama-care revision	N	5. Family planning regs	N	9. Guantanamo prisoners	Y
2. Tax Cuts	N	6. Body cameras/immigration	Y	10. Ground missiles, limit	Y
3. Omnibus appropriations	Y	7. Abortion ban	N	11. Defense Dept. spending	Y
4. Dodd-Frank revision	N	8. Concealed carry	N	12. FISA rules	N

Election Results

Election	Name (Party)	Vote (%)		Cand. Spent	Ind. Exp. Support	Ind. Exp. Oppose
2018 General	Suzan DelBene (D)............................	197,209	(59%)	$966,358	$2,092	$240
	Jeffrey Beeler (R)................................	135,534	(41%)	$16,489		
2018 Primary	Suzan DelBene (D)............................	106,107	(59%)			
	Jeffrey Beeler (R).................................	45,830	(26%)			
	Scott Stafne (R)....................................	20,354	(11%)			

Prior winning percentages: 2016 (55%), 2014 (55%), 2012 (54%)

Democrat Suzan DelBene, a former Microsoft executive, was elected to an open seat in 2012. With her corporate experience, she settled in with the dwindling ranks of business-oriented Democrats and has been a leader of the New Democrat Coalition. She got a coveted seat on the Ways and Means Committee. Following the 2018 election, she fell short in her bid to chair the Democratic Congressional Campaign Committee, but took on other party assignments.

DelBene was born in Selma Alabama. When she was a toddler, her parents divorced and DelBene lived with her mother, who married an airline pilot. The family moved often. When she was in high school, DelBene's stepfather got a job with Iran Air and her parents relocated overseas. She majored in biology at Reed College, originally hoping to become a veterinarian. Changing her career interests, her first job after college was with a biotechnology firm in Seattle. She got her master's degree in business administration and interned at Microsoft. She landed a full-time job there, where she met and married her husband, Kurt, then-president of Microsoft's Office division. She spent 12 years at Microsoft, rising to the position of corporate vice president of the company's mobile communications business. (Later, Kurt spent about a year with the Obama administration in the challenging assignment of managing the government website for citizen enrollment in the Affordable Care Act. He returned to Microsoft, where he is the chief digital officer and executive vice president for corporate strategy.)

DelBene left Microsoft in 1998 and joined two high-tech startups. She later worked on microfinance with an international nonprofit, a job that she said taught her the ways in which policy could create opportunities for families. Inspired to run for Congress, she spent more than $2 million of her own money in a 2010 challenge to Republican Rep. Dave Reichert in the east Seattle suburbs. Her narrow 52%-48% loss in the GOP-leaning district was impressive during a disastrous year for national Democrats. Democratic Gov. Christine Gregoire appointed her director of the state Department of Revenue, where she helped to enact a tax amnesty program that generated $345 million.

That job didn't last long. In 2012, DelBene was one of five Democrats running in the newly drawn 1st District. With a reported net worth of more than $50 million, her personal wealth was a prime topic. Her Democratic opponents cast her as just another millionaire running for Congress. Endorsed by Gregoire and Rep. Rick Larsen, her campaign ads focused on the financial struggles of her youth. The only Republican in the all-party primary was state legislator John Koster, who had lost two contests a decade apart in the adjacent 2nd District. Koster finished first with 45 percent of vote. DelBene won the battle to enter the runoff with 22 percent to 14 percent for liberal Darcy Burner, also a Microsoft executive. DelBene consolidated support among Democrats and won in November, 54%-46%. She got 60 percent in King County, and 52 percent in Snohomish; Koster took 55 percent in Whatcom.

DelBene spent much of her time during her first year tending to two unexpected local disasters and their follow-up: the collapse of a bridge on Interstate 5 in Skagit Valley and a destructive mudslide in rural Oso that killed 43 people. Later, she introduced the National Landslide Preparedness Act, which would create a national program to identify and reduce losses from landslide hazards. The Natural Resources Committee approved an amended version in December 2017, but the House took no action.

In 2015, DelBene was one of 28 House Democrats who voted to give trade promotion authority to Obama, noting that "Washington is the most trade-dependent state in the nation and 40 percent of our jobs depend on trade." In 2018, the farm bill was enacted with a section authored by DelBene to encourage additional research and development of wood products by the Forest Service. In the Almanac vote ratings, she has ranked near the center of House Democrats. Her scores were centrist on the economy and liberal on social issues.

In 2016, DelBene served on the temporary Panel on Infant Lives that House Republicans created to investigate Planned Parenthood and the procuring of fetal tissue. When Republicans issued their final report, she said, "this so-called investigation has repeatedly shown contempt for the facts and disdain for the truth."

In 2017, DelBene joined Ways and Means, while Republicans retained House control. Like other committee Democrats for the next two years, she had little opportunity to shape health care or tax legislation. In November 2017, she claimed that the committee-approved bill would "increase taxes on America's middle class," but was on firmer ground with her assertion that "ultra-wealthy and well-connected Americans receive the majority of the tax cuts." When Democrats took House control in January 2019, DelBene said that she would focus on international trade issues, including steps to respond to Trump's "reckless trade and tariff policies." She also pressed her economic views as vice chair for policy coordination of the New Democrat Coalition.

In 2017-18, DelBene was finance co-chair of the DCCC during the party's successful campaign cycle. Following the election, she fell short in a bid to chair the full committee, but was named a co-chair of the Frontline program to assist Democrats defending competitive districts. DelBene has had relatively easy reelection campaigns. In 2018, she got 59 percent of the vote — her strongest performance.

WA-1: Interior Northwest Washington

Cook Partisan Voting Index: D+6

Population		Race and Ethnicity		Income	
Total	729,667	White	74.3%	Median Income	$90,029
Land area (sq. miles)	6,186	Black	1.2%	District Income Rank	30
Pop/ sq mi	118	Latino	8.9%	Poverty Rate	7.6%
Born in State	48.5%	Asian	10.5%	With health insurance	93.8%
		Two or more races	3.8%	Cash public assistance	2.6%
Age Groups		Other	1.3%	Food stamp/SNAP	8.3%
Under 18	23.6%				
18-34	21.1%	**Education**		**Work**	
35-64	42.3%	H.S grad or less	25.5%	White Collar	13%
Over 64	13%	Some college	31.8%	Sales and Service	34.4%
		College Degree, 4 yr	27.2%	Blue Collar	17.8%
Military		Post grad	15.5%	Government	12.2%
Veteran/ Active Duty	7.8%				

2012 Pres. Vote	Obama	183,802	(54%)	Romney	147,074	(43%)			
2016 Pres. Vote	Clinton	188,952	(52%)	Trump	132,109	(37%)	Johnson	19,396	(5%)

Seattle and Everett Suburbs: With the high-tech growth since the 1980s, metropolitan Seattle grew to the north and to the east, as a wave of newcomers arrived seeking the area's distinctive blend of natural beauty, robust and creative economic expansion, and freewheeling culture. The heart of the new Seattle is east of Lake Washington, in the edge city of Redmond. That is where you find the turquoise, pine-shaded, low-rise buildings of the 500-acre Microsoft campus — a tranquil environment for a booming and boisterously aggressive company. With 50,300 employees in the Puget Sound area in June 2018, the company leased major chunks of office space in Seattle and Bellevue. In 2017, officials announced plans for a huge expansion of the campus, with 18 new and taller buildings replacing 12 buildings scheduled for demolition and expected to house 8,000 additional workers. Microsoft has fueled Redmond's transformation from a sleepy hamlet of 1,426 people in 1960 to a hip center of commerce with a population of more than 64,000, of whom 34 percent are Asian. Mindful of the limited amount of affordable housing, which Microsoft president Brad Smith termed a "crisis," the company pledged in January 2019 to finance $500 million in low-interest loans for new housing in the Seattle area. Executives strongly opposed President Donald Trump's executive order restricting immigrants and refugees; following federal court endorsement of Trump's moves, they pledged continuing support for employees and their families.

The 1st Congressional District of Washington includes most of Redmond and many of the other King County suburbs east of Seattle. Technology is a huge factor in the local economy. Redmond is also home of Nintendo of North America and an expanding research facility for Facebook. In neighboring Kirkland, Google maintains its research and development center, which developed Google Maps; according to news reports in 2018, it was planning to expand that campus. On the eastern shore of Lake Washington are the homes and estates of the "Microsoft millionaires," many of whom exercised company stock options before the economic bust. The affluent suburbs include Medina, Clyde Hill, Yarrow Point and Hunts Point, as well as Bill Gates' $60 million, 66,000-square-foot home.

The 1st crosses the Cascades to take in the eastern extremities of King County. It also takes in the interior portions away from coastline of Snohomish, Skagit and Whatcom counties, all the way to the Canadian border. Along the way, the economy gradually shifts from software code to raspberries and dairy farming. At the far north end of the district is the fishing and lumber town of Blaine, with America's most attractively landscaped border crossing and the International Peace Arch, just south of British Columbia. About 40 percent of the population is in King, and nearly as many in Snohomish. The King County areas of the district are strongly Democratic, while the inland portions are swing territory. The resulting district leans Democratic, but can be competitive. Hillary Clinton won 52 percent of the vote in 2016.

Rick Larsen (D)

Elected 2000, 10th term, b. Jun 15, 1965; Arlington; Pacific Lutheran University (WA), B.A., 1987; University of Minnesota, M.P.A., 1990; Methodist; Married (Tiia Karlen Larsen); 2 children.

Elected Office: Snohomish City Council, 1998-2000, President, 1999-2000.

Professional Career: Econ. dev. official, Port of Everett, 1990-1991; Director pub. affairs, WA St. Dental Assn., 1991-1998.

DC Office: 2113 RHOB 20515, 202-225-2605, Fax: 202-225-4420, larsen.house.gov

State Offices: Bellingham, 360-733-4500; Everett, 425-252-3188.

Committees: *Armed Services*: Intelligence, Emerging Threats & Capabilities; Strategic Forces. *Transportation & Infrastructure*: Aviation (Chmn); Coast Guard & Maritime Transportation.

Group Ratings

	ADA	ACLU	AFL-CIO	LCV	ITI	COC	HAFA	ACU	CFG	FRC
2018	-	86%	-	89%	-	67%	8%	8%	8%	0%
2017	90%	C	95%	91%	C	54%	C	4%	0%	0%

Almanac Ratings 2017-18

	Economy	Social	Foreign	Composite
Liberal	95%	97%	92%	94%
Conservative	5%	4%	8%	6%

Key Votes of the 115th Congress

1. Obama-care revision	N	5. Family planning regs	N	9. Guantanamo prisoners	Y
2. Tax Cuts	N	6. Body cameras/immigration	Y	10. Ground missiles, limit	Y
3. Omnibus appropriations	Y	7. Abortion ban	N	11. Defense Dept. spending	Y
4. Dodd-Frank revision	Y	8. Concealed carry	N	12. FISA rules	N

Election Results

Election	Name (Party)	Vote (%)	Cand. Spent	Ind. Exp. Support	Ind. Exp. Oppose
2018 General	Rick Larsen (D)..................................210,187	(71%)	$785,915	$2,120	
	Brian Luke (Lib)....................................84,646	(29%)			

Prior winning percentages: 2016 (64%), 2014 (61%), 2012 (61%), 2010 (51%), 2008 (62%), 2006 (64%), 2004 (64%), 2002 (50%), 2000 (50%)

Rick Larsen, a moderate Democrat first elected in 2000, has been well-positioned in the House to deal with aviation, maritime and national security issues that are vital at home. As chairman of the Aviation Subcommittee, he has sought to assist Boeing Co., the largest employer in his district. The crash of two new 737 jets from Boeing increased the pressure on Larsen to take an evenhanded approach to the controversy in early 2019. In the state's tradition, he remains an outspoken proponent of international trade and has taken an avid interest in issues related to China, a country that does substantial business with his state.

Larsen grew up in Arlington, in Snohomish County, graduated from Pacific Lutheran University, and got a master's degree at the University of Minnesota. He spent a year doing research on economic development for the Port of Everett. For six years, he was director of public affairs for the Washington State Dental Association. In 1998, he won a seat on the Snohomish County Council and later became its president.

In 2000, Republican Jack Metcalf kept his promise to retire after three terms in Congress. The Democratic field was cleared for Larsen. Republicans nominated state Rep. John Koster. The general election became one of the premier contests in the nation. Anti-abortion rights groups and the National Rifle Association backed Koster, and unions and abortion-rights groups supported Larsen. Larsen criticized Koster for referring to "our American holocaust," a familiar term among anti-abortion activists. Larsen won 50%-46%.

Larsen has been a leader of the centrist New Democrat Coalition, although he became more reliably Democratic after President Barack Obama took office and he has taken progressive positions on most social issues. He voted for the Bush-era tax cuts in 2001, but later opposed extending the cuts for upper-income taxpayers. He was one of 22 Democrats in 2012 to support a failed plan for a budget along the lines of the Simpson-Bowles deficit reduction commission. In 2015, he was one of 28 House Democrats who voted to give trade promotion authority to Obama, especially for the prospective Trans-Pacific Partnership.

Larsen has co-chaired the U.S.-China Working Group, a group of House members that seeks to build lasting diplomatic ties with China. The working group has called for greater U.S. engagement with China on military issues. In 2016, Larsen applauded an agreement by China to reduce its export subsidies. In March 2019, he led a bipartisan House delegation to China, where they held discussions about the ongoing trade negotiations.

As the "Congressman from Boeing," Larsen has a plum assignment as chairman of the Transportation and Infrastructure Committee's Aviation panel. Boeing and its employees have been among Larsen's major campaign contributors. He has urged innovative technologies to advance air safety. When specific controversies have arisen, he often has deferred to federal regulators. He supported the Federal Aviation Administration's decision in 2013 to ground the company's new 787 Dreamliner fleet over concerns about the plane's fire-plagued batteries, saying that safety should be paramount. He said that Congress must assure that the FAA is "positioned to understand and challenge assumptions put forward by manufacturers regarding new technologies." He has warned against proposals to privatize the air traffic control system.

Following the overseas crashes of two 737-max jets, plus the subsequent questions about Boeing's rollout of the new planes and federal certification, Larsen in March 2019 joined committee Chairman Peter DeFazio of Oregon in asking the FAA to engage an "independent, third-party review" of Boeing's handling of its aircraft. They also called for the inspector general at the Transportation Department to review the FAA's certifying of the plane. Larsen was slow to launch a public investigation by his panel.

On the Armed Services Committee, Larsen works closely with Chairman Adam Smith, his home-state colleague. He has pushed to secure funds for upgraded border security at Bellingham and helped get a pipeline safety bill into law in 2002 after a lethal explosion in his district. He co-founded the Congressional Arctic Working Group, with the chief focus of protecting U.S. environmental, economic and strategic interests in the region.

Larsen has been vocal in opposing President Donald Trump's moves to restrict international trade and offered forceful reminders that "trade is a two-way street." In March 2018, with Democratic Reps. Ron Kind of Wisconsin and Gregory Meeks of New York, Larsen wrote a letter to relevant House committees in which they warned that Trump's trade policies and increased tariffs were "causing chaos and confusion for our nation's economy, national security and trade relations with our allies."

Larsen won reelection easily until 2010, when he was challenged by Koster, his opponent of a decade earlier. Koster won endorsements from leading national conservatives, which inspired tea party activists to pump hundreds of thousands of dollars into the Republican's campaign. Larsen outspent the challenger $2.1 million to $1.1 million. Larsen stressed job creation and expanding credit for small business. He declared victory a week after the election, 51%-49%, a margin of 6,500 votes.

After the 2011 redistricting boosted the Democratic base in the district by five percentage points, Larsen has won more than 60 percent of the vote in each general election. But he has faced a difficult political balance. In 2016, the State Labor Council withheld its endorsement and environmentalists objected to refineries in Puget Sound. Democrat Mike LaPointe, a coffee shop owner in Everett, challenged Larsen in the primary from the left, with objections to his international trade votes. In the all-party primary, Larsen got 53 percent and LaPointe had 10 percent, with the remainder going to Republicans. In the 2018 primary, Larsen faced five challengers from various parties, none of whom spent more than $5,000. He took the primary with 65 percent and in November defeated Libertarian Brian Luke, 71%-29%. Luke ran on the need to address fiscal issues, including the federal debt.

As a relatively youthful and senior Democrat on the Transportation committee, Larsen could chair the influential panel in coming years.

WA-2: Upper Puget Sound   Cook Partisan Voting Index: D+10

Population		Race and Ethnicity		Income	
Total	715,426	White	71.8%	Median Income	$64,663
Land area (sq. miles)	1,015	Black	2.9%	District Income Rank	136
Pop/ sq mi	704.8	Latino	10.6%	Poverty Rate	11.8%
Born in State	47.8%	Asian	8.4%	With health insurance	91.6%
		Two or more races	4.7%	Cash public assistance	3.3%
Age Groups		Other	1.6%	Food stamp/SNAP	12.8%
Under 18	21%				
18-34	24.8%	Education		Work	
35-64	39.1%	H.S grad or less	31.6%	White Collar	15.1%
Over 64	15.1%	Some college	37.5%	Sales and Service	41.7%
		College Degree, 4 yr	20.8%	Blue Collar	22.7%
Military		Post grad	10.2%	Government	14.3%
Veteran/ Active Duty	11.7%				

2012 Pres. Vote	Obama	185,771	(59%)	Romney	119,266	(38%)			
2016 Pres. Vote	Clinton	185,821	(55%)	Trump	113,670	(34%)	Johnson	16,880	(5%)
	Stein	7,477	(2%)						

Everett Metro: The Seattle metropolitan area has marched north along the shore of Puget Sound, beyond the old lumber port and railroad terminus of Everett. The huge Boeing assembly plant has produced 747s, 767s, 777s and the long-range 787s. The ramifications of President Donald Trump's trade wars have become apparent at the port. Total shipments in 2018 were down 14 percent from a year earlier, the local King broadcast station reported. In the past, China had purchased $18 billion of goods from the Seattle area. The trade controversy, combined with numerous challenges faced by Boeing, were a reminder that the international economy has consequences for a trade-dependent area such as the Puget Sound and its surrounding industries.

Overall, business has been booming. In 2018, Boeing increased its statewide payroll to 70,000 -- its first increase since 2012, when it peaked at 87,000 employees. Because of automation, it's not likely to return to the earlier level, even as the company increases production. At the port, the chief long-term concern — aside from the trade war — has been the widening of the Panama Canal. As expected, that has shifted some destinations in the United States for Asia-based shipping. From January to September 2018, annual container imports increased 3 percent on the West Coast, while imports at East Coast ports grew 6 percent and 10 percent on the Gulf of Mexico. The 20,000 jobs at the Port of Seattle in 2018 had an average salary of $95,000.

In the waters of Puget Sound are the 176 San Juan Islands, which were the last part of the continental United States to be turned over to this country. The waters were great whaling grounds, and not until 1860 did the British relinquish them. Today, ferryboats connect the islands to mainland Washington and to British Columbia, directly to the west. The publicly operated Washington State Ferries system in 2018 had 24.7 million passengers (the most since 2002) and 10.8 million vehicles on 22 auto-passenger vessels to 20 terminals, the largest ferry operator in the United States. With planned expansion of service, the system prepared to purchase 16 new vessels by 2040. This is some of the most beautiful coastline in North America: the steely blue sound with forested hills rising behind it, shielded from the full force of Pacific rains by the Olympic Mountains, though still seldom dry. The little towns, on bits of level land between the water and the mountains, have the look of pristine New England villages. Further north is Bellingham, which grew up as a supply station for gold miners in the 1850s and was the source of much of the lumber used to rebuild San Francisco after the 1906 earthquake and fire. It still plays an important role in the local fishing industry.

The 2nd Congressional District of Washington encompasses the San Juan Islands, including 45-mile-long Whidbey Island, and most of the mainland along the east side of the sound. The district has several military installations, including a Navy base at Everett and a naval air station on Whidbey. Increased aircraft training at Whidbey in 2018 led to protests over the noise. The political tradition in most of the lumbering and fishing areas here is Democratic, as is the political culture in Everett. In addition to Everett, the district takes in most of the major ports on Puget Sound. Nearly 60 percent of the population resides in Snohomish County, which is closest to Seattle. The remainder are spread among four other counties. North of Bellingham, the district line is a few miles short of the Canadian border. The 2nd leans strongly Democratic. Hillary Clinton took 55 percent of the vote in 2016.

Jaime Herrera Beutler (R)

Elected 2010, 5th term, b. Nov 03, 1978; Glendale, CA; Seattle Pacific University (WA), Att., 1998; Bellevue Community College (WA), A.A., 2003; University of Washington, B.A., 2004; Christian Church; Married (Daniel Beutler); 3 children.

Elected Office: WA House, 2007-2011.

Professional Career: Legislative aide, Rep. Cathy McMorris Rodgers, 2005-2007.

DC Office: 2352 RHOB 20515, 202-225-3536, Fax: 202-225-3478, herrerabeutler.house.gov

State Offices: Chehalis, 360-695-6292; Vancouver, 360-695-6292.

Committees: *Appropriations*: Labor, Health & Human Services, Education & Related Agencies; Legislative Branch (RMM). *Joint Economic. Science, Space & Technology*: Research & Technology.

Group Ratings

	ADA	ACLU	AFL-CIO	LCV	ITI	COC	HAFA	ACU	CFG	FRC
2018	-	18%	-	11%	-	92%	47%	76%	62%	100%
2017	5%	C	18%	9%	C	93%	C	63%	54%	89%

Almanac Ratings 2017-18

	Economy	Social	Foreign	Composite
Liberal	11%	11%	3%	8%
Conservative	89%	89%	97%	92%

Key Votes of the 115th Congress

1. Obama-care revision	N	5. Family planning regs	Y	9. Guantanamo prisoners	N
2. Tax Cuts	Y	6. Body cameras/immigration	Y	10. Ground missiles, limit	N
3. Omnibus appropriations	Y	7. Abortion ban	Y	11. Defense Dept. spending	Y
4. Dodd-Frank revision	Y	8. Concealed carry	Y	12. FISA rules	N

Election Results

Election	Name (Party)	Vote (%)		Cand. Spent	Ind. Exp. Support	Ind. Exp. Oppose
2018 General	Jaime Herrera Beutler (R)	161,819	(53%)	$2,971,586	$154,896	$737,682
	Carolyn Long (D)	145,407	(47%)	$3,611,390	$1,493,295	$906,591

Prior winning percentages: 2016 (62%), 2014 (62%), 2012 (60%), 2010 (53%)

Republican Jaime Herrera Beutler, elected in 2010, is a young Latina — the only woman of color in their ranks. She assists the GOP in its outreach while compiling a business-friendly centrist voting record. On the Appropriations Committee, she tends to fund local resources and health research. In the 2016 presidential campaign, Herrera Beutler said she was open to supporting Donald Trump. Following the early October release of a 2005 tape in which Trump made lewd comments about women, she said, "That door has now slammed shut." She split with President Trump on his immigration enforcement actions and on repeal of the Affordable Care Act. That independence may have helped her to survive a narrow reelection in 2018.

Herrera Beutler grew up in the region. Her father was a printer. Her parents raised six children and finances were tight. She took a job as a nanny to help pay for college. After concluding that nursing studies weren't the right field for her, Herrera Beutler got a degree in communications from the University of Washington. As a teenager, she knocked on doors for Republicans in 1994. During college, she had a White House internship. After graduating, she was a legislative aide to Rep. Cathy McMorris Rodgers of eastern Washington, who became her mentor. When a seat opened in the state legislature in 2007, she was appointed. She became the assistant floor leader, the only woman and minority on the Republican leadership team.

When six-term Democratic Rep. Brian Baird retired in 2010, Herrera Beutler was 31 and a newlywed. Her husband, Daniel Beutler, who was about to start law school, delayed his plans so she could run. In the all-party primary, Herrera Beutler led a crowded Republican field that included two tea party-backed candidates, with 28 percent of the vote. In the primary, the National Republican Congressional Committee put her on its "Young Guns" list of candidates worthy of funding.

In the general, media and technology entrepreneur Denny Heck spent $2 million, including $350,000 of his own money, to her $1.5 million. Heck ran as a moderate Democrat and emphasized his experience creating jobs. She criticized Heck for his support of the health care overhaul championed by Democrats and of President Barack Obama's economic stimulus bill. Her television ads concluded, "For fiscal sanity, Jaime Herrera for Congress." Riding that year's GOP tidal wave, she won 53%-47%. In 2012, Heck won a nearby district that was created by redistricting.

Herrera Beutler was among the moderate members of the Class of 2010. She has been loyal to the GOP leadership on most major votes. Oregon GOP Rep. Greg Walden appointed her vice chair of the minority outreach effort at the National Republican Congressional Committee. "I think we can do a better job of tone," she told The Columbian of Vancouver about her party's relationship with Hispanics. She expressed reservations about legislative proposals to restrict gun rights, citing her own experience in her early 20s when a man repeatedly tried to break into her home. She said owning a gun gave her peace of mind. On immigration, she favored comprehensive reform, but opposed Obama's unilateral efforts to impose changes. She joined Democrat Rep. Kurt Schrader of Oregon in leading objections to a federal court's 2011 decision that water runoff from forest roads must be regulated the same as runoff from factories and sewage treatment plants. The Supreme Court in 2013 reversed the decision.

In 2013, Herrera Beutler took six months away from the Capitol to be with her daughter Abigail, who was born premature and without kidneys; she unexpectedly survived with unprecedented surgical intervention and kidney dialysis. In March 2016, her husband provided a donor kidney to their daughter, whose health seemed miraculously robust. As a result of that experience, Herrera Beutler has pushed for several related health care bills, including measures to help create a nationwide network of providers to assist medically complex children and to assure insurance coverage for such children. Those proposals were enacted in December 2018. Herrera Beutler delivered their third child in May 2019.

With her plum seat on Appropriations, Herrera Beutler worked to secure funds for the nuclear waste cleanup at the Hanford plant in her home state. She took the lead on other health care initiatives, including organ-donor assistance and mental health awareness. With her increased seniority in 2019, she became the top Republican on the Legislative Branch Subcommittee.

In 2017, she voted against the House Republican proposal to repeal the Obamacare law. When Trump at a White House meeting urged Herrera Beutler to support the bill, she told him that that she was helping him to "keep your promise" to his supporters that he would not back a bill that failed to protect people with pre-existing conditions, she later told The (Longview) Daily News. She also took issue with the policy of separating immigrant families at the border. In 2018, Trump signed her bills to permit Native Americans to kill sea lions in order to preserve salmon on the Columbia River and to give tribes the authority to manufacture certain distilled liquors on their tribal lands.

Herrera Beutler had coasted to reelection with at least 60 percent of the vote and entrenched herself in the previously Democratic district. That changed in 2018, when Democratic challenger Carolyn Long, a political science professor at Washington State University, advocated expansion of the Affordable Care Act and said that Herrera Beutler was not accessible to her constituents. Long outspent her, $3.6 million to $3 million, but Herrera Beutler won, 53%-47%. Long took Clark County by 4,300 votes; the incumbent took the seven outlying counties.

WA-3: Southwest Washington   **Cook Partisan Voting Index: R+4**

Population		Race and Ethnicity		Income	
Total	708,507	White	80.9%	Median Income	$60,163
Land area (sq. miles)	9,114	Black	1.3%	District Income Rank	177
Pop/ sq mi	77.7	Latino	9.1%	Poverty Rate	12.3%
Born in State	41.4%	Asian	3.3%	With health insurance	92%
		Two or more races	3.9%	Cash public assistance	4.5%
Age Groups		Other	1.4%	Food stamp/SNAP	16.5%
Under 18	23.8%				
18-34	20.2%	**Education**		**Work**	
35-64	39.8%	H.S grad or less	36.2%	White Collar	16.2%
Over 64	16.2%	Some college	39.2%	Sales and Service	40.9%
		College Degree, 4 yr	16%	Blue Collar	25.4%
Military		Post grad	8.7%	Government	14.7%
Veteran/ Active Duty	10.9%				

2012 Pres. Vote	Romney	150,409	(50%)	Obama	145,442	(48%)		
2016 Pres. Vote	Trump	157,359	(48%)	Clinton	134,009	(41%)	Johnson	15,707	(5%)

Vancouver: From the Pacific Ocean to the majestic row of active and inactive volcanoes of the Cascades, southwest Washington was long one of America's most productive lumber areas. The moist air and almost constant rain blown in from the Pacific have kept the trees on the coast growing rapidly. Precipitation is heavy in the valleys just past the Coast Range, and the forests there are also fast-growing. Then come the high mountains. The Cascades are a genuine divide, wringing almost all the moisture out of the atmosphere and making an arid climate eastward for a thousand miles. Americans had long been taught that the lower 48 states had no active volcanoes, but Mount St. Helens in Skamania County proved that wrong in 1980 when it erupted after laying dormant for 123 years, killing 57 people (many from asphyxiation), destroying its own peak and paving the land around it with lava. In January 2018, seismologists reported an increased number of quakes, with intensity up to 3.9 on the Richter scale.

For many years, this part of Washington was sparsely settled, with lumber-mill and fishing-boat towns scattered between mountains and water. It was flannel shirt country, Democratic since New Deal days. In the early 1990s, its resource-based economy was threatened by the environmental movement, which restricted fishing practices and produced a court decision shutting down logging in old-growth forests to save spotted owl habitat. This roiled local politics and gave Republicans an opening. The GOP's efforts in the region have been assisted by the growth of Clark County, across the Columbia River from Portland Oregon; Vancouver has filled with new residents eager to avoid Oregon's income tax, one of the highest in the country, but who want to make big purchases in Oregon free of sales tax. Clark County, where one-third of the residents commute to work in Portland, grew by 38 percent from 2000 to 2017; 10 percent of the county population is Hispanic and the fast-growing Asian community is 5 percent. In December 2017, The Seattle Times profiled Vancouver as America's "hippest" city, which was based on a study of such factors as local microbreweries, tattoo shops and vegan stores. In January 2018, Gov. Jay Inslee rejected a permit for a proposal to build an oil-by-rail terminal in Vancouver, which would have been the largest in the nation. A year later, local shipbuilder Vigor announced a nearly $1 billion contract to build a new landing craft for the U.S. Army.

The 3rd Congressional District of Washington covers the southwestern corner of the state, between the ocean and the Cascades. Economic growth and diversification and the arrival of many new residents with no roots in the old industries have made the area politically marginal. Nearly two-thirds of the district's residents live in Clark County. To the north, the district includes a small slice of Thurston County, but not the state's capital, Olympia. Donald Trump won in 2016, 48%-41%.

Dan Newhouse (R)

Elected 2014, 3rd term, b. Jul 10, 1955; Sunnyside; Washington State University, B.S., 1977; Presbyterian; Married (Joan Galvin); 2 children (from previous marriage).

Elected Office: WA House, 2003-2009.

Professional Career: Farmer; WA Director of Agriculture, 2009-2013.

DC Office: 1414 LHOB 20515, 202-225-5816, Fax: 202-225-3251, newhouse.house.gov

State Offices: Richland, 509-713-7374; Twisp, 509-433-7760; Yakima, 509-452-3243.

Committees: *Appropriations*: Energy & Water Development & Related Agencies; Homeland Security; Legislative Branch. *Select Committee on the Modernization of Congress.*

Group Ratings

	ADA	ACLU	AFL-CIO	LCV	ITI	COC	HAFA	ACU	CFG	FRC
2018	-	12%	-	6%	-	92%	69%	60%	57%	100%
2017	0%	C	22%	0%	C	92%	C	80%	66%	100%

Almanac Ratings 2017-18

	Economy	Social	Foreign	Composite
Liberal	9%	8%	5%	7%
Conservative	91%	92%	95%	93%

Key Votes of the 115th Congress

1. Obama-care revision	NV	5. Family planning regs	Y	9. Guantanamo prisoners	N
2. Tax Cuts	Y	6. Body cameras/immigration	N	10. Ground missiles, limit	N
3. Omnibus appropriations	N	7. Abortion ban	Y	11. Defense Dept. spending	Y
4. Dodd-Frank revision	Y	8. Concealed carry	Y	12. FISA rules	Y

Election Results

Election	Name (Party)	Vote (%)		Cand. Spent	Ind. Exp. Support	Ind. Exp. Oppose
2018 General	Dan Newhouse (R)	141,551	(63%)	$830,760		
	Christine Brown (D)	83,785	(37%)	$453,217	$39,656	
2018 Primary	Dan Newhouse (R)	77,203	(63%)			
	Christine Brown (D)	44,868	(37%)			

Prior winning percentages: 2016 (58%), 2014 (51%)

Dan Newhouse, who won the seat in 2014 with a promise of greater bipartisanship to address local priorities, has grown comfortable as a leadership ally and House insider. He has been willing to buck conservative Republican renegades on issues that are vital to business.

Newhouse grew up in a Yakima Valley family that was active in local politics. His father, Irv, was a state legislator for 34 years. The younger Newhouse operated, with his late wife, a 600-acre farm that grows hops, grapes and alfalfa. He got his bachelor's degree in agricultural economics from Washington State University and is a former president of the Hop Growers of America. Newhouse won election to the state House in 2002. Six years later, Democratic Gov. Christine Gregoire named him state agriculture director, calling him "the best person for the job." He served four years in the position. When Gregoire's successor, Democrat Jay Inslee, declined to keep Newhouse in the position, he became a frequent television spokesman for the victorious opponents of a 2013 state ballot initiative that would have required labeling of genetically modified food products.

When Republican Rep. Doc Hastings, chairman of the Natural Resources Committee, announced his retirement, Clint Didier and Newhouse led the field in the all-party primary with 32 percent and 26 percent, respectively. It marked the first time in state history that two Republicans faced off in the general election. Didier, a former tight end in the National Football League, was a major figure in the state's tea party movement. He was endorsed by former Alaska Gov. Sarah Palin and former Rep. Ron Paul of Texas, and emphasized gun rights, patriotism and religion.

Newhouse won endorsements from Hastings as well as the National Rifle Association. In its endorsement of Newhouse, the Yakima Herald-Republic noted the importance of the federal government in the district, which includes multiple federal dams. "Newhouse by far shows a better grasp of the federal government's influence," the newspaper said. Newhouse outspent Didier, $982,000 to $579,000, and won the general election, 51%-49%, a margin of 2,465 votes. Didier led in six of the eight counties. Newhouse took Benton and Yakima counties, which cast 64 percent of the total votes.

When an opening occurred in early 2015 on the Rules Committee, which operates as an arm of the leadership, Speaker John Boehner tapped him as the only freshman on the panel. Newhouse supported renewal of the Export-Import Bank, a split with many junior Republicans but a popular move in his home state, where Boeing is a major beneficiary of the loans, as are many farmers. "It's something I've seen as a very effective tool to help increase the exports coming out of the state of Washington," Newhouse said. He enacted a bill in 2017 that extended the deadline to start construction of the hydroelectric project at the Enloe Dam near Oroville. In 2019, he failed in his bid to become ranking Republican on the Rules Committee and gave up his seat on the panel.

Newhouse has kept busy with his seat on the Appropriations Committee. His subcommittee assignments, Newhouse said, "ensure that federal responsibilities to support Hanford cleanup and the groundbreaking scientific research and development at the Pacific Northwest National Laboratory are fulfilled." On the Homeland Security Subcommittee, he said that he has worked to "improve the nation's broken immigration system," including House approval of his move to make a guest-worker program available for agriculture.

Newhouse has repeatedly voiced concerns about the impact of President Donald Trump's crackdown on immigration and he urged steps to grant legal status to young "dreamers" who are undocumented. He also criticized Trump's international trade actions, including increased tariffs that are "harmful" for the economy in his district, he said in March 2018.

In the 2016 campaign, Newhouse had a rematch with Didier. This time, Didier — who had a radio show on a Christian network — was an enthusiastic supporter of Trump, but he declared his candidacy shortly before the filing deadline and was less-prepared. Newhouse, who had a fundraising advantage of 15-to-1, won the general election, 58%-42%. In 2018, Newhouse ran without Republican opposition. Against Democratic challenger Christine Brown, a former local television news anchor who criticized his support of Republican efforts to repeal the Affordable Care Act, Newhouse won 63%-37%. He outspent the challenger, $1.1 million to $467,000.

WA-4: Central Washington   Cook Partisan Voting Index: R+13

Population		Race and Ethnicity		Income	
Total	711,057	White	54.5%	Median Income	$53,381
Land area (sq. miles)	19,250	Black	1%	District Income Rank	248
Pop/ sq mi	36.9	Latino	38.5%	Poverty Rate	16.7%
Born in State	55.9%	Asian	1.5%	With health insurance	86%
		Two or more races	2.2%	Cash public assistance	3.8%
Age Groups		Other	2.4%	Food stamp/SNAP	19.1%
Under 18	29.1%				
18-34	22.6%	Education		Work	
35-64	35.3%	H.S grad or less	48%	White Collar	13%
Over 64	13%	Some college	31.8%	Sales and Service	36.2%
		College Degree, 4 yr	12.7%	Blue Collar	34.2%
Military		Post grad	7.4%	Government	16.3%
Veteran/ Active Duty	8.1%				

2012 Pres. Vote	Romney	142,741	(60%)	Obama	90,612	(38%)		
2016 Pres. Vote	Trump	140,560	(56%)	Clinton	85,083	(34%)	Johnson	12,039 (5%)

Richland, Yakima: The rugged peaks of the Cascade Mountains divide the state of Washington into two starkly different climate zones and two almost as starkly different political cultures. West of the Cascades, Washington is moist, green and crammed with watery inlets. To the east, it is barren and brown, except where irrigation ditches channel the water of the Columbia River into thirsty valleys and where the mountaintop waters fall east, as they do above the apple orchards in the Yakima Valley.

As Washington has become mostly Democratic west of the Cascades, it has become mostly Republican on the eastern side. This shift in political inclinations has followed the development of national politics and the local economy. The federal government has been a presence east of the Cascades since the 1930s, when it began to build dams to provide cheap power and boost economic development in this forbidding landscape. A giant bust of Franklin D. Roosevelt gazes out from a bluff on the Columbia over 550-foot-high Grand Coulee Dam, one of Roosevelt's favorite projects. Other dams are strung along the Columbia to Bonneville Dam near Portland, where the river breaks through the Cascades. This was Democratic territory then; Grant County, which includes the dam, gave Roosevelt 86 percent of the vote in 1936. As the region became wealthier — in part because of the federal projects — and as the nation's politics took on a cultural cast, the area shifted to the Republicans. Lumber towns in the Cascades responded angrily when the logging business was harmed by efforts to preserve the spotted owl. Farmers in the Yakima Valley, which produces most of the nation's apples and many other crops, were enraged when environmentalists proposed breaching the Snake River dams upriver to save salmon. In recent years, these farmers have faced new problems with government policy. With the essential aid that they receive from migrant labor, they have opposed President Donald Trump's efforts to restrict immigration. Plus, Trump's trade wars have devastated some of the local crops, including an estimated loss of $86 million in sales of cherries to China in 2018.

The 4th Congressional District of Washington covers much of the center of the state east of the Cascades, running from the vast wilderness of Okanogan County, which has long been gold country, past the Grand Coulee and the Columbia River. The biggest population center here is the Tri-Cities of Richland, Kennewick and Pasco in Benton County. Like Benton, Yakima County has about one-third of the voters in the district. Yakima has a larger population, of which 49 percent is Hispanic. In 2017, ConAgra Foods opened its second French fry processing line at its manufacturing campus in Richland; it produces more fries than any other company. Benton is the location of the Hanford Nuclear Reservation. Since 1997, the federal government has spent more than $240 billion to clean up the residue from the nuclear weapons that had been produced here.

The district's population is 39 percent Hispanic. Many are farm workers or the children of farm workers who have picked fruit for generations. The area was narrowly split between the parties as recently as the 1990s, but the 4th has become the most Republican district in the state; the cultural liberalism of Seattle seems very far away from here. Donald Trump got 58 percent in 2016, the only district in the state where he got a majority of the vote.

Cathy McMorris Rodgers (R)

Elected 2004, 8th term, b. May 22, 1969; Salem, OR; Pensacola Christian College (FL), B.A., 1990; University of Washington, M.B.A., 2002; Evangelical; Married (Brian Rodgers); 3 children.

Elected Office: WA House, 1994-2004, Minority Leader, 2002-2004.

Professional Career: Owner-operator, Peachcrest Fruit Basket orchard, 1984-1998; St. Legislative aide, 1990-1994.

DC Office: 1035 LHOB 20515, 202-225-2006, Fax: 202-225-3392, mcmorris.house.gov

State Offices: Colville, 509-684-3481; Spokane, 509-353-2374; Walla Walla, 509-529-9358.

Committees: *Energy & Commerce*: Consumer Protection & Commerce (RMM); Energy; Environment & Climate Change.

Group Ratings

	ADA	ACLU	AFL-CIO	LCV	ITI	COC	HAFA	ACU	CFG	FRC
2018	-	11%	-	6%	-	92%	55%	76%	50%	100%
2017	0%	C	11%	0%	C	93%	C	85%	76%	100%

Almanac Ratings 2017-18

	Economy	Social	Foreign	Composite
Liberal	3%	0%	0%	1%
Conservative	97%	100%	100%	99%

Key Votes of the 115th Congress

1. Obama-care revision	Y	5. Family planning regs	Y	9. Guantanamo prisoners	N
2. Tax Cuts	Y	6. Body cameras/immigration	N	10. Ground missiles, limit	N
3. Omnibus appropriations	Y	7. Abortion ban	Y	11. Defense Dept. spending	Y
4. Dodd-Frank revision	Y	8. Concealed carry	Y	12. FISA rules	Y

Election Results

Election	Name (Party)	Vote (%)		Cand. Spent	Ind. Exp. Support	Ind. Exp. Oppose
2018 General	Cathy McMorris Rodgers (R)	175,422	(55%)	$5,598,601	$73,831	$40,495
	Lisa Brown (D)	144,925	(45%)	$5,496,573	$106,388	$11,905
2018 Primary	Cathy McMorris Rodgers (R)	99,689	(49%)			
	Lisa Brown (D)	91,738	(45%)			

Prior winning percentages: 2016 (60%), 2014 (61%), 2012 (62%), 2010 (68%), 2008 (65%), 2006 (56%), 2004 (60%)

Cathy McMorris Rodgers, elected in 2004, stepped down from her Republican leadership position as a trusted on-message lieutenant after the party lost House control in the 2018 election. Despite her interest in moving up, other Republicans had leap-frogged her in the leadership ranks. McMorris Rodgers has become a senior member of the Energy and Commerce Committee, where she is the top Republican on its consumer protection panel. In 2018, she had her first serious reelection challenge.

McMorris Rodgers spent much of her childhood in northern British Columbia but moved with her family to Kettle Falls, where her parents bought a fruit orchard. Her father was a county Republican chairman. She graduated from Pensacola Christian College in Florida and got an MBA from the University of Washington. After college, she became a legislative assistant and then was appointed to her state House seat at age 24. She served for 10 years and chaired the Commerce and Labor Committee. She rose to minority leader, the first woman to hold such a post in state history.

In 2004, George Nethercutt, who defeated Democratic House Speaker Tom Foley in 1994, ran for the Senate. McMorris Rodgers and two other Republicans competed in the primary. They agreed on most major issues. McMorris Rodgers won 50 percent of the vote in the primary to 27 percent for state Sen. Larry Sheahan. The Democratic nominee, businessman Don Barbieri, had a large financial advantage and no primary opposition. The National Republican Congressional Committee spent heavily for McMorris Rodgers, highlighting her pro-business credentials and agricultural background. She won, 60%-40%, a sign of the change in Foley's old district.

She leaned toward the center of the House on some issues. In 2007, she voted to expand the Children's Health Insurance Plan, a move favored by Democrats but opposed by President George W. Bush. She backed Bush's Iraq war policies, but also criticized the administration on veterans' health care and on a delay in rules for country-of-origin meat labeling. On Energy and Commerce, she has worked across the aisle on several issues. With Democratic Rep. Diana DeGette, she enacted in 2013 the Hydropower Regulatory Efficiency Act, which streamlined the permitting process for small hydropower projects as a tool to expand clean energy.

McMorris Rodgers became an ally of Republican Leader John Boehner. She served as the GOP Conference vice chair and took on several tasks. She helped to recruit women to run and served as a liaison to newly elected Republican women, including with fundraising. McMorris Rodgers has broadened her party's use of social media tools. During the 2012 presidential campaign, Mitt Romney tapped McMorris Rodgers to serve as his House liaison, partly as a reward for her early endorsement. After the 2012 election, McMorris took over as Republican Conference chair. She defeated Tom Price of Georgia, a favorite of the tea party who had the backing of Paul Ryan of Wisconsin.

Along with senior GOP leaders, she considered the party's perceived weaknesses to be less about its policies than about how it conveys its message. "I don't think it's about the Republican Party needing to become more moderate," she told CNN. "I really believe it's the Republican Party becoming more modern." She created video products for other members to use on social media and in their districts. Much of her work remained behind the scenes. "I'm trying to promote a Republican cause," she said. "And part of that is [about] message as well as messengers. ... It's about doing that which I think is going to help our overall effort to advance the conservative cause." In 2015, McMorris Rodgers was instrumental in crafting a compromise between GOP women and pro-life conservatives on a House-passed abortion bill that would have barred most abortions after 20 weeks.

Her voting record has become more conservative. Although House Republicans praised McMorris Rodgers for her hard work, she passed up several opportunities to try to move up the leadership ladder. When Majority Leader Eric Cantor's unexpected primary defeat in 2014 opened two GOP leadership seats, she quickly said she would not run for either of them. Her staffers said the timing wasn't right and that she remained open to pursuing a higher post. She showed a similar reticence in the 2015 leadership shuffle after Boehner's resignation as Speaker. She stepped down from the leadership following the 2018 election, when she was term-limited as Conference chair and the GOP lost the majority. As ranking Republican on the Energy and Commerce Subcommittee on Consumer Protection and Commerce, she said that she was ready to "drive the policy discussion" on issues such as technology, privacy and cybersecurity.

In April 2007, McMorris Rodgers and her husband had their first child, Cole McMorris Rodgers, who was born four weeks premature and was diagnosed with Down syndrome. She subsequently gave birth to two daughters, making her the first member of Congress to deliver multiple babies while in office. She formed the Congressional Down Syndrome Caucus in 2008 to raise awareness about institutional barriers that face individuals with Down syndrome, and she became a leader in the disabilities community. In 2013, she enacted her National Pediatric Research Network Act. In 2014, she helped to enact the Achieving a Better Life Experience (ABLE) Act, which was designed to empower individuals with disabilities.

Following the 2016 election, McMorris Rodgers reportedly was the frontrunner for Interior Secretary before Donald Trump gave the position to the junior Rep. Ryan Zinke. The Spokane Spokesman-Review earlier reported that she had a "tepid alliance" with Trump during the presidential campaign. With Trump as president, she occasionally found herself in an awkward position of avoiding criticism when she disagreed with his policies. In a June 2018 profile, The Washington Post reported that she deflected questions about Trump, though she said, "I have stood up to him when I thought that was appropriate."

In 2018, McMorris Rodgers was challenged by Democrat Lisa Brown, who had been majority leader during 20 years in the state Senate and then served as chancellor of the Spokane campus of Washington State University. Brown contrasted their actions on health care issues, saying McMorris Rodgers was out of touch with the district and complained that "Congress just isn't getting the job done." Democrats voiced hope that they could reverse the 1994 outcome, when local voters ousted Foley. McMorris Rodgers outspent Brown, $5.6 million to $5.5 million. McMorris Rodgers scored an impressive victory, 55%-45%, taking 52 percent of the vote in Spokane County. At age 49, she retained options to emulate Foley — who had been a committee chairman before he was a party leader in the House.

WA-5: Eastern Washington   **Cook Partisan Voting Index: R+8**

Population		Race and Ethnicity		Income	
Total	696,562	White	84.2%	Median Income	$50,693
Land area (sq. miles)	15,473	Black	1.5%	District Income Rank	296
Pop/ sq mi	45	Latino	6.4%	Poverty Rate	15.9%
Born in State	53.2%	Asian	2.4%	With health insurance	92.3%
		Two or more races	3.7%	Cash public assistance	4.5%
Age Groups		Other	1.9%	Food stamp/SNAP	16.7%
Under 18	21.6%				
18-34	25.2%	**Education**		**Work**	
35-64	37.3%	H.S grad or less	32.5%	White Collar	15.9%
Over 64	15.9%	Some college	38.6%	Sales and Service	43.4%
		College Degree, 4 yr	17.9%	Blue Collar	20.4%
Military		Post grad	11%	Government	18.4%
Veteran/ Active Duty	11.8%				

2012 Pres. Vote	Romney	168,671	(54%)	Obama	137,771	(44%)			
2016 Pres. Vote	Trump	166,765	(50%)	Clinton	125,112	(38%)	Johnson	18,499	(6%)

Spokane: Eastern Washington is a land of great rivers and bare parched land, where the Columbia, Spokane and Snake rivers wind among vast plateaus, bringing water from the Rockies to the desert. Spokane grew up at the falls of the Spokane River when the railroads first came through. It was initially a gold rush town, and later became a major wheat, mining and railroad center. Nearby are some of the most fascinating landscapes in the United States: undulating yellow wheat fields on the rolling ridges of the Palouse, where the wheat-growing topsoil is 200 feet deep; acres of protected forestland in Colville National Forest, home to the last surviving herd of caribou in the lower 48 states; and bare-rock coulees rising above dammed-up lakes and barren desert. Much of this area is remote and inhospitable. The summers can be blazingly hot and the winters bitterly cold. But the water from the Grand Coulee and other dams irrigates some of the richest farmland in the country.

The 5th Congressional District of Washington covers the easternmost part of the state. Nearly three-fourths of the people live in Spokane County, where the voting habits have grown apart from the Washington west of the Cascades, especially on natural resource issues. Spokane, with four local universities, has become a "second-tier" city where companies locate for quality of life and lower housing costs. From 2010 to 2017, the population of Spokane County grew 7 percent and exceeded 500,000. A prospective round of base closures has had residents concerned about the fate of Fairchild Air Force Base, the area's largest employer. Fairchild lost two bids to be the home for the new KC-46A aerial tankers; in 2017, it gained 12 additional KC-135s, the military's experienced refueling tanker. The area also is a farming center. Near the Oregon border is Walla Walla, long dependent on alfalfa, wheat and sweet onions. Its budding wine industry had 120 wineries in 2018. The city's name is an American Indian term for "many waters."

The district's political inclinations lean Republican. Spokane County voted for Democrat Bill Clinton in 1992 and 1996, but Republicans have won it since. In 2016, Donald Trump took 50 percent of the vote, his second-best district in the state. Democrat Tom Foley was the local congressman for 30 years and served as Speaker of the House from 1989 until 1994, when he lost his seat and Democrats lost their majority. Democrats have not been competitive for the seat since.

Derek Kilmer (D)

Elected 2012, 4th term, b. Jan 01, 1974; Port Angeles; Princeton University (NJ), A.B., 1996; University of Oxford (UK), Ph.D., 2003; Methodist; Married (Jennifer Kilmer); 2 children.

Elected Office: WA House, 2005-2007; WA Senate, 2007-2013.

Professional Career: Mgmt. consultant, McKinsey & Co., 1999-2002; Vice President., Economic Development Board, Tacoma Pierce County, 2002-2012.

DC Office: 1410 LHOB 20515, 202-225-5916, Fax: 202-226-3575, kilmer.house.gov

State Offices: Bremerton, 360-373-9725; Port Angeles, 360-797-3623; Tacoma, 253-272-3515.

Committees: *Appropriations*: Defense; Energy & Water Development & Related Agencies; Interior, Environment & Related Agencies. *Select Committee on the Modernization of Congress (Chmn).*

Group Ratings

	ADA	ACLU	AFL-CIO	LCV	ITI	COC	HAFA	ACU	CFG	FRC
2018	-	79%	-	94%	-	75%	6%	8%	7%	0%
2017	85%	C	95%	100%	C	64%	C	4%	0%	11%

Almanac Ratings 2017-18

	Economy	Social	Foreign	Composite
Liberal	95%	98%	92%	95%
Conservative	5%	2%	8%	5%

Key Votes of the 115th Congress

1. Obama-care revision	N	5. Family planning regs	N	9. Guantanamo prisoners	Y
2. Tax Cuts	N	6. Body cameras/immigration	Y	10. Ground missiles, limit	Y
3. Omnibus appropriations	Y	7. Abortion ban	N	11. Defense Dept. spending	Y
4. Dodd-Frank revision	N	8. Concealed carry	N	12. FISA rules	N

Election Results

Election	Name (Party)	Vote (%)		Cand. Spent	Ind. Exp. Support	Ind. Exp. Oppose
2018 General	Derek Kilmer (D)............................	206,409	(64%)	$831,268	$2,565	
	Douglas Dightman (R).................	116,677	(36%)	$40,401		
2018 Primary	Derek Kilmer (D)............................	117,848	(64%)			
	Douglas Dightman (R).................	60,651	(33%)			

Prior winning percentages: 2016 (62%), 2014 (63%), 2012 (59%)

Democrat Derek Kilmer, elected in 2012, has had a steady rise in influence with a seat on the Appropriations Committee and as chairman of the New Democrat Coalition. Kilmer has been a centrist and has shown interest in defense and resource issues. In 2019, he took on a challenging assignment as chairman of a select committee to consider steps to modernize Congress.

Kilmer grew up as the son of two public school teachers in Port Angeles. Watching the town's economic struggles in the wake of the timber industry's decline led Kilmer to pursue a career linking public policy and economic development. He got a bachelor's from Princeton University and a doctorate in social policy from the University of Oxford in England, with a focus on economic development. After working as a business consultant for McKinsey and Co., he went to work for the nonprofit Economic Development Board for Tacoma-Pierce County. As a vice president, he talked with 200 businesses a year in an effort to broaden the economies of communities like Port Angeles, long dependent on timber. Kilmer was elected to the state House in 2004 and two years later moved to the state Senate, where he was the chief author of the state's capital budget and promoted legislation to create jobs by borrowing money for public construction.

Rep. Norm Dicks, who was the senior Democrat on Appropriations, gave his protégé early word in 2012 that he would not seek a 19th term. "He told me, 'In about an hour I'm going to announce my retirement, and you should figure out what you're going to do,'" Kilmer recalled. He moved quickly and was the only Democratic contender. In the all-party primary, Kilmer got 53 percent of the total vote. Republican businessman Bill Driscoll, an ex-Marine who served in Iraq and Afghanistan, led the six Republican candidates with 18 percent. He called the federal deficit the biggest threat to national security and departed from Republican orthodoxy in supporting abortion rights and same-sex marriage. Kilmer made sure to let voters know that he was running with Dicks' backing. The Seattle Times endorsed him as "a problem solver who can be bipartisan." Each candidate spent close to $2 million. Kilmer won 59%-41%.

Kilmer made an early effort at consensus-building with the Bipartisan Working Group and the Problem Solvers Caucus, which have tried to forge greater consensus on a variety of issues. With Republican Rep. Doug Collins of Georgia, he filed the "Keeping American Jobs Act," which sought to assure that employers can't require American workers to train cheaper staff who are working with U.S. visas. He helped to organize the Puget Sound Recovery Caucus to bring increased focus and attention to cleanup work. Kilmer has sought to limit contributions and increase transparency in campaigns. His Almanac vote ratings have placed him near the center of House Democrats. With Rep. Joe Kennedy of Massachusetts following the 2016 election, Kilmer won Democratic Caucus approval of a requirement that Democrats add a "vice ranking member" to each House committee — with the goal of giving more leadership opportunities to junior Democrats. Fortuitously, Kilmer took that new position at Appropriations.

On Appropriations, he has added district-oriented provisions to subcommittee bills. He has begun to follow in Dicks' footsteps with a long run on the panel, much as Dicks earlier was mentored as an aide to Sen. Warren Magnuson of Washington, who chaired the Senate Appropriations Committee. In the Pentagon appropriations bill for fiscal 2019, he secured funding to upgrade facilities at the Puget Sound shipyard and got $2 million to review steps to reduce military jet noise at the Naval Air Station on Whidbey Island. In December 2017, the House passed his bill to continue cooperation between the National Aeronautics and Space Administration and the Israeli Space Agency. Kilmer has been active on the New Democrat Coalition. As vice chairman in 2017, he created task forces to prepare alternatives to Republican proposals. As chairman in 2019, he welcomed 30 freshman Democrats to the group.

After Speaker Nancy Pelosi agreed to demands by many House members for a review of and recommendations for reforms to congressional operations, the House on its opening day in 2019 created a bipartisan select committee to study ways to modernize Congress. Citing Kilmer as an "innovator and pioneer" with a "commitment to bipartisanship," she named him as chairman. Congress needs to do better," he said in taking the assignment. "Americans deserve a Congress that approaches its work in innovative new ways."

On local interests, Kilmer enacted a bill in 2014 that renamed a memorial on Bainbridge Island in honor of Japanese Americans who were forced from their homes during World War II. He has been reelected easily and appears to have settled in for a lengthy and productive career.

WA-6: Lower Puget Sound, Olympic Peninsula

Cook Partisan Voting Index: D+6

Population		Race and Ethnicity		Income	
Total	689,399	White	77.5%	Median Income	$59,898
Land area (sq. miles)	6,903	Black	3.3%	District Income Rank	180
Pop/ sq mi	99.9	Latino	7.4%	Poverty Rate	12.9%
Born in State	48.6%	Asian	4.1%	With health insurance	91.9%
		Two or more races	5.3%	Cash public assistance	4%
Age Groups		Other	2.3%	Food stamp/SNAP	14.5%
Under 18	19.8%				
18-34	22%	**Education**		**Work**	
35-64	39.4%	H.S grad or less	32.7%	White Collar	18.8%
Over 64	18.8%	Some college	38.1%	Sales and Service	42.4%
Military		College Degree, 4 yr	18.3%	Blue Collar	21%
Veteran/ Active Duty	17.4%	Post grad	10.9%	Government	23.1%

2012 Pres. Vote	Obama	184,820	(56%)	Romney	135,573	(41%)			
2016 Pres. Vote	Clinton	172,596	(50%)	Trump	131,449	(38%)	Johnson	19,038	(6%)
	Stein	6,950	(2%)						

Tacoma, Bremerton: The rainiest part of the continental United States is its far northwest corner, where the Olympic Mountains of Washington jut into the Pacific Ocean. The waters of the Pacific evaporate, condense, and then mist or rain on the hills and mountains along Puget Sound. The mountains here are always green, the trees that line the inlets towering, and during heavy rainfalls the rivers can rise six feet in a day. This has long been lumbering and fishing country, where people start work at 6 a.m. and where the vagaries of nature and environmental laws — like the ban on old-growth logging to protect the habitat of the spotted owl — have strengthened a traditional surly independence and suspicion of authority. Still, respect for the beauty of nature endures, including at the 3,310-square-mile Olympic Coast National Marine Sanctuary, a vast underwater reserve.

The many inlets of Puget Sound, winding sinuously through mountains, are among America's most picturesque waterways and strategically among its most important. During World War II, shipyards were built to shelter much of the Navy's Pacific fleet. During the Cold War, some of the nuclear submarine fleet was anchored at the giant Kitsap Navy base. The Puget Sound Naval Shipyard now has five installations. It employed more than 14,000 in 2018, with plans to add a few hundred more workers. The Tacoma Narrows Bridge replaced the original bridge which, in a scene preserved on newsreel and still viewed by civil engineering students, started vibrating on the wrong harmonic in high winds and collapsed in 1940. On the other side is Tacoma, long the second city on Puget Sound, with its massive docks, former pulp mills, pleasant hilly residential neighborhoods and recently revived waterfront. On the northern coast, across from British Columbia, Port Angeles been ranked among the nation's best small towns. A retooled paper mill was expected to reopen in late 2019 at the site of a 98-year-old factory. The Olympic Peninsula extends from the Pacific Ocean to Puget Sound, and from the Canadian border to Oregon. The national park in the Olympic Mountains covers 1,442 square miles.

The 6th Congressional District of Washington includes the Olympic Peninsula, Bremerton and about 40 percent of Tacoma, but not the port; Tacoma also is part of the 9th and 10th Districts. Kitsap County is the largest population center, including Bainbridge Island; in 2017, new "fast ferry" service began, with a 30-minute trip from Bremerton to downtown Seattle. (No bridges cross the sound.) Kitsap has become a popular residential area for residents who can't afford the housing costs in Seattle. About two-thirds of the 6th's residents live in Kitsap or in Tacoma's Pierce County. Politically, the Olympic Peninsula and Tacoma are working-class Democrat, as is the district overall, though not overwhelmingly. The district has the smallest racial-minority population of the seven Seattle-area districts. Hillary Clinton in 2016 got 50 percent of the vote. Coastal and blue-collar Grays Harbor County voted Republican in the 2016 presidential election for the first time since 1928.

Pramila Jayapal (D)

Elected 2016, 2nd term, b. Sep 21, 1965; Chennai, India; Georgetown University (DC), A.B., 1986; Northwestern University, M.B.A., 1990; Hinduism; Married (Steve Williamson); 1 child ; 1 stepchild.

Elected Office: WA Senate, 2015-2016.

Professional Career: Financial Analyst; Non Profit Executive.

DC Office: 1510 LHOB 20515, 202-225-3106, Fax: 202-225-6197

State Offices: Seattle, 206-674-0040.

Committees: *Budget. Education & Labor*: Higher Education & Workforce Investment; Workforce Protections. *Judiciary*: Antitrust, Commercial & Administrative Law; Immigration & Citizenship.

Group Ratings

	ADA	ACLU	AFL-CIO	LCV	ITI	COC	HAFA	ACU	CFG	FRC
2018	-	97%	-	94%	-	50%	9%	4%	22%	0%
2017	100%	C	97%	97%	C	36%	C	7%	5%	0%

Almanac Ratings 2017-18

	Economy	Social	Foreign	Composite
Liberal	100%	100%	100%	100%
Conservative	0%	0%	0%	0%

Key Votes of the 115th Congress

1. Obama-care revision	N	5. Family planning regs	N	9. Guantanamo prisoners	Y
2. Tax Cuts	N	6. Body cameras/immigration	Y	10. Ground missiles, limit	Y
3. Omnibus appropriations	N	7. Abortion ban	N	11. Defense Dept. spending	N
4. Dodd-Frank revision	N	8. Concealed carry	N	12. FISA rules	N

Election Results

Election	Name (Party)	Vote (%)		Cand. Spent	Ind. Exp. Support	Ind. Exp. Oppose
2018 General	Pramila Jayapal (D)...........................	329,800	(84%)	$1,585,055	$2,175	
	Craig Keller (R)....................................	64,881	(16%)	$22,731		

Prior winning percentages: 2016 (56%)

Pramila Jayapal of Washington, who won her seat in 2016 in a runoff against another Democratic state legislator, quickly emerged as an outspoken leader of House progressives. She has been out front on topics such as government-run health care and taxpayer-funded college tuition for many. Following the 2018 election, Jayapal fell short in her bid for a seat on the Ways and Means Committee, but gained prominence as co-chair of the Progressive Caucus. She was "steering the progressive legislative agenda" and was "becoming a force party leaders must reckon with," the Wall Street Journal reported in April 2019.

Jayapal, the first Indian-American woman elected to Congress, was born in Chennai, India, where her parents have continued to reside. Her father was in the oil business, and the family traveled in Asia when she was a child. At 16, she moved to the United States to attend Georgetown University. She worked on Wall Street for PaineWebber as a financial analyst in leveraged buyouts and got an MBA from Northwestern University. After briefly working on the sales of cardiac defibrillators in the medical equipment industry, she pursued a career in the nonprofit world, starting with a Seattle-based group working on international public health. During that time, she spent two years living in small towns in India. She wrote a book about that experience: Pilgrimage to India: A Woman Revisits Her Homeland.

Following the 9/11 terrorist attacks, Jayapal started and was executive director of Hate Free Zone, an advocacy group for South Asians, Arabs and Muslims. The organization, which changed its name to OneAmerica, worked on local and state issues. She led a national coalition, We Belong Together, which addressed gender-related issues in the Senate-passed immigration reform bill in 2013. She was recognized by President Barack Obama as a White House "Champion of Change." In 2014, Jayapal was elected as the first woman of color to the state Senate, where she worked on tuition-free community college, a state voting rights act, automatic voter registration and measures to help survivors of sexual assault. Her husband, Steve Williamson, has held senior positions with labor unions.

When Democratic Rep. Jim McDermott announced his retirement, five Democrats entered the contest to succeed him. In the first round of voting, in which Democrats received 85 percent of the total vote, Jayapal was the frontrunner with 42 percent. The runner-up with 21 percent was Brady Walkinshaw, an openly gay Democratic state representative who was a native of Whatcom County and styled himself as a bipartisan bridge-builder. In the general election, Jayapal was endorsed by EMILY's List, several labor unions and Sen. Bernie Sanders of Vermont. She raised $3 million to $1.9 million for Walkinshaw, who won endorsements from many local Democrats and had $353,000 in support from a Latino advocacy group; he is Cuban-American. Jayapal won the runoff, 56%-44%.

Jayapal didn't wait long to get attention. Three days after taking office, during the typically ceremonial count of the Electoral College vote, she raised objections to the 2016 presidential vote count in Georgia, which Donald Trump had easily won. Vice President Joe Biden, who was presiding over the joint session of Congress, gaveled her to silence and advised her, to some laughter, "It's over." Jayapal was one of seven House Democrats who objected to certifying the Trump victory. She later told The Seattle Times that she had hoped to state her full objections, though the rules required that at least one senator join her.

In April 2017, she filed in coordination with Sanders a bill to make public colleges and universities tuition-free for families with less than $125,000 in income and to significantly reduce student debt. "The College for All Act renews our compact with our young people," Jayapal said. Her centerpiece proposal became the "Medicare for All" plan, on which she took the lead with Rep. Debbie Dingell of Michigan. "One of the best ways to ensure health care for all is to use the system that already exists for millions of seniors over the last half century: Medicare," Jayapal said. She was the founding co-chair of the Medicare for All Caucus, which was organized in July 2018. Also that month, she filed with Reps. Mark Pocan of Wisconsin and Adriano Espaillat of New York a bill to abolish the Immigration and Customs Enforcement agency, and create a commission to develop a "human immigration system that upholds the dignity of all individuals."

Following the 2018 election, Jayapal was elected with Pocan as co-chair of the Progressive Caucus. She described her commitment to "ensuring our caucus is as bold and strategic as possible." Her chief responsibility was to "keep as much unity as possible" among the nearly 100 members of the caucus, the veteran organizer said in a January 2019 interview with The Nation. "It doesn't mean people shouldn't disagree, but we should find ways for everybody to do what they need to do." The profile headlined that Jayapal's "inside-outside strategy is changing the future of progressive politics."

Her chief setback was her failure in January 2019 to secure a seat on Ways and Means, despite support from many of her progressive allies. At the time, five other second-term House members joined the panel, whose jurisdiction includes Medicare.

WA-7: Seattle Metro   **Cook Partisan Voting Index: D+33**

Population		Race and Ethnicity		Income	
Total	746,893	White	70.3%	Median Income	$80,962
Land area (sq. miles)	144	Black	4.1%	District Income Rank	48
Pop/ sq mi	5182.1	Latino	7.6%	Poverty Rate	10.7%
Born in State	40%	Asian	11.4%	With health insurance	93.9%
		Two or more races	5.4%	Cash public assistance	2.2%
Age Groups		Other	1.2%	Food stamp/SNAP	7.8%
Under 18	15.9%				
18-34	30.9%	Education		Work	
35-64	40%	H.S grad or less	16.4%	White Collar	13.2%
Over 64	13.2%	Some college	24.2%	Sales and Service	32.5%
		College Degree, 4 yr	35%	Blue Collar	9.8%
Military		Post grad	24.4%	Government	13.4%
Veteran/ Active Duty	6.1%				

2012 Pres. Vote	Obama	310,828	(79%)	Romney	70,973	(18%)			
2016 Pres. Vote	Clinton	341,412	(80%)	Trump	50,615	(12%)	Johnson	13,495	(3%)
	Stein	8,374	(2%)						

Seattle: Seattle rises from the Puget Sound harbor of Elliott Bay on steep hills once covered with 300-foot-high Douglas firs. Behind the hills and buildings, on a clear day you can see the nimbus of Mount Rainier. On the picturesque waterfront, below gleaming high-rises, is Pike Place Market, where you can get fresh salmon and Dungeness crabs. Nearby, where the ferries from Bainbridge and Vashon islands and Bremerton dock in the nation's busiest ferry system, is Pioneer Square, where stores and warehouses from the turn of the 20th century have been restored. Yesler Way was America's original Skid Road — literally a path for skidding newly cut logs to transportation terminals. It remains a haven for the homeless and a frequent locale for open-air drug dealing.

Seattle has some old ethnic neighborhoods, like the once heavily Scandinavian Ballard, which now features boutiques and nightspots, and the countercultural Capitol Hill, where shoppers jam busy stores, galleries, and clubs. Highly educated, affluent single professionals have made the Victorian houses overlooking the harbor and the 1940s houses in Capitol Hill among the nation's highest-priced residential real estate. After six years of steep increases, property prices dipped in late 2018 — at least temporarily. The city has a new ethnic mix, with thousands of recent Asian immigrants boosting the total to 15 percent.

The city's economic foundation is sound, and parts are bustling. The number of families with annual income exceeding $200,000 was greater than the families earning less than $50,000. Rejecting Microsoft's local model of a suburban campus, robust Amazon expanded into a huge campus with three new office towers in the South Lake Union area. In 2018, the company had more than 40,000 local workers who occupy more than 20 percent of the city's prime office space. Amazon founder and CEO Jeff Bezos occasionally monitors his part-time investment property, The Washington Post, and his new corporate headquarters across the Potomac in Crystal City, Virginia; he has opened his personal life to unusual — and, at times, salacious — public scrutiny. Microsoft founder Bill Gates' decision to turn his attention to global health philanthropy has made Seattle the Davos of health care, drawing experts in malaria, tuberculosis, AIDS and other global scourges. Seattle is the headquarters, in an old industrial district, of Starbucks. From 2012 to 2018, the company had a growth spurt from 18,000 to nearly 30,000 stores worldwide; about half are in the United States. For 2019, Starbucks projected adding 2,100 new shops globally. In 2014, the city council spurred a nationwide movement when it increased Seattle's minimum wage to $15 per hour, on a phased timetable to 2021. Although the city has continued to boom, some conservative economists contend that there has been a subsequent dip in minimum-wage jobs. A further financial twist was the city's move in May 2018 to impose a corporate tax that would raise an estimated $50 million annually to finance steps to aid the homeless; one month later, large businesses — led by Amazon — successfully pressured the city to repeal the new fee.

Seattle ranks as one of the nation's most desirable cities, but it has its flaws and limitations. The Justice Department investigated the city's police after several episodes in which officers were accused of using unnecessary force and discriminating against minorities, and concluded that the department had engaged in a pattern of excessive force that violated the Constitution and federal law. The city is a growing haven for young singles, as married couples with children make up only 13 percent of Seattle households. As many as 40 percent of Seattle households have a single occupant.

The 7th Congressional District of Washington includes nearly all of Seattle, some industrial suburban fringe to the south, a white-collar suburban fringe to the north, and artsy, bucolic Vashon Island in Puget Sound. Less than 10 percent of the population is in the southwest corner of Snohomish County, in Lynnwood. Hillary Clinton got 80 percent of the vote in 2016.

Kim Schrier (D)

Elected 2018, 1st term, b. Aug 23, 1968; Los Angeles, CA; Universidad Complutense de Madrid (Spain); University of California, Berkeley, B.A., 1991; University of California, M.D., 1997; Jewish; Married (David Gowing); 1 child.

Professional Career: Pediatrician, Virginia Mason Medical Center (Issaquah, WA).

DC Office: 1123 LHOB 20515, 202-225-7761, schrier.house.gov

State Offices: Issaquah, 425-657-1001.

Committees: *Agriculture*: Biotechnology, Horticulture & Research; Subcommittee Nutrition, Oversight & Department Operations. *Education & Labor*: Civil Rights & Human Services; Early Childhood, Elementary & Secondary Education.

Election Results

Election	Name (Party)	Vote (%)		Cand. Spent	Ind. Exp. Support	Ind. Exp. Oppose
2018 General	Kim Schrier (D)....................................	164,089	(52%)	$7,779,846	$3,855,559	$6,482,384
	Dino Rossi (R).............................	148,968	(48%)	$4,781,977	$366,924	$8,636,814
2018 Primary	Dino Rossi (R)................................	73,388	(43%)			
	Kim Schrier (D)....................................	31,837	(19%)			
	Jason Rittereiser (D)............................	30,708	(18%)			
	Shannon Hader (D)...............................	21,317	(13%)			

Freshman Democrat Kim Schrier won a district that Republicans had held since 1982. A pediatrician, she said that Republican attempts to repeal the Affordable Care Act spurred her to launch her first political campaign. She became the first woman doctor to serve in Congress. Schrier defeated Dino Rossi, a well-known Republican who had run three competitive statewide campaigns. She replaced Republican Rep. Dave Reichert, who retired after serving seven terms and worked on health care issues as a member of the Ways and Means Committee.

Schrier, a native of Los Angeles, graduated from the University of California, Berkeley, with a degree in astrophysics and got her medical degree from the university's Davis campus. She practiced at a medical center in Issaquah Washington for 16 years. As Congress prepared to overhaul the healthcare law in early 2017, Schrier met with an aide to Reichert to describe the adverse impact of the legislation on her patients. Reichert's decision to support the bill led her to run for his seat.

"The [2016] election and the utter failure of this Congress to provide checks and balances, or to work together on just about anything has compelled me to step up," Schrier said. She made health care the centerpiece of her campaign and said that, if elected, "she'd work to cut drug costs and stabilize Obamacare while moving gradually toward a 'Medicare for all' system," The Seattle Times reported.

In Washington's "top two" primary, Rossi was the front runner with 43 percent of the vote. Schrier got 19 percent to edge out Democratic attorney Jason Rittereiser for second place. Rittereiser and other Democrats criticized Schrier for failing to take a more activist approach on health-care changes. The total vote in the primary split 50%-47% for the Democrats over the Republican candidates.

Rossi, a former state legislator and a commercial real estate investor, lost a bid for governor in 2004 by 139 votes, plus subsequent bids for governor and the Senate. He said that Schrier was too liberal for the district and did not share his interest in bipartisanship. Schrier described Rossi as a "career politician" and cited his opposition to abortion as out of step with local voters. In their only debate, Rossi cited his legislative experience and said that Schrier's approach to health care "will destroy Medicare as we know it." Schrier said that Rossi would place the interests of President Donald Trump above those of constituents.

In its editorial endorsing Rossi, The Seattle Times praised "his demonstrated record of working across the aisle with Democrats" and said that he could do that in the "hopelessly dysfunctional Congress." Schrier, according to the editorial, would require more time to show her influence and "falls short in explaining how to manage the cost" of her health care proposals.

Schrier was an impressive fundraiser, with nearly $8 million in spending, and she benefited from more than $12 million in spending by national Democrats…The combined spending of more than $30 million made the contest "the costliest House race in the nation," the Times reported.

In a prime example of suburban hostility to Trump across the nation, Schrier won, 52%-48%. Rossi won four of the five counties and ran best in areas more distant from the Seattle metro area. In King County, which cast about three-fifths of the vote, Schrier took 58 percent.

If Schrier survives reelection in 2020 and has allies on the state's redistricting commission, she likely would gain favorable changes in redistricting.

WA-8: Outer Seattle-Tacoma Suburbs   Cook Partisan Voting Index: EVEN

Population		Race and Ethnicity		Income	
Total	725,674	White	71.8%	Median Income	$79,632
Land area (sq. miles)	7,360	Black	2.8%	District Income Rank	55
Pop/ sq mi	98.6	Latino	11.2%	Poverty Rate	9.4%
Born in State	51.6%	Asian	8.4%	With health insurance	92.8%
Age Groups		Two or more races	4.3%	Cash public assistance	2.8%
Under 18	25.1%	Other	1.5%	Food stamp/SNAP	10.1%
18-34	20.8%	**Education**		**Work**	
35-64	41.7%	H.S grad or less	33.3%	White Collar	12.4%
Over 64	12.4%	Some college	33%	Sales and Service	38.3%
Military		College Degree, 4 yr	22%	Blue Collar	22.3%
Veteran/ Active Duty	9.5%	Post grad	11.7%	Government	14.7%

2012 Pres. Vote	Obama	155,982	(50%)	Romney	151,069	(48%)			
2016 Pres. Vote	Clinton	153,167	(46%)	Trump	143,403	(43%)	Johnson	17,644	(5%)

Auburn, Wenatchee: In the shadow of the majestic 14,410-foot Mount Rainier, Seattle in the last 50 years has spread out to all four points of the compass. In 1960, surrounding King County had 935,000 residents, 557,000 of whom lived in Seattle. Since then, the city has added about 127,000 people, but the county has more than doubled to 2.2 million. At first these newcomers moved into places like Bellevue, Redmond and Renton, on the flat lands to the north and west of Cougar Mountain. As those places have filled in, the metropolitan area expanded out past Lake Sammamish and into the foothills of the Cascades, the valleys between the peaks of the Issaquah Alps and the southern flatlands of the Puget Trough. Auburn, an old center for hop farming that became a factory town for Boeing in the 1960s, doubled its population from 1999 to 2017, as a new super mall attracted businesses, jobs and new residents.

The 8th Congressional District of Washington takes in much of this new frontier in greater Seattle's development, as well as some of its last remaining areas of undeveloped land. It encompasses all of Mount Rainier, as well as one of the nation's last inland old-growth rain forests. Other areas include the southern edge of King County, including Auburn and smaller towns like Algona, Milton and Lakeland North. The district extends into Pierce County, where it includes some of the suburbs around Tacoma. The risk of mud slides and volcanic debris at Rainier have led Pierce County officials to prepare improved detections and warnings. In 2018, Rainier was ranked as the third most-active volcano in the United States. The district also takes in three agricultural counties that extend east of the Cascades. Kittitas County is a major producer of hay, most of which is shipped overseas. In Chelan County, growers in 2015 opened a state-required $6 million facility to house seasonal workers who pick cherries, apples and pears. Wenatchee, the county seat of Chelan, has been discovered as the "go-to place for everything from wine tourism and real-estate speculation to cannabis farming and bitcoin mining," The Seattle Times wrote in August 2018. About 60 percent of the district is in King, nearly 25 percent in Pierce, and the remainder is in or beyond the Cascades.

Of the three districts that are based chiefly in King County, the 8th has the preponderance of Republican precincts. Even with redistricting changes in 2012 that increased the GOP vote by several percentage points, the district has remained competitive in presidential elections. In 2016, Hillary Clinton led, 46%-43%. In a profile of the district, Ronald Brownstein wrote in The Atlantic in October 2018, the area was a mix of "growing Democratic strength in white-collar suburbs recoiling from Trump [and] continued Republican dominance in rural places and blue-collar communities that flocked to Trump in 2016 and haven't wavered much since."

Adam Smith (D)

Elected 1996, 12th term, b. Jun 15, 1965; Washington, DC; Western Washington University, Att.; Fordham University (NY), B.A., 1987; University of Washington, J.D., 1990; Christian Church; Married (Sara Bickle-Eldridge Smith); 2 children.

Elected Office: WA Senate, 1990-1996.

Professional Career: Practicing attorney, 1991-1992; City prosecutor, 1993-1995.

DC Office: 2264 RHOB 20515, 202-225-8901, adamsmith.house.gov

State Offices: Renton, 425-793-5180.

Committees: *Armed Services (Chmn).*

Group Ratings

	ADA	ACLU	AFL-CIO	LCV	ITI	COC	HAFA	ACU	CFG	FRC
2018	-	96%	-	100%	-	50%	13%	8%	23%	0%
2017	100%	C	95%	97%	C	31%	C	8%	8%	0%

Almanac Ratings 2017-18

	Economy	Social	Foreign	Composite
Liberal	98%	100%	87%	95%
Conservative	2%	0%	14%	5%

Key Votes of the 115th Congress

1. Obama-care revision	N	5. Family planning regs	N	9. Guantanamo prisoners	Y
2. Tax Cuts	N	6. Body cameras/immigration	Y	10. Ground missiles, limit	Y
3. Omnibus appropriations	N	7. Abortion ban	N	11. Defense Dept. spending	Y
4. Dodd-Frank revision	N	8. Concealed carry	N	12. FISA rules	N

Election Results

Election	Name (Party)	Vote (%)		Cand. Spent	Ind. Exp. Support	Ind. Exp. Oppose
2018 General	Adam Smith (D)	163,345	(68%)	$1,290,149	$5,112	
	Sarah Smith (D)	77,222	(32%)	$103,840		
2018 Primary	Adam Smith (D)	71,035	(48%)			
	Sarah Smith (D)	39,409	(27%)			
	Doug Basler (R)	36,254	(25%)			

Prior winning percentages: 2016 (73%), 2014 (71%), 2012 (72%), 2010 (55%), 2008 (65%), 2006 (66%), 2004 (63%), 2002 (59%), 2000 (62%), 1998 (65%), 1996 (50%)

Adam Smith of Washington, a Democrat first elected in 1996, early in his career was a pro-business moderate who wasn't shy about expressing his irritations with both political parties. As the top Democrat on the Armed Services Committee, he has become an expert on military policy and logistics who often has been a blunt critic. Although he has joined the panel's tradition of bipartisanship, the polarization of Congress occasionally has led Smith to go his own way. His takeover as committee chairman in 2019, at age 53, could give him a lengthy tenure and enhance the clout of home-state defense facilities and industries.

Smith grew up in the Sea-Tac area. His father, a baggage handler for United Airlines who was active in the Machinists Union, died when Smith was 17. The family went on welfare. Smith worked his way through Fordham University driving trucks for UPS, and got his law degree at the University of Washington. He worked as a Seattle prosecutor, handling drunk-driving and domestic-abuse cases. In 1990, at age 25, he was elected to the state Senate, beating an incumbent Republican by canvassing the district door-to-door.

In 1996, he ran against first-term Republican Rep. Randy Tate. The two had similar backgrounds. They had been born in the same year to families of modest means, were elected to office at a young age and were firm believers in grassroots campaigning. Tate was a religious conservative and a strong supporter of House Speaker Newt Gingrich, while Smith campaigned as a moderate Democrat, supporting the death penalty and tougher penalties for criminals. He attacked Tate for his support of Gingrich and for backing cuts in Medicare. Tate attacked Smith for his opposition to assigning youthful offenders to adult courts and prisons and for voting for a tax increase in 1993. This was one of the closest races in the country. In the September all-party primary, Smith led 49%-48%. In November, he won 50%-47%.

Smith joined the New Democrat Coalition, established a moderate voting record and showed a willingness to take on established views and interests in his party. He voted to authorize military action in Iraq and sought to improve compensation and other quality-of-life benefits for military personnel. He supported the House-passed health care overhaul in 2009, but refused to commit publicly on the final version until the very end in March 2010, finally agreeing to back it after pleas from President Barack Obama and others. He joined Republicans in 2011 in voting to extend key expiring provisions of the Patriot Act anti-terrorism law. In 2012, he lamented "the hyper-partisanship that is making Congress so dysfunctional." In opposing the New Year's Day 2013 tax and spending deal to avoid the so-called fiscal cliff, he accused Obama of "bad math" and of being unrealistic. "His insistence that we only tax the rich has put us in a box," he told The Seattle Times. In 2015, in a switch of his customary free-trade views, Smith cited problems for workers and the environment when he voted against giving trade promotion authority to Obama.

On the Armed Services Committee, Smith earned praise for his work as chairman of two of its subcommittees. He served on the Intelligence Committee, further bolstering his credentials on military and foreign affairs issues. When Armed Services Chairman Ike Skelton of Missouri lost his reelection bid in 2010, Smith made a bid for ranking Democrat on the panel. Intelligence Committee Chairman Silvestre Reyes of Texas and California Rep. Loretta Sanchez — two Latinos -- also got into the race. In the Democratic Caucus, Sanchez and Smith tied at 64 votes apiece, while Reyes got 53. In the runoff, Smith won by 11 votes. (Reyes subsequently was defeated for reelection. Sanchez lost a bid for the Senate.)

Smith joined efforts to help the military adapt to automatic spending cuts that took effect in 2013. He introduced a bill calling for spending reductions to be split about evenly between defense and discretionary domestic spending programs. As Armed Services chairman, Republican Rep. Mac Thornberry of Texas said that Smith has helped make the committee less partisan. Ironically, Smith for the first time voted in May 2015 against passage of the defense spending bill, and called it "extremely damaging" to national security because it did not remove the budgetary spending caps and shifted some funding off-budget. In November, after a budget deal was reached, he rejoined the bipartisan majority on the defense bill. In 2016, he again switched his earlier opposition after hot-button social issues were removed and the bill made "positive improvements" to defense policy.

In 2014, Smith was appointed to the select committee investigating the terrorist attacks at U.S. facilities in Benghazi Libya. "This is a committee that should not have been formed," he said when it was unveiled. "But since the Republicans chose to form it, I think we have to participate to do our best to bring out the correct arguments." Earlier, he said Obama "could have done a better job" in working with Congress before taking military action against Libya in 2011, but he backed the president's strategy.

In the debate over the Islamic State, he dismissed hawks' calls for swift military action and emphasized the need to build coalitions. "We need reliable partners to work with in the region," Smith told CBS News. "We can't simply bomb first and ask questions later." He said that a formal request for authorization for use of military force (AUMF) should be sharply limited in how much power it gave to the president. "I don't think we should give the executive a blank check," he said. On the defense spending bill that was enacted in August 2018, Smith took credit for more public disclosure of civilian casualties in U.S. military operations, limits on military support of Saudi Arabia and restrictions on the military use of public lands. He secured additional funds plus safety measures for the continuing clean-up at the Hanford nuclear site in Washington.

After Donald Trump was elected, Smith voiced serious doubts about his national security views. "I don't think it's intellectually possible to digest what he's talking about, and I'm not just being a wise-ass here," he told McClatchy News in November 2016. As time passed, his fears about Trump deepened. Following his meeting with Russian President Vladimir Putin in Helsinki in July 2018, Smith said, "There is no sugar coating. It is hard to see … as anything other than treason" Trump's taking sides against the views of the U.S. intelligence community. Congress needed to "begin an impeachment investigation," he added. Smith said that Trump's demand for a wall along the border with Mexico was rooted in "xenophobia and racism."

As Armed Services chairman, Smith said that he would use his oversight authority to hold the Trump administration accountable for military operations overseas and for wasteful military spending. "We are absolutely going to bird-dog them to get accurate record-keeping, a full audit that tells us where you're spending your money and why," he told The Seattle Times in January 2019. He called the past approach by the Pentagon, "Scare the crap out of you and convince you to spend more money." He vowed to pursue "the lack of transparency and explanation" for Trump's actions.

Smith's independence has worked well for him at home and he usually has won reelection easily. His closest contest was a 55%-45% win over Pierce County Council member Dick Muri during the Republican wave in 2010. Redistricting changes in 2012 removed much of his base in Pierce County and gave him a King County-based district that was ethnically diverse and largely new to him, but more safely Democratic.

In 2016, Democrat Jesse Wineberry, an African American and former state representative, challenged Smith for not being a local advocate. "Diversity is under attack in this country," Wineberry said. "Let me utilize the power of the office to benefit the community." Smith responded that 160 languages were spoken in the district and said, "I consistently reach out to these communities." In the all-party primary, Smith got 56 percent to 23 percent for Republican Doug Basler and 15 percent for Wineberry. He defeated Basler in November, 73%-27%. Smith eagerly supported Pramila Jayapal in the neighboring 7th District. She was a resident of the 9th and might have been a serious threat if she had instead challenged Smith. In 2018, Smith faced a potentially more difficult contest when the runner-up in the three-candidate primary was Democrat Sarah Smith, a political newcomer and member of the Democratic Socialists of America. Styling himself as "progressive" and outspending the challenger by more than 10-to-1, he handily won, 68%-32%. His relationship with more outspoken local activists and the potential tensions with his responsibilities as Armed Services chairman bear watching.

WA-9: Southern and Eastern Seattle Metro   Cook Partisan Voting Index: D+21

Population		Race and Ethnicity		Income	
Total	726,425	White	46.4%	Median Income	$73,249
Land area (sq. miles)	183	Black	10.8%	District Income Rank	77
Pop/ sq mi	3960.2	Latino	12.2%	Poverty Rate	12.3%
Born in State	38.2%	Asian	23%	With health insurance	90.8%
		Two or more races	5.7%	Cash public assistance	3.5%
Age Groups		Other	2%	Food stamp/SNAP	14%
Under 18	21.6%				
18-34	25.6%	**Education**		**Work**	
35-64	40%	H.S grad or less	30.3%	White Collar	12.8%
Over 64	12.8%	Some college	28.1%	Sales and Service	39.2%
		College Degree, 4 yr	25.9%	Blue Collar	18.3%
Military		Post grad	15.6%	Government	11.4%
Veteran/ Active Duty	6.5%				

2012 Pres. Vote	Obama	195,863	(68%)	Romney	84,828	(30%)			
2016 Pres. Vote	Clinton	205,193	(69%)	Trump	67,956	(23%)	Johnson	11,178	(4%)

Bellevue, Renton: The misty shores of Puget Sound have seen some of America's most vibrant economic growth over the past two decades. It has spread south and west from Seattle, over suburban territory to the outskirts of the once-industrial city of Tacoma. The subdivisions along the sound, which have some of the loveliest views in the U.S., tend to be high-income. But much of greater Seattle's prime industrial territory lies between the ridges that run north and south inland. Weyerhaeuser, the world's largest private owner of softwood timber, is headquartered in Federal Way. A host of smaller factories cluster near the rail lines that are the terminus from Minneapolis-St. Paul across the Great Plains to Puget Sound.

Boeing is a major presence in Renton, on the south end of Lake Washington. Its aircraft and electronic components plants have made it the nation's No. 1 exporter for many years. Renton manufactures 737s, the best-selling commercial jet in history. In March 2017, Boeing unveiled the MAX version of its 737, with a capacity of 220 passengers. Three months earlier, the company reported a backlog of nearly 4,500 orders for the 737, including the MAX. Production at Renton had been scheduled to increase in 2019 to 57 planes per month. In September 2018, The Seattle Times reported, the delayed delivery and assembly of many parts for the new 737s had resulted in workers putting in long overtime hours and "struggling to get planes finished" to meet the company's far-flung sales commitments. Planes awaiting delivery filled the ramps at the edges of the nearby Renton airport, "spilled onto one of the taxiways, and were parked on all available spaces on the Boeing site," The Times wrote. In the next six months, two of those Boeing-manufactured passenger planes crashed — in Indonesia and Ethiopia — resulting in large loss of lives and a worldwide shutdown of the MAX until explanations and solutions were found.

The 9th Congressional District of Washington covers much of this area. It includes Sea-Tac Airport and Renton, just south of Seattle, as well as Des Moines, and most of Kent and Federal Way. It includes the container port of Tacoma, though most of the rest of that city is in the 6th and 10th Districts. The 9th extends northward from the south Seattle suburbs, where it takes in the southeastern neighborhoods of Seattle proper. It also pushes into the eastern suburbs. As the city grew over the years, newcomers crossed the pontoon bridge across Mercer Island to Bellevue and made that area one of the most vibrant parts of metropolitan Seattle. Bellevue, where the population doubled from 1970 to 2010, is the fastest-growing neighborhood in Seattle, with many large residential and business projects underway. Online auction house eBay has its operations there. With its vibrant downtown, including new office towers and residential high-rises, Bellevue today is an "edge city." The Seattle and Tacoma ports have unified management in an alliance to compete more effectively with other ports. Their container cargo made the combined ports the fourth-largest in the United States, supporting 58,400 jobs statewide. The port's new Terminal 5 was projected to combine deep-water and rail service to facilitate transfer of containers to and from ships, with completion scheduled for 2021. Passenger traffic at Sea-Tac in 2017 was the ninth-busiest in the nation. A new international arrivals facility was scheduled to open in 2020, at a cost of about $1 billion.

More than 95 percent of the district is in King County. The 9th takes in much of Seattle's minority population and is the city's first majority-minority district. It is 23 percent Asian, 12 percent Hispanic, 11 percent African American. In 2016, Hillary Clinton led, 69%-23%.

Denny Heck (D)

Elected 2012, 4th term, b. Jul 29, 1952; Vancouver; Evergreen State College (WA), B.A., 1973; Portland State University (OR), Att., 1975; Lutheran; Married (Paula Heck); 2 children; 1 grandchild.

Elected Office: WA House, 1976-1986.

Professional Career: Chief of Staff, Gov. Booth Gardner, 1989-1993; Co-founder & CEO, TVW, 1993-2003; Co-founder, bd. member, Intrepid Learning Solutions, 1999-2012.

DC Office: 2452 RHOB 20515, 202-225-9740, dennyheck.house.gov

State Offices: Lacey, 360-459-8514; Lakewood, 253-533-8332.

Committees: *Financial Services*: Consumer Protection & Financial Institutions; Housing, Community Development & Insurance; Nat'l Security, International Development & Monetary Policy. *Joint Economic. Permanent Select on Intelligence*: Defense Intelligence & Warfighter Support; Strategic Technologies & Advanced Research.

Group Ratings

	ADA	ACLU	AFL-CIO	LCV	ITI	COC	HAFA	ACU	CFG	FRC
2018	-	79%	-	94%	-	67%	9%	8%	10%	0%
2017	90%	C	95%	100%	C	57%	C	11%	5%	0%

Almanac Ratings 2017-18

	Economy	Social	Foreign	Composite
Liberal	98%	98%	89%	95%
Conservative	2%	2%	11%	5%

Key Votes of the 115th Congress

1. Obama-care revision	N	5. Family planning regs	N	9. Guantanamo prisoners	N
2. Tax Cuts	N	6. Body cameras/immigration	Y	10. Ground missiles, limit	Y
3. Omnibus appropriations	Y	7. Abortion ban	N	11. Defense Dept. spending	Y
4. Dodd-Frank revision	N	8. Concealed carry	N	12. FISA rules	N

Election Results

Election	Name (Party)	Vote (%)		Cand. Spent	Ind. Exp. Support	Ind. Exp. Oppose
2018 General	Denny Heck (D)	166,215	(62%)	$669,380	$1,778	
	Joseph Brumbles (R)	103,860	(38%)	$3,899		
2018 Primary	Denny Heck (D)	82,552	(58%)			
	Joseph Brumbles (R)	45,270	(32%)			
	Tamborine Borrelli (I)	7,997	(6%)			

Prior winning percentages: 2016 (59%), 2014 (55%), 2012 (59%)

Democrat Denny Heck was elected in 2012 and has settled into the Democratic-friendly 10th District. Two years earlier, he lost a tough open-seat race in a nearby marginal district to Republican Jaime Herrera Beutler. With his long and diverse career in politics and business, he has become a busy utility player in the House on banking and intelligence issues and in Democratic campaigns. Following the 2018 election, he lost a bid to chair the Democratic Congressional Campaign Committee.

Heck had a working-class upbringing in Vancouver. After graduating from Evergreen State College, he applied for a position as an assistant to a school district superintendent. At the school board meeting where Heck was officially hired, he met his wife, Paula, who was monitoring the meeting as a local union representative. In 1976, he was elected to the state House, where he was an author of the state's Basic Education Act and its funding formula. He became House majority leader before retiring at age 34. Two years later, he became chief of staff to Democratic Gov. Booth Gardner. In the 1990s, Heck cofounded TVW, a statewide public affairs network modeled after C-SPAN. He hosted a public affairs program and won an Emmy for a documentary he produced. He was an early investor in RealNetworks, one of the first audio and video internet services. Later, he cofounded an education and worker training company called Intrepid Learning Solutions.

By 2010, Heck hadn't worked in politics in years. He entered the race for the open 3rd District, which had been Democratic-held. He raised almost $2 million to $1.5 million for Herrera Beutler. Heck ran as a moderate Democrat and emphasized his business experience in creating jobs. Herrera Beutler criticized his support of the congressional Democrats' agenda and ran on a campaign of "fiscal sanity," a message that resonated that year, and won, 53%-47%. Not discouraged, Heck had another opportunity in 2012 when Washington gained a new district in more favorable territory. In the all-party primary with six candidates, he had a 40%-28% lead over Republican Dick Muri, a retired Air Force lieutenant colonel. Heck called for phasing out tax breaks for households earning more than $250,000 a year. He outspent Muri nearly 8-to-1 in the campaign, and national funding groups showed little interest. Heck won, 59%-41%.

He gained a seat on the Financial Services Committee and found some areas of bipartisan cooperation. Heck moved legislation that gave small businesses a formal advisory role at the Consumer Financial Protection Bureau. He was an outspoken advocate for extending the authority of the Export-Import Bank of the United States, which is a popular agency in the trade-friendly state of Washington. With Democratic Rep. Ed Perlmutter of Colorado, Heck has advocated steps to give access to the banking system for businesses dealing with marijuana. In February 2019, he spearheaded the first-ever hearing on the topic at the Financial Services panel. Denying such banking access leaves store owners in a "dangerous position" by forcing them to do all of their business in cash, Heck said. Some critics of his proposal have responded that the federal government continues to treat marijuana as an illegal substance.

Heck won enactment in 2018 of his legislation to encourage investment in stormwater infrastructure — in part to assist with clean-up of Puget Sound. "Stormwater is the biggest source of pollution in the sound, and combatting it requires all of us to step up and do our part," Heck said. His Almanac vote ratings have placed him close to the center of House Democrats; he was more conservative on foreign policy and liberal on social issues.

He has taken on party-related assignments. With the centrist New Democrat Coalition, he co-chairs the housing task force. At the DCCC in 2017-18, he had the vital role of recruitment chairman. Following the 2018 election, he was runner-up to Rep. Cheri Bustos in the Democratic Caucus vote for a new DCCC chairman.

At home, he under-performed in the 2014 election against Republican Joyce McDonald, a former member of the Pierce County Council. McDonald, a native of Scotland who served in the state House, called for tighter limits on federal spending. She raised only $88,000, while Heck raised $1.9 million. McDonald held him to a 55%-45% win. The two candidates were less than 400 votes apart in Pierce; Heck took 60 percent of the vote in his base of Thurston. Since then, he has breezed to reelection against Republican challengers who have spent scant money on their campaigns.

WA-10: Southwest Seattle Metro   **Cook Partisan Voting Index: D+5**

Population		Race and Ethnicity		Income	
Total	720,357	White	66.8%	Median Income	$61,351
Land area (sq. miles)	827	Black	6.1%	District Income Rank	161
Pop/ sq mi	871.4	Latino	11.3%	Poverty Rate	13%
Born in State	47.3%	Asian	6.4%	With health insurance	91.9%
		Two or more races	6.4%	Cash public assistance	3.8%
Age Groups		Other	3.1%	Food stamp/SNAP	14.6%
Under 18	23.8%				
18-34	25.1%	**Education**		**Work**	
35-64	37.6%	H.S grad or less	34.3%	White Collar	13.5%
Over 64	13.5%	Some college	38.2%	Sales and Service	42.3%
		College Degree, 4 yr	18.2%	Blue Collar	22.4%
Military		Post grad	9.4%	Government	23.8%
Veteran/ Active Duty	18%				

2012 Pres. Vote	Obama	164,505	(56%)	Romney	120,066	(41%)			
2016 Pres. Vote	Clinton	151,373	(50%)	Trump	117,861	(39%)	Johnson	17,003	(6%)
	Stein	6,481	(2%)						

Tacoma Metro, Olympia: Beginning at Deception Pass, near present-day Mount Vernon and Anacortes, Puget Sound winds its way southward from the Strait of Juan de Fuca for more than 100 miles, through an intricate latticework of bays, straits and islands. At the far southern end of the sound, off of Budd Inlet, is Olympia, the capital of Washington. In 1846, two New England natives, Lathrop Smith and Edmund Sylvester, hoping to take advantage of the location near the end of the Cowlitz Trail, platted a town in the New England style: a town square, carefully planned streets and land reserved for schools. They initially opted to name the town Smithster — a portmanteau of their surnames — but eventually opted for Olympia, after the mountains that are visible to the north on a clear day. It soon thereafter became the capital of Washington territory. As late as 1880, Olympia's population rivaled that of other major Washington cities. But the railroads passed it by, and other ports were developed in more advantageous positions closer to the mouth of Puget Sound. Olympia grew at a relatively slow but steady pace, sustained mostly by the lumber industry and state government. In 2018, the port supported 5,000 jobs and $300 million in business revenues in the area.

Today, the lumber industry is in decline in Olympia; the Georgia Pacific and St. Regis mills are all long closed. Olympia is a relatively small city, with an economy that revolves mostly around government. The city has tried to diversify into tourism and as a hub for hydraulic fracturing, known as "fracking," a technique for extracting oil and natural gas. In 2016 and again in 2017, environmentalists protested shipments through the Olympia port of materials for fracking in the oil fields of North Dakota. Percival Landing, one of three waterfront parks in Olympia, features a mile-long boardwalk, restaurants, and piers for boats.

Since 2000, Thurston County has grown 35 percent; nearby Lacey has grown almost as large as Olympia and has a higher median income. Pierce County, which has grown 25 percent since 2000, has become a destination for homeowners who cannot afford the real-estate prices in Seattle and King County. In 2018, Pierce was second in the number of persons migrating within the area; Snohomish County, which is north of Seattle, ranked first. In Tacoma, where 40 percent of the population is minority, the city decided in 2017 not to expand its immigrant detention center, out of fear that it might facilitate round-ups and deportations by the Trump administration.

The 10th Congressional District centers around Olympia-based Thurston County and Tacoma-based Pierce County. A small fraction lives in Mason County, to the northwest. The district leans comfortably toward Democrats. Hillary Clinton won 50%-39%, similar to the results in the adjacent 6th District.

WEST VIRGINIA

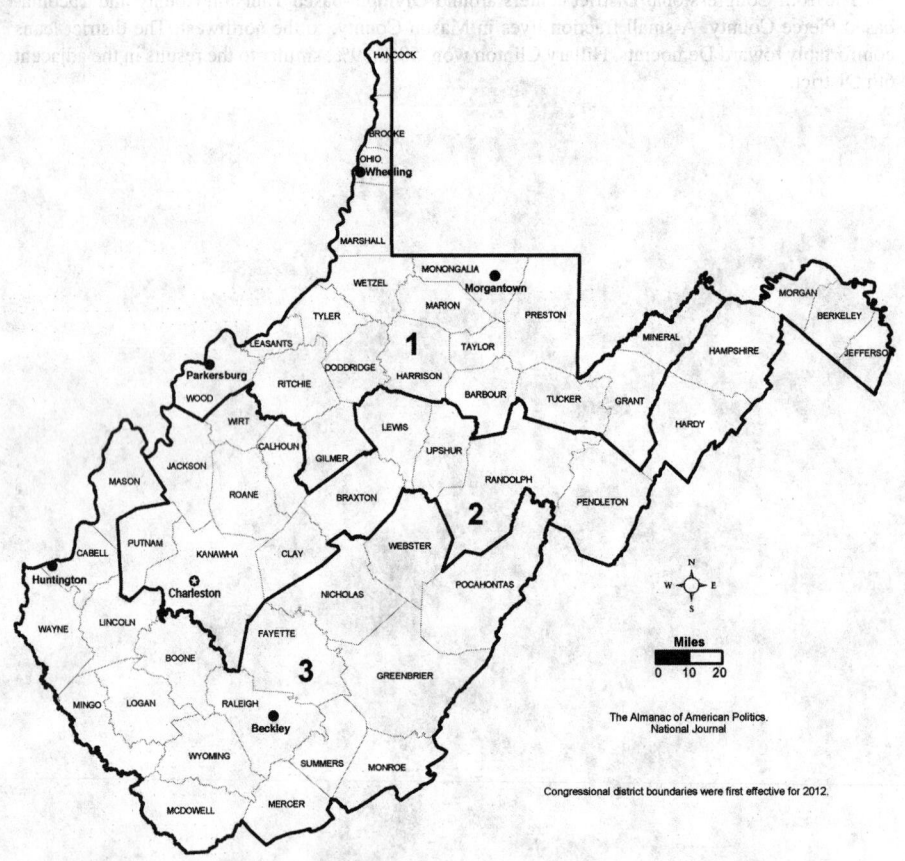

The Almanac of American Politics.
National Journal

Congressional district boundaries were first effective for 2012.

Few states have shifted more quickly, and more completely, from Democratic to Republican than West Virginia. Democratic presidential candidates haven't won the state since 1996. In 2016, Hillary Clinton – hobbled by an awkward comment about putting coal miners out of work – lost the state by a whopping 42-point margin, the second-widest margin for Donald Trump anywhere in the United States, trailing only Wyoming. All this has occurred while the state has grappled with severe industrial decline and the resulting economic and social woes.

"Almost heaven" is what the song says about West Virginia, and there's something to it, at least in the minds of West Virginians who have never lost their affection for the state's hills and hollers. Yet the state has had more than its share of tragedy and heartbreak. It was first settled by Scots-Irish immigrants, fresh from internecine fighting and determined to stake out comfortable homesteads. The state slogan is Montani semper liberi: Mountaineers are always free. West Virginia was created as a separate state during the Civil War, when a Republican Congress admitted to the union 55 mountain counties from Virginia that had few slaves. Since then, it has made a living first and foremost from coal. The state flag features a farmer and a coal miner, and the state's hills and mountains are laced with the black mineral. There are coal seams in 53 of its counties; coal kept the sons of large mountaineer families from leaving the state for much of the 20th century, and it brought immigrants from odd corners of Europe. People also came from adjacent areas of the South, where the local farming economies were stagnant as West Virginia's coal economy was booming. West Virginia today is 93 percent white – tied with Vermont for the second highest percentage in the nation, slightly behind Maine – and just 4 percent black and 2 percent Hispanic. In the mid-20th century, the availability of coal and local rock salt and brines led to the building of chemical plants in the Kanawha Valley around Charleston. Steel mills and glass factories went up in the Northern Panhandle and in the Monongahela River valley south of Pittsburgh.

The resource economy has been neither steady nor reliable. Demand for coal skyrocketed during World War II, and just after the war West Virginia coal production peaked at 179 million tons a year; not coincidentally, the state's population hit a record 2 million in the 1950 census. But demand for coal plunged as houses switched to oil for heat, and mechanization, especially in strip mines, reduced the demand for labor. To compensate, Democratic Sen. Robert Byrd leveraged his 50 years on the Senate Appropriations Committee to steer federal projects into the state, including the FBI's biggest division, with a growing workforce of 3,000 workers plus contractors in Clarksburg. But coal remains a major industry in the state, and it maintains a sizable, if declining, share of electricity generation. Where jobs still exist, miners can earn solid wages. However, the industry's decline has accelerated in recent years, as China has reduced its purchases, as U.S. natural gas production has expanded, and as production has shifted from the eastern United States to the West, where coal reserves have less sulfur and lie closer to the surface and thus can be removed more easily and cheaply.

Despite safety improvements, work in the mines remains gritty and dangerous. In 2006, an underground explosion at the Sago mine killed 12; the mine had been cited for 208 violations. Then, in 2010, another explosion, at the Upper Big Branch mine, killed 29 miners – the worst coal-mining disaster in decades. After the latter tragedy, the company's CEO, Don Blankenship was sentenced in April 2016 to a year in federal prison for conspiracy to willfully violate mine health and safety standards. But worker protections have declined, along with membership in the United Mine Workers. The union's rolls included 90 percent of the state's miners when it staged a black-lung strike in 1969, but that share has since crumbled. In 2016, the Republican-controlled legislature passed a right-to-work law detested by labor unions. West Virginia has some natural gas, too, in the Marcellus shale formation under several of the state's northern counties. This has helped ease the state's fiscal position, but "once the well is drilled, it doesn't take many people to manage that well," said John Deskins, director of WVU's Bureau of Business and Economic Research.

West Virginia offers a litany of grim statistics. Its median household income ranks dead last in the nation, and adjusting for inflation, median income hasn't grown in a decade. The poverty rate is 19.1 percent, fourth-highest in the country, with nearly one in five residents receiving food stamps. West Virginia has long had the lowest labor force participation rate in the nation. It ranks dead last in the percentage of residents with a bachelor's degree, and places in the bottom 10 for the percentage who graduated high school. Black-lung disease rates, historically a plague of miners, is now at a 25-year high. Perhaps most urgently, West Virginia is reeling from the opioid epidemic, with the highest overdose rate per capita of any state. Investigators have uncovered pain pills flooding into small-town pharmacies, such as the 21 million pills sent to Williamson and the 3 million sent to Kermit – both small towns in Mingo County near the Kentucky border. The cycle of addiction has affected all corners of life; since 2013, the number of children taken into foster care in West Virginia has increased by two-thirds.

In this difficult environment, West Virginia's population has contracted. Since the 2010 census, the state has lost 2.6 percent, dropping every year since 2012. The decline in impoverished coal counties has been even more stark; Mingo's population has fallen 6.7 percent and McDowell's has fallen 12.6 percent. The few growing areas of the state include the Eastern Panhandle, now a long-distance suburb of Washington D.C., and Morgantown, the home of West Virginia University, which has seen its population expand by 8 percent since 2010. Generations of out-migration by children raised in the state have left West Virginia with a higher percentage of residents 65 and older than any state but Maine and Florida.

West Virginia's political heritage from the Civil War days was Republican, though some counties tilted toward the Confederacy and Democrats. The United Mine Workers organized most of the West Virginia mines by 1902, and there were bloody strikes in 1912-13 and 1920-21. Under the UMW's John L. Lewis, coal country shifted toward New Deal Democrats, and for more than half a century, West Virginia was one of the most Democratic states. In the 21st century, it has swung back to the Republicans -- hard. A big reason has been the national party leaders' attitudes toward coal. In the 2000 presidential race, George W. Bush's strategist Karl Rove ignored precedent and targeted West Virginia, smartly calculating that Bush's support for mountaintop mining and his opposition to gun control could make the state winnable for a Republican. In office, Bush continued to push Congress to spend billions of dollars on clean coal technology and backed import quotas to help the steel industry, a major coal user.

After Barack Obama took office, the Environmental Protection Agency revoked a 2007 permit issued to Arch Coal for mountaintop mining in Logan County — the first time such a permit had been denied under clean water rules. Democratic Gov. Joe Manchin sued to overturn federal rules on mountaintop mining in October 2010, when he was running in the special election to fill Byrd's Senate seat. In 2012, West Virginians' anger at Obama administration policies was apparent in the May primary, in which 41 percent of registered Democrats voted for a convict instead of the president. Then, in 2014, the dominoes started falling. The legislature – which had been Democratic since the 1930s – fell to the GOP, first the state House on Election Night and then the state Senate after a post-election party switch. Republicans won all of the state's House seats for the first time since 1921, and flipped the seat held by retiring Democratic Sen. John (Jay) Rockefeller.

The swing toward the GOP continued in 2016. West Virginians recoiled from Clinton, who had blundered in a March televised town hall when she said, "We're going to put a lot of coal miners and coal companies out of business." While Clinton had said this in the context of urging new opportunities for ex-miners in renewable energy, the words stung in coal country, and they were easily turned into a cudgel by her critics. Trump widened the GOP's margin of victory from 26 points in 2012 to 42 points in 2016; Clinton underperformed even the unpopular Obama by 48,000 votes. Meanwhile, deep-pocketed businessman Jim Justice won the governorship in 2016 after distancing himself from Clinton, his Democratic ticket-mate. Less than a year later, amid a bromance with the billionaire president, Justice switched to the GOP, leaving state Treasurer John Perdue the only Democratic elected official on the state's board of public works. It was a far cry from just a few election cycles earlier, when Republicans had trouble fielding credible candidates for many legislative and statewide seats.

In 2018, Democrats could take some heart in Manchin's 50%-46% reelection victory. Earlier that year, striking teachers won a pay increase, suggesting that voters still favored elements of the Democratic platform even as they rejected the party's brand. At the same time, though, highly touted Democrat Richard Ojeda failed in his bid to win an open House seat by a 13-point margin, and voters approved a ballot measure to amend the state constitution to say that the right to an abortion is not protected in the state – a precursor to outlawing it if the Supreme Court overturns Roe v. Wade. All told, West Virginia has become solid Republican territory, with little evidence for now that Democrats are clawing their way back to long-term competitiveness.

Population		Race and Ethnicity		Income	
Total	1,836,843	White	92.3%	Median Income	$44,061
Land area (sq. miles)	24,038	Black	3.5%	State Income Rank	48
Pop/ sq mi	76.4	Latino	1.5%	Poverty Rate	17.8%
Born in state	69.8%	Asian	0.8%	With health insurance	92.0%
		Two or more races	1.6%	Cash public assistance	2.4%
Age Groups		Other	0.4%	Food stamp/SNAP	16.5%
Under 18	20.5%				
18-34	20.9%	**Education**		**Work**	
35-64	40.3%	H.S grad or less	54.7%	White Collar	32.8%
Over 64	18.3%	Some college	25.4%	Sales and Service	42.9%
		College Degree, 4 yr	12.0%	Blue Collar	24.2%
Military		Post grad	7.9%	Government	18.7%
Veteran/ Active Duty	9.6%				

Presidential Politics

2016 Primary (D)	Sanders (D)	124,700 (51%)	Clinton (D)	86,914 (36%)			
2016 Primary (R)	Trump (R)	157,238 (77%)	Cruz (R)	18,301 (9%)	Kasich (R)	13,721 (7%)
2016 Pres. Vote	Trump (R)	489,371 (69%)	Clinton (D)	188,794 (26%)	Johnson (L)	23,004 (3%)
2012 Pres. Vote	Romney (R)	417,655 (62%)	Obama (D)	238,269 (36%)			

From 1932 to 1996, the only Republicans who carried West Virginia were incumbents headed for landslide reelection victories — Dwight Eisenhower in 1956, Richard Nixon in 1972, and Ronald Reagan in 1984. But West Virginia has voted Republican in the last five presidential elections. That change in the new millennium can be explained by two factors: culture and coal. West Virginians tend to be more religious and tradition-minded than Americans generally. And national Democrats are bent on reducing carbon emissions to address climate change. Still, the state's voters can back Democrats and split their tickets. West Virginians elect their governor in the same year they cast their ballots for president. And in each of those past five elections, they have sent a Democrat to their statehouse in Charleston. But those Democrats were ones in tune with the West Virginia electorate.

The Democratic decline began when George W. Bush targeted West Virginia. Bush's support of mountaintop mining and his promotion of clean coal technology enabled him to beat Al Gore 52%-46% in 2000 and John Kerry 56%-43% in 2004. In 2012, Mitt Romney carried the state 62%-36%, winning all 55 counties — the first nominee of either party to do so since the Civil War. Donald Trump became the second, defeating Hillary Clinton 69%-27%.

West Virginia's presidential primary, held in May, has not attracted much attention since 1960, when John Kennedy took on Hubert Humphrey and beat him with 61 percent of the vote, proving that a Catholic could succeed in a virtually all-Protestant state. The 2008 Democratic contest was not an epic battle like 1960, but it was hard fought nonetheless. Turnout was a robust 356,000, well above the levels in recent primaries. Clinton defeated Obama 67%-26%, her biggest victory except for Arkansas, carrying every county. In the 2016 primary, Vermont Sen. Bernie Sanders defeated Clinton, 51%-36%. Not only did Sanders win every county, a majority of his supporters in the Democratic primary told the television network exit poll that they would vote for Trump in the general election. Coming right after Trump's remaining GOP rivals abandoned their bids, his 77%-9% victory over Texas Sen. Ted Cruz was anticlimactic.

Congressional Districts

116th Congress Lineup	3R	**115th Congress Lineup**	3R

West Virginia elected six members of the House in 1960 but only three in 1992. Current population projections show that it will lose another district in the 2020 reapportionment. As recently as 1998, the state elected three Democrats. With voter hostility to the national party, Republicans have taken all three. With only two districts, the map-drawers would have few options, even though

Republicans have gained control of state government. They could split the state with a line that goes roughly east-west, or one that goes north-south. In either case, the geographic realities appear to dictate one district that is Charleston-based and the other that hugs the Pennsylvania and Maryland state lines, with the remainder of the state split accordingly. When that happens, either two of the GOP incumbents will run against each other or one of them will bow out. It's not clear that any of the three has the personal influence to dictate the new map.

In 2011, Beltway Democratic strategists pressured West Virginia's legislators to be aggressive. Democratic state Sen. John Unger unveiled a proposal to keep untouched the district of Democrat Rep. Nick Rahall, who had held the southern 3rd District since 1976, and run the 1st and 2nd districts north-south rather than east-west, in effect pairing Republican Reps. Shelley Moore Capito and David McKinley and creating an open Eastern Panhandle seat. Furious Republicans pointed out that moving Mason County (population, 27,324) from the 2nd District to the 3rd District was all that was needed to equalize seats. The Unger plan earned tepid reception from Democrats, too. So, a few days later, the legislature passed and Democratic Gov. Earl Ray Tomblin signed the "Mason County flip" into law. Redistricting notwithstanding, in 2014, Rahall lost reelection and Republicans retained Capito's seat when she was elected to the Senate.

Jim Justice (R)

Elected 2016, term expires 2021, 1st term; b. Apr. 27, 1951, Raleigh County; Marshall University, BA & MBA; Married (Cathy); 2 children.

Professional Career: Entrepeneur.

Office: 1900 Kanawha Blvd., East #1, Charleston, 25305; 304-558-2000; Fax: 304-342-7025; Website: governor.wv.gov

Atty. Gen: Patrick Morrisey (R) **Sec. of State:** Mac Warner (R)

State Legislature: Senate: 14D, 20R **House:** 41D, 59R

Election Results

Election	Name (Party)	Vote (%)
2016 General	Jim Justice (D)...	350,408 (49%)
	Bill Cole (R)...	301,987 (42%)
	Charlotte Jean Pritt (MT)...	42,068 (6%)
	David Moran (L)..	15,354 (2%)
2016 Primary	Jim Justice (D)...	132,704 (51%)
	Booth Goodwin (D)..	65,416 (25%)
	Jeff Kessler (D)...	60,230 (23%)

Jim Justice, a billionaire often described as West Virginia's richest man, was elected governor in 2016, running as a Democrat in a state that, on the same Election Day, overwhelmingly backed Republican presidential nominee Donald Trump. Many observers noted that Justice and Trump shared key attributes, including their wealth, a range of controversies over their businesses, support for the coal industry, and an outspoken style – and less than a year after winning election, Justice, while appearing at a Trump rally in his state, dramatically announced that he was switching parties.

Justice was born in West Virginia and diversified his family's businesses. After earning a bachelor's and MBA at Marshall University, Justice started Bluestone Farms in 1977 and expanded it to cover 50,000 acres of corn, wheat and soybeans in West Virginia, Virginia, North Carolina and South Carolina. Following his father's death in 1993, Justice assumed control of Bluestone Industries Inc. and Bluestone Coal Corp. He proceeded to expand the company's operations in coal, Christmas tree farms, cotton gins, turfgrass, timber and golf courses. By the time he was elected governor, Justice was running approximately 100 companies. In 2009, he sold his coal company to the Russian firm Mechel OAO. But the new owner failed, and Justice purchased back his controlling interest in 2015 for a reported $5 million -- less than 1 percent of what he'd sold it for. In the meantime, Justice had purchased the Greenbrier – the debt-plagued resort in White Sulphur Springs that was one of the nation's finest and most storied getaways -- for $20.5 million in 2009. He added a casino and brought in such high-profile events as the PGA Tour and NFL and NBA training camps. He acquired other resorts and country clubs around the state. While running for governor, Justice had his daughter Jill run the Greenbrier while his son Jay oversaw the coal and agriculture businesses, though critics said Justice had not fully divested himself.

Despite his wealth, Justice cultivated a down-home image. He has been involved with Little League baseball in Beckley for a quarter-century, and the six-foot-seven Justice has coached girls and boys basketball teams for more than 35 years. Shortly after winning the governorship, he notched his 1,000th career win as a basketball coach. At times, Justice has shown little patience for political niceties. He rejected his Republican opponent's claim that he supported President Barack Obama as "complete dog snot" and, after winning the governorship, punctuated his veto of a budget passed by the Republican-controlled legislature by unveiling a copy of the budget topped by a pile of real-life bull feces.

Justice's business activities have been dogged by controversy. In 2014, NPR reported that his companies owed almost $2 million in unpaid fines. In 2015, Justice agreed to pay a $220,000 fine for failing to obtain Clean Water Act permits before building 20 dams at a hunting and fishing preserve. In September 2016, the Environmental Protection Agency announced a nearly $6 million agreement to settle thousands of pollution violations at coal facilities owned by Justice in West Virginia and other states. The violations included excess pollution, insufficient sampling, failure to file reports and inattention to federal requests, dating back to 2011. He and his companies have also faced problems with delinquent taxes in state and local jurisdictions in Kentucky, Virginia and West Virginia. A follow-up to the NPR investigation in October 2016 concluded that Justice had become "the nation's top mine-safety delinquent," owing $15 million from operations in six states, ranging from property and minerals taxes to unemployment taxes to mine-safety penalties. The NPR investigation found injury rates at Justice's mines to be twice the national average, with violation rates more than four times the national rate during the period of delinquency. In April 2019, the public-media project Ohio Valley ReSource reported that companies linked to the Justice family owed $4.3 million in delinquent debt for mine safety violations. And other controversies continued to dog him. In 2019, a federal judge ruled that a Justice family-controlled coal company had to turn over financial information and allow employees to testify concerning a $1.23 million contempt-of-court fine that stemmed from a lawsuit over nonpayment of a supplier.

Justice got into politics by running to succeed retiring Gov. Earl Ray Tomblin, a culturally conservative Democrat. The former president of the state Senate, Tomblin had succeeded Democrat Joe Manchin, who stepped down as governor to run successfully for the late Sen. Robert Byrd's seat in the Senate. Tomblin won an October 2011 special election and 13 months later won a four-year term of his own. Like many other West Virginia Democrats, Tomblin disdained many of the national Democratic Party's priorities. Justice did not have a clear path to the Democratic nomination, however. He faced a competitive three-way primary against former U.S. Attorney Booth Goodwin and state Senate Majority Leader Jeff Kessler. Goodwin touted his prosecution of cases stemming from one of the worst mine explosions in United States history, at West Virginia's Upper Big Branch mine that killed 29 men in 2010. Kessler, the candidate in the primary with the most extensive political experience, ran somewhat to the left of his rivals. But Justice, bolstered by his deep pockets and his statewide familiarity, won the primary with an outright majority of 51 percent.

In the general election, Justice positioned himself as a conservative Democrat, almost an independent – a necessity for any successful West Virginia Democrat in recent years, including Tomblin and Manchin. "I cannot be a supporter of Hillary Clinton," he said in a radio interview. "The reason I can't be is her position on coal is diametrically, completely wrong in many, many different ways." He also exhibited a higher tolerance for government spending than many politicians today. In the general election, Justice faced Republican state Senate President Bill Cole. Cole had attracted notice as a key player in state budget negotiations, but he preferred to emphasize his business background – he owned a car dealership and a share of a metal manufacturing plant in Tennessee.

Cole offered a traditional conservative agenda that included tax and spending cuts, curbs on abortion, and charter schools. He also tied himself to Trump. On the campaign trail, Cole attacked Justice's business record, which offered plenty of material. But Justice's ace in the hole was that he seemed to fit the national and state mood for an outsider willing to break up politics-as-usual, negating any drag from his Democratic party affiliation. Justice won 49%-42%. Ardent environmentalist Charlotte Pritt – no fan of Justice's support for mountaintop-removal mining -- took almost 6 percent running on the Mountain Party line, while Libertarian David Moran took 2 percent. Cole won only 19 counties, many of them in the historically Republican Eastern Panhandle region.

After his victory, Justice aligned himself with Trump, who had won the state overwhelmingly. At his inauguration, Justice said, "Whether you like it or don't like it, Donald Trump is our president. And let me just tell you this: I'm friends with the Trump family. I know 'em; I know them well. And I truly believe that he will provide us with opportunities in West Virginia." Inheriting a deficit of roughly $500 million, Justice didn't shy away from proposing revenue increases. Justice proposed a $4.5 billion budget, then reduced it to just under $4.3 billion. The proposal included a toll hike on the West Virginia Turnpike for out-of-state motorists, a gasoline tax increase, a tax on sugary drinks and an increase in motor-vehicle fees. In April, the legislature approved a $4.1 billion budget, which prompted a veto and Justice's bull-feces display. He eventually let a budget become law without his signature. In something of a surprise, the legislature passed and Justice signed a bill legalizing medical marijuana.

In August 2017, Justice made a move that, in retrospect, was probably inevitable: He became a Republican, making the announcement on the podium with Trump during a rally in the state. During another trip to the state a year later, Trump called Justice "the largest, most beautiful man," and in January 2019, when it looked like Trump wouldn't be able to deliver his State of the Union address at the Capitol, Justice invited him to give it in Charleston. Justice sought to work with the White House to bolster the coal industry, and with federal cooperation, West Virginia entered into an $83.7 billion shale gas and chemical manufacturing investment agreement with the China Energy Investment Corporation. While the deal could have far-reaching implications, details remained scarce in early 2019 and some worried that ongoing trade tensions with China posed an obstacle.

The biggest legislative battle of 2018 was prompted by a teacher strike in March that garnered national headlines. West Virginia teachers went on a nine-day strike and held large rallies at the capitol. The walkout ended after Justice and the legislature agreed to raise salaries by 5 percent. Meanwhile, with the state struggling with the nation's highest rate of opioid overdoses, Justice signed limits on opioid prescriptions for most types of patients, even though most overdoses were the result of non-prescription drugs such as fentanyl and heroin. The second half of the year was dominated by revelations that justices on the state's supreme court of appeals had misused more than $1 million in funds when they renovated their offices. Amid impeachment efforts, three justices resigned, allowing Justice to appoint temporary replacements. Democrats accused Justice of Court-packing, but all of Justice's appointees were ratified in special elections in November 2018.

Justice began 2019 with a record $185.9 million surplus covering the first six months of the fiscal year, and he proposed "Jim's Dream," a $45 million drug-addiction treatment program aimed at returning recovering addicts to the workforce. But the biggest controversy once again involved education. Justice had been pushing additional pay increases for teachers, but he objected to Republican legislators' efforts to pair the pay hikes with expanded options for families such as charter schools and education scholarship accounts. After another two-day teacher strike, the sides failed to reach an agreement.

In a January 2019 event at the White Sulphur Springs Civic Center, flanked by the Greenbrier East girls' basketball team, Justice announced that he would be seeking another term, flanked by the Greenbrier East girls basketball team. But in April, the Kanawha County Republican Executive Committee passed a resolution of no confidence for Justice's "lack of support" of GOP principles, and the Harrison County Republican Executive Committee and the West Virginia Federation of College Republicans followed suit. Woody Thrasher, who owned an engineering firm with 700 employees and previously served as Secretary of Commerce in West Virginia, announced his bid for the GOP nomination. Former Berkeley County Del. Mike Folk also voiced interest in challenging Justice. In an April interview with Politico, Manchin floated the idea of running against Justice in 2020. A Justice-Manchin matchup – which seemed far from a sure thing – would be an epic clash of West Virginia titans.

Joe Manchin (D)

Elected 2010, term expires 2024, 2nd full term, b. Aug 24, 1947; Farmington; West Virginia University, B.S., 1970; Catholic; Married (Gayle Conelly); 3 children; 8 grandchildren.

Elected Office: WV House, 1982-1986; WV Senate, 1986-1996; WV Secretary Of State, 2000-2004; WV Governor, 2004-2010.

Professional Career: Co-owner, Manchin's Carpet & Tile, 1968-1982; Owner, Enersystems, 1989-2000.

DC Office: 306 HSOB 20510, 202-224-3954, Fax: 202-228-0002, manchin.senate.gov

State Offices: Charleston, 304-342-5855; Fairmont, 304-368-0567; Martinsburg, 304-264-4626.

Committees: Senate Democratic Policy and Communications Center Vice Chairman. *Appropriations*: Commerce, Justice, Science & Related Agencies; Department of Homeland Security; DOL, HHS & Education & Related Agencies; Financial Services & General Government; Transportation, HUD & Related Agencies. *Armed Services*: Cybersecurity (RMM); Strategic Forces. *Energy & Natural Resources (RMM)*: Ex Officio membership on all subcommittees. *Veterans' Affairs*.

Group Ratings

	ADA	ACLU	AFL-CIO	LCV	ITI	COC	HAFA	ACU	CFG	FRC
2018	-	52%	-	43%	-	70%	26%	36%	28%	50%
2017	45%	C	87%	47%	C	57%	C	8%	13%	25%

Almanac Ratings 2017-18

	Economy	Social	Foreign	Composite
Liberal	49%	49%	9%	36%
Conservative	51%	51%	91%	65%

Key Votes of the 115th Congress

1. Obama-care revision	N	5. Gun regulations	Y	9. Kavanaugh confirmation	Y
2. Tax Cuts	N	6. Family planning regs	N	10. Saudi arms sales	N
3. Dodd-Frank revision	Y	7. Gorsuch confirmation	Y	11. FISA rules	Y
4. Omnibus appropriations	Y	8. Immigration restrictions	Y	12. Military aid in Yemen	Y

Election Results

Election	Name (Party)	Vote (%)		Cand. Spent	Ind. Exp. Support	Ind. Exp. Oppose
2018 General	Joe Manchin III (D)	290,510	(50%)	$7,374,158	$6,736,278	$11,428,094
	Patrick Morrisey (R)	271,113	(46%)	$5,581,599	$2,903,392	$12,148,307
	Rusty Hollen (Lib)	24,411	(4%)			
2018 Primary	Joe Manchin III (D)	112,658	(70%)			
	Paula Jean Swearengin (D)	48,594	(30%)			

Prior winning percentages: 2012 (61%), 2010 special (53%); Governor: 2008 (70%), 2004 (64%)

Democrat Joe Manchin, who won a special election in 2010 to succeed the late Robert Byrd, is West Virginia's senior senator. A popular former governor, he has sought to use his political capital to break through the Senate's gridlock, most notably on gun control. With his home state's tilt away from Democrats, he narrowly won a challenging re-election campaign in 2018. Manchin has turned down Republican entreaties to switch parties or join President Donald Trump's Cabinet but has continued to mull a return to the governor's mansion.

Manchin hails from a prominent political family. He grew up in Farmington, a few miles from the industrial city of Fairmont. Manchin took a semester off from college to help his father rebuild his carpet-and-furniture store after a fire. His grandfather and father both served as mayor of Farmington. His uncle, A. James Manchin, was elected to the West Virginia House of Delegates and was secretary of state and state treasurer. "As a child, Manchin never once left the state, and although he was recruited to play football by colleges across the country, there was never any doubt he'd go to West Virginia University," Jason Zengerle wrote in GQ. The idea of going farther was anathema to his father. "He's West Virginia," Manchin's sister Paula told Zengerle. "It's in his soul."

After graduating from WVU, Manchin went to work in the carpet-and-furniture business, helping send his four siblings to college. Then he started a coal-brokerage company and moved to Fairmont. Manchin was elected to the House of Delegates in 1982 and the state Senate in 1986. He ran for governor in 1996, only to lose in the Democratic primary to legislator Charlotte Pritt. When state Secretary of State Ken Hechler ran for the House in 2000, Manchin ran to succeed him — and so did Pritt. This time, Manchin beat her in the primary: 51% to 29%. He won the general election, too.

In 2003, Manchin announced that he would challenge Democratic Gov. Bob Wise in the 2004 primary. Later that month, Wise admitted that he'd had an extramarital affair and would not seek re-election. Manchin got support from both unions and businesses. His stands on cultural issues were impeccably conservative and in line with state preferences: He opposed abortion rights, gun control and same-sex marriage. Manchin won the Democratic primary with 53 percent of the vote, and he defeated Republican Monty Warner in the general election, 64% to 34%, carrying 52 of 55 counties.

Manchin had been in office for just one year when he gained renown as the public face of desperate attempts to rescue 13 trapped coal miners after the January 2006 explosion at the Sago Mine in central West Virginia. Manchin, whose uncle was killed in a 1968 mine accident that killed 78 people, gave numerous televised interviews from the mine site. He mistakenly announced "the miracle of all miracles" — that 12 of the miners had survived — when in fact they had died. The blunder could have been career-ending, but Manchin's standing skyrocketed in the polls, partly because West Virginia Republicans decided that invoking the disaster was a political line that they would not cross. In 2007, he signed laws mandating certain ventilation practices and giving the state authority to temporarily shut down mines with violations. After two other deadly mining tragedies, Manchin ordered safety inspections at all mines in the state.

In 2006, he signed into law eight health care bills, including giving low-income families basic care at clinics and creating a catastrophic health care insurance program and a mental health commission. His tenure was marred by a controversy involving his daughter and politically potent institutions in the state. The Pittsburgh Post-Gazette reported that the governor's daughter, Heather Bresch, falsely claimed to have earned a master's degree in business in 1998 at West Virginia University. The school then gave her the degree in 2007, even though she had completed only about half the required 48 credit hours. Under pressure, several top university officials, including the school's president, resigned. Bresch— by then a high-level executive at Mylan, a generic drugmaker that had donated heavily to the university and, through its top executives, to Manchin's campaigns — never admitted wrongdoing. Manchin expressed support for Bresch. In 2008, he was re-elected with 70 percent of the vote. In 2016, Bresch created new awkwardness for Manchin after Mylan began charging exorbitant sums for its EpiPen.

When Byrd died in June 2010 — after a record 51 years in the Senate plus six in the House — Manchin was considered the Democrats' best hope for keeping the seat. Although he could have appointed himself to the Senate pending a special election, Manchin declined to do so. Instead, he appointed his former chief counsel, Carte Goodwin, as a placeholder. His GOP opponent was John Raese, a wealthy businessman whom Byrd had defeated four years earlier by a nearly 2-to-1 margin. But Raese, who poured his own money into the contest, had the wind at his back in a strong election cycle for the GOP. He ran ads tying Manchin to President Barack Obama, and the National Republican Senate Committee launched its own ads portraying Manchin as a rubber stamp for Obama's agenda. Before long, the race was a toss-up.

Manchin distanced himself from the president, even to the extent of flip-flopping. Early in 2010, he supported Obama's health care overhaul. By October, Manchin was saying he would have voted against it had he been serving as a senator at the time. The Democrats' cap-and-trade bill to curb carbon emissions was highly unpopular in West Virginia coal country. Manchin famously ran an ad in which he shot a mock copy of the carbon emissions bill with a rifle. Manchin raised questions about Raese's commitment to the state, pointing out repeatedly on the stump and in television ads that the steel and limestone magnate owned a home in Palm Beach, Florida that had a pink marble driveway and that his wife was registered to vote there. Manchin hammered Raese for his support of eliminating the minimum wage and abolishing the Education Department. Although he was outspent $6.3 million to $4.4 million, Manchin won 53%-43%.

Taking office immediately after the election to begin serving the final two years of Byrd's term, he voted to extend the Bush-era tax cuts except for taxpayers earning more than $1 million. He was the only Democrat to vote against a proposal repealing the ban on openly gay members in the military. Still, Manchin was roundly criticized back home for missing a final vote on repealing "don't ask, don't tell" and a major vote on a bill to give legal status to the children of some undocumented immigrants. The Charleston Gazette called him "absolutely gutless." Manchin apologized publicly, saying he missed the December votes to be with his grandchildren over the holidays. He further angered the newspaper in 2012 when he declined to say whether he would vote to re-elect Obama. It refused to endorse him in that April's Democratic primary, questioning whether he was "on course to follow Connecticut's Joe Lieberman and register as independent." It hardly mattered; Manchin took 80 percent of the vote. His win set up a rematch with Raese for a six-year term. Raese resurrected his campaign theme that Manchin was an Obama rubber stamp, but the incumbent now had a voting record that demonstrated otherwise. Manchin easily improved upon his earlier victory, winning 61%-36%, even as GOP presidential nominee Mitt Romney captured 62 percent of the vote.

In April 2013, after several months of taking colleagues out on his Washington-docked houseboat for evenings of beer and pizza, Manchin announced a proposed compromise on gun control with Republicans Mark Kirk of Illinois — his best friend in the chamber — and Pat Toomey of Pennsylvania. Its most significant feature was a proposal to expand background checks to gun purchases at gun shows and online. The measure did not go as far as Obama wanted — it exempted sales between private citizens in some instances — but it was the best chance to advance gun control legislation in years. Manchin had previously boasted of his "A" rating from the National Rifle Association, but the group now attacked him. In the end, the measure couldn't attract enough votes to overcome a GOP filibuster. Manchin found greater success in a student loan debate during that summer. The two parties had spent months bickering about how to prevent an automatic doubling of student loan rates from 3.4 percent to 6.8 percent by a statutory deadline of July 1. Manchin was a key negotiator in a deal to bring down the rates and tie them to the market. The deal was signed into law.

On the Energy and Natural Resources Committee, Manchin backed the Keystone XL pipeline. He became the only Democrat to co-sponsor the Affordable Reliable Energy Now Act of 2015, a bill shepherded by West Virginia Republican Sen. Shelley Moore Capito. The bill — which Obama likely would have vetoed — pushed back against efforts by the administration's Environmental Protection Agency to curb carbon emissions. Manchin formed an unlikely partnership with liberal firebrand Elizabeth Warren to offer legislation that would publicize the details of trade deals before lawmakers were asked to approve presidential fast-track trade authority. In 2017, he joined the Appropriations Committee, where Capito already had a seat and Byrd earlier reigned as chairman.

After the Democrats lost the Senate in the 2014 elections — a development Manchin called "a real ass-whuppin'" — he expressed deep frustration to The Washington Post about Obama and Senate Democratic Leader Harry Reid of Nevada, and he said he might not back Reid for party leader. But he recommitted to remaining with his party rather than switching to the GOP. Manchin toyed with leaving the chamber two years early in 2016 to run for governor, a job that would provide him with executive powers he had enjoyed before. "My worst day as governor," Manchin has said, "was better than my best day as senator." But in spring 2015, Manchin announced that he would remain in the Senate — a big boost for Democrats, who had few other options for winning a seat in increasingly Republican West Virginia.

The Republican-controlled Senate gave Manchin opportunities to work on legislation and display his differences with Democrats. On a popular bill to attack opioid abuse, which was enacted in 2016, he contributed a section promoting public education about the crisis. Going his own way, he was one of two Democrats who voted in 2015 to force a vote to prohibit federal funding of Planned Parenthood. In 2017, he was the only Democrat to vote to confirm Jeff Sessions to be Trump's first attorney general, prompting backlash from liberal activists. He also voted for Scott Pruitt's nomination to head the EPA, but he voted against Wilbur Ross at Commerce, Tom Price at Health and Human Services and Betsy DeVos at Education. In April 2017, Manchin joined Joe Donnelly of Indiana and Heidi Heitkamp of North Dakota as the only Democratic senators to vote to confirm Neil Gorsuch to the Supreme Court.

Manchin rejected invitations to switch parties or join Trump's Cabinet and instead accepted a seat on the leadership team of Democratic Leader Chuck Schumer. He maintained a relationship — albeit rocky at times — with Trump, whom he praised for listening to him more thoroughly than Obama had. Manchin angered the White House by voting against the GOP-backed tax overhaul in 2017; he said the bill was too generous to the wealthy. He also criticized Republicans for closing off avenues for bipartisan input. "A couple, two, three other Democrats would have been easy pickups, if they had just made an effort," he said. Republicans weren't happy. By January 2018, Vice President Mike Pence was slamming Manchin with the hashtag #JoeVotedNo and Trump followed up with his own criticism in April. In October 2018, he was the only Democrat to vote to confirm Supreme Court nominee Brett Kavanaugh. But not even this satisfied Republicans, who assailed Manchin for announcing his support only after fellow swing senator Republican Susan Collins of Maine had announced that she would vote yes, making Manchin's support unnecessary.

In 2018, Manchin easily prevailed over a primary challenger from his left, political novice Paula Jean Swearengin, 70%-30%. But the GOP primary was a barnburner. The three main candidates were Rep. Evan Jenkins, state Attorney General Patrick Morrisey, and former coal magnate Don Blankenship. Some Republicans thought Jenkins would be best positioned to take on Manchin, although he had earlier in his career been a Democrat. Morrisey, meanwhile, had previously run for the House from New Jersey, opening him to criticism that he was a carpetbagger. Morrisey also fended off attacks on his record as a federal lobbyist.

The one thing most Republican officials were sure about is that they did not want Blankenship to be the nominee. A 2010 explosion at Blankenship's Upper Big Branch Mine had killed 29 workers, and in 2015, he was sentenced to a year in prison for conspiring to violate mine safety standards — a sentence that many West Virginians thought was too light. After his release, Blankenship channeled attempts at rehabilitation into a Senate bid, spending aggressively from his fortune to portray himself both as a victim of government run amuck and as the ultimate political outsider — a potentially resonant theme for Trump-supporting Republicans. Facing concerted opposition from Senate Majority Leader Mitch McConnell, Blankenship aired an ad attacking the Kentuckian as "Cocaine Mitch," based on an allegation that a shipping company owned by McConnell's father-in-law had once been connected to drug smuggling. Blankenship also called McConnell's wife, Transportation Secretary Elaine Chao, a "Chinaperson." As the primary approached, Republicans began panicking about the possibility that Blankenship could sneak past the two squabbling establishment candidates, and Trump urged voters not to support the former coal CEO. The alarm was unnecessary; Morrisey won with 35 percent of the vote, while Jenkins took 29 percent. Blankenship captured just 20 percent of the vote. McConnell celebrated by tweeting a photoshopped image of himself surrounded by cocaine with the caption, "Thanks for playing, Don."

The general election contest was competitive, but the GOP's momentum in West Virginia never quite matched what the party achieved in the other red-state contests that year. Trump aggressively touted Morrissey during rallies in the state and the GOP framed Manchin as a tool of Democratic congressional leaders. But Manchin benefited from voter concern about health care. In a state that had experienced tangible gains from the Affordable Care Act, Manchin attacked Morrisey for signing on to a lawsuit designed to repeal the law, contrasting his own efforts to protect the law as Senate Republicans sought to overturn it. Manchin echoed his memorable ad on carbon emissions by airing one in which he fired on a copy of the lawsuit that Morrisey had helped draft. Manchin won 50%-46% — a far narrower margin than his 25-point edge six years earlier but far better than any other Democrat could have expected in the state. Manchin's raw vote total dropped by more than one-quarter between the 2012 and 2018 elections.

After Manchin's victory, liberal activists objected when Schumer tapped him to be the top Democrat on the Energy and Natural Resources Committee, a crucial post for his state and one in which he could cause trouble for environmentalists. In April 2019, Manchin was considering a 2020 run for governor. "I think about it every minute of every day," he told Politico, saying he would decide on a run by the fall. He was sure to get intense pushback from Democratic senators who view his seat as essential for them to have a chance of seizing the majority.

Shelley Moore Capito (R)

Elected 2014, term expires 2020, 1st term, b. Nov 26, 1953; Glen Dale; Duke University (NC), B.S., 1975; University of Virginia, M.Ed., 1976; Presbyterian; Married (Dr. Charles Lewis Capito); 3 children; 4 grandchildren.

Elected Office: WV House, 1997-2001; US House, 2001-2015.

Professional Career: Career counselor, WV St. College, 1976-1978; Director, Education Information Center, WV Board of Regents, 1978-1981.

DC Office: 172 RSOB 20510, 202-224-6472, Fax: 202-224-7665, capito.senate.gov

State Offices: Beckley, 304-347-5372; Charleston, 304-347-5372; Martinsburg, 304-262-9285; Morgantown, 304-292-2310.

Committees: *Appropriations*: Commerce, Justice, Science & Related Agencies; Department of Homeland Security (Chmn); Department of the Interior, Environment & Related Agencies; DOL, HHS & Education & Related Agencies; Military Construction & Veteran Affairs & Related Agencies; Transportation, HUD & Related Agencies. *Commerce, Science & Transportation*: Communications, Technology, Innovation & the Internet; Manufacturing, Trade & Consumer Protection; Subcommittee on Aviation & Space; Subcommittee on Transportation & Safety. *Environment & Public Works*: Clean Air & Nuclear Safety; Fisheries, Water, and Wildlife; Transportation & Infrastructure (Chmn). *Rules & Administration*.

Group Ratings

	ADA	ACLU	AFL-CIO	LCV	ITI	COC	HAFA	ACU	CFG	FRC
2018	-	5%	-	7%	-	80%	56%	91%	54%	100%
2017	0%	C	0%	0%	C	86%	C	72%	67%	92%

Almanac Ratings 2017-18

	Economy	Social	Foreign	Composite
Liberal	0%	0%	2%	1%
Conservative	100%	100%	98%	99%

Key Votes of the 115th Congress

1. Obama-care revision	Y	5. Gun regulations	Y	9. Kavanaugh confirmation	Y
2. Tax Cuts	Y	6. Family planning regs	Y	10. Saudi arms sales	N
3. Dodd-Frank revision	Y	7. Gorsuch confirmation	Y	11. FISA rules	Y
4. Omnibus appropriations	Y	8. Immigration restrictions	Y	12. Military aid in Yemen	N

Election Results

Election	Name (Party)	Vote (%)		Cand. Spent	Ind. Exp. Support	Ind. Exp. Oppose
2014 General	Shelley Moore Capito (R)	281,820	(62%)	$8,779,918	$640,871	$227,388
	Natalie Tennant (D)	156,360	(35%)	$3,499,419	$34,000	$290,776
2014 Primary	Shelley Moore Capito (R)	74,655	(88%)			
	Matthew Dodrill (R)	7,072	(8%)			

Prior winning percentages: House: 2012 (70%), 2010 (69%), 2008 (57%), 2006 (57%), 2004 (58%), 2002 (60%), 2000 (49%)

Republican Shelley Moore Capito was elected West Virginia's junior senator in 2014 after serving seven terms in the House. The state's first Republican in the Senate since the 1950s and its first female senator, she is a well-liked insider who is unwavering in her advocacy of West Virginia's coal industry. She got along well with Majority Leader Mitch McConnell, another senator from coal country, and joined his leadership team. Her policy focus has been largely tied to home-state interests and needs. She appears politically secure at home.

Capito grew up in northern West Virginia and the Washington, D.C. area, where her father, Arch Moore, served in the House from 1957 to 1969. He was elected governor of West Virginia in 1968 and 1972, and then again in 1984. Capito graduated from Duke University with a degree in zoology and earned a master's degree in education from the University of Virginia. She worked for two years as a career counselor at West Virginia State University and then as director of the state's Educational Information Center from 1978 to 1981. She served two terms in the West Virginia House of Delegates.

Capito's opportunity to follow in her father's footsteps in the House came when Democratic Rep. Bob Wise ran for governor in 2000. She benefited from a divisive Democratic primary won by Jim Humphreys, a lawyer and former state senator. Capito, who supported abortion rights, started off as the underdog, but Humphreys proved to be a poor candidate, despite spending $6 million of his own money in the general election. Capito won 48% to 46%, becoming the first Cherry Blossom Princess elected to Congress. Capito has been the center of West Virginia's swing to the GOP. When she first ran for Congress in 2000, there were no Republicans in the delegation. By 2015, Sen. Joe Manchin — a longtime friend of Capito — was the only Democrat serving in federal office from West Virginia. A third generation of the family has emerged: Capito's son, Moore Capito, served in the House of Delegates.

In the House, Capito had a relatively moderate voting record; she was a member of the centrist Republican Main Street Partnership. She broke from conservatives to support programs important to her state, such as continued funding of rural air service and opposing drastic cutbacks in food stamps. In a rare encounter with controversy in 2006, she dealt with the fallout from revelations of inappropriate sexual advances by GOP Rep. Mark Foley of Florida, which included contact with House pages. Capito, a member of the three-lawmaker board that oversaw the teenage page program, said she was unaware of the allegations until after the scandal became public.

Capito grew more inclined to side with her party after the election of President Barack Obama, who was extremely unpopular in West Virginia. In 2011, she took over as chairwoman of the Financial Services Subcommittee on Financial Institutions and Consumer Credit. She focused on the regulatory burdens facing community banks and credit unions. Her husband, Charles, is a longtime banking executive, which raised eyebrows among watchdog groups. Capito said she makes her own decisions, telling Esquire magazine in 2010 that "no matter what your decisions are, no matter what your votes are, if you're not playing by the rules, you're taking a big risk."

After her re-election in 2012, Capito announced she would challenge Democratic Sen. Jay Rockefeller in 2014. Rockefeller, who was in his late-70s and had health problems, wanted no part of a tough race against Capito. During his 42 years as a statewide elected official, his only defeat came against her father in the 1972 contest for governor. Rockefeller announced his retirement after a poll showed her with a slight lead in a head-to-head matchup.

In the general, Capito faced Natalie Tennant, West Virginia's secretary of state and a former TV reporter. Tennant sought to make an issue of Capito and her spouse's close ties to banking interests, saying her own "West Virginia first" approach contrasted with Capito's record "working for Wall Street banks where her husband works." Capito ran a quietly effective campaign and was aided by Obama's deep unpopularity among West Virginians. Her move from the House to the Senate was such a certainty that by July, friends and colleagues reportedly began addressing her as "Senator." In November, she defeated Tennant 62%-35%.

Capito settled into the Senate with a seat on the Appropriations Committee, where she was the only freshman Republican tapped as a subcommittee chair. The assignment has outsize consequence for a state as poor as West Virginia. She took charge of the panel that funds congressional operations, a good way to make connections with Senate insiders. Since then, she has chaired the Financial Services and General Government Subcommittee and then the Homeland Security panel. She has been one of four senators to serve as counsel to McConnell, which could open the door down the road for her to move up as a leadership player. In a sensitive leadership assignment, Capito in 2018 worked with leaders of the Senate Rules and Administration Committee to craft a bipartisan plan to update the Senate's sexual harassment policy.

Capito joined two other panels of great importance to coal-producing West Virginia — the Energy and Natural Resources Committee and the Environment and Public Works Committee. On the latter, she chaired the Clean Air and Nuclear Safety Subcommittee. She was lead sponsor of the Affordable Reliable Energy Now Act, which sought to pre-empt the Obama administration's proposal to tackle climate change. "We're asking for a commonsense agreement that assures reliable and affordable energy, protects our economy and jobs and allows states to make their own decisions," she told reporters. The measure won co-sponsorship of nearly three dozen senators, including one Democrat: Manchin.

The election of Donald Trump became a vital opportunity for Capito and her allies to reverse regulations and enforcement by the Environmental Protection Agency. In April 2018, she wrote that she was encouraged that "the war on coal is over." In subsequent committee reorganization, she took over as chairwoman of the Transportation and Infrastructure Subcommittee. She gave up her seat on the Energy committee to join Commerce, Science and Transportation, where her interests include expanded broadband coverage in rural areas. She claimed success of her "Capito connect" initiative to reduce the urban-rural digital divide.

On a related topic, she advocated for giving health care coverage to retired miners. McConnell spearheaded a related plan that was enacted as part of a government funding bill in May 2017. Capito raised concerns about protecting her state's Medicaid funding amid GOP efforts to replace the Affordable Care Act. She joined three other GOP senators who wrote to McConnell about the need for "stability and certainty for individuals and families in Medicaid expansion programs or the necessary flexibility for states," including West Virginia. "I did not come to Washington to hurt people," she said during the health care debate. In the end, she supported the GOP's "skinny repeal" plan, though the Senate deadlocked.

As a House member, Capito was a founding member of the Congressional Women's Softball Team, a group that plays reporters in an annual faceoff. She eventually became a captain on the team and started at third base.

Capito is up for re-election in 2020. She often is criticized by the tea party pockets of the GOP, but given her family's name recognition and the conservative bent of the Mountain State, few political observers expected that she would face much of a challenge for a second term.

David McKinley (R)

Elected 2010, 5th term, b. Mar 28, 1947; Wheeling; Purdue University (IN), B.S., 1969; Episcopalian; Married (Mary McKinley); 4 children; 6 grandchildren.

Elected Office: WV House, 1980-1994.

Professional Career: Principal, McKinley & Association, 1981-2010; Chair, WV GOP, 1990-1994.

DC Office: 2239 RHOB 20515, 202-225-4172, Fax: 202-225-7564, mckinley.house.gov

State Offices: Morgantown, 304-284-8506; Parkersburg, 304-422-5972; Wheeling, 304-232-3801.

Committees: *Energy & Commerce*: Energy; Environment & Climate Change; Oversight & Investigations.

Group Ratings

	ADA	ACLU	AFL-CIO	LCV	ITI	COC	HAFA	ACU	CFG	FRC
2018	-	4%	-	11%	-	83%	41%	52%	36%	100%
2017	5%	C	29%	0%	C	93%	C	67%	53%	100%

Almanac Ratings 2017-18

	Economy	Social	Foreign	Composite
Liberal	12%	4%	3%	6%
Conservative	89%	97%	98%	94%

Key Votes of the 115th Congress

1. Obama-care revision	Y	5. Family planning regs	Y	9. Guantanamo prisoners	N
2. Tax Cuts	Y	6. Body cameras/immigration	N	10. Ground missiles, limit	N
3. Omnibus appropriations	Y	7. Abortion ban	Y	11. Defense Dept. spending	Y
4. Dodd-Frank revision	Y	8. Concealed carry	Y	12. FISA rules	Y

Election Results

Election	Name (Party)	Vote (%)		Cand. Spent	Ind. Exp. Support	Ind. Exp. Oppose
2018 General	David McKinley (R)............................ 127,997	(65%)	$1,151,701	$588,451	
	Kendra Fershee (D)............................. 70,217	(35%)	$270,548		
2018 Primary	David McKinley (R).......................................	(100%)			

Prior winning percentages: 2016 (69%), 2014 (64%), 2012 (62%), 2010 (50%)

Republican David McKinley, elected in 2010, is a coal-championing centrist. He has been an active legislator and has shown some independence from his party on big issues.

McKinley is a seventh-generation native of Wheeling. McKinley's great-grandfather ran for West Virginia governor as a Democrat in 1908. His father was a civil engineer who taught him to read blueprints when he was in third grade. He majored in civil engineering at Purdue University. After college, McKinley worked for several engineering and construction companies until he founded his own firm, McKinley & Associates, which restores historic properties and does other construction work. In West Virginia's House of Delegates, McKinley pushed for a bill to allow school and prison cafeterias to donate unused food to homeless shelters. He authored a law that prohibited insurance companies from canceling policies of people diagnosed with HIV. He ran for governor in 1996 but lost the primary to Cecil Underwood, who won the general election.

In his House bid in 2010, McKinley had the backing of national Republicans and won the primary with 35 percent of the vote. In the general election, he faced state Sen. Mike Oliverio, who had toppled 14-term Democratic Rep. Alan Mollohan in the primary after several newspaper accounts raised questions about whether Mollohan profited personally from business deals with people and nonprofit groups that got federal funds he earmarked in appropriations bills. McKinley emphasized his opposition to the Democrats' energy bill that would limit carbon emissions, arguing that it would hurt West Virginia's coal industry. Oliverio also opposed the bill. He charged that McKinley got rich from government contracts even as he criticized government spending, citing federal economic stimulus money that McKinley's architectural and engineering firm received to design a Marshall County school. McKinley eked out a victory of 1,440 votes, a split of 50.4%-49.6%.

McKinley was one of a handful of Republicans in 2011 and 2012 to vote against Budget Committee Chairman Paul Ryan's budget blueprint, complaining that it did not adequately protect Medicare. He got a plum seat on the Energy and Commerce Committee and co-founded a Marcellus Shale Caucus to oppose regulation of drilling in the oil-and-gas-rich area stretching along the Appalachians. In 2015, he took the lead for House Republicans in the enactment of tougher standards for energy efficiency. With Democratic Rep. Matt Cartwright of Pennsylvania, McKinley enacted a bill in 2016 that authorized the Bureau of Prisons to permit its officers to carry pepper spray for self-defense. He authored the bill after a federal correctional officer was murdered by an inmate. His 2017 bill to make it easier for corrections officers to carry firearms passed the House.

McKinley has spoken out about the state's growing opioid epidemic. When pharmaceutical executives testified before Congress in 2018 and refused to take responsibility for the worsening crisis, McKinley exploded at them. "I just want you to feel shame about your roles, respectively, in all of this," McKinley told them. McKinley, who is hearing-impaired, has worked with the Veterans Affairs Department to help more veterans get cochlear implants, often at a lower rate than for non-military persons. "Society doesn't recognize when you have hearing loss," he told Roll Call. "They're not very patient with you."

McKinley has aggressively fought so-called coal-ash rules that affect industries such as concrete production and manufacturing of wallboard. He introduced a bill to create an enforceable minimum standard for the regulation of coal ash by the states, allowing its use in a manner that he said would protect jobs. It passed the House but stalled in the Senate. In February 2017, the House rescinded on a nearly party-line vote the coal-ash rule that the Interior Department had written during the Obama administration; President Donald Trump signed the repeal measure.

McKinley cautioned that the coal industry would not be hiring nearly as many West Virginians as had worked in the mines a half-century ago, but he voiced hope that the coal industry would find new markets for overseas exports. In 2018, he got an amendment added to the Interior Department's appropriations bill that would add $160 million to the EPA's Brownfields Program to clean up abandoned industrial sites for a new use.

McKinley has strengthened himself politically. With a boost from serving on Energy and Commerce, he has stockpiled large contributions from coal interests. He has been reelected each time with at least 62 percent of the vote. In 2015, after extensive review, he ruled out a run for the open seat for governor. McKinley said he decided, "I can do much more for West Virginia right here in Congress." He's been a vocal supporter of President Donald Trump and credited him with the coal resurgence in West Virginia.

In 2016, the House Ethics Committee issued a letter of reproval — its mildest sanction — to McKinley because of his failure to remove his name from his engineering business, even after he had sold the company. In 2018, he faced a different kind of inquiry when he and Republican Rep. Scott Tipton of Colorado were questioned by Israeli police after taking an olive branch from a tree at the Temple Mount holy site in Jerusalem while on a trip sponsored by an evangelical group. Such an action is banned by the Muslim group that governs the area. The two said the branch was eventually dropped, though they weren't aware of such a prohibition.

WV-1: Northern West Virginia   Cook Partisan Voting Index: R+19

Population		Race and Ethnicity		Income	
Total	615,449	White	93.5%	Median Income	$45,670
Land area (sq. miles)	6,276	Black	2.5%	District Income Rank	369
Pop/ sq mi	98.1	Latino	1.3%	Poverty Rate	16.8%
Born in State	68.5%	Asian	1%	With health insurance	92.4%
		Two or more races	1.5%	Cash public assistance	2.3%
Age Groups		Other	0.2%	Food stamp/SNAP	13.6%
Under 18	19.5%				
18-34	23.2%	**Education**		**Work**	
35-64	39.2%	H.S grad or less	51.1%	White Collar	18.1%
Over 64	18.1%	Some college	26.5%	Sales and Service	41.8%
		College Degree, 4 yr	13.3%	Blue Collar	24.7%
Military		Post grad	9.1%	Government	17.8%
Veteran/ Active Duty	9.2%				

2012 Pres. Vote	Romney	141,736	(62%)	Obama	81,017	(36%)		
2016 Pres. Vote	Trump	165,934	(68%)	Clinton	64,384	(26%)	Johnson	8,862 (4%)

Morgantown, Parkersburg: The northern part of West Virginia is in many ways an extension of the Pittsburgh metropolitan area. People here are Steelers and Pirates fans, they drink Iron City and Rolling Rock beer, they watch Pittsburgh television, and they live in the crevasses between hills cut by the Monongahela and Ohio rivers. This has been one of America's prime industrial areas. Northern West Virginia is part of the same coal-and-steel economy that made Pittsburgh one of the nation's largest cities and filled the narrow bottomlands along the rivers with steel and glass factories, foundries and coal yards.

As in Pennsylvania, these industries have been declining and they have become far less labor-intensive. Local jobs and population have declined. Since 1980, the 12,000 mining jobs in this part of West Virginia have dropped by more than two-thirds, with comparable fall-offs in manufacturing. The Weirton tin and steel mill (now called ArcelorMittal and owned by an integrated steel and mining company headquartered in Luxembourg) employed 14,000 workers in the mid-1970s and was down to 880 in 2019. Service jobs have replaced some of these losses. Walmart has been West Virginia's second largest private employer since 1998, and the government has brought in thousands more jobs, compliments of the late Sen. Robert Byrd, the powerful Senate appropriator, whose legacy endures years after his death. One of the largest employers in Harrison County has been the Department of Justice, while the I-79 Technology Park in Fairmont houses offices for NASA, the National Oceanic and Atmospheric Association, the FBI and the Department of Homeland Security. Harrison County has become the state's leader in the Marcellus shale natural gas boom, with an influx of jobs and money that have resulted from more than 3,000 wells drilled in the state, though executives say more storage and pipelines are needed to help the industry grow. In 2017, China Energy announced an $84 billion investment in the state's natural gas and petrochemical industries.

The 1st Congressional District of West Virginia includes 20 counties in the northern third of the state. On the Panhandle along the Ohio River is Victorian Wheeling, once one of the richest cities in the country with its steel and glass companies. There is Weirton, named for Ernest T. Weir, the anti-union Pittsburgh industrialist who transformed it from a farming community to a steel town in the early 1900s. South of Pittsburgh on the Monongahela River is Morgantown, with human capital from West Virginia University, the largest employer in the state. On the Ohio River is the former oil-refining and shipping center of Parkersburg, which has become a plastics and manufacturing hub. Parts of the district are stagnant while others are on a growth path. Morgantown's population grew 7.8 percent from 2000 to 2017, while Wheeling and Parkersburg have continued consistent decline since the 1930s. Just to the east is Preston County, site of the Federal Correctional Institution Hazelton, a medium-security facility that has a growing problem with deaths and assaults.

For most of the 20th century, much of the territory in the 1st District was solidly Democratic. But dissatisfaction with the Clinton-Gore policies on coal mining and the environment helped Republican George W. Bush carry the district twice, and the local hostility accelerated with President Barack Obama's policies. Donald Trump in 2016 took at least 66 percent of the vote in each of West Virginia's three districts, with 68 percent in the 1st.

Alex Mooney (R)

Elected 2014, 3rd term, b. Jun 07, 1971; Washington, DC; Dartmouth College, A.B., 1993; Roman Catholic; Married (Grace Gonzalez); 3 children.

Elected Office: MD Senate, 1999-2010.

Professional Career: Aide, Rep. Roscoe Bartlett, 1993-1995; Executive, Council for National Policy Action, Inc, 1995-1998; Director, The National Journalism Center, 2005-2012; Chair, MD GOP, 2010-2013; Owner, consulting firm, 2011-2014.

DC Office: 2440 RHOB 20515, 202-225-2711, Fax: 202-225-7856, mooney.house.gov

State Offices: Charleston, 304-925-5964; Martinsburg, 304-264-8810.

Committees: *Financial Services*: Investor Protection, Entrepreneurship & Capital Markets; Subcommittee on Diversity & Inclusion.

Group Ratings

	ADA	ACLU	AFL-CIO	LCV	ITI	COC	HAFA	ACU	CFG	FRC
2018	-	18%	-	0%	-	75%	88%	96%	92%	100%
2017	0%	C	8%	0%	C	93%	C	85%	88%	100%

Almanac Ratings 2017-18

	Economy	Social	Foreign	Composite
Liberal	7%	7%	18%	11%
Conservative	93%	93%	82%	89%

Key Votes of the 115th Congress

1. Obama-care revision	Y	5. Family planning regs	Y	9. Guantanamo prisoners	N
2. Tax Cuts	Y	6. Body cameras/immigration	N	10. Ground missiles, limit	N
3. Omnibus appropriations	N	7. Abortion ban	Y	11. Defense Dept. spending	Y
4. Dodd-Frank revision	Y	8. Concealed carry	Y	12. FISA rules	N

Election Results

Election	Name (Party)	Vote (%)		Cand. Spent	Ind. Exp. Support	Ind. Exp. Oppose
2018 General	Alex Mooney (R)	110,504	(54%)	$1,200,669		
	Talley Sergent (D)	88,011	(43%)	$672,227		
	Daniel Lutz (M)	6,277	(3%)	$296		
2018 Primary	Alex Mooney (R)		(100%)			

Prior winning percentages: 2016 (58%), 2014 (47%)

Republican Alex Mooney, a onetime Marylander, found a receptive home in West Virginia in 2014 when he won an open seat. Mooney, who has run for office in three states, won a costly and contentious contest in the sprawling 2nd District. He has since been reelected more easily.

Mooney was born in Washington D.C. to a Cuban refugee mother and a father from an Irish immigrant family who served in Vietnam. He graduated from Dartmouth College, where he was president of the Coalition for Life; during his time there, he ran for the New Hampshire House of Representatives but got just 8 percent of the vote and finished last of the seven candidates in the general election. After college, he was an aide to GOP Rep. Roscoe Bartlett of Maryland. Mooney won a Maryland state Senate seat in 1998 at age 27 and became Maryland GOP chairman after he lost reelection to the Senate in 2010. (His official bio deleted reference to his service in Annapolis.) He then set his sights on his former boss' House seat and started raising money for a potential run in 2012 after most assumed Bartlett would retire. But Mooney abandoned the effort after Bartlett announced he would run in what turned out to be a losing effort in a tougher district post-redistricting. Mooney kept the campaign cash, saying he would run in 2014, and went back to work for Bartlett part-time in 2012.

But Mooney had a change of plan and crossed the state line to West Virginia, where he entered a seven-way GOP primary after Rep. Shelley Moore Capito ran successfully for the Senate. He won with 36 percent of the vote to 22 percent for Ken Reed, a pharmacist. In the general election, Mooney campaigned on an anti-Obama platform, vowing to repeal the Affordable Care Act and pledging to fight government overreach. Nick Casey, a former Democratic state chairman, said he wanted to scrap some parts of the health care law, such as the mandate for employers to provide coverage, and argued that Washington needed more moderate voices. The central fight was over whether geography or ideology mattered more. Casey, calling himself a "true West Virginian," branded Mooney a carpetbagger and opportunist. Mooney countered that he was a "West Virginian by choice," and therefore more committed to his adopted district's conservative values. He said that his Maryland state Senate seat bordered West Virginia and that the two areas are similar. The district agreed with Mooney, though some voters undoubtedly were turned off by his river-crossing. Each candidate spent about $2 million. Mooney benefited from more than $2.3 million in additional spending from Republican and conservative groups, compared with less than $900,000 that national Democrats delivered to Casey. Mooney won, 47%-44%.

In the House, Mooney joined the Budget Committee, where he supported the Republicans' spending plan and took credit for provisions that opposed funding of ozone standards by the Environmental Protection Agency and blocked regulations that would prohibit surface mining in West Virginia. On the Natural Resources Committee, he attacked Obama administration initiatives that were designed to limit the mining and use of coal. "West Virginia is blessed to be abundant in natural resources," Mooney said in 2015. "Unfortunately, the president is intent on destroying coal as a domestic energy source." He bucked party leaders during votes on trade promotion authority for the president, but he later received campaign support from Speaker Paul Ryan.

In 2017, Mooney got a seat on the Financial Services Committee, where he pursued his interest in community banking and housing issues. He introduced legislation to amend the Dodd-Frank banking law to repeal disclosures given to investors about the safety violations and worker deaths of publicly traded mining companies. In 2018, he filed a bill to end taxation of gold and silver coins and bars; he has voiced support for returning the United States to the gold standard.

After Casey decided not to seek a rematch, the Democratic Congressional Campaign Committee expressed interest in Cory Simpson — who had been an active-duty attorney in the Army, while residing in Silver Spring Maryland -- as its preferred choice in the primary in 2016. But Simpson finished second in the five-candidate primary to Mark Hunt, who self-financed $280,000 of the $480,000 that he raised. Hunt, a Charleston-area attorney, had served 14 years in the state House of Delegates, but received little support from national Democrats or their allies in the general election. Mooney won, 58%-42%.

In 2018, Democrats saw a glimmer of hope in their race against Mooney as the national environment was shifting in their favor. Talley Sergent, who served as Hillary Clinton's 2016 West Virginia state director, underscored her family's six-generation roots in the state compared to Mooney's weak ties. Sergent didn't mention her work for Clinton on her campaign bio and instead stressed her work for the State Department and former Democratic Sen. Jay Rockefeller. But Mooney played up those Clinton ties and his own support for Trump in an area where the president remained popular. The Democratic Congressional Campaign Committee and even EMILY's List, which backs women candidates who support abortion rights, steered clear of the contest. Sergent led in Kanawha County with 54 percent of the vote, but Mooney took the other 16 counties and won 54%-43%.

WV-2: Central West Virginia   Cook Partisan Voting Index: R+17

Population		Race and Ethnicity		Income	
Total	623,720	White	90.4%	Median Income	$49,173
Land area (sq. miles)	8,017	Black	4.4%	District Income Rank	326
Pop/ sq mi	77.8	Latino	2%	Poverty Rate	15.1%
Born in State	63.4%	Asian	0.8%	With health insurance	92.2%
		Two or more races	2%	Cash public assistance	2.4%
Age Groups		Other	0.4%	Food stamp/SNAP	14.6%
Under 18	21.5%				
18-34	19.6%	Education		Work	
35-64	41.2%	H.S grad or less	53.5%	White Collar	17.7%
Over 64	17.7%	Some college	25.2%	Sales and Service	42.2%
		College Degree, 4 yr	12.9%	Blue Collar	23.4%
Military		Post grad	8.4%	Government	19.9%
Veteran/ Active Duty	10.3%				

2012 Pres. Vote	Romney	140,783	(60%)	Obama	89,079	(38%)			
2016 Pres. Vote	Trump	164,674	(66%)	Clinton	73,487	(29%)	Johnson	8,232	(3%)

Charleston, Martinsburg: Not all of West Virginia has been coal country, and not all its hills have been scarred by strip mining. Large parts of this naturally beautiful state look as verdant and unchanged as they must have when George Washington was speculating in land here. For miles, there are gentle hills and rugged mountains. Yet over another hill you may find, amid scenery primeval and rural, sudden evidence of industrialization: a pulp mill or charcoal factory in a clearing scraped out of the forest; a small factory town, built close to a river in a cleft bordered with hills; the entrance to an underground coal mine or a mountaintop blasted open to allow surface mining.

The 2nd Congressional District of West Virginia is a central slice of the state, from Berkeley Springs and Harpers Ferry in the Washington D.C. exurbs, more than 300 miles to beyond Charleston and the Ohio River town of Ravenswood. The district includes fast-growing parts of the state: the Eastern Panhandle counties, which are part of the Washington metropolitan area, and chemical-producing Putnam County, which is increasingly home to suburbanites commuting to Charleston. The Toyota engine and transmission plant in Buffalo just outside Charleston, which employed 1,600 people, celebrated its 20th anniversary in 2016 with plans for a $400 million expansion; by 2020, the company planned another $115.3 million investment to produce its first American-made hybrid transaxles. In 2019, global tech company Infor added a location with 100 new jobs to help develop its cloud-based software. In Charleston, the state capitol sits on the banks of the Kanawha River, with a dome higher than that of the U.S. Capitol. When the city's two newspapers — The Charleston Gazette, which leans Democratic, and the Republican-tilting Charleston Daily Mail — combined into the Charleston Gazette-Mail in 2015, it created one news staff and two separate editorial pages. The family-owned newspaper declared bankruptcy in 2018 -- to the glee of the state's coal industry, often the subject of its investigations into safety and environmental practices -- but was later bought for nearly $11.5 million by HD Media.

In the 1940s, the area produced all of the nation's Lucite, polyethylene and nylon, as well as much of its artificial rubber and antifreeze. Today, the state boasts that it is home to more polymer producers than any other place on the planet; the chemical industry makes products used in the manufacturing of cosmetics, detergents, shampoo and other products. Those chemical plants employ thousands of workers in Kanawha and Putnam counties, but they can be hazardous. In 2014, a spill from a chemical tank farm on the Elk River just north of Charleston caused more than 300,000 people in the metropolitan area to lose fresh drinking water for days or weeks in some cases. Charleston is West Virginia's professional center, with a few downtown office towers and some affluent residential areas. Politically, this ancestrally Democratic district is trending Republican. Berkeley County, which has commuter rail to Washington, has grown over 50 percent since 2000 to become the second-largest county in the state. During that period, Kanawha County has dropped 7 percent, and Charleston is now the third-fastest shrinking city in the nation, with median home prices of just over $100,000. Donald Trump in 2016 won here with 66 percent of the vote.

Carol Miller (R)

Elected 2018, 1st term, b. Nov 04, 1950; Columbus, OH; Columbia College, B.S., 1972; Baptist; Married (Matt Miller); 2 children.

Elected Office: WV State House, 2006-2018.

Professional Career: Bison Farmer; Real Estate Manager.

DC Office: 1605 LHOB 20515, 202-225-3452, miller.house.gov

State Offices: Beckley, 304-250-6177; Bluefield, 304-325-6800; Huntington, 304-522-2201.

Committees: *Oversight & Reform*: Subcommittee on Civil Rights & Civil Liberties; Subcommittee on Economic & Consumer Policy. *Select Committee on the Climate Crisis. Transportation & Infrastructure*: Coast Guard & Maritime Transportation; Economic Dev't, Public Buildings & Emergency Management; Highways & Transit.

Election Results

Election	Name (Party)	Vote (%)		Cand. Spent	Ind. Exp. Support	Ind. Exp. Oppose
2018 General	Carol Miller (R).....................................	98,645	(56%)	$1,681,892	$74,280	$1,983,816
	Richard Ojeda (D).............................	76,340	(44%)	$2,633,500		$1,188,011
2018 Primary	Carol Miller (R).....................................	8,923	(24%)			
	Rupie Phillips (R).................................	7,319	(20%)			
	Marty Gearheart (R)............................	6,814	(18%)			
	Conrad Lucas (R).................................	6,771	(18%)			
	Rick Snuffer (R)...................................	3,987	(11%)			
	Ayne Amjad (R)....................................	2,795	(8%)			

Republican Carol Miller, elected in 2018, won competitive contests to take an open seat. She brought extensive political experience and embraced President Donald Trump, who was widely popular in her district. She faced Democrat Richard Ojeda, a feisty opponent who supported Trump in 2016 and distanced himself from his national party. Miller succeeded Rep. Evan Jenkins, who unsuccessfully sought the Republican nomination for the Senate in 2018 and later resigned to become a justice on the state Supreme Court. She was the only Republican in the large freshman class of women.

Miller has a congressional pedigree, as the daughter of GOP Rep. Samuel Devine of Ohio. He served 22 years, including two years as chairman of the House Republican Conference, before he lost reelection in 1980. Miller graduated from Columbia College in South Carolina. She was a real-estate property manager and managed the Swann Ridge Bison Farm, where she raised and processed buffalo meat. She served 12 years in the state House of Delegates, where she was majority whip and chaired the Small Business Committee. Her husband, Matt Miller, was a prominent automobile dealer.

The opening created by Jenkins resulted in a wide-open Republican primary. Each of the four leading contenders served in the Legislature or was a party official, and made clear their support for Trump. Miller ran ads that pledged "America First" principles. She gained backing from Rep. Susan Brooks of Indiana and Working for Women, a new group backing Republican women.

Miller won the primary with 24 percent of the vote. Rupie Phillips and Marty Gearhart, who both served with Miller in the House of Delegates, got 20 and 18 percent, respectively. Conrad Lucas, the former state party chairman who had support from the Republican Main Street Partnership, got 18 percent.

Ojeda, a state senator for two years, had an easier time in the Democratic primary, which he won with 52 percent against three opponents. He initially gained attention when he challenged 19-term Rep. Nick Rahall in 2014. Rahall got 66 percent of the vote in the Democratic primary and took every county except Logan, which was Ojeda's home ground. Jenkins defeated Rahall in November,

55%-45%. A retired Army captain and ally of organized labor, Ojeda voiced populist themes, including hostility to outside bankers and energy companies. His grandfather was an immigrant from Mexico.

Ojeda's distinctiveness included reversal of his earlier support for Trump. "All he's done is shown that he's taking care of the daggone people he's supposed to be getting rid of," Ojeda told Politico. During a campaign appearance in Wheeling in September, Trump responded by calling Ojeda "a total wacko" and "stone-cold crazy." Miller said that she welcomed Trump's support, though she would not have used those words.

With a boost from his national publicity, Ojeda outspent Miller in the campaign, $2.6 million to $1.7 million. But that wasn't enough to shift the increasingly entrenched Republican lean of southern West Virginia. Miller won 56%-44% and took 16 of 18 counties, losing only Boone and Fayette, both in the Charleston suburbs.

Taking her House seat at age 68, Miller faces a potentially significant challenge: the prospect that the state will lose one of its three districts as a result of the 2020 census and subsequent reapportionment. Because her district lacks the larger population centers of the other two districts, redistricting in West Virginia might leave her with less of a base than a potential competitor.

WV-3: Southern West Virginia   **Cook Partisan Voting Index: R+23**

Population		Race and Ethnicity		Income	
Total	597,674	White	93%	Median Income	$37,749
Land area (sq. miles)	9,745	Black	3.7%	District Income Rank	425
Pop/ sq mi	61.3	Latino	1%	Poverty Rate	21.6%
Born in State	77.8%	Asian	0.5%	With health insurance	91.5%
		Two or more races	1.4%	Cash public assistance	2.4%
Age Groups		Other	0.4%	Food stamp/SNAP	21.4%
Under 18	20.6%				
18-34	19.8%	**Education**		**Work**	
35-64	40.5%	H.S grad or less	59.5%	White Collar	19.1%
Over 64	19.1%	Some college	24.7%	Sales and Service	45.5%
		College Degree, 4 yr	9.7%	Blue Collar	24.7%
Military		Post grad	6.1%	Government	18.5%
Veteran/ Active Duty	9.1%				

2012 Pres. Vote	Romney	135,136	(65%)	Obama	68,173	(33%)		
2016 Pres. Vote	Trump	158,763	(73%)	Clinton	50,923	(23%)	Johnson	5,910	(3%)

Huntington, Beckley: Early in the 20th century, the coal fields of southern West Virginia were one of America's boom areas. Into rural farmland and hollows, inhabited by the same families that settled the mountains 100 years before, came coal company lawyers with mineral rights' leases to sign, coal company engineers to design and sink mineshafts, and men from other mountain counties to work the mines. Company houses were built, company stores were stocked with goods as the company dictated and company paymasters kept close tabs on the finances of every employee. These conditions bred discontent, which ignited into the fire of industrial unionism. The Battle of Blair Mountain in Logan County, where 10,000 armed unionists faced off against 3,000 law enforcement officers and strikebreakers, presaged later efforts at organization by John L. Lewis, president of the United Mine Workers. Lewis was not only a militant unionist, but also an isolationist. During and after World War II, he called out his coal miners on strikes, to the fury of Democratic Presidents Franklin Roosevelt and Harry Truman. The national war effort and postwar economic recovery were threatened by these labor stoppages involving some 300,000 workers.

Coal no longer is the dominant U.S. source of electricity. In 2016, it supplied 30 percent of the fuel to power utility plants, compared with 32 percent for natural gas. That share from coal has dropped markedly in recent years. Marion and Logan are the leading counties in this region for coal production, with at least 10 million tons each in 2017. Boone, Raleigh and Mingo counties, which were on that list a decade ago, have declined significantly in production. Marshall County in the northern part of the state is the county that produced the most coal. Production in the southern part of the state dropped from 116 million tons in 2008 to 46 million tons in 2017, which has become virtually the same total as in the northern counties. Statewide, the total of 13,000 jobs in the West Virginia mines in 2017 dropped from nearly 23,000 in 2011. Mingo and nearby counties have suffered among the highest rates in the nation for opioid drug addiction and deaths.

The 3rd Congressional District of West Virginia includes most of the mountainous coal country in the southern part of the state, which for years was heavily Democratic. But the coal mining counties make up less than half of the district. About a quarter of the population is in and around the industrial city of Huntington on the Ohio River, which includes Marshall University. Another quarter is to the east, in Beckley and the farming uplands. Also located there is the Greenbrier Resort, where the government built a massive secret fallout shelter, code-named "Project Greek Island," to house the entire Congress in the event of nuclear war. The district has shifted to Republicans in the past two decades. In 2016, Donald Trump won here, 73%-23%, among his strongest districts in the nation. This remarkable historical turnaround resulted largely from discontent with the energy, environmental and cultural policies of national Democrats.

WISCONSIN

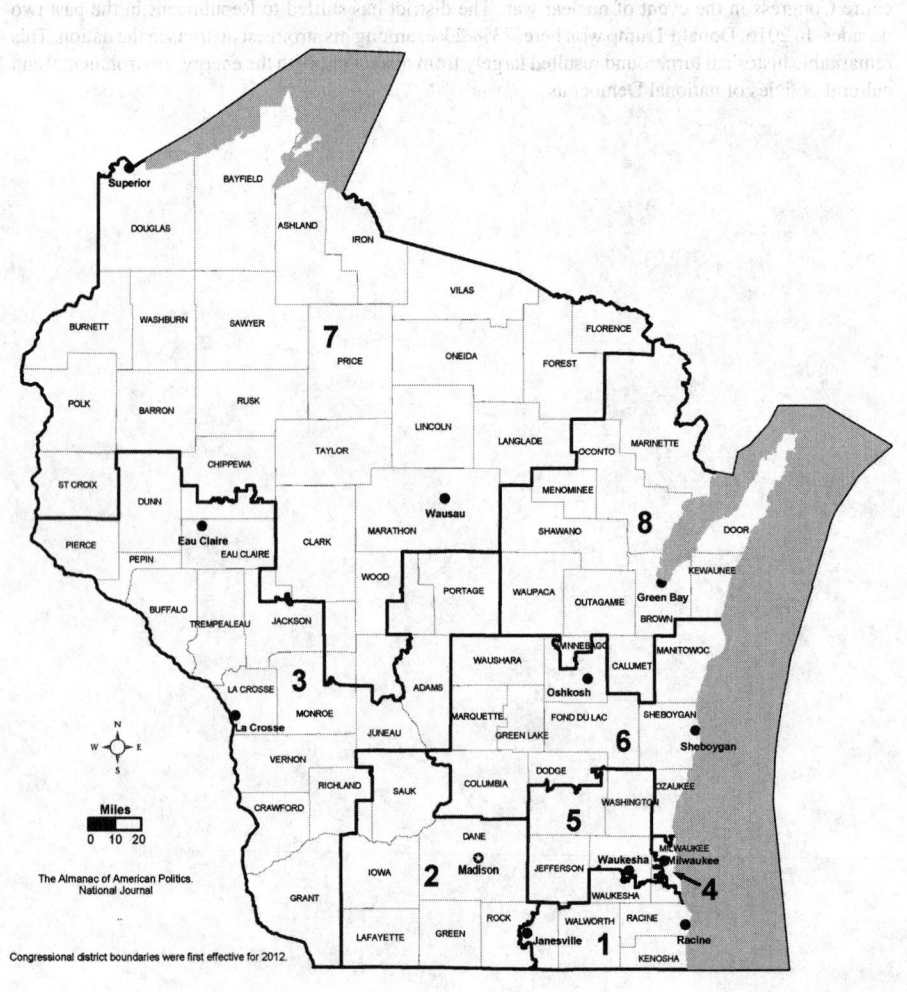

Heading into the 2016 presidential election, some considered Wisconsin one of the Democrats' "blue wall" states – a supposed bulwark against Republicans in the Electoral College. But they ignored that the state had turned to the right after the 2010 gubernatorial election of Scott Walker, who proceeded to enact a wish list of conservative policies. Donald Trump ended up winning the state, albeit by less than 23,000 votes, or about eight-tenths of a percentage point. Two years later, the state snapped back, again narrowly, as the Democrats ousted Walker, setting up perhaps the most pivotal battleground contest for Trump's reelection bid in 2020.

Wisconsin has long been one of America's premier "laboratories of reform," in Justice Louis Brandeis' phrase -- a state developing new public policies, debating them vigorously and even tumultuously, observing whether they worked, and serving as an example for other states. North of the dominant westward paths of migration, the state was sparsely settled, first by New England Yankees and then by waves of immigrants from Germany and Scandinavia. The German language is seldom heard now, but German place names and surnames are common and, like the once plainly German beer and brat brands, now seem quintessentially American. But from the 1840s into the 20th century, Germans were among the nation's most distinctive immigrants. On the rolling dairy land of Wisconsin and the orderly streets of Milwaukee, they built their own churches, kept their own language, and maintained old customs, from country weddings to Christmas trees to beer gardens — a source of friction in temperance-minded America. Wisconsin still has an orderliness and steadiness that owes something to its Germanic heritage, evident in its excellence in precision manufacturing, respect for higher learning, and its hold on its people. About half of Wisconsin residents, more than in any other state, reported in the 2010 census that they are of German descent.

Wisconsin's economy has been an outgrowth of its immigrant and manufacturing heritage. Its high-skill, precision production at companies like Johnson Controls and Rockwell Automation jumped into gear in the late 1980s and helped lead the nation's export boom of the 1990s. Wisconsin exceeded 100,000 tech jobs for the first time in 2016 and the state was poised to host an advanced Foxconn manufacturing plant near Racine (though both the billions of dollars in subsidies and doubts about the number of jobs to be created have made the project controversial). Wisconsin ranks either first or second in the nation in most categories of milk and cheese production. But due to improved productivity and competition from foreign countries -- and from California's giant agribusiness enterprises -- the number of milk-cow herds fell by 50 percent from 2003 to 2019, when the total was fewer than 8,000; that rate has accelerated in recent years. Wisconsin, of course, is also a prime source of beer and sausage. Pabst, which began in Milwaukee in 1844, closed its operations there in 1996, but reopened a brewery, taproom and restaurant in a former German Methodist church in 2017. Over time, Wisconsin's economy has ranked right around where the country is. "Wisconsin has suffered from the decline of manufacturing, but it isn't a Rust Belt sob story like Michigan or Ohio. It hasn't been among the places hardest hit by the opiate epidemic," wrote Bloomberg columnist Noah Smith.

Wisconsin's reputation for innovative public policy was established during the Progressive Era that began around 1900 and which owes its development to an extraordinary governor, Robert La Follette Sr., and the state's German heritage. This is one of the two states that gave birth to the Republican Party in 1854 (the other is Michigan), and Germans, then arriving in America in vast numbers, heavily favored the GOP. They opposed slavery and welcomed the free lands Republicans delivered in the Homestead Act, the educational opportunities provided by land grant colleges, and the transportation routes constructed by subsidized railroad builders. This was the seedbed from which sprouted the Progressive movement founded and symbolized by La Follette. At a time when Germany was the world's leader in graduate education and the application of science to government, La Follette had professors at the University of Wisconsin help develop the state workmen's compensation system and income tax. The Progressive movement favored the use of government to improve the lot of ordinary citizens, an idea borrowed partly from German liberals and adopted by the New Dealers a generation later. La Follette became a national figure and after he died in 1925, his sons, and then liberal Democrats such as Sens. William Proxmire and Gaylord Nelson and Gov. Patrick Lucey, carried on his tradition -- progressive at home and isolationist abroad.

Wisconsin also has a long history of labor activism. Before the violence of the 1892 Homestead steel strike in Pittsburgh and Colorado's Ludlow Massacre in 1914, Milwaukee saw bloodshed on May 5, 1886, when 1,500 tradesmen and Polish immigrants demanding an eight-hour workday marched on the Rolling Mills iron plant in the city's Bay View neighborhood. Gov. Jeremiah Rusk, who had served as a U.S. Army general in the Civil War, was in Milwaukee commanding 700 Wisconsin National Guard troops and gave the order to fire on the workers if they approached the iron works. Seven people, including a young boy, were killed. After the incident, Rusk famously said, "I seen my duty, and I done it." South of downtown Milwaukee, a memorial stands in the Bay View area not far from where the blood was spilled. Wisconsin became the first state to grant collective-bargaining rights to public employees, in 1959.

Starting in the 1990s, Wisconsin became a laboratory for conservative reforms driven by Republican Gov. Tommy Thompson, who beat a liberal Democrat in 1986 and was reelected three times. He cut taxes, sponsored a school choice program, and passed a series of welfare reforms — the nation's most sweeping — that cut caseloads by equipping recipients to work. The 1996 overhaul of federal welfare policy may not have passed without Wisconsin's example to give its backers confidence. When Thompson left to become George W. Bush's Health and Human Services secretary in 2001, Wisconsin moved back toward the Democrats. From 1992 to 2006, it elected only Democratic senators, although sometimes by narrow margins, and Democrat Jim Doyle was elected governor in 2002 and 2006. The 2010 election produced another experiment in conservative reform when Republican Scott Walker, a former Milwaukee County executive, took office and proceeded to set off a firestorm with a proposal to limit the power of unions. The effort was successful, and Walker turned back an energetic, labor-driven effort to recall him in 2012 before winning reelection in 2014. By 2017, shorn of the coercive power of closed shops, union membership in the state had fallen substantially. Walker joined two other national Republican figures from Wisconsin – Rep. Paul Ryan, the party's 2012 vice presidential nominee and later House Speaker, and Reince Priebus, the former Wisconsin GOP state chair who became chairman of the Republican National Committee and then White House chief of staff under Trump. Two years later, all three had left public life.

Wisconsin's population has grown, but at a modest rate – up only 2.2 percent since the 2010 census. The city of Milwaukee grew 1.6 percent, and its suburban counties – unlike many suburbs in other states – grew between 2 and 3 percent. The state's fastest growth has occurred in Dane County (Madison), which is home to a growing tech sector driven by the presence of the University of Wisconsin; the county has expanded by 9.4 percent since 2010, pushing growth to rural areas to the south and northeast. Another growth area has been Outagamie County (Appleton), expanding 5 percent since the last census. The state remains primarily white, with a small, if rising, foreign-born population. Overall, Wisconsin is 6 percent black, 7 percent Hispanic and 3 percent Asian.

Politically, the three large "WOW" counties in the Milwaukee suburbs — Washington, Ozaukee and Waukesha — have traditionally been Republican, sometimes enough to cancel out Milwaukee County and its lopsided Democratic margins. Eastern Wisconsin — the counties along Lake Michigan and two or three counties inland, with small industrial cities in the Fox River Valley like Kenosha, Sheboygan, Appleton and Green Bay — is historically Republican turf. Western Wisconsin — areas along the Mississippi River, the small inland cities such as Wausau and Eau Claire and the counties along Lake Superior — have tended to be more Democratic. These patterns stem from ethnic differences: Eastern Wisconsin is more German, and western Wisconsin more Scandinavian.

The most Democratic region by far is around Madison. Indeed, "what's going on in Dane County is gradually altering the electoral math in Wisconsin," the Milwaukee Journal Sentinel's Craig Gilbert has written in one of his fine-grained analyses of Wisconsin election results. "Dane has been growing about four points more Democratic with each presidential contest since 1980, while adding thousands more voters every year." La Crosse and Eau Claire host University of Wisconsin campuses, as does Rock County (Janesville), which is also home to Beloit College. The arc with this university belt has leaned Democratic. With statewide races in Wisconsin often won narrowly, a significant number of Wisconsinites are swing voters. A seven-county portion of southwest Wisconsin known as the Driftless Area (for its geology) "boasts the nation's greatest concentration of Obama-Trump counties -- places that voted for Obama in 2012 and Trump in 2016," Gilbert has written. Wisconsin has elected and re-elected both conservative Republican Ron Johnson and liberal Democrat Tammy Baldwin to the Senate.

The 2016 presidential election in Wisconsin was dramatic from start to finish. The state had not voted Republican for president since Ronald Reagan's 1984 landslide, and for much of the contest,

Trump seemed to test Republican voters' patience. Ted Cruz easily beat him in the primary, even though his Texas stylings were not an obvious fit for Wisconsin. After it became clear that Trump was going to be the GOP nominee, he and Ryan, by then the House Speaker, engaged in an on-again, off-again, awkward dance. The full extent of Clinton's struggles in the state were hard to spot and were largely ignored by her campaign team. Her key weakness was in the rural areas and small towns common in Wisconsin where Democrats had historically been competitive. On Election Day, a state Barack Obama had won by seven points in 2012 ended up voting for Trump by less than a point.

Wisconsin reasserted its swinginess in 2018. Walker lost a tough battle for a third term to Democrat Tony Evers. Walker improved his performance in 16 of Wisconsin's 20 least densely populated counties, but he lost ground in the state's 35 densest counties, a trade that wasn't enough to save his governorship. Then, just to stir the pot again, Wisconsin voters swung back to the right in an April 2019 judicial election. In the nominally nonpartisan judicial contest, the Republican base turned out just a little more, handing the conservative candidate a narrow win. Next up: The high-stakes 2020 presidential campaign, with both parties on tenterhooks.

Population		Race and Ethnicity		Income	
Total	5,763,217	White	81.8%	Median Income	$56,759
Land area (sq. miles)	54,158	Black	6.2%	State Income Rank	23
Pop/ sq mi	106.4	Latino	6.6%	Poverty Rate	12.3%
Born in state	71.4%	Asian	2.6%	With health insurance	93.5%
		Two or more races	1.8%	Cash public assistance	2.1%
Age Groups		Other	0.9%	Food stamp/SNAP	12.1%
Under 18	22.5%				
18-34	22.4%	Education		Work	
35-64	39.5%	H.S grad or less	39.6%	White Collar	35.5%
Over 64	15.6%	Some college	31.4%	Sales and Service	39.3%
		College Degree, 4 yr	19.2%	Blue Collar	25.1%
Military		Post grad	9.9%	Government	12.2%
Veteran/ Active Duty	7.9%				

Presidential Politics

2016 Primary (D)	Sanders (D)	570,192 (57%)	Clinton (D)	433,739 (43%)			
2016 Primary (R)	Cruz (R)	533,079 (48%)	Trump (R)	387,295 (35%)	Kasich (R)	155,902 (14%)	
2016 Pres. Vote	Trump (R)	1,405,284 (47%)	Clinton (D)	1,382,536 (46%)	Johnson (L)	106,674 (4%)	
2012 Pres. Vote	Obama (D)	1,620,985 (53%)	Romney (R)	1,407,966 (46%)			

Wisconsin has seen some very close presidential elections: Al Gore carried the state 47.8%-47.6%, a margin of only 5,708 votes in 2000, and John Kerry won it 49.7%-49.3%, a margin of only 11,384 votes in 2004. In 2016, the Badger State tipped the other way and Donald Trump defeated Hillary Clinton, 47.2%-46.5%, a relatively generous margin of 22,748 votes. Much of the blame for Clinton's loss of a state that had voted Democratic in the previous seven presidential elections was laid on her absentee performance there. The day before the election in 2012, Barack Obama's team staged a huge rally with the president and Bruce Springsteen in Madison. Clinton never returned to the state after her primary loss to Sanders in April. Veteran Democratic pollster Paul Maslin, who is based in Wisconsin, called that lack of attention "political malpractice." As Election Day neared, the Clinton campaign realized the state was a toss-up and pumped some $3 million in ads onto Wisconsin television and radio in the final week. But it was not enough to stem the erosion in the Democratic vote in this vital swing state.

There were a number of factors in Trump's victory, starting with the shift in the vote in Wisconsin's rural and non-metropolitan (and largely white) territory. Among the 34 counties that saw a 10-percentage point decline in the Democratic share of the two-party presidential vote, nearly every one of those counties was in the western half of the state or north of the Fox River Valley. All told, in these counties Clinton received roughly 109,000 fewer votes than Obama did in 2012. The total vote was down by just 4,569 in those counties. President Barack Obama carried 15 of these counties in 2012, and in another six he came within 2.5 percentage points of Mitt Romney. Clinton carried

Milwaukee County with 65 percent of the vote, but garnered roughly 43,600 fewer votes than Obama did in 2012. In the three suburban counties that make up the rest of the Milwaukee metropolitan area — Washington, Ozaukee and Waukesha (the locals refer to these as the WOW counties) — Clinton fared better, cutting the GOP margin from some 132,500 votes scored by Romney in 2012 to roughly 104,500 votes for Trump in 2016.

Clinton's other pockets of strength came in the University Belt stretching from Rock County — home to the University of Wisconsin-Rock County and liberal arts Beloit College — to La Crosse, Eau Claire, and Portage counties, which also have University of Wisconsin systems. But otherwise, Clinton carried only Menominee County, whose borders encompass the Menominee Indian Reservation, and three counties at the northern tip of the state: Ashland, Bayfield and Douglas, along the Gogebic iron range. In addition to the rural territory, Trump carried the Fox River Valley, which includes smaller industrial cities like Appleton, Fond du Lac, Green Bay and Oshkosh. He also won Kenosha and Racine counties with their blue-collar communities, which Obama won in 2012. Votes for third-party or independent candidates and write-ins grew to 188,330 in 2016 compared with 39,483 in 2012. Overall, turnout of eligible voters dipped to 70.5 percent, the lowest since 67.6 percent in 2000.

Wisconsin once had one of the nation's most influential presidential primaries. It knocked Wendell Willkie out of the race in 1944, helped John Kennedy establish his lead over Hubert Humphrey in 1960, prompted Lyndon Johnson to withdraw as Eugene McCarthy was about to beat him here in 1968, gave George McGovern his first victory in 1972, gave Jimmy Carter a key victory in 1976 and chose "New Democrat" Gary Hart over Minnesota neighbor Walter Mondale in 1984. In 2016, the "never Trump" movement coalesced around Texas Sen. Ted Cruz before the April 5 GOP primary. Conservative radio talk show host Charlie Sykes led the charge against Trump. Republican Gov. Scott Walker, who briefly sought his party's nomination, endorsed Cruz and appeared in television spots boosting the Texan's candidacy. It was enough to give Cruz a 48%-35% victory. But Wisconsin would be the last primary or caucus that Trump would lose on his way to the GOP nomination. On the Democratic side, Vermont Sen. Bernie Sanders held multiple rallies across the state and outspent Clinton on television advertising. She stumped primarily in the Milwaukee area. But on the Sunday before the primary she was speaking in black churches in New York City, basically conceding the state. Sanders won 56%-44% and carried 71 of the state's 72 counties. Clinton's lone win was Milwaukee County.

Congressional Districts

116th Congress Lineup	3D 5R	115th Congress Lineup	3D 5R

After Wisconsin lost a district in the 2000 census, the resulting consensus plan enabled all four Democrats and four Republicans running for reelection to win in 2002. The Green Bay-based 8th District has shifted twice since then and has returned to GOP control. Republican Sean Duffy picked up retiring Democrat David Obey's northwestern 7th District. In 2011, Republicans had total control over redistricting. With the state Senate under siege over a petition to oust six members in recall elections, Gov. Scott Walker quietly signed a pro-Republican map into law. The map shored up Duffy, giving him friendly St. Croix County in the Twin Cities exurbs and trading the liberal cities of Stevens Point and Wisconsin Rapids to 3rd District Democrat Ron Kind. It also boosted Republicans Paul Ryan in the 1st District and Tom Petri in the 6th District with an eye toward possible future open seats. In 2012, Republicans won 49 percent of all House votes but kept their 5-3 edge. Republican successors to Ryan and Petri later won with little difficulty.

In 2018, there were two significant developments. Democrat Tony Evers in November defeated Walker's bid for a third term as governor, thus breaking the Republican stranglehold on state governance. And after a three-judge federal panel found that the 2011 GOP plan was an unconstitutional "partisan gerrymander," the Supreme Court in June overturned that ruling and returned the case for further review. That next step likely will be affected by the Supreme Court's expected rulings in the spring of 2019 on alleged partisan gerrymanders in Maryland and North Carolina.

Whatever the dynamics in the courts and in the legislature, Democrats surely will seek at least a fair fight for a fourth seat in the delegation, which could be based in the suburbs and exurbs north and south of Milwaukee. That could place the 1st or the 6th, or both, in play. Although the 5th District, which separates the two other districts, likely will remain safely Republican in the western suburbs, the eventual retirement of veteran Rep. Jim Sensenbrenner could add further complications.

Tony Evers (D)

Elected 2018, term expires 2023, 1st term; b. Nov. 05,1951, Plymouth, WA; University of Wisconsin, Madison, B.A.,1973, M.A., 1976, PhD, 1986; Unknown; Married (Kathy); 3 children.

Elected Office: WI Superintendent, 2009-2019.

Professional Career: Teacher.

Office: 115 E. Capitol, Madison, 53702; 608-266-1212; Fax: 608-267-8983; Website: wisconsin.gov
Lt. Gov.: Mandela Barnes (D) **Atty. Gen:** Josh Kaul (D) **Sec. of State:** Doug La Follette (D)
State Legislature: Senate: 14D, 19R **House:** 36D, 63R

Election Results

Election	Name (Party)	Vote (%)
2018 General	Tony Evers (D)	1,324,307 (50%)
	Scott Walker (R)	1,295,080 (48%)
2018 Primary	Tony Evers (D)	225,082 (42%)
	Mahlon Mitchell (D)	87,926 (16%)
	Kelda Roys (D)	69,086 (13%)
	Kathleen Vinehout (D)	44,168 (8%)
	Michael McCabe (D)	39,885 (7%)
	Matthew Flynn (D)	31,580 (6%)
	Paul Soglin (D)	28,158 (5%)

Wisconsin's Tony Evers achieved one of the biggest Democratic victories of the 2018 midterm elections, ousting two-term Republican Gov. Scott Walker. The low-key career educator and administrator defeated Walker by just over one percentage point. But that was enough to lead a Democratic sweep of statewide offices and vindicate the Democratic argument that Wisconsin was experiencing fatigue from Walker's polarizing tenure. At the same time, the narrowness of Evers' victory reinforced the notion that Wisconsin would be a pivotal state in the 2020 presidential election.

Evers (it rhymes with "weavers") was born in Plymouth and met his wife Kathy there in kindergarten. His father practiced medicine at Rocky Knoll, a state tuberculosis sanitarium that also treated patients with silicosis, a disease often contracted by inhaling factory dust. His father would often testify on his patients' behalf. "It was about social justice," Evers told the New Yorker. "He could have gone into private practice, but he didn't. He decided to be a county employee and work with people who struggled." Evers earned a bachelor's, a master's and a Ph.D. from the University of Wisconsin-Madison and began his career in education as a science teacher in Baraboo, later becoming a principal in Tomah and running school districts in Oakfield and Verona. Eventually, Evers became deputy state superintendent of public instruction; during that time, he fought and beat esophageal cancer. In 2009 Evers was elected state superintendent, a nominally nonpartisan post, and was easily reelected in 2013 and 2017. After he won his third term, Evers began considering a run for governor.

"I realized that if I really wanted to make a difference for these kids in the state, I couldn't rely on this position to do it," he told the New Yorker. "The governor is the one who sets the tone."

The governor in Evers' mind was Walker, who had spent much of his time implementing a muscular conservative agenda. Not long after winning office, Walker called for curtailing collective bargaining rights for many of the state's public employees. Walker became an instant political celebrity – and a target. But Walker's collective bargaining changes survived court challenges and became law. He also signed laws tightening restrictions on abortion, enacted tough voter ID rules and eased restrictions on gun rights. Neither state Senate recall elections nor a recall attempt against Walker could vault Democrats into power; the incumbent notched a 53%-46% victory in the 2012 recall, becoming the first governor anywhere to survive such a vote. Walker won a second term in 2014, then flopped as a presidential candidate two years later, pushed aside by Donald Trump, who remade the party to be more rural and less suburban – a shift that hurt Walker's reelection bid two years later. As Walker's approval numbers sagged, his quest for a third term became a titanic battle in a politically energized and narrowly divided state.

As he prepared for his reelection bid, Walker touted the state's economic gains on his watch. He knew that Democrats were energized and sought to delay special elections in order to give GOP candidates a better shot. After Democrats won a hard-fought judicial race in April 2018, Walker tweeted, "Tonight's results show we are at risk of a #BlueWave in WI. The Far Left is driven by anger & hatred -- we must counter it with optimism & organization. Let's share our positive story with voters & win in November."

The Democratic primary field was larger than any in state history, and it was not predestined that Evers would prevail. His rivals included Mahlon Mitchell, president of the Professional Fire Fighters Association of Wisconsin; former legislator Kelda Roys; state Sen. Kathleen Vinehout; former state Democratic chair Matt Flynn; Madison Mayor Paul Soglin; and activists Mike McCabe and Josh Pade. (Businessman Andy Gronik and state Rep. Dana Wachs quit the race before Election Day.) Mahlon and Roys received support from progressive groups (Roys aired an ad in which she breast-fed her baby) while Evers portrayed himself as a steady pragmatist. In the end, Evers ran away with it, winning 42 percent, ahead of Mitchell (16 percent) and Roys (13 percent). Evers leveraged his decisive primary victory into fundraising gold: In the first nine days after the primary, he raised $1 million, about twice what he had collected in the previous six months.

Education became a major campaign issue. For years, Evers and Walker had tussled over education budgets, higher education politics and legal issues. Walker's sought to portray himself as the "education governor," touting his advocacy for school choice, but his record on school funding was one of consistent cuts for most of his tenure. Evers painted his record on school funding as a negative. Marquette Law School pollster Charles Franklin told The Washington Post that while Wisconsin voters had previously been evenly split between those supporting higher education spending and those backing lower property taxes, voters in 2018 were running at about 60 percent in favor of more education spending and about 35 percent in favor of lower taxes – a promising sign for Evers.

A major issue in the race was a deal Walker had negotiated in 2017 (with President Donald Trump's backing) to subsidize the building of a new, 13,000-employee factory complex in Mt. Pleasant for Foxconn Technology Group, the Taiwanese-based manufacturing partner for such tech giants as Apple, Sony, Microsoft and Nintendo. Trump joined Walker in Wisconsin to break ground, but as time went on – and as more details of the financing became known – voters in the state became less enthusiastic about the project and its cost. Walker and the legislature had approved some $4.5 billion in tax incentives to support the project – reportedly the nation's largest-ever subsidy for a foreign company. The nonpartisan Legislative Fiscal Bureau projected that a return on that investment might come as late as 2042.

Both candidates were charismatically challenged – Madison's newspaper, the Capital Times called the race "bland vs. bland" – but they differed sharply on policy. Evers backed driver's licenses and in-state tuition for undocumented residents, while Walker attacked Democratic-backed proposals for reforming the criminal justice system, saying in front of photographs of violent criminals, "I want to keep them in for their full terms." Evers, meanwhile, took Walker to task for supporting repeal of the Affordable Care Act. Several ex-Walker aides endorsed Evers, and national political figures flocked to campaign in the state – Trump, former President Barack Obama, former Vice President Joe Biden and a bevy of potential 2020 Democratic presidential candidates.

The result was in doubt until late absentee returns from Milwaukee County sealed the contest for Evers, 49.5%-48.4% -- a margin of just over 29,000 votes. Walker got 35,000 more votes than he had in 2014, but the Democratic nominee amassed more than 200,000 more votes than his predecessor.

Evers improved the Democratic showing in two key strongholds -- Milwaukee County, with 31,000 extra votes, and Dane County (Madison), with 44,115 additional votes. Walker bled support in the Republican bastions of suburban Milwaukee. In Waukesha County, his 45-point margin in 2014 shrank to 33 points in 2018; in Ozaukee County, his winning margin shrunk from 41 points to 27; and in Washington County, it shrunk from 53 points to 45. "Exit polls showed Walker lost ground with at least two key groups of voters compared with his 2014 re-election victory," the Milwaukee Journal-Sentinel's Craig Gilbert wrote. "One was independents. Walker had won independents in each of his three statewide victories, including the recall, by margins ranging from 9 to 14 points. But in the 2018 exit poll, he was trailing among independents by 7 points. A second group was college graduates. Walker won voters with college degrees by 1 point in 2014, according to the exit poll that year. He was losing them by 13 points this year."

The skirmishing didn't end on Election Day. To the outrage of the victorious Democrats, Republicans in a lame-duck session sought to tie Evers' hands as much as possible. Walker signed legislation that, among other things, hampered Evers' ability to modify the Walker-created Wisconsin Economic Development Corp.; made it harder for Evers and the newly elected Democratic attorney general, Josh Kaul, to withdraw from the anti-Affordable Care Act lawsuit; and placed tighter limits on early voting. Evers challenged the new legislation in court, and those battles played out for months; he also sought to expand Medicaid under the health care law despite Republican opposition. Meanwhile, in April 2019, the Legislative Fiscal Bureau brought unwelcome budget news with an estimate that the state could face a shortfall of almost $2 billion in the 2021-23 fiscal years.

Ron Johnson (R)

Elected 2010, term expires 2022, 2nd term, b. Apr 08, 1955; Mankato, MN; University of Minnesota, B.S., 1977; University of Minnesota, 1979; Lutheran; Married (Jane Johnson); 3 children; 2 grandchildren.

Professional Career: Owner, PACUR; Accountant, Josten's.

DC Office: 328 HSOB 20510, 202-224-5323, Fax: 202-228-6965, ronjohnson.senate.gov

State Offices: Madison, 608-240-9629; Milwaukee, 414-276-7282; Oshkosh, 920-230-7250.

Committees: *Budget. Commerce, Science & Transportation*: Communications, Technology, Innovation & the Internet; Manufacturing, Trade & Consumer Protection; Subcommittee on Science, Oceans, Fisheries & Weather; Subcommittee on Security. *Foreign Relations*: Africa & Global Health Policy; East Asia, the Pacific & International Cybersecurity Policy; Europe & Regional Security Cooperation (Chmn). *Homeland Security & Government Affairs (Chmn)*: Ex Officio membership on all subcommittees.

Group Ratings

	ADA	ACLU	AFL-CIO	LCV	ITI	COC	HAFA	ACU	CFG	FRC
2018	-	14%	-	0%	-	80%	86%	95%	93%	100%
2017	0%	C	0%	0%	C	86%	C	80%	91%	100%

Almanac Ratings 2017-18

	Economy	Social	Foreign	Composite
Liberal	0%	0%	0%	0%
Conservative	100%	100%	100%	100%

Key Votes of the 115th Congress

1. Obama-care revision	Y	5. Gun regulations	Y	9. Kavanaugh confirmation	Y
2. Tax Cuts	Y	6. Family planning regs	Y	10. Saudi arms sales	N
3. Dodd-Frank revision	Y	7. Gorsuch confirmation	Y	11. FISA rules	Y
4. Omnibus appropriations	N	8. Immigration restrictions	Y	12. Military aid in Yemen	N

Election Results

Election	Name (Party)	Vote (%)	Cand. Spent	Ind. Exp. Support	Ind. Exp. Oppose
2016 General	Ron Johnson (R)............................. 1,479,471	(50%)	$27,590,817	$2,187,944	$8,418,011
	Russ Feingold (D)........................ ... 1,380,335	(47%)	$25,190,356	$1,565,370	$16,527,845
	Phil Anderson (L)................................. 87,531	(3%)			
2016 Primary	Ron Johnson (R)............................ Unopposed				

Prior winning percentages: 2010 (52%)

Republican Ron Johnson, Wisconsin's senior senator, has twice defeated former Democratic Sen. Russ Feingold. With his business background, Johnson has shown independence on Senate legislation and in dealing with President Donald Trump. He has left open whether he will seek reelection in 2022

Johnson grew up in Mankato, Minnesota. He said he developed a strong work ethic at an early age, delivering newspapers, caddying at a golf course and baling hay on his uncle's dairy farm. He was a restaurant dishwasher at 15 and within a year won a promotion to night manager. Although Johnson didn't finish high school, he attended college, working full time and graduating with $7,000 in the bank. While working as an accountant, Johnson went to night school to earn an MBA. Just short of a degree in 1979, he decided to move to Oshkosh to start a plastics company, PACUR, with his brother-in-law. Their first customer was a company co-founded by his father-in-law. Since then, the business has become a major producer of specialty packaging for medical devices, employing about 120 workers. Johnson has said his political views have been influenced by Ayn Rand's 1957 novel "Atlas Shrugged," which argues that civilization cannot exist when people are slaves to society and government.

Johnson said that his motivation to run against Feingold was the senator's support of the Democrats' 2010 health care overhaul, which he called "the single greatest assault to our freedom in my lifetime." He entered the race in May, just days before the Republican State Convention. Three GOP candidates were already competing, including beer mogul and former state Commerce Secretary Dick Leinenkugel and Madison developer Terrence Wall. Johnson's ability to self-finance had an immediate effect. At the convention, Leinenkugel surprised everyone, including Johnson, by taking his turn at the lectern to drop out and endorse Johnson, saying, "It's not my time ... it's Ron Johnson's time." Wall reluctantly followed suit. Spending more than $4 million of his own money, Johnson went on to crush businessman Dave Westlake in the September primary.

The campaign between Johnson and Feingold — a liberal with a quirky, maverick streak — was nasty. Without a legislative record of his opponent to mine, Feingold sought to concentrate on Johnson's record in business, attempting to depict him as someone more concerned about profits than people — someone "with a country club view of reality." Feingold also called Johnson a hypocrite for opposing federal economic stimulus funds and then allegedly seeking those funds for renovation of an opera house. Johnson fought back, noting in an ad that the Senate had 57 lawyers, including Feingold, but just one accountant and no manufacturers like himself. Johnson's GOP allies depicted the incumbent as an entrenched Washington insider who supported deficit spending. Feingold had $21 million to Johnson's $15 million, but it was not enough in a Republican wave year. Johnson won 52% to 47%.

In 2011, Johnson did not support Wisconsin Republican Rep. Paul Ryan's budget plan to slash the deficit and transform Medicare, arguing that Ryan's proposal did not cut spending enough. Johnson blocked a resolution to support military action in Libya as a way of calling attention to debt reduction, saying on the floor that the debt is "the single most important issue facing this nation." In December 2011, Johnson launched a bid for a Senate Republican leadership post as conference vice chairman. The race was a classic outsider-vs.-insider battle, with Johnson the maverick running against the establishment candidate: Roy Blunt of Missouri. The conference selected Blunt over Johnson, 25-22.

Johnson has been blunt; one of his strategists, Brad Todd, has described him as "straight as a shot of uncut whiskey." He drew attention for grilling outgoing Secretary of State Hillary Clinton at a Foreign Relations Committee hearing in January 2013 on the deadly terrorist attack at the U.S. consulate in Benghazi, Libya. Johnson complained that lawmakers had been "misled" about the attack. When Clinton said it would have been inappropriate to contact diplomatic staff for details immediately afterward because the FBI was investigating, he replied, "I realize that's a good excuse." An exasperated Clinton retorted: "No, it's a fact. ... What difference, at this point, does it make?"

The footage of her incensed answer was unspooled repeatedly by conservatives during the 2016 presidential campaign to remind voters of Clinton's biggest foreign policy blemish.

Johnson occasionally has drawn attention for emphasizing pragmatism over political purity. When he became chairman of the Homeland Security and Governmental Affairs Committee in 2015, he became more engaged with domestic security issues. He won Senate passage of the Integrated Public Alert and Warning System Modernization Act of 2015, and he distanced himself from the tea party. "I sprang out of the tea party movement, no question," he told National Journal, but he emphasized, "I've never joined any kind of tea party caucus or tea party group."

The rematch with Feingold became a marquee Senate race in 2016. For much of Johnson's re-election campaign, polls showed Feingold was the front-runner. The widespread assumption was Feingold would do better in a presidential election year than a low-turnout midterm year. Johnson regrouped in September with help from his older brother, Dean, a veteran television executive producer and host and a new team of consultants. They took the gloves off against Feingold, relentlessly attacking him as a creature of Washington and painting Johnson in softer hues; they highlighted Johnson's work with the Joseph Project, a faith-oriented jobs program. Johnson targeted small, rural towns and worked to boost turnout in traditionally Republican areas that were lagging.

Johnson won 74,000 more votes than Trump did, and he defeated Feingold by 3 percentage points. Johnson's wider margin than Trump in the state can be traced chiefly to the "WOW" counties in the Milwaukee suburbs — Washington, Ozaukee and Waukesha. These counties are historically Republican, but their relatively high education and income levels made them less fertile ground for Trump's message. Johnson, a more conventional Republican, took a larger share of the GOP vote. In Ozaukee, Johnson won 65 percent of the vote; Trump took 57 percent. In Waukesha, Johnson nabbed 68 percent, while Trump won 61 percent. And in Washington County, Johnson garnered 72 percent, while Trump got 68 percent.

A significant ramification of Johnson's victory was his unhappiness that Senate Republicans — including Majority Leader Mitch McConnell — had apparently abandoned his campaign before his late comeback. "This has been a long-stewing simmer for him, and after they cut him loose, he was like, 'Screw them, I owe them nothing,'" the Daily Beast reported in June 2017, citing an anonymous Republican source.

After the elections, Johnson urged leveraging the newly all-Republican-controlled federal government to enact a conservative agenda. He complained that McConnell and other GOP senators did not push more aggressively. "Let's face it, the vast majority of members of Congress, their primary motivation is getting elected and unfortunately it's about maintaining majorities. But to what end?" Johnson told the Washington Examiner in October 2017. "We need leadership on these big issues. … We didn't get it with health care."

The Senate's failure to repeal the Affordable Care Act in 2017 was a sore spot for Johnson. He became a reluctant supporter of the limited repeal that McConnell presented to the Senate after extended closed-door negotiations in the Capitol. Johnson was especially unhappy that McConnell had bowed to pressure from other Republicans to defer cuts in Medicaid spending. During a meeting with business leaders in Green Bay in July 2017, Johnson said, "If our leader is basically saying, 'Don't worry about it, we've designed it so that these reforms will never take effect,' first of all, that's a pretty significant breach of trust," the Green Bay Press Gazette reported. He also complained about how McConnell crafted the alternative. "I kind of had to muscle my way into that core working group," he said. "I was shocked at the process. There was no information. Very little. It was the last step in the process. It doesn't surprise me that the result is far from what I'd like to see."

A few days later, when McConnell called for a Senate vote on his last-ditch alternative, the "skinny repeal," Johnson initially said that the plan would be "rather unsatisfying from my standpoint." Johnson subsequently had an unpleasant showdown with McConnell on the Senate floor before he reluctantly agreed to vote for the alternative. In the end, the opposition of three moderate Republicans torpedoed the deal.

Johnson continued his independence later in 2017 during debate of the Republican tax cuts. In the days before the Senate vote, he said he opposed the bill because it favored large companies over small businesses. He cited his own experience in the corporate world to complain that the Senate "doesn't understand numbers" in the tax bill, The Washington Post reported. Ultimately, Johnson said that he would vote for the bill after he secured changes to adjust the tax breaks for businesses. "No major piece of legislation is ever perfect. But this bill is a significant improvement over our current tax system," Johnson said.

As chairman of the Homeland Security Committee, he clashed with other Republicans over cybersecurity legislation. Johnson or his committee aides "have derailed many of the most significant cybersecurity-related bills in the past four years," Politico reported in February 2019. His objections often resulted from his opposition to excessive government regulation of business. Johnson's committee "is the place where legislation goes to die on cybersecurity," a national security expert told Politico. Aides to Johnson defended his work as chairman, including approval of legislation on federal procurement and reorganization of the Homeland Security Department.

Johnson voiced repeated concerns about Trump's tariffs and said Congress should consider restricting his authority to take unilateral actions. Of the trade war resulting from the tariffs Trump had levied on Chinese imports, he said, "There's some real damage being done" to companies, including in Wisconsin, The Associated Press reported in July 2018. Asked by CNN in April 2018 whether he would support Trump's re-election, Johnson said that it was "way too early to be talking about 2020."

During his 2016 campaign, Johnson announced that he would not run again in 2022. That became another explanation for his increased independence. GOP term-limit rules would force him to step down as Homeland Security Committee chairman after the 2020 elections — if Republicans retain Senate control. In May 2019, he reopened the door to a possible statewide contest in 2022, which could be a campaign for governor.

Tammy Baldwin (D)

Elected 2012, term expires 2024, 2nd term, b. Feb 11, 1962; Madison; Smith College (MA), A.B., 1984; University of Wisconsin Law School, J.D., 1989; Religion not stated; Single.

Elected Office: Dane County Board of Supervisors, 1986-1994; WI Assembly, 1992-1998; U.S. House, 1998-2012.

Professional Career: Practicing attorney, 1989-1992.

DC Office: 709 HSOB 20510, 202-224-5653, Fax: 202-224-9787, baldwin.senate.gov

State Offices: Ashland, 715-450-3754; Eau Claire, 715-832-8424; Green Bay, 920-498-2668; La Crosse, 608-796-0045; Madison, 608-264-5338; Milwaukee, 414-297-4451; Wausau, 715-261-2611.

Committees: Senate Democratic Conference Secretary. *Appropriations*: Agriculture, Rural Development, FDA & Related Agencies; Department of Defense; Department of Homeland Security; DOL, HHS & Education & Related Agencies; Military Construction & Veteran Affairs & Related Agencies. *Commerce, Science & Transportation*: Communications, Technology, Innovation & the Internet; Manufacturing, Trade & Consumer Protection; Subcommittee on Science, Oceans, Fisheries & Weather (RMM); Subcommittee on Transportation & Safety. *Health, Education, Labor & Pensions*: Employment & Workplace Safety (RMM); Primary Health & Retirement Security.

Group Ratings

	ADA	ACLU	AFL-CIO	LCV	ITI	COC	HAFA	ACU	CFG	FRC
2018	-	75%	-	100%	-	60%	3%	5%	5%	0%
2017	100%	C	100%	100%	C	29%	C	0%	4%	0%

Almanac Ratings 2017-18

	Economy	Social	Foreign	Composite
Liberal	93%	93%	86%	91%
Conservative	7%	7%	14%	9%

Key Votes of the 115th Congress

1. Obama-care revision	N	5. Gun regulations	N	9. Kavanaugh confirmation	N
2. Tax Cuts	N	6. Family planning regs	N	10. Saudi arms sales	Y
3. Dodd-Frank revision	N	7. Gorsuch confirmation	N	11. FISA rules	N
4. Omnibus appropriations	Y	8. Immigration restrictions	N	12. Military aid in Yemen	Y

Election Results

Election	Name (Party)	Vote (%)	Cand. Spent	Ind. Exp. Support	Ind. Exp. Oppose
2018 General	Tammy Baldwin (D)...................... ... 1,472,914	(55%)	$29,105,509	$3,727,282	$8,728,234
	Leah Vukmir (R)............................ 1,184,885	(45%)	$5,594,610	$1,886,430	$3,553,187
2018 Primary	Tammy Baldwin (D)...................	(100%)			

Prior winning percentages: 2012 (51%); House: 2010 (62%), 2008 (69%), 2006 (63%), 2004 (63%), 2002 (66%), 2000 (51%), 1998 (53%)

Democrat Tammy Baldwin of Wisconsin is the first openly gay member of the Senate and the first woman elected to the chamber from Wisconsin. After her initial close election in 2012 over former Gov. Tommy Thompson, she was re-elected easily in 2018 — a notable accomplishment in her polarized home state. In the Senate, she has focused on issues dealing with health, education and innovation and has had a strongly liberal voting record.

Baldwin grew up in Madison, where she was raised mostly by her maternal grandparents, a University of Wisconsin biochemist and the theater department's head costume designer. Her mother, who was 19 and a UW student when Baldwin was born, was "in the middle of a divorce and overwhelmed," Baldwin told The New York Times, adding that her mother had long battles with pain and addiction. "My grandparents were there, and I'm very, very grateful." Baldwin graduated first in her class at Madison West High School and went on to Smith College and UW law school. It was in college that it became "very clear" she was a lesbian.

Baldwin detailed her mother's health problems in 2018 for the first time, according to local news reports. Her mother had mental and physical illnesses, including pain for which she was prescribed narcotics. "At times in her life, she was addicted to the prescribed medication and she did not follow doctors' orders," the Appleton Post Crescent quoted Baldwin as saying in May 2018 after the senator participated in a roundtable about addiction. "She went through recovery and treatment multiple times." Her mother, Pamela Joan Bin-Rella, eventually got a master's degree and was a social worker. She died in August 2017 at 75. A week after the roundtable, Baldwin ran a campaign ad about her family history.

In 1986, at 24 and while in law school, Baldwin was elected to the Board of Supervisors of Dane County, which encompasses Madison. In 1992, she was elected to the Wisconsin State Assembly. Six years later, when moderate Republican Scott Klug honored his promise to serve only four terms in the House, Baldwin got into the race, along with three other Democrats and six Republicans. As a woman who favored abortion rights, she was supported by EMILY's List, which helped her raise about a quarter of her $1.5 million campaign chest. Baldwin won with 37 percent of the vote; then, in the general election, she beat former state Insurance Commissioner Jo Musser. This made her the first openly gay nonincumbent to win a seat in the House.

Baldwin's voting record was consistently one of the most liberal in the House. She secured a coveted seat on the Energy and Commerce Committee. With the chamber in Republican hands for 10 of her 14 years in the House, her ability to accomplish many of her progressive goals was limited. She was sharply critical of many GOP proposals and polices, including the budget proposed by Wisconsin Rep. Paul Ryan and Gov. Scott Walker's move to limit collective bargaining rights for state workers, an effort that touched off a recall campaign against Walker.

Baldwin's driving issue has been guaranteed health care for all Americans. The issue was personal: A serious illness, similar to spinal meningitis, kept her in the hospital for three months when she was a child, making her a patient with a pre-existing condition. Because she was living with her grandparents, they were unable to include her on their health insurance coverage and were forced to pay large costs for her medical care. Baldwin supported the Affordable Care Act even though it did not include a government-run "public option" to compete with private insurers, a provision she had favored.

Baldwin was a leading advocate for allowing same-sex marriages. In 2008, she and Massachusetts Democrat Barney Frank, another openly gay lawmaker, established the Congressional LGBT Equality Caucus. Baldwin told The New York Times that in the House, "I did a lot of sitting down with Republicans to talk about these bills. Often there was a real sort of intimacy in those conversations. People talked about gay brothers or a child who was gay, lesbian or transgender. I can't tell you how many of those stories I accumulated. I think I moved a number of my colleagues, and I think it at least caused a lot of internal conflict for those I didn't move." Baldwin is also one of a handful of lawmakers who haven't specified a religious affiliation. "They didn't let me put the phrase, 'It's complicated,' as Facebook might have," she told the Times.

Baldwin ran for the Senate when Democrat Herb Kohl retired after four terms. She was unchallenged in the Democratic primary, giving her ample time to organize her campaign and raise money. Thompson, a popular former governor known as a pragmatic conservative, won the GOP primary against three more conservative candidates and started with a lead over Baldwin in the general election campaign. But Baldwin and her allies outspent Thompson and his backers by 3-1 in the weeks after the primary, and the race got ugly.

Baldwin ran a disciplined campaign, seeking to convince voters that she would be more attuned to the needs of Wisconsin than the 70-year-old Thompson, a former Health and Human Services secretary under George W. Bush who hadn't been a candidate for office in 14 years. Realizing it made little sense to attack Thompson's gubernatorial record, which many Wisconsinites of both parties remembered fondly, Baldwin instead blasted Thompson with negative television ads about his post-gubernatorial career, highlighting his work for a Washington, D.C., lobbying firm. Meanwhile, Thompson and Republicans accused Baldwin of being a radical, but she downplayed her liberal views and highlighted her populist stands against China's trade policies and her efforts at bipartisanship. As the race neared its conclusion, Thompson veered to the right — he told a tea party group that he wanted to "do away with the Medicare and Medicaid," a stark departure from his previous positions — but the maneuver rang hollow with many swing voters. Baldwin won 51% to 46%.

In the Senate, Baldwin has continued to vote on a consistently liberal line, almost always taking the opposite stance from the state's senior senator, conservative Republican Ron Johnson. That has made Wisconsin one of the few remaining states with two senators of strongly divergent views. Craig Gilbert noted in the Milwaukee Journal Sentinel that Baldwin and Johnson split over the Affordable Care Act, fast-track trade authority for the president, the Keystone XL pipeline, gun control, immigration, the minimum wage and a host of other issues. A rare point of unison, Gilbert found, was a shared vote in favor of ensuring same-sex spouses have access to Social Security and veterans' benefits.

Baldwin worked with fellow Rust Belt Democratic Sens. Sherrod Brown of Ohio and Bob Casey of Pennsylvania to insert a "Buy America" provision in a major water resources bill, and she introduced a measure to end the carried-interest tax loophole that benefits hedge fund managers. After the Pulse nightclub shootings in Orlando, Florida, in 2016, Baldwin worked to make sure that LGBT concerns related to the site were not overlooked in the rush to discuss gun violence and terrorism. "They needed someone on the floor to come and say, 'This is all of these things. Do not just sweep away the hate crime aspect of it — give these people's lives, give them a voice," she told Glamour magazine. Baldwin was also among the leaders working to lift a longstanding Food and Drug Administration ban on men who've had sex with other men from donating blood. Language authored by Baldwin made it into the Comprehensive Addiction and Recovery Act signed by President Barack Obama in 2016. A strong supporter of Hillary Clinton in the 2016 Democratic presidential primary, Baldwin was reportedly among three dozen people considered for the vice presidential slot that eventually went to Virginia Sen. Tim Kaine.

Baldwin took an increased role in the health care debate. She co-sponsored in October 2017 the "Medicare for All" proposal filed by Sen. Bernie Sanders. "It would expand coverage to all the uninsured; make health care more affordable for working, middle-class families; and reduce growing prescription drug costs for taxpayers," she said. In October 2018, she voiced opposition to a Trump administration regulation on short-term health insurance plans that she said could hurt patients with pre-existing conditions. She demanded a Senate vote to veto the regulation, which she called "junk insurance." Her resolution was defeated on a 50-50 tie vote.

In 2017, Baldwin received an assignment in the Senate Democratic leadership: conference secretary. With a re-election campaign looming, she faced a balancing act between her party's drift to the left and her state's status as a linchpin of Donald Trump's presidential victory in 2016. She opposed more Trump nominees than most other Trump-state Democrats who were up for re-election in 2018. But back home, she emphasized more populist themes such as improving trade deals and lowering the cost of prescription drugs. Baldwin faced a competitive challenge in her politically polarized state. She got a break when two of the highest-profile Republicans who could have run opted against entering the race.

As was the case during her 2012 election, Baldwin benefited from a hard-fought contest among Republicans that was not resolved until the August primary. The chief contenders were state Sen. Leah Vukmir and Kevin Nicholson, an Iraq veteran and a former president of College Democrats of America who evolved in his political views. Vukmir was backed by most Republican leaders in

Wisconsin, including Walker. Nicholson had support from the Club for Growth and Steve Bannon, a former top aide to Trump. Vukmir won the primary 49%-43%, with three other candidates splitting the remainder. Meanwhile, conservative groups spent millions of dollars in ads attacking Baldwin. But she and her allies had even more money to respond and defend her record with key constituencies, including rural voters. She avoided discussing Trump.

In the general election, Baldwin had the wind at her back. The national mood favored Democrats, Vukmir was little-known beyond rank-and-file Republicans and the intense focus on Walker's bid for a third term worked in her favor. Vukmir embraced Trump. In her closing ads, Baldwin highlighted Vukmir's record in the Legislature in which she repeatedly voted against health care services. Baldwin spent more than $29 million, while Vulkmir spent $5.6 million for the entire campaign, including her primary.

Baldwin won 55%-45%. "Wisconsin voters went with Baldwin, a familiar figure who has been in public life for decades and has now built a personal brand that plays well around the state," the Journal Sentinel wrote.

Bryan Steil (R)

Elected 2018, 1st term, b. Mar 03, 1981; Janesville; Georgetown University (DC), B.S., 2003; University of Wisconsin, J.D., 2007; Catholic; Single.

Professional Career: Congressional Staffer; Attorney

DC Office: 1408 LHOB 20515, 202-225-3031, steil.house.gov

State Offices: Janesville, 608-752-4050.

Committees: *Financial Services*: Housing, Community Development & Insurance; Oversight & Investigations; Subcommittee on Diversity & Inclusion.

Election Results

Election	Name (Party)	Vote (%)		Cand. Spent	Ind. Exp. Support	Ind. Exp. Oppose
2018 General	Bryan Steil (R)	177,492	(55%)	$2,248,581	$40,001	
	Randy Bryce (D)	137,508	(42%)	$8,399,701	$436,440	$2,783,979
	Ken Yorgan (I)	10,006	(3%)			
2018 Primary	Bryan Steil (R)	30,885	(52%)			
	Nick Polce (R)	8,948	(15%)			
	Paul Nehlen (R)	6,638	(11%)			
	Kevin Steen (R)	6,262	(11%)			
	Jeremy Ryan (R)	6,226	(10%)			

Freshman Republican Bryan Steil in 2018 won a contest that received more than the customary attention, largely because he sought to succeed Republican Rep. Paul Ryan, who retired following three years as House Speaker and 20 years in the House. Steil had extensive political experience, as both a protégé of Ryan and a member of the Board of Regents of the University of Wisconsin. Democratic opponent Randy Bryce, a blue-collar ironworker, became a nationwide fundraising sensation among progressives when he announced his challenge before Ryan had retired. Both were first-time candidates, though Bryce eventually suffered from his inexperience.

Steil, like Ryan, was a native of Janesville, where their two families had close ties. He got his bachelor's degree from the business school at Georgetown University and a law degree from the University of Wisconsin. He was a legislative aide to Ryan in Washington. As an attorney with an expertise in business law, Steil worked for Regal Beloit Corp. and was general counsel for Wisconsin-based Charter NEX Films, which describes itself as "North America's leading independent producer of high-performance specialty polyethylene films used in flexible packaging." In 2016, Gov. Scott Walker appointed Steil to the Board of Regents, which had become controversial as it imposed major changes that Walker and his legislative allies made at the university.

When Ryan announced his retirement in April 2018, several prominent Republicans turned down invitations to run for his seat — including former White House chief of staff Reince Priebus and Assembly Speaker Robin Vos, the Milwaukee Journal Sentinel reported. Steil stepped forward and described himself as "a problem solver," based on his nine years in manufacturing. Downplaying his close ties to Ryan, and career politicians generally, he said that he would take on "the chattering class in Washington."

Steil faced five other candidates in the Republican primary. They included Paul Nehlen, who echoed the harsh criticism that he voiced about Ryan on immigration and international trade when he challenged him in the 2016 primary; Ryan won that contest, 84%-16%. Another opponent was Nick Polce, who served in the Army Special Forces and said that government had grown too large. Steil spent far more money than his opponents combined and won the primary with 52 percent of the vote; Polce was second, with 15 percent.

When Bryce initially took on Ryan, he unveiled a two-minute video that featured his blue-collar background, military service and success in battling cancer. He supported "Medicare for All," and an increase in the minimum wage to $15 per hour. His message to Ryan was: "You can come work the iron, and I'll go to D.C." With the resulting burst of attention, Bryce gained national media attention and raised more than $6 million prior to the Democratic primary. In a profile, the New Yorker reported that for many of his supporters, Bryce's "greatest appeal is that he is an ordinary worker, like them."

Other publications tracked down problems in Bryce's life, including his bankruptcy, delinquency in child-support payments to his ex-wife and nine arrests. Bryce's brother, a local police officer, criticized him and endorsed Steil. Bryce got 60 percent of the vote in the Democratic primary against Cathy Myers, a school-board member in Janesville.

During the closing weeks of the campaign, Steil largely drew the contrast with Bryce on their policy views, though outside groups ran ads that cited Bryce's personal problems. At local appearances with Ryan, Steil embraced his patron's easygoing demeanor and approach to the job. Despite tension between Ryan and President Donald Trump, Steil won 55%-42%, with big majorities in the Waukesha and Milwaukee parts of the district.

WI-1: Southeast Wisconsin   Cook Partisan Voting Index: R+5

Population		Race and Ethnicity		Income	
Total	716,303	White	80.8%	Median Income	$62,769
Land area (sq. miles)	1,728	Black	5.4%	District Income Rank	151
Pop/ sq mi	414.6	Latino	9.7%	Poverty Rate	10.4%
Born in State	67.5%	Asian	1.8%	With health insurance	93.7%
		Two or more races	1.8%	Cash public assistance	2.5%
Age Groups		Other	0.4%	Food stamp/SNAP	12%
Under 18	23.2%				
18-34	20%	**Education**		**Work**	
35-64	41.7%	H.S grad or less	39.5%	White Collar	15.1%
Over 64	15.1%	Some college	32.5%	Sales and Service	39.8%
		College Degree, 4 yr	18.6%	Blue Collar	25.2%
Military		Post grad	9.5%	Government	10.8%
Veteran/ Active Duty	8.3%				

2012 Pres. Vote	Romney	195,835	(52%)	Obama	179,872	(47%)		
2016 Pres. Vote	Trump	187,372	(52%)	Clinton	150,436	(42%)	Johnson	12,926	(4%)

Janesville, Kenosha: The southern tier of Wisconsin, from Lake Michigan to the Rock River Valley, has been some of America's prime industrial country. Settled by Yankee and German farmers 170 years ago, it was once primarily dairy land. By the early 20th century, the steady habits and high skills of the local dairy farmers had made them a good labor pool for factories. There are still major plants here, including the headquarters of S.C. Johnson in Racine, with its Frank Lloyd Wright-designed tower. But the collapse of the domestic auto industry had a powerful impact on the local economy. In 2008, General Motors closed its Janesville plant, laying off more than 5,000 workers, and in 2010 Chrysler shuttered its Kenosha plant, which once employed 14,000.

Local innovation remains alive. Kenosha, once primarily a factory town, has undergone a transformation, with some of the old smokestacks and shipyards along its lakefront replaced with museums, a marina, restaurants and boutiques that attract Chicagoans on weekends. Kenosha has competed with other towns in the region in trying to lure Chicago businesses north with lower tax rates. In 2017, Foxconn Technology, the Chinese company that manufactures screens for Apple phones, said that it was planning a $10 billion campus in Racine County, which initially was expected to hire 13,000 workers — a decision that was hailed by President Donald Trump and then-Gov. Scott Walker, who helped to secure $4 billion in state incentives. When a Foxconn official suggested in January 2019 that the company was considering turning that site into a research facility, Trump spoke to the company's chairman, who reportedly gave reassurances of its more expansive plans — though details remained uncertain. German candymaker Haribo planned a $242 million plant in Pleasant Prairie to produce gummy bears, with an accompanying museum and retail store; completion of the first phase was planned for 2020. Some old lake resorts continue to thrive, most notably on Lake Geneva, long a favorite weekend getaway for residents of Chicagoland. In nearby Williams Bay is the University of Chicago's historic Yerkes Observatory, one of the nation's largest astronomy research centers.

The 1st Congressional District of Wisconsin runs from Lake Michigan west to Janesville in the eastern part of Rock County and encompasses all of Racine and Kenosha counties on Lake Michigan as well as parts of Walworth County, including Lake Geneva. Janesville is the home of former House Speaker Paul Ryan. The 1st takes in the southern Milwaukee County suburbs of Oak Creek and Greenfield and the southern tier of townships in suburban Waukesha County, including New Berlin.

The district has been a competitive battleground. In 2008, Obama led, 51%-48%. Boosted a bit by Ryan's presence on the ticket, Mitt Romney in 2012 took the District, 52%-47%. Donald Trump doubled that margin, with his 52%-42% win in the 1st. Kenosha and Racine counties are the swing areas. Waukesha County is heavily Republican. Rock County gave Obama 61 percent of the vote in 2012. Four years later, Hillary Clinton won Rock with 52 percent. Though the overall change in four years was significant in the 1st, each of the four districts in the northern part of Wisconsin had a larger shift toward the GOP in 2016.

Mark Pocan (D)

Elected 2012, 4th term, b. Aug 14, 1964; Kenosha; University of Wisconsin - Madison, B.A., 1986; Married (Philip Frank).

Elected Office: Dane County Board of Supervisors, 1991-1996; WI Assembly, 1998-2012.

Professional Career: Owner, Budget Signs & Specialties, 1988-present; Public-relations specialist, WI Realtors Association, 1986-1988.

DC Office: 1421 LHOB 20515, 202-225-2906, Fax: 202-225-6942, pocan.house.gov

State Offices: Beloit, 608-365-8001; Madison, 608-258-9800.

Committees: *Appropriations*: Agriculture, Rural Development, FDA & Related Agencies; Energy & Water Development & Related Agencies; Labor, Health & Human Services, Education & Related Agencies. *Select Committee on the Modernization of Congress.*

Group Ratings

	ADA	ACLU	AFL-CIO	LCV	ITI	COC	HAFA	ACU	CFG	FRC
2018	-	93%	-	100%	-	50%	6%	4%	15%	0%
2017	85%	C	97%	89%	C	38%	C	4%	0%	0%

Almanac Ratings 2017-18

	Economy	Social	Foreign	Composite
Liberal	97%	94%	99%	96%
Conservative	3%	6%	1%	4%

Key Votes of the 115th Congress

1. Obama-care revision	N	5. Family planning regs	N	9. Guantanamo prisoners	Y
2. Tax Cuts	NV	6. Body cameras/immigration	Y	10. Ground missiles, limit	Y
3. Omnibus appropriations	N	7. Abortion ban	N	11. Defense Dept. spending	N
4. Dodd-Frank revision	N	8. Concealed carry	NV	12. FISA rules	N

Election Results

Election	Name (Party)	Vote (%)	Cand. Spent	Ind. Exp. Support	Ind. Exp. Oppose
2018 General	Mark Pocan (D)................................ 309,116 (100%)		$603,306		
2018 Primary	Mark Pocan (D)... (100%)				

Prior winning percentages: 2016 (69%), 2014 (68%), 2012 (68%)

Democrat Mark Pocan, elected in 2012, has gained influence in the House as co-chair of the Progressive Caucus, where he has worked with others to demand action by party leaders. He also has shown insider skills as a member of the Appropriations Committee. Like his predecessor Tammy Baldwin, who was elected to the Senate, Pocan is openly gay. He has taken up many of her issues, plus her outspoken advocacy.

Pocan was born and raised in Kenosha, the child of two small-business owners. Pocan's father served on the Kenosha City Council, and as a kid Pocan campaigned with him. At the University of Wisconsin, Pocan said, "I started out as a poli-sci major until I took my first poli-sci class that talked about the Ottoman Empire and not political campaigns. So I decided to switch" to journalism. After graduating, he opened a Madison-based print shop. Around that time, Pocan dealt with personal trauma. After leaving a gay bar one night, he was physically assaulted by two men and needed stitches. "That was kind of a turning point because after that happened, that's when I got very active with a number of LGBT nonprofits," he said. Since gay marriage was not legal in Wisconsin in 2006, Pocan married in Canada.

In 1991, Pocan won a seat on the Dane County Board of Supervisors. He spent 14 years in the state Assembly, where he succeeded Baldwin for the first time. He co-chaired the influential Joint Finance Committee. Pocan helped expand health care coverage for children and extend domestic-partner benefits for gay couples. Milwaukee Magazine named him "best legislator" in 2009. In an acrimonious contest for Baldwin's congressional seat, Pocan's chief rival was Kelda Helen Roys, also a Madison-area state representative. Pocan had support from unions and much of the party establishment, plus a roughly 2-to-1 fundraising advantage. Roys attacked him for compromising with Republicans and for taking money from political action committees. Pocan did not back away from his image as a strong progressive willing to work across the aisle. "There are those who scream and holler and put out a press release," he told the Wisconsin State Journal. "I decided I wanted to be the kind that gets things done." Pocan won 72%-22%. In the general election, he again won easily .

In the Republican-controlled House, Pocan sought opportunities for bipartisanship. He and conservative Republican Rep. Glenn Grothman of Wisconsin pursued steps to reduce student loan debt, including their bill to permit loan-holders to refinance at any time. His Almanac vote ratings have consistently ranked Pocan among the most liberal House members. In January 2017, he joined other gay House members in opposing the nomination of Betsy DeVos as secretary of Education, accusing her of supporting anti-gay causes. Also that month, he joined the Appropriations Committee, where he pledged to "fight for middle-class families and those aspiring to be in the middle class." He co-chaired the House Democrats' Labor Council. In 2015, Pocan joined New York City Mayor Bill de Blasio and others to launch The Progressive Agenda to Combat Income Inequality, which Pocan said would "put meat on the bone of our progressive values."

Pocan pursued his liberal agenda at the Progressive Caucus. As co-chair, he sought new opportunities to expand the group's membership and influence after Democrats won the House majority. Asked by The Washington Post whether his group would be a Democratic version of the House Freedom Caucus, which often forced confrontations within the Republican majority, he responded, "The question comes up often. ... The difference is the tea party liked to say no and we like to say yes."

He added that caucus members would seek to assure that party leaders shared their ambition. In the weeks following the 2018 election, he withheld his endorsement of Nancy Pelosi for House Speaker until she promised that progressives would have a prominent role in setting the House agenda. He included issues such as health care, the cost of prescription drugs, infrastructure projects and ethical standards, plus a proportional share of seats for progressives on key House committees. "We need to be big and bold and show people the path forward," he told the Wisconsin State Journal. Pelosi gave him a seat on the Select Committee on the Modernization of Congress, where he said he would seek to "advance a House that is diverse, dynamic and oriented toward the future."

Pocan has been reelected uneventfully. In 2018, he had no major-party opposition. Following the election, he said that he would no longer accept contributions from corporate political action committees.

WI-2: South-Central Wisconsin

Cook Partisan Voting Index: D+18

Population		Race and Ethnicity		Income	
Total	747,025	White	82.4%	Median Income	$63,850
Land area (sq. miles)	4,537	Black	4.4%	District Income Rank	146
Pop/ sq mi	164.7	Latino	6.4%	Poverty Rate	12.4%
Born in State	65%	Asian	4.2%	With health insurance	94.4%
		Two or more races	2.3%	Cash public assistance	1.8%
Age Groups		Other	0.4%	Food stamp/SNAP	10.2%
Under 18	21.8%				
18-34	26.4%	**Education**		**Work**	
35-64	38.3%	H.S grad or less	29.9%	White Collar	13.5%
Over 64	13.5%	Some college	29%	Sales and Service	37.3%
		College Degree, 4 yr	25.1%	Blue Collar	18%
Military		Post grad	16.1%	Government	18.2%
Veteran/ Active Duty	6.5%				

2012 Pres. Vote	Obama	284,084	(68%)	Romney	126,688	(30%)			
2016 Pres. Vote	Clinton	271,507	(65%)	Trump	119,608	(29%)	Johnson	14,385	(3%)

Madison: On a narrow isthmus between Lakes Mendota and Monona is the center of Madison, and in many ways, the center of Wisconsin. The state capitol rises at one end of State Street, and at the other end is the main campus of the University of Wisconsin, in a beautiful, park-like setting above Lake Mendota. For most of the 20th century, Wisconsin politics was dominated by the Madison-based LaFollettes and their liberal Democratic successors. University faculty were devoted to Robert LaFollette's "Wisconsin idea" of a supposedly apolitical bureaucracy and to his Wisconsin Tax Commission and workmen's compensation law — both firsts in the nation and conceived of by the former governor and senator.

Madison spawned an activist and sometimes violent student movement during the Vietnam War. The liberal campus opposed the welfare reform and school choice laws enacted while Republican Tommy Thompson was governor. The Madison community was the center of vocal opposition to Gov. Scott Walker's plan to end collective bargaining for most state workers and then led the unsuccessful recall effort to oust him in June 2012. Following his election to a second term, Walker took revenge of sorts with the 2015 enactment of a plan for the state to wield more control over the university, including faculty hiring, through its Board of Regents. Madison remains economically vibrant. The metropolitan area boasts one of the best-educated workforces in the country — 51 percent of residents hold a college degree and 17 percent have a graduate degree. The growth industries include health care (Madison is home to American Family Insurance) and biotechnology start-ups tied to the university.

Madison is the center of Wisconsin's 2nd Congressional District, nearly half of which is urban and the remainder split between suburban and rural. It includes surrounding Dane County and dairy and alfalfa country to the north and south, as well as several rural dairy counties that have traditionally been Republican. A local landmark disappeared in 2015 when the merger of Kraft and Heinz led to the shutdown of the Oscar Mayer meat headquarters and plant in Madison, after 96 years. Dodgeville, in Iowa County (not on the Iowa border), is the headquarters of Lands' End, the catalog retailer. Dane is about three-fourths of the district.

The rural areas of Dane County, which had been open to Republicans as recently as the 1990s, have become bluer as Madison-area liberals move to the countryside, even as other parts of the state have become more crimson. The strongly Democratic lean of the county, plus its nearly 50 percent population growth from 1990 to 2017 (while the population in the larger Milwaukee County has remained flat), has increased its voting power in the state. "Dane County is gradually altering the electoral math in Wisconsin," Craig Gilbert wrote in the Milwaukee Journal Sentinel in February 2018. As governor, Walker understood the threat. "The last thing we need is more Madison in our lives," he tweeted. In 2016, Hillary Clinton won the district, 65%-29%.

Ron Kind (D)

Elected 1996, 12th term, b. Mar 16, 1963; La Crosse; Harvard University, Bach. Deg., 1985; London School of Economics (England), M.A., 1987; University of Minnesota, J.D., 1990; Lutheran; Married (Tawni Zappa Kind); 2 children.

Professional Career: Practicing attorney, 1990-1992; Assistant State Prosecutor, La Crosse County, 1992-1996.

DC Office: 1502 LHOB 20515, 202-225-5506, Fax: 202-225-5739, kind.house.gov

State Offices: Eau Claire, 715-831-9214; La Crosse, 608-782-2558.

Committees: *Ways & Means*: Health; Trade.

Group Ratings

	ADA	ACLU	AFL-CIO	LCV	ITI	COC	HAFA	ACU	CFG	FRC
2018	-	81%	-	89%	-	60%	13%	13%	30%	0%
2017	70%	C	92%	94%	C	57%	C	7%	5%	0%

Almanac Ratings 2017-18

	Economy	Social	Foreign	Composite
Liberal	77%	70%	90%	79%
Conservative	23%	30%	10%	21%

Key Votes of the 115th Congress

1. Obama-care revision	N	5. Family planning regs	N	9. Guantanamo prisoners	Y
2. Tax Cuts	N	6. Body cameras/immigration	Y	10. Ground missiles, limit	Y
3. Omnibus appropriations	N	7. Abortion ban	N	11. Defense Dept. spending	Y
4. Dodd-Frank revision	Y	8. Concealed carry	Y	12. FISA rules	NV

Election Results

Election	Name (Party)	Vote (%)		Cand. Spent	Ind. Exp. Support	Ind. Exp. Oppose
2018 General	Ron Kind (D)	187,888	(60%)			
	Steve Toft (R)	126,980	(40%)	$304,107		
2018 Primary	Ron Kind (D)		(100%)			

Prior winning percentages: 2016 (99%), 2014 (57%), 2012 (64%) 2010 (50%), 2008 (63%), 2006 (65%), 2004 (56%), 2002 (63%), 2000 (64%), 1998 (72%), 1996 (52%)

Ron Kind, a Democrat elected in 1996, is a moderate who focuses on health and agriculture issues and seeks bipartisanship on the Ways and Means Committee. In contrast to the dominant liberal core of Wisconsin Democrats, he has been chairman of the New Democrat Coalition, a business-oriented group that attempts to break through partisan gridlock. In 2015, Kind was the leading Democratic proponent in the bitter intraparty battle to give trade promotion authority to President Barack Obama. He has called for new Democratic leaders and voted against Nancy Pelosi as House Speaker.

Kind grew up in a large family in La Crosse, the son of a telephone repairman and a secretary in the local schools. He went to Harvard University on a scholarship and played quarterback. He was a summer intern for Democratic Sen. William Proxmire, doing research for Proxmire's Golden Fleece awards pointing out wasteful government spending. Kind attended the London School of Economics and the University of Minnesota's law school, practiced law in a large firm in Milwaukee, then returned home to La Crosse to work as an assistant prosecutor on rape and sexual abuse cases.

Kind ran for an open seat that had been Republican-held. Former state Sen. Jim Harsdorf won the Republican primary and made a case for a balanced budget and for Republican Gov. Tommy Thompson's "Wisconsin Works" welfare reform program. Kind presented his own balanced budget proposal and urged reform of campaign finance. Kind won, 52%-48%.

Kind has taken a continuing interest in improving the health of the upper Mississippi River, which is vital to the well-being of his district. He has worked to restore the river, combat invasive species and ensure that it remains a resource for recreation and transportation.

Kind has been vitally interested in agriculture issues that affect dairy farmers in his district. In 2007, he joined with conservative deficit hawks and suburban and urban Democrats in seeking to add provisions to the farm bill that would have limited subsidies and provided more funds for land conservation and school nutrition. "For too long, we've had large taxpayer subsidies going to a few very large farming entities to the disadvantage of family farmers," Kind said. Democratic leaders were worried about angering farmers' groups in rural swing districts and refused to allow a House vote. Kind voted against the final version of the farm bill, calling it a "nightmare." In 2012, he complained in a letter to colleagues that the GOP-written farm bill "takes us backward in terms of budget-busting crop subsidies, unlimited insurance subsidies, and trade-distorting programs." Despite the farm subsidies that flow to his district, he said that most producers he represents don't get huge subsidies because they're not large agribusinesses. He voted against the 2018 farm bill, which he called "status quo" legislation that continued huge subsidies to encourage over-production. "Too many of our family farmers in Wisconsin are just going out of business and declaring bankruptcy," he said.

In the health care debate in 2009, Kind cosponsored a bill to put greater emphasis on quality and coordination of care in reimbursing providers. He was one of three Democrats who joined committee Republicans in opposing the version that Ways and Means approved. After lengthy meetings that he and others held with Speaker Pelosi on containing the spiraling costs of Medicare, he agreed to support the legislation.

As a leader of House moderates, Kind has chaired the New Democrat Coalition. "We want to work hard to find that sensible center on policy and move the ball," he told The Hill newspaper. Following the Democrats' disastrous 2010 election performance, he refused to support Pelosi in her bid for minority leader, though he subsequently backed her. But he was one of 15 Democrats who voted against her in the January 2019 House vote for Speaker. "I've been consistent in saying we're in desperate need of new leadership on both sides," Kind said.

On Obama's request in 2015 for trade promotion authority, Kind quietly and methodically assembled Democratic support. He faced fierce opposition from labor unions and many of his Democratic colleagues in his advocacy of Obama's top legislative priority of the year. Kind preserved cohesion among the depleted but still vital corps of 28 Democratic supporters of trade deals. He compared notes daily with White House officials. "Sometimes the phone rang and it was Obama himself," Roll Call reported. When President Donald Trump in 2017 withdrew the United States from the proposed Trans-Pacific Partnership, Kind objected that the move "will cost us jobs in Wisconsin." In January 2019, Kind challenged Rep. Bill Pascrell of New Jersey for chairman of the Trade Subcommittee; the more-senior Rep. Earl Blumenauer of Oregon pre-empted both. Kind said that Wisconsin's family farmers "are bearing the brunt of the president's trade war."

At home, Kind in 2004 had his first credible challenger, Republican state Sen. Dale Schultz, a moderate in the Wisconsin legislature. Schultz attacked Kind as a free trader who had sent jobs overseas. Kind affirmed his support for trade agreements, but criticized the Bush administration for supposedly failing to enforce their labor and environmental protection provisions. Kind won, 56%-43%. In 2010, another serious challenger emerged, Dan Kapanke, a Republican state senator who lambasted Kind for his support of the health care bill and Obama's economic agenda. Kind survived with a 50%-46% win. Since then, he has won comfortably with district lines that are more favorable for him. In 2018, Republican challenger Steve Toft — a retired army officer — criticized Kind as "a career politician. Kind outspent Toft, $2.3 million to $300,000, and won, 60%-40%.

Kind has considered runs for statewide office, including a run for governor in 2018. He likely would face problems in a primary with a liberal from Milwaukee or Madison.

WI-3: West-Central Wisconsin   Cook Partisan Voting Index: EVEN

Population		Race and Ethnicity		Income	
Total	718,086	White	92.1%	Median Income	$52,958
Land area (sq. miles)	11,112	Black	1.1%	District Income Rank	254
Pop/ sq mi	64.6	Latino	2.5%	Poverty Rate	13.3%
Born in State	71.6%	Asian	2.1%	With health insurance	92.8%
		Two or more races	1.5%	Cash public assistance	2.1%
Age Groups		Other	0.7%	Food stamp/SNAP	11.1%
Under 18	21.2%				
18-34	24.9%	**Education**		**Work**	
35-64	37.5%	H.S grad or less	41.6%	White Collar	16.4%
Over 64	16.4%	Some college	33.6%	Sales and Service	40.2%
		College Degree, 4 yr	16.4%	Blue Collar	27.8%
Military		Post grad	8.4%	Government	13.6%
Veteran/ Active Duty	8.8%				

2012 Pres. Vote	Obama	199,188	(55%)	Romney	159,205	(44%)		
2016 Pres. Vote	Trump	177,172	(49%)	Clinton	160,999	(44%)	Johnson	14,511 (4%)

Eau Claire, La Crosse: On the rolling land of western Wisconsin, in the knobby hills just east of the Mississippi River, is some of the most beautiful river landscape in the country. This is where author Laura Ingalls Wilder's family built their little house in the big woods in the 1870s, before the first railroad came steaming up the narrow floodplain alongside the Mississippi River. Today, it is hard to imagine the big woods. The trees have long since been cut down, and the hillsides are covered with grass grazed by placid dairy cattle. Where the pioneers tried to scratch out diversified crops, later generations of farmers created America's premier dairy region, producing milk, butter and cheese. Some Amish communities from Pennsylvania have relocated here in recent years because land is cheaper than in the East. Since 1980, the dairy economy here has been in flux. Numerous dairy farmers have gone out of business. Wisconsin also has had trouble competing against the European Union's subsidized cheese and butter, and more recently, with products from California's large-scale agribusiness. Cows have become more productive, and demand for milk has decreased. President Donald Trump's tariffs have been unpopular in this area, as his long-running trade negotiations with China raised additional worries. In the 44 counties of western Wisconsin, the 28 farm bankruptcies in 2017 were the highest in the nation. With young people less willing to stay on the farms, immigrant workers have played a growing role in the local dairy industry, the La Crosse Tribune reported in December 2017.

The 3rd Congressional District of Wisconsin follows the Mississippi from the border with Illinois north to Dunn County, covering the southern half of the western edge of the state. The district's two largest cities are La Crosse and Eau Claire, home to home-improvement giant Menards. Both cities have won recognition for their livability. Eau Claire has been rejuvenated by cleanup of the waterfront area and the opening of an arts center by the local campus of the University of Wisconsin. The population of Eau Claire County was 104,000 in 2017 — nearly double the total in 1950. The district stretches east to Democratic-leaning Portage County and Stevens Point, where the lakes, streams and trails make the area a recreational hotspot.

Settled largely by German and Scandinavian immigrants, the region once consistently voted for Wisconsin's LaFollette Progressives. In recent years, its voters have shown that they cannot be taken for granted. Western Wisconsin was one of the few segments of rural America where President Barack Obama in 2012 ran even with historic Democratic percentages; his 55 percent of the vote was vital to his statewide victory. In the district's current lines, Obama did even better in 2008, when he took 59 percent and won every county. This area was a bulwark for Republican Gov. Scott Walker in his 2010 election and June 2012 recall, when he won every county in the district except La Crosse. That shift continued in 2016. Trump won the district, 49%-44% -- a 15 percentage point drop for the Democrats in eight years. Eau Claire, La Crosse and Portage counties all voted for Hillary Clinton, but narrowly. The rural counties went heavily for Trump.

Gwen Moore (D)

Elected 2004, 8th term, b. Apr 18, 1951; Racine; Marquette University (WI), B.A., 1978; Milwaukee Area Technical College (WI), Att., 1983; Harvard University, Att., 2000; Baptist; Single; 3 children; 3 grandchildren.

Elected Office: WI Assembly, 1989-1992; WI Senate, 1992-2004, President pro tem, 1997-1998.

Professional Career: Housing & urban dev. specialist, 1985-1989.

DC Office: 2252 RHOB 20515, 202-225-4572, Fax: 202-225-8135, gwenmoore.house.gov

State Offices: Milwaukee, 414-297-1140.

Committees: *Ways & Means*: Oversight; Select Revenue Measures; Worker & Family Support.

Group Ratings

	ADA	ACLU	AFL-CIO	LCV	ITI	COC	HAFA	ACU	CFG	FRC
2018	-	93%	-	94%	-	64%	13%	8%	34%	0%
2017	95%	C	95%	100%	C	31%	C	8%	5%	0%

Almanac Ratings 2017-18

	Economy	Social	Foreign	Composite
Liberal	97%	100%	89%	95%
Conservative	3%	0%	12%	5%

Key Votes of the 115th Congress

1. Obama-care revision	N	5. Family planning regs	N	9. Guantanamo prisoners	NV
2. Tax Cuts	N	6. Body cameras/immigration	Y	10. Ground missiles, limit	NV
3. Omnibus appropriations	N	7. Abortion ban	N	11. Defense Dept. spending	N
4. Dodd-Frank revision	N	8. Concealed carry	N	12. FISA rules	N

Election Results

Election	Name (Party)	Vote (%)		Cand. Spent	Ind. Exp. Support	Ind. Exp. Oppose
2018 General	Gwen Moore (D)	206,487	(76%)	$961,874		
	Tim Rogers (R)	59,091	(22%)			
	Robert Raymond (I)	7,170	(3%)			
2018 Primary	Gwen Moore (D)	76,991	(89%)			
	Gary George (D)	9,468	(11%)			

Prior winning percentages: 2016 (77%), 2014 (70%), 2012 (72%), 2010 (69%), 2008 (88%), 2006 (71%), 2004 (70%)

Gwen Moore, a Democrat elected in 2004, has often recounted her personal struggles -- in candid detail -- as she has stood up for the poor, homeless and victims of domestic violence. As Wisconsin's first African-American member of Congress, she highlighted her selection to the Ways and Means Committee in 2019. She cited her recent treatment for small-cell lymphoma as "a living example of the life-saving value of essential health benefits."

Moore was born in Racine, the eighth of nine children, and raised on the North Side of Milwaukee. As an 18-year-old college freshman, she became a single mother who relied on welfare to help support her daughter. She graduated from Marquette University and worked as a housing and urban development specialist. Moore said she got active in politics when a rent-to-own center repossessed her washer and dryer even though she had paid three times their value in interest. She led an effort to establish a community credit union. Elected to the state Assembly in 1989 and the Senate in 1992, she was the state's first black woman senator. In 1990, she defeated Republican Scott Walker, who later served two terms as governor of Wisconsin.

In 2003, when blue-collar Democratic Rep. Gerald Kleczka announced that he was retiring, Moore was the frontrunner. She was challenged in the primary by two political veterans, state Sen. Tim Carpenter and former state Democratic Chairman Matt Flynn, both white. Moore took advantage of the energized black voter base and leveraged financial support from liberal women's organizations, teachers' unions, and other progressive groups. Flynn was endorsed by Kleczka. But he was damaged politically by his work as general counsel for the local Roman Catholic archdiocese in a priest sex abuse scandal. Carpenter was the only openly gay member of the Senate and had the support of national gay rights groups. Moore won 64 percent of the vote to 25 percent for Flynn and 10 percent for Carpenter. In the general election, Moore won easily, 70%-28%.

Moore has a staunchly liberal voting record, with Almanac vote ratings that have listed her in the top 5 percent of House progressives. She often has been hyperbolic in her criticism of Republican policies. She said in 2012 that a Wisconsin voter ID law "does nothing but attempt to return us to an era of Jim Crow politics." When House Republicans sought to defund Planned Parenthood during the 2011 budget debate, Moore drew on her own unwelcome experience of an unplanned pregnancy at age 18. "I just want to tell you a little bit about what it's like to not have Planned Parenthood," she said on the House floor. "You have to add water to the formula to make it stretch. You have to give your kids Ramen noodles at the end of the month to fill up their little bellies so they won't cry. You have to give them mayonnaise sandwiches."

In 2005, the House incorporated provisions of her Shield Act into the reauthorization of the Violence Against Women Act, to protect the identity of domestic-violence victims who receive homeless assistance. When the law came up in 2012, Moore stunned House colleagues by taking to the floor to graphically recount how a group of young men once discussed having sex with her. "The appointed boy, when he saw that I wasn't going to be so willing, completed a date rape and then took my underwear to display it to the rest of the boys. I mean, this is what American women are facing," she said.

On the Financial Services Committee, Moore took an interest in the World Bank and International Monetary Fund. In 2016, she wrote to the bank that she was "increasingly uneasy" with its funding and promotion of water privatization through public-private partnerships.

Moore harshly criticized Donald Trump's views of women when she spoke to the Democratic convention in 2016. She was more temperate when the CBC met with President Trump at the White House in March 2017. "It was important to sort of just clear the air," she said. "I don't think that our communities would be served well by our not engaging." Following Trump's response to the August 2017 white nationalist rally in Charlottesville Virginia, Moore said that he should be impeached "to restore our national dignity."

Prompted by her selection as the second Wisconsin Democrat on Ways and Means — Ron Kind, a leader of centrist Democrats, has served on the committee for two decades — Moore said that her recent treatments for cancer "quadrupled" her commitment to restore the individual mandate to the Affordable Care Act and expand coverage of health care. She told the Milwaukee Journal Sentinel that the committee handles "so many issues I care about and are important." Adding that her cancer is in remission, she called it "a cancer that I will live with for the rest of my life … not a cancer I will die from."

Moore remains firmly entrenched in her district. Former state Sen. Gary George has challenged her in the Democratic primary during the past three election cycles and criticized her failure to use the "bully pulpit" to address crime and economic issues. In 2018, Moore won the primary with 89 percent of the vote.

WI-4: Milwaukee

Cook Partisan Voting Index: D+25

Population		Race and Ethnicity		Income	
Total	715,308	White	42.7%	Median Income	$41,514
Land area (sq. miles)	128	Black	33.4%	District Income Rank	403
Pop/ sq mi	5573.1	Latino	16.7%	Poverty Rate	24.6%
Born in State	66.4%	Asian	3.9%	With health insurance	89.9%
		Two or more races	2.7%	Cash public assistance	3.4%
Age Groups		Other	0.5%	Food stamp/SNAP	25.8%
Under 18	25.4%				
18-34	27.7%	**Education**		**Work**	
35-64	35.7%	H.S grad or less	43.7%	White Collar	11.2%
Over 64	11.2%	Some college	28.9%	Sales and Service	44.3%
		College Degree, 4 yr	17.3%	Blue Collar	22.3%
Military		Post grad	10.1%	Government	12%
Veteran/ Active Duty	5.5%				

2012 Pres. Vote	Obama	268,440	(75%)	Romney	84,751	(24%)			
2016 Pres. Vote	Clinton	228,226	(73%)	Trump	67,287	(22%)	Johnson	8,501	(3%)

Milwaukee: Milwaukee is America's most German city, with an ethnic heritage noticeable not just in the names of its beers and its old German restaurants, but in the sturdiness of its houses and the orderliness of its streets. Until World War I inflamed sensitivities to all things German, the language was spoken on the streets and read in city newspapers; German beer was produced in dozens of breweries. A huge four-sided clock, nearly twice the size of London's Big Ben, rises above the Allen-Bradley factory, looking out over the industrial city. It is an apt symbol, a piece of precision engineering in this high-skill manufacturing town, with its skyline of smokestacks and church steeples — the closest thing in America to the German factory cities that inspired Milwaukee's early citizens. The city has led the nation in beer brewing, industrial control equipment, mining gear, cranes and independent foundries.

Downtown Milwaukee has seen major changes in the past few decades — with recent signs of an uptick. Many of the factories have shut down. It hemorrhaged population, with a drop from 740,000 in 1960 to 595,000. The city has stopped shrinking, thanks to its rapidly expanding Hispanic population. For the most part, the city has embraced Latinos. Many Hispanics have settled in the old immigrant neighborhoods of the city's South Side. The West Side and North Side are home to many of the city's African-American neighborhoods, such as Sherman Park and Bronzeville. Since 2000, its population has remained steady at 595,000 — though it initially dropped below that by 18,000 and then exceeded 600,000 in 2013. In July 2018, Vogue magazine profiled Milwaukee as "the Midwest's coolest (and most under-rated) city." Democrats will reinforce that theme when the city hosts their national convention in 2020 — the first Midwest city other than Chicago to host the party's convention since 1916.

That turnaround has been accompanied by a downtown building boom. The NBA Milwaukee Bucks in 2018 opened their $524 million arena, about half of which was financed by the state. Other new sites include Northwestern Mutual's office tower and apartment high-rise, the BMO Harris Financial Center office tower and the conversion of the Warner Grand Theater into the Milwaukee Symphony Orchestra's performance hall. Led by MillerCoors, the brewing industry continues to employ more than 7,000 in Milwaukee. The city has become a global hub for water technology and research, with many new tech start-ups. The University of Wisconsin-Milwaukee opened the first graduate school in the nation dedicated solely to the study of freshwater. In 2018, the Brookings Institution cited this development as one of the best industry clusters in the nation.

The 4th District of Wisconsin covers the entire city of Milwaukee and a few of its working-class suburbs — St. Francis, Cudahy and South Milwaukee on Lake Michigan, and West Milwaukee and part of West Allis. It includes to the north tonier suburbs along the lake, many with sizable Jewish populations — Shorewood, Whitefish Bay and Fox Point. These communities are politically competitive and closely attuned to state politics. About 25 percent of Milwaukee County voters reside in parts of three Republican-held districts in Wisconsin; that suggests potential redistricting options for Democrats. In the 4th, blacks make up 33 percent of the population, while Hispanics comprise another 17 percent. It is easily Wisconsin's most Democratic district, with Hillary Clinton getting 73 percent of the vote here in 2016. Turnout in Milwaukee County dropped by 50,000 voters from 2012. That reduced Clinton's lead in the county by 27,000 votes. She lost statewide by fewer than 23,000 votes. Democratic strategists have become mindful of those numbers.

Jim Sensenbrenner (R)

Elected 1978, 21th term, b. Jun 14, 1943; Chicago, IL; Milwaukee County Day School (WI), 1961; Stanford University (CA), B.A., 1965; University of Wisconsin Law School, J.D., 1968; Roman Catholic; Married (Cheryl Warren Sensenbrenner); 2 children; 1 grandchild.

Elected Office: WI Assembly, 1968-1974; WI Senate, 1974-1978.

Professional Career: Staff Assistant, U.S. Rep. Arthur Younger, 1965; Practicing attorney, 1968-1969.

DC Office: 2449 RHOB 20515, 202-225-5101, Fax: 202-225-3190, sensenbrenner.house.gov

State Offices: Brookfield, 262-784-1111.

Committees: *Foreign Affairs*: Africa, Global Health, Global Human Rights & Internat'l Orgs; Europe, Eurasia, Energy & the Environment. *Judiciary*: Antitrust, Commercial & Administrative Law (RMM); Crime, Terrorism & Homeland Security.

Group Ratings

	ADA	ACLU	AFL-CIO	LCV	ITI	COC	HAFA	ACU	CFG	FRC
2018	-	17%	-	6%	-	58%	83%	96%	89%	100%
2017	5%	C	3%	6%	C	93%	C	100%	95%	100%

Almanac Ratings 2017-18

	Economy	Social	Foreign	Composite
Liberal	4%	3%	15%	7%
Conservative	97%	97%	85%	93%

Key Votes of the 115th Congress

1. Obama-care revision	Y	5. Family planning regs	Y	9. Guantanamo prisoners	N
2. Tax Cuts	Y	6. Body cameras/immigration	N	10. Ground missiles, limit	N
3. Omnibus appropriations	N	7. Abortion ban	Y	11. Defense Dept. spending	Y
4. Dodd-Frank revision	Y	8. Concealed carry	Y	12. FISA rules	N

Election Results

Election	Name (Party)	Vote (%)		Cand. Spent	Ind. Exp. Support	Ind. Exp. Oppose
2018 General	Jim Sensenbrenner (R)................ 225,619	(62%)		$480,898	$1,383	$29,900
	Tom Palzewicz (D)............................. 138,385	(38%)		$241,165	$14,950	
2018 Primary	Jim Sensenbrenner (R)................ 73,397	(81%)				
	Jennifer Vipond (R)............................. 17,011	(19%)				

Prior winning percentages: 2016 (67%), 2014 (70%), 2012 (68%), 2010 (69%), 2008 (80%), 2006 (62%), 2004 (67%), 2002 (86%), 2000 (74%), 1998 (91%), 1996 (74%), 1994 (100%), 1992 (70%), 1990 (100%), 1988 (75%), 1986 (78%), 1984 (73%), 1982 (100%), 1980 (78%), 1978 (61%)

Republican Jim Sensenbrenner, first elected in 1978, is a forceful conservative whose prickly personality has rankled liberals even as he has racked up many impressive legislative accomplishments. With Republican Rep. Don Young of Alaska and Democratic Sen Patrick Leahy of Vermont, he is one of only three members of Congress who served before the election of Ronald Reagan. As something of an elder statesman in the House, he offers useful historical memory plus savvy in how to get things done. "Some would refer to me as the political 'Godfather'," he joked to the Milwaukee Journal Sentinel in 2017. That role shifted with the retirement of Speaker Paul Ryan, who served a neighboring district, and the Democratic takeover of the House.

Sensenbrenner was born in Chicago and grew up in the Milwaukee area, with strong Wisconsin roots. His great-grandfather was a founder of Kimberly-Clark, which invented the sanitary napkin, and Sensenbrenner is an heir to the paper and cellulose fortune. He graduated from Stanford University and the University of Wisconsin Law School, and has spent most of his adult life in politics. He served briefly as a staffer in the House, then was elected to the Wisconsin Assembly in

1968 and to the Senate in 1974. When Republican Rep. Bob Kasten ran for governor, Sensenbrenner won the Republican primary by 589 votes. At age 35, he was elected with 61 percent of the vote, which was the lowest of his career. In 2015, the most recent report of his net worth dropped to $13 million, according to the Center for Responsive Politics. In an example of the rich getting richer, he won $250,000 in the District of Columbia lottery after buying two tickets at a Capitol Hill liquor store.

Sensenbrenner's pugnaciousness has endeared him to conservatives. His legislative skills have earned him respect on Capitol Hill. He was one of the first to urge that Congress apply to itself the same laws it imposes on the rest of the country. A dependable conservative and something of an institutionalist, he occasionally opposes his party on principle. In 2003, he said he saw no need to amend the Constitution to ban same-sex marriages. He was one of 17 House Republicans to vote against a 2012 amendment to bar the Obama administration from using taxpayer funds to defend its health care law in court. That independence helps to explain why his Almanac vote ratings have been toward the center of the House and the least conservative of the Republicans from Wisconsin.

He chaired the Judiciary Committee from 2001 to 2006, where he was best known for his work after the September 11 attacks. Concerned about possible violations of civil liberties, he insisted on a sunset provision for the USA Patriot Act, the anti-terrorism law passed after the attacks on New York and Washington, ensuring it would expire in four years and giving Congress a chance to study its impact. By 2005, he decided that his concerns about civil liberties had been addressed and he pushed to make most of the law permanent. After a difficult conference committee with the Senate, he won an extension of the law for the Bush administration. Sensenbrenner had differences with Attorney General Alberto Gonzales over the scope of the domestic surveillance program and demanded steps to protect "the freedoms we cherish."

In 2015, he was instrumental in reducing the sweep of the Patriot Act, which had become unpopular with both tea party conservatives suspicious of government and civil libertarians. Following revelations of the National Security Agency's bulk collection of data, Sensenbrenner authored what became known as the USA Freedom Act, a comprehensive measure that put an end to collection of metadata, increased the transparency of the Foreign Intelligence Surveillance Court and found a new balance between national security and privacy. "Sensenbrenner could savor the kind of victory that doesn't come along too often in a polarized, party-line political world," the Milwaukee Journal-Sentinel wrote after the bill was enacted. "[President Barack Obama and I] both realized there was a problem that had to be fixed. And we worked together to fix it," he recounted.

Sensenbrenner worked steadily for years on some bills. Bankruptcy reform was enacted in 2005 after being held up by a Democratic abortion-related provision. He has backed limitations in tort law on class action, medical malpractice and asbestos liability, and has sought to increase penalties for frivolous lawsuits. He was instrumental in enacting in 2003 the Child Abduction Prevention Act, which enhanced the AMBER Alert system. One of his final actions as chairman was the bipartisan extension of the Voting Rights Act. In 2019, he became ranking Republican on the Antitrust, Commercial and Administrative Law Subcommittee.

With immigration, he successfully added to the 2004 intelligence reorganization bill provisions setting national standards for driver's licenses that denied licenses to illegal immigrants, prohibited the use of Mexican matricula consular cards for identification, tightened standards for asylum, and overrode state laws and regulations blocking border barriers. He was skeptical of bipartisan Senate passage in 2013 of a comprehensive immigration reform bill, saying, "extending amnesty to those who came here illegally or overstayed their visas is dangerous waters." He wants to use money forfeited by drug traffickers for increased security on the border wall.

After the House Republicans' six-year term limit for senior committee members forced Sensenbrenner to give up the top slot on Judiciary in 2007, he became ranking Republican on the Select Committee on Energy Independence and Global Warming. A skeptic of alarmist predictions about global warming, Sensenbrenner had voted against creation of the panel, saying it was nothing more than a publicity stunt, but he promised to participate in the debate. As chairman of the Science, Space, and Technology Committee in the late 1990s, he attacked the conclusions of some climate scientists.

Sensenbrenner has been reelected easily every two years and has been known for extensive contact with constituents. In 2017, he was among the few House Republicans who continued to hold frequent local meetings in the face of liberal protests of President Donald Trump. At a raucous town-hall meeting in Pewaukee soon after Trump took office, he urged his critics, "Be respectful."

Sensenbrenner has had reservations about Trump. "I'm not confident Trump will do the right thing, but I am confident Hillary Clinton will always do the wrong thing," he told the Journal Sentinel before the Wisconsin primary in 2016. That news story added, "Sensenbrenner says he doesn't view Trump as a conservative, disapproves of his language and tone, and fears a GOP disaster in November." He was two years early on his final point.

WI-5: East-Central Wisconsin   Cook Partisan Voting Index: R+13

Population		Race and Ethnicity		Income	
Total	720,844	White	87.6%	Median Income	$68,197
Land area (sq. miles)	1,891	Black	2.1%	District Income Rank	107
Pop/ sq mi	381.3	Latino	5.7%	Poverty Rate	7.5%
Born in State	76.4%	Asian	2.7%	With health insurance	95.6%
		Two or more races	1.6%	Cash public assistance	1.3%
Age Groups		Other	0.3%	Food stamp/SNAP	7.6%
Under 18	21.6%				
18-34	20.6%	**Education**		**Work**	
35-64	41.1%	H.S grad or less	33.2%	White Collar	16.7%
Over 64	16.7%	Some college	30.5%	Sales and Service	38.5%
		College Degree, 4 yr	24.4%	Blue Collar	20.6%
Military		Post grad	12%	Government	9.1%
Veteran/ Active Duty	7.5%				

2012 Pres. Vote	Romney	257,017	(61%)	Obama	158,226	(38%)			
2016 Pres. Vote	Trump	229,325	(57%)	Clinton	148,900	(37%)	Johnson	15,756	(4%)

Western Milwaukee Suburbs, Waukesha: For decades, the orderly, heavily German-American factory city of Milwaukee has spread, mostly west and north, into Wisconsin dairy country. There are high-income enclaves here, such as close-in Elm Grove and exurban Oconomowoc, halfway to Madison and tucked in around numerous lakes. There is office development in Brookfield, and subdivisions have spread to Menomonee Falls and farther, reaching small towns with roots in the 19th century. This is comfortable but not fancy territory, and the economy is still based heavily on skilled manufacturing. Not far from Milwaukee are West Bend, with West Bend kitchen appliances; and Pewaukee, with Harken sailboat hardware. Harley-Davidson began manufacturing on the city's West Side a century ago and has a payroll of about 1,000 employees who manufacture engines at the plant, now in Menomonee Falls. In July 2017, Harley announced local cutbacks, as it moved more of its production to Europe due to costly tariffs. GE shut down its engine plant in Waukesha and shifted its remaining employees to Canada in early 2019. A developer offered more positive news in 2018 with plans for an office, retail and residential site in West Allis.

The 5th Congressional District of Wisconsin includes most of the western and northwestern suburbs of Milwaukee, spanning the Milwaukee County suburbs of Wauwatosa, Greenfield and West Allis; the northern half of Waukesha County, including New Berlin; and Jefferson County farther west. To the north, it includes all of Washington County and much of Dodge County. Nearly half the population is in Waukesha. This has been the most Republican district in the state, and voters here tend to be better-off than Republicans elsewhere in Wisconsin. The median household income is $68,000, the highest of any district in the state, even the well-educated, Madison-based 2nd District.

Waukesha County, more than three-fourths of which is in the district, is the conservative core of the state, providing the grassroots energy that fueled Gov. Scott Walker's victory during the June 2012 recall campaign. Waukesha gave Walker 72 percent of the vote in the recall and reported the second highest countywide turnout in the state. Donald Trump, for his part, under-performed in Waukesha. His victory margin in the county was 63,000 votes with 61 percent of the vote, compared with Mitt Romney's 84,000-vote lead and 67 percent in 2012 — even though Trump won and Romney lost statewide. Overall, the district voted 57 percent for Trump in November, which was virtually the same as his share in the three districts to the north — which typically are more competitive than the 5th.

Glenn Grothman (R)

Elected 2014, 3rd term, b. Jul 03, 1955; Milwaukee; University of Wisconsin - Madison, B.B.A., 1977; University of Wisconsin Law School, J.D., 1983; Lutheran; Single.

Elected Office: WI Assembly, 1994-2004; Assistant Minority Leader, WI Senate, 2012-2013; Assistant Majority Leader, WI Senate 2013; WI Senate, 2004-2014.

Professional Career: Attorney.

DC Office: 1427 LHOB 20515, 202-225-2476, Fax: 202-225-2356, grothman.house.gov

State Offices: Fond du Lac, 920-907-0624.

Committees: *Education & Labor:* Early Childhood, Elementary & Secondary Education; Higher Education & Workforce Investment. *Oversight & Reform:* Government Operations; Subcommittee on Economic & Consumer Policy.

Group Ratings

	ADA	ACLU	AFL-CIO	LCV	ITI	COC	HAFA	ACU	CFG	FRC
2018	-	11%	-	3%	-	73%	84%	88%	67%	100%
2017	0%	C	5%	0%	C	93%	C	96%	91%	100%

Almanac Ratings 2017-18

	Economy	Social	Foreign	Composite
Liberal	5%	3%	0%	3%
Conservative	96%	97%	100%	97%

Key Votes of the 115th Congress

1. Obama-care revision	Y	5. Family planning regs	Y	9. Guantanamo prisoners	N
2. Tax Cuts	Y	6. Body cameras/immigration	N	10. Ground missiles, limit	N
3. Omnibus appropriations	N	7. Abortion ban	Y	11. Defense Dept. spending	Y
4. Dodd-Frank revision	Y	8. Concealed carry	Y	12. FISA rules	Y

Election Results

Election	Name (Party)	Vote (%)		Cand. Spent	Ind. Exp. Support	Ind. Exp. Oppose
2018 General	Glenn Grothman (R)	180,311	(56%)	$1,793,249	$9,745	$325,287
	Dan Kohl (D)	144,536	(44%)	$3,399,332	$61,072	$33,315
2018 Primary	Glenn Grothman (R)	(100%)				

Prior winning percentages: 2016 (57%), 2014 (57%)

Republican Glenn Grothman, elected in 2014, has been a staunch conservative with a lengthy record of provocative comments that raised national GOP concerns during his initial campaign. Since taking office, he has been relatively mainstream and has settled in with other Wisconsin Republicans. Democrats have continued to keep an eye on him.

Born in Milwaukee, Grothman earned his bachelor's and law degrees from the University of Wisconsin. He won a special election to the Wisconsin Assembly in 1993, then easily took the GOP nomination for a Senate seat in 2004, arguing that the incumbent was insufficiently conservative. He became assistant Republican leader in 2009 and was a vocal supporter of GOP Gov. Scott Walker's budget and policy changes.

In 2014, Grothman said that he would challenge the moderate, low-profile Rep. Tom Petri. After 35 years in the House, Petri decided to retire in the face of what likely would have been a competitive contest. Grothman won the primary over state Sen. Joe Leibham by 219 votes, with 36 percent each. State Rep. Duey Stroebel finished third with 25 percent.

Grothman was a dream candidate for opposition researchers. In the legislature, he supported Walker's decision to repeal the state's Equal Pay Enforcement Act, saying that "you could argue that money is more important for men." He introduced a bill that would have required a state board to list single parenthood as a contributor to child abuse. He told The Capital Times that when he was in high school, "Homosexuality was not on anybody's radar. And that's a good thing." He described welfare programs as "a bribe not to work that hard or a bribe not to marry someone with a full-time job."

Both Grothman and Winnebago County Executive Mark Harris, the Democratic nominee, argued that the other was too extreme for the district. Harris said Grothman was weak on "women's issues," while Grothman in a fundraising email labeled Harris a "far-left politician." Harris cast himself as being more like Petri — a "thoughtful, quiet moderate." Grothman spent $1.2 million, more than four times as much as Harris. Grothman won 57%-41%. He took nine of the 11 counties; Harris narrowly won Columbia and Winnebago.

Grothman attracted little attention in the House and kept busy with work on his committees. After his first two months, the Milwaukee Journal Sentinel reported, "we've hardly heard a word from him." He occasionally made provocative statements, but nothing sufficient to get him in trouble. During a TV interview in Milwaukee days before the Wisconsin presidential primary in April 2016, Grothman suggested that the state's new voter ID laws might reduce turnout by Democrats and increase the prospect that Republicans might win the presidential election in November. "Photo ID is going to make a little bit of a difference," he said. Martha Laning, the head of Wisconsin's Democratic Party responded that Grothman was accidentally telling the truth. "He might as well have said Republicans are working to rig elections to win," Laning said.

Grothman's candor extended to his dismissive comments about Donald Trump during the Wisconsin presidential primary. "You look at the way he behaves. If your 8-year-old child behaved that way, you'd wonder if there was something wrong with them," said Grothman, who had endorsed Ted Cruz. "So, he is not a human being who I think we want to emulate."

In 2017, he got some attention in education circles when he said at a congressional hearing that recipients of federal student aid chose not to marry to improve their prospects of qualifying for the program. An official of a higher education association told Inside Higher Ed, which covers those issues, there is anecdotal information for "everything under the sun."

Despite his tight primary when he was first elected, no Republican has challenged him since then. In 2016, Democratic challenger Sarah Lloyd was a dairy farmer who was on leave from a job at the Wisconsin Farmers Union. That rural background apparently did not strike a chord in this working-class district. Grothman won 57%-41%, nearly the same as his victory in 2014.

In 2018, the campaign financing escalated dramatically. Democrat Dan Kohl spent $3.7 million -- of which $600,000 was self-financed — to $1.9 million for Grothman. Kohl, a nephew of former Democratic Sen. Herb Kohl, had been a lobbyist in Washington for an advocacy group on Israel and was an executive for his uncle's Milwaukee Bucks NBA basketball franchise. Kohl spotlighted "the stalemate and the dysfunction in Washington," and voiced concerns about Trump's trade war. He cited a rating of congressional voting by the Washington-based Lugar Center, which showed that Grothman was among the most partisan members of the House in 2015. Grothman's margin of victory narrowed, but not significantly, 55%-44%. Kohl led with 52 percent in Winnebago, which had the highest turnout. Grothman took the next four largest counties, with between 56 and 60 percent of the vote.

WI-6: East-Central Wisconsin

Cook Partisan Voting Index: R+8

Population		Race and Ethnicity		Income	
Total	712,513	White	89.7%	Median Income	$57,150
Land area (sq. miles)	4,918	Black	1.6%	District Income Rank	201
Pop/ sq mi	144.9	Latino	4.4%	Poverty Rate	9.5%
Born in State	78.9%	Asian	2.4%	With health insurance	94.8%
		Two or more races	1.5%	Cash public assistance	1.9%
Age Groups		Other	0.4%	Food stamp/SNAP	10%
Under 18	21.5%				
18-34	20.6%	**Education**		**Work**	
35-64	40.8%	H.S grad or less	43%	White Collar	17.1%
Over 64	17.1%	Some college	31.3%	Sales and Service	38.5%
		College Degree, 4 yr	17.6%	Blue Collar	29.7%
Military		Post grad	8%	Government	10.6%
Veteran/ Active Duty	8.4%				

2012 Pres. Vote	Romney	202,979	(53%)	Obama	174,988	(46%)		
2016 Pres. Vote	Trump	203,433	(55%)	Clinton	141,917	(38%)	Johnson	14,291	(4%)

Oshkosh, Sheboygan: Central Wisconsin is a producer of basic commodities — milk, butter, cheese, Kleenex, Mercury Marine outboard motors and military trucks. This is where the rolling hills and prairies of southern Wisconsin begin to give way to the pine and hardwood forests and glacial lakes of the Northwoods. First settled by Yankee Protestants, the 1850s brought the first large surge of German migration into the United States, and central Wisconsin was a favorite destination. They built the dairy farms and factory towns that seemed steadfastly prosperous, and they developed a manufacturing economy. Central Wisconsin was one of the birthplaces of the Republican Party, when a group of Whigs, Free Soilers and anti-slavery Democrats met in February 1854 in a small white schoolhouse in Ripon and proclaimed themselves Republicans. (A similar gathering took place in Jackson Michigan, which also claims to be the birthplace of the party.) The party grew rapidly, winning an effective majority in the House in that year's elections.

The German influence is still felt. Sheboygan is the Bratwurst Capital of the World. Johnsonville Foods, which began as a small family-owned company in 1945, employs more than 2,700 workers (including vendors), sells more sausage than any of its national competitors and remains privately owned; in 2017, it expanded its local headquarters. In April 2018, a business website in Sheboygan claimed that almost 3,000 jobs were available in the area. In 2017, the county had the lowest poverty rate in the nation. New immigrant groups recently have moved into Sheboygan. The city and surrounding county are home to more than 6,300 Hispanics and 6,000 Asians, mostly Hmong. Sheboygan, which hosts an annual Hmong summer festival, is the site of the Lao, Hmong and American Veterans Memorial, which was dedicated in 2010 "to recognize and to honor the people who served and who died for the U.S. secret war." In 2017, more than 500 protesters successfully lobbied against a proposal to toughen Sheboygan's immigration enforcement. Oshkosh is no longer the place where children's clothing maker Oshkosh B'Gosh manufactures its products. It is home to the Oshkosh Corp., which produces everything from dump trucks to military vehicles. The blue-collar town historically has been the center of numerous paper mills, several of which have closed in recent years. Kimberly-Clark, which remained a large employer in the area, in January 2018 announced plans to shut down plants in Neenah and Fox Crossing.

The 6th Congressional District is a slice of central Wisconsin from Lake Michigan to the Wisconsin River. It takes in the conservative, northern Milwaukee suburbs in Ozaukee County, including Port Washington. It includes Oshkosh-based Winnebago, the largest city and county in the district and the most Democratic-leaning; Sheboygan and Manitowoc on Lake Michigan; and Fond du Lac on the south shore of Lake Winnebago. The district includes four rural counties plus the Wisconsin Dells and its giant water park. Overall, the district has been Republican territory since that first meeting in Ripon. As with the 7th and 8th Districts to the north, Donald Trump's victory margin in the 6th was at least 10 percentage points greater than Mitt Romney's victory in 2012. Barack Obama won each of the three districts in 2008.

Sean Duffy (R)

Elected 2010, 5th term, b. Oct 03, 1971; Hayward; St. Mary's University (MN), Bach. Deg., 1994; William Mitchell College of Law (MN), J.D., 1999; Roman Catholic; Married (Rachel Campos-Duffy); 8 children.

Elected Office: District Attorney, Ashland County, 2002-2010.

Professional Career: Practicing attorney, 1999-2000; Special prosecutor, Ashland County, 2000-2002.

DC Office: 1714 LHOB 20515, 202-225-3365, duffy.house.gov

State Offices: Hayward, 715-392-3984; Hudson, 715-808-8160; Wausau, 715-298-9344.

Committees: *Financial Services*: Housing, Community Development & Insurance (RMM); Investor Protection, Entrepreneurship & Capital Markets.

Group Ratings

	ADA	ACLU	AFL-CIO	LCV	ITI	COC	HAFA	ACU	CFG	FRC
2018	-	7%	-	0%	-	92%	55%	76%	56%	100%
2017	0%	C	21%	0%	C	93%	C	77%	71%	100%

Almanac Ratings 2017-18

	Economy	Social	Foreign	Composite
Liberal	5%	6%	3%	5%
Conservative	95%	94%	97%	95%

Key Votes of the 115th Congress

1. Obama-care revision	Y	5. Family planning regs	Y	9. Guantanamo prisoners	N
2. Tax Cuts	Y	6. Body cameras/immigration	N	10. Ground missiles, limit	N
3. Omnibus appropriations	Y	7. Abortion ban	Y	11. Defense Dept. spending	Y
4. Dodd-Frank revision	Y	8. Concealed carry	Y	12. FISA rules	N

Election Results

Election	Name (Party)	Vote (%)		Cand. Spent	Ind. Exp. Support	Ind. Exp. Oppose
2018 General	Sean Duffy (R)...............................	194,061	(60%)	$2,493,753	$1,870	
	Margaret Engebretson (D).................	124,307	(39%)	$122,637		
2018 Primary	Sean Duffy (R)...................................		(100%)			

Prior winning percentages: 2016 (62%), 2014 (59%), 2012 (56%), 2010 (52%)

When Republican Sean Duffy in 2010 succeeded retiring Democratic stalwart David Obey, the House Appropriations Committee chairman, it was a stunning turnaround for the district. The telegenic Duffy, a former prosecutor, tended to his work on the Financial Services Committee and has become an outspoken ally of President Donald Trump, despite occasional objections to his rhetoric. Duffy has kept the door open to a statewide bid in 2022.

Duffy hails from the thickly forested northern area of the state, the 10th of 11 children. He became adept at the local craft of lumberjacking, eventually earning multiple world-champion titles in the 60-foot and 90-foot pole speed climb. At St. Mary's College in Minnesota, he got his degree in business marketing. On a lark after graduation, Duffy joined the cast of MTV's The Real World: Boston. The program brought young people with diverse backgrounds together to live as roommates. Duffy was cast as the conservative in the show. He met his future wife, Rachel Campos-Duffy, an Arizona native who had been cast as the conservative foil in the Real World season taped in San Francisco. She later made many appearances on The View, the syndicated talk show, and wrote a book, Stay Home, Stay Happy: 10 Secrets to Loving At-Home Motherhood, which she calls "a love letter to at-home moms." The couple has eight children.

Duffy got a law degree from William Mitchell College of Law in St. Paul. He returned to Wisconsin to work briefly for his family's law firm. Appointed as Ashland County district attorney, he boasted a 90 percent success rate in jury trials and prosecuting child sex offenders. He resigned to challenge Obey in 2010. After Obey unexpectedly announced that he would not seek reelection after more than four decades as a powerful Washington insider, Duffy faced a young Washington outsider like himself, Democratic state Sen. Julie Lassa.

In his campaign, Duffy was adept at raising money, and he ran as an unabashedly family-values and small-government conservative. Lassa campaigned as a champion of the middle class but had difficulty connecting with voters. Duffy was at ease and won, 52%-44%.

Duffy has backed his party on big votes, especially on fiscal issues, but has been independent on constituent matters. He refused to join most other tea party-backed freshmen in voting to end subsidies to rural airports and to defund National Public Radio, which maintains a strong audience in some rural areas. He talked up conservative themes. In 2016, Duffy clashed on the House floor with Democratic Rep. Gwen Moore of Wisconsin, when he criticized the large number of abortions by black women. "Black lives matter," he said. "All those lives matter. We should fight for all life, including the life of the unborn." Moore responded, "It's painfully obvious that Rep. Duffy's concern for life ends as soon as the umbilical cord is cut." In January 2019, he warned that his local dairy farmers were "near depression." He filed a bill to give the president additional authority to impose tariffs.

On the Financial Services Committee, he gained influence as a subcommittee chairman. Duffy held hearings on allegations of discrimination and retaliation by managers of the Consumer Financial Protection Bureau against the agency's employees. At a September 2016 hearing with a State Department witness, Duffy demanded details of the Obama administration's cash payments to Iran as part of the nuclear deal a year earlier. In July 2018, as chairman of the Housing and Insurance Subcommittee, he won House passage of a bipartisan proposal to require greater oversight and transparency on international insurance standards.

He was an early and consistent supporter of Trump and served on the executive committee for Trump's presidential transition. In a January 2019 interview with a local broadcast station, Duffy said that Democratic leaders "hate Donald Trump so much and are so offended by his victory" that they won't support anything that Trump might call a victory. He cited immigration as an issue where "we also want to fix the problems." Duffy cautioned that Trump made comments that are "incredibly unfortunate" and "could do better if he was more targeted with his language."

At home, Duffy gained attention when he tried to show empathy with an economically struggling constituent at a 2011 town hall meeting. When the man pointed out that Duffy's salary was "three times what I make," Duffy responded, "If you think I'm living high off the hog, I've got one paycheck. ... I struggle to meet my bills right now." Democrats pounced on the comment, contending that it illustrated how out of touch Duffy was.

Pat Kreitlow, a former Democratic state senator, spent $1.3 million in his 2012 challenge. Duffy drew on the financial industry's largesse and spent twice that amount. Each national party spent more than $2 million for its candidate. Duffy won, 56%-44%. In 2014, Duffy faced Kelly Westlund, a 30-year-old liberal activist who served on the city council in Ashland and spent $527,000. Duffy increased his win to 59%-39%, carrying every county except Douglas. Democrats' opposition faded and they turned their attention elsewhere.

Duffy opened the door to additional political options. In 2017, he turned down the opportunity to challenge Democratic Sen. Tammy Baldwin in 2018. "This is not the right time for me to run for Senate," Duffy said, leaving the door open to a possible run in 2022, when GOP Sen. Ron Johnson has said he will not seek reelection. Duffy has also not ruled out a bid for governor.

WI-7: North-Central Wisconsin — Cook Partisan Voting Index: R+8

Population		Race and Ethnicity		Income	
Total	707,988	White	91.9%	Median Income	$52,826
Land area (sq. miles)	23,037	Black	0.7%	District Income Rank	259
Pop/ sq mi	30.7	Latino	2.2%	Poverty Rate	10.9%
Born in State	67.6%	Asian	1.6%	With health insurance	92.6%
		Two or more races	1.5%	Cash public assistance	2%
Age Groups		Other	1.9%	Food stamp/SNAP	11.4%
Under 18	22%				
18-34	17.7%	Education		Work	
35-64	41.4%	H.S grad or less	44%	White Collar	18.9%
Over 64	18.9%	Some college	33.4%	Sales and Service	38.5%
		College Degree, 4 yr	15.3%	Blue Collar	29.6%
Military		Post grad	7.4%	Government	12.1%
Veteran/ Active Duty	9.8%				

| 2012 Pres. Vote | Romney | 190,364 | (51%) | Obama | 178,841 | (48%) | | | |
| 2016 Pres. Vote | Trump | 213,467 | (57%) | Clinton | 137,874 | (37%) | Johnson | 12,613 | (3%) |

Wausau: In the late 19th century, thousands of migrants traveled the rail lines radiating northwest from Chicago and Milwaukee to settle the northern reaches of Wisconsin, the most thickly settled land this far north in the United States and east of the Mississippi. What attracted them was not cropland — there are no large wheat farms as in the Red River Valley of North Dakota — but trees, iron and cows. This was one of America's largest virgin timberlands, and the river towns are still dotted with paper mills. Farther north, iron brought Finns and Italians to the port of Superior, across St. Louis Bay from Duluth Minnesota, and to smaller towns on the chilly lake. Nearby Apostle Islands National Lakeshore has eight lighthouses and breeding grounds for 240 species of birds that migrate through the archipelago. The cleared forest lands became dairy farms. Dairy cattle, properly cared for, thrived in these northern uplands. Small cities grew, and some became home to big enterprises.

Those longstanding industries have encountered tough times. In Wausau, the city's eponymous paper industry has shrunk. The number of dairy farmers in the region is in sharp decline as the economics of their business have become less attractive. Prices have been low, as national consumption of milk has decreased. Cheese and butter consumption remained high, but those products are more costly to produce. Dairy farmers complained that the threats by President Donald Trump against undocumented immigrant workers jeopardized their workforce. Some farmers have turned to potatoes, vegetables and cranberries. Growing sales of high-quality ginseng in Marathon County were threatened by Trump's trade wars; in 2017, more than $14 million of the local crop was exported to China. Wausau, which the 1980 census found to be the most ethnically homogeneous city in the nation, now has a sizable immigrant community. Many Hmong refugees moved there in the 1980s; as of 2017, 12 percent of the city's population was Asian.

This region makes up Wisconsin's 7th Congressional District. Its 21 counties stretch more than 200 miles from Lake Superior in the north to part of Monroe County, next to La Crosse. Commuter-oriented St. Croix County, part of the Minneapolis-St. Paul metro area, was the fastest-growing county in Wisconsin from 2000 to 2010, with its population now 89,000. In northern Iron County, after a resource firm abandoned in 2015 a proposal for an open-pit mine in an area rich with iron ore that environmentalists and Native American tribes had fought, other developers explored opportunities. In 2017, Gov. Scott Walker signed a bill lifting a moratorium on gold and silver mining in the area. The state also loosened regulations on iron mining.

The politics of the 7th District have a rough-hewn quality, a lumberjack-populist flavor. Ancestrally Republican, the area favored the progressivism of Wisconsin's LaFollettes. Superior-based Douglas County has been the chief Democratic outpost, while Marathon, St. Croix and many of the smaller counties have leaned Republican. Barack Obama carried the new boundaries, 53%-45%, in 2008. There has been a remarkable transformation since then. Donald Trump's 57%-37% put the 7th in a tie with the 5th for his best district in the state. Douglas and two small neighboring counties, Bayfield and Ashland, were the only ones that supported Hillary Clinton.

Mike Gallagher (R)

Elected 2016, 2nd term, b. Mar 03, 1984; Green Bay; Princeton University Woodrow Wilson School of Public and International Affairs (NJ), B.A., 2006; National Intelligence University (DC), M.S., 2010; Georgetown University (DC), M.A., 2012; Georgetown University (DC), M.A., 2013; Georgetown University (DC), Ph.D., 2015; Catholic; Single.

Military Career: U.S. Marine Corps 2006-2013 (Iraq)

Professional Career: Staff, United States Senate Foreign Relations Committee, 2013-2016; Foreign Policy Advisor.

DC Office: 1230 LHOB 20515, 202-225-5665, Fax: 202-225-5729, gallagher.house.gov

State Offices: De Pere, 920-301-4500.

Committees: *Armed Services*: Intelligence, Emerging Threats & Capabilities; Seapower & Projection Forces. *Transportation & Infrastructure*: Aviation; Coast Guard & Maritime Transportation; Highways & Transit.

Group Ratings

	ADA	ACLU	AFL-CIO	LCV	ITI	COC	HAFA	ACU	CFG	FRC
2018	-	4%	-	0%	-	83%	83%	92%	70%	100%
2017	0%	C	3%	3%	C	93%	C	85%	80%	100%

Almanac Ratings 2017-18

	Economy	Social	Foreign	Composite
Liberal	2%	3%	5%	3%
Conservative	98%	97%	95%	97%

Key Votes of the 115th Congress

1. Obama-care revision	Y	5. Family planning regs	Y	9. Guantanamo prisoners	N
2. Tax Cuts	Y	6. Body cameras/immigration	N	10. Ground missiles, limit	N
3. Omnibus appropriations	Y	7. Abortion ban	Y	11. Defense Dept. spending	Y
4. Dodd-Frank revision	Y	8. Concealed carry	Y	12. FISA rules	Y

Election Results

Election	Name (Party)	Vote (%)	Cand. Spent	Ind. Exp. Support	Ind. Exp. Oppose
2018 General	Mike Gallagher (R)........................	209,410 (64%)	$2,046,785	$44,044	
	Beau Liegeois (D)...........................	119,265 (36%)	$340,523		
2018 Primary	Mike Gallagher (R)................................	(100%)			

Prior winning percentages: 2016 (63%)

Republican Mike Gallagher, elected in 2016 to an open seat in a district that has switched party control seven times since 1975, quickly established a reputation as a cerebral maverick who is eager to assert himself. A former Marine captain who worked in top-level intelligence circles, Gallagher has been easily elected — both with and without Donald Trump's coattails.

Gallagher was born in Green Bay. He moved with his mother to Costa Mesa California after his parents divorced when he was a toddler, though he spent summers with his father in Green Bay. He got his bachelor's from Princeton's Woodrow Wilson School of Public and International Affairs and joined the Marine Corps the day he graduated. He served seven years on active duty as a human intelligence and counterintelligence officer, and as a regional affairs officer for the Middle East and North Africa. During that time, he learned to speak Arabic, served on Gen. David Petraeus's Central Command Assessment Team in the Middle East and spent three years working in the intelligence community. During two tours in Iraq, he was deployed to Anbar Province and attempted to work with local Iraqis to identify both opportunities for action and threats to the safety of his Marine battalion. He later questioned the U.S. decisions both to invade Iraq and to remove troops from the region after it was pacified. "I do think it was an analytical failure and an intelligence failure," he told the Milwaukee Journal Sentinel. "The fact that we won the war and lost the peace I think is shameful."

Gallagher got a master's degree in strategic intelligence from the National Intelligence University, and another master's followed by a Ph.D in government from Georgetown University. After he left the Marines, Gallagher was a Republican aide for the Middle East, North Africa and counterterrorism on the Senate Foreign Relations Committee and later was the national security adviser for the presidential campaign of Wisconsin Gov. Scott Walker. He spent time in the private sector as the senior global market strategist at Breakthrough Fuel, a Green Bay-based energy and supply chain management company.

In the contest to replace GOP Rep. Reid Ribble, Gallagher won the Republican primary with 75 percent of the vote against Frank Lasee, a two-term state senator, who got 20 percent. Democratic nominee Tom Nelson, the Outagamie county executive and a former state legislator, was a prime recruit for his party. Nelson said that the limited time Gallagher had lived in Wisconsin combined with his support for international trade agreements showed that he was out of touch with local voters. Each candidate ran attack ads about his opponent's positions on taxes and Social Security. Fact-checking organizations pointed out that each side was not always truthful. The contest was a high-dollar affair. Gallagher outspent Nelson, $2.7 million to $1.8 million. Gallagher's unexpectedly wide 63%-37% win was part of a strong Republican performance in rural and small-town Wisconsin.

Gallagher quickly impressed many as a rising star in Congress. In April 2018, McClatchy News profiled his "unusually independent reputation in today's Republican Party." He filed with Democratic Rep. Ron Kind of Wisconsin a bill to reduce presidential authority to revise tariffs to achieve, he said, "a level and fair playing field for Wisconsin manufacturers and farmers." With Democratic Rep. Raja Krishnamoorthi of Illinois, he created the Middle-Class Jobs Caucus to encourage manufacturing and technical education. He worked with Democratic Rep. Seth Moulton of Massachusetts in the bipartisan "With Honor" group, to encourage military veterans to run for Congress. With his seat on the Armed Services Committee, Gallagher hosted Republican Rep. Rob Wittman of Virginia on a tour of the Marinette Marine Shipyard, a Pentagon contractor and a vital employer in his district; Wittman chaired the Seapower and Projection Forces Subcommittee, to which Gallagher was assigned. At age 32 when he entered the House, he won in 2018 the annual three-mile race for members of Congress. He defeated Republican Sen. Tom Cotton of Arkansas, who had won the previous four years.

Gallagher hasn't been afraid to challenge Trump. In an interview on Fox News in June 2018 about the "endless culture war," he criticized the president's penchant for "a side show distracting from real issues." Also that month, he told National Public Radio that he disagreed with Trump's unilateral decision to end joint military exercises with South Korea. "We're in a situation where we should be demanding concessions upfront from the North Koreans, who are of course in violation of international law."

With his professional and academic experiences, Gallagher offered insights on the problems with what he called the "broken Congress." In "How to Salvage Congress," a piece in The Atlantic in November 2018, Gallagher wrote, "It's much worse than you think." The problem, he said, is "a defective process and a power structure that, whichever party is in charge, funnels all power to leadership and stifles debate and initiative within the ranks." Congress is "no longer suited to making laws and providing oversight," he added. "It has instead become a theater used by both parties to stoke the outrage of their base." Among his recommendations: To strengthen House committees, chairmen should be selected by members of their committee rather than by leadership-dominated panels.

At home, Gallagher was reelected, 64%-36%, against Democrat Beau Liegeois, a prosecutor in Brown County. He outspent the challenger, $2 million to $341,000.

WI-8: Northeast Wisconsin   Cook Partisan Voting Index: R+7

Population		Race and Ethnicity		Income	
Total	725,150	White	87.3%	Median Income	$57,603
Land area (sq. miles)	6,807	Black	1.3%	District Income Rank	199
Pop/ sq mi	106.5	Latino	5.1%	Poverty Rate	10.1%
Born in State	78.3%	Asian	2.2%	With health insurance	94.1%
		Two or more races	1.8%	Cash public assistance	1.9%
Age Groups		Other	2.4%	Food stamp/SNAP	9.8%
Under 18	23.1%				
18-34	20.3%	**Education**		**Work**	
35-64	40.8%	H.S grad or less	42.3%	White Collar	15.8%
Over 64	15.8%	Some college	31.9%	Sales and Service	38.8%
		College Degree, 4 yr	18.1%	Blue Collar	28.6%
Military		Post grad	7.6%	Government	10.7%
Veteran/ Active Duty	8.5%				

2012 Pres. Vote	Romney	191,127	(51%)	Obama	177,346	(48%)		
2016 Pres. Vote	Trump	207,620	(56%)	Clinton	142,677	(38%)	Johnson	13,691	(4%)

Green Bay, Appleton: In 1673, the French Catholic missionary and explorer Jacques Marquette sailed from the open waters of Lake Michigan into what is now the expansive Green Bay. He had hoped to find the Northwest Passage to the Pacific. Instead, he found the Fox River, which leads to Lake Winnebago and, after a not-too-difficult portage, the Wisconsin River, which flows into the Mississippi. Green Bay and the Fox River Valley remained mostly wilderness and Indian country for more than 150 years. But once settled by Europeans, they became, as Father Marquette would have liked, one of the most heavily Catholic parts of the United States. The area thrived economically, with paper mills, a busy port and high-skill manufacturing in Green Bay and Appleton. The number of jobs in the paper and pulp industry in the Fox River Valley dropped from 51,000 in the late 1990s to 30,000 in 2017; plans were unveiled in 2018 for a $500 million overhaul of a mill in Green Bay, which would be the first new paper plant in the United States in 20 years. In Marinette County, located on the bay, the Marinette Marine shipyard has spurred an economic boomlet with a multibillion dollar Navy contract to build new littoral combat ships, with a workforce of about 2,000. In 2018, the shipyard got a Navy contract for work on a next-generation guided-missile frigate.

No reference to Green Bay is complete without a mention of professional football's Packers, the locally beloved franchise owned by 361,000 shareholders and unlikely ever to move. Under the team's quaint charter, if the Packers are sold, the proceeds would go to the local Sullivan-Wallen American Legion Post 11 "for the purposes of erecting a proper soldier's memorial." (In the unlikely event of a sale, the proceeds might be enough to rebuild the city!) Individual shares cannot be traded and they pay no dividend. The city, by far the smallest with an NFL franchise, has earned the nickname

"Titletown" for the Packers' numerous championships. In October 2017, the Packers and Microsoft announced a partnership to advance local innovation and technology. Thirty miles south is Appleton, which has produced famous, and infamous, Americans: novelist Edna Ferber, escape artist Harry Houdini and demagogue Sen. Joseph McCarthy, the central figure in the "red scare" of the 1950s and censured by the Senate. Both Green Bay and Appleton are growing, thanks in part to surging Hispanic populations. Green Bay's Latino community has increased from approximately 1,000 people in 1990 to nearly 15,000; the city is more than 14 percent Hispanic. Appleton officials said the city will operate as a "sanctuary city" in terms of national immigration policy, though it did not officially adapt the designation.

The 8th Congressional District of Wisconsin includes Green Bay and the Fox River Valley south to Appleton. It also includes the inland dairy counties and the Northwoods, which has hundreds of pine-ringed lakes. The Door County peninsula, which extends from Green Bay into Lake Michigan, is a more upscale summer destination, with art galleries, boutiques and restaurants. Green Bay-based Brown County is one-third of the population; Appleton-based Outagamie is about one-fourth. With other non-urban parts of Wisconsin, the 8th has shifted dramatically in its politics. Barack Obama carried the district with 54 percent of the vote in 2008. Eight years later, Donald Trump took 56 percent. Tiny Menominee County, the site of an Indian reservation, was the only county Trump lost.

WYOMING

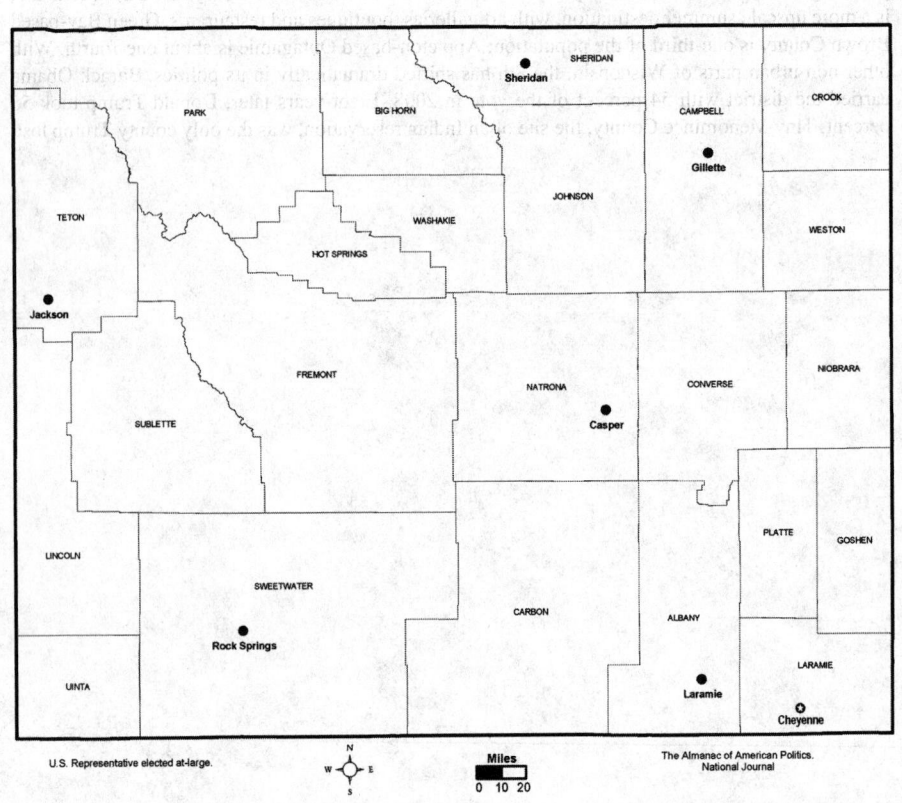

U.S. Representative elected at-large.

N
W ⊕ E
S

Miles
0 10 20

The Almanac of American Politics.
National Journal

As one might expect of a state that's the nation's leading producer of coal, Wyoming has the biggest Republican advantage in party affiliation of any state, and Hillary Clinton won a smaller percentage of Wyoming's vote than she did anywhere else.

America's frontier disappeared in 1890, according to the Census Bureau and historian Frederick Jackson Turner, but some people in Wyoming defy that historical consensus. The state – symbolized by the cowboy astride a bucking bronco that graces its license plates -- remains the most western of states in spirit. Largely unsettled even by western standards, its veneer of civilization stretches thinly across a forbidding and beautiful land. After the open range era, cattle ranches were made possible by the barbed wire that could fence in roaming herds and the steam locomotives that could carry cattle to markets in the East.

Wyoming is more than the land of the cowboy now. It produces about 40 percent of the nation's coal – more than three times the share of the second-ranking state, West Virginia – and it places eighth in natural gas production. Wyoming also ranks eighth in crude oil production, has the nation's largest uranium reserves, and has a substantial portion of the nation's helium reserves. Wyoming also produces at least half the world's supply – more than 4 million tons worth -- of bentonite, the highly absorbent mineral that comes from volcanic ash and is used to manufacture kitty litter, materials used in oil drilling, and cosmetics.

Wyoming's dependence on mining and minerals is not exactly new. It started with oil in 1884 – six years before statehood – with the drilling of the Mike Murphy No. 1 well. The first refinery followed in Casper in 1895, and the state's oil history was punctuated by the Teapot Dome scandal in the 1920s. The state boomed with oil prospectors during the energy price surge of the 1970s but was hit hard by steep drops in petroleum prices in the early 1980s and again in the late 1990s. As oil exploration slumped, the production of other minerals surged. The 1970 Clean Air Act put a premium on Wyoming's lower-sulfur coal, as did the Clean Air Act Amendments of 1990. In the Powder River Basin, 30-story-high machines blasted away the topsoil and scooped out coal. It was then hauled away by as many as 60 Burlington Northern Santa Fe and Union Pacific trains every day, each carrying 15,000 to 20,000 tons of coal. Much of the natural gas, meanwhile, is coal-bed methane, mixed with water next to coal seams. Only in 1989 did engineers figure out how to separate the natural gas from the water, and soon enough, 200-foot drilling rigs were sinking wells as deep as 25,000 feet.

The mineral industry helped make Wyoming a prosperous state. With fiber optic linkages, some of the nation's lowest electricity rates, and a cool climate, Wyoming has proved a good site for giant data centers — both Microsoft and the National Center for Atmospheric Research have a significant data-center presence around Cheyenne. The American Council for an Energy Efficient Economy ranked Wyoming among the worst states for energy efficiency, but renewable energy is gaining ground. Wind has been the primary focus; Wyoming has the nation's seventh-ranking wind capacity potential. With four new wind farms under development by Rocky Mountain Power and three by other companies, the state is poised to double its installed wind capacity within a few years. Legislators have periodically weighed increasing taxes on wind power generation but so far have decided against it. The state is dabbling in solar power as well; in 2018, the Bureau of Land Management green-lighted a 700-acre solar project on agency land.

While the energy sector buttressed the state during the Great Recession, Wyoming suffered when the sector experienced a downturn. The unemployment rate began edging above the national average, and between late 2014 and early 2019, the number of people employed in Wyoming's oil sector declined by about one-third. The decline hit the state budget particularly hard – the energy and mining sector typically provides the treasury with about two-thirds of its revenue, and despite gains in such fields as tourism and technology, these other fields haven't produced enough revenue to fill in the gaps. The revenue picture improved as the oil and gas sector recovered in 2018.

Wyoming is the nation's least populous state — Washington D.C. is 16 percent bigger in population despite being 1,400 times smaller in area. Its population grew by 14 percent in the decade ending in 2010, but only by an additional 2 percent through 2017, thanks to three consecutive years of shrinking population driven by declines in energy and mining payrolls. Some counties – including Casper-based Natrona, Gillette-based Campbell, Green River-based Sweetwater and Lander-based Fremont – all expanded by between 4 percent and 10 percent during the decade, much of that before the oil and gas downturn. Counties supported by other industries have seen steadier growth of 8 to

10 percent since 2010 – whether it's government (Laramie County, which includes the state capital of Cheyenne), higher education (Albany County, which includes Laramie, home of the University of Wyoming), or tourism (Teton County, which includes the resort area around Jackson Hole). Teton in particular has benefited from Wyoming's remarkable landscape. Yellowstone, established in 1872, was the nation's first national park; it has averaged about 4 million visitors annually in recent years, and Grand Teton National Park is a draw as well. Jackson Hole, just south of the parks, has become one of America's elite year-round resort areas since the early 1980s. Teton County now has a median income 31 percent higher than the state as a whole.

The juxtaposition of civilization and wilderness has created some thorny policy issues. For years, the state has run feeding grounds for elk near Jackson Hole, and the herd has grown to tens of thousands. Environmental groups, worried about the spread of chronic wasting disease, want the feeding stopped, though thousands of elk induced over generations to depend on the feeding grounds likely would die. Local ranchers want it continued, to keep the elk away from their cattle, especially in winter. Grizzly bears, once endangered and protected in Yellowstone, have now increased in number; they were initially removed from the endangered list in 2017, but that decision was overturned by a federal judge the following year. Reintroduction of the endangered gray wolf in Yellowstone in 1995 has also proven contentious, with several judicial decisions handed down over the years about whether the wolf should be taken off the protected list. In 2017, a federal judge ruled that the wolf should be managed by the state, which effectively allowed them to be hunted in most locations in Wyoming. Meanwhile, after protests from locals, the National Park Service agreed to allow snowmobiles and snow coaches into Yellowstone, and the National Forest Service permitted ice climbs on the Shoshone River to the east. Then there's the sage grouse, which has a habitat that covers about a quarter of the state's land area, including regions eyed for drilling. The federal government and private landowners have worked on conservation efforts, but some of those undertaken by the Obama administration have been reversed by the Trump administration.

The settled part of Wyoming consists of medium-sized towns, which are the state's largest cities. It is a small state, a single community really, where people remember who played what position, when and how well, and for what high school football team. Wyoming is 84 percent white and only 1 percent black, but it is almost 10 percent Hispanic. When it was still a territory in 1869, Wyoming was the first to give women the vote. (The exception: New Jersey allowed women with property to vote between 1776 and 1807, but there weren't many women with property.) Wyoming also had the nation's first woman governor, Nellie Tayloe Ross, in the 1920s.

There was once a sharp economic and regional split reflected in its partisan politics. The big economic interests — cattle ranchers, organized in the Wyoming Stock Growers Association, and the Union Pacific Railroad management — favored Republicans, as did the wildcatters, independent producers and oil company geologists. The main Democratic constituency was made up of Union Pacific Railroad workers who built the first transcontinental line across southern Wyoming in the 1860s. (Cheyenne was established because it was the midpoint between the UP's operations in Omaha and Ogden Utah.) The southern tier of counties, from Cheyenne through Laramie to Evanston, once voted Democratic. But now the Democrats are strongest in affluent Teton County, the only one to vote for Barack Obama in both 2008 and 2012, and in Albany County, home of Laramie and the University of Wyoming, which Obama carried in 2008.

Wyoming hasn't elected a Democrat to the Senate since 1970 or to the House since 1976, though it has had Democratic governors over that time. Given how much the GOP has tightened its hold on rural America, it may be a while before the Democrats win the governorship — or any statewide office — again. In 2014, the party couldn't even field a candidate for secretary of state, state treasurer and state auditor, and their candidate for education secretary, a credible business executive, won less than 40 percent of the vote. The Democratic caucuses in both chambers of the legislature number in the single digits.

Still, compared with other solidly Republican states where religious conservatives are dominant, Wyoming has a libertarian, live-and-let-live ethos. In 1994, on the same Election Day when the GOP was winning a competitive gubernatorial race by a 3-2 margin (and rolling to big gains nationally), Wyoming voters rejected a tough anti-abortion ballot measure by an equivalent 3-2 margin. Wyoming attracted negative attention with the gruesome 1998 murder of Matthew Shepard, a gay college student, in Laramie. Since then, Laramie, home of the University of Wyoming, approved an ordinance that banned discrimination on the basis of sexual orientation or gender identity. Wyoming's recent Republican governors, Matt Mead and the newly elected Mark Gordon, come from the GOP's establishment wing.

In the 2016 presidential election, Donald Trump's winning margins in the state's biggest counties all expanded in the GOP's direction, typically by seven to 14 points over 2012. The one that broke the pattern was Teton, which gave Clinton a winning margin 16 points bigger than Obama's in 2012. But in Wyoming, Teton County is the exception that proves the rule.

Cook Partisan Voting Index: R+25

Population		Race and Ethnicity		Income	
Total	583,200	White	84.3%	Median Income	$60,938
Land area (sq. miles)	97,093	Black	1.0%	State Income Rank	19
Pop/ sq mi	6.0	Latino	9.7%	Poverty Rate	11.1%
Born in state	41.8%	Asian	0.8%	With health insurance	88.1%
		Two or more races	2.0%	Cash public assistance	1.6%
Age Groups		Other	2.2%	Food stamp/SNAP	5.8%
Under 18	23.7%				
18-34	23.7%	**Education**		**Work**	
35-64	38.2%	H.S grad or less	35.9%	White Collar	33.6%
Over 64	14.4%	Some college	37.3%	Sales and Service	38.5%
		College Degree, 4 yr	17.4%	Blue Collar	27.9%
Military		Post grad	9.3%	Government	20.9%
Veteran/ Active Duty	11.1%				

Presidential Politics

2016 Caucus (D)	Sanders (D)	4,122 (57%)	Clinton (D)	3,131 (43%)					
2016 Conv. (R)	Cruz (R)	1,128 (69%)	Rubio (R)	231 (14%)	Trump (R)	112	(7%)		
2016 Pres. Vote	Trump (R)	174,419 (68%)	Clinton (D)	55,973 (22%)	Johnson (L)	13,287	(5%)		
2012 Pres. Vote	Romney (R)	170,962 (69%)	Obama (D)	69,286 (28%)	Johnson (L)	5,326	(2%)		

Wyoming was Donald Trump's best state in 2016: his 46-percentage point margin of victory over Hillary Clinton was his biggest of all 50. This wasn't a surprise. It was Mitt Romney's No. 2 state in 2012, when he carried it 69%-28%. Clinton did carry one of the state's 23 counties: Teton, 60%-32%, home to Jackson Hole, the outdoors playground of the super-rich.

Clinton fared only a little better when Wyoming Democrats held their caucuses on April 9. Bernie Sanders stumped in the state — he held a rally there on the night of his victory in the Wisconsin primary — and garnered 57 percent of the state convention delegates. Clinton captured Laramie (Cheyenne) and Natrona (Casper) counties. Sanders won Teton, Sweetwater, an old Democratic base of Union Pacific Railroad workers, and Albany, home of the University of Wyoming. Republicans held county conventions on March 11 and Texas Sen. Ted Cruz defeated Florida Sen. Marco Rubio 66%-20%. Trump finished third with 7 percent.

Congressional Districts

116th Congress Lineup	1R	115th Congress Lineup	1R

Mark Gordon (R)

Elected 2018, term expires 2023, 1st term; b. Mar. 14, 1957, New York, NY; Middlebury College, B.A., 1979; Unknown; Married (Jennie) 4 children.

Elected Office: WI Treasurer, 2012-2019.

Professional Career: Rancher.

Office: 2323 Carey Ave., Cheyenne, 82002-0010; 307-777-7434; Fax: 307-632-3909; Website: governor.wyo.gov

Sec. of State: Edward Buchanan (R)

State Legislature: Senate: 3D, 27R **House:** 9D, 50R, 1V

Election Results

Election	Name (Party)	Vote (%)
2018 General	Mark Gordon (R)	136,412 (67%)
	Mary Throne (D)	55,965 (28%)
	Rex Rammell (CNP)	6,751 (3%)
2018 Primary	Mark Gordon (R)	38,951 (33%)
	Foster Friess (R)	29,842 (25.6)
	Harriet Hageman (R)	25,052 (21.5)
	Sam Galeotos (R)	14,554 (12.5)
	Taylor Haynes (R)	6,511 (5.6)

Mark Gordon prevailed in a hard-fought, six-way Republican primary in 2018 and then easily won the general election to become governor of solidly red Wyoming. Gordon, previously the state treasurer, was the establishment choice in the primary, prevailing in a field that included prominent GOP donor Foster Friess, who lost despite receiving President Donald Trump's coveted endorsement.

Gordon grew up on a ranch near Kaycee and has continued to ranch throughout much of his career, currently running a cow-calf operation and growing hay with his wife, Jennie. He earned a bachelor's degree from Middlebury College and then ran several businesses in Buffalo and Sheridan, including two devoted to outdoor recreation and tourism. He also worked in the oil and gas industry. Gordon polished his financial skills as a member of the Board of the Federal Reserve Bank of Kansas City between 2008 and 2012; he also served as a board member of the Nature Conservancy of Wyoming. He was appointed state treasurer in 2012 following the death of the incumbent, Joseph Meyer. Gordon was elected to a term of his own in 2014. As treasurer, Gordon was named by the Sovereign Wealth Fund Institute as one of the top 100 "most significant and impactful asset owners and public executives."

Gordon entered a wide-open race to succeed outgoing, two-term Gov. Matt Mead. Mead, a Republican, had been elected in 2010 to succeed two-term Democratic Gov. Dave Freudenthal. Mead easily won a second term in 2014, though he grappled with declining revenues as the state's large energy sector experienced a slump. In a state in which the Republican Party is so dominant that most of the ideological debate occurs within the party, Mead tended to be a pragmatist. He worked to adapt Common Core standards for the state rather than junking them, and he repealed a ban on adopting science-education standards that say global warming is caused by humans. Mead also sought to expand Medicaid under the Affordable Care Act. But the GOP-dominated legislature put the kibosh on the idea.

In the primary, Gordon faced Friess, natural-resources attorney Harriet Hageman, businessman Sam Galeotos, rancher Taylor Haynes, and businessman Bill Dahlin. Friess, running as an outsider and with a relatively small footprint in state politics, sought to leverage his wealth and national connections within the conservative movement; several figures and groups he had backed previously returned the favor by endorsing and campaigning for him, including former Sen. Rick Santorum of Pennsylvania, Sen. Rand Paul of Kentucky and the Tea Party Patriots. Donald Trump Jr. gave Friess his endorsement, and his father, the president, followed up with the tweeted exhortation that Friess "will be a fantastic governor!" Friess told the New York Times, "We absolutely love this place, and now we have a half-billion-dollar deficit. And a lot of the elite here are treating my money, our money, the welders' money, the carpenters' money, nurses' money, truck drivers' money, as if it's Monopoly money." Friess topped his rivals in advertising spending. "He's got plenty of jack and he's using every cent of it. Every cent of it," Gordon supporter and former Sen. Alan Simpson told Politico. "We'll see whether you can really buy a governor's race." In the end, he couldn't. Gordon, touting a message of fiscal responsibility, won key in-state endorsements and secured 33 percent of the vote. Friess was second with 26 percent. It marked an unusual loss for a Trump-backed candidate in a Republican primary.

In such a Republican state, the general election was anticlimactic. The Democrats nominated a respected former legislator, Mary Throne, who agreed with Gordon on some issues – such as promoting carbon sequestration, securing a role for coal and natural gas, and criminal-justice reform – but differed on others, including nondiscrimination laws for sexual orientation and gender identity. Throne supported Medicaid expansion; Gordon wouldn't go that far, but he said he'd back a waiver program for the state's Medicaid program. Throne also proposed a tax overhaul. Rex ("T-Rex") Rammell of the Constitution Party attacked Gordon from the right, calling climate change the "greatest hoax in human history," while Larry Streumpf, of the Libertarian Party, took a more middle-of-the-road approach, backing wind power and a property tax increase to improve the state's financial picture. In the end, the share of the general election vote taken by third-party and write-in votes shrank from 13 percent in the 2014 gubernatorial race to 5 percent in 2018. Gordon defeated Throne, 67%-28%. Throne essentially matched her party's percentage from four years earlier, but she flipped affluent Teton County (Jackson), which had backed Mead by five points in 2014 and Throne by 15 points in 2018.

Once in office, Gordon prepared for negotiations with the GOP-dominated legislature on the state's revenue challenges and its strained education and infrastructure budgets. He proposed establishing a permanent fund for vocational and technical education, and he sought $10 million for a carbon capture test project.

Mike Enzi (R)

Elected 1996, term expires 2020, 4th term, b. Feb 01, 1944; Bremerton, WA; George Washington University (DC), B.B.A., 1966; University of Denver (CO), M.B.A., 1968; Presbyterian; Married (Diana Buckley Enzi); 3 children; 4 grandchildren.

Military Career: WY Air National Guard 1967-1973

Elected Office: Gillette Mayor, 1975-1982; WY House, 1986-1990; WY Senate, 1990-1996.

Professional Career: Owner, NZ Shoes, 1969-1995; Director & Chairman, First WY Bank of Gillette, 1978-1988; Accounting Manager & computer programmer, Dunbar Well Service, 1985-1997; Ed. Comm. of States, 1989-1993; Director, Black Hills Corporation, 1992-1996; Western Interstate Comm. for Higher Ed., 1995-1996.

DC Office: 379-A RSOB 20510, 202-224-3424, Fax: 202-228-0359, enzi.senate.gov
State Offices: Casper, 307-261-6572; Cheyenne, 307-772-2477; Cody, 307-527-9444; Gillette, 307-682-6268; Jackson, 307-739-9507.

Committees: *Budget (Chmn)*. *Finance*: Energy, Natural Resources & Infrastructure; Health Care; Taxation & IRS Oversight. *Health, Education, Labor & Pensions*: Primary Health & Retirement Security (Chmn). *Homeland Security & Government Affairs*: Federal Spending Oversight & Emergency Management; Regulatory Affairs & Federal Management. *Joint Taxation*.

Group Ratings

	ADA	ACLU	AFL-CIO	LCV	ITI	COC	HAFA	ACU	CFG	FRC
2018	-	19%	-	7%	-	70%	75%	86%	88%	100%
2017	0%	C	0%	0%	C	86%	C	80%	86%	100%

Almanac Ratings 2017-18

	Economy	Social	Foreign	Composite
Liberal	6%	6%	0%	4%
Conservative	94%	94%	100%	96%

Key Votes of the 115th Congress

1. Obama-care revision	Y	5. Gun regulations	Y	9. Kavanaugh confirmation	Y
2. Tax Cuts	Y	6. Family planning regs	Y	10. Saudi arms sales	N
3. Dodd-Frank revision	Y	7. Gorsuch confirmation	Y	11. FISA rules	Y
4. Omnibus appropriations	N	8. Immigration restrictions	N	12. Military aid in Yemen	N

Election Results

Election	Name (Party)	Vote (%)		Cand. Spent	Ind. Exp. Support	Ind. Exp. Oppose
2014 General	Mike Enzi (R)	121,554	(72%)	$3,486,953		
	Charlie Hardy (D)	29,377	(17%)	$88,284		
	Curt Gottshall (I)	13,311	(8%)	$76,431		
	Joe Porambo (L)	3,677	(2%)			
2014 Primary	Mike Enzi (R)	77,965	(82%)			
	Bryan Miller (R)	9,330	(10%)			

Prior winning percentages: 2008 (76%), 2002 (73%), 1996 (54%)

Mike Enzi, the senior senator from Wyoming, was elected in 1996. He is a mild-mannered conservative who has shown skills in working both sides of the aisle and winning backroom legislative battles. As chairman of the Budget Committee, he has had opportunities to assist in crafting a Republican game plan on fiscal issues. But he and Senate Republicans have taken little action to address mounting deficits since he took the post in 2015. Enzi's widespread support among Republicans helped thwart a 2014 primary challenge from Liz Cheney, who now serves in the House.

Enzi grew up in Thermopolis and Sheridan, the son of a shoe salesman. He earned degrees in accounting and retail marketing, moved to Gillette, and became an accountant for an oil well servicing company. He and his wife, Diana, started a small business, NZ Shoes. In the 1970s, at a meeting of his local Jaycee business group, Enzi met Republican Sen. Alan Simpson, who was impressed by his volunteerism and suggested he run for public office. In 1975, Enzi was elected mayor of Gillette, the center of Wyoming's coal belt and its fastest-growing town. He was mayor for eight years. In 1986, he was elected to the Wyoming state House and in 1990 to the state Senate.

After Simpson announced his retirement in December 1995, Enzi was one of nine Republicans and two Democrats who ran for the seat. With support from a grassroots network of conservatives, Enzi finished first in a straw poll at the Republican State Convention. His key difference with second-place finisher John Barrasso was on abortion rights — Enzi opposed abortion rights, and Barrasso favored them. Barrasso had more money, but Enzi won 32%-30%. Barrasso, later elected to the Senate, and Enzi have become friendly colleagues in the chamber. In the general election, the Democratic nominee, former Secretary of State Kathy Karpan, opposed gun control and abortion rights. Her support for President Bill Clinton and his Interior secretary, former Arizona Gov. Bruce Babbitt, doomed her candidacy in solidly Republican Wyoming. Enzi led from the outset and won 54%-42%.

Enzi offers several indices for his conservative credentials. He has been a conservative stalwart — his lifetime rating from the anti-tax American Conservative Union through 2018 was 91 percent, one of the highest among senators. The Almanac vote ratings have placed Enzi in the top one-third of the most conservative Republicans. Enzi has regularly introduced his "Repeal Amendment," a constitutional amendment enabling two-thirds of the states to overturn a federal law; tea party activists have applauded the proposal.

Enzi left his biggest mark on the Health, Education, Labor and Pensions Committee. Despite his ideological differences with the late Sen. Ted Kennedy of Massachusetts, with whom he alternated the chairmanship for years, Enzi forged a productive relationship with the liberal lion. They operated on the "80-20 principle" — reach broad agreement on 80 percent of an issue and leave out the 20 percent where no agreement can be found. The legislation that the two successfully pushed through the committee included a bill requiring insurance companies to treat mental illness the same as other ailments in coverage decisions, reauthorization of Head Start early education and renewal of college aid programs.

As chairman of the HELP panel in 2005, Enzi sided with Kennedy in opposing a proposal by the Bush administration to encourage more use of government vouchers for private school tuition in Gulf states recovering from Hurricane Katrina. On an issue of special interest with constituents, he helped enact a bill to expedite the cleanup of abandoned coal mines. He was instrumental in resolving conflicts over the funding formula to renew domestic AIDS programs.

Enzi participated in bipartisan negotiations in 2009 on President Barack Obama's health care proposal. His alternative called for tax credits for buying health insurance, assistance to help small businesses provide coverage for their employees and requirements for the states to reduce the cost of medical malpractice insurance. The "Gang of Six" group of senators that met during the summer that year failed to hammer out a solution acceptable to both parties.

In 2011, Democrat Tom Harkin of Iowa, then chairman of the HELP Committee, worked with Enzi to rewrite the No Child Left Behind education law. Some Republicans on the panel derailed a drafting session, complaining that they had been left out of the process. The bill passed the committee with Enzi and two other Republicans joining all committee Democrats in support, but it never came to a vote on the Senate floor.

On other legislation, Enzi regularly has sought common ground. As the only accountant in the Senate, Enzi played a key role in the enactment in 2002 of a corporate accountability bill. With Banking Chairman Paul Sarbanes of Maryland, he reached a compromise to establish an accounting board that had the power to oversee accounting firms and was independent of the Securities and Exchange Commission. The compromise was part of what became known as the Sarbanes-Oxley corporate accounting law.

For years, Enzi sought a seat on the Finance Committee. Twice in 2007, he was bypassed when GOP Senate leaders gave a committee vacancy to less senior Senators, who had their own political imperatives. An unhappy Enzi briefly considered retiring in 2008. Instead, he was re-elected that year and finally filled a vacant seat .

After Republicans took back the majority after the 2014 elections, Enzi was part of an unexpected battle for the chairmanship of the Budget Committee with Jeff Sessions of Alabama. Sessions had been the top Republican on the panel and was widely expected to take over as chairman. But the low-key Enzi startled fellow senators when he decided to use his edge in seniority over Sessions to claim the slot. Ultimately, Sessions deferred to Enzi, avoiding what could have been a nasty battle.

After taking over as Budget chairman, Enzi promised to offer a blueprint bringing the budget into balance within 10 years "without gimmicks and bad accounting." At the end of 2016, he unveiled a plan to move to a two-year appropriations process and eliminate the possibility of a shutdown by automatically funding the government if appropriations measures have not been enacted on time. He called the reforms "one of my top priorities."

Enzi worked in 2015 with House Budget Committee Chairman Tom Price of Georgia to win approval of a budget with big increases in defense spending and steep cuts in domestic programs. After the expected rejection from congressional Democrats and Obama, the bipartisan congressional leaders late that year agreed on a deal with a two-year budget framework. In February 2016, Enzi took the unusual step of refusing to invite officials from the Obama administration to present their annual budget to the Budget Committee. "It's not a significant budget, and holding a hearing on it doesn't do anything," he said.

In January 2017, Enzi filed a resolution in which he triggered the start of the annual budget process with a provision calling for repeal of the Affordable Care Act. The Republican-controlled Congress quickly agreed to his resolution, but the House and Senate failed to repeal the actual law. In October, Enzi worked with Republican leaders to agree on procedural steps that gave parliamentary protections to expedite the Republican tax-cut legislation. The accompanying budget resolution also projected more than $3 trillion in spending cuts — much of it from Medicaid and other health care programs and entitlements. But Republicans failed to enact most of those changes, which helped explain why the federal budget spiraled to an annual deficit exceeding $1 trillion.

In the face of that yawning federal deficit plus the difficulty of the Senate reaching agreement with the Democratic-controlled House, Enzi in early 2019 deferred action on his committee's chief responsibility of preparing an annual congressional budget. A year earlier, Enzi had suggested his committee, and his chairmanship, were irrelevant when he proposed eliminating the Budget panel. "It's getting very difficult to pass a budget," he told reporters. With no signs of his promised 10-year blueprint, his call to abolish the Budget Committee likely would worsen the fiscal challenges facing the nation and increase the deficit. Alternatively, Enzi supported a two-year cycle to handle spending bills, with greater oversight by congressional committees.

In July 2017, Enzi joined another part of the congressional Republican dysfunction when he conceded the failure of their efforts to repeal and revise the Affordable Care Act. "I am disappointed that we were unable to make more progress," he said. "We all know health care is complicated, but that doesn't change the need for us to find a way forward in order to provide relief for our constituents."

Amid those challenges, Enzi faced a decision whether to seek re-election in 2020 at 76. With little risk of a competitive Democratic opponent, Enzi's chief concern appeared to be another challenge from Cheney. In 2013, Cheney had taken steps toward such a primary contest. Cheney, who had been a State Department official and prominent conservative activist, ended her prospective bid in January 2014, citing "serious health issues" in her family. Enzi subsequently had another easy re-election. Cheney's election to the House two years later suggested that she was prepared to take a longer route to the Senate, though her selection to a House leadership position gave her some reason to remain in that chamber — especially if she would face a tough contest with Enzi.

For Enzi, the Senate Republican term-limit rules would require him to step down as Budget Committee chairman in 2021. But in 2019, he announced that he would not seek a fifth term in 2020.

John Barrasso (R)

Appointed 2007, term expires 2024, 2nd full term, b. Jul 21, 1952; Reading, PA; Georgetown University (DC), B.S., 1974; Georgetown University School of Medicine (DC), M.D., 1978; Presbyterian; Married (Bobbi Brown); 3 children (2 from previous marriage).

Elected Office: WY Senate, 2002-2007.

Professional Career: Orthopedic surgeon, 1983-2007; RNC Chairman, 1992-1996; Chief of staff, WY Med. Center, 2003-2005.

DC Office: 307 DSOB 20510, 202-224-6441, Fax: 202-224-1724, barrasso.senate.gov

State Offices: Casper, 307-261-6413; Cheyenne, 307-772-2451; Riverton, 307-856-6642; Rock Springs, 307-362-5012; Sheridan, 307-672-6456.

Committees: Senate Republican Conference Chairman. *Energy & Natural Resources*: National Parks; Public Lands, Forests & Mining; Water & Power. *Environment & Public Works (Chmn)*. *Foreign Relations*: Europe & Regional Security Cooperation; Internat'l Dev Instit & Internat'l Econ, Energy & Environ Policy; West Hem Crime Civ Sec Dem Rights & Women's Issues. *Indian Affairs*.

Group Ratings

	ADA	ACLU	AFL-CIO	LCV	ITI	COC	HAFA	ACU	CFG	FRC
2018	-	19%	-	7%	-	70%	73%	86%	77%	100%
2017	0%	C	0%	0%	C	86%	C	80%	87%	100%

Almanac Ratings 2017-18

	Economy	Social	Foreign	Composite
Liberal	6%	6%	0%	4%
Conservative	94%	94%	100%	96%

Key Votes of the 115th Congress

1. Obama-care revision	Y	5. Gun regulations	Y	9. Kavanaugh confirmation	Y
2. Tax Cuts	Y	6. Family planning regs	Y	10. Saudi arms sales	N
3. Dodd-Frank revision	Y	7. Gorsuch confirmation	Y	11. FISA rules	Y
4. Omnibus appropriations	N	8. Immigration restrictions	N	12. Military aid in Yemen	N

Election Results

Election	Name (Party)	Vote (%)		Cand. Spent	Ind. Exp. Support	Ind. Exp. Oppose
2018 General	John Barrasso (R)	136,210	(67%)	$4,267,798		
	Gary Trauner (D)	61,227	(30%)	$895,349		
	Joe Porambo (Lib)	5,658	(3%)			
2018 Primary	John Barrasso (R)	74,292	(65%)			
	David Dodson (R)	32,647	(29%)			

Prior winning percentages: 2012 (76%), 2008 special (73%)

Republican John Barrasso, Wyoming's junior senator, was appointed in June 2007 to fill a Senate vacancy. He has taken prime Senate leadership roles as chairman of both the Environment and Public Works Committee and the Republican Conference. He has used those platforms to identify policy priorities and move legislation, especially those serving the interests of Western states. In 2018, he spearheaded enactment of a nationwide water-resource bill. With a boost from the endorsement of President Donald Trump, Barrasso easily won a Republican primary in 2018 against a well-financed conservative.

Barrasso grew up in Reading, Pennsylvania, the son of a World War II veteran who made a living as a cement finisher and who took his family to Washington every four years for presidential inaugurations. Barrasso earned his undergraduate and medical degrees from Georgetown University, moved to Wyoming in the 1980s and set up practice as an orthopedic surgeon in Casper. Barrasso made his name in local Republican politics, serving as a Republican national committeeman and as state party treasurer. He was a local radio and television personality, dispensing practical medical advice on news programs and in public service announcements.

In 1996, a decade before his appointment to the Senate, Barrasso ran for an open seat when Republican Sen. Alan Simpson retired. He faced then-state Sen. Michael Enzi in a crowded GOP primary in which abortion played a key role. Running as a moderate, Barrasso favored abortion rights and had opposed a 1994 constitutional amendment to ban most abortions. Enzi, who had support from social conservatives, opposed abortion rights and edged out Barrasso 32%-30%. The two joined forces for the general election, with Barrasso serving as Enzi's finance chairman in the fall.

In 2002, Barrasso won election to the state Senate, where he worked on health care issues and chaired the Transportation, Highways, and Military Affairs Committee. He sponsored a bill to increase the criminal penalty for killing a pregnant woman, but Democratic Gov. Dave Freudenthal vetoed it. He occasionally crossed the political aisle to join with Democrats, backing a bill to exempt food from the state sales tax and supporting a ban on smoking in public buildings. He sponsored a law enabling physicians to talk freely with patients about medical complications without putting themselves at risk of the conversations being used against them in a lawsuit.

After Republican Sen. Craig Thomas died of leukemia in June 2007, Wyoming's Republican State Central Committee had 15 days to select three candidates to fill the vacancy; the governor was required to pick one of them. That triggered a scramble, as 31 candidates applied for consideration. Unlike in his Senate bid 11 years earlier, Barrasso emphasized his conservative credentials to the committee. "I believe in limited government, lower taxes, less spending, traditional family values, local control and a strong national defense," he told the committee. He noted that he had an "A" rating from the National Rifle Association, voted for prayer in public schools, sponsored legislation "to protect the sanctity of life" and opposed same-sex marriage.

The Republican committee named three finalists: Barrasso; Cynthia Lummis, who had served 14 years in the Legislature and two terms as state treasurer; and Tom Sansonetti, who had been Thomas' chief of staff and an assistant attorney general in the Bush administration. Lummis was not on good terms with the governor, and Sansonetti had been a lobbyist for mining and ranching interests. Barrasso, by contrast, had worked with Freudenthal on health care issues. The governor tapped him for the seat. He ran in 2008 to fill out Thomas' term and was unopposed in the Republican primary. In the general election, he defeated Democratic lawyer Nick Carter, an underfunded political newcomer, 73%-27%. Barrasso won a full six-year term in 2012 with 76 percent of the vote. Wyoming has not elected a Democrat to the Senate since 1970.

Barrasso has shown wide-ranging interests, though they often have a local tilt. In 2009, he showed his early interest in health care and regional issues when he won approval of a provision to benefit rural doctors and hospitals. He broke with many conservatives — but joined many farm groups — in calling for lifting the U.S. ban on travel to Cuba, saying U.S. citizens should be free to visit relatives in the communist country. He proposed legislation to protect undeveloped areas of the Wyoming range from oil and gas development and to preserve 387 miles around the Snake River. It became law as part of a larger land management bill in 2009. As Indian Affairs Committee chairman in 2015, he worked with Montana Democrat Jon Tester, the committee's vice chairman, to reintroduce a bill to streamline federal reviews of Native American energy projects.

As a veteran member of the Energy and Natural Resources Committee and the Environment and Public Works Committee, Barrasso has reflected the views of constituents and industries back home by expressing skepticism about federal regulation. In 2009, he said Democrats' cap-and-trade bill regulating carbon emissions would have unfairly punished his state's farmers and ranchers. In 2013, he lashed out at Obama's nominee to head the Environmental Protection Agency, Gina McCarthy, asserting that the agency was "making it impossible for our coal miners to feed their families." He filed legislation to bar the EPA from regulating greenhouse gases blamed for climate change.

He has found some success legislatively. Barrasso supported removing gray wolves from the Endangered Species List, telling The Associated Press: "This is a Wyoming concern that requires a Wyoming solution. It does not require interference from Washington." Barrasso loudly objected to a CIA center on climate change. The agency closed the center in 2012.

With Oklahoma Sen. Jim Inhofe term-limited as chairman of the Environment Committee, Barrasso took control in January 2017 — the same month President Donald Trump brought radical change in resource policies and enforcement. Barrasso supported Scott Pruitt's nomination to lead the EPA in the Trump administration. Pruitt, a former attorney general of Oklahoma, "will be the strong leader the EPA needs," Barrasso said.

As Pruitt ran into numerous ethical controversies, Barrasso stood by him — initially. "Administrator Pruitt has accomplished key priorities as head of the EPA," Barrasso said in April 2018. "With the support of the president, he has been instrumental in returning the agency to its original mission. American workers are benefiting from his reversal of punishing regulations." But he agreed in June to Democratic demands to hold an oversight hearing to review conflicts of interest at Pruitt's EPA. Three weeks later, in the face of declining support from Republicans, Pruitt resigned. Given that it had become "increasingly challenging for the EPA to carry out its mission with the administrator under investigation," Barrasso said, Trump made the right decision to accept his resignation

At a February 2017 hearing on proposals to "modernize" the Endangered Species Act, Barrasso said the law "is not working today" and he cited the many public officials and rural groups that have sought change. The law has not been reauthorized since 1992. In July 2018, he unveiled his proposal to revise the law by giving greater authority to states to manage wildlife within their borders. A highlight was a provision to form federal-state teams to create conservation strategies for a listed species. "We must do more than just keep listed species on life support," Barrasso said. "We need to see them recovered." His alternative included recommendations from the Western Governors Association. Some Democrats objected, saying his plan would undermine enforcement.

Barrasso turned his attention to legislation to fund water infrastructure projects by the Army Corps of Engineers — including inland waterways, dams, irrigation and water storage. The bill received broad bipartisan backing and was signed by Trump in October 2018. The measure was "good for our communities as well as the country, the economy as well as the environment," Barrasso told the Casper Star-Tribune. Included was modification of the Fontenelle Dam to permit increased storage along the Colorado River in Wyoming. With broad support, he also won enactment of a bill in January 2019 that was designed to increase transparency and overhaul internal operations at the Nuclear Regulatory Commission.

Barrasso has gained his broader partisan platform, becoming a firm ally of Republican Leader Mitch McConnell of Kentucky. In 2011, he took control of the Republican Policy Committee. In 2019, he moved up to become Republican Conference chairman, the No. 3 leadership position. At the same time, Rep. Liz Cheney of Wyoming became the chairwoman of the House Republican Conference — an unusual mark for one state.

In 2016, Barrasso chaired the Platform Committee of the Republican National Convention, where he worked with officials of the Trump campaign to find acceptable provisions. While reaching agreement on that document and afterward, Barrasso occasionally offered mild critiques or warnings to Trump. Asked in an interview on CNN whether Trump should release his tax returns, Barrasso said, "I think it would be a good idea. ... I'm somebody's who's in favor of transparency and openness." In response to Trump's travel ban on citizens from several Muslim-majority nations, which he issued a week after he took office, Barrasso said, "a religious test or ban is against everything our country stands for."

Those comments caught the attention of some conservatives in Wyoming. Erik Prince, the former head of the security contractor Blackwater USA, said that he was considering a challenge to Barrasso and had been encouraged by Stephen Bannon, a former executive chairman of Breitbart and former top Trump aide. "The people of Wyoming, they embrace very much Trump's agenda and its senator should too," Prince told NBC in October 2017. Prince, who had few ties to Wyoming, reportedly was promised ample conservative fundraising if he challenged Barrasso for working too closely with McConnell.

When Prince decided not to run, little-known businessman David Dodson self-financed nearly $2 million on a GOP primary challenge that sought to depict Barrasso as a Washington insider and advocated "a new way of doing business." Trump boosted Barrasso with a tweet that he was "absolutely outstanding in every way." Barrasso won the primary with 65 percent of the vote. In a November challenge from Democrat Gary Trauner, an executive at a medical center in Jackson Hole, Barrasso won 67%-30%. Trauner had run competitive campaigns for the House a decade earlier.

Liz Cheney (R)

Elected 2016, 2nd term, b. Jul 28, 1966; Madison, WI; Colorado College, B.A., 1988; University of Chicago Law School, J.D., 1996; Methodist; Married (Philip Perry); 5 children.

Professional Career: Staff, United States Agency for International Development, 1989-1992; Staff, United States Department of State, 1992; Attorney, International Finance Corporation, 199-2002; Deputy Assistant Secretary of State for Near Eastern Affairs, United States Department of State, 2002-2004; Presidential Campaign Staff, George W. Bush, 2004; Principal Deputy Assistant Secretary of State for Near Eastern Affairs, United States Department of State, 2005-2009; Non profit executive; Television commentator.

DC Office: 416 CHOB 20515, 202-225-2311, Fax: 202-225-3057, cheney.house.gov
State Offices: Casper, 307-261-6595; Cheyenne, 307-772-2595; Gillette, 307-414-1677; Riverton, 307-463-0482.

Committees: House Republican Conference Chairman. *Armed Services*: Military Personnel; Strategic Forces. *Natural Resources*: Energy & Mineral Resources.

Group Ratings

	ADA	ACLU	AFL-CIO	LCV	ITI	COC	HAFA	ACU	CFG	FRC
2018	-	4%	-	0%	-	82%	61%	77%	54%	100%
2017	0%	C	8%	0%	C	93%	C	81%	75%	100%

Almanac Ratings 2017-18

	Economy	Social	Foreign	Composite
Liberal	2%	3%	0%	2%
Conservative	98%	97%	100%	98%

Key Votes of the 115th Congress

1. Obama-care revision	Y	5. Family planning regs	Y	9. Guantanamo prisoners	N
2. Tax Cuts	Y	6. Body cameras/immigration	N	10. Ground missiles, limit	N
3. Omnibus appropriations	Y	7. Abortion ban	Y	11. Defense Dept. spending	Y
4. Dodd-Frank revision	Y	8. Concealed carry	Y	12. FISA rules	Y

Election Results

Election	Name (Party)	Vote (%)		Cand. Spent	Ind. Exp. Support	Ind. Exp. Oppose
2018 General	Liz Cheney (R).................................	127,963	(64%)	$4,315		
	Greg Hunter (D).............................	59,903	(30%)	$40,967		
	Richard Brubaker (Lib).................	6,918	(3%)			
	Daniel Cummings (CNP)................	6,070	(3%)	$486		

Prior winning percentages: 2016 (62%)

Liz Cheney of Wyoming was elected in 2016 to the seat that her father, Dick Cheney, held for a decade before he became secretary of Defense and, later, vice president. In November 2018, she was elected — without opposition — to chair the House Republican Conference. Her father, too, won that position during his second term in the House 38 years earlier. Liz Cheney made a quick impression on other Republicans with her informed and often outspoken style. That success and the opportunity to advance higher as a House GOP leader complicated her decision whether to run in 2020 for the seat of retiring Sen. Mike Enzi. Prior to her own electoral success, she worked closely with her father and shared many of his views, especially as a hawk on national security issues.

Growing up with the Cheney family, she resided chiefly in the Washington D.C. area and said that she split her time in Casper Wyoming. She got her bachelor's from Colorado College and her law degree from the University of Chicago. Before law school, she worked with the State Department and the U.S. Agency for International Development, then joined the consulting firm of Richard Armitage. Cheney practiced international law in the private sector. In 2002, she was appointed deputy assistant secretary of State for Near Eastern Affairs and remained at the State Department until the end of the Bush presidency, except for a break to work on the Bush-Cheney reelection campaign. With the change in administration, she served as chair of Keep America Safe, a nonprofit organization, and assisted her father with his writing.

In 2013, Cheney mounted a controversial challenge to Republican Sen. Mike Enzi of Wyoming. She was criticized as an outsider who had spent little time living in the state; she was distracted by an unexpected intra-family split over same-sex marriage with her sister Mary, who is a lesbian. Trailing by more than 50 points in a poll, Cheney withdrew from the race in January 2014, citing health issues in her family. Enzi was easily reelected.

When Republican Rep. Cynthia Lummis announced that she would retire in 2016, Cheney ran for the open seat. She was endorsed by a wide range of national Republicans and conservative leaders. In the eight-candidate GOP primary, her chief challenger was state Sen. Leland Christensen, a leader of the "constitutionalist" movement; he was endorsed by Sen. Rand Paul, who frequently clashed with the Cheneys on national security issues. Christensen accused Cheney of repeatedly lying or misleading voters about her campaign and experience in Wyoming. Cheney spent $2.1 million for the cycle, more than three times as much as her top three GOP opponents combined. Cheney took 40 percent of the vote to 22 percent for Christensen.

In the general election, Democrat Ryan Greene was a political newcomer who worked for an oil-field services company. He called himself a "persuader" and said that Cheney was "a-bomb-thrower" and "long on political ambition but short on Wyoming experience." He spent $184,000 and was largely ignored by national Democrats and liberal groups. Cheney supported Donald Trump for president, though she described as "appalling" his comments about groping women that were publicized in October. Cheney won, 62%-30%.

In the House, Cheney got committee assignments that catered to her local and national interests, on Natural Resources and Armed Services. In February 2017, the House passed her bill to repeal the Bureau of Land Management's land planning and management strategies, which were approved during the final days of the Obama administration. Trump signed the bill the following month. In November 2018, the Resources panel approved her bill to increase local input in enforcement of the federal Public Lands Act, including three wilderness areas of Wyoming that had been studied for four decades.

Revisiting an approach that her father had pursued years earlier, Cheney urged Trump to restore enhanced interrogation techniques in the war on terror. Working on the annual defense spending bill in 2017, she added a provision to assure that a minimum of 400 intercontinental ballistic missiles are retained at their site in Wyoming. With Republican Sen. Tom Cotton of Arkansas, she filed legislation that was designed to reduce Russia's advantage in tactical nuclear weapons. In December 2018, she said that Trump had made a "serious strategic error" in calling for the withdrawal of U.S. troops from

Syria, where they were supporting the fight against the ISIS caliphate. "American retreat will aid our adversaries, Russia and Iran, and hurt our allies, including Israel." Trump subsequently reversed himself and kept the troops in Syria.

Following the 2018 election, Cheney was elected without opposition to chair the House Republican Conference. Rep. Cathy McMorris Rodgers of Washington, who had held the position, decided not to seek another term. With direct criticism of her predecessor, Cheney wrote to other Republicans that the election results had shown that "our message isn't breaking through" and that "we must fundamentally overhaul and modernize our House GOP communications operation." In January 2019, she was an early proponent of the decision by Republican leaders to strip Rep. Steve King of Iowa of his committee assignments following his positive comments about "white supremacy."

At home, two Republicans challenged Cheney in the 2018 primary, but each spent less than $5,000. She won with 68 percent of the vote. In November, Cheney defeated Democrat Greg Hunter, 64%-30%, and took all but two counties — Laramie-based Albany and Jackson-based Teton. With Enzi's May 2019 retirement announcement, Cheney was the clear favorite to succeed him—if she decides to run. Even with her quick advance among House Republicans, it wasn't clear that she would have an early opportunity to replace the two top GOP leaders: Kevin McCarthy and Steve Scalise. As was the case with her father during his career, she had plenty of options.

THE INSULAR TERRITORIES

AMERICAN SAMOA

American Samoa, the only American territory south of the equator, remains almost as Polynesian today as it was when the United States took possession of it in 1900 at the request of tribal chiefs. These seven hot, rainy islands are 2,500 miles southwest of Hawaii, 1,700 miles northeast of New Zealand and have a land area slightly larger than the District of Columbia.

American Samoa has 51,000 people, the vast majority of them on the island of Tutuila. The islands' population had rapidly grown in recent decades, but since has dipped from a peak of 58,000 amid economic struggles. Fear that outsiders would change the culture prompted demands for stricter immigration standards, though the population remained 89% Samoan as of 2010. A federal law in 1940 classified American Samoans as U.S. nationals but not as U.S. citizens; they can serve in the military, but not as officers. That law was challenged in federal court as a violation of the 14th Amendment, but was upheld. The territory has had a non-voting delegate in Congress since 1981.

The Interior Department has overseen administration of American Samoa since 1956 and operates a National Park based in northern Tutuila, which attracts close to 14,000 visitors per year. Due to local customs that prohibit selling the land on which the park sits, the U.S. government has leased it from local villages. American Samoa adopted its own constitution in 1967. Residents elect a governor and a two-house legislature known as the Fono. The secretary of the Interior appoints the chief justice and associate justice of the High Court. About 16 percent of American Samoans are Mormon. Many are bilingual. Close to 90 percent of the population speaks Samoan at home. Government is mostly conducted in English. Fono proceedings are in Samoan, and court sessions are conducted in English but translated into Samoan. Within this governmental framework, older Samoan traditions and politics survive. Local chiefs, or matai, oversee communal lands and kinship systems called aigas.

Pago Pago, the largest town in American Samoa, has one of the finest natural harbors in the Pacific. But the market economy has not made much progress here. American Samoa leans heavily on the federal government, which contributes more than half of its revenues. The territorial government employs almost 45 percent of the workforce.

The tuna canning industry, the only real private sector work in the territory, has suffered in the past decade. Two big tuna canneries owned by StarKist and Chicken of the Sea once provided one-third of U.S. canned tuna and employed more than 5,000 workers. But dipping demand, international competition, regularly enforced minimum wage increases and regulatory issues have decimated the industry and hurt the local economy. American Samoa saw a 5.3 percent decrease in its Gross Domestic Product in 2017 after a 2.6 percent drop in 2016. Chicken of the Sea closed its plant and laid off 2,100 workers in 2009. StarKist, owned by the Korean firm Dongwon, reduced its workforce from 3,000 to 1,200 in 2010, though that had grown to 2,300 by 2018. In 2017, StarKist agreed to pay $6.9 million to settle a wastewater pollution case. Samoa Tuna Processors shuttered 2016, leading to doubling of the unemployment rate in 2017, from 10.5% to 21.5% A tax break that the tuna companies say is crucial to keeping operations in the territory was not included in the final version of Republicans' massive 2017 tax cut package.

The Bank of Hawaii, the only bank serving the territory, said in 2012 it planned to leave but agreed to stay on at a reduced capacity until a replacement could be found. The territory responded by chartering its own bank, the first new U.S. public bank in almost a century. Its creation was approved by the Federal Reserve in 2018.

Wages have been a perpetual problem in the territory. Average household incomes in American Samoa hover around $22,000, less than half the national average. In 2007, Congress passed a law raising the minimum wage in American Samoa to $7.25 an hour by 2014, but federally mandated delays had frozen wages for cannery workers. As of 2019, it had risen to $5.56 an hour, making it hard for the territory to compete with nearby islands where workers make $1 an hour in canneries.

Health is a major issue in American Samoa. The territory has one of the highest obesity rates in the world. With obesity have come diabetes and heart disease. One in five babies born in American Samoa is overweight, and usually within a year most infants are obese, according to a Brown University study. One in three American Samoans suffer from diabetes. Still, American Samoans have developed a reputation for athleticism, most notably in American football. American Samoa has sent 30 players to the National Football League and more than 200 to colleges in the NCAA. Top coaches make the long flight to Pago Pago to scout high school players.

American Samoa does not cast electoral votes for president, but it does send delegates to the major parties' national conventions. In 2016, its nine Republican delegates were unpledged, but they lined up behind Donald Trump after his victory in Indiana. Hillary Clinton won the territory's Democratic caucuses in 2008 and 2016.

Governor

Democrat Lolo Letalu Matalasi Moliga was elected in 2012 to succeed term-limited Gov. Togiola Tulafono. He was a High Talking Chief (Lolo) in the village of Sili in the Manu'a islands and High Chief (Letalu) from Ta'u, the largest island in the Manu'a group. He received an education degree from Chadron State College in Nebraska and a Master's of Public Administration from San Diego State University. He worked as a teacher and principal at Manu'a High School. He later became a school administrator, head of the American Samoa budget office, and chief procurement officer for the territory. He was elected to four terms in the territorial House of Representatives and to the Senate. In the November 2012 election for governor, Moliga, running as an independent, defeated former Lt. Gov. Faoa Aitofele Sunia, 53%-47% in a runoff election. He faced Sunia again in 2016, this time defeating him in the general election 60%-35%. In the territory's 2016 Democratic caucuses, he endorsed Hillary Clinton for president.

As governor, Moliga has sought increased autonomy for the territorial government in American Samoan affairs. He supported the decisions of federal courts in 2015 and 2016 not to grant automatic citizenship rights to American Samoans, saying that the territory should "determine for itself the political relationship it wishes to establish with the United States." He opposed the Obama administration's expansion of protected marine reserves in the Pacific Ocean and has been critical of federal aviation laws that limit accessibility to American Samoa. He's also been vocal in opposition to federally mandated minimum wage hikes. "We face the consequences of decisions made in Washington with insufficient consideration given to local conditions," he said in 2019 Senate testimony.

His administration views immigration reform as a way to bolster the territory's stagnant population growth. Under Moliga, American Samoa has granted amnesty to more than 4,000 foreigners living illegally on the islands. He supported federal legislation increasing the number of foreigners who may receive permanent residency status in the territory.

DELEGATE

Aumua Amata Coleman Radewagen (R)

Elected 2014, term expires 2020, 3rd term, b. Dec 29, 1947; Pago Pago, American Samoa; Sacred Hearts Academy (HI); Loyola Marymount University; George Mason University; University of Guam, B.S., 1975; Roman Catholic; Married (Fred Radewagen); 3 children; 1 grandchild.

Professional Career: Journalist; Trainer; Staff, U.S. Rep. Philip Crane (IL), 1997-1999; Staff, U.S. Rep. J.C. Watts Jr. (OK), 1999-2003; White House Commissioner for Asian Americans & Pacific Islanders, 2001.

DC Office: 1339 LHOB 20515, 202-225-8577, Fax: 202-225-8757, radewagen.house.gov

Committees: *Natural Resources*: Indigenous Peoples of the United States, Water, Oceans & Wildlife. *Small Business*: Economic Growth, Tax & Capital Access, Rural Development, Agriculture, Trade & Entrepreneurship. *Veterans' Affairs*: Health, Oversight & Investigations.

Amata Catherine Coleman Radewagen, a Republican, became the first woman to represent American Samoa in Congress after defeating 13-term Democrat Eni F. H. Faleomavaega in 2014. A former Capitol Hill GOP leadership staffer and cancer survivor commonly known as Auma Amata, Radewagen grew up with 12 siblings and earned a degree from the University of Guam.

Her family has deep roots in Samoan politics. Peter Tali Coleman, her father, was the first Samoan appointed to serve as governor of the territory and its first popularly elected governor. He ruled from 1956 to 1993 and he founded the territory's Republican Party. Radewagen has served on the Executive Council and Rules Committee of the Republican National Committee. She supported Donald Trump as a delegate to the 2016 Republican National Convention. She backed Trump's withdrawal of the. United States from the Trans-Pacific Partnership, his push for a United States-Mexico border wall and his pulling the U.S. out of the Paris Climate Accords, while seeking to reverse President Barack Obama's expansion of marine reserves in the Pacific Ocean.

In the House, Radewagen is the ranking member a Small Business subcommittee on health and technology and is a member of a Natural Resources panel responsible for insular affairs. Despite being a non-voting member of Congress, she has had some legislative successes. In October 2016, Obama signed into law her bill raising the minimum wage in American Samoa 40 cents every three years until it aligned with the federal minimum. Obama signed into law another bill from Radewagen related to international fishery management agreements. In 2015 and 2016, she supported decisions by federal courts not to grant birthright citizenship status to American Samoans, saying in a press release that the courts had reaffirmed "the bedrock principle that the American Samoan people, and not outside interest groups or federal courts, should have the final say in matters concerning their political status."

Radewagen challenged Faleomavaega eight times before finally winning the seat in 2014. In In 2014, Radewagen won 42 percent of the vote to Faleomavaega's 30 percent. Radewagen has easily won reelection in 2016 and 2018. Faleomavaega died in 2017.

GUAM

Some 6,300 miles west of Los Angeles and 3,800 miles west of Hawaii, 17 hours of flying time from Washington D.C., is Guam, an American possession since 1898. Geographically, this island is in the center of the Marianas Islands, though Guam is legally separate. It was acquired from Spain after the Spanish-American War, while the United States permitted Germany to purchase the rest of the Mariana chain. It was ruled by Navy captains from 1898 to 1949, except for 31 months of Japanese occupation during World War II. In 1950, the Guam Organic Act made Guamanians U.S. citizens. Carlton Skinner, who as a captain integrated the crew of his Navy ship in 1943, became the first civilian governor in 1949 and helped write the territorial constitution. The local government is known as GovGuam, but Congress retains final power over the territory. It gave Guam a non-voting delegate to the House in 1972.

Guam is 36 miles long by four to nine miles wide, with167,772 people as of mid-2018. Some 37 percent of the population is Chamorro (descendants of the original islanders) or from elsewhere in Micronesia; 26 percent is Filipino; 12 percent other Pacific Islander; 6 percent other Asian; and 7 percent white. The population is politically mixed and overwhelmingly Catholic, yet in 2015 Guam became the first U.S. territory to recognize same-sex marriage. The island's Catholic church has been wracked with scandal. Its previous archbishop was forced from his position in 2016 after numerous former altar boys accused him of sexual abusing them as minors. The diocese filed for bankruptcy in 2019 to avoid payments in dozens of sexual abuse lawsuits.

The island's tropical environment can be dangerous. In August 1993, Guam experienced an earthquake measuring 8.2 on the Richter scale, comparable to San Francisco's in 1906. Guam suffers from almost 300 invasive species, the most problematic of which is the brown tree snake. It has killed off nearly all of the island's bird population. In addition to using traps and repellants to eradicate the species, the Agriculture Department has dropped mice packed with acetaminophen from helicopters.

Guam depends heavily on tourism — especially from Japan — and service businesses, but especially on the U.S. military. Guam is America's forward position in Asia. Anderson Air Force Base is one of the busiest in the world with the largest stockpile of bombs, missiles and bullets. North Korean dictator Kim Jong Un threatened to destroy the island in "an enveloping fire" in 2017 after the U.S. deployed bombers there. President Donald Trump told Guam's governor he was with them

"1000 percent" in response, while predicting the infamy Guam would get from the threats would boost tourism "tenfold." Bases occupy one-third of the land, and an estimated 60 percent of the island's income is derived from the federal government. In 2013, the Pentagon announced plans to relocate 5,000 marines and 1,300 dependents from Okinawa to Guam by 2026, a move that defense officials predicted would add upwards of $37 million per year to Guam's economy. In 2017, the federal government announced that it will begin paying reparations to Guam residents who experienced wartime atrocities under Japan's occupation of the island during World War II.

The island is far from the U.S. mainland, but American policies have a direct impact on its economy. The Trump administration's decision to stop issuing temporary unskilled visas to workers from the Philippines risked a major work shortage on the island.

Guam does not cast any electoral votes for president, but elects delegates to national party conventions. In the 2016 Democratic caucuses, Hillary Clinton defeated Bernie Sanders 60%-40%. Guam Republicans held a convention in 2016, and all nine delegates pledged to back Trump. In lieu of a general election, Guam began holding non-binding straw polls every four years in 1984. For the first time in its history, the straw poll in 2016 did not accurately predict the next president. About 72 percent of Guam voters chose Clinton over Trump. In 2018, Democrats swept to power across the island, gaining a supermajority in the legislature and electing the first female governor and first openly gay lieutenant governor in Guam's history.

Governor

Democrat Lou Leon Guerrero was elected Guam's governor in 2018, making her the first female governor in the island's history, the first Pacific Islander to serve as governor in any of the U.S. territories, and only the third Democrat to hold the office since the territory began voting for governor a half-century ago; the other six were Republicans.

The election was a watershed moment in other ways: Her running mate, Joshua Tenorio, is Guam's first openly gay lieutenant governor, and the legislature is majority-female for the first time.

Guerrero, a former nurse, was a five-term territorial senator and president of the Bank of Guam. Her views matched mainland Democrats on many issues, something that's not always a given in the territories: She supported abortion rights and legalizing recreational marijuana, which became legal on the island in April 2019.

She campaigned on a pledge for more government investment to boost tourism and scrapping the island's sales tax, while supporting a task force to collect an estimated $200 million in unpaid taxes on the island. She ran against President Donald Trump, who caused a stir on the island by telling Guam's previous governor in a phone call that North Korea's threat to bomb Guam would help bring it attention and boost tourism.

Guerrero won the race with 50.8 percent of the vote, just barely avoiding a runoff, with the GOP ticket pulling 26.4 percent and write-ins pulling 22.8 percent.

DELEGATE

Michael San Nicolas (D)

Elected 2018, term expires 2020, 1st term, b. Jan 30, 1981; Talofofoam; University of Guam, B.A., 2004; Not Known; Married (Kathryn Santos Ko); 2 children.

DC Office: 1632 LHOB 20515, 202-225-1188, sannicolas.house.gov

Committees: *Financial Services*: Investor Protection, Entrepreneurship & Capital Markets, Nat'l Security, International Development & Monetary Policy. *Natural Resources*: Indigenous Peoples of the United States, Oversight & Investigations.

Michael San Nicolas defeated longtime delegate Madeleine Bordallo in a primary en route to becoming Guam's new member of Congress in 2018.

Nicolas, a former territorial senator, is a scion of a local political family: Both of his grandfathers were local legislators. As a teenager, he introduced then-President Bill Clinton at a 1998 rally in the territory. He went on to become a teacher, financial adviser, and a vice president at the Bank of Guam, where newly elected territorial governor Lou Leon Guerrero served as president.

Bordallo had been the territory's delegate in Congress since 2002, but was dogged by a House Ethics Committee investigation into whether she broke the law by leasing a home to the government of Japan and accepting more than 600 nights of free lodging at a beachfront hotel in Guam. He defeated her in the Democratic primary with 51.5 percent of the vote and won the general election with 55 percent in a good year for Democrats across the territory.

San Nicolas joined the House Hispanic Caucus and Congressional Asian Pacific American Caucus, and landed seats on the Financial Services and Natural Resources Committees. Delegates can vote in committee, but not in the full House.

In February, he criticized President Donald Trump's emergency declaration to build a wall on the border with Mexico, which Nicolas said would divert $749 million from military funding for Guam. "Readiness in our region grossly understates the real threat of a perceived waning in American commitment to the Asian Pacific," San Nicolas said.

NORTHERN MARIANA ISLANDS

The Commonwealth of the Northern Mariana Islands, in American hands since 1944, is a chain of 14 islands, only three permanently inhabited, running north from Guam in the Western Pacific. The northern islands are volcanic and the southern islands are limestone and fringed with coral reefs. They are closer to mainland Asia than to the mainland United States, sitting roughly 2,100 miles southeast of Hong Kong and some 7,800 miles southwest of Los Angeles.

The Northern Marianas were first peopled by Micronesians three millennia ago and were visited by Magellan in 1521. Spanish Jesuits arrived in 1668, and the islands were a possession of Spain until the Spanish-American War in 1898. Over the centuries, they became depopulated, and then in the middle 19th century, began to be settled by Chamorros from Guam. In 1898, the United States acquired Guam as a coaling station but was content to see the Northern Marianas sold to Germany in 1899. They were seized by Japan in 1914 soon after it entered World War I, and the League of Nations gave Japan legal claim to them in 1920. They were occupied by U.S. forces in 1944, in the midst of World War II. In August 1945, the Enola Gay took off from Tinian on its mission to drop the atomic bomb on Hiroshima. That same year, the Northern Marianas were put in the custody of the new United Nations Security Council, and in 1947 they were declared part of the U.S. Trust Territory of the Pacific Islands.

While the other islands in time opted for independence, the Northern Marianas voted in 1975 to approve a covenant with the United States creating the Commonwealth of the Northern Mariana Islands, which went into effect in 1976. Under its terms, the CNMI was not subject to federal immigration or labor laws and not obliged to pay U.S. taxes, but it deferred entirely to the United States in foreign and military affairs. Foreign investors were limited to a 49 percent share of businesses or property, and land could be owned only by "persons of Northern Marianas descent." The CNMI government started operating after the 1977 elections.

In the early 1970s, the Northern Marianas had only 12,000 people. The airport had no modern runways and only one rickety flight a day from Guam. Then, in the mid-1980s, the CNMI government opened up the economy to foreign investment and rewrote its immigration laws to permit an influx of guest workers. This resulted in heavy investment in garment factories that imported workers, mostly female, from low-wage countries such as the Philippines, China and Vietnam. Products made here could be labeled "Made in U.S.A." and imported into the United States without being subject to textile import quotas. By the mid-1990s, there were 34 garment factories, employing 17,000 guest workers. Japanese investors began building tourist destinations, with low-wage jobs for guest workers. The result was a population boom, which grew to 69,000 people in 2000.

The tiny island chain has faced major swings in economic prosperity depending on seemingly minor shifts in its treatment by the United States or by nearby countries — as well as shifts in the weather. In January 2005, a treaty that set quotas on textile imports into the U.S. expired. Suddenly the CNMI's exemption from those quotas became irrelevant, and Saipan was subject to lower-wage competition from Vietnam, Cambodia and China. By 2009, all of the islands' garment factories were shuttered. The second major blow occurred in October 2005 when Japan Airlines canceled its daily flights to Saipan, badly damaging the tourism industry. Gross domestic product dropped about 20 percent in 2009, and the CNMI's population decreased to less than 52,000 as of 2018.

The islands rallied in recent years, with booming tourism and gambling industries fueling rapid growth — a 28.2 percent increase in GDP in 2016 and 25 percent GDP growth in 2017. Part of that growth was from an Imperial Pacific mega-casino opened by Chinese investors. That construction led to serious allegations of human rights and immigration violations, plus accusations of money laundering. The parent company's Saipan offices were raided by U.S. agents in early 2018, and its construction contractors reached a $13.9 million settlement with the Department of Labor for wages and damages for 2,400 workers.

The Marianas were the first of the territories to legalize recreational marijuana in 2018. The islands have also become a destination for "birth tourism," where hundreds of wealthy Chinese women go to Saipan annually to give birth to children who automatically receive U.S. birthright citizenship. The islands are the only part of the U.S. that Chinese people can visit without a visa, and Saipan has become a more popular choice in recent years due to immigration crackdowns on the mainland.

In October 2018, the islands were ravaged by Super Typhoon Yutu, one of the worst storms ever to hit U.S. soil. Much of Saipan and Titian lost power for months, more than 5,000 houses were destroyed or severely damaged, and more than a quarter of the islands' population were displaced. The storm ravaged tourism, with only 6,000 tourists visiting in November, the month after the storm, down from 49,000 the year before. Reconstruction was hampered when the Trump administration eliminated the Philippines from the list of countries whose citizens can receive temporary worker visas, limiting the pool of available construction workers.

In response to concerns about labor abuses and national security issues, Congress brought the CNMI under federal immigration law in 2008. The transition established a guest worker system to ensure an adequate labor supply to support the tourism and garment industries. Most CNMI politicians opposed the bill but had little power to stop it. It also gave the CNMI its first-ever delegate in Congress, replacing the territory's Resident Representative, a position funded by the CNMI that had been in place since 1978. In 2014, the guest worker program and all other elements of the transition program were extended for five years to help CNMI businesses meet their labor needs; in 2018, it was extended through 2029. In 2007, legislation required the CNMI to increase the minimum wage — it's more than doubled from $3.05 an hour in 2007 to $7.25 an hour, the same as the rest of the U.S., as of 2018.

After the CIA closed its covert training base on Saipan in 1962, the U.S. military presence in the Northern Marianas became more limited than in nearby Guam. But the realignment of U.S. military operations in the Pacific could change that. The Marine Corps announced its intention to use the islands of Pagan and Tinian for live-fire amphibious training. Locals have hotly protested the plan, citing historical and environmental concerns. In response, the Navy = has been preparing alternative plans. A final decision about the training ranges was expected in 2020.

Governor

Republican Ralph Torres became governor of the CNMI in December 2015, following the death of Gov. Eloy Inos, and was elected to a full term in 2018. Torres ran as Inos' running mate in 2014. Inos won that election 57%-43%, defeating former CNMI House Speaker Heinz Sablan Hofschneider, an independent.

Torres was born in Saipan and attended high school and college in Idaho. After returning to the CNMI, he won election to the territory's legislature in 2008 and served as senate president from 2013 to 2015. In 2016, he drew national attention for his support of a law restricting ownership of some types of semi-automatic weapons. In the 2016 presidential race, Torres and Gov. Eddie Calvo of Guam co-chaired the Asian-Pacific Advisory Committee for Donald Trump's presidential campaign.

As governor, Torres has sought to boost tourism and grow the territory's workforce, and he has supported raising the cap on permits for foreign workers. He played a role in getting the Marianas' foreign guest worker program extended through 2029, and signed into law a bill authorizing recreational marijuana use.

Torres has been a vocal supporter of the growing casino tourism industry, helping to legalize gaming on the islands when he was in the state senate and defending the Chinese conglomerate that came in to build new casinos. The government gave the Imperial Pacific International company building repeated extensions to complete the work. Torres' opponents accused his family of receiving kickbacks, while pointing out that Torres' brothers were on the Chinese company's payroll as attorneys for the deal. Torres did say that foreign construction workers protesting for their back wages should be paid in 2017, but largely defended the company, according to local reports.

Torres faced former Gov. Juan Babauta, who ran as an independent, in the 2018 election. The election was delayed a week due to Typhoon Yutu. Torres prevailed easily, with 7,053 votes to Babuata's 4,293.

DELEGATE

Gregorio Kilili Camacho Sablan (D)

Elected 2008, term expires 2020, 5th term, b. Jan 19, 1955; Saipan; University of Guam, Att.; University of Hawaii, Manoa, Att., 1990; Roman Catholic; Married (Andrea C. Sablan); 6 children.

Elected Office: N. Marianas Islands Legislature, 1982-1986.

Professional Career: Gov.'s deputy chief admin. officer, CNMI Government, 1980-1981; Special Assistant for Management & budget, CNMI Government, 1994-1995; Executive Director, Commonwealth Election Commission, 1999-2008.

DC Office: 2411 RHOB 20515, 202-225-2646, Fax: 202-226-4249, sablan.house.gov

Committees: *Education & Labor*: Early Childhood, Elementary & Secondary Education (Chmn), Higher Education & Workforce Investment. *Natural Resources*: Water, Oceans & Wildlife. *Veterans' Affairs*: Disability Assistance & Memorial Affairs.

Gregorio Kilili Camacho Sablan, the first delegate to the House from the Commonwealth of the Northern Mariana Islands, was elected in 2008.

Sablan grew up in Saipan in an extended family much involved in politics. His grandfather was the first elected mayor of Saipan, and his uncle was the city's longest-serving mayor. He attended the University of Guam and the University of California, Berkeley, but did not get a degree. He worked for Democratic Gov. Carlos Camacho, the CNMI's first elected governor, then served in the legislature from 1982 to 1986. Sablan worked for 18 months on the Washington staff of Democratic Sen. Daniel Inouye of Hawaii, who had a long interest in the Pacific territories. When he returned to Saipan, Sablan worked as special assistant for management and budget for Democratic Gov. Froilan Tenorio. Later, he was appointed executive director of the Commonwealth Election Commission.

After Congress voted in April 2008 to give the CNMI a non-voting delegate in Congress, Sablan joined a field of nine candidates seeking the seat. He ran as an independent rather than as a Democrat because, he said, the local Democratic Party was poorly organized. Of 10,161 votes cast, Sablan led the field with 2,474 votes, edging Republican Pete A. Tenorio by 357 votes. In 2018, Sablan won with 9,150 votes to 5,199 for his opponent, Republican Angel Demapan. Sablan, who caucuses with House Democrats, endorsed Hillary Clinton for president in 2016.

Sablan has had some legislative successes, including enactment of a measure in 2013 giving the CNMI ownership of submerged lands three miles out to sea and a December 2012 amendment to the defense authorization bill requiring that the flags of the CNMI and other territories be displayed whenever military units display all of the states' flags. In 2014, he helped to prolong a visa program that allows long-term foreign investors to reside on the islands. In 2016 and 2017, the House passed his bills increasing caps on foreign workers in the CNMI. The Trump administration reversed course on those visas, lowering the cap on foreign workers in 2018 and reducing it by more than half for

2019 to 4,999. Sablan worked with his rival, Republican Gov. Ralph Torres, as well as Sen. Lisa Murkowski of Alaska and Rep. Rob Bishop of Utah, both Republicans, to increase that cap and extend the program to 2029. , The success was due more to Torres, who had more pull with the Trump administration. Sablan unsuccessfully fought a new federal ban on cockfighting in the territories that passed as part of the 2018 Farm Bill. As of early 2019, he was fighting the Trump administration as it considered eliminating policies that allow Chinese and Russian tourists onto the islands without visas.

After years of trying to create a national park on the island of Rota, Sablan came a step closer in 2017 when the National Park Service a study to determine if Rota is suitable as a unit of the national park system. Sablan has called for extending U.S. voting rights protections to the territories and has supported increases in the minimum wage.

PUERTO RICO

From Columbus' landing in 1493 until the Spanish-American War of 1898, Puerto Rico was a Spanish colony—and an important one in the three centuries when the port of San Juan was the gathering place for its annual convoy of gold and silver from the Americas to Spain. From the time it became an American territory in 1898 to the 1950s, it was considered "the poorhouse of the Caribbean," a sugar-producing island with a tiny elite. In the second half of the 20th century, it developed a recognizably first world economy and a solidly democratic—though sometimes turbulent—political system. In the 21st century, however, Puerto Rico's forward momentum has ground to a halt. Its economic woes, financial instability and declining population created a tinderbox ready to explode the moment a match was struck. The match came in September 2017, when Hurricane Maria unleashed its fury on the island, causing thousands of deaths and bringing widespread destruction that likely set Puerto Rico back years, if not decades.

Puerto Rico's economic crisis largely began when the federal government ended tax breaks that brought corporations and big businesses, particularly pharmaceutical companies, to the island. Spurred by the pharmaceutical manufacturing boom, the island's economy increased nearly 20 percent from 2000 to 2004. However, companies left as the tax breaks phased out. By 2017, a decade of recession had erased the island's economic gains. Total employment dropped from 1.25 million in 2007 to less than a million in 2017. When Hurricane Maria hit, Puerto Rico's poverty rate was around 45 percent, and just 40 percent of the population was participating in the labor force. It had half the per capita income of Mississippi, the poorest state in the union.

In the face of rapid economic decline and dwindling tax revenue, the government borrowed to make ends meet. By May 2017, the island had racked up $123 billion in bond debt and unfunded pension obligations, forcing it to take an unprecedented step toward insolvency. Although U.S. bankruptcy law prohibits Puerto Rico from restructuring its debt, Puerto Rico used a provision from a 2016 federal law to seek relief from its Wall Street creditors in a proceeding similar to bankruptcy. That law also established a seven-member oversight board to manage the territory's finances and restructuring debts. The broad powers granted to the board attracted criticism among Puerto Ricans, with some characterizing it as colonialism and calling the board a "junta."

Population loss and a brain drain of professionals leaving for the mainland tracked with Puerto Rico's financial troubles. From 2004 to 2016, Puerto Rico's population dropped by 11 percent, from roughly 3.8 million to 3.4 million. In 2014, an estimated 230 people left per day—most of them relocating to Florida. From 2006 to 2016, the number of doctors in Puerto Rico fell from 14,000 to 9,000.

These struggles left Puerto Rico ill-prepared for Hurricane Maria, a Category 4 storm that hit the southeastern shore on September 20, 2017. For an entire day Maria moved northwest across the island and wreaked havoc. With its 155 mph winds, Maria caused around $100 billion in damage, fully destroying 70,000 homes and partially destroying another 300,000. The Puerto Rican government initially said 64 people died in the storm. After independent estimates put the death toll as high as 4,500, the government revised its estimate to 2,975 dead. Maria also caused the island's power grid to collapse. It took one year to restore power to the entire island. With the island and its economy wrecked by the storm, many Puerto Ricans headed to the mainland. The Census Bureau estimated that 130,000 people left in the following year, with many settling in central Florida.

The federal government's response to Maria was widely panned by Puerto Rican officials and congressional Democrats, who argued that Puerto Rico received less aid and attention than mainland areas struck by disasters in 2017. President Donald Trump disagreed, calling the response "an incredible, unsung success." He feuded with the mayor of San Juan, threatening to cut off assistance to the island over its debt and saying the number of deaths was inflated by his political enemies. Congress responded by passing $15.8 billion in disaster relief in early 2018. Puerto Rican officials said the island needs $139 billion to recover, but Trump objected.

As they recovered from Maria, some Puerto Ricans said, "Puerto Rico se levanta," which roughly translates to "Puerto Rico is rising." The island's tourism industry began making a comeback as hotels were repaired, power was restored and cruise ships docked in San Juan again. However, critics said these were cosmetic fixes that masked deeper issues outside tourist hubs. Puerto Ricans living in impoverished and rural areas still had FEMA blue tarps serving as roofs on their homes. Across the island, many residents were suffering from post-traumatic stress disorder or living amid crumbling infrastructure.

The island's precarious financial situation deepened. In April 2018, the island's financial oversight board approved an austerity plan that cut public pensions and reduced benefits, setting up a legal battle with the island's governor, Ricardo Rosselló. A federal judge ruled in August that the board has the power to impose its fiscal plans on the island, but policy measures governed by Puerto Rican law must be approved by Puerto Rican officials. Rosselló sparred with the oversight board over a five-year austerity plan it approved in October. That same month, Trump said the federal government would not bail out the island. Experts said Trump misunderstood the situation and that no relief funds would go directly toward debt payments. In the midst of the fight over austerity, Puerto Rico restructured its debt under the bankruptcy proceedings initiated in May 2017. In November 2018, the island announced it had completed its first debt restructuring deal by closing out $4 billion owed by the defunct Government Development Bank.

Hurricane Maria and the financial crisis have given new life to the fundamental question of whether Puerto Rico should seek statehood, continue its current commonwealth status or, in what has traditionally been a minority view, declare independence. A transition to statehood requires congressional approval. Puerto Rico has elected a resident commissioner to Congress since 1900 with a four-year term, and residents of Puerto Rico have been American citizens since 1917. But they didn't elect their own governor until 1948. From the 1940s until the early 1960s, Puerto Rico was transformed by Gov. Luis Muñoz Marín and his Popular Democratic Party. Muñoz initiated "Operation Bootstrap" to lure businesses to Puerto Rico with promises of low-wage labor, government-built factories and tax exemptions. Muñoz also developed Puerto Rico's commonwealth form of government—in Spanish, Estado Libre Asociado, or, ELA, meaning Free Associated State —that was approved by referendum in 1952. Puerto Rico is part of the United States for purposes of international trade, foreign policy and war. But it has its own laws, taxes and representative government. It is not subject to federal income taxes and is not eligible for all federal benefits.

The island has developed its own political parties: Muñoz's Popular Democrats (the Spanish acronym is PPD), the New Progressive Party (PNP) which favors statehood, and two small pro-independence parties. PPD politicians have long been affiliated with the mainland Democratic Party, while PNP politicians have been split, with some favoring Democrats and some favoring Republicans. Gov. Rosselló, a PNP member elected in 2016, ran on a pro-statehood platform, arguing it would boost the territory's lagging economy.

Residents of Puerto Rico have voted on the issue of statehood five times. In the 1967 referendum, they voted to continue commonwealth status over statehood 60%-39%. In 1993, the vote was 48% for the commonwealth and 46% for statehood. In a 1998 referendum, the vote was 47% for statehood and 50% for "none of the above," the option favored by the PPD. In 2012, 52% voted against the current status and 44% voted for it. In a second question where voters were asked to choose between statehood, independence, and a "sovereign commonwealth," statehood won a plurality. In June 2017, 97 percent voted for statehood. However, only 23 percent of the island participated as opposition parties boycotted the vote.

After Maria, Rosselló renewed his push for statehood. He argued that the storm showed how Puerto Ricans are treated as second-class citizens by the United States. Trump came out against statehood in September 2018, citing his feud with the mayor of San Juan. Trump also likely shares the concern of other Republicans: as a state, Puerto Rico might elect five Democratic House members and two Democratic senators, and it would cast seven Democratic electoral votes. Rosselló disagreed. "If you look at Puerto Rico's electoral behavior, we're really a swing state. When we don't like something, we flip."

Governor

Ricardo Rosselló, a member of the New Progressive Party (PNP), was elected Puerto Rico's 12th governor in 2016. He came from a political family. His father, Pedro Rosselló, was governor from 1993 to 2001. But much of his life was spent in academia and in the scientific community. He studied at M.I.T., and earned a doctorate in biomedical engineering from the University of Michigan. He spent time as a neurobiology researcher at Duke. In 2010, he co-founded Beijing Prosperous Biopharm Co., a pharmaceutical research and development company.

Rosselló faced former Puerto Rico resident commissioner Pedro Pierluisi for the PNP nomination in 2016. The candidates sparred over the Puerto Rico Oversight, Management and Economic Stability Act (PROMESA), a bill passed by Congress in 2016 aimed at addressing Puerto Rico's economic crisis. Rosselló opposed the legislation, while Pierluisi tepidly supported it. Rosselló won the June primary, 51%-49% . In the general election, he defeated former Puerto Rico Secretary of State David Bernier, whose Popular Democratic Party was caught in a corruption scandal. Rosselló won 42%-39%, and an independent candidate took about 10% of the vote. Rosselló emphasized his support for Puerto Rican statehood.

Rosselló's plans were sidelined when Hurricane Maria hit Puerto Rico in September 2017, devastating the island and ensuring that much of the governor's time would be spent coordinating with the federal government on relief efforts. At first, he had warm words for the Trump and his administration's disaster response. However, he worried that the destruction in Puerto Rico would be viewed as a secondary problem because Texas and Florida were also hit by hurricanes that year. By April 2018, he said the Army Corps of Engineers was not acting with urgency to repair the energy grid. His relationship with Trump deteriorated. In June, Trump accused Rosselló, without evidence, of taking advantage of federal relief funds to rebuild a power plant that was defunct before Maria hit. Rosselló criticized Trump for claiming Puerto Rico's death toll was inflated and for opposing Puerto Rican statehood. Rosselló mobilized Latino voters against the Republican Party in the 2018 elections due to his opposition to the 2017 GOP tax bill, which he said treated Puerto Rico like a foreign country for tax purposes. He endorsed Florida Sen. Bill Nelson and gubernatorial candidate Andrew Gillum . Both Democrats lost to Trump allies.

Rosselló dealt with the island's dire fiscal situation. He opposed austerity plans proposed by the island's financial oversight board, which was established by PROMESA, and cheered efforts to restructure Puerto Rican debt. He privatized parts of the island's debt-ridden electrical authority. The authority drew scrutiny in October 2017 when it hired Whitefish Energy Holdings, a small Montana-based firm with ties to Secretary of the Interior Ryan Zinke, to restore Puerto Rico's power. Rosselló canceled the company's $300 million contract.

Despite these challenges , Rosselló was active on his signature issue of statehood, which he saw as the answer to the island's financial problems. He supported a statehood referendum in June 2017 that was approved by 97 percent of voters. But major opposition parties boycotted the vote, resulting in a turnout rate of just 23 percent. After Maria received enormous news coverage, Rosselló said more Americans were becoming aware of "second-class citizenship" for Puerto Ricans. He hoped that increased awareness of the island's issues and the exodus of Puerto Ricans to the mainland after Maria might help achieve statehood.

RESIDENT COMMISSIONER

Jenniffer González Colón (R)

Elected 2016, term expires 2020, 1st term, b. Aug 05, 1976; San Juan; University of Puerto Rico, Bach. Deg.; Inter-American University of Puerto Rico, J.D.; Inter-American University of Puerto Rico, LL.M.; Single.

Elected Office: President, Puerto Rico Republian Party, 2004-2016; Vice President, New Progressive Party, 2008-2016; PR House, 2002-2016, Speaker, 2009-2012, Minority Leader, 2012-2016.

DC Office: 1609 LHOB 20515, 202-225-2615, Fax: 202-225-2154, gonzalez-colon.house.gov

Committees: *Natural Resources*: Oversight & Investigations, Water, Oceans & Wildlife. *Science, Space & Technology*: Environment. *Transportation & Infrastructure*: Economic Dev't, Public Buildings & Emergency Management, Water Resources & Environment.

Jenniffer González-Colón, a member of Puerto Rico's pro-statehood New Progressive Party (PNP), was elected in 2016. At 40 when she was elected, González-Colón is the youngest person to serve as resident commissioner and the first woman to hold the position. She had been a legislator in Puerto Rico since 2002 and became the island's youngest speaker of the house seven years later. She got a law degree from Puerto Rico's Inter American University and worked in San Juan as an attorney. González-Colón succeeded two-term Resident Commissioner Pedro Pierluisi, who ran for governor. In November, she defeated Popular Democratic Party candidate Hector Ferrer, 48.8%-47.2%.

González-Colón chaired the territory's Republican Party. In the 2016 presidential campaign, she backed former Florida Gov. Jeb Bush and then Sen. Marco Rubio of Florida for the Republican nomination. She was a fierce critic of Donald Trump throughout the primary season, refusing to back him at the Republican National Convention because she didn't want to "validate the attack on the Latino community." She ended up supporting him in the general election. When Hurricane Maria devastated the island in 2017, González-Colón initially said she was "grateful" for the attention Trump paid to disaster response and traveled with him on Air Force One to survey disaster damage, even as other leading figures in Puerto Rico and on the mainland decried a botched disaster response. But after Trump threatened to cut short disaster aid a few weeks later she called his remarks "shocking."

"This is not the time to be talking about withdrawing the help," she told Politico in late 2017. "This is not the time to talk about how much it's costing the U.S., because we are American citizens." She sided with Trump and the GOP to accept partial funding for nutritional assistance in early 2019, rather than more robust reconstruction funds pushed for by Gov. Ricardo Rosselló and national Democrats.

In the House, González-Colón in 2017 filed a bill that would make Puerto Rico a state by 2025, and picked up support from then-Natural Resources Committee Chairman Rob Bishop of Utah, plus 51 other cosponsors. After Democrats took House control in 2019, she and Democratic Rep. Darren Soto of Florida, a Puerto Rico native, reintroduced a statehood bill. She mostly worked closely with Bishop, but sparred with him over how the federal oversight board regulating Puerto Rico's bankruptcy was forcing it to take actions that local officials opposed. She also filed legislation to expand health care access and preserve Medicaid in the commonwealth.

VIRGIN ISLANDS

The U.S. Virgin Islands, acquired from Denmark in 1917, are near the northern end of the Antilles chain between the Caribbean Sea and the Atlantic Ocean. They were settled by the Dutch and Danish and had a polyglot colonial society, with one of the oldest Jewish communities in the Western Hemisphere. Their most famous son is Alexander Hamilton, who grew up on St. Croix but moved to New York and never came back. Almost all of the territory's 107,000 people live on the three main islands of St. Thomas, St. John and St. Croix. Since the 1990s, there has been little net change. The Islands were devastated by two Category Five hurricanes, Irma and Maria, within two weeks in September 2017.

The Virgin Islands have lived primarily off tourism and, until 2013, an oil refinery. St. Thomas has long been one of the top cruise ship destinations in the world and the islands together receive nearly 3 million visitors each year. Tourism accounts for approximately 60 percent of the territory's Gross Domestic Product and the government continues to incentivize travel to the islands, with increased airplane flights from the mainland.

Even with its reliable tourism industry, the Virgin Islands' economy was weakened after Hovensa, an oil refinery built on St. Croix by Hess Oil in 1966, was closed. Once one of the largest refineries in the world, it closed in 2012, with a loss of 2,200 jobs and $100 million revenue to the territorial government. After nearly four years of inactivity, the Hovensa oil refinery was given a second chance in 2015 when the legislature approved a purchase agreement with Limetree Bay Holdings, a subsidiary of ArcLight Capital Partners. The refinery will act as an oil storage facility. Hovensa announced in July 2018 that it would spend $1.4 billion on the refinery and plan to reopen by 2020, with the use of lower sulfur petroleum. The project was expected to add 1,000 construction jobs and 750 permanent workers, in addition to 700 existing jobs at the terminal.

Rum sales in the Virgin Islands are a staple of the economy. Rum-producing U.S. territories have received $13.25 of the $13.50 per-gallon federal tax on rum since 1999. These payments have been used to incentivize rum producers to relocate to the Virgin Islands. In 2008, the Virgin Islands government made a deal with the British-based liquor company Diageo to move its Captain Morgan rum operations from Puerto Rico to a new $165 million distillery in the Virgin Islands. Puerto Rican politicians were unhappy with the plan to give a share of the revenue to Diageo and argued that it was illegitimate to use rum tax funds to lure a distillery operation from one territory to another. The rum tax rebate has been renewed since then, as criticism of the practice from fiscal hawks in Congress has grown louder. Island leaders have viewed the rum revenue as vital to local finances.

More than one quarter of workers on the islands are employed by the government. In addition to a budget deficit, the islands have a crushing burden of $2.4 billion in bond debt. In February 2017, the territory's legislature passed the Revenue Enhancement and Economic Recovery Act, taxing alcohol, tobacco and carbonated beverages to generate new revenue. Following the hurricanes later that year, reconstruction was slowed, in part, by the delay of disaster funding by the Federal Emergency Management Agency. The relief woes compounded the debt crisis. Local officials sought to avoid comparisons to Puerto Rico, whose finances seemed to be more desperate. By late 2018, tourism had revived, including cruise ships.

The Virgin Islands usually play a small role in the presidential selection process. The territory gained attention in 2016 when two factions within the local GOP disputed which slate of at-large delegates would attend the Republican National Convention in Cleveland. Ultimately, the GOP reinstated the original delegates, who had been disqualified for failing to file proper paperwork. Eight delegates backed Donald Trump and one abstained. In the Democratic caucus, Hillary Clinton defeated Bernie Sanders, 84-12%, securing all seven pledged delegates.

Governor

Albert Bryan, a Democrat, defeated incumbent Kenneth Mapp, an independent, with 55 percent of the vote in the November 20, 2018 runoff. Two weeks earlier, Bryan led Mapp, 38%-34%, among the seven candidates. Running on the "Change Course Now" theme, Bryan took advantage of many "self-inflicted wounds" by Mapp during his four years as governor, the Virgin Islands Consortium wrote. They included Mapp's insults of his opponents and harsh rhetoric about local residents. Bryan, who had wide experience in government on the Virgin Islands, styled himself as younger and more activist. Mapp was the third incumbent governor to lose a bid for a second term since 1974. In 2014, he was elected to replace a term-limited Democrat in an upset over Donna Christensen, the territory's long-time delegate to Congress; in that contest, Mapp got 62 percent in the runoff.

Bryan, a native of St. Thomas, got his bachelor's degree at Wittenberg University in Ohio and a Master's of Business Administration from the University of the Virgin Islands. He had a lengthy career in the private sector, including executive positions with Hess Oil Corp. and Innovative Communications. In 2002, he co-founded Generation Now!, a non-profit group that educated the public on political issues. He was a leader of Young Democrats. In 2007, he was appointed as Commissioner of Labor for the Islands, a position that he held for eight years. After Mapp was elected governor, Bryan became chief executive of Aabra Group, a business consulting firm. His campaign in 2018 was his first bid for elected office. He won the Democratic primary with 39 percent of the vote against two opponents.

During his campaign, Bryan said that the Islands needed to establish "realistic and conservative budget practices" and that they could no longer spend more than available revenue. He opposed a congressional oversight board like that for Puerto Rico to deal with strained public finances. "If there are tough decisions to be made, we should be courageous enough to make them by and for ourselves," including steps to address the long-standing deficit, he told the St. Thomas Source on the eve of the election. He voiced concern about the shrinking middle class and the continued migration from the Islands.

After taking office, Bryan moved quickly to deliver on a campaign promise to legalize marijuana for medical treatment, which Mapp had opposed. He also initiated steps to improve public-utility service and disaster preparedness in the wake of recent devastating hurricanes.

DELEGATE

Stacey Plaskett (D)

Elected 2014, term expires 2020, 3rd term, b. May 13, 1964; New York, NY; Georgetown University Foreign Service School (DC), B.S., 1984; American University, Washington College of Law, J.D., 1994; Lutheran; Married (Jeremy Buckney Small); 5 children.

Professional Career: Assistant District Attorney, Bronx; Consultant & legal counsel, Mitchel Madison Group; Practicing attorney; Staff, U.S. Department of Justice, 2002-2004; General counsel, Virgin Isl. econ. dev't. auth. 2007-2014.

DC Office: 2404 RHOB 20515, 202-225-1790, Fax: 202-225-5517, plaskett.house.gov

Committees: *Agriculture*: Biotechnology, Horticulture & Research (Chmn), Commodity Exchanges, Energy & Credit, Livestock & Foreign Agriculture. *Oversight & Reform*: Government Operations, National Security. *Transportation & Infrastructure*: Aviation, Coast Guard & Maritime Transportation, Highways & Transit.

Stacey Plaskett, a Democrat, was elected delegate from the Virgin Islands in 2014. Plaskett grew up in Brooklyn, raised by parents who migrated to New York from the Virgin Islands in the 1950s. She attended Choate Rosemary Hall, a boarding school in Connecticut. She earned a degree in history and diplomacy from Georgetown University and a law degree from American University. Afterwards, she worked as an assistant district attorney in the Bronx and later as counsel to the House Ethics Committee. Before relocating to the Virgin Islands, Plaskett was a political appointee in the Department of Justice from 2002 to 2004 and served on the staff of Deputy Attorney General Larry Thompson.

Plaskett first ran for the delegate seat in 2012 when she lost to incumbent Donna Christensen in the Democratic primary, 57%-42%. In 2014, when Christensen ran unsuccessfully for governor, Plaskett ran again and won the general election with more than 90 percent of the vote. She has been reelected easily.

In the House, Plaskett serves on the Oversight and Reform Committee and is the first delegate from the Virgin Islands to hold a seat on the Agriculture Committee. She has been active on territorial issues, including advocating expanded voting rights for the insular territories. In 2015, Plaskett introduced legislation to increase the rebate the Virgin Islands receives from federal taxes on rum sales. The bill failed, but she continued to argue that the territory may be owed $100 million in revenues. After the two huge hurricanes struck the Islands in September 2017, Plaskett criticized President Donald Trump for his slow response to the local crises. In an open letter to Trump in January 2019, she criticized his plan to transfer disaster funds to build the wall on the border with Mexico. "Any such action will create a national risk to these communities whose infrastructure and economy were severely compromised by the impact of those disasters."

Plaskett said in February 2019 that climate change was the most important issue facing Congress.

LEADERSHIP

The 116th Congress
2018-2019

U.S. Senate

53R, 45D, 2I

Republicans

Majority Leader...Mitch McConnell (KY)

Majority Whip & Assistant Majority Leader.....................................John Thune (SD)

President Pro Tempore..Chuck Grassley (IA)

Republican Conference Chairman...John Barrasso (WY)

Republican Conference Vice Chairman..Joni Ernst (IA)

Republican Policy Committee Chairman...Roy Blunt (MO)

National Republican Senatorial Committee Chairman........................Todd Young (IN)

Democrats

Minority Leader..Chuck Schumer (NY)

Minority Whip..Dick Durbin (IL)

Assistant Minority Leader..Patty Murray (WA)

Democratic Policy and Communications Center Chairman..............Debbie Stabenow (MI)

Democratic Conference Vice Chairman..Elizabeth Warren (MA)

Democratic Conference Vice Chairman..Mark Warner (VA)

Democratic Steering Committee Chairman...Amy Klobuchar (MN)

Democratic Outreach Committee Chairman..Bernie Sanders (VT)

Democratic Policy and Communications Center Vice Chairman. .....Joe Manchin (WV)

Democratic Conference Secretary...Tammy Baldwin (WI)

Democratic Senatorial Campaign Committee Chairman.....................Catherine Cortez Masto (NV)

U.S. House of Representatives

235D, 198R, 2 Vacant

Democrats

Speaker of the House...Nancy Pelosi (CA-12)

Majority Leader..Steny Hoyer (MD-5)

Majority Whip..James Clyburn (SC-6)

Assistant Speaker...Ben Ray Lujan (NM-3)

Democratic Caucus Chairman..Hakeem Jeffries (NY-8)

Democratic Caucus Vice Chairman..Katherine Clark (MA-5)

Democratic Steering and Policy Committee Co-Chair.........................Rosa DeLauro (CT-3)

Democratic Steering and Policy Committee Co-Chair.........................Eric Swalwell (CA-15)

Democratic Congressional Campaign Committee chairman..............Cheri Bustos (IL-17)

Republicans

Minority Leader..Kevin McCarthy (CA-23)

Minority Whip..Steve Scalise (LA-1)

Republican Conference Chairman..Liz Cheney (WY-A.L.)

Republican Policy Committee Chairman..Gary Palmer (AL-6)

Republican Chief Deputy Whip...Drew Ferguson (GA-3)

National Republican Congressional Committee Chairman...............Tom Emmer (MN-6)

Republican Conference Vice Chairman..Mark Walker (NC-6)

Republican Conference Secretary..Jason Smith (MO-8)

SENATE SENIORITY

Senators are ranked by length of consecutive service in the Senate. If necessary, ties are broken based on previous public service and state population. The Senate seniority list was compiled from Senate Historical Office records. It is current as of Jun 20, 2019.

Senator (Party and State)	Start of Service	Senator (Party and State)	Start of Service
Patrick Leahy (D-VT)	Jan 03, 1975	Rand Paul (R-KY)	Jan 03, 2011
Chuck Grassley (R-IA)	Jan 03, 1981	Richard Blumenthal (D-CT)	Jan 03, 2011
Richard Shelby (R-AL)	Jan 03, 1987	Mike Lee (R-UT)	Jan 03, 2011
Dianne Feinstein (D-CA)	Nov 10, 1992	Brian Schatz (D-HI)	Dec 27, 2012
Patty Murray (D-WA)	Jan 03, 1993	Tim Scott (R-SC)	Jan 02, 2013
Jim Inhofe (R-OK)	Nov 17, 1994	Tammy Baldwin (D-WI)	Jan 03, 2013
Ron Wyden (D-OR)	Feb 06, 1996	Chris Murphy (D-CT)	Jan 03, 2013
Pat Roberts (R-KS)	Jan 03, 1997	Mazie Hirono (D-HI)	Jan 03, 2013
Dick Durbin (D-IL)	Jan 03, 1997	Martin Heinrich (D-NM)	Jan 03, 2013
Jack Reed (D-RI)	Jan 03, 1997	Angus King (I-ME)	Jan 03, 2013
Susan Collins (R-ME)	Jan 03, 1997	Tim Kaine (D-VA)	Jan 03, 2013
Mike Enzi (R-WY)	Jan 03, 1997	Ted Cruz (R-TX)	Jan 03, 2013
Mike Crapo (R-ID)	Jan 03, 1999	Elizabeth Warren (D-MA)	Jan 03, 2013
Tom Carper (D-DE)	Jan 03, 2001	Deb Fischer (R-NE)	Jan 03, 2013
Debbie Stabenow (D-MI)	Jan 03, 2001	Ed Markey (D-MA)	Jul 16, 2013
Maria Cantwell (D-WA)	Jan 03, 2001	Cory Booker (D-NJ)	Oct 31, 2013
John Cornyn (R-TX)	Dec 01, 2002	Shelley Moore Capito (R-WV)	Jan 03, 2015
Lisa Murkowski (R-AK)	Dec 20, 2002	Gary Peters (D-MI)	Jan 03, 2015
Lindsey Graham (R-SC)	Jan 03, 2003	Bill Cassidy (R-LA)	Jan 03, 2015
Lamar Alexander (R-TN)	Jan 03, 2003	Cory Gardner (R-CO)	Jan 03, 2015
Richard Burr (R-NC)	Jan 03, 2005	James Lankford (R-OK)	Jan 03, 2015
John Thune (R-SD)	Jan 03, 2005	Tom Cotton (R-AR)	Jan 03, 2015
Johnny Isakson (R-GA)	Jan 03, 2005	Steve Daines (R-MT)	Jan 03, 2015
Bob Menendez (D-NJ)	Jan 18, 2006	Mike Rounds (R-SD)	Jan 03, 2015
Ben Cardin (D-MD)	Jan 03, 2007	David Perdue (R-GA)	Jan 03, 2015
Bernie Sanders (I-VT)	Jan 03, 2007	Thom Tillis (R-NC)	Jan 03, 2015
Sherrod Brown (D-OH)	Jan 03, 2007	Joni Ernst (R-IA)	Jan 03, 2015
Bob Casey (D-PA)	Jan 03, 2007	Ben Sasse (R-NE)	Jan 03, 2015
Amy Klobuchar (D-MN)	Jan 03, 2007	Dan Sullivan (R-AK)	Jan 03, 2015
Sheldon Whitehouse (D-RI)	Jan 03, 2007	Chris Van Hollen (D-MD)	Jan 03, 2017
Jon Tester (D-MT)	Jan 03, 2007	Todd Young (R-IN)	Jan 03, 2017
John Barrasso (R-WY)	Jun 25, 2007	Tammy Duckworth (D-IL)	Jan 03, 2017
Roger Wicker (R-MS)	Dec 31, 2007	Maggie Hassan (D-NH)	Jan 03, 2017
Tom Udall (D-NM)	Jan 03, 2009	Kamala Harris (D-CA)	Jan 03, 2017
Jeanne Shaheen (D-NH)	Jan 03, 2009	John Kennedy (R-LA)	Jan 03, 2017
Mark Warner (D-VA)	Jan 03, 2009	Catherine Cortez Masto (D-NV)	Jan 03, 2017
Jim Risch (R-ID)	Jan 03, 2009	Tina Smith (D-MN)	Jan 03, 2018
Jeff Merkley (D-OR)	Jan 03, 2009	Doug Jones (D-AL)	Jan 03, 2018
Michael Bennet (D-CO)	Jan 21, 2009	Cindy Hyde-Smith (R-MS)	Apr 02, 2018
Kirsten Gillibrand (D-NY)	Jan 26, 2009	Marsha Blackburn (R-TN)	Jan 03, 2019
Joe Manchin (D-WV)	Nov 15, 2010	Kyrsten Sinema (D-AZ)	Jan 03, 2019
Chris Coons (D-DE)	Nov 15, 2010	Kevin Cramer (R-ND)	Jan 03, 2019
Roy Blunt (R-MO)	Jan 03, 2011	Martha McSally (R-AZ)	Jan 03, 2019
Jerry Moran (R-KS)	Jan 03, 2011	Jacky Rosen (D-NV)	Jan 03, 2019
Rob Portman (R-OH)	Jan 03, 2011	Mitt Romney (R-UT)	Jan 03, 2019
John Boozman (R-AR)	Jan 03, 2011	Mike Braun (R-IN)	Jan 03, 2019
Pat Toomey (R-PA)	Jan 03, 2011	Josh Hawley (R-MO)	Jan 03, 2019
John Hoeven (R-ND)	Jan 03, 2011	Rick Scott (R-FL)	Jan 08, 2019
Marco Rubio (R-FL)	Jan 03, 2011		
Ron Johnson (R-WI)	Jan 03, 2011		

HOUSE SENIORITY

Representatives are ranked by the total length of time served in the House. Members are given credit for prior service, and ties are broken alphabetically. The House seniority list was provided was compiled from information records and rules provided by the office of the Clerk of the House. It is current as of Jun 20, 2019.

Member (Party and State)	Start of Service	Member (Party and State)	Start of Service
Don Young (R-AK)	Mar 06, 1973	Jim McGovern (D-MA)	Jan 03, 1997
Jim Sensenbrenner (R-WI)	Jan 03, 1979	Bill Pascrell (D-NJ)	Jan 03, 1997
Hal Rogers (R-KY)	Jan 03, 1981	Brad Sherman (D-CA)	Jan 03, 1997
Chris Smith (R-NJ)	Jan 03, 1981	John Shimkus (R-IL)	Jan 03, 1997
Steny Hoyer (D-MD)	May 19, 1981	Adam Smith (D-WA)	Jan 03, 1997
Marcy Kaptur (D-OH)	Jan 03, 1983	Gregory Meeks (D-NY)	Feb 03, 1998
Pete Visclosky (D-IN)	Jan 03, 1985	Barbara Lee (D-CA)	Apr 07, 1998
Peter DeFazio (D-OR)	Jan 03, 1987	Steve Chabot (R-OH)[3]	Jan 03, 2011
John Lewis (D-GA)	Jan 03, 1987	John Larson (D-CT)	Jan 03, 1999
Fred Upton (R-MI)	Jan 03, 1987	Grace Napolitano (D-CA)	Jan 03, 1999
Nancy Pelosi (D-CA)	Jun 02, 1987	Jan Schakowsky (D-IL)	Jan 03, 1999
Frank Pallone (D-NJ)	Nov 08, 1988	Mike Simpson (R-ID)	Jan 03, 1999
Eliot Engel (D-NY)	Jan 03, 1989	Mike Thompson (D-CA)	Jan 03, 1999
Nita Lowey (D-NY)	Jan 03, 1989	Greg Walden (R-OR)	Jan 03, 1999
Richard Neal (D-MA)	Jan 03, 1989	Lacy Clay (D-MO)	Jan 03, 2001
Jose Serrano (D-NY)	Mar 20, 1990	Susan Davis (D-CA)	Jan 03, 2001
David Price (D-NC)[1]	Jan 03, 1997	Sam Graves (R-MO)	Jan 03, 2001
Rosa DeLauro (D-CT)	Jan 03, 1991	Jim Langevin (D-RI)	Jan 03, 2001
Collin Peterson (DFL-MN)	Jan 03, 1991	Rick Larsen (D-WA)	Jan 03, 2001
Maxine Waters (D-CA)	Jan 03, 1991	Betty McCollum (DFL-MN)	Jan 03, 2001
Jerrold Nadler (D-NY)	Nov 03, 1992	Adam Schiff (D-CA)	Jan 03, 2001
Jim Cooper (D-TN)[2]	Jan 03, 2003	Stephen Lynch (D-MA)	Oct 16, 2001
Sanford Bishop (D-GA)	Jan 03, 1993	Joe Wilson (R-SC)	Dec 18, 2001
Ken Calvert (R-CA)	Jan 03, 1993	Rob Bishop (R-UT)	Jan 03, 2003
James Clyburn (D-SC)	Jan 03, 1993	Michael Burgess (R-TX)	Jan 03, 2003
Anna Eshoo (D-CA)	Jan 03, 1993	John Carter (R-TX)	Jan 03, 2003
Alcee Hastings (D-FL)	Jan 03, 1993	Tom Cole (R-OK)	Jan 03, 2003
Eddie Bernice Johnson (D-TX)	May 08, 1991	Mario Diaz-Balart (R-FL)	Jan 03, 2003
Pete King (R-NY)	Jan 03, 1993	Raul Grijalva (D-AZ)	Jan 03, 2003
Carolyn Maloney (D-NY)	Jan 03, 1993	Steve King (R-IA)	Jan 03, 2003
Lucille Roybal-Allard (D-CA)	Jan 03, 1993	Devin Nunes (R-CA)	Jan 03, 2003
Bobby Rush (D-IL)	Jan 03, 1993	Mike Rogers (R-AL)	Jan 03, 2003
Bobby Scott (D-VA)	Jan 03, 1993	Dutch Ruppersberger (D-MD)	Jan 03, 2003
Nydia Velázquez (D-NY)	Jan 03, 1993	Tim Ryan (D-OH)	Jan 03, 2003
Bennie Thompson (D-MS)	Apr 13, 1993	Linda Sánchez (D-CA)	Jan 03, 2003
Frank Lucas (R-OK)	May 10, 1994	David Scott (D-GA)	Jan 03, 2003
Lloyd Doggett (D-TX)	Jan 03, 1995	Michael Turner (R-OH)	Jan 03, 2003
Mike Doyle (D-PA)	Jan 03, 1995	G.K. Butterfield (D-NC)	Jul 20, 2004
Sheila Jackson Lee (D-TX)	Jan 03, 1995	Emanuel Cleaver (D-MO)	Jan 03, 2005
Zoe Lofgren (D-CA)	Jan 03, 1995	Mike Conaway (R-TX)	Jan 03, 2005
Mac Thornberry (R-TX)	Jan 03, 1995	Jim Costa (D-CA)	Jan 03, 2005
Elijah Cummings (D-MD)	Apr 16, 1996	Henry Cuellar (D-TX)	Jan 03, 2005
Earl Blumenauer (D-OR)	May 21, 1996	Jeff Fortenberry (R-NE)	Jan 03, 2005
Robert Aderholt (R-AL)	Jan 03, 1997	Virginia Foxx (R-NC)	Jan 03, 2005
Kevin Brady (R-TX)	Jan 03, 1997	Louie Gohmert (R-TX)	Jan 03, 2005
Danny Davis (D-IL)	Jan 03, 1997	Al Green (D-TX)	Jan 03, 2005
Diana DeGette (D-CO)	Jan 03, 1997	Brian Higgins (D-NY)	Jan 03, 2005
Kay Granger (R-TX)	Jan 03, 1997	Daniel Lipinski (D-IL)	Jan 03, 2005
Ron Kind (D-WI)	Jan 03, 1997	Kenny Marchant (R-TX)	Jan 03, 2005

Member (Party and State)	Start of Service	Member (Party and State)	Start of Service
Michael McCaul (R-TX)	Jan 03, 2005	Sean Duffy (R-WI)	Jan 03, 2011
Patrick McHenry (R-NC)	Jan 03, 2005	Jeff Duncan (R-SC)	Jan 03, 2011
Gwen Moore (D-WI)	Jan 03, 2005	Chuck Fleischmann (R-TN)	Jan 03, 2011
Cathy McMorris Rodgers (R-WA)	Jan 03, 2005	Bill Flores (R-TX)	Jan 03, 2011
Debbie Wasserman Schultz (D-FL)	Jan 03, 2005	Bob Gibbs (R-OH)	Jan 03, 2011
Doris Matsui (D-CA)	Mar 08, 2005	Paul Gosar (R-AZ)	Jan 03, 2011
Albio Sires (D-NJ)	Nov 07, 2006	Morgan Griffith (R-VA)	Jan 03, 2011
Gus Bilirakis (R-FL)	Jan 03, 2007	Andy Harris (R-MD)	Jan 03, 2011
Vern Buchanan (R-FL)	Jan 03, 2007	Vicky Hartzler (R-MO)	Jan 03, 2011
Kathy Castor (D-FL)	Jan 03, 2007	Jaime Herrera Beutler (R-WA)	Jan 03, 2011
Yvette Clarke (D-NY)	Jan 03, 2007	Bill Huizenga (R-MI)	Jan 03, 2011
Steve Cohen (D-TN)	Jan 03, 2007	Bill Johnson (R-OH)	Jan 03, 2011
Joe Courtney (D-CT)	Jan 03, 2007	Bill Keating (D-MA)	Jan 03, 2011
Hank Johnson (D-GA)	Jan 03, 2007	Mike Kelly (R-PA)	Jan 03, 2011
Jim Jordan (R-OH)	Jan 03, 2007	Adam Kinzinger (R-IL)	Jan 03, 2011
Doug Lamborn (R-CO)	Jan 03, 2007	Billy Long (R-MO)	Jan 03, 2011
Dave Loebsack (D-IA)	Jan 03, 2007	David McKinley (R-WV)	Jan 03, 2011
Kevin McCarthy (R-CA)	Jan 03, 2007	Steven Palazzo (R-MS)	Jan 03, 2011
Jerry McNerney (D-CA)	Jan 03, 2007	Cedric Richmond (D-LA)	Jan 03, 2011
Ed Perlmutter (D-CO)	Jan 03, 2007	Martha Roby (R-AL)	Jan 03, 2011
John Sarbanes (D-MD)	Jan 03, 2007	David Schweikert (R-AZ)	Jan 03, 2011
Adrian Smith (R-NE)	Jan 03, 2007	Austin Scott (R-GA)	Jan 03, 2011
Peter Welch (D-VT)	Jan 03, 2007	Terri Sewell (D-AL)	Jan 03, 2011
John Yarmuth (D-KY)	Jan 03, 2007	Steve Stivers (R-OH)	Jan 03, 2011
Bob Latta (R-OH)	Dec 11, 2007	Scott Tipton (R-CO)	Jan 03, 2011
Rob Wittman (R-VA)	Dec 11, 2007	Daniel Webster (R-FL)	Jan 03, 2011
Andre Carson (D-IN)	Mar 11, 2008	Frederica Wilson (D-FL)	Jan 03, 2011
Jackie Speier (D-CA)	Apr 08, 2008	Steve Womack (R-AR)	Jan 03, 2011
Steve Scalise (R-LA)	May 03, 2008	Rob Woodall (R-GA)	Jan 03, 2011
Marcia Fudge (D-OH)	Nov 18, 2008	Mark Amodei (R-NV)	Sep 13, 2011
Gerald Connolly (D-VA)	Jan 03, 2009	Suzanne Bonamici (D-OR)	Jan 31, 2012
Brett Guthrie (R-KY)	Jan 03, 2009	Suzan DelBene (D-WA)	Nov 06, 2012
Jim Himes (D-CT)	Jan 03, 2009	Thomas Massie (R-KY)	Nov 06, 2012
Duncan Hunter (R-CA)	Jan 03, 2009	Donald Payne (D-NJ)	Nov 06, 2012
Blaine Luetkemeyer (R-MO)	Jan 03, 2009	Dina Titus (D-NV)[6]	Jan 03, 2013
Ben Ray Luján (D-NM)	Jan 03, 2009	Andy Barr (R-KY)	Jan 03, 2013
Tom McClintock (R-CA)	Jan 03, 2009	Joyce Beatty (D-OH)	Jan 03, 2013
Pete Olson (R-TX)	Jan 03, 2009	Ami Bera (D-CA)	Jan 03, 2013
Chellie Pingree (D-ME)	Jan 03, 2009	Susan Brooks (R-IN)	Jan 03, 2013
Bill Posey (R-FL)	Jan 03, 2009	Julia Brownley (D-CA)	Jan 03, 2013
Phil Roe (R-TN)	Jan 03, 2009	Cheri Bustos (D-IL)	Jan 03, 2013
Kurt Schrader (D-OR)	Jan 03, 2009	Tony Cárdenas (D-CA)	Jan 03, 2013
Glenn Thompson (R-PA)	Jan 03, 2009	Matthew Cartwright (D-PA)	Jan 03, 2013
Paul Tonko (D-NY)	Jan 03, 2009	Joaquin Castro (D-TX)	Jan 03, 2013
Mike Quigley (D-IL)	Apr 07, 2009	Chris Collins (R-NY)	Jan 03, 2013
Judy Chu (D-CA)	Jul 14, 2009	Doug Collins (R-GA)	Jan 03, 2013
John Garamendi (D-CA)	Nov 03, 2009	Paul Cook (R-CA)	Jan 03, 2013
Ted Deutch (D-FL)	Apr 13, 2010	Rodney Davis (R-IL)	Jan 03, 2013
Tom Graves (R-GA)	Jun 08, 2010	Lois Frankel (D-FL)	Jan 03, 2013
Tom Reed (R-NY)	Nov 02, 2010	Tulsi Gabbard (D-HI)	Jan 03, 2013
Tim Walberg (R-MI)[4]	Jan 03, 2011	Denny Heck (D-WA)	Jan 03, 2013
Bill Foster (D-IL)[5]	Jan 03, 2013	George Holding (R-NC)	Jan 03, 2013
Justin Amash (R-MI)	Jan 03, 2011	Richard Hudson (R-NC)	Jan 03, 2013
Karen Bass (D-CA)	Jan 03, 2011	Jared Huffman (D-CA)	Jan 03, 2013
Mo Brooks (R-AL)	Jan 03, 2011	Hakeem Jeffries (D-NY)	Jan 03, 2013
Larry Bucshon (R-IN)	Jan 03, 2011	Dave Joyce (R-OH)	Jan 03, 2013
David Cicilline (D-RI)	Jan 03, 2011	Joe Kennedy (D-MA)	Jan 03, 2013
Rick Crawford (R-AR)	Jan 03, 2011	Dan Kildee (D-MI)	Jan 03, 2013
Scott DesJarlais (R-TN)	Jan 03, 2011	Derek Kilmer (D-WA)	Jan 03, 2013

Member (Party and State)	Start of Service	Member (Party and State)	Start of Service
Ann Kuster (D-NH)	Jan 03, 2013	John Ratcliffe (R-TX)	Jan 03, 2015
Doug LaMalfa (R-CA)	Jan 03, 2013	Kathleen Rice (D-NY)	Jan 03, 2015
Alan Lowenthal (D-CA)	Jan 03, 2013	David Rouzer (R-NC)	Jan 03, 2015
Sean Maloney (D-NY)	Jan 03, 2013	Elise Stefanik (R-NY)	Jan 03, 2015
Mark Meadows (R-NC)	Jan 03, 2013	Norma Torres (D-CA)	Jan 03, 2015
Grace Meng (D-NY)	Jan 03, 2013	Mark Walker (R-NC)	Jan 03, 2015
Markwayne Mullin (R-OK)	Jan 03, 2013	Bonnie Watson Coleman (D-NJ)	Jan 03, 2015
Scott Perry (R-PA)	Jan 03, 2013	Bruce Westerman (R-AR)	Jan 03, 2015
Scott Peters (D-CA)	Jan 03, 2013	Lee Zeldin (R-NY)	Jan 03, 2015
Mark Pocan (D-WI)	Jan 03, 2013	Trent Kelly (R-MS)	Jun 02, 2015
Tom Rice (R-SC)	Jan 03, 2013	Darin LaHood (R-IL)	Sep 10, 2015
Raul Ruiz (D-CA)	Jan 03, 2013	Warren Davidson (R-OH)	Jun 07, 2016
Chris Stewart (R-UT)	Jan 03, 2013	James Comer (R-KY)	Nov 08, 2016
Eric Swalwell (D-CA)	Jan 03, 2013	Dwight Evans (D-PA)	Nov 08, 2016
Mark Takano (D-CA)	Jan 03, 2013	Brad Schneider (D-IL)[9]	Jan 03, 2017
Juan Vargas (D-CA)	Jan 03, 2013	Jodey Arrington (R-TX)	Jan 03, 2017
Marc Veasey (D-TX)	Jan 03, 2013	Don Bacon (R-NE)	Jan 03, 2017
Filemon Vela (D-TX)	Jan 03, 2013	Jim Banks (R-IN)	Jan 03, 2017
Ann Wagner (R-MO)	Jan 03, 2013	Nanette Barragán (D-CA)	Jan 03, 2017
Jackie Walorski (R-IN)	Jan 03, 2013	John Bergman (R-MI)	Jan 03, 2017
Randy Weber (R-TX)	Jan 03, 2013	Andy Biggs (R-AZ)	Jan 03, 2017
Brad Wenstrup (R-OH)	Jan 03, 2013	Lisa Blunt Rochester (D-DE)	Jan 03, 2017
Roger Williams (R-TX)	Jan 03, 2013	Anthony Brown (D-MD)	Jan 03, 2017
Ted Yoho (R-FL)	Jan 03, 2013	Ted Budd (R-NC)	Jan 03, 2017
Robin Kelly (D-IL)	Apr 09, 2013	Salud Carbajal (D-CA)	Jan 03, 2017
Jason Smith (R-MO)	Jun 04, 2013	Liz Cheney (R-WY)	Jan 03, 2017
Katherine Clark (D-MA)	Dec 10, 2013	Lou Correa (D-CA)	Jan 03, 2017
Bradley Byrne (R-AL)	Dec 17, 2013	Charlie Crist (D-FL)	Jan 03, 2017
Alma Adams (D-NC)	Nov 04, 2014	Val Demings (D-FL)	Jan 03, 2017
Donald Norcross (D-NJ)	Nov 04, 2014	Neal Dunn (R-FL)	Jan 03, 2017
Ann Kirkpatrick (D-AZ)[7]	Jan 03, 2019	Adriano Espaillat (D-NY)	Jan 03, 2017
Ed Case (D-HI)[8]	Jan 03, 2019	Drew Ferguson (R-GA)	Jan 03, 2017
Ralph Abraham (R-LA)	Jan 03, 2015	Brian Fitzpatrick (R-PA)	Jan 03, 2017
Pete Aguilar (D-CA)	Jan 03, 2015	Matt Gaetz (R-FL)	Jan 03, 2017
Rick Allen (R-GA)	Jan 03, 2015	Mike Gallagher (R-WI)	Jan 03, 2017
Brian Babin (R-TX)	Jan 03, 2015	Vicente Gonzalez (D-TX)	Jan 03, 2017
Don Beyer (D-VA)	Jan 03, 2015	Josh Gottheimer (D-NJ)	Jan 03, 2017
Mike Bost (R-IL)	Jan 03, 2015	Clay Higgins (R-LA)	Jan 03, 2017
Brendan Boyle (D-PA)	Jan 03, 2015	Trey Hollingsworth (R-IN)	Jan 03, 2017
Kenneth Buck (R-CO)	Jan 03, 2015	Pramila Jayapal (D-WA)	Jan 03, 2017
Buddy Carter (R-GA)	Jan 03, 2015	Mike Johnson (R-LA)	Jan 03, 2017
Mark DeSaulnier (D-CA)	Jan 03, 2015	Ro Khanna (D-CA)	Jan 03, 2017
Debbie Dingell (D-MI)	Jan 03, 2015	Raja Krishnamoorthi (D-IL)	Jan 03, 2017
Thomas Emmer (R-MN)	Jan 03, 2015	David Kustoff (R-TN)	Jan 03, 2017
Ruben Gallego (D-AZ)	Jan 03, 2015	Al Lawson (D-FL)	Jan 03, 2017
Garret Graves (R-LA)	Jan 03, 2015	Roger Marshall (R-KS)	Jan 03, 2017
Glenn Grothman (R-WI)	Jan 03, 2015	Brian Mast (R-FL)	Jan 03, 2017
Jody Hice (R-GA)	Jan 03, 2015	A. Donald McEachin (D-VA)	Jan 03, 2017
French Hill (R-AR)	Jan 03, 2015	Paul Mitchell (R-MI)	Jan 03, 2017
Will Hurd (R-TX)	Jan 03, 2015	Stephanie Murphy (D-FL)	Jan 03, 2017
John Katko (R-NY)	Jan 03, 2015	Tom O'Halleran (D-AZ)	Jan 03, 2017
Brenda Lawrence (D-MI)	Jan 03, 2015	Jimmy Panetta (D-CA)	Jan 03, 2017
Ted Lieu (D-CA)	Jan 03, 2015	Jamie Raskin (D-MD)	Jan 03, 2017
Barry Loudermilk (R-GA)	Jan 03, 2015	Francis Rooney (R-FL)	Jan 03, 2017
John Moolenaar (R-MI)	Jan 03, 2015	John Rutherford (R-FL)	Jan 03, 2017
Alex Mooney (R-WV)	Jan 03, 2015	Lloyd Smucker (R-PA)	Jan 03, 2017
Seth Moulton (D-MA)	Jan 03, 2015	Darren Soto (D-FL)	Jan 03, 2017
Dan Newhouse (R-WA)	Jan 03, 2015	Thomas Suozzi (D-NY)	Jan 03, 2017
Gary Palmer (R-AL)	Jan 03, 2015	Ron Estes (R-KS)	Apr 11, 2017

Member (Party and State)	Start of Service	Member (Party and State)	Start of Service
Greg Gianforte (R-MT)	May 25, 2017	Lucy McBath (D-GA)	Jan 03, 2019
Jimmy Gomez (D-CA)	Jun 06, 2017	Daniel Meuser (R-PA)	Jan 03, 2019
Ralph Norman (R-SC)	Jun 20, 2017	Carol Miller (R-WV)	Jan 03, 2019
John Curtis (R-UT)	Nov 07, 2017	Debbie Mucarsel-Powell (D-FL)	Jan 03, 2019
Conor Lamb (D-PA)	Mar 13, 2018	Joe Neguse (D-CO)	Jan 03, 2019
Debbie Lesko (R-AZ)	Apr 24, 2018	Alexandria Ocasio-Cortez (D-NY)	Jan 03, 2019
Michael Cloud (R-TX)	Jun 30, 2018	Ilhan Omar (DFL-MN)	Jan 03, 2019
Troy Balderson (R-OH)	Aug 07, 2018	Chris Pappas (D-NH)	Jan 03, 2019
Kevin Hern (R-OK)	Nov 06, 2018	Greg Pence (R-IN)	Jan 03, 2019
Joseph Morelle (D-NY)	Nov 06, 2018	Dean Phillips (DFL-MN)	Jan 03, 2019
Mary Gay Scanlon (D-PA)	Nov 06, 2018	Katie Porter (D-CA)	Jan 03, 2019
Susan Wild (D-PA)	Nov 06, 2018	Ayanna Pressley (D-MA)	Jan 03, 2019
Steven Horsford (D-NV)[10]	Jan 03, 2019	Guy Reschenthaler (R-PA)	Jan 03, 2019
Colin Allred (D-TX)	Jan 03, 2019	Denver Riggleman (R-VA)	Jan 03, 2019
Kelly Armstrong (R-ND)	Jan 03, 2019	John Rose (R-TN)	Jan 03, 2019
Cindy Axne (D-IA)	Jan 03, 2019	Max Rose (D-NY)	Jan 03, 2019
Jim Baird (R-IN)	Jan 03, 2019	Harley Rouda (D-CA)	Jan 03, 2019
Anthony Brindisi (D-NY)	Jan 03, 2019	Chip Roy (R-TX)	Jan 03, 2019
Tim Burchett (R-TN)	Jan 03, 2019	Kim Schrier (D-WA)	Jan 03, 2019
Sean Casten (D-IL)	Jan 03, 2019	Donna Shalala (D-FL)	Jan 03, 2019
Gil Cisneros (D-CA)	Jan 03, 2019	Mikie Sherrill (D-NJ)	Jan 03, 2019
Benjamin Cline (R-VA)	Jan 03, 2019	Elissa Slotkin (D-MI)	Jan 03, 2019
T.J. Cox (D-CA)	Jan 03, 2019	Abigail Spanberger (D-VA)	Jan 03, 2019
Angie Craig (DFL-MN)	Jan 03, 2019	Ross Spano (R-FL)	Jan 03, 2019
Daniel Crenshaw (R-TX)	Jan 03, 2019	Greg Stanton (D-AZ)	Jan 03, 2019
Jason Crow (D-CO)	Jan 03, 2019	Pete Stauber (R-MN)	Jan 03, 2019
Joe Cunningham (D-SC)	Jan 03, 2019	Bryan Steil (R-WI)	Jan 03, 2019
Sharice Davids (D-KS)	Jan 03, 2019	Greg Steube (R-FL)	Jan 03, 2019
Madeleine Dean (D-PA)	Jan 03, 2019	Haley Stevens (D-MI)	Jan 03, 2019
Antonio Delgado (D-NY)	Jan 03, 2019	Van Taylor (R-TX)	Jan 03, 2019
Veronica Escobar (D-TX)	Jan 03, 2019	William Timmons (R-SC)	Jan 03, 2019
Abby Finkenauer (D-IA)	Jan 03, 2019	Rashida Tlaib (D-MI)	Jan 03, 2019
Lizzie Fletcher (D-TX)	Jan 03, 2019	Xochitl Torres Small (D-NM)	Jan 03, 2019
Russ Fulcher (R-ID)	Jan 03, 2019	Lori Trahan (D-MA)	Jan 03, 2019
Jesús Garcia (D-IL)	Jan 03, 2019	David Trone (D-MD)	Jan 03, 2019
Sylvia Garcia (D-TX)	Jan 03, 2019	Lauren Underwood (D-IL)	Jan 03, 2019
Jared Golden (D-ME)	Jan 03, 2019	Jeff Van Drew (D-NJ)	Jan 03, 2019
Anthony Gonzalez (R-OH)	Jan 03, 2019	Michael Waltz (R-FL)	Jan 03, 2019
Lance Gooden (R-TX)	Jan 03, 2019	Steve Watkins (R-KS)	Jan 03, 2019
Mark Green (R-TN)	Jan 03, 2019	Jennifer Wexton (D-VA)	Jan 03, 2019
Michael Guest (R-MS)	Jan 03, 2019	Ronald Wright (R-TX)	Jan 03, 2019
Debra Haaland (D-NM)	Jan 03, 2019	Fred Keller (R-PA)	Jun 03, 2019
Jim Hagedorn (R-MN)	Jan 03, 2019		
Josh Harder (D-CA)	Jan 03, 2019		
Jahana Hayes (D-CT)	Jan 03, 2019		
Katie Hill (D-CA)	Jan 03, 2019		
Kendra Horn (D-OK)	Jan 03, 2019		
Chrissy Houlahan (D-PA)	Jan 03, 2019		
Dusty Johnson (R-SD)	Jan 03, 2019		
John Joyce (R-PA)	Jan 03, 2019		
Andrew Kim (D-NJ)	Jan 03, 2019		
Susie Lee (D-NV)	Jan 03, 2019		
Andy Levin (D-MI)	Jan 03, 2019		
Mike Levin (D-CA)	Jan 03, 2019		
Elaine Luria (D-VA)	Jan 03, 2019		
Tom Malinowski (D-NJ)	Jan 03, 2019		
Ben McAdams (D-UT)	Jan 03, 2019		

[1]Also served 1987-1995.

[2]Also served 1983-1995.

[3]Also served 1995-2009.

[4]Also served 2007-2009.

[5]Also served 2008-2011.

[6]Also served 2009-2011.

[7]Also served 2009-2011, 2013-2017.

[8]Also served 2002-2007.

[9]Also served 2013-2015.

[10]Also served 2013-2015.

SENATE COMMITTEES

Agriculture, Nutrition & Forestry
agriculture.senate.gov

328A RSOB
202-224-2035

Majority (R 11): Roberts (KS), Chmn; McConnell (KY), Boozman (AR), Hoeven (ND), Ernst (IA), Hyde-Smith (MS), Braun (IN), Perdue (GA), Grassley (IA), Thune (SD), Fischer (NE)
Minority (D 9): Stabenow (MI), RMM; Leahy (VT), Brown (OH), Klobuchar (MN), Bennet (CO), Gillibrand (NY), Casey (PA), Smith (MN), Durbin (IL)

SUBCOMMITTEES

Commodities, Risk Management & Trade
Majority (R 7): Boozman (AR), Chmn; McConnell (KY), Hoeven (ND), Hyde-Smith (MS), Perdue (GA), Grassley (IA), Roberts (KS)
Minority (D 6): Brown (OH), RMM; Bennet (CO), Gillibrand (NY), Smith (MN), Durbin (IL), Stabenow (MI)

Conservation, Forestry & Natural Resources
Majority (R 7): Braun (IN), Chmn; Boozman (AR), Hyde-Smith (MS), Perdue (GA), Grassley (IA), Thune (SD), Roberts (KS)
Minority (D 6): Bennet (CO), RMM; Leahy (VT), Klobuchar (MN), Casey (PA), Durbin (IL), Stabenow (MI)

Livestock, Marketing & Agriculture Security
Majority (R 7): Hyde-Smith (MS), Chmn; Ernst (IA), Braun (IN), Perdue (GA), Grassley (IA), Fischer (NE), Roberts (KS)
Minority (D 6): Gillibrand (NY), RMM; Leahy (VT), Klobuchar (MN), Casey (PA), Smith (MN), Stabenow (MI)

Nutrition, Agricultural Research & Specialty Crops
Majority (R 7): Fischer (NE), Chmn; McConnell (KY), Boozman (AR), Hoeven (ND), Ernst (IA), Thune (SD), Roberts (KS)
Minority (D 6): Casey (PA), RMM; Leahy (VT), Brown (OH), Klobuchar (MN), Gillibrand (NY), Stabenow (MI)

Rural Development & Energy
Majority (R 7): Ernst (IA), Chmn; McConnell (KY), Hoeven (ND), Braun (IN), Thune (SD), Fischer (NE), Roberts (KS)
Minority (D 6): Smith (MN), RMM; Brown (OH), Klobuchar (MN), Bennet (CO), Durbin (IL), Stabenow (MI)

Appropriations
appropriations.senate.gov

S-128 The Capitol
202-224-7257

Majority (R 16): Shelby (AL), Chmn; McConnell (KY), Alexander (TN), Collins (ME), Murkowski (AK), Graham (SC), Blunt (MO), Moran (KS), Hoeven (ND), Boozman (AR), Capito (WV), Kennedy (LA), Hyde-Smith (MS), Daines (MT), Rubio (FL), Lankford (OK)
Minority (D 15): Leahy (VT), RMM; Murray (WA), Feinstein (CA), Durbin (IL), Reed (RI), Tester (MT), Udall (NM), Shaheen (NH), Merkley (OR), Coons (DE), Schatz (HI), Baldwin (WI), Murphy (CT), Manchin (WV), Van Hollen (MD)

SUBCOMMITTEES

Agriculture, Rural Development, FDA & Related Agencies
Majority (R 8): Hoeven (ND), Chmn; McConnell (KY), Collins (ME), Blunt (MO), Moran (KS), Hyde-Smith (MS), Kennedy (LA), Shelby (AL)
Minority (D 6): Merkley (OR), RMM; Feinstein (CA), Tester (MT), Udall (NM), Leahy (VT), Baldwin (WI)

Commerce, Justice, Science & Related Agencies
Majority (R 10): Moran (KS), Chmn; Alexander (TN), Murkowski (AK), Collins (ME), Graham (SC), Boozman (AR), Capito (WV), Kennedy (LA), Rubio (FL), Shelby (AL)
Minority (D 8): Shaheen (NH), RMM; Leahy (VT), Feinstein (CA), Reed (RI), Coons (DE), Schatz (HI), Manchin (WV), Van Hollen (MD)

Department of Defense
Majority (R 10): Shelby (AL), Chmn; McConnell (KY), Alexander (TN), Collins (ME), Murkowski (AK), Graham (SC), Blunt (MO), Moran (KS), Hoeven (ND), Boozman (AR)
Minority (D 9): Durbin (IL), RMM; Leahy (VT), Feinstein (CA), Murray (WA), Reed (RI), Tester (MT), Udall (NM), Schatz (HI), Baldwin (WI)

Department of Homeland Security
Majority (R 7): Capito (WV), Chmn; Shelby (AL), Murkowski (AK), Hoeven (ND), Kennedy (LA), Hyde-Smith (MS), Lankford (OK)
Minority (D 6): Tester (MT), RMM; Shaheen (NH), Leahy (VT), Murray (WA), Baldwin (WI), Manchin (WV)

Department of the Interior, Environment & Related Agencies
Majority (R 9): Murkowski (AK), Chmn; Alexander (TN), Blunt (MO), McConnell (KY), Capito (WV), Hyde-Smith (MS), Daines (MT), Rubio (FL), Shelby (AL)
Minority (D 7): Udall (NM), RMM; Feinstein (CA), Leahy (VT), Reed (RI), Tester (MT), Merkley (OR), Van Hollen (MD)

DOL, HHS & Education & Related Agencies
Majority (R 10): Blunt (MO), Chmn; Shelby (AL), Alexander (TN), Graham (SC), Moran (KS), Capito (WV), Kennedy (LA), Hyde-Smith (MS), Rubio (FL), Lankford (OK)
Minority (D 10): Murray (WA), RMM; Durbin (IL), Reed (RI), Shaheen (NH), Merkley (OR), Schatz (HI), Baldwin (WI), Murphy (CT), Manchin (WV), Leahy (VT)

Energy & Water Development
Majority (R 9): Alexander (TN), Chmn; McConnell (KY), Shelby (AL), Collins (ME), Murkowski (AK), Graham (SC), Hoeven (ND), Kennedy (LA), Hyde-Smith (MS)
Minority (D 9): Feinstein (CA), RMM; Murray (WA), Tester (MT), Durbin (IL), Udall (NM), Shaheen (NH), Merkley (OR) Coons (DE), Leahy (VT)

Financial Services & General Government
Majority (R 6): Kennedy (LA), Chmn; Moran (KS), Boozman (AR), Daines (MT), Lankford (OK), Shelby (AL)
Minority (D 5): Coons (DE), RMM; Durbin (IL), Manchin (WV), Van Hollen (MD), Leahy (VT)

Legislative Branch
Majority (R 3): Hyde-Smith (MS), Chmn; Shelby (AL), Lankford (OK)
Minority (D 3): Murphy (CT), RMM; Van Hollen (MD), Leahy (VT)

Military Construction & Veteran Affairs & Related Agencies
Majority (R 9): Boozman (AR), Chmn; McConnell (KY), Murkowski (AK), Hoeven (ND), Collins (ME), Capito (WV), Rubio (FL), Daines (MT), Shelby (AL)
Minority (D 8): Schatz (HI), RMM; Tester (MT), Murray (WA), Reed (RI), Udall (NM), Baldwin (WI), Murphy (CT), Leahy (VT)

State, Foreign Operations & Related Programs
Majority (R 9): Graham (SC), Chmn; McConnell (KY), Blunt (MO), Boozman (AR), Moran (KS), Rubio (FL), Lankford (OK), Daines (MT), Shelby (AL)
Minority (D 7): Leahy (VT), RMM; Durbin (IL), Shaheen (NH), Coons (DE), Merkley (OR), Murphy (CT), Van Hollen (MD)

Transportation, HUD & Related Agencies
Majority (R 9): Collins (ME), Chmn; Shelby (AL), Alexander (TN), Blunt (MO), Boozman (AR), Capito (WV), Graham (SC), Hoeven (ND), Daines (MT)
Minority (D 9): Reed (RI), RMM; Murray (WA), Durbin (IL), Feinstein (CA), Coons (DE), Schatz (HI), Murphy (CT), Manchin (WV), Leahy (VT)

Armed Services   **228 RSOB**
armed-services.senate.gov   **202-224-3871**

Majority (R 14): Inhofe (OK), Chmn; Wicker (MS), Fischer (NE), Cotton (AR), Rounds (SD), Ernst (IA), Tillis (NC), Sullivan (AK), Perdue (GA), Cramer (ND), McSally (AZ), Scott (FL), Blackburn (TN), Hawley (MO)
Minority (D 13): Reed (RI), RMM; Shaheen (NH), Gillibrand (NY), Blumenthal (CT), Hirono (HI), Kaine (VA), King (ME), Heinrich (NM), Warren (MA), Peters (MI), Manchin (WV), Duckworth (IL), Jones (AL)

SUBCOMMITTEES

Airland
Majority (R 7): Cotton (AR), Chmn; Wicker (MS), Tillis (NC), Sullivan (AK), Cramer (ND), McSally (AZ), Scott (FL)
Minority (D 6): King (ME), RMM; Blumenthal (CT), Warren (MA), Peters (MI), Duckworth (IL), Jones (AL)

Cybersecurity
Majority (R 5): Rounds (SD), Chmn; Wicker (MS), Perdue (GA), Scott (FL), Blackburn (TN)
Minority (D 4): Manchin (WV), RMM; Gillibrand (NY), Blumenthal (CT), Heinrich (NM)

Emerging Threats & Capabilities
Majority (R 5): Ernst (IA), Chmn; Fischer (NE), Cramer (ND), Blackburn (TN), Hawley (MO)
Minority (D 4): Peters (MI), RMM; Shaheen (NH), Hirono (HI), Heinrich (NM)

Personnel
Majority (R 4): Tillis (NC), Chmn; Rounds (SD), McSally (AZ), Scott (FL)
Minority (D 3): Gillibrand (NY), RMM; Warren (MA), Duckworth (IL)

Readiness & Management Support
Majority (R 6): Sullivan (AK), Chmn; Fischer (NE), Ernst (IA), Perdue (GA), McSally (AZ), Blackburn (TN)
Minority (D 5): Kaine (VA), RMM; Shaheen (NH), Hirono (HI), Duckworth (IL), Jones (AL)

Seapower
Majority (R 6): Perdue (GA), Chmn; Wicker (MS), Cotton (AR), Ernst (IA), Tillis (NC), Hawley (MO)
Minority (D 5): Hirono (HI), RMM; Shaheen (NH), Blumenthal (CT), Kaine (VA), King (ME)

Strategic Forces
Majority (R 6): Fischer (NE), Chmn; Cotton (AR), Rounds (SD), Sullivan (AK), Cramer (ND), Hawley (MO)
Minority (D 5): Heinrich (NM), RMM; King (ME), Warren (MA), Manchin (WV), Jones (AL)

Banking, Housing & Urban Affairs   **534 DSOB**
banking.senate.gov   **202-224-7391**

Majority (R 13): Crapo (ID), Chmn; Shelby (AL), Toomey (PA), Scott (SC), Sasse (NE), Cotton (AR), Rounds (SD), Perdue (GA), Tillis (NC), Kennedy (LA), McSally (AZ), Moran (KS), Cramer (ND)
Minority (D 12): Brown (OH), RMM; Reed (RI), Menendez (NJ), Tester (MT), Warner (VA), Warren (MA), Schatz (HI), Van Hollen (MD), Cortez Masto (NV), Jones (AL), Smith (MN), Sinema (AZ)

SUBCOMMITTEES

Economic Policy
Majority (R 7): Cotton (AR), Chmn; Cramer (ND), Sasse (NE), Perdue (GA), Tillis (NC), Kennedy (LA), Crapo (ID)
Minority (D 6): Cortez Masto (NV), RMM; Menendez (NJ), Jones (AL), Smith (MN), Sinema (AZ), Brown (OH)

Financial Institutions & Consumer Protection
Majority (R 10): Scott (SC), Chmn; Rounds (SD), Tillis (NC), Kennedy (LA), Moran (KS), Cramer (ND), Shelby (AL), Toomey (PA), Sasse (NE), Crapo (ID)
Minority (D 9): Warren (MA), RMM; Reed (RI), Tester (MT), Warner (VA), Schatz (HI), Van Hollen (MD), Cortez Masto (NV), Jones (AL), Brown (OH)

Housing, Transportation & Community Development
Majority (R 8): Perdue (GA), Chmn; Shelby (AL), Cotton (AR), Rounds (SD), McSally (AZ), Moran (KS), Cramer (ND), Crapo (ID)
Minority (D 7): Menendez (NJ), RMM; Reed (RI), Warren (MA), Cortez Masto (NV), Jones (AL), Smith (MN), Brown (OH)

National Security & International Trade & Finance
Majority (R 6): Sasse (NE), Chmn; McSally (AZ), Moran (KS), Toomey (PA), Scott (SC), Crapo (ID)
Minority (D 5): Warner (VA), RMM; Schatz (HI), Van Hollen (MD), Sinema (AZ), Brown (OH)

Securities, Insurance & Investment
Majority (R 10): Toomey (PA), Chmn; Shelby (AL), McSally (AZ), Scott (SC), Cotton (AR), Rounds (SD), Perdue (GA), Tillis (NC), Kennedy (LA), Crapo (ID)
Minority (D 9): Van Hollen (MD), RMM; Reed (RI), Menendez (NJ), Tester (MT), Warner (VA), Warren (MA), Smith (MN), Sinema (AZ), Brown (OH)

Budget
budget.senate.gov

624 DSOB
202-224-0642

Majority (R 11): Enzi (WY), Chmn; Grassley (IA), Crapo (ID), Graham (SC), Toomey (PA), Johnson (WI), Perdue (GA), Braun (IN), Scott (FL), Kennedy (LA), Cramer (ND)
Minority (D 10): Sanders (VT), RMM; Murray (WA), Wyden (OR), Stabenow (MI), Whitehouse (RI), Warner (VA), Merkley (OR), Kaine (VA), Van Hollen (MD), Harris (CA)

Commerce, Science & Transportation
commerce.senate.gov

512 DSOB
202-224-1251

Majority (R 14): Wicker (MS), Chmn; Thune (SD), Blunt (MO), Cruz (TX), Fischer (NE), Moran (KS), Sullivan (AK), Gardner (CO), Blackburn (TN), Capito (WV), Lee (UT), Johnson (WI), Young (IN), Scott (FL)
Minority (D 12): Cantwell (WA), RMM; Klobuchar (MN), Blumenthal (CT), Schatz (HI), Markey (MA), Udall (NM), Peters (MI), Baldwin (WI), Duckworth (IL), Tester (MT), Sinema (AZ), Rosen (NV)

SUBCOMMITTEES

Communications, Technology, Innovation & the Internet
Majority (R 14): Thune (SD), Chmn; Blunt (MO), Cruz (TX), Fischer (NE), Moran (KS), Sullivan (AK), Gardner (CO), Blackburn (TN), Capito (WV), Lee (UT), Johnson (WI), Young (IN), Scott (FL), Wicker (MS)
Minority (D 12): Schatz (HI), RMM; Klobuchar (MN), Blumenthal (CT), Markey (MA), Udall (NM), Peters (MI), Baldwin (WI), Duckworth (IL), Tester (MT), Sinema (AZ), Rosen (NV), Cantwell (WA)

Manufacturing, Trade & Consumer Protection
Majority (R 10): Moran (KS), Chmn; Thune (SD), Fischer (NE), Sullivan (AK), Blackburn (TN), Capito (WV), Lee (UT), Johnson (WI), Young (IN), Wicker (MS)
Minority (D 9): Blumenthal (CT), RMM; Klobuchar (MN), Schatz (HI), Markey (MA), Udall (NM), Baldwin (WI), Sinema (AZ), Rosen (NV), Cantwell (WA)

Subcommittee on Aviation & Space
Majority (R 9): Cruz (TX), Chmn; Thune (SD), Blunt (MO), Moran (KS), Gardner (CO), Blackburn (TN), Capito (WV), Lee (UT) Wicker (MS)
Minority (D 8): Sinema (AZ), RMM; Schatz (HI), Udall (NM), Peters (MI), Duckworth (IL), Tester (MT), Rosen (NV), Cantwell (WA)

Subcommittee on Science, Oceans, Fisheries & Weather
Majority (R 6): Gardner (CO), Chmn; Cruz (TX), Sullivan (AK), Johnson (WI), Scott (FL), Wicker (MS)
Minority (D 5): Baldwin (WI), RMM; Blumenthal (CT), Schatz (HI), Peters (MI), Cantwell (WA)

Subcommittee on Security
Majority (R 10): Sullivan (AK), Chmn; Blunt (MO), Cruz (TX), Fischer (NE), Blackburn (TN), Lee (UT), Johnson (WI), Young (IN), Scott (FL), Wicker (MS)
Minority (D 9): Markey (MA), RMM; Klobuchar (MN), Blumenthal (CT), Schatz (HI), Udall (NM), Duckworth (IL), Sinema (AZ), Rosen (NV), Cantwell (WA)

Subcommittee on Transportation & Safety
Majority (R 9): Fischer (NE), Chmn; Thune (SD), Blunt (MO), Moran (KS), Gardner (CO), Capito (WV), Young (IN), Scott (FL), Wicker (MS)
Minority (D 8): Duckworth (IL), RMM; Klobuchar (MN), Blumenthal (CT), Markey (MA), Udall (NM), Peters (MI), Baldwin (WI), Cantwell (WA)

Energy & Natural Resources
energy.senate.gov

304 DSOB
202-224-4971

Majority (R 11): Murkowski (AK), Chmn; Barrasso (WY), Risch (ID), Lee (UT), Daines (MT), Cassidy (LA), Gardner (CO), Hyde-Smith (MS), McSally (AZ), Alexander (TN), Hoeven (ND)
Minority (D 9): Manchin (WV), RMM; Wyden (OR), Cantwell (WA), Sanders (VT), Stabenow (MI), Heinrich (NM), Hirono (HI), King (ME), Cortez Masto (NV)

SUBCOMMITTEES

Energy
Majority (R 10): Cassidy (LA), Chmn; Risch (ID), Lee (UT), Daines (MT), Gardner (CO), Hyde-Smith (MS), McSally (AZ), Alexander (TN), Hoeven (ND), Murkowski (AK)
Minority (D 9): Heinrich (NM), RMM; Wyden (OR), Cantwell (WA), Sanders (VT), Stabenow (MI), Hirono (HI), King (ME), Cortez Masto (NV), Manchin (WV)

National Parks
Majority (R 8): Daines (MT), Chmn; Barrasso (WY), Lee (UT), Gardner (CO), Hyde-Smith (MS), Alexander (TN), Hoeven (ND), Murkowski (AK)
Minority (D 6): King (ME), RMM; Sanders (VT), Stabenow (MI), Heinrich (NM), Hirono (HI), Manchin (WV)

Public Lands, Forests & Mining
Majority (R 10): Lee (UT), Chmn; Barrasso (WY), Risch (ID), Daines (MT), Cassidy (LA), Gardner (CO), Hyde-Smith (MS), McSally (AZ), Hoeven (ND), Murkowski (AK)
Minority (D 8): Wyden (OR), RMM; Cantwell (WA), Stabenow (MI), Heinrich (NM), Hirono (HI), King (ME), Cortez Masto (NV), Manchin (WV)

Water & Power
Majority (R 7): McSally (AZ), Chmn; Barrasso (WY), Risch (ID), Cassidy (LA), Gardner (CO), Alexander (TN), Murkowski (AK)
Minority (D 5): Cortez Masto (NV), RMM; Wyden (OR), Cantwell (WA), Sanders (VT), Manchin (WV)

Environment & Public Works
epw.senate.gov
410 DSOB
202-224-6176

Majority (R 11): Barrasso (WY), Chmn; Inhofe (OK), Capito (WV), Cramer (ND), Braun (IN), Rounds (SD), Sullivan (AK), Boozman (AR), Wicker (MS), Shelby (AL), Ernst (IA)
Minority (D 10): Carper (DE), RMM; Cardin (MD), Sanders (VT), Whitehouse (RI), Merkley (OR), Gillibrand (NY), Booker (NJ), Markey (MA), Duckworth (IL), Van Hollen (MD)

SUBCOMMITTEES

Clean Air & Nuclear Safety
Majority (R 9): Braun (IN), Chmn; Inhofe (OK), Capito (WV), Cramer (ND), Rounds (SD), Sullivan (AK), Boozman (AR), Wicker (MS), Ernst (IA)
Minority (D 8): Whitehouse (RI), RMM; Cardin (MD), Sanders (VT), Merkley (OR), Gillibrand (NY), Booker (NJ), Markey (MA), Duckworth (IL)

Fisheries, Water, and Wildlife
Majority (R 7): Cramer (ND), Chmn; Capito (WV), Braun (IN), Sullivan (AK), Boozman (AR), Wicker (MS), Shelby (AL)
Minority (D 6): Duckworth (IL), RMM; Cardin (MD), Sanders (VT), Whitehouse (RI), Merkley (OR), Van Hollen (MD)

Superfund, Waste Management, & Regulatory Oversight
Majority (R 4): Rounds (SD), Chmn; Inhofe (OK), Shelby (AL), Ernst (IA)
Minority (D 3): Booker (NJ), RMM; Gillibrand (NY), Markey (MA)

Transportation & Infrastructure
Majority (R 9): Capito (WV), Chmn; Inhofe (OK), Cramer (ND), Braun (IN), Rounds (SD), Sullivan (AK), Boozman (AR), Wicker (MS), Shelby (AL)
Minority (D 8): Cardin (MD), RMM; Sanders (VT), Whitehouse (RI), Merkley (OR), Gillibrand (NY), Booker (NJ), Markey (MA), Van Hollen (MD)

Finance
finance.senate.gov
219 DSOB
202-224-4515

Majority (R 15): Grassley (IA), Chmn; Crapo (ID), Roberts (KS), Enzi (WY), Cornyn (TX), Thune (SD), Burr (NC), Isakson (GA), Portman (OH), Toomey (PA), Scott (SC), Cassidy (LA), Lankford (OK), Daines (MT), Young (IN)
Minority (D 13): Wyden (OR), RMM; Stabenow (MI), Cantwell (WA), Menendez (NJ), Carper (DE), Cardin (MD), Brown (OH), Bennet (CO), Casey (PA), Warner (VA), Whitehouse (RI), Hassan (NH), Cortez Masto (NV)

SUBCOMMITTEES

Energy, Natural Resources & Infrastructure
Majority (R 8): Scott (SC), Chmn; Grassley (IA), Crapo (ID), Roberts (KS), Enzi (WY), Cornyn (TX), Burr (NC), Daines (MT)
Minority (D 6): Bennet (CO), RMM; Wyden (OR), Cantwell (WA), Carper (DE), Whitehouse (RI), Hassan (NH)

Fiscal Responsibility & Economic Growth
Majority (R 4): Cassidy (LA), Chmn; Scott (SC), Lankford (OK), Grassley (IA)
Minority (D 2): Hassan (NH), RMM; Wyden (OR)

Health Care
Majority (R 12): Toomey (PA), Chmn; Grassley (IA), Roberts (KS), Enzi (WY), Thune (SD), Burr (NC), Isakson (GA), Scott (SC), Cassidy (LA), Lankford (OK), Daines (MT), Young (IN)
Minority (D 12): Stabenow (MI), RMM; Cantwell (WA), Menendez (NJ), Carper (DE), Cardin (MD), Brown (OH), Casey (PA), Warner (VA), Whitehouse (RI), Hassan (NH), Cortez Masto (NV), Wyden (OR)

International Trade, Customs & Global Competitiveness
Majority (R 12): Cornyn (TX), Chmn; Crapo (ID), Roberts (KS), Thune (SD), Isakson (GA), Portman (OH), Toomey (PA), Scott (SC), Cassidy (LA), Daines (MT),Young (IN), Grassley (IA)
Minority (D 9): Casey (PA), RMM; Wyden (OR), Stabenow (MI), Cantwell (WA), Menendez (NJ), Cardin (MD), Brown (OH), Warner (VA), Cortez Masto (NV)

Social Security, Pensions & Family Policy
Majority (R 5): Portman (OH), Chmn; Grassley (IA), Cassidy (LA), Lankford (OK), Young (IN)
Minority (D 5): Brown (OH), RMM; Bennet (CO), Casey (PA), Cortez Masto (NV), Wyden (OR)

Taxation & IRS Oversight
Majority (R 9): Thune (SD), Chmn; Crapo (ID), Enzi (WY), Cornyn (TX), Burr (NC), Isakson (GA), Portman (OH), Toomey (PA), Grassley (IA)
Minority (D 7): Warner (VA), RMM; Menendez (NJ), Carper (DE), Cardin (MD), Bennet (CO), Whitehouse (RI), Wyden (OR)

Foreign Relations	**423 DSOB**
foreign.senate.gov	**202-224-4651**

Majority (R 12): Risch (ID), Chmn; Rubio (FL), Johnson (WI), Gardner (CO), Romney (UT), Graham (SC), Isakson (GA), Barrasso (WY), Portman (OH), Paul (KY), Young (IN), Cruz (TX)
Minority (D 10): Menendez (NJ), RMM; Cardin (MD), Shaheen (NH), Coons (DE), Udall (NM), Murphy (CT), Kaine (VA), Markey (MA), Merkley (OR), Booker (NJ)

SUBCOMMITTEES

Africa & Global Health Policy
Majority (R 5): Graham (SC), Chmn; Isakson (GA), Portman (OH), Johnson (WI), Cruz (TX)
Minority (D 4): Kaine (VA), RMM; Coons (DE), Booker (NJ), Murphy (CT)

East Asia, the Pacific & International Cybersecurity Policy
Majority (R 5): Gardner (CO), Chmn; Rubio (FL), Johnson (WI), Isakson (GA), Young (IN)
Minority (D 4): Markey (MA), RMM; Coons (DE), Merkley (OR), Udall (NM)

Europe & Regional Security Cooperation
Majority (R 5): Johnson (WI), Chmn; Barrasso (WY), Portman (OH), Paul (KY), Romney (UT)
Minority (D 4): Shaheen (NH), RMM; Murphy (CT), Cardin (MD), Coons (DE)

Internat'l Dev Instit & Internat'l Econ, Energy & Environ Policy
Majority (R 5): Young (IN), Chmn; Romney (UT), Paul (KY), Barrasso (WY), Graham (SC)
Minority (D 4): Merkley (OR), RMM; Udall (NM), Markey (MA), Booker (NJ)

Near East, South Asia, Central Asia & Counterterrorism
Majority (R 5): Romney (UT), Chmn; Cruz (TX), Graham (SC), Gardner (CO), Paul (KY)
Minority (D 4): Murphy (CT), RMM; Cardin (MD), Shaheen (NH), Kaine (VA)

State Dept & USAID Mngmnt, Internat'l Ops & Internat'l Dev
Majority (R 5): Isakson (GA), Chmn; Young (IN), Paul (KY), Portman (OH), Rubio (FL)
Minority (D 4): Booker (NJ), RMM; Markey (MA), Merkley (OR), Udall (NM)

West Hem Crime Civ Sec Dem Rights & Women's Issues
Majority (R 5): Rubio (FL), Chmn; Portman (OH), Cruz (TX), Gardner (CO), Barrasso (WY)
Minority (D 4): Cardin (MD), RMM; Udall (NM), Shaheen (NH), Kaine (VA)

Health, Education, Labor & Pensions   428 DSOB
help.senate.gov   202-224-5375

Majority (R 12): Alexander (TN), Chmn; Enzi (WY), Burr (NC), Isakson (GA), Paul (KY), Collins (ME), Cassidy (LA), Roberts (KS), Murkowski (AK), Scott (SC), Romney (UT), Braun (IN)
Minority (D 11): Murray (WA), RMM; Sanders (VT), Casey (PA), Baldwin (WI), Murphy (CT), Warren (MA), Kaine (VA), Hassan (NH), Smith (MN), Jones (AL), Rosen (NV)

SUBCOMMITTEES
Children & Families
Majority (R 8): Paul (KY), Chmn; Murkowski (AK), Burr (NC), Cassidy (LA), Roberts (KS), Scott (SC), Romney (UT), Alexander (TN)
Minority (D 7): Casey (PA), RMM; Sanders (VT), Murphy (CT), Kaine (VA), Hassan (NH), Smith (MN), Murray (WA)

Employment & Workplace Safety
Majority (R 8): Isakson (GA), Chmn; Scott (SC), Paul (KY), Romney (UT), Braun (IN), Burr (NC), Cassidy (LA), Alexander (TN)
Minority (D 7): Baldwin (WI), RMM; Casey (PA), Warren (MA), Smith (MN), Jones (AL), Rosen (NV), Murray (WA)

Primary Health & Retirement Security
Majority (R 10): Enzi (WY), Chmn; Burr (NC), Collins (ME), Cassidy (LA), Roberts (KS), Romney (UT), Braun (IN), Murkowski (AK), Scott (SC), Alexander (TN)
Minority (D 9): Sanders (VT), RMM; Baldwin (WI), Murphy (CT), Warren (MA), Kaine (VA), Hassan (NH), Jones (AL), Rosen (NV), Murray (WA)

Homeland Security & Government Affairs   340 DSOB
hsgac.senate.gov   202-224-4751

Majority (R 8): Johnson (WI), Chmn; Portman (OH), Paul (KY), Lankford (OK), Romney (UT), Scott (FL), Enzi (WY), Hawley (MO)
Minority (D 6): Peters (MI), RMM; Carper (DE), Hassan (NH), Harris (CA), Sinema (AZ), Rosen (NV)

SUBCOMMITTEES
Federal Spending Oversight & Emergency Management
Majority (R 5): Paul (KY), Chmn; Scott (FL), Enzi (WY), Hawley (MO), Johnson (WI)
Minority (D 4): Hassan (NH), RMM; Harris (CA), Sinema (AZ), Peters (MI)

Investigations
Majority (R 6): Portman (OH), Chmn; Paul (KY), Lankford (OK), Romney (UT), Hawley (MO), Johnson (WI)
Minority (D 5): Carper (DE), RMM; Hassan (NH), Harris (CA), Rosen (NV), Peters (MI)

Regulatory Affairs & Federal Management
Majority (R 6): Lankford (OK), Chmn; Portman (OH), Romney (UT), Scott (FL), Enzi (WY), Johnson (WI)
Minority (D 4): Sinema (AZ), RMM; Carper (DE), Rosen (NV), Peters (MI)

Indian Affairs   838 HSOB
indian.senate.gov   202-224-2251

Majority (R 7): Hoeven (ND), Chmn; Barrasso (WY), Murkowski (AK), Lankford (OK), Daines (MT), McSally (AZ), Moran (KS)
Minority (D 6): Udall (NM), Cantwell (WA), Tester (MT), Schatz (HI), Cortez Masto (NV), Smith (MN)

Judiciary   224 DSOB
judiciary.senate.gov   202-224-5225

Majority (R 12): Graham (SC), Chmn; Grassley (IA), Cornyn (TX), Lee (UT), Cruz (TX), Sasse (NE), Hawley (MO), Tillis (NC), Ernst (IA), Crapo (ID), Kennedy (LA), Blackburn (TN)

Minority (D 10): Feinstein (CA), RMM; Leahy (VT), Durbin (IL), Whitehouse (RI), Klobuchar (MN), Coons (DE), Blumenthal (CT), Hirono (HI), Booker (NJ), Harris (CA)

SUBCOMMITTEES

Antitrust, Competition Policy & Consumer Rights
Majority (R 5): Lee (UT), Chmn; Grassley (IA), Hawley (MO), Crapo (ID), Blackburn (TN)
Minority (D 4): Klobuchar (MN), RMM; Leahy (VT), Blumenthal (CT), Booker (NJ)

Border Security & Immigration
Majority (R 9): Cornyn (TX), Chmn; Graham (SC), Grassley (IA), Lee (UT), Cruz (TX), Hawley (MO), Tillis (NC), Ernst (IA), Kennedy (LA)
Minority (D 8): Durbin (IL), RMM; Feinstein (CA), Leahy (VT), Klobuchar (MN), Coons (DE), Blumenthal (CT), Hirono (HI), Booker (NJ)

Constitution
Majority (R 6): Cruz (TX), Chmn; Cornyn (TX), Lee (UT), Sasse (NE), Crapo (ID), Blackburn (TN)
Minority (D 5): Hirono (HI), RMM; Durbin (IL), Whitehouse (RI), Coons (DE), Harris (CA)

Crime & Terrorism
Majority (R 7): Hawley (MO), Chmn; Graham (SC), Cornyn (TX), Cruz (TX), Tillis (NC), Ernst (IA), Kennedy (LA)
Minority (D 6): Whitehouse (RI), RMM; Feinstein (CA), Durbin (IL), Klobuchar (MN), Coons (DE), Booker (NJ)

Oversight, Agency Action, Federal Rights & Federal Courts
Majority (R 6): Sasse (NE), Chmn; Grassley (IA), Tillis (NC), Ernst (IA), Crapo (ID), Kennedy (LA)
Minority (D 5): Blumenthal (CT), RMM; Leahy (VT), Whitehouse (RI), Klobuchar (MN), Hirono (HI)

Subcommittee on Intellectual Property
Majority (R 8): Tillis (NC), Chmn; Graham (SC), Grassley (IA), Cornyn (TX), Lee (UT), Sasse (NE), Crapo (ID), Blackburn (TN)
Minority (D 7): Coons (DE), RMM; Leahy (VT), Durbin (IL), Whitehouse (RI), Blumenthal (CT), Hirono (HI), Harris (CA)

Rules & Administration
rules.senate.gov

305 RSOB
202-224-6352

Majority (R 10): Blunt (MO), Chmn; McConnell (KY), Alexander (TN), Roberts (KS), Shelby (AL), Cruz (TX), Capito (WV), Wicker (MS), Fischer (NE), Hyde-Smith (MS)
Minority (D 9): Klobuchar (MN), RMM; Feinstein (CA), Schumer (NY), Durbin (IL), Udall (NM), Warner (VA), Leahy (VT), King (ME), Cortez Masto (NV)

Small Business & Entrepreneurship
sbc.senate.gov

428A RSOB
202-224-5175

Majority (R 10): Rubio (FL), Chmn; Risch (ID), Paul (KY), Scott (SC), Ernst (IA), Inhofe (OK), Young (IN), Kennedy (LA), Romney (UT), Hawley (MO)
Minority (D 9): Cardin (MD), RMM; Cantwell (WA), Shaheen (NH), Markey (MA), Booker (NJ), Coons (DE), Hirono (HI), Duckworth (IL), Rosen (NV)

Veterans' Affairs
veterans.senate.gov

412 RSOB
202-224-9126

Majority (R 9): Isakson (GA), Chmn; Moran (KS), Boozman (AR), Cassidy (LA), Rounds (SD), Tillis (NC), Sullivan (AK), Blackburn (TN), Cramer (ND)
Minority (D 8): Tester (MT), RMM; Murray (WA), Sanders (VT), Brown (OH), Blumenthal (CT), Hirono (HI), Manchin (WV), Sinema (AZ)

SPECIAL AND SELECT

Aging
aging.senate.gov

G-31 DSOB
202-224-5364

Majority (R 8): Collins (ME), Chmn; Scott (SC), Burr (NC), McSally (AZ), Rubio (FL), Hawley (MO), Braun (IN), Scott (FL)

Minority (D 7): Casey (PA), RMM; Gillibrand (NY), Blumenthal (CT), Warren (MA), Jones (AL), Sinema (AZ), Rosen (NV)

Ethics	**220 HSOB**
ethics.senate.gov	**202-224-2981**

Majority (R 3): Isakson (GA), Chmn; Roberts (KS), Risch (ID)
Minority (D 3): Coons (DE), RMM; Schatz (HI), Shaheen (NH)

Intelligence	**211 HSOB**
intelligence.senate.gov	**202-224-1700**

Majority (R 8): Burr (NC), Chmn; Risch (ID), Rubio (FL), Collins (ME), Blunt (MO), Cotton (AR), Cornyn (TX), Sasse (NE)
Minority (D 7): Warner (VA), RMM; Feinstein (CA), Wyden (OR), Heinrich (NM), King (ME), Harris (CA), Bennet (CO)

HOUSE COMMITTEES

Agriculture
agriculture.house.gov

1301 LHOB
202-225-2171

Majority (D 26): Peterson (MN), Chmn; Scott (GA), Costa (CA), Fudge (OH), McGovern (MA), Vela (TX), Plaskett (VI), Adams (NC), Spanberger (VA), Hayes (CT), Delgado (NY), Cox (CA), Craig (MN), Brindisi (NY), Van Drew (NJ), Harder (CA), Schrier (WA), Pingree (ME), Bustos (IL), Maloney (NY), Carbajal (CA), Lawson (FL), O'Halleran (AZ), Panetta (CA), Kirkpatrick (AZ), Axne (IA)
Minority (R 21): Conaway (TX), RMM; Thompson (PA), Scott (GA), Crawford (AR), DesJarlais (TN), Hartzler (MO), LaMalfa (CA), Davis (IL), Yoho (FL), Allen (GA), Bost (IL), Rouzer (NC), Abraham (LA), Kelly (MS), Comer (KY), Marshall (KS), Bacon (NE), Dunn (FL), Johnson (SD), Baird (IN), Hagedorn (MN)

SUBCOMMITTEES

Biotechnology, Horticulture & Research
Majority (D 13): Plaskett (VI), Chmn; Delgado (NY), Cox (CA), Harder (CA), Brindisi (NY), Van Drew (NJ), Schrier (WA), Pingree (ME), Carbajal (CA), Panetta (CA), Maloney (NY), Lawson (FL), Peterson (MN)
Minority (R 10): Dunn (FL), RMM; Thompson (PA), Hartzler (MO), LaMalfa (CA), Davis (IL), Yoho (FL), Bost (IL), Comer (KY), Baird (IN), Conaway (TX)

Commodity Exchanges, Energy & Credit
Majority (D 11): Scott (GA), Chmn; Van Drew (NJ), Vela (TX), Plaskett (VI), Spanberger (VA), Delgado (NY), Craig (MN), Maloney (NY), Kirkpatrick (AZ), Axne (IA), Peterson (MN)
Minority (R 9): Scott (GA), RMM; Crawford (AR), Bost (IL), Rouzer (NC), Marshall (KS), Dunn (FL), Johnson (SD), Baird (IN), Conaway (TX)

Conservation & Forestry
Majority (D 6): Spanberger (VA), Chmn; Fudge (OH), O'Halleran (AZ), Pingree (ME), Axne (IA), Peterson (MN)
Minority (R 5): LaMalfa (CA), RMM; Allen (GA), Abraham (LA), Kelly (MS), Conaway (TX)

General Farm Commodities & Risk Management
Majority (D 6): Vela (TX), Chmn; Craig (MN), Scott (GA), Lawson (FL), Van Drew (NJ), Carbajal (CA), Peterson (MN) Minority (R 6): Thompson (PA), RMM; Scott (GA), Crawford (AR), Allen (GA), Abraham (LA), Conaway (TX)

Livestock & Foreign Agriculture
Majority (D 12): Costa (CA), Chmn; Brindisi (NY), Hayes (CT), Cox (CA), Craig (MN), Harder (CA), Vela (TX), Plaskett (VI), Carbajal (CA), Bustos (IL), Panetta (CA) Peterson (MN)
Minority (R 10): Rouzer (NC), RMM; Thompson (PA), DesJarlais (TN), Hartzler (MO), Kelly (MS), Comer (KY), Marshall (KS), Bacon (NE), Hagedorn (MN), Conaway (TX)

Subcommittee Nutrition, Oversight & Department Operations
Majority (D 9): Fudge (OH), Chmn; McGovern (MA), Adams (NC), Hayes (CT), Schrier (WA), Van Drew (NJ), Lawson (FL), Panetta (CA), Peterson (MN)
Minority (R 7): Johnson (SD), RMM; DesJarlais (TN), Davis (IL), Yoho (FL), Bacon (NE), Hagedorn (MN), Conaway (TX)

Appropriations
appropriations.house.gov

H-307 The Capitol
202-225-2771

Majority (D 30): Lowey (NY), Chmn; Kaptur (OH), Visclosky (IN), Serrano (NY), DeLauro (CT), Price (NC), Roybal-Allard (CA), Bishop (GA), Lee (CA), McCollum (MN), Ryan (OH), Ruppersberger (MD), Wasserman Schultz (FL), Cuellar (TX), Pingree (ME), Quigley (IL), Kilmer (WA), Cartwright (PA), Meng (NY), Pocan (WI), Clark (MA), Aguilar (CA), Frankel (FL), Bustos (IL), Watson Coleman (NJ), Lawrence (MI), Torres (CA), Crist (FL), Kirkpatrick (AZ), Case (HI)
Minority (R 23): Granger (TX), RMM; Rogers (KY), Aderholt (AL), Simpson (ID), Carter (TX), Calvert (CA), Cole (OK), Diaz-Balart (FL), Graves (GA), Womack (AR), Fortenberry (NE), Fleischmann (TN), Herrera Beutler (WA), Joyce (OH), Harris (MD), Roby (AL), Amodei (NV), Stewart (UT), Palazzo (MS), Newhouse (WA), Moolenaar (MI), Rutherford (FL), Hurd (TX)

SUBCOMMITTEES

Agriculture, Rural Development, FDA & Related Agencies
Majority (D 8): Bishop (GA), Chmn; DeLauro (CT), Pingree (ME), Pocan (WI), Lee (CA), McCollum (MN), Cuellar (TX), Lowey (NY)
Minority (R 4): Fortenberry (NE), RMM; Aderholt (AL), Harris (MD), Moolenaar (MI)

Commerce, Justice, Science & Related Agencies
Majority (D 8): Serrano (NY), Chmn; Cartwright (PA), Meng (NY), Lawrence (MI), Crist (FL), Case (HI), Kaptur (OH), Lowey (NY)
Minority (R 4): Aderholt (AL), RMM; Roby (AL), Palazzo (MS), Graves (GA)

Defense
Majority (D 12): Visclosky (IN), Chmn; McCollum (MN), Ryan (OH), Ruppersberger (MD), Kaptur (OH), Cuellar (TX), Kilmer (WA), Aguilar (CA), Bustos (IL), Crist (FL), Kirkpatrick (AZ), Lowey (NY)
Minority (R 7): Calvert (CA), RMM; Rogers (KY), Cole (OK), Womack (AR), Aderholt (AL), Carter (TX), Diaz-Balart (FL)

Energy & Water Development & Related Agencies
Majority (D 8): Kaptur (OH), Chmn; Visclosky (IN), Wasserman Schultz (FL), Kirkpatrick (AZ), Kilmer (WA), Pocan (WI), Frankel (FL), Lowey (NY)
Minority (R 4): Simpson (ID), RMM; Calvert (CA), Fleischmann (TN), Newhouse (WA)

Financial Services & General Government
Majority (D 8): Quigley (IL), Chmn; Serrano (NY), Cartwright (PA), Bishop (GA), Torres (CA), Crist (FL), Kirkpatrick (AZ), Lowey (NY)
Minority (R 4): Graves (GA), RMM; Amodei (NV), Stewart (UT), Joyce (OH)

Homeland Security
Majority (D 8): Roybal-Allard (CA), Chmn; Cuellar (TX), Ruppersberger (MD), Price (NC), Wasserman Schultz (FL), Meng (NY), Aguilar (CA), Lowey (NY)
Minority (R 4): Fleischmann (TN), RMM; Palazzo (MS), Newhouse (WA), Rutherford (FL)

Interior, Environment & Related Agencies
Majority (D 8): McCollum (MN), Chmn; Pingree (ME), Kilmer (WA), Serrano (NY), Quigley (IL), Watson Coleman (NJ), Lawrence (MI), Lowey (NY)
Minority (R 4): Joyce (OH), RMM; Simpson (ID), Stewart (UT), Amodei (NV)

Labor, Health & Human Services, Education & Related Agencies
Majority (D 9): DeLauro (CT), Chmn; Roybal-Allard (CA), Lee (CA), Pocan (WI), Clark (MA), Frankel (FL), Bustos (IL), Watson Coleman (NJ), Lowey (NY)
Minority (R 5): Cole (OK), RMM; Harris (MD), Herrera Beutler (WA), Moolenaar (MI), Graves (GA)

Legislative Branch
Majority (D 5): Ryan (OH), Chmn; Ruppersberger (MD), Clark (MA), Case (HI), Lowey (NY)
Minority (R 2): Herrera Beutler (WA), RMM; Newhouse (WA)

Military Construction, Veterans Affairs & Related Agencies
Majority (D 8): Wasserman Schultz (FL), Chmn; Bishop (GA), Case (HI), Ryan (OH), Pingree (ME), Cartwright (PA), Bustos (IL), Lowey (NY)
Minority (R 4): Carter (TX), RMM; Roby (AL), Rutherford (FL), Hurd (TX)

State, Foreign Operations & Related Programs
Majority (D 6): Lowey (NY), Chmn; Lee (CA), Meng (NY), Price (NC), Frankel (FL), Torres (CA)
Minority (R 3): Rogers (KY), RMM; Fortenberry (NE), Roby (AL)

Transportation, HUD & Related Agencies
Majority (D 8): Price (NC), Chmn; Quigley (IL), Clark (MA), Watson Coleman (NJ), Lawrence (MI), Torres (CA), Aguilar (CA), Lowey (NY)
Minority (R 4): Diaz-Balart (FL), RMM; Womack (AR), Rutherford (FL), Hurd (TX)

Armed Services
armedservices.house.gov

2216 RHOB
202-225-4151

Majority (D 31): Smith (WA), Chmn; Davis (CA), Langevin (RI), Larsen (WA), Cooper (TN), Courtney (CT), Garamendi (CA), Speier (CA), Gabbard (HI), Norcross (NJ), Gallego (AZ), Moulton (MA), Carbajal (CA), Brown (MD), Khanna (CA), Keating (MA), Vela (TX), Kim (NJ), Horn (OK), Cisneros (CA), Houlahan (PA), Crow (CO), Torres-Small (NM), Slotkin (MI), Sherrill (NJ), Hill (CA), Escobar (TX), Haaland (NM), Golden (ME), Trahan (MA), Luria (VA)

Minority (R 26): Thornberry (TX), RMM; Wilson (SC), Bishop (UT), Turner (OH), Rogers (AL), Conaway (TX), Lamborn (CO), Wittman (VA), Hartzler (MO), Scott (GA), Brooks (AL), Cook (CA), Byrne (AL), Graves (MO), Stefanik (NY), DesJarlais (TN), Abraham (LA), Kelly (MS), Gallagher (WI), Gaetz (FL), Bacon (NE), Banks (IN), Cheney (WY), Mitchell (MI), Bergman (MI), Waltz (FL)

SUBCOMMITTEES

Intelligence, Emerging Threats & Capabilities
Majority (D 12): Langevin (RI), Chmn; Larsen (WA), Cooper (TN), Gabbard (HI), Brown (MD), Khanna (CA), Keating (MA), Kim (NJ), Houlahan (PA), Crow (CO), Slotkin (MI), Trahan (MA)
Minority (R 10): Stefanik (NY), RMM; Graves (MO), Abraham (LA), Conaway (TX), Scott (GA), DesJarlais (TN), Gallagher (WI), Waltz (FL), Bacon (NE), Banks (IN)

Military Personnel
Majority (D 8): Speier (CA), Chmn; Davis (CA), Gallego (AZ), Cisneros (CA), Escobar (TX), Haaland (NM), Trahan (MA), Luria (VA)
Minority (R 6): Kelly (MS), RMM; Abraham (LA), Cheney (WY), Mitchell (MI), Bergman (MI), Gaetz (FL)

Readiness
Majority (D 10): Garamendi (CA), Chmn; Gabbard (HI), Kim (NJ), Horn (OK), Houlahan (PA), Crow (CO), Torres-Small (NM), Slotkin (MI), Escobar (TX), Haaland (NM)
Minority (R 8): Lamborn (CO), RMM; Scott (GA), Wilson (SC), Bishop (UT), Rogers (AL), Brooks (AL), Stefanik (NY), Bergman (MI)

Seapower & Projection Forces
Majority (D 11): Courtney (CT), Chmn; Langevin (RI), Cooper (TN), Norcross (NJ), Moulton (MA), Vela (TX), Cisneros (CA), Sherrill (NJ), Hill (CA), Golden (ME), Luria (VA)
Minority (R 9): Wittman (VA), RMM; Conaway (TX), Gallagher (WI), Bergman (MI), Waltz (FL), Hartzler (MO), Cook (CA), Byrne (AL), Kelly (MS)

Strategic Forces
Majority (D 10): Cooper (TN), Chmn; Davis (CA), Larsen (WA), Garamendi (CA), Speier (CA), Moulton (MA), Carbajal (CA), Khanna (CA), Keating (MA), Horn (OK)
Minority (R 8): Turner (OH), RMM; Wilson (SC), Bishop (UT), Rogers (AL), Brooks (AL), Byrne (AL), DesJarlais (TN), Cheney (WY)

Tactical Air & Land Forces
Majority (D 11): Norcross (NJ), Chmn; Langevin (RI), Courtney (CT), Gallego (AZ), Carbajal (CA), Brown (MD), Vela (TX), Torres-Small (NM), Sherrill (NJ), Hill (CA), Golden (ME)
Minority (R 9): Hartzler (MO), RMM; Cook (CA), Gaetz (FL), Bacon (NE), Banks (IN), Mitchell (MI), Turner (OH), Lamborn (CO), Wittman (VA)

| **Budget** | **204-E CHOB** |
| budget.house.gov | **202-226-7200** |

Majority (D 22): Yarmuth (KY), Chmn; Moulton (MA), Jeffries (NY), Higgins (NY), Boyle (PA), Khanna (CA), DeLauro (CT), Doggett (TX), Price (NC), Schakowsky (IL), Kildee (MI), Panetta (CA), Morelle (NY), Horsford (NV), Scott (VA), Jackson Lee (TX), Lee (CA), Jayapal (WA), Omar (MN), Sires (NJ), Peters (CA), Cooper (TN)
Minority (R 14): Womack (AR), RMM; Woodall (GA), Johnson (OH), Smith (MO), Flores (TX), Holding (NC), Stewart (UT), Norman (SC), Roy (TX), Meuser (PA), Timmons (SC), Crenshaw (TX), Hern (OK), Burchett (TN)

| **Commission Congressional Mailing Standards (Franking Commission)** | **1307 LHOB** |
| cha.house.gov/franking-commission | **202-225-9337** |

Majority (D 3): Davis (CA), Sherman (CA), McEachin (VA)
Minority (R 2): Davis (IL), RMM; Latta (OH)

| **Education & Labor** | **2176 RHOB** |
| edlabor.house.gov | **202-225-3725** |

Majority (D 28): Scott (VA), Chmn; Davis (CA), Grijalva (AZ), Courtney (CT), Fudge (OH), Sablan (MP), Wilson (FL), Bonamici (OR), Takano (CA), Adams (NC), DeSaulnier (CA), Norcross (NJ), Jayapal (WA), Morelle (NY), Wild (PA), Harder (CA), McBath (GA), Schrier (WA), Underwood (IL), Hayes (CT), Shalala (FL), Levin (MI), Omar (MN), Trone (MD), Stevens (MI), Lee (NV), Trahan (MA), Castro (TX)

Minority (R 22): Foxx (NC), RMM; Roe (TN), Thompson (PA), Walberg (MI), Guthrie (KY), Byrne (AL), Grothman (WI), Stefanik (NY), Allen (GA), Rooney (FL), Smucker (PA), Banks (IN),Walker (NC), Comer (KY), Cline (VA), Fulcher (ID), Taylor (TX), Watkins (KS), Wright (TX), Meuser (PA), Timmons (SC), Johnson (SD)

SUBCOMMITTEES

Civil Rights & Human Services
Majority (D 7): Bonamici (OR), Chmn; Grijalva (AZ), Fudge (OH), Schrier (WA), Hayes (CT), Trone (MD), Lee (NV)
Minority (R 4): Comer (KY), RMM; Thompson (PA), Stefanik (NY), Johnson (SD)

Early Childhood, Elementary & Secondary Education
Majority (D 8): Sablan (MP), Chmn; Schrier (WA), Hayes (CT), Shalala (FL), Davis (CA), Wilson (FL), DeSaulnier (CA), Morelle (NY)
Minority (R 5): Allen (GA), RMM; Thompson (PA), Grothman (WI), Taylor (TX), Timmons (SC)

Health, Employment, Labor & Pensions
Majority (D 14): Wilson (FL), Chmn; Norcross (NJ), Morelle (NY), Wild (PA), McBath (GA), Underwood (IL), Stevens (MI), Courtney (CT), Fudge (OH), Harder (CA), Shalala (FL), Levin (MI), Trahan (MA), Scott (VA)
Minority (R 11): Walberg (MI), RMM; Roe (TN), Allen (GA), Rooney (FL), Banks (IN), Fulcher (ID), Taylor (TX), Watkins (KS), Wright (TX), Meuser (PA), Johnson (SD)

Higher Education & Workforce Investment
Majority (D 16): Davis (CA), Chmn; Courtney (CT), Takano (CA), Jayapal (WA), Harder (CA), Levin (MI), Omar (MN), Trone (MD), Lee (NV), Trahan (MA), Castro (TX), Grijalva (AZ), Sablan (MP), Bonamici (OR), Adams (NC), Norcross (NJ)
Minority (R 12): Smucker (PA), RMM; Guthrie (KY), Grothman (WI), Stefanik (NY), Banks (IN), Walker (NC), Comer (KY), Cline (VA), Fulcher (ID), Watkins (KS), Meuser (PA), Timmons (SC)

Workforce Protections
Majority (D 8): Adams (NC), Chmn; DeSaulnier (CA), Takano (CA), Jayapal (WA), Wild (PA), McBath (GA), Omar (MN), Stevens (MI)
Minority (R 5): Byrne (AL), RMM; Rooney (FL), Walker (NC), Cline (VA), Wright (TX)

Energy & Commerce
energycommerce.house.gov

2125 RHOB
202-225-2927

Majority (D 31): Pallone (NJ), Chmn; Rush (IL), Eshoo (CA), Engel (NY), DeGette (CO), Doyle (PA), Schakowsky (IL), Butterfield (NC), Matsui (CA), Castor (FL), Sarbanes (MD), McNerney (CA), Welch (VT), Lujan (NM), Tonko (NY), Clarke (NY), Loebsack (IA), Schrader (OR), Kennedy (MA), Cardenas (CA), Ruiz (CA), Peters (CA), Dingell (MI), Veasey (TX), Kuster (NH), Kelly (IL), Barragan (CA), McEachin (VA), Blunt Rochester (DE), Soto (FL), O'Halleran (AZ)
Minority (R 24): Walden (OR), RMM; Upton (MI), Shimkus (IL), Burgess (TX), Scalise (LA), Latta (OH), McMorris Rodgers (WA), Guthrie (KY), Olson (TX), McKinley (WV), Kinzinger (IL), Griffith (VA), Bilirakis (FL), Johnson (OH), Long (MO), Bucshon (IN), Flores (TX), Brooks (IN), Mullin (OK), Hudson (NC), Walberg (MI), Carter (GA), Duncan (SC), Gianforte (MT)

SUBCOMMITTEES

Communications & Technology
Majority (D 18): Doyle (PA), Chmn; McNerney (CA), Clarke (NY), Loebsack (IA), Veasey (TX), McEachin (VA), Soto (FL), O'Halleran (AZ), Eshoo (CA), DeGette (CO), Butterfield (NC), Matsui (CA), Welch (VT), Lujan (NM), Schrader (OR), Cardenas (CA), Dingell (MI), Pallone (NJ)
Minority (R 13): Latta (OH), RMM; Shimkus (IL), Scalise (LA), Olson (TX), Kinzinger (IL), Bilirakis (FL), Johnson (OH), Long (MO), Flores (TX), Brooks (IN), Walberg (MI), Gianforte (MT), Walden (OR)

Consumer Protection & Commerce
Majority (D 14): Schakowsky (IL), Chmn; Castor (FL), Veasey (TX), Kelly (IL), O'Halleran (AZ), Lujan (NM), Cardenas (CA), Blunt Rochester (DE), Soto (FL), Rush (IL), Matsui (CA), McNerney (CA), Dingell (MI), Pallone (NJ)
Minority (R 10): McMorris Rodgers (WA), RMM; Upton (MI), Burgess (TX), Latta (OH), Guthrie (KY), Bucshon (IN), Hudson (NC), Carter (GA), Gianforte (MT), Walden (OR)

Energy

Majority (D 19): Rush (IL), Chmn; Peters (CA), Doyle (PA), Sarbanes (MD), McNerney (CA), Tonko (NY), Loebsack (IA), Butterfield (NC), Welch (VT), Schrader (OR), Kennedy (MA), Veasey (TX), Kuster (NH), Kelly (IL), Barragan (CA), McEachin (VA), O'Halleran (AZ), Blunt Rochester (DE), Pallone (NJ)
Minority (R 14): Upton (MI), RMM; Latta (OH), McMorris Rodgers (WA), Olson (TX), McKinley (WV), Kinzinger (IL), Griffith (VA), Johnson (OH), Bucshon (IN), Flores (TX), Hudson (NC), Walberg (MI), Duncan (SC), Walden (OR)

Environment & Climate Change

Majority (D 14): Tonko (NY), Chmn; Clarke (NY), Peters (CA), Barragan (CA), McEachin (VA), Blunt Rochester (DE), Soto (FL), DeGette (CO), Schakowsky (IL), Matsui (CA), McNerney (CA), Ruiz (CA), Dingell (MI), Pallone (NJ)
Minority (R 10): Shimkus (IL), RMM; McMorris Rodgers (WA), McKinley (WV), Johnson (OH), Long (MO), Flores (TX), Mullin (OK), Carter (GA), Duncan (SC), Walden (OR)

Health

Majority (D 19): Eshoo (CA), Chmn; Engel (NY), Butterfield (NC), Matsui (CA), Castor (FL), Sarbanes (MD), Lujan (NM), Schrader (OR), Kennedy (MA), Cardenas (CA), Welch (VT), Ruiz (CA), Dingell (MI), Kuster (NH), Kelly (IL), Barragan (CA), Blunt Rochester (DE), Rush (IL), Pallone (NJ)
Minority (R 14): Burgess (TX), RMM; Upton (MI), Shimkus (IL), Guthrie (KY), Griffith (VA), Bilirakis (FL), Long (MO), Bucshon (IN), Brooks (IN), Mullin (OK), Hudson (NC), Carter (GA), Gianforte (MT), Walden (OR)

Oversight & Investigations

Majority (D 11): DeGette (CO), Chmn; Schakowsky (IL), Kennedy (MA), Ruiz (CA), Kuster (NH), Castor (FL), Sarbanes (MD), Tonko (NY), Clarke (NY), Peters (CA), Pallone (NJ)
Minority (R 8): Guthrie (KY), RMM; Burgess (TX), McKinley (WV), Griffith (VA), Brooks (IN), Mullin (OK), Duncan (SC), Walden (OR)

Ethics	**1015 LHOB**
ethics.house.gov	**202-225-7103**

Majority (D 5): Deutch (FL), Chmn; Meng (NY), Wild (PA), Phillips (MN), Brown (MD)
Minority (R 5): Marchant (TX), RMM; Ratcliffe (TX), Holding (NC), Walorski (IN), Guest (MS)

Financial Services	**2129 RHOB**
financialservices.house.gov	**202-225-4247**

Majority (D 34): Waters (CA), Chmn; Maloney (NY), Velazquez (NY), Sherman (CA), Meeks (NY), Clay (MO), Scott (GA), Green (TX), Cleaver (MO), Perlmutter (CO), Himes (CT), Foster (IL), Beatty (OH), Heck (WA), Vargas (CA), Gottheimer (NJ), Gonzalez (TX), Lawson (FL), San Nicolas (GU), Tlaib (MI), Porter (CA), Axne (IA), Casten (IL), Pressley (MA), McAdams (UT), Ocasio-Cortez (NY), Wexton (VA), Lynch (MA), Gabbard (HI), Adams (NC), Dean (PA), Garcia (IL), Garcia (TX), Phillips (MN)
Minority (R 26): McHenry (NC), RMM; King (NY), Lucas (OK), Posey (FL), Luetkemeyer (MO), Huizenga (MI), Duffy (WI), Stivers (OH), Wagner (MO), Barr (KY), Tipton (CO), Williams (TX), Hill (AR), Emmer (MN), Zeldin (NY), Loudermilk (GA), Mooney (WV), Davidson (OH), Budd (NC), Kustoff (TN), Hollingsworth (IN), Gonzalez (OH), Rose (TN), Steil (WI), Gooden (TX), Riggleman (VA)

SUBCOMMITTEES

Consumer Protection & Financial Institutions

Majority (D 13): Meeks (NY), Chmn; Scott (GA), Velazquez (NY), Clay (MO), Heck (WA), Foster (IL), Lawson (FL), Tlaib (MI), Porter (CA), Pressley (MA), McAdams (UT), Ocasio-Cortez (NY), Wexton (VA)
Minority (R 10): Luetkemeyer (MO), RMM; Tipton (CO), Lucas (OK), Posey (FL), Barr (KY), Williams (TX), Loudermilk (GA), Budd (NC), Kustoff (TN), Riggleman (VA)

Housing, Community Development & Insurance

Majority (D 13): Clay (MO), Chmn; Velazquez (NY), Cleaver (MO), Sherman (CA), Beatty (OH), Green (TX), Gonzalez (TX), Maloney (NY), Heck (WA), Vargas (CA), Lawson (FL), Tlaib (MI), Axne (IA)
Minority (R 10): Duffy (WI), RMM; Gooden (TX), Luetkemeyer (MO), Huizenga (MI), Tipton (CO), Zeldin (NY), Kustoff (TN), Gonzalez (OH), Rose (TN), Steil (WI)

Investor Protection, Entrepreneurship & Capital Markets
Majority (D 14): Maloney (NY), Chmn; Sherman (CA), Scott (GA), Himes (CT), Foster (IL), Meeks (NY), Vargas (CA), Gottheimer (NJ), Gonzalez (TX), San Nicolas (GU), Porter (CA), Axne (IA), Casten (IL), Ocasio-Cortez (NY)
Minority (R 10): Huizenga (MI), RMM; Hollingsworth (IN), King (NY), Duffy (WI), Stivers (OH), Wagner (MO), Hill (AR), Emmer (MN), Mooney (WV), Davidson (OH)

Nat'l Security, International Development & Monetary Policy
Majority (D 13): Cleaver (MO), Chmn; Perlmutter (CO), Himes (CT), Heck (WA), Sherman (CA), Vargas (CA), Gottheimer (NJ), San Nicolas (GU), McAdams (UT), Wexton (VA), Lynch (MA), Gabbard (HI), Garcia (IL)
Minority (R 9): Stivers (OH), RMM; Riggleman (VA), King (NY), Lucas (OK), Williams (TX), Hill (AR), Emmer (MN), Gonzalez (OH), Rose (TN)

Oversight & Investigations
Majority (D 10): Green (TX), Chmn; Beatty (OH), Lynch (MA), Velazquez (NY), Perlmutter (CO), Vargas (CA), Casten (IL), Dean (PA), Garcia (TX), Phillips (MN)
Minority (R 7): Barr (KY), RMM; Zeldin (NY), Posey (FL), Loudermilk (GA), Davidson (OH), Rose (TN), Steil (WI)

Subcommittee on Diversity & Inclusion
Majority (D 12): Beatty (OH), Chmn; Clay (MO), Green (TX), Gottheimer (NJ), Gonzalez (TX), Lawson (FL), Pressley (MA), Gabbard (HI), Adams (NC), Dean (PA), Garcia (TX), Phillips (MN)
Minority (R 9): Wagner (MO), RMM; Gonzalez (OH), Lucas (OK), Mooney (WV), Budd (NC), Kustoff (TN), Hollingsworth (IN), Steil (WI), Gooden (TX)

Foreign Affairs
foreignaffairs.house.gov

2170 RHOB
202-225-5021

Majority (D 26): Engel (NY), Chmn; Sherman (CA), Meeks (NY), Sires (NJ), Connolly (VA), Deutch (FL), Bass (CA), Keating (MA), Cicilline (RI), Bera (CA), Castro (TX), Titus (NV), Espaillat (NY), Lieu (CA), Wild (PA), Phillips (MN), Omar (MN), Allred (TX), Levin (MI), Spanberger (VA), Houlahan (PA), Malinowski (NJ), Trone (MD), Costa (CA), Vargas (CA), Gonzalez (TX)
Minority (R 21): McCaul (TX), RMM; Smith (NJ), Chabot (OH), Wilson (SC), Perry (PA), Yoho (FL), Kinzinger (IL), Zeldin (NY), Sensenbrenner (WI), Wagner (MO), Mast (FL), Rooney (FL), Fitzpatrick (PA), Curtis (UT), Buck (CO), Wright (TX), Reschenthaler (PA), Burchett (TN), Pence (IN), Watkins (KS), Guest (MS)

SUBCOMMITTEES

Africa, Global Health, Global Human Rights & Internat'l Orgs
Majority (D 5): Bass (CA), Chmn; Wild (PA), Phillips (MN), Omar (MN), Houlahan (PA)
Minority (R 4): Smith (NJ), RMM; Sensenbrenner (WI), Wright (TX), Burchett (TN)

Asia, the Pacific & Nonproliferation
Majority (D 7): Sherman (CA), Chmn; Titus (NV), Houlahan (PA), Connolly (VA), Bera (CA), Levin (MI), Spanberger (VA)
Minority (R 5): Yoho (FL), RMM; Perry (PA), Wagner (MO), Mast (FL), Curtis (UT)

Europe, Eurasia, Energy & the Environment
Majority (D 12): Keating (MA), Chmn; Spanberger (VA), Meeks (NY), Sires (NJ), Deutch (FL), Cicilline (RI), Castro (TX), Titus (NV), Wild (PA), Trone (MD), Costa (CA), Gonzalez (TX)
Minority (R 10): Kinzinger (IL), RMM; Wilson (SC), Wagner (MO), Sensenbrenner (WI), Rooney (FL), Fitzpatrick (PA), Pence (IN), Wright (TX), Guest (MS), Burchett (TN)

Middle East, North Africa & International Terrorism
Majority (D 10): Deutch (FL), Chmn; Connolly (VA), Cicilline (RI), Lieu (CA), Allred (TX), Malinowski (NJ), Trone (MD), Sherman (CA), Keating (MA), Vargas (CA)
Minority (R 8): Wilson (SC), RMM; Chabot (OH), Kinzinger (IL), Zeldin (NY), Mast (FL), Fitzpatrick (PA), Reschenthaler (PA), Watkins (KS)

Oversight & Investigations
Majority (D 6): Bera (CA), Chmn; Omar (MN), Espaillat (NY), Lieu (CA), Malinowski (NJ), Cicilline (RI)
Minority (R 4): Zeldin (NY), RMM; Perry (PA), Buck (CO), Reschenthaler (PA)

Western Hemisphere, Civilian Security, & Trade
Majority (D 8): Sires (NJ), Chmn; Meeks (NY), Castro (TX), Espaillat (NY), Phillips (MN), Levin (MI), Gonzalez (TX), Vargas (CA)
Minority (R 6): Rooney (FL), RMM; Smith (NJ), Yoho (FL), Curtis (UT), Buck (CO), Guest (MS)

Homeland Security	**H2-176 FHOB**
homeland.house.gov	**202-226-2616**

Majority (D 18): Thompson (MS), Chmn; Jackson Lee (TX), Langevin (RI), Richmond (LA), Payne (NJ), Rice (NY), Correa (CA), Torres-Small (NM), Underwood (IL), Rose (NY), Slotkin (MI), Cleaver (MO), Green (TX), Clarke (NY), Titus (NV), Watson Coleman (NJ), Barragan (CA), Demings (FL)
Minority (R 13): Rogers (AL), RMM; King (NY), McCaul (TX), Katko (NY), Ratcliffe (TX), Walker (NC), Higgins (LA), Lesko (AZ), Green (TN), Taylor (TX), Joyce (PA), Crenshaw (TX), Guest (MS)

SUBCOMMITTEES

Border Security, Facilitation & Operations
Majority (D 7): Rice (NY), Chmn; Payne (NJ), Correa (CA), Torres-Small (NM), Green (TX), Clarke (NY), Thompson (MS)
Minority (R 5): Higgins (LA), RMM; Lesko (AZ), Joyce (PA), Guest (MS), Rogers (AL)

Cybersecurity, Infrastructure Protection & Innovation
Majority (D 7): Richmond (LA), Chmn; Jackson Lee (TX), Langevin (RI), Rice (NY), Underwood (IL), Slotkin (MI), Thompson (MS)
Minority (R 5): Katko (NY), RMM; Ratcliffe (TX), Walker (NC), Taylor (TX), Rogers (AL)

Emergency Preparedness, Response & Recovery
Majority (D 7): Payne (NJ), Chmn; Richmond (LA), Rose (NY), Underwood (IL), Green (TX), Clarke (NY), Thompson (MS)
Minority (R 5): King (NY), RMM; Joyce (PA), Crenshaw (TX), Guest (MS), Rogers (AL)

Intelligence & Counterterrorism
Majority (D 5): Rose (NY), Chmn; Jackson Lee (TX), Langevin (RI), Slotkin (MI), Thompson (MS)
Minority (R 4): Walker (NC), RMM; King (NY), Green (TN), Rogers (AL)

Oversight, Management & Accountability
Majority (D 5): Torres-Small (NM), Chmn; Titus (NV), Watson Coleman (NJ), Barragan (CA), Thompson (MS)
Minority (R 4): Crenshaw (TX), RMM; Higgins (LA), Taylor (TX), Rogers (AL)

Transportation & Maritime Security
Majority (D 7): Correa (CA), Chmn; Cleaver (MO), Titus (NV), Watson Coleman (NJ), Barragan (CA), Demings (FL), Thompson (MS)
Minority (R 5): Lesko (AZ), RMM; Katko (NY), Ratcliffe (TX), Green (TN), Rogers (AL)

House Administration	**1309 LHOB**
cha.house.gov	**202-225-2061**

Majority (D 6): Lofgren (CA), Chmn; Raskin (MD), Davis (CA), Butterfield (NC), Fudge (OH), Aguilar (CA)
Minority (R 3): Davis (IL), RMM; Walker (NC), Loudermilk (GA)

SUBCOMMITTEES

Elections
Majority (D 3): Marcia Fudge (OH), Chmn; G.K. Butterfield (NC), Pete Aguilar (CA)
Minority (R 1): Rodney Davis (IL)

Judiciary	**2138 RHOB**
judiciary.house.gov	**202-225-3951**

Majority (D 24): Nadler (NY), Chmn; Scanlon (PA), Lofgren (CA), Jackson Lee (TX), Cohen (TN), Johnson (GA), Deutch (FL), Bass (CA), Richmond (LA), Jeffries (NY), Cicilline (RI), Swalwell (CA), Lieu (CA), Raskin (MD), Jayapal (WA), Demings (FL), Correa (CA), Garcia (TX), Neguse (CO), McBath (GA), Stanton (AZ), Dean (PA), Mucarsel-Powell (FL), Escobar (TX)

Minority (R 17): Collins (GA), RMM; Sensenbrenner (WI), Chabot (OH), Gohmert (TX), Jordan (OH), Buck (CO), Ratcliffe (TX), Roby (AL), Gaetz (FL), Johnson (LA), Biggs (AZ), McClintock (CA), Lesko (AZ), Reschenthaler (PA), Cline (VA), Armstrong (ND), Steube (FL)

SUBCOMMITTEES

Antitrust, Commercial & Administrative Law
Majority (D 8): Cicilline (RI), Chmn; Neguse (CO), Johnson (GA), Raskin (MD), Jayapal (WA), Demings (FL), Scanlon (PA), McBath (GA)
Minority (R 5): Sensenbrenner (WI), RMM; Gaetz (FL), Buck (CO), Armstrong (ND), Steube (FL)

Constitution, Civil Rights & Civil Liberties
Majority (D 8): Cohen (TN), Chmn; Raskin (MD), Swalwell (CA), Scanlon (PA), Dean (PA), Garcia (TX), Escobar (TX), Jackson Lee (TX)
Minority (R 6): Johnson (LA), RMM; Gohmert (TX), Jordan (OH), Reschenthaler (PA), Cline (VA), Armstrong (ND)

Courts, Intellectual Property & Internet
Majority (D 11): Johnson (GA), Chmn; Correa (CA), Deutch (FL), Richmond (LA), Jeffries (NY), Lieu (CA), Stanton (AZ), Lofgren (CA), Cohen (TN), Bass (CA), Swalwell (CA)
Minority (R 9): Roby (AL), RMM; Chabot (OH), Jordan (OH), Ratcliffe (TX), Gaetz (FL), Johnson (LA), Biggs (AZ), Reschenthaler (PA), Cline (VA)

Crime, Terrorism & Homeland Security
Majority (D 12): Bass (CA), Chmn; Demings (FL), Jackson Lee (TX), McBath (GA), Deutch (FL), Richmond (LA), Jeffries (NY), Cicilline (RI), Lieu (CA), Dean (PA), Mucarsel-Powell (FL), Cohen (TN)
Minority (R 9): Ratcliffe (TX), RMM; Sensenbrenner (WI), Chabot (OH), Gohmert (TX), McClintock (CA), Lesko (AZ), Reschenthaler (PA), Cline (VA), Steube (FL)

Immigration & Citizenship
Majority (D 9): Lofgren (CA), Chmn; Jayapal (WA), Correa (CA), Garcia (TX), Neguse (CO), Mucarsel-Powell (FL), Escobar (TX), Jackson Lee (TX), Scanlon (PA)
Minority (R 6): Buck (CO), RMM; Biggs (AZ), McClintock (CA), Lesko (AZ), Armstrong (ND), Steube (FL)

Natural Resources
naturalresources.house.gov

1324 LHOB
202-225-6065

Majority (D 25): Grijalva (AZ), Chmn; Napolitano (CA), Costa (CA), Sablan (MP), Huffman (CA), Lowenthal (CA), Gallego (AZ), Cox (CA), Neguse (CO), Levin (CA), Haaland (NM), Van Drew (NJ), Cunningham (SC), Velazquez (NY), DeGette (CO), Clay (MO), Dingell (MI), Brown (MD), McEachin (VA), Soto (FL), Case (HI), Horsford (NV), San Nicolas (GU), Cartwright (PA), Tonko (NY)
Minority (R 19): Bishop (UT), RMM; Cheney (WY), Radewagen (AS), Cook (CA), Curtis (UT), Fulcher (ID), Gonzalez-Colon (PR), Gosar (AZ), Graves (LA), Gohmert (TX), Hern (OK), Hice (GA), Johnson (LA), Lamborn (CO), McClintock (CA), Webster (FL), Westerman (AR), Wittman (VA),Young (AK)

SUBCOMMITTEES

Energy & Mineral Resources
Majority (D 9): Lowenthal (CA), Chmn; Levin (CA), Cunningham (SC), McEachin (VA), DeGette (CO), Brown (MD), Huffman (CA), Cartwright (PA), Grijalva (AZ)
Minority (R 7): Gosar (AZ), RMM; Lamborn (CO), Westerman (AR), Graves (LA), Cheney (WY), Hern (OK), Bishop (UT)

Indigenous Peoples of the United States
Majority (D 7): Gallego (AZ), Chmn; Soto (FL), San Nicolas (GU), Haaland (NM), Case (HI), Cartwright (PA), Grijalva (AZ)
Minority (R 6): Cook (CA), RMM; Young (AK), Radewagen (AS), Curtis (UT), Hern (OK), Bishop (UT)

National Parks, Forests & Public Lands
Majority (D 11): Haaland (NM), Chmn; Lowenthal (CA), Gallego (AZ), DeGette (CO), Dingell (MI), Horsford (NV), Huffman (CA), Case (HI), Neguse (CO), Tonko (NY), Grijalva (AZ)
Minority (R 10): Young (AK), RMM; Gohmert (TX), McClintock (CA), Cook (CA), Westerman (AR), Hice (GA), Webster (FL), Curtis (UT), Fulcher (ID), Bishop (UT)

Oversight & Investigations
Majority (D 5): Cox (CA), Chmn; Dingell (MI), San Nicolas (GU), Grijalva (AZ), McEachin (VA)
Minority (R 5): Gohmert (TX), RMM; Gosar (AZ), Johnson (LA), Gonzalez-Colon (PR), Bishop (UT)

Water, Oceans & Wildlife
Majority (D 14): Huffman (CA), Chmn; Napolitano (CA), Costa (CA), Sablan (MP), Van Drew (NJ), Velazquez (NY), Brown (MD), Case (HI), Lowenthal (CA), Cox (CA), Neguse (CO), Levin (CA), Cunningham (SC), Grijalva (AZ)
Minority (R 11): McClintock (CA), RMM; Lamborn (CO), Wittman (VA), Graves (LA), Hice (GA), Radewagen (AS), Webster (FL), Johnson (LA), Gonzalez-Colon (PR), Fulcher (ID), Bishop (UT)

Oversight & Reform   **2157 RHOB**
oversight.house.gov   **202-225-5051**

Majority (D 24): Cummings (MD), Chmn; Maloney (NY), Norton (DC), Clay (MO), Lynch (MA), Cooper (TN), Connolly (VA), Krishnamoorthi (IL), Raskin (MD), Rouda (CA), Hill (CA), Wasserman Schultz (FL), Sarbanes (MD), Welch (VT), Speier (CA), Kelly (IL), DeSaulnier (CA), Lawrence (MI), Plaskett (VI), Khanna (CA), Gomez (CA), Ocasio-Cortez (NY), Pressley (MA), Tlaib (MI)
Minority (R 18): Jordan (OH), RMM; Amash (MI), Gosar (AZ), Foxx (NC), Massie (KY), Meadows (NC), Hice (GA), Grothman (WI), Comer (KY), Cloud (TX), Gibbs (OH), Norman (SC), Higgins (LA), Roy (TX), Miller (WV), Green (TN), Armstrong (ND), Steube (FL)

SUBCOMMITTEES

Government Operations
Majority (D 9): Connolly (VA), Chmn; Norton (DC), Sarbanes (MD), Speier (CA), Lawrence (MI), Plaskett (VI), Khanna (CA), Lynch (MA), Raskin (MD)
Minority (R 7): Meadows (NC), RMM; Massie (KY), Hice (GA), Grothman (WI), Comer (KY), Norman (SC), Steube (FL)

National Security
Majority (D 9): Lynch (MA), Chmn; Cooper (TN), Welch (VT), Rouda (CA), Wasserman Schultz (FL), Kelly (IL), DeSaulnier (CA), Plaskett (VI), Lawrence (MI)
Minority (R 7): Hice (GA), RMM; Amash (MI), Gosar (AZ), Foxx (NC), Meadows (NC), Cloud (TX), Green (TN)

Subcommittee on Civil Rights & Civil Liberties
Majority (D 9): Raskin (MD), Chmn; Maloney (NY), Clay (MO), Wasserman Schultz (FL), Kelly (IL), Gomez (CA), Ocasio-Cortez (NY), Pressley (MA), Norton (DC)
Minority (R 7): Roy (TX), RMM; Amash (MI), Massie (KY), Meadows (NC), Hice (GA), Cloud (TX), Miller (WV)

Subcommittee on Economic & Consumer Policy
Majority (D 7): Krishnamoorthi (IL), Chmn; DeSaulnier (CA), Hill (CA), Khanna (CA), Pressley (MA), Tlaib (MI), Connolly (VA)
Minority (R 5): Cloud (TX), RMM; Grothman (WI), Comer (KY), Roy (TX), Miller (WV)

Subcommittee on Environment
Majority (D 7): Rouda (CA), Chmn; Hill (CA), Tlaib (MI), Krishnamoorthi (IL), Speier (CA), Gomez (CA), Ocasio-Cortez (NY)
Minority (R 5): Comer (KY), RMM; Gosar (AZ), Gibbs (OH), Higgins (LA), Armstrong (ND)

Rules   **H-312 The Capitol**
rules.house.gov   **202-225-9091**

Majority (D 9): McGovern (MA), Chmn; Hastings (FL), Torres (CA), Perlmutter (CO), Raskin (MD), Scanlon (PA), Morelle (NY), Shalala (FL), DeSaulnier (CA)
Minority (R 4): Cole (OK), RMM; Woodall (GA), Burgess (TX), Lesko (AZ)

SUBCOMMITTEES

Legislative & Budget Process

Majority (D 5): Hastings (FL), Chmn; Morelle (NY), Scanlon (PA), Shalala (FL), McGovern (MA)
Minority (R 2): Woodall (GA), RMM; Burgess (TX)

Rules & Organization of the House

Majority (D 5): Torres (CA), Chmn; Perlmutter (CO), Scanlon (PA), Morelle (NY), McGovern (MA) Minority (R 2): Lesko (AZ), Chmn; Woodall (GA)

Expedited Procedures

Majority (D 5): Raskin (MD), Chmn; Shalala (FL), Torres (CA), DeSaulnier (CA), McGovern (MA)
Minority (R 2): Burgess (TX), RMM; Lesko (AZ)

Science, Space & Technology
science.house.gov

2321 RHOB
202-225-6375

Majority (D 22): Johnson (TX), Chmn; Lofgren (CA), Lipinski (IL), Bonamici (OR), Bera (CA), Lamb (PA), Fletcher (TX), Stevens (MI), Horn (OK), Sherrill (NJ), Sherman (CA), Cohen (TN), McNerney (CA), Perlmutter (CO), Tonko (NY), Foster (IL), Beyer (VA), Crist (FL), Casten (IL), Hill (CA), McAdams (UT), Wexton (VA)
Minority (R 16): Lucas (OK), RMM; Brooks (AL), Posey (FL), Weber (TX), Babin (TX), Biggs (AZ), Marshall (KS), Norman (SC), Cloud (TX), Balderson (OH), Olson (TX), Gonzalez (OH), Waltz (FL), Baird (IN), Herrera Beutler (WA), Gonzalez-Colon (PR)

SUBCOMMITTEES

Energy

Majority (D 8): Lamb (PA), Chmn; Lipinski (IL), Fletcher (TX), Stevens (MI), Horn (OK), McNerney (CA), Foster (IL), Casten (IL)
Minority (R 4): Weber (TX), RMM; Biggs (AZ), Norman (SC), Cloud (TX)

Environment

Majority (D 8): Fletcher (TX), Chmn; Bonamici (OR), Lamb (PA), Tonko (NY), Crist (FL), Casten (IL), McAdams (UT), Beyer (VA)
Minority (R 5): Marshall (KS), RMM; Babin (TX), Gonzalez (OH), Baird (IN), Gonzalez-Colon (R)

Investigations & Oversight

Majority (D 5): Sherrill (NJ), Chmn; Bonamici (OR), Cohen (TN), Beyer (VA), Wexton (VA)
Minority (R 3): Norman (SC), RMM; Biggs (AZ), Waltz (FL)

Research & Technology

Majority (D 8): Stevens (MI), Chmn; Lipinski (IL), Sherrill (NJ), Sherman (CA), Tonko (NY), McAdams (UT), Cohen (TN), Foster (IL)
Minority (R 5): Baird (IN), RMM; Marshall (KS), Balderson (OH), Gonzalez (OH), Herrera Beutler (WA)

Space & Aeronautics

Majority (D 8): Horn (OK), Chmn; Lofgren (CA), Bera (CA), Perlmutter (CO), Beyer (VA), Crist (FL), Hill (CA), Wexton (VA)
Minority (R 5): Babin (TX), RMM; Brooks (AL), Posey (FL), Olson (TX), Waltz (FL)

Small Business
smallbusiness.house.gov

2361 RHOB
202-225-4038

Majority (D 13): Velazquez (NY), Chmn; Finkenauer (IA), Golden (ME), Kim (NJ), Crow (CO), Davids (KS), Chu (CA), Veasey (TX), Evans (PA), Schneider (IL), Espaillat (NY), Delgado (NY), Houlahan (PA), Craig (MN)
Minority (R 10): Chabot (OH), RMM; Radewagen (AS), Kelly (MS), Balderson (OH), Hern (OK), Hagedorn (MN), Stauber (MN), Burchett (TN), Spano (FL), Joyce (PA)

SUBCOMMITTEES

Contracting & Infrastructure

Majority (D 3): Golden (ME), Chmn; Veasey (TX), Chu (CA)
Minority (R 3): Stauber (MN), RMM; Hagedorn (MN), Balderson (OH)

Economic Growth, Tax & Capital Access

Majority (D 6): Kim (NJ), Chmn; Davids (KS), Schneider (IL), Espaillat (NY), Delgado (NY), Crow (CO)
Minority (R 4): Hern (OK), RMM; Spano (FL), Radewagen (AS), Stauber (MN)

Innovation & Workforce Development

Majority (D 6): Crow (CO), Chmn; Veasey (TX), Houlahan (PA), Finkenauer (IA), Kim (NJ), Davids (KS)
Minority (R 3): Balderson (OH), RMM; Burchett (TN), Hern (OK)

Investigations, Oversight & Regulations
Majority (D 3): Chu (CA), Chmn; Evans (PA), Craig (MN)
Minority (R 3): Spano (FL), RMM; Kelly (MS), Burchett (TN)

Rural Development, Agriculture, Trade & Entrepreneurship
Majority (D 4): Finkenauer (IA), Chmn; Golden (ME), Crow (CO), Craig (MN)
Minority (R 4): Joyce (PA), RMM; Radewagen (AS), Kelly (MS), Hagedorn (MN)

Transportation & Infrastructure	**2165 RHOB**
transportation.house.gov	202-225-4472

Majority (D 37): DeFazio (OR), Chmn; Norton (DC), Johnson (TX), Cummings (MD), Larsen (WA), Napolitano (CA), Lipinski (IL), Cohen (TN), Sires (NJ), Garamendi (CA), Johnson (GA), Carson (IN), Titus (NV), Maloney (NY), Huffman (CA), Brownley (CA), Wilson (FL), Payne (NJ), Lowenthal (CA), DeSaulnier (CA), Plaskett (VI), Lynch (MA), Carbajal (CA), Brown (MD), Espaillat (NY), Malinowski (NJ), Stanton (AZ), Mucarsel-Powell (FL), Fletcher (TX), Allred (TX), Davids (KS), Finkenauer (IA), Garcia (IL), Delgado (NY), Pappas (NH), Craig (MN), Rouda (CA)
Minority (R 30): Graves (MO), RMM; Young (AK), Crawford (AR), Gibbs (OH), Webster (FL), Massie (KY), Meadows (NC), Perry (PA), Davis (IL), Woodall (GA), Katko (NY), Babin (TX), Graves (LA), Rouzer (NC), Bost (IL), Weber (TX), LaMalfa (CA), Westerman (AR), Smucker (PA), Mitchell (MI), Mast (FL), Gallagher (WI), Palmer (AL), Fitzpatrick (PA), Gonzalez-Colon (PR), Balderson (OH), Spano (FL), Stauber (MN), Miller (WV), Pence (IN)

SUBCOMMITTEES

Aviation
Majority (D 22): Larsen (WA), Chmn; Carson (IN), Plaskett (VI), Lynch (MA), Norton (DC), Lipinski (IL), Cohen (TN), Johnson (GA), Titus (NV), Brownley (CA), Brown (MD), Stanton (AZ), Allred (TX), Garcia (IL), Johnson (TX), Maloney (NY), Payne (NJ), Davids (KS), Craig (MN), Napolitano (CA), Carbajal (CA), DeFazio (OR)
Minority (R 17): Graves (LA), RMM; Young (AK), Webster (FL), Massie (KY), Perry (PA), Woodall (GA), Katko (NY), Rouzer (NC), Smucker (PA), Mitchell (MI), Mast (FL), Gallagher (WI), Fitzpatrick (PA), Balderson (OH), Spano (FL), Stauber (MN), Graves (MO)

Coast Guard & Maritime Transportation
Majority (D 9): Maloney (NY), Chmn; Cummings (MD), Larsen (WA), Plaskett (VI), Garamendi (CA), Lowenthal (CA), Brown (MD), Pappas (NH), DeFazio (OR)
Minority (R 7): Gibbs (OH), RMM; Young (AK), Weber (TX), Mast (FL), Gallagher (WI), Miller (WV), Graves (MO)

Economic Dev't, Public Buildings & Emergency Management
Majority (D 9): Titus (NV), Chmn; Mucarsel-Powell (FL), Davids (KS), Norton (DC), Johnson (GA), Garamendi (CA), Brown (MD), Fletcher (TX), DeFazio (OR)
Minority (R 6): Meadows (NC), RMM; Palmer (AL), Gonzalez-Colon (PR), Miller (WV), Pence (IN), Graves (MO)

Highways & Transit
Majority (D 31): Norton (DC), Chmn; Johnson (TX), Cohen (TN), Garamendi (CA), Johnson (GA), Huffman (CA), Brownley (CA), Wilson (FL), Lowenthal (CA), DeSaulnier (CA), Carbajal (CA), Brown (MD), Espaillat (NY), Malinowski (NJ), Stanton (AZ), Allred (TX), Davids (KS), Finkenauer (IA), Garcia (IL), Delgado (NY), Pappas (NH), Craig (MN), Rouda (CA), Napolitano (CA), Sires (NJ), Maloney (NY), Payne (NJ), Lipinski (IL), Titus (NV), Plaskett (VI), DeFazio (OR)
Minority (R 25): Davis (IL), RMM; Young (AK), Crawford (AR), Gibbs (OH), Webster (FL), Massie (KY), Meadows (NC), Woodall (GA), Katko (NY), Babin (TX), Rouzer (NC), Bost (IL), LaMalfa (CA), Westerman (AR), Smucker (PA), Mitchell (MI), Gallagher (WI), Palmer (AL), Fitzpatrick (PA), Balderson (OH), Spano (FL), Stauber (MN), Miller (WV), Pence (IN), Graves (MO)

Railroads, Pipelines & Hazardous Materials
Majority (D 19): Lipinski (IL), Chmn; Sires (NJ), Payne (NJ), Fletcher (TX), Cummings (MD), Carson (IN), Wilson (FL), DeSaulnier (CA), Lynch (MA), Malinowski (NJ), Napolitano (CA), Cohen (TN), Garcia (IL), Norton (DC), Johnson (TX), Lowenthal (CA), Allred (TX), Craig (MN), DeFazio (OR)
Minority (R 15): Crawford (AR), RMM; Perry (PA), Davis (IL), Babin (TX), Bost (IL), Weber (TX), LaMalfa (CA), Smucker (PA), Mitchell (MI), Fitzpatrick (PA), Balderson (OH), Spano (FL), Stauber (MN), Pence (IN), Graves (MO)

Water Resources & Environment

Majority (D 18): Napolitano (CA), Chmn; Mucarsel-Powell (FL), Johnson (TX), Garamendi (CA), Huffman (CA), Lowenthal (CA), Carbajal (CA), Espaillat (NY), Fletcher (TX), Finkenauer (IA), Delgado (NY), Pappas (NH), Craig (MN), Rouda (CA), Wilson (FL), Lynch (MA), Malinowski (NJ), DeFazio (OR)

Minority (R 14): Westerman (AR), RMM; Webster (FL), Massie (KY), Woodall (GA), Babin (TX), Graves (LA), Rouzer (NC), Bost (IL), Weber (TX), LaMalfa (CA), Mast (FL), Palmer (AL), Gonzalez-Colon (PR), Graves (MO)

Veterans' Affairs
veterans.house.gov

B234 LHOB
202-225-9756

Majority (D 16): Takano (CA), Chmn; Brownley (CA), Rice (NY), Lamb (PA), Levin (CA), Rose (NY), Brindisi (NY), Cisneros (CA), Lee (NV), Underwood (IL), Cunningham (SC), Luria (VA), Pappas (NH), Allred (TX), Peterson (MN), Sablan (MP)

Minority (R 12): Roe (TN), RMM; Bilirakis (FL), Radewagen (AS), Bost (IL), Dunn (FL), Bergman (MI), Banks (IN), Barr (KY), Meuser (PA), Watkins (KS), Roy (TX), Steube (FL)

SUBCOMMITTEES

Disability Assistance & Memorial Affairs
Majority (D 5): Luria (VA), Chmn; Cisneros (CA), Sablan (MP), Allred (TX), Underwood (IL)
Minority (R 4): Bost (IL), RMM; Bilirakis (FL), Watkins (KS), Steube (FL)

Economic Opportunity
Majority (D 7): Levin (CA), Chmn; Rice (NY), Brindisi (NY), Pappas (NH), Luria (VA), Lee (NV), Cunningham (SC)
Minority (R 5): Bilirakis (FL), RMM; Bergman (MI), Banks (IN), Barr (KY), Meuser (PA)

Health
Majority (D 7): Brownley (CA), Chmn; Lamb (PA), Levin (CA), Brindisi (NY), Rose (NY), Cisneros (CA), Peterson (MN)
Minority (R 5): Dunn (FL), RMM; Radewagen (AS), Barr (KY), Meuser (PA), Steube (FL)

Oversight & Investigations
Majority (D 5): Pappas (NH), Chmn; Rice (NY), Rose (NY), Cisneros (CA), Peterson (MN)
Minority (R 4): Bergman (MI), RMM; Radewagen (AS), Bost (IL), Roy (TX)

Technology Modernization
Majority (D 4): Lee (NV), Chmn; Brownley (CA), Lamb (PA), Cunningham (SC)
Minority (R 3): Banks (IN), RMM; Watkins (KS), Roy (TX)

Ways & Means
waysandmeans.house.gov

1102 LHOB
202-225-3625

Majority (D 25): Neal (MA), Chmn; Lewis (GA), Doggett (TX), Thompson (CA), Larson (CT), Blumenauer (OR), Kind (WI), Pascrell (NJ), Davis (IL), Sanchez (CA), Higgins (NY), Sewell (AL), DelBene (WA), Chu (CA), Moore (WI), Kildee (MI), Boyle (PA), Beyer (VA), Evans (PA), Schneider (IL), Suozzi (NY), Panetta (CA), Murphy (FL), Gomez (CA), Horsford (NV)

Minority (R 17): Brady (TX), RMM; Nunes (CA), Buchanan (FL), Smith (NE), Marchant (TX), Reed (NY), Kelly (PA), Holding (NC), Smith (MO), Rice (SC), Schweikert (AZ), Walorski (IN), LaHood (IL), Wenstrup (OH), Arrington (TX), Ferguson (GA), Estes (KS)

SUBCOMMITTEES

Health
Majority (D 11): Doggett (TX), Chmn; Thompson (CA), Kind (WI), Blumenauer (OR), Higgins (NY), Sewell (AL), Chu (CA), Evans (PA), Schneider (IL), Gomez (CA), Horsford (NV)
Minority (R 7): Nunes (CA), RMM; Buchanan (FL), Smith (NE), Marchant (TX), Reed (NY), Kelly (PA), Holding (NC)

Oversight
Majority (D 7): Lewis (GA), Chmn; DelBene (WA), Sanchez (CA), Suozzi (NY), Chu (CA), Moore (WI), Boyle (PA)
Minority (R 4): Kelly (PA), RMM; Walorski (IN), LaHood (IL), Wenstrup (OH)

Select Revenue Measures
Majority (D 9): Thompson (CA), Chmn; Doggett (TX), Larson (CT), Sanchez (CA), DelBene (WA), Moore (WI), Boyle (PA), Beyer (VA), Suozzi (NY)
Minority (R 6): Smith (NE), RMM; Rice (SC), Schweikert (AZ), LaHood (IL), Arrington (TX), Ferguson (GA)

Social Security
Majority (D 7): Larson (CT), Chmn; Pascrell (NJ), Sanchez (CA), Kildee (MI), Boyle (PA), Schneider (IL), Higgins (NY)
Minority (R 4): Reed (NY), RMM; Arrington (TX), Ferguson (GA), Estes (KS)

Trade
Majority (D 11): Blumenauer (OR), Chmn; Pascrell (NJ), Kind (WI), Davis (IL), Higgins (NY), Kildee (MI), Panetta (CA), Murphy (FL), Sewell (AL), DelBene (WA), Beyer (VA)
Minority (R 7): Buchanan (FL), RMM; Nunes (CA), Holding (NC), Rice (SC), Marchant (TX), Smith (MO), Schweikert (AZ)

Worker & Family Support
Majority (D 7): Davis (IL), Chmn; Sewell (AL), Chu (CA), Moore (WI), Evans (PA), Murphy (FL), Gomez (CA)
Minority (R 4): Walorski (IN), RMM; Wenstrup (OH), Estes (KS), Reed (NY)

OTHER COMMITTEES

Permanent Select on Intelligence   **HVC-304 The Capitol Visitors Center**
intelligence.house.gov   **202-225-7690**

Majority (D 13): Schiff (CA), Chmn; Himes (CT), Sewell (AL), Carson (IN), Speier (CA), Quigley (IL), Swalwell (CA), Castro (TX), Heck (WA), Welch (VT), Maloney (NY), Demings (FL), Krishnamoorthi (IL)
Minority (R 9): Nunes (CA), RMM; Conaway (TX), Turner (OH), Wenstrup (OH), Stewart (UT), Crawford (AR), Stefanik (NY), Hurd (TX), Ratcliffe (TX)

SUBCOMMITTEES

Counterterrorism, Counterintelligence & Counterproliferation
Majority (D 6): Carson (IN), Chmn; Speier (CA), Quigley (IL), Castro (TX), Welch (VT), Sean Maloney (NY)
Minority (R 4): Crawford (AR), RMM; Conaway (TX), Wenstrup (OH), Stewart (UT)

Defense Intelligence & Warfighter Support
Majority (D 6): Sewell (AL), Chmn; Himes (CT), Heck (WA), Welch (VT), Maloney (NY), Demings (FL)
Minority (R 4): Wenstrup (OH), RMM; Conaway (TX), Turner (OH), Hurd (TX)

Intelligence Modernization & Readiness
Majority (D 6): Swalwell (CA), Chmn; Sewell (AL), Speier (CA), Castro (TX), Demings (FL), Krishnamoorthi (IL)
Minority (R 4): Hurd (TX), RMM; Conaway (TX), Stefanik (NY), Ratcliffe (TX)

Strategic Technologies & Advanced Research
Majority (D 6): Himes (CT), Chmn; Carson (IN), Quigley (IL), Swalwell (CA), Heck (WA), Krishnamoorthi (IL)
Minority (R 4): Stewart (UT), RMM; Turner (OH), Stefanik (NY), Ratcliffe (TX)

Select Committee on the Climate Crisis   **2052 RHOB**
climatecrisis.house.gov   **202-225-3376**

Majority (D 9): Castor (FL), Chmn; Lujan (NM), Bonamici (OR), Brownley (CA), Huffman (CA), McEachin (VA), Levin (CA), Casten (IL), Neguse (CO)
Minority (R 6): Graves (LA), RMM; Griffith (VA), Palmer (AL), Carter (GA), Miller (WV), Armstrong (ND)

Select Committee on the Modernization of Congress   **1410 LHOB**
modernizecongress.house.gov   **202-225-5916**

Majority (D 6): Kilmer (WA), Chmn; Cleaver (MO), DelBene (WA), Lofgren (CA), Pocan (WI), Scanlon (PA)
Minority (R 6): Graves (GA), RMM; Woodall (GA), Brooks (IN), Davis (IL), Newhouse (WA), Timmons (SC)

JOINT COMMITTEES

Joint Economic   **G-01 DSOB**
jec.senate.gov   **202-224-5171**

House (D 6; R 4): Maloney (D-NY), VChmn; Beyer (D-VA), Heck (D-WA), Trone (D-MD), Beatty (D-OH), Frankel (D-FL); Schweikert (R-AZ), Herrera Beutler (R-WA), Lahood (R-IL), Marchant (R-TX)
Senate (R 6; D 4): Lee (R-UT), Chmn; Cotton (R-AR), Sasse (R-NE), Portman (R-OH), Cruz (R-TX), Cassidy (R-LA); Heinrich (D-NM), Klobuchar (D-MN), Peters (D-MI), Hassan (D-NH)

Joint Library
cha.house.gov/jointcommittees/joint-committee-library

House (D 3; R 2): Lofgren (D-CA), VChmn; Ryan (D-OH), Butterfield (D-NC), Rodney Davis (R-IL), Barry Loudermilk (R-GA)
Senate (R 3; D 2): Roy Blunt (R-MO), Chmn; Pat Roberts (R-KS), Richard Shelby (R-AL); Amy Klobuchar (D-MN), Patrick Leahy (D-VT)

Joint Printing
cha.house.gov/jointcommittees/joint-committee-on-printing

House (D 5;): Lofgren (CA), Chmn; Jamie Raskin (MD), Susan Davis (CA), Rodney Davis (IL), Barry Loudermilk (GA)
Senate (R 5;): Roy Blunt (MO), VChmn; Pat Roberts (KS), Roger Wicker (MS), Amy Klobuchar (MN), Tom Udall (NM)

Joint Taxation   **502 FHOB**
jct.gov   **202-225-3621**

House (D 3;R 2): Neal (MA), Chmn; Lewis (GA), Doggett (TX), Brady (R-TX), Nunes (R-CA)
Senate (R 3; D 2): Grassley (R-IA), VChmn; Crapo (R-ID), Enzi (R-WY), Wyden (D-OR), Stabenow (D-MI)

2016 VOTES CAST FOR THE U.S. HOUSE OF REPRESENTATIVES BY PARTY

The Federal Election Commission compiles every two years data on the total votes cast, by party, for all federal elections. This table shows the state-by-state turnout for each party in House contests—both primary and general elections—for 2016, which were the most recent results released by the FEC, as of June 2019.

This table is enhanced by a separate table on the following page that shows the total of citizen voting age population (CVAP), registered voters, plus voter turnout in each state in 2012, 2016 and 2018.

State	PRIMARY ELECTION			GENERAL ELECTION		
	Democratic	Republican	Other	Democratic	Republican	Other
AL		445,851		621,911	1,222,018	45,756
AK	25,057	54,528	5,543	111,019	155,088	42,091
AS				2,740	8,923	171
AZ	297,348	627,258	1,287	1,034,687	1,264,378	112,999
AR				111,347	760,415	196,815
CA	4,925,449	2,624,761	151,065	8,624,432	4,682,033	107,553
CO	257,032	312,551		1,263,791	1,288,618	149,152
CT				916,815	558,162	100,206
DE	63,794			233,554	172,301	14,785
DC	93,465	564	403	265,178		35,728
FL	527,988	850,366		3,985,050	4,733,630	118,746
GA	264,931	570,693		1,498,437	2,272,460	1,965
GU	12,834	7,727	4	18,345	15,617	206
HI	186,764	26,970	1,695	460,805	129,716	20,743
ID	26,200	128,241	82	208,992	447,544	25,058
IL	1,611,789	1,351,107	417	2,810,536	2,397,436	33,795
IN	550,226	917,165		1,052,901	1,442,989	162,477
IA	94,221	94,817		673,969	813,153	28,433
KS	76,227	276,896		317,635	694,240	161,861
KY	79,212	135,156		597,717	1,457,950	332
LA				610,643	1,424,567	41,428
ME	47,146	39,915		386,627	357,447	500
MD	843,292	380,855		1,636,200	962,088	109,457
MA	261,262	36,515		2,344,518	451,121	145,049
MI	496,213	637,949		2,193,980	2,243,402	233,523
MN	134,000	83,657		1,434,590	1,334,686	91,156
MS	44,533	344,632		449,896	680,810	51,567
MO	307,877	656,524	3,618	1,041,306	1,600,524	108,249
MT	112,821	144,662		205,919	285,358	16,554
NE	49,232	189,863	234	221,069	557,557	9,640
NV	97,474	62,715		508,113	498,104	72,280
NH	69,727	100,095		336,575	316,149	76,216
NJ	653,291	381,599		1,821,620	1,541,631	87,897
NM	183,460	92,139		436,932	343,124	70
NY	193,635	45,695	42	4,202,198	2,140,911	773,313
NC	110,537	229,518		2,142,661	2,447,326	8,471
ND	17,122	97,276	1,113	80,377	233,980	24,102
MP						10,605
OH	912,108	1,525,525	460	2,154,523	2,996,017	67,815
OK	122,292	222,737		305,222	781,691	46,331
OR	538,164	301,621	12,938	1,026,851	809,048	75,966
PA	1,128,201	1,300,252		2,905,596	3,126,237	40,832
PR			624,503			1,478,816
RI	61,074	1,270		263,648	141,324	26,553
SC	19,317	67,183		778,125	1,193,711	67,626
SD				132,810	237,163	
TN	148,761	332,050		814,181	1,493,740	83,140
TX	1,058,715	2,392,495		3,160,535	4,877,605	490,386
UT				356,290	710,656	47,224
VT	67,630	3,428	211	264,414		30,920
VI	4,796			14,531		371
VA	15,728	72,903		1,859,426	1,843,010	79,812
WA	759,737	545,259	67,262	1,736,145	1,404,890	

WV	187,827	165,067		224,449	445,017	16,883
WI	303,570	233,113	801	1,379,996	1,270,279	123,387
WY	18,936	148,443	455	75,466	156,176	20,134
Total:	18,061,015	19,259,606	872,133	62,315,293	63,422,020	5,915,145

Voter Registration and Turnout: 2012-2018

The voter registration table was compiled by Almanac staff from various sources to demonstrate trends in voter registration and turnout at the state level in federal elections from 2012-2018. Voter registration figures were retrieved from Secretary of State websites for each state and includes only individuals registered eligible to vote in the 2012, 2016, and 2018 federal elections respectively. Voter turnout for 2012 and 2016 elections "CVAP" indicates Civilian Age Voting Population. Citizen voting age population was retrieved from the U.S Census Bureau and is defined as citizens in the given geography that as U.S. citizens and meet all criteria to be eligible to vote.

Sources: U.S. Census Bureau, American Community Survey, 2012-17; Secretary of State websites, all states; The Almanac of American Politics, 2016.

State	2012 CVAP	2012 Total Registered	2012 Total Pres. Vote	2016 CVAP	2016 Total Registered	2016 Total Pres. Vote	2017 CVAP	2018 Total Registered
Alabama	3,481,375	3,166,202	2,051,621	3,639,493	2,990,533	2,092,269	3,651,914	3,476,676
Alaska	483,060	361,000	294,708	527,811	361,000	298,566	530,553	573,647
Arizona	4,110,890	3,124,712	2,258,886	4,613,575	3,588,466	2,519,895	4,690,177	3,716,263
Arkansas	2,090,150	1,610,364	1,042,153	2,175,338	1,759,982	1,095,195	2,183,895	1,784,014
California	23,802,577	18,245,970	12,694,243	24,875,293	19,411,771	13,994,764	25,200,451	19,696,371
Colorado	3,403,805	2,635,000	2,508,345	3,824,440	3,292,062	2,685,475	3,893,361	3,354,273
Connecticut	2,493,095	2,218,662	1,539,975	2,582,883	2,357,733	1,619,463	2,599,794	2,290,400
Delaware	638,160	632,805	408,068	689,653	681,950	435,487	697,329	694,572
Florida	12,812,525	12,166,959	8,401,203	14,195,896	12,971,305	9,329,904	14,461,395	13,396,112
Georgia	6,476,090	6,066,961	3,852,515	7,063,804	6,637,939	4,092,373	7,155,973	6,935,816
Hawaii	941,595	705,668	427,673	1,006,727	749,917	424,429	1,016,468	756,751
Idaho	1,156,869	896,234	666,290	1,148,895	813,218	673,627	1,168,167	867,840
Illinois	8,717,365	6,425,000	5,154,728	9,003,481	6,665,000	5,446,340	9,043,520	8,758,953
Indiana	4,649,340	4,555,257	2,663,368	4,824,553	3,270,000	2,724,405	4,850,327	4,526,663
Iowa	2,222,850	2,166,539	1,553,161	2,295,040	2,171,165	1,513,838	2,302,495	2,170,013
Kansas	1,989,385	1,771,252	1,133,360	2,061,775	1,817,920	1,176,935	2,069,337	1,841,848
Kentucky	3,189,845	3,037,152	1,766,560	3,313,798	2,253,000	1,885,577	3,325,139	3,409,688
Louisiana	3,241,185	2,962,999	1,961,403	3,432,034	3,022,075	1,958,792	3,447,638	2,990,267
Maine	1,029,240	1,025,444	693,582	1,051,867	787,000	745,684	1,055,130	1,026,715
Maryland	3,964,250	3,756,806	2,649,713	4,212,263	3,900,090	2,700,702	4,248,702	3,954,027
Massachusetts	4,602,185	4,342,841	3,109,604	4,887,325	4,534,974	3,224,107	4,931,669	4,574,967
Michigan	7,266,065	5,620,000	4,679,825	7,408,626	5,620,000	4,720,518	7,435,282	7,488,934
Minnesota	3,783,730	3,059,234	2,866,392	3,980,474	3,269,260	2,804,041	4,010,716	3,246,893
Mississippi	2,146,420	1,794,000	1,273,695	2,217,764	1,725,000	1,185,845	2,220,809	1,599,000
Missouri	4,384,195	4,190,936	2,706,236	4,547,880	4,223,787	2,762,938	4,567,241	4,194,223
Montana	742,845	681,608	483,932	789,499	694,370	484,986	794,084	579,000
Nebraska	1,284,815	1,164,166	777,145	1,341,016	1,211,101	819,401	1,350,097	1,220,679
Nevada	1,701,525	1,500,818	994,940	1,902,282	1,679,254	1,088,702	1,943,710	1,775,311
New Hampshire	987,480	905,957	699,479	1,027,630	752,000	725,093	1,034,685	974,077
New Jersey	5,838,035	5,497,322	3,602,669	6,087,275	5,819,276	3,750,211	6,142,332	5,937,432
New Mexico	1,383,780	1,255,273	778,911	1,464,241	1,291,905	779,442	1,471,669	1,266,629
New York	13,004,815	11,969,192	6,976,172	13,605,854	12,493,250	7,552,299	13,741,921	12,706,050
North Carolina	6,607,030	5,295,000	4,448,786	7,203,790	6,918,150	4,682,073	7,309,766	7,092,686
North Dakota	503,755	383,000	312,990	555,691	424,000	331,986	560,530	397,000
Ohio	8,547,605	7,987,203	5,489,146	8,734,125	7,861,025	5,409,673	8,761,633	8,070,917
Oklahoma	2,647,105	2,000,610	1,334,872	2,787,654	2,157,450	1,452,992	2,802,583	2,120,843
Oregon	2,692,195	2,199,360	1,724,663	2,911,330	2,553,808	1,928,742	2,948,763	2,751,512
Pennsylvania	9,475,230	8,508,015	5,670,708	9,725,847	8,722,977	6,043,889	9,740,191	8,602,457
Rhode Island	761,675	725,309	436,881	780,248	552,000	447,814	784,492	789,950
South Carolina	3,312,715	2,876,951	1,937,586	3,620,829	3,153,521	2,059,966	3,673,580	3,173,652
South Dakota	590,645	528,621	355,649	627,070	544,428	366,029	629,704	545,308
Tennessee	4,582,660	3,370,094	2,423,039	4,876,605	4,110,318	2,464,017	4,916,862	4,163,302
Texas	15,276,965	13,646,226	7,877,967	17,177,623	15,101,087	8,846,407	17,512,737	15,793,257
Utah	1,696,060	1,283,526	992,413	1,903,497	1,576,494	1,109,205	1,942,342	1,641,489

2008 2016 Votes Cast for the U.S. House of Representatives by Party

Vermont	481,700	461,237	291,937	493,535	471,619	290,778	493,441	490,074
Virginia	5,578,950	5,428,833	3,794,342	5,998,907	5,619,151	3,869,190	6,051,620	5,691,064
Washington	4,593,030	3,917,963	3,046,066	5,008,035	4,284,936	3,125,344	5,081,381	4,360,774
West Virginia	1,440,480	1,246,559	655,924	1,453,212	1,274,887	701,169	1,446,498	1,155,290
Wisconsin	4,160,995	3,515,813	3,028,951	4,313,304	3,619,995	2,894,494	4,328,520	3,252,407
Wyoming	405,100	268,000	245,574	432,377	304,000	243,679	432,814	276,696

NBC Exit Polls: Vote by Party Candidate

The national exit polls, which have been conducted in recent presidential elections by several national news organizations, have been a gold mine of information about the voters and their choices. The data on the following four pages were compiled by NBC News from the results of the exit polls that were taken from 1992 to 2016, as voters exited polling booths on Election Day. In addition to voter preferences on the candidates, the data provide a unique demographic and ideological breakdown of the electorate.

NBC News generously provided the exit-poll data for the past seven presidential elections to the Almanac for the unique publication in this book. On close examination, the shifts during that time offer significant insight into the remarkable political changes in the nation since 1992. They also provide vital measures about the opportunities and hazards for each party in the 2020 presidential election. Many thanks to John Lapinski and his colleagues at NBC for their extensive assistance in preparing the data.

Source: NBC News Exit Polls

OVERALL	1992		1996		2000		2004		2008		2012		2016	
Exit Poll Topline	Clinton (D)	43	Clinton (D)	49	Gore (D)	48	Kerry (D)	48	Obama (D)	53	Obama (D)	50	Clinton (D)	48
	Bush (R)	38	Dole (R)	41	Bush (R)	48	Bush (R)	51	McCain (R)	45	Romney (R)	48	Trump (R)	46
	Perot (I)	19	Perot (I)	8	Ind.	2	Ind.	*	Ind.	--	Ind.	--	Ind.	4
SEX	**1992**		**1996**		**2000**		**2004**		**2008**		**2012**		**2016**	
Men	Clinton (D)	41	Clinton (D)	43	Gore (D)	42	Kerry (D)	44	Obama (D)	49	Obama (D)	45	Clinton (D)	41
	Bush (R)	38	Dole (R)	44	Bush (R)	53	Bush (R)	55	McCain (R)	48	Romney (R)	52	Trump (R)	52
	Perot (I)	21	Perot (I)	10	Ind.	3	Ind.	*	Ind.	--	Ind.	--	Ind.	5
Women	Clinton (D)	45	Clinton (D)	54	Gore (D)	54	Kerry (D)	51	Obama (D)	56	Obama (D)	55	Clinton (D)	54
	Bush (R)	37	Dole (R)	38	Bush (R)	43	Bush (R)	48	McCain (R)	43	Romney (R)	44	Trump (R)	41
	Perot (I)	17	Perot (I)	7	Ind.	2	Ind.	*	Ind.	--	Ind.	--	Ind.	4
RACE & ETHNICITY	**1992**		**1996**		**2000**		**2004**		**2008**		**2012**		**2016**	
White	Clinton (D)	39	Clinton (D)	43	Gore (D)	42	Kerry (D)	41	Obama (D)	43	Obama (D)	39	Clinton (D)	37
	Bush (R)	40	Dole (R)	46	Bush (R)	54	Bush (R)	58	McCain (R)	55	Romney (R)	59	Trump (R)	57
	Perot (I)	20	Perot (I)	9	Ind.	3	Ind.	*	Ind.	--	Ind.	--	Ind.	5
Black	Clinton (D)	83	Clinton (D)	84	Gore (D)	90	Kerry (D)	88	Obama (D)	95	Obama (D)	93	Clinton (D)	89
	Bush (R)	10	Dole (R)	12	Bush (R)	9	Bush (R)	11	McCain (R)	4	Romney (R)	6	Trump (R)	8
	Perot (I)	7	Perot (I)	4	Ind.	1	Ind.	*	Ind.	--	Ind.	--	Ind.	3
Latino	Clinton (D)	61	Clinton (D)	72	Gore (D)	62	Kerry (D)	58	Obama (D)	67	Obama (D)	71	Clinton (D)	66
	Bush (R)	25	Dole (R)	21	Bush (R)	35	Bush (R)	40	McCain (R)	31	Romney (R)	27	Trump (R)	28
	Perot (I)	14	Perot (I)	6	Ind.	2	Ind.	0	Ind.	--	Ind.	--	Ind.	5
Asian	Clinton (D)	31	Clinton (D)	43	Gore (D)	55	Kerry (D)	56	Obama (D)	62	Obama (D)	73	Clinton (D)	65
	Bush (R)	55	Dole (R)	48	Bush (R)	41	Bush (R)	44	McCain (R)	35	Romney (R)	26	Trump (R)	27
	Perot (I)	15	Perot (I)	8	Ind.	3	Ind.	0	Ind.	--	Ind.	--	Ind.	6
AGE	**1992**		**1996**		**2000**		**2004**		**2008**		**2012**		**2016**	
18-29	Clinton (D)	43	Clinton (D)	53	Gore (D)	48	Kerry (D)	54	Obama (D)	66	Obama (D)	60	Clinton (D)	55
	Bush (R)	34	Dole (R)	34	Bush (R)	46	Bush (R)	45	McCain (R)	32	Romney (R)	37	Trump (R)	36
	Perot (I)	22	Perot (I)	10	Ind.	5	Ind.	*	Ind.	--	Ind.	--	Ind.	8
30-44	Clinton (D)	41	Clinton (D)	48	Gore (D)	48	Kerry (D)	46	Obama (D)	52	Obama (D)	52	Clinton (D)	51
	Bush (R)	38	Dole (R)	41	Bush (R)	49	Bush (R)	53	McCain (R)	46	Romney (R)	45	Trump (R)	41
	Perot (I)	21	Perot (I)	9	Ind.	2	Ind.	1	Ind.	--	Ind.	--	Ind.	7
45-59	Clinton (D)	41	Clinton (D)	48	Gore (D)	48	Kerry (D)	48	Obama (D)	49	Obama (D)	47	Clinton (D)	43
	Bush (R)	40	Dole (R)	41	Bush (R)	49	Bush (R)	51	McCain (R)	49	Romney (R)	52	Trump (R)	53
	Perot (I)	19	Perot (I)	9	Ind.	2	Ind.	*	Ind.	--	Ind.	--	Ind.	3
60+	Clinton (D)	50	Clinton (D)	48	Gore (D)	51	Kerry (D)	46	Obama (D)	47	Obama (D)	46	Clinton (D)	46
	Bush (R)	38	Dole (R)	44	Bush (R)	47	Bush (R)	54	McCain (R)	51	Romney (R)	54	Trump (R)	51
	Perot (I)	12	Perot (I)	7	Ind.	2	Ind.	*	Ind.	--	Ind.	--	Ind.	3
IDEOLOGY	**1992**		**1996**		**2000**		**2004**		**2008**		**2012**		**2016**	
Liberals	Clinton (D)	68	Clinton (D)	78	Gore (D)	80	Kerry (D)	85	Obama (D)	89	Obama (D)	86	Clinton (D)	84
	Bush (R)	14	Dole (R)	11	Bush (R)	13	Bush (R)	13	McCain (R)	10	Romney (R)	11	Trump (R)	10
	Perot (I)	18	Perot (I)	7	Ind.	6	Ind.	1	Ind.	--	Ind.	--	Ind.	5

	1992	1996	2000	2004	2008	2012	2016
Moderates	Clinton (D) 47	Clinton (D) 57	Gore (D) 52	Kerry (D) 54	Obama (D) 60	Obama (D) 56	Clinton (D) 52
	Bush (R) 31	Dole (R)	Bush (R) 33	Bush (R) 44	McCain (R) 39	Romney (R) 41	Trump (R) 40
	Perot (I) 21	Perot (I) 9	Ind. 2	Ind. *	Ind. --	Ind. --	Ind. 6
Conservatives	Clinton (D) 18	Clinton (D) 20	Gore (D) 17	Kerry (D) 15	Obama (D) 20	Obama (D) 17	Clinton (D) 16
	Bush (R) 64	Dole (R) 71	Bush (R) 81	Bush (R) 84	McCain (R) 78	Romney (R) 82	Trump (R) 81
	Perot (I) 18	Perot (I) 8	Ind. 1	Ind. *	Ind. --	Ind. --	Ind. 2

RELIGION	1992	1996	2000	2004	2008	2012	2016
All Protestant / Other Christian	Clinton (D) 37	Clinton (D) 42	Gore (D) 42	Kerry (D) 40	Obama (D) 45	Obama (D) 42	Clinton (D) 39
	Bush (R) 44	Dole (R) 47	Bush (R) 56	Bush (R) 59	McCain (R) 54	Romney (R) 57	Trump (R) 56
	Perot (I) 19	Perot (I) 9	Ind. 2	Ind. *	Ind. --	Ind. --	Ind. 3
White Protestant	Clinton (D) 33	Clinton (D) 36	Gore (D) 34	Kerry (D) 32	Obama (D) 34	Obama (D) 30	Clinton (D) 26
	Bush (R) 47	Dole (R) 53	Bush (R) 63	Bush (R) 67	McCain (R) 65	Romney (R) 69	Trump (R) 69
	Perot (I) 21	Perot (I) 10	Ind. 2	Ind. *	Ind. --	Ind. --	Ind. 3
Catholic	Clinton (D) 44	Clinton (D) 53	Gore (D) 50	Kerry (D) 47	Obama (D) 54	Obama (D) 50	Clinton (D) 46
	Bush (R) 35	Dole (R) 37	Bush (R) 47	Bush (R) 52	McCain (R) 45	Romney (R) 48	Trump (R) 50
	Perot (I) 20	Perot (I) 9	Ind. 2	Ind. *	Ind. --	Ind. --	Ind. 3
Jewish	Clinton (D) 80	Clinton (D) 78	Gore (D) 79	Kerry (D) 74	Obama (D) 78	Obama (D) 69	Clinton (D) 71
	Bush (R) 11	Dole (R) 16	Bush (R) 19	Bush (R) 25	McCain (R) 21	Romney (R) 30	Trump (R) 23
	Perot (I) 9	Perot (I) 3	Ind. 1	Ind. 0	Ind. --	Ind. --	Ind. 6
Mormon	Clinton (D) n/a	Clinton (D) n/a	Gore (D) n/a	Kerry (D) 19	Obama (D) 24	Obama (D) 21	Clinton (D) 28
	Bush (R) n/a	Dole (R) n/a	Bush (R) n/a	Bush (R) 80	McCain (R) 76	Romney (R) 78	Trump (R) 56
	Perot (I) n/a	Perot (I) n/a	Ind. n/a	Ind. 1	Ind. --	Ind. --	Ind. 8
None	Clinton (D) 62	Clinton (D) 59	Gore (D) 61	Kerry (D) 67	Obama (D) 75	Obama (D) 70	Clinton (D) 67
	Bush (R) 18	Dole (R) 23	Bush (R) 30	Bush (R) 31	McCain (R) 23	Romney (R) 26	Trump (R) 25
	Perot (I) 20	Perot (I) 13	Ind. 7	Ind. 1	Ind. --	Ind. 5	Ind. 7
Att. church at least once/week	Clinton (D) 36	Clinton (D) n/a	Gore (D) 39	Kerry (D) 39	Obama (D) 43	Obama (D) 39	Clinton (D) 41
	Bush (R) 48	Dole (R) n/a	Bush (R) 59	Bush (R) 61	McCain (R) 55	Romney (R) 59	Trump (R) 55
	Perot (I) 15	Perot (I) n/a	Ind. 2	Ind. *	Ind. --	Ind. --	Ind. 2
White Evangelical	Clinton (D) 22	Clinton (D) n/a	Gore (D) n/a	Kerry (D) 21	Obama (D) 26	Obama (D) 20	Clinton (D) 16
	Bush (R) 64	Dole (R) n/a	Bush (R) n/a	Bush (R) 79	McCain (R) 73	Romney (R) 79	Trump (R) 80
	Perot (I) 15	Perot (I) n/a	Ind. n/a	Ind. *	Ind. --	Ind. --	Ind. 2

SIZE OF PLACE	1992	1996	2000	2004	2008	2012	2016
Population over 500,000	Clinton (D) 58	Clinton (D) 68	Gore (D) 71	Kerry (D) 60	Obama (D) 70	Obama (D) 69	Clinton (D) 72
	Bush (R) 29	Dole (R) 25	Bush (R) 26	Bush (R) 39	McCain (R) 28	Romney (R) 29	Trump (R) 22
	Perot (I) 13	Perot (I) 6	Ind. 3	Ind. 0	Ind. --	Ind. --	Ind. 4
Population 50,000-500,000	Clinton (D) 50	Clinton (D) 50	Gore (D) 57	Kerry (D) 49	Obama (D) 59	Obama (D) 58	Clinton (D) 53
	Bush (R) 33	Dole (R) 39	Bush (R) 40	Bush (R) 49	McCain (R) 39	Romney (R) 40	Trump (R) 41
	Perot (I) 16	Perot (I) 8	Ind. 2	Ind. *	Ind. --	Ind. --	Ind. 5
Suburbs	Clinton (D) 41	Clinton (D) 47	Gore (D) 47	Kerry (D) 47	Obama (D) 50	Obama (D) 48	Clinton (D) 45
	Bush (R) 39	Dole (R) 42	Bush (R) 49	Bush (R) 52	McCain (R) 48	Romney (R) 50	Trump (R) 49
	Perot (I) 21	Perot (I) 8	Ind. 3	Ind. *	Ind. --	Ind. --	Ind. 4
Population 10,000-50,000	Clinton (D) 39	Clinton (D) 48	Gore (D) 38	Kerry (D) 48	Obama (D) 45	Obama (D) 42	Clinton (D) 46
	Bush (R) 42	Dole (R) 41	Bush (R) 59	Bush (R) 50	McCain (R) 53	Romney (R) 56	Trump (R) 51
	Perot (I) 20	Perot (I) 9	Ind. 2	Ind. 1	Ind. --	Ind. --	Ind. 3
Rural areas	Clinton (D) 39	Clinton (D) 44	Gore (D) 37	Kerry (D) 40	Obama (D) 45	Obama (D) 37	Clinton (D) 32
	Bush (R) 40	Dole (R) 46	Bush (R) 59	Bush (R) 59	McCain (R) 53	Romney (R) 61	Trump (R) 63
	Perot (I) 20	Perot (I) 10	Ind. 2	Ind. 1	Ind. --	Ind. --	Ind. 3

FAMILY INCOME	1992	1996	2000	2004	2008	2012	2016
Under $30,000	Clinton (D) 50	Clinton (D) 55	Gore (D) 55	Kerry (D) 59	Obama (D) 65	Obama (D) 63	Clinton (D) 53
	Bush (R) 31	Dole (R) 33	Bush (R) 40	Bush (R) 40	McCain (R) 33	Romney (R) 35	Trump (R) 40
	Perot (I) 20	Perot (I) 10	Ind. 4	Ind. *	Ind. --	Ind. --	Ind. --
$30,000-$49,999	Clinton (D) 41	Clinton (D) 48	Gore (D) 49	Kerry (D) 50	Obama (D) 55	Obama (D) 57	Clinton (D) 52
	Bush (R) 38	Dole (R) 40	Bush (R) 48	Bush (R) 49	McCain (R) 43	Romney (R) 42	Trump (R) 41
	Perot (I) 21	Perot (I) 10	Ind. 2	Ind. *	Ind. --	Ind. --	Ind. 5
$50,000-$99,999	Clinton (D) n/a	Clinton (D) 46	Gore (D) 46	Kerry (D) 44	Obama (D) 49	Obama (D) 46	Clinton (D) 46
	Bush (R) n/a	Dole (R) 46	Bush (R) 51	Bush (R) 56	McCain (R) 49	Romney (R) 52	Trump (R) 49

$100,000 and over	1992		1996		2000		2004		2008		2012		2016	
	Perot (I)	n/a	Perot (I)	7	Ind.	2	Ind.	*	Ind.	--	Ind.	--	Ind.	--
	Clinton (D)	n/a	Clinton (D)	38	Gore (D)	43	Kerry (D)	41	Obama (D)	49	Obama (D)	44	Clinton (D)	47
	Bush (R)	n/a	Dole (R)	54	Bush (R)	54	Bush (R)	58	McCain (R)	49	Romney (R)	54	Trump (R)	47
	Perot (I)	n/a	Perot (I)	6	Ind.	2	Ind.	1	Ind.	--	Ind.	--	Ind.	4

FAMILY'S FINANCIAL SITUATION	1992		1996		2000		2004		2008		2012		2016	
Better today	Clinton (D)	24	Clinton (D)	66	Gore (D)	61	Kerry (D)	19	Obama (D)	37	Obama (D)	84	Clinton (D)	72
	Bush (R)	61	Dole (R)	26	Bush (R)	36	Bush (R)	80	McCain (R)	60	Romney (R)	15	Trump (R)	23
	Perot (I)	14	Perot (I)	6	Ind.	2	Ind.	*	Ind.	--	Ind.	--	Ind.	3
About the same	Clinton (D)	41	Clinton (D)	46	Gore (D)	35	Kerry (D)	50	Obama (D)	45	Obama (D)	58	Clinton (D)	47
	Bush (R)	42	Dole (R)	45	Bush (R)	60	Bush (R)	49	McCain (R)	53	Romney (R)	40	Trump (R)	45
	Perot (I)	17	Perot (I)	8	Ind.	3	Ind.	1	Ind.	--	Ind.	--	Ind.	6
Worse today	Clinton (D)	61	Clinton (D)	27	Gore (D)	33	Kerry (D)	79	Obama (D)	71	Obama (D)	18	Clinton (D)	19
	Bush (R)	14	Dole (R)	57	Bush (R)	63	Bush (R)	20	McCain (R)	28	Romney (R)	80	Trump (R)	77
	Perot (I)	25	Perot (I)	13	Ind.	4	Ind.	*	Ind.	--	Ind.	--	Ind.	3

EDUCATION	1992		1996		2000		2004		2008		2012		2016	
High school or less	Clinton (D)	46	Clinton (D)	53	Gore (D)	50	Kerry (D)	48	Obama (D)	54	Obama (D)	52	Clinton (D)	46
	Bush (R)	34	Dole (R)	34	Bush (R)	47	Bush (R)	52	McCain (R)	44	Romney (R)	46	Trump (R)	51
	Perot (I)	20	Perot (I)	12	Ind.	1	Ind.	*	Ind.	--	Ind.	--	Ind.	--
Some college	Clinton (D)	41	Clinton (D)	48	Gore (D)	45	Kerry (D)	46	Obama (D)	51	Obama (D)	49	Clinton (D)	43
	Bush (R)	37	Dole (R)	40	Bush (R)	51	Bush (R)	54	McCain (R)	47	Romney (R)	48	Trump (R)	51
	Perot (I)	21	Perot (I)	10	Ind.	3	Ind.	*	Ind.	--	Ind.	--	Ind.	5
College graduate or more	Clinton (D)	44	Clinton (D)	47	Gore (D)	48	Kerry (D)	49	Obama (D)	53	Obama (D)	50	Clinton (D)	52
	Bush (R)	39	Dole (R)	44	Bush (R)	48	Bush (R)	49	McCain (R)	45	Romney (R)	48	Trump (R)	42
	Perot (I)	17	Perot (I)	7	Ind.	3	Ind.	1	Ind.	--	Ind.	--	Ind.	4
College graduate	Clinton (D)	39	Clinton (D)	44	Gore (D)	45	Kerry (D)	46	Obama (D)	50	Obama (D)	47	Clinton (D)	49
	Bush (R)	41	Dole (R)	46	Bush (R)	51	Bush (R)	52	McCain (R)	48	Romney (R)	51	Trump (R)	44
	Perot (I)	20	Perot (I)	8	Ind.	3	Ind.	1	Ind.	--	Ind.	--	Ind.	5
Post graduate study	Clinton (D)	50	Clinton (D)	52	Gore (D)	52	Kerry (D)	55	Obama (D)	58	Obama (D)	55	Clinton (D)	58
	Bush (R)	36	Dole (R)	40	Bush (R)	44	Bush (R)	44	McCain (R)	40	Romney (R)	42	Trump (R)	37
	Perot (I)	14	Perot (I)	5	Ind.	3	Ind.	1	Ind.	--	Ind.	--	Ind.	4

GENDER and RACE	1992		1996		2000		2004		2008		2012		2016	
White men	Clinton (D)	37	Clinton (D)	38	Gore (D)	36	Kerry (D)	37	Obama (D)	41	Obama (D)	35	Clinton (D)	31
	Bush (R)	40	Dole (R)	49	Bush (R)	60	Bush (R)	62	McCain (R)	57	Romney (R)	62	Trump (R)	62
	Perot (I)	22	Perot (I)	11	Ind.	3	Ind.	*	Ind.	--	Ind.	--	Ind.	5
White women	Clinton (D)	41	Clinton (D)	48	Gore (D)	48	Kerry (D)	44	Obama (D)	46	Obama (D)	42	Clinton (D)	43
	Bush (R)	41	Dole (R)	43	Bush (R)	49	Bush (R)	55	McCain (R)	53	Romney (R)	56	Trump (R)	52
	Perot (I)	19	Perot (I)	8	Ind.	2	Ind.	*	Ind.	--	Ind.	--	Ind.	4
Black men	Clinton (D)	77	Clinton (D)	78	Gore (D)	85	Kerry (D)	86	Obama (D)	95	Obama (D)	87	Clinton (D)	82
	Bush (R)	14	Dole (R)	15	Bush (R)	12	Bush (R)	13	McCain (R)	5	Romney (R)	11	Trump (R)	13
	Perot (I)	9	Perot (I)	5	Ind.	1	Ind.	*	Ind.	--	Ind.	--	Ind.	5
Black women	Clinton (D)	87	Clinton (D)	88	Gore (D)	94	Kerry (D)	90	Obama (D)	96	Obama (D)	96	Clinton (D)	94
	Bush (R)	8	Dole (R)	8	Bush (R)	6	Bush (R)	10	McCain (R)	3	Romney (R)	3	Trump (R)	4
	Perot (I)	6	Perot (I)	2	Ind.	*	Ind.	0	Ind.	--	Ind.	--	Ind.	1
Latino men	Clinton (D)	63	Clinton (D)	65	Gore (D)	60	Kerry (D)	50	Obama (D)	64	Obama (D)	65	Clinton (D)	63
	Bush (R)	24	Dole (R)	25	Bush (R)	37	Bush (R)	47	McCain (R)	33	Romney (R)	33	Trump (R)	32
	Perot (I)	13	Perot (I)	8	Ind.	3	Ind.	2	Ind.	--	Ind.	--	Ind.	5
Lation women	Clinton (D)	55	Clinton (D)	78	Gore (D)	63	Kerry (D)	57	Obama (D)	68	Obama (D)	76	Clinton (D)	69
	Bush (R)	28	Dole (R)	17	Bush (R)	34	Bush (R)	41	McCain (R)	30	Romney (R)	23	Trump (R)	25
	Perot (I)	17	Perot (I)	4	Ind.	2	Ind.	2	Ind.	--	Ind.	--	Ind.	5

AGE by RACE	1992		1996		2000		2004		2008		2012		2016	
Whites 18-29	Clinton (D)	38	Clinton (D)	45	Gore (D)	39	Kerry (D)	44	Obama (D)	54	Obama (D)	44	Clinton (D)	43
	Bush (R)	38	Dole (R)	41	Bush (R)	55	Bush (R)	55	McCain (R)	44	Romney (R)	51	Trump (R)	47
	Perot (I)	24	Perot (I)	11	Ind.	5	Ind.	*	Ind.	--	Ind.	--	Ind.	
Blacks 18-29	Clinton (D)	85	Clinton (D)	83	Gore (D)	91	Kerry (D)	88	Obama (D)	95	Obama (D)	91	Clinton (D)	85
	Bush (R)	7	Dole (R)	11	Bush (R)	8	Bush (R)	12	McCain (R)	4	Romney (R)	8	Trump (R)	9

	1992	1996	2000	2004	2008	2012	2016
	Perot (I) 8	Perot (I) 6	Ind. 1	Ind. *	Ind. --	Ind. --	Ind. 5
Whites 30-44	Clinton (D) 36	Clinton (D) 41	Gore (D) 41	Kerry (D) 37	Obama (D) 41	Obama (D) 38	Clinton (D) 37
	Bush (R) 41	Dole (R) 47	Bush (R) 56	Bush (R) 62	McCain (R) 57	Romney (R) 59	Trump (R) 54
	Perot (I) 23	Perot (I) 10	Ind. 2	Ind. 1	Ind. --	Ind. --	Ind. 7
Blacks 30-44	Clinton (D) 81	Clinton (D) 84	Gore (D) 91	Kerry (D) 88	Obama (D) 96	Obama (D) 94	Clinton (D) 89
	Bush (R) 12	Dole (R) 11	Bush (R) 7	Bush (R) 11	McCain (R) 4	Romney (R) 5	Trump (R) 7
	Perot (I) 7	Perot (I) 3	Ind. *	Ind. *	Ind. --	Ind. --	Ind. 3
Whites 45-59	Clinton (D) 37	Clinton (D) 43	Gore (D) 42	Kerry (D) 42	Obama (D) 42	Obama (D) 37	Clinton (D) 32
	Bush (R) 42	Dole (R) 46	Bush (R) 54	Bush (R) 58	McCain (R) 56	Romney (R) 62	Trump (R) 64
	Perot (I) 21	Perot (I) 9	Ind. 2	Ind. *	Ind. --	Ind. --	Ind. 3
Blacks 45-59	Clinton (D) 79	Clinton (D) 85	Gore (D) 89	Kerry (D) 88	Obama (D) 97	Obama (D) 93	Clinton (D) 89
	Bush (R) 14	Dole (R) 12	Bush (R) 9	Bush (R) 12	McCain (R) 3	Romney (R) 7	Trump (R) 9
	Perot (I) 7	Perot (I) 3	Ind. 1	Ind. *	Ind. --	Ind. --	Ind. 1
Whites 60 and older	Clinton (D) 47	Clinton (D) 45	Gore (D) 46	Kerry (D) 42	Obama (D) 41	Obama (D) 40	Clinton (D) 39
	Bush (R) 40	Dole (R) 47	Bush (R) 52	Bush (R) 58	McCain (R) 57	Romney (R) 59	Trump (R) 57
	Perot (I) 13	Perot (I) 7	Ind. 2	Ind. *	Ind. --	Ind. --	Ind. 3
Blacks 60 and older	Clinton (D) 88	Clinton (D) 82	Gore (D) 87	Kerry (D) 90	Obama (D) 95	Obama (D) 93	Clinton (D) 92
	Bush (R) 8	Dole (R) 16	Bush (R) 11	Bush (R) 9	McCain (R) 4	Romney (R) 7	Trump (R) 7
	Perot (I) 5	Perot (I) 1	Ind. 1	Ind. 0	Ind. --	Ind. --	Ind. 0
REGION	**1992**	**1996**	**2000**	**2004**	**2008**	**2012**	**2016**
From the East	Clinton (D) 47	Clinton (D) 55	Gore (D) 56	Kerry (D) 56	Obama (D) 59	Obama (D) 57	Clinton (D) 56
	Bush (R) 35	Dole (R) 34	Bush (R) 39	Bush (R) 43	McCain (R) 40	Romney (R) 42	Trump (R) 39
	Perot (I) 18	Perot (I) 9	Ind. 3	Ind. 1	Ind. --	Ind. --	Ind. 4
From the Midwest	Clinton (D) 42	Clinton (D) 48	Gore (D) 48	Kerry (D) 48	Obama (D) 54	Obama (D) 49	Clinton (D) 44
	Bush (R) 37	Dole (R) 41	Bush (R) 49	Bush (R) 51	McCain (R) 44	Romney (R) 49	Trump (R) 50
	Perot (I) 21	Perot (I) 10	Ind. 2	Ind. *	Ind. --	Ind. --	Ind. 5
From the South	Clinton (D) 41	Clinton (D) 46	Gore (D) 43	Kerry (D) 42	Obama (D) 45	Obama (D) 44	Clinton (D) 43
	Bush (R) 43	Dole (R) 46	Bush (R) 55	Bush (R) 58	McCain (R) 54	Romney (R) 54	Trump (R) 53
	Perot (I) 16	Perot (I) 7	Ind. 1	Ind. --	Ind. --	Ind. --	Ind. 4
From the West	Clinton (D) 43	Clinton (D) 48	Gore (D) 48	Kerry (D) 50	Obama (D) 57	Obama (D) 56	Clinton (D) 53
	Bush (R) 34	Dole (R) 40	Bush (R) 46	Bush (R) 49	McCain (R) 40	Romney (R) 42	Trump (R) 39
	Perot (I) 23	Perot (I) 8	Ind. 4	Ind. 1	Ind. --	Ind. --	Ind. --
REGION and RACE	**1992**	**1996**	**2000**	**2004**	**2008**	**2012**	**2016**
Whites in the East	Clinton (D) 44	Clinton (D) 51	Gore (D) 52	Kerry (D) 50	Obama (D) 52	Obama (D) 46	Clinton (D) 45
	Bush (R) 36	Dole (R) 37	Bush (R) 44	Bush (R) 49	McCain (R) 47	Romney (R) 52	Trump (R) 49
	Perot (I) 19	Perot (I) 10	Ind. 4	Ind. *	Ind. --	Ind. --	Ind. 4
Blacks in the East	Clinton (D) 78	Clinton (D) 85	Gore (D) 90	Kerry (D) 86	Obama (D) 97	Obama (D) 94	Clinton (D) 93
	Bush (R) 13	Dole (R) 12	Bush (R) 9	Bush (R) 13	McCain (R) 2	Romney (R) 6	Trump (R) 5
	Perot (I) 9	Perot (I) 3	Ind. 1	Ind. *	Ind. --	Ind. --	Ind. 2
Whites in the Midwest	Clinton (D) 40	Clinton (D) 45	Gore (D) 44	Kerry (D) 43	Obama (D) 47	Obama (D) 41	Clinton (D) 37
	Bush (R) 39	Dole (R) 43	Bush (R) 53	Bush (R) 56	McCain (R) 51	Romney (R) 57	Trump (R) 57
	Perot (I) 22	Perot (I) 10	Ind. 2	Ind. *	Ind. --	Ind. --	Ind. 5
Blacks in the Midwest	Clinton (D) 88	Clinton (D) 79	Gore (D) 89	Kerry (D) 90	Obama (D) 96	Obama (D) 95	Clinton (D) 85
	Bush (R) 8	Dole (R) 16	Bush (R) 8	Bush (R) 10	McCain (R) 4	Romney (R) 5	Trump (R) 11
	Perot (I) 4	Perot (I) 4	Ind. 1	Ind. 0	Ind. --	Ind. --	Ind. 4
Whites in the South	Clinton (D) 34	Clinton (D) 36	Gore (D) 31	Kerry (D) 29	Obama (D) 30	Obama (D) 28	Clinton (D) 28
	Bush (R) 49	Dole (R) 56	Bush (R) 67	Bush (R) 70	McCain (R) 69	Romney (R) 70	Trump (R) 68
	Perot (I) 18	Perot (I) 8	Ind. 1	Ind. *	Ind. --	Ind. --	Ind. 4
Blacks in the South	Clinton (D) 83	Clinton (D) 87	Gore (D) 91	Kerry (D) 90	Obama (D) 95	Obama (D) 92	Clinton (D) 88
	Bush (R) 11	Dole (R) 10	Bush (R) 8	Bush (R) 9	McCain (R) 3	Romney (R) 8	Trump (R) 9
	Perot (I) 6	Perot (I) 3	Ind. *	Ind. *	Ind. --	Ind. --	Ind. 3
Whites in the West	Clinton (D) 39	Clinton (D) 43	Gore (D) 43	Kerry (D) 45	Obama (D) 49	Obama (D) 46	Clinton (D) 45
	Bush (R) 37	Dole (R) 44	Bush (R) 51	Bush (R) 54	McCain (R) 48	Romney (R) 51	Trump (R) 47
	Perot (I) 24	Perot (I) 9	Ind. 4	Ind. 1	Ind. --	Ind. --	Ind. 5
Blacks in the West	Clinton (D) 84	Clinton (D) 77	Gore (D) 85	Kerry (D) 80	Obama (D) 91	Obama (D) 89	Clinton (D) 90
	Bush (R) 5	Dole (R) 14	Bush (R) 11	Bush (R) 18	McCain (R) 8	Romney (R) 5	Trump (R) 7
	Perot (I) 10	Perot (I) 7	Ind. 1	Ind. 0	Ind. --	Ind. --	Ind. 3

Vital Statistics on Congress

Vital Statistics on Congress, first published in 1980, long ago became the go-to source of impartial data on the United States Congress. Vital Statistics' purpose is to collect and provide useful data on America's first branch of government, including data on the composition of its membership, its formal procedure (such as the use of the filibuster), informal norms, party structure, and staff. With some chapters of data dating back nearly 100 years, Vital Statistics also documents how Congress has changed over time, illustrating, for example, the increasing polarization of Congress and the diversifying demographics of those who are elected to serve.

Vital Statistics began as a joint effort undertaken by Thomas E. Mann of Brookings and Norman J. Ornstein of the American Enterprise Institute, in collaboration with Michael Malbin of the Campaign Finance Institute. The datasets were published in print until 2013 when the project migrated online for the first time. This year, Brookings' Molly E. Reynolds spearheaded Vital Statistics' most recent update.

The Almanac team obtained permission from the Brookings Institution to provide select tables of data relevant to Almanac readers. The following tables can be found in this section:

- 1-1 Apportionment of Congressional Seats, by Region and State, 1910 - 2010 (435 seats)
- 1-3 Democratic and Republican Seats in the House, by Region, 69th - 116th Congresses, 1925–2019
- 1-5 Democratic and Republican Seats in the Senate, by Region, 69th-116th Congresses, 1925-2019
- 1-16 African Americans in Congress, 41st - 116th Congresses, 1869 - 2019
- 1-17 Asian Americans in Congress, 58th - 116th Congresses, 1903-2019
- 1-18 Hispanic Americans in Congress, 41st - 116th Congresses, 1869 - 2019
- 1-19 Women in Congress, 65th - 116th Congresses, 1917 - 2019
- 1-20 Political Parties of Senators and Representatives, 34th - 116th Congresses, 1855 – 2019
- 2-4 Losses by the President's Party in Midterm Elections, 1862 - 2018
- 2-5 House Seats That Changed Party, 1954 - 2018
- 2-6 Senate Seats That Changed Party, 1954 - 2018
- 2-7 House Incumbents Retired, Defeated, or Reelected, 1946 - 2018
- 2-8 Senate Incumbents Retired, Defeated, or Reelected, 1946 - 2018
- 2-9 House and Senate Retirements by Party, 1930 - 2018
- 2-10 Defeated House Incumbents, 1946 - 2018
- 2-11 Defeated Senate Incumbents, 1946 – 2018

The full Vital Statistics on Congress report contains a great deal more data and information that Almanac readers may find useful. For more information, visit www.brookings.edu/multi-chapter-report/vital-statistics-on-congress.

Supplemental text, which includes any footnote definitions, is available for all tables on pages 2035-2039.

Table 1-1 Apportionment of Congressional Seats, by Region and State, 1910-2010 (435 seats)

Region and State	1910	1920	1930	1940	1950	1960	1970	1980	1990	2000	2010
South	104	-	102	105	106	106	108	116	125	131	138
Alabama	10	-	9	9	9	8	7	7	7	7	7
Arkansas	7	-	7	7	6	4	4	4	4	4	4
Florida	4	-	5	6	8	12	15	19	23	25	27
Georgia	12	-	10	10	10	10	10	19	11	13	14
Louisiana	8	-	8	8	8	8	8	8	7	7	6
Mississippi	8	-	7	7	6	5	5	5	5	4	4
North Carolina	10	-	11	12	12	11	11	11	12	13	13
South Carolina	7	-	6	6	6	6	6	6	6	6	7
Tennessee	10	-	19	10	9	9	8	9	9	9	9
Texas	18	-	21	21	22	23	24	27	30	32	36
Virginia	10	-	9	9	10	10	10	10	11	11	11
Border	47	-	43	42	38	36	35	34	32	31	30
Kentucky	11	-	9	9	8	7	7	7	6	6	6
Maryland	6	-	6	6	7	8	8	8	8	8	8
Missouri	16	-	13	13	11	10	10	9	9	9	8
Oklahoma	8	-	9	8	6	6	6	6	6	5	5
West Virginia	6	-	6	6	6	5	4	4	3	3	3
New England	32	-	29	28	28	25	25	24	23	22	21
Connecticut	5	-	6	6	6	6	6	6	6	5	5
Maine	4	-	3	3	3	2	2	2	2	2	2
Massachusetts	16	-	13	13	11	10	10	9	9	9	9
New Hampshire	2	-	2	2	2	2	2	2	2	2	2
Rhode Island	3	-	2	2	2	2	2	2	2	2	2
Vermont	2	-	1	1	1	1	1	1	1	1	1
Mid-Atlantic	32	-	94	93	88	84	80	72	66	62	58
Delaware	1	-	1	1	1	1	1	1	1	1	1
New Jersey	12	-	14	14	14	15	15	4	13	3	2
New York	43	-	45	45	43	41	39	34	31	29	27
Pennsylvania	36	-	44	33	30	27	80	72	66	62	58
Midwest	86	-	90	87	87	88	86	80	74	69	65
Illinois	27	-	27	26	25	24	24	22	20	19	18
Indiana	13	-	12	11	11	11	11	10	10	9	9
Michigan	13	-	17	17	18	19	19	18	16	15	14
Ohio	22	-	24	23	23	24	23	21	22	18	16
Wisconsin	11	-	10	10	10	10	9	9	11	8	8

Region and State	1910	1920	1930	1940	1950	1960	1970	1980	1990	2000	2010
Plains	41	-	32	31	31	27	25	24	22	22	21
Iowa	11	-	9	8	8	7	6	6	5	5	4
Kansas	8	-	7	6	6	5	5	5	4	4	4
Minnesota	10	-	9	9	9	8	8	8	8	8	8
Nebraska	6	-	5	4	4	3	3	3	3	3	3
North Dakota	3	-	2	2	2	2	1	1	1	1	1
South Dakota	3	-	2	2	2	2	2	1	1	1	1
Rocky Mountains	14	-	14	16	16	17	11	19	24	28	31
Arizona	1	-	1	2	2	3	4	5	6	8	9
Colorado	4	-	4	4	4	4	5	6	6	7	7
Idaho	2	-	2	2	2	2	2	2	2	2	2
Montana	2	-	2	2	2	2	2	2	1	1	1
Nevada	1	-	1	1	1	1	1	4	3	2	2
New Mexico	1	-	1	2	2	2	2	3	3	3	3
Utah	2	-	2	2	2	2	2	3	3	3	4
Wyoming	1	-	1	1	1	1	1	1	1	1	1
Pacific Coast	19	-	29	33	43	52	57	61	69	70	71
Alaska	-	-			1	1	1	1	1	1	1
California	11	-	20	23	30	38	43	45	52	53	53
Hawaii	-	-			1	2	2	2	2	2	2
Oregon	3	-	3	4	4	4	4	5	5	5	5
Washington	5	-	6	6	7	7	7	8	9	9	10

Table 1-3 Democratic and Republican Seats in the House, by Region, 69th - 116th Congresses, 1925 – 2019

Congress	69th 1925-1926		75th 1937-1938		81st 1949-1950		87th 1961-1962		93rd 1973-1974		96th 1979-1980		97th 1981-1982		98th 1983-1984		101st 1989-1990		102nd 1991-1992		103rd 1993-1994	
Region	D	R	D	R	D	R	D	R	D	R	D	R	D	R	D	R	D	R	D	R	D	R
South																						
Percent	54.9	1.2	29.8	2.2	39.2	1.2	37.8	3.4	30.4	17.7	27.9	19.7	28.4	20.3	30.2	21.0	29.3	22.4	28.8	23.4	29.8	27.3
Seats	101	3	99	2	103	2	99	6	73	34	77	31	69	39	81	35	76	39	77	39	77	48
Border																						
Percent	14.7	7.8	12.0	2.2	14.1	2.9	12.2	3.4	11.3	4.2	9.8	5.1	9.9	5.7	9.7	4.8	8.9	6.3	8.6	6.6	8.1	6.3
Seats	27	19	40	2	37	5	32	6	27	8	27	8	24	11	26	8	23	11	23	11	21	11
New England																						
Percent	2.2	11.4	3.9	17.6	4.2	9.9	5.3	8.0	6.3	5.2	6.5	4.5	6.6	4.7	6.0	4.8	5.4	5.7	6.0	4.2	5.4	4.5
Seats	4	28	13	16	11	17	14	14	15	10	18	7	16	9	16	8	14	10	16	7	14	8
Mid-Atlantic																						
Percent	13.0	26.9	19.3	33.0	17.1	27.5	16.4	25.9	17.9	19.3	18.5	18.5	17.7	19.3	16.0	17.4	16.2	17.2	15.4	18.6	14.0	17.0
Seats	24	66	64	30	45	47	43	45	43	37	51	29	43	37	43	29	42	30	41	31	36	30
Midwest																						
Percent	7.6	28.2	19.6	19.8	14.4	28.7	13.4	29.3	13.3	27.6	17.0	24.2	17.7	22.4	16.4	21.6	18.1	18.4	18.4	18.6	16.7	17.6
Seats	14	69	65	18	38	49	35	51	32	53	47	38	43	43	44	36	47	32	49	31	43	31
Plains																						
Percent	3.3	13.5	3.9	17.6	1.9	15.2	2.3	14.4	3.8	8.3	3.6	9.6	3.7	8.3	4.5	7.2	4.6	6.9	4.9	6.6	4.7	5.7
Seats	6	33	13	16	5	26	6	25	9	16	10	15	9	16	12	12	12	12	13	11	12	10
Rocky Mountains																						
Percent	2.2	4.1	4.2	1.1	4.6	2.3	4.2	2.9	3.3	5.7	3.3	6.4	2.9	6.3	3.0	9.6	3.5	8.6	4.1	7.8	4.3	7.4
Seats	4	10	14	1	12	4	11	5	8	11	9	10	7	12	8	16	9	15	11	13	11	13
Pacific Coast																						
Percent	2.2	6.9	7.2	6.6	4.6	12.3	8.4	12.1	13.8	12.0	13.4	12.1	13.2	13.0	14.2	13.8	13.9	14.4	13.9	14.4	17.1	14.2
Seats	4	17	24	6	12	21	22	21	33	23	37	19	32	25	38	23	36	25	37	24	44	25
Total Seats	184	245	332	91	263	171	262	174	240	192	276	157	243	192	268	167	259	174	267	167	258	176

Table 1-3 Democratic and Republican Seats in the House, by Region, 69th - 116th Congresses, 1925 – 2019 (continued)

Congress	104th 1995-1996		105th 1997-1998		106th 1999-2000		107th 2001-2002		108th 2003-2004		109th 2005-2006		110th 2007-2008		111th 2009-2010		112th 2011-2012		113th 2013-2014		114th 2015-2016		115th 2017-2018		116th 2019-2020	
Region	D	R	D	R	D	R	D	R	D	R	D	R	D	R	D	R	D	R	D	R	D	R	D	R	D	R
South																										
Percent	29.9	27.8	26.1	31.3	25.6	31.5	25.1	32.3	26.8	33.2	24.4	35.3	23.2	38.1	23.0	40.4	19.2	38.8	20.0	41.6	19.7	40.9	20.1	41.1	20.4	45.0
Seats	61	64	54	71	54	70	53	71	55	76	49	82	54	77	59	72	37	94	40	97a	37	101	39	99	48	90
Border																										
Percent	7.8	7.0	6.3	8.4	6.2	8.6	5.7	9.1	6.8	7.4	7.0	7.3	6.4	7.9	6.3	8.4	6.7	7.4	5.5	8.2	5.3	8.1	5.2	8.3	4.7	9.5
Seats	16	16	13	19	13	19	12	20	14	17	14	17	15	16	16	15	13	18	11	19	10	20	10	20	11	19
New England																										
Percent	6.9	3.5	8.7	1.8	8.5	1.8	8.1	2.3	7.8	2.2	8.0	2.2	9.0	0.5	8.6	0.0	10.4	0.8	10.5	0.0	10.1	0.8	10.3	0.4	8.9	0.0
Seats	14	8	18	4	18	4	17	5	16	5	16	5	21	1	22	0	20	2	21	0	19	2	20	1	21	0
Mid-Atlantic																										
Percent	16.2	14.3	16.9	13.7	17.1	13.5	17.1	13.6	16.1	12.7	16.9	12.1	17.6	10.4	18.0	9.0	18.7	10.7	16.5	10.7	16.0	11.3	16.0	1.2	17.9	8.0
Seats	33	33	35	31	36	30	36	30	33	29	34	28	41	21	46	16	36	26	33	25	30	28	31	27	42	16
Midwest																										
Percent	15.7	18.3	17.9	16.3	17.5	16.7	17.5	16.8	13.7	17.9	13.9	17.7	14.2	17.8	15.2	16.3	13.0	18.2	12.4	16.7	12.8	16.6	12.9	16.6	12.3	18.0
Seats	32	42	37	37	37	37	37	37	28	41	28	41	33	36	39c	29	25	44	25b	39	24	41	25	40	29	36
Plains																										
Percent	3.9	6.1	3.9	6.2	4.3	5.9	3.8	6.4	3.4	6.6	4.0	6.0	5.2	5.0	4.3	6.2	3.6	6.2	3.5	6.0	3.7	5.7	3.1	6.2	3.8	6.0
Seats	8	14	8	14	9	13	8	14	7	15	8	14	12	10	11	11	7	15	7	14	7	14	6	15	9	12
Rocky Mountains																										
Percent	2.9	7.8	1.9	8.8	2.4	8.6	2.8	8.2	3.4	9.2	4.0	8.6	4.7	8.4	6.6	6.2	5.2	7.4	6.5	7.7	5.3	8.5	6.2	7.9	6.8	7.5
Seats	6	18	4	20	5	19	6	18	7	21	8	20	11	17	17	11	10	18	13	18	10	21	12	19	16	15
Pacific Coast																										
Percent	16.7	15.2	18.4	13.7	18.5	13.5	19.9	11.4	22.0	10.9	21.9	10.8	19.7	11.9	18.0	13.5	23.3	10.3	25.0	9.0	27.1	8.1	26.3	8.3	25.1	6.0
Seats	34	35	38	31	39	30	42	25	45	25	44	25	46	24	46	24	45	25	50	21	51	20	51	20	59	12
Total Seats	204	230	207	227	211	222	211	220	205	229	201	232	233	202	256	178	193	242	202	233	188	247	194	241	235	199

Table 1-5 Democratic and Republican Seats in the Senate, by Region, 69th-116th Congresses, 1925-2019

Congress	1925-1926		1937-1938		1949-1950		1961-1962		1973-1974		1981-1982		1989-1990		1991-1992		1993-1994		1995-1996		1997-1998	
Region	D	R	D	R	D	R	D	R	D	R	D	R	D	R	D	R	D	R	D	R	D	R
South																						
Percent	53.7	0	28.9	0	40.7	0	33.8	0	25	16.7	23.9	18.9	27.3	15.6	26.8	15.9	22.8	20.9	19.1	24.5	15.6	27.3
Seats	22	0	22	0	22	0	22	0	14	7	11	10	15	7	15	7	13	9	9	13a	7	15
Border																						
Percent	12.2	9.3	13.2	0	14.8	4.8	9.2	11.4	8.9	11.9	15.2	5.7	10.9	8.9	10.7	9.1	10.5	9.3	10.6	9.4	11.1	9.1
Seats	5	5	10	0	8	2	6	4	5	5	7	3	6	4	6	4	6	4	5	5	5	5
New England																						
Percent	2.4	20.4	7.9	37.5	5.6	21.4	7.7	20	12.5	11.9	13	11.3	12.7	11.1	12.5	11.4	12.3	11.6	12.8	11.3	13.3	10.9
Seats	1	11	6	6	3	9	5	7	7	5	6	6	7	5	7	5	7	5	6	6	6	6
Mid-Atlantic																						
Percent	7.3	9.3	7.9	12.5	5.6	11.9	3.1	17.1	3.6	11.9	8.7	7.5	7.3	8.9	7.1	9.1	8.8	7	8.5	7.5	8.9	7.3
Seats	3	5	6	2	3	5	2	6	2	5	4	4	4	4	4	4	5	3	4	4	4	4
Midwest																						
Percent	2.4	16.7	10.5	6.3	3.7	19.0	10.8	8.6	10.7	9.5	13	7.5	12.7	6.7	12.5	6.8	14	4.7	12.8	7.5	13.3	7.3
Seats	1	9	8	1	2	8	7	3	6	4	6	4	7	3	7	3	8	2	6	4	6	4
Plains																						
Percent	0	20.4	7.9	18.8	3.7	23.8	4.6	25.7	12.5	11.9	6.5	17	10.9	13.3	12.5	11.4	12.3	11.6	14.9	9.4	15.6	9.1
Seats	0	11	6	3	2	10	3	9	7	5	3	9	6	6	7	5	7	5	7	5	7	5
Rocky Mountains																						
Percent	19.5	14.8	19.7	6.3	22.2	9.5	18.5	11.4	16.1	16.7	10.9	20.8	10.9	22.2	10.7	22.7	10.5	23.3	10.6	20.8	8.9	21.8
Seats	8	8	15	1	12	4	12	4	9	7	5	11	6	10	6	10	6	10	5	11	4	12
Pacific Coast																						
Percent	2.4	9.3	3.9	18.8	3.7	9.5	12.3	5.7	10.7	9.5	8.7	11.3	7.3	13.3	7.1	13.6	8.8	11.6	10.6	9.4	13.3	7.3
Seats	1	5	3	3	2	4	8	2	6	4	4	6	4	6	4	6	5	5	5	5	6	4
Total Seats	41	54	76	16	54	42	65	35	56	42	46	53	55	45	56	44	57	43	47	53	45	55

Table 1-5 Democratic and Republican Seats in the Senate, by Region, 69th-116th Congresses, 1925-2019 (continued)

Congress	1999-2000		2001-2002		2003-2004		2005-2006		2007-2008		2009-2010		2011-2012		2013-2014		2015-2016		2017-2018		2019-2020	
Region	D	R	D	R	D	R	D	R	D	R	D	R	D	R	D	R	D	R	D	R	D	R
South																						
Percent	17.8	25.5	16	28	18.8	25.5	9.1	32.7	10.2	34.7	12.7	36.6	11.8	34	11.3	35.6	6.8	35.2	6.5	36.5	6.7	35.8
Seats	8	14	8	14	9	13	4	18	5	17	7	15	6	16	6	16	3	19	3	19	3	19
Border																						
Percent	8.9	10.9	10	10	8.3	11.8	9.1	10.9	10.2	10.2	9.1	12.2	9.8	10.6	9.4	11.1	9.1	11.1	8.7	11.5	6.7	13.2
Seats	4	6	5	5	4	6	4	6	5	5	5	5	5	5	5	5	4	6	4	6	3	7
New England																						
Percent	13.3	10.9	12	12	12.5	9.8	13.6	9.1	12.2	8.2	12.7	7.3	11.8	8.5	15.1	4.4	18.2	3.7	19.5	1.9	20	1.9
Seats	6	6	6	6	6	5	6	5	6	4	7	3	6	4	8	2	8	2	9	1	9	1
Mid-Atlantic																						
Percent	11.1	5.5	12	4	12.5	3.9	13.6	3.6	14.3	2	12.7	2.4	13.7	2.1	13.2	2.2	15.9	1.9	15.2	1.9	15.6	1.9
Seats	5	3	6	2	6	2	6	2	7	1	7	1	7	1	7	1	7	1	7	1	7	1
Midwest																						
Percent	11.1	9.1	12	8	12.5	7.8	15.9	5.5	16.3	4.1	12.7	4.9	9.8	10.6	11.3	8.9	13.6	7.4	15.0	5.7	13.3	7.5
Seats	5	5	6	4	6	4	7	3	8	2	7b	2	5	5	6	4	6	4	7	3	6	4
Plains																						
Percent	15.6	9.1	16	8	14.6	9.8	13.6	10.9	12.2	12.2	10.9	12.2	11.8	12.8	9.4	15.6	6.8	16.7	6.5	17.3	4.4	18.9
Seats	7	5	8	4	7	5	6	6	6	6	6c	5	6	6	5	7	3	9	3	9	2	10
Rocky Mountains																						
Percent	8.9	21.8	8	24	6.3	25.5	9.1	21.8	10.2	22.4	12.7	22	13.7	19.1	13.2	20	11.4	20.4	10.9	21.2	15.6	17
Seats	4	12	4	12	3	13	4	12	5	11	7	9	7	9	7	9	5	11	5	11	7	9
Pacific Coast																						
Percent	13.3	7.3	14	6	14.6	5.9	15.9	5.5	14.3	6.1	16.4	2.4	17.6	2.1	17.0	2.2	18.2	3.7	17.3	3.9	17.8	3.8
Seats	6	4	7	3	7	3	7	3	7	3	9	1	9	1	9	1	8	2	8	2	8	2
Total Seats	45	55	50	50	48	51	44	55	49	49	55	41	51	47	53	45	44	54	46	52	45	t53

Table 1-16 African Americans in Congress, 41st - 116th Congresses, 1869 – 2019

Congress	House D	House R	Senate D	Senate R	Congress	House D	House R	Senate D	Senate R
41st (1869)		2		1	86th (1959)	3			
42nd (1871)		5			87th (1961)	3			
43rd (1873)		7			88th (1963)	4			
44th (1875)		7		1	89th (1965)	5			
45th (1877)		3		1	90th (1967)	5			1
46th (1879)				1	91st (1969)	9			1
47th (1881)		2			92nd (1971)	13			1
48th (1883)		2			93rd (1973)	16			1
49th (1885)		2			94th (1975)	16			1
50th (1887)					95th (1977)	15			1
51st (1889)		3			96th (1979)	15			
52nd (1891)		1			97th (1981)	17			
53rd (1893)		1			98th (1983)	20			
54th (1895)		1			99th (1985)	20			
55th (1897)		1			100th (1987)	22			
56th (1899)a		1			101st (1989)	23			
71st (1929)		1			102nd (1991)	25	1		
72nd (1931)		1			103rd (1993)	38	1	1	
73rd (1933)		1			104th (1995)	37	2	1	
74th (1935)	1				105th (1997)	36	1	1	
75th (1937)	1				106th (1999)	36	1		
76th (1939)	1				107th (2001)	35	1		
77th (1941)	1				108th (2003)	37			
78th (1943)	1				109th (2005)	40		1	
79th (1945)	2				110th (2007)	40		1	
80th (1947)	2				111thb (2009)	39			
81st (1949)	2				112th (2011)	40	2		
82nd (1951)	2				113thc (2013)	41			
83rd (1953)	2				114th (2015)	42	2	1	1
84th (1955)	3				115th (2017)	45	2	2	1
85th (1957)	3				116th (2019)	52	1	2	1

Table 1-17 Asian Americans in Congress, 58th - 116th Congresses, 1903-2019

Congress	House D	House R	Senate D	Senate R
58th (1903)				
59th (1905)				
60th (1907)				
61st (1909)				
62nd (1911)				
63rd (1913)				
64th (1915)				
65th (1917)				
66th (1919)				
67th (1921)				
68th (1923)				
69th (1925)				
70th (1927)				
71st (1929)				
72nd (1931)				
73rd (1933)				
74th (1935)				
75th (1937)				
76th (1939)				
77th (1941)				
78th (1943)				
79th (1945)				
80th (1947)				
81st (1949)				
82nd (1951)				
83rd (1953)				
84th (1955)				
85th (1957)	1			
86th (1959)	2			1
87th (1961)	2			1

Congress	House D	House R	Senate D	Senate R
88th (1963)	1		1	1
89th (1965)	2		1	1
90th (1967)	2		1	1
91st (1969)	2		1	1
92nd (1971)	2		1	1
93rd (1973)	2			1
94th (1975)	2		1	1
95th (1977)	2		2	1
96th (1979)	3		2	1
97th (1981)	3		2	1
98th (1983)	3		2	
99th (1985)	3		2	
100th (1987)	3	1	2	
101st (1989)	3	1	3	
102nd (1991)	3		2	
103rd (1993)	4	1	2	
104th (1995)	4	1	2	
105th (1997)	4	1	2	
106th (1999)	4		2	
107th (2001)	5		2	
108th (2003)	4		2	
109th (2005)	4	1	2	
110th (2007)	5	1	2	
111th (2009)	4	1	2	
112th (2011)	7	1	2	
113th (2013)	10	0	1	0
114th (2015)	11	0	1	0
115th (2017)	12	0	3	0
116th (2019)	12	0	3	0

Table 1-18 Hispanic Americans in Congress, 41st - 116th Congresses, 1869 – 2019

Congress	House D	House R	Senate D	Senate R
41st (1869)				
42nd (1871)				
43rd (1873)				
63rd (1913)	1			
64th (1915)	1	1		
65th (1917)	1			
66th (1919)	1	1		
67th (1921)	1	1		
68th (1923)	1			
69th (1925)	1			
70th (1927)	1			1
71st (1929)				
72nd (1931)	2			
73rd (1933)	2			
74th (1935)	1		1	
75th (1937)	1		1	
76th (1939)	1		1	
77th (1941)			1	
78th (1943)	1		1	
79th (1945)	1		1	
80th (1947)	1		1	
81st (1949)	1		1	
82nd (1951)	1		1	
83rd (1953)	1		1	
84th (1955)	1		1	
85th (1957)	1		1	
86th (1959)	1		1	
87th (1961)	2		1	
88th (1963)	3		1	

Congress	House D	House R	Senate D	Senate R
89th (1965)	3		1	
90th (1967)	3		1	
91st (1969)	3	1	1	
92nd (1971)	4	1	1	
93rd (1973)	4	1	1	
94th (1975)	4	1		
95th (1977)	4	1		
96th (1979)	5	1		
97th (1981)	6	1		
98th (1983)	9	1		
99th (1985)	10	1		
100th (1987)	10	1		
101st (1989)	10	1		
102nd (1991)	10	1		
103rd (1993)	14	3		
104th (1995)	14	3		
105th (1997)	14	3		
106th (1999)	16	3		
107th (2001)	16	3		
108th (2003)	18	4		
109th (2005)	19	4	1	1
110th (2007)	20	3	2	1
111th (2009)	21	3	1	1
112th (2011)	21	3	1	1
113th (2013)	23	5	1	2
114th (2015)	23	9	1	2
115th (2017)	28	10	2	2
116th (2019)	32	7	2	2

Table 1-19 Women in Congress, 65th - 116th Congresses, 1917 – 2019

Congress	House D	House R	Senate D	Senate R	Congress	House D	House R	Senate D	Senate R
65th (1917)		1			91st (1969)	6	4		1
66th (1919)					92nd (1971)	10	3		1
67th (1921)		2		1	93rd (1973)	14	2	1	
68th (1923)		1			94th (1975)	14	5		
69th (1925)	1	2			95th (1977)	13	5		
70th (1927)	2	3			96th (1979)	11	5	1	1
71st (1929)	4	5			97th (1981)	10	9		2
72nd (1931)	4	3	1		98th (1983)	13	9		2
73rd (1933)	4	3	1		99th (1985)	13	9		2
74th (1935)	4	2	2		100th (1987)	12	11	1	1
75th (1937)	4	1	2		101st (1989)	14	11	1	1
76th (1939)	4	4	1		102nd (1991)	19	9	1	1
77th (1941)	4	5	1		103rd (1993)	36	12	5	1
78th (1943)	2	6	1		104th (1995)	31	17	5	3
79th (1945)	6	5			105th (1997)	35	16	6	3
80th (1947)	3	4		1	106th (1999)	40	16	6	3
81st (1949)	5	4		1	107th (2001)	41	18	10	3
82nd (1951)	4	6		1	108th (2003)	38	21	9	5
83rd (1953)	5	7		1	109th (2005)	42	23	9	5
84th (1955)	10	7		1	110th (2007)	50	21	11	5
85th (1957)	9	6		1	111th (2009)	57	17	13	4
86th (1959)	9	8		1	112th (2011)	52	24	12	5
87th (1961)	11	7	1	1	113th (2013)	56	20	16	4
88th (1963)	6	6	1	1	114th (2015)	62	22	14	6
89th (1965)	7	4	1	1	115th (2017)	62	21	16	5
90th (1967)	5	5		1	116th (2019)	89	13	17	8

Table 1-20 Political Parties of Senators and Representatives, 34th - 116th Congresses, 1855 – 2019

Congress	Senate					House of Representatives				
	# of Senators	D	R	Other	Vacant	# of Representatives	D	R	Other	Vacant
34th (1855 - 1857)	62	42	15	5		234	83	108	43	
35th (1857 - 1859)	64	39	20	5		237	131	92	14	
36th (1859 - 1861)	66	38	26	2		237	101	113	23	
37th (1861 - 1863)	50	11	31	7	1	178	42	106	28	2
38th (1863 - 1865)	51	12	39			183	80	103		
39th (1865 - 1867)	52	10	42			191	46	145		
40th (1867 - 1869)	53	11	42			193	49	143		1
41st (1869 - 1871)	74	11	61		2	243	73	170		
42nd (1871 - 1873)	74	17	57			243	104	139		
43rd (1873 - 1875)	74	19	54		1	293	88	203		2
44th (1875 - 1877)	76	29	46		1	293	181	107	3	2
45th (1877 - 1879)	76	36	39	1		293	156	137		
46th (1879 - 1881)	76	43	33			293	150	128	14	1
47th (1881 - 1883)	76	37	37	2		293	130	152	11	
48th (1883 - 1885)	76	36	40			325	200	119	6	
49th (1885 - 1887)	76	34	41		1	325	182	140	2	1
50th (1887 - 1889)	76	37	39			325	170	151	4	
51st (1889 - 1891)	84	37	47			330	156	173	1	
52nd (1891 - 1893)	88	39	47	2		333	231	88	14	
53rd (1893 - 1895)	88	44	38	3	3	356	220	126	10	
54th (1895 - 1897)	88	39	44	5		357	104	246	7	
55th (1897 - 1899)	90	34	46	10		357	134	206	16	1
56th (1899 - 1901)	90	26	53	11		357	163	185	9	
57th (1901 - 1903)	90	29	56	3	2	357	153	198	5	1
58th (1903 - 1905)	90	32	58			386	178	207		1
59th (1905 - 1907)	90	32	58			386	136	250		
60th (1907 - 1909)	92	29	61		2	386	164	222		
61st (1909 - 1911)	92	32	59		1	391	172	219		
62nd (1911 - 1913)	92	42	49		1	391	228	162	1	
63rd (1913 - 1915)	96	51	44	1		435	290	127	18	
64th (1915 - 1917)	96	56	39	1		435	231	193	8	3
65th (1917 - 1919)	96	53	42	1		435	210[a]	216	9	
66th (1919 - 1921)	96	47	48	1		435	191	237	7	
67th (1921 - 1923)	96	37	59			435	132	300	1	2
68th (1923 - 1925)	96	43	51	2		435	207	225	3	
69th (1925 - 1927)	96	40	54	1	1	435	183	247	5	
70th (1927 - 1929)	96	47	48	1		435	195	237	3	
71st (1929 - 1931)	96	39	56	1		435	163	267	1	4
72nd (1931 - 1933)	96	47	48	1		435	216[b]	218	1	
73rd (1933 - 1935)	96	59	36	1		435	313	117	5	
74th (1935 - 1937)	96	69	25	2		435	322	103	10	
75th (1937 - 1939)	96	75	17	4		435	333	89	13	
76th (1939 - 1941)	96	69	23	4		435	262	169	4	
77th (1941 - 1943)	96	66	28	2		435	267	162	6	
78th (1943 - 1945)	96	57	38	1		435	222	209	4	
79th (1945 - 1947)	96	57	38	1		435	243	190	2	
80th (1947 - 1949)	96	45	51			435	188	246	1	

Table 1-20 Political Parties of Senators and Representatives, 34th - 116th Congresses, 1855 – 2019 (continued)

| Congress | Senate | | | | | House of Representatives | | | | |
	# of Senators	D	R	Other	Vacant	# of Representatives	D	R	Other	Vacant
81st (1949 - 1951)	96	54	42			435	263	171	1	
82nd (1951 - 1953)	96	48	47	1		435	234	199	2	
83rd (1953 - 1955)	96	46	48	2		435	213	221	1	
84th (1955 - 1957)	96	48	47	1		435	232	203		
85th (1957 - 1959)	96	49	47			435	234	201		
86th (1959 - 1961)	98	63	34			436[c]	283	153		
87th (1961 - 1963)	100	64	36			437[d]	262	175		
88th (1963 - 1965)	100	67	33			435	258	176		1
89th (1965 - 1967)	100	68	32			435	295	140		
90th (1967 - 1969)	100	64	36			435	246	187		2
91st (1969 - 1971)	100	58	42			435	243	192		
92nd (1971 - 1973)	100	54	44	2		435	255	180		
93rd (1973 - 1975)	100	56	42	2		435	239	192	1	3
94th (1975 - 1977)	100	61	37	2		435	291	144		
95th (1977 - 1979)	100	61	38	1		435	292	143		
96th (1979 - 1981)	100	58	41	1		435	276	157		2
97th (1981 - 1983)	100	46	53	1		435	243	192		
98th (1983 - 1985)	100	46	54			435	268	166		1
99th (1985 - 1987)	100	47	53			435	252	182		1
100th (1987 - 1989)	100	55	45			435	258	177		
101st (1989 - 1991)	100	55	45			435	259	174		2
102nd (1991 - 1993)	100	56	44			435	267	167	1	
103rd (1993 - 1995)	100	57	43			435	258	176	1	
104th (1995 - 1997)	100	47	53			435	204	230	1	
105th (1997 - 1999)	100	45	55			435	207	227	1	
106th (1999 - 2001)	100	45	55			435	211	223	1	
107th (2001 - 2003)	100	50	50			435	211	221	2	1
108th (2003 - 2005)	100	48	51	1		435	205	229	1	
109th (2005 - 2007)	100	44	55	1		435	201	232	1	1
110th (2007 - 2009)	100	49	49	2		435	233	202		
111th (2009 - 2011)	100	55	41	2	1	435	256	178		1
112th (2011 - 2013)	100	51	47	2		435	193	242		
113th (2013 - 2015)	100	53	45	2		435	200	233		2
114th (2015 - 2017)	100	44	54	2		435	188	247		
115th (2017 - 2019)	100	46	52	2		435	194	241		
116th (2019 - 2021)	100	45	53	2		434[e]	235	199		1

Table 2-4 Losses by the President's Party in Midterm Elections, 1862 - 2018

Year	Party holding presidency	President's party gain/loss of seats in House	President's party gain/lose of seats in Senate
1902	R	9[a]	2
1906	R	-28	3
1910	R	-57	-8
1914	D	-61	5
1918	D	-22	-6
1922	R	-77	-6
1926	R	-9	-6
1930	R	-52	-8
1934	D	9	10
1938	D	-72	-7
1942	D	-44	-9
1946	D	-55	-12
1950	D	-28	-5
1954	R	-18	-1
1958	R	-48	-12
1962	D	-4	2
1966	D	-48	-4
1970	R	-12	1
1974	R	-48	-4
1978	D	-15	-3
1982	R	-26	1
1986	R	-5	-8
1990	R	-8	-1
1994	D	-54	-8[b]
1998	D	-4	0
2002	R	8	1
2006	R	-30	-6
2010	D	-64	-6
2014	D	-13	-9
2018	R	-42	1

Table 2-5 House Seats That Changed Party, 1954 – 2018

Year	Total Changes	Incumbent defeated		Open Seat	
		D → R	R → D	D → R	R → D
1954	26	3	18	2	3
1956	20	7	7	2	4
1958	49	1	34	0	14
1960	37	23	2	6	6
1962	19	9	5	2	3
1964	55	5	39	3	8
1966	47	38	2	5	2
1968	11	5	0	2	4
1970	25	2	9	6	8
1972	21	8	3	6	4
1974	55	4	36	2	13
1976	22	7	5	3	7
1978	32	15	5	7	5
1980	41	28	3	9	1
1982	31	1	23	3	4
1984	22	13	3	5	1
1986	22	2	7	7	6
1988	9	2	4	1	2
1990	20	6	8	0	6
1992	43	19	12	10	2
1994	60	35	0	21	4
1996	31	3	16	9	3
1998	18	1	5	5	7
2000	18	2	4	6	6
2002	15	2	2	6	5
2004	13	6	2	2	3
2006	31	0	22	0	9
2008	31	5	14	0	12
2010	69	52	2	14	1
2012	29	4	15	7	3
2014	19	11	2	5	1
2016	13	1	6	2	3
2018	44	0	30	2	12

Table 2-6 Senate Seats That Changed Party, 1954 – 2018

Year	Total Changes	Incumbent defeated		Open Seat	
		D → R	R → D	D → R	R → D
1954	7	2	3	1	0
1956	8	1	3	3	1
1958	14	0	10	0	3
1960	3	1	1	1	0
1962	8	2	4	0	2
1964	4	1	3	0	0
1966	3	2	0	1	0
1968	9	5	1	2	1
1970	6	3	2	1[a]	0
1972	10	2	4	2	2
1974	6	0	2	1	3
1976	14	5	4	2	3
1978	13	5	3	3	2
1980	12	12	0	0	0
1982	3	1	1	0	1
1984	4	1	2	0	1
1986	10	0	7	1	2
1988	7	1	3	2	1
1990	1	0	1	0	0
1992	4	1	3	0	0
1994	8[b]	2	0	6	0
1996	3	0	1	2	0
1998	6	1	2	2	1
2000	8	1	5	1	1
2002	3	1	1	1[c]	0
2004	8	1	0	5	2
2006	6	0	6	0	0
2008	7	0	4[d]	0	3
2010	6[e]	2[f]	0	4	0
2012	1	0	1	0	0
2014	9	5	0	4[g]	0
2016	2	0	2	0	0
2018	6	4	1	0	1

Table 2-7 House Incumbents Retired, Defeated, or Reelected, 1946 – 2018

Year	Retired[a]	Total seeking reelection	Defeated in primaries	Defeated in general election	Total reelected	Percentage of those seeing reelection	Reelected as persentage of House membership
1946	32	398	18	52	328	82.4	75.4
1948	29	400	15	68	317	79.3	72.9
1950	29	400	6	32	362	90.5	83.2
1952	42	389	9	26	354	91.0	81.4
1954	24	407	6	22	379	93.1	87.1
1956	21	411	6	16	389	94.6	89.4
1958	33	396	3	37	356	89.9	81.8
1960	26	405	5	25	375	92.6	86.2
1962	24	402	12	22	368	91.5	84.6
1964	33	397	8	45	344	86.6	79.1
1966	22	411	8	41	362	88.1	83.2
1968	23	409	4	9	396	96.8	91.0
1970	29	401	10	12	379	94.5	87.1
1972	40	393	11	13	365	92.9	83.9
1974	43	391	8	40	343	87.7	78.9
1976	47	384	3	13	368	95.8	84.6
1978	49	382	5	19	358	93.7	82.3
1980	34	398	6	31	361	90.7	83.0
1982	40	393	10	29	354	90.1	81.4
1984	22	411	3	16	392	95.4	90.1
1986	40	394	3	6	385	97.7	88.5
1988	23	409	1	6	402	98.3	92.4
1990	27	406	1	15	390	96.1	89.7
1992	65	368	19	24	325	88.3	74.7
1994	48	387	4	34	349	90.2	80.0
1996	49	384	2	21	361	94.0	83.0
1998	33	402	1	6	395	98.3	90.8
2000	30	403	3	6	394	97.8	90.6
2002	35	398[b]	8	8	383[c]	96.2	88.0
2004	29	404	2	7	395	97.8	90.8
2006	28	403	2	22	379	94.0	87.1
2008	32	402	4[d]	19	379	94.3	87.1
2010	36	397	4	54	339	85.4	77.9
2012	39	391	13	27	351	89.8	80.7
2014	41	392	5	13	374	95.4	86.0
2016	41	392	4	8	380	96.9	87.4
2018	52	376	4	30	342	91.0	78.6

Table 2-8 Senate Incumbents Retired, Defeated, or Reelected, 1946 – 2018

Year	Not seeing reelection	Total seeking reelection[a]	Defeated in primaries	Defeated in general election	Total reelected	Reelected as percentage of those seeking reelection
1946	9	30	6	7	17	56.7
1948	8	25	2	8	15	60.0
1950	4	32	5	5	22	68.8
1952	4	29	1	10	18	62.1
1954	6	32	2	5	25	78.1
1956	5	30	0	4	26	86.7
1958	6	27	0	10	17	63.0
1960	5	29	0	2	27	93.1
1962	4	35	1	5	29	82.9
1964	3	32	0	4	28	87.5
1966	3	32	3	1	28	87.5
1968	7	27	4	4	19	70.4
1970	4	31	1	6	24	77.4
1972	6	27	2	5	20	74.1
1974	7	27	2	2	23	85.2
1976	8	25	0	9	16	64.0
1978	10	25	3	7	15	60.0
1980	5	29	4	9	16	55.2
1982	3	30	0	2	28	93.3
1984	4	29	0	3	26	89.7
1986	6	28	0	7	21	75.0
1988	6	27	0	4	23	85.2
1990	4	32	0	1	31	96.9
1992	9	28	1	4	23	82.1
1994	9	26	0	2	24	92.3
1996	13	21	1[b]	1	19	90.5
1998	5	29	0	3	26	89.7
2000	5	29	0	6	23	79.3
2002	7	27	1	2	24	88.9
2004	8	26	0	1	25	96.2
2006	5	28	1[c]	6	22	78.6
2008	5	30	0	5	25	83.3
2010	12	25	3[d]	2	21	84.0
2012	10	23	1	1	21[e]	91.3
2014	7[f]	29	0	5	23[g]	79.3
2016	5	29	0	2	27	93.1
2018	3	32	0	5	27	84.4

Table 2-9 House and Senate Retirements by Party, 1930 – 2018

Year	House		Senate	
	D	R	D	R
1930	8	15	2	5
1932	16	23	1	1
1934	29	9	3	1
1936	29	3	4	2
1938	21	5	3	1
1940	16	6	1	2
1942	20	12	0	0
1944	17	5	3	2
1946	17	15	4	3
1948	17	12	3	4
1950	12	17	3	1
1952	25	17	2	1
1954	11	13	1	1
1956	7	13	4	1
1958	6	27	0	6
1960	11	15	3	1
1962	10	14	2	2
1964	17	16	1	1
1966	14	8	1	2
1968	13	10	4	3
1970	11	19	3	1
1972	20	20	3	3
1974	23	21	3	4
1976	31	16	4	4
1978	31	18	4	5
1980	21	13	2	3
1982	19	21	1	2
1984	9	13	2	2
1986	20	20	3	3
1988	10	13	3	3
1990	10	17	0	3
1992	41	24	4	3
1994	28	20	6	3
1996	28	21	8	5
1998	17	16	3	2
2000	7	23	4	1
2002	13	22	1	5[a]
2004	12	17	5	3
2006	9	17	2	1
2008	3	24	0	5
2010	17	15	6	6
2012	20	18	7[b]	3
2014	10	14	4	3
2016	16	25	3	2
2018	18	34	0	3

Table 2-10 Defeated House Incumbents, 1946 – 2018

Election	Party	Incumbents lost	Average Terms	Consecutive terms served						
				1	2	3	1-3	4-6	7-9	10+
1946	Democrat	62	2.7	35	5	4	44	11	5	2
	Republican	7	3.6	2	0	1	3	3	1	0
	Total	69	2.8	37	5	5	47	14	6	2
1948	Democrat[a]	9	2.7	4	1	1	6	3	0	0
	Republican	73	2.2	41	3	12	56	14	2	1
	Total	82	2.3	45	4	13	62	17	2	1
1958	Democrat[b]	6	5.0	1	1	0	2	2	1	1
	Republican	34	4.3	9	0	4	13	14	6	1
	Total	40	4.4	10	1	4	15	16	7	2
1966	Democrat	43	3.3	26	6	0	32	4	1	6
	Republican	2	11.0	1	0	0	1	0	0	1
	Total	45	3.6	27	6	0	33	4	1	7
1974	Democrat	9	4.7	1	1	1	3	3	2	1
	Republican	39	3.8	11	2	6	19	15	2	3
	Total	48	4.0	12	3	7	22	18	4	4
1978	Democrat	19	4.0	3	8	2	13	2	1	3
	Republican	5	5.4	2	0	0	2	2	0	1
	Total	24	4.3	5	8	2	15	4	1	4
1980	Democrat	32	5.2	5	2	10	17	5	4	6
	Republican	5	5.3	1	0	1	2	1	1	1
	Total	37	5.2	6	2	11	19	6	5	7
1982	Democrat	4	2.9	1	0	1	2	2	0	0
	Republican[c]	23	3.0	12	3	2	17	2	2	2
	Total	27	3.0	13	3	3	19	4	2	2
1984	Democrat	16	4.1	6	1	2	9	4	1	2
	Republican	3	3.7	0	0	2	2	1	0	0
	Total	19	4.0	6	1	4	11	5	1	2
1986	Democrat	3	1.8	2	0	0	2	1	0	0
	Republican	6	1.5	4	1	1	6	0	0	0
	Total	9	1.6	6	1	1	8	1	0	0
1988	Democrat	2	12.0	0	0	0	0	0	0	2
	Republican	5	1.6	2	3	0	5	0	0	0
	Total	7	4.6	2	3	0	5	0	0	2
1990	Democrat	6	6.3	0	1	0	1	3	1	1
	Republican[d]	10	3.6	2	3	0	5	4	1	0
	Total	16	4.6	2	4	0	6	7	2	1
1992	Democrat	30	5.6	2	1	4	7	12	10	1
	Republican	13	6.8	2	0	2	4	1	6	2
	Total	43	6.0	4	1	6	11	13	16	3
1994	Democrat	37	4.2	16	3	5	24	7	2	4
	Republican	0	0.0	0	0	0	0	0	0	0
	Total	37	4.2	16	3	5	24	7	2	4
1996	Democrat[e]	3	4.7	1	0	1	2	0	0	1
	Republican	18	1.8	12	4	1	17	0	1	0
	Total	21	2.2	13	4	2	19	0	1	1
1998	Democrat	1	1.0	1	0	0	1	0	0	0
	Republican	6	1.7	3	2	1	6	0	0	0
	Total	7	1.6	4	2	1	7	0	0	0

Table 2-10 Defeated House Incumbents, 1946 – 2018 (continued)

Election	Party	Incumbents lost	Average Terms	Consecutive terms served						
				1	2	3	1-3	4-6	7-9	10+
2000	Democrat	4	6.5	0	0	1	1	1	1	1
	Republican	5	2.4	1	2	1	4	1	0	0
	Total	9	4.2	1	2	2	5	1	1	1
2002	Democratf	12	4.6	0	2	2	4	5	3	0
	Republican	5	4.8	2	0	0	2	1	1	1
	Total	17	4.7	2	2	2	6	6	4	1
2004	Democratg	5	3	1	0	2	3	2	0	0
	Republican	2	9	1	0	0	1	0	0	1
	Total	7	4.7	2	0	2	4	2	0	1
2006	Democrat	0	0	0	0	0	0	0	0	0
	Republican	22	5.9	2	2	2	6	9	3	4
	Total	22	5.9	2	2	2	6	9	3	4
2008	Democrath	6	3.2	4	0	0	4	1	1	0
	Republican	17	4.4	3	2	4	6	4	3	1
	Total	23	4.1	7	2	4	13	5	4	1
2010	Democrat	54	3.8	23	15	3	41	1	4	7
	Republicani	4	1.5	3	0	1	4	0	0	0
	Total	58	3.6	26	15	4	45	1	4	7
2012	Democrat	10	6.2	2	2	1	5	2	1	2
	Republican	17	2.5	12	0	1	13	1	2	1
	Total	27	3.9	14	2	2	18	3	3	
2014	Democrat	12	4.3	7	1	0	8	2	1	1
	Republican	6	6	2	1	0	3	0	2	1
	Total	18j	4.8	9	2	0	11	2	3	2
2016	Democrat	3	7	1	0	0	1	0	1	1
	Republican	9	4.2	3	1	2	6	0	2	1
	Total	12	4.9	4	0	0	7	0	3	2
2018	Democrat	2	10.0	0	0	0	0	0	0	2
	Republican	32	3.3	5	12	5	22	7	1	2
	Total	34	3.7	5	12	5	22	7	1	4

Table 2-11 Defeated Senate Incumbents, 1946 – 2018

Election	Party	Incumbents lost	Average Terms	Consecutive terms served					
				1	2	3	4	5	6+
1946	Democrat	11	1.6	7	2	1	1	0	0
	Republican	2	4.0	0	0	0	2	0	0
	Total	13	2.0	7	2	1	3	0	0
1948	Democrat	2	1.5	1	1	0	0	0	0
	Republican	8	1.0	8	0	0	0	0	0
	Total	10	1.1	9	1	0	0	0	0
1958	Republican	10	1.4	6	4	0	0	0	0
	Total	10	1.4	6	4	0	0	0	0
1966	Democrat	4	2.0	2	0	2	0	0	0
	Total	4	2.0	2	0	2	0	0	0
1974	Democrat	2	3.0	1	0	0	0	1	0
	Republican	2	1.5	1	1	0	0	0	0
	Total	4	2.2	2	1	0	0	1	0
1978	Democrat	7	0.9	6	0	1	0	0	0
	Republican	3	2.7	0	2	0	1	0	0
	Total	10	1.4	6	2	1	1	0	0
1980	Democrat	12	2.4	5	1	3	2	0	1
	Republican	1	4.0	0	0	0	1	0	0
	Total	13	2.6	5	1	3	3	0	1
1982	Democrat	1	4.0	0	0	0	1	0	0
	Republican	1	1.0	1	0	0	0	0	0
	Total	2	2.5	1	0	0	1	0	0
1984	Democrat	1	2.0	0	1	0	0	0	0
	Republican	2	2.0	1	0	1	0	0	0
	Total	3	2.0	1	1	1	0	0	0
1986	Republican[a]	7	0.9	7	0	0	0	0	0
	Total	7	0.9	7	0	0	0	0	0
1988	Democrat	1	2.0	0	1	0	0	0	0
	Republican	3	1.4	2	0	1	0	0	0
	Total	4	1.6	2	1	1	0	0	0
1990	Republican	1	2.0	0	1	0	0	0	0
	Total	1	2.0	0	1	0	0	0	0
1992	Democrat	3	1.3	2	1	0	0	0	0
	Republican	2	1.2	1	1	0	0	0	0
	Total	5	1.3	3	2	0	0	0	0
1994	Democrat	2	1.8	1	0	1	0	0	0
	Total	2	1.8	1	0	1	0	0	0
1996	Republican[c]	2	1.5	1	0	1	0	0	0
	Total	2	1.5	1	0	1	0	0	0
1998	Democrat	1	1.0	1	0	0	0	0	0
	Republican	2	2.0	1	1	0	0	0	0
	Total	3	1.7	2	1	0	0	0	0
2000	Democrat	1	2.0	0	1	0	0	0	0
	Republican	5	2.0	3	1	0	0	1	0
	Total	6	2.0	3	2	0	0	1	0
2002	Democrat[d]	2	0.7	2	0	0	0	0	0
	Republican	2	1.5	1	1	0	0	0	0
	Total	4	1.3	3	1	0	0	0	0

Table 2-11 Defeated Senate Incumbents, 1946 – 2018 (continued)

Election	Party	Incumbents lost	Average Terms	Consecutive terms served					
				1	2	3	4	5	6+
2004	Democrat	1	3.0	0	0	1	0	0	0
	Republican	0	0.0	0	0	0	0	0	0
	Total	1	3.0	0	0	1	0	0	0
2006	Republican	5	1.8	2	2	1	0	0	0
	Total	5	1.8	2	2	1	0	0	0
2008	Republican	5	2.2	3	1	0	0	0	1
	Total	5	2.2	3	1	0	0	0	1
2010	Democrat	3	3.3	0	1	1	0	1	0
	Republican	1	3.0	0	0	1	0	0	0
	Total	4	3.3	0	1	2	0	1	0
2012	Republican	1	1	1	0	0	0	0	0
	Total	1	1	1	0	0	0	0	0
2014	Democrat[e]	5	2.0	3	0	1	1	0	0
	Republican	0	0.0	0	0	0	0	0	0
	Total	5	2.0	3	0	1	1	0	0
2016	Republican	2	1	2	0	0	0	0	0
	Total	2	1	2	0	0	0	0	0
2018	Democrat	4	1.8	2	1	1	0	0	0
	Republican	1	2	0	1	0	0	0	0
	Total	5	1.8	2	2	1	0	0	0

Supplemental Text:

1-1 Apportionment of Congressional Seats, by Region and State, 1910 - 2010 (435 seats)

a. New Mexico became a state in 1912; in 1910 it had a nonvoting delegate in Congress.
b. Alaska became a state on January 3, 1959. In 1950 Alaska had a nonvoting delegate in Congress, making the total for that year 437; subsequent reapportionment reduced the total to 435.
c. Hawaii became a state on August 21, 1959. In 1950 Hawaii had a nonvoting delegate in Congress, making the total for that year 437; subsequent reapportionment reduced the total to 435.

Source: Congressional Quarterly's Guide to U.S. Elections (Washington, D.C.: Congressional Quarterly, various editions); Congressional Quarterly Weekly Report, various issues; U.S. Census data 2000, www.census.gov.

1-2 Democratic and Republican Seats in the House, by Region, 69th - 116th Congresses, 1925 – 2019

Note: D indicates Democrats; R indicates Republicans. Third parties are omitted. Figures represent the makeup of Congress on the first day of the session.

a. Excludes South Carolina's 1st District - Tim Scott vacated the seat prior to the start of the 113th Congress after being appointed to the Senate and Mark Sanford did not assume office until May 7, 2013.
b. Excludes Illinois's 2nd District - Jesse Jackson Jr. resigned on November 21, 2012 and Robin Kelly did not assume office until April 11, 2013.
c. Excludes Illinois's 5th District - Rahm Emanuel resigned to become White House Chief of Staff and Mike Quigley did not assume office until April 7, 2009.

Source: Congressional Directory, various editions; Congressional Quarterly Weekly Report, various issues; Clerk of the U.S. House of Representatives, http://clerk.house.gov; The Almanac of American Politics (Washington, D.C.: National Journal Group, various editions).

1-3 Democratic and Republican Seats in the House, by Region, 69th - 116th Congresses, 1925 – 2019

Note: D indicates Democrats; R indicates Republicans. Third parties are omitted. Figures represent the makeup of Congress on the first day of the session.

a. Excludes South Carolina's 1st District - Tim Scott vacated the seat prior to the start of the 113th Congress after being appointed to the Senate and Mark Sanford did not assume office until May 7, 2013.
b. Excludes Illinois's 2nd District - Jesse Jackson Jr. resigned on November 21, 2012 and Robin Kelly did not assume office until April 11, 2013.
c. Excludes Illinois's 5th District - Rahm Emanuel resigned to become White House Chief of Staff and Mike Quigley did not assume office until April 7, 2009.

Source: Congressional Directory, various editions; Congressional Quarterly Weekly Report, various issues; Clerk of the U.S. House of Representatives, http://clerk.house.gov; The Almanac of American Politics (Washington, D.C.: National Journal Group, various editions).

1-5 Democratic and Republican Seats in the Senate, by Region, 69th-116th Congresses, 1925-2019

Note: D indicates Democrats; R indicates Republicans. Third parties are omitted. Figures represent the makeup of Congress on the first day of the session.

a. Includes Richard Shelby (AL) who switched from the Democratic to the Republican Party on the day following the election and before the beginning of the 104th Congress.
b. Excludes Barack Obama (D-IL) who resigned from office prior to the beginning of the 111th Congress.
c. Excludes Al Franken (D-MN) who was not sworn in until July 7, 2009.

Source: Congresional Directory, various editions; Congressional Quarterly Weekly Report, various issues; US Senate, http://www.senate.gov; The Almanac of American Politics (Washington, D.C.: National Journal Group, various editions).

1-16 African Americans in Congress, 41st - 116th Congresses, 1869 – 2019

Note: The data do not include nonvoting delegates or commissioners. Figures represent the makeup of Congress on the first day of the session.

a. After the 56th Congress, there were no African American members in either the House or Senate until the 71st Congress.
b. Roland Burris was not seated on the first day of the 111th session.
c. Tim Scott, who was appointed on December 17th to replace outgoing Senator Jim DeMint, is included in the Senate totals.

Source: Black Americans in Congress, 1870-1977, H. Doc. 95-258, 95th Cong., 1st sess., 1977; Congressional Quarterly Almanac (Washington, D.C.: Congressional Quarterly, various editions); Congressional Quarterly Weekly Report, various issues; Clerk of the U.S. House of Representatives, http://clerk.house.gov; "Membership of the 114th Congress: A Profile," Congressional Research Service

1-17 Asian Americans in Congress, 58th - 116th Congresses, 1903-2019

Note: The data do not include nonvoting delegates or commissioners. Figures represent the makeup of Congress on the first day of the session.

Source: "Asian Pacific Americans in the United States Congress;" "Membership of the 114th Congress: A Profile", Congressional Research Service

1-18 Hispanic Americans in Congress, 41st - 116th Congresses, 1869 – 2019

Note: The data do not include nonvoting delegates or commissioners. Figures represent the makeup of Congress on the first day of the session.

Source: Biographical Directory of the United States Congress 1774-1989; Congressional Quarterly Almanac (Washington, D.C.: Congressional Quarterly, various editions); Congressional Quarterly Weekly Report, various issues; Clerk of the U.S. House of Representatives, http://clerk.house.gov; http://www.senate.gov/galleries/daily/minority.htm; "Membership of the 114th Congress: A Profile", Congressional Research Service

1-19 Women in Congress, 65th - 116th Congresses, 1917 – 2019

Note: The data include only women who were sworn in as members and served more than one day. Figures represent the makeup of Congress on the first day of the session.

Source: Women in Congress, H. Rept. 94-1732, 94th Cong., 2nd sess., 1976; Congressional Quarterly Almanac (Washington, D.C.: Congressional Quarterly, various editions); Congressional Quarterly Weekly Report, various issues; Clerk of the U.S. House of Representatives, http://clerk.house.gov; US Senate, http://www.senate.gov.; "Membership of the 114th Congress: A Profile", Congressional Research Service

1-20 Political Parties of Senators and Representatives, 34th - 116th Congresses, 1855 – 2019

Note: Figures represent the makeup of Congress on the first day of the session.

a. Democrats organized House with help of other parties.
b. Democrats organized House because of Republican deaths.
c. Alaska was admitted as a state in 1958. The total figure includes the addition of Alaska's representative.
d. Alaska was admitted as a state in 1958 and Hawaii in 1959. The total figure includes the addition of Alaska's and Hawaii's representatives.
e. North Carolina's 9th District was not seated at the start of the 116th Congress as the election results had not been certified.

Source: Congressional Directory, various editions; Congressional Quarterly Weekly Report, various issues; Clerk of the U.S. House of Representatives, http://clerk.house.gov; US Senate, http://www.senate.gov; The Almanac of American Politics (Washington, D.C.: National Journal Group, various editions).

2-4 Losses by the President's Party in Midterm Elections, 1862 - 2018

Note: D indicates Democrats; R indicates Republicans.
Each entry is the difference between the number of seats won by the president's party in that midterm election and the number of seats won by that party in the preceding general election. Because of changes in the overall number of seats in the Senate and House, in the number of seats won by third parties, and in the number of vacancies, a Republican loss is not always matched precisely by a Democratic gain, or vice versa. Data reflects immediate election results.

a. Although the Republicans gained nine seats in the 1902 elections, they actually lost ground to the Democrats, who gained twenty-five seats after the increase in the overall number of Representatives after the 1900 census.
b. Sen. Richard Shelby (AL) switched from the Democratic to the Republican Party the day following the election, so that the total loss was nine seats.

Source: Biographical Directory of the United States Congress 1774–1989 (Washington, D.C.: Government Printing Office, 1989); Congressional Quarterly Almanac (Washington, D.C.: Congressional Quarterly, various years); National Journal, various issues; The Almanac of American Politics (Washington, D.C.: National Journal Group, various years), Clerk of the U.S. House of Representatives, http://clerk.house.gov; Clerk of the U.S. Senate, http://clerk.senate.gov.

2-5 House Seats That Changed Party, 1954 – 2018

Note: This table reflects shifts in party control of seats from immediately before to immediately after the November elections. It does not include party gains resulting from the creation of new districts and does not account for situations in which two districts were reduced to one, thus forcing incumbents to run against each other. Party gains that resulted from an incumbent being defeated in either a primary or general election are classified as incumbent defeats. In situations where the incumbent declined to run again, ran for another political office, or died or resigned before the end of the term are classified as open seats.

Source: Biographical Directory of the United States Congress 1774–1989 (Washington, D.C.: Government Printing Office, 1989); Congressional Quarterly Almanac (Washington, D.C.: Congressional Quarterly, various years); National Journal, various issues; The Almanac of American Politics (Washington, D.C.: National Journal Group, various years); Election 2012 Data: The Impact on the House (The Brookings Institution)., The Green Papers, http://thegreenpapers.com

2-6 Senate Seats That Changed Party, 1954 – 2018

Note: D indicates Democrat; R indicates Republican.
This table reflects shifts in party control of seats from immediately before to immediately after the November election. Party gains that resulted from an incumbent being defeated in either a primary or general election are classified as incumbent defeats. In situations where the incumbent declined to run again, ran for another political office, or died or resigned before the end of the term are classified as open seats.

a. Includes John Durkin (D-NH). After a contested election in which incumbent Sen. Norris Cotton did not run, the Senate declared the seat vacant as of August 8, 1975. Sen. Durkin was then elected by special election, September 16, 1975, to fill the vacancy.
b. Sen. Richard Shelby (AL) switched from the Democratic to the Republican Party the day after the election and brought the total change to nine.
c. Includes Norm Coleman (R-MN) who beat Walter Mondale (D-MN) after the death of Sen. Paul Wellstone (D-MN).
d. Does not include Al Franken (D-MN), who was declared on 30 June 2009 to have won the US Senate contest defeating Incumbent Senator Norm Coleman (R-MN). This brings the R#D Incumbent Defeat up to 5, and the Total Changes up to 8.

e. Does not include Incumbent Senator Lisa Murkowski (R-AK), who lost her primary to Joe Miller (R-AK) but won the general election as a Republican write-in candidate.
f. Includes Pat Toomey (R-PA), who defeated Senator Arlen Specter (D-PA). Specter had changed his affiliation from Republican to Democrat in office on April 30, 2009.
g. Includes Montana Senate race, in which incumbent John Walsh withdrew from race after winning Democratic primary and was replaced at party convention.

Source: Congressional Quarterly Almanac (Washington, D.C.: Congressional Quarterly, various years); Congressional Quarterly Weekly Report, various issues; National Journal, various issues, The Green Papers, http://thegreenpapers.com.

2-7 House Incumbents Retired, Defeated, or Reelected, 1946 – 2018

Note: Some data from previous versions of Vital Statistics have been updated. See errata for more detail.

a. This entry does not include persons who died or resigned before the election.
b. Includes Jim Traficant (D- OH), who ran as an Independent in the election despite being expelled from the House of Representatives in July 2002.
c. Includes Patsy Mink (D-HI) who died shortly before the election yet remained on the ballot.
d. Includes Albert R. Wynn (D-MD) who lost his primary on February 13, 2008, and promptly resigned his seat effective May 31, 2008. Donna Edwards (D-MD) who won the primary and then won the special election to fill Wynn's seat for the remainder of the term is not counted as an incumbent in this table.

Source: Biographical Directory of the United States Congress 1774–1989 (Washington, D.C.: Government Printing Office, 1989); Congressional Quarterly Almanac (Washington, D.C.: Congressional Quarterly, various years); National Journal, various issues; The Almanac of American Politics (Washington, D.C.: National Journal Group, various years), Center for Responsive Politics, http://opensecrets.org.

Most recent update source: Tabulations of data from Federal Election Commission, http://www.fec.gov

2-8 Senate Incumbents Retired, Defeated, or Reelected, 1946 – 2018

Note: Table includes all Senate contests in a given year, whether for full or partial terms.

a. This entry includes Senators who died or resigned before the election and those retiring at the end of their terms.
b. Sheila Frahm, appointed to fill Robert Dole's term, is counted as an incumbent in Kansas's "B" seat.
c. Sen. Joe Lieberman (CT) lost in the Democratic primary, but ran in the general election as an independent and won reelection.
d. Sen. Lisa Murkowski (R-AK) lost her primary to Joe Miller (R-AK), but ran in the general election as a Republican write-in candidate and won reelection.
e. Total includes Dean Heller (R-NV), who was appointed on May 9, 2011 and won reelection.
f. Includes the resignation of Tom Coburn (R-OK) and the resulting special election to finish his term.
g. John Walsh (D-MT) withdrew from race after primary and was replaced on the ballot at a party convention.

Source: Congressional Quarterly Almanac (Washington, D.C.: Congressional Quarterly, various years); Congressional Quarterly Weekly Report, various issues; National Journal, various issues, Center for Responsive Politics, http://opensecrets.org.

Most recent update source: Tabulations of data from Federal Election Commission, http://www.fec.gov

2-9 House and Senate Retirements by Party, 1930 – 2018

Note: D indicates Democrat; R indicates Republican.
These figures include members who did not run again for the office they held and members who sought other offices; the figures do not include members who died or resigned before the end of the particular Congress.

a. Includes Frank Murkowski (R-AK) who ran for governor, won and appointed Lisa Murkoswki to finish the last two years of his term.
b. This total includes Sen. Joe Lieberman (I-CT), who caucused with Democrats.

Source: Mildred L. Amer, "Information on the Number of House Retirees, 1930–1992," (Washington, D.C.: Congressional Research Service, Staff Report, May 19, 1992); Congressional Quarterly Weekly Report, various issues; National Journal, various issues; Roll Call, Casualty List: 112th Congress., Center for Responsive Politics, http://opensecrets.org

2-10 Defeated House Incumbents, 1946 - 2018

Note: The 1966 and 1982 numbers do not include races where incumbents ran against incumbents due to redistricting. We counted incumbents who lost in the primary as their party's incumbent but then ran in the general election as a write-in or third-party candidate as an incumbent loss.

a. This includes Leo Isacson (NY), who was a member of the American Labor Party.
b. This includes Vincent Dellay (NJ), who was elected as a Republican but switched to a Democrat. He ran for reelection as an Independent.
c. This includes Eugene Atkinson (PA), who began his House service January 3, 1979, as a Democrat. He became a Republican on October 14, 1981.
d. This includes Donald Lukens (OH) who was defeated in the primary and then resigned on October 24, 1990 and Bill Grant (Fla.) who began his House service January 6, 1987, as a Democrat, but later switched parties. The Republican Conference let his seniority count from 1987.
e. One Democratic incumbent, who served more than ten terms in office, was defeated.
f. Includes Jim Traficant (OH) who ran as an Independent after being expelled from the House.
g. Excludes two 13-term representatives, Charles Stenholm (TX) and Martin Frost (TX), that ran against incumbents as a result of redistricting.
h. Includes Albert R. Wynn (D-MD) who lost his primary on February 13, 2008, and promptly resigned his seat effective May 31, 2008.
i. Includes Parker Griffith (AL) who began his House service January 3, 2009, as a Democrat but switched to a Republican on December 22, 2009.
j. Excludes the defeat of Eni Faleomavaega (D-Samoa) seeking 14th term as a non-voting delegate.

Source: Biographical Directory of the United States Congress 1774-2012, http://bioguide.congress.gov; Congressional Quarterly Almanac (Washington, D.C.: Congressional Quarterly, various years); National Journal, various issues; The Almanac of American Politics (Washington, D.C.: National Journal Group, various years); Roll Call, Casualty List: 112th Congress, Center for Responsive Politics, http://opensecrets.org

2-11 Defeated Senate Incumbents, 1946 – 2018

Note: Some data from previous versions of Vital Statistics have been updated. See errata for more detail.

a. This includes James Broyhill (R-NC) who was appointed on July 14, 1986, until November 14, 1986. He lost to Terry Sanford (D-NC) who took over the seat on November 5, 1986.
b. Includes John Seymour (R-CA) who was appointed on January 7, 1991, until November 3, 1992.
c. Includes Sheila Frahm (R-KS) who was appointed on June 11, 1996 until November 7, 1996.
d. Includes Jean Carnahan (D-MO) who was appointed to fill her husband's seat in 2001.
e. Does not include John Walsh (D-MT) who withdrew from the race after the primary and was replaced on the ballot.

Source: Biographical Directory of the United States Congress 1774–1989 (Washington, D.C.: Government Printing Office, 1989); Congressional Quarterly Almanac (Washington, D.C.: Congressional Quarterly, various years); National Journal, various issues; The Almanac of American Politics (Washington, D.C.: National Journal Group, various years).

Most recent update source: Tabulations of data from Federal Election Commission, http://www.fec.gov

PROFILE LIST